THE SERIALS DIRECTORY

AN INTERNATIONAL REFERENCE BOOK

Editorial Advisory Board

Susan A. Cady
Associate Director
of Technical Services
Linderman Library
Lehigh University Libraries

Mary Elizabeth Clack
Serial Records Librarian
Harvard College Library

Genevieve Clay
Head, Central Serials
Eastern Kentucky University
Crabbe Library

Claude Daris
Head of Serials Department
Universite Libre de Bruxelles
Belgium

Kenneth E. Dowlin
Director, San Francisco Public Library
City Librarian
Main Library Civic Center

Ludo Holans
Librarian
Campus Bibliotheekdienst
Katholieke Universiteit Leuven
Belgium

Sul H. Lee
Dean, University Libraries
University of Oklahoma

Lois N. Upham
Uncle Remus Regional Library
Madison, Georgia

The 9th Edition of *The Serials Directory: An International Reference Book* was compiled and published by EBSCO Publishing, division of EBSCO Industries, Inc.

J.T. Stephens, President-EBSCO Industries, Inc.
Tim Collins, Vice President, Division General Manager-EBSCO Publishing
Mary Beth Vanderpoorten, M.S.L.S., Vice President-EBSCO Subscription Services, General Manager-Title Information

EDITORIAL / PRODUCTION

Leanne Wofford, Editorial Manager
Jill Hinds, Special Projects Editor
Stefanie Letanosky, Titles Editor

Jean Bowick, Editorial Assistant
Joe B. Crowe, Editorial Assistant
Kathy Entrekin, Editorial Assistant

Loyd McIntosh, Editorial Assistant
Mona Powell, Editorial Assistant
Kelly Rogers, Editorial Assistant

Database and publishing software
provided by Syscomp, Inc., Atlanta, Georgia, using Advanced Revelation®

Typesetting software provided by
Laser Solutions, Inc., Atlanta, Georgia using FrameMaker®

AN INTERNATIONAL REFERENCE BOOK

NINTH EDITION 1995
VOLUME II

En-L

Division of EBSCO Industries Inc., Birmingham, Alabama

Published by EBSCO Publishing
division of EBSCO Industries, Inc.
P.O. Box 1943, Birmingham, AL 35201-1943   USA

Copyright © 1995 by EBSCO Industries, Inc.
Printed and bound in the United States of America.

All rights reserved. Reproduction of this Directory, in whole or in part, by any method, without prior written permission of the publisher is prohibited.

Direct all editorial inquiries to EBSCO Publishing, P.O. Box 1943, Birmingham, AL 35201-1943.

Direct all other inquiries to EBSCO Publishing, 83 Pine Street, PO Box 2250, Peabody, MA 01960-7250

International Standard Book Number (5-Volume Set) 0-913956-86-4
International Standard Book Number (Volume-1) 0-913956-81-3
International Standard Book Number (Volume-2) 0-913956-82-1
International Standard Book Number (Volume-3) 0-913956-83-X
International Standard Book Number (Volume-4) 0-913956-84-8
International Standard Book Number (Volume-5) 0-913956-85-6

International Standard Serial Number 0886-4179

Every effort has been made to ensure the accuracy of information in *The Serials Directory* and since no payment has been made for the inclusion of any entries, the publisher cannot accept liability for errors or omissions, regardless of the cause.

CONTENTS

Preface vii
User's Guide ix
Filing Rules... xvi
Subject Headings.. xvii
Subject Cross References xxi
Tables xxxvii
    Frequency... xxxviii
    Document Delivery xxxviii
    Wire Services.. xxxix
    Country of Publication by Code.......................... xl
    Country of Publication by Country xli
    Unit of Currency xlii
    Indexes/Abstracts................................... xliii

Volume 1
    Serial Listings (A–Em) 3
Volume 2
    Serial Listings (En-L).................................. 1923
Volume 3
    Serial Listings (M-Z) 3475
Volume 4
  Newspapers
      US Newspapers..................................... 5625
      International Newspapers 5777
  Alphabetical Title Index................................ 5815
Volume 5
  ISSN Index.. 7607
  Peer Reviewed Index 7987
  Serials on CD-ROM Index.............................. 8051
  Serials Online Index................................... 8075
  Book Review Index 8113
  Advertising Accepted Index............................. 8275
  Controlled Circulation Index 8465
  Copyright Clearance Center Index....................... 8601
  New Title Index 8675

PREFACE

At EBSCO Publishing it is our goal to produce the primary serial reference source available. We have directed our energies toward obtaining the most up-to-date and accurate information on every title -- from the most familiar to the most obscure. In working toward this goal, several additions and changes have been made to the newest edition of **The Serials Directory: An International Reference Book**.

Eight new bibliographic elements are included in this edition to provide information professionals with a means for quick and easy serial research. In the newspaper section, Full and Half-page ad rates are now listed along with Publication Size, Wire Service Affiliations, and a notation for the inclusion of Photographs. Also included is data on document delivery availability/vendors, "Acid Free" notations and both Internet and E-mail addresses when provided by the publisher.

This edition of **The Serials Directory** contains approximately 151,000 serial titles with up to 60 bibliographic elements available for each one. Included in Volumes I, II and III are over 6,500 new titles, 2,800 titles available on CD-ROM or an online database, 10,600 titles registered with the Copyright Clearance Center, 24,000 serials publishing book reviews, and over 27,000 serials accepting advertising. This Edition contains verified information for over 100,000 serial titles representing approximately 65,000 publishers worldwide.

EBSCO Publishing is a sister division to EBSCO Subscription Services; therefore, gaining access to serial information on an ongoing basis is more simplified. EBSCO remains in constant contact with publishers throughout the world ensuring the accuracy of title and publisher information as well as providing the latest pricing and subscription data.

Information found in **The Serials Directory** is maintained through four sources.

First, through the internal EBSCO Subscription Services database, updated daily as a result of continuous contact with publishers worldwide. The second source is The Library of Congress' CONSER file of which EBSCO is an affiliate member. The CONSER file is maintained by the National Serials Data Program, National Library of Canada, National Library of Medicine, Chemical Abstracts Service, and the National Agricultural Library. The third source is The ISSN Register (formerly ISDS) which provides extensive coverage of international serials. The fourth source for data is direct correspondence with thousands of publishers throughout the world.

With this edition, you will receive two cumulative Updates throughout 1995 to keep you abreast of changes in title status, publisher and subscription addresses, format changes or additions, price and frequency changes, as well as information on new titles. With a subscription to **The Serials Directory: EBSCO CD-ROM**, you will receive four quarterly updated discs containing all historical serial data that may not be included in the print version.

Our other international offering is **The Index and Abstract Directory: An International Guide to Services and Serials Coverage**. This valuable reference tool, which is now contained in two volumes, consists of information on over 950 "active" Indexing/Abstracting services and includes bibliographic information on the more than 56,000 serials that are monitored by each.

You will also find that we go beyond just providing reference products alone. As always, we will continue to offer free serials research to any of our customers needing assistance in locating the more ambiguous serial publications. We receive thousands of calls each year and have proven very successful in pinpointing the answers to a variety of serials questions.

At EBSCO Publishing, we continue to grow -- to change -- to improve. **The Serials Directory** and the **Index and Abstract Directory** reflect this growth and, combined with EBSCO's valued reputation within the library community, provide the highest standard of quality available in serials reference.

Leanne Wofford
Editorial Manager

EBSCO Publishing, PO Box 1943, Birmingham, AL 35201-1943 USA
(800)826-3024 / (205)980-2773 / FAX (205)995-1582

AN INTERNATIONAL REFERENCE BOOK

USER'S GUIDE

USER'S GUIDE

How to Use The Serials Directory.
Twelve sections comprise The Serials Directory. Each of these sections allows the user to access information easily. The following is a brief explanation of each section.

- **Serial Listings (Subjects A-Z)**
  (Volumes I, II and III)
- **Newspaper Listings**
  (Volume IV)
- **Alphabetical Title Index**
  (Volume IV)
- **ISSN Index**
  (Volume V)
- **Peer Reviewed Index**
  (Volume V)
- **Serials Available on CD-ROM Index**
  (Volume V)
- **Serials Available Online Index**
  (Volume V)
- **Book Review Index**
  (Volume V)
- **Advertising Accepted Index**
  (Volume V)
- **Controlled Circulation Index**
  (Volume V)
- **Copyright Clearance Center Index**
  (Volume V)
- **New Title Index**
  (Volume V)

● Serial Listings—
The Serial Listings are arranged alphabetically by subject category. Titles given under each subject heading are in alphabetical order (See Filing Rules—page xvi). The Serial Listing arrangement enables the user to quickly locate the relevant subject area and to review all serial titles relating to that subject. There are over 18,000 "see notes" throughout the 146 major subject headings and 330 subheadings in the Serial Listings. These notes refer the user from related subject areas to the primary subject heading under which the full title listing appears. See pages xvii-xxxvi for a list of subject headings and subject cross references.

● Newspaper Listings—
This section lists all US and international newspapers included in our database. US newspapers will be listed alphabetically by state. International titles will follow and are arranged alphabetically, by country. Newspaper listings can be found in the Alphabetical Title Index as well as the ISSN Index along with the regular listings in Volume IV.

● Alphabetical Title Index—
Arranged alphabetically by title, this index lists the primary title, along with Country of Publication/ISSN, and MARC control number, when available.

The following notations are made in the Alphabetical Title Index:

1. New Titles— Titles are denoted with a bullet "●". Bullets will appear in both the Serial Listing, as well as the Alphabetical Title Index. This edition includes over 6,500 new titles which began publication after 1992 and were active at the time data was secured for publication.

2. Ceased Titles— Titles that have ceased publication and do not have a "succeeding entry." Ceased titles are denoted with "*CEASED*" in bold italics, following the primary title in the Serial Listing, as well as the Alphabetical Title Index. Ceased titles are included in the Directory for two consecutive editions after EBSCO is notified of the status change. This edition contains over 4,700 cessations.

3. Title Changes— Titles which have a succeeding entry, MARC field 785. These entries are included in the Alphabetical Title Index with a reference to the current title(s). Title changes are included in the Directory for two consecutive editions based on the "ending date of publication," MARC field 008/11-14. This edition contains over 4,840 title changes. See the User's Guide/Sample Listing for more information.

4. Suspended Titles— Titles for which EBSCO has received notification of suspension. Suspended titles are denoted in both the Serial Listing and the index with "*SUSPENDED*" in bold italics, following the primary title. These titles will remain suspended until EBSCO is notified otherwise.

5. Preceding Entries— Preceding entries print with a "see" note to the primary title provided the primary title has a MARC publication start date (008/7-10) later than 1992. Preceding entries will remain in the Directory for two consecutive editions with a reference to the newer title(s).

6. Main Entry - Corporate Name— A corporate name used as a main entry, this element prints in the Alphabetical Title Index as another access point to the publication in question. To further aid the user, the Main Entry-Corporate Name is listed with a "see" note to the primary title in the Serial Listings. Over 24,000 Main Entry-Corporate Names are included in the Directory.

USER'S GUIDE

- **ISSN Index—**

The ISSN Index contains current as well as preceding ISSN's, arranged in numerical order. The ISSN will be followed by a "see" note giving the title under which the ISSN will appear. The preceding ISSN is included with a "see" note to the primary title provided the MARC publication start date (field 008/7-10) is later than 1992. Preceding ISSN will appear in italicized typeface in order to distinguish it from the current ISSN. The page number for which the Serial Listing appears prints in boldface. There are over 100,400 titles included in the ISSN Index.

- **Peer Reviewed Index—**

Arranged alphabetically by title, the Peer Reviewed Index lists all active serials found in Volumes I, II and III which contain peer reviewed articles. Country of Publication/ISSN and MARC control number are provided, when available. The page number for which the Serial Listing appears prints in boldface. There are over 8,800 titles included in the Peer Reviewed Index.

- **Serials Available on CD-ROM Index—**

Arranged alphabetically by title, this index lists all active serial titles in Volumes I, II and III that are available on CD-ROM, either as the primary format, or as an "additional" available format. Included in this index are the Country of Publication/ISSN and publisher address/telephone number(s) when available. The page number for which the Serial Listing appears prints in boldface. There are over 1,300 titles included in the Serials Available on CD-ROM Index.

- **Serials Available Online Index—**

Arranged alphabetically by title, this index lists all active serials found in Volumes I, II and III that are available online, either as the primary format, or as an "additional" available format. Included in this index are the Country of Publication/ISSN and publisher address/telephone number(s) when available. The page number for which the Serial Listing appears prints in boldface. There are over 2,500 titles included in the Serials Available Online Index.

- **Book Review Index—**

Arranged alphabetically by title, this index lists all active serials found in Volumes I, II and III that contain book reviews. Included in this index are Country of Publication/ISSN and the quantity of book reviews published "per year" (unless otherwise specified). The page number for which the Serial Listing appears prints in boldface. There are over 24,000 titles included in the Book Review Index.

- **Advertising Accepted Index—**

Arranged alphabetically by title, this index contains all active serials found in Volumes I, II and III that accept advertising. The Country of Publication/ISSN and advertising manager/telephone number(s) are also provided, when supplied by the publisher. The page number for which the Serial Listing appears prints in boldface. There are over 27,000 titles included in the Advertising Accepted Index.

- **Controlled Circulation Index—**

Arranged alphabetically by title, this index lists all active titles in the Directory that have a controlled circulation. The Country of Publication/ISSN and circulation figures [printing in brackets] are provided when available. The page number for which the Serial Listing appears prints in boldface. There are over 19,000 titles included in the Controlled Circulation Index.

- **Copyright Clearance Center Index—**

Arranged alphabetically by title, this index lists all active serials found in Volumes I, II and III that are registered with the Copyright Clearance Center (CCC). The Country of Publication/ISSN are provided when available. The page number for which the Serial Listing appears prints in boldface. There are over 10,600 titles included in the Copyright Clearance Center Index.

- **New Title Index—**

Arranged by subject, then alphabetically by title, this index consists of all active titles that have a MARC "beginning date" of "1992" or greater, as well as, "non-MARC" titles where the start date has been verified by the publisher. Country of Publication/ISSN follow the title, with the page number on which the Serial Listing appears. There are over 6,500 titles included in the New Title Index.

USER'S GUIDE/SAMPLE LISTING

SAMPLE LISTING

Country of Publication/ISSN
● **KEY TITLE.** *CEASED/SUSPENDED.* (TITLE STATEMENT). [Abbreviated Title]. **Main/Conf** Main Entry—Meeting. **Main/Corp** Main Entry—Corporate Name. **Added/Corp** Added Entry—Corporate Name. **Series/Conf** Series Statement—Meeting Name. **VFOAT** Varying Form of a Title. **VAT** Variant Access Title. Date of Publication. Type of Serial. Language(s). Frequency. Price. Publisher Name & Address. **Tel** Telephone/Telex Number/Fax/Internet Address/Email Address. (subscription address:) **ED** Editor. **LC** Library of Congress Classification. **DD** Dewey Decimal Classification. **UDC** Universal Decimal Classification. **NLM** National Library of Medicine Classification. **CODEN** CODEN Designation. **[CCC]** Copyright Clearance Center. Index Availability. cum. index (Cumulative Index Availability). **Bk Rev** (Book reviews published), (Qty: Quantity Published). **Photos** [Photographs published]. **Ad Acc** (Advertising accepted), **Adv. Mgr**: Advertising Manager. **Tel** Telephone. Full Page (B&W) - Full page black and white ad rates. Half Page (B&W) - Half page black and white ad rates. Full Page (Color) - Full page color ad rates. Half Page (Color) - Half page color ad rates. **Pub. Size** [Publication trim size]. **Wire Svcs** [Newspaper wire services]. **Pr Rev.** (Peer Reviewed or Refereed). **Acid Free** [Acid free paper]. Circulation. (ctrl) - Controlled circulation. Document Delivery Available. Additional Physical Forms Available. *Preceding Entry-Title, Preceding Entry-ISSN. Succeeding Entry-Title, Succeeding Entry-ISSN.*
   Desc: Descriptive listing.
   Ind/Abst Indexes/Abstracts. Dates of Coverage. Full Text. Full/Selective Coverage

SERIAL LISTING CONTENTS

For the purpose of defining a serial, the definition as given in the USMARC Bibliographic Format is used: a bibliographic item issued in successive parts bearing numerical or chronological designations and intended to be continued indefinitely. Serials include periodicals; newspapers; annuals (reports, yearbooks, etc.); the journals, memoirs, proceedings, transactions, etc., of societies; and numbered monographic series, etc.

The following data elements (when available) are shown in order of appearance within a listing. Some definitions are taken in part from USMARC Formats Bibliographic Data.

Country of Publication. A two letter code indicating the place of publication, production, or execution. See Country of Publication Table, Page xxxvi for additions/changes.

ISSN. International Standard Serial Number, a unique identification number assigned to a serial title by national centers under the auspices of the ISSN Register (formerly ISDS).

●Denotes new titles beginning after 1992, that were active at the time data was secured for publication.

Key Title. Key Title is assigned by various national centers under the auspices of the ISSN Register (formerly International Serials Data System /ISDS). It is formed from title information transcribed from a piece of the serial and is constructed with qualifiers to make it unique when necessary. Since serial titles are taken from both the CONSER and ISSN Register databases, the primary title has not been altered to differentiate the alternative format from the original. In cases where CONSER or the ISSN Register has included a notation for the alternative format within the primary title, the primary title will reflect that notation. Serials in an alternative format (microfiche, microfilm, CD-ROM, etc.) are included in the Directory. Also in cases where multiple language entries appear, the user must refer to the primary language of the publication to ensure that the correct title is located. These titles may appear to be identical with the primary language being the only unique qualifier.

Ceased. This element is present only when a title has ceased publication. This does not include titles that have a succeeding entry or have had a title change. The word "*CEASED*" in bold italics, follows the primary title in the Serial Listing. Ceased titles are included in the Directory for two consecutive editions after the actual date of cessation. This edition contains over 4,700 cessations.

Suspended. Denotes temporary suspension of a title. The word "*SUSPENDED*" in bold italics, follows the primary title in the Serial Listing to denote suspended titles. These titles remain suspended in the database until the publisher notifies EBSCO otherwise.

Title Statement. Title Statement is present only when it differs from Key Title in any way, other than initial articles and prepositions. It consists of the title proper (including short title and alternative title, the numerical designation of a part/section and the name of a part/section) and may also contain the medium, remainder of title, other title information, and the statement of responsibility/remainder of title page transcription. Title Statement will follow Key Title in uppercase and will be enclosed in parentheses.

Abbreviated Title. Assigned by the ISSN Register (formerly ISDS), in accordance with ISO 4-1984, Documentation - Rules for the Abbreviation of Title Words and Titles of Publications and List of Serial Title Word Abbreviations. The Abbreviated Title is based on the Key Title and files in [brackets].

USER'S GUIDE/SAMPLE LISTING

Main Entry-Meeting. A meeting or conference name used as a main entry. Main entry under a meeting name is assigned to works that contain proceedings, reports, etc. Main Entry-Meeting will be preceded by the prefix "**Main/Conf**" in boldface.

Main Entry-Corporate Name. A corporate name used as a main entry. Main entry under corporate name is assigned to works that represent the collective thought of a body, including conference and meeting names that are entered subordinately to a corporate body. Main Entry-Corporate Name is preceded by the prefix "**Main/Corp**" in boldface.

Added Entry-Corporate Name. Contains a corporate heading used as main entry. A corporate body is identified by a name that acts or may act as an entity. Included in this definition are: associations, institutions, business firms, governments and their agencies, ships, churches and programs. The Added Entry-Corporate Name will be preceded by a prefix of "**Added/Corp**" in boldface.

Series Statement-Meeting Name. Series statement entered under a named conference or meeting. Series Statement-Meeting is preceded by "**Series/Conf**" in boldface.

Varying Form of a Title. Titles which may appear on different parts of a serial, or consisting of portions of the title proper or alternative forms of titles. Varying Form of a Title differs substantially from Key Title/Title Statement and contributes to the further identification of the serial. It is preceded by the prefix "**VFOAT**" in boldface. Additional titles are separated by commas.

Variant Access Title. A variant form of the title that does not appear on the serial. It is used when the title contains an initialism, non-roman alphabet character, etc. It provides additional access for searching purposes when access is not provided by any other title. Variant Access Title is preceded by the prefix of "**VAT**" in boldface. Additional titles are separated by commas.

Dates of Publication and Volume Information. Beginning (and ending) dates of publication and volume designation. The date may consist of the year, month, or day; month or season and year; or year alone, depending upon the frequency of publication and the usage of the publisher. Dates may appear in the vernacular and/or may be abbreviated.

Type of Serial. Indicates if the serial is a periodical, monographic series, or newspaper. When available, more specific types will be used such as bibliography, catalog, bulletin, directory, government publication, newsletter, proceedings, trade publication, consumer publication, corporate report, academic scholarly publication and abstracting/indexing publication.

Language(s). If the serial is published in more than one language, the predominant language will appear first and any additional languages will follow in parentheses (including languages for translations, summaries, tables of contents, etc.) with appropriate explanation if necessary.

Frequency. Indicated by a two letter code - see Frequency Table, page xxxviii. Exceptions to frequency are noted and in parentheses following code.

Price. The current annual subscription price at the time information was secured for publication. Prices are usually given in US dollars and currency of Country of Publication, if other than US. Exceptions are noted and explained.

Publisher Name and Address/Telecommunications Numbers. The complete name and address of the publisher when available. Telephone, telex and/or facsimile number as well as Internet and E-mail addresses are given for serials. Preceded by a prefix of "**Tel**" in boldface.

Subscription Address. The complete name and subscription/fulfillment address. Telecommunication numbers are listed when available.

Editor(s). Name, address and telephone number(s), when available. Preceded by a prefix of "**ED**" in boldface.

Library of Congress Classification. Contains an LC class/call number, shelf number, or pseudo-call-number assigned by The Library of Congress or one of its authorized agencies. Preceded by a prefix of "**LC**" in boldface.

Dewey Decimal Classification. Assigned according to the Dewey Decimal schedules maintained by The Library of Congress. Preceded by a prefix of "**DD**" in boldface.

Universal Decimal Classification. Derived from the Dewey Decimal Classification, the UDC differs in arrangement and philosophy. The UDC is distinguished from the DDC by its extensive expansions. Preceded by a prefix of "**UDC**" in boldface.

National Library of Medicine Classification. Contains either a complete NLM call number or an NLM classification number. Preceded by a prefix of "**NLM**" in boldface.

CODEN Designation. Abbreviation for periodical titles, which is assigned by the CODEN section of Chemical Abstracts Service. It is a unique identifier for scientific and technical publications. Preceded by a prefix of "**CODEN**" in boldface.

Copyright Clearance Center. [CCC] indicates titles registered with the Copyright Clearance Center. The Copyright Clearance Center has been authorized to give photocopy permission and to collect any pre-set royalty fees set by the publisher.

Index Availability. Shows the existence of an index, or a table of contents issued as an index, and the method of acquisition.

Cumulative Index Availability. Specifies if a cumulative index, or a table of contents issued as a cumulative index, is published.

USER'S GUIDE/SAMPLE LISTING

Appears in abbreviated form as "cum. index."

Book Reviews. If book reviews are published, "**Bk Rev**" will appear in the Serial Listing.

Book Review Quantity. Quantity of book reviews published "per year," unless otherwise specified. Quantity is preceded by "Qty:" and prints in parentheses.

Photos. If photographs are included within the serial, "**Photos**" will appear in the listing.

Advertising. If advertising is accepted in a serial, the abbreviation "**Ad Acc**" will appear in boldface.

Advertising Manager/Telephone. Lists the name and telephone number of the Advertising Manager, when available. Advertising Manager name is preceded by "**Adv Mgr:**" in boldface. Telephone is preceded by the prefix "**Tel**" in boldface.

Advertising Rates. Advertising rates for full and half-page ads. (B&W) designates rates for ads in black and white. (Color) designates ads printed in color.

Publication Size. The trim size of the serial or newspaper. Preceded by the abbreviation **Pub. Size**. Common publication sizes include Tabloid, Standard and Broadsheet.

Wire Services. Lists the news and photograph wire services affiliated with any given newspaper. These are preceded by a prefix of "**Wire Svcs**" in boldface. A chart of abbreviations used can be found on page xxxix.

Peer Reviewed. If a journal is peer reviewed or refereed, the abbreviation "**Pr Rev**" will appear.

Acid Free. If a publication is available on acid free paper, "**Acid Free**" will be seen in boldface.

Circulation. Annual circulation of publication, unless noted otherwise. Multiple circulation figures are separated by a comma.

Controlled Circulation. If circulation of a serial is controlled by the publisher, the abbreviation "ctrl" in parentheses follows the circulation figures. If no circulation figures are given, but the publisher has notified us that circulation is controlled, "ctrl circ" will appear.

Document Delivery. Indicates the availability of that serial for document delivery through the specified service(s). Refer to the chart on page xxxviii.

Additional Physical Forms Available. Additional media in which a serial is published, other than its original or conventional form.

Preceding Entry - Title/Preceding Entry - ISSN. The immediate predecessor(s) for the title, along with ISSN, appears in italics. Depending on indicators taken from the CONSER 780 field, a title's preceding entry will be preceded by one of the following: Continues, Continues in part, Supersedes, Supersedes in part, Formed by the union of... and..., Absorbed, Absorbed in part, or Separated from. If the title Continues in part, another title which is current, both titles will then be listed. Additional titles and ISSN are separated by semicolons and are preceded by one of the above, in boldface.

Succeeding Entry Title/Succeeding Entry - ISSN. The immediate successor(s) for the serial title (along with corresponding ISSN) will be listed. Multiple titles and ISSN are separated by semicolons, and preceded by a prefix of one of the following: Continued by, Continued in part by, Superseded by, Superseded in part by, Absorbed by, Absorbed in part by, Split into... and..., Merged with... to form..., Merged into, or Changed back to. In cases where CONSER did not give an ending date or a title was only continued "in part" both titles will be listed.

Descriptive Listing. Description of content submitted by publisher or by CONSER. Descriptions may have been edited for clarity. Description is preceded by "**Desc:**" in boldface.

Indexes/Abstracts. Specifies the publication(s) in which a serial has been indexed and/or abstracted. These are preceded by a prefix of "**Ind/Abst**" in boldface. Over 920 "active" Indexing/Abstracting services are used for the purposes of this Directory and can be found within the Serial Listings. See Indexes/Abstracts Abbreviations Table on page xliii.

Dates of Coverage. Dates of coverage are included for each index or abstract, when available. Dates are enclosed in parentheses and follow the abbreviation as used in the Serial Listing for each Indexing/Abstracting service. If no dates are provided by the Indexing/Abstracting service publisher, and we have been notified that a serial is no longer covered by a particular service, question marks will be used to notify the user that coverage of the particular serial by the service has been discontinued.

Full Text. Specifies if a journal is covered by an Indexing/Abstracting service in "Full Text." Full Text coverage indicates that all articles in the journal are indexed/abstracted completely, with any pertinent graphics, charts etc. For the purposes of this Directory, "Full Text" and "Full Image" are treated as if they were the same. These will be coded in the Serial Listing as [Full Txt.]. This notation will follow the dates of coverage in the Serial Listing.

Full/Selective Coverage — Full coverage indicates that journals are indexed/abstracted cover to cover. Selective coverage specifies serials in which the Indexing / Abstracting service selects only articles relevant to their publication. These will be coded in the Serial Listing as [Full Cov.] or [Select. Cov.]. This notation will follow the dates of coverage, when available, or will precede the Index or Abstract abbreviation when no dates of coverage are noted in the Serial Listing.

FILING RULES

A. General Rules— Filing is word for word with exceptions noted below. The order of characters applies the principle "nothing files before something," with numerals before letters, file A to Z.

1. Spaces, hyphens, diagonal slashes, and periods are filed as blanks:

> AAG-AAG
>
> AAG Directory / Association of American Geographers
>
> AAG Newsletter
>
> AAHA Directory of Membership

2. Variant spellings are filed as written:

> Ageing and Society
> Aging and Aging Disorders

B. Special Rules and Exceptions.

1. Modified letters and diacritics— Modified letters are written as their plain English alphabet equivalents.

2. Punctuation— Punctuation and non-alphabetic symbols (except those noted in A above) are ignored for filing purposes:

> "A" Magazine
>
> A Magyar Talalkozo Kronikaja
>
> A.N.A. Audiologia Protesica

3. Abbreviations— Filed exactly as written.

> Dr. McBirnie's Newsletter
>
> St. Louis Review
>
> U.N. Observer & International Report
>
> U.S. Census Report

4. Numerals— Filed character by character according to the numeric value of each string of characters.
Numerals precede letters:

> 33 Metal Producing
>
> 35/70; Journal of the Feature Film Industry
>
> 35MM Photography London England : 1983)
>
> 36 Cities : Real Estate Forecast and Review

5. Initials, initialisms, acronyms— Those in which each letter is separated by a space, dash, hyphen, period, or diagonal slash are regarded as a series of separate words. Those in which characters are separated by other marks or symbols, or which are not separated in any way, are regarded as single words:

> A. C. C. L. Union List of Serials
>
> A C E Q-A C G R Information
>
> A/C Flyer, The
>
> A.C.G.C.-Information : Bulletin d'Information de l'Association des Cadres et Gerants des Colleges du Quebec
>
> A C I S
>
> A. C. L. : Agence Cambodge Laos

6. Initial Articles— The following words are ignored when they appear at the beginning of an entry.

A	Eine	Hio	'n
al	Eit	Hin	Na
An	el-	Hinar	Nje
As	El	Hinir	Nji
Az	Els	Hinn	O
Bir	En	Ho	Os
Das	Et	Hoi	't
De	Ett	I	Ta
Dei	Gl'	Il	The
Den	Gli	Ka	To
Der	ha-	Ke	Um
Di	Hai	L'	Uma
Die	He	La	Un
Dos	he-	Las	Un'
Een	Heis	Le	Una
Eene	Hen	Les	Une
Egy	Hena	Lo	Uno
Ei	Henas	Los	Y
Ein	Het	Mia	Yr

Exceptions— Titles composed entirely of words on the list above are filed as written, as well as place names.
Hence:

> A Tavola
>
> A to Z of Who is Who in Australia's History, The
>
> A Traverso

7. Names and prefixes— A prefix that is part of the name of a person or place is treated as a separate word unless it is joined to the rest of the name:

> De Paul Law Review
>
> McCall's Book for Brides
>
> Van Buren Register

SUBJECT HEADINGS

The following section lists the subject headings used throughout the Directory. The list is arranged alphabetically, by subject, with the major subject (printing in boldface) followed by specific subheadings within the same category.

CROSS REFERENCES

This section combines all subject headings into one alphabetical list, regardless of whether it is a general, main subject or specific, subordinate subject. Cross references from a subject or topic not used in the Directory are made to that which is used. "See also" notes from one subject to a similar subject are included as well.

SUBJECT HEADINGS

Aeronautics, Astronautics 3
Agriculture 42
   Agricultural Equipment 158
   Crop Production and Soil 161
   Dairy Industry 191
   Feed Grain and Milling 199
   Livestock and Poultry 204
Animal Welfare 225
Anthropology 227
Antiques 248
Archaeology 253
Architecture 286
Arts, The 311
   Art 335
   Crafts and Decorative Arts 369
   Graphic Arts 376
   Performing Arts 383
Astrology 389
Astronomy 391
Beauty and Cosmetics 402
Bibliographies 406
Bicycles and Bicycling 427
Biographies 429
Biology 439
   Biochemistry 479
   Biophysics 494
   Botany 496
   Cytology and Histology 531
   Embryology 541
   Genetics 541
   Marine Biology 552
   Microbiology 558
   Microscopy 572
   Mycology 574
   Physiology 577
Birth Control 587
Boats and Boating 591
Building and Construction 597
   Carpentry and Woodwork 633
Business 636
   Accounting 735
   Advertising and Public Relations . . . 753
   Banking and Finance 768
   Chamber of Commerce 817
   Commerce 821
   General Management 858
   Investments 890
   Marketing 920
   Personnel Management 938
   Purchasing 948
   Retail 952
Chemistry 958
   Analytical Chemistry 1012
   Chemical Technology 1020
   Crystallography 1031
   Electrochemistry 1033
   Inorganic Chemistry 1035
   Organic Chemistry 1038
   Physical and Theoretical Chemistry . 1049
Children and Youth Interests 1059
Civil Defense 1072
Classical Studies 1073
Clothing Industry and Fashion 1081
College and School Publications . . . 1088
   Alumni 1096

Communication 1103
   Broadcasting 1125
   Postal Communications 1144
   Telecommunications 1148
Computers 1169
   Artificial Intelligence 1210
   Automation 1217
   Computer Assisted Instruction 1222
   Computer Crimes and Security 1225
   Computer Engineering 1227
   Computer Games 1230
   Computer Graphics and Design 1231
   Computer Industry and Industry
      Directories 1235
   Computer Music 1240
   Computer Networks 1240
   Computer Sales, Service
      and Supply 1244
   Computer Systems 1246
   Cybernetics 1250
   Data Base Management 1252
   Data Processing 1255
   Desktop Publishing 1263
   Hardware 1264
   Microcomputers, Personal
      Computers 1265
   Minicomputers 1273
   Online Computing and
      Information 1274
   Optical Storage, CD-ROM
      Applications 1276
   Programs and Programming 1277
   Simulation 1282
   Software 1283
   Word Processing 1292
Consumer Interests 1293
Copyright, Intellectual Property 1300
Dance 1310
Dentistry 1314
Drug Abuse and Alcoholism 1338
Earth Sciences 1351
   Geology 1364
   Geophysics 1402
   Hydrology 1412
   Meteorology 1419
   Mineralogy 1437
   Oceanography 1445
   Petrology 1458
Economics 1459
   Cooperatives 1541
   Economic History, Conditions 1544
   Economic Theory 1589
   Industry and Production 1596
   International Economics 1632
   Labor 1642
Education 1720
   Adult and Continuing Education 1799
   Early Childhood and
      Primary Education 1802
   Higher Education 1806
   Physical Education and
      Training 1854
   School Organization and
      Administration 1859
   Special Education and
      Rehabilitation 1874
   Teaching and Curriculum 1887
   Vocational Education 1909

Emigration and Immigration 1918
Encyclopedias and General
   Reference Books 1923
Energy 1930
Engineering 1963
   Chemical Engineering 2007
   Civil Engineering 2018
   Electricity, Electrical
      Engineering, Electronics 2034
   Hydraulic Engineering 2087
   Industrial Engineering
      and Design 2096
   Materials Engineering and
      Mechanics 2100
   Mechanical Engineering and
      Machinery 2108
   Mines and Mining Engineering 2132
   Nuclear Engineering 2153
Environmental Issues 2159
   Conservation and Natural
      Resources 2185
   Ecology 2210
   Pollution and Waste
      Management 2222
Ethics 2248
Ethnic Interests 2253
Family and Marriage 2276
Fire Prevention 2287
Fish and Fisheries 2293
Folklore 2318
Food and Food Industry 2325
   Beverage Industry 2363
Forestry 2373
   Lumber and Wood 2399
Funeral Service 2406
Gardening and Horticulture 2407
   Florist Trade 2434
Genealogy and Heraldry 2436
   Archives 2478
General Interest 2484
   General Interest-Africa 2497
   General Interest-Asia 2501
   General Interest-Australia
      and Oceania 2510
   General Interest-Central
      America 2511
   General Interest-Europe 2513
   General Interest-Middle East . . . .
   General Interest-North America 2526
   General Interest-South America . . . 2551
Geography 2553
   Cartography 2580
Gifts, Toys 2583
Glass and Ceramics 2585
Health and Personal Fitness 2595
Heating, Plumbing, and
   Refrigeration 2602
History (General) 2609
   History of Africa 2636
   History of Asia 2644
   History of Australia and
      Oceania 2668
   History of Europe 2671
   History of North, South, and
      Central America 2717
   History of the Middle East 2767

SUBJECT HEADINGS

Hobbies	2770
Numismatics	2779
Philately	2784
Home Economics	2788
Homosexuality	2793
Horses and Horsemanship	2796
Hotels/Motels	2803
Household Hardware and Appliances	2810
Housing and Urban Development	2812
Humanities	2841
Hypnosis	2857
Industrial Health and Safety	2858
Insurance	2872
Interior Design	2898
Home Furnishings	2904
International Assistance and Development	2907
Jewelry	2913
Clocks and Watches	2916
Journalism	2917
Law	2926
Banking Law	3084
Civil Law	3088
Constitutional Law	3091
Corporate Law	3094
Criminal Law	3104
Environmental Law	3109
Estate Planning	3117
Family Law	3119
International Law	3122
Judicial Systems	3138
Labor Law	3143
Law Enforcement and Criminology	3156
Legal Aid	3179
Maritime Law	3180
Military Law	3182
Leather and Fur Industry	3183
Library and Information Sciences	3186
Linguistics	3260
Literary and Political Reviews	3337
Literature	3357
Poetry	3459
Manufacturing	3475
Mathematics	3490
Medical Science and Technology	3543
Allergy and Immunology	3662
Anatomy	3678
Anesthesiology	3680
Biotechnology	3685
Cardiology	3697
Communicable Diseases	3711
Dermatology	3717
Emergency Medicine	3723
Endocrinology	3726
Epidemiology	3733
Family Practice	3736
Forensic Medicine, Medical Jurisprudence	3739
Gastroenterology	3743
Geriatrics	3748
Gynecology and Obstetrics	3755
Hematology	3769
Homeopathy	3774
Hospital Administration and Medical Centers	3775
Internal Medicine	3794
Musculoskeletal System	3802
Neoplasma, Neoplastic	3808
Neurology	3825
Nuclear Medicine	3847
Nursing	3849
Ophthalmology	3871
Orthopedics	3880
Otorhinolaryngology	3885
Pathology	3891
Pediatrics	3899
Physicians and Medical Personnel	3912
Podiatry	3917
Psychiatry	3918
Radiology	3938
Respiratory System	3947
Sports Medicine	3953
Surgery	3957
Toxicology	3978
Tropical Medicine	3985
Urology and Nephrology	3987
Men's Interests	3994
Metals and Metallurgy	3996
Welding	4026
Metrology and Standardization	4029
Military and Defense	4033
Motion Picture	4062
Motorcycles	4080
Museums and Galleries	4083
Music	4098
Natural History	4161
Naval Science, Navigation	4174
New Age Publications	4185
Newspapers	5625
Nutrition and Dietetics	4186
Occupations and Careers	4201
Office Equipment and Services	4210
Optometry	4214
Packaging	4217
Paints and Painting	4222
Paleontology	4226
Paper and Pulp Industry	4232
Parapsychology and Occultism	4240
Pest Control	4243
Petroleum and Natural Gas	4248
Pets	4285
Pharmacy and Pharmacology	4288
Philanthropy	4334
Philosophy	4339
Photography and Video	4366
Physical Therapy	4378
Physically Impaired	4382
Physics	4395
Analytic and Experimental Mechanics	4427
Heat	4430
Light, Optics, Radiation	4432
Magnetism	4443
Nuclear Physics	4445
Sound	4451
Plastics	4453
Political Science	4461
Civil Rights	4503
International Relations	4514
Socialism, Communism, Anarchism, Utopianism	4539
Population Studies	4549
Printing Industry	4563
Psychology	4570
Public Administration	4623
Civil Service	4701
Parks and Recreation	4705
Public Finance and Taxation	4708
Public Utilities	4759
Public Health and Safety	4763
Publishing	4811
Books and Bookmaking	4822
Real Estate	4833
Recreation, Leisure	4848
Games and Amusements	4856
Outdoor Life	4868
Sports	4881
Religion and Theology	4931
Bible	5013
Buddhism	5020
Catholicism	5022
Eastern Christian Churches	5039
Hinduism	5040
Islam, Bahaism, Theosophy	5041
Judaism	5045
Protestantism	5054
Restaurants	5070
Romance and Adventure	5073
Rubber	5075
Science and Technology	5078
Security Systems and Alarms	5176
Senior Citizens	5177
Sewing and Needlework	5182
Sexual Life	5186
Social Sciences	5189
Societies and Clubs	5228
Sociology	5237
Manners and Customs	5267
Social Services and Welfare	5269
Sound Recordings and Systems	5315
Statistics	5320
Textiles	5347
Theater	5361
Tobacco	5372
Transportation	5375
Automobiles	5403
Railroads	5429
Roads and Traffic	5438
Ships and Shipping	5447
Travel and Tourism	5458
Veterinary Sciences	5501
Water Resources	5528
Women's Interests	5550
Zoology	5572
Entomology	5604
Ornithology	5614

SUBJECT HEADINGS

The 117 subject headings listed below all contain a sub-heading for "Abstracting, Bibliographies, and Statistics." This sub-heading, which follows the major heading in the Serial Listing, contains serials which abstract and/or index publications in the applicable subject area. Bibliographies and statistical publications pertaining to each subject are also included.

Subject	Page
Aeronautics, Astronautics	3
Agriculture	42
Anthropology	227
Antiques	248
Archaeology	253
Architecture	286
Arts, The	311
Astronomy	391
Bicycles and Bicycling	427
Biographies	429
Biology	439
Birth Control	587
Boats and Boating	591
Building and Construction	597
Business	636
Chemistry	958
Children and Youth Interests	1059
Classical Studies	1073
Clothing Industry and Fashion	1081
Communication	1103
Computers	1169
Consumer Interests	1293
Copyright, Intellectual Property	1300
Dance	1310
Dentistry	1314
Drug Abuse and Alcoholism	1338
Earth Sciences	1351
Economics	1459
Education	1720
Encyclopedias and General Reference Books	1923
Energy	1930
Engineering	1963
Environmental Issues	2159
Ethnic Interests	2253
Family and Marriage	2276
Fire Prevention	2287
Fish and Fisheries	2293
Folklore	2318
Food and Food Industry	2325
Forestry	2373
Gardening and Horticulture	2407
Genealogy and Heraldry	2436
General Interest	2484
Geography	2553
Glass and Ceramics	2585
Health and Personal Fitness	2595
History (General)	2609
Hobbies	2770
Homosexuality	2793
Horses and Horsemanship	2796
Hotels/Motels	2803
Household Hardware and Appliances	2810
Housing and Urban Development	2812
Humanities	2841
Industrial Health and Safety	2858
Insurance	2872
International Assistance and Development	2907
Journalism	2917
Law	2926
Library and Information Sciences	3186
Linguistics	3260
Literary and Political Reviews	3337
Literature	3357
Manufacturing	3475
Mathematics	3490
Medical Science and Technology	3543
Metals and Metallurgy	3996
Metrology and Standardization	4029
Military and Defense	4033
Motion Picture	4062
Motorcycles	4080
Museums and Galleries	4083
Music	4098
Natural History	4161
Naval Science, Navigation	4174
New Age Publications	4185
Newspapers	5625
Nutrition and Dietetics	4186
Occupations and Careers	4201
Packaging	4217
Paints and Painting	4222
Paleontology	4226
Paper and Pulp Industry	4232
Parapsychology and Occultism	4240
Pest Control	4243
Petroleum and Natural Gas	4248
Pharmacy and Pharmacology	4288
Philosophy	4339
Photography and Video	4366
Physically Impaired	4382
Physics	4395
Plastics	4453
Political Science	4461
Population Studies	4549
Printing Industry	4563
Psychology	4570
Public Administration	4623
Public Health and Safety	4763
Publishing	4811
Real Estate	4833
Recreation, Leisure	4848
Religion and Theology	4931
Restaurants	5070
Rubber	5075
Science and Technology	5078
Social Sciences	5189
Sociology	5237
Sound Recordings and Systems	5315
Textiles	5347
Theater	5361
Tobacco	5372
Transportation	5375
Travel and Tourism	5458
Veterinary Sciences	5501
Water Resources	5528
Women's Interests	5550
Zoology	5572

SUBJECT CROSS REFERENCES

Abortion –See **Medical Science and Technology -- Gynecology and Obstetrics** pg 3755

Abrasives –See **Metals and Metallurgy** pg 3996

Accessories –See **Clothing Industry and Fashion** pg 1081

Accident Prevention –See **Industrial Health and Safety** pg 2858; **Public Health and Safety** pg 4763; **Transportation -- Roads and Traffic** pg 5438

Accounting –pg 735; see also Law pg 2926; Public Administration -- Public Finance and Taxation pg 4708

Acoustics –See **Physics -- Sound** pg 4451

Acquired Immune Deficiency Syndrome (AIDS) –See **Medical Science and Technology -- Allergy and Immunology** pg 3662; see also Medical Science and Technology -- Communicable Diseases pg 3711; Public Health and Safety pg 4763

Acting –See **Motion Picture** pg 4062; **The Arts -- Performing Arts** pg 383; **Theater** pg 5361

Actuarial Science –See **Insurance** pg 2872

Acupuncture –See **Medical Science and Technology** pg 3543

Addictions –See **Drug Abuse and Alcoholism** pg 1338; see also Psychology pg 4570

Adhesives –See **Chemistry -- Physical and Theoretical Chemistry** pg 1049; see also Chemistry -- Chemical Technology pg 1020; Engineering -- Chemical Engineering pg 2007; Engineering -- Materials Engineering and Mechanics pg 2100; Metals and Metallurgy -- Welding pg 4026; Paints and Painting pg 4222; Plastics pg 4453

Administrative Law –See **Law -- Constitutional Law** pg 3091

Adoption –See **Sociology -- Social Services and Welfare** pg 5269

Adult and Continuing Education –pg 1799

Adventure –See **Romance and Adventure** pg 5073

Advertising –See **Business -- Advertising and Public Relations** pg 753

Advertising and Public Relations –pg 753

Aerobics –See **Health and Personal Fitness** pg 2595

Aerodynamics –See **Aeronautics, Astronautics** pg 3

Aeronautics, Astronautics –pg 3; see also Military and Defense pg 4033; Transportation pg 5375

Aerospace Medicine –See **Aeronautics, Astronautics** pg 3; **Medical Science and Technology** pg 3543

Aesthetics –See **The Arts -- Art** pg 335; see also Philosophy pg 4339

Africa –See **General Interest -- General Interest-Africa** pg 2497; **History(General) -- History of Africa** pg 2636

African Studies –See **History(General) -- History of Africa** pg 2636; **Literature** pg 3357

Aging –See **Medical Science and Technology -- Geriatrics** pg 3748; **Sociology -- Social Services and Welfare** pg 5269; see also Senior Citizens pg 5177

Agricultural Aviation –See **Aeronautics, Astronautics** pg 3; see also Agriculture pg 42

Agricultural Chemistry –See **Agriculture** pg 42; see also Chemistry pg 958

Agricultural Economics –See **Agriculture** pg 42; see also Economics pg 1459

Agricultural Engineering –See **Agriculture** pg 42; see also Engineering pg 1963

Agricultural Equipment –pg 157

Agricultural Marketing –See **Agriculture** pg 42; see also Business -- Marketing pg 920

Agricultural Meteorology –See **Earth Sciences -- Meteorology** pg 1419; see also Agriculture pg 42

Agriculture –pg 42; see also Food and Food Industry pg 2325; Gardening and Horticulture pg 2407

Agronomy –See **Agriculture** pg 42; see also Agriculture -- Crop Production and Soil pg 161

AIDS –See **Medical Science and Technology -- Allergy and Immunology** pg 3662; see also Medical Science and Technology -- Communicable Diseases pg 3711; Public Health and Safety pg 4763

Air Cargo –See **Transportation** pg 5375; see also Aeronautics, Astronautics pg 3

Air Conditioning –See **Heating, Plumbing, and Refrigeration** pg 2810

Air Force –See **Aeronautics, Astronautics** pg 3; **Military and Defense** pg 4033

Air Pollution –See **Environmental Issues -- Pollution and Waste Management** pg 2222

Air Travel –See **Aeronautics, Astronautics** pg 3; **Travel and Tourism** pg 5458

Airplanes –See **Aeronautics, Astronautics** pg 3

Airports –See **Aeronautics, Astronautics** pg 3

Alarm/Security Systems –See **Engineering -- Electricity, Electrical Engineering, Electronics** pg 2034

Alcoholic Beverages –See **Food and Food Industry -- Beverage Industry** pg 2363

Alcoholism –See **Drug Abuse and Alcoholism** pg 1338

Alimony –See **Law -- Family Law** pg 3119

Allergy and Immunology –pg 3662

Almanacs –See **Encyclopedias and General Reference Books** pg 1923

Alumni –pg 1096

Amateur Radio –See **Communication -- Broadcasting** pg 1125; see also Communication pg 1103

American Studies –See **History(General) -- History of North, South, and Central America** pg 2717

Amusements –See **Recreation, Leisure -- Games and Amusements** pg 4856

Analytic and Experimental Mechanics –pg 4427

Analytical Chemistry –pg 1012

Anarchism –See **Political Science -- Socialism, Communism, Anarchism, Utopianism** pg 4539

Anatomy –See **Medical Science and Technology -- Anatomy** pg 3543; see also Biology -- Embryology pg 541; Medical Science and Technology -- Pathology pg 3891

Anesthesia –See **Medical Science and Technology -- Anesthesiology** pg 3680; see also Medical Science and Technology -- Surgery pg 3957; Pharmacy and Pharmacology pg 4288

Anesthesiology –pg 3680; see also Medical Science and Technology -- Surgery pg 3957

Angiology –See **Medical Science and Technology -- Cardiology** pg 3697

Anglo-Saxon Studies –See **History(General) -- History of Europe** pg 2671; **Literature** pg 3357

Animal Husbandry –See **Agriculture** pg 42; **Veterinary Sciences** pg 5501

Animal Science –See **Veterinary Sciences** pg 5501; see also Zoology pg 5572

SUBJECT CROSS REFERENCES

Animal Welfare –pg 225; see also Ethics pg 2248

Animals –See **Horses and Horsemanship** pg 2796; **Pets** pg 4285; see also Veterinary Sciences pg 5501; Zoology pg 5572

Anthropology –pg 227; see also Archaeology pg 253; Paleontology pg 4226; Sociology pg 5237

Antibiotics –See **Medical Science and Technology** pg 3543; **Pharmacy and Pharmacology** pg 4288; see also Chemistry pg 958

Antiques –pg 248; see also Hobbies pg 2770; Museums and Galleries pg 4083

Antitrust Law –See **Law -- Corporate Law** pg 3094

Anxiety –See **Medical Science and Technology -- Psychiatry** pg 3918; see also Psychology pg 4570

Apartments –See **Housing and Urban Development** pg 2812

Apparel –See **Clothing Industry and Fashion** pg 1081; see also Business -- Retail pg 952; Textiles pg 5347

Appliances –See **Household Hardware and Appliances** pg 2810

Applied Mechanics –See **Engineering -- Materials Engineering and Mechanics** pg 2100; **Physics -- Analytic and Experimental Mechanics** pg 4427; see also Engineering -- Mechanical Engineering and Machinery pg 2108

Apprenticeship –See **Economics -- Labor** pg 1642

Aquaculture –See **Fish and Fisheries** pg 2293; see also Biology pg 439; Biology -- Marine Biology pg 552

Archaeology –pg 253; see also Anthropology pg 227; History(General) pg 2609; Paleontology pg 4226

Archery –See **Recreation, Leisure -- Sports** pg 4881

Architecture –pg 286; see also Building and Construction pg 597; Engineering pg 1963; Interior Design pg 2898

Archives –pg 2478; see also History(General) pg 2609; Library and Information Sciences pg 3186

Army –See **Military and Defense** pg 4033

Aromatherapy –See **Beauty and Cosmetics** pg 402

Art –pg 335; see also Humanities pg 2841

Art Galleries –See **Museums and Galleries** pg 4083; see also The Arts -- Art pg 335

Art History –See **The Arts -- Art** pg 335; see also Humanities pg 2841; Museums and Galleries pg 4083; The Arts pg 311

Arthritis –See **Medical Science and Technology -- Musculoskeletal System** pg 3802

Artificial Intelligence –pg 1210; see also Computers -- Automation pg 1217; Science and Technology pg 5078

Arts and Sciences –See **The Arts** pg 311; see also Humanities pg 2841; Social Sciences pg

Asbestos –See **Building and Construction** pg 597; **Engineering -- Mines and Mining Engineering** pg 2132; see also Public Health and Safety pg 4763

Asia –See **General Interest -- General Interest-Asia** pg 2501; **History(General) -- History of Asia** pg 2644

Asian Studies –See **History(General) -- History of Asia** pg 2644; **Literature** pg 3357

Associations –See **Societies and Clubs** pg 5228

Asthma –See **Medical Science and Technology -- Respiratory System** pg 3947

Astrology –pg 389

Astronautics –See **Aeronautics, Astronautics** pg 3

Astronomy –pg 391

Atheism –See **Philosophy** pg 4339

Athletic Clubs –See **Health and Personal Fitness** pg 2595; see also Recreation, Leisure -- Sports pg 4881

Athletics –See **Recreation, Leisure -- Sports** pg 4881; see also Health and Personal Fitness pg 2595

Atlas –See **Geography** pg 2553

Atmospheric Science –See **Earth Sciences -- Meteorology** pg 1419; see also Science and Technology pg 5078

Atomic Energy –See **Energy** pg 1930; **Engineering -- Nuclear Engineering** pg 2153

Attorney General –See **Law -- Judicial Systems** pg 3138

Audio-Visual Education –See **Education -- Teaching and Curriculum** pg 1887

Audiology –See **Medical Science and Technology -- Otorhinolaryngology** pg 3885

Auditing –See **Business -- Accounting** pg 735; see also Public Administration -- Public Finance and Taxation** pg 4708

Audubon Society –See **Environmental Issues -- Conservation and Natural Resources** pg 2185; see also Natural History pg 4161

Australia –See **General Interest -- General Interest-Australia and Oceania** pg 2510; **History(General) -- History of Australia and Oceania** pg 2668

Authors –See **Biographies** pg 429; **Literature** pg 3357; see also Literature -- Poetry pg 3459; Publishing pg 4811

Automation –pg 1217

Automobile Racing –See **Recreation, Leisure -- Sports** pg 4881

Automobiles –pg 5403

Aviation –See **Aeronautics, Astronautics** pg 3

Bacteriology –See **Biology** pg 439; **Biology -- Microbiology** pg 558

Badminton –See **Recreation, Leisure -- Sports** pg 4881

Bahaism –See **Religion and Theology -- Islam, Bahaism, Theosophy** pg 5041

Bakers and Bakeries –See **Food and Food Industry** pg 2325

Balkan Studies –See **History(General) -- History of Europe** pg 2671

Banking –See **Business -- Banking and Finance** pg 768

Banking and Finance –pg 768; see also Business -- Cooperatives pg 1541; Business -- Investments pg 890; Economics pg 1459; Public Administration -- Public Finance pg 4708

Banking Law –pg 3084; see also Business -- Banking and Finance pg 768; Law -- Corporate Law pg 3094

Bankruptcy –See **Law -- Banking Law** pg 3084; see also Business -- Banking and Finance pg 768

Baptist –See **Religion and Theology -- Protestantism** pg 5054

Baseball –See **Recreation, Leisure -- Sports** pg 4881

Baseball Cards –See **Hobbies** pg 2770; **Recreation, Leisure -- Sports** pg 4881

Beauty and Cosmetics –pg 402

Beekeeping –See **Agriculture** pg 42

Behavior Therapy –See **Psychology** pg 4570

Behavioral Science –See **Medical Science and Technology -- Psychiatry** pg 3918; **Psychology** pg 4570; see also Sociology pg 5237

SUBJECT CROSS REFERENCES

Belizean Studies –See **History(General) -- History of North, South, and Central America** pg 2717

Beverage Industry –pg 2363

Bible –pg 5013

Bibliographies –pg 406; see also Library and Information Sciences pg 3186

Bicycles and Bicycling –pg 427

Bilingual –See **Education -- Special Education and Rehabilitation** pg 1874; **Linguistics** pg 3260; see also Education pg 1720

Biochemistry –pg 479

Bioengineering –See **Medical Science and Technology -- Biotechnology** pg 3685

Biofeedback –See **Psychology** pg 4570; see also Biology -- Physiology pg 577; Medical Science and Technology pg 3543

Biographies –pg 429

Biology –pg 439; see also Medical Science and Technology pg 3543; Zoology pg 5572

Biomechanics –See **Medical Science and Technology -- Biotechnology** pg 3685

Biomedical Engineering –See **Medical Science and Technology -- Biotechnology** pg 3685

Biomedicine –See **Medical Science and Technology -- Biotechnology** pg 3685

Biophysics –pg 494

Biotechnology –pg 3685

Birds –See **Zoology -- Ornithology** pg 5614; see also Environmental Issues -- Conservation and Natural Resources pg 2185; Natural History pg 4161

Birth Control –pg 587; see also Population Studies pg 4549

Blind –See **Physically Impaired** pg 4382; see also Education -- Special Education and Rehabilitation pg 1874; Medical Science and Technology -- Ophthalmology pg 3871; Sociology -- Social Services and Welfare pg 5269

Blood –See **Medical Science and Technology -- Hematology** pg 3769

Blood Groups –See **Medical Science and Technology -- Hematology** pg 3769

Blood Preservation –See **Medical Science and Technology -- Hematology** pg 3769

Blood Transfusions –See **Medical Science and Technology -- Hematology** pg 3769; see also Medical Science and Technology pg 3543; Medical Science and Technology -- Internal Medicine pg 3794; Medical Science and Technology -- Surgery pg 3957

Boats and Boating –pg 591

Bodybuilding –See **Health and Personal Fitness** pg 2595; see also Recreation, Leisure -- Sports pg 4881

Books and Bookmaking –pg 4822

Booksellers –See **Publishing -- Books and Bookmaking** pg 4822; see also Publishing pg 4811

Botany –pg 496; see also Agriculture -- Crop Production and Soil pg 161; Gardening and Horticulture pg 2407

Bowling –See **Recreation, Leisure -- Sports** pg 4881

Boxing –See **Recreation, Leisure -- Sports** pg 4881

Brahmanism –See **Hinduism** pg 5040

Braille –See **Physically Impaired** pg 4382; see also Education -- Special Education and Rehabilitation pg 1874

Breast-feeding –See **Medical Science and Technology -- Gynecology and Obstetrics** pg 3755; see also Medical Science and Technology -- Pediatrics pg 3899

Breweries –See **Food and Food Industry -- Beverage Industry** pg 2363

Bricks –See **Building and Construction** pg 597

Bride –See **Family and Marriage** pg 2276

Bridges –See **Transportation** pg 5375; see also Engineering -- Civil Engineering pg 2018; Transportation -- Roads and Traffic pg 5438

British Studies –See **History(General) -- History of Europe** pg 2671; **Literature** pg 3357

Broadcasting –pg 1125

Buddhism –pg 5020

Budget –See **Public Administration -- Public Finance and Taxation** pg 4708; see also Business -- Banking and Finance pg 768

Building and Construction –pg 597; see also Engineering -- Civil Engineering pg 2018; Housing and Urban Development pg 2812

Burns –See **Medical Science and Technology** pg 3543

Buses –See **Transportation** pg 5375

Business –pg 636

Business Education –See **Business** pg 636; see also Education pg 1720

Business Law –See **Business** pg 636; **Law -- Corporate Law** pg 3094; see also Law -- International Law pg 3122

Buying –See **Business -- Purchasing** pg 948

Cable Television –See **Communication -- Broadcasting** pg 1125

CAD/CAM –See **Computers -- Computer Graphics and Design** pg 1231; see also Computers -- Computer Engineering pg 1227

Calligraphy –See **The Arts -- Graphic Arts** pg 376

Cameras –See **Photography and Video** pg 4366; see also Hobbies pg 2770; Motion Picture pg 4062

Camping –See **Recreation, Leisure -- Outdoor Life** pg 4868

Canadian Studies –See **History(General) -- History of North, South, and Central America** pg 2717

Cancer –See **Medical Science and Technology -- Neoplasma, Neoplastic** pg 3808

Candy –See **Food and Food Industry** pg 2325

Canning and Preserving –See **Food and Food Industry** pg 2325; see also Gardening and Horticulture pg 2407

Canoeing –See **Boats and Boating** pg 591

Canon Law –See **Religion and Theology** pg 4931

Cardiology –pg 3697; see also Medical Science and Technology -- Hematology pg 3769

Careers –See **Occupations and Careers** pg 4201

Cargo –See **Transportation** pg 5375

Caribbean Studies –See **History(General) -- History of North, South, and Central America** pg 2717

Carpentry and Woodwork –pg 633; see also Hobbies pg 2770; Interior Design -- Home Furnishings pg 2904

Carpet, Rugs –See **Interior Design -- Home Furnishings** pg 2904

Cartography –pg 2580

Cartoons –See **The Arts -- Graphic Arts** pg 376; see also Recreation, Leisure -- Games and Amusements pg 4856

Catalogues –See **Bibliographies** pg 406

Catalysis –See **Chemistry -- Physical and Theoretical Chemistry** pg 1049

SUBJECT CROSS REFERENCES

Catalysts –See **Chemistry -- Physical and Theoretical Chemistry** pg 1049

Catering –See **Food and Food Industry** pg 2325; **Hotels/Motels** pg 2803; **Restaurants** pg 5070

Catholicism –pg 5022

Cattle –See **Agriculture -- Livestock and Poultry** pg 204; see also Agriculture pg 42; Agriculture -- Dairy Industry pg 191; Veterinary Sciences pg 5501

Caves –See **Earth Sciences -- Geophysics** pg 1402; see also Earth Sciences -- Geology pg 1364

CD-ROM –See **Computers -- Optical Storage, CD-ROM Applications** pg 1276

Celebrity Interests –See **General Interest** pg 2484; see also Motion Picture pg 4062

Celtic Studies –See **History(General) -- History of Europe** pg 2671; **Literature** pg 3357

Cement –See **Building and Construction** pg 597; **Chemistry -- Chemical Technology** pg 1020; see also Engineering -- Civil Engineering pg 2018; Industry and Production pg 1596

Cemeteries –See **Funeral Service** pg 2406

Central America –See **General Interest -- General Interest-Central America** pg 2511; **History(General) -- History of North, South, and Central America** pg 2717

Ceramics –See **Glass and Ceramics** pg 2585

Cereals –See **Agriculture -- Feed Grain and Milling** pg 199; see also Food and Food Industry pg 2325

Cerebral Palsy –See **Medical Science and Technology -- Neurology** pg 3825

Chamber of Commerce –pg 817

Charities –See **Philanthropy** pg 4334; see also Sociology -- Social Services and Welfare pg 5269

Chemical Engineering –pg 2007; see also Chemistry pg 958; Chemistry -- Chemical Technology pg 1020

Chemical Technology –pg 1020; see also Chemistry pg 958; Engineering -- Chemical Engineering pg 2007; Medical Science and Technology -- Biotechnology pg 3685

Chemistry –pg 958; see also Engineering -- Chemical Engineering pg 2007

Chemotherapy –See **Medical Science and Technology -- Neoplasma, Neoplastic** pg 3808; see also Pharmacy and Pharmacology pg 4288

Chess –See **Recreation, Leisure -- Games and Amusements** pg 4856

Child Development –See **Education -- Early Childhood and Primary Education** pg 1802

Child Psychology –See **Psychology** pg 4570

Child Welfare –See **Sociology -- Social Services and Welfare** pg 5269

Children and Youth Interests –pg 1059

China, Tableware –See **Glass and Ceramics** pg 2585; see also Gifts, Toys pg 2583

Chinese Studies –See **History(General) -- History of Asia** pg 2644; **Literature** pg 3357

Chiropractor –See **Medical Science and Technology -- Musculoskeletal System** pg 3802; **Physical Therapy** pg 4378

Christianity –See **Religion and Theology** pg 4931

Chromatography –See **Chemistry -- Analytical Chemistry** pg 1012; see also Chemistry pg 958

Churches –See **Religion and Theology** pg 4931; see also Religion and Theology -- Eastern Christian Churches pg 5039; Religion and Theology -- Protestantism pg 5054

Cinema –See **Motion Picture** pg 4062

Cinematography –See **Photography and Video** pg 4366; see also Motion Picture pg 4062

Citrus Industry –See **Agriculture -- Crop Production and Soil** pg 161; **Food and Food Industry** pg 2325; **Gardening and Horticulture** pg 2407

City Directory –See **Geography** pg 2553

City Planning –See **Housing and Urban Development** pg 2812

Civil Defense –pg 1072

Civil Engineering –pg 2018

Civil Law –pg 3088

Civil Rights –pg 4503

Civil Service –pg 4701; see also Public Administration pg 4623

Classical Studies –pg 1073; see also Archaeology pg 253; History(General) pg 2609; Linguistics pg 3260; Literature pg 3357

Climatology –See **Earth Sciences -- Meteorology** pg 1419

Clinical Medicine –See **Medical Science and Technology** pg 3543; **Medical Science and Technology** pg 3543

Clocks –See **Jewelry -- Clocks and Watches** pg 2916

Clocks and Watches –pg 2916

Clothing Industry and Fashion –pg 1081; see also Leather and Fur Industry pg 3183; Textiles pg 5347

Clubs –See **Societies and Clubs** pg 5228

Coaching –See **Recreation, Leisure -- Sports** pg 4881

Coal –See **Earth Science -- Mineralogy** pg 1437; see also Energy pg 1930; Engineering -- Mines and Mining Engineering pg 2132

Coast Guard –See **Naval Science, Navigation** pg 4174

Coins –See **Hobbies -- Numismatics** pg 2779

Collectors and Collecting –See **Antiques** pg 248; see also Hobbies pg 2770

College and School Publications –pg 1088; see also Education -- Higher Education pg 1806

Colleges and Universities –See **Education -- Higher Education** pg 1806; see also College and School Publications pg 1088

Combustion –See **Chemistry -- Physical and Theoretical Chemistry** pg 1049; **Energy** pg 1930; **Engineering** pg 1963

Comics –See **Recreation, Leisure -- Games and Amusements** pg 4856

Commerce –pg 821

Commercial Art –See **The Arts -- Graphic Arts** pg 376

Commercial Law –See **Law -- Corporate Law** pg 3094

Commodities –See **Business -- Commerce** pg 821

Common Law –See **Law -- Civil Law** pg 3088

Communicable Diseases –pg 3711; See also **Medical Science and Technology -- Epidemiology** pg 3733; Public Health and Safety pg 248

Communication –pg 1103

Communism –See **Political Science -- Socialism, Communism, Anarchism, Utopianism** pg 4539

Community Affairs –See **Public Administration** pg 4623

SUBJECT CROSS REFERENCES

Community Development –See **Housing and Urban Development** pg 2812

Compact Disc –See **Computers -- Optical Storage, CD-ROM Applications** pg 1276

Company Law –See **Law -- Corporate Law** pg 3094

Comparative Law –See **Law -- International Law** pg 3122

Composite Materials –See **Engineering -- Materials Engineering and Mechanics** pg 2100

Computer Architecture –See **Computers -- Computer Graphics and Design** pg 1231

Computer Assisted Instruction –pg 1222; see also Education -- Teaching and Curriculum pg 1887

Computer Crimes –See **Computers -- Computer Crimes and Security** pg 1225

Computer Crimes and Security –pg 1225

Computer Directories –See **Computers -- Computer Industry and Industry Directories** pg 1235

Computer Engineering –pg 1227

Computer Games – pg 1230; see also Recreation, Leisure -- Games and Amusements pg 4856

Computer Graphics and Design –pg 1231

Computer Industry –See **Computers -- Computer Industry and Industry Directories** pg 1235

Computer Industry and Industry Directories –pg 1235; see also Computers -- Computer Sales, Service and Supply pg 1244

Computer Music –pg 1240; see also Music pg 4098

Computer Networks –pg 1240

Computer Products –See **Computers -- Computer Sales, Service and Supply** pg 1244

Computer Sales, Service and Supply –pg 1244

Computer Science –See **Computers** pg 1169

Computer Simulation –See **Computers -- Simulation** pg 1282

Computer Systems –pg 1246

Computers –pg 1169

Confectioners –See **Food and Food Industry** pg 2325

Congress –See **Public Administration** pg 4623

Conservation and Natural Resources –pg 2185; see also Environmental Issues -- Ecology pg 2210; Natural History pg 4161; Public Administration -- Parks and Recreation pg 4705; Water Resources pg 5528

Constitutional Law –pg 3091

Construction –See **Building and Construction** pg 597; see also Engineering -- Civil Engineering pg 2018

Consumer Interests –pg 1293; see also Economics pg 1459

Consumer Protection –See **Consumer Interests** pg 1293; see also Law -- Corporate Law pg 3094

Contact Lenses –See **Medical Science and Technology -- Ophthalmology** pg 3871; **Optometry** pg 4214

Continuing Education –See **Education -- Adult and Continuing Education** pg 1799

Contraception –See **Birth Control** pg 587

Contractors –See **Building and Construction** pg 597; **Engineering -- Civil Engineering** pg 2018; see also Architecture pg 286

Conventions –See **Business -- Advertising and Public Relations** pg 753; **Science and Technology** pg 5078

Cookbooks, Cooking –See **Home Economics** pg 2788

Cooperatives –pg 1541; see also Agriculture pg 42; Business -- Banking and Finance pg 768

Copyright, Intellectual Property –pg 1300

Corporate Law –pg 3094

Corporation Law –See **Law -- Corporate Law** pg 3094

Corrosion –See **Engineering -- Chemical Engineering** pg 2007; see also Metals and Metallurgy pg 3996

Cosmetic Surgery –See **Medical Science and Technology -- Surgery** pg 3957

Cosmetics –See **Beauty and Cosmetics** pg 402

Cotton –See **Agriculture -- Crop Production and Soil** pg 161; see also Textiles pg 5347

Counseling –See **Psychology** pg 4570; see also Family and Marriage pg 2276; Religion and Theology pg 4931; Sociology -- Social Services and Welfare pg 5269

Court Rules –See **Law -- Judicial Systems** pg 3138

Courts –See **Law -- Judicial Systems** pg 3138

Crafts and Decorative Arts –pg 369; see also Gifts, Toys pg 2583; Glass and Ceramics pg 2585; Hobbies pg 2770; Sewing and Needlework pg 5182

Credit Unions –See **Business -- Banking and Finance** pg 768

Crime Prevention –See **Law -- Law Enforcement and Criminology** pg 3156

Crime Statistics –See **Law -- Law Enforcement and Criminology** pg 3156; see also Statistics pg 5320

Criminal Justice –See **Law -- Law Enforcement and Criminology** pg 3156; see also Law -- Criminal Law pg 3104

Criminal Law –pg 3104; see also Law -- Law Enforcement and Criminology pg 3156

Criminal Procedure –See **Law -- Judicial Systems** pg 3138; **Law -- Law Enforcement and Criminology** pg 3156; see also Law -- Criminal Law pg 3104

Criminology –See **Law -- Law Enforcement and Criminology** pg 3156

Croatian Studies –See **History(General) -- History of Europe** pg 2671

Crop Production and Soil –pg 161

Crystallography –pg 1031

Currency –See **Business -- Banking and Finance** pg 768; **Business -- Investments** pg 890; see also Economics -- International Economics pg 1632

Curriculum –See **Education -- Teaching and Curriculum** pg 1887

Customs –See **Sociology -- Manners and Customs** pg 5267

Customs and Excise –See **Public Administration -- Public Finance and Taxation** pg 4708; see also Law pg 2926

Cybernetics –pg 1250

Cystic Fibrosis –See **Medical Science and Technology -- Musculoskeletal System** pg 3802

Cytology –See **Biology -- Cytology and Histology** pg 531

Cytology and Histology –pg 531

Dairy Industry –pg 191

Dance –pg 1310; see also The Arts -- Performing Arts pg 383

Data Base Management –pg 1252

Data Processing –pg 1255

Data Protection –See **Computers -- Computer Crimes and Security** pg 1225

Daycare –See **Sociology -- Social Services and Welfare** pg 5269

SUBJECT CROSS REFERENCES

Deaf –See **Physically Impaired** pg 4382; see also Medical Science and Technology -- Otorhinolaryngology pg 3885

Decorative Arts –See **The Arts -- Crafts and Decorative Arts** pg 369

Defense –See **Military and Defense** pg 4033; see also Civil Defense pg 1072

Demography –See **Population Studies** pg 4549; see also Statistics pg 5320

Dentistry –pg 1314

Department Stores –See **Business -- Retail** pg 952; see also Business -- Marketing pg 920

Dermatology –pg 3717

Desktop Publishing –pg 1263; see also Publishing pg 4811

Diabetes –See **Endocrinology** pg 3726

Diagnostic Imaging –See **Medical Science and Technology -- Radiology** pg 3938

Dialysis –See **Medical Science and Technology -- Urology and Nephrology** pg 3987; see also Medical Science and Technology pg 3543; Medical Science and Technology -- Internal Medicine pg 3794

Dictionaries –See **Encyclopedias and General Reference Books** pg 1923

Dietetics –See **Nutrition and Dietetics** pg 4186

Directories –See **Encyclopedias and General Reference Books** pg 1923

Disarmament –See **Military and Defense** pg 4033; see also Law -- International Law pg 3122

Divorce –See **Family and Marriage** pg 2276; **Law -- Family Law** pg 3119

Doctrinal Theology –See **Religion and Theology** pg 4931

Dog Racing –See **Recreation, Leisure -- Sports** pg 4881

Domestic Relations –See **Law -- Family Law** pg 3119

Drama –See **Theater** pg 5361; see also The Arts -- Performing Arts pg 383

Drink –See **Food and Food Industry -- Beverage Industry** pg 2363

Drug Abuse and Alcoholism –pg 1338

Dyes and Dyeing –See **Chemistry -- Chemical Technology** pg 1020; **Textiles** pg 5347; see also The Arts -- Crafts and Decorative Arts pg 369

Early Childhood and Primary Education –pg 1802

Early Childhood Education –See **Education -- Early Childhood and Primary Education** pg 1802

Earth Sciences –pg 1351

Eastern Christian Churches –pg 5039

Ecology –pg 2210; see also Natural History pg 4161

Economic Conditions –See **Economics -- Economic History, Conditions** pg 1544

Economic History –See **Economics -- Economic History, Conditions** pg 1544

Economic History, Conditions –pg 1544

Economic Theory –pg 1589

Economics –pg 1459

Editing –See **Publishing** pg 4811; see also Journalism pg 2917; Literature pg 3357

Education –pg 1720

Educational Psychology –See **Education -- Teaching and Curriculum** pg 1887; **Psychology** pg 4570; see also Education pg 1720; Education -- Special Education and Rehabilitation pg 1874

Elections –See **Political Science** pg 4461; see also Public Administration pg 4623

Electric Power –See **Engineering -- Electricity, Electrical Engineering and Electronic** pg 2034

Electricity, Electrical Engineering, Electronics –pg 2034; see also Energy pg 1930; Heating, Plumbing and Refrigeration pg 2602; Public Administration -- Public Utilities pg 4759; Sound Recordings and Systems pg 5315

Electrochemistry –pg 1033; see also Chemistry -- Analytical Chemistry pg 1012; Chemistry -- Physical and Theoretical Chemistry pg 1049

Electronic Publishing –See **Desktop Publishing** pg 1263

Electronics –See **Engineering -- Electricity, Electrical Engineering, Electronics** pg 2034

Embroidery –See **Sewing and Needlework** pg 5182

Embryology –pg 541; see also Medical Science and Technology -- Anatomy pg 3678

Emergencies –See **Medical Science and Technology -- Emergency Medicine** pg 3723

Emergency Health Services –See **Medical Science and Technology -- Emergency Medicine** pg 3723

Emergency Medicine –pg 3723

Emigration and Immigration –pg 1918

Employment Law –See **Law -- Labor Law** pg 3143

Encyclopedias and General Reference Books –pg 1923

Endocrinology –pg 3726

Energy –pg 1930; see also Engineering -- Electricity, Electrical Engineering, Electronics pg 2034; Engineering -- Nuclear Engineering pg 2153; Petroleum and Natural Gas pg 4248; Physics -- Nuclear Physics pg 4445; Public Administration -- Public Utilities pg 4759

Engineering –pg 1963; see also Computers -- Artificial Intelligence pg 1210

Entomology –pg 5604

Environmental Health –See **Environmental Issues** pg 2159; see also Public Health and Safety pg 4763

Environmental Issues –pg 2159

Environmental Law –pg 3109; see also Environmental Issues pg 2159

Environmental Protection –See **Environmental Issues** pg 2159; see also Environmental Issues -- Pollution and Waste Management pg 2222

Environmental Studies –See **Environmental Issues** pg 2159; see also Environmental Issues -- Conservation and Natural Resources pg 2185; Environmental Issues -- Ecology pg 2210; Environmental Issues -- Pollution and Waste Management pg 2222

Environmental Technology –See **Environmental Issues** pg 2159; see also Science and Technology pg 5078

Environmental Waste Management –See **Environmental Issues** pg 2159

Enzymes –See **Biology -- Biochemistry** pg 479

Epidemiology –pg 3733; see also Medical Science and Technology -- Epidemiology pg 3711; Public Health and Safety pg 4763

Epilepsy –See **Medical Science and Technology -- Neurology** pg 3825

Episcopal –See **Religion and Theology -- Protestantism** pg 5054

Ergonomics –See **Engineering -- Mechanical Engineering and Machinery** pg 2108; see also Computers -- Cybernetics pg 1250

Esperanto –See **Linguistics** pg 3260; see also Education -- Teaching and Curriculum pg 1887

SUBJECT CROSS REFERENCES

Estate Planning –pg 3117; see also Business -- Banking and Finance pg 768; Business -- Investments pg 890

Ethics –pg 2248

Ethnic Interests –pg 2253

Ethnology –See **Anthropology** pg 227

Europe –See **General Interest-Europe** pg 2513; **History(General) -- History of Europe** pg 2671

European Studies –See **History(General) -- History of Europe** pg 2671; **Literature** pg 3357

Evangelism –See **Religion and Theology** pg 4931

Exceptional Children –See **Education -- Special Education and Rehabilitation** pg 1874

Exercise –See **Health and Personal Fitness** pg 2595

Exhibits/Exhibitions –See **Business -- Advertising and Public Relations** pg 753; **Science and Technology** pg 5078

Experimental Mechanics –See **Physics -- Analytic and Experimental Mechanics** pg 4427

Expert Systems –See **Computers -- Artificial Intelligence** pg 1210

Expositions –See **Business -- Advertising and Public Relations** pg 753; **Recreation, Leisure -- Games and Amusements** pg 4856; **Science and Technology** pg 5078

Fabric –See **Textiles** pg 5347; see also Clothing Industry and Fashion pg 1081; Sewing and Needlework pg 5182

Fairs –See **Recreation, Leisure -- Games and Amusements** pg 4856

Family and Marriage –pg 2276; see also Home Economics pg 2788

Family Law –pg 3119

Family Medicine –See **Medical Science and Technology -- Family Practice** pg 3736

Family Physicians –See **Medical Science and Technology -- Family Practice** pg 3736; see also Medical Science and Technology -- Physicians and Medical Personnel pg 3912

Family Planning –See **Birth Control** pg 587; **Family and Marriage** pg 2276

Family Practice –pg 3736

Fashion –See **Clothing Industry and Fashion** pg 1081

Federal Aid to Education –See **Education -- Higher Education** pg 1806; see also Education -- School Organization and Administration pg 1859

Federal Employees –See **Public Administration -- Civil Service** pg 4701

Federal Government –See **Public Administration** pg 4623; see also Political Science pg 4461

Feed Grain and Milling –pg 199

Feminism –See **Women's Interests** pg 5550

Fencing –See **Recreation, Leisure -- Sports** pg 4881

Fertility –See **Birth Control** pg 587; **Population Studies** pg 4549; see also Biology -- Physiology pg 577; Medical Science and Technology -- Gynecology and Obstetrics pg 3755

Fertilizers –See **Agriculture -- Crop Production and Soil** pg 161; **Chemistry -- Chemical Technology** pg 1020

Fiber Optics –See **Communication -- Telecommunications** pg 1148; **Physics -- Light, Optics, Radiation** pg 4432

Fiction –See **Literature** pg 3357; see also Literary and Political Reviews pg 3337

Films and Filmmaking –See **Motion Picture** pg 4062; see also Photography and Video pg 4366

Finance –See **Business -- Banking and Finance** pg 768; **Public Administration -- Public Finance and Taxation** pg 4708

Fire Prevention –pg 2287

Fish and Fisheries –pg 2293

Fishing –See **Fish and Fisheries** pg 2293

Floor Coverings –See **Building and Construction** pg 597; **Interior Design -- Home Furnishings** pg 2904

Florist Trade –pg 2434

Flowers –See **Gardening and Horticulture -- Florist Trade** pg 2434

Fluid Mechanics –See **Engineering -- Hydraulic Engineering** pg 2087; **Physics -- Analytic and Experimental Mechanics** pg 4427

Folk Music –See **Folklore** pg 2318; **Music** pg 4098

Folklore –pg 2318; see also History(General) pg 2609; Literature pg 3357; Sociology -- Manners and Customs pg 5267

Food and Food Industry –pg 2325; see also Agriculture pg 42; Home Economics pg 2788; Restaurants pg 5070

Food Production –See **Agriculture -- Crop Production and Soil** pg 3475; see also Food and Food Industry pg 2325

Football –See **Recreation, Leisure -- Sports** pg 4881

Footwear –See **Clothing Industry and Fashion** pg 1081; see also Leather and Fur Industry pg 3183

Foreign Affairs –See **International Relations** pg 4514; see also Law -- International Law pg 3122

Foreign Trade –See **Business -- Commerce** pg 821; see also Economics -- International Economics pg 1632

Forensic Medicine –See **Medical Science and Technology -- Forensic Medicine, Medical Jurisprudence** pg 3739

Forensic Medicine, Medical Jurisprudence –pg 3739

Forestry –pg 2373; see also Environmental Issues -- Conservation and Natural Resources pg 2185; Gardening and Horticulture pg 2407; Paper and Pulp Industry pg 4232

Franchises –See **Business** pg 636

Fraternities –See **Societies and Clubs** pg 5228

Freight –See **Transportation** pg 5375; see also Aeronautics, Astronautics pg 3; Business -- Commerce pg 821; Transportation - Ships and Shipping pg 5447; Transportation -- Railroads pg 5429

French Studies –See **History(General) History of Europe** pg 2671; **Literature** pg 3357

Frozen Foods –See **Food and Food Industry** pg 2325

Fruit –See **Agriculture -- Crop Production and Soil** pg 161; **Food and Food Industry** pg 2325; **Gardening and Horticulture** pg 2407

Fuel –See **Petroleum and Natural Gas** pg 4248; see also Energy pg 1930; Engineering -- Electricity, Electrical Engineering, Electronics pg 2034

Fund Raising –See **Philanthropy** pg 4334; see also Sociology -- Social Services and Welfare pg 5269

Funeral Service –pg 2406

Fungi –See **Biology -- Mycology** pg 574

Fur –See **Leather and Fur Industry** pg 3183

Furniture –See **Interior Design -- Home Furnishings** pg 2904; see also Antiques pg 248; Building and Construction -- Carpentry and Woodwork pg 633; Interior Design pg 2898

Galleries –See **Museums and Galleries** pg 4083

SUBJECT CROSS REFERENCES

Gambling –See **Recreation, Leisure -- Games and Amusements** pg 4856; see also Psychology pg 4570; Public Administration pg 4623

Games and Amusements –pg 4856; see also Children and Youth Interests pg 1059

Gardening and Horticulture –pg 2407

Gastroenterology –pg 3743

Gay/Lesbian –See **Homosexuality** pg 2793

Genealogy and Heraldry –pg 2436; see also History(General) pg 2609

General Interest –pg 2484

General Interest-Africa –pg 2497

General Interest-Asia –pg 2501

General Interest-Australia and Oceania –pg 2510

General Interest-Central America –pg 2511

General Interest-Europe –pg 2513

General Interest-Middle East –pg 2525

General Interest-North America –pg 2526

General Interest-South America –pg 2551

General Management –pg 858

General Management and Administration –See **Business -- General Management** pg 858

General Practice –See **Medical Science and Technology -- Family Practice** pg 3736

General Reference Books –See **Encyclopedias and General Reference Books** pg 1923

Genetic Engineering –See **Medical Science and Technology -- Biotechnology** pg 3685; see also Biology -- Genetics pg 541

Genetics –pg 541

Geochemistry –See **Chemistry** pg 958

Geodesy –See **Earth Sciences -- Geophysics** pg 1402; **Geography** pg 2553

Geography –pg 2553; see also Travel and Tourism pg 5458

Geology –pg 1364

Geophysics –pg 1402

Geriatrics –pg 3748; see also Senior Citizens pg 5177

Germanic Studies –See **History(General) -- History of Europe** pg 2671; **Literature** pg 3357

Gifted Children –See **Education -- Special Education and Rehabilitation** pg 1874

Gifts, Toys –pg 2583; see also Glass and Ceramics pg 2585; Recreation, Leisure -- Games and Amusements pg 4856; The Arts -- Crafts and Decorative Arts pg 369

Glass and Ceramics –pg 2585; see also The Arts -- Crafts and Decorative Arts pg 369

Golf –See **Recreation, Leisure -- Sports** pg 4881

Government –See **Public Administration** pg 4623; see also Political Science pg 4461

Government Employees –See **Public Administration -- Civil Service** pg 4701

Graphic Arts –pg 376; see also Printing Industry pg 4563

Grocery Trade –See **Food and Food Industry** pg 2325

Guns –See **Recreation, Leisure -- Sports** pg 4881; see also Military and Defense pg 4033

Gymnastics –See **Recreation, Leisure -- Sports** pg 4881

Gynecology and Obstetrics –pg 3755

Handicrafts –See **The Arts -- Crafts and Decorative Arts** pg 369

Hardware –pg 1264; **Household Hardware and Appliances** pg 2810; see also Building and Construction pg 597

Hazardous Waste –See **Environmental Issues -- Pollution and Waste Management** pg 2222; see also Environmental Issues pg 2159

Health and Personal Fitness –pg 2595; see also Physical Education and Training pg 1854; Recreation, Leisure -- Sports pg 4881

Hearing Disorders –See **Medical Science and Technology -- Otorhinolaryngology** pg 3885; **Physically Impaired** pg 4382

Heat –pg 4430

Heating, Plumbing, and Refrigeration –pg 2602; see also Electricity, Electrical Engineering, Electronics pg 2034; Household Hardware and Appliances pg 2810

Helicopters –See **Aeronautics, Astronautics** pg 3

Helminthology –See **Zoology** pg 5572

Hematologic Diseases –See **Medical Science and Technology -- Hematology** pg 3769

Hematology –pg 3769; see also Biology -- Physiology pg 577; Medical Science and Technology -- Cardiology pg 3697; Medical Science and Technology -- Internal Medicine pg 3794

Hemodialysis –See **Medical Science and Technology -- Hematology** pg 3769

Heraldry –See **Genealogy and Heraldry** pg 2436

Herbs and Spices –See **Food and Food Industry** pg 2325; see also Gardening and Horticulture pg 2407

Heredity –See **Biology -- Genetics** pg 541

Higher Education –pg 1806

Hinduism –pg 5040

Histology –See **Biology -- Cytology and Histology** pg 531

History of Africa –pg 2636

History of Asia –pg 2644

History of Australia and Oceania –pg 2668

History of Europe –pg 2671

History of North, South, and Central America –pg 2717

History of the Middle East –pg 2767

History(General) –pg 2609

Hobbies –pg 2770; see also Recreation, Leisure -- Sports pg 4881; Sewing and Needlework pg 5182; The Arts -- Crafts and Decorative Arts pg 369

Hockey –See **Recreation, Leisure -- Sports** pg 4881

Home and Gardening Publications –See **Gardening and Horticulture** pg 2407

Home Computing –See **Computers -- Microcomputers, Personal Computers** pg 1265

Home Economics –pg 2788; see also Family and Marriage pg 2276

Home Furnishings –pg 2904; see also Building and Construction -- Carpentry and Woodwork pg 633; Interior Design pg 2898

Homeopathy –pg 3774

Homosexuality –pg 2793

Hormones –See **Endocrinology** pg 3726; see also Biology -- Biochemistry pg 479; Biology -- Physiology pg 577

Horse Racing –See **Horses and Horsemanship** pg 2796; see also Recreation, Leisure -- Sports pg 4881

Horses and Horsemanship –pg 2796; see also Recreation, Leisure -- Sports pg 4881

Horticulture –See **Gardening and Horticulture** pg 2407; see also Agriculture -- Crop Production and Soil pg 161; Biology -- Botany pg 496; Forestry pg 2373

SUBJECT CROSS REFERENCES

Hospital Administration –See **Medical Science and Technology -- Hospital Administration and Medical Centers** pg 3775

Hospital Administration and Medical Centers –pg 3775

Hospitals –See **Medical Science and Technology -- Hospital Administration and Medical Centers** pg 3775

Hotels/Motels –pg 2803; see also Travel and Tourism pg 5458; see also Restaurants pg 5070

Household Hardware and Appliances –pg 2810; see also Electricity, Electrical Engineering, Electronics pg 2034; Heating, Plumbing, and Refrigeration pg 2602

Housing and Urban Development –pg 2812; see also Building and Construction pg 597; Real Estate pg 4833

Human Sexuality –See **Sexual Life** pg 5186

Humane Society –See **Animal Welfare** pg 225

Humanities –pg 2841; see also Social Sciences pg 5189; The Arts pg 311

Hunting –See **Recreation, Leisure -- Outdoor Life** pg 4868

Hydraulic Engineering –pg 2087; see also Earth Sciences -- Hydrology pg 1412; Energy pg 1930; Water Resources pg 5528

Hydrobiology –See **Biology -- Marine Biology** pg 552; see also Earth Sciences -- Oceanography pg 1445

Hydrology –pg 1412; see also Engineering -- Hydraulic Engineering pg 2087; Water Resources pg 5528

Hygiene –See **Industrial Health and Safety** pg 2858; **Public Health and Safety** pg 4763

Hypertension –See **Medical Science and Technology -- Cardiology** pg 3697; see also Medical Science and Technology -- Internal Medicine pg 3794

Hypnosis –pg 2857

Immigration –See **Emigration and Immigration** pg 1918

Immunology –See **Medical Science and Technology -- Allergy and Immunology** pg 3662

Imports/Exports –See **Business -- Commerce** pg 821

Income Tax –See **Public Administration -- Public Finance and Taxation** pg 4708; see also Business -- Accounting pg 735

Industrial Arts –See **Education -- Vocational Education** pg 1909; see also Science and Technology pg 5078

Industrial Design –See **Engineering -- Industrial Engineering and Design** pg 2096; see also Manufacturing pg 3475

Industrial Engineering and Design –pg 2096

Industrial Health and Safety –pg 2858

Industrial Medicine –See **Industrial Health and Safety** pg 2858

Industry –See **Economics -- Industry and Production** pg 1596

Industry and Production –pg 1596

Infectious Diseases –See **Medical Science and Technology -- Communicable Diseases** pg 3711; see also Medical Science and Technology -- Epidemiology pg 3733; Public Health and Safety pg 4763

Information Retrieval –See **Library and Information Sciences** pg 3186

Information Science –See **Library and Information Sciences** pg 3186

Inheritance –See **Law -- Estate Planning** pg 3117

Inorganic Chemistry –pg 1035

Insecticide –See **Pest Control** pg 4243

Insects –See **Zoology -- Entomology** pg 5604; see also Pest Control pg 4243

Insulation –See **Building and Construction** pg 597; see also Engineering -- Electricity, Electrical Engineering, Electronics pg 2034

Insurance –pg 2872

Insurance Law –See **Insurance** pg 2872; **Law -- Corporate Law** pg 3094

Integrated Circuits –See **Engineering -- Electricity, Electrical Engineering, Electronics** pg 2034

Intellectual Property –See **Copyright, Intellectual Property** pg 1300

Intensive Care –See **Medical Science and Technology** pg 3543; see also Medical Science and Technology -- Nursing pg 3849

Interior Design –pg 2898; see also Architecture pg 286

Internal Medicine –pg 3794

International Assistance and Development –pg 2907; see also Economics -- International Economics pg 1632; Sociology -- Social Services and Welfare pg 5269

International Economics –pg 1632

International Law –pg 3122; see also Political Science -- International Relations pg 4514

International Relations –pg 4514; see also History(General) pg 2609; Law -- International Law pg 3122; Military and Defense pg 4033

Invertebrates/Vertebrates –See **Zoology** pg 5572

Investing –See **Business -- Investments** pg 890

Investments –pg 890; see also Business -- Banking and Finance pg 768

Irish Slavonic Studies –See **History(General) -- History of Europe** pg 2671; **Literature** pg 3357

Irish Studies –See **History(General) -- History of Europe** pg 2671; **Literature** pg 3357

Irrigation –See **Engineering -- Hydraulic Engineering** pg 2087; see also Agriculture -- Crop Production and Soil pg 161

Islam –See **Religion and Theology -- Islam, Bahaism, Theosophy** pg 5041

Islam, Bahaism, Theosophy –pg 5041

Jails –See **Law -- Law Enforcement and Criminology** pg 3156

Jewelry –pg 2913

Journalism –pg 2917; see also Communication -- Broadcasting pg 1125; Publishing pg 4811

Judaism –pg 5045; see also Ethnic Interests pg 2253

Judges –See **Law -- Judicial Systems** pg 3138

Judicial Ethics –See **Law -- Judicial Systems** pg 3138

Judicial Statistics –See **Law -- Judicial Systems** pg 3138

Judicial Systems –pg 3138

Judo/Karate –See **Recreation, Leisure -- Sports** pg 4881; see also Health and Personal Fitness pg 2595

Juvenile Delinquency –See **Law -- Law Enforcement and Criminology** pg 3156; see also Sociology -- Social Services and Welfare pg 5269

Kidneys –See **Medical Science and Technology -- Urology and Nephrology** pg 3987

Kindergarten –See **Education -- Early Childhood and Primary Education** pg 1802

Knitting –See **Sewing and Needlework** pg 5182; see also Textiles pg 5347

SUBJECT CROSS REFERENCES

Korean Studies –See **History(General) -- History of Asia** pg 2644; see also Literature pg 3357

Labels/Labelling –See **Packaging** pg 4217

Labor –pg 1642; see also Business -- Personnel Management pg 938; Industrial Health and Safety pg 2858

Labor Law –pg 3143; see also Law pg 2926; see also Economics -- Labor pg 1642

Labor Unions –See **Economics -- Labor** pg 1642

LAN (Local Area Networks) –See **Computers -- Computer Networks** pg 1240

Land –See **Economics** pg 1459; **Environmental Issues -- Conservation and Natural Resources** pg 2185; **Public Administration** pg 4623; **Real Estate** pg 4833; see also Geography pg 2553

Landscape Architecture –See **Gardening and Horticulture** pg 2407

Language –See **Linguistics** pg 3260

Lasers –See **Physics -- Light, Optics, Radiation** pg 4432; see also Chemistry pg 958; Engineering pg 1963; Medical Science and Technology -- Surgery pg 3957; Physics pg 4395

Latin American Studies –See **History(General) -- History of North, South, and Central America** pg 2717; see also Literature pg 3357

Laundry –See **Chemistry -- Chemical Technology** pg 1020; see also Textiles pg 5347

Law –pg 2926; see also Public Administration pg 4623

Law Enforcement –See **Law -- Law Enforcement and Criminology** pg 2926

Law Enforcement and Criminology –pg 3156

Law Offices –See **Law** pg 2926; see also Business -- General Management pg 858

Learning Disabilities –See **Education -- Special Education and Rehabilitation** pg 1874

Leather and Fur Industry –pg 3183; see also Clothing Industry and Fashion pg 1081

Legal Aid –pg 3179

Legislation –See **Law** pg 2926; see also Public Administration pg 4623

Leisure –See **Recreation, Leisure** pg 4848

Leukemia –See **Medical Science and Technology -- Neoplasma, Neoplastic** pg 3808; see also Medical Science and Technology -- Internal Medicine pg 3794

Library and Information Sciences –pg 3186; see also Archives pg 2478; Bibliographies pg 406

Life/Death –See **Philosophy** pg 4339

Light, Optics, Radiation –pg 4432

Linguistics –pg 3260; see also Literature pg 3357

Liquor –See **Food and Food Industry -- Beverage Industry** pg 2363

Literacy –See **Education -- Special Education and Rehabilitation** pg 1874

Literary and Political Reviews –pg 3337; see also Literature pg 3357

Literary Criticism –See **Literary and Political Reviews** pg 3337

Literary Theory –See **Literary and Political Reviews** pg 3337

Literature –pg 3357; see also Linguistics pg 3260; Literary and Political Reviews pg 3337; Romance and Adventure pg 5073

Livestock and Poultry –pg 204

Local Area Networks –See **Computers -- Computer Networks** pg 1240

Local Government –See **Political Science** pg 4461; **Public Administration** pg 4623; **Public Administration** pg 4708

Lotteries –See **Public Administration** pg 4623

Lumber and Wood –pg 2399; see also Paper and Pulp Industry pg 4232

Lutheran –See **Religion and Theology -- Protestantism** pg 5054

Machinery –See **Engineering -- Mechanical Engineering and Machinery** pg 2108

Macroeconomics –See **Economics -- Economic Theory** pg 1589; see also Economics pg 1459; Economics -- International Economics pg 1632

Magic –See **Recreation, Leisure -- Games and Amusements** pg 4856; see also Parapsychology and Occultism pg 4240

Magnetic Resonance Imaging –See **Medical Science and Technology -- Radiology** pg 3938

Magnetism –pg 4443

Mainframe Computing –See **Computers -- Data Processing** pg 1255

Manners and Customs –pg 5267

Manufacturing –pg 3475; see also Industry and Production pg 1596

Maps and Mapmaking –See **Geography -- Cartography** pg 2580

Marine Biology –pg 552; see also Earth Sciences -- Oceanography pg 1445; Zoology pg 5572

Marine Engineering –See **Engineering** pg 1963

Marine Pollution –See **Environmental Issues -- Pollution and Waste Management** pg 2222

Marine Toxins –See **Biology -- Marine Biology** pg 552

Marines –See **Naval Science, Navigation** pg 4174

Maritime Law –pg 3180

Marketing –pg 920

Marriage –See **Family and Marriage** pg 2276

Marriage Law –See **Law -- Family Law** pg 3119

Martial Arts –See **Health and Personal Fitness** pg 2595

Marxism –See **Political Science -- Socialism, Communism, Anarchism, Utopianism** pg 4539; see also Sociology pg 5237

Masonry –See **Building and Construction** pg 597

Materials Engineering and Mechanics –pg 2100

Mathematical Geography –See **Geography** pg 2553

Mathematics –pg 3490

Matrimonial Actions –See **Law -- Family Law** pg 3119

Meat –See **Food and Food Industry** pg 2325; see also Agriculture -- Livestock and Poultry pg 204

Mechanical Engineering and Machinery –pg 2108

Media –See **Communication** pg 1103; see also Journalism pg 2917

Medical Centers –See **Medical Science and Technology -- Hospital Administration and Medical Centers** pg 3775

Medical Jurisprudence –See **Medical Science and Technology -- Forensic Medicine, Medical Jurisprudence** pg 3739

Medical Malpractice –See **Law** pg 2926; see also Medical Science and Technology pg 3543

Medical Personnel –See **Medical Science and Technology -- Physicians and Medical Personnel** pg 3912

Medical Science and Technology –pg 3543; see also Public Health and Safety pg 4763

SUBJECT CROSS REFERENCES

Medieval Studies –See **History(General) -- History of Europe** pg 2671; see also Classical Studies pg 1073

Meetings –See **Business** pg 636

Memory –See **Psychology** pg 4570

Men's Interests –pg 3994

Mental Health –See **Medical Science and Technology -- Psychiatry** pg 3918; **Psychology** pg 4570; **Public Health and Safety** pg 4763; **Sociology -- Social Services and Welfare** pg 5269

Mentally Disabled –See **Education -- Special Education and Rehabilitation** pg 1874; see also Medical Science and Technology -- Psychiatry pg 3918; Psychology pg 4570

Mergers/Acquisitions –See **Business** pg 636

Metabolic Diseases –See **Medical Science and Technology -- Allergy and Immunology** pg 3662

Metallurgy –See **Metals and Metallurgy** pg 3996

Metals and Metallurgy –pg 3996; see also Mines and Mining Engineering pg 2132

Meteorology –pg 1419

Methodist –See **Religion and Theology -- Protestantism** pg 5054

Metrology and Standardization –pg 4029

Microbiology –pg 558

Microcomputers –See **Computers -- Microcomputers, Personal Computers** pg 1265

Microcomputers, Personal Computers –pg 1265

Microscopy –pg 572

Midwifery –See **Medical Science and Technology -- Gynecology and Obstetrics** pg 3755

Migration –See **Emigration and Immigration** pg 1918; **Population Studies** pg 4549; see also Economics -- Labor pg 1642; Zoology pg 5572

Military Administration –See **Military and Defense** pg 4033

Military and Defense –pg 4033; see also Political Science -- International Relations pg 4514

Military History –See **Military and Defense** pg 4033

Military Law –pg 3182

Military Medicine –See **Medical Science and Technology** pg 3543; see also Military and Defense pg 4033

Milling –See **Agriculture -- Feed Grain and Milling** pg 199

Mineralogy –pg 1437

Mines and Mining Engineering –pg 2132; see also Earth Sciences -- Mineralogy pg 1437; Metals and Metallurgy pg 4026; Petroleum and Natural Gas pg 4248

Minicomputers –pg 1273; see also Computers -- Microcomputers, Personal Computers pg 1265

Mobile Homes –See **Building and Construction** pg 597; **Housing and Urban Development** pg 2812; **Transportation** pg 5375

Money –See **Business -- Banking and Finance** pg 768; **Economics** pg 1459

Monuments –See **History(General)** pg 2609; see also Architecture pg 286; The Arts -- Art pg 335

Mormons –See **Religion and Theology** pg 4931

Morphology –See **Biology -- Botany** pg 496

Motels –See **Hotels/Motels** pg 2803

Motion Picture –pg 4062

Motorcycles –pg 4080

Mountain Climbing –See **Recreation, Leisure -- Outdoor Life** pg 4868; see also Recreation, Leisure -- Sports pg 4881

Movies –See **Motion Picture** pg 4062

Multiple Sclerosis –See **Medical Science and Technology -- Neurology** pg 3825

Muscular Dystrophy –See **Medical Science and Technology -- Musculoskeletal System** pg 3802; see also Medical Science and Technology -- Neurology pg 3825

Musculoskeletal System –pg 3802

Museums and Galleries –pg 4083; see also Natural History pg 4161; The Arts -- Art pg 335

Music –pg 4098; see also Computers -- Computer Music pg 1240; Sound Recordings and Systems pg 5315; The Arts -- Performing Arts pg 383

Music Therapy –See **Medical Science and Technology** pg 3543; **Music** pg 4098; see also Psychology pg 4570

Mutual Funds –See **Business -- Investments** pg 890; see also Business -- Banking and Finance pg 768

Mycology –pg 574; see also Biology -- Botany pg 496

Mysticism –See **Parapsychology and Occultism** pg 4240; see also Literature pg 3357; Religion and Theology pg 4931

Mythology –See **Folklore** pg 2318

Narcotics –See **Drug Abuse and Alcoholism** pg 1338; see also Law -- Law Enforcement and Criminology pg 3156; Pharmacy and Pharmacology pg 4288

Natural Gas –See **Petroleum and Natural Gas** pg 4248

Natural History –pg 4161; see also Biology pg 4570; Environmental Issues -- Conservation and Natural Resources pg 2185; Environmental Issues -- Ecology pg 2185

Natural Resources –See **Environmental Issues -- Conservation and Natural Resources** pg 2185

Naturalist –See **Natural History** pg 4161; see also Environmental Issues -- Ecology pg 2210

Naval Architecture –See **Architecture** pg 286; **Naval Science and Navigation** pg 4174

Naval Science, Navigation –pg 4174; see also Transportation -- Ships and Shipping pg 5447

Navigation –See **Naval Science, Navigation** pg 4174

Navy –See **Naval Science, Navigation** pg 4174

Needlework –See **Sewing and Needlework** pg 5182

Neoplasma –See **Medical Science and Technology -- Neoplasma, Neoplastic** pg 3808

Neoplasma, Neoplastic –pg 3808; see also Medical Science and Technology -- Radiology pg 3938

Neoplastic –See **Medical Science and Technology -- Neoplasma, Neoplastic** pg 3808

Nephrology –See **Medical Science and Technology -- Urology and Nephrology** pg 3987

Neural Networks –See **Computers -- Artificial Intelligence** pg 1210

Neurology –pg 3825; see also Medical Science and Technology -- Psychiatry pg 3918; Psychology pg 4570

New Age Publications –pg 4185

Newspapers –pg 5625

Noise Control –See **Environmental Issues** pg 2159

North America –See **General Interest -- General Interest-North America** pg 2526; **History(General) -- History of North, South, and Central America** pg 2717

Nuclear Engineering –pg 2153

Nuclear Medicine –See **Medical Science and Technology -- Internal Medicine** pg 3794; Medical Science and Technology -- Radiology pg 3938

SUBJECT CROSS REFERENCES

Nuclear Physics –pg 4445

Nuclear Waste –See **Environmental Issues -- Pollution and Waste Management** pg 2222

Numismatics –pg 2779

Nursing –pg 3849; see also Medical Science and Technology -- Surgery pg 3849

Nursing Homes –See **Medical Science and Technology -- Hospital Administration and Medical Centers** pg 3775; see also Sociology -- Social Services and Welfare pg 5269

Nutrition and Dietetics –pg 4186; see also Food and Food Industry pg 2325

Nutritional Disorders –See **Nutrition and Dietetics** pg 4186

Obstetrics –See **Medical Science and Technology -- Gynecology and Obstetrics** pg 3755

Occultism –See **Parapsychology and Occultism** pg 4240

Occupational Health –See **Industrial Health and Safety** pg 2858

Occupational Therapy –See **Industrial Health and Safety** pg 2858; see also Education -- Special Education and Rehabilitation pg 1874; Medical Science and Technology -- Psychiatry pg 3918

Occupations and Careers –pg 4201; see also Economics -- Labor pg 1642; Education -- Special Aspects of Education pg 1874

Ocean Engineering –See **Engineering -- Hydraulic Engineering** pg 2087; see also Earth Sciences -- Oceanography pg 1445

Oceania –See **General Interest -- General Interest-Australia and Oceania** pg 2510; see also History(General) -- History of Australia and Oceania pg 2668

Oceanography –pg 1445

Office Equipment and Services –pg 4210; see also Computers pg 1169

Oil –See **Petroleum and Natural Gas** pg 4248

Oncology –See **Medical Science and Technology -- Neoplasma, Neoplastic** pg 3808

Online Computing and Information –pg 1274

Opera –See **The Arts -- Performing Arts** pg 383; see also Music pg 4098

Ophthalmology –pg 3871

Optical Storage, CD-ROM Applications –pg 1276

Optics –See **Physics -- Light, Optics, Radiation** pg 4432

Optometry –pg 4214

Oral Surgery –See **Medical Science and Technology -- Surgery** pg 3957; see also Dentistry pg 1314

Organic Chemistry –pg 1038

Oriental Studies –See **History(General) -- History of Asia** pg 2644; see also Literature pg 3357

Ornithology –pg 5614; see also Natural History pg 4161

Orthodontics –See **Dentistry** pg 1314

Orthopedics –pg 3880

Otorhinolaryngology –pg 3885

Outdoor Life –pg 4868; see also Environmental Issues -- Conservation and Natural Resources pg 2185; Fish and Fisheries pg 2293; Recreation, Leisure -- Sports pg 4881

Pacific Studies –See **History(General) -- History of Australia and Oceania** pg 2671; see also Literature pg 3357

Packaging –pg 4217

Pain –See **Medical Science and Technology -- Neurology** pg 3825

Paints and Painting –pg 4222

Paleontology –pg 4226

Paper and Pulp Industry –pg 4232

Parachuting –See **Recreation, Leisure -- Sports** pg 4881

Paramedics –See **Medical Science and Technology -- Emergency Medicine** pg 3723

Parapsychology and Occultism –pg 4240

Parenting –See **Family and Marriage** pg 2276

Parks –See **Environmental Issues -- Conservation and Natural Resources** pg 2185; Recreation, Leisure pg 4848

Parks and Recreation –pg 4705; see also Environmental Issues -- Conservation and Natural Resources pg 2185

Parliament/House of Commons –See **Public Administration** pg 4623; see also Political Science pg 4461

Patents –See **Copyright, Intellectual Property** pg 1300

Pathology –pg 3891; see also Medical Science and Technology -- Anatomy pg 3678

Pediatric Surgery –See **Medical Science and Technology -- Pediatrics** pg 3899; see also Medical Science and Technology -- Surgery pg 3957

Pediatrics –pg 3899

Penology –See **Law -- Law Enforcement and Criminology** pg 3156

Pensions –See **Business -- Investments** pg 890; see also Economics -- Labor pg 1642; Insurance pg 2872

Performing Arts –pg 383; see also Motion Picture pg 4062; Music pg 4098; The Arts -- Dance pg 1310; Theater pg 5361

Perfumes –See **Beauty and Cosmetics** pg 402; see also Chemistry -- Chemical Technology pg 1020

Perinatology –See **Medical Science and Technology -- Gynecology and Obstetrics** pg 3755; see also Medical Science and Technology -- Pediatrics pg 3899

Personal Computers –See **Computers -- Microcomputers, Personal Computers** pg 1265

Personal Hygiene –See **Health and Personal Fitness** pg 2595

Personnel Management –pg 938; see also Economics -- Labor pg 1642

Pest Control –pg 4243

Petroleum and Natural Gas –pg 4248; see also Energy pg 1930; Engineering -- Mines and Mining Engineering pg 2132

Petrology –pg 1458

Pets –pg 4285

Pharmaceutical Industry –See **Pharmacy and Pharmacology** pg 4288

Pharmacy and Pharmacology –pg 4288; see also Medical Science and Technology -- Toxicology pg 3978

Philanthropy –pg 4334; see also Sociology -- Social Services and Welfare pg 5269

Philately –pg 2784

Philology –See **Linguistics** pg 3260; see also Classical Studies pg 1073

Philosophy –pg 4339

Phonetics –See **Linguistics** pg 3260

Photography and Video –pg 4366

Physical and Theoretical Chemistry –pg 1049

Physical Education –See **Education -- Physical Education and Training** pg 2595; **Education -- Physical Education and Training** pg 1854; see also Health and Personal Fitness pg 2595

Physical Education and Training –pg 1854

Physical Fitness –See **Health and Personal Fitness** pg 2595

Physical Therapy –pg 4378

Physical Training –See **Education -- Physical Education and Training** pg 1854

SUBJECT CROSS REFERENCES

Physically Impaired –pg 4382; see also Education -- Special Education and Rehabilitation pg 1874; Sociology -- Social Services and Welfare pg 5269

Physician's Assistants –See **Medical Science and Technology -- Physicians and Medical Personnel** pg 3912

Physicians –See **Medical Science and Technology -- Physicians and Medical Personnel** pg 3912; see also Medical Science and Technology -- Family Practice pg 3736

Physicians and Medical Personnel –pg 3912

Physics –pg 4395

Physiology –pg 577

Phytopathology –See **Biology -- Botany** pg 496; **Gardening and Horticulture** pg 2407

Planned Parenthood –See **Birth Control** pg 587; see also Family and Marriage pg 2276

Plant Breeding –See **Biology -- Botany** pg 496; see also Agriculture -- Crop Production and Soil pg 161; Gardening and Horticulture pg 2407

Plant Culture –See **Gardening and Horticulture** pg 2407

Plastic Surgery –See **Medical Science and Technology -- Surgery** pg 3957

Plastics –pg 4453; see also Engineering -- Materials Engineering and Mechanics pg 2100

Plays –See **Literature** pg 3357; **The Arts -- Performing Arts** pg 383; **Theater** pg 5361

Plumbing –See **Heating, Plumbing, and Refrigeration** pg 2602

Podiatry –pg 3917

Poetry –pg 3459; see also Literary and Political Reviews pg 3337

Political Reviews –See **Literary and Political Reviews** pg 3337

Political Science –pg 4461; see also Military and Defense pg 4033; Public Administration pg 4623

Polling –See **Public Administration** pg 4623; see also Sociology pg 5237; Statistics pg 5320

Pollution and Waste Management –pg 2222; see also Earth Sciences -- Ecology pg 2210; Environmental Issues -- Ecology pg 2210

Polymers –See **Chemistry -- Organic Chemistry** pg 1038; see also Paints and Painting pg 4222; Plastics pg 4453

Population Studies –pg 4549; see also Birth Control pg 587; Statistics pg 5320

Portable Computers –See **Computers -- Microcomputers, Personal Computers** pg 1265

Postage Stamps –See **Hobbies -- Philately** pg 2784

Postal Communications –pg 1144; see also Public Administration -- Civil Service pg 4701

Pottery –See **Glass and Ceramics** pg 2585

Poultry –See **Agriculture -- Livestock and Poultry** pg 204

Poverty –See **Sociology -- Social Services and Welfare** pg 5269; see also International Assistance and Development pg 2907

Power –See **Engineering -- Electricity, Electrical Engineering, Electronics** pg 2034

Powerlifting –See **Health and Personal Fitness** pg 2595; see also Recreation, Leisure -- Sports pg 4881

Practical Theology –See **Religion and Theology** pg 4931

Presbyterian –See **Religion and Theology -- Protestantism** pg 5054

Preschool Education –See **Education -- Early Childhood and Primary Education** pg 1802

Preventive Medicine –See **Medical Science and Technology** pg 3543; see also Public Health and Safety pg 4763

Primary Care –See **Medical Science and Technology -- Family Practice** pg 3736

Primary Education –See **Education -- Early Childhood and Primary Education** pg 1802

Printing Industry –pg 4563; see also The Arts -- Graphic Arts pg 376

Prisons –See **Law -- Law Enforcement and Criminology** pg 3156

Private Schools –See **Education** pg 1720

Probation –See **Law -- Law Enforcement and Criminology** pg 3156

Production –See **Economics -- Industry and Production** pg 1596

Programs and Programming –pg 1277; see also Computers -- Software pg 1283

Protestantism –pg 5054

Psychiatry –pg 3918; see also Medical Science and Technology -- Neurology pg 3825; Psychology pg 4570

Psychoanalysis –See **Medical Science and Technology -- Psychiatry** pg 3918; **Psychology** pg 4570

Psychology –pg 4570; see also Medical Science and Technology -- Psychiatry pg 3918; Sociology pg 5237

Psychopathology –See **Medical Science and Technology -- Psychiatry** pg 3918

Psychosomatic Medicine –See **Medical Science and Technology** pg 3543; **Psychology** pg 4570

Psychotherapy –See **Medical Science and Technology -- Psychiatry** pg 3918; see also Family and Marriage pg 2276; Psychology pg 4570

PTA –See **Education -- School Organization and Administration** pg 1859

Public Administration –pg 4623; see also Political Science pg 4461

Public Affairs –See **Public Administration** pg 4623

Public Finance and Taxation –pg 4708; see also Law pg 2926

Public Health and Safety –pg 4763; see also Environmental Issues -- Pollution and Waste Management pg 2222; Medical Science and Technology -- Communicable Diseases pg 3711; Medical Science and Technology -- Epidemiology pg 3733

Public Opinion –See **Sociology** pg 5237

Public Relations –See **Business -- Advertising and Public Relations** pg 753

Public Transportation –See **Transportation** pg 5375; see also Public Administration pg 4623

Public Utilities –pg 4759

Publishing –See **Computers -- Desktop Publishing** pg 1263; Journalism pg 2917

Pulp Industry –See **Paper and Pulp Industry** pg 4232

Puppetry –See **The Arts -- Performing Arts** pg 383

Purchasing –pg 948

Puzzles –See **Recreation, Leisure -- Games and Amusements** pg 4856

Quarries –See **Engineering -- Mines and Mining Engineering** pg 2132; see also Industrial Health and Safety pg 2858

Race Relations –See **Sociology** pg 5237; see also Ethnic Interests pg 2253

Radiation –See **Physics -- Light, Optics, Radiation** pg 4432

Radio –See **Communication -- Broadcasting** pg 1125

SUBJECT CROSS REFERENCES

Radiology –pg 3938; see also Medical Science and Technology -- Neoplasma, Neoplastic pg 3808; Medical Science and Technology -- Nuclear Medicine pg 3847

Railroads –pg 5429

Rationalism –See **Philosophy** pg 4339

Real Estate –pg 4833; see also Housing and Urban Development pg 2812

Record Industry –See **Music** pg 4098; see also Communication -- Broadcasting pg 1125; Sound Recordings and Systems pg 5315

Recreation, Leisure –pg 4848; see also Hobbies pg 2770; Travel and Tourism pg 5458

Recreational Vehicles –See **Transportation** pg 5375; see also Recreation, Leisure pg 4848

Recycling –See **Environmental Issues -- Pollution and Waste Management** pg 2222

Red Cross –See **Sociology -- Social Services and Welfare** pg 5269; see also Medical Science and Technology pg 3543

Reformed Church –See **Religion and Theology -- Protestantism** pg 5054

Refrigeration –See **Heating, Plumbing, and Refrigeration** pg 2602

Regional Planning –See **Housing and Urban Development** pg 2812

Rehabilitation –See **Education -- Special Education and Rehabilitation** pg 1874; **Physically Impaired** pg 4382; see also Drug Abuse and Alcoholism pg 1338; Physical Therapy pg 4378; Sociology -- Social Services and Welfare pg 5269

Religion and Theology –pg 4931

Religious Education –See **Religion and Theology** pg 4931

Religious Music –See **Music** pg 4098

Research –See **Science and Technology** pg 5078; see also Education -- Higher Education pg 1806

Residential Homes –See **Housing and Urban Development** pg 2812

Resorts –See **Hotels/Motels** pg 2803; **Travel and Tourism** pg 5458

Respiratory System –pg 3947

Restaurants –pg 5070; see also Food and Food Industry pg 2325; Hotels/Motels pg 2803

Retail –pg 952

Rheumatology –See **Medical Science and Technology -- Musculoskeletal System** pg 3802; see also Pharmacy and Pharmacology pg 4288

Roads and Traffic –pg 5438

Robotics –See **Computers -- Artificial Intelligence** pg 1210; see also Computers -- Automation pg 1217

Roman Catholic Church –See **Religion and Theology -- Catholicism** pg 5022

Romance and Adventure –pg 5073; see also Literature pg 3357

Rubber –pg 5075

Rugby –See **Recreation, Leisure -- Sports** pg 4881

Running –See **Health and Personal Fitness** pg 2595

Safety –See **Industrial Health and Safety** pg 2858; see also Public Health and Safety pg 4763

Safety Engineering –See **Engineering -- Industrial Engineering and Design** pg 2096

Sailing –See **Boats and Boating** pg 591

Salary/Wages –See **Economics** pg 1459; **Economics -- Labor** pg 1642

Sanitation/Municipal Engineering –See **Environmental Issues -- Pollution and Waste Management** pg 2222; **Public Health and Safety** pg 4763; see also Environmental Issues -- Conservation and Natural Resources pg 2185; Environmental Issues -- Ecology pg 2210

Scholarships –See **Education -- Higher Education** pg 1806

School Counseling –See **Education -- Special Education and Rehabilitation** pg 1874

School Law/Legislation –See **Education -- School Organization and Administration** pg 1859

School Organization and Administration –pg 1859

Science –See **Science and Technology** pg 5078

Science and Technology –pg 5078; see also Chemistry -- Chemical Technology pg 1020; Engineering pg 1963

Science Fiction –See **Literature** pg 3357; see also Literary and Political Reviews pg 3337

Scuba Diving –See **Recreation, Leisure -- Sports** pg 4881

Sculpture –See **The Arts -- Art** pg 335; see also Architecture pg 286

Secondary Education –See **Education** pg 1720

Securities Law –See **Law -- Corporate Law** pg 3094

Security –See **Computers -- Computer Crimes and Security** pg 1225

Security Systems and Alarms –pg 5176; see also Engineering -- Electricity, Electrical Engineering, Electronics pg 2034

Sedimentology –See **Earth Sciences -- Geology** pg 1364; see also Earth Sciences -- Geophysics pg 1402

Seismology –See **Earth Sciences -- Geophysics** pg 1402

Semantics –See **Linguistics** pg 3260

Senior Citizens –pg 5177; see also Medical Science and Technology -- Geriatrics pg 3748; Sociology -- Social Services and Welfare pg 5269

Sewage –See **Environmental Issues -- Pollution and Waste Management** pg 2222; see also Water Resources pg 5528

Sewing and Needlework –pg 5182; see also Hobbies pg 2770; The Arts -- Crafts and Decorative Arts pg 369

Sexual Life –pg 5186

Sexually Transmitted Diseases –See **Medical Science and Technology -- Communicable Diseases** pg 3711; **Public Health and Safety** pg 4763

Ship Design –See **Engineering** pg 1459; **Naval Science, Navigation** pg 4174; see also Transportation -- Ships and Shipping pg 5447

Shipbuilding –See **Naval Science, Navigation** pg 4174; **Transportation -- Ships and Shipping** pg 5447

Ships and Shipping –pg 5447; see also Business -- Commerce pg 821; Naval Science, Navigation pg 4174

Shoes –See **Clothing Industry and Fashion** pg 1081

Simulation –pg 1282

Skiing –See **Recreation, Leisure -- Sports** pg 4881

Slavery –See **Civil Rights** pg 4503

Slavic Studies –See **History(General) -- History of Europe** pg 2671; **Literature** pg 3357

Small Business –See **Business** pg 636; see also Economics pg 1459

Smoking –See **Public Health and Safety** pg 4763; **Tobacco** pg 5372

Soap Operas –See **General Interest** pg 2484

Soccer –See **Recreation, Leisure -- Sports** pg 4881

Social Sciences –pg 5189; see also Humanities pg 2841

SUBJECT CROSS REFERENCES

Social Security –See **Sociology -- Social Services and Welfare** pg 5269; see also Economics -- Labor pg 1642; Insurance pg 2872

Social Services –See **Sociology -- Social Services and Welfare** pg 5269

Social Services and Welfare –pg 5269

Socialism –See **Political Science -- Socialism, Communism, Anarchism, Utopianism** pg 1589

Socialism, Communism, Anarchism, Utopianism –pg 4539

Societies and Clubs –pg 5228

Sociology –pg 5237

Software –pg 1283; see also Computer Industry and Industry Directories pg 1235; Programs and Programming pg 1277

Soil –See **Agriculture -- Crop Production and Soil** pg 161

Solar Energy –See **Energy** pg 1930; see also Engineering -- Mechanical Engineering and Machinery pg 2108

Sound –pg 4451

Sound Recordings and Systems –pg 5315; see also Engineering -- Electricity, Electrical Engineering, Electronics pg 2034; Music pg 4098

South America –See **General Interest -- General Interest-South America** pg 2551; History(General) -- History of North, South, and Central America pg 2717

Special Education –See **Education -- Special Education and Rehabilitation** pg 1874

Special Education and Rehabilitation –pg 1874

Spectroscopy –See **Physics -- Light, Optics, Radiation** pg 4432

Speech Disorders –See **Medical Science and Technology -- Otorhinolaryngology** pg 3885; see also Education -- Special Education and Rehabilitation pg 1874; Physically Impaired pg 4382

Speech Pathology –See **Physically Impaired** pg 4382; see also Education -- Special Education and Rehabilitation pg 1874

Speleology –See **Earth Sciences -- Geophysics** pg 1402

Sports –pg 4881; see also Recreation, Leisure -- Games and Amusements pg 4856; Recreation, Leisure -- Health and Personal Fitness pg 2595; Recreation, Leisure -- Outdoor Life pg 4868

Sports Medicine –pg 3953

Stained Glass –See **Glass and Ceramics** pg 2585

Standardization –See **Metrology and Standardization** pg 4029

State Government –See **Public Administration** pg 4623; see also Public Administration -- Public Finance and Taxation pg 4708

Statistics –pg 5320

Stomatology –See **Dentistry** pg 1314

Stress –See **Medical Science and Technology** pg 3543; **Psychology** pg 4570

Sugar –See **Agriculture -- Crop Production and Soil** pg 161; see also Food and Food Industry pg 2325

Surface Chemistry –See **Chemistry -- Physical and Theoretical Chemistry** pg 1049

Surgeons –See **Medical Science and Technology -- Physicians and Medical Personnel** pg 3912

Surgery –pg 3957

Surveying –See **Engineering -- Civil Engineering** pg 2018; **Geography** pg 2553

Swimming –See **Recreation, Leisure -- Sports** pg 4881

Tax Planning –See **Law -- Estate Planning** pg 3117

Taxation –See **Public Administration -- Public Finance and Taxation** pg 4708; see also Business -- Accounting pg 735; Law -- Estate Planning pg 3117

Taxidermy –See **Hobbies** pg 2770

Tea –See **Food and Food Industry -- Beverage Industry** pg 2363; see also Agriculture pg 42

Teaching and Curriculum –pg 1887

Teaching Materials –See **Education -- Teaching and Curriculum** pg 1887

Technical Education –See **Education -- Vocational Education** pg 1909

Technology –See **Science and Technology** pg 5078

Telecommunications –pg 1148

Telegraph –See **Communication -- Telecommunications** pg 1148

Telephone –See **Communication -- Telecommunications** pg 1148

Telephone Directories –See **Communication -- Telecommunications** pg 1148

Television –See **Communication -- Broadcasting** pg 1125

Tennis –See **Recreation, Leisure -- Sports** pg 4881

Textbooks –See **Education** pg 1720

Textiles –pg 5347; see also Clothing Industry and Fashion pg 1081

The Arts –pg 311

Theater –pg 5361; see also The Arts -- Performing Arts pg 383

Theology –See **Religion and Theology** pg 4931

Theoretical Chemistry –See **Chemistry -- Physical and Theoretical Chemistry** pg 1049

Theosophy –See **Religion and Theology -- Islam, Bahaism, Theosophy** pg 5041

Thrombosis –See **Medical Science and Technology -- Internal Medicine** pg 3794; see also Medical Science and Technology -- Cardiology pg 3697; Medical Science and Technology -- Hematology pg 3769; Medical Science and Technology -- Pathology pg 3891

Tobacco –pg 5372

Total Quality Management –See **Business -- General Management** pg 858; **Business -- Personnel Management** pg 938

Tourism –See **Travel and Tourism** pg 5458

Toxicology –pg 3978; see also Pharmacy and Pharmacology pg 4288

Toys –See **Gifts, Toys** pg 2583

Track and Field –See **Recreation, Leisure -- Sports** pg 4881

Trade –See **Business -- Commerce** pg 821

Trade Regulation –See **Business -- Commerce** pg 821; see also Law -- Corporate Law pg 3094

Trade Schools –See **Education -- Vocational Education** pg 1909

Trade Shows –See **Business -- Advertising and Public Relations** pg 753

Trade Unions –See **Economics -- Labor** pg 1642

Trademarks –See **Copyright, Intellectual Property** pg 1300

Traffic –See **Transportation -- Roads and Traffic** pg 5438

Transportation –pg 5375; see also Business -- Commerce pg 821

Travel and Tourism –pg 5458; see also Geography pg 2553; Recreation, Leisure pg 4848

Trees –See **Gardening and Horticulture** pg 2407; see also Forestry pg 2373

Tropical Diseases –See **Medical Science and Technology -- Tropical Medicine** pg 3985

Tropical Medicine –pg 3985

Trucks and Trucking –See **Transportation** pg 5375

Trustees –See **Law -- Estate Planning** pg 3117

SUBJECT CROSS REFERENCES

Trusts –See **Law -- Estate Planning** pg 3117

Ukrainian Studies –See **History(General) -- History of Europe** pg 2671; see also Literature pg 3357

Ultrafication –See **Medical Science and Technology -- Hematology** pg 3769

Ultrasonic Therapy –See **Medical Science and Technology -- Radiology** pg 3938

Ultrasound –See **Medical Science and Technology -- Radiology** pg 3938

Unemployment –See **Economics -- Labor** pg 1642; see also Law pg 2926

Unions –See **Economics -- Labor** pg 1642

Universities and Colleges –See **Education -- Higher Education** pg 1806; see also College and School Publications pg 1088

Urban Development –See **Housing and Urban Development** pg 2812

Urinary Tract –See **Medical Science and Technology -- Urology and Nephrology** pg 3987

Urology –See **Medical Science and Technology -- Urology and Nephrology** pg 3987

Urology and Nephrology –pg 3987

Utopianism –See **Political Science -- Socialism, Communism, Anarchism, Utopianism** pg 4539

Vacations –See **Travel and Tourism** pg 5458; see also Recreation,Leisure pg 4848

Veterans –See **Military and Defense** pg 4033; see also Naval Science, Navigation pg 4174

Veterinary Sciences –pg 5501; see also Zoology pg 5572

Video –See **Communication -- Broadcasting** pg 1125; **Photography and Video** pg 4366; see also Motion Picture pg 4062

Video Games/Arcades –See **Recreation, Leisure -- Games and Amusements** pg 4856

Virology –See **Biology -- Microbiology** pg 558

Virtual Reality –See **Computers -- Artificial Intelligence** pg 1210; see also Computers -- Automation pg 1217

Visual Arts –See **The Arts -- Art** pg 335

Vitamins –See **Nutrition and Dietetics** pg 4186

Vocational Education –pg 1909

Vocational Guidance –See **Education -- Vocational Education** pg 1909; see also Occupations and Careers pg 4201

Volcanoes –See **Earth Sciences -- Geophysics** pg 1402

Volunteer Work –See **Philanthropy** pg 4334

Voting –See **Political Science** pg 4461; see also Public Administration pg 4623

WAN (Wide Area Networks) –See **Computer** pg 1240

War –See **History(General)** pg 2609; see also Political Science pg 4461

Waste Management –See **Environmental Issues -- Pollution and Waste Management** pg 2222

Watches –See **Jewelry -- Clocks and Watches** pg 2916

Water Pollution –See **Environmental Issues -- Pollution and Waste Management** pg 2222; see also Water Resources pg 5528

Water Resources –pg 5528; see also Earth Sciences -- Hydrology pg 1412; Engineering -- Hydraulic Engineering pg 2087; Environmental Issues -- Conservation and Natural Resources pg 2185

Water Utilities –See **Public Administration -- Public Utilities** pg 4759; see also Water Resources pg 5528

Weaponry –See **Military and Defense** pg 4033

Weather –See **Earth Sciences -- Meteorology** pg 1419

Weightlifting –See **Health and Personal Fitness** pg 2595; see also Recreation, Leisure -- Sports pg 4881

Weights and Measures –See **Metrology and Standardization** pg 4029

Welding –pg 4026

Welfare –See **Sociology -- Social Services and Welfare** pg 5269

Western Australian Studies –See **History(General) -- History of Australia and Oceania** pg 2668

Who's Who –See **Biographies** pg 429

Wide Area Networks –See **Computers -- Computer Networks** pg 1240

Wildlife –See **Environmental Issues -- Conservation and Natural Resources** pg 2185; see also Environmental Issues -- Ecology pg 2210; Recreation, Leisure -- Outdoor Life pg 4868

Wills –See **Law -- Estate Planning** pg 3117

Wine –See **Food and Food Industry -- Beverage Industry** pg 2363

Women's Interests –pg 5550

Wood –See **Forestry -- Lumber and Wood** pg 2399

Woodwork –See **Building and Construction -- Carpentry and Woodwork** pg 633

Word Processing –pg 1292

Workmen's Compensation –See **Economics -- Labor** pg 1642; see also Insurance pg 2872

World Politics –See **Political Science** pg 4461

Wrestling –See **Recreation, Leisure -- Sports** pg 4881

Writing –See **Journalism** pg 2917; see also Literature pg 3357

Yachts and Yachting –See **Boats and Boating** pg 591; see also Travel and Tourism pg 5458

Yearbooks –See **Encyclopedias and General Reference Books** pg 1923

Youth –See **Children and Youth Interests** pg 1059

Zoning –See **Housing and Urban Development** pg 2812; **Law** pg 2926; see also Real Estate pg 4833

Zoology –pg 5572; see also Veterinary Sciences pg 5501

TABLES

Frequency
Document Delivery
Wire Services
Country of Publication
Unit of Currency
Indexes/Abstracts

FREQUENCY TABLE

an	Annual	sa	Semiannual
be	Biennial	sm	Semimonthly
bm	Bimonthly	sw	Semiweekly
bw	Biweekly	te	Triennial
da	Daily	tm	Three times a month
ir	Irregular	tq	Tri-quarterly
mo	Monthly	tw	Three times a week
qt	Quarterly	wk	Weekly

Additional frequencies may appear in the Serial Listing when provided by the publisher.

DOCUMENT DELIVERY

The following document supplier notations, when noted in a Serial Listing, indicate the availability of that serial for document delivery through the specified service. Permission has been granted by the copyright owner and is subject to change without notice. Only the portion in boldface will appear in the listing.

ADONIS™
ADONIS B.V.
Spuistraat 112D
1012VA Amsterdam, The Netherlands

Article Express International
Engineering Information Inc.
469 Union Avenue
Westbury, New York 11590

Ask*IEEE
(in cooperation with EBSCOdoc™)
1722 Gilbreth Road
Burlingame, CA 94010

BIOSIS Document Express™
(in cooperation with EBSCOdoc™)
1722 Gilbreth Road
Burlingame, CA 94010

BLDSC
British Library Document Supply Centre - Customer Services
Boston Spa, Wetherby
LS23 7BQ, United Kingdom

CASDDS ®
Chemical Abstracts Service Document Delivery Service
PO Box 3012
Columbus, Ohio 43210-0012

Documents on Demand
Congressional Information Service
4520 East-West Highway
Bethesda, MD 20814-3389

FAXON Xpress
FAXON Research Services, Inc.
15 Southwest Park
Westwood, MA 02090

Haworth Document Delivery Service
The Haworth Press, Inc.
10 Alice Street
Binghamton, New York 13904-1580

Magazine Collection™
Information Access Company
362 Lakeside Drive
Foster City, CA 94404

Petroleum Abstracts Document Delivery Service
University of Tulsa
600 South College
Tulsa, OK 74104-3189

Quick Copies
Williams and Wilkins Company
428 East Preston Street
Baltimore, MD 21202-3993

SWETSCAN-SWETDOC
Swets & Zeitlinger bv
Heereweg 347, PO Box 830
2160 SZ Lisse, The Netherlands

The Genuine Article®
Institute for Scientific Information
3501 Market Street
Philadelphia, PA 19104

The Uncover Company
3801 East Florida Avenue
Suite 200
Denver, CO 80210

UMI Article Clearinghouse
300 North Zeeb Road
PO Box 1346
Ann Arbor, MI 48106-1346

WIRE SERVICES

The following abbreviations represent the news and photograph wire services found in the Directory. Each code is followed by the complete name of the service.

CODE:	SERVICE:
AF	Agence France Presse
AN	Alternet
AP	Associated Press
API	Associated Press International
BU	British United Press
CA	Canadian Press
CH	Chicago Tribune - New York
CN	Capital News
CM	Christian Science Monitor
CO	Copley News Service
CP	Colorado Press
CQ	Congressional Quarterly
CS	Catholic News Service
CT	Chicago Sun Times
CP	China and Taiwan News Age
CU	Canadian United Press
DJ	Dow Jones
EI	Empire Information Service
ER	Editorial Research Service
FN	Federation News Service
GN	Gannett News Service
GP	Georgia Press Association
HH	Hearst Headline Service
HN	Harris News Service
IT	Independent Television Network
IM	Iowa Medialink
JT	Jewish Telegraphic Agency
KF	King Features
KN	Knight News Service
KR	Knight-Ridder
LA	Los Angeles Times
LO	London Daily News
LT	Times of London
MG	Manchester Guardian
ML	MediaLink
MN	Morris News Service
MP	Montana Press Association
NC	NEWSCOM
NE	Newspaper Enterprises Association
NF	Newsfinder
NM	Notimex
NN	Newhouse News Service
NP	NNAP
NU	News USA
NW	National Weather Service
NY	New York Times
ON	Ottawa News Service
PN	Pacific News Service
RN	Reuters News Service
SH	Scripps-Howard Newspaper Alliance-Scripps Howard News Service
SS	SportsStats
WN	World News
WP	Washington Post Writer's Guild
WS	Women's News Service
WW	Women's Wear Daily

COUNTRY OF PUBLICATION TABLE

The following lists of country codes have been taken directly from the USMARC Bibliographic Format, with the exception being that the United States and Canada state and province codes have been grouped under their respective countries, rather than being listed individually.

COUNTRY OF PUBLICATION BY CODE

Code	Country	Code	Country	Code	Country
AA	Albania	GS	Georgia (Republic)	PY	Paraguay
AE	Algeria	GT	Guatemala	QA	Qatar
AF	Afghanistan	GU	Guam	RE	Reunion
AG	Argentina	GV	Guinea	RH	Zimbabwe
AI	Armenia	GW	Germany	RM	Romania
AJ	Azerbaijan	GY	Guyana	RW	Rwanda
AM	Anguilla	GZ	Gaza Strip	RU	Russia (Republic)
AN	Andorra	HK	Hong Kong	SA	South Africa
AO	Angola	HM	Heard and McDonald Islands	SE	Seychelles
AQ	Antigua and Barbuda	HO	Honduras	SF	Sao Tome and Principe
AS	American Samoa	HT	Haiti	SG	Senegal
AT	Australia	HU	Hungary	SH	Spanish North Africa
AU	Austria	IC	Iceland	SI	Singapore
AW	Aruba	IE	Ireland	SJ	Sudan
AY	Antarctica	II	India	SL	Sierra Leone
BA	Bahrain	IO	Indonesia	SM	San Marino
BB	Barbados	IQ	Iraq	SO	Somalia
BD	Burundi	IR	Iran	SP	Spain
BE	Belgium	IS	Israel	SQ	Swaziland
BF	Bahamas	IT	Italy	SR	Surinam
BG	Bangladesh	IV	Ivory Coast	SS	Western Sahara
BH	Belize	IY	Iraq-Saudi Arabia Neutral Zone	SU	Saudi Arabia
BI	British Indian Ocean Territory			SW	Sweden
BL	Brazil	JA	Japan	SX	Namibia
BM	Bermuda Islands	JI	Johnson Atoll	SY	Syria
BN	Bosnia Hercegovina	JM	Jamaica	SZ	Switzerland
BO	Bolivia	JO	Jordan	TA	Tajikstan
BP	Solomon Islands	KE	Kenya	TC	Turks and Caicos Islands
BR	Burma	KG	Kyrgyzstan	TG	Togo
BS	Botswana	KN	Korea (North)	TH	Thailand
BT	Bhutan	KO	Korea (South)	TI	Tunisia
BU	Bulgaria	KU	Kuwait	TK	Turkmenistan
BV	Bouvet Island	KZ	Kazakhstan	TL	Tokelau Islands
BW	Byelarus	LB	Liberia	TO	Tonga
BX	Brunei	LE	Lebanon	TR	Trinidad and Tobago
CB	Cambodia	LH	Liechtenstein	TS	Trucial States (United Arab Emirates)
CC	China	LI	Lithuania		
CD	Chad	LO	Lesotho	TU	Turkey
CE	Sri Lanka	LS	Laos	TZ	Tanzania
CF	Congo (Brazzaville)	LU	Luxembourg	UA	Egypt
CG	Zaire	LV	Latvia	UC	United States Misc. Caribbean Islands
CH	China (Republic: 1949)	LY	Libya		
CI	Croatia	MC	Monaco	UG	Uganda
CJ	Cayman Islands	MF	Mauritius	UK	United Kingdom (Including Scotland)
CK	Colombia	MG	Madagascar		
CL	Chile	MH	Macão	UN	Ukraine
CM	Cameroon	MJ	Montserrat	UP	United States Misc. Pacific Islands
CN	Canada	MK	Oman		
CP	Canton and Enderbury Islands	ML	Mali	UR	USSR
CQ	Comorus	MM	Malta	US	United States
CR	Costa Rica	MP	Mongolia	UV	Burkina Faso
CS	Czechoslovakia	MQ	Martinique	UY	Uruguay
CU	Cuba	MR	Morocco	UZ	Uzbekistan
CV	Cape Verde	MU	Mauritania	VB	Virgin Islands (British V.I.)
CW	Cook Islands	MV	Moldova	VC	Vatican City
CX	Central African Republic	MW	Malawi	VE	Venezuela
CY	Cyprus	MX	Mexico	VI	Virgin Islands (U.S.)
DK	Denmark	MY	Malaysia	VM	Vietnam
DM	Benin	MZ	Mozambique	WF	Wallis and Futuna
DQ	Dominica	NA	Netherlands Antilles	WJ	West Bank of the Jordan River
DR	Dominican Republic	NE	Netherlands	WK	Wake Island
EC	Ecuador	NG	Niger	WS	Western Samoa
EG	Equatorial Guinea	NL	New Caledonia	XA	Christmas Island (Indian Ocean)
ER	Estonia	NN	Vanuatu		
ES	El Salvador	NO	Norway	XB	Cocos (Keeling) Islands
ET	Ethiopia	NP	Nepal	XC	Maldives
FA	Faroe Islands	NQ	Nicaragua	XD	Saint Kitts-Nevis
FG	French Guiana	NR	Nigeria	XE	Marshall Islands
FI	Finland	NU	Nauru	XF	Midway Island
FJ	Fiji	NW	Northern Mariana Islands	XH	Niue
FM	Micronesia (Federated States)	NX	Norfolk Island	XJ	Saint Helena
FP	French Polynesia	NZ	New Zealand	XK	Saint Lucia
FR	France	OT	Mayotte	XL	Saint Pierre and Miquelon
FS	Terres Australes et Antarctiques Francaises	PC	Pitcairn Island	XM	Saint Vincent and the Grenadines
		PE	Peru		
FT	Djibouti	PF	Paracel Islands	XN	Macedonia
GB	Kiribati	PG	Guinea-Bissau	XO	Slovakia
GD	Grenada	PH	Philippines	XP	Spratly Islands
GH	Ghana	PK	Pakistan	XR	Czech Republic
GI	Gibraltar	PL	Poland	XS	Falkland Islands
GL	Greenland	PN	Panama	XV	Slovenia
GM	Gambia	PO	Portugal	YE	Yemen
GO	Gabon	PP	Papua New Guinea	YU	Yugoslavia
GP	Guadeloupe	PR	Puerto Rico	ZA	Zambia
GR	Greece	PW	Palau		

COUNTRY OF PUBLICATION TABLE

COUNTRY OF PUBLICATION BY COUNTRY

Country	Code	Country	Code	Country	Code
Afghanistan	AF	Greenland	GL	Paracel Islands	PF
Albania	AA	Grenada	GD	Paraguay	PY
Algeria	AE	Guadeloupe	GP	Peru	PE
American Samoa	AS	Guam	GU	Philippines	PH
Andorra	AN	Guatemala	GT	Pitcairn Island	PC
Angola	AO	Guinea	GV	Poland	PL
Anguilla	AM	Guinea-Bissau	PG	Portugal	PO
Antarctica	AY	Guyana	GY	Puerto Rico	PR
Antigua and Barbuda	AQ	Haiti	HT	Qatar	QA
Argentina	AG	Heard and McDonald Islands	HM	Reunion	RE
Armenia	AI	Honduras	HO	Romania	RM
Aruba	AW	Hong Kong	HK	Russia (Republic)	RU
Australia	AT	Hungary	HU	Rwanda	RW
Austria	AU	Iceland	IC	Saint Helena	XJ
Azerbaijan	AJ	India	II	Saint Kitts-Nevis	XD
Bahamas	BF	Indonesia	IO	Saint Lucia	XK
Bahrain	BA	Iran	IR	Saint Pierre and Miquelon	XL
Bangladesh	BG	Iraq	IQ	Saint Vincent and the Grenadines	XM
Barbados	BB	Iraq-Saudi Arabia Neutral Zone	IY	San Marino	SM
Belgium	BE	Ireland	IE	Sao Tome and Principe	SF
Belize	BH	Israel	IS	Saudi Arabia	SU
Benin	DM	Italy	IT	Senegal	SG
Bermuda Islands	BM	Ivory Coast	IV	Seychelles	SE
Bhutan	BT	Jamaica	JM	Sierra Leone	SL
Bolivia	BO	Japan	JA	Singapore	SI
Bosnia Hercegovina	BN	Johnson Atoll	JI	Slovakia	XO
Botswana	BS	Jordan	JO	Slovenia	XV
Bouvet Island	BV	Kazakhstan	KZ	Solomon Islands	BP
Brazil	BL	Kenya	KE	Somalia	SO
British Indian Ocean Territory	BI	Kiribati	GB	South Africa	SA
Brunei	BX	Korea (North)	KN	Spain	SP
Bulgaria	BU	Korea (South)	KO	Spanish North Africa	SH
Burkina Faso	UV	Kuwait	KU	Spratly Island	XP
Burma	BR	Kyrgyzstan	KG	Sri Lanka	CE
Burundi	BD	Laos	LS	Sudan	SJ
Byelarus	BW	Latvia	LV	Surinam	SR
Cambodia	CB	Lebanon	LE	Swaziland	SQ
Cameroon	CM	Lesotho	LO	Sweden	SW
Canada	CN	Liberia	LB	Switzerland	SZ
Canton and Enderbury Islands	CP	Libya	LY	Syria	SY
Cape Verde	CV	Liechtenstein	LH	Tajikistan	TA
Cayman Islands	CJ	Lithuania	LI	Tanzania	TZ
Central African Republic	CX	Luxembourg	LU	Terres Australes et Antarctiques Francaises	FS
Chad	CD	Macao	MH		
Chile	CL	Macedonia	XN	Thailand	TH
China	CC	Madagascar	MG	Togo	TG
China (Republic: 1949)	CH	Malawi	MW	Tokelau Islands	TL
Christmas Island (Indian Ocean)	XA	Malaysia	MY	Tonga	TO
Cocos (Keeling) Islands	XB	Maldives	XC	Trinidad and Tobago	TR
Colombia	CK	Mali	ML	Trucial States (United Arab Emirates)	TS
Comoros	CQ	Malta	MM		
Congo (Brazzaville)	CF	Marshall Islands	XE	Tunisia	TI
Cook Islands	CW	Martinique	MQ	Turkey	TU
Costa Rica	CR	Mauritania	MU	Turkmenistan	TK
Croatia	CI	Mauritius	MF	Turks and Caicos Islands	TC
Cuba	CU	Mayotte	OT	Uganda	UG
Cyprus	CY	Mexico	MX	Ukraine	UN
Czech Republic	XR	Micronesia (Federated States)	FM	United Kingdom (Including Scotland)	UK
Czechoslovakia	CS	Midway Island	XF		
Denmark	DK	Moldova	MV	United States	US
Djibouti	FT	Monaco	MC	United States (Misc. Caribbean Islands)	UC
Dominica	DQ	Mongolia	MP		
Dominican Republic	DR	Montserrat	MJ	United States (Misc. Pacific Islands)	UP
Ecuador	EC	Morocco	MR	Uruguay	UY
Egypt	UA	Mozambique	MZ	USSR	UR
El Salvador	ES	Namibia	SX	Uzbekistan	UZ
Equatorial Guinea	EG	Nauru	NU	Vanuatu	NN
Estonia	ER	Nepal	NP	Vatican City	VC
Ethiopia	ET	Netherlands	NE	Venezuela	VE
Falkland Islands	XS	Netherlands Antilles	NA	Vietnam	VM
Faroe Islands	FA	New Caledonia	NL	Virgin Islands (British V.I.)	VB
Fiji	FJ	New Zealand	NZ	Virgin Islands (U.S.)	VI
Finland	FI	Nicaragua	NQ	Wake Island	WK
France	FR	Niger	NG	Wallis and Futuna	WF
French Guiana	FG	Nigeria	NR	West Bank of the Jordan River	WJ
French Polynesia	FP	Niue	XH	Western Sahara	SS
Gabon	GO	Norfolk Island	NX	Western Samoa	WS
Gambia	GM	Northern Mariana Islands	NW	Yemen	YE
Gaza Strip	GZ	Norway	NO	Yugoslavia	YU
Georgia (Republic)	GS	Oman	MK	Zaire	CG
Germany	GW	Pakistan	PK	Zambia	ZA
Ghana	GH	Palau	PW	Zimbabwe	RH
Gibraltar	GI	Panama	PN		
Greece	GR	Papua New Guinea	PP		

UNIT OF CURRENCY TABLE

In the Serial Listing, prices are given in country of publication currency and are one-year library subscription rates, unless designated otherwise.

Country	Currency	Country	Currency	Country	Currency
Afghanistan	afghanin	Greece	Greek drachma	Papua New Guinea	kina
Albania	lek	Guadeloupe	French franc	Paraguay	guarani
Algeria	Algerian dinar	Guatemala	quetzal	Peru	sole
Angola	kwanza	Guyana	Guyana dollar	Philippines	peso
Antigua and Barbuda	East Caribbean dollar	Haiti	gourde	Papua New Guinea	kina
		Honduras	lempira	Paraguay	guarani
Argentina	peso argentino	Hong Kong	Hong Kong dollar	Peru	sole
Australia	Australian dollar	Hungary	forint	Philippines	peso
Austria	schilling	Iceland	krona	Poland	zloty
Bahamas	Bahamian dollar	India	rupee	Portugal	escudo
Bangladesh	taka	Indonesia	rupiah	Qatar	Qatar riyal
Barbados	Barbados dollar	Iran	rial	Reunion	French franc
Belgium	Belgian franc	Iraq	Iraqi dinar	Romania	lei
Bermuda Islands	Bermuda dollar	Ireland	Irish pound	Rwanda	Rwanda franc
Bolivia	peso	Israel	shekel	San Marino	Italian lira
Botswana	pula	Italy	lira	Saudi Arabia	Saudi riyal
Brazil	cruzeiro	Ivory Coast	CFA franc	Senegal	CFA franc
Belize	Belize dollar	Jamaica	Jamaican dollar	Sierra Leone	leone
Benin	CFA franc	Japan	yen	Singapore	Singapore dollar
Bulgaria	lev	Jordan	Jordanian dinar	Somalia	Somali shilling
Burkina Faso	CFA franc	Kenya	Kenya shilling	South Africa	South African rand
Burma	kyat	Korea (North)	won	Southern Yemen	dinar
Cameroon	CFA franc	Korea (South)	won	Spain	pesata
Canada	Canadian dollar	Kuwait	Kuwaiti dinar	Sri Lanka	rupee
Cayman Islands	cordoba/dollar	Lebanon	Lebanese pound	Sudan	Sudanese pound
Central African Republic	CFA franc	Liberia	U.S. dollar	Surinam	Surinam guilder
		Libya	Libyan dinar	Swaziland	emalangeni
Chad	CFA franc	Liechtenstein	Swiss franc	Sweden	krona
Chile	peso	Luxembourg	Luxembourg franc	Switzerland	franc
China	renminbi yuan	Madagascar	Malagasy franc	Syria	Syrian pound
China (Republic: 1949)	New Taiwan dollar	Malawi	Malawi kwacha	Tanzania	Tanzanian shilling
		Malaysia	ringgit	Thailand	baht
Colombia	peso	Mali	CFA franc	Togo	CFA franc
Cook Islands	New Zealand dollar	Malta	Maltese pound	Trinidad and Tobago	Trinidad and Tobago dollar
Costa Rica	colon	Martinique	French franc		
Cuba	peso	Mauritius	Mauritian rupee	Tunisia	Tunisian dinar
Cyprus	Cyprus pound	Mexico	peso	Turkey	Turkish lira
Czechoslovakia	korona	Monaco	French franc	Uganda	Uganda shilling
Benin	CFA franc	Morocco	dirham	United Kingdom	pound sterling
Denmark	krone	Mozambique	meticais	United States	U.S. dollar
Djibouti	Djibouti franc	Nauru	Australian dollar	Uruguay	new peso
Dominican Republic	peso	Nepal	Nepalese rupee	USSR	ruble
Ecuador	sucre	Netherlands	guilder	Vatican City	lira
Egypt	Egyptian pound	New Caledonia	CFP franc	Venezuela	bolivare
El Salvador	colon	New Zealand	New Zealand dollar	Vietnam	dong
Ethiopia	Ethiopian birr	Nicaragua	cordoba	Yemen (Yemen (Sana))	riyal
Fiji	Fiji dollar	Niger	CFA franc		
Finland	fim (finnmark)	Nigeria	naira	Yugoslavia	dinar
France	French franc	Norway	krone	Zaire	CFA franc
Gambia	dalasi	Oman	rial	Zambia	Zambian kwacha
Germany	mark	Pakistan	rupee	Zimbabwe	Zimbabwean dollar
Ghana	cedi	Panama	balboa		

INDEXES/ABSTRACTS TABLE

The following is a list of all publications which may index, or contain an abstract of, titles in the Directory. The Abbreviated Title in boldface is the abbreviation of the index or abstract as used in the Serial Listing. The complete title of the index or abstract follows. Succeeding information or a Ceased/Suspended indicator will follow the complete title for those serials where it applies. For services that share the same journal source list, a reference will be made to that service which will appear in the Serial Listing. This table includes over 1,300 Indexing/Abstracting services, 921 of which are active.

A.I.D. RES. DEV. ABSTR.
[US/0096-1507]
A.I.D. RESEARCH AND DEVELOPMENT ABSTRACTS.
(**Continues** A.I.D. Reference Center. A.I.D. Research Abstracts.)

ABC POL SCI
[US/0001-0456]
ABC POL SCI. ADVANCE BIBLIOGRAPHY OF CONTENTS: POLITICAL SCIENCE & GOVERNMENT.

ABI/INFORM ONDISC
[US/1062-5127]
ABI/INFORM ONDISC.

ABI/INFORM ONDISC: EXPR. ED.
[US]
ABI/INFORM ONDISC: EXPRESS EDITION [COMPUTER FILE].

ABI/INFORM GLOB. ED.
[US]
ABI/INFORM GLOBAL EDITION [COMPUTER FILE].

ABR. CATHOL. PERIOD. LIT. INDEX
[US/0737-3457]
ABRIDGED CATHOLIC PERIODICAL AND LITERATURE INDEX, THE.

ABR. INDEX MED.
[US/0001-3331]
ABRIDGED INDEX MEDICUS.
(**Continues** American Medical Association. Abridged Index Medicus.)

ABR. READ. GUIDE PERIOD. LIT.
[US/0001-334X]
ABRIDGED READERS' GUIDE TO PERIODICAL LITERATURE.

ABS INT. GUIDE CLASSICAL STUD.
[US]
ABS INTERNATIONAL GUIDE TO CLASSICAL STUDIES.
(**Continued by** International Guide to Classical Studies (1966).)

ABSTR. ABSTR. BOOK REV. CUR. LEG. PERIOD.
[US]
ABSTRACTS : ABSTRACTS OF BOOK REVIEWS IN CURRENT LEGAL PERIODICALS.
(**Continues** Abstracts of Book Reviews in Current Legal Periodicals.)

ABSTR. AIT REP. PUBL. ENERGY
[TH/0857-6181]
ABSTRACTS OF AIT REPORTS AND PUBLICATIONS ON ENERGY.
(**Continues** Abstracts of AIT Reports and Publications on Renewable Energy Resources.)

ABSTR. ANTHROPOL.
[US/0001-3455]
ABSTRACTS IN ANTHROPOLOGY.

ABSTR. BIOCOMMER.
[UK/0263-6778]
ABSTRACTS IN BIOCOMMERCE.

ABSTR. BOOK REV. CURR. LEG. PERIOD.
[US/0362-1065]
ABSTRACTS OF BOOK REVIEWS IN CURRENT LEGAL PERIODICALS.
(**Continued by** Abstracts : Abstracts of Book Reviews in Current Legal Periodicals.)

ABSTR. BULL. INST. PAP. SCI. TECH.
[US/1047-2088]
ABSTRACT BULLETIN OF THE INSTITUTE OF PAPER SCIENCE AND TECHNOLOGY.
(**Continues** Institute of Paper Chemistry (Appleton, Wis.) Abstract Bulletin of the Institute of Paper Chemistry.)

ABSTR. BULL. INST. PAPER CHEM.
[US]
ABSTRACT BULLETIN OF THE INSTITUTE OF PAPER CHEMISTRY.
(**Continued by** Abstract Bulletin of the Institute of Paper Science and Technology.)

ABSTR. CLIN. CARE GUIDEL.
[US/1042-4423]
ABSTRACTS OF CLINICAL CARE GUIDELINES.

ABSTR. CRIMINOL. PENOL.
[NE/0001-3684]
ABSTRACTS ON CRIMINOLOGY AND PENOLOGY.
(**Continued by** Criminology & Penology Abstracts.)

ABSTR. ENGL. STUD.
[US/0001-3560]
ABSTRACTS OF ENGLISH STUDIES.
(Suspended)

ABSTR. ENTOMOL.
[US/0001-3579]
ABSTRACTS OF ENTOMOLOGY.
***Refer to Biological Abstracts for complete source list.

ABSTR. FOLK. STUD.
[US/0001-3587]
ABSTRACTS OF FOLKLORE STUDIES.
(Ceased)

ABSTR. GRAPHIC ARTS TECH. FOUND.
[US]
ABSTRACTS (GRAPHIC ARTS TECHNICAL FOUNDATION).
(**Continues** Graphic Arts Abstracts (Pittsburgh, PA. : 1968).)

ABSTR. HEALTH CARE MANAGE. STUD.
[US/0194-4908]
ABSTRACTS OF HEALTH CARE MANAGEMENT STUDIES.
(**Continues** Abstracts of Hospital Management Studies.)

ABSTR. HEALTH ENVIRON. POLLUTANTS
[US/0044-5819]
ABSTRACTS ON HEALTH EFFECTS OF ENVIRONMENTAL POLLUTANTS.
(Ceased)

ABSTR. HOSPIT. MANAGE. STUD.
[US/0001-3595]
ABSTRACTS OF HOSPITAL MANAGEMENT STUDIES.
(**Continued by** Abstracts of Health Care Management Studies.)

ABSTR. HUM. COMPUT. INTERACT.
[US/1042-0193]
ABSTRACTS IN HUMAN-COMPUTER INTERACTION.
(Suspended)

ABSTR. HYG.
[UK/0001-3692]
ABSTRACTS ON HYGIENE.
(**Continued by** Abstracts on Hygiene and Communicable Diseases.)

ABSTR. HYG. COMMUN. DIS.
[UK/0260-5511]
ABSTRACTS ON HYGIENE AND COMMUNICABLE DISEASES.
(**Continues** Abstracts on Hygiene.)
***Refer to Tropical Diseases Bulletin for complete source list.

ABSTR. J. EARTHQ. ENG.
[US/0363-5732]
ABSTRACT JOURNAL IN EARTHQUAKE ENGINEERING.

ABSTR. MIL. BIBLIOGR.
[AG]
ABSTRACTS OF MILITARY BIBLIOGRAPHY.
(**Continues** Resumenes Analiticos Sobre Defensa y Seguridad Nacional.)

ABSTR. NEW WORLD ARCHAEOL.
[US]
ABSTRACTS OF NEW WORLD ARCHAEOLOGY.
(Ceased)

ABSTR. NORTH AM. GEOL.
[US/0001-3625]
ABSTRACTS OF NORTH AMERICAN GEOLOGY.
(Ceased)

ABSTR. OF MYCOL.
[US/0001-3617]
ABSTRACTS OF MYCOLOGY.
***Refer to Biological Abstracts for complete source list.

ABSTR. PHOTOGR. SCI. ENG. LIT.
[US/0001-3633]
ABSTRACTS OF PHOTOGRAPHIC SCIENCE & ENGINEERING LITERATURE.
(**Continues** Monthly Abstract Bulletin from the Kodak Research Laboratories; ANSCO Abstracts.)

ABSTR. POP. CULT.
[US/0147-2615]
ABSTRACTS OF POPULAR CULTURE.
(Ceased)

ABSTR. RES. PASTOR. CARE COUNS.
[US/0733-2599]
ABSTRACTS OF RESEARCH IN PASTORAL CARE AND COUNSELING.
(**Continues** Pastoral Care and Counseling Abstracts.)

INDEXES/ABSTRACTS TABLE

ABSTR. SOC. GERONTOL.
[US/1047-4862]
ABSTRACTS IN SOCIAL GERONTOLOGY.
(*Continues* Current Literature on Aging.)

ABSTR. SOC. WORK.
[US/0001-3412]
ABSTRACTS FOR SOCIAL WORKERS.
(*Continued by* Social Work Research & Abstracts.)

ABSTR. TROP. AGRIC.
[NE/0304-5951]
ABSTRACTS ON TROPICAL AGRICULTURE.
(*Supersedes* Tropical Abstracts.)

ABSTR. WORLD MED.
[UK]
ABSTRACTS OF WORLD MEDICINE.
(*Absorbed* Abstracts of World Surgery, Obstetrics and Gynaecology.)

ACAD. ABSTR.
[US/1056-7496]
ACADEMIC ABSTRACTS.

ACAD. ABSTR. FULL TEXT ELITE
[US/1060-6750]
ACADEMIC ABSTRACTS FULL TEXT ELITE.

ACAD. IND. [COMPUTER FILE]
[US]
ACADEMIC INDEX. [COMPUTER FILE].

ACAD. SEARCH
[US/1071-2720]
ACADEMIC SEARCH.

ACCESS
[US/0095-5698]
ACCESS (SYRACUSE).
(*Absorbed* Monthly Periodical Index.)

ACCESS INDEX LITTLE MAG.
[US/0363-065X]
ACCESS INDEX TO LITTLE MAGAZINES.
(Ceased)

ACCOUNT. ART.
[US]
ACCOUNTING ARTICLES.

ACCOUNT. DATA PROCESS. ABSTR.
[UK/0001-4796]
ACCOUNTING + DATA PROCESSING ABSTRACTS.
(*Continued by* Accounting + Finance Abstracts.)

ACCOUNT. INDEX
[US]
ACCOUNTANTS INDEX.
(*Continued by* Accounting & Tax Index.)

ACCOUNT. INDEX SUPPL.
[US/0748-7975]
ACCOUNTANTS' INDEX. SUPPLEMENT.
(*Continued by* Accounting & Tax Index.)

ACCOUNT. TAX DATAB.
[US]
ACCOUNTING AND TAX DATABASE [ONLINE DATABASE].

ACCOUNT. TAX INDEX
[US/1063-0287]
ACCOUNTING AND TAX INDEX.
(*Continues* Accountants' Index. Supplement.)
***Refer to Accounting and Tax Database for complete source list.

ACCUMU. VET. INDEX
[US/0567-7033]
ACCUMULATIVE VETERINARY INDEX.
(Ceased)

ACID RAIN ABSTR.
[US/0882-1402]
ACID RAIN ABSTRACTS.
(*Absorbed by* Environment Abstracts.)

ACM GUIDE COMPUT. LIT.
[US/0149-1199]
ACM GUIDE TO COMPUTING LITERATURE.
(*Continues* Computing Reviews. Bibliography and Subject Index of Current Computing Literature.)

ACOUST. ABSTR.
[UK/0001-4974]
ACOUSTICS ABSTRACTS.

ADOLESC. MENT. HEALTH ABSTR.
[US]
ADOLESCENT MENTAL HEALTH ABSTRACTS.
(Ceased)

ADONIS
[NE]
ADONIS CD-ROM.

AERO. DEF. MARK. TECHNOL.
[US/0885-2286]
AEROSPACE/DEFENSE MARKETS & TECHNOLOGY.
(*Continues* Defense Markets & Technology.)

AESIS Q.
[AT/0313-704x]
AESIS QUARTERLY.

AFR. ABSTR.
[UK/0568-1200]
AFRICAN ABSTRACTS.
(Ceased)

AGBIOTECH NEWS INF.
[UK/0954-9897]
AGBIOTECH NEWS AND INFORMATION.

AGRIC. ENG. ABSTR.
[UK/0308-8863]
AGRICULTURAL ENGINEERING ABSTRACTS.

AGRIC. ENVIRON. BIOTECHNOL. ABSTR.
[US/1063-1151]
AGRICULTURAL & ENVIRONMENTAL BIOTECHNOLOGY ABSTRACTS.
(*Continues in part* Biotechnology Research Abstracts.)
***Refer to Biotechnology Research Abstracts for complete source list.

AGRIC. INDEX
[US/0196-5883]
AGRICULTURAL INDEX.
(*Continued by* Biological & Agricultural Index.)

AGRICOLA
[US/1050-6810]
AGRICOLA.

AGRINDEX
[IT/0254-8801]
AGRINDEX.

AGROFOR. ABSTR.
[UK/0952-1453]
AGROFORESTRY ABSTRACTS.

AIDS ABSTR.
[US/1066-1107]
AIDS ABSTRACTS (ATLANTA, GA.).

AIR POLLUT. TITLES
[US/0002-2497]
AIR POLLUTION TITLES.
(Ceased)

AIR UNIV. LIBR. INDEX MIL. PERIOD.
[US/0002-2586]
AIR UNIVERSITY LIBRARY INDEX TO MILITARY PERIODICALS.
(*Continues* Air University Periodical Index.)

AIR UNIV. PERIOD. INDEX
[US]
AIR UNIVERSITY PERIODICAL INDEX.
(*Continued by* Air University Library Index to Military Periodicals.)

ALCOHOL CLIN. UPDATE
[US/0740-1035]
ALCOHOL CLINICAL UPDATE.
(Ceased)

ALCOHOL. DIG.
[US/0093-7010]
ALCOHOLISM DIGEST.
(Ceased)

ALTERN. PRESS INDEX
[US/0002-662X]
ALTERNATIVE PRESS INDEX.

ALUM. IND. ABSTR.
[US/1066-0623]
ALUMINIUM INDUSTRY ABSTRACTS.
(*Continues* World Aluminum Abstracts.)

AM. BIBLIOGR. SLAVIC EAST EUROP. STUD.
[US/0094-3770]
AMERICAN BIBLIOGRAPHY OF SLAVIC AND EAST EUROPEAN STUDIES.
(*Continues* American Bibliography of Russian and East European Studies.)

AM. HIST. LIFE
[US/0002-7065]
AMERICA, HISTORY AND LIFE (SANTA BARBARA, CALIF. : 1989).
(*Formed by the union of* America, History and Life. Part A, Article Abstracts and Citations *and* America, History and Life. Part B, Index to Book Reviews America, History and Life. Part C, American History Bibliography, Books, Articles and Dissertations America, History and Life. Part D, Annual Index.)

AM. HIST. LIFE PART B
[US/0002-7065]
AMERICA: HISTORY AND LIFE. PART B: INDEX TO BOOK REVIEWS.
(*Merged with* America, History and Life. Part A, Article Abstracts and Citations; America, History and Life. Part C, American History Bibliography, Books, Articles and Dissertations *and* America, History and Life. Part D, Annual Index *to form* America, History and Life.)

AM. HUMANIT. INDEX
[US/0361-0144]
AMERICAN HUMANITIES INDEX, THE.

AM. INDIAN INDEX
[US/0569-5244]
AMERICAN INDIAN INDEX.
(Ceased)

AM. STAT. INDEX
[US/0091-1658]
AMERICAN STATISTICS INDEX.

ANAL. ABSTR.
[UK/0003-2689]
ANALYTICAL ABSTRACTS.
(*Continues* British Abstracts. Section C, Analysis and Apparatus.)

INDEXES/ABSTRACTS TABLE

ANBAR ACCOUNT. FINAN. ABSTR.
[UK/0961-2742]
ANBAR ACCOUNTING & FINANCE ABSTRACTS.
(*Continues* Accounting + Data Processing Abstracts.)

ANBAR MANAG. SERV. ABSTR.
[UK]
ANBAR MANAGEMENT SERVICES ABSTRACTS.
(*Superseded in part by* Accounting + Data Processing Abstracts; Marketing + Distribution Abstracts; Personnel + Training Abstracts *and* Top Management Abstracts.)

ANBAR MARK. DISTR. ABSTR.
[UK/0305-0661]
ANBAR MARKETING & DISTRIBUTION ABSTRACTS.
(*Continues* Marketing + Distribution Abstracts.)

ANBAR TOP MANAG. ABSTR.
[UK]
ANBAR TOP MANAGEMENT ABSTRACTS.
(*Continues* Top Management Abstracts.)

ANIM. BEHAV. ABSTR.
[US/0301-8695]
ANIMAL BEHAVIOR ABSTRACTS.
(*Continues* Animal Behaviour Abstracts.)

ANIM. BREED. ABSTR.
[UK/0003-3499]
ANIMAL BREEDING ABSTRACTS.
(*Formed by the union of* Imperial Bureau of Animal Breeding and Genetics. Quarterly Bulletin *and* Imperial Bureau of Animal References to Literature Contained in Periodicals Received.)

ANIM. DISEASE OCCURR.
[UK/0144-3879]
ANIMAL DISEASE OCCURRENCE.
(Ceased)

ANNALS BEHAV. MED.
[US/0883-6612]
ANNALS OF BEHAVIORAL MEDICINE.
(*Continues* Behavioral Medicine Update; **Absorbed** Behavioral Medicine Abstracts.)

ANNOT. BIBLIOGR. ECON. GEOL.
[US/0003-5076]
ANNOTATED BIBLIOGRAPHY OF ECONOMIC GEOLOGY.
(Ceased)

ANNU. BIBLIOGR. ENGL. LANG. LIT.
[UK/0066-3786]
ANNUAL BIBLIOGRAPHY OF ENGLISH LANGUAGE AND LITERATURE.
(*Continues* Bibliography of English Language and Literature.)

ANNU. INDEX POP. MUSIC REC. REV.
[US/0092-3486]
ANNUAL INDEX TO POPULAR MUSIC RECORD REVIEWS.
(*Continues* Annual Index to Popular Music Record Reviews.)

ANNU. LEG. BIBLIOGR.
[US/0073-0793]
ANNUAL LEGAL BIBLIOGRAPHY.
(Ceased)

ANTHROPOL. INDEX
[UK/0003-5467]
ANTHROPOLOGICAL INDEX TO CURRENT PERIODICALS IN THE LIBRARY OF THE ROYAL ANTHROPOLOGICAL INSTITUTE.
(*Continues* Anthropological Index to Current Periodicals in the Museum of Mankind (Library Incorporating the Royal Anthropological Institute Library).)

ANTHROPOL. LIT.
[US/0190-3373]
ANTHROPOLOGICAL LITERATURE.
(*Continues* Anthropological Literature (Cambridge, Mass. : 1984).)

ANTHROPOL. LIT. MICRO.
[US/0190-3373]
ANTHROPOLOGICAL LITERATURE.
(*Continued by* Anthropological Literature (Cambridge, Mass. : 1989).)

APAIS, AUST. PUBLIC AFF. INF. SER.
[AT/0727-8926]
APAIS. AUSTRALIAN PUBLIC AFFAIRS INFORMATION SERVICE.

API ABSTR. HEALTH ENVIRON.
[US]
API ABSTRACTS. HEALTH & ENVIRONMENT.
(*Continued by* Literature Abstracts. Health & Environment.)

API ABSTR. OIL. CHEM.
[US]
API ABSTRACTS : OILFIELD CHEMICALS.
(*Continued by* Literature & Patent Abstracts. Oilfield Chemicals.)

APIBIZ
[US]
APIBIZ [ONLINE DATABASE].
***Refer to Petroleum/Energy Business News Index for complete source list.

APIC. ABSTR.
[UK/0003-648X]
APICULTURAL ABSTRACTS.

APILIT
[US]
APILIT [ONLINE DATABASE].
***Refer to Literature & Patent Abstracts Oilfield Chemicals for a complete source list.

APPL. ECOL. ABSTR.
[UK/0305-3040]
APPLIED ECOLOGY ABSTRACTS.
(*Continued by* Ecology Abstracts.)

APPL. MECH. REV.
[US/0003-6900]
APPLIED MECHANICS REVIEWS.

APPL. SCI. TECHNOL. INDEX
[US/0003-6986]
APPLIED SCIENCE & TECHNOLOGY INDEX.
(*Continues in part* Industrial Arts Index.)

APPL. SOC. SCI. INDEX ABSTR.
[UK/0950-2238]
ASSIA. APPLIED SOCIAL SCIENCES INDEX & ABSTRACTS.

AQUALINE ABSTR.
[UK/0263-5534]
AQUALINE ABSTRACTS.
(*Continues* Water Research Centre (Great Britain). WRC Information.)

AQUAREF
[CN]
AQUAREF.
(*Continues* Canadian Environment; Environnement.)

AQUAT. SCI. FISH. ABSTR.
[UK/0044-8516]
AQUATIC SCIENCES & FISHERIES ABSTRACTS.
(*Split into* Aquatic Sciences and Fisheries Abstracts. Part 1, Biological Sciences and Living Resources *and* Aquatic Sciences and Fisheries Abstracts. Part 2, Ocean Technology, Policy and Non-Living Resources.)

AQUAT. SCI. FISH. ABSTR. (COMPUTER FILE)
[US/1064-0460]
AQUATIC SCIENCES & FISHERIES ABSTRACTS (CD-ROM ED.).

AQUAT. SCI. FISH. ABSTR. PART 1
[US/0140-5373]
AQUATIC SCIENCES AND FISHERIES ABSTRACTS. PART 1 : BIOLOGICAL SCIENCES AND LIVING RESOURCES.
(*Continued in part by* Aquatic Sciences and Fisheries Abstracts. Part 3, Aquatic Pollution and Environmental Quality.)
***Refer to Aquatic Science & Fisheries Abstracts [Computer File]: ASFA / Cambridge Scientific Abstracts for complete source list.

AQUAT. SCI. FISH. ABSTR. 2, OCEAN TECHNOL. POLICY NON-LIVING RESOUR.
[US/0140-5381]
AQUATIC SCIENCES AND FISHERIES ABSTRACTS. PART 2 : OCEAN TECHNOLOGY, POLICY AND NON-LIVING RESOURCES.
(*Continued in part by* Aquatic Sciences and Fisheries Abstracts. Part 3, Aquatic Pollution and Environmental Quality.)
***Refer to Aquatic Sciences & Fisheries Abstracts [Computer File] : ASFA / Cambridge Scientific Abstracts for complete source list.

AQUAT. SCI. FISHER. ABSTR. 3, AQUAT. POLLUT. ENVIRO. QUAL.
[US/1045-6031]
AQUATIC SCIENCES AND FISHERIES ABSTRACTS. PART 3 : AQUATIC POLLUTION AND ENVIRONMENTAL QUALITY.
(*Continues in part* Aquatic Sciences and Fisheries Abstracts. Part 1, Biological Sciences & Living Resources *and* Aquatic Sciences and Fisheries Abstracts. Part 2, Ocean Technology, Policy and Non-Living Resources.)
***Refer to Aquatic Sciences & Fisheries Abstracts [Computer File] : ASFA / Cambridge Scientific Abstracts for complete source list.

ARCHIT. PERIOD. INDEX
[UK/0266-4380]
API. ARCHITECTURAL PERIODICALS INDEX.
(*Supersedes* Royal Institute of British Architects. RIBA Library Bulletin; Royal Institute of British Architects. RIBA Annual Review of Periodical Articles.)

ARCT. BIBLIOGR.
[CN/0066-6947]
ARCTIC BIBLIOGRAPHY.
(Ceased)

ARECO Q. INDEX PERIOD. LIT. AGING
[US/0734-5569]
ARECO'S QUARTERLY INDEX TO PERIODICAL LITERATURE ON AGING.
(*Continued by* Index to Periodical Literature on Aging.)

ART ARCHAEOL. TECH. ABSTR.
[US/0004-2994]
ART AND ARCHAEOLOGY TECHNICAL ABSTRACTS.
(*Continues* I.I.C. Abstracts.)

ART DES. PHOTO
[UK/0306-817X]
ART, DESIGN, PHOTO.
(Ceased)

ART INDEX
[US/0004-3222]
ART INDEX.

INDEXES/ABSTRACTS TABLE

ART INTELL. ABSTR.
[US/0882-1410]
ARTIFICIAL INTELLIGENCE ABSTRACTS.
(**Ceased**)

ARTBIBLIOGR. CURR. TITLES
[UK/0307-9961]
ARTBIBLIOGRAPHIES. CURRENT TITLES.

ARTBIBLIOGR. MOD.
[UK/0300-466X]
ARTBIBLIOGRAPHIES MODERN.
(**Continues** LOMA; Literature on Modern Art.)

ARTS HUMANIT. CITATION INDEX
[US/0162-8445]
ARTS & HUMANITIES CITATION INDEX (PRINT ED.).

ASCATOPICS
[US/0730-8574]
ASCATOPICS.
(**Continued by** Research Alert.)

ASCE
[US/0730-3149]
ASCE.
(**Continued by** ASCE Annual Combined Index.)

ASCE ANNU. COMB. INDEX
[US/0742-1753]
ASCE ANNUAL COMBINED INDEX.
(**Continues** American Society of Civil Engineers. ASCE.)

ASCE PUBL. INF.
[US/0734-1962]
ASCE PUBLICATIONS INFORMATION.
(**Continues** ASCE Publications Abstracts.)

ASIA.-PAC. ECON. LIT.
[UK/0818-9935]
ASIAN-PACIFIC ECONOMIC LITERATURE.

ASSIA PLUS
[UK]
ASSIA PLUS [COMPUTER FILE].
***Refer to Applied Social Sciences Index & Abstracts for complete source list.

ASTIS BIBLIOGR.
[CN/0226-1685]
ASTIS BIBLIOGRAPHY.

ASTIS CURR. AWARE. BULL.
[CN/0705-8454]
A S T I S CURRENT AWARENESS BULLETIN.
(**Continues** Arctic Institute of North America. Library Accessions.)

ASTRON. ASTROPHYS. ABSTR.
[GW/0067-0022]
ASTRONOMY AND ASTROPHYSICS ABSTRACTS.
(**Continues** Astronomischer Jahresbericht.)

AUST. EDUC. INDEX
[AT/0004-9026]
AUSTRALIAN EDUCATION INDEX.

AUST. LEG. MON. DIG.
[AT/0004-9646]
AUSTRALIAN LEGAL MONTHLY DIGEST.

AUST. LIBR. INF. SCI. ABSTR.
[AT/0810-9265]
ALISA. AUSTRALIAN LIBRARY AND INFORMATION SCIENCE ABSTRACTS.

AUST. SCI. INDEX
[AT/0005-0229]
AUSTRALIAN SCIENCE INDEX.
(**Continues** C.S.I.R.O. Science Abstracts.)

AUTOM. SUBJ. CITATION ALERT
[US]
AUTOMATIC SUBJECT CITATION ALERT.
(**Continued by** Research Alert.)

AVERY INDEX ARCHIT. PERIOD. SUPPL.
[US/0588-540X]
AVERY INDEX TO ARCHITECTURAL PERIODICALS. SUPPLEMENT.
(**Continued by** Avery Index to Architectural Periodicals. Supplement / Columbia University.)

AVERY INDEX ARCHIT. PERIOD. SUPPL. COLUM. UNIV.
[US/0196-0008]
AVERY INDEX TO ARCHITECTURAL PERIODICALS. SECOND EDITION. REVISED AND ENLARGED. SUPPLEMENT.
(**Continues** Avery Library. Avery Index to Architectural Periodicals. Supplement.)

AVIAT. TRADESCAN
[US/0899-1928]
AVIATION TRADESCAN.

BEHAV. ABSTR.
[UK/0262-236X]
BEHAVIOURAL ABSTRACTS.
(**Ceased**)

BEHAV. MED. ABSTR.
[US/0197-7717]
BEHAVIORAL MEDICINE ABSTRACTS.
(**Absorbed by** Annals of Behavioral Medicine.)

BER. BIOCHEM. BIOL.
[GW/0005-9013]
BERICHTE BIOCHEMIE UND BIOLOGIE.
(**Continues** Berichte uber die Wissenschaftliche Biologie.)

BHA : BIBLIO. HIST. ART
[FR/1150-1588]
BIBLIOGRAPHY OF THE HISTORY OF ART : BHA.
(**Formed by the union of** Repertoire International de la Litterature de l'Art **and** Repertoire d'Art et d'Archeologie.)

BHI PLUS
[UK/0966-8772]
BHI PLUS [COMPUTER FILE].
***Refer to British Humanities Index for complete source list.

BIBLIOGR. AGRIC.
[US/0006-1530]
BIBLIOGRAPHY OF AGRICULTURE.
(**Continues** Bibliography of Agriculture with Subject Index.)
***Refer to AGRICOLA for complete source list.

BIBLIOGR. BRAS. CIEN. INF.
[BL/0102-2865]
BIBLIOGRAFIA BRASILEIRA DE CIENCIA DA INFORMACAO.
(**Ceased**)

BIBLIOGR. BRAS. MED.
[BL/0067-6675]
BIBLIOGRAFIA BRASILEIRA DE MEDICINA.
(**Continues** Indice-Catalogo Medico Brasileiro.)

BIBLIOGR. CARTO.
[GW/0340-0409]
BIBLIOGRAPHIA CARTOGRAPHICA.
(**Supersedes** Bibliotheca Cartographica.)

BIBLIOGR. ENGL. LIT.
[UK]
BIBLIOGRAPHY OF ENGLISH LANGUAGE AND LITERATURE.
(**Continued by** Annual Bibliography of English Language and Literature.)

BIBLIOGR. HIST. MED.
[US/0067-7280]
BIBLIOGRAPHY OF THE HISTORY OF MEDICINE.
***Refer to Index Medicus for complete source list.

BIBLIOGR. INDEX GEOL.
[US/0098-2784]
BIBLIOGRAPHY AND INDEX OF GEOLOGY.
(**Continues** Bibliography and Index of Geology Exclusive of North America; **Absorbed** Bibliography of North American Geology.)
***Refer to GeoRef [Computer File] for complete source list.

BIBLIOGR. INDEX GEOL. EXCLUS. NORTH AM.
[US/0376-1673]
BIBLIOGRAPHY AND INDEX OF GEOLOGY EXCLUSIVE OF NORTH AMERICA.
(**Continued by** Bibliography and Index of Geology.)

BIBLIOGR. INDEX HEALTH EDUC. PERIOD.
[US/0278-2340]
BIBLIOGRAPHIC INDEX OF HEALTH EDUCATION PERIODICALS : BIHEP.
(**Ceased**)

BIBLIOGR. INDEX MICROPALEONTOLOGY
[US/0300-7227]
BIBLIOGRAPHY AND INDEX OF MICROPALEONTOLOGY.
***Refer to GeoRef [Computer File] for complete source list.

BIBLIOGR. MISSION.
[IT]
BIBLIOGRAFIA MISSIONARIA.
(**Continued by** Bibliographia Missionaria.)

BIBLIOGR. MISSION.
[VC/0394-9869]
BIBLIOGRAPHIA MISSIONARIA / PONTIFICAL MISSIONARY LIBRARY OF THE CONGREGATION FOR THE EVANGELIZATION OF PEOPLES.
(**Continues** Bibliografia Missionaria.)

BIBLIOGR. NORTH AM. GEOL.
[US/0740-6347]
BIBLIOGRAPHY OF NORTH AMERICAN GEOLOGY.
(**Absorbed by** Bibliography and Index of Geology.)

BIOBUSINESS
[US]
BIOBUSINESS.

BIOCONT. NEWS INF.
[UK/0143-1404]
BIOCONTROL NEWS AND INFORMATION.

BIODETER. ABSTR.
[UK/0951-0621]
BIODETERIORATION ABSTRACTS.
(**Separated from** International Biodeterioration.)

BIOENG. ABSTR.
[US/0093-8378]
BIOENGINEERING ABSTRACTS.
(**Continued by** Engineering Index Bioengineering Abstracts.)

INDEXES/ABSTRACTS TABLE

BIOENG. ABSTR.
[US/1068-5693]
BIOENGINEERING ABSTRACTS (1993).
(*Continues* Engineering Index Bioengineering and Biotechnology Abstracts.)

BIOGR. INDEX
[US/0006-3053]
BIOGRAPHY INDEX.

BIOL. ABSTR. RRM
[US/0192-6985]
BIOLOGICAL ABSTRACTS / RRM.
(*Continues* Bioresearch Index.)
***Refer to Biological Abstracts for complete source list.

BIOL. ABSTR.
[US/0006-3169]
BIOLOGICAL ABSTRACTS.
(*Formed by the union of* Abstracts of Bacteriology *and* Botanical Abstracts.)

BIOL. ABSTR. ON COMPACT DISC
[US/1058-4129]
BIOLOGICAL ABSTRACTS ON COMPACT DISC.
***Refer to Biological Abstracts for complete source list.

BIOL. AGRIC. INDEX
[US/0006-3177]
BIOLOGICAL & AGRICULTURAL INDEX.
(*Continues* Agricultural Index.)

BIOL. DIG.
[US/0095-2958]
BIOLOGY DIGEST.

BIOSTATISTICA
[US/1041-7648]
BIOSTATISTICA (DAVENPORT, IOWA).

BIOTECHNOL. ABSTR.
[UK/0262-5318]
DERWENT BIOTECHNOLOGY ABSTRACTS.
(*Continued by* Biotechnology Abstracts.)

BIOTECHNOL. ABSTR.
[UK]
BIOTECHNOLOGY ABSTRACTS.
(*Continues* Derwent Biotechnology Abstracts.)
***Refer to PESTDOC for complete source list.

BIOTECHNOL. RES. ABSTR.
[US/0733-5709]
BIOTECHNOLOGY RESEARCH ABSTRACTS.
(*Continued in part by* Medical & Pharmaceutical Biotechnology Abstracts *and* Agricultural & Environmental Biotechnology Abstracts.)

BLACK INF. INDEX
[US/0045-2173]
BLACK INFORMATION INDEX.
(Ceased)

BMT ABSTR.
[UK/0268-9650]
BMT ABSTRACTS : BRITISH MARITIME TECHNOLOGY ABSTRACTS.
(*Continues* Journal of Abstracts of the British Ship Research Association.)

BOOK REV. DIGEST
[US/0006-7326]
BOOK REVIEW DIGEST.
(*Continues* Cumulative Book Review Digest.)

BOOK REV. INDEX
[US/0524-0581]
BOOK REVIEW INDEX.

BOOK REV. MON.
[US/0006-7342]
BOOK REVIEWS OF THE MONTH.
(Ceased)

BOSTON GLOBE INDEX
[US/0893-2727]
BOSTON GLOBE INDEX (1987), THE.
(*Continues* Bell & Howell Newspaper Index to the Boston Globe.)

BOWNE DIG. CORP. SEC. LAWYERS
[US/0896-906X]
BOWNE DIGEST FOR CORPORATE & SECURITIES LAWYERS.
(*Continues* Abstracts of Legal Periodicals (Corporate & Securities Ed.).)

BR. ARCHAEOL. ABSTR.
[UK/0007-0270]
BRITISH ARCHAEOLOGICAL ABSTRACTS.
(*Continued by* British Archaeological Bibliography.)

BR. ARCHAEOL. BIBLIOGR.
[UK/0964-7104]
BRITISH ARCHAEOLOGICAL BIBLIOGRAPHY.
(*Continues* British Archaeological Abstracts.)

BR. CERAM. ABSTR.
[UK/0300-4570]
BRITISH CERAMIC ABSTRACTS.
(*Continued by* World Ceramics Abstracts.)

BR. EDUC. INDEX
[UK/0007-0637]
BRITISH EDUCATION INDEX.

BR. HUMANIT. INDEX
[UK/0007-0815]
BRITISH HUMANITIES INDEX.
(*Supersedes in part* Subject Index to Periodicals.)

BR. TECHNOL. INDEX
[UK/0007-1889]
BRITISH TECHNOLOGY INDEX.
(*Continued by* Current Technology Index.)

BULL. ANAL. ENTOMOL. MED. VET.
[FR/0007-4098]
BULLETIN ANALYTIQUE D'ENTOMOLOGIE MEDICALE ET VETERINAIRE.
(Ceased)

BULL. SIGNAL.
[FR]
BULLETIN SIGNALETIQUE.
(Ceased)

BUS. ASAP
[US]
BUSINESS ASAP [COMPUTER FILE].

BUS. DATELINE
[US]
BUSINESS DATELINE.

BUS. EDUC. INDEX
[US/0068-4414]
BUSINESS EDUCATION INDEX.

BUS. INDEX
[US/0273-3684]
BUSINESS INDEX.

BUS. PERIOD. INDEX
[US/0006-6961]
BUSINESS PERIODICALS INDEX.
(*Continues in part* Industrial Arts Index.)

BUS. SOURCE
[US]
BUSINESS SOURCE. [COMPUTER FILE].

CA QUICK SEARCH
[US]
CA QUICK SEARCH [COMPUTER FILE].
***Refer to Concrete Abstracts for complete source list.

CA SEL., ACID RAIN ACID AIR
[US/0885-0097]
CA SELECTS: ACID RAIN & ACID AIR.
***Refer to Chemical Abstracts for complete source list.

CA SEL., ADHESIVES
[US/0162-7686]
CA SELECTS: ADHESIVES.
***Refer to Chemical Abstracts for complete source list.

CA SEL., AIDS RELAT. IMMUNODEFIC.
[US/1040-7111]
CA SELECTS: AIDS & RELATED IMMUNODEFICIENCIES.
***Refer to Chemical Abstracts for complete source list.

CA SEL., AIR POLLUT. BOOKS REV.
[US/0895-5980]
CA SELECTS: AIR POLLUTION (BOOKS & REVIEWS).
***Refer to Chemical Abstracts for complete source list.

CA SEL., ALKYL. CATAL.
[US/0895-5964]
CA SELECTS: ALKYLATION & CATALYSTS.
***Refer to Chemical Abstracts for complete source list.

CA SEL., ALUMIN. LITH. ALUMIN. CER. ALLOYS
[US/1066-1166]
CA SELECTS: ALUMINUM-LITHIUM & ALUMINUM-CERIUM ALLOYS.
***Refer to Chemical Abstracts for complete source list.

CA SEL., ALZHEIMER'S DIS. RELAT. MEM. DYSFUNC.
[US/1047-8183]
CA SELECTS: ALZHEIMER'S DISEASE & RELATED MEMORY DYSFUNCTIONS.
***Refer to Chemical Abstracts for complete source list.

CA SEL., AMINO ACIDS PEP. PROT.
[US/0275-701X]
CA SELECTS: AMINO ACIDS, PEPTIDES & PROTEINS.
***Refer to Chemical Abstracts for complete source list.

CA SEL., ANALYT. ELECTROCHEM.
[US/0160-8959]
CA SELECTS: ANALYTICAL ELECTROCHEMISTRY.
***Refer to Chemical Abstracts for complete source list.

CA SEL., ANIMAL LONG. AGING
[US/0162-7694]
CA SELECTS: ANIMAL LONGEVITY & AGING.
***Refer to Chemical Abstracts for complete source list.

CA SEL., ANTI INFLAM. AGENTS ARTHRIT.
[US/0148-2394]
CA SELECTS: ANTI-INFLAMMATORY AGENTS & ARTHRITIS.
***Refer to Chemical Abstracts for complete source list.

CA SEL., ANTIBAC. AGENTS
[US/1045-8522]
CA SELECTS: ANTIBACTERIAL AGENTS.
(*Continues* CA Selects. Bactericides, Disinfectants & Antiseptics.)
***Refer to Chemical Abstracts for complete source list.

CA SEL., ANTIOXID.
[US/0275-7028]
CA SELECTS: ANTIOXIDANTS.
***Refer to Chemical Abstracts for complete source list.

INDEXES/ABSTRACTS TABLE

CA SEL., ANTITUMOR AGENTS
[US/0148-2386]
CA SELECTS: ANTITUMOR AGENTS.
***Refer to Chemical Abstracts for complete source list.

CA SEL., ARTIF. SWEETEN.
[US/0890-1813]
CA SELECTS: ARTIFICIAL SWEETENERS.
***Refer to Chemical Abstracts for complete source list.

CA SEL., ASYMMET. SYNTH. INDUC.
[US/0890-183X]
CA SELECTS: ASYMMETRIC SYNTHESIS & INDUCTION.
***Refer to Chemical Abstracts for complete source list.

CA SEL., AT. SPECTROSC.
[US/0195-4911]
CA SELECTS: ATOMIC SPECTROSCOPY.
***Refer to Chemical Abstracts for complete source list.

CA SEL., ATHEROSCL. HEART DIS.
[US/0148-2378]
CA SELECTS: ATHEROSCLEROSIS & HEART DISEASE.
***Refer to Chemical Abstracts for complete source list.

CA SEL., AUTOM. CHEM. ANAL.
[US/0740-0683]
CA SELECTS: AUTOMATED CHEMICAL ANALYSIS.
***Refer to Chemical Abstracts for complete source list.

CA SEL., B-LACTAM ANTIB.
[US/0148-2459]
CA SELECTS: B-LACTAM ANTIBIOTICS.
***Refer to Chemical Abstracts for complete source list.

CA SEL., BACTER. DISINFECT. ANTISEP.
[US/0890-1848]
CA SELECTS: BACTERICIDES, DISINFECTANTS & ANTISEPTICS.
(*Continued by* CA Selects: Antibacterial Agents.)

CA SEL., BATTER. FUEL CELLS
[US/0162-7708]
CA SELECTS: BATTERIES & FUEL CELLS.
***Refer to Chemical Abstracts for complete source list.

CA SEL., BIOGEN. AMINES NERV. SYST.
[US/0162-7716]
CA SELECTS: BIOGENIC AMINES & THE NERVOUS SYSTEM.
***Refer to Chemical Abstracts for complete source list.

CA SEL., BIOL. INFO. TRANSF.
[US/0162-7724]
CA SELECTS: BIOLOGICAL INFORMATION TRANSFER.
(Ceased)

CA SEL., BISMUTH CHEM.
[US/1061-5342]
CA SELECTS: BISMUTH CHEMISTRY.
***Refer to Chemical Abstracts for complete source list.

CA SEL., BLOCK GRAFT POLYM.
[US/0734-8851]
CA SELECTS: BLOCK & GRAFT POLYMERS.
***Refer to Chemical Abstracts for complete source list.

CA SEL., BLOOD COAG.
[US/0162-7732]
CA SELECTS: BLOOD COAGULATION.
***Refer to Chemical Abstracts for complete source list.

CA SEL., CARBOHYDR. (CHEM. ASP.)
[US/0740-0756]
CA SELECTS: CARBOHYDRATES (CHEMICAL ASPECTS).
***Refer to Chemical Abstracts for complete source list.

CA SEL., CARBON FIBER COMPOS.
[US/0895-5956]
CA SELECTS: CARBON FIBER COMPOSITES.
***Refer to Chemical Abstracts for complete source list.

CA SEL., CARBON GRAPH. FIB.
[US/0890-1856]
CA SELECTS: CARBON & GRAPHITE FIBERS.
***Refer to Chemical Abstracts for complete source list.

CA SEL., CARBON HETERO. NMR
[US/0190-9401]
CA SELECTS: CARBON & HETEROATOM NMR.
(*Continues in part* CA Selects. Nuclear Magnetic Resonance, Chemical Aspects.)
***Refer to Chemical Abstracts for complete source list.

CA SEL., CARCIN. MUT. TERATO.
[US/0148-2408]
CA SELECTS: CARCINOGENS, MUTAGENS & TERATOGENS.
***Refer to Chemical Abstracts for complete source list.

CA SEL., CATAL. (APPL. PHYS. ASP.)
[US/0146-440X]
CA SELECTS: CATALYSIS (APPLIED AND PHYSICAL ASPECTS).
***Refer to Chemical Abstracts for complete source list.

CA SEL., CATAL. (ORG. REACT.)
[US/0146-4396]
CA SELECTS: CATALYSIS (ORGANIC REACTIONS).
***Refer to Chemical Abstracts for complete source list.

CA SEL., CATAL. KINET. ANAL.
[US/0890-1864]
CA SELECTS: CATALYTIC & KINETIC ANALYSIS.
***Refer to Chemical Abstracts for complete source list.

CA SEL., CATAL. REGEN.
[US/0734-8800]
CA SELECTS: CATALYST REGENERATION.
***Refer to Chemical Abstracts for complete source list.

CA SEL., CERAM. MATER. J.
[US/0895-5948]
CA SELECTS: CERAMIC MATERIALS (JOURNALS).
***Refer to Chemical Abstracts for complete source list.

CA SEL., CERAM. METER. PAT.
[US/0885-0100]
CA SELECTS: CERAMIC MATERIALS (PATENTS).
***Refer to Chemical Abstracts for complete source list.

CA SEL., CHELATING AGENTS
[US/0734-8797]
CA SELECTS: CHELATING AGENTS.
***Refer to Chemical Abstracts for complete source list.

CA SEL., CHEM. ENG. OPER.
[US/1040-712X]
CA SELECTS: CHEMICAL ENGINEERING OPERATIONS.
***Refer to Chemical Abstracts for complete source list.

CA SEL., CHEM. HAZ. HEALTH SAFETY
[US/0190-9398]
CA SELECTS: CHEMICAL HAZARDS, HEALTH, & SAFETY.
(*Continues* CA Selects. Chemical Hazards.)
***Refer to Chemical Abstracts for complete source list.

CA SEL., CHEM. INSTRUM.
[US/0195-4938]
CA SELECTS: CHEMICAL INSTRUMENTATION.
***Refer to Chemical Abstracts for complete source list.

CA SEL., CHEM. IR OS RH RU
[US/1040-7146]
CA SELECTS: CHEMISTRY OF IR, OS, RH, & RU.
***Refer to Chemical Abstracts for complete source list.

CA SEL., CHEM. PROCESS. APPAR.
[US/0195-4946]
CA SELECTS: CHEMICAL PROCESSING APPARATUS.
***Refer to Chemical Abstracts for complete source list.

CA SEL., CHEM. VAPOR DEPOS.
[US/0885-0119]
CA SELECTS. CHEMICAL VAPOR DEPOSITION.
***Refer to Chemical Abstracts for complete source list.

CA SEL., CHEMILUMIN.
[US/1040-7138]
CA SELECTS: CHEMILUMINESCENCE.
***Refer to Chemical Abstracts for complete source list.

CA SEL., COAL SCI. PROC. CHEM.
[US/0146-4426]
CA SELECTS: COAL SCIENCE & PROCESS CHEMISTRY.
***Refer to Chemical Abstracts for complete source list.

CA SEL., COAT. INKS REALT. PROD.
[US/0275-7036]
CA SELECTS: COATINGS, INKS, & RELATED PRODUCTS.
***Refer to Chemical Abstracts for complete source list.

CA SEL., COLLOIDS (APPL. ASP.)
[US/0160-8967]
CA SELECTS: COLLOIDS (APPLIED ASPECTS).
(*Continued by* CA Selects. Colloids (Macromolecular Aspects).)

CA SEL., COLLOIDS (MACROMOL. ASP.)
[US/0190-9444]
CA SELECTS: COLLOIDS (MACROMOLECULAR ASPECTS).
(*Supersedes in part* CA Selects. Colloids (Applied Aspects).)
***Refer to Chemical Abstracts for complete source list.

CA SEL., COLLOIDS (PHYSICO. ASP.)
[US/0160-8975]
CA SELECTS: COLLOIDS (PHYSICOCHEMICAL ASPECTS).
***Refer to Chemical Abstracts for complete source list.

CA SEL., COLOR SCI.
[US/0885-0127]
CA SELECTS: COLOR SCIENCE.
***Refer to Chemical Abstracts for complete source list.

CA SEL., COLOR. DYES
[US/0734-8789]
CA SELECTS: COLORANTS & DYES.
***Refer to Chemical Abstracts for complete source list.

CA SEL., COMPOS. MATER. (CERAM.)
[US/1066-1158]
CA SELECTS: COMPOSITE MATERIALS (CERAMIC).
***Refer to Chemical Abstracts for complete source list.

CA SEL., COMPOS. MATER. (MET.)
[US/1066-114X]
CA SELECTS: COMPOSITE MATERIALS (METALLIC).
***Refer to Chemical Abstracts for complete source list.

CA SEL., COMPOS. MATER. (POLYM.)
[US/1040-7154]
CA SELECTS: COMPOSITE MATERIALS (POLYMERIC).
***Refer to Chemical Abstracts for complete source list.

CA SEL., COMPUT. CHEM.
[US/0160-9025]
CA SELECTS: COMPUTERS IN CHEMISTRY.
***Refer to Chemical Abstracts for complete source list.

INDEXES/ABSTRACTS TABLE

CA SEL., CONDUCT. POLYM.
[US/0885-0135]
CA SELECTS: CONDUCTIVE POLYMERS.
***Refer to Chemical Abstracts for complete source list.

CA SEL., CONTROL. RELEASE TECHNOL.
[US/0740-0748]
CA SELECTS: CONTROLLED RELEASE TECHNOLOGY.
***Refer to Chemical Abstracts for complete source list.

CA SEL., CORROS.
[US/0146-4434]
CA SELECTS: CORROSION.
***Refer to Chemical Abstracts for complete source list.

CA SEL., CORROS.-INHIB. COAT.
[US/0749-7296]
CA SELECTS: CORROSION-INHIBITING COATINGS.
***Refer to Chemical Abstracts for complete source list.

CA SEL., COSMET. CHEM.
[US/0275-7044]
CA SELECTS: COSMETIC CHEMICALS.
***Refer to Chemical Abstracts for complete source list.

CA SEL., COSMOCHEM.
[US/0195-4954]
CA SELECTS: COSMOCHEMISTRY.
(Ceased)

CA SEL., CROSSLINK. REACT.
[US/0740-0721]
CA SELECTS: CROSSLINKING REACTIONS.
***Refer to Chemical Abstracts for complete source list.

CA SEL., CRYS. GROWTH
[US/0162-7740]
CA SELECTS: CRYSTAL GROWTH.
***Refer to Chemical Abstracts for complete source list.

CA SEL., DETER. SOAPS, SURFAC.
[US/0162-7767]
CA SELECTS: DETERGENTS, SOAPS, & SURFACTANTS.
***Refer to Chemical Abstracts for complete source list.

CA SEL., DISTILL. TECHNOL.
[US/0275-7052]
CA SELECTS: DISTILLATION TECHNOLOGY.
***Refer to Chemical Abstracts for complete source list.

CA SEL., DRILL. MUDS
[US/0749-730X]
CA SELECTS: DRILLING MUDS.
***Refer to Chemical Abstracts for complete source list.

CA SEL., DRUG COSMET. TOXIC.
[US/0162-7775]
CA SELECTS: DRUG & COSMETIC TOXICITY.
***Refer to Chemical Abstracts for complete source list.

CA SEL., DRUG DELIV. SYST. DOS. FORMS
[US/1040-7162]
CA SELECTS: DRUG DELIVERY SYSTEMS & DOSAGE FORMS.
***Refer to Chemical Abstracts for complete source list.

CA SEL., ELECT. AUG. SPECTRO.
[US/0146-4450]
CA SELECTS: ELECTRON & AUGER SPECTROSCOPY.
***Refer to Chemical Abstracts for complete source list.

CA SEL., ELECT. SPIN RESON. (CHEM. ASP.)
[US/0146-4469]
CA SELECTS: ELECTRON SPIN RESONANCE (CHEMICAL ASPECTS).
***Refer to Chemical Abstracts for complete source list.

CA SEL., ELECTR. CONDUCT. ORG.
[US/0885-0143]
CA SELECTS: ELECTRICALLY CONDUCTIVE ORGANICS.
***Refer to Chemical Abstracts for complete source list.

CA SEL., ELECTROCHEM. ORG. SYNTH.
[US/0734-8770]
CA SELECTS: ELECTROCHEMICAL ORGANIC SYNTHESIS.
***Refer to Chemical Abstracts for complete source list.

CA SEL., ELECTROCHEM. REAC.
[US/0146-4442]
CA SELECTS: ELECTROCHEMICAL REACTIONS.
***Refer to Chemical Abstracts for complete source list.

CA SEL., ELECTRODEPOSIT.
[US/0162-7783]
CA SELECTS: ELECTRODEPOSITION.
***Refer to Chemical Abstracts for complete source list.

CA SEL., ELECTRON. CHEM. MATER.
[US/0885-0151]
CA SELECTS: ELECTRONIC CHEMICALS & MATERIALS.
***Refer to Chemical Abstracts for complete source list.

CA SEL., ELECTROPHOR.
[US/0195-4962]
CA SELECTS: ELECTROPHORESIS.
***Refer to Chemical Abstracts for complete source list.

CA SEL., EMULS. POLYM.
[US/0195-4970]
CA SELECTS: EMULSION POLYMERIZATION.
***Refer to Chemical Abstracts for complete source list.

CA SEL., EMULSIF. & DEMULSIF.
[US/0734-8754]
CA SELECTS: EMULSIFIERS & DEMULSIFIERS.
***Refer to Chemical Abstracts for complete source list.

CA SEL., ENERGY REV. BOOKS
[US/0162-7791]
CA SELECTS: ENERGY REVIEWS & BOOKS.
***Refer to Chemical Abstracts for complete source list.

CA SEL., ENGINE EXH.
[US/0160-9033]
CA SELECTS: ENGINE EXHAUST.
(Ceased)

CA SEL., ENHANC. PETRO. RECOV.
[US/0734-8746]
CA SELECTS: ENHANCED PETROLEUM RECOVERY.
***Refer to Chemical Abstracts for complete source list.

CA SEL., ENVIRON. POLLUT.
[US/0160-9041]
CA SELECTS: ENVIRONMENTAL POLLUTION.
***Refer to Chemical Abstracts for complete source list.

CA SEL., ENZYM. APPL.
[US/0895-593X]
CA SELECTS: ENZYME APPLICATIONS.
***Refer to Chemical Abstracts for complete source list.

CA SEL., ENZYM. ASSAYS
[US/0895-5808]
CA SELECTS: ENZYME ASSAYS.
***Refer to Chemical Abstracts for complete source list.

CA SEL., EPOXY RESINS
[US/0275-7060]
CA SELECTS: EPOXY RESINS.
***Refer to Chemical Abstracts for complete source list.

CA SEL., FATS OILS
[US/0275-7079]
CA SELECTS: FATS & OILS.
***Refer to Chemical Abstracts for complete source list.

CA SEL., FERMENT. CHEM.
[US/0740-0713]
CA SELECTS: FERMENTATION CHEMICALS.
***Refer to Chemical Abstracts for complete source list.

CA SEL., FIBER OPT. OPT. COMMUN.
[US/0890-1872]
CA SELECTS: FIBER OPTICS & OPTICAL COMMUNICATION.
***Refer to Chemical Abstracts for complete source list.

CA SEL., FIBER-REINFOR. PLAST.
[US/0734-869X]
CA SELECTS: FIBER-REINFORCED PLASTICS.
***Refer to Chemical Abstracts for complete source list.

CA SEL., FLAMMABIL.
[US/0162-7805]
CA SELECTS: FLAMMABILITY.
***Refer to Chemical Abstracts for complete source list.

CA SEL., FLAV. FRAGR.
[US/0148-2327]
CA SELECTS: FLAVORS & FRAGRANCES.
***Refer to Chemical Abstracts for complete source list.

CA SEL., FLUID. SOLIDS TECHNOL.
[US/0195-4989]
CA SELECTS: FLUIDIZED SOLIDS TECHNOLOGY.
***Refer to Chemical Abstracts for complete source list.

CA SEL., FLUOROPOLY.
[US/0895-5921]
CA SELECTS: FLUOROPOLYMERS.
***Refer to Chemical Abstracts for complete source list.

CA SEL., FOOD DRUGS COSMET.
[US/1051-3914]
CA SELECTS: FOOD, DRUGS, & COSMETICS.
***Refer to Chemical Abstracts for complete source list.

CA SEL., FOOD FEED ANAL.
[US/0895-5913]
CA SELECTS: FOOD & FEED ANALYSIS.
***Refer to Chemical Abstracts for complete source list.

CA SEL., FOOD TOXIC.
[US/0162-7813]
CA SELECTS: FOOD TOXICITY.
***Refer to Chemical Abstracts for complete source list.

CA SEL., FORENS. CHEM.
[US/0362-9880]
CA SELECTS: FORENSIC CHEMISTRY.
***Refer to Chemical Abstracts for complete source list.

CA SEL., FORMUL. CHEM.
[US/0890-1880]
CA SELECTS: FORMULATION CHEMISTRY.
***Refer to Chemical Abstracts for complete source list.

CA SEL., FREE RADIC.
[US/0885-016X]
CA SELECTS: FREE RADICALS.
(**Continued by** CA Selects: Free Radicals (Organic Aspects).)

CA SEL., FREE RADIC. (BIOCHEM. ASP.)
[US/0895-5905]
CA SELECTS: FREE RADICALS (BIOCHEMICAL ASPECTS).
***Refer to Chemical Abstracts for complete source list.

INDEXES/ABSTRACTS TABLE

CA SEL., FREE RADIC. (ORG. ASP.)
[US/0895-5972]
CA SELECTS: FREE RADICALS (ORGANIC ASPECTS).
(*Continues* CA Selects. Free Radicals.)
***Refer to Chemical Abstracts for complete source list.

CA SEL., FUEL LUBR. ADDIT.
[US/0195-4997]
CA SELECTS: FUEL & LUBRICANT ADDITIVES.
***Refer to Chemical Abstracts for complete source list.

CA SEL., FUNGICID.
[US/0160-9068]
CA SELECTS: FUNGICIDES.
***Refer to Chemical Abstracts for complete source list.

CA SEL., GAS CHROMAT.
[US/0146-4477]
CA SELECTS: GAS CHROMATOGRAPHY.
***Refer to Chemical Abstracts for complete source list.

CA SEL., GAS. WASTE TREAT.
[US/0160-9076]
CA SELECTS: GASEOUS WASTE TREATMENT.
***Refer to Chemical Abstracts for complete source list.

CA SEL., GEL PERM. CHROMAT.
[US/0146-4485]
CA SELECTS: GEL PERMEATION CHROMATOGRAPHY.
***Refer to Chemical Abstracts for complete source list.

CA SEL., GEOCHEM.
[US/1066-5730]
CA SELECTS: GEOCHEMISTRY.
***Refer to Chemical Abstracts for complete source list.

CA SEL., HEAT-RESIST. ABLAT. POLYM.
[US/0162-7821]
CA SELECTS: HEAT-RESISTANT & ABLATIVE POLYMERS.
***Refer to Chemical Abstracts for complete source list.

CA SEL., HERBIC.
[US/0160-9084]
CA SELECTS: HERBICIDES.
***Refer to Chemical Abstracts for complete source list.

CA SEL., HIGH PERFORM. LIQ. CHROMATOGR.
[US/0195-5217]
CA SELECTS: HIGH PERFORMANCE LIQUID CHROMATOGRAPHY.
(*Continues* CA Selects. High Speed Liquid Chromatography.)
***Refer to Chemical Abstracts for complete source list.

CA SEL., HOT-MELT ADHES.
[US/0895-5891]
CA SELECTS: HOT-MELT ADHESIVES.
***Refer to Chemical Abstracts for complete source list.

CA SEL., HYPERTENS. ANTIHYPERTENS.
[US/1051-3922]
CA SELECTS: HYPERTENSION & ANTIHYPERTENSIVES.
***Refer to Chemical Abstracts for complete source list.

CA SEL., INFR. SPECTRO. (ORG. ASP.)
[US/0190-9428]
CA SELECTS: INFRARED SPECTROSCOPY (ORGANIC ASPECTS).
(*Continues in part* CA Selects. Infrared Spectroscopy.)
***Refer to Chemical Abstracts for complete source list.

CA SEL., INFR. SPECTRO. (PHYSICOCHEM. ASP.)
[US/0190-9436]
CA SELECTS: INFRARED SPECTROSCOPY (PHYSICOCHEMICAL ASPECTS).
(*Continues in part* CA Selects. Infrared Spectroscopy.)
***Refer to Chemical Abstracts for complete source list.

CA SEL., INIT. POLYMER.
[US/0734-8843]
CA SELECTS: INITIATION OF POLYMERIZATION.
***Refer to Chemical Abstracts for complete source list.

CA SEL., INORG. ANAL. CHEM.
[US/0275-7087]
CA SELECTS: INORGANIC ANALYTICAL CHEMISTRY.
***Refer to Chemical Abstracts for complete source list.

CA SEL., INORG. CHEM. REACT.
[US/0275-7095]
CA SELECTS: INORGANIC CHEMICALS & REACTIONS.
***Refer to Chemical Abstracts for complete source list.

CA SEL., INORG. FLOUR. CHEM.
[US/0195-5004]
CA SELECTS: INORGANIC FLOURINE CHEMISTRY.
(Ceased)

CA SEL., INORG. ORGANOMET. REACT. MECHAN.
[US/0195-5012]
CA SELECTS: INORGANIC & ORGANOMETALLIC REACTION MECHANISMS.
***Refer to Chemical Abstracts for complete source list.

CA SEL., INSECTIC.
[US/0160-9092]
CA SELECTS: INSECTICIDES.
***Refer to Chemical Abstracts for complete source list.

CA SEL., ION CHROMATOGR.
[US/0890-1899]
CA SELECTS: ION CHROMATOGRAPHY.
***Refer to Chemical Abstracts for complete source list.

CA SEL., ION EXCHANGE
[US/0146-4493]
CA SELECTS: ION EXCHANGE.
***Refer to Chemical Abstracts for complete source list.

CA SEL., ION-CONTAIN. POLYM.
[US/0195-5020]
CA SELECTS: ION-CONTAINING POLYMERS.
***Refer to Chemical Abstracts for complete source list.

CA SEL., ISOMERI. CATAL.
[US/0895-5883]
CA SELECTS: ISOMERIZATION & CATALYSTS.
***Refer to Chemical Abstracts for complete source list.

CA SEL., LASER APPL.
[US/0195-5039]
CA SELECTS: LASER APPLICATIONS.
***Refer to Chemical Abstracts for complete source list.

CA SEL., LASER-INDUC. CHEM REACT.
[US/0885-0178]
CA SELECTS: LASER-INDUCED CHEMICAL REACTIONS.
***Refer to Chemical Abstracts for complete source list.

CA SEL., LASERS MASERS
[US/0195-5047]
CA SELECTS: LASERS & MASERS.
(Ceased)

CA SEL., LIQ. CRYST.
[US/0148-2351]
CA SELECTS: LIQUID CRYSTALS.
***Refer to Chemical Abstracts for complete source list.

CA SEL., LIQ. WASTE TREAT.
[US/0160-9106]
CA SELECTS: LIQUID WASTE TREATMENT.
***Refer to Chemical Abstracts for complete source list.

CA SEL., LUBR. GREAS. LUBRICAT.
[US/0734-8738]
CA SELECTS: LUBRICANTS, GREASES & LUBRICATION.
***Refer to Chemical Abstracts for complete source list.

CA SEL., MACROCYCL. ANTIBIOT.
[US/0195-5055]
CA SELECTS: MACROCYCLIC ANTIBIOTICS.
(Ceased)

CA SEL., MASS SPECTRO.
[US/0362-9872]
CA SELECTS: MASS SPECTROMETRY.
***Refer to Chemical Abstracts for complete source list.

CA SEL., MEM. REC. DEVICES MATER.
[US/0890-1821]
CA SELECTS: MEMORY & RECORDING DEVICES & MATERIALS.
***Refer to Chemical Abstracts for complete source list.

CA SEL., MEMBR. SEP.
[US/1040-7197]
CA SELECTS: MEMBRANE SEPARATION.
***Refer to Chemical Abstracts for complete source list.

CA SEL., METAL. GLASS.
[US/1062-8681]
CA SELECTS: METALLIC GLASSES.
***Refer to Chemical Abstracts for complete source list.

CA SEL., METALLO ENZ. METALLO COENZ.
[US/0160-9114]
CA SELECTS: METALLO ENZYMES & METALLO COENZYMES.
***Refer to Chemical Abstracts for complete source list.

CA SEL., MOLEC. MODEL. (BIOCHEM. ASP.)
[US/1059-2784]
CA SELECTS: MOLECULAR MODELING (BIOCHEMICAL ASPECTS).
***Refer to Chemical Abstracts for complete source list.

CA SEL., NAT. PROD. SYNTH.
[US/0740-0691]
CA SELECTS: NATURAL PRODUCT SYNTHESIS.
***Refer to Chemical Abstracts for complete source list.

CA SEL., NEW ANTIBIOT.
[US/0895-5875]
CA SELECTS: NEW ANTIBIOTICS.
***Refer to Chemical Abstracts for complete source list.

CA SEL., NEW BOOKS CHEM.
[US/0148-2416]
CA SELECTS: NEW BOOKS IN CHEMISTRY.
***Refer to Chemical Abstracts for complete source list.

CA SEL., NEW PLAST.
[US/0734-8673]
CA SELECTS: NEW PLASTICS.
***Refer to Chemical Abstracts for complete source list.

CA SEL., NITROGEN FIXAT.
[US/1047-8108]
CA SELECTS: NITROGEN FIXATION.
***Refer to Chemical Abstracts for complete source list.

CA SEL., NONLINEAR OPT. MATER.
[US/0895-5867]
CA SELECTS: NONLINEAR OPTICAL MATERIALS.
***Refer to Chemical Abstracts for complete source list.

INDEXES/ABSTRACTS TABLE

CA SEL., NOV. PESTIC. HERBIC.
[US/0749-7318]
CA SELECTS: NOVEL PESTICIDES & HERBICIDES.
***Refer to Chemical Abstracts for complete source list.

CA SEL., NOVEL NAT. PROD.
[US/0734-872X]
CA SELECTS: NOVEL NATURAL PRODUCTS.
***Refer to Chemical Abstracts for complete source list.

CA SEL., NOVEL POLYM. PAT.
[US/0734-8819]
CA SELECTS: NOVEL POLYMERS FROM PATENTS.
***Refer to Chemical Abstracts for complete source list.

CA SEL., NOVEL SULFUR HETEROCYCL.
[US/0275-7109]
CA SELECTS: NOVEL SULFUR HETEROCYCLES.
***Refer to Chemical Abstracts for complete source list.

CA SEL., OMEGA THREE FAT. ACID. FISH OIL
[US/1052-1984]
CA SELECTS: OMEGA THREE FATTY ACIDS & FISH OIL.
***Refer to Chemical Abstracts for complete source list.

CA SEL., OPT. PHOTOSENSIT. MATER.
[US/0195-5063]
CA SELECTS: OPTICAL & PHOTOSENSITIVE MATERIALS.
***Refer to Chemical Abstracts for complete source list.

CA SEL., OPTIMIZ. ORG. REACT.
[US/0195-5071]
CA SELECTS: OPTIMIZATION OF ORGANIC REACTIONS.
***Refer to Chemical Abstracts for complete source list.

CA SEL., ORAGNOPHOS. CHEM.
[US/0162-783X]
CA SELECTS: ORGANOPHOSPHORUS CHEMISTRY.
***Refer to Chemical Abstracts for complete source list.

CA SEL., ORG. ANAL. CHEM.
[US/0275-7117]
CA SELECTS: ORGANIC ANALYTICAL CHEMISTRY.
***Refer to Chemical Abstracts for complete source list.

CA SEL., ORG. OPT. MATER.
[US/0885-0186]
CA SELECTS: ORGANIC OPTICAL MATERIALS.
***Refer to Chemical Abstracts for complete source list.

CA SEL., ORG. REACT. MECHAN.
[US/0162-7848]
CA SELECTS: ORGANIC REACTION MECHANISMS.
***Refer to Chemical Abstracts for complete source list.

CA SEL., ORG. STEREOCHEM.
[US/0195-508X]
CA SELECTS: ORGANIC STEREOCHEMISTRY.
***Refer to Chemical Abstracts for complete source list.

CA SEL., ORG.-TRANS. MET. COMPL.
[US/0160-9130]
CA SELECTS: ORGANO-TRANSITION METAL COMPLEXES.
***Refer to Chemical Abstracts for complete source list.

CA SEL., ORGANOBOR. CHEM. BORAN.
[US/0195-5098]
CA SELECTS: ORGANOBORON CHEMISTRY & BORANES.
(Ceased)

CA SEL., ORGANOFLOUR. CHEM.
[US/0160-905X]
CA SELECTS: ORGANOFLUORINE CHEMISTRY.
***Refer to Chemical Abstracts for complete source list.

CA SEL., ORGANOMET. ORG. SYNTH.
[US/0895-5859]
CA SELECTS: ORGANOMETALLICS IN ORGANIC SYNTHESIS.
***Refer to Chemical Abstracts for complete source list.

CA SEL., ORGANOSIL. CHEM.
[US/0362-9899]
CA SELECTS: ORGANOSILICON CHEMISTRY.
***Refer to Chemical Abstracts for complete source list.

CA SEL., ORGANOSUL. CHEM. J.
[US/1040-7189]
CA SELECTS: ORGANOSULFUR CHEMISTRY (JOURNALS).
***Refer to Chemical Abstracts for complete source list.

CA SEL., ORGANOTIN CHEM.
[US/0195-5101]
CA SELECTS: ORGANOTIN CHEMISTRY.
***Refer to Chemical Abstracts for complete source list.

CA SEL., OXID. CATAL.
[US/1040-7170]
CA SELECTS: OXIDATION CATALYSTS.
***Refer to Chemical Abstracts for complete source list.

CA SEL., OXIDE SUPERCOND.
[US/1040-7219]
CA SELECTS: OXIDE SUPERCONDUCTORS.
***Refer to Chemical Abstracts for complete source list.

CA SEL., PAINT ADDIT.
[US/0734-8762]
CA SELECTS: PAINT ADDITIVES.
***Refer to Chemical Abstracts for complete source list.

CA SEL., PAP. CHEM.
[US/1040-7200]
CA SELECTS: PAPER CHEMISTRY.
***Refer to Chemical Abstracts for complete source list.

CA SEL., PAP. THIN-LAY. CHROMATOGR.
[US/0146-4515]
CA SELECTS: PAPER & THIN-LAYER CHROMATOGRAPHY.
***Refer to Chemical Abstracts for complete source list.

CA SEL., PAPER ADDIT.
[US/0734-8711]
CA SELECTS: PAPER ADDITIVES.
***Refer to Chemical Abstracts for complete source list.

CA SEL., PHARM. ANAL.
[US/0890-1902]
CA SELECTS: PHARMACEUTICAL ANALYSIS.
***Refer to Chemical Abstracts for complete source list.

CA SEL., PHARM. CHEM. (PAT.)
[US/0890-1929]
CA SELECTS: PHARMACEUTICAL CHEMISTRY (PATENTS).
***Refer to Chemical Abstracts for complete source list.

CA SEL., PHARM. CHEM. J.
[US/0890-1910]
CA SELECTS: PHARMACEUTICAL CHEMISTRY (JOURNALS).
***Refer to Chemical Abstracts for complete source list.

CA SEL., PHASE TRANSF. CATAL.
[US/0885-0194]
CA SELECTS: PHASE TRANSFER CATALYSIS.
***Refer to Chemical Abstracts for complete source list.

CA SEL., PHOTOBIOCHEM.
[US/0148-2335]
CA SELECTS: PHOTOBIOCHEMISTRY.
***Refer to Chemical Abstracts for complete source list.

CA SEL., PHOTOCHEM.
[US/0362-9856]
CA SELECTS: PHOTOCHEMISTRY.
***Refer to Chemical Abstracts for complete source list.

CA SEL., PHOTOCHEM. ORG. SYNTH.
[US/0885-0208]
CA SELECTS: PHOTOCHEMICAL ORGANIC SYNTHESIS.
***Refer to Chemical Abstracts for complete source list.

CA SEL., PHOTORESIS.
[US/0885-0216]
CA SELECTS: PHOTORESISTS.
***Refer to Chemical Abstracts for complete source list.

CA SEL., PHOTOSENSIT. POLYM.
[US/0749-7326]
CA SELECTS: PHOTOSENSITIVE POLYMERS.
***Refer to Chemical Abstracts for complete source list.

CA SEL., PLAS. REACT. ION ETCHING
[US/0749-7334]
CA SELECTS: PLASMA & REACTIVE ION ETCHING.
***Refer to Chemical Abstracts for complete source list.

CA SEL., PLAST. ADDIT.
[US/0734-8681]
CA SELECTS: PLASTICS ADDITIVES.
***Refer to Chemical Abstracts for complete source list.

CA SEL., PLAST. FABR. USES
[US/0275-7125]
CA SELECTS: PLASTICS FABRICATION & USES.
***Refer to Chemical Abstracts for complete source list.

CA SEL., PLAST. FILMS
[US/0195-511X]
CA SELECTS: PLASTIC FILMS.
***Refer to Chemical Abstracts for complete source list.

CA SEL., PLAST. MANUF. PROCESS.
[US/0275-7133]
CA SELECTS: PLASTICS MANUFACTURING & PROCESSING.
***Refer to Chemical Abstracts for complete source list.

CA SEL., PLAT. PALLAD. CHEM.
[US/0890-1937]
CA SELECTS: PLATINUM & PALLADIUM CHEMISTRY.
***Refer to Chemical Abstracts for complete source list.

CA SEL., POLLUT. MONIT.
[US/0160-9149]
CA SELECTS: POLLUTION MONITORING.
***Refer to Chemical Abstracts for complete source list.

CA SEL., POLYACRYL. J.
[US/0890-1945]
CA SELECTS: POLYACRYLATES (JOURNALS).
***Refer to Chemical Abstracts for complete source list.

CA SEL., POLYEST.
[US/0734-8703]
CA SELECTS: POLYESTERS.
***Refer to Chemical Abstracts for complete source list.

CA SEL., POLYIMIDES
[US/0895-5840]
CA SELECTS: POLYIMIDES.
***Refer to Chemical Abstracts for complete source list.

CA SEL., POLYM. BLENDS
[US/0734-8827]
CA SELECTS: POLYMER BLENDS.
***Refer to Chemical Abstracts for complete source list.

CA SEL., POLYM. DEGRAD.
[US/0734-8835]
CA SELECTS: POLYMER DEGRADATION.
***Refer to Chemical Abstracts for complete source list.

INDEXES/ABSTRACTS TABLE

CA SEL., POLYM. KINET. PROCESS CONTROL
[US/0885-0224]
CA SELECTS: POLYMERIZATION KINETICS & PROCESS CONTROL.
***Refer to Chemical Abstracts for complete source list.

CA SEL., POLYM. MORPHOL.
[US/0195-5128]
CA SELECTS: POLYMER MORPHOLOGY.
***Refer to Chemical Abstracts for complete source list.

CA SEL., POLYURETH.
[US/0740-0705]
CA SELECTS: POLYURETHANES.
***Refer to Chemical Abstracts for complete source list.

CA SEL., PORPHYR.
[US/0195-5136]
CA SELECTS: PORPHYRINS.
***Refer to Chemical Abstracts for complete source list.

CA SEL., PROSTAGLAND.
[US/0148-2343]
CA SELECTS: PROSTAGLANDINS.
***Refer to Chemical Abstracts for complete source list.

CA SEL., PROT. MAG. RESON.
[US/0190-941X]
CA SELECTS: PROTON MAGNETIC RESONANCE.
(*Continues in part* CA Selects. Nuclear Magnetic Resonance, Chemical Aspects.)
***Refer to Chemical Abstracts for complete source list.

CA SEL., PSYCHOBIOCHEM.
[US/0362-9848]
CA SELECTS: PSYCHOBIOCHEMISTRY.
***Refer to Chemical Abstracts for complete source list.

CA SEL., QUAT. AMMON. COMP.
[US/0890-1953]
CA SELECTS: QUATERNARY AMMONIUM COMPOUNDS.
***Refer to Chemical Abstracts for complete source list.

CA SEL., RADIAT. CHEM.
[US/0146-4523]
CA SELECTS: RADIATION CHEMISTRY.
***Refer to Chemical Abstracts for complete source list.

CA SEL., RADIAT. CURING
[US/0749-7342]
CA SELECTS: RADIATION CURING.
***Refer to Chemical Abstracts for complete source list.

CA SEL., RAMAN SPECTROS.
[US/0148-2432]
CA SELECTS: RAMAN SPECTROSCOPY.
***Refer to Chemical Abstracts for complete source list.

CA SEL., RECOV. RECYCL. WASTES
[US/0160-9157]
CA SELECTS: RECOVERY & RECYCLING OF WASTES.
***Refer to Chemical Abstracts for complete source list.

CA SEL., SELEN. TELLUR. CHEM.
[US/0749-7350]
CA SELECTS: SELENIUM & TELLURIUM CHEMISTRY.
***Refer to Chemical Abstracts for complete source list.

CA SEL., SHAPE MEM. ALLOYS
[US/1062-869X]
CA SELECTS: SHAPE MEMORY ALLOYS.
***Refer to Chemical Abstracts for complete source list.

CA SEL., SILICAS SILICAT.
[US/0890-1961]
CA SELECTS: SILICAS & SILICATES.
***Refer to Chemical Abstracts for complete source list.

CA SEL., SILOX. SILIC.
[US/0895-5832]
CA SELECTS: SILOXANES & SILICONES.
***Refer to Chemical Abstracts for complete source list.

CA SEL., SILVER CHEM.
[US/0148-2440]
CA SELECTS: SILVER CHEMISTRY.
***Refer to Chemical Abstracts for complete source list.

CA SEL., SOL. ENERGY
[US/0148-236X]
CA SELECTS: SOLAR ENERGY.
***Refer to Chemical Abstracts for complete source list.

CA SEL., SOLID RADIOACT. WASTE TREAT.
[US/0160-9165]
CA SELECTS: SOLID & RADIOACTIVE WASTE TREATMENT.
***Refer to Chemical Abstracts for complete source list.

CA SEL., SOLID STATE NMR
[US/0895-5824]
CA SELECTS: SOLID STATE NMR.
***Refer to Chemical Abstracts for complete source list.

CA SEL., SOLV. EXTRACT.
[US/0146-4531]
CA SELECTS: SOLVENT EXTRACTION.
***Refer to Chemical Abstracts for complete source list.

CA SEL., SPECTROCHEM. ANAL.
[US/0885-0232]
CA SELECTS: SPECTROCHEMICAL ANALYSIS.
***Refer to Chemical Abstracts for complete source list.

CA SEL., STEROIDS (BIOCHEM. ASP.)
[US/0160-9173]
CA SELECTS: STEROIDS (BIOCHEMICAL ASPECTS).
***Refer to Chemical Abstracts for complete source list.

CA SEL., STEROIDS (CHEM. ASP.)
[US/0160-9181]
CA SELECTS: STEROIDS (CHEMICAL ASPECTS).
***Refer to Chemical Abstracts for complete source list.

CA SEL., STRESS CORROS.-MET.
[US/1066-1174]
CA SELECTS: STRESS CORROSION - METALS.
***Refer to Chemical Abstracts for complete source list.

CA SEL., STRUCT.-ACT. RELAT.
[US/0895-5816]
CA SELECTS: STRUCTURE-ACTIVITY RELATIONSHIPS.
***Refer to Chemical Abstracts for complete source list.

CA SEL., SUBSTIT. EFFECTS LIN. FREE ENERGY RELAT.
[US/0162-7856]
CA SELECTS: SUBSTITUENT EFFECTS & LINEAR FREE ENERGY RELATIONSHIPS.
(Ceased)

CA SEL., SURF. ANAL.
[US/0195-5152]
CA SELECTS: SURFACE ANALYSIS.
***Refer to Chemical Abstracts for complete source list.

CA SEL., SURF. CHEM. (PHYSICOCHEM. ASP.)
[US/0146-454X]
CA SELECTS: SURFACE CHEMISTRY (PHYSICOCHEMICAL ASPECTS).
***Refer to Chemical Abstracts for complete source list.

CA SEL., SYNFUELS
[US/0195-5160]
CA SELECTS: SYNFUELS.
***Refer to Chemical Abstracts for complete source list.

CA SEL., SYNTH. HIGH POLYM.
[US/0275-7168]
CA SELECTS: SYNTHETIC HIGH POLYMERS.
***Refer to Chemical Abstracts for complete source list.

CA SEL., SYNTH. MACROCY. COMP.
[US/0195-5179]
CA SELECTS: SYNTHETIC MACROCYCLIC COMPOUNDS.
***Refer to Chemical Abstracts for complete source list.

CA SEL., TECH. CERAM.
[US/1062-8703]
CA SELECTS: TECHNICAL CERAMICS.
***Refer to Chemical Abstracts for complete source list.

CA SEL., THERM. ANAL.
[US/0195-5187]
CA SELECTS: THERMAL ANALYSIS.
***Refer to Chemical Abstracts for complete source list.

CA SEL., THERMOCHEM.
[US/0162-7864]
CA SELECTS: THERMOCHEMISTRY.
***Refer to Chemical Abstracts for complete source list.

CA SEL., TRACE ELEM. ANAL.
[US/0160-919X]
CA SELECTS: TRACE ELEMENT ANALYSIS.
***Refer to Chemical Abstracts for complete source list.

CA SEL., ULTRAFILTR.
[US/0195-5195]
CA SELECTS: ULTRAFILTRATION.
***Refer to Chemical Abstracts for complete source list.

CA SEL., ULTRAVIOL. VISI. SPECTRO.
[US/0195-5209]
CA SELECTS: ULTRAVIOLET & VISIBLE SPECTROSCOPY.
***Refer to Chemical Abstracts for complete source list.

CA SEL., WATER TREAT.
[US/0740-073X]
CA SELECTS: WATER TREATMENT.
***Refer to Chemical Abstracts for complete source list.

CA SEL., WATER-BASED COAT.
[US/0749-7369]
CA SELECTS: WATER-BASED COATINGS.
***Refer to Chemical Abstracts for complete source list.

CA SEL., X-RAY ANAL. SPECTRO.
[US/0162-7872]
CA SELECTS: X-RAY ANALYSIS & SPECTROSCOPY.
***Refer to Chemical Abstracts for complete source list.

CA SEL., ZEOLITES
[US/0190-4949]
CA SELECTS: ZEOLITES.
***Refer to Chemical Abstracts for complete source list.

CALCIUM CALCIF. TISSUE ABSTR.
[US/1069-5540]
CALCIUM AND CALCIFIED TISSUE ABSTRACTS.
(*Continues* Calcified Tissue Abstracts.)

CALIF. PERIOD. INDEX
[US/0730-1367]
CALIFORNIA PERIODICALS INDEX.
(Ceased)

CALIF. PERIOD. MICROFI.
[US]
CALIFORNIA PERIODICALS ON MICROFILM.
(Ceased)

INDEXES/ABSTRACTS TABLE

CAN. BUS. INDEX
[CN/0227-8669]
CANADIAN BUSINESS INDEX.
(*Merged with* Canadian News Index *and* Canadian Magazine Index (Toronto, Ont.) *to form* Canadian Index (Toronto, Ont.).)

CAN. BUS. PERIOD. INDEX
[CN/0318-6717]
CANADIAN BUSINESS PERIODICALS INDEX.
(*Continued by* Canadian Business Index.)

CAN. CURR. LAW
[CN/0835-9768]
CANADIAN CURRENT LAW.
(*Split into* Jurisprudence (Scarborough, Ont.); Legislation (Scarborough, Ont.) *and* Canadian Legal Literature.)

CAN. EDUC. INDEX
[CN/0008-3453]
CANADIAN EDUCATION INDEX.
(*Absorbed* Directory of Education Studies in Canada.)

CAN. ENVIRON.
[CN]
CANADIAN ENVIRONMENT.
(*Continued by* AQUAREF.)

CAN. ESSAY LIT. INDEX
[CN/0316-0696]
CANADIAN ESSAY AND LITERATURE INDEX.
(Ceased)

CAN. INDEX
[CN/1192-4160]
CANADIAN INDEX (TORONTO).
(*Formed by the union of* Canadian Business Index *and* Canadian News Index Canadian Magazine Index (Toronto, Ont.).)

CAN. LEGAL LIT.
[CN/0832-9257]
CANADIAN LEGAL LITERATURE.
(*Continues in part* Canadian Current Law (1988).)

CAN. LIT. INDEX
[CN/0838-6021]
CANADIAN LITERATURE INDEX.
(Ceased)

CAN. MAG. INDEX
[CN/0829-8777]
CANADIAN MAGAZINE INDEX.
(*Merged with* Canadian Business Index *and* Canadian News Index *to form* Canadian Index (Toronto, Ont.).)

CAN. NEWS INDEX
[CN/0225-7459]
CANADIAN NEWS INDEX TORONTO.
(*Merged with* Canadian Business Index *and* Canadian Magazine Index (Toronto, Ont.) *to form* Canadian Index (Toronto, Ont.).)

CAN. PERIOD. INDEX
[CN/0008-4719]
CANADIAN PERIODICAL INDEX (1964).
(*Continues* Canadian Index to Periodicals and Documentary Films.)

CAN., MICROFICHE
[CN/0225-3216]
CANADIANA. MICROFICHE.
(Ceased)

CANON LAW ABSTR.
[UK/0008-5650]
CANON LAW ABSTRACTS.

CATCH. TRADE NAME INDEX : CATNI
[UK]
CATCHWORD AND TRADE NAME INDEX : CATNI.
***Refer to Current Technology Index for complete source list.

CATHOL. PERIOD. INDEX
[US/0363-6895]
CATHOLIC PERIODICAL INDEX.
(*Continued by* Catholic Periodical and Literature Index.)

CATHOL. PERIOD. LIT. INDEX
[US/0008-8285]
CATHOLIC PERIODICAL AND LITERATURE INDEX, THE.
(*Continues* Catholic Periodical Index; *Absorbed* Guide to Catholic Literature.)

CCLP CONTENTS CURR. LEG. PERIOD.
[US/0300-7391]
CCLP. CONTENTS OF CURRENT LEGAL PERIODICALS.
(*Continued by* Legal Contents.)

CERAM. ABSTR.
[US/0095-9960]
CERAMIC ABSTRACTS.
(*Continues in part* American Ceramic Society. Journal of the American Ceramic Society.)

CHEM INFORM
[GW/0931-7597]
CHEM INFORM.
(*Continues* Chemischer Informationsdienst.)

CHEM. ABSTR.
[US/0009-2258]
CHEMICAL ABSTRACTS.
(*Supersedes* Review of American Chemical Research.)

CHEM. BUS. BULL.
[UK]
CHEMICAL BUSINESS BULLETINS.

CHEM. BUS. NEWSBASE
[UK]
CHEMICAL BUSINESS NEWSBASE [ONLINE DATABASE].

CHEM. BUS. UPDATE
[UK/0950-6144]
CHEMICAL BUSINESS UPDATE.

CHEM. ENG. ABSTR.
[UK/0262-6438]
CHEMICAL ENGINEERING ABSTRACTS.
(*Continued by* Process & Chemical Engineering.)

CHEM. HAZARDS IND.
[UK/0265-5721]
CHEMICAL HAZARDS IN INDUSTRY.

CHEM. IND. NOTES
[US/0045-639X]
CHEMICAL INDUSTRY NOTES.
(*Supersedes* Plastics Industry Notes.)

CHEM. INF. DIENST.
[GW/0009-2975]
CHEMISCHER INFORMATIONSDIENST.
(*Continued by* Chem Inform.)

CHEM. TITLES
[US/0009-2711]
CHEMICAL TITLES.

CHEMORECEPT. ABSTR.
[US/0300-1261]
CHEMORECEPTION ABSTRACTS.

CHICAGO PSYCHOANAL. LIT. INDEX.
[US/0009-3661]
CHICAGO PSYCHOANALYTIC LITERATURE INDEX.
(Ceased)

CHICANO INDEX
[US/1044-3487]
CHICANO INDEX, THE.
(*Continues* Chicano Periodical Index.)

CHICOREL INDEX MENT. HEALTH BOOK REV.
[US/0149-4090]
CHICOREL INDEX TO MENTAL HEALTH BOOK REVIEWS.
(*Continues* Mental Health Book Review Index.)

CHILD DEV. ABSTR. BIBLIOGR.
[US/0009-3939]
CHILD DEVELOPMENT ABSTRACTS AND BIBLIOGRAPHY.
(*Continues* Selected Child Development Abstracts Currently Published in the Journal of Nervous and Mental Disease, the Wistar Institute Bibliographic Service, American Journal of Diseases of Children, Archives of Neurology and Psychiatry, Psychological Abstracts, Physiological Abstracts, Biological Abstracts, Chemical Abstracts, Endocrinology.)

CHILD. LIT. ABSTR.
[UK/0306-2015]
CHILDREN'S LITERATURE ABSTRACTS.

CHILD. MAG. GUIDE
[US/0743-9873]
CHILDREN'S MAGAZINE GUIDE.
(*Continues* Subject Index to Children's Magazines.)

CHRIST. PERIOD. INDEX
[US/0069-3871]
CHRISTIAN PERIODICAL INDEX.

CIS ABSTR.
[US/0302-7651]
CIS ABSTRACTS.
(*Continued by* Safety and Health at Work.)

CIS INDEX PUBL. U.S. CONGR.
[US/0007-8514]
CIS INDEX TO PUBLICATIONS OF THE UNITED STATES CONGRESS.

CIV. STRUCT. ENG. ABSTR.
[US/1063-7338]
CIVIL AND STRUCTURAL ENGINEERING ABSTRACTS.
(Ceased)

CLARK'S DIG.-ANNOT.
[US]
CLARK'S DIGEST-ANNOTATOR.
(*Continued by* New York Law Journal Digest-Annotator.)

CLASSIFIED ABSTR. ARCH. ALCOHOL LIT.
[US]
CLASSIFIED ABSTRACT ARCHIVE OF THE ALCOHOL LITERATURE.
(Ceased)

CLIN. BEHAV. THERAPY REV.
[US/0162-2269]
CLINICAL BEHAVIOR THERAPY REVIEW.
(Ceased)

COAL ABSTR.
[UK/0309-4979]
COAL ABSTRACTS.
(Ceased)

INDEXES/ABSTRACTS TABLE

COLL. STUD. PERS. ABSTR.
[US/0010-1168]
COLLEGE STUDENT PERSONNEL ABSTRACTS.
(*Continued by* Higher Education Abstracts.)

COMB. CUMUL. INDEX CARDIOL.
[US/0747-5330]
COMBINED CUMULATIVE INDEX TO CARDIOLOGY.
(Ceased)

COMB. CUMUL. INDEX OB. GYN.
[US/0884-8092]
COMBINED CUMULATIVE INDEX TO OBSTETRICS AND GYNECOLOGY.

COMB. CUMUL. INDEX PEDIATR.
[US/0190-4981]
COMBINED CUMULATIVE INDEX TO PEDIATRICS.

COMM. FISH. ABSTR.
[US/0010-2970]
COMMERCIAL FISHERIES ABSTRACTS.
(*Continued by* Marine Fisheries Abstracts.)

COMMUN. ABSTR.
[US/0162-2811]
COMMUNICATION ABSTRACTS.

COMMUNITY DEV. ABSTR.
[US]
COMMUNITY DEVELOPMENT ABSTRACTS.
(Ceased)

COMMUNITY MENT. HEALTH REV.
[US/0363-1605]
COMMUNITY MENTAL HEALTH REVIEW.
(*Continued by* Prevention in Human Services.)

COMPEND. PLUS
[US/1063-8709]
COMPENDEX PLUS.
***Refer to Engineering Index for complete source list.

COMPUMATH CIT. INDEX
[US/0730-6199]
COMPUMATH CITATION INDEX : CMCI.

COMPUT-A-CAL
[US/0742-5686]
COMPUT-A-CAL.
(Ceased)

COMPUT. ABSTR.
[UK/0010-4469]
COMPUTER ABSTRACTS.
(*Continues* Computer Bibliography.)

COMPUT. ASAP
[US]
COMPUTER ASAP [ONLINE DATABASE].

COMPUT. BUS.
[US/0732-8346]
COMPUTER BUSINESS (LOS ANGELES, CALIF.).

COMPUT. CONTENTS
[US/0747-0193]
COMPUTER CONTENTS.
(Ceased)

COMPUT. CONTROL ABSTR.
[UK/0036-8113]
COMPUTER & CONTROL ABSTRACTS.
(*Continues* Control Abstracts.)
***Refer to INSPEC [Online Database] for a complete source list.

COMPUT. DATABASE
[US]
COMPUTER DATABASE [ONLINE DATABASE].

COMPUT. IND. UPDATE
[US/0744-0081]
COMPUTER INDUSTRY UPDATE.

COMPUT. INF. SYST.
[US/0010-4507]
COMPUTER & INFORMATION SYSTEMS.
(*Continued by* Computer and Information Systems Abstracts Journal.)

COMPUT. INF. SYST. ABSTR. J.
[US/0191-9776]
COMPUTER AND INFORMATION SYSTEMS ABSTRACTS JOURNAL.
(*Continued by* Computer and Information Systems Abstracts.)

COMPUT. LIT. INDEX
[US/0270-4846]
COMPUTER LITERATURE INDEX.
(*Continues* Quarterly Bibliography of Computers and Data Processing.)

COMPUT. REV.
[US/0010-4884]
COMPUTING REVIEWS.

COMPUT. REV. INDEX
[US/1040-5003]
COMPUTER REVIEW INDEX.

COMPUT. REV., BIBLIOGR. SUBJ. INDEX CURR. COMPUT. LIT.
[US/0149-1202]
COMPUTING REVIEWS. BIBLIOGRAPHY AND SUBJECT INDEX OF CURRENT COMPUTING LITERATURE.
(*Continued by* ACM Guide to Computing Literature.)

CONCR. ABSTR.
[US/0045-8007]
CONCRETE ABSTRACTS.

CONSTR. INDEX
[US/0892-2047]
CONSTRUCTION INDEX.

CONSUM. HEALTH NUTR. INDEX
[US/0883-1963]
CONSUMER HEALTH & NUTRITION INDEX.

CONSUM. INDEX PROD. EVAL. INF. SOURCE
[US/0094-0534]
CONSUMERS INDEX TO PRODUCT EVALUATIONS AND INFORMATION SOURCES.

CONTENTS CONTEMP. MATH. J.
[US/0010-759X]
CONTENTS OF CONTEMPORARY MATHEMATICAL JOURNALS.
(*Merged with* New Publications - American Mathematical Society *to form* Contents of Contemporary Mathematical Journals and New Publications.)

CONTENTS CONTEMP. MATH. J. NEW PUBL.
[US]
CONTENTS OF CONTEMPORARY MATHEMATICAL JOURNALS AND NEW PUBLICATIONS.
(*Continued by* Current Mathematical Publications.)

CONTENTS CURR. LEG. PERIOD.
[US/0300-7391]
CONTENTS OF CURRENT LEGAL PERIODICALS.
(*Continued by* CCLP. Contents of Current Legal Periodicals.)

CONTENTS PAGES EDUC.
[UK/0265-9220]
CONTENTS PAGES IN EDUCATION.

CONTENTS RECENT ECON. J.
[UK]
CONTENTS OF RECENT ECONOMICS JOURNALS.
(Ceased)

CORROS. ABSTR.
[US/0010-9339]
CORROSION ABSTRACTS.
(*Supersedes in part* Corrosion.)

COT. TROP. FIBR. ABSTR. BIBLIOGR.
[UK]
COTTON AND TROPICAL FIBRES ABSTRACTS BIBLIOGRAPHY.
(*Continues* Cotton and Tropical Fibres Abstracts.)

CRIM. JUSTICE ABSTR.
[US/0146-9177]
CRIMINAL JUSTICE ABSTRACTS.
(*Continues* Crime and Delinquency Literature.)

CRIM. JUSTICE PERIOD. INDEX
[US/0145-5818]
CRIMINAL JUSTICE PERIODICAL INDEX.

CRIM. PENOL. POLICE SCI. ABSTR.
[NE/0928-8759]
CRIMINOLOGY, PENOLOGY AND POLICE SCIENCE ABSTRACTS.
(*Formed by the union of* Criminology & Penology Abstracts *and* Police Science Abstracts.)

CRIME DELINQ. ABSTR.
[US/0045-902X]
CRIME AND DELINQUENCY ABSTRACTS.
(*Continues* International Bibliography on Crime and Delinquency.)

CRIME DELINQ. LIT.
[US/0037-1327]
CRIME AND DELINQUENCY LITERATURE.
(*Continued by* Criminal Justice Abstracts.)

CRIMINOL. PENOL. ABSTR.
[NE/0166-6231]
CRIMINOLOGY & PENOLOGY ABSTRACTS.
(*Merged with* Police Science Abstracts *to form* Criminology, Penology, and Police Science Abstracts.)

CROP PHYSIOL. ABSTR.
[UK/0306-7556]
CROP PHYSIOLOGY ABSTRACTS.

CSA NEURO. ABSTR.
[US/0141-7711]
CSA NEUROSCIENCES ABSTRACTS.

CTI PLUS
[UK]
CTI PLUS [COMPUTER FILE].
***Refer to Current Technology Index for complete source list.

CUMUL. INDEX MED.
[US/0090-1423]
CUMULATED INDEX MEDICUS.
(*Continues* Quarterly Cumulative Index Medicus.)
***Refer to Index Medicus for complete source list.

CUMUL. INDEX NURS. ALLIED HEALTH LIT.
[US/0146-5554]
CUMULATIVE INDEX TO NURSING & ALLIED HEALTH LITERATURE.
(*Continued in part by* Nursing and Allied Health Index.)

CUMUL. INDEX NURS. LIT.
[US/0011-3018]
CUMULATIVE INDEX TO NURSING LITERATURE.
(*Continued by* Cumulative Index to Nursing & Allied Health Literature.)

INDEXES/ABSTRACTS TABLE

CURR. ABSTR. CHEM. INDEX CHEM.
[US/0161-455X]
CURRENT ABSTRACTS OF CHEMISTRY AND INDEX CHEMICUS.
(*Continued by* Index Chemicus : IC.)

CURR. ADV. APPL. MICROBIOL. BIOTECHNOL.
[UK/0964-8712]
CURRENT ADVANCES IN APPLIED MICROBIOLOGY & BIOTECHNOLOGY.
(*Continues* Current Advances in Microbiology.)
***Refer to Current Awareness in Biological Sciences : CABS for complete source list.

CURR. ADV. BIOCHEM.
[UK/0741-1618]
CURRENT ADVANCES IN BIOCHEMISTRY.
(*Continued by* Current Advances in Protein Biochemistry.)

CURR. ADV. CANCER RES.
[UK/0895-9803]
CURRENT ADVANCES IN CANCER RESEARCH.
***Refer to Current Awareness in Biological Sciences : CABS for complete source list.

CURR. ADV. CELL DEV. BIOL.
[UK/0741-1626]
CURRENT ADVANCES IN CELL AND DEVELOPMENTAL BIOLOGY.
(*Continues in part* Current Awareness in Biological Sciences.)
***Refer to Current Awareness in Biological Sciences : CABS for complete source list.

CURR. ADV. CLIN. CHEM.
[UK/0885-1980]
CURRENT ADVANCES IN CLINICAL CHEMISTRY.
(*Continues* Current Clinical Chemistry.)
***Refer to Current Awareness in Biological Sciences : CABS for complete source list.

CURR. ADV. ECOL. ENVIRON. SCI.
[UK/0955-6648]
CURRENT ADVANCES IN ECOLOGICAL & ENVIRONMENTAL SCIENCES.
(*Continues* Current Advances in Ecological Sciences.)
***Refer to Current Awareness in Biological Sciences : CABS for complete source list.

CURR. ADV. ECOL. SCI.
[UK/0306-3291]
CURRENT ADVANCES IN ECOLOGICAL SCIENCES.
(*Continued by* Current Advances in Ecological & Environmental Sciences.)

CURR. ADV. ENDOCRIN.
[UK/0741-1634]
CURRENT ADVANCES IN ENDOCRINOLOGY.
(*Continues in part* Current Awareness in Biological Sciences.)

CURR. ADV. ENDOCRIN. METAB.
[UK/0964-8720]
CURRENT ADVANCES IN ENDOCRINOLOGY AND METABOLISM.
(*Continues* Current Advances in Physiology.)
***Refer to Current Awareness in Biological Sciences : CABS for complete source list.

CURR. ADV. GENET. MOL. BIOL.
[UK/0741-1642]
CURRENT ADVANCES IN GENETICS & MOLECULAR BIOLOGY.
(*Continues* Current Advances in Genetics.)
***Refer to Current Awareness in Biological Sciences : CABS for complete source list.

CURR. ADV. IMMUNOL.
[UK/0741-1650]
CURRENT ADVANCES IN IMMUNOLOGY.
(*Continued by* Current Advances in Immunology & Infectious Diseases.)

CURR. ADV. IMMUNOL. INFECT. DISEAS.
[UK/0964-8747]
CURRENT ADVANCES IN IMMUNOLOGY & INFECTIOUS DISEASES.
(*Continues* Current Advances in Immunology.)
***Refer to Current Awareness in Biological Sciences : CABS for complete source list.

CURR. ADV. MICROBIOL.
[UK/0741-1669]
CURRENT ADVANCES IN MICROBIOLOGY.
(*Continued by* Current Advances in Applied Microbiology & Biotechnology.)

CURR. ADV. NEUROSCI.
[UK/0741-1677]
CURRENT ADVANCES IN NEUROSCIENCE.
(*Continues in part* Current Awareness in Biological Sciences.)
***Refer to Current Awareness in Biological Sciences : CABS for complete source list.

CURR. ADV. PHARMACOL. TOXICOL.
[UK/0741-1685]
CURRENT ADVANCES IN PHARMACOLOGY & TOXICOLOGY.
(*Continued by* Current Advances in Toxicology.)

CURR. ADV. PHYSIOL.
[UK/0741-1693]
CURRENT ADVANCES IN PHYSIOLOGY.
(*Continued by* Current Advances in Endocrinology & Metabolism.)

CURR. ADV. PLANT SCI.
[UK/0306-4484]
CURRENT ADVANCES IN PLANT SCIENCE.
***Refer to Current Awareness in Biological Sciences : CABS for complete source list.

CURR. ADV. PROT. BIOCHEM.
[UK/0965-0504]
CURRENT ADVANCES IN PROTEIN BIOCHEMISTRY.
(*Continues* Current Advances in Biochemistry.)
***Refer to Current Awareness in Biological Sciences : CABS for complete source list.

CURR. ADV. PROT. CHEM.
[UK/0965-0504]
CURRENT ADVANCES IN PROTEIN CHEMISTRY.
(*Continues* Current Advances in Biochemistry.)
***Refer to Current Awareness in Biological Sciences : CABS for complete source list.

CURR. ADV. TOXICOL.
[UK/0965-0512]
CURRENT ADVANCES IN TOXICOLOGY.
(*Continues* Current Advances in Pharmacology & Toxicology.)
***Refer to Current Awareness in Biological Sciences : CABS for complete source list.

CURR. AUST. NEW Z. LEG. LIT. INDEX
[AT]
CURRENT AUSTRALIAN AND NEW ZEALAND LEGAL LITERATURE INDEX.
(Ceased)

CURR. AWARE. BIOL. SCI., CABS
[UK/0733-4443]
CURRENT AWARENESS IN BIOLOGICAL SCIENCES.
(*Continued in part by* Current Advances in Neuroscience; Current Advances in Cell & Developmental Biology.)

CURR. AWARENESS LIBR. LIT., CALL
[US/0091-5270]
CURRENT AWARENESS-LIBRARY LITERATURE : CALL.
(Ceased)

CURR. BIOTECHNOL.
[UK/0960-5037]
CURRENT BIOTECHNOLOGY.
(*Continues* Current Biotechnology Abstracts.)

CURR. BIOTECHNOL. ABSTR.
[UK/0264-3391]
CURRENT BIOTECHNOLOGY ABSTRACTS.
(*Continued by* Current Biotechnology.)

CURR. BOOK REV. CITATIONS
[US/0360-1250]
CURRENT BOOK REVIEW CITATIONS.
(Ceased)

CURR. CHEM. REACT.
[US/0163-6278]
CURRENT CHEMICAL REACTIONS.

CURR. CONTENTS
[US/0272-1430]
CURRENT CONTENTS.
(*Continued by* Current Contents of Pharmaceutical Publications.)

CURR. CONTENTS AFR.
[UK/0721-5207]
CURRENT CONTENTS AFRICA.
(*Continues* CCA, Current Contents Afrika.)

CURR. CONTENTS AGRIC. BIOL. ENVIRON. SCI.
[US/0090-0508]
CURRENT CONTENTS. AGRICULTURE, BIOLOGY, & ENVIRONMENTAL SCIENCES.
(*Continues* Current Contents. Agricultural, Food & Veterinary Sciences.)

CURR. CONTENTS AGRIC. FOOD VET. SCI.
[US/0011-3379]
CURRENT CONTENTS : AGRICULTURAL, FOOD AND VETERINARY SCIENCES.
(*Continued by* Current Contents. Agriculture, Biology & Environmental Sciences.)

CURR. CONTENTS ARTS HUMANIT.
[US/0163-3155]
CURRENT CONTENTS. ARTS & HUMANITIES.

CURR. CONTENTS BEHAV. SOC. EDUC. SCI.
[US/0011-3387]
CURRENT CONTENTS: BEHAVIORAL, SOCIAL & EDUCATIONAL SCIENCES.
(*Continued by* Current Contents. Social & Behavioral Sciences.)

CURR. CONTENTS BEHAV. SOC. MANAGE. SCI.
[US/0590-384X]
CURRENT CONTENTS: BEHAVIORAL, SOCIAL & MANAGEMENT SCIENCES.
(*Continued by* Current Contents. Behavioral, Social & Educational Sciences.)

CURR. CONTENTS CLIN. MED.
[US/0891-3358]
CURRENT CONTENTS. CLINICAL MEDICINE.
(*Continues* Current Contents. Clinical Practice.)

CURR. CONTENTS CLIN. PRACT.
[US/0091-1704]
CURRENT CONTENTS. CLINICAL PRACTICE.
(*Continued by* Current Contents. Clinical Medicine.)

INDEXES/ABSTRACTS TABLE

CURR. CONTENTS EDUC.
[US/0590-3866]
CURRENT CONTENTS. EDUCATION.
(*Absorbed by* Current Contents: Behavioral, Social & Management Sciences.)

CURR. CONTENTS ENG. TECH. APPL. SCI.
[US/0095-7917]
CURRENT CONTENTS. ENGINEERING, TECHNOLOGY & APPLIED SCIENCES.
(*Continues* Current Contents: Engineering & Technology.)

CURR. CONTENTS ENG. TECH.
[US/0011-3395]
CURRENT CONTENTS: ENGINEERING & TECHNOLOGY.
(*Continued by* Current Contents. Engineering, Technology & Applied Sciences.)

CURR. CONTENTS LIFE SCI.
[US/0011-3409]
CURRENT CONTENTS. LIFE SCIENCES.
(*Continues* Current Contents. Your Weekly Guide to the Chemical, Pharmaco-Medical & Life Sciences.)

CURR. CONTENTS PHARM. PUBL.
[US/0272-1422]
CURRENT CONTENTS OF PHARMACEUTICAL PUBLICATIONS.
(*Superseded by* Current Contents of Pharmaco-Medical Publications.)

CURR. CONTENTS PHARM.-MED. PUBL.
[US/0272-1414]
CURRENT CONTENTS OF PHARMACO-MEDICAL PUBLICATIONS.
(*Continued by* Current Contents: Your Weekly Survey of Chemical, Pharmacological & Clinical Publications.)

CURR. CONTENTS PHYS. CHEM. EARTH SCI.
[US/0163-2574]
CURRENT CONTENTS. PHYSICAL, CHEMICAL & EARTH SCIENCES.
(*Continues* Current Contents. Physical and Chemical Sciences.)

CURR. CONTENTS PHYS. CHEM. SCI.
[US/0011-3417]
CURRENT CONTENTS. PHYSICAL & CHEMICAL SCIENCES.
(*Continued by* Current Contents. Physical, Chemical & Earth Sciences.)

CURR. CONTENTS SOC. BEHAV. SCI.
[US/0092-6361]
CURRENT CONTENTS. SOCIAL & BEHAVIORAL SCIENCES.
(*Continues* Current Contents. Behavioral, Social & Educational Sciences.)

CURR. CONTENTS YOUR WKLY. GUIDE CHEM. PHARM.-MED. LIFE SCI.
[US/0272-1503]
CURRENT CONTENTS: YOUR WEEKLY GUIDE OF THE CHEMICAL, PHARMACO-MEDICAL & LIFE SCIENCES.
(*Continued by* Current Contents. Life Sciences.)

CURR. CONTENTS YOUR WKLY. SURV. CHEM. PHARMACOL. CLIN. PUBL.
[US/0272-1449]
CURRENT CONTENTS: YOUR WEEKLY SURVEY OF CHEMICAL, PHARMACOLOGICAL & CLINICAL PUBLICATIONS.
(*Continued by* Current Contents. Your Weekly Guide to the Chemical, Pharmaco-Medical & Life Sciences.)

CURR. DIG. POST SOV. PRESS
[US/1067-7542]
CURRENT DIGEST OF THE POST-SOVIET PRESS, THE.
(*Continues* Current Digest of the Soviet Press.)

CURR. GEOGR. PUBL.
[US/0011-3514]
CURRENT GEOGRAPHICAL PUBLICATIONS.

CURR. INDEX J. EDUC.
[US/0011-3565]
CURRENT INDEX TO JOURNALS IN EDUCATION.

CURR. INDEX STAT.
[US/0364-1228]
CURRENT INDEX TO STATISTICS.

CURR. LAW INDEX
[US/0196-1780]
CURRENT LAW INDEX.

CURR. LIT. AGING
[US/0011-3662]
CURRENT LITERATURE ON AGING.
(*Continued by* Abstracts in Social Gerontology.)

CURR. LIT. BLOOD
[US/0001-7108]
CURRENT LITERATURE OF BLOOD.
(**Ceased**)

CURR. LIT. FAM. PLAN.
[US/0092-6000]
CURRENT LITERATURE IN FAMILY PLANNING.
(*Continues* Acquisitions List - Katharine Dexter McCormick Library.)

CURR. LIT. SCI. SCI.
[II]
CURRENT LITERATURE ON SCIENCE OF SCIENCE.
(*Supersedes* Index to Literature on Science of Science.)

CURR. MATH. PUBL.
[US/0361-4794]
CURRENT MATHEMATICAL PUBLICATIONS.
(*Continues* Contents of Contemporary Mathematical Journals and New Publications.)
***Refer to Mathematical Reviews for complete source list.

CURR. MIL. POL. LIT.
[UK/0954-3589]
CURRENT MILITARY & POLITICAL LITERATURE.
(*Continues* Current Military Literature.)

CURR. PAP. COMPUT. CONTROL
[UK/0011-3794]
CURRENT PAPERS ON COMPUTERS & CONTROL.
(*Continues* Current Papers on Control.)
***Refer to INSPEC [Online Database] for complete source list.

CURR. PAP. ELECTR. ELECTRON. ENG.
[UK/0011-3778]
CURRENT PAPERS IN ELECTRICAL & ELECTRONICS ENGINEERING.
(*Continues* Current Papers in Eletrotechnology.)
***Refer to INSPEC [Online Database] for complete source list.

CURR. PAP. PHYS.
[UK/0011-3786]
CURRENT PAPERS IN PHYSICS.
***Refer to INSPEC [Online Database] for complete source list.

CURR. PHYS. INDEX
[US/0098-9819]
CURRENT PHYSICS INDEX.

CURR. PRIMATE REF.
[US/0590-4102]
CURRENT PRIMATE REFERENCES.
(*Supersedes* Unverified Primate References.)

CURR. REF. FISH RES.
[US/0739-540X]
CURRENT REFERENCES IN FISH RESEARCH.

CURR. TECHNOL. INDEX
[UK/0260-6593]
CURRENT TECHNOLOGY INDEX : CTI.
(*Continues* British Technology Index.)

CURR. THOUGHTS TRENDS
[US/1054-8688]
CURRENT THOUGHTS AND TRENDS.
(*Continues* Current Christian Abstracts.)

CURR. TITL. DENT.
[DK/0903-3483]
CURRENT TITLES IN DENTISTRY.

CURR. TITLES ELECTROCHEM.
[II/0300-4376]
CURRENT TITLES IN ELECTROCHEMISTRY.
(*Absorbed* Electrochemical News.)

DAIRY SCI. ABSTR.
[UK/0011-5681]
DAIRY SCIENCE ABSTRACTS.

DATA PROCESS. DIG.
[US/0011-6858]
DATA PROCESSING DIGEST.

DEEP-SEA OCEANOGR. ABSTR.
[UK/0011-7471]
DEEP-SEA RESEARCH AND OCEANOGRAPHIC ABSTRACTS.
(*Continued by* Deep-Sea Research.)

DEEP-SEA RES.
[UK/0146-6291]
DEEP-SEA RESEARCH.
(*Continued by* Deep-Sea Research. Part A. Oceanographic Research Papers.)

DEEP-SEA RES., B, OCEANOGR. LIT. REV.
[UK/0198-0254]
DEEP-SEA RESEARCH. PART B. OCEANOGRAPHIC LITERATURE REVIEW.
(*Continued by* Oceanographic Literature Review.)

DENT. ABSTR.
[US/0011-8486]
DENTAL ABSTRACTS (CHICAGO).

DESALIN. ABSTR.
[IS/0011-9202]
DESALINATION ABSTRACTS.
(*Continued by* Desalination and Recycling Abstracts.)

DESALIN. RECYC. ABSTR.
[IS/0011-9172]
DESALINATION AND RECYCLING ABSTRACTS.
(*Continues* Desalination Abstracts.)

DEV. DISABIL. ABSTR.
[US/0191-1600]
DEVELOPMENTAL DISABILITIES ABSTRACTS.
(*Continues* Mental Retardation & Developmental Disabilities Abstracts.)

DEV. MED. CHILD NEUROL.
[UK/0012-1622]
DEVELOPMENTAL MEDICINE & CHILD NEUROLOGY.
(*Continued in part by* American Academy For Cerebral Palsy & Developmental Medicine. Meeting. Abstracts.)

INDEXES/ABSTRACTS TABLE

DIABETES LIT. INDEX
[US/0012-1819]
DIABETES LITERATURE INDEX.
(*Supersedes* Diabetes-Related Literature Index.)

DOANE INF. CENT. INDEX. SYST. SUBJ. INDEX
[US]
DICIS, DOANE INFORMATION CENTER INDEXING SYSTEM : SUBJECT INDEX.
(Ceased)

DOK. GEFAHRDUNG ALKOHOL, RAUCH., DROGEN, ARZNEIMITTEL
[GW/0341-8022]
DOKUMENTATION GEFAHRDUNG DURCH ALKOHOL, RAUCHEN, DROGEN, ARZNEIMITTEL.
(*Continues* Dokumentation Drogengefahrdung und Alkoholmissbrauch.)

DOK. RAUMENTWICKL.
[GW]
DOKUMENTATION ZUR RAUMENTWICKLUNG.
(*Continues* Documentatio Geographica.)

DSH ABSTR.
[US/0011-5150]
DSH ABSTRACTS.
(Ceased)

ECOL. ABSTR.
[UK/0305-196X]
ECOLOGICAL ABSTRACTS.

ECOLOGY ABSTR.
[US/0143-3296]
ECOLOGY ABSTRACTS.
(*Continues* Applied Ecology Abstracts.)

ECON. LIT. INDEX
[US]
ECONOMIC LITERATURE INDEX.

ECONLIT
[US]
ECONLIT [COMPUTER FILE].
***Refer to Economic Literature Index for a complete source list.

EDUC. ADM. ABSTR.
[US/0013-1601]
EDUCATIONAL ADMINISTRATION ABSTRACTS.

EDUC. INDEX
[US/0013-1385]
EDUCATION INDEX.

EDUC. TECHNOL. ABSTR.
[UK/0266-3368]
EDUCATIONAL TECHNOLOGY ABSTRACTS.

EI PAGE ONE
[US]
EI PAGE ONE [COMPUTER FILE].

ELECT. COMM. ABSTR.
[US/1069-5303]
ELECTRONICS AND COMMUNICATIONS ABSTRACTS.
(*Continues* Electronics & Communications Abstracts Journal.)

ELECTR. ELECTRON. ABSTR.
[UK/0036-8105]
ELECTRICAL & ELECTRONICS ABSTRACTS.
(*Continues* Science Abstracts. Electrical & Electronics Abstracts.)
***Refer to INSPEC [Online Database] for a complete source list.

ELECTROANAL. ABSTR.
[SZ/0013-4775]
ELECTROANALYTICAL ABSTRACTS.
(*Continues* Journal of Electroanalytical Chemistry. Abstracts Section.)

ELECTRON. COMMUN. ABSTR. J.
[US/0361-3313]
ELECTRONICS AND COMMUNICATIONS ABSTRACTS JOURNAL (RIVERDALE, MD.).
(*Continued by* Electronics and Communications Abstracts.)

ELECTRON. PUB. ABSTR.
[UK/0739-2907]
ELECTRONIC PUBLISHING ABSTRACTS.
(*Continued by* World Publishing Monitor.)

EMBASE LIST J. INDEXED
[NE]
EMBASE LIST OF JOURNALS INDEXED.
(*Continues* List of Journals Abstracted (1983).)
***Refer to EMBASE [Online Database] for complete source list.

EMBASE
[NE]
EMBASE [ONLINE DATABASE].

EMPLOY. RELAT. ABSTR.
[US]
EMPLOYMENT RELATIONS ABSTRACTS.
(*Continued by* Work Related Abstracts.)

ENERGY INDEX
[US/0094-6281]
ENERGY INDEX.
(*Absorbed by* Energy Information Abstracts Annual.)

ENERGY INF. ABSTR.
[US/0147-6521]
ENERGY INFORMATION ABSTRACTS.
(Ceased)

ENERGY INF. ABSTR. ANNU.
[US/0739-3679]
ENERGY INFORMATION ABSTRACTS ANNUAL.
(*Absorbed* Energy Index.)
***Refer to Energy Information Abstracts for complete source list.

ENERGY RES. ABSTR.
[US/0160-3604]
ENERGY RESEARCH ABSTRACTS.
(*Continues* ERDA Energy Research Abstracts.)

ENG. INDEX
[US/0739-4624]
ENGINEERING INDEX (1919), THE.
(*Continued by* Engineering Index Annual.)

ENG. INDEX ANNU.
[US/0360-8557]
ENGINEERING INDEX ANNUAL.
(*Continues* Engineering Index (New York, N.Y. : 1919).)

ENG. INDEX BIOENG. ABSTR.
[US/0736-6213]
ENGINEERING INDEX BIOENGINEERING ABSTRACTS.
(*Continued by* Engineering Index Bioengineering and Biotechnology Abstracts.)

ENG. INDEX ENERGY ABSTR.
[US/0093-8408]
ENGINEERING INDEX ENERGY ABSTRACTS.
. ***Refer to Engineering Index Annual for a complete source list.

ENG. INDEX MON.
[US/0742-1974]
ENGINEERING INDEX MONTHLY.
(*Continues* Engineering Index Monthly and Author Index.)
***Refer to Engineering Index Annual for a complete source list.

ENG. INDEX MON. AUTHOR INDEX
[US/0162-3036]
ENGINEERING INDEX MONTHLY AND AUTHOR INDEX.
(*Continued by* Engineering Index Monthly (1984).)

ENG. MATER. ABSTR.
[US/0951-9998]
ENGINEERED MATERIALS ABSTRACTS.

ENTOMOL. ABSTR.
[US/0013-8924]
ENTOMOLOGY ABSTRACTS.

ENVIRO ENERGYLINE PLUS
[US/1076-6464]
ENVIRO/ENERGYLINE ABSTRACTS PLUS.
(*Continued by* Environment Abstracts.)
***Refer to Environment Abstracts and Energy Infomation Abstracts for complete source list.

ENVIRON.
[CN/0709-8847]
ENVIRONNEMENT (MONTREAL).
(*Continues* Journal l'Environnement.)

ENVIRON. ABSTR.
[US/0093-3287]
ENVIRONMENT ABSTRACTS.
(*Continues* Environment Information Access; *Absorbed* Acid Rain Abstracts.)

ENVIRON. ABSTR.
[US]
ENVIRONMENT ABSTRACTS [COMPUTER FILE].
(*Continues* Enviro/Energyline Abstracts Plus.)
***Refer to Environment Abstracts and Energy Infomation Abstracts for complete source list.

ENVIRON. ABSTR. ANNU.
[US/0000-1198]
ENVIRONMENT ABSTRACTS ANNUAL.
(*Absorbed* Environment Index *and* Acid Raid Abstracts Annual.)
***Refer to Environment Abstracts for complete source list.

ENVIRON. ENG. ABSTR.
[US/1063-7346]
ENVIRONMENTAL ENGINEERING ABSTRACTS.
(Ceased)

ENVIRON. INDEX
[US/0090-791X]
ENVIRONMENT INDEX.
(*Absorbed by* Environment Abstracts Annual.)

ENVIRON. PERIOD. BIBLIOGR.
[US/0145-3815]
ENVIRONMENTAL PERIODICALS BIBLIOGRAPHY.
(*Continues* Environmental Periodicals.)

ERGON. ABSTR.
[UK/0046-2446]
ERGONOMICS ABSTRACTS.
(*Continues* Ergonomics Abstracts (1959).)

ETHNIC STUD. BIBLIOGR.
[US/0149-1555]
ETHNIC STUDIES BIBLIOGRAPHY.
(Ceased)

INDEXES/ABSTRACTS TABLE

ETHNOARTS INDEX
[US/0893-0120]
ETHNOARTS INDEX.
(*Continues* Tribal Arts Review.)

EUR. RES.
[NE/0304-4297]
EUROPEAN RESEARCH.
(*Continued by* Marketing and Research Today.)

EXCEPT. CHILD EDUC. RESOUR.
[US/0160-4309]
EXCEPTIONAL CHILD EDUCATION RESOURCES.
(*Continues* Exceptional Child Education Abstracts.)

EXCEPT. CHILD EDUC. ABSTR.
[US/0014-4010]
EXCEPTIONAL CHILD EDUCATION ABSTRACTS.
(*Continued by* Exceptional Child Education Resources.)

EXCEPT. HUM. EXP.
[US/1053-4768]
EXCEPTIONAL HUMAN EXPERIENCE.
(*Continues* Parapsychology Abstracts International.)

EXCERPTA MED. LIST J. ABSTR.
[US]
EXCERPTA MEDICA : LIST OF JOURNALS ABSTRACTED.
(*Continued by* List of Journals Abstracted.)

EXCERPTA MED., SECT. 06B, ARTHR. RHEUM.
[NE]
EXCERPTA MEDICA. SECTION 06B. ARTHRITIS AND RHEUMATISM.
(Ceased)

EXCERPTA MEDICA., SECT. 1, ANATOM. ANTHROPOL. EMBRYOL. HISTOL.
[NE/0014-4053]
EXCERPTA MEDICA. SECTION 1. ANATOMY, ANTHROPOLOGY, EMBRYOLOGY AND HISTOLOGY.
***Refer to EMBASE [Online Database] for complete source list.

EXCERPTA MED., SECT. 2, PHYSIOL.
[NE/0367-1089]
EXCERPTA MEDICA. SECTION 2A. PHYSIOLOGY.
(*Continues* Excerpta Medica. Section 2A. Physiology.)
***Refer to EMBASE [Online Database] for complete source list.

EXCERPTA MED., SECT. 2A, PHYSIOL.
[NE/0367-1089]
EXCERPTA MEDICA. SECTION 2A. PHYSIOLOGY.
(*Continued by* Excerpta Medica. Section 2. Physiology.)

EXCERPTA MED., SECT. 3, ENDOCRINOL.
[NE/0014-407X]
EXCERPTA MEDICA. SECTION 3. ENDOCRINOLOGY.
(*Continues* Excerpta Medica. Section 3. Endocrinology, Experimental and Clinical.)
***Refer to EMBASE [Online Database] for complete source list.

EXCERPTA MED., SECT. 4, MICROBIOL.
[NE/0167-4285]
EXCERPTA MEDICA. SECTION 4. MICROBIOLOGY.
(*Continued by* Excerpta Medica. Section 4, Microbiology, Bacteriology, Mycology, Parasitology, and Virology.)

EXCERPTA MED., SECT. 4, MICROBIOL. BACTERIOL. MYCOL. PARASITOL. VIROL.
[NE]
EXCERPTA MEDICA. SECTION 4. MICROBIOLOGY, BACTERIOLOGY, MYCOLOGY, PARASITOLOGY, AND VIROLOGY.
(*Continues* Excerpta Medica. Section 4, Microbiology; *Absorbed* Virology.)
***Refer to EMBASE [Online Database] for complete source list.

EXCERPTA MED., SECT. 5, GEN. PATHOL. PATHOLOGIC. ANAT.
[NE/0014-4096]
EXCERPTA MEDICA. SECTION 5. GENERAL PATHOLOGY AND PATHOLOGICAL ANATOMY.
***Refer to EMBASE [Online Database] for complete source list.

EXCERPTA MED., SECT. 6, INTERN. MED.
[NE/0014-410X]
EXCERPTA MEDICA. SECTION 6. INTERNAL MEDICINE.
***Refer to EMBASE [Online Database] for complete source list.

EXCERPTA MED., SECT. 7, PEDIATR. PEDIATR. SUR.
[NE/0373-6512]
EXCERPTA MEDICA. SECTION 7. PEDIATRICS AND PEDIATRIC SURGERY.
(*Continues* Excerpta Medica. Section 7. Pediatrics.)
***Refer to EMBASE [Online Database] for complete source list.

EXCERPTA MED., SECT. 8, NEUROL. NEUROSURG.
[NE/0014-4126]
EXCERPTA MEDICA. SECTION 8. NEUROLOGY AND NEUROSURGERY.
(*Continues* Excerpta Medica. Section 8A. Neurology and Neurosurgery.)
***Refer to EMBASE [Online Database] for complete source list.

EXCERPTA MED., SECT. 8A, NEUROL. NEUROSURG.
[NE/0014-4126]
EXCERPTA MEDICA. SECTION 8A. NEUROLOGY AND NEUROSURGERY.
(*Continued by* Excerpta Medica. Section 8. Neurology and Neurosurgery.)

EXCERPTA MED., SECT. 9, SURG.
[NE/0014-4134]
EXCERPTA MEDICA. SECTION 9. SURGERY.
(*Continued by* Excerpta Medica. Section 28, Urology.)

EXCERPTA MED., SECT. 9B, ORTHO. TRAUMATOL.
[NE]
EXCERPTA MEDICA. SECTION 9B. ORTHOPAEDICS AND TRAUMATOLOGY.
(*Continued by* Orthopedic Surgery.)

EXCERPTA MED., SECT. 10, OBSTETR. GYNECOL.
[NE/0014-4142]
EXCERPTA MEDICA. SECTION 10. OBSTETRICS AND GYNECOLOGY.
***Refer to EMBASE [Online Database] for complete source list.

EXCERPTA MED., SECT. 12, OPHTHALMOL.
[NE/0014-4169]
EXCERPTA MEDICA. SECTION 12. OPHTHALMOLOGY.
***Refer to EMBASE [Online Database] for complete source list.

EXCERPTA MED., SECT. 13, DERMATOL.
[NE/0014-4177]
EXCERPTA MEDICA. SECTION 13. DERMATOLOGY AND VENEREOLOGY.
***Refer to EMBASE [Online Database] for complete source list.

EXCERPTA MED., SECT. 14, RADIOL.
[NE/0014-4185]
EXCERPTA MEDICA. SECTION 14. RADIOLOGY.
***Refer to EMBASE [Online Database] for complete source list.

EXCERPTA MED., SECT. 16, CANCER
[NE/0014-4207]
EXCERPTA MEDICA. SECTION 16. CANCER.
(*Continues* Cancer, Experimental and Clinical.)
***Refer to EMBASE [Online Database] for complete source list.

EXCERPTA MED., SECT. 17, PUBL. HEALTH SOC. MED EPIDEM.
[NE]
EXCERPTA MEDICA. SECTION 17. PUBLIC HEALTH, SOCIAL MEDICINE AND EPIDEMIOLOGY.
(*Continues* Excerpta Medica. Section 17, Public Health, Social Medicine and Hygiene.)
***Refer to EMBASE [Online Database] for complete source list.

EXCERPTA MED., SECT. 17, PUBL. HEALTH SOC. MED. HYG.
[NE/0014-4215]
EXCERPTA MEDICA. SECTION 17. PUBLIC HEALTH, SOCIAL MEDICINE AND HYGIENE.
(*Continued by* Excerpta Medica. Section 17, Public Health, Social Medicine and Epidemiology.)

EXCERPTA MED., SECT. 18, CARDIOVASC. DISEAS. CARDIOVASC. SURG.
[NE/0014-4223]
EXCERPTA MEDICA. SECTION 18. CARDIOVASCULAR DISEASES AND CARDIOVASCULAR SURGERY.
(*Continues* Excerpta Medica. Section 18. Cardiovascular Diseases.)
***Refer to EMBASE [Online Database] for complete source list.

EXCERPTA MED., SECT. 19, REHABIL. PHYS. MED.
[NE/0014-4231]
EXCERPTA MEDICA. SECTION 19. REHABILITATION AND PHYSICAL MEDICINE.
(*Continues* Excerpta Medica. Section 19. Rehabilitation.)
***Refer to EMBASE [Online Database] for complete source list.

EXCERPTA MED., SECT. 20, GERONTOL. GERIATR.
[NE/0014-424X]
EXCERPTA MEDICA. SECTION 20. GERONTOLOGY AND GERIATRICS.
***Refer to EMBASE [Online Database] for complete source list.

INDEXES/ABSTRACTS TABLE

EXCERPTA MED., SECT. 21, DEVELOP. BIOL. TERATOL.
[NE/0014-4258]
EXCERPTA MEDICA. SECTION 21. DEVELOPMENTAL BIOLOGY AND TERATOLOGY.
(*Continues* Excerpta Medica. Section 21. Human Developmental Biology.)
***Refer to EMBASE [Online Database] for complete source list.

EXCERPTA MED., SECT. 22, HUMAN GENET.
[NE/0014-4266]
EXCERPTA MEDICA. SECTION 22. HUMAN GENETICS.
(*Continues* Human Genetics Abstracts.)
***Refer to EMBASE [Online Database] for complete source list.

EXCERPTA MED., SECT. 23, NUCL. MED.
[NE/0014-4274]
EXCERPTA MEDICA. SECTION 23. NUCLEAR MEDICINE.
***Refer to EMBASE [Online Database] for complete source list.

EXCERPTA MED., SECT. 24, ANESTHESIOL.
[NE/0014-4282]
EXCERPTA MEDICA. SECTION 24. ANESTHESIOLOGY.
***Refer to EMBASE [Online Database] for complete source list.

EXCERPTA MED., SECT. 25, HEMATOL.
[NE/0014-4290]
EXCERPTA MEDICA. SECTION 25. HEMATOLOGY.
***Refer to EMBASE [Online Database] for complete source list.

EXCERPTA MED., SECT. 26, IMMUNOL. SEROL. TRANSPLANT.
[NE/0014-4304]
EXCERPTA MEDICA. SECTION 26. IMMUNOLOGY, SEROLOGY AND TRANSPLANTATION.
(*Supersedes in part* Excerpta Medica. Section 4, Medical Microbiology, Immunology and Serology.)
***Refer to EMBASE [Online Database] for complete source list.

EXCERPTA MED., SECT. 27, BIOPHYS. BIOENG. MED. INSTRUMEN.
[NE/0014-4312]
EXCERPTA MEDICA. SECTION 27. BIOPHYSICS, BIOENGINEERING AND MEDICAL INSTRUMENTATION.
(*Continues* Excerpta Medica. Section 27. Medical Instrumentation.)
***Refer to EMBASE [Online Database] for complete source list.

EXCERPTA MED., SECT. 28, UROL.
[NE]
EXCERPTA MEDICA. SECTION 28. UROLOGY.
(*Continued by* Excerpta Medica. Section 28, Urology and Nephrology.)

EXCERPTA MED., SECT. 28, UROL. NEPHROL.
[NE/0014-4320]
EXCERPTA MEDICA. SECTION 28. UROLOGY AND NEPHROLOGY.
(*Continues* Excerpta Medica. Section 28, Urology.)
***Refer to EMBASE [Online Database] for complete source list.

EXCERPTA MED., SECT. 29, CLIN. BIOCHEM.
[NE/0300-5372]
EXCERPTA MEDICA. SECTION 29. CLINICAL BIOCHEMISTRY.
(*Continues* Excerpta Medica. Section 29. Biochemistry.)
***Refer to EMBASE [Online Database] for complete source list.

EXCERPTA MED., SECT. 30, CLIN. EXPER. PHARMACOL.
[NE]
EXCERPTA MEDICA. SECTION 30. CLINICAL AND EXPERIMENTAL PHARMACOLOGY.
(*Formed by the union of* Excerpta Medica. Section 30, Pharmacology *and* Excerpta Medica. Section 130, Clinical Pharmacology.)
***Refer to EMBASE [Online Database] for complete source list.

EXCERPTA MED., SECT. 30, PHARMACOL.
[IE/0167-9643]
EXCERPTA MEDICA. SECTION 30. PHARMACOLOGY.
(*Continued in part by* Excerpta Medica. Section 130, Clinical Pharmacology; *Merged into* Excerpta Medica. Section 30. Clinical and Experimental Pharmacology.)
***Refer to EMBASE [Online Database] for complete source list.

EXCERPTA MED., SECT. 32, PSYCH.
[NE/0014-4363]
EXCERPTA MEDICA. SECTION 32. PSYCHIATRY.
(*Continues* Excerpta Medica. Section 8B, Psychiatry.)
***Refer to EMBASE [Online Database] for complete source list.

EXCERPTA MED., SECT. 35, OCCUPAT. HEALTH INDUSTR. MED.
[NE/0014-4398]
EXCERPTA MEDICA. SECTION 35. OCCUPATIONAL HEALTH AND INDUSTRIAL MEDICINE.
***Refer to EMBASE [Online Database] for complete source list.

EXCERPTA MED., SECT. 36, HEALTH POLICY ECON. MANAG.
[NE]
EXCERPTA MEDICA. SECTION 36. HEALTH POLICY, ECONOMICS, AND MANAGEMENT.
(*Continues* Health Economics and Hospital Management.)
***Refer to EMBASE [Online Database] for complete source list.

EXCERPTA MED., SECT. 37, DRUG LIT. INDEX
[NE/0167-9171]
EXCERPTA MEDICA. SECTION 37. DRUG LITERATURE INDEX.
(*Continues* Drug Literature Index.)

EXCERPTA MED., SECT. 38, ADVERSE REACT. TITLES
[NE/0167-9090]
EXCERPTA MEDICA. SECTION 38. ADVERSE REACTIONS TITLES.
(*Continues* Adverse Reactions Titles.)
***Refer to EMBASE [Online Database] for complete source list.

EXCERPTA MED., SECT. 40, DRUG DEPEND. ALCOHOL ABUSE ALCOHOL.
[NE/0304-4041]
EXCERPTA MEDICA. SECTION 40. DRUG DEPENDENCE, ALCOHOL ABUSE, AND ALCOHOLISM.
(*Continues* Excerpta Medica. Section 40, Drug Dependence.)
***Refer to EMBASE [Online Database] for complete source list.

EXCERPTA MED., SECT. 46, ENVIRON. HEALTH POLLUT. CONT.
[NE/0300-5194]
EXCERPTA MEDICA. SECTION 46. ENVIRONMENTAL HEALTH AND POLLUTION CONTROL.
(*Continues* Environmental Health and Pollution Control.)
***Refer to EMBASE [Online Database] for complete source list.

EXCERPTA MED., SECT. 50, EPILEP. ABSTR.
[NE/0303-8459]
EXCERPTA MEDICA. SECTION 50. EPILEPSY ABSTRACTS.
(*Continues* Epilepsy Abstracts.)
***Refer to EMBASE [Online Database] for complete source list.

EXCERPTA MED., SECT. 52, TOXICOL.
[NE/0167-8353]
EXCERPTA MEDICA. SECTION 52. TOXICOLOGY.
(*Continues in part* Excerpta Medica. Section 30, Pharmacology and Toxicology.)
***Refer to EMBASE [Online Database] for complete source list.

EXCERPTA MED., SECT. 54, AIDS
[NE/0922-6532]
EXCERPTA MEDICA. SECTION 54. AIDS (ACQUIRED IMMUNE DEFICIENCY SYNDROME).
(Ceased)

EXCERPTA MED., SECT. 65, CANCER IMMUNOL. LIT. INDEX
[NE/0304-3789]
EXCERPTA MEDICA. SECTION 65. CANCER IMMUNOLOGY. LITERATURE INDEX.
***Refer to EMBASE [Online Database] for complete source list.

EXCERPTA MED., SECT. 130, CLINIC. PHARMACOL.
[NE/0921-4496]
EXCERPTA MEDICA. SECTION 130. CLINICAL PHARMACOLOGY.
(*Separated from* Excerpta Medica. Section 30, Pharmacology.)

EXCERPTA MED., SECT. 151, MYCOBACTER. DISEAS. LEPROSY TUBERCUL. RELATED SUBJ.
[NE/0168-8944]
EXCERPTA MEDICA. SECTION 151. MYCOBACTERIAL DISEASES--LEPROSY, TUBERCULOSIS, AND RELATED SUBJECTS.
(*Continues* Excerpta Medica. Section 51, Mycobacterial Diseases--Leprosy, Tuberculosis, and Related Subjects.)

EXPAND. ACAD. INDEX
[US]
EXPANDED ACADEMIC INDEX [COMPUTER FILE].

INDEXES/ABSTRACTS TABLE

F & S INDEX CORP. IND.
[US/0014-567X]
F & S INDEX OF CORPORATIONS AND INDUSTRIES.
(*Continued by* Predicasts F & S Index United States (Annual Edition).)

F & S INDEX PLUS TEXT, INT.
[US/1065-5956]
F & S INDEX PLUS TEXT. INTERNATIONAL.

F & S INDEX PLUS TEXT, U.S.
[US/1065-5964]
F & S INDEX PLUS TEXT. UNITED STATES.
***Refer to F&S Index Plus Text International for complete source list.

FABA BEAN ABSTR.
[UK/0260-8456]
FABA BEAN ABSTRACTS.
(Ceased)

FAMLI, FAM. MED. LIT. INDEX
[CN/0227-2393]
FAMLI : FAMILY MEDICINE LITERATURE INDEX.
(Ceased)

FARM GARD. INDEX
[US/0736-9980]
FARM & GARDEN INDEX.
(Ceased)

FDA CLIN. EXP. ABSTR.
[US/0429-9442]
FDA CLINICAL EXPERIENCE ABSTRACTS.
(Ceased)

FED. PRINT
[US/0891-2769]
FED IN PRINT.
(*Continued by* Fed in Print: Economics and Banking Topics.)

FED. PRINT ECON. BANK. TOP.
[US]
FED IN PRINT: ECONOMICS AND BANKING TOPICS.
(*Continues* Fed in Print: Business and Banking Topics.)

FED. TAX ARTIC.
[US]
FEDERAL TAX ARTICLES: INCOME, ESTATE, GIFT, EXCISE, EMPLOYMENT TAXES.

FERT. ABSTR.
[US/0015-0290]
FERTILIZER ABSTRACTS.
(Ceased)

FIELD CROP ABSTR.
[UK/0015-069X]
FIELD CROP ABSTRACTS.

FILM LIT. INDEX
[US/0093-6758]
FILM LITERATURE INDEX.

FISH REV.
[US/1042-6199]
FISHERIES REVIEW (FORT COLLINS, COLO.).
(*Continues* Sport Fishery Abstracts; **Absorbed** Fish Health News.)

FLUID ABSTR. CIVIL ENG.
[UK/0962-7170]
FLUID ABSTRACTS. CIVIL ENGINEERING.
(*Formed by the union of* Civil Engineering Hydraulics Abstracts; Industrial Aerodynamics Abstracts; Offshore Engineering Abstracts *and* World Ports & Harbours Abstracts (Incorporating International Dredging Abstracts).)

FLUID ABSTR. PROC. ENG.
[UK/0962-7162]
FLUID ABSTRACTS. PROCESS ENGINEERING.
(*Formed by the union of* Fluid Flow Measurements Abstracts; Fluid Power Abstracts; Fluid Sealing Abstracts; Pipelines Abstracts; Pumps and Other Fluids Machinery Abstracts; Solid-Liquid Flow Abstracts; Computer-Aided Process Control Abstracts *and* Mixing and Separation Technology Abstracts.)

FLUIDEX
[UK]
FLUIDEX [ONLINE DATABASE].

FOOD SCI. TECHNOL. ABSTR.
[UK/0015-6574]
FOOD SCIENCE AND TECHNOLOGY ABSTRACTS.

FOODS ADLIBRA
[US/0146-9304]
FOODS ADLIBRA (1975).

FOR. ABSTR.
[UK/0015-7538]
FORESTRY ABSTRACTS.

FOR. PROD. ABSTR.
[UK/0140-4784]
FOREST PRODUCTS ABSTRACTS.

FOREIGN LANG. INDEX
[US/0048-5810]
FOREIGN LANGUAGE INDEX.
(*Continued by* PAIS Foreign Language Index.)

FRESH. AQUA. CONTENTS TABLES
[IT]
FRESHWATER AND AQUACULTURE CONTENTS TABLES. ACTUALITES DES EAUX DOUCES ET DE L'AQUACULTURE.

FUNK & SCOTT ANNU. INDEX CORP. LIB.
[US]
FUNK & SCOTT ANNUAL INDEX OF CORPORATIONS & INDUSTRIES, THE.
(*Continued by* F & S Index of Corporations and Industries.)

FUNK & SCOTT INDEX CORP. IND.
[US/0532-8705]
FUNK & SCOTT INDEX OF CORPORATIONS AND INDUSTRIES.
(*Continued by* Funk & Scott Annual Index of Corporations & Industries.)

FUT. SURV.
[US/0190-3241]
FUTURE SURVEY.
(*Continues* Public Policy Book Forecast.)

GARDEN LIT.
[US/1061-3722]
GARDEN LITERATURE.

GAS ABSTR.
[US/0016-4844]
GAS ABSTRACTS.

GASTROENTEROL. ABSTR. CITATIONS
[US/0016-5093]
GASTROENTEROLOGY: ABSTRACTS & CITATIONS.
(Ceased)

GEN. BUSINESSFILE
[US]
GENERAL BUSINESSFILE [COMPUTER FILE].

GEN. PERIOD. INDEX
[US]
GENERAL PERIODICALS INDEX [COMPUTER FILE].

GEN. PERIOD. ONDISC
[US/1064-8380]
GENERAL PERIODICALS ONDISC (RESEARCH 1 ED.).
***Refer to Newspaper and Periodical Abstracts for complete source list.

GEN. SCI. INDEX
[US/0162-1963]
GENERAL SCIENCE INDEX.

GEN. SCI. SOURCE
[US/1073-1954]
GENERAL SCIENCE SOURCE.

GENEALOGICAL PERIOD. ANNU. INDEX
[US/0072-0593]
GENEALOGICAL PERIODICAL ANNUAL INDEX.

GENET. ABSTR.
[US/0016-674X]
GENETICS ABSTRACTS.

GEO ABSTR.
[UK]
GEO ABSTRACTS.
(*Continued by* Geographical Abstracts : Physical Geography; Geographical Abstracts. Human Geography.)

GEOGR. ABSTR.
[UK]
GEOGRAPHICAL ABSTRACTS.
(*Continued by* Geo Abstracts.)

GEOGR. ABSTR. HUMAN GEOGR.
[UK/0953-9611]
GEOGRAPHICAL ABSTRACTS. HUMAN GEOGRAPHY.
(*Formed by the union of* Geographical Abstracts. C, Economic Geography (1986); Geographical Abstracts. D, Social and Historical Geography *and* Geographical Abstracts. F, Regional and Community Planning.)

GEOGR. ABSTR. PHYS. GEOGR.
[UK/0954-0504]
GEOGRAPHICAL ABSTRACTS : PHYSICAL GEOGRAPHY.
(*Formed by the union of* Geographical Abstracts. A, Landforms and the Quaternary; Geographical Abstracts. B, Climatology and Hydrology; Geographical Abstracts. E, Sedimentology *and* Geographical Abstracts. G, Remote Sensing, Photogrammetry, and Cartography.)

GEOL. ABSTR.
[UK/0954-0512]
GEOLOGICAL ABSTRACTS.
(*Formed by the union of* Geological Abstracts. Economic Geology; Geological Abstracts. Geophysics & Tectonics Abstracts; Geological Abstracts. Palaeontology & Stratigraphy *and* Geological Abstracts. Sedimentary Geology.)

GEOL. ABSTR. ECON. GEOL.
[UK]
GEOLOGICAL ABSTRACTS. ECONOMIC GEOLOGY.
(*Merged with* Geological Abstracts. Geophysics & Tectonics Abstracts; Geological Abstracts. Palaeontology & Stratigraphy *and* Geological Abstracts. Sedimentary Abstracts *to form* Geological Abstracts.)

GEOL. ABSTR. GEOPHYS. TECTON.
[UK/0262-0847]
GEOLOGICAL ABSTRACTS. GEOPHYSICS & TECTONICS.
(*Merged with* Geological Abstracts. Economic Geology; Geological Abstracts. Palaeontology & Stratigraphy *and* Geological Abstracts. Sedimentary Geology *to form* Geological Abstracts.)

INDEXES/ABSTRACTS TABLE

GEOL. ABSTR. PALAEON. STRAT.
[UK/0268-8018]
GEOLOGICAL ABSTRACTS. PALAEONTOLOGY & STRATIGRAPHY.
(*Merged with* Geological Abstracts. Economic Geology; Geological Abstracts. Geophysics & Tectonics Abstracts *and* Geological Abstracts. Sedimentary Geology *to form* Geological Abstracts.)

GEOL. ABSTR. SEDIMEN. GEOL.
[UK/0268-8026]
GEOLOGICAL ABSTRACTS. SEDIMENTARY GEOLOGY.
(*Merged with* Geological Abstracts. Economic Geology; Geological Abstracts. Geophysics & Tectonics Abstracts *and* Geological Abstracts. Palaeontology & Stratigraphy *to form* Geological Abstracts.)

GEOPHYS. ABSTR.
[UK/0309-4332]
GEOPHYSICAL ABSTRACTS.
(*Continued by* Geological Abstracts. Geophysics & Tectonics Abstracts.)

GEOREF
[US/0197-7482]
GEOREF (CD-ROM).

GEOSCI. ABSTR.
[US/0435-5628]
GEOSCIENCE ABSTRACTS.
(*Supersedes* Geological Abstracts.)

GEOSCI. DOC.
[UK/0016-8483]
GEOSCIENCE DOCUMENTATION.

GEOTECH. ABSTR.
[US/0016-8491]
GEOTECHNICAL ABSTRACTS.
(Ceased)

GERONTOL. ABSTR.
[US/0736-4342]
GERONTOLOGICAL ABSTRACTS.
(Ceased)

GRAPH. ARTS ABSTR.
[US/0017-3282]
GRAPHIC ARTS ABSTRACTS.
(*Continued by* Abstracts (Graphic Arts Technical Foundation).)

GRAPH. ARTS BULL. INST. PAP. SCI. TECHNOL.
[US/1064-9638]
GRAPHIC ARTS BULLETIN OF THE INSTITUTE OF PAPER SCIENCE AND TECHNOLOGY.
(*Continues* Graphic Arts Literature Abstracts.)

GRAPH. ARTS LIT. ABSTR.
[US/0090-8207]
GRAPHIC ARTS LITERATURE ABSTRACTS.
(*Continued by* Graphic Arts Bulletin of the Institute of Paper Science and Technology.)

GUIDE PERFORM. ARTS
[US/0072-873X]
GUIDE TO THE PERFORMING ARTS.
(*Absorbed* Guide to Dance Periodicals.)

GUIDE REV. BOOKS HISP. AM.
[US/0716-0348]
GUIDE TO REVIEWS OF BOOKS FROM AND ABOUT HISPANIC AMERICA.
(Ceased)

GUIDE SOC. SCI. RELIG.
[US/1054-0946]
GUIDE TO SOCIAL SCIENCE AND RELIGION.
(*Continues* Guide to Social Science and Religion in Periodical Literature.)

GUIDE SOC. SCI. RELIG. PERIOD. LIT.
[US/0017-5307]
GUIDE TO SOCIAL SCIENCE AND RELIGION IN PERIODICAL LITERATURE.
(*Continued by* Guide to Social Science and Religion.)

HEALTH DEVICES ALERTS
[US/0163-0458]
HEALTH DEVICES ALERTS.

HEALTH INDEX
[US]
HEALTH INDEX [COMPUTER FILE].

HEALTH PERIOD. DATABASE
[US]
HEALTH PERIODICALS DATABASE [ONLINE DATABASE].

HEALTH PLAN. ADMINIS.
[US/1065-0679]
HEALTH PLANNING AND ADMINISTRATION.

HEALTH SAF. SCI. ABSTR.
[US/0892-9351]
HEALTH AND SAFETY SCIENCE ABSTRACTS.
(*Continues* Safety Science Abstracts Journal.)

HEALTH SERV. ABSTR.
[UK/0268-0459]
HEALTH SERVICE ABSTRACTS.
(*Formed by the union of* Current Literature on Health Services; Current Literature on General Medical Practice *and* Hospital Abstracts.)

HEALTH SOURCE
[US/1063-9810]
HEALTH SOURCE (PEABODY, MASS.).

HELMINTHOL. ABSTR.
[UK/0957-6789]
HELMINTHOLOGICAL ABSTRACTS.
(*Continues* Helminthological Abstracts. Series A, Animal and Human Helminthology.)

HELMINTHOL. ABSTR. SER. A, ANIM. HUM. HELMINTHOL.
[UK/0300-8339]
HELMINTHOLOGICAL ABSTRACTS. SERIES A, ANIMAL AND HUMAN HELMINTHOLOGY.
(*Continued by* Helminthological Abstracts.)

HELMINTHOL. ABSTR. SER. B, PLANT NEMATOLOGY
[UK/0300-8320]
HELMINTHOLOGICAL ABSTRACTS. SERIES B, PLANT NEMATOLOGY.
(*Continued by* Nematological Abstracts.)

HERB. ABSTR.
[UK/0018-0602]
HERBAGE ABSTRACTS.
(*Continued by* Grasslands and Forage Abstracts.)

HIGH. EDUC. ABSTR.
[US/0748-4364]
HIGHER EDUCATION ABSTRACTS.
(*Continues* College Student Personnel Abstracts.)

HIGHW. RES. ABSTR.
[US/0018-1730]
HIGHWAY RESEARCH ABSTRACTS.
(*Continued by* Transportation Research Abstracts.)

HIGHW. RES. ABSTR.
[US/1050-0804]
HIGHWAY RESEARCH ABSTRACTS (1990).
(*Continues* HRIS Abstracts.)

HILITES
[US]
HILITES DATABASE [ONLINE DATABASE].

HISP. AM. PERIOD. INDEX
[US/0270-8558]
HISPANIC AMERICAN PERIODICALS INDEX (LOS ANGELES, CALIF.).

HIST. ABSTR.
[US/0018-2435]
HISTORICAL ABSTRACTS.
(*Split into* Historical Abstracts. Part A, Modern History Abstracts *and* Historical Abstracts. Part B, Twentieth Century Abstracts.)

HIST. ABSTR., PART A, MOD. HIST. ABSTR.
[US/0363-2717]
HISTORICAL ABSTRACTS. PART A, MODERN HISTORY ABSTRACTS.
(*Continues in part* Historical Abstracts.)
***Refer to America: History and Life for complete source list.

HIST. ABSTR., PART B, TWENT. CENTURY ABSTR.
[US/0363-2725]
HISTORICAL ABSTRACTS. PART B, TWENTIETH CENTURY ABSTRACTS.
(*Continues in part* Historical Abstracts.)
***Refer to America: History and Life for complete source list.

HIST. SOURCE
[US/1063-9799]
HISTORY SOURCE.
(*Merged into* Humanities Source CD-ROM.)

HORTIC. ABSTR.
[UK/0018-5280]
HORTICULTURAL ABSTRACTS.

HOSPIT. ABSTR.
[UK/0018-5507]
HOSPITAL ABSTRACTS.
(*Merged with* Current Literature on Health Services *and* Current Literature on General Medical Practice *to form* Health Service Abstracts.)

HOSPIT. HEALTH ADMIN. INDEX
[US/1077-1719]
HOSPITAL AND HEALTH ADMINISTRATION INDEX.
(*Continues* Hospital Literature Index.)

HOSPIT. LIT. INDEX
[US/0018-5736]
HOSPITAL LITERATURE INDEX.
(*Continued by* Hospital and Health Administration Index.)

HOSPIT. MANAGE. REV.
[US/0737-903X]
HOSPITAL MANAGEMENT REVIEW.

HRIS ABSTR.
[US/0017-6222]
HRIS ABSTRACTS.
(*Continued by* Highway Research Abstracts (Washington, D.C. : 1990).)

HTFS DIG.
[UK/0952-2654]
HTFS DIGEST (1987).
(*Continues* Heat Transfer & Fluid Flow Digest; *Absorbed* Fouling Prevention Research Digest.)

INDEXES/ABSTRACTS TABLE

HUM. GENOME ABSTR.
[US/1045-4470]
HUMAN GENOME ABSTRACTS.

HUM. RESOUR. ABSTR.
[US/0099-2453]
HUMAN RESOURCES ABSTRACTS.
(*Continues* Poverty and Human Resources Abstracts.)

HUM. RIGHTS INTERN. REP.
[US/0275-049X]
HUMAN RIGHTS INTERNET REPORTER.
(*Continues* Human Rights Internet Newsletter.)

HUMANIT. INDEX
[US/0095-5981]
HUMANITIES INDEX.
(*Supersedes in part* Social Sciences & Humanities Index.)

HUMANIT. SOURCE
[US/1073-1962]
HUMANITIES SOURCE.
(*Absorbed* History Source CD-ROM.)

HUNGAR. LIBR. INFO. SCI. ABSTR.
[HU/0046-8304]
HUNGARIAN LIBRARY AND INFORMATION SCIENCE ABSTRACTS.

IAG, LIT. AUTO.
[NE/0376-9666]
IAG - LITERATURE ON AUTOMATION.
(*Continued by* New Literature on Automation.)

IMAGING ABSTR.
[US/0896-100X]
IMAGING ABSTRACTS.
(*Continues* Photographic Abstracts.)

IMMUNOL. ABSTR.
[US/0307-112X]
IMMUNOLOGY ABSTRACTS.

IND. ARTS INDEX
[US/0275-1682]
INDUSTRIAL ARTS INDEX.
(*Split into* Business Periodicals Index *and* Applied Science & Technology Index.)

IND. HYG. DIG.
[US/0019-8382]
INDUSTRIAL HYGIENE DIGEST.

INDEX AM. PERIOD. VERSE
[US/0090-9130]
INDEX OF AMERICAN PERIODICAL VERSE.

INDEX BLACK PERIOD.
[US/0899-6253]
INDEX TO BLACK PERIODICALS.
(*Continues* Index to Periodical Articles by and About Blacks.)

INDEX BOOK REV. HUMANIT.
[US/0073-5892]
INDEX TO BOOK REVIEWS IN THE HUMANITIES.
(Ceased)

INDEX BOOK REV. RELIG.
[US/0887-1574]
INDEX TO BOOK REVIEWS IN RELIGION.
(*Continues in part* Religion Index One. Periodicals.)

INDEX BUS. REPORTS
[UK]
INDEX TO BUSINESS REPORTS.
(*Continues* Index to Special Reports in UK Newspapers and Selected Periodicals.)

INDEX CAN. LEG. PERIOD. LIT.
[CN/0316-8891]
INDEX TO CANADIAN LEGAL PERIODICAL LITERATURE.

INDEX CHEM.
[US/0891-6055]
INDEX CHEMICUS (1987).
(*Continues* Current Abstracts of Chemistry and Index Chemicus (Philadelphia, Pa. : 1978).)

INDEX DENT. LIT.
[US/0019-3992]
INDEX TO DENTAL LITERATURE.
(*Continues* Index to Dental Literature in the English Language.)

INDEX ECON. ARTIC. J. COLLECT. VOL.
[US/0536-647X]
INDEX OF ECONOMIC ARTICLES IN JOURNALS AND COLLECTIVE VOLUMES.
(*Formed by the union of* Index of Economic Journals *and* Index of Economic Articles in Collective Volumes.)
***Refer to Journal of Economic Literature for complete source list.

INDEX ECON. J.
[US/0893-9527]
INDEX OF ECONOMIC JOURNALS.
(*Merged with* Index of Economic Articles in Collective Volumes *to form* Index of Economic Articles in Journals and Collective Volumes.)

INDEX FOREIGN LEG. PER.
[UK/0019-400X]
INDEX TO FOREIGN LEGAL PERIODICALS.

INDEX FREE PERIOD.
[US/0147-5630]
INDEX TO FREE PERIODICALS.
(*Merged into* Matter of Fact.)

INDEX IEEE PUBL.
[US/0099-1368]
INDEX TO IEEE PUBLICATIONS.
(*Supersedes* Institute of Electrical and Electronics Engineers. Index to IEEE Periodicals.)

INDEX INF.
[US/0073-5930]
INDEX TO HOW TO DO IT INFORMATION.

INDEX ISLAM.
[UK]
INDEX ISLAMICUS.
(*Continues* Index Islamicus. Supplement.)

INDEX ISLAM. LIT.
[UK]
INDEX OF ISLAMIC LITERATURE.

INDEX JEW. PERIOD.
[US/0019-4050]
INDEX TO JEWISH PERIODICALS.

INDEX LEG. PERIOD.
[US/0019-4077]
INDEX TO LEGAL PERIODICALS.

INDEX LIT. AM. INDIAN
[US/0091-7346]
INDEX TO LITERATURE ON THE AMERICAN INDIAN.
(Ceased)

INDEX MATH. PAP.
[US/0019-3917]
INDEX OF MATHEMATICAL PAPERS.
(Ceased)

INDEX MED.
[US/0019-3879]
INDEX MEDICUS (1960).
(*Continues* Current List of Medical Literature; *Absorbed* Monthly Bibliography of Medical Reviews.)

INDEX NEW Z. PERIOD.
[NZ]
INDEX TO NEW ZEALAND PERIODICALS.
(Ceased)

INDEX PERIOD. ARTIC. BLACKS
[US/0161-8245]
INDEX TO PERIODICAL ARTICLES BY AND ABOUT BLACKS.
(*Continued by* Index to Black Periodicals.)

INDEX PERIOD. ARTIC. NEGROES
[US/0073-5973]
INDEX TO PERIODICAL ARTICLES BY AND ABOUT NEGROES.
(*Continued by* Index to Periodical Articles by and About Blacks.)

INDEX PERIOD. ARTIC. RELAT. LAW
[US/0019-4093]
INDEX TO PERIODICAL ARTICLES RELATED TO LAW.

INDEX PERIOD. LIT. AGING
[US/0882-3405]
INDEX TO PERIODICAL LITERATURE ON AGING.
(*Continues* ARECO's Quarterly Index to Periodical Literature on Aging.)

INDEX PHILIP. PERIOD.
[PH/0073-599X]
INDEX TO PHILIPPINE PERIODICALS.

INDEX RELIG. PERIOD. LIT.
[US/0019-4107]
INDEX TO RELIGIOUS PERIODICAL LITERATURE.
(*Continued by* Religion Index One. Periodicals.)

INDEX SCI. REV.
[US/0360-0661]
INDEX TO SCIENTIFIC REVIEWS.

INDEX U.S. GOV. PERIOD.
[US/0098-4604]
INDEX TO U.S. GOVERNMENT PERIODICALS.
(Ceased)

INDEX VET.
[UK/0019-4123]
INDEX VETERINARIUS.

INDIAN GEOSCI. ABSTR.
[II]
INDIAN GEOSCIENCE ABSTRACTS.

INDIAN LIBR. SCI. ABSTR.
[II/0019-5790]
INDIAN LIBRARY SCIENCE ABSTRACTS.

INDIAN SCI. ABSTR.
[II/0019-6339]
INDIAN SCIENCE ABSTRACTS.
(*Continues* Bibliography of Scientific Publications of South and South East Asia.)

INDICE AGRICOLA AM. LAT. CARIBE
[CR/0304-0119]
INDICE AGRICOLA DE AMERICA LATINA Y EL CARIBE.
(*Continues* Bibliografia Agricola Latinoamericana y del Caribe.)

INDICE HIST. ESP.
[SP/0537-3522]
INDICE HISTORICO ESPANOL.

INDEXES/ABSTRACTS TABLE

INDICE MED. ESP.
[SP]
INDICE MEDICO ESPANOL.

INF. INSTRUC. TECHNOL.
[US]
INFORMATION & INSTRUCTION TECHNOLOGIES.

INF. MANAGE. TECHNOL.
[UK]
INFORMATION MANAGEMENT & TECHNOLOGY.
(*Continues* Information Media & Technology.)

INF. SCI. ABSTR.
[US/0020-0239]
INFORMATION SCIENCE ABSTRACTS.
(*Continues* Documentation Abstracts and Information Science Abstracts.)

INFO-SOUTH ABSTR.
[US/1059-5910]
INFO-SOUTH ABSTRACTS.

INFOBANK
[IO]
INFOBANK.

INFOMAT INT. BUS.
[US]
INFOMAT INTERNATIONAL BUSINESS [ONLINE DATABASE].

INIS ATOMINDEX
[AU/0004-7139]
INIS ATOMINDEX.
(*Continued by* INIS Atomindex.)

INIS ATOMINDEX [MICRO.]
[AU]
INIS ATOMINDEX [MICROFORM].
(*Continues* INIS Atomindex.)

INS. PERIOD. INDEX
[US/0074-073X]
INSURANCE PERIODICALS INDEX.

INSPEC
[UK]
INSPEC [ONLINE DATABASE].

INT. ABSTR. BIOL. SCI.
[UK/0020-5818]
INTERNATIONAL ABSTRACTS OF BIOLOGICAL SCIENCES.
(*Continued by* Current Awareness in Biological Sciences : CABS.)

INT. ABSTR. OPER. RES.
[UK/0020-580X]
INTERNATIONAL ABSTRACTS IN OPERATIONS RESEARCH.

INT. AEROSP. ABSTR.
[US/0020-5842]
INTERNATIONAL AEROSPACE ABSTRACTS.
(*Supersedes in part* Aerospace Engineering.)

INT. BIBLIOGR. BOOK REV.
[GW]
INTERNATIONAL BIBLIOGRAPHY OF BOOK REVIEWS.
(*Continued by* Internationale Bibliographie der Rezensionen Wissenschaftlicher Literatur (Osnabruck, Germany : 1984).)

INT. BIBLIOGR. HIST. RELIG.
[NE/0538-5105]
INTERNATIONAL BIBLIOGRAPHY OF THE HISTORY OF RELIGIONS.
(Ceased)

INT. BIBLIOGR. PERIOD. LIT.
[GW]
INTERNATIONAL BIBLIOGRAPHY OF PERIODICAL LITERATURE.
(*Continued by* Internationale Bibliographie der Zeitschriftenliteratur aus Allen Gebieten des Wissens (Osnabruck, Germany : 1984).)

INT. BIBLIOGR. REZEN. WISSEN. LIT.
[GW/0020-918X]
INTERNATIONALE BIBLIOGRAPHIE DER REZENSIONEN WISSENSCHAFTLICHER LITERATUR.
(*Continues* Internationale Bibliographie der Rezensionen.)

INT. BIBLIOGR. SOCIOL.
[UK/0085-2066]
INTERNATIONAL BIBLIOGRAPHY OF SOCIOLOGY.
(*Continues in part* Current Sociology (Paris, France).)

INT. BIBLIOGR. ZEITSCHRIFTENLITERATUR ALLEN GEBIETEN WISSENS
[GW]
INTERNATIONALE BIBLIOGRAPHIE DER ZEITSCHRIFTENLITERATUR AUS ALLEN GEBIETEN DES WISSENS.
(*Continues* Internationale Bibliographie der Zeitschriftenliteratur.)

INT. BUILD. SERV. ABSTR.
[UK/0140-4237]
INTERNATIONAL BUILDING SERVICES ABSTRACTS.
(*Continues* Thermal Abstracts.)

INT. CIVIL ENG. ABSTR.
[IE/0332-4095]
INTERNATIONAL CIVIL ENGINEERING ABSTRACTS.
(*Continues* Institution of Civil Engineers (Great Britain). I.C.E. Abstracts.)

INT. COPPER INF. BULL.
[UK/0309-2216]
INTERNATIONAL COPPER INFORMATION BULLETIN.
(*Formed by the union of* Selected Abstracts of Recent Literature on Copper and Copper Alloys *and* Kupfer-Mitteilungen.)

INT. DEV. ABSTR.
[UK/0262-0855]
INTERNATIONAL DEVELOPMENT ABSTRACTS.
(*Absorbed* International Development Index.)

INT. EXEC.
[US/0020-6652]
INTERNATIONAL EXECUTIVE.

INT. GUIDE CLASSICAL STUD.
[US/0020-6849]
INTERNATIONAL GUIDE TO CLASSICAL STUDIES.
(*Continues* ABS International Guide to Classical Studies.)

INT. INDEX
[US/0363-0382]
INTERNATIONAL INDEX.
(*Continued by* Social Sciences & Humanities Index.)

INT. INDEX FILM PERIOD.
[US/0000-0388]
INTERNATIONAL INDEX TO FILM PERIODICALS.

INT. INDEX MULTI MEDIA INF.
[US/0094-6818]
INTERNATIONAL INDEX TO MULTI-MEDIA INFORMATION.
(*Continues* Film Review Index.)

INT. INDEX PERIOD.
[US]
INTERNATIONAL INDEX TO PERIODICALS.
(*Continued by* International Index.)

INT. LABOUR DOC.
[SZ/0020-7756]
INTERNATIONAL LABOUR DOCUMENTATION.
(*Continues* International Labour Office. Library. International Labour Documentation.)

INT. NURS. INDEX
[US/0020-8124]
INTERNATIONAL NURSING INDEX.

INT. PACKAG. ABSTR.
[UK/0260-7409]
INTERNATIONAL PACKAGING ABSTRACTS.
(*Continues* PIRA Packaging Abstract.)

INT. PET. ABSTR.
[UK/0309-4944]
INTERNATIONAL PETROLEUM ABSTRACTS.
(*Continued by* International Petroleum Abstracts Incorporating Offshore Abstracts.)

INT. PHARM. ABSTR.
[US/0020-8264]
INTERNATIONAL PHARMACEUTICAL ABSTRACTS.

INT. POLIT. SCI. ABSTR.
[FR/0020-8345]
INTERNATIONAL POLITICAL SCIENCE ABSTRACTS.

INT. POLYM. SCI. TECH.
[UK/0307-174X]
INTERNATIONAL POLYMER SCIENCE AND TECHNOLOGY.
(*Formed by the union of* Soviet Plastics *and* Soviet Rubber Technology.)

INT. RISK CONTROL REV.
[US/0739-389X]
INTERNATIONAL RISK CONTROL REVIEW.
(*Continued by* International Loss Control Review.)

INT. ZEITSCHRIFTENSCHAU BIBELWISS. GRENZGEB.
[GW/0074-9745]
INTERNATIONALE ZEITSCHRIFTENSCHAU FUER BIBELWISSENSCHAFT UND GRENZGEBIETE.

IOWA DRUG INF. SERV.
[US]
IOWA DRUG INFORMATION SERVICE.

IRR. DRAIN. ABSTR.
[UK/0306-7327]
IRRIGATION AND DRAINAGE ABSTRACTS / COMMONWEALTH AGRICULTURAL BUREAUX.

ISMEC BULL.
[US/0306-0039]
ISMEC BULLETIN.
(*Continued by* ISMEC, Mechanical Engineering Abstracts.)

ISMEC MECH. ENG. ABSTR.
[US/0896-7113]
ISMEC, MECHANICAL ENGINEERING ABSTRACTS.
(*Continued by* Mechanical Engineering Abstracts.)

J. ABSTR. ARTIC. INT. EDUC.
[US/1064-0746]
JOURNAL OF ABSTRACTS (AND ARTICLES) IN INTERNATIONAL EDUCATION.
(*Continues* Journal of Abstracts in International Education.)

INDEXES/ABSTRACTS TABLE

J. ABSTR. BR. SHIP RES. ASSOC.
[UK/0141-903X]
JOURNAL OF ABSTRACTS OF THE BRITISH SHIP RESEARCH ASSOCIATION.
(*Continued by* BMT Abstracts.)

J. ABSTR. INT. EDUC.
[US/0094-2383]
JOURNAL OF ABSTRACTS IN INTERNATIONAL EDUCATION.
(*Continued by* Journal of Abstract (and Articles) in International Education.)

J. CONTENTS QUAN. METHODS
[UK/0142-5951]
JOURNAL CONTENTS IN QUANTITATIVE METHODS.

J. ECON. ABSTR.
[US/0364-281X]
JOURNAL OF ECONOMIC ABSTRACTS.
(*Continued by* Journal of Economic Literature.)

J. ECON. LIT.
[US/0022-0515]
JOURNAL OF ECONOMIC LITERATURE.
(*Continues* Journal of Economic Abstracts.)

J. FERROCEMENT
[TH/0125-1759]
JOURNAL OF FERROCEMENT.

J. PLAN. LIT.
[US/0885-4122]
JOURNAL OF PLANNING LITERATURE.

J. WATCH
[US/0896-7210]
JOURNAL WATCH.

JAZZ INDEX
[GW/0344-5399]
JAZZ INDEX.
(Ceased)

JMR ABSTR.
[US/1066-2375]
JMR ABSTRACTS.
(*Absorbed by* MRS Bulletin.)

JR. HIGH MAG. ABSTR.
[US/1045-5493]
JUNIOR HIGH MAGAZINE ABSTRACTS.
(Ceased)

KEY ABSTR., ADV. MATER.
[UK/0950-4753]
KEY ABSTRACTS. ADVANCED MATERIALS.
***Refer to INSPEC [Online Database] for complete source list.

KEY ABSTR., ANTENNAS PROPAG.
[UK/0950-4761]
KEY ABSTRACTS. ANTENNAS & PROPAGATION.
(*Continues in part* Key Abstracts. Communication Technology.)
***Refer to INSPEC [Online Database] for complete source list.

KEY ABSTR., ARTIF. INTELL.
[UK/0950-477X]
KEY ABSTRACTS. ARTIFICIAL INTELLIGENCE.
(*Continues* Key Abstracts. Systems Theory.)
***Refer to INSPEC [Online Database] for complete source list.

KEY ABSTR., BUS. AUTOMAT.
[UK/0954-9153]
KEY ABSTRACTS. BUSINESS AUTOMATION.
(*Continues* IT Focus.)
***Refer to INSPEC [Online Database] for complete source list.

KEY ABSTR., COMPUT. COMMUN. STOR.
[UK/0950-4788]
KEY ABSTRACTS. COMPUTER COMMUNICATIONS & STORAGE.
***Refer to INSPEC [Online Database] for complete source list.

KEY ABSTR., COMPUT. ELECTRON. POWER
[UK/0950-4796]
KEY ABSTRACTS. COMPUTING IN ELECTRONICS AND POWER.
***Refer to INSPEC [Online Database] for complete source list.

KEY ABSTR., ELECTR. MEAS. INSTRUM.
[UK/0307-7977]
KEY ABSTRACTS : ELECTRICAL MEASUREMENTS AND INSTRUMENTATION.
(*Continued by* Key Abstracts. Electronic Instrumentation.)

KEY ABSTR., ELECTRON. CIRC.
[UK/0306-557X]
KEY ABSTRACTS. ELECTRONIC CIRCUITS.
***Refer to INSPEC [Online Database] for complete source list.

KEY ABSTR., ELECTRON. INSTRUM.
[UK/0950-480X]
KEY ABSTRACTS. ELECTRONIC INSTRUMENTATION.
(*Continues* Key Abstracts. Electrical Measurements and Instrumentation.)
***Refer to INSPEC [Online Database] for complete source list.

KEY ABSTR., FACTORY AUTOMAT.
[UK]
KEY ABSTRACTS. FACTORY AUTOMATION.
***Refer to INSPEC [Online Database] for complete source list.

KEY ABSTR., HIGH-TEMP. SUPERCONDUC.
[UK/0953-1262]
KEY ABSTRACTS. HIGH-TEMPERATURE SUPERCONDUCTORS.
***Refer to INSPEC [Online Database] for complete source list.

KEY ABSTR., HUMAN-COMPUT. INTERACT.
[UK]
KEY ABSTRACTS. HUMAN-COMPUTER INTERACTION.
***Refer to INSPEC [Online Database] for complete source list.

KEY ABSTR., MACH. VISION
[UK/0952-7052]
KEY ABSTRACTS. MACHINE VISION.
***Refer to INSPEC [Online Database] for complete source list.

KEY ABSTR., MEAS. PHYS.
[UK/0950-4818]
KEY ABSTRACTS. MEASUREMENTS IN PHYSICS.
(*Continues* Key Abstracts. Physical Measurements and Instrumentation.)
***Refer to INSPEC [Online Database] for complete source list.

KEY ABSTR., MICROELECTRON. PRINT. CIRC.
[UK/0952-7060]
KEY ABSTRACTS. MICROELECTRONICS AND PRINTED CIRCUITS.
***Refer to INSPEC [Online Database] for complete source list.

KEY ABSTR., MICROWAVE TECHNOL.
[UK/0952-7079]
KEY ABSTRACTS. MICROWAVE TECHNOLOGY.
***Refer to INSPEC [Online Database] for complete source list.

KEY ABSTR., NEUR. NETWORKS
[UK]
KEY ABSTRACTS. NEURAL NETWORKS.
***Refer to INSPEC [Online Database] for complete source list.

KEY ABSTR., OPTOELECTRON.
[UK/0950-4826]
KEY ABSTRACTS. OPTOELECTRONICS.
(*Continues in part* Key Abstracts. Solid State Devices.)
***Refer to INSPEC [Online Database] for complete source list.

KEY ABSTR., PHYS. MEAS. INSTRUM.
[UK/0307-7969]
KEY ABSTRACTS : PHYSICAL MEASUREMENTS AND INSTRUMENTATION.
(*Continued by* Key Abstracts. Measurements in Physics.)

KEY ABSTR., POWER SYST. APPL.
[UK/0950-4834]
KEY ABSTRACTS. POWER SYSTEMS AND APPLICATIONS.
(*Continues* Key Abstracts. Power Transmission and Distribution.)
***Refer to INSPEC [Online Database] for complete source list.

KEY ABSTR., ROBOT. CONTROL
[UK/0950-4842]
KEY ABSTRACTS. ROBOTICS & CONTROL.
(*Continues* Key Abstracts. Industrial Power and Control Systems.)
***Refer to INSPEC [Online Database] for complete source list.

KEY ABSTR., SEMICOND. DEVICES
[UK/0950-4850]
KEY ABSTRACTS. SEMICONDUCTOR DEVICES.
(*Continues in part* Key Abstracts. Solid State Devices.)
***Refer to INSPEC [Online Database] for complete source list.

KEY ABSTR., SOFTW. ENG.
[UK/0950-4869]
KEY ABSTRACTS. SOFTWARE ENGINEERING.
***Refer to INSPEC [Online Database] for complete source list.

KEY ABSTR., TELECOM.
[UK/0950-4877]
KEY ABSTRACTS. TELECOMMUNICATIONS.
(*Continues* Key Abstracts. Communication Technology.)
***Refer to INSPEC [Online Database] for complete source list.

KEY ECON. SCI.
[NE]
KEY TO ECONOMIC SCIENCE.
(*Continued by* Key to Economic Science and Managerial Sciences.)

KEY ECON. SCI. MANAGE. SCI.
[NE/0165-4748]
KEY TO ECONOMIC SCIENCE AND MANAGERIAL SCIENCES.
(*Continues* Key to Economic Science.)

KEY WORD INDEX WILDL. RES.
[SZ]
KEY-WORD-INDEX OF WILDLIFE RESEARCH.

INDEXES/ABSTRACTS TABLE

KEY WORD INDEX MED. LIT.
[US/0145-9716]
KEY-WORD INDEX FOR THE MEDICAL LITERATURE.
(*Continues* Keyword Index in Internal Medicine.)

KEYWORD INDEX INTERN. MED.
[US/0097-0220]
KEYWORD INDEX IN INTERNAL MEDICINE.
(*Continued by* Key-Word Index for the Medical Literature.)

LAB. HAZARDS BULL.
[UK/0261-2917]
LABORATORY HAZARDS BULLETIN.

LABORDOC
[SZ]
LABORDOC [ONLINE DATABASE].

LANG. LANG. BEHAV. ABSTR.
[US/0023-8295]
LANGUAGE AND LANGUAGE BEHAVIOR ABSTRACTS : LLBA.
(*Continued by* Linguistics and Language Behavior Abstracts.)

LANG. TEACH.
[UK/0261-4448]
LANGUAGE TEACHING.
(*Continues* Language Teaching & Linguistics. Abstracts.)

LANG. TEACH. LINGUIST. ABSTR.
[UK/0306-6304]
LANGUAGE TEACHING & LINGUISTICS ABSTRACTS.
(*Continued by* Language Teaching.)

LAW OFFICE INF. SERV.
[US/0164-5390]
LAW OFFICE INFORMATION SERVICE.
(Ceased)

LEAD ABSTR.
[US/0023-9569]
LEAD ABSTRACTS.
(*Continued by* Leadscan.)

LEADSCAN
[UK/0950-1584]
LEADSCAN.
(*Continues* Lead Abstracts (London, England : 1962).)

LEFT INDEX
[US/0733-2998]
LEFT INDEX.

LEG. CONTENTS, LC
[US/0279-5787]
LEGAL CONTENTS : LC.
(*Continues* CCLP, Contents of Current Legal Periodicals.)

LEG. INF. MANAGE. INDEX
[US/0747-9298]
LEGAL INFORMATION MANAGEMENT INDEX.

LEG. RESOUR. INDEX
[US/0272-9296]
LEGAL RESOURCE INDEX.

LEGALTRAC
[US]
LEGALTRAC [COMPUTER FILE].

LEIS. RECREAT. TOUR. ABSTR.
[UK/0261-1392]
LEISURE, RECREATION, AND TOURISM ABSTRACTS.
(*Continues* Rural Recreation and Tourism Abstracts.)

LEUKEMIA ABSTR.
[US/0024-1466]
LEUKEMIA ABSTRACTS.
(Ceased)

LIBR. INF. SCI. ABSTR.
[UK/0024-2179]
LIBRARY & INFORMATION SCIENCE ABSTRACTS.
(*Supersedes* Library Science Abstracts.)

LIBR. LIT.
[US/0024-2373]
LIBRARY LITERATURE.

LIBR. SCI. ABSTR.
[UK/0459-262X]
LIBRARY SCIENCE ABSTRACTS.
(*Continued by* Library & Information Science Abstracts.)

LIFE SCI. COLLECT.
[US/0891-3889]
PERIODICALS SCANNED AND ABSTRACTED. LIFE SCIENCES COLLECTION.

LINGUIST. LANG. BEHAV. ABSTR.
[US/0888-8027]
LINGUISTICS AND LANGUAGE BEHAVIOR ABSTRACTS.
(*Continues* Language and Language Behavior Abstracts; *Absorbed* Reading Abstracts.)

LISA PLUS
[UK/0966-8799]
LISA PLUS [COMPUTER FILE].
***Refer to Library and Information Science Abstracts for complete source list.

LIST J. ABSTR.
[NE/0923-5582]
LIST OF JOURNALS ABSTRACTED.
(*Continued by* EMBASE List of Journals Indexed.)

LIT. ABSTR., CATAL. CATAL.
[US/1065-0539]
LITERATURE ABSTRACTS. CATALYSTS & CATALYSIS.
(*Continued by* Literature Abstracts. Catalysts/Zeolites.)

LIT. ABSTR., HEALTH ENVIRON.
[US/1065-0490]
LITERATURE ABSTRACTS. HEALTH & ENVIRONMENT.
(*Continues* API Abstracts. Health & Environment.)

LIT. ABSTR., PET. REFIN. PETROCHEM.
[US/1065-0512]
LITERATURE ABSTRACTS. PETROLEUM REFINING & PETROCHEMICALS.
(*Continues* Petroleum Refining and Petrochemicals.)

LIT. ABSTR., PET. SUBSTIT.
[US/1065-0504]
LITERATURE ABSTRACTS. PETROLEUM SUBSTITUTES.
(*Continues* Petroleum Substitutes.)

LIT. ABSTR., TRANSP. STORAGE
[US/1065-0520]
LITERATURE ABSTRACTS. TRANSPORTATION & STORAGE.
(*Continues* Transportation and Storage.)

LIT. ANALY. MICROCOMPUT. PUBL.
[US/0735-9721]
LITERATURE ANALYSIS OF MICROCOMPUTER PUBLICATIONS : LAMP.
(Ceased)

LIT. CRIT. REGIST.
[US/0733-2165]
LITERARY CRITICISM REGISTER.

LIT. PAT. ABSTR., OILFIELD CHEM.
[US/1065-0547]
LITERATURE & PATENT ABSTRACTS. OILFIELD CHEMICALS.
(*Continued in part by* Literature Abstracts. Oilfield Chemicals **and** Patent Abstracts. Oilfield Chemicals.)

LOMA LIT. MOD. ART
[US/0090-7235]
LOMA; LITERATURE ON MODERN ART.
(*Continued by* ARTbibliographies Modern.)

MAG. ARTIC. SUMMAR.
[US/0895-3376]
MAGAZINE ARTICLE SUMMARIES (PRINT ED.).
(*Continues* Popular Magazine Review.)

MAG. ARTIC. SUMMAR. CD-ROM
[US/1041-1151]
MAGAZINE ARTICLE SUMMARIES (CD-ROM ED.).

MAG. ARTIC. SUMMAR. ELITE
[US/1060-6769]
MAGAZINE ARTICLE SUMMARIES FULL TEXT ELITE.

MAG. ARTIC. SUMMAR. SELECT
[US/1058-0255]
MAGAZINE ARTICLE SUMMARIES FULL TEXT SELECT.

MAG. ASAP PLUS
[US]
MAGAZINE ASAP PLUS [COMPUTER FILE].

MAG. ASAP SEL.
[US]
MAGAZINE ASAP SELECT [COMPUTER FILE].

MAG. EXPRESS
[US]
MAGAZINE EXPRESS [COMPUTER FILE].

MAG. INDEX
[US]
MAGAZINE INDEX, THE.

MAG. INDEX PLUS
[US]
MAGAZINE INDEX PLUS [COMPUTER FILE].

MAG. INDEX SEL. MICROFICHE
[US]
MAGAZINE INDEX SELECT MICROFICHE.

MAG. INDEX. SEL.
[US]
MAGAZINE INDEX SELECT [COMPUTER FILE].

MAG. SEARCH
[US/1071-2739]
MAGAZINE SEARCH.

MAGYAR KONYV. SZAK. BIBLIO.
[HU/0133-736X]
MAGYAR KONYVTARI SZAKIRODALOM BIBLIOGRAFIAJA, A.

MAIZE ABSTR.
[UK/0267-2987]
MAIZE ABSTRACTS.
(*Continues* Maize Quality Protein Abstracts.)

MANAGE. BIBLIOGR. REV.
[UK/0309-0582]
MANAGEMENT BIBLIOGRAPHIES & REVIEWS.
(*Continues* Business Education.)

MANAGE. CONTENTS
[US/0360-2400]
MANAGEMENT CONTENTS.
(Ceased)

INDEXES/ABSTRACTS TABLE

MANAGE. CONTENTS
[US]
MANAGEMENT CONTENTS [ONLINE DATABASE].

MANAGE. INDEX
[US]
MANAGEMENT INDEX.
(Ceased)

MANAGE. MARKET. ABSTR.
[UK/0308-2172]
MANAGEMENT AND MARKETING ABSTRACTS.

MANAGE. RES.
[US/0099-2224]
MANAGEMENT RESEARCH.
(*Continues* Bi-Monthly Review of Management Research.)

MANUF. PROCESS ENG. ABSTR.
[US/1063-7354]
MANUFACTURING AND PROCESS ENGINEERING ABSTRACTS.
(Ceased)

MAR. FISH. ABSTR.
[US/0735-3782]
MARINE FISHERIES ABSTRACTS.
(*Continues* Commercial Fisheries Abstracts.)

MAR. SCI. CONTENTS TABLES
[IT/0025-3308]
MARINE SCIENCE CONTENTS TABLES. ACTUALITES DES SCIENCES DE LA MER. INDICES DE REVISTAS SOBRE CIENCIAS MARINAS.
(*Continues* Current Contents in Marine Sciences; *Continues in part* International Marine Science.)

MARK. ADVERT. REF. SERV.
[US]
MARKETING AND ADVERTISING REFERENCE SERVICE [ONLINE DATABASE].

MARK. DISTR. ABSTR.
[UK]
MARKETING + DISTRIBUTION ABSTRACTS.
(*Continued by* Anbar Marketing & Distribution Abstracts.)

MARK. INF. GUIDE
[US/0025-374X]
MARKETING INFORMATION GUIDE.
(*Continues* Marketing Information Guide (Washington : 1961).)

MARK. RES. ABSTR.
[UK/0025-3596]
MARKET RESEARCH ABSTRACTS.

MARK. RES. TODAY
[NE/0923-5957]
MARKETING AND RESEARCH TODAY : THE JOURNAL OF THE EUROPEAN SOCIETY FOR OPINION AND MARKETING RESEARCH.
(*Continues* European Research.)

MASS SPECT. BULL.
[UK/0025-4738]
MASS SPECTROMETRY BULLETIN.

MATER. SCI. ENG. ABSTR.
[US/1063-732X]
MATERIALS SCIENCE AND ENGINEERING ABSTRACTS.
(Ceased)

MATH. REV.
[US/0025-5629]
MATHEMATICAL REVIEWS.

MECH. ENG. ABSTR.
[US/1063-7311]
MECHANICAL ENGINEERING ABSTRACTS.
(*Continues* ISMEC, Mechanical Engineering Abstracts.)

MED. ABSTR. NEWSL.
[US/0730-7810]
MEDICAL ABSTRACTS NEWSLETTER.

MED. ELECTRON. COMMUN. ABSTR.
[UK/0025-7222]
MEDICAL ELECTRONICS AND COMMUNICATIONS ABSTRACTS.
(Ceased)

MED. PHARM. BIOTECHNOL. ABSTR.
[US/1063-1178]
MEDICAL & PHARMACEUTICAL BIOTECHNOLOGY ABSTRACTS.
(*Continues in part* Biotechnology Research Abstracts.)
***Refer to Biotechnology Research Abstracts for complete source list.

MED. REV. DIG.
[US/0363-7778]
MEDIA REVIEW DIGEST.
(*Continues* Multi Media Reviews Index.)

MED. SOCIOECON. RES. SOURCE
[US/0025-7540]
MEDICAL SOCIOECONOMIC RESEARCH SOURCES.
(*Supersedes* Weekly Bulletin *and* Index to Medical Socioeconomic Literature.)

MEDOC
[US/0097-9732]
MEDOC.
(Ceased)

MENT. HEALTH BOOK REV. INDEX
[US/0076-6445]
MENTAL HEALTH BOOK REVIEW INDEX.
(*Continued by* Chicorel Index to Mental Health Book Reviews.)

MENT. RETARD. ABSTR.
[US/0025-9691]
MENTAL RETARDATION ABSTRACTS.
(*Continued by* Mental Retardation & Developmental Disabilities Abstracts.)

MENT. RETARD. DEV. DISABIL. ABSTR.
[US/0361-3798]
MENTAL RETARDATION & DEVELOPMENTAL DISABILITIES ABSTRACTS.
(*Continued by* Developmental Disabilities Abstracts.)

MET. ABSTR.
[UK/0026-0924]
METALS ABSTRACTS.
(*Formed by the union of* Metallurgical Abstracts *and* Review of Metal Literature.)

MET. ABSTR. INDEX
[UK/0026-0932]
METALS ABSTRACTS INDEX.
(*Formed by the union of* Metallurgical Abstracts *and* Review of Metal Literature.)
***Refer to Metals Abstracts for complete source list.

MET. FINISHING ABSTR.
[UK/0026-0584]
METAL FINISHING ABSTRACTS.
(*Continued by* Surface Treatment Technology Abstracts.)

METEOROL. GEOASTROPHYS. ABSTR.
[US/0026-1130]
METEOROLOGICAL AND GEOASTROPHYSICAL ABSTRACTS.
(*Continues* Meteorological Abstracts and Bibliography.)

METEOROL. GEOASTROPHYS. ABSTR. [CD-ROM]
[US/1066-2707]
METEOROLOGICAL & GEOASTROPHYSICAL ABSTRACTS.
***Refer to Meteorological and Geoastrophysical Abstracts for a complete source list.

METHODIST PERIOD. INDEX
[US]
METHODIST PERIODICAL INDEX.
(*Continued by* United Methodist Periodical Index.)

METHODS ORGAN. SYNTH.
[UK/0265-4245]
METHODS IN ORGANIC SYNTHESIS.

MICROBIOL. ABSTR. SECT. A
[US/0300-838X]
MICROBIOLOGY ABSTRACTS. SECTION A : INDUSTRIAL & APPLIED MICROBIOLOGY.
(*Continues* Microbiology Abstracts. Section A. Industrial Microbiology.)

MICROBIOL. ABSTR. SECT. B
[US/0300-8398]
MICROBIOLOGY ABSTRACTS. SECTION B, BACTERIOLOGY.
(*Continues* Microbiology Abstracts. Section B: General Microbiology and Bacteriology.)

MICROBIOL. ABSTR. SECT. C
[US/0301-2328]
MICROBIOLOGY ABSTRACTS. SECTION C, ALGOLOGY, MYCOLOGY & PROTOZOOLOGY.

MICROCOMPUT. IND. UPDATE
[US/0741-6016]
MICROCOMPUTER INDUSTRY UPDATE.

MICROCOMPUT. INDEX
[US/8756-7040]
MICROCOMPUTER INDEX.
(*Continued by* Microcomputer Abstracts.)

MID. SEARCH
[US/1071-2755]
MIDDLE SEARCH.
(*Continues* Junior Search.)

MIDDLE EAST ABSTR. INDEX
[US/0162-766X]
MIDDLE EAST, ABSTRACTS AND INDEX.

MIDDLE EAST J.
[US/0026-3141]
MIDDLE EAST JOURNAL, THE.

MINERAL. ABSTR.
[UK/0026-4601]
MINERALOGICAL ABSTRACTS.

MINPROC
[CN/0828-8461]
MINPROC : MINERAL PROCESSING ABSTRACTS.
(Ceased)

MINTEC, MIN. TECHNOL. ABSTR.
[CN/0823-0773]
MINTEC : MINING TECHNOLOGY ABSTRACTS.
(Ceased)

INDEXES/ABSTRACTS TABLE

MISSIONALIA
[SA/0256-9507]
MISSIONALIA.
(*Formed by the union of* Lux Mundi (Pretoria, South Africa) *and* Missionaria.)

MLA INT. BIBL. BOOKS ARTIC. MOD. LANG. LIT.
[US/0024-8215]
MLA INTERNATIONAL BIBLIOGRAPHY OF BOOKS AND ARTICLES ON THE MODERN LANGUAGES AND LITERATURES (COMPLETE ED.).
(*Continues* MLA International Bibliography of Books and Articles on the Modern Languages and Literatures.)

MOD. MED.
[US/0026-8070]
MODERN MEDICINE (MINNEAPOLIS).

MON. PERIOD. INDEX
[US/0197-6567]
MONTHLY PERIODICAL INDEX.
(*Absorbed by* Access.)

MOSHER PERIOD. INDEX
[US/0194-0716]
MOSHER PERIODICAL INDEX.
(*Continues* Subject Index to Select Periodical Literature.)

MRS BULL.
[US/0883-7694]
MRS BULLETIN.
(*Absorbed* JMR Abstracts.)

MULTI MEDIA REV. INDEX
[US/0091-5858]
MULTI MEDIA REVIEWS INDEX.
(*Continued by* Media Review Digest.)

MULTICULT. EDUC. ABSTR.
[UK/0260-9770]
MULTICULTURAL EDUCATION ABSTRACTS.

MUSCULAR DYSTROPHY ABSTR.
[US/0027-3732]
MUSCULAR DYSTROPHY ABSTRACTS.
(Ceased)

MUSEUM ABSTR.
[UK/0267-8594]
MUSEUM ABSTRACTS.

MUSIC ARTIC. GUIDE
[US/0027-4240]
MUSIC ARTICLE GUIDE.

MUSIC INDEX
[US/0027-4348]
MUSIC INDEX, THE.

N. Y. LAW J. DIG.-ANNOT.
[US/0745-4406]
NEW YORK LAW JOURNAL DIGEST-ANNOTATOR.
(*Continues* Clark's Digest-Annotator.)

NAPRALERT
[US]
NAPRALERT [ONLINE DATABASE].

NAT. PROD. UPDATES
[UK/0950-1711]
NATURAL PRODUCT UPDATES.

NATL. NEWSP. INDEX
[US/0273-3676]
NATIONAL NEWSPAPER INDEX.

NEMATOL. ABSTR.
[UK/0957-6797]
NEMATOLOGICAL ABSTRACTS.
(*Continues* Helminthological Abstracts. Series B, Plant Nematology.)

NEW LIT. AUTOMAT.
[NE]
NEW LITERATURE ON AUTOMATION.
(*Continues* IAG-Literature on Automation.)

NEW PERIOD. INDEX
[US/0146-5716]
NEW PERIODICALS INDEX.
(Ceased)

NEW TESTAM. ABSTR.
[US/0028-6877]
NEW TESTAMENT ABSTRACTS.

NEWSP. ABSTR.
[US/1064-993X]
NEWSPAPER ABSTRACTS ONDISC.

NEWSP. ABSTR.
[US]
NEWSPAPER ABSTRACTS.

NEWSP. PERIOD. ABSTR.
[US]
NEWSPAPER & PERIODICAL ABSTRACTS [ONLINE DATABASE].

NEXIS
[US]
NEXIS.

NONWOVENS ABSTR.
[UK/9036-1234]
NONWOVENS ABSTRACTS.

NUCL. ACIDS ABSTR.
[US/1070-2466]
NUCLEIC ACIDS ABSTRACTS (1994).
(*Continues* Cambridge Scientific Biochemistry Abstracts, Part 2: Nucleic Acids.)

NUCL. SCI. ABSTR.
[US/0029-5612]
NUCLEAR SCIENCE ABSTRACTS.
(*Continues* Abstracts of Declassified Documents; Guide to Published Research on Atomic Energy.)

NUMIS. LIT.
[US/0029-6031]
NUMISMATIC LITERATURE.

NURS. ABSTR.
[US/0195-3354]
NURSING ABSTRACTS.

NURS. ALLIED HEALTH INDEX
[US/0744-8732]
NURSING AND ALLIED HEALTH INDEX.
(*Absorbed by* Cumulative Index to Nursing & Allied Health Literature.)

NURS. DIG.
[US/0091-4215]
NURSING DIGEST.
(*Continued by* Nursing Dimensions.)

NURS. DIMEN.
[US/0164-0232]
NURSING DIMENSIONS.
(*Continues* Nursing Digest.)

NUTR. ABSTR. REV.
[UK/0029-6619]
NUTRITION ABSTRACTS AND REVIEWS.
(*Split into* Nutrition Abstracts and Reviews. Series A. Human and Experimental **and** Nutrition Abstracts and Reviews. Series B, Livestock Feeds and Feeding.)

NUTR. ABSTR. REV., SER. A, HUM. EXP.
[UK/0309-1295]
NUTRITION ABSTRACTS AND REVIEWS. SERIES A: HUMAN & EXPERIMENTAL.
(*Continues in part* Nutrition Abstracts and Reviews.)

NUTR. ABSTR. REV., SER. B, LIVE FEEDS AND FEED.
[UK/0309-135X]
NUTRITION ABSTRACTS AND REVIEWS. SERIES B. LIVESTOCK FEEDS AND FEEDING.
(*Continues in part* Nutrition Abstracts and Reviews.)

NUTR. RES. NEWSL.
[US/0736-0037]
NUTRITION RESEARCH NEWSLETTER.

OCCUP. MENT. HEALTH
[US/0090-1679]
OCCUPATIONAL MENTAL HEALTH.
(*Supersedes* Occupational Mental Health News.)

OCCUP. MENT. HEALTH NOTES
[US/0029-795X]
OCCUPATIONAL MENTAL HEALTH NOTES.
(*Superseded by* Occupational Mental Health.)

OCEAN. ABSTR.
[US/0748-1489]
OCEANIC ABSTRACTS (BETHESDA, MD.).
(*Continues* Oceanic Abstracts with Indexes.)

OCEAN. ABSTR. INDEXES
[US/0093-6901]
OCEANIC ABSTRACTS WITH INDEXES.
(*Continued by* Oceanic Abstracts (Bethesda, Md.).)

OCEANIC CIT. J. ABSTR.
[US]
OCEANIC CITATION JOURNAL WITH ABSTRACTS / OCEANIC RESEARCH INSTITUTE.
(*Merged with* Oceanic Index *to form* Oceanic Abstracts with Indexes.)

OCEANIC INDEX CIT. J. ABSTR.
[US]
OCEANIC INDEX CITATION JOURNAL WITH ABSTRACTS.
(*Continued by* Oceanic Citation Journal with Abstracts.)

OCEANOGR. LIT. REV.
[UK/0967-0653]
OCEANOGRAPHIC LITERATURE REVIEW.
(*Continues* Deep-Sea Research. Part B, Oceanographic Literature Review.)

OLD TESTAM. ABSTR.
[US/0364-8591]
OLD TESTAMENT ABSTRACTS.

ONCOG. GROWTH FACTORS ABSTR.
[US/1043-8963]
ONCOGENES AND GROWTH FACTORS ABSTRACTS.

OPER. PROD. MANAGE. ABSTR.
[UK]
OPERATIONS & PRODUCTION MANAGEMENT ABSTRACTS.
(*Continues* Management Services and Production Abstracts.)

OPER. RES. MANAG. SCI.
[US/0030-3658]
OPERATIONS RESEARCH/MANAGEMENT SCIENCE.

ORAL RES. ABSTR.
[US/0030-4212]
ORAL RESEARCH ABSTRACTS.
(Ceased)

ORNAMENTAL HORT.
[UK/0305-4934]
ORNAMENTAL HORTICULTURE.

INDEXES/ABSTRACTS TABLE

ORTHO. SUR.
[NE/0014-4371]
ORTHOPEDIC SURGERY.
(*Continues* Orthopedics and Traumatology.)
***Refer to EMBASE [Online Database] for complete source list.

OZARK PERIOD. INDEX
[US/0275-9713]
OZARK PERIODICAL INDEX.

PAIS BULL.
[US/0898-2201]
PAIS BULLETIN.
(*Merged with* PAIS Foreign Language Index *to form* PAIS International in Print.)

PAIS FOREIGN LANG. INDEX
[US/0896-792X]
PAIS FOREIGN LANGUAGE INDEX.
(*Merged with* PAIS Bulletin *to form* PAIS International in Print.)

PAIS INT. PRINT
[US/1051-4015]
PAIS INTERNATIONAL IN PRINT.
(*Formed by the union of* PAIS Bulletin *and* PAIS Foreign Language Index.)

PAP. BOARD ABSTR.
[UK/0307-0778]
PAPER & BOARD ABSTRACTS.
(*Continues in part* Kenley Abstracts.)

PARAPSYCHOL. ABSTR. INT.
[US/0740-7629]
PARAPSYCHOLOGY ABSTRACTS INTERNATIONAL.
(*Continued by* Exceptional Human Experience.)

PASTOR. CARE COUNS. ABSTR.
[US]
PASTORAL CARE AND COUNSELING ABSTRACTS.
(*Continued by* Abstracts of Research in Pastoral Care and Counseling.)

PEACE RES. ABSTR. J.
[US/0031-3599]
PEACE RESEARCH ABSTRACTS JOURNAL.

PERIODEX
[CN]
PERIODEX: INDEX ANALYTIQUE DE PERIODIQUES DE LANGUE FRANCAISE.
(*Merged with* Radar *to form* Point de Repere.)

PERSON. MANAGE. ABSTR.
[US/0031-577X]
PERSONNEL MANAGEMENT ABSTRACTS.

PERSON. TRAIN. ABSTR.
[UK/0305-067X]
PERSONNEL + TRAINING ABSTRACTS.
(*Continues in part* Anbar Management Services Abstracts.)

PESTDOC
[UK]
PESTDOC.

PET. ABSTR.
[US/0031-6423]
PETROLEUM ABSTRACTS (TULSA, OKLA.).

PET. ENERGY BUS. NEWS INDEX
[US/0098-7743]
PETROLEUM/ENERGY BUSINESS NEWS INDEX.

PET. REFIN. PETROCHEM.
[US]
PETROLEUM REFINING AND PETROCHEMICALS.
(*Continued by* Literature Abstracts. Petroleum Refining & Petrochemicals.)

PET. SUBS.
[US]
PETROLEUM SUBSTITUTES.
(*Continued by* Literature Abstracts. Petroleum Substitutes.)

PHARM. NEWS INDEX
[US/0362-4439]
PHARMACEUTICAL NEWS INDEX.

PHILIP. ABSTR.
[PH/0031-7438]
PHILIPPINE ABSTRACTS.
(*Continued by* Philippine Science & Technology Abstracts.)

PHILIP. SCI. TECHNOL. ABSTR.
[PH/0115-8724]
PHILIPPINE SCIENCE & TECHNOLOGY ABSTRACTS.
(*Continues* Philippine Science and Technology Abstract Bibliography.)

PHILOS. INDEX
[US/0031-7993]
PHILOSOPHER'S INDEX.

PHOTOGR. ABSTR.
[UK/0031-8701]
PHOTOGRAPHIC ABSTRACTS.
(*Continued by* Imaging Abstracts.)

PHYS. ABSTR.
[UK/0036-8091]
PHYSICS ABSTRACTS.
(*Continues* Science Abstracts. Physics Abstracts.)
***Refer to INSPEC [Online Database] for a complete source list.

PHYS. BRIEFS
[UK/0170-7434]
PHYSICS BRIEFS.
(*Supersedes* Physikalische Berichte.)

PHYS. EDUC. INDEX
[US/0191-9202]
PHYSICAL EDUCATION INDEX (CAPE GIRARDEAU).

PHYS. MED. BIOL.
[UK/0031-9155]
PHYSICS IN MEDICINE & BIOLOGY.

PHYSIC. MEDLINE PLUS
[US/1065-6545]
PHYSICIAN'S MEDLINE PLUS.

PIG NEWS INF.
[UK/0143-9014]
PIG NEWS AND INFORMATION.

PINPOINTER
[AT/0031-9910]
PINPOINTER.
(Ceased)

PLANT BREED. ABSTR.
[UK/0032-0803]
PLANT BREEDING ABSTRACTS.

PLANT GROW. REG. ABSTR.
[UK/0305-9154]
PLANT GROWTH REGULATOR ABSTRACTS.

POINT REPERE
[CN/0822-8833]
POINT DE REPERE (MONTREAL).
(*Continued by* Repere.)

POLICE SCI. ABSTR.
[NE/0166-6282]
POLICE SCIENCE ABSTRACTS.
(*Merged with* Criminology & Penology Abstracts *to form* Criminology, Penology, and Police Science Abstracts.)

POLLUT. ABSTR. INDEXES
[US/0032-3624]
POLLUTION ABSTRACTS WITH INDEXES.

POLYMER CONTENTS
[UK/0883-153X]
POLYMER CONTENTS.
(*Continues* PRA Report: Polymer Contents.)

POP. MAG. REV.
[US/0740-3763]
POPULAR MAGAZINE REVIEW : PMR.
(*Continued by* Magazine Article Summaries.)

POP. PERIOD. INDEX
[US/0092-9727]
POPULAR PERIODICAL INDEX.
(Ceased)

POPUL. INDEX
[US/0032-4701]
POPULATION INDEX.
(*Continues* Population Literature.)

POTATO ABSTR.
[UK/0308-7344]
POTATO ABSTRACTS.

POULT. ABSTR.
[UK/0306-1582]
POULTRY ABSTRACTS.

POVER. HUM. RESOUR.
[US/0032-5864]
POVERTY & HUMAN RESOURCES.
(*Continued by* Poverty and Human Resources Abstracts.)

POVER. HUM. RESOUR. ABSTR.
[US/0094-4394]
POVERTY & HUMAN RESOURCES ABSTRACTS.
(*Continued by* Human Resources Abstracts.)

PREDICASTS
[US/0032-7166]
PREDICASTS.
(*Continued by* Predicasts Forecasts.)

PREDICASTS F & S INDEX INT.
[US/0270-4528]
PREDICASTS F & S INDEX INTERNATIONAL.
(*Continued by* F&S Index International (Foster City, Calif.).)
***Refer to Predicasts Forecasts for a complete source list.

PREDICASTS F&S INDEX, U. S. ANNU. ED.
[US/0277-9676]
PREDICASTS F&S INDEX. UNITED STATES ANNUAL EDITION.
(*Continued by* F&S Index United States Annual.)

PREDICASTS FORECASTS
[US/0278-0135]
PREDICASTS FORECASTS.
(*Continues* Predicasts.)

PREV. HUM. SERV.
[US/0270-3114]
PREVENTION IN HUMAN SERVICES.
(*Continues* Community Mental Health Review.)

PRIM. SEARCH
[US/1065-2485]
PRIMARY SEARCH.

PRINT. ABSTR.
[UK/0031-109X]
PRINTING ABSTRACTS.

INDEXES/ABSTRACTS TABLE

PROC. CHEM. ENG.
[UK/0960-5045]
PROCESS AND CHEMICAL ENGINEERING.
(*Continues* Chemical Engineering Abstracts.)

PROMT
[US/0161-8032]
PROMT / PREDICASTS OVERVIEW OF MARKETS AND TECHNOLOGY.
(*Formed by the union of* Chemical Market Abstracts *and* EMA, Equipment Market Abstracts.)

PROTOZOOLOG. ABSTR.
[UK/0309-1287]
PROTOZOOLOGICAL ABSTRACTS.

PSYCHEDELIC REV.
[US/0033-2631]
PSYCHEDELIC REVIEW.
(Ceased)

PSYCHOANAL. ABSTR.
[US/1066-9884]
PSYCHOANALYTIC ABSTRACTS.
(*Continues* Psycscan. Psychoanalysis.)

PSYCHOL. ABSTR.
[US/0033-2887]
PSYCHOLOGICAL ABSTRACTS.

PSYCHOL. READ. GUIDE
[SZ/0300-0443]
PSYCHOLOGICAL READER'S GUIDE.
(Ceased)

PSYCHOPHARMACOLOGY ABSTR.
[US/0033-3166]
PSYCHOPHARMACOLOGY ABSTRACTS.
(Ceased)

PSYCINFO
[US]
PSYCINFO.

PSYCLIT
[US]
PSYCLIT DATABASE.

PSYCSCAN PSYCHOANAL.
[US/0889-5236]
PSYCSCAN: PSYCHOANALYSIS.
(*Continued by* Psychoanalytic Abstracts.)

PSYCSCAN: APPL. EXP. ENG. PSYCH.
[US/0891-0685]
PSYCSCAN: APPLIED EXPERIMENTAL AND ENGINEERING PSYCHOLOGY.

PSYCSCAN: APPL. PSYCH.
[US/0271-7506]
PSYCSCAN. APPLIED PSYCHOLOGY.

PSYCSCAN: CLIN. PSYCH.
[US/0197-1484]
PSYCSCAN. CLINICAL PSYCHOLOGY.

PSYCSCAN: DEVELOP. PSYCH.
[US/0197-1492]
PSYCSCAN. DEVELOPMENTAL PSYCHOLOGY.

PSYCSCAN: LD/MR
[US/0730-1928]
PSYCSCAN. LD/MR.

PSYCSCAN: NEUROPSYCH.
[US/1058-6660]
PSYCSCAN. NEUROPSYCHOLOGY.

PTS NEWSL. DATABASE
[US]
PTS NEWSLETTER DATABASE [ONLINE DATABASE].

PUBLIC ADM. ABSTR. INDEX ARTIC. INDIA
[II/0033-331X]
PUBLIC ADMINISTRATION ABSTRACTS AND INDEX OF ARTICLES (INDIA).
(Ceased)

PUBLIC AFF. INF. SERV. BULL.
[US/0033-3409]
PUBLIC AFFAIRS INFORMATION SERVICE BULLETIN.
(*Continued by* PAIS Bulletin (Annual).)

Q. BIBLIOGR. COMPUT. DATA PROCESS.
[US/0048-6132]
QUARTERLY BIBLIOGRAPHY OF COMPUTERS AND DATA PROCESSING.
(*Continued by* Computer Literature Index.)

Q. INDEX ISLAM.
[UK/0308-7395]
QUARTERLY INDEX ISLAMICUS.
***Refer to Index Islamicus for complete source list.

QUAL. CONTROL APPL. STAT.
[US/0033-5207]
QUALITY CONTROL AND APPLIED STATISTICS.

RAPRA ABSTR.
[UK/0033-6750]
RAPRA ABSTRACTS.
(*Formed by the union of* Plastics. RAPRA Abstracts *and* Rubbers. RAPRA Abstracts.)

READ. ABSTR.
[US/0361-6118]
READING ABSTRACTS.
(*Continued by* Linguistics and Language Behavior Abstracts.)

READ. GUIDE ABSTR.
[US/0899-1553]
READERS' GUIDE ABSTRACTS (PRINT EDITION).
(*Continued by* Readers' Guide Abstracts (School and Public Library Ed. : Monthly).)

READ. GUIDE ABSTR.
[US/1058-1219]
READERS' GUIDE ABSTRACTS (SCHOOL AND PUBLIC LIBRARY ED.).
(*Continued by* Readers' Guide Abstracts Select Edition.)

READ. GUIDE ABSTR. SELECT ED.
[US]
READERS' GUIDE ABSTRACTS SELECT EDITION.
(*Continues* Readers' Guide Abstracts School and Public Library Edition.)

READ. GUIDE PERIOD. LIT.
[US/0034-0464]
READERS' GUIDE TO PERIODICAL LITERATURE.
(*Continues* Monthly Cumulative Index to ... Important Periodicals; *Absorbed* Cumulative Index to a Selected List of Periodicals (Annual).)

RECENT. PUBL. ARTIC.
[US/0145-5311]
RECENTLY PUBLISHED ARTICLES - AMERICAN HISTORICAL ASSOCIATION.
(Ceased)

RECIPE PERIOD. INDEX
[US/0743-3484]
RECIPE PERIODICAL INDEX.
(Ceased)

REF. BOOK REV. INDEX
[US]
REFERENCE BOOK REVIEW INDEX.
(Ceased)

REF. SOURCES
[US/0163-3546]
REFERENCE SOURCES.
(Ceased)

REF. UPD. BASIC ED.
[US]
REFERENCE UPDATE BASIC EDITION [COMPUTER FILE].

REF. UPD. CLINICAL ED.
[US]
REFERENCE UPDATE CLINICAL EDITION [COMPUTER FILE].

REF. UPD. DELUXE ED.
[US]
REFERENCE UPDATE DELUXE EDITION [COMPUTER FILE].

REFER. Z.
[RU]
REFERATIVNYI ZHURNAL: ORGANIZATSIIA I BEZOPASNOST DOROZHNOGO DVIZHENIIA.

REHABIL. LIT.
[US/0034-3579]
REHABILITATION LITERATURE.
(Ceased)

RELIG. INDEX ONE PERIOD.
[US/0149-8428]
RELIGION INDEX ONE. PERIODICALS.
(*Continued in part by* Index to Book Reviews in Religion.)

RELIG. PERIOD. INDEX
[US/0034-4117]
RELIGIOUS PERIODICALS INDEX.
(Ceased)

RELIG. THEOL. ABSTR.
[US/0034-4044]
RELIGIOUS AND THEOLOGICAL ABSTRACTS.

REPERT. ANAL. ARTIC. REV. QUE.
[CN/0315-2316]
RADAR: REPERTOIRE ANALYTIQUE D'ARTICLES DE REVUES DU QUEBEC.
(*Merged with* Periodex *to form* Point de Repere.)

RES. ALERT
[US]
RESEARCH ALERT.
(*Continues* Ascatopics.)

RES. HIGH. EDUC. ABSTR.
[UK/0034-5326]
RESEARCH INTO HIGHER EDUCATION ABSTRACTS.

RESOURCE/ONE ONDISC
[US]
RESOURCE/ONE ONDISC [COMPUTER FILE].

REV. AGRIC. ENTOMOL.
[UK/0957-6762]
REVIEW OF AGRICULTURAL ENTOMOLOGY.
(*Continues* Review of Applied Entomology. Series A, Agricultural.)

REV. APPL. ENTOMOL. SER. A, AGRIC.
[UK/0305-0076]
REVIEW OF APPLIED ENTOMOLOGY. SERIES A: AGRICULTURAL.
(*Continued by* Review of Agricultural Entomology.)

INDEXES/ABSTRACTS TABLE

REV. APPL. ENTOMOL. SER. B, MED. VET.
[UK/0305-0084]
REVIEW OF APPLIED ENTOMOLOGY. SERIES B, MEDICAL AND VETERINARY.
(*Continued by* Review of Medical and Veterinary Entomology.)

REV. MED. VET. ENTOMOL.
[UK/0957-6770]
REVIEW OF MEDICAL AND VETERINARY ENTOMOLOGY.
(*Continues* Review of Applied Entomology. Series B, Medical and Veterinary.)

REV. MED. VET. MYCOLOGY
[UK/0034-6624]
REVIEW OF MEDICAL AND VETERINARY MYCOLOGY.
(*Continues* Annotated Bibliography of Medical Mycology.)

REV. PLANT PATHOL.
[UK/0034-6438]
REVIEW OF PLANT PATHOLOGY.
(*Continues* Review of Applied Mycology.)

RIBA LIB. BULL.
[UK]
RIBA LIBRARY BULLETIN.
(*Superseded by* Architectural Periodicals Index.)

RILA, INT. REP. LIT. ART
[US/0145-5982]
RILA : INTERNATIONAL REPERTORY OF THE LITERATURE OF ART.
(*Merged with* Repertoire d'Art et d'Archeologie *to form* Bibliography of the History of Art.)

RILM ABSTR.
[US/0033-6955]
RILM ABSTRACTS.

RINGDOC
[UK]
RINGDOC.
***Refer to PESTDOC for complete source list.

RISK ABSTR.
[CN/0824-3336]
RISK ABSTRACTS.

ROBOMATIX REPORT.
[US/0748-1624]
ROBOMATIX REPORTER.
(*Continued by* Robotics Abstracts.)

ROBOTICS ABSTR.
[US/0000-1139]
ROBOTICS ABSTRACTS.
(*Continues* Robomatix Reporter.)

ROMANT. MOVE.
[US/0557-2738]
ROMANTIC MOVEMENT.

ROTHS AM. POETRY ANNUAL
[US/1040-5461]
ROTH'S AMERICAN POETRY ANNUAL.
(*Formed by the union of* Annual Survey of American Poetry; Annual Index to Poetry in Periodicals **and** American Poetry Index.)

RURAL EXT. EDUC. TRAIN. ABSTR.
[UK/0140-4776]
RURAL EXTENSION, EDUCATION AND TRAINING ABSTRACTS.
(Ceased)

RURAL RECREAT. TOUR. ABSTR.
[UK/0308-0137]
RURAL RECREATION AND TOURISM ABSTRACTS.
(*Continued by* Leisure, Recreation and Tourism Abstracts.)

SAF. HEALTH WORK
[SZ/1010-7053]
SAFETY AND HEALTH AT WORK : ILO-CIS BULLETIN.
(*Continues* International Occupational Safety and Health Information Centre. CIS Abstracts.)

SAF. SCI. ABSTR.
[US/0092-542X]
SAFETY SCIENCE ABSTRACTS.
(*Continued by* Safety Science Abstracts Journal.)

SAF. SCI. ABSTR. J.
[US/0160-1342]
SAFETY SCIENCE ABSTRACTS JOURNAL.
(*Continued by* Health and Safety Science Abstracts.)

SAGE FAM. STUD. ABSTR.
[US/0164-0283]
SAGE FAMILY STUDIES ABSTRACTS.

SAGE PUBLIC ADM. ABSTR.
[US/0094-6958]
SAGE PUBLIC ADMINISTRATION ABSTRACTS.

SAGE RACE RELAT. ABSTR.
[UK/0307-9201]
SAGE RACE RELATIONS ABSTRACTS.
(*Continues* Race Relations Abstracts.)

SAGE URBAN STUD. ABSTR
[US/0090-5747]
SAGE URBAN STUDIES ABSTRACTS.

SCHOOL ORGAN. MANAGE. ABSTR.
[UK/0261-2755]
SCHOOL ORGANISATION & MANAGEMENT ABSTRACTS.

SCI. ABSTR. PHYS. ABSTR.
[UK]
SCIENCE ABSTRACTS. PHYSICS ABSTRACTS.
(*Continued by* Science Abstracts. Series A, Physics Abstracts.)

SCI. ABSTR. SECT. A. PHYS. ABSTR.
[UK]
SCIENCE ABSTRACTS. SECTION A, PHYSICS ABSTRACTS / EDITED AND ISSUED MONTHLY BY THE INSTITUTION OF ELECTRICAL ENGINEERS, IN ASSOCIATION WITH THE PHYSICAL SOCIETY, THE AMERICAN PHYSICAL SOCIETY, THE AMERICAN INSTITUTE OF ELECTRICAL ENGINEERS.
(*Continued by* Science Abstracts. Physics Abstracts.)

SCI. ABSTR. SER. A, PHYS. ABSTR.
[UK]
SCIENCE ABSTRACTS. SERIES A, PHYSICS ABSTRACTS.
(*Continued by* Physics Abstracts.)

SCI. CIT. INDEX
[US/0036-827X]
SCIENCE CITATION INDEX (PRINT ED.).

SCI. CIT. INDEX ABSTR.
[US/1061-1290]
SCIENCE CITATION INDEX WITH ABSTRACTS.
***Refer to Science Citation Index (US/0036-827X) for a complete source list.

SCI. CIT. INDEX [CD-ROM]
[US/1044-6052]
SCIENCE CITATION INDEX (COMPACT DISC ED.).
***Refer to Science Citation Index (US/0036-827X) for a complete source list.

SCI. CIT. INDEX, ABR. ED.
[US/0737-2108]
SCIENCE CITATION INDEX. ABRIDGED EDITION.
(Ceased)

SCI. FICT. FANTASY BOOK REV. INDEX
[US/1046-1922]
SCIENCE FICTION AND FANTASY BOOK REVIEW INDEX.
(*Continues* Science Fiction Book Review Index.)

SCI. RES. ABSTR. J.
[US/0731-0943]
SCIENCE RESEARCH ABSTRACTS JOURNAL.
(*Absorbed by* Solid State Abstracts Journal.)

SCI. RES. ABSTR. J. PART A.
[US/0194-7486]
SCIENCE RESEARCH ABSTRACTS JOURNAL. PART A: SUPERCONDUCTIVITY, MAGNETOHYDRODYNAMICS AND PLASMAS, THEORETICAL PHYSICS.
(*Merged with* Science Research Abstracts Journal. Part B: Laser and Electro-Opticreviews, Quantum Electronics and Unconventional Energy Sources *to form* Science Research Abstracts Journal.)

SCISEARCH
[US]
SCISEARCH [ONLINE DATABASE].

SEA ABSTR.
[PH]
SEA ABSTRACTS.

SEED ABSTR.
[UK/0141-0180]
SEED ABSTRACTS.

SEL. PHILIP. PERIOD. INDEX
[PH/0037-1335]
SELECTED PHILIPPINE PERIODICAL INDEX.
(Ceased)

SEL. WATER RESOUR. ABSTR.
[US/0037-136X]
SELECTED WATER RESOURCES ABSTRACTS (WASHINGTON, D.C.).
(Ceased)

SELEC. COOP. INDEX MANAGE. PERIOD.
[FI/0782-2979]
SCIMP SELECTIVE CO-OPERATIVE INDEX OF MANAGEMENT PERIODICALS.
(Ceased)

SEVENTH-DAY ADVENTIST PERIOD. INDEX
[US/0270-3599]
SEVENTH-DAY ADVENTIST PERIODICAL INDEX.

SHIP ABSTR.
[NO/0346-1025]
SHIP ABSTRACTS.
(*Absorbed by* Journal of Abstracts of the British Ship Research Association.)

SHOCK VIBR. DIG.
[US/0583-1024]
SHOCK AND VIBRATION DIGEST, THE.

SMALL ANIM. ABSTR. BIBLIOGR.
[UK]
SMALL ANIMAL ABSTRACTS BIBLIOGRAPHY.
(*Continues* Small Animal Abstracts.)

SOC. PLANN. POLICY DEV. ABSTR.
[US/1042-8380]
SOCIAL PLANNING, POLICY & DEVELOPMENT ABSTRACTS.
(*Continues* Social Welfare, Social Planning/Policy & Social Development.)

INDEXES/ABSTRACTS TABLE

SOC. RES. METHODOL. ABSTR.
[NE/0167-8477]
SOCIAL RESEARCH METHODOLOGY ABSTRACTS.
(*Continues in part* SRM Abstract Bulletin.)

SOC. SCI. CIT. INDEX
[US/0091-3707]
SOCIAL SCIENCES CITATION INDEX (PRINT ED.).

SOC. SCI. HUMANIT. INDEX
[US/0037-7899]
SOCIAL SCIENCES & HUMANITIES INDEX.
(*Split into* Social Sciences Index *and* Humanities Index.)

SOC. SCI. INDEX
[US/0094-4920]
SOCIAL SCIENCES INDEX.
(*Supersedes in part* Social Sciences & Humanities Index.)

SOC. SCI. INDEX FULLTEXT
[US]
SOCIAL SCIENCES INDEX / FULLTEXT.

SOC. SCI. SOURCE
[US/1063-9802]
SOCIAL SCIENCE SOURCE.

SOC. WELF. SOC. PLAN./POLICY SOC. DEV.
[US/0195-7988]
SOCIAL WELFARE, SOCIAL PLANNING/POLICY & SOCIAL DEVELOPMENT.
(*Continued by* Social Planning, Policy & Development Abstracts.)

SOC. WORK ABSTR.
[US/1070-5317]
SOCIAL WORK ABSTRACTS.
(*Continues in part* Social Work Research and Abstracts.)

SOC. WORK RES.
[US/1070-5309]
SOCIAL WORK RESEARCH.
(*Continues in part* Social Work Research and Abstracts.)
***Refer to Social Work Abstracts for a complete source list.

SOC. WORK RES. ABSTR.
[US/0148-0847]
SOCIAL WORK RESEARCH & ABSTRACTS.
(*Split into* Social Work Abstracts *and* Social Work Research.)

SOCIOL. ABSTR.
[US/0038-0202]
SOCIOLOGICAL ABSTRACTS.

SOCIOL. EDUC. ABSTR.
[UK/0038-0415]
SOCIOLOGY OF EDUCATION ABSTRACTS.

SOFT. ABSTR. ENG.
[IE/0790-150X]
SOFTWARE ABSTRACTS FOR ENGINEERS : SAFE.

SOILS FERT.
[UK/0038-0792]
SOILS AND FERTILIZERS.
(*Supersedes* Imperial Bureau of Soil Science. Monthly Letter.)

SOLID STATE ABSTR. J.
[US/0038-108X]
SOLID STATE ABSTRACTS JOURNAL.
(*Continued by* Solid State and Superconductivity Abstracts.)

SOLID STATE SUPERCOND. ABSTR.
[US/0896-5900]
SOLID STATE AND SUPERCONDUCTIVITY ABSTRACTS.
(*Continues* Solid State Abstracts Journal.)

SORGHUM MILL. ABSTR.
[UK/03082970]
SORGHUM AND MILLETS ABSTRACTS.
(Ceased)

SOUTH. BAPTIST PERIOD. INDEX
[US/0081-3028]
SOUTHERN BAPTIST PERIODICAL INDEX.

SOYABEAN ABSTR.
[UK/0141-0172]
SOYABEAN ABSTRACTS.

SPEC. EDUC. NEEDS ABSTR.
[UK/0954-0822]
SPECIAL EDUCATIONAL NEEDS ABSTRACTS.

SPIN
[US]
SPIN.

SPORT DISCUS
[US]
SPORT DISCUS [COMPUTER FILE].

SPORT FISH. ABSTR.
[US/0038-786X]
SPORT FISHERY ABSTRACTS.
(*Continued by* Fisheries Review.)

SPORTSEARCH
[US/0882-553X]
SPORTSEARCH.

STAT. REF. INDEX
[US/0885-6834]
STATISTICAL REFERENCE INDEX.

STAT. THEORY METHOD ABSTR.
[UK/0039-0518]
STATISTICAL THEORY AND METHOD ABSTRACTS.
(*Continues* International Journal of Abstracts: Statistical Theory and Method.)

STUD. WOMEN ABSTR.
[UK/0262-5644]
STUDIES ON WOMEN ABSTRACTS.

SUBJ. INDEX CHILD. MAG.
[US/0039-4351]
SUBJECT INDEX TO CHILDREN'S MAGAZINES.
(*Continued by* Children's Magazine Guide.)

SUBJ. INDEX PERIOD.
[UK]
SUBJECT INDEX TO PERIODICALS.
(*Split into* British Humanities Index *and* British Technology Index.)

SUBJ. INDEX SEL. PERIOD. LIT.
[US/0194-0708]
SUBJECT INDEX TO SELECT PERIODICAL LITERATURE.
(*Continued by* Mosher Periodical Index.)

SUG. INDUS. ABSTR.
[UK/0957-5022]
SUGAR INDUSTRY ABSTRACTS / [CAB INTERNATIONAL, BUREAU OF HORTICULTURE AND PLANTATION CROPS IN ASSOCIATION WITH TATE & LYLE PLC].
(*Continues* Tate & Lyle's Sugar Industry Abstracts.)

SURF. TREAT. TECHNOL. ABSTR.
[UK]
SURFACE TREATMENT TECHNOLOGY ABSTRACTS.
(*Continues* Metal Finishing Abstracts.)

TECH. DATA DIG.
[US]
TECHNICAL DATA DIGEST.
(Ceased)

TECH. EDUC. ABSTR.
[UK/0040-0920]
TECHNICAL EDUCATION ABSTRACTS.
(*Continued by* Technical Education & Training Abstracts.)

TECH. EDUC. TRAIN. ABSTR.
[UK]
TECHNICAL EDUCATION & TRAINING ABSTRACTS.
(*Continues* Technical Education Abstracts.)

TELEGEN ABSTR.
[US/0000-118X]
TELEGEN ABSTRACTS.
(*Continues* Telegen Reporter.)

TELEGEN REPORT.
[US/0743-8443]
TELEGEN REPORTER.
(*Continued by* Telegen Abstracts.)

TERMITE ABSTR.
[UK/0144-5995]
TERMITE ABSTRACTS.
(Ceased)

TEXT. TECHNOL. DIG.
[US/0040-5191]
TEXTILE TECHNOLOGY DIGEST.

THEOL. RELIG. INDEX
[UK]
THEOLOGICAL AND RELIGIOUS INDEX.
(Ceased)

THEOR. CHEM. ENG.
[UK/0960-5053]
THEORETICAL CHEMICAL ENGINEERING.
(*Continues* Theoretical Chemical Engineering Abstracts.)

THEOR. CHEM. ENG. ABSTR.
[UK/0040-5787]
THEORETICAL CHEMICAL ENGINEERING ABSTRACTS.
(*Continued by* Theoretical Chemical Engineering.)

TOM GEN. INDEX
[US]
TOM GENERAL INDEX.

TOP MANAGE. ABSTR.
[UK/0049-4100]
TOP MANAGEMENT ABSTRACTS.
(*Continued by* Anbar Top Management Abstracts.)

TOPICATOR
[US/0040-9340]
TOPICATOR.

TOXICOL. ABSTR.
[US/0140-5365]
TOXICOLOGY ABSTRACTS.

TRADE IND. ASAP
[US]
TRADE & INDUSTRY ASAP [ONLINE DATABASE].

TRADE IND. INDEX
[US]
TRADE & INDUSTRY INDEX [ONLINE DATABASE].

INDEXES/ABSTRACTS TABLE

TRANS. AM. SOC. CIV. ENG.
[US/0066-0604]
TRANSACTIONS OF THE AMERICAN SOCIETY OF CIVIL ENGINEERS.

TRANSP. RES. ABSTR.
[US/0095-2648]
TRANSPORTATION RESEARCH ABSTRACTS.
(*Absorbed in part by* HRIS Abstracts.)

TRANSP. STORAGE
[US]
TRANSPORTATION AND STORAGE.
(*Continued by* Literature Abstracts. Transportation & Storage.)

TROP. ABSTR.
[NE/0041-3208]
TROPICAL ABSTRACTS.
(*Superseded by* Abstracts on Tropical Agriculture.)

TROP. DIS. BULL.
[UK/0041-3240]
TROPICAL DISEASES BULLETIN.
(*Supersedes* Bulletin of the Sleeping Sickness Bureau and the Kala Azar Bulletin.)

U.S. POLIT. SCI. DOC.
[US/0148-6063]
UNITED STATES POLITICAL SCIENCE DOCUMENTS.
(*Absorbed* Asian Studies Indexed Journal Reference Guide.)

UMI ABI/INFORM--BUS. PERIOD. ONDISC
[US/1064-5381]
UMI ABI/INFORM--BUSINESS PERIODICALS ONDISC.

UNITED METHODIST PERIOD. INDEX
[US/0041-7319]
UNITED METHODIST PERIODICAL INDEX.
(*Continues* Methodist Periodical Index.)

URBAN AFF. ABSTR.
[US/0300-6859]
URBAN AFFAIRS ABSTRACTS.

VET. BULL.
[UK/0042-4854]
VETERINARY BULLETIN (LONDON).
(*Supersedes* Tropical Veterinary Bulletin; *Absorbed* Veterinary Reviews.)

VETDOC
[UK]
VETDOC.
***Refer to PESTDOC for complete source list.

VIROL. ABSTR.
[US/0042-6830]
VIROLOGY ABSTRACTS.
(*Continued by* Virology and AIDS Abstracts.)

VIROL. AIDS ABSTR.
[US/0896-5919]
VIROLOGY & AIDS ABSTRACTS.
(*Continues* Virology Abstracts.)

VIS. INDEX
[US/0049-6510]
VISION INDEX.
(Ceased)

VITIS VITIC. ENOL. ABSTR.
[GW/0175-8292]
VITIS, VITICULTURE AND ENOLOGY ABSTRACTS.
(*Separated from* Vitis.)

VOCAT. SEARCH
[US/1071-2747]
VOCATIONAL SEARCH.

WALL STREET J. INDEX
[US/0083-7075]
WALL STREET JOURNAL INDEX.
(Ceased)

WATER POLLUT. ABSTR.
[UK/0043-1281]
WATER POLLUTION ABSTRACTS.
(*Merged with* Water Research Association Library List *to form* WRC Information.)

WEED ABSTR.
[UK/0043-1729]
WEED ABSTRACTS.

WEST. HIST. Q.
[US/0043-3810]
WESTERN HISTORICAL QUARTERLY.

WHEAT BARLEY TRIT. ABSTR.
[UK/0265-7880]
WHEAT, BARLEY AND TRITICALE ABSTRACTS.
(*Continues* Triticale Abstracts.)

WILDL. REV.
[US/0043-5511]
WILDLIFE REVIEW (FORT COLLINS).

WILSON BUS. ABSTR.
[US/1057-6533]
WILSON BUSINESS ABSTRACTS.

WOMEN MANAG. REV. ABSTR.
[UK/0955-8357]
WOMEN IN MANAGEMENT REVIEW & ABSTRACTS.
(*Continued by* Women in Management Review.)

WOMEN MANAGE. REV.
[UK/0964-9425]
WOMEN IN MANAGEMENT REVIEW.
(*Continues* Women in Management Review & Abstracts.)

WOMEN STUD. ABSTR.
[US/0049-7835]
WOMEN STUDIES ABSTRACTS.

WORK RELAT. ABSTR.
[US/0273-3234]
WORK RELATED ABSTRACTS.
(*Continues* Employment Relations Abstracts.)

WORLD AGRIC. ECON. RURAL SOCIOL. ABSTR.
[UK/0043-8219]
WORLD AGRICULTURAL ECONOMICS AND RURAL SOCIOLOGY ABSTRACTS.

WORLD ALUM. ABSTR.
[US/0002-6697]
WORLD ALUMINUM ABSTRACTS.
(*Continued by* Aluminium Industry Abstracts.)

WORLD CERAM. ABSTR.
[UK/0957-8897]
WORLD CERAMICS ABSTRACTS.
(*Continues* British Ceramic Abstracts.)

WORLD FISH. ABSTR.
[IT/0043-8472]
WORLD FISHERIES ABSTRACTS.
(Ceased)

WORLD PUBL. MONIT.
[UK/0960-653X]
WORLD PUBLISHING MONITOR.
(*Continues* Electronic Publishing Abstracts.)

WORLD SURF. COAT. ABSTR.
[UK/0043-9088]
WORLD SURFACE COATINGS ABSTRACTS.
(*Continues* Review of Current Literature Relating to the Paint, Colour, Varnish and Allied Industries.)

WORLD TEXT. ABSTR.
[UK/0043-9118]
WORLD TEXTILE ABSTRACTS.
(*Supersedes* Textile Abstracts.)

WRC INF.
[UK/0306-6649]
WRC INFORMATION.
(*Continued by* Aqualine Abstracts.)

WRIT. AM. HIST.
[US/0364-2887]
WRITINGS ON AMERICAN HISTORY.
(Ceased)

ZENTRALBL. MATH. IHRE GRENZGEB.
[GW/0044-4235]
ZENTRALBLATT FUER MATHEMATIK UND IHRE GRENZGEBIETE.
(*Superseded in part by* Zentralblatt fuer Mechanik.)

ZOOL. REC.
[UK/0144-3607]
ZOOLOGICAL RECORD (LONDON).
(*Continues* Record of Zoological Literature.)

ENCYCLOPEDIAS AND GENERAL REFERENCE BOOKS

UK/0065-3896
AFRICA SOUTH OF THE SAHARA. [Afr. south Sahara]. **Added/Corp** Europa Publications Limited. (1971)-. Directory. English. an (October). $320.00. Europa Publications Ltd, 18 Bedford Square, London WC1B 3JN England. **Tel** 011 44 71 5808236, telex 21540 EUROPA G. **LC** DT351; .A37. **DD** 916.7. **NLM** DT 351 A258. **[CCC].**
Desc: Expert, informed essays on topics of concern to Africa as a whole, details on international and regional organizations active in Africa, and surveys and directories for each African nation. For each country, signed articles cover its physical and social geography, recent history, and economy. Following the articles are statistical surveys covering the country's agriculture, demographics, finance, external trade and other areas. Each country's directory section gives important names and addresses for social, cultural, political, and economic contacts.

US/0277-1373
AFRICANA DIRECTIONS. 81-1 (Sept. 1981)-. Periodical. English. ir. Free. Library of Congress / African and Middle Eastern Division, African Section, Washington DC 20540. **Tel** (202)287-5528. **LC** Z3503; .A368; DT348. **DD** 016.967. **Circ:** 1,500.

PL/0002-3787
AKTUALNE PROBLEMY INFORMACJI I DOKUMENTACJI. [Aktual. probl. inf. dok.]. **Added/Corp** Centralny Instytut Informacji Naukowo-Technicznej i Ekonomicznej (Poland). (1962)-. Periodical. Polish. Six times a year. $93.00 (latest edition). **(Subscription address:** ARS Polona, PO Box 1001, 00068 Warsaw Poland.**) LC** AG500; .A4. **CODEN** APDKAG. Documents available from Ask*IEEE. ***Continues*** *Aktualne Problemy Dokumentacji.*
Ind/Abst INSPEC (Sept.-Oct. 1969-); Libr. Inf. Sci. Abstr. (Sept.-Oct. 1969-).

AU
ALLEMEINE ENZYKLOPADIE DER WISSENSCHAFTEN UND KUNSTE. (19??)-. German. ir. S1380.00 each vol. Akademische Druck & Verlag, Neufeldweg 75, Postfach 598, A-8010 Graz Austria. **Tel** 011 43 316 41153.
Desc: Published in three sections, each with separate volume numbering.

US/0194-3766
ALLIED HEALTH EDUCATION DIRECTORY. **Added/Corp** American Medical Association. Committee on Allied Health Education and Accreditation. American Medical Association. 7th Ed. (1978)-. English. ir. $46.00. American Medical Association, 515 North State Street, Chicago IL 60610. **Tel** (312)464-5000, (800)262-2350, FAX (312)464-5831. **(Subscription address:** American Medical Association, PO Box 109050, Chicago IL 60610.**) ED** John Boberg. **LC** R847; .D57. **DD** 610/.7/1073. **NLM** W 22 AA1 D5. ***Continues*** *Allied Medical Education Directory, 0163-2590.*

US/0887-0519
ALMANAC OF THE 50 STATES. [Alm. 50 states]. **VFOAT** Almanac of the Fifty States. Vol. 1 (1985)-. English. an (March). $55.00 (cloth edition). Information Publications, 3790 El Camino Real/Suite 162, Palo Alto CA 94306. **Tel** (415)965-4449. **ED** E. R. Hornor. **LC** HA203; .A5. **DD** 317.3. **Bk Rev.** ctrl circ.
Desc: Contains an 8 page profile for each state in summary format with information in 13 categories.

UK/0083-9256
ALMANACK FOR THE YEAR OF OUR LORD ... (LONDON, ENGLAND). (AN ALMANACK FOR THE YEAR OF OUR LORD ... / BY JOSEPH WHITAKER.). **VFOAT** Whitaker's Almanack. (1869)-. Periodical. English. an. £25.00. J. Whitaker & Sons Ltd, 12 Dyott Street, London WC1A 1DF England. **Tel** 011 44 71 8368911, FAX 011 44 71 836 2909. **LC** AY754; .W5. **DD** 314.2. **NLM** AY 754 W577A. Index available. **Ad Acc. Circ:** 35,000.
Desc: Presents facts and figures concentrating on Great Britain and the rest of the world.

US/0883-7368
ALMANAKH UKRAINSKOHO NARODNOHO SOIUZU. (ALMANAKH UKRAINSKOHO NARODNOHO SOIUZU NA ...). **Added/Corp** Ukrainian National Association. **VFOAT** Ukrainska Zamorska Tverdynia; Almanakh; Almanakh UNS; Almanac of the Ukrainian National Association for the ... . (1968)-. Periodical. Ukrainian (English). an. Svoboda, 30 Montgomery Street, PO Box 346, Jersey City NJ 07302. **Tel** (201)434-0237. **LC** AY76; .K22. **DD** 057. ***Continues*** *Kalendar-Almanakh Ukrainskoho Narodnoho Soiuzu Na ... Rik (1966).*
Ind/Abst MLA Int. Bibl. Books Artic. Mod. Lang. Lit.

BL
ALMANAQUE ABRIL. (19??)-. Portuguese. an. Editora Abril SA, Rua do Curtume 769 Lapa, 05066 900 Sao Paulo SP Brazil. **Tel** 011 55 11 8239222, 011 55 11 2623322, FAX 011 55 11 8643796. **(Subscription address:** A C Cida, Comercial Guias 4 Ro, Rua Geraldo Flausino Gomes 61, CEP 04575 Sao Paulo Brazil.**) LC** AY624; .A53. **DD** 056/.9.

US
ALMANAQUE MUNDIAL. (19??)-. Spanish. an. $8.35 (latest edition). Editorial America SA, 6355 Northwest 36th Street, Miami FL 33166. **Tel** (305)871-6400. **(Subscription address:** Spanish Periodical & Book Sale, 10100 Northwest 25th Street, Miami FL 33172.**) LC** AY515; .A52. **DD** 056/.1.

US/0065-9959
AMERICAN REFERENCE BOOKS ANNUAL. [Am. ref. books annu.]. **VFOAT** ARBA. 1st Ed. (1970), 5th Ed. (1974), Vol 6 (1975)-. English. an. $90.00. Libraries Unlimited Inc., PO Box 6633, Department 920, Englewood CO 80155. **Tel** (800)237-6124. **ED** Bohdan S. Wynar and Anna Grace Patterson. **LC** Z1035.1; .A55. **DD** 011/.02. **NLM** Z 1035 A522. cum. index. **Bk Rev. Circ:** 2,000.
Desc: The only comprehensive review source for North American reference works, ARBA 90, through its authoritative reviews, continues to offer librarians a reference and acquisitions tool without parallel in an easy-to-use, reasonably priced package. The approximately 1,700 entries cover reference books published or distributed in the United States and Canada.
Ind/Abst Book Rev. Index; Leg. Inf. Manage. Index.

US/0196-0180
AMERICANA ANNUAL, THE. (THE AMERICANA ANNUAL; AN ENCYCLOPEDIA OF CURRENT EVENTS.). **VFOAT** Yearbook of the Encyclopedia Americana. (1923)-. English. an. Grolier Enterprises Inc, Sherman Turnpike, Danbury CT 06816. **Tel** (203)797-3500. **ED** A. H. McDannald and Others. **LC** AE5; .A55. **DD** 031. cum. index.

UK
AMERICAS REVIEW / WORLD OF INFORMATION, THE. **Added/Corp** World of Information (Firm). 11th Ed. (1990)-. English. an (Aug.). $109.00. Kogan Page Ltd., 120 Pentonville Road, London N1 9BR England. **Tel** 011 44 71 2780433, FAX 011 44 71 8376348, telex 263088 KOGAN G. **(Subscription address:** Kogan Page / North America Subscriptions, PO Box 830430, Birmingham AL 35283-0430.**) ED** Richard Green. **LC** HC121; .L2713. **DD** 330.97/0005. **Ad Acc. Circ:** 7,329. ***Continues*** *Latin America & Caribbean Review.*
Desc: A country-by-country review of Latin American and Caribbean economic trends, business opportunities and financial issues combined in one timely, informative source.
Ind/Abst Acad. Abstr. Full Text Elite (July 1993-); Acad. Search (July 1993-); Mag. Artic. Summar. Elite (Jan. 1993-); Mag. Artic. Summar. CD-ROM (July 1993-).

CN
ANNUAIRE DU CANADA. [Annu. Can.]. (1905)-. French. an. 65.00Can$ Canada; $72.00 US; $84.00 other. Statistics Canada, Publications Sales & Services, Main Building Room 1710, Ottawa Ontario K1A 0T6 Canada. **Tel** (613)951-5078, (800)267-6677, FAX (613)951-1584, telex 053-3585. **LC** HA744; .S82. **DD** 317.1. ***Continues*** *Annuaire Statistique du Canada, 0840-2590.*
Desc: Annual statistics of resources, demographics, economics situation and socials in Canada.

BL
ANUARIO DELTA. **VFOAT** Anuario Delta Universal. Portuguese. an. Editora Delta SA, Av Almirante Barroso, 63 - 260 Andar, Rio de Janeiro Brazil. **LC** AE37; .A55. **DD** 036/.9. ***Continues*** *Anuario Delta-Larousse.*

US
ARGONNE NEWS : ABOUT THE PEOPLE AND PROGRAMS OF ARGONNE NATIONAL LABORATORY. **Added/Corp** Argonne National Laboratory. Argonne National Laboratory. Office of Public Affairs. English. Argonne National Laboratory, 9700 South Cass Aveue, Argonne IL 60439. **Tel** (708)972-2000, FAX (708)972-5510.

US/1054-4070
ASSOCIATIONS YELLOW BOOK. (ASSOCIATIONS YELLOW BOOK : A PUBLICATION OF MONITOR PUBLISHING COMPANY.). [Assoc. yellow book]. Vol. 1, No. 1 (Summer 1991)-. Directory. English. sa. $180.00. Monitor Leadership Directories, 104 Fifth Avenue, Second Floor, New York NY 10011. **Tel** (212)627-4140, FAX (212)645-0931. **LC** HD2425; .A88. **DD** 061/.3/025. **[CCC].**
Desc: Provides information on over 40,000 officers, managers, professional staff and top administrators of the major trade and professional organizations in the U.S.

AT/1031-0541
AUSTRALIA AT A GLANCE. [Aust. glance]. **Added/Corp** Australian Bureau of Statistics. (1971)-. English. an. 2.00Aus$. Australian Bureau of Statistics, PO Box 10, Belconnen Australian Capital Territory, 2616 Australia. **Tel** 011 61 6 2527911, FAX 011 61 6 2516009. **DD** 319.4.
Desc: Condensed information about agriculture, foreign transactions, building, climate, demography, education, exchange rates, finance, health, labour force, mining, manufacturing, national accounts, price indexes, retail trade, tourist accommodation, transport, and earnings.

US/0199-3844
BAKER STREET MISCELLANEA. ***Ceased.*** **Added/Corp** Northeastern Illinois University. Advisory Committee on Popular Culture. Northeastern Illinois University. English Dept. No. 1, (April 1975)-(19??). Periodical. English. qt. Socialist Press, PO Box 2579, Chicago IL 60690. **LC** PAR.

US/0736-1122
BARNHART DICTIONARY COMPANION, THE. [Barnhart dict. companion]. **VFOAT** Dictionary Companion. Vol. 1, No. 1 (Jan. 1982). Periodical. English. Four times a year. $56.50 academic public & government libraries; $75.00 others. Lexik House Publishers, PO Box 247, Cold Spring NY 10516. **Tel** (914)265-2822, FAX (914)265-9018. **ED** David Barnhart. **LC** PE1630; .B28. **DD** 523/.05. **[CCC].** Index available. cum. index. **Bk Rev**, (Qty: 12). **Circ:** 1,000.
Desc: The only publication devoted to updating general dictionaries. Features new words and meanings not in current dictionaries, word usage and commentary, explanations of word formation and comprehensive classifications of usage features.
Ind/Abst Annu. Bibliogr. Engl. Lang. Lit.

CN/1184-2989
BOOK OF SPECIAL DAYS. [Book spec. days]. **Added/Corp** Canadian Association of Broadcasters. (1990)-. English. an (Published in Jan.). 165.00Can$. Canadian Association of Broadcasters, PO Box 627, Station A, Ottawa, Ontario K1P 5S2 Canada. **Tel** (613)233-4035. **DD** 902/.02. ***Continues*** *Special Days (Ottawa, Ont.), 0849-4851.*

US/0891-9607
BORGO REFERENCE GUIDES. (1990)-. Monographic series. English. ir. Price varies per volume. Borgo Press, PO Box 2845, San Bernardino CA 92406. **Tel** (714)884-5813, (714)885-1161. **ED** Michael Burgess.
Desc: Modern reference and information guides and indexes on current affairs and other topics of interest.

US/0068-1156
BRITANNICA BOOK OF THE YEAR. **VFOAT** Britannica World Data Annual. (1938)-. English. an. $37.95. Encyclopedia Britannica Inc, Britannica Centre, 310 South Michigan Avenue, Chicago IL 60604. **Tel** (312)347-7453, FAX (312)347-7914, (312)289-2178. **ED** Charles P. Trumbull. **LC** AE5; .E364. **DD** 030.2. **NLM** AE 5 E561. Index available (Indexed in each volume). cum. index (Partial ten-year). **Bk Rev**, (Qty: 100-125).
Desc: Provides up-to-date information on all aspects of human activity worldwide in the previous calendar year. Topics include every country in the world; economics and business, religion and social issues, science, medicine, technology, and engineering projects, literature and arts, and sports.

UK
BRITISH TAX ENCYCLOPEDIA. **See** Public Administration-Public Finance and Taxation.

US
BROWARD STREET ATLAS. (19??)-. English. $9.95. South Florida Map Co., 3930 North East 5th Avenue, Oakland Park FL 33334. **Tel** (305)568-5664.

AT
BUSINESS & STREET DIRECTORY FOR PERTH CITY & SUBURBS. **See** Business.

US/0068-5771
CALIFORNIA PUBLIC SCHOOL DIRECTORY. **Added/Corp** California. State Dept. of Education. (1970)-. English. an. $16.00. California State Department of Education, PO Box 944272, 721 Capitol Mall, Sacramento CA 94244. **Tel** (916)657-2451, (916)445-7608, FAX (916)657-3000. **(Subscription address:** California State Department of Education, PO Box 271, Sacramento CA 95812.**) LC** L903.C2; C28. **DD** 371/.01/025794. ***Continues*** *Directory of Administrative and Supervisory Personnel of California Public Schools.*

CN/0068-8142
CANADA YEARBOOK. (THE CANADA YEAR BOOK.). [Can. year b.]. **Added/Corp** Canada. Census and Statistics Office. Canada. Dominion Bureau of Statistics. Canada. Dominion Bureau of Statistics. General Statistics Branch. Canada. Dominion Bureau of Statistics. Information Services Division. Canada. Canada Year Book Section. Canada. Canada Year Book, Handbook and Library Division. Canada. Canada Year Book Division. Statistics Canada. (1905)-. English (French). be. 65.00Can$ Canada; $72.00 US; $84.00 other. Statistics Canada, Publications Sales & Services, Main Building Room 1710, Ottawa Ontario K1A 0T6 Canada. **Tel** (613)951-5078, (800)267-6677, FAX (613)951-1584, telex 053-3585. **ED** Jonina Wood, Margaret Smith and Chantal Prevost. **LC** HA744; .S81. **DD** 317.1. **NLM** HA 744 S81. Index available. **Bk Rev. Ad Acc. Circ:** 10,000 (ctrl). ***Continues*** *Statistical Year-Book of Canada for ... .*
Desc: Reference work giving textual and tabular

information on Canada's physical and natural resources, social and economic conditions, government organizations, industry, finance and legal system.

CN/0068-8193
CANADIAN ALMANAC & DIRECTORY. [Can. alm. dir.]. **VFOAT** Canadian Almanac and Directory. 101st Year (1948)-. Directory. English. an. $134.00. Gale Research Inc., 835 Penobscot Building, Detroit MI 48226. **Tel** (800)877-GALE, (313)961-2242, FAX (313)961-6083, telex TWX 810-221-7086. **ED** Susan Bracken. **DD** 971/.0025. available on microfiche from University Microfilms International (UMI); and Micromedia Limited. ***Continues*** *Canadian Almanac and Legal and Court Directory, 0316-277X.*
Desc: The standard authoritative reference enables users to answer virtually any question on Canada, either directly from the book itself or from any of the thousands of bodies listed in its directory.

●CN/1187-4570
CANADIAN GLOBAL ALMANAC, THE. [Can. glob. alm.]. (1992)-. English. an. 14.95Can$. Macmillan Canada, 29 Birch Avenue, Toronto Ontario M4V 1E2 Canada. **Tel** (416)963-8830, FAX (416)923-4821. **ED** John Robert Colombo. **DD** 031.02. Index available. **Circ:** 40,000. ***Continues*** *The Canadian World Almanac and Book of Facts., 0833-532X.*
Desc: Provides facts and figures about Canada and the world. Includes information on geography, history, population and economic statistics, arts and science news, current events, sports, and more.

●US/1045-4543
CAPTN. JACK'S TIDE AND ... CURRENT ALMANAC. **See** Naval Science, Navigation.

US/0732-6696
CATALOG SOURCES FOR CREATIVE PEOPLE, NEWS & UPDATES. Catalog. English. qt. Boyd's, PO Box 6232-ED, Augusta GA 30906. **Tel** (404)798-3157.

US/1043-8939
CITY & STATE DIRECTORIES IN PRINT. ***Ceased.*** [City state dir. print]. **VFOAT** City and State Directories in Print. (1989)-1st Edition (Sept. 1992). English. be. Gale Research Inc., 835 Penobscot Building, Detroit MI 48226. **Tel** (800)877-GALE, (313)961-2242, FAX (313)961-6083, telex TWX 810-221-7086. **ED** Julie E Towell and Charles B Montney. **LC** Z5771; .C54; AY2001. **DD** 015.73.
Desc: Detailed entries list 4,500 state, city and other local directories published in the US to cover hundreds of thousands of manufacturers, chambers of commerce, exporters, minority businesses, attorneys, banks, hospitals, parks and a wide range of other businesses, organizations, facilities and individuals.

●US/1053-0460
CLEARINGHOUSE DIRECTORY, THE. [Clgh. dir.]. (1992)-. Directory. English. be. $89.50. Gale Research Inc., 835 Penobscot Building, Detroit MI 48226. **Tel** (800)877-GALE, (313)961-2242, FAX (313)961-6083, telex TWX 810-221-7086. **ED** Donna Batten. **LC** Z674.5.U5; C54. **DD** 020/.25/73.
Desc: Valuable resource of relevant information specific to issues of current human interest and concern. Helps connect readers who need information with organizations dedicated to providing it. Over 600 entries include name, address, phone, services, resources and publications of clearinghouses with areas of diverse interest in education, senior citizens, homelessness, and nuclear safety. Important special features, such as bilingual staff, hotline and toll-free numbers, or services for the hearing impaired are noted.

MX
COLIBRI. **Added/Corp** Mexico. Direccion General de Publicaciones y Bibliotecas. **VFOAT** Enciclopedia Infantil Colibri. (1979)-. Spanish. wk. Salvat Mexicana de Ediciones for Direccion General de Publicaciones y Bibliotecas, Mariano Escobedo No 438-20 Piso, Mexico Mexico. **LC** Discard.

●US
COMMERCIAL LIBRARY PUBLICATIONS LIST / UNITED STATES DEPARTMENT OF STATE LIBRARY. **Added/Corp** United States. Dept. of State. Library. United States. Dept. of State. Office of Information Services. **VFOAT** Publications List; Department of State Library Commercial Library Program, Publications List. (1991-1992)-. English. Office of Reports and Information Services, Securities and Exchange Commission, Washington DC 20549.

US/0191-1422
CONGRESSIONAL YELLOW BOOK (QUARTERLY ED.). (CONGRESSIONAL YELLOW BOOK.). [Congr. yellow book]. **VFOAT** CYB; Washington Monitor's Congressional Yellow Book. (1976)-. Directory. English. qt. $235.00. Monitor Leadership Directories, 104 Fifth Avenue, Second Floor, New York NY 10011. **Tel** (212)627-4140, FAX (212)645-0931. **ED** Jodi Scheiber. **LC** JK1083; .B55. **DD** 328.73/0761/025. **NLM** JK 1083; C749. **[CCC].** Index available. **Circ:** 12,500. ***Continues*** *Bimonthly Directory of Key Congressional Aides, 0099-1376.*
Desc: Complete listings, including all U.S. Senators and Representatives, their staffs, committees and sub committees and their staffs, with titles and addresses. Maps giving district boundaries and congressional delegations; zip code by congressional district and top staff in congressional support agencies are also included.

●US
CONTINUING MEDICAL EDUCATION DIRECTORY / AMERICAN MEDICAL ASSOCIATION. **Added/Corp** American Medical Association. (1993)-. Directory. English. an. $49.00 (nonmember), $36.00 (member of AMA). American Medical Association, 515 North State Street, Chicago IL 60610. **Tel** (312)464-5000, (800)262-2350, FAX (312)464-5831. **NLM** W 22; AA1 C75.

IT
CONTINUITA E SCUOLA. Italian. Five times a year. L50000.00 Italy; L100000.00 other. Salvatore Sciascia Editore, Corso Unmerto 111, 93100 Caltanissetta Italy. **Tel** 011 39 934 551509.

●US/1058-2908
CORPORATE YELLOW BOOK. (CORPORATE YELLOW BOOK : WHO'S WHO AT THE LEADING LISTED U.S. COMPANIES.). [Corp. yellow book]. Vol. 8, No. 1 (Winter 1992)-. Directory. English. qt. $235.00. Monitor Leadership Directories, 104 Fifth Avenue, Second Floor, New York NY 10011. **Tel** (212)627-4140, FAX (212)645-0931. **LC** HG4057; .A15646. **DD** 338.7/4/02573. **[CCC].** Index available. ***Continues*** *Corporate 1000 Yellow Book, 1049-7943.*
Desc: Provides listings of names, titles, addresses, facsimile and telephone numbers of over 40,000 executives who run America's leading corporations. Four indexes include directory entries by state, industry type, individual name or executive and by company subsidiary.

CN/0823-1133
CORPUS ALMANAC & CANADIAN SOURCEBOOK. [Corpus alm. Can. sourceb.]. **Added/Corp** Corpus Information Services. **VFOAT** Corpus Almanac and Canadian Sourcebook. **VAT** Corpus almanac and Canadian sourcebook. 18th Ed. (1983)-. English. an. 157.50Can$. Southam Information and Technology Group Inc., 1450 Don Mills Road, Don Mills Ontario M3B 2X7 Canada. **Tel** (416)445-6641, (800)668-2374, FAX (416)442-2261. **ED** Gordon Sova. **LC** F1004.7; .M3. **DD** 971/.0025. **Circ:** 5,000. ***Continues*** *Corpus Almanac of Canada, 0315-7083.*
Desc: Covers a range of Canadian topics from astronomy to a review of the economy, with special attention to government (federal, provincial and municipal governments are listed).

US/1058-3734
COUNTRY ALMANAC (NEW YORK, N.Y.). (COUNTRY ALMANAC.). [Ctry. alm.]. (1982)-. Periodical. English. qt. $14.97 (two year). Harris Publications, 1115 Broadway/8th Floor, New York NY 10010. **Tel** (212)807-7100. **DD** 747.

US
COURIER PLUS. English. ir. University Microfilms International, 300 North Zeeb Road, Ann Arbor MI 48106-1346. **Tel** (313)761-4700, (800)521-0600 Exts. 2490, 2491, FAX (313)973-1540.
Desc: Online service containing indexing and abstracts for 350 general interest periodicals and 25 national, international and regional newspapers. CD-ROM products containing information from Courier Plus include Periodical Abstracts Ondisc, Newspapers Abstracts Ondisc and Resource One.

US
CRITICAL GUIDE TO CATHOLIC REFERENCE BOOKS. **See** Religion and Theology-Catholicism.

UK/0070-1602
CRONER'S REFERENCE BOOK FOR IMPORTERS. **See** Business-Commerce.

US
CRUSADER'S ALMANAC, THE. Periodical. English. Crusader's Almanac, 1400 Quincy Street NE, Washington DC 20017.

UK
CURRENT EUROPEAN DIRECTORIES. (1969)-. Periodical. English. ir. price varies per issue. CBD Research Ltd, 15 Wickham Road, Beckenham Kent BR3 2JS England. **Tel** 011 44 81 6507745, FAX 011 44 81 6500768. **ED** G. P. Henderson. **DD** 940.
Desc: A guide to international, national, city and specialised directories and similar reference works for all countries of continental Europe.

US
DADE STREET ATLAS. (19??)-. English. $9.95. South Florida Map Co., 3930 North East 5th Avenue, Oakland Park FL 33334. **Tel** (305)568-5664.

AT/0813-4057
DAWSON'S LOCAL PINK PAGES. BANKSTOWN. **VFOAT** Bankstown Pink Pages. (1984)-. English. an. Dawson Publications Pty Ltd., PO Box 173 Frenchs Forest, New South Wales 2087 Australia. **Tel** 011 61 2 452-1999, FAX 011 61 2 975-2316.

AT/0812-1176
DAWSON'S LOCAL PINK PAGES. BLACKTOWN. **VFOAT** Blacktown Pink Pages. (1983)-. English. an. Dawson Publications Pty Ltd., PO Box 173 Frenchs Forest, New South Wales 2087 Australia. **Tel** 011 61 2 452-1999, FAX 011 61 2 975-2316.

AT/1034-4888
DAWSON'S LOCAL PINK PAGES. BRISBANE WATERS. **VFOAT** Brisbane Waters Pink Pages. (1985)-. English. an. Dawson Publications Pty Ltd., PO Box 173 Frenchs Forest, New South Wales 2087 Australia. **Tel** 011 61 2 452-1999, FAX 011 61 2 975-2316.

AT/0813-4049
DAWSON'S LOCAL PINK PAGES. CRONULLA-SUTHERLAND. **VFOAT** Cronulla-Sutherland Pink Pages. (1984)-. English. an. Dawson Publications Pty Ltd., PO Box 173 Frenchs Forest, New South Wales 2087 Australia. **Tel** 011 61 2 452-1999, FAX 011 61 2 975-2316.

AT/0810-4670
DAWSON'S LOCAL PINK PAGES. EASTERN SUBURBS. **VFOAT** Eastern Suburbs Pink Pages. (1983)-. English. an. Dawson Publications Pty Ltd., PO Box 173 Frenchs Forest, New South Wales 2087 Australia. **Tel** 011 61 2 452-1999, FAX 011 61 2 975-2316.

AT/0812-5643
DAWSON'S LOCAL PINK PAGES. FAIRFIELD. **VFOAT** Fairfield Pink Pages. (1984)-. English. an. Dawson Publications Pty Ltd., PO Box 173 Frenchs Forest, New South Wales 2087 Australia. **Tel** 011 61 2 452-1999, FAX 011 61 2 975-2316.

AT/0810-2643
DAWSONS LOCAL PINK PAGES. HILLS DISTRICT. [Dawsons local pink pages, Hills dist.]. (1982)-. English. an. Dawson Publications Pty Ltd., PO Box 173 Frenchs Forest, New South Wales 2087 Australia. **Tel** 011 61 2 452-1999, FAX 011 61 2 975-2316. **DD** 919.4410025. ***Continues*** *Dawsons Local Directory Covering the Parramatta and Hills District.*

AT/0811-479X
DAWSON'S LOCAL PINK PAGES. KU-RING-GAI. **VFOAT** Ku-Ring-Gai Pink Pages. (1983)-. English. an. Dawson Publications Pty Ltd., PO Box 173 Frenchs Forest, New South Wales 2087 Australia. **Tel** 011 61 2 452-1999, FAX 011 61 2 975-2316.

AT/0811-7276
DAWSON'S LOCAL PINK PAGES. LIVERPOOL. **VFOAT** Liverpool Pink Pages. (1983)-. English. an. Dawson Publications Pty Ltd., PO Box 173 Frenchs Forest, New South Wales 2087 Australia. **Tel** 011 61 2 452-1999, FAX 011 61 2 975-2316.

AT/0811-0360
DAWSON'S LOCAL PINK PAGES. LOWER NORTH SHORE. **VFOAT** Lower North Shore Pink Pages. (1983)-. English. an. Dawson Publications Pty Ltd., PO Box 173 Frenchs Forest, New South Wales 2087 Australia. **Tel** 011 61 2 452-1999, FAX 011 61 2 975-2316.

AT/1034-4896
DAWSON'S LOCAL PINK PAGES. MACARTHUR. **VFOAT** Macarthur Pink Pages. (198?)-. English. an. Dawson Publications Pty Ltd., PO Box 173 Frenchs Forest, New South Wales 2087 Australia. **Tel** 011 61 2 452-1999, FAX 011 61 2 975-2316.

AT/0812-7050
DAWSON'S LOCAL PINK PAGES. MANLY-WARRINGAH. **VFOAT** Manly-Warringah Pink Pages. (1982)-. English. an. Dawson Publications Pty Ltd., PO Box 173 Frenchs Forest, New South Wales 2087 Australia. **Tel** 011 61 2 452-1999, FAX 011 61 2 975-2316.

AT/1034-4918
DAWSON'S LOCAL PINK PAGES. NEWCASTLE. **VFOAT** Newcastle Pink Pages. (1985)-. English. an. Dawson Publications Pty Ltd., PO Box 173 Frenchs Forest, New South Wales 2087 Australia. **Tel** 011 61 2 452-1999, FAX 011 61 2 975-2316.

AT/0810-4689
DAWSON'S LOCAL PINK PAGES. NORTHERN DISTRICTS. **VFOAT** Northern Districts Pink Pages. (1983)-. English. an. Dawson

Publications Pty Ltd., PO Box 173 Frenchs Forest, New South Wales 2087 Australia. **Tel** 011 61 2 452-1999, FAX 011 61 2 975-2316.

AT/0813-4030
DAWSON'S LOCAL PINK PAGES. PARRAMATTA AND HOLROYD. **VFOAT** Parramatta and Holroyd Pink Pages. (1984)-. English. an. Dawson Publications Pty Ltd., PO Box 173 Frenchs Forest, New South Wales 2087 Australia. **Tel** 011 61 2 452-1999, FAX 011 61 2 975-2316.

AT/0814-1770
DAWSON'S LOCAL PINK PAGES. PENRITH AND LOWER BLUE MOUNTAINS. **VFOAT** Penrith and Lower Blue Mountains Pink Pages. (1985)-. English. an. Dawson Publications Pty Ltd., PO Box 173 Frenchs Forest, New South Wales 2087 Australia. **Tel** 011 61 2 452-1999, FAX 011 61 2 975-2316.

AT/0810-2465
DAWSONS LOCAL PINK PAGES. RYDE, HUNTERS HILL. [Dawsons local pink pages, Ryde Hunters Hill]. (1982)-. English. an. Dawson Publications Pty Ltd., PO Box 173 Frenchs Forest, New South Wales 2087 Australia. **Tel** 011 61 2 452-1999, FAX 011 61 2 975-2316. **DD** 919.4410025. ***Continues*** *Dawsons Everyday Directory Covering the Ryde Municipality, 0726-6871.*

AT/1034-490X
DAWSON'S LOCAL PINK PAGES. ST. GEORGE. **VFOAT** St. George Pink Pages. (1984)-. English. an. Dawson Publications Pty Ltd., PO Box 173 Frenchs Forest, New South Wales 2087 Australia. **Tel** 011 61 2 452-1999, FAX 011 61 2 975-2316.

AT/1034-4926
DAWSON'S LOCAL PINK PAGES. WOLLONGONG. **VFOAT** Wollongong Pink Pages. (1986)-. English. an. Dawson Publications Pty Ltd., PO Box 173 Frenchs Forest, New South Wales 2087 Australia. **Tel** 011 61 2 452-1999, FAX 011 61 2 975-2316.

GW
DEUTSCHES WOERTERBUCH. (19??)-. German. ir. Price varies per volume. S. Hirzel Verlag Stuttgart, Postfach 101061, D 70009 Stuttgart Germany. **Tel** 011 49 711 25820, FAX 0711/2582 290, telex 723636 daz d.

US/0270-3750
DICTIONARY ENCYCLOPEDIA HANDBOOK REVIEW. [Dict. encycl. handb. rev.]. Vol. 1, No. 1 (Spring 1981)-. English. sa. $5.00. Translation Research Institute, 5914 Pulaski Avenue, Philadelphia PA 19144. **LC** Z5848; .D53; AE5. **DD** 016.031.

US/0270-7543
DIRECTORS ENCYCLOPEDIA OF NEWSPAPERS, THE. English. an. Poston & Poston, 13940 North Dale Mabry, Tampa FL 33618. **LC** Z6951; .D58; PN4867. **DD** 071/.3025.

US
DIRECTORY OF OFFICIALS AND STAFF / AMERICAN MEDICAL ASSOCIATION. **Main/Corp** American Medical Association. **VFOAT** AMA Directory, Directory of Officials and Staff. (1990)-. English. an (Dec.). $42.00 (nonmember), $21.00 (member of AMA). American Medical Association, 515 North State Street, Chicago IL 60610. **Tel** (312)464-5000, (800)262-2350, FAX (312)464-5831. ***Continues*** *American Medical Association. AMA Directory of Officials and Staff.*

●US
DIRECTORY OF PHYSICIANS IN THE UNITED STATES / AMERICAN MEDICAL ASSOCIATION. **Added/Corp** American Medical Association. American Medical Association. Survey & Data Resources. 33rd Ed. (1992)-. Directory. English. ir. $545.00. American Medical Association, 515 North State Street, Chicago IL 60610. **Tel** (312)464-5000, (800)262-2350, FAX (312)464-5831. **(Subscription address:** American Medical Association, PO Box 109050, Chicago IL 60610.**)** **DD** 610/.25/73. **NLM** W 22; AA1 A512. available on CD-ROM from the publisher. ***Continues*** *American Medical Directory, 0065-9339.*

US
DIRECTORY OF POETRY PUBLISHERS. **See** Literature-Poetry.

SA
DIRECTORY OF SOUTH AFRICAN ASSOCIATIONS. Directory. English (Afrikaans). R160.00. Directory of South African Associations, PO Box 395, Pretoria 0001 South Africa. **Tel** 27-12-8414408, FAX 27-12-862869. **ED** Ingrid de Bont. **Circ:** 800. available on an online database.
Desc: Comprehensive listing of associations in South Africa with contact addresses, telephone and FAX numbers, publications, major conferences, and library collections.

US/0196-6545
DIRECTORY OF THE AMERICAN PSYCHOLOGICAL ASSOCIATION (1978). (DIRECTORY OF THE AMERICAN PSYCHOLOGICAL ASSOCIATION.). [Dir. Am. Psychol. Assoc.]. **Main/Corp** American Psychological Association. **VFOAT** Directory. (1978)-. English. ir. $50.00 (members), $70.00 (nonmembers). American Psychological Association, 750 First Street Northeast, Washington DC 20002. **Tel** (800)374-2721, (202)336-5600, (subscriptions - (202)336-5600. **(Subscription address:** American Psychological Association, Order Department, PO Box 2710, Hyattsville MD 20784.**)** **LC** BF11; .A67. **DD** 150/.25/73. **NLM** BF 11 A51D. **Ad Acc. Circ:** 10,000. ***Continues*** *American Psychological Association. Biographical Directory of the American Psychological Association, 0090-9076.*
Desc: Lists the names and addresses of American Psychological Association members, with home and office phone numbers, current major fields, areas of specialization, licensure as a psychologist, ABPP and ABPH diplomat status.

IT
DIZIONARIO ENCICLOPEDICO D'INFORMAZIONI, IL. 1977-. Italian. an. Rusconi Editori Spa, Via Vitruvio 43, 20124 Milan Italy. **Tel** 02/6964. **LC** AG35; .D47. **DD** 035/.1.

●UK/0962-1040
EASTERN EUROPE AND THE COMMONWEALTH OF INDEPENDENT STATES. **Added/Corp** Europa Publications Limited. 1st Ed. (1992)-. English. an. $390.00. Europa Publications Ltd, 18 Bedford Square, London WC1B 3JN England. **Tel** 011 44 71 5808236, telex 21540 EUROPA G. **(Subscription address:** Gale Research Co., 835 Penobscot Building, Detroit MI 48226.**)** **LC** HC244.A1; E29. **DD** 330.947/005.
Desc: Expert essays, directory, statistical and political profile sections help to put this volatile region into perspective.

NE
EMTREE THESAURUS. **Added/Corp** Excerpta Medica (Firm). **VFOAT** EMBASE EMTREE Thesaurus; EMBASE EMTREE. (1991)-. English. Eleven times a year. $121.00. Excerpta Medica Publishing Group, PO Box 548, 1000 AM Amsterdam Netherlands. **Tel** 011 31 20 5803243.

SP
ENCICLOPEDIA UNIVERSAL ILUSTRADA EUROPEO-AMERICANA. SUPLEMENTO ANUAL. **VFOAT** Suplemento Anual. (1934)-. Spanish. **LC** AE61; .E6 Suppl.

US/0071-0202
ENCYCLOPEDIA OF ASSOCIATIONS. [Encycl. assoc.]. **Added/Corp** Gale Research Company. 3rd. Ed. (1961)-. English. an. $375.00. Gale Research Inc., 835 Penobscot Building, Detroit MI 48226. **Tel** (800)877-GALE, (313)961-2242, FAX (313)961-6083, telex TWX 810-221-7086. **ED** Carol A. Schwartz. **LC** AS22; .E5. **DD** 060. **NLM** HD 2425 E56. cum. index. available on CD-ROM; available on diskette; available on magnetic tape; available on an online database (file 114/Full-Text) from DIALOG. ***Continues*** *Encyclopedia of American Associations, 0190-3071.* ***Continued in part by*** *Encyclopedia of Associations. International Organizations, 1041-0023.*
Desc: Entries offer, when available, complete name, address and phone number together with the primary official's name and title, fax number, founding date, purpose, activities and dues, national and international conferences and more.
Ind/Abst Curr. Lit. Fam. Plan.

US/1070-2318
ENCYCLOPEDIA OF ASSOCIATIONS CD-ROM. (ENCYCLOPEDIA OF ASSOCIATIONS CD-ROM [COMPUTER FILE].). [Encycl. assoc. CD-ROM]. **Added/Corp** Gale Research Inc. **VFOAT** Encyclopedia of Associations. (199?)-. English. an. Gale Research Inc., 835 Penobscot Building, Detroit MI 48226. **Tel** (800)877-GALE, (313)961-2242, FAX (313)961-6083, telex TWX 810-221-7086. **LC** AS2. **DD** 060. ***Continues*** *Gale Global Access. Associations, 1065-5050.*
Desc: Contains descriptions of national organizations of the United States, international organizations, regional, state and local organizations and supplements. Coverage includes trade and professional associations, national organizations of the United States and other countries, social welfare and public affairs organizations, religious, and sports and hobby groups.

US/1041-0023
ENCYCLOPEDIA OF ASSOCIATIONS. INTERNATIONAL ORGANIZATIONS. [Encycl. assoc., Int. organ.]. **Added/Corp** Gale Research Inc. **VFOAT** International Organizations. 23rd Ed. (1989)-. English. sa. $475.00. Gale Research Inc., 835 Penobscot Building, Detroit MI 48226. **Tel** (800)877-GALE, (313)961-2242, FAX (313)961-6083, telex TWX 810-221-7086. **ED** Grant Eldridge. **LC** AS8; .E53. **DD** 060. ***Separated from*** *Encyclopedia of Associations, 0071-0202.*
Desc: List over 13,500 international organizations. Gives organizations with international memberships, binational organizations, and national organizations in more than 180 countries of the world. Detailed entries furnish each association's full name, address, executive, and other contact information. Additional information includes budgets, publications, meeting and convention dates and locations, scope and purpose, and other facts helpful in matching your information needs to the appropriate organization.

UK
ENCYCLOPEDIA OF FORMS AND PRECEDENTS OTHER THAN COURT FORMS. English. Butterworth & Co. Ltd. / Kent, England, Borough Green, Sevenoaks Kent TN15 8PH England. **Tel** 011 44 732-884567, FAX 011 44 732-885996. **(Subscription address:** Butterworth Heinemann Publishers, 225 Wildwood Avenue, Unit B, Woburn MA 01801.**)**

UK
ENCYCLOPEDIA OF VALUE ADDED TAX. ***Ceased.*** (19??)-(Dec. 1993). English. Sweet & Maxwell Ltd., South Quay Plaza, 183 Marsh Wall, London E14 9FT England. **Tel** 011 44 264 342899, FAX 011 44 264 342723, telex 929089 ITPINF G.
Desc: This loose-leaf reference work draws together all the relevant sources which make up VAT law.

GW/0304-0089
ENCYCLOPEDIA OF WORLD PROBLEMS AND HUMAN POTENTIAL / EDITED BY UNION OF INTERNATIONAL ASSOCIATIONS. **Added/Corp** Union of International Associations. **VFOAT** World Problems and Human Potential; World Problems & Human Potential. 2nd Ed. (1986)-. English. ir. $575.00. K.G. Saur Verlag KG, A Reed Reference Publishing Company, Part of Reed International PLC, Ortlerstrasse 8, D 81373 Munich Germany. **Tel** 011 49 89 769020, FAX 011 49 89 76902150, telex 5212067-SAUR-D. **LC** AS2.5; .Y4. **DD** 050. Index available. **Circ:** 3,000. ***Continues*** *Year-Book of World Problems and Human Potential, 0304-0089.*
Desc: A sourcebook of over 4,700 recognized world problems. Describes ways in which these problems interconnect, and identifies the organizational human resources that can analyze, challenge, and ultimately resolve them.

●UK
ENVIRONMENT ENCYCLOPEDIA AND DIRECTORY, THE. (1994)-. English. an. $325.00. Europa Publications Ltd, 18 Bedford Square, London WC1B 3JN England. **Tel** 011 44 71 5808236, telex 21540 EUROPA G. **(Subscription address:** Gale Research Co., 835 Penobscot Building, Detroit MI 48226.**)**
Desc: Details the global movement to protect the environment.

GW
ENZYKLOPAEDIE DES MAERCHENS. **See** Folklore.

●UK
EUROPEAN COMMUNITIES ENCYCLOPEDIA & DIRECTORY. (1992)-. English. sa. $325.00. Europa Publications Ltd, 18 Bedford Square, London WC1B 3JN England. **Tel** 011 44 71 5808236, telex 21540 EUROPA G. **(Subscription address:** Gale Research Co., 835 Penobscot Building, Detroit MI 48226.**)** **LC** HC241.2; .E8334. **DD** 341.24/22/05.
Desc: Statistics, essays, and information on the European Communities.

GW
FACHWORTERBUCHER UND LEXIKA. **VFOAT** International Bibliography of Dictionaries. (Aug. 5, 1972)-. German (English). ir. K.G. Saur Verlag KG, A Reed Reference Publishing Company, Part of Reed International PLC, Ortlerstrasse 8, D 81373 Munich Germany. **Tel** 011 49 89 769020, FAX 011 49 89 76902150, telex 5212067-SAUR-D. **(Subscription address:** 175 Fifth Avenue, New York, NY 10010**)** **LC** Z7004.D5; F33. ***Continues*** *Technik, Wissenschaft und Wirtschaft in Fremden Sprachen; Techniques, Science and Economics in Foreign Languages.*

UK/0071-3791
FAR EAST AND AUSTRALASIA, THE. **Added/Corp** Europa Publications Limited. (1969)-. English. an. $360.00. Europa Publications Ltd, 18 Bedford Square, London WC1B 3JN England. **Tel** 011 44 71 5808236, telex 21540 EUROPA G. **(Subscription address:** Gale Research Co., 835 Penobscot Building, Detroit MI 48226.**)** **LC** DS1; .F3. **DD** 950/.05. **NLM** DS 5 F219.
Desc: Survey and reference book providing the latest facts and figures on all the countries and territories of East Asia, Southeast Asia, Australasia and the Pacific Islands. Gives basic reference material and specialist essays on such topics as development problems of Asia, major commodities of Asia and the Pacific, and the religions of Asia. Includes background essays, statistical surveys and a directory of essential names and addresses.

●US/1061-3153
FEDERAL REGIONAL YELLOW BOOK. (FEDERAL REGIONAL YELLOW BOOK : WHO'S WHO IN THE FEDERAL GOVERNMENT'S DEPARTMENTS, AGENCIES, COURTS, MILITARY INSTALLATIONS, AND SERVICE ACADEMIES OUTSIDE OF WASHINGTON, DC.). [Fed. reg. yellow book]. **VFOAT** Yellow Book. (Winter 1993)-. Directory. English. sa. $180.00. Monitor Leadership Directories, 104 Fifth Avenue, Second Floor, New York NY 10011. **Tel** (212)627-4140, FAX (212)645-0931. **ED** Debra Mayberry. **LC** JK6; .F425. **DD** 353.04/025. Index available. **Circ:** 1000.
Desc: Identifies key federal decision-makers at departments and agencies, courts, military installations and service academies outside of Washington, D.C. Provides titles, addresses, telephone and facsimile numbers. Three indexes organized by key words, locations and names.

US/0145-6202
FEDERAL YELLOW BOOK. **VFOAT** Yellow Book; Washington Monitor's Federal Yellow Book. (1976)-. Directory. English. qt. $235.00. Monitor Leadership Directories, 104 Fifth Avenue, Second Floor, New York NY 10011. **Tel** (212)627-4140, FAX (212)645-0931. **ED** Mary Forschler. **LC** JK6; .F45. **DD** 353/.00025. **NLM** JK 6 F293. **[CCC]. Circ:** 11,000.
Desc: Lists over 35,000 top level decision-makers in the White House, the Executive Office of the President, the O.M.B. and in the federal departments and agencies, including regional offices. Complete with telephone numbers, titles and mailing addresses.

●US/1058-2878
FINANCIAL YELLOW BOOK. [Financ. yellow book]. **Added/Corp** Monitor Publishing Company. **VFOAT** Yellow Book. Vol. 5, No. 1 (Winter 1992)-. Directory. English. sa. $180.00. Monitor Leadership Directories, 104 Fifth Avenue, Second Floor, New York NY 10011. **Tel** (212)627-4140, FAX (212)645-0931. **LC** HG65; .F52. **DD** 332. **[CCC]**. Index available. ***Continues*** *Financial 1000 Yellow Book, 1049-7935.*
Desc: Provides listings of names, titles, addresses, facsimile and telephone numbers of over 35,000 executives who run America's financial institutions. Five indexes organized by executive name, state location, financial service segment, parent company and a master index of financial institutions by organization.

US/1051-242X
FLORIDA MUNICIPAL PROFILES. [Fla. munic. profiles]. (1991)-. English. ir. $57.00 (latest edition). Information Publications, 3790 El Camino Real/Suite 162, Palo Alto CA 94306. **Tel** (415)965-4449. **ED** Louise L. Hornor. **LC** HA311; .F547. **DD** 317.59/05. available on diskette.
Desc: Contains a one-page profile on every county and municipality in state of Florida, including demographics, finance, school information, local officials, registered voters, and public safety information.

UK
GEIRIADUR PRIFYSGOL CYMRU. Multiple languages. £2.00. University of Wales Press, 6 Gwennyth Street, Cathays Cardiff CF2 4YD Wales United Kingdom. **Tel** 011 44 222 231919. **(Subscription address:** University of Wales Press, Freepost, Cardiff CF1 1YZ United Kingdom**) ED** Gareth A Beran. **Circ:** 1,500.

US
GOODE'S WORLD ATLAS. (19??)-. English. ir. $29.95. Rand McNally & Company, PO Box 32, Skokie IL 60076. **Tel** (708)673-0813, (800)444-4062. Index available (includes "pronouncing" index).
Desc: Includes 55 world thematic maps, large-scale maps of major world cities, and geographic tables.

US/0072-5188
GOVERNMENT REFERENCE BOOKS. **See** Public Administration.

●US
GRADUATE MEDICAL EDUCATION DIRECTORY. **Added/Corp** American Medical Association. Accreditation Council for Graduate Medical Education (U.S.). (1994)-. Directory. English. an. $54.00 (nonmember), $48.00 (member of AMA). American Medical Association, 515 North State Street, Chicago IL 60610. **Tel** (312)464-5000, (800)262-2350, FAX (312)464-5831. **(Subscription address:** American Medical Association, PO Box 109050, Chicago IL 60610.**) NLM** WX 22; AA1 D595. ***Continues*** *Directory of Graduate Medical Education Programs, 0892-0109.*

UK/0261-572X
GRAMPIAN DIRECTORY. [Grampian dir.]. (1981)-. English. an. £7.50. Grampian Regional Council, Economic Development and Planning Dept, Woodhill House Westburn Road, Aberdeen AB9 2LU Scotland. **Tel** 11 44 224 643322, FAX 0224 697445, telex 739277. **DD** 380.10254121. **Ad Acc. Circ:** 9,000. ***Formed by the union of*** *Offshore Directory* ***and*** *Manufacturers & Processors Directory - North East Scotland Development Authority.*

US/0072-7288
GREAT IDEAS TODAY, THE. (GREAT IDEAS TODAY.). (1961)-. English. an. $28.95. Encyclopedia Britannica Inc, Britannica Centre, 310 South Michigan Avenue, Chicago IL 60604. **Tel** (312)347-7453, FAX (312)347-7914, (312)289-2178. **ED** Mortimer J. Adler and John Van Doren. **LC** AY59; .G7. **DD** 909.82082. (Every ten years). cum. index.
Desc: Reviews intellectual developments of significance throughout the world and presents ideas of the Western tradition in their contemporary aspect. Each issue offers essays on the arts and sciences, commentaries on authors of the great books, and reprints of worthwhile books and essays.

US/0271-9509
GREENWOOD ENCYCLOPEDIA OF AMERICAN INSTITUTIONS, THE. [Greenwood encycl. Am. inst.]. (1977)-. Monographic series. English. ir. Price varies per volume. Greenwood Press Inc., PO Box 5007, Westport CT 06881-5007. **Tel** (203)226-3571, FAX (203)222-1502.

US/0533-5248
GUIDE TO AMERICAN DIRECTORIES. 4th Edition (1960)-. English. ir. $85.00. B. Klein Publications, PO Box 8503, Coral Springs FL 33065. **Tel** (305)752-1708, FAX (305)752-2547. **ED** Barry Klein and Bernard Klein. Index available. cum. index. **Bk Rev.** available on labels. ***Continues*** *Guide to American Directories for Compiling Mailing Lists.*
Desc: List the classifications of business, industry, and professions. Contains 9,000 directories of virtually every conceivable kind and tells you who publishes directories in any given field of endeavor, describes their contents, frequency of publication and its cost, if any.

US
GUIDE TO INTERNATIONAL SUBSCRIPTION AGENCIES. English. $95.00. Direct International Inc, 1501 3rd Avenue, New York NY 10028. **Tel** (212)861-4188, FAX (212)988-3537, telex 237818SVP.
Desc: In-depth information on agencies eager to help you boost sales in foreign markets. It also addresses many agencies to contact if you want to broaden your worldwide coverage.

US/1057-4557
GUINNESS BOOK OF RECORDS (NEW YORK, N.Y.). (THE GUINNESS BOOK OF RECORDS. [HARDCOVER]). [Guinness book rec.]. (1991)-. English. an. $22.95. Facts on File Publications, 460 Park Avenue South, New York NY 10016. **Tel** (212)683-2244, (800)322-8755, FAX (212)683-3633, telex 238 552 FACTS UR. **ED** Mark Young. **LC** AG243; .G87. **DD** 031. **Circ:** 450,000. ***Continues*** *Guinness Book of World Records, 0072-9000.*

US
GUINNESS DISC OF RECORDS [COMPUTER FILE], THE. ***Ceased.*** (19??)-(19??). English. Comptons Newmedia, 722 Genevieve, Suite M, Solana Beach CA 92075. **Tel** (800)532-3766, (415)597-5555. **LC** AG243; .G96.
Desc: System requirements: IBM PC, PS/2 or compatible; 640K RAM; CD-ROM player with external audio-out socket; external speakers or headphones; MS-DOS 3.1 or higher; CD-ROM extensions; VGA monitor; mouse, and Microsoft Windows 3.0 recommended.

US
HANDBOOK OF INTERNATIONAL DOCUMENTATION AND INFORMATION. Monographic series. English. Price varies per volume. K.G. Saur Verlag KG, A Reed Reference Publishing Company, Part of Reed International PLC, Ortlerstrasse 8, D 81373 Munich Germany. **Tel** 011 49 89 769020, FAX 011 49 89 76902150, telex 5212067-SAUR-D. **(Subscription address:** 175 Fifth Avenue, New York, NY 10010**)** ***Continues*** *Handbuch der Internationalen Dokumentation und Information.*
Desc: A very varied series of titles, mostly reference, information science or encyclopedia format and orientation.

US
HILL COUNTRY ALMANAC. Vol. 1, No. 1 (Winter 1991)-. English. **LC** WMLC 91/3324.

AT/1038-6424
HISTORICAL MICROFICHE SERIES. **VFOAT** Statistical Publications Since Federation. (1984)-. English. ir. 16000.00Aus$. Australian Bureau of Statistics, PO Box 10, Belconnen Australian Capital Territory, 2616 Australia. **Tel** 011 61 6 2527911, FAX 011 61 6 2516009.
Desc: Contains publications released by the Central Office of the ABS.

CN/0841-2200
HRVATSKI GODNISNJAK ZA GODINU. [Hrvat. god. god.]. (1982)-. Serbo-Croatian (Roman). an. $3.00 per vol. Hrvatski Glas, PO Box 596, Nanaimo British Columbia V9R 5LS Canada. **DD** 057/.82.

TU
HURRIYET INSANLAR, OLAYLAR, SAYLARYLA ... YLLG. **VFOAT** Insanlar, Olaylar, Saylaryla ... Yllg; Hurriyet Yllg; Saylar, Olaylar, Insanlaryla ... Yllg. Turkish. ***Continues*** *Hurriyet Ansiklopedik Yllg.*

US/1041-2778
ILLINOIS FACTS. [Ill. facts]. **VFOAT** Illinois Facts, Flying the Colors; Illinois Facts--Flying the Colors Series. 1989-. English. te. $59.50. Clements Research Inc, 16850 Dallas Parkway, Dallas TX 75248. **Tel** (214)931-8827. **ED** John Clements. **LC** F536; .I14. **DD** 977.3/005.
Desc: Book of facts on a state, county-by-county.

US/0145-1790
ILLUSTRATED ENCYCLOPAEDIA YEARBOOK, THE. **Added/Corp** Encyclopaedia Britannica, Inc. (19??)-. English. an. Britannica Home Library Service, 310 South Michigan Avenue, Chicago IL 60604. **Tel** (800)323-1229. **LC** AY12; .I43. **DD** 031.

US/0192-6969
INDEX TO AMERICAN REFERENCE BOOKS ANNUAL. **VFOAT** Index to ARBA. (1974)-. English. ir. $60.00. Libraries Unlimited Inc., PO Box 6633, Department 920, Englewood CO 80155. **Tel** (800)237-6124. **ED** Bohdan S. Wyunar. **Bk Rev.**
Desc: Provides both a subject index and an author/title index. Subjects reflect those used at The Library of Congress. A guide to the reference literature of the last five years.

●US
INDEX TO MARQUIS WHO'S WHO PUBLICATIONS. **See** Biographies.

AT/1038-6300
INDEX TO THE HISTORICAL MICROFICHE SERIES. **VFOAT** Statistical Publications Since Federation. (1990)-. English. an. 75.00Aus$. Australian Bureau of Statistics, PO Box 10, Belconnen Australian Capital Territory, 2616 Australia. **Tel** 011 61 6 2527911, FAX 011 61 6 2516009.
Desc: Lists publications released by the Central Office of the ABS.

AT/0817-9344
INFORMATION PAPER - AUSTRALIAN BUREAU OF STATISTICS. (1986)-. Monographic series. English. ir. Free on request. Australian Bureau of Statistics, PO Box 10, Belconnen Australian Capital Territory, 2616 Australia. **Tel** 011 61 6 2527911, FAX 011 61 6 2516009.
Desc: Provides information relevant to the analysis and interpretation of movements in ABS time series. Gives definitions and graphical representations to explain the influences present.

US/0073-7860
INFORMATION PLEASE ALMANAC, ATLAS AND YEARBOOK. (INFORMATION PLEASE ALMANAC, ATLAS AND YEARBOOK / PLANNED AND SUPERVISED BY DAN GOLENPAUL ASSOCIATES.). **Added/Corp** Dan Golenpaul Associates. **VFOAT** Information Please Almanac, Atlas & Yearbook; Information Please Almanac. 15th (1961)-. English. an. $9.95. Houghton Mifflin Company, Wayside Road, Burlington MA 01803. **Tel** (800)225-3362, (617)272-1500. **ED** Otto T. Johnson. **LC** AY64; .I55. **DD** 031. Index available. **Circ:** 350,000. ***Continues*** *Information Please Almanac.*
Desc: United States and world facts, current events, sports, articles by experts on business, economy, science, space, consumer interests and political affairs.

FR/0020-5613
INTERMEDIAIRE DES CHERCHEURS ET CURIEUX, L'. (April 1951)-. Periodical. French. Twelve times a year. 625.00F. Dawson France SA, BP 40, 91121 Palaiseau Cedex France. **Tel** 011 33 1 69104700, telex 220064F. **LC** AG305; .I64. **DD** 034. ***Supersedes*** *Intermediaire des Chercheurs et Curieux.*

US
INTERNATIONAL ATLAS. [EDITORS: RUSSEL L. VOISIN AND OTHERS]. **Main/Corp** Rand McNally and Company. Multiple languages. ir (once every 3 years). $125.00. Rand McNally & Company, PO Box 32, Skokie IL 60076. **Tel** (708)673-0813, (800)444-4062.

US/0092-3974
INTERNATIONAL DIRECTORY OF LITTLE MAGAZINES & SMALL PRESSES. [Int. dir. little mag. small presses]. 9th Ed. (1974)-. Directory. English. an. $29.95. Dustbooks, PO Box 100, Paradise CA 95969. **Tel** (916)877-6110. **ED** Len Fulton. **LC** Z6944.L5; D5. **DD** 051/.025. **Ad Acc. Circ:** 6,000. ***Continues*** *Directory of Little Magazines and Small Presses, 0363-2016.*
Desc: Reference for writers, librarians, contemporary and literature students.

NE
INTERNATIONAL ENCYCLOPAEDIA OF LAWS. **See** Law.

US
INTERNATIONAL YEAR BOOK COVERING THE YEAR... . **Added/Corp** Macmillan Educational Company. **VFOAT** International

Year Book; Collier's Year Book. (1990)-. English. ***Continues*** *Year Book Covering the Year ... (Macmillan Educational Company).*

IC
ISLENSK SAMT,I : ALFRIARBOK VOKU-HELGAFELLS. **Added/Corp** Vaka-Helgafell hf. (1991)-. English. **LC** AY960.A3; I84.

●IS
ISRAEL YEARBOOK AND ALMANAC. **VFOAT** Israel Yearbook & Almanac. Vol. 46 (1991/1992)-. Consumer Publication. English. an. $35.00. IBRT Translation Documentation Ltd., 8 207 Hata Asiya Street, 93420 Jerusalem Israel. **Tel** 011 972 2 720107. **ED** Naftali Greenwood. **LC** DS101; .I68. **Ad Acc.** available with illustrations. ***Continues*** *Israel Yearbook, 0075-1413.*

US
KALENDARZ POLSKI NA ROK ... . Periodical. Polish. an. Wydawn Promyk, 4566 Bermuda Street, Philadelphia PA 19137. **ED** Antoni Gadysz. **LC** AY934; .K34.

GW
KRITISCHES LEXIKON ZUR DEUTSCHSPRACHIGEN GEGENWARTSLITERATUR. Dutch. Three times a year. Edition Text & Kritik GmbH, Levelingstrasse 6A, Postfach 800529, D 81605 Munich Germany. **Tel** 011 49 89 432929, FAX 011 49 89 433997. **ED** H L Arnold.

US/1054-4054
LAW FIRMS YELLOW BOOK. (LAW FIRMS YELLOW BOOK : WHO'S WHO IN THE MANAGEMENT OF THE LEADING U.S. LAW FIRMS.). [Law firms yellow book]. **VFOAT** Who's Who in the Management of the Leading U.S. Law Firms; Yellow Book. (Summer 1991)-. Directory. English. sa. $180.00. Monitor Leadership Directories, 104 Fifth Avenue, Second Floor, New York NY 10011. **Tel** (212)627-4140, FAX (212)645-0931. **LC** KF190; .L3615. **DD** 338.7/6134973. **[CCC].**
Desc: Concentrates on law firms' organizational structure and specifically on the key individuals who manage their operations. Provides information on the major law firms in the U.S.

RU
LETOPIS RETSENZII. **Added/Corp** Vesoiuznaia Knizhnaia Palata. (19??)-. Periodical. Russian. mo. $119.95. **(Subscription address:** East View Publications Inc., 3020 Harbor Lane North, Suite 110, Minneapolis MN 55447.**)** **NLM** Z 2495 L649.

GW
LEXIKON DES MITTELALTERS. **VFOAT** Encyclopedia of the Middle Ages. (19??)-. Monographic series. German. ir. Price varies per volume. Artemis & Winkler, Hackenstrasse 5, D 80331 Munich Germany. **Tel** 011 49 89 2311980.

US/1055-632X
LIBRO DEL ANO (CHICAGO, ILL.). (LIBRO DEL ANO.). (1991)-. Periodical. English. $45.00. EBP Latin America Group, 310 South Michigan Avenue, Station 2101, Chicago IL 60604.

CN/0380-8246
LIVRE DE L'ANNEE. (LE LIVRE DE L'ANNEE.). **Added/Corp** Encyclopedie Grolier. (1950)-. French. an. 21.40Can$. Entreprises Grolier, 2925 Chemin Cote de Liesse, St. Laurent Quebec H4N 2X1 Canada. **DD** 034/.1.

UK
LOCAL GOVERNMENT COMPANION. **See** Public Administration.

US/0896-6206
LOUISIANA ALMANAC. [La. alm.]. English. be. 13.95 US; $16.50 other. Pelican Publishing Company, PO Box 3110, Gretna LA 70054. **Tel** (504)368-1175, (800)843-1724, FAX (504)368-1195. **ED** Nina Kooij. **LC** F375; .L9435. **DD** 976.3/005. Index available. ***Continues*** *Louisiana Almanac and Fact Book.*
Desc: Invaluable for those interested in Louisiana's government, natural resources, history, and people. With charts, maps, graphs, and tables. Over 500 pages at your fingertips.

JA
MAINICHI NYUSU JITEN. **Added/Corp** Mainichi Shimbun Sha. Chosabu. Vol. 1 (1973)-. Japanese. an. ¥7900. Mainichi Shimbun Sha, (Mainichi Newspapers), 1-1-1 Hitotsubashi Chiyoda-ku, Tokyo 100-51 Japan. **Tel** 03 3212 0321, FAX 03 3216 2574. **LC** AY1155.T6; M3.

US
MAMMALS : A MULTIMEDIA ENCYCLOPEDIA. **See** Zoology.

II/0542-5778
MANORAMA YEAR BOOK. (1965)-. English. an. Rs25.00 India, Rs50.00 other (surface mail); Rs105.00 (airmail). Manorama Publishing House, PO Box 26, Kottayam 686 001 Kerala India. **Tel** 3615, telex 0888-201 MNR-IN. **ED** K. M. Mathew. **LC** DS401; .M35. **DD** 315.4. **Bk Rev. Ad Acc. Circ:** 60,000.
Desc: This general reference publication consists of four parts: (1) science and technology, (2) world panorama, (3) India and states and, (4) the world of sports.

US/0076-4418
MARCONI'S INTERNATIONAL REGISTER. **See** Communication.

US/0884-7118
MARQUIS WHO'S WHO INDEX TO WHO'S WHO BOOKS. ***Title Change.*** **See** Biographies.

US
MCGRAW-HILL DICTIONARY OF SCIENTIFIC AND TECHNICAL TERMS. **Main/Corp** McGraw-Hill Book Company. **VFOAT** Dictionary of Scientific and Technical Terms. (1974)-. Monographic series. English. ir. price varies per volume. McGraw Hill Publishing Company, Inc., 1221 Avenue of the Americas, New York NY 10020. **Tel** (212)512-6410, (800)525-5003, FAX (212)512-6111. **(Subscription address:** McGraw Hill / Pennsylvania, 13311 Monterey Avenue, Blue Ridge Summit PA 17294.**)**

US
MCGRAW-HILL ENCYCLOPEDIA OF SCIENCE & TECHNOLOGY. **VFOAT** Encyclopedia of Science and Technology. **VAT** McGraw-Hill Encyclopedia of Science and Technology. (1960)-. English. ir. $1900.00. McGraw Hill Publishing Company, Inc., 1221 Avenue of the Americas, New York NY 10020. **Tel** (212)512-6410, (800)525-5003, FAX (212)512-6111. **(Subscription address:** McGraw Hill, 1221 Avenue of the Americas, 41st Floor, New York, NY 10020; telephone: (212)512-2000**)**

US/0363-0366
MEDICAL AND HEALTH ANNUAL. **Added/Corp** Encyclopaedia Britannica, inc. (1977)-. English. an. $32.95. Encyclopedia Britannica Inc, Britannica Centre, 310 South Michigan Avenue, Chicago IL 60604. **Tel** (312)347-7453, FAX (312)347-7914, (312)289-2178. **ED** Ellen Bernstein. **LC** R5; .M38. **DD** 362.1/05. **NLM** W1; ME18D. Index available (In each volume). cum. index (Three-year). **Pr Rev.**
Desc: Comprehensive review of recent developments in medicine and health internationally. Articles are written by authorities and medical specialists.

US/1053-0967
MEMBERSHIP DIRECTORY / AMERICAN COLLEGE OF PHYSICIANS. [Membersh. dir. - Am. Coll. Physicians]. **Main/Corp** American College of Physicians. (19??)-. English. an. $115.00 (hard copy), $109.00 (soft copy). American College of Physicians, 6th Street and Race Street, Independence Mall West, Philadelphia PA 19106-1572. **Tel** (215)351-2600, (800)523-1546. **(Subscription address:** American College of Physicians, PO Box 7777 R 0320, Philadelphia PA 19175.**)** **LC** R15; .A4. **DD** 610.69/52/02573. ***Continues*** *American College of Physicians. Directory (1949), 0197-5455.*

UK/0076-8502
MIDDLE EAST AND NORTH AFRICA, THE. **Added/Corp** Europa Publications Limited. 11th Ed. (1964/1965)-. English. an. $310.00. Europa Publications Ltd, 18 Bedford Square, London WC1B 3JN England. **Tel** 011 44 71 5808236, telex 21540 EUROPA G. **(Subscription address:** Gale Research Co., 835 Penobscot Building, Detroit MI 48226.**)** **NLM** DS 49 M627. ***Continues*** *Middle East.*
Desc: Presents topics of concern to the region as a whole, details on international and regional organizations active there, and surveys and directories for each nation and territory. For each country, signed articles cover physical and social geography, recent history, economy and more.

US
MIDDLE ENGLISH DICTIONARY. (19??)-. English. ir. $15.00. University of Michigan Press, PO Box 1104, Ann Arbor MI 48106. **Tel** (313)764-4392.

GW
MITTELLATEINISCHES WORTERBUCH BIS ZUM AUSGEHENDEN 13 JAHRHUNDERT. CH Beck Verlagsbuchhandlung, D 80791 Munich Germany. **Tel** 011 49 89 381891.

US/1054-4062
MUNICIPAL YELLOW BOOK. (MUNICIPAL YELLOW BOOK : WHO'S WHO IN THE LEADING CITY AND COUNTY GOVERNMENTS AND LOCAL AUTHORITIES.). [Munic. yellow book]. **VFOAT** Yellow Book; Who's Who in the Leading City and County Governments and Local Authorities. Vol. 1, No. 1 (Summer 1991)-. Directory. English. sa. $180.00. Monitor Leadership Directories, 104 Fifth Avenue, Second Floor, New York NY 10011. **Tel** (212)627-4140, FAX (212)645-0931. **LC** JS39; .M79; JS141; .M86. **DD** 352/.00025/73.
Desc: Complete names, titles and telephone numbers of nearly 20,000 decision-makers in the leading city and county governments and local authorities. Includes comprehensive listings of all departments, agencies, subdivisions and branches.

US
NATIONAL DIRECTORY OF MAILING LISTS, THE. (1990)-. Directory. English. $245.00. Gale Research Inc., 835 Penobscot Building, Detroit MI 48226. **Tel** (800)877-GALE, (313)961-2242, FAX (313)961-6083, telex TWX 810-221-7086.
Desc: List some 200 interest categories and some 33,000 listings of individual mailing lists, 13,000 actively marketed lists, plus 20,000 that are not actively marketed, but may be available to rent or swap. Gives descriptions of catalog lists, magazine subscriber lists, newsletter lists, and other mailing lists.

US
NEW ELECTRONIC ENCYCLOPEDIA. [COMPUTER FILE], THE. English. an. $395.00. Grolier Electronic Publishing, Sherman Turnpike, Danbury CT 06816. **Tel** (203)797-3500, FAX (203)797-3835. **ED** Maryanne Piazza (contact person). Index available. cum. index. **Bk Rev. Ad Acc, Adv Mgr:** Maryanne Piazza, **Tel** (203)797-3365. **Pr Rev.**
Desc: Contains over 33,000 articles, ten million words as well as pictures, maps and CD-quality audio on one compact disc.

●US/1071-8931
NEWS MEDIA YELLOW BOOK. [News media yellow book]. **Added/Corp** Monitor Leadership Directories, Inc. Vol. 5, No. 1 (Winter 1994)-. Directory. English. qt. $235.00. Monitor Leadership Directories, 104 Fifth Avenue, Second Floor, New York NY 10011. **Tel** (212)627-4140, FAX (212)645-0931. **LC** PN4899.W304; N49. **DD** 302. ***Continues*** *News Media Yellow Book of Washington and New York, 1043-2620.*
Desc: Access to journalists and opinion-makers at news media organizations that cover national news.

US/0733-6586
NEWS TALK. (NEWS TALK. SOUND RECORDING). [News talk]. Broadcast No. 1 (1983)-. Monographic series. English. mo. Price varies per volume. Magnatape Broadcasting System, 116 Washington Street, Brighton MA 02135. **DD** 051.

●US/1065-8947
NEWSPAPERS ONLINE. [Newsp. .nline]. **VFOAT** Newspapers Online from BiblioData; BiblioData Newspapers Online. (Feb. 1992)-. Directory. English. an. $104.00. Bibliodata, PO Box 61, Needham Heights MA 02194. **Tel** (617)444-1154, FAX (617)449-4584. **LC** Z6941; .N4; IN PROCESS. **DD** 071/.025.
Desc: Directory and research guide for newspapers that are available online and the services that cover these newspapers.

GW
NIEDERSAECHSISCHES WOERTERBUCH. Monographic series. German. ir. Price varies per volume. Karl Wachholtz Verlag, Postfach 2769, Gansemarkt 1-3, W-2350 Neumunster F R Germany. **Tel** 011 49 4321 5670, FAX 011 49 4321 56778, telex 299 618 CURIR.

US
NORTH AMERICA FACSIMILE BOOK. CD-ROM. English (Spanish and French). $495.00. Quanta Press, Inc., 1313 Fifth Street Southeast, Suite 208C, Minneapolis MN 55414. **Tel** (612)379-3956, FAX (612)623-4570.
Desc: Over 150,000 fax numbers for companies and locations in the United States, Canada and Mexico. Complete addresses are included for easy mailing list generation. Available in MAC or DOS formats.

RU
NOVOE V RUSSKOI LEKSIKE : SLOVARNYE MATERIALY / AKADEMIIA NAUK SSSR, INSTITUT RUSSKOGO IAZYKA. **See** Linguistics.

●US
OKLAHOMA ALMANAC. **Added/Corp** Oklahoma. Dept. of Libraries. (1994)-. English. an. $13.00 (two years). Oklahoma Department of Libraries, 200 Northeast 18th Street, Oklahoma City OK 73105. **Tel** (405)521-2502, FAX (405)525-7804. **ED** Patricia Lester. **Ad Acc, Adv Mgr:** P. Lester. ***Continues*** *Directory of Oklahoma.*

US/0078-4516
OLD FARMER'S ALMANAC, THE. [(Old) farmer's alm.]. No. 199 (1991)-. English. $19.95. Grey Castle Press, Pocket Knife Square, Lakeville CT 06039. **ED** The Farmer's Almanack (1793-1847) was founded and edited by Robert B. Thomas, whose name continues to appear after his death. **DD** 032.

US/0276-3060
OLD FARMER'S ALMANAC. SPECIAL CANADIAN EDITION, THE. (THE OLD FARMER'S ALMANAC.). [Old farmer's alm., Spec. Can. ed.]. **VFOAT** Old Farmer's Almanack. (1983)-. English. an (published Sept. of the previous year). $5.45. Yankee Publishing Inc., Main Street, Dublin NH 03444. **Tel** (603)563-8111, (800)736-1100. **(Subscription address:** CDS / SIFD Agency Control, 1901 Bell Avenue, Des Moines IA 50315.**)** **ED** Jud Hale. **DD** 032/.02. **Ad Acc. Circ:** 2,500,000.
Desc: This American tradition is an interesting collection of facts, entertaining features, astrological information and weather predictions.

●US/1054-4585
ORIGINAL ... HIGHWAY 17 ALMANAC & GAZETTEER, THE. **VFOAT** Original Highway 17 Almanac and Gazetteer; Original Highway Seventeen Almanac & Gazetteer. (1992)-. Periodical. English. sa. $2.00. Cogitator Publishing Company, PO Box 3602, Anta Cruz CA 95063-3602.

US
OUR EARTH. (19??)-. English. $99.95. National Geographic Society, 11555 Darnestown, Gaithersburg MD 20878. **Tel** (202)857-7000, (800)638-4077, FAX (202)429-5727, telex 64194 NATGEO. **(Subscription address:** National Geographic Society / CD-ROM Products, 1145 17th Street NW, Educational Media Division, Washington DC 20036.**)**

UK
OXFORD ILLUSTRATED ENCYCLOPAEDIA. ***Ceased.*** (19??)-Series complete with Vol. 9. English. ir. Oxford University Press / New York, 200 Madison Avenue, New York NY 10016. **Tel** (212)679-7300, (919)677-0977, (800)451-7556, (800)445-9714, FAX (919)677-1303. **(Subscription address:** Oxford University Press USA, Journals Department, 2001 Evans Road, Cary, NC 27513; telephone: (800)852-7323 or (919)677-0977; Fax: (919)677-8828; E-mail: jrnl_orders@oup-usa.org**) LC** AE5. **DD** 032.

CC
PAI KO CHIH SHIH. **VFOAT** Baike Zhishi. (May 1979)-. Periodical. Chinese. mo. $27.36. **(Subscription address:** China International Book Trading Corporation, PO Box 399, Library Service Department, Beijing 100044 People's Republic of China.**) LC** AP95.C4; P27. **DD** 039/.951.

US/1042-637X
PALM BEACH BOOKS OF FACTS & FIRSTS, THE. [Palm Beach book facts firsts]. 1st Ed. (March 1989)-. Periodical. English. an. $12.95. Palm Beach Social Pictorial, 240 Worth Avenue, Palm Beach CA 33480. **DD** 975.

UK
PEAR'S CYCLOPAEDIA. (19??)-. English. an. Viking Penguin Inc, 40 West 23rd Street, New York NY 10010.

FR
PETIT LAROUSSE ILLUSTRE. (1973)-. French (Portuguese and Spanish). an (Sept.). $54.95. Livres Dix Larousse, 15 rue Rigaud, 94855 Ivry Sur Seine France. **Tel** 011 33 1 49596091. **(Subscription address:** Centrale des Revues, 11 rue Gossin, 92543 Montrouge Cedex France.**) LC** AG25; .P43. **DD** 034/.1. ***Continues*** *Nouveau Petit Larousse.*

US/0276-8283
PHYSICIANS' CURRENT PROCEDURAL TERMINOLOGY. (PHYSICIANS' CURRENT PROCEDURAL TERMINOLOGY : CPT / AMERICAN MEDICAL ASSOCIATION.). [Physicians' curr. proced. terminol.]. **Added/Corp** American Medical Association. **VFOAT** CPT. 3rd Ed. (1973)-. Directory. English. an. American Medical Association, 515 North State Street, Chicago IL 60610. **Tel** (312)464-5000, (800)262-2350, FAX (312)464-5831. **(Subscription address:** American Medical Association, PO Box 109050, Chicago IL 60610.**) LC** RB115; .C17. **DD** 616/.001/4. **NLM** W 39; P578. **[CCC]. *Continues*** *Current Procedural Terminology, 0590-4129.*
Desc: Authoritative source for procedure codes, contains the most widely accepted system for reporting physician procedures and services to both government and private insurance programs.

US
PICTURE ATLAS OF THE WORLD. (19??)-. English. ir. $99.95. National Geographic Society, 11555 Darnestown, Gaithersburg MD 20878. **Tel** (202)857-7000, (800)638-4077, FAX (202)429-5727, telex 64194 NATGEO. **(Subscription address:** National Geographic Society / CD-ROM Products, 1145 17th Street NW, Educational Media Division, Washington DC 20036.**)**

CC
PING CHOU WEN HUA. (19??)-. Periodical. Chinese. mo. RMBY0.20. Ping Chou Wen Hua, Post Office, Tai-Yuan Shih, People's Republic of China. **LC** AP95.C4; P56. **DD** 039/.951.

AT
POCKET YEAR BOOK, AUSTRALIA. **Added/Corp** Australian Bureau of Statistics. **VFOAT** Australian Pocket Year Book. No. 64 (1979)-. English. an. 8.00Aus$. Australian Bureau of Statistics, PO Box 10, Belconnen Australian Capital Territory, 2616 Australia. **Tel** 011 61 6 2527911, FAX 011 61 6 2516009. **LC** HA3001; .A65. **DD** 319.4. ***Continues*** *Australian Bureau of Statistics. Pocket Compendium of Australian Statistics.*
Desc: A pocket year book emulating Year Book Australia in comprehensiveness without the detail. Emphasis is on basic statistics.

AT/0159-9321
POCKET YEAR BOOK OF NEW SOUTH WALES, AUSTRALIA, THE. ***Ceased.*** **Added/Corp** New South Wales. Bureau of Statistics and Economics. Australia. Commonwealth Bureau of Census and Statistics. New South Wales Office. Australian Bureau of Statistics. New South Wales Office. **VFOAT** Pocket Year Book for ...; New South Wales Pocket Year Book. (19??)-(1992). English. an. Australian Bureau of Statistics, PO Box 10, Belconnen Australian Capital Territory, 2616 Australia. **Tel** 011 61 6 2527911, FAX 011 61 6 2516009. **LC** HA3012; .A4. ***Continues*** *Statesman's Year Book of New South Wales, Australia.*

AT
POCKET YEAR BOOK OF SOUTH AUSTRALIA. **Added/Corp** Australian Bureau of Statistics. South Australian Office. (1968)-. English. an. 8.50Aus$. Australian Bureau of Statistics, PO Box 10, Belconnen Australian Capital Territory, 2616 Australia. **Tel** 011 61 6 2527911, FAX 011 61 6 2516009. **LC** HA3095; .P63. **DD** 319.42/3. ***Continues*** *Statesman's Pocket Year Book of South Australia.*
Desc: Compact tables covering most fields of statistics collected by the ABS; it also lists the State Government Ministry.

CN/0822-4706
PWACONTACT. [PWAContact]. **Added/Corp** Periodical Writers Association of Canada. **VFOAT** PWAC contact. **VAT** Periodical Writers Association of Canada Contact. No. 67 (Nov./Dec. 1988)-. Periodical. English. bm. $125.00 per year. Periodical Writers Association of Canada, 24 Ryerson Avenue, Toronto Ontario M5T 2P3 Canada. **Tel** (416)868-6914, (416)504-1645, FAX (416)860-0826. **ED** Kathe Lieber. **DD** 070.1/75/06071. **Ad Acc, Adv Mgr:** Paulette Pelletier-Kelly. ***Continues*** *P.W.A.C. National Newsletter., 0822-4706.*

AT
QUEENSLAND POCKET YEAR BOOK, THE. **Added/Corp** Queensland. Government Statistician's Office. No. 1 (1950)-. English. an. 8.50Aus$. Australian Bureau of Statistics, PO Box 10, Belconnen Australian Capital Territory, 2616 Australia. **Tel** 011 61 6 2527911, FAX 011 61 6 2516009. **LC** HA3072; .A33. **DD** 319.43. **Circ:** 2,000.
Desc: A pocket-sized reference to the state's official statistics. Covers most areas of statistics in concise tabular form.

AT/0085-5359
QUEENSLAND YEAR BOOK. **Added/Corp** Australia. Bureau of Census and Statistics. Queensland Office. No. 1 (1937)-. English. an. 38.95Aus$. Australian Bureau of Statistics, PO Box 10, Belconnen Australian Capital Territory, 2616 Australia. **Tel** 011 61 6 2527911, FAX 011 61 6 2516009. **Ad Acc.**
Desc: A general reference book for any person who wishes to acquire a broad knowledge of the State of Queensland.

FR/0532-6656
QUID?. **Main/Corp** Fremy, Dominique. (1963)-. French. an. $70.00 US & Canada; $65.52 others. Editions Robert Laffont, 6 Place Saint Sulpice, 75006 Paris France. **Tel** 011 33 1 43291233. **LC** AE25; .F75. **DD** 034/.1.

US
RAND MCNALLY ... COMMERCIAL ATLAS & MARKETING GUIDE. **Main/Corp** Rand McNally and Company. **VFOAT** Rand McNally ... Commercial Atlas and Marketing Guide; Commercial Atlas & Marketing Guide; Commercial Atlas and Marketing Guide. 114th ed. (1983)-. English. an. $395.00. Rand McNally & Company, PO Box 32, Skokie IL 60076. **Tel** (708)673-0813, (800)444-4062. **LC** IN PROCESS. **DD** 912. ***Continues*** *Rand McNally and Company. Commercial Atlas and Marketing Guide, 0361-9923.*
Desc: Geographic and economic data for over 128,000 US places, including population trends, transportation, communications, and postal information.

US
RAND MCNALLY COSMOPOLITAN WORLD ATLAS. (19??)-. English. an. $70.00. Rand McNally & Company, PO Box 32, Skokie IL 60076. **Tel** (708)673-0813, (800)444-4062. Index available (place-name index).
Desc: Contains large-scale maps of continents, countries, states and provinces. Aims to present the world in detail and reflect world changes.

US
RAND MCNALLY INTERSTATE ROAD ATLAS. **Added/Corp** Rand McNally and Company. **VFOAT** Interstate Road Atlas. (1971)-. Periodical. English. an. Available in retail stores only. Rand McNally & Company, PO Box 32, Skokie IL 60076. **Tel** (708)673-0813, (800)444-4062.

US/1057-9834
RAND MCNALLY WORLD FACTS & MAPS. [Rand McNally world facts maps]. **Added/Corp** Rand McNally and Company. **VFOAT** Rand McNally World Facts and Maps; World Facts & Maps; World Facts and Maps. (19??)-. English. ir. $9.95. Rand McNally & Company, PO Box 32, Skokie IL 60076. **Tel** (708)673-0813, (800)444-4062. **LC** D843; .R258.
Desc: Reviews issues and places of current news relevance.

US
RAND MCNALLY ZIP CODE FINDER. **See** Communication-Postal Communications.

US/0277-5948
RECOMMENDED REFERENCE BOOKS FOR SMALL AND MEDIUM-SIZED LIBRARIES AND MEDIA CENTERS. (1981)-. English. an. $45.00. Libraries Unlimited Inc., PO Box 6633, Department 920, Englewood CO 80155. **Tel** (800)237-6124. **ED** Bohdan S. Wynar. **LC** Z1035.1; .R438. **DD** 011/.02. **Ad Acc.**
Desc: Reviews over 550 titles chosen by the editor as the most valuable reference titles published in 1986.

US/0362-7683
RECORD-A-REF. SUPPLEMENT; COMMERCIAL RECORD REFERENCE. **Main/Corp** SESAC, Inc. English. an. SESAC Inc, 156 West 56th Street, New York NY 10019.

CN/0381-7229
RED BOOK. NUMERICAL PHONE INDEX OF GREATER MONTREAL. (THE RED BOOK : NUMERICAL PHONE INDEX OF GREATER MONTREAL. THE RED BOOK : INDEX NUMERIQUE DE TELEPHONE DU GRAND MONTREAL.). **Added/Corp** John Lovell & Son. **VFOAT** The Red Book : Index Numerique de Telephone du Grand Montreal. (1962/63)-. English (French and English). an. J Lovell, 423 rue St Nicolas, Montreal Quebec H2Y 2P4 Canada. **Tel** (514)849-2578. **DD** 917.14/281/0025. ***Supersedes*** *Lovell's Numerical Phone Index of Greater Montreal, 0381-7210.*

US/0272-1988
REFERENCE BOOK REVIEW, THE. [Ref. book rev.]. (1976)-. Periodical. English. Twice a year. $11.00. Reference Book Review, PO Box 190954, Dallas TX 75219. **Tel** (214)690-5882. **ED** Cameron and Donna Northouse. **LC** Z1035.1; .R44. **DD** 011/.02. **Bk Rev. Circ:** 1,000.
Desc: Reviews of reference publications in all fields. Approximately 100 reviews per issue.
Ind/Abst Book Rev. Index.

US
REFERENCE BOOK REVIEW INDEX. ***Ceased.*** **See** Encyclopedias and General Reference Books-Abstracting, Bibliographies and Statistics.

US/1055-4777
REFERENCE DESK : QUARTERLY JOURNAL OF THE ENCYCLOPEDISTS: INTERNATIONAL ENCYCLOPEDIA SOCIETY. [Ref. desk]. **Added/Corp** Encyclopedists: International Encyclopedia Society. Vol. 1, No. 1 (Spring 1991)-. Periodical. English. qt. $20.00. International Encyclopedia Society, Reference Desk, Box 519, Baldwin Place NY 10505-0519. **LC** Z1035.1; .R443. **DD** 028.1/2.

US
REFERENCE GUIDE TO HANDBOOKS AND ANNUALS. (1975)-. English. te (every three years). $63.70. Pfeiffer & Company International Publishers, Roggestraat 15, 2153 GC Nieuw Venn Netherlands. **Tel** 011 31 2526 89840, FAX 011 31 2526 86885. **LC** HM134; .R44. **DD** 016.158/2.
Desc: Indexes the contents of a handbook of structured experiences for human relations training and the annual handbook for group facilitators.

UK/0950-4125
REFERENCE REVIEWS. Vol. 1, No. 1 (March 1987)-. Periodical. English. Eight times a yearAnnual ((Vol. 7 with 7 issues)). $1629.00. MCB University Press, 60 62 Toller Lane, Bradford West Yorkshire BD8 9BX England. **Tel** 011 44 274 499821, FAX 011 44 274 547143, telex 51317 MCBUNI G. **(Subscription address:** MCB University Press / US and Canada Subscriptions, PO Box 10812, Birmingham AL 35201-0812.**) ED** Stuart James. **LC** Z1035.1; .R448. **DD** 028.1/2. Index available. **Bk Rev. Ad Acc. Circ:** 250. available on microfilm and microfiche from University Microfilms International (UMI).
Desc: Features hundreds of new reference works, reviewed impartially and in-depth, by a review of senior librarians.

US/0090-7324
REFERENCE SERVICES REVIEW. (RSR: REFERENCE SERVICES REVIEW.). [Ref. serv. rev.]. Vol. 1 (Jan./Mar. 1973)-. Periodical. English. qt. $65.00 (institutions), $40.00 (individuals) US; $79.00 (institutions), $54.00 (individuals) other. Pierian Press, PO Box 1808, Ann Arbor MI 48106. **Tel** (313)434-5530, (800)678-2435, FAX (313)434-6409. **ED** Ilene F. Rockman. **LC** Z1035.1; .R43. **DD** 011/.02/05. **NLM** Z 1035 R111. **Bk Rev. Ad Acc, Adv Mgr:** Annette Ferguson and Ken Wachsberger. **Pr Rev.** available on microfilm and microfiche from University Microfilms International (UMI); available in machine readable format.
Desc: Devoted to the enrichment of reference knowledge and the advancement of reference services in libraries. Features reviews, current surveys, core collections, reference serials, and bibliographic instruction.
Ind/Abst Abstr. Engl. Stud.; Acad. Abstr.; Acad. Search (July 1993-); Am. Hist. Life; Book Rev. Index; Child. Lit. Abstr. (19??-); Curr. Index J. Educ.; INFO-SOUTH Abstr.;

Inf. Instruc. Technol.; Inf. Sci. Abstr.; Leg. Inf. Manage. Index (19??-); Libr. Inf. Sci. Abstr.; Libr. Lit.; Mag. Search; Med. Rev. Dig.; Trade Ind. Index.

UK
REGIONAL SURVEYS OF THE WORLD. (19??)-. English. an. Europa Publications Ltd, 18 Bedford Square, London WC1B 3JN England. **Tel** 011 44 71 5808236, telex 21540 EUROPA G. **(Subscription address:** Gale Research Co., 835 Penobscot Building, Detroit MI 48226.)
Desc: Aimed at businesses, libraries, universities, government departments, embassies, newspapers and international organizations.

CN/0705-5455
REPERTOIRE DE VEDETTES-MATIERE. (REPERTOIRE DE VEDETTES-MATIERE [MICROFORM].). [Repert. vedett.-matiere]. **Added/Corp** Universite Laval. Bibliotheque. National Library of Canada. (Dec. 1988)-. Periodical. English (French). sa. 175.00Can$. Bibliotheque de l'Universite Laval, Serv Tech Pavillon Bonenfant, Ste-Foy Quebec G1K 7P4 Canada. **Tel** (418)656-2871. **DD** 025.4/9/0005. ***Continues*** *Repertoire de Vedettes-Matieres. Supplement, 0705-5455.*
Desc: Lists French subject headings.

FR/0987-6030
REPERTOIRE (MONTPELLIER, FRANCE). (REPERTOIRE.). **Added/Corp** Universite Paul Valery. **VFOAT** Catalogue Descriptif des Periodiques Francais d'Etudes Anglaises et am,ericaines; Descriptive Catalogue of French Periodicals of English and American Studies. (1987)-. Academic Scholarly Publication. French (English). be. 30.00F. Publications de la Recherche, Universite de Montpellier, BP 5043, 032 Montpellier Cedex 1 France. **Tel** 011 33 67142406, 011 33 67142393, FAX 011 33 67 142432. **LC** Z6956.F8; R388; PN5184.P4. **DD** 015.44034. Index available. **Acid Free. Circ:** 1,000 (ctrl).

US
REPORT ON ACTIVE AND PLANNED SPACECRAFT AND EXPERIMENTS. See Aeronautics, Astronautics.

US
RESEARCH & DEVELOPMENT. TELEPHONE DIRECTORY. VFOAT Telephone Directory; Research and Development. Telephone Directory; Research and Development Telephone Directory; Research & Development Telephone Directory. (1984)-. English. an (Feb.). Included with subscription to R&D; $50.00 US; $65.00 other (single copy, nonsubscriber). Cahners Publishing Company, 249 West 17th Street, New York NY 10011. **Tel** (212)645-0067, FAX (212)242-6987. **(Subscription address:** Cahners Publishing Company / Colorado, Paid Subscription Service Center, PO Box 7610, Highlands Ranch CO 80126-7610.) **ED** Robert Jones. **Ad Acc. Circ:** 107,000 (ctrl). ***Continues*** *Industrial Research & Development Telephone Directory.*

US/0361-6509
ROAD ATLAS : UNITED STATES, CANADA, AND MEXICO. Main/Corp Rand McNally and Company. **VFOAT** Road Atlas of the United States, Canada, and Mexico.; Road Atlas : United States, Canada, Mexico. (1932)-. English. an. $8.95. Rand McNally & Company, PO Box 32, Skokie IL 60076. **Tel** (708)673-0813, (800)444-4062. **LC** G1201.P2; R35 date. **DD** 629.281. ***Continues*** *Rand McNally and Company. Auto Road Atlas of the United States.*

US/1053-2374
ROSTER OF MEMBERSHIP AND RESOURCE GUIDE / EMPLOYEE RELOCATION COUNCIL. [Roster membersh. resour. guide - Empl. Relocat. Counc.]. **Main/Corp** Employee Relocation Council. (198?)-. Directory. English. ir. Comes with Employee Relocation Council membership; $150.00 (membership). Employee Relocation Council, 1720 North Street Northwest, Washington DC 20036. **Tel** (202)857-0905, FAX (202)467-4012. **LC** HF5549.5.R47; E46a. **DD** 658.3/83. ***Continues*** *Employee Relocation Council. Roster of Members, 0732-8168.*

PH
RR'S PHILIPPINE ALMANAC. VFOAT Philippine Almanac. (1990)-. English. **LC** DS651; .P338. **DD** 959.9/046. ***Continues*** *Philippine Almanac.*

●SZ
SCHWEIZER LOGISTIK-KATALOG / SWISS LOGISITICS CATALOGUE. (1993)-. German (English). an. 25.00F. Verlag Binkert AG, Baslerstrasse 15, CH-4335 Laufenburg Switzerland. **Tel** 011 41 64 697272, FAX 011 41 64 697333. **Bk Rev. Ad Acc, Adv Mgr:** W. Meier. **Circ:** 4,150. ***Continues*** *Conveying Material Catalogue.*
Desc: News and trends from the howle field of logistics, conveying, stockage, etc. Reference book for industrials and specialists.

CH
SHIH YUNG CHIH SHIH. Periodical. Chinese. NT$0.20. Kuang-Chou Shih Chiao Yu Kung, Yeh Kung SSU, Kung Hsiao Ching Li Pu Yu Kou Tsu 502, Li wan N Rd, Kung-Chou Shih, People's Republic of China. **LC** AG117; .S55. **DD** 039/.951.

JA
SHINBUN NO KOTOBA JITEN / ASAHI SHINBUNSHA HEN. Japanese. an. ¥1000. Asahi Sonorama, c/o Dai 2 Asahi Building 2-6 Ginza 4 Chuo-ku, Tokyo-to 104 Japan.

SI/0377-7928
SINGAPORE PERIODICALS INDEX. Added/Corp National Library (Singapore). (1970)-. Abstracting/Indexing Service. English (English and Malay). ir. Admin National Library, Stamford Road, Singapore 0617 Singapore. **Tel** 011 65 33 09 630. **LC** AI3; .S57. ***Continues in part*** *Indeks Majallah Kini Malaysia Singapura dan Brunei.*

AT/0085-6428
SOUTH AUSTRALIAN YEAR BOOK. Added/Corp Australia. Commonwealth Bureau of Census and Statistics. South Australian Office. Australian Bureau of Statistics. South Australian Office. No. 1 (1966)-. English. an. 29.50Aus$. Australian Bureau of Statistics, PO Box 10, Belconnen Australian Capital Territory, 2616 Australia. **Tel** 011 61 6 2527911, FAX 011 61 6 2516009. **LC** HC636; .S6. **DD** 309.1/94/2.
Desc: A general reference work providing a comprehensive statistical and descriptive portrayal of South Australia's physiography, history, institutions and social and economic conditions.

RU
SOVETSKAIA ISTORICHESKAIA ENTSIKLOPEDIIA. (1961)-. Russian. ir. **(Subscription address:** Victor Kamkin, 4956 Boiling Brook Parkway, Rockville MD 20852.)

US
STANDARD HIGHWAY MILEAGE GUIDE. Main/Corp Rand McNally and Company. (1934)-. English. ir. $135.00. Rand McNally & Company, PO Box 32, Skokie IL 60076. **Tel** (708)673-0813, (800)444-4062.
Desc: Geographic and mileage information for calculating expense account reimbursement, sales travel, logistics analysis and educational research.

US
STATE OF FLORIDA TELEPHONE DIRECTORY. (19??)-. Directory. English. $7.00. Department of Management Services / Florida, Suite 110, Knight Building, 2737 Centerview Drive, Tallahassee FL 32399.

US/0899-2207
STATE YELLOW BOOK. [State yellow book]. **Added/Corp** Monitor Publishing Company. **VFOAT** Yellow Book. Vol. 1, No. 1 (Winter 1989)-. Directory. English. qt. $235.00. Monitor Leadership Directories, 104 Fifth Avenue, Second Floor, New York NY 10011. **Tel** (212)627-4140, FAX (212)645-0931. **ED** Imogene Aikins. **LC** JK2403; .S77. **DD** 353.9/025. **[CCC].** Index available. **Circ:** 2,700. ***Continues*** *State Information Book, 0896-8128.*
Desc: Listings of names, addresses, titles and telephone numbers of more than 35,000 key decision-makers within the executive, and legislative branches of the 50 states and the District of Columbia. Also includes profiles for each state with census data and historical background.

US/0361-0764
STATISTICAL REFERENCE BOOK OF INTERNATIONAL ACTIVITIES. See Encyclopedias and General Reference Books-Abstracting, Bibliographies and Statistics.

AT/1031-9573
TASMANIAN POCKET YEAR BOOK. Added/Corp Australian Bureau of Statistics. Tasmanian Office. **VFOAT** Tasmanian Pocket Yearbook. (1988)-. English. an. 8.50Aus$. Australian Bureau of Statistics, PO Box 10, Belconnen Australian Capital Territory, 2616 Australia. **Tel** 011 61 6 2527911, FAX 011 61 6 2516009. ***Continues*** *Pocket Year Book of Tasmania, 0314-1640.*
Desc: Presents a basic summary of Tasmania.

GW
THEOLOGISCHE REALENZYKLOPADIE. Walter De Gruyter Inc, 200 Saw Mill River Road, Hawthorne NY 10532. **Tel** (914)747-0110.

CN/0383-2910
THESAURUS DE DESCRIPTEURS SUR L'EDUCATION. LISTE ROTATIVE ET ADDITIONS ET CORRECTIONS. April 1974-. Periodical. French. Centre d'Animation de Developpement et de Recherche en Education, 1940 Est Boul Henri-Bourassa, Montreal Quebec H2B 1S2 Canada. **Tel** (514)381-8891, FAX (514)381-4086. **DD** 025.3/3/37.

GW
THESAURUS LINGUAE LATINAE. (1900)-. Latin. ir. price varies per volume. BSB BG Teubner Verlagsgesellsc, PO Box 930, D 70510 Leipzig Germany. **Tel** 011 49 341 293158. **(Subscription address:** BG Teubner Stuttgart, Postfach 801069, D 70510 Stuttgart Germany.) **Bk Rev. Ad Acc. Circ:** 1,800 (ctrl).
Desc: Comprehensive Latin dictionary is an indispensable resource and working aid for philological and historical research.

US
THESAURUS OF ERIC DESCRIPTORS. SUPPLEMENT. Main/Corp Educational Resources Information Center. No. 1 (March 1968)-. Periodical. English. ir. Available to specific ERIC affiliates only (via Internet). Oryx Press, 4041 North Central Avenue, #700, Phoenix AZ 85012-3397. **Tel** (800)279-ORYX, (602)265-2651, FAX (602)265-6250, (800)279-4663, (800)279-6799.

UK
TOP 3,000 DIRECTORIES & ANNUALS : A GUIDE TO THE MAJOR TITLES USED IN BRITISH LIBRARIES, THE. VFOAT Top 3,000 Directories and Annuals; Top Three Thousand Directories and Annuals; Top 3000. (1986)-. Directory. English. an. $102.81. Dawson UK Ltd, Cannon House, Folkestone Kent CT19 5EE England. **Tel** 011 44 303-850101, FAX 011 44 303-850440, telex 96392. **(Subscription address:** Dawson UK Book Division, Crane Close, Denington Road, Wellingborough NN8 2QG United Kingdom.) **LC** Z5771; .T76; AY2001. **DD** 011/.02. ***Continues*** *Top 2,000 Directories & Annuals.*

CN
TYOKANSAN KALENTERI. (19??)-. Finnish.

AT
UBD AUSTRALIA WIDE BUSINESS AND STREET DIRECTORY : GOLD COAST. See Business.

US/1055-4246
UNDERGROUND STORAGE TANK GUIDE. [Undergr. storage tank guide]. **Added/Corp** Thompson Publishing Group. (198?)-. Periodical. English. mo. $279.00 (includes updates). Thompson Publishing Group, 7711 Anderson Road, Tampa FL 33634. **Tel** (800)677-3789, (813)282-8607. **DD** 344. **[CCC].**
Desc: A reference guide to help UST owners to stay in compliance with EPA's federal regulations. Dealing with US cities, the guide explains operational, financial and reprinting standards. Also gives timely hints for meeting compliance guidelines and explanations of federal and state regulations in state programs and state trust funds.

FR
UNESCO SOURCES. Added/Corp UNESCO. **VFOAT** Sources; Sources UNESCO. No. 1 (Feb. 1989)-. Periodical. English. Eleven times a year. Free on request. UNESCO / France, 31 rue Francois Bonvin, 75732 Paris Cedex 15 France. **Tel** 011 33 1 45684564, 011 33 1 45684565, FAX 011 33 1 42733007, telex 204461 Paris. **LC** AS4.U8; A565.
Ind/Abst Mag. Artic. Summar. Elite (July 1994-); Museum Abstr.

US/1045-9820
UNIVERSAL ALMANAC, THE. (1991)-. English. an. $19.95. Andrews McNeel & Parker Inc, 4900 Main Street, Kansas City MO 64112. **Tel** (816)932-6600, (800)826-4216.

FR
UNIVERSALIA; LES EVENEMENTS, LES HOMMES, LES PROBLEMES. 1st-1974-. French. ir. $30.92. Encyclopaedia Universalis, PO Box 2249, 175 Holiday Inn Drive, Cambridge Ontario N3C 3N4 Canada. **Tel** (519)658-4621, FAX (519)658-8181. Index Available in first issue of next volume--loose--separately paged.
Desc: This is a yearbook for Encyclopaedia Universalis.

US/0503-6291
VALIS-EESTLASE KALENDER. VFOAT Valis Eestlase Kalender; Valiseestlase Kalender; Waliseestlase Kalender. (19??)-. Estonian. an. Nordic Press Inc, 243 East 34th Street, PO Box 123, New York NY 10016. **Tel** (212)686-3356. **LC** AY78.E6; V3. **DD** 059.

US
VAN NOSTRAND'S SCIENTIFIC ENCYCLOPEDIA. ***Ceased.*** (1938)-(19??). English. ir. Litton Educational Publishing, 7625 Empire Drive, Florence KY 41042. **Tel** (800)354-9815.

US/1055-4610
VIET NAM HAI NGOAI. [Viet Nam hai ngoai]. (1977)-. Periodical. Vietnamese. mo. Vie Nam Hai Ngoai, PO Box 33627, San Diego CA 92103. **Tel** (619)280-0181. **DD** 059.

GW
WARENVERZEICHNIS FUER DIE AUSSENHANDELSSTATISTIK. Main/Corp Germany (Federal Republic). Statistisches Bundesamt. (19??)-. Periodical. German. an. Metzler Poeschel Verlag Veroeffen, Statist Bundesamt Kernerstr 43, D 70182 Stuttgart Germany. **Tel** 011 49 7071 935350. **(Subscription address:** Metzler Poeschel H Leins GmbH, Postfach 1152, D 72125 Kusterdingen Germany.)

Encyclopedias and General Reference Books

GW/0043-0331
WARENZEICHENBLATT. TEIL 1, (ANGEMELDETE ZEICHEN). AUSGABE A. [Warenzeich.bl., Tl. 1 (Angemeld. Zeich.), Ausg. A]. (1950)-. Periodical. German. sm. DM200.00. Wila Verlag/Wilhelm Lampl GMBH, Landsberger Str 191A, D-80687 Munich Germany. **Tel** 011 49 89 5795285. **UDC** 347.772.

GW/0043-034X
WARENZEICHENBLATT. TEIL 2, (EINGETRAGENE ZEICHEN). AUSGABE A. [Warenzeich.bl., Tl. 2 (Eingetrag. Zeich.), Ausg. A]. (1950)-. Periodical. German. sm. DM240.00. Wila Verlag/Wilhelm Lampl GMBH, Landsberger Str 191A, D-80687 Munich Germany. **Tel** 011 49 89 5795285. **UDC** 347.772.

US
WEBSTERS NINTH NEW COLLEGIATE DICTIONARY. CD-ROM. English. $199.95 (CD-ROM). Highlighted Data Inc., 6628 Medhill Place, Falls Church VA 22043. **Tel** (703)516-9211. Index available.

AT/0083-8772
WESTERN AUSTRALIAN YEAR BOOK / COMMONWEALTH BUREAU OF CENSUS AND STATISTICS, WESTERN AUSTRALIAN OFFICE. Added/Corp Australia. Commonwealth Bureau of Census and Statistics. Western Australian Office. Australian Bureau of Statistics. Western Australian Office. **VFOAT** Western Australian Yearbook. No. 6 (1967)-. English. an. 29.00Aus$. Australian Bureau of Statistics, PO Box 10, Belconnen Australian Capital Territory, 2616 Australia. **Tel** 011 61 6 2527911, FAX 011 61 6 2516009. **LC** HA3153; .A45. *Continues* Official Year Book of Western Australia.
Desc: Provides a general reference for Western Australia in terms of its geography, climate and geology, plant and animal life and the activities and background of its people in relation to the environment.

US/0084-1382
WORLD ALMANAC AND BOOK OF FACTS, THE. [World alm. book facts]. **VAT** World Almanac and Book of Facts. (1923)-. English. an. $8.95 (soft cover), $24.95 (hard cover). World Almanac, c/o C. Buckosh, 1278 West 9th Street, Cleveland OH 44113-1067. **Tel** (216)621-7300, 800 521-6600, FAX (216)621-1366. **ED** Hana Umlauf Lane. **LC** AY67.N5; W7. **DD** 317. **NLM** AY 67.N5 W927. **Bk Rev. Circ:** 1,000,000 (ctrl). available on microfilm and microfiche from University Microfilms International (UMI). *Continues* World Almanac and Encyclopedia.
Desc: The reference book to have on hand for all the up-to-date facts, statistics, events and information about the past year.

US/0084-1439
WORLD BOOK YEAR BOOK, THE. [World book year bookl]. (1962)-. English. an (Feb.). $27.90. World Book Encyclopedia Inc., 2515 East 43rd Street, Chattanooga TN 37422. **Tel** (800)874-0520, (615)867-9081. **LC** AE5; .W564. **DD** 031. *Supersedes* World Book Encyclopedia Annual Supplement.

AT
WORLD DATA : BOOK OF THE YEAR (AUSTRALIA). English. an. 45.95Aus$. Encyclopaedia Britannica, Private Bag 33, Castle Hill New South Wales 2154 Australia. **Tel** 02 680 5666, FAX 02 899 3231.

US/0000-0604
WORLD DICTIONARIES IN PRINT. *Ceased.* [World dict. print]. English. R R Bowker, A Reed Reference Publishing Company, Part of Reed International PLC, PO Box 31, 121 Chanlon Drive, New Providence NJ 07974. **Tel** (908)464-6800, (800)521-8110, FAX (908)665-6688, telex 138-755. **LC** Z7043.D5; W64; P361. **DD** 016.403.

UK
WORLD GUIDE TO ABBREVIATIONS OF ORGANIZATIONS. Added/Corp Gale Research Company. 1st Ed. (1954)-. English. ir. $140.00. Gale Research Inc., 835 Penobscot Building, Detroit MI 48226. **Tel** (800)877-GALE, (313)961-2242, FAX (313)961-6083, telex TWX 810-221-7086. **ED** F. A. Buttress and Henry J. Heaney.
Desc: Reveals the full names behind the plethora of initials and abbreviations currently used to identify the names of companies, institutions, international agencies, and governmental departments throughout the world.

US
WORLD GUIDE TO UNIVERSITIES. INTERNATIONALES UNIVERSITATS-HANDBUCH. VFOAT Internationales Universitats-Handbuch. (1971)-. English. ir. $130.00 (part 1), $104.50 (part 2). R R Bowker, A Reed Reference Publishing Company, Part of Reed International PLC, PO Box 31, 121 Chanlon Drive, New Providence NJ 07974. **Tel** (908)464-6800, (800)521-8110, FAX (908)665-6688, telex 138-755.

GW/0084-1889
WORLD LIST OF UNIVERSITIES, OTHER INSTITUTIONS OF HIGHER EDUCATION AND UNIVERSITY ORGANISATIONS. LISTE MONDIALE DES UNIVERSITES, AUTRES ETABLISSEMENTS D'ENSEIGNEMENT SUPERIEUR ET ORGANISATIONS UNIVERSITAIRES. Added/Corp International Association of Universities. **VFOAT** Liste Mondiale des Universites, Autres Etablissements d'Enseignement Superieur et Organisations Universitaires. (19??)-. Multiple languages. be (every two years). $130.00. Walter de Gruyter Inc., PO Box 303421, D 10728 Berlin Germany. **Tel** 011 49 30 260050, FAX 011 49 30 26005251. **(Subscription address:** Stockton Press, PO Box 6277, Church Street Station, New York NY 10010.) *Absorbed in part* International Handbook of Universities and Other Institutions of Higher Education, 0074-6215.
Desc: A concise world-wide directory covering all universities and other institutes of higher learning.

US
WORLDMARK ENCYCLOPEDIA OF THE NATIONS. (1960)-. English. ir. $335.00. Gale Research Inc., 835 Penobscot Building, Detroit MI 48226. **Tel** (800)877-GALE, (313)961-2242, FAX (313)961-6083, telex TWX 810-221-7086. Index available (Bound in each volume).
Desc: Covers two hundred countries and dependencies from around the world. Entries range from four to thirty pages in length and reveal details on fifty different categories. Contains a comprehensive overview of a country's size, scope, economic, political and social situation.

US/8756-3460
YEAR BOOK OF REHABILITATION, THE. *Ceased.* See Medical Science and Technology.

US/1051-4058
YEARBOOK OF EXPERTS, AUTHORITIES & SPOKESPERSONS. AN ENCYCLOPEDIA OF SOURCES. [Yearb. experts auth. spokesp.]. **VFOAT** Yearbook of Experts, Authorities and Spokespersons. 8th Ed. (1990)-. English. an (Aug.). $47.50 (one year). Broadcast Interview Source, 2233 Wisconsin Avenue NW, #540, Washington DC 20007-4104. **Tel** (800)955-0311, (202)333-4904, FAX (202)342-5411. **ED** Mitchell Davis. **LC** AS29.5; .B76. **DD** 791. **Ad Acc.** ctrl circ. *Continues* Directory of Experts, Authorities & Spokespersons, 1045-9537.
Desc: Profiles 869 national associations, Fortune 500 corporations, non-profit organizations and notable experts available for background information and commentary on today's most pressing issues. Includes an index of more than 7,000 topics cross-referenced to the profiles. Full contact information, including name, complete mailing address, and phone number, is provided for each listed organization or expert.

BE/0084-3814
YEARBOOK OF INTERNATIONAL ORGANIZATIONS. See Encyclopedias and General Reference Books-Abstracting, Bibliographies and Statistics.

ABSTRACTING, BIBLIOGRAPHIES AND STATISTICS

US
REFERENCE BOOK REVIEW INDEX. *Ceased.* (1???-19??). Abstracting/Indexing Service. English. ir. Pierian Press, PO Box 1808, Ann Arbor MI 48106. **Tel** (313)434-5530, (800)678-2435, FAX (313)434-6409.

US/0361-0764
STATISTICAL REFERENCE BOOK OF INTERNATIONAL ACTIVITIES. Main/Corp John E Fogarty International Center for Advanced Study in the Health Sciences. International Cooperation and Geographic Studies Branch. **VFOAT** National Institutes of Health Statistical Reference Book of International Activities. Began with fiscal year 1972. Statistical Publication. English. an. John E Fogarty International Center for Advanced Study in the Health Sciences, 9000 Rockville Pike, Bethesda MD 20205. **NLM** W2 A J6S. *Continues* Statistical Reference Book of International Activities.

BE/0084-3814
YEARBOOK OF INTERNATIONAL ORGANIZATIONS. [Yearb. int. organ.]. **Added/Corp** Union of International Associations. 11th Ed. (1966/67)-. English (French and German; summaries and/or abstracts in French and German). an. $875.00 (complete set). K.G. Saur Verlag KG, A Reed Reference Publishing Company, Part of Reed International PLC, Ortlerstrasse 8, D 81373 Munich Germany. **Tel** 011 49 89 769020, FAX 011 49 89 76902150, telex 5212067-SAUR-D. **LC** JX1904; .A42. **DD** 314.2. **NLM** JX 1904 A61. Index available. cum. index. available on CD-ROM from K G Saur. *Continues* Annuaire des Organisations Internationales.
Desc: Provides detailed information for over 28,000 organizations active in over 200 countries, and is accompanied by a comprehensive, computer-generated multilingual index.

ENERGY

AT
AAEC NUCLEAR NEWS. Added/Corp Australian Atomic Energy Commission. **VFOAT** Nuclear News. **VAT** Australian Atomic Energy Commission Nuclear News. No. 1 (March 1979)-. Periodical. English. qt. Australian Nuclear Science and Technology Organisation, Private Mailbag 1, Menai 2234 New South Wales Australia.

TH/0857-6181
ABSTRACTS OF AIT REPORTS AND PUBLICATIONS ON ENERGY. See Energy-Abstracting, Bibliographies and Statistics.

US/0890-8265
ACCESS TO ENERGY. [Access energy]. Vol. 1 (Sept. 1973)-. Periodical. English. mo (12 issues). $50.00 US: $52.00 Canada; $58.00 other. Access to Energy, Box 2298, Boulder CO 80306. **Tel** (303)444-0841. **ED** Pete Beckmaun. **DD** 531. Index available ($20.00). cum. index. **Bk Rev. Circ:** 4,000.
Desc: Information on power resources.
Ind/Abst Energy Res. Abstr. (Feb. 1977-).

US/0738-4882
ACTIVE SOLAR INSTALLATIONS SURVEY. (ACTIVE SOLAR INSTALLATIONS SURVEY / ENERGY INFORMATION ADMINISTRATION, OFFICE OF COAL, NUCLEAR, ELECTRIC, AND ALTERNATE FUELS, U.S. DEPT. OF ENERGY ; [PREPARED BY APPLIED MANAGEMENT SCIENCES, INC.].). [Act. solar install. surv.]. **Added/Corp** United States. Office of Coal, Nuclear, Electric, and Alternate Fuels. Applied Management Sciences, Inc. (1980)-. Government Publication. English. an. $5.50. Department of Energy / Energy Information Administration, Office of Coal Nuclear and Alternate Fuels, 1000 Independence Avenue SW, Washington DC 20585. **Tel** (202)586-5000. **ED** Peter Holihan (editor's telephone: (202)254-5432). **LC** TJ810; .A2. **DD** 338.4/769778/0973. **Pr Rev. Circ:** 500.

AG/0326-6672
ACTIVIDAD MINERA. See Engineering-Mines and Mining Engineering.

US
ACTIVITIES / FLORIDA SOLAR ENERGY CENTER. Main/Corp Florida Solar Energy Center. (19??)-. English. an. $1.14. Florida Solar Energy Center, 300 State Road 401, Cape Canaveral FL 32920. **LC** TJ810; .F58a. **DD** 333.79/23/09759.

US
ADDITIONS TO GENERATING CAPACITY ... FOR THE CONTIGUOUS UNITED STATES / AS PROJECTED BY THE REGIONAL ELECTRIC RELIABILITY COUNCILS IN THEIR ... LONG-RANGE COORDINATED PLANNING REPORTS TO THE DEPARTMENT OF ENERGY. Added/Corp United States. Dept. of Energy. Division of Power Supply and Reliability. (19??)-. English. an. National Technical Information Service - NTIS, Room 2027S, 5285 Port Royal Road, Springfield VA 22161. **Tel** (703)487-4630, (703)487-4660, (703)487-4650, FAX (703)321-8547, telex 89-9405.

US/0896-520X
ADVANCED FOSSIL ENERGY TECHNOLOGIES. (ADVANCED FOSSIL ENERGY TECHNOLOGIES : CURRENT REPORTS / U.S. DEPARTMENT OF ENERGY ; PREPARED FOR OFFICE OF FOSSIL ENERGY ; PREPARED BY OFFICE OF SCIENTIFIC AND TECHNICAL INFORMATION.). [Adv. foss. energy technol.]. **Added/Corp** United States. Dept. of Energy. Office of Scientific and Technical Information. United States. Office of Fossil Energy. **VFOAT** FET. Vol. 88, No. 1 (Jan. 15, 1988)-. Government Publication. English. sm. $175.00 US; $350.00 other. US Department of Energy, 1000 Independence Avenue SW, Washington DC 20585. **Tel** (202)586-5000, FAX (202)586-4073. **(Subscription address:** National Technical Information Service, 5285 Port Royal Road, Springfield, VA 22161) **DD** 662.

US/0896-5188
ADVANCED OIL AND GAS RECOVERY TECHNOLOGIES. (ADVANCED OIL AND GAS RECOVERY TECHNOLOGIES : CURRENT ABSTRACTS / U.S. DEPARTMENT OF ENERGY ; PREPARED FOR OFFICE OF FOSSIL ENERGY ;

PREPARED BY OFFICE OF SCIENTIFIC AND TECHNICAL INFORMATION.). [Adv. oil gas recovery technol.]. **Added/Corp** United States. Dept. of Energy. Office of Scientific and Technical Information. United States. Office of Fossil Energy. **VFOAT** OGT. Vol. 88, No. 1 (Jan. 1988)-. Government Publication. English. mo. $160.00 US; $320.00 other. US Department of Energy, 1000 Independence Avenue SW, Washington DC 20585. **Tel** (202)586-5000, FAX (202)586-4073. **(Subscription address:** National Technical Information Service, 5285 Port Royal Road, Springfield, VA 22161**) DD** 665.

UK/0276-2412
ADVANCES IN HYDROGEN ENERGY. [Adv. hydrogen energy]. 1-. Academic Scholarly Publication. English. ir. Price varies per volume. Pergamon Press, An Imprint of Elsevier Science Ltd., The Boulevard, Langford Lane, Kidlington, Oxford OX5 1GB United Kingdom. **Tel** 011 44 865 843000, 011 44 865 843699, FAX 011 44 865 843010. **(Subscription address:** US/ 395 Saw Mill River Road, Elmsford, NY 10523; Can/ 150 Consumers Road/Suite 104, Willowdale Ontario M2J 1P9; Aus-NZ/ POB 544, Potts Point NSW 2011**) CODEN** AHENDB. Documents available from Article Express International, CASDDS.
Ind/Abst Bioeng. Abstr.; Chem. Abstr.; Ei Page One; Eng. Index Annu.

US/0731-8618
ADVANCES IN SOLAR ENERGY. [Adv. sol. energy]. **Added/Corp** American Solar Energy Society. Vol. 1 (1982)-. Monographic series. English. ir. Price varies per volume. American Solar Energy Society, 2400 Central Avenue, Unit G-1, Boulder CO 80301. **Tel** (303)433-3130, FAX (303)443-3212. **LC** TJ809; .A38. **DD** 621.47/05.

US/0192-558X
ADVANCES IN THE ECONOMICS OF ENERGY AND RESOURCES. Vol. 1 (1979)-. Monographic series. English. ir. $73.25. JAI Press Inc., 55 Old Post Road, Suite 2, PO Box 1678, Greenwich CT 06836-1678. **Tel** (203)661-7602, FAX (203)661-0792. **ED** John R. Moroney. **LC** HD9502.A1; A38. **DD** 333.7. **[CCC].** Documents available from Article Express International.
Ind/Abst AESIS Q.; Eng. Index Annu. [Select. Cov.].

US
AEI STUDIES. Added/Corp American Enterprise Institute for Public Policy Research. **VAT** American Enterprise Institute Studies. (1976)-. Monographic series. English. ir. Price varies per volume. American Enterprise Institute, 1150 17th Street Northwest, Department 260, Washington DC 20036. **Tel** (202)862-5800, (800)269-6267. **(Subscription address:** University Press America, 4720 Boston Way, Lanham, MD 20706, (800)462-6420 or (301)459-3366**)**

US/1046-0993
AERO SUN-TIMES. [AERO sun times]. **Added/Corp** Alternative Energy Resources Organization (Helena, Mont.). **VFOAT** AERO Sun Times. **VAT** Alternative Energy Resources Organization Sun-Times. (19??)-. Periodical. English. qt. $15.00. Alternative Energy Resources, 44 North Last Chance Gulch 9, Helena MT 59601. **Tel** (406)443-7272. **DD** 333.
Ind/Abst Energy Inf. Abstr.

US/1071-6947
AES (SERIES). (AES.). [AES]. **Added/Corp** American Society of Mechanical Engineers. American Society of Mechanical Engineers. Advanced Energy Systems Division. Vol. 1 (1985)-. Monographic series. English. ir. price varies per volume. American Society of Mechanical Engineers, 22 Law Drive, Fairfield NJ 07007. **Tel** (201)882-1167, (212)705-7722 (editorial). **DD** 621. **CODEN** AMEAE8. Documents available from CASDDS.
Ind/Abst Chem. Abstr.

US
AFDC UPDATE : NEWS OF THE ALTERNATIVE FUELS DATA CENTER. Main/Corp Alternative Fuels Data Center (National Renewable Energy Laboratory). **Added/Corp** National Renewable Energy Laboratory (U.S.). Vol. 1, Issue 1 (Sept. 1991)-. Periodical. English. qt. Free. National Renewable Energy Laboratory, 1617 Cole Boulevard, Building 15/1, Golden CO 80401-3393. **Tel** (303)231-1000. **(Subscription address:** National Alternative Fuels Hotline, PO Box 12316, Arlington VA 22209.**)**

GW
AFGHANISTAN, PAKISTAN : ENERGIEWIRTSCHAFT. Main/Corp Bundesstelle fur Aussenhandelsinformation (Germany). German. DM2.00. Bundesstelle fuer Aussenhandelsinformation, Agrippastr 87 93, D 50676 Cologne Germany. **Tel** 011 49 221 2057316, FAX 011 49 221 2057212. **LC** HD9502.A47.

FR/0994-0235
AFRICA ENERGY & MINING. (1988)-. Periodical. English. Twenty-three times a year. 3672.87F France; 3750.00F other. Indigo Publications, 10 rue du Sentier, 75002 Paris France. **Tel** 011 33 1 45081480, FAX 011 33 1 45085983, telex 215405. **ED** Joel Delafond. **UDC** 622 (6) = 20. **Circ:** 23.
Desc: Energy and mining in Africa.

GW
AGUPTEM : ENERGIEWIRTSCHAFT. Main/Corp Bundesstelle fur Aussenhandelsinformation (Germany). German. 2.00. Bundesstelle fuer Aussenhandelsinformation, Agrippastr 87 93, D 50676 Cologne Germany. **Tel** 011 49 221 2057316, FAX 011 49 221 2057212. **LC** HD9502.E3; G47A.

CN/0380-4321
ALBERTA COAL INDUSTRY ANNUAL STATISTICS. See Energy-Abstracting, Bibliographies and Statistics.

CN/0706-1420
ALBERTA ELECTRIC INDUSTRY. ANNUAL STATISTICS. See Energy-Abstracting, Bibliographies and Statistics.

CN/0710-6874
ALBERTA ENERGY RESOURCE INDUSTRIES, MONTHLY STATISTICS. See Energy-Abstracting, Bibliographies and Statistics.

CN/0706-1412
ALBERTA'S ENERGY RESOURCES. (ALBERTA'S ENERGY RESOURCES, A SUMMARY.). [Alta. energy resour.]. **Added/Corp** Alberta. Energy Resources Conservation Board. (1973)-. English. an. 5.00Can$. Energy Resources Conservation Board, 640 Fifth Avenue Southwest, Calgary Alberta T2P 3G4 Canada. **Tel** (403)297-8311, (403)297-8190, telex 03-821717. **LC** TN873.C22; A442 subser.; TJ163.25.C3. **DD** 333.7.
Desc: Summary of Alberta's ultimate potential and remaining established reserves of energy resources including oil, gas, coal, and hydroelectric energy.

US
ALCOHOL FUELS PROGRAM TECHNICAL REVIEW. Summer 1981-. English. sa. Solar Energy Research Institute / Colorado, 1617 Cole Boulevard, Golden CO 80401. **Tel** (303)231-7303. ***Continues*** *Alcohol Fuels Process R/D Newsletter.*

US/0191-2585
ALI-ABA COURSE OF STUDY : ENERGY AND THE LAW, PROBLEMS AND CHALLENGES OF THE LATE 70'S : MATERIALS. See Law.

US/0272-8990
ALI-ABA COURSE OF STUDY. ENERGY LAW : MATERIALS. See Law.

US/0732-7099
ALTERNATE ENERGY SOURCES. (ALTERNATE ENERGY SOURCES MICROFORM.). Vol. 1, No. 1-. Monographic series. English. ir. Price varies per volume. Comtex, 850 3rd Avenue, New York NY 10017.

US/0886-828X
ALTERNATIVE ENERGY (BEVERLY HILLS, CALIF.). (ALTERNATIVE ENERGY : TRENDS AND FORECASTS.). [Altern. energy]. (19??)-. Periodical. English. Twelve times a year. $90.00 US & Mexico; $93.00 Canada; $104.00 other. Alternative Energy, 205 South Beverly Drive, Suite 208, Beverly Hills CA 90212. **Tel** (310)273-3486. **DD** 333.
Desc: Reports on important trends and developments in alternative energy sources including biomass, solar energy and hydrogen. Also presents information related to environmental pollution and global warming.

US/1050-3145
ALTERNATIVE ENERGY DIGESTS. (ALTERNATIVE ENERGY DIGESTS: AED ENVIRONMENTAL STUDIES INSTITUTE.). [Altern. energy dig.]. **Added/Corp** International Academy at Santa Barbara. Environmental Studies Institute. **VFOAT** AED. Vol. 1, No. 1 (Jan./Feb. 1990)-. Periodical. English. Eight times a year. $247.00 US; $257.00 other. International Academy at Santa Barbara, 800 Garden Street, Suite D, Santa Barbara CA 93101. **Tel** (805)965-5010, FAX (805)965-6071. **ED** Mary Ann Short. **DD** 333. **[CCC].** available on an online database from Predicasts, Inc.
Desc: Provides digests of important current articles, books, news releases, documents, reports, and announcements relating to alternative energy sources, plus listings of upcoming conferences and trade shows, newly released videos, CD-ROMs, online files, and computer programs.
Ind/Abst PTS Newsl. Database [Full Txt.].

US/0273-8163
ALTERNATIVE ENERGY RETAILER. VFOAT AER. (Nov. 1980)-. Periodical. English. mo. $32.00. Zackin Publications Inc, PO Box 2180, Waterbury CT 06722. **Tel** (203)755-0158. **ED** Ed Easley. **Bk Rev. Ad Acc. Circ:** 16,000 (ctrl).
Desc: Business and industry advice for dealers of alternative energy products.

CN/1186-6918
AMENAGEMENT HYDROELECTRIQUE D'EASTMAN 1, L'. [Amenage. hydroelectr. Eastman 1]. **Added/Corp** Hydro-Quebec. **VAT** Amenagement Hydroelectrique d'Eastman Un. No 1 (Jan 1991)-. Periodical. French. Hydro-Quebec, 14E Etage, 75 Ouest Boul Dorchester, Montreal Quebec H2Z 1A4 Canada. **DD** 333.79.

US/0747-5500
AMERICAN WIND ENERGY ASSOCIATION WIND ENERGY WEEKLY, THE. [Am. Wind Energy Assoc. wind energy wkly.]. **Added/Corp** American Wind Energy Association. **VFOAT** Wind Energy Weekly. (198?)-. Periodical. English. Fifty times a year. $225.00 US, Canada and Mexico; $255.00 other. American Wind Energy Association, 777 North Capitol Street NE, Suite 805, Washington DC 20002. **Tel** (202)408-8988, FAX (202)408-8536. **ED** Randall Swisher and Tom Gray. **Circ:** 400. ***Continues*** *AWEA Update.*
Desc: The most up-to-date information on wind industry activities. It covers industry developments, legislative and regulatory issues, state and local decisions affecting the industry, wind power projects and national and international business opportunities.
Ind/Abst Energy Inf. Abstr.

US
ANALYSES OF TIPPLE AND DELIVERED SAMPLES OF COAL. (ANALYSES OF TIPPLE AND DELIVERED SAMPLES OF COAL : COLLECTED DURING FISCAL YEAR.). 1948/50-. English. an. US Department of the Interior / Bureau of Mines, Publications Department, PO Box 18070, Cochrans Mill Road, Pittsburgh PA 15236. **Tel** (412)892-6400.

GW
ANGOLA, ENERGIEWIRTSCHAFT / BUNDESSTELLE FUR AUSSENHANDELSINFORMATION. German. an. DM3.00. Bundesstelle fuer Aussenhandelsinformation, Agrippastr 87 93, D 50676 Cologne Germany. **Tel** 011 49 221 2057316, FAX 011 49 221 2057212. **LC** HD9502.A63.

BE/0003-4290
ANNALES DES MINES DE BELGIQUE. ***Ceased.*** **See** Engineering-Mines and Mining Engineering.

FR
ANNUAL COAL STATISTICS. VFOAT Statistiques Annuelles du Charbon. English (French). an. $745.00 (magnetic tape). OECD Publications and Information Center, 2 rue Andre-Pascal, 75775 Paris Cedex 16 France. **Tel** 011 33 1 45248167, US:(202)785-6323, FAX 011 33 1 45248500 OR 45248176, telex 620 160 OCDE. **(Subscription address:** OECD Publications Center, 2001 L Street, Suite 700, Washington DC 20036.**)** available on magnetic tape.
Desc: Includes extensive statistical information on production , consumption, imports and exports and examines environmental and shipping issues.

US/0270-7586
ANNUAL COLLECTION AND STORAGE OF SOLAR ENERGY FOR THE HEATING OF BUILDINGS. (ANNUAL COLLECTION AND STORAGE OF SOLAR ENERGY FOR THE HEATING OF BUILDINGS; REPORT.). [Annu. collect. storage solar energy heat. build.]. **Main/Corp** United States. Dept. of Energy. Division of Solar Energy. (19??)-. English. sa. National Technical Information Service - NTIS, Room 2027S, 5285 Port Royal Road, Springfield VA 22161. **Tel** (703)487-4630, (703)487-4660, (703)487-4650, FAX (703)321-8547, telex 89-9405. **ED** Prepared for the United States Division of Solar Research by: J. T. Beard, F. A. Iachetta, L. U. Lilleleht and J. W. Dicky. **LC** TH7413; .U52f. **DD** 697/.78/05.

FR
ANNUAL ELECTRICITY STATISTICS. VFOAT Statistiques Annuelles de l'Electricite. English (French). an. $745.00 (magnetic tape). OECD Publications and Information Center, 2 rue Andre-Pascal, 75775 Paris Cedex 16 France. **Tel** 011 33 1 45248167, US:(202)785-6323, FAX 011 33 1 45248500 OR 45248176, telex 620 160 OCDE. **(Subscription address:** OECD Publications Center, 2001 L Street, Suite 700, Washington DC 20036.**)** available on magnetic tape.
Desc: Annual data on electricity supply and consumption in the OECD countries.

US/0278-5951
ANNUAL ENERGY BALANCE (U.S.). Main/Corp United States. Energy Information Administration. Government Publication. English. an. US Department of Energy, 1000 Independence Avenue SW, Washington DC 20585. **Tel** (202)586-5000, FAX (202)586-4073. **LC** TJ163.25.U6; U532D. **DD** 333.79/0973.

US/0273-7000
ANNUAL ENERGY LITIGATION INSTITUTE : EFFECTIVE STRATEGIES & TECHNIQUES. See Law.

US/0740-4190
ANNUAL ENERGY OUTLOOK. [Annu. energy outlook]. (1982)-. Government Publication. English. an. $7.50 (single copy) US; $9.38 (single copy) other. US Department of Energy, 1000 Independence Avenue SW, Washington DC 20585. **Tel** (202)586-5000, FAX (202)586-4073. **LC** TJ163.25.U6; A55. **DD** 333.79/0973.

Continues in part *United States. Energy Information Administration. Annual Report to Congress, 0161-5807.* ***Continued in part by*** *International Energy Outlook.*
Desc: This forecast report examines four different scenarios which, taken as a group, present a range of possible outcomes, which diverge over a 20-year projection. The report presents trends in energy supply and demand, based upon assumptions about world oil prices, ecohnomic growth, and other factors affecting energy markets.
Ind/Abst Energy Inf. Abstr.; F&S Index Plus Text, Int. [Select. Cov.]; Predicasts Forecasts.

US/0740-3909
ANNUAL ENERGY REVIEW (WASHINGTON, D.C.). (ANNUAL ENERGY REVIEW.). [Annu. energy rev.]. **Added/Corp** United States. Office of Energy Markets and End Use. (1982)-. English. an. $25.00. National Energy Information Center, Energy Information Administration, Forrestal Building, Room 1F-048, Washington DC 20585. **Tel** (202)586-8800. **ED** Diane Whited. **LC** TJ163.25.U6; U532a. **DD** 333.79/0973. ***Continues in part*** *United States. Energy Information Administration. Annual Report to Congress, 0161-5807.*
Desc: Presents historical energy data summaries as well as complete data coverage of the principal energy commodities.
Ind/Abst Energy Inf. Abstr.; Predicasts Forecasts.

US/0736-4997
ANNUAL ENERGY SUMMARY. [Annu. energy summ.]. Government Publication. English. an. US Department of Energy, 1000 Independence Avenue SW, Washington DC 20585. **Tel** (202)586-5000, FAX (202)586-4073. **LC** TJ163.25.U6; A56. **DD** 333.79/0973.

US
ANNUAL HIGHLIGHTS OF THE ENERGY TECHNOLOGY PROGRAMS. **Main/Corp** Brookhaven National Laboratory. Dept. of Energy and Environment. English. an. US Department of Energy Office of Energy Research, 1000 Independence Avenue SW, Room 7B-058, Washington DC 20585. **Tel** (202)586-5430, FAX (202)586-4120.

CN/0706-1293
ANNUAL INTERNATIONAL CONFERENCE / CANADIAN NUCLEAR ASSOCIATION. **See** Engineering-Nuclear Engineering.

US
ANNUAL MEETING & INTERNATIONAL CONFERENCE ON NUCLEAR ENERGY. (19??)-. English. an. $100.00. World Nuclear Fuel Market, 655 Engineering Drive, Suite 200, Norcross GA 30092. **Tel** (404)447-1144, FAX (404) 447-1797. Index available. **Circ:** 250 (ctrl).
Desc: Speeches and discussions from yearly meetings on nuclear energy.

US/0277-478X
ANNUAL PROGRAM INFORMATION NOTICE. [Annu. program inf. not.]. Government Publication. English. an. US Department of Energy, 1000 Independence Avenue SW, Washington DC 20585. **Tel** (202)586-5000, FAX (202)586-4073. **LC** TK23; .A66. ***Continues*** *Program Information Notice.*

CN
ANNUAL REPORT. **Main/Corp** Atomic Energy Control Board. 1st (1946/1947)-. Periodical. English (French). an. Free. Atomic Energy Control Board, 270 Albert Street, PO Box 1046, Ottawa Ontario K1P 5S9 Canada. **Tel** (613)996-8211, FAX (613)995-5086, telex 053-3771. **Circ:** 3,000.
Desc: Describes the organization and functions of the Atomic Energy Control Board and records its significant activities and financial position for one fiscal year ending March 31; lists major nuclear facilities.

CN/0846-5029
ANNUAL REPORT / CANMET. **See** Earth Sciences-Mineralogy.

FR
ANNUAL REPORT / CEA, FRENCH ATOMIC ENERGY COMMISSION. (19??)-. French. CEA Department des Relations Publiques et de la Communication, 31-33 rue de la Federation, 75752 Paris Cedex 15 France.
Ind/Abst AESIS Q.

AT/1036-1367
ANNUAL REPORT - CSIRO. COAL AND ENERGY TECHNOLOGY. ***Title Change.*** (ANNUAL REPORT.). [Annu. rep. - CSIRO. Coal Energy Technol.]. (1990)-(199?). English. an. Division of Coal and Energy Technology, Box 136, North Ryde New South Wales 2113 Australia. **Tel** (02)543-3979. **DD** 662.6006094. **Circ:** 800 (ctrl). ***Continues*** *Coal Technology Division Annual Report, 1031-6728* ***and*** *Annual Report - Division of Fuel Technology, 1033-2472.* ***Continued by*** *Interface Quarterly Newsletter.*

AT/0725-9727
ANNUAL REPORT - DEPARTMENT OF MINES AND ENERGY, NORTHERN TERRITORY. **See** Engineering-Mines and Mining Engineering.

US
ANNUAL REPORT - FEDERAL POWER COMMISSION. **Main/Corp** United States. Federal Power Commission. **VFOAT** Annual Report of the Federal Power Commission. (1920/1921)-. English. an. Superintendent of Documents, US Government Printing Office, Washington DC 20402. **Tel** (202)275-3328, FAX (202)786-2377.

II
ANNUAL REPORT / GOVERNMENT OF INDIA, DEPARTMENT OF NON-CONVENTIONAL ENERGY SOURCES, MINISTRY OF ENERGY. **Main/Corp** India. Dept. of Non-Conventional Energy Sources. (1982/83)-. English. an. Information Cell Department of Non-Conventional Energy Sources, Block No 14/Central Government Offices Complex, Lodi Road, New Delhi-110003 India. **LC** TJ807.9.I4; I53a. **DD** 954.54008/23.

AT/1032-111X
ANNUAL REPORT / MINERALS AND ENERGY RESEARCH INSTITUTE OF WESTERN AUSTRALIA. **Main/Corp** Minerals and Energy Research Institute of Western Australia. (1988/1989)-. English. **LC** IN PROCESS. ***Continues*** *Solar Energy Research Institute of Western Australia. Annual Report; Western Australian Mining and Petroleum Research Institute. Annual Report.*
Ind/Abst AESIS Q.

AT/0725-0827
ANNUAL REPORT - NATIONAL ENERGY ADVISORY COMMITTEE CANBERRA. [Annu. rep. - Natl. Energy Advis. Comm. Canberra]. (1979)-. English. an. Australian Bureau of Statistics, PO Box 10, Belconnen Australian Capital Territory, 2616 Australia. **Tel** 011 61 6 2527911, FAX 011 61 6 2516009. **DD** 354.94008232.
Ind/Abst AESIS Q.

US
ANNUAL REPORT / NEW MEXICO RESEARCH AND DEVELOPMENT INSTITUTE. **Main/Corp** New Mexico Research and Development Institute. (1986)-. English. New Mexico Energy Research and Development Institute, Room 358, Pinon Building, 1220 South Street Francis Drive, Santa Fe NM 87501. **LC** HD9502.U53; N4976a. **DD** 353.97890082/3. ***Continues*** *New Mexico Energy Research and Development Institute. Annual Report, 0739-3962.*

US/0161-5807
ANNUAL REPORT TO CONGRESS - UNITED STATES DEPARTMENT OF ENERGY, ENERGY INFORMATION ADMINISTRATION. (ANNUAL REPORT TO CONGRESS.). [Annu. rep. Congr. - U. S. Dep. Energy Energy Inf. Admin.]. **Main/Corp** United States. Energy Information Administration. (1977)-. English. an. National Energy Information Center, Energy Information Administration, Forrestal Building, Room 1F-048, Washington DC 20585. **Tel** (202)586-8800. **LC** TJ163.25.U6; U532a. **DD** 353.008/232. available on microfiche (Vols. for (1986-) distributed to depository libraries). ***Continued in part by*** *Annual Energy Review, 0740-3909* ***and*** *Annual Energy Outlook, 0740-4190.*
Desc: Discusses accomplishments of EIA and describes the responsibilities of EIA.

US/0161-1674
ANNUAL REPORT TO THE PRESIDENT AND THE CONGRESS ON THE STATE ENERGY CONSERVATION PROGRAM. (ANNUAL REPORT TO THE PRESIDENT AND THE CONGRESS ON THE STATE ENERGY CONSERVATION PROGRAM FOR CALENDAR YEAR ... / PREPARED BY U.S. DEPARTMENT OF ENERGY, ASSISTANT SECRETARY FOR CONSERVATION AND SOLAR APPLICATION, OFFICE OF STATE AND LOCAL PROGRAMS.). **Added/Corp** United States. Dept. of Energy. Office of Conservation and Solar Applications. Office of State and Local Programs. United States. Office of State Energy Conservation Programs. United States. Dept. of Energy. Office of Energy Management and Extension. United States. Dept. of Energy. Office of State and Local Assistance Programs. (1978)-. English. an. National Technical Information Service - NTIS, Room 2027S, 5285 Port Royal Road, Springfield VA 22161. **Tel** (703)487-4630, (703)487-4660, (703)487-4650, FAX (703)321-8547, telex 89-9405. **LC** TJ163.4.U6; U57a. **DD** 353.0082/32. ***Continues*** *United States. Dept. of Energy. Office of Conservation and Solar Application. Office of State and Local Programs. Annual Report to the President and the Congress on the State Energy Conservation Program, 0161-1674.*

US/0195-4806
ANNUAL REPORT TO THE PRESIDENT AND THE CONGRESS ON THE WEATHERIZATION ASSISTANCE PROGRAM. **Main/Corp** United States. Dept. of Energy. Office of Conservation and Solar Applications. Office of State and Local Programs. (19??)-. English. an. $4.50. National Technical Information Service - NTIS, Room 2027S, 5285 Port Royal Road, Springfield VA 22161. **Tel** (703)487-4630, (703)487-4660, (703)487-4650, FAX (703)321-8547, telex 89-9405. **LC** TH1715.A1; U54a. **DD** 363.5/82.

US/0197-0496
ANNUAL REPORT - WYOMING ENERGY CONSERVATION OFFICE. [Annu. rep. - Wyo. Energy Conserv. Off.]. **Main/Corp** Wyoming. Energy Conservation Office. 1977/78-. English. an. Wyoming Energy Conservation Office, Capitol Hill Office Building, 320 West 25th Street, Cheyenne WY 82002. **LC** TJ163.4.U6; W88A. **DD** 353.97870082/3.

US/1056-3466
ANNUAL REVIEW OF ENERGY AND THE ENVIRONMENT. [Annu. rev. energy environ.]. **Added/Corp** Annual Reviews, Inc. (1991)-. Academic Scholarly Publication. English. an (October). $71.00 US; $76.00 other. Annual Reviews Inc., 4139 El Camino Way, PO Box 10139, Palo Alto CA 94303-0139. **Tel** (415)493-4400, (800)523-8635, FAX (415)855-9815. **ED** Robert H. Socolow. **LC** TJ163.2; .A55. **DD** 333.7. **NLM** W1; AN77L. **CODEN** ANEEER. Each issue contains an index to its own contents (no volume index)--loose. available on microfilm and microfiche from University Microfilms International (UMI). Documents available from The Genuine Article, Ask*IEEE, CASDDS. ***Continues*** *Annual Review of Energy, 0362-1626.*
Ind/Abst Bioeng. Abstr.; Chem. Abstr.; Coal Abstr.; Curr. Contents Eng. Tech. Appl. Sci.; Energy Inf. Abstr.; GeoRef; INIS Atomindex [Micro.]; INSPEC; Life Sci. Collect.; Res. Alert [Full Cov.]; Sci. Cit. Index; SCISEARCH; Soc. Sci. Cit. Index [Select. Cov.].

US
ANNUAL SUMMARY OF PROGRAMS IN ENERGY SCIENCES. **Main/Corp** Brookhaven National Laboratory. Dept. of Energy and Environment. English. an. US Department of Energy Office of Energy Research, 1000 Independence Avenue SW, Room 7B-058, Washington DC 20585. **Tel** (202)586-5430, FAX (202)586-4120.

IT
ANNUARIO NAZIONALE DELL ENERGIA E DELL AMBIENTE. **VFOAT** Italian Energy and Environment Directory; Italian Energy & Environment Directory. 6A Ed. (1988)-. Italian (Italian). an. L300000. INTER-ED Srl, Via Cassia 1134/A, 00189 Rome Italy. **Tel** 011 39 6 3767922. **ED** Ludovico A Salvi. **LC** HD9502.I8; A55. **Bk Rev**. **Ad Acc**. ***Continues*** *Annuario Nazionale dell'Energia.*

BL
ANUARIO ESTATISTICO DE ENERGIA ELECTRICA / COMPANIA ENERGETICA DE SAO PAULO, DIVISAO DE ESTUDOS DO MERCADO DE ENERGIA ELETRICA. **See** Energy-Abstracting, Bibliographies and Statistics.

UK/0306-2619
APPLIED ENERGY. [Appl. energy]. Vol. 1 (Jan. 1975)-. Academic Scholarly Publication. English. Twelve times a year (3 Volumes). $1006.00 The Americas; £675.00 other. Elsevier Applied Science, An Imprint of Elsevier Science Ltd., The Boulevard, Langford Lane, Kidlington, Oxford OX5 1GB United Kingdom. **Tel** 011 44 865 843000, 011 44 865 843699, FAX 011 44 865 843010. **(Subscription address:** Elsevier Science Ltd. Oxford Fulfillment Centre, PO Box 800, Kidlington, Oxford OX5 1DX United Kingdom.**)** **ED** S. D. Probert. **LC** TJ1; .A83. **DD** 621. **CODEN** APENDX. **[CCC]**. **Bk Rev**. **Ad Acc**. **Pr Rev**. available on microfilm and microfiche from University Microfilms International (UMI). Documents available from Article Express International, The Genuine Article, Ask*IEEE, CASDDS, Documents on Demand.
Desc: Aims at bridging the gap between the fundamental scientist who rarely considers the problems of translating his research into practical applications and the manager/chief engineer who feels that the general run of scientific papers is too specialised to concern his own company.
Ind/Abst Abstr. AIT Rep. Publ. Energy; AESIS Q.; AGRICOLA; Bioeng. Abstr.; Chem. Abstr.; Coal Abstr.; Curr. Contents Eng. Tech. Appl. Sci.; Ei Page One; EMBASE; Energy Inf. Abstr.; Energy Res. Abstr. (July 1975-); Eng. Index Annu.; Environ. Abstr.; Fluid Abstr., Civil Eng.; Fluid Abstr. Proc. Eng.; FLUIDEX; Gas Abstr.; Geogr. Abstr. Human Geogr. (Jan. 1975-); GeoRef; HTFS Dig.; INSPEC (Jan. 1975-); Int. Aerosp. Abstr.; Int. Build. Serv. Abstr.; Int. Dev. Abstr. (Jan. 1975-); Ornamental Hort.; Life Sci. Collect.; Res. Alert [Full Cov.]; Rice Abstr.; Sci. Cit. Index; SCISEARCH; Soc. Sci. Cit. Index [Select. Cov.].

US/0003-701X
APPLIED SOLAR ENERGY. [Appl. sol. energy]. **Added/Corp** Uzbek Academy of Sciences. Vol. 1 (Jan./Feb. 1965)-. Academic Scholarly Publication.

English (Russian). bm. $895.00. Allerton Press, Inc., 150 Fifth Avenue, New York NY 10011. **Tel** (212)924-3950, FAX (212)463-9684, telex 427441 ALPRES. **LC** TJ810; .G413. **CODEN** ASOEA6. **[CCC].** Index available. **Bk Rev.** Documents available from Article Express International, Ask*IEEE.
Ind/Abst Agric. Eng. Abstr. (1991-); Bioeng. Abstr.; Ei Page One; Energy Res. Abstr. (June 1972-); Eng. Index Annu.; Environ. Period. Bibliogr. (?-?); Hortic. Abstr.; INIS Atomindex [Micro.]; INSPEC (1968-); Int. Aerosp. Abstr.; Ornamental Hort. (1991-); Pollut. Abstr. Indexes.

GW
ARABISCHE REPUBLIK JEMEN, ENERGIEWIRTSCHAFT / BUNDESSTELLE FUR AUSSENHANDELSINFORMATION. German. an. 3.00. Bundesstelle fuer Aussenhandelsinformation, Agrippastr 87 93, D 50676 Cologne Germany. **Tel** 011 49 221 2057316, FAX 011 49 221 2057212. **LC** HD9502.Y45; A72. **DD** 333.79/0953/32.

US/0741-6237
ARIZONA ENERGY JOURNAL. No. 1 (May 1979)-. Periodical. English. mo. $120.00. Energy Publications, PO Box 13433, Phoenix AZ 85002. **Tel** (602)234-3781, FAX (602)234-1410. **Bk Rev.**
Desc: Energy management, energy conservation, and energy rate design.

CN/0707-5588
ASCENT. [Ascent]. Vol. 1 (Spring 1979)-. Periodical. English. Three times a year. Free on Request. Atomic Energy of Canada Ltd, 344 Slater Street, Ottawa Ontario, K1A OS4 Canada. **Tel** (613)237-3270, FAX (613)782-2023, telex 053-4867. **ED** Lynn Gawker. **Bk Rev. Circ:** 15,000 (ctrl). ***Supersedes** AECL Review, 0001-1029.*
Ind/Abst Energy Res. Abstr. (Aug. 1980-); INIS Atomindex [Micro.].

MY
ASIAN PETROLEUM. English. Energy Publishing Services Sdn Bhd, 15A SG 3/4, Taman Sri Gombak, 68100 Batu Cave, Selangor Malaysia. **Tel** 60 03 689 0571/689 9576, FAX 60 03 689 3518. **ED** Ravi Krishnan.
Desc: Provides reports and analysis on Asian/Australian energy exploration and production news and technical articles relating to the upstream oil and gas industry.
Ind/Abst Pet. Energy Bus. News Index (1992).

US
ASSUMPTIONS FOR THE ANNUAL ENERGY OUTLOOK. Added/Corp United States. Office of Energy Markets and End Use. United States. Energy Information Administration. Office of Integrated Analysis and Forecasting. (19??)-. English. an. National Energy Information Center, Energy Information Administration, Forrestal Building, Room 1F-048, Washington DC 20585. **Tel** (202)586-8800. **LC** TJ163.25.U6; A88. **DD** 333.79/0973. Index available. cum. index.
Desc: Presents a detailed discussion of the assumptions underlying the forecasts of the AEO. These forecasts were developed for four alternative cases and consist of energy supply, consumption, and price projection by major fuel and end-use sector, which are published at a national level of aggregation.

CN/0821-2600
ATLANTIC ENERGY NEWS. [Atl. energy news]. Vol. 1, No. 1 (May 1982)-. Periodical. English. mo. $24.00 Canada and US; $38.00 other. Atlantic Energy News, Unit 14, 192 Joseph Zatzman Drive, Dartmouth Nova Scotia B3B 1N4 Canada. **Tel** (902)463-2661. **DD** 333.79/09715.

UK/0004-7015
ATOM (LONDON, ENGLAND). See Physics-Nuclear Physics.

US/0519-3389
ATOMIC ENERGY CLEARING HOUSE.
Added/Corp Congressional Information Bureau. (19??)-. English. wk. $525.00 US, Canada, and Mexico; $650.00 other. Congressional Information Bureau, 3030 Clarendon Boulevard, Suite 202, Arlington VA 22201. **Tel** (703)516-4801. **[CCC].**

AT/0004-7090
ATOMIC ENERGY IN AUSTRALIA. Vol. 1 (1957)-. Periodical. English. qt.
Ind/Abst AESIS Q.

US/0004-7104
ATOMIC ENERGY LAW JOURNAL. See Law.

US/0519-3486
ATOMIC INDUSTRY, THE. Added/Corp Atomic Industrial Forum. Periodical. English. **LC** HD9698.U5; A83. **DD** 338.39; 621.48; 338.4762148.

RU/0004-7163
ATOMNAIA ENERGIIA. [At. energ.].
Added/Corp Akademiia Nauk SSSR. Soviet Union. Glavnoe Upravlenie po Ispolzovaniiu Atomnoi Energii. Gosudarstvennyi Komitet po Ispolzovaniiu Atomnoi Energii SSSR. Vol. 1 (1956)-. Periodical. Russian. mo. $229.95. Ministry of the Russian Federation on Atomic Energy, Ulitsa Miasnitskaia 18, 101000 Moscow Russia. **Tel** 925 8670, FAX 943 0074. **(Subscription address:** East View Publications Inc., 3020 Harbor Lane North, Suite 110, Minneapolis MN 55447.) **LC** QC770; .A83. **CODEN** AENGAB. **[CCC].** Documents available from Article Express International, Ask*IEEE, CASDDS, Documents on Demand.
Ind/Abst Chem. Abstr.; Energy Inf. Abstr.; Energy Res. Abstr.; Eng. Index Annu.; Environ. Abstr.; GeoRef; INSPEC (1968-); Int. Aerosp. Abstr.

RU/0320-9326
ATOMNAIA TEKHNIKA ZA RUBEZHOM. [At. tekh. rub.]. (1957)-. Periodical. Russian. mo. $179.95. **(Subscription address:** East View Publications Inc., 3020 Harbor Lane North, Suite 110, Minneapolis MN 55447.)
Ind/Abst Energy Res. Abstr. (Feb. 1974-).

JA
ATOMS IN JAPAN. Added/Corp Nihon Genshiryoku Sangyo Kaigi. (1957)-. Periodical. English. mo. $921.50. Nihon Genshiryoku Sangyo Kaigi, (Japan Atomic Industrial Forum), 1-13, Shinbashi, 1 Chome, Minatoku, Tokyoto 105 Japan. **(Subscription address:** Japan Publications Trading Company, Ltd., PO Box 5030, Tokyo International, Tokyo 100-31 Japan.) **LC** QC770; .A96.
Ind/Abst EMBASE; Energy Res. Abstr. (Mar. 1972-).

GW
AUSGEWAHLTE ZAHLEN ZUR ENERGIEWIRTSCHAFT / HERAUSGEBER STATISTISCHES BUNDESAMT. Added/Corp Germany (West). Statistisches Bundesamt. (19??)-. German. Twelve times a year. DM121.20. Metzler Poeschel Verlag Veroeffen, Statist Bundesamt Kernerstr 43, D 70182 Stuttgart Germany. **Tel** 011 49 7071 935350. **(Subscription address:** Metzler Poeschel H Leins GmbH, Postfach 1152, D 72125 Kusterdingen Germany.) **LC** TJ163.25.G3; A87. **DD** 333.79.
Desc: Provides topical data on power production. For the various sources of energy are shown data on supply and utilization, imports and exports, price indices and prices as well as establishments, employment and production indices.

AT/0157-4566
AUSTRALIAN COAL REPORT. [Aust. coal rep.]. (1979)-. Periodical. English. Twelve times a year. 450.00Aus$. Australian Coal Report, Level 9, 16 O'Connell Stree, Sydney New South Wales 2000 Australia. **Tel** 011 61 2 2218440, FAX 011 62 2 2218592. **ED** Mr. J. Barlow. **DD** 382.4220994. Index available (Bound in next issue). cum. index. **Ad Acc, Adv Mgr:** Mr. J. Barton, **Tel** 221-8440. **Circ:** 500.
Desc: Comprehensive information on the export and domestic coal industries of Australia and Asian countries.

AT/0817-4113
AUSTRALIAN ENERGY MANAGEMENT NEWS. [Aust. energy manag. news]. **Added/Corp** Australia. Dept. of Resources and Energy. (1986)-. English. ir. Australian Government Publishing Service, GPO Box 84, Canberra ACT 2601 Australia. **Tel** 011 61 6 2954411, FAX 011 61 6 2954455. **DD** 333.79160994. ***Continues** Energy Manager (Melbourne), 0814-0782.*
Ind/Abst AESIS Q.

AT/0815-0575
AUSTRALIAN ENERGY RESEARCH. [Aust. energy res.]. **Added/Corp** Australia. Dept. of Resources and Energy. (1985)-. Periodical. English. qt. Australian Government Publishing Service, GPO Box 84, Canberra ACT 2601 Australia. **Tel** 011 61 6 2954411, FAX 011 61 6 2954455. **DD** 333.79150994.
Ind/Abst AESIS Q.

AT/0727-2596
AUSTRALIAN ENERGY STATISTICS / DEPARTMENT OF NATIONAL DEVELOPMENT AND ENERGY. See Energy-Abstracting, Bibliographies and Statistics.

GW
AUSTRALIEN ENERGIEWIRTSCHAFT / BUNDESSTELLE FUR AUSSENHANDELSINFORMATION. German. DM2.00. Bundesstelle fuer Aussenhandelsinformation, Agrippastr 87 93, D 50676 Cologne Germany. **Tel** 011 49 221 2057316, FAX 011 49 221 2057212. **LC** HD9502.A87; A9. **DD** 333.79/0994.

BL
BALANCO ENERGETICO NACIONAL. ***Title Change.*** **Main/Corp** Brazil. Ministerio das Minas e Energia. Portuguese. an. **LC** HD9502.B7; B72A. ***Continued by** Boletim do Balanco Energetico Nacional.*

FR
BASIC ENERGY STATISTICS. MAGNETIC TAPE. VFOAT Statistiques de Base de l'Energie. French. an. $745.00 (magnetic tape). OECD Publications and Information Center, 2 rue Andre-Pascal, 75775 Paris Cedex 16 France. **Tel** 011 33 1 45248167, US:(202)785-6323, FAX 011 33 1 45248500 OR 45248176, telex 620 160 OCDE. **(Subscription address:** OECD Publications Center, 2001 L Street, Suite 700, Washington DC 20036.) available on magnetic tape.
Desc: Annual statistical data on energy supply and consumption in OECD countries.

US/0005-6359
BATTERY MAN. [Battery man]. **Added/Corp** Independent Battery Manufacturers Association. Independent Battery Manufacturers of America. (1921)-. Periodical. English. mo. $20.00 (one year), $32.00 (two year), $42.00 (three year). Independent Battery Manufacturers Association Inc., 100 Larchwood Drive, Largo FL 34640. **Tel** (813)586-1408, FAX (813)586-1400. **ED** Celwyn Hopkins. Index available. cum. index. **Bk Rev. Ad Acc, Adv Mgr:** Suzanne Kellerman. **Circ:** 5,500 (ctrl).
Ind/Abst Curr. Titles Electrochem.; Energy Res. Abstr. (Oct. 1976-); Leadscan.

GW
BELGIEN : ENERGIEWIRTSCHAFT.
Main/Corp Bundesstelle fur Aussenhandelsinformation (Germany). German. DM3.00. Bundesstelle fuer Aussenhandelsinformation, Agrippastr 87 93, D 50676 Cologne Germany. **Tel** 011 49 221 2057316, FAX 011 49 221 2057212. **LC** HD9502.B3.

US
BENCHMARK PAPERS ON ENERGY. v. 1- 1975-. Periodical. English. ir. Price varies per volume. Van Nostrand Reinhold Company Inc., 115 5th Avenue, New York NY 10003. **Tel** (212)254-3232, FAX (212)673-1239, telex 272562. **(Subscription address:** Academic Press Inc., PO Box 620000, Orlando FL 32891-8340.)

US/0270-8930
BIENNIAL REPORT - CALIFORNIA ENERGY COMMISSION. [Bienn. rep. - Calif. Energy Comm.]. **Main/Corp** California Energy Commission. **VFOAT** Biennial Report to the Governor and the Legislature. 1979-. English. be. California Energy Commission, 1516 9th Street, Sacramento CA 95814. **Tel** (916)324-3014. **LC** HD9502.U53; C319A. **DD** 333.79/09794. ***Continues** California Energy Commission. Biennial Report of the State Energy Commission, 0160-032X.*

US/0363-6410
BIENNIAL REPORT OF THE OFFICE OF EMERGENCY ENERGY ASSISTANCE.
Main/Corp Wisconsin. Office of Emergency Energy Assistance. English. be. State of Wisconsin, PO Box 7840, Document Sales, Madison WI 53707. **Tel** (608)266-3358. **LC** HD9502.U53; W588A. **DD** 353.9/775/00872.

AT
BIENNIAL RESEARCH REPORT / DIVISION OF ENERGY CHEMISTRY, CSIRO. Main/Corp Institute of Energy and Earth Resources (Australia). Division of Energy Chemistry. (1985)-. English. be. CSIRO Publications, PO Box 89, 314 Albert Street, East Melborne Victoria 3002 Australia. **Tel** 011 61 3 4187333, 4187217, FAX 011 61 3 4190459, telex AA 30236. **LC** TJ163.25.A8; I57a. **DD** 621.042/072094. ***Continues** Institute of Energy and Earth Resources (Australia). Division of Energy Chemistry. Research Review.*

CN/0708-1936
BIO-JOULE. ***Ceased.*** Vol. 1 (Sept. 1978)-(May 1993). English. bm. Biomass Energy Institute, 1329 Niakwa Road East, Winnipeg Manitoba R2J 3T4 Canada. **Tel** (204)257-3891. **ED** Beth Candlish. **DD** 662/.6. **Ad Acc. Circ:** 2,000. ***Supersedes** Biomass Energy Institute. Newsletter, 0315-3223.*
Ind/Abst Energy Inf. Abstr.

US/1046-0411
BIOLOGUE AND THE REGIONAL BIOMASS ENERGY PROGRAM REPORTS. (BIOLOGUE AND THE REGIONAL BIOMASS ENERGY PROGRAM REPORTS : THE OFFICIAL PUBLICATION OF THE NATIONAL WOOD ENERGY ASSOCIATION.). [Biol. Reg. Biomass Energy Program rep.]. **Added/Corp** National Wood Energy Association (U.S.) Regional Biomass Energy Program. **VFOAT** Biologue. (July/Aug. 1988)-. Periodical. English. qt. $20.00. National Wood Energy Association, 777 North Capitol Street, Suite 805, Washington DC 20002. **DD** 662. ***Continues** Biologue (Portsmouth, N.H.).*

UK/0961-9534
BIOMASS & BIOENERGY. VFOAT Biomass and Bioenergy. Vol. 1, No. 1 (1991)-. Periodical. English. mo. $558.00 The Americas; £374.00 other. Pergamon Press, An Imprint of Elsevier Science Ltd., The Boulevard, Langford Lane, Kidlington, Oxford OX5 1GB United Kingdom. **Tel** 011 44 865 843000, 011 44 865 843699, FAX 011 44 865 843010. **(Subscription address:** Elsevier Science Ltd. Oxford Fulfillment Centre, PO Box 800, Kidlington, Oxford OX5 1DX United Kingdom.) **ED** J. Coombs, D. Hall, R. Overend, and W. Smith. **LC** TP360; .B5854. **DD** 662/.88/05. **CODEN** BMSBEO. **[CCC].** available on microfilm and microfiche from University Microfilms International (UMI). Documents available from Article Express International, The Genuine Article.
Ind/Abst Curr. Aware. Biol. Sci., CABS; Eng. Index Annu. [Select. Cov.]; Environ. Period. Bibliogr.; Res. Alert [Select. Cov.]; SCISEARCH.

UK/0262-7183
BIOMASS BULLETIN. Vol. 1, No. 1 (Sept. 1981)-. Periodical. English. qt (Jan., Apr., July, Oct.). £114.00 UK and Europe; £126.00 other, add £11.00 (airmail) for postage. Multi Science Publishing Company Ltd., 107 High Street, Brentwood, Essex CM14 4RX England. **Tel** 011 44 277 224632, FAX 011 44 277 223453, telex 89-8452. **[CCC].** available on microfiche.
Desc: Journal of news items, report and article summaries, book reviews and abstracts of conference proceedings, which offers an unrivalled synoptic survey of current and projected activity in this important area, including laboratory research and field trials on both the fuel potential and recycling aspects of biomass.

●US
BIOMASS BULLETIN/ WESTERN REGIONAL BIOMASS ENERGY PROGRAM. **Added/Corp** Western Regional Biomass Energy Program (U.S.). (1992)-. Periodical. English. qt. Western Regional Biomass Energy Program, A0410, PO Box 80401, Golden CO 80401.

●US
BIOMASS DIGEST / WESTERN REGIONAL BIOMASS ENERGY PROGRAM. **Added/Corp** Western Regional Biomass Energy Program (U.S.). Vol. 1, No. 1 (Winter 1992)-. Periodical. English. qt. Western Regional Biomass Energy Program, A0410, PO Box 80401, Golden CO 80401.

●US/1064-7651
BIOMASS ENERGY DIRECTORY. (BIOMASS ENERGY DIRECTORY / BY THE PUBLISHERS OF INDEPENDENT ENERGY MAGAZINE.). **VFOAT** Biomass Directory. (1992)-. Directory. English. $27.00. Independent Energy, 620 Central Avenue North, Milaca MN 56353. **LC** HD9502.5.B543; B56. **DD** 333.

US/0738-4114
BIOMASS ENERGY INCL. ALCOHOL FUELS MONTHLY UPDATE. ***Title Change.*** [Biomass energy incl. alcohol fuels mon. update]. **VFOAT** Biomass Energy Including Alcohol Fuels Monthly Update; Biomass Energy Incl. Alcohol Fuels. English. mo. GV Olsen Associates, 170 Broadway/Suite 201, New York NY 10038. ***Continued by*** *Olsen's Biomass Energy Report.*

US
BLOOMBERG ENERGY HANDBOOK. (19??)-. English. an. $125.00 US; $140.00 other. Bloomberg Financial Markets, 100 Business Park Drive, Princeton NJ 08542. **Tel** (609)279-4261. ***Continues*** *Petroleum Marketer's Handbook.*

FR/1153-3072
BOIS DE FEU & ENERGIE NOGENT-SUR-MARNE. (BOIS DE FEU & ENERGIE.). **VFOAT** Bois de Feu et Energie (Nogent-sur-Marne). (1989)-. Periodical. French. sa. $100.00. Assn Bois de Feu, 45 Bis Avenue de la Belle Gabriell, 94736 Nogent Marne CDX France. **Tel** 011 33 1 4877754. **UDC** 620.91. ***Continues*** *Bois de Feu Informations, 0766-5474.*

BL
BOLETIM ESTATISTICO DE ENERGIA ELETRICA. **See** Energy-Abstracting, Bibliographies and Statistics.

GW
BOLIVIEN : ENERGIEWIRTSCHAFT. **Main/Corp** Bundesstelle fur Aussenhandelsinformation (Germany). German. DM2.00. Bundesstelle fuer Aussenhandelsinformation, Agrippastr 87 93, D 50676 Cologne Germany. **Tel** 011 49 221 2057316, FAX 011 49 221 2057212. **LC** HD9502.B6.

UK/0263-9815
BP STATISTICAL REVIEW OF WORLD ENERGY. **See** Energy-Abstracting, Bibliographies and Statistics.

GW/0341-1060
BRAUNKOHLE (DUSSELDORF. 1972). (BRAUNKOHLE.). [Braunkohle]. (1972)-. Periodical. German. mo. DM280.20 Germany; DM259.20 other. Verlag die Braunkohle, Zeitschriftenverlag RBDV, D-440196 Dusseldorf Germany. **Tel** 011 49 211 5050, FAX 011 49 211 5052555, telex 8582495. **LC** TN831; .B697. **CODEN** BRUKAO. **[CCC]. Bk Rev. Ad Acc. Circ:** 1,400. Documents available from CASDDS. ***Continues*** *Braunkohle, Warme und Energie.*
Desc: Considers all aspects of open cast mining for brown coal in West Germany and internationally, including machinery technology, mining mechanics, slag technology, safety, conservation and environmental concerns.
Ind/Abst Chem. Abstr.; Coal Abstr.; EMBASE; Energy Res. Abstr.; GeoRef; MINPROC; Mintec, Min. Technol. Abstr.; Saf. Health Work.

GW/0006-9612
BRENNSTOFF-WAERME-KRAFT. (BRENNSTOFF-WAERME-KRAFT : BWK.). [Brennst.-Warme-Kraft]. **Added/Corp** Vereinigung der Technischen Ueberwachungs-Vereine. Verein Deutscher Ingenieure. Ausschuss fur Waerme- und Kraftwirtschaft (Germany). **VFOAT** BWK; Brennstoff, Waerme, Kraft. Vol. 1 (April 1949)-. Academic Scholarly Publication. German (summaries and/or abstracts in English). Ten times a year. DM365.00 Germany; DM395.00 other. VDI Verlag GmbH, Postfach 101054, D 40001 Dusseldorf Germany. **Tel** 011 49 211 6188313, FAX 011 49 211 6188133. **ED** Siegfried Binder. **LC** TJ260.A1; B7. **CODEN** BRWKAY. **[CCC]. Ad Acc. Pr Rev.** Documents available from The Genuine Article, Ask*IEEE, CASDDS. ***Formed by the union of*** *Waerme (Berlin, Germany); Archiv fuer Waermewirtschaft und Dampfkesselwesen, 0365-8422; Feuerungstechnik* ***and*** *Waerme- und Kaeltetechnik.*
Desc: Contains information about existing and future systems of obtaining, converting and distributing energy, and the economics of energy.
Ind/Abst Chem. Abstr.; Coal Abstr.; Curr. Contents Eng. Tech. Appl. Sci.; Ei Page One; EMBASE; Energy Res. Abstr.; Eng. Mater. Abstr.; INSPEC (1968-May 1985); Int. Aerosp. Abstr.; Lit. Pat. Abstr., Oilfield Chem. (1954-); Lit. Abstr., Catal. Catal.; Lit. Abstr., Health Environ.; Lit. Abstr., Pet. Refin. Petrochem.; Lit. Abstr., Pet. Substit.; Lit. Abstr., Transp. Storage; Met. Abstr.; Proc. Chem. Eng.; Res. Alert [Full Cov.]; Saf. Health Work; Sci. Cit. Index; SCISEARCH; Soc. Sci. Cit. Index [Select. Cov.]; Theoret. Chem. Eng.

CN/0706-1056
BRITEQ PRESSE. **Main/Corp** Bureau de Recherche sur l'Industrie de la Tourbe dans l'est du Quebec. **VAT** Bureau de Recherche sur l'Industrie de la Tourbe de l'Est du Quebec. V. 1- March 1979-. Periodical. French. mo. Bureau de Recherche Sur l Industrie de la Troube dans l East du Quebec, 78 rue Frontenac, CP 1270, Riviere-du-Loup Quebec G5R 1S8 Canada. **Tel** (418)867-1151. **DD** 338.2/7/21097147. **Ad Acc. Circ:** 200.
Desc: This is a documentation center for peat industry. Peat like energy, and many other transformations.

CN/0827-0333
BRITISH COLUMBIA ENERGY SUPPLY AND REQUIREMENTS FORECAST. SUMMARY REPORT. ***Title Change.*** [B.C. energy supply require. forecast, Summ. rep.]. **Added/Corp** British Columbia Energy Commission. British Columbia. Energy Resources Branch. Analysis and Forecasting Division. British Columbia. Energy Resources Branch. Forecasts and Special Projects Division. (1992)-(19??). English. British Columbia Energy Supply and Requirements Forecast, 21st Floor, 1177 West Hastings Street, Vancouver. **DD** 333.79/09711. ***Merged with*** *British Columbia Energy Supply and Requirements Forecast. Technical Report, 0827-0325* ***to form*** *British Columbia Energy Supply and Requirements Forecast, 0832-820X.*

CN/0827-0325
BRITISH COLUMBIA ENERGY SUPPLY AND REQUIREMENTS FORECAST. TECHNICAL REPORT. ***Title Change.*** (BRITISH COLUMBIA ENERGY SUPPLY AND REQUIREMENTS FORECAST. TECHNICAL REPORT/ PREPARED BY BRITISH COLUMBIA ENERGY COMMISSION.). [B.C. energy supply requir. forecast, Tech. rep.]. **Added/Corp** British Columbia Energy Commission. British Columbia. Energy Resources Branch. Analysis and Forecasting Division. British Columbia. Energy Resources Branch. Forecasts and Special Projects Division. British Columbia. Energy Resources Division. Forecasts and Special Projects Branch. (1992)-(2000). English. British Columbia Energy Supply and Requirements Forecast, 21st Floor, 1177 West Hastings Street, Vancouver. **DD** 333.79/09711. ***Continues*** *British Columbia Energy Supply and Demand Forecast, 0827-0317.* ***Merged with*** *British Columbia Energy Supply and Requirements Forecast. Summary Report, 0827-0333* ***to form*** *British Columbia Energy Supply and Requirements Forecast, 0832-820X.*

US/0891-3730
BUILDINGS ENERGY TECHNOLOGY. [Build. energy technol.]. **Added/Corp** United States. Dept. of Energy. Technical Information Center. **VFOAT** BET. DOE/BET-87/1 (Jan. 15, 1987)-. Government Publication. English. sm. $160.00 US; $320.00 other. US Department of Energy, 1000 Independence Avenue SW, Washington DC 20585. **Tel** (202)586-5000, FAX (202)586-4073. **(Subscription address:** National Technical Information Service, 5285 Port Royal Road, Springfield, VA 22161) **ED** Lila Smith and Barry C Steele. **DD** 697. **Bk Rev. Ad Acc.** ctrl circ. ***Continues*** *Buildings Energy Conservation, 8755-0237.*
Desc: Technology required for energy conservation in buildings of all types.

SZ
BULLETIN ASPEA. **VFOAT** SVA Bulletin. (19??)-. Bulletin. French (German). Twenty-one times a year. 320.00F Switzerland; 380.00F Europe; 430.00F other. Swiss Association for Atomic Energy, Belpstrasse 23, Postfach 5032, CH-3001 Bern, Switzerland. **Tel** 011 41 31 3115882. **ED** Peter Zuhlke. Index available (bound in Jan. issue). cum. index. **Bk Rev. Ad Acc. Circ:** 2,200.
Desc: News about developments in the field of nuclear energy, worldwide.

US/0160-7782
BULLETIN / GEOTHERMAL RESOURCES COUNCIL. [Bull. - Geotherm. Resour. Counc.]. (19??)-. Bulletin. English. Eleven times a year. $80.00 US membership; $115.00 other membership. Geothermal Resources Council, PO Box 1350, Davis CA 95617-1350. **Tel** (916)758-2360, FAX (916)758-2839. **ED** David N Anderson. **LC** GB1199.6; .B84. **DD** 333.8/8/0973. **CODEN** BGRCDD. cum. index. **Bk Rev. Ad Acc, Adv Mgr:** same as editor. **Circ:** 1,200 (ctrl). Documents available from Article Express International.
Ind/Abst AESIS Q.; Ei Page One; Energy Res. Abstr. (March 1976-); Eng. Index Annu.; GeoRef.

FI/0355-1008
BULLETIN OF THE INTERNATIONAL PEAT SOCIETY. [Bull. Int. Peat Soc.]. **Main/Corp** International Peat Society. **VFOAT** Mitteilungen der Internationale Moor-und Torf-Gesellschaft; Biulleten Mezhdunarodnogo Obschestva po Torfu. (1970)-. Bulletin. English. an. $15.00. International Peat Society, Kuokkalantie 4, SF 40420, Jyska, Finland. **Tel** 358 41 674042. **CODEN** BIPSDV. **Ad Acc. Circ:** 1,500 (ctrl).
Desc: Activities of the International Peat Society dealing with all aspects of peat and peatlands study and utilization.
Ind/Abst Coal Abstr.; GeoRef; Index Book Rev. Relig.

US/0509-7754
BULLETIN - STATE OF WASHINGTON DIVISION OF POWER RESOURCES. **Main/Corp** Washington (State). Division of Power Resources. No. 1- 1959-. Bulletin. English. Price varies per volume. State of Washington Division of Power Resources, Olympia WA 98504. **DD** 380.

CN/0823-1486
BULLETIN SUR L'ENERGIE (OTTAWA, ONT.). (BULLETIN SUR L'ENERGIE.). [Bull. energ.]. Autumn 1982-. Bulletin. French. Free. NPD Caucus Resource Office, 742 Edifice Confederation, Ottawa Ontario K1A 0A6 Canada. **DD** 333.79/0971.

US/0078-2610
BUYER'S GUIDE (HINSDALE, ILL.). **See** Engineering-Nuclear Engineering.

US/0148-236X
CA SELECTS: SOLAR ENERGY. **See** Chemistry-Abstracting, Bibliographies and Statistics.

NE
CADDET NEWSLETTER. **Added/Corp** Centre for the Analysis and Dissemination of Demonstrated Energy Technologies. International Energy Agency. Organisation for Economic Co-operation and Development. **VAT** Center for the Analysis and Dissemination of Demonstrated Energy Technologies Newsletter. No. 1 (Sept. 1988)-. Periodical. English. qt (Mar., June, Sept., Dec.). Free for member countries; F50.00 other. Centre for the Analysis and Dissemination of Demonstrated Energy Technologies (CADDET), Swentiboldstraat 21, 6137 AE Sittard Netherlands. **Tel** 011 31 46 595224. **CODEN** CTNWEK. Index available. cum. index. **Bk Rev.** ctrl circ.
Desc: Covers energy conservation and development.

FR
CAHIERS DE L'AFEDES. **Main/Corp** Association Francaise pour l'Etude et le Developpement des Applications de l'Energie Solaire. **VFOAT** Cahiers AFEDES. No. 1 (Jan. 1968)-. French (English). Twelve times a year. 1280.00F. Ed Eur Thermique and Industrie, 3 Rue Henri Heine, 75016 Paris France. **Tel** 011 33 1 44304176.

US/0748-8246
CALIFORNIA ENERGY PRICES. [Calif. energy prices]. English. be. California Energy Commission, 1516 9th Street, Sacramento CA 95814. **Tel** (916)324-3014. **LC** HD9502.U53; C3196. **DD** 338.4/3621042/09794.

CN/0319-3403
CANADIAN ENERGY NEWS. **Added/Corp** Capital Communications Limited. C C H Canada Limited. Vol. 9/72-Vol. 3/80, (Sept. 1972)-(March 1980); Vol. 1-. Periodical. English. bm. 335.00Can$. E L Littlejohn and Assoc. Ltd., Minto Pl Pstl Outlet, Box 56067, Ottawa Ontario K1R 7Z1 Canada. **Tel** (613)235-9183, FAX (613)594-3857. **DD** 333.79/0971. ***Supersedes*** *Energy News, 0319-339X;* ***Absorbed*** *Northern Reporter, 0380-5573; Pipelines, Politics & People, 0383-7017; Canadian Nuclear News, 0706-6783.*
Ind/Abst INIS Atomindex [Micro.].

CN/1196-0833
CANADIAN ENERGY TRENDS MONTHLY (1991). (199?)-. English. mo. Canadian Enerdata Limited, Suite 204 7030 Woodbine Avenue, Markham Ontario L3R 1A2 Canada. **Tel** (905)479-9697. ***Continues*** *Energytrends, 0848-9106.*

CN/0823-0226
CANADIAN SOLAR DIRECTORY (1983). (CANADIAN SOLAR DIRECTORY / ANNUAIRE DE L'ENERGIE SOLAIRE AU CANADA.). [Can. sol. dir.]. **Added/Corp** Solar Energy Society of Canada. **VFOAT** Annuaire de l'Energie Solaire au Canada. (1983)-. English (French). an. $4.00 per volume. Solar Energy

Society of Canada Inc, PO Box No. 1353, Winnipeg Man R3C 2Z1. **Tel** (613)596-1067, FAX (613)596-1120. **DD** 338.4/762147/02571. ***Continues*** *SESCI Canadian Solar Directory, 0710-1384.*

US/0195-5292
CAPITAL ENERGY LETTER. ***Ceased.*** Periodical. English. wk. PennWell Publishing Company, 1421 South Sheridan, PO Box 1260, Tulsa OK 74101. **Tel** (918)835-3161, (800)331-4463, FAX (918)831-9497. **ED** Ronald M Harris. **[CCC]. Bk Rev. Ad Acc.** ctrl circ.
Desc: Political, legislative, and regulatory intelligence and analysis on behind the scenes machines in energy (oil and gas), from Washington.

IT/0393-0971
CH4 ENERGIA METANO. [Ch4 energ. metano]. **VFOAT** Chquatro Energia Metano. (1984)-. Periodical. Italian (summaries and/or abstracts in English). qt. L100000 Italy; L200000 other. Ventus SNC, Via Palmieri 25, 10138 Turin Italy. **Tel** 011 39 11 434-5965. **UDC** 553.981.

FR/0009-2029
CHAUFFAGE, VENTILATION, CONDITIONNEMENT. **See** Heating, Plumbing, and Refrigeration.

FR
CHIFFRES CLES DE L'ENERGIE, LES. ***Ceased.*** **Added/Corp** France. Delegation Generale a l'Energie. France. Ministere de l'Industrie. France. Observatoire de l'Energie. **VFOAT** Chiffres Cles, Energie. (19??)-(19??). French. an. Documentation Francaise, 29 Quai Voltaire, 75344 Paris Cedex 7 France. **Tel** 011 33 1 40157000, FAX 011 33 1 40157230, telex 204 826 DOCFRAN. **LC** HD9502.F7; C48. **DD** 333.79/0944.

GW
CHILE : ENERGIEWIRTSCHAFT. **Main/Corp** Bundesstelle fur Aussenhandelsinformation (Germany). German. DM2.00. Bundesstelle fuer Aussenhandelsinformation, Agrippastr 87 93, D 50676 Cologne Germany. **Tel** 011 49 221 2057316, FAX 011 49 221 2057212. **LC** HD9502.C5.

HK
CHINA ENERGY REPORT. **Added/Corp** American Chamber of Commerce in Hong Kong. Energy Committee. **VFOAT** China Energy Report and Hong Kong Energy Directory; Hong Kong Energy Directory. (198?)-. English. an. American Chamber of Commerce Hong Kong, 1030 Swire House, Hong Kong Hong Kong. **LC** HD9502.C6; C483. **DD** 333.79/0951.

JA/0385-7034
CHINETSU. **See** Earth Sciences.

CN/0826-0206
CIE NATIONAL NEWS. (CIE NATIONAL NEWS / CANADIAN INSTITUTE OF ENERGY.). [CIE natl. news]. **Added/Corp** Canadian Institute of Energy. **VAT** Canadian Institute of Energy National News. Vol. 3, No. 2 (Mar./Apr. 1984)-. Periodical. English. Five times a year. 12.00Can$. Canadian Institute of Energy, 229 640 5th Avenue Southwest, Calgary Alberta Canada. **Tel** (403)262-6969. **DD** 333.79/0971. ***Continues*** *CIE National Newsletter, 0825-0219.*

US/0896-517X
CLEAN COAL TECHNOLOGIES. (CLEAN COAL TECHNOLOGIES : CURRENT ABSTRACTS / U.S. DEPARTMENT OF ENERGY ; PREPARED FOR OFFICE OF FOSSIL ENERGY ; PREPARED BY OFFICE OF SCIENTIFIC AND TECHNICAL INFORMATION.). [Clean coal technol.]. **Added/Corp** United States. Dept. of Energy. Office of Scientific and Technical Information. United States. Office of Fossil Energy. **VFOAT** CCT. Vol. 88, No. 1 (Jan. 1988)-. Government Publication. English. mo. $160.00 US; $320.00 other. US Department of Energy, 1000 Independence Avenue SW, Washington DC 20585. **Tel** (202)586-5000, FAX (202)586-4073. **(Subscription address:** National Technical Information Service, 5285 Port Royal Road, Springfield, VA 22161**)** **DD** 662.

US/1051-3116
CLEAN FUELS REPORT, THE. **See** Petroleum and Natural Gas.

TR/0253-0538
CLEC. CARIB-LATIN ENERGY CONSULTANT. (CARIB-LATIN ENERGY CONSULTANT.). [CLEC, Carib-Lat. Energy Consult.]. **Added/Corp** Carib-Latin Energy Consultants Limited. **VFOAT** CLEC. Vol. 1 (Jan. 1977)-. Periodical. English. Six times a year (Feb., Apr., June, Aug., Oct., Dec.). $195.00 (one year); $380.00 (two years); $570.00 (three years). Carib Latin Energy Consultant, PO Box 3074, St. James Post Office, Trinidad West Indies. **Tel** (809)637-9038, FAX (809)637-9038. **ED** C. Phelps and R. Appleton. **LC** HD9502.C37; C37. **DD** 338.4. **Circ:** 2,000.
Desc: An analysis of energy developments in oil, gas, nuclear, biomass, solar, thermal, etc. in Latin America and the Caribbean region, by energy experts from the region.
Ind/Abst GeoRef.

UK/0309-4979
COAL ABSTRACTS. ***Ceased.*** **See** Energy-Abstracting, Bibliographies and Statistics.

UK/0306-8544
COAL AND ENERGY QUARTERLY. [Coal energy Q.]. **Added/Corp** Great Britain. National Coal Board. No. 1 (1974)-. Periodical. English. qt. **CODEN** CENQDW.
Ind/Abst Energy Inf. Abstr.

UK/0143-6287
COAL CALENDAR. ***Ceased.*** **Added/Corp** IEA Coal Research. Technical Information Service. International Energy Agency. (Jan./Feb. 1980)-(1993). Periodical. English. bm. IEA Coal Research, 10-18 Putney Hill, Gemini House, London SW15 6AA England. **Tel** 011 41 81 780 2111, FAX 011 41 81 780 1746, telex 917624. **ED** Anne Carpenter. **CODEN** CLCLEC. Index available. **Ad Acc. Circ:** 1,200. available on microfiche.
Desc: Provides a comprehensive, descriptive listing of recently held and forthcoming meetings, exhibitions, and courses of interest to the coal industry worldwide.

US
COAL CONVERSION SYSTEMS TECHNICAL DATA BOOK. English. US Department of Energy Office of Energy Technology, 1000 Independence Avenue SW, Washington DC 20585.

US/0145-417X
COAL DATA. [Coal data]. **Main/Corp** National Coal Association. Dept. of Economics and Statistics. **Added/Corp** National Coal Association. Economics and Statistical Services. National Coal Association. Information and Statistical Services. National Coal Association. Statistical Services. National Coal Association. Economics and Statistics Dept. (19??)-. English. an. $50.00 nonprofit organizations; $75.00 other. National Coal Association, 1130 17th Street Northwest, Washington DC 20036. **Tel** (202)463-2640. **LC** HD9564; .N26a. **DD** 338.2/7/20973. Index available. available on diskette. ***Continues*** *Bituminous Coal Data.*
Desc: Contains detailed data on coal production, consumption, stocks, distribution and safety for a five year period. Contains several tables on federally leased coal reserves. Also contains tables which divide production between states east and west of the Mississippi river. It reports on reserves, production and consumption of crude oil, natural gas and natural gas liquids.
Ind/Abst GeoRef; Stat. Ref. Index.

FR
COAL INFORMATION / INTERNATIONAL ENERGY AGENCY. **Added/Corp** International Energy Agency. International Energy Agency. Secretariat. Organisation for Economic Co-Operation and Development. (1986)-. English. an. OECD Publications and Information Center, 2 rue Andre-Pascal, 75775 Paris Cedex 16 France. **Tel** 011 33 1 45248167, US:(202)785-6323, FAX 011 33 1 45248500 OR 45248176, telex 620 160 OCDE. **(Subscription address:** OECD Publications Center, 2001 L Street, Suite 700, Washington DC 20036.**)** **LC** HD9540.1; .C52. **DD** 338.8/22/05. ***Continues*** *Coal Information Report.*
Desc: Includes the latest international comparable information on coal reserves, production, trade, demand, prices, transport infrastructure, coal-fired power stations, emission standards, and more.
Ind/Abst F&S Index Plus Text, Int. [Select. Cov.]; Predicasts Forecasts.

US/0162-2714
COAL OUTLOOK. [Coal outl.]. (Oct. 1975)-. Periodical. English. wk (50 issues). $775.00 US; $805.00 other. Pasha Publications Inc., 1616 North Fort Myer Drive, Suite 1000, Arlington VA 22209. **Tel** (800)424-2908, (703)528-1244, FAX (703)528-3742, (703)528-1253. **ED** Harry Baisden. **[CCC].** available on an online database (files 636,648/Full-Text) from DIALOG.
Desc: Reports on coal market trends, legislation affecting the coal industry, transportation issues, export data, United Mine Workers organizing activities and contract negotiations. A statistical supplement gives coal prices and consumption data.
Ind/Abst Coal Abstr.; NEXIS (Oct. 13, 1975-); PTS Newsl. Database [Full Txt.].

US
COAL PATROL. Periodical. English. Brophy Associates, 915 15th Street NW/Suite 500, Washington DC 20005. **Tel** (202)234-6466.

US/0737-6499
COAL SITUATION, THE. (THE COAL SITUATION : A QUARTERLY REVIEW FROM ENERGY ECONOMICS--THE CHASE MANHATTAN BANK, N.Y.). [Coal situat.]. **Added/Corp** Chase Manhattan Bank, N.A. Energy Economics Division. (July 1980)-. Periodical. English. qt. Chase Manhattan Bank, One New York Plaza, New York NY 10081. **Tel** (212)552-7069.
Ind/Abst Coal Abstr.

US/1043-1845
COALDAT MARKETING REPORT. PRODUCING DISTRICT FORMAT (1988). (COALDAT MARKETING REPORT. PRODUCING DISTRICT FORMAT.). [COALDAT mark. rep., Prod. dist. format]. **Added/Corp** Resource Data International. **VFOAT** Producing District Format. (Aug. 1988)-. Periodical. English. mo. $595.00 US; $635.00 other. Pasha Publications Inc., 1616 North Fort Myer Drive, Suite 1000, Arlington VA 22209. **Tel** (800)424-2908, (703)528-1244, FAX (703)528-3742, (703)528-1253. **LC** HD9541; .C634. **DD** 338.2/74/0973021. ***Continues*** *COALDAT. Producing District Format, 1041-0988.*

US/1043-0474
COALDAT MARKETING REPORT. SUPPLIER FORMAT (1988). (COALDAT MARKETING REPORT. SUPPLIER FORMAT.). [COALDAT mark. rep., Supplier format]. **Added/Corp** Resource Data International. **VFOAT** Supplier Format. (Aug. 1988)-. Periodical. English. mo. $595.00 US; $635.00 other. Pasha Publications Inc., 1616 North Fort Myer Drive, Suite 1000, Arlington VA 22209. **Tel** (800)424-2908, (703)528-1244, FAX (703)528-3742, (703)528-1253. **LC** HD9541; .C635. **DD** 338.2/724/0973021. ***Continues*** *COALDAT. Supplier Format, 1041-097X.*

US/0895-2361
COALDAT MARKETING REPORT. UTILITY FORMAT. [COALDAT mark. rep., Util. format]. **Added/Corp** Resource Data International. **VFOAT** Utility Format. (198?)-. Periodical. English. mo. $595.00 US; $635.00 other. Pasha Publications Inc., 1616 North Fort Myer Drive, Suite 1000, Arlington VA 22209. **Tel** (800)424-2908, (703)528-1244, FAX (703)528-3742, (703)528-1253. **LC** HD9541; .C636. **DD** 338.2/724/0973021. ***Continues*** *COALDAT. Utility Format, 1041-0996.*

UK/0269-381X
COALTRANS WORCESTER PARK. (COALTRANS). [CoalTrans Worcest. Park]. **VFOAT** CoalTrans International. (1986)-. Periodical. English. bm. £64.00 (1 year), £102.00 (2 year), £149.00 (3 year) Europe; £70.00 (1 year), £128.00 (2 year), £168.00 (3 year) other. General Publishing Limited, 42 Rutherwyke Epsom, Surrey KT17 2NB England. **Tel** 011 44 81 786 8202, FAX 011 44 81 786 8175, telex 46690. **ED** Norman Parwanden. **DD** 338.272405. **Bk Rev. Ad Acc. Pr Rev.** ctrl circ. ***Continues*** *Bulk Systems International, 0143-7852.*
Desc: Covers the international seaborne coal market, concerned exclusively with coal trading, transport, and technology.
Ind/Abst Fluid Abstr., Civil Eng.; Fluid Abstr. Proc. Eng.; FLUIDEX.

US
CODE OF FEDERAL REGULATIONS. 10, ENERGY. **Added/Corp** United States. Office of the Federal Register. **VFOAT** Energy; CFR. 10, Energy. (19??)-. English. $345.00. Regulations Management Corporation, 1505 Arlington Road, Bloomington IN 47404. **Tel** (812)333-7347.

US
COGENERATION & RESOURCE RECOVERY. English. bm. $225.00. 747 Leigh Mill Road, Great Falls VA 22066. **Tel** (703)759-5060, FAX (703)759-6354. **ED** Scott Spiewak. **Bk Rev. Ad Acc.** ***Continues*** *Cogeneration World, 0738-5706.*

US/0749-5617
COGENERATION LETTER, THE. Vol. 1, No. 1 (Oct. 1984)-. Periodical. English. mo. $165.00 U.S. and Canada; $185.00 other. Energy Engineering, 700 Indian Trail, Lilburn GA 30247. **Tel** (404)925-9388. **ED** Anna Fay Williams. **DD** 338. **Circ:** 400.
Desc: Each issue brings ready-to-use information on cogeneration. Information on current federal and state regulatory actions and court decisions assessed for impact on project development.

US
COLORADO ENERGY FOCUS. **Added/Corp** Colorado Energy Research Institute. Vol. 1, No. 1 (Feb. 1981)-. Periodical. English. CERI, 3000 Youngfield Street, Suite 153, Lakewood CO 80215.

US
COMBUSTION RESEARCH. **Main/Corp** Lawrence Berkeley Laboratory. Energy and Environment Division. English. an. Lawrence Berkeley Laboratory, University of California, Berkeley CA 94720. **Tel** (415)486-4000.

US/1052-6331
COMMON SENSE ON ENERGY AND OUR ENVIRONMENT. [Common sense energy our environ.]. Vol. 1, No. 1 (Sept. 1990)-. Periodical. English. bm (6 issues). $34.00 (one year), $54.00 (two years). Common Sense, PO Box 215, Morrisville PA 19067. **Tel** (215)321-6479. **ED** Jason Makansi. **DD** 363. **Bk Rev**, (Qty: 5-10). **Circ:** 200.
Desc: Covers energy and environmental business and technology for the non-specialist.

US
COMPENDIUM OF PUBLICLY AVAILABLE REPORTS ON PROCUREMENT AND FINANCIAL ASSISTANCE AWARDS - (DEPT OF ENERGY). **Main/Corp** United States. Dept of Energy. Procurement Management Systems and Analysis Division. Government Publication. English. US Department of Energy, 1000 Independence Avenue SW, Washington DC 20585. **Tel** (202)586-5000, FAX

(202)586-4073.
Desc: Report covers three major sections: Published reports,unpublished reports and special reports.

UK/0306-7874
CONFERENCE - INTERNATIONAL SOLAR ENERGY SOCIETY UK SECTION. (CONFERENCE / UK SECTION OF THE INTERNATIONAL SOLAR ENERGY SOCIETY (UK-ISES).). [Conf. - Int. Sol. Energy Soc. UK Sect.]. **Main/Corp** International Solar Energy Society. UK Section. Conference. Academic Scholarly Publication. English. ir. King's College London, Atkins Building South (128), Campden Hill Road, London W8 7AH England. **Tel** 01-938-2919, FAX 01-937-7783. **CODEN** CUSSD5. Index available. cum. index. **Circ:** 300. Documents available from Article Express International, Ask*IEEE, CASDDS.
Ind/Abst Bioeng. Abstr.; Chem. Abstr. (1974-1984); Ei Page One; Eng. Index Annu.; INSPEC.

US/0198-0351
CONGRESSIONAL BUDGET REQUEST. **Main/Corp** United States. Dept. of Energy. Government Publication. English. an. US Department of Energy, 1000 Independence Avenue SW, Washington DC 20585. **Tel** (202)586-5000, FAX (202)586-4073. **LC** HD9502.U5; U523A. **DD** 353.0072/224. available on microfiche (Vols. for (1988) distributed to depository libraries).

CN/0848-984X
CONNEXIONS (ASSOCIATION CANADIENNE DE L'ELECTRICITE). (CONNEXIONS.). [Connex. - Assoc. can. electr.]. **Added/Corp** Association Canadienne de l'Electricite. Vol. 60, No. 7 (Sept. 1989)-. Periodical. French. Ten times a year. $35.00 North America; $65.00 other. Association Canadienne l'Electricite, 1 Westmount Square, Suite 1600, Montreal Que H3Z 2P9 Canada. **DD** 333.79/32/0971. ***Continues*** *Bulletin (Association Canadienne de l'Electricite). Francais, 0820-3229.*

FR
CONSOMMATIONS D'ENERGIE DANS LE COMMERCE DE DETAIL ET LES SERVICES A CARACTERE COMMERCIAL EN ..., LES. **Added/Corp** Institut National de la Statistique et des Etudes Economiques (France) France. Observatoire de l'Energie. (19??)-. French. Institut National de la Statistique et des Etudes Economiques, 18 Bd Adolphe Pinard, 75675 Paris 14 France.

IT/1120-2351
CONTATTO ELETTRICO. [Contatto elettr.]. (1988)-. Periodical. Italian. Nine times a year. L9000.00. Alberto Greco Editore, Via Del Fusaro 8, 20146 Milan Italy. **Tel** 011 39 2 4819086 or 4691895, FAX 011 39 2 4819091, telex 315367. **UDC** 537.

CN/0226-952X
COOPERATIVE ENERGY. [Coop. energy]. **Added/Corp** Appropriate Home Energy Co-operative. (June 1980)-. Periodical. English. ir. $5.00. Cooperative Energy, PO Box 11152 Station H, Nepean Ontario K2H 7T9 Canada. **DD** 333.79/16/0971384.

US/0069-9977
CORAL GABLES CONFERENCE ON FUNDAMENTAL INTERACTIONS AT HIGH ENERGY. PROCEEDINGS. **VFOAT** Proceedings; Fundamental Interactions at High Energy. 1st- 1969-. Proceedings. English. an. Gordon & Breach Science Publishers, Inc., PO Box 786, Cooper Station, New York NY 10276. **Tel** (212)206-8900, FAX (212)645-2459. **(Subscription address:** International Publishers Distributor at one of the following addresses: 820 Town Center Drive, Langhorne, PA 19047; or PO Box 90, Reading Berkshire RG1 8JL UK; or Kent Ridge PO Box 1180, Singapore 9111, Republic of Singapore**)** **LC** QC794. **DD** 539.76. ***Supersedes*** *Coral Gables Conference on Symmetry at High Energy.*

GW
COSTA RICA, ENERGIEWIRTSCHAFT / BUNDESSTELLE FUR AUSSENHANDELSINFORMATION. German. an. DM2.00. Bundesstelle fuer Aussenhandelsinformation, Agrippastr 87 93, D 50676 Cologne Germany. **Tel** 011 49 221 2057316, FAX 011 49 221 2057212. **LC** HD9502.C8; C67. **DD** 333.79/097286.

SP/0211-2213
COYUNTURA ENERGETICA. (COYUNTURA ENERGETICA / MINISTERIO DE INDUSTRIA Y ENERGIA, COMISARIA DE LA ENERGIA, COMISARIA DE LA ENERGIA Y RECURSOS MINERALES, CENTRO DE ESTUDIOS DE LA ENERGIA.). [Coyunt. energ.]. **Added/Corp** Centro de Estudios de la Energia (Spain). (1976)-. Spanish. mo. Centro De Estudios De La Energia, Agustin De Foxa, 29, Madrid 16. **LC** HD9502.S66; C69. **DD** 333.79/13/0946.
Ind/Abst GeoRef.

US/0883-2943
CURRENT ALTERNATIVE ENERGY RESEARCH AND DEVELOPMENT IN ILLINOIS. [Curr. altern. energy res. dev. Ill.]. **VFOAT** Alternative Energy. 1982-. English. sa. Energy Information Clearinghouse, 325 West Adams/Room #300, Springfield IL 62706. **LC** TJ808.7.U6; C87. **DD** 621.042.

US/0273-298X
CURRENT ENERGY PATENTS. ***Ceased.*** [Current energy pat.]. **Added/Corp** United States. Dept. of Energy. Technical Information Center. ( )-(1982). English. mo. National Technical Information Service - NTIS, Room 2027S, 5285 Port Royal Road, Springfield VA 22161. **Tel** (703)487-4630, (703)487-4660, (703)487-4650, FAX (703)321-8547, telex 89-9405. **LC** TJ163.2; .C87. **DD** 621.042/0272.
Ind/Abst INIS Atomindex [Micro.].

GW
DANEMARK, ENERGIEWIRTSCHAFT / BUNDESSTELLE FUR AUSSENHANDELSINFORMATION. German. an. DM2.00. Bundesstelle fuer Aussenhandelsinformation, Agrippastr 87 93, D 50676 Cologne Germany. **Tel** 011 49 221 2057316, FAX 011 49 221 2057212. **LC** HD9502.D4; D36. **DD** 333.79/09489.

CN/0823-9584
DATA RESOURCES MODEL OF CANADIAN ENERGY MARKETS, THE. [Data Resour. model Can. energy mark.]. **VFOAT** Energy Model Documentation. June 1982-. Periodical. English. Data Resources of Canada, 80 Bloor Street West/Suite 505, Toronto Ontario M5S 2V1 Canada. **DD** 025/.0633379/0971. ctrl circ.

GW
DEMOKRATISCHE VOLKSREPUBLIK JEMEN: ENERGIEWIRTSCHAFT. **Main/Corp** Bundesstelle fur Aussenhandelsinformation (Germany). (19??)-. German. **LC** TJ163.25.Y45; G47a.

US
DEPARTMENT OF ENERGY FY ... OBLIGATIONS AND COSTS BY STATE. **Main/Corp** United States. Dept. of Energy. Office of the Controller. Government Publication. English. an. US Department of Energy, 1000 Independence Avenue SW, Washington DC 20585. **Tel** (202)586-5000, FAX (202)586-4073.

UK
DEPARTMENT OF ENERGY PRESS RELEASES. ***Ceased.*** (19??)-(19??). English. Department of Trade and Industry, Room 3 3 15 1 Palace Street, London SW1E 5HE England. **Tel** 011 44 71 238 3576, FAX 011 44 71 238 3121, telex 91877 EZEGY G.

US/0275-3014
DEPARTMENT OF ENERGY RED BOOK. (19??)-. English. ir. $115.00. Government R & D Reports, MIT Branch Box 85, Cambridge MA 01938. **Tel** (603)436-3167.

US
DEPARTMENT OF ENERGY SOLAR ENERGY OBJECTIVES. **Main/Corp** United States. Dept. of Energy. **VFOAT** Solar Energy Objectives. 1980-. Government Publication. English. an. US Department of Energy, 1000 Independence Avenue SW, Washington DC 20585. **Tel** (202)586-5000, FAX (202)586-4073.

UK/0307-0603
DIGEST OF UNITED KINGDOM ENERGY STATISTICS. **See** Energy-Abstracting, Bibliographies and Statistics.

US
DIRECTORY OF COMPUTER SOFTWARE APPLICATIONS. ENERGY, A. **See** Computers-Software.

US
DIRECTORY OF ENERGY DATA COLLECTION FORMS / ENERGY INFORMATION ADMINISTRATION, OFFICE OF STATISTICAL STANDARDS. **Main/Corp** United States. Energy Information Administration. Office of Statistical Standards. (198?)-. Statistical Publication. English. an (Dec.). Free on request. National Energy Information Center, Energy Information Administration, Forrestal Building, Room 1F-048, Washington DC 20585. **Tel** (202)586-8800. ***Continues*** *United States. Energy Information Administration. Office of the National Energy Information System. Directory of Energy Data Collection Forms.*
Desc: Contains abstracts of forms used by EIA to collect energy data.

US/0273-1525
DIRECTORY OF SOLAR ENERGY RESEARCH ACTIVITIES IN THE UNITED STATES. [Dir. sol. energy res. act. U. S.]. 1st- Ed.; 1980-. Directory. English. an. Solar Energy Research Institute / Virginia, Academic and University Programs Branch, 5285 Port Royal Road, Springfield VA 22161. **LC** TJ810; .D57. **DD** 621.47/072073.

US
DISPATCH (OLYMPIA, WASH.). (DISPATCH / WASHINGTON STATE ENERGY OFFICE.). **Added/Corp** Washington State Energy Office. **VFOAT** Washington State Energy Office Dispatch; WSEO Dispatch. Vol. 8, No. 6 (Nov. 1985)-. Periodical. English. Six times a year (Jan., Mar., May, July, Sept., Nov.). Free. WSEO Dispatch, 809 Legion Way Southeast, Olympia WA 98504-1211. **Tel** (206)586-5047. **ED** Jim Erickson. **Circ:** 5,500. Documents available from Documents on Demand. ***Continues*** *WSEO Newsletter.*
Desc: Contains articles on energy research programs, conservation and renewable energy projects, and policy issues.
Ind/Abst Energy Inf. Abstr.; Environ. Abstr.

FR
DOC IFE PROFILS. French. ir. 750.00F France; 860.00F other (first title ordered). Institut Francais de l'Energie, 3 rue Henri Heine, 75016 Paris France. **Tel** 011 33 1 45244614.

US/0270-6512
DOE/ER (UNITED STATES. DEPT. OF ENERGY. OFFICE OF ENERGY RESEARCH). (DOE/ER.). [DOE/ER]. **Main/Corp** United States. Dept. of Energy. Office of Energy Research. (1977)-. Academic Scholarly Publication. English. Price varies per volume. National Technical Information Service - NTIS, Room 2027S, 5285 Port Royal Road, Springfield VA 22161. **Tel** (703)487-4630, (703)487-4660, (703)487-4650, FAX (703)321-8547, telex 89-9405. **CODEN** USDDDZ. available on microfiche. Documents available from Article Express International, CASDDS.
Ind/Abst Bioeng. Abstr.; Chem. Abstr.; Ei Page One; Eng. Index Annu.; GeoRef.

US/1058-9767
DOE NEW TECHNOLOGY. **Main/Corp** United States. Dept. of Energy. **Added/Corp** United States. Dept. of Energy. Office of Scientific and Technical Information. **VAT** Department of Energy New Technology. (1991)-. English. sa. $23.00 (single issue, U.S.), $46.00 (single issue, other). National Technical Information Service - NTIS, Room 2027S, 5285 Port Royal Road, Springfield VA 22161. **Tel** (703)487-4630, (703)487-4660, (703)487-4650, FAX (703)321-8547, telex 89-9405. ***Continues*** *DOE Patents Available for Licensing, 0277-3074.*

US
DOE NEWS / U.S. DEPARTMENT OF ENERGY. **Main/Corp** United States. Dept. of Energy. (19??)-. Periodical. English. ir. Free on request (accredited press only). US Department of Energy Office of Public Affairs, Washington DC 20585.

US/0730-3025
DOE STATE & LOCAL ASSISTANCE PROGRAMS. [DOE state local assist. programs]. **Main/Corp** United States. Dept. of Energy. Office of Conservation and Solar Energy. Office of State and Local Assistance Programs. **VFOAT** D.O.E. State and Local Assistance Programs; Program Activities; DOE State and Local Assistance Programs. **VAT** Department of Energy State and Local Assistance Programs. Government Publication. English. US Department of Energy, 1000 Independence Avenue SW, Washington DC 20585. **Tel** (202)586-5000, FAX (202)586-4073. **LC** HD9502.U5; U523G. **DD** 333.79.

US
DOE TELEPHONE DIRECTORY. **See** Public Administration.

US/1057-5782
DOE THIS MONTH. (DOE THIS MONTH / U.S. DEPARTMENT OF ENERGY.). [DOE month]. **Added/Corp** United States. Dept. of Energy. United States. Dept. of Energy. Office of Public Affairs. Editorial Services Branch. United States. Dept. of Energy. Office of Public Affairs. **VFOAT** D.O.E. This Month. **VAT** Department of Energy this Month. Vol. 7, No. 2 (Feb. 1984)-. Government Publication. English. mo. $21.00 domestic; $26.25 other. Superintendent of Documents, US Government Printing Office, Washington DC 20402. **Tel** (202)275-3328, FAX (202)786-2377. **ED** Martin Moon. **DD** 353. **Pr Rev. Circ:** 27,000 (ctrl). Documents available from Documents on Demand. ***Continues*** *Energy Insider, 0886-3539.*
Desc: Reports on new and continuing Department of Energy research and development projects, including fission, fusion, weapons, physics, renewables and synthetics, and on DOE publications and policy.
Ind/Abst Energy Inf. Abstr.; Environ. Abstr.

US/0147-5665
DRI ENERGY BULLETIN. **Main/Corp** Data Resources, Inc. **VAT** Data Resources Incorporated Energy Bulletin. Bulletin. English. DRI McGraw Hill, 24 Hartwell Avenue, Lexington MA 02173. **Tel** (617)863-5100. **LC** HD9502.A1; D37A. **DD** 333.7.

US
E-DIVISION SEMIANNUAL REPORT. **Main/Corp** Los Alamos Scientific Laboratory. E-Division. (19??)-. Government Publication. English. sa. US Department of Energy, 1000 Independence Avenue SW, Washington DC 20585. **Tel** (202)586-5000, FAX (202)586-4073.

US/0739-4233
E-LAB. [E-lab]. **Main/Corp** Massachusetts Institute of Technology. Energy Laboratory. **VFOAT** E Lab. (197?)-. Periodical. English. qt. Free. Massachusetts Institute of Technology, Energy Laboratory, Room E40-495, Cambridge MA 02139-4307. **Tel** (617)253-3400. **ED** Nancy W. Stauffer. **CODEN** ELABES.
Desc: Discusses recycling and environmental issues.

US
E-NOTES : QUARTERLY NEWSLETTER OF THE INTERNATIONAL INSTITUTE FOR ENERGY CONSERVATION. **Added/Corp** International Institute for Energy Conservation. **VFOAT** E Notes. (Fall 1991)-. Newsletter. English. qt. Free. International Institute for Energy Conservation, 750 1st Street NE, Suite 940, Washington DC 20002.

US/0731-4930
EARTH ENERGY. (EARTH ENERGY : NAFPA NEWSMAGAZINE.). [Earth energy]. Began with: Vol. 1, No. 1 (Oct. 1979). Periodical. English. mo. National Alcohol Fuel Producers Association, 1700 South 24th Street, Box 2756, Lincoln NE 68502.

UK/0954-2981
EASTERN BLOC ENERGY. [East. bloc energy]. (1988)-. English. mo. £288.00 Europe; £294.00 US; £296.00 other. Eastern Bloc Research Ltd., Newton Kyme, Tadcaster, North Yorkshire LS24 9LS England. **Tel** 011 44 937 835691, FAX 011 44 937 835756. **ED** David Cameron Wilson. **DD** 333.790947. **Ad Acc, Adv Mgr:** n. **Circ:** 500 (ctrl).
Desc: Developments in the oil and energy sectors of Russia and Eastern Europe.

US/1054-1608
EASTERN EUROPEAN ENERGY REPORT. [East. Eur. energy rep.]. **Added/Corp** Strategic Marketing Inc. East European Marketing Group. Vol. 1, No. 1 (Nov. 1990)-. Periodical. English. mo. $325.00 (charter), $375.00 (repeat). Strategic Marketing Communications, 550 North Maple Avenue, Ridgewood NJ 07450. **Tel** (201)444-1061, (800)443-4188, FAX (201)444-9171. **DD** 333. available on an online database (files 16,636/Full-Text) from DIALOG.
Ind/Abst PROMT [Full Txt.]; PTS Newsl. Database [Full Txt.].

UK/0957-3666
EC ENERGY MONTHLY. [EC energy mon.]. **VFOAT** European Communities Energy Monthly; EC Energy. (1989)-. Periodical. English. mo. Financial Times Business Information Ltd., Tower House, Southampton Street, London WC2E 7HA England. **Tel** 011 44 71 353 1040. available on microfiche; available on an online database from DIALOG.
Ind/Abst PROMT [Full Txt.]; PTS Newsl. Database [Full Txt.].

US/0270-823X
ECD. ENERGY CONSERVATION DIGEST. (ENERGY CONSERVATION DIGEST.). [ECD, Energy conserv. dig.]. Vol. 1 (197?)-. Periodical. English. Twenty-four times a year (1st and 3rd Monday). $189.00. Editorial Resources Inc, PO Box 20754, Seattle WA 98102. **Tel** (206)322-8387. **ED** David L. Howell. **Bk Rev.**
Desc: Features include state and local conservation programs, news of research and new products and a calendar of events.

IT
ECONOMIA DELLE FONTI DI ENERGIA. **Added/Corp** Universita Commerciale Luigi Bocconi. Istituto di Economia delle Fonti di Energia. (1975)-. Periodical. Italian. Three times a year. L87000 Italy; L120000 other. Franco Angeli Riviste SRL, Viale Monza 106, 20127 Milan Italy. **Tel** 011 39 2 2827651, 011 39 2 289562. **ED** Franco Angeli. **LC** HD9540.1; .E3. **Bk Rev. Ad Acc. Circ:** 3,300 (ctrl). ***Continues** Economia Internazionale delle Fonti di Energia.*
Desc: Publishes articles and essays from Italy and abroad concerning energy economics and energy policy. Includes English abstracts.
Ind/Abst Coal Abstr.

US
ECONOMIC & ENERGY INDICATORS / NATIONAL FOREIGN ASSESSMENT CENTER. ***Ceased.*** **See** Economics-Economic History, Conditions.

US/0364-3840
ECP REPORT. **Main/Corp** Environmental Law Institute. State and Local Energy Conservation Project. **VAT** Energy Conservation Project Report. Began with Aug. 1975 issue. English. ir (every 5 weeks). Free. Energy Conservation Project, 1346 Connecticut Avenue NW, Suite 620, Washington DC 20036. **LC** TJ163.3; .E58A. **DD** 333.7.

GW
ECUADOR : ENERGIEWIRTSCHAFT. **Main/Corp** Bundesstelle fur Aussenhandelsinformation (Germany). German. DM2.00. Bundesstelle fuer Aussenhandelsinformation, Agrippastr 87 93, D 50676 Cologne Germany. **Tel** 011 49 221 2057316, FAX 011 49 221 2057212. **LC** HD9502.E2.

US
EDISON TIMES. **Added/Corp** Edison Electric Institute. (19??)-. English. mo. $165.00 (nonmembers), $132.00 (members). Edison Electric Institute, 701 Pennsylvania Avenue Northwest, Washington DC 20004. **Tel** (202)508-5607, (202)508-5610, FAX (202)508-5030. **(Subscription address:** Edison Electric Institute, PO Box 2800, Kearneysville WV 25430.**)**

US/0737-349X
EEI WASHINGTON LETTER. [EEI Washington lett.]. **Added/Corp** Edison Electric Institute. **VFOAT** E.E.I. Washington Letter; Washington Letter. **VAT** Edison Electric Institute Washington Letter. (1983)-. Periodical. English. ir (weekly when congress is in session). $125.00 (nonmembers), $100.00 (members). Edison Electric Institute, 701 Pennsylvania Avenue Northwest, Washington DC 20004. **Tel** (202)508-5607, (202)508-5610, FAX (202)508-5030. **(Subscription address:** Edison Electric Institute, PO Box 2800, Kearneysville WV 25430.**)**

US/0889-0854
EEPA NEWS BULLETIN. **See** Engineering-Electricity, Electrical Engineering, Electronics.

US
EIA DATA INDEX / U.S. DEPARTMENT OF ENERGY, ENERGY INFORMATION ADMINISTRATION, OFFICE OF ENERGY INFORMATION SERVICES. **Added/Corp** United States. Energy Information Administration. Office of Energy Information Services. United States. Energy Information Administration. Office of the National Energy Information System. (Dec. 1980)-. Government Publication. English. sa. Superintendent of Documents, US Government Printing Office, Washington DC 20402. **Tel** (202)275-3328, FAX (202)786-2377. **LC** Z5853.P83; E43; TJ163.2. **DD** 016.33379.
Desc: Indexes the tables, graphs, and formatted data presented in the statistical publications of the EIA.

US
EIA PUBLICATIONS DIRECTORY / U.S. DEPARTMENT OF ENERGY, ENERGY INFORMATION ADMINISTRATION, OFFICE OF ENERGY INFORMATION SERVICES. **Added/Corp** United States. Energy Information Administration. Office of Energy Information Services. National Energy Information Center (U.S.). **VFOAT** Energy Information Administration Ppublications Directory. **VAT** Energy Information Administration Publications Directory. (1978)-. English. an (June). National Energy Information Center, Energy Information Administration, Forrestal Building, Room 1F-048, Washington DC 20585. **Tel** (202)586-8800. **LC** Z5853.P83; U53a; TJ163.2. **DD** 016.33379.
Desc: Contains abstracts and ordering information for EIA publications released each year.

GW
EL SALVADOR : ENERGIEWIRTSCHAFT. **Main/Corp** Bundesstelle fuer Aussenhandelsinformation (Germany). German. DM2.00. Bundesstelle fuer Aussenhandelsinformation, Agrippastr 87 93, D 50676 Cologne Germany. **Tel** 011 49 221 2057316, FAX 011 49 221 2057212. **LC** HD9502.S1.

US/0745-4651
ELECTRIC CONSUMER. [Electri. consum.]. **Added/Corp** Indiana Statewide Association of Rural Electric Cooperatives. (198?)-. Periodical. English. mo. $2.00. Indiana Statewide Association of Rural Electric Cooperatives, PO Box 24517, Indianapolis IN 46224. **Tel** (317)248-9453. **ED** Emily Born and Tim Brown. **Bk Rev. Ad Acc. Circ:** 260,000 (ctrl). ***Continues** Indiana Rural News. Electric Consumer, 0279-9952.*
Desc: News and feature stories of concern to rural electric co-op members, sections include recipes, poetry, health information and energy briefs.

US/0896-5196
ELECTRIC ENERGY SYSTEMS. (ELECTRIC ENERGY SYSTEMS : CURRENT ABSTRACTS / U.S. DEPARTMENT OF ENERGY ; PREPARED FOR OFFICE OF CONSERVATION AND RENEWABLE ENERGY ; PREPARED BY OFFICE OF SCIENTIFIC AND TECHNICAL INFORMATION.). [Electr. energy syst.]. **Added/Corp** United States. Dept. of Energy. Office of Conservation and Renewable Energy. United States. Dept. of Energy. Office of Scientific and Technical Information. **VFOAT** EES. Vol. 88, No. 1 (Jan./Feb. 1988)-. Government Publication. English. Twenty-four times a year. $150.00 North America; $300.00 other. US Department of Energy, 1000 Independence Avenue SW, Washington DC 20585. **Tel** (202)586-5000, FAX (202)586-4073. **(Subscription address:** National Technical Information Service, 5285 Port Royal Road, Springfield, VA 22161**)** **DD** 621. **CODEN** EESYE2.

●CN/1198-4848
ELECTRIC POWER STATISTICS. ANNUAL STATISTICS. **See** Energy-Abstracting, Bibliographies and Statistics.

CN/0380-951X
ELECTRIC POWER STATISTICS. VOLUME 1. ANNUAL ELECTRIC POWER SURVEY OF CAPABILITY AND LOAD. **See** Energy-Abstracting, Bibliographies and Statistics.

CN/0702-6609
ELECTRIC POWER STATISTICS. VOLUME 3. INVENTORY OF PRIME MOVER AND ELECTRIC GENERATING EQUIPMENT. **See** Energy-Abstracting, Bibliographies and Statistics.

US
ELECTRIC RATE BOOK. **See** Public Administration-Public Utilities.

II/0970-2318
ELECTRICITY CONSERVATION QUARTERLY. [Electr. Conserv. Q.]. (1980)-. Periodical. English. qt. $30.00. **(Subscription address:** Prints India, 11 Darya Ganj, New Delhi 110002 India.**)** **UDC** 621.31.

CN/0843-7343
ELECTRICITY TODAY (PICKERING). **See** Engineering-Electricity, Electrical Engineering, Electronics.

GW/0170-2033
ELEKTRISCHE ENERGIE-TECHNIK. [Elektr. Energ.-Tech.]. (1976)-. Periodical. German. bm (6 issues). DM112.00 Germany; DM123.00 other. Dr. Alfred Huethig Verlag GmbH, Postfach 102869, D 69018 Heidelberg Germany. **Tel** 011 49 6221 489281. **(Subscription address:** WEPF Publishing Services GmbH, Auf Dem Wolf 4, CH 4018 Basel Switzerland.**)** **ED** Volkmar Dipling (06221)489-273. **UDC** 621.31/.32. **[CCC]. Bk Rev. Ad Acc. Pr Rev. Circ:** 12,500 (ctrl). Documents available from Ask*IEEE. ***Continues** Elektro-Energie, 0343-6179.*
Desc: Technical CC-journal for plants and equipment of energy and industrial works.
Ind/Abst INSPEC (Jan. 1981-).

GW
ELFENBEINKUSTE : ENERGIEWIRTSCHAFT. **Main/Corp** Germany (Federal Republic, 1949-). Bundesstelle fur Aussenhandelsinformation. German. DM2.00. Bundesstelle fuer Aussenhandelsinformation, Agrippastr 87 93, D 50676 Cologne Germany. **Tel** 011 49 221 2057316, FAX 011 49 221 2057212. **LC** HD9502.I92.

US/1059-6631
EMF KEEPTRACK. **See** Law.

CN
EMR; ACTIVITIES OF THE SCIENCE AND TECHNOLOGY SECTOR. **Main/Corp** Canada. Dept. of Energy, Mines and Resources. Science and Technology Sector. **VAT** Energy Mines Resources. 1972/73-. English. Energy Mines and Resources Canada, 580 Booth Street, Ottawa Ontario K1A 0E4 Canada. **LC** QE48.C2; C35A. **DD** 354/.71/0082305.

US
ENERCOM. **Added/Corp** New York (State). State Energy Office. Office of Communications. (Fall 1983)-. Periodical. English. qt. New York State Energy Office, Office of Communications, Two Rockefeller Plaza, Albany NY 12223.
Ind/Abst Energy Inf. Abstr.

RM/0423-1082
ENERGETICA. [Energetica]. **Added/Corp** Asociatia Stiintifica a Ingenerilor si Tehnicienilor din Romania. Romania. Ministerul Energiei Electrice si Industriei Electrotehnice. (1953)-. Periodical. Romanian. mo. $62.00. **(Subscription address:** Ilexim Press Department, PO Box 1, 136-1-137, Bucharest, Romania.**)** Documents available from Ask*IEEE.
Desc: Studies on energetics.
Ind/Abst Coal Abstr.; INSPEC (1968-); Saf. Health Work.

RU
ENERGETICHESKOE STROITELJSTVO. Russian. mo. $129.95. **(Subscription address:** East View Publications Inc., 3020 Harbor Lane North, Suite 110, Minneapolis MN 55447.**)** Documents available from CASDDS.
Ind/Abst Chem. Abstr.

RU/0131-1328
ENERGETICHESKOE STROITELSTVO ZA RUBEZHOM : ORGAN MINISTERSTVA ENERGETIKI I ELEKTROTEKHNICHESKOI PROMYSHLENNOSTI. [Energ. stroit. rubezom]. **Added/Corp** Soviet Union. Ministerstvo Energetiki i Elektrotekhnicheskoi Pomyshlennosti. (1959)-. Academic Scholarly Publication. Russian. bm. $171.00 domestic airmail; $178.00 international airmail. **(Subscription address:** Victor Kamkin, 4956 Boiling Brook Parkway, Rockville MD 20852.**)** **CODEN** ESRBBN. Documents available from CASDDS.
Ind/Abst Chem. Abstr.; Coal Abstr.

MX
ENERGETICOS. Yearly V. 1- August 1977-. Periodical. Spanish. Secretaria de Patrimonio Y Fomento Industrial, Rio Rhin No 22, Ler Piso Mexico 5 DF Mexico. **LC** HD9502.A1; E52.

PL/0013-7294
ENERGETYKA. (ENERGETYKA [ORGAN STOWARZYSZENIA ELEKRYKOW POLSKICH].). [Energetyka]. **Added/Corp** Stowarzyszenie Elekrykow Polskich. (1947)-. Academic Scholarly Publication. Polish (summaries and/or abstracts in English, German and Russian). mo. $81.00. **(Subscription address:** ARS Polona, PO Box 1001, 00068 Warsaw Poland.**) CODEN** EGYAA4. Documents available from Ask*IEEE, CASDDS.
Ind/Abst Chem. Abstr.; INSPEC (1968-).

SI/0126-2696
ENERGI INDONESIA. Periodical. English (Indonesian). qt. World Energy Conference, Komite National Indonesia Seksi Publikasi Kni-Wec, D/A Badan Tenaga Atom Nasional 85, Jakarta Indonesia. **LC** TJ163.25.I5; E53. **DD** 333.79/.09598.

BL
ENERGIA. No. 1-. Periodical. English (Portuguese). $75.00. Apec Editora S A, rua Sorocaba 316 Botafogo, ZX 02 22.271 Rio de Janeiro Brazil. **Tel** 266-4449. **ED** Victor da Silva. **LC** TJ163.25.B6; E54. **DD** 333.79/0981. **Circ:** 2,000.
Desc: Articles on energy signed by Brazilian experts who analyze economical and technical aspects of the energetic sector of Brazil.

IT
ENERGIA. 80/1-. Periodical. Italian. qt. Editrice Del Automobile, V Le Regina Margherita 290, 00198 Rome Italy. **Tel** 011 39 6 4402061.

IT
ENERGIA E MATERIE PRIME. Vol. 1 No. 1 (May/June 1978)-. Periodical. Italian. Twelve times a year. L80000 Italy; L100000 others. Energia e Materie Prime SRL, VLE XXI Aprile 81, 00162 Rome Italy. **Tel** 011 39 6 44244094. **Ad Acc. Circ:** 2,500.
Desc: The main Italian review involved in energy's and raw material's problems.
Ind/Abst Coal Abstr.

HU/0013-7316
ENERGIA ES ATOMTECHNIKA. (ENERGIA ES ATOMTECHNIKA : AZ ENERGIAGAZDALKODASI TUDOMANYOS EGYESUELET LAPJA.). [Energ. atomtech.]. **Added/Corp** Energiagazdalkodasi Tudomamyos Egyesulet. **VFOAT** Energiia I Atomnaia Tekhnika; Energetics and Nuclear. Vol. 10 (1957)-. Hungarian (summaries and/or abstracts in English, German and Russian; table of contents in English, German and Russian). bm (6 issues). $23.00. **(Subscription address:** Kultura, PO Box 149, H 1389 Budapest 62 Hungary.**) LC** TJ4; .E56. **CODEN** ENATAO. cum. index. Documents available from The Genuine Article, Ask*IEEE, CASDDS. ***Continues*** *Magyar Energiagazdasag.*
Ind/Abst Alum. Ind. Abstr.; Chem. Abstr.; Coal Abstr.; Curr. Contents Eng. Tech. Appl. Sci.; Energy Inf. Abstr.; Energy Res. Abstr.; Eng. Mater. Abstr.; Gas Abstr.; INSPEC (June 1969-); Int. Aerosp. Abstr.; Leadscan; Met. Abstr.; Res. Alert [Select. Cov.]; SCISEARCH.

SP/0210-2056
ENERGIA MADRID. [EnergiaMadrid]. (1975)-. Periodical. Spanish. bm. $103.00 Europe; $164.00 other. Ingenieria Quimica SA, Triana 53, 28016 Madrid Spain. **Tel** 011 34 1 3456400. **UDC** 620. **[CCC].** Documents available from CASDDS.
Ind/Abst Chem. Abstr.

IT/0013-7332
ENERGIA NUCLEARE (MILANO). See Engineering-Nuclear Engineering.

HU/0021-0757
ENERGIAGAZDALKODAS. [Energiagazdalkodas]. Vol. 10 (1969)-. Periodical. Hungarian (table of contents in English). mo. **CODEN** ENGGAF. Documents available from CASDDS. ***Continues*** *Ipari Energiagazdalkodas.*
Ind/Abst Chem. Abstr.; Gas Abstr.

HU/0231-0678
ENERGIAIPARI ES ENERGIAGAZDALKODASI SZAKIRODALMI TAJEKOZTATO. (1983)-. Periodical. Hungarian. mo. 9.900ft. Orszagos Muszaki Informacios Kozpont es Konyvtar (O.M.I.K.K.), National Technical Information Centre and Library Museum, u 17, PO Box 12, 1428 Budapest, Hungary. **Tel** (361)118-1994, FAX (361)138-2414, telex 22-4944 OMIKK H. **ED** Denes Bernad. **UDC** 016. **Circ:** 175.
Desc: All questions concerning energy.

FI/0786-0021
ENERGIAN TUOTANTO JA VESIHUOLTO. VFOAT Energiproduktion Och Vattenforsorjning. Finnish (Swedish). an. Tilastokeskus, PL 504, Annankatu 44, 00101 Helsinki Finland. **Tel** 358-0-17341, FAX 358-0-17342474, telex 1002111 TILASTO SF. **LC** TJ163.25.F5; E537.

FI/0785-3165
ENERGIATILASTOT / KAUPPA- JA TEOLLISUUSMINISTERIO, ENERGIAOSASTO. VFOAT Energistatistik; Energy Statistics. 1960-1976-. English (Finnish and Swedish). an. Valtion Painatuskeskus, PO Box 516, SF 00101 Helsinki Finland. **Tel** 011 358 0 5660266. **LC** HD9502.F5; E54. **DD** 333.79/094897.

FR
ENERGIE. French. CNRS / Institut d'Information Scientifique et Technique, (Centre National de la Recherche Scientifique), 15 Quai Anatole France, Paris 75700 France. **Tel** 011 33 1 47531515, telex 299 356 F.
Ind/Abst Soils Fert.

CN/0844-7152
ENERGIE AU QUEBEC EN PRIMEUR, L'. [Energ. Que. primeur]. **Added/Corp** Quebec (Province). Secteur Energie. Direction Generale de L'Analyse Economique et Financiere. No. 19 (Jan. 1987)-. Periodical. French. ir. Free. Ministrie Energie & Resources, 1530 Boul de Entente, Dist Publ, Quebec Que G1S 4N6 Canada. **Tel** (418)643-1809. **DD** 333.79/09714. ***Continues*** *Statistiques de l'Energie au Quebec en Primeur, 0844-7144.*

NE
ENERGIE CONSULENT. Dutch. bm. DE Ferrante & Bakker BV, Postbus 77, 1200 AB Hilversum Netherlands.

FR
ENERGIE DANS LES SECTEURS ECONOMIQUES, L'. Began with 1983 Vol. French. an. 101 rue de Grenelle, 75700 Paris France. **LC** HD9502.F7; E55. **DD** 333.79/13/0944021.

GW
ENERGIE DIALOG. (19??)-. German. qt. DM8.50. Schiffahrts Verlag Hansa, Schroedter & Co., Postfach 520365, D 22605 Hamburg Germany. **Tel** 011 49 40 8228070. **(Subscription address:** Maximilian Verlagsgruppe, Postfach 2352, D 32045 Herford Germany**) Bk Rev. Ad Acc. Circ:** 6,750 (ctrl).
Desc: Journal for national energy use, future energy, and energy management.

FR
ENERGIE FLUIDE ET LUBRIFICATION. (19??)-. French. 300.00F France; 415.00F other. Societe Ulysse Boucoiran, rue Gustave Joublier #6, 75010 Paris France. **Tel** 011 33 1 42471205.

FR/0336-9811
ENERGIE FLUIDE, L'AIR INDUSTRIEL. [Energ. fluide air ind.]. **VFOAT** Energie Fluide. 20E Year No. 1 (Jan./Feb. 1981)-. Periodical. French. mo. 350.00F France; 480.00F other. Societe Ulysse Boucoiran, rue Gustave Joublier #6, 75010 Paris France. **Tel** 011 33 1 42471205. **LC** TJ840; .E49. **DD** 620.1/06/05. **CODEN** EFAID6. ***Continues*** *Energie Fluide Hydraulique, Pneumatique, Asservissement, Lubrication.*
Desc: Covers fluid power technology and compressed air.
Ind/Abst Coal Abstr.; Energy Res. Abstr. (Feb. 1983-); Fluid Abstr., Civil Eng.; Fluid Abstr. Proc. Eng.; FLUIDEX.

FR/0154-0335
ENERGIE. LEXIQUE. English (French). an. Informascience, Centre de Documentation Scientifique et Technique Service des Abonnements, 26 rue Boyer, 75971 Paris Cedex 20 France. **LC** Z695.1.P68; E53. **DD** 025.4/9621042.

SZ/0304-2065
ENERGIE (PFAFFHAUSEN). (ENERGIE.). V. 1, 1974-. Periodical. German. ir. 35.00 overseas. **LC** TK3; .E89.

FR/0292-1731
ENERGIE PLUS. [Energ. plus]. (1981)-. Periodical. French. mo (10 issues - not published in July & Dec.). 560.00F France; 650.00F other. ATEE - Association technique pour l'Efficacite Energetique, 47 Avenue La Place, 94117 Arcueil Cedex France. **Tel** 011 33 1 46569143, FAX 011 33 1 49850627. **ED** Michel Hoez. **UDC** 620.9. **Ad Acc. Circ:** 4,000 (ctrl). ***Continues*** *Informations - A.T.E.E, 0244-8858.*
Desc: Focuses on energy sources that are more efficient and less pollutant.

GW/0179-9932
ENERGIE SPEKTRUM. [Energ.-Spektrum]. No. 4 (April 1986)-. Periodical. German. mo (12 issues). DM204.00. Resch Media Mail Verlag GmbH, Postfach 1260, D 82166 Graefelfing Germany. **Tel** 011 49 89 8580710. **LC** TJ163.13; .E514. **CODEN** ENSPE4. Documents available from Ask*IEEE. ***Separated from*** *Energie (Munich, Germany);* ***Absorbed*** *Warme, 0372-7114.*
Ind/Abst INSPEC (April 1986-Dec. 1986).

FR
ENERGIE. T230. French. ir. 1837.80F France; 1910.00F other. Institut de l'Information Scientique et Technique (INIST), 2 Allee du Parc de Brabois, 54514 Vandoeuvre Nancy Cedex France. **Tel** 011 33 83 504600, FAX 011 33 83 504650. ***Continues*** *Pascal Thema. T230: Energie.*

GW/0013-7405
ENERGIEANWENDUNG. German. mo. $135.00. Georg Thieme Verlag Stuttgart, Postfach 301120, D 70451 Stuttgart Germany. **Tel** 011 49 711 89310, FAX 011 49 711 8931298, telex 7 252 275 GTVD. **(Subscription address:** Thieme Medical Publishers Inc., 381 Park Avenue South, New York NY 10016.**)** ***Continues*** *Energietechnik.*

GW
ENERGIEBILANZEN DER BUNDESREPUBLIK DEUTSCHLAND. (19??)-. German. ir. DM35.00 (latest issue). Verlag Wirtschaftsgesellschaft VWEW, Stresemannallee 23, D 60596 Frankfurt Germany. **Tel** 011 49 69 6304325.

GW/0013-7421
ENERGIETECHNIK. ***Title Change.*** [Energietechnik]. 1. Yearly Volume (July 1951)-(19??). Academic Scholarly Publication. German. mo. Deutscher Judo Verband, Redaktion Ippon Segewaldweg 40, D 12557 Berlin Germany. **Tel** 011 49 711 210770, telex 051 678. **LC** TJ3; .K343. **CODEN** ETNKA2. Documents available from Article Express International, Ask*IEEE, CASDDS. ***Merged into*** *Energieanwendung.*
Ind/Abst Bioeng. Abstr.; Chem. Abstr.; Coal Abstr.; Ei Page One; EMBASE; Eng. Index Annu.; INSPEC (1968-); Int. Aerosp. Abstr.

SW/0348-9493
ENERGIMAGASINET. [Energimagasinet]. (1979)-. Periodical. Swedish. Seven times a year. Kr245.00. Teknikforlaget, Box 104, 30102 Halmstad Sweden. **Tel** 011 46 35 104150, FAX 011 46 35 104154. **UDC** 620.9.

LU
ENERGISTATISTISK ARBOG. JAHRBUCH ENERGIESTATISTIK. ENERGY STATISTICS YEARBOOK. See Energy-Abstracting, Bibliographies and Statistics.

CN/0833-3505
ENERGY ALBERTA. (ENERGY ALBERTA : ENERGY RESOURCES CONSERVATION BOARD REVIEW OF ALBERTA ENERGY RESOURCES IN ...). [Energy Alta.]. **Added/Corp** Alberta. Energy Resources Conservation Board. (1984)-. English. an. Free upon request. Energy Resources Conservation Board, 640 Fifth Avenue Southwest, Calgary Alberta T2P 3G4 Canada. **Tel** (403)297-8311, (403)297-8190, telex 03-821717. **LC** TN873.C22; A442 subser.; TJ163.25.C3. **DD** 333.79/097123. ***Continues*** *Alberta Energy, 0825-1525.*
Desc: Provides details of the current status and anticipated future trends of Alberta's energy industry.

CN/0835-5266
ENERGY ALERT (TORONTO). (ENERGY ALERT.). [Energy alert]. **Added/Corp** Energy Educators of Ontario. **VFOAT** Alerte Energetique. Vol. 1, No. 1 (Fall 1982)-. Periodical. English. tq (Jan., Apr., Oct.). 15.00Can$. Energy Educators of Ontario, 517 College Street, Suite 406, Toronto ONT M6G 4A2 Canada. **Tel** (416)323-9216, FAX (416)323-0689. **ED** Doug Hahve. **DD** 531/.6/07013. **Bk Rev. Circ:** 400 (ctrl). available on an online database (files 16,636/Full-Text) from DIALOG.
Ind/Abst PROMT [Full Txt.]; PTS Newsl. Database [Full Txt.].

AT/0813-5215
ENERGY ALTERNATIVES. [Energy altern.]. (1982)-. Monographic series. English. ir. Price varies per volume. **DD** 333.79.
Ind/Abst AESIS Q.

CN/0315-1654
ENERGY ANALECTS. [Energy analects]. (June 1972)-. Periodical. English. Fifty times a year. 569.00Can$. C.O. Nickle Publications, 999 8th Street Southwest, Suite 300, Calgary, Alberta T2R 1N7 Canada. **Tel** (403)244-6111. **DD** 338.4/7/621. **[CCC].** available on microfilm and microfiche from University Microfilms International (UMI); available on an online database (file 16/Full-Text) from DIALOG. ***Absorbed*** *Canada's Executive Petroleum Report, 0315-1255; Electric Power Communicator, 0317-8943* ***and*** *Energy Update, 0709-647X.*
Ind/Abst PROMT [Full Txt.]; PTS Newsl. Database [Full Txt.].

US
ENERGY ANALYSIS. Monographic series. English. Price varies per volume. American Gas Association / Virginia, 1515 Wilson Boulevard, Arlington VA 22209. **Tel** (703)841-8400, (703)841-8559, FAX (703)841-8697. **LC** HD9581.U49; E53. **DD** 333.79/0973.

US/0748-5972
ENERGY ANALYST. [Energy anal.]. Vol. 1, No. 1 (July 30, 1984)-. Periodical. English. bw. $285.00. Thompson Publishing Group / Washington DC, PO Box 76927, Washington DC 20013. **DD** 338.

US/1045-5728
ENERGY ANALYST (SILVER SPRING, MD.). (ENERGY ANALYST [COMPUTER FILE].). [Energy anal.]. (Oct. 1989)-. Periodical. English. mo. $18,950.00. Quick Source Inc., 700 Roeder Road, Silver Spring MD 20910. **DD** 333.

SZ/0378-7788
ENERGY AND BUILDINGS. See Building and Construction.

US/1050-5326
ENERGY & CONSCIOUSNESS. (ENERGY & CONSCIOUSNESS : INTERNATIONAL JOURNAL OF CORE ENERGETICS.). [Energy conscious.]. **Added/Corp** Institute of Core Energetics. **VFOAT** Energy and Consciousness; International Journal of Core Energetics. Vol. 1, No. 1 (Winter 1991)-. Periodical. English. sa. $12.00. Institute of Core Energetics, 115 East 23rd Street, New York NY 10010. **DD** 150.

US/0891-0979
ENERGY & EDUCATION. ***Ceased.*** (ENERGY & EDUCATION / NATIONAL SCIENCE TEACHERS ASSOCIATION.). [Energy educ.]. **Added/Corp** United States. Dept. of Energy. National Science Teachers Association. **VFOAT** Energy and Education. Vol. 1, No. 1 (Oct. 1977)-(June 1989). Periodical. English. bm (October-June). National Science Teachers Association/Special Projects, 5112 Berwyn Road, College Park MD 20740. **Tel** (301)220-0874. **ED** Laura Bohor Roth. **DD** 338. **Bk Rev. Circ:** 3,000 (ctrl).
Desc: A newsletter serving the serving the energy education community. Features editorials by prominent figures in energy or education, book and material reviews, freebies, workshop/event notices, and new films.

UK/0958-305X
ENERGY & ENVIRONMENT. **VFOAT** Energy and Environment. Vol. 1, No. 1 (1990)-. Periodical. English. qt. $167.00. Multi Science Publ Co Ltd, 107 High Street, Brentwood, Essex CM14 4RX England. **Tel** 011 44 277 244632. **ED** Dr. David Everest. **CODEN** EENVE2. available on an online database (files 16,636/Full-Text) from DIALOG. Documents available from Documents on Demand.
Desc: An interdisciplinary journal aimed at natural scientists, social scientists, technologists and the international policy community covering the direct and indirect environmental impacts of energy acquisition, transport, production and use. A particular objective is to cover the social, economic and political dimensions of such issues at local, national and international level.
Ind/Abst Energy Inf. Abstr.; Environ. Abstr.; PROMT [Full Txt.]; PTS Newsl. Database [Full Txt.].

US/0147-8850
ENERGY AND ENVIRONMENT ANNUAL REPORT. **Main/Corp** Lawrence Berkeley Laboratory. Energy and Environment Division. **Added/Corp** Lawrence Berkeley Laboratory. Energy Environment Division. Annual Report. (19??)-. English. an (Jan., Apr., July, Oct.). $90.00 UK and Europe; $167 other. National Technical Information Service - NTIS, Room 2027S, 5285 Port Royal Road, Springfield VA 22161. **Tel** (703)487-4630, (703)487-4660, (703)487-4650, FAX (703)321-8547, telex 89-9405. **LC** TJ163.2; .L37a. **DD** 621.

II/0039-0828
ENERGY & FUEL USERS' JOURNAL. **Added/Corp** Energy & Fuel Users' Association of India. **VFOAT** Energy and Fuel Users' Journal. (19??)-. English. qt. $20.00. Energy & Fuel Users' Association of India, Madras, India. **(Subscription address:** Prints India, 11 Darya Ganj, New Delhi 110002 India.**)** **LC** TJ275; .S82. **DD** 621.042/0954. ***Continues*** *Steam & Fuel Users' Journal.*

US/0887-0624
ENERGY & FUELS. [Energy fuels]. **Added/Corp** American Chemical Society. **VFOAT** Energy and Fuels. Vol. 1, No. 1 (Jan. 1987)-. Academic Scholarly Publication. English. Six times a year. $395.00 (institution) US. American Chemical Society, 1155 Sixteenth Street Northwest, Washington DC 20036. **Tel** (800)333-9511, (800)227-5558, (614)447-3776, FAX (202)833-7736. **(Subscription address:** American Chemical Society / Ohio, Department L 0011, Columbus OH 43268-0011.**)** **ED** John W. Larsen. **LC** TP315; .E518. **DD** 662/.6/05. **CODEN** ENFUEM. **[CCC]. Bk Rev. Ad Acc. Pr Rev. Acid Free.** available on microfilm and microfiche from University Microfilms International (UMI). Documents available from Article Express International, The Genuine Article, CASDDS.
Desc: Covers all aspects of the transformation, utilization, formation, and production of fuels and non-nuclear energy in addition to studies of fuel structure and properties.
Ind/Abst Chem. Abstr. (1987-); Chem. Titles; Coal Abstr.; Curr. Contents Eng. Tech. Appl. Sci.; Ei Page One; Eng. Index Annu.; Gas Abstr.; GeoRef; Lit. Pat. Abstr., Oilfield Chem. (1990-); Lit. Abstr., Catal. Catal.; Lit. Abstr., Health Environ.; Lit. Abstr., Pet. Refin. Petrochem.; Lit. Abstr., Pet. Substit.; Lit. Abstr., Transp. Storage; Res. Alert [Full Cov.]; Sci. Cit. Index; SCISEARCH.

UK
ENERGY & NUCLEAR SCIENCES INTERNATIONAL WHO'S WHO. See Physics-Nuclear Physics.

US/0884-5050
ENERGY AND TECHNOLOGY REVIEW. [Energy technol. rev.]. **VFOAT** E&TR. (197?)-. Periodical. English. Twelve times a year. Free. Lawrence Livermore National Laboratory, PO Box 808, Livermore CA 94550. **Tel** (510)422-4859. **DD** 621.
Ind/Abst Int. Aerosp. Abstr.

HK/0253-0783
ENERGY ASIA. [Energy Asia]. Periodical. English. wk. Energynews Asia Services, 15A Jalan SG3 4 Taman, Sri Gombak, 68100B Caves Selangor Malaysia. **Tel** 011 60 3 688-8184, 011 60 3 689-7862.
Ind/Abst Pet. Energy Bus. News Index (1981).

FR
ENERGY BALANCE. English (French). an. $675.00 (magnetic tape). OECD Publications and Information Center, 2 rue Andre-Pascal, 75775 Paris Cedex 16 France. **Tel** 011 33 1 45248167, US:(202)785-6323, FAX 011 33 1 45248500 OR 45248176, telex 620 160 OCDE. **(Subscription address:** OECD Publications Center, 2001 L Street, Suite 700, Washington DC 20036.**)**

FR
ENERGY BALANCES OF OECD COUNTRIES ... AND MAIN SERIES FROM 1960 BILANS ENERGETIQUES DES PAYS DE L'OCDE ... ET SERIES PRINCIPALES DEPUIS 1960. **Added/Corp** International Energy Agency. Organization for Economic Co-operation and Development. **VFOAT** ilans Energetiques des Pays de l'OCDE ... et Series Principales Depuis 1960. (1970-1985)-. English (French). International Energy Agency, 2 rue Andre Pascal, 75775 Paris Cedex 16 France.

FR
ENERGY BALANCES OF OECD COUNTRIES. BILANS ENERGETIQUES DES PAYS DE L'OCDE. **Main/Corp** International Energy Agency. **Added/Corp** Organisation for Economic Co-Operation and Development. International Energy Agency. Bilans Energetiques des pays de l'OCDE. **VFOAT** Bilans Energetiques des pays de l'OCDE. (1976)-. English (French). an. $37.00 all except Europe. OECD Publications and Information Center, 2 rue Andre-Pascal, 75775 Paris Cedex 16 France. **Tel** 011 33 1 45248167, US:(202)785-6323, FAX 011 33 1 45248500 OR 45248176, telex 620 160 OCDE. **(Subscription address:** OECD Publications Center, 2001 L Street, Suite 700, Washington DC 20036.**)** **LC** HD9502.A1; O74a. ***Continues*** *Organisation for Economic Co-Operation and Development. Energy Balances of OECD Countries.*
Desc: Data on energy production/consumption balances in million tons of oil equivalent. Data is broken down by 7 major energy types and 12 sectors.

US/0886-8514
ENERGY BUSINESS. (ENERGY BUSINESS : A PUBLICATION OF EBASCO SERVICES INCORORATED.). [Energy bus.]. **Added/Corp** Ebasco Services Incorporated. (19??)-. Periodical. English. qt. Ebasco Services Inc., Two World Trade Center, New York NY 10048. **Tel** (212)839-1256. **DD** 333.
Ind/Abst Energy Inf. Abstr.

US/0273-3102
ENERGY CLEARINGHOUSE. [Energy clgh.]. **Added/Corp** United States. Federal Energy Regulatory Commission. U.S. Nuclear Regulatory Commission. United States. Environmental Protection Agency. World Bank United States. Dept. of the Interior. Vol. 1 (Jan. 14, 1980)-. Periodical. English. wk. Comes with Energy Minerals and Resources. Business Publishers Inc., 951 Pershing Drive, Silver Spring MD 20910-4464. **Tel** (301)587-6300, (800)274-0122, FAX (301)585-9075. ***Absorbed*** *Energy Register, 0270-8221.*

US/0147-4359
ENERGY CONSERVATION ANNUAL REPORT. **Main/Corp** Louisiana. Division of Natural Resources and Energy. Project Engineering Section. (19??)-. English. an. Louisiana Department of Conservation, 1260 Havenwood, Baton Rouge LA 70815. **LC** TJ163.4.U6; L68a. **DD** 353.9/763/008232.

US/0747-9638
ENERGY CONSERVATION BULLETIN (WASHINGTON, D.C.). (ENERGY CONSERVATION BULLETIN / ENERGY CONSERVATION COALITION.). [Energy conserv. bull.]. Bulletin. English. bm. $25.00. Energy Conservation Coalition, 1525 New Hampshire Avenue NW, Washington DC 20036. **Tel** (202)745-4870. **DD** 333.

FR
ENERGY CONSERVATION IN THE INTERNATIONAL ENERGY AGENCY; REVIEW. **Main/Corp** Organisation for Economic Co-Operation and Development. (1976)-. English. ir. OECD Publications and Information Center, 2 rue Andre-Pascal, 75775 Paris Cedex 16 France. **Tel** 011 33 1 45248167, US:(202)785-6323, FAX 011 33 1 45248500 OR 45248176, telex 620 160 OCDE. **(Subscription address:** OECD Publications Center, 2001 L Street, Suite 700, Washington DC 20036.**)** **LC** TJ163.3; .O73a. **DD** 333.79/16.

US/0161-6595
ENERGY CONSERVATION NEWS. [Energy conserv. news]. Vol. 1 (Aug. 1978)-. Periodical. English. mo. $325.00. Business Communications Inc., 25 Van Zant Street, Suite 13, Norwalk CT 06855. **Tel** (203)853-4266. **ED** Gail Greenberg. **Bk Rev. Ad Acc.** ctrl circ. available on an online database (file 636/Full-Text) from DIALOG.
Desc: Energy conservation information for the energy manager regarding industrial and commercial energy, conservation innovations, government influence, and who's doing what.
Ind/Abst PTS Newsl. Database [Full Txt.].

US
ENERGY CONSERVATION PROGRAM GUIDE FOR INDUSTRY AND COMMERCE, EPIC. (ENERGY CONSERVATION PROGRAM GUIDE FOR INDUSTRY AND COMMERCE.). **Added/Corp** Center for Building Technology. Office of Energy Conservation. United States. Federal Energy Administration. **VFOAT** EPIC. (1974)-. Government Publication. English. $2.25. US Department of Commerce, 14th Street & Constitution Avenue NW, Washington DC 20230. **Tel** (202)482-2000, FAX (202)482-3772. **CODEN** NBSHAP.

US
ENERGY CONSERVATION RESOURCE DIRECTORY. **Added/Corp** Washington State Energy Office. (19??)-. Directory. English. an. Washington State Energy Office, Library, 809 Legion Way SE, Olympia WA 98504-1211. **LC** HD9502.U53; W1925. **DD** 333.79/16/025797.

US/0162-1475
ENERGY CONSERVATION UPDATE. Periodical. English. mo. $27.50. National Technical Information Service - NTIS, Room 2027S, 5285 Port Royal Road, Springfield VA 22161. **Tel** (703)487-4630, (703)487-4660, (703)487-4650, FAX (703)321-8547, telex 89-9405. **LC** TJ163.3; .E543. **DD** 333.7.

UK/0196-8904
ENERGY CONVERSION AND MANAGEMENT. [Energy convers. manage.]. Vol. 20, No. 1 (1980)-. Academic Scholarly Publication. English. mo. $1114.00 The Americas; £747.00 other. Pergamon Press, An Imprint of Elsevier Science Ltd., The Boulevard, Langford Lane, Kidlington, Oxford OX5 1GB United Kingdom. **Tel** 011 44 865 843000, 011 44 865 843699, FAX 011 44 865 843010. **(Subscription address:** Elsevier Science Ltd. Oxford Fulfillment Centre, PO Box 800, Kidlington, Oxford OX5 1DX United Kingdom.**)** **ED** Jesse C. Denton. **LC** TK2896; .E48. **DD** 621.31/24/05. **CODEN** ECMADL. **[CCC]. Pr Rev.** available on microfilm and microfiche from University Microfilms International (UMI). Documents available from Article Express International, The Genuine Article, BIOSIS Document Express, Ask*IEEE, CASDDS, Documents on Demand. ***Continues*** *Energy Conversion, 0013-7480.*
Desc: Provides a medium through which energy conversion and management can be treated as a coherent subject.
Ind/Abst Abstr. AIT Rep. Publ. Energy; AgBiotech News Inf.; Agric. Eng. Abstr.; Appl. Sci. Technol. Index; Biodeter. Abstr.; Bioeng. Abstr.; Biol. Abstr. (1985-); Chem. Abstr.; Coal Abstr.; Curr. Biotechnol.; Curr. Contents Eng. Tech. Appl. Sci.; Ei Page One; Energy Inf. Abstr.; Energy Res. Abstr. (Dec. 1980-); Eng. Index Annu.; Environ. Abstr.; Environ. Period. Bibliogr.; Fluid Abstr., Civil Eng.; Fluid Abstr. Proc. Eng.; FLUIDEX (1980-); Gas Abstr.; Health Saf. Sci. Abstr.; Hortic. Abstr.; HTFS Dig.; INIS Atomindex [Micro.]; INSPEC (1980-); Int. Aerosp. Abstr.; J. Plan. Lit.; Ornamental Hort. (19??-19??); Pollut. Abstr. Indexes; Postharvest News Inf.; Proc. Chem. Eng.; Res. Alert [Select. Cov.]; Rice Abstr.; Rural Dev. Abstr.; SCISEARCH; Soc. Sci. Cit. Index [Select. Cov.]; Soils Fert.; SportSearch; Theoret. Chem. Eng.; Wheat Barley Trit. Abstr.

US/0277-6103
ENERGY COST CUTTER, THE. ***Suspended.*** [Energy cost cut.]. Began in Aug. (1981)-Suspended. Periodical. English. mo. Syntonic Systems Inc, PO Box 78, Cambridge MA 02138.

US/0364-5274
ENERGY DAILY, THE. [Energy dly.]. Vol. 4, No. 35 (Aug. 2, 1976)-. Periodical. English. da (Mon.-Fri.). $1495.00. King Publishing Group, 627 National Press Building, Washington DC 20045. **Tel** (202)638-4260, FAX (202)662-9744. **ED** John McCaughey. **[CCC]. Bk Rev. Ad Acc. Circ:** 20,000. available on an online database (files 16,636/Full-Text) from DIALOG. ***Continues*** *Weekly Energy Report, 0363-1591.*
Desc: Covering the spectrum of energy sources: oil and gas, nuclear, coal, electricity and synthetic fuels. Includes coverage of energy finance.
Ind/Abst Coal Abstr.; INIS Atomindex [Micro.]; PROMT [Full Txt.]; PTS Newsl. Database [Full Txt.].

US
ENERGY DATA BASE. SUBJECT THESAURUS, PERMUTED LISTING. **VFOAT** EDB. Subject Thesaurus, Permuted Listing. Oct. 1981-. English. National Technical Information Service - NTIS, Room 2027S, 5285 Port Royal Road, Springfield VA 22161. **Tel** (703)487-4630, (703)487-4660, (703)487-4650, FAX (703)321-8547, telex 89-9405.

US/0741-3629
ENERGY DESIGN UPDATE. [Energy des. update]. Vol. 1, No. 1 (July 1982)-. Periodical. English. mo. $327.00 (standard), $157.00 (educator/contractor) US, Canada, & Mexico. Cutter Information Corporation, 37 Broadway, Arlington MA 02174-5539. **Tel** (617)648-8700, (800)964-5118, FAX (617)648-8707, (617)648-1950, telex 650 100 9891. **[CCC].**
Ind/Abst AGRICOLA.

US
ENERGY DEVELOPMENT AND DEMONSTRATION PROGRAM : YEAR END REPORT. **Main/Corp** Wisconsin. Energy Development and Demonstration Program. **Added/Corp** Wisconsin. Division of State Energy. (1981)-. English. an. Wisconsin Energy Division, 101 South Webster Street, 6th Floor, Madison WI 53702. **Tel** (608)266-8234, FAX (608)267-0200. **ED** Barbara Samuel. **LC** TJ163.25.U6; W57a. **DD** 353.97750082/3. **Circ:** 400 (ctrl).

GW/0342-5665
ENERGY DEVELOPMENTS. [Energy dev.]. Vol. 1; April 1977-. Periodical. English. mo. 30.00. Resch Media Mail Verlag GmbH, Postfach 1260, D 82166 Graefelfing Germany. **Tel** 011 49 89 8580710. **ED** Helmut Sendner. **CODEN** EDEVDH. **Bk Rev. Ad Acc. Circ:** 7,400. Documents available from Article Express International, Ask*IEEE.
Ind/Abst Bioeng. Abstr.; Coal Abstr.; Ei Page One; EMBASE; Energy Res. Abstr. (May 1978-); Eng. Index Annu.; INSPEC (April 1977-); Int. Aerosp. Abstr.

US/0013-7502
ENERGY DEVELOPMENTS (NEW YORK, N.Y. 1957). (ENERGY DEVELOPMENTS / IRS.). [Energy dev.]. **Added/Corp** International Review Service (Firm). (1957)-. Periodical. English. bm. $375.00. International Review Service, 15 Washington Place, New York NY 10003.
Ind/Abst INIS Atomindex [Micro.].

UK/0367-1119
ENERGY DIGEST. [Energy dig.]. Vol.1 (Aug./Sept. 1972)-. Periodical. English. bm (6 issues). £54.00 UK; £69.00 airmail; £59.00 seamail. Springfield Information Services / Petersborough, PO Box 31, Cross Street Court, Peterborough PE1 1SD England. **Tel** 011 44 733 267272. **ED** J Perkins. **LC** TJ153; .E4784. **DD** 621./05. **CODEN** ENDGBZ. **Bk Rev. Ad Acc. Circ:** 1,000 (ctrl). available on microfilm and microfiche from University Microfilms International (UMI). Documents available from Article Express International, Documents on Demand. ***Supersedes*** *Journal of Fuel & Heat Technology.*
Desc: Contains the latest developments of all types of energy-related technology in the UK and overseas.
Ind/Abst Bioeng. Abstr.; Coal Abstr.; Curr. Technol. Index; Ei Page One; Energy Inf. Abstr.; Energy Res. Abstr. (Sept. 1973-); Eng. Index Annu.; Environ. Abstr.; Gas Abstr.

UK/0140-9883
ENERGY ECONOMICS. [Energy econ.]. Vol. 1 (Jan. 1979)-. Academic Scholarly Publication. English. qt. $351.00 The Americas; £235.00 other. Butterworth Heinemann Publishers, Linacre House, Jordan Hill, Oxford OX2 8DP England. **Tel** 011 44 865 310366. **(Subscription address:** Elsevier Science Ltd. Oxford Fulfillment Centre, PO Box 800, Kidlington, Oxford OX5 1DX United Kingdom.**)** **ED** Homa Motamen. **LC** HD9502.A1; E5345. **DD** 333.7. **CODEN** EECODR. **[CCC].** Index available. **Bk Rev. Ad Acc. Pr Rev. Circ:** 3,600 (ctrl). available on microfilm and microfiche from University Microfilms International (UMI). Documents available from Article Express International, The Genuine Article.
Desc: Provides a forum for papers dealing with economic theory and its statistical analysis, application, mathematical modelling and methodology. It reports on new energy publications and includes a comprehensive listing of recent energy economics papers. Critical rejoinders to published articles are also included. It is oriented to professional economists both in the academic world and in business.
Ind/Abst AESIS Q.; Bioeng. Abstr.; Coal Abstr.; Contents Recent Econ. J.; Curr. Contents Soc. Behav. Sci.; Econ. Lit. Index; Ei Page One; EMBASE; Energy Inf. Abstr.; Energy Res. Abstr. (July 1979-); Eng. Index Annu.; Gas Abstr.; Geogr. Abstr. Human Geogr.; Highw. Res. Abstr.; Int. Dev. Abstr.; J. Econ. Lit.; PAIS Int. Print (1991-); Res. Alert [Full Cov.]; Rural Dev. Abstr.; Selec. Coop. Index Manage. Period; Soc. Sci. Cit. Index [Full Cov.]; World Agric. Econ.

US/1059-5813
ENERGY, ECONOMICS AND CLIMATE CHANGE. (ENERGY, ECONOMICS AND CLIMATE CHANGE / FROM CUTTER INFORMATION CORP.). [Energy econ. clim. change]. **Added/Corp** Cutter Information Corp. Vol. 1, No. 1 (Oct. 1991)-. Periodical. English. mo. $547.00 US, Canada, & Mexico; $647.00 other. Cutter Information Corporation, 37 Broadway, Arlington MA 02174-5539. **Tel** (617)648-8700, (800)964-5118, FAX (617)648-8707, (617)648-1950, telex 650 100 9891. **LC** IN PROCESS. **DD** 344. **CODEN** EECCEQ. **[CCC].** available on an online database (file 636/Full-Text) from DIALOG.
Ind/Abst PTS Newsl. Database [Full Txt.].

UK/0262-7108
ENERGY ECONOMIST. (ENERGY ECONOMIST / FINANCIAL TIMES.). [Energy econ.]. **Added/Corp** Financial Times Business Information Ltd. **VFOAT** Financial Times Energy Economist; FTEE. (1981)-. Periodical. English. Twelve times a year. £265.00. Financial Times England, 8 16 Great New Street, London EC4A 3BN England. **Tel** 011 44 71 353 0305, 353 1040, FAX 011 44 353 0846. **ED** Chris Cragg. **Bk Rev.**
Desc: A newsletter providing a regular overview of factors affecting world energy patterns.
Ind/Abst Coal Abstr.; Energy Res. Abstr. (April 1982-); J. Plan. Lit.; PAIS Int. Print.

US/0199-8595
ENERGY ENGINEERING : JOURNAL OF THE ASSOCIATION OF ENERGY ENGINEERS. [Energy eng.]. **Added/Corp** Association of Energy Engineers. Vol. 77, No. 1 (Dec. 1979/Jan. 1980)-. Academic Scholarly Publication. English. bm. $99.00 (1 year), $178.00 (2 year) US and Canada; $125.00 (1 year), $230.00 (2 year) other. Fairmont Press, 700 Indian Trail, Lilburn GA 30247. **Tel** (404)925-9388, FAX (404)381-9865. **ED** Anna Fay Williams. **LC** TJ163.6; .E53. **DD** 621.042/05. **CODEN** EENGDO. **[CCC].** Index available. cum. index. **Bk Rev. Circ:** 9,000. available on microfilm and microfiche from University Microfilms International (UMI). Documents available from Article Express International, Ask*IEEE. ***Continues*** *Building Systems Design, 0002-2284.*
Desc: Brings regular in-depth coverage of new developments essential for engineering professionals in the energy field. Topics include cogeneration technology, heat recovery and load management.
Ind/Abst Appl. Sci. Technol. Index; Bioeng. Abstr.; CIS Abstr.; Coal Abstr.; Ei Page One; EMBASE; Energy Inf. Abstr.; Energy Res. Abstr. (Jan. 1981-); Eng. Index Annu.; Environ. Period. Bibliogr.; Fluid Abstr., Civil Eng.; Fluid Abstr. Proc. Eng.; FLUIDEX; Gas Abstr.; INIS Atomindex [Micro.]; INSPEC (1982-); Int. Build. Serv. Abstr.; Int. Civil Eng. Abstr.; J. Plan. Lit.; Leadscan; Ref. Sources; Saf. Health Work; Soft. Abstr. Eng.

US
ENERGY ENTS. V. 1- Fall 1980-. English. Governor's Energy Awareness Advisory Committee, 6545 Mercantile Way, Lansing MI 48910. **LC** TJ163.3; .E527. **DD** 333.79/16/05.

II/0970-3446
ENERGY ENVIRONMENT MONITOR. [Energy Environ. Monit.]. (1985)-. Periodical. English. sa. Free. Tata Energy Research Institute, 9 Jor Bagh Publications Unit, New Delhi 110 003 India. **Tel** 011 91 11 4623983, FAX 011 91 11 4621770, telex 31-6159 TERI IN. **UDC** 614.7. Documents available from Documents on Demand.
Ind/Abst Environ. Abstr.

US
ENERGY EQUIPMENT. (19??)-. English. mo. $225.00. Predicasts Inc., A Ziff Communications Company, 11001 Cedar Avenue, Cleveland OH 44106. **Tel** (800)321-6388, (216)795-3000, FAX (216)229-9944, telex 985 604. **(Subscription address:** Information Access Company, PO Box 61000, Department 1851, San Francisco, CA 94161; Phone: (800)321-6388**)**

UK/0144-5987
ENERGY EXPLORATION & EXPLOITATION. [Energy explor. exploit.]. **VFOAT** Energy Exploration and Exploitation. Vol. 1, No. 1- (1981)-. Academic Scholarly Publication. English. qt. £133.00 UK; £145.00 Europe; £162.00 (airmail) other. Multi Science Publishing Company Ltd., 107 High Street, Brentwood, Essex CM14 4RX England. **Tel** 011 44 277 224632, FAX 011 44 277 223453, telex 89-8452. **ED** D Abbot and G Jenkins. **LC** TJ163.13; .E525. **DD** 333.79/05. **CODEN** EEEXDU. **[CCC]. Bk Rev. Ad Acc. Circ:** 500. available on microfilm and microfiche from University Microfilms International (UMI). Documents available from Petroleum Abstracts Document Delivery Service, CASDDS.
Desc: Provides up-to-date and informative reviews of key issues in the exploration and exploitation of world's energy resources. Covers oil, gas, minerals, petroleum, geophysics, economics, etc.
Ind/Abst AESIS Q.; Chem. Abstr.; Coal Abstr.; EMBASE; Energy Res. Abstr. (March 1982-); Gas Abstr.; Geogr. Abstr. Human Geogr. (?-?); GeoRef; Pet. Abstr.

PH
ENERGY FORUM (PHILIPPINE NATIONAL OIL COMPANY). (ENERGY FORUM : A PUBLICATION OF THE PHILIPPINE NATIONAL OIL COMPANY.). **Added/Corp** Philippine National Oil Company. Vol. 1, No. 1 (July/Aug./Sept. 1981)-. Periodical. English. qt. Philippine National Oil Company, 7901 Makati Avenue, Makati Metro Manila Philippines. **LC** HD9502.P6; E53. **DD** 333.79/09599.
Ind/Abst AESIS Q.; Index Philip. Period. (-199?); Philip. Sci. Technol. Abstr.

US/0277-7851
ENERGY FROM BIOMASS AND WASTES. **See** Petroleum and Natural Gas.

LU/0256-6141
ENERGY IN EUROPE. **Added/Corp** Commission of the European Communities. Directorate-General for Energy. **VFOAT** Energia en Europa; Energie en Europa; Energie en Europe. No. 1 (April 1985)-. Periodical. English (French, German and Spanish). Three times a year. £38.40 UK; 41.60p Ireland. Office for Official Publications of the European Communities, 2 Rue Mercier, 2985 Luxembourg Luxembourg. **Tel** 011 352 499281, FAX 011 352 488573. **LC** TJ163.25.E86; E56. **DD** 333.79/094. ***Absorbed*** *Energia en Europa, 0257-9529; Energie in Europa, 0256-6133* ***and*** *Energie en Europe, 0256-615X.*
Ind/Abst Coal Abstr.; F&S Index Plus Text, Int. [Select. Cov.]; Predicasts Forecasts.

JA/0919-6080
ENERGY IN JAPAN. (ENERGY IN JAPAN / IEEJ.). **Added/Corp** Nihon Enerugi Keizai Kenkyujo. **VFOAT** Energy in Japan, Quarterly Report. (1966)-. Periodical. English. Six times a year. $200.00. Institute of Energy Economics, Japan, Shuwa Kamiyacho Building, 4-3-13 Toranomon, Minato-ku, Tokyo 105 Japan. **Tel** 011 81 03 5401 4322, FAX 011 81 03 5401 4310, telex 2225427 IEETKY J. **ED** Toshiaki YUASA. **LC** IN PROCESS.
Desc: News and information on the power resources and energy conservation in Japan.
Ind/Abst Coal Abstr.

US/0147-6521
ENERGY INFORMATION ABSTRACTS. ***Ceased.*** **See** Energy-Abstracting, Bibliographies and Statistics.

US/0739-3679
ENERGY INFORMATION ABSTRACTS ANNUAL. ***Ceased.*** **See** Energy-Abstracting, Bibliographies and Statistics.

AT/0729-3739
ENERGY INFORMATION ADELAIDE. [Energy inf. Adel.]. (1981)-. Periodical. English. tw. **DD** 333.79099423.
Ind/Abst AESIS Q.

US
ENERGY INFORMER. (19??)-. English. mo. $250.00 institutions; $200.00 individuals; $100.00 self employed and small businesses. Energy Efficiency Inc., 1120 Trinity Drive, Menlo Park CA 94025. **Tel** (415)854-9445, FAX (415)854-3616. **ED** Fereidoon P. Sioshansi. Index available (published in Feb. issue). cum. index. **Bk Rev**, (Qty: 12).

US/0195-6574
ENERGY JOURNAL (CAMBRIDGE, MASS.). (THE ENERGY JOURNAL / INTERNATIONAL ASSOCIATION OF ENERGY ECONOMISTS.). [Energy j.]. **Added/Corp** International Association of Energy Economists. Vol. 1, No. 1 (Jan. 1980)-. Periodical. English. qt. $175.00 US & Canada; $200.00 other. International Association for Energy Economics, 28790 Chagrin Boulevard, Suite 210, Cleveland OH 44122. **Tel** (216)464-5365, FAX (216)464-5365. **ED** Helmut Frank. **LC** HD9502.A1; E536. **DD** 333.79/05. **[CCC]. Bk Rev. Ad Acc. Circ:** 2,000. available on microfilm and microfiche from University Microfilms International (UMI). Documents available from UMI Article Clearinghouse.
Desc: Major articles dealing with theoretical or applied problems of continuing interest in energy economics and related disciplines.
Ind/Abst ABI/INFORM Glob. Ed.; ABI Inform Ondisc (Jan. 1988-); Abstr. AIT Rep. Publ. Energy; Acad. Search (July 1993-); AESIS Q.; Bus. ASAP (1990-) [Full Txt.]; Bus. Index (1985-); Bus. Period. Index; Bus. Source (Jul. 1993-); Coal Abstr.; Econ. Lit. Index (1981-); Energy Inf. Abstr.; Energy Res. Abstr. (1980-); Environ. Period. Bibliogr.; Gas Abstr.; Gen. BusinessFile (1985-); Gen. Period. Index (1985-); INFO-SOUTH Abstr.; INIS Atomindex [Micro.]; J. Econ. Lit.; Mag. Search; PAIS Int. Print; Trade Ind. Index (1981-?); Wilson Bus. Abstr.

US/0270-9163
ENERGY LAW JOURNAL. **See** Law.

US/1049-7420
ENERGY LIBRARY. (ENERGY LIBRARY [COMPUTER FILE].). [Energy libr.]. **Added/Corp** OCLC. (1989)-. English. an. OCLC Asia Pacific Services, 6565 Frantz Road, Dublin OH 43017. **Tel** (800)848-5878, (614)764-6394 or 6000, FAX (614)764-6096. **DD** 333. ***Continues*** *Energy (Dublin, Ohio), 0897-1374.*

CN/0821-4913
ENERGY MANAGEMENT (OTTAWA, ONT.). (ENERGY MANAGEMENT.). [Energy management]. **VFOAT** Gestion Energie; Gestion de l'Energie. **VAT** Energy Management Quarterly Newsletter. Fall 1981-. Periodical. English (French). qt. Free. Buildings and Equipment Branch Road, Ottawa Ontario K1Y 2C5 Canada. **DD** 333.79/17/0971384. Documents available from Documents on Demand.
Ind/Abst Abstr. Bull. Inst. Pap. Sci. Tech.; Alum. Ind. Abstr.; Energy Inf. Abstr.; Environ. Abstr.; Fluid Abstr., Civil Eng.; Fluid Abstr. Proc. Eng.; FLUIDEX; Int. Packag. Abstr.; Manage. Market. Abstr.; Met. Abstr.; Pap. Board Abstr.; Print. Abstr.; World Ceram. Abstr.; World Surf. Coat. Abstr.

II/0970-289X
ENERGY MANAGEMENT : QUARTERLY JOURNAL OF NATIONAL PRODUCTIVITY COUNCIL. **Added/Corp** National Productivity Council (India). **VFOAT** Quarterly Journal of National Productivity Council. (19??)-. Periodical. English. qt. $60.00. National Productivity Council, Productivity House, Lodi Road, New Delhi 110003 India. **(Subscription address:** Prints India, 11 Darya Ganj, New Delhi 110002 India.**)** **LC** HD9502.I4; E52. **DD** 333.79/0954/05.

CN/1183-7179
ENERGY MARKET UPDATE. [Energy mark. update]. **Added/Corp** British Columbia. Energy Resources Division. Vol. 3, No. 1 (Mar. 1991)-. Periodical. English. qt. Free (on request). BC Min Energy Mines Petr Resources, 402A 617 Goverment Street, Victoria British Columbia V8X 4S2 Canada. **Tel** (604)387-6407. **DD** 354.7110082. ***Continues*** *Energy Sector Update., 1183-7160.*

CN/0823-1478
ENERGY NEWS (OTTAWA. 1982). (ENERGY NEWS.). [Energy news]. Summer 1982-. Periodical. English. NDP Caucus Resource Office, 742 Confederation Building, Ottawa Ontario K1A 0A6 Canada. **DD** 333.79/0971.
Ind/Abst AESIS Q.

US/1059-289X
ENERGY NEWSBRIEF, THE. (THE ENERGY NEWSBRIEF / IRT.). [Energy newsbr.]. **Added/Corp** IRT Environment, Inc. Vol. 6, Issue No. 14 (July 22, 1991)-. Periodical. English. Thirty-five times a year. $295.00 (for profit organizations), $195.00 (non-profit organizations). IRT Environment Inc, PO Box 10990, Aspen CO 81612. **Tel** (303)927-3155, FAX (303)927-9428. **ED** Ted Flanigan. **DD** 333. **Bk Rev**, (Qty: 1-2). ***Continues*** *Issues Review and Tracking, 1056-1404.*

US/0276-1858
ENERGY NEWSLETTER INDEX. ***Ceased.*** [Energy newsl. index]. **Added/Corp** National Energy Researchers (Firm). Vol. 1, No. 1 (Jan. 1981)-?. Newsletter. English. mo. National Energy Researchers, PO Box 35286, Houston TX 77235. **Tel** (713)723-1921. **LC** Z5853.P83; E49; TJ163.2. **DD** 333.79/016.

II/0970-1583
ENERGY OPPORTUNITIES. [Energy Oppor.]. **VFOAT** Scoare's Energy Opportunities. (1986)-. Periodical. English. qt. $30.00. **(Subscription address:** Prints India, 11 Darya Ganj, New Delhi 110002 India.**)** **UDC** 620.9.

UK/0360-5442
ENERGY (OXFORD). (ENERGY.). [Energy]. Vol. 1 (March 1986)-. Periodical. English. mo. $775.00 The Americas; £520.00 other. Pergamon Press, An Imprint of Elsevier Science Ltd., The Boulevard, Langford Lane, Kidlington, Oxford OX5 1GB United Kingdom. **Tel** 011 44 865 843000, 011 44 865 843699, FAX 011 44 865 843010. **ED** S. S. Penner. **LC** HD9502.A1; E533. **DD** 333.7. **CODEN** ENEYDS. **[CCC]. Pr Rev.** available on microfilm and microfiche from University Microfilms International (UMI). Documents available from Article Express International, The Genuine Article, BIOSIS Document Express, Ask*IEEE, CASDDS, Documents on Demand.
Desc: Provides a medium through which energy conversion and management can be treated as a coherent subject. Papers of technical merit are published in areas dealing with primary energy sources and systems, both direct and dynamic conversion processes and problems associated with regulations and control. Subjects discussed include magnetohydrodynamics, nuclear and geothermal design principles, and much more.
Ind/Abst Abstr. AIT Rep. Publ. Energy; AESIS Q.; Agric. Eng. Abstr.; Appl. Sci. Technol. Index; Biodeter. Abstr.; Bioeng. Abstr.; Biol. Abstr.; Chem. Abstr.; Civ. Struct. Eng. Abstr.; Coal Abstr.; Curr. Contents Eng. Tech. Appl. Sci.; Ei Page One; EMBASE; Energy Inf. Abstr.; Energy Res. Abstr. (July 1976-); Eng. Index Annu.; Environ. Abstr.; Environ. Eng. Abstr.; Environ. Period. Bibliogr.; Fluid Abstr., Civil Eng.; Fluid Abstr. Proc. Eng.; FLUIDEX (1976-); For. Prod. Abstr.; Gas Abstr.; GeoRef; Health Saf. Sci. Abstr.; INIS Atomindex [Micro.]; INSPEC (March 1976-); Int. Aerosp. Abstr.; Lit. Pat. Abstr., Oilfield Chem. (1982-); Lit. Abstr., Catal. Catal.; Lit. Abstr., Health Environ.; Lit. Abstr., Pet. Refin. Petrochem.; Lit. Abstr., Pet. Substit.; Lit. Abstr., Transp. Storage; Mater. Sci. Eng. Abstr.; Mech. Eng. Abstr.; Life Sci. Collect. (1985-); Postharvest News Inf.; Res. Alert [Full Cov.]; Rural Dev. Abstr.; Sci. Cit. Index; SCISEARCH; Soc. Sci. Cit. Index [Select. Cov.]; Solid State Supercond. Abstr.

UK/0301-4215
ENERGY POLICY. [Energy policy]. Vol. 1 (June 1973)-. Periodical. English. mo. $589.00 The Americas; £395.00 other. Butterworth Heinemann Publishers, Linacre House, Jordan Hill, Oxford OX2 8DP England. **Tel** 011 44 865 310366. **(Subscription address:** Elsevier Science Ltd. Oxford Fulfillment Centre, PO Box 800, Kidlington, Oxford OX5 1DX United Kingdom.**)** **ED** Lyndon Driscoll. **LC** HD9502.A1; E54. **DD** 333.7/05. **CODEN** ENPYAC. **[CCC].** Index available. **Bk Rev. Ad Acc. Pr Rev. Circ:** 7,000. available on microfilm and microfiche from University Microfilms International (UMI). Documents available from The Genuine Article, UMI Article Clearinghouse, Ask*IEEE, Documents on Demand.
Desc: Coverage of energy policy issues worldwide. The scope of the journal encompasses economics, planning, politics, pricing, forecasting, investment, conservation, substitution and environment.
Ind/Abst ABI/INFORM Glob. Ed.; ABI Inform Ondisc (March 1981-); AESIS Q.; Bioeng. Abstr.; Coal Abstr.; Contents Recent Econ. J.; Curr. Contents Eng. Tech. Appl. Sci.; Curr. Contents Soc. Behav. Sci.; Ei Page One; EMBASE; Energy Res. Abstr. (1973-); Environ. Abstr.; Environ. Period. Bibliogr.; Expand. Acad. Index (1992-); Gas Abstr.; Gen. BusinessFile (1992-); Geogr. Abstr. Phys. Geogr.; Geogr. Abstr. Human Geogr.; GeoRef; Highw. Res. Abstr.; INSPEC (June 1973-); Int. Build. Serv. Abstr.; Int. Dev. Abstr.; J. Plan. Lit.; Newsp. Period. Abstr. (1992-); PAIS Int. Print (1991-); Res. Alert [Full Cov.]; Selec. Coop. Index Manage. Period; SCISEARCH; Soc. Sci. Cit. Index [Full Cov.]; World Ceram. Abstr.

US/0882-3537
ENERGY POLICY STUDIES (NEWARK, DEL.). (ENERGY POLICY STUDIES.). [Energy policy stud.]. **Added/Corp** Energy Policy Research Group (University of Delaware). Vol. 1 (1983)-. Monographic series. English. ir. Price varies per volume. Transaction Publishers / Rutgers State University, New Brunswick NJ 08903. **Tel** (908)932-2280 Ext. 105, FAX (908)932-3138. **ED** John Byrne and Daniel Rich. **DD** 363.
Desc: Examines social, political, and economic dimensions of energy technology, resources, and use. Covers issues of technological scale, resource allocation, environmental quality, and international relations.

US
ENERGY, POWER, AND ENVIRONMENT. (1977)-. Monographic series. English. Price varies per volume. Marcel Dekker Inc., 270 Madison Avenue, New York NY 10016. **Tel** (212)696-9000, (800)228-1160, FAX (212)685-4540, telex 421419. **(Subscription address:** Marcel Dekker Inc, PO Box 5017, Monticello NY 12701.**)**
Desc: Topics in the series include energy management, energy conservation and nuclear power.

FR/0256-2332
ENERGY PRICES AND TAXES. (ENERGY PRICES AND TAXES / INTERNATIONAL ENERGY AGENCY.). [Energy prices taxes]. **Added/Corp** International Energy Agency. 2nd Quarter (1984)-. Periodical. English. qt. $180.00. OECD Publications and Information Center, 2 rue Andre-Pascal, 75775 Paris Cedex 16 France. **Tel** 011 33 1 45248167, US:(202)785-6323, FAX 011 33 1 45248500 OR 45248176, telex 620 160 OCDE. **(Subscription address:** OECD Publications Center, 2001 L Street, Suite 700, Washington DC 20036.**)** **LC** HD9502.A1; E545. **DD** 338.2/3. **CODEN** EPRTEP.
Desc: Provides statistics on prices and taxes on oil products, gas, coal and electricity generation in national currencies. Included are comprehensive notes on sources and methods.

CN/0319-5759
ENERGY PROCESSING CANADA. [Energy process. Can.]. Vol. 66 (Sept./Oct. 1973)-. Periodical. English. bm (6 issues). 30.00Can$ (one year), 50.00Can$ (two year), 75.00Can$ (three year) Canada; 35.00Can$ (one year), 55.00Can$ (two year) US; 60.00Can$ other. Northern Star Communication, 1609700 4th Avenue SW, Calgary Alberta T2P 3J4 Canada. **Tel** (403)265-4750, FAX (408)263-6886. **ED** Scott Jeffrey. **CODEN** EPCADS. **[CCC]. Bk Rev. Ad Acc, Adv Mgr:** Jim Graham. **Circ:** 6,000 (ctrl). Documents available from Article Express International, Petroleum Abstracts Document Delivery Service, CASDDS. ***Continues*** *Gas Processing Canada, 0016-4968.*
Desc: Written and edited for the hydrocarbons processing and related industries and the presentation of changing technology in these fields.
Ind/Abst Bioeng. Abstr.; Chem. Abstr.; Coal Abstr.; Ei Page One; Energy Res. Abstr. (1977-); Eng. Index Annu.; Lit. Pat. Abstr., Oilfield Chem. (1977-); Lit. Abstr., Catal. Catal.; Lit. Abstr., Health Environ.; Lit. Abstr., Pet. Refin. Petrochem.; Lit. Abstr., Pet. Substit.; Lit. Abstr., Transp. Storage; Pet. Abstr.

US/0740-3496
ENERGY-RELATED MANPOWER. (ENERGY-RELATED MANPOWER / PREPARED FOR U.S. DEPARTMENT OF ENERGY, OFFICE OF ENERGY RESEARCH, MANPOWER ASSESSMENT PROGRAM ; PREPARED BY OAK RIDGE ASSOCIATED UNIVERSITIES, MANPOWER EDUCATION, RESEARCH, AND TRAINING DIVISION, LABOR AND POLICY STUDIES PROGRAM.). [Energy-relat. manpow.]. **Added/Corp** Manpower Assessment Program (U.S.) Oak Ridge Associated Universities. Labor and Policy Studies Program. (1982)-. English. an. Oak Ridge Associated Universities, PO Box 117, Oak Ridge TN 37831. **Tel** (615)576-3000, telex TWX 810-572-1076. **LC** HD5718.E472; U63. **DD** 331.12/5214/0973.

US
ENERGY REPORT. English. Energy Report, 215 East Lane Street, Raleigh NC 27611.

US/0888-8183
ENERGY REPORT (ARLINGTON, VA.). (THE ENERGY REPORT.). [Energy rep.]. Vol. 14, No. 25 (June 23, 1986)-. Periodical. English. Fifty times a year. $695.00 US; $769.00 other. Pasha Publications Inc., 1616 North Fort Myer Drive, Suite 1000, Arlington VA 22209. **Tel** (800)424-2908, (703)528-1244, FAX (703)528-3742, (703)528-1253. **LC** TJ153; .E4788. **DD** 333.79/0973. **CODEN** ENRPEX. **[CCC].** available on an online database from DIALOG. ***Continues*** *BNA's Energy Report, 8756-307X;* ***Absorbed*** *Health Facilities Energy.*
Desc: Reports on all types of energy, government decisions affecting energy, energy statistics and forecasts, technological innovations, cogeneration and fuel conservation.
Ind/Abst Abstr. Bull. Inst. Pap. Sci. Tech.; Trade Ind. ASAP [Full Txt.]; Trade Ind. Index [Full Txt.].

UK
ENERGY REPORT : ENERGY POLICY & TECHNOLOGY NEWS BULLETIN. (19??)-. Bulletin. English. mo. £82.50 UK; £87.50 other. Springfield Information Services / Peterborough, PO Box 31, Cross Street Court, Peterborough PE1 1SD England. **Tel** 011 44 733 267272.

US/0196-7754
ENERGY REPORT - TEXAS. COMPTROLLER'S OFFICE. (ENERGY REPORT.). [Energy rep. - Tex., Comptrol. Off.]. **Main/Corp** Texas. Comptroller's Office. April 1976-. English. qt. Texas Comptroller of Public Accounts, 111 East 17th Street, Austin TX 78774. **LC** HJ11; .T44423B subser; TJ163.25. **DD** 353.7640072 S; 353.97640072.
Ind/Abst F&S Index Plus Text, Int. [Select. Cov.]; PROMT; PTS Newsl. Database [Full Txt.].

NE/0167-692X
ENERGY RESEARCH. [Energy res.]. 1-. Academic Scholarly Publication. English. Price varies per volume. Elsevier Science Publishers BV, PO Box 211, 1000 AE Amsterdam Netherlands. **Tel** 011 31 20 5803642, FAX 011 31 20 5862696, telex 15682. **CODEN** ENRSD7. Documents available from Ask*IEEE, CASDDS.
Ind/Abst Abstr. AIT Rep. Publ. Energy; Chem. Abstr.; INSPEC.

US/0160-3604
ENERGY RESEARCH ABSTRACTS. **See** Energy-Abstracting, Bibliographies and Statistics.

US
ENERGY RESEARCH AND RESOURCE DEVELOPMENT IN KANSAS, FISCAL YEAR ... . English. an. **LC** HD9502.U53; K23. **DD** 333.79/0720781.

US/0360-1609
ENERGY RESEARCH AND TECHNOLOGY. English. National Technical Information Service - NTIS, Room 2027S, 5285 Port Royal Road, Springfield VA 22161. **Tel** (703)487-4630, (703)487-4660, (703)487-4650, FAX (703)321-8547, telex 89-9405. **LC** Z5853.P83; E5; TJ163.2. **DD** 016.621.

US/0098-518X
ENERGY RESEARCH PROGRAM OF THE U.S. DEPARTMENT OF THE INTERIOR. **Main/Corp** United States. Dept. of the Interior. Office of Research and Development. **VAT** Energy Research Program of the United States Department of the Interior. English. $5.70. US Department of the Interior / Bureau of Mines, Publications Department, PO Box 18070, Cochrans Mill Road, Pittsburgh PA 15236. **Tel** (412)892-6400. **LC** TJ163.25.U6; U53A. **DD** 621.

US/0195-699X
ENERGY RESEARCH PROGRAMS. [Energy res. programs]. **Added/Corp** Jaques Cattell Press. 1st Ed. (1980)-. English. ir. $75.00. R R Bowker, A Reed Reference Publishing Company, Part of Reed International PLC, PO Box 31, 121 Chanlon Drive, New Providence NJ 07974. **Tel** (908)464-6800, (800)521-8110, FAX (908)665-6688, telex 138-755. **LC** TJ163.25.U6; E52. **DD** 621.042/072073.

US/0270-0115
ENERGY RESOURCE NOTES. [Energy resour. notes]. V. 1- Apr. 1980-. Periodical. English. mo. $15.00. Energy Resource Notes, Center for Energy Policy and Research Technology, Old Westbury NY 11568.

US
ENERGY RESOURCES. (19??)-. English. mo. $225.00. Predicasts Inc., A Ziff Communications Company, 11001 Cedar Avenue, Cleveland OH 44106. **Tel** (800)321-6388, (216)795-3000, FAX (216)229-9944, telex 985 604. **(Subscription address:** Information Access Company, PO Box 61000, Department 1851, San Francisco, CA 94161; Phone: (800)321-6388**)**

US/0149-6263
ENERGY RESOURCES (DENVER). (ENERGY SOURCES.). Began in 1976. English. an. $10.95. United Black Fund, Inc. of Greater Washington, D.C., 1343 H Street NW, Washington DC 20005. **LC** TJ163.13; .E53. **DD** 338.2.

PH
ENERGY RESOURCES DEVELOPMENT IN THE PHILIPPINES. Began with Vol. for 1977/78. English. Energy Centre, Merritt Road, Fort

Bonifacio Metro Manila Philippines. **LC** TJ163.25.P6; E54. **DD** 333.79/15/09599. ***Continues*** *Energy Development Board Report.*

US/0270-1294
ENERGY RESOURCES SERIES. [Energy resour. ser.]. 1-. Monographic series. English. ir. Price varies per volume. Kansas Geological Survey, 1930 Constant Avenue, University of Kansas, Lawrence KS 66046. **Tel** (913)864-3965.
Ind/Abst GeoRef.

US/0749-6362
ENERGY REVIEW (ALBANY, N.Y.). (ENERGY REVIEW.). [Energy rev.]. **Added/Corp** New York State Energy Research and Development Authority. (Summer 1982)-. Periodical. English. sa. Energy Review, Two Rockefeller Plaza, Albany NY 12223. **LC** CURRENT ISSUES ONLY. **DD** 333. ***Continues*** *ERDA Review.*
Ind/Abst Energy Inf. Abstr.; Energy Res. Abstr. (1982-).

US/0147-9660
ENERGY REVIEW (LEXINGTON). (ENERGY REVIEW.). [Energy rev.]. **Added/Corp** Data Resources, inc. Vol. 1 (Summer 1977)-. Periodical. English. DRI McGraw Hill, 24 Hartwell Avenue, Lexington MA 02173. **Tel** (617)863-5100. **(Subscription address:** Data Resources, PO Box 5 0210, Woburn MA 01815.**) LC** HD9502.U5; E534. **DD** 333.7.

US/0094-8063
ENERGY REVIEW (SANTA BARBARA). (ENERGY REVIEW.). [Energy rev.]. **Added/Corp** Energy Research Corporation. (Jan./Feb. 1974)-. Periodical. English. mo. $485.00 (4-year college and university research libraries); $387.00 (surface mail), $401.00 (air mail) other. International Academy at Santa Barbara, 800 Garden Street, Suite D, Santa Barbara CA 93101. **Tel** (805)965-5010, FAX (805)965-6071. **ED** Miriam Flucks. **LC** TJ153; .E47857. **DD** 621. **CODEN** EGYRBM. **[CCC].** Index available. **Bk Rev. Circ:** 10,000. available on microfilm. Documents available from Documents on Demand.
Desc: Digests of current articles, reports, documents, and books on facets of energy and waste management. Covers scientific, technical, economic and popular materials.
Ind/Abst Energy Inf. Abstr.; Environ. Abstr.; GeoRef; Life Sci. Collect.

US/0090-8312
ENERGY SOURCES. [Energy sources]. Vol. 1 (Fall 1973)-. Periodical. English. bm. £205.00 UK; $339.00 other. Taylor & Francis Ltd., Rankine Road, Basingstoke Hampshire, RG24 8PR United Kingdom. **Tel** 011 44 256 840366, FAX 011 44 256 479438, telex 858540. **(Subscription address:** Taylor & Francis Inc., 1900 Frost Road, Suite 101, Bristol PA 19007-1598.**) ED** G. Ali Mansoori. **LC** TJ153; .E4786. **DD** 621/.05. **CODEN** EGYSAO. **[CCC]. Bk Rev. Ad Acc. Pr Rev. Circ:** 600. available on microfilm and microfiche from University Microfilms International (UMI). Documents available from Article Express International, The Genuine Article, Ask*IEEE, Petroleum Abstracts Document Delivery Service, CASDDS, Documents on Demand. ***Absorbed*** *Energy Systems & Policy, 0090-8347.*
Desc: An important forum for scientists, engineers and technologists researching conventional and new sources of energy, and developing these sources into practical fuels. Atmospheric-gradients, biomass, coal, geo-gradients, hydro-gradients, natural gas, nuclear energy, oil shale, petroleum, solar energy, and tar sand constitute the energy sources presently available to mankind.
Ind/Abst Abstr. AIT Rep. Publ. Energy; AESIS Q.; AGRICOLA [Select. Cov.]; Appl. Sci. Technol. Index; BioBusiness; Bioeng. Abstr.; Chem. Abstr.; Coal Abstr.; Curr. Contents Eng. Tech. Appl. Sci.; Ei Page One; Energy Inf. Abstr.; Energy Res. Abstr. (April 1974-); Eng. Index Annu.; Environ. Abstr.; Environ. Period. Bibliogr.; For. Prod. Abstr. (1991-); Gas Abstr.; GeoRef; Health Saf. Sci. Abstr.; INIS Atomindex [Micro.]; INSPEC (Fall 1973-); Int. Aerosp. Abstr.; Lit. Pat. Abstr., Oilfield Chem. (1975-); Lit. Abstr., Catal. Catal.; Lit. Abstr., Health Environ.; Lit. Abstr., Pet. Refin. Petrochem.; Lit. Abstr., Pet. Substit.; Lit. Abstr., Transp. Storage; Pet. Abstr.; Res. Alert [Full Cov.]; Sci. Cit. Index; SCISEARCH.

US/0149-9386
ENERGY (STAMFORD, CONN. 1975). (ENERGY.). [Energy]. **Added/Corp** Business Communications Co. Vol. 1 (Fall 1975)-. Periodical. English. Five times a year. $225.00. Business Communications Inc., 25 Van Zant Street, Suite 13, Norwalk CT 06855. **Tel** (203)853-4266. **ED** Louis Naturman. **LC** TJ163.2; .E44. **DD** 333.7. **CODEN** ENGYD4. **[CCC]. Bk Rev. Ad Acc.** ctrl circ. available on microfilm and microfiche from University Microfilms International (UMI). Documents available from Article Express International.
Desc: Energy news, interpretation, analyses written by people deeply involved and aware of what's really happening in the energy field.
Ind/Abst Bioeng. Abstr.; Coal Abstr.; Ei Page One; Energy Res. Abstr. (March 1976-);; Eng. Index Annu.; For. Prod. Abstr.; GeoRef; Highw. Res. Abstr.; INIS Atomindex [Micro.]; Int. Aerosp. Abstr.; Public Aff. Inf. Serv. Bull.; World Agric. Econ.

US/0739-3075
ENERGY STATISTICS (CHICAGO, ILL.). ***Ceased.*** **See** Energy-Abstracting, Bibliographies and Statistics.

●CN/1188-665X
ENERGY STATISTICS HANDBOOK. **Added/Corp** Statistics Canada. Industry Division. Canada. Energy Sector. **VFOAT** Guide Statistique Sur l'Energie. (Apr. 1992)-. English (French). mo. 300.00Can$ Canada; $360.00 US; $420.00 other. Statistics Canada, Publications Sales & Services, Main Building Room 1710, Ottawa Ontario K1A 0T6 Canada. **Tel** (613)951-5078, (800)267-6677, FAX (613)951-1584, telex 053-3585. **LC** HD9502.C3; E538. **DD** 333.79/0971/021.

●CN/1188-665X
ENERGY STATISTICS HANDBOOK. **Added/Corp** Statistique Canada. Division de l'Industrie. Canada. Secteur e l'Energie. **VFOAT** Guide Statistique Sur l'Energie. (Apr. 1992)-. Periodical. French (English). mo. 300.00Can$ Canada; $360.00 US; $420.00 other. Statistics Canada, Publications Sales & Services, Main Building Room 1710, Ottawa Ontario K1A 0T6 Canada. **Tel** (613)951-5078, (800)267-6677, FAX (613)951-1584, telex 053-3585. **DD** 333.79/0971/05.

FR
ENERGY STATISTICS (INTERNATIONAL ENERGY AGENCY). (ENERGY STATISTICS / STATISTIQUES DE L'ENERGIE.). **Added/Corp** International Energy Agency. **VFOAT** Statistiques de l'Energie. (1974/1976)-. English (French). International Energy Agency, 2 rue Andre Pascal, 75775 Paris Cedex 16 France. ***Continues*** *Energy Statistics (Organisation for Economic Co-Operation and Development).*

AS
ENERGY STATISTICS REPORT FOR FISCAL YEAR. **Added/Corp** American Samoa. Territorial Energy Office. (1983)-. English. an. Territorial Energy Office, Samoa Energy House, Tafuna, American Samoa Government, Pago Pago, American Samoa 96799. **LC** HD9502.A57; E53. **DD** 333.79/13/099613021. ***Continues*** *Energy Statistics Booklet.*

US/0889-5260
ENERGY STATISTICS SOURCEBOOK. **See** Energy-Abstracting, Bibliographies and Statistics.

US
ENERGY STATISTICS YEARBOOK (UNITED NATIONS. STATISTICAL OFFICE). **See** Energy-Abstracting, Bibliographies and Statistics.

US/0731-0927
ENERGY STATUS REPORT. [Energy status rep.]. **Added/Corp** Ohio. Dept. of Energy. (19??)-. English. an. Public Utilities Commission / Ohio, 180 East Broad Street, 11th Floor, Columbus OH 43266. **Tel** (614)466-0327. **LC** HD9502.U53; O4234. **DD** 333.79/09771.

US/0896-5145
ENERGY STORAGE SYSTEMS. (ENERGY STORAGE SYSTEMS : CURRENT ABSTRACTS / U.S. DEPARTMENT OF ENERGY ; PREPARED FOR OFFICE OF CONSERVATION AND RENEWABLE ENERGY ; PREPARED BY OFFICE OF SCIENTIFIC AND TECHNICAL INFORMATION.). [Energy storage syst.]. **Added/Corp** United States. Dept. of Energy. Office of Scientific and Technical Information. United States. Dept. of Energy. Office of Conservation and Renewable Energy. **VFOAT** EST. Vol. 88, No. 1 (Jan./Feb. 1988)-. Government Publication. English. bm. $155.00 US; $310.00 other. US Department of Energy, 1000 Independence Avenue SW, Washington DC 20585. **Tel** (202)586-5000, FAX (202)586-4073. **(Subscription address:** National Technical Information Service, 5285 Port Royal Road, Springfield, VA 22161**) LC** TJ165; .E526. **DD** 621.042.

US/0743-829X
ENERGY STUDIES (AUSTIN, TEX.). (ENERGY STUDIES.). [Energy stud.]. **Added/Corp** University of Texas at Austin. Center for Energy Studies. Vol. 1 (1975)-. Periodical. English. Six times a year. Free. Center for Energy Studies / University of Texas at Austin, Austin TX 78712. **Tel** (512)471-7792.
Ind/Abst Energy Inf. Abstr.

CN/0843-4379
ENERGY STUDIES REVIEW. [Energy stud. rev.]. **Added/Corp** McMaster Institute for Energy Studies. Vol. 1, No. 1 (1989)-. Periodical. English (summaries and/or abstracts in French). Three times a year. 55.00Can$ (1 year), 105.00Can$ (2 year) institutions Canada; 33.00Can$ (1 year), 60.00Can$ (2 year) individuals Canada; $45.00 (1 year), $85.00 (2 year) institutions US; $27.00 (1 year), $50.00 (2 year) individuals US. McMaster University / Institute for Energy Studies, Hamilton Ontario L8S 4M4 Canada. **Tel** (905)525-9140, FAX (905)521-8232. **ED** Mel Kliman. **DD** 333.79/0971. Index available. cum. index. **Bk Rev. Ad Acc. Pr Rev. Circ:** 500 (ctrl). Documents available from Documents on Demand. ***Continues*** *Energy Newsletter (Hamilton, Ont. : 1980)., 0711-3366.*
Desc: An interdisciplinary journal on energy matters covering all aspects of production and use of energy, policy, technology, experimental and theoretical research, environmental and social impacts.
Ind/Abst Econ. Lit. Index; Energy Inf. Abstr.; Environ. Abstr.; Environ. Period. Bibliogr.; INIS Atomindex [Micro.].

US/0270-8256
ENERGY SYSTEMS GUIDEBOOK. [Energy syst. guideb.]. Periodical. English. $10.00 per copy. McGraw Hill Publishing Company, Inc., 1221 Avenue of the Americas, New York NY 10020. **Tel** (212)512-6410, (800)525-5003, FAX (212)512-6111. **LC** TJ163.9; .E537. **DD** 621.042/05.

US/0093-500X
ENERGY TODAY. [Energy today]. Vol. 1 (Sept. 17, 1973)-. Periodical. English. mo. $795.00 (one year), $1,390.00 (two year). Trends Publishing Inc., 1079 National Press Building, Washington DC 20045. **Tel** (202)393-0031, FAX (202)393-1732. **ED** A Kranish. **LC** HD9502.A1; E55. **DD** 333.7/05. **Bk Rev.**
Desc: General energy information, including availability of resources, environmental effects, etc.
Ind/Abst Coal Abstr.; Energy Res. Abstr. (July 1975-).

UK/0308-1222
ENERGY TRENDS. **Added/Corp** Great Britain. Dept. of Energy. Economics and Statistics Division. (Aug. 1974)-. Periodical. English. Twelve times a year. £20.00 UK: £27.00 Europe; £38.00 others. Department of Trade and Industry, Room 3 3 15 1 Palace Street, London SW1E 5HE England. **Tel** 011 44 71 238 3576, FAX 011 44 71 238 3121, telex 91877 EZEGY G. **ED** Mike Ward. **[CCC]. Circ:** 2,500 (ctrl). ***Supersedes in part*** *Trade and Industry / Britain.*
Desc: UK statistics on energy production, consumption, exports and imports and fuel and power prices.
Ind/Abst Manage. Market. Abstr.; World Ceram. Abstr.

US/0279-621X
ENERGY UNLIMITED. ***Ceased.*** Ceased (Dec. 1987). Periodical. English. qt. Energy Unlimited Publications, PO Box 3110, Laredo TX 78044. **ED** Rhetta Jacobson. **DD** 621. **Bk Rev. Ad Acc. Circ:** 1,000 (ctrl).
Desc: Articles and reports on non-conventional energy technology from independent researchers around the world.

CN/0713-9144
ENERGY UPDATE (ENERGY, MINES AND RESOURCES CANADA). (ENERGY UPDATE.). [Energy update]. 1976-. English. Information EMR, Department of Energy, Mines and Resources, Ottawa Ontario K1A 0E4 Canada.

US
ENERGY USE, STATE OFFICE BUILDINGS. **Main/Corp** Wisconsin. Division of Buildings and Grounds. 1982-. English. an. Wisconsin Department of Administration, 101 South Webster Street, Madison WI 53702. **LC** JK1651.W5; A36A. **DD** 353.97750086/2.

US/0162-9131
ENERGY USER NEWS. [Energy user news]. Vol. 1 (Oct. 4, 1976)-. English. Twelve times a year. $69.50 US; $91.00 other. Chilton Company, 201 King of Prussia Road, Radnor PA 19089. **Tel** (610)964-4122, (800)695-1214, FAX (610)964-4978, telex 6851035 CHILTON UW. **(Subscription address:** Chilton Co., PO Box 2165, Radnor, PA 19089**) ED** Richard Mullin. **DD** 696. **[CCC]. Bk Rev. Ad Acc. Circ:** 150,000 (ctrl). available on an online database (files 16,648/Full-Text) from DIALOG. Documents available from Documents on Demand.
Desc: Serves information needs of energy managers from industrial commercial and institutional sectors who are responsible for conservation management control or purchase of fuel and power for their facilities.
Ind/Abst Bus. ASAP (1990-) [Full Txt.]; Bus. Index (1985-); Coal Abstr.; Energy Inf. Abstr.; Energy Res. Abstr. (Feb. 1977-); Environ. Abstr.; F&S Index Plus Text, Int. [Full Txt.] [Select. Cov.]; Gen. BusinessFile (1985-); Gen. Period. Index (1985-); PROMT [Full Txt.]; Trade Ind. ASAP [Full Txt.]; Trade Ind. Index (1981-) [Full Txt.].

UK/0959-0196
ENERGY UTILITIES. **See** Economics.

US/0887-610X
ENERGY WATCH (SACRAMENTO, CALIF.). (ENERGY WATCH / CALIFORNIA ENERGY COMMISSION.). [Energy watch]. **Added/Corp** California Energy Commission. (April 1978)-. Periodical. English. Twelve times a year. Free. California Energy Commission, 1516 9th Street, Sacramento CA 95814. **Tel** (916)324-3014. **LC** HD9502.U53; C336. **DD** 333.79/09794/05.

US/0894-4180
ENERGY WEST (SAN CLEMENTE, CALIF.). (ENERGY WEST.). [Energy west]. **Added/Corp** Frank Kester Associates. Vol. 5, No. 20 (Oct. 24, 1986)-. Periodical. English. wk. $445.00. Frank Kester Associates, 1709 Avenue Salvador, San Clemente CA 92672. **Tel** (714)492-1340, FAX (714)492-6556. **DD** 338. ***Formed by the union of*** *Energy Business Update* ***and*** *Enhanced Oil & Gas Recovery Report.*

US
ENERGY WHO'S WHO DIRECTORY, THE. **Added/Corp** Heidrick and Struggles. National Energy Resources Organization. 1st Ed. (1990/91)-.

Energy

Directory. English. be. $59.95 (hardbound copy), $39.95 (softbound copy). Energy Who's Who, 1629 K Street NW, Suite 1100, Washington DC 20006. **Tel** (202)785-6713. **LC** HD9502.U5; E63.

UK/0307-7942
ENERGY WORLD. [Energy world]. **Added/Corp** Institute of Fuel (Great Britain). (July 1973)-. Periodical. English. Ten times a year (Jan/Feb. and July/Aug. issues combined). £60.00 UK; £70.00 other. H Howland Associates, The Martins, East Street, Harrietsham Kent ME17 1HH England. **Tel** 011 44 622 850100, FAX 0622 850100. **ED** Johanna Fender. **LC** TP315; .E53. **DD** 333.7. **CODEN** EGYWA2. cum. index. **Bk Rev**, (Qty: 30). **Ad Acc**, **Adv Mgr**: H. Howland. **Circ**: 7,000 (ctrl). Documents available from Article Express International.
Desc: These articles are pertaining to the fields of energy.
Ind/Abst Bioeng. Abstr.; Coal Abstr.; Curr. Biotechnol.; Curr. Technol. Index; Ei Page One; EMBASE; Energy Res. Abstr. (Aug. 1974-); Eng. Index Annu. [Select. Cov.]; Gas Abstr.; GeoRef; HTFS Dig.; J. Plan. Lit.; PAIS Int. Print (1991-); Proc. Chem. Eng.; Theoret. Chem. Eng.; World Ceram. Abstr.

PK
ENERGY YEAR BOOK. Added/Corp Pakistan. Directorate General of Energy Resources. Vol. 1, (1979)-. English. **LC** HD9502.P27; E53. **DD** 353.79/09549/1.

US/0731-6291
ENERGYGRAMS (OAK RIDGE, TENN.). (ENERGYGRAMS / TECHNICAL INFORMATION CENTER, U.S. DEPT. OF ENERGY.). [Energygrams]. **Added/Corp** United States. Dept. of Energy. Technical Information Center. (Dec. 1981)-. Periodical. English. qt. $55.00 (U.S., Canada, & Mexico) $100.00 (foreign). National Technical Information Service – NTIS, Room 2027S, 5285 Port Royal Road, Springfield VA 22161. **Tel** (703)487-4630, (703)487-4660, (703)487-4650, FAX (703)321-8547, telex 89-9405.

US/1049-9296
ENERGYLETTERS (CORAL GABLES, FLA.). (ENERGYLETTERS.). [Energy Lett.]. **Added/Corp** International Energy Society. **VFOAT** Energy Letters. (1991)-. Periodical. English. qt. Free to members, $25.00 other. International Energy Society, PO Box 248514, Coral Gables FL 33124. **DD** 333.

US
ENERGYTALK. Added/Corp Colorado. Office of Energy Conservation. **VFOAT** Energy Talk. (19??)-. Periodical. English. mo. free. Colorado Ofc Energy Conservation, 114 E 14th Avenue, Denver CO 80203. **Tel** (303)866-5505.

CN/0848-9114
ENERGYTRENDS. [Energytrends]. **Added/Corp** Canadian Enerdata Limited. **VFOAT** Energy Trends; Canadian Energy Trends Quarterly. Vol. 7, No. 3 (Nov. 1989)-. Periodical. English. qt. 800.00Can$. Canadian Enerdata Limited, Suite 204 7030 Woodbine Avenue, Markham Ontario L3R 1A2 Canada. **Tel** (905)479-9697. **DD** 333.79/0971. **Continues** Canadian Energy Trends, 0711-3242.

FR/0153-9442
ENERPRESSE. [Enerpresse]. (1970)-. Periodical. French. da. 12047.00F France; 12650.00F other. Bureau d'Info Professionnelles, 142 rue Montmartre, 75073 Paris Cedex 02 France. **Tel** 011 33 1 40268321, FAX 011 33 1 40399752, telex 220528 BIP. **ED** Patruik Lavilleon. **UDC** 338.98 : 621. **Bk Rev**. **Circ**: 700.
Desc: Comprehensive coverage of energy in the world with emphasis on nuclear energy, classic electricity, coal, petroleum and gas, and renewable energy.

JA/0388-5267
ENERUGI FORAMU. [Enerugi foramu]. **VFOAT** Energy Forum (Tokyo. 1980); Gekkan Enerugi Foramu. (1980)-. Periodical. Japanese. mo. Denryoku Shinposha Company Ltd., 10-13 Ginza 5 chome, Chuoku Tokyoto 104 Japan. **Tel** 03-572-6871, FAX 03-574-1649. **DD** 338.4. **Continues** Denryoku Shinpo, 0388-5259.

JA/0288-5417
ENERUGI HENKAN GIJUTSU. [Enerugi henkan gijutsu]. **VFOAT** Frontier Science. Began with 1977 issue. Academic Scholarly Publication. Japanese (Japanese). an. ¥50000 membership. Enerugi Henkan Konwakai, c/o Nihon Kagaku Gijutsu Shinko, Zaidan 1 Kitanomaru Koen, 2 Chiyoda-ku Tokyo-to 102 Japan. **LC** TK2896; .E53. **CODEN** EHGIDG. Documents available from CASDDS.
Ind/Abst Chem. Abstr. (1977-1982).

JA
ENERUGI SEISAN JUKYU TOKEI GEPPO / [HENSHU] TSUSHO SANGYO [SHO] DAIJIN KAMBO CHOSA TOKEIBU. Added/Corp Japan. Tsusho Sangyosho. Chosa Tokeibu. (1981)-. Japanese. mo. Tsusho Sangyo Chosakai, (Research Institute on International Trade and Industry), Kobikikan Ginza Biru, 8-9 Ginza 2 chome Chuoku, Tokyoto 104 Japan. **LC** HD9502.J3; J35a.
Continues Enerugi Tokei Geppo.

JA
ENERUGI TOKEI NEMPO. YEARBOOK OF COAL, PETROLEUM AND COKE STATISTICS. See Energy-Abstracting, Bibliographies and Statistics.

JA/0285-5437
ENERUGI (TOKYO. 1968). (ENERUGI.). [Enerugi]. **VFOAT** Energy. Periodical. Japanese (Japanese). mo. ¥900 single issue. Nihon Kogyo Shimbun, Sankei Building, 7 2 1 Chome Ohtemachi, Chiyoda-Ku Tokyo 100 Japan. **Tel** 11 81 3 231 7111 ext. 3558, FAX 11 81 3 3295-3991. **LC** HD9502.J3 /B E53.
Ind/Abst Coal Abstr.

US/0093-8408
ENGINEERING INDEX ENERGY ABSTRACTS. See Engineering-Abstracting, Bibliographies and Statistics.

US/0271-7085
ENHANCED ENERGY RECOVERY NEWS. Added/Corp Business Communications Co. (1980)-. Periodical. English. mo. $325.00. Business Communications Inc., 25 Van Zant Street, Suite 13, Norwalk CT 06855. **Tel** (203)853-4266. available on an online database (file 636/Full-Text) from DIALOG.
Ind/Abst PTS Newsl. Database [Full Txt.].

KO
ENOJI YONGU. VFOAT Journal of Energy Research. Periodical. Korean (summaries and/or abstracts in English). qt. Korea Institute of Energy and Resources / Taejon, South Korea, PO Box 14, Taeduk Science Town, Taejon South Korea. **Tel** 042 861-9700, FAX 042 861-9734, telex KIERSK K45509. **LC** HD9502.A1; E57.
Ind/Abst Coal Abstr.

US
ENVIRONMENTAL AND ENERGY STUDY SPECIAL REPORTS. See Environmental Issues.

US
ENVIRONMENTAL DEVELOPMENT PLAN. BIOMASS ENERGY SYSTEMS. See Environmental Issues.

US
ENVIRONMENTAL DEVELOPMENT PLAN (EDP). DIRECT COMBUSTION PROGRAM. Main/Corp United States. Dept. of Energy. Office of Energy Technology. **VFOAT** Direct Combustion Program. 1977-. English. an. US Department of Energy Office of Energy Technology, 1000 Independence Avenue SW, Washington DC 20585.

US
ENVIRONMENTAL DEVELOPMENT PLAN (EDP). ENERGY STORAGE SYSTEMS. Main/Corp United States. Dept. of Energy. Office of Energy Technology. **VFOAT** Energy Storage Systems. 1977-. English. an. US Department of Energy Office of Energy Technology, 1000 Independence Avenue SW, Washington DC 20585.

US
ENVIRONMENTAL DEVELOPMENT PLAN (EDP). INDUSTRIAL ENERGY CONSERVATION. Main/Corp United States. Dept. of Energy. Office of Energy Technology. **Added/Corp** United States. Dept. of Energy. Office of the Assistant Secretary for Environment. **VFOAT** Industrial Energy Conservation. (1977)-. English. ir. $103.00. National Technical Information Service – NTIS, Room 2027S, 5285 Port Royal Road, Springfield VA 22161. **Tel** (703)487-4630, (703)487-4660, (703)487-4650, FAX (703)321-8547, telex 89-9405.

US
ENVIRONMENTAL DEVELOPMENT PLAN (EDP). WIND ENERGY CONVERSION. Main/Corp United States. Dept. of Energy. Office of Energy Technology. **VFOAT** Wind Energy Conversion. 1977-. English. an. US Department of Energy Office of Energy Technology, 1000 Independence Avenue SW, Washington DC 20585.

US
ENVIRONMENTAL DEVELOPMENT PLAN. INDUSTRIAL PROGRAMS. Main/Corp United States. Dept. of Energy. Office of Solar Applications. **VFOAT** Industrial Programs. 1979-. Government Publication. English. US Department of Energy, 1000 Independence Avenue SW, Washington DC 20585. **Tel** (202)586-5000, FAX (202)586-4073.
Continues Environmental Development Plan (EDP). Industrial Energy Conservation.

US
ENVIRONMENTAL DEVELOPMENT PLAN. OCEAN THERMAL ENERGY CONVERSION. Main/Corp United States. Dept. of Energy. Office of Energy Technology. **VFOAT** Ocean Thermal Energy Conversion. 1979-. English. US Department of Energy Office of Energy Technology, 1000 Independence Avenue SW, Washington DC 20585.
Continues Environmental Development Plan (EDP). Ocean Thermal Energy Conversion.

US
ENVIRONMENTAL DEVELOPMENT PLAN. SOLAR HEATING AND COOLING OF BUILDINGS. Main/Corp United States. Dept. of Energy. Office of Energy Technology. **VFOAT** Solar Heating and Cooling of Buildings. 1979-. Government Publication. English. US Department of Energy, 1000 Independence Avenue SW, Washington DC 20585. **Tel** (202)586-5000, FAX (202)586-4073. **Continues** Environmental Development Plan (EDP). Solar Heating and Cooling of the Buildings.

US
ENVIRONMENTAL DEVELOPMENT PLAN. WIND ENERGY CONVERSION. Main/Corp United States. Dept. of Energy. Office of Energy Technology. **Added/Corp** United States. Dept. of Energy. Office of the Assistant Secretary for Environment. **VFOAT** Wind Energy Conversion. (1979)-. English. an. US Department of Energy Office of Energy Technology, 1000 Independence Avenue SW, Washington DC 20585.
Continues Environmental Development Plan (EDP). Wind Energy Conversion.

US/0148-6004
ENVIRONMENTAL MONITORING AT MAJOR U.S. ENERGY RESEARCH & DEVELOPMENT ADMINISTRATION CONTRACTOR SITES. See Environmental Issues.

US
ENVIRONMENTAL MONITORING REPORT, UNITED STATES DEPARTMENT OF ENERGY, PADUCAH GASEOUS DIFFUSION PLANT. Main/Corp Paducah Gaseous Diffusion Plant. Periodical. English. an. PO Box Y, Oak Ridge TN 37830.

●US
ENVIRONMENTAL RADON PROGRAM, SUMMARIES OF RESEARCH IN FY ... / ENVIRONMENTAL SCIENCES DIVISION, OFFICE OF HEALTH AND ENVIRONMENTAL RESEARCH [AND] OFFICE OF ENERGY RESEARCH, DEPARTMENT OF ENERGY. Added/Corp United States. Dept. of Energy. Office of Health and Environmental Research. United States. Dept. of Energy. Environmental Sciences Division. United States. Dept. of Energy. Office of Energy Research. (1992)-. Government Publication. English. an. $44.50 US, Canada & Mexico; $82.00 other. US Department of Energy, 1000 Independence Avenue SW, Washington DC 20585. **Tel** (202)586-5000, FAX (202)586-4073. (**Subscription address**: National Technical Information Service, 5285 Port Royal Road, Springfield, VA 22161) **LC** TD885.5.R33; R327. **DD** 628.5/35. **Continues** Radon Research Program.

US
EPR ANNUAL REVIEW. English. an. $775.00. 9579 White Pillar Terrace, Gaithersburg MD 20882. **Tel** (301)253-3050, FAX (301)916-6281. **ED** John C Gehman. available on diskette.
Desc: Features the total spectrum of line-of-business financial and operating data reported on major companies for the most recent year relative to a 6-year comparative period

US
EPR QUARTERLY REVIEW. English. qt. $575.00. 9579 White Pillar Terrace, Gaithersburg MD 20882. **Tel** (301)253-3050, FAX (301)916-6281. **ED** John C Gehman. available on diskette.
Desc: Features revenues and earnings, energy output and average realized price data for the most recent quarter and year-to-date period relative to prior-year comparative periods.

FR
EQUIPEMENT ENERGETIQUE DES LOGEMENTS NEUFS, L'. See Housing and Urban Development.

US
ER NEWS : ENERGY RESEARCH. Added/Corp United States. Dept. of Energy. **VFOAT** Energy Research; Energy Research News. Vol. 1, No. 1 (July 1991)-. Government Publication. English. bm. US Department of Energy, 1000 Independence Avenue SW, Washington DC 20585. **Tel** (202)586-5000, FAX (202)586-4073.

SP/0212-4157
ERA SOLAR. [Era solar]. (1983)-. Periodical. Spanish. Five times a year. 5700ptas. Publicaciones Tecnicas SA, Costa Rica 13, Plt 4 A2, 28016 Madrid Spain. **Tel** 011 34 1 3505885. **UDC** 620.97.

CN
ESTIMATES. PART III, NATIONAL ENERGY BOARD. **Main/Corp** Canada. **VFOAT** Budget des Depenses. Partie III, Office National de l'Energie. (19??)-. English (French). $3.00 Canada; $3.60 other. Canada Communication Group Publishers, Order Processing, Ottawa Ontario K1A 0S9 Canada. **Tel** (819)956-4800, (819)956-4802. **LC** HD9502.C3; C32a. **DD** 354.710082/3.

GW/0720-6240
ET. ENERGIEWIRTSCHAFTLICHE TAGESFRAGEN. **VFOAT** Energiewirtschaftliche Tagesfragen (1980). (1980)-. Periodical. German. mo (11 issues). DM227.50 Germany; DM247.50 other. Energiewirtschaft Technik Verlagsges GmbH, Oberrather Str. 2, D 40472 Duesseldorf Germany. **Tel** 011 49 211 658070, FAX 011 49 211 652129, telex 841/8587177. **(Subscription address:** Presse Marketing Service, Postfach 290180, D 47261 Duisburg Germany**)** **UDC** 621.31. Documents available from Ask*IEEE.
Ind/Abst INSPEC (Nov. 1969-).

BE/0423-6734
EUR RAPPORT - COMMUNAUTE EUROPEENNE DE L'ENERGIE ATOMIQUE. (1958)-. Periodical. French. ir.
Ind/Abst Agric. Eng. Abstr.; Agrofor. Abstr.; Biocont. News Inf.; Biodeter. Abstr.; For. Prod. Abstr.; For. Abstr.; Hortic. Abstr.; Rev. Plant Pathol.; Seed Abstr.

BE
EUROPE ENERGY. English and French. bm. 21100.00F Belgium; (add 1000.00F postage) Europe; (add 1400.00F postage) North Africa, Israel, and Turkey; (add 1600.00F postage) North, South, and Central America; (add 1900.00F postage) Asia; (add 2100.00F postage) Australia. Europe Information Service, rue de Geneve 6, 1140 Brussels Belgium. **Tel** 011 32 2 242 6020, FAX 011 32 2 242 9549. **Bk Rev. Circ:** 1,000. available on an online database (file 636/Full-Text) from DIALOG.

UK
EUROPEAN ENERGY REPORT. English. sm. Financial Times Business Information Ltd., Tower House, Southampton Street, London WC2E 7HA England. **Tel** 011 44 71 353 1040. available on an online database (files 16,636/Full-Text) from DIALOG.
Ind/Abst PROMT; PTS Newsl. Database [Full Txt.].

UK/0261-8214
EUROPEAN POWER NEWS. [Eur. power news]. (1981)-. Periodical. English. Eight times a year. £31.75 UK; £34.00, $52.70 other. Argus Press Group, Queensway House, 2 Queensway Redhill, Surrey RH1 1QS England. **Tel** 011 44 737 768611, 011 44 737 761685, FAX 011 44 737 760510, telex 948669 TOPJNL G. **ED** Derek Downing. **Bk Rev. Ad Acc. Circ:** 5,100. available on an online database (file 16/Full-Text) from DIALOG. ***Continues** Power Generation Industrial, 0308-0897.*
Desc: A publication serving the power generation market, reporting on all types of generating plant and ancillary equipment. Includes petrol, diesel, gas turbines, AC generators, CHP and cogeneration plants, control monitoring, batteries and chargers, welding, lighting, compressors, and communications and aircraft handling sectors.
Ind/Abst F&S Index Plus Text, Int. [Full Txt.] [Select. Cov.]; Infomat Int. Bus.; PROMT [Full Txt.].

CN/0848-5712
EXPLOSIVE SAFETY AND CONTROL IN CANADA. **See** Engineering-Chemical Engineering.

US/0731-7190
FEDERAL LANDS. (FEDERAL LANDS : AN EXCLUSIVE NEWS WEEKLY COVERING FUEL AND MINERALS ONSHORE AND OFFSHORE.). [Fed. lands]. April 23, 1981-. Periodical. English. wk. $640.00 US; $665.00 other. McGraw Hill Publishing Company, Inc., 1221 Avenue of the Americas, New York NY 10020. **Tel** (212)512-6410, (800)525-5003, FAX (212)512-6111. **ED** Bill Loveless.
Ind/Abst NEXIS (1981-).

US
FERC DATA ON CD-ROM. (1992)-. English. $1995.00 (one year), $2995.00 (two year), $3995.00 (three year). OPRI, PO Box 1433, Manhattan Beach CA 90266. **Tel** (310)372-0722, FAX (310)374-0259. **ED** Donald Liebson. available on CD-ROM and diskette from the publisher. Documents available.
Desc: Includes a six year database of FERC Form 1 (Electric Utilities), Form 2 (Gas Pipelines), and Form 6 (Oil Pipeline). Also includes system maps, officers and directories, owners, and description of assets.

US/0745-6131
FERC PRACTICE AND PROCEDURE MANUAL. [FERC pract. proced. man.]. **Added/Corp** United States. Federal Energy Regulatory Commission. Federal Programs Advisory Service. **VFOAT** F.E.R.C. Practice and Procedure Manual. **VAT** Federal Energy Regulatory Commission Practice and Procedure Manual. Vol. 1, No. 1 (Jan. 1983)-. Periodical. English. Four times a year (Jan., Apr., Jul., Oct.). $897.00. Thompson Publishing Group, 7711 Anderson Road, Tampa FL 33634. **Tel** (800)677-3789, (813)282-8607. **ED** Roger Smith. **[CCC].** Index available (free). **Circ:** 450.
Desc: A guide to federal energy regulatory commission's rules of practice and procedures.

US
FIELDSTON COAL TRANSPORTATION MANUAL. **Added/Corp** Fieldston Company. (1985)-. English. be. $255.00. Fieldston Publications, 1920 North Street Northwest, Suite 210, Washington DC 20036. **Tel** (202)775-0240, FAX (202)872-8045.

AU
FILM AND VIDEO CATALOGUE / VIENNA INTERNATIONAL CENTRE LIBRARY. **Main/Corp** VIC Library. **Added/Corp** International Atomic Energy Agency. (1991)-. English. Free on request. International Atomic Energy Agency / IAEA, Wagramerstrasse 5, PO Box 100, A-1400 Vienna Austria. **Tel** 011 43 1 2360 ext. 2530, FAX 011 43 1 234564. **(Subscription address:** UNIPUB, 4611 F Assembly Drive, Lanham MD 20706.**)** **LC** QC792.72.Z9; I56a. **DD** 016.62148. ***Continues** VIC Library. Film Catalogue.*

US/0362-5192
FINANCIAL REPORT - ENERGY RESEARCH AND DEVELOPMENT ADMINISTRATION. **Main/Corp** United States. Energy Research and Development Administration. 1st-1975-. English. an. Free. US Energy Research and Development Administration, Washington DC 20402. **LC** TJ163.25.U6; U533A. **DD** 353.008/23.
Desc: Traces key financial trends in the US energy industry and several of the industry's major segments for the fourth quarter of the year. Financial data for companies are included in two broad groups--fossil fuel production and rate-regulated utilities.

UK/0950-1037
FINANCIAL TIMES NORTH SEA LETTER AND EUROPEAN OFFSHORE NEWS. [Financ. times North Sea lett. Eur. offshore news]. **Added/Corp** Financial Times Business Information Ltd. **VFOAT** North Sea Letter and European Offshore News; North Sea Letter. (19??)-. Newsletter. English. wk. £690.00 UK; £640.00 other. Financial Times England, 8 16 Great New Street, London EC4A 3BN England. **Tel** 011 44 71 353 0305, 353 1040, FAX 011 44 353 0846. **ED** David Tudball. **Bk Rev. Ad Acc.** ctrl circ.
Desc: A record with comments on events in the oil and gas industry on Europe's north-west continental shelf.
Ind/Abst PROMT [Full Txt.]; PTS Newsl. Database [Full Txt.].

FI
FINLAND AND ENERGY. English. an. Ministry of Trade and Industry / Finland, Energy Department, POB 37, SF-00131 Helsinki Finland. **LC** TJ163.25.F5; F57. **DD** 333.79/094897/05.

GW
FINNLAND : ENERGIEWIRTSCHAFT. **Main/Corp** Germany (Federal Republic, 1949-). Bundesstelle fur Aussenhandelsinformation. German. DM2.00. Bundesstelle fuer Aussenhandelsinformation, Agrippastr 87 93, D 50676 Cologne Germany. **Tel** 011 49 221 2057316, FAX 011 49 221 2057212. **LC** HD9502.F5.

US
FISSION ENERGY PROGRAM OF THE U.S. DEPARTMENT OF ENERGY. **Main/Corp** United States. Dept. of Energy. Deputy Assistant Secretary for Nuclear Reactor Programs. 1980/81-. Government Publication. English. an. US Department of Energy, 1000 Independence Avenue SW, Washington DC 20585. **Tel** (202)586-5000, FAX (202)586-4073. ***Continues** Fission Energy Program of The U.S. Department of Energy.*

US/0276-9964
FLORIDA SOLAR COALITION NEWSLETTER. **Added/Corp** Florida Solar Coalition. (19??)-. Newsletter. English. qt. $25.00. Environmental Information Center / Florida, 1251-B Miller Avenue, Winter Park FL 32789. **Tel** (407)644-5377.

SW
FORSKNING, UTVECKLING OCH DEMONSTRATION INOM ENERGIOMRADET--EN GLOBAL OVERSIKT. **Main/Corp** Sweden. Delegationen for Energiforskning. 1977-. Swedish. an. Delegationen for Energiforskning, Forsaljning Liberforlag Liber Distribution, 162 89 Vallingby, Stokholm Sweden. **LC** TJ163.2; .S9A.

US/0887-8218
FORUM FOR APPLIED RESEARCH AND PUBLIC POLICY. [Forum appl. res. public policy]. **Added/Corp** Tennessee Valley Authority. University of Tennessee, Knoxville. Energy, Environment, and Resources Center. Vol. 1, No. 1 (Spring 1986)-. Periodical. English. qt (4 issues). $36.00 US; $44.00 other. Executive Sciences Institute, 1005 Mississippi Avenue, PO Box 4318, Davenport IA 52808-4318. **Tel** (319)324-4463, FAX (319)322-3725. **(Subscription address:** Executive Sciences Institute, PO Box 4318, Davenport, IA 52808**)** **LC** H96; .F67. **DD** 320.6/05. Index available in last issue of volume--attached. available on CD-ROM; available on microfilm and microfiche from University Microfilms International (UMI). Documents available from Documents on Demand.
Desc: Publishes independent views on policy issues in energy, environment and economic development written by leading researchers and thinkers in universities, research institutes, government agencies, and corporations.
Ind/Abst AgBiotech News Inf.; Coal Abstr.; Dairy Sci. Abstr.; Ecol. Abstr.; Ei Page One; Energy Inf. Abstr.; Environ. Abstr.; Environ. Period. Bibliogr.; Geogr. Abstr. Phys. Geogr.; Geogr. Abstr. Human Geogr.; Geol. Abstr.; GeoRef; INIS Atomindex [Micro.]; Int. Polit. Sci. Abstr.; J. Plan. Lit.; Maize Abstr.; PAIS Int. Print (1991-); Sage Public Adm. Abstr. (?-?); Soc. Plann. Policy Dev. Abstr.; Sociol. Abstr.; Soyabean Abstr.; U.S. Polit. Sci. Doc. (199?-).

US/0146-1931
FOSSIL ENERGY PROGRAM REPORT. **Main/Corp** United States. Office of Fossil Energy. 1976/1977-. Government Publication. English. an. US Department of Energy, 1000 Independence Avenue SW, Washington DC 20585. **Tel** (202)586-5000, FAX (202)586-4073. **LC** TP315; .U48A. **DD** 662/.6/05. ***Continues** Fossil Energy Program Report, 0146-1931.*

US/0190-1141
FOSSIL ENERGY RESEARCH AND DEVELOPMENT PROGRAM OF THE U.S. DEPARTMENT OF ENERGY. **Main/Corp** United States. Dept. of Energy. Office of Energy Technology. **VAT** Fossil Energy Research and Development Program of the United States Department of Energy. 1978/79-. Government Publication. English. an. US Department of Energy, 1000 Independence Avenue SW, Washington DC 20585. **Tel** (202)586-5000, FAX (202)586-4073. **LC** TP315; .U47A. **DD** 662/.6/0973. ***Continues** Fossil Energy Research Program of the Energy Research and Development Administration.*

JA/0288-691X
FOTON FAKUTORI NYUSU. **VFOAT** P.F. News; PF News. 1st Edition-. Periodical. Japanese. ir (five issues per year). Free. Foton Fakutori Nyusu Henshu Iinkai, Koenerugi Butsurigaku Kenkyujo Hoshako Jikken Shisetsu, 1 Uehara, 1 Oho-Machi, Isukuba-gun, Ibaraki-ken 305 Japan. **Tel** 0298-64-1171. **ED** Hirohito Fukutani. **LC** QC793.5.P42; F67. Index available. **Circ:** 1,700 (ctrl).
Desc: Describes the conditions of the PF (linac, ring and instrumentations) with practical information for general users. Includes technical advice, machine time and personal experiences and opinions, with domestic and overseas information.

GW
FRANKREICH : ENERGIEWIRTSCHAFT. **Main/Corp** Bundesstelle fur Aussenhandelsinformation (Germany). German. DM2.00. Bundesstelle fuer Aussenhandelsinformation, Agrippastr 87 93, D 50676 Cologne Germany. **Tel** 011 49 221 2057316, FAX 011 49 221 2057212. **LC** HD9502.F7.

UK/0140-6701
FUEL AND ENERGY ABSTRACTS. [Fuel energy abstr.]. **Added/Corp** Institute of Fuel (Great Britain). Vol. 19 (Jan. 1978)-. Periodical. English. bm. $723.00 The Americas; £485.00 other. Butterworth Heinemann Publishers, Linacre House, Jordan Hill, Oxford OX2 8DP England. **Tel** 011 44 865 310366. **(Subscription address:** Elsevier Science Ltd. Oxford Fulfillment Centre, PO Box 800, Kidlington, Oxford OX5 1DX United Kingdom.**)** **ED** D. Edwards. **LC** TP315; .G8522. **DD** 662/.6/05. **CODEN** FEABDN. **[CCC].** Index available. available on microfilm and microfiche from University Microfilms International (UMI). ***Continues** Fuel Abstracts and Current Titles.*
Desc: Summary of world literature on all scientific, technical, commercial and environmental aspects of fuel and energy. Each issue contains 1500 abstracts and titles from international publications, special reports, monographs conference proceedings, surveys and statistical analyses, dealing with all scientific, economic, technical and policy aspects of fuel and energy.
Ind/Abst Anal. Abstr.; Fluid Abstr., Civil Eng.; Fluid Abstr. Proc. Eng.; FLUIDEX (1978-); World Ceram. Abstr.

US/0884-3759
FUEL SCIENCE & TECHNOLOGY INTERNATIONAL. [Fuel sci. technol. int.]. **VFOAT** Fuel Science and Technology International. Vol. 4, No. 1 (Feb. 1986)-. Academic Scholarly Publication. English. Ten times a year. $1,075.00 US; $1,110.00 other. Marcel Dekker Inc., 270 Madison Avenue, New York NY 10016. **Tel** (212)696-9000, (800)228-1160, FAX (212)685-4540, telex 421419. **(Subscription address:** Marcel Dekker Inc, PO Box 5017, Monticello NY 12701.**)** **ED** James G. Speight and Richard H. Schlosberg. **LC** TP343; .L6787. **DD** 662/.6. **CODEN** FSCTEG. **[CCC].** available on microfiche. Documents available from Article Express International, CASDDS, Documents on Demand. ***Continues** Liquid Fuels Technology, 0737-7266.*
Desc: This journal provides an international forum for the science and technology of fuels by offering articles that relate to the fundamental scientific and technological aspects of fuel sources such as heavy oils, tar sands, residual, coal, oil shale, and biomass. In addition, 'Fuel Science and Technology International' presents articles

on the scientific and technological aspects of products (including in situ production) from these source materials, as well as on the character and properties of the products. **Ind/Abst** Chem. Abstr. (1986-); Coal Abstr.; Ei Page One; Energy Inf. Abstr.; Eng. Index Annu.; Environ. Abstr.; Environ. Period. Bibliogr.; Gas Abstr.; GeoRef; Lit. Pat. Abstr., Oilfield Chem. (1983-); Lit. Abstr., Catal. Catal.; Lit. Abstr., Health Environ.; Lit. Abstr., Pet. Refin. Petrochem.; Lit. Abstr., Pet. Substit.; Lit. Abstr., Transp. Storage; Proc. Chem. Eng.; Theoret. Chem. Eng.

US/1051-8738
FUSION FACTS (SALT LAKE CITY, UTAH). (FUSION FACTS : A MONTHLY NEWSLETTER PROVIDING FACTUAL REPORTS ON COLD FUSION DEVELOPMENTS.). [Fusion facts]. **Added/Corp** Fusion Information Center. (1989)-. Newsletter. English. Twelve times a year. $300.00 one year; $800.00 three years. University of Utah Research Park, PO Box 58639, Salt Lake City UT 84158. **Tel** (801)583-6232, FAX (801)583-6245. **(Subscription address:** Fusion Information Center, PO Box 58639, Salt Lake City, UT 84158) **ED** Hal Fox. **DD** 539. **Bk Rev**, (Qty: 8). **Ad Acc**, **Adv Mgr:** E. Call. **Circ:** 500. available on diskette.
Desc: Technical summary of scientific news developments in the field of cold fusion and enhanced energy worldwide.

US
FUSION POWER ASSOCIATES EXECUTIVE NEWSLETTER. Newsletter. English. mo. $150.00 library, $40.00 other. Fusion Power Associates, 2 Professional Drive, Suite 248, Gaithersburg MD 20879. **Tel** (301)258-0545, FAX (301)975-9869. **Circ:** 1,500.
Desc: Provides a synopsis of current events related to fusion energy including research and experimental data, political news, personnel news and planned meetings and symposia.

US
FUSION POWER PROGRAM QUARTERLY PROGRESS REPORT. **Main/Corp** Argonne National Laboratory. English. qt. US Department of Energy Office of Energy Research, 1000 Independence Avenue SW, Room 7B-058, Washington DC 20585. **Tel** (202)586-5430, FAX (202)586-4120.

US/0276-2919
FUSION POWER REPORT. (FUSION POWER REPORT / BUSINESS PUBLISHERS, INC.). [Fus. power rep.]. (198?)-. Periodical. English. mo. $714.00. Business Publishers Inc., 951 Pershing Drive, Silver Spring MD 20910-4464. **Tel** (301)587-6300, (800)274-0122, FAX (301)585-9075. **DD** 539. **[CCC]**. available on an online database (file 636/Full-Text) from DIALOG.
Desc: Monthly report on scientific engineering, economic and political development in fusion energy in the US and worldwide.
Ind/Abst PTS Newsl. Database [Full Txt.].

US/0897-9138
FUTURE ENERGY CONFERENCES AND SYMPOSIA. (FUTURE ENERGY CONFERENCES AND SYMPOSIA / U.S. DEPT. OF ENERGY, OFFICE OF SCIENTIFIC AND TECHNICAL INFORMATION.). [Future energy conf. symp.]. **Added/Corp** United States. Dept. of Energy. Office of Scientific and Technical Information. **VFOAT** Energy Conferences and Symposia. (1988)-. Government Publication. English. mo. $165.00 US; $330.00 other. US Department of Energy, 1000 Independence Avenue SW, Washington DC 20585. **Tel** (202)586-5000, FAX (202)586-4073. **(Subscription address:** National Technical Information Service, 5285 Port Royal Road, Springfield, VA 22161) **DD** 621. **CODEN** ECSYE. ***Continues*** *Future Energy Conferences, 0896-7644.*
Ind/Abst Energy Inf. Abstr.

US/0730-6954
FY ANNUAL REPORT ON IN-HOUSE ENERGY MANAGEMENT. (FY ... ANNUAL REPORT ON IN-HOUSE ENERGY MANAGEMENT / ASSISTANT SECRETARY, MANAGEMENT AND ADMINISTRATION, OFFICE OF FACILITY PLANNING AND SUPPORT.). **Main/Corp** United States. Dept. of Energy. Office of Facility Planning and Support. **VFOAT** Annual Report on In-House Energy Management. English. an. National Technical Information Service - NTIS, Room 2027S, 5285 Port Royal Road, Springfield VA 22161. **Tel** (703)487-4630, (703)487-4660, (703)487-4650, FAX (703)321-8547, telex 89-9405. **LC** HD9502.U5; U523. **DD** 333.79. available on microfiche (Vols. for (1980-) distributed to depository libraries).

US
GAO WORK INVOLVING TITLE V OF THE ENERGY POLICY AND CONSERVATION ACT OF 1975. **See** Law.

US/0194-2468
GAS INDUSTRIES (1978). **See** Petroleum and Natural Gas.

UZ/0130-0997
GELIOTEHNIKA (TASKENT). (GELIOTEKHNIKA / AKADEMIIA NAUK UZBEKSKOI SSR.). [Geliotehnika]. **Added/Corp** Uzbekiston SSR Fanlar Akademiiasi. Akademiia nauk SSSR. (1965)-. Periodical. Russian (summaries and/or abstracts in English; table of contents in English and Uzbek). bm. Akademiia Nauk Uzbekskoi, Ulitsa Gogolya 70, K 105, 700000 Tashkent, Uzbeckistan. **CODEN** GLOTAY. Documents available from Ask*IEEE, CASDDS.
Ind/Abst Agric. Eng. Abstr.; Chem. Abstr.; Ei Page One; Hortic. Abstr.; INSPEC (1968-); Int. Aerosp. Abstr.; Ornamental Hort. (1991-).

JA
GENSHIRYOKU KISEI KANKEI HOREISHU / KAGAKU GIJUTSUCHO GENSHIRYOKU ANZENKYOKU KANSHU. **See** Engineering-Nuclear Engineering.

CN/0273-1371
GEOPOLITICS OF ENERGY. [Geopolit. energy]. **Added/Corp** Canadian Energy Research Institute. (19??)-. Periodical. English. mo. $375.00 US; $385.00 other. Canadian Energy Research Institute, 3512 33rd Street Northwest #150, Calgary Alberta T2L 2A6 Canada. **Tel** (403)282-1231, FAX (403)284-4181, (403)289-2344. **ED** Tony Reinsch. **DD** 333. **Circ:** 200.
Desc: Provides information on the political, economic, and pricing factors affecting access to energy worldwide. Includes quarterly price forecast, national energy profiles, and new energy technologies.
Ind/Abst Geogr. Abstr. Human Geogr.; Int. Dev. Abstr.

US/0896-6257
GEOTHERMAL ENERGY (OAK RIDGE, TENN.). (GEOTHERMAL ENERGY : CURRENT ABSTRACTS / U.S. DEPARTMENT OF ENERGY ; PREPARED FOR OFFICE OF CONSERVATION AND RENEWABLE ENERGY ; PREPARED BY OFFICE OF SCIENTIFIC AND TECHNICAL INFORMATION.). [Geotherm. energy]. **Added/Corp** United States. Dept. of Energy. Office of Scientific and Technical Information. United States. Dept. of Energy. Office of Conservation and Renewable Energy. **VFOAT** GET. Vol. 88, No. 1 (Jan./Feb. 1988)-. Government Publication. English. bm. $155.00 US; $310.00 other. US Department of Energy, 1000 Independence Avenue SW, Washington DC 20585. **Tel** (202)586-5000, FAX (202)586-4073. **(Subscription address:** National Technical Information Service, 5285 Port Royal Road, Springfield, VA 22161) **DD** 621. **CODEN** GTENEQ. ***Continues*** *Geothermal Energy Technology, 0736-6620.*

US/0735-0503
GEOTHERMAL HOT LINE. [Geotherm. hot line]. **Added/Corp** California. Division of Oil and Gas. **VFOAT** Geothermal Hot Line Newsletter. Vol. 1 (Jan. 21, 1971)-. Periodical. English. sa (July & Dec.). Free on request. Division of Oil & Gas, 801 K Street, 20th Floor MS 20, Sacramento CA 95814. **Tel** (916)445-9686, FAX (916)323-0424. **ED** Susan F. Hodgson. **DD** 333. Index available (bound in Dec. issue). **Bk Rev. Circ:** 2,000.
Desc: Worldwide geothermal resources and developments with emphasis on geothermal development in California.
Ind/Abst Energy Res. Abstr. (Aug. 1976-); GeoRef.

US/0733-9100
GEOTHERMAL REPORT. [Geotherm. rep.]. 1972. Periodical. English. sm. $200.00 US; $225.00 other. Warne and Blanton Publishers, 3225 Freeport Boulevard/#601, Sacramento CA 95818. **Tel** (916)442-4338. **ED** William E Warne. **Bk Rev. Circ:** 120 (ctrl).
Desc: Coverage of geothermal energy activities in government industry and internationally.
Ind/Abst Energy Res. Abstr. (April 1976-).

FJ/0250-7277
GEOTHERMAL REPORT. MINERAL RESOURCES DIVISION, FIJI. (GEOTHERMAL REPORT / MINERAL RESOURCES DEPT., MINISTRY OF LANDS AND MINERAL RESOURCES.). [Geotherm. rep., Miner. resour. div., Fiji]. No. 1-. Monographic series. English. Price varies per volume. Mineral Resources Division / Fiji Islands, Private Mail Bag GPO, Suva Fiji Islands. **Tel** 011 679 381 611, FAX 011 679 370 039, telex 2330 SOPAC PRO FJ. **Circ:** 120.
Desc: Results of investigations of geothermal areas or work related to geothermal energy.
Ind/Abst GeoRef.

GW
GHANA: ENERGIEWIRTSCHAFT. **Main/Corp** Bundesstelle fuer Aussenhandelsinformation (Germany). (19??)-. German. DM2.00. Bundesstelle fuer Aussenhandelsinformation, Agrippastr 87 93, D 50676 Cologne Germany. **Tel** 011 49 221 2057316, FAX 011 49 221 2057212. **LC** HD9502.G49; G47a.

US/0883-363X
GOVERNOR'S OFFICE OF ENERGY RESOURCES ANNUAL REPORT. [Gov. Off. Energy Resour. annu. rep.]. **Main/Corp** Georgia. Governor's Office of Energy Resources. **VFOAT** Annual Report. (1983)-. English. an. Free. Office of Energy Resources, 270 Washington Street Southwest, Room 401, Atlanta GA 30334. **Tel** (404)656-5176. **LC** TJ163.25.U6; G46a. **DD** 353.97580082/32. ***Continues*** *Georgia Office of Energy Resources. Georgia Office of Energy Resources Annual Report, 0196-710X.*

CN/1183-417X
GREEN ENERGY UPDATE. [Green energy update]. **Added/Corp** Canadian Renewable Fuels Association. Vol. 1, No. 1 (Winter 1991)-. Periodical. English. qt. Free to members (membership $40.00 per year). Canadian Renewable Fuels Association, 190 Nicklin Road, Guelph Ontario N1H 7L5 Canada. **DD** 333.79/4/0971. ***Continues*** *Renewable Fuels Report.*

GW
GRIECHENLAND : ENERGIEWIRTSCHAFT. **Main/Corp** Germany (Federal Republic, 1949-). Bundesstelle fur Aussenhandelsinformation. German. DM2.00. Bundesstelle fuer Aussenhandelsinformation, Agrippastr 87 93, D 50676 Cologne Germany. **Tel** 011 49 221 2057316, FAX 011 49 221 2057212. **LC** HD9502.G75.

GW
GROSSBRITANNIEN : ENERGIEWIRTSCHAFT. **Main/Corp** Germany (Federal Republic, 1949-). Bundesstelle fur Aussenhandelsinformation. German. DM2.00. Bundesstelle fuer Aussenhandelsinformation, Agrippastr 87 93, D 50676 Cologne Germany. **Tel** 011 49 221 2057316, FAX 011 49 221 2057212. **LC** HD9502.G7.

GW
GUATEMALA : ENERGIEWIRTSCHAFT. **Main/Corp** Germany (Federal Republic, 1949-). Bundesstelle fur Aussenhandelsinformation. German. DM2.00. Bundesstelle fuer Aussenhandelsinformation, Agrippastr 87 93, D 50676 Cologne Germany. **Tel** 011 49 221 2057316, FAX 011 49 221 2057212. **LC** HD9502.G9.

BE
GUIDE DE L'ENERGIE / ENERGIEGIDS / ENERGY HANDBOOK. **VFOAT** Energiegids; Energy Handbook; Energie. (19??)-. Directory. French (Dutch, English and French). an. $90.00. Addax Consultance, 173 rue de la Vignette, 1160 Brussels Belgium. **Tel** 011 32 2 672 6716. **LC** TJ163.235; .G85. **DD** 621.042/05. **Bk Rev**, (Qty: 20). **Ad Acc, Adv Mgr:** Jacques Culot. Full Page (B&W) $1650.00. Half Page (B&W) $900.00. Full Page (Color) $2200.00. Half Page (Color) $1300.00. **Acid Free. Circ:** 2,500.
Desc: Covers everything professionals need to know about energy in Belgium and Luxembourg. Provides information on education, research, statistics, power plants, equipment and services suppliers, and more.

US
GUIDE FOR THE PREPARATION OF PROPOSALS FOR FACULTY DEVELOPMENT PROJECTS IN ENERGY EDUCATION. **Main/Corp** United States. Dept. of Energy. Education Programs Division. 1980-. Government Publication. English. US Department of Energy, 1000 Independence Avenue SW, Washington DC 20585. **Tel** (202)586-5000, FAX (202)586-4073. ***Continues*** *Guide for the Preparation of Proposals for Faculty Development Projects in Energy.*

US
GUIDE TO COAL CONTRACTS. (19??)-. English. be. $257.00 (two years). Pasha Publications Inc., 1616 North Fort Myer Drive, Suite 1000, Arlington VA 22209. **Tel** (800)424-2908, (703)528-1244, FAX (703)528-3742, (703)528-1253. **LC** HD9541; .G84. **DD** 338.2/724/0975.

US/0270-000X
GUIDE TO PRACTICE AND PROCEDURE, U.S. DEPARTMENT OF ENERGY, BOARD OF CONTRACT APPEALS, CONTRACT ADJUSTMENT BOARD, FINANCIAL ASSISTANCE APPEALS BOARD, INVENTION LICENSING APPEALS BOARD. **Main/Corp** United States. Dept. of Energy. Board of Contract Appeals. **VFOAT** Guide, Energy Board of Contract Appeals and Contract Adjustment Board, Financial Assistance Appeals Board, Invention Licensing Appeals Board. 1979-. Government Publication. English. an. US Department of Energy, 1000 Independence Avenue SW, Washington DC 20585. **Tel** (202)586-5000, FAX (202)586-4073. **LC** KF869.5.E5; A843. **DD** 346.73/023; 347.30623. ***Continues*** *Guide of the U.S. Department of Energy, Board of Contract Appeals and Contract Adjustment Board.*

US/0732-7366
GUIDE TO THE ENERGY INDUSTRIES. [Guide energy ind.]. **Added/Corp** Harfax (Firm) Ballinger Publishing Company. 1st Ed. (1983)-. English. an. Ballinger Publishing Company, 10 E 53rd Street, New York NY 10022-5244. **LC** Z5853.P83; G8; HD9502.A1. **DD** 016.3384/7621042.

US/0503-3772
HALF-YEARLY BULLETIN OF ELECTRIC ENERGY STATISTICS FOR EUROPE. BULLETIN SEMESTRIEL DE STATISTIQUES DE L'ENERGIE ELECTRIQUE POUR L'EUROPE. POLUGODOVOI BIULLETEN EVROPEISKOI STATISTIKI ELECTROENERGII. **See** Energy-Abstracting, Bibliographies and Statistics.

US/0272-8443
HEALTH FACILITIES ENERGY REPORT. ***Title Change.*** [Health facil. energy rep.]. (Nov. 1980)-(19??). Periodical. English. mo. Health Resources Publishing, 3100 Highway 138, Wall Township NJ 07719-1442. **Tel** (908)681-1133, FAX (908)681-0490. **ED** Robert K. Jenkins. **NLM** W1; HE335NC. **Bk Rev. Ad Acc.** ctrl circ. ***Merged into*** *Energy Report.*
Desc: Presents up-to-date developments in energy conservation, specifically for hospitals.

US/0273-5695
HEARTH AND HOME (GILFORD, N.H. : 1989). (HEARTH AND HOME.). **VFOAT** Hearth & Home. Vol. 9, No. 4 (March 1989)-. Periodical. English. mo. $30.00. Hearth and Home, PO Box 2008, Laconia NH 03247. **Tel** (603)528-4285, FAX (603)524-0643. **ED** Richard Wright. **Ad Acc, Adv Mgr:** Jackie Avignone, **Tel** (800)258-3772. **Circ:** 17,000 (ctrl). Documents available from Documents on Demand. ***Continues*** *Wood 'N Energy, 0273-5695.*
Desc: Covering topics of interest to those in the hearth products industry and or the casual furnishings industry.
Ind/Abst Energy Inf. Abstr.; Environ. Abstr.

US/0017-9329
HEAT ENGINEERING (LIVINGSTON). (HEAT ENGINEERING.). [Heat eng.]. Periodical. English. qt. Free. Foster Wheeler Corporation, Perryville Corporate Park, Clinton NJ 08809. **ED** Dean L Muskevich. **LC** TH7121; .A2. **Circ:** 30,000.
Desc: Technical articles on power and process engineering and related fields.
Ind/Abst Coal Abstr.; Energy Res. Abstr. (April 1974-); Pollut. Abstr. Indexes.

US
HIGH ENERGY PHYSICISTS & GRADUATE STUDENTS / PREPARED BY U.S. DEPARTMENT OF ENERGY, DIRECTORATE, OFFICE OF ENERGY RESEARCH, DIVISION OF HIGH ENERGY PHYSICS. **Added/Corp** United States. Division of High Energy Physics. United States. Energy Research and Development Administration. Division of Physical Research. **VFOAT** Census of High Energy Physicists and Graduate Students. **VAT** High Energy Physicists and Graduate Students. (19??)-. English. National Technical Information Service - NTIS, Room 2027S, 5285 Port Royal Road, Springfield VA 22161. **Tel** (703)487-4630, (703)487-4660, (703)487-4650, FAX (703)321-8547, telex 89-9405.

US
HISTORICAL ENERGY STATISTICS. **See** Energy-Abstracting, Bibliographies and Statistics.

US/0896-9442
HOME ENERGY (BERKELEY, CALIF.). (HOME ENERGY MAGAZINE.). [Home energy]. **VFOAT** Home Energy Magazine. Vol. 5, No. 1 (Jan./Feb. 1988)-. Periodical. English. bm (Jan., Mar., May, July, Sept., Nov.). $49.00 US; $54.00 Canada; $59.00 other. Home Energy, 2124 Kittredge/Suite 95, Berkeley CA 94704. **Tel** (510)524-5405. **ED** Cyril Penn. **LC** TJ163.5.D86; H64. **DD** 696. Index available. cum. index (1984-1994 index). **Bk Rev**, (Qty: 1-6). **Ad Acc, Adv Mgr:** Emily Polsby, **Tel** (510)524-5405. **Pr Rev. Circ:** 10,000. ***Continues*** *Energy Auditor & Retrofitter Retrofitter, 8756-3339.*
Desc: Provides an informative, highly readable look at the world of residential energy conservation. Examines the latest energy conservation products, technologies and programs for today's homes.
Ind/Abst INIS Atomindex [Micro.].

US/0195-1874
HOME ENERGY DIGEST, WOOD BURNING QUARTERLY. **VFOAT** Wood Burning Quarterly; Home Energy Digest and Wood Burning Quarterly; Home Energy Digest; Home Energy Digest & Wood Burning Quarterly. Vol. 2 No. 4 (Spring 1978)-. Periodical. English. qt. $7.95. Investment Rarities Inc, 8009 34th Avenue South, Minneapolis MN 55420. **LC** TP324; .W66. **DD** 696/.05. ***Continues*** *Wood Burning Quarterly & Home Energy Digest, 0163-0385.*

US/1050-2416
HOME POWER. [Home power]. **VFOAT** Home Power Magazine. (1987)-. Periodical. English. bm (6 issues). $15.00 US; $20.00 (suface mail) other. Home Power, PO Box 520, Ashland OR 97520. **Tel** (916)475-3179, FAX (916)475-3179. **ED** Richard Perez. **LC** WMLC 93/1443. **DD** 621. Index available. cum. index. **Bk Rev**, (Qty: 4-6). **Ad Acc, Adv Mgr:** K. Perez. **Pr Rev. Circ:** 12,500. available on diskette; available on an online database from BRS.
Desc: Publishes do-it-yourself information about using solar wind, water, hydrogen, and other sources of renewable energy in your home. Everything is written by actual renewable energy users.

US
HOUSEHOLD ENERGY CONSUMPTION AND EXPENDITURES. PART I, NATIONAL DATA. **Added/Corp** United States. Office of Energy Markets and End Use. (1987)-. English. te (Feb.). $21.00. National Energy Information Center, Energy Information Administration, Forrestal Building, Room 1F-048, Washington DC 20585. **Tel** (202)586-8800. **LC** HD9502.U52; H675. ***Continues in part*** *Residential Energy Consumption Survey. Consumption and Expenditures, 0741-8302.*
Desc: Contains national level household energy consumption, expenditures, and the price households pay for electricity, natural gas, fuel oil and kerosene, and liquefied petroleum gas.

US
HOUSEHOLD ENERGY CONSUMPTION AND EXPENDITURES. SUPPLEMENT: REGIONAL. **Added/Corp** United States. Office of Energy Markets and End Use. United States. Energy Information Administration. **VFOAT** Supplement: Regional. (1990)-. English. te. $21.00. National Energy Information Center, Energy Information Administration, Forrestal Building, Room 1F-048, Washington DC 20585. **Tel** (202)586-8800. **LC** HD9502.U5; H68. **DD** 333.79/13/0973021. ***Continues*** *Household Energy Consumption and Expenditures. Part 2, Regional Data.*
Desc: Supplemental document that contains household energy consumption, expenditures and price data for Census regions and nine Census divisions.

US/1057-5006
HOUSEHOLD VEHICLES ENERGY CONSUMPTION. [Househ. veh. energy consum.]. **Added/Corp** United States. Office of Energy Markets and End Use. (1988)-. English. te. $14.00. National Energy Information Center, Energy Information Administration, Forrestal Building, Room 1F-048, Washington DC 20585. **Tel** (202)586-8800. **LC** HE5623; .A197. **DD** 333.79/6813/0973021. ***Continues*** *Residential Transportation Energy Consumption Survey. Consumption Patterns of Household Vehicles, 0894-6752.*
Desc: Energy used in household vehicles is compared with energy used in the home.

US/0888-661X
HUDSON VALLEY GREEN TIMES. **See** Environmental Issues.

US/8755-3058
HYDROGEN ENERGY COORDINATING COMMITTEE ANNUAL REPORT-SUMMARY OF DOE HYDROGEN PROGRAMS. (HYDROGEN ENERGY COORDINATING COMMITTEE ANNUAL REPORT-SUMMARY OF DOE HYDROGEN PROGRAMS FOR FY ...). **VFOAT** Annual Report-Summary of DOE Hydrogen Programs for FY ...; Summary of DOE Hydrogen Programs for FY ....; Annual Program-Summary of D.O.E. Hydrogen Programs for F.Y. ...; Summary of DOE Hydrogen Program. 1982-. English. an. National Technical Information Service - NTIS, Room 2027S, 5285 Port Royal Road, Springfield VA 22161. **Tel** (703)487-4630, (703)487-4660, (703)487-4650, FAX (703)321-8547, telex 89-9405. **LC** TP359.H8; H87. **DD** 665.8/1/072073. available on microfiche (Vols. for 1982- distributed to depository libraries). ***Continues*** *Summary of DOE Hydrogen Program.*

US
HYDROGEN ENERGY QUARTERLY LITERATURE REVIEW / ASSEMBLED AND DISSEMINATED BY THE TECHNOLOGY TRANSFER OFFICE OF GLOBAL RESOURCES AND ASSOCIATES]. **Added/Corp** Global Resources & Associates. (Jan.- March 1983)-. Periodical. English. Global Resources & Associates, University of New Mexico, Albuquerque NM 87131. **Tel** (505)242-2313. ***Continues*** *Hydrogen Energy : A Bibliography with Abstracts, 0364-5231.*

AU
IAEA NEWSBRIEFS : INTERNATIONAL ATOMIC ENERGY AGENCY. **Added/Corp** International Atomic Energy Agency. Division of Public Information. **VFOAT** International Atomic Energy Agency Newsbriefs. Vol. 1, No. 1 (Oct. 1986)-. Periodical. English. sm (24 issues per year). Free. International Atomic Energy Agency / IAEA, Wagramerstrasse 5, PO Box 100, A-1400 Vienna Austria. **Tel** 011 43 1 2360 ext. 2530, FAX 011 43 1 234564. **(Subscription address:** UNIPUB, 4611 F Assembly Drive, Lanham MD 20706.**)**
Ind/Abst AESIS Q.

US/0730-7209
ILLINOIS ENERGY CONSUMPTION. (ILLINOIS ENERGY CONSUMPTION / ILLINOIS DEPARTMENT OF BUSINESS AND ECONOMIC DEVELOPMENT, OFFICE OF RESEARCH, AND DIVISION OF ENERGY.). **Added/Corp** Illinois. Dept. of Business and Economic Development. Office of Research. Illinois. Division of Energy. (1975)-. English. an. National Technical Information Service - NTIS, Room 2027S, 5285 Port Royal Road, Springfield VA 22161. **Tel** (703)487-4630, (703)487-4660, (703)487-4650, FAX (703)321-8547, telex 89-9405. **LC** HD9502.U53; I4553. **DD** 333.79/13/09773.

US/1043-7320
INDEPENDENT ENERGY. [Indep. energy]. **VFOAT** Energy. Vol. 19, No. 4 (Apr. 1989)-. Periodical. English. Ten times a year (May/June & July/Aug. issues combined). $78.00 US & Canada & Mexico; $102.00 other. Marier Communications Inc., 620 Central Avenue North, Milaca MN 56353. **Tel** (612)983-6892, FAX (612)983-6893. **ED** John Anderson (phone: (612)983-6892). **LC** TJ163.2; .A46. **DD** 338.4/562042. **CODEN** IDPEEW. **Ad Acc, Adv Mgr:** Rick Huntzicker, **Tel** (612)983-6892. available on microfilm and microfiche from University Microfilms International (UMI). ***Continues*** *Independent Power, 1042-5829.*
Desc: Provides the senior executives at companies that develop, own and operate independent power production facilities with news and critical insights that help them better manage their growing businesses. Also provides companies that service the industry with information and analysis which is vital to their marketing plans. Technologies covered include: cogeneration, hydropower, resource recovery, photovoltaics and windpower.
Ind/Abst AESIS Q.; Appl. Sci. Technol. Index (-1990); BioBusiness (1990-); Energy Inf. Abstr.; Environ. Period. Bibliogr.; INIS Atomindex [Micro.]; PAIS Int. Print (1991-).

II
INDIAN ENERGY AND POWER UPDATE. (19??)-. English. sa. Rs240.00 India; $45.00 other. Technical Press Publications, 5-1 Convent Street, Colaba, Bombay 400 039 India. **Tel** 2021156, 2021446, 2026361, 3479 CHEM IN, telex 11-3479 CHEM IN. **ED** J P de Sousa. Index available. cum. index. **Bk Rev. Ad Acc.** ctrl circ. available on microfiche; available on microfilm.
Desc: Features Indian and worldwide developments in Energy, power, industry, and production.

GW
INDONESIEN : ENERGIEWIRTSCHAFT. **Main/Corp** Bundesstelle fur Aussenhandelsinformation (Germany). German. DM2.00. Bundesstelle fuer Aussenhandelsinformation, Agrippastr 87 93, D 50676 Cologne Germany. **Tel** 011 49 221 2057316, FAX 011 49 221 2057212. **LC** HD9502.I5.

US/1056-7194
INDUSTRIAL BIOPROCESSING. [Ind. bioprocess.]. **Added/Corp** Technical Insights, Inc. Vol. 13, No. 6 (June 1991)-. Periodical. English. mo. $545.00 North America; $605.00 other. Technical Insights Inc., PO Box 1304, Fort Lee NJ 07024-9967. **Tel** (201)568-4744, FAX (201)568-8247, telex 425900 SWIFT UI. **LC** TP360; .B565. **DD** 660. **CODEN** INBOES. **[CCC].** available on an online database (file 636/Full-Text) from DIALOG. ***Continues*** *Bioprocessing Technology, 0885-5625.*
Ind/Abst Abstr. Bull. Inst. Pap. Sci. Tech.; Abstr. BioCommer.; PTS Newsl. Database [Full Txt.].

US/0094-1646
INDUSTRIAL ENERGY. **See** Petroleum and Natural Gas.

US/0732-9776
INDUSTRIAL ENERGY EFFICIENCY IMPROVEMENT PROGRAM, THE. (THE INDUSTRIAL ENERGY EFFICIENCY IMPROVEMENT PROGRAM : ANNUAL REPORT.). [Ind. Energy Effic. Improv. Program]. **Main/Corp** Industrial Energy Efficiency Improvement Program (U.S.). (1979)-. English. an. National Technical Information Service - NTIS, Room 2027S, 5285 Port Royal Road, Springfield VA 22161. **Tel** (703)487-4630, (703)487-4660, (703)487-4650, FAX (703)321-8547, telex 89-9405. **LC** TJ163.25.U6. **DD** 333.79/16/0973. available on microfiche. ***Continues*** *Industrial Energy Efficiency Improvement Program (U.S.). Annual Report to the Congress and the President, 0278-9280.*

US/1057-4247
INDUSTRIAL ENERGY TECHNOLOGY. (INDUSTRIAL ENERGY TECHNOLOGY / U.S. DEPT. OF ENERGY ; PREPARED FOR OFFICE OF CONSERVATION AND RENEWABLE ENERGY, OFFICE OF INDUSTRIAL TECHNOLOGIES ; PREPARED BY OFFICE OF SCIENTIFIC AND TECHNICAL INFORMATION.). [Ind. energy technol.]. **Added/Corp** United States. Dept. of Energy. Office of Scientific and Technical Information. United States. Dept. of Energy. Office of Conservation and Renewable Energy. Office of Industrial Technologies. (July/Aug. 1991)-. Government Publication. English. Twelve times a year. $165.00 US; $330.00 other. US Department of Energy, 1000 Independence Avenue SW, Washington DC 20585. **Tel** (202)586-5000, FAX (202)586-4073. **(Subscription address:** National Technical Information Service, 5285 Port Royal Road, Springfield, VA 22161**)** **DD** 333. **CODEN** IETEEP. ***Continues*** *Industrial Energy Conservation, 0896-5161.*

US
INFORMATION DIGEST (U.S. NUCLEAR REGULATORY COMMISSION : POCKET REFERENCE ED.). **See** Public Administration.

CU/0253-5645
INGENIERIA ENERGETICA. [Ing. energ.]. Vol. 1, No. 1 (1980)-. Academic Scholarly Publication. Spanish (summaries and/or abstracts in English and Spanish). Three times a year. 35.93Can$ North America; 37.13Can$ South America; 39.52Can$ other. Ediciones Cubanas, Obispo 527, Altos ESQ Bernaza, CP 10100 Havana Cuba. **Tel** 011 632980, 631942, FAX 011 631011, telex 512337, 6540. **CODEN** INEEDC. Documents available from CASDDS. ***Continues*** *Ciencias Tecnicas Ingenieria Energetica, 0254-8496.*
Ind/Abst Chem. Abstr. (1980-1981); Ei Page One; Sug. Indus. Abstr.

AU
INIS GUIDELINES FOR STANDARDIZED ENTRY OF CORPORATE BODIES. **See** Energy-Abstracting, Bibliographies and Statistics.

UK
INSIDE ENERGY. (19??)-. English. Twenty-four times a year. $573.50. Reed Business Publishing / West Sussex, England, Perrymount Road, Haywards Heath, West Sussex RH16 3DH England. **Tel** 011 44 81 6523500.
Desc: A business to business newsletter which will help to create awareness of the commercial potential of electricity privatization and related energy issues.
Ind/Abst Infomat Int. Bus.

US
INSIDE ENERGY/WITH FEDERAL LANDS. **VAT** Inside Energy with Federal lands. (Aug. 23, 1982)-. Newsletter. English. wk. $1115.00 US and Canada; $1140.00 other. McGraw Hill Publishing Company, Inc., 1221 Avenue of the Americas, New York NY 10020. **Tel** (212)512-6410, (800)525-5003, FAX (212)512-6111. **ED** William E. Loveless. available on an online database (through Dialog). ***Formed by the union of*** *Federal Lands* ***and*** *Inside Energy.*
Desc: Federal policy regarding energy and federal lands mineral development.
Ind/Abst NEXIS (Aug. 1982-).

US/0163-948X
INSIDE F.E.R.C. [Inside F.E.R.C.]. **VAT** Inside Federal Energy Regulatory Commission. (Jan. 1, 1979)-. Newsletter. English. wk. $1125.00 US, Canada, and Mexico; $1175.00 other. McGraw Hill Publishing Company, Inc., 1221 Avenue of the Americas, New York NY 10020. **Tel** (212)512-6410, (800)525-5003, FAX (212)512-6111. **LC** HD9502.U5; I57. **DD** 333.7. available on an online database from DIALOG. ***Continued in part by*** *Inside F.E.R.C.'s Gas Market Report, 8756-3711.*
Ind/Abst NEXIS (Jan. 5, 1981-).

US/0194-0252
INSIDE N.R.C. [Inside N.R.C.]. **VAT** Inside Nuclear Regulatory Commission. (19??)-. Newsletter. English. Twenty-six times a year. $1445.00 US and Canada; $1540.00 other. McGraw Hill Publishing Company, Inc., 1221 Avenue of the Americas, New York NY 10020. **Tel** (212)512-6410, (800)525-5003, FAX (212)512-6111. **(Subscription address:** McGraw Hill Management Information Center, 1221 Avenue of the Americas, 36th Floor, New York NY 10020.**)** **ED** Michael Knapik. Index available. available on an online database from DIALOG.
Desc: Nuclear power plant safety regulation in the US and elsewhere.
Ind/Abst NEXIS (Jan. 12, 1981-).

US
INSTITUTE FOR ENERGY ANALYSIS NEWS. **Main/Corp** Oak Ridge Associated Universities. Institute for Energy Analysis. Vol. 1 (June 1978)-. Periodical. English. qt. Free on request. Institute for Energy Analysis, Oak Ridge Association and University, PO Box 117, Oak Ridge TN 37830.

US
INSTRUMENTATION AND CONTROLS DIVISION ANNUAL PROGRESS REPORT. **Main/Corp** Oak Ridge National Laboratory. Instrumentation and Controls Division. **VFOAT** I & C Instrumentation and Controls Division Annual Progress Report. 1957-. English. an. Oak Ridge National Laboratory, PO Box 2008, Oak Ridge TN 37831. **Tel** (615)574-6755, (615)574-5845, FAX (615)574-0334.

US/0737-2817
INSULATION GUIDE. [Insul. guide]. Vol. 1, No. 1 (Midsummer 1983)-. Periodical. English. ir (8 issues yearly). $24.00. Insulation International, Inc., Box 53132, Temple Heights Station, Washington DC 20009. **ED** D M Humphrey. **DD** 338. **Bk Rev**. **Ad Acc. Circ:** 8,000 (ctrl).
Desc: Independent magazine serving those who specify, purchase or apply thermal insulation for industrial, power and process, marine, utility, and commercial applications.

AT
INTERFACE QUARTERLY NEWSLETTER. (199?)-. Newsletter. English. qt. Division of Coal and Energy Technology, Box 136, North Ryde New South Wales 2113 Australia. **Tel** (02)543-3979. **Circ:** 800 (ctrl). ***Continues*** *Annual Report, 1036-1367.*
Desc: Informs clients of research advances in coal preparation, coal utilization as well as environmental programs relating to mineral and energy areas.

AU/0020-6067
INTERNATIONAL ATOMIC ENERGY AGENCY BULLETIN. (IAEA BULLETIN : QQUARTERLY JOURNAL OF THE INTERNATIONAL ATOMIC ENERGY AGENCY.). [Int. At. Energy Agency bull.]. **Added/Corp** International Atomic Energy Agency. International Atomic Energy Agency. Division of Public Information. **VAT** International Atomic Energy Agency Bulletin. Vol. 31 No. 1 (1989)-. Bulletin. English (French, Spanish, Chinese, Japanese and Russian). qt. Free on request. International Atomic Energy Agency - IAEA, Wagramerstrasse 5, PO Box 100, A-1400 Vienna Austria. **Tel** 011 43 222 2360. **ED** Lothar H. Wedekind. **LC** QC770; .I4955. **DD** 333.792/4/05. **CODEN** IAEBAB. **Ad Acc.** Documents available from Ask*IEEE. ***Continues*** *International Atomic Energy Agency Bulletin, 0020-6067.*
Desc: Strives to accelerate and enlarge the contribution of atomic energy to peace, health, and prosperity throughout the world.
Ind/Abst Energy Inf. Abstr.; GeoRef; INSPEC (1989-); Int. Aerosp. Abstr.; Risk Abstr.

AU
INTERNATIONAL ATOMIC ENERGY AGENCY PUBLICATIONS. CATALOGUE. **Main/Corp** International Atomic Energy Agency. **Added/Corp** International Atomic Energy Agency. Catalogue. (1972)-. English (French, Russian and Spanish). Free on request. International Atomic Energy Agency / IAEA, Wagramerstrasse 5, PO Box 100, A-1400 Vienna Austria. **Tel** 011 43 1 2360 ext. 2530, FAX 011 43 1 234564. **(Subscription address:** UNIPUB, 4611 F Assembly Drive, Lanham MD 20706.**)** **LC** Z5160; .I47; QC776. **DD** 016.5397. ***Continues*** *International Atomic Energy Agency. Publications in the Nuclear Sciences.*
Desc: Catalog of nuclear energy publications from the International Atomic Energy Agency.

BE
INTERNATIONAL COAL LETTER. **See** Engineering-Mines and Mining Engineering.

UK/0260-4299
INTERNATIONAL COAL REPORT. (INTERNATIONAL COAL REPORT / FINANCIAL TIMES.). [Int. coal rep.]. **VFOAT** ICR; I.C.R. Issue No. 1 (Sept. 1980)-. Periodical. English. Twenty-four times a year. £610.00 UK; £630.00 other. Financial Times England, 8 16 Great New Street, London EC4A 3BN England. **Tel** 011 44 71 353 0305, 353 1040, FAX 011 44 353 0846. **ED** Gerard McCloskey. **LC** Discard. **Bk Rev.** available on an online database (files 16,636/Full-Text) from DIALOG.
Desc: Covers prices and freight rates, economic trends/political developments, leasing agreements and mine developments world wide.
Ind/Abst Coal Abstr.; Fluid Abstr., Civil Eng.; Fluid Abstr. Proc. Eng.; FLUIDEX (1973-); PROMT [Full Txt.]; PTS Newsl. Database [Full Txt.].

UK
INTERNATIONAL COAL REPORT'S COAL YEAR / FINANCIAL TIMES. **Added/Corp** Financial Times Business Information Ltd. **VFOAT** Coal Year. (1984)-. English. an. Free to subscribers of International Coal Report. Financial Times England, 8 16 Great New Street, London EC4A 3BN England. **Tel** 011 44 71 353 0305, 353 1040, FAX 011 44 353 0846. **ED** Gerard McCloskey. **LC** HD9540.1; .I55. **DD** 338.2/724/05. Index available. available on microfiche.
Desc: A newsletter covering coal prices, coal deals, etc.

US/0742-5821
INTERNATIONAL DIRECTORY OF NUCLEAR UTILITIES. **See** Engineering-Nuclear Engineering.

●UK
INTERNATIONAL DIRECTORY OF POWER GENERATION. (1994)-. Directory. English. an. £75.00. Turret Group, 177 Hagden Lane, Watford Herts WD1 8LN United Kingdom. **Tel** 011 44 923 228577, FAX 011 44 923 221346.

US/0731-5341
INTERNATIONAL ENERGY ANNUAL. [Int. energy annu.]. **Added/Corp** United States. Energy Information Administration. International Statistics Division. United States. Energy Information Administration. United States. Office of Energy Markets and End Use. (19??)-. Government Publication. English. an. $24.00 US; $27.50 other. Superintendent of Documents, US Government Printing Office, Washington DC 20402. **Tel** (202)275-3328, FAX (202)786-2377. **(Subscription address:** US Government Bookstore / O'Neil Building, 2023 3rd Avenue North, Birmingham AL 35203.**)** **LC** TJ163.13; .I573. **DD** 333.79/11/0212. ***Continues*** *International Petroleum Annual, 0074-7319.*
Desc: Presents current data and trends for production, consumption, stocks, imports, and exports for primary energy commodities over 190 countries, dependencies and areas of special sovereignty.
Ind/Abst Energy Inf. Abstr.

US/1051-6360
INTERNATIONAL ENERGY OUTLOOK. (INTERNATIONAL ENERGY OUTLOOK / ENERGY INFORMATION ADMINISTRATION, OFFICE OF ENERGY MARKETS AND END USE, U.S. DEPARTMENT OF ENERGY.). [Int. energy outlook]. **Added/Corp** United States. Office of Energy Markets and End Use. United States. Energy Information Administration. Office of Integrated Analysis and Forecasting. (1985)-. English. an (Apr.). National Energy Information Center, Energy Information Administration, Forrestal Building, Room 1F-048, Washington DC 20585. **Tel** (202)586-8800. **LC** HD9502.A1; I565. **DD** 333.79/0973. ***Continues in part*** *Annual Energy Outlook, 0740-4190.*
Desc: This report presents the current EIA assessment of the long-term outlook for international energy markets.
Ind/Abst Energy Inf. Abstr.; F&S Index Plus Text, Int. [Select. Cov.]; Predicasts Forecasts.

US/0163-3724
INTERNATIONAL ENERGY STATISTICAL REVIEW. ***Suspended.*** **See** Energy-Abstracting, Bibliographies and Statistics.

US/1058-2487
INTERNATIONAL ENERGY STATISTICS SOURCEBOOK. **See** Energy-Abstracting, Bibliographies and Statistics.

UK/0143-0750
INTERNATIONAL JOURNAL OF AMBIENT ENERGY. [Int. j. ambient energy]. **VFOAT** Ambient Energy. Vol. 1, No. 1 (Jan. 1980)-. Academic Scholarly Publication. English. qt. $268.00. Ambient Press Ltd, PO Box 25, Lutterworth Leics LE17 4FF England. **Tel** 44 455 202281, telex 81259. **ED** J C McVeigh. **LC** TJ163 .13; .I58. **DD** 621.042/05. **CODEN** IJAEDW. **[CCC]. Bk Rev. Circ:** 250. available in microform (Back issues from William S Hein). Documents available from Article Express International, Ask*IEEE, CASDDS.
Desc: Renewable energy, applications and fundamental science-solar, wind, wave, tidal and geothermal energy policy, emphasis is on renewable energy in buildings.
Ind/Abst Abstr. AIT Rep. Publ. Energy; Archit. Period. Index (1980-); Bioeng. Abstr.; Chem. Abstr.; Ei Page One; EMBASE; Energy Inf. Abstr.; Energy Res. Abstr. (Nov. 1980-); Eng. Index Annu.; Fluid Abstr., Civil Eng.; Fluid Abstr. Proc. Eng.; FLUIDEX (1980-); Geogr. Abstr. Human Geogr.; INSPEC (Jan. 1982-); Int. Aerosp. Abstr.; Int. Build. Serv. Abstr.; Int. Dev. Abstr.

US/1054-853X
INTERNATIONAL JOURNAL OF ENERGY, ENVIRONMENT, ECONOMICS. [Int. j. energy environ. econ.]. **VFOAT** IJEEE. Vol. 1, No. 1 (1991)-. Periodical. English. Four times a year. $215.00. Nova Science Publishers Inc., 6080 Jericho Turnpike, Suite 207, Commack NY 11725-2808. **Tel** (516)499-3103, (516)499-3106, FAX (516)499-3146. **LC** TD195.E49; I57. **DD** 333.79/14. **CODEN** IJEEEJ.
Ind/Abst Energy Inf. Abstr.

UK/0363-907X
INTERNATIONAL JOURNAL OF ENERGY RESEARCH. [Int. j. energy res.]. **VFOAT** Energy Research. Vol. 1 Jan./March (1977)-. Academic Scholarly Publication. English. Nine times a year. $1,095.00. John Wiley & Sons Ltd., Baffins Lane, Chichester West Sussex PO19 1UD England. **Tel** 0243 779777, FAX 0243 776128 BTG:JWP001, telex 86290 WIBOOKG. **ED** J. T. McMullan and D. E. Claridge. **LC** TJ163.13; .I59. **DD** 621.042. **CODEN** IJERDN. **[CCC]. Pr Rev. Circ:** 800. available on microfilm and microfiche from University Microfilms International (UMI). Documents available from Article Express International, The Genuine Article, Ask*IEEE, CASDDS, Documents on Demand.
Desc: Covers the development and uses of traditional and new fuels and other sources of energy. It provides an inter-disciplinary platform for all aspects of energy research and development, including feasibility.
Ind/Abst Abstr. AIT Rep. Publ. Energy; AGRICOLA; Appl. Mech. Rev.; Bioeng. Abstr.; Chem. Abstr.; Coal Abstr.; Curr. Contents Eng. Tech. Appl. Sci.; Curr. Technol. Index; Ei Page One; Energy Inf. Abstr.; Energy Res. Abstr. (Sept. 1977-); Eng. Index Annu.; Environ. Abstr.; Environ. Eng. Abstr.; Environ. Period. Bibliogr.; Fluid Abstr., Civil Eng.; Fluid Abstr. Proc. Eng.; FLUIDEX (1977-); Gas Abstr.; Geogr. Abstr. Phys. Geogr.; Geogr. Abstr. Human Geogr.; Geol. Abstr.; GeoRef; Health Saf. Sci. Abstr.; HTFS Dig.; INSPEC (Jan./March 1977-); Int. Aerosp. Abstr.; Int. Build. Serv. Abstr.; Int. Dev. Abstr.; Leadscan; Lit. Pat. Abstr., Oilfield Chem. (1979-); Lit. Abstr., Catal. Catal.; Lit. Abstr., Health Environ.; Lit. Abstr., Pet. Refin. Petrochem.; Lit. Abstr., Pet. Substit.; Lit. Abstr., Transp. Storage; Mater. Sci. Eng. Abstr.; Mech. Eng. Abstr.; Life Sci. Collect. (1985-); Pollut. Abstr. Indexes; Res. Alert [Select. Cov.]; SCISEARCH; Soc. Sci. Cit. Index [Select. Cov.].

US/0226-1472
INTERNATIONAL JOURNAL OF ENERGY SYSTEMS. ***Title Change.*** (INTERNATIONAL JOURNAL OF ENERGY SYSTEMS : A JOURNAL OF THE INTERNATIONAL ASSOCIATION OF SCIENCE AND TECHNOLOGY FOR DEVELOPMENT-IASTED.). [Int. j. energy syst.]. **Added/Corp** International Association of Science and

Technology for Development. **VFOAT** Energy Systems. **VAT** Energy Systems (Calgary). Vol. 1, No. 1 (1981)-Vol. 13, No. 3 (1993). Academic Scholarly Publication. English (French). an. IASTED- International Association of Science and Technology for Development, PO Box 2481, Anaheim CA 92814. **Tel** (714)778-3230, (800)995-2161, FAX (714)535-2662. **ED** Dr. Christopher Garbacz. **LC** TJ163.13; .I6. **DD** 333.79/05. **CODEN** IJSYDC. Index available. **Bk Rev. Ad Acc. Circ:** 300 (ctrl). Documents available from Ask*IEEE, CASDDS. ***Continued by*** *International Journal of Power & Energy Systems.*
Desc: Covers policy, planning, economics, simulation, modelling, decision, technology, alternative energy sources, energy and power systems. Includes book reviews, conferences, new publications, and advertisements.
Ind/Abst Chem. Abstr.; Cot. Trop. Fibr. Abstr. Bibliogr.; Health Saf. Sci. Abstr.; INSPEC (1986-).

SZ/0954-7118
INTERNATIONAL JOURNAL OF GLOBAL ENERGY ISSUES. [Int. j. glob. energy issues]. **Added/Corp** Unesco. **VFOAT** Global Energy Issues. Vol. 1, Nos. 1/2 (1989)-. Periodical. English. Six times a year. £170.00 UK; $250.00 North America; DM420.00 other. Inderscience Enterprises Ltd, World Trade Center Building, 110 Avenue Louis Casai, Case Postale 306, CH-1215 Geneva-Aeroport Switzerland. **Tel** 011 41 22 7383437, FAX 011 41 22 7910885, telex 28 99 50. **LC** TJ163.13; .I584. **CODEN** IJGIE7. Documents available from Article Express International, The Genuine Article, Ask*IEEE, Documents on Demand.
Desc: Covers energy policy, management and planning; energy resources and economics; energy conservation and efficiency; alternative and renewable energy; environmental protection and pollution control.
Ind/Abst Ei Page One; Energy Inf. Abstr.; Eng. Index Annu.; Environ. Abstr.; Environ. Period. Bibliogr.; INSPEC (1989-); Pollut. Abstr. Indexes; Res. Alert [Select. Cov.]; Soc. Sci. Cit. Index [Select. Cov.].

UK/0360-3199
INTERNATIONAL JOURNAL OF HYDROGEN ENERGY. [Int. j. hydrogen energy]. **Added/Corp** International Association for Hydrogen Energy. Vol. 1 (1976)-. Academic Scholarly Publication. English. mo. $872.00 The Americas; £585.00 other. Pergamon Press, An Imprint of Elsevier Science Ltd., The Boulevard, Langford Lane, Kidlington, Oxford OX5 1GB United Kingdom. **Tel** 011 44 865 843000, 011 44 865 843699, FAX 011 44 865 843010. **(Subscription address:** Elsevier Science Ltd. Oxford Fulfillment Centre, PO Box 800, Kidlington, Oxford OX5 1DX United Kingdom.**) ED** T. N. Veziroglu and J. W. Sheffield. **LC** TP360; .I57. **DD** 665/.81/05. **CODEN** IJHEDX. **[CCC]. Pr Rev.** available on microfilm and microfiche from University Microfilms International (UMI). Documents available from Article Express International, The Genuine Article, Ask*IEEE, CASDDS, Documents on Demand.
Desc: Provides a central vehicle for the exchange and dissemination of ideas in the field of hydrogen energy, between research scientists and engineers throughout the world.
Ind/Abst Bioeng. Abstr.; Chem. Abstr.; Chem. Titles; Coal Abstr.; Curr. Contents Eng. Tech. Appl. Sci.; Curr. Titles Electrochem.; Ei Page One; Elect. Comm. Abstr.; Energy Inf. Abstr.; Energy Res. Abstr. (Aug. 1976-); Eng. Index Annu.; Environ. Abstr.; Environ. Eng. Abstr.; Environ. Period. Bibliogr.; Gas Abstr.; INIS Atomindex [Micro.]; INSPEC (1978-); Int. Aerosp. Abstr.; Int. Build. Serv. Abstr.; Leadscan; Manuf. Process Eng. Abstr.; Mater. Sci. Eng. Abstr.; Mech. Eng. Abstr.; Res. Alert [Full Cov.]; Sci. Cit. Index; SCISEARCH; Solid State Supercond. Abstr.

●US/1078-3466
INTERNATIONAL JOURNAL OF POWER & ENERGY SYSTEMS. (INTERNATIONAL JOURNAL OF POWER & ENERGY SYSTEMS : A JOURNAL OF THE INTERNATIONAL ASSOCIATION OF SCIENCE AND TECHNOLOGY FOR DEVELOPMENT-IASTED.). [Int. j. power energy syst.]. **Added/Corp** International Association of Science and Technology for Development. **VFOAT** International Journal of Power and Energy Systems. Vol. 14, No. 1 (1994)-. Periodical. English. Three times a year. $200.00. IASTED- International Association of Science and Technology for Development, PO Box 2481, Anaheim CA 92814. **Tel** (714)778-3230, (800)995-2161, FAX (714)535-2662. **LC** TJ163.13; .I6. **DD** 333.79/05. ***Continues*** *International Journal of Energy Systems, 0226-1472.*

SZ/0142-5919
INTERNATIONAL JOURNAL OF SOLAR ENERGY. [Int. j. sol. energy]. Vol. 1, No. 1 (1982)-. Academic Scholarly Publication. English. bm. $425.00 (academic institutions), $662.00 (corporate institutions). Harwood Academic Publishers, PO Box 90, Reading RG1 8JL England. **Tel** 011 44 734 560080. **(Subscription address:** International Publishers Distributor at one of the following addresses: 820 Town Center Drive, Langhorne, PA 19047; or PO Box 90, Reading Berkshire RG1 8JL UK; or Kent Ridge PO Box 1180, Singapore 9111, Republic of Singapore**) ED** Wolfgang Palz. **LC** TJ810; .I467. **DD** 621.47/05. **CODEN** IJSEEL. **[CCC]. Bk Rev. Ad Acc.** ctrl circ. Documents available from Article Express International, Ask*IEEE, CASDDS.
Ind/Abst Chem. Abstr.; Ei Page One; Energy Inf. Abstr.; Energy Res. Abstr. (Dec. 1982-); Eng. Index Annu.; Environ. Period. Bibliogr.; INSPEC (1982-); Int. Aerosp. Abstr.; Int. Build. Serv. Abstr. (1982-).

FI/0782-7784
INTERNATIONAL PEAT JOURNAL. See Agriculture.

US/1045-6325
INTERNATIONAL SOLAR ENERGY INTELLIGENCE REPORT. [Int. solar energy intell. rep.]. Vol. 12, No. 1 (Jan. 7, 1986)-. Periodical. English. Twenty-six times a year. $416.00. Business Publishers Inc., 951 Pershing Drive, Silver Spring MD 20910-4464. **Tel** (301)587-6300, (800)274-0122, FAX (301)585-9075. **DD** 333. **[CCC].** available on an online database (files 636,648/Full-Text) from DIALOG. ***Formed by the union of*** *Solar Energy Intelligence Report, 0148-4095* ***and*** *World Solar Markets.*
Desc: Dedicated to the business, technology and politics of renewable energy.

US
IOWA ENERGY BULLETIN. Added/Corp Iowa. Energy Policy Council. Vol. 1 (Feb. 1975)-. Periodical. English. Six times a year. $6.00. Department of Natural Resources / Iowa, 900 East Grand, Wallace State Building, Des Moines IA 50319. **Tel** (515)281-3887.

GW
IRAK : ENERGIEWIRTSCHAFT. Main/Corp Germany (Federal Republic, 1949-). Bundesstelle fur Aussenhandelsinformation. German. DM2.00. Bundesstelle fuer Aussenhandelsinformation, Agrippastr 87 93, D 50676 Cologne Germany. **Tel** 011 49 221 2057316, FAX 011 49 221 2057212. **LC** HD9502.I717.

GW
IRAN : ENERGIEWIRTSCHAFT. Main/Corp Germany (Federal Republic, 1949-). Bundesstelle fur Aussenhandelsinformation. German. DM2.00. Bundesstelle fuer Aussenhandelsinformation, Agrippastr 87 93, D 50676 Cologne Germany. **Tel** 011 49 221 2057316, FAX 011 49 221 2057212. **LC** HD9502.I7.

GW
ISLAND: ENERGIEWIRTSCHAFT. Main/Corp Bundesstelle fur Aussenhandelsinformation (Germany). (197?)-. German. DM2.00. Bundesstelle fuer Aussenhandelsinformation, Agrippastr 87 93, D 50676 Cologne Germany. **Tel** 011 49 221 2057316, FAX 011 49 221 2057212. **LC** HD9502.I2; G47a.

GW
ITALIEN : ENERGIEWIRTSCHAFT. Main/Corp Germany (Federal Republic, 1949-). Bundesstelle fur Aussenhandelsinformation. (19??)-. German. DM2.00. Bundesstelle fuer Aussenhandelsinformation, Agrippastr 87 93, D 50676 Cologne Germany. **Tel** 011 49 221 2057316, FAX 011 49 221 2057212. **LC** HD9502.I8; G47a.

●RU
IZVESTIIA AKADEMII NAUK. ENERGETIKA. Added/Corp Rossiiskaia Akademiia Nauk. Otdelenie Fiziko-Tekhnicheskikh Problem Energetiki. **VFOAT** Energetika; Izvestiia Rossiiskoi Akademii Nauk. Energetika; Izvestiia RAN. Energetika. (1992)-. Academic Scholarly Publication. Russian (table of contents in English). Six times a year. $169.95. Izdatelstvo Nauka / Akademiia Nauk, Publishing House of the Russian Academy of Sciences, Leninskii Porspekt 14, 117901 Moscow Russia. **Tel** 011 95 954-21-53, FAX 011 95 938-21-44, telex 411964. **(Subscription address:** East View Publications Inc., 3020 Harbor Lane North, Suite 110, Minneapolis MN 55447.**) CODEN** IRAEEL. ***Continues*** *Izvestiia Akademii Nauk SSSR. Energetika i Transport, 0002-3310.*

RU
IZVESTIIA VNIIG IMENI B.E. VEDENEEVA / MINISTERSTVO ENERGETIKI I ELEKTRIFIKATSII SSSR GLAVNIPROEKT, VSESOIUZNYI ORDENA TRUDOVO KRASNOGO ZNAMENI NAUCHNO-ISSLEDOVATELSKII INSTITUT GIDROTEKHNIKI IMEMI B.E. VEDENEEVA. Added/Corp Vsesoiuznyi Nauchno-Issledovatelskii Institut Gidrotekhniki im. B.E. Vedeneeva. **VFOAT** Izvestiia V.N.I.I.G. Imeni BE Vedeneeva; Izvestiia VNIIG. (1978)-. Periodical. Russian. bm. **(Subscription address:** Victor Kamkin, 4956 Boiling Brook Parkway, Rockville MD 20852.**) CODEN** IVIVD3. Documents available from CASDDS.
Ind/Abst Chem. Abstr.

BW/0579-2983
IZVESTIJA VYSSIH UCEBNYH ZAVEDENIJ, ENERGETIKA. (IZVESTIIA VYSSHIKH UCHEBNYKH ZAVEDENII. ENERGETIKA.). [Izv. vyss. ucebn. zaved., Energ.]. **Added/Corp** Soviet Union. Ministerstvo Vysshego Obrazovaniia. Soviet Union. Ministerstvo Vysshego i Srednego Spetsialogo Obrazovaniia. Belorusskii Politekhnicheskii Institut Imeni I.V. Stalina. Belaruski Palitekhnichny Instytut. Soviet Union. Gosudarstvennyi Komitet po Narodnomu Obrazovaniiu. **VFOAT** Energetika; Izvestiia Vysshikh Uchebnykh Zavedenii Ministerstva Vysshego Obrazovaniia SSSR. Energetika; Izvestiia Vysshikh Uchebnykh Zavedenii. Energetika. No. 1 (1958)-. Academic Scholarly Publication. Russian. mo. $56.00. **(Subscription address:** Victor Kamkin, 4956 Boiling Brook Parkway, Rockville MD 20852.**) CODEN** IVZEAY. Documents available from Article Express International, Ask*IEEE, CASDDS. ***Absorbed*** *Nauchnye Doklady Vysshei Shkoly. Energetika.*
Ind/Abst Bioeng. Abstr.; Chem. Abstr.; Coal Abstr.; Ei Page One; Energy Res. Abstr.; Eng. Index Annu.; GeoRef; INSPEC (1968-); Int. Aerosp. Abstr.

XR/0448-116X
JADERNA ENERGIE. [Jad. energ.]. (1955)-. Academic Scholarly Publication. Czech. mo. **(Subscription address:** Artia Pegas Press Ltd., Palac Metro Narodni Trida 25, 11210 Prague 1 Czech Republic.**) CODEN** JADEAQ. Documents available from Ask*IEEE, CASDDS.
Ind/Abst Chem. Abstr.; HTFS Dig.; INSPEC (1969-); Saf. Health Work.

GW
JAPAN : ENERGIEWIRTSCHAFT. Main/Corp Bundesstelle fur Aussenhandelsinformation (Germany). German. DM3.00. Bundesstelle fuer Aussenhandelsinformation, Agrippastr 87 93, D 50676 Cologne Germany. **Tel** 011 49 221 2057316, FAX 011 49 221 2057212. **LC** HD9502.J3.

JA
JAPAN PETROLEUM & ENERGY TRENDS. See Petroleum and Natural Gas.

JA
JAPAN PETROLEUM & ENERGY TRENDS. MONTHLY STATISTICAL SUPPLEMENT. See Petroleum and Natural Gas.

UA
JIME REVIEW. Added/Corp Chuto Keizai Kenkyujo. (19??)-. Periodical. English. qt. **LC** DS41; .J53. **DD** 956/.005.
Ind/Abst Middle East J.

GW
JORDANIEN : ENERGIEWIRTSCHAFT. Main/Corp Germany (Federal Republic, 1949-). Bundesstelle fur Aussenhandelsinformation. German. DM2.00. Bundesstelle fuer Aussenhandelsinformation, Agrippastr 87 93, D 50676 Cologne Germany. **Tel** 011 49 221 2057316, FAX 011 49 221 2057212. **LC** HD9502.J67.

US/0732-8087
JOURNAL OF COAL QUALITY, THE. (THE JOURNAL OF COAL QUALITY : CQ.). [J. coal qual.]. **Added/Corp** Standard Laboratories. Coal Testing Conference Division. Western Kentucky University. Center for Coal Science. **VFOAT** CQ; C.Q. Vol. 1, No. 1 (Winter 1981)-. Academic Scholarly Publication. English. Four times a year (Jan., Apr., July, Oct.). $51.00 (institutions); $43.00 (individuals). The Journal of Coal Quality, 313 TCNW, Western Kentucky University, Bowling Green KY 42101. **Tel** (502)745-6244, FAX (502)745-6293. **ED** George Vourvopoulos (phone: (502)745-5277). **LC** TP325; .J76. **DD** 662.6/22. **CODEN** JCQUDK. **Bk Rev. Ad Acc. Pr Rev. Circ:** 500. Documents available from CASDDS.
Desc: News on coal quality for technical professionals.
Ind/Abst Chem. Abstr.; Coal Abstr.; Energy Inf. Abstr.; Energy Res. Abstr. (Aug. 1982-); Gas Abstr.; GeoRef.

US/0361-4476
JOURNAL OF ENERGY AND DEVELOPMENT, THE. [J. energy dev.]. **Added/Corp** International Research Center for Energy and Economic Development. University of Colorado, Boulder. Vol. 1 (Autumn 1975)-. Periodical. English. sa. $20.00 individual; $30.00 library; $38.00 institutional. ICEED, 909 14th Street, Suite 201, Boulder CO 80302. **Tel** (303)492-7667, (303)541-9504, FAX (303)442-5042. **ED** Dorothea El Mallakh. **LC** HD9502.A1; J67. **DD** 333.7. Index available. cum. index. **Bk Rev. Ad Acc. Pr Rev. Circ:** 1,500. available on an online database from DATA-STAR; BRS; and DIALOG. Documents available from Article Express International.
Desc: Addresses professionals, business and industrial communities, government officials, and academicians in economics and areas related to energy and economic development. Brings together and facilitates data presentation on relevant projects, research, programs, policies, and concepts. Content largely economic but also interdisciplinary approach, emphasizing domestic and international energy and development issues.
Ind/Abst ABC POL SCI; AESIS Q.; AGRICOLA [Select. Cov.]; Bioeng. Abstr.; Coal Abstr.; Contents Recent Econ. J.; Econ. Lit. Index; Ei Page One; Energy Inf. Abstr.; Energy Res. Abstr. (April 1976-); Eng. Index Annu.; Environ. Period. Bibliogr.; Index Period. Artic. Relat. Law; INIS Atomindex [Micro.]; Int. Aerosp. Abstr.; J. Econ. Lit.; J. Plan. Lit.; Middle East Abstr. Index; PAIS Int. Print (1991-); Middle East J.

UK/0264-6811
JOURNAL OF ENERGY & NATURAL RESOURCES LAW. See Law.

US/0733-9402
JOURNAL OF ENERGY ENGINEERING. **See** Engineering-Mechanical Engineering and Machinery.

II/0970-9991
JOURNAL OF ENERGY, HEAT AND MASS TRANSFER. **Added/Corp** Regional Centre for Energy, Heat, and Mass Transfer for Asia and the Pacific. (1990)-. Periodical. English. qt. $40.00. Scientific Secretary, Regional Centre for Energy Heat and Mass Transfer for Asia and the Pacific, Department of Mechanical Engineering, Indian Institute of Technology, Madras 600 036 India. **(Subscription address:** Prints India, 11 Darya Ganj, New Delhi 110002 India.**)** **CODEN** JEHTEL. **Bk Rev. Circ:** 300. Documents available from CASDDS. ***Continues*** *Regional Journal of Energy, Heat and Mass Transfer.*
Ind/Abst Chem. Abstr.

US/0164-0313
JOURNAL OF FUSION ENERGY. [J. fusion energy]. Vol. 1, No. 1 (Jan. 1981)-. Academic Scholarly Publication. English. Four times a year. $335.00 institutions, $65.00 individuals US; $390.00 institutions, $76.00 individuals other. Plenum Press, 233 Spring Street, New York NY 10013-1578. **Tel** (212)620-8000, (800)221-9369, FAX (212)463-0742, (212)807-1047, telex 23/421139. **ED** Daniel Cohn. **LC** TK9001; .J68. **DD** 621.48/4. **CODEN** JFENDS. **[CCC].** Index available. **Pr Rev.** available on microfilm and microfiche from University Microfilms International (UMI). Documents available from Article Express International, The Genuine Article, Ask*IEEE, CASDDS, Documents on Demand.
Desc: Features contributed and review papers pertinent to the development of thermo-nuclear fusion as a useful power source.
Ind/Abst Bioeng. Abstr.; Chem. Abstr.; Curr. Contents Eng. Tech. Appl. Sci.; Ei Page One; Energy Inf. Abstr.; Energy Res. Abstr. (Jan. 1981-); Eng. Index Annu.; Environ. Abstr.; INIS Atomindex [Micro.]; INSPEC (Jan. 1981-); Int. Aerosp. Abstr.; Pollut. Abstr. Indexes; Ref. Z.; Res. Alert [Select. Cov.]; SCISEARCH.

US/0199-6231
JOURNAL OF SOLAR ENERGY ENGINEERING. [J. sol. energy eng.]. **Added/Corp** American Society of Mechanical Engineers. Vol. 102, No. 1 (Feb. 1980)-. Periodical. English. qt. $130.00 (nonmember), $40.00 (member) US and Canada. American Society of Mechanical Engineers, 22 Law Drive, Fairfield NJ 07007. **Tel** (201)882-1167, (212)705-7722 (editorial). **ED** Cornelia Monahan. **LC** TJ810; .T69. **DD** 621.47/05. **CODEN** JSEEDO. **[CCC]. Bk Rev. Ad Acc. Pr Rev. Circ:** 880. available on microfilm and microfiche from University Microfilms International (UMI). Documents available from Article Express International, The Genuine Article, Ask*IEEE, CASDDS.
Desc: Testing and simulation, solar thermal power, wind energy, conservation, bio-conversion, ocean energy systems, photovoltaics, materials, system analysis and optimization.
Ind/Abst Appl. Sci. Technol. Index; Bibliogr. Mission. (1980-); Bioeng. Abstr.; Chem. Abstr.; Curr. Contents Eng. Tech. Appl. Sci.; Ei Page One; Energy Inf. Abstr.; Energy Res. Abstr. (June 1980-); Eng. Index Annu.; Expand. Acad. Index (1992-); Fluid Abstr., Civil Eng.; Fluid Abstr. Proc. Eng.; FLUIDEX (1980-); HTFS Dig.; INSPEC (Feb. 1980-); Int. Aerosp. Abstr.; Proc. Chem. Eng.; Res. Alert [Full Cov.]; Sci. Cit. Index; SCISEARCH; Theoret. Chem. Eng.

IQ/0256-7911
JOURNAL OF SOLAR ENERGY RESEARCH / SOLAR ENERGY RESEARCH CENTER, SCIENTIFIC RESEARCH COUNCIL, BAGHDAD. [J. solar energy res.]. Vol. 1, No. 1 (Sept. 1983)-. Academic Scholarly Publication. English. sa. Editorial Secretary, Journal of Solar Energy Research, POB 13026, Joderiyah Baghdad Iraq. **CODEN** JSEREU. Documents available from Ask*IEEE, CASDDS.
Ind/Abst Chem. Abstr. (1983-); Ei Page One; INSPEC (Sept. 1983-).

US/0276-3486
JOURNAL OF SOLAR SCIENCES. [J. solar sci.]. Vol. 1, No. 1 (Spring 1982)-. Periodical. English. qt. $96.00 US; $112.00 other. Van Nostrand Reinhold Company Inc., 115 5th Avenue, New York NY 10003. **Tel** (212)254-3232, FAX (212)673-1239, telex 272562. **LC** TJ810; .J7. **DD** 621.47/05.
Ind/Abst Pollut. Abstr. Indexes.

UK/0144-2600
JOURNAL OF THE INSTITUTE OF ENERGY. [J. Inst. Energy]. **Main/Corp** Institute of Energy (Great Britain). Vol. 52, No. 410; (March 1979)-. Academic Scholarly Publication. English. qt (4 issues). £125.00. Institute of Energy, 18 Devonshire Street, London W1N 2AU England. **Tel** 011 44 71 580 7124, FAX 011 44 74 580 4420, telex 265871. **ED** C. Payne. **LC** TP315; .I6. **DD** 621.042/05. **CODEN** JINEDX. Index available. **Circ:** 3,000. Documents available from Article Express International, The Genuine Article, Ask*IEEE, CASDDS, Documents on Demand. ***Continues*** *Journal of the Institute of Fuel, 0020-2886.*
Desc: Learned society journal publishing research papers from the whole energy field.
Ind/Abst Acad. Search (July 1993-); Alum. Ind. Abstr.; Appl. Sci. Technol. Index; Bioeng. Abstr.; Chem. Abstr.; Coal Abstr.; Curr. Contents Eng. Tech. Appl. Sci.; Curr. Technol. Index; Ei Page One; Electron. Commun. Abstr. J.; EMBASE; Energy Inf. Abstr.; Energy Res. Abstr. (March 1980-);; Eng. Mater. Abstr.; Eng. Index Annu.; Environ. Abstr.; Environ. Period. Bibliogr.; GeoRef; INSPEC (March 1979-); Int. Aerosp. Abstr.; Int. Build. Serv. Abstr.; ISMEC Bull.; Met. Abstr.; Pollut. Abstr. Indexes; Res. Alert [Select. Cov.]; Saf. Sci. Abstr. J.; SCISEARCH; World Ceram. Abstr.

JA
KAGAKU GIJUTSU KENKYU CHOSA NI FUTAISURU ENERUGI KENKYU CHOSA HOKOKU / HENSHU, SORIFU TOKEIKYOKU. **VFOAT** Energi Kenkyu Chose Hokuku; Report on the Survey of Research and Development of Energy Taken as a Supplement of the Survey of Research and Development. Japanese. Sorifu Tokeikyoku, 95 Wakamatsu-cho Shinjuku-ku, Tokyo-to 162 Japan. **LC** HD9502.J3; K33.

GW
KAMERUN : ENERGIEWIRTSCHAFT. **Main/Corp** Germany (Federal Republic, 1949-). Bundesstelle fur Aussenhandelsinformation. German. DM2.00. Bundesstelle fuer Aussenhandelsinformation, Agrippastr 87 93, D 50676 Cologne Germany. **Tel** 011 49 221 2057316, FAX 011 49 221 2057212. **LC** HD9502.C27.

●PL
KARBO, ENERGOCHEMIA, EKOLOGIA. **See** Earth Sciences-Mineralogy.

FI
KAUPPA- JA TEOLLISUUSMINISTERION ENERGIAOSASTON JULKAISUJA SARJA B, ENERGIATALOUDELLISET SELVITYKSET. **VFOAT** Sarja B, Energiataloudelliset Selvitykset. Vol. 22 (1983)-. Monographic series. Finnish (summaries and/or abstracts in English and Swedish). Price varies per volume. Valtion Painatuskeskus, PO Box 516, SF 00101 Helsinki Finland. **Tel** 011 358 0 5660266. ***Continues*** *Kauppa- Ja Teollisuusministerion Energiaosaston Julkaisuja. Sarja B, Selvitykset Ja Tutkimukset, 0356-9284.*

GW
KENIA : ENERGIEWIRTSCHAFT. **Main/Corp** Germany (Federal Republic, 1949-). Bundesstelle fur Aussenhandelsinformation. German. DM2.00. Bundesstelle fuer Aussenhandelsinformation, Agrippastr 87 93, D 50676 Cologne Germany. **Tel** 011 49 221 2057316, FAX 011 49 221 2057212. **LC** HD9502.K4.

JA
KINKI DAIGAKU GENSHIRYOKU KENKYUJO NENPO. **See** Physics.

GW
KOLUMBIEN : ENERGIEWIRTSCHAFT. **Main/Corp** Germany (Federal Republic, 1949-). Bundesstelle fur Aussenhandelsinformation. German. Bundesstelle fuer Aussenhandelsinformation, Agrippastr 87 93, D 50676 Cologne Germany. **Tel** 011 49 221 2057316, FAX 011 49 221 2057212. **LC** HD9502.C7.

FR/0754-5215
L.A.E. LA LETTRE AFRIQUE ENERGIES. [L.A.E. Lett. Afr. energ.]. **VFOAT** Lettre Afrique Energie. (1983)-. Periodical. French. Twenty-three times a year. 3672.87F France; 3750.00F other. Indigo Publications, 10 rue du Sentier, 75002 Paris France. **Tel** 011 33 1 45081480, FAX 011 33 1 45085983, telex 215405. **ED** Joel Delafond. **UDC** 620.91. **Circ:** 23.
Desc: Energy, mining and petroleum in Africa.

AU/0074-1868
LEGAL SERIES. **See** Law-International Law.

CN/0840-7827
LIAISON ENERGIE FRANCOPHONIE. (LIAISON ENERGIE-FRANCOPHONIE / INSTITUT DE L'ENERGIE DES PAYS EN COMMUN USAGE DU FRANCAIS (EPF).). [Liaison energ. francoph.]. **Added/Corp** Institut de l'Energie des Pays en Commun Usage du Francais. No. 1 (Sept./Oct. 1988)-. Periodical. French. Four times a year (Mar., June, Sept., Dec.). 30.00Can$. Institute de L'Energie, 56 rue St. Pierre, 3E Etage, Quebec QUE G1K 4A1 Canada. **Tel** (418)692-5727, FAX (418)692-5644, telex 051-3024. **ED** Jean-Marc de Comarmond. **DD** 333.79/06/17541. **Bk Rev**, (Qty: 10). **Ad Acc. Circ:** 4,000 (ctrl).
Desc: Promotes the exchanges of information on energy among francophone countries.

US
LICENSED FUEL FACILITY STATUS REPORT. ***Ceased.*** English. sa. Nuclear Regulatory Commission, 1717 H Street NW, Washington DC 20555. **Tel** (301)492-7000. available on microfiche (Vols. for (1986-) distributed to depository libraries). Documents available from Documents on Demand.
Desc: Provides information on licensed fuel facilities. The information consists of NRC inspection results, license event reports, radioactive effluent data, facility data and inventory difference data.
Ind/Abst Am. Stat. Index; Energy Inf. Abstr.

US/1056-9057
LICENSEE EVENT REPORT (LER) COMPILATION. ***Ceased.*** **See** Law.

AT/0817-6191
LIPSCOMBE REPORT. (1969)-. Newspaper. English. wk. $2600.00 (per year), 700.00 (per quarter) Lipscombe Report Fax; $1650.00 (per year), $500.00 (per quarter) Lipscombe Report Fax, Backgrounder, and the Drilling Report (full service set). Pex Publications Pty Ltd, PO Box 158, Claremont Western Australia 6010. **Tel** (09)383-3477, FAX (09)385 1485. **ED** Don Lipscombe.
Desc: Monitors oil exploration and development in Australia, PNG and New Zealand.

FR/0398-9275
LISTE DES PUBLICATIONS DU COMMISSARIAT A L'ENERGIE ATOMIQUE / CENTRE D'ETUDES NUCLEAIRES DE SACLAY, SERVICE DE DOCUMENTATION. [Liste mens. publ. Commis. energ. at.]. **Main/Corp** France. Commissariat a l'Energie Atomique. 1977-. French. an. **NLM** Z 5160 F815L.

●US/1065-0504
LITERATURE ABSTRACTS. PETROLEUM SUBSTITUTES. **See** Petroleum and Natural Gas-Abstracting, Bibliographies and Statistics.

US/0024-581X
LOG ANALYST, THE. [Log anal.]. (1960)-. Periodical. English. bm. $130.00. Society of Professional Well Log Analysts, 8866 Gulf Freeway, Suite 320, Houston TX 77023. **Tel** (713)947-8727, FAX (713)928-9061. **ED** Stephen Prensky. **CODEN** LGALAS. Index available. **Ad Acc. Circ:** 4,000 (ctrl). Documents available from Article Express International, Petroleum Abstracts Document Delivery Service.
Desc: Technical articles on formation evaluation, news of members, chapter news, board of directors minutes, etc.
Ind/Abst AESIS Q.; Bioeng. Abstr.; Coal Abstr.; Ei Page One; Eng. Index Annu.; GeoRef; Pet. Abstr.

US/0882-8334
LONG-TERM BENTHIC MONITORING PROGRAMS NEAR THE MORGANTOWN AND CALBERT CLIFFS POWER PLANTS. **VFOAT** Long Term Benthic Monitoring Programs Near the Morgantown and Calvert Cliffs Power Plants. English. an. Environmental Center, Martin Marietta Corporation, 1450 South Rolling Road, Baltimore MD 21227-3898. **LC** QH545.E38; L66. **DD** 333.79/24.

US/0733-5903
LONG TERM ENERGY PLAN. [Long term energy plan]. English. Alaska Department of Commerce Division of Energy, Divsion of Energy, 338 Denali Street, 7th Floor, Mackay Building, Anchorage AK 99501. **LC** HD9502.U53; A46. **DD** 333.79/09798.

US/0733-592X
LONG TERM ENERGY PLAN. APPENDICES. [Long term energy plan, Append.]. English. Division of Energy and Power Development, 338 Denali Street, 7th Floor, Mackay Building, Anchorage AK 99501. **LC** HD9502.U53; A46 SUPPL. **DD** 333.79/09798.

US/0733-5911
LONG TERM ENERGY PLAN. EXECUTIVE SUMMARY. (LONG TERM ENERGY PLAN. / EXECUTIVE SUMMARY / PREPARED BY APPLIED ECONOMICS ASSOCIATES, INC. ... [ET AL.] FOR THE STATE OF ALASKA, DEPARTMENT OF COMMERCE & ECONOMIC DEVELOPMENT, DIVISION OF ENERGY & POWER DEVELOPMENT.). [Long term energy plan, Exec. summ.]. **Added/Corp** Applied Economics Associates. Alaska. Division of Energy and Power Development. (19??)-. Periodical. English. Alaska Department of Commerce Division of Energy, Divsion of Energy, 338 Denali Street, 7th Floor, Mackay Building, Anchorage AK 99501. **LC** HD9502.U53; A46 Suppl. 2. **DD** 333.79/09798.

UK
LONGMAN WORLD ENERGY CD-ROM. English. sa. £550.00. Longman Group Ltd., Fourth Avenue, Longman House, Harlow Essex CM19 5SR England. **Tel** 011 44 279 429655, FAX 011 44 279 431059, telex 81259. **(Subscription address:** Longman Cartermill, St. Andrews, Fife KY16 9EA Scotland**)**

US/8756-9000
LOW INCOME HOME ENERGY ASSISTANCE PROGRAM. [Low income home energy assist. program]. **Added/Corp** United States. Office of Family Assistance. Office of Energy Assistance. (198?)-. English. an. Office of Family Assistance, Welfare Management Institute/Transpoint Building, 2100 Second Street SW, Washington DC 20201. **LC** HC110.P63; L68. **DD** 363.5/8. available on microfiche (Vols. for (1983-) distributed to depository libraries).

GW
LUXEMBURG : ENERGIEWIRTSCHAFT. **Main/Corp** Germany (Federal Republic, 1949-). Bundesstelle fur Aussenhandelsinformation. German.

Energy

DM2.00. Bundesstelle fuer Aussenhandelsinformation, Agrippastr 87 93, D 50676 Cologne Germany. **Tel** 011 49 221 2057316, FAX 011 49 221 2057212. **LC** HD9502.L9.

GW
MADAGASKAR : ENERGIEWIRTSCHAFT. Main/Corp Germany
(Federal Republic, 1949-). Bundesstelle fur Aussenhandelsinformation. German. DM2.00. Bundesstelle fuer Aussenhandelsinformation, Agrippastr 87 93, D 50676 Cologne Germany. **Tel** 011 49 221 2057316, FAX 011 49 221 2057212. **LC** HD9502.M28.

US
MAGNETIC FUSION ENERGY; PROGRAM SUMMARY DOCUMENT.
Main/Corp United States. Dept. of Energy. Office of Fusion Energy. (1981)-. English. US Department of Energy Office of Energy Technology, 1000 Independence Avenue SW, Washington DC 20585. **Continues** United States. Dept. of Energy. Office of Fusion Energy. Magnetic Fusion Program Summary Document.

CN/0831-4667
MAITRISE DE L'ENERGIE (MONTREAL). (LA MAITRISE DE L'ENERGIE.).
[Maitrise energ.]. **Added/Corp** Association Quebecoise Pour la Maitrise de L'energie. Vol. 1, No 1 (1986)-. Periodical. French. qt. 25.00 Can$ Canada; 80.00 Can$ other. Assn Quebecoise Maitrise Energ, 5 Pl Vil Marie, 9E Etage, B 903, Montreal Que H3B 2G2 Canada. **Tel** (514)866-5584, FAX (514)874-1272. **DD** 333.79/16/09714. **Circ:** 10,000.

UK
MAJOR ENERGY COMPANIES OF EUROPE.
(1986)-. English. $180.00. Gale Research Inc., 835 Penobscot Building, Detroit MI 48226. **Tel** (800)877-GALE, (313)961-2242, FAX (313)961-6083, telex TWX 810-221-7086. **LC** HD9502.E8; M34. **DD** 338.7/621042/0254.
Desc: Gives information about the finances, personnel, structure, products, and profitability of over 1,000 major energy companies of Western Europe.

GW
MALAWI : ENERGIEWIRTSCHAFT.
Main/Corp Germany (Federal Republic, 1949-). Bundesstelle fur Aussenhandelsinformation. German. DM2.00. Bundesstelle fuer Aussenhandelsinformation, Agrippastr 87 93, D 50676 Cologne Germany. **Tel** 011 49 221 2057316, FAX 011 49 221 2057212. **LC** HD9502.M3.

GW
MALAYSIA : ENERGIEWIRTSCHAFT.
Main/Corp Bundesstelle fur Aussenhandelsinformation (Germany). German. DM2.00. Bundesstelle fuer Aussenhandelsinformation, Agrippastr 87 93, D 50676 Cologne Germany. **Tel** 011 49 221 2057316, FAX 011 49 221 2057212. **LC** HD9502.M36.

CN/0828-4334
MEDIUM-TERM PLANNING GUIDELINES.
[Medium-term plann. guidel.]. **Main/Corp** Ontario. Ministry of Energy. **VFOAT** Medium Term Planning Guidelines. July 1983-. English. an. Ministry of Energy, Queen's Park, Toronto Ontario M7A 2B7 Canada. **LC** HD9502.C33; O56B. **DD** 333.79/09713.

AU/0047-6641
MEETINGS ON ATOMIC ENERGY.
Added/Corp International Atomic Energy Agency. Vol 1 (Jan. 1969)-. English. qt. $720.00 . International Atomic Energy Agency / IAEA, Wagramerstrasse 5, PO Box 100, A-1400 Vienna Austria. **Tel** 011 43 1 2360 ext. 2530, FAX 011 43 1 234564. **(Subscription address:** UNIPUB, 4611 F Assembly Drive, Lanham MD 20706.) **LC** QC770; .M4. **DD** 539.7/06. **Supersedes** Conferences, Meetings, and Training Courses in Atomic Energy.
Desc: Presents a list of future conferences, exhibitions and training courses on subjects related, directly or indirectly, to nuclear energy and its peaceful uses. This information is collected by reviewing announcements as they appear and from correspondence with organizers of such meetings.

RU
MEZHVUZOVSKII TEMATICHESKII SBORNIK / MOSKOVSKII ORDENA LENINA I ORDENA OKTIABRSKOI REVOLIUTSII ENERGETICHESKII INSTITUT. Added/Corp Moskovskiĕi
Energeticheskiĕi Institut. Soviet Union. Ministerstvo Vysshego i Srednego Obrazovaniia. **VFOAT** Mezhvedomstvennyi Tematicheskii Sbornik; Mezhvuzovskii Sbornik Trudov. (1982)-. Monographic series. Russian. Price varies per volume. **CODEN** MTSIEB. Documents available from CASDDS.
Ind/Abst Chem. Abstr.

US/0196-9064
MIDWEST REGIONAL SOLAR ENERGY PLANNING VENTURE.
V. 1- Sept. 1977-. Periodical. English. Central Solar Energy Research Corporation / Michigan, 328 Executive Plaza, 1200 6th Street, Detroit MI 48226.

US
MINERAL & ENERGY INFORMATION SOURCES.
See Engineering-Mines and Mining Engineering.

US/0749-9876
MINERAL INFORMATION SOURCES.
See Earth Sciences.

AT
MINERALS & ENERGY JOURNAL / OFFICE OF MINERALS AND ENERGY (VICTORIA).
Added/Corp Victoria. Office of Minerals and Energy. **VFOAT** Minerals and Energy Journal. Vol. 1, No. 1 (June 1985)-. Periodical. English. sa. **Continues** Minning, Geology and Energy Journal of Victoria.
Ind/Abst AESIS Q.

AT/1031-556X
MINERALS AND ENERGY RESEARCH NEWS.
See Engineering-Mines and Mining Engineering.

CN
MINES DE CHARBON.
See Engineering-Abstracting, Bibliographies and Statistics.

UK/0260-7840
MODERN POWER SYSTEMS.
[Mod. power syst.]. Vol. 1, No. 1 (Jan. 1981)-. Academic Scholarly Publication. English. Twelve times a year. $140.00 US and Canada; £69.00 UK. Wilmington Publishing Ltd., PO Box 200, Field End Road, Ruislip Middx HA4 0SY England. **Tel** 011 44 81 841 3970, FAX 011 44 81 841 9676. **ED** L. D. Smith. **LC** TJ1; .E47. **DD** 621.4/005. **CODEN** MPSYDU. **[CCC]**. **Bk Rev**. **Ad Acc**. **Circ**: 13,000 (ctrl). available in microform from Xerox; available on an online database (file 648/Full-Text) from DIALOG. Documents available from Ask*IEEE. **Continues** Energy International, 0013-7529.
Desc: Electricity generation transmission and distribution, large scale utility and small scale private. Emphasis on cogeneration. Nuclear, hypro, renewables and fluidized bed combustion, etc.
Ind/Abst Bus. Abstr. (1990-) [Full Txt.]; Bus. Index (1985-); Bus. Period. Index (19??-); Coal Abstr. (19??-); EMBASE (19??-); Energy Inf. Abstr. (19??-); Energy Res. Abstr. (April 1981-); Gen. BusinessFile (1985-); Gen. Period. Index (1985-); HTFS Dig. (19??-); Infomat Int. Bus. (19??-); INSPEC (Jan. 1981-); Mag. Search (19??-); Life Sci. Collect. (19??-); Trade Ind. ASAP (19??-) [Full Txt.]; Trade Ind. Index (1981-) [Full Txt.].

US
MONTANA HISTORICAL ENERGY STATISTICS.
See Energy-Abstracting, Bibliographies and Statistics.

US/0095-7356
MONTHLY ENERGY REVIEW.
[Mon. energy rev.]. **Added/Corp** United States. Office of Energy Information and Analysis. United States. Energy Information Administration. United States. Energy Information Administration. Office of Energy Data. United States. Energy Information Administration. Office of Energy Data Operations. United States. Office of Energy Markets and End Use. (19??)-. Periodical. English. mo. $77.00 domestic; $96.25 other. National Energy Information Center, Energy Information Administration, Forrestal Building, Room 1F-048, Washington DC 20585. **Tel** (202)586-8800. **LC** HD9564; .M66. **DD** 333.7. available on microfilm and microfiche from University Microfilms International (UMI). Documents available from UMI Article Clearinghouse, Documents on Demand. **Formed by the union of** PIMS Monthly Petroleum Report, 0099-0914 **and** Monthly Energy Indicators, 0095-1897 **Quarterly Report**. Energy Information Report by Congress ... Required by Public Law 93-319, Amended by Public Law 94-163, 0148-494X.
Desc: Provides a complete overview of the Nation's energy picture. It provides data on petroleum, natural gas, coal, electricity, nuclear energy, oil and gas resource development, prices, consumption, and the international energy situation.
Ind/Abst Am. Stat. Index; Energy Inf. Abstr.; Expand. Acad. Index (1992-); GeoRef; Newsp. Period. Abstr. (1992-); Predicasts Forecasts.

US
MONTHLY ENERGY REVIEW DATABASE [COMPUTER FILE].
Added/Corp United States. Energy Information Administration. **VFOAT** Monthly Energy Review Data Base; MERDB. (Jan. 1990)-. Periodical. English. mo. National Energy Information Center, Energy Information Administration, Forrestal Building, Room 1F-048, Washington DC 20585. **Tel** (202)586-8800. **LC** TJ163.25.U6; M6.
Desc: List of all feature articles published in the Monthly Energy Review and the text of the latest article to have been published. It is updated monthly.

CN/0382-2168
MONTHLY STATISTICS. ALBERTA COAL INDUSTRY.
See Energy-Abstracting, Bibliographies and Statistics.

CN/0319-3705
MONTHLY STATISTICS. ALBERTA ELECTRIC ENERGY INDUSTRY. Main/Corp
Alberta. Energy Resources Conservation Board. (19??)-. Periodical. English. mo. 15.00Can$, 2.00Can$ (per issue). Energy Resources Conservation Board, 640 Fifth Avenue Southwest, Calgary Alberta T2P 3G4 Canada. **Tel** (403)297-8311, (403)297-8190, telex 03-821717.
Desc: Energy generation by thermal and hydroelectric plants; fuel consumption and conversion efficiency of thermal plants; generation and fuel consumption of isolated utility plants; generation interchanges and distribution; deliveries to ultimate customers by type of account.

GW
MOSAMBIK : ENERGIEWIRTSCHAFT.
Main/Corp Germany (Federal Republic, 1949-). Bundesstelle fur Aussenhandelsinformation. German. DM2.00. Bundesstelle fuer Aussenhandelsinformation, Agrippastr 87 93, D 50676 Cologne Germany. **Tel** 011 49 221 2057316, FAX 011 49 221 2057212. **LC** HD9502.M85.

US/0376-6454
MYERS' FINANCE & ENERGY. No. 151
(Sept. 28, 1972)-. Periodical. English. mo. $149.00 (one year), $240.00 (two year). Myers Finance & Energy, PO Box 3082, Spokane WA 99220. **Tel** (509)534-7132. **ED** C.V. Myers. **Continues** Myers' Finance & Petroleum, 0384-5435.

US/0279-4357
NATIONAL ENERGY JOURNAL, THE.
[Natl. energy j.]. Vol. 4, No. 1 (Oct. 1981)-. Periodical. English. mo. $21.00. National Energy Journal, 21640 N 19th Avenue/Suite C 3, Phoenix AZ 85027. **LC** TH7438; .N37. **DD** 697/.02. **Continues** National Wood Stove & Fireplace Journal, 0164-8241.

PH
NATIONAL NONCONVENTIONAL ENERGY RESOURCES DEVELOPMENT PROGRAM PROGRESS REPORT / MINISTRY OF ENERGY, THE. Added/Corp
Philippines. Ministry of Energy. Center for Nonconventional Energy Development (Philippines) Center for Nonconventional Energy Development (Philippines). Technology Promotions Division. (19??)-. Periodical. English. an. The Administrator Center for Nonconventional, Energy Development, Metro Manila Philippines. **LC** HD9502.P6; N38. **DD** 333.79/15/09599.

US
NATIONAL TELEPHONE DIRECTORY / DEPARTMENT OF ENERGY. See Public
Administration.

US/0739-1811
NATURAL GAS INTELLIGENCE. See
Petroleum and Natural Gas.

US/0251-723X
NATURAL RESOURCES & ENERGY. See
Environmental Issues-Conservation and Natural Resources.

GW/0341-0323
NDZ. NEUE DELIWA-ZEITSCHRIFT.
(NEUE DELIWA-ZEITSCHRIFT.). [ndz. Neue Deliwa-Z.]. **VFOAT** Neue Deliwa Zeitschrift. Began 1949. Academic Scholarly Publication. German. mo. DM80.00. Deliwa Verein, Hohenzollernstrasse 49, W-3000 Hannover 1 Germany. **CODEN** NEUDAA. Documents available from CASDDS. **Continues** Deutsche Licht- und Wasserfach-Zeitung.
Ind/Abst Chem. Abstr.; EMBASE; Energy Res. Abstr.

FR
NEA NEWSLETTER. Added/Corp OECD
Nuclear Energy Agency. **VFOAT** N.E.A. Newsletter; Nuclear Energy Agency Newsletter. No. 1 (Dec. 1983)-. Periodical. English (French). sa. $30.00. OECD Publications and Information Center, 2 rue Andre-Pascal, 75775 Paris Cedex 16 France. **Tel** 011 33 1 45248167, US;(202)785-6323, FAX 011 33 1 45248500 OR 45248176, telex 620 160 OCDE. **(Subscription address:** OECD Publications Center, 2001 L Street, Suite 700, Washington DC 20036.) **ED** Jacques de la Ferte, Zabel Cheghikian, and Roxanne Goldsmith. **LC** TK9001; .N4. **DD** 621.48/3/05. **Circ:** 1,550 (English), 600 (French) (ctrl).
Desc: Publishes articles concerning key issues in the field of nuclear energy and information on current programs and policies of the NEA.

NE
NEDERLANDSE ENERGIEHUISHOUDING / CENTRAAL BUREAU VOOR DE STATISTIEK, DE. See
Energy-Abstracting, Bibliographies and Statistics.

CH/0379-7376
NENG YUAN CHI KAN. VFOAT Energy
Quarterly. Academic Scholarly Publication. Chinese (English). qt. Room 405/109 Section 1 Hankow Street, Taiwan. **LC** TJ153; .N45. **CODEN** NYCKAD. Documents available from CASDDS.
Ind/Abst Chem. Abstr.

JA/0369-3783
NENRYO OYOBI NENSHO. [Nenryo oyobi nensho]. **Added/Corp** NenryÂo Oyobi NenshÂosha. **VFOAT** Fuel and Combustion. (1934)-. Academic Scholarly Publication. Japanese. mo. $160.00. Nenryo Oyobi Nenshosha, (Fuels & Combustion Co., Ltd.), 3-5, Kitayamacho, Tennojiku, Osakashi, Osakafu 543, Japan. **(Subscription address:** Kyowa Book Company Inc., 1 38 Kanda Jinbocho Chiyoda-ku, Tokyo 101 Japan.**)** **LC** IN PROCESS. **CODEN** NEONAA. Documents available from CASDDS. ***Absorbed*** *Boira Gishi, 0385-941X.*
Ind/Abst Chem. Abstr.; Coal Abstr.

JA/0286-6501
NENSHO KENKYU. [Nensho kenkyu]. **Added/Corp** Nihon Nensho Kenkyukai. (1959)-. Academic Scholarly Publication. Japanese. Nihon Nensho Kenkyukai, (Combustion Soc. of Japan), Kyoto Daigaku Kogakubu Kogyo, Kagaku Kyoshitsu, Yoshida, Honcho, Sakyoku, Kyotoshi, Kyotofu 606 Japan. **CODEN** NEKEBW. Documents available from CASDDS.
Ind/Abst Chem. Abstr.; Coal Abstr.

●US/1075-0045
NEW ENERGY NEWS. (NEW ENERGY NEWS : MONTHLY NEWSLETTER OF THE INSTITUTE FOR NEW ENERGY.). [New energy news]. **Added/Corp** Institute for New Energy. Fusion Information Center. (May 1993)-. Periodical. English. mo. $35.00 (individuals) US; $40.00 (individuals), Canada, $50.00 (individuals) other; 60.00 Corporations, Universities, Libraires, and Institutions. Fusion Information Center, PO Box 58639, Salt Lake UT 84158-0639. **Tel** (801)583-6232, FAX (801)583-2963. **ED** Hal Fox. **DD** 621. **Bk Rev. Ad Acc, Adv Mgr Tel** (801)583-6232. **Circ:** 300. ***Continues*** *Fusion Briefings.*
Desc: Covers all aspects of research from universities, government and commerical research facilities, and private scientific groups, as well as independent researchers and inventors. It is designed to inform both the scientist and the technically inclined layperson about new ideas in all energy fields, covering topics ranging from theory to commerical application.

US
NEW MEXICO'S ENERGY RESOURCES ... : ANNUAL REPORT OF BUREAU OF GEOLOGY IN THE MINING AND MINERALS DIVISION OF NEW MEXICO ENERGY AND MINERALS DEPARTMENT / COMPILED BY EMERY C. ARNOLD, DIRECTOR, (MINING AND MINERALS DIVISION), AND JAMES M. HILL, CHIEF (BUREAU OF GEOLOGY). **Main/Corp** New Mexico. Bureau of Geology. **Added/Corp** New Mexico. Bureau of Mines and Mineral Resources. New Mexico. Bureau of Geology. Annual Report of Bureau of Geology in the Mining and Minerals Division of New Mexico Energy and Minerals Department. (19??)-. English. an. $3.00. New Mexico Bureau of Mines, Campus Station, Socorro NM 87801. **Tel** (505)835-5410, FAX (505)835-6333. **LC** TN24.N6; A235 subser; TJ163.25.U6. **DD** 553/.09789 S; 338.8/09789. ***Continues*** *New Mexico. Office of State Geologist. New Mexico's Energy Resources.*

US
NEW RELEASES / ENERGY INFORMATION ADMINISTRATION. **Added/Corp** United States. Energy Information Administration. **VFOAT** EIA New Releases; New Releases Energy Information Administration; Energy Information Administration New Releases. (Sept/Oct. 1986)-. Periodical. English. Six times a year. Free on request. National Energy Information Center, Energy Information Administration, Forrestal Building, Room 1F-048, Washington DC 20585. **Tel** (202)586-8800. **Circ:** 16,000. ***Continues*** *EIA Publications, New Releases.*
Desc: The latest available EIA publications and upcoming reports are listed and described in this publication. Availability and ordering information are provided.

NZ/0110-1668
NEW ZEALAND ENERGY JOURNAL. (THE ENERGY JOURNAL.). [N.Z. energy j.]. Vol. 54, No. 4 (Apr. 1981)-. Periodical. English. mo. $8.44. Technical Publishing Company / New Zealand, PO Box 14 116, Panmurb Auchland New Zealand. **LC** TK1; .N57. **DD** 333.79/05. **CODEN** EJOUD4. Documents available from Article Express International, Ask*IEEE. ***Continues*** *New Zealand Energy Journal.*
Ind/Abst Alum. Ind. Abstr.; Bioeng. Abstr.; Coal Abstr.; Ei Page One; Energy Res. Abstr. (June 1981-); Eng. Index Annu.; INSPEC (April 1981-); Int. Labour Doc.; J. Plan. Lit.; Met. Abstr.

CN/0708-918X
NEWSLETTER - PLANETARY ASSOCIATION FOR CLEAN ENERGY. [Newsl. - Planet. Assoc. Clean Energy]. **Main/Corp** Planetary Association for Clean Energy. Vol. 1 (May 1979)-. Newsletter. English. ir (4 to 6 per year). 35.00Can$. Planetary Association for Clean Energy, 100 Bronson, Suite 1001, Ottawa ONT K1R 6G8 Canada. **Tel** (613)236-6265. **ED** Monique Michaud. **DD** 363.6. **Bk Rev. Ad Acc. Circ:** 2,500.
Desc: Forum for advanced scientific thinking merging latest conventional research with unconventional approaches for a clean technology.
Ind/Abst Energy Res. Abstr. (Oct. 1979-).

CN/0835-1996
NICKLE'S CANADIAN ENERGY INDEX. [Nickle's Can. energy index]. **Added/Corp** C.O. Nickle Publications. **VFOAT** Canadian Energy Index. (1986)-. English. an. 145.00Can$ Canada; 147.00Can$ US. C.O. Nickle Publications, 999 8th Street Southwest, Suite 300, Calgary, Alberta T2R 1N7 Canada. **Tel** (403)244-6111. **DD** 016.3382/0971.
Desc: Cites more than 6,000 articles published by Southam's Energy Group of Publications for the year just ended.

GW
NIEDERLANDE : ENERGIEWIRTSCHAFT. **Main/Corp** Bundesstelle fur Aussenhandelsinformation (Germany). German. DM2.00. Bundesstelle fuer Aussenhandelsinformation, Agrippastr 87 93, D 50676 Cologne Germany. **Tel** 011 49 221 2057316, FAX 011 49 221 2057212. **LC** TJ163.25.N4.

GW
NIGERIA : ENERGIEWIRTSCHAFT. **Main/Corp** Bundesstelle fur Aussenhandelsinformation (Germany). German. DM2.00. Bundesstelle fuer Aussenhandelsinformation, Agrippastr 87 93, D 50676 Cologne Germany. **Tel** 011 49 221 2057316, FAX 011 49 221 2057212. **LC** HD9502.N55.

JA/0004-7120
NIHON GENSHIRYOKU GAKKAISHI. (NIHON GENSHIRYOKU GAKKAISHI. JOURNAL OF THE ATOMIC ENERGY SOCIETY OF JAPAN.). [Nihon Genshiryoku Gakkaishi]. **Main/Corp** Nihon Genshiryoku Gakkai. **VFOAT** Journal of the Atomic Energy Society of Japan; Nihon Genshiryoku Gakkai Shi. Vol. 1 (1959)-. Academic Scholarly Publication. English (Japanese). mo. $210.00. **(Subscription address:** Kyowa Book Company Inc., 1-38 Kanda Jinbo-Cho, Chiyoda-Ku Tokyo 101, Japan**)** **CODEN** NGEGAL. **Pr Rev.** Documents available from Article Express International, The Genuine Article, Ask*IEEE, CASDDS.
Ind/Abst Alum. Ind. Abstr.; Chem. Abstr.; Ei Page One; Eng. Mater. Abstr.; Eng. Index Annu.; INSPEC (1968-); Leadscan; Met. Abstr.; Res. Alert [Select. Cov.]; SCISEARCH; Soc. Sci. Cit. Index [Select. Cov.].

CN
NON-FUEL MINERAL INDUSTRY / CANADA DEPARTMENT OF ENERGY, THE. (1990)-. English. an. Canada Department of Energy, Mines and Resources, Communications Branch/8th Floor, 580 Booth Street, Ottawa Ontario K1A 0E4 Canada. **Tel** (613)995-5030, FAX (613)996-9094.

US/0275-3898
NORTH AMERICAN ENERGY REVIEW, THE. [Nor. Am. energy rev.]. Vol. 1, No. 1 (1980)-. Periodical. English. $2.25 (per copy). Performance Publications Inc, PO Box 99, Amawalk NY 10501. **LC** TJ163.25.N77; N67. **DD** 621.042/05.

US/0738-971X
NORTHEAST SUN. (NORTHEAST SUN : THE OFFICIAL PUBLICATION OF THE NEW ENGLAND SOLAR ENERGY ASSOCIATION AND THE MID-ATLANTIC SOLAR ENERGY ASSOCIATION.). [Northeast sun]. **Added/Corp** New England Solar Energy Association. Mid-Atlantic Solar Energy Association. Metropolitan Solar Energy Society (New York, N.Y.). Vol. 1, No. 1 (Feb. 1983)-. Periodical. English. qt. (comes with Northeast Solar Association Membership). Northeast Solar Energy Association, 23 Ames Street, Greenfield MA 01301. **Tel** (413)774-6051, FAX (413)774-6053. **ED** Peg Smeltz. **LC** TJ809.96.N8; N67. **DD** 621.47/0974. Index available. cum. index. **Bk Rev. Ad Acc. Circ:** 2,500. ***Formed by the union of*** *Newsletter of the New England Solar Energy Association* ***and*** *Solar News.*
Desc: Major regional magazine promoting the use of energy through the quality application of solar and renewable resources, energy efficient construction and energy management.

US/8755-8866
NORTHERN CALIFORNIA SUN. [North. Calif. sun]. Periodical. English. qt. $20.00 (individuals), $50.00 (small business), $100.00 (corporates). Northern California Solar Energy Association, PO Box 3008, Berkeley CA 94703-0008. **ED** Robin Mitchell. **DD** 621. **Bk Rev. Ad Acc. Circ:** 1,000. ***Continues*** *Solar Energy Newsletter.*
Desc: Feature articles from energy professionals on a broad range of energy related topics such as energy conservation, daylighting, photovoltaics, wind and biomass. Regular columns on energy software, a calender of events and news clips.

US/1055-6761
NORTHWEST PUBLIC POWER BULLETIN. ***Title Change.*** [Northwest public power bull.]. **Added/Corp** Northwest Public Power Association. Vol. 20, No. 6 (June/July 1966)-Vol. 46, No. 5 (May 1992). Bulletin. English. ir. Northwest Public Power Association, PO Box 4576, Vancouver WA 98662. **Tel** (206)254-0109. **ED** Rick Kellogg. **DD** 333. **Bk Rev. Ad Acc. Circ:** 3,700 (ctrl). ***Continues*** *Pacific Northwest Public Power Bulletin.* ***Continued by*** *Bulletin (Northwest Public Power Association).*
Desc: Brings information about electrical industry to public power elected officials, managers and key staff members located in Pacific Northwest and Western Canada.

●US
NORTHWEST REGIONAL FORECAST OF POWER LOADS AND RESOURCES FOR ... / COMPILED BY PACIFIC NORTHWEST UTILITIES CONFERENCE COMMITTEE, SYSTEM PLANNING OFFICE. **Added/Corp** Pacific Northwest Utilities Conference Committee. System Planning Office. **VFOAT** Northwest Regional Forecast. (1992)-. English. PNUCC, 101 SW Main/Suite 810, Portland OR 97204. ***Continues*** *West Group Forecast of Power Loads and Resources for ... .*

GW
NORWEGEN : ENERGIEWIRTSCHAFT. **Main/Corp** Germany (Federal Republic, 1949-). Bundesstelle fur Aussenhandelsinformation. German. DM2.00. Bundesstelle fuer Aussenhandelsinformation, Agrippastr 87 93, D 50676 Cologne Germany. **Tel** 011 49 221 2057316, FAX 011 49 221 2057212. **LC** HD9502.N6. **DD** 333.7.

US/1071-2267
NRC CALENDAR, THE. **See** Law.

CN/0711-270X
NRC SOLAR INFORMATION SERIES. ***Title Change.*** [NRC sol. inf. ser.]. **VFOAT** L'Energie Solaire : Le CNRC Fait le Point. **VAT** National Research Council Solar Information Series; Energie Solaire: Le Conseil National de Recherches Canada Fait le Point (Edition Anglaise et Francaise); Energie Solaire: Le CNRC Fait le Point (Edition Analaise et Francaise). 1-. Monographic series. English (French). ir. Statistics Canada, Publications Sales & Services, Main Building Room 1710, Ottawa Ontario K1A 0T6 Canada. **Tel** (613)951-5078, (800)267-6677, FAX (613)951-1584, telex 053-3585. **DD** 621.47/05. ***Continued by*** *L'Energie Solaire (Conseil National de Recherches Canada), 0711-2726.*

●US
NREL SCIENCE & TECHNOLOGY IN REVIEW. **Added/Corp** National Renewable Energy Laboratory (U.S.). **VFOAT** In Review; National Renewable Energy Laboratory Science & Technology in Review; NREL Science and Technology in Review; Science & Technology in Review; NREL Science and Technology in Review. Vol. 14, No. 1 (Feb. 1992)-. Periodical. English. qt. NREL, 1617 Cole Blvd., Golden CO 80401-3393. ***Continues*** *SERI Science & Technology in Review.*

US
NTIS ALERT. ENERGY. **Added/Corp** United States. National Technical Information Service. (19??)-. Periodical. English. Twenty-four times a year. $175.00 US; $245.00 other. National Technical Information Service - NTIS, Room 2027S, 5285 Port Royal Road, Springfield VA 22161. **Tel** (703)487-4630, (703)487-4660, (703)487-4650, FAX (703)321-8547, telex 89-9405. Index available. ***Continues*** *Energy / NTIS, 0148-446X.*

CN/0383-8536
NUCLEAR CANADA YEARBOOK. [Nucl. Can. yearb.]. **Added/Corp** Canadian Nuclear Association. (1976)-. English. an (May). 12.00Can$ member, 21.00Can$ nonmember. Canadian Nuclear Association, 144 Front Street West, Suite 725, Toronto Ontario M5J 2L7 Canada. **Tel** (416)977-6152, (416)977-7620, FAX (416)979-8356, telex 06-23741. **ED** J. A. Weller. **LC** TK9026; .N83. **DD** 338.4/7/621480971. **Ad Acc. Circ:** 2,500.
Desc: Includes articles, statistics, and Canadian Buyers' Guide to Nuclear Products and Services.
Ind/Abst Energy Res. Abstr. (April 1982-).

AU/0257-6376
NUCLEAR DATA NEWSLETTER. (1979)-. Periodical. English. ir. Free on request. International Atomic Energy Agency / IAEA, Wagramerstrasse 5, PO Box 100, A-1400 Vienna Austria. **Tel** 011 43 1 2360 ext. 2530, FAX 011 43 1 234564. **(Subscription address:** UNIPUB, 4611 F Assembly Drive, Lanham MD 20706.**)** **UDC** 341.67.
Ind/Abst AESIS Q.

UK/0140-4067
NUCLEAR ENERGY (1978). (NUCLEAR ENERGY.). [Nucl. energy]. Vol. 17 (Jan 1978)-. Academic Scholarly Publication. English. Six times a year. £101.00 UK; £123.00 Europe; £137.00 other. Thomas Telford Ltd, Thomas Telford House, 1 Heron Quay, London E14 9XF England. **Tel** 011 44 71 987 6999, FAX 011 44 71 538 4101, telex 298105. **ED** J. M. Hutcheon. **LC** TK9001.B7; A182. **DD** 333.79/24/05. **CODEN** NEBSDV. **[CCC].** Index available. **Bk Rev. Ad Acc. Pr Rev. Circ:** 2,000.

Documents available from Article Express International, The Genuine Article, Ask*IEEE, CASDDS, Documents on Demand. ***Continues*** *Journal of the British Nuclear Energy Society, 0007-1587.*
Desc: Contains high quality technical papers on all aspects of the problems of nuclear energy, design, operation, safety and control.
Ind/Abst Alum. Ind. Abstr.; Bioeng. Abstr.; Ceram. Abstr.; Chem. Abstr.; Curr. Technol. Index; Ei Page One; EMBASE; Energy Inf. Abstr.; Energy Res. Abstr. (Dec. 1979-); Eng. Mater. Abstr.; Eng. Index Annu.; Environ. Abstr.; Fluid Abstr., Civil Eng.; Fluid Abstr. Proc. Eng.; FLUIDEX (1978-); HTFS Dig.; INSPEC (Jan. 1978-); Manuf. Process Eng. Abstr.; Mech. Eng. Abstr.; Met. Abstr.; PAIS Int. Print (1991-); Res. Alert [Select. Cov.]; SCISEARCH.

FR
NUCLEAR ENERGY DATA / OECD.
Added/Corp OECD Nuclear Energy Agency. **VFOAT** Donnees sur l'Energie Nucleaire. (1989)-. English (French). an. OECD Publications and Information Center, 2 rue Andre-Pascal, 75775 Paris Cedex 16 France. **Tel** 011 33 1 45248167, US:(202)785-6323, FAX 011 33 1 45248500 OR 45248176, telex 620 160 OCDE. **(Subscription address:** OECD Publications Center, 2001 L Street, Suite 700, Washington DC 20036.**) LC** HD9698.A1; E4. ***Continues*** *Electricity, Nuclear Power, and Fuel Cycle in OECD Countries.*
Ind/Abst Predicasts Forecasts.

US/0735-2506
NUCLEAR FUEL CYCLE. ***Ceased.*** (NUCLEAR FUEL CYCLE : A CURRENT AWARENESS BULLETIN.). [Nucl. fuel cycle]. **Added/Corp** United States. Department of Energy. Technical Information Center. (Jan. 1982)-(Jan. 1994). Government Publication. English. Twelve times a year. US Department of Energy, 1000 Independence Avenue SW, Washington DC 20585. **Tel** (202)586-5000, FAX (202)586-4073. **(Subscription address:** National Technical Information Service, 5285 Port Royal Road, Springfield, VA 22161**)** cum. index.

US
NUCLEAR INDEX, THE. Vol. 2, No. 1 (Jan. 1985)-. Periodical. English. mo. $380.00. McGraw Hill Publishing Company, Inc., 1221 Avenue of the Americas, New York NY 10020. **Tel** (212)512-6410, (800)525-5003, FAX (212)512-6111. **(Subscription address:** McGraw Hill Management Information Center, 1221 Avenue of the Americas, 36th Floor, New York NY 10020.**) LC** Z5160.A1; M35; TK9145. **DD** 016.33379/24. ***Continues*** *McGraw-Hill's Nuclear Publications News catalog, 0742-0048.*

FR/0304-3428
NUCLEAR LAW BULLETIN. See Law.

US/0889-3411
NUCLEAR MONITOR, THE. See Physics-Nuclear Physics.

US/0892-2055
NUCLEAR PLANT JOURNAL. [Nucl. plant j.]. Vol. 5, No. 1 (Jan./Feb. 1987)-. Periodical. English. Seven times a year. $102.00. Equipment Engineering & Sales Inc., 799 Roosevelt Road Building 6, Suite 208, Glen Ellyn IL 60137. **Tel** (708)858-6161, FAX (708)858-8787. **ED** Newal K. Agnihotri. **LC** TK1078; .N817. **DD** 621.48/3/05. **[CCC]. Bk Rev. Ad Acc. Circ:** 22,000 (ctrl). Documents available from Article Express International. ***Continues*** *Nuclear Plant Safety, 0742-4868.*
Desc: Covers computer application, health physics, plant maintenance, radwaste management, plant services and nondestructive testing and evaluation related technical papers, reports and departments for nuclear plants.
Ind/Abst Ei Page One; Eng. Index Annu.; Health Saf. Sci. Abstr.; Pollut. Abstr. Indexes; Risk Abstr.

US/0360-7690
NUCLEAR REGULATION REPORTS. See Law-Environmental Law.

US/0147-2909
NUCLEAR REGULATORY COMMISSION ISSUANCES. Main/Corp U.S. Nuclear Regulatory Commission. **Added/Corp** U.S. Nuclear Regulatory Commission. Division of Rules and Records. U.S. Nuclear Regulatory Commission. Division of Technical Information and Document Control. U.S. Nuclear Regulatory Commission. Division of Publications Services.U.S. Nuclear Regulatory Commission. Division of Freedom of Information and Publications Services. (1975)-. Government Publication. English. mo. $56.00 US; $70.00 other. Superintendent of Documents, US Government Printing Office, Washington DC 20402. **Tel** (202)275-3328, FAX (202)786-2377. **LC** CURRENT ISSUES ONLY. **DD** 343.73/0925; 347.30925. cum. index. ***Continues*** *Atomic Energy Commission Reports.*
Desc: A monthly publication containing opinions, decisions, denials, memorandum and orders of the Commission, the Atomic Safety and Licensing Appeal Board, the Atomic Safety and Licensing Board, and the Administrative Law Judge.

US
NUCLEAR REGULATORY COMMISSION ISSUANCES : OPINIONS AND DECISIONS OF THE NUCLEAR REGULATORY COMMISSION WITH SELECTED ORDERS. See Public Administration.

US
NUCLEAR REMEDIATION REPORT. (19??)-. Periodical. English. wk. $549.00. King Publishing Group, 627 National Press Building, Washington DC 20045. **Tel** (202)638-4260, FAX (202)662-9744.

CN/0838-3871
NUCLEAR SECTOR FOCUS. [Nucl. sect. focus]. **Added/Corp** Atomic Energy of Canada Limited. Energy Sector Research. (19??)-. Periodical. English. an. Free on request. Atomic Energy of Canada Ltd, 344 Slater Street, Ottawa Ontario, K1A OS4 Canada. **Tel** (613)237-3270, FAX (613)782-2023, telex 053-4867. **ED** Julie Montgomery. **DD** 333.79/24/0971. **Circ:** 600.
Desc: Energy, electricity, and nuclear energy facts and figures worldwide and with focus on Canada.

CK/0120-7067
NUCLEARES (BOGOTA). (NUCLEARES : REVISTA TECNICO-CIENTIFICA DEL INSTITUTO DE ASUNTOS NUCLEARES.). [Nucleares]. **Added/Corp** Instituto de Asuntos Nucleares. Vol. 1, No. 1 (1986)-. Academic Scholarly Publication. Spanish (English). sa. Instituto Asuntos Nucleares, Bibliotecay Publicaciones, Avenida Eldorado, Carrera 50, Apartado Aereo 8595, Bogota, Columbia. **CODEN** NCLREV. Documents available from CASDDS.
Ind/Abst Chem. Abstr. (1986-).

US/0048-105X
NUCLEONICS WEEK. [Nucleon. week]. (1960)-. Newsletter. English. wk. $1425.00 US and Canada; $1525.00 other. McGraw Hill Publishing Company, Inc., 1221 Avenue of the Americas, New York NY 10020. **Tel** (212)512-6410, (800)525-5003, FAX (212)512-6111. **(Subscription address:** McGraw Hill Management Information Center, 1221 Avenue of the Americas, 36th Floor, New York NY 10020.**) LC** HD9698.A1; N8. **DD** 338.4/7624483/0973. available on an online database (file 624/Full-Text) from DIALOG. ***Absorbed*** *Nucleonics, 0096-6207.*
Ind/Abst NEXIS (Jan. 8, 1981-).

PK/0029-5698
NUCLEUS (KARACHI). (THE NUCLEUS.). [Nucleus]. V. 1- Jan./Mar. 1964-. Academic Scholarly Publication. English (summaries and/or abstracts in French and German). qt. $8.00. Editor Nucleus Pakistan Atomic Energy Commission, PO Box 3112. **LC** TK9001.P3. **CODEN** NCLEAM. Documents available from Ask*IEEE, CASDDS.
Ind/Abst Chem. Abstr.; Energy Res. Abstr.; Food Sci. Technol. Abstr.; GeoRef; Hortic. Abstr.; INSPEC (Jan./April 1970-); Maize Abstr.; Postharvest News Inf.; Soils Fert.; Soyabean Abstr.

GW/0723-0893
NUKLEARE ENTSORGUNG. VFOAT Nuclear Fuel Cycle. (1981)-. Academic Scholarly Publication. German (summaries and/or abstracts in English). **LC** TK9360; .N88. **DD** 621.48/335/05. **CODEN** NUKEDA. Documents available from CASDDS.
Ind/Abst Chem. Abstr.

US
OCEAN THERMAL ENERGY CONVERSION REPORT TO CONGRESS.
Main/Corp United States. Office of Ocean and Coastal Resource Management. Ocean Minerals and Energy Division. English. Office of Ocean and Coastal Resource Management, Ocean and Minerals and Energy Division, 2001 Wisconsin Avenue NW, Washington DC 20235. available on microfiche (Vols. for (1983-) distributed to depository libraries). ***Continues*** *Ocean Thermal Energy Conversion Report to Congress, 0732-7323.*

AU
OEKV INFORMATIONEN. Main/Corp Osterreichischer Energiekonsumenten-Verband. **Added/Corp** Osterreichischer Energiekonsumenten-Verband. Informationen. (1976)-. German. ir. Osterreichischer Energiekonsumenten-Verband, 1090 Kolingasse 6, Vienna, Austria. **LC** HD9502.A9; O84a.

UK/0950-1045
OIL & ENERGY TRENDS. See Petroleum and Natural Gas.

US/0731-4620
OIL & GAS TAX ALERT / THE RESEARCH INSTITUTE OF AMERICA.
See Public Administration-Public Finance and Taxation.

US/0276-5977
OIL/ENERGY STATISTICS BULLETIN AND CANADIAN OIL REPORTS. See Energy-Abstracting, Bibliographies and Statistics.

US/0733-0200
OLIPHANT WASHINGTON SERVICE.
[Oliphant Washington serv.]. (19??)-. Periodical. English. da. $2,350.00. Oliphant Washington Service, 1729 H Street Northwest, Suite 330, Washington DC 20006. **Tel** (202)296-0924. **ED** John Oliphant. **Circ:** 200.
Desc: Factual personalized information service meeting needs of energy industries for actions in all branches of Federal Government affecting them so informed decisions can be made.

US/0733-0219
OLIPHANT WASHINGTON SERVICE. ENERGY SUMMARY. [Oliphant Wash. serv., Energy summ.]. Periodical. English. wk. $250.00. Oliphant Washington Service, 1729 H Street Northwest, Suite 330, Washington DC 20006. **Tel** (202)296-0924.

GW
OMAN: ENERGIEWIRTSCHAFT.
Main/Corp Bundesstelle fur Aussenhandelsinformation (Germany). (19??)-. German. DM2.00. Bundesstelle fuer Aussenhandelsinformation, Agrippastr 87 93, D 50676 Cologne Germany. **Tel** 011 49 221 2057316, FAX 011 49 221 2057212. **LC** HD9502.O46; G47a.

CN/0226-9392
ONTARIO ENERGY REVIEW. [Ont. energy rev.]. June 1979-. English. $2.50 each copy. Ontario Ministry of Energy, 56 Wellesley Street West, Toronto Ontario M7A 2B7 Canada. **LC** HD9502.C3; O58A. **DD** 333.79/09713. ***Continues*** *Ontario's Energy Future, 0715-6707.*

US
ORDER / UNITED STATES OF AMERICA, FEDERAL ENERGY REGULATORY COMMISSION. Main/Corp United States. Federal Energy Regulatory Commission. Publication began with No. 1, Oct. 6, 1977. Periodical. English. US Federal Energy Regulatory Commission, Washington DC 20426.

UK/0959-7727
OXFORD ENERGY FORUM. [Oxf. energy forum]. (1990)-. Periodical. English. Four times a year (Feb., May, Aug., Nov.). $34.00 US; £22.00 other. Oxford Institute of Energy Studies, 57 Woodstock Road, Oxford OX2 6FA England. **Tel** (0865)311377, FAX (0865)310527, telex 838771 ENERGY Q. **ED** Jeremy Turk and Leonie Archer. **DD** 531.6. **Circ:** 500 (ctrl).
Desc: Debates on current issues within the sphere of energy.

US/0737-1926
PACE SYNTHETIC FUELS REPORT.
[Pace synth. fuels rep.]. **Added/Corp** Pace Company Consultants & Engineers. Rocky Mountain Division. **VFOAT** Synthetic Fuels Report. Vol. 19, No. 1 (Mar. 1982)-. English. qt. Pace Company Consultants & Engineers, Rock Mountain Division, Cherry Creek Plaza II, 650 South Cherry Street/Suite 400, Denver CO 80222. **LC** TP355; .S97. **DD** 662.66/05. ***Continues*** *Cameron Synthetic Fuels Report, 0276-8941.*
Ind/Abst Coal Abstr.

II/0970-3888
PACIFIC AND ASIAN JOURNAL OF ENERGY. Added/Corp Tata Energy Research Institute. Vol. 1, Issue 1 (Jan. 1987)-. Periodical. English. sa. $50.00. Tata Energy Research Institute, 9 Jor Bagh Publications Unit, New Delhi 110 003 India. **Tel** 011 91 11 4623983, FAX 011 91 11 4621770, telex 31-6159 TERI IN. **(Subscription address:** Prints India, 11 Darya Ganj, New Delhi 110002 India.**) LC** HD9502.A1; P3.
Ind/Abst Agric. Eng. Abstr.; Rice Abstr.; Sug. Indus. Abstr.; Wheat Barley Trit. Abstr.

GW
PAKISTAN : ENERGIEWIRTSCHAFT.
Main/Corp Bundesstelle fur Aussenhandelsinformation (Germany). German. DM2.00. Bundesstelle fuer Aussenhandelsinformation, Agrippastr 87 93, D 50676 Cologne Germany. **Tel** 011 49 221 2057316, FAX 011 49 221 2057212. **LC** HD9502.P27.

AU/0074-1876
PANEL PROCEEDINGS SERIES - INTERNATIONAL ATOMIC ENERGY AGENCY. (PANEL PROCEEDINGS SERIES.). [Panel proc. ser. - Int. At. Energy Agency PNEXDA]. **Main/Corp** International Atomic Energy Agency. (1970)-. Proceedings. English. **CODEN** PNEXDA. Documents available from Ask*IEEE.
Ind/Abst Index Vet.; INSPEC; Vet. Bull.

GW
PARAGUAY : ENERGIEWIRTSCHAFT.
Main/Corp Germany (Federal Republic, 1949-). Bundesstelle fur Aussenhandelsinformation. German. DM2.00. Bundesstelle fuer Aussenhandelsinformation, Agrippastr 87 93, D 50676 Cologne Germany. **Tel** 011 49 221 2057316, FAX 011 49 221 2057212. **LC** HD9502.P3.

US/0191-9830
PASSIVE SYSTEMS. Main/Corp International Solar Energy Society. American Section. English. American Section of the International Solar Energy Society Inc, PO Box 1416, Killeen TX 76541. **LC** TH7413; .I56A. **DD** 697/.78.

US
PENNSYLVANIA ENERGY. Added/Corp Pennsylvania Energy Office. **VFOAT** Energy. Vol. 1, No. 1 (July 1987)-. Periodical. English. qt. **LC** HD9502.U53; P4567. **DD** 333.79/09748/05.
Ind/Abst Energy Inf. Abstr.

US/0163-6952
PEOPLE & ENERGY. [People energy]. **VAT** People and Energy. Periodical. English. $18.00. Institute for Ecological Policies, 1413 K Street NW, Washington DC 20005.
Ind/Abst GeoRef.

UK/0961-1347
PERSPECTIVES IN ENERGY. [Perspect. energy]. (1991)-. Periodical. English. qt. £104.00 UK; $200.00 US. Pion Ltd., 207 Brondesbury Park, London NW2 5JN England. **Tel** 011 44 81 459 0066, FAX 011 44 81 451 6454, telex 94016265 PION G. **ED** A. Sheindlin. **DD** 333.79.
Desc: Scholarly journal of the Moscow International Energy Club which aims to serve as an effective channel of international scientific communication and dissemination of information, reflecting not only the views of experts on energy problems but those of other scientists, politicians, businessmen, writers, artists, religious leaders, and laymen.

UK
PETROCOMPANIES. English. an. £550.00. Petroguide Ltd, 8 Balham Hill, Nightingale Center, London SW12 9EA England. **Tel** (81)673 5611. **ED** Richard Krijgsman. **Bk Rev. Circ:** 150. available on diskette.
Desc: Guide to the financial and operating performance of the international oil industry.

AT
PETROFAX. **See** Petroleum and Natural Gas.

FR/0298-6027
PETROSTRATEGIES ENGLISH ED. (1986)-. Periodical. English. wk (except Aug.). $1375.00. Petrostrategies, 4 rue Boulitte, 75014 Paris France. **Tel** 011 33 1 40446667, FAX 40446672. **ED** Pierre Terzian. **UDC** 531(656). **CODEN** 533(656). **Bk Rev.**
Desc: News and analysis on energy worldwide.

GW
PHILIPPINEN : ENERGIEWIRTSCHAFT. **Main/Corp** Germany (Federal Republic, 1949-). Bundesstelle fur Aussenhandelsinformation. German. DM2.00. Bundesstelle fuer Aussenhandelsinformation, Agrippastr 87 93, D 50676 Cologne Germany. **Tel** 011 49 221 2057316, FAX 011 49 221 2057212. **LC** HD9502.P6.

US/0896-5129
PHOTOVOLTAIC ENERGY. (PHOTOVOLTAIC ENERGY : CURRENT ABSTRACTS / U.S. DEPARTMENT OF ENERGY ; PREPARED FOR OFFICE OF CONSERVATION AND RENEWABLE ENERGY ; PREPARED BY OFFICE OF SCIENTIFIC AND TECHNICAL INFORMATION.). [Photovolt. energy]. **Added/Corp** United States. Dept. of Energy. Office of Scientific and Technical Information. United States. Dept. of Energy. Office of Conservation and Renewable Energy. **VFOAT** PHV. Vol. 88, No. 1 (Jan./Feb. 1988)-. Government Publication. English. bm. $155.00 US; $310.00 other. US Department of Energy, 1000 Independence Avenue SW, Washington DC 20585. **Tel** (202)586-5000, FAX (202)586-4073. **(Subscription address:** National Technical Information Service, 5285 Port Royal Road, Springfield, VA 22161**) DD** 621.

US/0731-4671
PHOTOVOLTAIC INSIDER'S REPORT. Vol. 1, No. 1 (Mar. 1982)-. Periodical. English. Twelve times a year. $127.00 US, Canada, & Mexico; $167.00 others. PV Publishing Company, 1011 West Colorado Boulevard, Dallas TX 75208. **Tel** (214)942-5248. **ED** Richard Curry. **LC** Discard. **[CCC].** Index available. cum. index. **Bk Rev. Circ:** 1,000.
Desc: Newsletter that keeps subscribers updated on progress and commercialization of solar photovoltaic technology worldwide.

US
PLANECON ENERGY REPORT. (19??)-. English. Four times a year. $950.00. PlanEcon Inc., 1111 14th Street Northwest, Suite 801, Washington DC 20005. **Tel** (202)898-0471.
Desc: A review of the energy situation in Eastern Europe and the former Soviet republics. Includes information on energy production, trade, and consumption.

GW
PORTUGAL : ENERGIEWIRTSCHAFT. **Main/Corp** Bundesstelle fur Aussenhandelsinformation (Germany). German. DM2.00. Bundesstelle fuer Aussenhandelsinformation, Agrippastr 87 93, D 50676 Cologne Germany. **Tel** 011 49 221 2057316, FAX 011 49 221 2057212. **LC** HD9502.P8. **DD** 333.7.

US/0190-5597
POST-SUMMER ELECTRIC POWER SURVEY. **Main/Corp** Edison Electric Institute. Electric Power Survey Committee. (1976)-. English. an. $10.00 (members), $8.00 (nonmembers). Edison Electric Institute, 701 Pennsylvania Avenue Northwest, Washington DC 20004. **Tel** (202)508-5607, (202)508-5610, FAX (202)508-5030. **(Subscription address:** Edison Electric Institute, PO Box 2800, Kearneysville WV 25430.**) ED** Carl Tobie. **LC** TK23; .E342a. **Circ:** 400. ***Supersedes in part** Semi-Annual Electric Power Survey, 0190-5589.*
Desc: First actual regional capability, peak load, and percent margin values for the summer just completed. Actual additions and new orders for generating units and scheduled additions as of July.

US/0032-5929
POWER. [Power]. Vol. 33 (Jan. 3, 1911)-. Academic Scholarly Publication. English. mo. $55.00 (one year), $95.00 (two year) US; $60.00 (one year), $110.00 (two year) Canada; $150.00 (one year), $260.00 (two year) other. McGraw Hill Publishing Company, Inc., 1221 Avenue of the Americas, New York NY 10020. **Tel** (212)512-6410, (800)525-5003, FAX (212)512-6111. **(Subscription address:** Power, PO Box 521, Hightstown NJ 08520.**) LC** TJ1; .P7. **DD** 621.042/05. **CODEN** POWEAD. **[CCC]. Ad Acc.** available on microfilm and microfiche from University Microfilms International (UMI). Documents available from Article Express International, Ask*IEEE, CASDDS, Documents on Demand. ***Continues** Power and the Engineer.*
Desc: Created for engineers who design, construct and manage the energy systems in utility central stations, manufacturing and process plants, and for the consultants who serve them. Readers' prime interests: fuels and fuel handling, steam generation, pollution control, plant electric systems, turbines and diesels, instrumentation and control management.
Ind/Abst Abstr. Bull. Inst. Pap. Sci. Tech.; Acad. Search (July 1993-); Acoust. Abstr.; Appl. Sci. Technol. Index; Bioeng. Abstr.; Bus. Index (1985-); Chem. Abstr.; Coal Abstr.; Ei Page One; EMBASE; Energy Inf. Abstr.; Energy Res. Abstr.; Eng. Index Annu.; Environ. Abstr.; Fluid Abstr., Civil Eng.; Fluid Abstr. Proc. Eng.; FLUIDEX (1973-); Gas Abstr.; Gen. BusinessFile (1985-); Gen. Period. Index (1985-); Health Saf. Sci. Abstr.; INSPEC (April 1969-); Int. Aerosp. Abstr.; Lit. Pat. Abstr., Oilfield Chem. (1972-); Lit. Abstr., Catal. Catal.; Lit. Abstr., Health Environ.; Lit. Abstr., Pet. Refin. Petrochem.; Lit. Abstr., Pet. Substit.; Lit. Abstr., Transp. Storage; Mag. Search; Shock Vibr. Dig.; Trade Ind. Index.

US/1071-2445
POWER DELIVERY PRODUCT NEWS. [Power deliv. prod. news]. **VFOAT** PDPN. (1992)-. Periodical. English. Six times a year. $24.00 US; $39.75 other. PennWell Publishing Company, 1421 South Sheridan, PO Box 1260, Tulsa OK 74101. **Tel** (918)835-3161, (800)331-4463, FAX (918)831-9497. **(Subscription address:** Power Delivery Product News, Publishing Services, PO Box 3223, Tulsa OK 74101.**) DD** 621.
Desc: Serves the needs of the total power delivery market, with new product information on transmission, distribution, substations, construction, maintenance and energy management.

US/0738-5676
POWER LINE (WASHINGTON, D.C.), THE. ***Suspended.*** (THE POWER LINE.). [Power line]. **Added/Corp** Environmental Action Foundation. Utility Action Foundation. (197?)-Suspended with Vol. 18. No. 1. Periodical. English. bm. $25.00. Environmental Action, 6930 Carroll Avenue, Suite 600, Takoma Park MD 20912. **Tel** (301)891-1100, FAX (301)891-2218. **ED** Christina Nichols. **Bk Rev. Ad Acc. Circ:** 1,400.
Desc: Provides coverage of electric utility, nuclear power, energy conservation and energy legislation issues.
Ind/Abst Altern. Press Index; Coal Abstr.; Energy Res. Abstr. (July 1979-).

●CN/1192-2354
POWER SMART ANNUAL REPORT. [Pow. Smart annu. rep.]. **Main/Corp** B.C. Hydro. Power Smart. (1991/1992)-. English. **DD** 333.79. ***Continues** B.C. Hydro. Power Smart. Times., 1183-7772.*

US
POWER SOURCE. (19??)-. English. ir (25 issues). $395.00 US and Europe. HCI Publications, 410 Archibald Street, Kansas City MO 64111. **Tel** (816)931-1311. Index available. ***Continues** Purpa Lines, 0886-7178.*

●US/1075-0592
PRIVATE POWER EXECUTIVE. [Priv. power exec.]. Vol. 1, No. 1 (May/June 1993)-. Periodical. English. bm (6 issues). $75.00. Pequot Publishing Inc., PO Box 447, Southport CT 06490. **Tel** (203)259-1812. **LC** IN PROCESS. **DD** 621. ***Continues in part** Cogeneration, 0884-7339.*

FR
PRIX DES ENERGIES. French. sa. Free on Request. Observatoire de l'Energie, 97 99 rue de Grenelle, 75353 Paris Cedex 7 France. **Tel** 011 33 45563284.

US/1075-7961
PROCEEDINGS - ANNUAL PITTSBURGH COAL CONFERENCE. (PROCEEDINGS.). **Added/Corp** University of Pittsburgh. Dept. of Chemical and Petroleum Engineering. Pittsburgh Energy Technology Center. (199?)-. Proceedings. English. an. School of Engineering / University of Pittsburgh, Pittsburgh PA 15261. Documents available from CASDDS. ***Continues** Proceedings ... Annual Pittsburgh Coal Conference, 1075-8313.*
Ind/Abst Chem. Abstr. (?-?).

US/1075-8313
PROCEEDINGS ... ANNUAL PITTSBURGH COAL CONFERENCE. ***Title Change.*** [Proc. - Pittsburgh Coal Conf.]. **Added/Corp** University of Pittsburgh. Dept. of Chemical and Petroleum Engineering. Pittsburgh Energy Technology Center. **VFOAT** Annual Pittsburgh Coal Conference. (1984)-(199?). Academic Scholarly Publication. English. an. **DD** 553. **CODEN** PAPCEE. Documents available from CASDDS. ***Formed by the union of** International Conference on Coal Gasification, Liquefaction and Conversion to Electricity. Proceedings, 0733-8988 **and** Industrial Coal Utilization Symposium. Proceedings. **Continued by** International Pittsburgh Coal Conference. Proceedings, 1075-7961.*
Ind/Abst Chem. Abstr. (?-?).

US/0730-7985
PROCEEDINGS / FRONTIERS OF POWER CONFERENCE. [Proc.- Front. Power Conf.]. **Main/Conf** Frontiers of Power Conference. **Added/Corp** Oklahoma State University. Engineering Energy Laboratory. Oklahoma State University. School of Electrical Engineering. Oklahoma State University. Engineering Extension. Oklahoma State University. School of Electrical and Computer Engineering. (1979)-. Academic Scholarly Publication. English. an (Oct.). $25.00. Engineering Energy Laboratory, Oklahoma State University, 216 Engineering South, Stillwater OK 74078. **Tel** (405)744-5151 or, 9912, FAX (405)744-6187. **ED** R. Ramakumar and Dan Lingelbach. **LC** TJ163.9; .F76a. **DD** 621.042/05. **CODEN** PFCODJ. **Circ:** 150. Documents available from Article Express International, CASDDS. ***Continues** Proceedings - Frontiers of Power Technology Conference, 0161-5319.*
Desc: The primary topics are devoted almost exclusively to the problems associated with large scale electric power generation.
Ind/Abst Chem. Abstr.; Eng. Index Annu.

US
PROCEEDINGS - INTERNATIONAL CONFERENCE ON THE PEACEFUL USES OF ATOMIC ENERGY. **Main/Conf** International Conference on the Peaceful Uses of Atomic Energy. **VFOAT** Peaceful Uses of Atomic Energy. 1st-1955-. Proceedings. English (French, Russian and Spanish; summaries and/or abstracts in Russian and Spanish). UNIPUB, 4611-F Assembly Drive, Lanham MD 20706-4391. **Tel** (800)274-4888, FAX (301)459-0056, telex 28787 GATT CH.

UK
PROCEEDINGS - INTERNATIONAL POWER SOURCES SYMPOSIUM. **See** Engineering-Electricity, Electrical Engineering, Electronics.

US
PROCEEDINGS OF THE ERDA SEMIANNUAL PHOTOVOLTAIC ADVANCED MATERIALS PROGRAM. **Main/Conf** ERDA Semiannual Photoboltaic Advanced Materials Program Review Meeting. Proceedings. English. sa. Energy Research and Development Administration, 20 Massachusetts Avenue Northwest, Washington DC 20545. ***Continues** Proceedings of the ERDA Semiannual Solar Photovoltaic Program Review Meeting.*

US/0146-955X
PROCEEDINGS OF THE ... INTERSOCIETY ENERGY CONVERSION ENGINEERING CONFERENCE. **Main/Conf** Intersociety Energy Conversion Engineering Conference. **Added/Corp** American Nuclear Society. Society of Automotive Engineers. American Chemical Society. American Institute of Aeronautics and Astronautics. **VFOAT** Intersociety Energy Conversion; Energy to the 21st Century. 12th (1977)-. Academic Scholarly Publication. English. ir. $350.00 (nonmembers), $295.00 (members). American Institute of Chemical Engineers, 345 East 47th Street, New York NY 10017. **Tel** (212)705-7663, (212)705-7703, FAX (212)705-8400. **CODEN** PIECDE. **[CCC].** Documents available from Article Express International, CASDDS. ***Continues** Intersociety Energy Conversion Engineering Conference Proceedings.*
Ind/Abst Bioeng. Abstr.; Chem. Abstr.; Coal Abstr.; Ei Page One; Eng. Index Annu.; GeoRef; Lit. Pat. Abstr., Oilfield Chem. (1976-); Lit. Abstr., Catal. Catal.; Lit. Abstr., Health Environ.; Lit. Abstr., Pet. Refin. Petrochem.; Lit. Abstr., Pet. Substit.; Lit. Abstr., Transp. Storage.

US
PROCEEDINGS OF THE ... NATIONAL PASSIVE SOLAR CONFERENCE. **Added/Corp** American Solar Energy Society. **VFOAT** Conference Proceedings. Vol. 9 (Sept. 24-26, 1984)-. Proceedings. English. an. $50.00 members, American Solar Energy Society; $100.00 other. American Solar Energy Society, 2400 Central Avenue, Unit G-1, Boulder CO 80301. **Tel** (303)433-3130, FAX (303)443-3212. **LC** TH7413; .N367a. **DD** 621.47. ***Continues** National Passive Solar Conference. Progress in Passive Solar Energy Systems.*

GW
PRODUZIERENDES GEWERBE. REIHE 4.1.1 : BESCHAFTIGUNG, UMSATZ UND ENERGIEVERSORGUNG DER UNTERNEHMEN UND BETRIEBE IM BERGBAU UND IM VERARBEITENDEN GEWERBE. **See** Economics-Labor.

US
PROGRAM REPORT - ATOMIC INDUSTRIAL FORUM. **Main/Corp** Atomic Industrial Forum. (19??)-. English.
Ind/Abst Energy Inf. Abstr.

UK/0360-1285
PROGRESS IN ENERGY AND COMBUSTION SCIENCE. [Progr. energy combust. sci.]. Vol. 1 (1975)-. Periodical. English. Six times a year. $594.00 The Americas; £398.00 other. Pergamon Press, An Imprint of Elsevier Science Ltd., The Boulevard, Langford Lane, Kidlington, Oxford OX5 1GB United Kingdom. **Tel** 011 44 865 843000, 011 44 865 843699, FAX 011 44 865 843010. **(Subscription address:** Elsevier Science Ltd. Oxford Fulfillment Centre, PO Box 800, Kidlington, Oxford OX5 1DX United Kingdom.**)** **ED** Norman Chigier. **LC** TJ163.9; .P75. **DD** 621. **CODEN** PECSDO. **[CCC]. Pr Rev.** available on microfilm and microfiche from University Microfilms International (UMI). Documents available from Article Express International, The Genuine Article, CASDDS, Documents on Demand.
Ind/Abst AESIS Q.; Appl. Mech. Rev.; Bioeng. Abstr.; Chem. Abstr.; Coal Abstr.; Curr. Contents Eng. Tech. Appl. Sci.; Ei Page One; EMBASE; Energy Inf. Abstr.; Energy Res. Abstr. (May 1977-); Eng. Index Annu.; Environ. Abstr.; Environ. Period. Bibliogr.; Gas Abstr.; HTFS Dig.; Index Sci. Rev. [Full Cov.]; Int. Aerosp. Abstr. (1984-); Lit. Pat. Abstr., Oilfield Chem. (1977-); Lit. Abstr., Catal. Catal.; Lit. Abstr., Health Environ.; Lit. Abstr., Pet. Refin. Petrochem.; Lit. Abstr., Pet. Substit.; Lit. Abstr., Transp. Storage; Res. Alert [Full Cov.]; Sci. Cit. Index; SCISEARCH.

US
PUBLICATIONS AND STAFF REPORTS LISTING - OFFICE OF CONGRESSIONAL AND PUBLIC AFFAIRS, FEDERAL ENERGY REGULATORY COMMISSION. **Main/Corp** United States. Federal Energy Regulatory Commission. Office of Congressional and Public Affairs. **VFOAT** Federal Energy Regulatory Commission Publications and Staff Reports List. 1979-. Government Publication. English. tw. US Department of Energy, 1000 Independence Avenue SW, Washington DC 20585. **Tel** (202)586-5000, FAX (202)586-4073.

CN/0711-9917
PUBLICATIONS CATALOGUE - ATOMIC ENERGY CONTROL BOARD. (PUBLICATIONS CATALOGUE.). [Publ. cat. - At. Energy Control Board]. **Main/Corp** Canada. Atomic Energy Control Board. **VFOAT** Catalogue des Publications. **VAT** Catalogue des Publications - Commission de Controle de l'Energie Atomique. English (French). an (with quartley supplements). Free. Atomic Energy Control Board, 270 Albert Street, PO Box 1046, Ottawa Ontario K1P 5S9 Canada. **Tel** (613)996-8211, FAX (613)995-5086, telex 053-3771. **DD** 016.33379/24. **Circ:** 600.
Desc: Lists all publications produced in past five years: technical reports, papers, and speeches, regulatory regulatory documents, news releases, notices, information bulletins and miscellaneous, e.g. annual report.

US
PUBLISHED SEARCH BIBLIOGRAPHIES FROM THE NTIS BIBLIOGRAPHIC DATA BASE. ENERGY / U.S. DEPARTMENT OF COMMERCE, NATIONAL TECHNICAL INFORMATION SERVICE. **See** Energy-Abstracting, Bibliographies and Statistics.

US/0886-7178
PURPA LINES. ***Title Change.*** (PURPA LINES : ALTERNATIVE ENERGY BUSINESS NEWS.). [PURPA lines]. **Added/Corp** Hydro Consultants, Inc. (1985)-(19??). Periodical. English. bw. HCI Publications, 410 Archibald Street, Kansas City MO 64111. **Tel** (816)931-1311. **ED** Carl Vansant. **DD** 343. ***Continued by*** *Power Source, 1072-9569.*
Desc: Covers US independent power business news including cogeneration, waste-to-energy, biomass and other independent power projects. Coverage includes the latest business and regulatory news on a national and regional basis.

US/0739-4829
PV NEWS. (PV NEWS : PHOTOVOLTAIC NEWS.). [PV news]. **Added/Corp** PV Energy Systems, Inc. **VFOAT** P.V. News; Photovoltaic News. (Aug. 1981)-. Periodical. English. mo. $100.00 (one year), $170.00 (two year), $220.00 (three year) US; $120.00 (one year), $210.00 (two year), $280.00 (three year) other. Photovoltaic Energy Systems Inc, PO Box 290, Casanova VA 22017. **Tel** (703)788-9626, FAX (703)788-9626. **ED** Paul D Maycock. Index available. cum. index. **Bk Rev. Circ:** 1,000.
Desc: International newsletter on photovoltaic energy (making electricity from sun light). Covers all industry news, markets, products, economics, government programs, key people, and annual market survey.

GW
QATAR : ENERGIEWIRTSCHAFT. **Main/Corp** Bundesstelle fur Aussenhandelsinformation (Germany). German. DM2.00. Bundesstelle fuer Aussenhandelsinformation, Agrippastr 87 93, D 50676 Cologne Germany. **Tel** 011 49 221 2057316, FAX 011 49 221 2057212. **LC** HD9502.Q2.

US/0736-4598
QUARTERLY COAL REPORT (WASHINGTON, D.C.). (QUARTERLY COAL REPORT / ENERGY INFORMATION ADMINISTRATION, OFFICE OF COAL, NUCLEAR, ELECTRIC, AND ALTERNATE FUELS, U.S. DEPARTMENT OF ENERGY.). [Q. coal rep.]. **Added/Corp** United States. Office of Coal, Nuclear, Electric, and Alternate Fuels. (Jan/March 1982)-. Academic Scholarly Publication. English. Four times a year. $26.00 US; $32.50 other. National Energy Information Center, Energy Information Administration, Forrestal Building, Room 1F-048, Washington DC 20585. **Tel** (202)586-8800. **DD** 338. **CODEN** QCREDK. Documents available from CASDDS. ***Continues*** *Coke Plant Report, 0730-7543;* ***Absorbed in part*** *Coal Distribution, 0737-4399.*
Desc: Written for a wide audience, including Congress, federal and state agencies, the coal industry, and the general public. The quarterly report provides comprehensive information about coal production, exports, imports, receipts, consumption and stocks in the United States.
Ind/Abst Chem. Abstr. (1982-1984); F&S Index Plus Text, Int. [Select. Cov.]; Predicasts Forecasts.

FR
QUARTERLY ENERGY BALANCE. French. Four times a year. $1,745.00 (magnetic tape). OECD Publications and Information Center, 2 rue Andre-Pascal, 75775 Paris Cedex 16 France. **Tel** 011 33 1 45248167, US:(202)785-6323, FAX 011 33 1 45248500 OR 45248176, telex 620 160 OCDE. **(Subscription address:** OECD Publications Center, 2001 L Street, Suite 700, Washington DC 20036.**)**

US
QUARTERLY REPORT OF FOREIGN AND DOMESTIC DEVELOPMENTS AFFECTING ENERGY. English. qt. Energy Research and Development Administration, 20 Massachusetts Avenue Northwest, Washington DC 20545.

CN
QUARTERLY REPORT ON ENERGY RELATED SOFTWARE IN CALGARY. **See** Computers-Software.

CN/0702-0465
QUARTERLY REPORT ON ENERGY SUPPLY-DEMAND IN CANADA. (QUARTERLY REPORT ON ENERGY SUPPLY-DEMAND IN CANADA / STATISTICS CANADA, MANUFACTURING AND PRIMARY INDUSTRIES DIVISION.). [Q. rep. energy supply-demand Can.]. **Added/Corp** Statistics Canada. Manufacturing and Primary Industries Division. Statistics Canada. Industry Division. Statistics Canada. Energy Section. **VFOAT** Bulletin Trimestriel- Disponibilite et Ecoulement d'Energie au Canada. Vol. 1, No. 1 (1976)-. English (French). qt. 136.00Can$ Canada; $164.00 US; $191.00 other. Statistics Canada, Publications Sales & Services, Main Building Room 1710, Ottawa Ontario K1A 0T6 Canada. **Tel** (613)951-5078, (800)267-6677, FAX (613)951-1584, telex 053-3585. **LC** TJ163.25.C3; Q37. **DD** 363.6/2/0971021. ***Absorbed*** *Detailed Energy Supply and Demand in Canada.*
Desc: Energy balance sheets in natural units and heat equivalents in primary and secondary forms, by province, each showing data on production, trade, interprovincial movements, conversion and consumption by sectors. Analytical tables and details on non-energy products are shown.

PH
QUARTERLY REVIEW / BUREAU OF ENERGY UTILIZATION. **Main/Corp** Philippines. Bureau of Energy Utilization. (19??)-. Periodical. English. qt. Bureau of Energy Utilization, Manila, Philippines. **LC** HD9502.P6; P45a. **DD** 333.79/09599.
Ind/Abst Philip. Sci. Technol. Abstr.

US/8756-9655
QUARTERLY REVIEW OF METHANE FROM COAL SEAMS TECHNOLOGY. **See** Earth Sciences-Geology.

US
QUARTERLY TRACKING SYSTEM, ENERGY USING AND CONSERVATION EQUIPMENT IN HOMES. **Main/Corp** United States. Energy Information Administration. Office of Applied Analysis. July 1978-. Government Publication. English. qt. US Department of Energy, 1000 Independence Avenue SW, Washington DC 20585. **Tel** (202)586-5000, FAX (202)586-4073.

CC/0253-2409
RANLIAO HUAXUE XUEBAO. **See** Chemistry.

LU
RAPID REPORTS. ENERGY AND INDUSTRY / EUROSTAT. **Added/Corp** Statistical Office of the European Communities. **VFOAT** Energy and Industry. (1989)-. Periodical. English. ir. ECU 206.00 (complete set). Office for Official Publications of the European Communities, 2 Rue Mercier, 2985 Luxembourg Luxembourg. **Tel** 011 352 499281, FAX 011 352 488573. ***Continues*** *Rapid Reports. Energy.*

CN
RAPPORT ANNUEL - ENERGIE QUEBEC. **Main/Corp** Quebec (Province). Direction Generale de l'Energie. French. an. Editeur Officiel du Quebec, 1283 Boul Charest Ouest, Quebec Quebec G1N 2C9 Canada. **LC** HD9502.C33; Q442A. **DD** 354.7140082/3.

FR
RAPPORT ANNUEL SUR L'ENERGIE: RECHERCHE, DEVELOPPEMENT ET DEMONSTRATION. **Main/Corp** International Energy Agency. (1978)-. French. OECD Publications and Information Center, 2 rue Andre-Pascal, 75775 Paris Cedex 16 France. **Tel** 011 33 1 45248167, US:(202)785-6323, FAX 011 33 1 45248500 OR 45248176, telex 620 160 OCDE. **(Subscription address:** OECD Publications Center, 2001 L Street Northwest, Suite 700, Washington, DC 20036; telephone: (202)785-6323**)** **LC** TJ163.13; .I57b. **DD** 333.79/05.

GW/0936-5893
RDE. RECHT DER ELEKTRIZITATSWIRTSCHAFT. [RdE, Recht Elektr.wirtsch.]. **VFOAT** Recht der Elektrizitatswirtschaft (1989). (1989)-. Trade Publication. German. bm (6 issues). DM138.00. Carl Heymanns Verlag KG, Luxemburger Strasse 449, D 50939 Cologne Germany. **Tel** 011 49 221 460100, telex 8 881 888. **UDC** 34. ***Continues*** *Recht der Elektrizitatswirtschaft, 0171-712X.*

US/0895-5700
RE NEWS DIGEST. ***Ceased.*** [Re news dig.]. **VFOAT** Renewable Energy News Digest; RE News. Vol. 1, No. 3 (March 1987)-(19??). Periodical. English. mo. Sunwords, 14 South Church Street, Schenectady NY 12305. **Tel** (518) 372-1799. **ED** Sandra Oddo. **DD** 351. **Circ:** 500.
Desc: Digest of news pertinent to renewable energy - sun, wind, hydro, geothermal, photovoltaics. Of interest to solar professionals, government offices and interested individuals.

GW/0171-712X
RECHT DER ELEKTRIZITATSWIRTSCHAFT. ***Title Change.*** [Recht Elektr.wirtsch.]. **Added/Corp** Vereinigung Deutscher Elektrizitatswerke. (1979)-(1993). Periodical. German. mo. Verlags und Wirtschaftsgesellschaft der Elektricitatswerke mbh, VWEW, M Stresemannallee 23, W-6000 Frankfurt 70 Germany. **Tel** 069 63 04-1, FAX 069 6 30 43 59, telex 4 11 284 VDEW. **LC** KK6852.A13; R4. **DD** 343.43/0929; 344.303929. **[CCC].** ***Continued by*** *R D E - Recht der Energiewirtschaft.*
Ind/Abst Coal Abstr.; Energy Res. Abstr. (Dec. 1979-).

●CN/1193-1442
REGULATORY TIMES, THE. [Regul. times]. **Added/Corp** C.O. Nickle Publications. Southam Communications. **VFOAT** Nickle's the Regulatory Times; Nickle's Regulatory Times. Vol. 1, No. 1 (Jan. 29, 1992)-. Periodical. English. bw. 578.00Can$. C.O. Nickle Publications, 999 8th Street Southwest, Suite 300, Calgary, Alberta T2R 1N7 Canada. **Tel** (403)244-6111. **DD** 343.7109.
Desc: Dedicated to regulatory issues affecting the energy industry.

UK/0960-1481
RENEWABLE ENERGY. [Renew. energy]. **Added/Corp** Unesco. International Centre for Theoretical Physics. Federation of Arab Councils of Scientific Research. Vol. 1, No. 1 (1991)-. Periodical. English. Eight times a year. $529.00 The Americas; £355.00 other. Pergamon Press, An Imprint of Elsevier Science Ltd., The Boulevard, Langford Lane, Kidlington, Oxford OX5 1GB United Kingdom. **Tel** 011 44 865 843000, 011 44 865 843699, FAX 011 44 865 843010. **(Subscription address:** Elsevier Science Ltd. Oxford Fulfillment Centre, PO Box 800, Kidlington, Oxford OX5 1DX United Kingdom.**)** **ED** A. A. Sayigh. **LC** TJ809; .S6. **DD** 621.042. **CODEN** RNENE3. **[CCC].** available on microfilm and microfiche from University Microfilms International (UMI). Documents available from Article Express International, Ask*IEEE. ***Continues*** *Solar & Wind Technology, 0741-983X.*
Ind/Abst Energy Inf. Abstr.; Eng. Index Annu.; Environ. Period. Bibliogr.; Fluid Abstr., Civil Eng.; Fluid Abstr. Proc. Eng.; FLUIDEX (19??-); INSPEC (1991-).

UK/0306-364X
RENEWABLE ENERGY BULLETIN. Vol. 1-6 (Jan./Mar. 1974)-. Bulletin. English. bm. £192.00 UK and Europe; £203.00 other. Multi Science Publishing Company Ltd., 107 High Street, Brentwood, Essex CM14 4RX England. **Tel** 011 44 277 224632, FAX 011 44 277 223453, telex 89-8452. **LC** Z5853.P83; R46. **DD**

Energy

016.3337. **[CCC]**. **Bk Rev**.
 Desc: Brings together information on the non-fossil sources of energy. Summarizes and classifies contributions yearly from periodicals and conference proceedings; book notices and items of interest from the lay and technical press are also published.
 Ind/Abst Energy Inf. Abstr.

CN/0827-2093
RENEWABLE ENERGY NEWS (CANADIAN ED.). (RENEWABLE ENERGY NEWS.). [Renew. energy news]. **VFOAT** ENFOR. Vol. 6, No. 6 (Sept. 1983)-. Periodical. English. mo. 28.00Can$. Renewable Energy News Canadian Edition, 58 Arthur Street, Ottawa Ontario K1R 7B9 Canada. **ED** Wendy L. Peters. **DD** 333.79/0971. *Continues in part* Renewable Energy News, 0714-8615.

US/0714-8615
RENEWABLE ENERGY NEWS NORTHEAST. **VFOAT** REN Northeast. Mar. 1983-. Periodical. English. mo. $60.00. Cren Publishing Company, M Geary, PO Box 408, Ashfield MA 01330. **Tel** (603)827-3347. *Continues in part* New Roots (1981).
 Ind/Abst Energy Res. Abstr. (March 1983-).

IE/0790-0619
RENEWABLE SOURCES OF ENERGY.
VFOAT Renewable Sources of Energy. Vol. 1, No. 1 (April 1983)-. Periodical. English. qt. Tycooly International Publishing, 6 Crofton Terrace, Dun Laoghaire Dublin Ireland. **ED** E. Hinnawi.
 Ind/Abst Ei Page One.

FR
REPERTOIRE DES CENTRES D'INFORMATION SUR L'ENERGIE DANS LE MONDE. French. ir. 350.00F. Institut Francaise de l'Energie, 3 Rue Henri Heine, 75016 Paris France. **Tel** 011 33 1 45244614.

US
REPORT OF REGISTRATIONS. **Added/Corp** Pennsylvania. Bureau of Motor Vehicles and Licensing. **VFOAT** Report of Registration by Type Vehicle by County. (1983)-. Periodical. English (German). mo. 20,500F. International Coal Letter, Rue Capouillet 19 21 Box 1, 1060 Brussels Belgium. **Tel** 011 32 2 536 86 11. **ED** Peter E Doerell 2/536 86 82, 2/657 98 75. **LC** HE5633.P4; B73. **DD** 353.97480087/834. *Continues Breakdown of Registration by Type Vehicle by County.*
 Desc: Energy newsletter on coal and general energy policy, coal and other energy market developments, coal and environment.

US
REPORT OF THE JOINT ENERGY COMMITTEE. **Main/Corp** Vermont. General Assembly. Joint Energy Committee. English. **LC** KFV286; .A243. **DD** 328.743/07658. *Continues* Annual Report of the Joint Energy Committee, 0734-8886.

US/0272-4774
REPORT ORO. (ORO / UNITED STATES ATOMIC ENERGY COMMISSION.). [Rep. ORO]. **Added/Corp** U.S. Atomic Energy Commission. United States. Energy Research and Development Administration. United States. Dept. of Energy. United States. Dept. of Energy. Division of Geothermal Energy. **VFOAT** Fossil Energy. **VAT** Oak Ridge Operations. (194?)-. Periodical. English. National Technical Information Service - NTIS, Room 2027S, 5285 Port Royal Road, Springfield VA 22161. **Tel** (703)487-4630, (703)487-4660, (703)487-4650, FAX (703)321-8547, telex 89-9405. **CODEN** ROROD9. available on microfiche. Documents available from CASDDS.
 Ind/Abst Chem. Abstr.

CN/0527-8503
REPORT - ROYAL COMMISSION ON ENERGY (OTTAWA). (REPORT - ROYAL COMMISSION ON ENERGY.). **Main/Corp** Canada. Royal Commission on Energy. **VFOAT** Royal Commission on Energy. Report. 1st (Oct. 1958)-. Periodical. English. Queens Printer Publications Branch, Ottawa Ontario Canada. **LC** HD9554.C29; A46. **DD** 338.9; 338.272.

US/0361-6126
REPORT TO CONGRESS ON THE ECONOMIC IMPACT OF ENERGY ACTIONS. *Ceased.* **Main/Corp** United States. Dept. of Energy. Office of Analytical Services. (1978)-(19??). English. sa. National Technical Information Service - NTIS, Room 2027S, 5285 Port Royal Road, Springfield VA 22161. **Tel** (703)487-4630, (703)487-4660, (703)487-4650, FAX (703)321-8547, telex 89-9405. **LC** HD9581.U49; U54a. **DD** 333.7. *Continues* Report to the Congress on the Economic Impact of Energy Actions, 0361-6126.

UK/0141-9676
REPORT - WATT COMMITTEE ON ENERGY. (REPORT.). [Rep. - Watt Comm. Energy]. **VFOAT** Watt Committee Report. (1977)-. Academic Scholarly Publication. English. Documents available from CASDDS.
 Ind/Abst Chem. Abstr.

GW
REPUBLIK KOREA : ENERGIEWIRTSCHAFT. **Main/Corp** Bundesstelle fur Aussenhandelsinformation (Germany). German. DM2.00. Bundesstelle fuer Aussenhandelsinformation, Agrippastr 87 93, D 50676 Cologne Germany. **Tel** 011 49 221 2057316, FAX 011 49 221 2057212. **LC** HD9502.K8.

GW
REPUBLIK SUDAFRIKA : ENERGIEWIRTSCHAFT. **Main/Corp** Bundesstelle fur Aussenhandelsinformation (Germany). German. DM2.00. Bundesstelle fuer Aussenhandelsinformation, Agrippastr 87 93, D 50676 Cologne Germany. **Tel** 011 49 221 2057316, FAX 011 49 221 2057212. **LC** HD9502.S55. **DD** 33.7.

TH
RERIC HOLDINGS LIST : / AN OCCASIONAL PUBLICATION OF RERIC.
Main/Corp Renewable Energy Resources Information Center (Thailand). **VFOAT** Holdings List. **VAT** Renewable Energy Resources Information Center Holdings List. 1st Edition (1982)-. English. an. $75.00 (individuals), $120.00 (institutions) US, Canada, Europe, Australia, Japan, New Zealand and the Middle East; $45.00 (individuals), $70.00 (institutions) other Comes with Regional Energy Resources Information Center membership. Asian Institute of Technology / Regional Energy Resources Information Center / RERIC, PO Box 2754, 10501 Bangkok, Thailand. **Tel** 011 66 2 516-0110-29, 011 66 2 516-0130-44, FAX 011 66 2 516-2126. **ED** H. A. Vespry, R. H. B. Exell and On-Anong Suraniranat. **LC** Z5853.P8; R46a; TJ808. **DD** 016.33379. Index available. **Bk Rev**. **Ad Acc. Circ:** 600 (ctrl).
 Desc: Publications on energy and renewable energy resources available at the Asian Institute of Technology Library and Regional Documentation Center.

TH
RERIC INTERNATIONAL ENERGY JOURNAL. **Added/Corp** Regional Energy Resources Information Center (Thailand). **VAT** Regional Energy Resources Information Center International Energy Journal. Vol. 10, No. 1 (June 1988)-. Periodical. English. Twice a year. $120.00 (institutions), $75.00 (individuals) US; $70.00 (institutions), $45.00 (individuals) other. Asian Institute of Technology / Regional Energy Resources Information Center / RERIC, PO Box 2754, 10501 Bangkok, Thailand. **Tel** 011 66 2 516-0110-29, 011 66 2 516-0130-44, FAX 011 66 2 516-2126. Documents available from Article Express International, Documents on Demand. *Continues* Renewable Energy Review Journal.
 Ind/Abst Abstr. AIT Rep. Publ. Energy; Energy Inf. Abstr.; Eng. Index Annu.; Environ. Abstr.; Environ. Period. Bibliogr.; SEA Abstr.

TH
RERIC NEWS. **Main/Corp** Renewable Energy Resources Information Center. Vol. 1 (Oct. 1978)-. Periodical. English. Asian Institute of Technology / Regional Energy Resources Information Center / RERIC, PO Box 2754, 10501 Bangkok, Thailand. **Tel** 011 66 2 516-0110-29, 011 66 2 516-0130-44, FAX 011 66 2 516-2126. Documents available from Documents on Demand.
 Ind/Abst Abstr. AIT Rep. Publ. Energy; Energy Inf. Abstr.; Environ. Abstr.

JA/0386-0752
RESEARCH ACTIVITIES OF THE INSTITUTE OF ATOMIC ENERGY, KYOTO UNIVERSITY. Began with Mar. 1972 Issue. Periodical. English. an. Kyoto University / Faculty of Science, Yoshida Honmachi Sakyo Ku, Kyotoshi Kyotofu 606 Japan. **Tel** (075)751-2111, telex 5422693 LIBKYU J. **LC** TA1; .K93. **DD** 621.48/05. *Continues* Kyoto Daigaku. Kogaku Kenkyujo. Research Activities.

CN/0825-0162
RESEARCH REPORT / ATOMIC ENERGY CONTROL BOARD. [Res. rep. - At. Energy Control Board]. **Added/Corp** Atomic Energy Control Board. (19??)-. Monographic series. English. Atomic Energy Control Board, 270 Albert Street, PO Box 1046, Ottawa Ontario K1P 5S9 Canada. **Tel** (613)996-8211, FAX (613)995-5086, telex 053-3771. **CODEN** RRABE9. Documents available from CASDDS. *Formed by the union of* Report (Atomic Energy Control Board), 0714-0207 *and* Rapport (Commission de Controle de l'Energie, 0715-8645.
 Ind/Abst Chem. Abstr.

FR
RESEAUX DE CHALEUR FRANCAIS.
French. an. Free. Observatoire de l'Energie, 97 99 rue de Grenelle, 75353 Paris Cedex 7 France. **Tel** 011 33 45563284.

FR/0993-3522
RESEAUX ET CHALEUR (ORLEANS).
Ceased. (RESEAUX ET CHALEUR.). **Added/Corp** International Reseaux de Chaleur et de la Geothermie. (19??)-No. 2 (1993). Periodical. English (summaries and/or abstracts in English). qt. Agence Fran Maitrise Energie, BP 20, 78611 Perray En Yvelins France. **Tel** 011 33 1 38643161. *Continues* Geothermie Actualites, 0755-6365.

CN/0380-4275
RESERVES OF COAL, PROVINCE OF ALBERTA. [Reserves coal, Prov. Alta.]. **Main/Corp** Alberta. Energy Resources Conservation Board. (1972)-. English. an. 110.00Can$. Energy Resources Conservation Board, 640 Fifth Avenue Southwest, Calgary Alberta T2P 3G4 Canada. **Tel** (403)297-8311, (403)297-8190, telex 03-821717. **LC** TN873.C22; A442 subser; TN806.C3A6. **DD** 333.7 S; 553/.2/09713.
 Desc: Designates coal fields and coal deposits in Alberta; contains detailed tabulation by fields and deposits of established reserves, and of reserves within mine permit boundaries.
 Ind/Abst GeoRef.

US
RESIDENTIAL ENERGY CONSUMPTION SURVEY [COMPUTER FILE] / ENERGY INFORMATION ADMINISTRATION, OFFICE OF ENERGY MARKETS AND END USE, ENERGY END USE DIVISION. **Added/Corp** United States. Office of Energy Markets and End Use. Energy End Use Division. **VFOAT** Res. Energy Consumption Survey; Residential Buildings Energy Consumption Survey (dBase Version). (1987)-. Government Publication. English. te. US Department of Energy, 1000 Independence Avenue SW, Washington DC 20585. **Tel** (202)586-5000, FAX (202)586-4073. **LC** HD7293.A1; R474.
 Desc: Contains data concerning residential building characteristics, annualized fuel consumption and expenditures and end-use estimates for space heating, air conditioning, water heating, and appliances. Intended for use in conjunction with: Residential Energy Consumption Survey. Housing Characteristics; Housing Energy Consumption and Expenditures. Part 1, National Data; and: Housing Energy Consumption and Expenditures. Part 2, Regional Data. System requirements: IBM PC or compatible; database management program; high density 1.2MB disk drive(s) and hard disk. Also available in ASCII format.

US
RESIDENTIAL ENERGY CONSUMPTION SURVEY [COMPUTER FILE] / ENERGY INFORMATION ADMINISTRATION, OFFICE OF ENERGY MARKETS AND END USE, ENERGY END USE DIVISION. **Added/Corp** United States. Office of Energy Markets and End Use. Energy End Use Division. **VFOAT** Res. Energy Consumption Survey; Residential Buildings Energy Consumption Survey (ASCII Version). (1987)-. Government Publication. English. te. US Department of Energy, 1000 Independence Avenue SW, Washington DC 20585. **Tel** (202)586-5000, FAX (202)586-4073.
 Desc: Contains data concerning residential building characteristics, annualized fuel consumption and expenditures and end-use estimates for space heating, air conditioning, water heating, and appliances. System requirements: IBM PC or compatible; database management program; high density (1.2MB) disk drive(s); hard disk. Also in dBase format.

●NE/0928-7655
RESOURCE AND ENERGY ECONOMICS. Vol. 15, No. 1 (Mar. 1993)-. Academic Scholarly Publication. English. qt (1 volume). Fl530.00. Elsevier Science Publishers BV, PO Box 211, 1000 AE Amsterdam Netherlands. **Tel** 011 31 20 5803642, FAX 011 31 20 5862696, telex 15682. **LC** HD9502.A1; R43. **CODEN** REEEEF. *Continues* Resources and Energy, 0165-0572.
 Ind/Abst Soc. Sci. Cit. Index [Select. Cov.].

US/0748-7231
RESOURCE DIRECTORY OF DOE INFORMATION ORGANIZATIONS. [Resour. dir DOE inf. organ.]. **Main/Corp** United States. Dept. of Energy. Technical Information Center. **VFOAT** Resource Directory of D.O.E. Information Organizations. **VAT** Resource Directory of Department of Energy Information Organizations. Jan. 1982-. Directory. English. ir. US Department of Energy Office of Scientific & Technical Information, PO Box 62, Oak Ridge TN 37831. **Tel** (615)576-1302. **(Subscription address:** National Technical Information Service, US Department of Commerce, Springfield, VA 22161) **LC** HD9502.U52; U5125A. **DD** 026/.33379/02573. *Continues* Directory of Librarians and Information Specialists in DOE and its Contractor Organizations.

US
RESULTS FROM THE WIND PROJECT PERFORMANCE REPORTING SYSTEM.
Added/Corp California Energy Commission. **VFOAT** Wind Project Performance Reporting System. 1st Quarter (Dec. 1985)-. English. ir. Free on request. California Energy Commission, 1516 9th Street, Sacramento CA 95814. **Tel** (916)324-3014.

AU
REVIEW / QUEENSLAND ENERGY ADVISORY COUNCIL. **Added/Corp** Queensland Energy Advisory Council. (1985)-. English. an. Free

(qualified). Secretariat Queensland Energy Advisory Council, Queensland Department of Mines, GPO Box 194, Brisbane 4001 Australia. **Tel** +61 7 224 2191, +61 8 229 7770, telex AA43040. **LC** TJ163.25.A8; A55. **Circ:** 1,000. ***Continues*** *Annual Review (Queensland Energy Advisory Council).*
Desc: A review of energy reserves, production and use in the state of Queensland.

UK
REVIEW : THE QUARTERLY JOURNAL OF RENEWABLE ENERGY. Issue 1 (Sept. 1987)-. Periodical. English. qt. Department of Trade and Industry, Room 3 3 15 1 Palace Street, London SW1E 5HE England. **Tel** 011 44 71 238 3576, FAX 011 44 71 238 3121, telex 91877 EZEGY G. **LC** WMLC L 83/6946. ***Continues*** *RE News.*

US/8756-5501
REVIEWS OF RENEWABLE ENERGY RESOURCES. [Rev. renew. energy resour.]. Vol. 1-. English. John Wiley & Sons, Inc., 605 Third Avenue, New York NY 10158-0012. **Tel** (212)850-6000, (212)850-6645, FAX (212)850-6088, telex 12-7063. **(Subscription address:** John Wiley & Sons / England, Baffins Lane, Chichester, West Sussex PO19 1UD England.**) LC** TJ807; .R48. **DD** 621.042.

FR/0303-240X
REVUE DE L'ENERGIE. [Rev. energ.]. Vol. 25 (Aug./Sept. 1974)-. Periodical. French. Ten times a year. 925.00F France; 1050.00F other. Les Editions Techniques et Economiques, 3 rue Soufflot, 75005 Paris France. **Tel** 33 1 46341030, FAX 33 1 46345583, telex 260 717 F. **ED** G Epstein. **LC** TJ2; .R43. **DD** 621/.05. **CODEN** REEND7. Index available. cum. index. **Bk Rev**, (Qty: 10). **Ad Acc**, **Adv Mgr:** Epstein. **Circ:** 2,500 (ctrl). Documents available from Article Express International, Ask*IEEE, CASDDS. ***Continues*** *Revue Francaise de l'Energie, 0035-2934.*
Ind/Abst Bioeng. Abstr.; Chem. Abstr.; Coal Abstr.; Ei Page One; Energy Res. Abstr. (Aug./Sept. 1974-); Eng. Index Annu.; F&S Index Plus Text, Int. [Select. Cov.]; Gas Abstr.; Geogr. Abstr. Human Geogr.; GeoRef; INSPEC (Aug./Sept. 1974-); Int. Aerosp. Abstr.; Int. Dev. Abstr.; PAIS Int. Print; PROMT; Saf. Health Work.

FR/0255-0830
REVUE ECONOMIQUE DE L'OCDE (PARIS). (REVUE ECONOMIQUE DE L'OCDE.). [Rev. econ. OCDE Paris]. **VFOAT** Revue Economique de l'Organisation de Cooperation et de Developpement Economiques (Paris). (1983)-. Periodical. French. sa. $48.00. OECD Publications and Information Center, 2 rue Andre-Pascal, 75775 Paris Cedex 16 France. **Tel** 011 33 1 45248167, US:(202)785-6323, FAX 011 33 1 45248500 OR 45248176, telex 620 160 OCDE. **(Subscription address:** OECD Publications Center, 2001 L Street, Suite 700, Washington DC 20036.**) UDC** 330.87 (44). available on magnetic tape.
Desc: Includes extensive statistical information on production, consumption, imports and exports and examines environmental and shipping issues.

BE/0556-7734
REVUE ENERGIE PRIMAIRE. ***Ceased.*** [Rev. energ. prim.]. **VFOAT** Tijdschrift Primaire Energie. Ceased (Jan. 1990). Academic Scholarly Publication. French (English, Dutch and German). qt. Union Revues Techn Belges, CP 165/ Avenue FR Roosevelt 50, 1050 Brussels Belgium. **Tel** 011 32 2 6502674. **LC** TK2931; .R45. **CODEN** RETPAH. Documents available from Ask*IEEE, CASDDS.
Ind/Abst Chem. Abstr.; INSPEC (1979-); Int. Aerosp. Abstr.

FR/0335-5004
REVUE GENERAL NUCLEAIRE. (RGN, REVUE GENERAL NUCLEAIRE.). [Rev. gen. nucl.]. **Added/Corp** Societe Francaise d'Energie Nucleaire. **VFOAT** Revue General Nucleaire. (Jan./Feb. 1976)-. Periodical. French (summaries and/or abstracts in English). Six times a year. 538.69F France; 666.00F EEC countries excpet France; 680.00F other. Revue Generale Electricite SA, 48 rue de la Procession, 75724 Paris Cedex 15 France. **Tel** 011 33 1 44496000. **ED** Francis Sorin. **LC** TK9001; .R354. **DD** 338.4/7/6214805. **CODEN** RGNEE6. **[CCC].** Index available. cum. index. **Bk Rev. Ad Acc. Circ:** 6,500 (ctrl). Documents available from Article Express International, Ask*IEEE. ***Continues*** *Revue Generale Nucleaire, 0335-5004.*
Desc: Civilian nuclear energy under all its aspects; science, developments, economy, industry, health, physics, medicine and environment. International relation and cooperation news about nuclear energy in France.
Ind/Abst Bioeng. Abstr.; Ei Page One; EMBASE; Energy Res. Abstr. (July 1976-); Eng. Index Annu.; Fluid Abstr., Civil Eng.; Fluid Abstr. Proc. Eng.; FLUIDEX (19??-); INSPEC (Jan./Feb. 1976-).

DK/0106-2840
RIS-R. **Added/Corp** Forsgsanlg Ris. **VFOAT** Ris R; Ris [Report]; Ris. No. 391 (Oct. 1979)-. Monographic series. English (Danish). ir. Price varies per volume. RIS National Laboratory, DK4000 Roskilde Denmark. **Tel** 46774677, FAX 46755627, telex 43116. **CODEN** RNLRDF. Documents available from CASDDS, BLDSC. ***Continues*** *Ris Report, 0418-6443.*
Desc: Contains scientific reports on material, the environment, and energy.

US/0730-0891
ROCKY MOUNTAIN ENERGY DIRECTORY. [Rocky Mt. energy dir.]. Directory. English. $22.00. Golden Bell Press, 2403 Champa Street, Denver CO 80205. **Tel** (303)296-1600. **LC** TJ163.165; .R63. **DD** 338.7/621042/02578.

XO/0035-8231
ROPA A UHLIE. **See** Petroleum and Natural Gas.

AO
SADCC ENERGY. **Added/Corp** Southern African Development Coordination Conference. Energy Sector. **VFOAT** SADCC Energy Bulletin. **VAT** Southern African Development Coordination Conference Energy. (19??)-. Periodical. English (Portuguese). Four times a year. $20.00 SADCC countries; $24.00 Africa; $28.00 others. SADCC Energy, PO Box 3217, Luanda Angola. **Tel** 34 14 31, telex 4090. **LC** HD9502.A4999; S24. **DD** 338.79/0968.

II/0971-118X
SAFE ENERGY & ENVIRONMENT. [Safe Energy Environ.]. **VFOAT** Safe Energy and Environment. (1990)-. Periodical. English. qt. $32.00. **(Subscription address:** Prints India, 11 Darya Ganj, New Delhi 110002 India.**) UDC** 620.9.

GW
SAUDI-ARABIEN: ENERGIEWIRTSCHAFT. **Main/Corp** Germany (Federal Republic, 1949-). Bundesstelle fur Aussenhandelsinformation. (19??)-. German. Bundesstelle fuer Aussenhandelsinformation, Agrippastr 87 93, D 50676 Cologne Germany. **Tel** 011 49 221 2057316, FAX 011 49 221 2057212. **LC** HD9502.S33; G47a.

US/0279-2338
SAVING ENERGY. [Sav. energy]. (197?)-. Periodical. English. Twelve times a year. $75.00 (one year); $140.00 (two years); $200.00 (three years). Saving Energy, 5411 - 117th Avenue Southeast, Bellevue WA 98006. **Tel** (206)643-4248, FAX (206)643-4248. **ED** Larry Libbman.
Desc: Energy conservation tips and case studies for business, industry and institutions.

DK/0905-5606
SCAN-ENERGY ENGLISH ED. (SCAN-ENERGY). [Scan-Energy Eng. Ed.]. (1988)- Vol. 6 (1993)-. Periodical. English. Eleven times a year. kr800.00. Scan-Energy APS, Aabenraavej 69, DK 6100 Haderslev Denmark. **Tel** 011 45 1 74535395, FAX 011 45 1 74535396. **DD** 621.042 094 8.

GW
SCHWEIZ : ENERGIEWIRTSCHAFT. **Main/Corp** Bundesstelle fur Aussenhandelsinformation (Germany). German. DM2.00. Bundesstelle fuer Aussenhandelsinformation, Agrippastr 87 93, D 50676 Cologne Germany. **Tel** 011 49 221 2057316, FAX 011 49 221 2057212. **LC** HD9502.S85. **DD** 333.7.

IR
SCIENTIFIC BULLETIN OF THE ATOMIC ENERGY ORGANIZATION OF IRAN. **See** Physics.

US
SECURING CALIFORNIA'S ENERGY FUTURE : ... BIENNIAL REPORT TO THE GOVERNOR AND THE LEGISLATURE / CALIFORNIA ENERGY COMMISSION. **Main/Corp** California Energy Commission. 1983-. English. be. California Energy Commission, 1516 9th Street, Sacramento CA 95814. **Tel** (916)324-3014. ***Continues*** *Energy Tomorrow, Challenges and Opportunities for California, 0732-3131.*

US/0736-0657
SELECTED ATOMIC ENERGY PRODUCTS. (CURRENT INDUSTRIAL REPORTS. MA-38Q, SELECTED ATOMIC ENERGY PRODUCTS.). [Sel. at. energy prod.]. Began in 1965. Government Publication. English. an. $1.25. US Department of Commerce / Bureau of the Census, Data User Services Division, Customer Services, Washington DC 20233-0800. **Tel** (301)763-4100. **(Subscription address:** Superintendent of Documents, US Government Printing Office, Washington DC 20402.**) LC** HD9698.U5; C87. **DD** 380.1/4562148/0973. ***Continues*** *Current Industrial Reports. M38Q, Selected Atomic Energy Products.*
Desc: Presents timely data on the production, inventories, and orders of approximately 5,000 products, which represents 40 percent of all US manufacturing.

SA
SELECTED ENERGY STATISTICS : SOUTH AFRICA. **See** Energy-Abstracting, Bibliographies and Statistics.

US
SEMIANNUAL REPORT / NEW YORK STATE ENERGY RESEARCH AND DEVELOPMENT AUTHORITY. **Main/Corp** New York State Energy Research and Development Authority. 198?. English. sa. ***Continues*** *Report to the Director of the Budget.*

GW
SENEGAL : ENERGIEWIRTSCHAFT. **Main/Corp** Germany (Federal Republic, 1949-). Bundesstelle fur Aussenhandelsinformation. German. DM2.00. Bundesstelle fuer Aussenhandelsinformation, Agrippastr 87 93, D 50676 Cologne Germany. **Tel** 011 49 221 2057316, FAX 011 49 221 2057212. **LC** HD9502.S38.

US/0278-601X
SERI JOURNAL. [SERI j.]. **VFOAT** S.E.R.I. Journal. **VAT** Solar Energy Research Institute Journal. Spring 1981-. Periodical. English. qt. Editor SERI Journal, Public Information Office, Solar Energy Research Institute, 1617 Cole Boulevard, Golden CO 80401. **LC** TJ810; .S46. **DD** 621.47/05.

US/0746-312X
SHEPARD'S FEDERAL ENERGY LAW CITATIONS (QUARTERLY). **See** Law.

CN/0713-6196
SHIPMENTS OF SOLID FUEL BURNING HEATING PRODUCTS. [Shipm. solid fuel burn. heat. prod.]. **Added/Corp** Statistics Canada. **VFOAT** Livraisons des Produits de Chauffage a Combustible Solide. Vol. 1, No. 1 (Mar. 1982)-. Periodical. English (French). qt. 24.00Can$ Canada; $29.00 US; $34.00 other. Statistics Canada, Publications Sales & Services, Main Building Room 1710, Ottawa Ontario K1A 0T6 Canada. **Tel** (613)951-5078, (800)267-6677, FAX (613)951-1584, telex 053-3585. **LC** HD9502.C3; S52. **DD** 381/4569707.
Desc: Provides detailed information on solid fuel burning heating products. Contains quarterly and year-to-date data on the number of units shipped and their value.

JA/0387-1819
SHO ENERUGI. [Sho enerugi]. **VFOAT** Energy Conservation. (1978)-. Academic Scholarly Publication. Japanese (Japanese). Four times a year. $190.00. **(Subscription address:** Maruzen Company Ltd., PO Box 5050, Import & Export Department, Tokyo 100 31 Japan.**) ED** Michitoshi Kono. **LC** TJ163.3; .S48. **CODEN** SHOEDS. **Circ:** 18,000 (ctrl). Documents available from CASDDS.
Desc: This journal reports about information of energy-saving of heat and electricity.
Ind/Abst Chem. Abstr.; Coal Abstr.

JA
SHO-ENERUGI SORAN / SHIGEN ENERUGICHO SHO-ENERUGI TAISAKUKA KANSHU. Japanese. ¥19000. Tsusan Shiryo Chosakai, 5-ban 12-go Fujimicho 2-chome, Chiyoda-ku, Tokyo-to 102 Japan. **LC** TJ163.4.J3; S466 .

US/0743-0604
SHORT-TERM ENERGY OUTLOOK. QUARTERLY PROJECTIONS. (SHORT-TERM ENERGY OUTLOOK. QUARTERLY PROJECTIONS / ENERGY INFORMATION ADMINISTRATION, OFFICE OF ENERGY MARKETS AND END USE, U.S. DEPARTMENT OF ENERGY.). [Short-term energy outlook, Q. project.]. **Added/Corp** United States. Office of Energy Markets and End Use. **VFOAT** Short Term Energy Outlook. Quarterly Projections. (Aug. 1982)-. Periodical. English. qt (Jan., Apr., July, Oct.). $17.00 US; $21.25 other. National Energy Information Center, Energy Information Administration, Forrestal Building, Room 1F-048, Washington DC 20585. **Tel** (202)586-8800. **ED** Diane Whited. **LC** TJ163.25.U6; S45. **DD** 333.79/0973. ***Continues*** *Short-Term Energy Outlook. Volume 1, Quarterly Projections, 0743-0612.*
Desc: Forecasts of energy supply, demand, and prices at the national level, including seasonal patterns and immediate impacts of unforeseen events affecting energy markets.
Ind/Abst Energy Inf. Abstr.; Energy Res. Abstr. (Nov. 1981-); F&S Index Plus Text, Int. [Select. Cov.]; Predicasts Forecasts.

US/0743-0620
SHORT-TERM ENERGY OUTLOOK. VOLUME II, METHODOLOGY. [Short-term energy outlook, II, methodol.]. **Added/Corp** United States. Office of Energy Markets and End Use. **VFOAT** Short Term Energy Outlook. Volume 2, Methodology. (19??)-. Government Publication. English. sa. $18.00. Superintendent of Documents, US Government Printing Office, Washington DC 20402. **Tel** (202)275-3328, FAX (202)786-2377. **LC** TJ163.25.U6; S452. **DD** 333.78/0723. ***Continues in part*** *Short-Term Energy Outlook, 0270-8205.*
Ind/Abst Energy Res. Abstr. (Nov. 1981-).

JA
SHOSHIGEN/SHOENERUGI GIJUTSU KOGAI BOSHI GIJUTSU RISUTO. **See** Environmental Issues-Conservation and Natural Resources.

NE
SIGE ENERGIE BULLETIN. Bulletin. Six times a year. Fl72.00. Sige, Postbus 77, 1200 AB Hilversum Netherlands. **Tel** 035-231940, FAX 035-231240. ctrl circ. **Desc:** Information bulletin of SIGE.

GW
SIMBABWE, ENERGIEWIRTSCHAFT / BUNDESSTELLE FUER AUSSENHANDELSINFROMATION. **Added/Corp** Bundesstelle fËur Aussenhandelsinformation (Germany). (19??)-. German. Bundesstelle fuer Aussenhandelsinformation, Agrippastr 87 93, D 50676 Cologne Germany. **Tel** 011 49 221 2057316, FAX 011 49 221 2057212. **LC** HD9502.Z55; S56. **DD** 333.79/096891.

GW
SINGAPUR : ENERGIEWIRTSCHAFT. **Main/Corp** Bundesstelle fur Aussenhandelsinformation (Germany). German. DM2.00. Bundesstelle fuer Aussenhandelsinformation, Agrippastr 87 93, D 50676 Cologne Germany. **Tel** 011 49 221 2057316, FAX 011 49 221 2057212. **LC** HD9502.S54. **DD** 333.79/095957.

AT/0810-1434
SOFT TECHNOLOGY. [Soft technol.]. (1980)-. Periodical. English. Four times a year (Mar., June, Sept., Dec.). 18.00Aus$ Australia; 28.50Aus$ others. Alternative Technology Association, 247 Flinders Lane, Melbourne Victoria 3000 Australia. **Tel** 011 61 3 6507883, FAX 011 61 3 6504175. **ED** Claire Beaumont. **DD** 600. **Bk Rev**, (Qty: 16-20). **Ad Acc, Adv Mgr:** Jo Wick, **Tel** (03)853 8055. **Circ:** 12,000.
Desc: News of environmentally friendly energy and technology, such as solar, wind, hydro, living with alternative technology, non-toxic cleaning and gardening.

CN/0709-504X
SOL (WINNIPEG). (SOL.). [Sol]. Periodical. English (French). bm (Feb., Apr., Jun., Aug., Oct., Dec.). 40.00Can$ Canada, 45.00Can$ other, 200.00Can$ Corporate (including membership), 400.00Can$ Supporting Corporate (including membership). Solar Energy Society of Canada Inc, PO Box No. 1353, Winnipeg Man R3C 2Z1. **Tel** (613)596-1067, FAX (613)596-1120. **ED** D. Rutherford. **DD** 621.47/06/071. **Bk Rev**, (Qty: 6). **Ad Acc. Circ:** 1,500. ***Absorbed** Solar Report (Ottawa, Ont.), 0827-5009.*
Desc: Magazine on scientific breakthroughs and current political happenings within the renewable energy environment.

US/0272-9776
SOLAR CENSUS. [Solar census]. English. be. $14.95. AATEC Publications, PO Box 7119, Ann Arbor MI 48107. **Tel** (313)995-1470. **LC** TJ810; .S48815. **DD** 621.47/025/73.
Desc: Directory of the photovoltaics field. Alphabetical listing of organizations, giving address, phone number, contact, activity/product descriptions. Cross referenced; contact and name subject and geographical indexes.

US/0197-2022
SOLAR COLLECTOR MANUFACTURING ACTIVITY. **See** Energy-Abstracting, Bibliographies and Statistics.

US/0741-5419
SOLAR ENERGY AND NONFOSSIL FUEL RESEARCH. **See** Agriculture.

US/0148-0871
SOLAR ENERGY & RESEARCH DIRECTORY. **VAT** Solar Energy and Research Directory. Directory. English. Ann Arbor Science Publishers Inc, PO Box 1425, Ann Arbor MA 48106. **LC** TJ810; .S616. **DD** 621.47/025.

US/0149-9238
SOLAR ENERGY HANDBOOK. 1978-. English. $1.95 each issue. Popular Science, 380 Madison Avenue, New York NY 10017. **LC** TJ810; .S624. **DD** 621.47/05.

●NE/0927-0248
SOLAR ENERGY MATERIALS AND SOLAR CELLS : AN INTERNATIONAL JOURNAL DEVOTED TO PHOTOVOLTAIC, PHOTOTHERMAL, AND PHOTOCHEMICAL SOLAR ENERGY CONVERSION. Vol. 25, No. 1 & 2 (Jan. 1992)-. Academic Scholarly Publication. English. Twenty times a year (5 volumes). Fl1900.00. Elsevier Science Publishers BV, PO Box 211, 1000 AE Amsterdam Netherlands. **Tel** 011 31 20 5803642, FAX 011 31 20 5862696, telex 15682. **LC** TJ812.7; .S64. **DD** 621.47/05. **CODEN** SEMCEQSOEMDH. **[CCC].** Documents available from The Genuine Article, CASDDS. ***Formed by the union of** Solar Energy Materials, 0165-1633 **and** Solar Cells, 0379-6787.*
Ind/Abst Chem. Abstr.; Curr. Contents Eng. Tech. Appl. Sci.; Curr. Contents Phys. Chem. Earth Sci.; Energy Inf. Abstr.; Environ. Period. Bibliogr.; Res. Alert [Full Cov.]; Sci. Cit. Index.

US/0038-092X
SOLAR ENERGY (PHOENIX, ARIZ.). (SOLAR ENERGY.). [Sol. energy]. **Added/Corp** Association for Applied Solar Energy. International Solar Energy Society. Vol. 2, No. 1 (Jan. 1958)-. Academic Scholarly Publication. English. mo. $634.00 The Americas; £425.00 other. Pergamon Press, An Imprint of Elsevier Science Ltd., The Boulevard, Langford Lane, Kidlington, Oxford OX5 1GB United Kingdom. **Tel** 011 44 865 843000, 011 44 865 843699, FAX 011 44 865 843010. **(Subscription address:** Elsevier Science Ltd. Oxford Fulfillment Centre, PO Box 800, Kidlington, Oxford OX5 1DX United Kingdom.**)** **ED** J. Duffie. **LC** TJ810; .S6. **DD** 621.47/05. **CODEN** SRENA4. **[CCC].** cum. index. **Pr Rev.** available on microfilm from Microfilms International Marketing Corp.; available on microfilm and microfiche from University Microfilms International (UMI); available on microfiche from the publisher. Documents available from Article Express International, The Genuine Article, BIOSIS Document Express, Ask*IEEE, UMI Article Clearinghouse, CASDDS, Documents on Demand. ***Continues** Journal of Solar Energy, Science, and Engineering.*
Desc: Provides an international forum for workers involved in all aspects of the science and technology of solar energy application, reflecting current research into the sun at work in agriculture, engineering, industry, power and environmental disciplines, with the ultimate aim of making extensive practical use of the knowledge gained.
Ind/Abst Abstr. AIT Rep. Publ. Energy; AGRICOLA [Select. Cov.]; Alum. Ind. Abstr.; Appl. Mech. Rev.; Appl. Sci. Technol. Index; Archit. Period. Index; Bioeng. Abstr.; Biol. Abstr.; Ceram. Abstr.; Chem. Abstr.; Civ. Struct. Eng. Abstr.; Coal Abstr.; Comput. Inf. Syst. Abstr. J. [Full Cov.]; Curr. Aware. Biol. Sci., CABS; Curr. Contents Eng. Tech. Appl. Sci.; Curr. Technol. Index; Ei Page One; Elect. Comm. Abstr.; Energy Inf. Abstr.; Energy Res. Abstr.; Eng. Index Annu.; Environ. Abstr.; Environ. Eng. Abstr.; Environ. Period. Bibliogr.; Expand. Acad. Index (1992-); Fluid Abstr., Civil Eng.; Fluid Abstr. Proc. Eng.; FLUIDEX (-19??); INSPEC (1968-); Int. Aerosp. Abstr.; Int. Build. Serv. Abstr.; Mater. Sci. Eng. Abstr.; Mech. Eng. Abstr.; Meteorol. Geoastrophys. Abstr.; Newsp. Period. Abstr. (1992-); Res. Alert [Full Cov.]; Sci. Cit. Index; SCISEARCH; Soc. Sci. Cit. Index [Select. Cov.].

AT
SOLAR ENERGY PROGRESS IN AUSTRALIA AND NEW ZEALAND. **Added/Corp** International Solar Energy Society. Australian & New Zealand Section. Solar Energy Society. Australian and New Zealand Section. (196?)-(197?). English. an. $7.00. International Solar Energy Society / Australia, PO Box 124, Caulfield East Victoria 3145 Australia. **Tel** 011 61 3 571 7557, FAX 61 3 563 5173, telex AA 154087 CITVIC. **LC** TJ810; .S625. **DD** 621.47/0994.

US/0194-1046
SOLAR, GEOTHERMAL, ELECTRIC AND STORAGE SYSTEMS PROGRAM, SUMMARY DOCUMENT. **Main/Corp** United States. Dept. of Energy. Office of Energy Technology. (1979)-. English. $9.00 each. National Technical Information Service - NTIS, Room 2027S, 5285 Port Royal Road, Springfield VA 22161. **Tel** (703)487-4630, (703)487-4660, (703)487-4650, FAX (703)321-8547, telex 89-9405. **LC** TJ163.25.U6; U528b. **DD** 621.042.

US/0735-6862
SOLAR INDEX. [Sol. index]. 1981-. English. an. $18.00. Solar Index Inc, Box 6933, Denver CO 80206. **LC** Z5853.S63; S65; TJ810. **DD** 016.33379/23.

US/1050-5660
SOLAR INDUSTRY JOURNAL. [Sol. ind. j.]. **Added/Corp** Solar Energy Industries Association. **VFOAT** Solar Energy Journal. Vol. 1, Issue 1 (1990)-. Periodical. English. qt. $25.00. Solar Energy Industry Association, 777 North Capitol Street, Suite 805, Washington DC 20002. **Tel** (202)408-0660. **LC** HD9681.U6; S65. **DD** 333.792/3/097305.
Desc: Descriptions of current solar projects, new products and services, feature articles on primary markets, industry news and announcements.

US
SOLAR LAW : CUMULATIVE SUPPLEMENT / PRESENT AND FUTURE : WITH PROPOSED FORMS. SANDY F. KRAEMER. **See** Law.

US
SOLAR PROBE NEWSLETTER. **Added/Corp** Jet Propulsion Laboratory (U.S.). No. 1 (1990)-. Newsletter. English.

AT/0729-6436
SOLAR PROGRESS. [Solar prog.]. (1980)-. Periodical. English (Multiple languages). Four times a year (Mar., June, Sept., Dec.). 50.00Aus$ Australia & New Zealand; 60.00Aus$ other. International Solar Energy Society / Australia, PO Box 124, Caulfield East Victoria 3145 Australia. **Tel** 011 61 3 571 7557, FAX 61 3 563 5173, telex AA 154087 CITVIC. **(Subscription address:** Bibliotec, GPO Box 4, Canberra ACT 2601 Australia**)** **ED** Trevor Lee (phone: (06)231-7313). **DD** 333.7923. Index available. **Bk Rev**, (Qty: 8). **Ad Acc, Adv Mgr:** T. Lee. **Pr Rev. Circ:** 2,000 (ctrl).

CN/0709-4043
SOLAR TECHNICAL SERIES (OTTAWA). (SOLAR TECHNICAL SERIES.). **Added/Corp** National Research Council Canada. **VAT** National Research Council Solar Technical Series (Ottawa). No. 1 (1978)-. Monographic series. English (French). ir. Price varies per volume. Canada Communication Group Publishers, Order Processing, Ottawa Ontario K1A 0S9 Canada. **Tel** (819)956-4800, (819)956-4802.

US/0741-5249
SOLAR THERMAL ENERGY TECHNOLOGY. [Sol. therm. energy technol.]. **Added/Corp** United States. Dept. of Energy. Technical Information Center. DOE/STT-83/1 (Oct. 30, 1983)-. Government Publication. English. Six times a year. $145.00 US; $290.00 other. US Department of Energy, 1000 Independence Avenue SW, Washington DC 20585. **Tel** (202)586-5000, FAX (202)586-4073. **(Subscription address:** National Technical Information Service, 5285 Port Royal Road, Springfield, VA 22161**)**

US/0146-6909
SOLAR THERMAL ENERGY UTILIZATION. CUMULATIVE VOLUME. (1974)-. English. Global Resources & Associates, University of New Mexico, Albuquerque NM 87131. **Tel** (505)242-2313. **LC** Z5853.P83; S66; TJ810. **DD** 016.62147.

US
SOLAR THERMAL POWER SYSTEMS. PROGRAM SUMMARY. **Main/Corp** United States. Dept. of Energy. Assistant Secretary for Conservation and Solar Energy. Dec. 1979-. English. an. National Technical Information Service - NTIS, Room 2027S, 5285 Port Royal Road, Springfield VA 22161. **Tel** (703)487-4630, (703)487-4660, (703)487-4650, FAX (703)321-8547, telex 89-9405. ***Continues** Solar Thermal Power Systems. Program Summary, 0193-1695.*

US/0888-4048
SOLAR TIMES (MADISON, CONN.). (SOLAR TIMES.). [Sol. times]. V. 1- Sept. 1979-. Periodical. English. mo. Cren Publishing Ltd, Box 4869 Station E, Ottawa Ontario K1S 5B4 Canada. **Tel** (203)245-9680. **DD** 338.

US/1042-0630
SOLAR TODAY. [Solar today]. **Added/Corp** American Solar Energy Society. Vol. 1, No. 1 (Jan./Feb. 1987)-. Periodical. English. Six times a year. $29.00 (one year); $53.00 (two years). American Solar Energy Society, 2400 Central Avenue, Unit G-1, Boulder CO 80301. **Tel** (303)433-3130, FAX (303)443-3212. **ED** Maureen McIntyre. **LC** WMLC 93/3323; TJ809; .S65. **DD** 621. **[CCC]. Bk Rev. Ad Acc, Adv Mgr:** McFadden, **Tel** (303)443-4308. **Circ:** 5,500 (ctrl).
Desc: Keeps scientists, engineers, educators, practicioners, researchers, and consumers current with developments in solar energy related fields.
Ind/Abst AESIS Q.; Energy Inf. Abstr.

US/0734-3949
SOLAR WASHINGTON. [Solar Washington]. **Added/Corp** Citizens for a Solar Washington. Washington Solar Council. (1980)-. Periodical. English. Six times a year. $15.00 (individuals), $30.00 (small business or organization less than 50 members), $50.00 (large business or organization). Citizens for a Solar Washington, 1932 1st Avenue 917, Seattle WA 98101. **Tel** (206)622-4046.

US/0361-5219
SOLID FUEL CHEMISTRY. **See** Chemistry-Chemical Technology.

CN/0229-1959
SOLWEST. (SOLWEST : CHAPTER NEWSLETTER.). [Solwest]. **Added/Corp** Solar Energy Society of Canada. British Columbia Chapter. Solar Energy Society of Canada. Northern Alberta Chapter. (1977)-. Newsletter. English. mo. $8.00. British Columbia Chapter, Solar Energy Society of Canada British Columbia Canada. **DD** 621.47/06/0711. ***Continues** Newsletter (Solar Energy Society. British Columbia Chapter).*

GW/0172-5912
SONNENENERGIE & WARMEPUMPE. [Sonnenenerg. & warmepumpe]. **Added/Corp** Deutsche Gesellschaft fuer Sonnenenergie. Vol. 4, No. 2/3 (March/June 1979)-. Periodical. German. bm. DM72.00. Bielefelder Verlagsanstalt KG, Niederwall 53, D 33602 Bielefeld Germany. **Tel** 011 49 521 595520. ctrl circ. ***Continues** Sonnenenergie.*
Ind/Abst Energy Res. Abstr. (April 1980-)(Apr. 1980-).

SZ/0275-7893
SOVIET TECHNOLOGY REVIEWS. SECTION A, ENERGY REVIEWS. ***Ceased.*** [Sov. technol. rev., Sect. A, Energy rev.]. **VFOAT** Section A. Energy Reviews; Energy Reviews. Vol. 1 (1982)-Vol. 6. English. an. Harwood Academic Publishers, PO Box 90, Reading RG1 8JL England. **Tel** 011 44 734 560080. **(Subscription address:** International Publishers Distributor at one of the following addresses: 820 Town Center Drive, Langhorne, PA 19047; or PO Box 90,

Reading Berkshire RG1 8JL UK; or Kent Ridge PO Box 1180, Singapore 9111, Republic of Singapore) **ED** L. A. Melentiev. **LC** TJ163.25.S68; S67. **DD** 333.79/0947. **[CCC].** Documents available from Ask*IEEE.
Desc: Outlines energy trends in the former Soviet Union and presents the reasons for the fundamental change in the fuel base for electrical power plants in the European regions of the USSR.
Ind/Abst INSPEC.

US/0883-6272
SPACE POWER. [Space power]. Vol. 6, No. 1 (1986)-. Academic Scholarly Publication. English. qt (Mar., June, Sept., Dec.). $144.00 (individuals); $288.00 (institutions). Council on Social and Economic Studies, PO Box 34070, Washington DC 20043. **Tel** (202)371-2700. **ED** Andrew Cutler. **LC** TK1056; .S66. **DD** 629.47/4. **CODEN** SPAPEE. **[CCC].** Index available. **Ad Acc.** available on microfilm and microfiche from University Microfilms International (UMI). Documents available from The Genuine Article, Ask*IEEE, CASDDS. ***Continues*** *Space Solar Power Review, 0191-9067.*
Desc: Publishes both pure and applied research papers on advanced materials science and engineering which relate to the production, deployment and use of structures and power systems in space.
Ind/Abst Chem. Abstr.; Curr. Contents Eng. Tech. Appl. Sci.; Energy Res. Abstr.; INSPEC (1986-); Int. Aerosp. Abstr.; Res. Alert [Select. Cov.].

GW
SPANIEN, ENERGIEWIRTSCHAFT / BUNDESSTELLE FUER AUSSENHANDELSINFORMATION. German. DM3.00. Bundesstelle fuer Aussenhandelsinformation, Agrippastr 87 93, D 50676 Cologne Germany. **Tel** 011 49 221 2057316, FAX 011 49 221 2057212. **LC** HD9502.S66. **DD** 333.79/0946.

UK/0372-4255
SRD REPORT. UNITED KINGDOM ATOMIC ENERGY AUTHORITY, SAFETY AND RELIABILITY DIRECTORATE. **See** Physics.

GW
SRI LANKA : ENERGIEWIRTSCHAFT. **Main/Corp** Bundesstelle fur Aussenhandelsinformation (Germany). German. DM2.00. Bundesstelle fuer Aussenhandelsinformation, Agrippastr 87 93, D 50676 Cologne Germany. **Tel** 011 49 221 2057316, FAX 011 49 221 2057212. **LC** HD9502.S72.

US
STATE ENERGY DATA REPORT / PREPARED BY STATISTICS BRANCH. **Added/Corp** United States. Office of Energy Markets and End Use. Statistics Branch. United States. Energy Information Administration. Energy Statistics Branch. United States. Office of Energy Markets and End Use. (1978)-. English. ir. $33.00. National Energy Information Center, Energy Information Administration, Forrestal Building, Room 1F-048, Washington DC 20585. **Tel** (202)586-8800. **LC** HD9502.U5; S82. **DD** 333.79/13/0973.

US
STATE ENERGY PRICE AND EXPENDITURE REPORT. **Added/Corp** United States. Office of Energy Markets and End Use. **VFOAT** Energy Price and Expenditure Data Report. (1981)-. English. an. $18.00 US and Canada. National Energy Information Center, Energy Information Administration, Forrestal Building, Room 1F-048, Washington DC 20585. **Tel** (202)586-8800. **LC** HD9502.U5; E529. **DD** 333.79/0973. ***Continues*** *Energy Price and Expenditure Data Report ... (State and U.S. Total).*
Desc: Presents energy price and expenditure estimates for the 50 states, the District of Columbia, and the United States for selected years, from 1970 forward.

US
STATE OF TEXAS PLAN FOR ENERGY CRISIS ASSISTANCE PROGRAM (ECAP). **Added/Corp** Texas. Economic Opportunity Division. (1979/80)-. English. an. Texas Department of Community Affairs, PO Box 13166 Capitol Station, Austin TX 78711.

US/0742-8235
STATE-OWNED ENERGY ENTERPRISES. [State-owned energy enterp.]. **VFOAT** State Owned Energy Enterprises. Periodical. English. bm. $525.00. International Review Service, 15 Washington Place, New York NY 10003. **LC** HD9502.A1; S73. **DD** 351.82/3.

US/0273-1916
STATISTICAL REPORT - STATE OF ALASKA, ALASKA OIL AND GAS CONSERVATION COMMISSION. **See** Environmental Issues-Conservation and Natural Resources.

US/1055-9698
STATISTICS ON FUEL USED TO GENERATE ELECTRICITY BY THE ELECTRIC UTILITY INDUSTRY. ***Title Change.*** [Stat. fuel used gener. electr. electr. util. ind.]. **Added/Corp** Edison Electric Institute. Economics and Finance Group. Edison Electric Institute. Finance and Regulation Group. (1983)-. English. an. Edison Electric Institute, 701 Pennsylvania Avenue Northwest, Washington DC 20004. **Tel** (202)508-5607, (202)508-5610, FAX (202)508-5030. **LC** HD9685.U4; S73. **DD** 333.79/32. ***Continues*** *Analysis of Fuel for Electric Generation by the Electric Utility Industry. Fuel Burned Under Boilers and by Internal Combustion Engines, 0422-5775.* ***Continued by*** *Electric Utility Fuel Statistics, 1075-6817.*

IO
STATISTIK ENERGI. **See** Energy-Abstracting, Bibliographies and Statistics.

FR
STATISTIQUE MENSUELLE DE L'ENERGIE / MINISTERE DU DEVELOPPEMENT INDUSTRIEL ET SCIENTIFIQUE, SECRETARIAT GENERAL DE L'ENERGIE ET SERVICE CENTRAL DE LA STATISTIQUE ET DES INFORMATIONS INDUSTRIELLES. **See** Energy-Abstracting, Bibliographies and Statistics.

US/0884-1810
STATUS REPORT ON THE ENERGY-RELATED INVENTIONS PROGRAM. (STATUS REPORT ON THE ENERGY-RELATED INVENTIONS PROGRAM AS OF ... / UNITED STATES DEPARTMENT OF COMMERCE, NATIONAL BUREAU OF STANDARDS.). [Status rep. Energy-Relat. Invent. Program]. **VFOAT** Status Report. English. qt. US Department of Commerce / National Bureau of Standards / Maryland, Gaithersburg MD 20899. **LC** TJ163.6; .S73. **DD** 621.042.

US/1045-3148
STEAM ELECTRIC MARKET ANALYSIS. [Steam electr. mark. anal.]. Began in 1977. Periodical. English. mo. $300.00 US; $350.00 other. NCA, 1130 17th Street NW, Washington DC 20036. **Tel** (202)463-2631. **DD** 338. ***Continues*** *Monthly Steam-Electric Plant Generation and Fuel Consumption Report.*
Desc: A report on coal consumption, stockpiles, fossil generation and percent generation by type of fuel for some 400 major electric power plants capable of burning coal. Generations at all nuclear plants are also shown for the month reported.

US/0090-3884
STEAM-ELECTRIC PLANT FACTORS. (STEAM-ELECTRIC PLANT FACTORS / AN ANNUAL STUDY BY THE DEPARTMENT OF COAL ECONOMICS, NATIONAL COAL ASSOCIATION.). [Steam-electr. plant factors]. **Added/Corp** National Coal Association. Dept. of Coal Economics. National Coal Association. Dept. of Economics and Transportation. National Coal Association. Division of Economics and Statistics. National Coal Association. Economics and Statistics Division. National Coal Association. Economics and Statistical Services. National Coal Association. Economics, Planning, and Foreign Trade. National Coal Association. Transportation and Computer Services. National Coal Association. Publication and Statistical Services. National Coal Association. Statistical Services. National Coal Association. Computer Services. National Coal Association. Economics and Statistics Dept. National Coal Association. Policy and Economic Analysis Dept. **VFOAT** Steam Electric Plant Factors. 7th Edition (1956)-25th Edition (1975)-(1976)-. English. an. $100.00 (non-profit); $125.00 others. National Coal Association, 1130 17th Street Northwest, Washington DC 20036. **Tel** (202)463-2640. **LC** HD9685.U4; N26. **DD** 338.4/3. ***Continues*** *Steam-Electric Plant Fuel Consumption and Costs.*
Desc: Contains detailed data on capacity, fuel consumption, quality and costs of fuel deliveries for essentially the entire steam electric generating system in the US on a plant by plant basis.

US/8750-3204
STRATEGIC PLANNING AND ENERGY MANAGEMENT. ***Title Change.*** [Strateg. plann. energy manage.]. **VFOAT** SP & EM. Vol. 4, No. 1 (Summer 1984)-?. Periodical. English. qt. Fairmont Press, 700 Indian Trail, Lilburn GA 30247. **Tel** (404)925-9388, FAX (404)381-9865. **ED** F William Payne. **LC** HD9502.A1; E5347. **DD** 333.79/05. **CODEN** SPEMEP. **[CCC].** **Bk Rev.** ctrl circ. available on microfilm from University Microfilms International (UMI). ***Continues*** *Energy Economics, Policy, and Management, 0275-7966.* ***Continued by*** *Strategic Planning for Energy and the Environment, 1048-5236.*
Desc: Addressed to managers and professionals responsible for developing and executing strategic plans that will enable businesses, industries and institutions to control their energy future.
Ind/Abst Coal Abstr.

US/1048-5236
STRATEGIC PLANNING FOR ENERGY AND THE ENVIRONMENT. [Strateg. plan. energy environ.]. **Added/Corp** Association of Energy Engineers. Environmental Engineers & Managers Institute. Vol. 9, No. 4 (Spring 1990)-. Periodical. English. qt. $99.00 (1 year), $178.00 (2 year) US and Canada; $125.00 (1 year), $230.00 (2 year) other. Fairmont Press, 700 Indian Trail, Lilburn GA 30247. **Tel** (404)925-9388, FAX (404)381-9865. **LC** HD9502.A1; E5347. **DD** 333.79/05. **CODEN** SEENEJ. **Ad Acc. Circ:** 8,600. available on microfilm and microfiche from University Microfilms International (UMI). Documents available from Article Express International. ***Continues*** *Strategic Planning and Energy Management, 8750-3204.*
Desc: Concentrates on the background, new developments and policy issues which impact corporate planning for energy and environmental concerns. You will learn the latest facts on such topics as CFC recycling and reclamation, ozone depletion, power generation alternatives, global warming, hazardous materials handling, indoor air pollution and approaches to preventing the "sick building" syndrome.
Ind/Abst Coal Abstr.; Ei Page One; Energy Inf. Abstr.; Eng. Index Annu.; Environ. Period. Bibliogr.; PAIS Int. Print.

CN/0709-3713
SUMMARY OF ORDERS AND APPROVALS - ENERGY RESOURCES CONSERVATION BOARD. **Main/Corp** Alberta. Energy Resources Conservation Board. Oct. (1978)-. Periodical. English. mo. Energy Resources Conservation Board, 640 Fifth Avenue Southwest, Calgary Alberta T2P 3G4 Canada. **Tel** (403)297-8311, (403)297-8190, telex 03-821717. ***Continues*** *Alberta. Energy Resources Conservation Board. Orders and Approvals., 0709-3705.*

US
SUMMARY REPORT - FEDERAL WIND ENERGY PROGRAM. **Main/Corp** United States. Energy Research and Development Administration. Federal Wind Energy Program. 1975-. Periodical. English. an. Energy Research and Development Administration, 20 Massachusetts Avenue Northwest, Washington DC 20545.

US
SUMMARY REPORT - SOLAR THERMAL ENERGY CONVERSION PROGRAM. **Main/Corp** United States. Energy Research and Development Administration. Solar Thermal Energy Conversion Program. **VFOAT** Solar Thermal Energy Conversion Program Summary. English. Energy Research and Development Administration, 20 Massachusetts Avenue Northwest, Washington DC 20545.

UK/0269-1159
SUN AT WORK IN EUROPE. **Added/Corp** International Solar Energy Society. Scottish Solar Energy Group. No. 1 (April 1986)-. Academic Scholarly Publication. English. Four times a year. £60.00. Franklin Company, 192 Franklin Road, Birmingham B30 2HE England. **Tel** 021-459-4826, FAX 021 459 8206. **ED** L. F. Jesch. **LC** TJ809.5.E85; S85. **DD** 333.79/23/094. **Bk Rev.** **Ad Acc.** **Pr Rev.** **Circ:** 3,000.
Desc: Journal of solar energy in Europe.
Ind/Abst Int. Build. Serv. Abstr.

AT/0149-1938
SUNWORLD. [Sunworld]. **VFOAT** Sun World. No. 1 (July 1976)-No. 6 (Nov. 1977); Vol. 2, No. 1 (Feb. 1978)-. Periodical. English. qt. $40.00 (one year), $70.00 (two year), $95.00 (three year) institutions; $30.00 (one year), $50.00 (two year), $72.00 (three year) individuals. International Solar Energy Society / New Mexico, PO Box 8364, Santa FE NM 87504-8364. **Tel** (505)471-0691. **ED** Debra D Carroll and Everett D Howe. **LC** TJ810; .S92. **DD** 621.47/05. **CODEN** SUNWDW. **[CCC].** **Bk Rev.** **Ad Acc. Circ:** 5,000 (ctrl). available on microfilm and microfiche from University Microfilms International (UMI). Documents available from Article Express International.
Desc: The official news and information magazine of the International Solar Energy Society, featuring the latest developments and applications of renewable energy resources.
Ind/Abst AGRICOLA; Bioeng. Abstr.; Ei Page One; Energy Res. Abstr. (Oct. 1977-); Eng. Index Annu.; Int. Aerosp. Abstr.; Microcomput. Index (July 1991-).

US/1062-1776
SUPERCONDUCTIVITY BULLETIN. (SUPERCONDUCTIVITY BULLETIN : PROGRESS IN HTS ELECTRIC POWER APPLICATIONS / DEPARTMENT OF ENERGY, CONSERVATION AND RENEWABLE ENERGY, OFFICE OF UTILITY TECHNOLOGIES.). [Supercond. bull.]. **Added/Corp** United States. Dept. of Energy. Office of Conservation and Renewable Energy. Office of Utility Technologies. Argonne National Laboratory. (Dec 1991)-. Bulletin. English. qt. Argonne National Laboratory, 9700 South Cass Aveue, Argonne IL 60439. **Tel** (708)972-2000, FAX (708)972-5510. **DD** 621.

US/0742-7328
SUPPLEMENT TO THE ANNUAL ENERGY OUTLOOK. (SUPPLEMENT TO THE ... ANNUAL ENERGY OUTLOOK / ENERGY INFORMATION ADMINISTRATION, OFFICE OF ENERGY MARKETS AND END USE, U.S. DEPARTMENT OF ENERGY.). [Suppl. Annu. energy outlook]. **Added/Corp** United States. Office of Energy Markets and End Use. United States. Energy Information Administration. Office of Integrated Analysis and Forecasting. **VFOAT** Annual Energy Outlook. (1982)-.

English. an. $17.00. National Energy Information Center, Energy Information Administration, Forrestal Building, Room 1F-048, Washington DC 20585. **Tel** (202)586-8800. **LC** TJ163.25.U6; S87. **DD** 333.79/0973. **Desc:** A companion document to the Annual Energy Outlook. These tables provide the regional projections underlying the national data and projections in the AEO.

CN/0833-9600
SURVEY OF MINES AND ENERGY RESOURCES. **See** Engineering-Mines and Mining Engineering.

US/0163-2183
SYNERJY. (SYNERJY; A DIRECTORY OF ENERGY ALTERNATIVES.). [Synerjy]. Vol. 1 (1974)-. Directory. English. sa (Mar., Sept.). $50.00 US; $56.00 other. Synerjy, PO Box 1854, Cathedral Station, New York NY 10025. **Tel** (212)865-9595. **ED** Jeff Twine. **LC** TJ163.2; .S97. **DD** 333.7. **Circ:** 400.
Desc: Bibliographic directory of energy alternatives. Features publications, products and facilities in solar, biomass, geothermal and hydrogen energy, wind and water power and energy storage.
Ind/Abst Energy Res. Abstr. (Dec. 1980-).

FR/0295-5873
SYSTEMES SOLAIRES. (1985)-. French. Eleven times a year. 405.00F France; 540.00F other. Societe d'Information sur les Energies Renouvelables SIER, 45 rue de Richelieu, 75001 Paris France. **Tel** 011 33 1 42962477, FAX 011 33 1 42962643. **ED** Yves-Bruno Civel; telephone: 42962477. Index available (bound in May issue). cum. index. **Bk Rev. Ad Acc, Adv Mgr:** Liebard.

FR
TABLEAU DE BORD DE L'ENERGIE. French. mo. 70.00F. Imprimerie Nationale / France, BP 514, 59505 Douai Cedex France. **Tel** 011 33 27 937090.

KO/0253-3103
TAINYAN NEINJI. (TAEYANG ENOJI. JOURNAL OF SOLAR ENERGY SOCIETY OF KOREA.). [Tainyan neinji]. **Added/Corp** Hanguk Taeyang Enoji Hakhoe. Hanguk Taeyang Enoji Hakhoe. Journal. **VFOAT** Journal of Solar Energy Society of Korea. Vol. 1 (1978)-. Academic Scholarly Publication. Korean (English). Feuilles Familiales, Rue du Congres 27 Charme, 1000 Brussels Belgium. **Tel** (514)274-5468. **LC** TJ810; .T315. **CODEN** TAEED8. Documents available from CASDDS.
Ind/Abst Chem. Abstr.

CC/0254-0096
TAIYANG NENG XUEBAO. (TAI YANG NENG HSUEH PAO.). [Taiyang neng xuebao]. **Added/Corp** Chung-kuo Tai Yang Neng Hsueh Hui. **VFOAT** Acta Energiae Solaris Sinica; Taiyangneng Xuebao. (1980)-. Academic Scholarly Publication. Chinese (summaries and/or abstracts in English). qt. **(Subscription address:** China International Book Trading Corporation, PO Box 399, Library Service Department, Beijing 100044 People's Republic of China.) **LC** TJ809; .T35. **DD** 333.792/3/05. **CODEN** TYNPDG. Documents available from Article Express International, Article Express International, CASDDS.
Ind/Abst Chem. Abstr.; Ei Page One; Eng. Index Annu.

JA/0388-9564
TAIYO ENERUGI (TOKYO. 1975). (TAIYO ENERUGI.). [Taiyo enerugi]. **Added/Corp** Nihon Taiyo Energi Gakkai. **VFOAT** Journal of JSES. **VAT** Journal of Japan Solar Energy Society. (19??)-. Academic Scholarly Publication. Japanese. Nihon Taiyo Enerugi Gakkai, (Japan Solar Energy Soc.), 1-5-322, Takadanobaba 3 Chome, Shinjukuku, Tokyoto 160, Japan. **CODEN** TAENAW. Documents available from CASDDS.
Ind/Abst Chem. Abstr. (1986-).

GW
TANSANIA, ENERGIEWIRTSCHAFT / BUNDESSTELLE FUER AUSSENHANDELSINFORMATION. German. DM3.00. Bundesstelle fuer Aussenhandelsinformation, Agrippastr 87 93, D 50676 Cologne Germany. **Tel** 011 49 221 2057316, FAX 011 49 221 2057212. **LC** HD9502.T35; T36. **DD** 333.79/09678.

AU/0074-1914
TECHNICAL REPORTS SERIES / INTERNATIONAL ATOMIC ENERGY AGENCY. [Tech. rep. ser. - Int. At. Energy Agency]. **Added/Corp** International Atomic Energy Agency. Began with No. 1 (1959)-. Monographic series. English. ir. Price varies per volume. UNIPUB, 4611-F Assembly Drive, Lanham MD 20706-4391. **Tel** (800)274-4888, FAX (301)459-0056, telex 28787 GATT CH. **LC** HD9698.A1; I6. **CODEN** TRAEA2. Documents available from BIOSIS Document Express, Ask*IEEE, CASDDS.
Ind/Abst Biol. Abstr. (1962-1978); Chem. Abstr.; Geogr. Abstr. Phys. Geogr.; GeoRef; INSPEC.

US/0884-1780
TERA ANALYSIS. (TERA ANALYSIS : TOTAL ENERGY RESOURCE ANALYSIS MODEL / AGA, AMERICAN GAS ASSOCIATION.). [TERA anal.]. **VFOAT** Total Energy Resource Analysis Model; TERA. Monographic series. English. Price varies per volume. Policy Evaluation & Analysis Group, American Gas Association, 1515 Wilson Boulevard, Arlington VA 22209. **Tel** (703)841-8400. **LC** HD9581.U49; T47. **DD** 338.2/7285/0973.

US/1050-7116
TEXAS ENERGY (1989). (TEXAS ENERGY.). [Tex. energy]. **Added/Corp** Texas A & M University. Center for Energy and Mineral Resources. Vol. 15, No. 6 (Oct./Dec. 1989)-. Periodical. English. bm. Free. Texas Energy Extension Service, Texas A&M University, College Station TX 77843. **Tel** (409)845-8025. **DD** 621. ***Continues*** *Texas Energy and Mineral Resources, 0745-094X.*

US/0273-396X
TEXAS ENERGY ISSUES. [Texas energy issu.]. English. an. Lyndon B Johnson School of Public Affairs, University of Texas, Austin TX 79112. **LC** HD9502.U53; T483. **DD** 333.79/09764.

US/0739-8050
TEXAS ENERGY REPORTER. ***Ceased.*** [Tex. energy report.]. Vol. 1, No. 1 (July 1983)-Vol. 10 (19??). Periodical. English. mo. Texas Energy Reporter, 5926 Balcones Drive, Suite 220, Austin TX 78731. **Tel** (512)452-9872. **DD** 338.

II/0971-085X
TIDE : TERI INFORMATION DIGEST ON ENERGY. **Added/Corp** Tata Energy Research Institute. **VFOAT** Information Digest on Energy; TERI Information Digest on Energy; Tata Energy Research Institute Information Digest on Energy. Vol. 1, No. 1 (Jan.-Mar. 1991)-. Periodical. English. qt (4 issues). $40.00. Tata Energy Research Institute, 9 Jor Bagh Publications Unit, New Delhi 110 003 India. **Tel** 011 91 11 4623983, FAX 011 91 11 4621770, telex 31-6159 TERI IN. **(Subscription address:** Prints India, 11 Darya Ganj, New Delhi 110002 India.) **ED** Mrs. Nalini Rangnathan. **LC** TJ163.13; .T53. **DD** 621.042. Index available (bound in issue). **Bk Rev. Ad Acc, Adv Mgr Tel** same as publisher. **Pr Rev. Circ:** 800.
Desc: Contains information on power resources.

GW
TOGO : ENERGIEWIRTSCHAFT. **Main/Corp** Bundesstelle fur Aussenhandelsinformation (Germany). German. DM2.00. Bundesstelle fuer Aussenhandelsinformation, Agrippastr 87 93, D 50676 Cologne Germany. **Tel** 011 49 221 2057316, FAX 011 49 221 2057212. **LC** HD9502.T6.

KO
TONGNYOK CHAWON. Periodical. Korean (English). mo. Korea Institute of Energy and Resources / Seoul, South Korea, 219-5 Garibong-dong Guro-gu, Seoul South Korea. **Tel** 042 861-9700, FAX 042 861-9734, telex KIERSK K45509. **LC** HD9506.A1; T66. **Circ:** 600.

US/0739-0971
TRANET. **See** Environmental Issues-Conservation and Natural Resources.

US/0193-5933
TRANSACTIONS - GEOTHERMAL RESOURCES COUNCIL. [Trans. - Geotherm. Resour. Counc.]. **Main/Corp** Geothermal Resources Council. Vol. 1 (1977)-. Academic Scholarly Publication. English. an. $55.00. Geothermal Resources Council, PO Box 1350, Davis CA 95617-1350. **Tel** (916)758-2360, FAX (916)758-2839. **ED** David N. Anderson. **LC** GB1199.5; .G457a. **DD** 621.44. **CODEN** TGRCD7. **Circ:** 1,600. Documents available from Article Express International, CASDDS.
Desc: Book series promoting the research, exploration, development and understanding of geothermal resources.
Ind/Abst Bioeng. Abstr.; Chem. Abstr.; Ei Page One; Eng. Index Annu.; GeoRef; Int. Aerosp. Abstr. (1983-).

UK/0372-3666
TRANSLATION - UNITED KINGDOM ATOMIC ENERGY AUTHORITY, RESEARCH GROUP, CULHAM LABORATORY. **See** Physics.

US
TRANSPORTATION AND STORAGE. ***Title Change.*** **See** Energy-Abstracting, Bibliographies and Statistics.

US/0885-8330
TRANSPORTATION ENERGY RESEARCH. **See** Transportation.

US
TRANSURANIUM PROCESSING PLANT SEMIANNUAL REPORT OF PRODUCTION, STATUS, AND PLANS. **Main/Corp** Oak Ridge National Laboratory. Chemical Technology Division. English. sa. US Department of Energy Office of Energy Technology, 1000 Independence Avenue SW, Washington DC 20585.

GW
TRINIDAD UND TOBAGO : ENERGIEWIRTSCHAFT. **Main/Corp** Bundesstelle fur Aussenhandelsinformation (Germany). German. DM2.00. Bundesstelle fuer Aussenhandelsinformation, Agrippastr 87 93, D 50676 Cologne Germany. **Tel** 011 49 221 2057316, FAX 011 49 221 2057212. **LC** HD9502.T75. **DD** 333.79/0972983.

GW
TURKEI, ENERGIEWIRTSCHAFT / BUNDESSTELLE FUER AUSSENHANDELSINFORMATION. German. an. DM3.00. Bundesstelle fuer Aussenhandelsinformation, Agrippastr 87 93, D 50676 Cologne Germany. **Tel** 011 49 221 2057316, FAX 011 49 221 2057212. **LC** HD9502.T9. **DD** 333.79/09561.

US/0193-1040
U.S. DEPARTMENT OF ENERGY BUDGET TO CONGRESS : BUDGET HIGHLIGHTS. **See** Public Administration.

US
U.S. ENERGY INDUSTRY FINANCIAL DEVELOPMENTS. **Added/Corp** United States. Energy Information Administration. United States. Office of Energy Markets and End Use. (1990)-. Periodical. English. qt. $9.00 US; $11.25 other. National Energy Information Center, Energy Information Administration, Forrestal Building, Room 1F-048, Washington DC 20585. **Tel** (202)586-8800.
Desc: Traces key financial trends in the US energy industry by quarter. Financial data is presented for companies in two broad groups; fossil fuel producing companies and rate regulated utilities.

US
U.S. STEP NEWSLETTER. **Added/Corp** U.S. STEP (Program) World Data Center A for Rockets and Satellites. National Space Science Data Center. **VFOAT** US STEP Newsletter. **VAT** United States Solar-Terrestrial Energy Program Newsletter; U.S. Solar-Terrestrial Energy Program Newsletter. Vol. 1, No. 1 (Mar. 1991)-. Newsletter. English. bm. National Space Science Data Center (NSSDC), World Data Center A for Rockets and Satellites (WDC-A-R & S), National Aeronautics and Space Administration, Greenbelt MD 20771. **Tel** (301)286-6695.

GW
UGANDA : ENERGIEWIRTSCHAFT. **Main/Corp** Germany (Federal Republic, 1949-). Bundesstelle fur Aussenhandelsinformation. German. DM2.00. Bundesstelle fuer Aussenhandelsinformation, Agrippastr 87 93, D 50676 Cologne Germany. **Tel** 011 49 221 2057316, FAX 011 49 221 2057212. **LC** HD9502.U33.

UK
UKAEA UNDERLYING RESEARCH PROGRAMME, ANNUAL REPORT. **Main/Corp** United Kingdom Atomic Energy Authority. Programme Planning Group. **VFOAT** Underlying Research Programme; Annual Report. **VAT** United Kingdom Atomic Energy Authority Underlying Research Programme, Annual Report. English. an. Harwell Laboratory, Oxfordshire OX11 ORA England. **LC** QC791.95.G7; U54A. **DD** 333.792/4/0941.

GW/0173-8720
UMWELT UND ENERGIE. [Umw. Energ.]. (1980)-. German. ir. Price varies. Rudolf Haufe Verlag, Hindenburgstrasse 64, D 79102 Freiburg I BR Germany. **Tel** 011 49 761 36830, FAX 011 49 761 3683236, telex 841 772442. **UDC** (625.5 + 658.26) (03).

UK/0142-288X
UNITED KINGDOM ATOMIC ENERGY AUTHORITY NORTHERN DIVISION REPORT. [U.K. At. Energy Auth. North. Div. rep.]. (1977)-. Academic Scholarly Publication. English. ir. Price varies per volume. Her Majesty's Stationery Office, 51 Nine Elms Lane, London SW8 5DR England. **Tel** 011 44 71 873 8459, 011 44 71 873 8499, FAX 011 44 71 873 8499, 011 44 71 873 8456, telex 297138. Documents available from CASDDS.
Ind/Abst Chem. Abstr.

US
UNITED STATES NUCLEAR REGULATORY COMMISSION STAFF PRACTICE AND PROCEDURE DIGEST. ***Ceased.*** **See** Public Administration.

CN/0828-2544
UPDATE ..., ENERGY ACTIVITIES, PROVINCE OF PRINCE EDWARD ISLAND. [Update energy act. prov. P.E.I.]. **VFOAT** Update ..., Energy Activities, Prince Edward Island. English. Department of Energy and Forestry, PO Box 2000, Charlottetown Prince Edward Island C1A 7N8 Canada. **LC** HD9502.C33; P748. **DD** 333.79/09717.

CN/0715-3740
UPDATE, MARKET FORECAST, ELECTRIC ENERGY REQUIREMENTS IN THE NORTHWEST TERRITORIES. [Update, mark. forecast, electr. energy requir. Northwest. Territ.]. 1979/80-. English. an. Northern Canada Power Commission, PO Box 5700 Station L, Edmonton Alberta T6C 4J8 Canada. **DD** 333.79/3212/097192. ***Continues*** *Market Forecast, Electric Energy Requirements in the Northwest Territories, 0715-3732.*

US
UPDATE! / NORTHWEST POWER PLANNING COUNCIL. **Main/Corp** Northwest Power Planning Council (U.S.). (Nov. 14, 1984)-. Periodical. English. mo. Northwest Power Planning Council, 851 Southwest 6th, Suite 1100, Portland OR 97204. **Tel** (503)222-5161, FAX (503)222-9246.
Ind/Abst Energy Inf. Abstr.

UK/0265-430X
URANIUM AND NUCLEAR ENERGY. (URANIUM AND NUCLEAR ENERGY : PROCEEDINGS OF THE ... INTERNATIONAL SYMPOSIUM HELD BY THE URANIUM INSTITUTE.). [Uranium nucl. energy]. **Main/Corp** Uranium Institute. International Symposium. 4th (Sept. 10-12, 1979)-. Academic Scholarly Publication. English. an. £74.50. Uranium Institute, 68 Knightsbridge, Bowater House, London SW1X 7LT England. **Tel** 011 44 71 2250303, FAX 011 44 71 2250308, telex 931211389. **LC** HD9539.U69; I57. **DD** 333.79/24. **CODEN** UNENDZ. Documents available from Article Express International, Ask*IEEE, CASDDS. ***Continues*** *Uranium Supply and Demand, 0951-3450.*
Ind/Abst Chem. Abstr. (1979-1982); Ei Page One; Eng. Index Annu.; GeoRef; INSPEC.

II/0378-9535
URJA. [Urja]. Vol. 1 (Jan. 1977)-. Academic Scholarly Publication. English. mo. $60.00. D B Chaudhuri Urja, PO Box 3008, G-82 Sujan Singh Park, New Delhi 110003 India. **Tel** (011)611536, telex 31-74111 VRJAIN. **(Subscription address:** Prints India, 11 Darya Ganj, New Delhi 110002 India.**)** **ED** Dipak Basu Chaudhuri. **LC** TJ163.2; .U75. **DD** 333.7. **CODEN** URJADF. Index available. cum. index. **Bk Rev. Ad Acc. Circ:** 6,273. Documents available from CASDDS.
Desc: Comprehensive newsmagazine on all energy resources, energy conversion, energy management and conservation.
Ind/Abst Chem. Abstr.; Coal Abstr.; Energy Inf. Abstr.; Energy Res. Abstr. (Nov. 1977-); Field Crop Abstr.; For. Prod. Abstr.; Rice Abstr.; Soils Fert.; Sug. Indus. Abstr.; Wheat Barley Trit. Abstr.

GW
URUGUAY: ENERGIEWIRTSCHAFT. **Main/Corp** Germany (Federal Republic, 1949-). Bundesstelle fur Aussenhandelsinformation. (19??)-. German. Bundesstelle fuer Aussenhandelsinformation, Agrippastr 87 93, D 50676 Cologne Germany. **Tel** 011 49 221 2057316, FAX 011 49 221 2057212. **LC** HD9502.U8; G47a.

GW
USA : ENERGIEWIRTSCHAFT. **Main/Corp** Bundesstelle fur Aussenhandelsinformation (Germany). German. DM3.00. Bundesstelle fuer Aussenhandelsinformation, Agrippastr 87 93, D 50676 Cologne Germany. **Tel** 011 49 221 2057316, FAX 011 49 221 2057212. **LC** HD9502.U5.

US/8755-7827
UTAH ENERGY STATISTICAL ABSTRACT. **See** Energy-Abstracting, Bibliographies and Statistics.

SW
VERKSAMHETSBERATTELSE / ENERGIEKONOMISKA FORENINGEN. **Main/Corp** Energiataloudellinen Yhdistys (Finland). Swedish. an. Energiekonomiska Foreningen, 13 Sodra Kajen 2, 001300 Helsinki Finland. **Tel** 358-0-601655. **LC** HD9502.F5; E48A. **Circ:** 1,000 (ctrl).
Desc: Covers national energy statistics.

US
VERMONT ENERGY STATISTICS. **See** Energy-Abstracting, Bibliographies and Statistics.

GW/0722-3951
VGB-TB. (VGB-TB / VGB TECHNISCHE VEREINIGUNG DER GROSSKRAFTWERKSBETREIBER E.V.). [VGB-TB]. **Added/Corp** VGB Technische Vereinigung der Grosskraftwerksbetreiber. **VFOAT** VGB TB. Academic Scholarly Publication. German. Price varies per volume. VGB Kraftwerkstechnik GmbH, Postfach 103932, D 45039 Essen Germany. **Tel** 011 49 201 4862682, telex 857507. **CODEN** VTVVDR. Documents available from CASDDS.
Ind/Abst Chem. Abstr.

US/0192-5016
VOLUNTARY INDUSTRIAL ENERGY CONSERVATION. **Main/Corp** United States. Dept. of Energy. Office of Conservation and Solar Applications. Office of Business Assistance Programs. Government Publication. English. US Department of Energy, 1000 Independence Avenue SW, Washington DC 20585. **Tel** (202)586-5000, FAX (202)586-4073. **LC** TJ163.4.U6; U545D. **DD** 333.7. ***Continues*** *Voluntary Industrial Energy Conservation, 0192-5016.*

US/0191-2631
WASHINGTON PUBLIC POWER SUPPLY SYSTEM ANNUAL REPORT. **Main/Corp** Washington Public Power Supply System. English. an. Washington Public Power Supply System, PO Box 968, 3000 George Washington Way, Richland WA 99352. **LC** HD9685.U7; W348. **DD** 353.9/797/008722.

US/0734-7294
WASHINGTON STATE ENERGY USE PROFILE. (WASHINGTON STATE ENERGY USE PROFILE / PREPARED BY GEORGE HINMAN ... [ET AL.] (ENVIRONMENTAL RESEARCH CENTER, WASHINGTON STATE UNIVERSITY), CONTRACT NO. 78-01-03 FOR THE WASHINGTON STATE ENERGY OFFICE.). [Wash. State energy use profile]. **Added/Corp** Washington State Energy Office. Washington State University. Office of Applied Energy Studies. Washington State University. Environmental Research Center. (1960/1978)-. English. an. Washington State Energy Office, Library, 809 Legion Way SE, Olympia WA 98504-1211. **LC** HD9502.U53; W1973a. **DD** 333.79/13/09797.

US/0163-5883
WATER FOR WESTERN ENERGY DEVELOPMENT UPDATE. **Main/Corp** Western States Water Council. (19??)-. English. 220 South 2nd Street East, Chancellor Building/Suite 220, Salt Lake City UT 84111. **LC** TK1193.U5; W47a. **DD** 333.9/14.

US
WEPS [COMPUTER FILE] : ARCHIVAL OF WORLD ENERGY PROJECTION SYSTEM. **Added/Corp** United States. Energy Information Administration. **VFOAT** Archival of Wworld Energy Projection System; World Energy Projection System. (1991)-. English. National Technical Information Service - NTIS, Room 2027S, 5285 Port Royal Road, Springfield VA 22161. **Tel** (703)487-4630, (703)487-4660, (703)487-4650, FAX (703)321-8547, telex 89-9405.
Desc: Disk characteristics: double sided, high density, soft sectored.

US/1062-4147
WESTERN ENERGY. [West. energy]. (1991)-. Periodical. English. qt. $3.00 (single issue). Chapman Publication Service, PO Box 4185, Glendale CA 91222-0185. **DD** 333.

US/0277-2140
WIND ENERGY ABSTRACTS. [Wind energy abstr.]. Vol. 1, No. 1 (Jan. 1982)-. English. bm. $190.00 (US); $210.00 (other). Wind Books, PO Box 4008, St Johnsbury VT 05819. **Tel** (802)748-5148, FAX (802)748-3286. **ED** F S Seiler. **[CCC]. Bk Rev**, (Qty: 30+ /yr). **Ad Acc. Circ:** 500 (ctrl).
Desc: Covers topics related to wind energy: aerodynamics; materials; electrical, mechanical, electronic engineering; meteorology; environment; economics; standards; bibliography; manufacturing; operation and maintenance.

US/0886-2818
WIND ENERGY NEWS. [Wind energy news]. **Added/Corp** Wind Energy News Service. (198?)-. Periodical. English. mo. $170.00. Wind Books, PO Box 4008, St Johnsbury VT 05819. **Tel** (802)748-5148, FAX (802)748-3286. **ED** F S Seiler. **DD** 621. **Bk Rev. Ad Acc. Circ:** 900 (ctrl).
Desc: Economic and Business articles on wind energy conversion systems (windmills): including news and events, projects, marketing and sales activities.

US/0162-8623
WIND ENERGY REPORT. ***Title Change.*** [Wind energy rep.]. (July 1978)-?. Periodical. English. qt. Wind Books, PO Box 4008, St Johnsbury VT 05819. **Tel** (802)748-5148, FAX (802)748-3286. **ED** F S Seiler. **[CCC]. Bk Rev. Ad Acc. Circ:** 1,000 (ctrl). available on an online database. ***Continued by*** *Wind Energy Abstracts, 0277-2140.*
Desc: Covers economics, business, projects, finance, management, manufacturing, marketing, sales, activities of manufacturers and suppliers of wind energy conversion systems (windmills) and their markets.
Ind/Abst Energy Res. Abstr. (July 1979-).

US/0896-5102
WIND ENERGY TECHNOLOGY. (WIND ENERGY TECHNOLOGY : CURRENT ABSTRACTS / U.S. DEPARTMENT OF ENERGY ; PREPARED FOR OFFICE OF CONSERVATION AND RENEWABLE ENERGY ; PREPARED BY OFFICE OF SCIENTIFIC AND TECHNICAL INFORMATION.). [Wind energy technol.]. **Added/Corp** United States. Dept. of Energy. Office of Scientific and Technical Information. United States. Dept. of Energy. Office of Conservation and Renewable Energy. **VFOAT** WET. Vol. 88, No. 1 (Jan./Feb. 1988)-. Government Publication. English. bm. $145.00 US; $290.00 other. US Department of Energy, 1000 Independence Avenue SW, Washington DC 20585. **Tel** (202)586-5000, FAX (202)586-4073. **(Subscription address:** National Technical Information Service, 5285 Port Royal Road, Springfield, VA 22161**)** **LC** TK1541; .W555. **DD** 621.4/5/05. **CODEN** WENTEO.

GW/0720-8073
WIND KRAFT JOURNAL. **Added/Corp** Deutsche Gesellschaft fuer Windenergie (Germany) Verein fuer Windenergie Hannover. **VFOAT** W.K.J.; WKJ. (19??)-. Periodical. German. qt. DM47.50. Verlag Naturliche Energie GmbH / Wind Kraft Journal, D 24811 Brekendorf Germany. **Tel** 011 49 4353 551. **LC** TJ825; .W553. **DD** 621.4/5/05.

UK/0950-0642
WINDIRECTIONS. [Windirections]. **VFOAT** Wind Directions. (1978)-. Periodical. English. Four times a year. £16.00. British Wind Energy Association, 4 Hamilton Place, London W1V OBQ England. **Tel** 11 44 0753 882447, FAX 11 44 7149 96230, telex 262826. **ED** Dr. D. Lindsey. **DD** 621.45. **Bk Rev**, (Qty: 4). **Ad Acc. Circ:** 2,000 (ctrl).
Desc: Contains the latest information behind energy developments with world-wide sources.
Ind/Abst Fluid Abstr., Civil Eng.; Fluid Abstr. Proc. Eng.; FLUIDEX (19??-).

DK/0109-7318
WINDPOWER MONTHLY. (WINDPOWER MONTHLY NEWSMAGAZINE.). [Windpower monthly]. **VFOAT** Wind Power Monthly Newsmagazine; Windpower Monthly News Magazine. Vol. 1, No. 1 (Jan. 1985)-. Periodical. English. mo. $105.00 (one year), $200.00 (two year), $285.00 (three year). Windpower Monthly, Vrinners Hoved, DK 8420 Knebel Denmark. **Tel** 011 45 8 6365465. **ED** Lyn Harrison. **CODEN** WIMOEW. **Bk Rev. Ad Acc. Circ:** 4,000. Documents available from Ask*IEEE.
Ind/Abst Environ. Period. Bibliogr.; INSPEC (1987-).

US
WINTER FUELS REPORT / ENERGY INFORMATION ADMINSTRATION, OFFICE OF OIL AND GAS, U.S. DEPT. OF ENERGY. **Added/Corp** United States. Energy Information Administration. Office of Oil and Gas. (Sept. 28, 1990)-. Periodical. English. wk (Oct.-Apr.). Free on request. National Energy Information Center, Energy Information Administration, Forrestal Building, Room 1F-048, Washington DC 20585. **Tel** (202)586-8800.
Desc: Contains monthly and weekly propane and fuel oil data, natural gas supply and disposition data, and selected price information.
Ind/Abst Energy Inf. Abstr.

KO
WONJARYOK YONGU. **VFOAT** Atomic Energy Research. Periodical. Korean (summaries and/or abstracts in English). Choson Taehakkyo Wonjaryok Yonguso, 17 Pullo-dong, Tong-ku Wangju Korea. **LC** QC770; .W634.

US/0273-5695
WOOD 'N ENERGY (CONCORD, N.H. : 1980). ***Title Change.*** (WOOD 'N ENERGY.). [Wood energy]. **VFOAT** Wood and Energy. Vol. 1, No. 1 (Dec. 1980)-?. Periodical. English. mo. Wood 'N Energy, PO Box 2008, Laconia NH 03247. ***Continued by*** *Hearth and Home, 0273-5695.*

CN/1192-2958
WOODSIDE REPORT, THE. [Woodside rep.]. **Added/Corp** Woodside Research. (1987)-. English. an. 600.00Can$ Canada; $490.00 US; $500.00 other. Woodside Research Ltd., c/o John Shiry, PO Box 6359 Station D, Calgary ALTA T2P 2C9 Canada. **Tel** (403)269-6003, FAX (403)269-6019. **DD** 338.2. **Bk Rev**, (Qty: 2-4 per year). **Circ:** 100-200 (ctrl).
Desc: Review of the upstream end of the Canadian oil and gas industry by segment, including financial and operating results.

CN/0225-3828
WORKING PAPER - CANADIAN ENERGY RESEARCH INSTITUTE. No. 78/1-. English. Free. Canadian Energy Research Institute, 3512 33rd Street Northwest #150, Calgary Alberta T2L 2A6 Canada. **Tel** (403)282-1231, FAX (403)284-4181, (403)289-2344. **DD** 338.4/7621.

US
WORKING PAPER (UNIVERSITY OF TEXAS AT AUSTIN. CENTER FOR ENERGY STUDIES). (WORKING PAPER - UNIVERSITY OF TEXAS AT AUSTIN. CENTER FOR ENERGY STUDIES.). Monographic series. English. sa. Price varies per volume. University of Texas at Austin / Jester Center, A231A Jester Center, AFR AFO Amer, Austin TX 78784. **Tel** (512)471-1784.

US
WORLD AUTOMOTIVE ALTERNATIVE ENERGY & FUELS BULLETIN. (19??)-. Bulletin. English. Twelve times a year. $525.00. Forecast International / DMS Inc., 22 Commerce Road, Newtown CT 06470. **Tel** (203)426-0800, FAX (203)426-1964, telex 467615.

●US/1048-2288
WORLD DIRECTORY OF ENERGY CONSERVATION AND RENEWABLE ENERGY SOFTWARE FOR MICROCOMPUTERS. (1992)-. Directory. English. $69.50. Energy Books, PO Box 254, Littleton NH 03561-0254.

UK
WORLD ENERGY AND NUCLEAR DIRECTORY : ORGANIZATIONS AND RESEARCH ACTIVITIES IN ATOMIC AND NON-ATOMIC ENERGY. 1st Ed. (1990)-. Directory. English. $450.00. Longman Group Ltd., Fourth

Avenue, Longman House, Harlow Essex CM19 5SR England. **Tel** 011 44 279 429655, FAX 011 44 279 431059, telex 81259. **(Subscription address:** US and Canada: Gale Research Co., 835 Penobscot Building, Detroit, MI 48226) **LC** TJ163.165; .W66. **DD** 621.042/025. ***Formed by the union of*** *World Nuclear Directory (Harlow, England)* ***and*** *World Energy Directory.*
Desc: Entries describe organizations involved in a wide range of energy-related scientific research.

CN/0843-2295
WORLD ENERGY NEWS (CALGARY). **See** Petroleum and Natural Gas.

US/0197-789X
WORLD ENERGY OUTLOOK. [World energy outlook]. **Main/Corp** Exxon Corporation. **Added/Corp** Exxon Corporation. Public Affairs Dept. Exxon Corporation. Corporate Planning Dept. (19??)-. English. be. $61.00. OECD Publications and Information Center, 2 rue Andre-Pascal, 75775 Paris Cedex 16 France. **Tel** 011 33 1 45248167, US:(202)785-6323, FAX 011 33 1 45248500 OR 45248176, telex 620 160 OCDE. **(Subscription address:** OECD Publications Center, 2001 L Street, Suite 700, Washington DC 20036; Phone: (202)822-3873) **LC** HD9502.A1; W67. **DD** 333.79/05.
Ind/Abst F&S Index Plus Text, Int. [Select. Cov.]; Predicasts Forecasts.

US/0891-4435
WORLD NUCLEAR PERFORMANCE. [World nucl. perform.]. Vol. 1, No. 1 (Nov. 15, 1986)-. Newsletter. English. mo. $1190.00. McGraw Hill Publishing Company, Inc., 1221 Avenue of the Americas, New York NY 10020. **Tel** (212)512-6410, (800)525-5003, FAX (212)512-6111. **LC** TK1078; .W64. **DD** 621.48/3/021.

UK
WORLD SOLID FUELS, ELECTRICITY, GAS, IRON AND STEEL AND PETROLEUM STATISTICS. **Added/Corp** Great Britain. Ministry of Power. Statistics Branch. (1957)-. Periodical. English. Ministry of Power, Statistics Branch, London WC1 England. **DD** 338.2; 338.39. ***Continues*** *World Solid Fuels, Electricity, Gas and Petroleum Statistics,, 0432-4676.*

US
WORLDWIDE REPORT. NUCLEAR DEVELOPMENT AND PROLIFERATION. **VFOAT** Nuclear Development and Proliferation. No. 1- July 1979-. Periodical. English. National Technical Information Service - NTIS, Room 2027S, 5285 Port Royal Road, Springfield VA 22161. **Tel** (703)487-4630, (703)487-4660, (703)487-4650, FAX (703)321-8547, telex 89-9405.

CC/1000-6931
YUANZINENG KEXUE JISHU. **See** Engineering-Nuclear Engineering.

CC/0253-3596
YUANZINENG NONGYE YINGYONG. (YUAN TZU NENG NUNG YEH YING YUNG.). [Yuanzineng nongye yingyong]. **Added/Corp** Chung-kuo Yuan Tzu Neng Nung Hsueh Hui. **VFOAT** Application of Atomic Energy in Agriculture. (19??)-. Academic Scholarly Publication. Chinese (English). qt. $1.30 (per issue). Yuanzineng Chubanshe / Atomic Energy Press, 43 Fucheng Road, Haidian District, Beijing 100037 People's Republic of China. **(Subscription address:** China International Book Trading Corporation, PO Box 399, Library Service Department, Beijing 100044 People's Republic of China.) **CODEN** YTNYDT. **Ad Acc. Circ:** 2,000. Documents available from CASDDS.
Desc: The application of nuclear technology in agriculture and science.
Ind/Abst Chem. Abstr.

GW
ZAIRE : ENERGIEWIRTSCHAFT. **Main/Corp** Bundesstelle fur Aussenhandelsinformation (Germany). German. DM2.00. Bundesstelle fuer Aussenhandelsinformation, Agrippastr 87 93, D 50676 Cologne Germany. **Tel** 011 49 221 2057316, FAX 011 49 221 2057212. **LC** HD9502.Z3.

GW/0343-5377
ZEITSCHRIFT FUER ENERGIEWIRTSCHAFT. [Z. Energiewirtsch.]. (Nov 1977)-. Periodical. German. qt. DM280.00. Vieweg Publishing, PO Box 5829, D 65048 Wiesbaden Germany. **Tel** 011 49 611 160230, FAX 011 49 611 160229. **ED** Hans K. Schneider and C. Christian von Weizsacker. **LC** HD9502.A1; Z44. **[CCC].** Index available. cum. index. **Bk Rev. Ad Acc. Circ:** 1,450.
Desc: Covers important current issues relating to energy use and regulation from economic and legal mid-long-term perspectives.
Ind/Abst Coal Abstr.; Energy Res. Abstr. (Feb. 1979-).

PL/0372-9796
ZESZYTY NAUKOWE POLITECHNIKI SLASKIEJ. ENERGETYKA. [Zesz. nauk. - Politech. Sl., Energ.]. **Added/Corp** Politechnika Slaska im. W. Pstrowskiego. **VFOAT** Energetyka. (1956)-. Academic Scholarly Publication. Polish. **LC** TJ4; .G53. **CODEN** ZPSEA8. Documents available from CASDDS.
Ind/Abst Chem. Abstr.

GW
ZYPERN : ENERGIEWIRTSCHAFT. **Main/Corp** Bundesstelle fur Aussenhandelsinformation (Germany). German. DM2.00. Bundesstelle fuer Aussenhandelsinformation, Agrippastr 87 93, D 50676 Cologne Germany. **Tel** 011 49 221 2057316, FAX 011 49 221 2057212. **LC** HD9502.C93.

ABSTRACTING, BIBLIOGRAPHIES AND STATISTICS

TH/0857-6181
ABSTRACTS OF AIT REPORTS AND PUBLICATIONS ON ENERGY. **Added/Corp** Renewable Energy Resources Information Center (Thailand). Vol. 7 (1987)-. Abstracting/Indexing Service. English. an. $75.00 (individuals), $120.00 (institutions) US, Canada, Europe, Australia, New Zealand, Japan & Middle East; $45.00 (individuals), $70.00 (institutions). Asian Institute of Technology / Regional Energy Resources Information Center / RERIC, PO Box 2754, 10501 Bangkok, Thailand. **Tel** 011 66 2 516-0110-29, 011 66 2 516-0130-44, FAX 011 66 2 516-2126. **ED** H. A. Vespry, R. H. B. Exell, and On-Anong Suraniranat. **Bk Rev. Ad Acc. Circ:** 500 (ctrl). available on microfiche. ***Continues*** *Abstracts of AIT Reports and Publications on Renewable Energy Resources.*
Desc: Provides information services on energy conservation, energy planning, solar energy, biomass energy, small-scale hydropower and wind energy. Publishes newsletter, journal, abstracts, directories, research reports and proceedings on the subjects covered.

CN/0380-4321
ALBERTA COAL INDUSTRY ANNUAL STATISTICS. [Alta. coal ind., Annu. stat.]. **Main/Corp** Alberta. Energy Resources Conservation Board. **VFOAT** Alberta's Coal Industry Annual Statistics. (1974)-. English. an. $30.00 Canada; $36.00 US; $39.00 other. Energy Resources Conservation Board, 640 Fifth Avenue Southwest, Calgary Alberta T2P 3G4 Canada. **Tel** (403)297-8311, (403)297-8190, telex 03-821717. ***Continues*** *Alberta. Energy Resources Conservation Board. Cumulative Annual Statistics. Alberta Coal Industry, 0837-2608.*
Ind/Abst GeoRef.

CN/0706-1420
ALBERTA ELECTRIC INDUSTRY. ANNUAL STATISTICS. **Added/Corp** Alberta. Energy Resources Conservation Board. (1977)-. English. an. 30.00Can$ Canada; 36.00Can$ US; 39.00Can$ other. Energy Resources Conservation Board, 640 Fifth Avenue Southwest, Calgary Alberta T2P 3G4 Canada. **Tel** (403)297-8311, (403)297-8190, telex 03-821717. **LC** TN873.C22; A442 Subser; HD9685.C3; A42. **DD** 333.79/16/0971231 S; 363.6/2/097123. ***Continues*** *Alberta. Energy Resources Conservation Board. Cumulative Annual Statistics: Alberta Electric Industry., 0704-4356.*
Desc: Capacity and generation of major power plants by unit, type and energy resource.

CN/0710-6874
ALBERTA ENERGY RESOURCE INDUSTRIES, MONTHLY STATISTICS. [Alta. energy resour. ind., Mon. stat.]. **Added/Corp** Alberta. Energy Resources Conservation Board. (1980)-. Periodical. English. Twelve times a year. 50.00Can$. Energy Resources Conservation Board, 640 Fifth Avenue Southwest, Calgary Alberta T2P 3G4 Canada. **Tel** (403)297-8311, (403)297-8190, telex 03-821717. **DD** 333.79/097123. ***Continues*** *Alberta. Energy Resources Conservation Board. Monthly Statistics, 0706-1447.*
Desc: Contains supply and disposition of crude oil, natural gas, gas plant products, refinery products, coal, electric energy; comparison with previous year for months and cumulative year to month-end; and activity data.

US/0066-3808
ANNUAL BULLETIN OF COAL STATISTICS FOR EUROPE. (ANNUAL BULLETIN OF COAL STATISTICS FOR EUROPE / ECONOMIC COMMISSION FOR EUROPE.). **Main/Corp** United Nations. Economic Commission for Europe. **Added/Corp** United Nations. Economic Commission for Europe. **VFOAT** Bulletin Annuel de Statistiques du Charbon pour l'Europe; Ezhegodnyi Biulleten Evropeiskoi Statistiki Uglia. (1966)-. Government Publication. English (French and Russian). an. $35.00. United Nations Publications, 2 United Nations Plaza, Room DC2 0853, Department 007C, New York NY 10017. **Tel** (212)963-8303, (800)253-9646. **LC** HD9555.A1; A56. **CODEN** ABCEEZ.
Desc: Provides basic data on developments and trends in the field of solid fuels, giving statistics for Europe, Canada and the United States.

US
ANNUAL BULLETIN OF GENERAL ENERGY STATISTICS FOR EUROPE / ECONOMIC COMMISSION FOR EUROPE. **Main/Corp** United Nations. Economic Commission for Europe. **Added/Corp** United Nations. Economic Commission for Europe. **VFOAT** Bulletin Annuel de Statistiques Generales de l'Energie pour l'Europe; Ezhegodnyi Biulleten Evropeiskoi Statistiki Obshchei Energetiki; General Energy Statistics for Europe. (1968)-. Government Publication. English (French and Russian). an. $40.00 (lates issue). United Nations Publications, 2 United Nations Plaza, Room DC2 0853, Department 007C, New York NY 10017. **Tel** (212)963-8303, (800)253-9646. **LC** HD9555.A1; U42. **DD** 333.8/094. **CODEN** ABGEEL.
Desc: Provides basic data on the energy situation as a whole as well as details on the production of energy for the European countries, Canada and the United States.

BL
ANUARIO ESTATISTICO DE ENERGIA ELECTRICA / COMPANIA ENERGETICA DE SAO PAULO, DIVISAO DE ESTUDOS DO MERCADO DE ENERGIA ELETRICA. Portuguese. an. Av Angelica 2565, 150 Andar 01227, Sao Paulo SP Brazil. **LC** HD9685.B82; S317C. ***Continues*** *Boletim Estatistico, Consumo e Consumidores por Classe e Municipio, Estado de Sao Paulo.*

AT/0727-2596
AUSTRALIAN ENERGY STATISTICS / DEPARTMENT OF NATIONAL DEVELOPMENT AND ENERGY. **Added/Corp** Australia. Dept. of National Development and Energy. (1981)-. Government Publication. English. ir. 6.95Aus$ Australia; 8.15Aus$ other. Australian Government Publishing Service, GPO Box 84, Canberra ACT 2601 Australia. **Tel** 011 61 6 2954411, FAX 011 61 6 2954455. **LC** HD9502.A87; A89. **DD** 333.79/0994. **[CCC].**
Desc: Covers energy consumption, energy industries, and power resources.

IT
BIBLIOGRAFIA ITALIANA DI ELETTROTECNICA. (1943)-. Periodical. Italian. mo. $44.55. Ente Nazionale Energia Elect, Casella Postale 386, Rome Italy.

BL
BOLETIM ESTATISTICO DE ENERGIA ELETRICA. Bulletin. Portuguese. qt. Coordenacao de Energia da Secretaria das Minas e Energia do Estado da Bahia, Centro Administrativo da Bahis, Av Luiz Viana Filho S/No 40.000, Bahia Salvador. **LC** TK42.B3; A2A. **DD** 333.79/32/098142. ***Continues*** *Boletim Estatistico Mensal de Energia Eletrica.*

UK/0263-9815
BP STATISTICAL REVIEW OF WORLD ENERGY. [BP stat. rev. world energy]. **Added/Corp** British Petroleum Company. **VFOAT** B.P. Statistical Review of World Energy. (1981)-. Statistical Publication. English. an. Free on request. British Petroleum Company, Britannic House, 1 Finsbury Circus, London EC2M 7B8 England. **Tel** 011 44 071 4964205. **LC** HD9560.4; .B74a. **DD** 333.79/05. **Circ:** 40,000 (ctrl). ***Continues*** *BP Statistical Review of the World Oil Industry.*
Desc: Statistics of oil, gas, coal, production and consumption, nuclear, hydroelectric and primary energy consumption.
Ind/Abst F&S Index Plus Text, Int. [Select. Cov.].

UK/0309-4979
COAL ABSTRACTS. ***Ceased.*** [Coal abstr.]. **Added/Corp** IEA Coal Research. Technical Information Service. (19??)-(Jan. 1995). Abstracting/Indexing Service. English. Eighteen times a year. IEA Coal Research, 10-18 Putney Hill, Gemini House, London SW15 6AA England. **Tel** 011 41 81 780 2111, FAX 011 41 81 780 1746, telex 917624. **ED** Robert Davidson. **LC** TP325; .C5143. **DD** 553.2/4/05. Index available. cum. index. **Ad Acc. Circ:** 1,200. available on an online database from CAN/OLE; QL Systems Ltd; and Belindis; available on microfiche.
Desc: Comprehensive computer based collection of indexed and abstracted references to the world's literature on coal including books, journals, reports, dissertations and conference proceedings.
Ind/Abst AESIS Q.; GeoRef; MINPROC; Mintec, Min. Technol. Abstr.

UK/0307-0603
DIGEST OF UNITED KINGDOM ENERGY STATISTICS. (DIGEST OF UNITED KINGDOM ENERGY STATISTICS / DEPARTMENT OF ENERGY.). **Main/Corp** Great Britain. Dept. of Energy. **Added/Corp** Great Britain. Dept. of Energy. Great Britain. Government Statistical Service. Great Britain. Dept. of Trade and Industry. (1974)-. English. an. £19.95. Her Majesty's Stationery Office, 51 Nine Elms Lane, London SW8 5DR England. **Tel** 011 44 71 873 8459, 011 44 71 873 8499, FAX 011 44 71 873 8499, 011 44 71 873 8456, telex 297138. **(Subscription address:** Her Majesty's Stationery Office, PO Box 276, Publications Centre, London SW8 5DT England.) **LC** HD9551.4; .A34. **DD** 333.8/0941. **[CCC].** ***Continues*** *Great Britain. Dept. of Trade and Industry. United Kingdom Energy Statistics.*

FR/0046-1202
ECONOMIE DE L'ENERGIE. **Added/Corp** France. Centre Nationale de la Recherche Scientifique.

Energy — Abstracting, Bibliographies and Statistics

(1971)-. Periodical. French. mo. Dunod Gauthier Villars, 15 rue Gossin, 92543 Montrouge cedex France. **Tel** 011 33 1 46 56 52 66, FAX 011 33 1 46 57 40 69. **(Subscription address:** Centrale des Revues, 11 rue Gossin, 92543 Montrouge Cedex France.**)** LC HD9540.1; .E35.
Desc: Comprehensive bibliographic report reprinting information on energetics from private and government organizations.

●CN/1198-4848
ELECTRIC POWER STATISTICS. ANNUAL STATISTICS.
(ELECTRIC POWER STATISTICS. ANNUAL STATISTICS / STATISTICS CANADA, INDUSTRY DIVISION, ENERGY SECTION / STATISTIQUES DE L'ENERGIE ELECTRIQUE. STATISTIQUES ANNUELLES / STATISTIQUE CANADA, DIVISION DE L'INDUSTRIE, SECTION DE L'ENERGIE.). [Electr. power stat., Annu. stat.]. **Added/Corp** Statistics Canada. Energy Section. **VFOAT** Statistiques de l'Energie Electrique. Statistiques Annuelles. (1992)-. English (French). an. 29.00Can$ Canada; $35.00 US; $41.00 other. Statistics Canada, Publications Sales & Services, Main Building Room 1710, Ottawa Ontario K1A 0T6 Canada. **Tel** (613)951-5078, (800)267-6677, FAX (613)951-1584, telex 053-3585. **DD** 333.79/32/0971021. **Continues** Electric Power Statistics. Volume II, Annual Statistics.
Desc: Supply and disposition of electricity together with number of customers and value of sales; also covers employees' salaries and wages, financial statistics, fuels used to generate electricity and historical tabulation of supply and disposal of electric energy, by province.

CN/0380-951X
ELECTRIC POWER STATISTICS. VOLUME 1. ANNUAL ELECTRIC POWER SURVEY OF CAPABILITY AND LOAD.
(ELECTRIC POWER STATISTICS. VOLUME I, ANNUAL ELECTRIC POWER SURVEY OF CAPABILITY AND LOAD / DOMINION BUREAU OF STATISTICS, INDUSTRY DIVISION, ENERGY STATISTICS SECTION.). [Electr. power stat., Vol. 1 Annu. electr. power surv. capabil. load]. **Added/Corp** Statistics Canada. Energy and Minerals Section. Canada. Dominion Bureau of Statistics. Energy and Minerals Section. Canada. Dominion Bureau of Statistics. Energy Statistics Section. **VFOAT** Annual Electric Power Survey of Capability and Load; Statistique de l'Energie Electrique. Volume I, Enquete Annuelle sur la Puissance Maximate et sur la Charge des Reseaux. (1966/1970)-. English (French). an. 29.00Can$ Canada; $35.00 US; $41.00 other. Statistics Canada, Publications Sales & Services, Main Building Room 1710, Ottawa Ontario K1A 0T6 Canada. **Tel** (613)951-5078, (800)267-6677, FAX (613)951-1584, telex 053-3585. **ED** Dave Madsen. **LC** TK26; .E44. **DD** 363.6/2/0971. **Circ:** 400. **Continues** Annual Electric Power Survey of Capability and Load.
Desc: Current and projected data of capability and load of producers of electric energy, by province.

CN/0702-6609
ELECTRIC POWER STATISTICS. VOLUME 3. INVENTORY OF PRIME MOVER AND ELECTRIC GENERATING EQUIPMENT.
(ELECTRIC POWER STATISTICS. VOLUME III, INVENTORY OF PRIME MOVER AND ELECTRIC GENERATING EQUIPMENT / DOMINION BUREAU OF STATISTICS, MANUFACTURING AND PRIMARY INDUSTRIES DIVISION, ENERGY STATISTICS SECTION.). [Electr. power stat., 3 Inventory prime mov. electr. gener. equip.]. **Added/Corp** Canada. Dominion Bureau of Statistics. Energy Statistics Section. Canada. Dominion Bureau of Statistics. Energy and Minerals Section. Statistics Canada. Energy Section. **VFOAT** Statistique de l'Energie Electrique. Volume III, Inventaire des Moteurs Primaires et des Generateurs Electriques. (1966)-. English (French). an. 29.00Can$ Canada; $35.00 US; $41.00 other. Statistics Canada, Publications Sales & Services, Main Building Room 1710, Ottawa Ontario K1A 0T6 Canada. **Tel** (613)951-5078, (800)267-6677, FAX (613)951-1584, telex 053-3585. **LC** TK26; .E445. **DD** 621.31/21/0971. **Continues** Inventory of Prime Mover and Electric Generating Equipment.
Desc: A list of generating plants in Canada by ownership, showing the location, year of installation, name-plate rating and other technical details of each unit as at year-end.

AT/1037-9886
ELECTRICITY AND GAS, AUSTRALIA.
(19??)-. English. an. 10.70Aus$. Australian Bureau of Statistics, PO Box 10, Belconnen Australian Capital Territory, 2616 Australia. **Tel** 011 61 6 2527911, FAX 011 61 6 2516009. **Continues** Electricity and Gas Establishments Details of Operations, Australia, States and Territories.
Desc: Structural variables: number of establishments, management units; employment at end of June; wages and salaries; industry gross product; and more.

LU
ENERGISTATISTISK ARBOG. JAHRBUCH ENERGIESTATISTIK. ENERGY STATISTICS YEARBOOK.
Added/Corp Statistical Office of the European Communities. **VFOAT** Jahrbuch Energiestatistik; Energy Statistics Yearbook. (1975)-. Danish (Dutch, English, French, German and Italian). an. Office for Official Publications of the European Communities, 2 Rue Mercier, 2985 Luxembourg Luxembourg. **Tel** 011 352 499281, FAX 011 352 488573. **(Subscription address:** Moniteur Belge Belg Staatsbald, rue de Louvain 40-42, 1000 Brussels Belgium.**)** LC HD9502.E79; E53. **Continues** Energistatistisk, 0081-4881.

US/0892-5461
ENERGY BOOKS QUARTERLY. Ceased.
[Energy books q.]. **Added/Corp** International Academy at Santa Barbara. Vol. 1, No. 1 (Spring 1987)-(Dec. 1993). Periodical. English. qt. International Academy at Santa Barbara, 800 Garden Street, Suite D, Santa Barbara CA 93101. **Tel** (805)965-5010, FAX (805)965-6071. **ED** Miriam Flacks. **DD** 333. **[CCC]. Bk Rev. Circ:** 1,000. available on an online database (file 636/Full-Text) from DIALOG.
Desc: Contains abstracts and bibliographic citations for approximately 30 new energy books, conference volumes, and reports in each issue, plus brief descriptions on selected nonprint materials.
Ind/Abst PTS Newsl. Database [Full Txt.].

US/0147-6521
ENERGY INFORMATION ABSTRACTS.
Ceased. [Energy inf. abstr.]. **Added/Corp** Environment Information Center. Vol. 1 (Jan./Feb. 1976)-(Dec. 1993). Abstracting/Indexing Service. English. mo (except bimonthly May/June and Nov./Dec.). R R Bowker, A Reed Reference Publishing Company, Part of Reed International PLC, PO Box 31, 121 Chanlon Drive, New Providence NJ 07974. **Tel** (908)464-6800, (800)521-8110, FAX (908)665-6688, telex 138-755. **ED** Leigh C Yuster, David Packer, Tim Mahrer, Sue Himmelstein, and Mindy Fleisher. **LC** TJ163.2; .E482. **DD** 333.7. **[CCC].** Index available. cum. index. available on microfiche and CD-ROM (SuperTech Abstracts Plus); available on an online database from Fiz-Technik; ESA-ISA; LEXIS; DATA-STAR; and DIALOG.
Desc: Contains abstracts and indexes to worldwide energy literature covering the latest developments in energy resources, production, consumption, economics, and more. Abstracts and indexes information from scientific, technical, and business journals; conference and symposium proceedings; newsletters; and academic corporate, and government reports.

US/0739-3679
ENERGY INFORMATION ABSTRACTS ANNUAL. Ceased.
[Energy inf. abstr. annu.]. **Added/Corp** Environment Information Center. Bowker A&I Publishing. Vol. 8 (1980)-(Dec. 1993). Abstracting/Indexing Service. English. an. R R Bowker, A Reed Reference Publishing Company, Part of Reed International PLC, PO Box 31, 121 Chanlon Drive, New Providence NJ 07974. **Tel** (908)464-6800, (800)521-8110, FAX (908)665-6688, telex 138-755. **LC** TJ163.2; .E4822. **DD** 016.33379. **[CCC].** Index available. cum. index. available on microfiche; available on an online database from ESA-ISA; ORBIT; DATA-STAR; DIALOG; and Fiz-Technik. **Absorbed** Energy Index, 0094-6281.
Desc: Focuses on research and developments, resources, consumption, conservation, economics, and industrial application of energy sources and technologies.

LU/0258-3569
ENERGY (LUXEMBOURG, LUXEMBOURG).
(ENERGY : MONTHLY STATISTICS.). **Added/Corp** Statistical Office of the European Communities. **VFOAT** Energie. (1986)-. English (French and German). mo. £59.00 UK; 64.00p Ireland. Office for Official Publications of the European Communities, 2 Rue Mercier, 2985 Luxembourg Luxembourg. **Tel** 011 352 499281, FAX 011 352 488573. **LC** HD9502.E862; E5. **DD** 333.79/094/021. **Formed by the union of** Kohle, 0378-357X; Statistical Office of the European Communities. Elektrizitat **and** Statistical Office of the European Communities. Kohlenwasserstoffe.
Desc: Statistics broken down by sector, country, and year showing the short-term developments in the energy economy.

US/0160-3604
ENERGY RESEARCH ABSTRACTS.
[Energy res. abstr.]. **Added/Corp** United States. Dept. of Energy. Technical Information Center. United States. Dept. of Energy. Office of Scientific and Technical Information. Vol. 2, No. 20 (Oct. 31, 1977)-. Abstracting/Indexing Service. English. mo. $164.00 domestic; $205.00 other. Superintendent of Documents, US Government Printing Office, Washington DC 20402. **Tel** (202)275-3328, FAX (202)786-2377. **ED** Robert Rutkowski. **LC** Z5853.P83; U544b; TJ163.2. **DD** 621. **NLM** ZW 1 E106. **CODEN** ERABDZ. Index available. cum. index. available on microfilm and microfiche from University Microfilms International (UMI). Documents available from CASDDS. **Continues** ERDA Energy Research Abstracts, 0361-9869.
Desc: Provides abstracting coverage of all scientific and technical reports, journal articles, conference papers and proceedings, books, patents, theses, and monographs originated by the United States Department of Energy, its laboratories energy centers, and contractors.
Ind/Abst Ceram. Abstr.; Chem. Abstr.; Coal Abstr.; Corros. Abstr.; GeoRef.

US/0739-3075
ENERGY STATISTICS (CHICAGO, ILL.).
Ceased. (ENERGY STATISTICS.). [Energy stat.]. **Added/Corp** Institute of Gas Technology. Technical Information Center. (1978)-(Vol.15, No. 3, 1993). English. qt. Institute of Gas Technology, 3424 South State Street, Chicago IL 60616. **Tel** (312)949-3970, (312)949-3650, FAX (312)949-3776, telex 25-6189. **ED** Harold L Mensch. **LC** HD9502.A1; E56. **DD** 333.79/0212. **Circ:** 800 (ctrl). available on an online database.
Desc: Covers statistics on reserves, production, consumption, imports, exports, and prices for energy, natural gas, crude oil, heating fuel, coal electricity and uranium US and world-wide by individual country.
Ind/Abst INIS Atomindex [Micro.].

FR
ENERGY STATISTICS OF OECD COUNTRIES / INTERNATIONAL ENERGY AGENCY.
Added/Corp International Energy Agency. **VFOAT** Statistiques de l'Energie des Pays de l'OCDE. **VAT** Energy Statistics of Organisation for Economic Co-Operation and Development Countries. (1988)-. English (French). an. $50.00. OECD Publications and Information Center, 2 rue Andre-Pascal, 75775 Paris Cedex 16 France. **Tel** 011 33 1 45248167, US;(202)785-6323, FAX 011 33 1 45248500 OR 45248176, telex 620 160 OCDE. **(Subscription address:** OECD Publications Center, 2001 L Street, Suite 700, Washington DC 20036.**)** LC HD9502.A1; E5615. **DD** 333.79/021. **Continues** Energy Statistics (Paris, France : 1988).

US/0889-5260
ENERGY STATISTICS SOURCEBOOK.
[Energy stat. sourceb.]. **Added/Corp** PennWell Publishing Company. **VFOAT** Energy Statistics Source Book. (1986)-. Statistical Publication. English. an. $229.50 US and Canada; $300.00 other. PennWell Publishing Company, 1421 South Sheridan, PO Box 1260, Tulsa OK 74101. **Tel** (918)835-3161, (800)331-4463, FAX (918)831-9497. **(Subscription address:** PennWell Books, PO Box 21288, Tulsa OK 74121.**)** LC HD9502.A1; E562. **DD** 338.2/728/021. **[CCC].**

US
ENERGY STATISTICS YEARBOOK (UNITED NATIONS. STATISTICAL OFFICE).
(ENERGY STATISTICS YEARBOOK.). **Added/Corp** United Nations. Statistical Office. **VFOAT** Energy Statistics Year Book; Annuaire des Statistiques de l'Energie. (1982)-. Government Publication. English (French). an. price varies per volume. United Nations Publications, 2 United Nations Plaza, Room DC2 0853, Department 007C, New York NY 10017. **Tel** (212)963-8303, (800)253-9646. **LC** HD9502.A1; Y42. **DD** 333.79/021. **Continues** Yearbook of World Energy Statistics.
Desc: Provides a global framework of comparable data on trends and developments in the supply of all forms of energy.

JA
ENERUGI TOKEI NEMPO. YEARBOOK OF COAL, PETROLEUM AND COKE STATISTICS.
Added/Corp Japan. Tsusho Sangyosho. Chosa Tokeibu. **VFOAT** Yearbook of Coal, Petroleum and Coke Statistics. (1975)-. Japanese. Tsusho Sangyo Chosakai, (Research Institute on International Trade and Industry), Kobikikan Ginza Biru, 8-9 Ginza 2 chome Chuoku, Tokyoto 104 Japan. **LC** HD9556.J29; E53. **Formed by the union of** Sekitan Kokusu Nempo **and** Sekiyu Tokei Nempo.

US/0741-5656
GEOTHERMAL TECHNOLOGY PUBLICATIONS AND RELATED REPORTS, A BIBLIOGRAPHY.
[Geotherm. technol. publ. relat. rep., bibliogr.]. 1977/1980-. Bibliography. English. an. National Technical Information Service – NTIS, Room 2027S, 5285 Port Royal Road, Springfield VA 22161. **Tel** (703)487-4630, (703)487-4660, (703)487-4650, FAX (703)321-8547, telex 89-9405. **DD** 621. available on microfiche.

US/0503-3772
HALF-YEARLY BULLETIN OF ELECTRIC ENERGY STATISTICS FOR EUROPE. BULLETIN SEMESTRIEL DE STATISTIQUES DE L'ENERGIE ELECTRIQUE POUR L'EUROPE. POLUGODOVOI BIULLETEN EVROPEISKOI STATISTIKI ELECTROENERGII.
Main/Corp United Nations. Economic Commission for Europe. **VFOAT** Bulletin Semestriel de Statistiques de l'Energie Electrique pour l'Europe; Polugodovoi Biulleten Evropeiskoi Statistiki Electroenergii. Vol. 10 (1965)-. Government Publication. English (Russian and French). ir. United Nations Publications, 2 United Nations Plaza, Room DC2 0853, Department 007C, New York NY 10017. **Tel** (212)963-8303, (800)253-9646. **Continues** Quarterly Bulletin of Electric Energy Statistics for Europe.

US
HISTORICAL ENERGY STATISTICS. V. 3-1979-. English. Department of Natural Resources and Conservation / Montana, Energy Division, Helena MT 59601. **ED** R Itami. **LC** HD9502.U53; M95. **DD** 333.79/09786. ***Continues*** *Montana Historical Energy Statistics.*

AU
INIS GUIDELINES FOR STANDARDIZED ENTRY OF CORPORATE BODIES. (19??)-. English. S80.00. International Atomic Energy Agency / IAEA, Wagramerstrasse 5, PO Box 100, A-1400 Vienna Austria. **Tel** 011 43 1 2360 ext. 2530, FAX 011 43 1 234564. **(Subscription address:** UNIPUB, 4611 F Assembly Drive, Lanham MD 20706.**)**
Desc: Provides guidelines for entering the names of corporate bodies in a standardized form. Includes the definition of the corporate body and how to identify, select and enter its name.

US/0163-3724
INTERNATIONAL ENERGY STATISTICAL REVIEW. ***Suspended.*** (Apr. 1978)-(19??). Statistical Publication. English. mo. $50.00. National Technical Information Service - NTIS, Room 2027S, 5285 Port Royal Road, Springfield VA 22161. **Tel** (703)487-4630, (703)487-4660, (703)487-4650, FAX (703)321-8547, telex 89-9405. **LC** HD9560.4; .U485A. **DD** 333.7. available on microfiche (Vols. for 1985-distributed to depository libraries). Documents available from Documents on Demand. ***Continues*** *International Energy Biweekly Statistical Review, 0160-1512.* ***Continued in part by*** *International Economic & Energy Statistical Review.*
Ind/Abst Am. Stat. Index; Energy Inf. Abstr.

US/1058-2487
INTERNATIONAL ENERGY STATISTICS SOURCEBOOK. [Int. energy stat. sourceb.]. (Dec. 1991)-. Statistical Publication. English. an (October). $220.00. PennWell Publishing Company, 1421 South Sheridan, PO Box 1260, Tulsa OK 74101. **Tel** (918)835-3161, (800)331-4463, FAX (918)831-9497. **(Subscription address:** PennWell Books, PO Box 21288, Tulsa OK 74121.**)** **ED** Sandra Meyer (editor's telephone: (918)832-9343). **LC** TJ163.13; .I575. **DD** 333.79/021. Index available. cum. index. **Ad Acc, Adv Mgr:** Jay Kilburn, **Tel** (918)831-9416. **Pr Rev. Circ:** 650 (ctrl).

US
MONTANA HISTORICAL ENERGY STATISTICS. 1976-. English. an. Montana Energy Office, Capitol Station, Helena MT 59601. **LC** HD9502.U53; M95. **DD** 333.79/09786.

CN/0382-2168
MONTHLY STATISTICS. ALBERTA COAL INDUSTRY. **Main/Corp** Alberta. Energy Resources Conservation Board. (1???)-. Periodical. English. mo. 18.00Can$ US and Canada; 19.50Can$ other. Energy Resources Conservation Board, 640 Fifth Avenue Southwest, Calgary Alberta T2P 3G4 Canada. **Tel** (403)297-8311, (403)297-8190, telex 03-821717.
Desc: Coal production by type of mine; processing by plant; disposition of coal and coal products by type; inventory changes and market.

NE
NEDERLANDSE ENERGIEHUISHOUDING / CENTRAAL BUREAU VOOR DE STATISTIEK, DE. **Added/Corp** Netherlands. Centraal Bureau voor de Statistiek. Netherlands. Centraal Bureau voor de Statistiek. Hoofdafdeling Statistieken van Industrie en Bouwnijverheid. **VFOAT** Energy Supply in the Netherlands. (19??)-. Dutch. qt (4 issues). Fl257.42. SDU Uitgeverij, Postbus 20014, Christoffel Plan, 2500 EA Den Haag Netherlands. **Tel** 011 31 70 3789911. **LC** HD9555.N4; A3.

US/0276-5977
OIL/ENERGY STATISTICS BULLETIN AND CANADIAN OIL REPORTS. [Oil/energy stat. bull. Can. oil rep.]. **VFOAT** Oil/Energy Statistics Bulletin. **VAT** Oil, Energy Statistics Bulletin and Canadian Oil Reports. (19??)-. Bulletin. English. bw. $185.00. Oil Statistics Company Inc, Box 189, Whitman MA 02382. **Tel** (617)447-6407. **ED** John J McGilvray. Index available.
Desc: Discussions and recommendations on a wide range of oil and other energy stocks. Discussions of energy industry trends.

US
PUBLISHED SEARCH BIBLIOGRAPHIES FROM THE NTIS BIBLIOGRAPHIC DATA BASE. ENERGY / U.S. DEPARTMENT OF COMMERCE, NATIONAL TECHNICAL INFORMATION SERVICE. **Added/Corp** United States. National Technical Information Service. **VFOAT** Published Search Bibliographies from the N.T.I.S. Bibliographic Data Base. Energy; Energy. (19??)-. English. ir. Free on request. National Technical Information Service - NTIS, Room 2027S, 5285 Port Royal Road, Springfield VA 22161. **Tel** (703)487-4630, (703)487-4660, (703)487-4650, FAX (703)321-8547, telex 89-9405. **LC** Discard.

FR
QUARTERLY OIL STATISTICS AND ENERGY BALANCES. **Added/Corp** Organisation for Economic Co-Operation and Development. International Energy Agency. **VFOAT** Statistiques Trimestrielles du Petrole et Bilans Energetiques. (2nd Quarter 1988)-. English (French). qt (4 issues). $185.00 (surface mail). OECD Publications and Information Center, 2 rue Andre-Pascal, 75775 Paris Cedex 16 France. **Tel** 011 33 1 45248167, US:(202)785-6323, FAX 011 33 1 45248500 OR 45248176, telex 620 160 OCDE. **(Subscription address:** OECD Publications Center, 2001 L Street, Suite 700, Washington DC 20036.**)** **LC** HD9560.1; .O5715. **DD** 338.2/728/021. ***Continues*** *Oil Statistics and Energy Balances.*
Desc: Statistics on oil and gas supply and demand in the OECD area. The statistics include trade, production, refinery intake and output, the final consumption as well as stock intake and output. Separate data for crude oil, NGL, feedstocks and nine product groups. Included is import/export data.
Ind/Abst Energy Inf. Abstr.

SA
SELECTED ENERGY STATISTICS : SOUTH AFRICA. English. qt. R300.00. Energy Research Institute Information Service, University of Cape Town, PO Box 33, Plumstead 7800 South Africa. **Tel** (021)705 0120, FAX (021)705 6266. **ED** Y Blomkamp. **Circ:** 75 (ctrl).
Desc: Statistical information on South African energy.

US/0197-2022
SOLAR COLLECTOR MANUFACTURING ACTIVITY. [Solar collect. manuf. act.]. **Added/Corp** United States. Energy Information Administration. Office of Energy Data. United States. Energy Information Administration. Office of Interfuel, International, and Emerging Energy Statistics. United States. Energy Information Administration. Emerging Energies Branch. United States. Office of Coal, Nuclear, Electric, and Alternate Fuels. (June 1977/July 1978)-. Periodical. English. an (Nov.). $5.00. National Energy Information Center, Energy Information Administration, Forrestal Building, Room 1F-048, Washington DC 20585. **Tel** (202)586-8800. available on microfiche (from NTIS). ***Continues*** *Solar Collector Manufacturing Activity and Applications in the Residential Sector, 0197-2030.*
Desc: This report presents a statistical profile of the solar thermal collector and photovoltaic cell/module manufacturing industry.
Ind/Abst Predicasts Forecasts.

IO
STATISTIK ENERGI. **VFOAT** Energy Statistics. English (Indonesian). an. Biro Pusat Statistik, JLN Dr Sutomo 8 Kotak, Pos 1003, Jakarta 10710 Indonesia. **Tel** 3728007, 374908. **LC** HD9502.I5; S7. **DD** 333.79/09598. **Bk Rev. Ad Acc.**

FR
STATISTIQUE MENSUELLE DE L'ENERGIE / MINISTERE DU DEVELOPPEMENT INDUSTRIEL ET SCIENTIFIQUE, SECRETARIAT GENERAL DE L'ENERGIE ET SERVICE CENTRAL DE LA STATISTIQUE ET DES INFORMATIONS INDUSTRIELLES. **Added/Corp** France. Service d'Etudes des Strategies et des Statistiques Industrielles. France. Service du Traitement de l'Information et des Statistiques Industrielles. France. Bureau de l'Energie et des Matieres Premieres. France. Bureau Statistique de l'Energie. France. Service Central de la Statistique et des Informations Industrielles. France. Secretariat General de l'Energie. (Jan. 1973)-. French. mo. 83 Bd du Montparnasse, 75270 Paris Cedex 06 France. **LC** HD9502.F7; F78. **DD** 333.79/0944/021. ***Continues*** *Statistiques Mensuelles de l'Energie.*

FR/0984-5259
STATISTIQUES ENERGETIQUES PARIS. [Stat. energ. Paris]. (1983)-. Periodical. French. sa. Free on request. Observatoire de l'Energie, 97 99 rue de Grenelle, 75353 Paris Cedex 7 France. **Tel** 011 33 45563284. **UDC** 620.

US
TRANSPORTATION AND STORAGE. ***Title Change.*** **Added/Corp** American Petroleum Institute. (1978-1992). Abstracting/Indexing Service. English. mo. American Petroleum Institute, 275 Seventh Avenue, New York NY 10001. **Tel** (212)366-4040, FAX (212)366-4298. **ED** Monica Peronin. ***Continues*** *Abstracts of Transportation and Storage Literature.* ***Continued by*** *Literature Abstracts. Transportation & Storage, 1065-0520.*
Desc: Information on power resources.

US/8755-7827
UTAH ENERGY STATISTICAL ABSTRACT. [Utah energy stat. abstr.]. 2nd Ed.-. Statistical Publication. English. an. Utah Energy Office, 3 Triad Center/Suite 450, Salt Lake City UT 84180-1204. **Tel** (801)538-5428, FAX (801)521-0657. **LC** HD9502.U53; U815. **DD** 333.79/09792/021. ***Continues*** *Annual Utah Energy Statistical Abstract, 0740-915X.*

US
VERMONT ENERGY STATISTICS. **VFOAT** Energy Statistics. English. an. State Energy Office, Fuel Management Division, State Office Building, Montpelier VT 05602. **LC** TJ163.25.U6; V48. **DD** 333.79/09743.

ENGINEERING

US
A-E BUSINESS REVIEW. See Architecture.

US/0090-2411
A.E. LEGAL NEWSLETTER. See Architecture.

US/0732-7943
A/E MARKETING JOURNAL. See Business-Marketing.

AT/0045-0731
A.N.C.O.L.D. BULLETIN. [ANCOLD bull.]. **VFOAT** Ancold Bulletin; Australian National Committee on Large Dams Bulletin. (1961)-. Periodical. English. Three times a year (Apr., Aug., Dec.). 59.00Aus$ Australia; 64.00Aus$ New Zealand, Papua New Guinea, Fiji, Indonesia, Malaysia, India & Japan; 66.00Aus$ others. ANCOLD, NSW Department of Water Resources, PO Box 3720, Parramatta 2124 Australia. **Tel** 011 61 2 8957430. **DD** _a627.806.
Ind/Abst AESIS Q.

BU/0204-577X
ABSTRACTS OF BULGARIAN SCIENTIFIC LITERATURE. INDUSTRY, BUILDING AND TRANSPORT. STATE COMMITTEE FOR SCIENCE AND TECHNICAL PROGRESS, CENTRAL INSTITUTE FOR SCIENTIFIC AND TECHNICAL INFORMATION. **Added/Corp** Bulgaria. Durzhaven Komitet za Nauka i Tekhnicheski Progres. Bulgaria. Ministerstvo na Ikonomikata i Planiraneto. TSentralen Institut za Nauchna i Tekhnicheska Informatsiia. **VFOAT** Industry, Building and Transport. Vol. 1 (Oct./Dec. 1971)-. Periodical. English. qt. 1.6olv. Tsentr IN-T ZA Nauchna i Tekhnicheska Informatsiia, 1040 Sofia, 52 A G. A. Nassyr Str. **LC** Z7911; .A34. **DD** 016. **CODEN** ASLTD5.

FR
ACHATS ET ENTRETIEN DU MATERIEL INDUSTRIEL. **VFOAT** Achats et Entretien; Industrie Francaise - Achats et Entretien. No. 1 (1952)-. Periodical. French. mo. Societe les Nouvelles du Monde, 13 rue de Liege, 75009 Paris France. **CODEN** AEEIEA. Documents available from Ask*IEEE. ***Absorbed*** *Automation.*
Ind/Abst INSPEC (1988-).

FI/0001-6853
ACTA POLYTECHNICA SCANDINAVICA. CHEMICAL TECHNOLOGY AND METALLURGY SERIES. No. 153 (1983) -. Periodical. English. ir. Fmk1300.00. The Finnish Academy of Technology, Tekniikantie 12, Fin 02150 Espoo Finland. **Tel** 011 358 0 4554565, FAX 011 358 0 6945041. **ED** Seppo Palosaari. Index available. **Circ:** 600. available on microfilm from University Microfilms International (UMI). Documents available from Article Express International, The Genuine Article, Ask*IEEE. ***Continues*** *Acta Polytechnica Scandinavica. Chemistry Including Metallurgy Series.*
Desc: Scientific research report series consisting of monographs.
Ind/Abst Curr. Contents Eng. Tech. Appl. Sci.; Ei Page One; Eng. Index Annu.; INSPEC (1983-); Res. Alert [Full Cov.]; SCISEARCH.

US/0360-9960
ADVANCES IN BIOENGINEERING. [Adv. bioeng.]. **Added/Corp** American Society of Mechanical Engineers. (197?)-. English. an (published in Dec.). $90.00 non-member, $72.00 member. American Society of Mechanical Engineers, 22 Law Drive, Fairfield NJ 07007. **Tel** (201)882-1167, (212)705-7722 (editorial). **LC** R856.A1; A29. **DD** 610/.28. **NLM** W1 AD437L. **CODEN** ADBIDL. **[CCC]**. Documents available from Article Express International, BIOSIS Document Express, CASDDS.
Desc: Covers biomedical engineering and bioengineering.
Ind/Abst Bioeng. Abstr.; Biol. Abstr.; Chem. Abstr.; Ei Page One; Eng. Index Annu.

GW
ADVANCES IN CONTROL SYSTEMS AND SIGNAL PROCESSING. Vol. 1 (1980)-. Monographic series. English. ir. Price varies per volume. Vieweg Publishing, PO Box 5829, D 65048 Wiesbaden Germany. **Tel** 011 49 611 160230, FAX 011 49 611 160229. Documents available from Article Express International.
Ind/Abst Ei Page One; Eng. Index Annu.; Math. Rev.

US/0065-2482
ADVANCES IN CRYOGENIC ENGINEERING. [Adv. cryog. eng.]. **VFOAT** International Advances in Cryogenic Engineering; Advances in Cryogenic Engineering Materials. Vol. 1 (1960)-. Proceedings. English. ir. Price varies per volume. Plenum Press, 233 Spring Street, New York NY 10013-1578. **Tel** (212)620-8000, (800)221-9369, FAX (212)463-0742, (212)807-1047, telex 23/421139. **LC** TP490; .A3. **DD** 660.29368. **CODEN** ACYEAC. Documents available from Article Express International, Ask*IEEE, CASDDS.
Ind/Abst Bioeng. Abstr.; Chem. Abstr.; Ei Page One; Energy Inf. Abstr.; Eng. Index Annu.; INIS Atomindex [Micro.]; INSPEC.

US/0886-1587
ADVANCES IN CRYOGENIC ENGINEERING MATERIALS. [Adv. cryog. eng. mater.]. **VFOAT** Advances in Cryogenic Engineering. Vol. 26 (1980)-. Monographic series. English. an. Price varies per volume. Plenum Press, 233 Spring Street, New York NY 10013-1578. **Tel** (212)620-8000, (800)221-9369, FAX (212)463-0742, (212)807-1047, telex 23/421139. **LC** TP490; .A3. **DD** 621.5/9. ***Continues*** *Advances in Cryogenic Engineering, 0065-2482.*
Ind/Abst Bioeng. Abstr.

US/0065-2555
ADVANCES IN ENGINEERING.
Added/Corp Society of Automotive Engineers. (1962)-. Monographic series. English. ir. Price varies per volume. Society of Automotive Engineers, 400 Commonwealth Drive, Warrendale PA 15096. **Tel** (412)776-4841, (412)772-7106, FAX (412)776-5760. **(Subscription address:** SAE / Society of Automotive Engineers, Department L1094P, Pittsburgh PA 15264.**)**

●UK/0965-9978
ADVANCES IN ENGINEERING SOFTWARE (1992). (ADVANCES IN ENGINEERING SOFTWARE.). [Adv. eng. softw.]. **Added/Corp** International Society for Boundary Elements. Vol. 14 No. 1 (1992)-. Academic Scholarly Publication. English. Nine times a year. $626.00 The Americas; £420.00 other. Elsevier Applied Science, An Imprint of Elsevier Science Ltd., The Boulevard, Langford Lane, Kidlington, Oxford OX5 1GB United Kingdom. **Tel** 011 44 865 843000, 011 44 865 843699, FAX 011 44 865 843010. **(Subscription address:** Elsevier Science Ltd. Oxford Fulfillment Centre, PO Box 800, Kidlington, Oxford OX5 1DX United Kingdom.**) [CCC].** Documents available from Article Express International, Ask*IEEE. ***Continues*** *Advances in Engineering Software and Workstations, 0961-3552.*
Ind/Abst Bioeng. Abstr. (1992-); Compumath Citation Index [Full Cov.]; Comput. Lit. Index; Ei Page One (1992-); Eng. Index Annu.; Fluid Abstr., Civil Eng.; Fluid Abstr. Proc. Eng.; FLUIDEX (1992-); INSPEC (1992-).

●US/1054-0032
ADVANCES IN INSTRUMENTATION AND CONTROL. **See** Science and Technology.

US/1054-0032
ADVANCES IN INSTRUMENTATION AND CONTROL. ***Title Change.*** **See** Science and Technology.

GW/0932-593X
ADVANCES IN SYSTEM ANALYSIS. [Adv. syst. anal.]. Vol. 1 (1986)-. Monographic series. English. ir. Price varies per volume. Vieweg Publishing, PO Box 5829, D 65048 Wiesbaden Germany. **Tel** 011 49 611 160230, FAX 011 49 611 160229. **NLM** W1; AD879E. **CODEN** ASAYEY.
Ind/Abst Math. Rev.; Zentralbl. Math. Ihre Grenzgeb.

US/0192-2734
ADVANCES IN THERMAL ENGINEERING. [Adv. therm. eng.]. (197?)-. Academic Scholarly Publication. English. ir. Price varies per volume. John Wiley & Sons Inc / New Jersey, 1 Wiley Drive, Somerset NJ 08875. **Tel** (800)225-5945, (908)469-4400. **(Subscription address:** John Wiley & Sons / England, Baffins Lane, Chichester, West Sussex PO19 1UD England.**) CODEN** ATREBT. Documents available from CASDDS.
Ind/Abst Chem. Abstr.

UK
AEU (LONDON, ENGLAND). (AEU.). **Added/Corp** Amalgamated Engineering Union. **VFOAT** AEU Journal. (April 1986)-. Periodical. English. Amalgamated Union ENGG Workers, 110 Peckham Road, London SE15 5EL England. **Tel** 011 44 71 7034231. **LC** HD6661; .A64. **DD** 331.88/12/000941. ***Continues*** *AUEW.*

UK/0308-5732
AGRICULTURAL ENGINEER, THE. **See** Agriculture.

US/0002-1458
AGRICULTURAL ENGINEERING. ***Title Change.*** [Agric. eng.]. **Added/Corp** American Society of Agricultural Engineers. Vol. 1 (Sept. 1920)-(Mar. 1994). Periodical. English. Six times a year. American Society of Agricultural Engineers, Department 2510, 2950 Niles Road, St. Joseph MI 49085-9659. **Tel** (616)429-0300, FAX (616)429-3852. **ED** Mark Zimmerman. **LC** S671; .A3. **DD** 630. **CODEN** AGENAZ. **[CCC].** Index available. cum. index. **Bk Rev. Ad Acc. Pr Rev.** available on microfilm and microfiche from University Microfilms International (UMI). Documents available from Article Express International, The Genuine Article, Ask*IEEE, UMI Article Clearinghouse, Documents on Demand. ***Merged with*** *Within ASAE, 0741-0387* ***to form*** *Resource (Saint Joseph, Mich.), 1076-3333.*
Desc: Broad interest articles and continuing departments spotlight agricultural process with emphasis on mechanization, plus trends influencing contemporary events.
Ind/Abst AgBiotech News Inf.; Agric. Eng. Abstr. (19??-19??); BioBusiness; Bioeng. Abstr.; Biogr. Index; Biol. Agric. Index; Curr. Aware. Biol. Sci., CABS; Curr. Contents, Agric. Biol. Environ. Sci.; Dairy Sci. Abstr.; Educ. Index; Ei Page One; EMBASE; Eng. Index Annu. [Select. Cov.]; Environ. Abstr.; Environ. Period. Bibliogr.; Expand. Acad. Index (1992-); Field Crop Abstr.; Grasslands For. Abstr.; Hortic. Abstr.; INIS Atomindex [Micro.]; INSPEC (Aug. 1971-Feb. 1973); Int. Aerosp. Abstr.; Irr. Drain. Abstr.; Newsp. Period. Abstr. (1992-); Life Sci. Collect.; Protozoolog. Abstr.; Res. Alert [Select. Cov.]; SCISEARCH; Soc. Sci. Cit. Index [Select. Cov.]; Soils Fert.

UK/0308-8863
AGRICULTURAL ENGINEERING ABSTRACTS. **See** Agriculture-Abstracting, Bibliographies and Statistics.

AT/0044-6807
AGRICULTURAL ENGINEERING AUSTRALIA. **See** Agriculture.

II
AGRICULTURAL ENGINEERING TODAY. **See** Agriculture.

US/1054-8645
AI REVIEW OF PRODUCTS, SERVICES, AND RESEARCH. [AI rev. prod. serv. res.]. **Added/Corp** American Association for Artificial Intelligence. **VFOAT** Review of Products, Services, and Research; AI Review. **VAT** Artificial Intelligence Review of Products, Services, and Research. (19??)-. English. American Association for Artificial Intelligence, 445 Burgess Drive, Menlo Park CA 94025-3496. **Tel** (415)328-3123, FAX (415)321-4457. **LC** Q334; .A517. **DD** 006.3/05. Documents available from Article Express International.
Ind/Abst Ei Page One; Eng. Index Annu. [Select. Cov.].

US/1054-7541
AIPE FACILITIES. (AIPE FACILITIES : THE JOURNAL OF PLANT AND FACILITIES MANAGEMENT & ENGINEERING.). [AIPE facil.]. **Added/Corp** American Institute of Plant Engineers. **VFOAT** Journal of Plant and Facilities Management & Engineering. **VAT** American Institute of Plant Engineers Facilities. (19??)-. Periodical. English. Six times a year (Jan., Mar., May, July, Sept., Nov.). $42.00 US; $60.00 other. American Institute of Plant Engineers, 8180 Corporate Park Drive, Suite 305, Cincinnati OH 45242. **Tel** (513)489-2473, FAX (513)247-7422. **ED** Michael A. Fening. **LC** TS184; .A35. **DD** 658.2/05. **CODEN** AIFAEJ. Index available. cum. index. **Bk Rev. Ad Acc, Adv Mgr:** M. Fening. **Pr Rev. Circ:** 10,000 (ctrl). Documents available from Ask*IEEE. ***Continues*** *AIPE Facilities Management, Operations & Engineering, 0747-1289.*
Desc: Caters to plant engineers and facilites managers and topics that they would enjoy reading about, such as CMMS, CFCs, roofing, and HVAC.
Ind/Abst INSPEC (1992-).

US/8750-2046
AIPE NEWSLINE. (AIPE NEWSLINE : THE NEWSLETTER OF THE AMERICAN INSTITUTE OF PLANT ENGINEERS.). [AIPE newsline]. **Main/Corp** American Institute of Plant Engineers. **VFOAT** A.I.P.E. Newsline; AIPE News Line. **VAT** American Institute of Plant Engineers Newsline. Newsletter. English. bm. $7.00. AIPE, 3975 Erie Avenue, Cincinnati OH 45208. **Tel** (513)561-6000. **ED** Sherrie L Hogueland. **DD** 658. **Circ:** 9,200 (ctrl). ***Continues*** *AIPE Newsletter, 0745-5712.*
Desc: Five issues that cover individual AIPE chapters, their leaders, activities and achievements.

●US/1064-3818
AIR TRAFFIC CONTROL QUARTERLY. **See** Aeronautics, Astronautics.

US
AIR TRAFFIC RESEARCH QUARTERLY. (1993)-. English. qt. $165.00 US; $185.00 Canada and Mexico; $220.00 other. John Wiley & Sons, Inc., 605 Third Avenue, New York NY 10158-0012. **Tel** (212)850-6000, (212)850-6645, FAX (212)850-6088, telex 12-7063. **(Subscription address:** John Wiley & Sons / England, Baffins Lane, Chichester, West Sussex PO19 1UD England.**) ED** Anand Mundra.
Desc: International journal of traffic and systems engineering and operations serving the needs of the global air transportation control community.

●UK/0967-439X
AIRCRAFT TECHNOLOGY ENGINEERING & MAINTENANCE. [Aircr. technol. eng. maint.]. **VFOAT** Aircraft Technology Engineering and Maintenance. (1992)-. Periodical. English. Six times a year (Feb., Mar., May, July, Oct., Dec.). £55.00 UK; £65.00 others. Aviation Industry Press Ltd., 31 Palace Street, London SW1E 5HW England. **Tel** 011 44 71 8284376, FAX 011 44 71 8289154. **ED** Paul Copping. **DD** 629.13334. **Ad Acc, Adv Mgr:** Lesley White. ctrl circ.

US/0401-1457
ALABAMA ENGINEER, THE. [Ala. eng.]. **Added/Corp** Engineers Club of Birmingham. Engineering Council of Birmingham and Jefferson County. Alabama Society of Professional Engineers. (June 1958)-. Periodical. English. mo. $18.00. Alabama Society of Professional Engineers, 1150 10th Avenue South, Suite 255, Birmingham AL 35294. **Tel** (205)934-8470, FAX (205)934-8437. **ED** George E. Shofner Jr., PE. **DD** 620. **Ad Acc. Circ:** 1,100.

GW
ALLGEMEINE VERMESSUNGS-NACHRICHTEN (1985). **See** Geography.

US
ALPHABETICAL ROSTER, PROFESSIONAL ENGINEERS AND PROFESSIONAL LAND SURVEYORS. **Added/Corp** Wyoming. Board of Registration for Professional Engineers and Professional Land Surveyors. **VFOAT** Alphabetical Roster. (1989)-. English. State Board of Examining Engineers, Barrett Building, Cheyenne WY 82002. **LC** IN PROCESS. ***Continues in part*** *Roster of Professional Engineers and Land Surveyors.*

US/1050-3145
ALTERNATIVE ENERGY DIGESTS. **See** Energy.

US
ALUMNAE/I DIRECTORY / BOSTON UNIVERSITY, COLLEGE OF ENGINEERING. **See** College and School Publications-Alumni.

US
ALUMNI DIRECTORY / COLLEGE OF ENGINEERING, UNIVERSITY OF MASSACHUSETTS AT AMHERST. **See** College and School Publications-Alumni.

GW/0340-7551
AMTS- UND MITTEILUNGSBLATT / BAM, BUNDESANSTALT FUER MATERIALFORSCHUNG UND -PRUFUNG. **Main/Corp** Bundesanstalt fur Materialforschung und -Prufung (Germany). (198?)-. Academic Scholarly Publication. German. qt. DM150.00. Bundesanstalt fur Materialforschung und Prufung, Unter den Eichen 87, 1000 Berlin 45 Germany. **Tel** (030)8104-5201, FAX (030)8 112 029, telex 183 261 BAMB D. **LC** TA410; .B38a. **CODEN** AMBBEU. **Circ:** 350. Documents available from CASDDS. ***Continues*** *Bundesanstalt fur Materialprufung (Germany). Amts- und Mitteilungsblatt der Bundesanstalt fuer Materialprufung, 0340-7551.*
Ind/Abst Chem. Abstr. (?-1988).

RM
ANAELE UNIVERSITATII DIN GALATI. FASCICULA VIII. Bulletin. Rundi (English and French). an. Price varies. Redactia Analelor, 6200 Galati, Str Domneasca Nr. 47 Romania. **Tel** 40 93 413602, FAX 40 93 412328.

RM
ANALELE UNIVERSITATII DIN GALATI. FASCICULA IV. Bulletin. Romanian (English and French). an. Price varies. Redactia Analelor, 6200 Galati, Str Domneasca Nr. 47 Romania. **Tel** 40 93 413602, FAX 40 93 412328.

CK
ANALES DE INGENIERIA. V. 1- August 1887-. Periodical. Spanish. mo. **LC** TA4; .A5.
Ind/Abst Int. Civil Eng. Abstr.; Soft. Abstr. Eng.

BE/0373-0891
ANNALES DES TRAVAUX PUBLICS DE BELGIQUE. ***Ceased.*** [Ann. trav. publics Belg.]. **VFOAT** Tijdschrift der Openbare Werken van Belgie. Vol. 1-52 (1843-96)-(June 1990). Academic Scholarly Publication. French. bm. Dawson France SA, BP 40, 91121 Palaiseau Cedex France. **Tel** 011 33 1 69104700, telex 220064F. **LC** TA2; .A7. **CODEN** ATRBAJ.
Ind/Abst Ei Page One; EMBASE; GeoRef; Int. Civil Eng. Abstr.; Soft. Abstr. Eng.

US/0885-3916
ANNALS (SOCIETY OF LOGISTICS ENGINEERS). ***Suspended.*** (ANNALS / SOCIETY OF LOGISTICS ENGINEERS.). [Ann. Soc. Logist. Eng.]. Vol. 1, No. 1 (Oct. 1986)-Suspended. Academic Scholarly Publication. English. an. $10.00. The Society of Logistics Engineers, 125 West Park Loop/Suite 201, Huntsville AL 35806-1745. **Tel** (205)837-1092, FAX (205)837-5283, telex 469527. **ED** Benjamin Ostrotsky. **DD** 355. **[CCC].** Index available. cum. index. **Circ:** 2,000 (ctrl).
Desc: Forum for research and exchange of scholarly opinions in logistics disciplines. Seeks to present the cutting edge of logistics theory and practice.

US/0732-6173
ANNUAL CONFERENCE PROCEEDINGS - STANDARDS ENGINEERING SOCIETY. CONFERENCE. (ANNUAL CONFERENCE PROCEEDINGS / STANDARDS ENGINEERING SOCIETY, INC.). [Annu. conf. proc. - Stand. Eng. Soc., Conf.]. **Main/Corp** Standards Engineering Society Conference. (19??)-. Proceedings. English. bm. $35.00 (nonmembers), $25.00 (members). Standards Engineering Society, 1706 Darst Avenue, Dayton OH 45403-3104. **Tel** (513)258-1955, FAX (513)256-9919. **CODEN** SDEPAE. Documents available from Article Express International.
Ind/Abst Eng. Index Annu.

AT
ANNUAL REPORT. **Main/Corp** Standards Association of Australia. 1st (1929/1930)-. English. **LC** TA368; .S7.
Ind/Abst AESIS Q.

UK
ANNUAL REPORT - GREATER LONDON COUNCIL. DEPT. OF PUBLIC HEALTH ENGINEERING. **See** Public Health and Safety.

US/0275-8008
ANNUAL REPORT OF THE NEBRASKA STATE BOARD OF EXAMINERS FOR PROFESSIONAL ENGINEERS AND ARCHITECTS. **Main/Corp** Nebraska. State Board of Examiners for Professional Engineers and Architects. 1st- 1937/38-. English. an. State Board of Examiners for Professional Engineers and Architects, 512 Terminal Building, 941 O Street, Lincoln NE 68508. **LC** TA24.N2; A3. **DD** 620.07.

INT/0255-9293
ANNUAL REVIEW OF ENGINEERING INDUSTRIES AND AUTOMATION .... . (1979)-. Government Publication. English. an. $50.00. United Nations Publications, 2 United Nations Plaza, Room DC2 0853, Department 007C, New York NY 10017. **Tel** (212)963-8303, (800)253-9646. **UDC** 62.
Desc: Analyses data on production, investments, manpower and price indicies in Europe, Canada and the United States.

BL
ANUARIO DO INSTITUTO DE ENGENHARIA. **Main/Corp** Instituto de Engenharia de S‰ao Paulo. (19??)-. Portuguese. Cr$50.00. Instituto de Engenharia, CP 2186, 20001 Rio de Janeiro RJ Brazil. **LC** TA4; .I4952.

US/0893-0457
APEC JOURNAL. [APEC j.]. (19??)-. Periodical. English. Three times a year. $15.00 North America; $20.00 other. APEC Journal, 40 West Fourth Street, Suite 2100, Dayton OH 45402. **Tel** (513)228-2602, FAX (513)228-5652. **ED** Doris J. Wallace. **DD** 621. **Pr Rev. Circ:** 1,500 (ctrl).
Desc: APEC Software development efforts, program applications by users, technology advancements to educate the membership, meeting announcements and other information.

GW/0938-1279
APPLICABLE ALGEBRA IN ENGINEERING, COMMUNICATION AND COMPUTING. **See** Mathematics.

GW/0942-251X
APPLIED DATA AND KNOWLEDGE ENGINEERING. ***Suspended.*** (1992)-(199?). English. qt. DM182.00. Springer-Verlag GmbH & Company KG, Heidelberger Platz 3, D 14197 Berlin Germany. **Tel** 011 49 30 8207223, FAX 011 49 30 8214091, telex 183 319 SPBLN D. **(Subscription address:** Springer Verlag New York Inc. / for North America, 44 Hartz Way, Secaucus NJ 07096.**) [CCC].**

US/0883-8542
APPLIED ENGINEERING IN AGRICULTURE. [Appl. eng. agric.]. **Added/Corp** American Society of Agricultural Engineers. Vol. 1, No. 1 (June 1985)-. Periodical. English. Six times a year. $71.00 (nonmember), $37.50 (member). American Society of Agricultural Engineers, Department 2510, 2950 Niles Road, St. Joseph MI 49085-9659. **Tel** (616)429-0300, FAX (616)429-3852. **DD** 630. **[CCC].** Index available (free). **Pr Rev.** Documents available from Article Express International.
Desc: Contributors representing industry, education, agricultural extension, and government research share studies of unique installations and applications, successful methods of technology transfer, and critical reviews of new technology.
Ind/Abst AgBiotech News Inf.; AGRICOLA [Full Cov.]; Agric. Eng. Abstr. (1991-); Biodeter. Abstr. (19??-19??); Cot. Trop. Fibr. Abstr. Bibliogr.; Dairy Sci. Abstr.; Eng. Index Annu.; Field Crop Abstr.; Food Sci. Technol. Abstr.; Grasslands For. Abstr.; Hortic. Abstr.; Index Vet.; Irr. Drain. Abstr.; Maize Abstr.; Nematol. Abstr.; Ornamental Hort. (19??-19??); Pig News Inf.; Plant Genet. Resour. Abstr.; Postharvest News Inf.; Rev. Agric. Entomol.; Rice Abstr.; Seed Abstr.; Soils Fert.; Sorghum Mill. Abstr.; Soyabean Abstr.; Vet. Bull.; Weed Abstr.; Wheat Barley Trit. Abstr.; World Agric. Econ.

UK/0003-6870
APPLIED ERGONOMICS. [Appl. ergon.]. **Added/Corp** Ergonomics Society (Great Britain) Ergonomics Research Society. Vol. 1 (Dec. 1969)-. Academic Scholarly Publication. English. Six times a year. $358.00 The Americas; £240.00 other. Butterworth Heinemann Publishers, Linacre House, Jordan Hill, Oxford OX2 8DP England. **Tel** 011 44 865 310366. **(Subscription address:** Elsevier Science Ltd. Oxford Fulfillment Centre, PO Box 800, Kidlington, Oxford OX5 1DX United Kingdom.**) ED** Stephen Bailey. **LC** TA166; .A66. **DD** 620.8/05. **NLM** W1 AP524. **CODEN** AERGBW. **[CCC].** Index available. **Bk Rev. Ad Acc. Pr Rev. Circ:** 1,300. available on microfilm and microfiche from University Microfilms International (UMI). Documents available from Article Express International, The Genuine Article, BIOSIS Document Express, UMI Article Clearinghouse, Ask*IEEE.
Desc: Contains refereed articles and technical notes on the practical applications of ergonomic design and research. Areas covered include applications in the office, industry, consumer products, information technology and, military design.
Ind/Abst ABI/INFORM Glob. Ed.; Abstr. Hum. Comput. Interact.; Acoust. Abstr.; Agric. Eng. Abstr. (19??-19??); Bioeng. Abstr.; Biol. Abstr. (1985-); Curr. Contents Eng. Tech. Appl. Sci.; Curr. Contents Soc. Behav. Sci.; Ei Page One; EMBASE; Eng. Index Annu.; Ergon. Abstr.; Expand. Acad. Index (1992-); Health Saf. Sci. Abstr.; Highw. Res. Abstr.; HILITES; INSPEC (June 1978-); Int. Aerosp. Abstr.; Pollut. Abstr. Indexes; Psychol. Abstr. (1971-); PsycINFO; PsycLit; PsycScan: Appl. Psych.; Res. Alert [Full Cov.]; Risk Abstr.; Saf. Health Work; SCISEARCH; Soc. Sci. Cit. Index [Full Cov.]; Tech. Educ. Train. Abstr.; Weed Abstr.

UK/0950-5903
APPLIED MATHEMATICS AND ENGINEERING SCIENCE TEXTS. **See** Mathematics.

CL/0716-0348
APUNTES DE INGENIERIA. [Apunt. ing.]. **Added/Corp** Universidad Catolica de Chile. Escuela de Ingenieria. (19??)-. Spanish. **LC** TA4; .A64.
Ind/Abst Abstr. J. Earthq. Eng. (?-?).

CN/0846-8583
ARCHITECTURAL, ENGINEERING AND SCIENTIFIC SERVICES. **See** Science and Technology.

UK/0954-1810
ARTIFICIAL INTELLIGENCE IN ENGINEERING. **See** Computers-Artificial Intelligence.

US/0197-1662
ASAE PUBLICATION. [ASAE publ.]. **Main/Corp** American Society of Agricultural Engineers. **VAT** American Society of Agricultural Engineers Publication. (19??)-. Academic Scholarly Publication. English. American Society of Agricultural Engineers, Department 2510, 2950 Niles Road, St. Joseph MI 49085-9659. **Tel** (616)429-0300, FAX (616)429-3852. **CODEN** ASPUDS. Documents available from Article Express International, CASDDS.
Ind/Abst Biodeter. Abstr.; Bioeng. Abstr.; Chem. Abstr.; Ei Page One; Eng. Index Annu.; Maize Abstr.; Soyabean Abstr.

US/8755-1187
ASAE STANDARDS. (ASAE STANDARDS : STANDARDS, ENGINEERING PRACTICES AND DATA ADOPTED BY THE AMERICAN SOCIETY OF AGRICULTURAL ENGINEERS.). [ASAE stand.]. **Main/Corp** American Society of Agricultural Engineers. **VAT** American Society of Agricultural Engineers Standards. (1984)-. English. an (June). $130.00 (nonmember), $42.50 (member). American Society of Agricultural Engineers, Department 2510, 2950 Niles Road, St. Joseph MI 49085-9659. **Tel** (616)429-0300, FAX (616)429-3852. **ED** Russel Hahn. **LC** S671; .A32. **DD** 631/.0218. **CODEN** ASEPER. **[CCC].** Index available (free). cum. index. ***Continues** Agricultural Engineers Yearbook of Standards, 0882-1224.*
Desc: Presents performance criteria for products, materials, and systems; readily available design data; safety information; and a basis for codes and regulations.
Ind/Abst AgBiotech News Inf.; Agric. Eng. Abstr. (1991-); Dairy Sci. Abstr.; Ei Page One; Irr. Drain. Abstr.; Maize Abstr.; Nutr. Abstr. Rev., Ser. B, Live Feeds and Feed.; Pig News Inf.; Postharvest News Inf.; Soils Fert.

US/1056-8077
ASEE PRISM. [ASEE prism]. **Added/Corp** American Society for Engineering Education. **VFOAT** Prism. **VAT** American Society for Engineering Education Prism. (Sept. 1991)-. Periodical. English. mo. $75.00 (nonmember), $21.00 (member), $125.00 (libraries). American Society for Engineering Education, 1818 North Street Northwest, Suite 600, Washington DC 20036. **Tel** (202)331-3500. **LC** T61; .A78. **DD** 620/.0071/1. **[CCC].**
***Formed by the union of** Engineering Education, 0022-0809 **and** Engineering Education News, 0193-4139.*
Ind/Abst Contents Pages Educ.; Educ. Index; Stat. Ref. Index.

US/0001-2505
ASHRAE TRANSACTIONS. **See** Heating, Plumbing, and Refrigeration.

ES
ASIA : ORGANO DE DIVULGACION TECNICA E INFORMACION DE LA ASOCIACION SALVADORENA DE INGENIEROS Y ARQUITECTOS. Periodical. Spanish. La Asociacion, 75 Avenue North 632 Apartado, 06-743 San Salvador El Salvador.

US/0273-4737
ASSE SOCIETY UPDATE. [ASSE soc. update]. **Main/Corp** American Society of Safety Engineers. **VFOAT** Society Update. **VAT** American Society of Safety Engineers Society Update. V. 1- 1977-. Periodical. English. mo. American Society of Safety Engineers, 1800 East Oakton Street, Des Plaines IL 60018. **Tel** (312)692-4121. **ED** Christina Roman. **Circ:** 22,000.
Desc: Main purpose is to keep members updated on society actions, initiatives, programs, etc. and happenings in the safety field.

US/8756-5528
ASSEMBLY TECHNOLOGY BUYERS GUIDE. **VFOAT** ATBG. Consumer Publication. English. an. Hitchcock Publishing Company, 191 South Gary Avenue, Carol Stream IL 60188. **Tel** (708)665-1000. **(Subscription address:** PO Box 830409, Birmingham, AL 35283-0409**) LC** TS191; .A87. **DD** 670.42/029/473.

MY
ASSOCIATION OF CONSULTING ENGINEERS MALAYSIA YEARBOOK, THE. **Main/Corp** Association of Consulting Engineers (Malaysia). **VFOAT** ACEM Yearbook. (1985)-. English. an. The Association of Consulting Engineers Malaysia, 36B 2nd Floor, Jalan 20/16A, Paramount Garden, 46300 Petaling Jaya Malaysia. **LC** TA12; .A827a. **DD** 620/.0025/595. ***Continues** Association of Consulting Engineers (Malaysia). Directory.*

UK
ASSOCIATION OF CONSULTING ENGINEERS WHO'S WHO & YEAR BOOK. Vol. 41 (1988)-. English. an. Municipal Journal Ltd, 3 Clements Inn, Strand London WC2 England. **LC** TA1; .C774. **DD** 620/.0025/41. ***Continues** Consulting Engineers Who's Who & Year Book.*

US/0736-6140
ASTE NEWSLETTER. [ASTE newsl.]. **Added/Corp** American Society of Test Engineers. American Society of Test Engineers. Newsletter. **VFOAT** A.S.T.E. Newsletter. **VAT** American Society of Test Engineers Newsletter. Vol. 1, No. 1 (Sept. 1982)-. Periodical. English. Four times a year. $75.00 (individuals & libraries); $400.00 (institutions) Comes with American Society Test Engineers membership. American Society of Test Engineers, 1050 Commonwealth Avenue, Suite 200, Boston MA 02215. **Tel** (617)734-4473.

US/0149-6115
ASTM GEOTECHNICAL TESTING JOURNAL. (GEOTECHNICAL TESTING JOURNAL.). [ASTM geotech. test. j.]. **Added/Corp** American Society for Testing and Materials. American Society for Testing and Materials. ASTM Geotechnical Testing Journal. **VFOAT** ASTM Geotechnical Testing Journal. **VAT** American Society for Testing and Materials Geotechnical Testing Journal. Vol. 1 (March 1978)-. Academic Scholarly Publication. English. qt (4 issues). $95.00 North America; $142.00 other (non-member). American Society for Testing and Materials, 1916 Race Street, Philadelphia PA 19103. **Tel** (215)299-5585, FAX (215)299-9679, telex 710 670 1037. **ED** Vincent P. Drnevich. **LC** TA710.5; .G46. **DD** 620.1/91. **CODEN** GTJODJ. **[CCC].** Index available. **Bk Rev. Circ:** 1,200 (ctrl). available on microfilm and microfiche from University Microfilms International (UMI). Documents available from Article Express International, CASDDS.
Desc: Test methods and research papers on soils and rocks, for engineering purposes.
Ind/Abst Bioeng. Abstr.; Ceram. Abstr. (19??-); Chem. Abstr.; Civ. Struct. Eng. Abstr.; Coal Abstr.; Comput. Inf. Syst. Abstr. J. [Full Cov.]; Ei Page One; Eng. Index Annu.;

GeoRef; Geotech. Abstr.; Highw. Res. Abstr.; Mech. Eng. Abstr.; Mintec, Min. Technol. Abstr.; Soils Fert.; Solid State Supercond. Abstr.

US/0066-0558
ASTM SPECIAL TECHNICAL PUBLICATION. ***Title Change.*** **Added/Corp** American Society for Testing and Materials. American Society for Testing and Materials. Special Technical Publications. American Society for Testing Materials. **VFOAT** Special Technical Publication. No. 1 (1911)-(19??). Academic Scholarly Publication. English. ASTM - American Society fo Testing and Materials, 1916 Race Street, Philadelphia PA 19103. **Tel** (215)299-5585. **CODEN** ASTTA8. **[CCC]**. Documents available from Article Express International, CASDDS. ***Continued by*** *ASTM Special Technical Publication, 0066-0558.*
Ind/Abst Ceram. Abstr. (19??-); Chem. Abstr.; Comput. Inf. Syst. Abstr. J. [Full Cov.]; Energy Res. Abstr.; Eng. Index Annu.; Environ. Eng. Abstr.; GeoRef; Geotech. Abstr.; INIS Atomindex [Micro.]; Manuf. Process Eng. Abstr.; Mech. Eng. Abstr.; Soils Fert.; Solid State Supercond. Abstr.

IT/0373-3475
ATTI ERASSEGNA TECNICA - SOCIETA DEGLI INGEGNERI E DEGLI ARCHITETTI IN TORINO. [Atti Erassegna Tec. - Soc. Ing. Archit. Torino]. (1947)-. Periodical. Italian. bm. ***Continues*** *Atti della Societa degli Ingegneri e degli Architetti in Torino.*
Ind/Abst BHA : Biblio. Hist. Art.

CN/0829-6154
ATV CANADA. (ATV CANADA BUYER'S GUIDE.). [ATV Can.]. **VFOAT** Recreational Vehicle Life. **VAT** All Terrain Vehicles Canada. Vol. 1, No. 1 (Winter 1984)-. Periodical. English. sa. $2.50 per issue. CRV Publications, 2585 Skymark Ave, Suite 306, Mississauga Ontario L4W 4L5 Canada. **Tel** (416)624-8218, FAX (416)624-6764. **DD** 629.2/2042/0971.

AT
AUSTRALIAN CONSULTING ENGINEER / JOURNAL FO THE ASSOCIATION OF CONSULTING ENGINEERS. English. ir (Mar., June, Sept., Dec.). free on request. Association of Consulting Engineers Australia / National Office, PO Box 1002, North Sydney, 2059 Australia. **Tel** 011 02 922-4711, FAX 011 02 957-2484. **ED** Michael Berry. **Circ:** 4,000 (ctrl).

AT/1037-3535
AUSTRALIAN DRILLING. [Aust. drill.]. **Added/Corp** Australian Drilling Industry Association. (1991)-. Periodical. English. Six times a year (Jan., Mar., May, July, Sept., Nov.). 100.00Aus$. Australian Drilling Industry Association, PO Box 269, Mentone Victoria 3194 Australia. **Tel** 011 61 3 580 6222, FAX 011 61 3 580 6699. **ED** Alan Boardman. **DD** 628.1140994. **Ad Acc. Circ:** 5,000 (ctrl). ***Continues*** *WMD. Water Mineral Development, 0811-5931.*

AT
AUSTRALIAN JOURNAL OF INSTRUMENTATION AND CONTROL. **Added/Corp** Institute of Instrumentation and Control (Australia). Vol. 1, No. 1 (Feb. 1986)-. Periodical. English. Four times a year. 67.00Aus$. Institute of Instrumentation and Control Australia, c/o Australian Mineral Foundation, 63 Conyngham Street, Glenside SA 5065 Australia. **Tel** 011 61 8 2955900, FAX 011 61 8 2949997. **ED** H. Addis. **Ad Acc. Circ:** 1,000 (ctrl). ***Continues in part*** *Process and Control Engineering, 0816-8148.*

IT
AUTOMUNDO. Edizione AGM, Via L Manara 15, 20122 Milan Italy.

CN
B.C. PROFESSIONAL ENGINEER. ANNUAL DIRECTORY NUMBER, THE. (1951)-. Periodical. English. Ten times a year. 28.50Can$. The Association of Professional Engineers & Geoscienctists, 210 6400 Robert Street, Burnaby British Columbia V5G 4C9 Canada. **Tel** (604)299-7100, FAX (604)299-8006. **ED** Wayne Gibson. **DD** 620/.006/2711. **Bk Rev. Ad Acc, Adv Mgr:** Gillian Cobban, **Tel** (604)924-6733. **Circ:** 16,000 (ctrl).
Desc: Technical articles of interest to British Columbia Engineers and Geoscientists Association. New information regarding initiations, licensing, and professional practices.

US/0005-4496
BALTIMORE ENGINEER, THE. **Added/Corp** Engineers CLub of Baltimore. Vol. 1 (Apr. 1926)-. Periodical. English. mo. $12.00. Engineering Society of Baltimore, 11 West Mount Vernon Place, Baltimore MD 21201. **Tel** (301)539-6914, FAX (301)783-9372. **ED** John W. Duvall. **Ad Acc. Circ:** 6,500.
Desc: All types of engineering topics. Focus is engineering, architecture and technology in the Baltimore-Washington metropolitan area.

BG/0304-9809
BANGLADESH JOURNAL OF SCIENTIFIC AND INDUSTRIAL RESEARCH. **See** Science and Technology.

US/0005-884X
BENT OF TAU BETA PI, THE. **Added/Corp** Tau Beta Pi. (19??)-. Periodical. English. qt (Jan., Apr., July, Oct.). $3.00. Tau Beta Pi Association, PO Box 8840, University Station, Knoxville TN 37996-4800. **Tel** (615)546-4578. **ED** James D. Froula. **Bk Rev. Ad Acc. Circ:** 95,000 (ctrl).
Desc: The official publication of Tau Beta Pi Association Inc., the National Engineering Honor Society

GW/0409-2791
BETRIEBSTECHNIK. [Betr.-tech.]. (1960)-. Periodical. German. Twelve times a year. DM89.00 Germany; DM97.00 other. Resch Media Mail Verlag GmbH, Postfach 1260, D 82166 Graefelfing Germany. **Tel** 011 49 89 8580710. **[CCC]**.
Ind/Abst Coal Abstr.; EMBASE; Energy Res. Abstr. (July 1978-).

AU/0005-8912
BHM. BERG- UND HUTTENMANNISCHE MONATSHEFTE. [BHM. Berg- huttenmann. Monatsh.]. **VFOAT** Berg- und Huttenmannische Monatshefte. (1963)-. Periodical. German. Twelve times a year. DM276.00. Springer-Verlag Wien, Sachsenplatz 4 6, PO Box 89, A-1201 Vienna Austria. **Tel** 011 43 1 3302415. **(Subscription address:** Springer Verlag New York Inc. / for North America, 44 Hartz Way, Secaucus NJ 07096.) **ED** G.B. Fettweis, H. Hiebler, and W. Schwenzfeier. **CODEN** BHMMAM. **[CCC]**. Documents available from Article Express International, Ask*IEEE. ***Continues*** *Berg- und Huttenmannische Monatshefte, 0170-0278.*
Ind/Abst Alum. Ind. Abstr.; Art Archaeol. Tech. Abstr.; Bioeng. Abstr.; Ceram. Abstr. (19??-); Coal Abstr.; Ei Page One; Eng. Index Annu.; GeoRef; INSPEC (Jan. 1979-); Met. Abstr.; Saf. Health Work.

BL/0100-0705
BIBLIOGRAFIA BRASILEIRA DE ENGENHARIA. ***Ceased.*** **Added/Corp** Instituto Brasileiro de Bibliografia e Documentacao. (1970)-(19??). Portuguese. ir. Instituto Nacional de Estudos e Pesquisas Educacionais Coordenadoria de Editoracao e Divulgacao, Via N 2 Anexo I do MEC, Subsolo 70047, Brasilia D F Brazil. **Tel** 242-2915. **LC** Z5852; .B5.

US/0149-3825
BIBLIOGRAPHY ON COLD REGIONS SCIENCE AND TECHNOLOGY. **See** Science and Technology.

US/0146-1753
BIENNIAL ROSTER OF REGISTERED PROFESSIONAL ENGINEERS AND LAND SURVEYORS AND ALABAMA LAW REGULATING PRACTICE OF ENGINEERING AND LAND SURVEYING. **Main/Corp** Alabama. State Board of Registration for Professional Engineers and Land Surveyors. English. be. Alabama State Board of Registration for Foresters, Montgomery AL. **Tel** (205)240-9368. **LC** TA12; .A46. **DD** 620/.0025/761. ***Continues*** *Roster, Registered Engineers and Land Surveyors.*

US
BIENNIAL ROSTER OF REGISTRANTS FOR THE YEAR ENDING JUNE 30 ... : REPORT OF THE STATE BOARD OF REGISTRATION FOR PROFESSIONAL ENGINEERS OF WEST VIRGINIA. **Main/Corp** West Virginia. State Board of Registration for Professional Engineers. **VFOAT** Report of the State Board of Registration for Professional Engineers of West Virginia. English. be. State Board of Registration for Professional Engineers of West Virginia, 608 Union Building, Charleston WV 25301. **LC** TA12; .W47A. **DD** 620/.0025/754.

●US/1059-0153
BIOMIMETICS (NEW YORK, N.Y.). (BIOMIMETICS.). [Biomimetics]. Vol. 1 No. 1 (Mar. 1992)-. Academic Scholarly Publication. English. Four times a year. $125.00 institutions, $50.00 individuals US; $149.00 institutions, $59.00 individuals other. Plenum Press, 233 Spring Street, New York NY 10013-1578. **Tel** (212)620-8000, (800)221-9369, FAX (212)463-0742, (212)807-1047, telex 23/421139. **ED** J.F. Vincent. **LC** IN PROCESS. **DD** 500. **NLM** W1; BI862G. **CODEN** BIMIEL. **[CCC]**. **Bk Rev**. Documents available from CASDDS.
Desc: An international interdisciplinary forum for the publication of original papers in areas at the intersection of biology and engineering. The journal publishes research papers and short notes on: mechanical and chemical analysis of structural biological materials leading to an understanding of their performance; development and production of materials based on direct copying of nature; analysis of the mechanical performance of materials produced using biotechnical processes; novel applications of biomimetic materials; improvements in the design of current organisms based on mechanical analysis of their structure; and analysis of the optimization criteria used in natural materials and structures.
Ind/Abst Chem. Abstr.

US/0883-0878
BIOPROCESS ENGINEERING. **Added/Corp** Bioprocess Engineering Society International. **VFOAT** Bio-Process Engineering. **VAT** BioProcess Engineering (Tampa, Fla.). Vol. 1, No. 1 (1984)-. Periodical. English. mo. Bioprocess Engineering, 324 Monroe A, Dunedin FL 33528-5740. **LC** TP248.3; .B5585. **DD** 660/.63. Documents available from The Genuine Article.
Ind/Abst Curr. Contents, Agric. Biol. Environ. Sci.; PESTDOC; Res. Alert [Full Cov.]; SCISEARCH.

US/1064-2455
BIOREMEDIATION REPORT, THE. (THE BIOREMEDIATION REPORT / COGNIS.). [Bioremediat. rep.]. **Added/Corp** COGNIS, Inc. King Communications Group Inc. (1991)-. Periodical. English. ir (250 issues). $395.00 (one year), $729.00 (two year). King Publishing Group, 627 National Press Building, Washington DC 20045. **Tel** (202)638-4260, FAX (202)662-9744. **DD** 628.
Ind/Abst Abstr. BioCommer.

TU/0379-587X
BOGAZICI UNIVERSITESI DERGISI : MUHENDISLIK. [Bogazici Univ. derg., Muhendislik]. **Main/Corp** Bogazici Universitesi. **VFOAT** Bogazici University Journal Engineering. V. 1- 1973-. Academic Scholarly Publication. Multiple languages (English and Turkish). $3.00. Bogazici University, Public Relations Office, Harbiye-Istanbul Turkey. **LC** TA1; .B63A. **CODEN** BUDMD3. Documents available from CASDDS.
Ind/Abst Chem. Abstr.; Int. Aerosp. Abstr.

SP
BOLETIN DE LA NORMALIZACION ESPANOLA UNE. **Main/Corp** Instituto Nacional de Racionalizacion y Normalizacion. **VFOAT** Boletin de la Normalizacion Espanola. Vol. 1 (Jan. 1978)-. Spanish. $2.00 per issue. **LC** T59.2.S64; I57a. ***Formed by the union of*** *Instituto Nacional de Racionalizacion y Normalizacion. Boletin de la Normalizacion Espanola* ***and*** *Instituto Nacional de Racionalizacion y Normalizacion. Boletin Informativo IRANOR.*

SP/0214-8307
BOLETIN ICE ECONOMICO. [Bol. ICE econ.]. (1988)-. Periodical. Spanish. wk. Min Economia Hacienda Ctr Publ, Plaza Campillo Mundo Nuevo 3, 28005 Madrid Spain. **Tel** 011 34 1 5271437, or 5835665. **UDC** 33. ***Continues*** *Boletin Economico de Informacion Comercial Espanola, 0213-3768.*

IT/0391-7088
BOLLETTINO DEL'ISTITUTO STORICO E DI CULTURA DELL'ARMA DEL GENIO. **See** Military and Defense.

UK/0957-2902
BOUNDARY ELEMENTS ABSTRACTS AND NEWSLETTER. [Bound. elem. abstr. newsl.]. **VFOAT** BE Abstracts and Newsletter. (1990)-. English. bm. $59.00 (individuals or ISBE members), $115.00 (institutions or ISBE non-members) us; £39.00 other. Computational Mechanics, Ashurst Lodge, Ashurst, Southampton SO4 2AA, United Kingdom. **Tel** 011 44 703 293223. **ED** M H Aliabad, C A Brebbia, J Mackerle. **DD** 620.001515353. Index available. **Bk Rev. Ad Acc.**
Desc: Contains information on boundary element software, benchmarks, institution profiles, interviews with leading researchers, and calendar of events.

●UK
BOUNDARY ELEMENTS COMMUNICATIONS. (1994)-. English. Six times a year. $225.00 US, Canada & Mexico; £149.00 other. Computational Mechanics, Ashurst Lodge, Ashurst, Southampton SO4 2AA, United Kingdom. **Tel** 011 44 703 293223. **(Subscription address:** US: Computational Mechanics, Inc., 25 Bridge Street, Billerica, MA 01821)
Desc: Carries learned articles and comprehensive abstracts, as well as schedules of meetings and news about the technique of boundary elements for engineering analysis.

US/0737-6278
BRIDGE (WASHINGTON, D.C. : 1969), THE. (THE BRIDGE.). [Bridge]. Vol. 1 (1969)-. Periodical. English. qt. Free on request. National Academy Press, 2101 Constitution Avenue NW, Lockbox 285, Washington DC 20055. **Tel** (800)624-6242, (202)334-3313, FAX (202)334-2451. **(Subscription address:** National Academy of Engineering, PO Box 285, Washington DC 20055.) **ED** H. Dale Langford and Carol M. Levandoski. **Circ:** 4,600.
Desc: Features articles and information on programs and general activities of the National Academy of Engineering.
Ind/Abst Eng. Mater. Abstr.; GeoRef.

US/0271-6437
BROOKLYN ENGINEER, THE. [Brooklyn eng.]. Periodical. English. mo. Brooklyn Engineers Club of

Greater New York, c/o Lewis Drittany, 66 Rugby Road, Brooklyn NY 11226. **Tel** (718)282-3269. **ED** Lewis Drittany. cum. index. **Ad Acc. Circ:** 500.
Desc: Technical reviews of items related to all engineering disciplines.

DK/0007-2621
BRUEL & KJAER TECHNICAL REVIEW. ***Ceased.*** [Bruel Kjaer tech. rev.]. **VAT** Bruel and Kjaer Technical Review. No. 1 (1954)-(Jan. 1991). English. sa. Bruel & Kjaer Instruments, 185 Forest Street, Marlborough MA 01752. **Tel** (508)481-7000. **CODEN** BKTRAP. **Pr Rev. Circ:** 14,000 (ctrl). Documents available from Article Express International, Ask*IEEE.
Desc: Advance techniques in acoustical, electrical, and mechanical measurement.
Ind/Abst Bioeng. Abstr.; Ei Page One; Eng. Index Annu.; INSPEC (1969-); Int. Aerosp. Abstr.; Shock Vibr. Dig.

GW/0173-9980
BULK SOLIDS HANDLING. (BULK SOLIDS HANDLING : THE INTERNATIONAL JOURNAL OF STORING AND HANDLING BULK MATERIALS.). [Bulk solids handl.]. Vol. 1, No. 1 (Feb. 1981)-. Academic Scholarly Publication. English (table of contents in French, German and Spanish). qt. $210.00. Trans Tech Publications Ltd., Hardstr. 13, CH-4714 Aedermannsdorf Switzerland. **Tel** 011 41 62 741379, FAX 011 41 12 72 10 58. **ED** Reinhard Wohlbier. Index available. cum. index. **Bk Rev. Ad Acc. Circ:** 10,000-15,000. Documents available from Article Express International.
Ind/Abst Ceram. Abstr. (19??-); Coal Abstr.; EMBASE; Eng. Mater. Abstr.; Eng. Index Annu.; Fluid Abstr., Civil Eng.; Fluid Abstr. Proc. Eng.; FLUIDEX (1981-); MINPROC; Mintec, Min. Technol. Abstr.; Soyabean Abstr.

US
BULLETIN - BUREAU OF ENGINEERING RESEARCH (UNIVERSITY). (BULLETIN - BUREAU OF ENGINEERING RESEARCH.). **Main/Corp** University of Alabama. Bureau of Engineering Research. No. 4 (1957)-. Bulletin. English. ir. Price varies per volume. University of Alabama / Dr. Gary C. April, Assistant Dean of Research, PO Box 1968, Tuscaloosa AL 35486. **Tel** (205)348-1591. **ED** Bette Jefcoat. **LC** TA7; .A5. **Circ:** 1,000 (ctrl).
Desc: Engineering research summary sheets detailing title, author, abstract, reports available, status and implications of research results, sponsoring organization and period of study.

JA/0578-2228
BULLETIN - CHUO DAIGAKU, TOKYO. FACULTY OF SCIENCE AND ENGINEERING. **Main/Corp** Chuo Daigaku, Tokyo. Faculty of Science and Engineering. V. 1- 1958?-. Bulletin. English (Japanese). an. Faculty of Science and Engineering, Chuo University, Kasuga Bunkyo-ku Tokyo 112 Japan. **Tel** 03-813-4171. **Circ:** 1,000.
Ind/Abst Math. Rev.

FR/0458-5860
BULLETIN DE LIAISON DES LABORATOIRES DES PONTS ET CHAUSSEES. [Bull. liaison lab. ponts ch.]. (19??)-. Academic Scholarly Publication. French (summaries and/or abstracts in English, German, Spanish and Russian). bm. 819.00F surface mail; 963.00 airmail. Laboratoire Central des Ponts et Chaussees, 58 Boulevard Lefebvre, 75732 Paris Cedex 15 France. **Tel** 011 33 1 40435226, FAX 011 33 1 40 435495, telex LC PARI 200361 F. **CODEN** LBLLAE. Index available. **Bk Rev. Ad Acc. Circ:** 6,500 (ctrl). Documents available from Article Express International, CASDDS.
Desc: Public works research laboratory.
Ind/Abst Bioeng. Abstr.; Chem. Abstr.; Coal Abstr.; Concr. Abstr.; Ei Page One; EMBASE; Energy Res. Abstr. (May 1977-); Eng. Index Annu. [Select. Cov.]; GeoRef; Int. Civil Eng. Abstr.

JA
BULLETIN OF THE EARTHQUAKE RESISTANT STRUCTURE RESEARCH CENTER. Bulletin. English. Institute of Industrial Science, University of Tokyo, 22-1 Roppongi, 7-chome, Minato-ku, Tokyo 106, Japan.
Ind/Abst Abstr. J. Earthq. Eng.

JA/0513-2592
BULLETIN OF THE FACULTY OF ENGINEERING, YOKOHAMA NATIONAL UNIVERSITY. [Bull. Fac. Eng. Yokohama Natl. Univ.]. **VFOAT** Bulletin of the Faculty of Engineering; Yokohama Kokuritsu Daigaku Kogakubu Kiyo. Began in 1952. Academic Scholarly Publication. English (French and German). an. Yokohama National University, 41 Shimizugaoka Minami-ku, Yokohama Japan. **LC** TA4; .Y6. **DD** 620/.005. **CODEN** BFEYA4. Documents available from Ask*IEEE, CASDDS.
Ind/Abst Alum. Ind. Abstr.; Chem. Abstr.; Coal Abstr.; Ei Page One; INSPEC (1968-); Met. Abstr.

JA/0388-0079
BULLETIN OF THE MARINE ENGINEERING SOCIETY IN JAPAN. [Bull. Mar. Eng. Soc. Jpn.]. **Main/Corp** Marine Engineering Society in Japan. (1973)-. Bulletin. English. qt. $96.00. **(Subscription address:** Kyowa Book Company Inc., 1-38 Kanda Jinbo-Cho, Chiyoda-Ku Tokyo 101, Japan**)**
Ind/Abst BMT Abstr.; Life Sci. Collect.

JA/0474-7844
BULLETIN OF UNIVERSITY OF OSAKA PREFECTURE. SERIES A : ENGINEERING AND NATURAL SCIENCES. [Bull. Univ. Osaka Prefect., Ser. A, Eng. nat. sci.]. **Main/Corp** Osaka Furitsu Daigaku, Sakai, Japan. Vol. 4 (1956)-. Academic Scholarly Publication. English. Twice a year. University of Osaka Prefecture, Sakai Japan. **(Subscription address:** Maruzen Company Ltd., PO Box 5050, Import & Export Department, Tokyo 100 31 Japan.**)** **LC** TA1; .O76. **CODEN** BSKAAJ. Documents available from Article Express International, Ask*IEEE, CASDDS. ***Continues*** *Bulletin of Naniwa University. Series A: Engineering and Natural Sciences.*
Ind/Abst Bioeng. Abstr.; Chem. Abstr.; Ei Page One; Eng. Mater. Abstr.; Eng. Index Annu.; GeoRef; INSPEC (1968-); Int. Aerosp. Abstr.; Math. Rev.; Zentralbl. Math. Ihre Grenzgeb.

BE
BULLETIN SCIENTIFIQUE AIM. Bulletin. French. qt. 1200F Belgium; 1500F other. Association des Ingenieurs Montefiore, Rue Saint Gilles 31, B-4000 Liege Belgium. **Tel** 011 32 41 22946.

US/0097-5273
BULLETIN - UNIVERSITY OF ARKANSAS (FAYETTEVILLE CAMPUS). ENGINEERING EXPERIMENT STATION. (BULLETIN - ENGINEERING EXPERIMENT STATION.). [Bull. - Univ. Ark. (Fayettev. Campus), Eng. Exp. Stn.]. **Main/Corp** University of Arkansas (Fayetteville Campus). Engineering Experiment Station. (19??)-. Bulletin. English. **LC** UNC.
Ind/Abst Wheat Barley Trit. Abstr.

UK/0071-0288
BUYERS GUIDE (ENGINEER (LONDON, ENGLAND)). (BUYERS GUIDE.). **VFOAT** Engineer Buyers Guide. (1953)-. English. an. £62.00. Benn Business Information Service Ltd, Riverbank House, Angel Lane, Tonbridge Kent TN9 1SE England. **Tel** 011 44 732 362666, FAX 011 44 732 770483, telex 95454 BBIS. ***Continues*** *Directory and Buyers Guide (Engineer (London, England)).*

CN/0381-6486
C-C O R E NEWS. [C-C O R E news]. **Main/Corp** Memorial University of Newfoundland. Centre for Cold Ocean Resources Engineering. Vol. 1 (Mar. 1976)-. Periodical. English. Three times a year. Free upon request. Centre for Cold Ocean Resources Engineering, Memorial University, St John's Newfoundland A1B 3X5 Canada. **Tel** (709)737-8354, FAX (709)737-4706, telex 016-4101. **ED** Eleanor Nesbitt-Friis. **DD** 620/.416/2. **Circ:** 1,800.
Desc: Newsletter describing the research activities of the centre.
Ind/Abst ASTIS Curr. Aware. Bull. (1978-); ASTIS Bibliogr. (1978-); Ei Page One; GeoRef; Ocean. Abstr.

CN/0229-5628
C-CORE PUBLICATION. [C-CORE publ.]. **VAT** Centre for Cold Ocean Resources Engineering Publication. English. Memorial University of Newfoundland / Ocean Engineering Information Center, Ocean Engineering Information Center 3X5 Canada. **Tel** (709)737-8377. **DD** 620/.4162. **CODEN** CCPUE7.
Ind/Abst ASTIS Curr. Aware. Bull. (1978-); ASTIS Bibliogr. (1978-).

US/0896-3266
CAD EVOLUTION. [CAD evol.]. **Added/Corp** Evolution Computing User Group. **VAT** Computer Aided Design Evolution. Vol. 1, No. 1 (Nov./Dec. 1987)-. Periodical. English. bm. $24.00. Martin Publishing, 21300 68 W/Suite 203, Lynnwood WA 98036. **DD** 620.
Desc: User group publications for CAD software predesign - CAD.

FR
CAHIERS DE L'INGENIERIE. French. qt. Free. Cineli, Tour Atlantique, 92080 Paris La Df CDX 6 France. **Tel** 011 33 1 47781406.
Ind/Abst Dairy Sci. Abstr.

FR/0575-0865
CAHIERS DES INGENIEURS AGRONOMES. **See** Agriculture.

US/0008-1027
CALIFORNIA ENGINEER. [Calif. eng.]. **Added/Corp** California. University, Berkeley. Student Engineers Council. Vol. 1, (Feb. 1923)-. Periodical. English. Four times a year (Feb., Apr., Oct., Dec.). $5.00. California Engineer Publishing Company, 221 Bechtel Engineering Center, University of California, Berkeley CA 94720. **Tel** (510)642-8679. **ED** David Chen. **Ad Acc, Adv Mgr:** Ivan Choi, **Tel** (510)642-8679. **Circ:** 10,000 (ctrl). ***Supersedes*** *California Journal of Technology.*
Desc: Based in University of California , Berkeley, we publish student-submitted articles to a readership of alumni and student subscriber worldwide.
Ind/Abst Calif. Period. Index (19??-); Calif. Period. Microfi. (19??-).

CN/0045-432X
CANADIAN AGRICULTURAL ENGINEERING. **See** Agriculture-Agricultural Equipment.

CN/0008-3267
CANADIAN CONSULTING ENGINEER. [Can. consult. eng.]. **Added/Corp** Association of Consulting Engineers of Canada. A C E C News. **VFOAT** ACEC News. Vol. 1 (June 1959)-. Periodical. English. Six times a year. 34.00Can$ (one year), 44.00Can$ (two year), 55.00Can$ (three year) Canada; 40.00Can$ (one year), 57.00Can$ (two year) US; 61.00Can$ other. Southam Information and Technology Group Inc., 1450 Don Mills Road, Don Mills Ontario M3B 2X7 Canada. **Tel** (416)445-6641, (800)668-2374, FAX (416)442-2261. **DD** 620/.00971. **[CCC].** available on microfilm from Micromedia Limited; available on microfilm and microfiche from University Microfilms International (UMI).
Ind/Abst AQUAREF.

US/1055-7156
CAPABILITIES (CHICAGO, ILL.). (CAPABILITIES / NORTHWESTERN UNIVERSITY.). [Capabilities]. **Added/Corp** Northwestern University. Rehabilitation Engineering Program. Vol. 1, No. 1 (Apr. 1991)-. Periodical. English. qt. Free. Northwestern University / Engineering, Rehabilitation Engineering Program, 345 East Superior Street, Room 1441, Chicago IL 60611. **DD** 681.

US/0887-7491
CAPACITOR AND RESISTOR TECHNOLOGY SYMPOSIUM. (CAPACITOR AND RESISTOR TECHNOLOGY SYMPOSIUM : CARTS : PROCEEDINGS.). [Capacit. Resist. Technol. Symp.]. **Added/Corp** Components Technology Institute (Huntsville, Ala.) IEEE Components, Hybrids, and Manufacturing Technology Society. **VFOAT** CARTS. (198?)-. Proceedings. English. sa. $70.00. CARTS, 904 Bob Wallace Avenue, Suite 117, Huntsville AL 35801. **Tel** (205)536-1304. **DD** 621.

US
CAREERS AND THE ENGINEER. (Fall 1989)-. English. Twice a year (Feb., & Nov.). $12.95. Bob Adams Inc., 260 Center Street, Holbrook MA 02343. **Tel** (617)767-8100, (800)872-5627, FAX (617)767-0994. **ED** Gigi Ranno. **LC** TA157; .C278.
Desc: Up-to-date information providing the guidance through every step of job search, from career choice to the initial contact to a follow-up letter.

SZ
CARROSSIER. German. Eight times a year. 66.00F Switzerland; 74.00F other. Huber & Co Ag, Postfach, CH-8501 Frauenfeld Switzerland. **Tel** 011 41 54 271111. **ED** M. Hebeisen. **Ad Acc.**

US/0898-5022
CASE INDUSTRY DIRECTORY. **See** Computers.

FR/0245-0283
CATALOGUE DE L'INGENIERIE. **VFOAT** French Engineering Catalog. French. an. 11 rue de Madrid, 75008 Paris France. **LC** TA214; .C38. **DD** 620/.0025/44.

US/0884-0636
CAVITATION AND MULTIPHASE FLOW FORUM. (CAVITATION AND MULTIPHASE FLOW FORUM : PAPERS.). **Main/Conf** Cavitation and Multiphase Flow Forum. 1983-. Periodical. English. an. A.S.C.M.E., United Engineering Center, 345 East 47th Street, New York NY 10017. **LC** TA357; .C35A. **DD** 620.1/064. Documents available from Article Express International. ***Continues*** *Cavitation and Polyphase Flow Forum, 0195-8577.*
Ind/Abst Bioeng. Abstr.; Ei Page One; Eng. Index Annu.

CN/0822-5192
CCI NOUVELLES. **Main/Corp** Conseil Canadien des Ingenieurs. **VAT** Conseil Canadien des Ingenieurs. Nouvelles. (April 1983)-. Periodical. French (English). mo. Canadian Council Prof Engineers, 116 rue Albert Street / Suite 401, Ottawa Ontario KIP 5G3 Canada. **Tel** (613)232-2474, FAX (613)230-5759. **ED** Georges Lolano. **DD** 620/.006/071. **Circ:** 100 (ctrl). ***Continues*** *Conseil Canadien des Ingenieurs. Nouvelles du CCI, 0712-5860.*
Desc: A newsletter of association events personalities and issues, plus news from Ottawa. The newsletter is circulated to the engineering community in Canada as well as to international engineering organizations.

CN/0712-5844
CCPE NEWS. [CCPE news]. **Main/Corp** Canadian Council of Professional Engineers. **VAT** Canadian Council of Professional Engineers News. Vol. 24, No. 4 (April 1982)-. Periodical. English (French). mo. CCPE News, c/o Canadian Council of Professional Engineers, Suite 401/116 Albert Street, Ottawa Ontario K1P 5G3 Canada. **Tel** (613)232-2474, FAX (613)230-5759. **ED** Georges Lolano. **DD** 620/.006/071. **Circ:** 1,000 (ctrl). ***Continues*** *Canadian Council of Professional Engineers.*

Newsbrief, 0319-6194.
Desc: A newsletter of Association events, personalities and issues, plus news from Ottawa. The newsletter is circulated to the engineering community in Canada as well as to international engineering organizations.

US
CED DIRECTORY OF ENGINEERING AND ENGINEERING TECHNOLOGY CO-OP PROGRAMS. **VFOAT** Directory of Engineering and Engineering Technology Co-Op Programs; Engineering Co-Op Directory. 1983-. Directory. English. be. $20.00. Mississippi State University / Cooperative Education Program, PO Box 6046, Mississippi State MS 39762. **Tel** (601)325-3823. **ED** Luther Epting. **Circ:** 300 (ctrl).
Desc: A directory of educational institutions offering engineering and engineering technology cooperative education programs with pertinent data included.

SA/0009-0409
CERTIFICATED ENGINEER. ***Title Change.*** (CERTIFICATED ENGINEER. GEDIPLOMEERDE INGENIEUR.). [Certif. eng.]. **Added/Corp** Institution of Certified Mechanical and Electrical Engineers, S.A. **VFOAT** Gediplomeerde Ingenieur. (1959)-(19??). Periodical. English. mo. Keeble Publishing (Pty) Ltd, Sherwell St, Doornfontein, PO Box 3080, 2000 Johannesburg South Africa. **CODEN** CEENA9. Documents available from Article Express International, Ask*IEEE. ***Continues*** *Institution of Certified Engineers, South Africa. Journal.* ***Continued by*** *Ticket.*
Ind/Abst Bioeng. Abstr.; Ei Page One; Eng. Index Annu. [Select. Cov.]; INSPEC (July 1969-).

US/0746-6641
CERTIFIED ENGINEERING TECHNICIAN. [Certif. eng. tech.]. **Added/Corp** American Society of Certified Engineering Technicians. Vol. 16 (1979)-. Periodical. English. Six times a year (Feb., Apr., June, Aug., Oct., Dec.). $12.00. American Society of Certified Engineering Technicians, PO Box 1348, Flowery Branch GA 30542. **Tel** (404)967-9173. **ED** G. Thomas Wakeland, (editor's address: 2269 Richter Street, Palm Harbor, FL 34683, phone: (813)784-1754). **DD** 620. **Bk Rev**, (Qty: varies). **Ad Acc**, **Adv Mgr:** Kurt Schuler. **Circ:** 2,500 (ctrl).
Desc: Devoted to technical and management information within the engineering and engineering technology professions. News of local, regular, and student chapter activities is included.

JA/0577-6848
CHIBA DAIGAKU KOGAKUBU KENKYU HOKOKU. **See** Science and Technology.

US/0193-6174
CHILTON'S IAN (1977). ***Title Change.*** (CHILTON'S IAN.). [Chilton's IAN]. **Added/Corp** Chilton Company. **VFOAT** Chilton's I.A.N.; Instrumentation & Control News; Instrument & Apparatus News. **VAT** Chilton's Instrument and Apparatus News. (June 1977)-Vol. 41, No. 5 (May 1993). Periodical. English. mo. Chilton Company, 201 King of Prussia Road, Radnor PA 19089. **Tel** (610)964-4122, (800)695-1214, FAX (610)964-4978, telex 6851035 CHILTON UW. **ED** Terry Persun. **LC** Q184; .I25. **DD** 681/.029/4. **[CCC]**. **Ad Acc. Circ:** 112,000 (ctrl). available on microfilm and microfiche from University Microfilms International (UMI). ***Continues*** *IAN.* ***Continued by*** *Instrumentation & Automation News.*
Desc: Information relating to the ever changing high-tech world of industrial control with a wealth of product information; a showcase for products and services.

US/0746-2395
CHILTON'S I&CS. ***Title Change.*** (CHILTON'S I & C S : THE INDUSTRIAL AND PROCESS CONTROL MAGAZINE.). [Chilton's I CS]. **Added/Corp** Chilton Company. **VFOAT** Chilton's I and C S; Instruments and Control Systems; I and C S; I & C S; Instruments & Control Systems. **VAT** Chilton's Instruments and Control Systems. Vol. 56, No. 5 (May 1983)-Vol. 65, No. 2 (Feb. 1992). Periodical. English. mo. Chilton Company, 201 King of Prussia Road, Radnor PA 19089. **Tel** (610)964-4122, (800)695-1214, FAX (610)964-4978, telex 6851035 CHILTON UW. **ED** Jack Hickey. **LC** TA165; .A2. **DD** 629.8/05. **CODEN** CHISDY. **[CCC]**. **Bk Rev**. **Ad Acc**. **Pr Rev.** ctrl circ. available on microfilm and microfiche from University Microfilms International (UMI). Documents available from Ask*IEEE. ***Continues*** *Chilton's Instruments & Control Systems, 0164-0089.* ***Continued by*** *Instrumentation & Control Systems.*
Desc: In-depth technical information on process control and instrumentation developments edited for electrical, mechanical, design and other engineers.
Ind/Abst Appl. Sci. Technol. Index; Coal Abstr.; Ei Page One; Fluid Abstr., Civil Eng.; Fluid Abstr. Proc. Eng.; FLUIDEX (1983-1990); INSPEC (Aug. 1987-); Lit. Pat. Abstr., Oilfield Chem. (19??-1990); Lit. Abstr., Catal. Catal.; Lit. Abstr., Health Environ.; Lit. Abstr., Pet. Refin. Petrochem.; Lit. Abstr., Pet. Substit.; Lit. Abstr., Transp. Storage; Proc. Chem. Eng.; Theoret. Chem. Eng.

US/1044-064X
CHINESE JOURNAL OF AUTOMATION. [Chin. j. autom.]. **Added/Corp** Chinese Association of Automation. Vol. 1, No. 1 (1989)-. Periodical. English (translations available in Chinese). Four times a year. $410.00. Allerton Press, Inc., 150 Fifth Avenue, New York NY 10011. **Tel** (212)924-3950, FAX (212)463-9684, telex 427441 ALPRES. **LC** TJ212; .T9844. **DD** 629.8. **CODEN** CJAUEF. **[CCC]**.

US/0885-663X
CHRYSLER POWER. [Chrysler power]. **VFOAT** Chrysler Power Magazine. (19??)-. Periodical. English. Six times a year. $19.95. Chrysler Power, PO Box 1210, Azusa CA 91702. **Tel** (818)303-6220. **DD** 629.

JA/0910-8629
CHUBU DAIGAKU KOGAKUBU KIYO. [Chubu Daigaku Kogakubu kiyo]. **Added/Corp** Chubu Daigaku. Kogakubu. **VFOAT** Memoirs of College of Engineering, Chubu University. (1984)-. Periodical. Japanese (English). an. Chuba Daigaku Kogakubu, Matsumoto-cho, Kasugai-shi, Aichi-ken 487 Japan. **LC** TA4; .C356. **CODEN** CDKKER. Documents available from Ask*IEEE, CASDDS. ***Continues*** *Chubu Kogyo Daigaku Kiyo. A, 0386-1732;* ***Absorbed in part*** *Chubu Kogyo Daigaku Kiyo. B, 0386-1740.*
Ind/Abst Chem. Abstr.; INSPEC (Oct. 1984-).

JA
CHUGOKU KOGYO GIJUTSU SHIKENJO HOKOKU. **Main/Corp** Chugoku Kogyo Gijutsu Shikenjo. **VFOAT** Reports of the Government Industrial Research Institute, Chugoku. No. 1- 1976-. Periodical. Japanese (summaries and/or abstracts in English). Kogyo Gijutsuin Chugoku Kogyo Gijutsu Shikenjo, 15000 Hiromachi 737-01, Kure Japan. **LC** TA4; .C35713.

CH/0253-3839
CHUNG-KUO KUNG CH'ENG HSUEH KAN. [Zhongguo gongcheng xuekan]. **VFOAT** Journal of the Chinese Institute of Engineers. (1978)-. Academic Scholarly Publication. English (Chinese). qt. $40.00. Chung-kuo Kung Cheng Shih Hsueh Hui, #1 4th Floor/2nd Section Jen-Ai Road, Taipei Taiwan. **LC** TA4; .C3578. **DD** 620/.005. **CODEN** CKCKDZ. Documents available from Article Express International, Ask*IEEE, CASDDS.
Ind/Abst ACM Guide Comput. Lit.; Bioeng. Abstr.; Chem. Abstr.; Comput. Rev.; Ei Page One; Eng. Index Annu.; INSPEC (Jan. 1978-); Int. Aerosp. Abstr.; Math. Rev.

US/0160-3647
CIRCULAR - ENGINEERING EXPERIMENT STATION, OREGON STATE UNIVERSITY. (CIRCULAR - ENGINEERING EXPERIMENT STATION.). [Circ. - Or. State Univ., Eng. Exp. Stn.]. **Main/Corp** Oregon State University. Engineering Experiment Station. No. 28 March (1962)-. Monographic series. English. ir. Free on request. Engineering Experiment Station, Oregon State University, Corvallis OR 97331. **LC** TA7; .O75. **DD** 620. **CODEN** COSSDV. Documents available from CASDDS. ***Continues*** *Circular - Engineering Experiment Station, Oregon State College, 0192-2696.*
Ind/Abst Chem. Abstr.

NE
CIVIELE TECHNIEK. Dutch. qt. Stam Tijdschriften BV, Postbus 235, 2280 AE Rijswijk Netherlands. **Tel** +31 70 3988100, FAX +31 70 3988276, telex 33702 STAM NL. ***Continues*** *PT : Civiele Techniek.*

●AT
CIVIL ENGINEERS AUSTRALIA. **Added/Corp** Institution of Engineers, Australia. (Aug. 22, 1992)-. Periodical. English. bw. 46.50Aus$ (one edition), 93.00Aus$ (both editions) Australia; 74.30Aus$ (one edition), 148.60Aus$ (both editions) other. Engineers Australia Pty Ltd, 2 Ernest Street, Crows Nest Centre, Crows Nest New South Wales 2065, Australia. **Tel** 011 61 2 438-1533, FAX 011 61 2 438-5934, telex 27640. **LC** TA1; .C4543. **DD** 624/.05. ***Continues in part*** *Engineers Australia, 1032-1195.*
Desc: Information on civil engineering.

US/0009-8809
CLEVELAND ENGINEERING. Periodical. English. mo. $24.00. Cleveland Engineering, 3100 Chester Avenue, Cleveland OH 44114-4683. **Tel** (216)361-3100. **ED** Elaine Rybak. **Bk Rev**. **Ad Acc**. **Circ:** 2,000 (ctrl).
Desc: Information on companies, people, products, programs and technology relating to all engineering disciplines on a local and national basis.

FR/1161-1804
CLUB INFORMATIONS NANTERRE. (TELE-CONTACT : JOURNAL CLUB INFORMATIONS.). (1958)-. Periodical. French. Five times a year. 110.00F France; 130.00F others. Journal Club Informations, 5 rue Nadar, 92566 Rueil Malmaison France. **Tel** 011 33 1 4129 8334, FAX 011 33 1 4751 7384. **UDC** 331.82(085.3). **Bk Rev**. **Circ:** 7,000.
Desc: News and information to the association and other related topics.

US/0938-0949
COASTAL AND ESTUARINE STUDIES. [Coast. estuar. stud.]. (1989)-. Monographic series. English. ir. Price varies per volume. Springer Verlag New York Inc., PO Box 19386 Books, Newark NJ 07195. **Tel** (201)348-4033. **CODEN** CESTEX. ***Continues*** *Lecture Notes on Coastal and Estuarine Studies, 0724-5890.*
Desc: Information on coastal engineering and estuaries.

NE/0378-3839
COASTAL ENGINEERING (AMSTERDAM). (COASTAL ENGINEERING.). [Coastal eng.]. Vol. 1 (March 1977)-. Academic Scholarly Publication. English. Twelve times a year (3 volumes). Fl1365.00. Elsevier Science Publishers BV, PO Box 211, 1000 AE Amsterdam Netherlands. **Tel** 011 31 20 5803642, FAX 011 31 20 5862696, telex 15682. **ED** E W Bijker. **LC** TC203; .C57. **DD** 620/.414/605. **CODEN** COENDE. **[CCC]**. **Pr Rev.** available on microfilm and microfiche from University Microfilms International (UMI). Documents available from Article Express International, The Genuine Article, Documents on Demand.
Desc: Publishes fundamental studies as well as case histories on the following aspects of coastal, harbour and offshore engineering: studies on waves and currents; coastal morphology; estuary hydraulics; harbour and offshore structures.
Ind/Abst AQUAREF; Aquat. Sci. Fish. Abstr. (Computer File); Bioeng. Abstr.; BMT Abstr.; Civ. Struct. Eng. Abstr.; Comput. Inf. Syst. Abstr. J. [Full Cov.]; Ei Page One; Energy Res. Abstr. (March 1979-); Eng. Index Annu.; Environ. Abstr.; Environ. Eng. Abstr.; Fluid Abstr., Civil Eng.; Fluid Abstr. Proc. Eng.; FLUIDEX (1977-); Geogr. Abstr. Phys. Geogr.; Geol. Abstr.; GeoRef; Geotech. Abstr.; J. Plan. Lit.; Mar. Sci. Contents Tables; Mech. Eng. Abstr.; Meteorol. Geoastrophys. Abstr. (-19??); Ocean. Abstr.; Pollut. Abstr. Indexes; Res. Alert [Full Cov.]; Sci. Cit. Index; SCISEARCH.

NE/0165-232X
COLD REGIONS SCIENCE AND TECHNOLOGY. [Cold reg. sci. technol.]. Vol. 1 (June 1979)-. Academic Scholarly Publication. English. Four times a year (1 volume). Fl590.00. Elsevier Science Publishers BV, PO Box 211, 1000 AE Amsterdam Netherlands. **Tel** 011 31 20 5803642, FAX 011 31 20 5862696, telex 15682. **ED** Malcolm Mellor. **LC** GB641; .C63. **DD** 620/.411. **CODEN** CRSTDL. **[CCC]**. **Bk Rev**. **Ad Acc**. **Pr Rev.** available on microfilm and microfiche from University Microfilms International (UMI). Documents available from Article Express International, The Genuine Article, CASDDS.
Desc: Deals with the scientific and technical problems of cold environments, including both natural and artificial environments.
Ind/Abst ASTIS Curr. Aware. Bull. (1979-); AGRICOLA; AQUAREF; ASTIS Bibliogr. (1979-); Bioeng. Abstr.; Chem. Abstr.; Curr. Contents Eng. Tech. Appl. Sci.; Ei Page One; Eng. Index Annu.; Geogr. Abstr. Phys. Geogr.; Geol. Abstr.; GeoRef; Meteorol. Geoastrophys. Abstr.; Ocean. Abstr.; Life Sci. Collect.; Res. Alert [Full Cov.]; Sci. Cit. Index; SCISEARCH; Soils Fert.

US
COLD REGIONS TECHNICAL DIGEST. **Added/Corp** U.S. Army Cold Regions Research and Engineering Laboratory. (19??)-. Monographic series. English. ir. Free on request. US Army Cold Regions Research, 72 Lyne Road, Hanover NH 03755. **Tel** (603)646-4100.

US/0010-1583
COLORADO ENGINEER, THE. [Colo. eng.]. Periodical. English. qt. $6.00. University of Colorado / Boulder, Campus Box 421, Boulder CO 80309. **Tel** (303)492-8635. **ED** Jeff Jacot. **Bk Rev**. **Ad Acc. Circ:** 3,000 (ctrl). ***Continues*** *University of Colorado Journal of Engineering.*
Desc: Aimed at students, faculty and alumni of distinguished engineering and research institutes in order to communicate the latest in engineering and technology.
Ind/Abst GeoRef.

UK/0367-7850
COMMUNICATION / THE INSTITUTION OF GAS ENGINEERS. [Comm. - Inst. Gas Eng.]. **Added/Corp** Institution of Gas Engineers. (19??)-. Monographic series. English. Price varies per volume. Institution of Gas Engineers, 17 Grosvenor Crescent, London SW1 7ES England. **Tel** 011 44 71 2459811. **LC** UNC. **CODEN** IGECBN. Documents available from CASDDS.
Ind/Abst Ceram. Abstr. (19??-); Chem. Abstr. (1930-1982); Ei Page One; Gas Abstr.

UK/0748-8025
COMMUNICATIONS IN APPLIED NUMERICAL METHODS. ***Title Change.*** **See** Mathematics.

●UK/1069-8299
COMMUNICATIONS IN NUMERICAL METHODS IN ENGINEERING. **See** Mathematics.

●US/1072-3757
COMMUNICATIONS IN RELIABILITY, MAINTAINABILITY, AND SUPPORTABILITY. [Commun. reliab. maintain. support.]. **Added/Corp** Society of Automotive Engineers. Vol. 1, No. 1 (winter 1994)-. Periodical. English. sa. $37.00 North America; $42.00 other. Society of

Automotive Engineers, 400 Commonwealth Drive, Warrendale PA 15096. **Tel** (412)776-4841, (412)772-7106, FAX (412)776-5760. **DD** 620.

TU/0256-7865
COMMUNICATIONS: SERIES C BIOLOGY AND GEOLOGICAL ENGINEERING. **See** Biology.

US/0275-7486
COMPANY RECOGNITION STUDY. RETAILER EDITION. (COMPANY RECOGNITION STUDY.). **VFOAT** Hardware Age Company Recognition Study. (1978)-. English. be (once every two years). $40.00. Chilton Company, 201 King of Prussia Road, Radnor PA 19089. **Tel** (610)964-4122, (800)695-1214, FAX (610)964-4978, telex 6851035 CHILTON UW. **ED** Jack Hickey. **LC** HD9745.U4; C65a. **DD** 381/.45/00029473. **Ad Acc.** ctrl circ.
Desc: In-depth technical information on process and industrial control and instrumentation developments edited for electrical, mechanical, design and other engineers.

US/1056-182X
COMPARISON REPORT ON ENGINEERING DOCUMENT MANAGEMENT (EDMS) SYSTEMS. [Comp. rep. eng. doc. manage. EDMS syst.]. **Added/Corp** International Imaging, Inc. **VFOAT** EDMS Comparison Report. (Apr. 29, 1991)-. Periodical. English. qt. $490.00. International Imaging Inc, 701 West Foothill Boulevard, Azusa CA 91702. **DD** 621. ***Continues*** *Comparison Report on Engineering Scanning Systems, 1055-7652.*

US/1063-8709
COMPENDEX PLUS. **See** Engineering-Abstracting, Bibliographies and Statistics.

UK/0952-6919
COMPOSITE POLYMERS. ***Title Change.*** **See** Plastics.

US/1058-904X
COMPOSITES INDUSTRY MONTHLY. [Compos. ind. mon.]. **Added/Corp** Composite Market Reports, Inc. (1989)-. Periodical. English. mo. $1440.00. Composite Market Reports Inc., 7670 Opportunity Road, Suite 250, San Diego CA 92111. **Tel** (619)560-1085. **DD** 620. **[CCC].** available on an online database (files 16,636/Full-Text) from DIALOG.
Ind/Abst PTS Newsl. Database [Full Txt.].

FR/0223-6335
COMPTES RENDUS DES TRAVAUX DES COLLOQUES. **See** Physics.

US
COMPUTER AIDED ENGINEERING SERIES. Monographic series. English. ir. Price varies per volume. Marcel Dekker Inc., 270 Madison Avenue, New York NY 10016. **Tel** (212)696-9000, (800)228-1160, FAX (212)685-4540, telex 421419. **(Subscription address:** Marcel Dekker Inc, PO Box 5017, Monticello NY 12701.**)**
Desc: Topics covered have included integrated computer network systems and CAD/CAM/CAE systems.

●US/1061-3773
COMPUTER APPLICATIONS IN ENGINEERING EDUCATION. (JOURNAL OF COMPUTER APPLICATIONS IN ENGINEERING EDUCATION.). [Comput. appl. eng. educ.]. (1992)-. Periodical. English. Four times a year. $220.00 (US); $260.00 (Canada & Mexico); $275.00 (other). John Wiley & Sons, Inc., 605 Third Avenue, New York NY 10158-0012. **Tel** (212)850-6000, (212)850-6645, FAX (212)850-6088, telex 12-7063. **(Subscription address:** John Wiley & Sons / England, Baffins Lane, Chichester, West Sussex PO19 1UD England.**) ED** Magdy F. Iskander. **LC** T61; .C575. **DD** 620/.0071/1. **CODEN** CAPEED.
Desc: Provides a forum for publishing timely information on the innovative uses of computers and software tools in education, and for accelerating the intergration of computers into the engineering curriculum.

NE/0045-7825
COMPUTER METHODS IN APPLIED MECHANICS AND ENGINEERING. **See** Computers-Data Processing.

US/1065-3201
COMPUTERS IN ENGINEERING. (COMPUTERS IN ENGINEERING : PROCEEDINGS OF THE ... ASME INTERNATIONAL COMPUTERS IN ENGINEERING CONFERENCE AND EXPOSITION / SPONSORED BY COMPUTERS IN ENGINEERING DIVISION, ASME.). [Comput. eng.]. **Main/Conf** ASME International Computers in Engineering Conference and Exposition. **Added/Corp** American Society of Mechanical Engineers. Computers in Engineering Division. (1989)-. Proceedings. English. ir. Price varies. American Society of Mechanical Engineers, 22 Law Drive, Fairfield NJ 07007. **Tel** (201)882-1167, (212)705-7722 (editorial). **LC** TA345; .I5485a. **DD** 620. ***Continues*** *ASME International Computers in Engineering Conference and Exhibition. Computers in Engineering, 1065-3201.*

US/0010-4876
COMPUTING REPORT IN SCIENCE AND ENGINEERING. **See** Science and Technology.

US/0956-0521
COMPUTING SYSTEMS IN ENGINEERING. (COMPUTING SYSTEMS IN ENGINEERING : AN INTERNATIONAL JOURNAL.). [Comput. syst. eng.]. Vol. 1, No. 1 (1990)-. Periodical. English. bm. $447.00 The Americas; £300.00 other. Pergamon Press, An Imprint of Elsevier Science Ltd., The Boulevard, Langford Lane, Kidlington, Oxford OX5 1GB United Kingdom. **Tel** 011 44 865 843000, 011 44 865 843699, FAX 011 44 865 843010. **(Subscription address:** Elsevier Science Ltd. Oxford Fulfillment Centre, PO Box 800, Kidlington, Oxford OX5 1DX United Kingdom.**) ED** Ahmed Noor and Barry Topping. **LC** TA345; .C652. **DD** 620/.00285. **CODEN** COSEEO. **[CCC].** available on microfilm and microfiche from University Microfilms International (UMI). Documents available from Ask*IEEE.
Desc: Communicates recent and projected advances in computational technology to practising engineers and research workers in this field. The scope of this journal will include computational strategies and numerical algorithms for large-scale engineering problems.
Ind/Abst INSPEC (1990-).

US/0749-9191
CONCRETE ... SOURCEBOOK. [Concr. sourceb.]. **Added/Corp** Concrete Construction Publications, Inc. **VFOAT** Concrete ... Source Book. (19??)-. English. an. **LC** TA439; .C573. **DD** 620.1/36/029473.

●UK/1063-293X
CONCURRENT ENGINEERING : RESEARCH AND APPLICATIONS. (1993)-. Academic Scholarly Publication. English. Four times a year. $350.00. Academic Press Ltd., A Division of Harcourt Brace & Company Ltd., 24-28 Oval Road, London NW1 7DX England. **Tel** 071 267 4466, FAX 071 482 2293, 071 485 4752, telex 25775 ACPRES G. **(Subscription address:** Harcourt Brace & Company, Ltd., Foots Cray, High Street, Sidcup Kent DA14 5HP England.**) ED** B. Prasad.
Desc: International, multidisciplinary research and applications-oriented journal aiming to promote a better understanding of concurrency in enterprise modeling, information processing and computing.

UK
CONDITION MONITORING AND DIAGNOSTIC TECHNOLOGY. ***Title Change.*** (19??)-(1993). English. qt. British Institute of Non-Destructive Testing, 1 Spencer Parade, Northampton NN1 5AA England. **Tel** 0604 30124, FAX 0604 231489. **ED** J. Percival. **Bk Rev. Ad Acc. Pr Rev. Circ:** 500 (ctrl). Documents available from Article Express International. ***Absorbed by*** *British Journal of Non-Destructive Testing.*
Ind/Abst Eng. Index Annu.

US
CONFERENCE ON RELIABILITY AND MAINTAINABILITY. (19??)-. Proceedings. English. ir. IEEE, Institution of Electrical and Electronics Engineers, Inc., 345 East 47th Street, New York NY 10017-2394. **Tel** (908)981-1393, FAX (908)981-9667.

US/0162-704X
CONFERENCE PAPERS INDEX. **See** Science and Technology.

US
CONFERENCE PROCEEDINGS / ANTEC. **See** Plastics.

UK
CONFERENCE PROCEEDINGS / INSTITUTE OF MARINE ENGINEERS. Proceedings. English. ir. $120.00 Conference 1; $120.00 Conference 2; $140.00 Conference 3; $360.00 all three Conference Proceedings. Marine Management Holdings Ltd, Memorial Building, 76 Mark Lane, London EC3R 7JN England. **Tel** 011 44 71 4818493. **(Subscription address:** For North America: Learned Information Inc., 143 Old Marlton Pike, Medford, NJ 08055-8750**)**

RH
CONSTRUCTION AND ENGINEERING, ZIMBABWE. **VFOAT** Construction and Engineering; Construction & Engineering. Vol. 1, No. 1 (Feb. 1989)-. Periodical. English. mo. 40.00Zin$ Zimbabwe; 55.00Zin$ other. The Argosy Press (Pvt) Ltd, Islip House, Samora Machel Avenue, Harare Zimbabwe. **Tel** 735434. **ED** S Orange. **LC** TA1; .C765. **DD** 620/.005. **Ad Acc. Circ:** 3,000 (ctrl). ***Formed by the union of*** *Zimbabwe Engineer, 0251-1037* ***and*** *Construction Review (Harare, Zimbabwe).*
Desc: Engineering works in Zimbabwe and various disciplines.

CN/0712-9890
CONSULTANT (MONTREAL. 1974). (CONSULTANT : BULLETIN D'INFORMATION DE L'ASSOCIATION DES INGENIEURS-CONSEILS DU QUEBEC.). [Consultant]. **VFOAT** Consultant : Association of Consulting Engineers of Quebec Newsletter. Bulletin. English (French). Free to Members. Association of Consulting Engineers of Canada, 130 Albert Street/Suite 616, Ottawa Ontario K10 5G4 Canada. **DD** 620/.006/0714.

UK
CONSULTING ENGINEERS WHO'S WHO & YEAR BOOK, THE. **See** Biographies.

CN
CONTACT. **See** Science and Technology.

UK
CONTAINERISATION INTERNATIONAL YEARBOOK. (197?)-. English. an. $315.00. EMAP Response Publishing Ltd., 67 Clerkenwell Road, London EC1R 5BH England. **Tel** 011 44 71 404 2763, FAX 011 44 71 404 2765. **LC** TA1215; .C597. **DD** 385.1; 658.7. ***Continues*** *Container Guide.*

UK/0267-4718
CONTEMPORARY ERGONOMICS : PROCEEDINGS OF THE ERGONOMICS SOCIETY'S ANNUAL CONFERENCE. **Main/Corp** Ergonomics Society (Great Britain). Conference. **VFOAT** Proceedings of the Ergonomics Society's Annual Conference. (1984)-. English. an. $95.00. Taylor & Francis Ltd., Rankine Road, Basingstoke Hampshire, RG24 8PR United Kingdom. **Tel** 011 44 256 840366, FAX 011 44 256 479438, telex 858540. **(Subscription address:** Taylor & Francis Inc., 1900 Frost Road, Suite 101, Bristol PA 19007-1598.**) ED** E. D. Megaw. **LC** TA166; .E734a. **DD** 620.8/2/05. **[CCC].** ***Continues*** *Ergonomics Society (Great Britain). Conference. Proceedings of the Ergonomics Society's Conference.*

US/0069-9551
CONTINUING ENGINEERING STUDIES SERIES. MONOGRAPHS. Began with No. 1 in 1967. Monographic series. English. Price varies per volume. American Society for Engineering Education, 1818 North Street Northwest, Suite 600, Washington DC 20036. **Tel** (202)331-3500.

US/0090-5267
CONTROL AND DYNAMIC SYSTEMS. (CONTROL AND DYNAMIC SYSTEMS : ADVANCES IN THEORY AND APPLICATIONS.). [Control dyn. syst.]. Vol. 9 (1973)-. Monographic series. English. ir. Price varies per volume. Academic Press, Inc., 6277 Sea Harbor Drive, Orlando FL 32887. **Tel** (800)543-9534, (407)345-4100, FAX (407)363-9661. **ED** C. T. Leondes. **LC** QA402.3; .A35. **DD** 629.8/312/05. **CODEN** CDSYD6. **[CCC].** Documents available from Article Express International, BIOSIS Document Express, Ask*IEEE, CASDDS. ***Continues*** *Advances in Control Systems.*
Ind/Abst Bioeng. Abstr.; Biol. Abstr.; Chem. Abstr.; Ei Page One; Eng. Index Annu.; INSPEC; Zentralbl. Math. Ihre Grenzgeb.

US/0010-8790
CORNELL ENGINEER, THE. [Cornell eng.]. (Oct. 1935)-. Periodical. English. ir (twice an academic semester). $14.00 (one year), $24.00 (two year), $32.00 (three year). Cornell Engineer, 217 Carpenter Hall, Cornell University, Ithaca NY 14853. **Tel** (607)255-3312. **ED** Jonathon Kwoh, Avinash Mehrotra and Gerald Cheung. **LC** TA1; .C802. **DD** 620/.005. **CODEN** CNLEA. **Bk Rev. Ad Acc. Circ:** 4,000 (ctrl). available on microfilm and microfiche from University Microfilms International (UMI). ***Formed by the union of*** *Cornell Civil Engineer* ***and*** *Sibley Journal of Engineering, 0096-9265.*
Desc: Focuses on issues relating to the engineering profession and college students majoring in engineering.
Ind/Abst GeoRef.

US
CORROSION TECHNOLOGY. (1989)-. Monographic series. English. Price varies per volume. Marcel Dekker Inc., 270 Madison Avenue, New York NY 10016. **Tel** (212)696-9000, (800)228-1160, FAX (212)685-4540, telex 421419. **(Subscription address:** Marcel Dekker Inc, PO Box 5017, Monticello NY 12701.**)**
Desc: Covers topics in corrosion technology such as corrosion-resistant piping and the corrosion resistance of elastomers.

US
COST ENGINEERING. Vol. 1 (1978)-. Monographic series. English. Price varies per volume. Marcel Dekker Inc., 270 Madison Avenue, New York NY 10016. **Tel** (212)696-9000, (800)228-1160, FAX (212)685-4540, telex 421419. **(Subscription address:** Marcel Dekker Inc, PO Box 5017, Monticello NY 12701.**)**
Desc: Covers topics such as applied cost engineering and applied cost and schedule control.

US/0274-9696
COST ENGINEERING (MORGANTOWN. 1980). (COST ENGINEERING : A PUBLICATION OF THE AMERICAN ASSOCIATION OF COST

ENGINEERS.). [Cost eng.]. **Added/Corp** American Association of Cost Engineers. **VFOAT** Cost Engineering Newsletter. Vol. 22/No. 4-A (Sept. 1980)-. Periodical. English. mo. $48.00 US; $64.00 other. American Association of Cost Engineers, PO Box 1557, Morgantown WV 26507. **Tel** (304)296-8444, (800)858-2678, FAX (304)291-5728, telex 887612 AACE MORG UD. **ED** Sara Pritchard. **LC** TA183; .A6. **[CCC].** Index available. cum. index. **Bk Rev. Ad Acc. Circ:** 6,000. available on microfilm and microfiche from University Microfilms International (UMI); available on an online database (files 15,485/Full-Text) from DIALOG. Documents available from Article Express International, UMI Article Clearinghouse, Ask*IEEE. ***Continues*** *Cost Engineering Magazine, 0276-721X.*
Desc: Edited for engineers and estimators specializing in project management, cost estimation, cost control, business planning and management science. Contains technical articles, news articles, books reviews and specialized columns.
Ind/Abst ABI/INFORM Glob. Ed.; ABI Inform Ondisc (Sept. 1980-); Abstr. Bull. Inst. Pap. Sci. Tech.; Account. Tax Datab. (Mar. 1977-) [Full Txt.]; Coal Abstr.; Eng. Index Annu.; INSPEC (Sept. 1980-); PAIS Int. Print (1991-); UMI ABI/Inform--Bus. Period. Ondisc [Full Txt.].

NE
COST ENGINEERS HANDBOOK. (19??)-. English. Three times a year. Fl93.40. Samson Bedrijfsinformatie, Postbus 4, 2400 HA Alphen Rij Netherlands. **Tel** 011 31 1 72066633. **(Subscription address:** Intermedia BV, Postbus 4, 2400 MA Alphen Rijn Netherlands.**)**

US
CRREL BENCHNOTES : U.S. ARMY CORPS OF ENGINEERS INFORMATION EXCHANGE BULLETIN. VFOAT USA Crrel Benchnotes; Cold Regions Research and Engineering Laboratory Benchnotes. Publication began with May 1976. Bulletin. English. ir. Free. US Army Corps of Engineers Cold Regions, Cold Regions Research and Engineering Laboratory, Hanover NH 03755. **Tel** (603)646-4238. **ED** Steven Bowen. **Circ:** 500 (ctrl).

US/0095-7917
CURRENT CONTENTS. ENGINEERING, TECHNOLOGY & APPLIED SCIENCES. **See** Engineering-Abstracting, Bibliographies and Statistics.

US/1062-3132
CURRENT CONTENTS ON DISKETTE. ENGINEERING, TECHNOLOGY & APPLIED SCIENCES. (CURRENT CONTENTS ON DISKETTE. ENGINEERING, TECHNOLOGY & APPLIED SCIENCES [COMPUTER FILE].). [Curr. contents diskette, Eng. technol. appl. sci.]. **Added/Corp** Institute for Scientific Information. **VFOAT** Engineering, Technology & Applied Sciences; Engineering, Technology and Applied Sciences. Vol. 20, Issue 1 (Jan. 1, 1990)-. Periodical. English. wk. $525.00. Institute for Scientific Information, 3501 Market Street, Philadelphia PA 19104. **Tel** (215)386-0100, (800)523-1850, FAX (215)386-6362, telex 84-5305. **(Subscription address:** Institute for Scientific Information, PO Box 71416, Chicago IL 60694.**) LC** Z7913. **DD** 016. available in print (as: Current Contents. Engineering, Technology, & Applied Sciences); available on diskette.

BL/0102-9541
CVRD REVISTA. [CVRD rev.]. **Main/Corp** Companhia Vale do Rio Doce. **Added/Corp** Brazil. Ministerio das Minas e Energia. **VFOAT** C.V.R.D. Review. **VAT** Companhia Vale do Rio Doce Revista. Vol. 1, No. 1, (August 1980)-. Portuguese (summaries and/or abstracts in English). qt. Free. Companhia Vale do Rio Doce, Divisao de Informacoes Tecnicas, Avenida Graca Aranha, Rio de Janeiro RJ Brasil CEP 20.005. **ED** Carlos Braune. **LC** TA4; .C633a. **DD** 669/.005. cum. index. **Circ:** 3,500 (ctrl).
Desc: Publishing of projects and articles done by the technical staff of CVRD in the fields of: mining, mechanical and civil engineering and forestry.
Ind/Abst Alum. Ind. Abstr.; Eng. Mater. Abstr.; Met. Abstr.

US
DEADLINE. **See** Computers-Software.

RU/0130-3082
DEFEKTOSKOPIIA. [Defektoskopija]. (1965)-. Periodical. Russian. mo. $230.00. **(Subscription address:** East View Publications Inc., 3020 Harbor Lane North, Suite 110, Minneapolis MN 55447.**) DD** 620.1. **CODEN** DEFKAG. Documents available from Article Express International, Ask*IEEE, CASDDS.
Ind/Abst Alum. Ind. Abstr.; Chem. Abstr.; Eng. Index Annu.; INSPEC (Jan.-Feb. 1973-); Int. Aerosp. Abstr.; Met. Abstr.; Pollut. Abstr. Indexes.

UK/0308-8448
DESIGN ENGINEERING (LONDON, ENGLAND). (DESIGN ENGINEERING.). [Des. eng.]. (Jan. 1973)-. Periodical. English. mo. £69.00 UK and Northern Ireland; $165.00 other. Morgan Grampian, 40 Beresford Street Woolwich, London SE18 6BQ England. **Tel** 011 44 81 855 7777, FAX 011 44 81 855 5548, telex 896238. **ED** Andy Pye. **LC** TA174; .D465. **DD** 620/.00425/05. **CODEN** DEMCBS. **Bk Rev. Ad Acc. Circ:** 26,231 (ctrl). Documents available from Ask*IEEE. ***Continues in part*** *Design Engineering, Materials, and Components;* ***Absorbed*** *Sub-Assembly Components-Fastening;* ***Absorbed in part*** *Fluid Power International.*
Desc: The ideal journal for design engineers covering applications of mechanical, electronic and electrical components and materials in original equipment manufacture design.
Ind/Abst Ceram. Abstr.; Ei Page One; Fluid Abstr., Civil Eng.; Fluid Abstr. Proc. Eng.; FLUIDEX (1973-); INSPEC (Sept. 1969-); Saf. Health Work; Surf. Treat. Technol. Abstr.

CN/0011-9342
DESIGN ENGINEERING (TORONTO). (DESIGN ENGINEERING.). [Des. eng.]. Vol. 1 (Apr. 1955)-. Periodical. English. mo (10 issues). 36.00Can$ Canada; 75.00Can$ other. MacLean Hunter Ltd. Business Publishers / Canada, Box 9100, Station A, Toronto ONT M5W 1A5 Canada. **Tel** (416)946-8420, (800)567-0444. **(Subscription address:** Indas, 35 Riviera Drive, Building 17, Markham Ontario L3R 8N4 Canada.**) CODEN** DEENAK. **[CCC].**
Ind/Abst Can. Bus. Index; Nucl. Sci. Abstr.; Ref. Sources.

US/1045-7194
DESIGN MANAGEMENT JOURNAL. [Des. manage. j.]. **Added/Corp** Design Management Institute (Boston, Mass.). (Dec. 1989)-. Periodical. English. qt. $96.00 US; $126.00 other. Design Management Institute, 107 South Street, Boston MA 02111. **Tel** (617)338-6380, FAX (617)338-6570. **ED** Thomas Walton. **LC** T342; .D47. **DD** 745. **Bk Rev**, (Qty: 12-16). **Ad Acc, Adv Mgr:** Melissa Blanchette, **Tel** (617)338-6380. **Circ:** 800.
Desc: Devoted to articles and case studies exploring how design, in products, communication, and environment, is an essential resource.

UK
DESIGN NEWS. English. mo. £33.00 UK; £53.00 other. Findlay Publications Ltd, Franks Hall, Horton Kirby, Kent DA4 9LL England. **Tel** 011 44 (0322)222222, FAX 011 44 (0322)289577.

UK
DEVELOPMENTS IN FRACTURE MECHANICS. (1979)-. Monographic series. English. ir. Price varies per volume. Elsevier Science Publishing Company Inc, Madison Square Station, PO Box 882, New York NY 10159-0882. **Tel** (212)633-3950, FAX (212)633-3990. **(Subscription address:** Elsevier Science Inc. / New York Books, 655 Avenue of the Americas, New York NY 10010.**) LC** TA409; .D45. **DD** 620.1/66. **Pr Rev.**

NE/0165-1250
DEVELOPMENTS IN GEOTECHNICAL ENGINEERING. [Dev. geotech. eng.]. Vol. 1, (1972)-. Monographic series. English. ir. Price varies per volume. Elsevier Science Publishers BV, PO Box 211, 1000 AE Amsterdam Netherlands. **Tel** 011 31 20 5803642, FAX 011 31 20 5862696, telex 15682. **(Subscription address:** Elsevier Science Publishers Co., Inc., 655 Avenue of the Americas Books, New York, NY 10010**) LC** UNC. **CODEN** DGEND3. **[CCC].**
Ind/Abst Coal Abstr.; GeoRef; Zentralbl. Math. Ihre Grenzgeb.

UK/0269-0225
DIAGNOSTIC ENGINEERING : NEWSLETTER OF THE INSTITUTION OF DIAGNOSTIC ENGINEERS. Added/Corp Institution of Diagnostic Engineers. (1984)-. Newsletter. English. Six times a year (Jan., Mar., May, July, Sept., Nov.). £48.00. Institution of Diagnostic Engineers, 3 Wycliffe Street, Leicester LE1 5LR England. **Tel** (053)359-2552, FAX (053)-359-2444. **Bk Rev**, (Qty: 20-30). **Ad Acc. Acid Free. Circ:** 6,000. ***Continues*** *Journal of Condition Monitoring and Fault Diagnosis.*
Desc: Covers diagnosis of deterioration, development of faults, condition monitoring and reliability.

CN/1184-1737
DIALOGUE FOR ENGINEERS & GEOSCIENTISTS. [Dialogue eng. geosci.]. **Added/Corp** Association of Professional Engineers and Geoscientists of Newfoundland. **VFOAT** Dialogue for Engineers and Geoscientists. (Sept. 1990)-. Periodical. English. Three times a year. Free to members. Association of Professional Engineers and Geoscientists of Newfoundland, PO Box 9715, Station B, St. John's, Newfoundland A1A 4J6 Canada. **DD** 620/.006/0718. ***Continues*** *Dialogue for Engineers., 0831-8719.*

US/0742-3381
DIRECTORY & GUIDE - FLORIDA INSTITUTE OF CONSULTING ENGINEERS. (DIRECTORY & GUIDE.). **Main/Corp** Florida Institute of Consulting Engineers. **VFOAT** Directory and Guide; FICE Directory; F.I.C.E. Directory. Directory. English. an. $15.00 members, $10.00 nonmembers. Florida Institute of Consulting Engineers, PO Box 750, Tallahassee FL 32302. **Tel** (904)224-7121. **ED** Connie J Witt. **DD** 620. **Circ:** 1,000.
Desc: Comprehensive directory of 350 key Florida engineering firms, and firms licensed to perform engineering. Lists name, address, phone, summary of services, branch offices and principals.

US/0270-5311
DIRECTORY AND YEARBOOK - HUMAN FACTORS SOCIETY. [Dir. yearb. - Hum. Factors Soc.]. **Main/Corp** Human Factors Society. (19??)-. English. an (Spring). $57.00. Human Factors and Ergonomics Society, PO Box 1369, Journals Department, Santa Monica CA 90406-1369. **Tel** (310)394-1811, (310)394-9793, FAX (310)394-2410. **LC** TA166; .H82b. **DD** 620.82/06/073. **Ad Acc.**
Desc: An alphabetical and geographical listing of people engaged in human factor design, education, research and development and their areas of expertise.

CN/0833-305X
DIRECTORY / CONSULTING ENGINEERS OF ONTARIO. [Dir. - Consult. Eng. Ont.]. **Main/Corp** Consulting Engineers of Ontario. (Feb. 1977)-. Periodical. English. an. $53.50 contents only; $64.20 contents and binder. Consulting Engineers Ontario, 86 Overlea Boulevard, Toronto ONT M4H 1C6 Canada. **Tel** (416)425-8027, FAX (416)425-8035. **DD** 620/.0025/713.

UK/0141-7592
DIRECTORY / ENGINEERING EMPLOYERS' FEDERATION. Main/Corp Engineering Employers' Federation. **VFOAT** Engineering Employers' Federation Directory. 1987/88-. Directory. English (French, German and Spanish). an. Guardian Communications Ltd, Albany House, Hurst Street, Birmingham B54 4BD England. **Tel** 021-622 4011, FAX (021)622-5304, telex 948669 TOPJNL. **LC** TA157; .E6117A. **DD** 620/.006/041. Index available. **Ad Acc.**
Desc: Comprises list of members and comprehensive classified section, circulated to members and major reference centers.

CN/0712-7499
DIRECTORY OF CERTIFICATES OF AUTHORIZATION HOLDERS AUTHORIZED TO PRACTISE PROFESSIONAL ENGINEERING IN THE PROVINCE OF ONTARIO. Vol. 8 (Aug. 1981)-. Directory. English. an. Free. Association of Professional Engineers of Ontario, 1155 Yonge Street, Toronto Ontario M4T 2Y5 Canada. **Tel** (416)961-1100, FAX (416)961-1499. **DD** 620/.006/0713. ctrl circ. ***Continues*** *Directory of Firms and Corporations Authorized to Practice Professional Engineering in the Province of Ontario, 0316-8123.*

US
DIRECTORY OF COMPUTER SOFTWARE APPLICATIONS. MARINE ENGINEERING, A. **See** Computers-Software.

US/0148-1819
DIRECTORY OF CONTRACT SERVICE FIRMS. (19??)-. Directory. English. an (Jan.). $10.00 US; $12.00 Canada; $15.00 other. Contract Engineer Publications Inc, PO Box 97000, Kirkland WA 98083. **Tel** (206)823-2222, FAX (206)821-0942. **ED** Jerry A. Erickson. **LC** TA12; .D485. **DD** 620/.004/202573. **Ad Acc. Circ:** 18,000 (ctrl).
Desc: A directory of employers for contract (temporary) engineering and technical positions.

●US/1057-5286
DIRECTORY OF ENGINEERING AND ENGINEERING TECHNOLOGY UNDERGRADUATE PROGRAMS. (DIRECTORY OF ENGINEERING AND ENGINEERING TECHNOLOGY UNDERGRADUATE PROGRAMS / AMERICAN SOCIETY FOR ENGINEERING EDUCATION.). [Dir. eng. eng. technol. undergrad. programs]. **Added/Corp** American Society for Engineering Education. 3rd ed. (1992)-. Directory. English. $49.95. American Society for Engineering Education, 1818 North Street Northwest, Suite 600, Washington DC 20036. **Tel** (202)331-3500. **DD** 620.

●US/1067-9022
DIRECTORY OF ENGINEERING GRADUATE STUDIES & RESEARCH. [Dir. eng. grad. stud. res.]. **Added/Corp** American Society for Engineering Education. **VFOAT** Engineering Graduate Studies & Research; Engineering Graduate Studies and Research. (1992)-. Directory. English. an. $72.95 US and Canada; $75.95 other. American Society for Engineering Education, 1818 North Street Northwest, Suite 600, Washington DC 20036. **Tel** (202)331-3500. **LC** T61; .D57. **DD** 620/.0071/1. ***Continues*** *Directory of Graduate Programs in Engineering, 1057-5278.*

US
DIRECTORY OF ENGINEERS AND LAND SURVEYORS REGISTERED IN SOUTH CAROLINA. Added/Corp South Carolina State Board of Engineering Examiners. (19??)-. English.

Engineering

an. $15.00. South Carolina Board of Engineers and Examiners, PO Box 50408, Columbia SC 29250. **Tel** (803)734-9166. **LC** TA12; .S65. **DD** 620/.0025/757. *Continues* Roster of Registered Professional Engineers and Land Surveyors.

US
DIRECTORY OF ENVIRONMENTAL CONSULTANTS. See Environmental Issues.

CN/0316-8123
DIRECTORY OF FIRMS AND CORPORATIONS AUTHORIZED TO PRACTISE PROFESSIONAL ENGINEERING IN THE PROVINCE OF ONTARIO. V. 1- 1970-. Directory. English. an. Free. Association of Professional Engineers of Ontario, 1155 Yonge Street, Toronto Ontario M4T 2Y5 Canada. **Tel** (416)961-1100, FAX (416)961-1499. **DD** 620/.006/2713.

US/0738-0887
DIRECTORY OF INDUSTRIAL HEAT PROCESSING AND COMBUSTION EQUIPMENT. UNITED STATES MANUFACTURERS, THE. See Building and Construction.

SA
DIRECTORY OF MEMBERS' FIRMS - SOUTH AFRICAN ASSOCIATION OF CONSULTING ENGINEERS. **Main/Corp** South African Association of Consulting Engineers. **VFOAT** Gids Van Lede Se Firmas. Directory. Multiple languages (Afrikaans and English). Associated Scientific and Technical Societies of SA, Kelvin House, 2 Holland Street, Johannesburg South Africa. **LC** TA12; .S637A. **DD** 620.

CN/0701-1814
DIRECTORY OF PROFESSIONAL ENGINEERS OF ONTARIO. **VFOAT** Directory of the Association of Professional Engineers of Ontario (Title Varies Slightly). (196?)-. Directory. English. be. Free to members. Association of Professional Engineers of Ontario, 1155 Yonge Street, Toronto Ontario M4T 2Y5 Canada. **Tel** (416)961-1100, FAX (416)961-1499. **DD** 620/.006/2713. *Supersedes* Association of Professional Engineers of Ontario. List of Members.

US/0419-3350
DIRECTORY OF PUBLISHED PROCEEDINGS. SERIES SEMT, SCIENCE/ENGINEERING/MEDICINE/TECHNOLOGY. ANNUAL CUMULATIVE VOLUME / INTERDOK. See Science and Technology.

US
DIRECTORY OF PUBLISHED PROCEEDINGS. SERIES SEMT SCIENCE/ENGINEERING/MEDICINE/TECHNOLOGY. CUMULATED INDEX SUPPLEMENT. See Science and Technology.

CN/1187-2306
DIRECTORY OF THE ASSOCIATION OF PROFESSIONAL ENGINEERS AND GEOSCIENTISTS OF THE PROVINCE OF BRITISH COLUMBIA. [Dir. Assoc. Prof. Eng. Geosci. Prov. B.C.]. **Main/Corp** Association of Professional Engineers and Geoscientists of the Province of British Columbia. (1991)-. Directory. English. Association of Professional Engineers and Geoscientists of the Province of British Columbia, 2210 West 12th Avenue, Vancouver, British Columbia V6K 2N6 Canada. **DD** 620/.006/0711. *Continues* Directory of the Association of Professional Engineers of the Province of British Columbia., 0316-490X.

US
DIRECTORY / SOUTH CAROLINA STATE BOARD OF REGISTRATION FOR PROFESSIONAL ENGINEERS AND LAND SURVEYORS. **Added/Corp** South Carolina State Board of Registration for Professional Engineers and Land Surveyors. (19??)-. Directory. English. $10.00. 2221 Devine Street/Suite 404, PO Drawer 50408, Columbia SC 29250. **LC** TA12; .S65. **DD** 620/.0025/757. *Continues* Directory (South Carolina State Board of Engineering Examiners).

US/1040-0230
DISCRETE SEMICONDUCTORS. SURFACE-MOUNTED DISCRETE SEMICONDUCTORS. **Added/Corp** D.A.T.A. Business Publishing. **VFOAT** Surface Mounted Discrete Semiconductors; Surface Mounted Discrete Semiconductors; Discrete Semiconductors. Surface-Mounted Discretics. (199?)-. English. sa (2 issues). $218.63. DATA Business Publishing, PO Box 6510, 15 Inverness Way East, Englewood CO 80155. **Tel** (800)447-4666, (303)799-0381, FAX (303)799-4082. **LC** TK7871.85; .D5587. *Continues* Discrete Semiconductors. Surface-Mounted Discretes, 1051-7715.

US/1051-7715
DISCRETE SEMICONDUCTORS. SURFACE-MOUNTED DISCRETES. *Title Change*. [Discret. semicond., Surf.-mounted discret.]. **Added/Corp** D.A.T.A. Business Publishing. **VFOAT** Surface Mounted Discretes; Surface-Mounted Discretes. Ed. 1 (1991)-(199?). English. an. DATA Business Publishing, PO Box 6510, 15 Inverness Way East, Englewood CO 80155. **Tel** (800)447-4666, (303)799-0381, FAX (303)799-4082. **LC** TK7871.85; .D5587. **DD** 621.3815/2/0294. *Continues* Surface-Mounted Discrete Semiconductors. *Continued by* Discrete Semiconductors. Surface-Mounted Discrete Semiconductors, 1040-0230.

US/0733-2386
DISPLAY AND IMAGING TECHNOLOGY. [Disp. imaging technol.]. Vol. 1, No. 1 (1985)-. Periodical. English. bm. $318.00 (corporations), $196.00 (academic libraries). Gordon & Breach Science Publishers, Inc., PO Box 786, Cooper Station, New York NY 10276. **Tel** (212)206-8900, FAX (212)645-2459. **(Subscription address:** International Publishers Distributor at one of the following addresses: 820 Town Center Drive, Langhorne, PA 19047; or PO Box 90, Reading Berkshire RG1 8JL UK; or Kent Ridge PO Box 1180, Singapore 9111, Republic of Singapore) **DD** 621. **CODEN** DIMTD7. **[CCC].** Documents available from Ask*IEEE.
Ind/Abst INSPEC (1985-).

AT/0374-4957
DIVISION OF APPLIED GEOMECHANICS TECHNICAL PAPER. [Div. Appl. Geomech. tech. pap.]. **Added/Corp** Institute of Earth Resources (Australia). Division of Applied Geomechanics. **VFOAT** Technical Paper. No. 8 (1970)-. Monographic series. English. ir. Price varies per volume. CSIRO / Division of Geomechanics, Box 54, Mt. Waverly Victoria 3149 Australia. **LC** TA705; .A9. **DD** 624.1/51/05. **CODEN** AAGTCN. Documents available from Article Express International. *Continues* Commonwealth Scientific and Industrial Research Organization (Australia). Division of Soil Mechanics. Division of Soil Mechanics Technical Paper, 0155-347X.
Ind/Abst Bioeng. Abstr.; Ei Page One; Eng. Index Annu.; GeoRef.

UK
DIVISIONAL NOTE. English. AFRC Institute of Engineering Research, Wrest Park Silsoe, Bedford, MK45 4HS, United Kingdom.
Ind/Abst Postharvest News Inf.

UK/0267-5471
DIVISIONAL NOTE - NATIONAL INSTITUTE OF AGRICULTURAL ENGINEERING. See Agriculture.

US/1054-4615
DOCUMENT MANAGEMENT TECHNOLOGY SOURCEBOOK. *Ceased*. [Doc. manage. technol. sourceb.]. **Added/Corp** Pinnacle Peak Publishing. 1st Ed. (1991)-1992 Edition August (1993). Periodical. English. Pinnacle Peak Publishing Ltd., 8711 East Pinnacle Peak Road #249, Scottsdale AZ 85255-9978. **Tel** (602)224-9777, FAX (602)585-7417. **LC** TA345; .D57. **DD** 651.8/05.

TU
DOGA BILIM DERGISI. SERI B, MUHENDISLIK VE CEVRE. Vol. 4 (1980)-. Turkish (summaries and/or abstracts in English). $10.00 (overseas). Scientific and Technical Research Council of Turkey, Ataturk Bulvari 221, Kavaklidere Ankara Turkey. **Tel** 3420845, FAX 1175902, telex BTAK TR 43186.

GW/0012-5148
DOKUMENTATION STRASSE. See Engineering-Abstracting, Bibliographies and Statistics.

CC/1001-0505
DONGNAN DAXUE XUEBAO. See Science and Technology.

JA/0036-8172
DOSHISHA DAIGAKU RIKOGAKU KENKYU HOKOKU. See Science and Technology.

CN/0319-8413
DPN: DESIGN PRODUCT NEWS. **VFOAT** Design Product News. Vol. 1 (Nov. 1973)-. Periodical. English. bm (6 issues). 35.00Can$ (1 year), 65.00Can$ (2 year) Canada; $55.00 (1 year), $105.00 (2 year) surface mail other; $105.00 airmail other. Action Communications Inc, 135 Spy Ct, Markham Ontario L3R 5H6 Canada. **Tel** (416)477-3222. **ED** James C Young. **Ad Acc. Circ:** 19,000 (ctrl).
Desc: Includes product editorials and articles on fluid and mechanical power transmission, electronics, materials manufacturing and processing for OEM and in-plant design.

UK/0951-5704
DRAUGHTING & DESIGN. See Computers.

UK/0950-5490
DRIVERS AND CONTROLS. [Drives controls]. (1986)-. Periodical. English. Ten times a year (July/Aug. and Dec/Jan. issues combined). £65.00 Western Europe; £75.00 other. Kamtech Publishing Ltd, 2 Stanley Road, North Downs House, Carshalton Surrey SM5 4LF England. **Tel** 081-669-5227, FAX 011 44 81 669 6593. **ED** Bob Dobson. **DD** 621.8. **Bk Rev**, (Qty: 4). **Ad Acc. Circ:** 18,000 (ctrl). *Continues* Electric Drives & Controls, 0267-422X.
Desc: Engineering journal about covering drives, power transmission, and motion control.

US/0890-362X
DU PONT REGISTRY. [Du Pont regist.]. **VFOAT** Dupont Registry. (198?)-. English. Twelve times a year. Playboy Magazine, 747 Third Avenue, New York NY 10017. **Tel** (212)688-3030. **(Subscription address:** Du Pont Registry, 2325 Ulmerton Road, Suite 16, Clearwater FL 34622.) **DD** 629.

US/1053-1270
EASTERN EUROPEAN AND SOVIET ADVANCED MATERIALS REPORT, THE. **VFOAT** Advanced Materials Report. (1991)-. Periodical. English. mo. $195.00. Kiser Research Inc., 1233 20th Street NW, Suite 505, Washington DC 20036. *Continues* Eastern Bloc Polymer Access Report, 1041-7370.

JA/0385-096X
EBARA-INFIRUKO JIHO. (EBARA INFIRUKO JIHO.). [Ebara-Infiruko jiho]. **Added/Corp** Ebara Infiruko Kabushiki Kaisha. **VFOAT** Ebara Infilco Engineering Review; Ebara Infilco Engineering Review. (1974)-. Periodical. Japanese. qt. Ebara Seisakujo, 11-1 Haneda Asahi-cho Ota-ku, Tokyo 144 Japan. **Tel** 743-6111, FAX 745-3356, telex EBARATYO J22988. **CODEN** EIJID4. Documents available from CASDDS. *Continues* Infiruko Nyusu.
Ind/Abst Chem. Abstr.

JA/0385-3004
EBARA JIHO. (EHARA JIHO.). **Main/Corp** Ebara Seisakujo. **VFOAT** Ebara Times; Ebara Engineering Review. Began with June 1952 issue. Academic Scholarly Publication. Japanese (summaries and/or abstracts in English). Four times a year. Free to qualified applicants. Ebara Seisakujo, 11-1 Haneda Asahi-cho Ota-ku, Tokyo 144 Japan. **Tel** 743-6111, FAX 745-3356, telex EBARATYO J22988. **ED** Nobuhiro Harasawa. **LC** TA4; .E23A. **CODEN** EHJIAS. **Circ:** 4,000 (ctrl). Documents available from CASDDS.
Ind/Abst Chem. Abstr.; Coal Abstr.

US/0896-3169
ECA MAGAZINE. [ECA mag.]. **VFOAT** ECA Directory and Buyer's Guide. **VAT** Engineering Contractors' Association Magazine. Periodical. English. mo. Free to members and current advertisers, $10.00 other. 8310 Florence Avenue, Downey CA 90240. **DD** 338. *Continues* Engineering Contractors' Association Magazine.

●NE/0925-8574
ECOLOGICAL ENGINEERING. Vol. 1, No. 1/2 (Mar. 1992)-. Academic Scholarly Publication. English. Eight times a year (2 vols.). Fl754.00. Elsevier Science Publishers BV, PO Box 211, 1000 AE Amsterdam Netherlands. **Tel** 011 31 20 5803642, FAX 011 31 20 5862696, telex 15682. **LC** TD1; .E26. **[CCC].** Documents available from Article Express International.
Ind/Abst Curr. Aware. Biol. Sci., CABS; Ecology Abstr.; Eng. Index Annu. [Select. Cov.]; Pollut. Abstr. Indexes; Sci. Cit. Index.

US
EDDY-CURRENT INSPECTION FOR STEAM GENERATOR TUBING PROGRAM QUARTERLY PROGRESS REPORT FOR PERIOD ENDING ... / OAK RIDGE NATIONAL LABORATORY, METALS AND CERAMICS DIVISION. Periodical. English. qt. National Technical Information Service - NTIS, Room 2027S, 5285 Port Royal Road, Springfield VA 22161. **Tel** (703)487-4630, (703)487-4660, (703)487-4650, FAX (703)321-8547, telex 89-9405. available on microfiche (Vols. for (Mar. 1983-) distributed to depository libraries).

●US/1061-9550
EDMS COMPARISON REPORT. (EDMS COMPARISON REPORT: REVIEWING ENGINEERING DOCUMENT MANAGEMENT SYSTEMS.). [EDMS comp. rep.]. **Added/Corp** International Imaging, Inc. (Feb. 28, 1992)-. Periodical. English. qt. International Imaging Inc, 701 West Foothill Boulevard, Azusa CA 91702. **DD** 621. *Continues* Comparison Report on Engineering Document Management (EDMS) Systems, 1056-182X.

US
EI PAGE ONE [COMPUTER FILE]. See Engineering-Abstracting, Bibliographies and Statistics.

GW/0071-0075
EISENBAHN INGENIEUR KALENDER.
See Transportation-Railroads.

US/0148-9046
ELECTRO-OPTICS SERIES. [Electro-opt. ser.]. (1976)-. Academic Scholarly Publication. English. Price varies per volume. Marcel Dekker Inc., 270 Madison Avenue, New York NY 10016. **Tel** (212)696-9000, (800)228-1160, FAX (212)685-4540, telex 421419. **(Subscription address:** Marcel Dekker Inc, PO Box 5017, Monticello NY 12701.**) CODEN** EOSEDB. Documents available from CASDDS.
Desc: Covers topics such as fiber optics in communication systems and electro-optics theory and methods.
Ind/Abst Chem. Abstr.

US/1051-5690
ELEKTOR ELECTRONICS USA. ***Ceased.***
See Physics.

AU/0302-2560
ELIN-ZEITSCHRIFT. [ELIN-Z.]. **VFOAT** Elin Zeitschrift. (1949)-. Periodical. German (summaries and/or abstracts in English). Twice a year. S160.00 Austria; S200.00 other. Elin-Union AG, Postfach 5, A-1141 Vienna Austria. **CODEN** ELNZAP. Documents available from Article Express International, Ask*IEEE.
Ind/Abst Bioeng. Abstr.; Coal Abstr.; Ei Page One; Eng. Index Annu.; INSPEC (1968-); Saf. Health Work.

VE/0378-9578
ENERGIA E INDUSTRIA. [Energ. ind.]. No. 1-Sept. 1972-. Spanish. **LC** TA4; .E38. **CODEN** EINEDC. Documents available from CASDDS.
Ind/Abst Chem. Abstr.

BL/0100-6916
ENGENHARIA AGRICOLA. See Agriculture.

BL
ENGENHARIA DE HOJE. Portuguese. $120.00. Bloch Editoras SA, Rua do Russell 766 804, 22210 Rio de Janeiro Brazil. **Tel** 011 51 21 2652012, 011 51 21 2850033. **LC** TA4; .E47117.

CE
ENGINEER. V. 1 (March 1973)-. Periodical. English. qt. Rs1.50 single issue. Institution of Engineers / Sri Lanka, Lower Chatham Street 1, Colombo Sri Lanka. **LC** TA104.7; .E54. **DD** 620/.009549/3.
Ind/Abst Eng. Mater. Abstr.; Int. Civil Eng. Abstr.

US/0046-1989
ENGINEER (FORT BELVOIR), THE. (THE ENGINEER.). [Eng.]. **Added/Corp** Army Engineer Center and Fort Belvoir. U.S. Army Engineer School. United States Army Engineer Center and Fort Leonard Wood. (Spring/Summer 1971)-. Government Publication. English. qt. $8.50 US; $10.65 other. Superintendent of Documents, US Government Printing Office, Washington DC 20402. **Tel** (202)275-3328, FAX (202)786-2377. **LC** UG1; .E52. **DD** 358/.2/0973. available on microfilm and microfiche from University Microfilms International (UMI). Documents available from Ask*IEEE.
Desc: Provides timely and authoritative information on Army engineering concepts, plans, policies, doctrine, procedures, operations, equipment, and developments.
Ind/Abst Air Univ. Libr. Index Mil. Period. (19??-); Energy Res. Abstr. (May 1978-); INSPEC.

CN/0849-2913
ENGINEER (HALIFAX). (ENGINEER : NEWSLETTER OF THE ASSOCIATION OF PROFESSIONAL ENGINEERS OF NOVA SCOTIA.). [Engineer]. **Added/Corp** Association of Professional Engineers of Nova Scotia. **VFOAT** APENS Newsletter. Vol. 1, No. 1 (May/June 1990)-. Newsletter. English. bm. Association of the Professional Engineers of Nova Scotia, PO Box 129, 1888 Brunswick Street/Suite 902, Halifax Nova Scotia B3J 1S6 Canada. **DD** 620/.006/0716.
Formed by the union of *Professional Engineer, 0225-851X; APENS Newsletter (1984), 0826-7472* ***and*** *Professional Engineer, 0225-851X.*

UK/0013-7758
ENGINEER (LONDON). (THE ENGINEER.). [Engineer]. Vol. 1 (1856)-. Periodical. English. Thirty-two times a year. £87.00 UK and Northern Ireland; $222.00 other. Morgan Grampian, 40 Beresford Street Woolwich, London SE18 6BQ England. **Tel** 011 44 81 855 7777, FAX 011 44 81 855 5548, telex 896238. **CODEN** ENGIAL. **[CCC].** cum. index. available on microfilm and microfiche from University Microfilms International (UMI). Documents available from Ask*IEEE.
Ind/Abst Alum. Ind. Abstr.; Appl. Sci. Technol. Index; Art Archaeol. Tech. Abstr.; BMT Abstr. (-199?); Coal Abstr.; Curr. Biotechnol.; Ei Page One; Energy Res. Abstr.; F&S Index Plus Text, Int. [Select. Cov.]; Fluid Abstr., Civil Eng.; Fluid Abstr. Proc. Eng.; FLUIDEX (1973-); Infomat Int. Bus.; INSPEC (Oct. 1977-); Int. Aerosp. Abstr.; Int. Civil Eng. Abstr.; J. Ferrocement; Met. Abstr.; Proc. Chem. Eng.; PROMT [Full Txt.]; Soft. Abstr. Eng.; Theoret. Chem. Eng.

US/0277-1233
ENGINEER OF CALIFORNIA. [Eng. Calif.]. Vol. 29, No. 10 (Oct. 1976)-. Periodical. English. Ten times a year. $12.00 (one year); $17.00 (two years). Engineer of California, PO Box 991, Alhambra CA 91802. **Tel** (213)283-3188. **ED** Annette Schilling (editor's address: 626 North Garfield, Alhambra, CA 91801, phone: (800)362-3162). **Bk Rev. Ad Acc, Adv Mgr:** A. Schilling, **Tel** 799-1246. **Circ:** 3,500 (ctrl). ***Continues*** *Engineer of Southern California, 0013-7766.*
Desc: Reporting the news and activities of engineers.

UK/0955-7997
ENGINEERING ANALYSIS WITH BOUNDARY ELEMENTS. [Eng. anal. bound. elem.]. **Added/Corp** International Society for Computational Methods in Engineering. Vol. 6 No. 1 (Mar. 1989)-. Academic Scholarly Publication. English. Eight times a year. $671.00 The Americas; £450.00 other. Elsevier Applied Science, An Imprint of Elsevier Science Ltd., The Boulevard, Langford Lane, Kidlington, Oxford OX5 1GB United Kingdom. **Tel** 011 44 865 843000, 011 44 865 843699, FAX 011 44 865 843010. **(Subscription address:** Elsevier Science Ltd. Oxford Fulfillment Centre, PO Box 800, Kidlington, Oxford OX5 1DX United Kingdom.**) ED** C. A. Brebbia, M. Tanaka, R. Shaw, W. L. Wendland. **LC** TA347.B69; E53. **DD** 620/.001/51535. **CODEN** EABAEL. **[CCC]. Bk Rev. Ad Acc. Pr Rev.** Documents available from Article Express International, The Genuine Article, Ask*IEEE. ***Continues*** *Engineering Analysis, 0264-682X.*
Desc: Contains innovations in boundary elements and computation techniques.
Ind/Abst Curr. Contents Eng. Tech. Appl. Sci.; Ei Page One; Eng. Index Annu.; INSPEC (Mar. 1989-); Int. Aerosp. Abstr.; Res. Alert [Full Cov.]; SCISEARCH.

GW/0931-6221
ENGINEERING & AUTOMATION.
Added/Corp Siemens Aktiengesellschaft. **VFOAT** Engineering and Automation. Vol. 13, 1/91 (Jan./Feb. 1991)-. Periodical. English. Six times a year. $97.00. Siemens AG ZWD V Verlag, Naegelsbachstrasse 26, D 91052 Erlangen Germany. **Tel** 011 49 9131 723004, FAX 011 49 9131 725022. **(Subscription address:** VCH Publishers Inc., 303 Northwest 12th Avenue, Journals Department, Deerfield FL 33442.**) CODEN** ENATES. **[CCC].** Documents available from Article Express International, Ask*IEEE. ***Continues*** *Energy & Automation.*
Ind/Abst Ei Page One; Eng. Index Annu.; INSPEC (Jan.-Feb. 1991).

US/0013-7812
ENGINEERING & SCIENCE. [Eng. sci.]. **Added/Corp** California Institute of Technology. Alumni Association. **VFOAT** Engineering & Science. **VAT** Engineering and Science. Vol. 6, No. 9 (Sept. 1943)-. Academic Scholarly Publication. English. Four times a year (Seasonally). $8.00 US; $20.00 others. California Institute of Technology, Engineering, and Science, 315 South Hill Avenue, Pasadena CA 91125. **Tel** (818)395-6327. **ED** Jane Dietrich. **LC** T171; .C217. **Bk Rev. Ad Acc. Circ:** 15,300 (ctrl). Documents available from CASDDS. ***Continues*** *Alumi Review.*
Desc: Contains faculty and staff written articles about Cal Tech research.
Ind/Abst Chem. Abstr.; EMBASE; GeoRef; Int. Aerosp. Abstr.; Surf. Treat. Technol. Abstr.

US/0071-0393
ENGINEERING AND TECHNOLOGY DEGREES. (ENGINEERING AND TECHNOLOGY DEGREES / ENGINEERING MANPOWER COMMISSION.). **Added/Corp** Engineers Joint Council. Engineering Manpower Commission. American Association of Engineering Societies. Engineering Manpower Commission. (19??)-. English. an. $140.00 (members), $230.00 (nonmembers). American Association of Engineering Societies-EJC, 1111 19th Street NW, Suite 608, Washington DC 20036. **Tel** (202)296-2237, FAX (202)296-1151. **LC** TA157; .E662. **DD** 620/.007/1173. **Bk Rev. Ad Acc. Circ:** 400. ***Continues*** *Engineering Degrees, 0275-7303.*
Desc: Contains degree data for accredited and nonaccredited schools, detailed data broken down into six minority groups, and major curricula are examined in detail.

US/0278-8985
ENGINEERING AND TECHNOLOGY ENROLLMENTS. Added/Corp Engineers Joint Council. Engineering Manpower Commission. American Association of Engineering Societies. Engineering Manpower Commission. (1974)-. English. an. $120.00 (members), $195.00 (nonmembers). American Association of Engineering Societies-EJC, 1111 19th Street NW, Suite 608, Washington DC 20036. **Tel** (202)296-2237, FAX (202)296-1151. **ED** Richard A Ellis. **LC** TA157; .E67b. **DD** 620/.0071173. **Circ:** 400. ***Continues*** *Engineering and Technician Enrollments, 0071-0407.*
Desc: Presents a statistical overview of the next generation of engineers, technologists and technicians.

●US/1065-6952
ENGINEERING AUTOMATION REPORT. (ENGINEERING AUTOMATION REPORT / TECHNOLOGY AUTOMATION SERVICES.). [Eng. Autom. Rep.]. **Added/Corp** Technology Automation Services. Vol. 1, No. 1 (Mar. 1992)-. Periodical. English. Twelve times a year. $225.00 (one year); $390.00 (two years); $570.00 (three years). Technology Automation Services, PO Box 3593, Englewood CO 80155-3593. **Tel** (303)770-1728, FAX (303)770-3660. **ED** David Weisberg. **DD** 004. **Bk Rev**, (Qty: 12).
Desc: Covers computer hardware and software for engineering management including CAD, CAM, and CAE.

UK/0264-4401
ENGINEERING COMPUTATIONS. Vol. 1, No. 1 (March 1984)-. Periodical. English. bm. £333.00 UK; $560.00 other. Pineridge Press Ltd, Journals Division, 54 Newton Road, Mumbles Swansea SA3 4BQ Wales. **Tel** 011 44 792 361557, FAX 011 44 792 295532. **ED** D R J Owen and E Hinton (editors' address: Department of Civil Engineering, University College of Swansea SA2 8PP United Kingdom). **LC** TA345; .E54. **DD** 620/.0028/5425. **Bk Rev**, (Qty: 5-10). **Circ:** 500. Documents available from Article Express International, Ask*IEEE.
Desc: Papers primarily deal with the numerical modelling of engineering problems, development of computer software and computer aided design.
Ind/Abst Abstr. J. Earthq. Eng.; Civ. Struct. Eng. Abstr.; Comput. Inf. Syst. Abstr. J. [Full Cov.]; Ei Page One; Eng. Index Annu.; Environ. Eng. Abstr.; Fluid Abstr., Civil Eng.; Fluid Abstr. Proc. Eng.; FLUIDEX; INSPEC (March 1990-); Int. Aerosp. Abstr. (1984-); J. Ferrocement; Manuf. Process Eng. Abstr.; Mech. Eng. Abstr.

II
ENGINEERING DESIGN. Added/Corp Institution of Engineers (India). National Design and Research Forum. (19??)-. Periodical. English. qt. $20.00. No 3 Vidhana Veedhi, Bangalore-1 India. **(Subscription address:** Prints India, 11 Darya Ganj, New Delhi 110002 India.**) LC** TA174; .E52. **DD** 620/.004/2.

US/0046-2012
ENGINEERING DESIGN GRAPHICS JOURNAL. [Eng. des. graph. j.]. **Added/Corp** American Society for Engineering Education. Engineering Design Graphics Division. Vol. 34 (Winter 1970)-. Periodical. English. tq (Feb., May, Nov.). $6.00 (members); individual, $10.00 (members) institution; $20.00 (non-members) US; $25.00 (non-members) Canada and Mexico; $30.00 (non-members) other. Engineering Design Graphics Division, Ohio State University, 2070 Neil Avenue, Columbus OH 43210. **Tel** (614)292-2893, FAX (614)292-9021. **ED** Mary A. Sadowski. **DD** 604. **Ad Acc, Adv Mgr:** Craig Miller. **Pr Rev. Circ:** 700. available on microfilm and microfiche from University Microfilms International (UMI). ***Continues*** *Journal of Engineering Graphics.*
Desc: Articles are devoted to the fundamentals of engineering graphics education and graphic technology. Topics include engineering graphics, computer graphics, descriptive geometry, geometric modeling, computer-aided drafting and design, graphic data processing, and graphics instruction.

UK/0141-5573
ENGINEERING DESIGN GUIDES. ***Ceased.*** [Eng. des. guides]. **VFOAT** Materials Engineering Design Guides. Ceased (May 1987). Academic Scholarly Publication. English. ir. Oxford University Press, Walton Street, Oxford OX2 6DP England. **Tel** 011 44 865 56767, FAX 011 44 865 267773, telex 837330 OXPRES G. **CODEN** EDGUDO. Documents available from CASDDS.
Ind/Abst Chem. Abstr. (1974-1979).

CN/0013-7901
ENGINEERING DIGEST (TORONTO). ***Suspended.*** (ENGINEERING DIGEST.). [Eng. dig.]. Vol. 1, No. 1 (Nov. 1954)-(19??). Periodical. English. Six times a year. 35.00Can$ Canada; 45.00Can$ other. Canadian Engineering Publications Ltd., 204 Richmond Street West / Suite 415, Toronto ONT M5V 1V6 Canada. **Tel** (416)599-3737, FAX (416)599-3730. **ED** Ronald M Farrell. **DD** 620/.005. **CODEN** EDIGAN. **[CCC]. Ad Acc, Adv Mgr:** Fran Hetherington. **Circ:** 67,000 (ctrl). available on microfiche from Micromedia Limited; available on microfilm from Micromedia Limited; available on microfilm and microfiche from University Microfilms International (UMI). ***Absorbed*** *Engineering Journal, 0013-8010.*
Desc: Technical magazine read by engineers in Canadian manufacturing, business, consulting practices, construction companies, utilities, transportation, mining, pulp and paper, government and defense.
Ind/Abst Alum. Ind. Abstr.; Appl. Sci. Technol. Index; AQUAREF; Coal Abstr.; Ei Page One; Fluid Abstr., Civil Eng.; Fluid Abstr. Proc. Eng.; FLUIDEX (1973-); INIS Atomindex [Micro.]; Met. Abstr.; MINPROC; Mintec, Min. Technol. Abstr.; Risk Abstr.

CN/0820-8190
ENGINEERING DIMENSIONS. (ENGINEERING DIMENSIONS / APEO.). [Eng. dimens.]. **Added/Corp** Association of Professional Engineers of Ontario. **VAT** Dimensions (Toronto. 1981). Vol. 2, No. 5 (Sept./Oct. 1981)-. Periodical. English. bm (Jan., Mar., May, July, Sept., Nov.). 20.00Can$ Canada; 25.00Can$ other. Association of Professional Engineers of Ontario, 1155 Yonge Street, Toronto Ontario M4T 2Y5 Canada. **Tel** (416)961-1100, FAX (416)961-1499. **ED** Conne Mucklestone. **DD** 620/.006/0713. **Bk Rev**, (Qty: 6). **Ad Acc, Adv Mgr:** Susan Browne, **Tel** (416)886-6640. **Circ:** 59,000. available on an online database from Canadian Business and Public Affairs Database. ***Continues*** *Dimensions (Association of Professional Engineers of*

*Ontario), 0227-5147. **Continued in part by** Association of Professional Engineers of Ontario. APEO Membership Salary Survey, 1193-6606.*
Desc: Official publication of the Association of Professional Engineers of Ontario. Covers business, professional and ethical issues of interest to licensed engineers. Each issue has an engineering theme and regular features, including management, safety factors, and book reviews.
Ind/Abst Coal Abstr.

●US/1062-8800
ENGINEERING DOCUMENTATION ADVISOR, THE. [Eng. doc. adv.]. **Added/Corp** CAE Consultants, Inc. (May 1992)-. Periodical. English. mo. $60.00. Cae Consultants, Inc., 41 Tavers Avenue, Yonkers NY 10705. **DD** 651.

UK
ENGINEERING ECONOMIC TRENDS / ENGINEERING EMPLOYERS' FEDERATION. **Added/Corp** Engineering Employers' Federation. (1978)-. Periodical. English. sa. Free. Engineering Employers Federation, Broadway House, Tothill Street, London SW1H 9NQ England. **Tel** 011 71 222 7777, FAX 011 71 222 2782. **Circ:** 10,000.

US/0013-791X
ENGINEERING ECONOMIST, THE. [Eng. econ.]. **Added/Corp** American Society for Engineering Education. Engineering Economy Committee. American Society for Engineering Education. Engineering Economy Division. Vol. 1 (June 1955)-. Periodical. English. qt. $55.00 (institutions), $24.00 (individuals) US; $78.00 (institutions), $34.00 (individuals) other. Institute of Industrial Engineers, 25 Technology Park-Atlanta, Norcross GA 30092. **Tel** (404)449-0460, FAX (404)263-8532. **ED** Gerald Thuesen. **LC** HD28; .E5. **CODEN** ENECAR. **[CCC].** cum. index. **Circ:** 2,000. available on microfilm and microfiche from University Microfilms International (UMI); available on an online database (file 15/Full-Text) from DIALOG. Documents available from Article Express International, Ask*IEEE, UMI Article Clearinghouse.
Desc: Devoted to the field of capital investment analysis and related topics in both the private and public sectors. Features articles on capital budgeting, project evaluation, economic design, equipment replacement analysis, resource allocation, and decision analysis.
Ind/Abst ABI/INFORM Glob. Ed.; ABI Inform Ondisc (Summer 1971-); Acad. Search (Jan. 1993-); Bioeng. Abstr.; Bus. ASAP (1992-) [Full Txt.]; Bus. Index (1985-); Bus. Period. Index; Bus. Source (Jan. 1993-); Contents Pages Manage.; Ei Page One; Energy Res. Abstr. (Feb. 1977-); Eng. Index Annu. [Select. Cov.]; Gas Abstr.; Gen. BusinessFile (1985-); Gen. Period. Index (1985-); INFO-SOUTH Abstr.; INIS Atomindex [Micro.]; INSPEC (Spring 1969-); Int. Abstr. Oper. Res. [Select. Cov.]; Int. Aerosp. Abstr.; J. Econ. Lit.; Mag. Search; Selec. Coop. Index Manage. Period; Trade Ind. ASAP [Full Txt.]; Trade Ind. Index (1981-) [Full Txt.]; UMI ABI/Inform--Bus. Period. Ondisc [Full Txt.]; Vocat. Search (Jan. 1993-); Wilson Bus. Abstr.

AT
ENGINEERING EDGE. (19??)-. English. Four times a year. 42.00Aus$ Australia; 50.00Aus$ New Zealand, Papua New Guinea; 54.00Aus$ Malaysia, Indonesia, Fiji; 55.00Aus$ Japan, India, Hong Kong; 65.00Aus$ US, Canada, Lebanon; 70.00Can$ Europe, Africa, former USSR. Thomson Publications / Australia, 47 Chippen Street, Chippendale New South Wales, 2008 Australia. **Tel** 011 61 2 6992411, FAX 011 61 2 698 3920, telex 122226. **(Subscription address:** Thomson Publications Australia, PO Box 815, Strawberry Hills, New South Wales, 2012 Australia.**)**

US
ENGINEERING EXTENSION DIVISION SERIES. **Added/Corp** Virginia Polytechnic Institute. Engineering Extension Division. **VFOAT** Bulletin. No. 19 (Apr. 1929)-. Periodical. English. Virginia Polytechnic Institute and State University, 617 North Main Street, Blacksburg VA 24060. **Tel** (313)764-4392. ***Continues** Bulletin of the Engineering Extension Division of the Virginia Polytechnic Institute.*

UK
ENGINEERING FAILURE ANALYSIS. (19??)-. English. Four times a year. $202.00 The Americas; £135.00 other. Pergamon Press, An Imprint of Elsevier Science Ltd., The Boulevard, Langford Lane, Kidlington, Oxford OX5 1GB United Kingdom. **Tel** 011 44 865 843000, 011 44 865 843699, FAX 011 44 865 843010. **(Subscription address:** Elsevier Science Ltd. Oxford Fulfillment Centre, PO Box 800, Kidlington, Oxford OX5 1DX United Kingdom.**)**

CN/0701-080X
ENGINEERING FORUM (TORONTO). (ENGINEERING FORUM.). No. 1- Mar. 1970-. Periodical. English. ir. Free. Liaison Office, Faculty of Applied Science & Engineering, University of Toronto, Toronto Ontario M5S 1A4 Canada. **DD** 620/.007/209713541. ctrl circ.

JA
ENGINEERING GEOLOGY. **See** Earth Sciences-Geology.

NE/0013-7952
ENGINEERING GEOLOGY. [Eng. geol.]. Vol. 1 (Aug. 1965)-. Academic Scholarly Publication. English (French and German; summaries and/or abstracts in French and German). Eight times a year (2 volumes). Fl882.00. Elsevier Science Publishers BV, PO Box 211, 1000 AE Amsterdam Netherlands. **Tel** 011 31 20 5803642, FAX 011 31 20 5862696, telex 15682. **ED** W R Judd and E L Krinitzsky. **LC** TA705; .E53. **CODEN** EGGOAO. **[CCC]. Pr Rev.** available on microfilm and microfiche from University Microfilms International (UMI). Documents available from Article Express International, The Genuine Article, CASDDS. ***Continues** Mining Science and Technology.*
Desc: Serves the needs of both geologists and foundation engineers. Particular attention is paid to problems in rock mechanics and earthquake engineering.
Ind/Abst Abstr. J. Earthq. Eng.; AESIS Q.; Appl. Mech. Rev.; Bioeng. Abstr.; Chem. Abstr.; Coal Abstr.; Curr. Contents Eng. Tech. Appl. Sci.; Ecol. Abstr.; Ei Page One; EMBASE; Energy Res. Abstr.; Eng. Index Annu.; Geogr. Abstr. Phys. Geogr.; Geogr. Abstr. Human Geogr.; Geol. Abstr.; GeoRef; Geotech. Abstr.; Highw. Res. Abstr.; Indian Geosci. Abstr.; Int. Civil Eng. Abstr.; Int. Dev. Abstr.; J. Plan. Lit.; MINPROC; Mintec, Min. Technol. Abstr.; Life Sci. Collect.; Res. Alert [Select. Cov.]; SCISEARCH; Soft. Abstr. Eng.

AT/0728-7224
ENGINEERING GEOLOGY SPECIALIST GROUP PAPERS. **See** Earth Sciences-Geology.

US/1040-1679
ENGINEERING HORIZONS (VAN NUYS, CALIF.). (ENGINEERING HORIZONS.). [Eng. horiz.]. (19??)-. Periodical. English. Four times a year (Jan, Mar, Sept, Oct). $35.80. Petersons / COG Publishing, 16030 Ventura Boulevard, Suite 560, Encino CA 91436. **Tel** (818)789-5293, FAX (818)789-5488. **ED** Al Austin. **LC** TA157; .E616. **DD** 620/.0023/73. **Ad Acc.** ctrl circ.
Desc: A career and job magazine for high school and college students preparing to enroll in or graduate from engineering or science programs.

US/0360-8557
ENGINEERING INDEX ANNUAL. **See** Engineering-Abstracting, Bibliographies and Statistics.

US/0093-8408
ENGINEERING INDEX ENERGY ABSTRACTS. **See** Engineering-Abstracting, Bibliographies and Statistics.

US/0742-1974
ENGINEERING INDEX MONTHLY. **See** Engineering-Abstracting, Bibliographies and Statistics.

UK
ENGINEERING INDUSTRIES REVIEW. ***Ceased.*** (1973/74)-(19??). English. Sombourne Press, 294 Leigh Road, Chandlers Ford, Eastleigh Hants SO5 3AU England. **LC** HD9680.G7; E53. **DD** 338.4/7/62000942.

JA
ENGINEERING INDUSTRY IN JAPAN. **Main/Corp** Nihon Kikai Kogyo Rengokai. (19??)-. Periodical. English. Japan Machinery Federation, 5-8, Shiba Koen, 3-chome, Minato-ku, Tokyo 105 Japan. **LC** HD9705.J3; N54b. **DD** 338.4/7/670952.

UK
ENGINEERING LASERS. ***Ceased.*** (19??)-(Dec. 1993). English. qt. Argus Press Group, Queensway House, 2 Queensway Redhill, Surrey RH1 1QS England. **Tel** 011 44 737 768611, 011 44 737 761685, FAX 011 44 737 760510, telex 948669 TOPJNL G. available on an online database (file 16/Full-Text) from DIALOG.
Desc: Dedicated to the practical, industrial applications of lasers for material processing.
Ind/Abst PROMT [Full Txt.].

US/0882-861X
ENGINEERING LITERATURE GUIDES. [Eng. lit. guides]. No. 1-. Monographic series. English. ir. Price varies per volume. American Society for Engineering Education, 1818 North Street Northwest, Suite 600, Washington DC 20036. **Tel** (202)331-3500. **DD** 620.

UK/0013-7782
ENGINEERING (LONDON). ***Ceased.*** (ENGINEERING.). [Engineering]. **Added/Corp** Design Council. Vol. 1 (Jan. 5, 1866)-(Feb. 1994). Periodical. English. Eleven times a year. Gillard Welch & Associates, Chester Court, High Street Knowlesolihull, West Midlands B93 0LL United Kingdom. **LC** TA1; .E55. **CODEN** ENGNA2. available on microfilm and microfiche from University Microfilms International (UMI). Documents available from Article Express International, The Genuine Article, Ask*IEEE, CASDDS, Documents on Demand.
Ind/Abst Alum. Ind. Abstr.; Appl. Sci. Technol. Index; Bioeng. Abstr.; BMT Abstr. (?-199?); Chem. Abstr.; Coal Abstr.; Curr. Biotechnol.; Curr. Technol. Index; Ei Page One; Eng. Mater. Abstr.; Eng. Index Annu.; Environ. Abstr.; Fluid Abstr., Civil Eng.; Fluid Abstr. Proc. Eng.; FLUIDEX (1973-); GeoRef; Highw. Res. Abstr.; INSPEC (Oct. 1981-); Int. Civil Eng. Abstr.; J. Ferrocement; Leadscan; Manage. Market. Abstr.; Met. Abstr.; Proc. Chem. Eng.; Res. Alert [Select. Cov.]; Saf. Health Work; Soft. Abstr. Eng.; Theoret. Chem. Eng.; World Text. Abstr.

US/1042-9247
ENGINEERING MANAGEMENT JOURNAL. (ENGINEERING MANAGEMENT JOURNAL : EMJ.). [Eng. manag. j.]. **Added/Corp** American Society for Engineering Management. **VFOAT** EMJ. Vol. 1, No. 1 (Mar. 1989)-. Periodical. English. Four times a year (Mar., June, Sept., Dec.). $40.00. American Society for Engineering Management, PO Box 820, Rolla MO 65401. **Tel** (314)341-2101, FAX (314)341-5522. **ED** Ted Eschenbach, (editor's address: University of Alaska, 3211 Providence Drive, Anchorage, Alaska 99308, phone: (907)786-1021). **LC** WMLC 93/1993. **DD** 620. **CODEN** EMJOEH. cum. index. **Bk Rev. Ad Acc, Adv Mgr:** Cathy Frank, **Tel** (314)364-7227. **Pr Rev. Circ:** 3,000.

UK/0960-7919
ENGINEERING MANAGEMENT JOURNAL. **Added/Corp** Institution of Electric Engineers. Vol. 1 (1991)-. Periodical. English. Six times a year. £83.00 EEC countries; £92.00 other. Institution of Electrical Engineers / IEE, Michael Faraday House, Six Hills Way, Stevenage Herts SG1 2AY UK. **Tel** 011 44 438 313311, FAX 011 44 438 742840, telex 825578 IEESTV G. **(Subscription address:** IEE / UK, Publications Sales Department, PO Box 96, Stevenage, Herts, SG1 2SD England.**) CODEN** EMAJEP. **[CCC].** Documents available from Ask*IEEE.
Ind/Abst INSPEC (Feb. 1991-).

US/0013-8037
ENGINEERING MANPOWER BULLETIN. ***Title Change.*** **Added/Corp** Engineers Joint Council. Engineering Manpower Commission. American Association of Engineering Societies. Engineering Manpower Commission. No. 1 (May 1965)-(1992). English. ir. American Association of Engineering Societies-EJC, 1111 19th Street NW, Suite 608, Washington DC 20036. **Tel** (202)296-2237, FAX (202)296-1151. **Bk Rev. Ad Acc. Circ:** 400 (ctrl). ***Continued by** Engineering Workforce Bulletin.*
Desc: Summaries of the major findings of the Engineering Manpower Commission. Corresponding to statistical surveys relating historical data and several summary tables and graphs.

UK/0967-7003
ENGINEERING MATERIALS. ***Ceased.*** (19??)-(1994). English. mo. Mechanical Engineering Publications, PO Box 24, Northgate Avenue, Bury St. Edmunds, Suffolk IP32 6BW England. **Tel** 011 44 284 763277, telex 817376. ***Continues** Material Matters.*

US
ENGINEERING MATERIALS SERIES. Monographic series. English. ir. Price varies per volume. Marcel Dekker Inc., 270 Madison Avenue, New York NY 10016. **Tel** (212)696-9000, (800)228-1160, FAX (212)685-4540, telex 421419. **(Subscription address:** Marcel Dekker Inc, PO Box 5017, Monticello NY 12701.**)**

II/0376-8872
ENGINEERING NEWS (CALCUTTA). (ENGINEERING NEWS.). Periodical. English. 48.00. Association of Indian Engineering Industry, Indian Exchange/7th Floor, Calcutta India. **LC** TA1; .E596. **DD** 620/.005.

UK/0952-8911
ENGINEERING OPTICS : AN INSTITUTE OF PHYSICS JOURNAL. ***Ceased.*** [Eng. opt.]. **Added/Corp** Institute of Physics (Great Britain) American Institute of Physics. (1988)-Vol. 6 (1993). Periodical. English. qt (February, May, August and November). Institute of Physics, Techno House, Redcliffe Way, Bristol BS1 6NX England. **Tel** 011 44 272 297481, FAX 011 44 272 294318, telex 449149 INSTP G. **ED** D William Swift. **CODEN** ENOPEI. Documents available from Article Express International.
Desc: Publishes papers, letters and review articles on all aspects of applied and engineering optics.
Ind/Abst Ei Page One; Eng. Index Annu. [Select. Cov.].

UK/0305-215X
ENGINEERING OPTIMIZATION. [Eng. optim.]. Vol. 1 (1974)-. Periodical. English. Four times a year. Price varies. Gordon & Breach Science Publishers, PO Box 90, Reading RG1 8JL England. **Tel** 011 44 734 560080, FAX 011 44 734 568211. **(Subscription address:** Gordon & Breach Science Publishers / US, 820 Town Center Drive, Langhorne PA 19047.**) ED** A. B. Templeman. **LC** TA174; .E55. **DD** 620/.004/2. **CODEN** EGOPAX. **[CCC]. Bk Rev. Ad Acc.** Documents available from Article Express International, Ask*IEEE.
Ind/Abst Bioeng. Abstr.; Ei Page One; Eng. Index Annu.; INSPEC (1974-); Int. Abstr. Oper. Res. [Select. Cov.].

US/0013-8088
ENGINEERING OUTLOOK. (ENGINEERING OUTLOOK - UNIVERSITY OF ILLINOIS AT URBANA-CHAMPAIGN, COLLEGE OF ENGINEERING.). [Eng. outlook]. **Added/Corp** University

of Illinois at Urbana-Champaign. College of Engineering. (197?)-. Periodical. English. Four times a year (Feb., May, Aug., Nov.). Free. Engineering Publications, 112 Engineering Hall, 1308 West Green Street, Urbana IL 61801. **Tel** (217)333-1510. **ED** Maureen L. Tan. **DD** 620. **Circ:** 24,000. ***Continues*** *Engineering Outlook at the University of Illinois.*
Desc: Describes the current research of the College of Engineering (including physics) in layman's terms for general readership and highly pictorial.
Ind/Abst Eng. Mater. Abstr. (1973-); Fluid Abstr., Civil Eng.; Fluid Abstr. Proc. Eng.; FLUIDEX (1973-); J. Ferrocement.

SZ
ENGINEERING REPORT. German. mo. 40.00F. Verlag Georg Moellerke, Kornweg 5, CH 5415 Nussbaumen, Switzerland. **Tel** 011 41 56 822351.

UK
ENGINEERING RESEARCH CENTRES : A WORLD DIRECTORY OF ORGANIZATIONS & PROGRAMMES. Directory. English. be. $400.00. Longman Group Ltd., Fourth Avenue, Longman House, Harlow Essex CM19 5SR England. **Tel** 011 44 279 429655, FAX 011 44 279 431059, telex 81259. **(Subscription address:** Fourth Avenue, Harlow Essex CM19 5AA England**)** Index available. available on CD-ROM.
Desc: Contains over 8,000 entries describing research and technology laboratories in over 70 countries. Provides details on industrial research centers and educational establishments with R & D activity.

US/0149-0605
ENGINEERING RESEARCH HIGHLIGHTS. Began with Fall 1975 issue. Periodical. English. Engineering Research Institute, Marston Hall, Ames IA 50011. **Tel** (515)294-1800. **ED** Janet R Greisch. **LC** TA160.4; .E53. **DD** 620/.007/20777. ctrl circ. ***Continues*** *Iowa State Engineering Research, 0075-0409.*
Desc: Various reports and bulletins describing engineering research projects at Iowa State University.

US
ENGINEERING SALARIES SURVEY / PREPARED BY D. DIETRICH ASSOCIATES, INC. Added/Corp D. Dietrich Associates. (199?)-. English. sa (Apr. & Oct.). $175.00. Dietrich Associates Inc, Box 511, Phoenixville PA 19460. **Tel** (215)935-1563. **LC** TA157; .S849. **DD** 331.2/82/000973. ***Continues*** *Survey of Engineering Salaries.*

●UK/0963-7346
ENGINEERING SCIENCE AND EDUCATION JOURNAL. Added/Corp Institution of Electrical Engineers. **VFOAT** Engineering Science & Education Journal. Vol. 1, No. 1 (Feb. 1992)-. Periodical. English. Six times a year. £83.00 EEC countries; £92.00 other. Institution of Electrical Engineers / IEE, Michael Faraday House, Six Hills Way, Stevenage Herts SG1 2AY UK. **Tel** 011 44 438 313311, FAX 011 44 438 742840, telex 825578 IEESTV G. **(Subscription address:** IEE / UK, Publications Sales Department, PO Box 96, Stevenage, Herts, SG1 2SD England.**) LC** IN PROCESS. Documents available from Article Express International, Ask*IEEE.
Ind/Abst Ei Page One; Eng. Index Annu. [Select. Cov.]; INSPEC (Feb. 1992-).

UK
ENGINEERING SCIENCES DATA UNIT : SUBSERIES AERODYNAMICS. (19??)-. English. ir. $7745.00. ESDU International Ltd., 27 Corsham Street, London N1 6UA England. **Tel** 011 44 71 4905151, telex 266168 ENDASAG.

UK
ENGINEERING SCIENCES DATA UNIT. SUBSERIES PERFORMANCE AND REVISION SERVICE. (19??)-. English. ir. $5300.00. ESDU International Ltd., 27 Corsham Street, London N1 6UA England. **Tel** 011 44 71 4905151, telex 266168 ENDASAG.

UK
ENGINEERING SCIENCES DATA UNIT. SUBSERIES TRANSONIC AERODYNAMICS AND REVISION SERVICE. (19??)-. English. ir. $2880.00. ESDU International Ltd., 27 Corsham Street, London N1 6UA England. **Tel** 011 44 71 4905151, telex 266168 ENDASAG.

US/0093-5735
ENGINEERING, SCIENTIFIC AND TECHNICAL SALARY SURVEY. Main/Corp Merchants and Manufacturers Association. English. 2300 Occidental Center, 1150 South Olive Street, Los Angeles CA 90015. **LC** TA157; .M383A. **DD** 331.2/82/000973.

UK/0951-7871
ENGINEERING SERVICES MANAGEMENT. [Eng. serv. manag.]. (1987)-. Periodical. English. Six times a year. £70.00 Europe; £98.00 other. Building Services Research and Information Association, Old Bracknell Lane West, Bracknell Berkshire RG12 7AH England. **Tel** 011 44 344 426511, FAX 011 44 344 487575, telex 848288. **ED** Stephen Loyd. **DD** 696. Index available. cum. index. **Bk Rev. Circ:** 400.
Desc: Provides a continuing awareness of information and developments in the engineering services relating to running a building or building estate. Includes news, events, technical summaries and tariffs. Topics covered are maintenance, energy management, fire protection, security, health and safety, electrical and lighting, hospitals, schools, sports buildings and case studies.

US
ENGINEERING TECHNOLOGY. (1979)-. Monographic series. English. Price varies per volume. Marcel Dekker Inc., 270 Madison Avenue, New York NY 10016. **Tel** (212)696-9000, (800)228-1160, FAX (212)685-4540, telex 421419. **(Subscription address:** Marcel Dekker Inc, PO Box 5017, Monticello NY 12701.**)**
Desc: Covers topics vital to those in the field of engineering technology.

US
ENGINEERING ; THE NEWSLETTER OF ENGINEERING AT CLEMSON UNIVERSITY. Added/Corp Clemson University. College of Engineering. Vol. 1, No. 1 (19??)-. Periodical. English. qt. Clemson University College of Engineering, Dean's Office, H Anne Bradbury, 22G Riggs Hall, Clemson SC 29634-0901. **Tel** (803)656-5711. **ED** H. Anne Bradbury. **Circ:** 16,800 (ctrl).
Desc: Features articles about current research and faculty achievements within the College of Engineering at Clemson University. Also included are articles of general interest about the university, engineering alumni activities, and courses offered through continuing engineering education.

US/0195-6876
ENGINEERING TIMES (WASHINGTON, D.C.). (ENGINEERING TIMES.). [Eng. times]. **Added/Corp** National Society of Professional Engineers. Vol. 1 (Sept. 1979)-. Periodical. English. mo. $30.00. Engineering Times, 1420 King Street, Alexandria VA 22314. **Tel** (703)684-2800. **ED** Stefan Jaeger. **LC** TA1; .E862. **DD** 620/.005. **Ad Acc, Adv Mgr Tel** (410)882-0050. **Circ:** 80,000 (ctrl).
Desc: Contains news and feature articles on the issues and events that engineers have in common, across various technical disciplines. It covers legislative and government affairs, quality of engineering, continuing competence, ethics, employment practices, industry policies relative to engineering, engineering society programs and cooperative activities, and employment opportunities and salary data.
Ind/Abst Alum. Ind. Abstr.; Eng. Mater. Abstr.; Met. Abstr.; Trade Ind. Index.

PL
ENGINEERING TRANSACTIONS. (19??)-. English (Portuguese). Four times a year. $120.00. **(Subscription address:** ARS Polona, PO Box 1001, 00068 Warsaw Poland.**) *Continues*** *Rozprawy Inzynierskie.*

US
ENGINEERING TROUBLESHOOTING. Vol. 1 (1980)-. Monographic series. English. Price varies per volume. Marcel Dekker Inc., 270 Madison Avenue, New York NY 10016. **Tel** (212)696-9000, (800)228-1160, FAX (212)685-4540, telex 421419. **(Subscription address:** Marcel Dekker Inc, PO Box 5017, Monticello NY 12701.**)**

US/0177-0667
ENGINEERING WITH COMPUTERS. [Eng. comput.]. Vol. 1, No. 1 (1985)-. Periodical. English. qt. £88.00. Springer-Verlag London Ltd., Springer House, 8 Alexandra Road Wimbledon, London SW19 7JZ England. **Tel** 011 44 81 9471280, or 9475885, FAX 011 44 81 9474651, telex 21531 SPRGB G. **(Subscription address:** North America: Springer Verlag, Journal Fulfillment Department, 44 Hartz Way, Secaucus, NJ 07096; Outside North America: Springer Verlag, Postfach 311340, D 10643 Berlin Germany**) ED** T Belytschko and S Fenves. **LC** TA174; .E56. **CODEN** ENGCE7. **[CCC]. Pr Rev.** Documents available from Article Express International, The Genuine Article, Ask*IEEE.
Desc: Publishes papers which creatively integrate analytical methods and numerical models with techniques of software engineering, including databases, geometric modeling, and computer graphics.
Ind/Abst Acoust. Abstr.; Civ. Struct. Eng. Abstr.; Compumath Citation Index [Full Cov.]; Comput. Inf. Syst. Abstr. J. [Full Cov.]; Curr. Contents Eng. Tech. Appl. Sci.; Ei Page One; Elect. Comm. Abstr.; Eng. Index Annu.; Inf. Sci. Abstr. (?-?); INSPEC (1987-); Int. Aerosp. Abstr.; Manuf. Process Eng. Abstr.; Mater. Sci. Eng. Abstr.; Res. Alert [Full Cov.]; SCISEARCH; Shock Vibr. Dig.; Zentralbl. Math. Ihre Grenzgeb.

●US
ENGINEERING WORKFORCE BULLETIN / EWC AAES. Added/Corp American Association of Engineering Societies. Engineering Workforce Commission. No. 124 (April 1993)-. Periodical. English. ir (8 issues). $117.00 (non-member), $69.00 (member). American Association of Engineering Societies-EJC, 1111 19th Street NW, Suite 608, Washington DC 20036. **Tel** (202)296-2237, FAX (202)296-1151. ***Continues*** *Engineering Manpower Bulletin, 0013-8037.*

UK
ENGINEERING WORLD (LONDON, ENGLAND). (ENGINEERING WORLD : THE JOURNAL OF THE SOCIETY OF ENGINEERS.). **Added/Corp** Society of Engineers (London, England). Vol. 80, No. 1 (Spring 1989)-. Academic Scholarly Publication. English. qt. £12.00 UK; $15.00 US. The Society of Engineers, Guinea Wiggs, Nayland Colchester, Essex CO6 4NF England. **Tel** 011 44 206 263332, FAX 011 44 206 262624. **ED** Peter Wilson. **LC** TA1; .S673b. **DD** 620/.005. **Bk Rev. Ad Acc.** ctrl circ. ***Continues*** *SoE Journal.*
Desc: Learned journal of The Society of Engineers, a multidisciplinary worldwide organization established in 1854.

●AT
ENGINEERS AUSTRALIA. Added/Corp Institution of Engineers, Australia. **VFOAT** Journal of the Institution of Engineers, Australia. Vol. 64, No. 16 (Aug. 21, 1992)-. Periodical. English. mo. 46.50Aus$ (one edition), 93.00Aus$ (both editions) Australia; 74.30Aus$ (one edition), 148.60Aus$ (both editions) other. Engineers Australia Pty Ltd, 2 Ernest Street, Crows Nest Centre, Crows Nest New South Wales 2065, Australia. **Tel** 011 61 2 438-1533, FAX 011 61 2 438-5934, telex 27640. **LC** TA1; .E69433. **DD** 620/.005. ***Continues in part*** *Engineers Australia, 1032-1195.*

AT/1032-1195
ENGINEERS AUSTRALIA. *Title Change.* [Eng. Aust.]. **Added/Corp** Institution of Engineers, Australia. **VFOAT** Journal of the Institution of Engineers, Australia. Vol. 60, No. 11 (May 27, 1988)-Vol. 64, No. 15 (Aug. 7, 1992). Periodical. English. mo. Engineers Australia Pty Ltd, 2 Ernest Street, Crows Nest Centre, Crows Nest New South Wales 2065, Australia. **Tel** 011 61 2 438-1533, FAX 011 61 2 438-5934, telex 27640. **ED** Dietrich Georg. **LC** TA1; .I72471. **DD** 620/.005. **CODEN** ENAUDU. **Bk Rev. Ad Acc. Circ:** 44,500 (ctrl). Documents available from Ask*IEEE. ***Continues*** *Journal of the Institution of Engineers, Australia, 0020-3319.* ***Split into*** *Engineers Australia General Edition* ***and*** *Engineers Australia Civil Edition.*
Desc: A news magazine covering all disciplines of engineering.
Ind/Abst AESIS Q.; Ceram. Abstr. (19??-Aug. 1992); Concr. Abstr.; INSPEC (Aug. 11, 1989-Aug. 1992); Int. Civil Eng. Abstr.; Soft. Abstr. Eng.

US/0199-0101
ENGINEER'S DIGEST (WILLOW GROVE). (ENGINEER'S DIGEST.). [Eng. dig.]. (19??)-. Periodical. English. mo. $55.00 US; $85.00 Canada and Mexico; $175.00 other. Huebcore Communications Inc., 1355 Mendiota Heights, Suite 210, Mendiota Heights MN 55120. **Tel** (612)686-0303. **(Subscription address:** Huebcore Communications Inc., 29100 Aurora Road, Suite 200, Solon OH 44139.**) [CCC].** available on microfilm from University Microfilms International (UMI). ***Continues*** *Plant & Industrial Engineer's Digest, 0192-1290.*

US/0071-0415
ENGINEERS' SALARIES : SPECIAL INDUSTRY REPORT. [Eng. salaries spec. ind. rep.]. **Added/Corp** American Association of Engineering Societies. Engineering Manpower Commission. Engineers Joint Council. Engineering Manpower Commission. (19??)-. English. an. $169.00 (members), $287.50 (nonmembers). American Association of Engineering Societies-EJC, 1111 19th Street NW, Suite 608, Washington DC 20036. **Tel** (202)296-2237, FAX (202)296-1151. **ED** R E Ellis. **LC** TA157; .E6627. **DD** 331.2/82/000973. **Circ:** 1,000. ***Continues*** *Engineering Salaries : Special Industry Report.*
Desc: Compilation of regional, national, and international technical and engineering organizations. Lists such information as addresses and telephone numbers, officers, membership, membership requirements, publications, and organizational objectives.

FR/0244-7118
ENQUETE ANNUELLE DE BRANCHE. INGENIERIE, ETUDES ET CONSEILS / MINISTERE DE L'INDUSTRIE ET DE LA RECHERCHE, SERVICE D'ETUDE DES STRATEGIES ET DES STATISTIQUES INDUSTRIELLES. **See** Engineering-Abstracting, Bibliographies and Statistics.

FR
ENQUETE ANNUELLE D'ENTERPRISE : MATERIEL DE MANUTENTION, MATERIEL POUR LES MINES, LA SIDERURGIE, LE GENIE CIVIL. Main/Corp Centre d'Enquetes Statistiques de Caen. French. mo.

$54.41. CEP Information Professions, 1 Cite Bergere, 75311 Paris Cedex 09 France. **Tel** 011 33 1 44695550. **LC** HD9705.F69; C45C. **DD** 338.4/768176.

US/0891-9526
ENR. [ENR]. **VFOAT** E.N.R. **VAT** Engineering News Record. Vol. 218, No. 1 (Jan. 1, 1987)-. Academic Scholarly Publication. English. wk. $69.00 (one year), $105.00 (two year) US and possessions; $75.00 (one year), $114.00 (two year) Canada; $180.00 (one year), $312.00 (two year) other. McGraw Hill Publishing Company, Inc., 1221 Avenue of the Americas, New York NY 10020. **Tel** (212)512-6410, (800)525-5003, FAX (212)512-6111. **(Subscription address:** ENR, PO Box 516, Hightstown NJ 08520.**) LC** TA1; .E6. **DD** 620/.005. **CODEN** ENRRE5. **[CCC]. Ad Acc.** available on microfilm and microfiche from University Microfilms International (UMI). Documents available from Article Express International, BIOSIS Document Express, UMI Article Clearinghouse, CASDDS. ***Continues** Engineering News-Record, 0013-807X.*
Desc: Reports on all aspects of construction; buildings, water and power, management and labor, economics and computer use. Offers full-run, regional and demographic advertising, plus four annual postcard decks.
Ind/Abst ABI/INFORM Glob. Ed.; ABI Inform Ondisc (Dec. 1987-); Acad. Search (July 1993-); Alum. Ind. Abstr.; Appl. Sci. Technol. Index; BioBusiness (1987-); Bioeng. Abstr.; Biol. Abstr.; Bus. Index (1988-); Bus. Period. Index; Bus. Source (Jul. 1993-); Chem. Abstr.; Coal Abstr.; Concr. Abstr.; Constr. Index; Ei Page One; EMBASE; Energy Res. Abstr.; Eng. Mater. Abstr.; Eng. Index Annu.; Expand. Acad. Index (1992-); F&S Index Plus Text, Int. [Select. Cov.]; Foods Adlibra (1987-); Gen. BusinessFile (1988-); Gen. Period. Index (1988-); GeoRef; Highw. Res. Abstr.; INFO-SOUTH Abstr.; INIS Atomindex [Micro.]; J. Ferrocement; Mag. Search; Met. Abstr.; NEXIS; Predicasts Forecasts; Stat. Ref. Index; Trade Ind. Index; UMI ABI/Inform--Bus. Period. Ondisc [Full Txt.]; Wilson Bus. Abstr.

US/0098-6305
ENR DIRECTORY OF DESIGN FIRMS. **VFOAT** Design Firms; Directory of Design Firms. **VAT** Engineering News-Record, Directory of Design Firms. (1974/75)-. Directory. English. be. $85.00. McGraw Hill Publishing Company, Inc., 1221 Avenue of the Americas, New York NY 10020. **Tel** (212)512-6410, (800)525-5003, FAX (212)512-6111. **ED** Paul Herrmannsfeldt. **LC** TA12; .E4. **DD** 620/.004/2. **Ad Acc. Circ:** 13,000 (ctrl).
Desc: Directory of engineering and design firms for the construction industry.

FR/0013-9084
ENTROPIE. [Entropie]. No. 1 (Jan./Feb. 1965)-. Academic Scholarly Publication. French (summaries and/or abstracts in French, English, German, Spanish and Portuguese; table of contents in French, English, German, Spanish and Portuguese). Seven times a year. 1439.61F France; 1760.00F other. Association Entropie, Boite Postale 63, 94002 Creteil Cedex France. **Tel** 011 33 1 48991058. **ED** Jean-Claude Charpentier and Georges Piar. **LC** TJ260; .E52. **DD** 621.4/005. **CODEN** ENTPA5. **[CCC].** Index available. cum. index. **Bk Rev. Ad Acc. Circ:** 2,000 (ctrl). available on diskette. Documents available from Article Express International, Ask*IEEE, CASDDS.
Desc: Covers thermodynamics, energetics, process engineering, state-of-the-art techniques and sciences.
Ind/Abst Bioeng. Abstr.; Chem. Abstr.; Coal Abstr.; Curr. Biotechnol.; Ei Page One; EMBASE; Energy Res. Abstr.; Eng. Index Annu.; Fluid Abstr., Civil Eng.; Fluid Abstr. Proc. Eng.; FLUIDEX (1973-); INSPEC (Jan./Feb. 1973-); Int. Aerosp. Abstr.; Proc. Chem. Eng.; Theoret. Chem. Eng.

CN/0705-9272
ENVIRONMENT SYSTEMS & INDUSTRIES. **See** Building and Construction.

US/1063-7346
ENVIRONMENTAL ENGINEERING ABSTRACTS. ***Ceased.*** **See** Environmental Issues-Abstracting, Bibliographies and Statistics.

UK/0954-5824
ENVIRONMENTAL ENGINEERING (BURY SAINT EDMUNDS, ENG. : 1988). (ENVIRONMENTAL ENGINEERING : THE JOURNAL OF THE SOCIETY OF ENVIRONMENTAL ENGINEERS.). Vol. 1, No. 1 (Sept. 1988)-. Periodical. English. qt (4 issues). $99.00. Mechanical Engineering Publications, PO Box 24, Northgate Avenue, Bury St. Edmunds, Suffolk IP32 6BW England. **Tel** 011 44 284 763277, telex 817376. **(Subscription address:** Mechanical Engineering Publications / Western Hemisphere Subscriptions, Subscription Office, PO Box 361, Birmingham AL 35201-0361.**) ED** Fred Whiteley. **NLM** W1; EN981S. **CODEN** ENENEU. **[CCC]. Bk Rev. Ad Acc. Circ:** 8,000. available on microfilm and microfiche from University Microfilms International (UMI). Documents available from Article Express International, Ask*IEEE. ***Continues** Journal of the Society of Environmental Engineers, 0374-356X.*
Desc: Reflects expert environmental engineers' concerns about all aspects of electrical, electronic, mechanical, chemical and civil engineering.
Ind/Abst Ei Page One; Eng. Index Annu.; Environ. Period. Bibliogr. (?-?); Highw. Res. Abstr.; INSPEC (1968-); Int. Aerosp. Abstr.; Int. Build. Serv. Abstr.; Int. Packag. Abstr.; Shock Vibr. Dig.

CN/0835-605X
ENVIRONMENTAL SCIENCE & ENGINEERING (AURORA). (ENVIRONMENTAL SCIENCE & ENGINEERING.). [Environ. sci. eng.]. **VAT** Environmental Science and Engineering (Aurora). Vol. 1, No. 1 (Jan./Feb. 1988)-. Periodical. English. bm. 45.00Can$ (one year), 80.00Can$ (two year) Canada; $55.00 (one year), $100.00 (two year) other. Davcom Communications, 220 Industrial Parkway South, Unit 30, Aurora Ontario L4G 3V6 Canada. **Tel** (905)727-4666, FAX (905)841-7271. **ED** Tom Davey. **DD** 620.8/0971. **Bk Rev. Ad Acc. Circ:** 20,000 (ctrl).

US/1055-9892
ENVISIONEERING. [Envisioneering]. **Added/Corp** Kyra Communications. Vol. 1, No. 1 (Mar 15, 1991)-. Periodical. English. sm. $395.00, $130.00 (public libraries, students). Kyra Communications, 3864 Bayberry Lane, Seaford NY 11783. **DD** 621.

FR/0184-9697
EQUIP-AFRIQUE. ***Title Change.*** (19??)-?. Periodical. French. sm. Ediafric la Documentation Africaine, 10 rue Vineuse, 75116 Paris France. **Tel** 011 33 1 44308100, FAX 011 33 1 45208174. **LC** HC800.A1; E68. **DD** 338.096. ***Continues** Equip-Afric.* ***Continued by** Afrique Entreprise.*
Desc: Unique source of information concerning the great projects of infrastructure in Africa. Also lists the activities of the societies and organizations in that sector-mines and heavy industry-ports.

US/0733-3056
EQUIPMENT MANAGEMENT. (EQUIPMENT MANAGEMENT : EM.). [Equip. manage.]. **VFOAT** EM; E.M. Vol. 10, No. 5 (May 1982)-. Periodical. English. mo. $4.00 (single issue); $40.00 US and Possessions; $50.00 other. Irving-Cloud Publishing Company, 417 North Hough Street, Barrington IL 60010. **Tel** (708)382-3405, FAX (708)674-7015. **(Subscription address:** 6201 W Howard Street, Room 207, Niles, IL 60648**) ED** Greg Sitek. **LC** TA725; .E5. **DD** 629.28/75. **Ad Acc. Circ:** 56,000 (ctrl). available on microfilm and microfiche from University Microfilms International (UMI). Documents available from UMI Article Clearinghouse. ***Continues** Heavy Duty Equipment Maintenance/Management, 0734-2640.*
Desc: Editorial content consists of information on how to purchase, select and maintain equipment used in construction, mining, forestry, utilities, government and oil/gas industries.
Ind/Abst ABI/INFORM Glob. Ed.; ABI Inform Ondisc (Jan. 1988-July 1991); UMI ABI/Inform--Bus. Period. Ondisc [Full Txt.].

●US/1064-8046
ERGONOMICS IN DESIGN. [Ergon. des.]. **Added/Corp** Human Factors and Ergonomics Society. (Jan. 1993)-. Periodical. English. qt (Jan, Apr, July, Oct). $28.00. Human Factors and Ergonomics Society, PO Box 1369, Journals Department, Santa Monica CA 90406-1369. **Tel** (310)394-1811, (310)394-9793, FAX (310)394-2410. **ED** Daryle J. Gardner-Bonneau, (Editor's Address: CTA, Inc, 2500 English Creek Avenue, #1000, McKee City, NJ, 08232). **LC** TA166; .E7253. **DD** 620.8/2. **[CCC].** Index available. **Bk Rev**, (Qty: 20-30). **Ad Acc, Adv Mgr:** Lois Smith. **Pr Rev. Circ:** 5100.
Desc: Includes articles, analysis, case studies, book and product reviews, news, and other items regarding how ergonomics is applied in real world systems and tools.
Ind/Abst Ergon. Abstr.

US/1043-982X
ESD TECHNOLOGY. [ESD technol.]. **VAT** Engineering Society of Detroit Technology. Vol. 49, No. 4 (April 1988)-. Periodical. English. mo. $2.00 members, $22.00 nonmembers US; $30.00 nonmembers other. ESD, 100 Farnsworth, Detroit MI 48202. **LC** TA1; .F69. **DD** 620/.005. ***Continues** De Technology, 8750-7811.*

●US/1064-2293
EURASIAN SOIL SCIENCE. **See** Earth Sciences.

UK
EUREKA : INNOVATIVE ENGINEERING DESIGN. (19??)-. Periodical. English. Twenty-five times a year. £385.00. Findlay Publications Ltd, Franks Hall, Horton Kirby, Kent DA4 9LL England. **Tel** 011 44 (0322)222222, FAX 011 44 (0322)289577. **CODEN** ERKAEF. Documents available from Ask*IEEE.
Ind/Abst INSPEC (1986-).

UK/0304-3797
EUROPEAN JOURNAL OF ENGINEERING EDUCATION. [Eur. j. eng. educ.]. **Added/Corp** European Society for Engineering Education. **VFOAT** EJEE. Vol. 1 (Summer 1975)-. Periodical. Multiple languages (English, French and German). qt (Mar., Jun., Sep., Dec.). £234.00. Carfax Publishing Company, PO Box 25 Abingdon, Oxfordshire OX14 3UE England. **Tel** 011 44 235 555335, FAX (0279)31067, telex 817484. **(Subscription address:** US and Canada/ PO Box 2025, Dunnellon, FL 34430-2025; telephone:(904)489-6996**) ED** Jean McChez. **LC** T61; .E78. **DD** 620/.007/114. **CODEN** EJEED8. **[CCC].** Index available (Bound in December issue). **Bk Rev. Ad Acc.** available on microfiche. Documents available from Ask*IEEE.
Desc: An examination of the factors influencing engineering education in different societies.
Ind/Abst Curr. Index J. Educ. (March 1990); Educ. Technol. Abstr.; INSPEC (Spring 1978-); Int. Civil Eng. Abstr.; Res. High. Educ. Abstr.; Soft. Abstr. Eng.; Tech. Educ. Train. Abstr.

●GW/0940-2470
EUROPEAN PRODUCTION ENGINEERING : EPE. [EPE, Eur. prod. eng.]. **VFOAT** EPE. (Mar. 1992)-. Periodical. English. sa. DM44.80. Carl Hanser Verlag, Postfach 860420, D 81631 Munich Germany. **Tel** 011 49 89 998300, FAX 011 49 89 984809. **LC** TS176; .I5436. **DD** 670.42/05. **CODEN** EPOEEX. Documents available from Ask*IEEE. ***Continues** Industrial & Production Engineering, 0343-334X.*
Ind/Abst INSPEC (1992-).

US/0895-7541
EW DESIGN ENGINEERS' HANDBOOK. ***Title Change.*** [EW des. eng. handb.]. **VFOAT** Design Engineers' Handbook. **VAT** Electronic Warfare Design Engineers' Handbook. (1987)-(19??). English. an. Horizon House, 685 Canton Street, Norwood MA 02062. **Tel** (617)365-4595. **LC** UG485; .E9. **DD** 623/.043/05. ***Continued by** EW Design Engineers' Handbook & Manufacturers Directory, 1069-708X.*

GW
EXPORT MARKT. ENGINEERING. Periodical. English. Vogel Verlag, Postfach 6740, D-97064 Wuerzburg Germany. **Tel** 011 49 931 4182145, 011 49 931 4182483, FAX 011 49 931 4182670, telex 841 680131. **LC** TS1; .E85. **DD** 670/.943. ***Continues** Export Market. Engineering Ed.*

US/0160-7464
EXTENDED ABSTRACTS AND PROGRAM - BIENNIAL CONFERENCE ON CARBON. [Ext. abstr. prog. - Bienn. Conf. Carbon]. **Added/Corp** American Carbon Society. University of Pittsburgh. School of Engineering. (19??)-. English. be. Electrochemical Society Inc, 215 Canal Street, Manchester NH 03108. **CODEN** EAPCDS. Documents available from Article Express International, CASDDS.
Ind/Abst Bioeng. Abstr.; Chem. Abstr. (-1985); Ei Page One; Eng. Index Annu.

UK/0144-8218
FAR EASTERN TECHNICAL REVIEW. ***Title Change.*** **See** Business-Commerce.

US
FEDERAL FORECAST FOR ENGINEERS. English. ir. Office of Personnel Management, 1900 East Street Northwest, OELR Room 7429, Washington DC 20415. **Tel** (202)632-6256.

NE/1830-2011
FINANCIAL ENGINEERING AND THE JAPANESE MARKETS. (19??)-. English. tq. $300.00. Kluwer Academic Publishers, Postbus 322, 3300 AH Dordrecht, The Netherlands. **Tel** 011 (31) 78 524400, FAX 011 31 78 183273, telex 20083.

US/0195-1076
FINISHING INTERNATIONAL. (19??)-. Periodical. English. qt.
Ind/Abst Ceram. Abstr. (19??-).

UK/0962-7170
FLUID ABSTRACTS. CIVIL ENGINEERING. **See** Engineering-Abstracting, Bibliographies and Statistics.

US
FLUID POWER AND CONTROL. Vol. 1 (1983)-. Monographic series. English. Price varies per volume. Marcel Dekker Inc., 270 Madison Avenue, New York NY 10016. **Tel** (212)696-9000, (800)228-1160, FAX (212)685-4540, telex 421419. **(Subscription address:** Marcel Dekker Inc, PO Box 5017, Monticello NY 12701.**)**
Desc: Each volume presents information to assist those involved with fluid power and control. Topics include hydraulic pumps and motors, hydraulic valves and electrohydraulic systems.

UK/0960-3085
FOOD AND BIOPRODUCTS PROCESSING : TRANSACTIONS OF THE INSTITUTION OF CHEMICAL ENGINEERS, PART C. **See** Food and Food Industry.

US/0146-6232
FOREFRONT (BERKELEY). (FOREFRONT.). English. an. University of California College of Engineering, Berkeley CA 94720. **LC** T171.C24; F67. **DD** 620/.007/2079465.

Engineering

GW/0015-7899
FORSCHUNG IM INGENIEURWESEN. (FORSCHUNG IM INGENIEURWESEN / VEREIN DEUTSCHER INGENIEURE.). [Forsch. ingenieurwes.]. **Added/Corp** Verein Deutscher Ingenieure. Vol. 30 (1964)-. Periodical. German. Nine times a year. DM1012.00 Germany; DM1039.00 other. VDI Verlag GmbH, Postfach 101054, D 40001 Dusseldorf Germany. **Tel** 011 49 211 6188313, FAX 011 49 211 6188133. **LC** TA1; .F68. **CODEN** FIGWA5. **[CCC]. Pr Rev.** Documents available from Article Express International, The Genuine Article, CASDDS. **Continues** Forschung auf dem Gebiete des Ingenieurwesens.
Desc: Features current technical developments and results of the latest experimental and theoretical investigations in engineering areas such as strength of materials, flow technology, heat technology, and process technology.
Ind/Abst Acoust. Abstr.; Alum. Ind. Abstr.; Bioeng. Abstr.; Chem. Abstr.; Coal Abstr.; Curr. Contents Eng. Tech. Appl. Sci.; Ei Page One; Energy Res. Abstr.; Eng. Mater. Abstr.; Eng. Index Annu.; Int. Aerosp. Abstr.; Leadscan; Met. Abstr.; Pollut. Abstr. Indexes; Res. Alert [Select. Cov.]; SCISEARCH.

GW
FORSCHUNGSBERICHT AGRARTECHNIK DES ARBEITSKREISES FORSCHUNG UND LEHRE DER MAX-EYTH-GESELLSCHAFT (MEG). See Agriculture.

GW
FORTSCHRITT BERICHTE DER VDI ZEITSCHRIFTEN. SERIES 1 : KONSTRUKTIONSTECHNIK. Monographic series. German. ir. Price varies per volume. VDI Verlag GmbH, Postfach 101054, D 40001 Dusseldorf Germany. **Tel** 011 49 211 6188313, FAX 011 49 211 6188133.

GW
FORTSCHRITT BERICHTE DER VDI ZEITSCHRIFTEN. SERIES 16 : TECHNIK UND WIRTSCHAFT. German. ir. Price varies per volume. VDI Verlag GmbH, Postfach 101054, D 40001 Dusseldorf Germany. **Tel** 011 49 211 6188313, FAX 011 49 211 6188133.

MX
FOTOGRAMETRIA, FOTOINTERPRETACION Y GEODESIA. See Photography and Video.

UK/0143-3598
FOULING PREVENTION RESEARCH DIGEST. Title Change. Vol. 1, No. 1-4 (Dec. 1979)-(19??). Periodical. English. qt. Lavis Marketing, 73 Lime Walk, Headington, Oxford OX3 7AD England. **Tel** 011 44 865 67575. Index available. **Circ:** 220. **Merged into** HTFS Digest, 0952-2654.
Desc: Bibliographic citations and indexes covering experimental and theoretical investigations about fouling of heat exchange surfaces and its preventions.
Ind/Abst Dairy Sci. Abstr.

PL/0324-8747
FOUNDATIONS OF CONTROL ENGINEERING. Title Change. [Found. control eng.]. Vol. 1 (1975)-(19??). Periodical. English. qt. (**Subscription address:** ARS Polona, PO Box 1001, 00068 Warsaw Poland). **CODEN** FCENDV. Documents available from Ask*IEEE. **Continued by** Foundations of Computing and Decision and Science.
Ind/Abst INSPEC (1978-); Math. Rev.; Pollut. Abstr. Indexes; Zentralbl. Math. Ihre Grenzgeb.

CH
FU JEN STUDIES. SCIENCE AND ENGINEERING. See Science and Technology.

JA/0016-2515
FUJITSU. Japanese. bm. $86.00. (**Subscription address:** Kyowa Book Company Inc., 1-38 Kanda Jinbocho Chiyoda Ku, Tokyo 101 Japan; Telephone: 011 81 3 3293 0727) Documents available from BLDSC.

JA/0429-8373
FUKUI DAIGAKU KOGAKUBU KENKYU HOKOKU. [Fukui Daigaku Kogakubu kenkyu hokoku]. **Added/Corp** Fukui Daigaku. Kogakubu. **VFOAT** Memoirs of the Faculty of Engineering, Fukui University. (1952)-. Periodical. Japanese (English; summaries and/or abstracts in English). sa. Fukui Dagaku Kogakubu, (Faculty of Engineering, Fukui University), 9-1, Bunkyo 3 Chome, Fukuishi, Fukuiken 910 Japan. **CODEN** FDKHAD. Documents available from Ask*IEEE, CASDDS.
Ind/Abst Chem. Abstr.; INSPEC (1984-).

NE
FUNDAMENTAL STUDIES IN ENGINEERING. Vol. 1 (1979)-. Monographic series. English. Elsevier Science Publishing Company Inc, Madison Square Station, PO Box 882, New York NY 10159-0882. **Tel** (212)633-3950, FAX (212)633-3990.
Ind/Abst Zentralbl. Math. Ihre Grenzgeb.

JA/0387-0863
FUNE NO KAGAKU. [Fune no kagaku]. **VFOAT** Marine Engineering. Vol. 1 (Nov. 1948)-. Periodical. Japanese. mo. $240.00. (**Subscription address:** Maruzen Company Ltd., PO Box 5050, Import & Export Department, Tokyo 100 31 Japan.)
Ind/Abst Aquat. Sci. Fish. Abstr. (Computer File).

SA
FWP : MATERIALS ENGINEERING JOURNAL. Ceased. VFOAT FWP Journal. Vol 31, No 11 (Nov. 1991)-(Nov. 1992). Periodical. English. mo. Founding Welding Production, PO Box 31548, 2017 Braamfontein South Africa. **Tel** 011 27 11 3396678. **Continues** FWP Journal, 0015-9026.

US/0747-1270
GATEWAY ENGINEER. (GATEWAY ENGINEER : OFFICIAL JOURNAL OF THE ENGINEERS' CLUB OF ST. LOUIS IN COOPERATION WITH PARTICIPATING SOCIETIES.). **Added/Corp** Engineers' Club of St. Louis. (19??)-. Periodical. English. Twelve times a year. $20.00. Admore Publishing Inc, 9701 Gravois Avenue, St Louis MO 63123. **Tel** (314)638-4050, FAX (314)638-3880. **DD** 620.

FR
GAZETTE DU CEFI. Ceased. (19??)-(Jan. 1992). French. Comite d Etudes Formations d Ingenieurs, 58 rue de Lisbonne, 75008 Paris France.

UK/0264-9187
GEC JOURNAL OF RESEARCH. (THE GEC JOURNAL OF RESEARCH.). [GEC J. Res.]. **Added/Corp** General Electric Company (Great Britain). **VFOAT** G.E.C. Journal of Research. **VAT** General Electric Company Journal of Research. Vol. 1, No. 1 (1983)-. Academic Scholarly Publication. English. Three times a year (Feb., June, Oct. (currently 10 months late)). £31.00 (Volume 12, Issues 1-3 to be published in mid-94 and continuing into 1995). GEC Journal of Research, GEC-Marconi Reasearch Centre, Great Baddow, Chelmsford, Essex CM2 8HN UK. **Tel** 011 44 1 245 473331, FAX 011 44 1 245 475244. **ED** A. J. Walkden. **LC** TK7800; .G47. **DD** 621.381/05. **CODEN** GJREES. Index available (Bound in 3rd issue). **Circ:** 8,000 (ctrl). available on microfilm and microfiche from University Microfilms International (UMI). Documents available from Article Express International, The Genuine Article, Ask*IEEE. **Absorbed** Marconi Review, 0025-2883.
Desc: Covers the research activities of the company and is largely, but not exclusively, concerned with electronics and engineering in all their aspects.
Ind/Abst Acoust. Abstr.; AESIS Q.; Alum. Ind. Abstr.; Bioeng. Abstr.; BMT Abstr.; Curr. Contents Eng. Tech. Appl. Sci.; Curr. Technol. Index; Ei Page One; EMBASE; Eng. Mater. Abstr.; Eng. Index Annu.; Ergon. Abstr.; Health Saf. Sci. Abstr.; INSPEC (1990-); Int. Aerosp. Abstr. (1984-); Leadscan; Met. Abstr.; Life Sci. Collect.; Pollut. Abstr. Indexes; Res. Alert [Select. Cov.]; SCISEARCH; Shock Vibr. Dig.

FR/0016-6812
GENIE CIVIL. (LE GENIE CIVIL : REVUE GENERALE DES TECHNIQUES.). [Genie civ.]. Vol. 151, No. 1 (Jan. 1976)-. Periodical. French. mo. **CODEN** GECIAS. **Continues** Revue Generale des Techniques.
Ind/Abst GeoRef.

CN/1183-7349
GENIE EN FORMATION. (LE GENIE EN FORMATION.). [Genie form.]. **Added/Corp** Ordre des Ingenieurs du Quebec. Services de Developpement Professionnel. Vol. 1, No 1 (Jun 1991)-. Periodical. French. qt. Free for members. Ordre des Ingenieurs du Quebec, A/S Serge Paquette, 14E Etage, 2020 Rue Universite, Montreal Quebec H3A 2A5 Canada. **DD** 620.

FR/0223-5293
GENIE INDUSTRIEL 1969. [Genie ind. 1969]. (1969)-. Periodical. French. mo. 980.00F France; 1120.00F other. Documentations Industrielles & Techniques, 11 rue de Madrid, 75008 Paris France. **Tel** 40 68 12 12, FAX 40 68 12 29. **UDC** 62. **Ad Acc, Adv Mgr:** Mr. Bernard.

HK/1010-6049
GEOCARTO INTERNATIONAL. See Geography.

•**RU/0869-7809**
GEOEKOLOGIIA, INZHENERNAIA GEOLOGIIA, GIDROGEOLOGIIA, GEOKRIOLOGIIA / ROSSIISKAIA AKADEMIIA NAUK. See Earth Sciences-Geology.

UK/0016-8505
GEOTECHNIQUE [MICROFORM]. **Added/Corp** Institution of Civil Engineers (Great Britain). Vol. 1 (1948/Dec. 1949)-. Periodical. English (French). Thomas Telford Ltd, Thomas Telford House, 1 Heron Quay, London E14 9XF England. **Tel** 011 44 71 987 6999, FAX 011 44 71 538 4101, telex 298105. **[CCC].** cum. index.

IT
GIORNALE DELL'INGEGNERE, IL. (19??)-. Italian. sm. L16.000 Italy. Editoriale PEG Spa, Via Fratelli Bressan 2, 20126 Milan Italy. **Tel** 011 39 2 2579841, FAX 011 39 2 255-2779, telex 323088 PEGMOS I. **ED** Giulio Galli. Index available. **Bk Rev. Ad Acc. Circ:** 24,000 (ctrl).
Desc: Professional, technical, class, normative and informative matters mostly addressed to engineers' category.

IT/1120-219X
GIORNALE DELL'INSTALLATORE TELEFONICO, IL. [G. install. telef.]. (1983)-. Periodical. Italian. Six times a year. L40000 Italy; L70000 other. Stammer Spa, Via della Liberazione 1, 20068 Peschiera Borromeo, Italy. **Tel** 011 39 2 55302606, FAX 011 39 2 55302700, telex 321083. **ED** Girolamo Bellina. **UDC** 654.15. **Bk Rev. Ad Acc. Pr Rev. Circ:** 4,500 (ctrl).
Desc: Electricity and telephone engineering and installation.

US/1058-4285
GLOBAL STANDARDS & SPECIFICATIONS BULLETIN. [Glob. stand. specif. bull.]. **Added/Corp** Global Engineering Documents (Firm). **VFOAT** Global Standards and Specifications Bulletin. (1991)-. Bulletin. English. Fifty-two times a year. $95.00. Global Engineering Documents Services, 15 Inverness Way East, Englewood CO 80112. **Tel** (800)624-3974. **DD** 620. **Continues** GED Bulletin.

BU/0205-0439
GODISNIK NA VISSIJA INSTITUT PO ARHITEKTURA I STROITELSTVO. SVITK II HISROTEHNIKA. (GODISHNIK NA VISSHIIA INSTITUT PO ARKHITEKTURA I STROITELSTVO, SOFIIA.). [God. Viss inst. arhit. Stroit., Svitk II hidroteh.]. **Added/Corp** Vissh Institut po Arkhitektura i Stroitelstvo, Sofia. **VFOAT** Annuaire de l'Institut d'Architecture et de Genie Civil, Sofia. Vol. 27 (1977/1978)-. Periodical. Bulgarian (summaries and/or abstracts in English, French, German and Russian; table of contents in English, French, German and Russian). an. 1.48лв. **LC** TA4; .S753. **CODEN** GVISD6. Documents available from CASDDS. **Continues** Godishnik na Visshiia Inzhenerno-Stroitelen Institut, Sofiia.
Ind/Abst Chem. Abstr.

US/0193-2276
GRADUATING ENGINEER. [Grad. eng.]. Vol 1 (Fall 1979)-. Periodical. English. Four times a year (Jan., Mar., Sept., Nov.). $16.00 (US), $18.00 (Canada & Mexico), $35.00 (other)-four regular issues; $28.00 (US), $30.00 (Canada & Mexico), $47.00 (other)-all eight issues. Petersons / COG Publishing, 16030 Ventura Boulevard, Suite 560, Encino CA 91436. **Tel** (818)789-5293, FAX (818)789-5488. **ED** Charlotte Thomas (phone: (818)789-5371). **LC** TA157; .G712. **DD** 620/.0023/73. **Ad Acc. Circ:** 70,000 (ctrl). available on microfilm and microfiche from University Microfilms International (UMI).
Desc: Edited and published to help meet the initial employment and career needs of upperclassmen and women in various engineering disciplines.

•**US/1057-2953**
GREEN COUNTRY SCIENCE & ENGINEERING JOURNAL. Added/Corp Tulsa Engineering Foundation. **VFOAT** Green Country Science and Engineering Journal. (1992)-. Periodical. English. mo. $20.00 (nonmembers). Landmark Publishing & Design, 2436 East 12th Street, Tulsa OK 74104. cum. index.

UK/0960-8796
GREEN ENGINEERING. Ceased. See Environmental Issues.

US/1060-7153
GTRI TECHNICAL JOURNAL. (GTRI TECHNICAL JOURNAL / GEORGIA TECH RESEARCH INSTITUTE.). [GTRI tech. j.]. **Added/Corp** Georgia Tech Research Institute. **VAT** Georgia Tech Research Institute Technical Journal. Vol. 1 (1991)-. English. Free. Georgia Tech Research Institute, Georgia Institute of Technology, Atlanta GA 30332. **DD** 605.

US
GUIDELINES LETTER. See Architecture.

TU/0379-5918
HACETTEPE BULLETIN OF NATURAL SCIENCES AND ENGINEERING. See Earth Sciences.

KO/0253-312X
HANGUG BUSIG HAGHOI JI. (HANGUK PUSIK HAKHOE CHI.). [Hangug busig haghoi ji]. **Added/Corp** Hanguk Pusik Hakhoe. **VFOAT** Journal of the Corrosion Science Society of Korea. (19??)-.

Academic Scholarly Publication. English (Korean). qt. Not for sale. Hanguk Pusik Hakhoe, 76-561 Yoksam-dong, Kangnam-ku 134-03, Seoul South Korea. **LC** TA462; .H35. **DD** 620.1/1223/05. **CODEN** HPHADI. Documents available from CASDDS.
Ind/Abst Chem. Abstr.; Corros. Abstr. (199?-).

KO
HANGUK UMHYANG HAKHOE CHI.
VFOAT The Journal of the Acoustical Society of Korea; Journal of the Acoustical Society of Korea. V. 1- No. 1- (March 1982)-. Periodical. English (Korean). Hanguk Umhyang Hakhoe, 134 Sinchon-dong, Sodaemun-ku, Seoul South Korea. **LC** TA365; .H29.

US/0017-9329
HEAT ENGINEERING (LIVINGSTON). See Energy.

US/0741-0808
HIGH-TECH MATERIALS ALERT. [High tech mater. alert]. **Added/Corp** Technical Insights, Inc. **VFOAT** High Tech Materials Alert. No. 1 (Jan. 1984)-. Periodical. English. mo. $570.00 North America; $630.00 other. Technical Insights Inc., PO Box 1304, Fort Lee NJ 07024-9967. **Tel** (201)568-4744, FAX (201)568-8247, telex 425900 SWIFT UI. **ED** Alan S. Brown and Richard Consolas. **[CCC].** available on an online database (file 636/Full-Text) from DIALOG.
Desc: Details on significant developments in high performance materials ranging from alloys and metallic whiskers to ceramic and graphite fibers, their fabrication and industrial applications.
Ind/Abst NEXIS (1984-); PTS Newsl. Database [Full Txt.].

JA
HIMEJI KOGYO DAIGAKU KOGAKUBU KENKYU HOKOKU. See Science and Technology.

JA/0018-1951
HINSHITSU KANRI. [Hinshitsu kanri]. **VFOAT** Statistical Quality Control. (1950)-. Periodical. Japanese. mo. $178.00. Nihon Kagaku Gijutsu Renmei, (Union of Japanese Scientists & Engineers), 10-11, Sendagaya 5 Chome, Shibuyaku, Tokyoto 151, Japan. **(Subscription address:** Maruzen Company Ltd., PO Box 5050, Import & Export Department, Tokyo 100 31 Japan.) **DD** 658.5.

JA/0018-2060
HIROSHIMA DAIGAKU KOGAKUBU KENKYU HOKOKU. [Hiroshima Daigaku Kogakubu kenkyu hokoku]. **Added/Corp** Hiroshima Daigaku. Kogakubu. **VFOAT** Bulletin of the Faculty of Engineering, Hiroshima University. (1952)-. Periodical. Japanese (summaries and/or abstracts in English). sa. Hiroshima Daigaku Kogakubu, (Faculty of Engineering, Hiroshima University), Shitami, Saijocho, Higashi, Hiroshimashi, Hiroshimaken 724 Japan. **CODEN** HIDKAA. Documents available from CASDDS.
Ind/Abst Chem. Abstr.

US
HISPANIC ENGINEER. Added/Corp Society of Hispanic Professional Engineers. Vol. 1, No. 1 (Fall 1984)-. Periodical. English. $15.00. Career Communications Group, 729 East Pratt Street, Suite 504, Baltimore MD 21202. **Tel** (410)244-7101 ext. 30, FAX (410)752-1837. **LC** TA1; .H58.

JA/0385-602X
HOKKAIDO DAIGAKU KOGAKUBU KENKYU HOKOKU. BULLETIN OF THE FACULTY OF ENGINEERING, HOKKAIDO UNIVERSITY. Main/Corp Hokkaido Daigaku. Kogakubu. **VFOAT** Bulletin of Faculty of Engineering, Hokkaido University. (1948)-. Bulletin. Japanese. Hokkaido University Faculty of Engineering, North 13 West 8, Sapporo Japan. **CODEN** HDKKAA. Documents available from CASDDS.
Ind/Abst Chem. Abstr.; Coal Abstr.; Concr. Abstr.; Ei Page One; Int. Aerosp. Abstr.

SP/0214-2422
HOSPITAL 2000. ***Suspended.*** **See** Architecture.

US/0163-3465
HOSPITAL ENGINEERING (CHICAGO). (HOSPITAL ENGINEERING.). **Added/Corp** American Hospital Association. American Society for Hospital Engineering. (1969)-. Periodical. English. bm. Comes with membership. American Hospital Association, 840 North Lake Shore Drive, Chicago IL 60611. **Tel** (312)280-6000, (800)242-2626. **NLM** W1 HO772K. ***Continues*** *Hospital Engineer's Newsletter.*
Ind/Abst Health Devices Alerts.

US/0898-6894
HPV NEWS (INDIANAPOLIS, IND.). (HPV NEWS.). [HPV news]. **Added/Corp** International Human Powered Vehicle Association. **VAT** Human Powered Vehicle News; Human-Powered-Vehicle News. (198?)-. Periodical. English. bm. Comes with International Human Power Vehicle Membership. International Human Powered Vehicle Association, PO Box 51255, Indianapolis IN 46251. **Tel** (317)876-9478, FAX (317)876-9470. **ED** Jean Anderson Seay. **LC** TL1; .H84. **DD** 629. **Bk Rev. Ad Acc. Circ:** 2,500 (ctrl).
Ind/Abst SPORT Discus; SportSearch (May 1987-).

CC/0253-987X
HSI-AN CHIAO TUNG TA HSUEH. [ERROR IN DATA]. **Main/Corp** Hsi-An Chiao Tung Ta Hsueh. (1978)-. Academic Scholarly Publication. Chinese (summaries and/or abstracts in English). bm. **LC** TA4; .H77a. **CODEN** HCTPDW. Documents available from Article Express International, CASDDS.
Ind/Abst Chem. Abstr.; Ei Page One; Eng. Index Annu.

CH/1017-4397
HSING TA KUNG CHENG HSUEH PAO. Added/Corp Kuo li Chung Hsing ta Hsueh. Kung Hsueh Yuan. **VFOAT** Journal of Engineering, National Chung Hsing University. No. 1 (Feb. 1990)-. Periodical. Chinese (English). an. **LC** TA4; .H79. **DD** 620/.005. **CODEN** XGXUEY. Documents available from CASDDS.
Ind/Abst Biodeter. Abstr.; Chem. Abstr.

CC
HSUEH PAO. TZU JAN KO HSUEH PAN. See Science and Technology.

CC/0253-2468
HUANJING KEXUE XUEBAO. (HUAN CHING KO HSUEH HSUEH PAO / ACTA SCIENTIAE CIRCUMSTANTIAE.). [Huanjing kexue xuebao]. **Added/Corp** Chung-Kuo ko Hsueh Yuan. Huan Ching ko Hsueh Wei Yuan Hui. **VFOAT** Acta Scientiae Circumstantiae. (1981)-. Academic Scholarly Publication. Chinese (English). qt. $80.40. Science Press, 16 Donghuangchenggen North Street, Beijing 100707, People's Republic of China. **Tel** 011 86 1 4019821, 011 86 1 4010642, FAX 011 86 1 4012180, 011 86 1 4019810, telex 210147. **LC** TD4; .H79. **DD** 620.8/05. **CODEN** HKXUDL. Documents available from CASDDS.
Ind/Abst Chem. Abstr.

US/0893-3529
HUFACT QUARTERLY. ***Suspended.*** [Hufact q.]. Vol. 1, No. 1 (Spring 1987)-Suspended Spring 1988. Periodical. English. qt (March, June, September, December). $100.00, $30.00 single issues US and Canada; $125.00, $35.00 (single issues) other. Ergosyst Associates Inc, 123 West Eighth Street, Suite 1012, Lawrence KS 66044-2605. **Tel** (913)842-7334, FAX (913)842-7348. **DD** 620. ***Continues*** *Report & Catalogue (Report Store (Firm)), 0883-5918.*
Desc: Provides international coverage of trends and issues about human factors and ergonomics, including conference calendar and reports; interviews; recommended reading lists of books, technical reports, and conference proceedings; reviews of books and journals, software and products.

US/0898-6908
HUMAN POWER. (HUMAN POWER : THE TECHNICAL JOURNAL OF THE IHPVA.). [Hum. power]. **Added/Corp** International Human Powered Vehicle Association. (19??)-. Periodical. English. qt. Free to members; $25.00 (membership) North America; $30.00 (membership) other. International Human Powered Vehicle Association, PO Box 51255, Indianapolis IN 46251. **Tel** (317)876-9478, FAX (317)876-9470. **ED** David Gordon Wilson. **LC** TL1; .H86. **DD** 629. Index available. cum. index. **Ad Acc. Circ:** 2,500 (ctrl).
Desc: The technical journal of the international human powered vehicle association, covering aircraft, helicopters, dirigibles; land vehicles; boats, hydrofoils and submarines, propelled by human power alone. Articles are aimed at the undergraduate and high-school levels, on scientific, research and development, and home-construction topics.
Ind/Abst SPORT Discus; SportSearch (May 1987-).

NE/0169-4200
I2-PROCESTECHNOLOGIE. (I2PROCESTECHNOLOGIE.). [I2-procestechnologie]. **Added/Corp** Nederlandse Ingenieursvereniging NIRIA. Koninklijk Instituut van Ingenieurs (Netherlands). **VAT** Ingenieurs Informatie Procestechnologie. (1985)-. Periodical. Dutch. mo. **CODEN** IPRTEZ. Documents available from CASDDS.
Ind/Abst Chem. Abstr.

FI/0786-9916
IACEE NEWSLETTER. (1989)-. Periodical. English. qt. $120.00 institutions; $40.00 individuals. IACEE - International Association of Continuing Engineering Education, Dipoli, Fin-02150 Espoo Finland. **Tel** 011 358 0 451-4024, FAX 011 358 0 451-4060, telex 125161 HTKK SF. **ED** Anders Hagstrom. **UDC** 37. **Bk Rev**, (Qty: 50-60). **Ad Acc. Circ:** 1,000.
Desc: International news in continuing engineering education and professional development.

JA/0367-7389
IBARAKI DAIGAKU KOGAKUBU KENKYU SHUHO. [Ibaraki Daigaku Kogakubu kenkyu shuho]. **Added/Corp** Ibaraki Daigaku. Kogakubu. **VFOAT** Journal of the Faculty of Engineering, Ibaraki University. (1948)-. Japanese (English). an. Ibaraki Daigaku Kogakubu, (Faculty of Engineering, Ibaraki University), 12-1, Nakanarusawacho 4 Chome, Hitachishi, Ibarakiken 316 Japan. **LC** TA4; .I118. **CODEN** IDKSAB. Documents available from Ask*IEEE, CASDDS.
Ind/Abst Chem. Abstr.; INSPEC (1971-).

NO
IBT-RAPPORT / [NORGES LANDBRUKSHGSKOLE, INSTITUTT FOR BYGNINGSTEKNIKK]. See Agriculture.

●US
IEEE/NPSS SYMPOSIUM FUSION ENGINEERING : PROCEEDINGS.
Added/Corp IEEE Nuclear and Plasma Sciences Society. Institute of Electrical and Electronics Engineers. **VFOAT** Fusion Engineering. (1993)-. Proceedings. English. be. IEEE, Institution of Electrical and Electronics Engineers, Inc., 345 East 47th Street, New York NY 10017-2394. **Tel** (908)981-1393, FAX (908)981-9667. **LC** TK9204; .S87a. ***Continues*** *Symposium on Fusion Engineering. Proceedings, 0886-8921.*
Ind/Abst Chem. Abstr.; Index IEEE Publ.

●US/1070-9908
IEEE SIGNAL PROCESSING LETTERS. [IEEE signal process. lett.]. **Added/Corp** Institute of Electrical and Electronics Engineers. **VFOAT** Institute of Electrical and Electronics Engineers Signal Processing letters; Signal Processing Letters. (1994)-. Periodical. English. mo. $100.00. IEEE, Institution of Electrical and Electronics Engineers, Inc., 345 East 47th Street, New York NY 10017-2394. **Tel** (908)981-1393, FAX (908)981-9667. **(Subscription address:** IEEE / Institute of Electrical and Electronics Engineers, 445 Hoes Lane, PO Box 1331, Piscataway NJ 08855-1331.) **ED** Katherine Wheeler. **LC** TK5102.9; .I32. **DD** 621.382/2/05. **CODEN** ISPLEMIESPEJ.
Desc: Publishes short papers in areas of signal processing, including recording, reproduction and measurement of speech; signals by digital, electronic, electrical, acoustic, mechanical and optical means.

US/0018-9340
IEEE TRANSACTIONS ON COMPUTERS. See Computers-Computer Systems.

●US/1063-6536
IEEE TRANSACTIONS ON CONTROL SYSTEMS TECHNOLOGY. (IEEE TRANSACTIONS ON CONTROL SYSTEMS TECHNOLOGY : A PUBLICATION OF THE IEEE CONTROL SYSTEMS SOCIETY.). [IEEE trans. control syst. technol.]. **Added/Corp** IEEE Control Systems Society. Institute of Electrical and Electronics Engineers. **VAT** Institute of Electrical and Electronics Engineers Transactions on Control Systems Technology. Vol. 1, No. 1 (Mar. 1993)-. Periodical. English. qt. $90.00. IEEE, Institution of Electrical and Electronics Engineers, Inc., 345 East 47th Street, New York NY 10017-2394. **Tel** (908)981-1393, FAX (908)981-9667. **(Subscription address:** IEEE / Institute of Electrical and Electronics Engineers, 445 Hoes Lane, PO Box 1331, Piscataway NJ 08855-1331.) **LC** TJ212; .I4813. **DD** 629.8. **CODEN** IETTE2.
Desc: Serve as a compendium for papers on the technological advances in control engineering and as an archival publication which will bridge the gap between theory and practice. Papers will highlight the latest knowledge, exploratory developments, and practical applications in all aspects of the technology needed to implement control systems from analysis and design through simulation and hardware.

JA/0018-9820
IHI ENGINEERING REVIEW. [IHI eng. rev.]. **Added/Corp** Ishikawajima-Harima Jukogyo Kabushiki Kaisha. **VFOAT** Engineering Review. **VAT** Ishikawajima-Harima Heavy Industries Engineering Review. Vol. 1, No. 1 (Sept. 1968)-. Academic Scholarly Publication. English. qt. Ishikawajima-Harima Heavy Industries Company, 2 16 3 Chome Toyosu, Koto Ku Tokyo Japan. **LC** TA1; .I9. **CODEN** IHERA6. available on microfilm from University Microfilms International (UMI). Documents available from Article Express International, CASDDS.
Ind/Abst Bioeng. Abstr.; BMT Abstr.; Chem. Abstr.; Coal Abstr.; Ei Page One; Eng. Index Annu.; Int. Aerosp. Abstr.; Pollut. Abstr. Indexes.

US/0019-2015
ILLINOIS ENGINEER. [Ill. eng.]. **Added/Corp** Illinois Society of Professional Engineers. (19??)-. Periodical. English. Six times a year. $10.00 US; $16.00 other. Illinois Society of Professional Engineers, 1304 South Lowell, Springfield IL 62704. **Tel** (217)544-7424. **ED** Chuck Stockus. **LC** TA1; .I28. **DD** 620. **Ad Acc. Circ:** 3,500 (ctrl).

PL/0208-6247
IM. INZYNIERIA MATERIALOVA. (INZYNIERIA MATERIALOVA.). [IM, Inz. mater.]. (1980)-. Periodical. Polish. bm. $87.00. **(Subscription address:** ARS Polona, PO Box 1001, 00068 Warsaw Poland.) **CODEN** INZME6.
Ind/Abst Alum. Ind. Abstr.; Met. Abstr.

UK
INDEX - ENGINEERING SCIENCES DATA UNIT. Main/Corp Engineering Sciences Data Unit, Ltd. **VFOAT** Engineering Sciences Data Unit Index. (19??)-. English. an (June). Price varies. ESDU International Ltd., 27 Corsham Street, London N1 6UA

Engineering

England. **Tel** 011 44 71 4905151, telex 266168 ENDASAG. **Continues** Royal Aeronautical Society. Engineering Sciences Data Unit. Index.
 Desc: A Key-Word Index referencing 1200 engineering data sheets.

II
INDIAN ENGINEER. Periodical. English. mo. $35.00. The Indian Engineer, 5 Clive Row R No 69 Government Printing Office 111, Calcutta 700001 India. **Tel** 22 8291. **(Subscription address:** Prints India, 11 Darya Ganj, New Delhi 110002 India.**)**

●II/0971-2356
INDIAN JOURNAL OF AGRICULTURAL ENGINEERING, THE. See Agriculture.

●II/0971-457X
INDIAN JOURNAL OF ENGINEERING & MATERIALS SCIENCES. (1994)-. Periodical. English. mo. $160.00. Council of Scientific & Industrial Research, Publications & Information Director, Hillside Road, New Delhi 110012 India. **Tel FAX** 011 91 11 5731353. **(Subscription address:** Prints India, 11 Darya Ganj, New Delhi 110002 India.**) Continues in part** Indian Journal of Technology, 0019-5669.

II/0368-0029
INDIAN SAFETY ENGINEER, THE. [Indian Saf. Eng.]. (1962)-. Periodical. English. mo. $20.00. **(Subscription address:** Prints India, 11 Darya Ganj, New Delhi 110002 India.**) UDC** 614.8.

CN/0828-7201
INDICATEUR (OTTAWA). Ceased.
(INDICATEUR: BULLETIN DU CONSEIL CANADIEN DE LA MAIN-D'OEUVRE EN GENIE.). **Added/Corp** Conseil Canadien de la Main-d'oeuvre en Genie. Conseil Canadien des Ingenieurs. Bureau Canadien de la Main-d'oeuvre en Genie. (1985)-Vol. 5, No. 1 (Dec. 1992). Bulletin. French. qt (published within the seasons of the year). Canadian Council Prof Engineers, 116 rue Albert Street / Suite 401, Ottawa Ontario KIP 5G3 Canada. **Tel** (613)232-2474, **FAX** (613)230-5759. **DD** 331.11/92/000971. **Continues** Main d'Oeuvre en Genie, Bulletin. Francais., 0826-1229.

IT/0019-7637
INDUSTRIA ITALIANA DEL CEMENTO, L'. [Ind. ital. cem.]. **Added/Corp** Associazione Italiana Tecnico-Economica del Cemento. Associazione dell'Industria Italiana del cemento, Fibro-Cemento, Calce e Gesso. Associazione Italiana Cemento, Armato, e Precompresso. (1929)-. Periodical. Italian (English and French). mo. Servizio Italiano Pubblicazioni International, Viale Pasteur 6, 00144 Rome Italy. **Tel** 011 39 6 5920509, telex 614567 SIPIRM I. **CODEN** IICEAW. Documents available from Article Express International.
 Ind/Abst Bioeng. Abstr.; Ceram. Abstr. (19??-); Concr. Abstr.; Ei Page One; Eng. Index Annu.; Int. Civil Eng. Abstr.; Soft. Abstr. Eng.

US
INDUSTRIAL R&D MANAGEMENT. VFOAT Industrial R and D Management. Vol. 1 (1982)-. Monographic series. English. Price varies per volume. Marcel Dekker Inc., 270 Madison Avenue, New York NY 10016. **Tel** (212)696-9000, (800)228-1160, **FAX** (212)685-4540, telex 421419. **(Subscription address:** Marcel Dekker Inc, PO Box 5017, Monticello NY 12701.**)**

●US/1064-5683
INDUSTRY ENGINEER. [Ind. eng.]. **Added/Corp** National Society of Professional Engineers. Professional Engineers in Industry Division. Vol. 9, No. 4 (Apr./May 1992)-. Periodical. English. bm. $1.00 (members), $5.00 (nonmembers). National Society of Professional Engineers, 1420 King Street, Alexandria VA 22314. **DD** 620. **Continues** NSPE PEI Industry Forum, 0746-6749.

US/8756-9825
INDUSTRY STANDARDS SERVICE. [Ind. stand. serv.]. English. bm. Information Marketing International, 80 Blanchard, Burlington MA 01803-5125. **LC** TA368; .I544. **DD** 602/.18.

PE
INFORMACIONES Y MEMORIAS DE LA SOCIEDAD DE INGENIEROS DEL PERU. Main/Corp Sociedad de Ingenieros, Lima. Periodical. Spanish. mo. $5.00. Sociedad de Ingenieros del Peru, Avda Nicolas de Pierola 788, Lima Peru. **(Subscription address:** Casilla Postal 1314, Lima Peru**) ED** Manuel Canepa Gonzalez. **LC** TA4; .S6513. Index available. **Bk Rev. Ad Acc. Circ:** 2,000 (ctrl).
 Desc: Provides articles about the advances of the national and word-wide engineering. Promotes technical-scientific competitions.

NE
INFORMATICA I. KWADRAAT INGENIEURS INFORMATIE. Dutch. mo. Ingenieurspers BV, Postbus 456 Netherlands. **Tel** 011 31 08340 5570.

CN/1182-0187
INFORMATION UPDATE - CANADIAN STANDARDS ASSOCIATION.
(INFORMATION UPDATE.). [Inf. update - Can. Stand. Assoc.]. **Main/Corp** Canadian Standards Association. **VFOAT** CSA Information Update. No. 1 (Feb. 1982)-. Periodical. English (summaries and/or abstracts in French). Eight times a year. 44.50Can$ Canada; 56.00Can$ US; 70.00Can$ other. Canadian Standards Association, 178 Rexdale Boulevard, Rexdale Ontario M9W 1R3 Canada. **Tel** (416)747-4000, (416)747-4044, telex 06-989344. **DD** 016.60218. ctrl circ. **Continues** C S A Information Update., 0702-7583.

GW/0724-1976
INFORMATIONSDIENST VDI : INSTANDHALTUNG. (19??)-. German. Six times a year. DM297.00 Germany; DM315.00 other. VDI Verlag GmbH, Postfach 101054, D 40001 Dusseldorf Germany. **Tel** 011 49 211 6188313, **FAX** 011 49 211 6188133. **[CCC].**

GW/0170-9550
INFORMATIONSDIENST - VEREIN DEUTSCHER INGENIEURE. KALTMASSIVUMFORMUNG. [Inf.dienst - Ver. Dtsch. Ing., Kaltmassivumform.]. (1978)-. German. bm (6 issues). DM297.00 Germany; DM315.00 other. VDI Verlag GmbH, Postfach 101054, D 40001 Dusseldorf Germany. **Tel** 011 49 211 6188313, **FAX** 011 49 211 6188133. **UDC** 621.77 (048.1). **[CCC]. Continues** VDI-Informationsdienst. Kaltmassivumformung, 0341-1605.

GW/0720-9886
INFORMATIONSDIENST - VEREIN DEUTSCHER INGENIEURE. MECHANISCHE VERBINDUNGSTECHNIK. (1981)-. Multiple languages. Four times a year. DM258.00 Germany; DM270.00 other. VDI Verlag GmbH, Postfach 101054, D 40001 Dusseldorf Germany. **Tel** 011 49 211 6188313, **FAX** 011 49 211 6188133. **UDC** 621.791/.795.

GW/0720-9878
INFORMATIONSDIENST - VEREIN DEUTSCHER INGENIEURE. NEUE FERTIGUNGSVERFAHREN. [Inf.dienst - Ver. Dtsch. Ing., Neue Fert.verfahr.]. (1981)-. Multiple languages. bm (6 issues). DM297.00 Germany; DM315.00 other. VDI Verlag GmbH, Postfach 101054, D 40001 Dusseldorf Germany. **Tel** 011 49 211 6188313, **FAX** 011 49 211 6188133. **UDC** 621.71.9. **Continues** VDI-Informationsdienst. Neue Fertigungverfahren, 0170-947X.

GW/0171-3647
INFORMATIONSDIENST - VEREIN DEUTSCHER INGENIEURE. SCHMIEDEN UND PRESSEN. [Inf.dienst - Ver. Dtsch. Ing., Schmied. Press.]. (1978)-. German. bm (6 issues). DM297.00 Germany; DM315.00 other. VDI Verlag GmbH, Postfach 101054, D 40001 Dusseldorf Germany. **Tel** 011 49 211 6188313, **FAX** 011 49 211 6188133. **[CCC]. Continues** VDI-Informationsdienst. Schmieden und Pressen, 0171-3639.

GW/0721-7242
INFORMATIONSDIENST - VEREIN DEUTSCHER INGENIEURE. STRANGPRESSEN VON METALLEN. [Inf.dienst - Ver. Dtsch. Ing., Strangpressen Met.]. (1981)-. Periodical. German. Three times a year. DM196.00 Germany; DM205.00 other. VDI Verlag GmbH, Postfach 101054, D 40001 Dusseldorf Germany. **Tel** 011 49 211 6188313, **FAX** 011 49 211 6188133. **UDC** 621.777.2:669.056. **Continues** VDI-Informationsdienst. Strangpressen von Metallen, 0170-9488.

PL
INFORMATOR I SKAD OSOBOWY NA ROK AKADEMICKI ... / POLITECHNIKA POZNANSKA. Main/Corp Politechnika Poananska. Polish. an. Wydawnictwo Politechniki Poznanskiej, PI M Skodowskiej-Curie, 60-965 Poznan Poland. **LC** T173.P795; A25.

UK
INFRARED PHYSICS AND ENGINEERING. Title Change. See Physics.

IT/0035-6263
INGEGNERIA. [Ingegneria]. No. 1- 1970-. Academic Scholarly Publication. Italian. bm. Ingegneria-Revista di, V Smareglia 9, 1020133 Milan Italy. **CODEN** IGGRBA. Documents available from CASDDS. **Continues** Rivista di Ingegneriao.
 Ind/Abst Chem. Abstr. (1970-1983); Int. Aerosp. Abstr.; Saf. Health Work.

IT/0020-0956
INGEGNERIA FERROVIARIA. [Ing. ferrov.]. Vol. 1 (July 15, 1946)-. Periodical. Italian. Eleven times a year. L110000 Italy; $100.00 others. Ingegneri Ferroviari, Via Giolitti 34, 00185 Rome Italy. **Tel** 011 39 6 4827116. **CODEN** INFEAE. Documents available from Article Express International.
 Ind/Abst Bioeng. Abstr.; Ei Page One; Eng. Index Annu.; Saf. Health Work.

IT
INGEGNERIA SANITARIA. Maggioli Editore, Casella Postale 290, 47037 Rimini, Italy. **Tel** 011 39 541 628666, **FAX** 011 39 541 742217.

MX
INGENIERIA. Added/Corp La Facultad de Ingenieria. Universidad Nacional Autonoma de Mexico. Vol. 1 (August 1927)-. Periodical. Spanish. qt. Unam Facultad Ingenieria, Apartado Postal M 6987, 04510 Mexico DF Mexico.
 Ind/Abst Int. Civil Eng. Abstr.; Soft. Abstr. Eng.

CL/0716-1174
INGENIERIA DE SISTEMAS. [Ing. Sist.]. (1975)-. Periodical. Spanish. ir. Departamento de Industrias, Universidad de Chile, Casilla 2777, Santiago, Chile. **UDC** 65.012.
 Ind/Abst Int. Abstr. Oper. Res.

FR
INGENIEUR CONSEIL DE FRANCE, L'. V.1- 1 -. Periodical. French. ir. **LC** TA2.
 Ind/Abst Int. Civil Eng. Abstr.; Saf. Health Work; Soft. Abstr. Eng.

NE/0020-1146
INGENIEUR (DEN HAAG). (DE INGENIEUR.). [Ingenieur]. Academic Scholarly Publication. Dutch. mo. Fl100.00 Netherlands; $70.00 US. VNU Business Publications BV, Postbus 9479, 1006 AC Amsterdam Netherlands. **Tel** 011 31 20 5102911, 011 31 20 5102879, **FAX** 011 31 20 6170291. **ED** J T Buma. **CODEN** INGRAO. Index available. **Bk Rev. Ad Acc. Circ:** 25,000 (ctrl). available on microfilm from University Microfilms International (UMI). Documents available from Ask*IEEE.
 Desc: Technical articles and general technical information for the members of the Royal Institution of Engineers in the Netherlands.
 Ind/Abst Acoust. Abstr.; Coal Abstr.; EMBASE; INSPEC (1968-1984); Int. Aerosp. Abstr.; Saf. Health Work.

●GW/0942-3915
INGENIEUR FUER POST UND TELEKOMMUNIKATION, DER. VFOAT Ingenieur (Bielefeld). (1992)-. Periodical. German. bm. DM48.00. Bielefelder Verlagsanstalt KG, Niederwall 53, D 33602 Bielefeld Germany. **Tel** 011 49 521 595520. **UDC** 656.8. **Continues** Der Ingenieur der Deutschen Bundespost, 0020-1170.

CN/0285-4166
INGENIEURS-CONSEILS CANADA (1981). (INGENIEURS-CONSEILS CANADA.). [Ing.-cons. Can.]. **VFOAT** Canada Consulting Engineers. **VAT** Canada Consulting Engineers (1981). 9E Ed. (1981)-. English (French). an. Free. Association of Consulting Engineers of Canada, 130 Albert Street/Suite 616, Ottawa Ontario K10 5G4 Canada. **ED** Pierre A H Franche. **DD** 620/.006/071. ctrl circ. **Continues** Consulting Engineers, Canada, 0317-6525.

BE/0020-1235
INGENIEURSBLAD. (HET INGENIEURSBLAD : ORGAN VAN DE KONINKLIJKE VLAAMSE INGENIEURSVERENIGING.). [Ingenieursblad]. **Added/Corp** Konin Klijke Vlaamse Ingenieursvereniging. Jaarg. 33 in (1964)-. Periodical. Dutch. ir. 1800F Europe; 2100F other. Koninklijke Vlaamse Ingenieurs K VIV, Desguinlei 214, 2018 Antwerpen Belgium. **Tel** 03/216 09 96, **FAX** 03/216 06 89. **CODEN** INBLAF. **Continues** Technisch-Wetenschappelijk Tijdschrift.

GW
INGENIEURWERKSTOFFE. Title Change. (19??)-(1994). German. Ten times a year. VDI Verlag GmbH, Postfach 101054, D 40001 Dusseldorf Germany. **Tel** 011 49 211 6188313, **FAX** 011 49 211 6188133. **Merged into** VDI Z.

GW
INGENIEURWISSEN. (1958)-. Monographic series. German. Price varies per volume. VDI Verlag GmbH, Postfach 101054, D 40001 Dusseldorf Germany. **Tel** 011 49 211 6188313, **FAX** 011 49 211 6188133.

GW/0173-0274
INGENIEURWISSENSCHAFTLICHE BIBLIOTHEK.
(INGENIEURWISSENSCHAFTLICHE BIBLIOTHEK ENGINEERING SCIENCE LIBRARY.). **VFOAT** Engineering Science Library. (1964)-. Monographic series. German. ir. Price varies per volume. Springer-Verlag New York Inc., 175 5th Avenue, New York NY 10010. **Tel** (212)460-1500, telex 232 235 SPB UR. **(Subscription address:** Springer Verlag New York Inc. / for North America, 44 Hartz Way, Secaucus NJ 07096.**)**
 Desc: Contains articles on engineering.

DK/0105-3205
INGENIREN (KBENHAVN. 1975).
(INGENIREN.). V. 1- ; Aug. 1, 1975-. Academic Scholarly

Publication. Danish. 140.00. Dansk Ingenirforening and Ingenir-Sammenlutningen, Skelbkgade 4, 1717 V Kbenhavn Denmark. **LC** TA4; .I413. **CODEN** INGNDF. Documents available from CASDDS. ***Formed by the union of*** *Ingenir- og Bygningsvsen (Copenhagen, Denmark : 1973)* ***and*** *Igeneirens Ugeblad;* ***Absorbed*** *Aret Rundt, 0105-631X.*
Ind/Abst Chem. Abstr.

UK/0264-9861
INNOVATION ST. ANDREWS. [InnovationSt. Andrews]. (1982)-. Periodical. English. Twice a year (June, Dec.). $780.00. Cartermill Publishing Ltd, PO Box 33, St Andrews, Fife KY16 9EA Scotland. **Tel** 011 44 334 77660, FAX 011 44 334 77180. **ED** A R Butler. **DD** 507.2041. **Circ:** 1,000 (ctrl).
Desc: Contains ideas from British universities, Polytechnic medical schools, and government research laboratories.

CN/0708-2215
INSTALLATION DES SYSTEMES DE GICLEURS, L'. 1975-. French. an. Free. Corporation des Maitres Entrepreneurs en Installations Contre l'Incendie dans la Province de Quebec, 620 Ouest Boulevard Lemoyne, Longueuil Quebec J4H 1X6 Canada. **DD** 628.9/252. ctrl circ. ***Continues*** *Installation des Extincteurs Automatiques, 0708-2207.*

GW
INSTITUTSVEROFFENTLICHUNGEN - INSTITUT FUR FESTKORPERMECHANIK DER FRAUNHOFER-GESELLSCHAFT.
Main/Corp Fraunhofer-Gesellschaft zur Forderung der Angewandten Forschung. Institut fur Festkorpermechanik. Multiple languages (English and German). **LC** TA405; .F67A.

●US
INSTRUMENTATION & AUTOMATION NEWS : IAN. **VFOAT** IAN; Instrumentation and Automation News. Vol. 41, No. 6 (June 1993)-. Periodical. English. mo. $35.00 US & Canada; $50.00 other. Chilton Company, 201 King of Prussia Road, Radnor PA 19089. **Tel** (610)964-4122, (800)695-1214, FAX (610)964-4978, telex 6851035 CHILTON UW. **LC** Q184; .I25. **DD** 681/.029/4. ***Continues*** *Chilton's IAN, 0193-6174.*

●US
INSTRUMENTATION & CONTROL SYSTEMS: I&CS. **Added/Corp** Chilton Company. **VFOAT** Instrumentation and Control Systems; I&CS; I&CS, Instrumentation & Control Systems. Vol. 65, No. 3 (Mar. 1992)-. Periodical. English. mo. $65.00 US; $99.00 other. Chilton Company, 201 King of Prussia Road, Radnor PA 19089. **Tel** (610)964-4122, (800)695-1214, FAX (610)964-4978, telex 6851035 CHILTON UW. **LC** TA165; .A2. **DD** 629.8/05. available on microfilm. Documents available from The Genuine Article, Ask*IEEE. ***Continues*** *Chilton's I&CS, 0746-2395.*
Ind/Abst Appl. Sci. Technol. Index (1983-); Coal Abstr. (1983-); Comput. ASAP [Full Txt.]; Comput. Database [Full Txt.]; Curr. Contents Eng. Tech. Appl. Sci.; Fluid Abstr., Civil Eng.; Fluid Abstr. Proc. Eng.; FLUIDEX (1983-); INSPEC (1983-); Res. Alert [Select. Cov.]; SCISEARCH; Soc. Sci. Cit. Index [Select. Cov.].

UK/0963-9640
INTELLIGENT SYSTEMS ENGINEERING. ***Ceased.*** [Intell. syst. eng.]. (1992)-Vol. 3 (1994). Periodical. English. qt (4 issues). Institution of Electrical Engineers / IEE, Michael Faraday House, Six Hills Way, Stevenage Herts SG1 2AY UK. **Tel** 011 44 438 313311, FAX 011 44 438 742840, telex 825578 IEESTV G. **(Subscription address:** IEE / UK, Publications Sales Department, PO Box 96, Stevenage, Herts, SG1 2SD England.**)** **DD** 620.0028563.

IT
INTERCONNECTIONS & CABLES. (19??)-. Italian. Nine times a year. L83000.00 Italy; L166000.00 other. Gruppo Editoriale JCE SRL, Via Ferri 6, 20092 Cinisello B Milan Italy. **Tel** 011 39 2 660251, FAX 011 39 2 66025343.

GW/0940-0117
INTERFERENZEN. [Interferenzen]. (1990)-. Periodical. German. bm (6 issues). DM40.00. DGH EV, Postfach 1722, W 29007 Osnabrueck Germany. **Tel** 011 49 541 7102199. **UDC** 655.

US/0197-1948
INTERNATIONAL ACTIVITIES. (INTERNATIONAL ACTIVITIES - NATIONAL ENGINEERING LABORATORY (U.S.).). [Int. act.]. **Main/Corp** National Engineering Laboratory (U.S.). English. $6.50. National Technical Information Service - NTIS, Room 2027S, 5285 Port Royal Road, Springfield VA 22161. **Tel** (703)487-4630, (703)487-4660, (703)487-4650, FAX (703)321-8547, telex 89-9405. **LC** TA160.4; .N37A. **DD** 620/.0072.

UK/0256-1840
INTERNATIONAL ARCHIVES OF PHOTOGRAMMETRY AND REMOTE SENSING. **VFOAT** Archives Internationales de Photogrammetrie et de Teledetection. Monographic series. English (French and German). Price varies per volume. Remote Sensing Society, Department of Geography, University of Nottingham, University Park, Nottingham NG7 2RD England. **Tel** (602)484848, telex 37346 UNINOT-G. **LC** TR693; .I5. **DD** 621.367/8. ***Continues*** *International Archives of Photogrammetry, 0252-8231.*

●US/1058-5796
INTERNATIONAL DIRECTORY OF CONSULTANTS AND CONTRACTORS ACTIVE IN THE UNITED STATES AND CANADA, AN. [Int. dir. consult. contract. active U.S. Can.]. **Added/Corp** Projects Research, Inc. **VFOAT** Directory of Consultants and Contractors Active in the United States and Canada. (1992)-. English. an (Jan.). $35.00. Projects Research, Inc., PO Box 2558, Falls Church VA 22042. **Tel** (703)698-9330, FAX (703)698-9837. **LC** HD69.C6; I592. **DD** 338.7/61001/02573.

●US/1067-9014
INTERNATIONAL DIRECTORY OF ENGINEERING SOCIETIES AND RELATED ORGANIZATIONS. [Int. dir. eng. soc. relat. organ.]. **Added/Corp** American Association of Engineering Societies. **VFOAT** Directory of Engineering Societies and Related Organizations. 14th Ed. (1993)-. Directory. English. an. $115.00 (members), $185.00 (nonmembers). American Association of Engineering Societies-EJC, 1111 19th Street NW, Suite 608, Washington DC 20036. **Tel** (202)296-2237, FAX (202)296-1151. **LC** TA1; .D48. **DD** 620. ***Continues*** *Directory of Engineering Societies and Related Organizations, 0070-5470.*
Desc: Lists over 960 not-for-profit engineering and technical organizations worldwide. Gives information on each organization's objectives, elected officers and terms of office, principal staff members, membership requirements and base, publications and federation memberships as well as other generalized information.

US/0737-8181
INTERNATIONAL DREDGING REVIEW. [Int. dredg. rev.]. Vol. 1, No. 1 (Oct. 1981)-. Trade Publication. English. Eight times a year. $45.00 US & Canada; $55.00 Central & South America; $75.00 other. International Dredging Review, PO Box 1487, Fort Collins CO 80522. **Tel** (303)484-9562, FAX (303)484-5778. **ED** Judith Powers. **[CCC].** Index available (December issue). cum. index. **Bk Rev. Ad Acc. Circ:** 3,300.
Desc: Glossy 4-C trade journal covering the dredging industry worldwide. Articles include updates on equipment, stories on use of equipment by contractors, and other news of interest to dredging contractors.
Ind/Abst Fluid Abstr., Civil Eng.; Fluid Abstr. Proc. Eng. (1981-); FLUIDEX (1981-).

GW
INTERNATIONAL ENCYCLOPEDIA OF COMPOSITES. ***Ceased.*** (19??)-Series complete with Vol. 6. Monographic series. English. ir. VCH Gesellschaft GmbH, Postfach 101161, D 69451 Weinheim Germany. **Tel** 011 49 6201 606459, FAX 011 49 6201 606184. **ED** Stuart Lee. Index available. cum. index. **Bk Rev. Pr Rev.**
Desc: The work combines the scholarship and practical knowledge of over 300 experts, academians and government researchers about composites for those desiring information for engineering.

US/0074-5774
INTERNATIONAL ENGINEERING DIRECTORY. **Added/Corp** American Consulting Engineers Council. Consulting Engineers Council. (19??)-. Directory. English. be. $50.00. American Consulting Engineers Council, 1015 15th Street Northwest, Suite 802, Washington DC 20005. **Tel** (202)347-7474, FAX (202)898-0068. **ED** Lillian Semples. **LC** TA12; .I57. **DD** 620/.0025/73. Index available. **Ad Acc. Circ:** 2,000 (ctrl).
Desc: A directory listing U.S. consulting engineering firms that provide international services. Each listing describes the firm and the types of engineering services offered.

UK/0029-5981
INTERNATIONAL JOURNAL FOR NUMERICAL METHODS IN ENGINEERING. [Int. j. numer. methods eng.]. **VFOAT** Numerical Methods in Engineering. Vol. 1 (1969)-. Periodical. English. Twenty-four times a year. $2,100.00. John Wiley & Sons Ltd., Baffins Lane, Chichester West Sussex PO19 1UD England. **Tel** 0243 779777, FAX 0243 776128 BTG:JWP001, telex 86290 WIBOOKG. **(Subscription address:** John Wiley / Philadelphia, PO Box 7247, Philadelphia PA 19170.**)** **ED** O. C. Zienkiewicz, R. H. Gallagher, and R. W. Lewis. **LC** TA335; .I57. **DD** 620/.001/517. **CODEN** IJNMBH. **[CCC]. Pr Rev. Circ:** 2,100. available on microfilm and microfiche from University Microfilms International (UMI). Documents available from Article Express International, The Genuine Article, Ask*IEEE. ***Continues*** *Numerical Methods in Engineering.*
Desc: Provides a common platform for the presentation of papers and exchange of views on numerical methods, used to solve a variety of engineering problems in such areas as heat transfer, structural analysis, fluid mechanics, and electronics.
Ind/Abst Abstr. Bull. Inst. Pap. Sci. Tech.; Abstr. J. Earthq. Eng.; Acoust. Abstr.; Appl. Mech. Rev.; Bioeng. Abstr.; Compumath Citation Index [Full Cov.]; Curr. Contents Eng. Tech. Appl. Sci.; Ei Page One; Eng. Index Annu.; Fluid Abstr., Civil Eng.; Fluid Abstr. Proc. Eng.; FLUIDEX (1973-); Geol. Abstr.; GeoRef; Geotech. Abstr.; HTFS Dig.; INSPEC (Jan./March 1969-); Int. Aerosp. Abstr.; Int. Civil Eng. Abstr.; J. Ferrocement; Math. Rev.; Res. Alert [Full Cov.]; Sci. Cit. Index; SCISEARCH; Shock Vibr. Dig.; Soft. Abstr. Eng.; Zentralbl. Math. Ihre Grenzgeb.

DK/0905-6866
INTERNATIONAL JOURNAL FOR THE JOINING OF MATERIALS, THE. **VFOAT** Joining of Materials. (1989)-. English. Four times a year. Kr1000.00. JOM Institute, Rasmus Knudsens VEJ 50, DK 3000 Helsingor Denmark. **UDC** 671.5. Documents available from Article Express International.
Ind/Abst Ei Page One; Eng. Index Annu.

UK/0890-6327
INTERNATIONAL JOURNAL OF ADAPTIVE CONTROL AND SIGNAL PROCESSING. [Int. j. adapt. control signal process.]. **VFOAT** Adaptive Control and Signal Processing. Vol. 1, No. 1 (Sept. 1987)-. Periodical. English. Six times a year. $450.00. John Wiley & Sons Ltd., Baffins Lane, Chichester West Sussex PO19 1UD England. **Tel** 0243 779777, FAX 0243 776128 BTG:JWP001, telex 86290 WIBOOKG. **(Subscription address:** John Wiley / Philadelphia, PO Box 7247, Philadelphia PA 19170.**)** **ED** Mike J. Grimble. **LC** TJ217; .I58. **DD** 629.8/36. **CODEN** IACPEDACPCEX. **[CCC].** available on microfilm and microfiche from University Microfilms International (UMI). Documents available from Article Express International, The Genuine Article, Ask*IEEE.
Desc: Concerned with the design, synthesis and application of estimators or controllers for uncertain systems. Papers which cover all aspects of the theory and application of adaptive systems are regulary featured.
Ind/Abst Compumath Citation Index [Full Cov.]; Ei Page One; Eng. Index Annu.; INSPEC (Sep. 1987-); Int. Aerosp. Abstr.; Res. Alert [Full Cov.]; SCISEARCH; Shock Vibr. Dig.; Zentralbl. Math. Ihre Grenzgeb.

SI/0218-1274
INTERNATIONAL JOURNAL OF BIFURCATION AND CHAOS IN APPLIED SCIENCES AND ENGINEERING. [Int. j. bifurc. chaos appl. sci. eng.]. Vol. 1, No. 1 (Mar. 1991)-. Periodical. English. bm. $295.00 individuals, $590.00 institutions. World Scientific Publishing Company, PO Box 128, Farrer Road, Singapore 9128 Singapore. **Tel** 011 65 3825663, FAX 011 65 3825919, telex RS 28561 WSPC. **(Subscription address:** US: World Scientific Publishing Co., Inc., 1060 Main Street, River Edge, NJ 07661 Telephone: (201)487-9655, Fax: (201)487-9656; Europe: World Scientific Publishing Co Ltd, 73 Lynton Mead, Totteridge, London N20 8DH United Kingdom Telephone: 011 44 81 4462461, Fax: 011 44 81 4463356; India: World Scientific Publishing Co Pte Ltd, 4911 9th Floor, High Point IV, 45 Palace Road, Bangalore 560 001 India Telephone: (80) 2205972, Fax: (80) 3344593, Telex: 0845-2900 PCO IN; Hong Kong: World Scientific Publishing (HK) Co, PO Box 72482, Kowloon Central Post Office, Hong Kong Telephone: 852-7718791, Fax: 852-7718155**)** **LC** Q172.5.C45; I58. **DD** 003/.7. **CODEN** IJBEE4. Documents available from Ask*IEEE.
Desc: Information on chaotic behavior in systems, bifurcation theory, dynamics and nonlinear theories.
Ind/Abst INSPEC (1991-); Math. Rev.

SZ/0957-4344
INTERNATIONAL JOURNAL OF CONTINUING ENGINEERING EDUCATION. (INTERNATIONAL JOURNAL OF CONTINUING ENGINEERING EDUCATION : OFFICIAL JOURNAL OF THE INTERNATIONAL ASSOCIATION FOR CONTINUING ENGINEERING EDUCATION (IACEE).). [Int. j. contin. eng. educ.]. **Added/Corp** International Association for Continuing Engineering Education. Unesco. Vol. 1 No. 1 (1990)-. Periodical. English. Twice a year. £70.00 UK; $95.00 North America; DM180.00 other. Inderscience Enterprises Ltd, World Trade Center Building, 110 Avenue Louis Casai, Case Postale 306, CH-1215 Geneva-Aeroport Switzerland. **Tel** 011 41 22 7383437, FAX 011 41 22 7910885, telex 28 99 50. **ED** M. A. Dorgham. **LC** T61; .I74. **DD** 620/.00715. **CODEN** ICEEE4. Index available. cum. index. **Bk Rev. Ad Acc. Pr Rev. Circ:** 6,000. Documents available from Article Express International, Ask*IEEE.
Desc: The journal of continuing engineering, engineering and technology management education; career development and training.
Ind/Abst Ei Page One; Eng. Index Annu.; INSPEC (1990-).

●US/1056-7895
INTERNATIONAL JOURNAL OF DAMAGE MECHANICS. [Int. j. damage mech.]. Vol. 1, no. 1 (Jan. 1992)-. Periodical. English. qt (Jan.,

Apr., July and Oct). $225.00 (one year), $440.00 (two year), $655.00 (three year). Technomic Publishing Company, Inc., 851 New Holland Avenue, Box 3535, Lancaster PA 17604. **Tel** (717)291-5609, (800)233-9936, FAX (717)295-4538. **LC** TA409; .I48. **DD** 620.1/126/05. **CODEN** IDMEEH. **[CCC].**
Desc: Publishes original research studies on the mechanics of fracture and damage in engineering materials and structures, including continuum damage mechanics. Topics include creep damage, low and high cycle fatigue damage, creep-fatigue interaction, brittle/elastic damage, ductile/plastic damage, strain softening, strain-rate sensitivity damage, and impact damage.
Ind/Abst Int. Aerosp. Abstr.

●GW
INTERNATIONAL JOURNAL OF ENGINEERING EDUCATION, THE. Vol. 8, No. 1 (1992)-. Periodical. English. bm (Jan., Mar., May, July, Sep., Nov.). $250.00 North America; £165.00 other. Tempus Publications, Berliner Tor 21, D 20099 Hamburg Germany. **Tel** 011 49 40 34882599. **ED** Michael S. Wald. **LC** T61; .I57. **CODEN** IEEDEF. **Bk Rev. Ad Acc.** ***Continues*** *International Journal of Applied Engineering Education, 0742-0269.*

UK/0020-7225
INTERNATIONAL JOURNAL OF ENGINEERING SCIENCE. [Int. j. eng. sci.]. Vol. 1 (Jan./March 1963)-. Periodical. English. Fifteen times a year. $1714.00 The Americas; £1150.00 other. Pergamon Press, An Imprint of Elsevier Science Ltd., The Boulevard, Langford Lane, Kidlington, Oxford OX5 1GB United Kingdom. **Tel** 011 44 865 843000, 011 44 865 843699, FAX 011 44 865 843010. **(Subscription address:** Elsevier Science Ltd. Oxford Fulfillment Centre, PO Box 800, Kidlington, Oxford OX5 1DX United Kingdom.**) ED** A. C. Eringen. **LC** TA1; .I749. **DD** 620/.005. **CODEN** IJESAN. **[CCC]. Pr Rev.** available on microfilm and microfiche from University Microfilms International (UMI). Documents available from Article Express International, The Genuine Article, Ask*IEEE, CASDDS, Documents on Demand. ***Absorbed*** *Letters in Applied & Engineering Sciences, 0090-6913.*
Desc: Publishes original research pertaining to the application of the physical, chemical and mathematical sciences to engineering.
Ind/Abst Abstr. J. Earthq. Eng.; Acoust. Abstr.; Alum. Ind. Abstr.; Appl. Mech. Rev.; Bioeng. Abstr.; Ceram. Abstr.; Chem. Abstr.; Civ. Struct. Eng. Abstr.; Curr. Contents Eng. Tech. Appl. Sci.; Curr. Technol. Index; Ei Page One; Energy Inf. Abstr.; Energy Res. Abstr.; Eng. Mater. Abstr.; Eng. Index Annu.; Environ. Abstr.; Fluid Abstr., Civil Eng.; Fluid Abstr. Proc. Eng.; FLUIDEX (1973-); GeoRef; INSPEC (1968-); Int. Aerosp. Abstr.; Int. Civil Eng. Abstr.; Leadscan; Manuf. Process Eng. Abstr.; Math. Rev.; Mech. Eng. Abstr.; Met. Abstr.; Pollut. Abstr. Indexes; Proc. Chem. Eng.; Res. Alert [Full Cov.]; Sci. Cit. Index; SCISEARCH; Shock Vibr. Dig.; Soft. Abstr. Eng.; Solid State Supercond. Abstr.; Theoret. Chem. Eng.; Zentralbl. Math. Ihre Grenzgeb.

SZ/0268-1900
INTERNATIONAL JOURNAL OF MATERIALS & PRODUCT TECHNOLOGY. [Int. j. mater. prod. technol.]. **Added/Corp** Unesco. **VFOAT** International Journal of Materials and Product Technology; Materials & & Product Technology; Materials and Product Technology; Internationale Zeitschrift fur Werkstoff- und Produkttechnologie. Vol. 1, No. 1 (July 1986)-. Academic Scholarly Publication. English (French, German and Japanese). Six times a year. £170.00 UK; $250.00 North America; DM420.00 other. Inderscience Enterprises Ltd, World Trade Center Building, 110 Avenue Louis Casai, Case Postale 306, CH-1215 Geneva-Aeroport Switzerland. **Tel** 011 41 22 7383437, FAX 011 41 22 7910885, telex 28 99 50. **ED** M. A. Dorgham. **LC** TA401; .I788. **DD** 620.1/1. **CODEN** IJMTE2. Index available. cum. index. **Bk Rev. Ad Acc. Pr Rev. Circ:** 15,000. Documents available from Article Express International, The Genuine Article, Ask*IEEE, CASDDS, Documents on Demand.
Desc: Provides a forum for an exchange of information and ideas between materials academics and engineers working in university research departments and research institutes, and manufacturing, marketing and process managers, designers, technologists and research and development engineers working in industry.
Ind/Abst Chem. Abstr. (1986); Ei Page One; Eng. Index Annu.; Environ. Abstr.; INSPEC (March 1987-); Oper. Prod. Manage. Abstr. [Full Txt.]; Res. Alert [Full Cov.]; Shock Vibr. Dig.; Soc. Sci. Cit. Index [Select. Cov.].

UK/0961-5539
INTERNATIONAL JOURNAL OF NUMERICAL METHODS FOR HEAT & FLUID FLOW. Vol. 1, No. 1 (Sept. 1990)-. Periodical. English. Ten times a year. £480.00 UK; $800.00 other. John Wiley & Sons Ltd., Baffins Lane, Chichester West Sussex PO19 1UD England. **Tel** 0243 779777, FAX 0243 776128 BTG:JWP001, telex 86290 WIBOOKG. **(Subscription address:** Pineridge Press Ltd., Journals Division, 54 Newton Rd., Mumbles,, Swansea SA3 4BQ Wales.**) ED** Roland W. Lewis and Cedric Taylor. **CODEN** INMFEM. **Bk Rev**, (Qty: 12-15). **Ad Acc.** Documents available from CASDDS.
Desc: The expressed intention of the journal is the dissemination of information relating to the development, refinement and application of computer-based numerical techniques for solving problems in heat and fluid flow.
Ind/Abst Chem. Abstr.; Fluid Abstr., Civil Eng.; Fluid Abstr. Proc. Eng.; FLUIDEX (19??-); Math. Rev.

US/1053-5381
INTERNATIONAL JOURNAL OF OFFSHORE AND POLAR ENGINEERING. (INTERNATIONAL JOURNAL OF OFFSHORE AND POLAR ENGINEERING / TRANSACTIONS OF THE ISOPE.). **Added/Corp** International Society of Offshore and Polar Engineers. **VFOAT** Journal of Offshore and Polar Engineering; IJOPE; ISOPE International Journal of Offshore and Polar Engineering. Vol. 1, No. 1 (Mar. 1991)-. Periodical. English. Four times a year. $120.00 US; $132.00 Canada; $136.00 other. International Society of Offshore and Polar Engineers, PO Box 1107, Golden CO 80402-1107. **Tel** (303)273-3673, FAX (303)420-3760. **ED** J. S. Chung (Editor's Address: Colorado School of Mines, 1500 Illinois Street, Golden, CO 80401). **LC** TC1665; .I577. **DD** 627/.98/05. **CODEN** IOPEE7. Index available. cum. index (available starting in 1995). **Ad Acc. Pr Rev. Circ:** 600. Documents available from Article Express International.
Desc: Research and engineering aspects of ocean, offshore, marine, polar, advanced ship technology, ocean energy and resources, environments, materials, and tubular structures.
Ind/Abst Civ. Struct. Eng. Abstr.; Comput. Inf. Syst. Abstr. J. [Full Cov.]; Ei Page One; Elect. Comm. Abstr.; Eng. Index Annu.; Environ. Eng. Abstr.; Manuf. Process Eng. Abstr.; Mech. Eng. Abstr.; Solid State Supercond. Abstr.

UK/0263-7863
INTERNATIONAL JOURNAL OF PROJECT MANAGEMENT. (INTERNATIONAL JOURNAL OF PROJECT MANAGEMENT : THE JOURNAL OF THE INTERNATIONAL PROJECT MANAGEMENT ASSOCIATION.). [Int. j. proj. manage.]. **Added/Corp** Association of Project Managers (Great Britain) International Project Management Association. **VFOAT** Project Management. Vol. 1, No. 1 (Feb. 1983)-. Periodical. English. Six times a year. $373.00 The Americas; £250.00 other. Butterworth Heinemann Publishers, Linacre House, Jordan Hill, Oxford OX2 8DP England. **Tel** 011 44 865 310366. **(Subscription address:** Elsevier Science Ltd. Oxford Fulfillment Centre, PO Box 800, Kidlington, Oxford OX5 1DX United Kingdom.**) ED** Angela Jamieson. **LC** T56.8; .I537. **DD** 658.4/04. **[CCC].** Index available. cum. index. **Bk Rev. Ad Acc.** available on microfilm and microfiche from University Microfilms International (UMI). Documents available from UMI Article Clearinghouse, Ask*IEEE, Documents on Demand. ***Continues*** *Project Manager.*
Desc: Offers wide ranging and comprehensive coverage of all facets of project management. Its scope includes project management concepts and methods, project controls, tools and training and motivation, techniques, management, contract law, project economics, national and international co-operation and communication.
Ind/Abst ABI/INFORM Glob. Ed.; Environ. Abstr.; INSPEC (May 1985-); Int. Abstr. Oper. Res. [Select. Cov.]; Oper. Res./Manag. Sci.; Qual. Control Appl. Stat.; Risk Abstr.; Selec. Coop. Index Manage. Period.

SI/0218-5393
INTERNATIONAL JOURNAL OF RELIABILITY, QUALITY & SAFETY ENGINEERING. English. Four times a year. $100.00 individuals, $220.00 institutions. World Scientific Publishing Company, PO Box 128, Farrer Road, Singapore 9128 Singapore. **Tel** 011 65 3825663, FAX 011 65 3825919, telex RS 28561 WSPC. **(Subscription address:** US: World Scientific Publishing Co., Inc., 1060 Main Street, River Edge, NJ 07661 Telephone: (201)487-9655, Fax: (201)487-9656; Europe: World Scientific Publishing Co Ltd, 73 Lynton Mead, Totteridge, London N20 8DH United Kingdom Telephone: 011 44 81 4462461, Fax: 011 44 81 4463356; India: World Scientific Publishing Co Pte Ltd, 4911 9th Floor, High Point IV, 45 Palace Road, Bangalore 560 001 India Telephone: (80) 2205972, Fax: (80) 3344593, Telex: 0845-2900 PCO IN; Hong Kong: World Scientific Publishing (HK) Co, PO Box 72482, Kowloon Central Post Office, Hong Kong Telephone: 852-7718791, Fax: 852-7718155**)**

UK/0143-1161
INTERNATIONAL JOURNAL OF REMOTE SENSING. [Int. j. remote sens.]. **Added/Corp** Remote Sensing Society. Vol. 1, No. 1 (Jan./March 1980)-. Academic Scholarly Publication. English. Eighteen times a year. £821.00 UK; $1355.00 other. Taylor & Francis Ltd., Rankine Road, Basingstoke Hampshire, RG24 8PR United Kingdom. **Tel** 011 44 256 840366, FAX 011 44 256 479438, telex 858540. **(Subscription address:** Taylor & Francis Inc., 1900 Frost Road, Suite 101, Bristol PA 19007-1598.**) ED** A. P. Cracknell. **LC** G70.4; .I56. **DD** 621.36/78. **CODEN** IJSEDK. **[CCC].** Index available. cum. index. **Bk Rev. Ad Acc. Pr Rev. Circ:** 800. available on microfilm and microfiche from University Microfilms International (UMI). Documents available from Article Express International, The Genuine Article, BIOSIS Document Express, Ask*IEEE.
Desc: Concerned with the science and technology of remote sensing and the applications of remotely sensed data in all major disciplines. Each issue contains primary papers on basic science, techniques and applications plus a technical news and information section and a section of remote sensing letters containing material which merits fast publication. This journal is the official journal of The Remote Sensing Society.
Ind/Abst AESIS Q.; Agrofor. Abstr. (1991-); Aquat. Sci. Fish. Abstr. (Computer File); Art Archaeol. Tech. Abstr.; Bioeng. Abstr.; Biol. Abstr.; BMT Abstr.; Civ. Struct. Eng. Abstr.; Cot. Trop. Fibr. Abstr. Bibliogr.; Curr. Contents Phys. Chem. Earth Sci.; Ecol. Abstr.; Ecology Abstr.; Ei Page One; Elect. Comm. Abstr.; Electron. Commun. Abstr. J.; EMBASE; Eng. Index Annu.; Environ. Eng. Abstr.; Field Crop Abstr.; Fish Rev.; For. Abstr.; Geogr. Abstr. Phys. Geogr.; Geogr. Abstr. Human Geogr.; Geol. Abstr.; GeoRef; Grasslands For. Abstr.; INSPEC (Jan./March 1982-); Int. Aerosp. Abstr.; Int. Dev. Abstr.; Irr. Drain. Abstr.; ISMEC Bull.; Maize Abstr.; Mech. Eng. Abstr.; Meteorol. Geoastrophys. Abstr. (199?-); Life Sci. Collect.; Pollut. Abstr. Indexes; Res. Alert [Full Cov.]; Rev. Med. Vet. Entomol.; Rev. Plant Pathol.; Rice Abstr.; Saf. Sci. Abstr. J.; Sci. Cit. Index; SCISEARCH; Soc. Sci. Cit. Index [Select. Cov.]; Soils Fert.; Sorghum Mill. Abstr.; Soyabean Abstr.; Wheat Barley Trit. Abstr.; Wildl. Rev.

UK/1049-8923
INTERNATIONAL JOURNAL OF ROBUST AND NONLINEAR CONTROL. [Int. j. robust nonlinear control]. Vol. 1 No. 1 (Jan/Mar. 1991)-. Periodical. English. Six times a year. $550.00. John Wiley & Sons Ltd., Baffins Lane, Chichester West Sussex PO19 1UD England. **Tel** 0243 779777, FAX 0243 776128 BTG:JWP001, telex 86290 WIBOOKG. **(Subscription address:** John Wiley / Philadelphia, PO Box 7247, Philadelphia PA 19170.**) ED** Mike J. Grimble and George Zames. **LC** TJ212; .I56. **DD** 629.8. **CODEN** IJRCEA. available on microfilm and microfiche from University Microfilms International (UMI). Documents available from Ask*IEEE.
Desc: Encourages the development of analysis and design techniques for uncertain systems. Provides a natural forum for papers on the theory and application of robust control system design, including contributions on the H oo design philosophy.
Ind/Abst INSPEC (Jan./Mar. 1991-); Zentralbl. Math. Ihre Grenzgeb.

II/0257-7828
INTERNATIONAL JOURNAL OF SCIENCE & ENGINEERING. [Int. j. sci. eng.]. **VFOAT** Journal of Science & Engineering; International Journal of Science and Engineering. Vol. 1, No. 1 (Apr. 1984)-. Academic Scholarly Publication. English. qt. $50.00. Euclidean Publishers, Allahabad, India. **(Subscription address:** Prints India, 11 Darya Ganj, New Delhi 110002 India.**) CODEN** ISENE7. Documents available from CASDDS.
Ind/Abst Chem. Abstr. (1984-); Math. Rev.; Zentralbl. Math. Ihre Grenzgeb.

●US/1061-3862
INTERNATIONAL JOURNAL OF SELF-PROPAGATING HIGH-TEMPERATURE SYSTEM. VFOAT International Journal of Self-Propagating High-Temperature Synthesis; Self-Propagating High-Temperature System; Self-Propagating High-Temperature Synthesis; SHS. (1992)-. Academic Scholarly Publication. English. qt. $340.00. Allerton Press, Inc., 150 Fifth Avenue, New York NY 10011. **Tel** (212)924-3950, FAX (212)463-9684, telex 427441 ALPRES. **CODEN** ISHSE3. **[CCC].** Documents available from CASDDS.
Ind/Abst Chem. Abstr.

JA
INTERNATIONAL JOURNAL OF THE JAPAN SOCIETY FOR PRECISION ENGINEERING. Added/Corp Seimitsu Kogakkai. Vol. 25, No. 1 (Mar. 1991)-. Periodical. English. qt. $130.00. Japan Society for Precision Engineering, Ceramics Building, 22-17 Hyakunin-Cho 2-Chome, Shinjuku-Ku, Tokyo 169 Japan. **(Subscription address:** Kyowa Book Company Inc., 1-38 Kanda Jinbo-Cho, Chiyoda-Ku Tokyo 101, Japan**) LC** TS500; .S37a. Documents available from The Genuine Article. ***Continues*** *Seimitsu Kogakkai Shi. English. Bulletin of the Japan Society of Precision Engineering, 0582-4206.*
Ind/Abst Curr. Contents Eng. Tech. Appl. Sci.; Res. Alert [Select. Cov.].

SZ/0143-3369
INTERNATIONAL JOURNAL OF VEHICLE DESIGN. See Transportation-Automobiles.

SZ/1351-7848
INTERNATIONAL JOURNAL OF VEHICLE DESIGN SERIES B : HEAVY VEHICLE SYSTEMS. See Transportation-Automobiles.

UK/1052-9268
INTERNATIONAL VIDEO JOURNAL OF ENGINEERING RESEARCH. ***Ceased.*** [Int. video j. eng. res.]. **VFOAT** Video Journal of Engineering

Research. Vol. 1 (1991)-Ceased with Vol. 2 (1992). Periodical. English. Twice a year (January and July). John Wiley & Sons Ltd., Baffins Lane, Chichester West Sussex PO19 1UD England. **Tel** 0243 779777, FAX 0243 776128 BTG:JWP001, telex 86290 WIBOOKG. **(Subscription address:** North, South and Central America/ John Wiley & Sons, Inc., PO Box 7247-8491, Philadelphia, PA 19170-8491**) ED** Vaughan Voller (editor's address: Army High Performance Computing Research Center, Institute of Technology, 1100 Washington Avenue South, Minneapolis MN 55415). **DD** 621. **CODEN** IVJREV.
Desc: The central theme of the journal will be modelling and analysis of engineering systems. The objective of the journal is to provide a forum, based on a video medium, in which video results can be presented to the engineering community at large.

CN/0710-2291
INTERPLAN. (INTERPLAN / ORDRE DES INGENIEURS DU QUEBEC.). [Interplan]. Periodical. English. bm. Order of Engineers of Quebec, Communications Department, Suite 1100, 2075 University Street, Montreal Quebec H3A 1K8, Canada. **DD** 620/.009714. ***Continues in part*** *Interplan. English & French, 0710-2291.*

PO
INVESTIGACAO OPERACIONAL. Portuguese. APDIO, CESUR Instituto Superior Tecnico, Avenida Rovisco Pais, 1000 Lisboa, Portugal.
Ind/Abst Int. Abstr. Oper. Res. [Full Cov.].

BW/0021-0285
INZENERNO-FIZICESKIJ ZURNAL. (INZHENERNO-FIZICHESKII ZHURNAL.). [Inz.-fiz. z.]. **Added/Corp** Akademiia Navuk Belaruskai SSR. **VFOAT** Journal of Engineering Physics. (1958)-. Periodical. Russian (summaries and/or abstracts in English). mo. $109.95. **(Subscription address:** East View Publications Inc., 3020 Harbor Lane North, Suite 110, Minneapolis MN 55447.**) CODEN** INFZA9. **[CCC].** Documents available from Article Express International, Ask*IEEE, CASDDS.
Ind/Abst Alum. Ind. Abstr.; Ceram. Abstr. (19??-); Chem. Abstr. (1968-); Ei Page One; Eng. Index Annu.; FLUIDEX; GeoRef; INSPEC (1968-); Int. Aerosp. Abstr.; Math. Rev.; Met. Abstr. (1968-); Proc. Chem. Eng.; Theoret. Chem. Eng.

RU
INZHENER. **Added/Corp** Soiuz Nauchnykh I Inzhenernykh Obshchestv SSSR. (1990)-. Periodical. Russian. mo. $99.95. **(Subscription address:** East View Publications Inc., 3020 Harbor Lane North, Suite 110, Minneapolis MN 55447.**) LC** T4; .T22843. **CODEN** INZHEP. ***Continues*** *Tekhnika I Nauka, 0321-3269.*

RU/0203-0292
INZHENERNAIA GEOLOGIIA / AKADEMIIA NAUK SSSR. ***Title Change.*** **See** Earth Sciences-Geology.

PL/0138-0540
INZYNIERIA MORSKA. (1980)-. Periodical. Multiple languages. mo. **UDC** 626.
Ind/Abst Geotech. Abstr.

JA/0578-7904
ISHIKAWAJIMA-HARIMA GIHO. [Ishikawajima-Harima giho]. **Added/Corp** Ishikawajima-Harima JukogyÂo Kabushiki Kaisha. **VFOAT** Ishikawajima-Harima Engineering Review; Ishikawajima Harima Giho. (1961)-. Periodical. Japanese (summaries and/or abstracts in English). bm. Ishikawakuma Harima Jukogyo K.K. Gijutsuhonbu Gyomubu, (Ishikawajima-Harima Heavy Industries, Co., Ltd.), 2-16, Toyosu 3 Chome, Kotoku, Tokyoto 135 Japan. **CODEN** ISHGAV. Documents available from Ask*IEEE, CASDDS. ***Supersedes*** *Ishikawajima Giho.*
Ind/Abst Alum. Ind. Abstr.; Chem. Abstr.; Coal Abstr.; INSPEC (July 1970-); Int. Aerosp. Abstr.; Met. Abstr.

SZ/0275-911X
ISSLEDOVANIE ZEMLI IZ KOSMOSA. (SOVIET JOURNAL OF REMOTE SENSING.). [Sov. j. remote sens.]. No. 1 (Sept. 1981)-. Periodical. English (Russian). bm. $1441.00 (academic institutions), $2249.00 (corporate institutions). Harwood Academic Publishers, PO Box 90, Reading RG1 8JL England. **Tel** 011 44 734 560080. **ED** A. V. Sidorenko. **LC** G70.4; .I882. **DD** 621.36/78. **CODEN** SJSEDS. **[CCC].** Index available. **Bk Rev. Ad Acc.** Documents available from Article Express International, The Genuine Article, Ask*IEEE.
Desc: Reports on the latest state-of-the-art assessments of theoretical and applied research developments in the field in the Soviet Union.
Ind/Abst Bioeng. Abstr.; Curr. Contents Eng. Tech. Appl. Sci.; Ei Page One; Eng. Index Annu.; Field Crop Abstr.; GeoRef; Grasslands For. Abstr.; INSPEC (1984-); Irr. Drain. Abstr.; Res. Alert [Full Cov.]; Sci. Cit. Index; SCISEARCH; Wheat Barley Trit. Abstr.

NE/0303-2434
ITC JOURNAL, THE. **See** Earth Sciences.

NO/0802-8532
ITF RAPPORT / NORGES LANDBRUKSHGSKOLE, INSTITUTT FOR TEKNISKE FAG. **See** Agriculture.

FR/0336-4410
IVF, INGENIEURS DES VILLES DE FRANCE. (INGENIEURS DES VILLES DE FRANCE.). [IVF. Ing. villes Fr.]. Periodical. French. mo. 400.00F France; 715.00F other. PYC Edition, 5 Avenue de Verdun, BP 105, 94208 Ivry S Seine Cedex France. **Tel** 011 33 1 49608636.
Ind/Abst EMBASE.

UZ/0516-2629
IZVESTIA AKADEMII NAUK UZBEKSKIJ SSR. SERIA TEHNICESKIH NAUK. ***Title Change.*** (IZVESTIIA AKADEMII NAUK UZSSR. SERIIA TEKHNICHESKIKH NAUK.). [Izv. Akad. nauk Uzb. SSR, Ser. teh. nauk]. **Added/Corp** Uzbekiston SSR Fanlar Akademiiasi. **VFOAT** Seriia Tekhnicheskikh Nauk; Tekhnika Fanlari Seriiasi; Tekhnika Fanlar Seriiasi; UzSSR Fanlar Akademiiasining Akhboroti. Tekhnika Fanlari Seriiasi; UzSSR Fanlar Akademiiasining Akhboroti. Tekhnika Fanlar Seriiasi. (1957)-(199?). Periodical. Russian (summaries and/or abstracts in Uzbek; table of contents in Uzbek). bm. **(Subscription address:** Victor Kamkin, 4956 Boiling Brook Parkway, Rockville MD 20852.**) LC** TA4.A375; A2. **CODEN** IUZTA4. Documents available from Ask*IEEE, CASDDS. ***Continues in part*** *Izvestiia Akademii Nauk UzSSR.* ***Continued by*** *Izvestiia Akademii Nauk UzSSR. Tekhnicheskie Nauki.*
Ind/Abst Chem. Abstr. (?-?); INSPEC (1971-).

AI
IZVESTIIA AKADEMII NAUK ARMENII. SERIIA TEKHNICHESKIKH NAUK. **Added/Corp** Hayastani Gitutyunneri Akademia. **VFOAT** Seriia Tekhnicheskikh Nauk; Tekhnikakan Gitutyunneri Seria; Hayastani Gitutyunneri Akademiayi Teghekagir. Tekhnikakan Gitutyunneri Seria; Izvestiia Akademii Nauk Armianskoi SSR. Seriia Tekhnicheskikh Nauk. Began in (1990)-. Periodical. Russian (summaries and/or abstracts in Armenian; table of contents in Armenian). bm. **LC** TA4.A35; A2. ***Continues*** *Izvestiia Akademii Nauk Armianskoi SSR. Seriia Tekhnicheskikh Nauk, 0002-306X.*

UZ
IZVESTIIA AKADEMII NAUK UZSSR. TEKHNICHESKIE NAUKI. **Added/Corp** Uzbekiston SSR Fanlar Akademiiasi. (199?)-. Periodical. Russian. bm. **(Subscription address:** Victor Kamkin, 4956 Boiling Brook Parkway, Rockville MD 20852.**) LC** TA4.A375; A2. ***Continues*** *Izvestiia Akademii Nauk UzSSR. Seriia Tekhnicheskikh Nauk.*

JA/0021-4647
JAPAN SHIPBUILDING & MARINE ENGINEERING. **See** Naval Science, Navigation.

JA/0448-8938
JAPANESE RAILWAY ENGINEERING. **See** Transportation-Railroads.

●US/1058-7322
JAPANESE TECHNOLOGY REVIEWS. SECTION D, MANUFACTURING ENGINEERING. **VFOAT** Manufacturing Engineering. (1992)-. Periodical. English. Twice a year (1 volume). $185.00 (academic institutions), $289.00 (corporate institutions). Gordon & Breach Science Publishers, Inc., PO Box 786, Cooper Station, New York NY 10276. **Tel** (212)206-8900, FAX (212)645-2459. **(Subscription address:** International Publishers Distributor at one of the following addresses: 820 Town Center Drive, Langhorne, PA 19047; or PO Box 90, Reading Berkshire RG1 8JL UK; or Kent Ridge PO Box 1180, Singapore 9111, Republic of Singapore**) [CCC].** ***Continues in part*** *Japanese Technology Reviews, 0898-5693.*

MY
JERNAL FAKULTI KEJURUTERAAN, UNIVERSITI MALAYA. **Main/Corp** University of Malaya (Founded 1962). Dept. of Engineering. Vol. 12 (June 1973)-. English. an. University of Malaya Faculty of Engineering, 59100 Kuala Lumpur Malaysia. **Tel** 7553466, telex UNIMAL MA 37453. **LC** TA1; .U677. **DD** 620/.005. **Circ:** 1,000. ***Continues*** *University of Malaya (Founded 1962). Dept. of Engineering. Journal.*
Desc: Publication of the latest research findings carried out at the Faculty of Engineering, University of Malaysia.

CC/0253-3219
JISHU, HE. [He Jishu]. **VFOAT** Nuclear techniques. (1978)-. Periodical. Multiple languages. mo. **UDC** 621.039.

●US
JOB CHOICES ... IN SCIENCE & ENGINEERING. **See** Occupations and Careers.

US/0270-5214
JOHNS HOPKINS APL TECHNICAL DIGEST. [Johns Hopkins APL tech. dig.]. **Main/Corp** Johns Hopkins University. Applied Physics Laboratory. **Added/Corp** Johns Hopkins University. Applied Physics Laboratory. APL Technical Digest. Johns Hopkins University. Applied Physics Laboratory. Technical Digest. **VAT** Johns Hopkins Applied Physics Laboratory Technical Digest. Vol. 1 No. 1 (Jan./March 1980)-. Academic Scholarly Publication. English. qt. Free. Johns Hopkins University / Physics, Applied Physics Laboratory, McClure Center, Johns Hopkins Road, Laurel MD 20707. **Tel** (301)338-6990. **LC** TA1; .J524. **DD** 620/.005. **NLM** W1; JO14P. **CODEN** JHADDQ. **Pr Rev.** Documents available from Article Express International, The Genuine Article, BIOSIS Document Express, Ask*IEEE, CASDDS. ***Supersedes*** *APL Technical Digest, 0001-2211.*
Ind/Abst Bioeng. Abstr.; Biol. Abstr.; Chem. Abstr.; Curr. Contents Eng. Tech. Appl. Sci.; Ei Page One; Eng. Index Annu.; GeoRef; INSPEC (Jan./March 1980-); Int. Aerosp. Abstr.; Meteorol. Geoastrophys. Abstr.; Ocean. Abstr.; Life Sci. Collect.; Res. Alert [Select. Cov.]; SCISEARCH; Soc. Sci. Cit. Index [Select. Cov.].

UK
JOINING SCIENCES. ***Ceased.*** (19??)-(1993). English. qt. Argus Press Group, Queensway House, 2 Queensway Redhill, Surrey RH1 1QS England. **Tel** 011 44 737 768611, 011 44 737 761685, FAX 011 44 737 760510, telex 948669 TOPJNL G.
Desc: Devoted to the science and technology of joining materials.

BE/0771-1107
JOURNAL A. [J. A]. **VFOAT** Revue A; Tijdschrift A; Zeitschrift A. Vol. 15 (1974)-. Periodical. Dutch (English, French and German; summaries and/or abstracts in English and French). qt (Mar., June, Sept., Dec.). 2200F. Koninklijke Vlaamse Ingenieurs, Jan viv Desguinlei 214, B-2018 Antwerpen Belgium. **Tel** 011 32 3 2160996. **CODEN** JRNAAD. Documents available from Ask*IEEE. ***Continues*** *Revue A - Review A - Zeitschrift A - Tijdschrift A, 0035-0656.*
Ind/Abst Comput. Rev.; INSPEC (Jan. 1974-).

BE/0021-8065
JOURNAL DES INGENIEURS (BRUSSELS, BELGIUM : 1984). (JOURNAL DES INGENIEURS.). [J. ing.]. (1984)-. Academic Scholarly Publication. French. Four times a year (Mar., June, Sept., Dec.). 1400.00F. Union Revues Techn Belges, CP 165/ Avenue FR Roosevelt 50, 1050 Brussels Belgium. **Tel** 011 32 2 6502674. **CODEN** JOINA6. **Bk Rev. Ad Acc, Adv Mgr:** Publicarto. Documents available from Ask*IEEE, CASDDS. ***Continues*** *Journal des Ingenieurs (Brussels, Belgium : 1957), 0021-8065.*
Ind/Abst Chem. Abstr.; EMBASE; INSPEC (1984-1986).

US/0015-4032
JOURNAL / FLORIDA ENGINEERING SOCIETY. [J. - Fla. Eng. Soc.]. **Main/Corp** Florida Engineering Society. **Added/Corp** Florida Engineering Society. **VFOAT** Florida Engineering Society Journal. (June 1947)-. Periodical. English. Eleven times a year (monthly except Dec). $53.50 Florida; $50.00 other. Florida Engineering Society, PO Box 750, Tallahassee FL 32302. **Tel** (904)224-7121, FAX (904)222-4349. **ED** Patti Sunseri. **DD** 620. **Ad Acc, Adv Mgr:** Nancy Taylor. **Circ:** 4,500. available on an online database.
Desc: Publishes legislative and professional information and news of interest to Florida's professional engineers, plus advertising in all related technical and professional areas.

US/0730-0050
JOURNAL OF ACOUSTIC EMISSION. [J. acoust. emiss.]. **Added/Corp** Acoustic Emission Group. Vol. 1, No. 1 (Jan. 1982)-. Academic Scholarly Publication. English. Four times a year (Mar., June, Sept., Dec.). $104.00. Acoustic Emission Group, Box 364, 308 Westwood Boulevard, Los Angeles CA 90024-1647. **Tel** (310)825-5233, FAX (310)368-8309. **ED** Kanji Ono. **LC** TA418.84; .J68. **DD** 620.2/05. **CODEN** JACEDO. Index available (Dec. iss.). **Bk Rev. Pr Rev. Circ:** 300. Documents available from Ask*IEEE, CASDDS.
Desc: Publishes articles covering research and engineering advances in all aspects of acoustic emission, from basic theory to all types of practical applications.
Ind/Abst Alum. Ind. Abstr.; Chem. Abstr.; Eng. Mater. Abstr.; INIS Atomindex [Micro.]; INSPEC (1986-); Int. Aerosp. Abstr. (1984-); Met. Abstr.; World Alum. Abstr.

●US/1070-9789
JOURNAL OF ADVANCED MATERIALS. (JOURNAL OF ADVANCED MATERIALS / SOCIETY FOR THE ADVANCEMENT OF MATERIAL AND PROCESS ENGINEERING.). [J. adv. mater.]. **Added/Corp** Society for the Advancement of Material and Process Engineering. Vol. 25, no. 1 (Oct. 1993)-. Periodical. English. qt. $60.00 (non-member), $18.00 (member) US; $68.00 (nonmember), $26.00 (member) Canada and Mexico; $75.00 (nonmember), $33.00 (member) other. Society for the Advancement of Material & Process Engineering, 1161 Parkview Drive, PO Box 2459, Covina CA 91724. **Tel** (818)331-0616 Ext 611, FAX (818)332-8929, telex 510/600 4889. **(Subscription address:** Society for Advancement Management, PO Box 2459, Covina CA 91722.**) LC** TL950; .S583. **DD** 620. ***Continues*** *SAMPE Quarterly, 0036-0821.*
Ind/Abst Bioeng. Abstr.; Chem. Abstr.; Coal Abstr.; Electron. Commun. Abstr. J.; Energy Inf. Abstr.; Energy Res. Abstr.; Eng. Index Annu.; Int. Aerosp. Abstr.; ISMEC Bull.; Met. Abstr.; Nucl. Sci. Abstr.; Pollut. Abstr. Indexes; Saf. Sci. Abstr. J.; World Alum. Abstr.

UK/0021-8634
JOURNAL OF AGRICULTURAL ENGINEERING RESEARCH. [J. agric. eng. res.]. Vol. 1 (1956)-. Academic Scholarly Publication. English. mo. $450.00. Academic Press Ltd., A Division of Harcourt Brace & Company Ltd., 24-28 Oval Road, London NW1 7DX England. **Tel** 071 267 4466, FAX 071 482 2293, 071 485 4752, telex 25775 ACPRES G. **(Subscription address:** Harcourt Brace & Company, Ltd., Foots Cray, High Street, Sidcup Kent DA14 5HP England.) **ED** D. J. White. **LC** S671; .J6. **DD** 631.305. **CODEN** JAERA2. **[CCC].** Index available (bound in last issue). **Pr Rev.** Documents available from The Genuine Article, BIOSIS Document Express, CASDDS.
Desc: Reflects the broad spectrum of interdisciplinary interests inherent in this field. Publishes mainly original research papers but also includes in-depth review articles and short research notes.
Ind/Abst AgBiotech News Inf.; AGRICOLA [Full Cov.]; Agric. Eng. Abstr. (19??-19??); Anim. Breed. Abstr.; Biodeter. Abstr. (19??-19??); Biol. Agric. Index; Biol. Abstr.; Chem. Abstr.; Curr. Contents, Agric. Biol. Environ. Sci.; Curr. Contents Eng. Tech. Appl. Sci.; Dairy Sci. Abstr.; EMBASE; Field Crop Abstr.; Fluid Abstr., Civil Eng.; Fluid Abstr. Proc. Eng.; FLUIDEX (1973-); Food Sci. Technol. Abstr.; For. Abstr.; Grasslands For. Abstr.; Hortic. Abstr.; Int. Abstr. Oper. Res. [Select. Cov.]; Irr. Drain. Abstr.; Maize Abstr.; Nutr. Abstr. Rev., Ser. B, Live Feeds and Feed.; Ornamental Hort. (19??-19??); Life Sci. Collect.; Pig News Inf.; Plant Genet. Resour. Abstr.; Postharvest News Inf.; Potato Abstr.; Res. Alert [Full Cov.]; Rev. Agric. Entomol.; Rice Abstr.; Sci. Cit. Index; SCISEARCH; Seed Abstr.; Soils Fert.; Soyabean Abstr.; Weed Abstr.

UK/0962-4694
JOURNAL OF DESIGN AND MANUFACTURING. **See** Manufacturing.

US/0022-0434
JOURNAL OF DYNAMIC SYSTEMS, MEASUREMENT, AND CONTROL. [J. dyn. syst. meas. control]. **Added/Corp** American Society of Mechanical Engineers. Vol. 93, No. 1 (March 1971)-. Periodical. English. Four times a year. $40.00 (members), $130.00 (nonmembers) US and Canada. American Society of Mechanical Engineers, 22 Law Drive, Fairfield NJ 07007. **Tel** (201)882-1167, (212)705-7722 (editorial). **ED** Cornelia Monahan. **LC** TJ212; .T68. **DD** 629.8/05. **CODEN** JDSMAA. **[CCC]. Bk Rev. Ad Acc. Pr Rev. Circ:** 1,492. available on microfilm and microfiche from University Microfilms International (UMI). Documents available from Article Express International, The Genuine Article, Ask*IEEE, CASDDS.
Desc: Covers transportation, bioengineering fluidics and fluid power control, control system components, instrumentation and economics system dynamics, urban dynamics and societal problems.
Ind/Abst Abstr. Bull. Inst. Pap. Sci. Tech.; Abstr. J. Earthq. Eng.; Appl. Sci. Technol. Index; Bioeng. Abstr.; Chem. Abstr.; Curr. Contents Eng. Tech. Appl. Sci.; Ei Page One; Eng. Index Annu.; Expand. Acad. Index (1992-); Fluid Abstr., Civil Eng.; Fluid Abstr. Proc. Eng.; FLUIDEX (1978-1989); INSPEC (March 1971-); Int. Aerosp. Abstr. (1991-); Math. Rev.; Proc. Chem. Eng.; Res. Alert [Full Cov.]; Robotics Abstr.; Sci. Cit. Index; SCISEARCH; Shock Vibr. Dig.; Theoret. Chem. Eng.; Zentralbl. Math. Ihre Grenzgeb.

UK/0191-9539
JOURNAL OF ENGINEERING AND APPLIED SCIENCES. ***Ceased.*** [J. eng. appl. sci.]. ( )-Vol. 3 (1984). Periodical. English. qt. Pergamon Press, An Imprint of Elsevier Science Ltd., The Boulevard, Langford Lane, Kidlington, Oxford OX5 1GB United Kingdom. **Tel** 011 44 865 843000, 011 44 865 843699, FAX 011 44 865 843010. **(Subscription address:** US/ 395 Saw Mill River Road, Elmsford, NY 10523; Can/ 150 Consumers Road/Suite 104, Willowdale Ontario M2J 1P9; Aus-NZ/ POB 544, Potts Point NSW 2011**) LC** TA1; .J633. **DD** 620/.005. **CODEN** JOASDI. available in microform. Documents available from Article Express International, Ask*IEEE.
Ind/Abst Bioeng. Abstr. (?-?); Ei Page One (?-?); Eng. Index Annu.; INIS Atomindex [Micro.]; INSPEC (1983); Int. Aerosp. Abstr. (?-?).

NE/0923-4748
JOURNAL OF ENGINEERING AND TECHNOLOGY MANAGEMENT. (JOURNAL OF ENGINEERING AND TECHNOLOGY MANAGEMENT : JET-M.). [J. eng. technol. manag.]. **VFOAT** JET-M. Vol. 6 No. 1 (Sept. 1989)-. Academic Scholarly Publication. English. qt (1 volume). Fl380.00. Elsevier Science Publishers BV, PO Box 211, 1000 AE Amsterdam Netherlands. **Tel** 011 31 20 5803642, FAX 011 31 20 5862696, telex 15682. **LC** TA190; .E55. **CODEN** JETMEQ. **[CCC].** available on microfilm and microfiche from University Microfilms International (UMI). Documents available from Article Express International, Ask*IEEE, Documents on Demand. ***Continues*** *Engineering Management International, 0167-5419.*
Ind/Abst Ei Page One; Energy Inf. Abstr.; Eng. Index Annu.; Environ. Abstr.; Gen. BusinessFile (1992-); INSPEC (Sep. 1989-)(Sept. 1989-); J. Ferrocement; Risk Abstr.

NZ/0377-7472
JOURNAL OF ENGINEERING EDUCATION IN SOUTHEAST ASIA. **Added/Corp** Association for Engineering Education in Southeast Asia. (19??)-. Periodical. English. Twice a year (June & Dec.). $50.00. Association of Engineering Education of Southeast Asia, University of Canterbury, School of Engineering, Private Bag 4800, Christchurch New Zealand. **Tel** 011 64 3 3667001, FAX 011 64 3 3642758. **LC** T149; .J67. **DD** 620/.007/1159. **Circ:** 250.
Desc: Distributing ideas and experience on engineering education. Among the areas covered are teaching techniques, educational philosophy, management issues, new initiatives, continuing engineering; education, relationships with industry and the use of new technology.
Ind/Abst J. Ferrocement.

●US/1069-4730
JOURNAL OF ENGINEERING EDUCATION (WASHINGTON, D.C.). (JOURNAL OF ENGINEERING EDUCATION / AMERICAN SOCIETY FOR ENGINEERING EDUCATION.). [J. eng. edu.]. **Added/Corp** American Society for Engineering Education. Vol. 82, No. 1 (Jan. 1993)-. Periodical. English. qt. $75.00. American Society for Engineering Education, 1818 North Street Northwest, Suite 600, Washington DC 20036. **Tel** (202)331-3500. **DD** 620. ***Continues*** *Engineering Education, 0022-0809.*

US/0022-0817
JOURNAL OF ENGINEERING FOR INDUSTRY. (TRANSACTIONS OF THE ASME. JOURNAL OF ENGINEERING FOR INDUSTRY.). [J. eng. ind.]. Vol. 1 (Feb. 1959)-. Academic Scholarly Publication. English. qt. $40.00 (members), $140.00 (nonmembers) US and Canada. American Society of Mechanical Engineers, 22 Law Drive, Fairfield NJ 07007. **Tel** (201)882-1167, (212)705-7722 (editorial). **ED** Cornelia Monahan. **LC** TA1; .J634. **DD** 620/.005. **CODEN** JEFIA8. **[CCC]. Bk Rev. Ad Acc. Pr Rev. Circ:** 1,563. available on microfilm and microfiche from University Microfilms International (UMI). Documents available from Article Express International, The Genuine Article, Ask*IEEE, CASDDS. ***Continues in part*** *Transactions of the American Society of Mechanical Engineers, 0097-6822.*
Desc: Aerospace, management, material handling, petroleum, plant engineering and maintenance process industry.
Ind/Abst Acoust. Abstr.; Alum. Ind. Abstr.; Appl. Sci. Technol. Index; Bioeng. Abstr.; Ceram. Abstr. (19??-); Chem. Abstr.; Coal Abstr.; Curr. Contents Eng. Tech. Appl. Sci.; Ei Page One; EMBASE; Energy Res. Abstr.; Eng. Mater. Abstr.; Eng. Index Annu.; Expand. Acad. Index (1992-); Fluid Abstr., Civil Eng.; Fluid Abstr. Proc. Eng.; FLUIDEX (1973-); INIS Atomindex [Micro.]; INSPEC (1968-); Int. Aerosp. Abstr.; Lit. Pat. Abstr., Oilfield Chem. (1960-1990); Lit. Abstr., Catal. Catal.; Lit. Abstr., Health Environ.; Lit. Abstr., Pet. Refin. Petrochem.; Lit. Abstr., Pet. Substit.; Lit. Abstr., Transp. Storage; Met. Abstr.; Res. Alert [Select. Cov.]; SCISEARCH; Shock Vibr. Dig.; Stat. Theory Method Abstr. (1978); Text. Technol. Dig.

CN/1183-7667
JOURNAL OF ENGINEERING FOR INTERNATIONAL DEVELOPMENT. [J. eng. int. dev.]. Vol. 1, No. 1 (Dec. 1991)-. Periodical. English. Three times a year. $35.00 (individuals), $75.00 (institutions) US. Journal of Engineering and International Development, Queens University Department of Mechanical Engineering, Kingston Ontario K7L 3N6 Canada. **Tel** (613)545-2563. **DD** 620/.009172/4.

II/0970-5317
JOURNAL OF ENGINEERING GEOLOGY. **See** Earth Sciences-Geology.

NE/0022-0833
JOURNAL OF ENGINEERING MATHEMATICS. [J. eng. math.]. Vol. 1 (Jan. 1967)-. Periodical. English. bm. $699.00. Kluwer Academic Publishers, Postbus 322, 3300 AH Dordrecht, The Netherlands. **Tel** 011 (31) 78 524400, FAX 011 31 78 183273, telex 20083. **ED** H.K. Kuiken and S.W. Rienstra. **LC** TA329; .J68. **DD** 620.001/51. **CODEN** JLEMAU. **[CCC].** cum. index. **Ad Acc. Pr Rev. Acid Free. Circ:** 600 (ctrl). available on microfilm and microfiche from University Microfilms International (UMI). Documents available from Article Express International, The Genuine Article, Ask*IEEE.
Desc: Original work in engineering science in which mathematical methods of solution are essential; promotes the application of mathematics to engineering problems and stresses intrinsic unity of fundamental problems of different branches of engineering.
Ind/Abst Bioeng. Abstr.; Civ. Struct. Eng. Abstr.; Compumath Citation Index [Full Cov.]; Curr. Contents Eng. Tech. Appl. Sci.; Ei Page One; Eng. Index Annu.; Environ. Eng. Abstr.; Fluid Abstr., Civil Eng.; Fluid Abstr. Proc. Eng.; FLUIDEX (1973-); GeoRef; INSPEC (Oct. 1968-); Int. Aerosp. Abstr.; Int. Civil Eng. Abstr. (Oct. 1968-); Math. Rev.; Mech. Eng. Abstr.; Pollut. Abstr. Indexes; Res. Alert [Full Cov.]; Sci. Cit. Index; SCISEARCH; Soft. Abstr. Eng.; Stat. Theory Method Abstr. (1972); Zentralbl. Math. Ihre Grenzgeb. (Oct. 1968-).

●US/1062-0125
JOURNAL OF ENGINEERING PHYSICS AND THERMOPHYSICS. **See** Physics.

KO
JOURNAL OF ENGINEERING RESEARCH, SEOUL NATIONAL UNIVERSITY. Korean (English). sa. Seoul National University College of Engineering, Kwanak ku Korea. **Tel** 82-2-880-700, FAX 82-2-887-9592. **ED** Hyochul Kim, Heonshik Shin, Seoug-Jo Kim, Chung-Hak Lee, and Jung-Joong Lee. cum. index. **Circ:** 500 (ctrl).
Desc: A faculty research journal devoted to fundamentals and technologies in Engineering.

SU/0377-9254
JOURNAL OF ENGINEERING SCIENCES. (JOURNAL OF ENGINEERING SCIENCES, KING SAUD UNIVERSITY.). [J. eng. sci.]. **Added/Corp** Jamiat Al-Malik Saud. Imadat Shuun Al-Maktabat. (1975)-. Periodical. English. sa. King Saud University, University Libraries, PO Box 22480, 11495 Riyadh Saudi Arabia. **CODEN** JESCDO. Documents available from Article Express International, Ask*IEEE, CASDDS. ***Continues*** *Journal of Engineering Sciences.*
Ind/Abst Chem. Abstr.; Civ. Struct. Eng. Abstr.; Comput. Inf. Syst. Abstr. J. [Full Cov.]; Ei Page One; Elect. Comm. Abstr.; Eng. Index Annu.; Environ. Eng. Abstr.; INSPEC (1982-); Manuf. Process Eng. Abstr.; Mater. Sci. Eng. Abstr.; Mech. Eng. Abstr.

US/0747-9964
JOURNAL OF ENGINEERING TECHNOLOGY. (JOURNAL OF ENGINEERING TECHNOLOGY : A PUBLICATION OF THE ENGINEERING TECHNOLOGY DIVISION AMERICAN SOCIETY FOR ENGINEERING EDUCATION / ASEE.). [J. eng. technol.]. **Added/Corp** American Society for Engineering Education. Engineering Technology Division. **VFOAT** Engineering Technology. Vol. 1, No. 1 (Mar. 1984)-. Periodical. English. Twice a year. $20.00. St Louis Community College, Florissant Val, Ferguson MO 63135. **Tel** (314)595-4314, FAX (314)595-4544. **ED** Carole Goodson, University of Houston, College of Technology, Houston, TX; (713)743-4046. **LC** TA1; .J68. Index available. **Ad Acc, Adv Mgr:** Richard Moore, **Tel** (503)725-3066. **Circ:** 2,000. Documents available from Article Express International.
Ind/Abst Appl. Sci. Technol. Index (1991-); Ei Page One; Eng. Index Annu. [Select. Cov.].

●US/1056-2702
JOURNAL OF ENVIRONMENTAL ENGINEERING. (1993)-. Periodical. English. qt. $110.00. Executive Enterprises, 22 West 21st Street, New York NY 10010-6990. **Tel** (800)332-8804, FAX (212)645-8689. Documents available from Documents on Demand.
Ind/Abst AESIS Q.; Environ. Abstr.; Expand. Acad. Index (1992-); Soc. Sci. Cit. Index [Select. Cov.].

US/0733-9372
JOURNAL OF ENVIRONMENTAL ENGINEERING (NEW YORK N.Y.). **See** Environmental Issues-Pollution and Waste Management.

US/0360-1226
JOURNAL OF ENVIRONMENTAL SCIENCE AND HEALTH. PART A, ENVIRONMENTAL SCIENCE AND ENGINEERING. **See** Environmental Issues.

US/0889-0668
JOURNAL OF EXPLOSIVES ENGINEERING, THE. [J. explos. eng.]. **Added/Corp** Society of Explosives Engineers. Vol. 1, No. 1 May (1983)-. Periodical. English. Six times a year (Jan., Mar., May, July, Sept., Nov.,). $25.00. Society of Explosives Engineers, 29100 Aurora Road, Cleveland OH 44139. **Tel** (216)349-4004, FAX (216)349-3788. **ED** Larry Trask and Joyce E. Linson. **DD** 620. **Bk Rev. Ad Acc. Circ:** 10,500 (ctrl). Documents available from Article Express International.
Desc: Technical articles, news, product information and practical application of explosives in mining, construction and demolition.
Ind/Abst Ei Page One; Eng. Index Annu. [Select. Cov.].

●US/1062-8924
JOURNAL OF FINANCIAL ENGINEERING, THE. [J. financ. eng.]. **Added/Corp** American Association of Financial Engineers. International Association of Financial Engineers. Vol. 1, No. 1 (June 1992)-. Periodical. English. Four times a year (Mar., June, Sept., Dec.). $180.00. International Association of Financial Engineers, St. John's University, Department of Finance, Jamaica NY 11439. **Tel** (718)990-6161 ext. 7381, FAX (718)990-1868. **LC** HG176.7; .J68. **DD** 658.15/224/05. **Ad Acc.**

US/1042-3915
JOURNAL OF FIRE PROTECTION ENGINEERING. **See** Fire Prevention.

●US/1068-3666
JOURNAL OF FRICTION AND WEAR. [J. frict. wear]. **Added/Corp** Akademiia Nauk SSSR. Akademiia Navuk Belaruskai SSR. **VFOAT** Soviet Journal of Friction and Wear. (1993)-. Periodical. English (translations available in Russian). Six times a year. $845.00. Allerton Press, Inc., 150 Fifth Avenue, New York NY 10011. **Tel** (212)924-3950, FAX (212)463-9684, telex 427441 ALPRES. **DD** 621. **CODEN** JFWEEO. **[CCC]**. ***Continues*** *Soviet Journal of Friction and Wear, 0733-1924.*

NE/0925-5001
JOURNAL OF GLOBAL OPTIMIZATION : AN INTERNATIONAL JOURNAL DEALING WITH THEORETICAL AND COMPUTATIONAL ASPECTS OF SEEKING GLOBAL OPTIMA AND THEIR APPLICATIONS IN SCIENCE, MANAGEMENT AND ENGINEERING. **See** Mathematics.

US/0022-1481
JOURNAL OF HEAT TRANSFER. (TRANSACTIONS OF THE ASME. JOURNAL OF HEAT TRANSFER.). [J. heat transfer]. Vol. 81 (Feb. 1959)-. Periodical. English. qt. $155.00 (nonmembers). ASME United Engineering Center, 345 East 47th Street, New York NY 10017. **LC** TA1; .J64. **DD** 621.4/022/05. **CODEN** JHTRAO. **[CCC]**. **Pr Rev.** available on microfilm and microfiche from University Microfilms International (UMI). Documents available from Article Express International, The Genuine Article, Ask*IEEE, Petroleum Abstracts Document Delivery Service, CASDDS. ***Continues in part*** *Transactions of the American Society of Mechanical Engineers, 0097-7788.*
Ind/Abst Abstr. Bull. Inst. Pap. Sci. Tech.; Appl. Sci. Technol. Index; Bioeng. Abstr.; Ceram. Abstr.; Chem. Abstr.; Coal Abstr.; Comput. Inf. Syst. Abstr. J. [Full Cov.]; Curr. Contents Eng. Tech. Appl. Sci.; Ei Page One; Elect. Comm. Abstr.; Energy Inf. Abstr.; Energy Res. Abstr.; Eng. Index Annu.; Environ. Eng. Abstr.; Expand. Acad. Index (1992-); Fluid Abstr., Civil Eng.; Fluid Abstr. Proc. Eng.; FLUIDEX (1978-); HTFS Dig.; INIS Atomindex [Micro.]; INSPEC (1968-); Int. Aerosp. Abstr. (1991-); Int. Build. Serv. Abstr.; Lit. Pat. Abstr., Oilfield Chem. (1960-); Lit. Abstr., Catal. Catal.; Lit. Abstr., Health Environ.; Lit. Abstr., Pet. Refin. Petrochem.; Lit. Abstr., Pet. Substit.; Lit. Abstr., Transp. Storage; Mater. Sci. Eng. Abstr.; Mech. Eng. Abstr.; Pet. Abstr.; Proc. Chem. Eng.; Res. Alert [Full Cov.]; Sci. Cit. Index; SCISEARCH; Solid State Supercond. Abstr.; SPIN (1977-); Theoret. Chem. Eng.

US/0742-597X
JOURNAL OF MANAGEMENT IN ENGINEERING. [J. manage. eng.]. **Added/Corp** American Society of Civil Engineers. Engineering Management Division. Vol. 1, No. 1 (Jan. 1985)-. Periodical. English. Six times a year. $135.00 (nonmember) US; $150.00 (nonmember) other. American Society of Civil Engineers / ASCE, 345 East 47th Street, New York NY 10017-2398. **Tel** (212)705-7179, FAX (212)705-7300, telex 422847 ASCE UI. **(Subscription address:** American Society of Civil Engineers, Publisher Fulfillment Agency, Box 828, Somerset NJ 08875.**) DD** 620. **CODEN** JMENEA. **[CCC]**. Index available. cum. index. **Circ:** 4,900. available on microfilm and microfiche from University Microfilms International (UMI); available on CD-ROM from American Society of Civil Engineers. Documents available from Article Express International.
Desc: Topics include project management; department, branch and office management; financial management; marketing; computer systems management; productivity management; budgeting; and management development.
Ind/Abst ASCE Annu. Comb. Index (1985-); ASCE Publ. Inf. (1985-); Ei Page One; Eng. Index Annu.; Expand. Acad. Index (1992-); Int. Civil Eng. Abstr.; Trans. Am. Soc. Civ. Eng.

UK
JOURNAL OF OFFSHORE TECHNOLOGY. English. Four times a year. $80.00 US. Marine Management Holdings Ltd, Memorial Building, 76 Mark Lane, London EC3R 7JN England. **Tel** 011 44 71 4818493. **(Subscription address:** North America: Learned Information Inc., 143 Marlton Pike, Medford, NJ 08055-8750**)**

US
JOURNAL OF SURFACE MOUNT TECHNOLOGY. (19??)-. Periodical. English. qt. Free to members; $295.00 (corporate user membership), $60.00 (individual membership). Surface Mount Technology Association / SMTA, 5200 Willson Road, Suite 100, Edina MN 55424. **Tel** (612)920-7682, FAX (612)926-1819.

US/0938-7706
JOURNAL OF SYSTEMS ENGINEERING. Vol. 1 (1991)-. English. qt. £144.00. Springer-Verlag New York Inc., 175 5th Avenue, New York NY 10010. **Tel** (212)460-1500, telex 232 235 SPB UR. **(Subscription address:** Springer Verlag New York Inc. / for North America, 44 Hartz Way, Secaucus NJ 07096.**) ED** D.T. Pham. Documents available from Ask*IEEE.
Desc: Encompassing all subjects pertinent to systems engineering: systems analysis, modeling, simulation, optimization, synthesis, operation, monitoring, identification, evaluation diagnosis, and control.
Ind/Abst INSPEC (1991-); Math. Rev.

US/0090-3973
JOURNAL OF TESTING AND EVALUATION. [J. test. eval.]. **Added/Corp** American Society for Testing and Materials. Vol. 1 (Jan. 1973)-. Periodical. English. bm (6 issues). $109.00 North America; $120.00 other (non-member). American Society for Testing and Materials, 1916 Race Street, Philadelphia PA 19103. **Tel** (215)299-5585, FAX (215)299-9679, telex 710 670 1037. **LC** TA401; .J672. **DD** 620/.004/405. **CODEN** JTEVAB. **[CCC]**. **Pr Rev.** available on microfilm and microfiche from University Microfilms International (UMI). Documents available from Article Express International, The Genuine Article, Ask*IEEE, CASDDS. ***Continues*** *Journal of Materials, 0022-2453.*
Ind/Abst Abstr. Bull. Inst. Pap. Sci. Tech.; Abstr. J. Earthq. Eng. (?-?); AGRICOLA; Alum. Ind. Abstr.; Appl. Sci. Technol. Index; Bioeng. Abstr.; Ceram. Abstr.; Chem. Abstr.; Coal Abstr.; Curr. Contents Eng. Tech. Appl. Sci.; Ei Page One; EMBASE; Energy Res. Abstr. (June 1973-); Eng. Mater. Abstr.; Eng. Index Annu.; Fluid Abstr., Civil Eng.; Fluid Abstr. Proc. Eng.; FLUIDEX (1973-); Geotech. Abstr.; INIS Atomindex [Micro.]; INSPEC (Jan. 1973-); Int. Aerosp. Abstr.; Int. Civil Eng. Abstr.; Int. Packag. Abstr.; J. Ferrocement; Met. Abstr.; Polymer Contents; Res. Alert [Full Cov.]; Sci. Cit. Index; SCISEARCH; Soft. Abstr. Eng.; World Ceram. Abstr.; World Surf. Coat. Abstr.

US/0013-8150
JOURNAL OF THE ENGINEERS' CLUB OF ST. LOUIS. A MONTHLY PERIODICAL DEVOTED TO THE INTERESTS OF THE ENGINEERING PROFESSION IN ST. LOUIS. **Main/Corp** Engineers' Club of St. Louis. English. mo. $24.00. Journal of the Engineers Club, 4359 Lindall Boulevard, St Louis MO 63108. **Tel** (314)534-4175. **ED** Michael Wild.
Desc: A comprehensive view of upcoming meetings, seminars and classes of interest to the engineering community. Feature articles of important happenings are also included.

JA/0037-3818
JOURNAL OF THE FACULTY OF ENGINEERING. SHINSHU UNIVERSITY. (SHINSHU DAIGAKU KOGAKUBU KENKYU HOHOKU.). [J. Fac. Eng., Shinshu Univ.]. **Added/Corp** Shinshu Daigaku. Kogakubu. (1951)-. Periodical. Japanese (summaries and/or abstracts in English). sa. **CODEN** SDKKBU. Documents available from Ask*IEEE. ***Absorbed*** *Shinshu Daigaku Kogakubu Kenkyu Hokoku, 0583-0915.*
Ind/Abst Abstr. J. Earthq. Eng.; INSPEC (Dec. 1971-).

JA/0563-7945
JOURNAL OF THE FACULTY OF ENGINEERING, UNIVERSITY OF TOKYO. SERIES A, ANNUAL REPORT. (JOURNAL OF THE FACULTY OF ENGINEERING, UNIVERSITY OF TOKYO. SERIES A.). [J. Fac. Eng., Univ. Tokyo Ser. A, Annu. rep.]. **Main/Corp** Tokyo Daigaku. Kogakubu. **Added/Corp** Tokyo Daigaku. Kogakubu. Kiyo. A. **VFOAT** Tokyo Daigaku Kogakubu Kiyo. P.A. No 1 (1963)-. English. Tokyo Daigaku Kogakubu, (Faculty of Engineering, University of Tokyo), 3-1, Hongo 7 Chome, Bunkyoku, Tokyoto 113 Japan. **CODEN** JETAAK. Documents available from Ask*IEEE, CASDDS, Documents on Demand. ***Continues in part*** *Tokyo Daigaku. Kogakubu. Journal of the Faculty of Engineering, University of Tokyo.*
Ind/Abst Alum. Ind. Abstr.; Chem. Abstr. (1963-1976); Ei Page One; Energy Inf. Abstr.; Energy Res. Abstr. (Mar. 1979-); Environ. Abstr.; GeoRef; INSPEC (1968-); Int. Aerosp. Abstr.; Met. Abstr.

JA/0563-7937
JOURNAL OF THE FACULTY OF ENGINEERING, UNIVERSITY OF TOKYO. SERIES B. [J. Fac. Eng., Univ. Tokyo, Ser. B]. **Main/Corp** Tokyo Daigaku. Kogakubu. **Added/Corp** Tokyo Daigaku. Kogakubu. Kiyo B. **VFOAT** Tokyo Daigaku Kogakubu Kiyo. P.B. (1964)-. Periodical. English. sa. Free on request. University of Tokyo Press, 7 3 1 Hongo Bunkyo-ku, Tokyo 113 Japan. **Tel** 011 81 3 3811 0964. **CODEN** JETBAN. Documents available from Article Express International, Ask*IEEE, CASDDS. ***Supersedes in part*** *Tokyo Daigaku. Kogakubu. Journal of the Faculty of Engineering, University of Tokyo.*
Ind/Abst Bioeng. Abstr.; Chem. Abstr.; Ei Page One; Eng. Index Annu.; GeoRef; INSPEC (1968-); Int. Aerosp. Abstr.; Int. Civil Eng. Abstr.; Math. Rev.

JA
JOURNAL OF THE ILLUMINATING ENGINEERING INSTITUTE OF JAPAN. **VFOAT** Shomei Gakkai. (19??)-. Japanese. mo. $188.00. **(Subscription address:** Kyowa Book Company, Inc., 1 38 Kanda Jinbocho Chiyoda Ku, Tokyo 101 Japan**)**

II/0019-4964
JOURNAL OF THE INDIAN INSTITUTE OF SCIENCE. **See** Science and Technology.

II
JOURNAL OF THE INDIAN INSTITUTE OF SCIENCE. SECTION A: ENGINEERING AND TECHNOLOGY. **See** Science and Technology.

UK/0269-6924
JOURNAL OF THE INSTITUTE OF REFRACTORIES ENGINEERS. [J. Inst. Refract. Eng.]. (1971)-. Periodical. English. qt. £22.50. Institute of Refractories Engineers, 15 St Benedicts Road, Wombourne West Midlands, WV5 9HP England. **Tel** 011 44 0902 894799. **ED** J. B. Traynor. **Bk Rev**, (Qty: 1). **Ad Acc. Circ:** 1,500. Documents available from BLDSC.
Ind/Abst Ceram. Abstr. (19??-).

BG/0379-4318
JOURNAL OF THE INSTITUTION OF ENGINEERS, BANGLADESH. [J. Inst. Eng., Bangladesh]. **VFOAT** Journal of the I.E.B.; Journal of the IEB. Vol. 1, No. 1 (Apr. 1973)-. Academic Scholarly Publication. English. qt. Institution of Engineers / Bangladesh, Bangladesh Headquarters, Ramna Dacca Bangladesh. **Tel** 234066. **LC** TA1; .J69. **DD** 620/.005. **CODEN** JIEBAA. Documents available from CASDDS. ***Continues in part*** *Pakistan Engineer, 0030-9753.*
Ind/Abst Chem. Abstr.

II/0257-3431
JOURNAL OF THE INSTITUTION OF ENGINEERS (INDIA). AGRICULTURAL ENGINEERING DIVISION. **See** Agriculture.

II/0970-9843
JOURNAL OF THE INSTITUTION OF ENGINEERS (INDIA). INTERDISCIPLINARY PANELS. [J. Inst. Eng., India, Interdiscip. Panels]. **Added/Corp** Institution of Engineers (India). Inter-Disciplinary Panels. **VFOAT** Interdisciplinary Panels; IE (I) Journal-IDP. Vol. 66, Pt. IDP 1 (Oct. 1985)-. Periodical. English. Twice a year. $4.00. Institution of Engineers India, 8 Gokhale Road, Calcutta 700020 India. **Tel** 011 91 33 288311, telex 21 7885 IEIC IN. **LC** TA1; .J72. **DD** 620/.005. Documents available from Ask*IEEE. ***Continues*** *Journal of the Institution of Engineers (India). Interdisciplinary & General Engineering, 0251-1118.*
Ind/Abst INSPEC (Oct. 1987-).

II/0251-110X
JOURNAL OF THE INSTITUTION OF ENGINEERS (INDIA). PART EN CALCUTTA, ENVIRONMENTAL ENGINEERING DIVISION, THE. **See** Environmental Issues.

US/0892-6298
JOURNAL OF THE INTERNATIONAL SOCIETY FOR RESPIRATORY PROTECTION. [J. Int. Soc. Respir. Prot.]. **Added/Corp** International Society for Respiratory Protection. **VFOAT** Journal of the ISRP. (198?)-. Periodical. English. qt. $65.00. International Society for Respiratory Protection, PO Box 158, Jonesborough TN 37659. **Tel** (301)838-3001. **DD** 620.

KO
JOURNAL OF THE KOREAN INSTITUTE OF SURFACE ENGINEERING. (19??)-. Korean (English). qt. W20,000 Korea; $33.00 other. Korean Institute of Surface Engineering, Korean Federation of Science and Technology, Building/Room 308, 635-4 Yeoksam-dong Kangnam-ku Seoul 135-703 Korea. **Tel** 02-563-0935/02-558-2230. **ED** K.J. Park and J.K. Han. Index available. **Bk Rev. Ad Acc. Circ:** 3,500 (ctrl).
Desc: Editorial covers surface physics and chemistry, electrochemistry, electroplating, CVD/PVD and ion beam processes, and nonmetallic coatings.

US
JOURNAL OF THE SOCIETY OF LOGISTICS ENGINEERING. English. qt (Mar., June, Sept., Dec.). $50.00 (North America); $60.00 (other) including postage. Society of Logistics Engineers, 8100 Professional Pl, Suite 211, Hyattsville MD 20785. **Tel** (301)459-8446, FAX (301)459-1522.

US
JOURNAL OF VIBRATION AND CONTROL. English. SAGE Periodical Press, 2455 Teller Road, Thousand Oaks CA 91320. **Tel** (805)499-0721, FAX (805)499-0871, telex 100799.

NE/0167-6105
JOURNAL OF WIND ENGINEERING AND INDUSTRIAL AERODYNAMICS. [J. wind eng. ind. aerodyn.]. **Added/Corp** International Association for Wind Engineering. (July 1980)-. Academic Scholarly Publication. English. Eighteen times a year (6 volumes). FI2562.00. Elsevier Science Publishers BV, PO Box 211, 1000 AE Amsterdam Netherlands. **Tel** 011 31 20 5803642, FAX 011 31 20 5862696, telex 15682. **ED** R I Harris. **LC** TA654.5; .J68. **DD** 621.4/5. **CODEN** JWEAD6. **[CCC]. Bk Rev. Ad Acc. Pr Rev.** available on microfilm and microfiche from University Microfilms International (UMI). Documents available from Article Express International, The Genuine Article, Ask*IEEE, Documents on Demand. ***Continues*** *Journal of Industrial Aerodynamics.*
Desc: Provides a means for the publication and interchange of information, on an international basis, of all those aspects of wind engineering included in the activities of the International Association for Wind Engineering.
Ind/Abst Agric. Eng. Abstr. (1991-); Bioeng. Abstr.; BMT Abstr.; Curr. Contents Eng. Tech. Appl. Sci.; Ei Page One; Energy Inf. Abstr.; Energy Res. Abstr. (May 1982-); Eng. Index Annu.; Environ. Abstr.; Fluid Abstr., Civil Eng.; Fluid Abstr. Proc. Eng.; FLUIDEX (1980-); Geogr. Abstr. Phys. Geogr.; Geogr. Abstr. Human Geogr. (?-?); Geol. Abstr.; INSPEC (July 1980-); Ornamental Hort.; Postharvest News Inf.; Res. Alert [Full Cov.]; Sci. Cit. Index; SCISEARCH.

SI/0377-7464
JOURNAL - THE INSTITUTION OF ENGINEERS, SINGAPORE. [IES j.]. **Main/Corp** Institution of Engineers, Singapore. English. qt. $3.60. Graphic Publications, 15th Floor/Selegie Complex, Singapore Singapore. **LC** TA1; .I728A. **DD** 620/.005. **CODEN** IEJOD4. Documents available from Ask*IEEE.
Ind/Abst INSPEC (Dec. 1979-).

●US
JPRS REPORT. SCIENCE & TECHNOLOGY. CENTRAL EURASIA. ENGINEERING & EQUIPMENT [MICROFORM] / FOREIGN BROADCAST INFORMATION SERVICE. **Added/Corp** United States. Foreign Broadcast Information Service. **VFOAT** Joint Publications Research Service Report. Engineering & Equipment; Science & Technology. Engineering & Equipment.; JPRS Report. Engineering and Equipment; Central Eurasia. Engineering & Equipment; Engineering & Equipment. JPRS-UEQ-92-002 (31 Jan. 1992)-. English (translations available in Russian). ***Continues*** *JPRS Report. Science & Technology. USSR. Engineering & Equipment.*

US
JPRS REPORT. SCIENCE & TECHNOLOGY. USSR. ENGINEERING & EQUIPMENT. ***Title Change.*** **Added/Corp** United States. Joint Publications Research Service. United States. Foreign Broadcast Information Service. **VFOAT** JPRS Report. Engineering and Equipment; Science & Technology. Engineering & Equipment; USSR. Engineering & Equipment; Engineering & Equipment. **VAT** Joint Publications Research Service Report. Science and Technology. Union of Soviet Socialist Republics. Engineering and Equipment. (198?)-JPRS-UEQ-92-001 2 (Jan. 1992). English (translations available in Russian). National Technical Information Service - NTIS, Room 2027S, 5285 Port Royal Road, Springfield VA 22161. **Tel** (703)487-4630, (703)487-4660, (703)487-4650, FAX (703)321-8547, telex 89-9405. **LC** Microfiche (o) 90/6273. ***Continues*** *USSR Report. Engineering and Equipment.* ***Continued by*** *JPRS Report. Science & Technology. Central Eurasia. Engineering & Equipment.*

MY/0126-513X
JURNAL INSTITUSI JURUTERA MALAYSIA. **Added/Corp** Institution of Engineers, Malaysia. **VFOAT** Journal of the Institution of Engineers, Malaysia. Vol. 34 (June 1984)-. English. sa (2 issues). 6.00Mal$ Malaysia; 10.00Mal$ other. Institution of Engineers, PO Box 223, Petaling Jaya Malaysia. **LC** TA1; .I7267. ***Continues*** *Journal of the Institution of Engineers, Malaysia, 0538-0057.*

HU/0302-8720
K.G.M.T.I. KOZLEMENYEI. [KGMTI kozl.]. **Main/Corp** Hungary. Koho- Es Gepipari Miniszterium. Tervezo Irodai. Hungarian. an. 1,000ft Hungary; $20.00 other. Koho-es Gepipari Tervezo Vallalat, Budapest I Krisztina Korut 55, Budapest 1013 Hungary. **Tel** (36-1)752-122, FAX (36-1)754-282, telex 22-4123. **ED** Istvan Havel. **LC** TN600; .H85A. available on microfilm.

JA
KAGAKU GIJUTSUCHO MUKI ZAISHITSU KENKYUJO YORAN. ***Ceased.*** **Main/Corp** Muki Zaishitsu Kenkyujo. (19??)-?. Japanese. Niihari-Gun Sakuramura, Muki Zaishitsu Kenkyujo, Tsukuba Kenkyi Gakuen Toshi 300-31, Ibaraki-ken Japan. **LC** TA417.M8; M84b.

JA
KAIGAI SEIKATSU NO TEBIKI. **Added/Corp** Nihon Denshin Denwa Kosha. Kaigai Renrakushitsu. (19??)-. Japanese. Nihon Denshin Denwa Kosha Kaigui Renrakushitsu, 1-1-6 Uchisaiwaicho Chiyoda-ku, Tokyo Japan. **LC** JV8721.Z8; K34.

JA/0287-2951
KAIJO HOAN DAIGAKKO KENKYU HOKOKU. RIKOGAKU-KEI. **See** Science and Technology.

JA/0387-0324
KANAGAWA DAIGAKU KOGAKU KOGAKU KENKYUJO SHOHO. **See** Science and Technology.

JA/0368-5381
KANAGAWA DAIGAKU KOGAKUBU KENKYU HOKOKU. [Kanagawa Daigaku Kogakubu kenkyu hokoku]. **Added/Corp** Kanagawa Daigaku. Kogakubu. **VFOAT** Reports of Faculty of Engineering, Kanagawa University. (1962)-. Japanese. an. Kangagawa University, Faculty of Engineering, 3-27 Rokkakubashi, Yokohama 221 Japan. **CODEN** KGDKBU. Documents available from CASDDS.
Ind/Abst Chem. Abstr.; Math. Rev.; Zentralbl. Math. Ihre Grenzgeb.

●II
KANCH. NEW DELHI. (1992)-. English. sa. $8.00. **(Subscription address:** Prints India, 11 Darya Ganj, New Delhi 110002 India.**)** ***Continues*** *Glass Udyog, 0379-0460.*

JA/0388-9459
KANKYO GIJUTSU. **See** Environmental Issues-Conservation and Natural Resources.

JA
KANTO GAKUIN DAIGAKU KOGAKUBU KOGAKKAI KOEN ROMBUN SHU. **Main/Corp** Kanto Gakuin Daigaku. Kogakkai. **Added/Corp** Kanto Gakuin Daigaku. Kogakubu. **VFOAT** Kanto Gakuin Daigaku Kogakubu Kenkyu Happyo Koenkai. (19??)-. Japanese. Kanto Gakuin Daigaku Kogakubu, 4834 Mutsuuracho Kanazawa-ku 236, Yokohama Japan. **LC** TA4; .K293a.

JA/0286-4215
KEIO SCIENCE AND TECHNOLOGY REPORTS. [Keio sci. technol. rep.]. **Added/Corp** Keio Gijuku Daigaku. Vol. 34, No. 1 (Sept. 1981)-. Periodical. English. Keio Gijuku Daigaku Rikogakubu, (Faculty of Science & Technology, Keio University), 14-1, Hiyoshicho 3 Chome, Kohokuku, Yokohamashi, Kanagawaken 223 Japan. **CODEN** KSTREE. Documents available from Ask*IEEE, CASDDS. ***Continues*** *Keio Engineering Reports.*
Ind/Abst Chem. Abstr.; Ei Page One; INSPEC (1984-); Int. Aerosp. Abstr.; Math. Rev. (?-1985); Zentralbl. Math. Ihre Grenzgeb.

JA
KEISOKU JIDO SEIGYO GAKKAI ROMBUNSHI. TRANSACTIONS OF THE SOCIETY OF INSTRUMENT AND CONTROL ENGINEERS. **Added/Corp** Keisoku Jido Seigyo Gakkai (Japan). **VFOAT** Transactions of the Society of Instrument and Control Engineers. Vol. 1 (March 1965)-. Monographic series. Japanese. mo. $220.00. **(Subscription address:** Kyowa Book Company Inc., 1-38 Kanda Jinbo-Cho, Chiyoda-Ku Tokyo 101, Japan**) CODEN** TSICA9.

JA/0453-4662
KEISOKU TO SEIGYO. **Added/Corp** Keisoku Jido Seigyo Gakkai (Japan). **VFOAT** Journal of the Society of Instrument and Control Engineers. (1962)-. Periodical. Japanese (summaries and/or abstracts in English). mo. $314.00. **(Subscription address:** Kyowa Book Company Inc., 1-38 Kanda Jinbo-Cho, Chiyoda-Ku Tokyo 101, Japan**) LC** WMLC L 83/5181. ***Formed by the union of*** *Keisoku* ***and*** *Jido Seigyo.*

UK/0075-5400
KEMPE'S ENGINEER'S YEAR-BOOK. (1894)-. Periodical. English. an. £99.00 UK; £109.00 other. Morgan Grampian, 40 Beresford Street Woolwich, London SE18 6BQ England. **Tel** 011 44 81 855 7777, FAX 011 44 81 855 5548, telex 896238. **(Subscription address:** Benn Business Information Services, Riverbank House Angel Lane, Tonbridge Kent TN9 1SE England.**) ED** C. Sharpe. **LC** TA151.A1; E6. Index available. **Ad Acc. Circ:** 5,200.
Desc: Classic engineering reference work.

UK/0075-5400
KEMPE'S ENGINEERS YEAR-BOOK FOR .... **VFOAT** Kempe's Engineers Year Book for .... . **VAT** Kempe's engineers year book for .... . (195?)-. English. an. Morgan Grampian, 40 Beresford Street Woolwich, London SE18 6BQ England. **Tel** 011 44 81 855 7777, FAX 011 44 81 855 5548, telex 896238. **LC** TA151.A1; E6. ***Continues*** *Engineer's Year-Book of Formulae, Rules, Tables, Data, and Memoranda in Civil, Mechanical, Electrical, Marine, and Mine Engineering.*

JA/0368-5373
KENKYU HOKOKU - KANTO GAKUIN DAIGAKU KOGAKUBU. **Main/Corp** Kanto Gakuin Daigaku Kogakubu. **VFOAT** Journal of Technological Researches of the College of Engineering, Kanto Gakuin University; Journal of Technological Researches. Academic Scholarly Publication. Japanese (summaries and/or abstracts in English). $30.00 (members), $60.00 (nonmembers). 4834 Mutsuuracho Kanazawa-ku, Yokohama 236 Japan. **LC** TA4; .K29A. **CODEN** KGDKAT. Documents available from CASDDS.
Ind/Abst Chem. Abstr.

JA/0286-0902
KENKYU HOKOKU / NAGASAKI DAIGAKU KOGAKUBU. [Nagasaki Daigaku Kogakubu kenkyu hokoku]. **VFOAT** Reports of the Faculty of Engineering, Nagasaki University; Nagasaki Daigaku Kogakubu Kenkyu Hokoku. Academic Scholarly Publication. Japanese (summaries and/or abstracts in English). ir. Nagasaki Daigaku Kogakubu, 1-ban 14-go Bunkyo-cho, Nagasaki-shi Japan. **LC** TA4; .K42. **CODEN** NDKHD2. Documents available from Ask*IEEE, CASDDS.
Ind/Abst Chem. Abstr.; INSPEC (Jan. 1984-).

US/0746-2255
KENTUCKY ENGINEER. [Ky. eng.]. **Added/Corp** Kentucky Society of Professional Engineers. Consulting Engineers Council of Kentucky. (19??)-. Periodical. English. mo (with Sept. and Oct. combined). $330.00. Kentucky Engineer, 3161 Custer Drive, Lexington KY 40502. **Tel** (602)271-1778.

KE
KENYA ENGINEER : JOURNAL OF THE INSTITUTION OF ENGINEERS OF KENYA. Periodical. English. bm. Institution of Engineers of Kenya, Mow Building, PO Box 41346, Nairobi Kenya. **LC** TA1; .K35. **DD** 620/.009676/2.

●US/1064-2145
KEY SOLUTIONS. [Key solut.]. **Added/Corp** Valve Engineering Associates. Vol. 1, No. 1 (Sept./Oct. 1992)-. Periodical. English. Six times a year. $28.95 (latest volume). Value Engineering Assoicates, PO Box 11978, Spokane WA 99211. **Tel** (509)928-5169. **LC** TS155.6; .K49. **DD** 670/.285. **CODEN** KESOE4.

JA/0386-491X
KINKI DAIGAKU KOGAKUBU KENKYU HOKOKU. [Kinki Daigaku Kogakubu kenkyu hokoku]. **Added/Corp** Kinki Daigaku. Kogakubu. **VFOAT** Research Reports of the Faculty of Engineering, Kinki University. (1966)-. Japanese (English). an. Kinki Daigaku Kogakubu, Shinaki Yasunaga Hiro-machi Kure, Hiroshima-ken 737-01 Japan. **CODEN** KDKHD3. Documents available from CASDDS.
Ind/Abst Chem. Abstr.

JA/0288-738X
KINKI DAIGAKU KYUSHU KOGAKUBU KENKYU HOKOKU. RIKOGAKU-HEN. [Kinki Daigaku Kyushu Kogakubu kenkyu hokoku. Rikogaku-hen]. **VFOAT** Reports of the Faculty of Engineering (Kyushu), Kinki University. Science and Technology Section. (1972)-. Periodical. Multiple languages. an. Kinki Daiagaku Kyushu Kogakubu, (Faculty of Engineering (Kyushu Campus), Kinki University), 11-6, Kashinomori, Iizukashi, Fukuokaken 820 Japan. **DD** 620. Documents available from CASDDS.
Ind/Abst Chem. Abstr.

JA/0286-4835
KINO ZAIRYO. [Kino zairyo]. **VFOAT** Function and Materials; Function and Material; Function & Material. (19??)-. Academic Scholarly Publication. Japanese (Japanese). mo. $612.00. Shi Emu Shi, (CMC Co., Ltd.), Miyako Biru, 5-4, Uchikanda, 1 Chome, Chiyodaku, Tokyoto 101 Japan. **(Subscription address:** Kyowa Book Company Inc., 1-38 Kanda Jinbo-Cho, Chiyoda-Ku, Tokyo 101, Japan (Phone: 03-3293-0727)**) LC** TA401; .K5. **CODEN** KIZAEP. Documents available from CASDDS.
Ind/Abst Chem. Abstr.; Eng. Mater. Abstr.

US
KLUWER INTERNATIONAL SERIES IN ENGINEERING AND COMPUTER SCIENCE, THE. (1984)-. Monographic series. English. **LC** UNC.
Ind/Abst Math. Rev. (1987-); Zentralbl. Math. Ihre Grenzgeb.

JA/0452-2311
KOATSU GASU. (KOATSU GASU / KOATSU GASU HOAN KYOKAI.). [Koatsu gasu]. **Added/Corp** Koatsu Gasu Hoan Kyokai. **VFOAT** Journal of the Institution for Safety of High Pressure Gas Engineering. Vol. 1, No. 1 (Sept. 1964)-. Japanese. Jitsugyo Koho Sha, Tokyo Japan. **CODEN** KOGAA2. Documents available from CASDDS. ***Continues*** *Koatsu Gasu Kyokaishi.*
Ind/Abst Chem. Abstr.

JA/0452-2834
KOGYO ZAIRYO. [Kogyo Zairyo]. **VFOAT** Engineering Materials. (1943)-. Periodical. Japanese. mo.

Engineering

$240.00. Nikkan Kogyo Shinbunsha, (Nikkan Kogyo Shinbun, Ltd.), 8-10, Kudan Kita 1 Chome, Chiyodaku, Tokyoto 102, Japan. **(Subscription address:** Maruzen Company Ltd., PO Box 5050, Import & Export Department, Tokyo 100 31 Japan.**) LC** TA401; .K85. **CODEN** KZAIA5. Documents available from CASDDS.
Ind/Abst Chem. Abstr.

KO
KONGHAK NONJIP. Added/Corp Koryo Taehakkyo. Kongkwa Taehak. **VFOAT** Journal of Engineering Science and Technology. (19??)-. Periodical. Korean (summaries and/or abstracts in English). Koryo Taehakkyo Kongkwa Taehak, Koryo Taehakkyo Chulpanbu 1, 5-ka Anam-dong, Songbuk-ku, Seoul Korea. **LC** TA4; .K5945. **CODEN** KONOEF. Documents available from CASDDS.
Ind/Abst Chem. Abstr.

●KO
KONGHAK YON'GU POGO. [Gondai nyengu bogo, Senur daihaggyo]. **Main/Corp** Soul Taehakkyo. Kongkwa Taehak. **Added/Corp** Soul Taehakkyo. Kongkwa Taehak. **VFOAT** Journal of Engineering Research; Soul Taehakkyo Kongkwa Haksul Nonmunjip; Soul Taehakkyo Konghak Yongu Pogo. (1993)-. Periodical. Korean (English). sa. Soul Taehakkyo Kongkwa Taehak / Chung Ryang, Chung Ryang, PO Box 105, Seoul 131 South Korea. **LC** T4; .S7127a. **DD** 620/.005. Documents available from CASDDS.
Continues Soul Taehakkyo. Kongkwa Taehak. Kongdae Yongu Pogo, 0253-3049.
Ind/Abst Chem. Abstr. (?-?); Energy Res. Abstr. (Sept. 1980-?).

CC/1000-8152
KONGZHI LILUN YU YINGYONG. (KUNG CHIH LI LUN YU YING YUNG.). [Kongzhi lilun yu yingyong]. **Added/Corp** Hua Nan Kung Hsueh Yuan. Chung-Kuo Ko Hsueh Yuan. Hsi Tung Ko Hsueh Yen Chiu So. **VFOAT** Control Theory & Applications; Control Theory and Applications. (Jan. 1984)-. Academic Scholarly Publication. Chinese (summaries and/or abstracts in English). bm. Zhongguo Kexueyuan / Xitong Kexue Yanjiusuo, Chinese Academy of Sciences, Institute of System Science, Huanan Ligong Daxue, Guangzhou, Guangdong 510641 People's Republic of China. **Tel** 20 7111464. **ED** Li Botian. **LC** QA402.3; .K763. **DD** 629.8/312. **CODEN** KLYYEB. Documents available from Article Express International.
Ind/Abst Ei Page One; Eng. Index Annu. [Select. Cov.]; Math. Rev. (1984-).

KO/0023-4052
KOREAN SCIENTIFIC ABSTRACTS. See Science and Technology.

SW
KOY. KORROSION OCH YTSKYDD. VFOAT Korrosion Och Ytskydd. (19??)-. Periodical. Swedish (summaries and/or abstracts in English). ir. Reed Business Publishing / West Sussex, England, Perrymount Road, Haywards Heath, West Sussex RH16 3DH England. **Tel** 011 44 81 6523500. **LC** TA418.74; .K18.

CC
KUO LI CHUNG HSING TA HSUEH LI KUNG HSUEH PAO / KUO LI CHUNG HSING TA HSUEH LI KUNG HSUEH PAO PIEN CHI WEI YUAN HUI. See Science and Technology.

CH/0404-5360
KUO LI TAI-WAN TA HSUEH KUNG CHENG HSUEH KAN. Main/Corp Tai-Wan Ta Hsueh, Tai-Pei. Kung Hsueh Yuan. **Added/Corp** Tai-Wan Ta Hsueh, Tai-Pei. Kung Hsueh Yuan. Bulletin Kuo Li Tai-Wan Ta Hsueh Kung Ko Li Tai-Wan Ta Hsueh Kung Cheng Hsueh Kan. **VFOAT** Bulletin of the College of Engineering, National Taiwan University. No. 1 (1956)-. Chinese (English). an. National Taiwan University / College of Engineering, Taipei, Taiwan. **LC** TA4; .T3. Documents available from CASDDS.
Ind/Abst Chem. Abstr.

JA
KURASHI NO TECHO. (1953)-. Periodical. Japanese. Six times a year (Jan., Mar., May, July, Sept., Nov.). $90.50 California; $93.50 elsewhere US; $107.00 Europe; $119.00 Asia; $95.00 other. **(Subscription address:** Kinokuniya Book Stores of America, 1581 Webster Street, San Francisco CA 94115.**) Continues** Utsukushii Kurashi no Techo.

JA/0388-1717
KYUSHU DAIGAKU DAIGAKUIN SOGO RIKOGAKU KENKYUKA HOKOKU. Added/Corp Kyushu Daigaku. Daigakuin. Kyushu Daigaku. Sogo Rikogaku Kenkyuka. **VFOAT** Engineering Sciences Reports, Kyushu University; Kyushu Daigaku Sogorikogaku Kenkyuka Hokoku; Sogo Rikogaku Hokoku. (19??)-. Academic Scholarly Publication. Japanese (summaries and/or abstracts in English). qt. Kyushu Daigaku Daigakuin Sogo Rikogaku Kenkyuka, 1-Banchi, Kasuga Koen 6-Chome, Kasuga-shi, Fukuoka 816 Japan. **LC** IN PROCESS. Documents available from CASDDS.
Ind/Abst Chem. Abstr.

JA/0023-2718
KYUSHU DAIGAKU KOGAKU SHUHO. [Kyushu Daigaku kogaku shuho]. **Added/Corp** Kyushu Daigaku. Kogakubu. **VFOAT** Technology Reports of the Kyushu University. (1952)-. Periodical. Japanese. bm. Kyushu Daigaku, (Faculty of Engineering, Kyushu University), 10-1, Hakozaki 6 Chome, Higashiku, Fukuokashi, Fukuokaken 812 Japan. **CODEN** KDKSAX. Documents available from Ask*IEEE, CASDDS.
Continues Kyushu Daigaku Kogaku Iho.
Ind/Abst Chem. Abstr.; Coal Abstr.; INSPEC (Aug. 1971-); Int. Aerosp. Abstr.

JA/0911-9485
KYUSHU KYORITSU DAIGAKU KENKYU HOKOKU. KOGAKUBU. [Kyushu Kyoritsu Daigaku kenkyu hokoku. Kogakubu]. **VFOAT** Bulletin of Kyushu Kyoritsu University. Faculty of Engineering; Bulletin of Faculty of Engineering, Kyushu Kyoritsu University. (1976)-. Periodical. Multiple languages. an. Kyushu Kyoritsu Daigaku, (Faculty of Engineering, Kyushu Kyoritsu University), 1-8, Orio Jiyugaoka, Yawata Nishiku, Kitakyushushi, Fukuokakend 807, Japan. **DD** 620. Documents available from CASDDS.
Ind/Abst Chem. Abstr.

JA/0286-7826
KYUSHU SANGYO DAIGAKU KOGAKUBU KENKYU HOKOKU. [Kyushu Sangyo Daigaku Kogakubu kenkyu hokoku]. **VFOAT** Bulletin of the Faculty of Engineering, Kyushu Sangyo. Began in 1964. Academic Scholarly Publication. Japanese (summaries and/or abstracts in English). Kyushu Sangyo Daigaku, 327-banchi Matsukadai 2-chome Higashi-ku, Fukuoka-shi 813 Japan. **LC** TA4 /B .K84. **CODEN** KSDKDE. Documents available from CASDDS.
Ind/Abst Chem. Abstr.

JA/0286-4002
KYUSHU TOKAI DAIGAKU KIYO. KOGAKUBU. [Kyushu Tokai Daigaku kiyo. Kogakubu]. **Added/Corp** Kyushu Tokai Daigaku. Kogakubu. **VFOAT** Bulletin of Faculty of Engineering, Kyushu Tokai University; Kyushu Tokai Daigaku Kogakubu Kiyo. (1980)-. Japanese (English). Kyushu Tokai Daigaku, Nogakubu Nawayo, Choyo-mura, Aso-Gun, Kumamoto-ken 869-14 Japan. **LC** TA4; .K85. **CODEN** KTDKEM. Documents available from Ask*IEEE.
Continues in part Kyushu Tokai Daigaku Kiyo.
Ind/Abst INSPEC (1986-).

SZ
LABORSCOPE. (19??)-. Trade Publication. English. bm. 47.00F. Verlag Binkert AG, Baslerstrasse 15, CH-4335 Laufenburg Switzerland. **Tel** 011 41 64 697272, FAX 011 41 64 697333. **Ad Acc.** ctrl circ.
Desc: Trade journal for laboratory and process engineering.

US/0898-1507
LASERS IN ENGINEERING. [Lasers eng.]. Vol. 1, No. 1 (1991)-. Periodical. English. qt. $339.00 (academic institutions), $529.00 (corporate institutions). Gordon & Breach Science Publishers, Inc., PO Box 786, Cooper Station, New York NY 10276. **Tel** (212)206-8900, FAX (212)645-2459. **(Subscription address:** International Publishers Distributor at one of the following addresses: 820 Town Center Drive, Langhorne, PA 19047; or PO Box 90, Reading Berkshire RG1 8JL UK; or Kent Ridge PO Box 1180, Singapore 9111, Republic of Singapore**) LC** IN PROCESS. **DD** 621. **CODEN** LAENEG. **[CCC].**

CN/0704-5689
LAVALIN. Main/Corp Lavalin Inc. Nov. 1976-. Periodical. French. mo. Free. Lavalin Inc, Suite 1526, 1130 Sherbrooke Street West, Montreal Quebec H3A 2R5. **Tel** (514)876-4455. **DD** 620/.006/271. ctrl circ.

CN/0227-7964
LAVALIN (ENGLISH EDITION). (LAVALIN.). **Main/Corp** Lavalin Inc. Mar. 1979-. Periodical. English. mo. Free. Lavalin Inc, Suite 1526, 1130 Sherbrooke Street West, Montreal Quebec H3A 2R5. **Tel** (514)876-4455. **DD** 620/.006/071. ctrl circ.

US/0176-5035
LECTURE NOTES IN ENGINEERING. [Lect. notes eng.]. 1-. Monographic series. English. ir. Price varies per volume. Springer-Verlag New York Inc., 175 5th Avenue, New York NY 10010. **Tel** (212)460-1500, telex 232 235 SPB UR. **(Subscription address:** Springer Verlag New York Inc. / for North America, 44 Hartz Way, Secaucus NJ 07096.**) CODEN** LNENE5. Documents available from Article Express International, Ask*IEEE.
Ind/Abst Ei Page One; Eng. Index Annu.; GeoRef; INSPEC (1986); Math. Rev.; Zentralbl. Math. Ihre Grenzgeb.

CN/1186-7043
LEMOYNE-TILLY 735-KV LINE. [Lemoyne-Tilly 735-kV line]. **Added/Corp** Hydro-Quebec. **VAT** Lemoyne-Tilly Seven Hundred Thirty Five-Kilovolts Line. No. 1 (Feb. 1990)-. Periodical. English. Hydro-Quebec, 14E Etage, 75 Ouest Boul Dorchester, Montreal Quebec H2Z 1A4 Canada. **DD** 333.79.

US
LETTERS, EI. Added/Corp Engineering Information, Inc. **VFOAT** Engineering Information Letters. Vol. 1, No. 1 (1991)-. Periodical. English. qt. Engineering Information Inc., Castle Point on the Hudson, Hoboken NJ 07030. **Tel** (800)221-1044, (201)216-8500, FAX (201)216-8526, telex 4990438. **CODEN** EILEE3.
Continues Notes & Comment.

AT/0810-5669
LOCAL GOVERNMENT ENGINEERS ASSOCIATION OF NEW SOUTH WALES JOURNAL. (1982)-. English. qt (Feb., May, Aug., Nov.). 25.00Aus$. Institute Municipal Eng/New South Wales Division, 215-217 Clarence Street 7th floor, Sydney, New South Wales, 2000 Australia. **Tel** 011 61 2 2996200.

US/0898-8625
LOCOMOTIVE ENGINEER NEWSLETTER, THE. See Transportation-Railroads.

US/0024-6794
LOUISIANA ENGINEER. Periodical. English. bm. Louisiana Engineering Society, Box 2683, Baton Rouge LA 70821.

UK/0954-0075
LUBRICATION SCIENCE. [Lubr. sci.]. (1988)-. English. qt. $185.00, £105.00. Leaf Coppin Publishing Ltd., 6 Coppin Street, Subscription Department, Deal Kent CT14 6JL England. **Tel** 011 44 304 360241. **DD** 621.89. **[CCC].** Documents available from Article Express International, CASDDS.
Ind/Abst Chem. Abstr.; Ei Page One; Eng. Index Annu.; Fluid Abstr., Civil Eng.; Fluid Abstr. Proc. Eng.; FLUIDEX (19??-); Lit. Pat. Abstr., Oilfield Chem. (1991-); Lit. Abstr., Catal. Catal.; Lit. Abstr., Health Environ.; Lit. Abstr., Pet. Refin. Petrochem.; Lit. Abstr., Pet. Substit.; Lit. Abstr., Transp. Storage.

●US/1048-8693
LYCEUM TECHNICAL JOURNAL. (1992)-. Periodical. English. bm. $139.00. Lyceum Engineering Technologies, Inc., PO Box 668, Franklin MI 48025.

II
MAGAZINE - COLLEGE OF ENGINEERING, TRIVANDRUM, INDIA. Main/Corp College of Engineering, Trivandrum, India. Multiple languages (English and Malayalam). Rs5.00. University of Kerala College of Engineering, Trivandrum 695581 India. **LC** TA1; .T88A. **DD** 620/.005.

FR/1154-6433
MAINTENANCE & ENTREPRISE PARIS. (MAINTENANCE & ENTREPRISE.). **VFOAT** Maintenance et Entreprise (Paris). (1991)-. Periodical. French. mo (11 issues). 381.98F France; 630.00F other. Edipresse, 16 rue Guillaume Tell, 75017 Paris France. **Tel** 011 33 1 47660005 ext. 246. **UDC** 62. **Formed by the union of** Maintenance (Paris), 0025-0880 **and** Equipement Industriel, Achats et Entretien, 0396-6666.

UK/0953-2110
MAINTENANCE FARNHAM. (MAINTENANCE.). [MaintenanceFarnham]. (1986)-. Periodical. English. Five times a year (Jan., March, June, Sep., Dec.). £42.00 UK; £49.00 Europe; £59.00 other. IBE Conferences Ltd, Monks Hill, Tilford Farnham, Surrey GU10 2AJ England. **Tel** 44 252 783111, FAX 44 252 783143. **ED** John Harris, David Wilson Tony Kelly. **DD** 658.202. **Bk Rev. Ad Acc. Circ:** 1,000. **Continues** Maintenance News.
Desc: Quarterly journal for all those concerned with the maintenance and servicing of physical assets.

US/0890-1775
MAINTENANCE (NEWSLETTER FOR PROFESSIONAL TRUCK EQUIPMENT MANAGERS). See Transportation.

US/0890-1767
MAINTENANCE : THE NEWSLETTER FOR PROFESSIONAL TRUCK EQUIPMENT EXECUTIVES. See Transportation.

CN/0025-2271
MANITOBA PROFESSIONAL ENGINEER. (THE MANITOBA PROFESSIONAL ENGINEER.). **Added/Corp** Association of Professional Engineers of the Province of Manitoba. Vol. 1 (July 1956)-. Periodical. English. Association Professional Engineer Manitoba, 530 330 Saint Mary Avenue, Winnipeg Manitoba R3C 3Z5 Canada. **Tel** (204)942-6481.

US/1063-7354
MANUFACTURING AND PROCESS ENGINEERING ABSTRACTS. ***Ceased.*** **See** Environmental Issues-Abstracting, Bibliographies and Statistics.

UK/0956-9944
MANUFACTURING ENGINEER. (MANUFACTURING ENGINEER : ME.). **Added/Corp** Institution of Producation Engineers (Great Britain). **VFOAT** ME; M.E. Vol. 68, No. 5 (May 1989)-. Periodical. English. Six times a year. £83.00 EEC countries; £92.00 other. Institution of Electrical Engineers / IEE, Michael Faraday House, Six Hills Way, Stevenage Herts SG1 2AY UK. **Tel** 011 44 438 313311, FAX 011 44 438 742840, telex 825578 IEESTV G. **(Subscription address:** IEE / UK, Publications Sales Department, PO Box 96, Stevenage, Herts, SG1 2SD England.**)** **ED** Ron Hewit. **DD** 338. **CODEN** MFENES. Index available (bound in Dec. issue). **Bk Rev. Ad Acc. Circ:** 20,000. available on microfilm and microfiche from University Microfilms International (UMI). ***Continues*** *Production Engineer, 0032-9851.*
Ind/Abst Ei Page One.

US/0361-0853
MANUFACTURING ENGINEERING. [Manuf. eng.]. **Added/Corp** Society of Manufacturing Engineers. Vol. 75, No. 2 (Aug. 1975)-. Periodical. English. mo. $75.00 US companies and libraries; $80.00 Canada and Mexico companies and libraries; $90.00 (sea mail), $170.00 (airmail) other. Society of Manufacturing Engineers, One SME Drive, PO Box 930, Member's Records Dept., Dearborn MI 48121-0930. **Tel** (313)271-1500, FAX (313)271-2861, telex 297742 SME UR (VIA RCA). **LC** TJ1180.A1; A6. **DD** 670/.5. **CODEN** MAENDQ. **[CCC].** available on microfilm and microfiche from University Microfilms International (UMI). Documents available from Article Express International, The Genuine Article, Ask*IEEE, UMI Article Clearinghouse. ***Continues*** *Manufacturing Engineering & Management, 0040-9219.*
Ind/Abst ABI/INFORM Glob. Ed.; ABI Inform Ondisc (Jan. 1988-); Alum. Ind. Abstr.; Appl. Sci. Technol. Index; Bioeng. Abstr.; Ceram. Abstr.; Comput. Lit. Index; Curr. Contents Eng. Tech. Appl. Sci.; Ei Page One; Eng. Mater. Abstr.; Eng. Index Annu.; Health Saf. Sci. Abstr.; INSPEC (1987-); Leadscan; Met. Abstr.; Oper. Res./Manag. Sci.; Qual. Control Appl. Stat.; Res. Alert [Select. Cov.]; Robotics Abstr.; SCISEARCH; Soc. Sci. Cit. Index [Select. Cov.].

US
MANUFACTURING ENGINEERING AND MATERIALS PROCESSING. (1977)-. Monographic series. English. Price varies per volume. Marcel Dekker Inc., 270 Madison Avenue, New York NY 10016. **Tel** (212)696-9000, (800)228-1160, FAX (212)685-4540, telex 421419. **(Subscription address:** Marcel Dekker Inc, PO Box 5017, Monticello NY 12701.**)** **LC** UNC.
Desc: Topics include computers in manufacturing, cold rolling of steel, and adhesives in manufacturing.

CN/0824-734X
MARINE ENGINEERING DIGEST. ***Suspended.*** (MARINE ENGINEERING DIGEST / THE CANADIAN INSTITUTE OF MARINE ENGINEERS.). [Mar. eng. dig.]. Vol. 1, No. 1 (July 1981)-?. Periodical. English (French). qt. 15.00Can$ North America; 30.00Can$ other. Marine Media Ltd, Suite 706/116 Albert Street, Ottawa Ontario K1P 5G3 Canada. **Tel** (613)234-3374, FAX (613)234-4039. **ED** H Arnsdorf. **DD** 623.8/7/0971. Index available. **Bk Rev. Ad Acc. Circ:** 3,100 (ctrl).
Desc: This maritime journal interests those associated with the seas, oceans and inland waterways and their use be it in design, construction, operation, maintenance, repair or support of vessels and waterborne structures and their equipments. It also contains editorial opinion, timely items of national/international interest and learned papers.

●US/1064-119X
MARINE GEORESOURCES & GEOTECHNOLOGY. [Mar. georesour. geotechnol.]. **VFOAT** Marine Georesources and Geotechnology. (1993)-. Academic Scholarly Publication. English. qt. £90.00 UK; $149.00 other. Taylor & Francis Ltd., Rankine Road, Basingstoke Hampshire, RG24 8PR United Kingdom. **Tel** 011 44 256 840366, FAX 011 44 256 479438, telex 858540. **(Subscription address:** Taylor & Francis Inc., 1900 Frost Road, Suite 101, Bristol PA 19007-1598.**)** **ED** Ronald C. Chaney and J. Robert Moore. **DD** 551. **CODEN** MGGEEI. Documents available from BIOSIS Document Express, Petroleum Abstracts Document Delivery Service, CASDDS, Documents on Demand. ***Formed by the union of*** *Marine Mining, 0149-0397* ***and*** *Marine Geotechnology, 0360-8867.*
Desc: Publishes research devoted to all scientific, georesource management and utilization, and engineering aspects of seafloor sediment and rocks. The journal is intended for researchers and engineers, in both academia and industry, who seek solutions to marine problems in civil engineering and the earth sciences. Includes contributions on such topics as shipboard mining systems, seafloor lodes and placers, pipelines, platforms, and transportation, as well as analytical techniques related to marine mining. Case studies will also be featured.
Ind/Abst Biol. Abstr.; Chem. Abstr.; Curr. Contents Phys. Chem. Sci.; Electron. Commun. Abstr. J.; Energy Inf. Abstr.; Environ. Abstr.; GeoRef; ISMEC Bull.; MINPROC; Mintec, Min. Technol. Abstr.; Life Sci. Collect.; Pet. Abstr.; Pollut. Abstr. Indexes; Saf. Sci. Abstr. J.; Sci. Cit. Index; Ship Abstr.

GW/0025-4509
MASCHINENMARKT. (MASCHINENMARKT : M.M.). [Maschinenmarkt]. **VFOAT** M.M.; MM. Vol. 1 (1895)-. Academic Scholarly Publication. German. wk. DM275.00 Germany; DM350.00 other. Vogel Verlag, Postfach 6740, D-97064 Wuerzburg Germany. **Tel** 011 49 931 4182145, 011 49 931 4182483, FAX 011 49 931 4182670, telex 841 680131. Documents available from Ask*IEEE.
Ind/Abst Alum. Ind. Abstr.; EMBASE; Energy Res. Abstr. (1971-); Fluid Abstr., Civil Eng.; Fluid Abstr. Proc. Eng.; FLUIDEX (19??-); INSPEC (1968-); Met. Abstr.

GW/0025-5270
MATERIAL UND ORGANISMEN. [Mater. Org.]. **VFOAT** Materials and Organisms; Materiaux et Organismes. (1965)-. Periodical. German (summaries and/or abstracts in English, French and Spanish). qt. DM384.40 Europe; DM398.40 other. Duncker und Humblot Verlag, Postfach 410329, D-12113 Berlin Germany. **Tel** 011 49 30 79000612, 011 49 30 79000613. **LC** TA418.74; .M37a. **CODEN** MTOGAF. **[CCC].**

US
MATERIALS ENGINEERING SERIES. Monographic series. English. ir. Price varies per volume. Marcel Dekker Inc., 270 Madison Avenue, New York NY 10016. **Tel** (212)696-9000, (800)228-1160, FAX (212)685-4540, telex 421419. **(Subscription address:** Marcel Dekker Inc, PO Box 5017, Monticello NY 12701.**)**
Desc: Topics covered have included adhesive bonding of aluminum alloys and thermal analysis of ceramics.

AT/0883-2900
MATERIALS FORUM. [Mater. forum]. **Added/Corp** Institute of Metals and Materials Australasia. Australian Ceramic Society. Vol. 9, No. 1 & 2 (1986)-. Academic Scholarly Publication. English. an. 200.00Aus$. Institute of Metals and Materials Australasia, PO Box 19, Parkville Victoria 3052 Australia. **Tel** 011 61 03 3472544, FAX 011 61 03 3481208. **ED** B. C. Muddle (editor's address: Dept. Materials Engineering, Monash University, Wellington Rd, Clayton VIC 3168). **LC** TN1; .A934. **DD** 669. **CODEN** MFOREM. **[CCC].** Index available. cum. index. **Bk Rev. Ad Acc. Acid Free. Circ:** 2,000. available on microfilm and microfiche from University Microfilms International (UMI). Documents available from Ask*IEEE, CASDDS. ***Continues*** *Metals Forum, 0160-7952.*
Desc: Publishes original research papers and review articles concerned with the science and technology of engineering materials. Short communications are published to offer authors rapid publication of exciting developments.
Ind/Abst Ceram. Abstr.; Chem. Abstr. (1986-); INSPEC (1987-); Leadscan.

SZ/0928-4931
MATERIALS SCIENCE & ENGINEERING. C, BIOMIMETIC MATERIALS, SENSORS AND SYSTEMS. Volume C1 (1993)-. English. Four times a year (1 volume). 340.00F; 8190.00F combined subscription with Materials Science and Engineering A & B, and Materials Science and Engineering Reports. Elsevier Sequoia SA, PO Box 564, CH-1001 Lausanne 1 Switzerland. **Tel** 011 41 21 3207381. **ED** D. DeRossi, P. Calvert, T. Tateishi. **[CCC].** Documents available from Article Express International, Ask*IEEE.
Desc: Reports on scientific and technical contributions dealing with all aspects of conceiving, designing, constructing and testing man-made materials, structures, devices and systems which replicate or are inspired by biological entities and processes.
Ind/Abst Eng. Mater. Abstr.; Eng. Index Annu.; Fluid Abstr., Civil Eng.; Fluid Abstr. Proc. Eng.; FLUIDEX; INSPEC (Aug. 1988-); Met. Abstr.; Surf. Treat. Technol. Abstr.

SZ/0927-796X
MATERIALS SCIENCE AND ENGINEERING : R-REPORTS. **VFOAT** Materials Science and Engineering. R, Reports; Reports. Vol. 10, Nos. 1-2 (July 1, 1993)-. Periodical. English. Sixteen times a year (2 volumes). 680.00F; 8190.00F combined subscription with Materials Science and Engineering A, B, and C. Elsevier Sequoia SA, PO Box 564, CH-1001 Lausanne 1 Switzerland. **Tel** 011 41 21 3207381. **ED** S.S. Lau, F.W. Saris. **LC** TA401; .M3846. **[CCC].** Documents available from Ask*IEEE. ***Continues*** *Materials Science Reports, 0920-2307.*
Desc: Publishes invited review papers covering the full spectrum of materials science and engineering. The reviews, both experimental and theoretical, provide general background information as well as assessments on topics in a state of flux.
Ind/Abst Eng. Mater. Abstr.; Index Sci. Rev.; INSPEC; Met. Abstr.; Res. Alert; Sci. Cit. Index; SCISEARCH.

NE/0166-6010
MATERIALS SCIENCE MONOGRAPHS. [Mater. sci. monogr.]. (1978)-. Monographic series. English. ir. Price varies per volume. Elsevier Science Publishers BV, PO Box 211, 1000 AE Amsterdam Netherlands. **Tel** 011 31 20 5803642, FAX 011 31 20 5862696, telex 15682. **(Subscription address:** Elsevier Science Inc. / New York Books, 655 Avenue of the Americas, New York NY 10010.**)** **CODEN** MSMODP. Documents available from BIOSIS Document Express, Ask*IEEE, CASDDS.
Ind/Abst Biol. Abstr. (1986-); Ceram. Abstr. (19??-); Chem. Abstr.; Ei Page One; GeoRef; INSPEC.

NE/0169-121X
MATHEMATICAL ENGINEERING IN INDUSTRY. **See** Mathematics.

GW/0170-4214
MATHEMATICAL METHODS IN THE APPLIED SCIENCES. **See** Mathematics.

US/0076-5392
MATHEMATICS IN SCIENCE AND ENGINEERING. **See** Mathematics.

US/0932-4194
MATHEMATICS OF CONTROL, SIGNALS, AND SYSTEMS : MCSS. [MCSS, Math. control signals syst.]. **VFOAT** MCSS. Vol. 1, No. 1 (1988)-. Periodical. English. Three times a year. £130.00. Springer-Verlag London Ltd., Springer House, 8 Alexandra Road Wimbledon, London SW19 7JZ England. **Tel** 011 44 81 9471280, or 9475885, FAX 011 44 81 9474651, telex 21531 SPRGB G. **(Subscription address:** North America: Springer Verlag, Journal Fulfillment Department, 44 Hartz Way, Secaucus, NJ 07096; Outside North America: Springer Verlag, Postfach 311340, D 10643 Berlin Germany**)** **ED** B W Dickinson and E D Sontag. **LC** QA402.3; .M3483. **DD** 629.8/312/05. **[CCC].** available on microfilm and microfiche from University Microfilms International (UMI). Documents available from Article Express International, The Genuine Article, Ask*IEEE.
Desc: An international interdisciplinary journal on mathematical problems in engineering. Covers areas of mathematical system theory, control theory and signal processing, etc.
Ind/Abst Compumath Citation Index [Full Cov.]; Curr. Contents Eng. Tech. Appl. Sci.; Ei Page One; Eng. Index Annu.; INSPEC (1989-); Math. Rev. (1988-); Res. Alert [Full Cov.]; SCISEARCH; Zentralbl. Math. Ihre Grenzgeb.

US/0271-1982
MATHEMATICS OF FINITE ELEMENTS AND APPLICATIONS, THE. **See** Mathematics.

US/0161-5106
MCGRAW-HILL ENGINEERING ADVANCEMENT. **VFOAT** Engineering Advancement. V. 1- Sept./Oct. 1978-. Periodical. English. bm. $36.00. McGraw Hill Publishing Company, Inc., 1221 Avenue of the Americas, New York NY 10020. **Tel** (212)512-6410, (800)525-5003, FAX (212)512-6111. **LC** TA1; .M1815A. **DD** 620/.005.

US
MEASURING & CONTROL DEVICES. (19??)-. English. mo. $225.00. Predicasts Inc., A Ziff Communications Company, 11001 Cedar Avenue, Cleveland OH 44106. **Tel** (800)321-6388, (216)795-3000, FAX (216)229-9944, telex 985 604. **(Subscription address:** Information Access Company, PO Box 61000, Department 1851, San Francisco, CA 94161; Phone: (800)321-6388**)**

US
MECHANICAL PARTS/LABOR ESTIMATING GUIDE. TRANSMISSION. **VFOAT** Transmission; Mitchell Mechanical Parts/Labor Estimating Guide. Transmission. (1986)-. English. an. $155.00. Mitchell International Inc, PO Box 26260, San Diego CA 92126-0260. **Tel** (619)578-6550, (800)648-8010, FAX (619)578-4752. **LC** TL262; .T73. **DD** 629.2/44/029473. ***Continues*** *Transmission Mechanical Parts/Labor Estimating Guide, 0884-4658.*

NE
MECHANICS OF SURFACE STRUCTURES. (1975)-. Monographic series. English. ir. Price varies per volume. Sijthoff & Noordhoff International Publishers BV, PO Box 4, Alphen an der Rijn Leyden Netherlands.
Ind/Abst Math. Rev. (1987-); Zentralbl. Math. Ihre Grenzgeb.

NE/0924-3992
MECHATRONIC SYSTEMS ENGINEERING. ***Title Change.*** **See** Computers-Automation.

SW/0368-3419
MEDDELANDE - JORDBRUKSTEKNISKA INSTITUTET. **See** Agriculture.

PK/0254-7821
MEHRAN UNIVERSITY RESEARCH JOURNAL OF ENGINEERING AND TECHNOLOGY. [Mehran Univ. res. j. eng. technol.]. **Added/Corp** Mehran University of Engineering and Technology. **VFOAT** Research Journal of Engineering and Technology. (1982)-. Periodical. English. qt. Mehran University, Jamshoro, Sind, Pakistan. **CODEN** MURTDB. Documents available from Ask*IEEE.
Ind/Abst Concr. Abstr.; Ei Page One; INSPEC (July 1982-).

JA/0388-130X
MEISEI DAIGAKU KENKYU KIYO. RIKO GAKUBU. **See** Science and Technology.

RU/0202-1927
MEKHANIZATSIIA I ELEKTRIFIKASIIA SEL'SKOGO KHOZIAISTVA. **Added/Corp** Ukraine. Ministerstvo Sil's'koho Hospodarstva. (19??)-. Periodical. Russian. Agropromizdat, Sadovo-Spasskaia, 18, 107807 Moscow Russia.
Ind/Abst Postharvest News Inf.

JA/0082-4747
MEMOIRS OF FACULTY OF TECHNOLOGY, TOKYO METROPOLITAN UNIVERSITY. [Mem. Fac. Technol., Tokyo Metrop. Univ.]. **Main/Corp** Tokyo Toritsu Daigaku. Kogakubu. No. 1 (1951)-. English. an. **LC** TA7; .T6. **DD** 620.82. **CODEN** MTTMAO. Documents available from CASDDS.
Ind/Abst Chem. Abstr.

JA/0475-0071
MEMOIRS OF THE FACULTY OF ENGINEERING. **Added/Corp** Okayama Daigaku. Keogakubu. Vol. 22 (Mar. 1988)-. Academic Scholarly Publication. English. an. Okayama University / School of Engineering, Okayama 700 Japan. **CODEN** MFEUEF. Documents available from CASDDS. ***Continues*** *Memoirs of the School of Engineering, Okayama University.*
Ind/Abst Chem. Abstr.

JA/0073-2311
MEMOIRS OF THE FACULTY OF ENGINEERING, HIROSHIMA UNIVERSITY. [Mem. Fac. Eng., Hiroshima Univ.]. **VFOAT** Hiroshima Daigaku Kogakubu Obun Kiyo. (1957)-. Periodical. English. an. Hiroshima University / Engineering, Faculty of Engineering, Hiroshima Japan. **DD** 607/.11764/847. **CODEN** MFEHA6. Documents available from Ask*IEEE.
Ind/Abst INSPEC (Jan. 1970-); Math. Rev.; SEA Abstr.

JA/0368-9379
MEMOIRS OF THE FACULTY OF ENGINEERING, HOKKAIDO UNIVERSITY. **Main/Corp** Hokkaido Daigaku. Kogakubu. (1926)-. English (French and German). Hokkaido University Faculty of Engineering, North 13 West 8, Sapporo Japan. **CODEN** MEHUAJ. cum. index. Documents available from Article Express International, Ask*IEEE, CASDDS.
Ind/Abst Alum. Ind. Abstr.; Bioeng. Abstr.; Chem. Abstr.; Coal Abstr.; Ei Page One; Eng. Index Annu.; INSPEC (1968-); Int. Aerosp. Abstr. (1984-); Met. Abstr.

JA/0368-9638
MEMOIRS OF THE FACULTY OF ENGINEERING, KOBE UNIVERSITY. [Mem. Fac. Eng., Kobe Univ.]. **Main/Corp** Kobe Daigaku. Kogakubu. **VFOAT** Kobe Daigaku Kogakubu Kenkyu Hokoku. Began in 1950. English. Dean of the Faculty of Engineering, Kobe University, Rokkodai-cho Nada-ku, Kobe Japan. **LC** TA1; .K64A. **DD** 620/.005. **CODEN** MFEKAF. Documents available from Article Express International, Ask*IEEE, CASDDS.
Ind/Abst Bioeng. Abstr.; Chem. Abstr.; Ei Page One; Energy Inf. Abstr.; Eng. Mater. Abstr.; Eng. Index Annu.; INSPEC (1969-).

JA/0023-5334
MEMOIRS OF THE FACULTY OF ENGINEERING, KUMAMOTO UNIVERSITY. [Mem. Fac. Eng., Kumamoto Univ.]. **Main/Corp** Kumamoto Daigaku. Kogakubu. **Added/Corp** Kumamoto Daigaku. Kogakubu. Kiyo. **VFOAT** Kumamoto Daigaku Kogakubu Kiyo. Vol. 1 (March 1954)-. English. Kumamoto Daigaku Kogakubu, (Faculty of Engineering, Kumamoto University), 39-1, Kurokami 2 Chome, Kumamotoshi, Kumamotoken 860, Japan. **CODEN** MEKMAA. Documents available from Ask*IEEE.
Ind/Abst Energy Inf. Abstr.; INSPEC (Dec. 1968-).

JA/0023-6063
MEMOIRS OF THE FACULTY OF ENGINEERING, KYOTO UNIVERSITY. [Mem. Fac. Eng., Kyoto Univ.]. **Main/Corp** Kyoto Daigaku. Kogakubu. (1949)-. Academic Scholarly Publication. English. qt. Kyoto University / Faculty of Science, Yoshida Honmachi Sakyo Ku, Kyotoshi Kyotofu 606 Japan. **Tel** (075)751-2111, telex 5422693 LIBKYU J. **CODEN** MEKYAC. Documents available from Article Express International, Ask*IEEE, CASDDS. ***Continues*** *Memoirs of the College of Engineering, Kyoto Imperial University, 0368-9425.*
Ind/Abst Alum. Ind. Abstr.; Bioeng. Abstr.; Chem. Abstr.; Ei Page One; EMBASE; Eng. Index Annu.; FLUIDEX (1973-); GeoRef; INSPEC (1968-); Int. Aerosp. Abstr.; Math. Rev.; Met. Abstr.

JA/0023-6160
MEMOIRS OF THE FACULTY OF ENGINEERING KYUSHU UNIVERSITY. [Mem. Fac. Eng. Kyushu Univ.]. **Added/Corp** KyushÂu Daigaku. (1943)-. Periodical. English. Kyushu Daigaku Kogakubu, (Faculty of Engineering, Kyushu University), 10-1, Hakozaki 6 Chome, Higashiku, Fukuokashi, Fukuokaken 812 Japan. **CODEN** MEKSAS. Documents available from Article Express International, Ask*IEEE, CASDDS.
Ind/Abst Alum. Ind. Abstr.; Bioeng. Abstr.; Chem. Abstr.; Civ. Struct. Eng. Abstr.; Comput. Inf. Syst. Abstr. J. [Full Cov.]; Curr. Biotechnol.; Ei Page One; Eng. Index Annu.; INSPEC (1968-); Int. Aerosp. Abstr.; Mech. Eng. Abstr.; Met. Abstr.

JA/0027-7657
MEMOIRS OF THE FACULTY OF ENGINEERING, NAGOYA UNIVERSITY. [Mem. Fac. Eng., Nagoya Univ.]. **Main/Corp** Nagoya Daigaku. Kogakubu. **Added/Corp** Nagoya Daigaku. Kogakubu. **VFOAT** Memoirs of the School of Engineering, Nagoya University; Nagoya Daigaku Kogakubu Kiyo. Vol. 1 (April 1949)-. Periodical. English. sa. Nagoya Daigaku Kogakubu, (Faculty of Engineering, Nagoya University), Furocho, Chikusaku, Nagoyashi, Aichiken 464, Japan. **LC** TA4; .N27. **CODEN** MENAAN. Documents available from Article Express International, Ask*IEEE, CASDDS.
Ind/Abst Bioeng. Abstr.; Chem. Abstr.; Ei Page One; Eng. Index Annu.; FLUIDEX (1973-); INSPEC (1968-); Int. Aerosp. Abstr.

JA/0078-6659
MEMOIRS OF THE FACULTY OF ENGINEERING, OSAKA CITY UNIVERSITY. [Mem. Fac. Eng., Osaka City Univ.]. **Main/Corp** Osaka Shiritsu Daigaku. Kogakubu. Vol. 1 (Dec. 1959)-. Periodical. English. an. Free upon request. Osaka City University, Faculty of Engineering, 3 138 Sugimoto 3 Chome, Osaka 558 Japan. **LC** TA7; .O77. **DD** 620/.005. **CODEN** MFEOAR. Documents available from CASDDS.
Ind/Abst Chem. Abstr.

JA/0369-1950
MEMOIRS OF THE SCHOOL OF SCIENCE AND ENGINEERING. WASEDA UNIVERSITY. (MEMOIRS.). [Mem. Sch. Sci. Eng., Waseda Univ.]. **Main/Corp** Waseda Daigaku, Tokyo. Rikogakubu. **Added/Corp** Waseda Daigaku. Riko Gakubu. **VFOAT** Memoirs of the Faculty of Science and Engineering, Waseda University; Memoirs of the School of Science and Engineering, Waseda University; Waseda Daigaku Riko Gakubu Kiyo. No. 1 (1922)-. Periodical. English (Japanese). an. Waseda University, Institute of Comparative Law-647 Totsuka, Shinjuku-ku Tokyo 16 Japan. **Tel** 011 81 3 203 2034141. **LC** T4; .W32. **CODEN** MSEWA6. Documents available from Ask*IEEE, CASDDS. ***Continues*** *Waseda Daigaku Riko Gakubu Kiyo.*
Ind/Abst Alum. Ind. Abstr.; Chem. Abstr.; Coal Abstr.; Ei Page One; INSPEC (1983-); Math. Rev.; Met. Abstr.; Zentralbl. Math. Ihre Grenzgeb.

UK/0047-5955
MER. MARINE ENGINEERS REVIEW. (MARINE ENGINEERS REVIEW.). [MER, Mar. eng. rev.]. **Added/Corp** Institute of Marine Engineers. (Jan. 1971)-. Periodical. English. mo. $110.00 (surface mail), $170.00 (airmial) US. Marine Management Holdings Ltd, Memorial Building, 76 Mark Lane, London EC3R 7JN England. **Tel** 011 44 71 4818493. **(Subscription address:** North America: Learned Information Inc., 143 Old Marlton Pike, Medford, NJ 08055-8750**)** **LC** VM1; .M32. **DD** 623.8/05. **CODEN** MRERBJ. **[CCC]**. Index available. cum. index. **Bk Rev. Ad Acc. Circ:** 16,000. Documents available from Article Express International.
Desc: Covers all aspects of marine engineering, from ship and machinery design to off shore structures, use of equipment, regulations, engines, fuel, safety, buildings, systems, communications, procedures, and new ideas.
Ind/Abst Alum. Ind. Abstr.; Aquat. Sci. Fish. Abstr. (Computer File); Bioeng. Abstr.; BMT Abstr.; Curr. Technol. Index; Ei Page One; EMBASE; Eng. Index Annu.; Fluid Abstr., Civil Eng.; Fluid Abstr. Proc. Eng.; FLUIDEX (1973-); Lit. Pat. Abstr., Oilfield Chem. (1972-); Lit. Abstr., Catal. Catal.; Lit. Abstr., Health Environ.; Lit. Abstr., Pet. Refin. Petrochem.; Lit. Abstr., Pet. Substit.; Lit. Abstr., Transp. Storage; Met. Abstr.; Ocean. Abstr.; Life Sci. Collect.; Pollut. Abstr. Indexes; Shock Vibr. Dig.

GW/0937-3446
MESSEN & PRUFEN (1990). **VFOAT** Messen und Prufen (1990); Messen & Prufen (Munchen). (1990)-. Periodical. German. mo. DM167.14. Iva Intl Ges Intern Kommunika, Kistlerhofstrasse 119, W 8000 Munich 70 Germany. **Tel** 49 89 788032, or 788037. **UDC** 53.08. **CODEN** 620.16. ***Continues*** *Messen, Prufen, Automatisiern, 0177-7297.*
Ind/Abst Fluid Abstr., Civil Eng.; Fluid Abstr. Proc. Eng.; FLUIDEX (19??-).

FR/0755-219X
MESURES (PARIS, FRANCE : 1983). (MESURES.). [Mesures]. Vol. 48, No. 1 (Jan. 24, 1983)-. Academic Scholarly Publication. French. Fifteen times a year. 656.22F France; 797.00F other. Groupe Tests, 26 Rue d'Oradour sur Glane, 75504 Paris Cedex 15 France. **Tel** 011 33 1 44253131. **LC** T2; .M48. **DD** 620/.0044. Documents available from Ask*IEEE. ***Continues*** *Mesures, Regulation, Automatisme.*
Ind/Abst Alum. Ind. Abstr.; EMBASE; Eng. Mater. Abstr.; INSPEC (May 1983-); Met. Abstr.

JA/0911-9647
METALWORKING, ENGINEERING AND MARKETING. **See** Metals and Metallurgy.

FR/1152-0647
METHODES ET TECHNIQUES DE L'INGENIEUR PARIS. (METHODES ET TECHNIQUES DE L'INGENIEUR.). **VFOAT** Methodes et Pratiques de l'Ingenieur (Paris); Collection Methodes et Pratiques de l'Ingenieur; Collection Methodes et Techniques de l'Ingenieur. (1990)-. Monographic series. French. Price varies per volume. **UDC** 62.002.
Ind/Abst Zentralbl. Math. Ihre Grenzgeb.

GW/0173-752X
METHODS OF OPERATIONS RESEARCH (1980). (METHODS OF OPERATIONS RESEARCH.). [Methods oper. res.]. Vol. 36 (Oct. 1978)-. Monographic series. English (German). ir. price varies per volume. Verlag Anton Hain Athenaeum, Wormer Strasse 99, D 55294 Bodenheim Germany. **Tel** 011 49 6135 3057. Documents available from Ask*IEEE. ***Continues*** *Operations Research-Verfahren. Methods of Operations Research, 0078-5318.*
Ind/Abst INSPEC (1980-); Int. Abstr. Oper. Res. [Select. Cov.]; Math. Rev.; Zentralbl. Math. Ihre Grenzgeb.

US/1054-5840
MICHIGAN PROFESSIONAL ENGINEER (1990). (MICHIGAN PROFESSIONAL ENGINEER : OFFICIAL PUBLICATION OF THE MICHIGAN SOCIETY OF PROFESSIONAL ENGINEERS.). **Added/Corp** Michigan Society of Professional Engineers. Vol. 42, No. 7 (Sept. 1990)-. Periodical. English. Nine times a year. $35.00. Michigan Society of Professional Engineers, 215 North Walnut Street, Lansing MI 48933. **Tel** (517)487-9388, FAX (517)487-0635. **ED** Nancy A. Carpenter. **Ad Acc, Adv Mgr:** Jim Hagerty, **Tel** (414)466-0610. **Circ:** 2,500 (ctrl). ***Continues*** *Professional Engineer.*

US/1050-0324
MIDNIGHT ENGINEERING. (MIDNIGHT ENGINEERING : THE JOURNAL OF PERSONAL PRODUCT DEVELOPMENT.). [Midnight eng.]. Vol. 1, No. 1 (Jan./Feb. 1990). Periodical. English. bm. $24.00. Midnight Engineering, 111 East Drake Road, Suite 7041. **Tel** (303)491-9092. **LC** QA76.76.D47; M53. **DD** 005.1.
Desc: Engineering magazine for the individual developing and marketing high tech products. Covers hardware/software engineering and small business from the garage to a million in sales.
Ind/Abst ACM Guide Comput. Lit.; Comput. Rev.

US/0026-3370
MIDWEST ENGINEER. **Added/Corp** Western Society of Engineers (Chicago, Ill.) Western Society of Engineers (Chicago, Ill.). Yearbook. Vol. 1, (Sept. 1948)-. Periodical. English. Five times a year (Jan., Mar., May, Sept., Nov.). $15.00 US & Canada; $20.00 other. Western Society of Engineers, 176 West Adams Street, Midland Building, Chicago IL 60603. **Tel** (312)372-3760, FAX (312)372-3761. **ED** James Kepler. **LC** TA1; .M6835. **DD** 620.5. cum. index. **Ad Acc. Circ:** 1,000 (ctrl). available on microfilm and microfiche from University Microfilms International (UMI). ***Supersedes*** *Journal of the Western Society of Engineers, 0096-3585.*
Ind/Abst Ceram. Abstr.

US/0026-3982
MILITARY ENGINEER, THE. [Mil. eng.]. **Added/Corp** Society of American Military Engineers. Vol. 12, No. 61 (Jan./Feb. 1920)-. Academic Scholarly Publication. English. Six times a year. $46.00 US; $54.00 other. Society of American Military Engineers, 607 Prince Street, Century House, PO Box 21289, Alexandria VA 22314. **Tel** (703)549-3800, (800)336-3097. **ED** John J. Kern. **LC** TA1; .P85. **DD** 623. **Ad Acc. Circ:** 30,000. Documents available from Article Express International. ***Continues*** *Professional Memoirs, Corps of Engineers, United States Army and Engineer Department at Large.*
Desc: Engineering, technical and managerial information to keep abreast of civil and military engineering to improve communication between engineers and

architects in civil and military practice.
Ind/Abst Air Univ. Libr. Index Mil. Period.; Bibliogr. Carto.; Bioeng. Abstr.; Coal Abstr.; Concr. Abstr.; Ei Page One; EMBASE; Energy Res. Abstr. (Sept. 1975-); Eng. Index Annu.; GeoRef; Highw. Res. Abstr.; Int. Aerosp. Abstr.

GW/0341-1893
MINERALOLTECHNIK. **See** Earth Sciences-Mineralogy.

US/0884-1829
MINORITY ENGINEER : ME, THE. [Minor. eng.]. **VFOAT** ME. (198?)-. Periodical. English. Four times a year (March, April, Sept., Dec.). $17.00 (1 year), $33.00 (2 year), $48.00 (3 year); $30.00 (1 year), $55.00 (2 year), $75.00 (3 year) combined with Woman Engineer. Equal Opportunity Publications Inc, 150 Motor Parkway Suite 420, Hauppage NY 11788. **Tel** (516)273-0066, FAX (516)273-8936. **ED** James Schneider, Anne Kelly. **LC** TA157; .M52. **DD** 620/.0023/73. **Bk Rev. Ad Acc. Circ:** 16,000 (ctrl).
Desc: An affirmative action recruitment magazine serving graduating and professional minority engineers (black, hispanic, native american and Asian American) career areas: scientific, engineering and systems positions in business, industry, armed forces and government.

JA/0026-6825
MITSUI ZOSEN GIHO. **VFOAT** Mitsui Technical Review; Mitsui Zosen Technical Review. (1952)-. Academic Scholarly Publication. Japanese (summaries and/or abstracts in English). Three times a year. Free on request. Mitsui Engineering and Shipbuilding Company Ltd, 6-4 Tsukiji 5-Chomechuo Ku, Tokyo 104 Japan. **CODEN** MIZGAR. cum. index. Documents available from Ask*IEEE, CASDDS.
Ind/Abst BMT Abstr.; Chem. Abstr.; Coal Abstr.; INSPEC (1970-).

JA/0540-4932
MIYAZAKI DAIGAKU KOGAKUBU KENKYU HOKOKU. [Miyazaki Daigaku Kogakubu kenkyu hokoku]. **Added/Corp** Miyazaki Daigaku. Kogakubu. **VFOAT** Bulletin of the Faculty of Engineering, Miyazaki University. (1955)-. Japanese (summaries and/or abstracts in English). an. Miyazaki Daigaku Kogakubu, (Faculty of Engineering, Miyazaki University), 7710, Kumano, Miyazakishi, Miyazakiken 889-21 Japan. **CODEN** MDKHAM. Documents available from CASDDS.
Ind/Abst Chem. Abstr.

NE/0925-5125
MOLECULAR ENGINEERING. Vol. 1 No. 1 (1991)-. Academic Scholarly Publication. English. qt. $416.00. Kluwer Academic Publishers, Postbus 322, 3300 AH Dordrecht, The Netherlands. **Tel** 011 (31) 78 524400, FAX 011 31 78 183273, telex 20083. **NLM** W1; MO196GL. **CODEN** MOLEEV. **[CCC].** available on microfilm and microfiche from University Microfilms International (UMI). Documents available from CASDDS.
Ind/Abst Chem. Abstr.

US/0899-5834
MORE POWER. (POWER.). [More power]. **VFOAT** Power Magazine; More Power Magazine; More Power. (Apr. 1989)-. Periodical. English. qt. $9.99. Power, PO Box 6068, Syracuse NY 13217. **DD** 629.

US/1060-488X
MORRISON ENVIRONMENTAL DIRECTORY. [Morrison environ. dir.]. **VFOAT** Environmental Directory. (1991)-. Directory. English. Morrison Environmental Directory, Inc., 226 North Emporia, Suite A, Wichita KS 67202. **LC** TD23; .M67. **DD** 628/.025/73.

CH/1010-2744
MRL BULLETIN OF RESEARCH AND DEVELOPMENT. (MRL BULLETIN OF RESEARCH AND DEVELOPMENT / MATERIALS RESEARCH LABORATORIES, INDUSTRIAL TECHNOLOGY RESEARCH INSTITUTE, TAIWAN, REPUBLIC OF CHINA.). [MRL bull. res. dev.]. **Added/Corp** Kung Yeh Chi Shu Yen Chiu Yuan. Kung Yeh Tsai Liao Yen Chiu So. **VFOAT** Bulletin of Research and Development; Tsai Yen Hsueh Kan. **VAT** Materials Research Laboratory Bulletin of Research and Development. Vol. 1, No. 1 (Mar. 1987)-. Academic Scholarly Publication. English (summaries and/or abstracts in Chinese). sa. **LC** TA404.2; .M75. **DD** 620.1/1. **CODEN** MBRDEZ. Documents available from Article Express International, Ask*IEEE, CASDDS.
Ind/Abst Ceram. Abstr. (19??-); Chem. Abstr.; Ei Page One; Eng. Index Annu.; INSPEC (1989-); Int. Aerosp. Abstr.

UK
MULTIHULL INTERNATIONAL. (1992)-. English. Twelve times a year. £20.00 UK; £26.00 other; $52.00 US. Chandler Publications Ltd, 10 South Street, Totnes Devon TQ9 5DZ England. **Tel** 0803 864668, FAX 0803 805049, telex 42928. **ED** Jack R. D. Heming. Index available. **Bk Rev. Ad Acc. Circ:** 6,500 (ctrl).
Desc: The only monthly magazine in the world devoted entirely to news and views of multihulls, from dinghies to ships, cruising and racing, design and construction.

UK/0957-4484
NANOTECHNOLOGY (BRISTOL). (NANOTECHNOLOGY.). [Nanotechnology]. **Added/Corp** American Institute of Physics. Vol. 1, No. 1 (July 1990)-. Periodical. English. qt (January, April, July and October). $258.00. Institute of Physics, Techno House, Redcliffe Way, Bristol BS1 6NX England. **Tel** 011 44 272 297481, FAX 011 44 272 294318, telex 449149 INSTP G. **(Subscription address:** American Institute of Physics, Publishing Sales, 500 Sunnyside Blvd., Woodbury NY 11797.) **ED** E C Teague. **LC** T174.7; .N37. **DD** 620/.4. **CODEN** NNOTER. **[CCC].** Index available in last issue of volume--attached. available on microfiche. Documents available from Article Express International, Ask*IEEE.
Desc: Aimed at promoting the dissemination of research and improving understanding amongst the engineering, fabrication, optics, electronics, materials science, biological and medical communities.
Ind/Abst Ei Page One; Eng. Index Annu.; INSPEC (July 1990-).

AT/0313-6922
NATIONAL CONFERENCE PUBLICATION - INSTITUTION OF ENGINEERS, AUSTRALIA. [Natl. conf. pub. - Inst. Eng. Aust.]. **Main/Corp** Institution of Engineers, Australia. **VFOAT** National Conference Publication. (1973)-. Academic Scholarly Publication. English. ir. Price varies per volume. Engineers Australia Pty Ltd, 2 Ernest Street, Crows Nest Centre, Crows Nest New South Wales 2065, Australia. **Tel** 011 61 2 438-1533, FAX 011 61 2 438-5934, telex 27640. **(Subscription address:** Accent Publications SVC Inc., 911 Silver Spring Avenue, Suite 202, Silver Spring, MD 20910, telephone: (301)588-5496) **DD** 551.47. **CODEN** NPIEDX. Documents available from Article Express International, CASDDS.
Ind/Abst Bioeng. Abstr.; Chem. Abstr. (1973-1979); Ei Page One; Eng. Index Annu.; GeoRef.

US/0738-1670
NATIONAL DEVELOPMENT. MIDDLE EAST/AFRICA. **See** Building and Construction.

US/0027-9218
NATIONAL ENGINEER, THE. [Natl. eng.]. **Added/Corp** National Association of Power Engineers (U.S.) National Association of Stationary Engineers (U.S.) National Association of Power Engineers (U.S.) N.A.P.E. Official Directory. Vol. 1 (Jan. 1897)-. Periodical. English. Twelve times a year. $23.40 US; $32.50 Mexico & Canada. National Association of Power Engineers, 5-7 Springfield Street, Chicopee MA 01013. **Tel** (413)592-6273, FAX (413)592-1998. **ED** William Judd, (editor's address: 1 Springfield Street, Chicopee, MA 01013). **LC** TJ1; .N2. **DD** 621. **CODEN** NAENAY. **Bk Rev. Ad Acc. Circ:** 5,000. Documents available from Article Express International, CASDDS.
Desc: Current developments in the field of power and plant technology, use of new techniques and equipment, fuels and combustion, and new information on plant safety.
Ind/Abst Bioeng. Abstr.; Chem. Abstr. (1897-1983); Coal Abstr.; Ei Page One; EMBASE; Eng. Index Annu. [Select. Cov.].

US
NATIONAL PATTERNS OF R&D RESOURCES. **See** Science and Technology.

SI
NATIONAL SURVEY OF ENGINEERING MANPOWER. **See** Economics-Labor.

UK/1351-3249
NATURAL LANGUAGE ENGINEERING. **See** Computers.

RU/0540-9691
NAUCHNYE TRUDY / MOSKOVSKII LESOTEKHNICHESKII INSTITUT. **See** Forestry.

US/0199-8994
NCEE REGISTRATION BULLETIN. **Main/Corp** National Council of Engineering Examiners. **Added/Corp** National Council of Engineering Examiners. **VFOAT** Registration Bulletin. **VAT** National Council of Engineering Examiners Registration Bulletin. (19??)-. Periodical. English. Five times a year. National Council of Engineering Examiners, PO Drawer 1686, Clemson SC 29633. **Tel** (803)654-6824. **ED** Barbara Robinson. **LC** WMLC L 83/8415. **Circ:** 4,000 (ctrl).
Desc: A newsletter for engineers.

UK/0963-8695
NDT & E INTERNATIONAL : INDEPENDENT NONDESTRUCTIVE TESTING AND EVALUATION. **VFOAT** NDT and E International. **VAT** Non-Destructive Testing and Evaluation International. Vol. 24, No. 2 (Apr. 1991)-. Academic Scholarly Publication. English. Six times a year. $261.00 The Americas; £175.00 other. Butterworth Heinemann Publishers, Linacre House, Jordan Hill, Oxford OX2 8DP England. **Tel** 011 44 865 310366. **(Subscription address:** Elsevier Science Ltd. Oxford Fulfillment Centre, PO Box 800, Kidlington, Oxford OX5 1DX United Kingdom.) **LC** TA417.2; .N65. **DD** 620.1/127/05. **CODEN** NDTIEH. Documents available from Article Express International, The Genuine Article, Ask*IEEE, CASDDS. ***Continues** NDT International, 0308-9126.*
Ind/Abst Abstr. Bull. Inst. Pap. Sci. Tech.; Alum. Ind. Abstr.; Bioeng. Abstr.; Chem. Abstr.; Coal Abstr.; Curr. Contents Eng. Tech. Appl. Sci.; Ei Page One; Eng. Index Annu.; INSPEC (April 1991-); Int. Aerosp. Abstr.; Met. Abstr.; Res. Alert [Full Cov.]; Sci. Cit. Index; SCISEARCH.

US/0739-697X
NEAS. NEWSLETTER OF ENGINEERING ANALYSIS SOFTWARE. [Newsl. eng. anal. softw.]. **VFOAT** Newsletter of Engineering Analysis Software. (19??)-. Newsletter. English. Twelve times a year. $205.00. Frank Maga & Associates, PO Box 2435, Sepulveda CA 91343. **Tel** (818)994-5179, FAX (818)994-6385. **ED** Frank Maga. **Bk Rev. Circ:** 5,000 (ctrl).
Desc: Abstracts of computer software, hardware, and methods in structures and structural mechanics and dynamics. Contains book reviews and comprehensive calendar of events worldwide.

JA
NENPO (KENSETSU KOGYO KENKYU SHINKOKAI). (NENPO / ANNUAL REPORT OF SOCIETY FOR THE PROMOTION OF CONSTRUCTION ENGINEERING. KENSETSU KOGYO KENKYU SHINKOKAI.). [Nenpo - Kensetsu Kogyo Kenkyu Shinkokai]. **Added/Corp** Kensetsu Kogyo Kenkyu Shinkokai (Japan). **VFOAT** Annual Report of Society for the Promotion of Construction Engineering. (1965)-. Academic Scholarly Publication. Japanese. an. Kensetsy Kogyo Kenkyu, Shinkokai Kitame-Machi 4-6, Sendai-shi 980 Japan. **CODEN** KKNMDE. Documents available from CASDDS.
Ind/Abst Chem. Abstr. (1965-1983).

PK
NESPAK PRICE INDEX : ESCALATION OF PRICES OF CONSTRUCTION INDUSTRY INPUTS. **VFOAT** Price Index. Began with issue for July 1974. English. sa. National Engineering Services, 417 Wapda House, PO Box 1351, Lahore Pakistan. **LC** HD9715.8.P18; N47. **DD** 338.4/3624/095491.

US/0047-9454
NEVADA ENGINEER, THE. Periodical. English. qt. Free to members of NSP-ASCE, $1.00 others. Jay Publishing, 445 Wright Way, Sparks NV 89431.

US/0047-9632
NEW ENGINEER. [New eng.]. Began with Oct. 1971 issue. Periodical. English. bm. Free to students, faculty and recent alumni of accredited engineering schools; $12.00 US; $14.00 other. New Engineer, 730 Third Avenue, New York NY 10017. **LC** TA1; .N34. **DD** 620/.005. available on microfilm and microfiche from University Microfilms International (UMI).
Ind/Abst Int. Aerosp. Abstr.

US/0274-6484
NEW ENGLAND ENGINEERING JOURNAL. V. 6- 1978-. Periodical. English. mo. $2.00. J Chisholm Associates, 14 Lakeside Ofc Pk, PO Box 289, Wakefield MA 01880. **Tel** (617)245-7070. ***Formed by the union of** Engineering Societies of New England. Journal **and** Massachusetts Professional Engineer.*

US/0149-1954
NEW MEXICO PROFESSIONAL ENGINEER (1977). (NEW MEXICO PROFESSIONAL ENGINEER.). **Added/Corp** New Mexico Society of Professional Engineers. Vol. 29, No. 2 (Feb. 1977)-. Periodical. English. Twelve times a year. $10.00. New Mexico Professional, 1615 University Boulevard NE, Albuquerque NM 87102. **Tel** (505)247-9181. **ED** Kate Warder. **LC** TA24.N6; N4. **DD** 620/.006/2789. **Bk Rev. Circ:** 800 (ctrl). ***Continues** New Mexico Engineer, 0148-463X.*
Desc: Intrasociety communication; articles of interest to the New Mexico engineering community.

US/0028-7458
NEW YORK PROFESSIONAL ENGINEER. **Added/Corp** New York State Society of Professional Engineers. Vol. 1 (1944)-. Periodical. English. Ten times a year. $2.00 members, $4.00 nonmembers. New York State Society of Professional Engineers, 150 State Street, Albany NY 12207. **Tel** (518)465-7386. **LC** TA1; .N38.

NZ/0028-808X
NEW ZEALAND ENGINEERING. [N.Z. eng.]. (1946)-. English. mo. 45.00NZ$ New Zealand; 60.00NZ$ other. Engineering Publications Company Ltd, PO Box 12241, Wellington New Zealand. **Tel** 011 64 4 739444, FAX 011 64 4 4732324. **ED** Peter King. **LC** TA1; .N44. **DD** 620.62931. **CODEN** NZENA5. **[CCC].** Index available (included in Feb. and Mar. issues). **Ad Acc, Adv Mgr:** Jackie Enright, **Tel** 011 64 4952399. **Circ:** 6,139 (ctrl). Documents available from Ask*IEEE.
Desc: Professional engineering.

Ind/Abst Alum. Ind. Abstr.; Ei Page One; Energy Res. Abstr. (April 1976-); Eng. Mater. Abstr.; Fluid Abstr., Civil Eng.; Fluid Abstr. Proc. Eng.; FLUIDEX (1973-); Health Saf. Sci. Abstr.; INSPEC (1968-); Int. Civil Eng. Abstr.; Met. Abstr.; Pollut. Abstr. Indexes; Soft. Abstr. Eng.

US/0028-9205
NEWS IN ENGINEERING. [News eng.]. **Added/Corp** Ohio State University. Engineering Experiment Station. Vol. 26, No. 2 (April 1954)-. Academic Scholarly Publication. English. bm. Free on request. Ohio State University / News in Engineering, 025 Hitchcock Hall, 27D Neil Avenue, Columbus OH 43210. **CODEN** NEEOAV. Documents available from CASDDS. ***Continues*** *Engineering Experiment Station News, 0097-5028.*
Ind/Abst Chem. Abstr.

JA/0285-6174
NIHON DAIGAKU KOGAKUBU KIYO. BUNRUI A. [Nihon Daigaku Kogakubu kiyo, Bunrui A, Kogaku-hen]. **VFOAT** Journal of the College of Engineering of Nihon University. Series A. Academic Scholarly Publication. Japanese (English). an. Nihon Daigaku Kogakubu, Tamura-cho Koriyama-shi, Fukushima-ken 9 Japan. **LC** TA4; .48. **CODEN** NDKADF. Documents available from CASDDS. ***Continues*** *Nihon Daigaku Kogakubu Kiyo. Dai 1-Shu, Kogaku Hen.*
Ind/Abst Chem. Abstr.; Eng. Mater. Abstr.

JA/0285-6182
NIHON DAIGAKU KOGAKUBU KIYO. BUNRUI B, IPPAN KYOIKU HEN. [Nihon Daigaku Kogakubu kiyo. Bunrui B, Ippan kyoiku hen]. **VFOAT** Journal of the College of Engineering, Nihon University. Series B. Periodical. English (Japanese; summaries and/or abstracts in German, Japanese and English). an. Hihon Daigaku Kogakubu, Tamura-cho Koriyama-shi, Fukushima-ken 9 Japan. **LC** AS552.K695; A35. ***Continues*** *Nihon Daigaku Kogakubu Kiyo. Dai 2-shu, Japan Kyoiku Hen.*
Ind/Abst Math. Rev.

JA
NIHON HAKUYO KIKAN GAKKAI SHI. JOURNAL OF THE MARINE ENGINEERING SOCIETY IN JAPAN. **Main/Corp** Nihon Hakuyo Kikan Gakkai. **Added/Corp** Nihon Hakuyo Kikan Gakkai. Journal of the Marine Engineering Society in Japan. **VFOAT** Journal of the Marine Engineering Society in Japan. (19??)-. Academic Scholarly Publication. Japanese (summaries and/or abstracts in English). mo. $500.00. Nihon Hakuyo Kikan Gakkai, c/o Osaoa Building, 2-Gokan Chiyoda-ku 2-2 Uchisaiwaicho 1, Tokyo Japan. **Tel** 03-503-5518. **(Subscription address:** Kyowa Book Company Inc., 1-38 Kanda Jinbo-Cho, Chiyoda-Ku Tokyo 101, Japan) **ED** M. Endo. **LC** VM595; .N53a. **CODEN** NHGADN. Index available. cum. index. **Bk Rev. Ad Acc. Circ:** 3,000 (ctrl). Documents available from CASDDS.
Desc: The purpose of the society is to strive for the advancement of marine engineering by investigating marine machinery and ocean machinery.
Ind/Abst Chem. Abstr.; Coal Abstr.

JA/0546-0794
NIHON KASAI GAKKAI RONBUNSHU. **VFOAT** Bulletin of Japanese Association of Fire Science and Engineering. Academic Scholarly Publication. Japanese. Nihon Kasai Gakkai, (Japanese Assoc. of Fire Science & Engineering), Gakkai Senta Biru, 4-16, Yayo 2 Chome, Bunkyoku, Tokyoto 113 Japan. **CODEN** NGKRAG. Documents available from CASDDS.
Ind/Abst Chem. Abstr.

JA
NIHON KAZE KOGAKKAI SHI. **Added/Corp** Nihon Kaze Kogakkai. **VFOAT** JWE; J.W.E.; Journal of Wind Engineering. (19??)-. Japanese (English). qt. ¥10000 Japan; $70.00 US. Nihon Kaze Kogakkai, c/o Business Center for Academic Societies Japan, 4-16 Yayoi 2-chome Bunkyo-ku, Tokyo 113 Japan. **Tel** 03-817-5801. **ED** Shuzo Murakami. **LC** TA654.5; N54. **Bk Rev. Ad Acc. Circ:** 350. Documents available from Documents on Demand.
Desc: Photo-graviure, technical papers, short reports and announcements from the Association.
Ind/Abst Energy Inf. Abstr.; Environ. Abstr.

JA
NIHON ROBOTTO GAKKAI. ROBOTTO SHINPOJUMU YOKOSHU / ROBOTICS SOCIETY OF JAPAN. PREPRINTS OF ROBOTICS SYMPOSIUM. (1991)-. Japanese (English). an. Nihon Robotto Gakkai, 15-4 Hongo 1-chome, Bunkyo-ku, Tokyo, 113 Japan.

JA/0374-4345
NIIGATA DAIGAKU KOGAKUBU KENKYU HOKOKU. [Niigata Daigaku Kogakubu kenkyu hokoku]. **Added/Corp** Niigata Daigaku. Kogakubu. **VFOAT** Reports of the Faculty of Engineering, Niigata University. (1952)-. Japanese (English). an. Niigata Daigaku Kogakubu, (Faculty of Engineering, Niigata University), 8050, Igarashi Ninocho, Niigatashi, Niigataken 950-21, Japan. **CODEN** NDKHAX. Documents available from CASDDS.
Ind/Abst Chem. Abstr.

JA/0286-2743
NIIHAMA KOGYO KOTO SENMON GAKKO KIYO. RIKOGAKU HEN. **See** Science and Technology.

JA/0287-0029
NOGYO DOBOKU SHIKENJO GIHO. HE, SUIKO. **See** Agriculture.

AT/0157-6461
NON-DESTRUCTIVE TESTING - AUSTRALIA. (NON-DESTRUCTIVE TESTING, AUSTRALIA.). [Non-destr. test. - Aust.]. **Added/Corp** Australian Institute for Non-destructive Testing. Vol. 13, No. 1/2 (Jan./Feb. 1976)-. Periodical. English. bm. 65.00Aus$. Australian Institute for Non-Destructive Testing, 71 73 Flemington Road Ndt Aust, North Mel Vic 3051 Australia. **Tel** 011 61 3 3291633, FAX 011 61 3 890 4490, telex 883 1604. **ED** Gary G. Martin. **LC** TA417.2; .T47. **DD** 620.1/127/05. **CODEN** NTAUDZ. cum. index. **Bk Rev. Ad Acc. Circ:** 1,000 (ctrl). Documents available from Article Express International. ***Continues*** *Testing, Instruments & Controls.*
Desc: Technical papers on Non-Destructive Testing Institute news, industry news, book reviews, latest literature, aerospace notes, new products, international news and conference reviews.
Ind/Abst Acoust. Abstr.; Alum. Ind. Abstr.; Bioeng. Abstr.; Ei Page One; Eng. Mater. Abstr.; Eng. Index Annu.; Met. Abstr.

US/0730-7152
NONDESTRUCTIVE TESTING MONOGRAPHS AND TRACTS. [Nondestr. test. monogr. tracts]. Vol. 1 (1982)-. Monographic series. English. ir. Price varies per volume. Gordon & Breach Science Publishers, Inc., PO Box 786, Cooper Station, New York NY 10276. **Tel** (212)206-8900, FAX (212)645-2459. **(Subscription address:** International Publishers Distributor at one of the following addresses: 820 Town Center Drive, Langhorne, PA 19047; or PO Box 90, Reading Berkshire RG1 8JL UK; or Kent Ridge PO Box 1180, Singapore 9111, Republic of Singapore)

NE/0924-090X
NONLINEAR DYNAMICS. [Nonlinear dyn.]. Vol. 1, No. 1 (1990)-. Periodical. English. Eight times a year. $960.00. Kluwer Academic Publishers, Postbus 322, 3300 AH Dordrecht, The Netherlands. **Tel** 011 (31) 78 524400, FAX 011 31 78 183273, telex 20083. **ED** A.H. Nayfeh. **CODEN** NODYES. **[CCC]. Pr Rev. Acid Free.** available on microfilm and microfiche from University Microfilms International (UMI). Documents available from Article Express International, Ask*IEEE.
Desc: The scope of the journal encompasses all nonlinear dynamic phenomena associated with mechanical, structural, civil, aeronautical, ocean, electrical and control systems.
Ind/Abst Ei Page One; Eng. Index Annu.; INSPEC (1990-).

US
NORTH CAROLINA ENGINEER. Began with Sept. 1944 issue. Periodical. English. qt. North Carolina Soc of Engr, PO Box 10614, Raleigh NC 27605. **LC** TA1; .N5723. **DD** 620.5. ***Supersedes*** *North Carolina Society of Engineers. Bulletin.*
Desc: Beginning in 1954 the July issue includes a Directory of Membership.

US/0029-3083
NORTHERN ENGINEER, THE. ***Suspended.*** [North. eng.]. **Added/Corp** University of Alaska, Fairbanks. Geophysical Institute. University of Alaska (College). College of Mathematics, Physical Sciences, and Engineering. (1968)-Suspended. Periodical. English. qt. $12.00. Institute of Northern Engineering, 539 Duckering, University of Alaska, Fairbanks AK 99775. **Tel** (907)474-7775. **LC** TA1; .N63. **DD** 620/.411. **CODEN** NOENDX. Documents available from Article Express International.
Ind/Abst ASTIS Curr. Aware. Bull.; ASTIS Bibliogr.; Bioeng. Abstr. (1978-); Ei Page One (1978-); Eng. Index Annu.; GeoRef; Highw. Res. Abstr.

AG/0325-5298
NOTICIERO - SOCIEDAD ARGENTINA DE INVESTIGACION OPERATIVA. [Not. - Soc. argent. invest. oper.]. (1969)-. Periodical. Spanish. mo. Sociedad Argentina de Investigacion Operativa, San Jose 317, Buenos Aires, Argentina. **UDC** 659.2.
Ind/Abst Int. Abstr. Oper. Res.

US/0730-8086
NTIAC NEWSLETTER. (NTIAC NEWSLETTER / NONDESTRUCTIVE TESTING INFORMATION ANALYSIS CENTER.). [NTIAC newsl.]. **Added/Corp** United States. Nondestructive Testing Information Analysis Center. **VFOAT** N.T.I.A.C. Newsletter. **VAT** Nondestructive Testing Information Analysis Center Newsletter. (19??)-. Periodical. English. qt. Free. NTIAC, Texas Research Institute Austin, Inc., 415 Crystal Creek Drive, Austin TX 78746. **Tel** (512)263-2106, FAX (512)263-3530, (512)263-5944. **ED** Gary W. Carriveau. **Bk Rev. Circ:** 2,000 (ctrl).
Desc: Current awareness in the area of nondestructive testing.

UK
NUMERICAL METHODS IN THERMAL PROBLEMS : PROCEEDINGS OF THE FIRST INTERNATIONAL CONFERENCE. Vol. 1 (1979)-. Proceedings. English. Pineridge Press Ltd, Journals Division, 54 Newton Road, Mumbles Swansea SA3 4BQ Wales. **Tel** 011 44 792 361557, FAX 011 44 792 295532.

CN/0318-5338
O A C E T T NEWSLETTER. **Main/Corp** Ontario Association of Certified Engineering Technicians and Technologists. (Jan. 1972)-. Newsletter. English. bm. Ontario Association of Certified Engineering Technicians and Technologists, 10 Four Seasons Place/Suite 404, Islington Ontario M9B 6H7 Canada. **Tel** (416)621-9621. **ED** Ruth M. Klein. **DD** 620/.0062/713. **Ad Acc. Circ:** 16,000 (ctrl).

BL
O EMPREITEIRO. Portuguese. $40.00. **LC** TA4; .E37. **DD** 620/.005.

US
OCEAN ENGINEERING. (1981)-. Monographic series. English. Price varies per volume. Marcel Dekker Inc., 270 Madison Avenue, New York NY 10016. **Tel** (212)696-9000, (800)228-1160, FAX (212)685-4540, telex 421419. **(Subscription address:** Marcel Dekker Inc, PO Box 5017, Monticello NY 12701.)
Desc: Each title presents some aspect of ocean engineering. Topics include undersea work systems and offshore pipeline design elements.

CN/0226-7683
OEIC INFORMATION BULLETIN. **See** Earth Sciences-Oceanography.

US/0749-3932
OFFICE SYSTEMS ERGONOMICS REPORT. ***Ceased.*** [Off. syst. ergon. rep.]. Vol. 2, No. 3 (May-June 1983)-(April 1987). Periodical. English. ir (6 times per year). The Koffler Group, 2103 Main Street, Santa Monica CA 90405-2215. **Tel** (310)453-1844, telex 181149 WEST LSA. **ED** Kathleen Potosnak. **DD** 651. **Bk Rev. Circ:** 1,000. ***Continues*** *Ergonomics Newsletter, 0732-524X.*
Desc: In-depth coverage of all people/technology issues found in today's offices.

US/0194-9276
OHIO ENGINEER, THE. **Added/Corp** Ohio Society of Professional Engineers. Vol. 1 (Nov. 1943)-. Periodical. English. Six times a year. $15.00. Ohio Society of Professional Engineers, 445 Kings Avenue, Columbus OH 43201. **Tel** (614)424-6640, FAX (614)421-1257. **ED** Judy A. Nagy. **LC** TA1; .O372. **DD** 620.62771. **Ad Acc. Circ:** 5,500 (ctrl).
Desc: Activities of society legislative and government affairs P.R. Programs that are continuing.

US/0892-354X
OPTICAL ENGINEERING (NEW YORK, N.Y.). (OPTICAL ENGINEERING.). [Opt. eng.]. Vol. 1 (1982)-. Academic Scholarly Publication. English. ir. Price varies per volume. Marcel Dekker Inc., 270 Madison Avenue, New York NY 10016. **Tel** (212)696-9000, (800)228-1160, FAX (212)685-4540, telex 421419. **(Subscription address:** Marcel Dekker Inc, PO Box 5017, Monticello NY 12701.) **DD** 621. **CODEN** OPENEI. Documents available from Ask*IEEE, CASDDS.
Desc: Covers topics such as integrated optical circuits, laser spectroscopy, optical computing and more.
Ind/Abst Chem. Abstr. (1989-); INSPEC (1986-).

UK/0143-8166
OPTICS AND LASERS IN ENGINEERING. **See** Physics-Light, Optics, Radiation.

SA/0259-191X
ORION JOHANNESBURG. [Orion Johannesbg.]. (1984)-. Periodical. Multiple languages. sa. Operations Research Society of South Africa, PO Box 3982, Johannesburg 2000 South Africa.
Ind/Abst Int. Abstr. Oper. Res. [Full Cov.].

JA/0472-1438
OSAKA KOGYO GIJUTSU SHIKENJO HOKOKU. (OSAKA KOGYO GIJUTSU SHIKENJO HOKOKU. REPORT OF THE GOVERNMENT INDUSTRIAL RESEARCH INSTITUTE, OSAKA.). [Osaka Kogyo Gijutsu Shikenjo hokoku]. **Main/Corp** Osaka Kogyo Gijutsu Shikenjo. **Added/Corp** Osaka Kogyo Gijutsu Shikenjo. Report of the Government Industrial Research Institute, Osaka. **VFOAT** Report of the Government Industrial Research Institute, Osaka. No. 299 (1953)-. Academic Scholarly Publication. English (Japanese). Four times a year. $158.00. Kogyo Gijutsuin Osaka Kogyo Gijutsu Shikenjo, (Government Industrial Research Inst., Osaka, Agency of Industrial Science & Technology), 8-31, Midorigaoka 1 Chome, Ikedashi, Osakafu 563, Japan. **(Subscription address:** Japan Publications Trading Company, Ltd., PO Box 5030, Tokyo

International, Tokyo 100-31 Japan.) **LC** TA4; .O86a. **CODEN** OKGHA5. Documents available from Ask*IEEE, CASDDS. ***Supersedes*** *Osaka Kogyo Shikenjo. Osaka Kogyo Shikenjo Hokoku.*
Ind/Abst Chem. Abstr.; INSPEC (Nov. 1983-).

UK/0953-3222
OXFORD ENGINEERING SCIENCE SERIES. [Oxf. eng. sci. ser.]. (1974)-. Monographic series. English. ir. Price varies per volume. Oxford University Press / New York, 200 Madison Avenue, New York NY 10016. **Tel** (212)679-7300, (919)677-0977, (800)451-7556, (800)445-9714, FAX (919)677-1303. **CODEN** OESSEQ.
Ind/Abst Math. Rev.; Zentralbl. Math. Ihre Grenzgeb.

US/0149-9890
PAPER - AMERICAN SOCIETY OF AGRICULTURAL ENGINEERS. [Pap. - Am. Soc. Agric. Eng.]. **Main/Corp** American Society of Agricultural Engineers. **VFOAT** Transcript; ASAE Paper; ASAE Technical Paper. (196?)-. Academic Scholarly Publication. English. sa. Price varies per volume. American Society of Agricultural Engineers, Department 2510, 2950 Niles Road, St. Joseph MI 49085-9659. **Tel** (616)429-0300, FAX (616)429-3852. **ED** James Basselman. **DD** 631. **CODEN** AAEPCZ. Index available. cum. index. available on microfiche. Documents available from Article Express International, CASDDS.
Desc: Papers presented at Summer and Winter meetings of the Society.
Ind/Abst AgBiotech News Inf.; AGRICOLA; Agric. Eng. Abstr.; Anim. Breed. Abstr.; Biodeter. Abstr. (19??-19??); Bioeng. Abstr.; Chem. Abstr.; Cot. Trop. Fibr. Abstr. Bibliogr.; Dairy Sci. Abstr.; Ei Page One; Energy Res. Abstr. (Sept. 1978-); Eng. Index Annu.; Field Crop Abstr.; For. Prod. Abstr. (19??-19??); For. Abstr.; GeoRef; Grasslands For. Abstr.; Hortic. Abstr.; Index Vet.; Irr. Drain. Abstr.; Maize Abstr.; Nematol. Abstr.; Nutr. Abstr. Rev., Ser. B, Live Feeds and Feed.; Nutr. Abstr. Rev., Ser. A, Hum. Exp.; Ornamental Hort. (1991-); Pig News Inf.; Plant Genet. Resour. Abstr.; Postharvest News Inf.; Potato Abstr.; Poult. Abstr.; Rice Abstr.; Seed Abstr.; Sorghum Mill. Abstr.; Soyabean Abstr.; Vet. Bull.; Weed Abstr.; Wheat Barley Trit. Abstr.; World Agric. Econ.

US/0272-4723
PAPER SUMMARIES - AMERICAN SOCIETY FOR NONDESTRUCTIVE TESTING. [Pap. summ. - Am. Soc. Nondestr. Test.]. **Main/Corp** American Society for Nondestructive Testing. (19??)-. English. an. $50.00 US; $55.00 other. American Society for Nondestructive Testing, 4153 Arlingate Plaza, Columbus OH 43228. **Tel** (614)274-6003, (800)222-2768, telex 245347. **ED** Patrick O. Moore. **CODEN** PSNTDA. Index available. cum. index. **Bk Rev**. **Ad Acc. Circ:** 10,000 (ctrl). Documents available from Article Express International.
Desc: Applied engineering technology of nondestructive testing. Containing technical papers, tutorial papers, book reviews, feature articles, products and literature, events, calendars, and society news.
Ind/Abst Bioeng. Abstr.; Ei Page One; Eng. Index Annu.

GW
PCIM EUROPE. (19??)-. English (summaries and/or abstracts in German and French). bm (6 issues). DM180.00 Europe; DM324.00 other. ZM Communications GmbH, Kleinreuther Weg 58, D 90408 Nuernberg Germany. **Tel** 011 49 911 367058, FAX 011 49 911 364522. **Ad Acc.**
Desc: Covers power conversion and intelligent motion.

CN/0030-7912
PEGG, THE. [Pegg]. **Added/Corp** Association of Professional Engineers, Geologists and Geophysicists of Alberta. Association of Professional Engineers of Alberta. **VFOAT** P E G G. **VAT** PEGG. Professional Engineer, Geologist, Geophysicist; Professional Engineer, Geologist, Geophysicist. Vol. 24 (Jan. 1970)-. Periodical. English. Ten times a year. 25.00Can$. Association of Professional Engineers Geologists and Geophysicists of Alberta, 10060 Jasper Avenue, Scotia Place, Edmonton Alberta T5J 4A2 Canada. **Tel** (403)426-3990, FAX (403)426-1877. **ED** Nordahl Flakstad. **Ad Acc. Circ:** 33,150 (ctrl). available with illustrations. ***Continues*** *Alberta Professional Engineer, 0380-6553.*
Desc: Features interesting and informative articles and comprises a vital source of information for members of the association.

CN/0823-1745
PEGG. ASSOCIATION OF PROFESSIONAL ENGINEERS, GEOLOGISTS AND GEOPHYSICISTS OF ALBERTA (MONTHLY ED.). (THE PEGG : ASSOCIATION OF PROFESSIONAL ENGINEERS, GEOLOGISTS AND GEOPHYSICISTS OF ALBERTA.). [PEGG, Assoc. Prof. Eng. Geol. Geophys. Alta.]. **Added/Corp** Association of Professional Engineers, Geologists and Geophysicists of Alberta. Vol. 10, No. 7 (Aug. 1982)-. Periodical. English. Ten times a year (Except July and Dec.). 21.40Can$. Association of Professional Engineers Geologists and Geophysicists of Alberta, 10060 Jasper Avenue, Scotia Place, Edmonton Alberta T5J 4A2 Canada. **Tel** (403)426-3990, FAX (403)426-1877. **ED** Nordahl Flakstad. **DD** 620/.006/07123. **Ad Acc. Circ:** 33,000 (ctrl). ***Continues*** *Mini PEGG., 0380-4674.*
Desc: Articles on engineering and earth sciences. Member achievements and activities, association affairs, government programs and continuing education are emphasized to enhance professional development.

US/1061-0235
PENTON'S CONTROLS & SYSTEMS. ***Title Change.*** **See** Manufacturing.

US
PERSPECTIVES IN ENGINEERING. English. qt. New Jersey Society of Professional Engineers, 407 West State Street, Trenton NJ 08618. **Tel** (609)393-0099, FAX (609)396-5361. **ED** Linda Maurice. **Ad Acc. Circ:** 3,200 (ctrl).
Desc: Publication for the members of the New Jersey Society of Professional Engineers.

US/0745-3485
PERSPECTIVES (RIDGEFIELD, CONN.). (PERSPECTIVES.). [Perspectives]. (19??)-. Periodical. English. bm. $15.00 US; $20.00 Canada. CPS Communications Inc, 7200 West Camino Road, Suite 215, Boca Raton FL 33433. **Tel** (407)368-9301, FAX (407)368-7870. **DD** 629.

PH/0031-7470
PHILIPPINE ARCHITECTURE, ENGINEERING, & CONSTRUCTION RECORD. **See** Architecture.

PH
PHILIPPINES JOURNAL OF OPERATIONS RESEARCH. English. Operations Research Society of the Philippines, San Miguel Corporation, 40 San Miguel Avenue, Namdaluyong, Metro Manila, The Philippines.
Ind/Abst Int. Abstr. Oper. Res. [Full Cov.].

UK/0962-8428
PHILOSOPHICAL TRANSACTIONS - ROYAL SOCIETY OF LONDON. PHYSICAL SCIENCES AND ENGINEERING. **See** Physics.

US/0099-1112
PHOTOGRAMMETRIC ENGINEERING AND REMOTE SENSING. [Photogramm. eng. remote sensing]. **Added/Corp** American Society of Photogrammetry. American Society for Photogrammetry and Remote Sensing. **VFOAT** Photogrammetric Engineering & Remote Sensing; PE & RS. Vol. 41 (Jan. 1975)-. Periodical. English. mo. $120.00 (non-members), $65.00 (members) US. American Society for Photogrammetry and Remote Sensing / Maryland, 5410 Grosvenor Lane, Suite 210, Bethesda MD 20814-2160. **Tel** (301)493-0290, FAX (301)493-0208. **ED** James B. Case. **LC** TA593.A2; P5. **DD** 526.9/82/05. **CODEN** PGMEA9. **[CCC]**. Index available (Dec.). **Bk Rev. Ad Acc. Pr Rev. Circ:** 11,000. available on CD-ROM; available on microfilm and microfiche from University Microfilms International (UMI); available on microfilm. Documents available from Article Express International, The Genuine Article, Ask*IEEE, Petroleum Abstracts Document Delivery Service, CASDDS. ***Continues*** *Photogrammetric Engineering, 0031-8671.*
Desc: The official journal of ASPRS. Devoted to the exchange of ideas and information about the application of photogrammetry, remote sensing and geographic information systems.
Ind/Abst AESIS Q.; AGRICOLA [Select. Cov.]; Agric. Eng. Abstr.; Appl. Sci. Technol. Index; AQUAREF; Bibliogr. Carto.; Bioeng. Abstr.; Chem. Abstr.; Comput. Inf. Syst. Abstr. J. [Full Cov.]; Curr. Contents Eng. Tech. Appl. Sci.; Curr. Geogr. Publ. (199?-); Ecol. Abstr.; Ei Page One; Elect. Comm. Abstr.; EMBASE; Eng. Index Annu.; Environ. Period. Bibliogr.; Field Crop Abstr.; For. Abstr.; Geogr. Abstr. Phys. Geogr.; Geogr. Abstr. Human Geogr.; GeoRef; Grasslands For. Abstr.; Hortic. Abstr.; INSPEC (March 1975-); Int. Aerosp. Abstr.; Int. Dev. Abstr.; Pet. Abstr.; Potato Abstr.; Res. Alert [Full Cov.]; Rev. Agric. Entomol.; Sci. Cit. Index; SCISEARCH; Soc. Sci. Cit. Index [Select. Cov.]; Soils Fert.; Soyabean Abstr.

US/0085-4581
PIE, PUBLICATIONS INDEXED FOR ENGINEERING. ***Title Change.*** **Main/Corp** Engineering Index, Inc. **VFOAT** Publications Indexed for Engineering. (19??)-(1993). Periodical. English. an. Engineering Information Inc., Castle Point on the Hudson, Hoboken NJ 07030. **Tel** (800)221-1044, (201)216-8500, FAX (201)216-8526, telex 4990438. **LC** Z7913; .P15. **DD** 016.6/05. **CODEN** PIEGAN. ***Continued by*** *PIE, Publications in Engineering.*

CN/0032-0536
PLAN (MONTREAL). (PLAN.). **Main/Corp** Order of Engineers of Quebec. Vol. 10, No. 2 (Feb. 1974)-. Periodical. French. Ten times a year. 30.00Can$. Ordre des Ingenieurs du Quebec, 2020 University, 18th Floor, Montreal Quebec H3A 2A5 Canada. **Tel** (514)845-6141. **ED** Jean Marc Papineau. **DD** 620/.006/0714. **Ad Acc, Adv Mgr:** France Cadieux. **Circ:** 40,000 (ctrl). ***Continues*** *Corporation of Engineers of Quebec. Plan, 0032-0536.*

UK
PLANT & WORKS ENGINEERING. (1983)-. Trade Publication. English. mo. £32.00 (one year), £60.00 (two year), £86.00 (three year). Industrial Trade Journals Ltd, Stakes House, Quebec Square, Westerham Kent TN161TD England. **Tel** 011 44 0959 564212, FAX 011 44 0959 562325. **ED** Rick Pendrous. **Ad Acc, Adv Mgr:** Steve Aslett. **Pr Rev. Circ:** 20,500 (ctrl).
Desc: Trade and technical journal aimed at updating workers, managers, directors, and engineers on maintenance matters .
Ind/Abst Infomat Int. Bus.

US/0032-082X
PLANT ENGINEERING. [Plant eng.]. Vol. 1 (Nov. 1947)-. Periodical. English. Sixteen times a year. $75.00 US; $112.00 Canada; $105.00 Mexico; $199.00 (surface mail) other. Cahners Publishing Company, 249 West 17th Street, New York NY 10011. **Tel** (212)645-0067, FAX (212)242-6987. **(Subscription address:** Cahners Publishing Company / Colorado, Paid Subscription Service Center, PO Box 7610, Highlands Ranch CO 80126-7610.**)** **ED** Leo Spector. **LC** TS155.A1; P53. **DD** 658.205. **CODEN** PLENAV. **[CCC]. Bk Rev. Ad Acc. Circ:** 128,668 (ctrl). available on microfilm and microfiche from University Microfilms International (UMI); available on an online database (file 648/Full-Text) from DIALOG. Documents available from Article Express International, UMI Article Clearinghouse, CASDDS.
Desc: Serves plant engineers and managers who are responsible for the design, construction, equipment and maintenance of the industrial plant. Features include job oriented, problem solving data on the equipment and services plant engineers use daily in the various manufacturing industries.
Ind/Abst ABI/INFORM Glob. Ed.; ABI Inform Ondisc (March 1988-); Acad. Search (July 1993-); Acoust. Abstr.; Appl. Sci. Technol. Index; Bioeng. Abstr.; Bus. Index (1985-); Chem. Abstr.; Chem. Hazards Ind.; Ei Page One; EMBASE; Energy Res. Abstr. (April 1976-); Eng. Index Annu.; Foods Adlibra; Gen. BusinessFile (1985-); Gen. Period. Index (1985-); Int. Build. Serv. Abstr.; Lab. Hazards Bull.; Proc. Chem. Eng.; Saf. Health Work; Shock Vibr. Dig.; Surf. Treat. Technol. Abstr.; Theoret. Chem. Eng.; Trade Ind. ASAP [Full Txt.]; Trade Ind. Index (1981-) [Full Txt.].

JA
PLANT ENGINEERING & TECHNOLOGY, PET. **Added/Corp** Kagaku KÂogyÂo NippÂo Sha. **VFOAT** PET. (19??)-. Periodical. English. Chemical Daily Company Ltd, 3 16 8 Nihonbashi Hama Cho, Chuo Ku Tokyo 103 Japan. **Tel** 011 81 3 36637932, FAX 03 6632550, telex 2422362 NIPPO J. **LC** TS184; .P57. **DD** 660.2/8/005.

US/1040-2527
PLASTICS ENGINEERING (NEW YORK, N.Y.). (PLASTICS ENGINEERING.). [Plast. eng.]. (1981)-. Monographic series. English. Price varies per volume. Marcel Dekker Inc., 270 Madison Avenue, New York NY 10016. **Tel** (212)696-9000, (800)228-1160, FAX (212)685-4540, telex 421419. **(Subscription address:** Marcel Dekker Inc, PO Box 5017, Monticello NY 12701.**)** **DD** 668. **CODEN** PLENEZ. Documents available from BIOSIS Document Express.
Desc: Covers topics in plastics engineering such as plastics waste recovery, polyester molding compounds, and metal filled polymers.
Ind/Abst Biol. Abstr. (1988-).

●US/1062-5674
POINT LINE POLY. HOST. (POINT LINE POLY. HOST : A TECHNICAL FRIEND FOR ARC/INFO USERS.). [Point line poly, Host]. **VFOAT** Point Line Poly; PLP; Host. Vol. 1, No. 1 (1992)-. Periodical. English. bm (6 issues). $35.00. Stover Publishing Company Inc., 19 South Street, Proctor VT 05765. **Tel** (802)459-6358. **ED** Dan Stover. **DD** 620. Index available (bound in Nov. issue). **Circ:** 300 (ctrl).

PL/0374-4078
POLISH ENGINEERING (1970). (POLISH ENGINEERING.). [Pol. eng.]. (19??)-. English. Six times a year. $30.00. **(Subscription address:** ARS Polona, PO Box 1001, 00068 Warsaw Poland.**)** **LC** TA4; .P57. **DD** 620/.005. **CODEN** PERGAQ. Documents available from Ask*IEEE.
Ind/Abst Eng. Mater. Abstr.; INSPEC (1972-).

●US/1054-3414
POLYMER REACTION ENGINEERING. [Polym. react. eng.]. Vol. 1, No. 1 (1992)-. Periodical. English. qt (4 issues). $265.00 US; $279.00 other. Marcel Dekker Inc., 270 Madison Avenue, New York NY 10016. **Tel** (212)696-9000, (800)228-1160, FAX (212)685-4540, telex 421419. **(Subscription address:** Marcel Dekker Inc, PO Box 5017, Monticello NY 12701.**)** **ED** Alexander Penlidis and Kenneth F. O'Driscoll. **LC** IN PROCESS. **DD** 660. **CODEN** PREEEG. **[CCC].**
Desc: Devoted to papers on polymerization and

post-polymerization reactions. Emphasizes engineering aspects such as reactor design and modelling, process optimization and process control.

UK/0967-3911
POLYMERS & POLYMER COMPOSITES. **See** Plastics.

US/0032-406X
POLYTECHNIC ENGINEER, THE. V. 1- Feb. 1960-. Periodical. English. sa. Polytechnic Institute of New York, 333 Jay Street, Brooklyn NY 11201. **LC** TA1; .P72.

US/0897-6627
POWDER AND BULK ENGINEERING. [Powder bulk eng.]. **VFOAT** PBE. Vol. 1, No. 1 (Jan. 1987)-. Periodical. English. mo. $60.00 US and possessions; $75.00 Canada and Mexico; $120.00 (surface mail), $180.00 (airmail) other. CSC Publishing Company Inc., 1300 East 66th Street, Minneapolis MN 55423. **Tel** (612)866-2242, FAX (612)866-1939. **DD** 620. **Circ:** 35,000.
Ind/Abst Ei Page One; Foods Adlibra.

US/1055-0259
POWDER COATING. [Powder coat.]. Vol. 1, No. 1 (Sept. 1990)-. Periodical. English. Seven times a year. $40.00 US; $55.00 Canada and Mexico; $80.00 (surface mail), $130.00 (air mail) other. CSC Publishing Company Inc., 1300 East 66th Street, Minneapolis MN 55423. **Tel** (612)866-2242, FAX (612)866-1939. **LC** TP1175.M4; P682. **DD** 667/.9. **Circ:** 20,000.

US/0885-7156
POWDER DIFFRACTION. **See** Metals and Metallurgy.

UK/0307-0697
POWER & WORKS ENGINEERING (1974). (POWER & WORKS ENGINEERING.). [Power works eng.]. No. 23- May 8, 1974-. Periodical. English. bw. £7.50. Power and Works Engineering, 54/55 Wilton Road, London SW1 1DE England. **LC** TS184; .W64. **DD** 621.7/05. ***Continues** Works Engineering, 0307-1618.*
Ind/Abst Eng. Mater. Abstr.; Fluid Abstr., Civil Eng.; Fluid Abstr. Proc. Eng.; FLUIDEX (1974-).

CN/0477-8626
POWER PROTECTION. [Power prot.]. V. 1- June 1951-. Periodical. English. qt. Free. The Boiler Inspection and Insurance Company of Canada, 8 King Street East, Toronto Ontario M5C 1B5 Canada. **DD** 621.1/84.

US/0748-8505
POWER TECHNOLOGY NEWS. [Power technol. news]. **Added/Corp** Darnell Research Inc. Vol. 1, No. 1 (July 1984)-. Periodical. English. Twelve times a year. $380.00 US; $445.00 other. Infortechnics Inc., PO Box 581, Norco CA 91760. **ED** Jeffrey Shepard. **DD** 621. **Circ:** 300.
Desc: The only newsletter devoted exclusively to world-wide developments in power conversion technology.

US/0885-0259
POWERCONVERSION & INTELLIGENT MOTION. [Powerconvers. intell. motion]. **VFOAT** Powerconversion and Intelligent Motion; Power Conversion & Intelligent Motion; Power Conversion and Intelligent Motion. Vol. 11, No. 8 (Aug. 1985)-. Periodical. English. mo. $72.00 (non-trade) US; Free on request (trade) US; $144.00 other. Intertec International, 2472 Eastman Avenue 33 34, Ventura CA 93003. **Tel** (805)650-7070. **(Subscription address:** Intertec International Directlink, PO Box 6209, West Lafayette IN 47903.**)** **DD** 621. **CODEN** PIMOEN. **[CCC].** Documents available from Article Express International, Ask*IEEE. ***Continues** Powerconversion International, 0199-1884.*
Ind/Abst Eng. Index Annu.; INSPEC (1985-).

PL/0137-3846
POWOKI OCHRONNE. [Powoki ochr.]. **Added/Corp** Warsaw. Instytut Mechaniki Precyzyjnej. Vol. 1 (April 1973)-. Academic Scholarly Publication. Polish (summaries and/or abstracts in English, German and Russian). bm. Price on Request. **(Subscription address:** ARS Polona, PO Box 1001, 00068 Warsaw Poland.**)** **LC** TA418.76; .P68. **CODEN** PLOCAE. Documents available from CASDDS.
Ind/Abst Alum. Ind. Abstr.; Chem. Abstr.; Eng. Mater. Abstr.; Met. Abstr.; Surf. Treat. Technol. Abstr.

PL
PRACE. SERIA B. **Main/Corp** Bydgoskie Towarzystwo Naukowe. Wydzial Nauk Technicznych. Vol. 1; 1969-. Academic Scholarly Publication. Polish. **(Subscription address:** ARS Polona, PO Box 1001, 00068 Warsaw Poland.**)** **CODEN** PWNBDI. Documents available from CASDDS.
Ind/Abst Chem. Abstr. (1969-1982).

US
PREPRINTS OF PAPERS OF THE SAE TRANSACTIONS. **Main/Corp** Society of Automotive Engineers. No. 1 (1???)-. English. Documents available from Article Express International.
Ind/Abst Energy Res. Abstr. (Dec. 1976-); Eng. Index Annu.

US
PRESENTATIONS. **Main/Corp** International Bridge, Tunnel, and Turnpike Association. Meeting. **Added/Corp** International Bridge, Tunnel, and Turnpike Association. (19??)-. English. an. **LC** TE5; .I515a. **DD** 388.1/22.

US/0269-9648
PROBABILITY IN THE ENGINEERING AND INFORMATIONAL SCIENCES. Vol. 1, No. 1 (1987)-. Academic Scholarly Publication. English. qt. $250.00 US, Canada and Mexico; £169.00 other. Cambridge University Press / New York, 40 West 20th Street, New York NY 10011-4211. **Tel** (212)924-3900, (800)221-4512. **(Subscription address:** Cambridge University Press / Outside of North America, Journal Fulfillment Department, The Edinburgh Building, Cambridge CB2 2RU United Kingdom.**)** **ED** Sheldon M Ross. **LC** TA340; .P74. **DD** 620/.0042. **[CCC].** available on microfilm from University Microfilms International (UMI).
Desc: Primary focus is on stochastic modelling in the physical and engineering sciences, with particular emphasis on queueing theory, reliability theory, inventory theory, simulation, stochastic control theory and probabilistic networks and graphs. Papers on analytic properties and related disciplines are also considered, as well as more general papers on applied and computational probability, if appropriate. Readers include academics working in statistics, operations research, computer science, engineering, management science and physical sciences as well as industrial practitioners engaged in telecommunications, computer science, engineering, operations research and management science.
Ind/Abst Abstr. Bull. Inst. Pap. Sci. Tech.; Biostatistica; Curr. Index Stat.; Math. Rev.; Oper. Res./Manag. Sci.; Qual. Control Appl. Stat.

UN/0555-2656
PROBLEMY BIONIKI. [Probl. bioniki]. **Added/Corp** Kharkovskii Institut Radioelektroniki. (1968)-. Academic Scholarly Publication. Russian. **LC** Q300; .P73. **NLM** W1 PR577K. **CODEN** PBNKAV. Documents available from CASDDS.
Ind/Abst Chem. Abstr. (1968-1983); Int. Aerosp. Abstr.; Zentralbl. Math. Ihre Grenzgeb.

UN/0556-171X
PROBLEMY PROCNOSTI (KIEV). (PROBLEMY PROCHNOSTI.). [Probl. procn.]. **Added/Corp** Instytut Problem Mitsnosti (Akademiia Nauk Ukrainskoi RSR). Vol. 1, No. 1 (July 1969)-. Academic Scholarly Publication. Russian (table of contents in English and Russian). Twelve times a year. $309.95 US & Canada; $319.95 Europe; $334.95 others. **(Subscription address:** East View Publications Inc., 3020 Harbor Lane North, Suite 110, Minneapolis MN 55447.**)** **CODEN** PPCNBG. **[CCC].** Index available in last issue of volume--attached. Documents available from Article Express International, Ask*IEEE, CASDDS.
Ind/Abst Alum. Ind. Abstr.; Bioeng. Abstr.; Chem. Abstr.; Ei Page One; Energy Res. Abstr.; Eng. Mater. Abstr.; Eng. Index Annu.; INSPEC (Jan. 1972-); Int. Aerosp. Abstr.; Met. Abstr.

US
PROCEEDINGS / ... ANNUAL WORKSHOP ON INTERACTIVE COMPUTING, CAD/CAM, ELECTRICAL ENGINEERING EDUCATION. **Main/Corp** Workshop on Interactive Computing. **Added/Corp** IEEE Computer Society. College CAD/CAM Consortium. Oct. 25-27, 1982-. Proceedings. English. an. IEEE Computer Society, 10662 Los Vaqueros Circle, PO Box 3014, Los Alamitos CA 90720-1264. **Tel** (714)821-8380, (800)272-6657, FAX (714)821-4641.
Ind/Abst Index IEEE Publ.

US/0190-5848
PROCEEDINGS - FRONTIERS IN EDUCATION CONFERENCE. [Proc. - Front. Educ. Conf.]. **Main/Conf** Frontiers in Education Conference. **Added/Corp** IEEE Education Society. IEEE Education Group. American Society for Engineering Education. Educational Research and Methods Division. **VFOAT** Frontiers in Education. (1973)-. Proceedings. English. an. Price varies. IEEE, Institution of Electrical and Electronics Engineers, Inc., 345 East 47th Street, New York NY 10017-2394. **Tel** (908)981-1393, FAX (908)981-9667. **(Subscription address:** IEEE Service Center, 445 Hoes Lane, Piscataway, NJ 08854; telephone: (201)981-1393 or (800)678-4333**)** **LC** T62; .F76a. **DD** 620/.007/11. **CODEN** PFECDR. **[CCC].** Documents available from Article Express International, Ask*IEEE. ***Continues** IEEE Conference on Frontiers in Education. Proceedings of the Conference on Frontiers in Education, 0190-583X.*
Ind/Abst Bioeng. Abstr.; Ei Page One; Eng. Index Annu.; Index IEEE Publ.; INSPEC.

US/1050-4729
PROCEEDINGS / IEEE INTERNATIONAL CONFERENCE ON ROBOTICS AND AUTOMATION. **See** Computers-Automation.

US/0090-0729
PROCEEDINGS / INSTITUTE OF ENVIRONMENTAL SCIENCES. **Main/Corp** Institute of Environmental Sciences. **Added/Corp** Institute of Environmental Sciences. (1959)-. Academic Scholarly Publication. English. an. IES, 940 East Northwest Highway, Mt. Prospect IL 60056. **LC** TA1; .I39813. **DD** 620. **NLM** W1 IN535J. **Circ:** 4,000. Documents available from CASDDS.
Ind/Abst Acoust. Abstr.; Chem. Abstr.; Coal Abstr.

AT/0312-1933
PROCEEDINGS - NATIONAL CONFERENCE OF THE AUSTRALIAN SOCIETY FOR OPERATIONS RESEARCH. [Proc. - Natl. Conf. Aust. Soc. Oper. Res.]. (1973)-. Periodical. English. be. Australian Society of OR, School of Mathematical Sciences, University of Technology, Sydney PO Box 123, Broadway, NSW 2007 Australia. **DD** 658.4034.
Ind/Abst Int. Abstr. Oper. Res. [Select. Cov.].

US/0277-786X
PROCEEDINGS OF SPIE--THE INTERNATIONAL SOCIETY FOR OPTICAL ENGINEERING. [Proc. SPIE int. soc. opt. eng.]. **Added/Corp** Society of Photo-Optical Instrumentation Engineers. **VFOAT** Proceedings; Proceedings of SPIE; SPIE. **VAT** Proceedings of Society of Photo-Optical Instrumentation Engineers--The International Society for Optical Engineering. Vol. 266 (1981)-. Academic Scholarly Publication. English. ir. International Society for Optical Engineering, PO Box 10, Bellingham WA 98227-0010. **Tel** (206)676-3290, FAX (206)647-1445, telex 46-7053. **DD** 621. **CODEN** PSISDG. **[CCC]. Circ:** 500-1,000. available on microfiche. Documents available from Article Express International, Ask*IEEE, CASDDS. ***Continues** Proceedings of the Society of Photo-Optical Instrumentation Engineers, 0361-0748.*
Ind/Abst Agric. Eng. Abstr.; Bioeng. Abstr.; Chem. Abstr.; Comput. Inf. Syst. Abstr. J. [Full Cov.]; Curr. Biotechnol.; Ei Page One; Elect. Comm. Abstr.; Eng. Index Annu.; GeoRef; INSPEC (1981-); Manuf. Process Eng. Abstr.; Mater. Sci. Eng. Abstr.; Mech. Eng. Abstr.; Microbiol. Abstr. Sect. C; Pig News Inf.; Plant Genet. Resour. Abstr.; Solid State Supercond. Abstr.

US/0743-1619
PROCEEDINGS OF THE AMERICAN CONTROL CONFERENCE. (PROCEEDINGS OF THE ... AMERICAN CONTROL CONFERENCE.). [Proc. Am. Control Conf.]. **Main/Conf** American Control Conference. **Added/Corp** American Automatic Control Council. (1982)-. English. an. Price varies per volume. Institution of Electrical Engineers / IEE, Michael Faraday House, Six Hills Way, Stevenage Herts SG1 2AY UK. **Tel** 011 44 438 313311, FAX 011 44 438 742840, telex 825578 IEESTV G. **(Subscription address:** IEE / UK, Publications Sales Department, PO Box 96, Stevenage, Herts, SG1 2SD England.**)** **LC** TJ212.2; .A48a. **DD** 629.8/05. ***Continues in part** Joint Automatic Control Conference. Proceedings of the Joint Automatic Control Conference.*

US
PROCEEDINGS OF THE AMERICAN SOCIETY FOR COMPOSITES ... TECHNICAL CONFERENCE. (1986)-. Proceedings. English. an. $175.00 (7th Conference). Technomic Publishing Company, Inc., 851 New Holland Avenue, Box 3535, Lancaster PA 17604. **Tel** (717)291-5609, (800)233-9936, FAX (717)295-4538.

US/0148-1002
PROCEEDINGS OF THE ANNUAL ROCKY MOUNTAIN BIOENGINEERING SYMPOSIUM. **See** Biology.

US/0361-5987
PROCEEDINGS OF THE ANNUAL SOUTHWESTERN PETROLEUM SHORT COURSE. **See** Petroleum and Natural Gas.

US/0732-619X
PROCEEDINGS OF THE CONFERENCE ON EXPLOSIVES AND BLASTING TECHNIQUES. **Main/Conf** Conference on Explosives and Blasting Techniques. **Added/Corp** Society of Explosives Engineers. (1975)-. Proceedings. English. an (August). $45.00. Society of Explosives Engineers, 29100 Aurora Road, Cleveland OH 44139. **Tel** (216)349-4004, FAX (216)349-3788. **ED** J. Deane. **LC** TP270.A1; C66. **DD** 662/.2/05. **CODEN** PCETDN. **Circ:** 1,000. available on audiocassette. Documents available from Article Express International.
Desc: Technical articles for domestic use of explosives and related products.
Ind/Abst Eng. Index Annu.

JA
PROCEEDINGS OF THE FACULTY OF ENGINEERING OF TOKAI UNIVERSITY. **Main/Corp** Tokai Daigaku. Kogakubu. V. 1- 1974-. Academic Scholarly Publication. English. Editorial

Committee of Proceedings of the Faculty of Engineering, Tokai University, 2-28 Tomigaya, Shibuya-ku Tokyo 151 Japan. **LC** TA1; .T6516. **DD** 620/.005. **CODEN** PFEUDD. Documents available from CASDDS.
Ind/Abst Chem. Abstr. (1974-1982); Eng. Mater. Abstr.

US
PROCEEDINGS OF THE ... IEEE/ASME JOINT RAILROAD CONFERENCE. **See** Transportation-Railroads.

UK
PROCEEDINGS OF THE INSTITUTION OF CIVIL ENGINEERS. GEOTECHNICAL ENGINEERING. (19??)-. English. qt (Jan., Apr., July, Oct.). £50.00 UK; £59.00 other. Thomas Telford Ltd, Thomas Telford House, 1 Heron Quay, London E14 9XF England. **Tel** 011 44 71 987 6999, FAX 011 44 71 538 4101, telex 298105.

US/0734-7499
PROCEEDINGS OF THE INTERNATIONAL CONFERENCE ON THERMAL INSULATION. [Proc. Int. Conf. Therm. Insul.]. **Main/Conf** International Conference on Thermal Insulation. **Added/Corp** Product Safety Corporation. Vol. 1 (1979)-. Academic Scholarly Publication. English. an. $190.00. Product Safety Corporation, 1457 Firebird Way, Sunnyvale CA 94087. **Tel** (408)732-5325. **CODEN** PCTNDC. Documents available from Article Express International, CASDDS.
Ind/Abst Bioeng. Abstr.; Chem. Abstr.; Ei Page One; Eng. Index Annu.

US/1046-672X
PROCEEDINGS OF THE INTERNATIONAL CONGRESS ON EXPERIMENTAL MECHANICS. (PROCEEDINGS OF THE ... INTERNATIONAL CONGRESS ON EXPERIMENTAL MECHANICS.). [Proc. Int. Congr. Exp. Mech.]. **Added/Corp** Society for Experimental Stress Analysis. (June 10-15, 1984)-. Proceedings. English. ir. price varies per volume. Society for Experimental Mechanics, 7 School Street, Bethel CT 06801-1405. **Tel** (203)790-6373, FAX (203)790-4472. **DD** 620. ***Continues*** *International Congress on Experimental Mechanics. Proceedings of the ... SESA International Congress on Experimental Mechanics, 0734-7111.*

UK/0308-5422
PROCEEDINGS OF THE ... INTERNATIONAL CRYOGENIC ENGINEERING CONFERENCE. **Main/Conf** International Cryogenic Engineering Conference. (19??)-. Academic Scholarly Publication. English. ir. Price varies. Butterworth Heinemann / Woburn, MA, 225 Wildwood Avenue, Unit B, Woburn MA 01801. **Tel** (800)366-2665, FAX (617)928-2620, telex 880052. **LC** TP480; .I47a. **DD** 621.5/9/05. **CODEN** PICCD4. Documents available from CASDDS.
Ind/Abst Chem. Abstr.

US/1046-6770
PROCEEDINGS OF THE ... INTERNATIONAL MODAL ANALYSIS CONFERENCE & EXHIBIT. [Proc. Int. Modal Anal. Conf. Exhib.]. **Added/Corp** Society for Experimental Mechanics (U.S.) Union College (Schenectady, N.Y.) Society of Photo-Optical Instrumentation Engineers. **VFOAT** Proceedings of the ... International Modal Analysis Conference. (Nov. 8-10, 1982)-. English. ir. price varies per volume. Society for Experimental Mechanics, 7 School Street, Bethel CT 06801-1405. **Tel** (203)790-6373, FAX (203)790-4472. **LC** TA654.15; .I57a. **DD** 620. **CODEN** PMCNEW.

US/0146-955X
PROCEEDINGS OF THE ... INTERSOCIETY ENERGY CONVERSION ENGINEERING CONFERENCE. **See** Energy.

JA/0368-3141
PROCEEDINGS OF THE JAPAN CONGRESS ON MATERIALS RESEARCH. (PROCEEDINGS OF THE JAPAN CONGRESS ON MATERIALS RESEARCH / COMPILED BY THE EDITORIAL COMMITTEE OF THE JAPAN CONGRESS ON MATERIALS RESEARCH, WITH COOPERATION OF THE SCIENCE COUNCIL OF JAPAN.). [Proc. Jpn. Congr. Mater. Res.]. **Added/Corp** Nihon Gakujutsu Kaigi. Zairyo Kenkyu Renraku Iinkai. Nihon Zairyo Gakkai. 11th (Sept. 1967)-. Academic Scholarly Publication. English. an. $176.00. Nihon Zairyo Kenkyu Rengo, (Japan Congress on Materials Research), 1-101, Yoshida Izumidonocho, Sakyoku, Kyotoshi, Kyotofu 606, Japan. **(Subscription address:** Kyowa Book Company Inc., 1-38 Kanda Jinbo-Cho, Chiyoda-Ku, Tokyo 101, Japan**)** **LC** TA401.3; .Z3. **DD** 620.1/12. **CODEN** JMRPA9. cum. index. Documents available from Article Express International, CASDDS. ***Continues*** *Zairyo Shiken Rengo Koenkai. Proceedings.*
Ind/Abst Bioeng. Abstr.; Chem. Abstr.; Ei Page One; Eng. Index Annu.

US
PROCEEDINGS OF THE ... SYMPOSIUM ON ENGINEERING ASPECTS OF MAGNETOHYDRODYNAMICS. **Main/Conf** Symposium on the Engineering Aspects of Magnetohydrodynamics. **VFOAT** Engineering Aspects of Magnetohydrodynamics; Proceedings. (19??)-. Proceedings. English. an. $40.00. Universtiy of Tennessee, Space Institute, Attn L Crawford, Tullahoma TN 37388. **LC** QC809.M3; S92. **DD** 621.31/245. ***Continues*** *Engineering Aspects of Magnetohydrodynamics, 0270-2576.*

US/0080-3278
PROCEEDINGS - ROAD BUILDERS CLINIC. [Proc. - Road Build. Clin.]. **Added/Corp** University of Idaho. College of Engineering. Washington State University. Engineering Extension Service. Road Builders Clinic. Proceedings. (1951)-. Proceedings. English. $20.00. Washington State University / Enginerrig Extension Service, Engineering Extension Service, Pullman WA 99164. **CODEN** ABCPDX. Documents available from Article Express International.
Ind/Abst Bioeng. Abstr.; Ei Page One; Eng. Index Annu.

US/8756-8470
PROCEEDINGS - SOCIETY OF AUTOMOTIVE ENGINEERS. (PROCEEDINGS.). [Proc. - Soc. Automot. Eng.]. Academic Scholarly Publication. English. ir. Society of Automotive Engineers, 400 Commonwealth Drive, Warrendale PA 15096. **Tel** (412)776-4841, (412)772-7106, FAX (412)776-5760. **DD** 629. **CODEN** PSOED4. Documents available from Article Express International, CASDDS.
Ind/Abst Chem. Abstr.; Civ. Struct. Eng. Abstr.; Eng. Index Annu.; Environ. Eng. Abstr.; Mater. Sci. Eng. Abstr.; Mech. Eng. Abstr.

AT/0159-3935
PROCESS ENGINEERING. Vol. 7, No. 10 (Oct. 1979)-. Periodical. English. mo (11 issues). 60.00Aus$ Australia; 100.00Aus$ other. Reed Business Publishing Pty Ltd. / Australia, 1 5 Railway Street, Level 12 North Tower, Chatswood W 2067 NSW Australia. **Tel** 011 61 2 3725222, FAX 011 61 2 4197533. **CODEN** PROEDV. ***Continues*** *Australian Process Engineering.*
Ind/Abst AESIS Q.

CN/0555-3105
PRODUCT DESIGN AND VALUE ENGINEERING. March/April 1964-. Periodical. English. 50.00Can$ each number. Southam Information and Technology Group Inc., 1450 Don Mills Road, Don Mills Ontario M3B 2X7 Canada. **Tel** (416)445-6641, (800)668-2374, FAX (416)442-2261. **DD** 620/.0042. ***Continues*** *Product Design and Engineering, 0381-8209.*

GW
PRODUCTION ENGINEERING : RESEARCH AND DEVELOPMENTS IN GERMANY. (19??)-. English. Twice a year. DM398.00. Carl Hanser Verlag, Postfach 860420, D 81631 Munich Germany. **Tel** 011 49 89 998300, FAX 011 49 89 984809.
Desc: Publication of the German Academic Society for Production Engineering. Contains contributions from all fields of production engineering, dealing with basic questions and research results closely related to industrial application.

US/0735-7850
PROFESSIONAL INCOME OF ENGINEERS (1981). (PROFESSIONAL INCOME OF ENGINEERS.). [Prof. income eng.]. **Added/Corp** American Association of Engineering Societies. Engineering Manpower Commission. (1981)-. English. an. $70.00 (members), $115.00 (nonmembers). American Association of Engineering Societies-EJC, 1111 19th Street NW, Suite 608, Washington DC 20036. **Tel** (202)296-2237, FAX (202)296-1151. **ED** Carolyn J Heydt. **LC** TA157; .E683. **DD** 331.2/82/000973. **Circ:** 500. ***Continues*** *Engineers' Salaries. Professional Income of Engineers, 0735-7842.*
Desc: Contains breakdowns for broad industry groups, without degree level breakdowns. Data for engineers employed by state, local and federal governments included.

CN/0828-9239
PROJECT MAGAZINE. [Proj. mag.]. Vol. 1 (Dec. 1984)-. Periodical. English (French). ir. 3.00Can$ each number. Project Magazine, Clark Hall / Queens University, Kingston Ontario K7L 3N6 Canada. **DD** 620/.007/1171.

NE/0032-4094
PT. PROCESTECHNIEK. [Pt, Procestech.]. **Added/Corp** Nederlandse Ingenieursvereniging. **VFOAT** Procestechniek. **VAT** Polytechnisch Tijdschrift. Volume 37, No. 1 (Jan. 1982)-. Academic Scholarly Publication. Dutch. mo. Fl177.36. Ten Hagen and Stam BV, Postbus 34, 2501 AG The Hague Netherlands. **Tel** 011 31 70 3569100. **CODEN** PTPTBP. Documents available from Ask*IEEE, CASDDS. ***Continues*** *Polytechnisch Tijdschrift. Procestechniek.*
Desc: Covers production engineering.

Ind/Abst Chem. Abstr.; Coal Abstr.; Curr. Biotechnol.; EMBASE; INSPEC (Jan. 1982-); Proc. Chem. Eng.; Theoret. Chem. Eng.

US/0033-3840
PUBLIC WORKS. [Public works]. Vol. 48, No. 4 (Feb. 7, 1920)-. Periodical. English. Thirteen times a year (plus 1 manual in April). $45.00 (one year); $85.00 (two year). Public Works Journal Corporation, 200 South Broad Street, Ridgewood NY 07451. **Tel** (201)445-5800, FAX (201)445-5170. **ED** Edward B. Rodie. **LC** TD1; .P8. **CODEN** PUWOAH. Index available. **Bk Rev. Ad Acc. Circ:** 50,400 (ctrl). available on microfilm and microfiche from University Microfilms International (UMI). Documents available from Article Express International, CASDDS. ***Continues*** *Municipal Journal & Public Works, 0096-6169;* ***Absorbed*** *Contracting; Public Works Manual.*
Ind/Abst Acad. Search (Jan. 1993-); Appl. Sci. Technol. Index; Bioeng. Abstr.; Bus. ASAP (1992-) [Full Txt.]; Bus. Index (1985-); Chem. Abstr.; Coal Abstr.; Ei Page One; EMBASE; Energy Res. Abstr. (April 1976-); Eng. Index Annu. [Select. Cov.]; Gen. BusinessFile (1985-); Gen. Period. Index (1985-); GeoRef; Geotech. Abstr.; Highw. Res. Abstr.; J. Plan. Lit.; Mag. Search; Trade Ind. ASAP [Full Txt.]; Trade Ind. Index [Full Txt.]; Urban Aff. Abstr.; Vocat. Search (Jan. 1993-).

US
PUBLICATIONS IN ENGINEERING : PIE : PUBLICATIONS ABSTRACTED AND INDEXED IN THE ... ENGINEERING INFORMATION DATABASES. **Added/Corp** Engineering Information, Inc. **VFOAT** PIE; Engineering Information Inc. (1993)-. Periodical. English. an. Engineering Information Inc., Castle Point on the Hudson, Hoboken NJ 07030. **Tel** (800)221-1044, (201)216-8500, FAX (201)216-8526, telex 4990438. **LC** TA145; .P83. **CODEN** PIEGAN. ***Continues*** *Engineering Index, Inc. PIE, Publications Indexed for Engineering, 0085-4581.*

●US/1064-4733
PUBLICITY DIRECTORY FOR THE DESIGN, ENGINEERING, AND BUILDING INDUSTRIES, THE. **See** Building and Construction.

CN/0840-6170
QST CANADA. ***Ceased.*** (QST CANADA : OFFICIAL JOURNAL OF THE CANADIAN RADIO RELAY LEAGUE.). [QST Can.]. **VFOAT** Journal Officiel de la Ligue Canadienne de la Radio Amateur. (June 1988)-(June 1993). Periodical. English. mo. Canadian Radio Relay League, PO Box 7009, Station E, London Ontario N5Y 4J9 Canada. **DD** 621.3841/66/0971. **Ad Acc. Circ:** 5,800.

US
QUALITY AND RELIABILITY. (1985)-. Monographic series. English. ir. Price varies per volume. Marcel Dekker Inc., 270 Madison Avenue, New York NY 10016. **Tel** (212)696-9000, (800)228-1160, FAX (212)685-4540, telex 421419. **(Subscription address:** Marcel Dekker Inc, PO Box 5017, Monticello NY 12701.**)**
Desc: Topics covered have included quality control for profit, statistical process control, and integrated product testing and evaluation.

UK/0748-8017
QUALITY AND RELIABILITY ENGINEERING INTERNATIONAL. [Qual. reliab. eng. int.]. **VFOAT** QRE International. Vol. 1, No. 1 (Jan.-Mar. 1985)-. Periodical. English. Six times a year. $575.00. John Wiley & Sons Ltd., Baffins Lane, Chichester West Sussex PO19 1UD England. **Tel** 0243 779777, FAX 0243 776128 BTG:JWP001, telex 86290 WIBOOKG. **(Subscription address:** John Wiley / Philadelphia, PO Box 7247, Philadelphia PA 19170.**)** **ED** F. Jensen, P. D. T. O'Connor, and H. A. Malec. **LC** TA169; .Q34. **DD** 620/.00452. **CODEN** QREIE5. **[CCC]. Bk Rev. Ad Acc. Circ:** 1,000. available on microfilm and microfiche from University Microfilms International (UMI). Documents available from Article Express International, Ask*IEEE.
Desc: Devoted to practical engineering problems from the fields of quality and reliability, it is designed to bridge the gap between existing theoretical methods, scientific research and current industrial practices.
Ind/Abst Ei Page One; Eng. Index Annu.; INSPEC (Oct./Dec. 1986-); Int. Aerosp. Abstr.; Qual. Control Appl. Stat.

US/0480-9068
QUALITY CONTROL AND APPLIED STATISTICS YEARBOOK. [Qual. control appl. stat. yearb.]. **Added/Corp** Executive Sciences Institute. (1956)-. English. an. $185.00 US; $195.00 other. Executive Sciences Institute, 1005 Mississippi Avenue, PO Box 4318, Davenport IA 52808-4318. **Tel** (319)324-4463, FAX (319)322-3725. **(Subscription address:** Executive Sciences Institute, PO Box 4318, Davenport, IA 52808**)** **ED** Bruce Brocka. **DD** 658. Index available.
Desc: Contains digest summaries of journal articles and books related to quality control and applied statistics.

US/0898-2112
QUALITY ENGINEERING. [Qual. eng.]. **Added/Corp** American Society for Quality Control. Vol. 1, No. 1 (1988)-. Periodical. English. Four times a year. $225.00 US; $239.00 other. Marcel Dekker Inc., 270 Madison Avenue, New York NY 10016. **Tel** (212)696-9000, (800)228-1160, FAX (212)685-4540, telex 421419. **(Subscription address:** Marcel Dekker Inc, PO Box 5017, Monticello NY 12701.**) ED** Frank Caplan and Ichiro Miyauchi. **LC** TS156.A1; Q364. **DD** 658.5/62/05. **CODEN** QUENE7. **[CCC].** available in microform (from Research Publications). Documents available from Ask*IEEE.
Desc: Directed to professionals in all engineering and management fields interested in quality improvement, this journal provides the widest-ranging coverage of "how-we-did-it" accomplishments focusing on comprehensive quality science applications throughout the entire economy and society. Contains the latest thinking on quality control and quality assurance management, related physical technology, associated statistical tools, standards information, and more. Co-published by American Society for Quality Control.
Ind/Abst Foods Adlibra; INSPEC (1988-1989).

US/0033-524X
QUALITY PROGRESS. [Qual. prog.]. **Added/Corp** American Society for Quality Control. Vol. 1 (Jan. 1968)-. Periodical. English. mo. $50.00 US; $85.00 other. American Society for Quality Control, 611 East Wisconsin Avenue, PO Box 3005, Milwaukee WI 53201. **Tel** (414)272-8575, (800)248-1946, FAX (414)272-1734, telex 316567. **ED** Nancy A Karabatsos, Robert D Brezenski, Paul E Borawski. **LC** TS156.A1; Q35. **CODEN** QUPRB3. **[CCC].** Index available (bound in Dec. issue). cum. index. **Bk Rev. Ad Acc. Pr Rev. Circ:** 55,000. available on microfilm and microfiche from University Microfilms International (UMI). Documents available from Article Express International, The Genuine Article, Ask*IEEE, UMI Article Clearinghouse. ***Continues in part*** *Industrial Quality Control.*
Desc: Techniques and philosophies used by QA/QC professionals in manufacturing and service industries. Topics range from product development to use of customer information in engineering.
Ind/Abst ABI/INFORM Glob. Ed.; ABI Inform Ondisc (Sept. 1982-); Anbar Account. Finan. Abstr. [Full Txt.]; Anbar Mark. Distr. Abstr. [Full Txt.]; Anbar Top Manage. Abstr. [Full Txt.]; Appl. Sci. Technol. Index; Bioeng. Abstr.; Curr. Contents Eng. Tech. Appl. Sci.; Ei Page One; EMBASE; Eng. Mater. Abstr.; Eng. Index Annu.; Expand. Acad. Index (1992-); Gen. BusinessFile (1992-); Graph. Arts Bull. Inst. Pap. Sci. Technol. (June 1989, Sept. 1989-Oct. 1989, Dec. 1989); INSPEC (May 1968-); Manage. Bibliogr. Rev.; Oper. Prod. Manage. Abstr. [Full Txt.]; Oper. Res./Manag. Sci.; Person. Train. Abstr. [Full Txt.]; Qual. Control Appl. Stat.; Res. Alert [Select. Cov.]; Soc. Sci. Cit. Index [Select. Cov.]; Women Manage. Rev. [Full Txt.].

SP/0210-8054
QUESTIIO. VFOAT Quaderns d'Estadistica, Sistemes, Informatica i Investigacio Operativa; Questio. (1977)-. Periodical. Multiple languages. qt. Universidad Politecnica de Barcelona, Av. Gregorio Maranon S/N, Barcelona-28, Spain. **UDC** 519.2.
Ind/Abst Int. Abstr. Oper. Res. [Select. Cov.].

NE/0257-0130
QUEUEING SYSTEMS. [Queuing syst.]. **Added/Corp** Operations Research Society of America. Vol. 1, No. 1 (June 1986)-. Periodical. English. mo. 1123.50F (includes distribution costs). Baltzer Science Publishers BV, Asterweg 1A, 1031 HL Amsterdam Netherlands. **Tel** 011 31 20 6370061, FAX 011 31 20 6323651. **CODEN** QUSYE8. Documents available from Ask*IEEE.
Ind/Abst ACM Guide Comput. Lit.; Biostatistica; Comput. Rev.; INSPEC (1986-); Zentralbl. Math. Ihre Grenzgeb.

US/0163-321X
R.F. DESIGN. [R.F. des.]. **VFOAT** RF Design; RFDesign. V. 1 (Nov./Dec. 1978)-. Periodical. English. mo (plus one extra issue). $30.00. Cardiff Publishing Company, 6300 South Syracuse Way, Suite 650, Englewood CO 80111. **Tel** (303)220-0600, telex 450726. **(Subscription address:** PO Box 6228, Duluth, MN 55806**) ED** Gary Breed. **LC** TK6540; .R123. **DD** 621.3841/05. **CODEN** RFDEDG. **[CCC]. Bk Rev. Ad Acc. Circ:** 33,382 (ctrl). available on microfilm and microfiche from University Microfilms International (UMI). Documents available from Ask*IEEE.
Desc: Magazine for radio frequency engineers and design engineers.
Ind/Abst INSPEC (Sept./Oct. 1981-).

US/0163-9838
RAC NEWSLETTER. See Engineering-Abstracting, Bibliographies and Statistics.

UK/0961-1096
RACECAR ENGINEERING. See Transportation-Automobiles.

SZ
RAPPORTS DES COMMISSIONS DE TRAVAIL. Main/Corp International Association for Bridge and Structural Engineering. **VFOAT** Berichte der Arbeitskommissionen; Reports of the Working Commissions. V. 1- 1965-. Multiple languages. ir. International Association for Bridge and Structural Engineering, Eth-Honggerberg, CH 8093 Zurich Switzerland. **Tel** 011 41 1 3772647, FAX 011 41 1 371213, telex 822186.

GW
REALLEXIKON DER ASSYRIOLOGIE UND VORDERASIATISCHEN ARCHEOLOGIE. See Archaeology.

GW
REALLEXIKON ZUR DEUTSCHEN KUNSTGESCHICHTE. See The Arts.

US/1057-0225
REBOOTING (PITTSBURGH, PA.). (REBOOTING.). [Rebooting]. Issue #1 (Feb. 1, 1991)-. Periodical. English. Free. Rebooting, PO Box 6598, Pittsburgh PA 15212-0598. **DD** 620.

US/0736-7090
RECENT AWARDS IN ENGINEERING. (RECENT AWARDS IN ENGINEERING / NATIONAL SCIENCE FOUNDATION.). [Recent awards eng.]. First quarter fiscal year 1982-. Periodical. English. qt. National Science Foundation / Engineering, Directorate for Engineering, Program Analyst for Communications, 1800 G Street Northwest/Room 110B, Washington DC 20550. **Tel** (202)357-9859. **LC** TA160.4; .R4. **DD** 620/.0072073. **Circ:** 3,000 (ctrl).
Desc: Abstracts and bibliographic data on engineering grants awarded by the National Science Foundation's Directorate for Engineering.

US/0196-402X
RECORD (NORWOOD). (RECORD.). **Added/Corp** Factory Mutual System. Vol. 48 (Jan./Feb. 1971)-. Periodical. English. bm. Factory Mutual Engineering Corporation, PO Box 9102, Norwood MA 02062. **Tel** (617)762-4300. **LC** TH9201; .F3. **DD** 693.8/05. ***Continues*** *Factory Mutual Record, 0014-6595.*

GW/0722-0057
REFERATEORGAN MESSEN MECHANISCHER GROSSEN. VFOAT Measurement of Mechanical Quantities; Messen Mechanischer Grossen; MMG. Referateorgan Messen Mechanischer Grossen. (1981)-. German (English). bm. DM218.95 Germany; DM218.00 Europe; DM215.00 North America. Fachinformationszent Technik, Ostbahnhofstrasse 13, D 60314 Frankfurt Germany. **Tel** 011 49 69 4308234, 011 49 69 4308254. **UDC** 531.75/8(01). **CODEN** 53.08(01).

US/0363-7034
REGISTRY OF ENGINEERS AND LAND SURVEYORS AND REPORT OF THE STATE BOARD OF ENGINEERING EXAMINERS OF OREGON. Main/Corp Oregon. State Board of Engineering Examiners. English. be. Oregon State Board of Engineering Examiners, 750 Front Street NE/Suite 240, Salem OR 97310. **Tel** (503)378-4180. **ED** Edward B Graham. **LC** TA12; .O73A. **DD** 620/.0025/795. **Circ:** 7,500 (ctrl).
Desc: List of registrants.

GW/0080-0791
REINE UND ANGEWANDTE METALLKUNDE IN EINZELDARSTELLUNGEN. (1937)-. Monographic series. German. ir. Price varies per volume. Springer-Verlag New York Inc., 175 5th Avenue, New York NY 10010. **Tel** (212)460-1500, telex 232 235 SPB UR. **(Subscription address:** Springer Verlag New York Inc. / for North America, 44 Hartz Way, Secaucus NJ 07096.**) CODEN** RAMEDQ.
Desc: Materials research and engineering.

SP
RELACION DE INGENIEROS DE CAMINOS, CANALES Y PUERTOS. Added/Corp Colegio de Ingenieros de Caminos, Canales y Puertos. (19??)-. Spanish. 950. Colegio de Ingenieros de Caminos, Montalban 3 40 IZQDA, Madrid Spain. **LC** TA12; .R38. **DD** 609/.2/2.

UK/0951-8320
RELIABILITY ENGINEERING & SYSTEM SAFETY. [Reliab. eng. syst. saf.]. **VFOAT** Reliability Engineering and System Safety. Vol. 20, No. 1 (1988)-. Academic Scholarly Publication. English. Twelve times a year. $1520.00 The Americas; £1020.00 other. Elsevier Applied Science, An Imprint of Elsevier Science Ltd., The Boulevard, Langford Lane, Kidlington, Oxford OX5 1GB United Kingdom. **Tel** 011 44 865 843000, 011 44 865 843699, FAX 011 44 865 843010. **(Subscription address:** Elsevier Science Ltd. Oxford Fulfillment Centre, PO Box 800, Kidlington, Oxford OX5 1DX United Kingdom.**) ED** G. E. Apostolakis, F. R. Farmer and R. W. van Otterloo. **CODEN** RESSEP. **[CCC]. Pr Rev.** available on microfilm and microfiche from University Microfilms International (UMI). Documents available from Article Express International, The Genuine Article, Ask*IEEE. ***Continues*** *Reliability Engineering.*
Desc: Devoted to the development and application of methods for the enhancement of safety and reliability of complex technological systems, like nuclear power plants, chemical plants, hazardous waste facilities and space systems.
Ind/Abst Curr. Contents Eng. Tech. Appl. Sci.; Ei Page One; Eng. Index Annu.; INSPEC (1988-); Qual. Control Appl. Stat.; Res. Alert [Full Cov.]; Risk Abstr.; Sci. Cit. Index; SCISEARCH; Soc. Sci. Cit. Index [Select. Cov.]; Zentralbl. Math. Ihre Grenzgeb.

US/0277-9633
RELIABILITY REVIEW (MILWAUKEE, WIS.). (RELIABILITY REVIEW.). [Reliab. rev.]. **Added/Corp** American Society for Quality Control. Reliability Division. Vol. 1, No. 1-4 (Dec. 1981)-. Periodical. English. qt. $35.00 US; $40.00 Canada and Mexico. Reliability Division ASQC, c/o H W Williams, 2678 Brown Bear Court, Cool CA 95614. **Tel** (916)885-5322. **ED** H. W. Williams. **LC** TA169; .R45. **DD** 620/.00452. Index available. **Bk Rev**, (Qty: 3). **Ad Acc. Circ:** 7,000 (ctrl). available on diskette.
Desc: Reliability engineering and quality assurance are two of the topics often covered. Other major topics are systems effectiveness, human engineering, maintainability engineering, parts, materials and processes, and system safety engineering.
Ind/Abst Qual. Control Appl. Stat.

SZ/0275-7257
REMOTE SENSING REVIEWS. [Remote sens. rev.]. **VFOAT** Remote Sensing Device. Vol. 1, Part 1 (June 1983)-. Periodical. English. Four times a year. $441.00 (academic institutions), $688.00 (corporate institutions). Harwood Academic Publishers, PO Box 90, Reading RG1 8JL England. **Tel** 011 44 734 560080. **(Subscription address:** International Publishers Distributor at one of the following addresses: 820 Town Center Drive, Langhorne, PA 19047; or PO Box 90, Reading Berkshire RG1 8JL UK; or Kent Ridge PO Box 1180, Singapore 9111, Republic of Singapore**) LC** G70.4; .R466. **DD** 621.36/78/05. **CODEN** RSRVEP. **[CCC]. Bk Rev. Ad Acc.** Documents available from Ask*IEEE.
Ind/Abst Field Crop Abstr.; GeoRef; Grasslands For. Abstr.; INSPEC (1983-); Int. Aerosp. Abstr. (1984-); Potato Abstr.; Soils Fert.

US/0034-4508
RENSSELAER ENGINEER. [Rensselaer eng.]. (19??)-. Periodical. English. tq. $10.00 (1 year), $18.00 (2 year). Rensselaer Union, Rensselaer Polytechnic Inst, Troy NY 12180-3590. **Tel** (518)276-6515. **ED** Anthony M Szema. **Bk Rev. Ad Acc. Circ:** 5,000 (ctrl).
Desc: Student-run engineering and science journal of Rensselaer Polytechnic Institute. Research at RPI is reported, and nontechnical articles which relate to RPI are discussed.

CN/0709-4787
REPERTOIRE - ASSOCIATION DES INGENIEURS-CONSEILS DU QUEBEC. (REPERTOIRE - ASSOCIATION DES INGENIEURS-CONSEILS DU QUEBEC. ROSTER - ASSOCIATION OF CONSULTING ENGINEERS OF QUEBEC.). [Repert. - Assoc. ing.-cons. Que.]. **Main/Corp** Association of Consulting Engineers of Quebec. **VFOAT** Roster - Association of Consulting Engineers of Quebec; Roster; AICQ Repertoire des Membres; ACEQ Roster of Members. 1st Ed. (1975)-. English (French). an. 75.00Can$. AICQ, 2050 rue Mansfield, Bureau 600, Montreal Quebec H3A 1Y9 Canada. **Tel** (514)288-2032. **DD** 620/.0025/714. ctrl circ.

CN/0229-9534
REPERTOIRE DES LABORATOIRES D'ESSAIS ET D'ANALYSES DU QUEBEC ... . Added/Corp Centre de Recherche Industrielle du Quebec. (1979)-. Directory. French. ir. 19.50Can$. Centre de Recherche Industrielle du Quebec / CRIQ, 333 rue Franquet, CP 9038, Sainte-Foy Quebec G1V 4C7 Canada. **Tel** (418)659-1550, FAX (418)652-2251, telex 051-31569. **DD** 620/.0044/025714. Index available. **Ad Acc. Circ:** 1,800.
Desc: Directory of testing laboratories located in province of Quebec, Canada.

US/0736-6639
REPORT - BROWN UNIVERSITY. DIVISION OF ENGINEERING. (REPORT / DIVISION OF ENGINEERING, BROWN UNIVERSITY.). [Rep. - Brown Univ., Div. Eng.]. Monographic series. English. Price varies per volume. Brown University /

Division of Engineering, Providence RI 02912. ctrl circ. ***Continues*** *Engineering Research Report.*
Ind/Abst GeoRef.

US/0145-0093
REPORT - CENTER FOR ENERGY STUDIES, KANSAS STATE UNIVERSITY. [Rep. Cent. Energy Stud., Kans. State Univ.]. **Main/Corp** Kansas. State University of Agriculture and Applied Science, Manhattan. Center for Energy Studies. Academic Scholarly Publication. English. Price varies per volume. Center for Energy Studies / Kansa State University, Manhattan KS 66506. **LC** TA168; .K35 subser. **DD** 620/.7/08. **CODEN** RSUSDU. Documents available from CASDDS.
Ind/Abst Chem. Abstr.; GeoRef.

UK/0305-4055
REPORT - CIRIA UNDERWATER ENGINEERING GROUP. Main/Corp Construction Industry Research and Information Association. Underwater Engineering Group. (19??)-. Monographic series. English. Price varies per volume.
Ind/Abst Aquat. Sci. Fish. Abstr. (Computer File).

UK
REPORT OF THE RESEARCH COMMITTEE. Main/Corp Institution of Civil Engineers (Great Britain). Research Committee. (1935/36)-. English.

CN/0318-3734
REPORT ON SALARIES. See Economics-Labor.

JA/0023-6195
REPORTS OF RESEARCH INSTITUTE FOR APPLIED MECHANICS, KYUSHU UNIVERSITY. [Rep. Res. Inst. Appl. Mech., Kyushu Univ.]. **Main/Corp** Kyushu Daigaku, Fukuoka, Japan. OYo Rikigaku Kenkyujo. V. 1- (No. 1-); Jan. 1952-. English. Kyushu University / Research Institute for Applied Mechanics, 33 Fukuoka 812 Japan. **LC** TA350; .K9. **DD** 620.10072. **CODEN** RMKUA9. Documents available from Article Express International, Ask*IEEE, CASDDS. ***Formed by the union of*** *Kyusheu Daigaku Dansei Keogaku Kenkyujo Hokoku* ***and*** *Ryutai Kogaku Kenkyujo Hokoku.*
Ind/Abst Bioeng. Abstr.; BMT Abstr.; Chem. Abstr.; Ei Page One; Eng. Index Annu.; Fluid Abstr., Civil Eng.; Fluid Abstr. Proc. Eng.; FLUIDEX (1973-); INSPEC (Jan. 1972-); Int. Aerosp. Abstr.

JA/0563-6590
REPORTS OF THE RESEARCH INSTITUTE FOR STRENGTH AND FRACTURE OF MATERIALS, TOHOKU UNIVERSITY. (REPORTS.). [Rep. Res. Inst. Strength Fract. Mater., Tohoku Univ.]. **Main/Corp** Tohoku Daigaku, Sendai, Japan. Kogakubu. Zairyo Kyodo Kenkyu Shisetsu. Vol. 1 (May 1965)-. Periodical. English. an. Free on request. Research Institute for Strength and Fracture Materials, Tohoku University, Faculty Engineer, Sendai 980 Japan. **CODEN** TDSKBD. Documents available from Ask*IEEE.
Ind/Abst Alum. Ind. Abstr.; Eng. Mater. Abstr.; INSPEC (1968-); Met. Abstr.

US/0934-9839
RESEARCH IN ENGINEERING DESIGN. Vol. 1, No. 1 (1989)-. Periodical. English. Four times a year. £88.00. Springer-Verlag London Ltd., Springer House, 8 Alexandra Road Wimbledon, London SW19 7JZ England. **Tel** 011 44 81 9471280, or 9475885, FAX 011 44 81 9474651, telex 21531 SPRGB G. **(Subscription address:** North America: Springer Verlag, Journal Fulfillment Department, 44 Hartz Way, Secaucus, NJ 07096; Outside North America: Springer Verlag, Postfach 311340, D 10643 Berlin Germany**) ED** John R Dixon and Susan Finger. **LC** TA174; .R47. **DD** 620/.0042/0285. **CODEN** REEDEC. **[CCC]. Bk Rev.** available on microfilm and microfiche from University Microfilms International (UMI). Documents available from Article Express International, Ask*IEEE.
Desc: Provides an international forum for research papers on design theory and methodology in mechanical, civil, chemical, electrical, architectural and manufacturing engineering, and computer science.
Ind/Abst Eng. Index Annu.; Ergon. Abstr.; INSPEC (1990-).

US/0934-9847
RESEARCH IN NONDESTRUCTIVE EVALUATION. (RESEARCH IN NONDESTRUCTIVE EVALUATION : A JOURNAL OF THE AMERICAN SOCIETY FOR NONDESTRUCTIVE TESTING.). [Res. nondestruct. eval.]. **Added/Corp** American Society for Nondestructive Testing. Vol. 1, No. 1 (1989)-. Periodical. English. Four times a year. $117.00. Springer-Verlag New York Inc., 175 5th Avenue, New York NY 10010. **Tel** (212)460-1500, telex 232 235 SPB UR. **(Subscription address:** Springer Verlag New York Inc. / for North America, 44 Hartz Way, Secaucus NJ 07096.**) ED** H Thomas Yolken. **LC** TA417.2; .R46. **DD** 620.1/127/05. **CODEN** RNEVER. **[CCC]. Ad Acc. Pr Rev. Circ:** 1,000 (ctrl). available in microform from University Microfilms International (UMI). Documents available from Article Express International, Ask*IEEE.
Desc: Publishes experimental and theoretical investigations into the scientific and engineering bases of nondestructive evaluation, its measurement methodology, and a wide range of applications of materials and structures that relate to the entire life cycle from manufacture to use and retirement.
Ind/Abst Eng. Index Annu.; INSPEC (1989-); Int. Aerosp. Abstr.

JA
RESEARCH NOTES AND MEMORANDA OF APPLIED GEOMETRY FOR PREVENIENT NATURAL PHILOSOPHY. See Science and Technology.

US/0503-5562
RESEARCH REPORT - U. S. LAND LOCOMOTION RESEARCH LABORATORY, CENTER LINE, MICHIGAN. Main/Corp United States. Land Locomotion Research Laboratory, Center Line, Michigan. No. 1 (1956?)-. English. **DD** 356.

JA
RESEARCH REPORTS OF THE FACULTY OF ENGINEERING, MIE UNIVERSITY. Added/Corp Mie Daigaku. Kogakubu. **VFOAT** Mie Daigaku KÂogakubu Kenkyu Hokoku. Vol. 1 (Dec. 1976)-. Periodical. English. an. Mie University / Engineering, Faculty of Engineering, Tsu Japan. **LC** TA1; .R47. Documents available from CASDDS.
Ind/Abst Chem. Abstr.

US
RESEARCH TECHNIQUES IN NONDESTRUCTIVE TESTING. Began with Vol. 1 (197?)-. Academic Scholarly Publication. English. Academic Press Ltd., A Division of Harcourt Brace & Company Ltd., 24-28 Oval Road, London NW1 7DX England. **Tel** 071 267 4466, FAX 071 482 2293, 071 485 4752, telex 25775 ACPRES G. **(Subscription address:** Harcourt Brace Jovanovich Limited, Footscray High Street, Sidcup, Kent DA14 5HP UK, (Phone: 081-300-3322)**) ED** R.S. Sharpe. **DD** 620.

●US/1076-3333
RESOURCE (SAINT JOSEPH, MICH.). (RESOURCE : ENGINEERING & TECHNOLOGY FOR A SUSTAINABLE WORLD.). [Resource]. **Added/Corp** American Society of Agricultural Engineers. Vol. 1, No. 1 (May 1994)-. Periodical. English. mo. $49.50 (nonmember), $22.00 (member). American Society of Agricultural Engineers, Department 2510, 2950 Niles Road, St. Joseph MI 49085-9659. **Tel** (616)429-0300, FAX (616)429-3852. **DD** 630. Index available (free). ***Formed by the union of*** *Agricultural Engineering, 0002-1458* ***and*** *Within ASAE, 0741-0387.*
Desc: Contains information on technology for food, agriculture and biological industries. Broad interest articles and continuing departments spotlight technological progress with emphasis on mechanization, plus trends influencing engineering procedures.

FR
RESULTATS : SOCIETES D'ETUDES ET DE CONSEILS, INGENIEURS-CONSEILS. Main/Corp France. Service du Traitement de l'Information et des Statistiques Industrielles. French. Ministere de l'Industrie et de la Recherche, 280, BD Saint-Germain, Paris 75700 France. **LC** TA71; .F7A. **DD** 331.1/1.

US/0743-0760
REVIEW OF PROGRESS IN QUANTITATIVE NONDESTRUCTIVE EVALUATION. [Rev. prog. quant. nondestruct. eval.]. **Added/Corp** United States. Air Force. United States. Defense Advanced Research Projects Agency. (1981)-. Academic Scholarly Publication. English. an. Plenum Press, 233 Spring Street, New York NY 10013-1578. **Tel** (212)620-8000, (800)221-9369, FAX (212)463-0742, (212)807-1047, telex 23/421139. **LC** TA417.2; .R48. **DD** 620.1/127. **CODEN** RPQEDF. Documents available from Ask*IEEE, CASDDS.
Ind/Abst Chem. Abstr. (1983-); INSPEC.

CK/0590-9120
REVISTA - CALI, COLOMBIA. UNIVERSIDAD DEL VALLE. DIVISION DE INGENIERIA. Main/Corp Cali, Colombia. Universidad del Valle. Division de Ingenieria. 1- Sept. 1969-. Periodical. Spanish. Universidad del Valle, Division de Ingenieria, Apartados Aereo 2188, Cali Colombia.

CU
REVISTA CIENCIAS TECNICAS AGROPECUARIAS. See Agriculture.

CL/0034-9089
REVISTA DEL IDIEM. (1962)-. Spanish. Editorial Universitaria SA de Chile, Casilla 10220, Santiago Chile. **Tel** 011 56 2 223-4555.
Ind/Abst Ceram. Abstr. (19??-); Concr. Abstr.; Int. Civil Eng. Abstr.

SP/0213-1315
REVISTA INTERNACIONAL DE METODOS NUMERICOS PARA CALCULO Y DISE*f*NO EN INGENIERIA. [Rev. int. metodos numer. calc. dise*f*no ing.]. **VFOAT** Metodos Numericos para Calculo y Dise*f*no en Ingenieria. (1985)-. Periodical. Spanish. qt. $110.00. Univ Politecnica Cataluna, Apartado de Correos 30250, 08034 Barcelona Spain. **Tel** 011 34 3 4016200. **UDC** 519:620. Index available. cum. index. **Bk Rev. Ad Acc. Pr Rev. Circ:** 200 (ctrl).

MX/0035-0028
REVISTA MEXICANA DE INGENIERIA Y ARQUITECTURA : ORGANO DE LA ASSOCIACION DE INGENIEROS Y ARQUITECTOS DE MEXICO. Added/Corp Asociacion de Ingenieros y Arquitectos de Mexico. Centro Nacional de Ingenieros (Mexico). Vol. 1, No. 1 (Mar. 15, 1923)-. Periodical. Spanish. ir. Asociacion de Ingenieros Minas, Jaime Torres Bodet No. 176, CP06400 Mexico DF Mexico. **Tel** 011 52 5 5471094, 011 52 5 5471473. **LC** TA4; .R5. **DD** 620.5. cum. index.

VE/0254-0770
REVISTA TECNICA DE LA FACULTAD DE INGENIERIA, UNIVERSIDAD DEL ZULIA. [Rev. tec. Fac. ing., Univ. Zulia]. **Added/Corp** Universidad del Zulia. Facultad de Ingenieria. (1978)-. Periodical. Spanish. Universidad del Zulia, Apartado 1490, Maracaibo Venezuela. **CODEN** RTFZDH. Documents available from CASDDS.
Ind/Abst Chem. Abstr.; Gas Abstr.

MX
REVISTA UPADI. Main/Corp Pan American Federation of Engineering Societies. **VAT** Revista Union Panamericana de Asociaciones de Ingenieros. Multiple languages (English and Spanish). Pan American Federation of Engineering Societies, Insurgentes Sur No 753, Torre Dorada 11 Piso, Mexico DF Mexico. **LC** TA1; .P2516. **DD** 620/.009181/2.

IT/0034-916X
RIVISTA DI INGEGNERIA AGRARIA. Added/Corp Associazione Italiana de Genio Rurale. Utenti Motori Agricoli. Vol. 1 (Mar 1970)-. Periodical. Italian (summaries and/or abstracts in English, French and German). qt. $23.76. Edagricole, PO Box 2157, 40100 Bologna Italy. **Tel** 011 39 51 492211 Ext. 22, FAX 011 39 51 493660, telex 510336 EDAGRI.
Ind/Abst AgBiotech News Inf.; Agric. Eng. Abstr. (1991-); Dairy Sci. Abstr.; Food Sci. Technol. Abstr.; For. Prod. Abstr. (1991-); For. Abstr.; Hortic. Abstr.; Irr. Drain. Abstr.; Maize Abstr.; Nutr. Abstr. Rev., Ser. A, Hum. Exp.; Plant Breed. Abstr.; Postharvest News Inf.; Rev. Agric. Entomol.; Rice Abstr.; Seed Abstr.; Soils Fert.; Soyabean Abstr.; World Agric. Econ.

US/0035-7405
ROCHESTER ENGINEER, THE. Added/Corp Rochester Engineering Society, Rochester, N. Y. Vol. 1, No. 2 (Dec. 1922)-. Periodical. English. mo. $13.00. Rochester Engineering Society Inc, 170 Moutn Read Boulevard, Rochester NY 14604. **Tel** (716)328-2310. **LC** TA1; .R6. ***Continues*** *Publication of the Rochester Engineering Society.*

AU/0080-3375
ROCK MECHANICS. SUPPLEMENT. *Ceased.* [Rock mec., Suppl.]. **VFOAT** Felsmechanik Supplementum; Mecanique des Roches Supplementum. Monographic series. German. ir. Springer-Verlag Wien, Sachsenplatz 4 6, PO Box 89, A-1201 Vienna Austria. **Tel** 011 43 1 3302415. **(Subscription address:** Springer Verlag New York Inc. / for North America, 44 Hartz Way, Secaucus NJ 07096.**) ED** K Kovari. **DD** 642/.151. **CODEN** RMESDA. **[CCC]. Bk Rev. Ad Acc.** available on microfilm from University Microfilms International (UMI). Documents available from Article Express International. ***Continues*** *Felsmechanik und Ingenieur Geologie. Supplementum, 0591-2768.*
Desc: The subject matter of the journal covers the experimental and theoretical aspects of rock mechanics, including laboratory and field testing, methods of computation and field observation of structural behavior.
Ind/Abst Bioeng. Abstr.; Ei Page One; Eng. Index Annu.; GeoRef; Indian Geosci. Abstr.

US/0149-3035
ROSTER OF LICENSED PROFESSIONAL ENGINEERS. English. Delaware Association of Professional Engineers, 1508 Pennsylvania Avenue, Wilmington DE 19806. **LC** TA12; .R67. **DD** 620/.0025/751.

US
ROSTER OF PROFESSIONAL ENGINEERS AND LAND SURVEYORS. Main/Corp California. Board of Registration for Professional Engineers. **VFOAT** Roster, Professional Engineers. (1982)-. English. $20.00. California Department of General Services, Publication Division, PO

Box 1015, North Highlands CA 95660. **Tel** (916)445-1020. **LC** TA24.C2; A37. **DD** 620/.0025/794. ***Continues*** *Professional Engineers' Act, Land Surveyors' Act, with Rules and Regulations and Directory, 0092-2072.*

US/0147-555X
ROSTER OF WOMEN AND MINORITY ENGINEERING AND TECHNOLOGY STUDENTS. Periodical. English. an. Engineers Joint Council, 345 East 47th Street, New York NY 10017. **Tel** (212)644-7840. **LC** T73; .R67. **DD** 620/.007/1173.

US
ROSTER - STATE BOARD OF REGISTRATION OF PROFESSIONAL ENGINEERS, ARCHITECTS AND LAND SURVEYORS. **Main/Corp** Hawaii. State Board of Registration of Professional Engineers, Architects and Land Surveyors. English. Department of Treasury and Regulation, Board of Registration of Professional Engineers Architects and Land Surveyors, Professional and Vocational Licensing Division, PO Box 3469, Honolulu HI 96801. **LC** TA12; .H38A. **DD** 620/.0025/969.

US/0737-2329
ROSTER - TENNESSEE STATE BOARD OF ARCHITECTURAL AND ENGINEERING EXAMINERS. See Architecture.

FR/1011-1891
ROUTES PARIS. 1986. (ROUTES ROADS.). [Routes Paris, 1986]. **VFOAT** Roads. (1986)-. Periodical. English (French). Three times a year. Free to members, 210.00F other. Permanent International Association of Road Congresses Paris France, 27 Rue Guenegaud, 75006 Paris France. **Tel** 011 33 1 46337190, FAX 011 33 1 46338460. **ED** Patrice Retour. **UDC** 656. **Circ:** 3,000. ***Continues*** *Bulletin de l'Association Internationale Permanente des Congres de la Route, 0004-556X.*

UK/0035-8878
ROYAL ENGINEERS JOURNAL, THE. [R. eng. j.]. **Added/Corp** Great Britain. Army. Royal Engineers. Institution of Royal Engineers (Great Britain) Royal Engineers' Institute (Great Britain). (Aug. 1870)-. Periodical. English. Three times a year (Apr., Aug., Dec.). £15.52. Institution of Royal Engineers, Brompton Barracks, Chatham Kent ME4 4UG England. **Tel** 44 634 842669, FAX 44 634 844555. **ED** G W A Napier. **LC** UG1; .R8. **DD** 623/.04/05. Index available. cum. index. **Bk Rev. Ad Acc. Circ:** 3,500 (ctrl).
Desc: Technical and general interest articles describing the work history and role of the royal engineers.
Ind/Abst GeoRef.

CC/0254-0150
RUNHUA YU MIFENG. (JUN HUA YU MI FENG : MO TSA HSUEH HSUEH HUI HUI KAN.). [Runhua yu mifeng]. **Added/Corp** Chung-Kuo Chi Hsieh Kung Cheng Hsueh Hui (Peking, China). Mo Tsa Hsueh Hsueh Hui. Kuang-Chou Chi Chuang Yen Chiu So (China). **VFOAT** Lubrication Engineering. (19??)-. Periodical. Chinese. bm. **LC** TJ1075.A2; J85. **CODEN** RYMID2. Documents available from CASDDS.
Ind/Abst Chem. Abstr.

US/1051-8053
RUSSIAN JOURNAL OF ENGINEERING THERMOPHYSICS. ***Ceased.*** [Russ. j. eng. thermophys.]. Vol. 1 (1991)-(1992). Academic Scholarly Publication. English. qt. Elsevier Science Publishing Company Inc, Madison Square Station, PO Box 882, New York NY 10159-0882. **Tel** (212)633-3950, FAX (212)633-3990. **ED** V E Nakoryakov. **LC** TJ265; .R93. **DD** 621.402/1/05. **CODEN** RJETER. Documents available from Article Express International, CASDDS.
Desc: Latest developments and research in engineering thermophysics. Presenting current accomplishments at the Institute of Thermophysics of the USSR Academy of Sciences and other major institutions in the USSR, the journal's coverage includes: heat transfer, mass transfer, two-phase flow, radiation, multiphase flow, plasma physics, conduction and convection, thermo-gas-dynamics, thermal-power-engineering and rarefied gas flow.
Ind/Abst Chem. Abstr.; Eng. Index Annu.

US/0036-0821
S.A.M.P.E. QUARTERLY. ***Title Change.*** (SAMPE QUARTERLY.). [S.A.M.P.E. q.]. **Main/Corp** Society for the Advancement of Material and Process Engineering. **Added/Corp** Society of Aerospace Material and Process Engineers. Society for the Advancement of Material and Process Engineering. (19??)-(1993). Periodical. English. Four times a year (Jan., Apr., July, Oct.). Society for the Advancement of Material & Process Engineering, 1161 Parkview Drive, PO Box 2459, Covina CA 91724. **Tel** (818)331-0616 Ext 611, FAX (818)332-8929, telex 510/600 4889. **LC** TL950; .S583. **DD** 620.1/1/05. **CODEN** SAMQA2. **[CCC].** Index available (4th iss. (July)). **Pr Rev.** ctrl circ. Documents available from Article Express International, The Genuine Article, CASDDS, Documents on Demand. ***Continues*** *SAMPE Quarterly.* ***Continued by*** *Journal of Advanced Materials, 1070-9789.*
Ind/Abst Alum. Ind. Abstr. (?-?); Bioeng. Abstr. (?-?); Ceram. Abstr. (?-?); Chem. Abstr. (?-?); Coal Abstr. (?-?); Curr. Contents Eng. Tech. Appl. Sci. (?-?); Ei Page One (?-?); Electron. Commun. Abstr. J. (?-?); Energy Inf. Abstr. (?-?); Energy Res. Abstr. (Nov. 1971-); Eng. Mater. Abstr. (?-?); Eng. Index Annu. (?-?); Environ. Abstr. (?-?); Int. Aerosp. Abstr. (?-?); ISMEC Bull. (?-?); Mech. Eng. Abstr. (?-?); Met. Abstr. (?-?); Nucl. Sci. Abstr. (?-?); Pollut. Abstr. Indexes (?-?); Polymer Contents (?-?); Res. Alert (?-?) [Full Cov.]; Saf. Sci. Abstr. J. (?-?); Text. Technol. Dig. (?-?); World Alum. Abstr. (?-?).

II/0256-2499
SADHANA (BANGALORE). (SADHANA. ACADEMY PROCEEDINGS IN ENGINEERING SCIENCES.). [Sadhana]. **Added/Corp** Indian Academy of Sciences. **VFOAT** Academy Proceedings in Engineering Sciences. Vol. 7, Pt. 1 (June 1984)-. Academic Scholarly Publication. English. qt. $75.00. Indian Academy of Sciences Circulation, PO Box 8005, Department of Sadashivanagar, Bangalore 560 080 India. **Tel** 011 91 812 342546, 342310, telex 0845-2178 ACAD IN. **(Subscription address:** Prints India, 11 Darya Ganj, New Delhi 110002 India.**)** **ED** R Narasimha. **CODEN** SAPSER. Index available. **Circ:** 500. Documents available from The Genuine Article, Ask*IEEE, CASDDS. ***Continues*** *Proceedings. Engineering Sciences, 0253-4096.*
Desc: A journal covering mathematics, computer science, electronics, energy, aerospace technology, materials science, nuclear engineering, systems analysis, alternative technologies, etc.
Ind/Abst Chem. Abstr. (1984-); Coal Abstr.; Curr. Contents Eng. Tech. Appl. Sci.; Ei Page One; Fluid Abstr., Civil Eng.; Fluid Abstr. Proc. Eng.; FLUIDEX; INSPEC; Math. Rev.; Res. Alert [Select. Cov.]; Soc. Sci. Cit. Index [Select. Cov.].

US/0741-2029
SAE TECHNICAL LITERATURE ABSTRACTS. ***Title Change.*** [SAE tech. lit. abstr.]. **Added/Corp** Society of Automotive Engineers. **VFOAT** S.A.E. Technical Literature Abstracts; Technical Literature Abstracts. Vol. 7, No. 1 (Jan./March 1981)-(19??). English. qt. Society of Automotive Engineers, 400 Commonwealth Drive, Warrendale PA 15096. **Tel** (412)776-4841, (412)772-7106, FAX (412)776-5760. **[CCC].** ***Continues*** *Technical Literature Abstracts.* ***Continued by*** *Technical Literature Abstracts (Warrendale, PA. : 1987).*
Ind/Abst Corros. Abstr. (1981-); Fluid Abstr., Civil Eng.; Fluid Abstr. Proc. Eng.; FLUIDEX (1981-19??); HTFS Dig.

US
SAE TRANSACTIONS. See Transportation-Automobiles.

US
SAE TRANSACTIONS AND LITERATURE DEVELOPED DURING. See Transportation-Automobiles.

JA/0385-6186
SAGA DAIGAKU RIKOGAKUBU SHUHO. **Main/Corp** Saga Daigaku. Rikogakubu. **VFOAT** Reports of the Faculty of Science and Engineering, Saga University. No. 1- ; 1973-. Academic Scholarly Publication. Japanese (English). 1 Honjomachi, Saga 830 Japan. **Tel** (0952)24-5191. **ED** Toru Nakahara. **LC** Q4; .S22A. **CODEN** RFSSDV. **Circ:** 365 (ctrl). Documents available from Ask*IEEE, CASDDS.
Desc: Publishes prompt reports or full papers related to engineering or mathematics.
Ind/Abst Chem. Abstr.; INSPEC (March 1983-).

US/0742-6143
SALARIES OF ENGINEERS IN EDUCATION. **Added/Corp** American Association of Engineering Societies. Engineering Manpower Commission. (1981)-. Periodical. English. be. $70.00 (members), $115.00 (nonmembers). American Association of Engineering Societies-EJC, 1111 19th Street NW, Suite 608, Washington DC 20036. **Tel** (202)296-2237, FAX (202)296-1151. **ED** Richard A Ellis. **LC** TA157; .S33. **DD** 331.2/82/00071173. **Circ:** 400. ***Continues*** *Salaries of Engineers in Education, Special Report, 0271-7697.*
Desc: Reports median, quartile, decile and mean salaries of engineers in educational institutions by rank, length of contract and years of experience.

US/0091-1062
SAMPE JOURNAL. [S.A.M.P.E. j.]. **Main/Corp** Society for the Advancement of Material and Process Engineering. **VAT** Society for the Advancement of Material and Process Engineering Journal. Vol. 8, No. 6 (Dec./Jan. 1972/73)-. Periodical. English. bm. $65.00 US; $73.00 Canada and Mexico; $105.00 other. Society for the Advancement of Material & Process Engineering, 1161 Parkview Drive, PO Box 2459, Covina CA 91724. **Tel** (818)331-0616 Ext 611, FAX (818)332-8929, telex 510/600 4889. **ED** Dr. Stuart Lee. **LC** TL950; .S5825. **DD** 620.1/1/05. **CODEN** SAJUAX. **[CCC].** Index available. cum. index. **Ad Acc. Pr Rev. Circ:** 15,000. Documents available from Article Express International, The Genuine Article, CASDDS. ***Continues*** *Society of Aerospace Material and Process Engineers. SAMPE Journal, 0091-1062.*
Desc: Provides technical information on materials and processes, news of the society, members and chapters, industry news, international happenings.
Ind/Abst Abstr. Bull. Inst. Pap. Sci. Tech.; Alum. Ind. Abstr.; Bioeng. Abstr.; Ceram. Abstr. (19??-); Chem. Abstr.; Civ. Struct. Eng. Abstr.; Coal Abstr.; Corros. Abstr.; Curr. Contents Eng. Tech. Appl. Sci.; Ei Page One; Eng. Mater. Abstr.; Eng. Index Annu.; Int. Aerosp. Abstr.; Manuf. Process Eng. Abstr.; Mater. Sci. Eng. Abstr.; Mech. Eng. Abstr.; Met. Abstr.; Pollut. Abstr. Indexes; Polymer Contents; Res. Alert [Full Cov.]; Solid State Supercond. Abstr.

KO
SANOP KISUL YON'GUSO NONMUNJIP. **Main/Corp** Yonse Taehakkyo, Seoul, Korea. Sanop Kisul Yon'Guso. **VFOAT** Yonsei Engineering Review. (19??)-. Academic Scholarly Publication. English (Korean). **LC** TA4; .Y64a. **CODEN** NSKYEN. Documents available from CASDDS.
Ind/Abst Chem. Abstr.; Energy Res. Abstr. (Aug. 1976-).

CN
SASKATCHEWAN SCHEDULE OF WELLS. See Earth Sciences-Geology.

YU/0350-2953
SAVREMENA POLJOPRIVREDNA TEHNIKA. See Agriculture.

RU
SBORNIK ASPIRANTSKIKH RABOT: TEORIIA PLASTIN I OBOLOCHEK. **Main/Corp** Kazan, Russia (City). Universitet. **VFOAT** Teoriia Plastin i Obolochek. Vol. 1 (1971)-. Russian. 0.67rub single issue. Izdatelstvo Kazanskogo Universiteta SFSR. **LC** TA660.P6; K383a.

XO/0452-6171
SBORNIK VEDECKYCH PRAC. **Main/Corp** Kosice, Czechoslovak Republic. Vysoka Skola Technicka. 1- 1957-. Academic Scholarly Publication. Czech (summaries and/or abstracts in Russian and German). **LC** TA4; .K6. Documents available from CASDDS.
Ind/Abst Chem. Abstr.

GW/0343-9356
SCHOTT-FORSCHUNGSBERICHTE. [Schott-Forschungsbr.]. (197?)-. Periodical. Multiple languages. be. **UDC** 666.1.
Ind/Abst Ceram. Abstr.

AU/0253-5262
SCHWEISSTECHNIK (VIENNA). (SCHWEISSTECHNIK : ORGAN DER OSTERREICHISCHEN GESELLSCHAFT FUER SCHWEISSTECHNIK UND DER SCHWEISSTECHNISCHEN ZENTRALANSTALT WIEN.). [Schweisstechnik]. **Added/Corp** Osterreichische Gesellschaft fur Schweisstechnik. Schweisstechnische Zentralanstalt Wien. (1947)-. Academic Scholarly Publication. German. Twelve times a year. S730.00 Austria; S910.00 other. Oesterr Gesellschaft Schweiss Technik, Arsenal Objekt 12, A 1030 Vienna Austria. **Tel** 011 43 222 1 782168 or 784398, FAX 011 43 222 1 784398-15. **LC** WMLC L 83/8734. **CODEN** SWTEAJ. Documents available from Article Express International, CASDDS.
Ind/Abst Alum. Ind. Abstr.; Bioeng. Abstr.; Chem. Abstr.; Ei Page One; EMBASE; Eng. Index Annu.; Met. Abstr.

SZ/0251-0960
SCHWEIZER INGENIEUR UND ARCHITEKT. [Schweiz. Ing. Archit.]. **Added/Corp** Gesellschaft Ehemaliger Studierender der ETH Zurich. Schweizerischer Ingenieur- und Architekten-Verein. Schweizerische Vereinigung Beratender Ingenieure. **VFOAT** Ingenieurs et Architectes Suisses; Ingegneri e Architetti Svizzeri. Vol. 97 (Jan. 8 1979)-. Academic Scholarly Publication. German (French and Italian). wk. 198.00F Switzerland; $215.00 US. Imprimerie Bron SA, CP 508, CH-1001 Lausanne Switzerland. **Tel** 011 41 21 6529944, FAX 011 41 21 6527323. **CODEN** SIARD4. Index available in last issue of volume--attached. cum. index. **Bk Rev. Ad Acc. Circ:** 10,500 (ctrl). Documents available from Article Express International. ***Continues*** *Schweizerische Bauzeitung, 0036-7524.*
Desc: Reports of technological development and documentary articles in civil engineering, architecture and mechanical engineering.
Ind/Abst Alum. Ind. Abstr.; Art Archaeol. Tech. Abstr.; Bioeng. Abstr.; Ei Page One; EMBASE; Eng. Mater. Abstr.; Eng. Index Annu.; Int. Civil Eng. Abstr.; Met. Abstr.; Saf. Health Work; Soft. Abstr. Eng.

SZ
SCHWEIZER LANDTECHNIK. See Agriculture.

II/0036-8164
SCIENCE & ENGINEERING. **See** Science and Technology.

US/1048-6313
SCIENCE & ENGINEERING INDICATORS. [Sci. eng. indic.]. **Added/Corp** National Science Board (U.S.). **VFOAT** Science and Engineering Indicators. (1987)-. English. be (every 2 years). $39.00. Superintendent of Documents, US Government Printing Office, Washington DC 20402. **Tel** (202)275-3328, FAX (202)786-2377. **(Subscription address:** US Government Bookstore / O'Neil Building, 2023 3rd Avenue North, Birmingham AL 35203.**) LC** Q172.5.S34; S34. **DD** 509.73. **NLM** W1; SC665. **CODEN** SENIEF. ***Continues** Science Indicators, 0092-315X.*

US
SCIENTIFIC DRILLER, THE. **Added/Corp** James L. Ruhle and Associates. (19??)-. Periodical. English. mo. $100.00. James L. Ruhle and Associates, PO Box 4301, Fullerton CA 92634. **Tel** (714)526-6120. **ED** James L. Ruhle. **LC** TN281; .S34. **Circ:** 40.
Desc: Newsletter on the subject of drilling technology research and the various scientific drilling programs.

US/0036-8768
SCIENTIFIC, ENGINEERING, TECHNICAL MANPOWER COMMENTS. **See** Science and Technology.

JA/0912-0289
SEIMITSU KOGAKKAI SHI. **Added/Corp** Seimitsu Kogakkai. **VFOAT** Journal of the Japan Society of Precision Engineering. (1986)-. Periodical. Japanese (summaries and/or abstracts in English). Twelve times a year. $372.00. Japan Society for Precision Engineering, Ceramics Building, 22-17 Hyakunin-Cho 2-Chome, Shinjuku-Ku, Tokyo 169 Japan. **(Subscription address:** Kyowa Book Company Inc., 1 38 Kanda Jinbocho Chiyoda-ku, Tokyo 101 Japan.**) LC** TS500; .S38. **CODEN** SKKAEI. Documents available from Article Express International, CASDDS. ***Continues** Seimitsu Kikai, 0374-3543.*
Ind/Abst Chem. Abstr. (-1987); Ei Page One; Eng. Index Annu.

US/0891-3218
SELECTED ACQUISITIONS - ENGINEERING SOCIETIES LIBRARY. ACQUISITIONS DEPT. ***Ceased.*** (SELECTED ACQUISITION.). **Main/Corp** Engineering Societies Library. Acquisitions Dept. (19??)-(1992). Periodical. English. mo. Engineering Societies Library, 345 East 47th Street, New York NY 10017. **Tel** (212)705-7608. **ED** Dan Wood. **Circ:** 225.

JA/0371-0807
SENI KOBUNSHI ZAIRYO KENKYUSHO KENKYU HOKOKU. ***Title Change.*** **See** Textiles.

JA/0914-4935
SENSORS AND MATERIALS. [Sens. mater.]. (1988)-. Periodical. English. bm. $250.00. Myu K.K., 32-3, Sendagi 2 Chome, Bunkyoku, Tokyoto 113, Japan. **(Subscription address:** Maruzen Company Ltd., PO Box 5050, Import & Export Department, Tokyo 100 31 Japan.**) DD** 620. Documents available from CASDDS.
Ind/Abst Chem. Abstr.

US/1042-2757
SENSORS BUYER'S GUIDE. **See** Manufacturing.

US/0746-9462
SENSORS (PETERSBOROUGH, N.H.). (SENSORS.). [Sensors]. Vol. 1, No. 1 (Jan. 1984)-. Periodical. English. mo (includes Buyers Guide). $55.00. Helmers Publishing Inc., 174 Concord Street, PO Box 874, Peterborough NH 03458-0874. **Tel** (603)924-9631, FAX (603)924-7408. **(Subscription address:** ID Systems Subscriptions, PO Box 1226, Northbrook, IL 60062; telephone:(708)564-8900**) ED** Dorothy Rosa. **LC** TA165; .S458. **DD** 681.2. **[CCC].** Index available. **Bk Rev. Ad Acc. Circ:** 50,000 (ctrl). Documents available from Article Express International, Ask*IEEE.
Desc: Covers a broad spectrum of established and emerging sensor technologies including new product reviews, applications, what's new in research, market trends, sensor conference announcements and a reader wish list.
Ind/Abst Eng. Index Annu.; HTFS Dig.; Infomat Int. Bus.; INSPEC (Dec. 1991-); Robotics Abstr.

US/0956-9618
SEPARATIONS TECHNOLOGY. Vol. 1, No. 1 (1990)-. Periodical. English. qt. $225.00 (institution), $60.00 (individual) US and Canada; $265.00 (institution), $70.00 (individual) other. Butterworth Heinemann / Woburn, MA, 225 Wildwood Avenue, Unit B, Woburn MA 01801. **Tel** (800)366-2665, FAX (617)928-2620, telex 880052. **ED** Chi Tien. **LC** TP156.S45; S46. **DD** 660/.2842. **CODEN** SETEEX. **[CCC].** Index available. **Bk Rev. Ad Acc. Pr Rev. Circ:** 150. available on microfilm and microfiche from University Microfilms International (UMI). Documents available from Article Express International, CASDDS.
Desc: Focuses on the field of separation and purification principally from an engineering point of view. It provides a forum for work in the field of separations technology and its future development in areas such as genetic engineering, fossil fuels, the environment and ultrapure substances.
Ind/Abst Chem. Abstr.; Eng. Index Annu.; Food Sci. Technol. Abstr.

US/0272-3980
SERIES IN GEOTECHNICAL ENGINEERING. [Ser. geotech. eng.]. Monographic series. English. Price varies per volume. John Wiley & Sons, Inc., 605 Third Avenue, New York NY 10158-0012. **Tel** (212)850-6000, (212)850-6645, FAX (212)850-6088, telex 12-7063. **(Subscription address:** John Wiley & Sons / England, Baffins Lane, Chichester, West Sussex PO19 1UD England.**)**

US
SERIES OF SPECIAL REPORTS, A. Report No. 1 (1977)-. Monographic series. English. Price varies per volume. Marcel Dekker Inc., 270 Madison Avenue, New York NY 10016. **Tel** (212)696-9000, (800)228-1160, FAX (212)685-4540, telex 421419. **(Subscription address:** Marcel Dekker Inc, PO Box 5017, Monticello NY 12701.**)**
Desc: Presents special reports in engineering. Topics include corporate risk assessment and making accurate initial cost estimates.

JA/0912-8859
SHIKOKU KOKENKAIHO. [Shikoku Kokenkaiho]. **VFOAT** Report of the Shikoku Engineering Association. (1949)-. Academic Scholarly Publication. Japanese. an. Shikoku Kogyo Kenkyukai, (Shikoku Engineering Assoc.), Shikoku Kogyo Gijutsu Shikenjo, 3-3, Hananomiyamachi 2 Chome, Takamatsushi, Kagawaken 761, Japan. **DD** 620. Documents available from CASDDS.
Ind/Abst Chem. Abstr.

JA
SHINAGAWA GIHO. **VFOAT** Shinagawa Technical Report; Shinagawa Fire Brick Technical Report; Shinagawa Refractories Technical Report. Academic Scholarly Publication. Japanese (Japanese). Shinagawa Shirorenga Kabushiki Kaisha Gijutsu Kenkyujo, 707 IBE, 705 Bizen Japan. **LC** TH7140; .S53. **CODEN** SHGHDV. Documents available from CASDDS.
Ind/Abst Chem. Abstr.; Coal Abstr.

JA/0583-0915
SHIZUOKA DAIGAKU KOGAKUBU KENKYU HOHOKU. [Shizuoka Daigaku Kogakubu kenkyu hohoku]. **Added/Corp** Shizuoka Daigaku. Kogakubu. **VFOAT** Reports of the Faculty of Engineering, Shizuoka University; Kogakubu Kenkyu Hohoku. (1950)-. Academic Scholarly Publication. Japanese (English). Shizuoka Daigaku Kogakubu, (Faculty of Engineering, Shizuoka University), 5-1, Johoku 3 Chome, Hamamatsushi, Shizuokaken 432 Japan. **CODEN** SDKKAT. Documents available from CASDDS.
Ind/Abst Chem. Abstr.

US/1070-9622
SHOCK AND VIBRATION. [Shock vib.]. Vol. 1, Issue 1 (1993)-. Periodical. English. bm. $198.00 US; $258.00 Canada and Mexico; $280.50 other. John Wiley & Sons, Inc., 605 Third Avenue, New York NY 10158-0012. **Tel** (212)850-6000, (212)850-6645, FAX (212)850-6088, telex 12-7063. **(Subscription address:** John Wiley & Sons / England, Baffins Lane, Chichester, West Sussex PO19 1UD England.**) LC** TA355; .S515. **DD** 620.1/04. **CODEN** SHVIE8.

US/1058-0670
SHOCK AND VIBRATION TECHNOLOGY REVIEW. [Shock vib. tech. rev.]. **Added/Corp** Shock and Vibration Information Analysis Center. **VFOAT** Technology Review. Vol. 1, No. 1 (Jan. 1991)-. Periodical. English. mo. Saviac/Booz Allen & Hamilton, Inc., 2711 South Jefferson Davis Highway, Arlington VA 22202-4158. **DD** 620.

●DK
SKIN RESEARCH AND TECHNOLOGY. **See** Biology.

SZ
SLM ENGINEERING JOURNAL. an. 15.00F. Buchhandlung Vogel AG, Marktgasse 41-43, CH-8400 Winterthur Switzerland. **Tel** 052 22 6588.

US
SME TECHNICAL DIGEST. **Main/Corp** Society of Manufacturing Engineers. (1969)-. Periodical. English. Society of Manufacturing Engineers, One SME Drive, PO Box 930, Member's Records Dept., Dearborn MI 48121-0930. **Tel** (313)271-1500, FAX (313)271-2861, telex 297742 SME UR (VIA RCA). Each issue contains an index to its own contents (no volume index)--loose. ***Continues** American Society of Tool and Manufacturing Engineers ASTME Technical Digest.*
Ind/Abst FLUIDEX (1973-1990).

US/0099-5908
SOCIETY OF AUTOMOTIVE ENGINEERS. (SPECIAL PUBLICATION.). **Main/Corp** Society of Automotive Engineers. (????)-. Academic Scholarly Publication. English. ir. Price varies. Society of Automotive Engineers, 400 Commonwealth Drive, Warrendale PA 15096. **Tel** (412)776-4841, (412)772-7106, FAX (412)776-5760. **(Subscription address:** SAE / Society of Automotive Engineers, Department L1094P, Pittsburgh PA 15264.**) CODEN** SAESA2. **[CCC].** Documents available from Article Express International, CASDDS.
Ind/Abst Bioeng. Abstr.; Chem. Abstr.; Coal Abstr.; Comput. Inf. Syst. Abstr. J. [Full Cov.]; Ei Page One; Eng. Index Annu.

US
SOCIETY OF TRIBOLOGISTS AND LUBRICATION ENGINEERS SPECIAL PUBLICATIONS. (19??)-. Monographic series. English. ir. Price varies per volume. Society of Tribologists and Lubrication Engineers, 840 Busse Highway, Park Ridge IL 60068. **Tel** (708)825-5536, FAX (708)825-1456.

US/1053-6760
SOFTWARE ENGINEERING. ***Ceased.*** (SOFTWARE ENGINEERING : TOOLS, TECHNIQUES, PRACTICE.). [Softw. eng.]. **Added/Corp** Auerbach Publishers. Vol. 1, No. 1 (May/June 1990)-(1992). Periodical. English. bm. Warren Gorham & Lamont Inc., Park Square Building, 31 St. James Avenue, Boston MA 02116-4112. **Tel** (617)423-2020, (800)950-1207, FAX (617)423-2026. **LC** QA76.758; .S6466. **DD** 005.1/05. **CODEN** SOENEL.

UK/0268-6961
SOFTWARE ENGINEERING JOURNAL. [Softw. eng. j.]. **Added/Corp** British Computer Society. Institution of Electrical Engineers. Vol. 1, No. 1 (Jan. 1986)-. Periodical. English. Six times a year. £125.00. Institution of Electrical Engineers / IEE, Michael Faraday House, Six Hills Way, Stevenage Herts SG1 2AY UK. **Tel** 011 44 438 313311, FAX 011 44 438 742840, telex 825578 IEESTV G. **(Subscription address:** IEE / UK, Publications Sales Department, PO Box 96, Stevenage, Herts, SG1 2SD England.**) LC** QA76.758; .S656. **DD** 005.1/05. **CODEN** SEJOED. **[CCC]. Pr Rev.** Documents available from Article Express International, The Genuine Article, Ask*IEEE. ***Continues** Software & Microsystems, 0261-3182.*
Ind/Abst Abstr. Hum. Comput. Interact.; ACM Guide Comput. Lit.; Compumath Citation Index [Full Cov.]; Comput. Rev.; Ei Page One; Eng. Index Annu.; HILITES; INSPEC (1986); Res. Alert [Full Cov.].

UK/0952-8768
SOFTWARE FOR ENGINEERING AND WORKSTATIONS. ***Title Change.*** **See** Computers.

JA/0371-3067
SOGO SHIKENSHO NEMPO. (SOGO SHIKENJO NENPO.). [Sogo Shikensho nempo]. **Added/Corp** Tokyo Teikoku Daigaku. Dai 1 Kogakubu. Sogo Shikenjo. Tokyo Daigaku. Dai 1 Kogakubu. Sogo Shikenjo. Tokyo Daigaku. Kogakubu. Sogo Shikenjo. **VFOAT** Annual Report of the Engineering Research Institute, First Faculty of Engineering, University of Tokyo; Annual Report of the Engineering Research Institute, Faculty of Engineering, University of Tokyo. (1942)-. Academic Scholarly Publication. Japanese (English; summaries and/or abstracts in English). Tokyo Daigaku Kogakubu Sogo Shikenjo Chokoatsu Denshi Kembikyoshitsu, 11-16 Yayoi 2, Bunkyo-ku 113, Tokyo Japan. **LC** TA4; .S756. **CODEN** SSNEAT. Documents available from CASDDS.
Ind/Abst Alum. Ind. Abstr.; Chem. Abstr.; Met. Abstr.

UK/0267-7261
SOIL DYNAMICS AND EARTHQUAKE ENGINEERING (1984). (SOIL DYNAMICS AND EARTHQUAKE ENGINEERING.). [Soil dyn. earthqu. eng.]. Vol. 3, No. 3 (July 1984)-. Academic Scholarly Publication. English. Six times a year. $582.00 The Americas; £390.00 other. Elsevier Applied Science, An Imprint of Elsevier Science Ltd., The Boulevard, Langford Lane, Kidlington, Oxford OX5 1GB United Kingdom. **Tel** 011 44 865 843000, 011 44 865 843699, FAX 011 44 865 843010. **(Subscription address:** Elsevier Science Ltd. Oxford Fulfillment Centre, PO Box 800, Kidlington, Oxford OX5 1DX United Kingdom.**) ED** A. S. Cakmak. **LC** TA710.A1; I53. **DD** 624.1/762/05. **Bk Rev. Ad Acc. Circ:** 1,000. Documents available from Article Express International, Ask*IEEE. ***Continues** International Journal of Soil Dynamics and Earthquake Engineering, 0261-7277.*
Desc: A single medium for both theoretical and applied aspects of geotechnical and earthquake engineering.
Ind/Abst Abstr. J. Earthq. Eng.; Acoust. Abstr.; Ei Page One; Eng. Index Annu.; Fluid Abstr., Civil Eng.; Fluid Abstr. Proc. Eng.; FLUIDEX; GeoRef; Geotech. Abstr.; Health Saf. Sci. Abstr.; INSPEC (July 1984-); Int. Civil Eng. Abstr.; Pollut. Abstr. Indexes; Risk Abstr.; Soft. Abstr. Eng.

JA/0385-1621
SOILS AND FOUNDATIONS. (DOSHITSU KOGAKKAI RONBUN-HOKOKUSH U = B.JOURNAL OF THE JAPANESE SOCIETY OF SOIL MECHANICS AND FOUNDATION ENGINEERING.). [Soils found.]. **Added/Corp** Doshitsu Kogakkai (Japan). **VFOAT** Journal

of the Japanese Society of Soil Mechanics and Foundation Engineering; Soil and Foundation. Vol. 1, No. 1 (April 1960)-. Periodical. Japanese (English). qt. Doshitsu Kogakkai, (Japanese Soc. of Soil Mechanics & Foundation Engineering), 2-23, Kanda Awajicho, Chiyodaku, Tokyoto 101, Japan. **LC** TA710.A1; D594. **DD** 624.1/5136/05.

US/0747-623X
SOLETTER. (SOLETTER : NEWS BULLETIN OF THE SOCIETY OF LOGISTICS ENGINEERS.). [Soletter]. **Added/Corp** Society of Logistics Engineers. (19??)-. Bulletin. English. Eleven times a year (Nov/Dec issue combined). $25.00 (US); $30.00 (other) includes postage. Society of Logistics Engineers, 8100 Professional Pl, Suite 211, Hyattsville MD 20785. **Tel** (301)459-8446, FAX (301)459-1522. **DD** 623. **[CCC]. Bk Rev. Ad Acc. Circ:** 9,500 (ctrl).
Desc: The newsletter of the Society of Logistics Engineers; covering news of the chapters, logistics education opportunities, logistics issues and technological developments.

KO
SOUL TAEHAKKYO KONGDAE SOSIK. **Main/Corp** Soul Taehakkyo. Kongkwa Taehak. **VFOAT** College of Engineering, Seoul National University Newsletter. Korean (Korean). Soul Taehakkyo, Kongnung-dong Tobong-ku, Seoul 130-02 Korea. **LC** T173.S4588; A35.

CN/0228-7781
SOUND HERITAGE SERIES. [Sound herit. ser.]. No. 28-. Monographic series. English. qt. Price varies per volume. Provincial Archives, Sound & Moving Image Division, Victoria British Columbia V8V 1X4 Canada. **Tel** 387-6748. **ED** Derek Reimer. **DD** 620.2/05. ***Continues*** *Sound Heritage, 0316-2826.*
Ind/Abst Am. Hist. Life (1977-1980).

US/8756-7008
SOVIET SURFACE ENGINEERING & APPLIED ELECTROCHEMISTRY. ***Title Change.*** **See** Chemistry-Electrochemistry.

US/0361-7866
SPARK (NEW YORK. 1971). (SPARK.). V. 1- Mar. 1971-. Periodical. English. sa. Committee for Social Responsibility in Engineering, 475 Riverside Drive, New York NY 10027.

UK/0957-7580
SPECIAL VEHICLE ENGINEER. [Spec. veh. eng.]. (1988)-. English. ir. **DD** 629.2240941.
Ind/Abst Agric. Eng. Abstr.

YU/0374-0803
SRPSKA AKADEMIJA NAUKA I UMETNOSTI. GLAS. ODELJENJE TEHNICKIH NAUKA. **See** Science and Technology.

US/1042-6019
STANDARDS AND RECOMMENDED PRACTICES FOR INSTRUMENTATION AND CONTROL. [Stand. recomm. pract. instrum. control]. **Added/Corp** Instrument Society of America. 10th ed. (1989)-. English. be. $279.50. Instrument Society of America, 67 Alexander Drive, Research Triangle NC 27709. **Tel** (919)549-8411, FAX (919)549-8288, telex 802 540. **LC** TA165; .S78. **DD** 620. ***Continues*** *Standards and Practices for Instrumentation, 0074-0527.*

US
STEEL INDUSTRY MONITOR. English. mo. McGraw Hill Publishing Company, Inc., 1221 Avenue of the Americas, New York NY 10020. **Tel** (212)512-6410, (800)525-5003, FAX (212)512-6111.

XO/0039-2472
STROJNICKY CASOPIS. Czech (summaries and/or abstracts in English, French, German and Russian). bm. DM166.00. Slovenska Akademia Vied / Slovak Academy of Sciences, PO Box 57, 81005 Bratislava Slovakia. **Tel** 011 42 7 3782715, 011 42 7 3782925, FAX 011 42 7 496849, telex 93261. **(Subscription address:** Slovart GTG Ltd., Krupinska 4, 852 99 Bratislava Slovakia.**)**
Ind/Abst Fluid Abstr., Civil Eng.; Fluid Abstr. Proc. Eng.; FLUIDEX; Shock Vibr. Dig.

KO/1225-4568
STRUCTURAL ENGINEERING AND MECHANICS. (1993)-. English. ir. $260.00 institution, $150.00 individual. Techno-Press, PO Box 33, Yusong, Taejon 305-600, Korea. **Tel** 011 82 42 869-8451, FAX 011 82 42 869-3690. **ED** Prof. Chang-Koon Choi and Prof. William C. Schnobrich (editors' telephone: 011 82 42 869-3611). Index available (bound in sixth issue). **Ad Acc, Adv Mgr:** N.H. Lee, **Tel** same as publisher. **Pr Rev.**
Desc: The main theme is structural engineering concerned with aspects of mechanics. Areas covered include structural mechanics, design of civil and building and mechanical structures, structural optimization and controls, new structural materials and applications, the effects of earthquake and wave loadings on structures, fluid-structure and soil-structure interactions, AI application and expert systems in structural engineering.

PL/0137-6365
STUDIA GEOTECHNICA ET MECHANICA. [Stud. geotech. mech.]. **Added/Corp** Politechnika Wrocawska. No. 1 (1979)-. Periodical. English (French and Russian). qt. $80.00. **(Subscription address:** ARS Polona, PO Box 1001, 00068 Warsaw Poland.**) LC** TA710.A1; S82. **DD** 624.1/51/05. **CODEN** SGMEDB. Documents available from Article Express International. ***Supersedes*** *Studia Geotechnica.*
Ind/Abst Bioeng. Abstr.; Ei Page One; Eng. Index Annu.; GeoRef; Math. Rev.

●UK/1062-3949
STUDIES ON MANUFACTURING ENGINEERING AND PRODUCTION MANAGEMENT. (1992)-. English. ir. prices vary. Gordon & Breach Science Publishers, Inc., PO Box 786, Cooper Station, New York NY 10276. **Tel** (212)206-8900, FAX (212)645-2459. **(Subscription address:** International Publishers Distributor at one of the following addresses: 820 Town Center Drive, Langhorne, PA 19047; or PO Box 90, Reading Berkshire RG1 8JL UK; or Kent Ridge PO Box 1180, Singapore 9111, Republic of Singapore**) ED** Prof. A. Villa and Prof. M.C. Bonney. Index available. **Pr Rev.**

US
SUNDIAL. **Added/Corp** Cornell University. College of Engineering. Premier Ed. (1991)-. English. Cornell University College of Engineering, Ithaca NY 14853.

US/0894-7635
SUPERCONDUCTOR WEEK. [Supercond. week]. (1987)-. Periodical. English. Forty times a year. $427.00. Atlantic Information Services Inc., 1050 17th Street Northwest, Suite 480, Washington DC 20036. **Tel** (202)775-9008, (800)521-4323, FAX (202)331-9542. **DD** 620. **[CCC].** available on an online database (file 636/Full-Text) from DIALOG.
Ind/Abst PTS Newsl. Database [Full Txt.].

US/0095-0416
SUPPLEMENTAL YEAR BOOK - STATE BOARD OF PROFESSIONAL ENGINEERS AND LAND SURVEYORS. **Main/Corp** Florida. State Board of Professional Engineers and Land Surveyors. **Added/Corp** Florida. State Board of Professional Engineers and Land Surveyors. Year Book - State Board of Professional Engineers and Land Surveyors. (19??)-. English. 6900 Lake Ellenor Drive, Suite 100, Orlando FL 32809. **LC** TA12; .F55a. **DD** 620/.0092/2.

UK/0267-0844
SURFACE ENGINEERING. [Surf. eng.]. **Added/Corp** Institute of Metals. Wolfson Institute for Surface Engineering. Vol. 1, No. 1 (1985)-. Academic Scholarly Publication. English. qt. £182.00 EEC; £209.30 other. The Institute of Materials, 1 Carlton House Terrace, London SW1Y 5DB England. **Tel** 011 44 71 839 4071, FAX (071)839 2078. **ED** Tom Bell. **LC** TA418.7; .S855. **DD** 621.3. **CODEN** SUENET. Index available. **Bk Rev. Ad Acc.** Documents available from Article Express International, Ask*IEEE, CASDDS.
Desc: Reports developments in processes, techniques and their industrial applications for the user and designer of engineering components. Contributions include articles covering aspects of surface engineering, industrial case studies, reviews, surface engineering news and a diary of forthcoming events.
Ind/Abst Ceram. Abstr. (19??-); Chem. Abstr. (1985-); Curr. Titles Electrochem.; Ei Page One; Eng. Index Annu.; Fluid Abstr., Civil Eng.; Fluid Abstr. Proc. Eng.; FLUIDEX; INSPEC (1985-); Surf. Treat. Technol. Abstr.

●US/1068-3755
SURFACE ENGINEERING AND APPLIED ELECTROCHEMISTRY. (1993)-. Periodical. English (translations available in Russian). Six times a year. $915.00. Allerton Press, Inc., 150 Fifth Avenue, New York NY 10011. **Tel** (212)924-3950, FAX (212)463-9684, telex 427441 ALPRES. **[CCC].** ***Continues*** *Soviet Surface Engineering and Applied Electrochemistry, 8756-7008.*

JA/0386-2240
SURI KAGAKU. **See** Mathematics.

US/1051-4716
SURVEY OF EXECUTIVE ENGINEERING COMPENSATION. [Surv. exec. eng. compens.]. **Added/Corp** D. Dietrich Associates. **VFOAT** Executive Engineering Compensation Survey. (1987)-. English. Dietrich Associates Inc, Box 511, Phoenixville PA 19460. **Tel** (215)935-1563. **LC** TA157; .E95. **DD** 331.2/82/000973021. ***Continues*** *Executive Engineering Compensation Survey, 0275-2859.*

UK
SURVEYOR (WALLINGTON, ENGLAND). (SURVEYOR.). Vol. 168, No. 4938 (April 2, 1987)-. Periodical. English. wk (50 issues). $129.60 US and Canada. Reed Business Publishing / West Sussex, England, Perrymount Road, Haywards Heath, West Sussex RH16 3DH England. **Tel** 011 44 81 6523500. ***Continues*** *Public Works Weekly Surveyor.*
Ind/Abst Fluid Abstr., Civil Eng.; Fluid Abstr. Proc. Eng.; FLUIDEX (-19??).

AU/0938-1953
SURVEYS ON MATHEMATICS FOR INDUSTRY. Vol. 1, No. 1 (1991)-. Periodical. English. qt. $185.00. Springer-Verlag Wien, Sachsenplatz 4 6, PO Box 89, A-1201 Vienna Austria. **Tel** 011 43 1 3302415. **(Subscription address:** Springer Verlag New York Inc. / for North America, 44 Hartz Way, Secaucus NJ 07096.**) [CCC].** Index available. cum. index. **Bk Rev. Ad Acc. Pr Rev.** available in microform.
Desc: Presents original articles, book reviews and conference news on the latest mathematical techniques relevant for industry, as well as exposing industrial problems of interest to mathematicians.
Ind/Abst Zentralbl. Math. Ihre Grenzgeb.

UN/0203-3119
SVERH-TVERDYE MATERIALY. (SVERKHTVERDYE MATERIALY.). [Sverh-tverd. mater.]. **Added/Corp** Akademiia Nauk SSSR. Otdelenie Fiziko-Khimii i Tekhnologii Neorganicheskikh Materialov. Akademiia Nauk Ukrainskoi RSR. Viddil Fizyko-Tekhnichnykh Problem Materialoznavstva. No. 1 (1979)-. Academic Scholarly Publication. Russian. bm. $99.95. Izdatelstvo Naukova Dumka / Ukrainian Academy of Sciences, Vladimirskaia Ulitsa 54, 252601 Kiev Ukraine. **Tel** 225-63-66, telex 131376. **(Subscription address:** East View Publications Inc., 3020 Harbor Lane North, Suite 110, Minneapolis MN 55447.**) LC** TA418.26; .S87. **CODEN** SVMAD2. Documents available from Article Express International, CASDDS.
Ind/Abst Ceram. Abstr. (19??-); Chem. Abstr.; Ei Page One; Eng. Index Annu.

●US/1070-6232
SWE (NEW YORK, N.Y.). (SWE / MAGAZINE OF THE SOCIETY OF WOMEN ENGINEERS.). **Added/Corp** Society of Women Engineers. **VFOAT** Society of Women Engineers. (1993)-. Periodical. English. Six times a year. $30.00. Society of Women Engineers, 120 Wall Street, 11th Floor, New York NY 10005. **Tel** (212)509-9577, (800)666-1793, FAX (212)319-0947. ***Continues*** *U.S. Woman Engineer, 0272-7838.*

US/1056-5272
SWEET'S INDUSTRIAL CONSTRUCTION & RENOVATION CATALOG FILE. [Sweet's ind. constr. renov. cat. file]. **Added/Corp** McGraw-Hill, Inc. Sweet's Group. **VFOAT** Sweet's Industrial Construction and Renovation Catalog File; Industrial Construction & Renovation; Industrial Construction and Renovation; Sweet's Catalog File. Industrial Construction & Renovation. (1991)-. Catalog. English. McGraw Hill Information Systems Company, 1221 Avenue of the Americas, New York NY 10020. **Tel** (212)512-2000, (800)525-5003, FAX (212)512-6111. **LC** TA215; .S85; TA215; .S85. **DD** 624/.029/4. ***Continues*** *Sweet's Catalog File. Products for Industrial Construction and Renovation, 0145-4870.*

SZ/1013-4476
SWISS MATERIALS. **Added/Corp** Schweizerischer Verband fur die Materialtechnik. Schweizerische Gesellschaft fur Zerstorungsfreie Technik. Schweizerischer Verband fur die Warmebehandlung der Werkstoffe. Vol. 1, (1989)-. Academic Scholarly Publication. German (English and French). Six times a year (Feb., Apr., June., Aug., Oct., Dec.). 100.00F Switzerland; 120.00F Europe; 200.00F other. Verlag Dr Felix Wust AG, Seestrasse 5, Postfach, CH-8700 Kusnacht ZH Switzerland. **Tel** (01)823-5511, FAX 91-9106080, telex 53817. **ED** Dr. Felix Wust. **CODEN** SWMAEA. Index available. **Ad Acc. Circ:** 3,000 (ctrl). Documents available from CASDDS. ***Continues*** *Material + Technik, 0376-6845.*
Desc: Swiss journal of materials, testing and measuring technics.
Ind/Abst Chem. Abstr.

US/0082-0784
SYMPOSIUM (INTERNATIONAL) ON COMBUSTION. PAPERS. [Symp., Int., Combust.]. **Main/Conf** Symposium (International) on Combustion. **Added/Corp** Combustion Institute (U.S.) Symposium (International) on Combustion. Standing Committee on Combustion Symposia. **VFOAT** Combustion and Detonation Waves; Combustion in Engines and Combustion Kinetics. 4th (Sept. 1-5, 1952)-. English. be. $210.00. The Combustion Institute, 5001 Baum Boulevard, Pittsburgh PA 15213. **Tel** (412)687-1366, FAX (412)687-0340. **LC** QD516; .S92. **DD** 541.39; 541.36*. **CODEN** SYMCAQ. cum. index. **Circ:** 2,000 (ctrl). Documents available from Article Express International, CASDDS. ***Continues*** *Symposium on Combustions and Flame, and Explosion Phenomena, 1062-2896.*
Desc: Collection of research results on combustion.
Ind/Abst Bioeng. Abstr.; Chem. Abstr.; Coal Abstr.; Ei Page One; Eng. Index Annu.; Lit. Pat. Abstr., Oilfield

Chem.; Lit. Abstr., Catal. Catal.; Lit. Abstr., Health Environ.; Lit. Abstr., Pet. Refin. Petrochem.; Lit. Abstr., Pet. Substit.; Lit. Abstr., Transp. Storage.

NE/0167-6911
SYSTEMS & CONTROL LETTERS. [Syst. control lett.]. **VAT** Systems and Control Letters. Vol. 1, No. 1 (1981)-. Academic Scholarly Publication. English. Fifteen times a year (3 vols.). Fl1095.00. Elsevier Science Publishers BV, PO Box 211, 1000 AE Amsterdam Netherlands. **Tel** 011 31 20 5803642, FAX 011 31 20 5862696, telex 15682. **ED** R W Brockett and J C Willems. **CODEN** SCLEDC. **[CCC]. Pr Rev.** available on microfilm and microfiche from University Microfilms International (UMI). Documents available from Article Express International, The Genuine Article, Ask*IEEE.
Desc: Publication for literature in all areas of systems and control and their applications in engineering.
Ind/Abst ACM Guide Comput. Lit.; Compumath Citation Index [Full Cov.]; Comput. Rev. (1984-); Ei Page One; Eng. Index Annu.; Inf. Sci. Abstr.; INSPEC (Nov. 1981-); Math. Rev.; Pollut. Abstr. Indexes; Res. Alert [Full Cov.]; Soc. Sci. Cit. Index [Select. Cov.]; Zentralbl. Math. Ihre Grenzgeb.

PL/0137-1223
SYSTEMS SCIENCE. See Computers-Computer Systems.

CC/1000-1611
TAIYUAN GONGYE DAXUE XUEBAO. See Science and Technology.

US/0146-8235
TAX GUIDE FOR ENGINEERS. See Public Administration-Public Finance and Taxation.

AT
TECHNICAL AND FURTHER EDUCATION. ENGINEERING. Main/Corp Western Australia. Technical Education Division. **VFOAT** Engineering. (19??)-. English. Nelson Wadsworth, PO Box 4725, Melbourne Victoria, 3001 Australia. **Tel** 03 329-5199. **LC** WMLC L 83/1794.

UK/0955-3835
TECHNICAL DIAGNOSTICS AND NONDESTRUCTIVE TESTING. VFOAT Tekhnicheskaya Diagnostika i Nerazrushayushchii Kontrol. Vol. 1, No. 1 (1989)-. English (Russian). qt. £79.00 UK; $130.00 other. Riecansky Science Publishing Company, 7 Meadow Walk, Great Abington, Cambridge CB1 6AZ England. **Tel** 011 44 223 893295, FAX 011 44 462 480947, telex 825372 TURPIN G. **ED** B E Paton. Index available. **Bk Rev. Ad Acc.**
Desc: Covers the latest developments in nondestructive testing and diagnostics.

US/0741-2029
TECHNICAL LITERATURE ABSTRACTS (WARRENDALE, PA. : 1987). (TECHNICAL LITERATURE ABSTRACTS.). **Added/Corp** Society of Automotive Engineers. (19??)-. Periodical. English. qt (Mar., Jun., Sep., Dec.). $110.00. Society of Automotive Engineers, 400 Commonwealth Drive, Warrendale PA 15096. **Tel** (412)776-4841, (412)772-7106, FAX (412)776-5760. **LC** TL1; .T43. **DD** 629.2/31. **[CCC]. *Continues*** *SAE Technical Literature Abstracts, 0741-2029.*
Ind/Abst Corros. Abstr.

US/0161-1852
TECHNICAL PAPER - SOCIETY OF MANUFACTURING ENGINEERS. EM. [Tech. pap., Soc. Manuf. Eng.]. **Main/Corp** Society of Manufacturing Engineers. Academic Scholarly Publication. English. Price varies per volume. Society of Manufacturing Engineers, One SME Drive, PO Box 930, Member's Records Dept., Dearborn MI 48121-0930. **Tel** (313)271-1500, FAX (313)271-2861, telex 297742 SME UR (VIA RCA). **CODEN** TSEMDM. Documents available from Article Express International, CASDDS.
Ind/Abst Bioeng. Abstr.; Chem. Abstr. (1970-1980); Ei Page One; Eng. Index Annu.

US/0161-1887
TECHNICAL PAPER - SOCIETY OF MANUFACTURING ENGINEERS. TE. [Tech. pap., Soc. Manuf. Eng.]. **Main/Corp** Society of Manufacturing Engineers. Academic Scholarly Publication. English. Price varies per volume. Society of Manufacturing Engineers, One SME Drive, PO Box 930, Member's Records Dept., Dearborn MI 48121-0930. **Tel** (313)271-1500, FAX (313)271-2861, telex 297742 SME UR (VIA RCA). **CODEN** TPSTDO. Documents available from Article Express International, CASDDS.
Ind/Abst Bioeng. Abstr.; Chem. Abstr. (1977); Ei Page One; Eng. Index Annu.

US/0271-499X
TECHNICAL PAPER - U.S. ARMY, CORPS OF ENGINEERS, COASTAL ENGINEERING RESEARCH CENTER. (TECHNICAL PAPER.). [Tech. paper - U.S. Army Corps of Eng., Coast. Eng. Res. Cent.]. **Main/Corp** Coastal Engineering Research Center (U.S.). **VAT** Technical Paper - United States Army, Corps of Engineers, Coastal Engineering Research Center. (19??)-. Monographic series. English. Price varies per volume. National Technical Information Service - NTIS, Room 2027S, 5285 Port Royal Road, Springfield VA 22161. **Tel** (703)487-4630, (703)487-4660, (703)487-4650, FAX (703)321-8547, telex 89-9405.
Ind/Abst Aquat. Sci. Fish. Abstr. (Computer File); GeoRef; Life Sci. Collect.

US/0749-9477
TECHNICAL REPORT CERC. (TECHNICAL REPORT CERC / U.S. ARMY ENGINEER WATERWAYS EXPERIMENT STATION.). [Tech. rep. CERC]. **Added/Corp** U.S. Army Engineer Waterways Experiment Station. Coastal Engineering Research Center (U.S.). **VFOAT** Technical Report C.E.R.C. **VAT** Technical Report Coastal Engineering Research Center. (1983)-. Monographic series. English. Price varies per volume. HQDA Office of the Chief of Engineers, Public Affairs Office, Washington DC 20314. **DD** 353. ***Continues*** *Coastal Engineering Research Center (U.S.). Technical Report -U.S. Army, Corps of Engineers, Coastal Engineering Research Center, 0271-4981.*
Ind/Abst Aquat. Sci. Fish. Abstr. (Computer File).

US/0271-4981
TECHNICAL REPORT - COASTAL ENGINEERING RESEARCH CENTER (U.S.). ***Title Change.*** (TECHNICAL REPORT - U.S. ARMY, CORPS OF ENGINEERS, COASTAL ENGINEERING RESEARCH CENTER.). [Tech. rep. - Coast. Eng. Res. Cent. (U. S.)]. **Main/Corp** Coastal Engineering Research Center (U.S.). **VAT** Technical Report - Coastal Engineering Research Center (United States). (19??)-(19??). Monographic series. English. ***Continues*** *United States. Beach Erosion Board. Technical Report - Beach Erosion Board.* ***Continued by*** *Technical Report CERC, 0749-9477.*
Ind/Abst Aquat. Sci. Fish. Abstr. (Computer File).

CN/0715-8629
TECHNICAL REPORT - UNIVERSITY OF GUELPH, SCHOOL OF ENGINEERING. (TECHNICAL REPORT - SCHOOL OF ENGINEERING, UNIVERSITY OF GUELPH.). [Tech. rep. - Univ. Guelph, Sch. Eng.]. **Main/Corp** Ontario Agricultural College. School of Engineering. **Added/Corp** Ontario Agricultural College. School of Engineering. Monographic series. English. Price varies per volume. University of Guelph School of Engineering, Guelph Ontario N1G 2W1 Canada. **DD** 631. ***Continues*** *Engineering Technical Publications.*
Ind/Abst Maize Abstr.

CN/0381-5366
TECHNIKAS APSKATS - LATVIESU INZENIERU APVIENIBA. Main/Corp Latviesu Inzenieru Apvieniba. **VFOAT** Technical Review. Periodical. Latvian (English). Three times a year. 12.00Can$ Canada. Association of Latvian Engineers, 2 Palieps, 4517 Oxford Avenue, Montreal Quebec H4A 2YG Canada. **Tel** (514)487-9093. **ED** J Palieps. **DD** 620/.005. Index available. **Bk Rev. Circ:** 530 (ctrl). ***Continues*** *Latviesu Inzenieur Apvieniba Arzemes. Technikas Apskats, 0497-0551.*

FR
TECHNIQUES DE L'INGENIEUR / GENERALITES GENIE INDUSTRIEL. French. Editions Techniques, 141 rue de Javel, 75747 Paris Cedex 15 France. **Tel** 011 33 1 45589100.

FR
TECHNIQUES DE L'INGENIEUR / GENIE ENERGETIQUE AND GENIE MECANIQUE. French. 12925.00F 13 basic volumes and updates; 2075.00F updates only. Editions Techniques, 141 rue de Javel, 75747 Paris Cedex 15 France. **Tel** 011 33 1 45589100.

FR/0399-4147
TECHNIQUES DE L'INGENIEUR. MESURES ET CONTROLE. [Tech. ing., mes. controle]. **VFOAT** Mesures et Controle. (1960)-. Academic Scholarly Publication. French. ir. 1490.00F. Editions Techniques, 141 rue de Javel, 75747 Paris Cedex 15 France. **Tel** 011 33 1 45589100. **CODEN** TIMCDU. Documents available from CASDDS.
Ind/Abst Chem. Abstr.

JA/0453-2198
TECHNOLOGY REPORTS OF KANSAI UNIVERSITY. [Technol. rep. Kansai Univ.]. **Main/Corp** Kansai Daigaku, Osaka. Kogakubu. No. 1 (1959)-. Academic Scholarly Publication. English. ir. Kansai Daigaku Kogakubu, (Faculty of Engineering, Kansai University), 3-35, Yamatecho 3 Chome, Suitashi, Osakafu 564, Japan. **LC** TA7; .K23. **CODEN** TRKUAW. Documents available from Article Express International, Ask*IEEE, CASDDS.
Ind/Abst Bioeng. Abstr.; Ceram. Abstr. (19??-); Chem. Abstr.; Ei Page One; Eng. Index Annu.; GeoRef; INSPEC (Feb. 1969-); Math. Rev.; Zentralbl. Math. Ihre Grenzgeb.

JA/0030-6177
TECHNOLOGY REPORTS OF THE OSAKA UNIVERSITY. [Technol. rep. Osaka Univ.]. **Main/Corp** Osaka Daigaku. Kogakubu. **Added/Corp** Osaka Daigaku. Kogakubu. **VFOAT** Technology Reports; Kogaku Hokoku; Osaka Daigaku Kogaku Hokoku. Vol. 1 (1951)-. Academic Scholarly Publication. English. ir. Free on request. Osaka Cty. University, Faculty of Engineering, 3 138 Sugimoto 3 Chome, Osaka 558 Japan. **Tel** 06 877 5111. **LC** TA4; .O85. **DD** 620.82. **CODEN** TROUAI. Documents available from Article Express International, Ask*IEEE, CASDDS.
Ind/Abst Alum. Ind. Abstr.; Bioeng. Abstr.; Chem. Abstr.; Coal Abstr.; Ei Page One; Eng. Index Annu.; Fluid Abstr., Civil Eng.; Fluid Abstr. Proc. Eng.; FLUIDEX (1973-); GeoRef; INSPEC (1968-); Int. Aerosp. Abstr.; Math. Rev.; Met. Abstr.; Pollut. Abstr. Indexes.

HK
TECHNOVA. Chinese. sa. HK$70.00 Hong Kong; $24.00 other. Adsale Publishing Company, 14/F Devon House Taikoo Place, 979 King's Road, Quarry Bay, Hong Kong. **Tel** 011 852 811 8897, FAX 011 852 516 5119. **ED** Josephine Cheng. **Ad Acc. Pr Rev. Circ:** 40,000 (ctrl).
Desc: A polytechnic industrial magazine designed to introduce to China advanced foreign technology, market trends and products of various industries.

PO/0040-1714
TECNICA LISBOA. [Tecnica Lisb.]. (1926)-. Portuguese (English). qt. $12.00. Assn Estudantes Inst Superior Tecnico, Av Rovisco Pais, 1000 Lisbon Portugal. **Tel** 351 1 881018 OR 889323. **CODEN** TECLAA. Documents available from Ask*IEEE.
Ind/Abst Ei Page One; INSPEC (1968-).

RU/0040-2230
TEHNICESKAJA ESTETIKA (MOSKVA). (TEKHNICHESKAIA ESTETIKA.). [Teh. estet.]. **Added/Corp** Vesesoiuznyi Nauchno-Issledovatelskii Institut Tekhnicheskoi Estetiki. (1964)-. Periodical. Russian. Twelve times a year. $99.95. **(Subscription address:** East View Publications Inc., 3020 Harbor Lane North, Suite 110, Minneapolis MN 55447.) **CODEN** TKESBG.
Ind/Abst BHA : Biblio. Hist. Art.

MY
TEKNOLOGI. See Science and Technology.

US/0744-4044
TENNESSEE PROFESSIONAL ENGINEER, THE. Added/Corp Tennessee Society of Professional Engineers. Consulting Engineers of Tennessee. (19??)-. Periodical. English. an. Free on request. Tennessee Society of Professional Engineers, 206 Capitol Boulevard, Nashville TN 37291. **Tel** (615)242-2486.

JA/0386-6831
TEREBIJON GAKKAISHI. Added/Corp Terebijon Gakkai (Japan). **VFOAT** Journal of the Institute of Television Engineers of Japan. Vol. 32, No. 1 (Jan. 1978)-. Periodical. Japanese (English). mo. $320.00. Terebijon Gakkai, (Inst. of Television Engineers of Japan), 5-8, Shiba Koen 3 Chome, Minatoku, Tokyoto 105 Japan. **(Subscription address:** Kyowa Book Company Inc., 1-38 Kanda Jinbo-Cho, Chiyoda-Ku, Tokyo 101, Japan) ***Continues*** *Terebijon.*

IT/0040-3725
TERMOTECNICA. (LA TERMOTECNICA.). [Termotecnica]. **Added/Corp** Associazione Termotecnica Italiana. (Apr. 1947)-. Academic Scholarly Publication. Italian. mo (10 issues). L60000 Italy; L80000 other. Editrice Bias, Viale Premuda 2, 20129 Milan Italy. **Tel** 011 39 2 55181842. **LC** TJ260.A1; T47. **CODEN** TERMAK. Documents available from Article Express International, CASDDS.
Ind/Abst Bioeng. Abstr.; Chem. Abstr.; Coal Abstr.; Ei Page One; EMBASE; Energy Res. Abstr.; Eng. Index Annu.; Fluid Abstr., Civil Eng.; Fluid Abstr. Proc. Eng.; FLUIDEX (1973-); Int. Aerosp. Abstr.; Int. Build. Serv. Abstr.; Proc. Chem. Eng.; Theoret. Chem. Eng.

US/0747-1262
TEXAS PROFESSIONAL ENGINEER (1981). (TEXAS PROFESSIONAL ENGINEER.). [Tex. prof. eng.]. **Added/Corp** Texas Society of Professional Engineers. (1981)-. Periodical. English. bm. $10.00. Texas Society of Professional Engineers, 3501 Manor Road, PO Box 2145, Austin TX 78768. **Tel** (512)472-9286, FAX (512)472-2934. **ED** Edd O'Donnell. **Ad Acc. Circ:** 7,500. ***Continues*** *TPE, 0195-2811.*

UK/0040-6015
THERMAL ENGINEERING. [Therm. eng.]. **Added/Corp** British Library. Lending Division. Great Britain. Dept. of Education and Science. Heating and Ventilating Research Association. Great Britain. Dept. of Scientific and Industrial Research. (1964)-. Academic Scholarly Publication. English (Russian). mo. $988.00 US and Canada; $1059.00 other. MAIK Nauka / Interperiodica, Ulitsa Profsoyuznaya 90, Moscow 117864 Russia. **(Subscription address:** Interperiodica Publishing, Subscription Office, PO Box 1831, Birmingham AL 35201-1831.) **CODEN** THENAD. **Pr Rev.** Documents available from Article Express International, The Genuine Article, Ask*IEEE, CASDDS, Documents on Demand.
Ind/Abst Alum. Ind. Abstr.; Chem. Abstr.; Coal Abstr.; Curr. Contents Eng. Tech. Appl. Sci.; Ei Page One; EMBASE; Energy Inf. Abstr.; Eng. Mater. Abstr. (1973-);

Eng. Index Annu.; Environ. Abstr.; Fluid Abstr., Civil Eng.; Fluid Abstr. Proc. Eng.; FLUIDEX (1973-1988)(1973-); HTFS Dig.; INSPEC (1969-); Int. Aerosp. Abstr.; Int. Build. Serv. Abstr.; Met. Abstr.; Proc. Chem. Eng.; Res. Alert [Full Cov.]; Sci. Cit. Index; SCISEARCH; Soc. Sci. Cit. Index [Select. Cov.]; Theoret. Chem. Eng.

●US
THESAURUS. **Added/Corp** Engineering Information, Inc. **VFOAT** Engineering Information Thesaurus. 1st Ed. (1992)-. English. $130.00 North America; $140.00 other. Engineering Information Inc., Castle Point on the Hudson, Hoboken NJ 07030. **Tel** (800)221-1044, (201)216-8500, FAX (201)216-8526, telex 4990438. ***Continues in part*** *EI Vocabulary.*

US
THESAURUS OF ENGINEERED MATERIALS / MATERIALS INFORMATION. **Added/Corp** Materials Information (Information Service) ASM International. (Jan. 1987)-. Periodical. English. an. $90.00 North America; £60.00 E.C. countries; $100.00 other. American Society for Metals International, c/o Deborah Barthelmes, Materials Park OH 44073-0002. **Tel** (216)338-5151, FAX (216)338-4634, telex 980-619. **(Subscription address:** ASM International, Materials Information, Materials Park OH 44073.**)** **LC** Z695.1.M39; T47. **DD** 025.4/9669.

CN/0707-3968
THOROUGH. V. 1- Jan. 1979-. Periodical. English. ir. Free. University of Saskatchewan College of Engineering, Saskatoon Saskatchewan S7N 0W0 Canada. **Tel** (306)966-6202, telex 074-2659. **ED** Wayne Eyre. **DD** 620/.007/1171242. **Circ:** 8,000.
Desc: College newsletter to alumni, engineering profession, and selected corporations.

CC
TI CHEN KUNG CHENG YU KUNG CHENG CHEN TUNG. **VFOAT** Earthquake Engineering and Engineering Vibration. (19??)-. Periodical. Chinese (summaries and/or abstracts in English). qt. Institute of Engineering Mechanics / Beijing, Earthquake Publishing House, Beijing, People's Republic of China. **LC** TA654.6; .T56. **DD** 551.2/2/05.
Ind/Abst Abstr. J. Earthq. Eng.

CH
TI CHI TSE LIANG. **VFOAT** Cadastral Survey; Annals of Chinese Society of Cadastral Survey. V. 1, (May 1982)-. Chinese. an. Chinese Society of Cadastral Survey 4, 469 Lane Sung-chiang Road, Taipei Taiwan. **LC** TA501; .T5. **DD** 526.9/05.

FR
TIERS MONDE INGENIERIE : TMI. French. ir. 4900.00F. IC Publications Ediafric, 10 rue Vineuse, 75116 Paris France. **Tel** 011 33 1 44308100.

US/0197-6753
TMR, TRAVEL MARKETING REPORT. [TMR. Travel mark. rep.]. **VFOAT** Travel Marketing Report; Directory of Engineering, Architectural & Construction Companies. 1st- Ed.; 1980/81-. English. be. $500.00. Travel Marketing Report, PO Box 66323, O'Hare International Airport, Chicago IL 60666. **LC** TA12; .T17. **DD** 338.4/762/0002573.

JA
TOA. **Added/Corp** Kazankai. (19??)-. Periodical. Japanese. mo. ¥2500. **(Subscription address:** Maruzen Company Ltd., PO Box 5050, Import & Export Department, Tokyo 100 31 Japan.**)** **LC** DS518.1; .T59. ***Continues*** *Kazan.*

JA/0288-6502
TOCHI ZOSEI KOGAKU KENKYU SHISETSU HOKOKU. No. 1-. Japanese. Kobe Daigaku Kogakubu Tochi Zosei Kogaku Kenkyu, Shisetsu Rokkodai-cho Nada-ku Kobe-shi 657 Japan.

US/1060-2534
TODAY'S PARTS MANAGER. [Today's parts manag.]. Vol. 1, Issue 1 (1991)-. Periodical. English. qt. Free. Management Computer Services, Inc., 2790 Fisher Road, Columbus OH 43204-3581. **DD** 629.

JA/0389-617X
TOKYO DENKI DAIGAKU KOGAKUBU KENKYU HOKOKU. [Tokyo Denki Daigaku Kogakubu kenkyu hokoku]. **Added/Corp** Tokyo Denki Daigaku. Kogakubu. **VFOAT** Research Reports of Faculty of Engineering, Tokyo Denki University; Kenkyu Hokoku. No. 27 (Dec. 1979)-. Periodical. Japanese. Tokyo Denki Daigaku Kogakubu, (Faculty of Engineering, Tokyo Denki University), 2-2, Kanda Nishikicho, Chiyodaku, Tokyoto 101, Japan. **CODEN** RPFUD8. Documents available from Ask*IEEE, CASDDS. ***Continues*** *Tokyo Denki Daigaku Kenkyu Hokoku.*
Ind/Abst Chem. Abstr. (1979-1981); INSPEC (Dec. 1980-); Int. Aerosp. Abstr.; Math. Rev.

UK/0952-5300
TOPICS IN ENGINEERING. Vol. 1 (1987)-. Monographic series. English.
Ind/Abst Zentralbl. Math. Ihre Grenzgeb.

IT/0394-512X
TP. IL GIORNALE DELLA TRASMISSIONE DI POTENZA. ***Ceased.*** [TP, g. trasm. potenza]. **VFOAT** Trasmissione Potenza. Il Giornale della Trasmissione di Potenza. (19??)-(Dec. 1993). Periodical. Italian. mo. Tecniche Nuove SPA, Via Ciro Menotti 14, 20129 Milan Italy. **Tel** 011 39 2 75701, FAX 011 39 2 7610351, telex 334647 TECHS I. **UDC** 621.3.

UK
TRANSACTIONS / INSTITUTE OF MARINE ENGINEERS. **Added/Corp** Institute of Marine Engineers. Vol. 1, Pt. 1 (1988)-. Periodical. English. bm. $230.00 US. Marine Management Holdings Ltd, Memorial Building, 76 Mark Lane, London EC3R 7JN England. **Tel** 011 44 71 4818493. **(Subscription address:** North America: Learned Information Inc., 143 Old Marlton Pike, Medford, NJ 08055-8750**)** **Circ:** 8,000. ***Continues*** *Transactions (TM), 0268-4152.*
Desc: Covers all aspects of marine engineering, from ship and machinery design to offshore structures, use of equipment, regulations, engines, fuel, safety, new ideas, buildings, systems and procedures.
Ind/Abst BMT Abstr.; Lit. Pat. Abstr., Oilfield Chem. (1989-); Lit. Abstr., Catal. Catal.; Lit. Abstr., Health Environ.; Lit. Abstr., Pet. Refin. Petrochem.; Lit. Abstr., Pet. Substit.; Lit. Abstr., Transp. Storage.

UK
TRANSACTIONS / INSTITUTION OF ENGINEERS AND SHIPBUILDERS IN SCOTLAND. **Main/Corp** Institution of Engineers and Shipbuilders in Scotland. Periodical. English. an. £20.00. Institute of Engineers and Shipbuilders in Scotland, 1 Atlantic Quay Broomielaw, Glasgow G2 8JE Scotland. **Tel** 011 44 41 2483721. ***Continues*** *Transactions of the Institution of Engineers in Scotland, with which is Incorporated the Scottish Shipbuilders' Association.*

IE
TRANSACTIONS - INSTITUTION OF ENGINEERS OF IRELAND. **Main/Corp** Institution of Engineers of Ireland. V. 96- 1969/71-. English. ir. $20.00. Institute of Engineers of Ireland, 22 Clyde Road, Ballsbridge, Dublin 4 Ireland. ***Continues*** *Institution of Civil Engineers of Ireland. Transactions.*

UK/0029-280X
TRANSACTIONS - NORTH EAST COAST INSTITUTION OF ENGINEERS AND SHIPBUILDERS. ***Ceased.*** [Trans. - North East Coast Inst. Eng. Shipbuild.]. **Main/Corp** North East Coast Institution of Engineers and Shipbuilders, Newcastle-Upon-Tyne. (1884)-Ceased with Vol. 108, No.4 (Sept. 1992). English. Four times a year. Northern Engineering Centre, Great North House, Sandyford Road, Newcastle Upon Tyne NE1 8ND United Kingdom. **Tel** (091)230 1514. **(Subscription address:** North East Coast Insititution of Engineers and Shipbuilders, 12 Windsor Terrace Jesmond, Newcastle Upon Tyne, NE2 4HE United Kingdon.**)** **ED** A J Rainsford. **CODEN** TNEEAS. Index available in last issue of volume--attached. cum. index. **Circ:** 1,200. Documents available from Article Express International, Ask*IEEE.
Desc: List of members in each volume.
Ind/Abst Bioeng. Abstr.; BMT Abstr. (-1992); Ei Page One (1984-1992); EMBASE; Eng. Index Annu.; INSPEC (March 1983-).

US
TRANSACTIONS OF THE AMERICAN INSTITUTE OF MINING, METALLURGICAL AND PETROLEUM ENGINEERS. **Main/Corp** American Institute of Mining, Metallurgical, and Petroleum Engineers. Vol. 1 (May 1871)-. English. mo. $752.00 (nonmember and institutional member), $50.00 (individual member). American Society for Metals International, c/o Deborah Barthelmes, Materials Park OH 44073-0002. **Tel** (216)338-5151, FAX (216)338-4634, telex 980-619. **(Subscription address:** ASM International, Materials Information, Materials Park OH 44073.**)** **LC** TN1; .A5. cum. index.
Ind/Abst AESIS Q.

US/0001-2351
TRANSACTIONS OF THE ASAE. [Trans. ASAE]. **Main/Corp** American Society of Agricultural Engineers. **VAT** Transactions of the American Society of Agricultural Engineers. Vol. 1 (1958)-. Academic Scholarly Publication. English. Six times a year. $202.00 (nonmember), $68.50 (member). American Society of Agricultural Engineers, Department 2510, 2950 Niles Road, St. Joseph MI 49085-9659. **Tel** (616)429-0300, FAX (616)429-3852. **ED** James Basselman. **LC** S671; .A452. **DD** 631.3/05. **CODEN** TAAEAJ. **[CCC]**. Index available ($6.25). cum. index. **Pr Rev. Circ:** 2,200 (ctrl). Documents available from Article Express International, The Genuine Article, BIOSIS Document Express, CASDDS, Documents on Demand. ***Supersedes*** *Transactions of the American Society of Agricultural Engineers.*
Desc: Full length technical articles describe the application of engineering principles to the solution of agricultural problems.
Ind/Abst AgBiotech News Inf.; AGRICOLA [Full Cov.]; Agric. Eng. Abstr.; Biodeter. Abstr. (1991-); Bioeng. Abstr.; Biol. Agric. Index; Biol. Abstr.; Chem. Abstr.; Civ. Struct. Eng. Abstr.; Coal Abstr.; Comput. Inf. Syst. Abstr. J. [Full Cov.]; Cot. Trop. Fibr. Abstr. Bibliogr.; Curr. Aware. Biol. Sci., CABS; Curr. Contents, Agric. Biol. Environ. Sci.; Curr. Contents Eng. Tech. Appl. Sci.; Dairy Sci. Abstr.; Ei Page One; Elect. Comm. Abstr.; EMBASE; Energy Inf. Abstr.; Eng. Index Annu.; Environ. Abstr.; Environ. Eng. Abstr.; Field Crop Abstr.; Fluid Abstr., Civil Eng.; Fluid Abstr. Proc. Eng.; FLUIDEX (1973-); Food Sci. Technol. Abstr.; For. Prod. Abstr. (19??-19??); For. Abstr.; Grasslands For. Abstr.; Hortic. Abstr.; Int. Abstr. Oper. Res. [Select. Cov.]; Irr. Drain. Abstr.; Maize Abstr.; Manuf. Process Eng. Abstr.; Mater. Sci. Eng. Abstr.; Mech. Eng. Abstr.; Nutr. Abstr. Rev., Ser. B, Live Feeds and Feed.; Ocean. Abstr.; Ornamental Hort. (19??-19??); Life Sci. Collect.; Pig News Inf.; Plant Genet. Resour. Abstr.; Postharvest News Inf.; Potato Abstr.; Poult. Abstr.; Res. Alert [Full Cov.]; Rev. Agric. Entomol.; Rev. Med. Vet. Entomol.; Rev. Med. Vet. Mycology; Rev. Plant Pathol.; Rice Abstr.; Sci. Cit. Index; SCISEARCH; Seed Abstr.; Soils Fert.; Solid State Supercond. Abstr.; Sorghum Mill. Abstr.; Soyabean Abstr.; Sug. Indus. Abstr.; Weed Abstr.

AT/0812-3314
TRANSACTIONS OF THE INSTITUTION OF ENGINEERS, AUSTRALIA. MULTI-DISCIPLINARY ENGINEERING. **Added/Corp** Institution of Engineers, Australia. **VFOAT** Multi-Disciplinary Engineering. Vol. 1 (1983)-. Academic Scholarly Publication. English. Twice a year (June & Dec.). 35.00Aus$ Australia; 50.00Aus$ others. Engineers Australia Pty Ltd, 2 Ernest Street, Crows Nest Centre, Crows Nest New South Wales 2065, Australia. **Tel** 011 61 2 438-1533, FAX 011 61 2 438-5934, telex 27640. **ED** Don J. Fraser. **Pr Rev. Circ:** 1,000 (ctrl). Documents available from Article Express International, Ask*IEEE. ***Continues*** *Transactions of the Institution of Engineers, Australia. General Engineering.*
Desc: Learned papers covering all aspects of engineering which are common to the major engineering disciplines such as management and heritage.
Ind/Abst Ei Page One; EMBASE; Energy Inf. Abstr.; Energy Res. Abstr. (1983-); Eng. Index Annu. [Select. Cov.]; INSPEC (1983-).

NZ/0111-946X
TRANSACTIONS OF THE INSTITUTION OF PROFESSIONAL ENGINEERS NEW ZEALAND, ELECTRICAL/MECHANICAL/CHEMICAL ENGINEERING SECTION. ***Title Change.*** [Trans. Inst. Prof. Eng. N.Z., Electr./Mech./Chem. Eng. Sect.]. **Main/Corp** Institution of Professional Engineers New Zealand. Electrical, Mechanical, Chemical, Engineering Section. **VFOAT** I.P.E.N.Z. Transactions; IPENZ Transactions. Vol. 9, No. 1 (Mar. 1982)-(198?). English. Institute of Professional Engineers New Zealand, PO Box 12241, Wellington New Zealand. **Tel** 011 64 4 4739444. **LC** TA1; .I745a. **DD** 620/.005. **CODEN** TPESDJ. Documents available from Article Express International, Ask*IEEE. ***Continues*** *New Zealand Institution of Engineers. Electrical, Mechanical, Chemical Engineering Section. Transactions of the New Zealand Institution of Engineers. Electrical/Mechanical/Chemical Engineering Section, 0111-2740.* ***Continued by*** *Transactions of the Institution of Professional Engineers New Zealand. General section, 0114-1562.*
Ind/Abst Alum. Ind. Abstr.; Bioeng. Abstr.; Coal Abstr.; Ei Page One; Eng. Mater. Abstr.; Eng. Index Annu. [Select. Cov.]; INSPEC (March 1982-); Met. Abstr.

UK/0020-3122
TRANSPORT ENGINEER, THE. **Added/Corp** Institute of Road Transport Engineers. (1970)-. Periodical. English. Twelve times a year. £24.00 Europe; £30.00 other. Institute of Road Transport Engineers / IRTE, 22 Greencoat Place, London SW1P 1PR United Kingdom. **Tel** 071 630 1111, FAX 071 630 6677. **ED** John Dickson-Simpson (editor's address: Transport Press Services, Pegasus House, 116-120 Golden Lane, London EC1Y 0TL England; editor's phone: 44 71 2511227). **LC** TL230.A1; T68. **DD** 629.22/4/05. Index available (April). **Bk Rev. Ad Acc. Circ:** 16,500 (ctrl). ***Continues*** *Institute of Road Transport Engineers. Journal of the Institute of Road Transport Engineers;* ***Absorbed*** *Transport Engineer Monthly Bulletin.*
Ind/Abst Curr. Technol. Index; Manage. Market. Abstr.

UK
TRANSPORT ENGINEER'S HANDBOOK, THE. (1983)-. English. Kogan Page Ltd., 120 Pentonville Road, London N1 9BR England. **Tel** 011 44 71 2780433, FAX 011 44 71 8376348, telex 263088 KOGAN G. **LC** TL230.A1; T684. **DD** 629.2/24/0941.
Desc: Provides a concise and practical guide for every keep up with the latest developments in the industry. Combines practical information and advice with detailed technical information for today's transport engineer.

FR/0041-1906
TRAVAUX. [Travaux]. Vol. 17 (Jan. 1933)-. Academic Scholarly Publication. French (summaries and/or abstracts in English, Spanish, German and Portuguese). mo (eleven issues per year). 650.00F France; 780.00F

other. Editions Science et Industrie, 6 Avenue Pierre 1 de Serbie, Paris 75116 France. **Tel** (1)40 75 03 95, FAX (1)42 56 48 31. **ED** Dominique Milleron. **LC** TA2; .T7. **DD** 620.5. **CODEN** TRAVAJ. **[CCC].** Index available. **Ad Acc. Circ:** 5,000. Documents available from Article Express International. ***Continues in part*** *Science et Industrie.*
Desc: Public works and associated disciplines. Mostly water drainage, special foundations, materials structure and industrial equipment, pipelaying, roads and aerodromes, earthworks, underground and railways.
Ind/Abst Bioeng. Abstr.; Coal Abstr.; Concr. Abstr.; Ei Page One; EMBASE; Eng. Index Annu.; GeoRef; Highw. Res. Abstr.

US/0362-0018
TREND IN ENGINEERING AT THE UNIVERSITY OF WASHINGTON, THE. [Trend eng. Univ. Wash.]. **Added/Corp** University of Washington. Office of Engineering Research. **VFOAT** Trend in Engineering; Trend in Engineering at the University of Washington Newsletter. Vol. 1 (Dec. 1948)-. Academic Scholarly Publication. English. sa. Free. Trend in Engineering, University of Washington, School of Engineering, Seattle WA 98195. **Tel** (206)543-2520. **LC** TA1; .T85. **DD** 620. **CODEN** TREEAM. ctrl circ. Documents available from CASDDS.
Ind/Abst Chem. Abstr.; Int. Aerosp. Abstr.

FI/0780-2285
TRIBOLOGIA. **VFOAT** Finnish Journal of Tribology. (1982)-. Multiple languages. qt.
Ind/Abst Ei Page One; Fluid Abstr., Civil Eng.; Fluid Abstr. Proc. Eng.; FLUIDEX (19??-).

US/1040-2004
TRIBOLOGY TRANSACTIONS. (TRIBOLOGY TRANSACTIONS : A PUBLICATION OF THE SOCIETY OF TRIBOLOGISTS AND LUBRICATION ENGINEERS.). [Tribol. trans.]. **Added/Corp** Society of Tribologists and Lubrication Engineers. **VFOAT** STLE Transactions. **VAT** Society of Tribologists and Lubrication Engineers Tribology Transactions. Vol. 31, No. 1 (Jan. 1988)-. Periodical. English. qt. $144.00 (one year), $271.00 (two years) US; $168.00 (one year), $328.00 (two years) other. Society of Tribologists and Lubrication Engineers, 840 Busse Highway, Park Ridge IL 60068. **Tel** (708)825-5536, FAX (708)825-1456. **LC** TJ1075.A2; A25. **DD** 621.8/9. **CODEN** TRTRE4. **[CCC].** available on microfilm and microfiche from University Microfilms International (UMI). Documents available from The Genuine Article, CASDDS. ***Continues*** *ASLE Transactions, 0569-8197.*
Desc: Reports worldwide progress in every aspect of lubrication research, design, and development. Is a continuing record of advanced original research by top authorities in the field of lubrication.
Ind/Abst Appl. Sci. Technol. Index (1988-); Chem. Abstr.; Curr. Contents Eng. Tech. Appl. Sci.; Fluid Abstr., Civil Eng.; Fluid Abstr. Proc. Eng.; FLUIDEX; Lit. Pat. Abstr., Oilfield Chem. (1960-); Lit. Abstr., Catal. Catal.; Lit. Abstr., Health Environ.; Lit. Abstr., Pet. Refin. Petrochem.; Lit. Abstr., Pet. Substit.; Lit. Abstr., Transp. Storage; Res. Alert [Full Cov.]; Sci. Cit. Index; SCISEARCH; Shock Vibr. Dig.

CC/1001-4055
TUIJIN JISHU. **VFOAT** Journal of Propulsion Technology. (1980)-. Periodical. Chinese. bm. Journal of Propulsion Technology, Editorial Department, PO Box 7208-26, 100074 Beijing China. **DD** 629.13238. Documents available from Article Express International.
Ind/Abst Ei Page One; Eng. Index Annu.; Int. Aerosp. Abstr.

GW
TUNNEL. **See** Building and Construction.

CN/0708-1995
U N B ENGINEERING NEWSLETTER. **Added/Corp** University of New Brunswick. Faculty of Engineering. **VAT** University of New Brunswick Engineering Newsletter. Vol. 1 (Jan. 1979)-. Periodical. English. Free. University of New Brunswick Electrical Engineering Department, PO Box 4400, Fredericton New Brunswick E3B 5A3 Canada. **DD** 621/.07/1171551.

US/0272-7838
U.S. WOMAN ENGINEER. ***Title Change.*** [U.S. woman eng.]. **Added/Corp** Society of Women Engineers. **VAT** United States Woman Engineer. Vol. 26, No. 4 (Mar./Apr. 1980)-(19??). Periodical. English. Six times a year. Society of Women Engineers, 120 Wall Street, 11th Floor, New York NY 10005. **Tel** (212)509-9577, (800)666-1793, FAX (212)319-0947. **ED** Anne E. Perusek. **LC** TA1; .S18. **DD** 620/.0088042. **Bk Rev. Ad Acc. Circ:** 15,000 (ctrl). Documents available from Article Express International. ***Continues*** *SWE Newsletter.* ***Continued by*** *SWE.*
Desc: Articles and issues relevant to women engineers.
Ind/Abst Ei Page One; Eng. Index Annu.

TZ
UHANDISI. Began with Dec. 1974 issue. Periodical. English. Faculty of Engineering, University of Dar es Salaam, PO Box 35131, Dar es Salaam Tanzania. **LC** TA1; .U45. **DD** 620/.005.

US/0270-6504
UKY BU (UNIVERSITY OF KENTUCKY). (UKY BULLETIN.). [UKY BU]. **Added/Corp** University of Kentucky. Office of Engineering Services. No. 95 (1971)-. Bulletin. English. IEEE, Institution of Electrical and Electronics Engineers, Inc., 345 East 47th Street, New York NY 10017-2394. **Tel** (908)981-1393, FAX (908)981-9667. **LC** UNC. **CODEN** UKOBDS. Documents available from Article Express International, CASDDS. ***Continues*** *Bulletin (University of Kentucky. Office of Research and Engineering Services), 0453-5650.*
Ind/Abst Bioeng. Abstr.; Chem. Abstr. (-1984); Ei Page One; Eng. Index Annu.

SP/0211-9099
ULTRASONIDOS. ***Ceased.*** Vol. 1, No. 1 (March 1982)-(1990). Periodical. Spanish. qt. Editorial Garsi SA, Juan Bravo 46, 28006 Madrid, Spain. **Tel** 011 34 1 4021212, telex 98358 GARSI E. **NLM** W1; UL748B.
Ind/Abst Indice Med. Esp.

US
UNDERGROUND TANK TECHNOLOGY UPDATE. (19??)-. English. bm (6 issues). $25.00. Department of Engineering and Professional Development, 432 North Lake Street, Madison WI 53706. **Tel** (800)442-4616, (608)262-3484. **ED** Pat Komor. **Circ:** 3,000 (ctrl).

AT
UNISURV REPORT S. **See** Earth Sciences.

UK/0309-6521
UNIVERSITY OF CAMBRIDGE. DEPARTMENT OF ENGINEERING. CUED/A-TURBO. **Main/Corp** Cambridge. University. Dept. of Engineering. **VFOAT** Cued/A-Turbo. Academic Scholarly Publication. English. Price varies per volume. Cambridge University Press, The Edinburgh Building, Shaftesbury Road, Cambridge CB2 2RU United Kingdom. **Tel** 011 44 223 312393, FAX 011 44 223 325959. **(Subscription address:** US/ 110 Midland Avenue, Port Chester, NY 10573**)** **CODEN** CUTUDG. Documents available from CASDDS.
Ind/Abst Chem. Abstr.; Ei Page One.

UK/0309-6505
UNIVERSITY OF CAMBRIDGE. DEPARTMENT OF ENGINEERING. CUED/C-MAT. **Main/Corp** Cambridge. University. Dept. of Engineering. **VFOAT** Cued/C-Mat. Academic Scholarly Publication. English. Price varies per volume. Cambridge University Press, The Edinburgh Building, Shaftesbury Road, Cambridge CB2 2RU United Kingdom. **Tel** 011 44 223 312393, FAX 011 44 223 325959. **(Subscription address:** US/ 110 Midland Avenue, Port Chester, NY 10573**)** **CODEN** UCDCDM. Documents available from CASDDS.
Ind/Abst Chem. Abstr.

JA
UNYUSHO KENKYU KIHON KEIKAKU. **Main/Corp** Japan. Unyusho. (19??)-. Periodical. Japanese. an. Unyusho, (Ministry of Transport), 1-3 Kasumigaseki 2 Chiyodaku, Tokyoto 100 Japan. **LC** TA160.6.J3; J36a.

US/1058-2428
US BLACK ENGINEER. **See** Ethnic Interests.

US
USSR REPORT. ENGINEERING AND EQUIPMENT. **Added/Corp** United States. Joint Publications Research Service. United States. Foreign Broadcast Information Service. **VFOAT** Engineering and Equipment. No. 57, (Aug. 1979)-. English. ***Continues*** *USSR and Eastern Europe Scientific Abstracts. Engineering and Equipment.*

US
UTILIZATION OF SHIPBUILDING AND REPAIR FACILITIES SERIES. **See** Naval Science, Navigation.

GW/0934-9758
VAKUUM IN DER PRAXIS. **See** Physics.

US/0275-4371
VALUE ENGINEERING & MANAGEMENT DIGEST. (VALUE ENGINEERING & MANAGEMENT DIGEST : DEFENSE CONTRACT GUIDE.). **VFOAT** Defense Contract Guide; Value Engineering Digest; Value Digest. **VAT** Value Engineering and Management Digest. (1960)-. Periodical. English. Twelve times a year. $180.00. Tufty Communications Inc, 499 National Press Building, Washington DC 20045. **Tel** (202)347-8998. **ED** Hal Tufty. **Ad Acc. Circ:** 5,000 (ctrl). ***Continues*** *Value Engineering Digest/Defense Contract Guide.*
Desc: Publishes extracts of books and articles about value engineering, analysis, management, and improvement to identify and solve problems, while maintaining quality, at the lowest total cost.

GW/0083-5560
VDI-BERICHTE. [VDI-Ber.]. **Main/Corp** Verein Deutscher Ingenieure. **Added/Corp** Verein Deutscher Ingenieure. **VAT** VDI Berichte; Verein Deutscher Ingenieure-Berichte. No. 1 (1955)-. Academic Scholarly Publication. German. ir. Price varies per volume. VDI Verlag GmbH, Postfach 101054, D 40001 Dusseldorf Germany. **Tel** 011 49 211 6188313, FAX 011 49 211 6188133. **LC** TA3; .V15. **CODEN** VDIBAP. **[CCC].** Documents available from Article Express International, Ask*IEEE, CASDDS.
Desc: Reports on international conferences of the various VDI technical groups. Contains lectures and discussions on special technical subjects dealing with the latest developments in a particular field.
Ind/Abst Bioeng. Abstr.; Chem. Abstr.; Coal Abstr.; Ei Page One; Energy Res. Abstr. (Aug. 1972-); Eng. Index Annu.; GeoRef; INSPEC (1986-); Int. Aerosp. Abstr.

GW/0042-174X
VDI-FORSHUNGSHEFT. ***Title Change.*** **VAT** Vereins Deutscher Ingenieure Forschungsheft. Vol. 1 (1901)-(1992). Academic Scholarly Publication. German. Six times a year. VDI Verlag GmbH, Postfach 101054, D 40001 Dusseldorf Germany. **Tel** 011 49 211 6188313, FAX 011 49 211 6188133. **[CCC].** Documents available from Article Express International, CASDDS. ***Merged into*** *Forschung im Ingenieurwesen.*
Desc: Contains extensive papers dealing with fields where the theory of solving technical problems does not suffice and attempts have to be made to solve unknown relationships.
Ind/Abst Acoust. Abstr.; Alum. Ind. Abstr.; Bioeng. Abstr.; Chem. Abstr.; Ei Page One; EMBASE; Energy Res. Abstr. (Aug. 1972-); Eng. Index Annu.; Int. Aerosp. Abstr.; Met. Abstr.; Proc. Chem. Eng.; Theoret. Chem. Eng.

GW
VDI INFORMATIONSDIENST REGELUNGSTECHNIK. **Added/Corp** Elektroinformation Berlin. **VFOAT** Informationsdienst Regelungstechnik. (1978)-. Periodical. German. mo. DM1291.00 Germany; DM1330.00 other. VDI Verlag GmbH, Postfach 101054, D 40001 Dusseldorf Germany. **Tel** 011 49 211 6188313, FAX 011 49 211 6188133. ***Continues*** *Dokumentation Regelungstechnik.*
Desc: Abstracting papers taken from German and other international literature on the following subjects: cybernetics, feedback control, process date processing, remote-action technology, switchboard technology, etc.

SZ/0252-9424
VERMESSUNG, PHOTOGRAMMETRIE, KULTURTECHNIK. (VERMESSUNG, PHOTOGRAMMETRIE, KULTURTECHNIK.). [Vermess. Photogramm. Kult.tech.]. **VFOAT** Mensuration, Photogrammetrie, Genie Rural. (Jan. 1978)-. Periodical. French (German). mo. 96.00F Switzerland; 120.00F other. SIGWERB AG, PF 173 Dorfmattenstr 26, CH 5612 Villmergen Switzerland. **Tel** 011 41 57 230505, FAX 011 41 57 231550. **LC** TA501; .M39. **DD** 526.9/05. Index Bound in First Issue (Jan.). **Bk Rev. Ad Acc, Adv Mgr:** Mr Signer. ctrl circ. ***Continues*** *Mensuration, Photogrammetrie, Genei Rural.*
Ind/Abst GeoRef.

GW/0372-5715
VGB-KRAFTWERKSTECHNIK. [VGB-Kraftwerkstech.]. **Main/Corp** Technische Vereinigung der Grosskraftwerksbetreiber E.V. (1972)-. Academic Scholarly Publication. English. mo. DM552.12 Germany; $379.70 US. VGB Kraftwerkstechnik GmbH, Postfach 103932, D 45039 Essen Germany. **Tel** 011 49 201 4862682, telex 857507. **CODEN** VGBKB5. Index available. cum. index. **Bk Rev. Ad Acc. Circ:** 3,600. Documents available from Article Express International, Ask*IEEE, CASDDS.
Desc: Power plant engineering, conventional and nuclear.
Ind/Abst Alum. Ind. Abstr. (19??-); Bioeng. Abstr. (19??-); Chem. Abstr. (19??-); Coal Abstr. (19??-); Ei Page One (19??-); EMBASE (19??-); Energy Res. Abstr. (Oct. 1972-); Eng. Mater. Abstr. (19??-); Eng. Index Annu. (19??-) [Select. Cov.]; INSPEC (Sept. 1980-); Met. Abstr. (19??-); Saf. Health Work (19??-).

II/0377-8487
VIGNANA BHARATHI. **See** Science and Technology.

US/0504-4251
VIRGINIA ENGINEER (1974), THE. (THE VIRGINIA ENGINEER.). (1974)-. Periodical. English. Twelve times a year. $15.00 one year; $27.00 two years; $37.00 three years. Richard Carden, Route 2 Box 58, Cumberland VA 23040. **Tel** (804)492-4578. **ED** Richard O. Carden. **Bk Rev. Ad Acc. Circ:** 3,450. ***Continues*** *Virginia Professional Engineer.*
Desc: News and features of multi-disclinary subjects for engineers and architects.

US/1054-481X
VITRO TECHNICAL JOURNAL. [Vitro tech. j.]. **Added/Corp** Vitro Corporation. (19??)-. Periodical. English. **LC** TA168; .V57. **DD** 620/.001/1. **CODEN** VTJOEF. Documents available from Article Express International, Ask*IEEE.
Ind/Abst Ei Page One; Eng. Index Annu. [Select. Cov.]; INSPEC (Winter 1990-); Int. Aerosp. Abstr.

RU
VOPROSY INZHENERNOI GEOLGII I GRUNTOVEDENIIA. **Main/Corp** Moscow. Universitet. Kafedra Gruntovedeniia i Inzhenernoi Geologii. Vol. 1 (1963)-. Academic Scholarly Publication. Russian. 4.19rub single issue. Izdatelstvo Moskovskogo Universiteta, K-9 Ulitsa Gertsena 5/7, Moscow Russia. **Tel** (301)881-5973. **LC** TA705; .M69a. **CODEN** VIGGAV. Documents available from CASDDS.
Ind/Abst Chem. Abstr. (?-1973).

GW/0340-5141
VR. VERMESSUNGSWESEN UND RAUMORDNUNG. **See** Geography.

GW/0042-3890
VTB. VERFAHRENSTECHNISCHE BERICHTE. [VtB, Verfahrenstech. Ber.]. **VFOAT** Verfahrenstechnische Berichte. (194?)-. German (English). wk. $2940.00. Verlag Hoppenstedt & Company, Postfach 100139, D 64201 Darmstadt Germany. **Tel** 011 49 6151 380436. **UDC** [66.0-54.03/.04-620.21/.22-678.01](01). **[CCC].**

XR/0139-9365
VYTVARNA KULTURA. **See** The Arts-Art.

JA
WASEDA DAIGAKU DAIGAKUIN RIKOGAKU KENKYU IHO. **Main/Corp** Waseda Daigaku, Tokyo. Daigakuin. Rikogaku Kenkyuka. **VFOAT** Synopses of Engineering Papers, Graduate School of Science and Engineering, Waseda University. Japanese (Japanese). Waseda Daigaku, 170 Nishi Okubo 4 Shinjuku-ku, Tokyo Japan. **LC** TA4; .W34A.

JA/0372-7181
WASEDA DAIGAKU RIKOGAKU KENKYUJO HOKOKU. (HOKOKU.). [Waseda Daigaku Rikogaku Kenkyujo Hokoku]. **Main/Corp** Waseda Daigaku, Tokyo. Rikogaku Kenkyujo. **Added/Corp** Waseda Daigaku, Tokyo. Rikogaku Kenkyujo. Bulletin. **VFOAT** Bulletin of Science and Engineering Research Laboratory, Waseda University. (1944)-. Periodical. Japanese (English). qt. **CODEN** WDRKA6. Documents available from CASDDS.
Ind/Abst Bioeng. Abstr.; Chem. Abstr.; Coal Abstr.; Math. Rev.; Sug. Indus. Abstr.

JA
WASEDA DAIGAKU SHISUTEMU KAGAKU KENKYUJO KIYO. **Main/Corp** Waseda Daigaku. Shisutemu Kagaku Kenkyujo. **VFOAT** Bulletin of the System Science Institute, Waseda University. Japanese (summaries and/or abstracts in Spanish). an. Waseda Daigaku Shisutemu Kagaku Kenkyujo, Okubo 3-4-1, Shinjuku-ku 160, Tokyo Japan. **Tel** 03-200-2436. **ED** Shinji Tsuchida. **LC** TA168; .W348A. **Circ:** 1,200.
Desc: The subjects are social system, management system and production system.

GW
WASSER, LUFT UND BODEN. HANDBUCH UMWELTTECHNIK. **See** Environmental Issues.

US
WEIGHT ENGINEERING. (1981)-. Periodical. English. tq. (Comes with Society of Allied Weight Engineers membership). Society of Allied Weight Engineers Inc, 344 East J Street, Chula Vista CA 91910. **Tel** (619)427-8262. **ED** Robert W. Ridenour. **Ad Acc. Circ:** 1,500 (ctrl). ***Continues** S.A.W.E. Journal, 0583-9270.*
Ind/Abst Int. Aerosp. Abstr. (19??-).

GW
WERKSTOFFE UND KONSTRUKTION. **VFOAT** Werkstoffe & Konstruktion; Engineering Materials Progress. Vol. 1, No. 1 (Jan. 1987)-. Periodical. German. qt. DM265.00. Sprechsaal Publishing Group, PO Box 2962, D-96418 Coburg Germany. **Tel** 011 49 9561 742810, FAX 011 49 9561 90009, telex 179561817. **LC** TA401; .W44. **DD** 620.1/1/05. **CODEN** WEKOES.
Ind/Abst Ceram. Abstr. (19??-).

US/0892-4015
WHAT EVERY ENGINEER SHOULD KNOW. Vol. 1 (1979)-. Monographic series. English. Price varies per volume. Marcel Dekker Inc., 270 Madison Avenue, New York NY 10016. **Tel** (212)696-9000, (800)228-1160, FAX (212)685-4540, telex 421419. **(Subscription address:** Marcel Dekker Inc, PO Box 5017, Monticello NY 12701.) **LC** UNC. **DD** 621. **[CCC].** Documents available from Ask*IEEE.
Desc: Presents information that is vital for the engineer. Covers microcomputer systems, ceramics, quality control, project management and more.
Ind/Abst INSPEC (1986-); Zentralbl. Math. Ihre Grenzgeb.

UK
WHAT'S NEW IN DESIGN. **See** Manufacturing.

US/0149-7537
WHO'S WHO IN ENGINEERING (NEW YORK. 1977). **See** Biographies.

PL/0509-6677
WIADOMOSCI INSTYTUTU MELORACJI I UZYTKOW ZIELONYCH. [Wiad. Inst. Melior. Uzyt. Ziel.]. **Added/Corp** Instytut Melioracji i Uzytkow Zielonych. (1958)-. Academic Scholarly Publication. Polish (summaries and/or abstracts in English and Russian). an. Panstwowe Wydawn Naukowe, Miodowa 10, PO Box 391, 00251 Warsaw Poland. **CODEN** WIMUAC. Documents available from CASDDS.
Desc: Covers problems and methods of forecasting and programming of drainage.
Ind/Abst Chem. Abstr. (-1986); Grasslands For. Abstr.; Nutr. Abstr. Rev., Ser. B, Live Feeds and Feed.; Potato Abstr.; Soils Fert.

US/0084-019X
WILEY SERIES ON SYSTEMS ENGINEERING AND ANALYSIS. [Wiley ser. syst. eng. anal.]. (19??)-. Monographic series. English. ir. Price varies per volume. John Wiley & Sons, Inc., 605 Third Avenue, New York NY 10158-0012. **Tel** (212)850-6000, (212)850-6645, FAX (212)850-6088, telex 12-7063. **(Subscription address:** John Wiley & Sons / England, Baffins Lane, Chichester, West Sussex PO19 1UD England.)

UK/0263-0915
WIND ENGINEERING ABSTRACTS. **Added/Corp** Multi Science Publishing Company. Vol. 1, No. 1 (1982)-. Periodical. English. qt. £98.00 UK & Europe, £105.00 other (surface mail), £117.00 (airmail). Multi Science Publishing Company Ltd., 107 High Street, Brentwood, Essex CM14 4RX England. **Tel** 011 44 277 224632, FAX 011 44 277 223453, telex 89-8452. **[CCC].** available on microfiche.
Desc: Offers several hundred summaries in each volume of contributions to the advancement of wind energy, drawn from a range of journals, government agency reports and conference proceedings.

US/0899-4013
WIND TURBINE WORLDWIDE CATALOG. [Wind turbine worldw. cat.]. (1989)-. Catalog. English. an. $75.00. Stadia Inc, PO Box 11068, Albany NY 12211-0068. **LC** TJ828; .W58. **DD** 621.4/5/05. **CODEN** WTWCEL. Documents available from Ask*IEEE.
Ind/Abst INSPEC.

GW/0934-5906
WIREWORLD. **VFOAT** Wire World. Vol. 30, No. 1 (Jan. 1988)-. Periodical. English. Six times a year. DM136.00. Vogel Verlag, Postfach 6740, D-97064 Wuerzburg Germany. **Tel** 011 49 931 4182145, 011 49 931 4182483, FAX 011 49 931 4182670, telex 841 680131. **ED** Dietmar Kuhn. **LC** IN PROCESS. **[CCC].** Index available. cum. index. **Bk Rev. Ad Acc. Circ:** 8,000 (ctrl). ***Continues** Wire World International, 0043-6046.*
Desc: International journals for the wire industry and all fields of wire working. It reports on the manufacture, working and application of wire, cable, rope, springs, bent parts, chains, mesh, fabric, netting, nuts, formed parts and all other wire products.

US/0043-6453
WISCONSIN ENGINEER. [Wis. eng.]. **Added/Corp** University of Wisconsin. College of Engineering. University of Wisconsin--Madison. College of Engineering. (1896)-. Periodical. English. Four times a year. $10.00 (one year), $18.00 (two years), $25.00 (three years). Wisconsin Engineer, 1513 University Avenue, Madison WI 53706. **Tel** (608)262-3494. **ED** Jerry Hill. **LC** TA1; .W8. **CODEN** WISEAS. **Ad Acc. Circ:** 2,000 (ctrl).
Desc: Journal focuses on science but includes engineering views on political, social, and economic issues and social life at the University.

US/0741-0387
WITHIN ASAE. ***Title Change.*** (WITHIN ASAE / AMERICAN SOCIETY OF AGRICULTURAL ENGINEERS.). [Within ASAE]. **Added/Corp** American Society of Agricultural Engineers. **VFOAT** Within A.S.A.E. **VAT** Within American Society of Agricultural Engineers. Vol. 1, No. 1 (Nov. 1983)-(Apr. 1994). Periodical. English. mo. American Society of Agricultural Engineers, Department 2510, 2950 Niles Road, St. Joseph MI 49085-9659. **Tel** (616)429-0300, FAX (616)429-3852. **DD** 630. ***Merged with** Agricultural Engineering, 0002-1458 **to form** Resource (Saint Joseph, Mich.), 1076-3333.*
Desc: Broad interest articles and continuing departments spotlight agricultural process with emphasis on mechanization, plus trends influencing contemporary events.

UK
WOMAN ENGINEER, THE. **Added/Corp** Women's Engineering Society. Vol. 1 (Dec. 1919)-. Periodical. English. Four times a year (published seasonally). £20.00. Women's Engineering Society, Imperial College of Science and Technology, Department of Civil Engineering, Imperial College Road, London SW7 2BU England. **Tel** 011 44 71 5895111 Ext. 4731. **ED** Rowena Plaser (editor's address: 26 Lime Road, Southville Bristol BS3 1LT England). **LC** TA1; .W85. **Bk Rev**, (Qty: varies). **Ad Acc. Circ:** 1,000 (ctrl).
Desc: Relevant to women engineers.
Ind/Abst Sociol. Educ. Abstr.

US/0887-2120
WOMAN ENGINEER. (GREENLAWN, N.Y.), THE. (WOMAN ENGINEER.). (198?)-. Periodical. English. Four times a year (March, May, Sept., Dec.). $17.00 (1 year), $33.00 (2 year), $48.00 (3 year); $30.00 (1 year), $55.00 (2 year), $75.00 (3 year), combined with Minority Engineer. Equal Opportunity Publications Inc, 150 Motor Parkway Suite 420, Hauppage NY 11788. **Tel** (516)273-0066, FAX (516)273-8936. **ED** Anne Kelly, James Schneider. **LC** TA157; .W64. **DD** 620/.0088042. **Bk Rev. Ad Acc. Circ:** 16,000 (ctrl).
Desc: An affirmative action recruitment magazine serving college graduating and professional women engineers. Career areas served: scientific, engineering and systems positions in business, industry, the Armed Forces and government.

US
WOOD DESIGN FOCUS. **See** Architecture.

US/1061-9240
WORLD SCANNER REPORT : A JOURNAL OF VHF-UHF SCANNER TECHNOLOGY & ENGINEERING, THE. [World scanner rep.]. (1991)-. Periodical. English. qt. $25.00. Commtronics Engineering, PO Box 262478, San Diego CA 92196. **DD** 338.

●US/0192-5512
WORLDWIDE PROJECTS. [Worldw. proj.]. Vol. 1, No. 1 (Spring 1993)-. Periodical. English. bm. $38.00 (nonmember) US; $48.00 (nonmember) other. American Society of Civil Engineers / ASCE, 345 East 47th Street, New York NY 10017-2398. **Tel** (212)705-7179, FAX (212)705-7300, telex 422847 ASCE UI. **(Subscription address:** American Society of Civil Engineers, Publisher Fulfillment Agency, Box 828, Somerset NJ 08875.) **ED** Virginia Fairweather. **LC** IN PROCESS. **DD** 338. **Bk Rev. Ad Acc. Circ:** 18,000 (ctrl). ***Continues** Worldwide Projects, 0192-5512.*
Desc: Covers the financial, legal, cultural, managerial, political aspects of working on large international design and construction projects, with a stress on marketing information.

CC/1000-6656
WUSUN JIANCE. (WU SUN CHIEN TSE.). [Wusun jiance]. **Added/Corp** Shang-Hai Tsai Liao Yen Chiu So. Chung-Kuo Chi Hsieh Kung Cheng Hsueh Hui (Peking, China). Wu Sun Chien Tse Hsueh Hui. **VFOAT** Nondestructive Testing. (19??)-. Academic Scholarly Publication. Chinese. bm. **LC** TA417.2; .W8. **DD** 620.1/127/05. **CODEN** WUJIDE. Documents available from CASDDS.
Ind/Abst Chem. Abstr. (1985-).

JA/0372-7661
YAMAGUCHI DAIGAKU KOGAKUBU KENKYU HOKOKU. [Yamaguchi Daigaku Kogakubu kenkyu hokoku]. **Main/Corp** Yamaguchi Daigku. Kogakubu. **VFOAT** Memoirs of the Faculty of Engineering, Yamaguchi University. Academic Scholarly Publication. Japanese (summaries and/or abstracts in English). sa. Yamaguchi Daigaku Kogakubu, Tokiwadai, Ube 755 Japan. **LC** T4; .Y36A. **CODEN** YDKGAF. Documents available from Ask*IEEE, CASDDS.
Ind/Abst Chem. Abstr.; Eng. Mater. Abstr.; INSPEC (Oct. 1983-); Int. Aerosp. Abstr.

US
YEAR BOOK - FLORIDA STATE BOARD OF ENGINEER EXAMINERS. **Main/Corp** Florida. State Board of Engineer Examiners. English. **LC** TA24.F6; A3. **DD** 620.58. ***Continues** Florida. State Board of Engineer Examiners. Year Book.*

CC
YING YUNG SHENG HSUEH. **VFOAT** Applied Acoustics. No. 1 (1982)-. Periodical. Chinese. qt. Science Press, 16 Donghuangchenggen North Street, Beijing 100707, People's Republic of China. **Tel** 011 86 1 4019821, 011 86 1 4010642, FAX 011 86 1 4012180, 011 86 1 4019810, telex 210147. **LC** TA365; .Y565. **DD** 620.2/05.

KO
YONGU NONMUNJIP (HANGUK KWAHAK KISURWON). (YONGU NONMUNJIP.). **VFOAT** Hanguk Kwahak Kisurwon Yongu Nonmunjip. 1983, Vol. 1-. Periodical. English (German and Korean). Hanguk Hwahak Kisurwon, 207-43 Chongnyangni-dong Tong Daemun-ku, Seoul Korea. **LC** Q4; .Y65.

JA/0514-5163
ZAIRYO. [Zairyo]. **VFOAT** Journal of the Society of Materials Science, Japan. Vol. 12, No. 112 (Jan. 1963)-. Periodical. Japanese. mo. $172.00 (surface mail); $188.30 (Asia & Oceania), $203.00 (North America), $217.60 (other) airmail. Nihon Zairyo Gakkai, (Society of Materials Science, Japan), 1-101, Yoshida Izumidonocho, Sakyoku, Kyotoshi, Kyotofu 606, Japan. **(Subscription address:** Japan Publications Trading Company, Ltd., PO

Box 5030, Tokyo International, Tokyo 100-31 Japan.) **[CCC].** cum. index. Documents available from Article Express International, Ask*IEEE, CASDDS. ***Continues*** *Zairyo Shiken.*
Ind/Abst Alum. Ind. Abstr.; Bioeng. Abstr.; BMT Abstr. (?-199?); Ceram. Abstr.; Chem. Abstr.; Coal Abstr.; Ei Page One; Eng. Index Annu.; GeoRef; INSPEC (Oct. 1971-); Int. Aerosp. Abstr.; Int. Civil Eng. Abstr.; Met. Abstr.

JA
ZAIRYO GIJUTSU NO GENJO TO TEMBO; SOGO REBYU. **Added/Corp** Japan. Kagaku Gijutsucho. **Series/Conf** z. (1973)-. Periodical. Japanese. Okurasho Insatukyoku, 2-4, Toranomon 2 chome, Minatoku, Tokyoto 105 Japan. **LC** TA401; .Z273.

JA/0917-0480
ZAIRYO TO KANKYO. [Zairyo to kankyo]. **Added/Corp** Fushoku Boshoku Kyokai (Japan). **VFOAT** Zairyo-to-Kankyo; Corrosion Engineering. No. 427 (1991)-. Periodical. Japanese (English). mo. **LC** TA418.74; .Z34. **CODEN** ZAKAEP. Documents available from Article Express International, Ask*IEEE, CASDDS. ***Continues*** *Boshoku Gijutsu, 0010-9355.*
Ind/Abst Alum. Ind. Abstr.; Bioeng. Abstr.; Chem. Abstr.; Coal Abstr. (Jan. 1991-); Ei Page One; Eng. Index Annu.; INSPEC (Jan. 1991-); Int. Aerosp. Abstr.; Met. Abstr. (Jan. 1991-).

JA/0914-6628
ZAIRYO TO PUROSESU. [Zairyo to purosesu]. **VFOAT** Current Advances in Materials and Processes; Report of the ISIJ Meeting; CAMP, ISIJ; Nippon Tekko Kyokai Koen Ronbunshu. (1988)-. Periodical. Multiple languages. bm (6 issues). $480.00. Nippon Tekko Kyokai, (Iron & Steel Institute of Japan), 9-4, Otemach 1 Chome, Chiyodaku, Tokyoto 100, Japan. **(Subscription address:** Japan Publications Trading Company, Ltd., PO Box 5030, Tokyo International, Tokyo 100-31 Japan.) **DD** 620.1. ***Continues in part*** *Tetsu-to-Hagane, 0021-1575.*

GW/0044-2267
ZEITSCHRIFT FUER ANGEWANDTE MATHEMATIK UND MECHANIK. **See** Mathematics.

PL/0324-9174
ZESZYTY NAUKOWE AKADEMII ROLNICZO-TECHNICZNEJ W OLSZTYNIE. GEODEZJA I URZADZENIA ROLNE. (GEODEZJA I URZADZENIA ROLNE.). [Zesz. nauk. akad. roln. - tech. Olszt. geod. urzadz. rolne]. Monographic series. Polish (summaries and/or abstracts in English, French and Russian). Price varies per volume. Akademii Rolniczo-Technicznej W Olsztynie, Ksiegarnia Akademicka, Olsztyn Poland. **LC** TA501; .G39. ***Supersedes*** *Zeszyty Naukowe Wyzszej Szkoty Rolniczej w Olsztynie. Seria F. Inzynieria; Zeszyty Naukowe Wyzszej Szkoty Rolniczej w Olsztynie. Seria F. Inzynieria. Suplement.*
Ind/Abst AGRICOLA.

PL/0372-9796
ZESZYTY NAUKOWE POLITECHNIKI SLASKIEJ. ENERGETYKA. **See** Energy.

CC/1000-209X
ZHEJIANG GONGXUEYUAN XUEBAO. **VFOAT** Journal of Zhejiang Engineering Institute. (1985)-. Academic Scholarly Publication. Chinese. qt. Zhejiang Gongxueyuan, Zhejiang Institute of Engineering, 6 District, Zhaohui Xinchun, Hangzhou, Zhejiang 310014, People's Republic of China. **Tel** 0571-5131816, FAX 0571-8074940. **ED** Z. Kangda. **DD** 605. Documents available from BLDSC, CASDDS.
Ind/Abst Chem. Abstr.

RH/1019-6404
ZIMBABWE ENGINEER (1992). (ZIMBABWE ENGINEER.). (1992)-. English. mo. 55.20Zin$ Zimbabwe; 59.20Zin$ Africa; 62.20Zin$ other. Thomson Publications Zimbabwe PVT Ltd., Box 1683, Harare Zimbabwe. **Tel** 011 263 4 736835, FAX 011 263 4 706055. ***Continues*** *Mining and Engineering, 0254-0304.*

ABSTRACTING, BIBLIOGRAPHIES AND STATISTICS

US/0363-5732
ABSTRACT JOURNAL IN EARTHQUAKE ENGINEERING. [Abstr. j. earthq. eng.]. **Added/Corp** University of California, Berkeley. Earthquake Engineering Research Center. Vol. 1 (1971)-. Abstracting/Indexing Service. English. Twice a year. $80.00 US and Canada; $100.00 other. Earthquake Engineering Research Center, Regents of University of California, 1301 South 46th Street, Richmond CA 94804. **Tel** (510)231-9468. **ED** Ruth C. Denton. **LC** TA658.44; .A25. **DD** 624/.176. **CODEN** AJEEDW. Index available. **Circ:** 450.
Desc: Abstracts, subject, title and author indexes of world's literature in earthquake hazards mitigation and earthquake engineering. Covers structural and soil dynamics, engineering seismology and earthquake-resistant design.
Ind/Abst GeoRef.

JA
ABSTRACTS OF SCIENCE AND TECHNOLOGY IN JAPAN. ELECTRONICS AND COMMUNICATION. ***Ceased.*** **Added/Corp** Nihon Kagaku Gijutsu Joho Senta. **VFOAT** Electronics and Communication. (Jan. 1985)-Vol. 9 (1993). Periodical. English. Four times a year. Nihon Kagaku Gijutsu Joho Senta, (Japan Information Center of Science & Technology), 5-2, Nagatacho 2 Chome, Chiyodaku, Tokyoto 100 Japan. **(Subscription address:** Japan Publications Trading Company, Ltd., PO Box 5030, Tokyo International, Tokyo 100-31 Japan.)

US
ANTIMONY IN ... . English. qt. US Department of the Interior / Bureau of Mines, Publications Department, PO Box 18070, Cochrans Mill Road, Pittsburgh PA 15236. **Tel** (412)892-6400.
Desc: Timely statistical and economic data on antimony.

CL
ANUARIO ESTADISTICO DE LA SIDERURGIA Y MINERIA DEL HIERRO DE AMERICA LATINA / INSTITUTO LATINOAMERICANO DEL FIERRO Y EL ACERO. **Added/Corp** Instituto Latinoamericano del Fierro y el Acero. **VFOAT** Statistical Yearbook of Steelmaking and Iron Ore Mining in Latin America. (19??)-. Spanish (English). an. $45.00. Instituto Latinoamericano del Fierro el Acero, Dario Urzua 1994, Santiago 9 Chile. **Tel** 011 56 2 2047764, FAX 011 56 2 2253111, telex 340.348 ILAFA CK. **LC** HD9524.L3; A58. **DD** 338.2/73/098021. **Circ:** 200.

AG
ANUARIO ESTADISTICO. ENERGIA ELECTRICA. **Main/Corp** Argentine Republic. Oficina Sectorial de Desarrollo de Energia. **Added/Corp** Argentine Republic. Direccion Nacional de Energia y Combustibles. **VFOAT** Energia Electrica. (19??)-. Spanish.

US/0003-6900
APPLIED MECHANICS REVIEWS. [Appl. mech. rev.]. **Added/Corp** American Society of Mechanical Engineers. Vol. 1 (Jan. 1948)-. Abstracting/Indexing Service. English. mo. $555.00 US and Canada, $672.00 other (non-member). American Society of Mechanical Engineers, 22 Law Drive, Fairfield NJ 07007. **Tel** (201)882-1167, (212)705-7722 (editorial). **ED** A. W. Kenneth Metzner. **LC** TA1; .A63953. **DD** 620.1/005. **CODEN** AMREAD. **[CCC].** cum. index. **Bk Rev. Pr Rev. Circ:** 1,800. available on microfilm and microfiche from University Microfilms International (UMI). Documents available from Article Express International, Ask*IEEE.
Desc: Serves engineering scientists worldwide by accessing, reviewing, and reporting on advances in a broad range of mechanical engineering sciences. Contains refereed review articles, book reviews, staff-prepared book notes and abstracts selected from journals in the field of applied mechanics.
Ind/Abst Abstr. Bull. Inst. Pap. Sci. Tech.; Abstr. J. Earthq. Eng. (?-?); Acoust. Abstr.; Eng. Index Annu. [Select. Cov.]; Fluid Abstr., Civil Eng.; Fluid Abstr. Proc. Eng.; FLUIDEX (1973-); GeoRef; HTFS Dig.; INSPEC (1968-April 1975); Int. Aerosp. Abstr.; Math. Rev.; Surf. Treat. Technol. Abstr.; Zentralbl. Math. Ihre Grenzgeb.

UK/0263-5534
AQUALINE ABSTRACTS. [Aqualine abstr.]. **Added/Corp** Water Research Centre (Great Britain). Vol. 1, No. 1 (Jan. 8, 1985)-. Abstracting/Indexing Service. English. Twenty-six times a year. £575.00. Water Research Centre, WRC PLC Frankland Road, Blagrove Swindon SN5 8YF England. **Tel** 011 44 793 511711, FAX 011 44 793 511712, telex 449541. **ED** Karen Gibbs. **DD** 627. Index available. cum. index. **Ad Acc. Circ:** 3,600 (ctrl). available on microfilm and microfiche from University Microfilms International (UMI); available on CD-ROM from Aqualine; available on an online database from ESA-IRS; and ORBIT. Documents available. ***Continues*** *Water Research Centre (Great Britain). WRC Information, 0306-6649.*
Desc: Offers comprehensive coverage of all aspects of water, wastewater, associated engineering services and the aquatic environment.
Ind/Abst Abstr. Bull. Inst. Pap. Sci. Tech.; Anal. Abstr.

US/0742-1753
ASCE ANNUAL COMBINED INDEX. [ASCE annu. comb. index]. **Main/Corp** American Society of Civil Engineers. **VFOAT** A.S.C.E. Annual Combined Index. **VAT** American Society of Civil Engineers Annual Combined Index. (1982)-. Abstracting/Indexing Service. English. an. $48.00 (non-member) US; $71.00 (non-member) other. American Society of Civil Engineers / ASCE, 345 East 47th Street, New York NY 10017-2398. **Tel** (212)705-7179, FAX (212)705-7300, telex 422847 ASCE UI. **(Subscription address:** American Society of Civil Engineers, Publisher Fulfillment Agency, Box 828, Somerset NJ 08875.) **LC** TA145; .A47a. **DD** 016.624. cum. index. **Circ:** 4,000. available on an online database (as Civil Engineering Database - CEDB) from STN International (Math) Database. ***Continues*** *American Society of Civil Engineers. ASCE, 0730-3149.*

US/0734-1962
ASCE PUBLICATIONS INFORMATION. [ASCE publ. inf.]. **Added/Corp** American Society of Civil Engineers. American Society of Civil Engineers. Publications Information. **VFOAT** A.S.C.E. Publications Information. **VAT** American Society of Civil Engineers Publications Information. Vol. 18, No. 1 (Jan./Feb. 1983)-. Abstracting/Indexing Service. English. bm. $180.00 (non-member) US; $207.00 (non-member) other (includes Combined Index). American Society of Civil Engineers / ASCE, 345 East 47th Street, New York NY 10017-2398. **Tel** (212)705-7179, FAX (212)705-7300, telex 422847 ASCE UI. **(Subscription address:** American Society of Civil Engineers, Publisher Fulfillment Agency, Box 828, Somerset NJ 08875.) **LC** Z5851; .A77; TA145. **DD** 016.624/05. **CODEN** ASPIDQ. **[CCC].** Index available (copy of ASCE Annual Combined Index included with subscription). cum. index. **Circ:** 1,300. available on an online database (as Civil Engineering Database - CEDB) from STI International. ***Continues*** *ASCE Publications Abstracts, 0001-2432.*
Desc: Contains abstracts and indexes for all articles, journals, technical notes, reference papers, conference papers, books, and publications of the American Society of Civil Engineers.
Ind/Abst ASCE Annu. Comb. Index (1983-); Trans. Am. Soc. Civ. Eng. (1983-).

UK
BCRA QUARTERLY : A REVIEW OF PUBLISHED LITERATURE ON COAL, COKA AND ALLIED TOPICS. No. 1 (Oct. 1983)-. English. qt. £75.00. BCRA Scientific Technical Services Ltd, Wingerworth, Chesterfield, Derbyshire S41 6NG England. **Tel** 011 44 246 209654, FAX 011 44 1246 272247, telex 547061. **ED** R.K. Smart. **Circ:** 150. Documents available from BLDSC. ***Continues*** *BCRA Review.*
Desc: Abstracts and lists of current literature on coal, coke, and allied topics. Also contains literature reviews in the same subject area, news items and statistics relevant to the coke industry.
Ind/Abst Coal Abstr.

CL/0577-7933
BOLETIN DE ESTADISTICA MINERA. **Main/Corp** Chile. Direccion de Estadistica y Censos. Statistical Publication. Spanish. Instituto Nacional de Estadisticas, Avenida Bulnes 418, Casilla 498, Correo 3 Santiago Chile. **Tel** 6991441. ctrl circ.
Desc: Contains statistics on mining property, production and accidents in mining and the international market.

US/0084-8174
BULLETIN OF STATISTICS ON WORLD TRADE IN ENGINEERING PRODUCTS. (BULLETIN OF STATISTICS ON WORLD TRADE IN ENGINEERING PRODUCTS ECONOMIC COMMISSION FOR EUROPE.). [Bull. Stat. World trade eng. prod.]. **Main/Corp** United Nations. Economic Commission for Europe. **Added/Corp** United Nations. Economic Commission for Europe. **VFOAT** Bulletin de Statistiques du Commerce Mondial des Produits des Industries Mechaniques et Electriquea. (1963)-. Government Publication. English (French and Russian). an. $55.00. United Nations Publications, 2 United Nations Plaza, Room DC2 0853, Department 007C, New York NY 10017. **Tel** (212)963-8303, (800)253-9646. **LC** PAR.
Desc: Statistics on flow of machinery, transport, scientific, medical, optical and measuring equipment, watches, and clocks in 36 countries, comprising about 90 per cent of total world trade.

MY
BULLETIN OF STATISTICS RELATING TO THE MINING INDUSTRY OF MALAYSIA. ***Title Change.*** **Main/Corp** Malaysia. Kementerian Pertanian dan Tanah. Bulletin. English (Malay). an. Jalan Gurney, Kuala Lumpur, Mines Department, Selangor Malaysia. **Tel** 2929797. **LC** HD9506.M36; M35A. **DD** 338.2/09595. **Circ:** 500. ***Continued by*** *Majallah Perangkaan Berkenaan Perusahaan Perkembongan Malaysia.*
Desc: Includes statistics relating to the mining industry, number of mines, production, employment and power. Does not include petroleum.

FR
BULLETIN SIGNALETIQUE. 140: ELECTROTECHNIQUE. **Added/Corp** Centre National de la Recherche Scientifique (France). Centre de Documentation. Vol. 33 (1972)-. Bulletin. French. Centre National de la Recherche Scientifique, Informascience, 26 rue Boyer, 75971 Paris France. **Tel** 61.41.11.05, telex CNRSDOC 220880 F. **LC** QC501; .B83. **DD** 016.537. ***Continues*** *Bulletin Signaletique. 140: Physique II-Electricite.*

US
CA QUICK SEARCH [COMPUTER FILE]. (1992)-. Abstracting/Indexing Service. English. $650.00 (members), $875.00 (nonmembers) CD-ROM single user

version; $2500.00 (members), $3250.00 (nonmembers) CD-ROM 1-5 user network license; $250.00 (members), $375.00 (nonmembers) floppy disk version - one year cumulative. American Concrete Institute, PO Box 19150, Detroit MI 48219. **Tel** (313)532-2600. available on diskette; available in print.
Desc: Machine-readable version of ACI's Concrete Abstracts. Provides worldwide coverage of journals plus selected reports and books. The 10-year database (1982-1991) on CD-ROM includes over 15,000 records. Current year floppy disk subscription contains 1,500 records.

AT
CENSUS OF MINING ESTABLISHMENTS: INDUSTRY CONCENTRATION STATISTICS, AUSTRALIA. **Main/Corp** Australian Bureau of Statistics. (19??)-. English. ir. 7.50Aus$. Australian Bureau of Statistics, PO Box 10, Belconnen Australian Capital Territory, 2616 Australia. **Tel** 011 61 6 2527911, FAX 011 61 6 2516009. **LC** HD9506.A7; A93e. **DD** 338.8/2622/0994.
Desc: Statistics relating to industry concentration concerned with providing measures of the extent to which a few firms are dominant in individual industries.

US/1063-7338
CIVIL AND STRUCTURAL ENGINEERING ABSTRACTS. ***Ceased.*** [Civ. struct. eng. abstr.]. **Added/Corp** Cambridge Scientific Abstracts, Inc. Engineering Information, Inc. **VFOAT** Civil and Structural Engineering Abstracts Journal; Civil & Structural Eng. Abstracts. Vol. 1, No. 1 (1993)-(1995). Abstracting/Indexing Service. English. mo. Cambridge Scientific Abstracts, 7200 Wisconsin Avenue, #601, Bethesda MD 20814-4823. **Tel** (301)961-6750, (800)843-7751, FAX (301)961-6720. **DD** 624. available on magnetic tape.
Desc: Published in collaboration with Engineering Information Inc., this journal focuses on scientific advances in the planning, testing, and building of major structures, from bridges and tunnels to industrial plants.

CN/0380-6847
COAL AND COKE STATISTICS. (COAL AND COKE STATISTICS / PREPARED IN THE MINING, METALLURGICAL AND CHEMICAL SECTION). [Coal coak stat.]. **Added/Corp** Canada. Dominion Bureau of Statistics. Mining, Metallurgical & Chemical Section. Canada. Bureau Federal de la Statistique. Division du Commerce International. Canada. Bureau Federal de la Statistique. Division de l'Industrie et du Commerce. Canada. Dominion Bureau of Statistics. Mineral Statistics Section. Canada. Bureau Federal de la Statistique. Division de l'Industrie. Canada. Bureau Federal de la Statistique. Division des Industries Manufacturieres et Primaires. Statistique Canada. Division des Industries Manufacturieres et Primaires. Statistique Canada. Division de l'Industrie. **VFOAT** Statistique du Charbon et du Coke. Vol. 29, No. 3 (March 1950)-. Periodical. French (English). mo. 110.00Can$ Canada; $132.00 US; $154.00 other. Statistics Canada, Publications Sales & Services, Main Building Room 1710, Ottawa Ontario K1A 0T6 Canada. **Tel** (613)951-5078, (800)267-6677, FAX (613)951-1584, telex 053-3585. **DD** 338.2/724/0971. ***Continues*** *Coal and Coke Statistics for Canada, 0829-9781.*
Desc: Covers production, imports, exports and disposition of coal by provinces; supply and disposition of coke in Canada.

US/1063-8709
COMPENDEX PLUS. (COMPENDEX PLUS [COMPUTER FILE].). [Compend. plus]. **Added/Corp** Engineering Information, Inc. **VFOAT** Dialog OnDisc Compendex Plus. (1985)-. Abstracting/Indexing Service. English. qt. $3450.00 US, Canada and South Africa; $3530.00 UK; $5175.00 Brazil; $4071.00 Argentina; $3450.00 Hong Kong, China, Taiwan, Southeast Asia and Korea. Dialog Information Services, 3460 Hillview Avenue, Palo Alto CA 94304. **Tel** (415)858-4240, (800)334-2564. **(Subscription address:** UK, Ireland, Western Europe/ Thompson Henry Ltd, London Road, Sunningdale Berks SL5 OEP England; Telephone- Ascot (0990)24615; Fax- (0990)26120**)** **LC** Z5851. **DD** 620. available in print (Engineering Index Monthly and Engineering Index Annual as part of El Chemdisc); available on magnetic tape; available on an online database from ESA-IRS; CEDOCAR; STN International; ORBIT; OCLC; Fiz-Technik; DIALOG; DATA-STAR; and CAN/OLE.
Desc: Indexes and abstracts over one million records of engineering and technical literature from more than 4,500 journals, professional societies' publications, approximately 2,000 conference proceedings per year, technical papers, and books. About 10% of the material indexed is not in English, and author-written abstracts are included when available. The CD-ROM version corresponds to the online version Ei Compendex*Plus as well as to the printed Engineering Index. Coverage is available from 1985 to the present and is updated quarterly.

US/0045-8007
CONCRETE ABSTRACTS. **Added/Corp** American Concrete Institute. Vol. 1 (July 1971)-. Abstracting/Indexing Service. English. bm. $185.00 (non-members), $158.00 (members) US; $197.00 (non-members), $169.00 (members) other. American Concrete Institute, PO Box 19150, Detroit MI 48219. **Tel** (313)532-2600. **(Subscription address:** American Concrete Institute, PO Box 32190, Detroit MI 48232**)** **ED** Helayne Beavers. **LC** TP875; .C65. **DD** 666/.89. **CODEN** CNASB. **[CCC].** Index available. **Bk Rev. Circ:** 650. available on CD-ROM and diskette.
Desc: Summarizes articles and publications that report developments in concrete and concrete technology. Covers civil and structural engineering, design, research, architecture, construction, and manufacturing.
Ind/Abst Corros. Abstr.; J. Ferrocement.

US
COPPER INDUSTRY ANNUAL SUPPLEMENT / U.S. DEPARTMENT OF THE INTERIOR, BUREAU OF MINES. **VFOAT** Copper in ... . English. mo. US Department of the Interior / Bureau of Mines, Publications Department, PO Box 18070, Cochrans Mill Road, Pittsburgh PA 15236. **Tel** (412)892-6400.
Desc: Timely statistical and economic data on copper.

US/0010-9339
CORROSION ABSTRACTS. [Corros. abstr.]. **Added/Corp** National Association of Corrosion Engineers. Vol. 1 (Jan. 1962)-. Abstracting/Indexing Service. English. bm (6 issues). $195.00 (NACE members); $230.00 (nonmembers) US, $250.00 (nonmembers) other. National Association of Corrosion Engineers, 1440 South Creek Drive, Houston TX 77084. **Tel** (713)492-0535, FAX (713)492-8254, telex 792310 NACE HOU. **(Subscription address:** National Association of Corrosion Engineers, PO Box 218340, Houston TX 77084.**)** **ED** Ray Lindberg. **LC** TA462; .C652. **DD** 620.1/1223/05. **CODEN** CRNAA. **[CCC]. Circ:** 850 (ctrl). available on diskette (COR AB and on CD-ROM); available on microfilm from University Microfilms International (UMI); available on CD-ROM. ***Supersedes in part*** *Corrosion, 0010-9312.*
Desc: Compilation of abstracts of the world's corrosion control literature.
Ind/Abst Abstr. Bull. Inst. Pap. Sci. Tech.; Surf. Treat. Technol. Abstr.; World Surf. Coat. Abstr.

US/0095-7917
CURRENT CONTENTS. ENGINEERING, TECHNOLOGY & APPLIED SCIENCES. [Curr. contents, Eng. tech. appl. sci.]. **Added/Corp** Institute for Scientific Information. **VFOAT** Current Contents. Engineering, Technology, and Applied Sciences; Engineering, Technology & Applied Sciences; Engineering, Technology, and Applied Sciences. (Jan. 6, 1975)-. Abstracting/Indexing Service. English. wk. $488.00 print; $779.00 combined with diskette. Institute for Scientific Information, 3501 Market Street, Philadelphia PA 19104. **Tel** (215)386-0100, (800)523-1850, FAX (215)386-6362, telex 84-5305. **(Subscription address:** Institute for Scientific Information, PO Box 71416, Chicago IL 60694.**)** **LC** Z7913; .C78; T45. **DD** 016.6. **NLM** Z 7911 C976. **CODEN** CCETA. available on diskette; available on magnetic tape and an online database (as Current Contents Search). Documents available from The Genuine Article. ***Continues*** *Current Contents: Engineering & Technology, 0011-3395.*
Desc: Reproduces the table of contents of the issues of journals in engineering, technology, and applied sciences.
Ind/Abst Abstr. Bull. Inst. Pap. Sci. Tech.; Curr. Contents Eng. Tech. Appl. Sci.; J. Ferrocement; Res. Alert [Full Cov.]; Sci. Cit. Index; SCISEARCH; Soc. Sci. Cit. Index [Full Cov.]; World Ceram. Abstr.

UK/0011-3778
CURRENT PAPERS IN ELECTRICAL & ELECTRONICS ENGINEERING. [Curr. pap. electr. electron. eng.]. **Added/Corp** Institution of Electrical Engineers. Institute of Electrical and Electronics Engineers. Vol. 54 (1969)-. Abstracting/Indexing Service. English. mo. £215.00. Institution of Electrical Engineers / IEE, Michael Faraday House, Six Hills Way, Stevenage Herts SG1 2AY UK. **Tel** 011 44 438 313311, FAX 011 44 438 742840, telex 825578 IEESTV G. **(Subscription address:** IEE / UK, Publications Sales Department, PO Box 96, Stevenage, Herts, SG1 2SD England.**)** **LC** Z5832; .C85. **[CCC].** ***Continues*** *Current Papers in Eletrotechnology.*
Desc: Gives the title and full details of the bibliographic reference of each article selected from the world's scientific and technical literature.

DK
DANSK ELFORSYNING. **Added/Corp** Danske Elvrkers Forening. (1976)-. Statistical Publication. Danish. an. Kr80.00. Danske Elvrkers Forening, Vodroffsvej 59, 1900 Kbenhavn V Denmark. **Tel** 095 31 39 01 11, FAX 045 31 39 59 58. **ED** Knud MoseKjaer Madsen. **LC** TK1193.D4; D36. **Pr Rev. Circ:** 3,000 (ctrl). ***Continues*** *Dansk Elvrksstatistik, 0070-2803.*
Desc: Statistic on electricity, production, consumption and distribution.

GW/0012-5148
DOKUMENTATION STRASSE. (1961)-. German. mo. DM162.00 Germany; DM167.00 other. Forschungsgesellschaft fuer Strassen-und Verkehrswesen, Konrad-Adenauer-Strasse 13, 50996 Koln, Postfach 50 1362, 50973 Koln Germany. **Tel** 011 49 221 397035, FAX 011 49 221 393747. **UDC** 625.7/.8 + 624 + 338.47 + 656.1.05 + 711.73] (048).

US
EI PAGE ONE [COMPUTER FILE]. **Added/Corp** Engineering Information, Inc. **VFOAT** Page One; Ei Page One Database. (198?)-. Abstracting/Indexing Service. English. an. Engineering Information Inc., Castle Point on the Hudson, Hoboken NJ 07030. **Tel** (800)221-1044, (201)216-8500, FAX (201)216-8526, telex 4990438. **(Subscription address:** UK, Ireland, and Western Europe/ Thompson Henry Ltd, London Road, Sunningdale Berks SL5 OEP England; Telephone- Ascot (0990)24615, Fax- (0990)26120**)** **LC** TA1; .E38.
Desc: A listing of the table of contents from the El database of serial publications that include journals, conferences, and report series.

US/0736-9352
ELECTRIC POWER ANNUAL. [Electr. power annu.]. (Nov. 1982)-. English. an (Feb.). $13.00. National Energy Information Center, Energy Information Administration, Forrestal Building, Room 1F-048, Washington DC 20585. **Tel** (202)586-8800. **ED** Dolores McCadney. **LC** HD9685.U4; E39. **DD** 333.79/32/0973. ***Formed by the union of*** *Electric Energy & Peak Load Data ... Annual, 0278-646X* ***and*** *Power Production, Fuel Consumption, & Installed Capacity Data ... Annual, 0178-1549.*
Desc: Presents a summary of electric utility statistics at the national, regional and state levels on various subjects.
Ind/Abst Energy Inf. Abstr.; Predicasts Forecasts.

US/0190-1729
ELECTRIC UTILITY STATISTICAL REFERENCE. **Main/Corp** Donaldson, Lufkin & Jenrette, Inc. Statistical Publication. English. Donaldson Lufkin & Jenrette Securities Corporation, 140 Broadway, New York NY 10005. **LC** HD9685.U4; D66A. **DD** 338.4/3.

UK/0036-8105
ELECTRICAL & ELECTRONICS ABSTRACTS. (SCIENCE ABSTRACTS. SERIES B, ELECTRICAL & ELECTRONICS ABSTRACTS.). [Electr. electron. abstr.]. **Added/Corp** Institution of Electrical Engineers. Institute of Electrical and Electronics Engineers. INSPEC (Information Service). **VFOAT** Electrical & Electronics Abstracts; Electrical and Electronics Abstracts. **VAT** Electrical and Electronics Abstracts. Vol. 70, No. 829 (Jan. 1967)-. Abstracting/Indexing Service. English. mo. $1400.00. Institution of Electrical Engineers / IEE, Michael Faraday House, Six Hills Way, Stevenage Herts SG1 2AY UK. **Tel** 011 44 438 313311, FAX 011 44 438 742840, telex 825578 IEESTV G. **(Subscription address:** IEE / UK, Publications Sales Department, PO Box 96, Stevenage, Herts, SG1 2SD England.**)** **LC** Z5833; .E37; TK145. **DD** 016.6213. **[CCC].** cum. index (published separately, twice per year and include subject/author and other indexes). available on CD-ROM. ***Continues*** *Science Abstracts. Electrical & Electronics Abstracts.*
Desc: Brings together summarised information of recent technical developments world-wide in all areas of electronics, radio, telecommunications, optoelectronics, and electrical power. Covers electronic components and technology, telecommunications, power engineering and instrumentation. This includes such subjects as aerospace electronics, antennas and propagation, biomedical engineering, electric machines, electron tubes, electronic circuits, energy conversion, image processing, insulation, lasers, superconductivity devices, etc.

US/0364-0124
ELECTRICITY SALES STATISTICS (MONTHLY). (ELECTRICITY SALES STATISTICS.). Periodical. English. mo. Tennessee Valley Authority / Chattanooga, 417 Edney Building, Chattanooga TN 37401. **Tel** (615)632-3257. Documents available from Documents on Demand.
Desc: Distribution of electricity at TVA wholesale and retail rates.
Ind/Abst Am. Stat. Index.

●US/1069-5303
ELECTRONICS AND COMMUNICATIONS ABSTRACTS. [Electron. commun. abstr.]. **Added/Corp** Cambridge Scientific Abstracts, Inc. Engineering Information, Inc. **VFOAT** Electronics & Communications Abstracts; Electronics & Comm. Abstracts. Vol. 26, No. 1 (1993)-. Abstracting/Indexing Service. English. mo. $975.00 US; $995.00 other. Cambridge Scientific Abstracts, 7200 Wisconsin Avenue, #601, Bethesda MD 20814-4823. **Tel** (301)961-6750, (800)843-7751, FAX (301)961-6720. **LC** TK7800; .E43859. **DD** 621.381/08. **Circ:** 320. available via Internet (to the current year's abstracts and five-year backfiles) from Cambridge Scientific Abstracts. ***Continues*** *Electronics & Communications Abstracts Journal, 0361-3313.*
Desc: Contains worldwide information on electronics, communications and the disciplines that contribute to their advancement.

US/0361-3313
ELECTRONICS AND COMMUNICATIONS ABSTRACTS JOURNAL (RIVERDALE, MD.). ***Title Change.*** (ELECTRONICS AND COMMUNICATIONS ABSTRACTS JOURNAL.). [Electron. commun. abstr. j.]. **Added/Corp** Cambridge Scientific Abstracts, Inc. **VFOAT** Electronics and Communications Abstracts Journal. Vol. 4, No. 1 (1972)- Vol. 25 (1992). Abstracting/Indexing Service. English. bm (plus annual index). Cambridge Scientific Abstracts, 7200 Wisconsin Avenue, #601, Bethesda MD 20814-4823. **Tel** (301)961-6750, (800)843-7751, FAX (301)961-6720. **ED** Evelyn Beck. **LC** TK7800; .E43859. **DD** 621.381/08. **NLM** Z 5836 E38. **CODEN** ECAJA. Index available. cum. index. **Bk Rev.** available on magnetic tape; available on an online database. ***Continues*** *Electronics Abstracts Journal, 0013-5097.* ***Continued by*** *Electronics and Communications Abstracts.*
Desc: Theoretical and applied research in electronics and communications. Includes electronics systems, physics, circuits, and devices. Business aspects are also covered.

US
ENCYCLOPEDIA OF FLUID POWER STANDARDS. VOL. J : BIBLIOGRAPHIES. **Main/Corp** National Fluid Power Association. (19??)-. English. $10.00. National Fluid Power Association, 3333 North Mayfair Road, Milwaukee WI 53222. **Tel** (414)778-3369, FAX (414)778-3361, telex 704557.

US/0951-9998
ENGINEERED MATERIALS ABSTRACTS. (ENGINEERED MATERIALS ABSTRACTS : EMA.). [Eng. mater. abstr.]. **Added/Corp** Materials Information (Information Service). **VFOAT** EMA. (198?)-. Abstracting/Indexing Service. English. mo. $1340.00 (nonsubscribers of Metals Abstracts), $1150.00 (subscribers of Metals Abstracts) North America. American Society for Metals International, c/o Deborah Barthelmes, Materials Park OH 44073-0002. **Tel** (216)338-5151, FAX (216)338-4634, telex 980-619. **(Subscription address:** ASM International, Materials Information, Materials Park OH 44073.**) LC** TA401; .E47. **DD** 620.1/1/05. **[CCC].** Index available (free). cum. index. available on an online database; available on CD-ROM.
Desc: Covers the development, production and processing of ceramic, polymeric and/or composite materials intended for engineering use. Each issue contains subject, trade name, materials, author and corporate author indexes.

US/0360-8557
ENGINEERING INDEX ANNUAL. [Eng. index annu.]. **VFOAT** Engineering Index; EI Annual. (1968)-. Abstracting/Indexing Service. English. an. $2,100.00 North America; £1,505.00 Europe; $1,125.00 other. Engineering Information Inc., Castle Point on the Hudson, Hoboken NJ 07030. **Tel** (800)221-1044, (201)216-8500, FAX (201)216-8526, telex 4990438. **(Subscription address:** Thompson Henry Ltd., London Road, Sunningdale, Berks SL5 OEP England.**) LC** Z5851; .E62. **DD** 016.62. **NLM** Z 5851 E57. **[CCC].** cum. index. available on CD-ROM (Compendex Plus); available on microfilm. ***Continues*** *Engineering Index (New York, N.Y. : 1919), 0739-4624.*
Desc: An organized compilation of bibliographic citations and abstracts covering the world's technological literature in all engineering disciplines.

US/1041-2913
ENGINEERING INDEX BIOENGINEERING AND BIOTECHNOLOGY ABSTRACTS. ***Title Change.*** [Eng. index bioeng. biotech. abstr.]. **Added/Corp** Engineering Information, Inc. **VFOAT** Bioengineering and Biotechnology Abstracts. Vol. 16, No. 1 (Jan. 1989)-Vol. 19, No. 12 (Dec. 1992). Abstracting/Indexing Service. English. mo. Engineering Information Inc., Castle Point on the Hudson, Hoboken NJ 07030. **Tel** (800)221-1044, (201)216-8500, FAX (201)216-8526, telex 4990438. **LC** R856.A1; E56. **DD** 610/.28. **NLM** ZQT 34; B616. **CODEN** EIBAD8. **[CCC].** available on magnetic tape. ***Continues*** *Engineering Index Bioengineering Abstracts, 0736-6213.* ***Continued by*** *BioEngineering Abstracts (Bethesda, Md.), 1068-5693.*

US/0093-8408
ENGINEERING INDEX ENERGY ABSTRACTS. [Eng. index energy abstr.]. **Added/Corp** Engineering Index, inc. **VFOAT** Energy Abstracts. (April 1974)-. Abstracting/Indexing Service. English (Dutch, French, German, Italian, Polish and Russian). mo. $1,075.00 North America; £75.00 Europe; $1,125.00 other. Engineering Information Inc., Castle Point on the Hudson, Hoboken NJ 07030. **Tel** (800)221-1044, (201)216-8500, FAX (201)216-8526, telex 4990438. **(Subscription address:** Thompson Henry Ltd., London Road, Sunningdale, Berks SL5 OEP England.**) LC** TJ163.13; .E54. **DD** 621. **[CCC].** available on microfilm.
Desc: A specialized monthly publication with an author and subject index, drawn from Engineering Index Monthly, covering the literature of conventional and alternative energy sources.

US/0742-1974
ENGINEERING INDEX MONTHLY. [Eng. index mon.]. **Added/Corp** Engineering Information, Inc. Vol. 22, No. 1 (Jan. 1984)-. Abstracting/Indexing Service. English. mo. $2,450.00 North America; £1,920.00 Europe; $2,750.00 other. Engineering Information Inc., Castle Point on the Hudson, Hoboken NJ 07030. **Tel** (800)221-1044, (201)216-8500, FAX (201)216-8526, telex 4990438. **(Subscription address:** Thompson Henry Ltd., London Road, Sunningdale, Berks SL5 OEP England.**) DD** 620. **CODEN** EIMOD3. **[CCC].** available on microfilm; available on CD-ROM from DIALOG. ***Continues*** *Engineering Index Monthly and Author Index, 0162-3036.*
Desc: A monthly compilation of abstracts with an author index and subject index covering the journal and conference literature of engineering and related technical disciplines.

FR/0244-7118
ENQUETE ANNUELLE DE BRANCHE. INGENIERIE, ETUDES ET CONSEILS / MINISTERE DE L'INDUSTRIE ET DE LA RECHERCHE, SERVICE D'ETUDE DES STRATEGIES ET DES STATISTIQUES INDUSTRIELLES. **VFOAT** Ingenierie, Etudes et Conseils. French. an. Documentation Francaise, 29 Quai Voltaire, 75344 Paris Cedex 7 France. **Tel** 011 33 1 40157000, FAX 011 33 1 40157230, telex 204 826 DOCFRAN. **LC** HD9680.F8; E56. available in microform.

AO/0301-6552
ESTATISTICA DA ACTIVIDADE MINEIRA NO ESTADO DE ANGOLA. (ESTATISTICA DA ACTIVIDADE MINEIRA.). [Estat. act. min. estado Angola]. **Main/Corp** Angola. Direccao Provincial dos Servicos de Geologia e Minas. (19??)-. Statistical Publication. Portuguese. **LC** HD9506.A58; A53a. **DD** 338.2/0967/3. **CODEN** EMAGDF.
Ind/Abst GeoRef.

●US
FINANCIAL STATISTICS OF MAJOR U.S. INVESTOR-OWNED ELECTRIC UTILITIES. **Added/Corp** United States. Office of Coal, Nuclear, Electric, and Alternate Fuels. **VFOAT** Financial Statistics of Major US Investor-Owned Electric Utilities. (1992)-. Government Publication. English. an. $47.00. Superintendent of Documents, US Government Printing Office, Washington DC 20402. **Tel** (202)275-3328, FAX (202)786-2377. ***Continues*** *Financial Statistics of Major Investor-Owned Electric Utilities.*
Desc: Presents summary and detailed financial accounting data on the investor-owned electric utilities.

UK/0962-7170
FLUID ABSTRACTS. CIVIL ENGINEERING. [Fluid abstr., Civil eng.]. **VFOAT** Civil Engineering. (1991)-. Abstracting/Indexing Service. English. mo. $686.00 The Americas; £460.00 other. Elsevier Geo Abstracts, An Imprint of Elsevier Science Ltd., The Boulevard, Langford Lane, Kidlington, Oxford OX5 1GB United Kingdom. **Tel** 011 44 865 843000, 011 44 865 843699, FAX 011 44 865 843010. **(Subscription address:** Elsevier Science Ltd. Oxford Fulfillment Centre, PO Box 800, Kidlington, Oxford OX5 1DX United Kingdom.**) [CCC].** available on an online database from ESA-IRS; and (as FLUIDEX) DIALOG. ***Formed by the union of*** *Civil Engineering Hydraulics Abstracts, 0305-9456; Industrial Aerodynamics Abstracts; Offshore Engineering Abstracts, 0268-1374* ***and*** *World Ports & Harbours Abstracts (Incorporating International Dredging Abstracts), 0264-0775.*
Desc: Covers civil engineering applications of fluid mechanics, hydraulics of open and closed systems, and related aspects of wind energy, the atmosphere and aerodynamics.

UK/0962-7162
FLUID ABSTRACTS. PROCESS ENGINEERING. **VFOAT** Process Engineering. Vol. 1, Issue 1 (1991)-. Abstracting/Indexing Service. English. Twelve times a year. $686.00 The Americas; £460.00 other. Elsevier Geo Abstracts, An Imprint of Elsevier Science Ltd., The Boulevard, Langford Lane, Kidlington, Oxford OX5 1GB United Kingdom. **Tel** 011 44 865 843000, 011 44 865 843699, FAX 011 44 865 843010. **(Subscription address:** Elsevier Science Ltd. Oxford Fulfillment Centre, PO Box 800, Kidlington, Oxford OX5 1DX United Kingdom.**) LC** TA357; .F545. **DD** 620.1/06/05. **[CCC].** available on microfilm and microfiche from University Microfilms International (UMI); available on an online database from DIALOG; and (as FLUIDEX) ESA-IRS. ***Formed by the union of*** *Fluid Flow Measurements Abstracts, 0305-9235; Fluid Power Abstracts, 0015-4644; Fluid Sealing Abstracts, 0015-4660; Pipelines Abstracts, 0265-3990; Pumps and Other Fluids Machinery Abstracts, 0302-2870; Solid-Liquid Flow Abstracts, 0038-1063; Computer-Aided Process Control Abstracts, 0955-4319* ***and*** *Mixing and Separation Technology Abstracts, 0955-7059.*
Desc: Covers all aspects of hydraulics of interest to process engineers, including fluid mechanics, fluid-solid flow, flow measurement, hydraulic and pneumatic applications and equipment, pumps and other turbomachinery, seals and sealing, piping systems and technology and mixing and separation equipment and processes. Each volume contains approximately 5,000 abstracts.

UK
FLUIDEX [ONLINE DATABASE]. (19??)-. Abstracting/Indexing Service. English. Available through Dialog and ESA/IRS. Elsevier Geo Abstracts, An Imprint of Elsevier Science Ltd., The Boulevard, Langford Lane, Kidlington, Oxford OX5 1GB United Kingdom. **Tel** 011 44 865 843000, 011 44 865 843699, FAX 011 44 865 843010. available in print.
Desc: A specialized database providing a comprehensive source of information on all aspects of fluid engineering and behavior and applications of fluids.

UK/0440-1905
HANDBOOK OF ELECTRICITY SUPPLY STATISTICS. ***Ceased.*** (1966)-Ceased (1991). English. an. Electricity Association Services Ltd, 30 Millbank, London SW1P 4RD England. **Tel** 011 44 71 834 2333. **LC** HD9685.G69; H35.

US/1050-0804
HIGHWAY RESEARCH ABSTRACTS (1990). (HIGHWAY RESEARCH ABSTRACTS.). [Highw. res. abstr.]. **Added/Corp** National Research Council (U.S.). Highway Research Information Service. National Research Council (U.S.). Transportation Research Board. National Research Council (U.S.). Transportation Research Information Services. Vol 23, No. 1 (Spring 1990)-. Abstracting/Indexing Service. English. qt. $100.00 North America; $115.00 other. Transportation Research Board, Box 289, Washington DC 20055. **Tel** (202)334-3218, FAX (202)334-2519. **LC** TE1; .N469a. **DD** 388.1/08. **Circ:** 2,500. ***Continues*** *HRIS Abstracts, 0017-6222.*
Desc: Contains research reports, technical papers from conference proceedings and journal articles on related topics.
Ind/Abst Highw. Res. Abstr.

UK/0952-2654
HTFS DIGEST (1987). (HTFS DIGEST.). [HTFS dig.]. **Added/Corp** Heat Transfer and Fluid Flow Service. **VFOAT** Heat Transfer and Fluid Flow Digest; Heat Transfer & Fluid Flow Digest; Heat Transfer & Fluid Flow Service. **VAT** Heat Transfer and Fluid Flow Service Digest. Vol. 18, No. 1 (Jan./Feb. 1985)-. Abstracting/Indexing Service. English. qt. £145.00 UK; £160.00 other. Heat Transfer and Fluid Flow Service, Harwell Laboratory Building 392 #7, Oxfordshire OX11 0RA England. **Tel** 011 44 235 432908, FAX 011 44 235 831981, telex 83135. **ED** P. Hicklin. **Circ:** 400. available on an online database from ESA-ISA. ***Continues*** *Heat Transfer & Fluid Flow Digest, 0309-1953;* ***Absorbed*** *Fouling Prevention Research Digest.*
Desc: Current awareness journal covering literature on design performance and operation of heat transfer and other equipment and processes occuring within such equipment.
Ind/Abst Fluid Abstr., Civil Eng.; Fluid Abstr. Proc. Eng.; FLUIDEX (1985-).

US/0099-1368
INDEX TO IEEE PUBLICATIONS. [Index IEEE publ.]. **Main/Corp** Institute of Electrical and Electronics Engineers. **VAT** Index to Institute of Electrical and Electronics Engineers Publications. (1973)-. Abstracting/Indexing Service. English. an. $430.00 (surface mail), $277.90 (airmail) all except Japan. IEEE, Institution of Electrical and Electronics Engineers, Inc., 345 East 47th Street, New York NY 10017-2394. **Tel** (908)981-1393, FAX (908)981-9667. **(Subscription address:** IEEE Service Center, 445 Hoes Lane, Piscataway, NJ 08854; telephone: (201)981-1393**) LC** Z5832; .I54; TK145. **DD** 621.3/01/6. available on CD-ROM (as IEEE/IEE Publications Ondisc - IPO) from University Microfilms International (UMI); available on an online database from DIALOG. ***Supersedes*** *Institute of Electrical and Electronics Engineers. Index to IEEE Periodicals.*
Desc: Index to all papers in IEEE journal, magazines and conference proceedings during the current year.

CN/0713-1445
INFOR-MER. MINES. (INFO-MER, MINES / CENTRE DE DOCUMENTATION ET DES RENSEIGNEMENTS.). [Info-MER, Mines]. **Main/Corp** Quebec (Province). Ministere de l'Energie et des Ressources. Centre de Documentation et de Renseignements. **VAT** Information - Ministere de l'Energie et des Ressources. Mines. Vol. 3, No. 13 Nov. 21, 1980-. French (English). Free. Gouvernement du Quebec, 600 St Amable 4E Etage, Quebec Quebec G1R 4Z1 Canada. **DD** 016.622/05. ctrl circ. ***Continues*** *Info-Biblio-Mines, 0704-1691.*

UK
INSPEC [ONLINE DATABASE]. Abstracting/Indexing Service. English. Varies according to usage. Institution of Electrical Engineers / IEE, Michael Faraday House, Six Hills Way, Stevenage Herts SG1 2AY UK. **Tel** 011 44 438 313311, FAX 011 44 438

742840, telex 825578 IEESTV G. **(Subscription address:** IEE / UK, Publications Sales Department, PO Box 96, Stevenage, Herts, SG1 2SD England.**)** available on CD-ROM from University Microfilms International (UMI).
Desc: Input to the INSPEC database is prepared from the world's literature in the fields if physics, electrical engineering, electronics, computers and control. The publications scanned include journals, conference proceedings, books, reports and theses.

IE/0332-4095
INTERNATIONAL CIVIL ENGINEERING ABSTRACTS. (Feb. 1982)-. Abstracting/Indexing Service. English. mo (except January and August). $660.00 US & Canada; £390.00 UK & Ireland; DM1325.00 other; Combined subscription with Software Abstracts for Engineers: £480.00 UK & Ireland; $880.00 US & Canada; DM1650.00 other. CITIS Ltd, 2 Rosemount Terrace, Blackrock Dublin Ireland. **Tel** 3531-886227, FAX 3531-885971, telex 30259 MSCH ET. **(Subscription address:** 80 8th Avenue, Suite 303, New York, NY 10011**) ED** D P Murphy. Index available. cum. index. **Ad Acc.** available on CD-ROM; available on diskette. ***Continues*** *Institution of Civil Engineers (Great Britain). I.C.E. Abstracts, 0305-2176.*
Desc: Gives abstracts of all major literature on civil engineering worldwide. Original papers may be obtained.

US/0272-3743
INVENTORY OF POWER PLANTS IN THE UNITED STATES. (INVENTORY OF POWER PLANTS IN THE UNITED STATES / [PREPARED BY THE DIVISION OF ELECTRIC POWER STATISTICS, OFFICE OF COAL AND ELECTRIC POWER STATISTICS, ENERGY INFORMATION ADMINISTRATION, DEPARTMENT OF ENERGY]). **Added/Corp** United States. Energy Information Administration. Division of Electric Power Statistics. United States. Energy Information Administration. Office of Coal and Electric Power Statistics. United States. Federal Energy Administration. United States. Dept. of Energy. Office of Utility Project Operations. United States. Energy Information Administration. Office of Energy Data. United States. Energy Information Administration. Office of Energy Data Operations. United States. Office of Coal, Nuclear, Electric, and Alternate Fuels. United States. Office of Coal, Nuclear, Electric, and Alternate Fuels. Electric Power Division. (June 1977)-. Statistical Publication. English. an. $25.00. National Energy Information Center, Energy Information Administration, Forrestal Building, Room 1F-048, Washington DC 20585. **Tel** (202)586-8800. **LC** TK1193.U5; I63. **DD** 338.4/7621312132/02573. ***Continues*** *Trends in Power Plant Capacity and Utilization, Inventory of Power Plants in the United States, 0272-3735.*
Desc: This report presents year-end statistics about electric generating units operated by electric utilities in the United States.

UK/0306-7327
IRRIGATION AND DRAINAGE ABSTRACTS / COMMONWEALTH AGRICULTURAL BUREAUX. Added/Corp Commonwealth Agricultural Bureaux. (May 1975)-. Abstracting/Indexing Service. English. bm. $263.00 US. CAB International Centre, Wallingford, Oxon OX10 8DE United Kingdom. **Tel** 44 491 832111, FAX 44 491 833508, telex 847964 (COMAGG G). **ED** J. R. Metcalfe. **LC** S612; .I73. **DD** 631.6/2/05. **Ad Acc. Circ:** 450.
Desc: Covers world literature on water management, soil-water relations, irrigation, plant-water relations, drainage, salinity and toxicity problems.
Ind/Abst Field Crop Abstr.; Grasslands For. Abstr.

US/0896-7113
ISMEC, MECHANICAL ENGINEERING ABSTRACTS. ***Title Change.*** [ISMEC mech. eng. abstr.]. **Added/Corp** Cambridge Scientific Abstracts, Inc. **VFOAT** Mechanical Engineering Abstracts; ISMEC; Ismec Bulletin. **VAT** Information Service in Mechanical Engineering Mechanical Engineering Abstracts. Vol. 21, No. 1 (Feb. 1988)-(1992). Abstracting/Indexing Service. English. bm (plus annual index). Cambridge Scientific Abstracts, 7200 Wisconsin Avenue, #601, Bethesda MD 20814-4823. **Tel** (301)961-6750, (800)843-7751, FAX (301)961-6720. **ED** Evelyn Beck. **LC** Z5853.M2; I54a; TJ145. **DD** 016.621. **CODEN** ISMECI. Index available. **Bk Rev.** available on magnetic tape; available on an online database. ***Continues*** *ISMEC Bulletin, 0306-0039.* ***Continued by*** *Mechanical Engineering Abstracts, 1063-7311.*
Desc: Mechanical and production engineering, engineering management, includes operations research, material testing, machine tools, energy and power, vehicle engineering, robotics, and CAD/CAM.

US/1066-2375
JMR ABSTRACTS. ***Title Change.*** [JMR abstr.]. (1992)-(199?). Abstracting/Indexing Service. English. mo. Materials Research Society, 9800 McKnight Road, Suite 327, Pittsburgh PA 15237-6006. **Tel** (412)367-3003, FAX (412)367-4373. **(Subscription address:** Kinokuniya Company Ltd., 38-1 Sakuragaoka 5, chome Setagaya-ku, Tokyo 156 Japan.**) DD** 620. **Pr Rev. Circ:** 11,500. ***Absorbed by*** *MRS Bulletin, 0883-7694.*
Desc: Includes an easy-to-scan table of contents and complete abstracts of papers appearing in the next issue of Journal of Materials Research. A convenient way to quickly identify and flag articles you don't want to miss.

JA/0011-3271
KAGAKU GIJUTSU BUNKEN SOKUHO. KAGAKU. KAGAKU KOGYO HEN : KOKUNAI-HEN. [Kagaku gijutsu bunken sokuho, Kagaku, Kagaku kogyo hen: Kokunai-hen]. **Added/Corp** Nihon Kagaku Gijutsu Joho Senta. **VFOAT** Current Bibliography on Science and Technology. Chemistry and Chemical Engineering. (19??)-. Academic Scholarly Publication. Japanese (English). ir. Nihon Kagaku Gijutsu Joho Senta, (Japan Information Center of Science & Technology), 5-2, Nagatacho 2 Chome, Chiyodaku, Tokyoto 100 Japan. **(Subscription address:** Japan Publications Trading Company, Ltd., PO Box 5030, Tokyo International, Tokyo 100-31 Japan.**) CODEN** KGBHDD. Documents available from CASDDS. ***Continues*** *Nihon Kagaku Soran.*
Ind/Abst Chem. Abstr.

UK/0950-4753
KEY ABSTRACTS. ADVANCED MATERIALS. [Key abstr., Adv. mater.]. **Added/Corp** INSPEC (Information Service) Institute of Electrical and Electronics Engineers. **VFOAT** Advanced Materials. (1987)-. Abstracting/Indexing Service. English. mo. $178.00. Institution of Electrical Engineers / IEE, Michael Faraday House, Six Hills Way, Stevenage Herts SG1 2AY UK. **Tel** 011 44 438 313311, FAX 011 44 438 742840, telex 825578 IEESTV G. **(Subscription address:** IEEE / Institute of Electrical and Electronics Engineers, 445 Hoes Lane, PO Box 1331, Piscataway NJ 08855-1331.**) ED** V. K. Royce. Index available. **Bk Rev.**
Desc: Abstracts journal with index. Provides details from recently published papers on fields such as: preparation, structure, properties and testing of ceramics, refractories, composite materials, polymers, glasses and porous materials.

UK/0950-4761
KEY ABSTRACTS. ANTENNAS & PROPAGATION. [Key abstr., Antennas propag.]. **Added/Corp** INSPEC (Information Service) Institute of Electrical and Electronics Engineers. **VFOAT** Antennas & Propagation; Key Abstracts. Antennas and Propagation. (1987)-. Abstracting/Indexing Service. English. mo. $178.00. Institution of Electrical Engineers / IEE, Michael Faraday House, Six Hills Way, Stevenage Herts SG1 2AY UK. **Tel** 011 44 438 313311, FAX 011 44 438 742840, telex 825578 IEESTV G. **(Subscription address:** IEEE / Institute of Electrical and Electronics Engineers, 445 Hoes Lane, PO Box 1331, Piscataway NJ 08855-1331.**)** ***Continues in part*** *Key Abstracts. Communication Technology.*
Desc: Covers radio links and equipment, EM and radio wave propagation, antennas, radar, radionaviation, and EM compatibility.

UK/0950-477X
KEY ABSTRACTS. ARTIFICIAL INTELLIGENCE. [Key abstr., Artif. intell.]. **Added/Corp** INSPEC (Information Service) Institute of Electrical and Electronics Engineers. **VFOAT** Artificial Intelligence. (Jan. 1987)-. Abstracting/Indexing Service. English. mo. $178.00. Institution of Electrical Engineers / IEE, Michael Faraday House, Six Hills Way, Stevenage Herts SG1 2AY UK. **Tel** 011 44 438 313311, FAX 011 44 438 742840, telex 825578 IEESTV G. **(Subscription address:** IEEE / Institute of Electrical and Electronics Engineers, 445 Hoes Lane, PO Box 1331, Piscataway NJ 08855-1331.**) LC** Q334; .K48. **DD** 006.3. ***Continues*** *Key Abstracts. Systems Theory, 0306-5553.*
Desc: Covers theory and applications of artificial intelligence, knowledge engineering and expert systems.
Ind/Abst HILITES.

UK/0954-9153
KEY ABSTRACTS. BUSINESS AUTOMATION. Added/Corp INSPEC (Information Service) Institute of Electrical and Electronics Engineers. **VFOAT** Business Automation. (Jan. 1989)-. Abstracting/Indexing Service. English. mo. $178.00. Institution of Electrical Engineers / IEE, Michael Faraday House, Six Hills Way, Stevenage Herts SG1 2AY UK. **Tel** 011 44 438 313311, FAX 011 44 438 742840, telex 825578 IEESTV G. **(Subscription address:** IEEE / Institute of Electrical and Electronics Engineers, 445 Hoes Lane, PO Box 1331, Piscataway NJ 08855-1331.**)** ***Continues*** *IT Focus, 0264-9152.*
Desc: Covers communications, computers and office systems in business and commerce including banking, financial markets and retailing.
Ind/Abst HILITES.

UK/0950-4788
KEY ABSTRACTS. COMPUTER COMMUNICATIONS & STORAGE. [Key abstr., Comput. commun. stor.]. **Added/Corp** INSPEC (Information Service) Institute of Electrical and Electronics Engineers. **VFOAT** Computer Communications & Storage; Computer Communications and Storage; Key Abstracts. Computer Communications and Storage. (1987)-. Abstracting/Indexing Service. English. mo. $178.00. Institution of Electrical Engineers / IEE, Michael Faraday House, Six Hills Way, Stevenage Herts SG1 2AY UK. **Tel** 011 44 438 313311, FAX 011 44 438 742840, telex 825578 IEESTV G. **(Subscription address:** IEEE / Institute of Electrical and Electronics Engineers, 445 Hoes Lane, PO Box 1331, Piscataway NJ 08855-1331.**)**
Desc: Covers multiprocesssor systems, modern storage media including optical discs, interfaces, networks network equipment.

UK/0950-4796
KEY ABSTRACTS. COMPUTING IN ELECTRONICS AND POWER. [Key abstr., Comput. electron. power]. **Added/Corp** INSPEC (Information Service) Institute of Electrical and Electronics Engineers. **VFOAT** Computing in Electronics and Power. (1987)-. Abstracting/Indexing Service. English. mo. $178.00. Institution of Electrical Engineers / IEE, Michael Faraday House, Six Hills Way, Stevenage Herts SG1 2AY UK. **Tel** 011 44 438 313311, FAX 011 44 438 742840, telex 825578 IEESTV G. **(Subscription address:** IEEE / Institute of Electrical and Electronics Engineers, 445 Hoes Lane, PO Box 1331, Piscataway NJ 08855-1331.**)**
Desc: Covers computer applications in communications and electrical, electronic and power engineering.

UK/0306-557X
KEY ABSTRACTS. ELECTRONIC CIRCUITS. Added/Corp Institution of Electrical Engineers. Institute of Electrical and Electronics Engineers. INSPEC (Information Service). **VFOAT** Electronic Circuits. (1975)-. Abstracting/Indexing Service. English. mo. $178.00. Institution of Electrical Engineers / IEE, Michael Faraday House, Six Hills Way, Stevenage Herts SG1 2AY UK. **Tel** 011 44 438 313311, FAX 011 44 438 742840, telex 825578 IEESTV G. **(Subscription address:** IEEE / Institute of Electrical and Electronics Engineers, 445 Hoes Lane, PO Box 1331, Piscataway NJ 08855-1331.**) LC** TK7800; .K49. **DD** 621.381/5.
Desc: Provides details of recently published papers chosen from 4,000 leading international journals on the subjects of: power electronics, amplifiers, signal generators, modulators, pulse circuits, digital electronics, and filters.

UK/0950-480X
KEY ABSTRACTS. ELECTRONIC INSTRUMENTATION. [Key abstr., Electron. instrum.]. **Added/Corp** INSPEC (Information Service) Institute of Electrical and Electronics Engineers. **VFOAT** Electronic Instrumentation. (Jan. 1987)-. Abstracting/Indexing Service. English. mo. $178.00. Institution of Electrical Engineers / IEE, Michael Faraday House, Six Hills Way, Stevenage Herts SG1 2AY UK. **Tel** 011 44 438 313311, FAX 011 44 438 742840, telex 825578 IEESTV G. **(Subscription address:** IEEE / Institute of Electrical and Electronics Engineers, 445 Hoes Lane, PO Box 1331, Piscataway NJ 08855-1331.**) LC** TK7869; .K49. **DD** 621.381. ***Continues*** *Key Abstracts. Electrical Measurements and Instrumentation, 0307-7977.*
Desc: Covers instrumentation and measurement systems, signal processing circuits and devices, transducers, bench instruments, display technology, measurement of electrical and magnetic variables.

UK/0953-1262
KEY ABSTRACTS. HIGH-TEMPERATURE SUPERCONDUCTORS. Added/Corp INSPEC (Information Service) Institute of Electrical and Electronics Engineers. **VFOAT** Key Abstracts. High Temperature Superconductors; High-temperature Superconductors; High Temperature Superconductors. (Jan. 1988)-. Abstracting/Indexing Service. English. mo. $178.00. Institution of Electrical Engineers / IEE, Michael Faraday House, Six Hills Way, Stevenage Herts SG1 2AY UK. **Tel** 011 44 438 313311, FAX 011 44 438 742840, telex 825578 IEESTV G. **(Subscription address:** IEEE / Institute of Electrical and Electronics Engineers, 445 Hoes Lane, PO Box 1331, Piscataway NJ 08855-1331.**)**

UK/0952-7060
KEY ABSTRACTS. MICROELECTRONICS AND PRINTED CIRCUITS. Added/Corp INSPEC (Information Service) Institute of Electrical and Electronics Engineers. **VFOAT** Microelectronics and Printed Circuits. (Jan. 1988)-. Abstracting/Indexing Service. English. mo. $178.00. Institution of Electrical Engineers / IEE, Michael Faraday House, Six Hills Way, Stevenage Herts SG1 2AY UK. **Tel** 011 44 438 313311, FAX 011 44 438 742840, telex 825578 IEESTV G. **(Subscription address:** IEEE / Institute of Electrical and Electronics Engineers, 445 Hoes Lane, PO Box 1331, Piscataway NJ 08855-1331.**)**
Desc: Covers semiconductor integrated circuits, thin film, thick film and hybrid integrated circuits, printed circuit design and manufacture.

UK/0952-7079
KEY ABSTRACTS. MICROWAVE TECHNOLOGY. Added/Corp INSPEC (Information Service) Institute of Electrical and Electronics Engineers. **VFOAT** Microwave Technology. (Jan. 1988)-. Abstracting/Indexing Service. English. mo. $178.00. Institution of Electrical Engineers / IEE, Michael Faraday House, Six Hills Way, Stevenage Herts SG1 2AY UK. **Tel** 011 44 438 313311, FAX 011 44 438 742840, telex 825578 IEESTV G. **(Subscription address:** IEEE /

Institute of Electrical and Electronics Engineers, 445 Hoes Lane, PO Box 1331, Piscataway NJ 08855-1331.) [CCC].

UK/0950-4826
KEY ABSTRACTS. OPTOELECTRONICS. **Added/Corp** Institution of Electrical Engineers. Information Services Division. Institute of Electrical and Electronics Engineers. **VFOAT** Optoelectronics. (1987)-. Abstracting/Indexing Service. English. mo. $178.00. Institution of Electrical Engineers / IEE, Michael Faraday House, Six Hills Way, Stevenage Herts SG1 2AY UK. **Tel** 011 44 438 313311, FAX 011 44 438 742840, telex 825578 IEESTV G. **(Subscription address:** IEEE / Institute of Electrical and Electronics Engineers, 445 Hoes Lane, PO Box 1331, Piscataway NJ 08855-1331.) ***Continues in part*** *Key Abstracts. Solid State Devices, 0306-5537.*
Desc: Covers articles on fibre optics, integrated optoelectronics, electro-optic devices, lasers and their applications, nonlinear optics, optical computing, holography.

UK/0950-4850
KEY ABSTRACTS. SEMICONDUCTOR DEVICES. [Key abstr., Semicond. devices]. **Added/Corp** INSPEC (Information Service) Institute of Electrical and Electronics Engineers. **VFOAT** Semiconductor Devices. (1987)-. Abstracting/Indexing Service. English. mo. $178.00. Institution of Electrical Engineers / IEE, Michael Faraday House, Six Hills Way, Stevenage Herts SG1 2AY UK. **Tel** 011 44 438 313311, FAX 011 44 438 742840, telex 825578 IEESTV G. **(Subscription address:** IEEE / Institute of Electrical and Electronics Engineers, 445 Hoes Lane, PO Box 1331, Piscataway NJ 08855-1331.) **LC** TK7871.85; .K43. **DD** 621.381/52/05. ***Continues in part*** *Key Abstracts. Solid State Devices, 0306-5537.*
Desc: Covers semiconductor devices technology, diodes, transistors and other semiconductor devices.

US/1063-732X
MATERIALS SCIENCE AND ENGINEERING ABSTRACTS. ***Ceased.*** [Mater. sci. eng. abstr.]. **Added/Corp** Cambridge Scientific Abstracts, Inc. Engineering Information, Inc. **VFOAT** Materials Science & Engineering Abstracts. Vol. 1, No. 1 (1993)-(1995). Abstracting/Indexing Service. English. mo. Cambridge Scientific Abstracts, 7200 Wisconsin Avenue, #601, Bethesda MD 20814-4823. **Tel** (301)961-6750, (800)843-7751, FAX (301)961-6720. **DD** 620. available on magnetic tape.
Desc: Published in collaboration with Engineering Information Inc., this journal focuses on mechanical and physical properties of materials and commercial or industrial applications for materials. In addition to properties of materials,topics highlighted include new methods for strength testing, effects of vibration and other stresses, corrosion and protective coatings, storage and handling, and ways of producing materials commercially are among the covered topics.

●US/1063-7311
MECHANICAL ENGINEERING ABSTRACTS. **Added/Corp** Cambridge Scientific Abstracts, Inc. (1993)-. Abstracting/Indexing Service. English. mo. $895.00 US; $995.00 other. Cambridge Scientific Abstracts, 7200 Wisconsin Avenue, #601, Bethesda MD 20814-4823. **Tel** (301)961-6750, (800)843-7751, FAX (301)961-6720. available on magnetic tape and an online database; available via Internet (to the current year's abstracts and five-year backfiles) from Cambridge Scientific Abstracts. ***Continues*** *ISMEC, Mechanical Engineering Abstracts, 0896-7113.*
Desc: Covers aspects of international mechanical engineering literature.

US/0160-5151
MINERAL COMMODITY SUMMARIES. [Miner. commod. summ.]. **Added/Corp** United States. Bureau of Mines. Geological Survey (U.S.). (1978)-. Government Publication. English. an. Free on request. US Department of the Interior / Bureau of Mines, 810 7th Street NW, Room 604, Washington DC 20241. **Tel** (202)501-9300. **(Subscription address:** Superintendent of Documents, US Government Printing Office, Washington DC 20402) **ED** A E Schreck. **LC** HD9506.U6; U48b. **DD** 338.2/0973. **Circ:** 7,000 (ctrl). available on microfiche (Vols. for 1982- distributed to depository libraries). ***Continues*** *Commodity Data Summaries, 0082-9137.*
Desc: Up-to-date summary of 85 nonfuel minerals. Earliest furnish estimates of previous years production, sales, trade data and reserves.
Ind/Abst F&S Index Plus Text, Int. [Select. Cov.]; GeoRef; Predicasts Forecasts.

CN
MINES DE CHARBON. **Main/Corp** Statistics Canada. Manufacturing and Primary Industries Division. **VFOAT** Mines de Charbon. Multiple languages (English and French). an. 24.00Can$ Canada; $29.00 US; $34.00 other. Statistics Canada, Publications Sales & Services, Main Building Room 1710, Ottawa Ontario K1A 0T6 Canada. **Tel** (613)951-5078, (800)267-6677, FAX (613)951-1584, telex 053-3585. **ED** Dave Madsen. **Circ:** 375.
Desc: Presents statistics on the number of mines or plants, average number of employees, salaries and wages, cost of fuel and electricity, cost of materials and gross selling value of products, with comparative totals for earlier years for Canada and breakdown by province.

CN
MINING STATISTICS : NORTH OF 60. **Main/Corp** Canada. Northern Economic Development Branch. Mining Section. **VFOAT** Statistiques Minieres: Au Nord du 60E. Multiple languages. National Economic Development Branch, Mining Section, Information Canada Receiver General Canada, Statistics Canada Publications, Ottawa Ontario K1A 0T6 Canada. **LC** HD9506.C2; A384. **DD** 338.2/09712.

AT
MINING TASMANIA. **Main/Corp** Australian Bureau of Statistics. Tasmanian Office. (19??)-. English. an. 12.00Aus$. Australian Bureau of Statistics, PO Box 10, Belconnen Australian Capital Territory, 2616 Australia. **Tel** 011 61 6 2527911, FAX 011 61 6 2516009. **LC** TN122.T3; A87a. **DD** 338.2/09946.
Desc: Covers number of mining establishments, average employment and employment at end of June by type of employment, wages and salaries paid, components and value of turnover, type and value of stocks, value of purchases, etc.

AT
MINING, WESTERN AUSTRALIA / AUSTRALIAN BUREAU OF STATISTICS, WESTERN AUSTRALIAN OFFICE. (19??)-. English. an. 15.00Aus$. Australian Bureau of Statistics, PO Box 10, Belconnen Australian Capital Territory, 2616 Australia. **Tel** 011 61 6 2527911, FAX 011 61 6 2516009. **LC** HD9506.A7; S85. **DD** 338.2/09941. ***Continues*** *Statistics of Western Australia. Mining.*
Desc: Census of mining establishments: summary of operations, employment, wages and salaries, turnover, stocks, purchases, capital expenditure and mineral royalties by industry class.

CN/0828-8461
MINPROC : MINERAL PROCESSING ABSTRACTS. ***Ceased.*** [MINPROC, Miner. process. abstr.]. **Added/Corp** Canada Centre for Mineral and Energy Technology. **VFOAT** Mineral Processing Abstracts. Vol. 1, No. 1 (Jan. 9, 1985)-Vol. 9. Abstracting/Indexing Service. English (French; summaries and/or abstracts in English and French). Twelve times a year. Canada Center Mineral & Energy Technology, 555 Booth Street, Ottawa ONT K1A OG1 Canada. **Tel** (613)992-8837, FAX (613)952-2587. **DD** 016.549. Index Bound in First Issue (Annually). cum. index. available on an online database from CAN/OLE.
Desc: A bulletin of abstracts of current literature on mineral processing. Subjects covered include separation processes, hydrometallurgy, pyrometallurgy, purification, plants and equipment, as well as waste disposal.

CN/0823-0773
MINTEC : MINING TECHNOLOGY ABSTRACTS. ***Ceased.*** [MINTEC, Min. technol. abstr.]. **Main/Corp** Canada Centre for Mineral and Energy Technology. **VFOAT** Mining Technology Abstracts. Vol. 1 (Feb. 18, 1983)-Vol. 11. Abstracting/Indexing Service. English (French; summaries and/or abstracts in French). bw. Canada Center Mineral & Energy Technology, 555 Booth Street, Ottawa ONT K1A OG1 Canada. **Tel** (613)992-8837, FAX (613)952-2587. **DD** 622. Index available. **Circ:** 500.
Desc: Subjects covered include production methods, ground control, plant construction and maintenance, drilling, blasting, tunnelling and mine geology.

UK
OPERATIONS & PRODUCTION MANAGEMENT ABSTRACTS. (19??)-. Abstracting/Indexing Service. English. mo. $2999.00. MCB University Press, 60 62 Toller Lane, Bradford West Yorkshire BD8 9BX England. **Tel** 011 44 274 499821, FAX 011 44 274 547143, telex 51317 MCBUNI G. **(Subscription address:** MCB University Press / US and Canada Subscriptions, PO Box 10812, Birmingham AL 35201-0812.) ***Continues*** *Management Services and Production Abstracts, 0952-4614.*

FR/1146-5093
PASCAL. T 295, BATIMENT TRAVAUX PUBLICS. **VFOAT** PASCAL. T 295, Buildings Public Works; PASCAL. T Deux-Cent-Quatre-Vingt-Quinze, Batiment Travaux Publics. (1990)-. Periodical. Multiple languages. Eleven times a year (10 issues plus cumulative index). 1030.00F France; 1085.00F others. CNRS / Institut d'Information Scientifique et Technique, (Centre National de la Recherche Scientifique), 15 Quai Anatole France, Paris 75700 France. **Tel** 011 33 1 47531515, telex 299 356 F. **(Subscription address:** Institut d'Information Scientifique et Technique Diffusion, 2 Allee du Parc de Brabois, 54514 Vandoeuvre Nancy France.) **UDC** 011. Index available. cum. index. ***Continues*** *PASCAL Thema. T295, Batiment, Travaux Publics, 0761-1722.*

US
PERIODICALS CURRENTLY RECEIVED. ***Ceased.*** **Main/Corp** Engineering Societies Library. **VFOAT** E.S.L. Periodicals Currently Received. (1978)-(19??). English. be. Engineering Societies Library, 345 East 47th Street, New York NY 10017. **Tel** (212)705-7608.

US
PERLITE. (PERLITE IN ...). English. an. US Department of the Interior / Bureau of Mines, Publications Department, PO Box 18070, Cochrans Mill Road, Pittsburgh PA 15236. **Tel** (412)892-6400.
Desc: Statistical and economic data on perlite.

UK/0960-5045
PROCESS AND CHEMICAL ENGINEERING. **Added/Corp** Royal Society of Chemistry (Great Britain). **VFOAT** Process & Chemical Engineering. Vol. 10, Issue 1 (Jan. 1991)-. Abstracting/Indexing Service. English. mo (12 issues). £336.00 EC; $610.00 US; £336.00 other. Royal Society of Chemistry, Thomas Graham House, Science Park, Cambridge CB4 4WF England. **Tel** 011 44 223 420066, FAX 011 44 223 423429, telex 818293 ROYAL. **(Subscription address:** Turpin Distribution Services Limited, Blackhorse Road, Letchworth, Hertfordshire SG6 1HN, United Kingdom.) **CODEN** PCEGEJ. Index available. **Ad Acc.** available on an online database from Fiz-Technik; STN International; ORBIT; ESA-IRS; DIALOG; and DATA-STAR. ***Continues*** *Chemical Engineering Abstracts, 0262-6438.*
Desc: A monthly current awareness bulletin giving full coverage of the published information needed by practicing chemical engineers, production and process chemists, plant managers and industrial engineering libraries.

US
QUARTZ CRYSTAL. 1976-. English. an. US Department of the Interior / Bureau of Mines, Publications Department, PO Box 18070, Cochrans Mill Road, Pittsburgh PA 15236. **Tel** (412)892-6400.
Desc: Statistical and economic data on industrial quartz crystal.

US/0163-9838
RAC NEWSLETTER. [RAC newsl.]. **Main/Corp** Reliability Analysis Center (U.S.). **VAT** Reliability Analysis Center Newsletter. (19??)-. Newsletter. English. qt (Jan, Apr, July, Oct). Free. Reliability Analysis Center, PO Box 4700, Rome NY 13440. **Tel** (315)337-0900, FAX (315)337-0900. **ED** N Pfrimmer. **Bk Rev. Circ:** 22,000 (ctrl).
Desc: Electrical and mechanical reliability and failure analysis. Consulting service and failure rate data basis. Statistical services, and this newsletter keeps VP up with state of art events.

BE
REPERTOIRE DES CENTRALES ELECTRIQUES. **Main/Corp** Federation Professionnelle des Producteurs et Distributeurs d'Electricite de Belgique. (19??)-. French (Dutch). an. 200F. Federation Professionnelle des Producteurs et Distributeurs d'Electriate de Belgique, Avenue de Tervuren 34 Bte 38, Bruxelles Belgium. **Tel** 02/733 96 07, FAX 02/733 95 65. **LC** TK1193.B5; F43a. **Circ:** 900.
Desc: A listing of all electricity plants in Belgium with their yearly production of electricity.

US/0583-1024
SHOCK AND VIBRATION DIGEST, THE. (THE SHOCK AND VIBRATION DIGEST : A PUBLICATION OF THE SHOCK AND VIBRATION INFORMATION CENTER, NAVAL RESEARCH LABORATORY.). [Shock vibr. dig.]. **Added/Corp** Shock and Vibration Information Center. Vibration Institute. (1969)-. Abstracting/Indexing Service. English. Six times a year. $250.00. The Vibration Institute, 6262 South Kingery Highway, Suite 212, Willowbrook IL 60514. **Tel** (708)654-2254, FAX (708)654-2271, telex (708)654-2271. **ED** Vicki M. Pate. **LC** Z5853.V6; S5; TA355. **CODEN** SHVDAN. Index available (free five-year index). **Bk Rev. Circ:** 1,000. available on microfilm and microfiche from University Microfilms International (UMI); available on an online database. Documents available from Article Express International.
Desc: Tracks technical progress in shock, vibration, acoustics and closely related technologies. Abstracts from a wide range of journals and proceedings are arranged in technical categories that allow the reader to follow specific areas of interest.
Ind/Abst Abstr. J. Earthq. Eng.; Acoust. Abstr.; Bioeng. Abstr.; Ei Page One; EMBASE; Eng. Index Annu.; Fluid Abstr., Civil Eng.; Fluid Abstr. Proc. Eng.; FLUIDEX (1973-1989); Int. Aerosp. Abstr.; Int. Packag. Abstr.

CN/0707-2767
STATISTICAL REVIEW OF COAL IN CANADA. 1977-. Statistical Publication. English. an. Canada Department of Energy, Mines and Resources, Communications Branch/8th Floor, 580 Booth Street, Ottawa Ontario K1A 0E4 Canada. **Tel** (613)995-5030, FAX (613)996-9094. **LC** TN806.C2; S72. **DD** 333.7. ***Continues*** *Coal in Canada.*

BE
STATISTIQUES: HOUILLE, COKES, AGGLOMERES, METALLURGIE, CARRIERES. STATISTIEKEN: STEENKOLEN, COKES, AGGLOMERATEN, METAALNIJVERHEID, GROVEN. **Main/Corp** Belgium. Administration des Mines. **Added/Corp** Belgium. Administration des Mines. Statistieken: Steenkolen, Cokes, Agglomeraten, Metaalnijverheid, Groven. **VFOAT** Statistieken : Steenkolen, Cokes, Agglomeraten, Metaalnijverheid, Groven. (19??)-. Multiple languages (Dutch and French). Ministere des Affaires Economiques Comite de Concertation et du Controle du Petrole, Rue de Mot, 1040 Brussels Belgium. **LC** HD9555.B4; B4b.

UK/0960-5053
THEORETICAL CHEMICAL ENGINEERING. [Theor. chem. eng.]. (1991)-. Abstracting/Indexing Service. English. mo (12 issues). £130.00 EC; $236.00 US; £130.00 other. Royal Society of Chemistry, Thomas Graham House, Science Park, Cambridge CB4 4WF England. **Tel** 011 44 223 420066, FAX 011 44 223 423429, telex 818293 ROYAL. **(Subscription address:** Turpin Distribution Services Limited, Blackhorse Road, Letchworth, Hertfordshire SG6 1HN, United Kingdom.**)** **DD** 016.6602. Index available (free). cum. index (annually). **Ad Acc.** available on an online database from Fiz-Technik; STN International; ORBIT; ESA-IRS; DIALOG; and DATA-STAR. ***Continues*** *Theoretical Chemical Engineering Abstracts, 0040-5787.*
Desc: Contains worldwide current awareness coverage of theoretical chemical engineering including theory and laboratory studies.

US/0066-0604
TRANSACTIONS OF THE AMERICAN SOCIETY OF CIVIL ENGINEERS. [Trans. Am. Soc. Civ. Eng.]. **Main/Corp** American Society of Civil Engineers. **Added/Corp** American Society of Civil Engineers. Journal. **VFOAT** Journal. Vol. 1 (1867)-. Abstracting/Indexing Service. English. an. $150.00 (nonmembers) US; $171.00 (nonmembers) other. American Society of Civil Engineers / ASCE, 345 East 47th Street, New York NY 10017-2398. **Tel** (212)705-7179, FAX (212)705-7300, telex 422847 ASCE UI. **(Subscription address:** American Society of Civil Engineers, Publisher Fulfillment Agency, Box 828, Somerset NJ 08875.**)** **LC** TA1; .A5. **DD** 624/.05. **CODEN** TACEAT. **[CCC].** cum. index. **Circ:** 6,500. available on an online database from STN International (Math) Database; available on microfilm and microfiche from University Microfilms International (UMI).
Desc: Contains abstracts for all ASCE journal papers and technical notes, feature articles and other ASCE publications issued during the year.
Ind/Abst Appl. Soc. Sci. Index Abstr.; GeoRef.

CHEMICAL ENGINEERING

FI/0781-2698
ACTA POLYTECHNICA SCANDINAVICA. CHEMICAL TECHNOLOGY AND METALLURGY SERIES. [Acta polytech. Scand., Chem. technol. metall. ser.]. **Added/Corp** Teknillisten Tieteiden Akatemia. **VFOAT** Chemical Technology and Metallurgy Series. No. 153 (1983)-. Monographic series. English. Finnish Academy of Technology, Kansakoulukatu 10A, SF-00100 Helsinki 10 Finland. **Tel** 358-0-6944262, FAX 358-0-6945041. **CODEN** APSSEH. available on microfilm. Documents available from CASDDS. ***Continues*** *Acta Polytechnica Scandinavica. Chemistry including Metallurgy Series, 0001-6853.*
Ind/Abst Chem. Abstr.; Leadscan.

US/0001-821X
ADHESIVES AGE. [Adhes. age]. Vol. 1 (Oct. 1958)-. Periodical. English. mo. $52.00. Argus Business, 6151 Powers Ferry Road, Atlanta GA 30339. **Tel** (404)995-2500, (800)233-3359. **ED** Ann Barker. **LC** TP967; .A5. **DD** 668.305. **CODEN** ADHAAO. **[CCC]. Bk Rev. Ad Acc. Circ:** 23,000 (ctrl). available on microfilm and microfiche from University Microfilms International (UMI); available on an online database (Full-Text) from DIALOG. Documents available from Article Express International, Ask*IEEE, UMI Article Clearinghouse, CASDDS. ***Continues*** *Adhesives Red Book.*
Desc: News and information about adhesives for manufacturers and end-users.
Ind/Abst ABI/INFORM Glob. Ed. (August 1991-); ABI Inform Ondisc (August 1991-); Abstr. Bull. Inst. Pap. Sci. Tech.; Appl. Sci. Technol. Index; Art Archaeol. Tech. Abstr.; Biodeter. Abstr.; Bioeng. Abstr.; Chem. Abstr.; Chem. Ind. Notes; Coal Abstr.; Ei Page One; EMBASE; Eng. Index Annu.; F&S Index Plus Text, Int. [Select. Cov.]; Fluid Abstr., Civil Eng.; Fluid Abstr. Proc. Eng.; FLUIDEX (1973-); Foods Adlibra; INSPEC (Vol. 12, No. 10 Oct. 1969-Vol. 22, No. 9 1979); Int. Packag. Abstr.; Print. Abstr.; PROMT; Robotics Abstr.; Text. Technol. Dig.; Trade Ind. ASAP [Full Txt.]; Trade Ind. Index [Full Txt.]; World Surf. Coat. Abstr.

UK/0263-6174
ADSORPTION SCIENCE & TECHNOLOGY. [Adsorp. sci. technol.]. **VFOAT** Adsorption Science and Technology. Vol. 1, No. 1 (Jan. 1984)-. Academic Scholarly Publication. English. qt. £98.00 UK; £113.00 Europe; £126.00 (airmail) other. Multi Science Publishing Company Ltd., 107 High Street, Brentwood, Essex CM14 4RX England. **Tel** 011 44 277 224632, FAX 011 44 277 223453, telex 89-8452. **LC** QD547; .A394. **DD** 541.3/453. **CODEN** ASTEEZ. **[CCC].** available in microform from University Microfilms International (UMI). Documents available from Article Express International, CASDDS.
Desc: Publishes original research papers and critical reviews relating to adsorption and desorption phenomena. Original papers are published dealing with adsorption theory, measurements and techniques at gas-solid, liquid-solid and liquid-gas interfaces. The journal emphasizes links between developments in these sciences to their practical and industrial applications, for example in corrosion processes, catalysis, etc.
Ind/Abst Chem. Abstr. (1984-); Chem. Titles; Ei Page One; Eng. Index Annu.; Proc. Chem. Eng.; Theoret. Chem. Eng.; World Surf. Coat. Abstr.

GW/0724-6145
ADVANCES IN BIOCHEMICAL ENGINEERING/BIOTECHNOLOGY. [Adv. biochem. eng. biotechnol.]. Vol. 26 (1983)-. Academic Scholarly Publication. English. ir. Price varies per volume. Springer-Verlag GmbH & Company KG, Heidelberger Platz 3, D 14197 Berlin Germany. **Tel** 011 49 30 8207223, FAX 011 49 30 8214091, telex 183 319 SPBLN D. **(Subscription address:** Springer Verlag New York Inc. / for North America, 44 Hartz Way, Secaucus NJ 07096.**)** **LC** TP248.3; .A38. **DD** 660/.63/05. **NLM** W1 AD436N. **CODEN** ABEBDZ. **[CCC].** Documents available from Article Express International, BIOSIS Document Express, CASDDS. ***Continues*** *Advances in Biochemical Engineering, 0065-2210.*
Ind/Abst AGRICOLA [Select. Cov.]; Biodeter. Abstr.; Bioeng. Abstr.; Biol. Abstr. (1986-); Chem. Abstr. (1983-); Ei Page One; Eng. Index Annu.; Index Med. (1983-); Life Sci. Collect.; PESTDOC.

US/0065-2377
ADVANCES IN CHEMICAL ENGINEERING. [Adv. chem. eng.]. Vol. 1 (1956)-. Monographic series. English. ir. Price varies per volume. Academic Press, Inc., 6277 Sea Harbor Drive, Orlando FL 32887. **Tel** (800)543-9534, (407)345-4100, FAX (407)363-9661. **ED** Thomas B. Drew, Giles R. Cokelet, John W. Hoopes Jr. and Theodore Vermeulen. **LC** TP145; .A4. **DD** 660.28. **CODEN** ACHEAT. **[CCC].** Documents available from BIOSIS Document Express, CASDDS.
Ind/Abst Biol. Abstr.; Chem. Abstr. (1956-1983); Proc. Chem. Eng.; Theoret. Chem. Eng.

US/0743-0183
AICHE APPLICATIONS SOFTWARE SURVEY FOR PERSONAL COMPUTERS. ***Ceased.*** **See** Computers-Software.

US/0569-5473
AICHE EQUIPMENT TESTING PROCEDURE. **Main/Corp** American Institute of Chemical Engineers. **VFOAT** Equipment Testing Procedure. **VAT** American Institute of Chemical Engineers Equipment Testing Procedure. (19??)-. Monographic series. English. ir. Price varies per volume. American Institute of Chemical Engineers, 345 East 47th Street, New York NY 10017. **Tel** (212)705-7663, (212)705-7703, FAX (212)705-8400. **[CCC].**
Desc: Reviewed and re-evaluated by specialists in the field in an effort to meet current standards and requirements.
Ind/Abst Ei Page One.

US/0001-1541
AICHE JOURNAL. [AIChE j.]. **Main/Corp** American Institute of Chemical Engineers. **Added/Corp** American Institute of Chemical Engineers. Journal. **VAT** American Institute of Chemical Engineers Journal. (1955)-. Periodical. English. Twelve times a year. $445.00 US; $515.00 other. American Institute of Chemical Engineers, 345 East 47th Street, New York NY 10017. **Tel** (212)705-7663, (212)705-7703, FAX (212)705-8400. **ED** Morton M. Denn. **LC** TP1; .A634. **DD** 660.6273. **CODEN** AICEAC. **[CCC].** Index available (bound in Nov. issue). **Bk Rev. Ad Acc. Pr Rev. Acid Free. Circ:** 4,300 (ctrl). available on microfilm and microfiche from University Microfilms International (UMI). Documents available from Article Express International, The Genuine Article, Ask*IEEE, Petroleum Abstracts Document Delivery Service, CASDDS.
Desc: Archival journal in chemical engineering. It is devoted to fundamental research and developments having immediate or potential value in chemical engineering. It provides comprehensive coverage of ongoing research and developing technologies in conventional chemical engineering areas. The journal also provides efficient analyses of data and current theoretical ideas, as well as an excellent reference source for researchers.
Ind/Abst Abstr. Bull. Inst. Pap. Sci. Tech.; Appl. Sci. Technol. Index; Biodeter. Abstr. (1991-); Bioeng. Abstr.; Chem. Abstr.; Chem. Titles; Coal Abstr.; Curr. Biotechnol.; Curr. Contents Eng. Tech. Appl. Sci.; Curr. Titles Electrochem. (1973-); Ei Page One; Elect. Comm. Abstr.; EMBASE; Energy Inf. Abstr.; Energy Res. Abstr.; Eng. Mater. Abstr.; Eng. Index Annu.; Environ. Eng. Abstr.; Fluid Abstr., Civil Eng.; Fluid Abstr. Proc. Eng. (1968-); FLUIDEX (1973-); Foods Adlibra; Gas Abstr.; HTFS Dig.; INIS Atomindex [Micro.]; INSPEC (1968-); Lit. Pat. Abstr., Oilfield Chem. (1956-); Lit. Abstr., Catal. Catal.; Lit. Abstr., Health Environ.; Lit. Abstr., Pet. Refin. Petrochem.; Lit. Abstr., Pet. Substit.; Lit. Abstr., Transp. Storage; Mater. Sci. Eng. Abstr.; Math. Rev.; Mech. Eng. Abstr.; MINPROC; Pet. Abstr.; Pollut. Abstr. Indexes; Polymer Contents; Proc. Chem. Eng.; Res. Alert [Full Cov.]; Sci. Cit. Index; SCISEARCH; Soils Fert.; Solid State Supercond. Abstr.; Sug. Indus. Abstr.; Theoret. Chem. Eng.

US/0065-8804
AICHE MONOGRAPH SERIES. [AIChE monogr. ser.]. **Added/Corp** American Institute of Chemical Engineers. **VAT** American Institute of Chemical Engineers Monograph Series. No. 7 (1972)-. Monographic series. English. ir. Price varies per volume. American Institute of Chemical Engineers, 345 East 47th Street, New York NY 10017. **Tel** (212)705-7663, (212)705-7703, FAX (212)705-8400. **CODEN** ACEMB5. **[CCC].** Documents available from CASDDS. ***Continues*** *Chemical Engineering Progress Monograph Series, 0577-6090.*
Desc: Institute lecture presented at AICHE's annual meeting.
Ind/Abst Chem. Abstr.; Proc. Chem. Eng.; Theoret. Chem. Eng.

US/0065-8812
AICHE SYMPOSIUM SERIES. [AIChE symp. ser.]. **Added/Corp** American Institute of Chemical Engineers. American Institute of Chemical Engineers. Symposium Series. **VAT** American Institute of Chemical Engineers Symposium Series. No. 116 (1971)-. Monographic series. English. Twelve times a year. Price varies per volume. American Institute of Chemical Engineers, 345 East 47th Street, New York NY 10017. **Tel** (212)705-7663, (212)705-7703, FAX (212)705-8400. **LC** UNC. **CODEN** ACSSCQ. **[CCC].** Documents available from Article Express International, BIOSIS Document Express, CASDDS. ***Continues*** *Chemical Engineering Progress Symposium Series, 0069-2948.*
Ind/Abst Bioeng. Abstr.; Biol. Abstr. (1985-); Chem. Abstr.; Coal Abstr.; Curr. Biotechnol.; Ei Page One; Energy Res. Abstr. (March 1973-); Eng. Index Annu.; GeoRef; HTFS Dig.; INIS Atomindex [Micro.]; Int. Aerosp. Abstr.; Lit. Pat. Abstr., Oilfield Chem. (1973-); Lit. Abstr., Catal. Catal.; Lit. Abstr., Health Environ.; Lit. Abstr., Pet. Refin. Petrochem.; Lit. Abstr., Pet. Substit.; Lit. Abstr., Transp. Storage; Pollut. Abstr. Indexes; Proc. Chem. Eng.; Theoret. Chem. Eng.

US/0569-5457
AICHE WORKSHOP. **Main/Corp** American Institute of Chemical Engineers. **Added/Corp** American Institute of Chemical Engineers. Workshop. **VFOAT** Workshop. **VAT** American Institute of Chemical Engineers Workshop. Vol. 1 (1967)-. Monographic series. English. ir. Price varies per volume. American Institute of Chemical Engineers, 345 East 47th Street, New York NY 10017. **Tel** (212)705-7663, (212)705-7703, FAX (212)705-8400. **CODEN** AIWOA. **[CCC].**

US/8755-3163
AMERICAN FIREWORKS NEWS. **VFOAT** F.N.; AFN. (198?)-. English. Twelve times a year. $19.95. American Fireworks News, SR Box 30, Dingmans Ferry PA 18328. **Tel** (717)828-8417, FAX (717)828-8695. **ED** J. M. Drewes. **DD** 662. **Bk Rev. Ad Acc.**
Desc: World's only newsletter for fireworks enthusiasts.

US/0360-7011
AMMONIA PLANT SAFETY (AND RELATED FACILITIES). [Ammon. plant saf. relat. facil.]. **Added/Corp** American Institute of Chemical Engineers. Vol. 12 (1970)-. English. ir. Price varies per volume. American Institute of Chemical Engineers, 345 East 47th Street, New York NY 10017. **Tel** (212)705-7663, (212)705-7703, FAX (212)705-8400. **LC** TP149; .S2. **DD** 661/.34. **CODEN** ASAFB8. **[CCC].** Documents available from Article Express International, CASDDS. ***Continues*** *Safety in Air and Ammonia Plants, 0069-293X.*
Ind/Abst Bioeng. Abstr.; Chem. Abstr.; Chem. Hazards Ind.; Ei Page One; Eng. Index Annu.; HTFS Dig.; Lab. Hazards Bull.; Soils Fert.

SP/0213-5469
ANALES DE CIENCIAS - UNIVERSIDAD DE MURCIA. **See** Chemistry.

US/0196-7282
ANNUAL MEETING - AMERICAN INSTITUTE OF CHEMICAL ENGINEERS. [Annu. meet. - Am. Inst. Chem. Eng.]. **Main/Corp** American Institute of Chemical Engineers. (19??)-. English. an. American Institute of Chemical Engineers, 345 East 47th Street, New York NY 10017. **Tel** (212)705-7663, (212)705-7703, FAX (212)705-8400.

Documents available from Article Express International.
Desc: An advance program of each meeting.
Ind/Abst Eng. Index Annu.

US/0198-9677
ANNUAL REPORT / POLYMER SCIENCE AND STANDARDS DIVISION. See Engineering-Materials Engineering and Mechanics.

UK/0003-5599
ANTI-CORROSION METHODS AND MATERIALS. [Anti-corros. methods mater.]. Vol. 1 (Jan. 1966)-. Academic Scholarly Publication. English. bm. $149.00. MCB University Press, 60 62 Toller Lane, Bradford West Yorkshire BD8 9BX England. **Tel** 011 44 274 499821, FAX 011 44 274 547143, telex 51317 MCBUNI G. **(Subscription address:** MCB University Press / US and Canada Subscriptions, PO Box 10812, Birmingham AL 35201-0812.**) LC** TA462; .A67. **DD** 620.1122. **CODEN** ACMEBL. Documents available from Article Express International, Petroleum Abstracts Document Delivery Service, CASDDS. ***Supersedes*** *Corrosion Technology.*
Ind/Abst Alum. Ind. Abstr.; Art Archaeol. Tech. Abstr.; Biodeter. Abstr. (1973-); Bioeng. Abstr.; BMT Abstr. (?-199?); Chem. Abstr.; Coal Abstr.; Curr. Technol. Index; Curr. Titles Electrochem.; Ei Page One; EMBASE; Eng. Mater. Abstr.; Eng. Index Annu.; Fluid Abstr., Civil Eng.; Fluid Abstr. Proc. Eng.; FLUIDEX (1973-); Gas Abstr.; Highw. Res. Abstr.; Int. Packag. Abstr.; Leadscan; Lit. Pat. Abstr., Oilfield Chem. (1969-); Lit. Abstr., Catal. Catal.; Lit. Abstr., Health Environ.; Lit. Abstr., Pet. Refin. Petrochem.; Lit. Abstr., Pet. Substit.; Lit. Abstr., Transp. Storage; Met. Abstr.; Life Sci. Collect. (1973-); Pet. Abstr.; World Surf. Coat. Abstr.

NE/0926-860X
APPLIED CATALYSIS A : GENERAL. VFOAT General. Vol. 79, No. 1 (Nov. 26, 1991)-. Academic Scholarly Publication. English. Twenty-six times a year (13 vols.). Fl5525.00; Fl6225.00 combination subscription with Applied Catalysis B. Elsevier Science Publishers BV, PO Box 211, 1000 AE Amsterdam Netherlands. **Tel** 011 31 20 5803642, FAX 011 31 20 5862696, telex 15682. **ED** B. Delmon. **LC** QD505; .A66. **CODEN** ACAGE4. **[CCC].** Documents available from Article Express International, The Genuine Article, CASDDS. ***Continues in part*** *Applied Catalysis, 0166-9834.*
Desc: Publishes papers on all aspects of applied catalysis.
Ind/Abst Chem Inform; Chem. Abstr.; Curr. Contents Eng. Tech. Appl. Sci.; Curr. Contents Phys. Chem. Earth Sci.; Eng. Index Annu.; Environ. Eng. Abstr.; Lit. Pat. Abstr., Oilfield Chem. (1992-); Lit. Abstr., Catal. Catal.; Lit. Abstr., Health Environ.; Lit. Abstr., Pet. Refin. Petrochem.; Lit. Abstr., Pet. Substit.; Lit. Abstr., Transp. Storage; Mater. Sci. Eng. Abstr.; Mech. Eng. Abstr.; Res. Alert [Full Cov.]; Sci. Cit. Index; Solid State Supercond. Abstr.

CL
AREA INGENIERIA QUIMICA. 1-. Periodical. Spanish (summaries and/or abstracts in English). Direccion de Investigaciones Cientificas y Tecnologicas de la Universidad Tecnica del Estado etc, Avda Ecuador 3469, Santiago Chile. **LC** TP1; .A68 PAR.

US/1044-5110
ATOMIZATION AND SPRAYS. [At. sprays]. (1991)-. Periodical. English. qt. $135.00 US; £75.00 UK. Begell House Inc., PO Box 1109, Pearl River NY 10965. **Tel** (212)725-1999. **ED** Norman Chigier (editor's address: Department of Mechanical Engineering, Carnegie-Mellon University, Pittsburgh PA 15213). **DD** 621. **CODEN** ATSPE2. **[CCC].** Index available. cum. index. **Bk Rev. Ad Acc. Circ:** 500. available on microfilm.
Desc: Features original papers reporting on experimental and theoretical investigations of physical phenomena occurring in the breakup of liquids and the development of sprays.
Ind/Abst Abstr. Bull. Inst. Pap. Sci. Tech.

AT/0004-833X
AUSTRALASIAN CORROSION ENGINEERING. ***Ceased.*** [Australas. corros. eng.]. (May 1962)-(October 1976). Academic Scholarly Publication. English. mo. Australasian Corrosion, PO Box 250, North Sydney New South Wales 2060 Australia. **CODEN** ACOEAU. Documents available from Article Express International, CASDDS. ***Continues*** *Australian Corrosion Engineering.*
Ind/Abst Alum. Ind. Abstr.; Chem. Abstr. (1962-1982); Ei Page One; EMBASE; Eng. Mater. Abstr.; Eng. Index Annu.; Int. Aerosp. Abstr.; Met. Abstr.; Life Sci. Collect.; World Surf. Coat. Abstr.

AT/0004-8828
AUSTRALIAN CHEMICAL ENGINEERING. [Aust. chem. eng.]. (1961)-. Academic Scholarly Publication. English. Ten times a year. Australian Chemical Engineering, PO Box 250, North Sydney New South Wales 2060 Australia. **LC** TP1; .A867. **DD** 660.2/05. Documents available from CASDDS. ***Continues*** *Australian Journal for Chemical Engineers.*
Ind/Abst Chem. Abstr.

CC/1000-5668
BEIJING HUAGONG XUEYUAN XUEBAO ZIRAN KEXUE BAN. See Chemistry-Chemical Technology.

GW/0178-515X
BIOPROCESS ENGINEERING (BERLIN, WEST). (BIOPROCESS ENGINEERING.). [Bioprocess eng.]. Vol. 1, No. 1 (1986)-. Academic Scholarly Publication. English. Twelve times a year. DM1320.00. Springer-Verlag GmbH & Company KG, Heidelberger Platz 3, D 14197 Berlin Germany. **Tel** 011 49 30 8207223, FAX 011 49 30 8214091, telex 183 319 SPBLN D. **(Subscription address:** Springer Verlag New York Inc. / for North America, 44 Hartz Way, Secaucus NJ 07096.**) ED** H Brauer. **NLM** W1; BI88P. **CODEN** BIENEU. **[CCC]. Pr Rev.** available on microfilm and microfiche from University Microfilms International (UMI). Documents available from BIOSIS Document Express, CASDDS, ADONIS.
Desc: Concerned with all technical and economical aspects of the processes in which natural or derived biological substances are the basic material.
Ind/Abst Abstr. BioCommer.; ADONIS; AGRICOLA [Select. Cov.]; Biodeter. Abstr.; Biol. Abstr. (1989-); Chem. Abstr. (1986); Curr. Aware. Biol. Sci., CABS; Ei Page One; EMBASE.

US
BLUE BOOK (NEW YORK, N.Y.). See Rubber.

UK/0007-0599
BRITISH CORROSION JOURNAL. [Br. corros. j.]. **Added/Corp** Metals Society. British Joint Corrosion Group. Vol. 1 (July 1965)-. Periodical. English. qt. £168.00 UK; £193.20 other. The Institute of Materials, 1 Carlton House Terrace, London SW1Y 5DB England. **Tel** 011 44 71 839 4071, FAX (071)839 2078. **ED** H.S. Campbell. **LC** TA462; .B73. **CODEN** BCRJA3BCRJA. cum. index. **Bk Rev. Ad Acc. Pr Rev. Circ:** 1,000. available on microfilm and microfiche from University Microfilms International (UMI). Documents available from Article Express International, Ask*IEEE, Petroleum Abstracts Document Delivery Service, CASDDS.
Desc: Concerned with aspects of the theory and practice of corrosion processes and corrosion control. Informs of developments in all parts of the corrosion field, with emphasis on practical problems and their solution. Includes notices of forthcoming conferences, including a calendar, and news of corrosion societies, including the European Federation of Corrosion.
Ind/Abst Abstr. Bull. Inst. Pap. Sci. Tech.; Alum. Ind. Abstr.; Anal. Abstr.; Aquat. Sci. Fish. Abstr. (Computer File); Art Archaeol. Tech. Abstr.; Bioeng. Abstr.; Chem. Abstr.; Chem. Hazards Ind.; Chem. Titles; Corros. Abstr.; Curr. Technol. Index; Curr. Titles Electrochem.; Ei Page One; EMBASE; Eng. Mater. Abstr.; Eng. Index Annu.; Fluid Abstr., Civil Eng. (1968-); Fluid Abstr. Proc. Eng. (1968-); FLUIDEX (1973-); Health Saf. Sci. Abstr.; HTFS Dig.; INSPEC (1968-); Int. Packag. Abstr.; Lab. Hazards Bull.; Leadscan; Lit. Pat. Abstr., Oilfield Chem. (1969-); Lit. Abstr., Catal. Catal.; Lit. Abstr., Health Environ.; Lit. Abstr., Pet. Refin. Petrochem.; Lit. Abstr., Pet. Substit.; Lit. Abstr., Transp. Storage; Met. Abstr.; Life Sci. Collect.; Pet. Abstr. (1973-); Pollut. Abstr. Indexes; Proc. Chem. Eng.; Soils Fert.; Surf. Treat. Technol. Abstr.; Theoret. Chem. Eng.; World Surf. Coat. Abstr.

RM/0378-9675
BULETINUL STIINTIFIC SI TEHNIC AL INSTITUTULUI POLITEHNIC "TRAIAN VUIA" TIMISOARA. SERIA CHIMIE. [Bul. stiint. teh. Inst. Politeh. "Traian Vuia" Timisoara. Ser. Chim.]. **Added/Corp** Institutul Politehnic "Traian Vuia" Timisoara. Vol. 1 No.1 (1978)-. Periodical. Romanian (English, French and German; summaries and/or abstracts in English, French, German and Russian). sa. **(Subscription address:** Orion Press SRL, SPL Independentei 202-A, Bucharest 6 Romania.**) CODEN** BTICBN. ***Continues in part*** *Buletinul Stiintific si Tehnic al Institutului Politehnic Timisoara.*

US/0888-6911
BULLETIN OF THE INTERNATIONAL CENTRE FOR HEAT AND MASS TRANSFER. ***Ceased.*** **See** Engineering-Mechanical Engineering and Machinery.

US/1049-1279
C2C ABSTRACTS JAPAN. CHEMICAL ENGINEERING. See Chemistry-Abstracting, Bibliographies and Statistics.

US/1040-712X
CA SELECTS: CHEMICAL ENGINEERING OPERATIONS. See Chemistry-Abstracting, Bibliographies and Statistics.

US/0195-4946
CA SELECTS: CHEMICAL PROCESSING APPARATUS. See Chemistry-Abstracting, Bibliographies and Statistics.

US/0146-4426
CA SELECTS: COAL SCIENCE & PROCESS CHEMISTRY. See Chemistry-Abstracting, Bibliographies and Statistics.

US/0146-4434
CA SELECTS: CORROSION. See Chemistry-Abstracting, Bibliographies and Statistics.

US/0749-7296
CA SELECTS: CORROSION-INHIBITING COATINGS. See Chemistry-Abstracting, Bibliographies and Statistics.

US/0749-730X
CA SELECTS: DRILLING MUDS. See Chemistry-Abstracting, Bibliographies and Statistics.

US/0160-9076
CA SELECTS: GASEOUS WASTE TREATMENT. See Chemistry-Abstracting, Bibliographies and Statistics.

US/0195-5039
CA SELECTS: LASER APPLICATIONS. See Chemistry-Abstracting, Bibliographies and Statistics.

US/0885-0178
CA SELECTS: LASER-INDUCED CHEMICAL REACTIONS. See Chemistry-Abstracting, Bibliographies and Statistics.

US/0195-5071
CA SELECTS: OPTIMIZATION OF ORGANIC REACTIONS. See Chemistry-Abstracting, Bibliographies and Statistics.

US/0885-0194
CA SELECTS: PHASE TRANSFER CATALYSIS. See Chemistry-Abstracting, Bibliographies and Statistics.

US/0890-1945
CA SELECTS: POLYACRYLATES (JOURNALS). See Chemistry-Abstracting, Bibliographies and Statistics.

US/0895-5840
CA SELECTS: POLYIMIDES. See Chemistry-Abstracting, Bibliographies and Statistics.

US/0885-0224
CA SELECTS: POLYMERIZATION KINETICS & PROCESS CONTROL. See Chemistry-Abstracting, Bibliographies and Statistics.

US/0160-9165
CA SELECTS: SOLID & RADIOACTIVE WASTE TREATMENT. See Chemistry-Abstracting, Bibliographies and Statistics.

US/0195-5152
CA SELECTS: SURFACE ANALYSIS. See Chemistry-Abstracting, Bibliographies and Statistics.

US/0195-5195
CA SELECTS: ULTRAFILTRATION. See Chemistry-Abstracting, Bibliographies and Statistics.

US/0740-073X
CA SELECTS: WATER TREATMENT. See Chemistry-Abstracting, Bibliographies and Statistics.

CN/0008-4034
CANADIAN JOURNAL OF CHEMICAL ENGINEERING, THE. [Can. j. chem. eng.]. **Added/Corp** Canadian Society for Chemical Engineering. Chemical Institute of Canada. Vol. 35 (June 1957)-. Periodical. English (French). bm (6 issues). 170.00Can$ Canada; 225.00Can$ other. Chemical Institute of Canada, 130 Slater Street/Suite 550, Ottawa Ontario K1P 6E2 Canada. **Tel** (613)232-6252, FAX (613)232-5862. **LC** TP1; .C25. **DD** 605. **NLM** W1 CA583. **CODEN** CJCEA7. **[CCC]. Pr Rev.** available on microfiche from Micromedia Limited; available on microfilm and microfiche from University Microfilms International (UMI). Documents available from Article Express International, The Genuine Article, Ask*IEEE, Petroleum Abstracts Document Delivery Service, CASDDS, Documents on Demand. ***Continues*** *Canadian Journal of Technology.*
Desc: An international journal dedicated to publishing original research dealing with chemical engineering and applied chemistry.
Ind/Abst Abstr. Bull. Inst. Pap. Sci. Tech.; AGRICOLA; Appl. Sci. Technol. Index; AQUAREF; Ceram. Abstr.; Chem. Abstr.; Chem. Titles; Coal Abstr.; Curr. Biotechnol.; Curr. Contents Eng. Tech. Appl. Sci.; EMBASE; Energy Inf. Abstr.; Eng. Mater. Abstr.; Eng. Index Annu.; Environ. Abstr.; Fluid Abstr., Civil Eng.; Fluid Abstr. Proc. Eng.; FLUIDEX (1973-); Gas Abstr.; HTFS Dig.; INIS Atomindex [Micro.]; INSPEC (Oct. 1971-); Leadscan; Lit. Pat. Abstr., Oilfield Chem. (1958-); Lit. Abstr., Catal. Catal.; Lit. Abstr., Health Environ.; Lit. Abstr., Pet. Refin. Petrochem.; Lit. Abstr., Pet. Substit.; Lit. Abstr., Transp. Storage; Met. Abstr.; MINPROC;

PESTDOC; Pet. Abstr.; Proc. Chem. Eng.; Res. Alert [Full Cov.]; Sci. Cit. Index; SCISEARCH; Soils Fert.; Theoret. Chem. Eng.

US/0161-4940
CATALYSIS REVIEWS : SCIENCE AND ENGINEERING. [Catal. rev., Sci. eng.]. Vol. 9 (1974)-. Periodical. English. qt. $475.00 US; $489.00 other. Marcel Dekker Inc., 270 Madison Avenue, New York NY 10016. **Tel** (212)696-9000, (800)228-1160, FAX (212)685-4540, telex 421419. **(Subscription address:** Marcel Dekker Inc, PO Box 5017, Monticello NY 12701.**)** **ED** Alexis T. Bell, Kamil Klier, Robert J. Madix, John B. Butt. **LC** QD501; .C4457. **DD** 541/.395/05. **NLM** W1 CA95J. **CODEN** CRSEC9. **[CCC]. Bk Rev. Ad Acc. Pr Rev.** available on microfiche. Documents available from Article Express International, The Genuine Article, CASDDS. ***Formed by the union of*** *Catalysis Reviews, 0360-2451* ***and*** *Catalysis Reviews, 0008-7645.*
Desc: This publication features an interdisciplinary view-point and is designed to stimulate progressive ideas throughout this broad science, offering articles in such areas as advances in technology and theory, engineering and chemical aspects of catalytic reactions, reactor design, computer models, analytical tools, and statistical evaluations.
Ind/Abst Alum. Ind. Abstr.; Bioeng. Abstr.; Chem Inform; Chem. Abstr.; Curr. Chem. React.; Curr. Contents Phys. Chem. Earth Sci.; Ei Page One; Energy Res. Abstr. (Apr. 1977-); Eng. Mater. Abstr.; Eng. Index Annu.; Gas Abstr.; Index Sci. Rev. [Full Cov.]; INIS Atomindex [Micro.]; Lit. Pat. Abstr., Oilfield Chem. (1969-); Lit. Abstr., Catal. Catal.; Lit. Abstr., Health Environ.; Lit. Abstr., Pet. Refin. Petrochem.; Lit. Abstr., Pet. Substit.; Lit. Abstr., Transp. Storage; Met. Abstr.; Phys. Briefs; Proc. Chem. Eng.; Res. Alert [Full Cov.]; Sci. Cit. Index; SCISEARCH; Theoret. Chem. Eng.

US/0190-4760
CEC CENSUS OF BUYERS IN THE CHEMICAL PROCESS INDUSTRIES. **See** Economics-Industry and Production.

II/0009-2517
CEW, CHEMICAL ENGINEERING WORLD. [Chem. eng. world]. (1966)-. English. Twelve times a year. $12.40 India; $50.00 other; $100.00 US; $80.00 airmail;. Industrial Publications, TAJ Building/3rd Floor, 210 Dive DN Road, Bombay-1 India. **Tel** 204-2044, FAX 91(22)2870502, telex 011-2775 JSCO IN. **(Subscription address:** Prints India, 11 Darya Ganj, New Delhi 110002 India.**)** **ED** Jasu Shah. **LC** TP1; .C12. **DD** 660.2/05. **CODEN** CEWOAY. Index available. **Bk Rev**, (Qty: 36-48). **Ad Acc, Adv Mgr:** Uday Rastogi, **Tel** 2042044. **Pr Rev. Circ:** 11,000. available on microfilm from University Microfilms International (UMI). Documents available from CASDDS.
Desc: Technical journal for chemical and processing industry.
Ind/Abst Chem. Abstr.; Coal Abstr.; Curr. Biotechnol.; Ei Page One; EMBASE; Fluid Abstr., Civil Eng.; Fluid Abstr. Proc. Eng.; FLUIDEX (1973-); For. Prod. Abstr. (1991-); Soils Fert.

US/0895-3384
CHAPTER ONE. **See** Education-Higher Education.

PL/0376-0898
CHEMIA STOSOWANA (1971). ***Title Change.*** (CHEMIA STOSOWANA.). [Chem. Stos.]. **Added/Corp** Polska Akademia Nauk. Komitet Nauk Chemicznych. **VFOAT** Polish Journal of Applied Chemistry. (19??)-(19??). Academic Scholarly Publication. Polish (summaries and/or abstracts in English). qt. **(Subscription address:** ARS Polona, PO Box 1001, 00068 Warsaw Poland.**)** **LC** TP1; .C3178. **CODEN** CHSWAP. Documents available from CASDDS. ***Continues*** *Chemia Stosowana. Seria A.* ***Continued by*** *Polish Journal of Applied Chemistry.*
Ind/Abst Ceram. Abstr.; Chem. Abstr. (-1990); Coal Abstr.; Surf. Treat. Technol. Abstr.

CI
CHEMICAL AND BIOCHEMICAL ENGINEERING QUARTERLY. (1987)-. Periodical. English (English). Four times a year (Mar., June, Sept., Dec.). $50.00. Croatian Society of Chemical Engineers, Berislavicevaul 61, Zagreb Croatia. **Tel** 011 38 41 422931, FAX 011 38 41 422931. **ED** Professor Egon Bauman. **NLM** W1; CH239. **CODEN** CBEQEZ. Index available (Bound in 4th iss.). **Pr Rev. Circ:** 800. Documents available from The Genuine Article, CASDDS.
Ind/Abst Chem. Abstr.; Coal Abstr.; PESTDOC; Res. Alert [Full Cov.].

US/0009-2347
CHEMICAL & ENGINEERING NEWS. **See** Chemistry-Chemical Technology.

US/0009-2355
CHEMICAL AND PETROLEUM ENGINEERING. [Chem. pet. eng.]. **Added/Corp** Consultants Bureau. (1965)-. Academic Scholarly Publication. English (Russian; translations available in Russian). mo. $1375.00 US; $1610.00 other. Consultants Bureau, A Division of Plenum Publishing Corporation, 233 Spring Street, New York NY 10013. **Tel** (212)620-8000, (212)620-8466, FAX (212)463-0742, telex 23/421139. **ED** A. M. Vasil'ev. **DD** 660. **CODEN** CPTEAW. **[CCC].** Index available. available in microform. Documents available from Article Express International, CASDDS.
Desc: Examines problems of design and operations of equipment for the basic technological processes of the chemical, petrochemical, petroleum refining and paper industries.
Ind/Abst Bioeng. Abstr.; Chem. Abstr.; Coal Abstr.; Ei Page One; EMBASE; Energy Res. Abstr.; Eng. Index Annu.; Fluid Abstr., Civil Eng.; Fluid Abstr. Proc. Eng.; FLUIDEX (1973-); HTFS Dig.; INIS Atomindex [Micro.]; Pollut. Abstr. Indexes.

II/0970-3136
CHEMICAL BUSINESS. (198?)-. Periodical. English. mo. $50.00. Colour Publications Private, 126A Dhuruwadi Off, c/o Dr. Nariman, Bombay 400025 India. **Tel** 011 91 22 4309318 6319, telex 71242 CEPE. **(Subscription address:** Prints India, 11 Darya Ganj, New Delhi 110002 India.**)** **ED** R.V. Raghavan. **Bk Rev. Ad Acc.** ***Continues*** *Chemical Business of India.*

UK/0302-0797
CHEMICAL ENGINEER (LONDON). (CHEMICAL ENGINEER.). [Chem. eng.]. **Added/Corp** Institution of Chemical Engineers. No. 238 (May 1970)-. Periodical. English. Twenty-three times a year. $188.00 US; £105.00 other. Taylor & Francis Ltd., Rankine Road, Basingstoke Hampshire, RG24 8PR United Kingdom. **Tel** 011 44 256 840366, FAX 011 44 256 479438, telex 858540. **(Subscription address:** Taylor & Francis Inc., 1900 Frost Road, Suite 101, Bristol PA 19007-1598.**)** **ED** Peter Varey (editor's address: The Institutions of Chemical Engineers, 165-171 Railway Terrace, Rugby CV21 3HQ United Kingdom). **DD** 660. **CODEN** CMERA9. **[CCC].** Index available. **Ad Acc. Pr Rev. Circ:** 20,000. available on microfilm and microfiche from University Microfilms International (UMI). Documents available from Article Express International, The Genuine Article, Ask*IEEE, CASDDS, Documents on Demand. ***Continues in part*** *Institution of Chemical Engineers. Transactions of the Institution of Chemical Engineers.*
Desc: Disseminates key information across the broad spectrum of the chemical process industries, including pharmaceuticals, food, petroleum, mining, water treatment, aquaculture, biotechnology, and loss prevention.
Ind/Abst Abstr. BioCommer.; AGRICOLA; Agric. Eng. Abstr. (1991-); Alum. Ind. Abstr.; Appl. Sci. Technol. Index (-1990); Bioeng. Abstr.; Ceram. Abstr.; Chem. Abstr.; Chem. Bus. Bull.; Chem. Bus. NewsBase (1989-); Chem. Bus. Update; Coal Abstr.; Curr. Biotechnol.; Curr. Contents Eng. Tech. Appl. Sci.; Curr. Technol. Index; Ei Page One; EMBASE; Energy Inf. Abstr.; Energy Res. Abstr.; Eng. Mater. Abstr.; Eng. Index Annu.; Environ. Abstr.; Fluid Abstr., Civil Eng.; Fluid Abstr. Proc. Eng.; FLUIDEX (1973-); HTFS Dig.; INSPEC (1970-); Lit. Pat. Abstr., Oilfield Chem. (1966-); Lit. Abstr., Catal. Catal.; Lit. Abstr., Health Environ.; Lit. Abstr., Pet. Refin. Petrochem.; Lit. Abstr., Pet. Substit.; Lit. Abstr., Transp. Storage; Met. Abstr.; PESTDOC; Pollut. Abstr. Indexes; Postharvest News Inf.; Proc. Chem. Eng.; Res. Alert [Select. Cov.]; Risk Abstr.; SCISEARCH; Sel. Water Resour. Abstr.; Theoret. Chem. Eng.; Trade Ind. Index; World Alum. Abstr.; World Ceram. Abstr.

SZ/0255-2701
CHEMICAL ENGINEERING AND PROCESSING. [Chem. eng. process.]. **VFOAT** Genie des Procedes; Verfahrenstechnik. Vol. 18, No. 1 (Jan./Feb. 1984)-. Academic Scholarly Publication. English (German). Six times a year (1 volume). 980.00F. Elsevier Sequoia SA, PO Box 564, CH-1001 Lausanne 1 Switzerland. **Tel** 011 41 21 3207381. **ED** Ernst U Schlunder and Volker Gnielinski. **LC** TP1; .C363. **DD** 660.2/05. **CODEN** CENPEU. **[CCC]. Ad Acc, Adv Mgr:** Ms. W van Cattenburch (Amsterdam). **Pr Rev.** available on microfilm and microfiche from University Microfilms International (UMI). Documents available from Article Express International, The Genuine Article, Ask*IEEE, CASDDS. ***Continues in part*** *VT. Verfahrenstechnik.*
Desc: The journal offers space for articles on any branch of chemical engineering and is particularly concerned with mechanical, thermal and chemical unit operations and their application in the process industries. Special emphasis has been placed on heat transfer, mass transfer and reaction kinetics.
Ind/Abst Alum. Ind. Abstr.; Chem. Abstr. (1984-); Comput. Inf. Syst. Abstr. J. [Full Cov.]; Curr. Contents Eng. Tech. Appl. Sci.; Elect. Comm. Abstr.; Eng. Mater. Abstr.; Eng. Index Annu.; Environ. Eng. Abstr.; Fluid Abstr., Civil Eng.; Fluid Abstr. Proc. Eng.; FLUIDEX; Foods Adlibra; INSPEC (Jan./Feb. 1984-); Manuf. Process Eng. Abstr.; Mech. Eng. Abstr.; Met. Abstr.; Proc. Chem. Eng.; Res. Alert [Full Cov.]; Sci. Cit. Index; SCISEARCH; Solid State Supercond. Abstr.; Theoret. Chem. Eng.

GW/0930-7516
CHEMICAL ENGINEERING & TECHNOLOGY. [Chem. eng. technol.]. **Added/Corp** Gesellschaft Deutscher Chemiker. Dechema. VDI-Gesellschaft Verfahrenstechnik und Chemieingenieurwesen. **VFOAT** Chemical Engineering and Technology. Vol. 10, No. 1 (Feb. 1987)-. Periodical. English. Six times a year. $545.00. VCH Gesellschaft GmbH, Postfach 101161, D 69451 Weinheim Germany. **Tel** 011 49 6201 606459, FAX 011 49 6201 606184. **(Subscription address:** VCH Publishers Inc., 303 Northwest 12th Avenue, Journals Department, Deerfield FL 33442.**)** **LC** TP1; .C333. **DD** 660/.2. **CODEN** CETEER. **[CCC].** Documents available from Article Express International, CASDDS. ***Continues*** *German Chemical Engineering, 0343-5539.*
Ind/Abst Abstr. Bull. Inst. Pap. Sci. Tech.; Bioeng. Abstr. (1987-); Chem. Abstr.; Chem. Hazards Ind.; Civ. Struct. Eng. Abstr.; Coal Abstr. (1987-); Comput. Inf. Syst. Abstr. J. [Full Cov.]; Curr. Biotechnol.; Ei Page One (1987-); Elect. Comm. Abstr.; Energy Res. Abstr. (1987-); Eng. Index Annu.; Environ. Eng. Abstr.; Fluid Abstr., Civil Eng.; Fluid Abstr. Proc. Eng.; FLUIDEX (1987-); Lab. Hazards Bull.; Lit. Pat. Abstr., Oilfield Chem. (1993-); Lit. Abstr., Catal. Catal.; Lit. Abstr., Health Environ.; Lit. Abstr., Pet. Refin. Petrochem.; Lit. Abstr., Pet. Substit.; Lit. Abstr., Transp. Storage; Mech. Eng. Abstr.; PESTDOC; Proc. Chem. Eng.; Sug. Indus. Abstr.; Theoret. Chem. Eng.

●US
CHEMICAL ENGINEERING BUYERS GUIDE FOR ... . **VFOAT** CEBG; Chemical Engineering CEBG Issue. (1993)-. Consumer Publication. English. an. McGraw Hill Publishing Company, Inc., 1221 Avenue of the Americas, New York NY 10020. **Tel** (212)512-6410, (800)525-5003, FAX (212)512-6111. ***Continues*** *Chemical Engineering Equipment Buyers' Guide.*

US/0276-8429
CHEMICAL ENGINEERING CATALOG. [Chem. eng. cat.]. **VFOAT** CEC . (1916)-. Catalog. English. an. $60.00 US; $65.00 Canada; $70.00 other. Penton Publishing, 1100 Superior Avenue, Cleveland OH 44114-2543. **Tel** (216)696-7000, FAX (216)696-0836. **(Subscription address:** Penton Publishing, PO Box 96732, Chicago IL 60693.**)** **LC** TP157; .C4. **DD** 660.78. **[CCC].** available on microfilm from University Microfilms International (UMI).
Desc: An annual reference source serving the Chemical Process Industries in the United States.

US/0098-6445
CHEMICAL ENGINEERING COMMUNICATIONS. [Chem. eng. commun.]. Vol. 1 (1973)-. Academic Scholarly Publication. English. ir. Gordon & Breach Science Publishers, Inc., PO Box 786, Cooper Station, New York NY 10276. **Tel** (212)206-8900, FAX (212)645-2459. **(Subscription address:** Gordon & Breach Science Publishers / US, 820 Town Center Drive, Langhorne PA 19047.**)** **LC** TP1; .C3653. **DD** 660/.05. **CODEN** CEGCAK. **[CCC]. Pr Rev.** Documents available from Article Express International, The Genuine Article, Petroleum Abstracts Document Delivery Service, CASDDS.
Desc: A forum for the rapid exchange of communications in all fields of chemical engineering. Publishes articles detailing completed research, and short communications announcing new theoretical concepts in data correlations. Also covers bioengineering, fluid mechanics, the molecular theory of equilibrium and transport properties, applied mathematics and computer aided design.
Ind/Abst Abstr. Bull. Inst. Pap. Sci. Tech.; Bioeng. Abstr.; Chem. Abstr.; Chem. Titles; Coal Abstr.; Curr. Biotechnol.; Curr. Contents Eng. Tech. Appl. Sci.; Ei Page One; EMBASE; Eng. Index Annu.; Fluid Abstr., Civil Eng.; Fluid Abstr. Proc. Eng.; FLUIDEX (1973-); HTFS Dig.; Int. Aerosp. Abstr.; PESTDOC; Pet. Abstr.; Proc. Chem. Eng.; Res. Alert [Full Cov.]; Sci. Cit. Index; SCISEARCH; Soils Fert.; Theoret. Chem. Eng.

US/0734-1644
CHEMICAL ENGINEERING, CONCEPTS AND REVIEWS. [Chem. eng. concepts rev.]. (1985)-. Monographic series. English. ir. Price varies per volume. Gordon & Breach Science Publishers, Inc., PO Box 786, Cooper Station, New York NY 10276. **Tel** (212)206-8900, FAX (212)645-2459. **(Subscription address:** Gordon & Breach Science Publishers / US, 820 Town Center Drive, Langhorne PA 19047.**)** **DD** 660.

US/0009-2479
CHEMICAL ENGINEERING EDUCATION. (CEE. CHEMICAL ENGINEERING EDUCATION.). [Chem. eng. educ.]. (1960)-. Periodical. English. qt (Feb., May, Aug., Nov.). $20.00 (non-members), $15.00 (members and chemical engineering departments) surface mail; $29.00 (nonmembers), $24.00 (members) airmail Canada and Mexico; $33.00 (nonmembers), $28.00 (members) airmail Central America, Columbia and Venezuela; $39.00 (nonmembers), $34.00 (members) South America and Europe; $45.00 (nonmembers), $40.00 (members) other. Chemical Engineering Education, University of Florida, Department of Chemical Engineering, Gainesville FL 32611. **Tel** (904)392-0861. **ED** Ray W Fahien. **LC** TP165; .C18. **DD** 660/.2/071. **CODEN** CHEDAY. cum. index. **Bk Rev. Ad Acc. Pr Rev. Circ:** 1,900 (ctrl). available on microfilm and microfiche from University Microfilms International (UMI). Documents available from Article Express International, CASDDS.
Desc: Articles written by chemical engineering educators for CEE educators describing courses, teaching methods, research.
Ind/Abst Abstr. Bull. Inst. Pap. Sci. Tech.; Bioeng. Abstr.; Chem. Abstr.; Coal Abstr.; Contents Pages Educ.; Curr. Biotechnol.; Curr. Index J. Educ.; Ei Page One; Energy Res. Abstr. (March 1979-); Eng. Index Annu. [Select. Cov.].

US/0272-4057
CHEMICAL ENGINEERING EQUIPMENT BUYERS' GUIDE. ***Title Change.*** [Chem. eng. equip. buy. guide]. **VFOAT** CEEBG. (1981)-(1992). Consumer Publication. English. an. McGraw Hill Publishing Company, Inc., 1221 Avenue of the Americas, New York NY 10020. **Tel** (212)512-6410, (800)525-5003, FAX (212)512-6111. **LC** TP158; .C47. **DD** 660.2/83/029473. **Ad Acc.** ***Continues*** *Chemical Engineering. Equipment Buyers' Guide Issue, 0094-9841.* ***Continued by*** *Chemical Engineering Buyers Guide for ...*

US/0569-5465
CHEMICAL ENGINEERING FACULTIES. [Chem. eng. fac.]. (19??)-. English. an (published in Sept.). $60.00. American Institute of Chemical Engineers, 345 East 47th Street, New York NY 10017. **Tel** (212)705-7663, (212)705-7703, FAX (212)705-8400. **LC** TP165; .C48. **DD** 660/.2/0711. **[CCC].**
Desc: Contains names, addresses, telephone numbers, degrees granted, accreditation status, department heads, and placement officers.

AT/0157-9762
CHEMICAL ENGINEERING IN AUSTRALIA : CEA. [CEA. Chem. eng. Aust.]. **Added/Corp** Institution of Engineers, Australia. College of Chemical Engineers. Institution of Chemical Engineers in Australia. **VFOAT** CEA; C.E.A. (1976)-. Academic Scholarly Publication. English. qt. 23.50Aus$ Australia; 32.10Aus$ other. Engineers Australia Pty Ltd, 2 Ernest Street, Crows Nest Centre, Crows Nest New South Wales 2065, Australia. **Tel** 011 61 2 438-1533, FAX 011 61 2 438-5934, telex 27640. **LC** TJ1; .C49. **DD** 660.2/05. **CODEN** CCEADR. Documents available from Article Express International, Ask*IEEE, CASDDS. ***Continues in part*** *Mechanical & Chemical Engineering Transactions, 0020-3327.*
Ind/Abst Alum. Ind. Abstr.; Bioeng. Abstr.; Ceram. Abstr. (19??-); Chem. Abstr.; Coal Abstr.; Ei Page One; Energy Inf. Abstr.; Eng. Index Annu. [Select. Cov.]; Fluid Abstr., Civil Eng.; Fluid Abstr. Proc. Eng.; FLUIDEX (1976-); INSPEC (1976-); Met. Abstr.; Pollut. Abstr. Indexes.

AT/0313-5527
CHEMICAL ENGINEERING IN AUSTRALIA / THE INSTITUTION OF ENGINEERS, AUSTRALIA. **Added/Corp** Institution of Engineers, Australia. College of Chemical Engineers, Australia. Institution of Chemical Engineers in Australia. **VFOAT** CEA. (1976)-. Periodical. English. qt. ***Continues in part*** *Mechanical & Chemical Engineering Transactions, 0020-3327.*
Ind/Abst AESIS Q.; Fluid Abstr., Civil Eng.; Fluid Abstr. Proc. Eng.; FLUIDEX.

SZ/0923-0467
CHEMICAL ENGINEERING JOURNAL AND THE BIOCHEMICAL ENGINEERING JOURNAL, THE. [Chem. eng. j. biochem. eng. j.]. **VFOAT** Biochemical Engineering Journal; Chemical Engineering Journal, The Biochemical Engineering Journal. Vol. 27, No. 1 (Aug. 1983)-. Academic Scholarly Publication. English (French and German). Twelve times a year (4 volumes). 1520.00F. Elsevier Sequoia SA, PO Box 564, CH-1001 Lausanne 1 Switzerland. **Tel** 011 41 21 3207381. **ED** R.C. Darton. **LC** TP1; .C334. **DD** 660/.05. **[CCC].** **Ad Acc, Adv Mgr:** Ms. W van Cattenburch (Amsterdam). **Pr Rev.** available on microfilm and microfiche from University Microfilms International (UMI). Documents available from Article Express International, The Genuine Article, BIOSIS Document Express, Ask*IEEE, CASDDS, Documents on Demand. ***Continues*** *Chemical Engineering Journal (Lausanne, Switzerland), 0300-9467.*
Desc: Provides an international forum for the presentation of original work and interpretative reviews and the discussion of the latest developments in chemical engineering. Provides international coverage of research and development in the expanding area of biochemical engineering.
Ind/Abst Alum. Ind. Abstr.; Bioeng. Abstr.; Biol. Abstr.; Chem. Abstr.; Curr. Aware. Biol. Sci., CABS; Curr. Contents Eng. Tech. Appl. Sci.; Ei Page One; Elect. Comm. Abstr.; EMBASE; Energy Inf. Abstr.; Energy Res. Abstr. (Aug. 1983-); Eng. Mater. Abstr.; Eng. Index Annu.; Environ. Abstr.; Fluid Abstr., Civil Eng.; Fluid Abstr. Proc. Eng.; FLUIDEX (1983-); INSPEC (Oct. 1983-); Mater. Sci. Eng. Abstr.; Math. Rev.; Mech. Eng. Abstr.; Met. Abstr.; Phys. Briefs; Res. Alert [Full Cov.]; Sci. Cit. Index; SCISEARCH.

NE/0167-4188
CHEMICAL ENGINEERING MONOGRAPHS. [Chem. eng. monogr.]. Vol. 1 (1975)-. Academic Scholarly Publication. English. ir. Price varies per volume. Elsevier Science Publishing Company Inc, Madison Square Station, PO Box 882, New York NY 10159-0882. **Tel** (212)633-3950, FAX (212)633-3990. **CODEN** CENMDK. **[CCC].** Documents available from Ask*IEEE, CASDDS.
Ind/Abst Chem. Abstr.; INSPEC.

US/0009-2460
CHEMICAL ENGINEERING (NEW YORK). **See** Chemistry-Electrochemistry.

US/0360-7275
CHEMICAL ENGINEERING PROGRESS. [Chem. eng. prog.]. **Added/Corp** American Institute of Chemical Engineers. **VFOAT** CEP. Vol. 43, No. 1 (Jan. 1947)-. Periodical. English. Twelve times a year. $75.00 US; $130.00 other. American Institute of Chemical Engineers, 345 East 47th Street, New York NY 10017. **Tel** (212)705-7663, (212)705-7703, FAX (212)705-8400. **ED** Agnes Dubberly. **LC** TP1; .A6. **DD** 660.6273. **NLM** W1 C264. **CODEN** CEPRA8. **[CCC].** Index available (bound in Dec. issue). **Ad Acc.** **Pr Rev.** **Circ:** 58,037. available on microfilm and microfiche from University Microfilms International (UMI). Documents available from Article Express International, The Genuine Article, Ask*IEEE, Petroleum Abstracts Document Delivery Service, CASDDS, Documents on Demand. ***Continues*** *American Institute of Chemical Engineers. Transactions of the American Institute of Chemical Engineers, 0096-7408.*
Desc: Contains up-to-date information on the latest advances in the chemical process and related industries.
Ind/Abst Abstr. Bull. Inst. Pap. Sci. Tech.; Abstr. BioCommer. (1973-); AGRICOLA [Select. Cov.]; Agric. Eng. Abstr. (1991-); Alum. Ind. Abstr.; Appl. Sci. Technol. Index; BioBusiness; Bioeng. Abstr.; Chem Inform; Chem. Abstr.; Chem. Bus. Bull.; Chem. Bus. NewsBase (1986-); Chem. Bus. Update; Chem. Hazards Ind.; Coal Abstr.; Curr. Biotechnol.; Curr. Contents Eng. Tech. Appl. Sci.; Ei Page One (1984-); EMBASE; Energy Res. Abstr.; Eng. Index Annu.; Environ. Abstr.; F&S Index Plus Text, Int. [Select. Cov.]; Fluid Abstr., Civil Eng.; Fluid Abstr. Proc. Eng.; FLUIDEX (1973-); Gas Abstr.; Health Saf. Sci. Abstr.; Hortic. Abstr.; HTFS Dig.; INIS Atomindex [Micro.]; INSPEC (1968-); Int. Aerosp. Abstr.; Lab. Hazards Bull.; Lit. Pat. Abstr., Oilfield Chem. (1954-); Lit. Abstr., Catal. Catal.; Lit. Abstr., Health Environ.; Lit. Abstr., Pet. Refin. Petrochem.; Lit. Abstr., Pet. Substit.; Lit. Abstr., Transp. Storage; Met. Abstr.; MINPROC; PESTDOC; Pet. Abstr.; Pollut. Abstr. Indexes; Postharvest News Inf.; PROMT; Res. Alert [Full Cov.]; Risk Abstr.; Saf. Health Work; Sci. Cit. Index; SCISEARCH; Soc. Sci. Cit. Index [Select. Cov.]; Soils Fert. (1988-).

UK/0263-8762
CHEMICAL ENGINEERING RESEARCH & DESIGN. (CHEMICAL ENGINEERING RESEARCH & DESIGN : TRANSACTIONS OF THE INSTITUTION OF CHEMICAL ENGINEERS.). [Chem. eng. res. des.]. **VFOAT** Chemical Engineering Research and Design. Vol. 61, No. 1 (Jan. 1983)-. Academic Scholarly Publication. English. Eight times a year. £258.00 UK; $425.00 other. Taylor & Francis Ltd., Rankine Road, Basingstoke Hampshire, RG24 8PR United Kingdom. **Tel** 011 44 256 840366, FAX 011 44 256 479438, telex 858540. **(Subscription address:** Taylor & Francis Inc., 1900 Frost Road, Suite 101, Bristol PA 19007-1598.**) ED** G. F. Hewitt. **LC** TP1; .I7. **DD** 660.2/81/05. **CODEN** CERDEE. **[CCC].** Index available. **Pr Rev.** available on microfilm and microfiche from University Microfilms International (UMI). Documents available from Article Express International, The Genuine Article, Ask*IEEE, Petroleum Abstracts Document Delivery Service, CASDDS. ***Continues*** *Transactions of the Institution of Chemical Engineers.*
Desc: Publishes papers on all aspects of experimental work, development and theory in chemical engineering. A proportion of each issue is devoted to a particular subject area. An overview or review highlights the recent advances in the area which is complemented by recent papers.
Ind/Abst Alum. Ind. Abstr.; Chem. Abstr. (1983-); Chem. Titles; Coal Abstr.; Comput. Abstr.; Curr. Biotechnol.; Curr. Contents Eng. Tech. Appl. Sci.; Curr. Technol. Index; EMBASE; Energy Res. Abstr. (Jan. 1983-); Eng. Mater. Abstr.; Eng. Index Annu.; Fluid Abstr., Civil Eng.; Fluid Abstr. Proc. Eng.; FLUIDEX (1983-); HTFS Dig.; INSPEC (Jan. 1983-); Lit. Pat. Abstr., Oilfield Chem. (1956-); Lit. Abstr., Catal. Catal.; Lit. Abstr., Health Environ.; Lit. Abstr., Pet. Refin. Petrochem.; Lit. Abstr., Pet. Substit.; Lit. Abstr., Transp. Storage; Met. Abstr.; Pet. Abstr.; Proc. Chem. Eng.; Res. Alert [Full Cov.]; Sci. Cit. Index; SCISEARCH; Theoret. Chem. Eng.; World Ceram. Abstr.

BG/0379-7678
CHEMICAL ENGINEERING RESEARCH BULLETIN. [Chem. eng. res. bull.]. **Added/Corp** Bangladesh University of Engineering and Technology. Chemical Engineering Dept. No. 1 (1977)-. Periodical. English. an. Free. Bangladesh University of Engineering & Technology, Department of Chemical Engineering, Dacca Bangladesh 500254. **CODEN** CERBD7. Documents available from CASDDS.
Ind/Abst Chem. Abstr.

UK/0009-2509
CHEMICAL ENGINEERING SCIENCE. [Chem. eng. sci.]. **VFOAT** Genie Chimique; Journal International de Genie Chimique. Vol. 1 (Oct. 1951)-. Periodical. Multiple languages (English, French and German). Twenty-four times a year. $2005.00 The Americas; £1345.00 other. Pergamon Press, An Imprint of Elsevier Science Ltd., The Boulevard, Langford Lane, Kidlington, Oxford OX5 1GB United Kingdom. **Tel** 011 44 865 843000, 011 44 865 843699, FAX 011 44 865 843010. **ED** J. Bridgewater. **LC** TP1; .C366. **DD** 660.5. **CODEN** CESCAC. **[CCC].** **Pr Rev.** available on microfilm from Microfilms International Marketing Corp.; available on microfilm and microfiche from University Microfilms International (UMI). Documents available from Article Express International, The Genuine Article, Ask*IEEE, Petroleum Abstracts Document Delivery Service, CASDDS, Documents on Demand.
Desc: Publishes papers on the fundamentals of chemical engineering, including applications of the basic sciences and of mathematics.
Ind/Abst Abstr. Bull. Inst. Pap. Sci. Tech.; Aqualine Abstr.; Biodeter. Abstr. (1991-); Bioeng. Abstr.; Chem Inform; Chem. Abstr.; Chem. Hazards Ind.; Chem. Titles; Coal Abstr.; Comput. Abstr.; Curr. Aware. Biol. Sci., CABS; Curr. Biotechnol.; Curr. Contents Eng. Tech. Appl. Sci.; Curr. Technol. Index; Ei Page One; EMBASE; Energy Inf. Abstr.; Energy Res. Abstr.; Eng. Index Annu. [Select. Cov.]; Environ. Abstr.; Fluid Abstr., Civil Eng.; Fluid Abstr. Proc. Eng.; FLUIDEX (1973-); Gas Abstr.; HTFS Dig.; INIS Atomindex [Micro.]; INSPEC (1968-); Int. Aerosp. Abstr.; Lab. Hazards Bull.; Lit. Pat. Abstr., Oilfield Chem. (1954-); Lit. Abstr., Catal. Catal.; Lit. Abstr., Health Environ.; Lit. Abstr., Pet. Refin. Petrochem.; Lit. Abstr., Pet. Substit.; Lit. Abstr., Transp. Storage; MINPROC; PESTDOC; Pet. Abstr.; Proc. Chem. Eng.; Res. Alert [Full Cov.]; Sci. Cit. Index; SCISEARCH; Soils Fert.; Surf. Treat. Technol. Abstr.; Theoret. Chem. Eng.

II/0304-1166
CHEMICAL INDIA ANNUAL. (19??)-. English. 5.00. S K Bharat, 640 Double Storey, New Rajinder Nagar India. **LC** TP1; .C3665. **DD** 338.4/7/66020973.

US/0146-681X
CHEMICAL PROCESSING AND ENGINEERING (NEW YORK). (CHEMICAL PROCESSING AND ENGINEERING.). [Chem. process. eng.]. Vol. 1 (1975)-. Academic Scholarly Publication. English. Price varies per volume. Marcel Dekker Inc., 270 Madison Avenue, New York NY 10016. **Tel** (212)696-9000, (800)228-1160, FAX (212)685-4540, telex 421419. **(Subscription address:** Marcel Dekker Inc, PO Box 5017, Monticello NY 12701.**) ED** McKetta/Cunningham. **DD** 660. **CODEN** CPENDL. Documents available from CASDDS.
Desc: Covers the following types of engineering: mechanical, processing control, chemical instrumentation, computer, management, process cost, energy, fuel, and design.
Ind/Abst Chem. Abstr. (1974-1977/1979).

II/0045-6500
CHEMICAL WEEKLY. **See** Chemistry.

GW/0009-2800
CHEMIE-ANLAGEN + VERFAHREN. [Chemie-Anlagen und Verfahren]. (1967)-. Academic Scholarly Publication. German. ir. Free. Konradin Verlags Gruppe, Robert Kohlhammer GmbH, D-70765 Leinfelden Germany. **Tel** 011 49 711 7594370, 011 49 711 7594229. **LC** TP1; .C4327. **DD** 660/.2/05. **CODEN** CHAVBZ. **[CCC].** Documents available from CASDDS.
Ind/Abst Chem. Abstr.; Coal Abstr.; EMBASE; Energy Res. Abstr. (July 1973-); PESTDOC; Sug. Indus. Abstr.

GW/0340-9961
CHEMIE-TECHNIK. [Chem.-Tech.]. (1974)-. Academic Scholarly Publication. German. mo. $149.00. Dr. Alfred Huethig Verlag GmbH, Postfach 102869, D 69018 Heidelberg Germany. **Tel** 011 49 6221 489281. **(Subscription address:** Huethig Publishing Inc., 29 Macintosh Drive, Oxford CT 06478.**) ED** Sieghard Neufeldt, Almuth Dekker, and Erik Zimmer. **LC** TP1; .C16. **CODEN** CMTKAT. **Bk Rev.** **Ad Acc.** **Circ:** 19,000 (ctrl). Documents available from Article Express International, CASDDS. ***Continues*** *CZ-Chemie-Technik, 0366-8509.*
Desc: Construction of machinery and installations, raw materials, chemical engineering, biotechnology, standards and norms.
Ind/Abst Anal. Abstr.; Chem. Abstr. (1974-1984); Chem. Hazards Ind.; Coal Abstr.; Comput. Inf. Syst. Abstr. J. [Full Cov.]; Curr. Biotechnol.; Ei Page One; EMBASE; Energy Res. Abstr. (April 1979-); Eng. Index Annu.; Environ. Eng. Abstr.; Lab. Hazards Bull.; Mater. Sci. Eng. Abstr.; Mech. Eng. Abstr.; PESTDOC; Proc. Chem. Eng.; Theoret. Chem. Eng.

GW/0009-286X
CHEMIEINGENIEURTECHNIK. (CHEMIE-INGENIEUR-TECHNIK.). [Chemieingenieurtech.]. **VFOAT** CIT; Chemie-Ingenieur-Technik. Vol. 21 (1949)-. Periodical. German (English). mo. $495.00. VCH Gesellschaft GmbH, Postfach 101161, D 69451 Weinheim Germany. **Tel** 011 49 6201 606459, FAX 011 49 6201 606184. **(Subscription address:** VCH Publishers Inc., 303 Northwest 12th Avenue, Journals Department, Deerfield FL 33442.**) CODEN** CITEAH. **[CCC].** **Pr Rev.** available on microfilm. Documents available from Article Express International, The Genuine Article, Ask*IEEE, Petroleum Abstracts Document Delivery Service, CASDDS, Documents on Demand. ***Continues*** *Angewandte Chemie. B, Technisch-Wirtschaftlicher Teil, 0170-9054;* ***Absorbed*** *Beihefte Verfahrenstechnik.*
Ind/Abst Alum. Ind. Abstr.; Bioeng. Abstr.; Chem Inform; Chem. Abstr.; Coal Abstr.; Curr. Biotechnol.; Dairy Sci. Abstr.; Ei Page One; Elect. Comm. Abstr.; EMBASE; Energy Inf. Abstr.; Energy Res. Abstr.; Eng. Index Annu.; Environ. Abstr.; Environ. Eng. Abstr.; Fluid Abstr., Civil Eng.; Fluid Abstr. Proc. Eng.; FLUIDEX (1973-1988);

HTFS Dig.; INSPEC (July 1971-); Int. Aerosp. Abstr.; Lit. Pat. Abstr., Oilfield Chem. (1954-); Lit. Abstr., Catal. Catal.; Lit. Abstr., Health Environ.; Lit. Abstr., Pet. Refin. Petrochem.; Lit. Abstr., Pet. Substit.; Lit. Abstr., Transp. Storage; Mater. Sci. Eng. Abstr.; Met. Abstr.; PESTDOC; Pet. Abstr.; Res. Alert [Full Cov.]; Saf. Health Work; Sci. Cit. Index; SCISEARCH; Soc. Sci. Cit. Index [Select. Cov.]; Solid State Supercond. Abstr.; Sug. Indus. Abstr.

GW/0009-2959
CHEMISCHE INDUSTRIE (DUSSELDORF). See Chemistry.

GW/0045-6519
CHEMISCHE TECHNIK. ***Ceased.*** [Chem. Tech.]. Vol. 1, (1949)-(Dec. 1994). Academic Scholarly Publication. German. bm. Deutscher Verlag Grundstoffind, Karl Heine Strasse 27, D 04211 Leipzig Germany. **Tel** 011 49 341 4081011. **LC** TP1; .C56. **CODEN** CHTEAA. Documents available from Article Express International, The Genuine Article, Ask*IEEE, CASDDS.
Ind/Abst Anal. Abstr.; Bioeng. Abstr.; Chem Inform; Chem. Abstr.; Chem. Hazards Ind.; Chem. Titles; Coal Abstr.; Curr. Biotechnol.; Curr. Contents Eng. Tech. Appl. Sci.; Ei Page One; EMBASE; Eng. Index Annu.; INSPEC (1968-); Lab. Hazards Bull.; Leadscan; Lit. Pat. Abstr., Oilfield Chem. (1960-); Lit. Abstr., Catal. Catal.; Lit. Abstr., Health Environ.; Lit. Abstr., Pet. Refin. Petrochem.; Lit. Abstr., Pet. Substit.; Lit. Abstr., Transp. Storage; Proc. Chem. Eng.; Res. Alert [Full Cov.]; Saf. Health Work; Sci. Cit. Index; SCISEARCH; Theoret. Chem. Eng.

SA/0379-4687
CHEMSA. ***Ceased.*** [CHEMSA]. **Added/Corp** South African Institute of Chemical Engineers. South African Chemical Institute. Transvaal Chemical Manufacturers Association. Vol. 1, (Nov. 1974)-(Aug. 1993). Periodical. Multiple languages (English and Afrikaans). Twelve times a year. Jim Cane, PO Box 14418, Dersley 1569 South Africa. **LC** TP1; .C4383. **DD** 660.2/05. **CODEN** CHEMDU. Documents available from Article Express International, CASDDS.
Ind/Abst Bioeng. Abstr.; Chem. Abstr.; Coal Abstr.; Ei Page One; EMBASE; Eng. Index Annu.

SZ/0590-8450
COATING. [Coating]. Vol. 1 (Oct. 1968)-. Academic Scholarly Publication. German. mo. 172.00F Switzerland; 197.00F other. Verlag Coating Thomas & Company, Bankgasse 8, CH-9001 St. Gallen Switzerland. **Tel** 011 41 71 223239, telex 719220 COAT CH. **LC** TA418.76; .C6. **CODEN** COTGAV. Index available. **Ad Acc. Circ:** 4,300. Documents available from CASDDS.
Desc: International magazine for chemical and technical coating, adhesives, printing inks' chemistry, wax-technology and abrasives.
Ind/Abst Abstr. Bull. Inst. Pap. Sci. Tech.; Alum. Ind. Abstr.; Art Archaeol. Tech. Abstr.; Chem. Abstr.; Eng. Mater. Abstr.; Int. Packag. Abstr.; Met. Abstr.; Pap. Board Abstr.; Print. Abstr.; World Surf. Coat. Abstr.

UK/0098-1354
COMPUTERS & CHEMICAL ENGINEERING. [Comput. chem. eng.]. **VFOAT** Computers and Chemical Engineering. Vol. 1 (1977)-. Periodical. English. Thirteen times a year. $917.00 The Americas; £615.00 other. Pergamon Press, An Imprint of Elsevier Science Ltd., The Boulevard, Langford Lane, Kidlington, Oxford OX5 1GB United Kingdom. **Tel** 011 44 865 843000, 011 44 865 843699, FAX 011 44 865 843010. **(Subscription address:** Elsevier Science Ltd. Oxford Fulfillment Centre, PO Box 800, Kidlington, Oxford OX5 1DX United Kingdom.**)** **ED** G.V. Reklaitis, D.W.T. Rippin. **LC** TP149; .C64. **DD** 660.2/028/5. **CODEN** CCENDW. **[CCC]. Pr Rev.** available on microfilm and microfiche from University Microfilms International (UMI). Documents available from Article Express International, The Genuine Article, Ask*IEEE, CASDDS.
Desc: Records new developments in the application of computing and systems technology to chemical engineering problems. Publishes full-length articles, survey papers, journal reviews, short notes and letters to the editor. Topics covered include: process synthesis, analysis and design; dynamic analysis and control of chemical processes.
Ind/Abst Abstr. Bull. Inst. Pap. Sci. Tech.; Appl. Sci. Technol. Index (1991-); Bioeng. Abstr.; Chem. Abstr.; Chem. Titles; Civ. Struct. Eng. Abstr.; Coal Abstr.; Compumath Citation Index [Full Cov.]; Comput. Abstr.; Comput. Inf. Syst. Abstr. J. [Full Cov.]; Comput. Rev.; Curr. Biotechnol.; Curr. Contents Eng. Tech. Appl. Sci.; Ei Page One; EMBASE; Eng. Index Annu.; Fluid Abstr., Civil Eng.; Fluid Abstr. Proc. Eng.; FLUIDEX; HTFS Dig.; Inf. Sci. Abstr.; INSPEC (1977-); Lit. Pat. Abstr., Oilfield Chem. (1979-); Lit. Abstr., Catal. Catal.; Lit. Abstr., Health Environ.; Lit. Abstr., Pet. Refin. Petrochem.; Lit. Abstr., Pet. Substit.; Lit. Abstr., Transp. Storage; Mater. Sci. Eng. Abstr.; Pollut. Abstr. Indexes; Proc. Chem. Eng.; Res. Alert [Full Cov.]; Sci. Cit. Index; SCISEARCH; Soc. Sci. Cit. Index [Select. Cov.]; Theoret. Chem. Eng.

AT/0729-2341
CONFERENCE - AUSTRALASIAN CORROSION ASSOCIATION. (CONFERENCE : PROCEEDINGS / THE AUSTRALASIAN CORROSION ASSOCIATION.). [Conf. - Australas. Corros. Assoc.]. **Main/Conf** Australasian Corrosion Association. Conference. (1979)-. Academic Scholarly Publication. English. an. 92.500Aus$ Australia; 130.00Aus$ other. The Australasian Corrosion Association, PO Box 250, Clayton VIC 3168 Australia. **Tel** 011 61 3 5440066. **DD** CEANDQ. **CODEN** CEANDQ. Documents available from Article Express International, CASDDS.
Ind/Abst Bioeng. Abstr.; Chem. Abstr. (1979-1983); Ei Page One; Eng. Index Annu.

US/0010-9339
CORROSION ABSTRACTS. See Engineering-Abstracting, Bibliographies and Statistics.

SA/0377-8711
CORROSION & COATINGS SOUTH AFRICA. [Corros. coat., S. Afr.]. **Added/Corp** South African Corrosion Institute. **VAT** Corrosion and Coatings South Africa. (1974)-. Academic Scholarly Publication. English. Ten times a year. R102.60 South Africa; R120.00 APU countries; R140.00 other. George Warman Publications Pty, PO Box 704, Cape Town 8000 South Africa. **Tel** 011 27 21 245320, FAX 011 27 21 261332, telex 5-21849. **ED** Tony Walker. **LC** TA418.74; .C59. **DD** 671.7/3/05. **CODEN** CCSADT. **Ad Acc. Circ:** 2,500 (ctrl). Documents available from CASDDS.
Desc: Official journal of the South African Corrosion Institute; devoted entirely to corrosion prevention and surface coatings.
Ind/Abst Alum. Ind. Abstr.; Chem. Abstr.; Coal Abstr.; Corros. Abstr.; Eng. Mater. Abstr.; Met. Abstr.; World Surf. Coat. Abstr.

AT/0155-6002
CORROSION AUSTRALASIA. [Corros. australas.]. **Added/Corp** Australasian Corrosion Association. (1976)-. Academic Scholarly Publication. English. bm (6 issues). 36.00Aus$ Australia; 42.00Aus$ other. Australasian Corrosion Association, PO Box 250, Clayton Victoria 3168 Australia. **Tel** 011 61 3 5440066, FAX 011 61 3 5435905. **ED** G. Sussex. **CODEN** COAUDF. Index available. **Bk Rev. Ad Acc. Circ:** 1,200 (ctrl). Documents available from CASDDS.
Desc: Publishes original papers in the fields of metallic corrosion surface treatments, coatings, linings, alloys, ceramics, plastics, corrosion preventives, water and fuel treatment, cathodic and anodic protection.
Ind/Abst Art Archaeol. Tech. Abstr.; Chem. Abstr.; Corros. Abstr.; World Surf. Coat. Abstr.

US/0892-4228
CORROSION ENGINEERING (NEW YORK, N.Y.). (CORROSION ENGINEERING / ZAIRYO TO KANKYO.). [Corros. eng.]. **Added/Corp** Fushoku Boshoku Kyokai (Japan). **VFOAT** Zairyo to Kankyo. Vol. 40, No. 1 (1991)-. Periodical. English (translations available in Japanese). mo (12 issues). $675.00. Allerton Press, Inc., 150 Fifth Avenue, New York NY 10011. **Tel** (212)924-3950, FAX (212)463-9684, telex 427441 ALPRES. **LC** TA418.74; .B673. **[CCC].** Documents available from Article Express International. ***Continues*** *Boshoku Gijutsu. English. Corrosion Engineering, 0892-4228.*
Ind/Abst Eng. Index Annu.

US/0010-9312
CORROSION (HOUSTON, TEX.). (CORROSION.). [Corrosion]. **Added/Corp** National Association of Corrosion Engineers. Vol. 1 (March 1945)-. Periodical. English. mo. $45.00 NACE members; $120.00 nonmembers mainland US; $150.00 nonmembers other. National Association of Corrosion Engineers, 1440 South Creek Drive, Houston TX 77084. **Tel** (713)492-0535, FAX (713)492-8254, telex 792310 NACE HOU. **(Subscription address:** National Association of Corrosion Engineers, PO Box 218340, Houston TX 77084.**)** **ED** Ira D. Perry. **LC** TA462; .C65. **DD** 620.1122. **CODEN** CORRAK. **[CCC].** Index available. cum. index. **Ad Acc. Pr Rev. Circ:** 4,000 (ctrl). available on microfilm and microfiche from University Microfilms International (UMI). Documents available from Article Express International, The Genuine Article, Ask*IEEE, Petroleum Abstracts Document Delivery Service, CASDDS.
Desc: Permanent record of the progress in the science and technology of corrosion control. Focuses on research as it applies to corrosion science and engineering.
Ind/Abst Abstr. Bull. Inst. Pap. Sci. Tech.; Alum. Ind. Abstr.; Appl. Sci. Technol. Index; Aquat. Sci. Fish. Abstr. (Computer File); Art Archaeol. Tech. Abstr.; Bioeng. Abstr.; BMT Abstr.; Ceram. Abstr.; Chem. Abstr.; Chem. Titles; Civ. Struct. Eng. Abstr.; Coal Abstr.; Comput. Inf. Syst. Abstr. J. [Full Cov.]; Concr. Abstr.; Corros. Abstr.; Curr. Contents Eng. Tech. Appl. Sci.; Curr. Titles Electrochem.; Ei Page One; Elect. Comm. Abstr.; EMBASE; Energy Res. Abstr.; Eng. Mater. Abstr.; Eng. Index Annu.; Environ. Period. Bibliogr. (?-?); Fluid Abstr., Civil Eng.; Fluid Abstr. Proc. Eng.; FLUIDEX (1973-); Health Saf. Sci. Abstr.; HTFS Dig.; INIS Atomindex [Micro.]; INSPEC (May 1971-); Int. Aerosp. Abstr.; Int. Packag. Abstr.; Leadscan; Lit. Pat. Abstr., Oilfield Chem. (1954-); Lit. Abstr., Catal. Catal.; Lit. Abstr., Health Environ.; Lit. Abstr., Pet. Refin. Petrochem.; Lit. Abstr., Pet. Substit.; Lit. Abstr., Transp. Storage; Manuf. Process Eng. Abstr.; Mater. Sci. Eng. Abstr.; Mech. Eng. Abstr.; Met. Abstr.; Ocean. Abstr.; Pet. Abstr.; Proc. Chem. Eng.; Res. Alert [Full Cov.]; Sci. Cit. Index; SCISEARCH; Soils Fert.; Solid State Supercond. Abstr.; Theoret. Chem. Eng.; World Surf. Coat. Abstr.

UK/0010-9371
CORROSION PREVENTION AND CONTROL. [Corros. prev. contr.]. Vol. 1 (March 1954)-. Academic Scholarly Publication. English. bm. £75.00. Scientific Press Ltd, PO Box 21, Beaconsfield Bucks HP9 1NS England. **Tel** 011 44 494 675139, 011 44 494 672614, FAX 011 44 494 670155. **ED** J.N.H. Tiratsoo. **LC** TA462; .C657. **DD** 620.1/1223. **CODEN** CRPCAK. Index available (bound in Dec. issue). **Bk Rev. Ad Acc.** ctrl circ. Documents available from Article Express International, CASDDS, Petroleum Abstracts Document Delivery Service.
Ind/Abst Abstr. Bull. Inst. Paper Chem.; Abstr. Bull. Inst. Pap. Sci. Tech.; Agric. Eng. Abstr.; Alum. Ind. Abstr.; Art Archaeol. Tech. Abstr.; Biodeter. Abstr.; Bioeng. Abstr.; BMT Abstr.; Chem. Abstr.; Coal Abstr.; Corros. Abstr. (199?-); Curr. Technol. Index; Curr. Titles Electrochem.; Ei Page One; Eng. Mater. Abstr.; Eng. Index Annu.; Fluid Abstr., Civil Eng.; Fluid Abstr. Proc. Eng.; FLUIDEX (1973-); Int. Civil Eng. Abstr.; Leadscan; Lit. Pat. Abstr., Oilfield Chem. (1969-); Lit. Abstr., Catal. Catal.; Lit. Abstr., Health Environ.; Lit. Abstr., Pet. Refin. Petrochem.; Lit. Abstr., Pet. Substit.; Lit. Abstr., Transp. Storage; Met. Abstr.; Nucl. Sci. Abstr.; Life Sci. Collect.; Pet. Abstr.; Ship Abstr.; Soft. Abstr. Eng.; Soils Fert.; Surf. Treat. Technol. Abstr.; World Alum. Abstr.; World Surf. Coat. Abstr.

US/0364-3301
CORROSION PREVENTION/INHIBITION DIGEST. [Corros. prev.-inhib. dig.]. **Added/Corp** American Society for Metals. Materials Science Division. (19??)-. English. mo. $175.00 (nonmember), $145.00 (member) North America. American Society for Metals International, c/o Deborah Barthelmes, Materials Park OH 44073-0002. **Tel** (216)338-5151, FAX (216)338-4634, telex 980-619. **(Subscription address:** ASM International, Materials Information, Materials Park OH 44073.**)** **LC** TA462; .C6574. **DD** 620.1/6/2305. **Bk Rev.**
Desc: One of a series of ten digests; each digest is a cost effective solution reproducing complete subject relevant abstracts as published in Metals Abstracts.
Ind/Abst Abstr. Bull. Inst. Pap. Sci. Tech.

IS/0048-7538
CORROSION REVIEWS. Vol. 6, No. 2 (1985)-. Academic Scholarly Publication. English. qt. $200.00. Freund Publishing House Ltd, PO Box 35010, 61 Nachmani Street, Tel Aviv 61350 Israel. **Tel** 011 972 3 5662925, FAX 011 972 3 5605335. **(Subscription address:** Freund Publishing House Ltd., Suite 500 Chesham House, 150 Regent Street, London W1R 5FA England.**)** **ED** M. Schorr. **CODEN** CORVE2. Documents available from CASDDS. ***Continues*** *Reviews on Coatings and Corrosion, 0048-7538.*
Ind/Abst Chem. Abstr. (1985-); Corros. Abstr.; Fluid Abstr., Civil Eng.; Fluid Abstr. Proc. Eng.; FLUIDEX; Pollut. Abstr. Indexes.

UK/0010-938X
CORROSION SCIENCE. [Corros. sci.]. **Added/Corp** Corrosion Science Society. Centre Belge d'Etude de la Corrosion. Vol. 1 (Aug. 1961)-. Periodical. Multiple languages (English, French and German; summaries and/or abstracts in English, French and German). mo. $1289.00 The Americas; £865.00 other. Pergamon Press, An Imprint of Elsevier Science Ltd., The Boulevard, Langford Lane, Kidlington, Oxford OX5 1GB United Kingdom. **Tel** 011 44 865 843000, 011 44 865 843699, FAX 011 44 865 843010. **(Subscription address:** Elsevier Science Ltd. Oxford Fulfillment Centre, PO Box 800, Kidlington, Oxford OX5 1DX United Kingdom.**)** **ED** J. C. Scully. **LC** TA462; .C659. **DD** 620.16205. **CODEN** CRRSAA. **[CCC]. Pr Rev.** available on microfilm and microfiche from University Microfilms International (UMI). Documents available from Article Express International, The Genuine Article, Ask*IEEE, Petroleum Abstracts Document Delivery Service, CASDDS, Documents on Demand.
Desc: Provides a medium for the communication of ideas, developments and research in all aspects of the field.
Ind/Abst Abstr. Bull. Inst. Pap. Sci. Tech.; Alum. Ind. Abstr.; Appl. Sci. Technol. Index; Aqualine Abstr.; Aquat. Sci. Fish. Abstr. (Computer File); Art Archaeol. Tech. Abstr.; Biodeter. Abstr.; Bioeng. Abstr.; BMT Abstr. (-199?); Ceram. Abstr. (19??-); Chem Inform; Chem. Abstr.; Chem. Hazards Ind.; Chem. Titles; Civ. Struct. Eng. Abstr.; Coal Abstr.; Corros. Abstr.; Curr. Contents Eng. Tech. Appl. Sci.; Curr. Technol. Index; Curr. Titles Electrochem.; Ei Page One; EMBASE; Energy Inf. Abstr.; Eng. Mater. Abstr.; Eng. Index Annu.; Environ. Abstr.; Environ. Period. Bibliogr. (?-?); Fluid Abstr., Civil Eng.; Fluid Abstr. Proc. Eng.; FLUIDEX; Health Saf. Sci. Abstr.; HTFS Dig.; INIS Atomindex [Micro.]; INSPEC (1968-); Int. Aerosp. Abstr.; Lab. Hazards Bull.; Leadscan; Lit. Pat. Abstr., Oilfield Chem. (1969-); Lit. Abstr., Catal. Catal.; Lit. Abstr., Health Environ.; Lit. Abstr., Pet. Refin. Petrochem.; Lit. Abstr., Pet. Substit.; Lit. Abstr., Transp. Storage; Manuf. Process Eng. Abstr.; Mass Spect. Bull.; Mater. Sci. Eng. Abstr.; Mech. Eng. Abstr.; Met. Abstr.; Ocean. Abstr.; Life Sci. Collect.; Pet. Abstr.; Pollut. Abstr. Indexes; Proc. Chem. Eng.; Res. Alert [Full Cov.]; Sci. Cit. Index; SCISEARCH; Solid State Supercond. Abstr.; Surf. Treat. Technol. Abstr.; Theoret. Chem. Eng.; World Surf. Coat. Abstr.

US/0010-938X
CORROSION SCIENCE [MICROFORM].
Vol. 1 (1961)-. Periodical. English (French and German). mo. $810.00. University Microfilms International, 300 North Zeeb Road, Ann Arbor MI 48106-1346. **Tel** (313)761-4700, (800)521-0600 Exts. 2490, 2491, FAX (313)973-1540. **CODEN** CRRSAA. **[CCC].** available in print.

SP/0045-8678
CORROSION Y PROTECCION. ***Title Change.*** [Corros. prot.]. Academic Scholarly Publication. Spanish. bm. Editorial Garsi SA, Juan Bravo 46, 28006 Madrid, Spain. **Tel** 011 34 1 4021212, telex 98358 GARSI E. **ED** Miguel Angel Guillen. **CODEN** CPTNAP. Index available. **Bk Rev. Ad Acc. Circ:** 1,000 (ctrl). Documents available from CASDDS. ***Continued by*** *Revista Iberoamericana de Corrosion y Proteccion, 0210-6604.*
Desc: Corrosion, naval, industrial, paints anodizing treatments.
Ind/Abst Alum. Ind. Abstr.; Chem. Abstr.; Eng. Mater. Abstr.; Met. Abstr.; Surf. Treat. Technol. Abstr.

UK
DECHEMA CORROSION HANDBOOK.
English. Twice a year. DM775.00. VCH Gesellschaft GmbH, Postfach 101161, D 69451 Weinheim Germany. **Tel** 011 49 6201 606459, FAX 011 49 6201 606184. **(Subscription address:** VCH Publishers Inc., 303 Northwest 12th Avenue, Journals Department, Deerfield FL 33442.**) ED** Dieter Behrens. Index available. cum. index. **Bk Rev. Circ:** 900.
Desc: Informs about the corrosion characteristics of materials, both important and frequently used. Possibilities for the prevention and cure of corrosion are described.

UK/0262-1576
DEVELOPMENTS IN ADHESIVES. [Dev. adhes.]. (1977)-. Academic Scholarly Publication. English. ir. Price varies. Elsevier Science Publishers Ltd, Crown House, Linton Road, Barking Essex IG11 8JU England. **Tel** 011 44 81 5947272, FAX 081-594-5942, telex 896950. **(Subscription address:** Elsevier Science Inc. / New York Books, 655 Avenue of the Americas, New York NY 10010.**) CODEN** DEADD7. Documents available from CASDDS.
Ind/Abst Chem. Abstr.

US/1075-2013
DIGEST OF POLYMER DEVELOPMENTS. SER. 3, STYRENICS AND ACRYLICS. (DIGEST OF POLYMER DEVELOPMENTS.). (19??)-. Periodical. English. ir. price varies per volume. Springborn Laboratories Inc., 10 Springborn Center, Enfield CT 06082. **Tel** (203)749-8371 Ext. 295, FAX (203)749-8234, telex 4436041. **DD** 547.

CN/0709-3438
DIRECTORY OF CHEMICAL ENGINEERING RESEARCH IN CANADIAN UNIVERSITIES (1979).
(DIRECTORY OF CHEMICAL ENGINEERING RESEARCH IN CANADIAN UNIVERSITIES.). [Dir. chem. eng. res. Can. univ. (1979)]. **VFOAT** Compte Rendu de la Recherche en Genie Chimique Dans les Universites Canadiennes. 18th- 1978/79-. Directory. English (French). an. Canadian Society for Chemical Engineering, 151 Slater Street, Ottawa K1P 5H3 Canada. **DD** 660.2/07/2071. ***Continues*** *Annual Directory of Chemical Engineering Research in Canadian Universities, 0315-9752.*

UK
EFCE PUBLICATION SERIES. Added/Corp European Federation of Chemical Engineering. Institution of Chemical Engineers (Great Britain) Dechema. Society of Chemical Industry (Great Britain). (1978)-. Monographic series. English. Institution of Chemical Engineers, Davis Building, 165-189 Railway Terrace, Rugby Warwickshire CV21 3HQ England. **Tel** 011 44 1788 578214, FAX 011 44 1788 560833, telex 311780. **CODEN** EPSEDI. Documents available from CASDDS.
Ind/Abst Chem. Abstr.

US/0886-5671
ELECTRONIC CHEMICALS NEWS. See Engineering-Electricity, Electrical Engineering, Electronics.

UK/0957-9052
ENVIRONMENTAL PROTECTION BULLETIN. See Environmental Issues-Pollution and Waste Management.

UK/0938-5807
EQUIPMENT, CORROSION, AND CORROSION PROTECTION. (19??)-. English. mo (12 issues). $214.00 US; £118.00 other. Royal Society of Chemistry, Thomas Graham House, Science Park, Cambridge CB4 4WF England. **Tel** 011 44 223 420066, FAX 011 44 223 423429, telex 818293 ROYAL. **(Subscription address:** Royal Society of Chemistry, Distribution Center, Blackhorse Road, Letchworth, SG6 1HN England.**)**
Desc: Contains abstracts on the related fields of construction, maintenance and corrosion within the chemical and processing industries.

UK/0938-5207
EQUIPMENT, CORROSION, AND CORROSION PROTECTION. (19??)-. Periodical. English. mo. £118.00 EC; $214.00 US; £118.00 other. Royal Society of Chemistry, Thomas Graham House, Science Park, Cambridge CB4 4WF England. **Tel** 011 44 223 420066, FAX 011 44 223 423429, telex 818293 ROYAL. **(Subscription address:** Turpin Distribution Services Limited, Blackhorse Road, Letchworth, Hertfordshire SG6 1HN, United Kingdom.**)**
Desc: Contains abstracts on the related fields of construction, maintenance and corrosion within the chemical and processing industries, as well as abstracts on corrosion protection.

GW/0014-2484
EUROPA CHEMIE. [Eur.-Chem.]. No. 1 (1963)-. Periodical. German. Thirty-six times a year. DM213.08 Germany; DM261.00 others Comes with Chemische Industrie. Handelsblatt GmbH, Postfach 102716, D-40018 Duesseldorf Germany. **Tel** 011 49 211 8871730. **ED** H. Seidel. **NLM** W1 EU583L. **CODEN** EUCHAD. **[CCC]. Ad Acc. Circ:** 5,000 (ctrl). Documents available from CASDDS. ***Continues*** *Chemie Markt.*
Desc: Topical news service for the European chemical industry. Appears at ten days intervals and gives last minute comprehensive summary of events in Europe's chemical markets.
Ind/Abst Biodeter. Abstr. (1991-); Chem. Abstr.; Chem. Bus. Bull.; Chem. Bus. NewsBase (1985-); Chem. Bus. Update; Chem. Ind. Notes; F&S Index Plus Text, Int. [Select. Cov.]; Infomat Int. Bus.; PROMT; World Surf. Coat. Abstr.

US
EVEREADY BATTERY ENGINEERING DATA / UNION CARBIDE. Added/Corp Union Carbide Corporation. (19??)-. English. Union Carbide Corporation, Battery Products Division, Danbury CT 06817.

CN/0848-5712
EXPLOSIVE SAFETY AND CONTROL IN CANADA. [Explos. saf. control Can.]. **Main/Corp** Canada. Explosives Branch. **VFOAT** Securite et Controle des Explosifs au Canada. (198?)-. English (French). Explosives Branch, Department of Energy Mines and Resources, 580 Booth Street, Ottawa Ontario K1A 0E4 Canada. **Tel** (613)995-7556. **DD** 354.710075/05. ***Continues*** *Report of the Explosives Branch. Canada. Explosives Branch, 0710-7129;* ***Absorbed*** *Securite et Controle des Explosifs au Canada. Canada. Explosives Branch.*

US/0014-505X
EXPLOSIVES AND PYROTECHNICS.
Added/Corp Franklin Institute, Philadelphia. Research Laboratories. Vol. 1 (Jan. 1968)-. Periodical. English. mo. $42.00 US; $46.00 other; $54.00 airmail. Franklin Applied Physics, 98 Highland Avenue, PO Box 313, Oaks PA 19456. **Tel** (215)666-6645, , FAX (215)666-0173. **ED** R. Thompson. **Bk Rev**, (Qty: 2). **Ad Acc. Circ:** 400.
Desc: Explosives and pyrotechnics news and research results. Advance notice of meetings, seminars, symposia, activities.

UK/0952-3960
EXPLOSIVES ENGINEERING. Added/Corp Institute of Explosives Engineers. Vol. 1, No. 1 (Autumn 1987)-. Periodical. English. qt. £19.00 UK; £26.00 Europe; £40.00 other. Sampson Publishing Ltd., 31 High Street, Witney Oxon, OX8 7RN England. **Tel** 011 44 865 300229. **LC** TP270.A1; E82. **DD** 662/.2/05. **CODEN** EXENEW. ***Continues*** *Explosives Engineer (London, England).*
Ind/Abst Coal Abstr.

GW/0933-5927
F & S. FILTRIEREN UND SEPARIEREN.
VFOAT F und S. Filtrieren und Separieren; Filtrieren und Separieren. (1987)-. Periodical. German. bm. DM89.60 Germany; DM98.00 other. Umschau Verlag, Postfach 110262, D-60037 Frankfurt Germany. **Tel** 011 49 69 2600692, FAX 011 49 69 2600223, telex 411964. **UDC** 628.33. **CODEN** 57.088.3.
Ind/Abst Fluid Abstr., Civil Eng.; Fluid Abstr. Proc. Eng.; FLUIDEX (199?-).

UK/0015-1882
FILTRATION & SEPARATION. [Filtr. sep.]. **Added/Corp** Filtration Society (Great Britain) Proceedings of the Filtration Society. **VAT** Filtration and Separation. (Jan./Feb. 1965)-. Academic Scholarly Publication. English (summaries and/or abstracts in French, German and Spanish). Ten times a year. $135.00 The Americas; £90.00 other. Elsevier Advanced Technology, An Imprint of Elsevier Science Ltd., The Boulevard, Langford Lane, Kidlington, Oxford OX5 1GB United Kingdom. **Tel** 011 44 865 843000, 011 44 865 843699, FAX 011 44 865 843010. **(Subscription address:** Elsevier Science Ltd. Oxford Fulfillment Centre, PO Box 800, Kidlington, Oxford OX5 1DX United Kingdom.**) ED** S. Barrett. **CODEN** FSEPAA. **[CCC].** Index available. cum. index. **Bk Rev. Ad Acc. Circ:** 4,000. available on microfilm and microfiche from University Microfilms International (UMI). Documents available from Article Express International, CASDDS. ***Absorbed*** *Dust Control and Air Cleaning;* ***Continues*** *Filtration.*
Desc: Worldwide coverage of filtration and separation technologies for liquids and air gases including news, case studies and new products. Feature articles and proceedings of the Filtration Society.
Ind/Abst Abstr. Bull. Inst. Pap. Sci. Tech.; Agric. Eng. Abstr.; Bioeng. Abstr.; Chem. Abstr.; Chem. Hazards Ind.; Coal Abstr.; Ei Page One; EMBASE; Eng. Index Annu.; F&S Index Plus Text, Int. [Select. Cov.]; Fluid Abstr., Civil Eng.; Fluid Abstr. Proc. Eng.; FLUIDEX (1973-); Infomat Int. Bus.; Lab. Hazards Bull.; Nonwovens Abstr.; Proc. Chem. Eng.; PROMT; Saf. Health Work; Text. Technol. Dig.; Theoret. Chem. Eng.; World Ceram. Abstr.; World Surf. Coat. Abstr.; World Text. Abstr.

UK
FOCUS ON CHEMICALS. English. bw. £400.00. Stuart H Wamsley, Burwash Weald, East Sussex TN19 7LQ England. **Tel** 44 435 882957, FAX 44 436 882965. **ED** Stuart Wamsley. Index available. cum. index. ctrl circ.
Desc: A commentary on the international chemical industry.

BU/0489-6211
GODISNIK NA VISSIJA HIMIKO-TEHNOLOGICESKI INSTITUT--SOFIJA. (GODISHNIK NA VISSHIIA KHIMIKO-TEKHNOLOGICHESKI INSTITUT--SOFIIA.). [God. viss. him.-tehnol. inst. Sofija]. **Main/Corp** Vissh Khimiko-Tekhnologicheski Institut (Sofia, Bulgaria). **VFOAT** Annuaire de l'Ecole Superieure de Chimie Industrielle--Sofia. (1965)-. Bulgarian (summaries and/or abstracts in English, French and German). **LC** TP1; .K485. **CODEN** GVKIAH. Documents available from CASDDS. ***Continues*** *Godishnik na Khimiko-Tekhnologicheski Institut.*
Ind/Abst Chem. Abstr.

MX
GUIA DE LA INDUSTRIA QUIMICA : PRODUCTOS QUIMICOS. (19??)-. Spanish. an. $44.20 US and Canada; $34.00 Mexico; $51.00 other. Editorial Cosmos / Mexico, Espana 396 Col Granjas Estrela, Mexico 13 DF Mexico. **Tel** 011 52 5829928, 5703485. **LC** HD9655.M4; G84.

US/0145-7632
HEAT TRANSFER ENGINEERING. [Heat transf. eng.]. Vol. 1 (July/Sept. 1979)-. Academic Scholarly Publication. English. qt. £121.00 UK; $200.00 other. Taylor & Francis Ltd., Rankine Road, Basingstoke Hampshire, RG24 8PR United Kingdom. **Tel** 011 44 256 840366, FAX 011 44 256 479438, telex 858540. **(Subscription address:** Taylor & Francis Inc., 1900 Frost Road, Suite 101, Bristol PA 19007-1598.**) ED** Kenneth J. Bell and Afshin J. Ghajar (coordinating editor). **LC** TJ260; .H39. **DD** 621.402/2/05. **CODEN** HTEND2HTEND3. **[CCC].** Index available. **Bk Rev. Ad Acc. Pr Rev. Circ:** 1,800. available on microfilm and microfiche from University Microfilms International (UMI). Documents available from Article Express International, The Genuine Article, CASDDS.
Desc: Offers a comprehensive presentation of the major advances in the field in a practical format. Included in the scope of developments are equipment, instrumentation and practice, as well as the latest reports from companies, universities, laboratories and educational programs. The journal is a forum for heat exchange, design, planning, operation, and practice.
Ind/Abst Abstr. Bull. Inst. Paper Chem.; Abstr. Bull. Inst. Pap. Sci. Tech.; Bioeng. Abstr.; Chem. Abstr.; Curr. Contents Eng. Tech. Appl. Sci.; Ei Page One; Electron. Commun. Abstr. J.; EMBASE; Energy Res. Abstr. (June 1980-); Eng. Mater. Abstr.; Eng. Index Annu.; Environ. Eng. Abstr.; Fluid Abstr., Civil Eng.; Fluid Abstr. Proc. Eng.; FLUIDEX (1979-); HTFS Dig.; INIS Atomindex [Micro.]; Int. Aerosp. Abstr.; ISMEC Bull.; Mech. Eng. Abstr.; Pollut. Abstr. Indexes; Proc. Chem. Eng.; Res. Alert [Full Cov.]; Saf. Sci. Abstr. J.; SCISEARCH; Theoret. Chem. Eng.

UN/0451-8306
HIMICESKOE MASINOSTROENIE (KIEV). (KHIMICHESKOE MASHINOSTROENIE / MINISTERSTVO VYSSHEGO I SREDNEGO SPETSIALNOGO OBRAZOVANIIA USSR.). [Him. masinostr.]. **Added/Corp** Ukraine. Ministerstvo Vyshchoi i Serednoi Spetsialnoi Osvity. (1965)-. Russian. **LC** TP157; .K45. **CODEN** kmmraz. Documents available from CASDDS.
Ind/Abst Chem. Abstr.

US
HISTORICAL PRICING--PETROCHEMICALS. See Chemistry-Chemical Technology.

UK/0952-2654
HTFS DIGEST (1987). See Engineering-Abstracting, Bibliographies and Statistics.

CC/1000-6613
HUAGONG JINZHAN. (HUA KUNG CHIN CHAN.). [Huagong jinzhan]. **Added/Corp** Chung-Kuo Hua Kung Hsueh Hui. **VFOAT** Chemical Industry and

Engineering Progress. (19??)-. Periodical. Chinese. bm. RMBY0.45. Chung-Kuo Hua Kung Hsueh Hui, Pei-Ching Shih Pao Kan Fa Hsing Chu, Beijing, People's Republic of China. **LC** TP1; .H83. **DD** 660.2/05. **CODEN** HUJIEK. Documents available from CASDDS.
Ind/Abst Chem. Abstr.

CC/0254-6094
HUAGONG JIXIE. (HUA KUNG CHI HSIEH.). [Huagong jixie]. **Added/Corp** Hua Hsueh Kung Yeh pu Hua Kung Chi Hsieh Yen Chiu Yuan (China). **VFOAT** Huagong Jixie; Chemical Engineering and Machinery; Chemical Engineering & Machinery. (19??)-. Academic Scholarly Publication. Chinese (summaries and/or abstracts in English). bm. $36.00. Institute of Chemical Engineering Machinery, Minister of Chemical Industry, 3 North Heshui Road, Xigu, Lanzhou, Gansu Province, People's Republic of China. **Tel** 0931-557401, FAX 0931-558554. **ED** Zhu Yue. **LC** TP155; .H775. **DD** 660/.05. **CODEN** HUJIDJ. Index available. **Ad Acc**, **Adv Mgr:** Z. Laimeng. **Circ:** 10,000. Documents available from CASDDS, BLDSC, CASDDS.
Ind/Abst Chem. Abstr.; Corros. Abstr. (199?-); Curr. Biotechnol.

CH/1001-2052
HUAGONG YEJIN. **VFOAT** Engineering Chemistry & Metallurgy. (1980)-. Periodical. Chinese. qt. Science Press, 16 Donghuangchenggen North Street, Beijing 100707, People's Republic of China. **Tel** 011 86 1 4019821, 011 86 1 4010642, FAX 011 86 1 4012180, 011 86 1 4019810, telex 210147. **DD** 669.9. Documents available from Article Express International, CASDDS.
Ind/Abst Chem. Abstr.; Ei Page One; Eng. Index Annu.

CC/1000-3932
HUAGONG ZIDONGHUA JI YIBIAO. (HUA KUNG TZU TUNG HUA CHI I PIAO.). [Huagong zidonghua ji yibiao]. **Added/Corp** Hua Hsueh Kung Yeh Pu Tzu Tung Hua Yen Chiu So. **VFOAT** Control and Instruments in Chemical Industry. (19??)-. Periodical. Chinese. bm. Hua Hsueh Kung Yeh Pu Tzu Tung Hua Yen Chiu So, Lan-Chou China, People's Republic of China. **CODEN** HZJYEZ. Documents available from CASDDS.
Ind/Abst Chem. Abstr.

CC/1001-7631
HUAXUE FANYING GONGCHENG YU GONGYI. (HUA HSUEH FAN YING KUNG CHENG YU KUNG I.). [Huaxue fanying gongcheng yu gongyi]. **VFOAT** Chemical Reaction Engineering and Technology. (198?)-. Academic Scholarly Publication. Chinese. qt. $48.00. Zhejiang Daxue / Huagong Xi, Zhejioang University, Department of Chemical Engineering, Zheda lu, Hangzhou, Zhejiang 310027, People's Republic of China. **Tel** 0571 572244, FAX 0571 571797. **ED** C. Gantang. **CODEN** HFGGEU. Documents available from CASDDS, BLDSC, CASDDS.
Ind/Abst Chem. Abstr. (1986-); Lit. Pat. Abstr., Oilfield Chem.; Lit. Abstr., Catal. Catal.; Lit. Abstr., Health Environ.; Lit. Abstr., Pet. Refin. Petrochem.; Lit. Abstr., Pet. Substit.; Lit. Abstr., Transp. Storage.

CC/1001-0017
HUAXUE YU ZHANHE. **VFOAT** Chemistry and Adhesion. (1982)-. Periodical. Chinese. qt. $1.50 (per issue). Heilongjiang Sheng Kexueyuan, Shiyou Huaxe Yanjiusuo, Heilongjiang Academy of Sciences, Institute of Petrochemistry, 160 Zhongshan lu, Harbin, Heilongjiang, 150040 People's Republic of China. **Tel** 0451 223691. **ED** Y. Zhaojian. **DD** 668.3. Documents available from CASDDS.
Ind/Abst Chem. Abstr.

KO
HWAHAK KWA HWAHAK KONGOP. **VFOAT** Hwahakgwa Hwahakgongop. (19??)-. Periodical. Korean (summaries and/or abstracts in English). **LC** TP1; .H89. Documents available from CASDDS.
Ind/Abst Chem. Abstr.

II/0019-4506
INDIAN CHEMICAL ENGINEER. [Indian chem. eng.]. **Added/Corp** Indian Institute of Chemical Engineers. (1959)-. Periodical. English. qt. $48.00. Indian Institute of Chemical Engineers, Calcutta, India. **(Subscription address:** Prints India, 11 Darya Ganj, New Delhi 110002 India.**)** **ED** A K Mitra. **CODEN** ICHEAF. **Bk Rev.** **Ad Acc.** **Circ:** 4,000 (ctrl). Documents available from CASDDS. ***Absorbed** Indian Institute of Chemical Engineers. Transactions.*
Ind/Abst Chem. Abstr.; Curr. Biotechnol.; Eng. Mater. Abstr.; Proc. Chem. Eng.; Theoret. Chem. Eng.

II/0019-5065
INDIAN JOURNAL OF APPLIED CHEMISTRY. (INDIAN JOURNAL OF APPLIED CHEMISTRY / INDIAN CHEMICAL SOCIETY.). (195?)-. English. **NLM** W1 IN206P. ***Continues** Industrial & News Edition of the Journal of the Indian Chemical Society.*
Ind/Abst Ceram. Abstr.

US/0888-5885
INDUSTRIAL & ENGINEERING CHEMISTRY RESEARCH. [Ind. eng. chem. res.]. **Added/Corp** American Chemical Society. **VFOAT** Industrial and Engineering Chemistry Research. Vol. 26, No. 1 (Jan. 1987)-. Academic Scholarly Publication. English. mo. $695.00 (institution) US. American Chemical Society, 1155 Sixteenth Street Northwest, Washington DC 20036. **Tel** (800)333-9511, (800)227-5558, (614)447-3776, FAX (202)833-7736. **(Subscription address:** American Chemical Society / Ohio, Department L 0011, Columbus OH 43268-0011.**)** **ED** Donald R. Paul. **LC** TP1; .I618. **DD** 660.2/05. **CODEN** IECRED. **[CCC].** Index available. **Bk Rev.** **Ad Acc.** **Pr Rev.** **Acid Free.** available on microfilm and microfiche from University Microfilms International (UMI). Documents available from Article Express International, The Genuine Article, Ask*IEEE, CASDDS. ***Formed by the union of** Industrial & Engineering Chemistry Fundamentals, 0196-4313; Industrial & Engineering Chemistry Process Design and Development, 0196-4305 **and** Industrial & Engineering Chemistry Product Research and Development, 0196-4321.*
Desc: Coverage focuses on fundamental and theoretical aspects of chemical engineering, design methods and their application to processes and process equipment, and new technology applicable to products involving chemical engineering.
Ind/Abst Abstr. Bull. Inst. Pap. Sci. Tech.; Appl. Sci. Technol. Index; Biodeter. Abstr. (1991-); Ceram. Abstr. (19??-); Chem Inform; Chem. Abstr.; Comput. Inf. Syst. Abstr. J. [Full Cov.]; Curr. Biotechnol.; Curr. Titles Electrochem.; Ei Page One; Elect. Comm. Abstr.; Energy Res. Abstr.; Eng. Index Annu.; Environ. Eng. Abstr.; Fluid Abstr., Civil Eng.; Fluid Abstr. Proc. Eng.; FLUIDEX; For. Prod. Abstr.; Gas Abstr.; HTFS Dig.; INIS Atomindex [Micro.]; INSPEC (1987-); Int. Aerosp. Abstr.; Leadscan; Lit. Pat. Abstr., Oilfield Chem. (1962-); Lit. Abstr., Catal. Catal.; Lit. Abstr., Health Environ.; Lit. Abstr., Pet. Refin. Petrochem.; Lit. Abstr., Pet. Substit.; Lit. Abstr., Transp. Storage; Manuf. Process Eng. Abstr.; Mater. Sci. Eng. Abstr.; Mech. Eng. Abstr.; Met. Abstr.; MINPROC; PESTDOC; Proc. Chem. Eng.; Res. Alert [Full Cov.]; Sci. Cit. Index; SCISEARCH; Soils Fert.; Solid State Supercond. Abstr.; Theoret. Chem. Eng.; Weed Abstr.; World Ceram. Abstr.; World Surf. Coat. Abstr.

UK/0955-7040
INDUSTRIAL CORROSION ABSTRACTS. ***Title Change.*** **Added/Corp** BHRA (Association). Vol. 1 (1989)-(19??). Periodical. English. qt. STI, 4 Kings Meadow, Ferry Hinksey Road, Oxford OX2 0DU United Kingdom. **Tel** (0865) 798898, FAX (0865) 798788. **ED** L S Gale. Index available. cum. index. **Bk Rev.** **Circ:** 100. ***Merged with** Tribos, 0041-2694 **to form** Tribology and Corrosion Abstracts, 0962-7189.*

MX/0185-3899
INGENIERIA PETROLERA. [Ing. pet.]. Periodical. Spanish. qt. $52.00. Asociacion des Ingenieros Petroleros Mexico, Tacuba N5, Palacio de Mineria Mexico DF Mexico. **CODEN** INGPAI. Documents available from Article Express International.
Ind/Abst Bioeng. Abstr.; Ei Page One; Energy Res. Abstr. (March 1981-); Eng. Index Annu.; GeoRef.

SP/0210-2064
INGENIERIA QUIMICA (MADRID). (INGENIERIA QUIMICA.). [Ing. quim.]. (1969)-. Academic Scholarly Publication. Spanish. mo. Ingenieria Quimica SA, Triana 53, 28016 Madrid Spain. **Tel** 011 34 1 3456400. **CODEN** INQUDI. **[CCC].** Documents available from CASDDS.
Ind/Abst Abstr. Bull. Inst. Pap. Sci. Tech.; Biodeter. Abstr. (1991-); Chem. Abstr.; Curr. Biotechnol.; Proc. Chem. Eng.; Sug. Indus. Abstr.; Theoret. Chem. Eng.

CR/0250-8303
INGENIERIA Y CIENCIA QUIMICA. [Ing. cienc. quim.]. **Added/Corp** Colegio Federado de Quimicos y de Ingenieros Quimicos de Costa Rica. (1977)-. Periodical. Spanish. tq. Colegio Federado de Quimicos y de Ingenieros Quimicos de Costa Rica, Av 8 C 7 Y 9, San Jose Coast Rica. **CODEN** ICQUD9. Documents available from CASDDS. ***Continues** Revista del Colegio de Quimicos e Ingenieros Quimicos de Costa Rica, 0378-2328.*
Ind/Abst Chem. Abstr.

GW
INORGANIC REACTIONS & METHODS. Monographic series. English. ir. Price varies per volume. VCH Gesellschaft GmbH, Postfach 101161, D 69451 Weinheim Germany. **Tel** 011 49 6201 606459, FAX 011 49 6201 606184. **(Subscription address:** VCH Publishers Inc., 303 Northwest 12th Avenue, Journals Department, Deerfield FL 33442.**)**

UK/0307-0492
INSTITUTION OF CHEMICAL ENGINEERS SYMPOSIUM SERIES, THE. (SYMPOSIUM SERIES.). [Inst. Chem. Eng. symp. ser.]. **Main/Corp** Institution of Chemical Engineers. (1947)-. Monographic series. English. ir. Price varies per volume. Hemisphere Publishing Corporation, 1900 Frost Road, Suite 101, Bristol PA 19007. **Tel** (800)821-8312. **CODEN** ICESDB. **[CCC].** Index available. cum. index. **Circ:** 1,000. Documents available from Article Express International, CASDDS.
Desc: Series of publications concerning the latest ideas and trends within the chemical engineering world.
Ind/Abst Bioeng. Abstr.; Chem. Abstr.; Curr. Biotechnol.; Ei Page One; Eng. Index Annu.

US/0020-6318
INTERNATIONAL CHEMICAL ENGINEERING. [Int. chem. eng.]. **Added/Corp** American Institute of Chemical Engineers. Vol. 1 (Oct. 1961)-. Academic Scholarly Publication. English (Multiple languages). qt. $349.00 US; $379.00 other. American Institute of Chemical Engineers, 345 East 47th Street, New York NY 10017. **Tel** (212)705-7663, (212)705-7703, FAX (212)705-8400. **ED** Renate Churchill. **LC** TP1; .I748. **DD** 660/.05. **NLM** W1 IN727. **CODEN** INCEAX. **[CCC].** Index available. **Bk Rev.** **Ad Acc.** **Circ:** 1,300 (ctrl). available on microfilm and microfiche from University Microfilms International (UMI). Documents available from Article Express International, Petroleum Abstracts Document Delivery Service, CASDDS.
Desc: This journal is devoted to English-language translations in important non-English language chemical engineering journals.
Ind/Abst Bibliogr. Mission. (1973-); Bioeng. Abstr.; Chem. Abstr.; Coal Abstr.; Comput. Abstr.; Curr. Biotechnol.; Ei Page One; EMBASE; Energy Res. Abstr.; Eng. Index Annu.; Fluid Abstr., Civil Eng.; Fluid Abstr. Proc. Eng.; FLUIDEX (1973-); Gas Abstr.; HTFS Dig.; INIS Atomindex [Micro.]; Int. Aerosp. Abstr.; Lit. Pat. Abstr., Oilfield Chem. (1964-); Lit. Abstr., Catal. Catal.; Lit. Abstr., Health Environ.; Lit. Abstr., Pet. Refin. Petrochem.; Lit. Abstr., Pet. Substit.; Lit. Abstr., Transp. Storage; MINPROC; Pet. Abstr.; Proc. Chem. Eng.; Soils Fert.; Theoret. Chem. Eng.

GW/0722-4087
INTERNATIONALE JAHRESTAGUNG / FRAUNHOFER-INSTITUT FUER TREIB-UND EXPLOSIVSTOFFE. [Int. Jahrestag. - Fraunhofer-Inst. Treib- Explosivst.]. **Main/Corp** Fraunhofer-Institut fur Treib- und Explosivstoffe. Internationale Jahrestagung. (1979)-. Academic Scholarly Publication. English (French and German). an. DM200.00. Fraunhofer-Institut fur Chemische Technologie, Postfach 1240, W-7507 Pfinztal 1 F R Germany. **Tel** 11 49 721 46400, 721 46121, FAX 11 49 721 4640111, telex 7826909 ICT D. **LC** TP270.A1; F73a. **DD** 662/.2/05. **CODEN** IFTEDV. Index available. Documents available from Article Express International, CASDDS. ***Continues** Institut fuer Chemie der Treib- und Explosivstoffe (Fraunhofer-Gesellschaft). Internationale Jahrestagung. Internationale Jahrestagung, 0172-8911.*
Ind/Abst Bioeng. Abstr.; Chem. Abstr.; Ei Page One; Eng. Index Annu.; Int. Aerosp. Abstr.

PL/0208-6425
INZYNIERIA CHEMICZNA I PROCESOWA. (INZYNIERIA CHEMICZNA I PROCESOWA / POLSKA AKADEMIA NUAK, KOMITET INZYNIERII CHEMICZNEJ I PROCESOWEJ.). [Inz. chem. procesowa]. **Added/Corp** Polska Akademia Nauk. Komitet Inzynierii Chemicznej i Procesowej. Vol. 1, No. 1 (1980)-. Academic Scholarly Publication. Polish (English; summaries and/or abstracts in English, Polish and Russian). qt. $70.00. **(Subscription address:** ARS Polona, PO Box 1001, 00068 Warsaw Poland.**)** **LC** TP1; .I7674. **CODEN** ICPRDT. **Pr Rev.** Documents available from The Genuine Article, CASDDS. ***Continues** Inzynieria Chemiczna.*
Ind/Abst Ceram. Abstr.; Chem. Abstr.; Ei Page One; Energy Res. Abstr. (Oct. 1982-); Proc. Chem. Eng.; Res. Alert [Full Cov.]; Sci. Cit. Index; SCISEARCH; Theoret. Chem. Eng.

RU
ITOGI NAUKI I TEKHNIKI: KORROZIIA I ZASHCHITA OT KORROZII. **Added/Corp** Vsesoiuznyi Institut Nauchnoi i Tekhnicheskoi Informatsii (Soviet Union). **VFOAT** Itogi Nauki i Tekhniki: Seriia Korroziia i Zashchita ot Korrozii; Korroziia i Zashchita ot Korrozii; Seriia Korroziia i Zashchita ot Korrozii. (1973)-. Russian. 1.56rub (single issue). VINITI - Vsesoyuznyi Institut Nauchno-Tekhnicheskoi Informatsii, All-Union Scientific and Technical Information Institute, Baltiiskaia Ulitsa 14, 125219 Moscow Russia. **Tel** 238-46-00, FAX 9430060, telex 411160. **LC** TA462; .I97. **CODEN** IKZKA9. Documents available from CASDDS. ***Continues** Itogi Nauki: Korroziia i Zashchita ot Korrozii.*
Ind/Abst Chem. Abstr.

RU
ITOGI NAUKI I TEKHNIKI. SERIIA PROTSESSY I APPARATY KHIMICHESKOI TEKHNOLOGII. **Added/Corp** Vsesoiuznyi Institut Nauchnoi i Tekhnicheskoi Informatsii (Soviet Union). (1980)-. Periodical. Russian. ir. VINITI - Vsesoyuznyi Institut Nauchno-Tekhnicheskoi Informatsii, All-Union Scientific and Technical Information Institute, Baltiiskaia Ulitsa 14, 125219 Moscow Russia. **Tel** 238-46-00, FAX 9430060, telex 411160. **LC** TP155.7; .I86. ***Continues** Itogi Nauki i Tekhniki. Protsessy i Apparaty Khimicheskoi Tekhnologii, 0202-8018.*

RU/0579-2991
IZVESTIJA VYSSIH UCEBNYH ZAVEDENIJ. HIMIJA I HIMICESKAJA TEHNOLOGIJA. **See** Chemistry.

US/0021-8995
JOURNAL OF APPLIED POLYMER SCIENCE. [J. appl. polym. sci.]. Vol. 1 (Jan./Feb. 1959)-. Academic Scholarly Publication. English (summaries and/or abstracts in French and German). Fifty-two times a year. $7,772.00 US; $6,292.00 Canada and Mexico; $6,487.00 other. John Wiley & Sons, Inc., 605 Third Avenue, New York NY 10158-0012. **Tel** (212)850-6000, (212)850-6645, FAX (212)850-6088, telex 12-7063. **(Subscription address:** John Wiley & Sons / England, Baffins Lane, Chichester, West Sussex PO19 1UD England.**) ED** Eric Baer. **LC** TP156.P6; J6. **DD** 678.705. **CODEN** JAPNAB. **[CCC]. Ad Acc. Pr Rev. Circ:** 2,000. available on microfilm and microfiche from University Microfilms International (UMI). Documents available from Article Express International, The Genuine Article, CASDDS. ***Supersedes in part*** *Journal of Polymer Science, 0022-3832.*
Desc: Provides scientists and engineers with coverage of up-to-date progress and significant results in the systematic practical application of polymer science. Areas of focus include testing of plastics, elastomers, films, fibers, coatings, and adhesives, studies of emulsions and lattices, aging of polymers, extrusion and molding, diffusion and permeability.
Ind/Abst Abstr. Bull. Inst. Pap. Sci. Tech.; AGRICOLA [Select. Cov.]; Appl. Mech. Rev.; Art Archaeol. Tech. Abstr.; Biodeter. Abstr.; Bioeng. Abstr.; Chem. Abstr.; Chem. Titles; Civ. Struct. Eng. Abstr.; Coal Abstr.; Comput. Inf. Syst. Abstr. J. [Full Cov.]; Curr. Biotechnol.; Curr. Contents Eng. Tech. Appl. Sci.; Curr. Contents Phys. Chem. Earth Sci.; Ei Page One; EMBASE; Energy Res. Abstr.; Eng. Index Annu.; Environ. Eng. Abstr.; For. Prod. Abstr. (19??-19??); Int. Aerosp. Abstr.; Manuf. Process Eng. Abstr.; Mater. Sci. Eng. Abstr.; Mech. Eng. Abstr.; Polymer Contents; Proc. Chem. Eng.; RAPRA Abstr.; Res. Alert [Full Cov.]; Sci. Cit. Index; SCISEARCH; Sug. Indus. Abstr.; Text. Technol. Dig.; Theoret. Chem. Eng.; World Surf. Coat. Abstr.; World Text. Abstr.

US/0146-4140
JOURNAL OF BALLISTICS. [J. ballist.]. **Added/Corp** Douglas Documentation Systems. **VFOAT** Ballistics. Vol. 1 (Oct. 1976)-. Academic Scholarly Publication. English. ir. $290.00. Douglas Documentation Systems, RD 5, Box 5105 A, Stroudsburg PA 18360. **Tel** (215)322-7845. **ED** Bruce W. Brodman. **LC** UF820; .J66. **DD** 623.5/1/05. **CODEN** BALLD2. **Ad Acc. Circ:** 200 (ctrl). Documents available from CASDDS.
Desc: Latest in ballistics theory, research and development. Propellant technology emphasized.
Ind/Abst Chem. Abstr.; Int. Aerosp. Abstr.

US/0021-9568
JOURNAL OF CHEMICAL AND ENGINEERING DATA. [J. chem. eng. data]. **Added/Corp** American Chemical Society. Vol. 4 (Jan. 1959)-. Periodical. English. bm. $395.00 (institution) US. American Chemical Society, 1155 Sixteenth Street Northwest, Washington DC 20036. **Tel** (800)333-9511, (800)227-5558, (614)447-3776, FAX (202)833-7736. **(Subscription address:** American Chemical Society / Ohio, Department L 0011, Columbus OH 43268-0011.**) ED** Bruno J. Zwolinski. **DD** 540. **NLM** W1 JO58J. **CODEN** JCEAAX. **[CCC].** Index available (free). **Bk Rev. Ad Acc. Pr Rev. Acid Free. Circ:** 1,785 (ctrl). available on microfilm and microfiche from University Microfilms International (UMI). Documents available from Article Express International, The Genuine Article, Petroleum Abstracts Document Delivery Service, CASDDS. ***Continues*** *I/E C. Industrial and Engineering Chemistry. Chemical and Engineering Data Series, 0095-9146.*
Desc: Experimental data relating to pure compounds of mixtures covering a range of states, manuscripts of published experimental information making tangible contributions, and experimental data aiding in identifying or utilizing new organic or inorganic compounds.
Ind/Abst Abstr. Bull. Inst. Pap. Sci. Tech.; Appl. Sci. Technol. Index; AQUAREF; Bioeng. Abstr.; Ceram. Abstr.; Chem Inform; Chem. Abstr.; Coal Abstr.; Curr. Chem. React.; Curr. Contents Eng. Tech. Appl. Sci.; Curr. Contents Phys. Chem. Earth Sci.; Ei Page One; Energy Inf. Abstr.; Energy Res. Abstr.; Eng. Index Annu.; Gas Abstr.; GeoRef; Index Chem.; INIS Atomindex [Micro.]; Int. Aerosp. Abstr.; Leadscan; Lit. Pat. Abstr., Oilfield Chem. (1959-); Lit. Abstr., Catal. Catal.; Lit. Abstr., Health Environ.; Lit. Abstr., Pet. Refin. Petrochem.; Lit. Abstr., Pet. Substit.; Lit. Abstr., Transp. Storage; Pet. Abstr.; Proc. Chem. Eng.; Res. Alert [Full Cov.]; Sci. Cit. Index; SCISEARCH; Soils Fert.; Theoret. Chem. Eng.

JA/0021-9592
JOURNAL OF CHEMICAL ENGINEERING OF JAPAN. [J. chem. eng. Jpn.]. **Added/Corp** Kagaku Kogaku Kyokai. Vol. 1 (Feb. 1968)-. Periodical. English. bm. $264.00. Society of Chemical Engineers, Kyoritsu Kaikan, 6-19, Kohinata 4 chome, Bunkyoku, Tokyo 112 Japan. **(Subscription address:** Maruzen Company Ltd., PO Box 5050, Import & Export Department, Tokyo 100 31 Japan.**) LC** TP1; .J68. **DD** 660/.2/05. **CODEN** JCEJAQ. **[CCC].** cum. index. **Pr Rev.** ctrl circ. Documents available from Article Express International, The Genuine Article, CASDDS. ***Supersedes*** *Kagaku Kogaku. Chemical Engineering, Japan.*
Desc: Provides chemical engineers an international forum for presentation of original papers and short communications, from fundamentals to practical application, having immediate or potential value in chemical engineering.
Ind/Abst Bioeng. Abstr.; Chem. Abstr.; Chem. Hazards Ind.; Chem. Titles; Civ. Struct. Eng. Abstr.; Coal Abstr.; Comput. Inf. Syst. Abstr. J. [Full Cov.]; Curr. Biotechnol.; Curr. Contents Eng. Tech. Appl. Sci.; Ei Page One; Elect. Comm. Abstr.; EMBASE; Energy Res. Abstr. (July 1976-); Eng. Index Annu.; Environ. Eng. Abstr.; Fluid Abstr., Civil Eng.; Fluid Abstr. Proc. Eng.; FLUIDEX (1973-); Gas Abstr.; HTFS Dig.; Int. Aerosp. Abstr.; Lab. Hazards Bull.; Leadscan; Lit. Pat. Abstr., Oilfield Chem. (1969-); Lit. Abstr., Catal. Catal.; Lit. Abstr., Health Environ.; Lit. Abstr., Pet. Refin. Petrochem.; Lit. Abstr., Pet. Substit.; Lit. Abstr., Transp. Storage; Manuf. Process Eng. Abstr.; Mater. Sci. Eng. Abstr.; Mech. Eng. Abstr.; MINPROC; PESTDOC; Proc. Chem. Eng.; Res. Alert [Full Cov.]; Sci. Cit. Index; SCISEARCH; Solid State Supercond. Abstr.; Theoret. Chem. Eng.

CC/1000-9027
JOURNAL OF CHEMICAL INDUSTRY AND ENGINEERING (CHINA). ***Ceased.*** [J. chem. ind. eng., China]. **Added/Corp** Chung-Kuo Hua Kung Hsueh Hui. **VFOAT** Hua Kung Hsueh Pao. Vol. 1, No. 1 (1986)-Vol. 6 (1991). Periodical. English (translations available in Chinese). Twice a year. Pergamon Press Inc., 660 White Plains Road, Tarrytown NY 10591-5153. **Tel** (914)524-9200, FAX (914)333-2444, telex 13-7328. **(Subscription address:** UK/ Headington Hill Hall, Oxford OX3 0BW; Can/ 150 Consumers Road/Suite 104, Willowdale Ontario M2J 1P9; Aus-NZ/ PO Box 544, Potts Point NSW 2011**) LC** TP1; .H84. **DD** 660.2/09. **[CCC].**
Desc: Features achievements in areas of chemical industries and engineering in China with a view to promoting scientific interchange between China and the rest of the world.
Ind/Abst Gas Abstr.

UK/0147-698X
JOURNAL OF POWDER & BULK SOLIDS TECHNOLOGY. ***Ceased.*** [J. powder bulk solids technol.]. **VAT** Journal of Powder and Bulk Solids Technology. Vol. 1 (Summer 1977)-(19??). Academic Scholarly Publication. English. ir (4 times a year). Childwall University Press Ltd, PO Box 78, London NW11 0PG England. **Tel** 011 41 81 14551040, telex 8954242 POWDER G. **ED** A S Goldberg. **LC** TA418.78; .J58. **DD** 620/.43/05. **CODEN** JPBTDX. **Bk Rev. Ad Acc.** ctrl circ. Documents available from Article Express International, CASDDS.
Desc: Original research, review and industrial technology papers on all aspects of powders, particles, and bulk solids.
Ind/Abst Bioeng. Abstr.; Ceram. Abstr.; Chem. Abstr.; Coal Abstr.; Ei Page One; Eng. Index Annu.; Gas Abstr. (?-?); Proc. Chem. Eng.; Theoret. Chem. Eng.

CH/0368-1653
JOURNAL OF THE CHINESE INSTITUTE OF CHEMICAL ENGINEERS. [J. Chin. Inst. Chem. Eng.]. **Main/Corp** Chinese Institute of Chemical Engineers. **Added/Corp** Chung Kuo Hua Hsuih Kung Cheng Hsueh Hui. Vol. 1, (Nov. 1970)-. Periodical. English (Chinese). Six times a year (Jan., Mar., May, July, Sept., Nov.). NT$24.00 (individual), NT$48.00 (institutions). Chemical Engineering Department, National Tsing Jua University, Hsinchu 300 Taiwan. **Tel** 011 886 35 715131 Ext. 3619. **ED** Chan Jen Lee. **CODEN** JCICAP. Index available. cum. index. **Circ:** 850 (ctrl). Documents available from Article Express International, CASDDS.
Desc: Devoted to theoretical development and research in chemical engineering and allied branches of engineering and science.
Ind/Abst Bioeng. Abstr.; Chem. Abstr.; Curr. Biotechnol.; Ei Page One; Eng. Index Annu.; Proc. Chem. Eng.; Stat. Theory Method Abstr. (1983); Theoret. Chem. Eng.

II/0020-3351
JOURNAL OF THE INSTITUTION OF ENGINEERS. INDIA. PART CH: CHEMICAL ENGINEERING DIVISION. (JOURNAL OF THE INSTITUTION OF ENGINEERS (INDIA). CHEMICAL ENGINEERING DIVISION.). [J. Inst. Eng., India, Part CH]. **Main/Corp** Institutions of Engineers (India). **Added/Corp** Institution of Engineers (India). Chemical Engineering Division. **VFOAT** Chemical Engineering Division; IE (I) Journal-CH. Vol. 41 (June 1961)-. Periodical. English. Three times a year. $30.00. Institution of Engineers India, 8 Gokhale Road, Calcutta 700020 India. **Tel** 011 91 33 288311, telex 21 7885 IEIC IN. **LC** TP1; .J7. **DD** 660/.05. **CODEN** JECEAF. Documents available from CASDDS. ***Continues in part*** *Journal of the Institution of Engineers (India), 0368-2498.*
Ind/Abst Chem. Abstr.; Coal Abstr.; Curr. Biotechnol.; Ei Page One; Energy Res. Abstr.

JA/0011-3271
KAGAKU GIJUTSU BUNKEN SOKUHO. KAGAKU. KAGAKU KOGYO HEN : KOKUNAI-HEN. **See** Engineering-Abstracting, Bibliographies and Statistics.

JA/0375-9253
KAGAKU KOGAKU. [Kagaku kogaku]. **Added/Corp** Kagaku Kogaku Kyokai (Japan). **VFOAT** Chemical Engineering. Vol. 17, No. 1 (1953)-. Periodical. Japanese (English). mo. Kagaku Kogaku Kyokai, c/o Kyoritsu Kaikan 6-19, Obinata 4-chome, Bunkyo-ku 112, Tokyo Japan. **CODEN** KKGKA4. Documents available from CASDDS. ***Continues*** *Kagaku Kikai.*
Ind/Abst Chem. Abstr.

JA/0386-216X
KAGAKU KOGAKU RONBUNSHU. (KAGAKU KOGAKU ROMBUN SHU. KAGAKU KOGAKU RONBUNSHU.). [Kagaku kogaku ronbunshu]. **Added/Corp** Kagaku Kogaku Kyokai. **VFOAT** Kagaku Kogaku Ronbunshu. (197?)-. Academic Scholarly Publication. Japanese (summaries and/or abstracts in English). bm (6 issues). $348.00. Kagaku Kogaku Kyokai, c/o Kyoritsu Kaikan 6-19, Obinata 4-chome, Bunkyo-ku 112, Tokyo Japan. **(Subscription address:** Japan Publications Trading Company, Ltd., PO Box 5030, Tokyo International, Tokyo 100-31 Japan.**) LC** TP1; .K26. **CODEN** KKRBAW. **Pr Rev.** Documents available from The Genuine Article, CASDDS.
Ind/Abst Biodeter. Abstr.; Chem. Abstr.; Coal Abstr.; Curr. Contents Eng. Tech. Appl. Sci.; Res. Alert [Full Cov.]; Sci. Cit. Index; SCISEARCH.

JA/0451-2014
KAGAKU KOGYO. [Kagaku kogyo]. **VFOAT** Chemical Industry. V. 1, No. 1, (March 1950)-. Academic Scholarly Publication. Japanese (Japanese). mo. Kagaku Kogyosha, (Kagaku Kogyosha, Inc.), 5-9, Sendagaya 4 Chome, Shibuyaku, Tokyoto 151 Japan. **CODEN** KAKOAY. Documents available from CASDDS.
Ind/Abst Chem. Abstr.; Coal Abstr.; Curr. Biotechnol.

JA/0387-1037
KEMIKARU ENGINIYARINGU. [Kemikaru enginiyaringu]. **VFOAT** Chemical Engineering. (1955)-. Periodical. Japanese. mo. Kagaku Kogyosha, (Kagaku Kogyosha, Inc.), 5-9, Sendagaya 4 Chome, Shibuyaku, Tokyoto 151 Japan. **LC** TP155; .K45. **CODEN** KEENAT. Documents available from CASDDS.
Ind/Abst Chem. Abstr.

KO/0256-1115
KOREAN JOURNAL OF CHEMICAL ENGINEERING, THE. **Added/Corp** Hanguk Hwahak Konghakhoe. Vol. 1, No. 1 (Mar. 1984)-. Periodical. English. qt. $17.90 Korea; $43.00 Japan; $35.00 other. Korean Institute of Chemical Engineers, 307 Regent River V 547 8 KUI, Seoul 133 200 Korea. **Tel** 011 82 2 4583078, 4583079. Documents available from The Genuine Article, CASDDS.
Ind/Abst Chem. Abstr.; Curr. Contents Eng. Tech. Appl. Sci.; HTFS Dig.; Res. Alert [Select. Cov.]; SCISEARCH.

AG/0327-0793
LATIN AMERICAN APPLIED RESEARCH. **Added/Corp** Asociacion Argentina de Investigadores en Ciencias de la Ingenieria Quimica y Quimica Aplicada. Comite Argentino de Transferencia de Calor y Materia. Centro Latino-Americano de Transferencia de Calor y Materia. **VFOAT** Pesquisa Aplicada Latino Americana; Investigacion Aplicada Latinoamericana. Vol. 18, No. 1 (1988)-. Academic Scholarly Publication. English (Portuguese and Spanish). qt. $80.00. Latin American Applied Research, Casilla 717, 8000 Bahia Blanca Argentina. **Tel** 011 54 91 4231602, FAX 011 51 91 25764. **ED** Esteban A Brignole. **CODEN** LAARE8. Index available. **Bk Rev. Circ:** 450. Documents available from CASDDS. ***Formed by the union of*** *Revista Latinoamericana de Ingenieria Quimica y Quimica Aplicada, 0325-0474* ***and*** *Revista Latinoamericana de Transferencia de Calor y Materia, 0325-4011.*
Desc: Seeks to provide a central vehicle for exchange of basic ideas in heat and/or mass transfer, thermodynamics and energy related problems between research workers, particularly Latin American countries.
Ind/Abst Chem. Abstr.

UK/0097-2312
LOSS PREVENTION. ***Title Change.*** [Loss prev.]. Vol. 1 (1967)-. English. bm. Institute of Chemical Engineers, 165-171 Railway Terrace, Rugby CY21 3HQ England. **Tel** 0788 578214, 0788 560833, telex 311780. **ED** Bernard M Hancock. **LC** TP149; .L69A. **DD** 660.2/804. **CODEN** LOPVAJ. Index available. cum. index. **Bk Rev. Circ:** 1,200 (ctrl). Documents available from Article Express International, CASDDS. ***Absorbed by*** *Plant Operations Progress, 0278-4513.*
Desc: Articles and case studies on chemical process engineering, hazards and consequences of fire, explosion, releases, emergency procedures and all aspects of maintenance and operations.
Ind/Abst Bioeng. Abstr.; Chem. Abstr. (1967-1981); Chem. Hazards Ind.; Ei Page One; Eng. Index Annu.; Lab. Hazards Bull.

UK/0260-9576
LOSS PREVENTION BULLETIN. **See** Industrial Health and Safety.

US/0197-3967
MANAGING CORROSION WITH PLASTICS. [Managing corros. plast.]. **Main/Conf** Intersociety Plastics Seminar. **Added/Corp** National Association of Corrosion Engineers. Vol. 1/2/3 (1977)-. Academic Scholarly Publication. English. ir. Price varies per volume. National Association of Corrosion Engineers, 1440 South Creek Drive, Houston TX 77084. **Tel** (713)492-0535, FAX (713)492-8254, telex 792310 NACE HOU. **(Subscription address:** National Association of Corrosion Engineers, PO Box 218340, Houston, TX 77084) **LC** TA455.P5; M34. **DD** 620.1/1223. **CODEN** MCWPDY. Documents available from CASDDS.
Ind/Abst Chem. Abstr. (1977-1979).

US
MARCO POLYMER NOTES. English. mo. $895.00 (one year), $1,611.00 (two year), $2,285.00 (three year). Technomic Publishing Company, Inc., 851 New Holland Avenue, Box 3535, Lancaster PA 17604. **Tel** (717)291-5609, (800)233-9936, FAX (717)295-4538.

US/0148-0529
MATERIALS PERFORMANCE : CORROSION ENGINEERING BUYER'S GUIDE. ***Title Change.*** **VFOAT** Corrosion Engineering Buyer's Guide. English. National Association of Corrosion Engineers, 1440 South Creek Drive, Houston TX 77084. **Tel** (713)492-0535, FAX (713)492-8254, telex 792310 NACE HOU. **LC** TA462; .M3685. **DD** 338.4/7/6201122302573. ***Continues*** *Materials Performance Buyer's Guide, 0095-7976.* ***Continued by*** *NACE Corrosion Engineering Buyer's Guide.*
Ind/Abst Soils Fert.

US
MEETING PAPERS ON MICROFICHE. **Main/Corp** American Institute of Chemical Engineers. (19??)-. English. Three times a year. $270.00 (complete set). American Institute of Chemical Engineers, 345 East 47th Street, New York NY 10017. **Tel** (212)705-7663, (212)705-7703, FAX (212)705-8400.
Desc: Unedited papers presented at AICHE meetings.

CN/1184-0218
MEMBERSHIP DIRECTORY / CANADIAN SOCIETY FOR CHEMICAL ENGINEERING. [Membsh. dir. - Can. Soc. Chem. Eng.]. **Main/Corp** Canadian Society for Chemical Engineering. **VFOAT** Repertoire des Membres; CSChE Membership Directory; Repertoire des Membres SCGCh. **VAT** Repertoire des Membres - Societe Canadienne du Genie Chimique. (Sept. 1990)-. Directory. English (French). Free to members. Canadian Society for Chemical Engineering, 151 Slater Street, Ottawa K1P 5H3 Canada. **DD** 660/.025/71.

US/0890-5444
MEMBRANCE SEPARATION ENGINEERING. ***Ceased.*** **See** Engineering-Civil Engineering.

FR/0026-1084
METAUX, CORROSION - INDUSTRIE. ***Suspended.*** [Met. Corros. ind.]. Vol. 41, No. 485 (Jan. 1966)-Suspended Nov-Dec 1989. Periodical. French. mo. Editions Metaux, 32 rue du Marechal Joffre, 78100 St Germn en Laye France. **Tel** 33 3 451 6211. ***Continues*** *Metaux, Corrision - Industries.*
Ind/Abst Energy Res. Abstr.

UK/0955-7059
MIXING AND SEPARATION TECHNOLOGY ABSTRACTS. ***Title Change.*** **Added/Corp** BHRA (Association). Vol. 1 (1989)-(19??). Periodical. English. qt. STI, 4 Kings Meadow, Ferry Hinksey Road, Oxford OX2 0DU United Kingdom. **Tel** (0865) 798898, FAX (0865) 798788. **ED** L S Gale. ***Merged with*** *Fluid Flow Measurements Abstracts, 0305-9235; Fluid Power Abstracts, 0015-4644; Fluid Sealing Abstracts, 0015-4660; Pipelines Abstracts, 0265-3990; Pumps and Other Fluids Machinery Abstracts, 0302-2870; Solid-liquid Flow Abstracts, 0038-1063* ***and*** *Computer-aided Process Control Abstracts, 0955-4319* ***to form*** *Fluid Abstracts. Process Engineering, 0962-7162.*

JA/0386-5495
MOL. (KAGAKU GIJUTSUSHI MOL.). [MOL]. **VFOAT** MOL Journal; Kagaku Gijutsushi M.O.L.; Kagaku Gijutsushi. (1963)-. Academic Scholarly Publication. Japanese. mo. $160.00. **(Subscription address:** Kyowa Book Company Inc., 1 38 Kanda Jinbocho Chiyoda-ku, Tokyo 101 Japan.) **ED** Isao Ishikawa. **CODEN** KGMOAI. **Ad Acc.** ctrl circ. Documents available from CASDDS.
Desc: Journal for the engineer and researcher in manufacturing, research and development, engineering, maintenance, control of various industries concerned with chemical industry and chemical technology.
Ind/Abst Chem. Abstr.; Coal Abstr.

US/0730-9155
MOLY CORROSION INHIBITORS. (MOLY CORROSION INHIBITORS : AN AMAX NEWSLETTER.). [Moly corros. inhib.]. Vol. 1, No. 1 (Oct. 1981)-. Newsletter. English. ir. Free. Climax Molybdenum Company, One Greenwich Plaza, Greenwich CT 06830. **Tel** (203)629-6474. **Circ:** 10,000 (ctrl).
Desc: This publication describes use of molybdenum chemicals as corrosion inhibitors, among applications such as water treatment, engine coolants, synthetic metalworking, fluids and oilfield fluids.

US
NACE CORROSION ENGINEERING BUYER'S GUIDE : OFFICIAL PUBLICATION OF NACE. **Added/Corp** National Association of Corrosion Engineers. **VFOAT** Corrosion Engineering Buyer's Guide. **VAT** National Association of Corrosion Engineers Corrosion Engineering Buyer's Guide. (19??)-. English. be. $18.00. National Association of Corrosion Engineers, 1440 South Creek Drive, Houston TX 77084. **Tel** (713)492-0535, FAX (713)492-8254, telex 792310 NACE HOU. **(Subscription address:** National Association of Corrosion Engineers, PO Box 218340, Houston, TX 77084) **Ad Acc. Circ:** 16,000 (ctrl). ***Continues*** *Material Performance: Corrosion Engineering Buyer's Guide.*

IR/1011-3509
NASHRIYYAH-I SHIMI VA-MUHANDISI-I SHIMI-I IRAN. **See** Chemistry.

US
NATIONAL MEETING; PROGRAM. **Main/Corp** American Institute of Chemical Engineers. (19??)-. English. an. Free. American Institute of Chemical Engineers, 345 East 47th Street, New York NY 10017. **Tel** (212)705-7663, (212)705-7703, FAX (212)705-8400.
Desc: Contains program information for the national meeting and information on continuing education courses offered by the Institute.

US/0030-1442
OIL MILL GAZETTEER. [Oil mill gazet.]. **Added/Corp** International Oil Mill Superintendents. Tri-States Oil Mill Superintendents Association. (19??)-. Periodical. English. Twelve times a year. $13.00 US; $20.00 other. Oil Mill Gazetteer, PO Box 590483, Houston TX 77259. **Tel** (713)480-7889, FAX (713)334-4619. **ED** Paula Kolmar. **CODEN** OMGAAW. cum. index. **Ad Acc. Circ:** 1,300.
Desc: Contains information on oilseed processing.
Ind/Abst BioBusiness (1988-); Food Sci. Technol. Abstr.; Rice Abstr.

US
OZONE CHEMISTRY AND TECHNOLOGY. **Added/Corp** Franklin Institute. Science Information Services. Vol. 14 No. 1 (1975)-. Periodical. English. bw. Franklin Institute Press, PO Box 2266, Philadelphia PA 19103.
Ind/Abst Pollut. Abstr. Indexes.

US
PAPER - CORROSION. **Main/Conf** Corrosion (Conference). **Added/Corp** National Association of Corrosion Engineers. (19??)-. Monographic series. English. Price varies per volume. NACE, PO Box 986, Katy TX 77450.

US
PAPERS PRESENTED AT THE SHORT COURSE IN PAINT TECHNOLOGY. **Main/Corp** Florida. University, Gainesville. Dept. of Chemical Engineering. **Added/Corp** Florida. University, Gainesville. Dept. of Chemistry. (Jan. 28/Feb. 1, 1957)-. English. $20.00. Chemical Engineering Education, University of Florida, Department of Chemical Engineering, Gainesville FL 32611. **Tel** (904)392-0861. **ED** R W Fahien. **LC** TA1; .F62. **DD** 667.6082. **Bk Rev. Ad Acc. Circ:** 1,850 (ctrl).
Desc: Articles by and for chemical engineering educators concerning courses, research, and developments in the field of chemical engineering.

US/0272-6351
PARTICULATE SCIENCE AND TECHNOLOGY. [Part. sci. technol.]. **Added/Corp** Fine Particle Society. Fine Particle Society. Proceedings of the Fine Particle Society. Vol. 1, No. 1 (Jan.-March 1983)-. Academic Scholarly Publication. English. qt. £108.00 UK; $179.00 other. Taylor & Francis Ltd., Rankine Road, Basingstoke Hampshire, RG24 8PR United Kingdom. **Tel** 011 44 256 840366, FAX 011 44 256 479438, telex 858540. **(Subscription address:** Taylor & Francis Inc., 1900 Frost Road, Suite 101, Bristol PA 19007-1598.) **LC** TP156.P3; P368. **DD** 620/.43/05. **CODEN** PTCHDS. **[CCC].** Index available. **Bk Rev. Ad Acc. Pr Rev. Circ:** 600. available on microfilm and microfiche from University Microfilms International (UMI). Documents available from CASDDS.
Desc: Covers both theoretical and applied aspects of particle sizing, morphology, physicochemical properties, fluid-particle and particle-particle separation, mixing, solids handling and storage, particle formation and production, agglomeration, instrumentation, and health hazards. This refereed publication will be of interest to persons working in both the theoretical and applied aspects of this field.
Ind/Abst Alum. Ind. Abstr.; Chem. Abstr. (1983-); Ei Page One; Health Saf. Sci. Abstr.; Met. Abstr.; Pollut. Abstr. Indexes; Proc. Chem. Eng.; Theoret. Chem. Eng.

HU/0324-5853
PERIODICA POLYTECHNICA. CHEMICAL ENGINEERING. HIMIJA. (PERIODICA POLYTECHNICA. CHEMICAL ENGINEERING. KHIMIIA.). [Period. polytech., Chem. eng., Him.]. **Added/Corp** Budapesti Muszaki Egyetem. **VFOAT** Chemical Engineering. Khimiia; Chemical Engineering. Chemisches Ingenieurwesen. (1957)-. English (German and Russian). qt. $12.00. **(Subscription address:** Kultura, PO Box 149, H 1389 Budapest 62 Hungary.) **LC** TP1; .P4. **DD** 660/.05. **CODEN** PDPTAE. Documents available from Article Express International, CASDDS.
Ind/Abst Alum. Ind. Abstr.; Bioeng. Abstr.; Ceram. Abstr.; Chem Inform; Chem. Abstr.; Ei Page One; Eng. Index Annu. [Select. Cov.]; Fluid Abstr., Civil Eng.; Fluid Abstr. Proc. Eng.; FLUIDEX (19??-); Int. Civil Eng. Abstr.; Met. Abstr.; Proc. Chem. Eng.; Soft. Abstr. Eng.; Theoret. Chem. Eng.; World Surf. Coat. Abstr.

US/0278-4513
PLANT/OPERATIONS PROGRESS. ***Title Change.*** [Plant/oper. prog.]. **Added/Corp** American Institute of Chemical Engineers. **VFOAT** Plant Operations Progress. **VAT** Plant Operations Progress. Vol. 1, No. 1 (Jan. 1982)-(1992). Academic Scholarly Publication. English. qt. American Institute of Chemical Engineers, 345 East 47th Street, New York NY 10017. **Tel** (212)705-7663, (212)705-7703, FAX (212)705-8400. **ED** T A Ventrone. **LC** TP155.6; .P56. **DD** 660.2/8/0068. **CODEN** POPPDE. **[CCC]. Ad Acc. Circ:** 1,400. available on microfilm and microfiche from University Microfilms International (UMI). Documents available from Article Express International, CASDDS. ***Absorbed*** *Loss Prevention, 0097-2312.* ***Continued by*** *Process Safety Progress, 1066-8527.*
Desc: Contains technical papers and reports presenting new techniques and advances in the promotion of loss prevention and efficient plant operation.
Ind/Abst Chem. Abstr.; Chem. Hazards Ind.; Eng. Index Annu.; Environ. Eng. Abstr.; Fluid Abstr., Civil Eng.; Fluid Abstr. Proc. Eng.; FLUIDEX (199?-); HTFS Dig.; Lab. Hazards Bull.; Lit. Pat. Abstr., Oilfield Chem. (1982-); Lit. Abstr., Catal. Catal.; Lit. Abstr., Health Environ.; Lit. Abstr., Pet. Refin. Petrochem.; Lit. Abstr., Pet. Substit.; Lit. Abstr., Transp. Storage; Mech. Eng. Abstr.; Proc. Chem. Eng.; Risk Abstr.; Theoret. Chem. Eng.

US/0272-4324
PLASMA CHEMISTRY AND PLASMA PROCESSING. [Plasma chem. plasma process.]. Vol. 1, No. 1 (March 1981)-. Academic Scholarly Publication. English. Four times a year. $325.00 US; $380.00 other. Plenum Press, 233 Spring Street, New York NY 10013-1578. **Tel** (212)620-8000, (800)221-9369, FAX (212)463-0742, (212)807-1047, telex 23/421139. **ED** E. Pfender and S. Veprek. **LC** QD581; .P62. **DD** 541/.0424. **CODEN** PCPPDW. **[CCC].** Index available. **Pr Rev.** available on microfilm and microfiche from University Microfilms International (UMI). Documents available from Article Express International, The Genuine Article, Ask*IEEE, CASDDS.
Desc: International journal for the publication of original papers on fundamental research and new developments in plasma chemistry and plasma processing.
Ind/Abst Bioeng. Abstr.; Chem. Abstr.; Curr. Contents Eng. Tech. Appl. Sci.; Curr. Contents Phys. Chem. Earth Sci.; Ei Page One; Energy Res. Abstr. (Feb. 1982-); Eng. Index Annu.; INSPEC (March 1983-); Life Sci. Collect. (1985-); Res. Alert [Full Cov.]; Sci. Cit. Index; SCISEARCH.

PL
POLISH JOURNAL OF APPLIED CHEMISTRY. **Added/Corp** Polska Akademia Nauk. Komitet Nauk Chemicznych. Vol. 135 No. 1/2 (1991)-. Periodical. English. qt. $78.00. **(Subscription address:** ARS Polona, PO Box 1001, 00068 Warsaw Poland.) **LC** TP1; .C3178. **CODEN** PJACE2. ***Continues*** *Chemia Stosowana.*

●UK/0966-7822
POLYMER GELS AND NETWORKS. Vol. 1, No. 1 (1993)-. Academic Scholarly Publication. English. Four times a year. $254.00 The Americas; £170.00 other. Elsevier Applied Science, An Imprint of Elsevier Science Ltd., The Boulevard, Langford Lane, Kidlington, Oxford OX5 1GB United Kingdom. **Tel** 011 44 865 843000, 011 44 865 843699, FAX 011 44 865 843010. **(Subscription address:** Elsevier Science Ltd. Oxford Fulfillment Centre, PO Box 800, Kidlington, Oxford OX5 1DX United Kingdom.) **ED** T. Tanaka. **LC** QD549.2.P64; P65. **DD** 547.7. **CODEN** PGNEEI. **[CCC].** Documents available from CASDDS.
Desc: Provides a venue for publication of research results dealing with the structure and properties of these materials.
Ind/Abst Chem. Abstr.

US/0360-2559
POLYMER-PLASTICS TECHNOLOGY AND ENGINEERING (SOFTCOVER ED.). (POLYMER-PLASTICS TECHNOLOGY AND ENGINEERING.). [Polym.-plast. technol. eng.]. **VFOAT** Polymer-Plastics. (19??)-. Academic Scholarly Publication. English. bm. $795.00 US; $816.00 other. Marcel Dekker Inc., 270 Madison Avenue, New York NY 10016. **Tel** (212)696-9000, (800)228-1160, FAX

(212)685-4540, telex 421419. **(Subscription address:** Marcel Dekker Inc, PO Box 5017, Monticello NY 12701.) **ED** Nicholas P. Cheremisinoff. **DD** 668. **CODEN** PPTEC7. **[CCC]. Bk Rev. Ad Acc.** available on microfiche. Documents available from Article Express International, The Genuine Article, Ask*IEEE, CASDDS. ***Absorbed*** *Polymer Process Engineering, 0735-7931.*
Desc: Includes original articles, state-of-the-art reviews, abstracts, notes, and letters on topics such as developing non-solution based polymerization processes; new generation catalysts for producing ultra-narrow molecular weight distribution polymers; reactor design and catalyst technology for compositional control of polymers; advanced manufacturing techniques and equipment; analytical tools for characterizing molecular properties, and other timely subjects.
Ind/Abst Appl. Mech. Rev. (1989-); Chem. Abstr. (1989-); Curr. Contents Eng. Tech. Appl. Sci.; EMBASE (1989-); Eng. Index Annu.; INSPEC (1989-); Polymer Contents; Res. Alert [Full Cov.]; SCISEARCH; Soc. Sci. Cit. Index [Select. Cov.].

SZ/0032-5910
POWDER TECHNOLOGY. [Powder technol.]. Vol. 1 (Feb. 1967)-. Periodical. English (French and German). Twelve times a year (4 vols.). 1720.00F. Elsevier Sequoia SA, PO Box 564, CH-1001 Lausanne 1 Switzerland. **Tel** 011 41 21 3207381. **ED** R. Clift. **LC** TP156.P3; P63. **CODEN** POTEBX. **[CCC]. Ad Acc, Adv Mgr:** Ms. W van Cattenburch (Amsterdam). **Pr Rev.** available on microfilm and microfiche from University Microfilms International (UMI). Documents available from Article Express International, The Genuine Article, Ask*IEEE, CASDDS.
Desc: An international journal on the science and technology of wet and dry particulate systems. It publishes papers on all aspects of the formation of particles and their characterization and on the study of systems containing particulate solids.
Ind/Abst Alum. Ind. Abstr.; Anal. Abstr.; Bioeng. Abstr.; Ceram. Abstr.; Chem. Abstr.; Chem. Hazards Ind.; Civ. Struct. Eng. Abstr.; Coal Abstr.; Comput. Inf. Syst. Abstr. J. [Full Cov.]; Curr. Contents, Agric. Biol. Environ. Sci.; Dairy Sci. Abstr.; Ei Page One; Energy Res. Abstr.; Eng. Mater. Abstr.; Eng. Index Annu.; Environ. Eng. Abstr.; Fluid Abstr., Civil Eng.; Fluid Abstr. Proc. Eng.; FLUIDEX (1973-); Gas Abstr.; GeoRef; HTFS Dig.; INSPEC (Sept. 1969-); Int. Aerosp. Abstr.; Lab. Hazards Bull.; Manuf. Process Eng. Abstr.; Mater. Sci. Eng. Abstr.; Mech. Eng. Abstr.; Met. Abstr.; MINPROC; Phys. Briefs; Proc. Chem. Eng.; Res. Alert [Full Cov.]; Sci. Cit. Index; SCISEARCH; Solid State Supercond. Abstr.; Sug. Indus. Abstr.; Theoret. Chem. Eng.; World Ceram. Abstr.; World Surf. Coat. Abstr.

SP
PREVIEW OF THE INSTITUTO NACIONAL DE HIDROCARBUROS ANNUAL REPORT FOR ... . See Public Administration.

US/0066-538X
PROCEEDINGS OF THE ... ANNUAL APPALACHIAN UNDERGROUND CORROSION SHORT COURSE. [Proc. annu. Appalach. Undergr.Corros. Short Course]. **Main/Conf** Appalachian Underground Corrosion Short Course. **Added/Corp** West Virginia University. Engineering Experiment Station. 1st (1956)-. Monographic series. English. an. Price varies per volume. AUCSC West Virginia University Mining Extension Service, Morgantown WV 26506. **Tel** (304)293-4212. **ED** Angela J. Durham. **LC** TA462; .A69a; T7; .W3 subser. **DD** 620.1/1223. **CODEN** PUCCEL. **Circ:** 1,400.
Desc: Provides both technical and non-technical presentations of the practical and theoretical aspects of corrosion.
Ind/Abst GeoRef.

UK/0144-8846
PROCEEDINGS OF THE ... EUROPEAN CONFERENCE ON MIXING. (PROCEEDINGS.). [Proc. Eur. Conf. Mix.]. **Added/Corp** BHRA (Association). (1977)-. Academic Scholarly Publication. English. **CODEN** PECMD6. Documents available from CASDDS. ***Continues*** *European Conference on Mixing and Centrifugal Separation. Proceedings.*
Ind/Abst Chem. Abstr. (1977-1982).

US/0074-4123
PROCEEDINGS OF THE INTERNATIONAL CONGRESS ON METALLIC CORROSION. Added/Corp National Association of Corrosion Engineers. 1st (1961)-. Proceedings. English. ir. Price varies per volume. National Association of Corrosion Engineers, 1440 South Creek Drive, Houston TX 77084. **Tel** (713)492-0535, FAX (713)492-8254, telex 792310 NACE HOU. **(Subscription address:** National Association of Corrosion Engineers, PO Box 218340, Houston, TX 77084) **LC** TA462; .I61.

JA/0368-3141
PROCEEDINGS OF THE JAPAN CONGRESS ON MATERIALS RESEARCH. See Engineering.

US/0197-727X
PROCEEDINGS - PACIFIC CHEMICAL ENGINEERING CONGRESS. [Proc. - Pac. Chem. Eng. Congr.]. **Main/Conf** Pacific Chemical Engineering Congress. **VFOAT** Pacific Chemical Engineering Congress. Academic Scholarly Publication. English. ir. **CODEN** PCEPDB. Documents available from CASDDS.
Ind/Abst Chem. Abstr.

US
PROCEEDINGS / THE INSTITUTE FOR BRIQUETTING AND AGGLOMERATION. Main/Corp Institute for Briquetting and Agglomeration. Biennial Conference. **VFOAT** IBA Proceedings. (1977)-. Academic Scholarly Publication. English. be (Publishes every two years). $35.00 (members); $50.00 (non-members). Institute for Briquetting and Agglomeration, 179 Riverview Acres Road, Hudson WI 54016. **Tel** (715)549-6342. Documents available from CASDDS. ***Continues*** *Institute for Briquetting and Agglomeration. Biennial Conference. Proceedings of the Biennial Conference, 0145-8701.*
Ind/Abst Chem. Abstr.

UK/0960-5045
PROCESS AND CHEMICAL ENGINEERING. See Engineering-Abstracting, Bibliographies and Statistics.

II
PROCESS & PLANT ENGINEERING. VFOAT Process and Plant Engineering. (19??)-. Periodical. English. qt. $75.00. Shanvik Publications, Bombay, India. **(Subscription address:** Prints India, 11 Darya Ganj, New Delhi 110002 India.) **LC** TP155.5; .P75.

UK
PROCESS BIOCHEMISTRY. Vol. 26 No. 1 (Feb. 1991)-. Academic Scholarly Publication. English. Eight times a year. $388.00 The Americas; £260.00 other. Elsevier Applied Science, An Imprint of Elsevier Science Ltd., The Boulevard, Langford Lane, Kidlington, Oxford OX5 1GB United Kingdom. **Tel** 011 44 865 843000, 011 44 865 843699, FAX 011 44 865 843010. **(Subscription address:** Elsevier Science Ltd. Oxford Fulfillment Centre, PO Box 800, Kidlington, Oxford OX5 1DX United Kingdom.) **ED** C.M. Brown. **LC** TP248.13; .P76. **NLM** W1; PR588AB. **CODEN** PBCHE5. Documents available from The Genuine Article, CASDDS. ***Continues*** *Process Biochemistry International, 0963-4940.*
Desc: Industry-orientated research journal devoted to reporting advances in the science and technology of the application of living organisms to the production of materials for the benefit of mankind.
Ind/Abst BioBusiness; Chem. Abstr.; Curr. Aware. Biol. Sci., CABS; PESTDOC; Res. Alert [Full Cov.]; Sci. Cit. Index; SCISEARCH.

US/0924-3089
PROCESS CONTROL & QUALITY. [Process control qual.]. Vol. 1, No. 1 (Nov. 1990)-. Academic Scholarly Publication. English. Eight times a year (2 volumes). Fl1040.00. Elsevier Science Publishers BV, PO Box 211, 1000 AE Amsterdam Netherlands. **Tel** 011 31 20 5803642, FAX 011 31 20 5862696, telex 15682. **ED** K.J. Clevett. **LC** TJ212; .P67. **CODEN** PCQUEJ. **[CCC].** Index available. **Bk Rev. Ad Acc. Pr Rev.** available in microform from University Microfilms International (UMI). Documents available from Article Express International, Ask*IEEE, CASDDS.
Desc: Covers the science and technology of process quality measurement systems and their use in process control.
Ind/Abst Chem. Abstr.; Eng. Index Annu.; Fluid Abstr., Civil Eng.; Fluid Abstr. Proc. Eng.; FLUIDEX (199?-); Food Sci. Technol. Abstr.; INSPEC (Nov. 1990-).

UK/0370-1859
PROCESS ENGINEERING. [Process eng.]. Vol. 53, No. 8 (Aug. 1972)-. Periodical. English. mo. £70.00 UK and Northern Ireland; $170.00 other. Morgan Grampian, 40 Beresford Street Woolwich, London SE18 6BQ England. **Tel** 011 44 81 855 7777, FAX 011 44 81 855 5548, telex 896238. **ED** Clive Tayler. **LC** TP1; .P6835. **DD** 660.2/05. **CODEN** PSEGAP. **[CCC]. Bk Rev. Ad Acc. Circ:** 19,168 (ctrl). available on microfilm and microfiche from University Microfilms International (UMI). Documents available from Article Express International, Ask*IEEE, CASDDS. ***Formed by the union of*** *Process Engineering Plant & Control* ***and*** *Chemical & Process Engineering, 0952-2751.*
Desc: Technical, cost and product information on the chemical and process industries.
Ind/Abst Appl. Sci. Technol. Index; Ceram. Abstr. (19??-); Chem. Abstr.; Chem. Bus. Bull.; Chem. Bus. NewsBase (1985-); Chem. Bus. Update; Chem. Hazards Ind.; Coal Abstr.; Curr. Biotechnol.; Curr. Technol. Index; Ei Page One; EMBASE; Energy Res. Abstr. (1975-); Eng. Index Annu. [Select. Cov.]; F&S Index Plus Text, Int. [Select. Cov.]; Fluid Abstr., Civil Eng.; Fluid Abstr. Proc. Eng.; FLUIDEX (1973-); Gas Abstr.; HTFS Dig.; INSPEC (1972-); Lab. Hazards Bull.; Leadscan; Lit. Pat. Abstr., Oilfield Chem. (1954-1959, 1969-); Lit. Abstr., Catal. Catal.; Lit. Abstr., Health Environ.; Lit. Abstr., Pet. Refin. Petrochem.; Lit. Abstr., Pet. Substit.; Lit. Abstr., Transp. Storage; Pap. Board Abstr.; Proc. Chem. Eng.; PROMT [Full Txt.]; Saf. Health Work; Theoret. Chem. Eng.; Trade Ind. ASAP [Full Txt.]; Trade Ind. Index [Full Txt.]; World Ceram. Abstr.; World Surf. Coat. Abstr.

UK/0264-7176
PROCESS ENGINEERING INDEX. [Process eng. index]. (1983)-. Periodical. English. sa (June and Dec.). $250.00 US. Technical Indexes Ltd, Willoughby Road, Bracknell, Berks RG12 4DW England. **Tel** 011 44 0344 426311. **(Subscription address:** Information Handling Services, 15 Inverness Way, Englewood CO 80150.) **ED** Naresh Saksena. **DD** 660.2800941. **Ad Acc. Circ:** 4,362. ***Continues*** *Chemical Engineering Index, 0308-8391.*
Desc: Comprehensive who makes what guide to suppliers and manufacturers of process equipment and instrumentation.

CN/0826-7243
PROCESS INDUSTRIES CANADA. ***Ceased.*** [Process ind. Can.]. **VFOAT** Chemical Buyers Guide and Bulk Handling Directory; Chemical Buyers Guide. (Oct./Nov. 1984)-(199?). Academic Scholarly Publication. English. bm (seven times a year). Southam Information and Technology Group Inc., 1450 Don Mills Road, Don Mills Ontario M3B 2X7 Canada. **Tel** (416)445-6641, (800)668-2374, FAX (416)442-2261. **ED** Arthur Kendrick. **LC** TP155.75; .P76. **DD** 660.2/81. **CODEN** PICAEX. **Ad Acc. Circ:** 24,500 (ctrl). available on microfiche from University Microfilms International (UMI); and Micromedia Limited; available on an online database (file 648/Full-Text) from DIALOG. Documents available from CASDDS. ***Absorbed*** *Chemical Buyers' Guide, 0069-2891;* ***Continues*** *Canadian Chemical Processing, 0008-3186.*
Desc: Documentary magazine sent to personnel engaged in processing operations in 18 process industries. Covers equipment, services, and technology common to all the process industries.
Ind/Abst Appl. Sci. Technol. Index (1984-); Chem. Abstr.; Chem. Ind. Notes (1984-); Gas Abstr. (?-?); Lit. Pat. Abstr., Oilfield Chem. (1954-1963, 1969-1991); Lit. Abstr., Catal. Catal. (?-?); Lit. Abstr., Health Environ. (?-?); Lit. Abstr., Pet. Refin. Petrochem. (?-?); Lit. Abstr., Pet. Substit. (?-?); Lit. Abstr., Transp. Storage (?-?); Trade Ind. ASAP [Full Txt.]; Trade Ind. Index [Full Txt.].

UK/0305-439X
PROCESSING. [Process.]. Vol. 20, No. 10 (Oct. 1974)-. Periodical. English. mo (11 issues). £55.00 UK; £75.00 Europe; £100.00 other. IML Group, Blair House, 184-186 High Street, Tonbridge Kent, TN9 1BQ England. **Tel** 011 44 732 359990, FAX 011 44 732 770049. **ED** Brian Matkins. **LC** TP1; .P684. **DD** 660.2/05. **CODEN** PCSNA4. **Ad Acc, Adv Mgr:** David Lewis. available on microfilm and microfiche from University Microfilms International (UMI). Documents available from CASDDS. ***Continues*** *Chemical Processing, 0009-2622.*
Ind/Abst Abstr. Bull. Inst. Pap. Sci. Tech.; Alum. Ind. Abstr.; Art Archaeol. Tech. Abstr.; Chem. Abstr. (1974-1983); Chem. Bus. Bull.; Chem. Bus. NewsBase (1985-); Chem. Bus. Update; Coal Abstr.; Curr. Biotechnol.; Curr. Technol. Index; EMBASE; Energy Res. Abstr. (July 1976-); F&S Index Plus Text, Int. [Select. Cov.]; Fluid Abstr., Civil Eng.; Fluid Abstr. Proc. Eng.; FLUIDEX (1974-); Food Sci. Technol. Abstr.; HTFS Dig.; Lit. Pat. Abstr., Oilfield Chem. (1974-); Lit. Abstr., Catal. Catal.; Lit. Abstr., Health Environ.; Lit. Abstr., Pet. Refin. Petrochem.; Lit. Abstr., Pet. Substit.; Lit. Abstr., Transp. Storage; Met. Abstr.; Proc. Chem. Eng.; PROMT; Saf. Health Work; Theoret. Chem. Eng.; World Surf. Coat. Abstr.

PL/0033-2496
PRZEMYS CHEMICZNY. [Przem. chem.]. **Added/Corp** Poland. Ministerstwo Wyznan Religijnych i Oswiecenia Publicznego. Wydzia Nauki. Chemiczny Instytut Badawczy (Warsaw, Poland) Polskie Towarzystwo Chemiczne. (1920)-. Periodical. Polish. mo. $144.00. **(Subscription address:** ARS Polona, PO Box 1001, 00068 Warsaw Poland.) **LC** TP1; .P77. **NLM** W1 PR945. **CODEN** PRCHAB. **Pr Rev.** Documents available from Article Express International, The Genuine Article, CASDDS. ***Continues*** *Methan.*
Ind/Abst Bioeng. Abstr.; Ceram. Abstr.; Chem Inform; Chem. Abstr.; Chem. Titles; Coal Abstr.; Curr. Biotechnol.; Curr. Chem. React.; Ei Page One; Eng. Index Annu.; Index Chem.; Leadscan; Proc. Chem. Eng.; Res. Alert [Full Cov.]; Soc. Sci. Cit. Index [Select. Cov.]; Surf. Treat. Technol. Abstr.; Theoret. Chem. Eng.; World Surf. Coat. Abstr.

BL
QUIMICA & DERIVADOS. VFOAT Exame. **VAT** Quimica e Derivados. (196?)-. Periodical. Portuguese. mo. Editora Abril SA, Rua do Curtume 769 Lapa, 05066 900 Sao Paulo SP Brazil. **Tel** 011 55 11 8239222, 011 55 11 2623322, FAX 011 55 11 8643796. **LC** TP1; .Q47.
Ind/Abst PROMT.

US/0090-3507
RECORD OF CONFERENCE PAPERS - PETROLEUM AND CHEMICAL INDUSTRY CONFERENCE. (RECORD OF CONFERENCE PAPERS.). [Rec. conf. pap. - Pet. Chem. Ind. Conf.]. **Main/Conf** Petroleum and Chemical Industry Conference. 20th (1973)-. English. an. IEEE, Institution of Electrical and Electronics Engineers, Inc., 345 East 47th

Engineering — Chemical Engineering

Street, New York NY 10017-2394. **Tel** (908)981-1393, FAX (908)981-9667. (**Subscription address:** IEEE Service Center, 445 Hoes Lane, Piscataway, NJ 08854; telephone: (201)981-1393) **LC** TP157; .P46. **DD** 660.2/83. **CODEN** PCIRAY. Documents available from Article Express International. *Continues* IEEE Conference Record of Annual Petroleum and Chemical Industry Technical Conference.
 Ind/Abst Bioeng. Abstr.; Coal Abstr.; Ei Page One; Eng. Index Annu.; Index IEEE Publ.

AT/0810-8862
REPORT / DIVISION OF MINERAL ENGINEERING. [Rep. - Div. Miner. Eng.].
Added/Corp Commonwealth Scientific and Industrial Research Organization (Australia). Division of Mineral Engineering. CE R/57 (1978)-. Academic Scholarly Publication. English. ir. Price varies per volume. CSIRO Publications, PO Box 89, 314 Albert Street, East Melborne Victoria 3002 Australia. **Tel** 011 61 3 4187333, 4187217, FAX 011 61 3 4190459, telex AA 30236. **CODEN** RCSED2. Documents available from CASDDS. *Continues* Report (Commonwealth Scientific and Industrial Research Organization (Australia). Division of Chemical Engineering).
 Ind/Abst Chem. Abstr. (1978-1982).

US/0453-249X
REPORT - KANSAS STATE UNIVERSITY. INSTITUTE FOR SYSTEMS DESIGN AND OPTIMIZATION. (REPORT - INSTITUTE FOR SYSTEMS DESIGN AND OPTIMIZATION.). [Rep. - Kans. State Univ., Inst. Syst. Des. Optim.]. **Added/Corp** Kansas State University. Institute for Systems Design and Optimization. No. 1 (1968)-. English. $20.00. Kansas State University Department of Chemical Engineering, Manhattan KS 66506. **Tel** (913)532-5584. **ED** L T Fan. **LC** TA168; .K35. **CODEN** KISDAT. Documents available from CASDDS.
 Ind/Abst Chem. Abstr.; Ei Page One.

UK/0264-8431
REVIEWS IN CHEMICAL ENGINEERING. [Rev. chem. eng.]. Vol. 1, No. 1 (Jan.-March 1983)-. Academic Scholarly Publication. English. ir. $220.00. Freund Publishing House Ltd, PO Box 35010, 61 Nachmani Street, Tel Aviv 61350 Israel. **Tel** 011 972 3 5662925, FAX 011 972 3 5605335. (**Subscription address:** Freund Publishing House Ltd., Suite 500 Chesham House, 150 Regent Street, London W1R 5FA England.) **ED** Dan Luss and Neal R. Amundson. **LC** TP1; .R358. **DD** 660.2/.005. **CODEN** RCEGD6. **Bk Rev. Ad Acc. Pr Rev.** Documents available from Article Express International, The Genuine Article, CASDDS.
 Desc: Develops new insights and to promote interest and research activity in chemical engineering and applied chemistry, as well as the application of new developments in these areas.
 Ind/Abst Chem. Abstr.; Eng. Index Annu.; Res. Alert [Full Cov.]; Sci. Cit. Index; SCISEARCH.

BL/0102-2687
REVISTA BRASILEIRA DE ENGENHARIA. CADERNO DE ENGENHARIA QUIMICA / ASSOCIACAO BRASILEIRA DE ENGENHARIA QUIMICA. **Added/Corp** Associacao Brasileira de Engenharia Quimica. **VFOAT** Caderno de Engenharia Quimica. (198?)-. Periodical. Portuguese. sa. Revista Brasileira de Engenharia Quimica, Caixa Postal 68506, Rio de Janeiro, CEP 21944 Brazil. **LC** TP1; .R359. **DD** 660/.05. Documents available from CASDDS.
 Ind/Abst Chem. Abstr.

BL/0102-9843
REVISTA BRASILEIRA DE ENGENHARIA QUIMICA. (REVISTA BRASILEIRA DE ENGENHARIA QUIMICA : ORGAO DA ASSOCIACAO BRASILEIRA DE ENGENHARIA QUIMICA.). [Rev. bras. eng. quim.]. **Added/Corp** Associacao Brasileira de Engenharia Quimica. (19??)-. Periodical. Portuguese. **CODEN** RBEQEU. Documents available from CASDDS.
 Ind/Abst Chem. Abstr.

SP/0210-6604
REVISTA IBEROAMERICANA DE CORROSION Y PROTECCION. *Ceased.* [Rev. iberoam. corros. prot.]. Vol. 10, Nos. 1-2 (Jan./Feb. 1979)-(1992). Academic Scholarly Publication. Spanish. Editorial Garsi SA, Juan Bravo 46, 28006 Madrid, Spain. **Tel** 011 34 1 4021212, telex 98358 GARSI E. **CODEN** RCPRDQ. Documents available from CASDDS. *Continues* Corrosion y Proteccion, 0045-8678.
 Ind/Abst Chem. Abstr.; World Surf. Coat. Abstr.

FR
REVUE HEBDOMADAIRE DES INDUSTRIES CHIMIQUES. French. wk. 1197.69F France; 1640.00F other. Soc Communication Europeenne, 22 rue du Martroi, BP 47, 45190 Beaugency France. **Tel** 011 33 38 445603.
 Ind/Abst PROMT.

US/0035-9572
RUBBER WORLD. *See* Rubber.

XR
SBORNIK. CHEMICKE INZENYRSTVI A AUTOMATIZACE. **Main/Corp** Vysoka Skola Chemicko-Technologicka V Praze. **VFOAT** Chemicke Inzenyrstvi A Automatizace; Protsessy I Apparaty, Avtomatizatsiia; Scientific Papers. Chemical Engineering and Automation. Began in 1967. Czech (English; summaries and/or abstracts in German, Russian and Russian). **LC** TP1; .P655.

XR/0139-973X
SBORNIK VYSOKE SKOLY CHEMICKO-TECHNOLOGICKE V PRAZE. AUTOMATIZOVANE SYSTEMY RIZENI A VYPOCETNI METODY. SBORNIK PRAZHSKOGO KHIMIKO-TEKHNOLOGICHESKOGO INSTITUTA. AVTOMATIZIROVANNYE SISTEMY UPRAVLENIIA I VYCHISLITELNYE METODY. SCIENTIFIC PAPERS OF THE PRAGUE INSTITUTE OF CHEMICAL TECHNOLOGY. AUTOMATIC CONTROL SYSTEMS AND COMPUTING METHODS. **Main/Corp** Vysoka Skola Chemicko-Technologicka v Praze. **Added/Corp** Vysoka Skola Chemicko-Technologicka v Praze. Sbornik Prazhskogo Khimiko-Tekhnologichesgo Instituta. Avtomatizirovannye Sistemy Upravleniia i Vychislitelnye Metody. Vysoka Skola Chemicko-Technologicka v Praze. Scientific Papers of the Prague Institute of Chemical Technology. Automatic Control Systems and Computing Methods. **VFOAT** Sbornik Prazhskogo Khimiko-Tekhnologicheskogo Instituta. Avtomatizirovannye Sistemy Upravleniia i Vychislitelnye Metody; Scientific Papers of the Prague Institute of Chemical Technology. Automatic Control Systems and Computing Methods; Automatizovane Systemy Rizeni a Vypocetni Metody. (1977)-. Periodical. Czech (English, German and Russian). Statni Pedagogicke Nakladatelstvi, Ostrovni 30, 113 01 Prague 1 Czech Republic. **Tel** (2)203787, FAX (2)293883. **LC** TP155; .P687a. **CODEN** SVSRDF. Documents available from CASDDS.
 Ind/Abst Chem. Abstr.

US/1043-4976
SIM INDUSTRIAL MICROBIOLOGY NEWS. [SIM ind. microbiol. news]. Vol. 39, No. 1 (Jan./Feb. 1989)-. Periodical. English. bm. $36.00 (nonmembers). SIM Headquarters, 4201 John Marr Drive, Annandale VA 22003. **DD** 660. *Continues* SIM News.
 Ind/Abst Abstr. BioCommer.

SA
SOUTH AFRICAN JOURNAL OF CHEMICAL ENGINEERING. **Added/Corp** South African Institution of Chemical Engineers. **VFOAT** Suid-Afrikaanse Tydskrif vir Chemiese Ingeniuerswese. (19??)-. Academic Scholarly Publication. Afrikaans (English). SA Tydskrif vir Chemiese Ingenieurswese, Postbus 36654, Menlopark 0102 South Africa. **LC** IN PROCESS. **CODEN** SACEEM. Documents available from CASDDS.
 Ind/Abst Chem. Abstr.

UK/0142-5811
SYMPOSIUM PAPERS / INSTITUTION OF CHEMICAL ENGINEERS, NORTH WESTERN BRANCH. [Symp. pap. - Inst. Chem. Eng., North West. Branch]. **Added/Corp** Institution of Chemical Engineers (Great Britain). North Western Branch. (19??)-. Academic Scholarly Publication. English. Institution of Chemical Engineers, Davis Building, 165-189 Railway Terrace, Rugby Warwickshire CV21 3HQ England. **Tel** 011 44 1788 578214, FAX 011 44 1788 560833, telex 311780. **CODEN** SPIBDB. Documents available from CASDDS.
 Ind/Abst Bioeng. Abstr.; Chem. Abstr.

BE
TECHNICAL REPORTS. **Main/Corp** Centre Belge d'Etude de la Corrosion. (19??)-. Academic Scholarly Publication. English. Documents available from CASDDS.
 Ind/Abst Chem. Abstr.

GR/0251-0324
TECHNIKA CHRONIKA EPISTEMONIKE EKDOSE T.E.E. EPISTEMONIKE PERIOCHE C. **Added/Corp** Technikon Epimeleterion Hellados. **VFOAT** Technika Chronika Epistemonike Ekdose TEE. Epistemonike Perioche C; Technika Chronika Scientific Journal of the Technical Chamber of Greece. Section C. Periodical. Greek, Modern (English and French). qt. Technical Chamber of Greece, rue Karageorgi Servias 4, Athens 125 Greece. **Tel** (01)32 54 590-9, telex TEEGR 218374. *Continues in part* Technika Chronika.

FR
TECHNIQUES DE L'INGENIEUR / ANALYSE CHIMIQUE & CARACTERISATION PA. French. Editions Techniques, 141 rue de Javel, 75747 Paris Cedex 15 France. **Tel** 011 33 1 45589100.

UK/0960-5053
THEORETICAL CHEMICAL ENGINEERING. *See* Engineering-Abstracting, Bibliographies and Statistics.

US/0040-5795
THEORETICAL FOUNDATIONS OF CHEMICAL ENGINEERING. [Theor. found. chem. eng.]. **Added/Corp** Consultants Bureau. Vol. 1 (Jan./Feb. 1967)-. Academic Scholarly Publication. English (translations available in Russian). bm (6 issues). $1160.00 US; $1350.00 other. Plenum Press, 233 Spring Street, New York NY 10013-1578. **Tel** (212)620-8000, (800)221-9369, FAX (212)463-0742, (212)807-1047, telex 23/421139. (**Subscription address:** Plenum Press Subscription Department, PO Box 730, Canal Street Station NY 10013-1578.) **ED** V. V. Kafarov. **LC** TP1; .T48. **DD** 660. **CODEN** TFCEAU. **[CCC].** Index available. available on microfilm and microfiche from University Microfilms International (UMI). Documents available from Article Express International, CASDDS.
 Desc: Publishes articles on scientific problems of chemical technology. Directed primarily to research workers, chemistry and chemical engineering. Useful reference in automation of chemical technology.
 Ind/Abst Bioeng. Abstr.; Chem. Abstr.; Coal Abstr.; Ei Page One; EMBASE; Eng. Index Annu.; Pollut. Abstr. Indexes; Proc. Chem. Eng.; Theoret. Chem. Eng.

US/0277-5883
TOPICS IN CHEMICAL ENGINEERING. [Top. chem. eng.]. (1982)-. Monographic series. English. ir. Price varies per volume. Gordon & Breach Science Publishers, Inc., PO Box 786, Cooper Station, New York NY 10276. **Tel** (212)206-8900, FAX (212)645-2459. (**Subscription address:** Gordon & Breach Science Publishers / US, 820 Town Center Drive, Langhorne PA 19047.)

UK/0962-7189
TRIBOLOGY AND CORROSION ABSTRACTS. *Ceased.* (19??)-(1992). Academic Scholarly Publication. English. mo. Elsevier Science Publishers Ltd, Crown House, Linton Road, Barking Essex IG11 8JU England. **Tel** 011 44 81 5947272, FAX 081-594-5942, telex 896950. **[CCC].** available on microfilm and microfiche from University Microfilms International (UMI). *Formed by the union of* Industrial Corrosion Abstracts, 0955-7040 *and* Tribos, 0041-2694.
 Desc: Covers all aspects of tribology and corrosion - friction wear, lubrication and lubricants, bearings and other machine components, corrosion problems, corrosion protection, corrosion resistant materials and applications, monitoring and test equipment and techniques, remedial techniques and processes. Each volume contains approximately 3,500 abstracts. Each issues includes full subject indexes.
 Ind/Abst Corros. Abstr. (199?-1992)9; FLUIDEX (?-?); World Ceram. Abstr.

HU/0231-0775
VEGYIPARI SZAKIRODALMI TAJEKOZTATO MUANYAG- ES GUMIIPARI KULONLENYOMATA. *See* Chemistry.

GW/0042-1084
VFDB ZEITSCHRIFT. [VFDB Z.]. **Added/Corp** Vereinigung zur FEorderung des Deutschen Brandschutzes. (1952)-. Periodical. German (summaries and/or abstracts in English and French). qt. DM130.00 Germany; $91.41 US. W Kohlhammer Verlag GmbH, Postfach 800430, D 70549 Stuttgart Germany. **Tel** 011 49 711 78631, FAX 011 49 711 7863263, telex 7-255820. Index available (Free).
 Ind/Abst Energy Res. Abstr. (19??-); Saf. Health Work (19??-).

UK/0042-7519
VITREOUS ENAMELLER. [Vitreous enameller]. **Added/Corp** Institute of Vitreous Enamellers. Institute of Vitreous Enamellers. Bulletin. (195?)-. Academic Scholarly Publication. English. Four times a year. $60.00 North America; £32.00 other. Institute of Vitreous Enamellers, Wych House / 37 Avenue Road, Redditch B96 6AQ England. **Tel** 011 44 527 893031, FAX 011 44 527 893031. **ED** M.A. Collins. **CODEN** VITEAM. Index available. **Bk Rev. Ad Acc. Circ:** 250 (ctrl). Documents available from CASDDS.
 Desc: Covers all aspects of vitreous and porcelain enamelling.
 Ind/Abst Ceram. Abstr.; Chem. Abstr.; World Ceram. Abstr.

UK/0263-6050
WORLD CEMENT. See Building and Construction.

UK
WORLD PATENT INDEX GAZETTE. SECTION CH-CHEMICAL. (19??)-. English. Fifty-two times a year. Derwent Publications Ltd., Derwent House 14, Great Queen Street, London WC2B 5DF England. **Tel** 011 44 71 3442800. **LC** TP210; .W63. **DD** 660.2/02/72.

CIVIL ENGINEERING

US/0363-5732
ABSTRACT JOURNAL IN EARTHQUAKE ENGINEERING. See Engineering-Abstracting, Bibliographies and Statistics.

US/0363-2296
ACI DIRECTORY. **Main/Corp** American Concrete Institute. **VAT** American Concrete Institute Directory. Directory. English. be. ACI Directory, PO Box 4754 Redford Station, Detroit MI 48219. **LC** TA680; .A6. **DD** 624/.1834/06273.

US/0889-325X
ACI MATERIALS JOURNAL. [ACI mater. j.]. **Added/Corp** American Concrete Institute. **VFOAT** Materials Journal. **VAT** American Concrete Institute Materials Journal. Vol. 84, No. 1 (Jan./Feb. 1987)-. Academic Scholarly Publication. English. bm. $104.00 US; $111.00 other. American Concrete Institute, PO Box 19150, Detroit MI 48219. **Tel** (313)532-2600. **(Subscription address:** American Concrete Institute, PO Box 32190, Detroit MI 48232**)** **ED** Robert G Wiedyke. **LC** TA439.A36. **DD** 620.1/36/05. **CODEN** AMAJEF. **[CCC].** Index available. **Pr Rev. Circ:** 18,000. available on microfilm and microfiche from University Microfilms International (UMI). Documents available from Article Express International, The Genuine Article, CASDDS. ***Continues in part*** *Journal of the American Concrete Institute, 0002-8061.*
Desc: Contains technical, archival type of articles and papers devoted to structural and materials research, design theory, structural analysis, and state-of-the-art reviews.
Ind/Abst Abstr. J. Earthq. Eng.; Appl. Sci. Technol. Index; Bioeng. Abstr.; Ceram. Abstr. (19??-); Chem. Abstr. (1987-); Coal Abstr.; Concr. Abstr.; Curr. Contents Eng. Tech. Appl. Sci.; Ei Page One; EMBASE; Eng. Index Annu.; Geotech. Abstr.; Mintec, Min. Technol. Abstr.; Res. Alert [Full Cov.]; Sci. Cit. Index; SCISEARCH.

US/0569-4027
ACI STANDARDS / AMERICAN CONCRETE INSTITUTE. **Main/Corp** American Concrete Institute. **VAT** American Concrete Institute Standards. (1948)-. English. ir. Price varies. American Concrete Institute, PO Box 19150, Detroit MI 48219. **Tel** (313)532-2600. **LC** TA439.

US/0889-3241
ACI STRUCTURAL JOURNAL. [ACI struct. j.]. **Added/Corp** American Concrete Institute. **VFOAT** Structural Journal. **VAT** American Concrete Institute Structural Journal. Vol. 84, No. 1 (Jan./Feb. 1987)-. Periodical. English. bm. $104.00 US; $111.00 other. American Concrete Institute, PO Box 19150, Detroit MI 48219. **Tel** (313)532-2600. **(Subscription address:** American Concrete Institute, PO Box 32190, Detroit MI 48232**)** **ED** Robert G Wredyke. **LC** TA680; .A25. **DD** 624.1/834/05. **CODEN** ASTJEG. **[CCC].** Index available. **Pr Rev. Circ:** 20,000. available on microfilm and microfiche from University Microfilms International (UMI). Documents available from Article Express International, The Genuine Article. ***Continues in part*** *Journal of the American Concrete Institute, 0002-8061.*
Desc: The journal contains technical, archival type of articles and papers devoted to structural and materials research, design theory, structural analysis, and state-of-the-art reviews.
Ind/Abst Abstr. J. Earthq. Eng.; Appl. Sci. Technol. Index; Civ. Struct. Eng. Abstr.; Comput. Inf. Syst. Abstr. J. [Full Cov.]; Concr. Abstr.; Curr. Contents Eng. Tech. Appl. Sci.; Ei Page One; Eng. Index Annu.; Geotech. Abstr.; Highw. Res. Abstr.; Manuf. Process Eng. Abstr.; Mater. Sci. Eng. Abstr.; Res. Alert [Full Cov.]; Sci. Cit. Index; SCISEARCH; Solid State Supercond. Abstr.

FI/0355-2705
ACTA POLYTECHNICA SCANDINAVICA. CIVIL ENGINEERING AND BUILDING CONSTRUCTION SERIES. CI. (ACTA POLYTECHNICA SCANDINAVICA. CIVIL ENGINEERING AND BUILDING CONSTRUCTION SERIES.). [Acta polytech. Scand., Civil eng. build. constr. ser., Ci]. **Added/Corp** Scandinavian Council for Applied Research. Teknillisten Tieteiden Akatemia. **VFOAT** Civil Engineering and Building Construction Series. Vol. 1-4, No. 10, (1947-1957)-. Academic Scholarly Publication. English. ir. Price varies per volume. The Finnish Academy of Technology, Tekniikantie 12, Fin 02150 Espoo Finland. **Tel** 011 358 0 4554565, FAX 011 358 0 6945041. **ED** Jussi Hyyppa. **CODEN** APCBAI. Index available. **Circ:** 600. available on microfilm from University Microfilms International (UMI). Documents available from Article Express International, CASDDS. ***Supersedes*** *Acta Polytechnica. Civil Engineering and Building Construction Series.*
Desc: Scientific research report series consisting of monographs.
Ind/Abst Bioeng. Abstr.; Chem. Abstr.; Ei Page One; Energy Res. Abstr.; Eng. Index Annu.; Geogr. Abstr. Phys. Geogr. (?-?); GeoRef; Leadscan.

●US/1065-7355
ADVANCED CEMENT-BASED MATERIALS. See Building and Construction.

US/0899-5788
AEG NEWS. (AEG NEWS / ASSOCIATION OF ENGINEERING GEOLOGISTS.). [AEG news]. **Main/Corp** Association of Engineering Geologists. **VAT** Association of Engineering Geologists News. Vol. 31, No.1 (Jan. 1988)-. Periodical. English. Four times a year (Jan., Apr., July, Oct.). $20.00 AEG News only; $435.00 US & Canada; $445.00 other, combination subscription for Bulletin, News, & Directory; $135.00 US & Canada; $145.00 other, combination subscription for Bulletin and News; $125.00 for Bulletin only. Association of Engineering Geologists, 323 Boston Post, Suite 2D, Sudbury MA 01776. **Tel** (508)443-4639. **LC** TA705; .A45. **DD** 624. cum. index. **Bk Rev**, (Qty: varies). **Ad Acc, Adv Mgr:** K. Rose, **Tel** (617)891-8597. **Circ:** 3,600. ***Continues*** *Association of Engineering Geologists. Association of Engineering Geologists Newsletter, 0888-305X.*
Ind/Abst Fluid Abstr., Civil Eng. (19??-); Fluid Abstr. Proc. Eng. (19??-); FLUIDEX (19??-); GeoRef.

US/0146-7557
AMERICAN PROFESSIONAL CONSTRUCTOR, THE. [Am. prof. constr.]. **Added/Corp** American Institute of Constructors. (19??)-. English. qt. $150.00. American Institute of Constructors, 9887 North Grandy Boulevard, Suite 104, St. Petersburg FL 33702. **Tel** (813)578-0317, FAX (813)578-9982. **ED** Roger Liska (editor's address: Dept. of Building Construction, Clemson University, Clemson South Carolina; editor's phone: (803)656-3916). **LC** TA1; .A37. **DD** 624/.05. Index available. cum. index. **Pr Rev. Circ:** 1,700 (ctrl).
Desc: Compiles articles on new construction technology, methodology and current research.

AU
AMTSBLATT FUER DAS VERMESSUNGSWESEN. **Main/Corp** Austria. Bundesamt fur Eich- und Vermessungswesen. (19??)-. German. ir. **LC** TA526.A8; A95a.

FR/0152-9668
ANNALES DES PONTS ET CHAUSSEES. [Ann. ponts chaussees]. **Added/Corp** France. Ministere des Travaux et des Transports. France. Commission des Annales des Ponts et Chaussees. Vol. 105 (1935)-. Academic Scholarly Publication. French. qt. $135.00. Lavoisier Abonnements, 14 rue de Provigny, F 94236 Cachan Cedex France. **Tel** 011 33 1 47406700. **CODEN** APCSAZ. Documents available from Article Express International. ***Formed by the union of*** *Annales des Ponts et Chaussees, 1re Partie, Partie Technique* ***and*** *Annales des Ponts et Chaussees, 2e Partie, Partie Administrative.*
Ind/Abst Bioeng. Abstr.; Ei Page One; EMBASE; Eng. Index Annu.; GeoRef; Int. Civil Eng. Abstr.; Soft. Abstr. Eng.; Stat. Theory Method Abstr. (1968).

UK
ANNUAL REPORT OF THE COUNCIL AND INSTITUTE ACCOUNTS. **Main/Corp** Institute of Road Transport Engineers. (1971)-. English. an. Free. 1 Cromwell Place, Kensington SW7 SJF England. **Tel** 01-589 3744, FAX 01-225-0494. **LC** TL1; .I57614. **DD** 629.04. **Circ:** 16,500 (ctrl). ***Continues*** *Report of the Council, Income and Expenditure Account and Balance Sheet.*

●PL
ARCHIVES OF CIVIL ENGINEERING / POLISH ACADEMY OF SCIENCES, INSTITUTE OF FUNDAMENTAL TECHNOLOGICAL RESEARCH [AND] COMMITTEE FOR CIVIL ENGINEERING. **Added/Corp** Instytut Podstawowych Problemow Techniki (Polska Akademia Nauk) Polska Akademia Nauk. Komitet Inzynierii Ladowej i Wodnej. **VFOAT** Archiwum Inzynierii Ladowej; ACE. Vol. 38, Issue 1-2 (1992)-. Periodical. English (summaries and/or abstracts in Polish). qt. ***Continues*** *Archiwum Inzynierii Ladowej, 0004-0797.*

US/0148-5768
ARIZONA'S FIVE-YEAR TRANSPORTATION CONSTRUCTION PROGRAM. ***Title Change.*** **Main/Corp** Arizona. Dept. of Transportation. 1975/76-?. English. an. Arizona Department of Transportation, 205 South 17th Avenue, 614 East, Phoenix AZ 85007. **Tel** (602)255-7724. **LC** TE24.A6; A78A. **DD** 388.1/09771. ***Continues*** *Arizona's Five-Year Highway Construction Program, 0095-8336.* ***Continued by*** *Five-Year Transportation Facilities Construction Program.*

FI/0355-3213
ARTES CONSTRUCTIONUM. No. 1- 1974-. Monographic series. Finnish (English). ir. Price varies per volume. University of Oulu, c/o Leo Hirvonen, 90100 Oulu 10 Finland. **Tel** 358-81-3332133. **ED** Matti Karras. cum. index. **Ad Acc. Circ:** 450 (ctrl).
Desc: Monographs, reviews, and dissertations in the field of engineering.

US/0742-1753
ASCE ANNUAL COMBINED INDEX. See Engineering-Abstracting, Bibliographies and Statistics.

US/0197-4076
ASCE NEWS. [ASCE news]. **Main/Corp** American Society of Civil Engineers. **Added/Corp** American Society of Civil Engineers. News. **VAT** American Society of Civil Engineers News. (197?)-. Periodical. English. mo. $36.00 (non-member) US; $55.00 (non-member) other. American Society of Civil Engineers / ASCE, 345 East 47th Street, New York NY 10017-2398. **Tel** (212)705-7179, FAX (212)705-7300, telex 422847 ASCE UI. **(Subscription address:** American Society of Civil Engineers, Publisher Fulfillment Agency, Box 828, Somerset NJ 08875.**)** **DD** 624. **CODEN** ANEWED.
Ind/Abst J. Ferrocement.

US/0734-1962
ASCE PUBLICATIONS INFORMATION. See Engineering-Abstracting, Bibliographies and Statistics.

SP
ASOCIACION TECNICA ESPANOLA DEL PRETENSADO. Spanish (summaries and/or abstracts in English). qt. 8.000ptas (individuals), 20.000ptas (institutions) Spain; $60.00 (individuals), $125.00 (institutions) other. Asociacion Tecnica Espanola del Pretensado, Inst Eduardo Torroja, Apr 19002, 28033 Madrid Spain. **Tel** (91)302-04 04, FAX (91)302 07 00. Index available. **Bk Rev. Ad Acc. Circ:** 1,000.
Desc: Articles about materials, research, methods of design, description of works of civil engineering in prestressed and reinforced concrete.

UK/0271-9231
ASPECTS OF MODERN LAND SURVEYING. [Asp. mod. land surv.]. Monographic series. English. Price varies per volume. John Wiley & Sons Ltd., Baffins Lane, Chichester West Sussex PO19 1UD England. **Tel** 0243 779777, FAX 0243 776128 BTG:JWP001, telex 86290 WIBOOKG. **(Subscription address:** North, South and Central America/ John Wiley & Sons, Inc., Subscription Department, 605 Third Avenue, New York, NY 10158-0012, USA; telephone: (212)850-6645; FAX: (212)850-6021**)**

US/0270-2932
ASPHALT PAVING TECHNOLOGY. [Asph. paving technol.]. **Main/Corp** Association of Asphalt Paving Technologists. **Added/Corp** Association of Asphalt Paving Technologists. Proceedings. Vol. 40 (1971)-. Academic Scholarly Publication. English. an (Feb.). $60.00. Association of Asphalt Paving Technologists, 1983 Sloan Place, Suite 10, St Paul MN 55117. **Tel** (612)776-7703. **CODEN** APATDV. Index available. cum. index. **Circ:** 100. available on microfilm from University Microfilms International (UMI). Documents available from Article Express International, CASDDS. ***Continues*** *Proceedings of the Association of Asphalt Paving Technologists, Technical Sessions, 0066-9466.*
Ind/Abst Bioeng. Abstr.; Chem. Abstr.; Ei Page One; Eng. Index Annu.; Lit. Pat. Abstr., Oilfield Chem. (1954-); Lit. Abstr., Catal. Catal.; Lit. Abstr., Health Environ.; Lit. Abstr., Pet. Refin. Petrochem.; Lit. Abstr., Pet. Substit.; Lit. Abstr., Transp. Storage.

AT
AUSTRALIAN CIVIL ENGINEERING TRANSACTIONS. Proceedings. English. qt. price varies. Engineers Australia Pty Ltd, 2 Ernest Street, Crows Nest Centre, Crows Nest New South Wales 2065, Australia. **Tel** 011 61 2 438-1533, FAX 011 61 2 438-5934, telex 27640. **Circ:** 5,000.
Ind/Abst AESIS Q.; Fluid Abstr., Civil Eng.; Fluid Abstr. Proc. Eng.; FLUIDEX (19??-); Geotech. Abstr.

AT/0159-8910
AUSTRALIAN JOURNAL OF GEODESY, PHOTOGRAMMETRY, AND SURVEYING. [Aust. j. geod., photogramm., surv.]. **Added/Corp** University of New South Wales. School of Surveying. No. 30 (June 1979)-. Periodical. English. Twice a year (Jun., Dec.). 20.00Aus$ (students), 35.00Aus$ (individuals), 55.00Aus$ (institutions). The Australian Surveyor - Institution of Surveyors, 27-29 Napie R Close, Deakin Australian Capital Territory 2600 Australia, 2600 Australia. **Tel** 11 61 6 2822282, FAX 11 691 6 2822576. **ED** A. H. W. Kearsley. **LC** QB301; .A87. **DD** 526. **CODEN** AJGSDG. **Bk Rev**, (Qty: varies). **Pr Rev. Circ:** 300. Documents available from Ask*IEEE. ***Continues*** *UNISURV G.*
Desc: Research in areas of geodesy, photogrammetry

and all other branches of surveying in the South West Pacific region, and to provide a vehicle for the publication of this research.
Ind/Abst AESIS Q.; Geogr. Abstr. Phys. Geogr. (June 1981-); Geogr. Abstr. Human Geogr.; GeoRef; INSPEC (June 1981-).

AT/0005-0326
AUSTRALIAN SURVEYOR. (THE AUSTRALIAN SURVEYOR : A QUARTERLY PUBLICATION DEVOTED TO THE INTERESTS OF THE SURVEYING PROFESSION IN AUSTRALIA.). [Aust. surv.]. **Added/Corp** Queensland Institute of Surveyors. Institution of Surveyors, New South Wales. Victorian Institute of Surveyors. Institution of Surveyors, Western Australia. Institute of Surveyors, Tasmania. South Australian Institute of Surveyors. Vol., No. 1 (Jan. 1928)-. Periodical. English. Four times a year (Mar., June, Sept., & Dec,). 53.00Aus$. The Australian Surveyor - Institution of Surveyors, 27-29 Napie R Close, Deakin Australian Capital Territory 2600 Australia, 2600 Australia. **Tel** 11 61 6 2822282, FAX 11 691 6 2822576. **ED** N. O. Ward and J. Sneddon. **LC** TA529.A1; A12. **DD** 526.905. **CODEN** AUSUAK. Index available. cum. index. **Bk Rev**, (Qty: varies). **Ad Acc, Adv Mgr:** C. Fuller, **Tel** (06)2822282. **Pr Rev. Circ:** 3,900. Documents available from Article Express International.
Desc: Publication of articles on the scientific, technical, and educational aspects of surveying and information regarding the activities of The Institution of Surveyors in Australia.
Ind/Abst Bibliogr. Carto.; Bioeng. Abstr.; Ei Page One; Eng. Index Annu.; Geogr. Abstr. Phys. Geogr.; Geogr. Abstr. Human Geogr.; Int. Aerosp. Abstr.; Int. Dev. Abstr.

GW/0002-5968
AVN. ALLGEMEINE VERMESSUNGS-NACHRICHTEN. ***Title Change.*** (ALLGEMEINE VERMESSUNGS-NACHRICHTEN.). [AVN, Allg. Vermess.-Nachr.]. (1889)-(1992). Periodical. English. Deutscher Judo Verband, Redaktion Ippon Segewaldweg 40, D 12557 Berlin Germany. **Tel** 011 49 711 210770, telex 051 678. **LC** TA501; .A63. **CODEN** ALVNAJ. **[CCC].** ***Absorbed*** *Bildmessung und Luftbildwesen; Vermessungstechnik.* ***Absorbed by*** *Zeitschrift fur Vermessungwesen.*
Ind/Abst Bibliogr. Carto.; GeoRef.

GW/0005-6650
BAUINGENIEUR, DER. [Bauingenieur]. **Added/Corp** Hafenbautechnische Gesellschaft (Germany). Vol. 1 (1920)-. Periodical. German. Twelve times a year. DM486.00. Springer-Verlag GmbH & Company KG, Heidelberger Platz 3, D 14197 Berlin Germany. **Tel** 011 49 30 8207223, FAX 011 49 30 8214091, telex 183 319 SPBLN D. **(Subscription address:** Springer Verlag New York Inc. / for North America, 44 Hartz Way, Secaucus NJ 07096.**) ED** J Scheer. **LC** TA3; .H33. **CODEN** BANGAS. **[CCC]. Bk Rev. Ad Acc.** available on microfilm from University Microfilms International (UMI). Documents available from Article Express International. ***Supersedes*** *Armieter Beton.*
Desc: Informs across the spectrum of construction engineers' specialties through carefully chosen and science-based articles. Reports on mechanical engineering and machinery, new building materials and outstanding building projects. Offers solutions to problems and a hardware-software column.
Ind/Abst Bioeng. Abstr.; Concr. Abstr.; Ei Page One; EMBASE; Energy Res. Abstr.; Eng. Index Annu.; GeoRef; Geotech. Abstr.; Int. Civil Eng. Abstr.; Phys. Briefs; Soft. Abstr. Eng.

GW/0171-5445
BAUPHYSIK. [Bauphysik]. Vol. 1 (Oct. 1979)-. Academic Scholarly Publication. German. bm. $170.00. Wilhelm Ernst & Sohn, Muehlenstr 33 34 170, D 13187 Berlin Germany. **Tel** 011 49 30 47889200. **(Subscription address:** VCH Publishers Inc., 303 Northwest 12th Avenue, Journals Department, Deerfield FL 33442.**) ED** Hans-Peter Luhr. **LC** TH6014; .B38. **CODEN** BAUPDP. **[CCC].** Documents available from CASDDS.
Ind/Abst Acoust. Abstr.; Chem. Abstr.; EMBASE; Int. Civil Eng. Abstr.; Soft. Abstr. Eng.

GW
BAUTECHNIK, DIE. (1923)-. Periodical. German. mo. $295.00. Wilhelm Ernst & Sohn, Muehlenstr 33 34 170, D 13187 Berlin Germany. **Tel** 011 49 30 47889200. **(Subscription address:** VCH Publishers Inc., 303 Northwest 12th Avenue, Journals Department, Deerfield FL 33442.**) LC** TH3; .B3. cum. index.
Ind/Abst Ei Page One; Geotech. Abstr.

GW
BD FUR BAUSTOFFE UND BAUMASCHINEN. Periodical. German. 4.30 single issue. Krafthand Verlag W Schulz, Anna-Strasse 26, Postfach 160, 8939 Bad Worishofen Germany. **LC** TA401; .B14. **DD** 624/.028.

US/0006-0208
BETTER ROADS. **See** Transportation-Roads and Traffic.

US
BIENNIAL REPORT OF THE STATE ENGINEER OF NEW MEXICO. Main/Corp New Mexico. State Engineer. 1st- 1912/14-. English. be. **LC** TA24.N6; A3. **DD** 352.8. ***Continues*** *New Mexico (Ter.). Engineer Dept. Biennial Report of the Territorial Engineer.*

DK
BILAG TIL GTO RAPPORT. Main/Corp Grnlands Tekniske Organisation. **Added/Corp** Grnlands Tekniske Organisation. Direktoratet. GTO Rapport. **VFOAT** Bilag Til G.T.O. Rapport. (19??)-. Danish. an. Grnlands Tekniske Organisation Direktoratet, Hauser Plads 20, 1127 Kbenhavn K Denmark. **LC** TA125.5; .G74a.

GW/0006-3916
BITUMEN. (19??)-. Periodical. German. qt. Free. Arbeitsgemeinschaft der Bitumen Industrie, Steindamm 71, W-2000 Hamburg 1 Germany. **Tel** 040 280 2439, FAX 040 280 2125. **ED** Rolf G Urbau. **CODEN** BITUAK. Index available. cum. index. **Bk Rev. Circ:** 9,000.
Ind/Abst Bioeng. Abstr.; Ei Page One; Int. Civil Eng. Abstr.; Soft. Abstr. Eng.

PL
BIULETYN INFORMACYJNY. ***Title Change.*** **Main/Corp** Warsaw. Instytut Techniki Budowlanej. (19??)-(19??). Academic Scholarly Publication. Polish. **(Subscription address:** ARS Polona, PO Box 1001, 00068 Warsaw Poland.**) LC** TA630; .W34a. Documents available from CASDDS. ***Continued by*** *Prace Instytutu Techniki Budowlanej, 0138-0796.*
Ind/Abst Chem. Abstr.

IT
BOLLETTINO ASSOCIAZIONE REGIONALE INGEGNERI E ARCHITETTI DI PUGLIA. Italian. ir. Assoc Reg Ingegneri Architetti Di Puglia, V Putignani 76, 70121 Bari Italy.

UK
BRE DIGEST. Added/Corp Building Research Establishment. **VAT** British Research Establishment Digest. (May 1988)-. Periodical. English. mo. £50.00. Building Research Establishment, BRE Bookshop, Garston Watford WD27JR England. **Tel** 011 44 923 664444, FAX 011 44 923 664400. **CODEN** BREDET. Index available. cum. index. **Circ:** 10,000. Documents available from BLDSC. ***Continues*** *Building Research Establishment Digest, 0144-8536.*
Ind/Abst Archit. Period. Index; Int. Civil Eng. Abstr.; J. Ferrocement.

II
BRIDGE & STRUCTURAL ENGINEER. English. Bridge & Structural Engineer, Jamnagar House, Ida Building, Shahjahan Road, New Delhi 110011, India.
Ind/Abst Concr. Abstr.

UK
BRUSSELS BRIEFING. (19??)-. English. £300.00. Thomas Telford Ltd, Thomas Telford House, 1 Heron Quay, London E14 9XF England. **Tel** 011 44 71 987 6999, FAX 011 44 71 538 4101, telex 298105.

UK/0960-5185
BUILDING AND CIVIL ENGINEERING RESEARCH FOCUS. [Build. civ. eng. res. focus]. **VFOAT** Research Focus - Institution of Civil Engineers. (1990)-. Periodical. English. qt (4 issues). Free on request. Institute of Civil Engineers, 1 Heron Quay Isle of Dogs, London E14 9XF England. **Tel** 11 44 71 253 9999. **DD** 624. ***Continues*** *Civil Engineering Research Newsletter, 0950-0324.*

UK/0142-310X
BUILDING SERVICES & ENVIRONMENTAL ENGINEER. [Build. serv. environ. eng.]. Vol. 1 (Sept. 1978)-. Periodical. English. mo. £40.00 UK; £56.00 other. Batiste Publications Ltd, Pembroke House, Campsbourne Road, Hornsey London N8 7PE England. **Tel** 011 44 81 3403291, FAX 011 44 81 3414840, telex 267727. **CODEN** BSENDV. Documents available from Ask*IEEE.
Ind/Abst BMT Abstr. (?-199?); Coal Abstr.; INSPEC (Sept. 1978-); Int. Build. Serv. Abstr.; Int. Civil Eng. Abstr.; Soft. Abstr. Eng.

AT/0728-9820
BUILDING SURVEYOR MELBOURNE. **See** Building and Construction.

RM/0378-1267
BULETINUL STIINTIFIC AL INSTITUTULUI POLITECHNIC CLUJ: SERIA CONSTRUCTII. [Bul. Stiint. Inst. Politeh., Cluj, Ser. Constr.]. **Added/Corp** Institutul Politehnic Cluj. Vol. 13 (1970)-. Periodical. Multiple languages (French, German, Romanian and Russian). an. ***Continues in part*** *Cluj, Transylvania. Institutul Politechnic. Buletinul Stiintific.*
Ind/Abst Math. Rev.; Zentralbl. Math. Ihre Grenzgeb.

RM/0524-8159
BULETINUL STIINTIFIC / INSTITUTUL DE CONSTRUCTII BUCURESTI. [Bul. stiint. - Inst. Constr. Bucur.]. **Main/Corp** Institutul de Constructii (Bucharest, Romania). **Added/Corp** Institutul de Constructii Bucuresti. (195?)-. Periodical. Romanian (summaries and/or abstracts in Russian, French, English and German). Twice a year. DM333.00. **(Subscription address:** Kubon & Sagner, ABT Zeitschriftenimport, D 80328 Munich Germany.**) LC** TA4; .B77. **CODEN** BUICAT. Documents available from Article Express International.
Ind/Abst Bioeng. Abstr.; Ei Page One; Eng. Index Annu.; GeoRef; Zentralbl. Math. Ihre Grenzgeb.

US/0090-8517
BULLETIN - CONNECTICUT RIVER VALLEY COVERED BRIDGE SOCIETY. (BULLETIN.). [Bull. - Conn. River Val. Covered Bridge Soc.]. **Main/Corp** Connecticut River Valley Covered Bridge Society. (19??)-. Bulletin. English. qt. $5.00. Bulletin of the Connecticut River Valley Covered Bridge Society, PO Box 63, Swanzey NH 03146. **LC** TG1; .C57. **DD** 917.46/04/405.

BE
BULLETIN DES COURS ET DES LABORATOIRES D'ESSAIS DES CONSTRUCTIONS DU GENIE CIVIL ET D'HYDRAULIQUE FLUVIALE. ***Title Change.*** **Main/Corp** Universite de Liege. Centre d'Etudes de Recherches et d'Essais Scientifiques des Constructions du Genie Civil et d'Hydraulique Fluviale. Vol. 1 (1940/41)-. Bulletin. French. qt. ***Continued by*** *Bulletin / Universite. Centre d'Etudes de Recherche et d'Essais Scientifiques du Genie.*

JA/0454-7675
BULLETIN OF THE DISASTER PREVENTION RESEARCH INSTITUTE. **Main/Corp** Kyoto Daigaku. Bosai Kenkyujo. No. 1 (Dec. 1951)-. Bulletin. Japanese. qt. Kyoto University / Disaster Prevention Research Institute, Kyoto Daigaku Bosai Kenkyujo, Gokasho Uji 611 Japan. **LC** TA495; .K9. **CODEN** DPKBAN. **Circ:** 650. Documents available from Article Express International.
Ind/Abst Abstr. J. Earthq. Eng.; Bioeng. Abstr.; Ei Page One; Eng. Index Annu.; GeoRef; J. Ferrocement.

GW/0074-1612
BULLETIN OF THE INTERNATIONAL ASSOCIATION OF ENGINEERING GEOLOGY. [Bull. Int. Assoc. Eng. Geol.]. **Main/Corp** International Association of Engineering Geology. **VFOAT** Bulletin de l'Association Internationale de Geologie de l'Ingenieur. No. 1 (Aug. 1970)-. Bulletin. English (French). sa. DM950.00. AIGI Laboratoire Central, Direction Scientifique, BP 6009, 05060 Orleans Cedex France. **Tel** (1)5323279. **ED** M L Primel and A Peter. **LC** TA705; .I48. **DD** 624/.151/05. **CODEN** BIEGB6. **Bk Rev. Ad Acc. Circ:** 4,500 (ctrl). Documents available from Article Express International, CASDDS.
Desc: Covers engineering, geology, applied hydrogeology, the environment, nuclear wastes engineering, civil engineering, aggregated soil and rock investigation, and geophysics.
Ind/Abst AESIS Q.; Bioeng. Abstr.; Chem. Abstr. (1970-1982); Coal Abstr.; Ei Page One; Eng. Index Annu.; Geogr. Abstr. Phys. Geogr.; GeoRef; Geotech. Abstr.

NZ/0110-0718
BULLETIN OF THE NEW ZEALAND NATIONAL SOCIETY FOR EARTHQUAKE ENGINEERING. [Bull. N.Z. Natl. Soc. Earthq. Eng.]. **Added/Corp** New Zealand National Society for Earthquake Engineering. Vol. 7, No. 1 (March 1974)-. Bulletin. English. qt (Mar., June, Sep., Dec.). 160.00NZ$. New Zealand Society for Earthquake Engineering, PO Box 17-268 Karori, Wellington New Zealand. **Tel** 011 64 4 766866. **ED** P J Moss. **LC** TH1095; .N46a. **DD** 624/.176. **CODEN** BNZED6. **[CCC].** Index available. cum. index. **Bk Rev. Circ:** 800 (ctrl). Documents available from Article Express International. ***Continues*** *Bulletin of the New Zealand Society for Earthquake Engineering, 0550-6743.*
Desc: To advance the science and practice of earthquake engineering.
Ind/Abst Abstr. J. Earthq. Eng.; Bioeng. Abstr.; Concr. Abstr.; Ei Page One; Eng. Index Annu.; GeoRef.

AT/0041-9966
BULLETIN - QUEENSLAND. UNIVERSITY, BRISBANE. DEPT. OF CIVIL ENGINEERING. ***Ceased.*** **Main/Corp** Queensland. University, Brisbane. Dept. of Civil Engineering. No. 1 (1962)-(Dec. 31, 1993). Bulletin. English. University of Queensland / Department of Civil Engineering, St. Lucia Queensland 4072 Australia. **Tel** (07)377 2486, FAX (07)371-5863, telex UNIVQLD AA40315. **DD** 624. **Circ:** 500.
Desc: One of a continuing series of bulletins by the Department of Civil Engineering at the University of Queensland.
Ind/Abst Ei Page One.

CN/0826-452X
BULLETIN TECHNIQUE / INSTIUT CANADIEN DE TOLE D'ACIER EN BATIMENT. [Bull. tech. - Inst. can. tole acier batim.]. **Added/Corp** Institut Canadien de Tole d'Acier en Batiment. (197?)-. Bulletin. French. Price varies per volume. ICTAB, 305-201 Chemin Consumers, Willowdale Ontario M2J 4G8 Canada. **DD** 624.1/821.

DK/0106-3715
BYGNINGSSTATISKE MEDDELELSER. [Bygningsstatiske medd.]. **Main/Corp** Dansk Selskab for Bygningsstatik. Began with Vol. for 1929. Danish (English). ir. kr120.00. Dansk Selskab for Bygningsstatik, Danmarks Tekniske Hjskole Bygning 118, 2800 Lyngby Kbenhavn Denmark. **LC** TA645; .D27A. **DD** 624/.171/05. **CODEN** BYMEAF. Documents available from Article Express International.
Ind/Abst Bioeng. Abstr.; Concr. Abstr.; Ei Page One; Eng. Index Annu.

US
CA QUICK SEARCH [COMPUTER FILE]. **See** Engineering-Abstracting, Bibliographies and Statistics.

US/0045-3900
CALIFORNIA BUILDER & ENGINEER. [Calif. build. eng.]. **VFOAT** CB & E. **VAT** California Builder and Engineer. Vol. 75 (Jan. 10, 1969)-. Periodical. English. Twenty-four times a year. $30.00 heavy construction contractors in California, Nevada, Arizona & Hawaii; $40.00 others. California Builder & Engineer Inc, 4110 Transport Street, Palo Alto CA 94303. **Tel** (415)494-8822. **ED** David W. Woods. **LC** TA1; .P114. **DD** 624/.05. **Circ:** 11,532. ***Continues** Pacific Builder & Engineer. California.*

CN/0825-7515
CANADIAN CIVIL ENGINEER. [Can. civ. eng.]. **Added/Corp** Canadian Society for Civil Engineering. **VFOAT** L'Ingenieur Civil Canadien; Ingenieur Civil Canadien. Vol. 1, No. 1 (July 1984)-. Periodical. English (French). bm. 30.00Can$ Canada; 40.00Can$ other. Canadian Society for Civil Engineering, 2050 Mansfield Street, Suite 700, Montreal Quebec H3A 1Z2 Canada. **Tel** (514)842-5653. **ED** Elizabeth A. Gormley and Leslie C. Lavigne. **DD** 624/.06/071. **Bk Rev. Ad Acc. Circ:** 7,500 (ctrl).
Desc: Covers news and articles of topical interest.

CN/0315-1468
CANADIAN JOURNAL OF CIVIL ENGINEERING. [Can. j. civ. eng.]. **Added/Corp** National Research Council Canada. **VFOAT** Revue Canadienne de Genie Civil. Vol. 1 (Sept. 1974)-. Periodical. English (French). bm. 287.00Can$ (institutions), 92.00Can$ (individuals) Canada; $287.00 (institutions), $97.00 (individuals) other. National Research Council of Canada, Receiver General for Canada, Ottawa Ontario K1A 0R6 Canada. **Tel** (613)993-0362, FAX (613)952-7656. **ED** R. A. Dorton. **LC** TA1; .N17513. **DD** 624/.05. **CODEN** CJCEB8. **[CCC].** Index available. **Bk Rev. Ad Acc. Pr Rev. Circ:** 5,474 (ctrl). available on microfilm and microfiche from University Microfilms International (UMI). Documents available from Article Express International, The Genuine Article.
Desc: The official journal of the Canadian Society for Civil Engineering. Papers are published in structural engineering and construction materials, hydrotechnical engineering, transportation and urban planning, environmental and sanitary engineering, and construction.
Ind/Abst ASTIS Curr. Aware. Bull. (1978-); Abstr. J. Earthq. Eng.; AQUAREF; ASTIS Bibliogr. (1978-); Bioeng. Abstr.; Ceram. Abstr. (199?-); Coal Abstr.; Concr. Abstr.; Curr. Contents Eng. Tech. Appl. Sci.; Ei Page One; EMBASE; Eng. Index Annu.; Fluid Abstr., Civil Eng.; Fluid Abstr. Proc. Eng.; FLUIDEX (1974-); Geogr. Abstr. Phys. Geogr.; Geogr. Abstr. Human Geogr.; Geol. Abstr.; GeoRef; Geotech. Abstr.; INIS Atomindex [Micro.]; Int. Civil Eng. Abstr.; J. Plan. Lit.; Environ.; Leadscan; Life Sci. Collect.; Res. Alert [Full Cov.]; Sci. Cit. Index; SCISEARCH; Soc. Sci. Cit. Index [Select. Cov.]; Soft. Abstr. Eng.

US/0743-1732
CASE 1. [Case 1]. **VFOAT** Case One. Vol. 1, No. 1 (May/June 1984)-. Periodical. English. bm. $30.00. EASI Inc, 220 Montgomery Street/Suite 482, San Francisco CA 94111-1011. **DD** 624.

IT
CATALOGO EDILE. (19??)-. Italian. an. L120000. BE MA Editrice, Via Teocrito 50, 20128 Milan, Italy. **Tel** 011 39 2 2552451.

SW/0346-6906
CBI FORSKNING. [CBI forsk.]. **VFOAT** CBI Research. Academic Scholarly Publication. Swedish (English). ir. **CODEN** CBIFDL. Documents available from Article Express International, CASDDS.
Ind/Abst Bioeng. Abstr.; Ceram. Abstr. (19??-); Chem. Abstr. (1974-1984); Ei Page One; Eng. Index Annu.

SW/0346-8240
CBI RAPPORTER. Main/Corp Svenska Forskingsinstitutet for Cement och Betong. **VFOAT** CBI Reports. **VAT** Cement och Betonginstitutet Rapporter. (197?)-. Academic Scholarly Publication. Multiple languages (English and Swedish). Price varies per volume. **CODEN** CBIRDN. Documents available from CASDDS.
Ind/Abst Ceram. Abstr. (19??-); Chem. Abstr.

US/1044-8179
CE COMPUTING REVIEW. *Ceased.* (CE COMPUTING REVIEW : ASCE'S NEWSLETTER ON COMPUTING IN CIVIL ENGINEERING.). [CE comput. rev.]. **Added/Corp** American Society of Civil Engineers. **VAT** Civil Engineering Computing Review. Vol. 1, No. 1 (June 1989)-(June 1994). Newsletter. English. mo. American Society of Civil Engineers / ASCE, 345 East 47th Street, New York NY 10017-2398. **Tel** (212)705-7179, FAX (212)705-7300, telex 422847 ASCE UI. **DD** 624. **CODEN** CERVEY.

US/0008-8846
CEMENT AND CONCRETE RESEARCH. [Cem. concr. res.]. **Added/Corp** American Concrete Institute. Vol. 1 (Jan. 1971)-. Periodical. Multiple languages (English, French, German and Russian; summaries and/or abstracts in English, French, German and Russian). Eight times a year. $656.00 The Americas; £440.00 other. Pergamon Press, An Imprint of Elsevier Science Ltd., The Boulevard, Langford Lane, Kidlington, Oxford OX5 1GB United Kingdom. **Tel** 011 44 865 843000, 011 44 865 843699, FAX 011 44 865 843010. **(Subscription address:** Elsevier Science Ltd. Oxford Fulfillment Centre, PO Box 800, Kidlington, Oxford OX5 1DX United Kingdom.**)** **LC** TA434; .C39. **CODEN** CCNRAI. **[CCC].** cum. index. **Pr Rev.** available on microfiche from Pergamon International Marketing Company; available on microfilm and microfiche from University Microfilms International (UMI). Documents available from Article Express International, The Genuine Article, Petroleum Abstracts Document Delivery Service, CASDDS.
Desc: Features fundamental research results and comprehensive reviews in the field of cement, cement composites, concrete and other allied materials incorporating cement.
Ind/Abst Appl. Mech. Rev.; Aqualine Abstr.; Art Archaeol. Tech. Abstr.; Bioeng. Abstr.; Ceram. Abstr.; Chem. Abstr.; Chem. Titles; Civ. Struct. Eng. Abstr.; Coal Abstr.; Concr. Abstr.; Curr. Contents Eng. Tech. Appl. Sci.; Ei Page One; EMBASE; Energy Res. Abstr.; Eng. Index Annu.; Environ. Eng. Abstr.; GeoRef; Health Saf. Sci. Abstr.; Int. Civil Eng. Abstr.; J. Ferrocement; Manuf. Process Eng. Abstr.; Mater. Sci. Eng. Abstr.; Mech. Eng. Abstr.; MINPROC; Mintec, Min. Technol. Abstr.; Pet. Abstr.; Res. Alert [Full Cov.]; Sci. Cit. Index; SCISEARCH; Soft. Abstr. Eng.; Soils Fert.; World Ceram. Abstr.

CI/0008-882X
CEMENT. ZAGREB. See Building and Construction.

UK/0142-5196
CHARTERED QUANTITY SURVEYOR. *Ceased.* [Chart. quant. surv.]. Vol. 1 (1979)-(Nov. 1993). Periodical. English. mo (with a mid-month supplement). The Builder Group, 1 Millharbour, London E14 9RA England. **Tel** 011 44 81 4028486, telex 25212 BUIKDA G. **ED** Lesley Davis. Index available. cum. index. **Bk Rev. Ad Acc. Circ:** 32,219 (ctrl). available on microfilm and microfiche from University Microfilms International (UMI).
Desc: Provides up to date information on construction and engineering for quantity surveyors and cost engineers in the U.K. and around the world.
Ind/Abst Archit. Period. Index (1979-); Int. Civil Eng. Abstr.; Soft. Abstr. Eng.

UK
CHARTERED SURVEYOR : RURAL QUARTERLY. VFOAT Rural Quarterly. V. 1- Oct. 1973-. Periodical. English. qt. Royal Institution of Chartered Surveyors, PO Box 87, London EC4P 4HL England. **Tel** 01 353 2300, telex 25212 BUILDA-G. **LC** TA501; .R6 SUPPL. **DD** 338.1/0941.

JA
CHIBA-KEN NO JIBAN CHINKA. Main/Corp Chiba-Ken Kogai Kenkyujo. **Added/Corp** Chiba-ken Kogai Kenkyujo. Researches on Landsubsidence in Chiba Prefecture. **VFOAT** Researches on Landsubsidence in Chiba Prefecture. (19??)-. Academic Scholarly Publication. Japanese (Japanese). an. Chibaken Suishitsu Hozen Kenkyujo, (Chiba Prefectural Laboratory of Water Pollution), 5-1 Inagekaigan 3-chome, Mihama-ku, Chiba-shi, Chiba-ken, 261, Japan. **LC** QE600; .C47a.

CC
CHIEN CHU CHIEH KOU HSUEH PAO. Added/Corp Chung-kuo Chien Chu Hsueh Hui. **VFOAT** Journal of Building Structures. (19??)-. Periodical. Chinese (summaries and/or abstracts in English). Science Press, 16 Donghuangchenggen North Street, Beijing 100707, People's Republic of China. **Tel** 011 86 1 4019821, 011 86 1 4010642, FAX 011 86 1 4012180, 011 86 1 4019810, telex 210147. **LC** TA630; .C48. **DD** 624.1.
Ind/Abst Abstr. J. Earthq. Eng.

CC
CHIEN CHU CHIEH KOU / JIANZHU JIEGOU. Added/Corp Chung-kuo Chien Chu Chi Shu Chiao Liu Chung Hsin. **VFOAT** Jianzhu Jiegou. (19??)-. Periodical. Chinese. bm. RMBY0.42. Zhongguo Jianzhu Jishu Fazhan Zhongxin, 19 Chegongzhuang Dajie, Beijing 100044, People's Republic of China. **Tel** 011 86 8317744. **ED** Huang Yuntian. **LC** TA630; .C47. **DD** 624.1/05.

CH
CHIEN TSAI NIEN CHIEN. VFOAT Chung-Hua Min Kuo Chien Tsai Nien Chien. 1982. Chinese. an. Tai-Wan Shen Chien Chu Tsai Liao Shang Yeh Tung Yeh Kung Hui Lien Ho Hui, 62-1 2nd Sec, 4th Floor Kai-Feng Street, Taipei Shih Taiwan. **LC** TA402.5.T28; C45. **DD** 691/.0951/249.

CC
CHINA CIVIL ENGINEERING JOURNAL. China Civil Engineering Society, 10 Fuxing Road, Beijing, People's Republic of China.
Ind/Abst Concr. Abstr.

IT
CIB : EDIFICI INTELLIGENTI. bm. L5000 (single issue); L25000 (one year), L35000 (two year) Italy; L50000 Europe; L700000 other. Tecniche Nuove SPA, Via Ciro Menotti 14, 20129 Milan Italy. **Tel** 011 39 2 75701, FAX 011 39 2 7610351, telex 334647 TECHS I.

MX
CIC. Main/Corp Colegio de Ingeniernos Civiles de Mexico. **VAT** Colegio de Ingeniernos Civiles. Periodical. Spanish. mo. **LC** TA4; .I274. ***Continues** Ingenieria Civil.*
Ind/Abst Int. Civil Eng. Abstr.

IE
CITIS CD-ROM. See Building and Construction.

US/1063-7338
CIVIL AND STRUCTURAL ENGINEERING ABSTRACTS. *Ceased.* See Engineering-Abstracting, Bibliographies and Statistics.

SA/0009-7845
CIVIL ENGINEER IN SOUTH AFRICA, THE. *Title Change.* [Civil eng. S. Afr.]. **Added/Corp** South African Institution of Civil Engineers. **VFOAT** Die Siviele Ingenieur in Suid-Afrika. Vol. 1 (Jan. 1959)- Vol. 34 (1992). Periodical. Multiple languages (English and Afrikaans). mo. South African Institution of Civil Engineers, Gillstraat 18A Gill Street, 93495 Yeoville 2143 South Africa. **Tel** 27 11 6481184, FAX 27 11 6487427. **ED** R.C. Boers (editor's address: Box 93495 Yeoville 2143 South Africa). **LC** TA4; .C38. **DD** 620. **CODEN** CESAA6. Index available. **Bk Rev. Ad Acc, Adv Mgr:** Mrs. Smith. **Pr Rev. Circ:** 7,200 (ctrl). available on microfilm from University Microfilms International (UMI). Documents available from Article Express International. ***Supersedes** South African Institution of Civil Engineers. Transactions. **Split into** Civil Engineering (Johannesburg, South Africa), 1021-2000 **and** Journal of the South African Institution of Civil Engineers, 1021-2019.*
Desc: Refereed papers and general editorial concerning civil engineering.
Ind/Abst Bioeng. Abstr.; Coal Abstr.; Ei Page One; Electron. Commun. Abstr. J.; EMBASE; Energy Res. Abstr. (Feb. 1976-?); Eng. Index Annu. [Select. Cov.]; Int. Civil Eng. Abstr.; ISMEC Bull.; J. Ferrocement; Pollut. Abstr. Indexes; Saf. Sci. Abstr. J.

II
CIVIL ENGINEERING, CONSTRUCTION & PUBLIC WORKS JOURNAL. Vol. 1, (March/April 1968)-. Periodical. English. bm. Chary Publications, 14 Sidh Prasad Ghatkopar Mahul Road, Tilak Nagar PO 89, Bombay India. **Tel** 5518254. **LC** TA1; .C4532. **DD** 624/.05.

SA/0009-7888
CIVIL ENGINEERING CONTRACTOR. [Civ. eng. contract.]. **VFOAT** Siviele - Ingenieurswerk Aannemer. (1966)-. Periodical. Multiple languages. mo. R88.00 South Africa; R11.00 Africa; R230.00 other. Brooke Pattrick Publishing Limited, PO Box 422, Bedfordview 2008 South Africa. **Tel** 011 27 11 6224666, FAX 011 27 11 6167196. **DD** 692.8.

US/0884-1926
CIVIL ENGINEERING EDUCATION. [Civil eng. educ.]. **Added/Corp** American Society for Engineering Education. Civil Engineering Division. Vol. 1 (Spring 1979)-. Periodical. English. Twice a year. American Society for Engineering Education, 1818 North Street Northwest, Suite 600, Washington DC 20036. **Tel** (202)331-3500. **ED** Jack Bakos, Jim McDonough, Roger Seals and Colby Ardis. **LC** T73; .C54. **DD** 624/.07/1173. **CODEN** CEEDDG. **Pr Rev. Circ:** 1,100 (ctrl). Documents available from Article Express International.
Desc: A publication of the civil engineering division of ASEE. Articles on any and all aspects of civil engineering education are welcome.
Ind/Abst Bioeng. Abstr.; Ei Page One; Eng. Index Annu.

JA/0578-3747
CIVIL ENGINEERING IN JAPAN. [Civ. eng. Jpn.]. **Added/Corp** Doboku Gakkai. (1961)-. Periodical.

English. an. $60.00. Japan Society of Civil Engineers, Yotsuya 1-chome Shinjuku-ku, Tokyo 160 Japan. **Tel** 03/278-9224, FAX (03)355-3446, telex J26517 MARUZEN. **(Subscription address:** Maruzen Company Ltd., PO Box 5050, Import & Export Department, Tokyo 100 31 Japan.**)** **LC** TA105; .D58. **DD** 624. **CODEN** CVEJAE. **Circ:** 1,000. Documents available from Article Express International.
Desc: Covers civil engineering technology, representative projects under construction or completed. Planned and research works in Japan are introduced with photos and figures.
Ind/Abst Abstr. J. Earthq. Eng. (?-?); Alum. Ind. Abstr.; Bioeng. Abstr.; Civ. Struct. Eng. Abstr.; Coal Abstr.; Concr. Abstr.; Ei Page One; Eng. Mater. Abstr.; Eng. Index Annu.; Environ. Eng. Abstr.; Int. Civil Eng. Abstr.; Mech. Eng. Abstr.; Met. Abstr.; Soft. Abstr. Eng.

●SA/1021-2000
CIVIL ENGINEERING : MAGAZINE OF THE SOUTH AFRICAN INSTITUTION OF CIVIL ENGINEERS / SIVIELE INGENIEURSWESE. **Added/Corp** South African Institution of Civil Engineers. **VFOAT** Siviele Ingenieurswese. Vol. 1, No. 1 (Jan./Feb. 1993)-. Periodical. Afrikaans (English). mo. South African Institution of Civil Engineers, Gillstraat 18A Gill Street, 93495 Yeoville 2143 South Africa. **Tel** 27 11 6481184, FAX 27 11 6487427. **LC** TA1; .C44. **DD** 624/.05. **CODEN** CIVNEO. ***Continues in part*** *Civil Engineer in South Africa, 0009-7845.*

US/0195-3664
CIVIL ENGINEERING (NEW YORK, N.Y. 1979). (CIVIL ENGINEERING.). [Civ. eng.]. (1979)-. Monographic series. English. ir. Price varies per volume. Marcel Dekker Inc., 270 Madison Avenue, New York NY 10016. **Tel** (212)696-9000, (800)228-1160, FAX (212)685-4540, telex 421419. **(Subscription address:** Marcel Dekker Inc, PO Box 5017, Monticello NY 12701.**)** **LC** TA1; .C4523. **DD** 624.
Desc: Covers topics in civil engineering such as chemical grouting and bridge maintenance.
Ind/Abst Biodeter. Abstr.; Int. Civil Eng. Abstr.; Shock Vibr. Dig.; Soft. Abstr. Eng.

US/0885-7024
CIVIL ENGINEERING (NEW YORK, N.Y. 1983). (CIVIL ENGINEERING.). [Civ. eng.]. **Added/Corp** American Society of Civil Engineers. **VFOAT** Civil Engineering-ASCE. Vol. 53, No. 1 (Jan. 1983)-. Periodical. English. mo. $89.00 (nonmember) US; $127.00 (nonmember) other. American Society of Civil Engineers / ASCE, 345 East 47th Street, New York NY 10017-2398. **Tel** (212)705-7179, FAX (212)705-7300, telex 422847 ASCE UI. **(Subscription address:** American Society of Civil Engineers, Publisher Fulfillment Agency, Box 828, Somerset NJ 08875.**)** **DD** 624. **CODEN** CIEGEK. **[CCC]. Pr Rev.** available on microfilm and microfiche from University Microfilms International (UMI). Documents available from UMI Article Clearinghouse. ***Continues*** *Civil Engineering ASCE, 0360-0556.*
Ind/Abst Acad. Abstr. Full Text Elite (July 1990-); Acad. Abstr. (July 1990-); Acad. Search (July 1990-); Appl. Sci. Technol. Index; Ceram. Abstr. (19??-); Coal Abstr.; Concr. Abstr.; Expand. Acad. Index (1992-); Geogr. Abstr. Phys. Geogr. (?-?); GeoRef; INFO-SOUTH Abstr.; Mag. Artic. Summar. Elite (July 1990-); Mag. Artic. Summar. Select (July 1990-); Mag. Artic. Summar. CD-ROM (July 1990-); Newsp. Period. Abstr. (1992-); Sci. Cit. Index; Soc. Sci. Cit. Index [Select. Cov.]; Vocat. Search (July 1990-).

US/1051-9629
CIVIL ENGINEERING NEWS (MARIETTA, GA.). (CIVIL ENGINEERING NEWS.). **VFOAT** CE News. (1989)-. Periodical. English. mo. $34.00 US; $46.00 other. Civil Engineering News, 795 Powder Springs Street STE 4D, Marietta GA 30064. **Tel** (404)499-1857, FAX (404)428-6418. **DD** 624. **Ad Acc. Circ:** 20,000.
Desc: Provides civil engineers the latest news coverage, industry-wide developments and business strategies. Monthly columns and feature articles cover topics such as project management, computers & CAD, public works, surveying & GIS, engineering perspective, project news and company profiles.

US/0886-9685
CIVIL ENGINEERING PRACTICE. (CIVIL ENGINEERING PRACTICE : JOURNAL OF THE BOSTON SOCIETY OF CIVIL ENGINEERS SECTION/ASCE.). [Civ. eng. pract.]. **Added/Corp** American Society of Civil Engineers. Boston Society of Civil Engineers Section. Vol. 1, No. 1 (Spring 1986)-. Periodical. English. sa. $30.00 (institutions), $25.00 (individuals) US; $35.00 (institutions), $30.00 (individuals) other. Boston Society of Civil Engineers, Engineering Center, One Walnut Street, Boston MA 02108. **Tel** (617)227-5551, FAX (617)227-6783. **ED** Gian Lombardi, (editor's phone: (413)268-3632). **LC** TA1; .B78. **DD** 624. **Ad Acc. Pr Rev. Circ:** 2,950. Documents available from Article Express International. ***Continues*** *American Society of Civil Engineers. Boston Society of Civil Engineers Section. Journal of the Boston Society of Civil Engineers Section, American Society of Civil Engineers, 0361-087X.*

Desc: Presents articles that emphasize techniques being applied successfully in civil engineering projects.
Ind/Abst Bioeng. Abstr. (1986-); Ei Page One (1986-); Eng. Index Annu. [Select. Cov.]; Geotech. Abstr.; J. Plan. Lit.

US/0095-1692
CIVIL ENGINEERING REPORT SERIES. English. $3.00. Texas Tech University / Water Resource Center, PO Box 4630, Lubbock TX 79409. **LC** TD224.T4; T422 subser. **DD** 333.9/1/09764.

US/1058-9929
CIVIL ENGINEERING STUDIES. CONSTRUCTION MATERIALS RESEARCH SERIES. (1991)-. Monographic series. English. Metz Reference Room, Department of Civil Engineering, 205 North Matthews Avenue, Urbana IL 61801.

US/0734-9971
CIVIL ENGINEERING STUDIES. GEOTECHNICAL RESEARCH SERIES. **VFOAT** Geotechnical Research Series. Began with No. 17?. Monographic series. English. ir. Price varies per volume. University of Illinois Engineering Document Center, 208 Engineering Hall, Urbana IL 61801. ***Continues*** *Civil Engineering Series. Soil Mechanics Series.*

UK/0266-139X
CIVIL ENGINEERING SURVEYOR. [Civil eng. surv.]. (1979)-. Periodical. English. Ten times a year. £29.00 UK; £34.00 Europe; £39.00 other. Institution of Civil Engineering Surveyors, 26 Market Street, Altrincham, Cheshire WA14 1PF England. **Tel** 011 44 0438 351465. **ED** S J Booth. **DD** 624.05. Index available. **Bk Rev. Ad Acc. Circ:** 3,100 (ctrl). ***Continues*** *ASCE Journal.*
Desc: Matters of professional and technical interests relevant to land surveys and quantity surveyors involved in civil engineering work.
Ind/Abst Int. Civil Eng. Abstr.

UK/0263-0257
CIVIL ENGINEERING SYSTEMS. Vol. 1, No. 1 (Sept. 1983)-. Periodical. English. qt. $339.00 (academic institutions), $529.00 (corporate institutions). Gordon & Breach Science Publishers, PO Box 90, Reading RG1 8JL England. **Tel** 011 44 734 560080, FAX 011 44 734 568211. **LC** WMLC 93/2724. **CODEN** CESYEE. **[CCC].** Index available. **Bk Rev. Ad Acc. Pr Rev. Circ:** 200. Documents available from The Genuine Article.
Desc: Provides a comprehensive approach to its subject matter ranging from fundamental research papers to case studies, and endeavours to offer working tools to the practicing civil engineer involved in planning, design, construction, maintenance or operation of such systems. It contains authoritative review articles that together form a a comprehensive view of the state-of-the-art.
Ind/Abst Curr. Contents Eng. Tech. Appl. Sci.; Fluid Abstr., Civil Eng.; Fluid Abstr. Proc. Eng.; FLUIDEX; Int. Civil Eng. Abstr.; J. Ferrocement; Res. Alert [Select. Cov.]; SCISEARCH; Soft. Abstr. Eng.

●SA/1021-2000
CIVIL ENGINEERING YEOVILLE. **VFOAT** Siviele Ingenieurs (Yeoville). (1993)-. Periodical. mo. R130.00. South African Institution of Civil Engineers, Gillstraat 18A Gill Street, 93495 Yeoville 2143 South Africa. **Tel** 27 11 6481184, FAX 27 11 6487427.

IT
CODICE CONDOMINIO. (19??)-. Periodical. Italian. tq. IPSOA Editore SRL, Casella Postale 12055, Mastrangelo, 20120 Milan Italy. **Tel** 011 39 2 82476248. Index available (Included).

IT
CODICE DELL EDILIZIA LOCAZIONI CONDOMINIO. (19??)-. Periodical. Italian. tq. IPSOA Editore SRL, Casella Postale 12055, Mastrangelo, 20120 Milan Italy. **Tel** 011 39 2 82476248. Index available.

US/0045-8007
CONCRETE ABSTRACTS. See Engineering-Abstracting, Bibliographies and Statistics.

JA
CONCRETE LIBRARY INTERNATIONAL / JAPAN SOCIETY OF CIVIL ENGINEERS. **Added/Corp** Doboku Gakkai. **VFOAT** Concrete Library. No. 2 (1984)-. Periodical. English (translations available in Japanese). sa. $64.00. Japan Society of Civil Engineers, Yotsuya 1-chome Shinjuku-ku, Tokyo 160 Japan. **Tel** 03/278-9224, FAX (03)355-3446, telex J26517 MARUZEN. **(Subscription address:** Maruzen Company Ltd., PO Box 5050, Import & Export Department, Tokyo 100 31 Japan.**)** **LC** TA680; .C773. **DD** 624.1/834/05. ***Continues*** *Concrete Library.*
Desc: Contains research papers, committee reports, new codes, and committee recommendations on concrete engineering related to civil engineering works.
Ind/Abst Abstr. J. Earthq. Eng.

UK/0010-5317
CONCRETE (LONDON). (CONCRETE.). [Concrete]. **Added/Corp** Concrete Society. Vol. 1 (Jan. 1967)-. Periodical. English. Six times a year. £50.00 UK; £55.00 (surface mail), £80.00 (airmail) overseas. Concrete Society Services Ltd., Framewood Road Wexham, Slough SL3 6PJ England. **Tel** 11 44 753 662226, FAX 11 44 753 662126. **ED** R J Barfoot. **DD** 693. **CODEN** CCRTAA. **Bk Rev. Ad Acc. Circ:** 8,700. available on microfilm and microfiche from University Microfilms International (UMI). Documents available from Article Express International, CASDDS. ***Formed by the union of*** *Concrete and Constructional Engineering* ***and*** *Structural Concrete.*
Desc: Covers all aspects of concrete design and construction.
Ind/Abst Archit. Period. Index; Avery Index Archit. Period. Suppl. Colum. Univ. (19??-199?); Bioeng. Abstr.; Ceram. Abstr. (19??-); Chem. Abstr.; Coal Abstr.; Concr. Abstr.; Ei Page One; EMBASE; Eng. Index Annu. [Select. Cov.]; Geotech. Abstr.; Highw. Res. Abstr.; Int. Civil Eng. Abstr.; J. Ferrocement; Soft. Abstr. Eng.

US
CONCRETE TECHNOLOGY TODAY. See Building and Construction.

UK
CONFERENCE REPORTS : ENGINEERING, TECHNOLOGY AND APPLIED SCIENCES. V. 1-. Academic Scholarly Publication. English. qt. Elsevier Science Publishers Ltd, Crown House, Linton Road, Barking Essex IG11 8JU England. **Tel** 011 44 81 5947272, FAX 081-594-5942, telex 896950. **LC** TA5; .C67. **DD** 016.6.

SZ
CONGRESS PUBLICATIONS. English. ir. 108.00F. Intl Assn Bridge & Struc Eng, Eth Hoenggerberg, CH8093 Zurich Switzerland. **Tel** 011 41 1 3772647. **Bk Rev. Pr Rev. Circ:** 2,000.

SZ
CONGRESS REPORT / CONGRESS. **Main/Corp** International Association for Bridge and Structural Engineering. Congress. **VFOAT** Rapport du Congres; Kongress-Bericht. 13th (June 6-10, 1988)-. English (French and German). ir. 150.00F (includes Post-Congress Report). International Association for Bridge and Structural Engineering, Eth-Honggerberg, CH 8093 Zurich Switzerland. **Tel** 011 41 1 3772647, FAX 011 41 1 371213, telex 822186. ***Continues in part*** *International Association for Bridge and Structural Engineering. Congress. Rapport Final.*

BL
CONSTRUCAO HOJE. Periodical. Portuguese. Corena, Caixa Postal 30, 493 Sao Paulo Brazil. **LC** TA41; .C63. ***Absorbed*** *Construcao Moderna.*

US
CONSTRUCTION MATERIALS INVENTORY / KANSAS DEPARTMENT OF TRANSPORTATION, BUREAU OF MATERIALS & RESEARCH, BUREAU OF TRANSPORTATION PLANNING. No. 36-. Monographic series. English. ir. Price varies per volume. Bureau of Transportation Planning, Kansas Department of Transportation, State Office Building/7th Floor, Topeka KS 66612. **LC** TE200; .C66. **DD** 625.7/35/09781. ***Continues*** *Construction Materials Inventory Report.*

UK/0268-5507
CONSTRUCTION TODAY. **Added/Corp** Institution of Civil Engineers (Great Britain). No. 1 (April 1985)-. Periodical. English. Twelve times a year. £55.00 UK; £68.00 other. Thomas Telford Ltd, Thomas Telford House, 1 Heron Quay, London E14 9XF England. **Tel** 011 44 71 987 6999, FAX 011 44 71 538 4101, telex 298105. ***Absorbed*** *New Civil Engineer International.*
Ind/Abst Int. Civil Eng. Abstr.; J. Ferrocement; Soft. Abstr. Eng.

UK
CONSTRUCTION WEEKLY. ***Title Change.*** Vol. 1, No. 1 (Apr. 5, 1989)-Vol. 6, No. 11 (Mar. 23, 1994). Periodical. English. wk. Reed Business Publishing / West Sussex, England, Perrymount Road, Haywards Heath, West Sussex RH16 3DH England. **Tel** 011 44 81 6523500. **CODEN** COWEEA. ***Continues*** *Civil Engineering, 0305-6473.* ***Merged into*** *Contract Journal, 0010-7859.*
Ind/Abst Curr. Technol. Index; Fluid Abstr., Civil Eng.; Fluid Abstr. Proc. Eng.; FLUIDEX; J. Ferrocement; World Ceram. Abstr.

IT
COSTRUTTORE EDILE DELLA MARCA TREVIGIANA. (19??)-. Italian. mo. L60000. Editrice Siceta, Via Bonifacio 8, 31100 Treviso Italy. **Tel** 011 39 422 545788.

IT/0589-8765
COSTRUTTORI ITALIANI NEL MONDO. [Costr. ital. mondo]. (1961)-. Periodical. Italian. mo. L90000 Italy; L130000 Europe; L200000 other. Editrice Edilstampa, Via Guattani 20, 00161 Rome Italy. **Tel** 011

39 6 84881. **UDC** 338.7. ***Continues*** *Bollettino Informativo - Associazione Nazionale Costruttori Edili. Settore Lavori all'Estero, 0393-1498.*

IT/0393-8220
COSTRUZIONI STRADE CANTIERI. [Costr. str. cantieri]. (1984)-. Periodical. Multiple languages. ir (9 issues per year). L99000 Italy; L148000 other. Gesto Srl, Via C Battisti 21, 20122 Milan Italy. **Tel** 011 39 2 55187581, FAX 011 39 2 5465310. **UDC** 624.

US
COVERED BRIDGE TOPICS. V. 1- Apr. 1943-. Periodical. English. qt. $6.50. National Society for the Preservation of Covered Bridges, 1611 Sandcastle Road, Sanibel FL 33957. **Tel** (813)472-3188. **ED** Joseph Cohen. **LC** TG1. **DD** 624.1. **Bk Rev. Ad Acc. Circ:** 300.

II
CRI ABSTRACTS. Added/Corp Cement Research Institute of India. National Council for Cement and Building Materials (India). (1968)-. Periodical. English. qt. Rs80.00 India; $40.00 other. National Council for Cement and Building Materials, M-10 South Extension II Ring Road, New Delhi 110049 India. **Tel** 6440133, FAX 91-11-6468868, telex 031-66261. **(Subscription address:** Prints India, 11 Darya Ganj, New Delhi 110002 India.) **ED** C. Rajkumar. **LC** TA680; .C513. **Circ:** 500.
Desc: A new concept in science communication, developed to provide quick, easy and inexpensive access to information from a selected set of the world's most significant journals in the field of cement and building materials. Enables one to be abreast of contemporary developments in one's line of specialty in the larger scheme of cement and building materials technology.

II/0253-5122
CURRENT PRACTICES IN GEOTECHNICAL ENGINEERING.
Added/Corp Geo-Environ Academia (Organization : Jodhpur, India). **VFOAT** Geotechnical Engineering. Vol. 1 (1985)-. English. an. International Book Traders, G 3 46 Model Town, Delhi 110009 India. **(Subscription address:** Prints India, 11 Darya Ganj, New Delhi 110002 India.) **LC** TA710.A1; C87. **DD** 624.1/513/05.

US/0165-1854
CURRENT TOPICS IN MATERIALS SCIENCE. ***Suspended.*** [Curr. top. mater. sci.]. Began in 1977-?. Academic Scholarly Publication. English. Price varies per volume. Elsevier Science Publishing Company Inc, Madison Square Station, PO Box 882, New York NY 10159-0882. **Tel** (212)633-3950, FAX (212)633-3990. **LC** TA403; .C87. **DD** 620.1/1/05. **CODEN** CTMSD2. **[CCC].** Documents available from Article Express International, Ask*IEEE, CASDDS.
Ind/Abst Bioeng. Abstr.; Chem. Abstr.; Ei Page One; Eng. Index Annu.; INSPEC; Leadscan.

NE/0304-985X
DELFT PROGRESS REPORT. ***Ceased.*** [Delft prog. rep.]. Vol. 2 (Oct. 1976)-(19??). Academic Scholarly Publication. English. qt. Delft University Press, Stevinweg 1, 2628 CN Delft The Netherlands. **Tel** 011 31 15 783254. **CODEN** DPRED2. Documents available from Article Express International, Ask*IEEE, CASDDS. ***Formed by the union of*** *Delft Progress Report. Series A. Chemistry and Physics, Chemical and Physical Engineering, 0165-2567; Delft Progress Report. Series B. Electrical, Electronic and Information Engineering; Delft Progress Report. Series C. Mechanical and Aeronautical Engineering and Shipbuilding, 0165-2311; Delft Progress Report. Series D. Architecture, Industrial Design, Social Sciences; Delft Progress Report. Series E. Geosciences, 0302-2307* ***and*** *Delft Progress Report. Series F. Mathematical Engineering, Mathematics and Information Engineering.*
Ind/Abst Alum. Ind. Abstr.; Bioeng. Abstr.; Chem. Abstr. (1976-1983); Ei Page One; Energy Res. Abstr. (April 1977-); Eng. Index Annu. [Select. Cov.]; Fluid Abstr., Civil Eng.; Fluid Abstr. Proc. Eng.; FLUIDEX (1976-); GeoRef; Highw. Res. Abstr.; INSPEC (Oct. 1976-); Int. Aerosp. Abstr.; Math. Rev.; Met. Abstr.; Zentralbl. Math. Ihre Grenzgeb.

JA/0386-2895
DENRYOKU DOBOKU. [Denryoku doboku]. **Added/Corp** Denryoku Doboku Gijutsu Kyokai (Japan). **VFOAT** Electric Power Civil Engineering. No. 151 (1977)-. Periodical. Japanese. bm. $148.00. **(Subscription address:** Kyowa Book Company Inc., 1 38 Kanda Jinbo-Cho, Chiyoda-Ku Tokyo 101, Japan**)** **LC** TK4; .H33. ***Continues*** *Hatsuden Suiryoku.*

NE/0924-5308
DEVELOPMENTS IN CIVIL AND FOUNDATION ENGINEERING. [Dev. civ. found. eng.]. (1986)-. Monographic series. English. ir. Price varies per volume. Martinus Nijhoff Publishers, Subsidiary of Kluwer Academic Publishers, Koraalrood 50, 2718 SC Zoetermeer Netherlands. **Tel** 011 31 79 684400. **UDC** 624.
Ind/Abst Zentralbl. Math. Ihre Grenzgeb.

UK
DEVELOPMENTS IN THIN-WALLED STRUCTURES. VAT Developments in Thin Walled Structures. 1-. Academic Scholarly Publication. English. Elsevier Science Publishers Ltd, Crown House, Linton Road, Barking Essex IG11 8JU England. **Tel** 011 44 81 5947272, FAX 081-594-5942, telex 896950. **LC** TA660.T5; D48. **DD** 624.1/77.

●US/1063-1232
DIRECTORY OF CALIFORNIA LICENSED CONTRACTORS (NORTHERN ED.). **See** Building and Construction.

US
DIRECTORY OF REGISTERED ARCHITECTS, PROFESSIONAL ENGINEERS, LAND SURVEYORS, AND ARCHITECTURAL, ENGINEERING AND LAND SURVEYING CORPORATIONS.
See Architecture.

VI/0732-782X
DIRECTORY OF REGISTERED PROFESSIONAL ARCHITECTS, ENGINEERS, AND LAND SURVEYORS.
See Architecture.

SZ
DISP. Added/Corp Eidgenossische Technische Hochschule Zurich. Institut fuer Orts-, Regional- und Landesplanung. **VFOAT** Dokumente und Informationen Zur Schweizerischen Orts-, Regional-und Landesplanung. (19??)-. Academic Scholarly Publication. German (French, English and Italian). qt. Free. Institut fur Orts-Regional und Landesplanung, Redaktion DISP, ORL-Institut ETH, 8093 Zurich Switzerland. **Tel** 01-377 29 56. **ED** M. Koch and B. Huber. **LC** HD791; .D6. **DD** 361.6/09494. Index available. **Bk Rev.** ctrl circ.
Desc: Covers environmental and economic planning for Switzerland on the local, regional and national level. Scholarly monographs are illustrated with charts and computer models. Related topics include cultural dynamics, urbanization, waste management and life cycles.

US/0012-4281
DIXIE CONTRACTOR, THE. (1926)-. Trade Publication. English. Twenty-four times a year. $20.00. Dixie Contractor Inc, 525 Marshall Street, PO Box 280, Decatur GA 30031. **Tel** (404)377-2683, FAX (404)371-1509. **ED** Steve Hudson. **LC** TA1; .D5. **DD** 620.5. **Ad Acc, Adv Mgr:** F J Aaron. **Circ:** 10,000 (ctrl).
Desc: Serves the highway and heavy construction industry primarily in the states of Alabama, Florida, Georgia, South Carolina, and central and eastern Tennessee.

JA/0385-5392
DOBOKU GAKKAI RONBUN HOKOKUSHU. (DOBOKU GAKKAI RONBUN HOKOKUSHU. PROCEEDINGS OF THE JAPAN SOCIETY OF CIVIL ENGINEERS.). [Doboku Gakkai ronbun hokokushu]. **Main/Corp** Doboku Gakkai. **VFOAT** Proceedings of the Japan Society of Civil Engineers. No. 161 (1969)-. Proceedings. Japanese (summaries and/or abstracts in English; table of contents in English). mo. $529.00. Japan Society of Civil Engineers, Yotsuya 1-chome Shinjuku-ku, Tokyo 160 Japan. **Tel** 03/278-9224, FAX (03)355-3446, telex J26517 MARUZEN. **(Subscription address:** Maruzen Company Ltd., PO Box 5050, Import & Export Department, Tokyo 100 31 Japan.) **CODEN** DGRHAD. ctrl circ. Documents available from Article Express International. ***Continues*** *Doboku Gakkai. Doboku Gakkai Ronbunsho.*
Desc: Main contents are theoretical field of mathematics, physics, chemistry, technology, medicine, agricultural sciences. Takes a premier stand in natural sciences in Japan.
Ind/Abst Abstr. J. Earthq. Eng.; Alum. Ind. Abstr.; Concr. Abstr.; Ei Page One; Eng. Index Annu.; Geotech. Abstr.; Met. Abstr.; SEA Abstr.

JA/0021-468X
DOBOKU GAKKAI SHI. Added/Corp Doboku Gakkai. **VFOAT** Journal of the Japan Society of Civil Engineers. (1915)-. Periodical. Japanese. mo. Japan Society of Civil Engineers, Yotsuya 1-chome Shinjuku-ku, Tokyo 160 Japan. **Tel** 03/278-9224, FAX (03)355-3446, telex J26517 MARUZEN. cum. index.
Ind/Abst Alum. Ind. Abstr.; Coal Abstr.; Concr. Abstr.; Ei Page One; Int. Civil Eng. Abstr.; J. Ferrocement; Met. Abstr.

JA/0387-0790
DOBOKU SEKO. VFOAT Doboku-Seko. (1960)-. Periodical. Japanese. mo. $188.00. Sankaido, 5-18, Hongo 5 Chome, Bunkyoku, Tokyoto 113 Japan. **(Subscription address:** Kuowa Book Company Inc., 1 38 Kanda Jinbo-Cho, Chiyoda-Ku Tokyo 101, Japan**)** **LC** TA4; .D63.

IT/1120-2505
DST (MILANO, ITALY : 1988). (DST : RASSEGNA DI STUDI E RICERCHE DEL DIPARTIMENTO DI SCIENZE DEL TERRITORIO DEL POLITECNICO DI MILANO.). **Added/Corp** Politecnico di Milano. Dipartimento di Scienze del Territorio. **VFOAT** DsT; Territorio. (Dec. 1988)-. Periodical. Italian. Three times a year. L40000 Italy; L80000 other. Grafo Edizioni, Via A Bassi 10, 25123 Brescia Italy. **Tel** 39 30 393221, FAX 39 30 307397. **ED** Prof. P Paolillo. **LC** HD671.A1; D76.

GW/0173-6280
DVW HESSEN MITTEILUNGEN. VFOAT D.V.W. Hessen Mitteilungen. German. sa. DM5.00 Germany; $2.50 US. Deutscher Verein fur Vermessungswesen, Landesverein Hessen, Postfach 22 40, 6200 Wiesbaden 1 Germany. **Tel** 06121/535-0 OR 535-241. **LC** TA501; .D47A. **DD** 526/.1/05. Index available. cum. index. **Bk Rev. Circ:** 1,100 (ctrl). ***Continues*** *Mitteilungen (Deutscher Verein fur Vermessungswesen. Laandesverein Hessen).*
Desc: Contains articles relating to surveying, mapping, topography, professional education, licensed surveyors and valuation.

UK/0098-8847
EARTHQUAKE ENGINEERING & STRUCTURAL DYNAMICS. [Earthquake eng. struct. dyn.]. **Added/Corp** International Association for Earthquake Engineering. **VFOAT** Earthquake Engineering and Structural Dynamics; International Journal of Earthquake Engineering and Structural Dynamics. Vol. 1; (July/Sept. 1972)-. Periodical. English. Twelve times a year. $1,025.00. John Wiley & Sons Ltd., Baffins Lane, Chichester West Sussex PO19 1UD England. **Tel** 0243 779777, FAX 0243 776128 BTG:JWP001, telex 86290 WIBOOKG. **(Subscription address:** John Wiley / Philadelphia, PO Box 7247, Philadelphia PA 19170.) **ED** G. B. Warburton, A. K. Chopra, and R. W. Clough. **LC** TA654.6; .E37. **DD** 624/.176. **CODEN** IJEEBG. **[CCC]. Pr Rev. Circ:** 1,250. available on microfilm and microfiche from University Microfilms International (UMI). Documents available from Article Express International, The Genuine Article, Ask*IEEE, Documents on Demand.
Desc: Concerned with all aspects of engineering related to earthquakes and other types of dynamic loading. Publishes papers from research workers and design engineers on such aspects of earthquake engineering as ground motion characteristics, seismic code requirements, experimental behaviour of structures and related areas of concern to designer and researchers.
Ind/Abst Abstr. J. Earthq. Eng.; Acoust. Abstr.; Appl. Mech. Rev.; Appl. Sci. Technol. Index; Bioeng. Abstr.; Civ. Struct. Eng. Abstr.; Comput. Inf. Syst. Abstr. J. [Full Cov.]; Curr. Contents Eng. Tech. Appl. Sci.; Ei Page One; Energy Res. Abstr. (Jan. 1975-); Eng. Index Annu.; Environ. Abstr.; Environ. Eng. Abstr.; Fluid Abstr., Civil Eng.; Fluid Abstr. Proc. Eng.; FLUIDEX (1973-); Geogr. Abstr. Human Geogr.; Geol. Abstr.; GeoRef; Geotech. Abstr.; INSPEC (April/June 1977-); Int. Civil Eng. Abstr.; J. Ferrocement; J. Plan. Lit.; Leadscan; Mater. Sci. Eng. Abstr.; Mech. Eng. Abstr.; Life Sci. Collect.; Res. Alert [Full Cov.]; Risk Abstr.; Sci. Cit. Index; SCISEARCH; Shock Vibr. Dig.; Soft. Abstr. Eng.

UK/1012-9243
EARTHQUAKE ENGINEERING - EUROPEAN SYMPOSIUM ON EARTHQUAKE ENGINEERING.
(EARTHQUAKE ENGINEERING: PROCEEDINGS OF THE EUROPEAN SYMPOSIUM ON EARTHQUAKE ENGINEERING.). [Earthq. eng. - Eur. Symp. Earthq. Eng.]. **Main/Conf** European Symposium on Earthquake Engineering. 1962-. Proceedings. English.
Ind/Abst Abstr. J. Earthq. Eng. (?-?); GeoRef.

US/8755-2930
EARTHQUAKE SPECTRA. (EARTHQUAKE SPECTRA : THE PROFESSIONAL JOURNAL OF THE EARTHQUAKE ENGINEERING RESEARCH INSTITUTE.). [Earthq. spectra]. Vol. 1, No. 1 (Nov. 1984)-. Periodical. English. qt. $120.00 (institutions), $75.00 (individual). Earthquake Engineering Research Institute / Oakland, CA, 499 14th Street, Suite 320, Oakland CA 94612. **Tel** (510)451-0905, FAX (510)451-5411. **ED** Charles C. Thiel. **LC** TA654.6; .E384. **DD** 624.1/762/05. **CODEN** EASPEF. Index available. **Bk Rev. Circ:** 1,600.
Desc: The journal of record for the professions in earthquake hazard mitigation-engineers, seismologists, planners, architects, social scientists, and policy makers.
Ind/Abst Abstr. J. Earthq. Eng.; Ei Page One; GeoRef; Shock Vibr. Dig.

IT
EDILIZIA. (19??)-. Italian. bw. L40000. Sepit Srl, Via San Francesco da Paola 37, 10123 Turin Italy. **Tel** 011 39 11 57491.

IT
EDILIZIA-EX PREFABBRICAZIONE.
(19??)-. Italian. Ten times a year. L110000.00 Italy; L165000.00 other. De Lettera Edizioni, Via A Bazzini 17, 20131 Milan Italy. **Tel** 011 39 2 2664781, FAX 011 39 2 2664781. ***Continues*** *Edizilia e Industrializzazione.*

JA/0285-6107
EHIME DAIGAKU KOGAKUBU KIYO.
VFOAT Memoirs of the Faculty of Engineering, Ehime University. Academic Scholarly Publication. English (Japanese). an. Ehime Daigaku Kogakubu, 3-ban Bunkyo-cho, Matsuyama-shi Japan. **LC** TA4; .E36. **CODEN** EDKKDE. Documents available from CASDDS. ***Continues*** *Ehime Daigaku Kiyo. Dai 3-Bu, Kogaku.*
Ind/Abst Chem. Abstr.

US/1062-9580
ELECTRONIC SWEET'S. See Building and Construction.

●US/1075-0495
EMERGING TECHNOLOGY (AMERICAN SOCIETY OF CIVIL ENGINEERS).
(EMERGING TECHNOLOGY : A PUBLICATION OF THE ASCE AND THE CIVIL ENGINEERING RESEARCH FOUNDATION.). [Emerg. technol.]. **Added/Corp** American Society of Civil Engineers. Civil Engineering Research Foundation. (1994)-. Periodical. English. bm (6 issues). $80.00 (non-members), $40.00 (members). American Society of Civil Engineers / ASCE, 345 East 47th Street, New York NY 10017-2398. **Tel** (212)705-7179, FAX (212)705-7300, telex 422847 ASCE UI. **(Subscription address:** American Society of Civil Engineers, Publisher Fulfillment Agency, Box 828, Somerset NJ 08875.**)**
Desc: A joint publication of ASCE and the Civil Engineering Research Foundation. Articles feature materials, methods, equipment, processes and software in the construction, transportation, water resources and environmental fields. Spotlights what is out of the lab and ready for industry.

US
EMPIRE STATE SURVEYOR. Added/Corp New York State Association of Professional Land Surveyors. Vol. 1 (1965)-. Periodical. English. bm (Jan., Mar., May, July, Sept., Nov.). $25.00. Empire State Surveyor, PO Box 2988, Syracuse NY 13220. **Tel** (315)455-1073, FAX (315)454-8117. **ED** Margaret A. Shields. **Bk Rev**, (Qty: rarely). **Ad Acc. Circ:** 1,970 (ctrl).

BL/0100-2201
ENGENHARIA CIVIL (SAO PAULO).
(ENGENHARIA CIVIL.). Yearly V. 1- Nov. 1974-. Academic Scholarly Publication. Portuguese. $100. Engetec, rua Nestor Pestana 125 50 Andar, Sao Paulo Brazil. **LC** TA4; .E47115. Documents available from CASDDS. ***Supersedes in part** Engenharia.*
Ind/Abst Chem. Abstr.

UK/0969-9988
ENGINEERING CONSTRUCTION & ARCHITECTURAL MANAGEMENT.
(199?)-. Academic Scholarly Publication. English. Four times a year. $205.00 (institutions), $94.00 (individuals) US & Canada; £120.00 (institutions), £55.00 (individuals) Europe; £132.00 (institutions), £60.50 (individuals) other. Blackwell Scientific Publications Ltd, Marston Book Services, PO Box 87, Oxford OX2 ODT UK. **Tel** 011 44 865 791155, FAX 011 44 865 791927, telex 837 515 MARDIS G.

US/0896-1735
ENGINEERING INTERNATIONAL.
Added/Corp American Society of Civil Engineers. (Jan. 1988)-. Periodical. English. mo. $30.00. American Society of Civil Engineers / ASCE, 345 East 47th Street, New York NY 10017-2398. **Tel** (212)705-7179, FAX (212)705-7300, telex 422847 ASCE UI. **(Subscription address:** American Society of Civil Engineers, Publisher Fulfillment Agency, Box 828, Somerset NJ 08875.**) DD** 624.

UK
ENGINEERING PAPERS. *Ceased.* Main/Corp Building Research Station (Great Britain). (19??)-(1994). English. Building Research Establishment, BRE Bookshop, Garston Watford WD27JR England. **Tel** 011 44 923 664444, FAX 011 44 923 664400.

UK/0141-0296
ENGINEERING STRUCTURES. [Eng. struct.]. Vol. 1, No. 1 (Oct. 1978)-. Periodical. English. Ten times a year. $582.00 The Americas; £390.00 other. Butterworth Heinemann Publishers, Linacre House, Jordan Hill, Oxford OX2 8DP England. **Tel** 011 44 865 310366. **(Subscription address:** Elsevier Science Ltd. Oxford Fulfillment Centre, PO Box 800, Kidlington, Oxford OX5 1DX United Kingdom.**) ED** P. L. Gould and A. E. Long. **LC** TA630; .E54. **DD** 624.1/05. **CODEN** ENSTDF. **[CCC].** Index available. **Bk Rev. Ad Acc. Pr Rev.** available on microfilm and microfiche from University Microfilms International (UMI). Documents available from Article Express International, The Genuine Article.
Desc: Provides board intergrated coverage of the dynamic effects of wind, earthquakes and waves and of the analytical methods whereby the structural response to these loadings may be computed. It features both theoretical and applied research papers describing original work not previously published. It also encourages submission of articles on the design and construction of significant structures.
Ind/Abst Abstr. J. Earthq. Eng.; Acoust. Abstr.; Agric. Eng. Abstr.; Alum. Ind. Abstr.; Bioeng. Abstr.; BMT Abstr.; Concr. Abstr.; Curr. Contents Eng. Tech. Appl. Sci.; Ei Page One; Energy Res. Abstr. (March 1981-); Eng. Mater. Abstr.; Eng. Index Annu.; Fluid Abstr., Civil Eng.; Fluid Abstr. Proc. Eng.; FLUIDEX (1978-); Int. Civil Eng. Abstr.; Met. Abstr.; Ocean. Abstr.; Life Sci. Collect.; Pollut. Abstr. Indexes; Res. Alert [Full Cov.]; Sci. Cit. Index; SCISEARCH; Shock Vibr. Dig.; Soft. Abstr. Eng.

IT/0394-5103
EUROPEAN EARTHQUAKE ENGINEERING. Vol. 1, No. 1 (Dec. 1987)-. Periodical. English. Three times a year. L156000. Patron Editore, Via Badini 12, 40050 Quarto Inf. Bologna Italy. **Tel** 011 39 51 767003, FAX 011 39 51 768252. **ED** Duilio Benedetti. **CODEN** EEENEZ. **Bk Rev. Circ:** 1,000 (ctrl).
Desc: For engineers, researchers and educators. Publishes research results obtained by European researchers in the fields of earthquake engineering and engineering seismology and informs about events and projects currently in progress.
Ind/Abst Abstr. J. Earthq. Eng.

AU
EVM, EICH- UND VERMESSUNGSMAGAZIN. Added/Corp Austria. Bundesamt fur Eich- und Vermessungswesen. **VFOAT** Eich- und Vermessungsmagazin. (19??)-. Periodical. German. **LC** TA165; .E15.

US/0882-4258
EXCELLENCE IN HIGHWAY DESIGN.
(EXCELLENCE IN HIGHWAY DESIGN / U.S. DEPARTMENT OF TRANSPORTATION, FEDERAL HIGHWAY ADMINISTRATION.). Began in 1980. English. be. US Department of Transportation - Federal Highway Administration, 400 Seventh Street Southwest, Washington DC 20590. **Tel** (202)366-0660. **LC** TE177; .H53. **DD** 625.7/079. ***Continues** Highway and its Environment, 0882-424X.*

IS/0440-0917
FACULTY PUBLICATION - TECHNION - ISRAEL INSTITUTE OF TECHNOLOGY, FACULTY OF CIVIL ENGINEERING. [Fac. publ. - Technion - Isr. Inst. Technol. Fac. Civ. Eng.]. (19??)-. Periodical. English.
Ind/Abst Irr. Drain. Abstr.

GS
FIZIKA I MEKHANIKA GORNYKH POROD. Main/Corp G. Culukizis Saxelobis Samto Mekanikis Instituti. (1974)-. Academic Scholarly Publication. Russian. 0.63rub single issue. Izdatelstvo Metsniereba / Science Publishers, Ulitsa Kutuzova 19, 380060 Tbilisi 60 Georgia (Republic). **LC** TA705; .A43a. **CODEN** FMGPDF. Documents available from CASDDS.
Ind/Abst Chem. Abstr. (?-1977).

US/0015-4628
FLUID DYNAMICS. [Fluid dyn.]. **Added/Corp** Consultants Bureau. Vol. 1 (Jan./Feb. 1966)-. Periodical. English (Russian). bm. $1265.00 US; $1480.00 other. Consultants Bureau, A Division of Plenum Publishing Corporation, 233 Spring Street, New York NY 10013. **Tel** (212)620-8000, (212)620-8466, FAX (212)463-0742, telex 23/421139. **ED** G. G. Chernyi. **LC** TA357; .F57. **CODEN** FLDYAH. **[CCC].** Index available. available on microfilm and microfiche from University Microfilms International (UMI). Documents available from Article Express International, Ask*IEEE, CASDDS.
Desc: Publishes articles on theoretical and applied research in aerodynamics, magnetohydrodynamics, fluid mechanics, problems of the motion of a gas with nonequilibrium chemical reactions, statistical methods.
Ind/Abst Appl. Mech. Rev.; Bioeng. Abstr.; Chem. Abstr.; Ei Page One; Eng. Index Annu.; Fluid Abstr., Civil Eng.; Fluid Abstr. Proc. Eng.; FLUIDEX (1973-); INIS Atomindex [Micro.]; INSPEC (Jan./Feb. 1970-); Int. Aerosp. Abstr.; Math. Rev.; Life Sci. Collect.; Pollut. Abstr. Indexes; Proc. Chem. Eng.; Theoret. Chem. Eng.; Zentralbl. Math. Ihre Grenzgeb.

FR
FORMES ET STRUCTURES : ARCHITECTURE, GENIE CIVIL, ENVIRONNEMENT. See Architecture.

GW/0532-2669
FORTSCHRITT-BERICHTE DER VDI-ZEITSCHRIFTEN. REIHE 4, BAUINGENIEURWESEN. [Fortschrittber. VDI-Z., 4, Bauingenieurwes.]. **Added/Corp** Verein Deutscher Ingenieure. **VFOAT** Bauingenieurwesen. **VAT** Fortschrittberichte der Verein Deutscher Ingenieure Zeitschriften. Reihe Vier: Bauingenieurwesen. (19??)-. Monographic series. German. ir. Price varies per volume. VDI Verlag GmbH, Postfach 101054, D 40001 Dusseldorf Germany. **Tel** 011 49 211 6188313, FAX 011 49 211 6188133. **LC** TA3; .F65. **DD** 624/.08. **CODEN** FBVBA2. ***Continues** Fortschritt-Berichte VDI-Zeitschrift. Reihe 4: Bauingenieurwesen.*
Ind/Abst Bioeng. Abstr.; Int. Aerosp. Abstr.

US/0015-8933
FOUNDATION FACTS. [Found. facts]. Vol. 1 (Spring 1965)-. Periodical. English. sa. Raymond International, Box 22718, Houston TX 77027. **Tel** (713)623-1446. **DD** 060. **CODEN** FDFTAO.
Ind/Abst Ei Page One.

JA
GAIYO - HOKKAIDO KAIHATSUKYOKU DOBOKU SHIKENJO. Main/Corp Japan. Hokkaido Kaihatsukyoku. Doboku Shikenjo. **VFOAT** Operational Outline of the Civil Engineering Research Institute. Japanese (Japanese). Hokkaido Kaihatsukyoku Dobuku Shikenjo, 2 Hiragishi Ichijo 3-chome Toyohira-ku, Sapporo 062 Japan. **LC** TA160.6.J3; J34B.

IT/0393-1641
GALLERIE E GRANDI OPERE SOTTERRANEE. [Gallerie grandi opere sotter.]. (1976)-. Periodical. Italian. tq. L40000 Italy; L50000 other. Dune Srl, Via Montemagno 15, 10132 Turin Italy. **Tel** 011 39 11 8195694. **UDC** 624.19.

US/0747-0622
GARDEN RAILWAYS. See Transportation-Railroads.

NE/0046-5577
GEMEETEWERKEN. *Title Change.*
[Gemeentewerken]. **Added/Corp** Bond van Hoofden van Gemeentewerken (Netherlands) Hinderwet en Bouwtoezichtvereniging (Netherlands) Vereniging van Directeuren en Ingenieurs van Gemeentewerken (Netherlands) Nederlands Instituut van Direkteuren en Ingenieurs van Gemeentewerken. Vol. 1 (1972)-(1992). Academic Scholarly Publication. Dutch. mo. Samson Bedrijfsinformatie, Postbus 4, 2400 HA Alphen Rij Netherlands. **Tel** 011 31 1 72066633. ***Formed by the union of** Publieke Werken **and** Technisch Gemeenteblad. **Continued by** Stadswerk.*
Ind/Abst Avery Index Archit. Period. Suppl. Colum. Univ. (19??-199?); EMBASE; Saf. Health Work.

FR/0016-6812
GENIE CIVIL, LE. *Title Change.* V. 1 (Nov. 1, 1880)-?. Periodical. French. mo. Monsieur Boblet, 22 Avenue Victoria, 75001 Paris France. **LC** TA2; .G3. **DD** 620/.005. cum. index. ***Superseded by** Revue Generale des Techniques.*

IT
GEOMETRA DELLA PROVINCIA GRANDA. (19??)-. Periodical. Italian. Four times a year. L50000 Italy. ICAP SPA, Piazza Galimberti 10, 12100 Cuneo, Italy. **Tel** 011 39 171 698989.

FR/0016-7967
GEOMETRE. [Geometre]. (Jan. 1952)-. Periodical. French. mo (with Aug. and Sept. combined). 500.00F France; 750.00F other. Publi Topex, 13 rue Leon Cogniet, 75017 Paris France. **Tel** 1 42 27 30 78, FAX 1 47 63 71 16. **LC** TA501; .R4. **CODEN** GRGTA2. ***Continues** Revue Mensuelle of the Ordre des Geometres-Experts Francais; Journal des Geometres Experts et Topographes Francais.*
Ind/Abst Bibliogr. Carto.; GeoRef.

TH/0046-5828
GEOTECHNICAL ENGINEERING.
Added/Corp Southeast Asian Society of Soil Engineering. Asian Institute of Technology. Southeast Asian Society of Soil Engineering. Journal of the Southeast Asian Society of Soil Engineering. Vol. 1 (June 1970)-. Periodical. English. Twice a year (June & Dec.). $20.00 (individuals), $30.00 (institutions). Asian Institute of Technology, PO Box 2754, 10501 Bangkok Thailand. **Tel** 011 66 2 5245429. **ED** D. Greenway. **LC** TA710.A1; G39. **DD** 624/.151/05. cum. index. **Bk Rev. Ad Acc.** ctrl circ. Documents available from Article Express International.
Ind/Abst Ei Page One; Eng. Index Annu. [Select. Cov.]; GeoRef; Geotech. Abstr.; Int. Civil Eng. Abstr.; Sci. Cit. Index (19??-19??); SCISEARCH; Soft. Abstr. Eng.

US/0895-0563
GEOTECHNICAL SPECIAL PUBLICATION. [Geotech. spec. publ.].
Added/Corp American Society of Civil Engineers. No. 1 (1986)-. Monographic series. English. ir. Price varies per volume. American Society of Civil Engineers / ASCE, 345 East 47th Street, New York NY 10017-2398. **Tel** (212)705-7179, FAX (212)705-7300, telex 422847 ASCE UI. **(Subscription address:** American Society of Civil Engineers, Publisher Fulfillment Agency, Box 828, Somerset NJ 08875.**) DD** 624. Documents available from Article Express International.
Ind/Abst Ei Page One; Eng. Index Annu.; GeoRef.

GW/0172-6145
GEOTECHNIK. (GEOTECHNIK : ORGAN DER DEUTSCHEN GESELLSHAFT FUER ERD- UND GRUNDBAU.). [Geotechnik]. (1978)-. Academic Scholarly Publication. German. Four times a year. DM50.00. Deutsche Gesellschaft fur Erd-und Grundbau, Hohenzollernstr 52, 45128 Essen Germany. **Tel** 49 201 782723, FAX 49 201 782743. **ED** Smoltczyk, Gudehus, Wittke, Krauter, Floss, Nubbaumer. **LC** TA710.A1; G396. **DD** 624.1/51/05. cum. index. **Bk Rev**, (Qty: 4). **Ad Acc. Circ:** 2,300 (ctrl).
Desc: Soil mechanics, foundation engineering, rock mechanics and engineering geology.
Ind/Abst EMBASE; GeoRef; Geotech. Abstr.; Int. Civil Eng. Abstr.; Soft. Abstr. Eng.

UK/0016-8505
GEOTECHNIQUE. [Geotechnique]. Vol. 1 (June 1948/Dec. 1949)-. Periodical. English (French). Four times a year (Mar., June, Sept., Dec.). £133.00 UK; £158.00 other. Thomas Telford Ltd, Thomas Telford House, 1 Heron Quay, London E14 9XF England. **Tel** 011

44 71 987 6999, FAX 011 44 71 538 4101, telex 298105. **ED** Martin Owen. **LC** TA710.A1; G4. **CODEN** GTNQA8. **[CCC].** Index available. **Bk Rev. Ad Acc. Pr Rev. Circ:** 3,000. Documents available from Article Express International, The Genuine Article, Petroleum Abstracts Document Delivery Service.
Desc: Soil/rock mechanics, offshore geotechnics, coastal engineering, mathematical modelling of soil properties, construction of dams and foundations, and landslides.
Ind/Abst Abstr. J. Earthq. Eng. (?-?); AESIS Q.; Agric. Eng. Abstr.; Bioeng. Abstr.; Coal Abstr.; Curr. Contents Eng. Tech. Appl. Sci.; Curr. Technol. Index; Ei Page One; Eng. Index Annu.; Fluid Abstr., Civil Eng.; Fluid Abstr. Proc. Eng.; FLUIDEX; Geogr. Abstr. Phys. Geogr.; Geol. Abstr.; GeoRef; Geotech. Abstr.; Highw. Res. Abstr.; Int. Civil Eng. Abstr.; Life Sci. Collect.; Pet. Abstr.; Res. Alert [Full Cov.]; Sci. Cit. Index; SCISEARCH; Soft. Abstr. Eng.; Soils Fert.; World Ceram. Abstr.

BL/0379-9522
GEOTECNIA. [Geotecnia]. **Added/Corp** Sociedade Portuguesa de Geotecnia. (19??)-. Periodical. Portuguese (French and English; summaries and/or abstracts in English). Three times a year (Mar., July, Dec.). $40.00. Sociedade Portuguesa de Geotecnia, Avenida do Brasil 5, Lisbon Portugal. **Tel** 011 351 1 8482131, FAX 011 351 1 8478187. **LC** TA710.A1; G44. **DD** 624.1/513/05. **CODEN** GEOTDM.
Ind/Abst GeoRef; Geotech. Abstr.

IT/0017-016X
GIORNALE DEL GENIO CIVILE. [G. genio civ.]. Vol. 83; 1945-. Periodical. Italian. qt. L90000 Italy; L130000 other. Istituto Poligrafico Zecca Stato, Piazza Verdi 10, 00198 Rome Italy. **Tel** 011 39 6 85082307, 011 39 6 85082221. **LC** TA4; .A6. **CODEN** GIGCAO. Documents available from Article Express International. ***Continues*** *Annali dei Lavori Pubblici.*
Ind/Abst Abstr. J. Earthq. Eng.; Bioeng. Abstr.; Ei Page One; Eng. Index Annu.; Int. Civil Eng. Abstr.; Soft. Abstr. Eng.

UK/0017-4653
GROUND ENGINEERING. [Ground eng.]. No. 1 (1968)-. Periodical. English. Ten times a year. £44.00 UK; £54.00 other. Thomas Telford Ltd, Thomas Telford House, 1 Heron Quay, London E14 9XF England. **Tel** 011 44 71 987 6999, FAX 011 44 71 538 4101, telex 298105. **ED** B. D. Johnson. **LC** TA715; .G74. **CODEN** GRENDB. **[CCC].** Index available. **Bk Rev. Ad Acc. Circ:** 4,048. Documents available from Article Express International.
Desc: The dissemination of information on techniques and equipment in geotechnical and geomorphological theory and practice, including site descriptions.
Ind/Abst AESIS Q.; Art Archaeol. Tech. Abstr.; Bioeng. Abstr.; Coal Abstr.; Ei Page One; Eng. Index Annu.; GeoRef; Geotech. Abstr.; Highw. Res. Abstr.; Int. Civil Eng. Abstr.; Soft. Abstr. Eng.; World Ceram. Abstr.

UK/0959-9959
GROUND ENGINEERING YEARBOOK. (19??)-. English. an. £55.00. Thomas Telford Ltd, Thomas Telford House, 1 Heron Quay, London E14 9XF England. **Tel** 011 44 71 987 6999, FAX 011 44 71 538 4101, telex 298105. **ED** D. M. Sanders. **LC** TA715; .G76. Index available. **Ad Acc. Circ:** 1,500. available on labels.
Desc: Directory of geotechnical and civil engineering products, plants and services.

●UK
GROUND IMPROVEMENT. (1995)-. English. qt (Jan., Apr., Jul., Oct.). £100.00 UK; £120.00 other. Thomas Telford Ltd, Thomas Telford House, 1 Heron Quay, London E14 9XF England. **Tel** 011 44 71 987 6999, FAX 011 44 71 538 4101, telex 298105.

AT
GUIDE SPECIFICATIONS FOR BRIDGE CONSTRUCTION. Added/Corp National Association of Australian State Road Authorities. **VFOAT** Specifications Bridge Construction. (1987)-. English. National Association of Australian State Road Authorities, PO Box 489, Milsons Point New South Wales 2061 Australia. **Tel** (02)957-6188, FAX (02)959-4756. **LC** TG310; .G85.

AT
GUIDE TO STABILISATION IN ROADWORKS / NATIONAL ASSOCIATION OF AUSTRALIAN STATE ROAD AUTHORITIES. See Transportation-Roads and Traffic.

NE/0046-7316
HERON. Vol. 17 (1970)-. Periodical. English. qt. Free. Stevinweg 1, PO Box 5048, 2600 GA Delft The Netherlands. **CODEN** HERNDU. Documents available from Article Express International. ***Supersedes*** *Heron. English Edition; Heron. Dutch Edition.*
Ind/Abst Bioeng. Abstr.; Concr. Abstr.; Ei Page One; Eng. Index Annu.; Int. Civil Eng. Abstr.; Soft. Abstr. Eng.

US
HIGHWAY BUILDER. Added/Corp Associated Pennsylvania Constructors. (Aug. 1922)-. Periodical. English. Four times a year (Mar., June, Sept., Dec.). $10.00. Association of Pennsylvania Construction, 800 North Third Street, Suite 500, Harrisburg PA 17102. **Tel** (717)238-2513, FAX (717)238-5060. **ED** Ron L. Geist. **Ad Acc, Adv Mgr:** Naylor Publications, **Tel** (800)879-1107. **Circ:** 3,500. ***Continues*** *Associated Pennsylvania Constructors. Bulletin.*
Desc: Publishes stories and features with photos of highway construction activities, including job stories on Pennsylvania contractors.

US/1050-0804
HIGHWAY RESEARCH ABSTRACTS (1990). See Engineering-Abstracting, Bibliographies and Statistics.

UK
HIGHWAYS (CROYDON, LONDON, ENGLAND). (HIGHWAYS.). Vol. 52, No. 1899 (March 1985)-. Periodical. English. Twelve times a year. £44.00 UK; £51.00 others. Thomas Telford Ltd, Thomas Telford House, 1 Heron Quay, London E14 9XF England. **Tel** 011 44 71 987 6999, FAX 011 44 71 538 4101, telex 298105. **LC** TE1; .H577. **DD** 625.7/05. Documents available from Article Express International. ***Continues*** *Highways + Public Works.*
Ind/Abst Curr. Technol. Index; Ei Page One; Eng. Index Annu.; Geotech. Abstr.; Int. Civil Eng. Abstr.

CC
HUN NING TU CHI CHIA CHIN HUN NING TU. Periodical. Chinese. bm. RMBY0.40. Post Office, Shen-Yang Shih, People's Republic of China. **LC** TA439; .H85. **DD** 624.1/834.

NQ
I & I.E. Y A. Added/Corp Asociacion Nicaraguense de Ingenieros y Arquitectos. **VAT** Ingenieria y Arquitectura. (19??)-. Periodical. Spanish. $2.00 single issue. Ingenieria y Arquitectura, Apartado No 3518, Managua Nicaragua. **LC** TA4; .T34. ***Continues*** *Ingenieria y Arquitectura.*

SZ
IABSE REPORTS. Added/Corp International Association for Bridge and Structural Engineering. **VFOAT** I.A.B.S.E. Reports. **VAT** International Association for Bridge and Structural Engineering Reports. Vol. 37 (1982)-. Monographic series. English (French and German). ir. Price varies per volume. International Association for Bridge and Structural Engineering, Eth-Honggerberg, CH 8093 Zurich Switzerland. **Tel** 011 41 1 3772647, FAX 011 41 1 371213, telex 822186. ***Continues*** *Reports of the Working Commissions (International Association for Bridge and Structural Engineering).*

US/0882-2115
ICES JOURNAL. *Ceased.* [ICES j.]. Vol. 1 (1968)-?. Periodical. English. sm. Ices User Group Inc, PO Box 8243, Cranston RI 02920. **Tel** (401)885-1688. **ED** Frederick E Hajjar. **DD** 001. **Ad Acc. Circ:** 500 (ctrl).
Desc: Contains papers presented at conferences and other information relevant to the civil engineering community.

US/0730-9244
IEEE CONFERENCE RECORD-ABSTRACTS. (IEEE CONFERENCE RECORD-ABSTRACTS / IEEE INTERNATIONAL CONFERENCE ON PLASMA SCIENCE.). [IEEE conf. rec.-abstr.]. **Main/Conf** IEEE International Conference on Plasma Science. 1976-. English. an. IEEE, Institution of Electrical and Electronics Engineers, Inc., 345 East 47th Street, New York NY 10017-2394. **Tel** (908)981-1393, FAX (908)981-9667. **(Subscription address:** IEEE Service Center, 445 Hoes Lane, Piscataway, NJ 08854; telephone: (201)981-1393**)** **LC** TA2005; .I56A. **DD** 621.044/05. **[CCC].** ***Continues*** *IEEE Conference Record-Abstracts, 0730-9244.*
Ind/Abst Index IEEE Publ.

VE/0376-723X
IMME BOLETIN TECNICO. [Bol. tec. - IMME]. **Main/Corp** Universidad Central de Venezuela. Instituto de Materiales y Modelos Estructurales. **VFOAT** Boletin Tecnico. (1962)-. Periodical. Spanish (English). ir. Institute d'Materiales y Modelos Estr Faculty Ingenieria UCV, Apartado 50 361, Carcas 1050A Venezuela. Index available. cum. index. **Bk Rev. Circ:** 1,200 (ctrl).
Ind/Abst GeoRef.

II/0019-4565
INDIAN CONCRETE JOURNAL, THE. See Building and Construction.

II/0046-8983
INDIAN GEOTECHNICAL JOURNAL. [Indian geotech. j.]. **Added/Corp** Indian Geotechnical Society. (Jan. 1971)-. Periodical. English. qt. $35.00. Indian Geotechnical Society, Civil Engineering Department, Indian Institute Technology, Hauz Khas New Delhi 110016 India. **(Subscription address:** Prints India, 11 Darya Ganj, New Delhi 110002 India.**)** **LC** TA710; .A1I42. **CODEN** IGTJAG. Documents available from Article Express International. ***Continues*** *Journal of the Indian National Society of Soil Mechanics and Foundation Engineering, 0537-233X.*
Ind/Abst Abstr. J. Earthq. Eng. (?-?); Bioeng. Abstr.; Ei Page One; Eng. Index Annu.; GeoRef; Geotech. Abstr.

US/0097-4560
INFORMATION SERIES - ASPHALT INSTITUTE. Main/Corp Asphalt Institute. Monographic series. English. Price varies per volume. Asphalt Institute, Asphalt Institute Building, College Park MD 20740-1802. **Tel** (301)277-4258, FAX (301)927-5226. **LC** TE270; .A74.
Desc: Concerns asphalt pavements for streets, parking lots, athletics and in railway roadbeds.

IT
INGEGNERI E COSTRUTTORI. (19??)-. Italian. mo. L67000. IST Promozionale Industria SRL, Piazza Castello 3, 36100 Vicenza Italy. **Tel** 011 39 444 542211.

IT/0393-1420
INGEGNERIA SISMICA. [Ing. sism.]. (1984)-. Periodical. Italian (English). tq. L75000 Italy L85000 other. Patron Editore, Via Badini 12, 40050 Quarto Inf. Bologna Italy. **Tel** 011 39 51 767003, FAX 011 39 51 768252. **ED** Alberto Castellani. **UDC** 550.34. **Ad Acc. Circ:** 5,000 (ctrl).
Desc: Journal of earthquake engineering and engineering seismology.

CU/0020-1022
INGENIERIA CIVIL (LA HABANA). (INGENIERIA CIVIL.). [Ing. civ.]. V. 1- Jan. 1950-. Periodical. Spanish. bm. Ediciones Cubanas, Obispo 527, Altos ESQ Bernaza, CP 10100 Havana Cuba. **Tel** 011 632980, 631942, FAX 011 631011, telex 512337, 6540. **LC** TA4; .C4553. **DD** 624./05. **CODEN** INCVAG. Index available in last issue of volume--attached.
Ind/Abst GeoRef; Int. Civil Eng. Abstr.; J. Ferrocement; Soft. Abstr. Eng.

SP/0213-8468
INGENIERIA CIVIL MADRID. [Ing. civ.Madr.]. (1987)-. Periodical. Spanish (summaries and/or abstracts in English). Four times a year (Jan., Apr., July, Oct.). 7000ptas Spain; $90.00 other. Centro Estudios Exper Obras, Calle Alfonso XII 3, 28014 Madrid Spain. **Tel** 011 34 1 335-7200. **UDC** 624. Index available. **Pr Rev.** ***Continues*** *Boletin Bibliografico de Ingenieria Civil, 0211-3147.*
Desc: Technical articles on highways, coastal hydrology, bridge structure, materials and geotechnics.

CU
INGENIERIA ESTRUCTURAL Y VIAL. Added/Corp Instituto Superior Politecnico "Jose Antonio Echeverria.". (1989)-. Periodical. Spanish (summaries and/or abstracts in English; table of contents in English). tq. Ediciones Cubanas, Obispo 527, Altos ESQ Bernaza, CP 10100 Havana Cuba. **Tel** 011 632980, 631942, FAX 011 631011, telex 512337, 6540. ***Continues*** *Ingenieria Estructural.*

IE/0790-5769
INTERNATIONAL BUILDING SCIENCE & CONSTRUCTION ABSTRACTS. *Title Change.* **VFOAT** International Building Science and Construction Abstracts. Pt. 1 (Mar. 1986)-(19??). Periodical. English. qt. CITIS Ltd, 2 Rosemount Terrace, Blackrock Dublin Ireland. **Tel** 3531-886227, FAX 3531-885971, telex 30259 MSCH ET. **Ad Acc.** ***Merged with*** *International Structural Engineering Abstracts* ***to form*** *International Building Science & Structural Abstracts.*
Desc: Conprises abstracts of the world's most important literature in the field of building and construction science.

UK/0959-6038
INTERNATIONAL CEMENT REVIEW. See Building and Construction.

IE/0332-4095
INTERNATIONAL CIVIL ENGINEERING ABSTRACTS. See Engineering-Abstracting, Bibliographies and Statistics.

UK/0020-6415
INTERNATIONAL CONSTRUCTION. [Int. constr.]. Vol. 1, No. 1 (Sept. 1962)-. Periodical. English (French, German, Italian and Spanish). Twelve times a year. $172.00 US and Canada. Maclean Hunter Ltd. / UK, Chalk Lane Cockfosters Road, Barnet Herts EN4 0BU England. **Tel** 011 44 81 2423000, FAX 011 44 81 9759753, telex 299072. **LC** TA1; .I747. **CODEN** INCOBU. available on microfilm and microfiche from University Microfilms International (UMI). Documents available from Article Express International. ***Absorbed*** *World Construction, 0043-8375* ***and*** *CII.*
Ind/Abst Bioeng. Abstr.; Ei Page One; Eng. Index Annu.; Fluid Abstr., Civil Eng.; Fluid Abstr. Proc. Eng.; FLUIDEX; Infomat Int. Bus.; Int. Civil Eng. Abstr.; Soft. Abstr. Eng.

IE/0791-4326
INTERNATIONAL DIRECTORY OF CIVIL ENGINEERING/CONSTRUCTION SOFTWARE. See Computers-Software.

US/1056-1099
INTERNATIONAL DIRECTORY OF CONSULTANTS AND CONTRACTORS ACTIVE IN WESTERN EUROPE, AN. **See** Building and Construction.

US/0191-9636
INTERNATIONAL DIRECTORY OF CONSULTING ENVIRONMENTAL AND CIVIL ENGINEERS. **VFOAT** Directory of Consulting Environmental and Civil Engineers. Directory. English. International Research Service, PO Box 225, Blue Bell PA 19422. **LC** TD169.6; .I57. **DD** 625/.025.

UK/0363-9061
INTERNATIONAL JOURNAL FOR NUMERICAL AND ANALYTICAL METHODS IN GEOMECHANICS. [Int. j. numer. anal. methods geomech.]. **VFOAT** Numerical and Analytical Methods in Geomechanics. Vol. 1 No. 1 (Jan./March 1977)-. Periodical. English. Twelve times a year. $1,075.00. John Wiley & Sons Ltd., Baffins Lane, Chichester West Sussex PO19 1UD England. **Tel** 0243 779777, FAX 0243 776128 BTG:JWP001, telex 86290 WIBOOKG. **(Subscription address:** John Wiley / Philadelphia, PO Box 7247, Philadelphia PA 19170.**) ED** C. S. Desai, I. M. Smith, and W. Wittke. **LC** TA710.A1; I5197. **DD** 624.1/513/0151. **CODEN** IJNGDZ. **[CCC]. Pr Rev. Circ:** 900. available on microfilm and microfiche from University Microfilms International (UMI). Documents available from Article Express International, The Genuine Article, Ask*IEEE.
Desc: Covers a wide range of subjects including soil and rock mechanics, mechanics of structures and foundations, earth-structure interaction, offshore and marine technology, oil and fluid flow, geothermal energy and ice mechanics.
Ind/Abst Abstr. J. Earthq. Eng.; Acoust. Abstr.; Appl. Mech. Rev.; Bioeng. Abstr.; Coal Abstr.; Comput. Inf. Syst. Abstr. J. [Full Cov.]; Curr. Contents Eng. Tech. Appl. Sci.; Ei Page One; Eng. Index Annu.; Fluid Abstr., Civil Eng.; Fluid Abstr. Proc. Eng.; FLUIDEX (19??-); Geogr. Abstr. Phys. Geogr.; Geol. Abstr.; GeoRef; Geotech. Abstr.; Highw. Res. Abstr.; INSPEC (Jan./March 1977-); Int. Civil Eng. Abstr.; Math. Rev.; Life Sci. Collect.; Pollut. Abstr. Indexes; Res. Alert [Full Cov.]; Sci. Cit. Index; SCISEARCH; Shock Vibr. Dig.; Soft. Abstr. Eng.; Zentralbl. Math. Ihre Grenzgeb.

US/0020-7683
INTERNATIONAL JOURNAL OF SOLIDS AND STRUCTURES. [Int. j. solids struct.]. Vol. 1 (Feb. 1965)-. Periodical. English (summaries and/or abstracts in Russian). Twenty-four times a year. $2273.00 The Americas; £1525.00 other. Pergamon Press, An Imprint of Elsevier Science Ltd., The Boulevard, Langford Lane, Kidlington, Oxford OX5 1GB United Kingdom. **Tel** 011 44 865 843000, 011 44 865 843699, FAX 011 44 865 843010. **(Subscription address:** Elsevier Science Ltd. Oxford Fulfillment Centre, PO Box 800, Kidlington, Oxford OX5 1DX United Kingdom.**) ED** Charles R. Steele and G. Herrmann. **LC** TA349; .I5. **CODEN** IJSOAD. **[CCC]. Pr Rev.** available on microfilm from Microfilms International Marketing Corp.; available on microfilm and microfiche from University Microfilms International (UMI); available on microfiche from the publisher. Documents available from Article Express International, The Genuine Article, Ask*IEEE, CASDDS.
Desc: Fosters the exchange of ideas among workers in different parts of the world and also among workers who emphasize different aspects of the foundations and applications of this field.
Ind/Abst Abstr. J. Earthq. Eng.; Acoust. Abstr.; Alum. Ind. Abstr.; Appl. Mech. Rev.; Bioeng. Abstr.; Ceram. Abstr.; Chem. Abstr.; Civ. Struct. Eng. Abstr.; Comput. Inf. Syst. Abstr. J. [Full Cov.]; Curr. Contents Eng. Tech. Appl. Sci.; Ei Page One; Elect. Comm. Abstr.; Eng. Index Annu.; Environ. Eng. Abstr.; Fluid Abstr., Civil Eng.; Fluid Abstr. Proc. Eng.; FLUIDEX (199?-); GeoRef; INSPEC (1968-); Int. Aerosp. Abstr.; Int. Civil Eng. Abstr.; J. Ferrocement; Manuf. Process Eng. Abstr.; Mater. Sci. Eng. Abstr.; Math. Rev.; Mech. Eng. Abstr.; Met. Abstr.; Pollut. Abstr. Indexes; Res. Alert [Full Cov.]; Sci. Cit. Index; SCISEARCH; Soft. Abstr. Eng.; Solid State Supercond. Abstr.; Zentralbl. Math. Ihre Grenzgeb.

●UK/1062-8002
INTERNATIONAL JOURNAL OF THE STRUCTURAL DESIGN OF TALL BUILDINGS, THE. [Struct. des. tall build.]. **VFOAT** Journal of the Structural Design of Tall Buildings. (1992)-. Periodical. English. Four times a year. $225.00. John Wiley & Sons Ltd., Baffins Lane, Chichester West Sussex PO19 1UD England. **Tel** 0243 779777, FAX 0243 776128 BTG:JWP001, telex 86290 WIBOOKG. **(Subscription address:** John Wiley / Philadelphia, PO Box 7247, Philadelphia PA 19170.**) ED** G.C. Hart. **LC** TH1611; .S77. **DD** 690. **CODEN** SDTBEH. **Ad Acc, Adv Mgr:** Michael Levermore, **Tel** 0243 770351.
Desc: Provides a forum for the publication of papers in all aspects of structural engineering, related to tall buildings. In the context of the journal, tall buildings will be defined as those that are at least six stories or 160 feet (49 meters) high. Presents papers on new innovative structural systems, materials and methods of analysis.

IE/0790-5750
INTERNATIONAL STRUCTURAL ENGINEERING ABSTRACTS. ***Title Change.*** Pt. 1 (Mar. 1986)-(19??). Periodical. English. qt. CITIS Ltd, 2 Rosemount Terrace, Blackrock Dublin Ireland. **Tel** 3531-886227, FAX 3531-885971, telex 30259 MSCH ET. **ED** D. P. Murphy. ***Merged with*** *International Building Science and Construction Abstracts* ***to form*** *International Building Science & Structural Abstracts.*
Desc: Composed of abstracts of papers, books and conference proceedings published internationally.

US/0021-163X
IRONWORKER, THE. **VFOAT** Bridgeman's Magazine. V. 1- 1901-. Periodical. English. mo. $5.00. International Association of Bridge Structural and Ornamental Iron Workers, Suite 400/1750 New York Avenue NW, Washington DC 20006. **Tel** (202)383-4864. **ED** Martin T Byrne. **Circ:** 134,000 (ctrl).

NE
JAARVERSLAG - PROVINCIALE WATERSTAAT IN LIMBURG. **Main/Corp** Limburg (Netherlands) Provinciale Waterstaat. Dutch. Societe Historique et Archaeologique, Bureau LGOG, PO Box 83, Maastricht 6200 AB Netherlands. **Tel** 011 31 43 212586. **LC** TA78.L5; L5A.

JA
JIGYO NO ARAMASHI - KENSETSUSHO CHUBU CHIHO KENSETSUKYOKU. **Main/Corp** Japan. Kensetsusho. Chubu Chiho Kensetsukyoku. (19??)-. Periodical. Japanese. Kensetsucho Chubu Chiho Kensetsukyoku, 2-29 Marunouchi 3-chome Naka-ku, Nagoya Japan. **LC** TA106.C45; J36a.

UK/0031-5524
JOURNAL AND REPORT OF PROCEEDINGS - PERMANENT WAY INSTITUTION. [J. rep. proc. - Perm. Way. Inst.]. (1893)-. Periodical. English. Three times a year (Apr., Aug., Dec.). £18.00. Permanent Way Institution, 22 Chervil Close, Meir Park, Stoke-on-Trent ST3 7YD England. **Tel** 011 44 782 396691. **ED** Alan Blower. Index available. cum. index. **Bk Rev. Ad Acc. Circ:** 8,000.
Desc: Technical papers on railway civil engineering and transportation.

●US/1076-0431
JOURNAL OF ARCHITECTURAL ENGINEERING. (March 1995)-. English. qt. $108.00 (nonmember), $24.00 (member). American Society of Civil Engineers / ASCE, 345 East 47th Street, New York NY 10017-2398. **Tel** (212)705-7179, FAX (212)705-7300, telex 422847 ASCE UI. **(Subscription address:** American Society of Civil Engineers, Publisher Fulfillment Agency, Box 828, Somerset NJ 08875.**)** available on CD-ROM.
Desc: Will provide a multidisciplinary forum for practice-based information on engineering and technical issues concerned with the architectural engineering of buildings.

US/0887-381X
JOURNAL OF COLD REGIONS ENGINEERING. [J. cold reg. eng.]. **Added/Corp** Technical Council on Cold Regions Engineering. **VFOAT** ASCE Cold Regions Engineering. Vol. 1, No. 1 (March 1987)-. Periodical. English. qt. $80.00 (nonmember) US; $88.00 (nonmember) other. American Society of Civil Engineers / ASCE, 345 East 47th Street, New York NY 10017-2398. **Tel** (212)705-7179, FAX (212)705-7300, telex 422847 ASCE UI. **(Subscription address:** American Society of Civil Engineers, Publisher Fulfillment Agency, Box 828, Somerset NJ 08875.**) ED** Bernard Alkire. **DD** 620. **CODEN** JCRGEI. **[CCC].** Index available. cum. index. **Circ:** 2,000. available on microfilm and microfiche from University Microfilms International (UMI); available on CD-ROM from American Society of Civil Engineers. Documents available from Article Express International.
Desc: Includes practice and research oriented articles from civil engineering areas substantially related to cold regions. Topics include ice engineering, ice forces and cold weather construction.
Ind/Abst Appl. Sci. Technol. Index; Aquat. Sci. Fish. Abstr. (Computer File); ASCE Annu. Comb. Index (1987-); ASCE Publ. Inf. (1987-); Civ. Struct. Eng. Abstr.; Ei Page One; Eng. Index Annu.; Expand. Acad. Index (1992-); Fluid Abstr., Civil Eng.; Fluid Abstr. Proc. Eng.; FLUIDEX; GeoRef; Geotech. Abstr.; Int. Civil Eng. Abstr.; Mater. Sci. Eng. Abstr.; Ocean. Abstr.; Trans. Am. Soc. Civ. Eng.

US/0887-3801
JOURNAL OF COMPUTING IN CIVIL ENGINEERING. [J. comput. civ. eng.]. **Added/Corp** American Society of Civil Engineers. Technical Council on Computer Practices. **VFOAT** ASCE Computing in Civil Engineering; Computing in Civil Engineering. Vol. 1, No. 1 (Jan. 1987)-. Periodical. English. qt. $122.00 (nonmember) US; $131.00 (nonmember) other. American Society of Civil Engineers / ASCE, 345 East 47th Street, New York NY 10017-2398. **Tel** (212)705-7179, FAX (212)705-7300, telex 422847 ASCE UI. **(Subscription address:** American Society of Civil Engineers, Publisher Fulfillment Agency, Box 828, Somerset NJ 08875.**) DD** 624. **CODEN** JCCEE5. **[CCC].** Index available. cum. index. **Circ:** 2,100. available on microfilm and microfiche from University Microfilms International (UMI); available on CD-ROM from American Society of Civil Engineers. Documents available from Article Express International.
Desc: Covers state of the art computing in civil engineering practices. Papers describe innovative projects that have implications for civil engineering practice.
Ind/Abst ASCE Annu. Comb. Index (1987-); ASCE Publ. Inf. (1987-); Ei Page One; Eng. Index Annu.; Expand. Acad. Index (1992-); Fluid Abstr., Civil Eng.; Fluid Abstr. Proc. Eng.; FLUIDEX; GeoRef; Inf. Sci. Abstr. (?-?); Int. Civil Eng. Abstr.; Trans. Am. Soc. Civ. Eng.

US/0733-9364
JOURNAL OF CONSTRUCTION ENGINEERING AND MANAGEMENT. [J. constr. eng. manage.]. **Added/Corp** American Society of Civil Engineers. Construction Division. **VFOAT** A.S.C.E. Construction Engineering and Management; ASCE Construction Engineering and Management; Construction Engineering and Management. Vol. 109, No. 1 (March 1983)-. Academic Scholarly Publication. English. qt. $144.00 (nonmember) US; $157.00 (nonmember) other. American Society of Civil Engineers / ASCE, 345 East 47th Street, New York NY 10017-2398. **Tel** (212)705-7179, FAX (212)705-7300, telex 422847 ASCE UI. **(Subscription address:** American Society of Civil Engineers, Publisher Fulfillment Agency, Box 828, Somerset NJ 08875.**) LC** TA1; .A5236. **DD** 624/.05. **CODEN** JCEMD4. **[CCC].** Index available. cum. index. **Circ:** 8,300. available on microfilm and microfiche from University Microfilms International (UMI); available on CD-ROM from American Society of Civil Engineers. Documents available from Article Express International, The Genuine Article. ***Continues*** *Journal of the Construction Division, 0569-7948.*
Desc: Reports on construction equipment and techniques, defines construction terms and encourages education and research in construction engineering and management.
Ind/Abst Appl. Sci. Technol. Index; Aquat. Sci. Fish. Abstr. (Computer File); ASCE Annu. Comb. Index (1983-); ASCE Publ. Inf. (1983-); Curr. Contents Eng. Tech. Appl. Sci.; Ei Page One; EMBASE; Energy Res. Abstr.; Eng. Index Annu.; Expand. Acad. Index (1992-); Fluid Abstr., Civil Eng.; Fluid Abstr. Proc. Eng.; FLUIDEX (1983-); GeoRef; Highw. Res. Abstr.; INIS Atomindex [Micro.]; Int. Civil Eng. Abstr.; J. Ferrocement; Life Sci. Collect.; Res. Alert [Select. Cov.]; SCISEARCH; Soft. Abstr. Eng.; Trans. Am. Soc. Civ. Eng. (1983-).

UK/0143-974X
JOURNAL OF CONSTRUCTIONAL STEEL RESEARCH. **See** Building and Construction.

US/0733-9410
JOURNAL OF GEOTECHNICAL ENGINEERING. **See** Earth Sciences-Geology.

●US/1076-0342
JOURNAL OF INFRASTRUCTURE SYSTEMS. (Feb. 1995)-. English. qt. $108.00 (nonmember), $24.00 (member). American Society of Civil Engineers / ASCE, 345 East 47th Street, New York NY 10017-2398. **Tel** (212)705-7179, FAX (212)705-7300, telex 422847 ASCE UI. **(Subscription address:** American Society of Civil Engineers, Publisher Fulfillment Agency, Box 828, Somerset NJ 08875.**)** available on CD-ROM.
Desc: Documents important advances in infrastructure engineering methodologies and technologies.

US/0899-1561
JOURNAL OF MATERIALS IN CIVIL ENGINEERING. [J. mater. civ. eng.]. **Added/Corp** American Society of Civil Engineers. Materials Engineering Division. **VFOAT** Materials in Civil Engineering; ASCE Materials in Civil Engineering. Vol. 1, No. 1 (Feb. 1989)-. Periodical. English. qt. $153.00 (nonmember) US; $162.00 (nonmember) other. American Society of Civil Engineers / ASCE, 345 East 47th Street, New York NY 10017-2398. **Tel** (212)705-7179, FAX (212)705-7300, telex 422847 ASCE UI. **(Subscription address:** American Society of Civil Engineers, Publisher Fulfillment Agency, Box 828, Somerset NJ 08875.**) ED** Frederick V. Lawrence and P. J. Sereda. **LC** TA401; .J677. **DD** 620.1/1. **CODEN** JMCEE7. **[CCC].** Index available. cum. index. available on microfilm and microfiche from University Microfilms International (UMI); available on CD-ROM from American Society of Civil Engineers. Documents available from Article Express International.
Ind/Abst ASCE Annu. Comb. Index; ASCE Publ. Inf.; Ceram. Abstr. (19??-); Ei Page One; Eng. Index Annu.; Expand. Acad. Index (1992-); GeoRef; Geotech. Abstr.; Int. Civil Eng. Abstr.; J. Ferrocement.

US/0887-3828
JOURNAL OF PERFORMANCE OF CONSTRUCTED FACILITIES. [J. perform. constr. facil.]. **Added/Corp** American Society of Civil Engineers. Technical Council on Forensic Engineering (American Society of Civil Engineers) Architecture and

Engineering Performance Information Center. Professional Engineers in Private Practice. **VFOAT** Performance of Constructed Facilities; ASCE Performance of Constructed Facilities. Vol. 1, No. 1 (Feb. 1987)-. Periodical. English. qt. $84.00 (nonmember) US; $92.00 (nonmember) other. American Society of Civil Engineers / ASCE, 345 East 47th Street, New York NY 10017-2398. **Tel** (212)705-7179, FAX (212)705-7300, telex 422847 ASCE UI. **(Subscription address:** American Society of Civil Engineers, Publisher Fulfillment Agency, Box 828, Somerset NJ 08875.**) DD** 624. **CODEN** JPCFEV. **[CCC].** Index available. cum. index. **Circ:** 2,000. available on microfilm and microfiche from University Microfilms International (UMI); available on CD-ROM from American Society of Civil Engineers. Documents available from Article Express International.
Desc: Examines the causes and costs of performance problems in constructed facilities. Catastrophic failures and more common service ability problems are examined.
Ind/Abst Appl. Sci. Technol. Index; ASCE Annu. Comb. Index (1987-); ASCE Publ. Inf. (1987-); Constr. Index; Ei Page One; Eng. Index Annu.; Expand. Acad. Index (1992-); Fluid Abstr., Civil Eng.; Fluid Abstr. Proc. Eng.; FLUIDEX; J. Ferrocement; Trans. Am. Soc. Civ. Eng.

US/1052-3928
JOURNAL OF PROFESSIONAL ISSUES IN ENGINEERING EDUCATION AND PRACTICE. [J. prof. issues eng. educ. pract.]. **Added/Corp** American Society of Civil Engineers. Vol. 117, No. 1 (Jan. 1991)-. Periodical. English. qt. $95.00 (nonmember) US; $104.00 (nonmember) other. American Society of Civil Engineers / ASCE, 345 East 47th Street, New York NY 10017-2398. **Tel** (212)705-7179, FAX (212)705-7300, telex 422847 ASCE UI. **(Subscription address:** American Society of Civil Engineers, Publisher Fulfillment Agency, Box 828, Somerset NJ 08875.**) LC** TA1; .A52322. **DD** 624/.023. **CODEN** JPEPE3. **[CCC].** available on microfilm and microfiche from University Microfilms International (UMI); available on CD-ROM from American Society of Civil Engineers. Documents available from Article Express International. ***Continues*** *Journal of Professional Issues in Engineering, 0733-9380.*
Ind/Abst ASCE Annu. Comb. Index (1983-); ASCE Publ. Inf. (1983-); Ei Page One; Eng. Index Annu.; Expand. Acad. Index (1992-); Highw. Res. Abstr.

II/0970-0137
JOURNAL OF STRUCTURAL ENGINEERING. [J. struct. eng.]. **Added/Corp** Structural Engineering Research Centre. Vol. 1 (Apr. 1973)-. Periodical. English. Four times a year (Jan., Apr., July, Oct.). $77.00. Structural Engineering Research Center, CSIR Campus, Taramani, Madras 600113 India. **Tel** 011 91 2352175, 011 91 2350489, FAX 011 91 44-2350508, telex 041-8906 CSIR IN, 041-8798 TTRS IN. **(Subscription address:** Prints India, 11 Darya Ganj, New Delhi 110002 India.**) ED** Dr. R. Narayanan, S. Gopalakrishnan and N. Jayaraman. **LC** TA630; .J67. **DD** 624/.1/05. **UDC** 624. **CODEN** JSENEI. Index available (published separately). **Bk Rev. Pr Rev. Circ:** 500 (ctrl). Documents available from Petroleum Abstracts Document Delivery Service.
Desc: Acts as an open forum publishing papers in research and development activities in structural mechanics. Devotes one issue to a particular current theme or topic.
Ind/Abst Agric. Eng. Abstr.; Appl. Mech. Rev.; Aquat. Sci. Fish. Abstr. (Computer File); Concr. Abstr.; Curr. Contents Eng. Tech. Appl. Sci.; Ei Page One; Highw. Res. Abstr.; Int. Civil Eng. Abstr.; J. Ferrocement; Ocean. Abstr.; Pet. Abstr.; Shock Vibr. Dig.; Soft. Abstr. Eng.

US/0733-9445
JOURNAL OF STRUCTURAL ENGINEERING (NEW YORK, N.Y.). (JOURNAL OF STRUCTURAL ENGINEERING.). [J. struct. eng.]. **Added/Corp** American Society of Civil Engineers. American Society of Civil Engineers. Structural Division. **VFOAT** Structural Engineering; ASCE Structural Engineering; A.S.C.E. Structural Engineering. Vol. 109, No. 1 (Jan. 1983)-. Periodical. English. mo. $356.00 (nonmember) US; $411.00 (nonmember) other. American Society of Civil Engineers / ASCE, 345 East 47th Street, New York NY 10017-2398. **Tel** (212)705-7179, FAX (212)705-7300, telex 422847 ASCE UI. **(Subscription address:** American Society of Civil Engineers, Publisher Fulfillment Agency, Box 828, Somerset NJ 08875.**) LC** TA1; .A5235. **DD** 624.1/05. **CODEN** JSENDH. **[CCC].** Index available. cum. index. **Circ:** 7,800. available on microfilm and microfiche from University Microfilms International (UMI); available on CD-ROM from American Society of Civil Engineers. Documents available from Article Express International, The Genuine Article, Petroleum Abstracts Document Delivery Service. ***Continues*** *Journal of the Structural Division, 0044-8001.*
Desc: Journal advances the science of structural design. Topics include design, erection and safety of structures ranging from bridges to transmission towers and tall buildings.
Ind/Abst Abstr. Bull. Inst. Pap. Sci. Tech.; Abstr. J. Earthq. Eng.; Acoust. Abstr.; Appl. Sci. Technol. Index; ASCE Annu. Comb. Index (1983-); ASCE Publ. Inf. (1983-); BMT Abstr.; Concr. Abstr.; Ei Page One; Eng. Index Annu.; Expand. Acad. Index (1992-); Fluid Abstr., Civil Eng.; Fluid Abstr. Proc. Eng.; FLUIDEX (1983-); For. Prod. Abstr. (19??-19??); Geol. Abstr.; GeoRef; Geotech. Abstr.; Highw. Res. Abstr.; J. Ferrocement; Life Sci. Collect.; Pet. Abstr.; Postharvest News Inf.; Res. Alert [Full Cov.]; Risk Abstr.; Sci. Cit. Index; SCISEARCH; Trans. Am. Soc. Civ. Eng. (1983-).

US/0733-9453
JOURNAL OF SURVEYING ENGINEERING. [J. surv. eng.]. **Added/Corp** American Society of Civil Engineers. Surveying and Mapping Division. American Society of Civil Engineers. Surveying Engineering Division. **VFOAT** Surveying Engineering. Vol. 109, No. 1 (Mar. 1983)-. Periodical. English. Four times a year. $80.00 (nonmember) US; $87.00 (nonmember) other. American Society of Civil Engineers / ASCE, 345 East 47th Street, New York NY 10017-2398. **Tel** (212)705-7179, FAX (212)705-7300, telex 422847 ASCE UI. **(Subscription address:** American Society of Civil Engineers, Publisher Fulfillment Agency, Box 828, Somerset NJ 08875.**) LC** TA501; .A655. **DD** 526.9/05. **CODEN** JSUED2. **[CCC].** Index available. cum. index. **Bk Rev. Ad Acc. Pr Rev. Circ:** 1,800 (ctrl). available on microfilm and microfiche from University Microfilms International (UMI); available on CD-ROM from American Society of Civil Engineers. Documents available from Article Express International, The Genuine Article. ***Continues*** *Journal of the Surveying and Mapping Division, 0569-8073.*
Desc: Covers developments in surveying and mapping; cartographic, geodetic, oceanographic and interplanetary surveying.
Ind/Abst Appl. Sci. Technol. Index; ASCE Annu. Comb. Index (1983-); ASCE Publ. Inf. (1983-); Curr. Contents Eng. Tech. Appl. Sci.; Ei Page One; Eng. Index Annu.; Expand. Acad. Index (1992-); Fluid Abstr., Civil Eng.; Fluid Abstr. Proc. Eng.; FLUIDEX (1983-); GeoRef; Highw. Res. Abstr.; Int. Civil Eng. Abstr.; J. Plan. Lit.; Life Sci. Collect.; Res. Alert [Full Cov.]; Sci. Cit. Index (19??-19??); SCISEARCH; Soft. Abstr. Eng.; Trans. Am. Soc. Civ. Eng. (1983-).

UK/0022-4898
JOURNAL OF TERRAMECHANICS. [J. terramech.]. **Added/Corp** International Society for Terrain Vehicle Systems. Vol. 1 (1964)-. Periodical. English. Six times a year. $400.00 The Americas; £268.00 other. Pergamon Press, An Imprint of Elsevier Science Ltd., The Boulevard, Langford Lane, Kidlington, Oxford OX5 1GB United Kingdom. **Tel** 011 44 865 843000, 011 44 865 843699, FAX 011 44 865 843010. **(Subscription address:** Elsevier Science Ltd. Oxford Fulfillment Centre, PO Box 800, Kidlington, Oxford OX5 1DX United Kingdom.**) LC** TE208.5; .J6. **DD** 625.7/32. **CODEN** JTRMAF. **[CCC]. Pr Rev.** available on microfilm and microfiche from University Microfilms International (UMI). Documents available from Article Express International, The Genuine Article.
Ind/Abst Agric. Eng. Abstr. (1991-); Appl. Mech. Rev.; Bioeng. Abstr.; Curr. Contents Eng. Tech. Appl. Sci.; Ei Page One; Energy Res. Abstr.; Eng. Index Annu.; For. Prod. Abstr. (1991-); For. Abstr.; GeoRef; Geotech. Abstr.; Res. Alert [Select. Cov.]; Rice Abstr.; SCISEARCH; Soils Fert.

PP
JOURNAL OF THE ASSOCIATION OF SURVEYORS OF PAPUA NEW GUINEA, THE. Main/Corp Association of Surveyors of Papua New Guinea. English. an. $10.00. Hon Secretary, Association of Surveyors of Papua New Guinea, PO Box 1422, Boroko Papua New Guinea. **Tel** NE 23000. **ED** M J Larmer. **LC** TA527.P25; A88A. **DD** 526.9/05. **Bk Rev. Ad Acc. Circ:** 300 (ctrl).
Desc: Publication covering events and items of interest and technical papers for members of the association and other interested persons.

II/0373-1995
JOURNAL OF THE INSTITUTION OF ENGINEERS (INDIA). CIVIL ENGINEERING DIVISION. Main/Corp Institution of Engineers (India). **Added/Corp** Institution of Engineers (India). Civil Engineering Division. **VFOAT** Civil Engineering Division; IE (I) Journal-Cl. Vol. 41, Pt. Cl 1 (July 1961)-. Periodical. English. Four times a year (Feb., May, Aug., Nov.). $18.00. Institution of Engineers India, 8 Gokhale Road, Calcutta 700020 India. **Tel** 011 91 33 288311, telex 21 7885 IEIC IN. **ED** B. D. Varma. **LC** TA1; .J7. **Ad Acc. Circ:** 15,000. ***Continues in part*** *Journal of the Institution of Engineers (India), 0368-2498.*
Desc: Covers original research papers on construction planning and management, earthquake engineering, geotechnical engineering, hydrology and hydraulic engineering, ocean engineering, structural engineering, transportation engineering, and general engineering.
Ind/Abst Ei Page One; Energy Res. Abstr. (Nov. 1976-); Fluid Abstr., Civil Eng.; Fluid Abstr. Proc. Eng.; FLUIDEX (19??-); Indian Geosci. Abstr.; J. Ferrocement.

SA/1021-2019
JOURNAL OF THE SOUTH AFRICAN INSTITUTION OF CIVIL ENGINEERS / JOERNAAL VAN DIE SUID-AFRIKAANSE INSTITUUT VAN SIVIELE INGENIEURS. Added/Corp South African Institution of Civil Engineers. **VFOAT** Joernaal van die Suid-Afrikaanse Instituut van Siviele Ingenieurs. Vol. 35, No. 1 (1st Quarter 1993)-. Periodical. Afrikaans (English). qt. South African Institution of Civil Engineers, Gillstraat 18A Gill Street, 93495 Yeoville 2143 South Africa. **Tel** 27 11 6481184, FAX 27 11 6487427. **LC** TA1; .C45. **CODEN** JSAEE5. ***Continues in part*** *Civil Engineer in South Africa, 0009-7845.*

US/0733-947X
JOURNAL OF TRANSPORTATION ENGINEERING. [J. transp. eng.]. **Added/Corp** American Society of Civil Engineers. American Society of Civil Engineers. Aerospace Division. **VFOAT** Transportation Engineering; A.S.C.E. Transportation Engineering; ASCE Transportation Engineering. Vol. 109, No. 1 (Jan. 1983)-. Academic Scholarly Publication. English. bm. $157.00 (nonmember) US; $171.00 (nonmember) other. American Society of Civil Engineers / ASCE, 345 East 47th Street, New York NY 10017-2398. **Tel** (212)705-7179, FAX (212)705-7300, telex 422847 ASCE UI. **(Subscription address:** American Society of Civil Engineers, Publisher Fulfillment Agency, Box 828, Somerset NJ 08875.**) LC** TA1001; .A512. **DD** 629.04/05. **CODEN** JTPEDI. **[CCC].** Index available. cum. index. **Bk Rev. Ad Acc. Pr Rev. Circ:** 4,400 (ctrl). available on microfilm and microfiche from University Microfilms International (UMI); available on CD-ROM from American Society of Civil Engineers. Documents available from Article Express International, The Genuine Article, Petroleum Abstracts Document Delivery Service, Documents on Demand. ***Continues*** *Transportation Engineering Journal of ASCE, 0569-7891.*
Desc: Technical and professional articles on aerospace, air transport, highway, pipeline and urban transportation. Divisions of ASCE are included.
Ind/Abst Appl. Sci. Technol. Index; ASCE Annu. Comb. Index (1983-); ASCE Publ. Inf. (1983-); Bioeng. Abstr.; Civ. Struct. Eng. Abstr.; Coal Abstr.; Comput. Inf. Syst. Abstr. J. [Full Cov.]; Curr. Contents Eng. Tech. Appl. Sci.; Ei Page One; Elect. Comm. Abstr.; EMBASE; Energy Inf. Abstr.; Energy Res. Abstr. (Jan. 1983-); Eng. Index Annu.; Environ. Abstr.; Expand. Acad. Index (1992-); Fluid Abstr., Civil Eng.; Fluid Abstr. Proc. Eng.; FLUIDEX (1983-); Gas Abstr.; GeoRef; Highw. Res. Abstr.; Int. Abstr. Oper. Res. [Select. Cov.]; Int. Civil Eng. Abstr.; Mater. Sci. Eng. Abstr.; Mech. Eng. Abstr.; Pet. Abstr.; Res. Alert [Select. Cov.]; SCISEARCH; Soc. Sci. Cit. Index [Select. Cov.]; Soft. Abstr. Eng.; Trans. Am. Soc. Civ. Eng. (1983-).

CC
JOURNAL OF TSINGHUA UNIVERSITY. Tsinghua University, Research Institute of Structural Engineering, Tsinghuayuau, Beijing, People's Republic of China.
Ind/Abst Concr. Abstr.; Math. Rev.

US/0733-9488
JOURNAL OF URBAN PLANNING AND DEVELOPMENT. [J. urban plann. dev.]. **Added/Corp** American Society of Civil Engineers. Urban Planning and Development Division. Vol. 109, No. 1 (May 1983)-. Periodical. English. Four times a year. $96.00 (nonmember) US; $102.00 (nonmember) other. American Society of Civil Engineers / ASCE, 345 East 47th Street, New York NY 10017-2398. **Tel** (212)705-7179, FAX (212)705-7300, telex 422847 ASCE UI. **(Subscription address:** American Society of Civil Engineers, Publisher Fulfillment Agency, Box 828, Somerset NJ 08875.**) LC** NA9000; .A5785. **DD** 711/.4/0973. **CODEN** JUPDDM. **[CCC].** Index available. cum. index. **Bk Rev. Ad Acc. Circ:** 4,000 (ctrl). available on microfilm and microfiche from University Microfilms International (UMI); available on CD-ROM from American Society of Civil Engineers. Documents available from Article Express International, The Genuine Article, Documents on Demand. ***Continues*** *Journal of the Urban Planning and Development Division, 0569-8081.*
Desc: Application of civil engineering to urban planning including transportation, public works, utilities, environmental assessment, renewal legislation and land use planning.
Ind/Abst Acad. Search (July 1993-); Appl. Sci. Technol. Index; ASCE Annu. Comb. Index (1983-); ASCE Publ. Inf. (1983-); Comput. Inf. Syst. Abstr. J. [Full Cov.]; Curr. Contents Eng. Tech. Appl. Sci.; Curr. Contents Soc. Behav. Sci.; Ei Page One; Energy Res. Abstr. (May 1983-); Eng. Index Annu.; Environ. Abstr.; Expand. Acad. Index (1992-); Fluid Abstr., Civil Eng.; Fluid Abstr. Proc. Eng.; FLUIDEX (1983-); GeoRef; Highw. Res. Abstr.; Int. Civil Eng. Abstr.; Mag. Search; Middle East Abstr. Index; PAIS Int. Print (1991-?); Res. Alert [Full Cov.]; Risk Abstr.; SCISEARCH; Soc. Sci. Cit. Index [Full Cov.]; Trans. Am. Soc. Civ. Eng. (1983-).

US/0733-9496
JOURNAL OF WATER RESOURCES PLANNING AND MANAGEMENT. **See** Water Resources.

US/0733-950X
JOURNAL OF WATERWAY, PORT, COASTAL, AND OCEAN ENGINEERING. **See** Engineering-Hydraulic Engineering.

US/0883-0061
KEEPER'S LOG. [Keep. log]. **Added/Corp** United States Lighthouse Society. Vol. 1, No. 1 (Fall 1984)-. Periodical. English. Four times a year (Jan., Apr., July, Oct.). $25.00. US Lighthouse Society, 244 Kearny Street,

5th Floor, San Francisco CA 94108. **Tel** (415)362-7255. **ED** Wayne Wheeler. **LC** VK1000; .K44. **DD** 387.1/55. Index available (Published separately , $5.00). cum. index. **Bk Rev**, (Qty: 4-5). **Ad Acc. Circ:** 5,500.
Desc: Membership includes newsletters, a bumper sticker and membership card, plus occasional mailings and lighthouse related events around the nation. Consists of historical and contemporary information about lighthouses, lightships and related aids to navigation.

PL
KONFERENCJE. **Main/Corp** Politechnika Wrocawska. Instytut Materiaoznawstwa i Mechaniki Technicznej. **VFOAT** Seria Konferencje. Polish (summaries and/or abstracts in English and Russian). Z20.00 single issue. Wojewodzka Ksiegarnia Techniczna, Ul Swidnicka 8, 50-064 Warsaw Poland. **LC** TA401; .B7 subser.

KO
KONSOL CHONGNAM. **Added/Corp** Konsol Kisul Yonguhoe. (1976)-. Korean. W13.000. **LC** HD9715.K8; K65.

GW/0023-3633
KONSTRUKTIVER IGENIEURBAU. **See** Building and Construction.

UK/0265-4210
LAND AND MINERALS SURVEYING. ***Ceased.*** [Land miner. surv.]. **VFOAT** Lams; L & MS. Vol. 1, No. 1 (Oct. 1983)-Ceased (July/Aug. 1991). Periodical. English. mo. Royal Institution of Chartered Surveyors, PO Box 87, London EC4P 4HL England. **Tel** 01 353 2300, telex 25212 BUILDA-G. **ED** Rita Virgo. **LC** TA501; .C48. **DD** 526.9/05. Index available. **Bk Rev. Ad Acc. Circ:** 2,760 (ctrl). available on microfilm. ***Continues*** *Chartered Land Surveyor, Chartered Minerals Surveyor, 0142-520X.*
Desc: Articles describe new products, new techniques, and new computer hardware and software. Features recent contracts and reports the major conferences and lectures.
Ind/Abst Coal Abstr.; Ecol. Abstr.; Geogr. Abstr. Phys. Geogr.; Geogr. Abstr. Human Geogr. (?-?); Geol. Abstr.; GeoRef; Life Sci. Collect.

NE
LAND + WATER / MILIEUTECHNIEK. Ten times a year. Fl2550.00. VNU Business Publications BV, Postbus 9479, 1006 AC Amsterdam Netherlands. **Tel** 011 31 20 5102911, 011 31 20 5102879, FAX 011 31 20 6170291. **ED** D Schols. Index available. **Ad Acc. Pr Rev.** ctrl circ.
Desc: Magazine for civil-technical engineers.

DK/0105-4570
LANDINSPEKTREN; TIDSSKRIFT FOR OPMALINGSOG MATRIKELVAESEN. **Added/Corp** Danske Landinspektrforening. Vol. 1 (Nov., 1891)-. Periodical. Danish. Five times a year. kr226.00. Danish Technical Press, Skelbaekgade 4, DK 1717 Copenhagen 5 Denmark. **Tel** 011 45 31216801. **ED** Kay Lauritzen. cum. index. **Bk Rev. Ad Acc. Circ:** 1,500 (ctrl).
Desc: Mathematics, mapping, land information systems (LIS) surveying instruments, EDB-equipment, laws about agriculture, land conservation and housing plans.

JA
LIST OF MEMBERS - THE ASSOCIATION OF JAPANESE CONSULTING ENGINEERS. **Main/Corp** Nihon Gijutsushikai. 1974-. English. Nogyo Doboku Kainkan, 34-4 Shinbashi 5 Minato-ku 105, Tokyo Japan. **LC** TA12; .N75A. **DD** 620/.0025/52.

FI
MAANKAYTTO. Periodical. Finnish. ir. 24.00. Maanmittausinsinoorien Liitto, Vanhanlinnankuja 1 E 94 00900 90, Helsinki Finland. **LC** TA501; .M3. ***Continues*** *Maanmittausinsinoori.*

FI
MAARAKENNUS JA KULJETUS. (19??)-. Periodical. Finnish. mo. Fmk160.00. Maarakentajain Kustannus, Oy Arkadiankatu 16 B, 00100 Helsinki 10 Finland. **Tel** 90-494743. **ED** Heikki Saarento. **LC** TA725; .M25. Index available. **Bk Rev. Circ:** 4,500 (ctrl).
Desc: Contracts road and water building, municipal technics, waste and environment service and other heavy transportation pertaining to these.

UK/0024-9831
MAGAZINE OF CONCRETE RESEARCH. [Mag. concr. res.]. **Added/Corp** Cement and Concrete Association. (Jan. 1949)-. Periodical. English. qt (Mar., June, Sept., Dec.). £100.00 UK; £150.00 (airmail) other. Thomas Telford Ltd, Thomas Telford House, 1 Heron Quay, London E14 9XF England. **Tel** 011 44 71 987 6999, FAX 011 44 71 538 4101, telex 298105. **ED** J. N. Clarke. **LC** TA680; .M27. **DD** 693.505*. **CODEN** MCORAV. **[CCC]**. cum. index. **Bk Rev. Pr Rev. Circ:** 1,200. available on microfilm from University Microfilms International (UMI). Documents available from Article Express International, The Genuine Article, Ask*IEEE, CASDDS.
Desc: Covers all aspects of research on concrete and allied materials, including performance and evaluation of materials, design and testing and the use of concrete in conjunction with other materials.
Ind/Abst Abstr. J. Earthq. Eng. (?-?); Bioeng. Abstr.; Ceram. Abstr.; Chem. Abstr.; Coal Abstr.; Concr. Abstr.; Curr. Technol. Index; Ei Page One; Eng. Index Annu.; Geotech. Abstr.; Highw. Res. Abstr.; INSPEC (1968-1985); Int. Civil Eng. Abstr.; J. Ferrocement; Res. Alert [Full Cov.]; Sci. Cit. Index; SCISEARCH; Soft. Abstr. Eng.; World Ceram. Abstr.

US/0734-7685
MANUALS AND REPORTS ON ENGINEERING PRACTICE. [Man. rep. eng. pract.]. **Added/Corp** American Society of Civil Engineers. (1962)-. Monographic series. English. ir. Price varies per volume. American Society of Civil Engineers / ASCE, 345 East 47th Street, New York NY 10017-2398. **Tel** (212)705-7179, FAX (212)705-7300, telex 422847 ASCE UI. **(Subscription address:** American Society of Civil Engineers, Publisher Fulfillment Agency, Box 828, Somerset NJ 08875.**)** **CODEN** MECEAE. Documents available from Article Express International. ***Continues*** *Manuals of Engineering Practice.*
Desc: A series of books covering all areas of civil engineering, dealing with specific topics in a direct way, more in-depth than journal publications.
Ind/Abst Eng. Index Annu.; GeoRef.

●UK
MATERIALS AND STRUCTURES / INTERNATIONAL UNION OF TESTING AND RESEARCH LABORATORIES FOR MATERIALS AND STRUCTURES (RILEM). **See** Building and Construction.

IS/0025-5912
MATI (TEL-AVIV). (MATI.). [Mati]. **Main/Corp** Mekhon Ha-Tekanim Ha-Yisreeli. No. 1- April 1968-. Hebrew. ir. Mekhon Ha-Tekanim Ha-Yisrali, Rehov Ha-Universitah 42 Ramat Aviv, Tel Aviv Israel. **LC** TA368; .M43A.

US/1050-270X
MCMAHON HEAVY CONSTRUCTION COST GUIDE. [McMahon heavy constr. cost guide]. **Added/Corp** Leonard McMahon, Incorporated. **VFOAT** Heavy Construction Cost Guide; McMahon ... Construction Guide. (1989)-. English. an. $70.00. Leonard McMahon Incorporated, PO Box 7422, Quincy MA 02269. **Tel** (617)471-3883. **LC** TA183; .M36. **DD** 624/.029/9. **Bk Rev. Circ:** 1,000. ***Continues*** *Dodge Heavy Construction Cost Data.*

RU/0025-8903
MEKHANIZATSIIA STROITELSTVA. **Added/Corp** Soviet Union. Ministerstvo Stroitelnogo i Dorozhnogo Mashinostroeniia. (Dec. 1939)-. Periodical. Russian. mo. $89.95. **(Subscription address:** East View Publications Inc., 3020 Harbor Lane North, Suite 110, Minneapolis MN 55447.**)**

HU/0231-0732
MELYEPITESI ES VIZEPITESI SZAKIRODALMI TAJEKOZTATO. (1983)-. Periodical. Hungarian. mo. 9.800ft. Orszagos Muszaki Informacios Kozpont es Konyvtar (O.M.I.K.K.), National Technical Information Centre and Library Museum, u 17, PO Box 12, 1428 Budapest, Hungary. **Tel** (361)118-1994, FAX (361)138-2414, telex 22-4944 OMIKK H. **ED** Janos Winter. **UDC** 016. **CODEN** 627. Index available. cum. index. **Bk Rev. Ad Acc. Circ:** 95 (ctrl).
Desc: Information about civil engineering, roads, bridges, hydraulic construction.

US
MEMBERSHIP DIRECTORY / AMERICAN SOCIETY OF CIVIL ENGINEERS. **Main/Corp** American Society of Civil Engineers. (1984)-. Directory. English. be. United Engineering Center, 345 East 47th Street, New York NY 10017. ***Continues*** *Directory / American Society of Civil Engineers, 0569-7883.*

US/0890-5444
MEMBRANCE SEPARATION ENGINEERING. ***Ceased.*** [Membr. sep. eng.]. (1989)-(1989). Periodical. English. qt. Marcel Dekker Inc., 270 Madison Avenue, New York NY 10016. **Tel** (212)696-9000, (800)228-1160, FAX (212)685-4540, telex 421419. **(Subscription address:** Marcel Dekker Inc, PO Box 5017, Monticello NY 12701.**)** **ED** Peter S Cartwright. available on microfiche.
Desc: Focuses on applications of microfiltration, ultrafiltration, reverse osmosis, electrodialysis and the latest improvements in fluid processing.

FR/0025-9195
MEMOIRES C.E.R.E.S. [Mem. CERES]. **Main/Corp** Universite de Liege. Centre d'Etudes, de Recherches et d'Essais Scientifique du Genie Civil. **VAT** Memoires Centre d'Etudes, de Recherches et d'Essais Scientifique du Genie Civil. (1961)-. Monographic series. French. ir. Price varies per volume. Centre d'Etudes de Recherches et d'Essais Scientifique, 6 Quai Banning, Liege France. **CODEN** MECEBF. ***Continues*** *Universite de Liege. Centre d'Etudes, de Recherches et d'Essais Scientifique du Genie Civil Bulletin.*
Ind/Abst Ei Page One; GeoRef.

UK/0885-9507
MICROCOMPUTERS IN CIVIL ENGINEERING. [Microcomput. civ. eng.]. Vol. 1, No. 1 (July 1986)-. Periodical. English. Six times a year (1 volume). $318.50 North America; $340.00 other. Blackwell Publishers, 238 Main Street, Cambridge MA 02142. **Tel** (617)547-7110, (800)835-6770, FAX (617)547-0789. **ED** H. Adeli. **LC** TA345; .M487. **DD** 624/.028/5416. **CODEN** MCENE7. **[CCC]**. available on microfilm and microfiche from University Microfilms International (UMI). Documents available from Article Express International, Ask*IEEE.
Desc: Acts as a bridge between advances being made in microcomputer technology and civil engineering and, in doing so, will aim to encourage the effective incorporation of microcomputers into civil engineering practice and instruction.
Ind/Abst Ei Page One; Eng. Index Annu.; Fluid Abstr., Civil Eng.; Fluid Abstr. Proc. Eng.; FLUIDEX (19??-); GeoRef; Geotech. Abstr.; INSPEC (1987-).

GW
NACHRICHTEN AUS DEM OFFENTLICHEN VERMESSUNGSDIENST NORDRHEIN-WESTFALEN. **Added/Corp** North Rhine-Westphalia. Innenministerium. Gruppe Vermessungswesen. (1980)-. Periodical. German. Twice a year. DM2.00. Innenministerium des Landes Nordrhein-Westfalen-Gruppe Vermessungswesen, Landesvermessungsamt, Nordhein Westfalen, Muffendorfer Str. 19-21, 53177 Bonn Germany. **LC** TA501; .N26. **Bk Rev**, (Qty: 5). **Pr Rev. Acid Free.**

GW/0939-2378
NACHRICHTENBLATT DER VERMESSUNGS- UND KATASTERVERWALTUNG RHEINLAND-PFALZ. **Added/Corp** Landesvermessungsamt Rheinland-Pfalz. Rhineland-Palatinate. Ministerium des Innern. Abteilung fuer Vermessungs- und Katasterwesen. (1958)-. Academic Scholarly Publication. German. qt. DM2.00 (single issue). Ferdinand-Sauerbruch, Strabe 15, Postfach 1428, 5400 Koblenz Germany. **Tel** 0261/492-232. **LC** TA501; .N27. Index available (once a year). **Circ:** 1,500 (ctrl).

CN/1186-9216
NATIONAL BULLETIN / MECHANICAL CONTRACTORS ASSOCIATION OF CANADA. [Natl. bull. - Mech. Contract. Assoc. Can.]. **Added/Corp** Mechanical Contractors Association of Canada. (1991)-. Bulletin. English. Naylor Communications Ltd, 100 Sutherland Avenue, Winnipeg Manitoba R2W 3C7 Canada. **Tel** (204)947-0222, FAX (604)985-7399. **DD** 338.4/769/006071.

US/0096-9419
NAVY CIVIL ENGINEER. [Navy civ. eng.]. **Added/Corp** United States. Navy. Civil Engineer Corps. United States. Naval Facilities Engineering Command. (Feb. 1960)-. Government Publication. English. qt. $6.50 US; $8.15 other. Superintendent of Documents, US Government Printing Office, Washington DC 20402. **Tel** (202)275-3328, FAX (202)786-2377. **LC** VG593; .A24. **DD** 623.8/05. available on microfilm and microfiche from University Microfilms International (UMI). ***Continues*** *U.S. Navy Civil Engineer Corps Bulletin; Budocks Technical Digest.*
Desc: Features articles on the Navy's worldwide shore establishments, including technical articles on planning and designing, construction, maintenance, public works, utilities, transportation, Navy housing and real estate, and the Naval Civil Engineering Laboratory. Covers research and development, disaster control, and features articles on Civil Engineer Corps officers and the Seabees.

UK/0307-7863
NEW CIVIL ENGINEER. (NEW CIVIL ENGINEER : NCE : MAGAZINE OF THE INSTITUTION OF CIVIL ENGINEERS.). [New civ. eng.]. **Added/Corp** Institution of Civil Engineers (Great Britain). **VFOAT** NCE, New Civil Engineer. No. 1 (May 1972)-. Trade Publication. English. Fifty times a year. £98.00 UK; £148.00 other. Thomas Telford Ltd, Thomas Telford House, 1 Heron Quay, London E14 9XF England. **Tel** 011 44 71 987 6999, FAX 011 44 71 538 4101, telex 298105. **ED** Hugh Ferguson. **Bk Rev. Ad Acc. Circ:** 54,000.
Desc: All aspects of the construction industry and professions in the UK and worldwide.
Ind/Abst Archit. Period. Index; Coal Abstr.; Curr. Technol. Index; Fluid Abstr., Civil Eng.; Fluid Abstr. Proc. Eng.; FLUIDEX (1973-); Highw. Res. Abstr.; Int. Civil Eng. Abstr.; Leadscan; Soft. Abstr. Eng.

JA/0910-8025
NIHON KENCHIKU GAKKAI KOZOKEI RONBUN HOKOKUSHU. **VFOAT** Journal of Structural and Construction Engineering. (1985)-. Periodical. Japanese (English). mo. Do Gakkai, Keto Tsushin 19-ban 30-go Mita, 2-chome Minato-ku, Tokyo 108 Japan. ***Continues in part*** *Nihon Kenchiku Gakkai Ronbun Hokokushu, 0387-1185.*
Ind/Abst Abstr. J. Earthq. Eng.; Coal Abstr.; Concr. Abstr.; SEA Abstr.

UK/0960-4405
NO-DIG INTERNATIONAL. (NO DIG INTERNATIONAL.). [No-dig int.]. **VFOAT** NDI; No-Dig International. (1990)-. Periodical. English. mo. £40.00, $72.00. Mining Journal Ltd., 60 Worship Street, London EC2A 2HD England. **Tel** 011 44 071 377 2020, FAX 071 247 4100, telex 8952809 MINING G. **ED** Ian Clarke. **Bk Rev. Ad Acc, Adv Mgr:** Mike Bellenger. **Circ:** 5,000 (ctrl).
Desc: This publication covers the civil engineering area of trenchless technology, including new installation of public utilities and services, renovation of existing utilities and services, and inspection of same with the use of major open cut excavations.
Ind/Abst Fluid Abstr., Civil Eng.; Fluid Abstr. Proc. Eng.; FLUIDEX (19??-).

JA
NOGYO DOBOKU SHIKENJO GIHO. C : ZOKO. See Agriculture.

●US/1021-643X
NOISE/NEWS INTERNATIONAL. [Noise/news int.]. **Added/Corp** International Institute of Noise Control Engineering. Institute of Noise Control Engineering. **VFOAT** Noise News International. Vol. 1, No. 1 (Mar. 1993)-. Periodical. English. Four times a year (Mar., June, Sept., Dec.). $40.00. Institute of Noise Control Engineering, PO Box 3206, Arlington Branch, Poughkeepsie NY 12603. **Tel** (914)462-4006. **DD** 620.
Desc: Covers acoustical noise and its effects on people. Of interest to individuals responsible for design of airports, highways, buildings and machinery.

RU
NOVOSTI TEKHNICHESKOI LITERATURY. RAZDEL A. SERIIA IX: INZHENERNYE IZYSKANIIA V STROITELSTVE. STROITELSTVO I ARKHITEKTURA. Added/Corp Moscow. Tsentralnyi Institut Nauchnoi Informatsii po Stroitelstvu i Arkhitekture. Moscow. Proizvodstvennyi Nauchno-Issledovatelskii Institu po Inzheneranym Izyskaniam v Stroitelstve. **VFOAT** Stroitelstvo I Arkhitektura. Seriia IX: Inzhenernye Izyskaniia v Stroitelstve; Inzhenernye Izyskaniia v Stroitelstve. (1974)-. Multiple languages (Russian and Multiple languages). mo. Izdatelstvo Kniga, 50 Gorky Ulitsa, 125047 Moscow Russia. **LC** Z5853.E43; N68; TA705. ***Continues*** *Novosti Tekhnicheskoi Literatury. Stroitelstvo I Arkhitektura. Razdel A. Seria XI: Inzhenernye Izyskaniia v Stroitelstve.*

RU
NOVOSTI TEKHNICHESKOI LITERATURY. RAZDEL A. SERIIA XI: TRANSPORTNOE STROITELSTVO. STROITELSTVO I ARKHITEKTURA. Added/Corp Moscow. Tsentralnyi Institut Nauchnoi Informatsii po Stroitelstvu i Arkhitekture. Tsentralnyi Institut Nauchnoi Informatsii po Stroitelstvu i Arkhitekture. **VFOAT** Stroitelstvo I Arkhitektura. Seriia XI: Transportnoe Stroitelstvo; Transportnoe Stroitelstvo. (1974)-. Multiple languages (Russian and Multiple languages). mo. Izdatelstvo Kniga, 50 Gorky Ulitsa, 125047 Moscow Russia. **LC** Z5851; .N67; TA145. ***Continues*** *Novosti Tekhnicheskoi Literatury. Stroitelstvo I Arkhitektura. Razdel A. Seriia V: Transportnoe Stroitelstvo.*

RU
NOVOSTI TEKHNICHESKOI LITERATURY. STROITELSTVO I ARKHITEKTURA. RAZDEL SERIIA VII. STROITELNYE MATERIALY I IZDELIIA, KHARAKTERISTIKA I PRIMENENIE. Added/Corp Moscow. Tsentralnyi Institut Nauchnoi Informatsii po Stritelstvu i Arkhitekture. Tsentralnaia Nauchno-Tekhnicheskaia Biblioteka po Stroitelstvu i Arkhitekture. Informatsionno-Bibliograficheskii Otdel. **VFOAT** Stroitelnyi Institut Nauchnoi Informatsii Po Stroitelstvu I Arkhitekture; Stroitelstvu I Arkhitektura. Seriia VII: Stroitelnye Materialy I Izdeliia, Kharakteristika I Primenenie. (1974)-. Multiple languages (Russian and Multiple languages). mo. Informatsii po Stroitelstvu I Arkhitekture, A-47 Ulitsa Gorkogo Dom 38, Moscow 125047 Russia. **LC** Z5853.N14; N68; TA403. ***Continues*** *Novosti Tekhnicheskoi Literatury. Stroitelstvu I Arkhitektura. Razdel A. Seriia X: Stroitelnye Materialy I Izdeliia.*

US
NTIS ALERT. CIVIL ENGINEERING. Added/Corp United States. National Technical Information Service. (19??)-. Periodical. English. Twenty-four times a year. $145.00 US; $210.00 other. National Technical Information Service - NTIS, Room 2027S, 5285 Port Royal Road, Springfield VA 22161. **Tel** (703)487-4630, (703)487-4660, (703)487-4650, FAX (703)321-8547, telex 89-9405. Index available. ***Continues*** *Civil Engineering / NTIS, 0145-0344.*
Desc: Provides information on construction equipment, materials and supplies, highway engineering, rock mechanics, etc.

PL/0473-7733
OCHRONA PRZED KOROZJA. [Ochr. przed korozja]. **Added/Corp** Polska Akademia Nauk. Komitet do Spraw Ochrony Tworzyw Przed Korozja. Stowarzyszenie Naukowo-Techniczne InAzynierow i Technikow Przemysow Chemicznego i Materiaow Budowlanych. (1958)-. Academic Scholarly Publication. Polish. mo. $105.00. **(Subscription address:** ARS Polona, PO Box 1001, 00068 Warsaw Poland.**) LC** TA418.74; .O24. **CODEN** OPZKA8. Documents available from CASDDS.
Ind/Abst Alum. Ind. Abstr.; Biodeter. Abstr. (1991-); Chem. Abstr.; Corros. Abstr. (199?-); For. Prod. Abstr. (1991-); Met. Abstr.; World Surf. Coat. Abstr.

US/0402-1142
OFFICIAL REGISTER - AMERICAN SOCIETY OF CIVIL ENGINEERS. [Off. regist. - Am. Soc. Civil Eng.]. **Main/Corp** American Society of Civil Engineers. **VFOAT** ASCE Official Register. (1948)-. English. an. Free on request. American Society of Civil Engineers / ASCE, 345 East 47th Street, New York NY 10017-2398. **Tel** (212)705-7179, FAX (212)705-7300, telex 422847 ASCE UI. **(Subscription address:** American Society of Civil Engineers, Publisher Fulfillment Agency, Box 828, Somerset NJ 08875.**) ED** Phyllis G. Lanz. **LC** TA1; .A484. **DD** 624/.06/073. **Circ:** 18,000 (ctrl).
Desc: Contains all authoritative data and statistics on the American Society of Civil Engineers, its functions, services and rules.

CN
ONTARIO HIGHWAY BRIDGE DESIGN CODE / ONTARIO MINISTRY OF TRANSPORTATION AND COMMUNICATIONS, HIGHWAY ENGINEERING DIVISION. English. ir. Ontario Government Bookstore, 880 Bay Street, Toronto Ontario M7A 1N8 Canada. **LC** TG27.O5; O57. **DD** 624/.250212.

CN/0316-2001
ONTARIO LAND SURVEYOR, THE. [Ont. land surv.]. **Added/Corp** Association of Ontario Land Surveyors. (July 1958)-. Periodical. English. Four times a year (Jan., Apr., July, Oct.). 40.00Can$. Association of Ontario Land Surveyor, 1043 McNicoll Avenue, Scarborough ONT M1W 3W6 Canada. **Tel** (416)491-9020, FAX (416)729-2673. **ED** Brian Munday. **Ad Acc. Circ:** 1,500 (ctrl). ***Absorbed*** *Association of Ontario Land Surveyors. OLS Blaze., 0315-8993.*

RU
OSNOVANIIA, FUNDAMENTY I MEKHANIKA GRUNTOV. Added/Corp Soviet Union. Gosudarstvennyi Komitet po Delam Stroitelstva. (1959)-. Academic Scholarly Publication. Russian. Six times a year. $69.95. **(Subscription address:** East View Publications Inc., 3020 Harbor Lane North, Suite 110, Minneapolis MN 55447.**) LC** TA710.A1; O8. **CODEN** OFMGAV. Documents available from CASDDS.
Ind/Abst Chem. Abstr. (?-1973).

NE
OTAR. Added/Corp Vereniging van Waterstaatkundige Ambtenaren van de Rijkswaterstaat. (19??)-. Periodical. Dutch. Eleven times a year (July/Aug. issue combined). Fl105.00 Netherlands; Fl140.00 others. Uitgeverij Debozet, van Poelgeestlaan 72, NL 2355 BE Hoogmade Netherlands. **Tel** 011 31 1712 2178. **ED** H. Verhey. **LC** TC77; .O83. Index available. **Bk Rev. Ad Acc. Circ:** 2,150 (ctrl).
Desc: News and information on highways and waterways engineering.

US/0030-8544
PACIFIC BUILDER & ENGINEER. [Pac. build. & eng.]. **VAT** Pacific Builder and Engineer. (1969)-. Trade Publication. English. Twenty-four times a year. $62.00 Washington residents (includes sales tax); $58.00 US; $78.00 other (surface mail). Vernon Publications Inc., 3000 Northup Way, Suite 200, Bellevue WA 98004. **Tel** (206)827-9900, FAX (206)827-9372. **ED** John Watkins. **DD** 338. **Ad Acc. Circ:** 12,400 (ctrl). available on microfilm from University Microfilms International (UMI). ***Continues*** *Northwest Pacific Builder and Engineer.*
Desc: Serving the heavy construction industry of Washington, Oregon, Idaho, Montana and Alaska.

US
PAVING FORUM. ***Title Change.*** Periodical. English. ir. National Asphalt Pavement Association, NAPA Building, 5100 Forbes Boulevard, Lanham MD 20706-4413. **Tel** (301)731-4748, FAX (301)731-4621. **ED** George Goggin. **Ad Acc. Circ:** 25,000 (ctrl). ***Continued by*** *HMAT Magazine.*
Desc: Profiles of paving projects utilizing hot mix asphalt in highways, streets, parking lots, recreation, and environmental usages. Also articles of interest affecting design and construction.

US/0887-9672
PCI JOURNAL. [PCI j.]. **VAT** Prestressed Concrete Institute Journal. Vol. 27, No. 4 (July/Aug. 1982)-. Periodical. English. bm. $75.00 (1 year), $205.00 (3 year) airmail, $29.00 (1 year), $69.00 (3 year) surface mail. Prestressed Concrete Institute, 175 West Jackson Boulevard, Suite 1859, Chicago IL 60604. **Tel** (312)786-0300, FAX (312)786-0353. **LC** TA680; .P83. **DD** 624.1/8341. Documents available from Article Express International, The Genuine Article. ***Continues*** *Journal - Prestressed Concrete Institute, 0032-793X.*
Ind/Abst Abstr. J. Earthq. Eng.; Concr. Abstr.; Eng. Index Annu.; Geotech. Abstr.; Int. Civil Eng. Abstr.; J. Ferrocement; Res. Alert [Full Cov.].

FR/0986-1793
PCM LE PONT. See Transportation-Roads and Traffic.

HU/0553-6626
PERIODICA POLYTECHNICA. CIVIL ENGINEERING. ***Ceased.*** **VFOAT** Periodica Polytechnica. Stroitel'Stvo; Periodica Polytechnica. Bauingenieurwesen; PP. Periodica Polytechnica. (1968)-(1992). Periodical. Multiple languages (German). qt. **(Subscription address:** Kultura, PO Box 149, H 1389 Budapest 62 Hungary**) UDC** 624. **CODEN** 627. Index available. **Bk Rev. Ad Acc.** ctrl circ. Documents available from Article Express International.
Ind/Abst Eng. Index Annu. [Select. Cov.]; J. Ferrocement.

UK/0031-868X
PHOTOGRAMMETRIC RECORD, THE. See Geography.

US/0095-6686
PHYSICAL RESEARCH REPORT. English. Illinois Department of Transportation, Auditorium, 2300 South Dirksen Parkway, Springfield IL 62764. **LC** TE1; .P48. **DD** 625.7/08.

US/0739-3865
POINT OF BEGINNING- POB. [Point begin.]. **VFOAT** POB; P.O.B. (19??)-. Periodical. English. Six times a year (Feb., Apr., June, Aug., Oct., Dec.). $26.00 US; $34.00 Canada and Mexico; $38.00 Central America; $46.00 South America and Europe; $54.00 other. P O B Publishing Company, 5820 Lilley Road, Suite 5, Canton MI 48187. **Tel** (313)981-4600, FAX (313)981-0048. **ED** Victoria Dickinson. **LC** TA501; .P59. **DD** 526.9/05. **Ad Acc, Adv Mgr:** Ed Miller. **Circ:** 59,000 (ctrl).
Desc: National magazine featuring information of a technical, business, professional, and general nature for the professionals and key technicians of the surveying and mapping community.

NE
POLYTECHNISCH TIJDSCHRIFT. Dutch. qt. Stam Tijdschriften BV, Postbus 235, 2280 AE Rijswijk Netherlands. **Tel** +31 70 3988100, FAX +31 70 3988276, telex 33702 STAM NL.
Ind/Abst Archit. Period. Index (Jan. 1977-Dec. 1981).

PL/0138-0796
PRACE INSTYTUTU TECHNIKI BUDOWLANEJ. [Pr. Inst. Tech. Budow.]. **Main/Corp** Warsaw. Instytutu Techniki Budowlanej. **VFOAT** Building Research Institute Quarterly; Kvartalnyi Zhurnal Instituta Stroitelnoi Tekhniki. (197?)-. Academic Scholarly Publication. Polish (summaries and/or abstracts in English and Russian). qt. Z20,000. Instytut Techniki Budowlanej, Ul Filtrowa 1 Skrytka Pocztowa 998, 00-950 Warszawa Poland. **Tel** 25-04-71, FAX 251303, telex 813022. **LC** TA630; .W34A. **CODEN** PITBDI. **Bk Rev. Circ:** 1,600. Documents available from CASDDS. ***Continues*** *Instytut Techniki Budowlanej. Biuletyn Informacyjny.*
Ind/Abst Chem. Abstr. (1975-1982); Concr. Abstr.

IT
PREZZARIO MATERIALI OPERE EDILI PROVINCIA GENOVA. Camera Comm Ind Art Agr / Genoa, Genova, Via Garibaldi 4, 16124 Genoa Italy. **Tel** 011 39 10 2094208.

IT
PREZZI INFORMATIVI DELL EDILIZIA MATERIALI ED OPERE COMPIUTE : OPERE DI URBANIZ E INFRASTRUTTURE. (19??)-. Italian. sa. L80000. Edizioni Dei, Via Nomentana 12, 00161 Rome Italy. **Tel** 011 39 6 4402046, FAX 011 39 06 4402034.

IT
PREZZI INFORMATIVI DELL EDILIZIA MATERIALI ED OPERE COMPIUTE : RECUPERO RISTRUT E MAUTEZIONE. Edizioni Dei, Via Nomentana 12, 00161 Rome Italy. **Tel** 011 39 6 4402046, FAX 011 39 06 4402034.

IT
PREZZI INFORMATIVI DELLE OPERE EDILI IN MILANO. (19??)-. Italian. qt. L250000.00. Camera Comm Ind Art Agr Milan, Via Meravigli 9/B, 20123 Milan Italy. **Tel** 011 39 2 85154516.

IT
PREZZI INFORMATIVI MATERIALI DA COSTRUZIONE E OPERE EDILI : REGGIO EMILIA. Cameta Comm Ind Art Agr, Reggio Piazza Vittoria, Palazzo Affari, 42100 Reggio Emilia Italy.

IT
PREZZI INFORMATIVI OPERE EDILI DI MANUTENZIONE. Italian. qt. L85000. Edilizia Pubblicazioni, Via Ponte Seveso 19, 20125 Milan Italy. **Tel** 011 39 2 606922.

IT
PREZZI INFORMATIVI OPERE EDILI DI VICENZA. (19??)-. Italian. Four times a year. L68000. Cam Comm Ind Agr Art Vicenza, C So Fogazzaro 37, 36100 Vicenza Italy. **Tel** 011 39 444 994811.

IT
PREZZIARIO DELLE OPERE EDILI DI BRESCIA E PROVINCIA. Italian. qt. L35000. CER Srl, Via Ugo Foscolo 6, 25128 Brescia Italy. **Tel** 011 39 30 399133.

UK
PROCEEDINGS. Main/Corp Institution of Civil Engineers (Great Britain). Vol. 1 (Jan. 1952)-. Proceedings. English. bm. Package of six titles: £350.00 UK; £410.00 other. Thomas Telford Ltd, Thomas Telford House, 1 Heron Quay, London E14 9XF England. **Tel** 011 44 71 987 6999, FAX 011 44 71 538 4101, telex 298105. ***Supersedes*** *Journal of the Institution of Civil Engineers.*
Ind/Abst Postharvest News Inf.

CN/0226-2053
PROCEEDINGS - CANADIAN SOCIETY FOR CIVIL ENGINEERING. [Proc.- Can. Soc. Civ. Eng.]. **Main/Corp** Canadian Society for Civil Engineering. Conference. **VFOAT** Compte Rendu - Societe Canadienne de Genie Civil. **VAT** Congres - Societe Canadienne de Genie Civil; Conference - Canadian Society for Civil Engineering. 1979-. Proceedings. English (French). an. Canadian Society for Civil Engineering, 2050 Mansfield Street, Suite 700, Montreal Quebec H3A 1Z2 Canada. **Tel** (514)842-5653. **DD** 624/.0971.

US/0091-5122
PROCEEDINGS - COMMITTEE ON COMPUTER TECHNOLOGY. See Transportation-Roads and Traffic.

US
PROCEEDINGS - FIRE SERVICE EXTENSION SCHOOL, WEST VIRGINIA UNIVERSITY. See Fire Prevention.

CN/0712-2470
PROCEEDINGS OF THE ANNUAL CONFERENCE OF CANADIAN TECHNICAL ASPHALT ASSOCIATION. (PROCEEDINGS OF THE ... ANNUAL CONFERENCE OF CANADIAN TECHNICAL ASPHALT ASSOCIATION.). [Proc. annu. conf. Can. Tech. Asph. Conf.]. **Main/Corp** Canadian Technical Asphalt Association. Conference. **VFOAT** Canadian Technical Asphalt Association Proceedings. (1956)-. Academic Scholarly Publication. English (French). an. 55.00Can$ Canada; 58.00Can$ other. Polyscience Publications Inc., PO Box 148, Morin Heights, Quebec J0R 1H0 Canada. **Tel** (514)226-5870, FAX (514)226-5866. **ED** Elaine Thompson. **LC** TE270; .C26a. **DD** 625.8/5. **CODEN** PACADA. cum. index. **Circ:** 800. Documents available from CASDDS.
Desc: All papers relate to asphalt in its various forms and uses.
Ind/Abst Chem. Abstr. (1956-1982).

US
PROCEEDINGS OF THE ... ANNUAL CONVENTION OF THE AMERICAN RAILWAY BRIDGE AND BUILDING ASSOCIATION. Main/Corp American Railway Bridge and Building Association. Convention. (1908)-. Proceedings. English. an (Mar.). $30.00. American Railway Bridge & Buildings Association, 18154 Harwood Avenue, Homewood IL 60430. **Tel** (708)799-4650, FAX (708)799-4703. **LC** TF1; .A76. **DD** 624/.2/05. ***Continues*** *Proceedings of the ... Annual Convention of the Association of Railway Superintendents of Bridges and Buildings.*

US
PROCEEDINGS OF THE ... ANNUAL ROAD SCHOOL. Main/Conf Road School. Purdue University. 10th- 1924-. Proceedings. English. an. Free. Purdue University / School of Civil Engineering, Lafayette IN 47907. **Tel** (317)494-2211. **ED** K C Sinha. **LC** TE191. **DD** 625.70715. **Circ:** 2,500 (ctrl).
Desc: A compilation of papers by federal, state and county officials and professors on the financing, planning, design, construction, maintenance and operation of federal, state and county highways.

●UK/0965-089X
PROCEEDINGS OF THE INSTITUTION OF CIVIL ENGINEERS. CIVIL ENGINEERING. Added/Corp Institution of Civil Engineers (Great Britain). **VFOAT** Civil Engineering; CE. Vol. 92, Issue 1 (Feb. 1992)-. Proceedings. English. qt (Plus 2 special issues). £52.00 US; £61.00 other. Thomas Telford Ltd, Thomas Telford House, 1 Heron Quay, London E14 9XF England. **Tel** 011 44 71 987 6999, FAX 011 44 71 538 4101, telex 298105. **LC** TA1; .I396d. **CODEN** PCCIEF. Documents available from Article Express International, The Genuine Article. ***Continues in part*** *Proceedings - Institution of Civil Engineers. Part 1, Design and Construction, 0307-8353; Proceedings - Institution of Civil Engineers. Part 2, Research and Theory, 0307-8361* ***and*** *Municipal Engineer (Institution of Civil Engineers (Great Britain)), 0263-788X.*
Ind/Abst Curr. Contents Eng. Tech. Appl. Sci.; Eng. Index Annu.; Fluid Abstr., Civil Eng.; Fluid Abstr. Proc. Eng.; FLUIDEX (19??-); Highw. Res. Abstr.; Int. Civil Eng. Abstr.; Leadscan; Res. Alert [Full Cov.]; Sci. Cit. Index; SCISEARCH; Soc. Sci. Cit. Index [Select. Cov.]; Sug. Indus. Abstr.

●UK/0965-0903
PROCEEDINGS OF THE INSTITUTION OF CIVIL ENGINEERS. MUNICIPAL ENGINEER. Added/Corp Institution of Civil Engineers (Great Britain). **VFOAT** Municipal Engineer. Vol. 93, Issue 1 (Mar. 1992)-. Proceedings. English. qt (Mar., June, Sept., Dec.). £50.00 UK; £59.00 other. Thomas Telford Ltd, Thomas Telford House, 1 Heron Quay, London E14 9XF England. **Tel** 011 44 71 987 6999, FAX 011 44 71 538 4101, telex 298105. **LC** TD159.A1; P76. **CODEN** PCEME3. Documents available from Article Express International, The Genuine Article. ***Continues in part*** *Institution of Civil Engineers (Great Britain)., 0307-8353; Proceedings - Institution of Civil Engineers. Part 1, Design and Construction, 0307-8361; Institution of Civil Engineers (Great Britain)., 0263-788X; Proceedings - Institution of Civil Engineers. Part 2, Research and Theory* ***and*** *Municipal Engineer (Institution of Civil Engineers (Great Britain)).*
Ind/Abst Curr. Contents Eng. Tech. Appl. Sci.; Eng. Index Annu.; Fluid Abstr., Civil Eng.; Fluid Abstr. Proc. Eng.; FLUIDEX (19??-); Int. Civil Eng. Abstr.; Res. Alert [Full Cov.]; Sci. Cit. Index; SCISEARCH; Soc. Sci. Cit. Index [Select. Cov.].

●UK/0965-0911
PROCEEDINGS OF THE INSTITUTION OF CIVIL ENGINEERS. STRUCTURES AND BUILDINGS. Added/Corp Institution of Civil Engineers (Great Britain). **VFOAT** Structures and Buildings. Vol. 94, Issue 1 (Feb. 1992)-. Proceedings. English. qt (Feb,m May, Aug., Nov.). £102.00 UK; £119.00 other. Thomas Telford Ltd, Thomas Telford House, 1 Heron Quay, London E14 9XF England. **Tel** 011 44 71 987 6999, FAX 011 44 71 538 4101, telex 298105. **LC** TA630; .P762. **CODEN** PCESEL. Documents available from Article Express International, The Genuine Article. ***Continues in part*** *Institution of Civil Engineers (Great Britain). Proceedings - Institution of Civil Engineers. Part 1, Design and Construction, 0307-8353; Institution of Civil Engineers (Great Britain). Proceedings - Institution of Civil Engineers. Part 2, Research and Theory, 0307-8361* ***and*** *Municipal Engineer (Institution of Civil Engineers (Great Britain)), 0263-788x.*
Desc: Covers structural engineering.
Ind/Abst Curr. Contents Eng. Tech. Appl. Sci.; Eng. Index Annu.; Fluid Abstr., Civil Eng.; Fluid Abstr. Proc. Eng.; FLUIDEX (19??-); Int. Civil Eng. Abstr.; Res. Alert [Full Cov.]; Sci. Cit. Index; SCISEARCH.

●UK/0965-092X
PROCEEDINGS OF THE INSTITUTION OF CIVIL ENGINEERS, TRANSPORT. Added/Corp Institution of Civil Engineers (Great Britain). **VFOAT** Transport. (1992)-. Proceedings. English. Four times a year (Feb., May, Aug., Nov.). £63.00 UK; £73.00 other. Thomas Telford Ltd, Thomas Telford House, 1 Heron Quay, London E14 9XF England. **Tel** 011 44 71 987 6999, FAX 011 44 71 538 4101, telex 298105. **LC** TA1001; .P76. Documents available from Article Express International, The Genuine Article. ***Continues in part*** *Proceedings - Institution of Civil Engineers. Part 1, Design and Construction, 0307-8353; Proceedings - Institution of Civil Engineers. Part 2, Research and Theory, 0307-8361* ***and*** *Municipal Engineer (Institution of Civil Engineers (Great Britain)), 0263-788x.*
Ind/Abst Curr. Contents Eng. Tech. Appl. Sci.; Eng. Index Annu.; Fluid Abstr., Civil Eng.; Fluid Abstr. Proc. Eng.; FLUIDEX (19??-); Int. Civil Eng. Abstr.; Res. Alert [Full Cov.]; Sci. Cit. Index; SCISEARCH.

US/0893-8717
PROCEEDINGS OF THE INTERNATIONAL CONFERENCE / ... COASTAL ENGINEERING CONFERENCE. [Proc. int. conf. - Coastal Eng. Conf.]. **Added/Corp** American Society of Civil Engineers. Coastal Engineering Research Council. **VFOAT** Coastal Engineering, ... Proceedings; Coastal Engineering. 19th (1984)-. Proceedings. English. be (every two years). $250.00 US & Canada; $300.00 other. American Society of Civil Engineers / ASCE, 345 East 47th Street, New York NY 10017-2398. **Tel** (212)705-7179, FAX (212)705-7300, telex 422847 ASCE UI. **(Subscription address:** American Society of Civil Engineers, Publisher Fulfillment Agency, Box 828, Somerset NJ 08875.**) DD** 627. ***Continues*** *Coastal Engineering Conference. Proceedings of the Coastal Engineering Conference, 0161-3782.*

SA
PROCEEDINGS OF THE NATIONAL CONFERENCE OF SOUTH AFRICAN SURVEYORS. VFOAT Verrigtinge van die Nasionale Konferensie van Suid-Afrikaanse Opmeters. (19??)-. English. Institute of Land Surveyors of the Cape Province, PO Box 462, Capetown South Africa. **LC** TA5; .N26a. **DD** 526/.9/05.

US
PROCEEDINGS OF THE ... PAVING AND TRANSPORTATION CONFERENCE ... . Main/Conf Paving and Transportation Conference. **Added/Corp** University of New Mexico. Dept. of Civil Engineering. (Jan. 10-12, 1983)-. Proceedings. English. an (Apr.). $15.00. University of New Mexico Department of Civil Engineering, UNM Paving Conference, Albuquerque NM 87131. **Tel** (505)277-6633, FAX (505)277-1988. **ED** Dr. James Brogan, (phone: (505)277-1314). cum. index. **Circ:** 300 (ctrl). Documents available from Article Express International. ***Continues*** *Proceedings of the Paving Conference .... .*
Ind/Abst Bioeng. Abstr.; Ei Page One; Eng. Index Annu.

US
PROFESSIONAL ENGINEERS AND LAND SURVEYORS REPORT / STATE BOARD OF REGISTRATION FOR PROFESSIONAL ENGINEERS AND LAND SURVEYORS. Added/Corp California. State Board of Registration for Professional Engineers and Land Surveyors. (19??)-. Periodical. English. Engineers-Surveyors, 142B Howe Avenue/#56, Sacramento CA 95825-3204. **LC** TA157; .P773. **DD** 344.794/01762. ***Continues*** *Professional Engineers Report.*

US/0278-1425
PROFESSIONAL SURVEYOR. [Prof. surv.]. Vol. 1, No. 1 (Sept. 1981)-. Periodical. English. Six times a year (Jan., Mar., May, July, Sept., Nov.). $10.00 members; $35.00 North America; $65.00 other. Harrison Communications, 2300 South 9th Street, Suite 501, Arlington VA 22204. **Tel** (703)892-0733, FAX (703)920-3652. **ED** Dinna Gorham, (phone: (703)892-0735). **LC** TA501; .P6245. **DD** 526/.05. **Bk Rev. Ad Acc. Circ:** 58,000 (ctrl).
Desc: Containing materials of interest to the professionals in land surveying, computer-based mapping, site planning, photogrammetry, geodesy and related civil engineering fields.
Ind/Abst Fish Rev. (Jan. 1989-July 1992); GeoRef; Wildl. Rev. (Jan. 1989-July 1992).

PL
PRZEGLAD GEODEZYJNY. Added/Corp Stowarzyszenie Geodetow Polskich. Vol. 1 (1928)-. Periodical. Polish. mo. $84.00. **(Subscription address:** ARS Polona, PO Box 1001, 00068 Warsaw Poland.**)**
Ind/Abst Energy Res. Abstr. (Feb. 1983-); Int. Aerosp. Abstr.

CN/0826-4538
PUB. - INSTITUT CANADIEN DE TOLE D'ACIER EN BATIMENT. (PUB.). [Pub. - Inst. can. tole acier batim.]. Monographic series. French. Price varies per volume. ICTAB, 305-201 Chemin Consumers, Willowdale Ontario M2J 4G8 Canada. **DD** 624.1/821.

US/0033-3735
PUBLIC ROADS. See Transportation-Roads and Traffic.

CN/0316-7968
PUBLICATION (UNIVERSITY OF TORONTO. DEPT. OF CIVIL ENGINEERING). (PUBLICATION - UNIVERSITY OF TORONTO, DEPARTMENT OF CIVIL ENGINEERING.). Began publication in 1971?. Monographic series. English. Price varies per volume. University of Toronto Department of Civil Engineering, Front Campus, Toronto Ontario M5S 1A6 Canada. **DD** 624.

KO
PUT I SAOBRACAJ. Began with Apr. 1955 issue. Periodical. Serbo-Croatian (Roman). **LC** TE4; .P8.

UK/0481-2085
QUARTERLY JOURNAL OF ENGINEERING GEOLOGY, THE. [Q. j. eng. geol.]. **Added/Corp** Geological Society of London. Vol. 1 (Sept. 1967)-. Academic Scholarly Publication. English. qt. £123.00 UK; $245.00 US; £148.00 other. Geological Society Publishing House, Unit 7 Brassmill Enterprise Centre, Brassmill Lane, Bath BA1 3JN England. **Tel** 011 44 225 445046, FAX 011 44 225 442836. **ED** A. L. Little.

LC TA705; .Q3. DD 624/.151/05. CODEN QJEGA7. [CCC]. Index available (bound in 4th issue). cum. index. **Bk Rev. Ad Acc. Pr Rev. Acid Free. Circ:** 2,700. available on microfilm and microfiche from University Microfilms International (UMI). Documents available from Article Express International, The Genuine Article.
Desc: Major topics of international interest in engineering geology.
Ind/Abst AESIS Q.; Bioeng. Abstr.; Coal Abstr.; Curr. Contents Eng. Tech. Appl. Sci.; Ei Page One; EMBASE; Eng. Index Annu.; Geogr. Abstr. Phys. Geogr. (?-?); Geol. Abstr.; GeoRef; Geotech. Abstr.; Highw. Res. Abstr.; Int. Dev. Abstr. (?-?); MINPROC; Mintec, Min. Technol. Abstr.; Res. Alert [Full Cov.]; Risk Abstr.; Sci. Cit. Index; SCISEARCH.

JA/0033-9008
QUARTERLY REPORTS - RAILWAY TECHNICAL RESEARCH INSTITUTE. See Transportation-Railroads.

FR/0222-8394
RAPPORT DE RECHERCHE LPC. [Rapp. Rech. - LPC]. No. 61 (Nov. 1976)-. Academic Scholarly Publication. French (summaries and/or abstracts in English, German, Russian and Spanish). ir. Price varies per volume. Laboratoire Central des Ponts et Chaussees, 58 Boulevard Lefebvre, 75732 Paris Cedex 15 France. **Tel** 011 33 1 40435226, FAX 011 33 1 40 435495, telex LC PARI 200361 F. **ED** Jean-Francois Coste. **LC** TE2; .L33. **CODEN** RRLPD3. **Bk Rev. Ad Acc.** ctrl circ. Documents available from Article Express International, CASDDS. ***Continues*** *Rapport de Recherche (Laboratoire Central des Ponts et Chaussees), 0085-2643.*
Ind/Abst Bioeng. Abstr.; Chem. Abstr.; Ei Page One; Eng. Index Annu.

FR
RAPPORT GENERAL D'ACTIVITE - LABORATOIRE CENTRAL DES PONTS ET CHAUSSEES. Main/Corp Laboratoire Central des Ponts et Chaussees. French. an. Free. Laboratoire Central des Ponts et Chaussees, 58 Boulevard Lefebvre, 75732 Paris Cedex 15 France. **Tel** 011 33 1 40435226, FAX 011 33 1 40 435495, telex LC PARI 200361 F. **LC** TE2; .L32. **DD** 625.7/33.

SP
RELACION DE LOS INGENIEROS DE CAMINOS, CANALES Y PUERTOS. (19??)-. Spanish. mo. 7500.00ptas Spain & Portugal; 10500.00ptas other. Colegio Ingenieros de Caminos, Canales y Puertos, Almagro 42, 28010 Madrid Spain. **Tel** (1)3081988, FAX (1)3191531. **LC** TA12; .R39. Index available. **Ad Acc, Adv Mgr:** Tonice Baeze. Documents available.
Desc: Covers civil engineering, public works, roads, harbors, hydraulic works, environmental protection, railways, and transport.

US/0484-4041
RENTAL RATE BLUE BOOK. See Engineering-Mechanical Engineering and Machinery.

US
REPORT. Main/Corp California. University, Berkeley. Earthquake Engineering Research Center. (1967)-. Monographic series. English. Price varies per volume.
Desc: Describes research projects associated with the center and detail testing methods, results and recommendations.

US/0097-8817
REPORT AND ROSTER : REGISTERED LAND SURVEYORS. Main/Corp Kansas. State Board of Engineering Examiners. English. State Board Of Engineering Examiners, 535 Kansas Avenue, Topeka KS 66603. **LC** TA522.K3; K27A. **DD** 526.9/092/2.

US/0271-0323
REPORT - EARTHQUAKE ENGINEERING RESEARCH CENTER, COLLEGE OF ENGINEERING, UNIVERSITY OF CALIFORNIA, BERKELEY, CALIFORNIA. (REPORT / EARTHQUAKE ENGINEERING RESEARCH CENTER.). [Rep. - Earthqu. Eng. Res. Cent., Coll. Eng., Univ. Calif., Berkeley, Calif.]. **Added/Corp** University of California, Berkeley. Earthquake Engineering Research Center. No. EERC 67-1 (1967)-. Periodical. English. ir (Published 12 to 40 times per year). $225.00 (educational libraries & educational institutions); $325.00 (others). Earthquake Engineering Research Center, Regents of University of California, 1301 South 46th Street, Richmond CA 94804. **Tel** (510)231-9468. **ED** Beverley Bolt. **LC** UNC. Index available. cum. index. **Circ:** 350 (ctrl). available on microfiche from National Technical Information Service.
Desc: Each report describes earthquake engineering research carried out by the University of California, Berkeley.
Ind/Abst GeoRef.

NZ
REPORT OF THE DEPARTMENT OF SURVEY AND LAND INFORMATION FOR THE YEAR ENDED. Main/Corp New Zealand. Dept. of Survey and Land Information. (March 31, 1988)-. English. an. Department of Survey and Land Information, Charles Fergusson Building, Bowen Street, Private Box 170, Wellington New Zealand. **Tel** 0-4-473 5022, FAX 0-4-472 2244. **LC** TA529.5; .N48a. ***Continues in part*** *New Zealand. Dept. of Lands and Survey. Report.*

US
REPORT OF THE PERIOD ... / VERMONT BOARD OF REGISTRATION FOR LAND SURVEYORS. Main/Corp Vermont. State Board of Registration for Land Surveyors. English. **LC** TA522.V45; V47B. **DD** 526.9/2/025743.

US/1069-1510
REPROGRAPHICS & DESIGN IMAGING. ***Ceased.* See** Printing Industry.

AT
RESEARCH REPORT / DEPARTMENT OF CIVIL ENGINEERING, UNIVERSITY OF QUEENSLAND. Added/Corp University of Queensland. Department of Civil Engineering. **VFOAT** Research Report Series; Civil Engineering Research Reports. No. 1 (1979)-. Monographic series. English. mo (ten issues per year). Price varies per volume. University of Queensland / Department of Civil Engineering, St. Lucia Queensland 4072 Australia. **Tel** (07)377 2486, FAX (07)371-5863, telex UNIVQLD AA40315. **LC** UNC. **CODEN** RRSED5. cum. index. **Pr Rev. Circ:** 360 (ctrl). Documents available from Article Express International.
Desc: One of a continuing series of research reports published by the Department of Civil Engineering of the University of Queensland.
Ind/Abst Bioeng. Abstr.; Ei Page One; Eng. Index Annu.

SP/0034-8619
REVISTA DE OBRAS PUBLICAS. [Rev. obras publicas]. **Added/Corp** Escuela Especial de Ingenieros de Caminos, Canales y Puertos (Madrid, Spain). (1853)-. Academic Scholarly Publication. Spanish. Eleven times a year. 7500ptas Spain & Portugal; 10500ptas other. Colegio de Ingenieros de Caminos Canales y Puertos, Almagro 42, 28010 Madrid Spain. **Tel** 34 1 3081988, FAX 34 1 3191531. **LC** HD4242; .R4. **DD** 351.8. **CODEN** RVOPA9. Index available. **Ad Acc, Adv Mgr:** Monica Baeza. **Circ:** 5,000 (ctrl). Documents available from CASDDS.
Desc: Technical review of Spanish civil engineers.
Ind/Abst Chem. Abstr.; Coal Abstr.; GeoRef; Highw. Res. Abstr.

FR/0397-9296
REVUE TECHNIQUE DE BATIMENT ET DES CONSTUCTIONS INDUSTRIELLES. [Rev. tech. batim. constr. ind.]. (1959)-. Periodical. French. Seven times a year. 900.00F. Diffusions Relations Offl Sa, 50 rue Championnet, 75018 Paris France. **Tel** 011 33 1 42541414, FAX 011 33 1 42522894. **UDC** 69. ***Continues*** *Revue Technique du Batiment (Paris), 0048-8186.*

TI
REVUE TUNISIENNE DE L'EQUIPEMENT. Periodical. French. Ministere de l'Equipement, Centre de Documentation, Cite-Jardins, Tunis Tunisia. **LC** TA2; .R39.

IT/0373-367X
RIVISTA DEL CATASTO E DEI SERVIZI TECNICI ERARIALI. ***Title Change.*** (RIVISTA DEL CATASTO E DEI SERVIZI TECNICI ERARIALI / MINISTERO DELLE FINANZE.). [Riv. catasto serv. tec. erar.]. **Main/Corp** Italy. Direzione Generale del Catasto. **Added/Corp** Italy. Ministero delle Finanze. Italy. Direzione Generale del Catasto. Italy. Direzione Generale del Catasto e dei Servizi Tecnici. Ufficio Centrale di Coordinamento e Studi. Italy. Direzione Generale del Catasto e dei Servizi Tecnici Erariali. (1934)-(1992). Periodical. Italian (summaries and/or abstracts in English). sa. Istituto Poligrafico Zecca Stato, Piazza Verdi 10, 00198 Rome Italy. **Tel** 011 39 6 85082307, 011 39 6 85082221. **LC** HD671; .A47; TA501; .I88. ***Continued by*** *Rivista del Dipartimento del Territorio.*
Ind/Abst GeoRef.

US/8750-9229
ROADS & BRIDGES (DES PLAINS, ILL.). (ROADS & BRIDGES.). [Roads bridges]. **VFOAT** Roads and Bridges; Roads and Bridges Magazine; Roads & Bridges Magazine. Vol. 23, No. 1 (Jan. 1985)-. Trade Publication. English. mo. $20.00 (one year), $30.00 (two year), $40.00 (three year), US; $45.00 (one year), $75.00 (two year), $90.00 (three year) other. Scranton Gillette Communications Inc., 380 East Northwest Highway, Des Plaines IL 60016-2282. **Tel** (708)298-6622, FAX (708)390-0408. **ED** Tom Kuennen, Deborah Hegg, and Alyce Vacha. **LC** TE1; .R78. **DD** 625.7/05. [CCC]. **Ad Acc. Circ:** 60,000 (ctrl). available on microfilm and microfiche from University Microfilms International (UMI). ***Continues*** *Roads (Des Plaines, Ill.), 0746-3111.*
Desc: The nation's largest road and bridge construction and maintenance magazine, read by public works professionals, contractors and consulting engineers whose primary work is in this industry.
Ind/Abst Concr. Abstr.; Geotech. Abstr.

US
ROSTER NO. ... OF LICENSED CONTRACTORS IN THE STATE OF ALABAMA / STATE LICENSING BOARD FOR GENERAL CONTRACTORS. VFOAT Licensed Contractors in the State of Alabama. English. an. State Licensing Board for General Contractors, 125 South Ripley Street, Montgomery AL 36130. **LC** TH13.A2; R67. **DD** 624/.025/761.

US/0561-0214
ROSTER OF LICENSED CONTRACTORS IN THE STATE OF SOUTH CAROLINA. Main/Corp South Carolina. Licensing Board for Contractors. English. an. South Carolina Licensing Board for Contractors, 1300 Pickens Street, Columbia SC 29250. **LC** TA12; .S64.

US/8756-2251
ROSTER OF QUALIFIED ENGINEERING AND LAND SURVEYING FIRMS / LOUISIANA STATE BOARD OF REGISTRATION FOR PROFESSIONAL ENGINEERS AND LAND SURVEYORS. 1983-. English. be. $10.00. Louisiana State Board of Registration for Professional Engineers and Land Surveyors, 1055 St Charles Avenue/Suite 415, New Orleans LA 70130. **Tel** (504)568-8450. **LC** TA157; .R66. **DD** 620/.0025/763. **Circ:** 3,000. ***Continues*** *Rosters of Qualified Engineering and Land Surveying Firms, 8756-2251.*
Desc: Roster, rules and law.

US
ROSTER OF REGISTERED PROFESSIONAL ENGINEERS AND LAND SURVEYORS. Main/Corp Connecticut. State Board of Registration For Professional Engineers and Land Surveyors. English. an. State Board of Registration for Professional Engineers & Land Surveyors, Hartford CT 06115. **LC** TA24.C8. **DD** 620.58.

US/0361-8161
ROSTER OF REGISTERED PROFESSIONAL ENGINEERS AND LAND SURVEYORS : ANNUAL REPORT. Main/Corp North Dakota. State Board of Registration for Professional Engineers and Land Surveyors. English. an. $3.00. North Dakota State Board of Registration for Professional Engineers and Land Surveyors, PO Box 1264, Minot ND 58701. **LC** TA12; .N83A. **DD** 620/.0025/784.

IT
SCHEDE. Main/Corp Centro di Documentazione d'Ingegneria Civile, Architettura e Pianificazione Territoriale. (19??)-. Periodical. Italian. mo. Cntro Docu Ingen Civil Archt, Planif Ter / Via Manara 11, Milan Italy. **DD** 016; 620; 720.

SZ/0251-0960
SCHWEIZER INGENIEUR UND ARCHITEKT. (INGENIEURS ET ARCHITECTES SUISSES.). [Schweiz. Ing. Archit.]. **Added/Corp** Schweizerischer Ingenieur- und Architekten-Verein. **VFOAT** Schweizer Ingenieur und Architekt Ingegneri e Architetti Svizzeri. Vol. 105e, 79/1 (Jan. 1979)-. Academic Scholarly Publication. French. bw. 152.00F. Imprimerie Bron SA, CP 508, CH-1001 Lausanne Switzerland. **Tel** 011 41 21 6529944, FAX 011 41 21 6527323. **LC** TA4; .B8. **DD** 624/.09494. **CODEN** IASUD5. Documents available from Article Express International. ***Continues*** *Bulletin Technique de la Suisse Romande (Lausanne, Switzerland), 0007-5744.*
Ind/Abst Bioeng. Abstr.; Ei Page One; EMBASE; Eng. Index Annu.

UK/0085-6002
SCOTTISH BUILDING AND CIVIL ENGINEERING YEAR BOOK. See Building and Construction.

US/0080-9004
SERIES ON ROCK AND SOIL MECHANICS. See Earth Sciences-Geology.

UK/0073-9847
SESSIONAL YEARBOOK ... AND DIRECTORY OF MEMBERS. Main/Corp Institution of Structural Engineers (Great Britain). **VFOAT** Sessional Year Book ... and Directory of Members. (1986)-. Directory. English. an. £100.00. Structural Engineers Trading Organization, Ltd., 11 Upper Belgrave Street, London SW1X 8BH England. **Tel** 011 44 71 235 4535, FAX 011 44 71 235 4294. **LC** TA680; .I52. **DD** 624.1/06041. **Ad Acc, Adv Mgr Tel** same as publisher. **Circ:** 2,000. ***Continues*** *Institution of Structural Engineers (Great Britain). Year Book and Directory of Members.*

FI
SFS-LUETTELO. **Main/Corp** Suomen Standardisoimisliitto. **VFOAT** SFS-Catalogue. Finnish (English). an. Fmk60.00. Finnish Standards Association SFS, PO Box 205, 00121 Helsinki Finland. **Tel** 358 0 645 601, FAX 350 0 643 147, telex 122303 STAND SF. **LC** TA368; .S94A. Index available. cum. index. **Circ:** 4,000.
Desc: Lists all SFS standards valid through 1987 in numerical order and in subject groups; includes other documents published by SFS.

US/1051-6441
SISMODINAMICA (DURHAM, N.H.). (SISMODINAMICA : REVISTA INTERNACIONAL DE SISMOINGENIERIA Y DINAMICA ESTRUCTURAL.). [Sismodinamica]. **Added/Corp** Universidad de Chile. Facultad de Ciencias Fisicas y Matematicas. University of New Hampshire. Dept. of Civil Engineering. University of New Hampshire. College of Engineering and Physical Sciences. No. 1 (March 1990)-. Periodical. Spanish (summaries and/or abstracts in English). Four times a year. $80.00. University of New Hampshire / Civil Engineering Department, Kingsbury Hall, Durham NH 03824. **Tel** (603)862-1234. **ED** Francis Medina and Pedro de Alba. **LC** TA654; .S57. **DD** 624.1/762/05. Index available. **Bk Rev.** **Ad Acc.** **Pr Rev.** **Circ:** 1,000 (ctrl).
Desc: Specializes in structural/geotechnical earthquake engineering and structural vibrations.
Ind/Abst Abstr. J. Earthq. Eng.

●UK
SMART MATERIALS AND STRUCTURES. See Engineering-Electricity, Electrical Engineering, Electronics.

US/0038-0741
SOIL MECHANICS AND FOUNDATION ENGINEERING. See Engineering-Mechanical Engineering and Machinery.

CN/0541-6329
SOIL MECHANICS SERIES (MONTREAL, QUEBEC). (SOIL MECHANICS SERIES.). [Soil mech. ser.]. **Added/Corp** McGill University. Soil Mechanics Laboratory. McGill University. Soil Mechanics Research Laboratory. McGill University. Geotechnical Research Centre. No. 1 (1962)-. Monographic series. English. ir. Price varies per volume. Geotechnical Research Center, McGill University, 817 Sherbrooke Street West, Montreal Quebec H34 2K6 Canada. **Tel** (514)392-4751, telex 05-268510. **ED** Raymond N. Yong. **DD** 624/.1513. Index available. **Bk Rev.** ctrl circ.
Desc: Waste management, geoscience, alleviation of pollution, off-road mobility, analytical modelling soil-vehicle interaction, cold temperature and compaction study of clays.

SA/0038-0806
SOILS AND FOUNDATIONS. [Soils found.]. V. 8 (1968)-. Periodical. English. qt. **(Subscription address:** Japan Publications Trading Company, Ltd., PO Box 5030, Tokyo International, Tokyo 100-31 Japan.) **CODEN** SOIFBE. **[CCC].** Documents available from Article Express International. ***Continues*** *Soil and Foundation.*
Ind/Abst Abstr. J. Earthq. Eng.; Bioeng. Abstr.; Civ. Struct. Eng. Abstr.; Ei Page One; Eng. Index Annu.; Environ. Eng. Abstr.; GeoRef; Geotech. Abstr.; Highw. Res. Abstr.; J. Plan. Lit.; Mater. Sci. Eng. Abstr.; Mech. Eng. Abstr.; Soils Fert.

FR/0038-1217
SOLS. **VFOAT** Soils. Vol. 1- (1-) 1962-. Periodical. Multiple languages (English and French). Editions Sols Soils, 16 Avenue Sadi Carnot, 91160 Longjumeau France.

SA/0255-058X
SOUTH AFRICAN TUNNELLING. [S. Afr. tunn.]. V. 1- June 1975-. Periodical. English. Three times a year. Pithead Press, 91 Mooi Street, PO Box 9002, Johannesburg South Africa. **LC** TA800; .S68. **DD** 624/.29/0968.
Ind/Abst Mintec, Min. Technol. Abstr.

US/1064-6914
SOUTHWEST CONTRACTOR (PHOENIX, ARIZ.). See Building and Construction.

US/0038-5492
SOVIET JOURNAL OF NONDESTRUCTIVE TESTING, THE. ***Title Change.*** [Sov. j. nondestr. test.]. No. 1- (Jan./Feb. 1968)-. Periodical. English (translations available in Russian). mo. Plenum Press, 233 Spring Street, New York NY 10013-1578. **Tel** (212)620-8000, (800)221-9369, FAX (212)463-0742, (212)807-1047, telex 23/421139. **ED** V E Shcherbinin. **LC** TA417.2. **DD** 620.1/127/05. **CODEN** SJNTAB. **[CCC].** **Pr Rev.** available in microform from University Microfilms International (UMI). Documents available from Article Express International, Ask*IEEE, CASDDS. ***Supersedes*** *Defectoscopy, 0418-4947.* ***Continued by*** *Russian Journal of Nondestructive Testing.*
Desc: This journal publishes articles on research in the theory and technique of non destructive quality control of materials and products.
Ind/Abst Acoust. Abstr.; Alum. Ind. Abstr.; Appl. Mech. Rev.; Bioeng. Abstr.; Chem. Abstr.; Coal Abstr.; Ei Page One; Energy Res. Abstr.; Eng. Mater. Abstr.; Eng. Index Annu.; INSPEC (Jan./Feb. 1973-); Int. Aerosp. Abstr.; Met. Abstr.; Pollut. Abstr. Indexes.

NE
SOVIET JOURNAL ON CONCRETE AND REINFORCED CONCRETE. **VFOAT** Beton and Zhelezobeton. English. qt. $250.00 US; Fl475.00 Netherlands. AA Balkema, Box 1675, 3000 BR Rotterdam Netherlands. **Tel** 011 31 10 4145822, FAX 011 31 10 4135947, telex 41605.
Desc: Contains papers which appeared in the original (Russian) journal's monthly issues of the preceding quarter. Papers are selected for inclusion based on their applicability outside the Soviet Union, no papers are included that deal with local interest and those dealing with management and economics of the Soviet Union.
Ind/Abst J. Ferrocement.

NE
SOVIET JOURNAL ON STRUCTURAL MECHANICS AND DESIGN OF STRUCTURES. **VFOAT** Stroitelnaya Mekhanika i Raschet Sooruzhenii. Oct. (1987)-. English. Three times a year (May, August, and December). Fl475.00 Netherlands; $250.00 US. AA Balkema, Box 1675, 3000 BR Rotterdam Netherlands. **Tel** 011 31 10 4145822, FAX 011 31 10 4135947, telex 41605. **ED** O I Thomson and A A Chiras.
Desc: A premier journal of the USSR State Committee on Civil Construction. The foremost Soviet journal in the field of structural mechanics and theory of structures. Of interest to structural engineers in developed as well as developing countries.

UK
SPON'S CIVIL ENGINEERING PRICE BOOK. English. an (includes three updates). £49.50. International Thompson Publishing Services Ltd, North Way, Cheriton House, Andover Hampshire SP10 5BE England. **Tel** 011 44 264 342840.

US
SPORT CONSTRUCTION BUYERS GUIDE. Consumer Publication. English. an. International Sport Summit, 200 West 60th Street, Suite 310, New York NY 10023-8510. **Tel** (212)502-5306, telex RCA 261239. **ED** Monica Hellerman. Index available. **Ad Acc.** ctrl circ.

CE
SRI LANKA SURVEYOR : JOURNAL OF THE SURVEYORS' INSTITUTE OF SRI LANKA. **Added/Corp** Surveyors' Institute of Sri Lanka. (19??)-. Periodical. English. Rs25.00 per issue to non-members. **LC** TA501; .S73.

●NE/0927-7641
STADSWERK. **Added/Corp** Vereniging Stadswerk Nederland. (May 1992)-. Periodical. Dutch. mo (11 issues). Fl92.92. Pers Media, Postbus 2107, 1620 EC Hoorn Netherlands. **Tel** 011 31 2290 13254. ***Continues*** *Gemeentewerken, 0046-5577.*

AU/0561-7855
STAHLBAU RUNDSCHAU. [Stahlbau Rundsch.]. **Added/Corp** Oesterreichischer Stahlbauverband. (19??)-. German. Twice a year. S294.55 Austria; S348.00 others. Bohmann Druck und Verlag Ges MBH, Leberstrasse 122, A-1110 Vienna Austria. **Tel** 011 43 1 74095174, FAX 011 43 1 741595-183, telex 132312. **LC** TA684; .S685. **Ad Acc.** **Circ:** 5,600 (ctrl).
Ind/Abst Ei Page One; Energy Res. Abstr. (Feb. 1982-).

US
STANDARD SPECIFICATIONS FOR HIGHWAY BRIDGES. **Main/Corp** American Association of State Highway and Transportation Officials. Began with 1st Ed. in 1931. English. ir. American Association of State Highway and Transportation Officials, 444 North Capital Street, Suite 249, Washington DC 20001. **Tel** (202)624-5800. ***Continues*** *Standard Specifications for Highway Bridges.*

US/0360-6902
STANDARD SPECIFICATIONS FOR TRANSPORTATION MATERIALS AND METHODS OF SAMPLING AND TESTING. **Main/Corp** American Association of State Highway and Transportation Officials. **Added/Corp** American Association of State Highway and Transportation Officials. **VFOAT** AASHTO Materials. 11th Ed. (1974)-. English. an. American Association of State Highway and Transportation Officials, 444 North Capital Street, Suite 249, Washington DC 20001. **Tel** (202)624-5800. **LC** TE200; .A615. **DD** 625.7/0218. ***Continues*** *Standard Specifications for Highway Materials and Methods of Sampling and Testing.*

US/0146-0633
STATE HIGHWAY IMPROVEMENT PROGRAM: PRIMARY SYSTEM. **Main/Corp** Maryland. State Highway Administration. (19??)-. English. an. Maryland State Department of Transportation, State Highway Administration, PO Box 717, Baltimore MD 21203. **LC** TE24.M3; M28a. **DD** 625.7/09752.

CN/0712-9092
STEEL DESIGN. [Steel des.]. **Added/Corp** Dofasco. (1971)-. Periodical. English. Twice a year. Free. Dofasco Inc, PO Box 2460, Hamilton Ontario L8N 2J5 Canada. **Tel** (905)544-3761. **DD** 624.1/821/05. ctrl circ.

US/0736-2994
STOCHASTIC ANALYSIS AND APPLICATIONS. See Mathematics.

GW/0039-2162
STRASSE UND AUTOBAHN. [Str. Autob.]. **Added/Corp** Forschungsgesellschaft fuer das Strassenwesen (Germany) Bundesvereinigung der Strassenbau- und Verkehrsingenieure. **VFOAT** Strasse + Autobahn. Vol. 1, No. 1 (Jan. 1950)-. Academic Scholarly Publication. German. Twelve times a year. DM176.60 Germany; DM195.00 others. Kirschbaum Verlag, Siegfriedstr 28, Postfach 210209, D 53157 Bonn Germany. **Tel** 011 49 228 954530. **LC** TE3; .S752. **[CCC].** Index available. **Bk Rev.** **Ad Acc.** **Circ:** 5,200 (ctrl).
Ind/Abst EMBASE; GeoRef; Int. Civil Eng. Abstr.; Soft. Abstr. Eng.

GW/0039-2197
STRASSEN- UND TIEFBAU. [Str.- Tiefbau]. (June 1947)-. Academic Scholarly Publication. German (English). mo. DM167.50 Germany; DM178.00 other. Giesel Verlag Publizitaet GmbH, Postfatch 120161, D 30907 Isernhagen Germany. **Tel** 011 49 511 7304146, FAX 011 49 511 7304157, telex 511889. **LC** TE3; .S758. **CODEN** STTBAN. Index available. **Circ:** 4,100 (ctrl). Documents available from Article Express International. ***Supersedes*** *Asphalt und Teer, Strassenbautechnik;* ***Absorbed*** *Strassenbau und Strassenbaustoffe; Bitumen, Terre, Asphalte, Peche; Strasse, Brucke, Tunnel, 0039-2197.*
Ind/Abst Bioeng. Abstr.; Coal Abstr.; Ei Page One; EMBASE; Energy Res. Abstr. (March 1982-); Eng. Index Annu.; GeoRef; Int. Civil Eng. Abstr.; Soft. Abstr. Eng.

UK
STRUCTURAL ENGINEER (LONDON, ENGLAND : 1988). (THE STRUCTURAL ENGINEER : JOURNAL OF THE INSTITUTION OF STRUCTURAL ENGINEERS.). **Added/Corp** Institution of Structural Engineers (Great Britain). Vol. 66, No. 1 (Jan. 5, 1988)-. Periodical. English. Twenty-four times a year. £132.00. The Structural Engineer, 11 Upper Belgrave Street, London SW1X 8BH England. **Tel** 44 71 2354535, FAX 44 71 2354294. Documents available from Article Express International. ***Formed by the union of*** *Structural Engineer. Part A. Journal of the Institution of Structural Engineers - Monthly, 0959-6577* ***and*** *Structural Engineer. Part B. Journal of the Institutions of Structural Engineers - R & D Quarterly, 0959-6585.*
Ind/Abst Agric. Eng. Abstr. (1991-); Archit. Period. Index; Concr. Abstr.; Ei Page One; Eng. Index Annu.; Geotech. Abstr.; Int. Civil Eng. Abstr.; Soft. Abstr. Eng.; World Ceram. Abstr.

JA/0289-8063
STRUCTURAL ENGINEERING/EARTHQUAKE ENGINEERING. **Added/Corp** Doboku Gakkai. **VFOAT** Structural Engineering, Earthquake Engineering; Proceedings of Structural Engineering/Earthquake Engineering; Proceedings of JSCE. Structural Engineering/Earthquake Engineering. Vol. 1, No. 1 (April 1984)-. Periodical. English (translations available in Japanese). sa. $72.00. Doboku Gakkai, (Japan Soc. of Civil Engineers), Yotsuya 1-chome, Shinjuku-ku, Tokyo 160 Japan. **(Subscription address:** Kyowa Book Company Inc., 1-38 Kanda Jinbo-Cho, Chiyoda-Ku Tokyo 101, Japan) **CODEN** SEEEEQ. Documents available from Article Express International.
Desc: Contains papers from the fields of engineering mechanics, structural engineering and earthquake engineering.
Ind/Abst Ei Page One; Eng. Index Annu.

SZ/1016-8664
STRUCTURAL ENGINEERING INTERNATIONAL : JOURNAL OF THE INTERNATIONAL ASSOCIATION FOR BRIDGE AND STRUCTURAL ENGINEERING (IABSE). See Transportation.

CN/0319-0110
STRUCTURAL ENGINEERING REPORT. [Struct. eng. rep.]. Began publication in 1968?. Monographic series. English. ir (five-six issues per year). Price varies per volume. University of Alberta Department of Civil Engineering, Edmonton Alberta T6G 2H5 Canada. **Tel** (403)492-0249. **DD** 624/.1. **CODEN** ASERCV. **Circ:** 50 (ctrl). Documents available from Article Express International.
Ind/Abst Bioeng. Abstr.; Ei Page One; Eng. Index Annu.

UK/0952-5807
STRUCTURAL ENGINEERING REVIEW. Vol. 1, No. 1 (March 1988)-. Periodical. English. qt.

$209.00 The Americas; £140.00 other. Pergamon Press, An Imprint of Elsevier Science Ltd., The Boulevard, Langford Lane, Kidlington, Oxford OX5 1GB United Kingdom. **Tel** 011 44 865 843000, 011 44 865 843699, FAX 011 44 865 843010. **(Subscription address:** Elsevier Science Ltd. Oxford Fulfillment Centre, PO Box 800, Kidlington, Oxford OX5 1DX United Kingdom.**) ED** B. H. V. Topping. **LC** TA630; .S834. **DD** 624.1/05. **CODEN** SENRE8. **[CCC].** Index available. **Bk Rev. Ad Acc. Pr Rev. Circ:** 150.
Desc: Covers all aspects of structural engineering theory and practice.

CN/0318-3378
STRUCTURAL RESEARCH SERIES; REPORT. Began publication in 1970. Monographic series. English. Price varies per volume. University of British Columbia, Vancouver British Columbia V6T 1W5 Canada. **DD** 620.1.

NE/0167-4730
STRUCTURAL SAFETY. See Building and Construction.

IT
SUMMARIES OF PUBLICATIONS / DIPARTIMENTO DI INGEGNERIA STRUTTURALE, POLITECNICO DI MILANO. Main/Corp Politecnico di Milano. Dipartimento di Ingegneria Strutturale. English. an. Dipartimento di Ingegneria Strutturale, Politecnico di Milan, Piazza Leonardo da Vinci 32, 20133 Milan Italy. **LC** TA630; .P63A. **DD** 624/.05.

UK/0039-6265
SURVEY REVIEW - DIRECTORATE OF OVERSEAS SURVEYS. (SURVEY REVIEW.). [Surv. rev. - Dir. Overseas Surv.]. **Added/Corp** Great Britain. Directorate of Overseas Surveys. Commonwealth Association of Surveying and Land Economy. No. 127 (Jan. 1963)-. Periodical. English. qt. £39.00 UK; $95.00 US; £47.00 other. Commonwealth Association Survey and Land, 12 Gr George Street, Parliament Square, London SW1P 3AD England. **Tel** 011 44 71 222 7000. **(Subscription address:** Turpin Transactions Ltd., Blackhorse Road, Letchworth, Herfordshire SG6 1HN United Kingdom; Telephone: (0462) 672555, FAX: (0462) 480947**) LC** TA501; .E6. **DD** 526.9/05. available on microfilm from University Microfilms International (UMI). ***Continues** Empire Survey Review.*
Ind/Abst Geogr. Abstr. Phys. Geogr.; Geogr. Abstr. Human Geogr.; Geol. Abstr.; GeoRef.

AT/0157-1672
SURVEYING AUSTRALIA. [Surv. Aust.]. (1979)-. Periodical. English. Four times a year (Mar., June, Sept., Dec.). 40.00Aus$ Australia; 46.00Aus$ U.S., Canada & Europe; 44.00Aus$ other. Instutute of Engineering Mining Survey, 725 South Road, Moorabbin Vic, 3001 Australia. **Tel** 011 61 3 7974715. **DD** 526.90994.

UK/0952-5793
SURVEYING TECHNICIAN. *Ceased.* [Surv. tech.]. (1970)-Vol. 21, No. 5 (Nov. 1993). Periodical. English. Six times a year. Society of Surveying Technicians, Drayton House, 30 Gordon Street, London WC1H 0BH England. **Tel** 011 44 1 388 8008, FAX 071 383 7554. **DD** 526.9. **Bk Rev. Ad Acc. Pr Rev. Circ:** 6,500 (ctrl).
Desc: Surveying technique and education in care of land and property.
Ind/Abst Geogr. Abstr. Phys. Geogr.

UK
SURVEYOR (WALLINGTON, ENGLAND : 1987). (SURVEYOR. MICROFORM.). Vol. 168, No. 4938 (April 2, 1987)-. English. ***Continues** Public Works Weekly Surveyor.*

SW
SVENSK LANTMATERITIDSKRIFT. *Title Change.* Added/Corp Sveriges Lantmatareforening. (1909)-(19??). Periodical. Swedish. bm. Sveriges Lantmatareforening, Box 40037, Stockholm S-10341 Sweden. **LC** TA501; .S9. **DD** 526.9062485. ***Continued by** Lantmateritidskriften.*

US/0146-8316
SWEET'S ENGINEERING MARKET. 1977-. English. McGraw Hill Information Systems Company, 1221 Avenue of the Americas, New York NY 10020. **Tel** (212)512-2000, (800)525-5003, FAX (212)512-6111. **LC** TA12; .S97. **DD** 338.4/7/620002573.

KO
TAEHAN TOMOK HAKHOE CHI. JOURNAL OF THE KOREAN SOCIETY OF CIVIL ENGINEERS. Main/Corp Taehan Tomok Hakhoe. **Added/Corp** Taehan Tomok Hakhoe. Journal. **VFOAT** Journal of the Korean Society of Civil Engineers. (19??)-. Periodical. Korean. **LC** TA4; .T25a.
Ind/Abst Energy Res. Abstr. (Sept. 1980-); J. Ferrocement.

JA/0374-4663
TAKENAKA GIJUTSU KENKYU HOKOKU. VFOAT Takenaka Technical Research Report. Japanese. an. Takenaka Komuten Kohobu, (Takenaka Komuten Co., Ltd.), 4-27, Honmachi, Higashiku, Osakashi, Osakafu 541 Japan. **LC** TA630. **CODEN** TGKHAI. Documents available from Article Express International, Ask*IEEE.
Ind/Abst Abstr. J. Earthq. Eng.; Bioeng. Abstr.; Ei Page One; Eng. Index Annu.; INSPEC (June 1971-).

CN/0077-5428
TECHNICAL MEMORANDUM - ASSOCIATE COMMITTEE ON GEOTECHNICAL RESEARCH (OTTAWA). (TECHNICAL MEMORANDUM - ASSOCIATE COMMITTEE ON GEOTECHNICAL RESEARCH, NATIONAL RESEARCH COUNCIL OF CANADA.). [Tech. memo. - Assoc. Comm. Geotech. Res.]. **Main/Corp** National Research Council of Canada. Associate Committee on Geotechnical Research. **VFOAT** Memoire Technique - Comite Associe de Recherches Geotechniques. No. 87-. Monographic series. English (summaries and/or abstracts in French). ir. Price varies per volume. Associate Committee on Geotechnical Research, National Research Council of Canada, Ottawa Ontario K1A 0R6 Canada. **Tel** (613)993-3801, telex 053-3145. **DD** 624.1/5136. **CODEN** NAGTAS. Index available. cum. index. **Circ:** 1,000 (ctrl). ***Continues** Technical Memorandum - National Research Council of Canada, Associate Committee on Soil and Snow Mechanics.*
Desc: Technical memorandum prepared by such committees on various topics: soil mechanics, snow and ice, urban terrain, permafrost, marine geotechnical engineering, peatlands, soil and rock.
Ind/Abst GeoRef.

US/0502-3262
TECHNICAL REPORT - CIVIL ENGINEERING LABORATORY, NAVAL CONSTRUCTION BATTALION CENTER, PORT HUENEME, CALIFORNIA. [Tec. rep. - Civ. Eng. Lab. Nav. Constr. Battalion Cent. Port Hueneme Calif.]. **Main/Corp** United States Naval Civil Engineering Laboratory, Port Hueneme, California. (19??)-. Monographic series. English.
Ind/Abst GeoRef; Int. Civil Eng. Abstr.; Ocean. Abstr.

CN/0709-9916
TECHNICAL REPORT (SASKATCHEWAN. SASKATCHEWAN HIGHWAYS AND TRANSPORTATION). (TECHNICAL REPORT / SASKATCHEWAN HIGHWAYS AND TRANSPORTATION.). [Tech. rep. - Sask. Highw. Transp.]. Monographic series. English. Price varies per volume. Saskatchewan Highways & Transportation, 9th Floor, 1855 Victoria Avenue, Regina Saskatchewan S4P 3V5 Canada. **Tel** (306)787-4756, FAX (306)787-1007. **LC** TE27.S3; S27A. **DD** 625.7. ***Continues** Technical Report (Saskatchewan. Dept. of Highways and Transportation).*

US/0585-0738
TECHNICAL REPORT (STANFORD UNIVERSITY. DEPT. OF CIVIL ENGINEERING). (TECHNICAL REPORT - DEPARTMENT OF CIVIL ENGINEERING, STANFORD UNIVERSITY.). [Tech. rep. Dep. Civ. Eng. Stanford Univ.]. **Main/Corp** Stanford University. Dept. of Civil Engineering. No. 1 (1956)-. Monographic series. English. Price varies per volume. Stanford University / Civil Engineering, Department of Civil Engineering, Stanford CA 94305. **DD** 620. **CODEN** SUCTAX. Documents available from Article Express International.
Ind/Abst Bioeng. Abstr.; Ei Page One; Eng. Index Annu.; Life Sci. Collect.

CN/0709-1222
TECHNICAL REPORT (UNIVERSITY OF NEW BRUNSWICK. DEPT. OF SURVEYING ENGINEERING). (TECHNICAL REPORT - DEPARTMENT OF SURVEYING ENGINEERING, UNIVERSITY OF NEW BRUNSWICK.). [Tech. rep. - Dep. Surv. Eng. Univ. N. B.]. **Added/Corp** University of New Brunswick. Dept. of Surveying Engineering. (19??)-. Monographic series. English. Seven times a year. 30.00Can$. Geodesy and Geomatics Engineering, University of New Brunswick, PO Box 4400, Fredericton, New Brunswick, Canada E3B 5A3. **Tel** (506)453-4698, FAX (506)453-4943. **DD** 526.9. **Circ:** 500.
Desc: Technical reports covering topics in surveying engineering: cadastral, geodetic, hydrographic surveying, mining and engineering surveys, photogrammetry, digital mapping, remote sensing, cartography, and land information management/systems.
Ind/Abst GeoRef.

GR/0250-9954
TECHNIKA CHRONIKA EPISTEMONIKE EKDOSE. T.E.E. EPISTEMONIKE PERIOCHE A. Added/Corp Technikon Epimeleterion Hellados. **VFOAT** Technika Chronika Epistemonike Ekdose TEE. Epistemonike Perioche A; Technika Chronika Scientific Journal of the Technical Chamber of Greece. Section A. Periodical. Greek, Modern (English and French). qt. Technical Chamber of Greece, rue Karageorgi Servias 4, Athens 125 Greece. **Tel** (01)32 54 590-9, telex TEEGR 218374. ***Continues in part** Technika Chronika.*

FR
TECHNIQUES DE L'INGENIEUR / CONSTRUCTION CA. French. Editions Techniques, 141 rue de Javel, 75747 Paris Cedex 15 France. **Tel** 011 33 1 45589100.

SZ
TECHNISCHE MITTEILUNGEN FUER SAPPEURE, PONTONIERE, UND MINEURE. Added/Corp Gesellschaft fuer Militarische Bautechnik. (1936)-. Periodical. German (French and Italian). Four times a year. 50.00F. Gesellschaft fuer Militaerische Bautechnik, Auf der Mauer 2, CH-8001 Zurich Switzerland. **Tel** 011 41 1 2526260, FAX 0/252 1667. **LC** UG1; .T4. Index available. cum. index. **Bk Rev. Ad Acc. Circ:** 1,300.
Desc: Application of civil engineering for military purposes.

IT/0040-1846
TECNICA ITALIANA. [Tec. ital.]. Vol. 1 (Oct. 1946)-. Academic Scholarly Publication. Italian (English). bm. L70000 Italy; L90000 other. Zorzut, Via Matteotti 55, 34071 Cormons Italy. **Tel** 39 481 60164. **ED** Zorzut Giovanni. **LC** TA4; .T42. **CODEN** TITLAL. **Ad Acc. Pr Rev. Circ:** 1,000. Documents available from Ask*IEEE, CASDDS.
Ind/Abst Chem. Abstr.; INSPEC (1968-); Int. Aerosp. Abstr.; Ship Abstr.; Surf. Treat. Technol. Abstr.

US
TENNESSEE VALLEY ENGINEER. V. 1- Apr. 1940-. Periodical. English. mo. $3.00 US; $4.00 other. Tennessee Valley Section, American Society of Civil Engineers, Box 1243, Knoxville TN 37901. **LC** TA1; .T395. **DD** 620.6273. ***Supersedes** Lookout Engineer; American Society of Civil Engineers. Tennessee Valley Section. Bulletin of the Knoxville Subsection.*

NE/0376-6411
TERRA ET AQUA. See Engineering-Hydraulic Engineering.

CN/0714-4091
TERRAVUE. [Terravue]. **Added/Corp** Canadian Council of Land Surveyors. (Autumn 1982)-. English (French). an. Free to members. Canadian Council of Land Surveyors, 210 14964-121 A Avenue, Edmonton Alta T5V 1A3 Canada. **DD** 526.9/0971.

UK/0263-8231
THIN-WALLED STRUCTURES. [Thin-walled struct.]. Vol. 1, No. 1 (March 1983)-. Academic Scholarly Publication. English. Twelve times a year. $760.00 The Americas; £510.00 other. Elsevier Applied Science, An Imprint of Elsevier Science Ltd., The Boulevard, Langford Lane, Kidlington, Oxford OX5 1GB United Kingdom. **Tel** 011 44 865 843000, 011 44 865 843699, FAX 011 44 865 843010. **(Subscription address:** Elsevier Science Ltd. Oxford Fulfillment Centre, PO Box 800, Kidlington, Oxford OX5 1DX United Kingdom.**) ED** J. Rhodes and K. P. Chong. **CODEN** TWASDE. **[CCC]. Bk Rev. Ad Acc.** available on microfilm and microfiche from University Microfilms International (UMI). Documents available from Article Express International, The Genuine Article, Ask*IEEE.
Desc: Covers such diverse engineering areas as pressure vessels, aircraft, ships, bridges, offshore structures, storage tanks, box girders, box columns, industrial buildings, and sheet structures.
Ind/Abst Alum. Ind. Abstr.; Civ. Struct. Eng. Abstr.; Comput. Inf. Syst. Abstr. J. [Full Cov.]; Curr. Contents Eng. Tech. Appl. Sci.; Ei Page One; Eng. Mater. Abstr.; Eng. Index Annu.; Fluid Abstr., Civil Eng.; Fluid Abstr. Proc. Eng.; FLUIDEX (19??-); INSPEC (1985-); Int. Aerosp. Abstr. (1983-); Manuf. Process Eng. Abstr.; Mech. Eng. Abstr.; Met. Abstr.; Res. Alert [Full Cov.]; Solid State Supercond. Abstr.

FI
TIE JA LIIKENNE. Vol. 44- ; 1974-. Finnish (English). mo (except January and July). Fmk104.00 Finland; Fmk128.00 other. Finnish Road Association, PO Box 131, 00701 Helsinki Finland. **Tel** 358-0-70010881. **ED** Jarmo Nupponen. **LC** TE4; .T5. **Ad Acc. Circ:** 7,000 (ctrl). ***Continues** Tielehti.*
Desc: Contains articles on planning, construction and maintenance of roads, road traffic, transportation and traffic engineering.

GW/0340-5079
TIEFBAU, INGENIEURBAU, STRASSENBAU. [Tiefbau. Ingenieurbau. Strassenbau]. **VFOAT** Tiefbau, Ingenieurbau, Strassenbau. Ausgabe A. (1970)-. Academic Scholarly Publication. German. mo. DM159.00. Bertelsmann Fachzeitschriften GmbH, Carl-Bertelsmann Strasse 270, D-33311 Frankfurt Germany. **Tel** 011 49 5241 802199. **(Subscription address:** Translibris GmbH, PO Box 301373, D 50783 Cologne Germany.**) LC** TA3; .T5.

CODEN TFBABE. Documents available from Article Express International, CASDDS. ***Continues*** *Tiefbau, 0040-7240.*
Desc: Concerned with civil engineering: road building, excavation and structural engineering.
Ind/Abst Bioeng. Abstr.; Chem. Abstr.; Coal Abstr.; Ei Page One; EMBASE; Energy Res. Abstr. (April 1981-); Eng. Index Annu.; Geotech. Abstr.; Highw. Res. Abstr.; Int. Civil Eng. Abstr.; Soft. Abstr. Eng.

US/1048-0935
TODAY'S REFINERY. See Petroleum and Natural Gas.

JA/0285-3817
TOHOKU KOGYO DAIGAKU KIYO. SERIES 1. RIKOGAKUEN. (TOHOKU KOGYO DAIGAKU KIYO. 1, RIKOGAKU HEN.). [Tohoku kogyo Daigaku kiyo. Ser. 1. Rikogaku-hen]. **VFOAT** Memoirs of the Tohoku Institute of Technology. Ser. 1, Science and Engineering. No. 1- (March, 1981)-. Periodical. Japanese (English, German and French). an. Tohoku Institute of Technology Taihaku-ku, Sendai 982 Japan. **Tel** 022-291-1151. **ED** Atsushi Numata. **LC** TA4; .T617. **DD** 605. **CODEN** TKDRDA. Index available. **Circ:** 740. Documents available from Ask*IEEE, CASDDS.
Ind/Abst Chem. Abstr.; Ei Page One; INSPEC (March 1985-).

CN/0226-9171
TOPOLOGIE STRUCTURALE / STRUCTURAL TOPOLOGY. See Mathematics.

US/0066-0604
TRANSACTIONS OF THE AMERICAN SOCIETY OF CIVIL ENGINEERS. See Engineering-Abstracting, Bibliographies and Statistics.

AT/0159-2068
TRANSACTIONS OF THE INSTITUTION OF ENGINEERS, AUSTRALIA. CIVIL ENGINEERING. [Trans. Inst. Eng., Aust., Civil eng.]. **Added/Corp** Institution of Engineers, Australia. **VFOAT** Civil Engineering; Australian Civil Engineering Transactions. (Sept. 1979)-. Periodical. English. qt. 55.00Aus$, 70.00Aus$. Engineers Australia Pty Ltd, 2 Ernest Street, Crows Nest Centre, Crows Nest New South Wales 2065, Australia. **Tel** 011 61 2 438-1533, FAX 011 61 2 438-5934, telex 27640. **ED** V. E. Schmidt. **LC** TA1; .C454. **DD** 624/.05. **CODEN** TEACDA. Index available (Bound in Oct. issue). ctrl circ. Documents available from Article Express International, Ask*IEEE. ***Continues*** *Civil Engineering Transactions, 0020-3297.*
Desc: Contains scientific and research papers prepared by Australian engineers dealing with civil engineering projects and research.
Ind/Abst Alum. Ind. Abstr.; Coal Abstr.; Concr. Abstr.; Ei Page One; Energy Inf. Abstr.; Eng. Index Annu.; Fluid Abstr., Civil Eng.; Fluid Abstr. Proc. Eng.; FLUIDEX (1979-); Geotech. Abstr.; Highw. Res. Abstr.; INSPEC (1979-); Int. Civil Eng. Abstr.; Met. Abstr.; Pollut. Abstr. Indexes; Soft. Abstr. Eng.

NZ/0111-9508
TRANSACTIONS OF THE INSTITUTION OF PROFESSIONAL ENGINEERS NEW ZEALAND, CIVIL ENGINEERING SECTION. [Trans. Inst. Prof. Eng. N.Z., Civ. Eng. Sect.]. **Main/Corp** Institution of Professional Engineers New Zealand. Civil Engineering Section. **VFOAT** IPENZ Transactions; I.P.E.N.Z. Transactions. Vol. 9, No. 1 (Mar. 1982)-. Periodical. English. ir (2 to 3 per year). 20.00NZ$. Institute of Professional Engineers New Zealand, PO Box 12241, Wellington New Zealand. **Tel** 011 64 4 4739444. **CODEN** TPCSD9. **[CCC].** Documents available from Article Express International, Ask*IEEE. ***Continues*** *New Zealand Institution of Engineers. Civil Engineering Section. Transactions of the New Zealand Institution of Engineers Incorporated, Civil Engineering Section, 0111-2759.*
Ind/Abst Alum. Ind. Abstr.; Bioeng. Abstr.; Ei Page One; Eng. Index Annu. [Select. Cov.]; INSPEC (1982-); Met. Abstr.

JA
TRANSACTIONS OF THE JAPAN CONCRETE INSTITUTE. Added/Corp Japan Concrete Institute. (1979)-. Periodical. English. an. $170.00. Japan Concrete Institute, Room 708/Shuwa-Kioicho TBR Building No 7, Kojimachi 5-chome Chiyoda-ku, Tokyo 102 Japan. **Tel** (03)263-1571, FAX (03)263-2115. **(Subscription address:** Maruzen Company Ltd., PO Box 5050, Import & Export Department, Tokyo 100 31 Japan.**) LC** TA680; .T68. **DD** 624.1/834. **Circ:** 500.
Desc: Research papers from the Japan Concrete Institute.

BW
TRENIE I IZNOS. VFOAT Friction and Wear. (Jan. 1980)-. Academic Scholarly Publication. Russian (summaries and/or abstracts in English). bm. $186.00 doemstic airmail; $194.00 international airmail. **(Subscription address:** Victor Kamkin, 4956 Boiling Brook Parkway, Rockville MD 20852.**) LC** TA418.72; .T733. **CODEN** TRIZD6. Documents available from Article Express International, Ask*IEEE, CASDDS.
Ind/Abst Bioeng. Abstr.; Chem. Abstr.; Ei Page One; Energy Res. Abstr. (Oct. 1982-); Eng. Index Annu.; Fluid Abstr., Civil Eng.; Fluid Abstr. Proc. Eng.; FLUIDEX (1980-); INSPEC (1985-).

CH
TSE LIANG CHI SHU TUNG PAO.
Added/Corp China. Lien ho chin wu Tsung ssu Ling pu. Tse Liang shu. China. Lien ho Chin wu Tsung ssu Ling pu. Tse Liang chu. China. Lien ho Chin wu Tsung ssu Ling pu. Tse Liang shu. CTS Bulletin. **VFOAT** CTS Bulletin. No. 8 (May 1955)-. Periodical. Chinese. Three times a year. **LC** TA501; .T779. ***Continues*** *Chung-Kuo Tse Liang.*

CH/0253-3804
TU MU SHUI LI. [Tumu shuili]. **Added/Corp** Chung-Kuo Tu Mu Shui Li Kung Cheng Hsueh Hui. **VFOAT** Journal of Civil and Hydraulic Engineering. (19??)-. Periodical. Chinese. NT$50.00. Chung-Kuo Tu Mu Shui Li Kung Cheng Hsueh Hui, PO Box 3067, Taipei Taiwan. **LC** TA4; .T767. **DD** 624/.05. **CODEN** TMSLDD. Documents available from CASDDS.
Ind/Abst Chem. Abstr.

US/0095-2664
TUNNELING TECHNOLOGY NEWSLETTER. *Ceased.* [Tunn. technol. newsl.]. (March 1973)-(1990). Newsletter. English. qt. National Academy Press, 2101 Constitution Avenue NW, Lockbox 285, Washington DC 20055. **Tel** (800)624-6242, (202)334-3313, FAX (202)334-2451. **(Subscription address:** National Academy of Sciences, Box 285, Washington DC 20055**) ED** Susan V. Heisler. **LC** TA800; .T79. **DD** 624/.19/05. **Circ:** 1,500.
Desc: Technical articles on various aspects of underground construction and mining technology, selected news items, list of meetings with program synopses, list of recent publications.
Ind/Abst Coal Abstr.; GeoRef.

UK/0886-7798
TUNNELLING AND UNDERGROUND SPACE TECHNOLOGY. [Tunn. undergr. space technol.]. **Added/Corp** International Tunnelling Association. Vol. 1, No. 1 (1986)-. Periodical. English. qt. $410.00 The Americas; £275.00 other. Pergamon Press, An Imprint of Elsevier Science Ltd., The Boulevard, Langford Lane, Kidlington, Oxford OX5 1GB United Kingdom. **Tel** 011 44 865 843000, 011 44 865 843699, FAX 011 44 865 843010. **(Subscription address:** Elsevier Science Ltd. Oxford Fulfillment Centre, PO Box 800, Kidlington, Oxford OX5 1DX United Kingdom.**) ED** E. Brock and C. Fairhurst. **LC** TA800; .T7893. **DD** 624.1/9. **[CCC]. Bk Rev. Ad Acc.** available on microfilm and microfiche from University Microfilms International (UMI). Documents available from Article Express International, The Genuine Article. ***Formed by the union of*** *Advances in Tunnelling Technology and Subsurface Use, 0275-5416* ***and*** *Underground Space, 0362-0565.*
Desc: Provides an effective vehicle for the improved worldwide exchange of information on developments in underground technology and the experience gained from its use; is strongly committed to publishing papers on the interdisciplinary aspects of creating, planning and regulating underground space.
Ind/Abst Coal Abstr.; Curr. Contents Eng. Tech. Appl. Sci.; Ei Page One; Eng. Index Annu.; Fluid Abstr., Civil Eng.; Fluid Abstr. Proc. Eng.; FLUIDEX (199?-); Geogr. Abstr. Phys. Geogr. (?-?); Geogr. Abstr. Human Geogr.; Geol. Abstr.; GeoRef; Geotech. Abstr.; Int. Build. Serv. Abstr.; Int. Civil Eng. Abstr.; Int. Dev. Abstr.; Res. Alert [Select. Cov.]; Soc. Sci. Cit. Index [Select. Cov.]; Soft. Abstr. Eng.

UK/0041-414X
TUNNELS & TUNNELLING. [Tunn. tunn.]. **VAT** Tunnels and Tunnelling. (May/June 1969)-. Academic Scholarly Publication. English. mo. £50.00 UK and Northern Ireland; $125.00 other (includes Micro-Tunnelling). Morgan Grampian, 40 Beresford Street Woolwich, London SE18 6BQ England. **Tel** 011 44 81 855 7777, FAX 011 44 81 855 5548, telex 896238. **ED** David Martin. **LC** TA800; .T8. **DD** 624/.19/05. **CODEN** TUTUBV. Index available. **Bk Rev. Ad Acc. Circ:** 3,349. available on microfilm and microfiche from University Microfilms International (UMI). Documents available from Article Express International.
Desc: The design, planning, construction, operation and maintenance of tunnels and underground excavations and latest techniques in this specialized branch of civil engineering.
Ind/Abst Bioeng. Abstr.; Coal Abstr.; Curr. Technol. Index; Ei Page One; EMBASE; Eng. Index Annu. [Select. Cov.]; Fluid Abstr., Civil Eng.; Fluid Abstr. Proc. Eng.; FLUIDEX (1973-); GeoRef; Geotech. Abstr.; Highw. Res. Abstr.; Int. Civil Eng. Abstr.; Mintec, Min. Technol. Abstr.; Soft. Abstr. Eng.

UK
TUNNELS & TUNNELLING. WORLD PROFILE OF CONTRACTORS. VFOAT Tunnels and Tunnelling; World Profile of Contractors. 1982-. English. an. Morgan Grampian, 40 Beresford Street Woolwich, London SE18 6BQ England. **Tel** 011 44 81 855 7777, FAX 011 44 81 855 5548, telex 896238.

FR
TUNNELS. ET OUVRAGES SOUTERRAINS. (1974)-. French. Six times a year (Jan., Mar., May, July, Sept., Nov.). 310.00F France; 470.00F Europe; 520.00F others. Sedip Communication, 49 Rue Servient, 69423 Lyon Cedex 03 France. **Tel** 011 33 72 352372. **ED** Jean Luc Reith. **Bk Rev. Circ:** 1,800.

FR/0399-0834
TUNNELS ET OUVRAGES SOUTERRAINS VILLEURBANNE. [Tunn. ouvrages souterr. Villeurbanne]. (1974)-. Periodical. French (summaries and/or abstracts in English). bm. 310.00F France; 470.00F Europe except France; 520.00 other. Specifique, 5 rue Juliette Recamier, 69006 Lyon France. **Tel** 011 33 7 2741034. **ED** Jean Luc Reith (telephone 72.35.23.72). **UDC** 624.1. **Ad Acc. Circ:** 1800 (ctrl).
Ind/Abst Highw. Res. Abstr.; Int. Civil Eng. Abstr.

AT
UNICIV REPORT. Main/Corp University of New South Wales. School of Civil Engineering. No. 1 (April 1963)-. Monographic series. English. ir. Price varies per volume. University of New South Wales / School of Civil Engineering, Sydney 2052 Australia. **Tel** 02 385 5033, FAX 02 663 2188. ctrl circ.

SW/0042-2177
VAG-OCH VATTEN BYGGAREN. [Vag-vatten bygg.]. **Added/Corp** Svenska Vag Och Vattensbyggares Riksforbund. **VFOAT** Journal of the Swedish Society of Civil Engineers. (195?)-. Periodical. Swedish. bm. $24.75. Svenska Vaeg Och Vatten Riksf, Box 1334, S 111 83 Stockholm Sweden. **Tel** 011 46 8 245450. **LC** WMLC L 83/4733. **CODEN** VVTBAZ. Documents available from Article Express International.
Ind/Abst Ei Page One (19??-); Energy Res. Abstr. (May 1973-); Eng. Index Annu. (19??-).

HU/0133-0314
VAROSI KOZLEKEDES. See Transportation.

NE
VERBRUIK BOUWMATERIALEN : NIEUWBOUW WONINGEN. Main/Corp Netherlands. Centraal Bureau Voor de Statistiek. **VFOAT** Consumption of Building Materials: New Construction of Dwellings. Dutch. Fl9.75. Centraal Bureau voor de Statistiek, AFD ALG Zaken, Postbus 959, 2270 AZ Voorburg Netherlands. **Tel** 011 31 70 3373800, FAX 011 31 038 7429, telex 32692 CBS NL. **LC** TA402.5.N4; N47A.

US/0273-6861
VIRGINIA CONTRACTOR. Vol. 1 (Sept. 1980)-. Periodical. English. mo. $24.00. Commonwealth Communications, GRP 5049, Admiral Wright Road, Suite 339, Virginia Beach VA 23462. **Tel** (804)490-9653. ***Supersedes*** *Tidewater Contractor, 0274-5712.*

UK/0364-7714
WATER SUPPLY & MANAGEMENT. *Ceased.* See Water Resources.

US
WEEKLY LETTING REPORT - IOWA. HIGHWAY DIVISION. Main/Corp Iowa. Highway Division. English. wk. Iowa Department of Transportation, 800 Lincoln Way, Ames IA 50010. **Tel** (515)239-1528. **LC** TE180; .I63A. **DD** 353.97770071/12.

NE/0043-2067
WEGEN. [Wegen]. **Added/Corp** Vereniging "Het Nederlandse Wegencongres." Permanent International Association of Road Congresses. (1925)-. Academic Scholarly Publication. Dutch. mo. Fl40.00. Stichting Crow, Postbus 37, 6710 BA EDE Netherlands. **Tel** 011 31 8380 20410. **LC** TE4; .W4. Index available. **Bk Rev. Ad Acc.**
Desc: Studies of roads, bridges, traffic, materials for building roads and bridges, engineering, etc.
Ind/Abst EMBASE (19??-); Highw. Res. Abstr. (19??-).

GW
WERKSTOFFE, BETRIEBSLEITUNG + TECHNIK. Added/Corp ERFA-Gruppe Betriebsleiter der Deutschen Wirtschaft. **VFOAT** Werkstoffe, Betriebsleitung und Technik. (19??)-. German. Six times a year. DM104.00. Holzverlag GmbH & Co KG, VdK Strasse 25, D 86438 Kissing Germany. **Tel** 011 44 8233 5029, telex 533 295. **LC** TA3; .W38. **DD** 620.1/1/05. **Bk Rev. Ad Acc.** ***Continues*** *Werkstoffe + Technik.*

GW/0863-0925
WISSENSCHAFTLISCHE ZEITSCHRIFT DER TECHNISCHEN UNIVERSITAT OTTO VON GUERICKE MAGDEBURG. [Wiss. Z. Tech. Univ. "Otto Guericke" Magdebg.]. (1987)-. Academic Scholarly Publication. German. bm. Buchexport, Postfach 160, DDR-7010 Leipzig Germany. **Tel** 011 37 41 71370. **LC** TA4; .M18. **DD** 670.42/05. **CODEN** WZTMEA. Documents available from Ask*IEEE, CASDDS. ***Continues*** *Wissenschaftliche Zeitschrift der Technischen Hochschule "Otto von Guericke" Magdeburg.*
Ind/Abst Chem. Abstr.; INSPEC (1987-); Math. Rev. (1988-).

KO
WOLGAN KONSOL. See Architecture.

UK
YEARBOOK - INSTITUTION OF CIVIL ENGINEERS. **Main/Corp** Institution of Civil Engineers (Great Britain). (19??)-. English. an. £22.00 (members), £75.00 (nonmembers) UK; £26.00 (members), £80.00 (nonmembers) other. Thomas Telford Ltd, Thomas Telford House, 1 Heron Quay, London E14 9XF England. **Tel** 011 44 71 987 6999, FAX 011 44 71 538 4101, telex 298105. **LC** TA1; .I6846. **DD** 624/.06/242. ***Absorbed*** *Institution of Civil Engineers (Great Britain). List of Members.*

CH
YING TSAO CHIEN TSAI TSUNG LAN. 1984-. Chinese. NT$300.00. Ching Chi Jih Pao, Kung Shang Fu Wu Pu 555, Chung Hsiao East Road, 4 Section/8th Floor, Taipei Shih Taiwan. **LC** TA402.5.T28; Y56. **DD** 338.4/7691/02551249.

GW/0340-4560
ZEITSCHRIFT FUER VERMESSUNGSWESEN. ZFV. [ZFV. Z. Vermessungswes.]. **Added/Corp** Deutscher Geometerverein. Deutscher Verein fuer Vermessungswesen. **VFOAT** ZFV. Vol. 1 (Jan. 1972)-. Periodical. German (English). mo. DM146.00. Konrad Wittwer Verlag, Nordbahnhofstr 16, W 70191 Stuttgart Germany. **Tel** 011 49 711 2507305. **ED** Holger Magel, Wolfgang Torge. **LC** TA501; .Z5. **DD** 526.9/05. **CODEN** ZTVRAM. **[CCC].** Index available. cum. index. **Bk Rev. Ad Acc. Circ:** 8,000 (ctrl). Documents available from Ask*IEEE. ***Absorbed*** *Allgemeine Vermessungs-Nachrichten; Bildmessung und Luftbildwesen; Photogrammetria.*
Desc: Surveying, land registering, cartography, photo and grammetry.
Ind/Abst Bibliogr. Carto.; Geogr. Abstr. Phys. Geogr. (?-?); INSPEC (Sept. 1971-); Int. Aerosp. Abstr.; Stat. Theory Method Abstr. (1972, 1984).

ELECTRICITY, ELECTRICAL ENGINEERING, ELECTRONICS

GW
A.G.T. DOKUMENTATION. **VFOAT** AGT Dokumentation; Doku. (19??)-. German. Four times a year. DM104.20. AGT Verlag Thum GmbH, Postfach 109, Teinacherstr 34, D 71601 714 Ludwigsburg 10 Germany. **Tel** 011 49 7141 223156. **LC** Discard. **Bk Rev. Ad Acc. Circ:** 10,000 (ctrl).

JA
ABSTRACTS OF SCIENCE AND TECHNOLOGY IN JAPAN. ELECTRONICS AND COMMUNICATION. ***Ceased.*** **See** Engineering-Abstracting, Bibliographies and Statistics.

US/1042-2617
ACCESS CONTROL. [Access control]. **VFOAT** Access Control Buyers' Guide. (1989)-. Periodical. English. Thirteen times a year (Plus 1 directory). $48.00. Argus Business, 6151 Powers Ferry Road, Atlanta GA 30339. **Tel** (404)995-2500, (800)233-3359. **(Subscription address:** Sunbelt Fulfillment Services, PO Box 41369, Nashville, TN 37204**) ED** Barbara Katinsky. **LC** TH9730; .A26. **DD** 621.389/28. **Circ:** 22,800. available on microfilm from University Microfilms International (UMI). ***Continues*** *Access Control, Fence Industry, 0894-6639.*

BE/0001-0669
ACEC REVIEW. [ACEC rev.]. **Added/Corp** Ateliers de Constructions Electriques de Charleroi. (1958)-. Periodical. English (French, Dutch and German). ir (Published three or four times per year). Free. ACEC PLG MK AP, BP 4, 6000 Charleroi Belgium. **CODEN** ACECA8. Documents available from Ask*IEEE. ***Continues*** *ACEC Charleroi.*
Ind/Abst Alum. Ind. Abstr.; Energy Res. Abstr.; INSPEC (1968-); Met. Abstr.

XR/0374-2474
ACTA POLYTECHNICA. III, PRACE CVUT V PRAZE / CESKE VYSOKE UCENI TECHNICKE V PRAZE. **Added/Corp** Ceske Vysoke Uceni Technicke v Praze. **VFOAT** Prace CVUT v Praze; Prace Ceskeho Vysokeho Uceni Technickeho v Praze. (196?)-. Periodical. Czech (summaries and/or abstracts in English and Russian). Acta Polytechnica, Prace CVUT v Praze, Prague Czech Republic. **LC** TK4; .P64917. Documents available from Article Express International, Ask*IEEE. ***Continues*** *Ceske Vysoke Uceni Technicke v Praze. Prace CVUT v Praze. Rada III: Elektrotechnicka.*
Ind/Abst Ei Page One; Eng. Index Annu. [Select. Cov.]; INSPEC (1968-).

FI/0001-6845
ACTA POLYTECHNICA SCANDINAVICA. ELECTRICAL ENGINEERING SERIES. [Acta polytech. Scand., Electr. eng. ser.]. **Added/Corp** Teknillisten Tieteiden Akatemia. Scandinavian Council for Applied Research. **VFOAT** Electrical Engineering Series. No. 1 (1958)-. Monographic series. English. ir. Fmk1350.00. The Finnish Academy of Technology, Tekniikantie 12, Fin 02150 Espoo Finland. **Tel** 011 358 0 4554565, FAX 011 358 0 6945041. **ED** Seppo Halme. **LC** TK4; .A26. **DD** 621.3/05. **CODEN** APSEA5. Index available. **Circ:** 600. available on microfilm and microfiche from University Microfilms International (UMI). Documents available from Article Express International, The Genuine Article, Ask*IEEE. ***Continues*** *Acta Polytechnica. Electrical Engineering Series.*
Desc: Scientific research report series consisting of monographs.
Ind/Abst Bioeng. Abstr.; Curr. Contents Eng. Tech. Appl. Sci.; Ei Page One; EMBASE; Energy Res. Abstr.; Eng. Index Annu. [Select. Cov.]; INSPEC (1980-); Int. Aerosp. Abstr.; Leadscan; Res. Alert [Full Cov.]; SCISEARCH.

US/0882-7516
ACTIVE AND PASSIVE ELECTRONIC COMPONENTS. [Act. passive electron. compon.]. Vol. 12, No. 1 (1985)-. Periodical. English. ir (4 issues per volume). Gordon & Breach Science Publishers, Inc., PO Box 786, Cooper Station, New York NY 10276. **Tel** (212)206-8900, FAX (212)645-2459. **ED** Josephine A. Castellano. **LC** QC176.8.T5; E4. **DD** 621.38. **[CCC]. Bk Rev. Ad Acc.** ctrl circ. Documents available from Ask*IEEE. ***Continues*** *Electrocomponent Science and Technology, 0305-3091.*
Ind/Abst Acoust. Abstr.; INSPEC (Vol. 12, No. 1 1985-).

SP/0210-6302
ACTUALIDAD ELECTRONICA. [Actual. electron.]. (1977)-. Periodical. Spanish (summaries and/or abstracts in English). Nine times a year. 4603ptas Spain & Portugal; 5575ptas other Europe; 6925ptas other (Comes with Mundo Electronico). Cetisa Boixareu Editores SA, C Concepcion Arsenal 5 7, 08027 Barcelona Spain. **Tel** 011 34 3 352-7061. **UDC** 621.38. **[CCC].**
Ind/Abst Infomat Int. Bus.

US/0742-9282
ADVANCE FORECAST REPORT TO THE MINNESOTA ENVIRONMENTAL QUALITY BOARD ... . 1980-. English. be. **LC** TK24.M6; A37. **DD** 363.6/2/09776. ***Continues*** *Advance Forecasting Report to the Minnesota Environmental Quality Council, 0742-9304.*

US
ADVANCE PROGRAM. **Main/Corp** Bonneville Power Administration. (196?)-. English. be. **LC** HD9685.U6; A195. **DD** 338.476213. ***Continues*** *Bonneville Power Administration. Advance Program: U.S. Columbia River Power System.*

US/0001-8627
ADVANCED BATTERY TECHNOLOGY. [Adv. battery technol.]. **VFOAT** ABT; A.B.T. Vol. 1 (1965)-. Periodical. English. mo. $135.00 North America; $165.00 (airmail) other. Robert Morey Associates, PO Box 30, Cooperstown NY 13326. **Tel** (607)547-5314, FAX (607)547-5314. **ED** Robert Morey. **Bk Rev**, (Qty: 6 per year). **Ad Acc, Adv Mgr:** R. Morey, **Tel** same as publisher. Documents available from Ask*IEEE.
Desc: Focuses exclusively on the international battery industry, with both business and technical news.
Ind/Abst INSPEC (Sept. 1982-); Leadscan.

●US/1065-0555
ADVANCED PACKAGING. (ADVANCED PACKAGING : AN IHS GROUP PUBLICATION.). [Adv. packag.]. Vol. 1, No. 1 (Summer 1992)-. Periodical. English. qt. $45.00 (one year), $58.00 (two year), $77.00 (three year) US; $24.00 (one year), $42.00 (two year), $54.00 (three year) other. IHS Publishing Group, 17730 West Peterson Road, Libertyville IL 60048. **Tel** (708)362-8711, FAX (708)362-3484. **ED** Tom Williams. **LC** IN PROCESS. **DD** 621. **[CCC]. Ad Acc, Adv Mgr:** Jackie Fanella. ctrl circ. ***Continues*** *Hybrid Circuit Technology, 0747-1599.*
Desc: Read by engineers involved in using leading-edge electronic packaging technologies like multichip modules, power packages, hybrids, ASICs, advanced thick film, wafer scale integration, microwave packages, chip-on-board, power substrates, optoelectronics, and superconductors.

UK/1061-8945
ADVANCES IN BIOSENSORS. **See** Biology.

US/0065-2539
ADVANCES IN ELECTRONICS AND ELECTRON PHYSICS. [Adv. electron. electron. phys.]. Vol. 6 (1954)-. Monographic series. English. ir. Price varies per volume. Academic Press, Inc., 6277 Sea Harbor Drive, Orlando FL 32887. **Tel** (800)543-9534, (407)345-4100, FAX (407)363-9661. **ED** L. Marton. **LC** TK7800; .A37. **DD** 621.381/05. **NLM** W1 AD552. **CODEN** AEEPAR. **[CCC].** cum. index. **Pr Rev.** Documents available from The Genuine Article, Ask*IEEE, CASDDS. ***Continues*** *Advances in Electronics, 0096-6002.*
Ind/Abst Chem. Abstr.; Ei Page One; Energy Res. Abstr.; INIS Atomindex [Micro.]; INSPEC; Mass Spect. Bull.; Res. Alert [Full Cov.]; Sci. Cit. Index; SCISEARCH; SPIN (1981-).

US/0065-2547
ADVANCES IN ELECTRONICS AND ELECTRON PHYSICS. SUPPLEMENT. [Adv. electron. electron phys., Suppl.]. (1963)-. Monographic series. English. ir. Price varies per volume. Academic Press, Inc., 6277 Sea Harbor Drive, Orlando FL 32887. **Tel** (800)543-9534, (407)345-4100, FAX (407)363-9661. **CODEN** AEPSAN. Documents available from Article Express International, CASDDS.
Ind/Abst Chem. Abstr.; Ei Page One; Energy Res. Abstr.; Eng. Index Annu.; Index Sci. Rev. [Full Cov.]; SPIN (1981-).

GW/0932-3031
ADVANCES IN ELECTROPHORESIS. [Adv. electrophor.]. Vol. 1 (1987)-. Academic Scholarly Publication. English. an. Price varies per volume. VCH Gesellschaft GmbH, Postfach 101161, D 69451 Weinheim Germany. **Tel** 011 49 6201 606459, FAX 011 49 6201 606184. **(Subscription address:** VCH Publishers Inc., 303 Northwest 12th Avenue, Journals Department, Deerfield FL 33442.**) LC** QP519.9.E434; A38. **DD** 541.3/72. **UDC** 543.545. **NLM** W1; AD554. **CODEN** ADELEC. Documents available from CASDDS.
Ind/Abst Chem. Abstr.

US/0882-6137
ADVANCES IN MAN-MACHINE SYSTEMS RESEARCH. ***Ceased.*** [Adv. man-mach. syst. res.]. **VFOAT** Advances in Man Machine Systems Research. Vol. 1 (1984)-(19??). English. an. JAI Press Inc., 55 Old Post Road, Suite 2, PO Box 1678, Greenwich CT 06836-1678. **Tel** (203)661-7602, FAX (203)661-0792. **LC** TA167; .A37. **DD** 620.8/05.

●IT/1122-2824
AEI. AUTOMAZIONE ENEGIA INFORMAZIONE. (1994)-. Italian. Twelve times a year. L10000 Italy; L12000 others Comes with Associazione Elettrotecnica ed Elettronica Italiana membership. Assn Elettrotecnica Elettronic, Italiana Viale Monza 259, 20126 Milan Italy. **Tel** 011 39 2 2550641, 011 39 2 25779223. ***Continues*** *L'Elettrotecnica.*

GW/0001-1096
AEU. ARCHIV. FUER ELEKTRONIK UND UBERTRAGUNGSTECHNIK. **See** Communication-Telecommunications.

JA/0385-0447
AEU : JOURNAL OF ASIA ELECTRONICS UNION. **Added/Corp** Asia Electronics Union. Vol. 6, No. 1 (1973)-. Periodical. English. bm. $65.00 North America and Central America; $60.00 Asia and Oceania; $70.00 Africa and South America. Dempa Publications Inc., 1 11 15 Higashi Gotanda, Shinagawa Ku Tokyo 141 Japan. **Tel** 011 81 3 34456111. **(Subscription address:** Dempa Publications, 400 Madison Avenue, New York, NY 10017**) ED** Mojiro Machida. **LC** TK7800; .J18. **DD** 621.381/05. **CODEN** AEUNAX. **Ad Acc.** Documents available from Ask*IEEE. ***Continues*** *JAEU;* ***Absorbed*** *Journal of Asia Electronics Union.* ***Continued in part by*** *Journal of Asia Electronics Union.*
Desc: Inside reports on the entire Asian electronics market. Covers emerging industry newcomers as well as established manufacturers.
Ind/Abst INSPEC (1973-).

US/0163-4496
ALMANACK - INSTITUTE OF ELECTRICAL AND ELECTRONICS ENGINEERS, INC. PHILADELPHIA SECTION. **Main/Corp** Institute of Electrical and Electronics Engineers. Philadelphia Section. (19??)-. Periodical. English. mo (Sept. to May). Institution of Electrical Engineers / IEE, Michael Faraday House, Six Hills Way, Stevenage Herts SG1 2AY UK. **Tel** 011 44 438 313311, FAX 011 44 438 742840, telex 825578 IEESTV G. **(Subscription address:** IEE / UK, Publications Sales Department, PO Box 96, Stevenage, Herts, SG1 2SD England.**)**

IT/1120-1908
ALTA FREQUENZA. RIVISTA DI ELETTRONICA. **Added/Corp** Associazione Elettrotecnica ed Elettronica Italiana. **VFOAT** Rivista di Elettronica. Vol. 1, No. 1 (Jan.-March 1989)-. Periodical. Italian. bm. L60000 nonmembers; L40000 members. Association Elettrotecnica Elettronic, Italiana Viale Monza 259, 20126 Milan Italy. **Tel** 011 39 2 25779223. **CODEN** ARELE8. Documents available from Ask*IEEE.
Ind/Abst INSPEC (Jan./Feb. 1989-).

RM
ANALELE UNIVERSITATII DIN CRAIOVA. MECANICA, ELECTROTEHNICA. **Added/Corp** Universitatea din Craiova. **VFOAT** Mecanica, Electrotehnica. (19??)-.

Periodical. English (French and Romanian). Al I Cuza Street No 13, Craiova The Socialist Republic of Romania. **LC** TA350.3; .A53.

RM
ANALELE UNIVERSITATII DIN GAGATI. FASCICULA III. Bulletin. Romanian (English and French). an. Price varies. Redactia Analelor, 6200 Galati, Str Domneasca Nr. 47 Romania. **Tel** 40 93 413602, FAX 40 93 412328.

RM
ANALELE UNIVERSITATII DIN GALATI. FASCICULA III. Bulletin. Romanian (English and French). an. Price varies. Redactia Analelor, 6200 Galati, Str Domneasca Nr. 47 Romania. **Tel** 40 93 413602, FAX 40 93 412328.

SP/0003-2506
ANALES DE MECANICA Y ELECTRICIDAD. [An. mec. electr.]. **Added/Corp** Instituto Catolico de Artes e Industrias. (1951)-. Periodical. Spanish. qt. $10.47. Assoc de Ingenieros del Icai, Reina 31, Madrid 4 Spain. **CODEN** AMEMA6. Documents available from Ask*IEEE.
Ind/Abst Alum. Ind. Abstr.; Eng. Mater. Abstr.; INSPEC (1968-); Met. Abstr.; Surf. Treat. Technol. Abstr.

US/0925-1030
ANALOG INTEGRATED CIRCUITS AND SIGNAL PROCESSING. [Analog integr. circuits signal process.]. Vol. 1, No. 1 (Sept. 1991)-. Periodical. English. bm. $704.00. Kluwer Academic Publishers / Massachusetts, PO Box 358, Accord Station, Hingham MA 02018. **Tel** (617)871-6600. **ED** Mohammed Ismail, David G. Haigh, and Nobuo Fujii. **LC** TK7874; .A56. **DD** 621.3815/05. **CODEN** AICPEF. **[CCC]. Pr Rev. Acid Free.** available on microfilm and microfiche from University Microfilms International (UMI). Documents available from Article Express International, The Genuine Article, Ask*IEEE.
Desc: Publishes research and tutorial papers on the design and applications of analog integrated circuits and signal processing circuits and systems. Promotes and expedites the dissemination of new research results and tutorial views in the analog field.
Ind/Abst ACM Guide Comput. Lit.; Compumath Citation Index [Full Cov.]; Comput. Rev.; Eng. Index Annu.; Inf. Sci. Abstr.; INSPEC (Sept. 1991-); Res. Alert [Full Cov.]; Soc. Sci. Cit. Index [Select. Cov.].

SZ
ANNUAIRE DE LA CEI. NORMES MONDIALES POUR L'EELECTRICITE ET L'ELECTRONIQUE / COMMISSION ELECTROTECHNIQUE INTERNATIONALE. **Added/Corp** International Electrotechnical Commission. **VFOAT** Normes Mondiales pour l'Electricite et l'Electronique; World Standards for Electrical and Electronic Engineering; IEC Yearbook. World Standards for Electrical and Electronic Engineering. (19??)-. Periodical. English (French). an. 50.00F. International Electrotechnical Commission, PO Box 131, 3 rue de Varembe, Ch 1211 Geneva 20 Switzerland. **Tel** 011 41 22 9190211. **LC** TK277; .A56. **DD** 621.3/0218.

SZ
ANNUAIRE - INTERNATIONAL ELECTROTECHNICAL COMMISSION. **Main/Corp** International Electrotechnical Commission. **VFOAT** Handbook. Multiple languages (English and French). 15.00. International Electrotechnical Commission, PO Box 131, 3 rue de Varembe, Ch 1211 Geneva 20 Switzerland. **Tel** 011 41 22 9190211. **LC** TK1; .I54A. **DD** 621.3/06/31.

US/0066-3816
ANNUAL BULLETIN OF ELECTRIC ENERGY STATISTICS FOR EUROPE. ***Title Change.*** (ANNUAL BULLETIN OF ELECTRIC ENERGY STATISTICS FOR EUROPE. / BULLETIN ANNUEL DE STATISTIQUES DE L'ENERGIE ELECTRIQUE POUR L'EUROPE. / EZHEGODNYI BIULLETEN EVROPEISKOI STATISTIKI ELEKTROENERGII.). **Main/Corp** United Nations. Economic Commission for Europe. **Added/Corp** United Nations. Economic Commission for Europe. Bulletin Annuel de Statistiques de l'Energie Electrique pour l'Europe. United Nations. Economic Commission for Europe. EzhegodnyÊi Biulleten Evropeiskoi Statistiki Elektroenergii. **VFOAT** Bulletin Annuel de Statistiques de l'Energie Electrique pour l'Europe; Ezhegodnyi Biulleten Evropeiskoi Statistiki Elektroenergii. (1956)-(1993). Government Publication. English (French and Russian). an. United Nations Publications, 2 United Nations Plaza, Room DC2 0853, Department 007C, New York NY 10017. **Tel** (212)963-8303, (800)253-9646. **LC** HD9685.A1; U53. **DD** 621.3. ***Continued by*** *Annual Bulletin of Electric Energy Statistics for Europe and North America.*
Desc: Basic data on developments and trends of electric energy.

●US
ANNUAL BULLETIN OF ELECTRIC ENERGY STATISTICS FOR EUROPE AND NORTH AMERICA / BULLETIN ANNUEL DE STATISTIQUES DE L'ENERGIE ELECTRIQUE POUR L'EUROPE ET L'AMERIQUE DU NORD / EZHEGODNYI BIULLETEN' STATISTIKI ELEKTROENERGII DLIA EVROPY I SEVERNOI AMERIKI. **Added/Corp** United Nations. Economic Commission for Europe. **VFOAT** Electric Energy Statistics for Europe and North America; Bulletin Annuel de Statistiques de l'Energie Electrique pour l'Europe et l'Amerique du nord; Ezhegodnyi Biulleten' Statistiki Elektroenergii dlia Evropy i Severnoi Ameriki. (1994)-. Government Publication. English (French and Russian). an. United Nations Publications, 2 United Nations Plaza, Room DC2 0853, Department 007C, New York NY 10017. **Tel** (212)963-8303, (800)253-9646. **LC** HD9685.A1; U53. ***Continues*** *United Nations. Economic Commission for Europe. Annual Bulletin of Electric Energy Statistics for Europe, 0066-3816.*

US
ANNUAL PROJECT HISTORY : PACIFIC NORTHWEST-PACIFIC SOUTHWEST INTERTIE, ARIZONA, CALIFORNIA, NEVADA. **Main/Corp** United States. Bureau of Reclamation. **Added/Corp** Parker-Davis Project Headquarters. **VFOAT** Pacific Northwest-Pacific Southwest Intertie, Arizona, California, Nevada; Project History: Pacific Northwest-Pacific Southwest Intertie, Arizona, California, Nevada. V. 1- 1965-. English.

II
ANNUAL REPORT. **Main/Corp** India (Republic). Dept. of Electronics. (19??)-. English. Government of India Press Department of Electronics, Minto Road, New Delhi India. **LC** HD9696.A3; I568a. **DD** 354/.54/008243.

UK
ANNUAL REPORT AND ACCOUNTS - NORTHERN IRELAND ELECTRICITY SERVICE. **Main/Corp** Northern Ireland Electricity Service. (19??)-. Corporate Report. English. an. Northern Ireland Electricity PLC, Danesfort 120 Malone Road, Belfast BT9 5HT Northern Ireland. **Tel** 0232 661100, FAX 0232 663579. **LC** HD9685.G73; N66a. **DD** 338.7/6136362.
Desc: Presents financial and operative information.

MW
ANNUAL REPORT AND STATEMENT OF ACCOUNTS FOR THE YEAR ENDED ... / ELECTRICITY SUPPLY COMMISSION OF MALAWI. **Main/Corp** Electricity Supply Commission of Malawi. English. an. Electricity Supply Commission of Malawi, PO Box 2047, Blantyre Malawi. **Tel** BLANTYRE 63600, telex 4246. **LC** HD9685.M24; E4A. **DD** 354.68970087/22/006. **Circ:** 2,000 (ctrl).
Desc: ESCOM is responsible for the generation and distribution of electricity throughout Malawi.

US/0898-3917
ANNUAL REPORT / BONNEVILLE POWER ADMINISTRATION. **Main/Corp** United States. Bonneville Power Administration. (1984)-. English. Uitgeverij De Schouw, Waterlandlaan 37, 1441 RS Purmerend Netherlands. **DD** 338. ***Continues*** *Report on the Federal Columbia River Power System.*

AT/0728-8069
ANNUAL REPORT - ELECTRICITY TRUST OF SOUTH AUSTRALIA. (19??)-. English.
Ind/Abst AESIS Q.

JA
ANNUAL REPORT ... FOR THE YEAR ENDED NOVEMBER 30 ... / SANYO DENKI KABUSHIKI KAISHA. **Main/Corp** Sanyo Denki Kabushiki Kaisha. **VFOAT** Annual Report. (1985)-. English. Sanyo Electric Company Ltd, Public Relations Department, 18 Keihan-Hondori 2-chome, Moriguchi City, Osaka 570 Japan. **Tel** (06)991-1181, J63353, J63565, FAX (06)991-6566, telex SANYO J63363. **LC** HD9696.A1; S26a. **DD** 338.7/621381/0952. ***Continues*** *Sanyo Electric Annual Report ... for the Year Ended November 30 ... .*

II
ANNUAL REPORT / IETE. **Main/Corp** Institution of Electronics and Telecommunication Engineers (India). English. an. Institution of Electronics and Telecommunication Engineers, 2 Institutional Area, Lodi Road, New Delhi 110003 India. **Tel** 617282, 618529. **LC** TK7812.I5; I57A. **DD** 621.3/06/054.

●DK
ANNUAL REPORT. MIKROELEKTRONIK CENTRET. (1992)-. English. an. Free. Mikroelektronik Centret, Technical University of Denmark, Building 345e, DK-2800 Lyngby, Denmark. **Tel** 45 4593 4610, FAX 45 4588 7762. **ED** Ove Poulsen. ***Continues*** *Arsberetning. / Laboratory for Semiconductor Technology.*

US/1048-4744
ANNUAL REPORT / NORTH AMERICAN ELECTRIC RELIABILITY COUNCIL. [Annu. rep. - North Am. Electr. Reliab. Counc.]. **Main/Corp** North American Electric Reliability Council. English. an. North American Electric Reliability Council, 101 College Road East, Princeton NJ 08540-6601. **Tel** (609)452-8060. **DD** 333.

US
ANNUAL REPORT ON ELECTRONICS RESEARCH AT THE UNIVERSITY OF TEXAS AT AUSTIN. **Main/Corp** Texas. University at Austin. Electronics Research Center. No. 1- 19 -. English. an. University of Texas at Austin Engineering Science Building, PO Box 7728, Room 316, Austin TX 78712.

CN/0382-2826
ANNUAL REPORT / ONTARIO HYDRO. [Annu. rep. - Ont. Hydro]. **Main/Corp** Ontario Hydro. **VFOAT** Ontario Hydro Annual Report. (1974)-. English. Ontario Hydro, 700 University Avenue, Toronto Ontario M5G 1X6 Canada. **Tel** (416)592-5111. **LC** HD9685.C3; O88. **DD** 354.7130087/22. ***Continues*** *Ontario Hydro. Ontario Hydro Annual Report., 0382-2826.*

US/0272-4693
ANTENNAS AND PROPAGATION. [Antennas propag.]. **Added/Corp** Institute of Electrical and Electronics Engineers. **VFOAT** AP-S International Symposium. **VAT** Antenna and Propagation Society International Symposium. (19??)-. English. IEEE, Institution of Electrical and Electronics Engineers, Inc., 345 East 47th Street, New York NY 10017-2394. **Tel** (908)981-1393, FAX (908)981-9667. **CODEN** IAPSBG. Documents available from Article Express International.
Ind/Abst Bioeng. Abstr.; Ei Page One; Eng. Index Annu.; Index IEEE Publ.

RU/0320-9601
ANTENNY (MOSKVA). (ANTENNY.). [Antenny]. **Added/Corp** Nachno-Tekhnicheskoe Obshchestvo Radiotekhniki i Elektrosviazi. Antennaia Sektsiia. (1966)-. Periodical. Russian. **LC** TK7871.6; .A55.
Ind/Abst Int. Aerosp. Abstr.

BL
ANUARIO DA INDUSTRIA ELETRICA E ELETRONICA DO BRASIL. Portuguese. an. Associacao Brasileira da Industria Eletrica e Eletronica, Av Paulista 1.313 7O. Andar Conj 703, CEP 01311 Sao Paulo Brasil. **LC** HD9685.B78; A58. **DD** 338.4/76213/0981. ***Continues*** *Anuario da Industria Eletro-Eletronica No Brasil.*

AG
ANUARIO ESTADISTICO. ENERGIA ELECTRICA. **See** Engineering-Abstracting, Bibliographies and Statistics.

II
ANUDANOM KI MANGEM (INDIA. DEPT. OF ELECTRONICS). **Main/Corp** India (Republic). Dept. of Electronics. **VFOAT** Demands for Grants. Multiple languages (Hindi and English). Government of India Press Department of Electronics, Minto Road, New Delhi India. **LC** HD9696.A3; I568B.

FR/0001-2122
APAVE. [APAVE]. **Added/Corp** Groupement des Associations de Proprietaires d'Appareils a Vapeur et Electriques. **VAT** Association de Proprietaires d'Appareils A Vapeur et Electriques. (1964)-. Academic Scholarly Publication. French. Four times a year. 297.75F France; 304.00F EEC; 359.00F other. SADAVE, 191 Rue de Vaugirard, 75015 Paris France. **Tel** 011 33 1 45669944. **LC** T2; .A16. **CODEN** APAVBZ. Documents available from CASDDS.
Ind/Abst Chem. Abstr.; Coal Abstr.; Energy Res. Abstr. (March 1976-); Saf. Health Work.

●UK/0964-1807
APPLIED SUPERCONDUCTIVITY. [Appl. supercond.]. Vol. 1, No. 1/2 (Jan./Feb. 1993)-. Periodical. English. mo. $649.00 The Americas; £435.00 other. Pergamon Press, An Imprint of Elsevier Science Ltd., The Boulevard, Langford Lane, Kidlington, Oxford OX5 1GB United Kingdom. **Tel** 011 44 865 843000, 011 44 865 843699, FAX 011 44 865 843010. **(Subscription address:** Elsevier Science Ltd. Oxford Fulfillment Centre, PO Box 800, Kidlington, Oxford OX5 1DX United Kingdom.**) ED** Roger Poeppel. **LC** TK7872.S8; A667. **DD** 621.3. **CODEN** ASUEE6. **[CCC].** Documents available from Ask*IEEE. ***Continues in part*** *Solid-State Electronics, 0038-1101.*
Desc: Strives to provide an international forum for the exchange of ideas concerning the large and small scale

application of superconductivity. The focus is on any process, device, equipment, component, system, machine or structure which incorporates a superconducting element or which in some way takes advantage of, or relies on, the unique electrical or magnetic properties of superconductors to achieve a useful function.
Ind/Abst Curr. Contents Eng. Tech. Appl. Sci.; Curr. Contents Phys. Chem. Earth Sci.; INSPEC (1993-); Res. Alert; Sci. Cit. Index; SCISEARCH; Soc. Sci. Cit. Index [Select. Cov.].

US/0148-9380
APPROVED WELDING ELECTRODE WIRE-FLUX AND WIRE-GAS COMBINATIONS. **See** Metals and Metallurgy-Welding.

US/0894-0436
ARCHITECTURAL LIGHTING. **See** Architecture.

GW/0003-9039
ARCHIV FUER ELEKTROTECHNIK (BERLIN). (ARCHIV FUER ELEKTROTECHNIK.). [Arch. Elektrotech.]. **Added/Corp** Verband Deutscher Elektrotechniker. Elektrotechnischer Verein (Berlin, Germany). Vol. 1 (1912)-. Periodical. German. Six times a year. DM768.00. Springer-Verlag GmbH & Company KG, Heidelberger Platz 3, D 14197 Berlin Germany. **Tel** 011 49 30 8207223, FAX 011 49 30 8214091, telex 183 319 SPBLN D. **(Subscription address:** Springer Verlag New York Inc. / for North America, 44 Hartz Way, Secaucus NJ 07096.) **ED** M Stiebler. **LC** TK3; .A6. **CODEN** AELTA6. **[CCC].** cum. index. **Pr Rev.** available on microfilm from University Microfilms International (UMI). Documents available from Article Express International, The Genuine Article, Ask*IEEE, CASDDS.
Desc: Publishes original articles drawn from the entire range of electrical and electronic engineering, including related fields in mathematics and physics.
Ind/Abst Alum. Ind. Abstr.; Bioeng. Abstr.; Chem. Abstr.; Curr. Contents Eng. Tech. Appl. Sci.; Ei Page One; Energy Res. Abstr.; Eng. Index Annu.; INSPEC (1968-); Int. Aerosp. Abstr.; Leadscan; Met. Abstr.; Res. Alert [Full Cov.]; Sci. Cit. Index.

PL/0004-0746
ARCHIWUM ELEKTROTECHNIKI. [Arch. elektrotech.]. **Added/Corp** Instytut Podstawowych Problemow Techniki (Polska Akademia Nauk). Polska Akademia Nauk. Zakad Badania Drgan. Polska Akademia Nauk. Zakad Elektroniki. Vol. 1 (1952)-. Periodical. Polish. qt. $80.00. **(Subscription address:** ARS Polona, PO Box 1001, 00068 Warsaw Poland.) **CODEN** ARELA4. Documents available from Article Express International, Ask*IEEE, CASDDS.
Ind/Abst Alum. Ind. Abstr.; Bioeng. Abstr.; Ceram. Abstr. (1968-); Chem. Abstr.; Ei Page One; Energy Res. Abstr.; Eng. Mater. Abstr.; Eng. Index Annu.; INSPEC (1968-); Int. Aerosp. Abstr.; Math. Rev.; Met. Abstr.

PL/0066-684X
ARCHIWUM ENERGETYKI. [Arch. energ.]. **Added/Corp** Polska Akademia Nauk. Komitet Energetyki. (1972)-. Polish (summaries and/or abstracts in English and Russian). qt. $40.00. **(Subscription address:** ARS Polona, PO Box 1001, 00068 Warsaw Poland.) **LC** TK95.P7; A83. **CODEN** AREGBO. Documents available from CASDDS.
Ind/Abst Chem. Abstr. (1972-1981); Coal Abstr.

CL
AREA ELECTRICIDAD. **VFOAT** Area de Electricidad. Spanish. Direccion de Investigaciones Cientificas y Tecnologicas de la Universidad Tecnica del Estado etc, Avda Ecuador 3469, Santiago Chile. **LC** TK4; .A38. **DD** 621.3/08.

US/1055-0097
ARIZONA HIGH TECH DIRECTORY. [Ariz. high tech dir.]. **VFOAT** Southwest Technology Report's Arizona High Tech Directory. (1988)-. Directory. English. $54.95. Keiland Corporation, 15207 North 75th Street, #106, Scottsdale AZ 85260. **LC** HC107.A63; H533. **DD** 338.7/62/00025791. ***Continues*** *Arizona Electronics & High Technology Directory.*

US/0362-5745
ARMY COMMUNICATOR, THE. **See** Military and Defense.

DK
ARSBERETNING / LABORATORY FOR SEMICONDUCTOR TECHNOLOGY. ***Title Change.*** **Main/Corp** Danmarks Tekniske Hjskole. Laboratoriet for Halvlederteknik. (19??)-(19??). Danish. an. Mikroelektronik Centret, Technical University of Denmark, Building 345e, DK-2800 Lyngby, Denmark. **Tel** 45 4593 4610, FAX 45 4588 7762. **LC** TK7871.85; .D35a. **DD** 621.3815/2/05. ***Continued by*** *Annual Report: Mikroelektronik Centret.*

SW/0346-6582
ASEA TIDNING. [Asea tidn.]. **Added/Corp** ASEA (Firm). (1924)-. Periodical. Swedish (English, French, German, Italian and Spanish). ABB Corporate Communications Ltd., Ruetistrasse 6, CH-5401 Baden Switzerland. **Tel** 011 41 56 754836, FAX 011 41 56 212274. **ED** Jan Wall. **LC** TK4; .A4. **Circ:** 90,000 (ctrl). ***Continues*** *ASEA's Tidning.*
Desc: Technical magazine describing the activities of the ASEA in electrical engineering and electronics.
Ind/Abst Coal Abstr.

SI/0129-5411
ASIA-PACIFIC ENGINEERING JOURNAL. PART A, ELECTRICAL ENGINEERING. ***Ceased.*** **VFOAT** Asia Pacific Engineering Journal. Part A, Electrical Engineering; Electrical Engineering. Vol. I, No. I (Sept. 1991)-Vol. 3, No. 4 (Dec. 1993). Periodical. English. qt. World Scientific Publishing Company, PO Box 128, Farrer Road, Singapore 9128 Singapore. **Tel** 011 65 3825663, FAX 011 65 3825919, telex RS 28561 WSPC. **LC** TK1; .A69. **DD** 621.3/05. **CODEN** APEJEM. Documents available from Ask*IEEE.
Ind/Abst INSPEC (1991-).

UK/0264-3340
ASIAN ELECTRICITY. [Asian electr.]. (1983)-. Periodical. English. mo. $215.30. Reed Business Publishing / West Sussex, England, Perrymount Road, Haywards Heath, West Sussex RH16 3DH England. **Tel** 011 44 81 6523500. **DD** 021.3095.
Ind/Abst Energy Inf. Abstr.

HK
ASIAN ELECTRONIC ENGINEER. English. mo. $69.00 (1 year), $119.00 (2 year), $159.00 (3 year) US; $159.00 (1 year) other. Trade Media Ltd / Hong Kong, GPO Box 11411, Hong Kong Hong Kong. **Tel** 011 852 555-4777, FAX 011 852 870-0637. **(Subscription address:** Wordright Enterprises Inc., PO Box 3062, Circulation Dept., Evanston, IL 60204**)**

HK/0254-1114
ASIAN SOURCES ELECTRONICS. [Asian sources electron.]. **VFOAT** Electronics. (19??)-. Trade Publication. English. mo. $80.00 (1 year), $130.00 (2 year) surface mail; $170.00 (air mail) Far East and India; $225.00 (air mail) other. Trade Media Ltd / Hong Kong, GPO Box 11411, Hong Kong Hong Kong. **Tel** 011 852 555-4777, FAX 011 852 870-0637. **Ad Acc.** ctrl circ. Documents available from Ask*IEEE.
Desc: Trade journal puts the importer in direct contact with the Asian manufacturer/supplier. About 25 percent editorials.
Ind/Abst F&S Index Plus Text, Int. [Select. Cov.]; INSPEC (Aug. 1968-Dec. 1988); PROMT.

US/0090-3590
AUERBACH DATA COMMUNICATIONS EQUIPMENT DIGEST. [Auerbach data commun. equip. dig.]. Periodical. English. sa. Auerbach Publishers Inc., Park Square Building, 31 St. James Avenue, Boston MA 02116. **Tel** (800)950-1207. **LC** TK5102.5; .A785. **DD** 621.38/05.

AT/1031-6914
AUSTRALIAN, ASIAN AND PACIFIC ELECTRICAL WORLD. [Aust. Asian Pac. electr. world]. (1988)-. Periodical. English. mo (11 issues). 50.00Aus$ Australia; 110.00Aus$ other. Reed Business Publishing Pty Ltd. / Australia, 1 5 Railway Street, Level 12 North Tower, Chatswood W 2067 NSW Australia. **Tel** 011 61 2 3725222, FAX 011 61 2 4197533. **DD** 621.305. ***Continues*** *Australian Electrical World (1981), 1031-6906.*

AT/0004-9042
AUSTRALIAN ELECTRONICS ENGINEERING. [Aust. electron. eng.]. (Oct. 1967)-. Periodical. English. mo. 75.00Aus$ Australia; 104.00Aus$ New Zealand, Papua New Guinea; 109.00Aus$ Malaysia, Indonesia, Fiji; 110.00Aus$ Japan, India, Hong Kong; 124.00Aus$ US, Canada, Lebanon; 134.00Aus$ Europe, Africa, former USSR. Thomson Publications / Australia, 47 Chippen Street, Chippendale New South Wales, 2008 Australia. **Tel** 011 61 2 6992411, FAX 011 61 2 698 3920, telex 122226. **(Subscription address:** Thomson Publications Australia, PO Box 815, Strawberry Hills, New South Wales, 2012 Australia.) **LC** TK7800; .A89. **DD** 621.381/05. **CODEN** AUEEB5. Documents available from Ask*IEEE.
Ind/Abst Ei Page One; INSPEC (Nov. 1972-).

US/1051-3396
AUTOMATED AGENCY REPORT, THE. [Autom. agency rep.]. Vol. 6, No. 6 (June 1990)-. Periodical. English. Twelve times a year. $175.00. Automation Management Group, PO Box 7024, Boulder CO 80306. **Tel** (303)449-9898. **DD** 004. ***Continues*** *Agency Automation Report, 0888-8205.*

HU/0865-7580
AUTOMATIZALAS ES ROBOTTECHNIKA. (1990)-. Multiple languages. mo. ***Continues*** *Automatizalas, 0133-1620.*
Ind/Abst Fluid Abstr., Civil Eng.; Fluid Abstr. Proc. Eng.; FLUIDEX (19??-).

UN/0005-111X
AVTOMATICESKAJA SVARKA (KIEV). (AVTOMATICHESKAIA SVARKA.). [Avtom. svarka]. **Added/Corp** Instytut Elektrozvariuvannia im. IE.O. Patona. (1950)-. Periodical. Russian. mo. $119.95. Izdatelstvo Naukova Dumka / Ukrainian Academy of Sciences, Vladimirskaia Ulitsa 54, 252601 Kiev Ukraine. **Tel** 225-63-66, telex 131376. **(Subscription address:** East View Publications Inc., 3020 Harbor Lane North, Suite 110, Minneapolis MN 55447.) **LC** TK4660.A1; A42. **CODEN** AVSVAU. Documents available from CASDDS. ***Continues*** *Trudy po Avtomaticheskoi Svarke pod Fliusom.*
Ind/Abst Chem. Abstr.

CC/0253-4177
BANDAOTI XUEBAO. (PAN TAO TI HSUEH PAO / JOURNAL OF CHINESE SEMICONDUCTORS.). [Bandaoti xuebao]. **Added/Corp** Chung-kuo Tien tzu Hsueh Hui. Pan Tao ti yu Chi Cheng Chi Shu Hsueh Hui. Chung-kuo ko Hsueh Yuan. Pan Tao ti Yen Chiu so. **VFOAT** Chinese Journal of Semiconductors. (1980)-. Periodical. Chinese (summaries and/or abstracts in English). mo. $164.80. Science Press, 16 Donghuangchenggen North Street, Beijing 100707, People's Republic of China. **Tel** 011 86 1 4019821, 011 86 1 4010642, FAX 011 86 1 4012180, 011 86 1 4019810, telex 210147. **(Subscription address:** China International Book Trading Corporation, PO Box 399, Library Service Department, Beijing 100044 People's Republic of China.) **LC** QC610.9; .P36. **DD** 621.381/52/05. **CODEN** PTTPDZ. **Ad Acc. Pr Rev. Circ:** 11,000. Documents available from Article Express International, Ask*IEEE, CASDDS.
Ind/Abst Bioeng. Abstr.; Chem. Abstr.; Ei Page One; Energy Res. Abstr. (Sept. 1982-); Eng. Index Annu.; INSPEC (Feb. 1980-); SPIN (1982-).

UK/0957-9249
BATTERIES INTERNATIONAL. [Batter. int.]. (1989)-. Periodical. English. Four times a year (Jan., Apr., July, Oct.). £40.00 Europe; £50.00 other. Batteries International Limited, Aberdeen House, Headley Road, Grayshott Hindhead Surrey GU26 6LA England. **Tel** 011 44 428 605536, FAX 011 44 428 606339. **ED** Don Gribble. Index available. cum. index. **Ad Acc, Adv Mgr:** H. Cullimore, **Tel** 011 44 276 856461. **Circ:** 6,000 (ctrl).
Desc: Battery manufacturing and usage worldwide.

GW/0005-2825
BBC NACHRICHTEN. [BBC nachr.]. **VFOAT** BBC-Nachrichten. Academic Scholarly Publication. German. mo. Buch Kober, Postfach 1301, W-6800 Mannheim 1 Germany. **CODEN** BBCNAZ. cum. index. Documents available from Ask*IEEE. ***Continues*** *BBC Mitteilungen, 0365-9232.*
Ind/Abst Alum. Ind. Abstr.; Coal Abstr.; EMBASE; Energy Res. Abstr.; INSPEC (1968-); Met. Abstr.; Saf. Health Work.

DK
BERETNING FRA LABORATORIET FOR ELEKTRONIK, DANMARKS TEKNISKE HJSKOLE. **Main/Corp** Copenhagen. Polyteknisk l'Reanstalt. Laboratoriet for Elektronik. Danish. Bygning 344, Danmarks Tekniske Hjskole, 2800 Lyngby Denmark. **LC** TK213.C66; C6A.

US/0738-0305
BIBLIOGRAPHY OF SOVIET LASER DEVELOPMENTS. [Bibliogr. Sov. laser dev.]. **VFOAT** Soviet Laser Developments; Soviet Lasers. Bibliography. English. Defense Intelligence Agency, Directorate for Scientific and Technical Intelligence, ATT: DT-1A, The Pentagon, Washington DC 20301. **LC** Z5838.L3; B52; TA1675. **DD** 016.62136/6/0947.

US
BIENNIAL REPORT OF EXAMINING AND LICENSING BOARDS - MINNESOTA. STATE BOARD OF ELECTRICITY. **Main/Corp** Minnesota. State Board of Electricity. English. be. Griggs Midway Building/Room N-191, 1821 University Avenue, St Paul MN 55104. **LC** TK224.M6; M56A. **DD** 353.97760082/42.

US
BIENNIAL SURVEY OF POWER EQUIPMENT REQUIREMENTS OF THE U.S. ELECTRIC UTILITY INDUSTRY. ***Ceased.*** Ceased 1986. English. be. National Electrical Manufacturers Association, 2101 L Street NW/Suite 300, Washington DC 20037. **LC** TK23; .B53. **DD** 338.4/762131042/0973.

●SZ/0302-4598
BIOELECTROCHEMISTRY AND BIOENERGETICS. Vol. 28, No. 3 (Oct. 1992)-. Periodical. English. Six times a year (3 volumes). 1200.00F. Elsevier Sequoia SA, PO Box 564, CH-1001 Lausanne 1 Switzerland. **Tel** 011 41 21 3207381. **ED** H. Berg, M. Blank. **LC** QP517.B53; B5. **[CCC].** ***Separated from*** *Journal of Electroanalytical Chemistry (Lausanne, Switzerland), 0022-0728.*
Desc: Provides an international forum where life scientists and electrochemists interested in biological problems can find ideas and results originating from scientists of different basic backgrounds and education.

PL
BIULETYN - POLSKI ZWIAZEK KROTKOFALOWCOW. **Main/Corp** Polski Zwiazek Krotkofalowcow. Polish. 78.00. Zarzad Gowny Polskiego Zwiazku Krotkofalowcow, Ul Nowy Zjazd 1, Warszawa Poland. **LC** TK6553; .P62A.

US
BLI FACSIMILE SPECIFICATIONS GUIDE. **See** Communication.

MX/0185-0059
BOLETIN DEL INSTITUTO DE INVESTIGACIONES ELECTRICAS. (BOLETIN IIE.). [Bol. Inst. Invest. Electr.]. V. 1- 1977-. Academic Scholarly Publication. Spanish. Instituto de Investigaciones Electricas, Leibnitz 14, 3Er Piso, Mexico 5 D F Mexico. **CODEN** BOIID8. Documents available from CASDDS.
Ind/Abst Chem. Abstr.

US/0734-1903
BOOK OF SEMI STANDARDS. [Book SEMI stand.]. **Main/Corp** Semiconductor Equipment and Materials Institute. **VFOAT** Book of S.E.M.I. Standards; B.O.S.S.; Specifications; BOSS. **VAT** Book of Semiconductor Equipment and Materials Institute Standards. (1978)-. Periodical. English (Japanese). an. $100.00 (single volume); $425.00 (set). Semiconductor Equipment and Materials Institute, 805 East Middlefield Road, Mountain View CA 94043. **Tel** (415)964-5111, (415)940-6960, telex 17-1977. **LC** TK7871.85; .S46a. **DD** 621.3815/2/0218. **Circ:** 1,000. available on microfiche.
Desc: Voluntary consensus specifications developed by producers and users of semiconductor production equipment and materials as well as general-interest volunteers.

UK
BRITAINS TOP 500 ELECTRONIC & ELECTRICAL COMPANIES. **VFOAT** Britains Top 500 Electronic and Electrical Companies; Britains Top Five Hundred Electronic and Electrical Companies. (19??)-. English. Jordan & Sons (Surveys), 44 Whitchurch Road, Cardiff South Wales CF4 3UQ UK. **LC** TK12; .B75. **DD** 338.7/6213/02541.

UK/0068-2276
BRITISH MINIATURE ELECTRONIC COMPONENTS DATA ANNUAL. 1961/62-. Periodical. English. an. Pergamon Press, An Imprint of Elsevier Science Ltd., The Boulevard, Langford Lane, Kidlington, Oxford OX5 1GB United Kingdom. **Tel** 011 44 865 843000, 011 44 865 843699, FAX 011 44 865 843010. **(Subscription address:** US/ 395 Saw Mill River Road, Elmsford, NY 10523; Can/ 150 Consumers Road/Suite 104, Willowdale Ontario M2J 1P9; Aus-NZ/ POB 544, Potts Point NSW 2011**)**

RM
BULETINUL UNIVERSITATII DIN GALATI. FASCICULA III, ELECTROTEHNICA, ELECTRONICA, AUTOMTICA [SIC], INFORMATICA. **Added/Corp** Universitatea din Galati. (19??)-. Periodical. English (French; summaries and/or abstracts in Romanian). an. Redactia Buletinului, 6200 Galati Str, Republicii Nr 47 Romania. **LC** TK4; .B763. **DD** 621.3.

FR/0037-9530
BULLETIN. [Bull. - Soc. R. Belge Electr.]. **Main/Corp** Societe Royale Belge des Electriciens. Bulletin. French. qt. Office Internationale des Periodiques, Kouterveld 14, B 1831 Diegem Belgium. **Tel** 011 32 2 7231158. **CODEN** BSREAW. Documents available from Article Express International, Ask*IEEE. ***Absorbed** Revue E;* ***Continues** Revue d'Electricite.*
Ind/Abst Bioeng. Abstr.; Ei Page One; Eng. Index Annu.; INSPEC (1968).

BE/0379-0401
BULLETIN - BISMUTH INSTITUTE. **See** Metals and Metallurgy.

FR/0013-4503
BULLETIN DE LA DIRECTION DES ETUDES ET RECHERCHES. SERIE B. RESEAUX ELECTRIQUES, MATERIELS ELECTRIQUES. [Bull. Dir. etud. rech., Ser. B]. **VFOAT** Reseaux Electriques, Materiels Electriques. No. 1 (1967)-. Academic Scholarly Publication. French (summaries and/or abstracts in English). qt. Free. Electricite de France, Direction des Etudes et Recherches, 2 rue Louis Murat, 75784 Paris Cedex 08 France. **Tel** 40 42 31 26 MME FIEVEZ. **ED** Israel. **CODEN** EFDBAV. **Circ:** 1,600 (ctrl). Documents available from Article Express International, Ask*IEEE, CASDDS. ***Continues in part** Bulletin du Centre de Recherches et d'Essais de Chatou.*
Ind/Abst Bioeng. Abstr.; Chem. Abstr. (1967-1982); Ei Page One; Energy Res. Abstr. (Oct. 1976-); Eng. Index Annu.; Fluid Abstr., Civil Eng.; Fluid Abstr. Proc. Eng.; FLUIDEX (1973-); INSPEC (1969-); Int. Civil Eng. Abstr.

CN/0715-7746
BULLETIN DE L'ASSOCIATION QUEBECOISE DE TELEDETECTION. [Bull. Assoc. que. teledetect.]. **VFOAT** Bulletin de l'A.Q.T. V. 1, No. 1 (April 1977)-. Bulletin. French. $7.50 Canada; $9.00 other. Association Quebecoise de Teledetection, C P 10047, Ste Foy Quebec G1V 4C6 Canada. **Tel** (819)821-7180. **DD** 621.36/78/060714.

SZ/0004-587X
BULLETIN DE L'ASSOCIATION SUISSE DES ELECTRICIENS. (BULLETIN.). [Bull. Assoc. Suisse Electr.]. **Main/Corp** l'Association Suisse des Electriciens. Vol. 1 (1910)-. Bulletin. French. sm. $79.17. Bulletin de l'Association Stauffacherquai, 36-40 Post 229, 8021 Zurich Switzerland. **CODEN** BUSEAH. Documents available from Article Express International.
Ind/Abst Bioeng. Abstr.; Ei Page One; Eng. Index Annu.; Saf. Health Work.

SZ/0036-1321
BULLETIN DES SCHWEIZERISCHEN ELEKTROTECHNISCHEN VEREINS (ZURICH). (BULLETIN DES SCHWEIZERISCHEN ELEKTROTECHNISCHEN VEREINS.). [Bull. Schweiz. Elektrotech. Ver.]. **Main/Corp** Schweizerischer Elektrotechnischer Verein. **Added/Corp** Verband Schweizerischer Elektrizitatswerke. Verband Schweizerischer Elektrizitatswerke. Bulletin. **VFOAT** Bulletin des Schweizerischen Elektrotechnischen Vereins des Verbandes Schweizerischer Elektrizitaetswerke; Bulletin de l'Association Suisse des Electriciens de l'Union des Centrales Suisses d'Electricite. (1910)-. Bulletin. German. Twenty-four times a year. 155.00F Switzerland, 185.00F others (latest volume). Schweizerischer Elektro Verein, Seefeldstr 301, 8008 Zurich Switzerland. **Tel** 011 41 1 3849111. **LC** TK3; .S3. **DD** 621.305. Documents available from Ask*IEEE.
Ind/Abst Coal Abstr.; EMBASE; INSPEC (March 1987-); Saf. Health Work; Surf. Treat. Technol. Abstr.

FR
BULLETIN D'HISTOIRE DE L'ELECTRICITE. **Added/Corp** Association pour l'Histoire de l'Electricite en France. (June 1983)-. Bulletin. French. Twice a year. 100.00F France; 120.00F other. Assn Histoire Elec en France, 9 Avenue Percier, F-75008 Paris France. **Tel** 011 33 1 40422453.

US/0433-342X
BULLETIN - GENERAL ELECTRIC COMPANY. RESEARCH LABORATORY. **Main/Corp** General Electric Company. Research Laboratory. (Spring 1958)-. Bulletin. English. General Electric Company, 120 Erie Boulevard, Schenectady NY 12305. **Tel** (502)685-6200. **DD** 621.3.

II/0020-3343
BULLETIN OF THE INSTITUTION OF ENGINEERS (INDIA). [Bull. Inst. Eng., India]. **Main/Corp** Institution of Engineers (India). **Added/Corp** Institution of Engineers (India) Journal. Supplement. (1951)-. Bulletin. English. Twelve times a year. $30.00. Institution of Engineers India, 8 Gokhale Road, Calcutta 700020 India. **Tel** 011 91 33 288311, telex 21 7885 IEIC IN. **ED** D. K. Ghosh, P. P. Sinha and S. Vincent. **LC** TA4; .I47. **Bk Rev. Ad Acc. Circ:** 50,000 (ctrl). ***Continues** Journal of the Institution of Engineers (India). Mechanical, Electrical and General Sections.*
Desc: Covers news, notes and activities of the centers of the institution.
Ind/Abst Abstr. J. Earthq. Eng. (?-?); Alum. Ind. Abstr.; Coal Abstr.; Ei Page One; Energy Res. Abstr. (Aug. 1976-); Eng. Mater. Abstr.; J. Ferrocement; Met. Abstr.

FR/0302-2676
BULLETIN SCIENTIFIQUE DE L'ASSOCIATION DES INGENIEURS ELECTRICIENS SORTIS DE L'INSTITUT ELECTROTECHNIQUE MONTEFIORE. [Bull. sci. - Assoc. ing. electr. sortis inst. electrotech. Montefiore]. **Main/Corp** Association des Ingenieurs Electriciens Sortis de l'institut Electrotechnique Montefiore. **VFOAT** Bulletin Mensuel - Association des Ingenieurs Electriciens Sortis de l'Institut Electrotechnique Montefiore; Bulletin Scientifique A.I.M. Jan. 1931-. Bulletin. Multiple languages (Dutch, English, French and German). ir. 650.00. Association des Ingenieurs Electriciens Sortis de l'Institut, 31 rue Saint-Gilles, Liege 4000 France. **LC** TK2; .A75. **CODEN** BURMA2. Documents available from Ask*IEEE. ***Continues** Association des Ingenieurs Electriciens Sortis de l'Institut Electrotechnique Montefiore. Bulletin.*
Ind/Abst Coal Abstr.; INSPEC (1968-).

FR
BULLETIN SIGNALETIQUE. 140: ELECTROTECHNIQUE. **See** Engineering-Abstracting, Bibliographies and Statistics.

FR/0301-3308
BULLETIN SIGNALETIQUE. [SECTION] 140. ELECTROTECHNIQUE. **Main/Corp** France. Centre National de la Recherche Scientifique. **Added/Corp** France. Centre National de la Recherche Scientifique. Bulletin Signaletique. [Section] 140. Physique II: Electricite. France. Centre National de la Recherche Scientifique. Bulletin Signaletique. [Section] 140. Electricite, Electronique. Vol. 22 (1961)-. Bulletin. French. ir. $79.82. Editions du CNRS, 22 rue Saint Armand, F 75015 Paris France. **Tel** 011 33 1 45075050. ***Continues in part** France. Centre National de la Recherche Scientifique. Bulletin Signaletique.*

CN/0822-5508
BULLETIN SPECIAL - INSTITUT TECCART. (BULLETIN SPECIAL.). [Bull. spec. - Inst. Teccart]. **Added/Corp** Institut Teccart. (19??)-. Bulletin. French. Institut Teccart, 3155 rue Hochelaga, Montreal Quebec H1W 1G4 Canada. **DD** 621.381/01/4.

US/0093-8270
C.O.S.-M.O.S. DIGITAL INTEGRATED CIRCUITS. (COS/MOS DIGITAL INTEGRATED CIRCUITS.). **Main/Corp** RCA Corporation. Solid State Division. (19??)-. English. RCA Corporation, Box 3200, Somerville NJ 08876. **Tel** (609)734-3222. **LC** TK7874; .R18b. **DD** 621.381/73/05.

US/1049-1236
C2C CURRENTS JAPAN. ELECTRONICS. [C2C curr. Jpn., Electron.]. **Added/Corp** Scan C2C, Inc. **VFOAT** Electronics. **VAT** Sea to sea currents Japan. Electronics. (1990)-. English. mo. $100.00. SCAN C2C Inc, Attn Carol G Heffernan Marketing Director, 500 E Street Southwest, Suite 800, 8th Floor, Washington DC 20024. **Tel** (202)863-3850, (800)525-3865, FAX (202)863-3855. **DD** 621. Index available. cum. index. available on an online database from DATA-STAR; and DIALOG; available on CD-ROM from DIALOG.
Desc: English content listings of the leading Japanese science, technical and business journals in the field of electronics.

US/0749-7334
CA SELECTS: PLASMA & REACTIVE ION ETCHING. **See** Chemistry-Abstracting, Bibliographies and Statistics.

US
CABLE REPORT. 1- Mar. 1972-. Periodical. English. PO Box 6119, 541 North Fairbank Court, Chicago IL 60611.

BL
CADASTRO DE ELECTRIFICACAO DO ESTADO DA BAHIA. **Main/Corp** Bahia (Brazil : State). Coordenacao de Energia. (19??)-. Portuguese. **LC** HD9685.B82; B325. **DD** 338.4/7/3636209814.

IT
CAMAC BULLETIN. **Added/Corp** ESONE Committee. No. 1 (June 1971)-. Bulletin. English. Three times a year. Commission des Communautes Europeenn, 200 rue de la Loi, B 1049 Bruxelles Belgium. **Tel** 011 32 2 2357639, 2351111. **LC** TK7870; .C24. **DD** 621.381.

UK
CAMINUS QUARTERLY POOL PRICE REVIEW. English. qt. £1100.00. Caminus Energy Limited, Caminus House Castle Park, Cambridge CB3 0RA England. **Tel** 011 44 223 322736, FAX 011 44 223 69599. **ED** M.B. Morrison. **Circ:** 50 (ctrl).

CN/0834-3977
CANADIAN AMATEUR (1987). (THE CANADIAN AMATEUR.). [Can. amat.]. **Added/Corp** Canadian Amateur Radio Federation. Vol. 15, No. 2 (Feb. 1987)-. Periodical. English (French). Eleven times a year. $51.00. Radio Amateurs of Canada Inc., PO Box 356, Kingston Ontario K7L 4W2 Canada. **Tel** (613)634-4184. **DD** 621.3841/66/05. **Bk Rev. Ad Acc. Circ:** 5,000 (ctrl). ***Continues** TCA : the Canadian Amateur, 0228-6513.*
Desc: Covers amateur radio stations.

CN/1186-1568
CANADIAN COMMENT. (CANADIAN COMMENT / IBEW, INTERNATIONAL BROTHERHOOD OF ELECTRICAL WORKERS). [Can. comment]. **Added/Corp** International Brotherhood of Electrical Workers. **VAT** IBEW Canadian Comment; FIOE Canadian Comment. (Oct. 1990)-. Periodical. English (summaries and/or abstracts in French). qt. Free to members. International Brotherhood of Electrical Workers / Canada, Suite 401, 45 Sheppard Avenue East, Willowdale, Ontario M2N 5Y1 Canada. **DD** 331.88.

CN
CANADIAN ELECTRONICS ENGINEERING ANNUAL BUYER'S GUIDE. 84-85-. English. an. $10.00. Maclean Hunter Canada / Montreal, 1001 bvd. de Maisonneuve W., Montreal, Quebec H3A 3E1 Canada. **Tel** 514-845-5141, FAX 514-845-4302, telex 055-60604. ***Continues** Canadian Electronics Engineering. Annual Buyers' Guide & Directory.*
Desc: A directory issue listing products and services for various electronic equipment, along with Canadian sources, U.S., U.K. and other manufacturers and Canadian distributors.

CN/0317-0292
CANADIAN ELECTRONICS ENGINEERING ANNUAL BUYERS' GUIDE AND CATALOG DIRECTORY. 1972/73-. Consumer Publication. English. an. Canadian Electronics Engineering, PO Box 9100 Station A, Toronto Ontario M5W 1V5 Canada. **DD** 338.4/7/62138102571. ***Supersedes*** *Canadian Electronics Engineering Directory and Buyers Guide.*

CN/0381-9396
CANADIAN ELECTRONICS MARKET, THE. 1976-. English. Maclean Hunter Canada / Montreal, 1001 bvd. de Maisonneuve W., Montreal, Quebec H3A 3E1 Canada. **Tel** 514-845-5141, FAX 514-845-4302, telex 055-60604. **DD** 380.1/45/6213810971.

CN/1187-6026
CANADIAN ELECTRONICS (WILLOWDALE). (CANADIAN ELECTRONICS.). [Can. electron.]. Vol. 5, No. 15 (Nov. 1990)-. Periodical. English. ir (11 issues). 75.00Can$ Canada; 110.00Can$ other. Action Communications Inc, 135 Spy Ct, Markham Ontario L3R 5H6 Canada. **Tel** (416)477-3222. **DD** 621.38. available on an online database (file 648/Full-Text) from DIALOG. ***Formed by the union of*** *CEE (Toronto, Ont.), 0008-3461* ***and*** *Electronics Times, 0832-1515.*
Ind/Abst PROMT.

CN/0840-8688
CANADIAN JOURNAL OF ELECTRICAL AND COMPUTER ENGINEERING. See Computers-Computer Engineering.

US/0272-7943
CAR STEREO (NEW YORK). (CAR STEREO.). Periodical. English. an. $2.50. Service Communications, 50 Rockefeller Plaza, New York NY 10020. **LC** TK7881.85; .C37. **DD** 629.2/77.

KO
CATALOG OF KOREA ELECTRONICS. **Added/Corp** Hanguk Chonja Kongop Chinhunghoe. (19??)-. Catalog. English. Electronic Industries Association of Korea, World Trade Center Korea/Room 1101, 10-1 2 Ka Hoehyun-dong Chung-ku, Seoul Korea. **LC** TK7870.3; .C37. **DD** 621.381/029/45195.

SZ
CATALOGUE OF IEC PUBLICATIONS COMPLETE TO ... / INTERNATIONAL ELECTROTECHNICAL COMMISSION. **Main/Corp** International Electrotechnical Commission. **VFOAT** Catalogue of IEC Publications. (Jan. 1988)-. English (French). an. 20.00F. International Electrotechnical Commission, PO Box 131, 3 rue de Varembe, Ch 1211 Geneva 20 Switzerland. **Tel** 011 41 22 9190211. **(Subscription address:** Standards Council of Canada, 350 Sparks Street, Suite 1200, Ottawa, Ontario K1P 6N7 Canada.**) LC** Z5832; .I55; TK152. **DD** 621.3/0218. ***Continues*** *International Electrotechnical Commission. Catalogue of Publications Complete to ... .*

NE
CBS ELEKTROTECHNISCHE INDUSTRIE / CENTRAAL BUREAU VOOR DE STATISTIEK, HOOFDAFDELING STATISTIEKEN VAN INDUSTRIE EN BOUWNIJVERHEID. **Added/Corp** Netherlands. Centraal Bureau voor de Statistiek. Hoofdafdeling Statistieken van Industrie en Bouwnijverheid. **VFOAT** C.B.S. Elektrotechnische Industrie; Electrical Engineering. (1979/80)-. Dutch (summaries and/or abstracts in English). an. Fl12.10. SDU Uitgeverij, Postbus 20014, Christoffel Plan, 2500 EA Den Haag Netherlands. **Tel** 011 31 70 3789911. **LC** HD9695.N2; A3. ***Continues*** *Produktiestatistieken, Elektrotechnische Industrie.*

US/0747-9948
CECON RECORD (1983). (CECON ... RECORD / CLEVELAND ELECTRICAL/ELECTRONICS CONFERENCE AND EXPOSITION RECORD.). [CECON rec.]. **Main/Conf** Cleveland Electrical/Electronics Conference and Exposition. **VFOAT** C.E.C.O.N. Record; CECON. **VAT** Cleveland Electrical Electronics Conference and Exposition Record. 1983-. Periodical. English. $20.00. IEEE, Institution of Electrical and Electronics Engineers, Inc., 345 East 47th Street, New York NY 10017-2394. **Tel** (908)981-1393, FAX (908)981-9667. **(Subscription address:** IEEE Service Center, 445 Hoes Lane, Piscataway NJ 08854; telephone: (201)981-1393**) LC** TK5; .C44A. **DD** 621.3/05. ***Continues*** *Cleveland Electrical/Electronics Conference and Exposition. Conference Record, 0278-7024.*
Ind/Abst Index IEEE Publ.

US/1045-2710
CEE NEWS. [CEE news]. **VAT** Contractors Electrical Equipment News. Vol. 41, No. 9 (Sept. 1989)-. Periodical. English. mo. $52.94 US; $92.94 other. Intertec Publishing Corporation, 9800 Metcalf, Overland Park KS 66212. **Tel** (913)341-1300. **(Subscription address:** Intertec Publishing Corporation, PO Box 2901, Overland Park KS 66282.**) ED** Stuart Lewis. **LC** TK1; .C65. **DD** 621.319/24. **[CCC]. Bk Rev. Ad Acc. Circ:** 109,000 (ctrl). ***Continues*** *Electrical Construction Technology, 1041-4061.*
Desc: News and new product magazine; covering electrical equipment.

UK
CEGB ABSTRACTS. ***Ceased.*** **Main/Corp** Central Electricity Generating Board. Central Library & Information Services. Vol. 1, No. 1 (Jan. 1985)-Ceased (May 1989). English. mo. Central Electricity Generating Board, Courtney House 18 Warwick Lane, London EC4P England. **LC** TK1041; .C46A. **DD** 621.3/1/05.

UK/0374-2792
CEGB DIGEST. [CEGB dig.]. **Main/Corp** Central Electricity Generating Board. Technical Information Unit. **Added/Corp** Central Electricity Generating Board. Technical Information Unit. Digest. **VFOAT** Digest. (19??)-. Periodical. English. mo. $84.28. Central Electricity Generating Board, Courtney House 18 Warwick Lane, London EC4P England. **LC** Z5832; .C45; TK145. **DD** 621.3/05. **CODEN** CEGDAN. Documents available from Ask*IEEE. ***Continues*** *Central Electricity Generating Board. Information Services. Digest.*
Ind/Abst Coal Abstr.; Fluid Abstr., Civil Eng.; Fluid Abstr. Proc. Eng.; FLUIDEX (1973-1990); INSPEC (June 1971-).

UK/0305-7194
CEGB RESEARCH. ***Ceased.*** [CEGB res.]. **Added/Corp** Central Electricity Generating Board. **VFOAT** C.E.G.B. Research. **VAT** Central Electricity Generating Board Research. No. 1 (Dec. 1974)-(19??). Periodical. English. ir. Marchwood Engineering Laboratories, Public Relations Office, I Martin, Southampton SO4 4ZB England. **LC** TK1; .C37. **DD** 621.3/05. **CODEN** CEREDG. Documents available from Ask*IEEE, CASDDS.
Ind/Abst Alum. Ind. Abstr.; Chem. Abstr. (1974-1983); Coal Abstr.; Curr. Technol. Index (1974-); Energy Res. Abstr. (April 1976-); Eng. Mater. Abstr. (1974-1983); Fluid Abstr., Civil Eng.; Fluid Abstr. Proc. Eng.; FLUIDEX (1974-1990); Geogr. Abstr. Phys. Geogr. (?-?); Geogr. Abstr. Human Geogr. (?-?); INSPEC (Dec. 1974-); Int. Aerosp. Abstr.; Met. Abstr.; Life Sci. Collect.; Risk Abstr. (19??-19??); World Ceram. Abstr.

BE
CENELEC CATALOGUE. (1973)-. Catalog. English (French and German). an. 800.00F. CENELEC, Rue de Stassart 35, 1050 Brussels Belgium. **Tel** 011 32 2 5196871, FAX 011 32 2 5196919.

●FR
CFE BATIMENT. **VFOAT** Cahiers Francais d'Electricite Batiment; Batiment. Vol. 3, No. 1 (Febr. 1992)-. Periodical. French. Six times a year. 380.00F France; 480.00F other. Edicom, 21 rue Tournefort, 75005 Paris France. **Tel** 33 1 47072929, FAX 33 1 47073066, 33 1 4703129. **ED** Marique Hemy. **Bk Rev. Ad Acc.** ***Continues*** *Batiment Cfe.*
Desc: Contains applications of electricity in industry.

●FR/1146-1497
CFE INDUSTRIE. **VFOAT** Cahiers Francais d'Electricite Industrie; Industrie. Vol. 3, No. 1 (Jan. 1992)-. Periodical. French. Four times a year. 650.00F France; 800.00F other. Edicom, 21 rue Tournefort, 75005 Paris France. **Tel** 33 1 47072929, FAX 33 1 47073066, 33 1 4703129. **ED** Marique Hemy. **Bk Rev. Ad Acc.** ***Continues*** *Industrie Cfe.*
Desc: Contains applications of electricity.

US/1050-1142
CHILTON FUEL INJECTION & ELECTRONIC ENGINE CONTROLS. ASIA. (CHILTON'S GUIDE TO FUEL INJECTION AND ELECTRONIC ENGINE CONTROLS. JAPANESE & ASIAN CARS AND TRUCKS.). [Chilton fuel inject. electron. engine controls, Asia]. **Added/Corp** Chilton Book Company. **VFOAT** Guide to Fuel Injection & Electronic Engine Controls; Fuel Injection & Electronic Engine Controls; Fuel Injection and Electronic Engine Controls; Chilton Fuel Injection and Electronic Engine Controls; Chilton's Guide to Fuel Injection & Electronic Engine Controls. (1988/90)-. English. be. $18.95 (single issue). Chilton Book Company, 1 Chilton Way, Radnor PA 19089. **Tel** (215)964-4000, (800)695-1214, FAX (215)964-4273, telex 6851035 CHILTON UW. **LC** TL214.F78; C45. **DD** 629.25/3.

US/1056-1285
CHILTON'S CHASIS ELECTRONICS SERVICE MANUAL. ASIAN CARS AND TRUCKS. See Transportation-Automobiles.

US/1056-1307
CHILTON'S CHASSIS ELECTRONICS SERVICE MANUAL. EUROPEAN. [Chilton's chass. elec. serv. man., Eur.]. **VFOAT** European; Chassis Electronics Service Manual; Motor/Age Professional Chassis Electronics Service Manual; Chilton Motor/Age Professional Chassis Electronics Service Manual. (1991)-. English. be. $72.00. Chilton Book Company, 1 Chilton Way, Radnor PA 19089. **Tel** (215)964-4000, (800)695-1214, FAX (215)964-4273, telex 6851035 CHILTON UW. **DD** 629. ***Continues in part*** *Chilton's Chassis Electronics Service Manual.*

US/0193-614X
CHILTON'S ELECTRONIC COMPONENT NEWS. [Chilton's electron. compon. news]. **VFOAT** Electronic Component News. Vol. 21, No. 2 (Feb. 1977)-. Periodical. English. mo. $70.00. Chilton Company, 201 King of Prussia Road, Radnor PA 19089. **Tel** (610)964-4122, (800)695-1214, FAX (610)964-4978, telex 6851035 CHILTON UW. **ED** Hy Natkin. **DD** 621. **[CCC]. Ad Acc. Circ:** 110,000 (ctrl). available on microfilm and microfiche from University Microfilms International (UMI). ***Continues*** *Electronic Component News (Radnor, Pa.).*
Desc: Product news publication for design engineers and engineering management working with electronics; encompasses new product advances in electronic components, discrete and integrated circuits, equipment and software.

KO
CHONGI ANJON. **VFOAT** The Electric Security; Electric Security. Periodical. Korean (Korean). qt. Hanguk Chongi Anjon Kongsa, 22-6 Sinsu-dong Mapo-ku, Seoul Korea. **LC** TK152; .C515.

KO
CHONJA KWAHAK. Periodical. Korean. W700 single issue. Chonja Kwahak Sa, 156-Lo Tonhhyo-dong, Mapo-ku 121, Seoul South Korea. **LC** TK7800; .C49.

US/1058-9317
CIRCUIT NEWS. (1991)-. Periodical. English. Twenty-four times a year. $100.00 (one year), $175.00 (two year) US; $150.00 (one year), $275.00 (two year) other. Circuit News Inc, PO Drawer 48, Joplin MO 64802-0048. **Tel** (417)673-2860, FAX (800)628-1705. **ED** Robert J Blanset. **Bk Rev. Ad Acc, Adv Mgr:** Irene Blanset. **Circ:** 22,000. ***Continues*** *Electronics Manufacturing Circuit News, 1058-9546.*
Desc: The only bi-weekly newspapers dedicated to the electronic manufacturing industry. Focusing on printed circuits, surface mount technology, packaging, production, quality and test, environmental, sales and marketing news. Publishers of the only daily newspaper for the electronics manufacturing industry ENN Daily News Report.

US/1058-9325
CIRCUIT NEWS ASSEMBLY. (1991)-. Periodical. English. mo. $50.00. Circuit News Inc, PO Drawer 48, Joplin MO 64802-0048. **Tel** (417)673-2860, FAX (800)628-1705. ***Continues*** *Electronics Manufacturing Assembly Circuit News Cotract Assembly SMT, 1058-9554.*

US/0164-5447
CIRCUIT NEWS (JERICHO). (CIRCUIT NEWS.). Vol. 1 (Jan. 15, 1979)-. Periodical. English. sm. Free to qualified engineers, buyers & managers, $15.00 others. Newsprint Inc., 125 Jericho Turnpike, Jericho NY 11753. **ED** John Tsantes.

●US/1058-9333
CIRCUIT NEWS MAGAZINE. (1992)-. English. Free to qualified subscribers. Circuit News Inc, PO Drawer 48, Joplin MO 64802-0048. **Tel** (417)673-2860, FAX (800)628-1705. ***Continues*** *Circuit Equipment Trader Magazine, 1058-9570.*

UK/0305-6120
CIRCUIT WORLD. [Circuit world]. Vol. 1 (Oct. 1974)-. Periodical. English. qt. $98.00. Wela Publications Ltd, Asahi House, 10 Church Road, Port Erin, Isle of Man., British Isles. **Tel** 011 44 0 624 836044, FAX 011 44 0 624 835400. **ED** Lorna Cullen. **CODEN** CIWODV. **[CCC].** Index available. cum. index. **Bk Rev. Ad Acc.** ctrl circ. Documents available from Article Express International, Ask*IEEE.
Desc: Specializes solely on the subject of printed circuits. International coverage.
Ind/Abst Appl. Sci. Technol. Index; Eng. Mater. Abstr.; Eng. Index Annu.; INSPEC (Jan. 1975-); Surf. Treat. Technol. Abstr.

US
CIRCUITREE MAGAZINE. English. mo. $48.00 North America; $128.00 other. Circuitree Magazine, 700 Gale Drive, Suite 200, Campbell CA 95050. **Tel** (408)986-1292, FAX (408)986-1873. **ED** Raymond A. Rasmussen. **Ad Acc. Pr Rev. Circ:** 8,000 (ctrl).
Desc: Dedicated to the business of manufacturing printed circuit boards.

IV
CIRCUITS. French. Service Commercial Division Relations, Publiques Commerciales, BP 1345, Abidjan Ivory Coast. **LC** TK119.I9; C57. **DD** 621.39/4/096668.

US/1054-0407
CIRCUITS ASSEMBLY. (CIRCUITS ASSEMBLY : THE MAGAZINE FOR SURFACE-MOUNT & BOARD-LEVEL ASSEMBLY.). [Circuits assem.]. Vol. 1, No. 1 (Oct. 1990)-. Academic Scholarly Publication. English. mo. $80.00 US and Canada; $135.00 other.

Miller Freeman Inc., 600 Harrison Street, San Francisco CA 94107. **Tel** (415)905-2337, FAX (415)905-2240, telex 278273. **(Subscription address:** Palm Coast Data, PO Box 420235, Agency Department, Palm Coast FL 32142.**)** **LC** TK7868.P7; C543. **DD** 621.381/531. **CODEN** CIATE5. **[CCC].** available on microfilm and microfiche from University Microfilms International (UMI). Documents available from Ask*IEEE. ***Formed by the union of*** *Circuits Manufacturing, 0009-7306* ***and*** *Printed Circuit Assembly, 0896-8489.*
Ind/Abst Alum. Ind. Abstr.; EMBASE (19??-); INSPEC (Oct. 1990-); Int. Aerosp. Abstr. (19??-); Met. Abstr. (19??-).

US/0278-081X
CIRCUITS, SYSTEMS, AND SIGNAL PROCESSING. (CIRCUITS, SYSTEMS, AND SIGNAL PROCESSING : CSSP.). [Circuits syst. signal process.]. **VFOAT** CSSP; C.S.S.P. Vol. 1, No. 1 (1982)-. Periodical. English. Six times a year. 561.10F Switzerland; 575.70F other. Birkhauser Boston, Inc., c/o Springer Publishers New York Inc., Customer Service Department, 333 Meadowlands Parkway, Secaucus NJ 07096-2491. **Tel** (201)348-4033, (800)777-4643. **ED** S. R. Parker and A. H. Zemanian. **LC** TK5102.5; .C49. **DD** 621.38/043/05. **[CCC]. Pr Rev.** Documents available from Article Express International, The Genuine Article, Ask*IEEE.
Desc: Includes topics such as linear and nonlinear network analysis and synthesis, lumped and distributed circuits, continuous and discrete time systems, one-dimensional and multidimensional signal processing, signal enhancement and identification, switching circuits, digital filters, computer-aided design, graph theory, large-scale systems, and fault analysis.
Ind/Abst ACM Guide Comput. Lit.; Acoust. Abstr.; Comput. Rev.; Curr. Contents Eng. Tech. Appl. Sci.; Eng. Index Annu.; INSPEC (1983-); Int. Aerosp. Abstr. (1983-); Math. Rev.; Pollut. Abstr. Indexes; Res. Alert [Full Cov.]; Sci. Cit. Index; SCISEARCH; Zentralbl. Math. Ihre Grenzgeb.

●US/1066-8683
COGENERATION AND COMPETITIVE POWER JOURNAL. [Cogener. compet. power j.]. **Added/Corp** AEE Cogeneration and Competitive Power Institute (U.S.). Vol. 8, No. 1 (Winter 1993)-. Trade Publication. English. qt. $99.00 (1 year), $178.00 (2 year) US and Canada; $125.00 (1 year), $230.00 (2 year) other. Fairmont Press, 700 Indian Trail, Lilburn GA 30247. **Tel** (404)925-9388, FAX (404)381-9865. **LC** TK1041; .C64. **DD** 621. **CODEN** CCPJE8. **Circ:** 2,200. ***Continues*** *Cogeneration Journal, 0883-5985.*
Desc: For engineers and executives involved in the assessment, planning, implementation, and management of cogeneration projects as well as wheeling and transmission of generated power.

US
COGENERATION AND RESOURCE RECOVERY. English. mo. $225.00. Cogeneration Information Services, 747 Leigh Mill Road, Great Falls VA 22066. **Tel** (703)759-5135, FAX (703)759-0232. **LC** TK. **DD** 338. **UDC** 33. ***Continues*** *Cogeneration and Small Power Monthly, 1042-6957.*

FR/0399-4198
COLLECTION DE LA DIRECTION DES ETUDES ET RECHERCHES D'ELECTRICITE DE FRANCE. Added/Corp Electricite de France. Direction des Etudes et Recherches. (19??)-. Monographic series. French. Price varies per volume.
Ind/Abst Zentralbl. Math. Ihre Grenzgeb.

US/1055-0461
COLLEGE BROADCASTER. See Communication-Broadcasting.

IE/0332-1649
COMPEL. [Compel]. Vol. 1, No. 1 (March 1982)-. Periodical. English. qt. £130.00 UK; $220.00 other. Taylor & Francis Ltd., Rankine Road, Basingstoke Hampshire, RG24 8PR United Kingdom. **Tel** 011 44 256 840366, FAX 011 44 256 479438, telex 858540. **(Subscription address:** Taylor & Francis Inc., 1900 Frost Road, Suite 101, Bristol PA 19007-1598.**) ED** Professor J. Penman. **LC** TK1.A1; C65. **DD** 621.3/0151. **CODEN** CODUDU. Index available. **Bk Rev. Ad Acc. Pr Rev. Circ:** 250. available on microfilm and microfiche from University Microfilms International (UMI). Documents available from Article Express International, The Genuine Article, Ask*IEEE.
Desc: Exists for the discussion and dissemination of computational and analytical methods in electrical and electronic engineering. The main emphasis of papers should be on methods and new techniques, or the application of existing techniques in a novel way.
Ind/Abst Compumath Citation Index [Full Cov.]; Comput. Inf. Syst. Abstr. J. [Full Cov.]; Ei Page One; Elect. Comm. Abstr.; Eng. Index Annu.; INSPEC (March 1990-); Math. Rev. (1984-); Res. Alert [Full Cov.]; SCISEARCH; Solid State Supercond. Abstr.; Zentralbl. Math. Ihre Grenzgeb. (March 1990-).

IT
COMPOLUX. (19??)-. Italian. bm (6 issues). L55000.00 Italy; L120000.00 other. Staff Editoriale SNC, Via Gabriele Rossetti 9, 20145 Milan Italy. **Tel** 011 39 2 48007493, FAX 011 39 2 4985508. **Ad Acc.** ctrl circ.
Desc: Publication on the components of light fixtures.

US
COMPUTER AIDED ENGINEERING REVIEW. Added/Corp CAE Consultants, Inc. Vol. 6, No. 12 Dec. (1987)-. Academic Scholarly Publication. English. mo. Elsevier Science Publishing Company Inc, Madison Square Station, PO Box 882, New York NY 10159-0882. **Tel** (212)633-3950, FAX (212)633-3990. ***Continues*** *Engineering Software Exchange, 0743-2984.*

US/0882-200X
COMPUTER & ELECTRONICS GRADUATE, THE. ***Ceased.*** **See** Occupations and Careers.

US/1053-9808
COMPUTER SCIENCE. VERY LARGE SCALE INTEGRATION. See Computers.

US/0045-7906
COMPUTERS & ELECTRICAL ENGINEERING. See Computers-Computer Engineering.

US
CONFERENCE PAPER [PREPRINTS]. Main/Corp Institute of Electrical and Electronics Engineers. (19??)-. English. ir. Institution of Electrical Engineers / IEE, Michael Faraday House, Six Hills Way, Stevenage Herts SG1 2AY UK. **Tel** 011 44 438 313311, FAX 011 44 438 742840, telex 825578 IEESTV G. **(Subscription address:** IEE / UK, Publications Sales Department, PO Box 96, Stevenage, Herts, SG1 2SD England.**)**
Desc: Papers recommended by the institute's various committees for conference presentation.

US
CONFERENCE PROCEEDINGS / ISTFA ..., INTERNATIONAL SYMPOSIUM FOR TESTING AND FAILURE ANALYSIS. **VFOAT** ISTFA Proceedings; Proceedings of the International Symposium on Testing and Failure Analysis; ISTFA. (1988)-. English. an (Dec.). $100.00 (nonmember), $81.20 (nonmember). American Society for Metals International, c/o Deborah Barthelmes, Materials Park OH 44073-0002. **Tel** (216)338-5151, FAX (216)338-4634, telex 980-619. ***Continues*** *International Symposium for Testing and Failure Analysis. Proceedings, 0890-1740.*
Desc: Covers electronics, semiconductors and electronic apparatus and appliances.

US/1058-6393
CONFERENCE RECORD / ASILOMAR CONFERENCE ON SIGNALS, SYSTEMS & COMPUTERS. [Conf. rec. - Asilomar Conf. Signals, Syst. Comput.]. **Main/Conf** Asilomar Conference on Signals, Systems & Computers. **Added/Corp** Naval Postgraduate School (U.S.) IEEE Acoustics, Speech, and Signal Processing Society. 20th (1986)-. Periodical. English. ir. $140.00 (26th edition). IEEE Computer Society, 10662 Los Vaqueros Circle, PO Box 3014, Los Alamitos CA 90720-1264. **Tel** (714)821-8380, (800)272-6657, FAX (714)821-4641. **LC** TK7801; .A8a. **DD** 621.38. **[CCC].** ***Continues*** *Asilomar Conference on Circuits, Systems, and Computers. Conference Record.*

US
CONFERENCE RECORD - INDUSTRIAL & COMMERCIAL POWER SYSTEM TECHNICAL CONFERENCE. See Engineering-Industrial Engineering and Design.

US/0164-2006
CONFERENCE RECORD OF IEEE INTERNATIONAL SYMPOSIUM ON ELECTRICAL INSULATION. [Conf. rec. IEEE Int. Symp. Electr. Insul.]. **Added/Corp** IEEE Society on Electrical Insulation. **VAT** Conference Record of Institute of Electrical and Electronics Engineers International Symposium on Electrical Insulation. (197?)-. English. IEEE, Institution of Electrical and Electronics Engineers, Inc., 345 East 47th Street, New York NY 10017-2394. **Tel** (908)981-1393, FAX (908)981-9667. **CODEN** CRIID6. **[CCC].** Documents available from CASDDS.
Ind/Abst Chem. Abstr.

US
CONFERENCE RECORD OF ... INTERNATIONAL DISPLAY RESEARCH CONFERENCE. Main/Conf International Display Research Conference. **VFOAT** Display Research Conference. (1982)-. English. an. IEEE, Institution of Electrical and Electronics Engineers, Inc., 345 East 47th Street, New York NY 10017-2394. **Tel** (908)981-1393, FAX (908)981-9667. **(Subscription address:** IEEE Service Center, 445 Hoes Lane, Piscataway, NJ 08854; telephone: (201)981-1393**)** ***Continues*** *Display Research Conference. Conference Record.*
Ind/Abst Index IEEE Publ.

US/0160-8371
CONFERENCE RECORD OF THE ... IEEE PHOTOVOLTAIC SPECIALISTS CONFERENCE. [Conf. rec. IEEE Photovolt. Spec. Conf.]. **Added/Corp** Institute of Electrical and Electronics Engineers. 8th (1970)-. Academic Scholarly Publication. English. ir. IEEE, Institution of Electrical and Electronics Engineers, Inc., 345 East 47th Street, New York NY 10017-2394. **Tel** (908)981-1393, FAX (908)981-9667. **LC** TK2960; .P48a. **DD** 537. **[CCC].** Documents available from Article Express International, CASDDS. ***Continues*** *Photovoltaic Specialists Conference. Conference Record of the Photovoltaics Specialists Conference, 0742-6666.*
Ind/Abst Ceram. Abstr. (19??-); Chem. Abstr.; Energy Res. Abstr. (June 1980-); Eng. Index Annu.; Index IEEE Publ.; INIS Atomindex [Micro.].

CN/0848-984X
CONNEXIONS (ASSOCIATION CANADIENNE DE L'ELECTRICITE). See Energy.

US/1056-7372
CONSUMER ELECTRONICS BUYER'S GUIDE. ***Ceased.*** [Consum. electron. buy. guide]. Vol. 1, No. 1 (Aug./Sept. 1991)-(19??). Periodical. English. ir. IDG Communications / New Hampshire, 86 Elm Street, Peterborough NH 03458. **Tel** (603)924-9471, (800)343-0728. **DD** 621.

●US/1065-7223
CONSUMER ELECTRONICS EDGE, THE. VFOAT Edge; CE Edge. (1992)-. Periodical. English. mo. $89.95. Twin Creeks Entertainment Inc., PO Box 410867, San Francisco CA 94141.

US/0097-8329
CONSUMER ELECTRONICS PRODUCT NEWS. VFOAT Inaugural Issue; CEPN. Vol. 1 (Jan. 1975)-. Periodical. English. mo. CES Publishing Company, 345 Park Avenue South, Bernard Rock, New York NY 10010. **Tel** (212)686-7744. **LC** HD9696.A3; U533. **DD** 338.4/7/62130973.

CN/0838-3340
CONTACT - CANADIAN ELECTROACOUSTIC COMMUNITY. (CONTACT!.). [Contact - Can. Electroacoust. Community]. **Added/Corp** Canadian Electroacoustic Community. **VFOAT** Discontact!; Lettre Sonore; Sound Letter. **VAT** Contact - Communaute Electroacoustique Canadienne. Mars (1988)-. Periodical. English (French). ir. Free to members. Canadian Electroacoustic Community, 4001 rue Berri 202, Montreal Quebec H2L 4H2 Canada. **Tel** (514)849-1564, FAX (514)849-0323. **DD** 621.38/0412.

NE
CONTEMPORARY TOPICS IN INFORMATION TRANSFER. Vol. 1 (1982)-. Monographic series. English. ir. Price varies per volume. Elsevier Science Publishers BV, PO Box 211, 1000 AE Amsterdam Netherlands. **Tel** 011 31 20 5803642, FAX 011 31 20 5862696, telex 15682. **CODEN** CTITEK. Documents available from Ask*IEEE.
Ind/Abst INSPEC.

US/1053-1017
CONTRACT AND CAPTIVE ELECTRONIC MANUFACTURING AND PRINTED CIRCUIT PRODUCTION. [Contract and captiv. electron. manuf. printed circuit prod.]. **VFOAT** Electronic Manufacturing. Vol. 35, No. 11 (Oct. 1989)-. Periodical. English. mo. Free to qualified professionals, $60.00 US; $90.00 other. IHS Publishing Group, 17730 West Peterson Road, Libertyville IL 60048. **Tel** (708)362-8711, FAX (708)362-3484. **LC** TK7836; .E465. **DD** 621.381/.05. available on microfilm and microfiche from University Microfilms International (UMI). ***Continues*** *Electronic Manufacturing, 0895-3708.*

US/0734-1695
CONTROL AND SYSTEMS THEORY. ***Ceased.*** Vol. 2 (1975)-?. Monographic series. English. ir. Marcel Dekker Inc., 270 Madison Avenue, New York NY 10016. **Tel** (212)696-9000, (800)228-1160, FAX (212)685-4540, telex 421419. **(Subscription address:** Marcel Dekker Inc, PO Box 5017, Monticello NY 12701.**) ED** J. M. Mendel. Each issue contains an index to its own contents (no volume index)--loose. ***Continues*** *Control Theory Series.*
Desc: This is an ongoing series. Each title has a different subject.
Ind/Abst Math. Rev. (?-?).

UK/0264-715X
CONVERTING TODAY. [Convert. today]. (1981)-. Periodical. English. mo (10 issues). £45.00 Europe; £56.00 other. Angel Publishing Ltd., 361 373 City Road, 5th Floor, London EC1V 1LR England. **Tel** 011 44 71 417 7400, FAX 011 44 71 417 7500.

US/0743-6815
COST AND QUALITY OF FUELS FOR ELECTRIC UTILITY PLANTS (ANNUAL). (COST AND QUALITY OF FUELS FOR ELECTRIC UTILITY PLANTS / [PREPARED BY THE DIVISION OF ELECTRIC POWER STATISTICS, OFFICE OF COAL AND ELECTRIC POWER STATISTICS, ENERGY INFORMATION ADMINISTRATION, DEPARTMENT OF ENERGY].). [Cost qual. fuels electr. util. plants]. **Added/Corp** United States. Energy Information Administration. Division of Electric Power Statistics. United States. Office of Coal, Nuclear, Electric, and Alternate Fuels. Electric Power Division. United States. Office of Coal, Nuclear, Electric, and Alternate Fuels. (1981)-. English. an. $13.00. National Energy Information Center, Energy Information Administration, Forrestal Building, Room 1F-048, Washington DC 20585. **Tel** (202)586-8800. **LC** HD9685.U4; C67. **DD** 338.4/336362/0973. ***Continues*** *Cost & Quality of Fuels for Electric Utility Plants, ... Annual, 0743-6815.*
Desc: Information on the cost and quality of fossil fuel receipts at electric utility plants is presented in a historical series.

US
CURRENT INDUSTRIAL REPORTS. ELECTRONIC BULLETIN BOARD. English. ir. US Department of Commerce / Bureau of the Census / Current Industrial Reports, 4 Room 2132, Washington DC 20233. **Tel** (301)763-7108.

US
CURRENT INDUSTRIAL REPORTS. MA-36M, RADIO AND TELEVISION RECEIVERS, PHONOGRAPHS, AND RELATED EQUIPMENT / U.S. DEPT. OF COMMERCE, BUREAU OF THE CENSUS. **VFOAT** Radio and Television Receivers, Phonographs and Related Equipment. Began in 1978. Government Publication. English. an. $1.25. US Department of Commerce / Bureau of the Census, Data User Services Division, Customer Services, Washington DC 20233-0800. **Tel** (301)763-4100. **(Subscription address:** Superintendent of Documents, US Government Printing Office, Washington DC 20402.**) LC** HD9696.R363; U67. **DD** 338.4/76213841/0973. ***Continues*** *Radio Receivers and Television Sets, Phonographs and Record Players, Speakers and Related Equipment.*
Desc: Presents timely data on the production, inventories, and orders of approximately 5,000 products, which represents 40 percent of all US manufacturing.

UK/0011-3778
CURRENT PAPERS IN ELECTRICAL & ELECTRONICS ENGINEERING. See Engineering-Abstracting, Bibliographies and Statistics.

US/0743-2402
CVC VIDEO REPORT. **VFOAT** C.V.C. Video Report. (1983)-. Periodical. English. Twenty-two times a year (published twice a month except Jan. and Aug.). $195.00. Creative Video Consulting, 648 Broadway, New York NY 10012. **Tel** (212)533-9870.

US/0097-3564
D.A.T.A.'S MICROWAVE TUBE. ***Ceased.*** **Main/Corp** Derivation and Tabulation Associates, Inc. **VFOAT** Microwave Tube. **VAT** Derivation and Tabulation Associates' Microwave Tube. -Ceased 54th Ed. (1987). English. an. DATA Business Publishing, PO Box 6510, 15 Inverness Way East, Englewood CO 80155. **Tel** (800)447-4666, (303)799-0381, FAX (303)799-4082. ***Continues*** *Microwave Tube List.*

FR/0767-4635
D.E.R. ... PANORAMA. **Added/Corp** Electricite de France. Direction des Etudes et Recherches. **VFOAT** DER ... Panorama; Panorama; Rapport d'Activite. (19??)-. French. an. Electricite de France, Direction des Etudes et Recherches, 2 rue Louis Murat, 75784 Paris Cedex 08 France. **Tel** 40 42 31 26 MME FIEVEZ.

DK
DANSK ELFORSYNING. See Engineering-Abstracting, Bibliographies and Statistics.

DK/0900-5579
DANTEC INFORMATION. [Dantec inf.]. **Added/Corp** Dantec Electronics, Inc. **VFOAT** Dantec Information, Measurement and Analysis. No. 1 (June 1985)-. Periodical. English. sa. Free on request. Disa Electronics, 6 Pearl Court, Allendale NJ 07401. **Tel** (201) 825-3339. **CODEN** DAINEG. Documents available from Ask*IEEE. ***Continues*** *DISA Information, 0070-6639.*
Ind/Abst INSPEC (1985-); Int. Aerosp. Abstr.

US/0882-2433
DATA-ACQUISITION DATABOOK. [Data-acquis. datab.]. **Main/Corp** Analog Devices, Inc. **VFOAT** Data Acquisition Databook; Databook. English. Analog Devices, 2 Technology Way, PO Box 280, Norwood MA 02062. **LC** TK7874.5; .A48A. **DD** 621.381/73/0294.
Desc: Provides detailed technical information and specifications for over 1,000 products.

US
DATA ENGINEERING / INTERNATIONAL CONFERENCE ON DATA ENGINEERING. **Main/Conf** International Conference on Data Engineering. **Added/Corp** IEEE Computer Society. **VFOAT** COMPDEC. 1st (1984)-. English. IEEE Computer Society, 10662 Los Vaqueros Circle, PO Box 3014, Los Alamitos CA 90720-1264. **Tel** (714)821-8380, (800)272-6657, FAX (714)821-4641.

US/0739-1013
DATA-TEK SEMICONDUCTOR PRICE GUIDE. **VFOAT** Semiconductor Price Guide. (19??)-. English. sa (May, Nov.). $175.00. Datatistics Publishing Co. Inc, PO Box 664, Hawthorne NJ 07507. **Tel** (201)427-0330, FAX (201)942-8203, (201)942-4594. **LC** Discard.

CN/0225-4034
DCS NEWSLETTER. [DCS newsl. - Dep. Comput. Serv., Univ. Waterloo]. **Added/Corp** University of Waterloo. Dept. of Computing Services. (1981-1982)-. Newsletter. English. mo. Users Services, Department of Computing Services, University of Waterloo, Waterloo Ontario N2L 3G1 Canada. **Tel** (519)885-1211. **DD** 004/.07/1171344. ***Continues*** *University of Waterloo. Dept. of Computing Services. Newsletter - Department of Computing Services, University of Waterloo., 0841-7644.*

US/1056-747X
DEFENSE & AEROSPACE ELECTRONICS. [Def. aerosp. electron.]. **VFOAT** Defense and Aerospace Electronics. (1991)-. Periodical. English. Fifty times a year. $497.00 US; $527.00 other. Pasha Publications Inc., 1616 North Fort Myer Drive, Suite 1000, Arlington VA 22209. **Tel** (800)424-2908, (703)528-1244, FAX (703)528-3742, (703)528-1253. **DD** 355. **[CCC].** available on an online database (files 16,80,636,648/Full-Text) from DIALOG. ***Formed by the union of*** *CP4SI Report, 1050-2483* ***and*** *Training Electronics & Cp4sl, 1054-6472.*
Ind/Abst Comput. Lit. Index; PROMT [Full Txt.]; PTS Newsl. Database [Full Txt.].

US/0278-3479
DEFENSE ELECTRONICS. [Def. electron.]. Vol. 13, No. 1 (Jan. 1981)-. Periodical. English. mo (12 issues). $39.00 (one year), $62.00 (two years). Argus Business, 6151 Powers Ferry Road, Atlanta GA 30339. **Tel** (404)995-2500, (800)233-3359. **(Subscription address:** Sunbelt Fulfillment Services, PO Box 41530, Nashville TN 37204.**) ED** Don Dougdale. **LC** UG485; .E53. **DD** 623/.043/05. **CODEN** DEELDH. **[CCC].** Index available. **Ad Acc. Circ:** 48,000 (ctrl). available on microfilm and microfiche from University Microfilms International (UMI); available on an online database (file 648/Full-Text) from DIALOG. Documents available from Ask*IEEE. ***Continues*** *Defense Electronics Including Electronic Warfare, 0194-7885;* ***Absorbed*** *Defence, 0142-6184.*
Ind/Abst Acad. Search (July 1993-); Air Univ. Libr. Index Mil. Period.; Bus. ASAP (1990-) [Full Txt.]; Bus. Index (1985-); Curr. Mil. Pol. Lit.; Ei Page One; F&S Index Plus Text, Int. [Select. Cov.]; Fluid Abstr., Civil Eng.; Fluid Abstr. Proc. Eng.; FLUIDEX; Gen. BusinessFile (1985-); Gen. Period. Index (1985-); Infomat Int. Bus.; INSPEC (Jan. 1981-); Mag. Search; NEXIS (1982-); PROMT; Trade Ind. ASAP [Full Txt.]; Trade Ind. Index (1981-) [Full Txt.].

US
DEMAND SIDE MONTHLY. See Public Administration-Public Utilities.

JA/0288-6103
DEMPA DIGEST. [Dempa dig.]. (1983)-. Periodical. English. wk (50 issues). $350.00. Dempa Publications Inc., 1 11 15 Higashi Gotanda, Shinagawa Ku Tokyo 141 Japan. **Tel** 011 81 3 34456111. **(Subscription address:** Dempa Publications, 275 Madison Avenue, New York, NY 10016**) ED** K. Ejiri.
Desc: A summary of events shaping the direction of the electronics industry.
Ind/Abst F&S Index Plus Text, Int. [Select. Cov.]; PROMT.

JA
DENGEN KAIHATSU NO GAIYO. **Main/Corp** Japan. Shigen Enerugicho. Koeki Jigyobu. (1973/74)-. Japanese. ir. Okumura Printing Company Ltd, 2-44 Kanda Jinbo-cho, Chiyoda-ku Tokyo 101 Japan. **LC** TK105; .J36a. ***Supersedes*** *Dengen Kaihatsu No Gaiyo.*

JA/0385-4205
DENKI GAKKAI RONBUNSHI. A, KISO ZAIRYO. [Denki Gakkai ronbunshi, A Kiso zairyÂo]. **Added/Corp** Denki Gakkai (1888). **VFOAT** Kiso Zairyo; Transactions of the Institute of Electrical Engineers of Japan. A. (1972)-. Periodical. Japanese. mo. $142.00. Denki Gakkai, (Institution of Electrical Engineers of Japan), 12-1, Yurakucho 1 Chome, Chiyodaku, Tokyoto 100 Japan. **(Subscription address:** Kyowa Book Company, Inc., 1 38 Kanda Jinbo-Cho, Chiyoda-Ku Tokyo 101, Japan**) LC** TK4; .D317. ***Separated from*** *Denki Gakkai Zasshi, 0020-2878.*

JA/0385-4213
DENKI GAKKAI RONBUNSHI. B, ENERUGI, DENKI KIKI, DENRYOKU. [Denki gakkai ronbunshi. B Enerugi, denki kiki, denryoku]. **Added/Corp** Denki Gakkai (1888). **VFOAT** Enerugi, Denki Kiki, Denryoku; Transactions of the Institute of Electrical Engineers of Japan. B. (1972)-. Periodical. Japanese. mo. $142.00. Denki Gakkai, (Institution of Electrical Engineers of Japan), 12-1, Yurakucho 1 Chome, Chiyodaku, Tokyoto 100 Japan. **(Subscription address:** Kyowa Book Company, Inc., 1 38 Kanda Jinbo-Cho, Chiyoda-Ku Tokyo 101, Japan**) LC** TK4; .D3174. ***Separated from*** *Denki Gakkai Zasshi, 0020-2878.*

JA/0385-4221
DENKI GAKKAI RONBUNSHI. C, EREKUTORONIKUSU, JOHO KOGAKU, SHISUTEMU. **Added/Corp** Denki Gakkai (1888). **VFOAT** Erekutoronikusu, Joho Kogaku, Shisutemu; Transactions of the Institute of Electrical Engineers of Japan. C. (1972)-. Periodical. Japanese. mo. $142.00. Denki Gakkai, (Institution of Electrical Engineers of Japan), 12-1, Yurakucho 1 Chome, Chiyodaku, Tokyoto 100 Japan. **(Subscription address:** Kyowa Book Company, Inc., 1 38 Kanda Jinbo-Cho, Chiyoda-Ku Tokyo 101, Japan**) LC** TK7800; .D37. ***Separated from*** *Denki Gakkai Zasshi, 0020-2878.*

JA/0913-6339
DENKI GAKKAI RONBUNSHI. D, SANGYO OYO BUMONSHI. **VFOAT** Transactions of the Institute of Electrical Engineers of Japan. D, A Publication of Industry Applications Society. (1987)-. Proceedings. Japanese. Twelve times a year. $170.00. Denki Gakkai, (Institution of Electrical Engineers of Japan), 12-1, Yurakucho 1 Chome, Chiyodaku, Tokyoto 100 Japan. **(Subscription address:** Japan Publications Trading Company, Ltd., PO Box 5030, Tokyo International, Tokyo 100-31 Japan.**) DD** 621.3. ***Continues in part*** *Denki Gakkai Zasshi, 0020-2878.*

JA
DENKI GAKKAI ZASSHI. [Denki Gakkai zasshi]. **Added/Corp** Denki Gakkai (Chiyoda-Ku, Tokyo, Japan). **VFOAT** The Journal of the Institute of Electrical Engineers of Japan; Journal of the Institute of Electrical Engineers of Japan. Academic Scholarly Publication. Japanese. mo. $282.00. Denki Gakkai, (Institution of Electrical Engineers of Japan), 12-1, Yurakucho 1 Chome, Chiyodaku, Tokyoto 100 Japan. **(Subscription address:** Kyowa Book Company, Inc., 1 38 Kanda Jinbo-Cho, Chiyoda-Ku Tokyo 101, Japan**) CODEN** DGZAAW. Documents available from CASDDS.
Ind/Abst Chem. Abstr.

JA
DENKI GIJUTSU: ELECTRICAL TECHNICS. Japanese. qt. $60.00. **(Subscription address:** Kyowa Book Company Inc., 1-38 Kanda Jinbo-Cho, Chiyoda-Ku, Tokyo 101, Japan (Phone: 03-3293-0727)**)**

JA
DENKI JIGYO YORAN. **Added/Corp** Japan. Tsushinkyoku. Japan. Denkikyoku. Japan. Denkicho. Japan. Koeki Jigyokyoku. Japan. Shigen Enerigicho. Koeki Jigyobu. No. 1 (1907)-. Japanese. ¥2000. Nihon Denki Kyokai, (Japan Electric Association), 7-1, Yurakucho 1 Chome, Chiyodaku, Tokyoto 100 Japan. **LC** HD9685.J3; D46.

JA/0387-0758
DENKI KYOKAI ZASSHI. **VFOAT** Journal of the Japan Electric Association. (194?)-. Periodical. Japanese. Twelve times a year. $64.00. Nihon Denki Kyokai, (Japan Electric Association), 7-1, Yurakucho 1 Chome, Chiyodaku, Tokyoto 100 Japan. **(Subscription address:** Maruzen Company Ltd., PO Box 5050, Import & Export Department, Tokyo 100 31 Japan.**) LC** TK4; .D32a. ***Continues*** *Dai Nihon Denkikai Shi.*
Ind/Abst Coal Abstr.

JA/0366-9084
DENSHI GIJUTSU SOGO KENKYUJO CHOSA HOKOKU. [Denshi Gijutsu Sogo Kenkyujo chosa hokoku]. **Added/Corp** Denshi Gijutsu Sogo Kenkyujo Chosa Hokoku. **VFOAT** Circulars of the Electrotechnical Laboratory. (1970)-. Monographic series. Japanese (English). Kogyo Gijutsuin Denshi Gijutsu Sogo Kenkyujo, (Electrotechnical Lab., Agency of Industrial Science & Technology), 1-4, Umezono 1 Chome, Tsukubashi, Ibarakiken 305 Japan. **CODEN** DGSCA3. Documents available from Article Express International, Ask*IEEE, CASDDS. ***Continues*** *Denki Shikenjo Chosa Hokoku.*
Ind/Abst Alum. Ind. Abstr.; Bioeng. Abstr.; Chem. Abstr. (-1987); Ei Page One; Eng. Index Annu.; INSPEC (1970-); Met. Abstr.

JA
DENSHI GIJUTSU SOGO KENKYUJO HOKOKURUI ICHIRAN. **Main/Corp** Kogyo Gijutsuin (Japan). Denshi Gijutsu Sogo Kenkyujo. No. 2-Issue 48- 1973-. Japanese. $331.00. **(Subscription address:** Japan Publications Trading Company, Ltd., PO

Box 5030, Tokyo International, Tokyo 100-31 Japan.) **LC** Z5837; .D46A. ***Continues*** *Denki Shikenjo Hokokurui Ichiran.*

JA/0366-9092
DENSHI GIJUTSU SOGO KENKYUJO IHO. [Denshi Gijutusu Sogo Kenkyujo iho]. **Added/Corp** Kogyo Gijutsuin (Japan). Denshi Gijutsu Sogo Kenkyujo. **VFOAT** Bulletin of the Electrotechnical Laboratory. No. 34 (Jan. 1970)-. Periodical. Japanese (summaries and/or abstracts in English). mo. $364.00. Kogyo Gijutsuin Denshi Gijutsu Sogo Kenkyujo, (Electrotechnical Lab., Agency of Industrial Science & Technology), 1-4, Umezono 1 Chome, Tsukubashi, Ibarakiken 305 Japan. **(Subscription address:** Japan Publications Trading Company, Ltd., PO Box 5030, Tokyo International, Tokyo 100-31 Japan.**) CODEN** DGSKAR. Documents available from Article Express International, Ask*IEEE. ***Continues*** *Denki Shikenjo Iho.*
Ind/Abst Alum. Ind. Abstr.; Comput. Inf. Syst. Abstr. J. [Full Cov.]; Eng. Index Annu.; INSPEC (1970-); Mech. Eng. Abstr.; Met. Abstr.; Solid State Supercond. Abstr.

JA/0366-9106
DENSHI GIJUTSU SOGO KENKYUJO KENKYU HOKOKU. [Denshi Gijutsu Sogo Kenkyujo kenkyu hokoku]. **Main/Corp** Kogyo Gijutsuin (Japan). Denshi Gijutsu Sogo Kenkyujo. **Added/Corp** Kogyo Gijutsuin (Japan). Denshi Gijutsu Sogo Kenkyujo. Researches of the Electrotechnical Laboratory. **VFOAT** Researches of the Electro-Technical Laboratory. (1970)-. Multiple languages (Japanese and English). Kogyo Gijutsuin Denshi Gijutsu Sogo Kenkyujo, (Electrotechnical Lab., Agency of Industrial Science & Technology), 1-4, Umezono 1 Chome, Tsukubashi, Ibarakiken 305 Japan. **LC** TK4; .D33. **DD** 621.3/08. **CODEN** DGSKBS. Documents available from Article Express International, Ask*IEEE, CASDDS. ***Continues*** *Denki Shikenjo, Tokyo. Denki Shikenjo Kenkyu Hokoku.*
Ind/Abst Alum. Ind. Abstr.; Bioeng. Abstr.; Chem. Abstr.; Ei Page One; Eng. Index Annu.; INSPEC (1970-); Int. Aerosp. Abstr.; Met. Abstr.

JA/0301-9845
DENSHI GIJUTSU SOGO KENKYUJO YORAN. **Main/Corp** Kogyo Gijutsuin (Japan). Denshi Gijutsu Sogo Kenkyujo. (19??)-. Japanese. **(Subscription address:** Japan Publications Trading Company, Ltd., PO Box 5030, Tokyo International, Tokyo 100-31 Japan.**) LC** TK7855; .D45a.

JA
DENSHI IGAKU / MEDICAL ELECTRONICS. **See** Medical Science and Technology.

JA/0913-5707
DENSHI JOHO TSUSHIN GAKKAI RONBUNSHI. A. **VFOAT** Transactions of the Institute of Electronics, Information and Communication Engineers. A. Vol. J70-A, No. 1 (Jan. 1987)-. Periodical. Japanese. mo. $220.00. Denshi Joho Tsushin Gakkai, (Inst. of Electronics, Information & Communication Engineers of Japan), Kikai Shinko Kaikan, 5-8, Shiba Koen 3 Chome, Minatoku Tokyoto 105 Japan. **(Subscription address:** Maruzen Company Ltd., PO Box 5050, Import & Export Department, Tokyo 100 31 Japan.**) CODEN** DJTAER. Documents available from Ask*IEEE. ***Continues*** *Denshi Tsushin Gakkai Ronbunshi A, 0373-6091.*
Ind/Abst INSPEC (1987-).

JA
DENSHI JOHO TSUSHIN GAKKAI RONBUNSHI. B. **Added/Corp** Denshi Joho Tsushin Gakkai (Japan). **VFOAT** Transactions of the Institute of Electronics, Information and Communication Engineers. B. Vol. J70-B, No. 1 (Jan. 1987)-. Periodical. Japanese. mo. $370.00. Denshi Joho Tsushin Gakkai, (Inst. of Electronics, Information & Communication Engineers of Japan), Kikai Shinko Kaikan, 5-8, Shiba Koen 3 Chome, Minatoku Tokyoto 105 Japan. **(Subscription address:** Maruzen Company Ltd., PO Box 5050, Import & Export Department, Tokyo 100 31 Japan.**) CODEN** DJTBEU. Documents available from Ask*IEEE. ***Continues*** *Denshi Tsushin Gakkai Rombunshi B, 0373-6105.*
Ind/Abst INSPEC (1987-).

JA
DENSHI JOHO TSUSHIN GAKKAI RONBUNSHI. C. **Added/Corp** Denshi Joho Tsushin Gakkai (Japan). **VFOAT** Transactions of the Institute of Electronics, Information and Communication Engineers. A. Vol. J70-C, No. 1 (Jan. 1987)-. Academic Scholarly Publication. Japanese. mo. $370.00. Denshi Joho Tsushin Gakkai, (Inst. of Electronics, Information & Communication Engineers of Japan), Kikai Shinko Kaikan, 5-8, Shiba Koen 3 Chome, Minatoku Tokyoto 105 Japan. **(Subscription address:** Maruzen Company Ltd., PO Box 5050, Import & Export Department, Tokyo 100 31 Japan.**) CODEN** DJTCEX. Documents available from Ask*IEEE, CASDDS. ***Continues*** *Denshi Tsushin Gakkai Rombunshi C, 0373-6113.*
Ind/Abst Chem. Abstr. (1987-); INSPEC (1987-).

JA/0374-468X
DENSHI JOHO TSUSHIN GAKKAI RONBUNSHI. D. **Added/Corp** Denshi Joho Tsushin Gakkai (Japan). **VFOAT** Transactions of the Institute of Electronics, Information and Communication Engineers. D. Vol. J70-D, No. 1 (Jan. 1987)-. Periodical. Japanese. mo. $370.00. Denshi Joho Tsushin Gakkai, (Inst. of Electronics, Information & Communication Engineers of Japan), Kikai Shinko Kaikan, 5-8, Shiba Koen 3 Chome, Minatoku Tokyoto 105 Japan. **(Subscription address:** Maruzen Company Ltd., PO Box 5050, Import & Export Department, Tokyo 100 31 Japan.**) CODEN** DJTDE2. Documents available from Ask*IEEE. ***Continues*** *Denshi Tsushin Gakkai Rombunshi D.*
Ind/Abst INSPEC (1987-).

JA
DENSHI KOGYO GEPPO. Periodical. Japanese. mo. $145.00. Nihon Denshi Kogyo Shinko Kyokai, c/o Kikai Shinko Kaikan, 5-8 Shiba Koen 3 Minato-ku, Tokyo-to Japan. **LC** HD9696.A3; J33324.

JA/0285-1903
DENSHI TOKYO. [Denshi Tokyo]. No. 19 (1980)-. Periodical. English. Fujitsu Laboratories Ltd., Publication Committee, 1015 Kamikodanaka Nakahara-ku, Kawasaki Kanagawa 211 Japan. **CODEN** DETODX. Documents available from Article Express International.
Ind/Abst Bioeng. Abstr.; Ei Page One; Eng. Index Annu.

JA/0413-6869
DENSHI TSUSHIN GAKKAI. DENSHI TSUSHIN GAKKAI ROMBUNSHI. **VFOAT** Transactions of the Institute of Electronics and Communication Engineers of Japan. Vol. 51 (1968)-. Periodical. Japanese (table of contents in English). mo. **(Subscription address:** Kyowa Book Company Inc., 1-38 Kanda Jinbo-Cho Chiyoda-Ku, Tokyo 101 Japan**)** ***Supersedes in part*** *Denshi Tsushin Gakkai Shi.*
Ind/Abst Int. Abstr. Oper. Res. [Select. Cov.].

JA/0387-0774
DENSHI ZAIRYO. [Denshi zairyo]. **VFOAT** Electronic Parts and Materials. (1962)-. Periodical. Japanese. mo. Kogyo Chosakai, (Kogyo Chosakai Publishing Co., Ltd.), 14-7, Hongo 2 Chome, Bunkyoku, Tokyoto 113, Japan. **(Subscription address:** US & Canada/ Overseas Courier Services America Inc., 5 East 44th St, New York, NY 10017, Tel. (212)599-4517; Elsewhere/ Overseas Courier Services Co., Ltd., 9 2 Shibaura Minato Ku, Tokyo 108 Japan, Tel. 81 3 453 8311**) DD** 621.38. Documents available from CASDDS.
Ind/Abst Chem. Abstr.

GW/0933-8667
DESIGN & ELEKTRONIK. **VFOAT** Design und Elektronik; Markt & Technik. Design & Elektronik. (1985)-. Periodical. German. bw. DM138.00 Germany; DM 214.00 other. Verlag Markt & Technik, Hans Pinsel Str 2, W-8013 Haar B Munich Germany. **Tel** 011 49 89 461300, FAX 11 49 89 4613774. **UDC** 621.38. **CODEN** 681.3.06.

NE/0925-1022
DESIGNS, CODES AND CRYPTOGRAPHY. [Designs codes cryptogr.]. **VFOAT** DCC. Vol. 1, No. 1 (May 1991)-. Periodical. English. bm. $704.00. Kluwer Academic Publishers / Massachusetts, PO Box 358, Accord Station, Hingham MA 02018. **Tel** (617)871-6600. **ED** Dieter Jungnickel, Ronald Mullin, and Scott Vanstone. **LC** IN PROCESS; QA279; .D4643. **CODEN** DCCREC. **Pr Rev. Acid Free.** available on microfilm and microfiche from University Microfilms International (UMI). Documents available from Ask*IEEE.
Desc: Publishes survey and original papers in the designated areas. The aim is to provide a forum for high quality papers of both a theoretical and practical nature which bridge more than one of these areas. Papers emphasize the algebraic and geometric aspects of any of the areas considered.
Ind/Abst ACM Guide Comput. Lit.; Comput. Rev.; Ei Page One; Inf. Sci. Abstr.; INSPEC (May 1991-); Math. Rev.; Zentralbl. Math. Ihre Grenzgeb.

II
DETAILED ESTIMATES OF IRRIGATION, ELECTRICITY AND PUBLIC WORKS FOR ... . **Main/Corp** Mysore (India : State). English. an.

UK
DIAL ELECTRICAL ELECTRONICS SALES CONTACTS. English. an. £198.00. Dial Industry Publications, Windsor Court, East Grinstead House, East Grinstead West Sussex, RH19 1XA England. **Tel** (0342)326972, FAX (0342)315130, telex 95127 INFSERG. **ED** D Lamin. **Ad Acc. Circ:** 3,000.
Desc: Details on 13,000 companies in the electrical/electronics industry with full contact information.

CC/1000-4742
DIANDU YU HUANBAO. (TIEN TU YU HUAN PAO.). [Diandu yu huanbao]. **Added/Corp** Shang-Hai Shih Ching Kung Yeh Yen Chiu So. Chuan Kuo Ching Kung Huan Pao Hsueh Hui. **VFOAT** Electroplating & Pollution Control; Electroplating and Pollution Control. (198?)-. Academic Scholarly Publication. Chinese. bm. $22.00. Shanghai Qinggongye-ju / Keji Qingbaosuo, Light Industry Bureau, Institute of Science and Technology Information, Room 506, No. 19/Lane 607 Yuyao Road, Shanghai 200042 People's Republic of China. **Tel** 021 2150691, FAX 021 4031633. **ED** Y. Xilu. **CODEN** DYHUEU. **Bk Rev. Ad Acc. Circ:** 12,000. Documents available from CASDDS, BLDSC, CASDDS.
Ind/Abst Chem. Abstr.

CC/0258-0934
DIANZIXUE YU TANCE JISHU, HE. [He dianzixue yu tance jishu]. **VFOAT** Nuclear Electronics and Detection Technology. (1981)-. Periodical. Chinese. bm. Zhongguo He Dianzixue Yu Tance Jishu Xuehui, Beijing, People's Republic of China. **UDC** 539. Documents available from CASDDS.
Ind/Abst Chem. Abstr.

SW
DIELECTRICS & EI NEWS BULLETIN. Bulletin. English. qt. Kr875.00 Sweden; Kr750.00 other. AK Intl El Consultants, c/o Dr A Kelen, PO Box 11043, S-72011 Vasteras Sweden. **Tel** 46 21 137888, FAX 46-21-138649. **ED** Audreas Kelen. cum. index. **Bk Rev. Ad Acc.**
Desc: Reports on conferences, organizations, presentations and laboratories, reviews of publications and coming events.

US/1064-3125
DIGEST - ANTENNAS AND PROPAGATION SOCIETY SYMPOSIUM. **See** Science and Technology.

UK
DIGEST OF INFORMATION ON FUSES PROTECTIVE AND SWITCHING DEVICES. English. bm. £440.00, £471.00 other. ERA Technology Ltd., Cleeve Road, Leatherhead Surrey KT22 7SA England. **Tel** 011 44 372 374151, FAX 011 44 372 374496, telex 264045. **ED** Dr. DJA Williams and Dr. C Turner. Index available. cum. index. **Bk Rev.**
Desc: Recent papers on fuses, switchgear, electrical protective devices in general, controlgear and contacts are studied by expers. Recent developments in standardisation are reported.

US/0097-966X
DIGEST OF TECHNICAL PAPERS. [Dig. tech. pap.]. **Main/Conf** SID International Symposium. **Added/Corp** Society for Information Display. (19??)-. English. an. $100.00. Society for Information Display, 8055 West Manchester Avenue, Suite 615, Playa del Ray CA 90293. **Tel** (310)305-1502. **LC** TK7882.I6; S18a. **DD** 621.38/0414. **CODEN** DTPSDS. **[CCC].** Documents available from Article Express International, Ask*IEEE.
Ind/Abst Bioeng. Abstr.; Ei Page One; Eng. Index Annu.; INSPEC.

US/0747-668X
DIGEST OF TECHNICAL PAPERS / IEEE INTERNATIONAL CONFERENCE ON CONSUMER ELECTRONICS. [Dig. tech. pap. - IEEE Int. Conf. Consum. Electron.]. **Main/Conf** IEEE International Conference on Consumer Electronics. 1st Ed. (1982)-. English. an. IEEE, Institution of Electrical and Electronics Engineers, Inc., 345 East 47th Street, New York NY 10017-2394. **Tel** (908)981-1393, FAX (908)981-9667. **(Subscription address:** IEEE Service Center, 445 Hoes Lane, Piscataway, NJ 08854**) LC** TK7869; .I33A. **DD** 621.381/05. Documents available from Article Express International.
Ind/Abst Eng. Index Annu.; Index IEEE Publ.

US/0193-6530
DIGEST OF TECHNICAL PAPERS / IEEE INTERNATIONAL SOLID-STATE CIRCUITS CONFERENCE. [Dig. tech. pap. - IEEE Int. Solid-State Circuits Conf.]. **Main/Conf** IEEE International Solid-State Circuits Conference. **Added/Corp** IEEE Solid-State Circuits Council. Institute of Electrical and Electronics Engineers. Philadelphia Section. University of Pennsylvania. **VAT** Digest of Technical Papers - Institute of Electrical and Electronics Engineers International Solid State Circuits Conference. (1969)-. Periodical. English. an. IEEE, Institution of Electrical and Electronics Engineers, Inc., 345 East 47th Street, New York NY 10017-2394. **Tel** (908)981-1393, FAX (908)981-9667. **(Subscription address:** IEEE / Institute of Electrical and Electronics Engineers, 445 Hoes Lane, PO Box 1331, Piscataway NJ 08855-1331.**) ED** L. Winner. **LC** TK7870; .I58. **DD** 621.3815/05. **CODEN** DTPCDE. **[CCC].** Documents available from Article Express International, Ask*IEEE. ***Continues*** *International Solid-State Circuits Conference. Digest of Technical Papers, 0074-8587.*
Ind/Abst Bioeng. Abstr.; Ei Page One; Eng. Index Annu.; Index IEEE Publ.; INSPEC.

US/0743-1562
DIGEST OF TECHNICAL PAPERS / SYMPOSIUM ON VLSI TECHNOLOGY. [Dig. tech. pap. - Symp. VLSI Technol.]. **Added/Corp** IEEE Electron Devices Society. Oyo Butsuri Gakkai. **VFOAT** VLSI Technology; V.L.S.I Technology. 1st (1981)-. English. IEEE, Institution of Electrical and Electronics Engineers, Inc., 345 East 47th Street, New

York NY 10017-2394. **Tel** (908)981-1393, FAX (908)981-9667. **DD** 621. Documents available from Article Express International.
Ind/Abst Ei Page One; Eng. Index Annu.

SZ/0301-4184
DIGITAL PROCESSES. ***Suspended.*** [Digit. process.]. Vol. 1 (Spring 1975)-. Periodical. English (French and German). $75.00. Georgi Publishing Co., CH-1813 St Saphorin Switzerland. **LC** TK7888.3; .D54. **DD** 001.6/4/05. **CODEN** DGPRBY. Index available in last issue of volume--attached. Documents available from Article Express International, Ask*IEEE.
Ind/Abst Bioeng. Abstr.; Comput. Abstr.; Comput. Rev.; Ei Page One; Energy Res. Abstr. (March 1982-); Eng. Index Annu.; INSPEC (Spring 1975-); Math. Rev.; Zentralbl. Math. Ihre Grenzgeb.

GW
DIODEN. **Main/Corp** Ag-Telefunken. Fachbereich Halbleiter. **VFOAT** Diodes. German (English). DM10.00. Telefunken Electronic, Theresienstrasse 2, 7100 Heilbronn Germany. **Tel** 07131-670, telex 728 746. **LC** TK7871.86; .A18A. **DD** 621.3815/22.
Desc: Databook with technical data on diodes for universal, switching, rectifier and other applications.

US/0890-1244
DIRECTORY - AMERICAN ELECTRONICS ASSOCIATION. ***Title Change.*** [Dir. - Am. Electron. Assoc.]. **Main/Corp** American Electronics Association. 30th Ed. (1978)-(19??). Directory. English. an. American Electronics Association, 5201 Great America Parkway, Santa Clara CA 95054. **Tel** (415)327-9300. **LC** TK7805; .W25. **DD** 338.4/7/62138102573. ***Continues*** *WEMA Directory.* ***Continued by*** *American Electronics Association. AEA ... Directory.*

US/0882-6064
DIRECTORY OF CONSULTANTS IN ELECTRONICS, THE. [Dir. consult. electron.]. **VFOAT** Consultants in Electronics; Directory of Consultants in Electronics (and Electrical Engineering). 1st Ed. (1985)-. English. ir. $85.00. Gale Research Inc., 835 Penobscot Building, Detroit MI 48226. **Tel** (800)877-GALE, (313)961-2242, FAX (313)961-6083, telex TWX 810-221-7086. **LC** TK7805; .D57. **DD** 621.3/025/73.

US
DIRECTORY OF DEFENSE ELECTRONIC PRODUCTS AND SERVICES : UNITED STATES SUPPLIERS, THE. **See** Military and Defense.

US
DIRECTORY OF EDUCATIONAL PROGRAMS (NEW YORK, N.Y. : 1984). **See** Physics-Sound.

AT/1322-350X
DIRECTORY OF ELECTRONIC SERVICES AND COMMUNICATION NETWORKS. **See** Communication-Telecommunications.

US/1040-0249
DISCRETE SEMICONDUCTORS. DIODES. [Discrete semicond., Diodes]. **Added/Corp** D.A.T.A. Business Publishing. **VFOAT** Diodes. (1988)-. English. sa. $205.00. DATA Business Publishing, PO Box 6510, 15 Inverness Way East, Englewood CO 80155. **Tel** (800)447-4666, (303)799-0381, FAX (303)799-4082. **LC** TK7871.86; .D47a. **DD** 621.381/522/0294. ***Continues*** *Diode, 0732-0353.*
Desc: Information on diodes and semiconductor rectifiers.

US/1043-6367
DISCRETE SEMICONDUCTORS. DIRECT ALTERNATE SOURCES. **Added/Corp** D.A.T.A. Business Publishing. **VFOAT** Direct Alternate Sources; Direct Alternate Sources Discrete Semiconductor. (1988)-. Periodical. English. sa. $135.00. DATA Business Publishing, PO Box 6510, 15 Inverness Way East, Englewood CO 80155. **Tel** (800)447-4666, (303)799-0381, FAX (303)799-4082. **LC** TK7871.85; .D558. **DD** 621.381/52/0294. ***Continues in part*** *Suggested Replacement/Alternate Source Guide, Discrete Semiconductors, 0887-0047.*

US/1040-0907
DISCRETE SEMICONDUCTORS. OPTOELECTRONICS. **Added/Corp** D.A.T.A. Business Publishing. **VFOAT** Optoelectronics. (1988)-. English. sa. $205.00. DATA Business Publishing, PO Box 6510, 15 Inverness Way East, Englewood CO 80155. **Tel** (800)447-4666, (303)799-0381, FAX (303)799-4082. **LC** TK8300; .O67. **DD** 621.381/542/0294. ***Continues*** *Optoelectronics (San Diego, Calif.), 1040-2462.*
Desc: Information photoelectronic and optoelectronic devices and semiconductors.

●US/1058-8566
DISCRETE SEMICONDUCTORS. SUGGESTED REPLACEMENTS. [Discrete semicond., Suggest. replace.]. **Added/Corp** D.A.T.A. Business Publishing. **VFOAT** Suggested Replacements. (1992)-. English. sa. $135.00. DATA Business Publishing, PO Box 6510, 15 Inverness Way East, Englewood CO 80155. **Tel** (800)447-4666, (303)799-0381, FAX (303)799-4082. **LC** TK7871.85; .D5585. **DD** 621.381/52/0294. ***Continues*** *Discrete Semiconductors. Suggested Replacement Alternate Sources, 1040-0915.*

US/0270-3807
DISCUSSIONS AND CLOSURES OF ABSTRACTED PAPERS FROM THE WINTER MEETING. **Main/Corp** IEEE Power Engineering Society. **Added/Corp** IEEE Power Engineering Society. IEEE PES Winter Meeting Discussions & Closures. **VFOAT** IEEE PES Winter Meeting Discussions & Closures. (19??)-. English. an. IEEE, Institution of Electrical and Electronics Engineers, Inc., 345 East 47th Street, New York NY 10017-2394. **Tel** (908)981-1393, FAX (908)981-9667. **(Subscription address:** IEEE Service Center, 445 Hoes Lane, Piscataway, NJ 08854; telephone: (201)981-1393**)** **LC** TK5; .I25d. **DD** 621.31/05.
Ind/Abst Index IEEE Publ.

UK/0305-0378
DISTRIBUTION DEVELOPMENTS. [Distrib. dev.]. (1974)-. Periodical. English. ir. £30.00. Electricity Association Services Ltd, 30 Millbank, London SW1P 4RD England. **Tel** 011 44 71 834 2333.

US/0160-0842
DISTRIBUTORS OF ELECTRONIC PARTS. **Main/Corp** National Credit Office, Inc. Marketing and Management Services. English. an. National Credit Office, 99 Church Street, New York NY 10007. **LC** HD9696.A3; U569. **DD** 381/.45/621310420973.

●US
DOCUMENT IMAGING REPORT. **See** Computers.

FR
DOSSIERS TECHNIQUES PAUL HUET. ELECTRICITE ELECTRONIQUE. French. ir. 610.00F France; 723.46F other. Editions Techniques Paul Huet, 185 rue Gallieni, 92100 Boulogne, Billancourt, France. **Tel** 011 33 1 46046633.

US
DREXEL INSULATION REPORT. **See** Building and Construction.

US
DSM LETTER. (19??)-. Newsletter. English. bw (published every other Friday). $195.00. DSM Letter, 111 Presidential Blvd., Suite 127, Bala Cynwyd PA 19004. **Tel** (610)667-2160, FAX (610)667-5593. **ED** Richard Smithers. Index available. **Bk Rev. Circ:** 250. ***Continues*** *TEL, The Electric Letter, 0093-5379.*

CN/0226-7748
E I C, ELECTRONIQUE, INDUSTRIELLE & COMMERCIALE. [EIC, Electron., ind. commer.]. **VFOAT** Electronique, Industrielle & Commerciale; Revue E I C, Electronique, Industrielle et Commerciale. V. 1 (March 1980)-. Periodical. French. bm. $14.00. EIC Magazine, Serpro International Inc, 963 est Hegerrdre, Montreal Quebec H2M 2J9 Canada. **Tel** (514)383-7700, FAX (514)383-7691. **ED** J J Pierre Tremblay. **DD** 338.4/762138/09714. **Bk Rev. Ad Acc. Circ:** 10,000 (ctrl).
Desc: Technology up-date, news, new products directly related to industrial and commercial production and use, electronics equipment and supplies.

NE/0921-5131
E.R.M. JOURNAAL. [E.R.M. j.]. **VFOAT** Electro Radio Mercuur Journaal. (1988)-. Periodical. Dutch. mo (12 issues). Fl193.00. Wegener Tijl Tijdschriften Group, Postbus 9943, 1006 AP Amsterdam Netherlands. **Tel** 011 31 20 5182828. **UDC** 621.3. ***Continues*** *ERM (Amsterdam), 0165-5205.*

UK
EC ELECTRONICS COMPONENTS EUROPE. **VFOAT** Electronics Components Europe; EC Europe. Periodical. English. bw. £10.00. United Trade Press Ltd, 33/35 Bowling Green Lane, London EC1R 0DA England. **Tel** (01)837-1212. **LC** TK7870; .E14. **DD** 621.381/028.

FR/0012-9283
ECHO DES RECHERCHES, L'. **See** Communication-Telecommunications.

FR/0013-0508
ECONOMIE ELECTRIQUE, L'. [Econ. electr.]. French. qt. $6.66. Unipede, 39 Avenue de Friedland, 75008 Paris France. **LC** HD9685.A1; E25. **DD** 338.4/7/62131.
Ind/Abst Coal Abstr.

US/1055-0399
EDI WORLD. [EDI world]. **VAT** Electronic Data Interchange World. Vol. 1, No. 1 (Jan. 1991)-. Periodical. English. mo. $45.00 U.S.; $55.00 Canada; $90.00 other. EDI World Inc, 2021 Coolidge Street, Hollywood FL 33020. **Tel** (305)925-5900, FAX (305)925-7533. **ED** Mike McGarr. **LC** HF5548.33; .E35. **DD** 658/.05. **Bk Rev. Ad Acc, Adv Mgr:** R. Sessa. **Pr Rev. Circ:** 42,000 (ctrl).
Desc: Dedicated to the furthering of electronic data interchange crossing all industries covering the practical, not the technical aspects of electronic data interchange.

US/0012-7515
EDN. [EDN]. **VFOAT** EDN, Electrical Design News; EDN/EEE; EDN with EEE. **VAT** Electrical Design News. Vol. 6, No. 3 (March 1961)-. Periodical. English. Twenty-six times a year. $120.00 US; $182.00 Canada; $170.00 Mexico; $210.00 (surface mail) other. Cahners Publishing Company, 249 West 17th Street, New York NY 10011. **Tel** (212)645-0067, FAX (212)242-6987. **(Subscription address:** Cahners Publishing Company / Colorado, Paid Subscription Service Center, PO Box 7610, Highlands Ranch CO 80126-7610.**)** **LC** TK1; .E266. **DD** 621.305. **CODEN** EDNSBH. **[CCC].** Index available (free). available on an online database from DIALOG. Documents available from Article Express International, The Genuine Article, Ask*IEEE. ***Continues*** *Electrical Design News, 0364-6637;* ***Absorbed*** *EEE, 0012-7582.*
Desc: Provides up-to-the minute data on American electric technology, as well as detailed samplings of design from all over the world. Features products, technology and applications. It also offers the reader a new look at computers and peripherals, test and measurement equipment, data communications, semiconductor technology and semicustom ICs.
Ind/Abst Acad. Search (July 1993-); Appl. Sci. Technol. Index; Bioeng. Abstr.; Bus. Index (1988-); Comput. ASAP [Full Txt.]; Comput. Database [Full Txt.]; Curr. Contents Eng. Tech. Appl. Sci.; Ei Page One; Eng. Index Annu.; Expand. Acad. Index (1992-); Gen. BusinessFile (1988-); Gen. Period. Index (1985-); INFO-SOUTH Abstr.; Infomat Int. Bus.; INSPEC (June 1976-); Mag. Search; Res. Alert [Select. Cov.]; SCISEARCH; Trade Ind. Index (1981-?).

●US
EDN ASIA. (May 1992)-. English. mo. $99.00. Cahners Publishing Company, 249 West 17th Street, New York NY 10011. **Tel** (212)645-0067, FAX (212)242-6987. **(Subscription address:** Cahners Publishing Company / Colorado, Paid Subscription Service Center, PO Box 7610, Highlands Ranch CO 80126-7610.**)**
Desc: Serves design engineers and engineering managers working in Asia's electronic original-equipment market. The in-depth editorial coverage concentrates on new products and technologies, how-to-design application articles, product articles and news relevant to Asian engineering professionals.

US
EDN CAREER NEWS. ***Title Change.*** (Oct. 1984)-(19??). Periodical. English. Cahners Publishing Company, 249 West 17th Street, New York NY 10011. **Tel** (212)645-0067, FAX (212)242-6987. **(Subscription address:** PO Box 173306, Denver, CO 80217-3306**)** available on microfilm from University Microfilms International (UMI). ***Continued by*** *EDN Products and Careers.*

US/0012-7515
EDN; ELECTRONIC ENGINEER'S DESIGN MAGAZINE. **VAT** Electrical Design News. Vol. 1 (May 1956)-. Periodical. English. mo. $60.00 US; $98.00 Canada; $90.00 Mexico; $105.00 (surface mail) other. Cahners Publishing Company, 249 West 17th Street, New York NY 10011. **Tel** (212)645-0067, FAX (212)242-6987. **(Subscription address:** Cahners Publishing Company / Colorado, Paid Subscription Service Center, PO Box 7610, Highlands Ranch CO 80126-7610.**)** **CODEN** EDNSBM. **[CCC].** available on microfilm and microfiche from University Microfilms International (UMI).
Desc: A product tabloid for electronics design engineers. Provides additional technology news and product information.
Ind/Abst Eng. Index Annu.

US
EDN NEWS. ***Title Change.*** (19??)-(19??). English. Twenty-two times a year. Cahners Publishing Company, 249 West 17th Street, New York NY 10011. **Tel** (212)645-0067, FAX (212)242-6987. available on microfilm from University Microfilms International (UMI). ***Continued by*** *EDN Products & Careers.*
Desc: News tabloid for electronics design engineers. Provides technology news, product information, and engineering career coverage.

US
EDN PRODUCTS AND CAREERS. (19??)-. English. Twelve times a year. $60.00 US; $91.59 Canada; $90.00 Mexico; $105.00 (surface mail) other. Cahners Publishing Company, 249 West 17th Street, New York NY 10011. **Tel** (212)645-0067, FAX (212)242-6987. **(Subscription address:** Cahners Publishing Company / Colorado, Paid Subscription Service Center, PO Box 7610, Highlands Ranch CO 80126-7610.**)** ***Continues*** *EDN Career News; EDN News.*

US/0899-952X
EE PRODUCT NEWS. [EE prod. news]. **VFOAT** EE. Vol. 48, No. 2 (Feb. 1988)-. Periodical. English. mo. $52.94 US; $92.94 other. Intertec Publishing Corporation, 9800 Metcalf, Overland Park KS 66212. **Tel** (913)341-1300. **(Subscription address:** Intertec Publishing Corporation, PO Box 2901, Overland Park KS 66282.) **LC** TK7800; .E438. **DD** 621.381. ***Continues*** *EE, 0364-9369.*

US/0889-0854
EEPA NEWS BULLETIN. (EEPA NEWS BULLETIN / ELECTROMAGNETIC ENERGY POLICY ALLIANCE.). [EEPA news bull.]. **Added/Corp** Electromagnetic Energy Policy Alliance (U.S.). **VFOAT** EEPA News / Bulletin. **VAT** Electromagnetic Energy Policy Alliance news bulletin. (1984)-. Periodical. English. Eight times a year. $95.00 library, $195.00 regular. Electromagnetic Energy Policy Alliance, 1255 23rd Street Northwest, Washington DC 20037. **Tel** (202)452-1070. **DD** 621.

US/0360-1757
EIA ELECTRONICS MULTIMEDIA HANDBOOK. **Main/Corp** Electronic Industries Association. **VFOAT** Electronics Multimedia Handbook. **VAT** Electronic Industries Association Electronics Multimedia Handbook. 1st- 1975-. English. Howard Sams & Company, Inc., 2647 Waterfront Parkway E Drive, Indianapolis IN 46214. **Tel** (800)428-7267, (317)298-5400. **LC** TK7860; .E43A. **DD** 016.6213.

US
EIA GUIDE. **See** Business-Purchasing.

XO
EKT : ELEKTROIZOLACNA A KABLOVA TECHNIKA / VYZKUMNY USTAV KABLOV A IZOLANTOV V BRATISLAVE. **Added/Corp** Vyzkumny ustav Kablov a Izolantov v Bratislave. **VFOAT** Elektroizolacna a Kablova Technika. (1966)-. Periodical. Slovak. qt. **LC** TK4; .B68a. Documents available from CASDDS. ***Continues*** *Bulletin VUKI.*
Ind/Abst Chem. Abstr.

US/1058-2460
EL&P ELECTRIC UTILITY INDUSTRY SOFTWARE DIRECTORY. ***Title Change.*** [EL&P electr. util. ind. softw. dir.]. **VFOAT** EL & P Electric Utility Industry Software Directory; EL and P Electric Utility Industry Software Directory; Electric Utility Industry Software Directory. **VAT** Electric Light and Power Electric Utility Industry Software Directory. 2nd Ed. (1992)-(1992). Directory. English. PennWell Publishing Company, 1421 South Sheridan, PO Box 1260, Tulsa OK 74101. **Tel** (918)835-3161, (800)331-4463, FAX (918)831-9497. **LC** HD9696.C6; E54. **DD** 621.3/0285. ***Continues*** *Electrical Industry Software Directory, 1051-3981.* ***Continued by*** *EL&P U.S. Electric Utility Industry Software Directory, 1069-0557.*

●US/1069-0557
EL&P U.S. ELECTRIC UTILITY INDUSTRY SOFTWARE DIRECTORY. [EL&P U.S. electr. util. ind. softw. dir.]. **VFOAT** Electric Light and Power United States Electric Utility Industry Software Directory; EL&P US Electric Utility Industry Software Directory; U.S. Electric Utility Industry Software Directory; EL and P U.S. Electric Utility Industry Software Directory; Electric Utility Industry Software Directory; Electric Utility Industry Software; EL&P Electric Utility Industry Software Directory. 3rd Edition (1993)-. Directory. English. an (Dec.). $204.50 US & Canada; $230.00 others. PennWell Publishing Company, 1421 South Sheridan, PO Box 1260, Tulsa OK 74101. **Tel** (918)835-3161, (800)331-4463, FAX (918)831-9497. **LC** HD9696.C6; E54. **DD** 621.3/0285. ***Continues*** *EL&P Electric Utility Industry Software Directory, 1058-2460.*
Desc: Information concerning computer software and electric utilities.

FR/0424-7701
ELECTRA (PARIS. 1948). [Electra Paris, 1948]. (1948)-. Periodical. Multiple languages. bm. Comes with Conference Internationale des Grands Reseaux Electrique a Haute Tension membership or US National Committee of CIGRE membership. CIGRE, 3 5 Rue de Metz, 75010 Paris France. **Tel** 011 33 1 42465085, FAX 011 33 1 42465827, telex 290006. **UDC** 621.497.74. Documents available from Article Express International, Ask*IEEE.
Ind/Abst Ei Page One; Eng. Index Annu.; INSPEC (1968-).

US/1054-3260
ELECTRIC GENERATING AND DISTRIBUTING COMPANIES. [Electr. gener. distrib. co.]. **Added/Corp** Midwest Oil Register (Firm : U.S.). English. Midwest Register Inc., 1345 East 15th Street, Tulsa OK 74120. **Tel** (800)829-2002, (918)582-2000. **DD** 333. ***Continues*** *Directory of Electric Light and Power Companies, 0092-4970.*

US/0273-4400
ELECTRIC LAMPS (ANNUAL). (ELECTRIC LAMPS.). [Electr. lamps]. **Main/Corp** United States. Bureau of the Census. Government Publication. English. qt (summary issue). $16.00; $1.00 (quarterly or monthly single issue), $1.25 (single summary issue) US; $20.00; $1.25 (quarterly or monthly single issue), $1.56 (single summary issue) other. US Department of Commerce / Bureau of the Census, Data User Services Division, Customer Services, Washington DC 20233-0800. **Tel** (301)763-4100. **(Subscription address:** Superintendent of Documents, US Government Printing Office, Washington DC 20402.) **LC** HD9697.L333; U68B. **DD** 338.4/7621322/0973.
Desc: Presents tables and statistics based on a survey of manufacturers on the total production, value, shipment, and consumption of the product manufactured by industries in the United States.

US/0013-4120
ELECTRIC LIGHT & POWER. [Electr. light power]. **VFOAT** EL and P; EL & P. **VAT** Electric Light and Power. Vol. 1, No. 1 (Jan. 1923)-. Trade Publication. English. Twelve times a year. $55.00 US; $60.00 Canada and Mexico; $150.00 other. PennWell Publishing Company, 1421 South Sheridan, PO Box 1260, Tulsa OK 74101. **Tel** (918)835-3161, (800)331-4463, FAX (918)831-9497. **(Subscription address:** Electric Light & Power, Publishing Services, PO Box 2680, Tulsa OK 74101.) **LC** TK1; .E213. **[CCC].** available on microfilm and microfiche from University Microfilms International (UMI); available on an online database (fle 648/Full-Text) from DIALOG. Documents available from Documents on Demand.
Desc: Serves the US electric utility industry - electrical power generation transmission and distribution operations, as well as the consulting engineering/construction firms building electric power plants.
Ind/Abst Bus. ASAP (1990-) [Full Txt.]; Bus. Index (1985-); Coal Abstr.; Energy Inf. Abstr.; Energy Res. Abstr.; Environ. Abstr.; Gen. BusinessFile (1985-); Gen. Period. Index (1985-); Mag. Search; Saf. Health Work; Trade Ind. ASAP [Full Txt.]; Trade Ind. Index (1981-) [Full Txt.]; Vocat. Search (Jan. 1993-).

US/0740-1698
ELECTRIC LIGHTING FIXTURES. ***Ceased.*** (CURRENT INDUSTRIAL REPORTS. MA-36L, ELECTRIC LIGHTING FIXTURES / BUREAU OF THE CENSUS, U.S. DEPARTMENT OF THE COMMERCE.). [Electr. light. fixt.]. **Added/Corp** United States. Bureau of the Census. ( )-(1987). Government Publication. English. an. US Department of Commerce, 14th Street & Constitution Avenue NW, Washington DC 20230. **Tel** (202)482-2000, FAX (202)482-3772. **LC** HD9697.L333; U62. **DD** 380.1/45621322/0973.
Desc: Presents timely data on the production, inventories, and orders of approximately 5,000 products, which represents 40 percent of all US manufacturing.

US/0895-2116
ELECTRIC LINES. ***Ceased.*** [Electr. lines]. **VFOAT** ElectricLines. Vol. 1, No. 1 (Nov./Dec. 1987)-(Aug. 1992). Periodical. English. bm. N J International Inc, 77 West Nicholai Street, Hicksville NY 11801. **Tel** (516)433-8720, FAX (516)938-5109. **Bk Rev. Ad Acc. Circ:** 5,000 (ctrl).

US/0731-356X
ELECTRIC MACHINES AND POWER SYSTEMS. [Electr. mach. power syst.]. Vol. 8, No. 1 (Jan.-Feb. 1983)-. Periodical. English. bm. £329.00 UK; $395.00 other. Taylor & Francis Ltd., Rankine Road, Basingstoke Hampshire, RG24 8PR United Kingdom. **Tel** 011 44 256 840366, FAX 011 44 256 479438, telex 858540. **(Subscription address:** Taylor & Francis Inc., 1900 Frost Road, Suite 101, Bristol PA 19007-1598.) **ED** S. A. Nasar (editor's address: University of Kentucky, Department of Electrical Engineering, Lexington, KY 40506). **LC** TK2000; .E3812. **DD** 621.31/042/05. **CODEN** EMPSDO. **[CCC]. Bk Rev. Ad Acc. Pr Rev. Circ:** 600. available on microfilm and microfiche from University Microfilms International (UMI). Documents available from Article Express International, The Genuine Article, Ask*IEEE. ***Continues*** *Electric Machines and Electromechanics, 0361-6967.*
Desc: Publishes original theoretical and applied papers of permanent reference value relating to the broad field of electromechanics, electric machines, and power systems. Some specific topics covered are: rotating electric machines, advances in materials used in electric machines, solid-state control of electric machines, linear motors, power system planning, reliability and security, high voltage of DC systems and power system protection.
Ind/Abst Civ. Struct. Eng. Abstr.; Comput. Inf. Syst. Abstr. J. [Full Cov.]; Curr. Contents Eng. Tech. Appl. Sci.; Elect. Comm. Abstr.; Electron. Commun. Abstr. J.; Eng. Index Annu.; INSPEC (Jan.-Feb. 1983-); ISMEC Bull.; Leadscan; Manuf. Process Eng. Abstr.; Mech. Eng. Abstr.; Pollut. Abstr. Indexes; Res. Alert [Select. Cov.]; Saf. Sci. Abstr. J.; SCISEARCH.

US/0277-1616
ELECTRIC OUTPUT. **Added/Corp** Edison Electric Institute. Vol. 1 (1933)-. Periodical. English. wk. $43.75. Edison Electric Institute, 701 Pennsylvania Avenue Northwest, Washington DC 20004. **Tel** (202)508-5607, (202)508-5610, FAX (202)508-5030. ***Supersedes*** *Weekly Electric Power Output.*
Desc: Provides data for nine geographic divisions and for the entire United States as a whole.

US/0364-474X
ELECTRIC PERSPECTIVES. [Electr. perspect.]. **Added/Corp** Edison Electric Institute. (1976)-. Periodical. English. qt. $42.00 (members), $44.10 (nonmembers). Edison Electric Institute, 701 Pennsylvania Avenue Northwest, Washington DC 20004. **Tel** (202)508-5607, (202)508-5610, FAX (202)508-5030. **(Subscription address:** Edison Electric Institute, PO Box 2800, Kearneysville WV 25430.) **LC** HD9685.U4; E38. **DD** 363.6/2. **[CCC].** cum. index. available on microfilm and microfiche from University Microfilms International (UMI). ***Supersedes*** *EEI Bulletin, 0012-7604.*
Ind/Abst Account. Art.; Bus. Index (1988-); Bus. Period. Index; Bus. Source (Jan. 1993-); Coal Abstr.; Energy Inf. Abstr.; Energy Res. Abstr. (April 1976-); F&S Index Plus Text, Int. [Select. Cov.]; Gen. BusinessFile (1988-); Gen. Period. Index (1988-); INIS Atomindex [Micro.]; Int. Aerosp. Abstr.; Mag. Search; Predicasts Forecasts; Stat. Ref. Index; Trade Ind. Index (1981-); Vocat. Search (Jan. 1993-); Wilson Bus. Abstr.

US
ELECTRIC POWER ALERT. Periodical. English. bw (26 issues). $503.50 (includes 6% sales tax) Washington DC; $475.00 other. Inside Washington Publishers, PO Box 7167, Benjamin Franklin Station, Washington DC 20044. **Tel** (703)416-8500, (800)424-9068.

US/0736-9352
ELECTRIC POWER ANNUAL. **See** Engineering-Abstracting, Bibliographies and Statistics.

US
ELECTRIC POWER IN ASIA AND THE PACIFIC. **Main/Corp** United Nations. Economic and Social Commission for Asia and the Pacific. (1971/72)-. Government Publication. English. an. $20.00. United Nations Publications, 2 United Nations Plaza, Room DC2 0853, Department 007C, New York NY 10017. **Tel** (212)963-8303, (800)253-9646. **LC** JX1977; .A2 subser. **DD** 300 S; 363.6/2. ***Continues*** *Electric Power in Asia and the Far East, 0501-2945.*
Desc: Contains data on energy resources of the region.

KO
ELECTRIC POWER IN KOREA / KOREA ELECTRIC POWER CORPORATION. **Main/Corp** Hanguk Chollyok Kongsa. English. an. Korea Electric Power Corporation, San-2 Cheongdam-dong Kangnam-ku, Seoul Korea. **LC** TK106.5; .H365A. **DD** 363.6/2.

US/0732-2305
ELECTRIC POWER MONTHLY. (ELECTRIC POWER MONTHLY / U.S. DEPARTMENT OF ENERGY, ENERGY INFORMATION ADMINISTRATION, OFFICE OF ENERGY DATA OPERATIONS, OFFICE OF COAL AND ELECTRIC POWER STATISTICS.). [Electr. power mon.]. **Added/Corp** United States. Energy Information Administration. United States. Office of Coal, Nuclear, Electric, and Alternate Fuels. United States. Office of Coal, Nuclear, Electric, and Alternate Fuels. Electric Power Division. United States. Energy Information Administration. Office of Coal and Electric Power Statistics. United States. Energy Information Administration. Division of Electric Power Statistics. **VFOAT** EPM. (June 1980)-. Periodical. English. mo. $87.00 US; $108.75 other. National Energy Information Center, Energy Information Administration, Forrestal Building, Room 1F-048, Washington DC 20585. **Tel** (202)586-8800. **LC** TK23; .E52. **DD** 363.6/2. Documents available from Documents on Demand. ***Formed by the union of*** *Preliminary Power Production, Fuel Consumption, and Installed Capacity Data; Report on Monthly Electric Energy and Peak Load Data;* ***Absorbed*** *EIA Report on 500 KWH Residential Electric Bills in Major Cities;* ***Formed by the union of*** *Quarterly Report on National Trends in Electric Energy Resources Use;* ***Absorbed*** *Sales, Revenue, and Income of Electric Utilities, 0742-1885;* ***Absorbed in part*** *Cost and Quality of Fuels for Electric Utility Plants (Monthly), 0743-7145.*
Desc: Presents monthly summaries of electric utility statistics on net operation, net energy for load, peak load and net capability, fuel consumption, fuel stocks, fuel deliveries, and prices.
Ind/Abst Am. Stat. Index; Energy Inf. Abstr.

US/0737-1845
ELECTRIC POWER SUPPLY AND DEMAND. ***Title Change.*** [Electr. power supply demand]. **Added/Corp** North American Electric Reliability Council. (1991)-(1994). English. an. North American Electric Reliability Council, 101 College Road East, Princeton NJ 08540-6601. **Tel** (609)452-8060. **LC** HD9685.U4; E32. **DD** 333.79/3211/0973. ***Continues*** *Electric Power Supply and Demand ... for the Regional Reliability Councils of NERC, 0735-2611.* ***Continued by*** *Electricity Supply & Demand for ... for the Regional Reliability Councils of the North American Electric Reliability Council, 1046-3186.*

US/0735-9446
ELECTRIC POWER SUPPLY AND DEMAND FOR THE CONTIGUOUS UNITED STATES. ***Ceased.*** (1978/87)-(1998). English. an. National Technical Information Service - NTIS, Room 2027S, 5285 Port Royal Road, Springfield

VA 22161. **Tel** (703)487-4630, (703)487-4660, (703)487-4650, FAX (703)321-8547, telex 89-9405. ***Continues*** *Electric Power Supply and Demand.*

JA
ELECTRIC POWER SURVEY (TOKYO, JAPAN). (ELECTRIC POWER SURVEY.). English. sa. Japan Electric Power Survey, Committee 4-2, 1-chome Uchisaiwai-cho Chiyoda-ku Tokyo Japan. **LC** TK1193.J3; N5. **DD** 363.6/2. ***Continues*** *Semi-Annual Electric Power Survey.*

SZ/0378-7796
ELECTRIC POWER SYSTEMS RESEARCH. [Electr. power syst. res.]. Vol. 1 (Sept. 1977)-. Academic Scholarly Publication. English. Twelve times a year (4 vols.). 1760.00F. Elsevier Sequoia SA, PO Box 564, CH-1001 Lausanne 1 Switzerland. **Tel** 011 41 21 3207381. **ED** M E Council. **LC** TK1; .E234. **DD** 621.31/05. **CODEN** EPSRDN. **[CCC]. Ad Acc, Adv Mgr:** Ms. W van Cattenburch (Amsterdam). available on microfilm and microfiche from University Microfilms International (UMI). Documents available from Article Express International, The Genuine Article, Ask*IEEE, CASDDS.
Desc: An international journal devoted to research and new applications in generation, transmission, distribution and utilization of electric power.
Ind/Abst Bioeng. Abstr.; Chem. Abstr.; Coal Abstr.; Curr. Contents Eng. Tech. Appl. Sci.; Ei Page One; Energy Inf. Abstr.; Energy Res. Abstr. (April 1978-); Eng. Index Annu.; INSPEC (Sept. 1977-); J. Plan. Lit.; Leadscan; Res. Alert [Select. Cov.]; SCISEARCH.

US
ELECTRIC POWER TRENDS. Added/Corp Arthur Andersen & Co. Cambridge Energy Research Associates. (1989)-. English. ir. Cambridge Energy Research Association, 20 University Road, Suite 450, Cambridge MA 02138. **Tel** (617)497-6446. **LC** IN PROCESS.

CN/0831-6899
ELECTRIC PROPULSION. (ELECTRIC PROPULSION / ELECTRIC VEHICLE ASSOCIATION OF CANADA.). [Electr. propuls.]. **Added/Corp** Electric Vehicle Association of Canada. Vol. 1, No. 1 (May 1986)-. Periodical. English (French; summaries and/or abstracts in French). qt. 50.00Can$ Canada; 75.00Can$ other. Electric Vehicle Association of Canada, 301 Moodie Drive, Suite 420, Nepean Ontario K2H 9C4 Canada. **Tel** (613)596-0827. **ED** Norman E. Wood. **DD** 629.2/293/05. **Bk Rev**.

US/0895-1853
ELECTRIC RD&D. ***Ceased.*** **VFOAT** Electric RD and D. **VAT** Electric Research, Development and Demonstration. Vol. 1, No. 1 (Oct. 7, 1987)-?. Periodical. English. sm. Electric RD&D, 2621 Ellesmere Drive, Midlothian VA 23113. **DD** 621.

US
ELECTRIC SALES AND REVENUE. Added/Corp United States. Office of Coal, Nuclear, Electric, and Alternate Fuels. **VFOAT** Electric $ales and Revenue. (1989)-. English. an. National Energy Information Center, Energy Information Administration, Forrestal Building, Room 1F-048, Washington DC 20585. **Tel** (202)586-8800. **LC** HD9685.U4; T95. **DD** 333.79/323/097305. ***Continues*** *Electric Sales, Revenue, and Bills.*

US/0737-2701
ELECTRIC UTILITY FORECASTING IN NEW JERSEY. [Electr. util. forecast. N. J.]. English. an. New Jersey Department of Energy, Office of Technical Assistance, 101 Commerce Street, Newark NJ 07102. **LC** HD9685.U6; N3925. **DD** 338.4/736362.

US/0270-0743
ELECTRIC UTILITY GENERATION PLANBOOK, THE. [Elect. util. gener. planb.]. **VFOAT** Generation Planbook. (1972)-. English. an. $10.00. McGraw Hill Publishing Company, Inc., 1221 Avenue of the Americas, New York NY 10020. **Tel** (212)512-6410, (800)525-5003, FAX (212)512-6111. **LC** TK1191; .E54. **DD** 621.312/13.

US/0190-1729
ELECTRIC UTILITY STATISTICAL REFERENCE. See Engineering-Abstracting, Bibliographies and Statistics.

US/0736-413X
ELECTRIC UTILITY WEEK. [Electr. util. week]. (Jan. 3, 1983)-. Newsletter. English. wk. $1325.00 US and Canada; $1345.00. McGraw Hill Publishing Company, Inc., 1221 Avenue of the Americas, New York NY 10020. **Tel** (212)512-6410, (800)525-5003, FAX (212)512-6111. available on an online database (file 624/Full-Text) from DIALOG. ***Continues*** *Electrical Week, 0046-1695.*
Ind/Abst Coal Abstr.; Energy Inf. Abstr.; NEXIS (Jan. 1983-).

AT/0818-8491
ELECTRIC VEHICLE NEWS MELBOURNE. See Transportation-Automobiles.

US/0190-4175
ELECTRIC VEHICLE PROGRESS.
Added/Corp Downtown/Urban Research Center. Vol. 1 (April 1, 1979)-. Periodical. English. sm (24 issues). $397.00 US, Canada and Mexico; $427.00 other. Alexander Research & Communications, Inc, 215 Park Avenue South, Suite 1301, New York NY 10003. **Tel** (212)228-0246, FAX (212)228-0376. **ED** Laurence A. Alexander. **CODEN** EVEPEO. available on an online database from NEWSNET.
Desc: Worldwide news of research and development and commercialization in the electric and hybrid vehicle industries.
Ind/Abst Leadscan.

US
ELECTRICAL ADVERTISER. English. mo. $34.00. Electrical Advertiser, 6500 Brooklyn Boulevard, Minneapolis MN 55429. **Tel** (612)566-4820, FAX (612)566-4826. **Ad Acc. Circ:** 60,000 (ctrl).

CN/0835-0159
ELECTRICAL AND ELECTRONIC PRODUCTS INDUSTRIES. (ELECTRICAL AND ELECTRONIC PRODUCTS INDUSTRIES / STATISTICS CANADA, INDUSTRY DIVISION, CENSUS OF MANUFACTURES SECTION.). [Elect. electron. prod. ind.]. **Added/Corp** Statistics Canada. Census of Manufactures Section. Statistics Canada. Industry Division. Statistics Canada. Annual Survey of Manufactures Section. **VFOAT** Industries des Produits Electriques et Electroniques. (1985)-. English (French). an. 38.00Can$ Canada; $46.00 US; $54.00 other. Statistics Canada, Publications Sales & Services, Main Building Room 1710, Ottawa Ontario K1A 0T6 Canada. **Tel** (613)951-5078, (800)267-6677, FAX (613)951-1584, telex 053-3585. **LC** HD9696.A3; C348. **DD** 338.4/76213/0971021. ***Formed by the union of*** *Communications and Other Electronic Equipment Industries, 0828-9824; Electrical Industrial Equipment Industries, 0831-4209; Communications and Energy Wire and Cable Industry, 0833-2002; Appliances, Radio and Television Manufacturers, 0319-8995* ***and*** *Miscellaneous Electrical Industries, 0319-9002.*
Desc: Annual census of manufacturers.

UK/0036-8105
ELECTRICAL & ELECTRONICS ABSTRACTS. See Engineering-Abstracting, Bibliographies and Statistics.

US/0190-1370
ELECTRICAL APPARATUS. [Electr. appar.]. (197?)-. Periodical. English. mo (Plus extra directory issue in Dec.). $75.00 (airmail), $40.00 (surface mail) US; $75.00 (surface mail), $85.00 (air mail) other; $15.00 Comes with Electromechnaical Bench Reference. Barks Publications Inc, 400 North Michigan Avenue, Suite 1016, Chicago IL 60611. **Tel** (312)321-9440, FAX (312)321-1288. **ED** Elsie Dickson and Kevin N Jones. **LC** TK1; .E2517. **DD** 621.31/042/05. **[CCC].** Index available. cum. index. **Bk Rev. Ad Acc. Circ:** 16,000 (ctrl). ***Continues*** *Electrical Apparatus Service Volt/Age;* ***Absorbed*** *Electric Heat and Air Conditioning.*
Desc: A professional business journal edited for electrical engineers and technicians involved with the application, maintenance and servicing of electrical/electronic systems.
Ind/Abst Energy Res. Abstr. (Feb. 1975-).

CN/0149-6174
ELECTRICAL BLUE BOOK, THE. VFOAT Mid-Atlantic Electrical Blue Book. English. an. 40.00Can$. Kerrwil Publications Ltd., 395 Matheson Boulevard E, Mississauga Ontario L4Z 2H2 Canada. **Tel** (905)890-1846. **LC** TK12; .E36. **DD** 338.4/7/62138102574. **Ad Acc. Circ:** 24,000 (ctrl).
Desc: Directory of electrical suppliers, distributors, manufacturer's agents and electrical products.

CN/0013-4244
ELECTRICAL BUSINESS. [Electr. bus.]. Vol. 1 (May 31, 1964)-. Periodical. English. Twelve times a year. $92.00. Kerrwil Publications Ltd., 395 Matheson Boulevard E, Mississauga Ontario L4Z 2H2 Canada. **Tel** (905)890-1846. ***Absorbed*** *Canadian Electrical Distributors Association. CEDA Current, 0315-8225.*
Ind/Abst Coal Abstr.

US/1057-0241
ELECTRICAL CODE WATCH. [Elect. code watch]. (1990)-. Periodical. English. mo. $97.50. Intertech Publishing Corporation, 888 7th Avenue, New York NY 10106. **DD** 621.

US/0013-4260
ELECTRICAL CONSTRUCTION AND MAINTENANCE. (EC & M : ELECTRICAL CONSTRUCTION AND MAINTENANCE.). [Electr. constr. maint.]. **VFOAT** EC and M. Vol. 80, No. 1 (Jan. 1981)-. Periodical. English. mo. $30.59 US; $45.88 Canada; $75.30 other. Intertec Publishing Corporation, 9800 Metcalf, Overland Park KS 66212. **Tel** (913)341-1300. **(Subscription address:** Intertec Publishing Corporation, PO Box 2901, Overland Park KS 66282.) **LC** TK1; .N27. **DD** 621.3/05. **[CCC].** available on microfilm and microfiche from University Microfilms International (UMI); available on an online database (file 648/Full-Text) from DIALOG. Documents available from Article Express International, Ask*IEEE. ***Continues*** *Electrical Construction and Maintenance, 0013-4260.*
Ind/Abst Appl. Sci. Technol. Index; Bus. Index (1985-); Eng. Index Annu.; Gen. BusinessFile (1985-); Gen. Period. Index (1985-); INSPEC (1981-); Trade Ind. ASAP [Full Txt.]; Trade Ind. Index (1981-) [Full Txt.].

US/1041-729X
ELECTRICAL CONSTRUCTION ESTIMATOR. [Electr. constr. estim.]. (1986)-. English. an. $28.50. Craftsman Book Company, PO Box 6500, 6058 Corte del Cedro, Carlsbad CA 92008. **Tel** (619)438-7828, (800)829-8123, FAX (619)438-0398. **LC** TK435; .E56. **DD** 621.319/24.

US
ELECTRICAL CONSTRUCTION MATERIALS DIRECTORY. Added/Corp Underwriters' Laboratories. (1977)-. Directory. English. an (June). $17.00. Underwriters Laboratories Inc., 333 Pfingsten Road, Northbrook IL 60062. **Tel** (708)272-8800 Ext.3542, FAX (708)272-8129, telex 6502543343. ***Continues*** *Electrical Construction Materials List.*

US/1062-6808
ELECTRICAL CONTACTS. [Electr. contacts]. **Added/Corp** Institute of Electrical and Electronics Engineers. IEEE Components, Hybrids, and Manufacturing Technology Society. Canadian Electrical Association. **VFOAT** Proceedings of the ... Meeting of the IEEE Holm Conference on Electric Contact Phenomena; Proceedings of the ... IEEE Holm Conference on Electrical Contacts. (1985)-. English. an. IEEE, Institution of Electrical and Electronics Engineers, Inc., 345 East 47th Street, New York NY 10017-2394. **Tel** (908)981-1393, FAX (908)981-9667. **LC** TK2821; .E498. **DD** 621.31/7. Documents available from CASDDS. ***Continues*** *Holm Conference on Electrical Contacts. Electrical Contacts.*
Ind/Abst Chem. Abstr.

UK/0308-7174
ELECTRICAL CONTRACTOR. (1903)-. English. mo. £34.00 UK; £43.00 other. The Builder Group, 1 Millharbour, London E14 9RA England. **Tel** 011 44 81 4028486, telex 25212 BUIKDA G. Documents available from Ask*IEEE.
Ind/Abst Infomat Int. Bus.; INSPEC (Sep. 1979-).

US/0033-5118
ELECTRICAL CONTRACTOR (WASHINGTON). (ELECTRICAL CONTRACTOR.). [Electr. contract.]. **Added/Corp** National Electrical Contractors Association. Vol. 35 (Jan. 1970)-. Periodical. English. mo. Electronic Construction, 3 Bethesda Metro Center, Suite 1100, Bethesda MD 20814. **Tel** (301)657-3110. **LC** HD9695.U5; Q3. **DD** 338.4/7/62130973. ***Continues*** *Qualified Contractor.*
Desc: Exclusively for the electrical contracting industry.
Ind/Abst Curr. Technol. Index; Int. Build. Serv. Abstr.

US/1065-7436
ELECTRICAL DESIGN & MFG. [Electr. des. mfg.]. **VFOAT** Electrical Design and Mfg.; Electrical Design and Manufacturing; ED&M. (19??)-. Periodical. English. bm. $45.00 (one year), $58.00 (two year), $77.00 (three year) US; $24.00 (one year), $42.00 (two year), $54.00 (three year) other. IHS Publishing Group, 17730 West Peterson Road, Libertyville IL 60048. **Tel** (708)362-8711, FAX (708)362-3484. **ED** Tom Williams. **LC** TK7869; .E37. **DD** 621.3. **CODEN** EDEMEP. **[CCC]. Ad Acc, Adv Mgr:** Jackie Fanella. ctrl circ. ***Continues*** *Electrical Manufacturing (Libertyville, Ill.), 0895-3716.*
Desc: Focuses on electrical product applications. Targets engineers involved in the design, fabrication, production, assembly and testing of mid-range electrical end products and subassemblies.

UK
ELECTRICAL DESIGN : BUILDING ELECTRICAL SERVICES & LIGHTING. English. mo. £33.00 UK; £51.00 other. Building Services Publ Ltd, 1 Millharbour, London E14 9RA England. **Tel** 011 44 71 537 2222.

US/0422-8707
ELECTRICAL DISTRIBUTOR, THE. ***Title Change.*** [Electr. distrib.]. **Added/Corp** National Association of Electrical Distributors (U.S.). **VFOAT** TED. Vol. 1, No. 1 (Aug. 1964)-(June 1992). Periodical. English. mo. Electrical Distributor, 28 Cross Street, c/o Evie Cavanaugh, Norwalk CT 06851. **LC** TK1; .E277. **DD** 338. ***Continued by*** *TED (Wilton, Conn.).*

AT
ELECTRICAL ENGINEER (CHIPPENDALE, N.S.W.). (ELECTRICAL ENGINEER.). Vol. 31, No. 1, (April 20, 1957)-. Periodical. English. mo. 77.00Aus$ Australia; 104.00Aus$ New Zealand, Papua New Guinea; 109.00Aus$ Malaysia, Indonesia, Fiji; 110.00Aus$ Japan, India, Hong Kong; 124.00Aus$ US, Canada, Lebanon; 134.00Aus$ Europe, Africa, former USSR. Thomson Publications / Australia, 47 Chippen Street, Chippendale New South Wales, 2008 Australia. **Tel** 011 61 2 6992411, FAX 011 61 2 698 3920, telex 122226. **(Subscription address:** Thomson Publications Australia, PO Box 815, Strawberry Hills, New

South Wales, 2012 Australia.) **CODEN** ELEMA9. available on microfilm from University Microfilms International (UMI). Documents available from Ask*IEEE. ***Continues** Electrical Engineer and Merchandiser).*
Ind/Abst INSPEC (1968-).

US/0891-6225
ELECTRICAL ENGINEERING AND ELECTRONICS. [Electr. eng. electron.]. (1977)-. Monographic series. English. ir. Price varies per volume. Marcel Dekker Inc., 270 Madison Avenue, New York NY 10016. **Tel** (212)696-9000, (800)228-1160, FAX (212)685-4540, telex 421419. **(Subscription address:** Marcel Dekker Inc, PO Box 5017, Monticello NY 12701.) **ED** Raymond G. Jacquot. **LC** UNC. **DD** 621. Documents available from Ask*IEEE.
Desc: Covers topics such as rational fault analysis, solid state electronics and systolic signal processing.
Ind/Abst Ei Page One; INSPEC (1985-); Math. Rev.; Zentralbl. Math. Ihre Grenzgeb.

US/0888-2134
ELECTRICAL ENGINEERING COMMUNICATIONS AND SIGNAL PROCESSING. [Electr. eng. commun. signal process.]. Monographic series. English. ir. Price varies per volume. Computer Science Press Inc, 9125 Fall River Lane, Potomac MD 20854. **Tel** (301)251-9050. **ED** Raymond L Pickholtz. **DD** 621. Index available. ctrl circ. Documents available from Ask*IEEE.
Desc: Emphasizes the broad impact of computers on modern electrical engineering, including communications and signal processing.
Ind/Abst INSPEC.

US/0424-7760
ELECTRICAL ENGINEERING IN JAPAN. [Electr. eng. Jpn.]. **Added/Corp** Denki Gakkai (1888). **VFOAT** Denki Gakkai Ronbunshi. Vol. 92, No. 1 (Jan.-Feb. 1972)-. Periodical. English (translations available in Japanese). Eight times a year. $1,496.00 US; $1,576.00 Canada and Mexico; $1,606.00 other. Scripta Technica, A Subsidiary of John Wiley & Sons, Inc., 7961 Eastern Avenue, Silver Spring MD 20910. **Tel** (301)588-0484, FAX (301)588-5278. **ED** Yasuji Sekine. **LC** TK4; .E2. **DD** 621. **[CCC].** Documents available from Article Express International. ***Continues** Denki Gakkai Zasshi. English. Electrical Engineering in Japan, 0424-7760.*
Desc: Translation of the Transactions of the Institute of Electrical Engineers of Japan publishing original research findings in power generation, transmission and conversion, electrical machinery, control theory and industrial controls, robotics, electrical transportation equipment, insulation, solar energy and high-power semiconductors.
Ind/Abst Ei Page One; Eng. Index Annu.

CN/0070-9662
ELECTRICAL ENGINEERING RESEARCH ABSTRACTS. CANADIAN UNIVERSITIES. (ELECTRICAL ENGINEERING RESEARCH ABSTRACTS, CANADIAN UNIVERSITIES. SOMMAIRES DE RECHERCHES EN GENIE ELECTRIQUE, UNIVERSITES CANADIENNES.). **Added/Corp** University of British Columbia. Dept. of Electrical Engineering. **VFOAT** Universites Canadiennes, Sommaires de Recherches, Genie Electrique; Sommaires de Recherches en Genie Electrique, Universites Canadiennes. No. 6 June (1965)-. French (summaries and/or abstracts in English and French). an. University of British Columbia Department of Electrical Engineering, Vancouver British Columbia V6T 1W5 Canada. **DD** 016.6213. ***Continues** Electrical Engineering, Canadian Universities, Research Abstracts and Reports, 0380-0865.*

UK/0013-4317
ELECTRICAL EQUIPMENT LONDON. [Electr. equip.Lond.]. (1961)-. Periodical. English. mo (10 issues per year). $99.00 US; £30.00 UK. Wilmington Publishing Ltd., PO Box 200, Field End Road, Ruislip Middx HA4 OSY England. **Tel** 011 44 81 841 3970, FAX 011 44 81 841 9676. **ED** Mark Healey. **CODEN** ELEQBMELEQBMELEQALELEQAL. **[CCC].** Index available. **Bk Rev. Ad Acc. Pr Rev. Circ:** 30,383 (ctrl). Documents available from Ask*IEEE.
Desc: Technical features and application stories, new equipment, industry news, energy saving products and systems and catalogues.
Ind/Abst INSPEC (Sep. 1972-).

CN/0013-4333
ELECTRICAL EQUIPMENT NEWS. [Electr. equip. news]. **VAT** EEN. Electrical Equipment News. Vol. 34, No. 6 (June 1989)-. Periodical. English. Ten times a year. Comes with Canadian Industrial Equipment News. Southam Information and Technology Group Inc., 1450 Don Mills Road, Don Mills Ontario M3B 2X7 Canada. **Tel** (416)445-6641, (800)668-2374, FAX (416)442-2261. **DD** 621.31/042/05. **[CCC]. *Continues** EEN., 0013-4333.*

II/0013-435X
ELECTRICAL INDIA. [Electr. India]. (1961)-. Periodical. English. Twenty-six times a year. $100.00. Chary Publications, 14 Sidh Prasad Ghatkopar Mahul Road, Tilak Nagar PO 89, Bombay India. **Tel** 5518254. **(Subscription address:** Prints India, 11 Darya Ganj, New Delhi 110002 India.) **ED** S T Chary. **CODEN** EIDAAF. **Bk Rev. Ad Acc. Circ:** 6,000 (ctrl). Documents available from Ask*IEEE.
Desc: Special articles pertaining to power generation distribution and utilization, plans and projects, staff charges, technology, new products, and processes.
Ind/Abst INSPEC (April 1969-).

US/0149-5771
ELECTRICAL MARKETING. (19??)-. Periodical. English. sm. $495.30. Intertec Publishing Corporation, 9800 Metcalf, Overland Park KS 66212. **Tel** (913)341-1300. **(Subscription address:** Intertec Publishing Corporation, PO Box 2901, Overland Park KS 66282.) **[CCC]. Ad Acc.** available on an online database from DIALOG.
Ind/Abst NEXIS (1982-).

US/0094-9434
ELECTRICAL PRACTICE. V. 1- July/Aug. 1974-. English. bm. $16.00. McGraw Hill Publishing Company, Inc., 1221 Avenue of the Americas, New York NY 10020. **Tel** (212)512-6410, (800)525-5003, FAX (212)512-6111. **LC** TK1; .E3618. **DD** 621.3/05. available on microfilm and microfiche from University Microfilms International (UMI).

UK/0260-1656
ELECTRICAL PRODUCTS TUNBRIDGE WELLS, KENT. [Electr. prod. Tunbridge Wells, Kent]. (1978)-. Periodical. English. mo. £55.00 UK; £75.00 Europe; £100.00 other. IML Group, Blair House, 184-186 High Street, Tonbridge Kent, TN9 1BQ England. **Tel** 011 44 732 359990, FAX 011 44 732 770049. **ED** James Hunt. **Ad Acc, Adv Mgr:** Stuart Wetherall.
Ind/Abst Infomat Int. Bus.

US/0093-3236
ELECTRICAL PRODUCTS YEARBOOK. **VFOAT** EC & M's Electrical Products Yearbook. English. $2.50. McGraw Hill Publishing Company, Inc., 1221 Avenue of the Americas, New York NY 10020. **Tel** (212)512-6410, (800)525-5003, FAX (212)512-6111. **LC** TK455; .E34. **DD** 338.4/7/6213028.

UK/0074-8714
ELECTRICAL RETAILING. English. Eleven times a year. £78.00 UK; £97.00, $180.00 other. Argus Press Group, Queensway House, 2 Queensway Redhill, Surrey RH1 1QS England. **Tel** 011 44 737 768611, 011 44 737 761685, FAX 011 44 737 760510, telex 948669 TOPJNL G.
Desc: Covers the UK domestic appliances and consumer electronics market.

UK
ELECTRICAL REVIEW. (19??)-. English. sm. £78.00 UK; $104.25 US; £110.00 other. Reed Business Publishing Group / England, Quadrant House, Quadrant Sutton Surrey, SM2 5AS England. **Tel** 011 44 81 652-3500. **(Subscription address:** Reed Electrical Review, Garrard House, 2-6 Homesdale Road, Bromley BR2 9WL England.)

UK/0965-5433
ELECTRICAL TECHNOLOGY. No. 1 (1991)-. Periodical. English (translations available in Russian). qt. $894.00 The Americas; £600.00 other. Pergamon Press, An Imprint of Elsevier Science Ltd., The Boulevard, Langford Lane, Kidlington, Oxford OX5 1GB United Kingdom. **Tel** 011 44 865 843000, 011 44 865 843699, FAX 011 44 865 843010. **(Subscription address:** Elsevier Science Ltd. Oxford Fulfillment Centre, PO Box 800, Kidlington, Oxford OX5 1DX United Kingdom.) **ED** F. B. Hinderwell. **LC** TK4; .E627. **[CCC].** Documents available from Article Express International, The Genuine Article. ***Continues** Electric Technology, 0013-4155.*
Ind/Abst Curr. Contents Eng. Tech. Appl. Sci.; Eng. Index Annu.; Leadscan; Res. Alert [Select. Cov.].

UK/0013-4414
ELECTRICAL TIMES. [Electr. times]. (1902)-. Periodical. English. mo. £38.25 UK; £40.50 Europe; $140.33 US and Canada; £81.50 other. Reed Business Publishing Group / England, Quadrant House, Quadrant Sutton Surrey, SM2 5AS England. **Tel** 011 44 81 652-3500. **LC** TK1; .E486. **CODEN** ELTIA4. **[CCC].** available on microfilm from University Microfilms International (UMI). Documents available from Ask*IEEE. ***Continues** Lightning.*
Ind/Abst Alum. Ind. Abstr. (19??-); Coal Abstr. (19??-); Curr. Technol. Index (19??-); Energy Inf. Abstr. (19??-); Eng. Mater. Abstr. (19??-); Infomat Int. Bus. (19??-); INSPEC (1973-); Int. Build. Serv. Abstr. (19??-); Leadscan (19??-); Met. Abstr. (19??-); Saf. Health Work (19??-).

UK/0013-4422
ELECTRICAL WHOLESALER. [Electr. wholesaler]. (1962)-. Periodical. English. mo. £30.00 UK; £35.00 other. Batiste Publishing Ltd, Pembroke House, Campsbourne Road, Hornsey, London N8 7PE England. **Tel** 011 44 81 340 3291.
Ind/Abst Infomat Int. Bus.

US/0013-4430
ELECTRICAL WHOLESALING. [Electr. wholesaling]. (1946)-. Periodical. English. mo. $20.00 US; $21.18 Canada; $37.65 other. Intertec Publishing Corporation, 9800 Metcalf, Overland Park KS 66212. **Tel** (913)341-1300. **(Subscription address:** Intertec Publishing Corporation, PO Box 2901, Overland Park KS 66282.) **LC** TK1; .J6. **DD** 621. **[CCC]. Ad Acc.** available on microfilm from University Microfilms International (UMI). ***Continues** Wholesaler's Salesman.*
Desc: Published for executives and sales personnel of wholesale distributors of electrical supplies and apparatus, electronic components and equipment purchased by electrical contractors, institutions, service industries, utilities and retail outlets.
Ind/Abst Stat. Ref. Index; Trade Ind. Index.

US/0013-4457
ELECTRICAL WORLD. [Electr. world]. Vol. 47 (Jan. 1906)-. Periodical. English. mo. $55.00 (one year), $95.00 (two year) US; $60.00 (one year), $100.00 (two year), $150.00 (one year), $260.00 (two year) other. McGraw Hill Publishing Company, Inc., 1221 Avenue of the Americas, New York NY 10020. **Tel** (212)512-6410, (800)525-5003, FAX (212)512-6111. **(Subscription address:** Electrical World, PO Box 513, Hightstown NJ 08520.) **ED** Herb Cavanaugh. **DD** 621. **CODEN** ELWOA3. **[CCC].** cum. index. **Bk Rev. Ad Acc. Circ:** 42,091. available on microfilm and microfiche from University Microfilms International (UMI); available on an online database (file 624/Full-Text) from DIALOG. Documents available from Article Express International, Ask*IEEE, UMI Article Clearinghouse, Documents on Demand. ***Formed by the union of** Electrical World and Engineer **and** American Electrician.*
Desc: A publication for management and engineering personnel in the electric utility industry.
Ind/Abst ABI/INFORM Glob. Ed.; ABI Inform Ondisc (Oct. 1987-); Acad. Ind. [Computer File] (1985-); Appl. Sci. Technol. Index; Bus. Index (1985-); Bus. Period. Index; Bus. Source (Jan. 1993-); Coal Abstr.; EMBASE; Energy Inf. Abstr.; Energy Res. Abstr.; Eng. Index Annu. [Select. Cov.]; Environ. Abstr.; Expand. Acad. Index (1985-); F&S Index Plus Text, Int. [Select. Cov.]; Gen. BusinessFile (1985-); Gen. Period. Index (1985-); INIS Atomindex [Micro.]; INSPEC (1968-); Mag. Index Plus (1989-); Mag. Search; Newsp. Period. Abstr. (1988-); Predicasts Forecasts; Saf. Health Work; Stat. Ref. Index; Mag. Index (1977-); Trade Ind. Index (1981-); UMI ABI/Inform--Bus. Period. Ondisc [Full Txt.]; Vocat. Search (July 1993-); Wilson Bus. Abstr.

US
ELECTRICAL WORLD DIRECTORY OF ELECTRIC UTILITIES. **VFOAT** Directory of Electric Utilities. (196?)-. English. an. $395.00. McGraw Hill Publishing Company, Inc., 1221 Avenue of the Americas, New York NY 10020. **Tel** (212)512-6410, (800)525-5003, FAX (212)512-6111. **(Subscription address:** McGraw Hill, 1221 Avenue of the Americas, 41st Floor, New York NY 10020.) ***Continues** McGraw-Hill Directory of Electric Utilities.*

US/0164-2804
ELECTRICIAN'S GUIDE. **Added/Corp** Massachusetts Electrical Contractors Association. (19??)-. Periodical. English. Massachusetts Electrical Contractors Association, 1616 Soldier Field Road, Brighton MA 02135. **LC** TK24.M4; E43. **DD** 352/.923/09744.

PO/0870-5364
ELECTRICIDADE. Portuguese. mo (except Aug.). $700.00. Empresa Editorial Electrotechi, Rua Dona Estefania 48 3 Esq, Lisbon 1000 Portugal. **Tel** 011 351 1 528608. **Ad Acc. Circ:** 4000 (ctrl). Documents available from Ask*IEEE.
Ind/Abst INSPEC (Sep./Oct. 1969-).

FR
ELECTRICIEN INDUSTRIEL, L'. Yearly V. 87- (No. 2157-); Jan. 1974-. French. 105.00. Dunod Gauthier Villars, 15 rue Gossin, 92543 Montrouge cedex France. **Tel** 011 33 1 46 56 52 66, FAX 011 33 1 46 57 40 69. **(Subscription address:** Centrale des Revues, 11 rue Gossin, Gauthier Villars, 92543, Montrouge Cedex France) **LC** TK2; .E5. **DD** 621.3/05. ***Continues** Electricien.*

BE/0013-4481
ELECTRICITE. ***Suspended.*** [Electricite]. Academic Scholarly Publication. French. sa. Union des Exploitations Electriques en Belgique, Galerie Ravenstein 4 Bte 6, 1000 Brussels Belgium. **CODEN** LCTRDE. Documents available from Ask*IEEE, CASDDS. ***Continues** Votre Electricite.*
Ind/Abst Chem. Abstr. (1930-1983); Coal Abstr.; INSPEC (1968-).

●AT
ELECTRICITY AUSTRALIA / ESAA. **Added/Corp** Electricity Supply Association of Australia. (1991)-. English. an (Apr.). 42.50Aus$. Electricity Supply Association of Australia, GPO Box 1823Q, Melbourne Victoria 3001 Australia. **Tel** 011 61 03 6700188, FAX 33272. **LC** HD9685.A8; E42a. **DD** 338.4/7/621310994. ***Continues** Electricity Supply Association of Australia. Electricity Supply Industry in Australia, 0312-8393.*

UK/0955-5439
ELECTRICITY INTERNATIONAL. [Elec. int.]. (1989)-. Periodical. English. mo (except combined

Dec./Jan.). $110.00 (1 year), $200.00 (2 year). ICOM Communications Limited, ICOM House, 17A Woodcote Road, Wallington SRY SM6 0LH England. **Tel** 011 44 81 7733773, FAX 011 44 81 7732019.

UK
ELECTRICITY POOL PRICES AND BID PRICES : DEMAND DATA MONTHLY FIGURES. DISKETTE. English. NGC Settlement Ltd, Fairham House, Green Lane, Clifton Notts NG11 9LN England. **Tel** 011 44 602 456692.

US/0364-0124
ELECTRICITY SALES STATISTICS (MONTHLY). See Engineering-Abstracting, Bibliographies and Statistics.

US/1046-3186
ELECTRICITY SUPPLY & DEMAND FOR ... THE REGIONAL RELIABILITY COUNCILS OF THE NORTH AMERICAN ELECTRIC RELIABILITY COUNCIL. See Public Administration-Public Utilities.

AT/0312-8393
ELECTRICITY SUPPLY INDUSTRY IN AUSTRALIA. ***Title Change.*** (THE ELECTRICITY SUPPLY INDUSTRY IN AUSTRALIA.). [Electr. supply ind. Aust.]. **Main/Corp** Electricity Supply Association of Australia. (1968)-(19??). English. an. Electricity Supply Association of Australia, GPO Box 1823Q, Melbourne Victoria 3001 Australia. **Tel** 011 61 03 6700188, FAX 33272. **LC** HD9685.A8; E42a. **DD** 338.4/7/621310994. ***Continues*** *Statistics of the Electricity Supply Industry in Australia.* ***Continued by*** *Electricity Australia.*

AT/0725-3125
ELECTRICITY SUPPLY INDUSTRY IN QUEENSLAND, FINANCIAL REPORT, THE. Main/Corp State Electricity Commission of Queensland. **VFOAT** Financial Report on the Electricity Supply Industry of Queensland for the Year ended 30 June ... . English. an. State Electricity Commission of Queensland, Herman Research Laboratory, Howard Street, Richmond Victoria 3121 Australia. **LC** HD9685.A84; S737A. **DD** 338.7/6136362/09943.

CN/0843-7343
ELECTRICITY TODAY (PICKERING). (ELECTRICITY TODAY.). [Electr. today]. Vol. 1, No. 1 (March/April 1989)-. Periodical. English. Ten times a year. Free to Canadian subscribers in the electrical or utility field; 32.10Can$ (includes GST) Canada; 36.00Can$ US. Canadian Electricity Forum, 900 McKay Road, Unit 3, Pickering Ontario L1W 3X8 Canada. **Tel** (416)428-2299, FAX (416)428-7040. **ED** Randolph Hurst. **DD** 621.31/0971. **CODEN** ELTDER. **Ad Acc, Adv Mgr:** Michele LeGresley. **Circ:** 14,000 (ctrl).

AT/1032-5565
ELECTRICITY WEEK. (1987)-. Periodical. English. ir (24 issues). 640.00Aus$ Australia; 690.00Aus$ other. EWN Publishing, 515 Kent Street, 1st Floor, Sydney NSW 2000 Australia. **Tel** 011/61/2/2612123, FAX 011/61/2/2672261. **ED** Bob Beatty. Index available (bound in each issue). **Ad Acc.**
Desc: Information on electricity and the power industry.

UK
ELECTRICS. 1972/73-. English. £4.00. The Electricity Council, Trafalgar Building, 1 Charing Cross, London SW1A 2DS England. **LC** TK3271; .E42. **DD** 621.319/24.

FR
ELECTRO ANNUAIRE. VFOAT Electro Annuaire de l'Electricite, Electronique, Electromenage. French. an. Societe Nouvelle d'Editions Publicitaires, 16 Av de Verdun, 75010 Paris France. **LC** TK12; .E53. **DD** 621.3/025/44. ***Continues*** *Electro.*

US/1040-0397
ELECTROANALYSIS (NEW YORK, N.Y.). See Chemistry-Analytical Chemistry.

UK/0963-5637
ELECTROCHEMICAL SCIENCE AND TECHNOLOGY OF POLYMERS. See Chemistry.

US/0275-7230
ELECTROCOMPONENT SCIENCE MONOGRAPHS. [Electrocompon. sci. monogr.]. Vol. 1; 1981-. Monographic series. English. Price varies per volume. Gordon & Breach Science Publishers, Inc., PO Box 786, Cooper Station, New York NY 10276. **Tel** (212)206-8900, FAX (212)645-2459. **(Subscription address:** International Publishers Distributor at one of the following addresses: 820 Town Center Drive, Langhorne, PA 19047; or PO Box 90, Reading Berkshire RG1 8JL UK; or Kent Ridge PO Box 1180, Singapore 9111, Republic of Singapore**) CODEN** ESMOD5. Documents available from Ask*IEEE.
Ind/Abst INSPEC.

UK
ELECTROLYTE SOLUTIONS BULLETIN. Bulletin. English. ir. $47.00. University Newcastle Upon Tyne, 1 Kensington Terrace, Newcastle Tyne NE1 7RU England. **Tel** 011 44 91 232 8511 ext. 6507.

US/0270-4935
ELECTROMAGNETIC NEWS REPORT. (ELECTROMAGNETIC NEWS REPORT : ENR.). [Electromagn. news rep.]. **VFOAT** ENR. (1971)-. Periodical. English. bm (6 issues). $59.00 US, Canada and Mexico; $75.00 other. Seven Mountains Scientific Inc., PO Box 650, 913 Tressler Street, Boalsburg PA 16827. **Tel** (814)466-6559, FAX (814)466-6559. **ED** Josephine Chesworth (Managing Editor) and Dr. E. Thomas Chesworth, P.E. (Technical Editor). **DD** 621. **Bk Rev. Ad Acc. Circ:** 1,200 (ctrl).
Desc: News, developments, techniques in reduction and control of electromagnetic interference; abstracts, technical articles, EMI instrumentation, government standards, and international EMI requirements.

US/0272-6343
ELECTROMAGNETICS. [Electromagnetics]. Vol. 1, No. 1 (Jan.-Mar. 1981)-. Periodical. English. bm. £158.00 UK; $260.00 other. Taylor & Francis Ltd., Rankine Road, Basingstoke Hampshire, RG24 8PR United Kingdom. **Tel** 011 44 256 840366, FAX 011 44 256 479438, telex 858540. **(Subscription address:** Taylor & Francis Inc., 1900 Frost Road, Suite 101, Bristol PA 19007-1598.**) ED** Nicolaos G. Alexopolous. **LC** QC759.6; .E4. **CODEN** ETRMDV. **[CCC].** Index available. **Bk Rev. Ad Acc. Pr Rev. Circ:** 450. available on microfilm and microfiche from University Microfilms International (UMI). Documents available from Article Express International, The Genuine Article, Ask*IEEE.
Desc: Publishes refereed papers of permanent archival value in the broad field of electromagnetics. Topics covered include electromagnetic theory, high frequency techniques, extra low frequency and very low frequency, antennas and randomes, arrays, numerical techniques and scattering and diffractions. Also serves as a forum for deliberations on innovations in the field. Additionally, special issues give more in-depth coverage to issues of immediate importance.
Ind/Abst Curr. Contents Eng. Tech. Appl. Sci.; Elect. Comm. Abstr.; Eng. Index Annu.; INSPEC (Jan.-March 1982-); Res. Alert [Select. Cov.]; SCISEARCH; Solid State Supercond. Abstr.

UK
ELECTROMAGNETICS NEWS. See Physics-Magnetism.

●US/1069-4595
ELECTROMAGNETOEFFECT (COMMACK, N.Y.). (ELECTROMAGNETOEFFECT.). [Electromagnetoeffect]. (1993)-. Periodical. English. Four times a year. $295.00. Nova Science Publishers Inc., 6080 Jericho Turnpike, Suite 207, Commack NY 11725-2808. **Tel** (516)499-3103, (516)499-3106, FAX (516)499-3146. **DD** 621.

US/0742-1532
ELECTRON DISPLAY WORLD. (ELECTRONIC DISPLAY WORLD: EDW.). [Electron. disp. world]. **Added/Corp** Stanford Resources, Inc. **VFOAT** EDW; E.D.W. (198?)-. Periodical. English. mo. $440.00. Information Associates, 1259 El Camino Real, Suite 231, Menlo Park CA 94025. **Tel** (415)322-0247, FAX (415)322-0469. **ED** Joseph A Castellano. **DD** 001. **[CCC].** Index available. cum. index. ctrl circ.
Desc: Report of events and up-to-date developments in the worldwide electronic display industry.

PL/0070-9816
ELECTRON TECHNOLOGY. [Electron technol.]. **Added/Corp** Polska Akademia Nauk. Instytut Technologii Elektronowej. Vol. 1, (1968)-. Academic Scholarly Publication. English (summaries and/or abstracts in Polish and Russian). ir. **(Subscription address:** ARS Polona, PO Box 1001, 00068 Warsaw Poland.**) LC** TK7800; .E428. **DD** 621.381/05. **CODEN** ETNTAT. Documents available from Article Express International, Ask*IEEE, CASDDS.
Ind/Abst Alum. Ind. Abstr.; Bioeng. Abstr.; Chem. Abstr.; Ei Page One; Eng. Mater. Abstr.; Eng. Index Annu. [Select. Cov.]; INSPEC (1968-); Int. Aerosp. Abstr.; Met. Abstr.; Pollut. Abstr. Indexes.

CN/0824-6912
ELECTRONIC AGE (TORONTO). ***Ceased.*** (ELECTRONIC AGE.). [Electron. age]. Vol. 1, No. 1 (Sept./Oct. 1983)-?. Periodical. English. bm. Electronic Age, Suite 1/3031 Queen Street East, Scarborough Ontario M1N 1A5 Canada. **DD** 338.4/762138/0971.

UK/0965-030X
ELECTRONIC AND ELECTRICAL ENGINEERING. [Electron. electr. eng.]. (1990)-. Periodical. English. mo. £6.00 UK and surface mail other; £11.00 airmail. Institution of Electronics and Electrical Incorporated Engineers, Savoy Hill House, Savoy Hill, London WC2R 0BS England. **Tel** 071 836 3357, FAX 071 497 9006. ***Continues*** *Electrical and Electronics Incorporated Engineer, 0952-8563.*

UK
ELECTRONIC & ELECTRICAL ENGINEERING RESEARCH STUDIES. LINES AND CABLES FOR POWER TRANSMISSION SERIES. VFOAT Electronic and Electrical Engineering Research Studies. Lines and Cables for Power Transmission Series. (1985)-. Monographic series. English. Price varies per volume. Research Studies Press, 24 Belvedere Road, Taunton, Somerset TA1 1HD England. **Tel** (0823)336197.

II/0013-4813
ELECTRONIC APPLICATION NEWS. (1964)-. Periodical. English. Six times a year (Jan., Mar., May, July, Sept., Nov.). Rs30.00. Peico Electronic and Electric Ltd, Ramon House, 169 Backbay Reclam, Bombay 400020 India. **Tel** 4930311/4930590. **ED** Kailash Sharma. **Bk Rev. Circ:** 2,000.
Desc: Brief specifications and application information on latest range of electronic components and materials from Philips Group companies worldwide.

US/0163-6197
ELECTRONIC BUSINESS. ***Title Change.*** [Electron. bus.]. Vol. 15, No. 10 (Oct. 24, 1975)-(Sept. 1993). Periodical. English. Twelve times a year. Cahners Publishing Company, 249 West 17th Street, New York NY 10011. **Tel** (212)645-0067, FAX (212)242-6987. **ED** Eric Lundquist. **LC** HD9696.A3; U5376. **DD** 338.4/7/62130973. **CODEN** ELBUDL. **[CCC]. Ad Acc.** available on microfilm and microfiche from University Microfilms International (UMI); available on an online database (files 648,675/Full-Text) from DIALOG. Documents available from UMI Article Clearinghouse, Ask*IEEE. ***Continues*** *Electronic Purchasing.* ***Continued by*** *Electronic Business Buyer.*
Desc: The magazine for management in electronic, computer and system companies worldwide. Features news, trends, figures and forecasts of vital interest.
Ind/Abst ABI/INFORM Glob. Ed.; ABI Inform Ondisc (Dec. 1987-); Acad. Search (July 1993-); Bus. Index (1985-); Bus. Period. Index; Bus. Source (Jul. 1993-); Comput. ASAP [Full Txt.]; Comput. Bus.; Comput. Database [Full Txt.]; F&S Index Plus Text, Int. [Select. Cov.]; Gen. BusinessFile (1985-); Gen. Period. Index (1985-); INFO-SOUTH Abstr.; Infomat Int. Bus.; INSPEC (April 1988-); Mag. Search; PROMT; Robotics Abstr.; Stat. Ref. Index; Trade Ind. ASAP [Full Txt.]; Trade Ind. Index [Full Txt.]; Wilson Bus. Abstr.

HK
ELECTRONIC BUSINESS ASIA. (19??)-. English. mo. $90.00. Cahners Publishing Company, 249 West 17th Street, New York NY 10011. **Tel** (212)645-0067, FAX (212)242-6987. **(Subscription address:** Cahners Publishing Company / Colorado, Paid Subscription Service Center, PO Box 7610, Highlands Ranch CO 80126-7610.**) Ad Acc. Circ:** 41,000 (ctrl).
Desc: Business magazine for managers in Asian electronics and computer systems companies. Features news, trends, analysis and issues of vital interest to the management buying team in corporate, engineering, operating, purchasing and marketing management throughout Asia.

●US/1073-1059
ELECTRONIC BUSINESS BUYER. [Electron. bus. buy.]. Vol. 19, No. 9 (Sept. 1993)-. Periodical. English. mo. $70.00 US; $102.00 Canada; $95.00 Mexico; $130.00 (surface mail) other. Cahners Publishing Company, 249 West 17th Street, New York NY 10011. **Tel** (212)645-0067, FAX (212)242-6987. **(Subscription address:** Cahners Publishing Company / Colorado, Paid Subscription Service Center, PO Box 7610, Highlands Ranch CO 80126-7610.**) DD** 338. **CODEN** EBBUEK. ***Continues*** *Electronic Business, 0163-6197.*
Desc: Provides strategic business information for manufacturing, purchasing, engineering, marketing and corporate managers in the electronics and computer industries.
Ind/Abst Bus. Period. Index.

US/0736-5705
ELECTRONIC BUSINESS FORECAST. [Electron. bus. forecast.]. Vol. 1, No. 1 (Jan. 1983)-. Periodical. English. sm (24 issues). $337.00 US and Canada; $387.00 (airmail) other. Cahners Publishing Company, 249 West 17th Street, New York NY 10011. **Tel** (212)645-0067, FAX (212)242-6987. **(Subscription address:** Cahners Publishing Company / Colorado, Paid Subscription Service Center, PO Box 7610, Highlands Ranch CO 80126-7610.**)**
Desc: Reports on emerging markets to enable readers to monitor and anticipate turning points in the fast paced electronics industry.

US/0164-6362
ELECTRONIC BUYERS' NEWS. [Electron. buy. news]. (19??)-. Periodical. English. Fifty times a year. $149.00 US. CMP Publications Inc., c/o B. Werner, One Jericho Plaza, Wing A, 2nd Floor, Jericho NY 11753. **Tel** (516)733-6700. **(Subscription address:** CMP Publications, Inc. / New York, PO Box 4037, Church Street Station, New York NY 10261-4037.**) ED** Eric Lundquist. **DD** 621. **[CCC]. Ad Acc. Circ:** 61,000 (ctrl). available on an online database (file 16/Full-Text) from

DIALOG.
Desc: High-technology purchasing newsweekly provides purchasing-oriented news, analysis and trend/product reports to more than 60,000 professionals in purchasing management, purchasing and other corporate positions directly involved in the purchase of electronic products and services.
Ind/Abst F&S Index Plus Text, Int. [Full Txt.] [Select. Cov.]; PROMT [Full Txt.].

US
ELECTRONIC BUYERS' NEWS HANDBOOK & DIRECTORY. ***Ceased.*** **VFOAT** Electronic Buyers' News Handbook and Directory; Buyers' News; EBN Handbook and Directory. (1986)-?. Directory. English. an. CMP Publications Inc., c/o B. Werner, One Jericho Plaza, Wing A, 2nd Floor, Jericho NY 11753. **Tel** (516)733-6700. **LC** TK7870.3; .E363. **DD** 621.381/0294.

US/0886-5671
ELECTRONIC CHEMICALS NEWS. [Electron. chem. news]. Vol. 1, No. 1 (Jan. 6, 1986)-. Periodical. English. Twenty-six times a year. $452.00. Chemical Week Association, 888 Seventh Avenue, 26th Floor, New York NY 10106. **Tel** (212)621-4900. **ED** Deborah Hairston and Maurice Martorella. **DD** 621. **[CCC].** available on an online database (files 16,636/Full-Text) from DIALOG. ***Continues*** *Electronic Chemicals & Materials News, 0884-9757.*
Desc: Covers the electronic chemicals and materials business, including acquisitions, marketing strategies, new products and price data. Covers patent activity in Europe, Japan, and U.S.
Ind/Abst PTS Newsl. Database [Full Txt.].

HK
ELECTRONIC COMPONENTS. (19??)-. English. mo. $75.00 (1 year), $120.00 (2 year) surface mail; $190.00 (air mail) Far East and India; $250.00 (air mail) other. Trade Media Ltd / Hong Kong, GPO Box 11411, Hong Kong Hong Kong. **Tel** 011 852 555-4777, FAX 011 852 870-0637. **(Subscription address:** Wordright Enterprises Inc., PO Box 3062, Circulation Dept., Evanston, IL 30204**)** **LC** TK7869; .A85. **DD** 621.381/095. ***Continues*** *Asian Sources Electronic Components, 0254-1122.*

US
ELECTRONIC COMPONENTS. (19??)-. English. mo. $225.00. Predicasts Inc., A Ziff Communications Company, 11001 Cedar Avenue, Cleveland OH 44106. **Tel** (800)321-6388, (216)795-3000, FAX (216)229-9944, telex 985 604. **(Subscription address:** Information Access Company, PO Box 61000, Department 1851, San Francisco, CA 94161; Phone: (800)321-6388**)**

NE/0141-6219
ELECTRONIC COMPONENTS & APPLICATIONS. ***Ceased.*** [Electron. compon. appl.]. **VAT** Electronic Components and Applications. Vol.1 (Oct. 1978)-(1992). Periodical. English. qt. N V Philips Gloeilampenfabrie, Elcoma Marketing Commission, 5600 MD Eindhoven Netherlands. **Tel** 31 40 72 34 12. **ED** I Crick. **LC** TK7869; .E42. **DD** 621.381/05. **CODEN** ECAPD6. Index available. cum. index. **Circ:** 12,000. Documents available from Article Express International, Ask*IEEE. ***Formed by the union of*** *Electronic Applications Bulletin, 0013-4821 and Mullard Technical Communications.*
Desc: In-depth information on important new Philips high technology components and their applications.
Ind/Abst Acoust. Abstr.; Agric. Eng. Abstr.; Bioeng. Abstr.; Ei Page One; Eng. Index Annu.; INSPEC (Oct. 1978-).

US
ELECTRONIC COMPONENTS - EXPORT LICENSING CONTROLS. **See** Business-Commerce.

US/0013-4872
ELECTRONIC DESIGN. [Electron. des.]. Vol. 1, No. 1 (Jan. 1953)-. Periodical. English. Twenty-six times a year. $100.00 US; $170.00 Canada; $180.00 Mexico; $200.00 other. Penton Publishing, 1100 Superior Avenue, Cleveland OH 44114-2543. **Tel** (216)696-7000, FAX (216)696-0836. **(Subscription address:** Penton Publishing, PO Box 96732, Chicago IL 60693.**)** **LC** TK7800; .E437. **DD** 621. **CODEN** ELODAW. **[CCC].** Index available in last issue of volume--attached. available on microfilm and microfiche from University Microfilms International (UMI); available on an online database (files 648,675/Full-Text) from DIALOG. Documents available from Article Express International, The Genuine Article, Ask*IEEE. ***Continued in part by*** *Microwaves (New York, N.Y.), 0026-2919.*
Desc: Electronic articles using schematics, graphs and photos; concentrates on the design problems faced by the electronics engineer and engineering manager.
Ind/Abst Abstr. Bull. Inst. Pap. Sci. Tech.; Acad. Search (July 1993-); Appl. Sci. Technol. Index; Bioeng. Abstr.; BMT Abstr. (-199?); Bus. ASAP (1990-) [Full Txt.]; Bus. Index (1985-); Bus. Source (Jul. 1993-); Comput. ASAP [Full Txt.]; Comput. Database [Full Txt.]; Comput. Rev. (1981-); Curr. Contents Eng. Tech. Appl. Sci.; Ei Page One; Energy Res. Abstr.; Eng. Index Annu.; Expand. Acad. Index (1992-); Gen. BusinessFile (1985-); Gen. Period. Index (1985-); Infomat Int. Bus.; INIS Atomindex [Micro.]; INSPEC (Oct. 1969-); Int. Aerosp. Abstr.; Leadscan; Mag. Search; Res. Alert [Full Cov.]; SCISEARCH; Trade Ind. Index (1981-?); World Publ. Monit.

US/0738-0399
ELECTRONIC DESIGN'S GOLD BOOK. ***Ceased.*** [Electron. des. Gold book]. **VFOAT** Gold Book. (1974)-(1988). Catalog. English. an. Hayden Publishing Company Inc, 10 Mulholland Drive, Hasbrouck Heights NJ 07604. **Tel** (201)393-6253. **ED** John R Tavaska. **LC** TK7870; .E47. **DD** 621.381/029/34. **Ad Acc. Circ:** 120,000 (ctrl). ***Continues*** *Electronic Designer's Catalog.*
Desc: Directory and master catalog of electronic components, pub-systems and systems.

US/0890-8699
ELECTRONIC DISPLAY NEWS. ***Ceased.*** [Electron. disp. news]. **VFOAT** EDN. Vol. 1, No. 1 (Sept./Oct. 1986)-(19??). Periodical. English. Six times a year. Electronic Display News, 134 Baltimore Street, PO Box 209, Cumberland MD 21501. **Tel** (301)777-0453. **DD** 338.

UK/0013-4902
ELECTRONIC ENGINEERING. **Added/Corp** Television Society (Great Britain). Vol. 1 (1928)-. Periodical. English. mo. £70.00 UK and Northern Ireland; $165.00 other. Morgan Grampian, 40 Beresford Street Woolwich, London SE18 6BQ England. **Tel** 011 44 81 855 7777, FAX 011 44 81 855 5548, telex 896238. **ED** Ron Neale. **[CCC].** Index available. **Ad Acc.** ctrl circ. available on microfilm and microfiche from University Microfilms International (UMI); available on an online database (file 648/Full-Text) from DIALOG. Documents available from Article Express International, The Genuine Article, Ask*IEEE.
Ind/Abst Appl. Sci. Technol. Index; BMT Abstr. (-199?); Curr. Contents Eng. Tech. Appl. Sci.; Curr. Technol. Index; Eng. Index Annu.; F&S Index Plus Text, Int. [Select. Cov.]; Infomat Int. Bus.; INSPEC (1968-); Leadscan; Predicasts F&S Index, U. S. Annu. Ed.; PROMT; Res. Alert [Select. Cov.]; SCISEARCH.

US/0192-1541
ELECTRONIC ENGINEERING TIMES. [Electron. eng. times]. (197?)-. Periodical. English. wk. $159.00 US. CMP Publications Inc., c/o B. Werner, One Jericho Plaza, Wing A, 2nd Floor, Jericho NY 11753. **Tel** (516)733-6700. **(Subscription address:** CMP Publications, Inc. / New York, PO Box 4037, Church Street Station, New York NY 10261-4037.**)** **DD** 621. **[CCC].** available on an online database (file 16/Full-Text) from DIALOG.
Desc: Delivers business and technological news of strategic importance to engineers and technical managers in the electronics industry.
Ind/Abst Acad. Search (July 1993-); Comput. Database; F&S Index Plus Text, Int. [Full Txt.] [Select. Cov.]; INFO-SOUTH Abstr.; Mag. Search; PROMT [Full Txt.]; Robotics Abstr.

US/0732-9016
ELECTRONIC ENGINEERS MASTER CATALOG. (ELECTRONIC ENGINEERS MASTER CATALOG : EEM.). [Electr. eng. master cat.]. **VFOAT** EEM. (19??)-. Catalog. English. an. $95.00 US; $160.00 Europe & Latin America; $175.00 other. Hearst Business Communications, 1790 Broadway, New York NY 10019. **Tel** (212)969-7500, FAX (212)969-7564. **LC** TK7870.3; .E37. **DD** 621.3/029/4. ***Continues*** *Electronic Engineers Master, 0423-9938.*

US/0164-3762
ELECTRONIC FIELD ENGINEER, THE. **VFOAT** Field Engineer. Periodical. English. mo. $6.00 US; $20.00 other. DF & M Communications, 360 North Michigan Avenue, Chicago IL 60601.

US/1057-0942
ELECTRONIC IMAGING REPORT. ***Title Change.*** **See** Computers.

US/0735-3316
ELECTRONIC INDUSTRY MANUFACTURERS REPRESENTATIVES LOCATOR. **See** Manufacturing.

US
ELECTRONIC INDUSTRY OUTLOOK. English. qt. $625.00. HTE Management, PO Box 621, Santa Cruz 95061-0621.
Desc: Forecasts and analyzes the electronics industry including exclusive components to equipment interrelationships and proprietary educators. Intensive use of computer generated charts and concise format.

US/0270-0093
ELECTRONIC MARKET DATA BOOK. [Electron. mark. data book]. 1970-. English. an. $100.00 US (add $12.00 for postage) other. Electronic Industries Association, 2001 Pennsylvania Avenue Northwest, Washington DC 20006. **Tel** (202)457-4900, telex 710-822-0148 EIA WSH. **LC** HD9696.A3; U539. **DD** 381/.45/62130973. ***Supersedes*** *Electronic Industries Yearbook; Electronic Industries Review, 0422-9045.*
Desc: Single most comprehensive source of information on the US electronic industries today. 140 pages of text, and over 100 tables, charts and graphs.
Ind/Abst Predicasts Forecasts.

US/0886-8506
ELECTRONIC MARKET TRENDS. (ELECTRONIC MARKET TRENDS / ELECTRONIC INDUSTRIES ASSOCIATION.). [Electron. mark. trends]. **Added/Corp** Electronic Industries Association. (19??)-. Periodical. English. Twelve times a year. $159.00 Washington, DC, $150.00 others (surface mail); $186.00 (airmail). Electronic Industries Association, 2001 Pennsylvania Avenue Northwest, Washington DC 20006. **Tel** (202)457-4900, telex 710-822-0148 EIA WSH. **ED** Shannon Brinkley (editor's telephone: (202)457-4981). **DD** 338. **Bk Rev.** ctrl circ.
Desc: Reports market trends and new technologies in the electronic industries. Includes statistical summary.

●US/1071-247X
ELECTRONIC MARKETPLACE REPORT. (ELECTRONIC MARKETPLACE REPORT / SIMBA INFORMATION COMMUNICATION TRENDS.). (1993)-. Periodical. English. mo. $432.00 (one year), $778.00 (two year). Simba Information Inc., 213 Danbury Road, Wilton CT 06897-7430. **Tel** (203)834-0033 ext. 133, FAX (203)884-1771. **(Subscription address:** Simba Information Inc., PO Box 7430, Wilton CT 06897.**)** ***Continues*** *Electronic Directory & Classified Report.*

UK
ELECTRONIC MATERIALS. English. mo. £249.00 UK; $435.00 other. World Business Publications Ltd., 960 High Road, Britannia 4th Floor, London N12 9RY England. **Tel** 11 44 81 446 5141, FAX 11 44 81 446 3659, telex 9419208.

UK/0957-9737
ELECTRONIC MATERIALS AND PROCESSING. [Electron. mater. process.]. (1990)-. Periodical. English. Six times a year. $388.00 The Americas; £260.00 other. Elsevier Advanced Technology, An Imprint of Elsevier Science Ltd., The Boulevard, Langford Lane, Kidlington, Oxford OX5 1GB United Kingdom. **Tel** 011 44 865 843000, 011 44 865 843699, FAX 011 44 865 843010. **(Subscription address:** Elsevier Science Ltd. Oxford Fulfillment Centre, PO Box 800, Kidlington, Oxford OX5 1DX United Kingdom.**)** available on microfilm from University Microfilms International (UMI). Documents available from Article Express International.
Desc: This newsletter covers developments in the field of electronic and optoelctronic materials, manufacturing techniques, and equipment, and new devices and applications.
Ind/Abst Eng. Index Annu.; PTS Newsl. Database [Full Txt.].

US/1045-0955
ELECTRONIC MATERIALS TECHNOLOGY NEWS. (ELECTRONIC MATERIALS TECHNOLOGY NEWS : A MONTHLY NEWSLETTER FROM BUSINESS COMMUNICATIONS COMPANY, INC.). [Electron. mater. technol. news]. **Added/Corp** Business Communications Company. (1986)-. Newsletter. English. mo. $325.00. Business Communications Inc., 25 Van Zant Street, Suite 13, Norwalk CT 06855. **Tel** (203)853-4266. **DD** 621. available on an online database (file 636/Full-Text) from DIALOG.
Ind/Abst PTS Newsl. Database [Full Txt.].

US/1044-9892
ELECTRONIC MESSAGING NEWS. **See** Communication.

US/0275-9136
ELECTRONIC MODELING. ***Title Change.*** [Electron. model.]. **VFOAT** Elektronnoe Modelirovanie. No. 1 (1981)-. Periodical. English (Russian). bm. Gordon & Breach Science Publishers, Inc., PO Box 786, Cooper Station, New York NY 10276. **Tel** (212)206-8900, FAX (212)645-2459. **(Subscription address:** International Publishers Distributor at one of the following addresses: 820 Town Center Drive, Langhorne, PA 19047; or PO Box 90, Reading Berkshire RG1 8JL UK; or Kent Ridge PO Box 1180, Singapore 9111, Republic of Singapore**)** **ED** G Y Pukhov. **LC** QA75.5; .E56. **CODEN** EMODD8. **[CCC]. Bk Rev. Ad Acc.** available in microform. Documents available from Article Express International, Ask*IEEE. ***Continued by*** *Engineering Simulation.*
Ind/Abst Bioeng. Abstr.; Ei Page One; Eng. Index Annu.; INSPEC (1985).

US/0197-2685
ELECTRONIC NEW PRODUCT DIRECTORY, THE. [Electron. new prod. dir.]. Directory. English. 402 Border Road, Concord MA 01742. **LC** TK7870.3; .E38. **DD** 621.381/029/473. ***Continues*** *New Electronic Products Directory, 0195-8984.*

AT
ELECTRONIC NEWS. English. 60.00Aus$ Australia; 110.00Aus$ other. Reed Business Publishing Pty Ltd. / Australia, 1 5 Railway Street, Level 12 North Tower, Chatswood W 2067 NSW Australia. **Tel** 011 61 2 3725222, FAX 011 61 2 4197533.

US/1061-6624
ELECTRONIC NEWS (1991). (ELECTRONIC NEWS.). [Electron. news]. Vol. 37, No. 1886 (Nov. 11, 1991)-. Periodical. English. wk. $69.00 (one year), $99.00 (two year) US; $149.00 Canada; $299.00 other. IDG Communications / New York, 488 Madison Avenue, 6th Floor, New York NY 10022. **Tel** (212)909-5900. **(Subscription address:** Electronic News, PO Box 1978, Danbury CT 06813.**) DD** 338. available on an online database (files 16,648,675/Full-Text) from DIALOG. ***Continues*** *Chilton's Electronic News, 1054-6847.*
Ind/Abst Acad. Ind. [Computer File] (1992-); Acad. Search (July 1993-); Bus. ASAP (199?-) [Full Txt.]; Bus. Period. Index; Bus. Source (Jul. 1993-); Comput. ASAP [Full Txt.]; Comput. Bus. (199?-); Comput. Database [Full Txt.]; Comput. Lit. Index; Expand. Acad. Index (1992-); INFO-SOUTH Abstr.; Infomat Int. Bus.; Mag. Search; Predicasts; Trade Ind. ASAP [Full Txt.]; Trade Ind. Index [Full Txt.]; Wilson Bus. Abstr.

US/0013-4945
ELECTRONIC PACKAGING AND PRODUCTION. [Electron. packag. prod.]. **VFOAT** Electronic Packaging & Production. Vol. 1 (July/Aug. 1961)-. Periodical. English. mo. $85.00 US; $123.00 Canada; $115.00 Mexico; $150.00 (surface mail) other. Cahners Publishing Company, 249 West 17th Street, New York NY 10011. **Tel** (212)645-0067, FAX (212)242-6987. **(Subscription address:** Cahners Publishing Company / Colorado, Paid Subscription Service Center, PO Box 7610, Highlands Ranch CO 80126-7610.**) LC** TK7870; .E54. **DD** 621.7/57. **CODEN** ELPPA5. **[CCC].** available on microfilm and microfiche from University Microfilms International (UMI). Documents available from Article Express International, Ask*IEEE. ***Absorbed*** *Electronic Production, 0306-333X.*
Desc: Brings the engineer and manufacturing executive a complete news and feature package on the business of assembly and design of electronic goods, including objective comparisons of products, and the processes and techniques intended to help the reader make purchasing and design decisions.
Ind/Abst Bioeng. Abstr.; Ceram. Abstr.; Ei Page One; Eng. Index Annu.; INSPEC (April 1977-).

JA
ELECTRONIC PARTS & MATERIALS. DENSHI ZAIRYO. Japanese. mo. $194.00. Kogyo Chosakai, (Kogyo Chosakai Publishing Co., Ltd.), 14-7, Hongo 2 Chome, Bunkyoku, Tokyoto 113, Japan. **(Subscription address:** Kyowa Book Company Inc., 1-38 Kanda Jinbo-Cho, Chiyoda-Ku, Tokyo 101, Japan (Phone: 03-3293-0727))

UK/0263-1474
ELECTRONIC PRODUCT DESIGN. [Electron. prod. des.]. (19??)-. Periodical. English. mo. £55.00 UK; £75.00 Europe; £100.00 other. IML Group, Blair House, 184-186 High Street, Tonbridge Kent, TN9 1BQ England. **Tel** 011 44 732 359990, FAX 011 44 732 770049. **ED** Graham Prophet. **CODEN** EPDEDB. **Ad Acc, Adv Mgr:** Patrick Flynn. ctrl circ. Documents available from Ask*IEEE.
Desc: Edited specifically for managers and engineers engaged in electronics design and research and development.
Ind/Abst Ei Page One; Fluid Abstr., Civil Eng.; Fluid Abstr. Proc. Eng.; FLUIDEX (1973-1991); INSPEC (1980-).

BE
ELECTRONIC PRODUCT NEWS. English. mo (13 times a year). 3.000F. Pan European Publishing Company, rue Verte 216, 1210 Brussels 21 Belgium. **Tel** 011 32 2 2420611.

BE
ELECTRONIC PRODUCT NEWS ASIA. English. Seven times a year. 3.000F. Pan European Publishing Company, rue Verte 216, 1210 Brussels 21 Belgium. **Tel** 011 32 2 2420611.

UK/0269-3216
ELECTRONIC PRODUCT REVIEW. [Electron. prod. rev.]. (198?)-. Periodical. English. mo. $159.00 US; £35.00 UK. Wilmington Publishing Ltd., PO Box 200, Field End Road, Ruislip Middx HA4 0SY England. **Tel** 011 44 81 841 3970, FAX 011 44 81 841 9676.
Ind/Abst Infomat Int. Bus. (19??-).

US/0013-4953
ELECTRONIC PRODUCTS (1981). (ELECTRONIC PRODUCTS.). [Electron. prod.]. Vol. 23, No. 10 (Mar. 1981)-. Periodical. English. mo. $50.00. Hearst Business Communications, 1790 Broadway, New York NY 10019. **Tel** (212)969-7500, FAX (212)969-7564. **(Subscription address:** NSC Limited, PO Box 2029, Sturminster Newton, Dorset, England DT10 1YE.**) ED** Frank Egan. **DD** 621. **CODEN** ELPOA2. **Bk Rev. Ad Acc. Pr Rev. Circ:** 126,000 (ctrl). available on microfilm and microfiche from University Microfilms International (UMI). Documents available from The Genuine Article, Ask*IEEE. ***Continues*** *Electronic Products Magazine.*
Desc: Information on electronic products and their application.
Ind/Abst Acoust. Abstr.; Curr. Contents Eng. Tech. Appl. Sci.; Ei Page One; F&S Index Plus Text, Int. [Select. Cov.]; INSPEC (Oct. 1985-); Res. Alert [Select. Cov.]; SCISEARCH; Trade Ind. Index.

CN/0708-4366
ELECTRONIC PRODUCTS AND TECHNOLOGY. (EP&T : ELECTRONIC PRODUCTS AND TECHNOLOGY.). [Electron. prod. technol.]. **VFOAT** Electronic Products and Technology; E P & T; Electronic Products & Technology. Vol. 7, No. 5 (Sept./Oct. 1985)-. Periodical. English. ir (7 issues). 42.00Can$ Canada; 66.00Can$ US; 78.00Can$ other. Electronic Products Technology, 27-1200 Aerowood Drive, Mississauga Ontario L4W 2S7 Canada. **Tel** (416)624-8100. **DD** 338.4/762138/0971. **Ad Acc, Adv Mgr:** R Luton, **Tel** (416)624-8100. **Circ:** 22,000 (ctrl). available on microfilm. ***Continues*** *Electronic Products and Technology., 0708-4366.*
Desc: Provides timely, comprehensive coverage of the latest worldwide developments and trends in electronic products, equipment and systems and interprets their significance to manufacturers and end users in the Canadian market place.

US
ELECTRONIC PROPERTIES OF MATERIALS; A GUIDE TO THE LITERATURE. (1965)-. English. ir. Plenum Press, 233 Spring Street, New York NY 10013-1578. **Tel** (212)620-8000, (800)221-9369, FAX (212)463-0742, (212)807-1047, telex 23/421139.

US/0887-4336
ELECTRONIC REPRESENTATIVES DIRECTORY. [Electron. represent. dir.]. **VFOAT** ERD. (19??)-. Directory. English. an (March). $30.00. Harris Publishing Company, 2057-2 Aurora Road, Twinsburg OH 44087. **Tel** (800)888-5900, (216)425-9000, FAX (216)425-7150, telex 510 601 1740. **ED** Frances L. Carlsen. **LC** TK7805; .E34. **DD** 381/.45621381/02573. available on CD-ROM and diskette.
Desc: Covers over 4,800 independent representative firms. Full data includes telephone number, address, personnel, territories served, lines handled, types of markets served and more.

US/0730-1189
ELECTRONIC RETAILING (NEW YORK, N.Y.). (ELECTRONICS RETAILING.). [Electron. retail.]. (1981)-. Periodical. English. bm. Fairchild Publications Inc, 7 West 34th Street, 4th Floor, New York NY 10001. **Tel** (212)630-4230. **LC** HD9696.A1; E54. **DD** 381/.4568383/0973. ***Continues in part*** *HFD/Retailing Home Furnishings, 0162-9158.*

US
ELECTRONIC SERVICES UPDATE. (19??)-. Periodical. English. mo. $495.00. International Data Corporation, 5 Speen Street, PO Box 9015, Framingham MA 01701. **Tel** (508)872-8200, (508)935-4443. **(Subscription address:** IDG News Letter Corp, 77 Franklin Street, Boston MA 02111.**)** available on an online database (file 636/Full-Text) from DIALOG.
Ind/Abst PTS Newsl. Database [Full Txt.].

US/0278-9922
ELECTRONIC SERVICING & TECHNOLOGY. [Electron. serv. technol.]. **VFOAT** Electronic Servicing and Technology. Vol. 1, No. 1 (Nov. 1981)-. Periodical. English. mo. $24.75 US & possessions; $30.75 other. CQ Communications Inc., 76 North Broadway, Hicksville NY 11801. **Tel** (516)681-2922, FAX (516)681-2926. **ED** Nils Conrad Persson. **LC** TK7870; .E547. **DD** 621.381/028/8. **Bk Rev. Ad Acc. Circ:** 49,450. available on microfilm and microfiche from University Microfilms International (UMI). ***Continues*** *Electronic Servicing, 0013-497X;* ***Absorbed*** *Electronic Technician/Dealer.*
Desc: How-to technical format is tailored for the professional consumer electronics servicer and the active servicing enthusiast; articles discuss the latest in test equipment, tools and replacement parts, and show step-by-step procedures for maintaining VCRs, CD players, televisions, personal computers and the entire realm of consumer electronics.

●US/1063-1100
ELECTRONIC SIMULATION. (1992)-. Periodical. English. bm (2 volumes). $1271.00 (academic institutions), $1983.00 (corporate institutions). Gordon & Breach Science Publishers, Inc., PO Box 786, Cooper Station, New York NY 10276. **Tel** (212)206-8900, FAX (212)645-2459. **(Subscription address:** International Publishers Distributor at one of the following addresses: 820 Town Center Drive, Langhorne, PA 19047; or PO Box 90, Reading Berkshire RG1 8JL UK; or Kent Ridge PO Box 1180, Singapore 9111, Republic of Singapore**) CODEN** ENSIEH. **[CCC].** Documents available from Article Express International, Ask*IEEE. ***Continues*** *Elektronnoe Modelirovanie. English, 0275-9136.*
Ind/Abst Bioeng. Abstr.; Ei Page One; Eng. Index Annu.; INSPEC.

US/8755-1527
ELECTRONIC SOURCE BOOK FOR SOUTHERN CALIFORNIA, THE. English. an. $19.50. Paramount Publishing Inc, 13422 Weymouth Street, Westminister CA 92683. **Tel** (714)897-9576, FAX (714)893-0820. **ED** Ilana Goldberg. **LC** TK7805; .E35. **DD** 338.4/7621381/0257949. Index available. cum. index. **Ad Acc. Circ:** 12,000 (ctrl). available on CD-ROM; available on diskette.
Desc: Regional procurement directory for buyers and engineers dealing with electronic components and subassemblies. Cross referenced by manufacturer, distributor, value-added services, products or representatives.

US
ELECTRONIC SYSTEMS FORECAST. (19??)-. English. Twelve times a year. $1390.00. Forecast International / DMS Inc., 22 Commerce Road, Newtown CT 06470. **Tel** (203)426-0800, FAX (203)426-1964, telex 467615. available on CD-ROM ($1595.00).

US/0895-8742
ELECTRONIC SYSTEMS INFORMATION BULLETIN. (ELECTRONICS SYSTEMS INFORMATION BULLETIN / U.S. DEPARTMENT OF TRANSPORTATION, UNITED STATES COAST GUARD.). [Electron. syst. inf. bull.]. **Added/Corp** United States. Coast Guard. **VFOAT** ESIB. (198?)-. Bulletin. English. mo. US Coast Guard, 2100 2nd Street Southwest, Washington DC 20590. **Tel** (202)267-1408. **DD** 621. cum. index. ***Continues*** *Electronics Engineering Information Bulletin, 0145-1316.*

UK/0141-061X
ELECTRONIC TECHNOLOGY (LONDON). ***Ceased.*** (ELECTRONIC TECHNOLOGY.). [Electron. technol.]. **Added/Corp** Society of Electronic and Radio Technicians. Vol. 12 (Jan. 1978)-Vol. 23 (Dec. 1990). Periodical. English. mo. Society of Electronic & Radio Technicians, 57-61 Newington Causeway, London SE1 6BL England. **Tel** 01-403 2351, FAX 01-378 0291. **ED** I.R.G. Channing. **CODEN** ETSTDN. Index available. **Bk Rev. Ad Acc. Circ:** 8,300. Documents available from Ask*IEEE. ***Continues*** *SERT Journal, 0308-2377.*
Desc: Articles, news, product news, and institution news.
Ind/Abst Curr. Technol. Index; INSPEC (Jan. 1978-1990); World Publ. Monit. (Jan. 1978-1990).

UK
ELECTRONIC TRADER. English. mo (July/Aug. combined). Hastings Hilton Ltd, 630 Chisusick High Road, Lindon W4 5BG. **Tel** 011 44 81 7422828. **(Subscription address:** BKT Subscription Services, 196 High Stret, Tonbridge Kent 7N9 1EF**) ED** Barnaby Harris. **Bk Rev. Ad Acc, Adv Mgr:** Kate Lauton. **Circ:** 5000 (ctrl).
Desc: Information relating to electronic data interchange. This is of interest to anyone involved in EDI. Covers European and world issues.

US/0013-5011
ELECTRONIC TRENDS INTERNATIONAL. (ELECTRONIC TRENDS INTERNATIONAL / PREPARED BY THE MARKETING SERVICES DEPARTMENT, ELECTRONIC INDUSTRIES ASSOCIATION.). [Electron. trends int.]. **Added/Corp** Electronic Industries Association. Marketing Services Dept. Vol. 1, No. 1 (Oct. 1967)-. Periodical. English. mo. Electronic Industries Association, 2001 Pennsylvania Avenue Northwest, Washington DC 20006. **Tel** (202)457-4900, telex 710-822-0148 EIA WSH. **ED** Karen E. Thuermer. **LC** HD9696.A1; E52. **DD** 382/.45621381/05.
Desc: Reports market trends and new technologies in the electronic industries.

US/0884-4828
ELECTRONIC WARFARE DIGEST. **See** Military and Defense.

US
ELECTRONIC WARFARE FORECAST. **See** Military and Defense.

US/1045-6627
ELECTRONIC WORLD NEWS. ***Ceased.*** [Elec. world news]. (198?)-(1993). Periodical. English. Twenty times a year. CMP Publications Inc., c/o B. Werner, One Jericho Plaza, Wing A, 2nd Floor, Jericho NY 11753. **Tel** (516)733-6700. **LC** HD9696.A1; E53. **DD** 338.4/7821381/05. Documents available from Ask*IEEE.
Desc: Serving the needs of electronics industry managers who do business worldwide. This global perspective includes news of technology developments and trends, new product information and industry news.
Ind/Abst Abstr. Hum. Comput. Interact.; F&S Index Plus Text, Int. [Full Txt.] [Select. Cov.]; INSPEC (Dec. 1989-); PROMT [Full Txt.].

SP/0213-0400
ELECTRONICA HOY. Spanish. mo. 7526.00ptas. VNU Business Publications / Spain, Cinca 13, 28002 Madrid Spain. **Tel** 011 34 1 563-8100, FAX 011 34 1 563-7572.

US/0883-4989
ELECTRONICS (1985). (ELECTRONICS.). [Electronics]. Vol. 58, No. 24 (June 17, 1985)-. Academic Scholarly Publication. English. Twenty-three times a year. $98.00 US; $120.00 Canada; $140.00 Mexico; $190.00 other. Penton Publishing, 1100 Superior Avenue, Cleveland OH 44114-2543. **Tel** (216)696-7000, FAX (216)696-0836. **(Subscription address:** Penton Publishing, PO Box 96732, Chicago IL 60693.**) LC** TK7800; .E4384. **DD** 621.381. **[CCC]. Ad Acc. Circ:** 97,116 (ctrl). available on microfilm and microfiche from University Microfilms International (UMI). Documents available from Article Express International, The Genuine Article, Ask*IEEE, UMI Article Clearinghouse. ***Continues*** *ElectronicsWeek, 0748-3252.*
Desc: Primary management publication devoted to covering the worldwide electronics industry. Audience is executives and engineers that design and manufacture electronic equipment or components.
Ind/Abst Abstr. Bull. Inst. Pap. Sci. Tech.; Acad. Abstr. Full Text Elite (Jan. 1991-); Acad. Abstr. (Jan. 1991-); Acad. Ind. [Computer File] (1985-); Acad. Search (Jan. 1991-); Appl. Sci. Technol. Index; Bioeng. Abstr.; Bus. ASAP (1990-) [Full Txt.]; Bus. Index (1985-); Ceram. Abstr.; Comput. ASAP [Full Txt.]; Comput. Bus.; Comput. Database [Full Txt.]; Ei Page One; EMBASE; Eng. Index Annu.; Expand. Acad. Index (1985-); F&S Index Plus Text, Int. [Select. Cov.]; Fluid Abstr., Civil Eng.; Fluid Abstr. Proc. Eng.; FLUIDEX (1985-); Gen. BusinessFile (1985-); Gen. Period. Index (1985-); INFO-SOUTH Abstr.; Infomat Int. Bus.; INIS Atomindex [Micro.]; INSPEC (?-1986); Mag. ASAP Plus [Full Txt.]; Mag. Index Plus (1989-); Mag. Search; Newsp. Period. Abstr. (1988-); PROMT; Res. Alert [Full Cov.]; Sci. Cit. Index; SCISEARCH; Soc. Sci. Cit. Index [Select. Cov.]; Stat. Ref. Index; Mag. Index (1985-); Trade Ind. ASAP [Full Txt.]; Trade Ind. Index (1985-) [Full Txt.].

UK/0013-5119
ELECTRONICS & COMMUNICATIONS ABSTRACTS. ***Ceased.*** [Electron. commun. abstr.]. **VFOAT** Electronics and Communications Abstracts. Vol. 1 (Sept./Oct. 1961)-Vol. 33, No. 4 (Dec. 1994). Periodical. English. mo. Multi Science Publishing Company Ltd., 107 High Street, Brentwood, Essex CM14 4RX England. **Tel** 011 44 277 224632, FAX 011 44 277 223453, telex 89-8452. **LC** TK5101.A1; E48. **CODEN** ECOAAS. **[CCC].**
Desc: Scans the world's major scientific and technical and periodicals, summarizes the most important papers from them, translating where necessary, and classifies them under 38 headings. Over 7,000 papers are summarized yearly to give a uniquely valuable synoptic survey of world activity in electronics, communications and the disciplines that contribute to their advancement.
Ind/Abst GeoRef.

●US/1069-5303
ELECTRONICS AND COMMUNICATIONS ABSTRACTS. See Engineering-Abstracting, Bibliographies and Statistics.

US/0361-3313
ELECTRONICS AND COMMUNICATIONS ABSTRACTS JOURNAL (RIVERDALE, MD.). ***Title Change.*** **See** Engineering-Abstracting, Bibliographies and Statistics.

UK/0954-0695
ELECTRONICS & COMMUNICATIONS ENGINEERING JOURNAL. Added/Corp Institution of Electrical Engineers. **VFOAT** Electronics and Communications Engineering Journal. Vol. 1, No. 1 (Jan./Feb. 1989)-. Periodical. English. Six times a year. £83.00 EEC countries; £92.00 other. Institution of Electrical Engineers / IEE, Michael Faraday House, Six Hills Way, Stevenage Herts SG1 2AY UK. **Tel** 011 44 438 313311, FAX 011 44 438 742840, telex 825578 IEESTV G. **(Subscription address:** IEE / UK, Publications Sales Department, PO Box 96, Stevenage, Herts, SG1 2SD England.**) LC** TK6540; .B838. **DD** 621.381/05. **CODEN** ECEJE9. **[CCC].** Documents available from Article Express International, The Genuine Article, Ask*IEEE. ***Continues*** *Journal of the Institution of Electronic and Radio Engineers, 0267-1689.*
Ind/Abst Eng. Index Annu.; INSPEC (Jan./Feb. 1989-); Res. Alert [Full Cov.]; Sci. Cit. Index; SCISEARCH.

US/8756-6621
ELECTRONICS & COMMUNICATIONS IN JAPAN. PART 1, COMMUNICATIONS. [Electron. commun. Jpn., Part 1, Commun.]. **Added/Corp** Denshi Tsushin Gakkai. Scripta Technica, inc. **VFOAT** Electronics and Communications in Japan. Vol. 68, No. 1 (Jan. 1985)-. Periodical. English (translations available in Japanese). Thirty-six times a year. $3,780.00 US; $4,140.00 Canada and Mexico; $4,275.00 other (Parts 1, 2 and 3). Scripta Technica, A Subsidiary of John Wiley & Sons, Inc., 7961 Eastern Avenue, Silver Spring MD 20910. **Tel** (301)588-0484, FAX (301)588-5278. **ED** Tatsuo Itoh. **LC** TK5101.A1; E47. **DD** 621.38/05. available on microfilm and microfiche from University Microfilms International (UMI). Documents available from Article Express International, Ask*IEEE. ***Continues in part*** *Electronics & Communications in Japan, 0424-8368.*
Desc: A translation of papers from Transactions of the Institute of Electronics, Information and Communications Engineers of Japan. Published in Part I, Part II, and Part III. Part I deals with areas within the communication field, Part II covers the electronics field, Part III deals with the fundamentals of electronic science. Topics of study include pattern recognition, circuits and networks, analysis and design, and information systems.
Ind/Abst Ei Page One; Eng. Index Annu.; INSPEC (1985-); Math. Rev. (?-199?).

US/8756-663X
ELECTRONICS & COMMUNICATIONS IN JAPAN. PART 2, ELECTRONICS. [Electron. commun. Jpn., Part 2, Electron.]. **VFOAT** Electronics and Communications in Japan. Vol. 68, No. 1 (Jan. 1985)-. Periodical. English (translations available in Japanese). Thirty-six times a year. $3,780.00 US, $4,140.00 Canada and Mexico, $4,275.00 other (Parts 1, 2 and 3). Scripta Technica, A Subsidiary of John Wiley & Sons, Inc., 7961 Eastern Avenue, Silver Spring MD 20910. **Tel** (301)588-0484, FAX (301)588-5278. **LC** TK7800. **DD** 621.381/05. **CODEN** ECJEEJ. available on microfilm and microfiche from University Microfilms International (UMI). Documents available from Article Express International, Ask*IEEE. ***Continues in part*** *Electronics & Communications in Japan, 0424-8368.*
Ind/Abst Comput. Inf. Syst. Abstr. J. [Full Cov.]; Ei Page One; Elect. Comm. Abstr.; Eng. Index Annu.; INSPEC (1985-); Manuf. Process Eng. Abstr.; Mater. Sci. Eng. Abstr.; Math. Rev.; Solid State Supercond. Abstr.

US/1042-0967
ELECTRONICS AND COMMUNICATIONS IN JAPAN. PART 3, FUNDAMENTAL ELECTRONIC SCIENCE. [Elec. commun. Jap. Part 3 Fundam. elec. sci.]. **VFOAT** Fundamental Electronic Science. (1989)-. Periodical. English. Thirty-six times a year. $3,780.00 US, $4,140.00 Canada and Mexico, $4,275.00 other (Parts 1, 2 and 3). Scripta Technica, A Subsidiary of John Wiley & Sons, Inc., 7961 Eastern Avenue, Silver Spring MD 20910. **Tel** (301)588-0484, FAX (301)588-5278. **ED** Tatsuo Itoh. **CODEN** ECJSER. available on microfilm and microfiche from University Microfilms International (UMI). Documents available from Article Express International, Ask*IEEE.
Desc: This journal is a comprehensive translation of papers from 'Transactions of the Institute of Electronics and Communications Engineers of Japan'. The topics of study include pattern recognition, circuits and networks, analysis and design, and information systems.
Ind/Abst Ei Page One; Eng. Index Annu.; INSPEC (Jan. 1989-); Math. Rev.

AT/1036-0212
ELECTRONICS AUSTRALIA WITH ETI. [Electron. Aust. ETI]. (1990)-. Periodical. English. Twelve times a year. 53.00Aus$ Australia; 88.00Aus$ New Zealand & Papua New Guinea; 112.00Aus$ US & Canada; 119.00Aus$ Europe & Africa; 94.00Aus$ Singapore, Malaysia & Indonesia; 103.00Aus$ other. Federal Publishing Co Pty Ltd, PO Box 199, 180 Bourke Road, Alexandria New South Wales, 2015 Australia. **Tel** 011 61 2 693 6666, FAX 011 61 2 693 9935. **(Subscription address:** Federal Publishing Co. Pty Ltd., PO Box 199, Alexandria NSW 2015 Australia.**) DD** 621.38405. ***Formed by the union of*** *Electronics Australia, 0313-0150* ***and*** *Electronics Today International (Sydney. 1972), 0811-0727.*

US/0090-5291
ELECTRONICS BUYERS' GUIDE. ***Ceased.*** ( )-(1987/88). Consumer Publication. English. an. McGraw Hill Publishing Company, Inc., 1221 Avenue of the Americas, New York NY 10020. **Tel** (212)512-6410, (800)525-5003, FAX (212)512-6111. **LC** TK7870; .E24. **DD** 338.4/7/621381025. **NLM** TK 7803 E38.

CN/0046-1733
ELECTRONICS COMMUNICATOR. (THE ELECTRONICS COMMUNICATOR.). (1970)-. Periodical. English. Forty times a year. 575.00Can$; 10.00Can$ single issue. Evert Communications Ltd, 1296 Carling Avenue, Ottawa, Ontario, K1Z 7K8 Canada. **Tel** (613)728-4621, FAX (613)728-0385. **ED** Gordon D. Hutchison. Index available.
Desc: News and analysis of the industrial, technical and financial aspects of the Canadian electronics industry.

US/0898-7149
ELECTRONICS DISTRIBUTION TODAY. ***Ceased.*** [Electron. distrib. today]. **Added/Corp** National Electronic Distributors Association (U.S.). Vol. 131, No. 5 May (1987)-(19??). Periodical. English. mo. Intertec Publishing Corporation, 9800 Metcalf, Overland Park KS 66212. **Tel** (913)341-1300. **LC** HD9696.A1; E37. **DD** 381/.45621381/0973. ***Continues*** *EE's Electronics Distributor, 0734-175X.*

UK/0957-2953
ELECTRONICS EDUCATION (LONDON). (ELECTRONICS EDUCATION). [Electron. educ. Lond.]. (1990)-. Periodical. English. Three times a year. £9.00. Institution of Electrical Engineers / IEE, Michael Faraday House, Six Hills Way, Stevenage Herts SG1 2AY UK. **Tel** 011 44 438 313311, FAX 011 44 438 742840, telex 825578 IEESTV G. **(Subscription address:** IEE / UK, Publications Sales Department, PO Box 96, Stevenage, Herts, SG1 2SD England.**) DD** 621.38101105. ***Continues*** *Electronic Systems News, 0265-0096.*

US/0897-7631
ELECTRONICS HANDBOOK. (ELECTRONICS HANDBOOK / C&E HOBBY HANDBOOKS.). [Electron. handb.]. **Added/Corp** C&E Hobby Handbooks, Inc. (1986)-. Periodical. English. sa. $7.50 (2 issues), $15.00 (4 issues) US; $9.00 (2 issues), $18.00 (4 issues) Canada; $12.50 (2 issues), $25.00 (4 issues) other. C&E Hobby Handbooks, PO Box 5148, North Branch NJ 08876. **Tel** (201)231-1518. **DD** 621. ***Absorbed*** *Budget Electronics.*
Desc: This publication is directed to lay people who are interested in electronics. It provides information on topics such as transistors, magnetism, radio receivers, and cathode ray tubes

II/0304-9876
ELECTRONICS INFORMATION & PLANNING. [Electron. inf. plann.]. **Added/Corp** India. Electronics Commission. Information, Planning, and Analysis Group. **VAT** Electronics Information and Planning. Vol. 1 (Oct. 1973)-. Academic Scholarly Publication. English. mo. $35.00. Chairman Electronics Commission, Department of Electronics Ipag, Electronics Niketan, CGO Complex/Lodi Road, New Delhi 110-003 India. **Tel** 011 91 11 4360107, FAX 011 91 11 4363083, 011 91 11 4363134. **(Subscription address:** Prints India, 11 Darya Ganj, New Delhi 110002 India.**) ED** Pronab Sen (phone: 4363085). **LC** TK7812.I5; E4. **DD** 338.4/7/6213810954. **CODEN** ELIPB5ELPLDU. **Bk Rev. Ad Acc. Pr Rev.** ctrl circ. Documents available from The Genuine Article, Ask*IEEE, CASDDS.
Ind/Abst Chem. Abstr.; Curr. Contents Eng. Tech. Appl. Sci.; INSPEC (Oct. 1973-); Res. Alert [Select. Cov.]; SCISEARCH; Soc. Sci. Cit. Index [Select. Cov.].

US/0733-1614
ELECTRONICS INSIGHT. ***Ceased.*** [Electron. insight]. **Added/Corp** Arthur D. Little Decision Resources. Vol. 1, No. 1 (Aug. 1982)-(19??). Periodical. English. mo. Garland Publishing Inc, 1000A Sherman Avenue, Hamden CT 06514. **Tel** 800-627-6273, (203)281-4487.

US/0149-5542
ELECTRONICS INTERNATIONAL. [Electron. int.]. **VFOAT** Electronics. Periodical. English. bw. $14.00 US; $16.00 Canada. Circulation Sales, Electronics, PO Box 418, Hightstown NJ 08520. ctrl circ.
Ind/Abst World Publ. Monit.

CC
ELECTRONICS INTERNATIONAL CHINA REPORT. bw. $240.00 (one year), $450.00 (two year) China; $265.00 (one year), $500.00 (two year) other. Electronics International Publishing House, PO Box 750, Beijing 100039, People's Republic of China. **Tel** 011 86 810431.
Desc: Offers complete and skillfully condensed coverage of information about China's policies, investment environment, policies and market trends of electronic equipment, components and other high-tech products.

KO
ELECTRONICS KOREA. Periodical. English. mo. $60.00 US, $72.00 Europe, $48.00 Asia. Fine Instruments Center, Gurodanji PO Box 27, Seoul Korea. **Tel** 863-0611. **ED** Hae Lee. **Ad Acc. Circ:** 5,000 (ctrl).
Desc: Furnishes information about promising products and lively features on Korea's heavy industries including machinery, metals, shipbuilding and vehicles.

UK/0013-5194
ELECTRONICS LETTERS. [Electron. lett.]. **Added/Corp** Institution of Electrical Engineers. Vol. 1 (Mar. 1965)-. Periodical. English. Twenty-five times a year. £470.00. Institution of Electrical Engineers / IEE, Michael Faraday House, Six Hills Way, Stevenage Herts SG1 2AY UK. **Tel** 011 44 438 313311, FAX 011 44 438 742840, telex 825578 IEESTV G. **(Subscription address:** IEE / UK, Publications Sales Department, PO Box 96, Stevenage, Herts, SG1 2SD England.**) ED** K. Westwood. **LC** TK7800; .E4395. **DD** 621.381/05. **CODEN** ELLEAK. **[CCC].** cum. index. **Ad Acc. Pr Rev. Circ:** 2,200. available on microfilm from University Microfilms International (UMI); available on an online database (as Electronics Letters Online). Documents available from Article Express International, The Genuine Article, Ask*IEEE, CASDDS.
Desc: Offers rapid publication of the very latest research results in electronics and communications.
Ind/Abst Acoust. Abstr.; Alum. Ind. Abstr.; Bioeng. Abstr.; Ceram. Abstr.; Chem. Abstr.; Comput. Inf. Syst. Abstr. J. [Full Cov.]; Curr. Contents Eng. Tech. Appl. Sci.; Ei Page One; Elect. Comm. Abstr.; Eng. Mater. Abstr.; Eng. Index Annu.; INSPEC (1968-); Int. Aerosp. Abstr.; Leadscan; Manuf. Process Eng. Abstr.; Mater. Sci. Eng. Abstr.; Math. Rev.; Mech. Eng. Abstr.; Met. Abstr.; Res. Alert [Full Cov.]; Sci. Cit. Index; SCISEARCH; Solid State Supercond. Abstr.; Zentralbl. Math. Ihre Grenzgeb.

UK
ELECTRONICS MANAGEMENT. v. 1- Apr. 1973-. Periodical. English. mo. £6.00. Trade News Ltd, Pembroke House 3291 London England. **LC** TK7870; .E556. **DD** 338.4/7/6213810942.

UK/0265-301X
ELECTRONICS MANUFACTURE & TEST. [Electron. manuf. test]. **VFOAT** Electronics Manufacture and Test. (1982)-. Periodical. English. mo (11 issues per year). £55.00 UK; $75.00 other Europe; £100.00 other. IML Group, Blair House, 184-186 High Street, Tonbridge Kent, TN9 1BQ England. **Tel** 011 44 732 359990, FAX 011 44 732 770049. **ED** Gordon Wong. **DD** 621.381. **Bk Rev. Ad Acc, Adv Mgr:** Simon Eliis. **Circ:** 12,000 (ctrl). Documents available from Ask*IEEE.
Desc: Features manufacturing, quality assurance, and test articles in a technical format.
Ind/Abst INSPEC (June 1983-).

●US/1067-9294
ELECTRONICS NOW. [Electron. now]. **VFOAT** Radio Electronics Combined with Electronics Now. Vol. 63, No. 7 (July, 1992)-. Periodical. English. mo. $19.97. Gernsback Publications Inc, 500 B Bi-County Boulevard, Farmingdale NY 11735. **Tel** (516)293-3000. **(Subscription address:** Neodata / Colorado, PO Box 2606, Boulder Boulder CO 80322.**) ED** Brian Fenton. **LC** TK6540; .R34. **DD** 621. **CODEN** ELNOEU. Documents available from UMI Article Clearinghouse. ***Continues*** *Radio Electronics., 0033-7862.*
Desc: Presents articles on new technology, electronics construction, video, audio, computers, and more. For the electronics professional who truly enjoys electronics and for whom electronics is more than just a job.
Ind/Abst Acad. Abstr. (Mar. 1993-); Acad. Search (Mar. 1993-); Appl. Sci. Technol. Index; INFO-SOUTH Abstr.; Mag. Artic. Summar. Elite (Mar. 1993-); Mag. Artic. Summar. CD-ROM (March 1993-); Newsp. Period. Abstr. (1986-); Read. Guide Period. Lit.

CN/0826-2179
ELECTRONICS PRODUCT NEWS. ***Ceased.*** [Electron. prod. news]. (1983)-?. Periodical. English. ir. Electric Product News, 777 Bay Street, Toronto Ontario M5W 1A7 Canada. **Tel** (416)596-5070. **ED** Peter J Thorne and Deidre McMuroy. **DD** 338.4/7621381/0971. **Circ:** 20,000. ***Continues*** *Electronics Products News, 0826-2179.*
Desc: Brings new product information to Canadian design engineers, purchasing influences, specifiers and management; colorful, informative and professionally edited publication includes coverage of world electronic news and profiles of the latest new products available. Tabloid format.

US/0889-0196
ELECTRONICS PURCHASING. ***Title Change.*** [Electron. purch.]. (Sept. 1986)-(Sept. 1993). Periodical. English. mo. Cahners Publishing Company, 249 West 17th Street, New York NY 10011. **Tel** (212)645-0067, FAX (212)242-6987. **(Subscription address:** Cahners Publishing Company, Paid Subscription Service Center, 44 Cook Street, Denver, CO 80206**) DD** 658. **CODEN** ELEPEM. **[CCC].** available on microfilm and microfiche from University Microfilms International (UMI). Documents available from Ask*IEEE. ***Merged into*** *Electronic Business Buyer.*
Desc: Provides information for purchasing managers and buyers in the OEM electronics market and covers such subjects as electronic componenet pricing, leadtimes, products, quality concerns and supplier trends, supplier evaluation, purchasing techniques, etc. It also provides interpretive analysis and forecasts aimed at helping readers make better purchasing decisions.
Ind/Abst INSPEC (1987-).

UK
ELECTRONICS RESEARCH CENTRES. English. ir. $475.00. Longman Group Ltd., Fourth Avenue, Longman House, Harlow Essex CM19 5SR England. **Tel** 011 44 279 429655, FAX 011 44 279 431059, telex 81259. **(Subscription address:** Fourth Avenue, Harlow Essex CM19 5AA England**)**
Desc: Reference guide to electronic research which includes 3,500 detailed profiles of corporate and academic laboratories in 60 countries.

US/0149-9203
ELECTRONICS RETAILING. See Business-Retail.

UK/0269-2309
ELECTRONICS SHOWCASE. (1985)-. English. mo.
Ind/Abst Fluid Abstr., Civil Eng.; Fluid Abstr. Proc. Eng.; FLUIDEX (19??-).

US
ELECTRONICS SOURCE BOOK FOR SOUTH ATLANTIC, THE. VFOAT Electronic Source Book for South Atlantic. English. an. $19.50. Paramount Publishing Inc, 13422 Weymouth Street, Westminister CA 92683. **Tel** (714)897-9576, FAX (714)893-0820. **ED** Ilana Goldberg. **LC** TK7805; .E43. **DD** 621.381/02575. Index available. cum. index. **Ad Acc. Circ:** 12,000 (ctrl). available on CD-ROM; available on diskette.
Desc: Regional procurement directory for buyers and engineers dealing with electronic components and subassemblies. Cross referenced by manufacturer, distributor, value-added services, products or representatives.

US
ELECTRONICS SOURCE BOOK. SOUTHWEST, THE. (19??)-. English. an. $22.00. Paramount Publishing Inc, 13422 Weymouth Street, Westminister CA 92683. **Tel** (714)897-9576, FAX (714)893-0820. **ED** Ilana Goldberg. **LC** TK7805; .E42. **DD** 621.381/02575. Index available. cum. index. **Circ:** 12,000 (ctrl). available on diskette; available on CD-ROM.
Desc: Regional procurement directory for buyers and engineers dealing with electronic components and subassemblies. Cross referenced by manufacturer, distributor, value-added services, products or representatives.

UK
ELECTRONICS TIMES. (1978)-. English. wk. £80.00 UK and Northern Ireland; $215.00 other. Morgan Grampian, 40 Beresford Street Woolwich, London SE18 6BQ England. **Tel** 011 44 81 855 7777, FAX 011 44 81 855 5548, telex 896238. **ED** John Taylor. **Bk Rev. Ad Acc. Circ:** 42,000 (ctrl). available on microfilm and microfiche from University Microfilms International (UMI).
Ind/Abst PROMT [Full Txt.].

II/0374-3063
ELECTRONICS TODAY BOMBAY. [Electron. Today Bombay]. (1968)-. Periodical. English. mo. $50.00. **(Subscription address:** Prints India, 11 Darya Ganj, New Delhi 110002 India.**) UDC** 621.38.

UK/0811-0727
ELECTRONICS TODAY INTERNATIONAL. [Electron. today int.]. (1972)-. Periodical. English. Twelve times a year. £23.40 UK; $56.00 other. Argus Specialist Publications, Queensway House, 2 Queensway Redhill, Surrey RH1 1QS England. **Tel** 0737 768611, FAX 0737 773993, telex 948669 TOPJNL G. **ED** David Kelly. **LC** TK7800; .E4396. **DD** 621.381/05. **CODEN** ETOIE5. **Bk Rev. Ad Acc. Circ:** 30,000. Documents available from Ask*IEEE. ***Continues*** *Electronics Today.*
Desc: Offers construction projects with detailed technical explanations, tutorial features on the world of electronics, and general features covering current affairs in science and technology.
Ind/Abst INSPEC (1972-).

UK/0013-5224
ELECTRONICS WEEKLY. [Electron. wkly.]. No. 1 (Sept. 7, 1960)-. Periodical. English. wk. Reed Business Publishing / West Sussex, England, Perrymount Road, Haywards Heath, West Sussex RH16 3DH England. **Tel** 011 44 81 6523500. **[CCC].** available on microfilm and microfiche from University Microfilms International (UMI); available on an online database (files 648,675,771,772,799/Full-Text) from DIALOG. Documents available from Ask*IEEE. ***Absorbed*** *Industrial Electronics, 0537-5185.*
Ind/Abst Comput. ASAP [Full Txt.]; Comput. Database [Full Txt.]; Curr. Technol. Index; F&S Index Plus Text, Int. [Select. Cov.]; Infomat Int. Bus.; INSPEC (Aug. 1984-); PROMT; Trade Ind. ASAP [Full Txt.]; Trade Ind. Index [Full Txt.]; World Text. Abstr.

US/1042-3508
ELECTRONICS WORLD (LAKE ZURICH, ILL.). (ELECTRONICS WORLD.). [Electron. world]. (1987)-. Periodical. English. Four times a year. W. Randal Vaughn, 1 Holly Court, Lake Zurich IL 60047. **Tel** (312)540-0618. **DD** 621.
Desc: Presents technical tutorials on applied electronic systems/circuits and current affairs affecting technical education and the profession. Written for undergraduate, practicing engineers.

UK/0959-8332
ELECTRONICS WORLD + WIRELESS WORLD. [Electron. world wirel. world]. **VFOAT** Electronics World and Wireless World; Electronics World Plus Wireless World. Vol. 95, No. 1644 (Oct. 1989)-. Periodical. English. mo (12 issues). $91.00. Reed Business Publishing / West Sussex, England, Perrymount Road, Haywards Heath, West Sussex RH16 3DH England. **Tel** 011 44 81 6523500. **LC** TK5700; .W55. **DD** 621.38/05. **CODEN** EWWWE6. **[CCC].** available on microfilm and microfiche from University Microfilms International (UMI). ***Continues*** *Electronics & Wireless World, 0266-3244.*
Ind/Abst Appl. Sci. Technol. Index; Expand. Acad. Index (1992-); SCISEARCH; Soc. Sci. Cit. Index [Select. Cov.].

FR
ELECTRONIQUE. French. Ten times a year. 636.63F France; 734.00F other. Groupe Tests, 26 Rue d'Oradour sur Glane, 75504 Paris Cedex 15 France. **Tel** 011 33 1 44253131. Documents available from Ask*IEEE.
Ind/Abst INSPEC (Oct. 1990-); Point Repere (1992-).

FR/0994-1894
ELECTRONIQUE EUROPE 2000 PARIS. ***Ceased.*** (ELECTRONIQUE EUROPE 2000.). **VFOAT** 2 E 2000; Electronique Europe Deux Mille (Paris). (1988)-(1993). Periodical. French. bm. Kathya Debrinon Editions, 18 Bis rue Violet, 75015 Paris France. **Tel** 011 33 1 47055811. **ED** Kathya De Brinon. **UDC** 681. **Bk Rev. Ad Acc. Circ:** 10,000.
Desc: Business and technical information on the electronics industry, with special emphasis on European news.

FR
ELECTRONIQUE FRANCAISE, L'. Main/Corp Federation Nationale des Industries Electroniques. French. 16 rue de Presles, Paris 75784 France. **LC** HD9696.A3; F725B. **DD** 338.4/7/6213810944.

FR/1157-4445
ELECTRONIQUE INTERNATIONAL HEBDO PARIS. (ELECTRONIQUE INTERNATIONAL HEBDO.). (1990)-. Periodical. French. Forty-one times a year. 773.75F France; 995.00F other. Groupe Tests, 26 Rue d'Oradour sur Glane, 75504 Paris Cedex 15 France. **Tel** 011 33 1 44253131. **UDC** 621.38. ***Absorbed*** *Electronique Actualites; Electronique Hebdo.*
Ind/Abst Infomat Int. Bus.; PROMT.

FR/1157-1152
ELECTRONIQUE PARIS. 1990. (ELECTRONIQUE). (1990)-. Periodical. French. mo. ***Formed by the union of*** *Electronique de Puissance (Paris), 0760-0259; Minis et Micros (Paris), 0336-4585* ***and*** *Electronique Industrielle & TE. Toute l'Electronique, 1154-3663.*

FR
ELECTRONIQUE PRATIQUE. New Series No. 1 (Jan. 1978)-. French. Eleven times a year. 238.00F France; 333.00F others. George Ventillard, 2A 12 rue Bellevue, 75019 Paris Cedex 19 France. **Tel** 011 33 1 42003305. **LC** TK7800; .E44186. **DD** 621.381/05.

FR/1144-5742
ELECTRONIQUE RADIO PLANS PARIS. (ELECTRONIQUE RADIO PLANS.). [Electron. radio plans Paris]. (1989)-. Periodical. French. mo. 253.67F France; 259.00F Tunisia; 364.00F other. Les Publ Georges Ventillard, 2 A 12 rue de Bellevue, 75019 Paris Cedex 19 France. **Tel** 011 33 1 44848484. **UDC** 537. ***Formed by the union of*** *Electronique Applications (Paris), 0243-489X* ***and*** *Radio-Plans (Paris), 0033-7668.*

FR
ELECTRONIQUE TECHNIQUES ET INDUSTRIES. No. 1 (Oct. 1983)-. Periodical. French. bm. $182.00. Masson Editeur, Box Postale 22, 41353 Vineuil 16 France. **Tel** 011 33 54 438994. **(Subscription address:** 7A Boulevard de Perolles, CH-1701 Fribourg Switzerland**) CODEN** EEINEL. available on microfilm and microfiche from University Microfilms International (UMI). Documents available from Ask*IEEE.
Ind/Abst INSPEC (Oct. 1983-).

CN/0826-192X
ELECTROSOURCE : PRODUCT REFERENCE GUIDE AND TELEPHONE DIRECTORY. [Electrosource]. (1984)-. Directory. English. an. 40.00Can$ Canada; 50.00Can$ other. Lakeview Publications Inc, 1200 Aerowood Drive/Unit 27, Mississauga Ontario L4W 2S7 Canada. **Tel** (416)624-8100, FAX (416)624-1760. **ED** E. D. Kerfoot. **DD** 338.4/762138/0971. **Ad Acc. Circ:** 22,000 (ctrl).
Desc: A comprehensive listing of Canadian sources of supply for all types of electronic products and equipment. Names, addresses and telephone numbers provided.

RM/0254-2242
ELECTROTECHNICA, ELECTRONICA, AUTOMATICA. AUTOMATICA SI ELECTRONICA. [Electroteh. electron. autom., Autom. electron.]. **Added/Corp** Romania. Ministerul Industriei Constructiilor de Masini-Unelte si Electrotechnicii. Consiliul National al Inginerilor si Technicienilor din Republica Socialista Romania. Romania. Ministerul Industriei Constructiilor de Masini. Institutul Central de Cercetari Pentru Electronica, Electrotechnica, Automatica, Masini-Unelte si Mecanica Fina. Vol. 18, No. 4/5 (Nov./Dec. 1974)-. Romanian (summaries and/or abstracts in English, French, German and Russian). mo. DM435.00. Cartimex Inc, 126 Calea Victoriei, Box 134-35, Bucharest Romania. **(Subscription address:** Kubon & Sagner, ABT Zeitschriftenimport, D 80328 Munich Germany.**) LC** TJ212; .A744. **CODEN** EAAEDR. Documents available from Ask*IEEE. ***Continues*** *Automatica si Electronica.*
Ind/Abst INSPEC (March 1975-).

UK/0306-8552
ELECTROTECHNOLOGY (LONDON). (ELECTROTECHNOLOGY.). [Electrotechnology]. Vol. 1, (Jan. 1973)-. Periodical. English. bm. £30.00 UK and surface mail other; £45.00 airmail. Institution of Electronics and Electrical Incorporated Engineers, Savoy Hill House, Savoy Hill, London WC2R OBS England. **Tel** 071 836 3357, FAX 071 497 9006. **(Subscription address:** IEEE Service Center, 445 Hoes Lane, Piscataway, NJ 08854**) CODEN** ENYBB. Documents available from Article Express International, Ask*IEEE. ***Supersedes*** *Electrical and Electronics Technician Engineers.*
Ind/Abst Ei Page One; Eng. Index Annu. [Select. Cov.]; INSPEC (Jan. 1973-).

US/0163-1462
ELECTROTECHNOLOGY (SPRINGFIELD, VA.). ***Title Change.*** (ELECTROTECHNOLOGY / NTIS.). [Electrotechnology]. **Added/Corp** United States. National Technical Information Service. (19??)-(19??). Periodical. English. Twenty-four times a year. National Technical Information Service - NTIS, Room 2027S, 5285 Port Royal Road, Springfield VA 22161. **Tel** (703)487-4630, (703)487-4660, (703)487-4650, FAX (703)321-8547, telex 89-9405. ***Continued by*** *NTIS Alert Electrotechnology.*
Ind/Abst Manage. Market. Abstr.; World Publ. Monit.

RM/0376-4745
ELECTROTEHNICA, ELECTRONICA, AUTOMATICA. ELECTROTEHNICA. ***Ceased.*** [Electroteh. electron. autom. Electroteh.]. **Added/Corp** Romania. Ministerul Industriei Constructiilor de Masini-Unelte si Electrotehnicii. Consiliul National al Inginerilor si Tehnicienilor din Republica Socialista Romania. Romania. Ministerul Industriei Constructiilor de Masini-Unelte si Electrotehnicii. Institutul Central de Cercetari Pentru Electronica, Electrotehnica, Automatica, Masini-Unelte si Mecanica Fina. Year 22, No. 7/8 (July/Aug. 1974)-(19??). Romanian (summaries and/or abstracts in English, French, German and Russian). **(Subscription address:** Orion Press SRL, SPL Independentei 202-A, Bucharest 6 Romania.**) LC** TK4; .E713. **DD** 621.3/05. **CODEN** EEAEDL. Documents available from Ask*IEEE. ***Continues*** *Electrotehnica.*
Ind/Abst Ceram. Abstr.; INSPEC (Jan. 1975-).

SI
ELECTSO, ELECTRICAL & ELECTRONIC ENGINEERING SOCIETY'S MAGAZINE, THE. **Main/Corp** Electrical & Electronic Engineering Society. **VFOAT** I An Kung I Hsueh Yuan Tien Chi Chi Tien Tzu Kung Cheng Hsueh Hui Hui Kan. 1972/73-. English (Chinese). $3.60. Electrical and Electronic Engineering Society, Ngee Ann Technical College, 535 Clementi Road 21, Singapore Singapore. **(Subscription address:** IEEE Service Center, 445 Hoes Lane, Piscataway, NJ 08854**) LC** TK1; .E251413. **DD** 621.3/05.

GW/0932-5468
ELEKTOR AACHEN. [Elektor Aachen]. (1986)-. Periodical. German. mo. £34.00 US and Canada; £28.00 other. Elector Verlag GmbH, Suesterfeldstr 25, D 52072 Aachen Germany. **Tel** 011 49 241 889090, FAX 011 49 241 8890988. **(Subscription address:** World-Wide Subscription Services, Unit 4, Gibbs Reed Farm Pashley Road, Ticehurst TN5 7HE England.**) ED** M. Landman. **UDC** 621.38. **Bk Rev. Ad Acc, Adv Mgr Tel** 749-241-8890911. **Circ:** 105,000. ***Continues*** *Elektor-Elektronik, 0177-7610.*

UK/0268-4519
ELEKTOR ELECTRONICS. [Elektor electron.]. **VFOAT** Elektor. No. 106 (Feb. 1984)-. Periodical. English (German, French, Spanish, Italian, Greek, Modern, Dutch and Portuguese, Swedish). mo. £35.00. Elektor Electronics Publishing, Down House, Broomhill Road, London SW18 4JQ England. **Tel** +44 8177 1688, FAX +44 8174 9153. **(Subscription address:** World Wide Subscription Service Ltd., Unit 4, Gibbs Reed Farm, Ticehurst TN5 7HE England**) ED** Len Seymour. **LC** TK7800; .E44196. **CODEN** ELELEA. cum. index. **Bk Rev. Ad Acc. Circ:** 26,000. Documents available from Ask*IEEE. ***Continues*** *Elektor, 0308-308X.*
Desc: Electronics in its widest sense.
Ind/Abst INSPEC (1986).

RU/0422-9274
ELEKTRICESKAJA I TEPLOVOZNAJA TJAGA. ***Title Change.*** **See** Transportation-Railroads.

RU/0013-5380
ELEKTRICESTVO. (ELEKTRICHESTVO.). [Elektricestvo]. **Added/Corp** Imperatorskoe Russkoe Tekhnicheskoe Obshchestvo. VI Otdiel. Vsesoiuznoe Elektrotekhnicheskoe Obedinenie (Soviet Union) Glavenergoprom NKTP (Soviet Union) Soviet Union. Narodnyi Komissariat Tiazheloi Promyshlennosti. Soviet Union. Narodnyi Komissariat Elektrostantsii i Elektropromyshlennosti. Akademiia Nauk SSSR. (1880)-. Academic Scholarly Publication. Russian (summaries and/or abstracts in English, French, German and Italian; table of contents in English). mo. $288.00. Izdatelstvo Nauka / Akademiia Nauk, Publishing House of the Russian Academy of Sciences, Leninskii Porspekt 14, 117901 Moscow Russia. **Tel** 011 95 954-21-53, FAX 011 95 938-21-44, telex 411964. **(Subscription address:** East View Publications Inc., 3020 Harbor Lane North, Suite 110, Minneapolis MN 55447.**) LC** TK4; .E73. **CODEN** ELEKA3. **[CCC].** Index available. **Bk Rev. Ad Acc.** Documents available from Article Express International, Ask*IEEE, CASDDS.
Ind/Abst Chem. Abstr.; Ei Page One; Eng. Index Annu.; GeoRef; INSPEC (1968-); Seed Abstr.

RU/0201-4564
ELEKTRICHESKIE STANTSII. [Elektr. stn.]. **Added/Corp** Energotsentr (Soviet Union) Soviet Union. Ministerstvo Energetiki i Elektrifikatsii. Soviet Union. Ministerstvo Elektrostantsii. Nauchno-Tekhnicheskoe Obshchestvo Energetiki i Elektrotekhnicheskoi Promyshlennosti (Soviet Union). (1930)-. Academic Scholarly Publication. Russian. mo. $189.95. Izdatelstvo Energiia, Slyuzovaia Nab., 10, Z-114, Moscow Russia. **(Subscription address:** East View Publications Inc., 3020 Harbor Lane North, Suite 110, Minneapolis MN 55447.**) LC** TK4; .E725. **CODEN** EKSTAP. Index available. **Bk Rev. Ad Acc.** Documents available from Ask*IEEE, CASDDS. ***Formed by the union of*** *Biulleten Inzhkollektivov MOGES* ***and*** *Izvestiia Elektrotoka.*
Ind/Abst Acoust. Abstr.; Chem. Abstr.; Coal Abstr.; Energy Res. Abstr.; INSPEC (1968-).

GW/0013-5399
ELEKTRIE. [Elektrie]. (June 1959)-. Academic Scholarly Publication. German. mo. DM160,00 Germany; DM173,20 other. Deutscher Judo Verband, Redaktion Ippon Segewaldweg 40, D 12557 Berlin Germany. **Tel** 011 49 711 210770, telex 051 678. **ED** Dr. Heide and Partner. **LC** TK3; .K34. **CODEN** EKTRAO. **Ad Acc.** Documents available from Article Express International, Ask*IEEE, CASDDS. ***Continues*** *Deutsche Elektrontechnik.*
Ind/Abst Alum. Ind. Abstr.; Bioeng. Abstr.; Chem. Abstr.; Coal Abstr.; Ei Page One; Eng. Mater. Abstr.; Eng. Index Annu.; INSPEC (1968-); Met. Abstr.; Saf. Health Work; Stat. Theory Method Abstr. (1967); Surf. Treat. Technol. Abstr.

GW/0170-2033
ELEKTRISCHE ENERGIE-TECHNIK. **See** Energy.

GW/0013-5496
ELEKTRIZITATSWIRTSCHAFT. (ELEKTRIZITATSWIRTSCHAFT : MITTEILUNGEN DER VEREINIGUNG DER ELEKTRIZITATSWERKE EV.). [Elektrizitatswirtschaft]. Vol. 25, No. 400 (Jan. 1, 1926)-. Periodical. German. ir. DM356.00. Verlags und Wirtschaftsgesellschaft der Elektricitatswerke mbh, VWEW, M Stresemannallee 23, W-6000 Frankfurt 70 Germany. **Tel** 069 63 04-1, FAX 069 6 30 43 59, telex 4 11 284 VDEW. **LC** TK3; .E716. **CODEN** EKZWAZ. **[CCC].** Documents available from Article Express International, Ask*IEEE. ***Absorbed*** *Oeffentliche Elektrizitatswerk;* ***Continues*** *Mitteilungen der Vereinigung der Elekticitatswerke.*
Ind/Abst Bioeng. Abstr.; Coal Abstr.; Ei Page One; EMBASE; Energy Res. Abstr.; Eng. Index Annu.; INSPEC (1968-).

NO/0013-550X
ELEKTRO. [Elektro]. **Added/Corp** Norsk Elektroteknisk Forening. Norske Elektrisitetsverkers Forening. Norges Energiverkforbund. Industriens Forening for Elektroteknikk og Automatisering (Norway). **VFOAT** Elektroteknisk Tidsskrift. (Jan. 1968)-. Periodical. Norwegian. sm. kr280.00. Ingeniorforlaget A S, Kronprinsens Gate 17, 0202 Oslo 2 Norway. **LC** TK4; .E75. **CODEN** EEROAV. **[CCC].** Documents available from Ask*IEEE. ***Continues*** *Elektroteknisk Tidsskrift.*
Ind/Abst Energy Res. Abstr. (Jan. 1971-); INSPEC (Jan. 1973-).

XR
ELEKTRO. (199?)-. Periodical. Czech. mo. **LC** TK4; .E765. **DD** 621.3. **CODEN** EKTRES. Documents available from Ask*IEEE. ***Formed by the union of*** *Elektrotechnicky Obzor* ***and*** *Elektrotechnik (Prague, Czechoslovakia).*
Ind/Abst INSPEC (1991-).

GW/0013-5518
ELEKTRO-ANZEIGER. ***Title Change.*** [Elektro-anz.]. (1950)-(1994). Periodical. German. bw. Konradin Verlags Gruppe, Robert Kohlhammer GmbH, D-70765 Leinfelden Germany. **Tel** 011 49 711 7594370, 011 49 711 7594229. **CODEN** EKANAJ. **[CCC].** Documents available from Ask*IEEE. ***Continued by*** *Elektro Automation.*
Ind/Abst Energy Res. Abstr. (April 1972-); INSPEC (Sept. 1968-).

GW
ELEKTRO AUTOMATION. (19??)-. Periodical. German. Twelve times a year. DM96.00 Germany; DM106.80 others. Konradin Verlags Gruppe, Robert Kohlhammer GmbH, D-70765 Leinfelden Germany. **Tel** 011 49 711 7594370, 011 49 711 7594229. **CODEN** EKANAJ. Documents available from Ask*IEEE. ***Continues*** *Elektro Anzeiger.*
Ind/Abst Energy Res. Abstr. (April 1972-); INSPEC (Sept. 1968-).

NE/0925-5397
ELEKTRO MAGAZINE EDITIE DETAIL. [Elektro mag., Ed. detail]. (1990)-. Periodical. Dutch. mo (11 issues per year). Fl53.40 Netherlands; Fl281.00 other. Kluwer BV, Postbus 23, 7400 GA Deventer Netherlands. **Tel** 011 31 5700 33155, 011 31 5700 48999, FAX 011 31 5700 11504, telex 42829. **UDC** 621.3. ***Continues*** *Elektro Magazine, 0169-0205.*

GW
ELEKTRO-VERKAUF + ELEKTRO NEUHEITEN. Periodical. German. ir. 16.00. U Pfriemer Verlag, Landwehrstrasse 68, W-8000 Munchen 2 Germany. **LC** TK7018; .E638. ***Supersedes*** *Elektro-Neuheiten.*

GW/0424-8562
ELEKTROFACH, DAS. (1959)-. Periodical. German. mo. DM96.00 Germany; DM102.00 other. Futura-Verlag R Stephan, Postfach 102464, D 40015 Dusseldorf Germany. **Tel** 011 49 211 387030, telex 8586486. **UDC** 628.973.1.

GW/0013-5542
ELEKTROHANDEL HEIDELBERG. ***Title Change.*** **VFOAT** EH. Elektrohandel. (1969)-(Jan. 1994). Periodical. German. mo. Dr. Alfred Huethig Verlag GmbH, Postfach 102869, D 69018 Heidelberg Germany. **Tel** 011 49 6221 489281. **UDC** 696.6. **CODEN** 621.396/.397. **[CCC].** ***Merged into*** *Elektrofach.*
Ind/Abst Infomat Int. Bus.

RU/0424-8570
ELEKTROHIMIA. (ELEKTROKHIMIIA.). [Elektrohimia]. **Added/Corp** Akademiia Nauk SSSR. (1965)-. Academic Scholarly Publication. Russian. mo. $279.95. Izdatelstvo Nauka / Akademiia Nauk, Publishing House of the Russian Academy of Sciences, Leninskii Porspekt 14, 117901 Moscow Russia. **Tel** 011 95 954-21-53, FAX 011 95 938-21-44, telex 411964. **(Subscription address:** East View Publications Inc., 3020 Harbor Lane North, Suite 110, Minneapolis MN 55447.**) CODEN** ELKKAX. **[CCC].** available on microfilm. Documents available from Ask*IEEE, CASDDS.
Ind/Abst Alum. Ind. Abstr.; Chem. Abstr.; Curr. Titles Electrochem.; Energy Res. Abstr.; Eng. Mater. Abstr.; INSPEC (1971-); Int. Aerosp. Abstr.; Met. Abstr.; World Alum. Abstr.

NE
ELEKTROMAGAZINE. INSTALLATIE. Dutch. ir. Kluwer BV, Postbus 23, 7400 GA Deventer Netherlands. **Tel** 011 31 5700 33155, 011 31 5700 48999, FAX 011 31 5700 11504, telex 42829.

GW/0012-1258
ELEKTROMEISTER + DEUTSCHES ELEKTROHANDWERK. [Elektromeister + Dtsch. elektrohandw.]. **VFOAT** DE. Vol. 46, No. 1 (Jan. 10, 1971)-. Periodical. English (German). Twenty-four times a year. DM183.10 Germany; DM197.80 others. Huethig and Pflaum Verlag Gmbh, Postfach 102869, D 69018 Heidelberg Germany. **Tel** 011 49 6221 4890. **(Subscription address:** WEPF Publishing Services GmbH, Auf Dem Wolf 4, CH 4018 Basel Switzerland.**) CODEN** EMDEAL. **[CCC]. Bk Rev. Ad Acc.** ctrl circ. Documents available from Ask*IEEE. ***Formed by the union of*** *Deutsches Elektrohandwerk* ***and*** *Elektromeister.*
Ind/Abst Energy Res. Abstr. (Sept. 1977-); INSPEC (Jan. 1971-); Saf. Health Work.

NE/0168-7840
ELEKTRONICA. [Elektronica]. (1981)-. Periodical. Dutch. sm (24 issues). Fl155.66. Kluwer BV, Postbus 23, 7400 GA Deventer Netherlands. **Tel** 011 31 5700 33155, 011 31 5700 48999, FAX 011 31 5700 11504, telex 42829. **UDC** 621.38. **[CCC].** Documents available from Ask*IEEE. ***Continues*** *Radio Electronica, 0033-7854;* ***Absorbed*** *Databus.*
Ind/Abst INSPEC (April 1981-).

NE/0165-7062
ELEKTRONICA + I.E. EN ELEKTROTECHNIEK. [Elektron. + elektrotech.]. Periodical. Dutch. 50.00. Uitgevensmij Diligentia, Tesselschadestraat 18-22, Amsterdam Netherlands. **LC** TK7800; .E4425. Documents available from Ask*IEEE. ***Continues*** *Elektronica.*
Ind/Abst INSPEC (1972-).

GW/0172-6153
ELEKTRONIK ENTWICKLUNG. [Elektron.-Entwickl.]. Began 1978. Periodical. German. mo. DM84.00. Verlag fur Technik und Wirtschaft VTW GmbH, Postfach 5769, Kaiser-Friedrich-Ring 49, 62 Wiesbaden Germany. **Tel** 06121/880438, FAX 06121/809465, telex 4186761. **ED** Gunter Haarmann. **LC** TK7800; .E4432. **DD** 621.381/05. **CODEN** ELEEDM. **Circ:** 16,000. available on diskette. Documents available from Ask*IEEE. ***Continues*** *Bauelemente der Elektrotechnik, 0374-2636.*
Ind/Abst INSPEC (Oct. 1978-); World Publ. Monit.

GW/0171-4198
ELEKTRONIK HEUTE. [Elektron. heute]. Apr. 1978-. Periodical. German. Kontron Elektronik GmbH, 8057 Eching Bei Munchen, Breslauer Strasse 2, Munchen Germany. **LC** TK7878.4; .M4. **CODEN** ELHED3. Documents available from Ask*IEEE. ***Continues*** *Messen, Zahlen, Registrieren.*
Ind/Abst INSPEC (April 1979-).

GW/0013-5658
ELEKTRONIK (MUNCHEN). (ELEKTRONIK.). [Elektronik]. (1954)-. Periodical. German. mo. Franzis Verlag GmbH, Postfach 200710, D 80007 Munich Germany. **Tel** 011 49 89 5117363. **CODEN** EKRKAR. **[CCC].** Documents available from Ask*IEEE.
Ind/Abst Ei Page One; INSPEC (1968-).

GW/0172-6250
ELEKTRONIK-PRODUKTION & PRUFTECHNIK. [Elektron.-Prod. & Pruftech.]. **VFOAT** Elektronik-Produktion und Pruftechnik. (1979)-. Periodical. German. ir (10 issues per year). DM120.00. Konradin Verlags Gruppe, Robert Kohlhammer GmbH, D-70765 Leinfelden Germany. **Tel** 011 49 711 7594370, 011 49 711 7594229. **UDC** 621.38. ***Continues*** *Elektronik Packaging & Produktion, 0343-673X.*

SW/0033-7749
ELEKTRONIK VARLDEN. VFOAT Elektronikvarlden. Periodical. Swedish. mo (ten issues per year). Kr310.00. Elektronikvarlden, Box 529, S-371 23 Karlskrona Sweden. **Tel** +46-455-258 00, FAX +46-455-149 88. **(Subscription address:** Press Data AB, Box 3263, S-103 65 Stockholm Sweden**) LC** TK6540; .P58. **DD** 621.381/05. **Ad Acc. Circ:** 21,000 (ctrl). ***Continues*** *Radio Och Television.*

PL/0033-2089
ELEKTRONIKA. [Elektronika]. **Added/Corp** Polska Akademia Nauk. Komitet Elektroniki i Telekomunikacji. Stowarzyszenie Elektrykow Polskich. Sekcja Elektroniki i Telekomunikacji. Naczelna Organizacja Techniczna (Poland). Wojewodzki Oddzia w Koszalinie. No. 11 (1970)-. Academic Scholarly Publication. Polish (summaries and/or abstracts in English, Polish and Russian). mo. $84.00. **(Subscription address:** ARS Polona, PO Box 1001, 00068 Warsaw Poland.**) LC** TK7850.A1P7. **CODEN** EKNTBZ. Documents available from Article Express International, Ask*IEEE, CASDDS. ***Continues*** *Przeglad Elektroniki.*
Ind/Abst Bioeng. Abstr.; Ceram. Abstr. (19??-); Chem. Abstr.; Ei Page One; Eng. Index Annu.; INSPEC (1970-).

RU
ELEKTRONIKA. Added/Corp Soviet Union. Ministerstvo Vysshego i Srednego Spetsialnogo Obrazovaniia. No. 1 (1974)-. Periodical. Russian. Twenty-four times a year. $189.95 US & Canada; $199.95 Europe; $214.95 others. **(Subscription address:** East View Publications Inc., 3020 Harbor Lane North, Suite 110, Minneapolis MN 55447.**) LC** TK7800; .E4433.

HU/0231-066X
ELEKTRONIKAI ES HRADASTECHNIKAI SZAKIRODALMI TAJEKOZTATO. (1983)-. Periodical. Hungarian. mo. 9.900ft. Orszagos Muszaki Informacios Kozpont es Konyvtar (O.M.I.K.K.), National Technical Information Centre and Library Museum, u 17, PO Box 12, 1428 Budapest, Hungary. **Tel** (361)118-1994, FAX (361)138-2414, telex 22-4944 OMIKK H. **(Subscription address:** OMIKK Budapest, POB 12, H-1428 Hungary**) ED** Elek Nagy. **UDC** 016. Index available. cum. index. **Bk Rev. Ad Acc. Circ:** 135 (ctrl).

SZ/0531-9218
ELEKTRONIKER. Began publication in 1962?. Periodical. German. ir. 102.00F. Grafische Betriebe, Aargauer Tagblatt AG/Bahnhfstr, 39 43 CH5001 Aarau Switzerland. **CODEN** ELKRBL. **[CCC].** Documents available from Ask*IEEE.
Ind/Abst INSPEC (Sept. 1968-).

GW/0374-3144
ELEKTRONIKINDUSTRIE. (ELEKTRONIK INDUSTRIE.). [Elektronikindustrie]. **VFOAT** Elektronik-Industrie; El. (1970)-. Periodical. German. mo. $127.00 North America. Dr. Alfred Huethig Verlag GmbH, Postfach 102869, D 69018 Heidelberg Germany. **Tel** 011 49 6221 489281. **(Subscription address:** Huethig Publishing Inc., 29 Macintosh Drive, Oxford CT 06478.**) CODEN** EKIDAT. **Circ:** 16,269. Documents available from Ask*IEEE.
Ind/Abst INSPEC (Dec. 1970-).

GW/0013-5674
ELEKTRONIKJOURNAL. [Elektronikjournal]. (1966)-. German. mo (10 issues per year). DM150.00. Europa Fachpresse Verlag GmbH, Thomas Dehler Strasse 27, D-81737 Munich Germany. **Tel** 011 49 89 67804273. **UDC** 621.3. **CODEN** EKTJAY. **[CCC].**

GW/0341-5589
ELEKTRONIKPRAXIS. [Elektronikpraxis]. (196?)-. Periodical. German. bw (26 issues per year). DM225.00 Germany; DM235.00 other. Vogel Verlag, Postfach 6740, D-97064 Wuerzburg Germany. **Tel** 011 49 931 4182145, 011 49 931 4182483, FAX 011 49 931 4182670, telex 841 680131. **UDC** 621.38.

SW/1102-7495
ELEKTRONIKTIDNINGEN. [Elektroniktidningen]. (1992)-. Periodical. Swedish. ir. Kr443.00. Ekonomi Teknik Forlag AB, Klara Soedra Kyrkogata 1, 106 12 Stockholm Sweden. **Tel** 011 46 8 7966661, 011 46 8 7966500. **UDC** 62. ***Formed by the union of*** *Elteknik (1989), 1101-6965* ***and*** *Modern Elektronik, 0345-7656.*

MV/0013-5739
ELEKTRONNAJA OBRABOTKA MATERIALOV. (ELEKTRONNAIA OBRABOTKA MATERIALOV.). [Elektron. obrab. mater.]. **Added/Corp** Institutul de Fizike Aplikate (Akademiia de Shtiintse a RSSM). (1965)-. Academic Scholarly Publication. Russian. Six times a year. $99.95. **CODEN** EOBMAF. Documents available from Article Express International, Ask*IEEE, CASDDS.
Ind/Abst Alum. Ind. Abstr.; Bioeng. Abstr.; Chem. Abstr.; Ei Page One; Eng. Index Annu.; INSPEC (July-Aug. 1967-); Met. Abstr.

RU/0013-5771
ELEKTROSVIAZ (MOSKVA. 1934). See Communication-Telecommunications.

XO/0013-578X
ELEKTROTECHNICKY CASOPIS. [Elektrotech. cas.]. Began with Vol. 10 in 1959. Academic Scholarly Publication. Slovak (Czech). mo. kcs180.00 Czechoslovakia; $92.00 US. Publishers House Slovak Acad Science, Klemensoya 19, 81430 Bratislava Slovakia. **Tel** 56621. **ED** Oldrich Benda, Ivan Puzjak. **CODEN** ELKCA9. Index available. cum. index. **Bk Rev.** ctrl circ. Documents available from Ask*IEEE, CASDDS. ***Continues in part*** *Strojnoelektrotechnicky Casopis.*
Desc: Covers semiconductors and microelectronics.
Ind/Abst Chem. Abstr.; INSPEC (1968-).

CS/0013-5798
ELEKTROTECHNICKY OBZOR. *Title Change.* [Elektrotech. obz.]. **Added/Corp** Czechoslovakia. Federalni Ministerstvo Hutnictvi, Strojirenstvi a Elektrotechniky. Elektrotechnicky svaz Ceskoslovensky. (1910)-(199?). Academic Scholarly Publication. Czech. mo. **(Subscription address:** Artia Pegas Press Ltd., Palac Metro Narodni Trida 25, 11210 Prague 1 Czech Republic.**) LC** TK4; .E745. **CODEN** EKOBAJ. Documents available from Article Express International, Ask*IEEE, CASDDS. ***Merged with*** *Elektrotechnik (Prague, Czechoslovakia)* ***to form*** *Elektro (Usti nad Labem, Czechoslovakia).*
Ind/Abst Alum. Ind. Abstr.; Bioeng. Abstr.; Chem. Abstr.; Ei Page One; Eng. Mater. Abstr.; Eng. Index Annu.; INSPEC (1968-); Met. Abstr.; Saf. Health Work.

GW/0013-581X
ELEKTROTECHNIK. [Elektrotechnik]. (1970)-. Academic Scholarly Publication. German. ir (10 issues per year). DM100.00 Germany; DM110.00 other. Vogel Verlag, Postfach 6740, D-97064 Wuerzburg Germany. **Tel** 011 49 931 4182145, 011 49 931 4182483, FAX 011 49 931 4182670, telex 841 680131. **CODEN** EKTCBE. **[CCC].** Documents available from Ask*IEEE. ***Absorbed*** *Elektrische Ausrustung.*
Ind/Abst EMBASE; Energy Res. Abstr. (Oct. 1977-); INSPEC (Nov. 1976-); Saf. Health Work; Surf. Treat. Technol. Abstr.

CS
ELEKTROTECHNIK : MESICNIK PRO VYCHOVU ELEKTROTECHNIKU. *Title Change.* **Added/Corp** Czechoslovakia. Federalni Ministerstvo Hutnictvi, Strojirenstvi a Elektrotechniky. Elektrotechnicky svaz Ceskoslovensky. (194?)-(199?). Periodical. Czech. mo. **(Subscription address:** Artia Pegas Press Ltd., Palac Metro Narodni Trida 25, 11210 Prague 1 Czech Republic.**) LC** TK4; .E74733. Documents available from Ask*IEEE. ***Merged with*** *Elektro (Usti nad Labem, Czechoslovakia)* ***to form*** *Elektrotechnicky Obzor.*
Ind/Abst INSPEC (1968-).

AU/0932-383X
ELEKTROTECHNIK UND INFORMATIONSTECHNIK : E&I. [E I, Elektrotech. Inf.tech.]. **Added/Corp** Osterreichischer Verband fur Elektrotechnik. **VFOAT** E&I; E & I; E und I. Vol. 105 No. 1 (Jan. 1988)-. Periodical. German. Twelve times a year. DM298.00. Springer-Verlag Wien, Sachsenplatz 4 6, PO Box 89, A-1201 Vienna Austria. **Tel** 011 43 1 3302415. **(Subscription address:** Springer Verlag New York Inc. / for North America, 44 Hartz Way, Secaucus NJ 07096.**) ED** H Birkner, H Ebenberger, F Smola and H Staerker. **LC** TK3; .E6. **CODEN** EIEIEE. **[CCC].** Documents available from Ask*IEEE. ***Continues*** *Elektrotechnik und Maschinenbau.*
Ind/Abst INSPEC (1988-).

HU/0367-0708
ELEKTROTECHNIKA. [Elektrotechnika]. **Added/Corp** Magyar Elektrotechnikai Egyesulet. (1908)-. Academic Scholarly Publication. Hungarian (summaries and/or abstracts in English, French, German and Russian). Twelve times a year. $73.00. Akademiai Kiado, Publishing House of the Hungarian Academy of Sciences, Prielle Kornelia u. 19-35, H-1117 Budapest Hungary. **Tel** 011 36 1 1811991, FAX 011 36 1 1811991, telex 22-6228 AKNYO H. **(Subscription address:** Kultura, Hungarian Foreign Trading Company, PO Box 149, H-1389 Budapest Hungary**) LC** TK4; .E74734. **CODEN** EKTTAU. Documents available from Article Express International, Ask*IEEE.
Ind/Abst Alum. Ind. Abstr.; Bioeng. Abstr.; Ei Page One; Eng. Mater. Abstr.; Eng. Index Annu.; INSPEC (1968-); Met. Abstr.

HU/0231-0783
ELEKTROTECHNIKAI SZAKIRODALMI TAJEKOZTATO. (1983)-. Periodical. Hungarian. mo. 9.900ft. Orszagos Muszaki Informacios Kozpont es Konyvtar (O.M.I.K.K.), National Technical Information Centre and Library Museum, u 17, PO Box 12, 1428 Budapest, Hungary. **Tel** (361)118-1994, FAX (361)138-2414, telex 22-4944 OMIKK H. **(Subscription address:** OMIKK Budapest, POB 12, H-1428 Hungary**) ED** Ottmar Kladiva. **UDC** 016. **Circ:** 135.
Desc: Articles on electrical engineering and electronics.

CI/0013-5844
ELEKTROTEHNIKA (ZAGREB). (ELEKTROTEHNIKA : CASOPIS SAVEZA ELEKTROTEHNICKIH INZENJERA I TEKNICARA HRVATSKE I UDRUZENIH IZDAVACA.). [Elektrotehnika]. **Added/Corp** Savey Elektrotehnickih Inzenjera i Tehnicara Hrvatske. (1958)-. Academic Scholarly Publication. Serbo-Croatian (Roman) (Serbian; summaries and/or abstracts in English and Serbian). bm (6 issues). $60.00. Electrotehnika, Berisloviceva 6 1, 41000 Zagreb Croatia. **Tel** 041 422 943. **ED** Stjepan A. Szabo. **CODEN** ELTHB2. Index available. cum. index. **Bk Rev. Ad Acc. Circ:** 1,000 (ctrl). Documents available from Ask*IEEE, CASDDS.
Desc: Scientific and technical journal in electrotechnics in all fields, telecommunications and computing (including computer science).
Ind/Abst Chem. Abstr.; INIS Atomindex [Micro.]; INSPEC (1968-).

YU/0013-5852
ELEKTROTEHNISKI VESTNIK. [Elektroteh. vestn.]. (1931)-. Periodical. Multiple languages. bm. **UDC** 621.3. **CODEN** ELVEA2. Documents available from Article Express International, Ask*IEEE.
Ind/Abst Comput. Inf. Syst. Abstr. J. [Full Cov.]; Ei Page One; Elect. Comm. Abstr.; Eng. Index Annu. [Select. Cov.]; Environ. Eng. Abstr.; INSPEC (1968-); Int. Aerosp. Abstr.; Mech. Eng. Abstr.; Solid State Supercond. Abstr.

RU/0013-5860
ELEKTROTEKHNIKA (MOSKVA, 1963). (ELEKTROTEKHNIKA.). [Elektrotekhnika]. (Sept. 1963)-. Periodical. Russian. mo. $149.95. **(Subscription address:** East View Publications Inc., 3020 Harbor Lane North, Suite 110, Minneapolis MN 55447.**) CODEN** ELKTAQ. **[CCC].** Documents available from Article Express International, Ask*IEEE, CASDDS. ***Continues*** *Vestnik Elektropromyshlennosti.*
Ind/Abst Chem. Abstr.; Ei Page One; Eng. Index Annu.; INSPEC (1968-); Int. Aerosp. Abstr.

PL/0459-682X
ELEKTRYKA. Main/Corp ODZ. Poland. Politechnika. 1- 1955-. Academic Scholarly Publication. summaries and/or abstracts in Russian, English and German. Panstwowe Wydawn Rolnicze i Lesne, Al Jerozolimskie 28, PO Box 374, 00 024 Warszawa Poland. **Tel** 34-21, telex 642410 IUNG PL. **LC** TK4. **CODEN** ZNPEAD. Documents available from CASDDS.
Ind/Abst Chem. Abstr. (1955-1982).

NE/0013-5895
ELEKTUUR. [Elektuur]. (1964)-. Periodical. Dutch (English, French, German, Italian, Spanish and Greek, Modern). Eleven times a year (Monthly with July/Aug. combined). F85.00 Netherlands and Belgium; F116.00 other. Uitgeversmij Elektuur BV, Postbus 75, 6190 AB Beek L Netherlands. **Tel** 011 31 46 389444, FAX 011 31 46 370161, telex 56617. **UDC** 621.38. **Bk Rev**, (Qty: 10). **Ad Acc. *Continues*** *Elektronica Aktueel, 0920-7015.*

BL/0100-2104
ELETRICIDADE MODERNA (SAO PAULO). (ELETRICIDADE MODERNA.). (19??)-. Periodical. Portuguese. mo. 40.00. Editora Abril SA, Rua do Curtume 769 Lapa, 05066 900 Sao Paulo SP Brazil. **Tel** 011 55 11 8239222, 011 55 11 2623322, FAX 011 55 11 8643796. **LC** TK4; .E6282.

IT/0013-6093
ELETTRIFICAZIONE. [Elettrificazione]. (1950)-. Academic Scholarly Publication. Italian. mo. L80000.00 Italy; L150000.00 other. Editoriale Delfino, Via Simone d'Orsenigo 25, 20135 Milan Italy. **Tel** 011-39-551-84932, FAX 011-39-551-84971. **CODEN** ELTZAL. Index available. cum. index. **Ad Acc.** Documents available from Ask*IEEE, CASDDS.
Ind/Abst Chem. Abstr.; Coal Abstr.; Ei Page One; INSPEC (Nov. 1969-); Saf. Health Work.

IT
ELETTRODOMESTICA. (19??)-. Italian. mo. L96000 Italy; L140000 other. Franco Angeli Riviste SRL, Viale Monza 106, 20127 Milan Italy. **Tel** 011 39 2 2827651, 011 39 2 289562.

IT/0013-6123
ELETTRONICA E TELECOMUNICAZIONI. [Elettron. telecomun.]. **Added/Corp** Radiotelevisione Italiana. STET-Societa Finanziaria Telefonica. Vol. 17, No. 1 (Jan./Feb. 1968)-. Periodical. Italian (summaries and/or abstracts in English). tq. L20000 Italy; L40000 other. Nuova Eri Edizioni RAI, Via Arsenale 41, 10121 Turin Italy. **Tel** 011 39 11 8102238. **ED** Eri Edizioni. **LC** TK7800; .E47. **CODEN** ETTCB9. **Bk Rev. Ad Acc. Circ:** 12,000 (ctrl). Documents available from Ask*IEEE. ***Continues*** *Elettronica.*
Desc: The review is sponsored by the STET and the RAI and presents articles of the above organizations (Cselt-Rai-Telespazio-Sip) which deal with electronics and telecommunications.
Ind/Abst INSPEC (1968-).

IT/0391-6391
ELETTRONICA OGGI. [Elettron. oggi]. (1969)-. Periodical. Italian. mo. Gruppo Editoriale Jackson Spa, Via Gorki 69, 20092 Cinisello Balsamo Italy. **Tel** 011 39 2 66034401. **ED** P. Palerma. **LC** Discard. **CODEN** ELOGDA. **Circ:** 15,030. Documents available from Ask*IEEE.
Ind/Abst INSPEC (Nov. 1976-); World Publ. Monit.

IT/0013-6131
ELETTROTECNICA, L'. ***Title Change.*** [Elettrotecnica]. **Added/Corp** Associazione Elettrotecnica ed Elettronica Italiana. Associazione Elettrotecnica Italiana. Vol. 1 (1914)-(Jan. 1993). Periodical. Italian. mo. Assn Elettrotecnica Elettronic, Italiana Viale Monza 259, 20126 Milan Italy. **Tel** 011 39 2 2550641, 011 39 2 25779223. **CODEN** ETRTAF. **[CCC].** Documents available from Article Express International, The Genuine Article, Ask*IEEE. ***Supersedes*** *Associazione Elettrotecnica Italiana. Atti dell'Associazione Elettrotecnica Italiana.* ***Continued by*** *Automazione Enegia Informazione AEI.*
Ind/Abst Bioeng. Abstr.; Ei Page One; Eng. Index Annu.; INSPEC (1968-); Res. Alert [Select. Cov.]; Saf. Health Work.

NE
ELEX. English. Twelve times a year. Fl62.50. Uitgeversmij Elektuur BV, Postbus 75, 6190 AB Beek L Netherlands. **Tel** 011 31 46 389444, FAX 011 31 46 370161, telex 56617. **ED** P Kersemaneas. cum. index. **Bk Rev**, (Qty: 5). **Ad Acc**, **Adv Mgr:** U Van Noordenne.
Desc: Aimed at those interested in electronics and having a lower and/or intermediate level of education or knowledge in the wide field of electronics/information studies, and at those keen on acquiring this knowledge.

GW/0170-1827
ELRAD. (1977)-. Periodical. German. mo. DM79.20 Germany; DM86.40 other. Verlag Heinz Heise GmbH und Co, Postfach 610407, D 30604 Hannover Germany. **Tel** 011 49 511 53520, FAX 011 49 511 5352129. **UDC** 621.317.

SW/0346-6310
ELTEKNIK MED AKTUELL ELEKTRONIK. [Eltek. aktuell elektron.]. (1972)-. Swedish. Twenty times a year. Kr554.00 Scandinavia; Kr773.00 Europe; Kr850.00 others. Ekonomi Teknik Forlag AB, Klara Soedra Kyrkogata 1, 106 12 Stockholm Sweden. **Tel** 011 46 8 7966661, 011 46 8 7966500. **ED** U. Skiden. **LC** TK4; .E764. **CODEN** ETAEBM. **Bk Rev. Ad Acc. Circ:** 11,600. Documents available from Ask*IEEE. ***Continues*** *Elteknik.*
Desc: Professional information for engineers in electronics and power electronics with emphasis on industrial applications.
Ind/Abst Energy Res. Abstr. (Aug. 1976-); INSPEC (Jan. 1978-).

GW/0013-5445
EMA. ELEKTRISCHE MASCHINEN. [EMA, Elektr. Masch.]. (1969)-. Periodical. German. mo. DM146.00 Germany; DM162.70 other. Huethig and Pflaum Verlag Gmbh, Postfach 102869, D 69018 Heidelberg Germany. **Tel** 011 49 6221 4890. **UDC** 621.313. **CODEN** ELMCAJ. **[CCC].**

GW
EMA, ELEKTRISCHE MASCHINEN. **VFOAT** Eliktrische Mashinen. Vol. 48, No. 4-. Periodical. German. mo. $60.00 (add $25.50 for postage). Huethig Publishing Ltd, 117 Spencer Place, Mamaroneck NY 10543. **Tel** (914)698-6655, telex 9102400802 LAWHUTH. **Bk Rev. Ad Acc. Circ:** 6,000. Documents available from Ask*IEEE. ***Continues*** *EMA, die Elektriche Maschine.*
Ind/Abst INSPEC (July 1969-).

US/1055-6230
EMC TECHNOLOGY. ***Ceased.*** [EMC technol.]. **VFOAT** EMC Technology Magazine; EMC Technology and Interference Control News; EMC Technology & Interference Control News. **VAT** Electromagnetic Compatibility Technology. Vol. 8, No. 5 (July/Aug. 1989)-(Jan. 1994). Periodical. English. bm (Jan./Feb. issue is the Gold Book). Don White Consultants, Inc., Route 3, Box 2000 D, Gainesville VA 22065. **Tel** (703)347-0030, FAX (703)347-5813. **ED** Donald White. **LC** TK6553; .E59. **DD** 621.382/24/05. **Bk Rev. Ad Acc, Adv Mgr:** Walter Loop, **Tel** (703)347-0030. **Circ:** 28,000 (ctrl). available on CD-ROM (full text) from Datadisc. ***Continues*** *EMC Technology & Interference Control News, 0278-4270.*
Desc: Information on electromagnetic interference.
Ind/Abst Int. Aerosp. Abstr.

US/0748-108X
EMC TECHNOLOGY ... ANTHOLOGY. [EMC technol. anthol.]. **VFOAT** E.M.C. Technology ... Anthology. **VAT** Electromagnetic Compatibility Technology Anthology. 1982-. Periodical. English. Don White Consultants, Inc., Route 3, Box 2000 D, Gainesville VA 22065. **Tel** (703)347-0030, FAX (703)347-5813. **ED** Don White. **LC** TK6553; .E594. **DD** 621.38/0436. **Bk Rev. Ad Acc. Circ:** 35,000 (ctrl).
Desc: Providing electrical engineers, working within the field of electromagnetic compatibility, with pragmatic solutions to real-life problems, as well as current news items and information.

US/1054-5816
EMC TEST & DESIGN. [EMC test des.]. **VFOAT** Electromagnetic Compatibility Test and Design; EMC Test and Design. **VAT** Electromagnetic Compatibility Test & Design. Vol. 1, No. 1 (Nov./Dec. 1990)-. Periodical. English. bm. $39.00. Argus Business, 6151 Powers Ferry Road, Atlanta GA 30339. **Tel** (404)995-2500, (800)233-3359. **(Subscription address:** Sunbelt Fulfillment Services, PO Box 41530, Nashville TN 37204.**) LC** TK6553; .E596. **DD** 621.382/24. **CODEN** ETDEE6. Documents available from Article Express International, Ask*IEEE.
Ind/Abst Ei Page One; Eng. Index Annu.; INSPEC (Jan.-Feb. 1991-).

BE
EMTP NEWS. ***Ceased.*** (19??)-(Dec. 1993). English. qt. Kathlke Univ. of Leuven / Department Elec, K. Mercierlaan 94 / Dommelen, B-3030 Louvain, Belgium. **Tel** 032-16-220931, FAX 032-16-221855, telex 25941. **ED** D. Van Dommelen and W. S. Meyer. **Ad Acc.** ctrl circ. ***Continues*** *EMTP Newsletter.*
Desc: Study of transient phemomena in electrical power systems.

RU/0013-7278
ENERGETIK (MOSKVA). (ENERGETIK.). [Energetik]. **Added/Corp** Soviet Union. Ministerstvo Elektrostantsii. Soviet Union. Ministerstvo Elektrostantsii i Elektropromyshlennosti. (1953)-. Periodical. Russian. mo. $199.95. **(Subscription address:** East View Publications Inc., 3020 Harbor Lane North, Suite 110, Minneapolis MN 55447.**) LC** TK4; .E774. **CODEN** EGTKA9. Documents available from Ask*IEEE, CASDDS. ***Supersedes*** *Rabochii Energetik.*
Ind/Abst Chem. Abstr.; INSPEC (1968-).

LI/0235-7208
ENERGETIKA. Added/Corp Lietuvos Mokslu Akademija. Prezidiumas. Fizikiniu-Techniniu Energetikos Problemu Institutas (Lietuvos Mokslu Akademija). **VFOAT** Power Engineering; Lietuvos Mokslu Akademija. Energetika. (1990)-. Periodical. Russian (summaries and/or abstracts in English and Lithuanian; table of contents in English and Lithuanian). ir. $199.95. **(Subscription address:** East View Publications Inc., 3020 Harbor Lane North, Suite 110, Minneapolis MN 55447.**) LC** TJ163.6; E47. **CODEN** ENEKEL. Documents available from Ask*IEEE. ***Continues in part*** *Lietuvos TSR Mokslu Akademijos Darbai. Serija B, 0132-2729.*
Ind/Abst INSPEC (1990-).

UN/0424-9879
ENERGETIKA I ELEKTRIFIKACIA KIEV. [Energ. elektrif.Kiev]. (1966)-. Periodical. Russian. Four times a year. $159.95. **(Subscription address:** East View Publications Inc., 3020 Harbor Lane North, Suite 110, Minneapolis MN 55447.**) UDC** 620.9+621.311. Documents available from CASDDS.
Ind/Abst Chem. Abstr.

BU/0324-1521
ENERGETIKA (SOFIJA). (ENERGETIKA : ORGAN NA KOMITETA PO ENERGETIKATA I GORIVATA I NAUCHNO-TEKHNICHESKIIA SUIUZ PO ELEKTROTEKHNIKA.). [Energetika]. **Added/Corp** Komitet po Energetikata i Gorivata (Bulgaria) Nauchno-Tekhnicheski Suiuz po Elektrotekhnika. Suiuz po Energetika, Elektrotekhnika i Suobshteniia (Bulgaria) Bulgaria. Ministerstvo na Energetikata. (1966)-. Periodical. Bulgarian (summaries and/or abstracts in German and Russian). Eight times a year. DM215.00. Suiuz Na Iuristite v Bulgaria, Ul Zhdanov No, 1000 Sofia Bulgaria. **(Subscription address:** Kubon & Sagner, ABT Zeitschriftenimport, D 80328 Munich Germany.**) LC** TK4; .E743. **CODEN** ENGTBL. Documents available from CASDDS. ***Continues*** *Elektroenergiia.*
Ind/Abst Chem. Abstr.

IT/0013-7308
ENERGIA ELETTRICA. (L'ENERGIA ELETTRICA.). [Energ. elettr.]. (1924)-. Academic Scholarly Publication. Italian (French, English and Spanish). Twelve times a year. L45000.00 (members), L90000.00 (nonmembers) Italy; L110000.00 other. Association Elettrotecnica Elettronic, Italiana Viale Monza 259, 20126 Milan Italy. **Tel** 011 39 2 25779223. **ED** "Fondatore: Giacinto Motta.". **LC** TK4; .E775. **CODEN** ENELAK. **[CCC].** Index available. cum. index. **Ad Acc. Circ:** 30,000 (ctrl). Documents available from Article Express International, Ask*IEEE, CASDDS. ***Absorbed*** *Annali delle Utilizzazioni delle Acque.*
Desc: Original scientific articles on electrotechnics and subjects concerning electrical energy generation (hydraulics, thermotechnics, structural engineering) as well as relevant main plants.
Ind/Abst Bioeng. Abstr.; Chem. Abstr. (1973-); Coal Abstr.; Ei Page One; Energy Res. Abstr.; Eng. Index Annu.; Fluid Abstr., Civil Eng.; Fluid Abstr. Proc. Eng.; FLUIDEX (1973-1990); GeoRef; INSPEC (Jan. 1981-); Int. Aerosp. Abstr.; Int. Civil Eng. Abstr.; Saf. Health Work; Soft. Abstr. Eng.

CG
ENERGIE ET PROGRES. Yearly V. 1- ; Jan. 1972-. Periodical. French. Societe Nationale d'Electricite, Building INSS, Boulevard du 30-Juin Boite, Postale 500, Kinshasa Zaire. **LC** TK119.Z3; E53. **DD** 621.39/4/096751.

US/0736-6582
ENGINEER (NEW YORK, N.Y. 1982), THE. (THE ENGINEER / WESTERN ELECTRIC.). [Engineer]. **Added/Corp** Western Electric Company. **VFOAT** Western Electric Engineer. Vol. 26, No. 3 (Summer 1982)-. Periodical. English. qt. Western Electric, 222 Broadway, NY NY 10038. **DD** 621. **CODEN** ENGRDH. Documents available from Article Express International, Ask*IEEE, CASDDS. ***Continues*** *Western Electric Engineer, 0043-3659.*
Ind/Abst Bibliogr. Mission.; Bioeng. Abstr.; Chem. Abstr. (1982-1983); Ei Page One; Eng. Index Annu.; INSPEC (1982-).

US
ENGINEERING MANAGEMENT CONFERENCE. English. an. Institute of Electrical and Electronics Engineers / IEEE, 445 Hoes Lane, Piscataway NJ 08855. **Tel** (908)981-0060.

US
ENVIRONMENTAL DEVELOPMENT PLAN (EDP). ELECTRIC ENERGY SYSTEMS. Main/Corp United States. Dept. of Energy. Office of Energy Technology. **VFOAT** Electric Energy Systems. 1977-. English. an. US Department of Energy Office of Energy Technology, 1000 Independence Avenue SW, Washington DC 20585.

IT/0394-6681
EO NEWS. [EO News]. (1987)-. Periodical. Italian. Nineteen times a year. L57000 Italy; L114000 other. Gruppo Editoriale Jackson Spa, Via Gorki 69, 20092 Cinisello Balsamo Italy. **Tel** 011 39 2 66034401. **UDC** 621 :38. ***Continues*** *Elettronica Strumentazione Product News.*

UK/0963-5920
EPE. VFOAT Electrical Power Engineer. (1990)-. English. mo. £25.00 UK; £30.00 other. Electrical Power Engineers Association, Station House, Fox Lane N, Chertsey, Surrey KT16 9HW England. **Tel** 011 0932 564131. **ED** Patricia Battams. Index available. **Bk Rev. Ad Acc. Circ:** 33,296. ***Continues*** *Electrical Power Engineer, 0013-4376.*
Desc: Magazine of the Engineers and Managers Association. Covers trade union members working in senior positions in electricity, shipbuilding, aerospace and general engineering industries.

UK/0954-3244
EPJOURNAL. See Publishing.

US/0362-3416
EPRI JOURNAL. [EPRI j.]. **Main/Corp** Electric Power Research Institute. **Added/Corp** Electric Power Research Institute. Journal. **VAT** Electric Power Research Institute Journal. No. 1 (Feb. 1976)-. Periodical. English. Eight times a year (Except Jan./Feb. and July/Aug.issues are combined). $29.00 US; $100.00 other. Electric Power Research Institute, PO Box 10412, Palo Alto CA 94303. **Tel** (415)855-2837, (415)855-2600, FAX (415)855-2041. **ED** Brent Barker. **LC** TK1; .E233a. **DD** 621.31/05. **CODEN** EPRJDS. Index available. cum. index. **Circ:** 25,000 (ctrl). Documents available from Article Express International, Ask*IEEE, UMI Article Clearinghouse, CASDDS, Documents on Demand.
Desc: Electrical power research and development, new technologies, environmental and economic issues.
Ind/Abst Abstr. Bull. Inst. Pap. Sci. Tech.; AESIS Q.; Appl. Sci. Technol. Index; Bioeng. Abstr.; Ceram. Abstr.; Chem. Abstr.; Coal Abstr.; Ei Page One; Energy Inf. Abstr.; Energy Res. Abstr. (March 1976-); Eng. Index Annu. [Select. Cov.]; Environ. Abstr.; Environ. Period. Bibliogr. (1976-); Expand. Acad. Index (1992-); Fluid Abstr., Civil Eng.; Fluid Abstr. Proc. Eng.; FLUIDEX (1976-1990); GeoRef; HTFS Dig.; INIS Atomindex [Micro.]; INSPEC (Sept. 1980-); Int. Aerosp. Abstr.; Int. Build. Serv. Abstr.; J. Plan. Lit.; Newsp. Period. Abstr. (1992-); Pollut. Abstr. Indexes; Risk Abstr.

US/1042-3737
EPSIG NEWS. [EPSIG news]. **Added/Corp** Association of American Publishers. Electronic Publishing Special Interest Group. **VAT** Electronic Publishing Special Interest Group News. Vol. 1 No. 1 (Sept. 1987)-. Periodical. English. qt. $25.00. Electronic Publishing Special Interest Group (EPSIG), c/o OCLC, 6565 Frantz Road, Dublin OH 43017-0702. **DD** 070. **CODEN** EPNWEE.

FR/0758-489X
EPURE. [Epure]. (1984)-. Periodical. French. qt. Free. Electricite France dir Etudes, 1 Ave du General de Gaulle, F 92140 Clamart France. **Tel** 011 33 1 47654321. **UDC** 621.3. Documents available from Article Express International, Ask*IEEE.
Ind/Abst Ei Page One; Eng. Index Annu. [Select. Cov.]; Fluid Abstr., Civil Eng.; Fluid Abstr. Proc. Eng.; FLUIDEX (19??-); INSPEC (1984-).

SP
EQUIPOS PRODUCTOS ELECTRONICOS. (19??)-. Spanish. Free. Elsevier Prensa SA, Avenida Paral Lel 180, 08015 Barcelona Spain. **Tel** 011 34 3 3255350, FAX 011 34 3 4252880. **Ad Acc.** Full Page (B&W) 385000ptas. Half Page (B&W) 235000ptas. Full Page (Color) 410000ptas. Half Page

(Color) 255000ptas.
Desc: New products publication for the Spanish electronics industry.

SW
ERA, ELEKTRICITETENS RATIONELLA ANVANDNING. **VFOAT** Elecktricitetens Rationella Anvandning. Jan. 15, 1928-. Periodical. Swedish. mo. Kr170.00 Sweden; Kr300.00 US. ERA, Box 3192, Stockholm 10363 Sweden. **Tel** +468 7916900, FAX 468 210352, telex 13848 SETS. **ED** Bo Gustrin. **LC** TK4. **CODEN** ERAFAA. Index available. **Bk Rev.** **Ad Acc.** **Circ:** 13,000 (ctrl). Documents available from Ask*IEEE.
Desc: Purely technical articles and original articles on questions of common interest for the electric branch such as surveys and reports on electrical engineering.
Ind/Abst Energy Res. Abstr. (Sept. 1974-); INSPEC (1968-).

IT
ERA ELETTRONICA. Italian. Six times a year. L300000.00. Edric Srl, Via Della Pigna 19, 00186 Rome Italy. **Tel** 011 39 6 6785789.

JA/0421-3513
EREKUTORONIKUSU. [Erekutoronikusu]. **VFOAT** Electronics. (1956)-. Academic Scholarly Publication. Japanese. mo. $246.50. Nihon Denshi Kikai Kogyokai Gijutsu Honiinkai, (Electronic Industries Assoc. of Japan), 3-1, Kanda Nishikicho, Chiyodaku, Tokyoto 101 Japan. **(Subscription address:** Maruzen Company Ltd., PO Box 5050, Import & Export Department, Tokyo 100 31 Japan.**)** **ED** Takeshi Suzuki. **CODEN** EREKDE. **Circ:** 25,000 (ctrl). Documents available from CASDDS.
Desc: Journal of explanation about all-around electronics: computers, system, materials and parts of information systems.
Ind/Abst Chem. Abstr.

GW/0720-6240
ET. ENERGIEWIRTSCHAFTLICHE TAGESFRAGEN. See Energy.

GW/0170-1711
ETZ. ELEKROTECHNISCHE ZEITSCHRIFT (BERLIN, WEST). (ETZ.). [Etz, Elekrotech. Z.]. **Added/Corp** Verband Deutscher Elektrotechniker. Energietechnische Gesellschaft im VDE. (Mar. 1987)-. Periodical. Greek, Modern. bw. DM151.78 (general), DM124.78 (VDE-members), DM84.58 (students). VDE Verlag GmbH, Postfach 122305, D 10591 Berlin Germany. **Tel** 011 49 30 3480010. **LC** TK3; .E84. **DD** 621.3. **CODEN** EEEFEB. **[CCC].** Documents available from Ask*IEEE. ***Continues*** *Elektrotechnische Zeitschrift (Berlin : 1979), 0170-1711.*
Ind/Abst Ei Page One; F&S Index Plus Text, Int. [Select. Cov.]; Infomat Int. Bus.; INSPEC (1987-); PROMT.

US/0277-898X
EUPHONY. [Euphony]. Periodical. English. Harrison Systems Inc, PO Box 22964, Nashville TN 37202. **LC** TK7881.4; .E93. **DD** 621.389/3/05.

SP/0211-2973
EUROFACH ELECTRONICA. [Eurofach electron.]. (1976)-. Periodical. Spanish. mo. 10810ptas Canary Islands; 11500ptas other Spain; 12500ptas other Europe; 13500ptas other. Pedeca, Maria Auxiliadora 5, 28040 Madrid Spain. **Tel** 011 34 1 4508837. **ED** Aridres Hennequet and Eloy Maestre. **UDC** 621.38. **Bk Rev.** **Ad Acc**, **Adv Mgr:** Carlos Gomez Yepes. **Acid Free.** **Circ:** 7,500 (ctrl).
Desc: Covers all aspects of the electronic industry.

UK/0952-956X
EUROPEAN ELECTRICAL APPLIANCES MARKETING DIRECTORY. [Eur. electr. appl. mark. dir.]. (1988)-. English. an. $335.00. Euromonitor Publications Ltd., 87-88 Turnmill Street, London EC1M 5QU England. **Tel** 011 44 71 2518024, FAX 011 44 71 6083149, telex 21120. **(Subscription address:** North America: Gale Research Co., 835 Penobscot Building, Detroit, MI 48226**)**
Desc: Contains extensive details on 3,600 manufacturers, retailers and wholesalers of electrical appliances in Europe.

UK/0905-2233
EUROPEAN GENERATING SET DIRECTORY. Directory. English. an. £52.25 UK; $89.00 other. Argus Press Group, Queensway House, 2 Queensway Redhill, Surrey RH1 1QS England. **Tel** 011 44 737 768611, 011 44 737 761685, FAX 011 44 737 760510, telex 948669 TOPJNL G.

UK
EUROPEAN MICROWAVE CONFERENCE; CONFERENCE PROCEEDINGS. **Main/Conf** European Microwave Conference. (1969)-. Proceedings. English. an. £57.00. Microwave Exhibitions and Publishers, 90 Calverley Road, Tunbridge Wells TN1 2UN England. **Tel** 0892 544027. **CODEN** CEMCDJ. Documents available from Article Express International.
Ind/Abst Bioeng. Abstr.; Ei Page One; Eng. Index Annu.

UK
EUROPEAN MINIATURE ELECTRONIC COMPONENTS AND ASSEMBLIES DATA : INCLUDING SIX-LANGUAGE GLOSSARIES OF ELECTRONIC COMPONENT AND MICROELECTRONICS TERMS. ***Title Change.*** English. an. Pergamon Press, An Imprint of Elsevier Science Ltd., The Boulevard, Langford Lane, Kidlington, Oxford OX5 1GB United Kingdom. **Tel** 011 44 865 843000, 011 44 865 843699, FAX 011 44 865 843010. **(Subscription address:** US/ 395 Saw Mill River Road, Elmsford, NY 10523; Can/ 150 Consumers Road/Suite 104, Willowdale Ontario M2J 1P9; Aus-NZ/ POB 544, Potts Point NSW 2011**)** **ED** G W A Dummer and J MacKenzie Robertson. ***Continues*** *Miniature Electronic Components Data Annual.* ***Continued by*** *German Miniature Electronic Components and Assemblies Data.*

UK/0261-8214
EUROPEAN POWER NEWS. See Energy.

UK/0957-5685
EUROPEAN SEMICONDUCTOR. (EUROPEAN SEMICONDUCTOR : DESIGN, PRODUCTION, ASSEMBLY.). [Eur. semicond.]. (1987)-. Periodical. English. Ten times a year. £49.00 Europe; £61.00 others; $162.00 US. Angel Publishing Ltd., 361 373 City Road, 5th Floor, London EC1V 1LR England. **Tel** 011 44 71 417 7400, FAX 011 44 71 417 7500. **ED** Andrew Hicklenton. **CODEN** EUSEEK. **Ad Acc.** **Circ:** 8,240 (ctrl). Documents available from Article Express International, Ask*IEEE. ***Continues*** *European Semiconductor Design & Production.*
Desc: Specialist publication aimed specifically at the European user of semiconductor manufacturing and test equipment.
Ind/Abst Ei Page One; Eng. Index Annu.; INSPEC (Sep. 1989-).

GW/0939-3072
EUROPEAN TRANSACTIONS ON ELECTRICAL POWER ENGINEERING. [Eur. trans. electr. power eng.]. **Added/Corp** Verband Deutscher Elektrotechniker. Convention of National Societies of Electrical Engineers of Western Europe. Commission of the European Communities. **VFOAT** ETEP. Vol. 1, No. 1 (Jan./Feb. 1991)-. Periodical. English. bm. VDE Verlag GmbH, Postfach 122305, D 10591 Berlin Germany. **Tel** 011 49 30 3480010. **CODEN** ETEEEB. **[CCC].** Documents available from The Genuine Article, Ask*IEEE. ***Continues*** *ETZ Archiv, 0170-1703.*
Ind/Abst Curr. Contents Eng. Tech. Appl. Sci.; INSPEC (Jan.-Feb. 1991-); Res. Alert [Select. Cov.].

CN/0837-3752
EV CIRCUIT - ELECTRIC VEHICLE CLUB OF OTTAWA. (EV CIRCUIT : NEWSLETTER OF THE ELECTRIC VEHICLE CLUB OF OTTAWA.). [EV circuit - Electr. Veh. Club Ott.]. **Added/Corp** Electric Vehicle Club of Ottawa. **VAT** Electric Vehicle Circuit - Electric Vehicle Club of Ottawa. June (1987)-. Periodical. English. bm. 15.00Can$. EV Circuit, PO Box 4044 Station B, Ottawa Ontario K1S 5B1 Canada. **Tel** (613)232-5950. **ED** Fred D. Green. **DD** 629.2/293/05. ctrl circ. ***Continues*** *EV Circuit (Ottawa, Ont. : 1982), 0822-5230.*

US/0149-0370
EVALUATION ENGINEERING. (EE, EVALUATION ENGINEERING.). [Eval. eng.]. **VFOAT** EE; Evaluation Engineering. (197?)-. Periodical. English. mo. $90.00 US; $115.00 Canada; $135.00 other; $85.00 (airmail) Brazil, Bulgaria, England, Czechoslovakia, Finland, France, Holland, Italy, Norway, Spain, Switzerland, Germany, North Africa, Caribbean, South America; $105.00 (airmail) Australia, India, Israel, Japan, Korea, Singapore, Taiwan, former USSR, Hong Kong, New Zealand, South Africa, Middle East. Nelson Publishing, 2504 North Tamiami Trail, Nokomis FL 34275. **Tel** (813)966-9521, FAX (813)966-2590. **ED** A. Verner Nelson. **LC** TK7869; .E3. **DD** 620. **[CCC].** **Bk Rev.** **Ad Acc.** **Circ:** 70,312 (ctrl). Documents available from Article Express International, Ask*IEEE. ***Continues*** *Evaluation Engineering, 0149-0370.*
Desc: Serves companies that test/evaluate, design, develop and manufacture electronics products, equipment and systems.
Ind/Abst Eng. Index Annu.; INSPEC (Sept./Oct. 1968-).

UK/0262-3617
EVERYDAY ELECTRONICS. ***Title Change.*** [Everyday electron.]. (1971)-(19??). Periodical. English. mo. Wimborne Publishing Ltd., 6 Church Street, Wimborne, Dorset BH21 1JH England. **Tel** 011 44 202 881749, FAX 011 44 202 841692. **ED** Mike Kenward. **DD** 537.5. Index available. **Ad Acc.** ***Continued by*** *Everyday with Practical Eletronics.*

UK
EVERYDAY WITH PRACTICAL ELECTRONICS. (19??)-. English. Twelve times a year. £24.00 UK; £30.00 other. Wimborne Publishing Ltd., 6 Church Street, Wimborne, Dorset BH21 1JH England. **Tel** 011 44 202 881749, FAX 011 44 202 841692. **ED** Mike Kenward (editor's address: Allen House, East Borough, Wimborne, Dorset BH21 1PF England). Index available in last issue of volume--attached. **Ad Acc**, **Adv Mgr:** P. Mew, **Tel** 0255 850596. **Circ:** 23,000. ***Formed by the union of*** *Everyday Electronic, 0262-3617* ***and*** *Practical Electronics, 0032-6372 Electronics Monthly.*

US/1069-708X
EW DESIGN ENGINEERS' HANDBOOK & MANUFACTURERS DIRECTORY. ***Title Change.*** See Military and Defense.

•US
EW REFERENCE & SOURCE GUIDE. See Military and Defense.

GW/0176-0920
EX MAGAZINE. [Ex mag.]. (197?)-. English. an. Free. R. Stahl Inc., 150 L New Boston Street, Woburn MA 01801. **Tel** (617)933-1844. **CODEN** EXMADW. Documents available from Ask*IEEE.
Ind/Abst INSPEC (June 1978-).

CN/0846-9105
FABRICANTS DE PRODUITS ELECTRIQUES ET ELECTRONIQUES AU QUEBEC, REPERTOIRE, LES. [Fabr. prod. electr. electron. Que. repert.]. **Added/Corp** Quebec (Province). Ministere de l'Industrie, du Commerce et de la Technologie. Quebec (Province). Direction des Produits Electriques et Electroniques. **VFOAT** Les Fabricants de Produits Electriques et Electroniques au Quebec. (June 1990)-. French. **DD** 338.4/76213/025714. ***Continues*** *Repertoire des Fabricants de Produits Electriques et Electroniques., 0839-9433.*

CN/0380-7061
FACTORY SALES OF ELECTRIC STORAGE BATTERIES. [Fact. sales electr. storage batteries]. **Main/Corp** Canada. Statistique Canada. Division des Indutries Manufacturieres et Primaires. **Added/Corp** Canada. Dominion Bureau of Statistics. Mining, Metallurgical & Chemical Section. Canada. Dominion Bureau of Statistics. Canada. Dominion Bureau of Statistics. Metal and Chemical Products Section. Canada. Bureau Federal de la Statistique. Division de l'Industrie et du Commerce. Canada. Bureau Federal de la Statistique. Division de l'Industrie. Canada. Bureau Federal de la Statistique. Division des Industries Manufacturieres et Primaires. Statistique Canada. Division des Industries Manufacturieres et Primaires. Statistique Canada. Division de l'Industrie. **VFOAT** Ventes a l'Usine de Batteries d'Accumulateurs Electriques. (May 1949)-. Periodical. French (English). mo. 60.00Can$ Canada; $72.00 US; $84.00 other. Statistics Canada, Publications Sales & Services, Main Building Room 1710, Ottawa Ontario K1A 0T6 Canada. **Tel** (613)951-5078, (800)267-6677, FAX (613)951-1584, telex 053-3585. **DD** 338.4/76292542/0971. ***Continues*** *Monthly Report on Factory Sales of Electric Storage Batteries.*
Desc: Contains data on Canadian factory sales of lead-acid and alkaline storage batteries. Includes the number of units sold and their factory selling value each month along with a cumulative total for the year.

US
FAIRCHILD'S ELECTRONICS INDUSTRY FINANCIAL DIRECTORY. ***Ceased.*** 30th Ed. (1991/1992)-(1993). Directory. English. an. Fairchild Publications Inc, 7 West 34th Street, 4th Floor, New York NY 10001. **Tel** (212)630-4230. ***Continues*** *Electronic News Financial Fact Book & Directory, 0070-9875.*

FR
FAITS MARQUANTS. French. an. 2 rue Louis-Murat, 75384 Paris Cedex 08 France. **LC** TK71; .E44. **DD** 621.3/072044. ***Continues*** *Electricite de France. Direction des Etudes et Recherches. Quelques Faits Marquants.*

IT
FARE ELETTRONICA. Italian. mo. L67.200 Italy; L134.400 other. Gruppo Editoriale Jackson Spa, Via Gorki 69, 20092 Cinisello Balsamo Italy. **Tel** 011 39 2 66034401. **(Subscription address:** Via Amendola 45, Paderno Dugnano, Milan Italy**)** **ED** Angelo Cattaneo. Index available. cum. index. **Ad Acc.** **Pr Rev.** **Circ:** 40,000 (ctrl).
Desc: Magazine dedicated to practical hobby electronics.

US/0731-5171
FERROELECTRICS. LETTERS SECTION. [Ferroelectr., Lett. sect.]. **VFOAT** Ferroelectrics Letters. Vol. 44, No. 1 (April 1982)-. Academic Scholarly Publication. English. mo. $373.00 (academic institutions), $582.00 (corporate institutions). Gordon & Breach Science Publishers, Inc., PO Box 786, Cooper Station, New York NY 10276. **Tel** (212)206-8900, FAX (212)645-2459. **(Subscription address:** International Publishers Distributor at one of the following addresses: 820 Town Center Drive, Langhorne, PA 19047; or PO Box 90, Reading Berkshire RG1 8JL UK; or Kent Ridge PO Box 1180, Singapore 9111, Republic of Singapore**)** **ED** George W. Taylor. **LC** QC596; .F47. **DD** 537/.2448. **CODEN** FELEDJ. **[CCC].** **Bk Rev.** **Ad Acc.** **Pr Rev.** Documents available from Article Express International, The Genuine Article, Ask*IEEE, CASDDS.

Ind/Abst Alum. Ind. Abstr. (1982-); Chem. Abstr. (1983-); Chem. Titles (1982-); Curr. Contents Clin. Med.; Ei Page One; Eng. Index Annu.; INSPEC (1982-); Leadscan; Met. Abstr. (1982-); Res. Alert [Full Cov.]; Sci. Cit. Index; SCISEARCH.

●US
FINANCIAL STATISTICS OF MAJOR U.S. INVESTOR-OWNED ELECTRIC UTILITIES. See Engineering-Abstracting, Bibliographies and Statistics.

UK/0266-7797
FINTECH. 2, ELECTRONIC OFFICE. [FinTech, 2 Electron. off.]. (1984)-. Periodical. English. bw. Financial Times Business Information Ltd., Tower House, Southampton Street, London WC2E 7HA England. **Tel** 011 44 71 353 1040. **DD** 651.2.
Ind/Abst Infomat Int. Bus.; PTS Newsl. Database [Full Txt.].

RU/0015-3222
FIZIKA I TECHNIKA POLUPROVODNIKOV. [Fiz. teh. poluprovodn.]. **Added/Corp** Akademiia Nauk SSSR. **VFOAT** Physics and Technics of Semiconductors. Vol. 1 (1967)-. Academic Scholarly Publication. Russian (table of contents in English). mo. $246.00. Izdatelstvo Nauka / Akademiia Nauk, Publishing House of the Russian Academy of Sciences, Leninskii Porspekt 14, 117901 Moscow Russia. **Tel** 011 95 954-21-53, FAX 011 95 938-21-44, telex 411964. **(Subscription address:** Victor Kamkin, 4956 Boiling Brook Parkway, Rockville, MD 20852**) CODEN** FTPPA4. Documents available from Ask*IEEE, CASDDS.
Desc: Information on semiconductors.
Ind/Abst Alum. Ind. Abstr.; Ceram. Abstr.; Chem. Abstr.; Chem. Titles; Eng. Mater. Abstr.; INSPEC (1968-); Int. Aerosp. Abstr.; Met. Abstr.

US/0734-7723
FLORIDA POWER & LIGHT COMPANY TEN YEAR POWER PLANT SITE REPORT. (FLORIDA POWER & LIGHT COMPANY TEN YEAR POWER PLANT SITE PLAN ...). **Main/Corp** Florida Power and Light Company. **VFOAT** Florida Power and Light Company Ten Year Power Plant Site Plan; Ten Year Power Plant Site Plan. English. an. Florida Power & Light Company, PO Box 529100, Miami FL 33152.

US
FLUORESCENT LAMP BALLASTS. (CURRENT INDUSTRIAL REPORTS. MQ-36C, FLUORESCENT LAMP BALLASTS (COMPUTER FILE).). [Fluoresc. lamp ballasts]. **Added/Corp** United States. Bureau of the Census. **VFOAT** Fluorescent Lamp Ballasts. (1992)-. Periodical. English. qt. US Department of Commerce, 14th Street & Constitution Avenue NW, Washington DC 20230. **Tel** (202)482-2000, FAX (202)482-3772. **LC** HD9697.L333; U68a. **DD** 338.4/76213273. Documents available from Documents on Demand. ***Continues** Current Industrial Reports. MQ36C, Flourescent Lamps Ballasts.*
Desc: Presents data on the production, inventories, and orders of approximately 5,000 products, which represents 40 percent of all US manufacturing.

US/0145-5184
FLUORESCENT LAMP BALLASTS. ***Title Change.*** (CURRENT INDUSTRIAL REPORTS. MQ-36C, FLUORESCENT LAMP BALLASTS.). [Fluoresc. lamp ballasts]. **Added/Corp** United States. Bureau of the Census. **VFOAT** Fluorescent Lamp Ballasts. (19??)-(1992). Government Publication. English. qt. US Department of Commerce, 14th Street & Constitution Avenue NW, Washington DC 20230. **Tel** (202)482-2000, FAX (202)482-3772. **LC** HD9697.L333; U68a. **DD** 338.4/76213273. Documents available from Documents on Demand. ***Continued by** Current Industrial Reports. MQ36C, Fluorescent Lamp Ballasts (Computer File).*
Desc: Presents timely data on the production, inventories, and orders of approximately 5,000 products, which represents 40 percent of all US manufacturing.
Ind/Abst Am. Stat. Index.

●UK/0969-6202
FOCUS ON ELECTRONICS CHEMICALS. See Chemistry.

US/0093-3155
FOREST H. BELT'S YEARBOOK OF CONSUMER ELECTRONICS. [Forest H. Belt's yearb. consum. electron.]. **VFOAT** Yearbook of Consumer Electronics. (1974)-. English. an. $2.50. Forest H. Belt's Yearbook of Consumer Electronics, PO Box 68351, Indianapolis IN 46268. **LC** TK7869; .B34. **DD** 621.38/05.

GW/0341-1672
FORTSCHRITT-BERICHTE DER VDI ZEITSCHRIFTEN. REIHE 8, MESS-, STEUERUNGS- UND REGELUNGSTECHNIK. [Fortschrittber. VDI-Z., 8, Mess-, Steuerungs- Regelungstech.]. **VFOAT** Mess-, Steuerungs- und Regelungstechnik. **VAT** Fortschritt-Berichte der Verein Deutscher Ingenieure-Zeitschriften. Reihe 8, Mess-, Steuerungs- und Regelungstechnik. Monographic series. German. Price varies per volume. VDI Verlag GmbH, Postfach 101054, D 40001 Dusseldorf Germany. **Tel** 011 49 211 6188313, FAX 011 49 211 6188133.
Ind/Abst Math. Rev.

US
FOSTER ELECTRIC REPORT. (19??)-. English. Twenty-six times a year. $650.00. Foster Associates Inc., 1015 15th Street Northwest, Suite 1100, Washington DC 20005-2697. **Tel** (202)408-7710, FAX (202)408-7723.

US/0197-2766
FRACTURE MECHANICS OF CERAMICS. See Glass and Ceramics.

GW/0016-1136
FREQUENZ ZEITSCHRIFT FUER SCHWINGUNGS-UND SCHWACHSTROMTECHNIK. [Frequenz]. Vol. 1 (Oct. 1947)-. Periodical. German. mo. DM588.00 Germany; DM640.20 other. Fachverlag Schiele & Schoen, Markgrafenstrasse 11, W-1000 Berlin 61 Germany. **Tel** 011/49/30/2516029, FAX 011/49/30/2517248, telex 841/181470. **CODEN** FONZA3. **[CCC]. Pr Rev.** Documents available from Article Express International, The Genuine Article, Ask*IEEE.
Ind/Abst Bioeng. Abstr.; Ei Page One; Energy Res. Abstr. (Oct. 1976-); Eng. Index Annu.; INSPEC (1968-); Int. Aerosp. Abstr.; Math. Rev.; Res. Alert [Select. Cov.]; SCISEARCH.

US/0532-744X
FRONTIERS IN FUEL CELLS. (Aug. 1, 1962)-. English. Venture-Technology Inc, 1015 Claymark Drive, St Louis MO 63131. **DD** 621.3.

US
FRONTIERS IN LASERS/MASERS. Periodical. English. bw. Venture-Technology Inc, 1015 Claymark Drive, St Louis MO 63131. **LC** TK7871.3; .F76. **DD** 621.36/6/05.

US
FUEL CELLS. Added/Corp American Chemical Society. Division of Fuel Chemistry. American Chemical Society Division of Petroleum Chemistry. Vol. 1. English. Van Nostrand Reinhold Company Inc., 115 5th Avenue, New York NY 10003. **Tel** (212)254-3232, FAX (212)673-1239, telex 272562. **ED** G J Young. **LC** TK2920; .F8. **DD** 621.3.
Desc: Vols 1- are presented at the American Chemical Society symopsia, 1959.

US/1050-1150
FUEL INJECTION & ELECTRONIC ENGINE CONTROLS. AUDI, BMW, JAGUAR, MERCEDES-BENZ, PEUGEOT, SAAB, STERLING, VOLKSWAGEN, VOLVO. [Fuel inject. electron. engine controls, Audi BMW Jaguar Mercedes-Benz Peugeot Saab Sterling Volkswagen Volvo]. **Added/Corp** Chilton Book Company. **VFOAT** Fuel Injection and Electronic Engine Controls. Audi, BMW, Jaguar, Mercedes-Benz, Peugeot, Saab, Sterling, Volkswagen, Volvo; Audi, BMW, Jaguar, Mercedes-Benz, Peugeot, Saab, Sterling, Volkswagen, Volvo; Europe; Chilton's Guide to Fuel Injection & Electronic Engine Controls. Audi, BMW, Jaguar, Mercedes-Benz, Peugeot, Saab, Sterling, Volkswagen, Volvo.; Chilton Fuel Injection & Electronic Engine Controls. Europe. (1990)-. English. be. $18.95 (single issue). Chilton Book Company, 1 Chilton Way, Radnor PA 19089. **Tel** (215)964-4000, (800)695-1214, FAX (215)964-4273, telex 6851035 CHILTON UW. **DD** 629.

JA/0429-8284
FUJI ELECTRIC REVIEW. [Fuji electr. rev.]. (1964)-. Periodical. English. Fuji Corporation, Han Ei, 2 Building 1 10 1 Shinjuku, Shinjuku-ku Tokyo 160 Japan. **Tel** 011 81 3 35087017. **CODEN** FUERBV. ***Continues** Fuji Denki Review.*

JA/0367-3332
FUJI JIHO. [Fuji jiho]. **VFOAT** Fuji Electric Journal. Began in 1923. Academic Scholarly Publication. Japanese (Japanese). mo. $105.50. Fuji Denki K.K., (Fuji Electric Co., Ltd.), 12-1, Yurakucho 1 Chome, Chiyodaku, Tokyoto 100 Japan. **(Subscription address:** Maruzen Company Ltd., PO Box 5050, Import & Export Department, Tokyo 100 31 Japan.**) CODEN** FUJIAS. ctrl circ. Documents available from CASDDS.
Desc: Public relations magazine of electrical technique.
Ind/Abst Chem. Abstr.

JA/0016-2523
FUJITSU SCIENTIFIC & TECHNICAL JOURNAL. [Fujitsu sci. tech. j.]. **Added/Corp** Fujitsu Kabushiki Kaisha. Fujitsu Kenkyujo. **VFOAT** Fujitsu Scientific and Technical Journal; Scientific & Technical Journal; Scientific and Technical Journal. **VAT** Fujitsu Scientific and Technical Journal. Vol. 1 (Apr. 1965)-. Periodical. English. Twice a year. $50.00. **(Subscription address:** Maruzen Company Ltd., PO Box 5050, Import & Export Department, Tokyo 100 31 Japan.**) ED** Hiroshi Yamada. **LC** TK1; .F9. **CODEN** FUSTA4. **Pr Rev. Circ:** 88,000. Documents available from Article Express International, The Genuine Article, Ask*IEEE, CASDDS.
Desc: Specific studies and reports on ultra high technological fields such as electrical engineering.
Ind/Abst Alum. Ind. Abstr.; Bioeng. Abstr.; Chem. Abstr.; Curr. Contents Eng. Tech. Appl. Sci.; Ei Page One; Eng. Mater. Abstr.; Eng. Index Annu.; INSPEC (1968-); Int. Aerosp. Abstr.; Leadscan; Met. Abstr.; Res. Alert [Select. Cov.]; SCISEARCH.

JA/0911-050X
FUKUOKA KOGYO DAIGAKU EREKUTORONIKUSU KENKYUJO SHOHO. [Fukuoka Kogyo Daigaku Erekutoronikusu Kenkyujo shoho]. **Added/Corp** Fukuoka Kogyo Daigaku. Erekutoronikusu Kenkyujo. **VFOAT** Erekutoronikusu Kenkyujo Shoho; Reports of the Electronics Research Laboratory, Fukuoka Institute of Technology. (1984)-. Japanese. an. Fukuoka Kogyo Daigaku Erekutoronikusu Kenkyujo, (Electronics Research Lab., Fukuoka Inst. of Technology), 30-1, Wajiro Higashi 3 Chome, Higashiku, Fukuokashi,, Fukuokaken 811-02 Japan. **CODEN** FKDSEU. Documents available from CASDDS.
Ind/Abst Chem. Abstr.

GW/0016-2841
FUNKSCHAU. [Funkschau]. (19??)-. Periodical. German. Twenty-six times a year. DM157.00 Germany; DM168.00 other. Franzis Verlag GmbH, Postfach 200710, D 80007 Munich Germany. **Tel** 011 49 89 5117363. **LC** TK7800; .F86. **CODEN** FUSHA2. **[CCC].** Index available. **Bk Rev. Ad Acc. Circ:** 75,000 (ctrl). available on microfilm. Documents available from Ask*IEEE.
Desc: Reports on audio and visual information, communications, and computer technology. Covers new developments, offers repair tips to the professional or serious amateur engineer.
Ind/Abst Energy Res. Abstr. (May 1973-); F&S Index Plus Text, Int. [Select. Cov.]; Infomat Int. Bus.; INSPEC (Feb. 1975-); PROMT.

GW/0172-2778
FUNKSCHAU. SONDERHEFT. **VFOAT** Sonderheft. (19??)-. Periodical. German. ir. DM15.60. Franzis Verlag GmbH, Postfach 200710, D 80007 Munich Germany. **Tel** 011 49 89 5117363. **LC** TK7800; .F862. **DD** 621.38/05.

JA/0429-9159
FURUKAWA REVIEW. [Furukawa rev.]. Vol. 1 (Sept. 1980)-. Academic Scholarly Publication. English. Furukawa Denki Kogyo K.K., (Furukawa Electric Co., Ltd.), 6-1, Marunouchi 2 Chome, Chiyodaku, Tokyoto 100 Japan. **LC** TK3301; .F87. **DD** 621.319/3/05. **CODEN** FUREDP. Documents available from Article Express International, Ask*IEEE, CASDDS.
Ind/Abst Chem. Abstr.; Ei Page One; Eng. Index Annu.; INSPEC (July 1969-).

JA
GAISHI REBYU. **VFOAT** NGK Review. No. 27- Jan. 1969-. Japanese (Japanese). Nihon Gaishi Kabushi Ki Kaisha 850 Nagoya, Japan. **LC** TK3246; .G33. ***Continues** Nichigai Rebyu.*

GW/0016-4232
GALVANOTECHNIK. [Galvanotechnik]. (1959)-. Academic Scholarly Publication. German. mo. S138.00 Austria; S142.80 other. Eugen G Leuze Verlag, Postfach 1352, D 88348 Saulgau F R Germany. **Tel** 011 49 7581 7617, FAX 011 49 7581 1756. **CODEN** GVTKAY. **[CCC].** Documents available from Article Express International, Ask*IEEE, CASDDS. ***Continues** Metallwaren-Industrie und Galvanotechnik.*
Ind/Abst Alum. Ind. Abstr.; Bioeng. Abstr.; Chem. Abstr.; Curr. Titles Electrochem.; Ei Page One; EMBASE; Energy Res. Abstr.; Eng. Mater. Abstr.; Eng. Index Annu.; INSPEC (1972-); Int. Aerosp. Abstr.; Met. Abstr.; Surf. Treat. Technol. Abstr.

US/0272-3212
GE NEWS. [GE news]. **Main/Corp** General Electric Company. **VAT** General Electric News. Periodical. English. wk. General Electric Company, 120 Erie Boulevard, Schenectady NY 12305. **Tel** (502)685-6200. ***Continues** Hotpoint News, 0272-3220.*

UK/0264-9187
GEC JOURNAL OF RESEARCH. See Engineering.

UK/0267-9337
GEC REVIEW. ***Title Change.*** [GEC rev.]. **Added/Corp** General Electric Company (Great Britain). **VFOAT** G.E.C. Review; General Electric Company Review. **VAT** General Electric Company review. (1985)-. Periodical. English. Three times a year (Apr., Aug., Dec.). GEC Journal of Research, GEC-Marconi Reasearch Centre, Great Baddow, Chelmsford, Essex CM2 8HN UK. **Tel** 011 44 1 245 473331, FAX 011 44 1 245 475244. **ED** A. J. Walkden. **LC** WMLC L 83/9138. **CODEN** GECREP. **Circ:** 12,000 (ctrl). available on microfilm from University Microfilms International (UMI). Documents available from Article Express International, Ask*IEEE. ***Formed by the union of** GEC Journal of Science & Technology,*

0264-0295 ***and*** *GEC Engineering GEC Journal for Industry.*
Desc: Covers the activities and products of the whole of GEC, at a technical level which will be of interest to the specialist, while still being intelligible to the non-specialist.
Ind/Abst BMT Abstr.; Civ. Struct. Eng. Abstr.; Coal Abstr.; Comput. Inf. Syst. Abstr. J. [Full Cov.]; Curr. Technol. Index; Ei Page One; Elect. Comm. Abstr.; Eng. Mater. Abstr.; Eng. Index Annu.; Ergon. Abstr.; INSPEC (1985-); Mech. Eng. Abstr.; Pollut. Abstr. Indexes.

UK/0533-7534
GERMAN PATENTS GAZETTE: SECTION II, ELECTRICAL. [Ger. pat. gaz., Sect. 2, electr.]. (19??)-. English (German). ir. $1800.00. Derwent Publications Ltd., Derwent House 14, Great Queen Street, London WC2B 5DF England. **Tel** 011 44 71 3442800. **(Subscription address:** Derwent Inc., 1420 Spring Hill Road Suite 525, McLean VA 22102.**) LC** TK257; .G45. **DD** 621.3/02/72.

IT
GIORNALE DELL ICE. ***Title Change.*** (19??)-(19??). Italian. wk. Edizioni Abete Srl, Via Tiburtina 655, 00159 Rome Italy. **Tel** 011 39 6 4389034. ***Continues*** *Informazioni per il Commercio Estero.* ***Continued by*** *Sistemi Italia.*

IT/0392-3630
GIORNALE DELL' INSTALLATORE ELETTRICO, IL. [G. Install. Elettr.]. (1979)-. Periodical. Italian. Eighteen times a year. L60000 Italy; L130000 other. Stammer Spa, Via della Liberazione 1, 20068 Peschiera Borromeo, Italy. **Tel** 011 39 2 55302606, FAX 011 39 2 55302700, telex 321083. **ED** Girolamo Bellina. **UDC** 696.6. **Bk Rev**. **Ad Acc**. **Pr Rev. Circ:** 17,200 (ctrl).
Desc: Electricity, electrical engineering and installations.

BU
GODISHNIK NA SOFIISKIIA UNIVERSITET "SV. KLIMENT OKHRIDSKI." INSTITUT PO FIZIKA I TEKHNIKA NA POLUPROVODNITSITE / ANNUAIRE DE L'UNIVERSITE DE SOFIA "ST. KLIMENT OHRIDSKI." INSTITUTE DE PHYSIQUE ET TECHNOLOGIE DES SEMI-CONDUCTEURS. **Added/Corp** Sofiiski Universitet "Sv. Kliment Okhridski." Institut po Fizika i Tekhnika na Poluprovodnitsite. **VFOAT** Institut po Fizika i Tekhnika na Poluprovodnitsite; Institute de Physique et Technologie des Semi-Conducteurs; Annuaire de l'Universite de Sofia "Sv. Kliment Ohridski." Institute de Physique et Technologie des Semi-Conducteurs. (19??)-. Periodical. English (summaries and/or abstracts in Russian). Izdatelstvo na Bulgarskata Akademiia Na Naukite, 6 Rouski Boulevard, Sofia Bulgaria. **Tel** FAX 80 13 41, telex 22267 HEMKIK. **LC** QC610.9; .G63. **CODEN** GUKPEZ. ***Continues*** *Godishnik na Sofiiskiia Universitet "Kliment Okhridski." Fizika i Tekhnika na Poluprovodnitsite.*
Ind/Abst Chem. Abstr.

US/0097-7721
GTE JOURNAL OF RESEARCH AND DEVELOPMENT. **VAT** General Telephone & Electronics Journal of Research and Development. V. 1 (June 1974)-. Periodical. English. qt. $12.00. GTE Laboratories Inc, 40 Sylvan Road, Waltham MA 02154. **LC** TK7800; .G17. **DD** 621.3/05.

US/0163-982X
GTE LENKURT DEMODULATOR. **Main/Corp** GTE Lenkurt. **VFOAT** Demodulator. Periodical. English. bm. Lenkurt Electric Company Inc, 1105 County Road, San Carlos CA 94070. ***Continues*** *Lenkurt Demodulator.*

US/0271-731X
GTE SYLVANIA NEWS. [GTE Sylvania news]. **VAT** General Telephone and Electronics Sylvania News. Periodical. English. GTE Sylvania Electronic Components, Johnston Street, Seneca Falls NY 13148.

IT
GTV L'ANTENNA. **VFOAT** Antenna. (19??)-. Periodical. Italian. mo. **LC** TK7800; .A54. **DD** 621.38/05. ***Continues*** *Antenna Nuova.*

II/0376-5229
GUIDE TO ELECTRONICS INDUSTRY IN INDIA. 2nd- Ed.; 1974-. English. ir. $35.00 seamail, $50.00 airmail. Statistics Investigations Bureau, 4-A Naaz Building, Lamington Road, Bombay India. **Tel** 360436 6260478, telex 011-75497 AECO IN. **ED** S Swarn. **LC** HD9999.R153; I5. **DD** 333.4/7/62138102554. Index available. **Bk Rev**. **Ad Acc. Circ:** 10,000. ***Continues*** *Guide to Radio Electronics & Components Trade & Industry in India.*
Desc: Gives statistical data, facts and figures about electronics, computer, telecommunications, industrial electronics, components and other related industries in India.

KO
HAN'GUK CHONJA KONGOP TONGGYE YON'GAM. **VFOAT** Korean Electronic Industry Statistics Yearbook. 1978-. English (Korean). Hanguk Chongmil Kigi Sento, 222-13 Kuro-dong, Yongdungpo-ku, Seoul South Korea. **LC** HD9696.A3; K758.

KO
HANGUK CHONJA YONGAM. 1985-. Korean. an. Chonja Sibosa, 44-13 Youido-Dong, Yongdungpo-ku, Seoul Korea. **LC** HD9696.A3; K759.

US/1040-1105
HANSEN REPORT ON AUTOMOTIVE ELECTRONICS, THE. [Hansen rep. automot. electron.]. **Added/Corp** Paul Hansen Associates. Began in (1988)-. Periodical. English. mo. $327.00 North America; $367.00 others. Paul Hansen Associates, 234 Parker Road, Goffstown NH 03045. **Tel** (603)497-2854, FAX (603)497-2858. **ED** Paul Hansen. **DD** 629. Index available. cum. index.
Desc: A business and technology newsletter that provides a complete picture of the automotive electronics industry today and a view of what it will be like in the future. The aim of the HANSEN REPORT is to promote and encourage , to bring together carmakers and suppliers.

FR/0178-7586
HARD AND SOFT. ***Ceased.*** **See** Computers.

●US/1064-2285
HEAT TRANSFER RESEARCH. [Heat transf. res.]. **Added/Corp** Scripta Technica, Inc. American Society of Mechanical Engineers. American Society of Mechanical Engineers. Heat Transfer Division. Vol. 24, No. 1 (1992)-. Academic Scholarly Publication. English (translations available in Russian). Eight times a year. $1,496.00 US; $1,576.00 Canada and Mexico; $1,606.00 other. Scripta Technica, A Subsidiary of John Wiley & Sons, Inc., 7961 Eastern Avenue, Silver Spring MD 20910. **Tel** (301)588-0484, FAX (301)588-5278. **(Subscription address:** John Wiley / Philadelphia, PO Box 7247, Philadelphia PA 19170.**) ED** James P. Hartnett. **LC** QC320; .H38. **DD** 536/.2/005. **CODEN** HTREE7HTSO24. Documents available from Article Express International, Ask*IEEE, CASDDS. ***Continues*** *Heat Transfer: Soviet Research, 0440-5749.*
Desc: Presents translations of important theoretical and experimental papers selected from the foremost Russian, Ukranian, and Belarus periodicals, conference proceedings and academic laboratory reports.
Ind/Abst Bioeng. Abstr.; Chem. Abstr.; Coal Abstr.; Ei Page One; Energy Res. Abstr.; Eng. Index Annu.; Eng. Index Energy Abstr.; Fluid Abstr., Civil Eng.; Fluid Abstr. Proc. Eng.; FLUIDEX; INIS Atomindex [Micro.]; INSPEC; Int. Aerosp. Abstr.; Nucl. Sci. Abstr.

US
HENDERSON ELECTRONIC MARKET FORECAST. English. Eleven times a year. $495.00 US; $545.00 other. Henderson Ventures, 101 First Street, Suite 444, Los Altos CA 94022. **Tel** (415)961-2900, FAX (415)961-3000. **ED** Edward Henderson. **UDC** 33.
Desc: Analyses and quantitative forecast of the global electronics industry with a focus on US hardware markets, including communications equipment, computers, industrial electronics, instruments, military, etc.
Ind/Abst F&S Index Plus Text, Int. [Select. Cov.]; PROMT.

GW/0938-7412
HERZSCHRITTMACHERTHERAPIE & ELEKTROPHYSIOLOGIE. [Herzschrittmach.ther. Elektrophysiol.]. **VFOAT** Herzschrittmachertherapie und Elektrophysiologie. (1990)-. Periodical. Multiple languages. qt. DM162.00. Dr Dietrich Steinkopff Verlag, PO Box 111442, D 64229 Darmstadt Germany. **Tel** 011 49 6151 17450. **(Subscription address:** Springer Verlag New York Inc. / for North America, 44 Hartz Way, Secaucus NJ 07096.**) UDC** 61. **[CCC].**

US/0899-8531
HIGH RELIABILITY ELECTRONIC COMPONENTS. [High reliab. electron. compon.]. **Added/Corp** D.A.T.A. Business Publishing. **VFOAT** D.A.T.A. High Reliability Electronic Components; High Reliability Electronic Components Digest; High Reliability Electronic Components Digest Update. (1988)-. English. ir (1 annual issue plus 3 updates per year). $245.00 US; $255.00 other. DATA Business Publishing, PO Box 6510, 15 Inverness Way East, Englewood CO 80155. **Tel** (800)447-4666, (303)799-0381, FAX (303)799-4082. **LC** UG485; .H5. **DD** 621. available on CD-ROM. ***Continues*** *Military Electronic Devices Guide, Microcircuits and Semiconductors, 0887-0063.*
Desc: Information on integrated circuits, semiconductors, and electronics in military engineering.

UK/0142-6192
HOBBY ELECTRONICS. [Hobby electron.]. (1978)-. Periodical. English. mo. Infonet Ltd, Industrial Area, Billets Lane, Berkhamsted HP4 1HL England. **CODEN** HOELDT. Documents available from Ask*IEEE.
Ind/Abst INSPEC (March 1981-).

JA
HOKKAIDO DAIGAKU OYO DENKI KENKYUJO YORAN. **Main/Corp** Hokkaido Daigaku. Oyo Denki Kenkyujo. (19??)-. Periodical. Japanese. Hokkaido Daigaku, Kita 12-jo Nishi 6-chome Kita-ku, Sapporo Japan. **LC** TK7855; .H64a.

JA
HOKURIKU NO DENKI TO KOGYO. 1970/71-. Japanese. Hokuriku Denki Kyokai, Sakurabashidori, Toyama 930 Japan. **LC** HD9685.J33; H64. ***Continues*** *Hokuriku No Denki Gasu Oyobi Kogyo.*

HK
HONG KONG ELECTRONICS. English. qt. $100.00. Hong Kong Trade Development Council, 38th Floor/Office Tower, Convention Plaza, 1 Harbour Road, Hong Kong. **Tel** 852 5844333, FAX 852 8240249, telex 7395 CONHK HX. **(Subscription address:** for North America; 219 East 16th Street, New York NY 10017**) ED** Saul Lockhart. **Ad Acc. Circ:** 40,000 (ctrl).
Desc: Information on electronic products as well as a directory sourcing guide to the people who make it work in Hong Kong.

HK
HONG KONG ENERGY STATISTICS. **Added/Corp** Hong Kong. Census and Statistics Dept. Industrial Production Statistics Section. (1980)-. Government Publication. English. ir. Hong Kong Government Information Service, Beaconsfield House, 4 Queens Road, Hong Kong Hong Kong. **Tel** 011 852 8428801 4, telex 61190 HKGIS. **LC** HD9502.H8; H66. **DD** 333.79/0951/25.

UK/0265-3028
HYBRID CIRCUITS : JOURNAL OF THE INTERNATIONAL SOCIETY FOR HYBRID MICROELECTRONICS-UK / INTERNATIONAL SOCIETY FOR HYBRID ELECTRONICS, UNITED KINGDOM. ***Title Change.*** (HYBRID CIRCUITS : JOURNAL OF THE INTERNATIONAL SOCIETY FOR HYBRID MICROELECTRONICS.). [Hybrid circuits]. **Added/Corp** International Society for Hybrid Microelectronics--UK. (19??)-(19??). Academic Scholarly Publication. English. Three times a year. Wela Publications Ltd, Asahi House, 10 Church Road, Port Erin, Isle of Man., British Isles. **Tel** 011 44 0 624 836044, FAX 011 44 0 624 835400. **ED** Lorna Cullen. **CODEN** HYCRD5. **[CCC].** Index available. cum. index. **Bk Rev. Ad Acc.** Documents available from Ask*IEEE, CASDDS. ***Continued by*** *Microelectronics International.*
Desc: Specializing in hybrid microelectronics and semiconductor industry items.
Ind/Abst Ceram. Abstr. (19??-); Chem. Abstr.; INSPEC (Spring 1983-).

US/0886-697X
HYDROWIRE. [Hydrowire]. **VFOAT** Hydro Wire. (19??)-. Periodical. English. bw. $295.00 US and Canada; $375.00 other. HCI Publications, 410 Archibald Street, Kansas City MO 64111. **Tel** (816)931-1311. **DD** 343.

US
I E E PUBLICATIONS BULLETIN. Bulletin. English. ir. Institution of Electrical Engineers / IEE, Michael Faraday House, Six Hills Way, Stevenage Herts SG1 2AY UK. **Tel** 011 44 438 313311, FAX 011 44 438 742840, telex 825578 IEESTV G. **(Subscription address:** IEE / UK, Publications Sales Department, PO Box 96, Stevenage, Herts, SG1 2SD England.**)**

UK/0018-9146
I.E.E.-I.E.R.E. PROCEEDINGS INDIA. **Main/Corp** Institution of Electrical Engineers. **VAT** Institution of Electrical Engineers-Institution of Electronic and Radio Engineers Proceedings India. Proceedings. English. bm. $3.45. Institution of Electrical and Radio Engineers, 8 Gokhale Road, Calcutta 20 India. **CODEN** IIPIB8. Documents available from Article Express International, Ask*IEEE.
Ind/Abst Ei Page One; Eng. Index Annu.; INSPEC (April/June 1970-1978).

UK
I.P.R.E. REVIEW, THE. **VFOAT** IPREReview. **VAT** Incorporated Practitioners in Radio and Electronics Review. Periodical. English. Incorporated Practitioners R & E, 32 Kidmore Road, Caversham Reading England. ***Absorbed*** *Radar and Electronics; Electronics.*

US/0020-5974
IAEI NEWS. **See** Fire Prevention.

US/0018-8646
IBM JOURNAL OF RESEARCH AND DEVELOPMENT. [IBM j. res. develop.]. **Added/Corp** International Business Machines Corporation. **VFOAT** Journal of Research and Development. **VAT** International Business Machines Journal of Research and Development. (Jan. 1957)-. Periodical. English. bm (Jan., Mar., May, July, Sept., Nov.). $74.50 US, Canada & Mexico; $89.50 other. IBM Corporate Technical Publications, PO Box 218, Yorktown Heights NY 10598. **Tel** (914)241-4184. **LC** TK7800; .I14.

DD 621.3072. **CODEN** IBMJAE. Index available in last issue of volume--attached. **Pr Rev.** available on microfilm and microfiche from University Microfilms International (UMI). Documents available from Article Express International, The Genuine Article, UMI Article Clearinghouse, Ask*IEEE, CASDDS, Documents on Demand.
Ind/Abst ABI/INFORM Glob. Ed.; ABI Inform Ondisc (Jan. 1976-Aug. 1979); Abstr. Bull. Inst. Paper Chem.; Abstr. Bull. Inst. Pap. Sci. Tech.; Acad. Search (Jan. 1994-); ACM Guide Comput. Lit.; Acoust. Abstr.; Alum. Ind. Abstr.; Appl. Sci. Technol. Index; Bioeng. Abstr.; BMT Abstr. (-199?); Bus. Source (Jul. 1993-); Ceram. Abstr.; Chem. Abstr.; Coal Abstr.; Comput. Abstr.; Comput. Database; Comput. Lit. Index; Comput. Rev.; Curr. Contents Eng. Tech. Appl. Sci.; Curr. Contents Phys. Chem. Earth Sci.; Educ. Index; Ei Page One; Electron. Pub. Abstr.; Energy Inf. Abstr.; Energy Res. Abstr.; Eng. Mater. Abstr.; Eng. Index Annu.; Environ. Abstr.; Ergon. Abstr.; Expand. Acad. Index (1992-); Graph. Arts Bull. Inst. Pap. Sci. Technol. (July 1989); INIS Atomindex [Micro.]; INSPEC (1968-); Int. Aerosp. Abstr.; Mag. Search; Math. Rev.; Met. Abstr.; Oper. Res./Manag. Sci.; Predicasts; Qual. Control Appl. Stat.; Res. Alert [Full Cov.]; Sci. Cit. Index; SCISEARCH; Ship Abstr.; Shock Vibr. Dig.; Text. Technol. Dig.; World Alum. Abstr.; World Publ. Monit.; Zentralbl. Math. Ihre Grenzgeb.

US/0894-6809
IC MASTER. [IC master]. **VAT** Integrated Circuits Master. (1977)-. English. an. $180.00 (print), $395.00 (CD-ROM). Hearst Business Communications, 1790 Broadway, New York NY 10019. **Tel** (212)969-7500, FAX (212)969-7564. **ED** Dave Howell and Tom Mays. **LC** TK7874; .I32. **DD** 621.381/73. **Ad Acc. Circ:** 30,000. available on CD-ROM (as IC Master CD-ROM Plus).
Desc: Devoted to integrated semiconductor circuits and related products. The editorial emphasis is on "problem-solution" as it relates to electronic engineering design work.

SW/0018-9138
IEC BULLETIN. [IEC bull.]. **Main/Corp** International Electrotechnical Commission. **VAT** International Electrotechnical Commission Bulletin. (June 1967)-. Bulletin. English (French). bm. Free on request. International Electrochemical Commission, PO Box 131, 3 rue de Varembe, CH-1211 Geneva 20 Switzerland. **Tel** 011 41 22 9190211. **LC** TK1.A1; I525. **DD** 621.3/05. **CODEN** IEBUAD. Documents available from Ask*IEEE.
Desc: Bulletin of the latest I.E.C. activities, including lists of recently issued publications.
Ind/Abst INSPEC (Sept. 1969-).

UK/0537-9989
IEE CONFERENCE PUBLICATION. [IEE conf. publ.]. **Main/Corp** Institution of Electrical Engineers. **Added/Corp** Institution of Electrical Engineers. Conference Publication. **VFOAT** Conference Publication. **VAT** Institution of Electrical Engineers Conference Publication. (1964)-. Academic Scholarly Publication. English. ir. Price varies per volume. Institution of Electrical Engineers / IEE, Michael Faraday House, Six Hills Way, Stevenage Herts SG1 2AY UK. **Tel** 011 44 438 313311, FAX 011 44 438 742840, telex 825578 IEESTV G. **(Subscription address:** IEE / UK, Publications Sales Department, PO Box 96, Stevenage, Herts, SG1 2SD England.**) CODEN** IECPB4. **[CCC].** Documents available from Article Express International, Ask*IEEE, CASDDS.
Ind/Abst Bioeng. Abstr.; Chem. Abstr.; Coal Abstr.; Ei Page One; Eng. Index Annu.; INSPEC.

UK/0262-1797
IEE CONTROL ENGINEERING SERIES. [IEE control eng. ser.]. **Main/Corp** Institution of Electrical Engineers. **Added/Corp** Institution of Electrical Engineers. Control Engineering Series. **VFOAT** Control Engineering Series. (1976)-. Monographic series. English. ir. Institution of Electrical Engineers / IEE, Michael Faraday House, Six Hills Way, Stevenage Herts SG1 2AY UK. **Tel** 011 44 438 313311, FAX 011 44 438 742840, telex 825578 IEESTV G. **(Subscription address:** IEE / UK, Publications Sales Department, PO Box 96, Stevenage, Herts, SG1 2SD England.**)**
Ind/Abst Math. Rev. (1987-); Zentralbl. Math. Ihre Grenzgeb.

UK
IEE DIGITAL ELECTRONICS AND COMPUTING SERIES. **Added/Corp** Institution of Electrical Engineers. (1981)-. Monographic series. English. ir. Price varies per volume. Institution of Electrical Engineers / IEE, Michael Faraday House, Six Hills Way, Stevenage Herts SG1 2AY UK. **Tel** 011 44 438 313311, FAX 011 44 438 742840, telex 825578 IEESTV G. **(Subscription address:** IEE / UK, Publications Sales Department, PO Box 96, Stevenage, Herts, SG1 2SD England.**)**
Ind/Abst Zentralbl. Math. Ihre Grenzgeb.

UK
IEE ELECTRICAL MEASUREMENT SERIES. **Added/Corp** Institution of Electrical Engineers. **VFOAT** Electrical Measurement Series. (1983)-. Monographic series. English. ir. Price varies per volume. Institution of Electrical Engineers / IEE, Michael Faraday House, Six Hills Way, Stevenage Herts SG1 2AY UK. **Tel** 011 44 438 313311, FAX 011 44 438 742840, telex 825578 IEESTV G. **(Subscription address:** IEE / UK, Publications Sales Department, PO Box 96, Stevenage, Herts, SG1 2SD England.**)**

UK
IEE ELECTROMAGNETIC WAVES SERIES. [IEE electromagn. waves ser.]. **Added/Corp** Institution of Electrical Engineers. **VFOAT** Institution of Electrical Engineers Electromagnetic Waves Series. **VAT** I. E. E. Electromagnetic Waves Series. (1976)-. Monographic series. English. ir. Price varies per volume. Institution of Electrical Engineers / IEE, Michael Faraday House, Six Hills Way, Stevenage Herts SG1 2AY UK. **Tel** 011 44 438 313311, FAX 011 44 438 742840, telex 825578 IEESTV G. **(Subscription address:** IEE / UK, Publications Sales Department, PO Box 96, Stevenage, Herts, SG1 2SD England.**)** Documents available from Article Express International.
Ind/Abst Ei Page One; Eng. Index Annu.

UK/0266-1721
IEE HISTORY OF TECHNOLOGY SERIES. (HISTORY OF TECHNOLOGY SERIES.). [IEE hist. technol. ser.]. **Added/Corp** Institution of Electrical Engineers. **VFOAT** IEE History of Technology Series. (1979)-. Monographic series. English. ir. Price varies per volume. Institution of Electrical Engineers / IEE, Michael Faraday House, Six Hills Way, Stevenage Herts SG1 2AY UK. **Tel** 011 44 438 313311, FAX 011 44 438 742840, telex 825578 IEESTV G. Documents available from Ask*IEEE.
Ind/Abst INSPEC.

UK
IEE MANAGEMENT OF TECHNOLOGY SERIES. **Added/Corp** Institution of Electrical Engineers. **VAT** Institution of Electrical Engineers Management of Technology Series. (1984)-. Monographic series. English. ir. Price varies per volume. Institution of Electrical Engineers / IEE, Michael Faraday House, Six Hills Way, Stevenage Herts SG1 2AY UK. **Tel** 011 44 438 313311, FAX 011 44 438 742840, telex 825578 IEESTV G. **(Subscription address:** IEE / UK, Publications Sales Department, PO Box 96, Stevenage, Herts, SG1 2SD England.**)**

UK/0953-5985
IEE MATERIALS & DEVICES SERIES. [IEE mater. devices ser.]. **Added/Corp** Institution of Electrical Engineers. **VFOAT** IEE Materials and Devices Series; IEE Materials & Devices. **VAT** Institution of Electrical Engineers Materials & Devices Series. Vol. 4 (1987)-. Monographic series. English. ir. Price varies per volume. Institution of Electrical Engineers / IEE, Michael Faraday House, Six Hills Way, Stevenage Herts SG1 2AY UK. **Tel** 011 44 438 313311, FAX 011 44 438 742840, telex 825578 IEESTV G. **(Subscription address:** IEE / UK, Publications Sales Department, PO Box 96, Stevenage, Herts, SG1 2SD England.**) CODEN** IMDSE9. Documents available from Ask*IEEE. ***Continues*** *IEE Electrical and Electronic Materials and Devices Series, 0264-5548.*
Ind/Abst INSPEC.

UK/0308-0684
IEE NEWS. [IEE news]. **Main/Corp** Institution of Electrical Engineers. New Series. No. 1 (Jan. 1976)-. Periodical. English. Twelve times a year. Comes with IEE Review. Institution of Electrical Engineers / IEE, Michael Faraday House, Six Hills Way, Stevenage Herts SG1 2AY UK. **Tel** 011 44 438 313311, FAX 011 44 438 742840, telex 825578 IEESTV G. **(Subscription address:** IEE / UK, Publications Sales Department, PO Box 96, Stevenage, Herts, SG1 2SD England.**) [CCC]. Ad Acc. Circ:** 90,000 (ctrl). ***Separated from*** *Electronics & Power.*
Desc: Reports institution news and provides overview of electrical and electronic engineering scene.
Ind/Abst BMT Abstr. (1976-199?); Fluid Abstr., Civil Eng.; Fluid Abstr. Proc. Eng.; FLUIDEX (1976-1990); HILITES.

UK/0960-7641
IEE PROCEEDINGS. A, SCIENCE, MEASUREMENT AND TECHNOLOGY. ***Title Change.*** [IEE proc., A Sci. meas. technol.]. **Added/Corp** Institution of Electrical Engineers. **VFOAT** Science, Measurement and Technology. **VAT** Institution of Electrical Engineers Proceedings. Part A, Science, Measurement and Technology. Vol. 138, No. 1 (Jan. 1991)-Vol. 140, No. 6 (Nov. 1993). Academic Scholarly Publication. English. Six times a year. Institution of Electrical Engineers / IEE, Michael Faraday House, Six Hills Way, Stevenage Herts SG1 2AY UK. **Tel** 011 44 438 313311, FAX 011 44 438 742840, telex 825578 IEESTV G. **(Subscription address:** IEE / UK, Publications Sales Department, PO Box 96, Stevenage, Herts, SG1 2SD England.**) LC** TK1; .I135. **DD** 621.3/05. **CODEN** IPATEI. Index available (free). available on microfilm from University Microfilms International (UMI). Documents available from Article Express International, The Genuine Article, Ask*IEEE, CASDDS. ***Continues*** *IEE Proceedings. A, Physical Science, Measurement and Instrumentation, Management and Education, Reviews, 0143-702X.* ***Continued by*** *IEE Proceedings. Science, Measurement and Technology.*
Ind/Abst Appl. Sci. Technol. Index; Chem. Abstr.; Comput. Inf. Syst. Abstr. J. [Full Cov.]; Curr. Contents Eng. Tech. Appl. Sci.; Ei Page One; Elect. Comm. Abstr.; Eng. Index Annu.; Environ. Eng. Abstr.; INSPEC (Jan. 1991-); Manuf. Process Eng. Abstr.; Mech. Eng. Abstr.; Res. Alert [Full Cov.]; Sci. Cit. Index; SCISEARCH; Soc. Sci. Cit. Index [Select. Cov.]; Solid State Supercond. Abstr.; World Ceram. Abstr.

UK/0143-7046
IEE PROCEEDINGS. C, GENERATION, TRANSMISSION, AND DISTRIBUTION. ***Title Change.*** [IEE proc. C]. **Added/Corp** Institution of Electrical Engineers. **VFOAT** I.E.E. Proceedings. C, Generation, Transmission, and Distribution; Generation, Transmission, and Distribution; I.E.E. Proceedings. Part C, Generation, Transmission, and Distribution; IEE Proceedings. Part C, Generation, Ttransmission, and Distribution. **VAT** Institution of Electrical Engineers. Part C, Generation, Transmission and Distribution. Vol. 127, Pt. C, No. 1 (Jan. 1980)-Vol. 140, No. 6 (Nov. 1993). Academic Scholarly Publication. English. Six times a year. Institution of Electrical Engineers / IEE, Michael Faraday House, Six Hills Way, Stevenage Herts SG1 2AY UK. **Tel** 011 44 438 313311, FAX 011 44 438 742840, telex 825578 IEESTV G. **(Subscription address:** IEE / UK, Publications Sales Department, PO Box 96, Stevenage, Herts, SG1 2SD England.**) LC** TK1; .I137. **DD** 621.31/05. **CODEN** IPPDDA. **[CCC]. Pr Rev.** available on microfilm from University Microfilms International (UMI). Documents available from Article Express International, The Genuine Article, Ask*IEEE. ***Continues in part*** *Proceedings of the Institution of Electrical Engineers, 0020-3270.* ***Continued by*** *IEE Proceedings. Generation, Transmission and Distribution, 1350-2360.*
Ind/Abst Appl. Sci. Technol. Index; Bioeng. Abstr.; Curr. Contents Eng. Tech. Appl. Sci.; Ei Page One; EMBASE; Energy Res. Abstr. (July 1980-); Eng. Index Annu.; INSPEC (Jan. 1980-); Int. Aerosp. Abstr.; Leadscan; Math. Rev.; Res. Alert [Full Cov.]; Sci. Cit. Index; SCISEARCH.

●UK/1350-2409
IEE PROCEEDINGS. CIRCUITS, DEVICES AND SYSTEMS. **Added/Corp** Institution of Electrical Engineers. **VFOAT** Circuits, Devices and Systems; IEE Proc.-Circuits Devices Syst. Vol. 141, No. 1 (Feb. 1994)-. Periodical. English. Six times a year. £340.00 (surface mail); £360.00 (airmail); £58.00 (single copy) Comes with combination of IEE Proceedings (all 11 parts). Institution of Electrical Engineers / IEE, Michael Faraday House, Six Hills Way, Stevenage Herts SG1 2AY UK. **Tel** 011 44 438 313311, FAX 011 44 438 742840, telex 825578 IEESTV G. **(Subscription address:** IEE / UK, Publications Sales Department, PO Box 96, Stevenage, Herts, SG1 2SD England.**) CODEN** ICDSE7. **Pr Rev.** ***Continues*** *IEE Proceedings. G, Circuits, Devices, and Systems, 0956-3768.*

●UK/1350-2379
IEE PROCEEDINGS. CONTROL THEORY AND APPLICATIONS. **Added/Corp** Institution of Electrical Engineers. **VFOAT** Control Theory and Applications; IEE Proc.-Control Theory Appl. **VAT** Institution of Electrical Engineers Proceedings. Control Theory and Applications. Vol. 141, No. 1 (Jan. 1994)-. Periodical. English. Six times a year. £340.00 (surface mail); £360.00 (airmail); £58.00 (single copy) Comes in combination of IEE Proceedings (all 11 parts). Institution of Electrical Engineers / IEE, Michael Faraday House, Six Hills Way, Stevenage Herts SG1 2AY UK. **Tel** 011 44 438 313311, FAX 011 44 438 742840, telex 825578 IEESTV G. **(Subscription address:** IEE / UK, Publications Sales Department, PO Box 96, Stevenage, Herts, SG1 2SD England.**) LC** TK1; .I1372. **CODEN** ICTAEX. **Pr Rev.** ***Continues*** *IEE Proceedings. D, Control Theory and Applications, 0143-7054.*

UK/0143-7054
IEE PROCEEDINGS. D, CONTROL THEORY AND APPLICATIONS. ***Title Change.*** [IEE proc. Part D]. **Added/Corp** Institution of Electrical Engineers. **VFOAT** Control Theory and Applications; I.E.E. Proceedings. D, Control Theory and Applications; I.E.E. Proceedings, Part D, Control Theory and Applications; IEE Proceedings. Part D, Control Theory and Applications. **VAT** Institution of Electrical Engineers Proceedings. Part D. Control Theory and Applications. Vol. 127, No. 1 (Jan. 1980)-Vol. 140, No. 6 (1993). Academic Scholarly Publication. English. Six times a year. Institution of Electrical Engineers / IEE, Michael Faraday House, Six Hills Way, Stevenage Herts SG1 2AY UK. **Tel** 011 44 438 313311, FAX 011 44 438 742840, telex 825578 IEESTV G. **(Subscription address:** IEE / UK, Publications Sales Department, PO Box 96, Stevenage, Herts, SG1 2SD England.**) LC** TK1; .I1372. **DD** 629.8/312/05. **CODEN** IPDAD9. **[CCC]. Pr Rev.** available on microfilm from University Microfilms International (UMI). Documents available from Article Express International, The Genuine Article, Ask*IEEE, CASDDS. ***Continues in part*** *Proceedings of the Institution of Electrical Engineers, 0020-3270.* ***Continued by*** *IEE Proceedings. Control Theory and Applications, 1350-2379.*
Ind/Abst Acoust. Abstr.; Appl. Sci. Technol. Index; Bioeng. Abstr.; Chem. Abstr.; Curr. Contents Eng. Tech.

Appl. Sci.; Curr. Technol. Index; Ei Page One; EMBASE; Energy Res. Abstr. (July 1980-); Eng. Index Annu.; INSPEC (Jan. 1980-); Int. Aerosp. Abstr.; Leadscan; Math. Rev.; Res. Alert [Full Cov.]; Sci. Cit. Index; SCISEARCH; Zentralbl. Math. Ihre Grenzgeb.

●UK/1350-2352
IEE PROCEEDINGS. ELECTRIC POWER APPLICATIONS. **Added/Corp** Institution of Electrical Engineers. **VFOAT** Electric Power Applications; IEE Proc.-Electr. Power Appl. Vol. 141, No. 1 (Jan. 1994)-. Periodical. English. Six times a year. £340.00 (surface mail); £360.00 (airmail); £58.00 (single copy) Comes in combination of IEE Proceedings (all 11 parts). Institution of Electrical Engineers / IEE, Michael Faraday House, Six Hills Way, Stevenage Herts SG1 2AY UK. **Tel** 011 44 438 313311, FAX 011 44 438 742840, telex 825578 IEESTV G. **(Subscription address:** IEE / UK, Publications Sales Department, PO Box 96, Stevenage, Herts, SG1 2SD England.**) CODEN** IEPAER. **Pr Rev.** ***Continues*** *IEE Proceedings. B, Electric Power Applications, 0143-7038.*

UK/0956-3768
IEE PROCEEDINGS. G, CIRCUITS, DEVICES, AND SYSTEMS. ***Title Change.*** [IEE proc., G. Circuits devices syst.]. **Added/Corp** Institution of Electrical Engineers. **VFOAT** Circuits, Devices, and Systems; IEE Proceedings. Part G, Circuits, Devices, and Systems. **VAT** Institution of Electrical Engineers Proceedings. G, Circuits, Devices, and Systems. Vol. 136, Pt. G, No. 1 (Feb. 1989)-Vol. 140, No. 6 (Dec. 1993). Periodical. English. Six times a year. Institution of Electrical Engineers / IEE, Michael Faraday House, Six Hills Way, Stevenage Herts SG1 2AY UK. **Tel** 011 44 438 313311, FAX 011 44 438 742840, telex 825578 IEESTV G. **(Subscription address:** IEE / UK, Publications Sales Department, PO Box 96, Stevenage, Herts, SG1 2SD England.**) LC** TK7867; .I368. **DD** 621.381/5. **CODEN** IPGSEB. **[CCC]. Pr Rev.** available on microfilm from University Microfilms International (UMI). Documents available from Article Express International, The Genuine Article, Ask*IEEE. ***Formed by the union of*** *IEE Proceedings. G, Electronic Circuits and Systems, 0143-7089* ***and*** *IEE Proceedings. I, Solid-State and Electron Devices, 0143-7100.* ***Continued by*** *IEE proceedings. Circuits, Devices and Systems, 1350-2409.*
Ind/Abst Appl. Sci. Technol. Index; Ei Page One; Eng. Index Annu.; INSPEC (Feb. 1989-); Leadscan; Res. Alert [Full Cov.]; Sci. Cit. Index; SCISEARCH.

●UK/1350-2360
IEE PROCEEDINGS. GENERATION, TRANSMISSION, AND DISTRIBUTION. **Added/Corp** Institution of Electrical Engineers. **VFOAT** Generation, Transmission, and Distribution; IEE Proc.-Gener. Transm. Distrib. Vol. 141, No. 1 (Jan. 1994)-. Periodical. English. Six times a year. £340.00 (surface mail); £360.00 (airmail); £58.00 (single copy) Comes in combination of IEE Proceedings (all 11 parts). Institution of Electrical Engineers / IEE, Michael Faraday House, Six Hills Way, Stevenage Herts SG1 2AY UK. **Tel** 011 44 438 313311, FAX 011 44 438 742840, telex 825578 IEESTV G. **(Subscription address:** IEE / UK, Publications Sales Department, PO Box 96, Stevenage, Herts, SG1 2SD England.**) LC** TK1; .I137. **DD** 621.31/05. **CODEN** IGTDE2. **Pr Rev.** ***Continues*** *IEE Proceedings. C, Generation, Transmission, and Distribution, 0143-7046.*

UK
IEE PROCEEDINGS INDEX. ***Ceased.*** (19??)-(19??). Proceedings. English. ir. Institution of Electrical Engineers / IEE, Michael Faraday House, Six Hills Way, Stevenage Herts SG1 2AY UK. **Tel** 011 44 438 313311, FAX 011 44 438 742840, telex 825578 IEESTV G. **(Subscription address:** IEE / UK, Publications Sales Department, PO Box 96, Stevenage, Herts, SG1 2SD England.**)** cum. index.

●UK/1350-2417
IEE PROCEEDINGS. MICROWAVES, ANTENNAS AND PROPAGATION. **Added/Corp** Institution of Electrical Engineers. **VFOAT** Microwaves, Antennas and Propagation; IEE Proc.-Microw. Antennas Propag. Vol. 141, No. 1 (Feb. 1994)-. Periodical. English. Six times a year. £340.00 (surface mail); £360.00 (airmail); £58.00 (single copy) Comes with combination of IEE Proceeding (all 11 parts). Institution of Electrical Engineers / IEE, Michael Faraday House, Six Hills Way, Stevenage Herts SG1 2AY UK. **Tel** 011 44 438 313311, FAX 011 44 438 742840, telex 825578 IEESTV G. **(Subscription address:** IEE / UK, Publications Sales Department, PO Box 96, Stevenage, Herts, SG1 2SD England.**) LC** TK1; .I138. **CODEN** IMIPEP. **Pr Rev.** ***Continues*** *IEE Proceedings. H, Microwaves, Antennas and Propagation, 0950-107X.*

●UK/1350-2433
IEE PROCEEDINGS. OPTOELECTRONICS. **Added/Corp** Institution of Electrical Engineers. **VFOAT** Optoelectronics; IEE proc.-Optoelectron. Vol. 141, No. 1 (Feb. 1994)-. Periodical. English. Six times a year. £340.00 (surface mail); £360.00 (airmail); £58.00 (single copy) Comes with combination of IEE Proceedings (all 11 parts). Institution of Electrical Engineers / IEE, Michael Faraday House, Six Hills Way, Stevenage Herts SG1 2AY UK. **Tel** 011 44 438 313311, FAX 011 44 438 742840, telex 825578 IEESTV G. **(Subscription address:** IEE / UK, Publications Sales Department, PO Box 96, Stevenage, Herts SG1 2SD England.**) LC** TA1750; .I33. **DD** 621.38/0414; 19. **CODEN** IPOPE8. **Pr Rev.** ***Continues*** *IEE Proceedings. J, Optoelectronics, 0267-3932.*

UK/0143-7038
IEE PROCEEDINGS. PART B. ELECTRIC POWER APPLICATIONS. ***Title Change.*** (IEE PROCEEDINGS. B, ELECTRIC POWER APPLICATIONS.). [IEE proc. B]. **Added/Corp** Institution of Electrical Engineers. **VFOAT** I.E.E. Proceedings. B, Electric Power Applications; Electric Power Applications; I.E.E. Proceedings. Part B, Electric Power Applications; IEE Proceedings. Part B, Electric Power Applications. **VAT** Institution of Electrical Engineers Proceedings. Part B, Electric Power Applications. Vol. 127, Pt. B, No. 1 (Jan. 1980)-Vol. 140, No. 6 (Nov. 1993). Academic Scholarly Publication. English. Six times a year. Institution of Electrical Engineers / IEE, Michael Faraday House, Six Hills Way, Stevenage Herts SG1 2AY UK. **Tel** 011 44 438 313311, FAX 011 44 438 742840, telex 825578 IEESTV G. **(Subscription address:** IEE / UK, Publications Sales Department, PO Box 96, Stevenage, Herts, SG1 2SD England.**) LC** TK4001; .I17. **DD** 621.3/05. **CODEN** IPPADZ. **[CCC]. Pr Rev.** available on microfilm from University Microfilms International (UMI). Documents available from Article Express International, The Genuine Article, Ask*IEEE. ***Continues in part*** *Proceedings of the Institution of Electrical Engineers, 0020-3270;* ***Absorbed*** *IEE Journal on Electric Power Applications.* ***Continued by*** *IEE Proceedings. Electric Power Applications, 1350-2352.*
Ind/Abst Appl. Sci. Technol. Index; Bioeng. Abstr.; Curr. Contents Eng. Tech. Appl. Sci.; Ei Page One; EMBASE; Energy Res. Abstr. (July 1980-); Eng. Index Annu.; INSPEC (Jan. 1980-); Int. Aerosp. Abstr.; Leadscan; Math. Rev.; Res. Alert [Full Cov.]; Sci. Cit. Index; SCISEARCH.

UK/0950-107X
IEE PROCEEDINGS. PART H, MICROWAVES, ANTENNAS, AND PROPAGATION. ***Title Change.*** (IEE PROCEEDINGS. H, MICROWAVES, ANTENNAS, AND PROPAGATION.). [IEE proc., H, Microw. antennas propag.]. **Added/Corp** Institution of Electrical Engineers. **VFOAT** Microwaves, Antennas, and Propagation; IEE Proceedings. Part H, Microwaves, Antennas, and Propagation. **VAT** Institution of Electrical Engineers Proceedings. Part H, Microwaves, Antennas, and Propagation. Vol. 132, No. 2 (Apr. 1985)-Vol. 140, No. 6 (Dec. 1993). Periodical. English. Six times a year. Institution of Electrical Engineers / IEE, Michael Faraday House, Six Hills Way, Stevenage Herts SG1 2AY UK. **Tel** 011 44 438 313311, FAX 011 44 438 742840, telex 825578 IEESTV G. **(Subscription address:** IEE / UK, Publications Sales Department, PO Box 96, Stevenage, Herts, SG1 2SD England.**) ED** J. Helszajn and A. D. Olver. **LC** TK1; .I138. **DD** 621.381/3/05. **[CCC].** Index available. **Bk Rev. Ad Acc. Pr Rev.** available on microfilm from University Microfilms International (UMI). Documents available from Article Express International, The Genuine Article, Ask*IEEE. ***Continues in part*** *IEE Proceedings. H, Microwaves, Optics, and Antennas, 0143-7097.* ***Continued by*** *IEE Proceedings. Microwaves, Antennas and Propagation, 1350-2417.*
Desc: Research papers in the areas of microwave components and techniques and in antennas and propagation of radio waves.
Ind/Abst Acoust. Abstr.; Appl. Sci. Technol. Index; Ei Page One; Eng. Index Annu.; INSPEC (April 1985-); Int. Aerosp. Abstr.; Res. Alert [Full Cov.]; Sci. Cit. Index; SCISEARCH.

UK/0143-7100
IEE PROCEEDINGS. PART I. SOLID-STATE AND ELECTRON DEVICES. [IEE proc., Part I., Solid-state electron devices]. **Main/Corp** Institution of Electrical Engineers. **VFOAT** Solid-State and Electron Devices. **VAT** Institution of Electrical Engineers Proceedings. Part I. Solid-State and Electron Devices. Vol. 127 (Feb. 1980)-. Academic Scholarly Publication. English. bm. $639.00. Institution of Electrical Engineers / IEE, Michael Faraday House, Six Hills Way, Stevenage Herts SG1 2AY UK. **Tel** 011 44 438 313311, FAX 011 44 438 742840, telex 825578 IEESTV G. **(Subscription address:** IEE / UK, Publications Sales Department, PO Box 96, Stevenage, Herts, SG1 2SD England.**)** Documents available from CASDDS. ***Formed by the union of*** *Proceedings of the Institution of Electrical Engineers, 0020-3270.*
Ind/Abst Ceram. Abstr. (19??-); Chem. Abstr.

UK/0267-3932
IEE PROCEEDINGS. PART J, OPTOELECTRONICS. ***Title Change.*** (IEE PROCEEDINGS. J, OPTOELECTRONICS.). [IEE pro., J Optoelectron.]. **Added/Corp** Institution of Electrical Engineers. **VFOAT** IEE Proceedings. Part J, Optoelectronics; Optoelectronics. **VAT** Institution of Electrical Engineers Proceedings. J, Optoelectronics. Vol. 132, No. 1 (Feb. 1985)-Vol. 140, No. 6 (Dec. 1993). Academic Scholarly Publication. English. Six times a year. Institution of Electrical Engineers / IEE, Michael Faraday House, Six Hills Way, Stevenage Herts SG1 2AY UK. **Tel** 011 44 438 313311, FAX 011 44 438 742840, telex 825578 IEESTV G. **(Subscription address:** IEE / UK, Publications Sales Department, PO Box 96, Stevenage, Herts, SG1 2SD England.**) LC** TA1750; .I33. **DD** 621.38/0414. **CODEN** IPJOEE. **[CCC]. Pr Rev.** available on microfilm from University Microfilms International (UMI). Documents available from Article Express International, The Genuine Article, Ask*IEEE, CASDDS. ***Continues in part*** *IEE Proceedings. H, Microwaves, Optics, and Antennas, 0143-7097.* ***Continued by*** *IEE Proceedings. Optoelectronics, 1350-2433.*
Ind/Abst Appl. Sci. Technol. Index; Ceram. Abstr. (19??-); Chem. Abstr. (1985-); Curr. Contents Eng. Tech. Appl. Sci.; Ei Page One; Eng. Index Annu.; INSPEC (Feb. 1985-); Int. Aerosp. Abstr.; Res. Alert [Full Cov.]; Sci. Cit. Index; SCISEARCH.

●UK/1350-2344
IEE PROCEEDINGS. SCIENCE, MEASUREMENT AND TECHNOLOGY. **Added/Corp** Institution of Electrical Engineers. **VFOAT** Science, Measurement and Technology; IEE Proc.-Sci. meas. Technol. Vol. 141, No. 1 (Jan. 1994)-. Periodical. English. Six times a year. £340.00 (surface mail); £360.00 (airmail); £58.00 (single copy) Comes in combination with IEE Proceedings (all 11 parts). Institution of Electrical Engineers / IEE, Michael Faraday House, Six Hills Way, Stevenage Herts SG1 2AY UK. **Tel** 011 44 438 313311, FAX 011 44 438 742840, telex 825578 IEESTV G. **(Subscription address:** IEE / UK, Publications Sales Department, PO Box 96, Stevenage, Herts, SG1 2SD England.**) CODEN** ISMTEV. ***Continues*** *IEE Proceedings. A, Science, Measurement and Technology, 0960-764X.*

GW
IEE PRODUCTRONIC. **VFOAT** I.E.E. Productronic. (19??)-. Periodical. German. Ten times a year. DM205.50 Germany; DM222.00 other. Dr. Alfred Huethig Verlag GmbH, Postfach 102869, D 69018 Heidelberg Germany. **Tel** 011 49 6221 489281. **(Subscription address:** WEPF Publishing Services GmbH, Auf Dem Wolf 4, CH 4018 Basel Switzerland.**) ED** S.W. Best and H. Beine. **LC** TK7836; .I37. **DD** 621.381/05. Index available. cum. index. **Bk Rev. Ad Acc. Circ:** 13,167 (ctrl).
Desc: Covers the manufacturing of electronic components and boards : semiconductor manufacturing, PCB-manufacturing, text of boards and components.

UK/0953-5683
IEE REVIEW. [IEE rev.]. **Added/Corp** Institution of Electrical Engineers. **VAT** Institution of Electrical Engineers Review. Vol. 34, No. 1 (Jan. 1988)-. Periodical. English. Six times a year. £65.00 EEC countries; £72.00 other (includes IEE News). Institution of Electrical Engineers / IEE, Michael Faraday House, Six Hills Way, Stevenage Herts SG1 2AY UK. **Tel** 011 44 438 313311, FAX 011 44 438 742840, telex 825578 IEESTV G. **(Subscription address:** IEE / UK, Publications Sales Department, PO Box 96, Stevenage, Herts, SG1 2SD England.**) LC** TK1; .I412. **DD** 621.3. **CODEN** IEREEF. Index available (free). available on microfilm from University Microfilms International (UMI). Documents available from The Genuine Article, Ask*IEEE. ***Continues*** *Electronics and Power, 0013-5127.*
Ind/Abst Appl. Sci. Technol. Index; Curr. Contents Eng. Tech. Appl. Sci.; Curr. Technol. Index; Energy Inf. Abstr.; Fluid Abstr., Civil Eng.; Fluid Abstr. Proc. Eng.; FLUIDEX; HILITES; INSPEC (Jan. 1988-); Res. Alert [Select. Cov.]; SCISEARCH; Soc. Sci. Cit. Index [Select. Cov.].

UK/0265-2986
IEE TOPICS IN CONTROL SERIES. [IEE topics control ser.]. **Added/Corp** Institution of Electrical Engineers. Vol. 1 (1983)-. Periodical. English. ir. Institution of Electrical Engineers / IEE, Michael Faraday House, Six Hills Way, Stevenage Herts SG1 2AY UK. **Tel** 011 44 438 313311, FAX 011 44 438 742840, telex 825578 IEESTV G. **(Subscription address:** IEE / UK, Publications Sales Department, PO Box 96, Stevenage, Herts, SG1 2SD England.**)**
Ind/Abst Math. Rev.; Zentralbl. Math. Ihre Grenzgeb.

US/0897-6813
IEEE 802.3 REPORT. [IEEE 802.3 rep.]. **VFOAT** IEEE Eight Zero Two-Point-Three Report. **VAT** Institute of Electrical and Electronics Engineers 802.3 Report. (1988)-. English. Three times a year. $750.00. Ship Star Associates Inc, 36 Woodhill Drive, Newark DE 19711. **DD** 621.

US/0885-8985
IEEE AEROSPACE AND ELECTRONIC SYSTEMS MAGAZINE. **See** Aeronautics, Astronautics.

US/1045-9243
IEEE ANTENNAS & PROPAGATION MAGAZINE. [IEEE antennas propag. mag.]. **Added/Corp** IEEE Antennas and Propagation Society. **VFOAT** Antennas & Propagation Magazine; IEEE Antennas and Propagation Magazine; Antennas and Propagation Magazine; AP-S Magazine; IEEE Antennas and Propagation Society Magazine. **VAT** Institute of Electrical and Electronics Engineers Antennas & Propagation Magazine. Vol. 32, No. 1 (Feb. 1990)-.

Periodical. English. bm. $85.00. IEEE, Institution of Electrical and Electronics Engineers, Inc., 345 East 47th Street, New York NY 10017-2394. **Tel** (908)981-1393, FAX (908)981-9667. **(Subscription address:** IEEE / Institute of Electrical and Electronics Engineers, 445 Hoes Lane, PO Box 1331, Piscataway NJ 08855-1331.**) LC** TK7871.6; .I35. **DD** 621.382/4. **CODEN** IAPMEZ. **[CCC].** Documents available from Article Express International, Ask*IEEE. ***Continues*** *Newsletter (IEEE Antennas and Propagation Society).*
Desc: Covers all areas relating to antenna theory, design, and practice; propagation, including theory, effects, and system considerations; analytical and computational electromagnetics, scattering, diffraction, and radar cross sections; and all relationships of these areas to applications, including telecommunications, broadcasting, electromagnetic effects on systems, and design and measurement techniques.
Ind/Abst Appl. Sci. Technol. Index (1991-); Ei Page One; Eng. Index Annu.; INSPEC (Feb. 1990-); Int. Aerosp. Abstr.

US/0162-3842
IEEE BULLETIN. [IEEE bull.]. **Main/Corp** Institute of Electrical and Electronics Engineers. Los Angeles Council. **VAT** Institute of Electrical and Electronics Engineers Bulletin. (19??)-. Periodical. English. mo. $8.00. IEEE Los Angeles Council, 20695 South Western Avenue, Suite 145, Torrance CA 90501. **Tel** (310)618-8314, FAX (310)618-1331. **ED** Erin Lipsitz. **DD** 620. **Ad Acc. Circ:** 16,000 (ctrl).
Desc: Membership periodical for electrical and electronic engineering members of IEEE Los Angeles Council.

US
IEEE/CHMT INTERNATIONAL ELECTRONIC MANUFACTURING TECHNOLOGY SYMPOSIUM : [PROCEEDINGS]. **Added/Corp** IEEE Components, Hybrids, and Manufacturing Technology Society. **VFOAT** Proceedings. 5th (Oct. 10-12, 1988)-. English. ir. IEEE, Institution of Electrical and Electronics Engineers, Inc., 345 East 47th Street, New York NY 10017-2394. **Tel** (908)981-1393, FAX (908)981-9667. **(Subscription address:** IEEE / Institute of Electrical and Electronics Engineers, 445 Hoes Lane, PO Box 1331, Piscataway NJ 08855-1331.**)** ***Continues*** *IEEE/CHMT European International Electronic Manufacturing Technology Symposium. IEEE/CHMT European International Electronic Manufacturing Technology Symposium : [Proceedings].*
Ind/Abst Ceram. Abstr. (19??-).

US/8755-3996
IEEE CIRCUITS AND DEVICES MAGAZINE. [IEEE circuits devices mag.]. **Added/Corp** Institute of Electrical and Electronics Engineers. **VFOAT** Circuits and Devices Magazine. **VAT** Institute of Electrical and Electronics Engineers Circuits and Devices Magazine. Vol. 1, No. 1 (Jan. 1985)-. Periodical. English. bm. $130.00. IEEE, Institution of Electrical and Electronics Engineers, Inc., 345 East 47th Street, New York NY 10017-2394. **Tel** (908)981-1393, FAX (908)981-9667. **(Subscription address:** IEEE / Institute of Electrical and Electronics Engineers, 445 Hoes Lane, PO Box 1331, Piscataway NJ 08855-1331.**) LC** TK1; .I395a. **DD** 621.3/05. **[CCC].** **Pr Rev.** available on microfiche. Documents available from Article Express International, The Genuine Article, Ask*IEEE. ***Continues*** *Institute of Electrical and Electronics Engineers. IEEE Circuits and Systems Magazine, 0163-6812.*
Desc: Contains assessments of emerging technologies and their continued impact on the man-machine interface, new products, new inventions and new books.
Ind/Abst Bioeng. Abstr.; Comput. Inf. Syst. Abstr. J. [Full Cov.]; Curr. Contents Eng. Tech. Appl. Sci.; Ei Page One; Elect. Comm. Abstr.; Eng. Index Annu.; Index IEEE Publ. (Jan. 1985-); INSPEC (1985-); Int. Aerosp. Abstr.; Mater. Sci. Eng. Abstr.; Mech. Eng. Abstr.; Pollut. Abstr. Indexes; Res. Alert [Full Cov.]; Sci. Cit. Index; SCISEARCH; Soc. Sci. Cit. Index [Select. Cov.]; Solid State Supercond. Abstr.

US/0895-0156
IEEE COMPUTER APPLICATIONS IN POWER. (IEEE COMPUTER APPLICATIONS IN POWER : CAP.). [IEEE comput. applic. power]. **Added/Corp** Institute of Electrical and Electronics Engineers. IEEE Power Engineering Society. **VFOAT** CAP; Computer Applications in Power; IEEE Computer Applications in Power Magazine. **VAT** Institute of Electrical and Electronics Engineers Computer Application in Power Magazine. Vol. 1, No. 1 (Jan. 1988)-. Periodical. English. qt. $75.00. IEEE, Institution of Electrical and Electronics Engineers, Inc., 345 East 47th Street, New York NY 10017-2394. **Tel** (908)981-1393, FAX (908)981-9667. **(Subscription address:** IEEE / Institute of Electrical and Electronics Engineers, 445 Hoes Lane, PO Box 1331, Piscataway NJ 08855-1331.**) LC** TK3091; .I17. **DD** 621.319. **[CCC].** available on microfiche. Documents available from Article Express International, Ask*IEEE.
Desc: Devoted to computer applications in the electric power field involving planning, design, construction, operation, maintenance and control of power systems. Articles cover energy management systems, transient network analysis, cable systems, economics, and contingency analysis.
Ind/Abst Ei Page One; Eng. Index Annu.; Index IEEE Publ.; INSPEC (Jan. 1988-).

US/0272-4685
IEEE CONFERENCE RECORD OF ... ANNUAL CONFERENCE OF ELECTRICAL ENGINEERING PROBLEMS IN THE RUBBER AND PLASTICS INDUSTRIES. [IEEE conf. rec. annu. Conf. Electr. Eng. Problem. Rubber Plast. Ind.]. **Main/Conf** Conference of Electrical Engineering Problems in the Rubber and Plastics Industries. **VFOAT** I.E.E.E. Conference Record of ... Annual Conference of Electrical Engineering Problems in the Rubber and Plastics Industries; Conference Record of ... Annual Conference of Electrical; I.E.E.E. ... Rubber and Plastics Industry; IEEE ... Rubber & Plastics Industry. **VAT** Institute of Electrical and Electronics Engineers Conference Record of Annual Conference of Electrical Engineering Problems in the Rubber and Plastics Industry. Began with 17th, 1965. Periodical. English. an. $40.00. IEEE, Institution of Electrical and Electronics Engineers, Inc., 345 East 47th Street, New York NY 10017-2394. **Tel** (908)981-1393, FAX (908)981-9667. **(Subscription address:** IEEE Service Center, 445 Hoes Lane, Piscataway, NJ 08854**) LC** TK5; .A2. **DD** 668.9. **CODEN** ICEPD2. Documents available from Article Express International. ***Continues*** *Electrical Engineering Problems in the Rubber and Plastics Industries, 0732-295X.*
Ind/Abst Ei Page One; Eng. Index Annu.; Index IEEE Publ.

US/0736-590X
IEEE CONFERENCE RECORD OF ... POWER MODULATOR SYMPOSIUM. [IEEE conf. rec. Power Modul. Symp.]. **Added/Corp** IEEE Electron Devices Society. United States. Advisory Group on Electron Devices. Palisades Institute for Research Services. **VFOAT** I.E.E.E. Conference Record of ... Power Modulator Symposium; IEEE ... Power Modulator. 15th (1982)-. English. be. IEEE, Institution of Electrical and Electronics Engineers, Inc., 345 East 47th Street, New York NY 10017-2394. **Tel** (908)981-1393, FAX (908)981-9667. **CODEN** ICRSD8. Documents available from Article Express International. ***Continues*** *Pulse Power Modulator Symposium. IEEE Conference Record of ... Pulse Power Modulator Symposium.*
Ind/Abst Bioeng. Abstr.; Ei Page One; Eng. Index Annu.; GeoRef; Index IEEE Publ.

US/1066-033X
IEEE CONTROL SYSTEMS. (IEEE CONTROL SYSTEMS / IEEE CONTROL SYSTEMS SOCIETY.). [IEEE control syst.]. **Added/Corp** IEEE Control Systems Society. **VFOAT** Control Systems; IEEE Control Systems Magazine. **VAT** Institute of Electrical and Electonics Engineers Control Systems. Vol. 11, No. 1 (Jan. 1991)-. Periodical. English. bm. $145.00. IEEE, Institution of Electrical and Electronics Engineers, Inc., 345 East 47th Street, New York NY 10017-2394. **Tel** (908)981-1393, FAX (908)981-9667. **(Subscription address:** IEEE / Institute of Electrical and Electronics Engineers, 445 Hoes Lane, PO Box 1331, Piscataway NJ 08855-1331.**) DD** 629. ***Continues*** *IEEE Control Systems Magazine, 0272-1708.*

US/0883-7554
IEEE ELECTRICAL INSULATION MAGAZINE. (IEEE ELECTRICAL INSULATION MAGAZINE : A PUBLICATION OF THE IEEE ELECTRICAL INSULATION SOCIETY.). [IEEE elec. insul. mag.]. **Added/Corp** IEEE Electrical Insulation Society. IEEE Dielectrics and Electrical Insulation Society. **VFOAT** Electrical Insulation Magazine; Electrical Insulation. **VAT** Institute of Electrical and Electronics Engineers, Electrical Insulation Magazine. Vol. 1, No. 1 (Sept. 1985)-. Periodical. English. bm. $115.00. IEEE, Institution of Electrical and Electronics Engineers, Inc., 345 East 47th Street, New York NY 10017-2394. **Tel** (908)981-1393, FAX (908)981-9667. **(Subscription address:** IEEE / Institute of Electrical and Electronics Engineers, 445 Hoes Lane, PO Box 1331, Piscataway NJ 08855-1331.**) LC** TK3421; .I37. **DD** 621.319/37/05. **CODEN** IIMAE6. **[CCC].** Documents available from Article Express International, Ask*IEEE.
Desc: A compilation of articles and news which relate to insulation and dielectrics; includes conference activities reporting and papers of general interest.
Ind/Abst Civ. Struct. Eng. Abstr.; Ei Page One; Elect. Comm. Abstr.; Eng. Index Annu.; Index IEEE Publ. (Sept. 1985-); INSPEC (Sept. 1985-); Mater. Sci. Eng. Abstr.

US/0748-9196
IEEE ELECTRO TECHNOLOGY REVIEW. [IEEE electroTechnol. rev.]. **VFOAT** Electro Technology Review; Electrotechnology Review. 1984-. English. an. IEEE, Institution of Electrical and Electronics Engineers, Inc., 345 East 47th Street, New York NY 10017-2394. **Tel** (908)981-1393, FAX (908)981-9667. **(Subscription address:** IEEE Service Center, 445 Hoes Lane, Piscataway, NJ 08854; telephone: (201)981-1393**) LC** TK7800; .I15. **DD** 621.3/05. Documents available from Ask*IEEE.
Ind/Abst Index IEEE Publ.; INSPEC (1986-).

US/0741-3106
IEEE ELECTRON DEVICE LETTERS. (IEEE ELECTRON DEVICE LETTERS : A PUBLICATION OF THE IEEE ELECTRON DEVICES SOCIETY.). [IEEE electron device lett.]. **Added/Corp** IEEE Electron Devices Society. **VFOAT** Electron Device Letters; I.E.E.E. Electron Device Letters. **VAT** Institute of Electrical and Electronics Engineers Electron Device Letters. Vol. EDL.-1, No. 2 (Feb. 1980)-. Academic Scholarly Publication. English. mo. $160.00. IEEE, Institution of Electrical and Electronics Engineers, Inc., 345 East 47th Street, New York NY 10017-2394. **Tel** (908)981-1393, FAX (908)981-9667. **(Subscription address:** IEEE / Institute of Electrical and Electronics Engineers, 445 Hoes Lane, PO Box 1331, Piscataway NJ 08855-1331.**) LC** TK7869; .E4. **DD** 621.3815/2. **CODEN** EDLEDZ. **[CCC].** available on microfilm and microfiche. Documents available from Article Express International, The Genuine Article, Ask*IEEE, CASDDS. ***Continues*** *Electron Device Letters, 0193-8576.*
Desc: Covers the theory, design, and performance of electron and ion devices, solid-state devices, integrated electronic devices, optoelectronic devices, and energy sources.
Ind/Abst Acoust. Abstr.; Bioeng. Abstr.; Chem. Abstr.; Comput. Inf. Syst. Abstr. J. [Full Cov.]; Curr. Contents Eng. Tech. Appl. Sci.; Ei Page One; Elect. Comm. Abstr.; Eng. Index Annu.; Index IEEE Publ.; INIS Atomindex [Micro.]; INSPEC (Feb. 1980-); Int. Aerosp. Abstr.; Manuf. Process Eng. Abstr.; Mater. Sci. Eng. Abstr.; Res. Alert [Full Cov.]; Sci. Cit. Index; SCISEARCH; Solid State Supercond. Abstr.

US/0360-8581
IEEE ENGINEERING MANAGEMENT REVIEW. [IEEE eng. manage. rev.]. **Main/Corp** IEEE Engineering Management Society. **VFOAT** Engineering Management Review. **VAT** Institute of Electrical and Electronic Engineers Engineering Management Review. Vol. 1 (March 1973)-. Periodical. English. qt. $108.00. IEEE, Institution of Electrical and Electronics Engineers, Inc., 345 East 47th Street, New York NY 10017-2394. **Tel** (908)981-1393, FAX (908)981-9667. **(Subscription address:** IEEE / Institute of Electrical and Electronics Engineers, 445 Hoes Lane, PO Box 1331, Piscataway NJ 08855-1331.**) CODEN** IEMRAP. **[CCC].** available on microfiche.
Desc: Papers are aimed at those engaged in managing research, development or engineering activities.
Ind/Abst Index IEEE Publ.; Oper. Res./Manag. Sci.; Pollut. Abstr. Indexes.

US/0018-9189
IEEE GRID. [IEEE grid]. **Main/Corp** Institute of Electrical and Electronics Engineers. **Added/Corp** Institute of Electrical and Electronics Engineers. San Francisco Bay Area Council. **VAT** Institute of Electrical and Electronics Engineers Grid. (19??)-. Periodical. English. mo. Comes with membership. Institute of Electrical and Electronics Engineers / IEEE, 445 Hoes Lane, Piscataway NJ 08855. **Tel** (908)981-0060. **ED** Doug Davalt.

US/0271-8308
IEEE IECI PROCEEDINGS. [IEEE IECI proc.]. **Main/Corp** Institute of Electrical and Electronics Engineers. **VFOAT** IECI Proceedings. **VAT** Institute of Electrical and Electronics Engineers Industrial Electronics and Control Instrumentation Society Proceedings. 1980-. Proceedings. English. an. IEEE Computer Society, 10662 Los Vaqueros Circle, PO Box 3014, Los Alamitos CA 90720-1264. **Tel** (714)821-8380, (800)272-6657, FAX (714)821-4641. **CODEN** IACPDC. Documents available from Article Express International. ***Continues*** *IECE Annual Conference Proceedings.*
Ind/Abst Bioeng. Abstr.; Ei Page One; Eng. Index Annu.

US/0274-8207
IEEE IMPACT. [IEEE impact]. **Main/Corp** Institute of Electrical and Electronics Engineers. **VFOAT** Impact. **VAT** Institute of Electrical and Electronics Engineers Impact. Periodical. English. bm. IEEE, Institution of Electrical and Electronics Engineers, Inc., 345 East 47th Street, New York NY 10017-2394. **Tel** (908)981-1393, FAX (908)981-9667. **(Subscription address:** IEEE Service Center, 445 Hoes Lane, Piscataway, NJ 08854; telephone: (201)981-1393**) LC** TK1; .I1414. **DD** 621.3/02373.
Ind/Abst Index IEEE Publ.

US/0161-1038
IEEE INSTRUMENTATION AND MEASUREMENT SOCIETY NEWSLETTER. **Main/Corp** IEEE Instrumentation and Measurement Society. **VAT** Institute on Electrical and Electronics Engineers Instrumentation and Measurement Society Newsletter. Newsletter. English. qt. IEEE, Institution of Electrical and Electronics Engineers, Inc., 345 East 47th Street, New York NY 10017-2394. **Tel** (908)981-1393, FAX (908)981-9667. **(Subscription address:** IEEE Service Center, 445 Hoes Lane, Piscataway, NJ 08854**)**
Ind/Abst Index IEEE Publ.

US
IEEE INTERNATIONAL SYMPOSIUM ON CIRCUITS AND SYSTEMS : [SELECTED PAPERS]. **Added/Corp** IEEE Circuits and Systems Society. (1989)-. English. IEEE, Institution of Electrical

and Electronics Engineers, Inc., 345 East 47th Street, New York NY 10017-2394. **Tel** (908)981-1393, FAX (908)981-9667. ***Continues*** *IEEE International Symposium on Circuits and Systems IEEE International Symposium on Circuits and Systems Proceedings.*
Ind/Abst Index IEEE Publ.

US/0018-9197
IEEE JOURNAL OF QUANTUM ELECTRONICS. [IEEE j. quantum electron.]. **Added/Corp** Institute of Electrical and Electronics Engineers. Electron Devices Group. IEEE Microwave Theory and Techniques Group. IEEE Quantum Electronics Council. IEEE Quantum Electronics and Applications Society. Lasers and Electro-Optics Society (Institute of Electrical and Electronics Engineers). **VFOAT** Journal of Quantum Electronics; I.E.E.E. Journal of Quantum Electronics. Vol. Ed. 1, No. 1 (Apr. 1965)-. Academic Scholarly Publication. English. mo. $535.00. IEEE, Institution of Electrical and Electronics Engineers, Inc., 345 East 47th Street, New York NY 10017-2394. **Tel** (908)981-1393, FAX (908)981-9667. **(Subscription address:** IEEE / Institute of Electrical and Electronics Engineers, 445 Hoes Lane, PO Box 1331, Piscataway NJ 08855-1331.**) LC** TK7800; .I53. **DD** 537.5/05. **CODEN** IEJQA7. **[CCC]. Pr Rev.** available on microfiche. Documents available from Article Express International, The Genuine Article, Ask*IEEE, CASDDS.
Desc: Covers the science and technology of quantum electronics devices, systems and applications.
Ind/Abst Acoust. Abstr.; Appl. Sci. Technol. Index; Bioeng. Abstr.; Ceram. Abstr.; Chem. Abstr.; Chem. Titles; Curr. Contents Eng. Tech. Appl. Sci.; Curr. Contents Phys. Chem. Earth Sci.; Ei Page One; Energy Res. Abstr.; Eng. Index Annu.; Index IEEE Publ.; INIS Atomindex [Micro.]; INSPEC (1968-); Int. Aerosp. Abstr.; Pollut. Abstr. Indexes; Res. Alert [Full Cov.]; Sci. Cit. Index; SCISEARCH.

US/0018-9200
IEEE JOURNAL OF SOLID-STATE CIRCUITS. [IEEE j. solid-state circuits]. **Added/Corp** IEEE Solid-State Circuits Council. **VFOAT** Journal of Solid-State Circuits. **VAT** IEEE Journal of Solid State Circuits; Journal of Solid State Circuits. Vol. SC-1 (Sept. 1966)-. Periodical. English. mo. $300.00. IEEE, Institution of Electrical and Electronics Engineers, Inc., 345 East 47th Street, New York NY 10017-2394. **Tel** (908)981-1393, FAX (908)981-9667. **(Subscription address:** IEEE / Institute of Electrical and Electronics Engineers, 445 Hoes Lane, PO Box 1331, Piscataway NJ 08855-1331.**) LC** TK7871.85; .I23. **CODEN** IJSCBC. **[CCC]. Pr Rev.** Documents available from Article Express International, The Genuine Article, Ask*IEEE, CASDDS.
Desc: Covers the area of solid-state circuits; emphasis is on practical applications.
Ind/Abst Acoust. Abstr.; Appl. Sci. Technol. Index; Bioeng. Abstr.; Chem. Abstr. (1966-1982); Comput. Inf. Syst. Abstr. J. [Full Cov.]; Curr. Contents Eng. Tech. Appl. Sci.; Ei Page One; Elect. Comm. Abstr.; Eng. Index Annu.; Index IEEE Publ.; INIS Atomindex [Micro.]; INSPEC (1968-); Int. Aerosp. Abstr.; Leadscan; Pollut. Abstr. Indexes; Res. Alert [Full Cov.]; Sci. Cit. Index; SCISEARCH; Solid State Supercond. Abstr.

US
IEEE JOURNAL ON SELECTED TOPICS IN QUANTUM ELECTRONICS. Periodical. English. qt. $300.00. IEEE, Institution of Electrical and Electronics Engineers, Inc., 345 East 47th Street, New York NY 10017-2394. **Tel** (908)981-1393, FAX (908)981-9667. **(Subscription address:** IEEE / Institute of Electrical and Electronics Engineers, 445 Hoes Lane, PO Box 1331, Piscataway NJ 08855-1331.**) ED** Steven Brueck.
Desc: Theory and applications of quantum electronics devices and technologies.

US/0073-9146
IEEE MEMBERSHIP DIRECTORY. [IEEE membsh. dir.]. **Main/Corp** Institute of Electrical and Electronics Engineers. **Added/Corp** Institute of Electrical and Electronics Engineers. Membership Directory. **VAT** Institute of Electrical and Electronics Engineers Membership Directory. (19??)-. Directory. English. an. $159.00. IEEE, Institution of Electrical and Electronics Engineers, Inc., 345 East 47th Street, New York NY 10017-2394. **Tel** (908)981-1393, FAX (908)981-9667. **(Subscription address:** IEEE / Institute of Electrical and Electronics Engineers, 445 Hoes Lane, PO Box 1331, Piscataway NJ 08855-1331.**) LC** TK1.A1; I47. **DD** 621.3/06/273.
Desc: Provides quick access to name, current location and title of all current IEEE members and society affiliates, excluding students.
Ind/Abst Index IEEE Publ.

US/1051-8207
IEEE MICROWAVE AND GUIDED WAVE LETTERS. (IEEE MICROWAVE AND GUIDED WAVE LETTERS : A PUBLICATION OF THE IEEE MICROWAVE THEORY AND TECHNIQUES SOCIETY.). [IEEE microw. guided wave lett.]. **Added/Corp** Institute of Electrical and Electronics Engineers. IEEE Microwave Theory and Techniques Society. **VFOAT** Microwave and Guided Wave Letters. **VAT** Institute of Electrical and Electronics Engineers Microwave and Guided Wave Letters. Vol. 1, No. 1 (Jan. 1991)-. Periodical. English. mo. $170.00. IEEE, Institution of Electrical and Electronics Engineers, Inc., 345 East 47th Street, New York NY 10017-2394. **Tel** (908)981-1393, FAX (908)981-9667. **(Subscription address:** IEEE / Institute of Electrical and Electronics Engineers, 445 Hoes Lane, PO Box 1331, Piscataway NJ 08855-1331.**) LC** TK7876; .I183. **DD** 621 381/3. **CODEN** IMGLE3. **[CCC].** Documents available from Article Express International, Ask*IEEE.
Desc: Covers research and engineering contributions in the electromagnetic spectrum from microwaves to infrared, including millimeter-waves, submillimeter-waves and guided wave structures, with emphasis on components, devices, circuits, systems and applications.
Ind/Abst Comput. Inf. Syst. Abstr. J. [Full Cov.]; Ei Page One; Elect. Comm. Abstr.; Eng. Index Annu.; Index IEEE Publ.; INSPEC (Jan. 1991-); Int. Aerosp. Abstr.; Solid State Supercond. Abstr.

US
IEEE ... MICROWAVE AND MILLIMETER-WAVE MONOLITHIC CIRCUITS SYMPOSIUM DIGEST OF PAPERS. **Main/Conf** IEEE Microwave and Millimeter-Wave Monolithic Circuits Symposium. **VFOAT** Microwave and Millimeter-Wave Monolithic Circuits Symposium Digest of Papers; Digest of Papers. (1982)-. English. an. IEEE, Institution of Electrical and Electronics Engineers, Inc., 345 East 47th Street, New York NY 10017-2394. **Tel** (908)981-1393, FAX (908)981-9667. **(Subscription address:** IEEE Service Center, 445 Hoes Lane, Piscataway NJ 08854; telephone: (201)981-1393**) LC** TK7876; .I185A. **DD** 621.381/73. **CODEN** DPISEY. Documents available from Article Express International.
Ind/Abst Ei Page One; Eng. Index Annu.; Index IEEE Publ.

US/0149-645X
IEEE MTT-S INTERNATIONAL MICROWAVE SYMPOSIUM DIGEST. [IEEE MTT-S Int. Microw. Symp. dig.]. **Added/Corp** Institute of Electrical and Electronics Engineers. **VFOAT** IEEE MTT International Microwave Symposium Digest. **VAT** Institute of Electrical and Electronics Engineers Microwave Theory and Techniques Society International Microwave Symposium Digest. (1977)-. English. an. $28.00. IEEE, Institution of Electrical and Electronics Engineers, Inc., 345 East 47th Street, New York NY 10017-2394. **Tel** (908)981-1393, FAX (908)981-9667. **(Subscription address:** IEEE Service Center, 445 Hoes Lane, Piscataway, NJ 08854**) LC** TK7876; .I18a. **DD** 621.381/3. **CODEN** IMIDDM. **[CCC].** Documents available from Article Express International, Ask*IEEE. ***Continues*** *IEEE MTT-S International Microwave Symposium Digest of Technical Papers, 0149-6298.*
Desc: Covers microwaves and microwave devices.
Ind/Abst Bioeng. Abstr.; Comput. Inf. Syst. Abstr. J. [Full Cov.]; Ei Page One; Elect. Comm. Abstr.; Eng. Index Annu.; Index IEEE Publ.; INSPEC; Manuf. Process Eng. Abstr.; Mech. Eng. Abstr.; Solid State Supercond. Abstr.

US/0746-7834
IEEE OCEANIC ENGINEERING SOCIETY. NEWSLETTER. [IEEE Ocean. Eng. Soc. newsl.]. **VFOAT** Newsletter; Oceanic Engineering Society Newsletter. **VAT** Institute of Electrical and Electronics Engineers Oceanic Engineering Society Newsletter. Began in 1983?. Newsletter. English. qt. IEEE, Institution of Electrical and Electronics Engineers, Inc., 345 East 47th Street, New York NY 10017-2394. **Tel** (908)981-1393, FAX (908)981-9667. **(Subscription address:** IEEE Service Center, 445 Hoes Lane, Piscataway, NJ 08854**) DD** 621. ***Continues*** *IEEE Council on Oceanic Engineering Newsletter, 0749-8039.*
Ind/Abst Index IEEE Publ.

●US
IEEE PARALLEL AND DISTRIBUTED TECHNOLOGY. **Added/Corp** Institute of Electrical and Electronics Engineers. **VAT** Institute of Electrical and Electronics Engineers Parallel and Distributed Systems Magazine. (1993)-. Periodical. English. qt. $210.00. IEEE, Institution of Electrical and Electronics Engineers, Inc., 345 East 47th Street, New York NY 10017-2394. **Tel** (908)981-1393, FAX (908)981-9667. **(Subscription address:** IEEE / Institute of Electrical and Electronics Engineers, 445 Hoes Lane, PO Box 1331, Piscataway NJ 08855-1331.**)**

US/0278-6648
IEEE POTENTIALS. [IEEE potentials]. **Added/Corp** Institute of Electrical and Electronics Engineers. **VFOAT** Potentials. **VAT** Institute of Electrical and Electronics Engineers Potentials. (Winter 1982)-. Periodical. English. qt. $40.00. IEEE, Institution of Electrical and Electronics Engineers, Inc., 345 East 47th Street, New York NY 10017-2394. **Tel** (908)981-1393, FAX (908)981-9667. **(Subscription address:** IEEE / Institute of Electrical and Electronics Engineers, 445 Hoes Lane, PO Box 1331, Piscataway NJ 08855-1331.**) DD** 629. **[CCC].** Documents available from Article Express International, Ask*IEEE.
Desc: Discusses career issues, the latest technical areas, and other subjects of general interest to the IEEE student member.
Ind/Abst Comput. Inf. Syst. Abstr. J. [Full Cov.]; Ei Page One; Elect. Comm. Abstr.; Eng. Index Annu.; Index IEEE Publ.; INSPEC (Feb. 1984-); Int. Aerosp. Abstr.; Manuf. Process Eng. Abstr.; Mater. Sci. Eng. Abstr.; Mech. Eng. Abstr.; Solid State Supercond. Abstr.

US/0272-1724
IEEE POWER ENGINEERING REVIEW. [IEEE power eng. rev.]. **Added/Corp** IEEE Power Engineering Society. **VFOAT** Power Engineering Review. **VAT** Institute of Electrical and Electronics Engineers Power Engineering Review. Vol. PER. 1 No. 1 (Jan. 1981)-. Periodical. English. mo. $115.00. IEEE, Institution of Electrical and Electronics Engineers, Inc., 345 East 47th Street, New York NY 10017-2394. **Tel** (908)981-1393, FAX (908)981-9667. **(Subscription address:** IEEE / Institute of Electrical and Electronics Engineers, 445 Hoes Lane, PO Box 1331, Piscataway NJ 08855-1331.**) LC** TK1001; .I235. **CODEN** IPERDV. **[CCC].** available on microfilm and microfiche. Documents available from Ask*IEEE.
Desc: Covers electric power system engineering; includes one-page summaries of all papers accepted for publication.
Ind/Abst Index IEEE Publ.; INSPEC (Jan. 1981-); Pollut. Abstr. Indexes.

US/0160-0141
IEEE POWER ENGINEERING SOCIETY DISCUSSIONS AND CLOSURES OF ABSTRACTED PAPERS FROM THE SUMMER MEETING. (DISCUSSIONS AND CLOSURES OF ABSTRACTED PAPERS FROM THE SUMMER MEETING.). **Main/Corp** IEEE Power Engineering Society. **Added/Corp** IEEE Power Engineering Society. IEEE PES Summer Meeting Discussions & Closures. IEEE Power Engineering Society. IEEE Summer Meeting Discussions and Closures. **VFOAT** IEEE PES Summer Meeting Discussions & Closures; IEEE Summer Meeting Discussions and Closures. **VAT** Institute of Electrical and Electronics Engineers Power Engineering Society Discussions and Closures of Abstracted Papers from the Summer Meeting. (19??)-. English. an. Institution of Electrical Engineers / IEE, Michael Faraday House, Six Hills Way, Stevenage Herts SG1 2AY UK. **Tel** 011 44 438 313311, FAX 011 44 438 742840, telex 825578 IEESTV G. **(Subscription address:** IEE / UK, Publications Sales Department, PO Box 96, Stevenage, Herts, SG1 2SD England.**) LC** TK5; .I25a. **DD** 621.31/05.

US/0046-8371
IEEE PUBLICATIONS BULLETIN. [IEEE publ. bull.]. **Main/Corp** Institute of Electrical and Electronics Engineers. (Oct. 1970)-. Newsletter. English. qt. Free on request. IEEE, Institution of Electrical and Electronics Engineers, Inc., 345 East 47th Street, New York NY 10017-2394. **Tel** (908)981-1393, FAX (908)981-9667. **(Subscription address:** IEEE / Institute of Electrical and Electronics Engineers, 445 Hoes Lane, PO Box 1331, Piscataway NJ 08855-1331.**) LC** CURRENT ISSUES ONLY. **DD** 621. **CODEN** IPBUDP. **[CCC].**
Desc: For librarians, announcing new IEEE publications and services.
Ind/Abst Index IEEE Publ.

US/1053-5888
IEEE SIGNAL PROCESSING MAGAZINE. [IEEE signal process. mag.]. **Added/Corp** Institute of Electrical and Electronics Engineers. IEEE Signal Processing Society. **VFOAT** Signal Processing Magazine; I.E.E.E. Signal Processing Magazine; IEEE SP Magazine. **VAT** Institute of Electrical and Electronics Engineers Signal Processing Magazine. Vol. 8, No. 1 (Jan. 1991)-. Periodical. English. qt. $75.00. IEEE, Institution of Electrical and Electronics Engineers, Inc., 345 East 47th Street, New York NY 10017-2394. **Tel** (908)981-1393, FAX (908)981-9667. **(Subscription address:** IEEE / Institute of Electrical and Electronics Engineers, 445 Hoes Lane, PO Box 1331, Piscataway NJ 08855-1331.**) LC** TK5981; .I143. **DD** 621.382/2/05. **CODEN** ISPRE6. **[CCC].** Documents available from Article Express International, Ask*IEEE. ***Continues*** *IEEE ASSP Magazine, 0740-7467.*
Desc: Contains full-length papers of practical use to engineers interested in audio, electroacoustics and signal processing. Also features tutorials of a light technical nature, news and notes, conferences, workshops, seminars and lectures.
Ind/Abst Ei Page One; Eng. Index Annu.; Index IEEE Publ.; INSPEC (Jan. 1991-); Int. Aerosp. Abstr.; Pollut. Abstr. Indexes.

US/0018-9235
IEEE SPECTRUM. [IEEE spectrum]. **Added/Corp** Institute of Electrical and Electronics Engineers. **VFOAT** Spectrum. Vol. 1, No. 1 (Jan. 1964)-. Periodical. English. mo. $157.00. IEEE, Institution of Electrical and Electronics Engineers, Inc., 345 East 47th Street, New York NY 10017-2394. **Tel** (908)981-1393, FAX (908)981-9667. **(Subscription address:** IEEE / Institute of Electrical and Electronics Engineers, 445 Hoes Lane, PO Box 1331, Piscataway NJ 08855-1331.**) ED** Donald Christiansen. **LC** TK1; .I15. **DD** 621.3/05. **CODEN** IEESAM. **[CCC]. Pr Rev.** available on microfiche. Documents available from Article Express International, The Genuine Article, Ask*IEEE, UMI Article

Clearinghouse, CASDDS. ***Continues*** *Electrical Engineering, 0095-9197.*
Desc: State-of-the-art, review, and applications articles chosen for their utility to a range of engineers and scientists in the electrical and electronics field.
Ind/Abst ABI/INFORM Glob. Ed.; ABI Inform Ondisc (Jan. 1979-); Abstr. Hum. Comput. Interact.; ACM Guide Comput. Lit.; Alum. Ind. Abstr.; Appl. Sci. Technol. Index; Chem. Abstr.; Coal Abstr.; Comput. Inf. Syst. Abstr. J. [Full Cov.]; Comput. Bus. (19??-); Comput. Database; Comput. Lit. Index; Comput. Rev.; Curr. Contents Eng. Tech. Appl. Sci.; Ei Page One; Elect. Comm. Abstr.; Energy Res. Abstr.; Eng. Mater. Abstr.; Eng. Index Annu.; Ergon. Abstr.; Expand. Acad. Index (1992-); Geogr. Abstr. Human Geogr. (?-?); HILITES; Index IEEE Publ. (Jan. 1964-); Inf. Sci. Abstr.; INIS Atomindex [Micro.]; INSPEC (1968-); Int. Aerosp. Abstr.; Law Office Inf. Serv.; Manuf. Process Eng. Abstr.; Mech. Eng. Abstr.; Met. Abstr.; Oper. Res./Manag. Sci.; Peace Res. Abstr. J. (1985-1988); Qual. Control Appl. Stat.; Res. Alert [Full Cov.]; Res. High. Educ. Abstr.; Saf. Health Work; Sci. Cit. Index; SCISEARCH; Soc. Sci. Cit. Index [Select. Cov.]; Solid State Supercond. Abstr.; World Publ. Monit.

US/0362-4536
IEEE STUDENT PAPERS. [IEEE stud. pap.]. **Main/Corp** Institute of Electrical and Electronics Engineers. **Added/Corp** Institute of Electrical and Electronics Engineers. Student Papers. **VAT** Institute of Electrical and Electronics Engineers Student Papers. (1975)-. English. an. Free on request. IEEE, Institution of Electrical and Electronics Engineers, Inc., 345 East 47th Street, New York NY 10017-2394. **Tel** (908)981-1393, FAX (908)981-9667. **(Subscription address:** IEEE Service Center, 445 Hoes Lane, Piscataway, NJ 08854**)** **LC** TK7800; .I525a. **DD** 621.3/05.
Ind/Abst Index IEEE Publ.

US/0360-8956
IEEE STUDENT PRIZE PAPERS, THE.
VAT Institute of Electrical and Electronics Engineers Student Prize Papers. English. an. University of Nevada Engineering Department, Reno NV 89557. **LC** TK1; .I17. **DD** 621.3/05.

US/0278-520X
IEEE TECHNICAL ACTIVITIES GUIDE. (IEEE TECHNICAL ACTIVITIES GUIDE / INSTITUTE OF ELECTRICAL AND ELECTRONICS ENGINEERS.). [IEEE tech. act. guide]. **Added/Corp** Institute of Electrical and Electronics Engineers. **VFOAT** Technical Activities Guide; IEEE TAG: A Guide to New Technical Horizons. **VAT** Institute of Electrical and Electronics Engineers Technical Activities Guide. Vol. 1, No. 3 (July 1980)-. Periodical. English. qt. $25.00. IEEE, Institution of Electrical and Electronics Engineers, Inc., 345 East 47th Street, New York NY 10017-2394. **Tel** (908)981-1393, FAX (908)981-9667. **(Subscription address:** IEEE / Institute of Electrical and Electronics Engineers, 445 Hoes Lane, PO Box 1331, Piscataway NJ 08855-1331.**)** **[CCC].** ***Continues*** *Institute of Electrical and Electronics Engineers. Technical Activities Guide, 0195-3273.*
Desc: A guide to all IEEE sponsored and co-sponsored technical conferences held each year.
Ind/Abst Index IEEE Publ.; Int. Aerosp. Abstr.

US/0018-9251
IEEE TRANSACTIONS ON AEROSPACE AND ELECTRONIC SYSTEMS. [IEEE trans. aerosp. electron. syst.]. **Added/Corp** IEEE Aerospace and Electronic Systems Society. Institute of Electrical and Electronics Engineers. Aerospace and Electronic Systems Group. **VFOAT** Transactions on Aerospace and Electronic Systems; Aerospace and Electronic Systems. **VAT** Institute of Electrical and Electronics Engineers Transactions on Aerospace and Electronic Systems. Vol. AES-1 (Aug. 1965)-. Academic Scholarly Publication. English. qt. $175.00. IEEE, Institution of Electrical and Electronics Engineers, Inc., 345 East 47th Street, New York NY 10017-2394. **Tel** (908)981-1393, FAX (908)981-9667. **(Subscription address:** IEEE / Institute of Electrical and Electronics Engineers, 445 Hoes Lane, PO Box 1331, Piscataway NJ 08855-1331.**)** **LC** TL3000.A1; I53. **DD** 629.1. **CODEN** IEARAX. **[CCC]. Pr Rev.** available on microfiche. Documents available from Article Express International, The Genuine Article, Ask*IEEE, CASDDS. ***Formed by the union of*** *IEEE Transactions on Aerospace, 0536-1516; IEEE Transactions on Space Electronics and Telemetry, 0096-2414; IEEE Transactions on Aerospace and Navigational Electronics, 0096-1957* ***and*** *IEEE Transactions on Military Electronics, 0536-1559.*
Desc: Covers the equipment, procedures and techniques applicable to the organization, installation, and operation of functional systems designed to meet the high performance requirements of earth and space systems.
Ind/Abst Acoust. Abstr.; Appl. Sci. Technol. Index; Bioeng. Abstr.; Chem. Abstr.; Curr. Contents Eng. Tech. Appl. Sci.; Ei Page One; EMBASE; Eng. Index Annu.; Expand. Acad. Index (1992-); Index IEEE Publ.; INSPEC (1968-); Int. Aerosp. Abstr.; Leadscan; Math. Rev.; Res. Alert [Full Cov.]; Sci. Cit. Index; SCISEARCH; Stat. Theory Method Abstr. (1980-1981).

US/0018-926X
IEEE TRANSACTIONS ON ANTENNAS AND PROPAGATION. [IEEE trans. antennas propag.]. **Added/Corp** IEEE Antennas and Propagation Society. Institute of Electrical and Electronics Engineers. Antennas and Propagation Group. **VFOAT** Transactions on Antennas and Propagation; Antennas and Propagation. Vol. AP-11 (Jan. 1963)-. Periodical. English. mo. $230.00. IEEE, Institution of Electrical and Electronics Engineers, Inc., 345 East 47th Street, New York NY 10017-2394. **Tel** (908)981-1393, FAX (908)981-9667. **(Subscription address:** IEEE / Institute of Electrical and Electronics Engineers, 445 Hoes Lane, PO Box 1331, Piscataway NJ 08855-1331.**)** **LC** TK7800; .I2. **CODEN** IETPAK. **[CCC].** cum. index. **Pr Rev.** available in microform. Documents available from Article Express International, The Genuine Article, Ask*IEEE, CASDDS. ***Continues*** *IRE Transactions on Antennas and Propagation, 0096-1973.*
Ind/Abst Acoust. Abstr.; Appl. Sci. Technol. Index (1991-); Bioeng. Abstr.; Chem. Abstr.; Coal Abstr.; Comput. Abstr.; Curr. Contents Eng. Tech. Appl. Sci.; Ei Page One; Energy Res. Abstr.; Eng. Index Annu.; Expand. Acad. Index (1992-); Index IEEE Publ.; INIS Atomindex [Micro.]; INSPEC (1968-); Int. Aerosp. Abstr.; Math. Rev.; Res. Alert [Full Cov.]; Sci. Cit. Index; SCISEARCH.

US/1051-8223
IEEE TRANSACTIONS ON APPLIED SUPERCONDUCTIVITY. (IEEE TRANSACTIONS ON APPLIED SUPERCONDUCTIVITY : A PUBLICATION OF THE IEEE SUPERCONDUCTIVITY COMMITTEE.). [IEEE trans. appl. supercond.]. **Added/Corp** IEEE Superconductivity Committee. **VAT** Institute of Electrical and Electronics Engineers Transactions on Applied Superconductivity. Vol. 1, No. 1 (Mar. 1991)-. Periodical. English. qt. $225.00. IEEE, Institution of Electrical and Electronics Engineers, Inc., 345 East 47th Street, New York NY 10017-2394. **Tel** (908)981-1393, FAX (908)981-9667. **(Subscription address:** IEEE / Institute of Electrical and Electronics Engineers, 445 Hoes Lane, PO Box 1331, Piscataway NJ 08855-1331.**)** **LC** TK7872.S8; I35. **DD** 621.3. **CODEN** ITASE9. **[CCC].** available on microfiche. Documents available from Article Express International, Ask*IEEE.
Desc: Materials and their application to electronics and power systems, where superconductivity is central to the work.
Ind/Abst Ei Page One; Eng. Index Annu.; Expand. Acad. Index (1992-); INSPEC (March 1991-); Int. Aerosp. Abstr.

●US/1057-7122
IEEE TRANSACTIONS ON CIRCUITS & SYSTEMS. PART 1, FUNDAMENTAL THEORY AND APPLICATIONS. [IEEE trans. circuits syst. 1, Fundam. theory appl.]. **Added/Corp** Institute of Electrical and Electronics Engineers. IEEE Circuits and Systems Society. **VFOAT** Fundamental Theory and Applications; Transactions on Circuits and Systems. N.1, Fundamental Theory and Applications. **VAT** Institute of Electrical and Electronics Engineers Transactions on Circuits and Systems. 1, Fundamental Theory and Applications. Vol. 39, No. 1 (Jan. 1992)-. Periodical. English. mo. $265.00. IEEE, Institution of Electrical and Electronics Engineers, Inc., 345 East 47th Street, New York NY 10017-2394. **Tel** (908)981-1393, FAX (908)981-9667. **(Subscription address:** IEEE / Institute of Electrical and Electronics Engineers, 445 Hoes Lane, PO Box 1331, Piscataway NJ 08855-1331.**)** **LC** TK7867 b .I373. **DD** 621.3815. **CODEN** ITCAEX. **[CCC].** available on microfiche. Documents available from Article Express International, The Genuine Article, Ask*IEEE. ***Continues in part*** *IEEE Transactions on Circuits and Systems, 0098-4094.*
Ind/Abst Appl. Sci. Technol. Index; Curr. Contents Eng. Tech. Appl. Sci.; Ei Page One; Elect. Comm. Abstr.; Eng. Index Annu.; Expand. Acad. Index (1992-); INSPEC (Jan. 1992-); Int. Aerosp. Abstr.; Res. Alert [Full Cov.]; Sci. Cit. Index; SCISEARCH; Solid State Supercond. Abstr.

●US/1057-7130
IEEE TRANSACTIONS ON CIRCUITS AND SYSTEMS. PART 2, ANALOG AND DIGITAL SIGNAL PROCESSING. (IEEE TRANSACTIONS ON CIRCUITS AND SYSTEMS. II, ANALOG AND DIGITAL SIGNAL PROCESSING : A PUBLICATION OF THE IEEE CIRCUITS AND SYSTEMS SOCIETY.). [IEEE trans. circuits syst., 2 Analog digit. signal process.]. **Added/Corp** Institute of Electrical and Electronics Engineers. IEEE Circuits and Systems Society. **VFOAT** Analog and Digital Signal Processing; Transactions on Circuits and Systems. N.2, Analog and Digital Signal Processing. **VAT** Institute of Electrical and Electronics Engineers Transactions on Circuits and Systems. 2, Analog and Digital Signal Processing. Vol. 39, No. 1 (Jan. 1992)-. Periodical. English. mo. $240.00. IEEE, Institution of Electrical and Electronics Engineers, Inc., 345 East 47th Street, New York NY 10017-2394. **Tel** (908)981-1393, FAX (908)981-9667. **(Subscription address:** IEEE / Institute of Electrical and Electronics Engineers, 445 Hoes Lane, PO Box 1331, Piscataway NJ 08855-1331.**)** **LC** TK7867; .I374. **DD** 621.3815. **CODEN** ICSPE5. **[CCC].** available on microfiche. Documents available from Article Express International, The Genuine Article, Ask*IEEE. ***Continues in part*** *IEEE Transactions on Circuits and Systems, 0098-4094.*
Ind/Abst Appl. Sci. Technol. Index; Curr. Contents Eng. Tech. Appl. Sci.; Ei Page One; Eng. Index Annu.; Expand. Acad. Index (1992-); INSPEC (Jan. 1991-); Int. Aerosp. Abstr.; Res. Alert [Full Cov.]; Sci. Cit. Index; SCISEARCH; Soc. Sci. Cit. Index [Select. Cov.].

US/0148-6411
IEEE TRANSACTIONS ON COMPONENTS, HYBRIDS AND MANUFACTURING TECHNOLOGY. ***Title Change.*** [IEEE trans. components hybrids manuf. technol.]. **Added/Corp** IEEE Components, Hybrids, and Manufacturing Technology Society. **VAT** Institute of Electrical and Electronics Engineers Transactions on Components, Hybrids, and Manufacturing Technology. Vol. CHMT 1-16 (Mar. 1978)-(1993). Academic Scholarly Publication. English. Six times a year. IEEE, Institution of Electrical and Electronics Engineers, Inc., 345 East 47th Street, New York NY 10017-2394. **Tel** (908)981-1393, FAX (908)981-9667. **LC** TK7869; .I18. **DD** 621.3/05. **CODEN** ITTEDR. **[CCC]. Pr Rev.** available on microfiche. Documents available from Article Express International, The Genuine Article, Ask*IEEE, CASDDS. ***Formed by the union of*** *IEEE Transactions on Manufacturing Technology, 0046-838X* ***and*** *IEEE Transactions on Parts, Hybrids, and Packaging, 0361-1000.* ***Split into*** *IEEE Transactions on Components, Packaging, and Manufacturing technology. Part A, 1070-9886* ***and*** *IEEE Transactions on Components, Packaging, and Manufacturing Technology. Part B, Advanced packaging, 1070-9894.*
Desc: Covers the fields of component parts, hybrid microelectronics, materials, packaging techniques, and manufacturing technology.
Ind/Abst Acoust. Abstr.; Bioeng. Abstr.; Ceram. Abstr.; Chem. Abstr.; Curr. Contents Eng. Tech. Appl. Sci.; Ei Page One; Eng. Index Annu.; Expand. Acad. Index (1992-); Index IEEE Publ.; INSPEC (March 1978-); Int. Aerosp. Abstr.; Leadscan; Res. Alert [Full Cov.]; Sci. Cit. Index (19??-19??); SCISEARCH; Soc. Sci. Cit. Index [Select. Cov.].

US/0278-0070
IEEE TRANSACTIONS ON COMPUTER-AIDED DESIGN OF INTEGRATED CIRCUITS AND SYSTEMS. (IEEE TRANSACTIONS ON COMPUTER-AIDED DESIGN OF INTEGRATED CIRCUITS AND SYSTEMS : A PUBLICATION OF THE IEEE CIRCUITS AND SYSTEMS SOCIETY.). [IEEE trans. comput.-aided des. integr. circuits syst.]. **Added/Corp** IEEE Circuits and Systems Society. Institute of Electrical and Electronics Engineers. **VFOAT** Transactions on Computer-Aided Design of Integrated Circuits and Systems. **VAT** IEEE Transactions on Computer Aided Design of Integrated Circuits and Systems. Vol. CAD-1, No. 1 (Jan. 1982)-. Periodical. English. mo. $376.00. IEEE, Institution of Electrical and Electronics Engineers, Inc., 345 East 47th Street, New York NY 10017-2394. **Tel** (908)981-1393, FAX (908)981-9667. **(Subscription address:** IEEE / Institute of Electrical and Electronics Engineers, 445 Hoes Lane, PO Box 1331, Piscataway NJ 08855-1331.**)** **LC** TK7874; .I327. **DD** 621.381/73/0285. **CODEN** ITCSDI. **[CCC]. Pr Rev.** available on microfiche. Documents available from Article Express International, The Genuine Article, Ask*IEEE.
Desc: Deals with algorithms, methods and man-machine interfaces for physical and logical design. Practical applications are emphasized.
Ind/Abst Acoust. Abstr.; Appl. Sci. Technol. Index (1991-); Compumath Citation Index [Full Cov.]; Comput. Abstr.; Curr. Contents Eng. Tech. Appl. Sci.; Ei Page One; Eng. Index Annu.; Expand. Acad. Index (1992-); Index IEEE Publ.; INSPEC (Jan. 1982-); Int. Aerosp. Abstr. (1983-); Res. Alert [Full Cov.]; Sci. Cit. Index; SCISEARCH.

US/0098-3063
IEEE TRANSACTIONS ON CONSUMER ELECTRONICS. [IEEE trans. consum. electron.]. **Added/Corp** IEEE Consumer Electronics Society. IEEE Broadcast, Cable, and Consumer Electronics Society. IEEE Consumer Electronics Group. **VAT** Institute of Electrical and Electronics Engineers Transactions on Consumer Electronics. (Feb. 1975)-. Periodical. English. qt. $150.00. IEEE, Institution of Electrical and Electronics Engineers, Inc., 345 East 47th Street, New York NY 10017-2394. **Tel** (908)981-1393, FAX (908)981-9667. **(Subscription address:** IEEE / Institute of Electrical and Electronics Engineers, 445 Hoes Lane, PO Box 1331, Piscataway NJ 08855-1331.**)** **LC** TK6563; .I2. **DD** 621.38. **CODEN** ITCEDA. **[CCC].** cum. index. **Pr Rev.** available on microfiche. Documents available from Article Express International, The Genuine Article, Ask*IEEE. ***Continues*** *IEEE Transactions on Broadcast and Television Receivers, 0018-9308.*
Desc: Covers the technical aspects of all consumer electronics products. Papers concentrate on new technology oriented to consumer electronics.
Ind/Abst Appl. Sci. Technol. Index (Feb. 1975-); Bioeng. Abstr.; Comput. Abstr.; Curr. Contents Eng. Tech. Appl. Sci.; Ei Page One; Eng. Index Annu.; Expand. Acad. Index (1992-); Index IEEE Publ. (Feb. 1975-); INSPEC (Feb. 1975-); Int. Aerosp. Abstr.; Leadscan; Res. Alert [Full Cov.]; Sci. Cit. Index; SCISEARCH.

●US/1070-9878
IEEE TRANSACTIONS ON DIELECTRICS AND ELECTRICAL INSULATION. [IEEE trans. dielectr. electr. insul.]. **Added/Corp** Institute of Electrical and Electronics Engineers. (1994)-. Periodical. English. bm. $195.00. IEEE, Institution of Electrical and Electronics Engineers, Inc., 345 East 47th Street, New York NY 10017-2394. **Tel** (908)981-1393, FAX (908)981-9667. **(Subscription address:** IEEE / Institute of Electrical and Electronics Engineers, 445 Hoes Lane, PO Box 1331, Piscataway NJ 08855-1331.**) LC** TK3421; .I38. **DD** 621.319/37/05. **CODEN** ITDIESITDEIS. ***Continues*** *IEEE Transactions on Electrical Insulation, 0018-9367.*

US/0018-9359
IEEE TRANSACTIONS ON EDUCATION. (IEEE TRANSACTIONS ON EDUCATION / PROFESSIONAL TECHNICAL GROUP ON EDUCATION.). [IEEE trans. ed.]. **Added/Corp** Institute of Electrical and Electronics Engineers. Institute of Electrical and Electronics Engineers. Professional Technical Group on Education. Institute of Electrical and Electronics Engineers. Education Group. IEEE Education Group. IEEE Education Society. **VFOAT** I.E.E.E. Transactions on Education; Transactions on Education. Vol. E-6, No. 1 (Mar. 1963)-. Periodical. English. qt. $115.00. IEEE, Institution of Electrical and Electronics Engineers, Inc., 345 East 47th Street, New York NY 10017-2394. **Tel** (908)981-1393, FAX (908)981-9667. **(Subscription address:** IEEE / Institute of Electrical and Electronics Engineers, 445 Hoes Lane, PO Box 1331, Piscataway NJ 08855-1331.**) LC** T61; .I2. **DD** 607. **CODEN** IEEDAB. **[CCC]. Pr Rev.** Documents available from Article Express International, The Genuine Article, Ask*IEEE, CASDDS. ***Continues*** *IRE Transactions on Education, 0893-7141.*
Desc: Covers electrical engineering education.
Ind/Abst Bioeng. Abstr.; Chem. Abstr.; Comput. Abstr.; Contents Pages Educ.; Curr. Contents Eng. Tech. Appl. Sci.; Educ. Technol. Abstr.; Ei Page One; Eng. Index Annu.; Expand. Acad. Index (1992-); Index IEEE Publ.; Inf. Sci. Abstr. (?-?); INSPEC (1968-); Int. Aerosp. Abstr.; Res. Alert [Full Cov.]; Res. High. Educ. Abstr.; Risk Abstr.; Sci. Cit. Index; SCISEARCH; Soc. Sci. Cit. Index [Select. Cov.]; Stud. Women Abstr.; Tech. Educ. Train. Abstr.

US/0018-9367
IEEE TRANSACTIONS ON ELECTRICAL INSULATION. ***Title Change.*** [IEEE trans. electr. insul.]. **Added/Corp** IEEE Society on Electrical Insulation. IEEE Group on Electrical Insulation. **VFOAT** Transactions on Electrical Insulation. Vol. EI-1 (March 1965)-(1993). Periodical. English. bm. IEEE, Institution of Electrical and Electronics Engineers, Inc., 345 East 47th Street, New York NY 10017-2394. **Tel** (908)981-1393, FAX (908)981-9667. **CODEN** IETIAX. **[CCC]. Pr Rev.** available on microfiche. Documents available from Article Express International, The Genuine Article, Ask*IEEE, CASDDS. ***Continued by*** *IEEE Transactions on Dielectrics and Electrical Insulation, 1070-9878.*
Desc: Covers electrical insulation common to the design and construction of components and equipment for use in electrical and electronic circuits and distribution systems at all frequencies.
Ind/Abst Acoust. Abstr. (?-?); Bioeng. Abstr. (?-?); Chem. Abstr. (?-?); Curr. Contents Eng. Tech. Appl. Sci. (?-?); Ei Page One (?-?); Eng. Index Annu. (?-?); Expand. Acad. Index (1992-?); Index IEEE Publ. (?-?); INSPEC (1968-?); Int. Aerosp. Abstr. (?-?); Leadscan (?-?); Pollut. Abstr. Indexes (?-?); Res. Alert (?-?) [Full Cov.]; Sci. Cit. Index (?-?); SCISEARCH (?-?); Soc. Sci. Cit. Index (?-?) [Select. Cov.].

US/0018-9375
IEEE TRANSACTIONS ON ELECTROMAGNETIC COMPATIBILITY. [IEEE trans. electromagn. compat.]. **Added/Corp** IEEE Electromagnetic Compatibility Society. Institute of Electrical and Electronics Engineers. Electromagnetic Compatibility Group. **VFOAT** Transactions on Electromagnetic Compatibility; Electromagnetic Compatibility. Vol. EMC-6 (Jan. 1964)-. Periodical. English. qt. $93.00. IEEE, Institution of Electrical and Electronics Engineers, Inc., 345 East 47th Street, New York NY 10017-2394. **Tel** (908)981-1393, FAX (908)981-9667. **(Subscription address:** IEEE / Institute of Electrical and Electronics Engineers, 445 Hoes Lane, PO Box 1331, Piscataway NJ 08855-1331.**) CODEN** IEMCAE. **[CCC]. Pr Rev.** available on microfiche. Documents available from Article Express International, The Genuine Article, Ask*IEEE, CASDDS. ***Continues*** *IEEE Transactions on Radio Frequency Interference.*
Desc: Covers all areas of electromagnetic compatibility.
Ind/Abst Acoust. Abstr.; Bioeng. Abstr.; Chem. Abstr.; Curr. Contents Eng. Tech. Appl. Sci.; Ei Page One; Elect. Comm. Abstr.; Eng. Index Annu.; Expand. Acad. Index (1992-); Index IEEE Publ.; INSPEC (1968-); Int. Aerosp. Abstr.; Res. Alert [Full Cov.]; Sci. Cit. Index; SCISEARCH; Solid State Supercond. Abstr.

US/0018-9383
IEEE TRANSACTIONS ON ELECTRON DEVICES. [IEEE trans. electron devices]. **Added/Corp** IEEE Electron Devices Society. Institute of Electrical and Electronics Engineers. Electron Devices Group. **VFOAT** Transactions on Electron Devices; Electron Devices. Vol. 10 (Jan. 1963)-. Periodical. English. mo. $395.00. IEEE, Institution of Electrical and Electronics Engineers, Inc., 345 East 47th Street, New York NY 10017-2394. **Tel** (908)981-1393, FAX (908)981-9667. **(Subscription address:** IEEE / Institute of Electrical and Electronics Engineers, 445 Hoes Lane, PO Box 1331, Piscataway NJ 08855-1331.**) NLM** W1 I223E. **CODEN** IETDAI. **[CCC]. Pr Rev.** available on microfiche. Documents available from Article Express International, The Genuine Article, Ask*IEEE, CASDDS. ***Continues*** *Institute of Radio Engineers. Professional Group on Electron Devices. IRE Transactions on Electron Devices, 0096-2430.*
Desc: Covers the theory, design, and performance of active electron and ion devices, integrated electron devices, and energy sources.
Ind/Abst Acoust. Abstr.; Bioeng. Abstr.; Chem. Abstr.; Comput. Abstr.; Comput. Inf. Syst. Abstr. J. [Full Cov.]; Curr. Contents Eng. Tech. Appl. Sci.; Ei Page One; Elect. Comm. Abstr.; EMBASE; Energy Res. Abstr.; Eng. Index Annu.; Expand. Acad. Index (1992-); Index IEEE Publ.; INIS Atomindex [Micro.]; INSPEC (1968-); Int. Aerosp. Abstr.; Leadscan; Mech. Eng. Abstr.; Res. Alert [Full Cov.]; Sci. Cit. Index; SCISEARCH; Solid State Supercond. Abstr.

US/0885-8969
IEEE TRANSACTIONS ON ENERGY CONVERSION. [IEEE trans. energy convers.]. **Added/Corp** IEEE Power Engineering Society. **VFOAT** Transactions on Energy Conversion. **VAT** Institute of Electrical and Electronics Engineers Transactions on Energy Conversion. Vol. EC-1, No. 1 (March 1986)-. Periodical. English. qt. $150.00. IEEE, Institution of Electrical and Electronics Engineers, Inc., 345 East 47th Street, New York NY 10017-2394. **Tel** (908)981-1393, FAX (908)981-9667. **(Subscription address:** IEEE / Institute of Electrical and Electronics Engineers, 445 Hoes Lane, PO Box 1331, Piscataway NJ 08855-1331.**) LC** TK1001; .I25. **DD** 621.31/24. **[CCC]. Pr Rev.** available on microfilm and microfiche. Documents available from Article Express International, The Genuine Article, Ask*IEEE. ***Continues in part*** *IEEE Transactions on Power Apparatus and Systems, 0018-9510.*
Desc: Covers research, development, design, application, construction, installation, and operation of electric power generating facilities (along with their conventional, nuclear, or renewable sources) for the safe, reliable, and economic generation, conversion, and control of electrical energy for general industrial, commercial, public, and domestic consumption.
Ind/Abst Appl. Sci. Technol. Index; Curr. Contents Eng. Tech. Appl. Sci.; Ei Page One; Energy Inf. Abstr.; Eng. Index Annu.; Expand. Acad. Index (1992-); Fluid Abstr., Civil Eng.; Fluid Abstr. Proc. Eng.; FLUIDEX; Index IEEE Publ. (March 1986-); INIS Atomindex [Micro.]; INSPEC (1986-); Int. Aerosp. Abstr.; Res. Alert [Full Cov.]; Sci. Cit. Index; SCISEARCH.

US/0018-9391
IEEE TRANSACTIONS ON ENGINEERING MANAGEMENT. (IEEE TRANSACTIONS ON ENGINEERING MANAGEMENT / PROFESSIONAL TECHNICAL GROUP ON ENGINEERING MANAGMENT.). [IEEE trans. eng. manage.]. **Added/Corp** Institute of Electrical and Electronics Engineers. Professional Technical Group on Engineering Management. Institute of Electrical and Electronics Engineers. Engineering Management Group. IEEE Engineering Management Group. IEEE Engineering Management Society. **VFOAT** Transactions on Engineering Management; Engineering Management. **VAT** Institute of Electrical and Electronics Engineers Transactions on Engineering Management. Vol. EM-10, No. 1 (Mar. 1963)-. Periodical. English. qt. $150.00. IEEE, Institution of Electrical and Electronics Engineers, Inc., 345 East 47th Street, New York NY 10017-2394. **Tel** (908)981-1393, FAX (908)981-9667. **(Subscription address:** IEEE / Institute of Electrical and Electronics Engineers, 445 Hoes Lane, PO Box 1331, Piscataway NJ 08855-1331.**) LC** T56; .I2. **CODEN** IEEMA4. **[CCC].** cum. index. **Pr Rev.** Documents available from Article Express International, The Genuine Article, UMI Article Clearinghouse, Ask*IEEE, CASDDS. ***Continues*** *IRE Transactions on Engineering Management, 0096-2252.*
Desc: Covers management of technical functions, such as research development, and engineering in industry, government, university and other settings.
Ind/Abst ABI/INFORM Glob. Ed.; ABI Inform Ondisc (Feb. 1976-); Acad. Search (Jan. 1994-); Bioeng. Abstr.; Bus. Index (1988-); Bus. Period. Index; Chem. Abstr.; Comput. Abstr.; Comput. Inf. Syst. Abstr. J. [Full Cov.]; Contents Pages Manage.; Curr. Contents Eng. Tech. Appl. Sci.; Curr. Contents Soc. Behav. Sci.; Curr. Lit. Sci. Sci.; Ei Page One; Elect. Comm. Abstr.; Eng. Index Annu.; Expand. Acad. Index (1992-); Gen. BusinessFile (1988-); Gen. Period. Index (1988-); Index IEEE Publ.; INFO-SOUTH Abstr.; INSPEC (1968-); Int. Aerosp. Abstr.; Manuf. Process Eng. Abstr.; Res. Alert [Full Cov.]; Sci. Cit. Index; SCISEARCH; Soc. Sci. Cit. Index [Full Cov.]; Trade Ind. Index.

●US/1057-7149
IEEE TRANSACTIONS ON IMAGE PROCESSING. (IEEE TRANSACTIONS ON IMAGE PROCESSING / A PUBLICATION OF THE IEEE SIGNAL PROCESSING SOCIETY.). [IEEE trans. image process.]. **Added/Corp** IEEE Signal Processing Society. Institute of Electrical and Electronics Engineers. **VFOAT** Image Processing. **VAT** Institute of Electrical and Electronics Engineers Transactions on Image Processing. Vol. 1, No. 1 (Jan. 1992)-. Periodical. English. mo. $350.00. IEEE, Institution of Electrical and Electronics Engineers, Inc., 345 East 47th Street, New York NY 10017-2394. **Tel** (908)981-1393, FAX (908)981-9667. **(Subscription address:** IEEE / Institute of Electrical and Electronics Engineers, 445 Hoes Lane, PO Box 1331, Piscataway NJ 08855-1331.**) LC** TA1632; .I37. **DD** 621.36/7/05. **CODEN** IIPRE4. **[CCC].** Documents available from Article Express International.
Desc: Focuses on signal processing, imaging systems and image scanning, display and printing. Includes theory, algorithms and architectures for image coding, filtering, enhancement, restoration, segmentation, and motion estimation.
Ind/Abst Ei Page One; Eng. Index Annu.; Expand. Acad. Index (1992-); Int. Aerosp. Abstr.

US/0278-0046
IEEE TRANSACTIONS ON INDUSTRIAL ELECTRONICS (1982). (IEEE TRANSACTIONS ON INDUSTRIAL ELECTRONICS : A PUBLICATION OF THE IEEE INDUSTRIAL ELECTRONICS SOCIETY.). [IEEE trans. ind. electron.]. **Added/Corp** IEEE Industrial Electronics Society. **VFOAT** Transactions on Industrial Electronics. Vol. IE-29, No. 1 (Feb. 1982)-. Periodical. English. bm. $175.00. IEEE, Institution of Electrical and Electronics Engineers, Inc., 345 East 47th Street, New York NY 10017-2394. **Tel** (908)981-1393, FAX (908)981-9667. **(Subscription address:** IEEE / Institute of Electrical and Electronics Engineers, 445 Hoes Lane, PO Box 1331, Piscataway NJ 08855-1331.**) LC** TK7800; .I22. **DD** 621.381/05. **CODEN** ITIED6. **[CCC].** available on microfiche. Documents available from Article Express International, The Genuine Article, Ask*IEEE. ***Continues*** *IEEE Transactions on Industrial Electronics and Control Instrumentation, 0018-9421.*
Desc: The application of electronics and electrical sciences to the control, treatment, and measurement of industrial processes.
Ind/Abst Acoust. Abstr.; Bioeng. Abstr.; Coal Abstr.; Comput. Abstr.; Comput. Rev.; Curr. Contents Eng. Tech. Appl. Sci.; Ei Page One; Eng. Index Annu.; Expand. Acad. Index (1992-); Index IEEE Publ.; INSPEC (Feb. 1982-); Int. Aerosp. Abstr.; Leadscan; Res. Alert [Select. Cov.].

US
IEEE TRANSACTIONS ON INDUSTRY APPLICATIONS. **Added/Corp** Institute of Electrical and Electronics Engineers. IEEE Industry Applications Society. **VFOAT** Transactions on Industry Applications. (Jan./Feb. 1972)-. Periodical. English. ir. $240.00. IEEE / Microfilm Service, 445 Hoes Lane, Piscataway NJ 08854. **Tel** (908)981-0060. **CODEN** ITIACR. ***Continues*** *IEEE Transactions on Industry and General Applications, 0018-943x.*

US/0093-9994
IEEE TRANSACTIONS ON INDUSTRY APPLICATIONS. [IEEE trans. ind. appl.]. **Added/Corp** Institute of Electrical and Electronics Engineers. IEEE Industry Applications Society. **VFOAT** Transactions on Industry Applications; Industry Applications. Vol. IA-8 (Jan./Feb. 1972)-. Academic Scholarly Publication. English. bm. $240.00. IEEE, Institution of Electrical and Electronics Engineers, Inc., 345 East 47th Street, New York NY 10017-2394. **Tel** (908)981-1393, FAX (908)981-9667. **(Subscription address:** IEEE / Institute of Electrical and Electronics Engineers, 445 Hoes Lane, PO Box 1331, Piscataway NJ 08855-1331.**) LC** TK1; .I39. **DD** 621.3/05. **CODEN** ITIACR. **[CCC].** cum. index. **Pr Rev.** available on microfiche. Documents available from Article Express International, The Genuine Article, Ask*IEEE, CASDDS, Documents on Demand. ***Continues*** *IEEE Transactions on Industry and General Applications, 0018-943X.*
Desc: Covers the development and application of electrical systems, apparatus, devices, and controls to the processes and equipment of industry and commerce; the promotion of safe, reliable, and economic installations.
Ind/Abst Appl. Sci. Technol. Index; Bioeng. Abstr.; Chem. Abstr.; Coal Abstr.; Comput. Abstr.; Curr. Contents Eng. Tech. Appl. Sci.; Ei Page One; EMBASE; Energy Inf. Abstr.; Energy Res. Abstr. (Feb. 1975-); Eng. Index Annu.; Environ. Abstr.; Expand. Acad. Index (1992-); HTFS Dig.; Index IEEE Publ.; INSPEC (Jan./Feb. 1972-); Int. Aerosp. Abstr.; Leadscan; Res. Alert [Full Cov.]; Robotics Abstr.; Saf. Health Work; Sci. Cit. Index; SCISEARCH.

US/0018-9448
IEEE TRANSACTIONS ON INFORMATION THEORY. (IEEE TRANSACTIONS ON INFORMATION THEORY / PROFESSIONAL TECHNICAL GROUP ON INFORMATION THEORY.). [IEEE trans. inf. theory]. **Added/Corp** Institute of Electrical and Electronics Engineers. Professional Technical Group on Information Theory. Institute of Electrical and Electronics Engineers. Information Theory Group. IEEE Information Theory Group. IEEE Information Theory Society. **VFOAT** Transactions on Information Theory; Information Theory. **VAT** Institute of Electrical and Electronics Engineers

Transactions on Information Theory. Vol. IT-9, No. 1 (Jan. 1963)-. Academic Scholarly Publication. English. Seven times a year. $350.00. IEEE, Institution of Electrical and Electronics Engineers, Inc., 345 East 47th Street, New York NY 10017-2394. **Tel** (908)981-1393, FAX (908)981-9667. **(Subscription address:** IEEE / Institute of Electrical and Electronics Engineers, 445 Hoes Lane, PO Box 1331, Piscataway NJ 08855-1331.**) LC** Q350; .I2. **DD** 001.53/9. **CODEN** IETTAW. **[CCC].** Documents available from Article Express International, The Genuine Article, Ask*IEEE, CASDDS. ***Continues*** *IRE Transactions on Information Theory, 0096-1000.*
Desc: Covers the theoretical and experimental aspects of information transmission, processing, and utilization.
Ind/Abst Acoust. Abstr.; Appl. Sci. Technol. Index (1991-); Bioeng. Abstr.; Chem. Abstr.; Compumath Citation Index [Full Cov.]; Comput. Abstr.; Comput. Database; Comput. Rev.; Curr. Contents Eng. Tech. Appl. Sci.; Ei Page One; EMBASE; Eng. Index Annu.; Expand. Acad. Index (1992-); Index IEEE Publ.; Inf. Sci. Abstr. [Full Cov.]; INSPEC (1968-); Int. Aerosp. Abstr.; Math. Rev.; Oper. Res./Manag. Sci.; Pollut. Abstr. Indexes; Res. Alert [Full Cov.]; Sci. Cit. Index; SCISEARCH; Stat. Theory Method Abstr. (1968-1981, 1983-1984); Zentralbl. Math. Ihre Grenzgeb.

US/0018-9456
IEEE TRANSACTIONS ON INSTRUMENTATION AND MEASUREMENT.
[IEEE trans. instrum. meas.]. **Added/Corp** IEEE Instrumentation and Measurement Society. IEEE Group on Instrumentation & Measurement. IEEE Professional Technical Group on Instrumentation and Measurement. **VFOAT** Transactions on Instrumentation and Measurement; Instrumentation and Measurement. Vol. IM L2- (June 1963)-. Periodical. English. bm. $190.00. IEEE, Institution of Electrical and Electronics Engineers, Inc., 345 East 47th Street, New York NY 10017-2394. **Tel** (908)981-1393, FAX (908)981-9667. **(Subscription address:** IEEE / Institute of Electrical and Electronics Engineers, 445 Hoes Lane, PO Box 1331, Piscataway NJ 08855-1331.**) DD** 621. **NLM** W1 I223T. **CODEN** IEIMAO. **[CCC]. Pr Rev.** Documents available from Article Express International, The Genuine Article, Ask*IEEE, CASDDS. ***Continues*** *IRE Transactions on Instrumentation, 0096-2260.*
Desc: Covers measurements and instrumentation utilizing electrical and electronic techniques.
Ind/Abst Acoust. Abstr.; Bioeng. Abstr.; Chem. Abstr.; Comput. Abstr.; Curr. Contents Eng. Tech. Appl. Sci.; Ei Page One; EMBASE; Eng. Index Annu.; Expand. Acad. Index (1992-); Fluid Abstr., Civil Eng.; Fluid Abstr. Proc. Eng.; FLUIDEX (1973-); Index IEEE Publ.; INSPEC (1968-); Int. Aerosp. Abstr.; Res. Alert [Full Cov.]; Sci. Cit. Index; SCISEARCH.

US/1041-4347
IEEE TRANSACTIONS ON KNOWLEDGE AND DATA ENGINEERING.
[IEEE trans. knowl. data eng.]. **Added/Corp** Institute of Electrical and Electronics Engineers. IEEE Computer Society. **VFOAT** Institute of Electrical and Electronics Engineers Transactions on Knowledge and Data Engineering; Transactions on Knowledge and Data Engineering; Knowledge and Data Engineering. **VAT** Institute of Electrical and Electronics Engineers Transactions on Knowledge and Data Engineering. Vol. 1, No. 1 (Mar. 1989)-. Periodical. English. bm. $340.00. IEEE, Institution of Electrical and Electronics Engineers, Inc., 345 East 47th Street, New York NY 10017-2394. **Tel** (908)981-1393, FAX (908)981-9667. **(Subscription address:** IEEE / Institute of Electrical and Electronics Engineers, 445 Hoes Lane, PO Box 1331, Piscataway NJ 08855-1331.**) ED** Gail S. Ferenc. **LC** QA76.76.E95; I36. **DD** 006/3/3/05. **CODEN** ITKEEH. **[CCC].** Index available. **Circ:** 6,000. available on microfiche. Documents available from Article Express International, The Genuine Article, Ask*IEEE.
Desc: Designed to provide an international and interdisciplinary forum to publish results on the research, design and development of data engineering methodologies, strategies and systems.
Ind/Abst Compumath Citation Index [Full Cov.]; Comput. Abstr.; Curr. Contents Eng. Tech. Appl. Sci.; Ei Page One; Eng. Index Annu.; Index IEEE Publ.; INSPEC (March 1989-); Int. Aerosp. Abstr.; Res. Alert [Full Cov.]; Soc. Sci. Cit. Index [Select. Cov.]; Zentralbl. Math. Ihre Grenzgeb.

US/0278-0062
IEEE TRANSACTIONS ON MEDICAL IMAGING.
See Medical Science and Technology-Radiology.

US/0018-9480
IEEE TRANSACTIONS ON MICROWAVE THEORY AND TECHNIQUES.
[IEEE trans. microwave theor. tech.]. **Added/Corp** Institute of Electrical and Electronics Engineers. Professional Technical Group on Microwave Theory and Techniques. Institute of Electrical and Electronics Engineers. Microwave Theory and Techniques Group. IEEE Microwave Theory and Techniques Group. IEEE Microwave Theory and Techniques Society. **VFOAT** I.E.E.E. Transactions on Microwave Theory and Techniques; Transactions on Microwave Theory and Techniques; Microwave Theory and Techniques. **VAT** Institute of Electrical and Electronics Engineers Transactions on Microwave Theory and Techniques. Vol. MTT-11, No. 1 (Jan. 1963)-. Academic Scholarly Publication. English. Sixteen times a year. $340.00. IEEE, Institution of Electrical and Electronics Engineers, Inc., 345 East 47th Street, New York NY 10017-2394. **Tel** (908)981-1393, FAX (908)981-9667. **(Subscription address:** IEEE / Institute of Electrical and Electronics Engineers, 445 Hoes Lane, PO Box 1331, Piscataway NJ 08855-1331.**) LC** TK7800; .I23. **DD** 621.381/3/05. **CODEN** IETMAB. **[CCC]. Pr Rev.** Documents available from Article Express International, The Genuine Article, Ask*IEEE, CASDDS. ***Continues*** *IRE Transactions on Microwave Theory and Techniques, 0097-2002.*
Ind/Abst Acoust. Abstr.; Appl. Sci. Technol. Index (1991-); Bioeng. Abstr.; Chem. Abstr.; Coal Abstr.; Curr. Contents Eng. Tech. Appl. Sci.; Ei Page One; EMBASE; Energy Res. Abstr.; Eng. Index Annu.; Expand. Acad. Index (1992-); Index IEEE Publ.; INSPEC (1968-); Int. Aerosp. Abstr.; Math. Rev.; Res. Alert [Full Cov.]; Sci. Cit. Index; SCISEARCH.

US
IEEE TRANSACTIONS ON POWER APPARATUS AND SYSTEMS.
No. 1-69, Aug. 1952-Dec. 1963; V. Pas 83- Jan. 1964-. Periodical. English. bm. IEEE, Institution of Electrical and Electronics Engineers, Inc., 345 East 47th Street, New York NY 10017-2394. **Tel** (908)981-1393, FAX (908)981-9667. **(Subscription address:** IEEE Service Center, 445 Hoes Lane, Piscataway, NJ 08854; telephone: (201)981-1393**) CODEN** IEPSA9. Documents available from Ask*IEEE. ***Continues*** *Transactions of the American Institute of Electrical Engineers, Pt. 3.*
Ind/Abst Coal Abstr.; Fluid Abstr., Civil Eng.; Fluid Abstr. Proc. Eng.; FLUIDEX; Index IEEE Publ.; INSPEC (1968-Dec. 1985).

US/0885-8977
IEEE TRANSACTIONS ON POWER DELIVERY.
(IEEE TRANSACTIONS ON POWER DELIVERY : A PUBLICATION OF THE POWER ENGINEERING SOCIETY.). [IEEE trans. power deliv.]. **Added/Corp** IEEE Power Engineering Society. Institute of Electrical and Electronics Engineers. **VFOAT** Transactions on Power Delivery. **VAT** Institute of Electrical and Electronics Engineers Transactions on Power Delivery. Vol. PWRD-1, No. 1 (Jan. 1986)-. Periodical. English. qt. $200.00. IEEE, Institution of Electrical and Electronics Engineers, Inc., 345 East 47th Street, New York NY 10017-2394. **Tel** (908)981-1393, FAX (908)981-9667. **(Subscription address:** IEEE / Institute of Electrical and Electronics Engineers, 445 Hoes Lane, PO Box 1331, Piscataway NJ 08855-1331.**) LC** TK1; .I18. **DD** 621. **CODEN** ITPDE5. **[CCC]. Pr Rev.** available on microfiche; available on microfilm. Documents available from Article Express International, The Genuine Article, Ask*IEEE, CASDDS. ***Continues in part*** *IEEE Transactions on Power Apparatus and Systems, 0018-9510.*
Desc: Covers research, development, design, application, construction, installation, and operation of apparatus, equipment, structures, materials, and systems for the safe, reliable, and economic delivery and control of electrical energy for general industrial, commercial, public, and domestic consumption.
Ind/Abst Appl. Sci. Technol. Index; Chem. Abstr.; Curr. Contents Eng. Tech. Appl. Sci.; Ei Page One; Eng. Index Annu.; Expand. Acad. Index (1992-); Index IEEE Publ. (Jan. 1986-); INIS Atomindex [Micro.]; INSPEC (Jan. 1986-); Res. Alert [Full Cov.]; Sci. Cit. Index; SCISEARCH.

US/0885-8993
IEEE TRANSACTIONS ON POWER ELECTRONICS.
[IEEE trans. power electron.]. **Added/Corp** Institute of Electrical and Electronics Engineers. Power Electronics Council (Institute of Electrical and Electronics Engineers) IEEE Power Electronics Society. **VFOAT** Transactions on Power Electronics. **VAT** Institute of Electrical and Electronics Engineers Transactions on Power Electronics. Vol. PE-1, No. 1 (Jan. 1986)-. Periodical. English. Six times a year. $160.00. IEEE, Institution of Electrical and Electronics Engineers, Inc., 345 East 47th Street, New York NY 10017-2394. **Tel** (908)981-1393, FAX (908)981-9667. **(Subscription address:** IEEE / Institute of Electrical and Electronics Engineers, 445 Hoes Lane, PO Box 1331, Piscataway NJ 08855-1331.**) LC** TK7881.15; .I34. **DD** 621.31/7. **CODEN** ITPEE8. **[CCC].** available on microfilm and microfiche. Documents available from Article Express International, Ask*IEEE.
Desc: Covers fundamental technologies used in the control and conversion of electric power.
Ind/Abst Coal Abstr.; Ei Page One; Eng. Index Annu.; Expand. Acad. Index (1992-); Index IEEE Publ. (Jan. 1986-); INIS Atomindex [Micro.]; INSPEC (Jan. 1986-); Int. Aerosp. Abstr.

US/0885-8950
IEEE TRANSACTIONS ON POWER SYSTEMS.
(IEEE TRANSACTIONS ON POWER SYSTEMS : A PUBLICATION OF THE POWER ENGINEERING SOCIETY.). [IEEE trans. power syst.]. **Added/Corp** IEEE Power Engineering Society. Institute of Electrical and Electronics Engineers. **VFOAT** Transactions on Power Systems. **VAT** Institute of Electrical and Electronics Engineers Transactions Power Systems. Vol. 1 No. 1 (Feb. 1986)-. Periodical. English. qt. $200.00. IEEE, Institution of Electrical and Electronics Engineers, Inc., 345 East 47th Street, New York NY 10017-2394. **Tel** (908)981-1393, FAX (908)981-9667. **(Subscription address:** IEEE / Institute of Electrical and Electronics Engineers, 445 Hoes Lane, PO Box 1331, Piscataway NJ 08855-1331.**) LC** TK1005; .I35. **DD** 621.31. **CODEN** ITPSEG. **[CCC]. Pr Rev.** available on microfiche. Documents available from Article Express International, The Genuine Article, Ask*IEEE. ***Continues in part*** *IEEE Transactions on Power Apparatus and Systems, 0018-9510.*
Desc: Covers the requirements, planning, analysis, reliability, operation and economics of electric generating, transmission, and distribution systems for general industrial, commercial, public and domestic consumption.
Ind/Abst Appl. Sci. Technol. Index; Coal Abstr.; Comput. Abstr.; Comput. Inf. Syst. Abstr. J. [Full Cov.]; Curr. Contents Eng. Tech. Appl. Sci.; Ei Page One; Elect. Comm. Abstr.; Energy Inf. Abstr.; Eng. Index Annu.; Environ. Eng. Abstr.; Expand. Acad. Index (1992-); Index IEEE Publ. (Feb. 1986-); INIS Atomindex [Micro.]; INSPEC (1986-); Mech. Eng. Abstr.; Res. Alert [Full Cov.]; Sci. Cit. Index; SCISEARCH; Soc. Sci. Cit. Index [Select. Cov.]; Solid State Supercond. Abstr.

US/0361-1434
IEEE TRANSACTIONS ON PROFESSIONAL COMMUNICATION.
[IEEE trans. prof. commun.]. **Added/Corp** IEEE Professional Communication Society. IEEE Professional Communication Group. **VFOAT** I.E.E.E. Transactions on Professional Communications; Transactions on Professional Communication; Professional Communication. (March 1972)-. Periodical. English. qt. $85.00. IEEE, Institution of Electrical and Electronics Engineers, Inc., 345 East 47th Street, New York NY 10017-2394. **Tel** (908)981-1393, FAX (908)981-9667. **(Subscription address:** IEEE / Institute of Electrical and Electronics Engineers, 445 Hoes Lane, PO Box 1331, Piscataway NJ 08855-1331.**) LC** T10.5; .I35. **DD** 601.4. **CODEN** IEPCBU. **[CCC].** available on microfilm. Documents available from Article Express International, Ask*IEEE, UMI Article Clearinghouse. ***Continues*** *IEEE Transactions on Engineering Writing and Speech, 0018-9405.*
Desc: The study, development, improvement, and promotion of techniques for preparing, organizing for use, processing, editing, collecting, conserving, and disseminating any form of information in the electrical and electronics fields.
Ind/Abst ABI/INFORM Glob. Ed.; ABI Inform Ondisc (March 1976-); Bioeng. Abstr.; Comput. Abstr.; Comput. Rev.; Ei Page One; Eng. Index Annu.; Ergon. Abstr.; Expand. Acad. Index (1992-); Gen. BusinessFile (1992-); Index IEEE Publ.; INSPEC (March 1972-); Int. Aerosp. Abstr.; Libr. Inf. Sci. Abstr.

US/0018-9529
IEEE TRANSACTIONS ON RELIABILITY.
(IEEE TRANSACTIONS ON RELIABILITY / PROFESSIONAL TECHNICAL GROUP ON RELIABILITY.). [IEEE trans. reliab.]. **Added/Corp** Institute of Electrical and Electronics Engineers. Professional Technical Group on Reliability. IEEE Reliability Group. IEEE Reliabilty Society. American Society for Quality Control. Electronics Division. **VFOAT** Transactions on Reliability; Reliability. **VAT** Institute of Electrical and Electronics Engineers Transactions on Reliability. Vol. R-12, No. 1 (Mar. 1963)-. Periodical. English. qt. $175.00. IEEE, Institution of Electrical and Electronics Engineers, Inc., 345 East 47th Street, New York NY 10017-2394. **Tel** (908)981-1393, FAX (908)981-9667. **(Subscription address:** IEEE / Institute of Electrical and Electronics Engineers, 445 Hoes Lane, PO Box 1331, Piscataway NJ 08855-1331.**) LC** TK7800; .I16. **CODEN** IEERAJ. **[CCC]. Pr Rev.** Documents available from Article Express International, The Genuine Article, Ask*IEEE, CASDDS. ***Continues*** *IRE Transactions on Reliability and Quality Control, 0097-4552.*
Desc: Covers the principles and practices of reliability, maintainability, and product liability pertaining to electrical and electronic equipment.
Ind/Abst Bioeng. Abstr.; Ceram. Abstr. (19??-); Chem. Abstr.; Coal Abstr.; Compumath Citation Index [Full Cov.]; Comput. Abstr.; Curr. Contents Eng. Tech. Appl. Sci.; Ei Page One; Eng. Index Annu.; Expand. Acad. Index (1992-); Index IEEE Publ.; INSPEC (1968-); Int. Aerosp. Abstr.; Math. Rev.; Res. Alert [Full Cov.]; Soc. Sci. Cit. Index [Select. Cov.]; Stat. Theory Method Abstr. (1968, 1970-1984, 1986-1987); Zentralbl. Math. Ihre Grenzgeb.

US/0894-6507
IEEE TRANSACTIONS ON SEMICONDUCTOR MANUFACTURING.
(IEEE TRANSACTIONS ON SEMICONDUCTOR MANUFACTURING : A PUBLICATION OF THE IEEE COMPONENTS, HYBRIDS, AND MANUFACTURING TECHNOLOGY SOCIETY, THE IEEE ELECTRON DEVICES SOCIETY, THE IEEE RELIABILITY SOCIETY, THE IEEE SOLID-STATE CIRCUITS COUNCIL.). [IEEE trans. semicond. manuf.]. **Added/Corp** IEEE Components, Hybrids, and Manufacturing Technology Society. IEEE Electron Devices Society. IEEE Reliability Society. IEEE Solid-State Circuits Council. Institute of Electrical and Electronics Engineers. **VFOAT** Transactions on Semiconductor Manufacturing; Semiconductor Manufacturing. **VAT** Institute of Electrical

and Electronics Engineers Transactions on Semiconductor Manufacturing. Vol. 1, No. 1 (Feb. 1988)-. Periodical. English. qt. $130.00. IEEE, Institution of Electrical and Electronics Engineers, Inc., 345 East 47th Street, New York NY 10017-2394. **Tel** (908)981-1393, FAX (908)981-9667. **(Subscription address:** IEEE / Institute of Electrical and Electronics Engineers, 445 Hoes Lane, PO Box 1331, Piscataway NJ 08855-1331.**) LC** TK7836; .I39. **DD** 621.3815/2. **[CCC]. Pr Rev.** available on microfilm and microfiche. Documents available from Article Express International, The Genuine Article, Ask*IEEE.
Desc: Covers papers describing techniques used in solving the problems of manufacturing complex microelectronic components. Coverage ranges from fundamental to applied.
Ind/Abst Curr. Contents Eng. Tech. Appl. Sci.; Ei Page One; Eng. Index Annu.; Index IEEE Publ.; INSPEC (Feb. 1988-); Oper. Res./Manag. Sci.; Qual. Control Appl. Stat.; Res. Alert [Full Cov.]; Robotics Abstr.; Soc. Sci. Cit. Index [Select. Cov.].

US/1053-587X
IEEE TRANSACTIONS ON SIGNAL PROCESSING. (IEEE TRANSACTIONS ON SIGNAL PROCESSING : A PUBLICATION OF THE IEEE SIGNAL PROCESSING SOCIETY.). [IEEE trans. signal process.]. **Added/Corp** IEEE Signal Processing Society. **VFOAT** Transactions on Signal Processing; Signal Processing. **VAT** Institute of Electrical and Electronics Engineers Transactions on Signal Processing. Vol. 39, No. 1 (Jan. 1991)-. Academic Scholarly Publication. English. mo. $420.00. IEEE, Institution of Electrical and Electronics Engineers, Inc., 345 East 47th Street, New York NY 10017-2394. **Tel** (908)981-1393, FAX (908)981-9667. **(Subscription address:** IEEE / Institute of Electrical and Electronics Engineers, 445 Hoes Lane, PO Box 1331, Piscataway NJ 08855-1331.**) LC** TK5981; .I2. **DD** 621.382/2/05. **CODEN** ITPRED. **[CCC].** Documents available from Article Express International, The Genuine Article, Ask*IEEE, CASDDS. ***Continues*** *IEEE Transactions on Acoustics, Speech, and Signal Processing, 0096-3518.*
Desc: Covers transmission, recording, reproduction, processing, and measurement of speech and other signals by digital, electronic, electrical, acoustic, mechanical and optical means; the components and systems to accomplish these and related aims; and the environmental, psychological and physiological factors concerned therewith.
Ind/Abst Appl. Sci. Technol. Index; Bioeng. Abstr. (Jan. 1991-); Chem. Abstr. (Jan. 1991-); Comput. Inf. Syst. Abstr. J. [Full Cov.]; Curr. Contents Eng. Tech. Appl. Sci.; Ei Page One; Elect. Comm. Abstr.; EMBASE (Jan. 1991-); Eng. Index Annu.; Index IEEE Publ. (Jan. 1991-); INSPEC (Jan. 1991-); Int. Aerosp. Abstr. (Jan. 1991-); Math. Rev. (Jan. 1991-); Mech. Eng. Abstr.; Res. Alert [Full Cov.]; Sci. Cit. Index; SCISEARCH; Zentralbl. Math. Ihre Grenzgeb.

US/0018-9545
IEEE TRANSACTIONS ON VEHICULAR TECHNOLOGY. [IEEE trans. veh. technol.]. **Added/Corp** Vehicular Technology Society. Institute of Electrical and Electronics Engineers. IEEE Vehicular Technology Group. **VFOAT** Transactions on Vehicular Technology; Vehicular Technology. (Oct. 1967)-. Academic Scholarly Publication. English. qt. $175.00. IEEE, Institution of Electrical and Electronics Engineers, Inc., 345 East 47th Street, New York NY 10017-2394. **Tel** (908)981-1393, FAX (908)981-9667. **(Subscription address:** IEEE / Institute of Electrical and Electronics Engineers, 445 Hoes Lane, PO Box 1331, Piscataway NJ 08855-1331.**) LC** TK7882.M6; I2. **DD** 621.3841/65. **CODEN** ITUTAB. **[CCC]. Pr Rev.** available on microfiche. Documents available from Article Express International, The Genuine Article, Ask*IEEE, CASDDS, Documents on Demand. ***Continues*** *IEEE Transactions on Vehicular Communications, 0096-2503.*
Desc: Covers land, airborne, and maritime mobile services; portable or hand carried and citizen's communications services, when used as an adjunct to a vehicular system; vehicular electrotechnology, equipment and systems ordinarily identified with the automotive industry, excluding systems associated with public transit.
Ind/Abst Acoust. Abstr.; Bioeng. Abstr.; Chem. Abstr.; Civ. Struct. Eng. Abstr.; Comput. Inf. Syst. Abstr. J. [Full Cov.]; Curr. Contents Eng. Tech. Appl. Sci.; Ei Page One; Elect. Comm. Abstr.; EMBASE; Energy Inf. Abstr.; Energy Res. Abstr.; Eng. Index Annu.; Environ. Abstr.; Expand. Acad. Index (1992-); Highw. Res. Abstr.; Index IEEE Publ.; INIS Atomindex [Micro.]; INSPEC (1968-); Int. Aerosp. Abstr.; Leadscan; Mech. Eng. Abstr.; Pollut. Abstr. Indexes; Res. Alert [Full Cov.]; Sci. Cit. Index; SCISEARCH.

US/0882-4959
IEEE TRANSLATION JOURNAL ON MAGNETICS IN JAPAN. ***Ceased.*** **See** Physics-Magnetism.

JA/0916-8516
IEICE TRANSACTIONS ON COMMUNICATIONS. **See** Communication.

•JA/0916-8524
IEICE TRANSACTIONS ON ELECTRONICS. **Added/Corp** Denshi Joho Tsushin Gakkai (Japan). **VFOAT** IEICE Transactions; Institute of Electronics, Information and Communication Engineers Transactions on Electronics; Transactions on Electronics. Vol. E75-C, No. 1 (Jan. 1992)-. Periodical. English. mo. $100.00. Institute of Electronics / Tokyo, Information and Communication Engineers, Tokyo Japan. **(Subscription address:** Maruzen Company Ltd., PO Box 5050, Import & Export Department, Tokyo 100 31 Japan.**) LC** IN PROCESS; TK7800; .I34. **CODEN** IELEEJ. **[CCC].** Documents available from The Genuine Article, Ask*IEEE. ***Continues in part*** *IEICE Transactions on Communications, Electronics, Information, and Systems, 0917-1673.*
Ind/Abst Curr. Contents Eng. Tech. Appl. Sci.; INSPEC (Jan. 1992-); Res. Alert [Select. Cov.]; SCISEARCH.

•JA/0916-8508
IEICE TRANSACTIONS ON FUNDAMENTALS OF ELECTRONICS, COMMUNICATIONS AND COMPUTER SCIENCES. **See** Communication-Telecommunications.

UK/0961-1290
III-VS REVIEW. **VAT** Three-Fives Review. Vol. 3, No. 4 (Aug. 1990)-. Periodical. English. Six times a year. $142.00 The Americas; £95.00 other. Elsevier Advanced Technology, An Imprint of Elsevier Science Ltd., The Boulevard, Langford Lane, Kidlington, Oxford OX5 1GB United Kingdom. **Tel** 011 44 865 843000, 011 44 865 843699, FAX 011 44 865 843010. **(Subscription address:** Elsevier Science Ltd. Oxford Fulfillment Centre, PO Box 800, Kidlington, Oxford OX5 1DX United Kingdom.**) CODEN** IVSRE8. **[CCC].** available on microfilm and microfiche from University Microfilms International (UMI). Documents available from Ask*IEEE. ***Continues*** *Euro III-Vs Review.*
Ind/Abst INSPEC (Feb. 1991-).

IT
ILLUMINITECNICA. (19??)-. Italian. Pitra Editoriale SNC, Via Luchino Del Maino 12, 20146 Milan Italy.

US/1050-7019
IMAGING BUSINESS REPORT, THE. ***Title Change.*** [Imaging bus. rep.]. Vol. 1, No. 1 (Mar. 1990)-(Oct. 1993). Periodical. English. mo. IW Publishing / Massachusetts, 1 Snow Road, Marshfield MA 02050. **Tel** (617)837-7202. **DD** 338. ***Merged into*** *Document Imaging Report.*

PE
IMERA. Periodical. Spanish. $18.00. A & F Producciones SCR Ltd, Jr Soledad 247 of 103 14, Lima Peru. **LC** TK4; .I4.

IT/0394-5634
IMPIANTO ELETTRICO, L'. [Impianto elettr.]. (1987)-. Periodical. Italian. mo. L95000.00 Italy; L150000.00 other. Etas SRL, Via Mecenate 89, 20138 Milan Italy. **Tel** 011 39 2 580841. **UDC** 621.3.

US/0888-9406
IN-STAT ELECTRONICS REPORT. [In-Stat electron. rep.]. **Added/Corp** In-Stat, Inc. (Scottsdale, Ariz.). **VFOAT** In Stat Electronics Report. (198?)-. Periodical. English. Twelve times a year. $795.00. In Stat, PO Box 8130, Scottsdale AZ 85252. **Tel** (602)860-8515, FAX (602)483-0400. **ED** Jack Beedle. **DD** 338. **Circ:** 300-500 (ctrl).
Desc: A popular monthly newsletter which keeps its reader abreast of current semiconductor and end-use market conditions as well as providing In-Stat forecasts. The past decade has proven the company's forecasting methods to be logical, solid and accurate.

US/0362-3858
INCREMENTAL MOTION CONTROL SYSTEMS AND DEVICES NEWSLETTER. [Increm. mot. control syst.devices newsl.]. Newsletter. English. an. Free. Incremental Motion Control Systems Society, PO Box 2772 Station A, Champaign IL 61825-2772. **Tel** (217)256-1523. **ED** Benjamin C Kuo. **CODEN** IMCNB. Index available. **Ad Acc. Circ:** 10,000 (ctrl). Documents available from Ask*IEEE.
Desc: The symposium encompasses a broad area on motion control systems, selection of motion control devices, electronic, machine tool, computer control; material science of motor design.
Ind/Abst INSPEC (Oct. 1972-).

US/1049-0744
INDEPENDENT POWER REPORT. [Indep. power rep.]. (Nov. 4, 1988)-. Newsletter. English. bw. $865.00 US and Canada; $890.00 other. McGraw Hill Publishing Company, Inc., 1221 Avenue of the Americas, New York NY 10020. **Tel** (212)512-6410, (800)525-5003, FAX (212)512-6111. **(Subscription address:** McGraw Hill Management Information Center, 1221 Avenue of the Americas, 36th Floor, New York NY 10020.**) DD** 338. available on an online database (file 624/Full-Text) from DIALOG. ***Continues*** *Cogeneration Report, 8756-372X.*

US
INDEX OF EIA & JEDEC STANDARDS & ENGINEERING PUBLICATIONS. **Main/Corp** Electronic Industries Association. Engineering Department. 1958. English. bm. $5.00. Electronic Industries Association, 2001 Pennsylvania Avenue Northwest, Washington DC 20006. **Tel** (202)457-4900, telex 710-822-0148 EIA WSH. **Circ:** 500.
Desc: Comprehensive listing describing all EIA and JEDEC standards and engineering publications.

US/0099-1368
INDEX TO IEEE PUBLICATIONS. **See** Engineering-Abstracting, Bibliographies and Statistics.

US/0897-151X
INDEX TO PROCEEDINGS OF THE IEEE. [Index proc. IEEE]. **VAT** Index to Proceedings of the Institute of Electrical and Electronics Engineers. Vol. 1 (1988)-. Proceedings. English. an. IEEE, Institution of Electrical and Electronics Engineers, Inc., 345 East 47th Street, New York NY 10017-2394. **Tel** (908)981-1393, FAX (908)981-9667. **(Subscription address:** IEEE Service Center, 445 Hoes Lane, Piscataway NJ 08854; telephone: (201)981-1393**) DD** 621.
Ind/Abst Index IEEE Publ.

II/0377-7340
INDIAN ELECTRONICS DIRECTORY. 1974-. Directory. English. Electronic Component Industries Association, C-40 South Extension 11, New Delhi India. **LC** TK7805; .I5. **DD** 338.7/62/138102554.

BL
INDICADOR DO SETOR ENERGETICO NACIONAL. (1975)-. Portuguese. M Gruenwald, Caixa Postal 30.556, Sao Paulo 01000 Brazil. **Tel** 280-9411, telex 1130410. **LC** TK41; .I53. ***Continues*** *Indicador de Fabricantes.*

GW/0019-9079
INDUSTRIE ELEKTRIK + ELEKTRONIK. **VFOAT** Industrie Elektrik und Elektronik; EW; Elektro-Welt. Ausg. (196?)-. Periodical. German. sm. DM180.00. Dr. Alfred Huethig Verlag GmbH, Postfach 102869, D 69018 Heidelberg Germany. **Tel** 011 49 6221 489281. **(Subscription address:** Huethig Publishing Inc., 29 Macintosh Drive, Oxford CT 06478.**) LC** TK3; .I5. ***Continues*** *Industrie-Elektrik, Elektrowelt.*

FR/0302-2609
INDUSTRIES ELECTRIQUES ET ELECTRONIQUES (PARIS, 1973). (INDUSTRIES ELECTRIQUES ET ELECTRONIQUES.). [Ind. electr. electron.]. No. 1, 2nd Quarter (1972)-. Periodical. French. 30F. 13 rue Hamelin, Paris 75783 France. **LC** HD9685.F8; I53. **CODEN** IEEQAG. Documents available from Article Express International.
Ind/Abst Ei Page One; Eng. Index Annu.

IT
INFORMATICA 70 [I.E. SETTANTA]. **See** Computers-Data Processing.

NE
INFORMATICA I. KWADRAAT ELEKTROTECHNIEK. Dutch. mo. Ingenieurspers BV, Postbus 456 Netherlands. **Tel** 011 31 08340 5570.

US/0362-0972
INFORMATION DISPLAY (1975). (INFORMATION DISPLAY : THE OFFICIAL JOURNAL OF THE SOCIETY FOR INFORMATION DISPLAY.). [Inf. disp.]. **Added/Corp** Society for Information Display. Vol. 1, No. 1 (Jan. 1985)-. Periodical. English. mo. $36.00 US and Canada; $72.00 other. Society for Information Display, 8055 West Manchester Avenue, Suite 615, Playa del Rey CA 90293. **Tel** (310)305-1502. **LC** TK7882.I6; I6. **DD** 621.38. **CODEN** INFDAB. **[CCC].** Documents available from Ask*IEEE. ***Continues*** *Information Display, 0362-0972.*
Ind/Abst INSPEC (1985-); Int. Aerosp. Abstr. (1985-); World Publ. Monit. (1985-).

GW/0170-9569
INFORMATIONSDIENST - VEREIN DEUTSCHER INGENIEURE. ELEKTRISCH ABTRAGENDE FERTIGUNGSVERFAHREN. [Inf.dienst - Ver. Dtsch. Ing., Elektr. abtrag. Fertig.verfahr.]. (1978)-. German. Four times a year. DM258.00 Germany; DM270.00 other. VDI Verlag GmbH, Postfach 101054, D 40001 Dusseldorf Germany. **Tel** 011 49 211 6188313, FAX 011 49 211 6188133. **UDC** 621.3 (048.1). **[CCC].** ***Continues*** *VDI-Informationsdienst. Elektrisch Abtragende Fertigungsverfahren, 0341-1621.*

IT/0390-2455
INFORMAZIONE ELETTRONICA. ***Ceased.*** [Inf. elettron.]. (1973)-No. 12 (1992). Periodical. Italian. mo (11 issues per year). Editrice Il Rostro Sas, 6A Via Monte Generoso, 20155 Milan Italy. **Tel** 011 39 2 39217306, 39262186. **UDC** 621. Documents available from Ask*IEEE.
Ind/Abst INSPEC (Dec. 1980-).

PE
INFORME - COMISION DE INTEGRACION ELECTRICA REGIONAL. SUBCOMITE DE DISTRIBUCION ENERGIA ELECTRICA. **Main/Corp** Comision de Integracion Electrica Regional Subcomite de Distribucion Energia Electrica. Spanish. Medios de Comunicacion S A, JR Cuaeo 440 OFC 702, Lima Peru. **LC** TK34; .C64A. **DD** 621.39/4/098.

IT
INGEGNERIA ELETTRONICA. (19??)-. Italian. L80000.00 Italy; L160000.00 other. Gammatrol Edizioni, Via Bitti #28, 20125 Milan Italy. **Tel** 011 39 2 6472381, telex 6473123. **Ad Acc. Circ:** 10,000.

CU
INGENIERIA ELECTRONICA, AUTOMATICA Y COMUNICACIONES. Vol. 1, No. 1 (1980)-. Periodical. Spanish (summaries and/or abstracts in English; table of contents in English). Three times a year. Ediciones Cubanas, Obispo 527, Altos ESQ Bernaza, CP 10100 Havana Cuba. **Tel** 011 632980, 631942, FAX 011 631011, telex 512337, 6540. **LC** TK7800; .C53. ***Continues*** *Ciencias Tecnicas. Ingenieria Electronica, Automatica y Comunicaciones.*

US
INSIDE ISHM MAGAZINE. (19??)-. English. Six times a year. $30.00 US; $50.00 other. International Society for Hybrid Microelectronics / Virginia, 1850 Centennial Park Drive, Suite 105, Reston VA 22091. **Tel** (703)758-1060, FAX (703)758-1066. **ED** Nancy Binkley. **Ad Acc, Adv Mgr:** Bob Stegle. **Circ:** 5,300 (ctrl).

UK
INSPEC MATTERS. **Added/Corp** Institution of Electrical Engineers. (19??)-. Periodical. English. ir. free. Institution of Electrical Engineers / IEE, Michael Faraday House, Six Hills Way, Stevenage Herts SG1 2AY UK. **Tel** 011 44 438 313311, FAX 011 44 438 742840, telex 825578 IEESTV G. **(Subscription address:** IEE / UK, Publications Sales Department, PO Box 96, Stevenage, Herts, SG1 2SD England.**)**

US/1063-7060
INSPEC ONDISC. (INSPEC ONDISC [COMPUTER FILE].). [INSPEC ondisc]. **Added/Corp** INSPEC (Information Service) University Microfilms International. **VFOAT** INSPEC on Disc; ProQuest INSPEC Ondisc; Pro Quest INSPEC on Disc. (19??)-. English. qt. $4,500.00 (subscriber); $7,500.00 (non-subscriber). University Microfilms International, 300 North Zeeb Road, Ann Arbor MI 48106-1346. **Tel** (313)761-4700, (800)521-0600 Exts. 2490, 2491, FAX (313)973-1540. **DD** 621.
Desc: Indexes and abstracts the literature from the Institute of Electrical Engineers (IEE). It covers more than 4,200 journals, 4,000 conference proceedings, books, dissertations, and unpublished reports. Coverage is from 1989 to the present and the disc corresponds to INSPEC [Online Database].

UK
INSPEC TOPICS. 390. POWER SYSTEM PROTECTION. (19??)-. English. bm. £115.00 UK and Northern Ireland; £125.00 Europe and Southern Ireland; £145.00 other. Institution of Electrical Engineers / IEE, Michael Faraday House, Six Hills Way, Stevenage Herts SG1 2AY UK. **Tel** 011 44 438 313311, FAX 011 44 438 742840, telex 825578 IEESTV G. **(Subscription address:** IEE / UK, Publications Sales Department, PO Box 96, Stevenage, Herts, SG1 2SD England.**)**
Desc: Abstracts on Power Systems Protection.

UK
INSPEC TOPICS. T0740. SEMICONDUCTOR LASERS. (19??)-. Abstracting/Indexing Service. English. bw (26 issues per year). $150.00 European Union; $170.00 other. Institution of Electrical Engineers / IEE, Michael Faraday House, Six Hills Way, Stevenage Herts SG1 2AY UK. **Tel** 011 44 438 313311, FAX 011 44 438 742840, telex 825578 IEESTV G. **(Subscription address:** IEE / UK, Publications Sales Department, PO Box 96, Stevenage, Herts, SG1 2SD England.**) ED** Geoff Jones. **Bk Rev**, (Qty: varies).
Desc: Summaries of recent articles from journals and conference proceedings, world-wide, on semiconductor lasers.

UK
INSPEC [ONLINE DATABASE]. **See** Engineering-Abstracting, Bibliographies and Statistics.

SP
INSTALADOR, EL. Spanish. mo (Jul./Aug. issue combined). $140.00. El Instalador, Navaleno 9, 28033 Madrid Spain. **Tel** 011 34 1 2028145, 011 34 1 2025240, FAX 011 34 1 7661664. **ED** Carlos Ocejo. Index available (published in Feb. issue). **Bk Rev. Ad Acc, Adv Mgr:** Jose Moreno, **Tel** 302 5240. **Pr Rev. Circ:** 7.000.
Desc: Covers technical installations.

NE
INSTALLATIE JOURNAAL. Wegener Tijl Tijdschriften Group, Postbus 9943, 1006 AP Amsterdam Netherlands. **Tel** 011 31 20 5182828.

GW/0723-4775
INSTALLATION, DKZ. **VFOAT** Installation, Deutsche Klempner-Zeitung. (1979)-. Periodical. German. Twelve times a year. DM121.49 Germany; DM150.00 other. Georg Siemens Verlagsbuchhandlung, Postfach 450169, D-12171 Berlin Germany. **Tel** 011 49 30 7699040, FAX 011 49 30 76990418. **UDC** 644. **CODEN** 696.1. **[CCC].**

US/1050-1797
INSTITUTE (NEW YORK, N.Y.), THE. (THE INSTITUTE.). [Institute]. **Added/Corp** Institute of Electrical and Electronics Engineers. Vol. 1 (Aug. 1977)-. Periodical. English. bm. $25.00. IEEE, Institution of Electrical and Electronics Engineers, Inc., 345 East 47th Street, New York NY 10017-2394. **Tel** (908)981-1393, FAX (908)981-9667. **(Subscription address:** IEEE / Institute of Electrical and Electronics Engineers, 445 Hoes Lane, PO Box 1331, Piscataway NJ 08855-1331.**)**
Desc: Provides coverage of activities that have an impact on the electrical engineer's career and profession.

US/0538-2351
INSTRUMENT MAINTENANCE MANAGEMENT. (INSTRUMENT MAINTENANCE MANAGEMENT; PROCEEDINGS.). [Instrum. maint. manage.]. **Main/Conf** International ISA Instrumentation Maintenance Management Symposium. **Added/Corp** Instrument Society of America. Instrument Society of America. Chemical and Petroleum Industries Division. Proceedings of the Second Joint Spring Conference. Vol. 6 (1971)-. Proceedings. English. an. Instrument Society of America, 67 Alexander Drive, Research Triangle NC 27709. **Tel** (919)549-8411, FAX (919)549-8288, telex 802 540. **LC** TA165; .N27; TP157; .I55. **DD** 681/.028. **CODEN** ISMMA6. ***Continues*** *National ISA Instrumentation Maintenance Management Symposium. Instrument Maintenance Management, 0538-2351.*

US/0020-4366
INSTRUMENTATION. [Instrumentation]. V. 1-1943-. Periodical. English. qt. **LC** TA165; .A15. **DD** 620.78. **CODEN** INSRAG. Documents available from Ask*IEEE.
Ind/Abst Acoust. Abstr.; INSPEC (1968-).

UK/0959-8286
INSTRUMENTATION & CONTROL ENGINEERING. ***Ceased.*** (19??)-(1992). Academic Scholarly Publication. English. Six times a year (1 volume). Elsevier Science Publishers Ltd, Crown House, Linton Road, Barking Essex IG11 8JU England. **Tel** 011 44 81 5947272, FAX 081-594-5942, telex 896950. **[CCC].** Documents available from Ask*IEEE.
Ind/Abst INSPEC (1988-).

US/0074-056X
INSTRUMENTATION IN THE POWER INDUSTRY. [Instrum. power ind.]. **Main/Conf** International ISA Power Instrumentation Symposium. **Added/Corp** Instrument Society of America. Power Industry Division. **VFOAT** Proceedings of the International ISA Power Instrumentation Symposium. Vol. 1, (1958)-. Academic Scholarly Publication. English. an (Nov.). $29.95 plus shipping. Instrument Society of America, 67 Alexander Drive, Research Triangle NC 27709. **Tel** (919)549-8411, FAX (919)549-8288, telex 802 540. **CODEN** IPWIAN. **[CCC].** Documents available from Article Express International, Ask*IEEE, CASDDS.
Ind/Abst Chem. Abstr.; Ei Page One; Eng. Index Annu.; INIS Atomindex [Micro.]; INSPEC.

US/0192-303X
INTECH. [InTech]. **Added/Corp** Instrument Society of America. **VFOAT** Instrumentation Technology. Vol. 26, No. 1 (Jan. 1979)-. Academic Scholarly Publication. English. mo. $75.00 US & Canda; $110.00 other. Instrument Society of America, 67 Alexander Drive, Research Triangle NC 27709. **Tel** (919)549-8411, FAX (919)549-8288, telex 802 540. **(Subscription address:** ISA Services, Inc. PO Box 3561, Durham NC 27702**) ED** Walter J. Maczka. **LC** TA165; .A14. **DD** 681/.2/05. **CODEN** INTCDD. **[CCC]. Pr Rev. Circ:** 51,000 (ctrl). available on microfilm and microfiche from University Microfilms International (UMI). Documents available from Article Express International, The Genuine Article, Ask*IEEE, Petroleum Abstracts Document Delivery Service, CASDDS. ***Continues*** *Instrumentation Technology, 0020-4382.*
Desc: The official journal of the Instrument Society of America, services the instrumentation and control field.
Ind/Abst Abstr. Bull. Inst. Pap. Sci. Tech.; ACM Guide Comput. Lit.; Alum. Ind. Abstr.; Anal. Abstr.; Appl. Sci. Technol. Index; Bioeng. Abstr.; Chem. Abstr.; Chem. Hazards Ind.; Coal Abstr.; Comput. Database; Comput. Rev.; Curr. Biotechnol.; Curr. Contents Eng. Tech. Appl. Sci.; Ei Page One; EMBASE; Eng. Mater. Abstr.; Eng. Index Annu.; F&S Index Plus Text, Int. [Select. Cov.]; Fluid Abstr., Civil Eng.; Fluid Abstr. Proc. Eng.; FLUIDEX; Gas Abstr.; INSPEC (1986-); Lab. Hazards Bull.; Lit. Pat. Abstr., Oilfield Chem. (1969-); Lit. Abstr., Catal. Catal.; Lit. Abstr., Health Environ.; Lit. Abstr., Pet. Refin. Petrochem.; Lit. Abstr., Pet. Substit.; Lit. Abstr., Transp. Storage; Met. Abstr.; Pet. Abstr.; Proc. Chem. Eng.; PROMT; Res. Alert [Select. Cov.]; SCISEARCH; Shock Vibr. Dig.; Soc. Sci. Cit. Index [Select. Cov.]; Theoret. Chem. Eng.

LV
INTEGRALNYE SKHEMY V DISKRETNOI TEKHNIKE. **Added/Corp** Elektronikas un Skaitlosanas Tehnikas Instituts (Latvijas PSR Zinatnu Akademija). Vol. 1 (1973)-. Russian. 1.08rub (single issue). Zinatne / Science Publishing House, Turgeneva Iela 19, Riga Latvia 1530. **Tel** 3712 212 797. **LC** TK7874; .I54.

US/0730-2290
INTEGRATED CIRCUIT DISCONTINUED DEVICES. (INTEGRATED CIRCUIT DISCONTINUED DEVICES D.A.T.A. BOOK.). [Integr. circuit discontin. devices]. **Added/Corp** Derivation and Tabulation Associates, Inc. **VFOAT** Integrated Circuit Discontinued Devices DATA Book. (1980)-. English. an. $195.00. DATA Business Publishing, PO Box 6510, 15 Inverness Way East, Englewood CO 80155. **Tel** (800)447-4666, (303)799-0381, FAX (303)799-4082. **LC** TK7874; .D47. **DD** 621.381/73/0216. ***Continues*** *Discontinued Integrated Circuit D.A.T.A. Book, 0271-0129.*

BE
INTEGRATED CIRCUITS. CIRCUITS INTEGRES. INTEGRIERTE SCHALTUNGEN. **Added/Corp** Association Internationale Pro Electron. **VFOAT** Circuits Integres; Integrierte Schaltungen. 1st Ed. (1975)-. Multiple languages (English, French and German). **LC** TK7874; .I545. **DD** 621.381/73.

US/1057-4530
INTEGRATED CIRCUITS. DIGITAL. [Integr. circuits, Digit.]. **Added/Corp** D.A.T.A. Business Publishing. **VFOAT** Digital; Digital Integrated Circuit Digest. (1990)-. English. sa (2 issues). $235.00 US; $275.00 other. DATA Business Publishing, PO Box 6510, 15 Inverness Way East, Englewood CO 80155. **Tel** (800)447-4666, (303)799-0381, FAX (303)799-4082. **LC** TK7874.5; .D55. **DD** 621.381/5/0294. ***Continues*** *Integrated Circuits. Digital Integrated Circuits, 0899-8523.*
Desc: Information on digital integrated circuits.

US/1057-4522
INTEGRATED CIRCUITS. INTERFACE. [Integr. circuits, Interface]. **Added/Corp** D.A.T.A. Business Publishing. **VFOAT** Interface; Interface Integrated Circuit Digest. (1990)-. English. an. $205.00. DATA Business Publishing, PO Box 6510, 15 Inverness Way East, Englewood CO 80155. **Tel** (800)447-4666, (303)799-0381, FAX (303)799-4082. **LC** TK7868.I58; D47a. **DD** 621.381/5/0294. ***Continues*** *Integrated Circuits. Interface Integrated Circuits, 0899-8515.*
Desc: Covers interfaced and integrated circuits.

UK/0263-6522
INTEGRATED CIRCUITS INTERNATIONAL. [Integr. circuits int.]. **VFOAT** IC International; I.C. International. Vol. 6, No. 5 (July 1982)-. Periodical. English. Twelve times a year. $453.00 The Americas; £304.00 other. Elsevier Advanced Technology, An Imprint of Elsevier Science Ltd., The Boulevard, Langford Lane, Kidlington, Oxford OX5 1GB United Kingdom. **Tel** 011 44 865 843000, 011 44 865 843699, FAX 011 44 865 843010. **(Subscription address:** Elsevier Science Ltd. Oxford Fulfillment Centre, PO Box 800, Kidlington, Oxford OX5 1DX United Kingdom.**) ED** Patricia Harris. **CODEN** ICIIDZ. **[CCC].** available on microfilm from University Microfilms International (UMI); available on an online database (file 636/Full-Text) from DIALOG. Documents available from Ask*IEEE. ***Continues*** *Microcomputer News International.*
Desc: Designed to keep all those involved with the design, manufacture and use of microtechnology up-to-date with the latest developments in the field.
Ind/Abst Comput. Lit. Index; INSPEC (July 1982-); PTS Newsl. Database [Full Txt.].

US/1059-3128
INTEGRATED CIRCUITS. LINEAR. [Integr. circuits, Linear]. **Added/Corp** D.A.T.A. Business Publishing. **VFOAT** Linear Integrated Circuits. (199?)-. English. sa. $205.00. DATA Business Publishing, PO Box 6510, 15 Inverness Way East, Englewood CO 80155. **Tel** (800)447-4666, (303)799-0381, FAX (303)799-4082. **LC** TK7874; .I54684. **DD** 621.381/5/0294. ***Continues*** *Integrated Circuits. Linear Integrated Circuits, 0899-854X.*

US/1048-2598
INTEGRATED CIRCUITS. MEMORY. [Integr. circuits. Mem.]. **Added/Corp** D.A.T.A. Business Publishing. **VFOAT** Memory; Memory Integrated Circuits. (1989)-. English. sa. $205.00. DATA Business Publishing, PO Box 6510, 15 Inverness Way East, Englewood CO 80155. **Tel** (800)447-4666, (303)799-0381, FAX (303)799-4082. **LC** TK7895.M4; D48a. **DD** 621.381/5/0294. ***Continues*** *Integrated Circuits. Memory Integrated Circuits, 1040-0796.*
Desc: Information on semiconductor storage devices and integrated circuits.

US/1049-2445
INTEGRATED CIRCUITS. MICROPROCESSORS. [Integr. circuits, Microprocess.]. **Added/Corp** D.A.T.A. Business Publishing. **VFOAT** Microprocessor Integrated Circuits. (1989)-. English. sa. $205.00. DATA Business Publishing,

PO Box 6510, 15 Inverness Way East, Englewood CO 80155. **Tel** (800)447-4666, (303)799-0381, FAX (303)799-4082. **DD** 621. ***Continues*** *Integrated Circuits. Microprocessor Integrated Circuits, 1040-0818.*
Desc: Information on microprocessors and integrated circuits.

US/1051-7707
INTEGRATED CIRCUITS. SURFACE-MOUNTED ICS. [Integr. circuits, Surf.-mounted ICs]. **Added/Corp** D.A.T.A. Business Publishing. **VFOAT** Surface-Mounted ICs; Surface Mounted Integrated Circuits; Integrated Circuits. Surface Mounted Integrated Circuits. (1991)-. English. an. $180.00. DATA Business Publishing, PO Box 6510, 15 Inverness Way East, Englewood CO 80155. **Tel** (800)447-4666, (303)799-0381, FAX (303)799-4082. **LC** TK7874; .I5453. **DD** 621.381/5/0294.
Desc: Information on integrated and printed circuits.

●US/1058-4587
INTEGRATED FERROELECTRICS. [Integr. ferroelectr.]. Vol. 1, No. 1 (Apr. 1992)-. Periodical. English. qt. $425.00 (academic institutions), $662.00 (corporate institutions). Gordon & Breach Science Publishers, Inc., PO Box 786, Cooper Station, New York NY 10276. **Tel** (212)206-8900, FAX (212)645-2459. **(Subscription address:** International Publishers Distributor at one of the following addresses: 820 Town Center Drive, Langhorne, PA 19047; or PO Box 90, Reading Berkshire RG1 8JL UK; or Kent Ridge PO Box 1180, Singapore 9111, Republic of Singapore**) LC** TK7872.F44; I57. **DD** 537/.2448. **CODEN** IFEREU. **[CCC].**

NE/0167-9260
INTEGRATION (AMSTERDAM). (INTEGRATION, THE VLSI JOURNAL.). [Integration]. **VFOAT** Integration, The V.L.S.I. Journal; Integration. **VAT** Integration, the Very Large Scale Integration Journal. Vol. 1, No. 1 (April 1983)-. Academic Scholarly Publication. English. Six times a year (2 vols.). Fl820.00. Elsevier Science Publishers BV, PO Box 211, 1000 AE Amsterdam Netherlands. **Tel** 011 31 20 5803642, FAX 011 31 20 5862696, telex 15682. **ED** L Spaanenburg. **[CCC]. Bk Rev. Ad Acc. Pr Rev.** available on microfilm and microfiche from University Microfilms International (UMI). Documents available from Article Express International, The Genuine Article, Ask*IEEE.
Desc: Journal covering every aspect of the VLSI design and testing field. Technical, commercial, legal, social, educational and managerial aspects of the business will be covered, with the technical aspects normally predominating.
Ind/Abst ACM Guide Comput. Lit.; Acoust. Abstr.; Compumath Citation Index [Full Cov.]; Comput. Abstr.; Comput. Rev.; Curr. Contents Eng. Tech. Appl. Sci.; Ei Page One; Eng. Index Annu.; INSPEC (April 1983-); Int. Polit. Sci. Abstr.; Res. Alert [Full Cov.]; SCISEARCH.

FR
INTER ELECTRONIQUE. ***Ceased.*** Vol. 21 (1966)-Ceased (Dec. 1984). Periodical. French. ir. CFIE, 23 rue Laugier, 75017 Paris France. **Tel** 766 01 57. ***Continues*** *Revue Generale d'Electronique.*

US
INTERFACE DISCONTINUED DEVICES. ***Ceased.*** English. an. D A T A Inc, 9889 Willow Creed Road, PO Box 26875, San Diego CA 92126. **Tel** (619)578-7600, telex 910 530606. **ED** Steven D'Adolf. **LC** TK7874.5; .I59. **DD** 621.381/73/0216.
Desc: Contains specifications on 20,300 devices from 119 manufacturers.

US/0190-0943
INTERFERENCE TECHNOLOGY ENGINEER'S MASTER. (INTERFERENCE TECHNOLOGY ENGINEER'S MASTER : ITEM.). [Interfer. technol. eng. master]. **VFOAT** ITEM. (197?)-. English. an (Mar.). $80.00. R & B Enterprises, 20 Clipper Road, West Conshohocken PA 19428. **Tel** (215)825-1960, FAX (215)825-1684, (510)660-8120. **ED** Leonard M. Levin. **LC** TK6553; .I614. **DD** 621.38/0436. **Ad Acc, Adv Mgr Tel** (610)825-1960 ext. 223. **Circ:** 25,000 (ctrl).
Desc: Directory and design guide to the reduction and control of electromagnetic interference. Covers measurement and shielding techniques, filtering, EMC regulations, ESD, fiber optics, lighting, EMP, power-line conditioning and index of related products and services.

US
INTERIM COLLECTION OF THE NATIONAL ELECTRICAL SAFETY CODE INTERPRETATIONS / NATIONAL ELECTRICAL SAFETY CODE COMMITTEE, ANSI C2. Main/Corp American National Standards Institute. National Electrical Safety Code Committee. **Added/Corp** Institute of Electrical and Electronics Engineers. **VFOAT** Interim Collection NESC ... Interpretations; National Electrical Safety Code. Interim Collection NESC ... Interpretations. (1988/1990)-. English. sa. Institution of Electrical Engineers / IEE, Michael Faraday House, Six Hills Way, Stevenage Herts SG1 2AY UK. **Tel** 011 44 438 313311, FAX 011 44 438 742840, telex 825578 IEESTV G. **(Subscription address:** IEE / UK, Publications Sales Department, PO Box 96, Stevenage, Herts, SG1 2SD England.**) LC** TK152; .A44b.

US
INTERNATIONAL CONTRACTORS. See Aeronautics, Astronautics.

US/0145-2584
INTERNATIONAL COUNTERMEASURES HANDBOOK, THE. ***Title Change.*** **See** Military and Defense.

US/0887-008X
INTERNATIONAL DIRECTORY OF DISCONTINUED ICS AND DISCRETE SEMICONDUCTORS. Added/Corp Derivation and Tabulation Associates, Inc. **VFOAT** International Directory of Discontinued Integrated Circuits and Discrete Semiconductors. (1986)-. Directory. English. sa (2 issues). $138.65 US; $160.00 US possessions; $170.00 other. DATA Business Publishing, PO Box 6510, 15 Inverness Way East, Englewood CO 80155. **Tel** (800)447-4666, (303)799-0381, FAX (303)799-4082. **ED** Steven D'Adolf. **LC** TK7867; .D58. **DD** 621.381/73/0216. available on CD-ROM. ***Continues*** *Discontinued Type Locator, 0730-4943.*
Desc: Consolidated listing of 600,000 ICs and semiconductors from over 600 manufacturers. Useful in determining what a device is and where to find additional information.

UK/0098-9886
INTERNATIONAL JOURNAL OF CIRCUIT THEORY AND APPLICATIONS. [Int. j. circuit theory appl.]. **VFOAT** Circuit Theory and Applications. Vol. 1 March (1973)-. Periodical. English. Six times a year. $1,250.00. John Wiley & Sons Ltd., Baffins Lane, Chichester West Sussex PO19 1UD England. **Tel** 0243 779777, FAX 0243 776128 BTG:JWP001, telex 86290 WIBOOKG. **(Subscription address:** John Wiley / Philadelphia, PO Box 7247, Philadelphia PA 19170.**) ED** J. O. Scanlan, A. Csurgay, L. O. Chua, and A. I. Petrenko. **LC** TK454; .I58. **DD** 621.319/2/05. **CODEN** ICTACV. **[CCC]. Pr Rev. Circ:** 800. available on microfilm and microfiche from University Microfilms International (UMI). Documents available from Article Express International, The Genuine Article, Ask*IEEE.
Desc: Covers all aspects of the theory and design of analog and digital circuits together with the application of the idea of circuit theory to a wide variety of problems.
Ind/Abst Acoust. Abstr.; Bioeng. Abstr.; Curr. Contents Eng. Tech. Appl. Sci.; Ei Page One; Eng. Index Annu.; INSPEC (March 1973-); Math. Rev. (?-199?); Pollut. Abstr. Indexes; Res. Alert [Full Cov.]; Sci. Cit. Index; SCISEARCH; Zentralbl. Math. Ihre Grenzgeb.

US/1042-7988
INTERNATIONAL JOURNAL OF COMPUTER AIDED VLSI DESIGN. ***Ceased.*** [Int. j. comput. aided VLSI des.]. **VFOAT** Journal of Computer Aided VLSI Design; Computer Aided VLSI Design. **VAT** International Journal of Computer Aided Very-Large-Scale Integrated Circuits Design. (1989)-?. Periodical. English. qt. Ablex Publishing Corporation, 355 Chestnut Street, Norwood NJ 07648. **Tel** (201)767-8450, (201)767-8455 (Customer Service), FAX (201)767-6717. **ED** George W Zobrist. **LC** TK7874; .I586. **DD** 621.39/5/05. Index available. cum. index. **Ad Acc. Circ:** 100. Documents available from Ask*IEEE.
Ind/Abst INSPEC.

UK/0020-7209
INTERNATIONAL JOURNAL OF ELECTRICAL ENGINEERING EDUCATION. [Int. j. electr. eng. educ.]. Vol. 1 (June 1963)-. Periodical. English (summaries and/or abstracts in French, German and Spanish). qt. £110.00 (institution), £40.00 (individual) UK; $220.00 (institution), $80.00 (individual) other. Manchester University Press, Journals Dept, Oxford Road, Manchester M13 9PL England. **Tel** 011 44 061 2735539, FAX 011 44 061 2743346, telex 668932. **ED** Michael G Hartley and Anne Buckley. **CODEN** IJEEAF. **Bk Rev. Ad Acc. Pr Rev. Circ:** 502. available on microfilm from University Microfilms International (UMI). Documents available from Article Express International, The Genuine Article, Ask*IEEE. ***Supersedes*** *Bulletin of Electrical Engineering Education.*
Desc: An international forum for educators at the university and technical college levels covering trends in curriculum development; includes technical articles.
Ind/Abst Bioeng. Abstr.; Comput. Inf. Syst. Abstr. J. [Full Cov.]; Curr. Contents Eng. Tech. Appl. Sci.; Curr. Technol. Index; Educ. Technol. Abstr.; Ei Page One; Elect. Comm. Abstr.; Eng. Index Annu.; INSPEC (1968-); Leadscan; Mech. Eng. Abstr.; Res. Alert [Select. Cov.]; Res. High. Educ. Abstr.; SCISEARCH; Soc. Sci. Cit. Index [Select. Cov.]; Solid State Supercond. Abstr.; Tech. Educ. Train. Abstr.

UK/0142-0615
INTERNATIONAL JOURNAL OF ELECTRICAL POWER & ENERGY SYSTEMS. [Electr. power energy syst.]. **VFOAT** Electrical Power & Energy Systems. Vol. 1 (April 1979)-. Periodical. English. bm. $515.00 The Americas; £345.00 other. Butterworth Heinemann Publishers, Linacre House, Jordan Hill, Oxford OX2 8DP England. **Tel** 011 44 865 310366. **(Subscription address:** Elsevier Science Ltd. Oxford Fulfillment Centre, PO Box 800, Kidlington, Oxford OX5 1DX United Kingdom.**) ED** Jemi Goss. **LC** TK1; .I55. **DD** 621.319/1/05. **CODEN** IEPSDC. **[CCC].** Index available. **Bk Rev. Ad Acc. Pr Rev.** available on microfilm and microfiche from University Microfilms International (UMI). Documents available from Article Express International, The Genuine Article, Ask*IEEE.
Desc: Covers theoretical developments in electrical power and energy systems and their applications, operations, online control, dynamics, network theory, reliability, protection, distribution systems.
Ind/Abst Bioeng. Abstr.; Curr. Contents Eng. Tech. Appl. Sci.; Ei Page One; Energy Inf. Abstr.; Energy Res. Abstr. (June 1980-); Eng. Index Annu.; INSPEC (Jan. 1980-); Res. Alert [Select. Cov.]; SCISEARCH; Soc. Sci. Cit. Index [Select. Cov.].

UK/0020-7217
INTERNATIONAL JOURNAL OF ELECTRONICS THEORETICAL & EXPERIMENTAL. (INTERNATIONAL JOURNAL OF ELECTRONICS.). [Int. j. electron. theor. exp.]. **VFOAT** Electronics. 1st Ser., Vol. 18, No. 1 (Jan. 1965)-. Academic Scholarly Publication. English. mo. £630.00 UK; $1040.00 other. Taylor & Francis Ltd., Rankine Road, Basingstoke Hampshire, RG24 8PR United Kingdom. **Tel** 011 44 256 840366, FAX 011 44 256 479438, telex 858540. **(Subscription address:** Taylor & Francis Inc., 1900 Frost Road, Suite 101, Bristol PA 19007-1598.**) ED** David J. Jefferies (editor's address: Department of Electronic and Electrical Engineering, University of Surrey, Guildford, Surrey GU2 5XH, UK. **LC** TK7800; .J6. **CODEN** IJELA2. **[CCC].** Index available. available on microfilm from University Microfilms International (UMI). Documents available from Article Express International, The Genuine Article, Ask*IEEE, CASDDS. ***Continues in part*** *Journal of Electronics and Control.* ***Continued in part by*** *International Journal of Control, 0020-7179.*
Desc: Publishes original papers in experimental and theoretical aspects of electronics. The scope is widely drawn and includes topics such as: fundamental electron conduction processes in near-vacuum, gases, vapors, and crystalline and amorphous solids, preparation and characterization of improved semiconductor materials and other kinds of solid for electronic device applications, molecular electronics and microwave circuit designs.
Ind/Abst Bioeng. Abstr.; Chem. Abstr.; Comput. Inf. Syst. Abstr. J. [Full Cov.]; Curr. Contents Eng. Tech. Appl. Sci.; Ei Page One; Elect. Comm. Abstr.; EMBASE; Eng. Index Annu.; INSPEC (1968-); Int. Aerosp. Abstr.; Leadscan; Mater. Sci. Eng. Abstr.; Math. Rev.; Mech. Eng. Abstr.; Pollut. Abstr. Indexes; Res. Alert [Full Cov.]; Sci. Cit. Index; SCISEARCH; Solid State Supercond. Abstr.; Zentralbl. Math. Ihre Grenzgeb.

SI/0129-1564
INTERNATIONAL JOURNAL OF HIGH SPEED ELECTRONICS. [Int. j. high speed electron.]. **VFOAT** High Speed Electronics. Vol. 1, No. 1 (March 1990)-. Periodical. English. qt. $140.00 individuals, $290.00 institutions. World Scientific Publishing Company, PO Box 128, Farrer Road, Singapore 9128 Singapore. **Tel** 011 65 3825663, FAX 011 65 3825919, telex RS 28561 WSPC. **(Subscription address:** US: World Scientific Publishing Co., Inc., 1060 Main Street, River Edge, NJ 07661 Telephone: (201)487-9655, Fax: (201)487-9656; Europe: World Scientific Publishing Co Ltd, 73 Lynton Mead, Totteridge, London N20 8DH United Kingdom Telephone: 011 44 81 4462461, Fax: 011 44 81 4463356; India: World Scientific Publishing Co Pte Ltd, 4911 9th Floor, High Point IV, 45 Palace Road, Bangalore 560 001 India Telephone: (80) 2205972, Fax: (80) 3344593, Telex: 0845-2900 PCO IN; Hong Kong: World Scientific Publishing (HK) Co, PO Box 72482, Kowloon Central Post Office, Hong Kong Telephone: 852-7718791, Fax: 852-7718155**) LC** IN PROCESS. **CODEN** IHSEE7. **[CCC].** Documents available from Ask*IEEE.
Ind/Abst INSPEC (1990-).

●US/1063-1674
INTERNATIONAL JOURNAL OF MICROCIRCUITS AND ELECTRONIC PACKAGING, THE. See Packaging.

US/1050-1827
INTERNATIONAL JOURNAL OF MICROWAVE AND MILLIMETER-WAVE COMPUTER-AIDED ENGINEERING. [Int. j. Microw. millim.-wave comput.-aided eng.]. **Added/Corp** University of Colorado, Boulder. Center for Microwave and Millimeter-Wave CAD. **VFOAT** International Journal of Microwave and Millimeter Wave Computer Aided Engineering. Vol. 1 No. 1 Jan. (1991)-. Periodical. English. Six times a year. $330.00 (US); $390.00 (Canada and Mexico); $412.50 (other). John Wiley & Sons, Inc., 605 Third Avenue, New York NY 10158-0012. **Tel** (212)850-6000, (212)850-6645, FAX (212)850-6088, telex 12-7063. **(Subscription address:** John Wiley & Sons / England, Baffins Lane, Chichester, West Sussex PO19 1UD England.**) ED** K. C. Gupta, Inder J. Bahl, and Ingo Wolff. **LC** TK7876; .I547. **DD** 621.381/3. **CODEN**

IMMEEC. available on microfilm and microfiche from University Microfilms International (UMI). Documents available from Article Express International, The Genuine Article.
Desc: Provides a common forum for the dissemination of research and development results in the areas of computer-aided design and engineering of microwave and millimeter-wave components, circuits, subsystems and antennas.
Ind/Abst Compumath Citation Index [Full Cov.]; Ei Page One; Eng. Index Annu.; Res. Alert [Full Cov.]; SCISEARCH.

UK/0301-9322
INTERNATIONAL JOURNAL OF MULTIPHASE FLOW. [Int. j. multiph. flow]. Vol. 1 (Oct. 1973)-. Periodical. English. Six times a year (1 supplement). $947.00 The Americas; £635.00 other. Pergamon Press, An Imprint of Elsevier Science Ltd., The Boulevard, Langford Lane, Kidlington, Oxford OX5 1GB United Kingdom. **Tel** 011 44 865 843000, 011 44 865 843699, FAX 011 44 865 843010. **(Subscription address:** Elsevier Science Ltd. Oxford Fulfillment Centre, PO Box 800, Kidlington, Oxford OX5 1DX United Kingdom.**)** **ED** G. Hetsroni. **LC** TA357; .I57. **DD** 620.1/064. **CODEN** IJMFBP. **[CCC]. Pr Rev.** available on microfilm and microfiche from University Microfilms International (UMI). Documents available from Article Express International, The Genuine Article, Ask*IEEE, Petroleum Abstracts Document Delivery Service, CASDDS. ***Formed by the union of** PCH. Physicochemical Hydrodynamics., 0191-9059.*
Desc: Publishes theoretical and experimental investigations of multiphase flow that are of relevance and permanent interest.
Ind/Abst Abstr. Bull. Inst. Pap. Sci. Tech.; Appl. Mech. Rev.; Bioeng. Abstr.; Chem. Abstr.; Coal Abstr.; Curr. Contents Eng. Tech. Appl. Sci.; Ei Page One; Energy Res. Abstr. (Nov. 1977-); Eng. Index Annu.; Fluid Abstr., Civil Eng.; Fluid Abstr. Proc. Eng.; FLUIDEX (1973-); Gas Abstr.; HTFS Dig.; INSPEC (April 1974-); Int. Aerosp. Abstr.; Lit. Pat. Abstr., Oilfield Chem. (1975-); Lit. Abstr., Catal. Catal.; Lit. Abstr., Health Environ.; Lit. Abstr., Pet. Refin. Petrochem.; Lit. Abstr., Pet. Substit.; Lit. Abstr., Transp. Storage; Pet. Abstr.; Proc. Chem. Eng.; Res. Alert [Full Cov.]; Sci. Cit. Index; SCISEARCH; Theoret. Chem. Eng.; Zentralbl. Math. Ihre Grenzgeb.

UK/0894-3370
INTERNATIONAL JOURNAL OF NUMERICAL MODELLING. [Int. j. numer.]. **VFOAT** Numerical Modelling. Vol. 1, No. 1 Mar. (1988)-. Periodical. English. Six times a year. $450.00. John Wiley & Sons Ltd., Baffins Lane, Chichester West Sussex PO19 1UD England. **Tel** 0243 779777, FAX 0243 776128 BTG:JWP001, telex 86290 WIBOOKG. **(Subscription address:** John Wiley / Philadelphia, PO Box 7247, Philadelphia PA 19170.**)** **ED** Wolfgang J. R. Hoefer and B. Tuck. **LC** TK3226; .I64. **DD** 621.3. **CODEN** IJNFEX. **[CCC].** available on microfilm and microfiche from University Microfilms International (UMI). Documents available from Article Express International, Ask*IEEE.
Desc: Provides a communication vehicle for numerical modelling methods and data preparation methods associated with electrical and electronic circuits and fields. It concentrates on numerical modelling rather than abstract numerical mathematics.
Ind/Abst Ei Page One; Eng. Index Annu.; INSPEC (March 1988-); Math. Rev. (1988-); Sci. Cit. Index.

NE/0020-7853
INTERNATIONAL LIGHTING REVIEW. [Int. light. rev.]. **VFOAT** ILR. (1949)-. Periodical. English. Four times a year (Mar., June, Sept., Dec.). F91.00 Europe, F108.00 others (airmail); F90.00 (surface mail). Stichting Prometheus, PO Box 721, 5600 AS Eindhoven Netherlands. **Tel** 011 31 40 755252, FAX 011 31 40 755861, telex 35000. **ED** J. F. Caminada. **LC** TK1; .I56.
Ind/Abst Archit. Period. Index (1950/1951-); Coal Abstr.; Ergon. Abstr.; Infomat Int. Bus.; Int. Build. Serv. Abstr.; Saf. Health Work.

US/0739-9898
INTERNATIONAL NETWORKS. ***Ceased.*** **See** Communication-Telecommunications.

UK/0141-1918
INTERNATIONAL POWER GENERATION. [Int. power gener.]. (1977)-. Academic Scholarly Publication. English. Seven times a year. £99.00 UK; £102.00, $198.00 other. Argus Press Group, Queensway House, 2 Queensway Redhill, Surrey RH1 1QS England. **Tel** 011 44 737 768611, 011 44 737 761685, FAX 011 44 737 760510, telex 948669 TOPJNL G. **CODEN** IPGED2. Documents available from Ask*IEEE.
Desc: Provides a technical and economic analysis of power systems particularly those of developing countries.
Ind/Abst Coal Abstr.; EMBASE; Energy Res. Abstr. (Jan. 1981-); Fluid Abstr., Civil Eng.; Fluid Abstr. Proc. Eng.; FLUIDEX; INSPEC (June 1979-).

●US/1070-2989
INTERNATIONAL PRIVATE POWER QUARTERLY. (INTERNATIONAL PRIVATE POWER QUARTERLY : A COUNTRY-BY-COUNTRY UPDATE OF MARKETS OUTSIDE THE U.S. AND CANADA.). [Int. priv. power q.]. (1993)-. Periodical. English. qt. $795.00. McGraw Hill Publishing Company, Inc., 1221 Avenue of the Americas, New York NY 10020. **Tel** (212)512-6410, (800)525-5003, FAX (212)512-6111. **LC** HD9685.A1; I474. **DD** 333.

UK/0538-9992
INTERNATIONAL SERIES OF MONOGRAPHS ON ELECTROMAGNETIC WAVES. ***Ceased.*** **VFOAT** International Series of Monographs in Electromagnetic Waves. (1965)-(19??). Monographic series. English. ir. Pergamon Press, An Imprint of Elsevier Science Ltd., The Boulevard, Langford Lane, Kidlington, Oxford OX5 1GB United Kingdom. **Tel** 011 44 865 843000, 011 44 865 843699, FAX 011 44 865 843010. **(Subscription address:** US/ 395 Saw Mill River Road, Elmsford, NY 10523; Can/ 150 Consumers Road/Suite 104, Willowdale Ontario M2J 1P9; Aus-NZ/ POB 544, Potts Point NSW 2011**)**

UK/0733-1940
INTERNATIONAL SERIES ON SYSTEMS AND CONTROL. [Int. ser. syst. control]. **VFOAT** Systems and Control. Vol. 1-. Monographic series. English. Price varies per volume. Pergamon Press, An Imprint of Elsevier Science Ltd., The Boulevard, Langford Lane, Kidlington, Oxford OX5 1GB United Kingdom. **Tel** 011 44 865 843000, 011 44 865 843699, FAX 011 44 865 843010. **(Subscription address:** US/ 395 Saw Mill River Road, Elmsford, NY 10523; Can/ 150 Consumers Road/Suite 104, Willowdale Ontario M2J 1P9; Aus-NZ/ POB 544, Potts Point NSW 2011**)** **DD** 629. Documents available from Ask*IEEE.
Ind/Abst INSPEC; Math. Rev.; Zentralbl. Math. Ihre Grenzgeb.

US
INTERNATIONAL SOCIETY FOR HYBRID MICROELECTRONICS. English. $50.00. International Society for Hybrid Microelectronics / Virginia, 1850 Centennial Park Drive, Suite 105, Reston VA 22091. **Tel** (703)758-1060, FAX (703)758-1066.

US/0272-3743
INVENTORY OF POWER PLANTS IN THE UNITED STATES. **See** Engineering-Abstracting, Bibliographies and Statistics.

US/1074-3715
IRP REPORT. (IRP REPORT : THE AUTHORITATIVE MONTHLY ON INTEGRATED RESOURCE PLANNING.). [IRP rep.]. Vol. 1, No. 1 (Oct. 1993)-. Newsletter. English. mo. $495.00. McGraw Hill Publishing Company, Inc., 1221 Avenue of the Americas, New York NY 10020. **Tel** (212)512-6410, (800)525-5003, FAX (212)512-6111. **DD** 333.

NE/0924-2716
ISPRS JOURNAL OF PHOTOGRAMMETRY AND REMOTE SENSING. (ISPRS JOURNAL OF PHOTOGRAMMETRY AND REMOTE SENSING : OFFICIAL PUBLICATION OF THE INTERNATIONAL SOCIETY FOR PHOTOGRAMMETRY AND REMOTE SENSING (ISPRS).). [ISPRS j. photogramm. remote sens.]. **Added/Corp** International Society for Photogrammetry and Remote Sensing. **VFOAT** Journal of Photogrammetry and Remote Sensing; Photogrammetry and Remote Sensing. **VAT** International Society for Photogrammetry and Remote Sensing Journal of Photogrammetry and Remote Sensing. Vol. 44, No. 1 (Sept. 1989)-. Academic Scholarly Publication. English (French and German). bm (1 volume). Fl455.00. Elsevier Science Publishers BV, PO Box 211, 1000 AE Amsterdam Netherlands. **Tel** 011 31 20 5803642, FAX 011 31 20 5862696, telex 15682. **LC** TA593.A2; P48. **DD** 621.36/78. **CODEN** IRSEE9. **[CCC].** available on microfilm and microfiche from University Microfilms International (UMI). Documents available from The Genuine Article, Ask*IEEE. ***Continues** Photogrammetria, 0031-8663.*
Ind/Abst Bibliogr. Carto.; Curr. Contents Eng. Tech. Appl. Sci.; Ecol. Abstr.; Ei Page One; Geogr. Abstr. Phys. Geogr.; GeoRef; INSPEC (Sept. 1989-); Int. Aerosp. Abstr.; Res. Alert [Select. Cov.]; SCISEARCH.

●US
ISSUE UPDATE / BONNEVILLE POWER ADMINISTRATION. **Main/Corp** United States. Bonneville Power Administration. (1992)-. English. **LC** TK23.7; .U55i. ***Continues** Issue Alert.*

IT
ITALIAN LIGHTING. (19??)-. Italian. Six times a year. L45000.00 Italy; L100000.00 other. Staff Editoriale SNC, Via Gabriele Rossetti 9, 20145 Milan Italy. **Tel** 011 39 2 48007493, FAX 011 39 2 4985508. **Ad Acc, Adv Mgr:** Renato Pisaniello. ctrl circ.

RU/0235-229X
ITOGI NAUKI I TEKHNIKI. SERIIA FIZICHESKIE OSNOVY LAZERNOI I PUCHKOVOI TEKHNOLOGII. **Added/Corp** Vsesoiuznyi Institut Nauchnoi i Tekhnicheskoi Informatsii (Soviet Union). **VFOAT** Seriia Fizicheskie Osnovy Lazernoi i Puchkovoi Tekhnologii; Fizicheskie Osnovy Lazernoi i Puchkovoi Tekhnologii; Itogi Nauki i Tekhniki. (1988)-. Monographic series. Russian. ir. Price varies per volume. VINITI - Vsesoyuznyi Institut Nauchno-Tekhnicheskoi Informatsii, All-Union Scientific and Technical Information Institute, Baltiiskaia Ulitsa 14, 125219 Moscow Russia. **Tel** 238-46-00, FAX 9430060, telex 411160. **LC** QC685; .I86.

RU
IZ ISTORII ENERGETIKI, ELEKTRONIKI I SVIAZI. **Added/Corp** Sovetskoe Natsionalnoe Obedinenie Istorii i Filosofii Estestvoznaniia i Tekhniki. (19??)-. Academic Scholarly Publication. Russian. 0.57rub. Izdatelstvo Nauka / Akademiia Nauk, Publishing House of the Russian Academy of Sciences, Leninskii Porspekt 14, 117901 Moscow Russia. **Tel** 011 95 954-21-53, FAX 011 95 938-21-44, telex 411964. **LC** TK15; .I9.

RU
IZBIRATELNYE SISTEMY S OBRATNOI SVIAZIU. **Added/Corp** Taganrogskii Radiotekhnicheskii Institut. (19??)-. Russian. 0.85rub (single issue). Taganrogskii Radiotekhn, Nekrasovskii Pereulok, Taganrog 44 Russia. **LC** TK7872.F5; I98.

RU
IZVESTIIA VNIIG IMENI B.E. VEDENEEVA / MINISTERSTVO ENERGETIKI I ELEKTRIFIKATSII SSSR GLAVNIPROEKT, VSESOIUZNYI ORDENA TRUDOVO KRASNOGO ZNAMENI NAUCHNO-ISSLEDOVATELSKII INSTITUT GIDROTEKHNIKI IMEMI B.E. VEDENEEVA. **See** Energy.

US/0735-2727
IZVESTIIA VYSSHIKH UCHEBMYKH ZAVEDENII. RADIOELEKTRONIKA. (RADIOELECTRONICS AND COMMUNICATIONS SYSTEMS.). [Radioelectron. commun. syst.]. (19??)-. Periodical. English (Russian). mo (12 issues). $1015.00. Allerton Press, Inc., 150 Fifth Avenue, New York NY 10011. **Tel** (212)924-3950, FAX (212)463-9684, telex 427441 ALPRES. **LC** TK7800; .R8713. **DD** 621.38/05. **CODEN** RCSYDS. **[CCC].** Documents available from Ask*IEEE. ***Continues** Radio Electronics and Communications Systems, 0735-2727.*
Ind/Abst INSPEC (1978-) [Full Cov.].

RU/0136-3360
IZVESTIIA VYSSHIKH UCHEBNYKH ZAVEDENII. ELEKTROMEKHANIKA. **Added/Corp** Novocherkasskii Politekhnicheskii Institut Imeni Sergo Ordzhonikidze. **VFOAT** Elektromekhanika; Izvestiia Vysshikh Uchebnykh Zabedenii. Elektromekhanika. Vol. 1 (1958)-. Academic Scholarly Publication. Russian. mo. **(Subscription address:** Victor Kamkin, 4956 Boiling Brook Parkway, Rockville MD 20852.**)** **LC** TK4; .R846. **CODEN** IVUEA9. Index available in last issue of volume--attached. Documents available from Article Express International, Ask*IEEE, CASDDS. ***Absorbed** Nauchnye Doklady Vysshei Shkoly. Elektromekhanika i Avomatika.*
Ind/Abst Bioeng. Abstr.; Chem. Abstr.; Ei Page One; Eng. Index Annu.; INSPEC (1968-); Math. Rev.

UN/0021-3470
IZVESTIJA VYSSIH UCEBNYH ZAVEDENIJ. RADIOELEKTRONIKA. (IZVESTIIA VYSSHIKH UCHEBNYKH ZAVEDENII. RADIOELEKTRONIKA.). [Izv. vyss. ucebn. zaved., Radioelektron.]. Vol. 10 (Jan. 1967)-. Periodical. Russian. mo. $148.00. **(Subscription address:** Victor Kamkin, 4956 Boiling Brook Parkway, Rockville MD 20852.**)** **LC** TK6540; .R96. **CODEN** IVUZB5. **Pr Rev.** Documents available from Article Express International, The Genuine Article, Ask*IEEE. ***Continues** Izvestiia Vysshikh Uchebnykh Zavedenii. Radiotekhnika.*
Ind/Abst Bioeng. Abstr.; Ei Page One; Energy Res. Abstr.; Eng. Index Annu.; INSPEC (1968-); Int. Aerosp. Abstr.; Res. Alert [Select. Cov.]; SCISEARCH.

FR/0758-3826
J3E L JOURNAL DE L EQUIPMENT ELECTRIQUE ET ELECTRONIQUE. **VFOAT** Journal de l'Equipement Ectrique et Electronique, Trois E. (1983)-. Periodical. French. Fourteen times a year (Publish 11 months + 3 Suppls). 610.00F France; 680.00F other; 790.00F airmail. SEPP, 13 rue Ganneron, 75018 Paris France. **Tel** 011 33 1 42932243, FAX 011 33 1 42875024. **UDC** 537. **[CCC].**

US/0360-2419
JACK DARR'S SERVICE CLINIC. [Jack Darr's serv. clin.]. No. 1- 1967-. English. Tab Books Inc., 11 West 19th Street, New York NY 10011. **Tel** (212)337-5025. **LC** TK6642; .D322. **DD** 621.388/8/705.

GW
JAHRESSCHAU DER DEUTSCHEN INDUSTRIE. DIE ELEKTRO-INDUSTRIE, ELEKTRONIK UND IHRE HELFER. **VFOAT** Elektro-Industrie, Elektronik und Ihre Helfer;

Elektro-Industrie. (19??)-. German. an. Industrieschau Verlagsgesellschaft MBH, PO Box 4034, Berliner Allee 8, W-6000 Darmstadt Germany. **Tel** (06151)33411, FAX (06151)33164, telex 419257. **(Subscription address:** US/ Western Hemisphere Publishing Corporation, PO Box 710, Newcastle, CA 95658**)** **LC** HD9696.A3; G454. **DD** 338.4/76213/02543. **Ad Acc. Circ:** 8,000. available on CD-ROM from ABC Database.
Desc: Covers the entire German electrical and electronic industry.

UK
JANE'S AVIONICS. See Military and Defense.

JA
JAPAN ANNUAL REVIEWS IN ELECTRONICS, COMPUTERS & TELECOMMUNICATIONS. ***Ceased.*** **VFOAT** Japan Annual Reviews in Electronics, Computers and Telecommunications. (198?)-Series complete. Monographic series. English. an. Elsevier Science Publishing Company Inc, Madison Square Station, PO Box 882, New York NY 10159-0882. **Tel** (212)633-3950, FAX (212)633-3990. Documents available from Ask*IEEE, CASDDS.
Ind/Abst Chem. Abstr.; INSPEC.

JA
JAPAN ELECTRONIC PARTS GUIDE. (19??)-. English. an. $9.00. Japan Trade Publications Ltd, Matsuo Building 7, Sanei-cho Shinjuku-ku, Tokyo 160 Japan. **LC** TK7805; .J36. **DD** 621.381/029/452.

JA
JAPAN ELECTRONICS ALMANAC. (1981)-. English. an. $68.00 North and Central America, Europe, and Middle East; $65.00 Asia and Oceania; $71.00 Africa and South America. Dempa Publications Inc., 1 11 15 Higashi Gotanda, Shinagawa Ku Tokyo 141 Japan. **Tel** 011 81 3 34456111. **LC** HD9696.A3; J3614. **DD** 338.4/7621381/0952. ***Continues*** *Japan Fact Book.*
Desc: Covers Japan's electronics industry by sector. It contains complete profiles of companies and forecasts of anticipated performance. There is an illustrated statistical review.
Ind/Abst F&S Index Plus Text, Int. [Select. Cov.]; PROMT.

JA/0448-861X
JAPAN ELECTRONICS BUYERS' GUIDE. (1962)-. Consumer Publication. English. an. $200.00 Asia; $210.00 North/Central America, Europe, Mideast; $220.00 Africa and South America. Dempa Publications Inc., 1 11 15 Higashi Gotanda, Shinagawa Ku Tokyo 141 Japan. **Tel** 011 81 3 34456111. **(Subscription address:** Dempa Publications, 275 Madison Avenue, New York, NY 10016**)** **ED** Tetsuo (Ted) Hirayama. **LC** TK7870; .J33.
Desc: Lists more than 1,600 products and more than 1,700 manufacturers and trading companies, plus their overseas affiliates and agents, in a revised format.

JA
JAPAN NEW MATERIALS LETTER. English. mo. $1000.00. IPI - Intl Planning Info Aps, Rugvaenget 21, DK 2630 Taastrup Denmark. **Tel** 011 45 43 712044, FAX 011 45 43 712025, telex 33576.
Desc: News and analysis of current developments in the area of new materials in Japan. New items are broken down into the following categories: Trend Watch; Industry; Products and Development.

SP
JAPANESE NEW MATERIALS IACA SERIES. ELECTRONIC MATERIALS. (19??)-. English. qt. £215.00 UK; $370.00 US. Newmedia International Japan, AV Infanta Carlota 123 5 A, 08029 Barcelona Spain. **Tel** 011 34 3 4195690, FAX 414 42 13. available on an online database (files 16,636/Full-Text) from DIALOG.
Ind/Abst PROMT [Full Txt.]; PTS Newsl. Database [Full Txt.].

US
JAPANESE SENSOR NEWSLETTER. Newsletter. English. Four times a year (Mar., June, Sept., Dec.). $160.00 US; $180.00 others. Case Western Reserve University / Elec Design Center, Bingham Buildings, Cleveland OH 44106. **Tel** (216)368-2934, (216)368-2000. **Circ:** 125 (ctrl).
Desc: These issues contains the most up-to-date information on Japanese Sensor technology.

●US/1058-7292
JAPANESE TECHNOLOGY REVIEWS. SECTION A, ELECTRONICS. **VFOAT** Electronics. (1992)-. Periodical. English. $185.00 (academic institutions), $289.00 (corporate institutions). Gordon & Breach Science Publishers, Inc., PO Box 786, Cooper Station, New York NY 10276. **Tel** (212)206-8900, FAX (212)645-2459. **(Subscription address:** International Publishers Distributor at one of the following addresses: 820 Town Center Drive, Langhorne, PA 19047; or PO Box 90, Reading Berkshire RG1 8JL UK; or Kent Ridge PO Box 1180, Singapore 9111, Republic of Singapore**)** **[CCC].** ***Continues in part*** *Japanese Technology Reviews, 0898-5693.*

US
JEC BATTERY NEWSLETTER. See Chemistry.

JA/0385-4515
JEI, JOURNAL OF THE ELECTRONICS INDUSTRY. [JEI, J. electron. ind.]. (1974)-. Periodical. English. mo. $135.00 Asia & Oceania; $150.00 North & Central America, Europe, Mideast; $165.00 Africa, South America. Dempa Publications Inc., 1 11 15 Higashi Gotanda, Shinagawa Ku Tokyo 141 Japan. **Tel** 011 81 3 34456111. **(Subscription address:** Dempa Publications, 275 Madison Avenue, New York NY 10016.**)** **ED** Tetsuo Hirayama. **LC** HD9696.A3; J36. **CODEN** JJEID7. **Ad Acc. Circ:** 108,500. Documents available from Ask*IEEE. ***Continues*** *JEI, Japan Electronic Industry, 0021-3616.*
Desc: Covers advanced consumer electronics, and reveals the latest events and topics through interviews with industry leaders and in-depth technical articles. Covers A/V products, home electronics, and components and devices.
Ind/Abst F&S Index Plus Text, Int. [Select. Cov.]; INSPEC (April 1982-); PROMT.

KO/0254-4172
JENGI HAGHOI RONMUN JI. (CHONGI NAKHOE NONMUNJI.). [Jengi haghoi ronmun ji]. **VFOAT** The Transactions of the Korean Institute of Electrical Engineers; Transactions of the Korean Institute of Electrical Engineers. Began in 1982. Academic Scholarly Publication. English (Korean). mo. Taehan Chongi Hakhoe, 11-4 Supyo-dong, Chung-ku Seoul Korea. **Tel** (02)274-1661/5, K23493, telex KEAYJ. **LC** TK4; .C47. **CODEN** CHNODD. Documents available from Ask*IEEE, CASDDS.
Ind/Abst Chem. Abstr.; INSPEC (1982-).

UK/0269-6533
JET CUTTING TECHNOLOGY. [Jet cutt. technol.]. **VFOAT** Proceedings of the ... International Symposium on Jet Cutting Technology (1986); International Symposium on Jet Cutting Technology. (1986)-. English. ir. BHR Group Ltd Brit Hydrom. Research, Cranfield, Bedford MK43 0AJ England. **Tel** 011 44 243 750422, FAX 011 44 243 750074, telex 825059. ***Continues*** *Papers Presented at the ... International Symposium on Jet Cutting Technology, 0263-435X.*

SI/0218-1266
JOURNAL OF CIRCUITS, SYSTEMS, AND COMPUTERS. Vol. 1, No. 1 (Mar. 1991)-. Periodical. English. qt. $98.00 individuals, $210.00 institutions. World Scientific Publishing Company, PO Box 128, Farrer Road, Singapore 9128 Singapore. **Tel** 011 65 3825663, FAX 011 65 3825919, telex RS 28561 WSPC. **(Subscription address:** US: World Scientific Publishing Co., Inc., 1060 Main Street, River Edge, NJ 07661 Telephone: (201)487-9655, Fax: (201)487-9656; Europe: World Scientific Publishing Co Ltd, 73 Lynton Mead, Totteridge, London N20 8DH United Kingdom Telephone: 011 44 81 4462461, Fax: 011 44 81 4463356; India: World Scientific Publishing Co Pte Ltd, 4911 9th Floor, High Point IV, 45 Palace Road, Bangalore 560 001 India Telephone: (80) 2205972, Fax: (80) 3344593, Telex: 0845-2900 PCO IN; Hong Kong: World Scientific Publishing (HK) Co, PO Box 72482, Kowloon Central Post Office, Hong Kong Telephone: 852-7718791, Fax: 852-7718155**)** **LC** TK7800; .J58. **CODEN** JCSME7. Documents available from Ask*IEEE.
Ind/Abst INSPEC (March 1991-).

●US/1064-2269
JOURNAL OF COMMUNICATIONS TECHNOLOGY & ELECTRONICS. [J. commun. technol. electron.]. **VFOAT** Journal of Communications Technology and Electronics. Vol. 38, No. 1 (1993)-. Periodical. English (translations available in Russian). Sixteen times a year. $1,728.00 US; $1,888.00 Canada and Mexico; $1,948.00 other. Scripta Technica, A Subsidiary of John Wiley & Sons, Inc., 7961 Eastern Avenue, Silver Spring MD 20910. **Tel** (301)588-0484, FAX (301)588-5278. **(Subscription address:** John Wiley / Philadelphia, PO Box 7247, Philadelphia PA 19170.**)** **ED** Reuben Glass, City University, London. **LC** TK7800; .R413. **DD** 621.381/05. **CODEN** JTELEJ. Documents available from Article Express International, Ask*IEEE. ***Continues*** *Radiotekhnika i Elektronika. English. Soviet Journal of Communications Technology & Electronics, 8756-6648.*
Desc: Devoted to the theory and physical fundamentals of communications and electronics engineering, this journal offers original work from research centers of the Russian Academy of Sciences, as well as frequent state-of-the-art reviews.
Ind/Abst Bioeng. Abstr.; Ei Page One; Electron. Commun. Abstr. J.; Eng. Index Annu.; INSPEC; Int. Aerosp. Abstr.; ISMEC Bull.; Math. Rev.; Pollut. Abstr. Indexes; Saf. Sci. Abstr. J.

AT/0725-2986
JOURNAL OF ELECTRICAL AND ELECTRONICS ENGINEERING, AUSTRALIA. [J. electr. electron. eng., Aust.]. **Added/Corp** Institution of Engineers, Australia. Institution of Radio and Electronics Engineers, Australia. Vol. 1, No. 1 (March 1981)-. Academic Scholarly Publication. English. qt. 55.00Aus$ Australia; 70.00Aus$ other. Institute of Radio and Electrical Engineering of Australia, PO Box 79, Edgecliff New South Wales 2027 Australia. **Tel** 011 61 2 3274822, FAX 011 61 2 3276770. **ED** Hugh F. Bartlett, D. Wong, and H. Harriman. **LC** TK1; .J78. **DD** 621.3/05. **CODEN** JEEADG. Index available. **Ad Acc. Circ:** 6,000 (ctrl). Documents available from Article Express International, Ask*IEEE, CASDDS. ***Formed by the union of*** *Proceedings of the IREE Australia, 0158-0736* ***and*** *Transactions of the Institution of Engineers, Australia. Electrical Engineering.*
Desc: Covers wide range of electrical and electronic engineering subjects by tutorial, research, overview state-of-the art and applications papers.
Ind/Abst Acoust. Abstr.; Bioeng. Abstr.; Chem. Abstr.; Ei Page One; Energy Res. Abstr. (Oct. 1981-); Eng. Index Annu.; Fluid Abstr., Civil Eng.; Fluid Abstr. Proc. Eng.; FLUIDEX (19??-); INSPEC (March 1981-); World Publ. Monit.

CH
JOURNAL OF ELECTRICAL ENGINEERING. English. Graduate Institute of Electrical Engineering, National University of Taiwan, Taipei Taiwan. **LC** TK1; .J79. **DD** 621.3/05.

NE/0920-5071
JOURNAL OF ELECTROMAGNETIC WAVES AND APPLICATIONS. [J. electromagn. waves appl.]. Vol. 1 No. 1 (1987)-. Periodical. English. mo. DM1080.00. VSP International Science Publishers, Godfried van Seystlaan 47, 3703 BR Zeist Netherlands. **Tel** 011 31 3404 25790, FAX 011 31 3404 32081, telex 40217 USP NL. **(Subscription address:** VSP International Science Publishers, PO Box 346, 3700 AH Zeist Netherlands.**)** **ED** J. A. Kong. **LC** QC660.5; .J68. **DD** 530.1/41. **CODEN** JEWAE5. **Pr Rev.** Documents available from The Genuine Article, Ask*IEEE.
Desc: Covers all aspects of electromagnetic wave theory and its various applications. Publishes original papers and review articles on new theories, methodology and computational techniques, and interpretations of both theoretical and experimental results.
Ind/Abst Curr. Contents Eng. Tech. Appl. Sci.; GeoRef; INSPEC (1988-); Int. Aerosp. Abstr.; Res. Alert [Select. Cov.]; SCISEARCH.

JA/0385-4507
JOURNAL OF ELECTRONIC ENGINEERING : JEE. [JEE, J. electron. eng.]. **VFOAT** JEE. No. 94 (Sept. 1974)-. Academic Scholarly Publication. English. mo. $115.00 North & Central America, Europe, Mideast; $105.00 Asia and Oceania; $120.00 Africa and South America. Dempa Publications Inc., 1 11 15 Higashi Gotanda, Shinagawa Ku Tokyo 141 Japan. **Tel** 011 81 3 34456111. **(Subscription address:** Dempa Publications, 275 Madison Avenue, New York, NY 10016**)** **ED** Tetsuo Hirayama. **LC** TK7800; .J2. **DD** 621.381/05. **CODEN** JEENDL. **Bk Rev. Ad Acc. Circ:** 51,000 (ctrl). Documents available from Article Express International, Ask*IEEE, CASDDS. ***Continues*** *JEE, 0021-3608.*
Desc: Provides technology reports, news on production and marketing trends, and information concerning components and devices, test and production equipment and materials.
Ind/Abst Chem. Abstr.; Comput. Inf. Syst. Abstr. J. [Full Cov.]; Ei Page One; Elect. Comm. Abstr.; Eng. Index Annu.; Environ. Eng. Abstr.; F&S Index Plus Text, Int. [Select. Cov.]; INSPEC (Dec. 1979-); Manuf. Process Eng. Abstr.; PROMT; Solid State Supercond. Abstr.

●US/1017-9909
JOURNAL OF ELECTRONIC IMAGING. [J. electron. imaging]. **Added/Corp** Society of Photo-Optical Instrumentation Engineers. IS&T--The Society for Imaging Science and Technology. **VFOAT** Electronic Imaging. Vol. 1, No. 1 (Jan. 1992)-. Periodical. English. qt. $100.00 (institutions), $60.00 (nonmember), $40.00 (member) (individuals) North America; $120.00 (institutions), $80.00 (nonmember), $60.00 (member) (individuals) other. International Society for Optical Engineering, PO Box 10, Bellingham WA 98227-0010. **Tel** (206)676-3290, FAX (206)647-1445, telex 46-7053. **(Subscription address:** Society for Imaging Science and Technology, 7003 Kilworth Lane, Springfield VA 22151.**)** **ED** Paul Roetling. **LC** TA1632; .J68. **DD** 621.36/7/05. **CODEN** JEIME5. **[CCC]. Ad Acc. Acid Free.** Documents available from Article Express International.
Desc: Publishes papers in all technology areas that make up the field of electronic imaging and are normally considered in the design, engineering, and application of an electronic imaging system.
Ind/Abst Ei Page One; Eng. Index Annu.

US/0968-2783
JOURNAL OF ELECTRONIC MATERIAL APPLICATIONS. ***Ceased.*** (1993)-(Dec. 1994). English. qt (Jan., Apr., July and Oct.). Technomic Publishing Company, Inc., 851 New Holland Avenue, Box 3535, Lancaster PA 17604. **Tel** (717)291-5609, (800)233-9936, FAX (717)295-4538. **[CCC].**

US/0361-5235
JOURNAL OF ELECTRONIC MATERIALS. [J. electron. mater.]. **Added/Corp** Minerals, Metals and Materials Society. Institute of

Electrical and Electronics Engineers. Metallurgical Society of AIME. Metallurgical Society of AIME. Electronic Materials Committee. IEEE Electron Devices Society. (1972)-. Academic Scholarly Publication. English. mo. $228.00 (institutions), $96.00 (individuals) US; $248.00 (institutions), $116.00 (individuals) other. Minerals, Metals and Materials Society, 420 Commonwealth Drive, Warrendale PA 15086-7514. **Tel** (412)776-9000 ext. 236, (800)759-4867, FAX (412)776-3770. **ED** T.C. Harman. **LC** TK7871; .J66. **DD** 621.381/028. **CODEN** JECMA5. **[CCC].** Index available. **Ad Acc. Pr Rev.** available on microfilm from University Microfilms International (UMI). Documents available from Article Express International, The Genuine Article, Ask*IEEE, CASDDS.
Desc: Provides a common forum for dissemination of the results of original research on all materials of interest in the field of electronics.
Ind/Abst ACM Guide Comput. Lit.; Acoust. Abstr.; Alum. Ind. Abstr.; Appl. Sci. Technol. Index (1991-); Bioeng. Abstr.; Ceram. Abstr. (Feb. 1973-); Chem. Abstr.; Chem. Titles; Comput. Rev. (Feb. 1973-); Curr. Contents Phys. Chem. Earth Sci.; Ei Page One; Elect. Comm. Abstr.; Eng. Mater. Abstr.; Eng. Index Annu.; INSPEC (Feb. 1973-); Int. Aerosp. Abstr.; Leadscan; Mech. Eng. Abstr.; Met. Abstr.; Print. Abstr. (1991-); Res. Alert [Full Cov.]; Sci. Cit. Index; SCISEARCH; Solid State Supercond. Abstr.

US/1043-7398
JOURNAL OF ELECTRONIC PACKAGING. [J. electron. packag.]. **Added/Corp** American Society of Mechanical Engineers. Vol. 111, No. 1 (March 1989)-. Periodical. English. qt. $130.00 (nonmember), $40.00 (member) US and Canada. American Society of Mechanical Engineers, 22 Law Drive, Fairfield NJ 07007. **Tel** (201)882-1167, (212)705-7722 (editorial). **LC** TK7870; .J656. **DD** 621.381/046. **CODEN** JEPAE4. **[CCC].** Index available. cum. index. **Bk Rev. Ad Acc.** available on microfilm and microfiche from University Microfilms International (UMI). Documents available from Article Express International, Ask*IEEE.
Ind/Abst Ei Page One; Eng. Index Annu.; Expand. Acad. Index (1992-); INSPEC (Mar. 1989-); Shock Vibr. Dig.

US/0923-8174
JOURNAL OF ELECTRONIC TESTING. (JOURNAL OF ELECTRONIC TESTING : THEORY AND APPLICATIONS (JETTA).). [J. electron. test]. **VFOAT** Electronic Testing; JETTA. Vol. 1, No. 1 (Feb. 1990)-. Periodical. English. bm. $704.00. Kluwer Academic Publishers / Massachusetts, PO Box 358, Accord Station, Hingham MA 02018. **Tel** (617)871-6600. **ED** Vishwani Agrawal. **CODEN** JTTAER. **[CCC]. Pr Rev. Acid Free.** available on microfilm and microfiche from University Microfilms International (UMI). Documents available from Article Express International, Ask*IEEE.
Desc: An international forum for the dissemination of research and application information in the area of electronic testing. This is the only journal devoted specifically to electronic testing. The journal will provide archival material, and through its quick publication cycle, will strive to bring recent results to researchers and practitioners. While it will emphasize publication of previously unpublished material, conference papers of exceptional merit that require wider exposure will, at the discretion of the editors, also be published provided they meet the journal's peer-review standard. It will also seek clearly written survey and review articles to promote improved understanding of the state of the art.
Ind/Abst ACM Guide Comput. Lit.; Comput. Rev.; Ei Page One; Eng. Index Annu.; INSPEC (Feb. 1990-).

CC/0217-9822
JOURNAL OF ELECTRONICS (CHINA). [J. Electron. (China)]. **VFOAT** Dianzi Kexue Xuekan. (1984)-. Academic Scholarly Publication. English. qt. $186.50 (institutions), $120.00 (individuals) US; $206.50 (institutions), $140.00 (individuals) other. Science Press, 16 Donghuangchenggen North Street, Beijing 100707, People's Republic of China. **Tel** 011 86 1 4019821, 011 86 1 4010642, FAX 011 86 1 4012180, 011 86 1 4019810, telex 210147. **DD** 537.5. **[CCC].**

UK/0960-3131
JOURNAL OF ELECTRONICS MANUFACTURING. Vol. 1, No. 1 (Sept. 1991)-. Academic Scholarly Publication. English. Four times a year. $245.00 US and Canada; £145.00 Europe; £160.00 other. Chapman & Hall, 2-6 Boundary Row, London SE1 8HN England. **Tel** 011 44 71 865 0066, FAX 011 44 71 522 9623, telex 290164 Chapmag. **(Subscription address:** Chapman & Hall, Cheriton House, North Way, Andover, Hampshire, SP10 5BE England.**) ED** David Williams, Eddie Lo, Keith Gardiner, David Upton. **CODEN** JELMEK. **[CCC]. Pr Rev.** Documents available from Ask*IEEE, CASDDS.
Desc: Vertically integrated journal aimed at providing a unique interface between managers, researchers and application engineers working both in the academic and industrial communities.
Ind/Abst Chem. Abstr. (Sept. 1991-); INSPEC (Sept. 1991-).

US/0892-1059
JOURNAL OF ELECTROPHYSIOLOGY. ***Title Change.*** [J. electrophysiol.]. (Feb. 1987)-?. Periodical. English. bm. Futura Publishing Company Inc., 135 Bedford Road, PO Box 418, Armonk NY 10504-0418. **Tel** (914)273-1014, (800)877-8761, FAX (914)273-1015, (914)273-1016. **ED** Richard Luceri. **DD** 616. **NLM** W1; JO633C. **Bk Rev. Ad Acc. Circ:** 2,000. ***Continues*** *Clinical Progress in Electrophysiology and Pacing, 8756-9264.* ***Continued by*** *Journal of Cardiovascular Electrophysiology, 1045-3873.*
Desc: Provides a forum for the study of arrhythmias, basic or clinical, in all their ramifications. Publishes abstracts of meetings as well as symposia dedicated to electrophysiology and arrhythmias.

NE/0304-3886
JOURNAL OF ELECTROSTATICS. [J. electrostat.]. Vol. 1 (Feb. 1975)-. Academic Scholarly Publication. English. Eight times a year (2 volumes). Fl1040.00. Elsevier Science Publishers BV, PO Box 211, 1000 AE Amsterdam Netherlands. **Tel** 011 31 20 5803642, FAX 011 31 20 5862696, telex 15682. **ED** T.B. Jones. **LC** QC570; .J68. **DD** 537.2/05. **CODEN** JOELDH. **[CCC]. Bk Rev. Ad Acc. Pr Rev.** available on microfilm and microfiche from University Microfilms International (UMI). Documents available from Article Express International, The Genuine Article, Ask*IEEE, CASDDS.
Desc: Disseminates knowledge of static electricity in its fundamental aspects, in its useful applications, and in its hazardous nature.
Ind/Abst Bioeng. Abstr.; Chem. Abstr.; Coal Abstr.; Curr. Contents Eng. Tech. Appl. Sci.; Ei Page One; Eng. Index Annu.; INSPEC (Feb. 1975-); Res. Alert [Select. Cov.]; SCISEARCH; World Text. Abstr.

AT
JOURNAL OF INSTRUMENTATION & CONTROL / INSTITUTE OF INSTRUMENTATION AND CONTROL, AUSTRALIA. Vol. 39, No. 5 (Oct. 1983)-. Periodical. English. bm. $48.08. Institute of Instrumentation and Control Australia, c/o Australian Mineral Foundation, 63 Conyngham Street, Glenside SA 5065 Australia. **Tel** 011 61 8 2955900, FAX 011 61 8 2949997. Documents available from Ask*IEEE. ***Continues*** *Australian Journal of Instrumentation and Control.*
Ind/Abst INSPEC.

US
JOURNAL OF MAGNETOHYDRODYNAMICS & PLASMA RESEARCH. (199?)-. English. qt (Jan., Apr., July, Oct.). $325.00. Nova Science Publishers Inc., 6080 Jericho Turnpike, Suite 207, Commack NY 11725-2808. **Tel** (516)499-3103, (516)499-3106, FAX (516)499-3146. ***Continues*** *Magnetohydrodynamics, 0891-9801.*

UK/0957-4522
JOURNAL OF MATERIALS SCIENCE. MATERIALS IN ELECTRONICS. [J. mater. sci., Mater. electron.]. **VFOAT** Materials in Electronics. Vol. 1, No. 1 (May 1990)-. Academic Scholarly Publication. English. bm. $275.00 US and Canada; £160.00 Europe; £175.00 other. Chapman & Hall, 2-6 Boundary Row, London SE1 8HN England. **Tel** 011 44 71 865 0066, FAX 011 44 71 522 9623, telex 290164 Chapmag. **(Subscription address:** Chapman & Hall, Cheriton House, North Way, Andover, Hampshire, SP10 5BE England.**) ED** A. Willoughby. **LC** TK7871; .J665. **DD** 621.381. **CODEN** JSMEEV. **[CCC].** Index available. cum. index. **Ad Acc. Pr Rev.** Documents available from Article Express International, The Genuine Article, Ask*IEEE, CASDDS.
Desc: Papers on materials and their applications in modern electronics. The journal covers the ground between the fundamental science such as semiconductor physics, and work concerned solely with applications. Features not only the growth and preparation of new materials, but also their processing, fabrication, bonding and encapsulation, together with reliability, failure analysis, quality assurance and characterisation related to the whole range of applications in electronics.
Ind/Abst Ceram. Abstr. (19??-); Chem. Abstr. (May 1990-); Curr. Contents Phys. Chem. Earth Sci.; Ei Page One; Eng. Index Annu.; INSPEC (May 1990-); Int. Aerosp. Abstr.; Res. Alert [Full Cov.]; SCISEARCH.

●US/1057-7157
JOURNAL OF MICROELECTROMECHANICAL SYSTEMS. (JOURNAL OF MICROELECTROMECHANICAL SYSTEMS : A JOINT IEEE/ASME PUBLICATION.). **Added/Corp** Institute of Electrical and Electronics Engineers. American Society of Mechanical Engineers. **VFOAT** Microelectromechanical Systems. Vol. 1, No. 1 (Mar. 1992)-. Academic Scholarly Publication. English. qt. $120.00. IEEE, Institution of Electrical and Electronics Engineers, Inc., 345 East 47th Street, New York NY 10017-2394. **Tel** (908)981-1393, FAX (908)981-9667. **(Subscription address:** IEEE / Institute of Electrical and Electronics Engineers, 445 Hoes Lane, PO Box 1331, Piscataway NJ 08855-1331.**) LC** TK7874; .J666. **DD** 621.381. **CODEN** JMIYET. **[CCC].** available on microfiche. Documents available from Article Express International, Ask*IEEE, CASDDS.
Desc: Devoted to the field of microelectromechanical systems (also called MEMS, micromechanics, and microdynamics); embraces all aspects of the science, engineering, design and applications in the MEMS area.
Ind/Abst Chem. Abstr.; Comput. Inf. Syst. Abstr. J. [Full Cov.]; Ei Page One; Eng. Index Annu.; INSPEC (March 1992-); Int. Aerosp. Abstr.; Mater. Sci. Eng. Abstr.; Mech. Eng. Abstr.

UK/0960-1317
JOURNAL OF MICROMECHANICS AND MICROENGINEERING : STRUCTURES, DEVICES, AND SYSTEMS. Added/Corp American Institute of Physics. Institute of Physics (Great Britain). Vol. 1 No. 1 (Mar. 1991)-. Periodical. English. qt. $245.00. Institute of Physics, Techno House, Redcliffe Way, Bristol BS1 6NX England. **Tel** 011 44 272 297481, FAX 011 44 272 294318, telex 449149 INSTP G. **(Subscription address:** American Institute of Physics, Publishing Sales, 500 Sunnyside Blvd., Woodbury NY 11797.**) ED** W. Carr. **LC** QC176.8.M5; J68. **DD** 530.4/1. **CODEN** JMMIEZ. **[CCC].** Index available in last issue of volume--attached. available on microfiche. Documents available from Article Express International, Ask*IEEE.
Desc: Devoted to all aspects of research and development for micro-electromechanical, micromechanical and vacuum microelectronic technology. It covers fundamental structures, application devices and systems within the following technology areas: Microsystems and controls; processing and fabrication; microstructures and devices; interface electronics and integration, related electron/photon devices and systems.
Ind/Abst Ei Page One; Eng. Index Annu.; Fluid Abstr., Civil Eng.; Fluid Abstr. Proc. Eng.; FLUIDEX (19??-); INSPEC (March 1991-).

US/0832-7823
JOURNAL OF MICROWAVE POWER AND ELECTROMAGNETIC ENERGY, THE. (THE JOURNAL OF MICROWAVE POWER AND ELECTROMAGNETIC ENERGY : A PUBLICATION OF THE INTERNATIONAL MICROWAVE POWER INSTITUTE.). [J. microw. power electromagn. energy]. **Added/Corp** International Microwave Power Institute. **VFOAT** Microwave Power. Vol. 20, No. 1 (1985)-. Periodical. English. qt. $95.00 US and Canada; $120.00 other. International Microwave Power Institute, 13542 Union Village Circle, Clifton VA 22024. **Tel** (703)830-5588, FAX (703)830-0281. **ED** George Freedman and L P Halbrook. **LC** TK7876; .J68. **DD** 621.381/3/05. **NLM** W1; JO765J. **CODEN** JMPEE4. Index available. **Bk Rev. Pr Rev. Circ:** 1,000 (ctrl). available on microfiche. Documents available from Article Express International, The Genuine Article, BIOSIS Document Express, Ask*IEEE, CASDDS. ***Continues*** *Journal of Microwave Power, 0022-2739.*
Ind/Abst AGRICOLA [Select. Cov.]; Appl. Sci. Technol. Index; Bioeng. Abstr.; Biol. Abstr.; Chem. Abstr. (1985-); Coal Abstr.; Ei Page One; Eng. Index Annu.; Food Sci. Technol. Abstr.; Foods Adlibra; INIS Atomindex [Micro.]; INSPEC (1986-); Int. Packag. Abstr.; Res. Alert [Select. Cov.]; SCISEARCH.

UK/0264-3375
JOURNAL OF SEMI-CUSTOM ICS. ***Title Change.*** [J. semi-custom ICs]. Vol. 1, No. 1 (Sept. 1983)-(1992). Periodical. English. qt. Benn Electronics Publishing Ltd, Sovereign Way Tonbridge, Kent TN9 1RW England. **Tel** 011 44 732 364422, telex 27844. **ED** S. Hurst. **[CCC].** Index available. cum. index. **Bk Rev. Ad Acc. Pr Rev.** available on microfilm and microfiche from University Microfilms International (UMI). Documents available from Ask*IEEE. ***Merged into*** *Microelectronics Journal.*
Desc: A powerful journal specifically for the semicustom industry. Covers developments in companies OEM interests and the expanding status of work stations and CAD activities.
Ind/Abst Acoust. Abstr.; INSPEC (Sept. 1983-).

US/0896-1107
JOURNAL OF SUPERCONDUCTIVITY. [J. supercond.]. Vol. 1, No. 1 (Mar. 1988)-. Periodical. English. Six times a year. $295.00 US; $345.00 other. Plenum Press, 233 Spring Street, New York NY 10013-1578. **Tel** (212)620-8000, (800)221-9369, FAX (212)463-0742, (212)807-1047, telex 23/421139. **ED** Stuart A. Wolf, Donald O. Gubser, and Vladimir Kresin. **LC** QC611.9; .J68. **DD** 537.6/23/05. **CODEN** JOUSEH. **[CCC].** available on microfilm and microfiche from University Microfilms International (UMI). Documents available from Article Express International, The Genuine Article, Ask*IEEE, CASDDS.
Desc: Includes topics on new materials, new mechanisms, new phenomena, technological properties, and small-scale and large-scale applications.
Ind/Abst Appl. Sci. Technol. Index (1991-); Chem. Abstr.; Curr. Contents Phys. Chem. Earth Sci.; Ei Page One; Eng. Index Annu.; INSPEC (March 1988-); Int. Aerosp. Abstr.; Res. Alert [Full Cov.]; SCISEARCH.

US/0099-4480
JOURNAL OF THE ILLUMINATING ENGINEERING SOCIETY. [J. Illum. Eng. Soc.]. **Main/Corp** Illuminating Engineering Society. **Added/Corp** Illuminating Engineering Society. Illuminating Engineering Society of North America. **VFOAT** Journal of IES. Vol. 1 (Oct. 1971)-. Periodical. English. sa. $195.00. Illuminating Engineering Society, 120 Wall Street, 17th Floor, New York NY 10005. **Tel** (212)248-5000 ext 111, FAX (212)248-5017, (212)248-5018. **ED** Kevin Heslin. **LC** TH7700; .I35. **DD**

621.32/05. **CODEN** JIESBS. **[CCC]**. Index available. cum. index. **Pr Rev. Circ:** 10,000 (ctrl). available on microfilm and microfiche from University Microfilms International (UMI). Documents available from Article Express International, The Genuine Article, Ask*IEEE, CASDDS. ***Continues*** *Illuminating Engineering, 0019-2333.*
Desc: Technical papers addressing topics of interest to illuminating engineers.
Ind/Abst Appl. Sci. Technol. Index; Art Archaeol. Tech. Abstr.; Bioeng. Abstr.; Chem. Abstr.; Curr. Contents Eng. Tech. Appl. Sci.; Ei Page One; Energy Res. Abstr. (July 1976-); Eng. Index Annu.; Ergon. Abstr.; Highw. Res. Abstr.; INSPEC (Oct. 1971-); Int. Build. Serv. Abstr.; Res. Alert [Select. Cov.]; Saf. Health Work; SCISEARCH.

II/0377-2063
JOURNAL OF THE INSTITUTION OF ELECTRONICS AND TELECOMMUNICATION ENGINEERS. **See** Communication-Telecommunications.

II/0020-3386
JOURNAL OF THE INSTITUTION OF ENGINEERS (INDIA). (JOURNAL OF THE INSTITUTION OF ENGINEERS (INDIA). ELECTRICAL ENGINEERING DIVISION.). [J. Inst. Eng., India, Electr. Eng. Div.]. **Main/Corp** Institution of Engineers (India). Electrical Engineering Division. (1961)-. Academic Scholarly Publication. English. Four times a year (Feb., May, Aug., Nov.). $18.00. Institution of Engineers India, 8 Gokhale Road, Calcutta 700020 India. **Tel** 011 91 33 288311, telex 21 7885 IEIC IN. **ED** D. K. Ghosh, P. P. Sinha and S. Ramaseshan. **LC** TK1; .J794. **CODEN** JEELAC. **Ad Acc. Circ:** 15,000 (ctrl). Documents available from Article Express International, Ask*IEEE. ***Continues in part*** *Journal of the Institution of Engineers (India). Mechanical, Electrical and General Sections.*
Desc: Contains original research papers on control and protection, electrical machinery and apparatus, high voltage engineering, transmission, distribution and utilization and power system loadflow, generation and station equipment.
Ind/Abst Abstr. J. Earthq. Eng. (?-?); Bioeng. Abstr.; Ei Page One; EMBASE; Energy Res. Abstr. (Oct. 1976-); Eng. Mater. Abstr.; Eng. Index Annu.; INSPEC (1968-); Int. Aerosp. Abstr.

II/0251-1096
JOURNAL OF THE INSTITUTION OF ENGINEERS (INDIA). ELECTRONICS & TELECOMMUNICATION ENGINEERING DIVISION. [J. Inst. Eng., India, Electron. tele-commun. eng. div.]. **Main/Corp** Institution of Engineers (India). **Added/Corp** Institution of Engineers (India). Electronics & Telecommunication Engineering Division. **VFOAT** Journal of the Institution of Engineers (India). Electronics and Telecommunication Engineering Division; Electronics and Telecommunication Engineering Division; Electronics & Telecommunication Engineering Division; IE (I) Publication-ET. Vol. 42, (Sept. 1961)-. Periodical. English. Twice a year (Mar., Sept.,). $5.00. Institution of Engineers India, 8 Gokhale Road, Calcutta 700020 India. **Tel** 011 91 33 288311, telex 21 7885 IEIC IN. **ED** D. K. Ghosh, P. P. Sinha and S. Ramaseshan. **LC** TK7800; .J7. **DD** 621.381/05. Index available. **Ad Acc. Circ:** 6,000 (ctrl). Documents available from Ask*IEEE. ***Continues in part*** *Journal of the Institution of Engineers (India), 0368-2498.*
Desc: Publishes technical papers on electronics and telecommunication engineering including electronmagnetics, radar, microwave, electronic devices and solid state devices.
Ind/Abst Ei Page One; INSPEC (1968-).

KO/0374-4876
JOURNAL OF THE KOREAN INSTITUTE OF ELECTRICAL ENGINEERS. (CHON'GI HAKHOE CHI.). [J. Korean Inst. Electr. Eng.]. **Main/Corp** Taehan Chon'Gi Hakhoe. Academic Scholarly Publication. English (Korean). Taehan Chongi Hakhoe, 11-4 Supyo-dong, Chung-ku Seoul Korea. **Tel** (02)274-1661/5, K23493, telex KEAYJ. **LC** TK4. **CODEN** CGHCA5. Documents available from Ask*IEEE, CASDDS.
Ind/Abst Chem. Abstr.; INSPEC (1968-).

US/0922-5773
JOURNAL OF VLSI SIGNAL PROCESSING. [J. VLSI process.]. **VAT** Journal of Very Large Scale Integration Signal Processing. Vol. 1, No. 1 (Aug. 1989)-. Periodical. English. Nine times a year. $1,026.00. Kluwer Academic Publishers / Massachusetts, PO Box 358, Accord Station, Hingham MA 02018. **Tel** (617)871-6600. **ED** Earl Swartzlander and S.Y. Kung. **LC** TK5102.5; .J67. **DD** 621.382/2. **CODEN** JVSPED. **[CCC]. Pr Rev. Acid Free.** available on microfilm and microfiche from University Microfilms International (UMI). Documents available from Article Express International, Ask*IEEE.
Desc: The key subject areas of interest to the journal are: design and analysis of signal processing algorithms and architecture, performance analysis (including measurement, modeling, and simulation) of signal processing systems, VLSI design methodology (including silicon compilation), design of arithmetic circuits and VLSI components used in signal processing (such as multipliers, dividers, and digital filter sections), specialized number systems (including on-line arithmetic, residue number systems, and logarithmic number systems), application of advanced technology to signal processing, generic and programmable signal processors, special purpose signal processor architectures (including parallel and pipeline signal processors), systolic/wave front arrays, and neutral nets.
Ind/Abst ACM Guide Comput. Lit.; Compumath Citation Index [Full Cov.]; Comput. Rev.; Ei Page One; Eng. Index Annu.; INSPEC (1989-); Zentralbl. Math. Ihre Grenzgeb.

UK/0950-4761
KEY ABSTRACTS. ANTENNAS & PROPAGATION. **See** Engineering-Abstracting, Bibliographies and Statistics.

UK/0950-477X
KEY ABSTRACTS. ARTIFICIAL INTELLIGENCE. **See** Engineering-Abstracting, Bibliographies and Statistics.

UK/0950-4796
KEY ABSTRACTS. COMPUTING IN ELECTRONICS AND POWER. **See** Engineering-Abstracting, Bibliographies and Statistics.

UK/0306-557X
KEY ABSTRACTS. ELECTRONIC CIRCUITS. **See** Engineering-Abstracting, Bibliographies and Statistics.

UK/0950-480X
KEY ABSTRACTS. ELECTRONIC INSTRUMENTATION. **See** Engineering-Abstracting, Bibliographies and Statistics.

UK/0953-1262
KEY ABSTRACTS. HIGH-TEMPERATURE SUPERCONDUCTORS. **See** Engineering-Abstracting, Bibliographies and Statistics.

UK/0952-7060
KEY ABSTRACTS. MICROELECTRONICS AND PRINTED CIRCUITS. **See** Engineering-Abstracting, Bibliographies and Statistics.

UK/0952-7079
KEY ABSTRACTS. MICROWAVE TECHNOLOGY. **See** Engineering-Abstracting, Bibliographies and Statistics.

UK/0950-4826
KEY ABSTRACTS. OPTOELECTRONICS. **See** Engineering-Abstracting, Bibliographies and Statistics.

UK/0950-4850
KEY ABSTRACTS. SEMICONDUCTOR DEVICES. **See** Engineering-Abstracting, Bibliographies and Statistics.

US/1050-1495
KING'S COALSTATS. MONTHLY COAL GUIDE. ELECTRIC UTILITIES REPORT. **See** Engineering-Mines and Mining Engineering.

GW/0172-8717
KONTAKTE. [Kontakte]. 1971-. Academic Scholarly Publication. German (English and French; summaries and/or abstracts in French and English). **CODEN** KONTDT. Documents available from CASDDS.
Ind/Abst Chem Inform; Chem. Abstr.

SW
KRAFTARET : SVENSKA KRAFTVERKSFORENINGENS VERKSAMHETSBERATTELSE. **Main/Corp** Svenska Kraftverksforeningen. **VFOAT** Svenska Kraftverkeforeningens Verksamhetsberattelse. Swedish. an. Svenska Kraftverksforeningen, Box 1704, 11187 Stockholm Sweden. **LC** HD9685.S85; S84A.

UN/0368-7155
KVANTOVAIA ELEKTRONIKA. [Kvantovaja elektron.]. **Added/Corp** Instytut Napivprovidnykiv (Akademiia Nauk Ukrainskoi RSR). (1966)-. Russian. mo. $379.95. Izdatelstvo Naukova Dumka / Ukrainian Academy of Sciences, Vladimirskaia Ulitsa 54, 252601 Kiev Ukraine. **Tel** 225-63-66, telex 131376. **(Subscription address:** East View Publications Inc., 3020 Harbor Lane North, Suite 110, Minneapolis MN 55447.**) LC** QC685; .K9. **CODEN** KVELA6. Documents available from Ask*IEEE, CASDDS.
Ind/Abst Chem. Abstr.; INSPEC (1972-); Int. Aerosp. Abstr.; Math. Rev.; Sci. Cit. Index.

RU/0368-7147
KVANTOVAJA ELEKTRONIKA (MOSKVA). (KVANTOVAIA ELEKTRONIKA.). [Kvant. elektron.]. (1974)-. Periodical. Russian (summaries and/or abstracts in English; table of contents in English). mo. $610.00. **(Subscription address:** East View Publications Inc., 3020 Harbor Lane North, Suite 110, Minneapolis MN 55447.**) CODEN** KVEKA3. Documents available from CASDDS. ***Continues*** *Kvantovaia Elektronika, 0368-7147.*
Ind/Abst Chem. Abstr.

PL
KWARTALNIK ELEKTRONIKI I TELEKOMUNIKACJI. **Added/Corp** Polska Akademia Nauk. Komitet Elektroniki i Telekomunikacji. **VFOAT** Electronics and Telecommunications Quarterly. Vol. 36, No. 1, (1990)-. Periodical. Polish (English). qt. $80.00. **(Subscription address:** ARS Polona, PO Box 1001, 00068 Warsaw Poland.**) LC** TK4; .R69. **CODEN** KETEED. ***Continues*** *Rozprawy Elektrotechniczne, 0035-9386.*

VM
KY THUAT IEN LC. Periodical. Vietnamese. bm. 20$00 single issue. Cong Ty Ien Lc Mien Bac, 20 Tran Nguyen Han, Hanoi Vietnam. **LC** TK4; .K9.

US
LAND & SEA-BASED ELECTRONICS FORECAST. (19??)-. English. Twelve times a year. $1390.00. Forecast International / DMS Inc., 22 Commerce Road, Newtown CT 06470. **Tel** (203)426-0800, FAX (203)426-1964, telex 467615. available on CD-ROM ($1595.00).

●US/1063-4002
LED LAMPS & DISPLAYS. [LED lamps disp.]. **Added/Corp** D.A.T.A. Business Publishing. **VFOAT** LED Lamps and Displays; LED Lamps and Displays Handbook; LED Lamps & Displays Handbook. **VAT** Light Emitting Diode Lamps and Displays. (1992)-. English. $99.00. DATA Business Publishing, PO Box 6510, 15 Inverness Way East, Englewood CO 80155. **Tel** (800)447-4666, (303)799-0381, FAX (303)799-4082. **LC** IN PROCESS. **DD** 621.

US/0273-6586
LEISURE TIME ELECTRONICS. ***Ceased.*** [Leis. time electron.]. -Ceased July/Aug. 1987. Periodical. English. mo. US Business Press, 11 West 19th Street, New York NY 10011-4202. **Tel** (212)953-9322. **ED** Dan Shannon. **LC** WMLC L 83/619. **DD** 338. **Ad Acc. Circ:** 15,466 (ctrl).
Desc: Consumer electronics trade publication specializing in audio, video, computer autosound, personal electronics, media magnetic, media satellites, and communications in general.

FR/0183-6552
LETTRE DE L'EQUIPEMENT ELECTRIQUE ET ELECTRONIQUE L. 3 E, LA. **VFOAT** Lettre de l'Equipement Electrique et Electronique L Trois E. (1978)-. Periodical. French. Forty-Four times a year. 3428.01F France; 3600.00F other. SEPP, 13 rue Ganneron, 75018 Paris France. **Tel** 011 33 1 42932243, FAX 011 33 1 42875024. **UDC** 66.

GW/0171-5496
LICHT (MUNCHEN). (LICHT.). [Licht]. 31.- Yearly volume; Jan. 1979-. Trade Publication. German. Eight times a year. DM65.40 Germany; DM69.00 other. Richard Pflaum Verlag Gmbh, Postfach 190737, D 80607 Munich Germany. **Tel** 011 49 89 126070, FAX 011 49 89 12607200, telex 5216075. **ED** Richard Pflaum. **LC** TH7700; .L47. **CODEN** LCHTAP. **[CCC]. Ad Acc. Circ:** 10,000 (ctrl). Documents available from Article Express International, Ask*IEEE. ***Supersedes in part*** *Lichttechnik.*
Desc: Only trade journal in German-speaking regions covering the full range of industrial lighting manufacturing and the planning, sales, installation and application of lighting.
Ind/Abst Bioeng. Abstr.; Coal Abstr.; Ei Page One; Eng. Index Annu.; Infomat Int. Bus.; INSPEC (1979-); SportSearch.

●US/1068-9761
LIGHT & ENGINEERING. [Light eng.]. **VFOAT** Light and Engineering. Vol. 1, No. 1 (1993)-. Periodical. English (translations available in Russian). qt. $145.00. Allerton Press, Inc., 150 Fifth Avenue, New York NY 10011. **Tel** (212)924-3950, FAX (212)463-9684, telex 427441 ALPRES. **DD** 744. **[CCC].**

AT
LIGHTING. (19??)-. English. Six times a year. 53.00Aus$ Australia; 60.00Aus$ others. Illuminating Engineering Society of New South Wales, PO Box 495, Kogarah New South Wales 2217 Australia. **Tel** 011 61 2 5883055. ***Continues*** *Lighting in Australia.*

US/0360-6325
LIGHTING DESIGN & APPLICATION. (LIGHTING DESIGN + APPLICATION : LD + A.). [Light. des. appl.]. **Added/Corp** Illuminating Engineering Society of North America. **VFOAT** Lighting Design Plus Application; L.D. and A; LD Plus A; L.D. + A; Lighting Design and Application. Vol. 12, No. 6 (June 1982)-. Periodical. English. mo. $39.00 (one year), $70.00 (two year), $90.00 (three year). Illuminating Engineering Society, 120 Wall Street, 17th Floor, New York NY 10005. **Tel** (212)248-5000 ext 111, FAX (212)248-5017, (212)248-5018. **ED** Kevin Heslin. **LC** TK1; .L23. **DD**

729/.28/05. **CODEN** LGDAAA. **[CCC].** Index available (December issue). cum. index. **Bk Rev**, (Qty: 10). **Ad Acc, Adv Mgr:** Beth Bay. **Circ:** 10,000 (ctrl). available on microfilm and microfiche from University Microfilms International (UMI). Documents available from Article Express International. ***Continues*** *Lighting Design & Application, 0360-6325.*
Desc: Magazine for lighting designers, interior designers, architects, consulting engineers, manufacturers, and all others concerned with illumination. Features articles on current lighting applications, including health care, industrial, theater, television recreation, outdoor, indoor, education behavior, office and computerized lighting. Latest news on energy, products, industry and IES activities.
Ind/Abst Appl. Sci. Technol. Index; Bioeng. Abstr.; Ei Page One; Eng. Index Annu.; Ergon. Abstr.; Int. Build. Serv. Abstr.; Saf. Health Work.

UK/0024-3418
LIGHTING EQUIPMENT NEWS. [Light. equip. news]. (1967)-. Periodical. English. Twelve times a year. £60.00. Maclean Hunter Ltd. / UK, Chalk Lane Cockfosters Road, Barnet Herts EN4 0BU England. **Tel** 011 44 81 2423000, FAX 011 44 81 9759753, telex 299072. Documents available from Ask*IEEE.
Ind/Abst INSPEC (1969-); Int. Build. Serv. Abstr.; Saf. Health Work.

US
LIGHTING HANDBOOK REFERENCE & APPLICATION. English. ir. $389.00. Illuminating Engineering Society, 120 Wall Street, 17th Floor, New York NY 10005. **Tel** (212)248-5000 ext 111, FAX (212)248-5017, (212)248-5018. **ED** Mark S. Rea, Rensselaer Polytechnic Institute, Lighting Research Center Troy, NY (518)276-6000.
Desc: Handbook covering topics realted to lighting including the science of lighting, lighting engineering, elements of design, and lighting applications.

AT/0728-5639
LIGHTING IN AUSTRALIA. ***Title Change.*** [Light. Aust.]. **Added/Corp** Illuminating Engineering Societies of Australia. Vol. 1, No. 1 (1981)-(19??). Periodical. English. bm. Illuminating Engineering Society of New South Wales, PO Box 495, Kogarah New South Wales 2217 Australia. **Tel** 011 61 2 5883055. **ED** Warren Julian. **CODEN** LIAUD4. **Ad Acc**. Documents available from Ask*IEEE. ***Continues*** *IES Lighting Review.* ***Continued by*** *Lighting.*
Ind/Abst Ergon. Abstr.; INSPEC (Aug. 1981-); Int. Build. Serv. Abstr.

UK
LIGHTING JOURNAL (RUGBY, WARWICKSHIRE). (THE LIGHTING JOURNAL : OFFICIAL JOURNAL OF THE INSTITUTION OF LIGHTING ENGINEERS.). **Added/Corp** Institution of Lighting Engineers (Great Britain). Vol. 51, No. 1 (March 1986)-. Periodical. English. bm. £36.00 UK; £48.00 (air mail) other. Institute of Lighting Engineers, Lennox House 9 Lawford Road, Rugby CV21 2DZ England. **Tel** 011 44 788 576492, FAX 011 44 788 540145. **ED** D Barnes. **LC** TK4188; .P8. **DD** 628.9/5/05. **CODEN** LIJOEW. Index available. **Bk Rev**. **Ad Acc**. **Circ:** 2,000. Documents available from Article Express International, Ask*IEEE. ***Continues*** *IPLE Lighting Journal, 0033-3603.*
Desc: Demonstrates various methods of using interior and exterior lighting; includes a trade section for providing information on new products. A mix of science and art.
Ind/Abst Curr. Technol. Index; Ei Page One; Eng. Index Annu. [Select. Cov.]; Ergon. Abstr.; Infomat Int. Bus.; INSPEC (1986); Int. Build. Serv. Abstr.

UK/0024-3426
LIGHTING RESEARCH & TECHNOLOGY. [Light. res. technol.]. **VAT** Lighting Research and Technology. (1969)-. Periodical. English. qt. £69.00 UK; £99.00 other. Chartered Institution of Building Services Engineers, 222 Balham High Road, Delta House, London SW12 9BS England. **Tel** 011 44 81 675 5211. **ED** Barry W Copping. **LC** TH7700.I4; A13. **DD** 621.32/0005. **CODEN** LRTEA9. Index available. cum. index. **Bk Rev**. **Pr Rev. Circ:** 1,000. available on microfilm and microfiche from University Microfilms International (UMI). Documents available from Article Express International, Ask*IEEE. ***Supersedes*** *Transactions of the Illuminating Engineering Society.*
Ind/Abst Bioeng. Abstr.; Ei Page One; Eng. Index Annu.; Ergon. Abstr.; Highw. Res. Abstr.; INSPEC (1969-); Int. Build. Serv. Abstr.; Saf. Health Work; SportSearch.

US/0741-4226
LINEAR CIRCUITS DATA BOOK. [Linear circuits data book]. **Added/Corp** Texas Instruments Incorporated. **VFOAT** Linear Circuits Databook. (1984)-. English. ir. $16.20 (per copy). Texas Instruments / Carrollton, PO Box 117692, Carrollton TX 75011. **Tel** (214)242-0864. **LC** TK7874.5; .L55. **DD** 621.381/73/0216.

US/0734-516X
LINEAR DISCONTINUED DEVICES. ***Ceased.*** [Linear discontin. devices]. Ed. 1 (Sept. 1982-Aug. 1983)-?. Periodical. English. an. DATA Business Publishing, PO Box 6510, 15 Inverness Way East, Englewood CO 80155. **Tel** (800)447-4666, (303)799-0381, FAX (303)799-4082. **ED** Steven d'Adolf. **LC** TK7874.5; .L56. **DD** 621.381/73/0216.
Desc: Contains specifications on 8,600 devices from 160 manufacturers.

US/0092-7201
LINEAR INTEGRATED CIRCUITS AND MOS DEVICES. **Main/Corp** RCA Corporation. Solid State Division. (1973)-. English. an. RCA Corporation, Box 3200, Somerville NJ 08876. **Tel** (609)734-3222. **LC** TK7874; .R18a. **DD** 621.381/73.

CN/0838-8539
LIST OF CERTIFIED ELECTRICAL EQUIPMENT (1988). (LIST OF CERTIFIED ELECTRICAL EQUIPMENT.). [List certif. electr. equip.]. **Main/Corp** Canadian Standards Association. 31st Ed. (1987/1988)-. English. Price varies per volume. Canadian Standards Association, 178 Rexdale Boulevard, Rexdale Ontario M9W 1R3 Canada. **Tel** (416)747-4000, (416)747-4044, telex 06-989344. **DD** 621.3/021/6. ***Continues*** *Canadian Standards Association. Certified Electrical Equipment., 0832-1825.*
Desc: Source of suppliers of certified products.

US
LIST OF MATERIALS ACCEPTABLE FOR USE ON SYSTEMS OF REA ELECTRIFICATION BORROWERS / RURAL ELECTRIFICATION ADMINISTRATION, U.S. DEPARTMENT OF AGRICULTURE. **Added/Corp** United States. Rural Electrification Administration. (19??)-. Government Publication. English. an (three quarterly supplements). $26.00 US; $32.50 other. Superintendent of Documents, US Government Printing Office, Washington DC 20402. **Tel** (202)275-3328, FAX (202)786-2377. **LC** TK453; .U55; TK4018; .U613 subser.
Desc: Contains listings of electrical materials acceptable for use on distribution transmission, and plant systems of REA borrowers.

NZ
LIVE LINES. **Added/Corp** Electrical Supply Authorities' Association of New Zealand. New Zealand Electrical Supply Authorities' Industrial Union of Employers. Electrical Supply Authorities' Association of New Zealand. Secretaries' Association. (19??)-. Periodical. English. ir (except January). Free. Electricity Supply Authority Association of New Zealand, PO Box 1017, Wellington New Zealand. **Tel** (04)859.632, FAX (04)842519. **ED** T. E. Hore. **LC** TK1; .L55. **Bk Rev**. **Ad Acc. Circ:** 1,600 (ctrl).
Desc: Received and read by elected members, officers and suppliers to electricity distribution industry.

FR/0024-7669
LUX; LA REVUE DE L'ECLAIRAGE. [Lux]. (1928)-. Periodical. French. Five times a year. 500.00F France; 560.00F (surface mail), 650.00F (air mail) other. Editions Lux, 52 Boulevard Malesherbes, 75008 Paris France. **Tel** 011 33 1 43872121, FAX 011 33 1 43871698. **ED** Jaques Valin. **Bk Rev**. **Ad Acc. Circ:** 3,500.
Ind/Abst Saf. Health Work.

US/0008-7882
MACHLETT CATHODE PRESS. **VFOAT** Cathode Press. Periodical. English. qt. **LC** TK7800; .M3. **DD** 621. **CODEN** CTPRAB. Documents available from Ask*IEEE.
Ind/Abst INSPEC (1968-).

US/0738-923X
MAGNETIC MEDIA INTERNATIONAL NEWSLETTER. **Added/Corp** Magnetic Media Information Services (Firm). (198?)-. Periodical. English. Six times a year (Every 10 weeks). $1,500. Magnetic Media Information Services, 841 Ikena Circle, Honolulu HI 96821. **Tel** (808)373-5330, FAX (808)377-5668. **ED** Laurence B. Lueck. **LC** TK7895.M3; I57. **DD** 621.397. ***Continues*** *International Newsletter (Magnetic Media Information Services (Firm)), 0738-923X.*
Desc: Concerned with technology, marketing and trends in all forms of recordable and recorded media, whether magnetic, optical or solid state.

US/0891-9801
MAGNETOHYDRODYNAMICS (NEW YORK, N.Y. 1989). ***Title Change.*** (MAGNETOHYDRODYNAMICS : THE JOURNAL OF THE INTERNATIONAL LIAISON GROUP ON MAGNETOHYDRODYNAMIC ELECTRICAL POWER GENERATION.). [Magnetohydrodynamics]. **Added/Corp** International Liaison Group on Magnetohydrodynamic Electrical Power Generation. Vol. 2, No. 1 (1989)-(199?). Periodical. English. qt. Taylor & Francis Ltd., Rankine Road, Basingstoke Hampshire, RG24 8PR United Kingdom. **Tel** 011 44 256 840366, FAX 011 44 256 479438, telex 858540. **(Subscription address:** Taylor & Francis Inc., 1900 Frost Road, Suite 101, Bristol PA 19007-1598.**) ED** William D. Jackson and A. E. Sheindlin. **LC** TK2970; .M327. **DD** 621.21/245. **CODEN** MPGEED. **[CCC].** Index available. **Bk Rev**. **Ad Acc. Circ:** 300. available on microfilm and microfiche from University Microfilms International (UMI). ***Continues*** *MHD Theory, Energy Conversion and Technology.* ***Continued by*** *Journal of Magnetohydrodynamics & Plasma Research.*
Desc: Provides international treatment of magnetohydrodynamics, implications for related technologies, and fundamental aspects of interest to engineers. As a means of keeping up to date on advances around the world, this journal is especially important for its English-language reports on developments in Eastern Europe and the Soviet Union.
Ind/Abst Zentralbl. Math. Ihre Grenzgeb.

RU
MAGNITO-POLUPROVODNIKOVYE I ELEKTROMASHINNYE ELEMENTY AVTOMATIKI. **Added/Corp** Riazanskii Radiotekhnicheskii Institut. No. 1 (1974)-. Russian. 0.52rub (single issue). Riazanskii Radiotekhn In-t, 390024 Ulitsa Gagarina 59/1, Riazan Russia. **LC** TJ212; .M28.

CN/0025-0988
MAITRE ELECTRICIEN, LE. [Maitre electr.]. **Added/Corp** Corporation des Maitres Electriciens du Quebec. Vol. 1 (May 1954)-. Periodical. French (English). mo (except Feb., Jul., Dec.). 26.00Can$ (one year), 42.00Can$ (two year). Corps of Master Electricians of Quebec, 5925 Boulevard Decarie, Montreal Quebec H3W 3C9 Canada. **Tel** (514)738-2184, FAX (514)738-2192. **ED** Chantale Baar. **Ad Acc.** Full Page (B&W) $495.00 (12 times). Half Page (B&W) $860.00 (12 times). **Circ:** 10,800 (ctrl).
Desc: Technical aspects of the electrical and electronics industry as it pertains to concepts, systems, installations, markets, economics, and current and forthcoming projects.
Ind/Abst Point Repere (1983-).

CN/0823-5198
MAITRE FRIGORISTE. ***Title Change.*** (LE MAITRE FRIGORISTE / CORPORATION DES MAITRES ENTREPRENEURS EN REFRIGERATION.). [Ma„itre frigoriste]. **Added/Corp** Corporation des Maitres Entrepreneurs en Refrigeration du Quebec. **VFOAT** Frigoriste. Vol. 1 (Nov. 1983)-(1993). Periodical. French. bm. Corporation des Maitres Entrepreneurs en Refrigeration Michel, Montreal Quebec H2A 3L9 Canada. **DD** 621.5/6/060714. ***Continued by*** *Clima Presse, 1198-1849.*

CN/0700-0774
MANUFACTURERS OF ELECTRIC WIRE AND CABLE (PRELIMINARY ED.). **See** Manufacturing.

GW/0344-8843
MARKT & TECHNIK. [Markt & Tech.]. **VFOAT** Markt und Technik. (197?)-. Periodical. German. wk. DM174.00 Germany; DM219.00 other. Verlag Markt & Technik, Hans Pinsel Str 2, W-8013 Haar B Munich Germany. **Tel** 011 49 89 461300, FAX 11 49 89 4613774. **UDC** 621.38. **[CCC].**
Ind/Abst Infomat Int. Bus.; PROMT.

US/0272-9172
MATERIALS RESEARCH SOCIETY SYMPOSIA PROCEEDINGS. [Mater. Res. Soc. symp. proc.]. **Main/Corp** Materials Research Society. **VFOAT** Symposia Proceedings. Vol. 1 (1980)-. Academic Scholarly Publication. English. ir. price varies per volume. Materials Research Society, 9800 McKnight Road, Suite 327, Pittsburgh PA 15237-6006. **Tel** (412)367-3003, FAX (412)367-4373. **DD** 620. **CODEN** MRSPDH. **[CCC].** Documents available from Article Express International, Ask*IEEE, CASDDS.
Ind/Abst Bioeng. Abstr.; Ceram. Abstr.; Chem. Abstr.; Ei Page One; Eng. Index Annu.; GeoRef; INIS Atomindex [Micro.]; INSPEC.

PL/0209-0058
MATERIAY ELEKTRONICZNE. (MATERIAY ELEKTRONICZNE / CENTRUM NAUKOWO-PRODUKCYJNE MATERIAOOW ELEKTRONICZNYCH.). [Mater. elektron.]. **Added/Corp** Poland. Centrum Naukowo-Produkcyjne Materiaoow Elektronicznych. (1973)-. Periodical. Polish (summaries and/or abstracts in English and Russian). **CODEN** MAELDK. Documents available from CASDDS.
Ind/Abst Chem. Abstr.

US/0885-9418
MATHEMATICAL CONCEPTS AND METHODS IN SCIENCE AND ENGINEERING. **See** Mathematics.

US/0277-6758
MCGRAW-HILL'S NATIONAL ELECTRICAL CODE HANDBOOK. ***Ceased.*** [McGraw-Hill's Natl. electr. code handb.]. **VFOAT** National Electrical Code Handbook. **VAT** McGraw Hill's National Electrical Code Handbook. 16th Ed.-?. English. ir. McGraw Hill Publishing Company, Inc., 1221 Avenue of the Americas, New York NY 10020. **Tel** (212)512-6410, (800)525-5003, FAX (212)512-6111. **ED** J F McPartland. **LC** TK260; .N2. **DD** 621.319/24/0218. ***Continues*** *NFPA Handbook of the National Electrical Code.*

US/1044-2812
MEANS ELECTRICAL CHANGE ORDER COST DATA. [Means electr. change order cost data]. **Added/Corp** Means (Firm). (1989)-. Periodical. English. an. $89.95. RS Means Company Inc. Trade

Sales, 100 Construction Plaza, PO Box 800, Kingston MA 02364. **Tel** (617)585-7880, (800)448-8182, FAX (617)585-7466. **LC** TK435; .M417. **DD** 621.319/24.

US/0748-7002
MEANS ELECTRICAL COST DATA. **See** Building and Construction.

JA/0387-5385
MEIDEN REVIEW. INTERNATIONAL EDITION. [Meiden rev., Int. ed.]. (1974)-. Periodical. English. Three times a year. Free. Meidensha Electric Manufacturing Company Limited, 2 1 2 Chome Ote Machi Chiyoda Ku, Tokyo 100 Japan. **Tel** 011 81 3 3490 3711. **DD** 621.3. ***Continues*** *Meidensha Review (International Edition), 0025-8741.*

US
MEMORY DISCONTINUED DEVICES. Ed. 1- (1987). English. an. $65.00. D A T A Inc, 9889 Willow Creed Road, PO Box 26875, San Diego CA 92126. **Tel** (619)578-7600, telex 910 530606. **ED** Steven D'Adolf. **LC** TK7874.5; .M45. **DD** 621.397/3.
Desc: Contains specifications on 10,000 devices from 119 manufacturers.

CN/0823-5430
MICROBITS. (MICROBITS : THE NEWSLETTER OF THE ONTARIO CENTRE FOR MICROELECTRONICS.). [Microbits]. Vol. 1, No. 1 (Mar. 1983)-. Newsletter. English. bm. Free. Ontario Centre for Microelectronics, Suite 400/1150 Morrison Drive, Ottawa Ontario K2H 9B8 Canada. **Tel** (613)596-6690, telex 053-4315. **ED** Ian Mumford. **DD** 001.64/06/0713. **Circ:** 15,000 (ctrl).
Desc: Newsletter about the Ontario Centre of Microelectronics and applications and developments in the field of microelectronics.

US/0738-713X
MICROCONTAMINATION. [Microcontamination]. **VFOAT** Micro Contamination. Vol. 1, No. 1 (June/July 1983)-. Periodical. English. mo. $125.00. Microcontamination, 3340 Ocean Park Boulevard/Suite 1000, Santa Monica CA 90405. **Tel** (310)392-5509, (312)762-2193, FAX (310)392-4920. **ED** Ed Bott. **LC** TK7870.27; .M53. **DD** 621.381/54. **CODEN** MCRCE5. **Circ:** 28,544. Documents available from Article Express International, Ask*IEEE.
Ind/Abst Ei Page One; Eng. Index Annu. [Select. Cov.]; INSPEC (Nov. 1989-); Trade Ind. Index.

NE/0167-9317
MICROELECTRONIC ENGINEERING. [Microelectron. eng.]. Vol. 1, No. 1 (Sept. 1983)-. Academic Scholarly Publication. English. Sixteen times a year (4 volumes). Fl1660.00. Elsevier Science Publishers BV, PO Box 211, 1000 AE Amsterdam Netherlands. **Tel** 011 31 20 5803642, FAX 011 31 20 5862696, telex 15682. **ED** John Kelly, Susumu Namba and Karel van der Mast. **LC** TK7871.85; .M516. **DD** 621.381/52. **CODEN** MIENEF. **[CCC].** available on microfilm and microfiche from University Microfilms International (UMI). Documents available from Article Express International, The Genuine Article, Ask*IEEE, CASDDS.
Desc: Brings together in one publication, the results of European, American and Japanese work in the rapidly expanding field of microelectronic devices.
Ind/Abst ACM Guide Comput. Lit.; Acoust. Abstr.; Chem. Abstr. (1983-); Comput. Rev.; Curr. Contents Eng. Tech. Appl. Sci.; Ei Page One; Eng. Mater. Abstr.; Eng. Index Annu.; INSPEC (Sept. 1983-); Res. Alert [Select. Cov.]; SCISEARCH.

UK/0026-2692
MICROELECTRONICS. (MICROELECTRONICS JOURNAL.). [Microelectronics]. **VFOAT** Microelectronics. Vol. 6, No. 2 (Dec. 1974)-. Academic Scholarly Publication. English. Eight times a year. $477.00 The Americas; £320.00 other. Elsevier Advanced Technology, An Imprint of Elsevier Science Ltd., The Boulevard, Langford Lane, Kidlington, Oxford OX5 1GB United Kingdom. **Tel** 011 44 865 843000, 011 44 865 843699, FAX 011 44 865 843010. **(Subscription address:** Elsevier Science Ltd. Oxford Fulfillment Centre, PO Box 800, Kidlington, Oxford OX5 1DX United Kingdom.) **ED** J. B. Butcher. **LC** TK7874; .M476. **DD** 621.381/7/05. **CODEN** MICEB9. **[CCC].** available on microfilm and microfiche from University Microfilms International (UMI). Documents available from Article Express International, Ask*IEEE, CASDDS. ***Continues*** *Microelectronics, 0026-2692;* ***Absorbed*** *The Journal of Semicustom ICS, 0264-3375.*
Desc: Worldwide coverage of the interchange between science and industry - new ideas, current opinion and practical applications. Covers the latest research and development projects, original research papers, abstracts, book reviews, current technology and future trends in the semiconductor component industry.
Ind/Abst Acoust. Abstr.; Bioeng. Abstr.; Chem. Abstr.; Ei Page One; Eng. Index Annu.; INSPEC (Jan./Feb. 1979-).

UK/0026-2714
MICROELECTRONICS AND RELIABILITY. [Microelectron. reliab.]. Vol 3, No. 1 (June 1964)-. Academic Scholarly Publication. English. mo. $1222.00 The Americas; £820.00 other. Pergamon Press, An Imprint of Elsevier Science Ltd., The Boulevard, Langford Lane, Kidlington, Oxford OX5 1GB United Kingdom. **Tel** 011 44 865 843000, 011 44 865 843699, FAX 011 44 865 843010. **(Subscription address:** Elsevier Science Ltd. Oxford Fulfillment Centre, PO Box 800, Kidlington, Oxford OX5 1DX United Kingdom.) **ED** G. W. Dummer and H. Reiche. **LC** TK7870; .M456. **DD** 621.381/05. **CODEN** MCRLAS. **[CCC].** **Bk Rev. Ad Acc. Pr Rev.** available on microfilm and microfiche from University Microfilms International (UMI). Documents available from Article Express International, The Genuine Article, Ask*IEEE, CASDDS. ***Continues*** *Electronics Reliability & Microminiaturization.*
Desc: Combines the practical, theoretical and statistical aspects of reliability with design, construction, engineering and testing of microelectronic systems, bringing an up to date continuity never previously achieved. It is the only regular international journal in the world covering this specific field.
Ind/Abst Acoust. Abstr.; Bioeng. Abstr.; Chem. Abstr.; Curr. Contents Eng. Tech. Appl. Sci.; Ei Page One; EMBASE; Eng. Index Annu.; Inf. Sci. Abstr.; INSPEC (1968-); Int. Aerosp. Abstr.; Oper. Res./Manag. Sci.; Pollut. Abstr. Indexes; Qual. Control Appl. Stat.; Res. Alert [Full Cov.]; Sci. Cit. Index; SCISEARCH; Soc. Sci. Cit. Index [Select. Cov.]; Stat. Theory Method Abstr. (1968).

UK/0736-6914
MICROELECTRONICS AND SIGNAL PROCESSING. **See** Computers.

UK
MICROELECTRONICS INTERNATIONAL. (19??)-. English. Three times a year. $98.00. Wela Publications Ltd, Asahi House, 10 Church Road, Port Erin, Isle of Man., British Isles. **Tel** 011 44 0 624 836044, FAX 011 44 0 624 835400. ***Continues*** *Hybrid Circuits.*

US/1054-9668
MICROELECTRONICS MANUFACTURING TECHNOLOGY. ***Ceased.*** [Microelectron. manuf. technol.]. Vol. 14, No. 1 (Jan. 1991)-Ceased (Jan. 1992). Periodical. English. mo. IHS Publishing Group, 17730 West Peterson Road, Libertyville IL 60048. **Tel** (708)362-8711, FAX (708)362-3484. **LC** TK7874; .M468. **DD** 621.381. **CODEN** MMATE7. Documents available from Ask*IEEE. ***Continues*** *Microelectronic Manufacturing and Testing, 0161-7427.*
Ind/Abst INSPEC (Jan. 1991-).

●US/1074-407X
MICROLITHOGRAPHY WORLD. [Microlithogr. world]. **Added/Corp** Society of Photo-optical Instrumentation Engineers. Vol. 1, No. 1 (Mar./Apr. 1992)-. Trade Publication. English. Four times a year. $31.50 US; $47.00 other. PennWell Publishing Company, 1421 South Sheridan, PO Box 1260, Tulsa OK 74101. **Tel** (918)835-3161, (800)331-4463, FAX (918)831-9497. **(Subscription address:** Microlithography World, Publishing Services, PO Box 1050, Tulsa OK 74101.) **LC** TK7871.85; .M519. **DD** 621.3815/31. **CODEN** MCWRE7.
Desc: Core technology in microelectronic chip manufacturing, flat panel display, microscopic sensors, micromechanical assembliers, bimedical electronics and other global high tech industries.

US/0895-2477
MICROWAVE AND OPTICAL TECHNOLOGY LETTERS. [Microw. opt. technol. lett.]. Vol. 1 (1988)-. English. Eighteen times a year. $375.00 US; $555.00 Canada and Mexico; $622.50 other. John Wiley & Sons, Inc., 605 Third Avenue, New York NY 10158-0012. **Tel** (212)850-6000, (212)850-6645, FAX (212)850-6088, telex 12-7063. **(Subscription address:** John Wiley & Sons / England, Baffins Lane, Chichester, West Sussex PO19 1UD England.) **ED** Kai Chang. **LC** TK7876; .M5235. **DD** 621.381/3/05. **CODEN** MOTLEO. **[CCC].** **Pr Rev.** available on microfilm and microfiche from University Microfilms International (UMI). Documents available from Article Express International, The Genuine Article, Ask*IEEE.
Desc: Answers the need for up-to-date information on the rapidly developing field of high frequency technology.
Ind/Abst Comput. Inf. Syst. Abstr. J. [Full Cov.]; Curr. Contents Eng. Tech. Appl. Sci.; Ei Page One; Elect. Comm. Abstr.; Eng. Index Annu.; INSPEC (1988-); Int. Aerosp. Abstr.; Mater. Sci. Eng. Abstr.; Mech. Eng. Abstr.; Res. Alert [Select. Cov.]; SCISEARCH; Solid State Supercond. Abstr.

UK/0960-667X
MICROWAVE ENGINEERING EUROPE. [Microw. eng. Eur.]. **VFOAT** Microwave Engineering. (1990)-. Periodical. English. bm. £60.00 UK and Northern Ireland; $130.00 other. Morgan Grampian, 40 Beresford Street Woolwich, London SE18 6BQ England. **Tel** 011 44 81 855 7777, FAX 011 44 81 855 5548, telex 896238. Documents available from Ask*IEEE. ***Continues*** *Microwave & RF Engineering, 0960-2267.*
Ind/Abst INSPEC (July/Aug. 1990-).

US/0192-6217
MICROWAVE JOURNAL (EURO-GLOBAL ED.). (MICROWAVE JOURNAL.). [Microw. j.]. (1964)-. Periodical. English. mo. $67.00 (one year) $110.00 (two year) US; $120.00 (one year), $175.00 (two year), other. Horizon House, 685 Canton Street, Norwood MA 02062. **Tel** (617)365-4595. **(Subscription address:** Microwave Journal, PO Box 9098, Braintree MA 02184.) **ED** Howard I Ellowitz. **DD** 621. **[CCC].** Index available. **Bk Rev. Ad Acc. Pr Rev. Circ:** 50,000 (ctrl). available on microfilm. Documents available from Ask*IEEE, Documents on Demand. ***Continues in part*** *Microwave Journal, 0026-2897.*
Desc: Edited for the microwave system designer, emphasizes design articles.
Ind/Abst Appl. Sci. Technol. Index; Energy Inf. Abstr.; Environ. Abstr.; F&S Index Plus Text, Int. [Select. Cov.]; INSPEC (1968-); Int. Packag. Abstr.; PROMT; Soc. Sci. Cit. Index [Select. Cov.].

US/0276-7961
MICROWAVE WORLD. [Microw. world]. Vol. 1 (Jan./Feb. 1980)-. Periodical. English. bm. $40.00. International Microwave Power Institute, 13542 Union Village Circle, Clifton VA 22024. **Tel** (703)830-5588, FAX (703)830-0281. **LC** TX657.O64; M5. **CODEN** MIWOD5. ***Continues*** *Microwave Energy Applications Newsletter, 0026-2889.*
Ind/Abst BioBusiness; Food Sci. Technol. Abstr.; Foods Adlibra; Int. Packag. Abstr.

US
MICROWAVES & RF PRODUCT DATA DIRECTORY. **VFOAT** Product Data Directory; Microwaves and RF Product Data Directory. (1984)-. English. an. Included with subscription to Microwaves & RF: $60.00 US; $100.00 Canada; $120.00 Mexico; $140.00 other. Penton Publishing, 1100 Superior Avenue, Cleveland OH 44114-2543. **Tel** (216)696-7000, FAX (216)696-0836. **(Subscription address:** Penton Publishing, PO Box 96732, Chicago IL 60693.) ***Continues*** *Microwaves Product Data Directory, 0194-7397.*

US
MICROWAVES & RF PRODUCT EXTRA. (19??)-. English. Six times a year. $20.00 US; $25.00 Canada; $35.00 Mexico; $55.00 other. Penton Publishing, 1100 Superior Avenue, Cleveland OH 44114-2543. **Tel** (216)696-7000, FAX (216)696-0836. **(Subscription address:** Penton Publishing, PO Box 96732, Chicago IL 60693.)

US/0194-7397
MICROWAVES PRODUCT DATA DIRECTORY. ***Title Change.*** (197?)-?. Directory. English. an. Hayden Publishing Company Inc, 10 Mulholland Drive, Hasbrouck Heights NJ 07604. **Tel** (201)393-6253. ***Continued by*** *Microwaves & RF Product Data Directory.*

UK/0309-4707
MIDDLE EAST ELECTRICITY. [Middle East electr.]. (1976)-. Periodical. English. ir (5 issues). $104.70 US and Canada. Reed Business Publishing / West Sussex, England, Perrymount Road, Haywards Heath, West Sussex RH16 3DH England. **Tel** 011 44 81 6523500. available on microfilm and microfiche from University Microfilms International (UMI). Documents available from Ask*IEEE.
Ind/Abst Energy Inf. Abstr.; INSPEC (Sept. 1984-).

GW
MIKROELEKTRONIK. **Main/Corp** Internationaler Elektronik-Arbeitskreis. Vol. 1 (1964)-. English (French and German). DM132.00 Germany; DM135.00 (surface mail), DM162.00 (airmail) other. VDE Verlag GmbH, Postfach 122305, D 10591 Berlin Germany. **Tel** 011 49 30 3480010. **LC** TK7874; .I595A. Index available. **Bk Rev. Ad Acc.**

RU/0544-1269
MIKROELEKTRONIKA. [Mikroelektronika]. **Added/Corp** Akademiia Nauk SSSR. Vol. 1, (1972)-. Academic Scholarly Publication. Russian. Six times a year. $115.00. Izdatelstvo Nauka / Akademiia Nauk, Publishing House of the Russian Academy of Sciences, Leninskii Porspekt 14, 117901 Moscow Russia. **Tel** 011 95 954-21-53, FAX 011 95 938-21-44, telex 411964. **(Subscription address:** East View Publications Inc., 3020 Harbor Lane North, Suite 110, Minneapolis MN 55447.) **CODEN** MKETA9. Documents available from Article Express International, Ask*IEEE, CASDDS.
Ind/Abst Chem. Abstr.; Ei Page One; Energy Res. Abstr. (Feb. 1979-); Eng. Index Annu.; INSPEC (May-June 1976-); Int. Aerosp. Abstr.

GW/0936-9104
MIKROWELLEN- & HF-MAGAZIN. [Mikrowellen- & HF-Mag.]. **VFOAT** Mikrowellen- und High-Fidelity-Magazin. (1988)-. Periodical. Multiple languages. ir. **UDC** 50/59. ***Continues*** *Mikrowellen- & Military-Electronics-Magazin, 0722-8244.*

US
MILITARY ELECTRONICS BRIEFING. **See** Military and Defense.

CL/0026-458X
MINERALES. [Minerales]. **Added/Corp** Instituto de Ingenieros de Minas de Chile. (Sept. 1945)-. Academic Scholarly Publication. Spanish. qt. $36.00 (one year), $70.00 (two year), $100.00 (three year). Instituto Ingenieros Minas Chile, Casilla 14668 Correo 21,

Santiago, Chile. **Tel** 011 56 2 717371. **LC** TN43; .M5. **CODEN** MINCAN. Index available (Free). Documents available from CASDDS.
Ind/Abst Chem. Abstr.

AT
MINGAY'S ELECTRICAL RETAILER. See Business-Retail.

US/0730-9775
MINUTES OF THE ... ANNUAL INTERNATIONAL CONFERENCE OF DOBLE CLIENTS. Main/Conf International Conference of Doble Clients. **VFOAT** Doble Client Conference Minutes. English. an. **LC** TK5; .D6. **DD** 621.3/05. ***Continues*** *Minutes of the Annual Conference on Doble Clients.*

JA/0369-2302
MITSUBISHI DENKI GIHO. [Mitsubishi Denki giho]. (1925)-. Periodical. Japanese. mo. $118.00. **(Subscription address:** Kyowa Book Company Inc., 1 38 Kanda Jinbocho Chiyoda-ku, Tokyo 101 Japan.**)** **LC** TK4; .M57. **CODEN** MTDNAF.

JA/0386-5096
MITSUBISHI ELECTRIC ADVANCE. Added/Corp Mitsubishi Denki Kabushiki Kaisha. (19??)-. Periodical. English. qt. $92.00. Mitsubishi Denki K.K., (Mitsubishi Electric Corp.), 2-3, Marunouchi 2 Chome, Chiyodaku, Tokyoto 100, Japan. **(Subscription address:** Maruzen Company Ltd., PO Box 5050, Import & Export Department, Tokyo 100 31 Japan.**)** Documents available from Article Express International, Ask*IEEE.
Ind/Abst Ei Page One; Eng. Index Annu.; INSPEC (Sept. 1977-).

SW
MODERN ELEKTRONIK. *Title Change.* (19??)-(19??). ir. Ekonomi Teknik Forlag AB, Klara Soedra Kyrkogata 1, 106 12 Stockholm Sweden. **Tel** 011 46 8 7966661, 011 46 8 7966500. ***Continued by*** *Elektroniktidningen, 1102-7495.*

US/0730-1197
MODULAR HI-FI COMPONENTS SERVICE DATA. VFOAT Sams Modular Hi-Fi Components Service Data; Sams Modular Hi-Fi Service Data. **VAT** Modular High Fidelity Components Service Data. MHF 205 (1981)-. English. sm. $9.95 per copy. Howard Sams & Company, Inc., 2647 Waterfront Parkway E Drive, Indianapolis IN 46214. **Tel** (800)428-7267, (317)298-5400. **LC** TK7881.7; .S233. **DD** 621.389/332/0288. **Bk Rev. Ad Acc.** ***Continues*** *Sams Modular Hi-Fi Components.*
Desc: Full service documentation for repair of modular hi-fi components.

US/0734-5178
MODULES/HYBRIDS. *Ceased.* [Modul./hybrids]. **Added/Corp** Derivation and Tabulation Associates, inc. **VAT** Modules Hybrids. Ed. 1 (Aug. 1982-Jan. 1983)-Ceased (1987). Periodical. English. an. DATA Business Publishing, PO Box 6510, 15 Inverness Way East, Englewood CO 80155. **Tel** (800)447-4666, (303)799-0381, FAX (303)799-4082. **ED** Steven d'Adolf. **LC** TK7874.5; .M6. **DD** 621.381/73.
Desc: Details 11,600 linear and interface solid-state modules and hybrid IC devices from over 84 manufacturers. Sections cover amplifiers, drivers, multiplexers, VCOs and more.

CN/0026-9379
MONDE DE L'ELECTRICITE, LE. [Monde electr.]. Vol.1 (Aug. 30, 1965). Periodical. French. mo. $32.00 Canada; $59.00 other. Kerrwil Publications Ltd., 395 Matheson Boulevard E, Mississauga Ontario L4Z 2H2 Canada. **Tel** (905)890-1846.

FR
MONITEUR PROFESSIONNEL DE L'ELECTRICITE, LE. Periodical. French. mo. Moniteur Professionnel, 2 A 12 rue de Bellerrie, Paris 19 France. **Tel** 200-33-05. **LC** TK2; .M65.

AT
MONITOR. VFOAT IREE Monitor. March 1979-. Periodical. English. mo (except January). 35.00Aus$. Institution Radio & Electronics Engineers, Commercial Unite 3, 2 New McLean Street, PO Box 79, Edgecliff Sydney New South Wales 2027 Australia. **Tel** (02)327 4822, FAX (02)327 6770. **ED** Heather Harriman. **LC** TK6540; .M67. **DD** 621.38/06/094. **Bk Rev. Ad Acc. Circ:** 3,000 (ctrl). Documents available from Ask*IEEE. ***Supersedes in part*** *Proceedings of the Institution of Radio and Electronics Engineers Australia.*
Desc: News magazine with information of general interest to electronics engineers including short technical articles, book reviews, conference and educational information, topical news and product details.
Ind/Abst INSPEC (Jan./Feb. 1976-).

US/1054-8483
MONTHLY DIGESTS OF SOVIET ELECTRONICS PAPERS. [Mon. dig. Sov. electr. pap.]. Periodical. English. mo. $200.00. Soviet Electronics Digest Dissemination Service, PO Box 857, Burtonsville MD 20866. **Tel** (301)384-5647. **ED** Iwao Pete Sugai. **LC** TK7800; .M585. **DD** 621.381.
Desc: Critical digests of Soviet electronics papers at MS and PhD levels.

US/0544-7259
MOSSBAUER EFFECT DATA INDEX. (1963)-. Monographic series. English. ir. Price varies per volume. Plenum Press, 233 Spring Street, New York NY 10013-1578. **Tel** (212)620-8000, (800)221-9369, FAX (212)463-0742, (212)807-1047, telex 23/421139. **LC** QC490; .M63. **DD** 537.5/352.

US/0736-2110
MOTORS AND GENERATORS. (CURRENT INDUSTRIAL REPORTS. MA-36H, MOTORS AND GENERATORS / U.S. DEPARTMENT OF COMMERCE, BUREAU OF THE CENSUS.). [Mot. gener.]. Began with 1965. Government Publication. English. an. $1.25. US Department of Commerce / Bureau of the Census, Data User Services Division, Customer Services, Washington DC 20233-0800. **Tel** (301)763-4100. **(Subscription address:** Superintendent of Documents, US Government Printing Office, Washington DC 20402.**)** **LC** HD9705.5.M673; U63. **DD** 338.4/76214/0973021. ***Continues*** *Current Industrial Reports. M36H, Motors and Generators.*
Desc: Presents timely data on the production, inventories, and orders of approximately 5,000 products, which represents 40 percent of all US manufacturing.

SP/0300-3787
MUNDO ELECTRONICO. EDICION INTERNACIONAL. (MUNDO ELECTRONICO.). [Mundo electron., Ed. int.]. (19??)-. Periodical. Spanish. Eleven times a year (Except Aug.). 9252ptas Andorra, Canarias, Ceuta Melilla & Portugal; 10640ptas Spain & Baleares; 11187ptas Europe; 17397ptas others. Cetisa Boixareu Editores SA, C Concepcion Arenal 5 7, 08027 Barcelona Spain. **Tel** 011 34 3 3527061. **LC** TK7800; .M85. **DD** 621.381/05. **CODEN** MUELCN. **[CCC].** Documents available from Ask*IEEE.
Ind/Abst GeoRef; Indice Med. Esp.; INSPEC (July 1974-).

BL
MUNDO ELETRICO. *Suspended.* Periodical. Portuguese. mo. $85.00. Editora Gruenwald Ltd, Caixa Postal 30 556, Sao Paulo Brazil. **Tel** 280-9411, telex 1130410. **LC** TK4; .M78. Index available. **Ad Acc. Circ:** 33,000.
Desc: Covers electricity, electrical engineering and electronics.

GW/0323-4657
NACHRICHTENTECHNIK - ELEKTRONIK. See Communication-Telecommunications.

US/0547-3578
NAECON. See Aeronautics, Astronautics.

US/0743-7072
NATIONAL DIRECTORY OF COMMUNICATION CUSTOMER PREMISE EQUIPMENT WIRING & EQUIPMENT INSTALLERS, WITH RATE INFORMATION BY CITY, STATE & REGION, THE. Directory. English. an. Carl D Southard Associates Inc, 27508. **LC** TK6011; .N37. **DD** 621.386/025/73.

US/0364-8095
NATIONAL ELECTRIC RATE BOOK. Main/Corp United States. Energy Information Admininstration. Office of Energy Data and Interpretation. (19??)-. Government Publication. English. ir. $22.50. Superintendent of Documents, US Government Printing Office, Washington DC 20402. **Tel** (202)275-3328, FAX (202)786-2377. **LC** HD9685.U4; U53c. **DD** 338.4/336362. ***Continues*** *National Electric Rate Book, 0364-8095.*
Desc: Consists of separate sections each representing a state.

US/0550-4406
NATIONAL ELECTRICAL CODE. See Fire Prevention.

US/0193-7324
NATIONAL ELECTRICAL CODE HANDBOOK (1978), THE. See Fire Prevention.

UK
NATIONAL POWER NEWS. (19??)-. English. Ten times a year. £20.00 UK; £24.00 Europe; £27.50 others. TG Scott Subscriber Services, 6 Bourne Enterprise Center, Wrotham Road, Borough Green, Kent TN15 8DG England. **Tel** 011 44 01 732 884023, FAX 011 44 01 732 884034.
Desc: The paper reports developments across the company which has a turnover in excess of ú4,000 million as well as significant developments across the privatised electricity supply industry.

JA/0048-0436
NEC RESEARCH & DEVELOPMENT. [NEC res. dev.]. **Added/Corp** Nippon Denki Kabushiki Kaisha. **VAT** Nippon Electric Company Research and Development. No. 1 (Oct. 1960)-. Academic Scholarly Publication. English. qt. $108.00. Nippon Electric Company, 33 1 5-Chome Shiba Minato-ku, Tokyo 108 Japan. **(Subscription address:** Maruzen Company Ltd., PO Box 5050, Import & Export Department, Tokyo 100 31 Japan.**)** **CODEN** NECRAU. cum. index. Documents available from Article Express International, The Genuine Article, Ask*IEEE, CASDDS.
Ind/Abst Bioeng. Abstr.; Chem. Abstr.; Comput. Inf. Syst. Abstr. J. [Full Cov.]; Curr. Contents Eng. Tech. Appl. Sci.; Ei Page One; Elect. Comm. Abstr.; Eng. Index Annu.; INSPEC (April 1968-); Int. Aerosp. Abstr.; Manuf. Process Eng. Abstr.; Mech. Eng. Abstr.; Res. Alert [Select. Cov.]; SCISEARCH; SEA Abstr.; Soc. Sci. Cit. Index [Select. Cov.]; Solid State Supercond. Abstr.

JA
NEMPO: NIHON DENSHIN DENWA KOSHA DENKI TSUSHIN KENKYUJO. Main/Corp Nihon Denshin Denwa Kosha. Musashino Denki Tsushin Kenkyujo. **Added/Corp** Nihon Denshin Denwa Kosha. Ibaraki Denki Tsushin. Kenkyujo. Nihon Denshin Denwa Kosha. Yokosuka Denki Tsushin Kenkyujo. Vol. 45 (1970)-. Periodical. Japanese. Nihon Denshin Denwa Kosha, 9-11 Midoricho 3-chome, Musashino 180 Japan. **LC** TK5101.A1; D44b. ***Continues*** *Denki Tsushin Kenkyujo (Japan). Nempo.*

UK/0047-9624
NEW ELECTRONICS. [New electron.]. (1968)-. Periodical. English. mo. £60.00 UK; £95.00 other. Findlay Publications Ltd, Franks Hall, Horton Kirby, Kent DA4 9LL England. **Tel** 011 44 (0322)222222, FAX 011 44 (0322)289577. **CODEN** NWELAC. **[CCC].** Documents available from Article Express International, Ask*IEEE. ***Absorbed*** *Electronics To-Day, 0013-483x.*
Ind/Abst Bioeng. Abstr.; Ei Page One; Eng. Index Annu.; Fluid Abstr., Civil Eng.; Fluid Abstr. Proc. Eng.; FLUIDEX (1973-); Infomat Int. Bus.; INSPEC (Oct. 1972-); Int. Aerosp. Abstr.; World Publ. Monit.; World Surf. Coat. Abstr.

NZ
NEW ELECTRONICS. English. Eleven times a year. 24.75NZ$ New Zealand; 33.00NZ$ Australia and Pacific Islands; 60.50NZ$ other. Associated Group Media Ltd, Private Bag 99915, Newmarket, Auckland 1031 New Zealand. **Tel** 11 64 9 3795393, FAX 11 64 9 3089523, telex 79121057. **ED** Christine Niven (Editor's Phone: 0064 9 3795393). **Ad Acc, Adv Mgr:** John Emmanuet. **Circ:** 8,000 (ctrl).
Desc: Covers electronics in New Zealand companies.

US
NEW ENGLAND ELECTRICAL BLUE BOOK. VFOAT Electrical Blue Book. (19??)-. English. an. $22.50. Trade Register & Data, 13 Main Street, Hingham MA 02043. **Tel** (617)729-0716. **ED** Timothy Marsac. **LC** TK12; .N48. **DD** 621.3/025/74. **Ad Acc. Circ:** 9,000 (ctrl).
Desc: Cross reference directory of products and services utilized in the electrical market in New England.

US/0744-1770
NEW GENERATING PLANTS. English. an. Power Engineering, 1250 Grove Avenue/Suite 302, Barrington IL 60010. **LC** TJ1; .P77 SUPPL. **DD** 621.31/213/05.

NZ/0549-026X
NEW ZEALAND ELECTRONICS REVIEW. *Ceased.* [N.Z. electron. rev.]. **VFOAT** Electronics Review. Vol. 1 (1967)-(1986). Periodical. English. Associated Group Media Ltd, Private Bag 99915, Newmarket, Auckland 1031 New Zealand. **Tel** 11 64 9 3795393, FAX 11 64 9 3089523, telex 79121057. **LC** TK7800; .N48. **CODEN** NZERBI. Documents available from Ask*IEEE.
Ind/Abst INSPEC (Nov. 1981-).

US/1043-433X
NEWSLETTER / IEEE PROFESSIONAL COMMUNICATION SOCIETY. [Newsl. - IEEE Prof. Commun. Soc.]. **Added/Corp** IEEE Professional Communication Society. **VFOAT** IEEE Professional Communication Society Newsletter; IEEE Professional Communication Society. **VAT** Institute of Electrical and Electronic Engineers Professional Communication Society Newsletter. (19??)-. Newsletter. English. qt. IEEE, Institution of Electrical and Electronics Engineers, Inc., 345 East 47th Street, New York NY 10017-2394. **Tel** (908)981-1393, FAX (908)981-9667. **DD** 808. ***Continues*** *IEEE Professional Communication Society. IEEE Professional Communication Society Newsletter, 0161-5718.*
Ind/Abst Index IEEE Publ.

US/0744-7531
NEWSLINE - NATIONAL RURAL ELECTRIC WOMEN'S ASSOCIATION (U.S.). (NEWSLINE.). **VFOAT** News Line. Periodical. English. qt. NREWA, 1800 Massachusetts Avenue NW, Washington DC 20036.

US
NFPA HANDBOOK OF THE NATIONAL ELECTRICAL CODE. *Title Change.* VFOAT Handbook of the National Electrical Code. 1932-. English. ir. National Fire Protection Association, 1 Batterymarch

Park, PO Box 9101, Quincy MA 02269-9101. **Tel** (617)770-3000, (800)344-3555. ***Continued by*** *National Electrical Code Handbook.*

JA/0285-3833
NIHON DENSHI ZAIRYO GIJUTSU KYOKAI KAIHO. [Nihon Denshi Zairyo Gijutsu Kyokai kaiho]. **Added/Corp** Nihon Denshi Zairyo Gijutsu Kyokai. **VFOAT** Bulletin of the Japan Electronic Materials Society. (1967)-. Academic Scholarly Publication. Japanese. Nihon Denshi Zairyo Gijutsu Kyokai, 1-38-2 Yoyogi, Shibuyu-ku, Tokyo 151 Japan. **CODEN** NDZKDI. Documents available from CASDDS.
Ind/Abst Chem. Abstr.

JA
NIKKEI EREKUTORONIKUSU. NIKKEI ELECTRONICS. **VFOAT** Nikkei Electronics. (1978)-. Periodical. Japanese (Japanese). Twenty-six times a year. $650.00. Overseas Courier Service Company Ltd., 9 Shibaura 2-Chome Minato-Ku, Tokyo 108 Japan. **Tel** 011 81 3 3453 8311. **(Subscription address:** Overseas Courier Service America Inc., 5 East 44th Street, New York, NY 10017 USA; telephone: (718)392-2330**)** **LC** TK7800; .N54.

US/1052-0716
NORTH AMERICAN DIRECTORY OF CONTRACT MANUFACTURERS IN ELECTRONICS. [North Am. dir. contract manuf. electron.]. **Added/Corp** Miller Freeman Publications, Inc. **VFOAT** Directory of Contract Manufacturers in Electronics. (1990)-. Directory. English. an. $177.00. Miller Freeman Inc., 600 Harrison Street, San Francisco CA 94107. **Tel** (415)905-2337, FAX (415)905-2240, telex 278273. **ED** Vincent Ridley. **LC** HD9696.A3; N676. **DD** 621.381/029/47. Index available. **Ad Acc. Circ:** 1,500. available on diskette.
Desc: Contains contract manufacturers, consultants and equipment manufacturers in electronics.

US/1049-0736
NORTHEAST POWER REPORT. [Northeast power rep.]. (19??)-. Newsletter. English. bw. $825.00 US and Canada; $875.00 other. McGraw Hill Publishing Company, Inc., 1221 Avenue of the Americas, New York NY 10020. **Tel** (212)512-6410, (800)525-5003, FAX (212)512-6111. **(Subscription address:** McGraw Hill Management Information Center, 1221 Avenue of the Americas, 36th Floor, New York NY 10020.**)** **DD** 338.

IT
NOTIZIARIO ELETTRICO. Italian. sa. Free. EPE-Editrice Publ Editoriale, Via La Spezia 33, 20142 Milan Italy. **Tel** 011 39 2 89500673.

US
NTIS ALERT. DETECTION & COUNTERMEASURES. **Added/Corp** United States. National Technical Information Service. (19??)-. Periodical. English. Twenty-four times a year. $140.00 US; $195.00 other. National Technical Information Service - NTIS, Room 2027S, 5285 Port Royal Road, Springfield VA 22161. **Tel** (703)487-4630, (703)487-4660, (703)487-4650, FAX (703)321-8547, telex 89-9405.

US
NTIS ALERT. ELECTROTECHNOLOGY. **Added/Corp** United States. National Technical Information Service. (19??)-. Periodical. English. Twenty-four times a year. $145.00 US; $210.00 other. National Technical Information Service - NTIS, Room 2027S, 5285 Port Royal Road, Springfield VA 22161. **Tel** (703)487-4630, (703)487-4660, (703)487-4650, FAX (703)321-8547, telex 89-9405. ***Continues*** *Electrotechnology. NTIS, 0163-1462.*

SP
NUEVA ELECTRONICA. Spanish. mo. 3150.00ptas (one year), 6300.00ptas (two year) Spain; 3535.00ptas Portugal; 3920.00ptas Europe; 4690.00ptas, $52.14 other. Comercial Electronica Rte SA, Manuel Luna 4, 28020 Madrid Spain. **Tel** 011 34 1 5716857.

IT
NUOVA ELETTRAUTO. (19??)-. Italian. Eleven times a year. L63000.00 Italy; L120000.00 other. Morales Srl, Via Spreafico 10, 20052 Monza Mi Italy. **Tel** 011 39 39 2302363. ***Continues*** *Elettrauto.*

IT
NUOVA ELETTRONICA. (19??)-. Italian (Greek, Modern and Spanish, French). ir. L60000 Italy; L90000 other. Nuova Elettronica, Via Cracovia 19, 40139 Bologna Italy. **Tel** 011 39 51 461109, 011 39 51 461207, FAX 011 39 51 450387. Index available. cum. index. **Ad Acc. Circ:** 16,000 (ctrl).

UK
OFFICE OF ELECTRICITY REGULATION ANNUAL REPORT. English. an. £12.50. Her Majesty's Stationery Office, 51 Nine Elms Lane, London SW8 5DR England. **Tel** 011 44 71 873 8459, 011 44 71 873 8499, FAX 011 44 71 873 8499, 011 44 71 873 8456, telex 297138. **(Subscription address:** PO Box 276, Public Centre, London SW8 5DT England**)**

JA/0386-5576
OHM. [Ohm]. **VFOAT** Denki Zasshi OHM. (1914)-. Periodical. Japanese. mo. $266.00. Omusha, (Ohm-Sha Ltd.), 3-1, Kanda Nishikicho, Chiyodaku, Tokyoto 101, Japan. **(Subscription address:** Maruzen Company Ltd., PO Box 5050, Import & Export Department, Tokyo 100 31 Japan.**)**
Ind/Abst Coal Abstr.

FR/0030-2430
ONDE ELECTRIQUE. (L'ONDE ELECTRIQUE.). [Onde electr.]. **Added/Corp** Societe des Radioelectriciens. Societe des Electriciens, des Electroniciens et des Radioelectriciens. (1920)-. Periodical. French (summaries and/or abstracts in English). Six times a year. 661.12F France; 847.20F EEC countries except France; 865.00F other. Revue Generale Electricite SA, 48 rue de la Procession, 75724 Paris Cedex 15 France. **Tel** 011 33 1 44496000. **ED** Lucien Boithias. **CODEN** ONELAS. **[CCC].** Index available. **Bk Rev. Ad Acc. Pr Rev. Circ:** 3,000 (ctrl). Documents available from Article Express International, The Genuine Article, Ask*IEEE, CASDDS.
Desc: Covers components, micro electronics, telecommunications, measurements, radiobroadcasting, television, navigation, and signal processing.
Ind/Abst Acoust. Abstr.; Bioeng. Abstr.; Ceram. Abstr.; Chem. Abstr. (1922-1983); Curr. Contents Eng. Tech. Appl. Sci.; Ei Page One; Energy Res. Abstr.; Eng. Index Annu. [Select. Cov.]; INSPEC (1968-); Int. Aerosp. Abstr.; Res. Alert [Select. Cov.]; SCISEARCH; Soc. Sci. Cit. Index [Select. Cov.].

CN/0711-3501
ONTARIO ELECTRICAL CONTRACTOR, THE. [Ont. electr. contract.]. **Main/Corp** Electrical Contractors Association of Ontario. **VFOAT** Annual Report. Periodical. English. bm. Free to members. Ontario Electrical Contractors East/Suite 605, Toronto Ontario M4P 1J5 Canada. **DD** 621.3.

FR/0247-4808
OPTO ELECTRONIQUE. [Opto electron.]. **VFOAT** Opto. (1980)-. Periodical. French (summaries and/or abstracts in English). Five times a year. $120.00. Masson Editeur, Box Postale 22, 41353 Vineuil 16 France. **Tel** 011 33 54 438994. **LC** TA1671; .O7. **DD** 621.38/0414. available on microfilm and microfiche from University Microfilms International (UMI).
Ind/Abst Energy Res. Abstr. (Aug. 1982-).

US/0732-4235
OPTOELECTRONICS DISCONTINUED DEVICES. ***Ceased.*** [Optoelectron. discontin. devices]. Ed. 4 (May 1981 through April 1982)-?. English. an. DATA Business Publishing, PO Box 6510, 15 Inverness Way East, Englewood CO 80155. **Tel** (800)447-4666, (303)799-0381, FAX (303)799-4082. **ED** Steven d'Adolf. **LC** TK8304; .O67. **DD** 621.3815/42/0216. ***Continues*** *Discontinued Devices. Optoelectronics, 0271-2121.*
Desc: Contains specifications on 12,600 devices from 118 manufacturers.

JA/0912-5434
OPTOELECTRONICS (TOKYO). (OPTOELECTRONICS--DEVICES & TECHNOLOGIES.). [Optoelectronics]. **VFOAT** Devices and Technologies; Optoelectronics. **VAT** Optoelectronics, Devices and Technologies. Vol. 1, No. 1 (June 1986)-. Periodical. English. Four times a year. $156.00. Mita Shuppankai, (Mita Press), Ochanomizu Senta Biru, 2-12, Hongo 3 Chome, Bunkyoku, Tokyoto 113, Japan. **(Subscription address:** Maruzen Company Ltd., PO Box 5050, Import & Export Department, Tokyo 100 31 Japan.**)** **LC** TA1750; .O6737. **DD** 621.381/045. **CODEN** ODTEEG. available on microfilm and microfiche from University Microfilms International (UMI). Documents available from Article Express International, Ask*IEEE.
Desc: Journal dealing with the interaction of photons and electrons, and related devices and technologies. The journal publishes original papers and review articles on all areas of optoelectronics.
Ind/Abst Ei Page One; Eng. Index Annu.; INSPEC (Dec. 1987-).

UN/1011-6559
OPTOELEKTRONIKA I POLUPROVODNIKOVAA TEHNIKA. (OPTOELEKTRONIKA I POLUPROVODNIKOVAIA TEKHNIKA / AKADEMIIA NAUK UKRAINSKOI SSR, INSTITUT POLUPROVODNIKOV.). [Optoelektron. poluprovodn. teh.]. **Added/Corp** Instytut Napivprovidnykiv (Akademiia nauk Ukrainskoi RSR). (1982)-. Periodical. Ukrainian. 1.50rub (single issue). **LC** TK7871.85; .O63. **DD** 621.38/0414. **CODEN** OPTEDV. Documents available from Ask*IEEE, CASDDS. ***Continues*** *Poluprovodnikovaia Tekhnika i Mikroelektronika, 0554-6222.*
Ind/Abst Chem. Abstr.; INSPEC (1982-); Int. Aerosp. Abstr.

GW
OPTOELEKTRONISCHE BAUELEMENTE. **VFOAT** Optoelectronic Devices. Multiple languages (English and German). AEG-Telefunken, Postfach 1109, Theresienstrasse 2, Heilbronn Germany. **LC** TK8300; .O68.

IT/1120-8724
OPTOLASER MILANO. ***Ceased.*** [Optolaser Milano]. (1990)-(1992). Periodical. Italian. bm. Masson S.P.A, Via Statuto 2/4, 20121 Milan Italy. **Tel** 011 39 2 63671, FAX 011 39 2 6367211. **UDC** 654. **Bk Rev. Ad Acc. Circ:** 5,000 (ctrl).

AU/0029-9618
OZE. OSTERREICHISCHE ZEITSCHRIFT FUER ELEKTRIZITATSWIRTSCHAFT. ***Ceased.*** [Osterr. Z. Elektr.wirtsch.]. **VFOAT** Osterreichische Zeitschrift fur Elektrizitatswirtschaft. (July/ Aug. 1948)-Vol. 46, No. 12 (Dec. 1993). Academic Scholarly Publication. German. Twelve times a year. Springer-Verlag GmbH & Company KG, Heidelberger Platz 3, D 14197 Berlin Germany. **Tel** 011 49 30 8207223, FAX 011 49 30 8214091, telex 183 319 SPBLN D. **(Subscription address:** Springer Verlag New York Inc. / for North America, 44 Hartz Way, Secaucus NJ 07096.**)** **ED** J Gartner. **LC** TK3; .O4. **DD** 621.3/05. **CODEN** OZELAA. **[CCC].** Documents available from Article Express International, Ask*IEEE.
Desc: Original articles focus on technical problems of construction and management of energy sources, economic aspects of large projects and new technologies of energy extraction. Supplementary numbers report on trends in energy technology. Inserts cover special problems of energy production and transfer.
Ind/Abst Bioeng. Abstr.; Coal Abstr.; Ei Page One; EMBASE; Eng. Index Annu.; INSPEC (1968-); Saf. Health Work.

US/0092-8828
P.B.X. SYSTEMS GUIDE. (PBX SYSTEMS GUIDE.). [P.B.X. syst. guide]. **Added/Corp** Marketing Programs and Services Group. (March 1972)-. English. ir. $595.00. The ARIES Group MPSG, 1350 Piccard Drive, Suite 300, Rockville MD 20850. **Tel** (301)840-0800. **LC** TK6195; .P18. **DD** 621.385.

US/0734-7464
PAPERS PRESENTED AT THE ... ANNUAL CONFERENCE / RURAL ELECTRIC POWER CONFERENCE. [Pap. present. annu. conf. - Rural Electr. Power Conf.]. **Main/Conf** Rural Electric Power Conference. **VFOAT** Rural Electric Power Conference. Began in 1957. English. an. IEEE, Institution of Electrical and Electronics Engineers, Inc., 345 East 47th Street, New York NY 10017-2394. **Tel** (908)981-1393, FAX (908)981-9667. **(Subscription address:** IEEE Service Center, 445 Hoes Lane, Piscataway, NJ 08854; telephone: (201)981-1393**)** **LC** TK4018; .R78A. **DD** 621.39/3/05. **CODEN** PEPCD7. Documents available from Article Express International, Ask*IEEE.
Ind/Abst Bioeng. Abstr.; Ei Page One; Eng. Index Annu.; Index IEEE Publ.; INSPEC.

UK
PAPERS PRESENTED AT THE INTERNATIONAL SYMPOSIUM OF JET CUTTING TECHNOLOGY. English. ir. £72.00. BHR Group Ltd Brit Hydrom. Research, Cranfield, Bedford MK43 0AJ England. **Tel** 011 44 243 750422, FAX 011 44 243 750074, telex 825059. **(Subscription address:** International Fluid Power Symposium, Conference Secy, Cranefield Bedford MK43 0AJ England**)**

US/0736-7805
PAPERS PRESENTED AT THE PICA CONFERENCE. (POWER INDUSTRY COMPUTER APPLICATIONS CONFERENCE, PICA : PAPERS PRESENTED AT THE ... PICA CONFERENCE. / SPONSORED BY IEEE POWER ENGINEERING SOCIETY AND THE IEEE TORONTO SECTION.). [Pap. presented PICA Conf.]. **Added/Corp** IEEE Power Engineering Society. **VFOAT** P.I.C.A. ... Conference Papers; PICA ... Conference Papers. **VAT** Papers Presented at the Power Industry Computer Applications Conference. (1977)-. Periodical. English. ir. IEEE, Institution of Electrical and Electronics Engineers, Inc., 345 East 47th Street, New York NY 10017-2394. **Tel** (908)981-1393, FAX (908)981-9667. **LC** TK5; .P68. **DD** 621.31/028/5. **CODEN** PICPEA. **[CCC].** Documents available from Ask*IEEE. ***Continues*** *Power Industry Computer Applications Conference. PICA Conference Proceedings (1971).*
Ind/Abst INSPEC.

FR/1146-5387
PASCAL. E29, SEMICONDUCTEURS, MATERIAUX ET COMPOSANTS. ***Ceased.*** **Added/Corp** Institut de l'Information Scientifique et Technique (France). **VFOAT** Semiconducteurs, Materiaux et Composants; Semiconductors, Materials, and Components; PASCAL. E29, Semiconductors, Materials, and Components. No. 1 (1990)-No. 10 (Dec. 1992). French. ir. CNRS / Institut d'Information Scientifique et Technique, (Centre National de la Recherche Scientifique), 15 Quai Anatole France, Paris 75700 France. **Tel** 011 33 1 47531515, telex 299 356 F. **(Subscription address:** Institut de l'Information Scientifique et Technique, 2 Allee du Parc de Brabois, 54514 Vandoeuvre Nancy France**)** ***Continues*** *PASCAL Explore. E29, Informatique.*

US/0363-1885
PC, PERSONAL COMMUNICATIONS SHOW DAILY. **VFOAT** Personal Communications Show Daily. V. 1- March 30, 1976-. English. St Regis Publications, 390 5th Avenue, New York NY 10018. **LC** TK6570.C5; P18. **DD** 621.3845/4/05.

HU/0031-532X
PERIODICA POLYTECHNICA: ELECTRICAL ENGINEERING. ELEKTROTECHNIK. [Period. polytech. Electr. eng. Elektrotech.]. **Added/Corp** Budapesti Muszaki Egyetem. **VFOAT** Electrical Engineering; Electrotechnik. Vol. 1 (1957)-. Periodical. English (German). qt. $12.00. **(Subscription address:** Kultura, PO Box 149, H 1389 Budapest 62 Hungary.**) ED** F. Szabadvary. **LC** TK4; .P4. **CODEN** PPYTA7. **[CCC]. Bk Rev. Circ:** 900 (ctrl). Documents available from Article Express International, Ask*IEEE.
Desc: All topics of electrical engineering, telecommunication and electrotechnics and electronics.
Ind/Abst Bioeng. Abstr.; Ei Page One; Eng. Index Annu. [Select. Cov.]; INSPEC (1968-); Int. Aerosp. Abstr.

US/0275-9306
PESC RECORD. [PESC rec.]. **Main/Conf** IEEE Power Electronics Specialists Conference. **VAT** Power Electronics Specialists Conference Record. 1973-. English. ir. Institute of Electrical and Electronics Engineers / IEEE, 445 Hoes Lane, Piscataway NJ 08855. **Tel** (908)981-0060. **(Subscription address:** IEEE / Institute of Electrical and Electronics Engineers, 445 Hoes Lane, PO Box 1331, Piscataway NJ 08855-1331.**) LC** TL1100; .P68. **DD** 621.31/3. **CODEN** PRICDT. **[CCC].** Bound Index published separately, free upon request. Documents available from Article Express International, Ask*IEEE. ***Continues*** *Record - I.E.E.E. Power Processing and Electronics Specialists Conference, 0090-2381.*
Ind/Abst Bioeng. Abstr.; Ei Page One; Eng. Index Annu.; Index IEEE Publ.; INSPEC.

CN/0711-5350
PHILIGRAM (1980). (PHILIGRAM.). [Philigram]. **Added/Corp** Philips Electronics. Electron Devices Division. (1980)-. Periodical. English. ir. Free. Philips Electronics Ltd, Electron Devices Division, 601 Milner Avenue, Scarborough Ontario M1B 1M8 Canada. **DD** 621.381/05. ***Continues*** *Philips Bulletin, 0709-5392.*

NE/0165-5817
PHILIPS JOURNAL OF RESEARCH. [Philips j. res.]. **Added/Corp** Philips Natuurkundig Laboratorium. Vol. 33 (1978)-. Academic Scholarly Publication. English. Four times a year. $142.00 The Americas; £95.00 other. Elsevier Advanced Technology, An Imprint of Elsevier Science Ltd., The Boulevard, Langford Lane, Kidlington, Oxford OX5 1GB United Kingdom. **Tel** 011 44 865 843000, 011 44 865 843699, FAX 011 44 865 843010. **(Subscription address:** Elsevier Science Ltd. Oxford Fulfillment Centre, PO Box 800, Kidlington, Oxford OX5 1DX United Kingdom.**) ED** P. J. Severin. **LC** Q1; .P47. **DD** 500.2/05. **CODEN** PHJRD9. **[CCC].** cum. index. **Circ:** 1,700 (ctrl). available on microfilm from University Microfilms International (UMI). Documents available from Article Express International, The Genuine Article, Ask*IEEE, CASDDS. ***Continues*** *Philips Research Reports, 0031-7918.*
Desc: Research papers describing work carried out in laboratories of Philips.
Ind/Abst Acoust. Abstr.; Alum. Ind. Abstr.; Ceram. Abstr.; Chem. Abstr.; Curr. Contents Eng. Tech. Appl. Sci.; Energy Inf. Abstr.; Eng. Mater. Abstr.; Eng. Index Annu.; Ergon. Abstr.; INSPEC (1978-); Int. Aerosp. Abstr.; Leadscan; Mass Spect. Bull.; Math. Rev.; Met. Abstr.; Pollut. Abstr. Indexes; Res. Alert [Full Cov.]; Sci. Cit. Index; SCISEARCH; World Ceram. Abstr.; Zentralbl. Math. Ihre Grenzgeb.

NE
PHILIPS' TECHNISCHE RUNDSCHAU. Began in 1936. Periodical. German. mo. Fl16.25 students, Fl62.50 others. N V Philips, Gloeilampenfabrieken Abt 862.89, Bankverbindung F Lanschot, Eindhoven Netherlands. **LC** TK1; .P53. **DD** 621.3/05.

US/1067-5345
PHOTONICS AND OPTOELECTRONICS. See Physics-Light, Optics, Radiation.

US/0731-4671
PHOTOVOLTAIC INSIDER'S REPORT. See Energy.

US/8750-8591
PLATEAU ELECTRIC NEWS. Periodical. English. qt. $0.60 members. Plateau Electric Cooperative, PO Drawer T, Oneida TN 37841.

US/0271-7166
PLS LISTING. POWER FACILITIES OPERATED BY THE BUREAU OF RECLAMATION. (PLS LISTING. POWER FACILITIES OPERATED BY THE BUREAU OF RECLAMATION.). [PLS listing, Power facil. oper. Bur. Reclam.]. **Main/Corp** United States. Bureau of Reclamation. **VFOAT** Power Facilities Operated by the Bureau of Reclamation. (19??)-. Government Publication. English. an. US Department of the Interior Bureau of Reclamation, 1849 C Street NW, Room 7654, Washington DC 20240. **Tel** (202)208-4157, FAX (202)343-3484. **LC** TK1; .U54. **DD** 363.6/2/0973. ***Continues*** *PLS Listing. Hydroelectric Plants, Transmission Lines and Substations Operated by the Bureau of Reclamation.*

RU
POLUPROVODNIKOVAIA ELEKTRONIKA V TEKHNIKE SVIAZI. (19??)-. Periodical. Russian. 0.90rub. Izdatelstvo Sviaz, Christoprudnyi Bulvar D 2, 101000 Moscow Russia. **LC** TK5103; .P56.

SZ
POLYSCOPE, COMPUTER, ELECTRONICS, COMMUNICATION. English. ir (forty times a year). 130.00F. Verlag Binkert AG, Baslerstrasse 15, CH-4335 Laufenburg Switzerland. **Tel** 011 41 64 697272, FAX 011 41 64 697333. **Ad Acc.** ctrl circ.
Desc: News and trend reports from automatic, electronic, data-technics, control techniques and measurement engineering in industrial environment.

NE/0925-5672
POLYTECHNISCH TIJDSCHRIFT. ELEKTRONICA ELEKTROTECHNIEK (1990). (POLYTECHNISCH TIJDSCHRIFT, ELEKTRONICA ELEKTROTECHNIEK.). [Polytec. tijdschr., Elektron. elektrotech. (1990)]. (1990)-. Periodical. Dutch. mo. Fl165.00. Ten Hagen and Stam BV, Postbus 34, 2501 AG The Hague Netherlands. **Tel** 011 31 70 3569100. **CODEN** PEELEEPTEEEU. Documents available from Ask*IEEE. ***Continues*** *Pt, Elektronica Elektrotechniek, 0925-5664.*
Ind/Abst INSPEC (May 1990-).

US/1042-170X
POPULAR ELECTRONICS (1989). (POPULAR ELECTRONICS.). [Pop. electron.]. **VFOAT** Popular Electronics Including Hands-On Electronics. Vol. 6, No. 2 (Feb. 1989)-. Periodical. English. mo. $21.95. Gernsback Publications Inc, 500 B Bi-County Boulevard, Farmingdale NY 11735. **Tel** (516)293-3000. **(Subscription address:** Kable Publishers Aide, 308 East Hitt Street, Subscription Department, Mt. Morris IL 61054-1473.**) LC** TK7800; .P65. **DD** 621.381/05. available on microfilm and microfiche from University Microfilms International (UMI). ***Absorbed*** *Hands-On Electronics, 0743-2968.*
Desc: The magazine for the electronics hobbyist.
Ind/Abst Abr. Read. Guide Period. Lit.; Index Inf.; Microcomput. Index (Jan. 1982-Oct. 1982); Read. Guide Period. Lit.; Mag. Index.

UK
POST NEWS. English. mo. £143.00 UK; $249.00 other. Post News, Stoke Sub Hamdon, Somerset TA14 6BR England. **Tel** 0935 88 1245, FAX 0935 88 1860. **ED** Ronald Brown.
Desc: Articles and latest news on electronics at the point of sale in retailing, banking, hotels, travel, etc.

US/1071-2445
POWER DELIVERY PRODUCT NEWS. See Energy.

US/0271-2652
POWER DIRECTORY. [Power dir.]. Directory. English. $75.00. Utility Data Inst, 1700 K Street NW/Suite 400, Washington DC 20006. **Tel** (202)466-3660. **LC** TK1223; .P67. **DD** 621.31/2132/02573.

US/0032-5961
POWER ENGINEERING (BARRINGTON, ILL.). See Engineering-Mechanical Engineering and Machinery.

●US/1069-4994
POWER ENGINEERING INTERNATIONAL. [Power eng. int.]. Vol. 1, No. 1 (Feb. 1993)-. Periodical. English. Six times a year. $27.00 US; $63.00 other. PennWell Publishing Company, 1421 South Sheridan, PO Box 1260, Tulsa OK 74101. **Tel** (918)835-3161, (800)331-4463, FAX (918)831-9497. **(Subscription address:** Power Engineering International, Publishing Services, PO Box 1440, Tulsa OK 74101.**) DD** 621.
Desc: Serves the global electric power generation and transmission industry. Includes electric utilities and power generation companies, industrial and independent power companies government energy departments, etc.

UK/0950-3366
POWER ENGINEERING JOURNAL. [Power eng. j.]. **Added/Corp** Institution of Electrical Engineers. Vol. 1, No. 1 (Jan. 1987)-. Periodical. English. Six times a year. £83.00 EEC countries; £92.00 other. Institution of Electrical Engineers / IEE, Michael Faraday House, Six Hills Way, Stevenage Herts SG1 2AY UK. **Tel** 011 44 438 313311, FAX 011 44 438 742840, telex 825578 IEESTV G. **(Subscription address:** IEE / UK, Publications Sales Department, PO Box 96, Stevenage, Herts, SG1 2SD England.**) LC** TK1; .P773. **DD** 621.31. **[CCC].** Documents available from Article Express International, Ask*IEEE.
Ind/Abst Eng. Index Annu.; INSPEC (1987-).

UK
POWER EUROPE. English. Power Europe, Tower House, Southampton Street, London WC2E 7HA England.
Ind/Abst PROMT [Full Txt.]; PTS Newsl. Database [Full Txt.].

UK
POWER IN ASIA, THE ASIAN ELECTRICITY MARKET. **VFOAT** The Asian Electricity Market. English. sm. Financial Times Business Information Ltd., Tower House, Southampton Street, London WC2E 7HA England. **Tel** 011 44 71 353 1040.
Ind/Abst PROMT [Full Txt.]; PTS Newsl. Database [Full Txt.].

US
POWER MARKETS WEEK. (19??)-. Newsletter. English. wk. $695.00 US and Canada; $745.00 other. McGraw Hill Publishing Company, Inc., 1221 Avenue of the Americas, New York NY 10020. **Tel** (212)512-6410, (800)525-5003, FAX (212)512-6111.

II
POWER SUPPLY POSITION IN THE COUNTRY. **Main/Corp** India. Central Electricity Authority. English. mo. Ministry of Energy, Department of Power, Delhi 110054 India. **LC** TK103; .I54A. **DD** 363.6/2.

UK/0951-9653
POWER TECHNOLOGY INTERNATIONAL. (POWER TECHNOLOGY INTERNATIONAL : THE INTERNATIONAL REVIEW OF ELECTRICAL POWER TRANSMISSION AND DISTRIBUTION.). [Power technol. int.]. (19??)-. English. an. £55.00. Sterling Publications Ltd., PO Box 799, Brunel House, London W2 1XR England. **Tel** 011 44 71 2580066, FAX 011 44 71 4026441, telex 295819 ESPEEL G. **LC** TK1001; .P692. **CODEN** PTEIE8.

US/0093-0296
POWER TRANSISTORS AND POWER HYBRID CIRCUITS. **Main/Corp** RCA Corporation. Solid State Division. (19??)-. English. $2.00. RCA Solid State Division, Box 3200, Somerville NJ 08876. **LC** TK7871.9; .R17b. **DD** 621.3815/3.

PL
PRACE INSTYTUTU ELEKTROENERGETYKI I STEROWANIA UKADOW POLITECHNIKI SLASKIEJ. **Main/Corp** Gliwice, Upper Silesia (City). Politechnika Slaska. Instytut Elektroenergetyki i Sterowania Ukadow. April 1976-. Periodical. Polish. Instytutu Elektroenergetyki I Sterowania Ukadow Politechniki Slaskiej, Ul Bolesawa Krzywoustego 2, Cliwice Poland. **LC** TK4; .G552A.

PL/0138-0915
PRACE INSTYTUTU TECHNOLOGII ELEKTRONOWEJ CEMI. **VFOAT** Prace ITE CEMI. (1978)-. Polish. ***Continues*** *Prace Instytutu Technologii Elektronowej, 0079-3248.*

PL
PRACE NAUKOWE INSTYTUTU METROLOGII ELEKTRYCZNEJ POLITECHNIKI WROCAWSKIEJ. SERIA MONOGRAFIE. **Added/Corp** Politechnika Wrocawska. Instytut Metrologii Elektrycznej. **VFOAT** Seria Monografie; Monografie; Scientific Papers of the Institute of Electrical Energy Metrology of Wrocaw Technical University. Monographs. (1974)-. Monographic series. Polish (summaries and/or abstracts in English and Russian). Price varies per volume. **(Subscription address:** ARS Polona, PO Box 1001, 00068 Warsaw Poland.**) LC** TK275; .B68 subser. **CODEN** PMWMER.

UK/0032-6372
PRACTICAL ELECTRONICS. (19??)-. Periodical. English. mo. £35.00 US and Canada; £18.00 UK; £22.00 other. Intra Press, Intra House, 193 Uxbridge Road, London W12 9RA England. **Tel** 011 44 81 7438888, FAX 011 44 81 7433062. **[CCC].** Documents available from Ask*IEEE.
Ind/Abst INSPEC (1975-1992).

US/0739-4489
PRECIS (DENVILLE, N.J.). (PRECIS.). Periodical. English. mo. $80.00. Point of View / New Jersey, 92 Broadway, Denville NJ 07834. **Tel** (201)625-8877.

US
PRINTED CIRCUIT DESIGN. (19??)-. English. mo. $55.00 North America; $110.00 other. Miller Freeman Inc., 600 Harrison Street, San Francisco CA 94107. **Tel** (415)905-2337, FAX (415)905-2240, telex 278273. **(Subscription address:** Palm Coast Data, PO Box 420235, Agency Department, Palm Coast FL 32142.**)**

US/0274-8096
PRINTED CIRCUIT FABRICATION. [Print. circuit fabr.]. **VFOAT** PC FAB. (19??)-. Periodical. English. mo. $60.00 North America; $115.00 other. Miller Freeman Inc., 600 Harrison Street, San Francisco CA 94107. **Tel** (415)905-2337, FAX (415)905-2240, telex 278273. **(Subscription address:** Palm Coast Data, PO Box 420235, Agency Department, Palm Coast FL 32142.**)** **ED** Donna J. Esposito. **CODEN** PCFAE6. **[CCC]. Bk Rev. Ad Acc. Circ:** 22,030 (ctrl). available on microfilm and microfiche from University Microfilms International (UMI). Documents available from Article Express International. ***Continues*** *Printed Circuit Exchange, 0194-9683.*
Desc: For manufacturers of bare printed circuit boards. Technical articles on processing, equipment and chemistry materials.
Ind/Abst Eng. Index Annu. (19??-); Surf. Treat. Technol. Abstr. (19??-).

US/0032-9460
PROBLEMS OF INFORMATION TRANSMISSION. [Probl. inf. transm.]. **Added/Corp** Consultants Bureau. Vol. 1 (Jan./Mar. 1965)-. Academic Scholarly Publication. English (Russian). qt (4 issues). $945.00 US; $1105.00 other. Consultants Bureau, A Division of Plenum Publishing Corporation, 233 Spring Street, New York NY 10013. **Tel** (212)620-8000, (212)620-8466, FAX (212)463-0742, telex 23/421139. **ED** V. I. Siforov. **LC** Q350; .P7213. **CODEN** PRITA9. **[CCC].** Index available. available on microfilm and microfiche from University Microfilms International (UMI). Documents available from Article Express International, Ask*IEEE, CASDDS.
Desc: Covers topics such as statistical information, theory coding, theories and techniques, noisy channels, theory of random process and bionics.
Ind/Abst Bioeng. Abstr.; Chem. Abstr.; Comput. Rev.; Ei Page One; Eng. Index Annu.; Inf. Sci. Abstr.; INSPEC (1968-); Math. Rev.; Pollut. Abstr. Indexes; Stat. Theory Method Abstr. (1986-1987); Zentralbl. Math. Ihre Grenzgeb.

US
PROCEEDINGS. Main/Corp Association of Iron and Steel Engineers. **Added/Corp** Association of Iron and Steel Electrical Engineers. (19??)-. Proceedings. English. an. Association of Iron and Steel Engineers, Three Gateway Centre, Suite 2350, Pittsburgh PA 15222. **Tel** (412)281-6323, FAX (412)281-4657. **LC** TK1; .A83.

US/0732-6181
PROCEEDINGS - ALLERTON CONFERENCE ON COMMUNICATION, CONTROL AND COMPUTING. [Proc. - Allerton Conf. Commun. Control Comput.]. **Main/Conf** Allerton Conference on Communication, Control, and Computing. **Added/Corp** University of Illinois at Urbana-Champaign. Dept. of Electrical Engineering. University of Illinois at Urbana-Champaign. Coordinated Science Laboratory. University of Illinois at Urbana-Champaign. Dept. of Electrical and Computer Engineering. (1977)-. Proceedings. English. an. $63.00. University of Illinois Coordinated Science Lab, 1101 West Springfield Avenue, Urbana IL 61801. **Tel** (217)333-0282. **CODEN** PCCCDU. Index available in last issue of volume--attached. Documents available from Article Express International. ***Continues*** *Proceedings - Annual Allerton Conference on Circuit and System Theory, 0569-0552.*
Ind/Abst Bioeng. Abstr.; Ei Page One; Eng. Index Annu.

US/0092-1661
PROCEEDINGS. ANNUAL SYMPOSIUM. INCREMENTAL MOTION CONTROL SYSTEMS AND DEVICES. (PROCEEDINGS.). **Main/Conf** Symposium of Incremental Motion Control Systems and Devices. **Added/Corp** Illinois. University at Urbana-Champaign. Dept. of Electrical Engineering. (197?)-. Monographic series. English. ir. Price varies per volume. Incremental Motion Control Systems Society, PO Box 2772 Station A, Champaign IL 61825-2772. **Tel** (217)256-1523. **ED** B. C. Kuo. **LC** TK4058; .S94a. **DD** 621.46/2. Index available. cum. index. **Ad Acc. Circ:** 1,000 (ctrl).
Desc: Motion control systems and devices. Incremental motion CONTRO/DC and step motion control systems and devices.

US/0161-3219
PROCEEDINGS - BIENNIAL CORNELL ELECTRICAL ENGINEERING CONFERENCE. [Proc., Bienn. Cornell Electr. Eng. Conf.]. **Main/Conf** Cornell Electrical Engineering Conference. **Added/Corp** Cornell University. School of Electrical Engineering. (1969)-. Academic Scholarly Publication. English. be. price varies per volume. Cornell University / School of Electrical Engineering, 224 Philips Hall, Ithaca NY 14853. **Tel** (607)256-1000. **CODEN** PBCCDN. Documents available from Article Express International, CASDDS. ***Continues*** *Cornell Conference on Engineering Applications of Electrical Phenomena. Proceedings.*
Ind/Abst Bioeng. Abstr.; Chem. Abstr.; Ei Page One; Eng. Index Annu.

US/0569-5503
PROCEEDINGS / ELECTRONIC COMPONENTS & TECHNOLOGY CONFERENCE. Added/Corp Institute of Electrical and Electronics Engineers. (1990)-. Academic Scholarly Publication. English. an. IEEE, Institution of Electrical and Electronics Engineers, Inc., 345 East 47th Street, New York NY 10017-2394. **Tel** (908)981-1393, FAX (908)981-9667. **LC** TK7801; .A5. **DD** 621.3815/1. **CODEN** PETCES. Documents available from CASDDS. ***Continues*** *Electronic Components Conference. Proceedings, 0569-5503.*
Ind/Abst Chem. Abstr.

US/0734-659X
PROCEEDINGS / ELECTRONICS TEST AND MEASUREMENT CONFERENCE. [Proc. - Electron. Test Measure. Conf.]. **Main/Conf** Electronics Test and Measurement Conference. 1st (Oct. 5-8, 1981)-. Proceedings. English. an. Benwill Publishing Corporation, 1050 Commonwealth Avenue, Boston MA 02215. **Tel** (413)499-2550. **LC** TK7870; .E557. **DD** 621.381/028/7.

US
PROCEEDINGS / IEEE IECON. Added/Corp Insititute of Electrical and Electronics Engineers. **VFOAT** IEEE IECON.; IECON. (198?)-. Proceedings. English. IEEE, Institution of Electrical and Electronics Engineers, Inc., 345 East 47th Street, New York NY 10017-2394. **Tel** (908)981-1393, FAX (908)981-9667. **LC** TK7885.A1; I334.
Ind/Abst Civ. Struct. Eng. Abstr.; Comput. Inf. Syst. Abstr. J. [Full Cov.]; Elect. Comm. Abstr.; Environ. Eng. Abstr.; Index IEEE Publ.; Manuf. Process Eng. Abstr.; Mater. Sci. Eng. Abstr.; Mech. Eng. Abstr.; Solid State Supercond. Abstr.

US/1051-0117
PROCEEDINGS / IEEE ... ULTRASONICS SYMPOSIUM. [Proc. - IEEE Ultrason. Symp.]. **Main/Conf** IEEE Ultrasonics Symposium. **Added/Corp** Institute of Electrical and Electronics Engineers. Institute of Electrical and Electronics Engineers. Sonics and Ultrasonics Group. IEEE Ultrasonics, Ferroelectrics, and Frequency Control Society. **VFOAT** Ultrasonics Symposium; Ultrasonics Symposium Proceedings. (1984)-. Academic Scholarly Publication. English. an. IEEE, Institution of Electrical and Electronics Engineers, Inc., 345 East 47th Street, New York NY 10017-2394. **Tel** (908)981-1393, FAX (908)981-9667. **ED** B R McAvoy. **LC** TA367; .U46. **DD** 620. Documents available from Article Express International, Ask*IEEE, CASDDS. ***Continues*** *Ultrasonics Symposium. Proceedings, 0090-5607.*
Ind/Abst Bioeng. Abstr.; Chem. Abstr.; Coal Abstr.; Ei Page One; Eng. Index Annu.; Eng. Index Energy Abstr.; Index IEEE Publ.; INSPEC.

FR/1016-2437
PROCEEDINGS - INTERNATIONAL CONFERENCE ON LARGE HIGH VOLTAGE ELECTRIC SYSTEMS (CIGRE). [Proc. - Int. Conf. Large High Electr. Syst.]. (1972)-. Proceedings. English. be (every 2 years). 3125.00F. CIGRE, 3 5 Rue de Metz, 75010 Paris France. **Tel** 011 33 1 42465085, FAX 011 33 1 42465827, telex 290006. **LC** TK5; .I57. **DD** 621.319/2. **CODEN** CRETAG. ***Continues*** *International Conference on Large Electric Systems. Proceedings.*
Ind/Abst Bioeng. Abstr.; Eng. Index Annu.

UK
PROCEEDINGS - INTERNATIONAL POWER SOURCES SYMPOSIUM. Main/Conf International Power Sources Symposium. **VFOAT** Batteries; Power Resources. 1st- 1958-. Academic Scholarly Publication. English. be. Electrochemical Society Inc, 215 Canal Street, Manchester NH 03108. **ED** D H Collins. Documents available from CASDDS.
Ind/Abst Chem. Abstr.

US/1012-0343
PROCEEDINGS - INTERNATIONAL SYMPOSIUM ON SUBSCRIBER LOOPS AND SERVICES. [Proc. - Int. Symp. Subscr. Loops Serv.]. **VFOAT** ISSLS Proceedings; IEEE Subscriber Loops and Services; Proceedings - ISSLS. (1980)-. Periodical. English. ir. IEEE, Institution of Electrical and Electronics Engineers, Inc., 345 East 47th Street, New York NY 10017-2394. **Tel** (908)981-1393, FAX (908)981-9667.

US/0884-5123
PROCEEDINGS - INTERNATIONAL TELEMETERING CONFERENCE. Main/Corp International Telemetering Conference. V. 1- 1965-. Proceedings. English. an. $169.95 plus shipping. Instrument Society of America, 67 Alexander Drive, Research Triangle NC 27709. **Tel** (919)549-8411, FAX (919)549-8288, telex 802 540. **LC** TK399. **DD** 621.37/9. **CODEN** ITCOD6. Documents available from Article Express International, Ask*IEEE.
Desc: Proceedings of the International Telemetering Conference describe recent technical advances in the field.
Ind/Abst Ei Page One; Eng. Index Annu.; INSPEC.

US/0077-5401
PROCEEDINGS - NATIONAL RELAY CONFERENCE. (PROCEEDINGS / RELAY CONFERENCE.). [Proc. - Natl. Relay Conf.]. **Main/Conf** National Relay Conference. Oklahoma State University. **Added/Corp** National Association of Relay Manufacturers. Oklahoma State University. School of Electrical Engineering. 20th (1972)-. English. an. $65.00. National Association of Relay Manufacture, 9459 North Broadmoor Road, Milwaukee WI 53217. **Tel** (414)351-4548. **LC** TK2851; .N33. **DD** 621/31/7. **CODEN** PRECD9. Index available. **Circ:** 500. Documents available from Article Express International. ***Continues*** *National Relay Conference. Papers, 0740-3747.*
Desc: Technical papers concerning relays, design, application and related subjects.
Ind/Abst Bioeng. Abstr.; Ei Page One; Eng. Index Annu.

IE
PROCEEDINGS OF INTERNATIONAL CONFERENCE ON NUMERICAL ANALYSIS OF SEMICONDUCTOR DEVICES INTEG CIR : NASECODE. (19??)-. Proceedings. English. be. Price varies per volume. Boole Press Ltd, 26 Temple Lane, Temple Bar Dublin 2 Ireland. **Tel** 011 353 1 6797655, telex 30547 SHCN E1.

US/0091-7702
PROCEEDINGS OF INTERNATIONAL WIRE AND CABLE SYMPOSIUM. (PROCEEDINGS.). [Proc. Int. Wire Cable Symp.]. **Main/Conf** International Wire and Cable Symposium. Academic Scholarly Publication. English. National Technical Information Service - NTIS, Room 2027S, 5285 Port Royal Road, Springfield VA 22161. **Tel** (703)487-4630, (703)487-4660, (703)487-4650, FAX (703)321-8547, telex 89-9405. **LC** TK3301; .I53A. **DD** 621.319/3/05. **CODEN** PIWSDG. Documents available from Article Express International, CASDDS.
Ind/Abst Bioeng. Abstr.; Chem. Abstr.; Ei Page One; Eng. Index Annu.

US/0192-494X
PROCEEDINGS OF POWERCON. *Ceased.* **Main/Conf** Powercon. Vol. 1 (March 1975)-Vol. 11 (Nov. 1984). Proceedings. English. an. Power Concepts Inc, 2515 Greencastle Court, Oxnard Ca 93030. **LC** TK7801; .P69a. **DD** 621.3815.

US/1075-7988
PROCEEDINGS OF THE AESF ANNUAL TECHNICAL CONFERENCE, THE. (PROCEEDINGS OF THE ... AESF ANNUAL TECHNICAL CONFERENCE.). [Proc. AESF annu. tech. conf.]. **Main/Corp** American Electroplaters and Surface Finishers Society. **VFOAT** AESF Annual Technical Conference Proceedings; SUR/FIN. (1986)-. Proceedings. English. an. $280.00. American Electroplaters Society, 12644 Research Parkway, Orlando FL 32826-3225. **Tel** (407)281-6441, (800)334-2052, FAX (407)281-6446, telex 510 601 6246. **DD** 671. **CODEN** PATCEY. Documents available from Article Express International, CASDDS. ***Continues*** *American Electroplaters' Society. Annual Technical Conference, 0270-2622.*
Ind/Abst Chem. Abstr.; Ei Page One; Eng. Index Annu.

US/0895-4097
PROCEEDINGS OF THE ANNUAL NORTH AMERICAN POWER SYMPOSIUM. (PROCEEDINGS OF THE ... ANNUAL NORTH AMERICAN POWER SYMPOSIUM : NAPS / JOINTLY SPONSORED BY IEEE POWER ENGINEERING SOCIETY ... [ET AL.].). [Proc. Annual North Am. Power Symp.]. **Added/Corp** IEEE Power Engineering Society. Institute of Electrical and Electronics Engineers. **VFOAT** NAPS. (198?)-. Proceedings. English. $80.00. IEEE Computer Society, 10662 Los Vaqueros Circle, PO Box 3014, Los Alamitos CA 90720-1264. **Tel** (714)821-8380, (800)272-6657, FAX (714)821-4641. **LC** TK5; .N63a. **DD** 621.31/05.

●US/1071-6270
PROCEEDINGS OF THE ELECTRICAL ELECTRONICS INSULATION CONFERENCE & ELECTRICAL MANUFACTURING & COIL WINDING. Added/Corp Institute of Electrical and Electronics Engineers. (1993)-. Proceedings. English. be. IEEE, Institution of Electrical and Electronics Engineers, Inc., 345 East 47th Street, New York NY 10017-2394. **Tel** (908)981-1393, FAX (908)981-9667.

UK
PROCEEDINGS OF THE EUROPEAN ELECTRO-OPTICS MARKETS AND TECHNOLOGY CONFERENCE. Main/Conf European Electro-Optics Markets and Technology Conference. 1st- 1972-. Proceedings. English. **NLM** W3 EU878; P34320000.

US/0018-9219
PROCEEDINGS OF THE IEEE. [Proc. I.E.E.E.]. **Main/Corp** Institute of Electrical and Electronics Engineers. Vol. 51, No. 1 (Jan. 1963)-. Academic Scholarly Publication. English. mo. $325.00. IEEE, Institution of Electrical and Electronics Engineers, Inc., 345 East 47th Street, New York NY 10017-2394. **Tel** (908)981-1393, FAX (908)981-9667. **(Subscription address:** IEEE / Institute of Electrical and Electronics Engineers, 445 Hoes Lane, PO Box 1331, Piscataway NJ 08855-1331.**)** **LC** TK5700; .W5. **DD** 621.381/05. **CODEN** IEEPAD. **[CCC]. Pr Rev.** available on microfiche. Documents available from Article Express International, The Genuine Article, Ask*IEEE, Petroleum Abstracts Document Delivery Service, CASDDS, Documents on Demand. ***Continues*** *Institute of Radio Engineers. Proceedings of the IRE, 0096-8390.*
Desc: Fundamental papers of broad significance and long-range interest in all areas of electrical and electronics science and technology.
Ind/Abst Acoust. Abstr.; Appl. Sci. Technol. Index; Bioeng. Abstr.; Chem. Abstr.; Coal Abstr.; Comput. Database; Comput. Rev.; Curr. Contents Eng. Tech. Appl. Sci.; EMBASE; Energy Inf. Abstr.; Energy Res. Abstr.; Eng. Index Annu.; Environ. Abstr.; Ergon. Abstr.; GeoRef; Index IEEE Publ.; Inf. Sci. Abstr.; INSPEC (1968-); Int. Aerosp. Abstr.; Math. Rev.; Oper. Res./Manag. Sci.; Pet. Abstr.; Qual. Control Appl. Stat.; Res. Alert [Full Cov.]; Sci. Cit. Index; SCISEARCH; Shock Vibr. Dig.; Soc. Sci. Cit. Index [Select. Cov.].

US/0743-1546
PROCEEDINGS OF THE ... IEEE CONFERENCE ON DECISION & CONTROL. [Proc. IEEE Conf. Decis. Control]. **Main/Conf** IEEE Conference of Decision & Control. 21st (Dec. 8-10, 1982)-. Proceedings. English. an. $160.00. IEEE, Institution of Electrical and Electronics Engineers, Inc., 345 East 47th Street, New York NY 10017-2394. **Tel** (908)981-1393, FAX (908)981-9667. **LC** TJ217; .I17A. **DD** 629.8. Documents available from Article Express International. ***Continues*** *Proceedings of the IEEE Conference on Decision & Control, Including the Symposium on Adaptive Processes.*
Ind/Abst Eng. Index Annu.; Index IEEE Publ.

UK/0020-3270
PROCEEDINGS OF THE INSTITUTION OF ELECTRICAL ENGINEERS. Main/Corp Institution of Electrical Engineers, London. **Added/Corp** Institution of Electrical Engineers, London. Journal. Vol. 1 (1872)-. Periodical. English. bm. $1,720.35. Institution of Electrical Engineers / IEE, Michael Faraday House, Six Hills Way, Stevenage Herts SG1 2AY UK. **Tel** 011 44 438 313311, FAX 011 44 438 742840, telex 825578 IEESTV G. **(Subscription address:** IEE / UK, Publications Sales Department, PO Box 96, Stevenage, Herts, SG1 2SD England.**) ED** B. Dunkley. **[CCC].** cum. index. **Bk Rev. Ad Acc. Circ:** 3,000. available on microfilm from University Microfilms International (UMI). Documents available from Ask*IEEE, Petroleum Abstracts Document Delivery Service.
Desc: Research level publication describing work across every area of electrical and electronic engineering.
Ind/Abst Appl. Mech. Rev.; Appl. Sci. Technol. Index; Ceram. Abstr. (19??-); Comput. Abstr.; INSPEC (1968-Dec. 1979); Int. Aerosp. Abstr.; Int. Build. Serv. Abstr.; Math. Rev.; Pet. Abstr.

JA
PROCEEDINGS OF THE INTERNATIONAL MICROELECTRONICS CONFERENCE. **Main/Conf** International Microelectronics Conference. **VFOAT** Proceedings of the ... International Microelectronics Conference. (1980)-. Proceedings. English. bm. International Society for Hybrid Microelectronics / Alabama, PO Box 3255, Montgomery AL 36109. **Tel** (205)272-3191. **LC** TK7874; .I5916A. **DD** 621.381.

US
PROCEEDINGS OF THE ... INTERNATIONAL SYMPOSIUM ON MICROELECTRONICS. Added/Corp International Society for Hybrid Microelectronics. **VFOAT** Proceedings, International Symposium on Microelectronics. (1984)-. English. an. $75.00 (members), $60.00 (non-members). International Society for Hybrid Microelectronics / Virginia, 1850 Centennial Park Drive, Suite 105, Reston VA 22091. **Tel** (703)758-1060, FAX (703)758-1066. ***Continues*** *International Microelectronics Symposium. Proceedings of the ... International Microelectronics Symposium, 0146-9525.*
Ind/Abst Ceram. Abstr.

US
PROCEEDINGS OF THE ... MIDWEST SYMPOSIUM ON CIRCUITS AND SYSTEMS. (Aug. 10-12, 1986)-. Proceedings. English. IEEE, Institution of Electrical and Electronics Engineers, Inc., 345 East 47th Street, New York NY 10017-2394. **Tel** (908)981-1393, FAX (908)981-9667. **LC** TK3226; .M55. ***Continues*** *Midwest Symposium on Circuits and Systems. Conference Proceedings.*

US/0163-917X
PROCEEDINGS OF THE TECHNICAL PROGRAM - INTERNATIONAL MICROELECTRONICS CONFERENCE. [Proc. tech. program - Int. Microelectron. Conf.]. **Main/Conf** International Microelectronics Conference. 1975-. Academic Scholarly Publication. English. an. $30.00. International Society for Hybrid Microelectronics / Virginia, 1850 Centennial Park Drive, Suite 105, Reston VA 22091. **Tel** (703)758-1060, FAX (703)758-1066. **CODEN** PPICDF. Documents available from Article Express International, CASDDS. ***Continues*** *International Microelectronics/Semiconductor Conference. Proceedings of the Technical Program.*
Ind/Abst Bioeng. Abstr.; Chem. Abstr.; Ei Page One; Eng. Index Annu.

US/0272-4677
PROCEEDINGS, REGION 6 CONFERENCE. (PROCEEDINGS, REGION 6 CONFERENCE - INSTITUTE OF ELECTRICAL AND ELECTRONIC ENGINEERS.). [Proc. - Reg. 6 conf.]. **Main/Corp** Institute of Electrical and Electronic Engineers. Region 6 Conference. **Added/Corp** Institute of Electrical and Electronics Engineers. San Diego Section. **VAT** Proceedings, Region Six Conference. (19??)-. English. ir. Institution of Electrical Engineers / IEE, Michael Faraday House, Six Hills Way, Stevenage Herts SG1 2AY UK. **Tel** 011 44 438 313311, FAX 011 44 438 742840, telex 825578 IEESTV G. **(Subscription address:** IEE / UK, Publications Sales Department, PO Box 96, Stevenage, Herts, SG1 2SD England.**) CODEN** IRCRDZ. Documents available from Article Express International.
Ind/Abst Bioeng. Abstr.; Ei Page One; Eng. Index Annu.

US/0080-0821
PROCEEDINGS - RELIABILITY PHYSICS SYMPOSIUM. ***Title Change.*** **Main/Conf** Reliability Physics Symposium. Vol. 1 (1962)-. Proceedings. English. an. Institution of Electrical Engineers / IEE, Michael Faraday House, Six Hills Way, Stevenage Herts SG1 2AY UK. **Tel** 011 44 438 313311, FAX 011 44 438 742840, telex 825578 IEESTV G. **(Subscription address:** IEE / UK, Publications Sales Department, PO Box 96, Stevenage, Herts, SG1 2SD England.**)** ***Continued by*** *Reliability Physics, 0735-0791.*

US/1063-0988
PROCEEDINGS / THE ... ANNUAL IEEE INTERNATIONAL ASIC CONFERENCE AND EXHIBIT. [Proc. - IEEE Int. ASIC Conf. Exhib.]. **Added/Corp** Institute of Electrical and Electronics Engineers. **VFOAT** Proceedings of ... Annual IEEE International ASIC Conference and Exhibit. 4th (Sept. 23-27, 1991)-. Proceedings. English. IEEE, Institution of Electrical and Electronics Engineers, Inc., 345 East 47th Street, New York NY 10017-2394. **Tel** (908)981-1393, FAX (908)981-9667. **LC** TK7874.6; I34a. **DD** 621.381/5. ***Continues*** *Proceedings.*

US/0749-6877
PROCEEDINGS - UNIVERSITY/GOVERNMENT/INDUSTRY MICROELECTRONICS SYMPOSIUM. (PROCEEDINGS.). [Proc. - Univ./Gov./Ind. Microelectron. Symp.]. **Main/Conf** University/Government/Industry Microelectronics Symposium. **VFOAT** University, Government, Industry Microelectronics Symposium; UGIM; University/Governmemt/Industry Microelectronics Symposium. 1983-. Proceedings. English. be. IEEE, Institution of Electrical and Electronics Engineers, Inc., 345 East 47th Street, New York NY 10017-2394. **Tel** (908)981-1393, FAX (908)981-9667. **(Subscription address:** IEEE Service Center, 445 Hoes Lane, Piscataway, NJ 08854; telephone: (201)981-1393**) LC** TK7874; .I48A. **DD** 621.381/7. ***Continues*** *University/Government/Industry Symposium Proceedings, 0734-2500.*
Ind/Abst Index IEEE Publ.

US
PROFESSIONAL ELECTRONICS / THE OFFICIAL JOURNAL OF NESDA AND ISCET. Vol. 8, No. 5 (Sept./Oct. 1982)-. English. bm. $12.00 (one year), $20.00 (two year), $26.00 (three year) US; $20.00 (one year), $28.00 (two year), $34.00 (three year) other. NESDA / National Electronics Serice Dealers, 2708 West Berry Street, Fort Worth TX 76109. **Tel** (817)921-9061. **ED** Wallace Harrison. **Bk Rev. Ad Acc. Circ:** 11,000 (ctrl). ***Continues*** *Service Shop.*
Desc: For owners, managers, operators and employees of retail electronics sales and service firms. Contains articles on improving management skills, technical articles to update and improve efficiency.

US/0198-7259
PROGRESS IN BATTERIES & SOLAR CELLS. [Prog. batteries sol. cells]. **VAT** Progress in Batteries and Solar Cells. Vol. 1, (1978)-. Academic Scholarly Publication. English. an. $125.00 + shipping. ITE Inc., 3398 Tyler Drive, Brunswick OH 44212. **Tel** (216)225-3834, FAX (216)941-9364. **CODEN** PBASDR. **Ad Acc. Circ:** 300. Documents available from CASDDS.
Desc: Recent progress in different battery types and solar cells.
Ind/Abst Chem. Abstr.; Ei Page One.

●UK/1062-7995
PROGRESS IN PHOTOVOLTAICS. [Prog. photovolt.]. (1993)-. Periodical. English. qt. $395.00. John Wiley & Sons Ltd., Baffins Lane, Chichester West Sussex PO19 1UD England. **Tel** 0243 779777, FAX 0243 776128 BTG:JWP001, telex 86290 WIBOOKG. **(Subscription address:** John Wiley / Philadelphia, PO Box 7247, Philadelphia PA 19170.**) ED** P. A. Lynn. **DD** 621. **CODEN** PPHOED.
Desc: Journal reaches all of those with an interest in the results of research work being undertaken in this field of rapid current development. It will also cover practical implementation, thus encouraging contributions from industrial practitioners.

UK/0079-6727
PROGRESS IN QUANTUM ELECTRONICS. [Prog. quantum electron.]. Vol. 1 (1969)-. English. Five times a year. $425.00 The Americas; £285.00 other. Pergamon Press, An Imprint of Elsevier Science Ltd., The Boulevard, Langford Lane, Kidlington, Oxford OX5 1GB United Kingdom. **Tel** 011 44 865 843000, 011 44 865 843699, FAX 011 44 865 843010. **(Subscription address:** Elsevier Science Ltd. Oxford Fulfillment Centre, PO Box 800, Kidlington, Oxford OX5 1DX United Kingdom.**) ED** P. T. Landsberg. M. Osinski. **LC** QC680; .P74. **DD** 537.5. **CODEN** PQUEAH. **[CCC]. Pr Rev.** available on microfilm and microfiche from University Microfilms International (UMI). Documents available from Article Express International, The Genuine Article, Ask*IEEE, CASDDS.
Desc: International review journal devoted to the dissemination of new, specialized topics at the forefront of quantum electronics and its applications.
Ind/Abst Bioeng. Abstr.; Chem. Abstr.; Ei Page One; Eng. Index Annu.; Index Sci. Rev. [Full Cov.]; INSPEC (April 1975-); Int. Aerosp. Abstr.; Res. Alert [Full Cov.]; Sci. Cit. Index; SCISEARCH.

IT/1121-371X
PROMOTEC. AGGIORNAMENTO ELETTRICO. [Promotec, Aggiorn, elettr.]. (1991)-. Periodical. Italian. mo. L230000.00 Italy; L460000.00 other. Promotec Editoriale Srl, Via Dei Cignoli 9, 20151 Milan Italy. **Tel** 011 39 2 38010450. **UDC** 696.6.

RU/0033-1155
PROMYSLENNAJA ENERGETIKA. (PROMYSHELENNAIA ENERGETIKA.). [Prom. energ.]. **Added/Corp** Soviet Union. Gosudarstvennaia Inspektsiia po Promyshlennoi Energetike i Energonadzoru. Vol. 1, (1944)-. Academic Scholarly Publication. Russian. mo. $79.95. **(Subscription address:** East View Publications Inc., 3020 Harbor Lane North, Suite 110, Minneapolis MN 55447.**) LC** TK4; .P67. **CODEN** PREGAI. Documents available from Ask*IEEE, CASDDS.
Ind/Abst Chem. Abstr.; Coal Abstr.; INSPEC (1968-); Int. Aerosp. Abstr.

PL/0033-2097
PRZEGLAD ELEKTROTECHNICZNY. [Prz. elektrotech.]. **Added/Corp** Stowarzyszenie Elektrykow Polskich. (1919)-. Periodical. Polish. mo. $87.00. **(Subscription address:** ARS Polona, PO Box 1001, 00068 Warsaw Poland.**) LC** TK4; .P7. **CODEN** PZELAL. Documents available from Article Express International, Ask*IEEE.
Ind/Abst Bioeng. Abstr.; Ei Page One; Eng. Index Annu.; INSPEC (1968-); Surf. Treat. Technol. Abstr.

NE/0032-4086
PT. ELEKTROTECHNIEK ELEKTRONICA. ***Title Change.*** [Pt, Elektrotech., elektron.]. **Added/Corp** Netherlandse Ingenieursvereniging. **VFOAT** Elektrotehniek Elektronica. Vol. 37, No. 1 (Jan. 1982)-(19??). Periodical. Dutch. mo. Stam Tijdschriften BV, Postbus 235, 2280 AE Rijswijk Netherlands. **Tel** +31 70 3988100, FAX +31 70 3988276, telex 33702 STAM NL. **CODEN** PEELDD. Documents available from Ask*IEEE. ***Continues*** *Polytechnisch Tijdschrift, Editie Elektrotechniek Elektronica.* ***Continued by*** *Polytechnisch Tijdschrift Elektronica Elecktrotechniek.*
Ind/Abst INSPEC (Jan. 1982-).

SZ/0351-4749
PUBLIKACIJE ELEKTROTEHNICKOG FAKULTETA. UNIVERZITET U BEOGRADU. SERIJA ELEKTROENERGETIKA. (PUBLIKACIJE ELEKTROTEHNICKOG FAKULTETA. SERIJA : ELEKTROENERGETIKA.). [Publ. Elektroteh. fak., Univ. Beogr., Ser. Elektroenerg.]. **Main/Corp** Univerzitet u Beogradu. Elektrotehnicki Fakultet. **VFOAT** Elektroenergetika; Serija : Elektroenergetika. Multiple languages (English, French and German). Univerzitet u Beogradu, Pravni Fakultet, Belgrade Stud TRG1 Yugoslavia. **LC** TK1.A1. **DD** 601.3/05. **CODEN** PEFEDV. Documents available from Ask*IEEE.
Ind/Abst INSPEC (1981-).

Engineering —Electricity, Electrical Engineering, Electronics

YU/0409-0179
PUBLIKACIJE. SERIJA : ELEKTRONIKA, TELEKOMUNIKACIJE, AUTOMATIKA. Main/Corp Belgrad. Univerzitet. Elektrotehnicki Fakultet. **VFOAT** Publications. Telecommunications et Electronique. No. 1- 1956-. Periodical. Serbo-Croatian (Roman) (summaries and/or abstracts in French). PO Box 36, Belgrad Yugoslavia.

US
PUBLISHED SEARCH BIBLIOGRAPHIES FROM THE NTIS BIBLIOGRAPHIC DATA BASE. COMMUNICATION AND ELECTROTECHNOLOGY / U.S. DEPARTMENT OF COMMERCE, NATIONAL TECHNICAL INFORMATION SERVICE. See Communication-Abstracting, Bibliographies and Statistics.

SA
PULSE BUYERS GUIDE. Consumer Publication. English. an. R171.00 South Africa; R150.00 other. Pulse Publications Pty Ltd, Box 1884, Johannesburg 2000 South Africa. **Tel** 27 21 8352221, FAX 27 21 8351943. **Ad Acc.**

SA/0256-6028
PULSE (KLOOF). (PULSE.). [Pulse]. **Added/Corp** South African Institute of Measurement and Control. (19??)-. Academic Scholarly Publication. English. mo. R54.54 South Africa; R90.54 other. Pulse Publications Pty Ltd, Box 1884, Johannesburg 2000 South Africa. **Tel** 27 21 8352221, FAX 27 21 8351943. **ED** Ian Roberts. **CODEN** PULSDB. **Ad Acc. Circ:** 4,000. Documents available from CASDDS.
Desc: Aimed at the electronic engineer. It embraces design, components, measurement techniques, computers, telecoms, broadcast radio and TV, radar, and production techniques.
Ind/Abst Chem. Abstr. (1977-1983); Fish Rev. (Jan. 1989-July 1992); Wildl. Rev. (Jan. 1989-July 1992).

JA/0917-5555
PURINTO KAIRO GAKKAI DENJI TOKUSEI KENKYU BUKAI KOKAI KENKYUKAI RONBUNSHU. VFOAT Denji Tokusei Kenkyu Bukai Kokai Kenkyukai Ronbunshu. (1991)-. Periodical. Japanese. tq. Japan Institute of Printed Circuit, Research Group on Electromagnetic Behaviors, Toyo Rika Daigaku, Rikogakubu Denki Kogakka, 2641 Yamazaki Noda-shi, Chiba-ken 278 Japan.

●US/1063-7818
QUANTUM ELECTRONICS (NEW YORK, N.Y. 1993). (QUANTUM ELECTRONICS.). **Added/Corp** American Institute of Physics. (1993)-. Academic Scholarly Publication. English (translations available in Russian). mo. $1990.00. **(Subscription address:** Turpin Distribution Services Limited, Blackhorse Road, Letchworth, Hertfordshire SG6 1HN, United Kingdom.) Documents available from Article Express International, Ask*IEEE, CASDDS. **Continues** Soviet Journal of Quantum Electronics, 0049-1748.
Ind/Abst Bioeng. Abstr.; Chem. Abstr.; Curr. Phys. Index; Ei Page One; Energy Res. Abstr.; Eng. Index Annu.; Eng. Index Energy Abstr.; INSPEC; Int. Aerosp. Abstr.; Nucl. Sci. Abstr.; SPIN.

JA
QUARTERLY ABSTRACTS (DENRYOKU CHUO KENKYUJO (TOKYO, JAPAN)). (QUARTERLY ABSTRACTS / CENTRAL RESEARCH INSTITUTE OF ELECTRIC POWER INDUSTRY.). **Added/Corp** Denryoku Chuo Kenkyujo (Tokyo, Japan). No. 1 (1977)-. Periodical. English. qt (4 issues). Free on request. Central Research Institute of Electric Power Industry, 1-6-1 Otemachi 1 Chome, Chiyodaku Tokyo 100 Japan.
Ind/Abst Fluid Abstr., Civil Eng.; Fluid Abstr. Proc. Eng.; FLUIDEX (1977-1990).

UK
QUARTERLY REPORT ON THE OPERATION AND BUSINESS OF THE ELECTRICITY POOL IN ENGLAND AND WALES. (19??)-. English. Four times a year. £40.00. Chief Executives's Office, 2nd Floor, 15 Bloomsbury Square, London WC1A 2LJ England. **Tel** 011 44 71 8314790, FAX 011 44 071 8314813.

XR
QUO VADIS ELEKTRONIKA. VFOAT Q.V.; QV. Periodical. Czech (Czech). an. TESLA--Vust, Novodvorska 994, Prague 4 Czech Republic. **LC** TK7800; .Q62.

UK
RADIO & ELECTRONICS CONSTRUCTOR. (1947)-(1981). Periodical. English. mo. $7.00. Data Publications Ltd., 45 Yeading Avenue, Rayners Lane, Harrow Middlesex HA2 9RL England. **LC** TK9956; .R17. **DD** 621.38/05. **Continues** Radio Constructor.

UK/0307-3165
RADIO AND TELEVISION SERVICING. English. an MacDonald and Jane's Publishers, Paulton House, 8 Shepherdess Walk, London N1 7LW England. **LC** TK6553.A1; R25. **DD** 621.38.

UK/0033-7803
RADIO COMMUNICATION. [Radio commun.]. Vol. 44 (Jan. 1968)-. Periodical. English. mo. £32.00. Radio Society of Great Britain England, Cranbourne Road, Potters Bar, Herts EN6 3JW England. **Tel** 44 707 59015, FAX 44 707 45105, telex 25280. **ED** Mike Demison. **LC** TK6540; .T15. **DD** 621.3841/05. **CODEN** RADCB7. Index available. **Bk Rev. Ad Acc. Circ:** 36,000 (ctrl). available on microfilm and microfiche from University Microfilms International (UMI). Documents available from Ask*IEEE. **Continues** R.S.G.B. Bulletin.
Desc: Amateur radio journal of the radio society of Great Britain.
Ind/Abst Curr. Technol. Index; INSPEC (Sept. 1971-).

US/0033-7862
RADIO-ELECTRONICS. Title Change. [Radio-electron.]. **VAT** Radio Electronics. Vol. 20, (Oct. 1948)-(1992). Periodical. English. mo. Gernsback Publications Inc, 500 B Bi-County Boulevard, Farmingdale NY 11735. **Tel** (516)293-3000. **(Subscription address:** Neodata, PO Box 2606, Boulder, CO 80322) **LC** TK6540. **CODEN** RAECAB. **[CCC].** available on microfilm and microfiche from University Microfilms International (UMI). Documents available from Ask*IEEE, Magazine Collection. **Continues** Radio-Craft, Radio-Electronics. **Continued by** Electronics Now.
Desc: A popular technical magazine covering all aspects of electronics, including video, television, radio, television, radio, computers, satellite tv, industrial electronics and high fidelity, including stereo. For service technicians, engineers, students, hi-fi fans, and electronic activists.
Ind/Abst Acad. Abstr. Full Text Elite (Jan. 1984-Feb. 1993); Acad. Abstr. (Jan. 1984-Feb. 1993); Acad. Search (Jan. 1984-Feb. 1993); Appl. Sci. Technol. Index; Comput. Rev. Index (1986-); Consum. Index Prod. Eval. Inf. Source; Gen. Period. Index (1985-); Index Inf.; INFO-SOUTH Abstr.; INSPEC (1968-); Mag. Artic. Summar. Elite (Jan. 1984-Feb. 1993); Mag. Artic. Summar. Select (July 1984-); Mag. Artic. Summar. CD-ROM (Jan. 1984-Feb. 1993); Mag. Index Plus (1989-); Mag. Index. Sel. (1986-); Mag. Search; Microcomput. Index (Jan. 1986-Feb. 1983); Read. Guide Abstr. Select Ed.; Read. Guide Period. Lit.; Mag. Index (1977-); Vocat. Search (Jan. 1984-Feb. 1993).

AU
RADIO ELEKTRONIK SCHAU. (1971)-. German. Resch Media Mail Verlag GmbH, Postfach 1260, D 82166 Graefelfing Germany. **Tel** 011 49 89 8580710. **Continues** Radioschau.

GW
RADIO-, FERNSEH-, PHONO-PRAXIS. VFOAT RP. (19??)-. Periodical. German. mo. Vogel Verlag, Postfach 6740, D-97064 Wuerzburg Germany. **Tel** 011 49 931 4182145, 011 49 931 4182483, FAX 011 49 931 4182670, telex 841 680131. **LC** TK6540; .R464.

RU/0033-8494
RADIOTEKHNIKA I ELEKTRONIKA. [Radioteh. elektron.]. Vol. 1 (1956)-. Academic Scholarly Publication. Russian. mo. $185.95. Izdatelstvo Nauka / Akademiia Nauk, Publishing House of the Russian Academy of Sciences, Leninskii Porspekt 14, 117901 Moscow Russia. **Tel** 011 95 954-21-51, FAX 011 95 938-21-44, telex 411964. **(Subscription address:** East View Publications Inc, 3020 Harbor Lane North, Suite 110, Minneapolis MN 55447.) **LC** TK7800; .R4. **CODEN** RAELA4. **[CCC]. Bk Rev. Ad Acc. Pr Rev. Circ:** 5,500. Documents available from Article Express International, The Genuine Article, Ask*IEEE, CASDDS.
Ind/Abst Chem. Abstr.; Curr. Contents Eng. Tech. Appl. Sci.; Eng. Index Annu.; INSPEC (1968-); Int. Aerosp. Abstr. (19??-19??); Math. Rev. (?-199?); Res. Alert [Full Cov.]; Sci. Cit. Index; SCISEARCH.

SZ
RAPPORT ANNUEL / CEI. Main/Corp International Electrotechnical Commission. **VFOAT** Annual Report. English (French). an. Commission Electrotechnique Internationale, 3 rue du Varembe, 1211 Geneve 20 Suisse Switzerland. **LC** TK275; .I53A. **DD** 621.3/06/01. **Continues** International Electrotechnical Committee. Central Office. Report on Activities.

GW
RAPPORT ANNUEL - UNION POUR LA COORDINATION DE LA PRODUCTION ET DU TRANSPORT DE L'ELECTRICITE. Main/Corp Union for the Coordination of the Production and Transport of Electric Power. **VFOAT** Jahresbericht - Union fur die Koordinierubg der Erzeugung und des Transportes Elektrischer Energie; Rapporto Annuale - Unione per il Coordinamento della Produzione e del Trasporto di Energia Elettrica; Jaarverslag - Unie voor de Coordinatie van de Produktie en het Transport van Elektriciteit. Multiple languages (Dutch, French, German and Italian). Ziegelhauser Landstrasse 5, W-6900 Heidelberg Germany. **LC** TK55; .U54A.

FR
RAPPORT D'ACTIVITE / DIVISION TECHNIQUE GENERALE. Main/Corp Electricite de France. Division Technique Generale. **VFOAT** Activite de la Division Technique Generale. French. an. 37 rue Diderot BP No 41 Centre de Tri, 38040 Grenoble Cedex France. **LC** TK71; .E44A. **DD** 621.3/0944. **Continues** Electricite de France. Division Technique Generale. Activite.

FR
RAPPORT D'ACTIVITE - ELECTRICITE DE FRANCE, DIRECTION DES AFFAIRES EXTERIEURES ET DE LA COOPERATION. Main/Corp Electricite de France. Direction des Affaires Exterieures et de la Cooperation. French. 68 rue du Faubourg Saint-Honore, Paris 75008 France. **LC** HD9685.F84; E48. **DD** 338.7/62/131.

FR
RAPPORT D'ACTIVITE - ELECTRICITE DE FRANCE, DIRECTION DES ETUDES ET RECHERCHES. Main/Corp Electricite de France. Direction des Etudes et Recherches. French. **LC** TK71; .E44c. **DD** 621.3/05.

LV
RASPOZNAVANIE OBRAZOV. Main/Corp Elektronikas un Skaitlosanas Tehnikas Instituts (Latvijas PSR Zinatnu Akademija). Vol. 1 (1971)-. Russian. Zinatne / Science Publishing House, Turgeneva Iela 19, Riga Latvia 1530. **Tel** 3712 212 797. **LC** TK7882.P3; L38a.
Desc: Information on pattern recognition systems and pattern perception.

NE
RB ELEKTRONICA MAGAZINE. Uitgeverij De Muiderkring BV, POB 313, 1380 AH Weesp Netherlands. **Tel** 011 31 2940 15210.

GW/0936-5893
RDE. RECHT DER ELEKTRIZITATSWIRTSCHAFT. See Energy.

US/0160-3264
REA BULLETIN. (REA BULLETIN / UNITED STATES DEPARTMENT OF AGRICULTURE, RURAL ELECTRIFICATION ADMINISTRATION.). [REA bull.]. **Added/Corp** United States. Rural Electrification Administration. **VFOAT** REA-Bulletin. **VAT** Rural Electrification Administration Bulletin. (1952)-. Monographic series. English. ir. Superintendent of Documents, US Government Printing Office, Washington DC 20402. **Tel** (202)275-3328, FAX (202)786-2377. **LC** TK4018; .U613. **DD** 621.39/3/0973.
Ind/Abst AGRICOLA.

US/8755-3619
REAL-TIME SIGNAL PROCESSING. [Real-time signal process.]. **VFOAT** Real Time Signal Processing. 1 (Aug. 28-29, 1978)-. English. an. 405 Fieldston Road, Bellingham WA 98225. **LC** TK5102.5; .R372. **DD** 621.38/043.

US
RECEIVING TUBE MANUAL. Main/Corp General Electric Company. Tube Dept. **VFOAT** Electronics Tube Manual: Receiving Tubes. English. bm. General Electric Company, 120 Erie Boulevard, Schenectady NY 12305. **Tel** (502)685-6200.

●US
RECENT ADVANCES IN ACTIVE CONTROL OF SOUND AND VIBRATION. (1992)-. Proceedings. English. an. $195.00. Technomic Publishing Company, Inc., 851 New Holland Avenue, Box 3535, Lancaster PA 17604. **Tel** (717)291-5609, (800)233-9936, FAX (717)295-4538.
Desc: Provides a forum for presentation and discussion of the latest developments in the key areas of physical systems, actuators and sensors and control approaches. Goal is to judge how much the field of active control has matured towards ultimate use in a number of applications.

GW/0171-712X
RECHT DER ELEKTRIZITATSWIRTSCHAFT. Title Change. See Energy.

US
RECORD - POSITION LOCATION AND NAVIGATION SYMPOSIUM. Added/Corp IEEE Aerospace and Electronic Systems Society. Institute of Electrical and Electronics Engineers. San Diego Section. **VFOAT** IEEE PLANS.; PLANS. (1976)-. English. ir. IEEE, Institution of Electrical and Electronics Engineers, Inc., 345 East 47th Street, New York NY 10017-2394. **Tel** (908)981-1393, FAX (908)981-9667.

RU
REFERATIVNYI ZHURNAL: ELEKTRONIKA. **Added/Corp** Vsesoiuznyi Institut Nauchnoi i Tekhnicheskoi Informatsii (Soviet Union). **VFOAT** Elektronika. (Jan. 1980)-. Periodical. Russian. mo. 87.96rub. VINITI - Vsesoyuznyi Institut Nauchno-Tekhnicheskoi Informatsii, All-Union Scientific and Technical Information Institute, Baltiiskaia Ulitsa 14, 125219 Moscow Russia. **Tel** 238-46-00, FAX 9430060, telex 411160. **(Subscription address:** V/O Mezhdunarodnaya Kniga, 113095 Dimitrova Ul 39, Moscow USSR**)** **ED** Professor Nesterov, D S Djakov. **LC** TK7800; .R47. Index available. cum. index. **Bk Rev. Ad Acc. Circ:** 5,900 (ctrl). ***Continues*** *Referativnyi Zhurnal: Elektronika i Ee Primenenie.*

RU/0203-5189
REFERATIVNYI ZHURNAL. ELEKTROTEKHNIKA / GOSUDARSTVENNYI KOMITET SSSR PO NAUKE I TEKHNIKE, AKADEMIIA NAUK SSSR, VSESOIUZNYI INSTITUT NAUCHNOI I TEKHNICHESKOI INFORMATSII. **Added/Corp** Vsesoiuznyi Institut Nauchnoi i Tekhnicheskoi Informatsii (Soviet Union). **VFOAT** Elektrotekhnika. (1982)-. Abstracting/Indexing Service. Russian. mo. $579.95. VINITI - Vsesoyuznyi Institut Nauchno-Tekhnicheskoi Informatsii, All-Union Scientific and Technical Information Institute, Baltiiskaia Ulitsa 14, 125219 Moscow Russia. **Tel** 238-46-00, FAX 9430060, telex 411160. **(Subscription address:** East View Publications Inc., 3020 Harbor Lane North, Suite 110, Minneapolis MN 55447.**)** **LC** TK4; .R32. Index available. ctrl circ. ***Continues in part*** *Referativnyi Zhurnal: Elektrotekhnika i Elektroenergetika.*

RU/0034-2327
REFERATIVNYI ZHURNAL: ELEKTROTEKHNIKA I ENERGETIKA. **Added/Corp** Akademiia Nauk SSSR. Institut Nauchnoi Informatsii. **VFOAT** Elektrotekhnika i Energetika. (Jan. 1961)-. Periodical. Russian. mo. VINITI - Vsesoyuznyi Institut Nauchno-Tekhnicheskoi Informatsii, All-Union Scientific and Technical Information Institute, Baltiiskaia Ulitsa 14, 125219 Moscow Russia. **Tel** 238-46-00, FAX 9430060, telex 411160. **LC** TK4; .R342. ***Supersedes in part*** *Referativnyi Zhurnal: Elektrotekhnika.*

RU/0203-5308
REFERATIVNYI ZHURNAL. ENERGETIKA / GOSUDARSTVENNYI KOMITET SSSR PO NAUKE I TEKHNIKE, AKADEMIIA NAUK SSSR, VSESOIUZNYI INSTITUT NAUCHNOI I TEKHNICHESKOI INFORMATSII. **Added/Corp** Vsesoiuznyi Institut Nauchnoi i Tekhnicheskoi Informatsii (Soviet Union). **VFOAT** Energetika. (1982)-. Abstracting/Indexing Service. Russian. mo. $719.95. VINITI - Vsesoyuznyi Institut Nauchno-Tekhnicheskoi Informatsii, All-Union Scientific and Technical Information Institute, Baltiiskaia Ulitsa 14, 125219 Moscow Russia. **Tel** 238-46-00, FAX 9430060, telex 411160. **(Subscription address:** East View Publications Inc., 3020 Harbor Lane North, Suite 110, Minneapolis MN 55447.**)** **LC** TK4; .R33. ***Continues in part*** *Referativnyi Zhurnal. Elektrotekhnika i Elektroenergetika.*

US/1066-2731
REFERENCE DATA FOR ENGINEERS : RADIO, ELECTRONICS, COMPUTER, AND COMMUNICATIONS. [Ref. data eng.]. (1985)-. English. ir. $99.95. Howard Sams & Company, Inc., 2647 Waterfront Parkway E Drive, Indianapolis IN 46214. **Tel** (800)428-7267, (317)298-5400. **ED** E C Jordan. **LC** TK6552; .F4. **DD** 621.38. ***Continues*** *Reference Data for Radio Engineers.*
Desc: Reference book containing charts, graphs, diagrams, tables, curves and illustrations.

FR
REGLES DE L'ART HAUTE ET BASSE TENSION. (19??)-. French. 8785.00F France; 9268.18F other. Union Technique de l'Electricite, Cedex 64, 92052 Paris La Defense France. **Tel** 011 33 1 46911111.

BL
RELATORIO - CEPISA. **Main/Corp** Centrais Eletricas do Piaui. Portuguese. Centrais Electricas do Piaui, Av Maranhao No 759, Teresina Brazil. **LC** TK42.P5; C46A.

US/0095-0815
RELAY MINIATURE AND SUBMINIATURE D.A.T.A. BOOK. **Main/Corp** Derivation and Tabulation Associates, Inc. **VAT** Relay Miniature and Subminiature Derivation and Tabulation Associates Book. Began with 1971 Vol. English. $27.50. 32 Lincoln Avenue, Orange NJ 07050. **LC** TK2861; .D47A. **DD** 621.31/7.

US/0898-3933
RELIABILITY ASSESSMENT. [Reliab. assess.]. **Added/Corp** North American Electric Reliability Council. (1987)-. English. an. Free on request. North American Electric Reliability Council, 101 College Road East, Princeton NJ 08540-6601. **Tel** (609)452-8060. **DD** 363. ***Continues*** *Reliability Review (Princeton, N.J.).*
Ind/Abst F&S Index Plus Text, Int. [Select. Cov.]; Predicasts Forecasts.

US/0735-0791
RELIABILITY PHYSICS. [Reliab. phys.]. **Main/Conf** International Reliability Physics Symposium. **Added/Corp** IEEE Electron Devices Society. IEEE Reliability Group. IEEE Reliability Society. Institute of Electrical and Electronics Engineers. Electron Devices Group. (1970)-. English. an. IEEE, Institution of Electrical and Electronics Engineers, Inc., 345 East 47th Street, New York NY 10017-2394. **Tel** (908)981-1393, FAX (908)981-9667. **(Subscription address:** IEEE / Institute of Electrical and Electronics Engineers, 445 Hoes Lane, PO Box 1331, Piscataway NJ 08855-1331.**)** **LC** TK7870; .S95. **DD** 621.381. **[CCC]. *Continues*** *Reliability Physics Symposium. Proceedings.*
Ind/Abst Index IEEE Publ.

SZ
REPERTOIRE / COMMISSION ELECTROTECHNIQUE INTERNATIONALE. **Main/Corp** International Electrotechnical Commission. **VFOAT** Directory. English. an. 0.15F. Commission Electrotechnique Internationale, 3 rue du Varembe, 1211 Geneve 20 Suisse Switzerland. **LC** TK12; .I53A. **DD** 621.3/06/01.

BE
REPERTOIRE DES CENTRALES ELECTRIQUES. **See** Engineering-Abstracting, Bibliographies and Statistics.

II
REPORT - GOVERNMENT OF INDIA, DEPARTMENT OF POWER. **Main/Corp** India (Republic). Dept. of Power. 1974/75-. English. Government of India / Ministry of Energy, Janpath New Delhi India. **LC** TK103; .A33A. **DD** 363.6/2/0954. ***Supersedes in part*** *Report - Government of India, Ministry of Irrigation and Power.*

UK
REPORT (GREAT BRITAIN. ELECTRICAL EQUIPMENT CERTIFICATION MANAGEMENT BOARD). (REPORT / HEALTH AND SAFETY EXECUTIVE, ELECTRICAL EQUIPMENT CERTIFICATION MANAGEMENT BOARD.). 1981-82-. English. £2.00. 49 High Holborn, London WC1V 6HB England. **LC** TK57; .R47. **DD** 621.3/028.

CN/0823-2660
RESEARCH REPORT / CANADIAN ELECTRICAL ASSOCIATION. [Res. Rep. - Can. Electr. Assoc.]. **Added/Corp** Canadian Electrical Association. Canadian Electrical Association. Research and Development. **VFOAT** CEA Research Report. (197?)-. Periodical. English. Canadian Electrical Association, 1 Westmount Square, Suite 1600, Montreal Quebec H3Z 2P9 Canada. **Tel** (514)937-6181, FAX (514)937-6498. **DD** 621.3.
Ind/Abst Ei Page One.

CN/0082-514X
RESEARCH REPORT - DEPARTMENT OF ELECTRICAL ENGINEERING. UNIVERSITY OF TORONTO. (RESEARCH REPORT - UNIVERSITY OF TORONTO, DEPT. OF ELECTRICAL ENGINEERING.). No. 1- 1954-. Monographic series. English. ir. Price varies per volume. University of Toronto Department of Electrical Engineering, Front Campus, Toronto Ontario M5S 7A6 Canada. **DD** 621.3.

FR
RESULTATS / ELECTRICITE DE FRANCE, DIRECTION REGIONALE POUR LES DEPARTEMENTS D'OUTRE-MER. **Main/Corp** Electricite de France. Direction Regionale pour led Departements d'Outre-mer. (19??)-. French. **LC** HD9688.F8; E43a. **DD** 363.6/2.

UY
REUNION. **Main/Corp** Comision de Integracion Electrica Regional. Subcomite de Distribucion de Energia Electrica. Spanish. Comision de Integracion Electrica Regional, Subcomite de Distribucion de Energia Electrica, Boulevar Artigas 996, 1040 Montevideo Uruguay. **Tel** 795359 - 790611, telex CIER UY 920. **LC** TK34; .C64F.

JA
REVIEW OF THE ELECTRICAL COMMUNICATION LAB. Japanese. ir. Must order direct. Nippon Tel & Tel Public Corporation, 9 11 3 Chome Modoricho, Tokyo, Japan.
Ind/Abst Ceram. Abstr. (19??-).

SP/0482-6396
REVISTA ESPANOLA DE ELECTRONICA. [Rev. esp. electron.]. (1972)-. Periodical. Spanish. Twelve times a year. $160.00 (two years). Ediciones Tecnicas Rede, Apartado 35400, 08029 Barcelona Spain. **Tel** 011 34 3 4103097, 011 34 3 4302872. **LC** TK7800; .R485. **CODEN** RVEEBT. Documents available from Ask*IEEE.
Ind/Abst INSPEC (Jan. 1972-); Ornamental Hort.

GW/0937-9649
REVISTA SIEMENS (PORTUGUESE EDITION). (19??)-. Portuguese. qt. $50.00. Siemens AG ZWD V Verlag, Naegelsbachstrasse 26, D 91052 Erlangen Germany. **Tel** 011 49 9131 723004, FAX 011 49 9131 725022. **(Subscription address:** VCH Publishers Inc., 303 Northwest 12th Avenue, Journals Department, Deerfield FL 33442.**)**

AG/0035-0516
REVISTA TELEGRAFICA ELECTRONICA. [Rev. telegr. electron.]. No. 412 (Jan. 1947)-. Periodical. Spanish. Twelve times a year. $45.00. ARBO Sac Ei, Avenida Martin Garcia 653, Buenos Aires Argentina. **Tel** (54)362-0747 OR362-0643. **ED** Ariel Arbo. **CODEN** RTELB2. Index available. cum. index. **Bk Rev. Ad Acc. Pr Rev. Circ:** 10,000. Documents available from Ask*IEEE. ***Continues*** *Revista Telegrafica.*
Desc: Provides updated information about new theories and practice resulting from research in the field of electronics, cybernetics, telecommunications and computers.
Ind/Abst INSPEC (Jan. 1973-).

BE/0777-2181
REVUE E 1989. **VFOAT** Revue d'Electricite et d'Electronique Industrielle. (1989)-. Periodical. French. qt. 1460.00F. Societe Royale Belge des Electriciens, Pleinlaan 2, B 1050 Brussels Belgium. **Tel** 011 32 2 6412819, FAX 011 32 2 6413620. **UDC** 621.35.

FR/0035-3116
REVUE GENERALE DE L'ELECTRICITE. [Rev. gen. electr.]. **Added/Corp** Societe Francaise des Electriciens. Union Technique des Syndicats de l'Electricite. Comite Electrotechnique Francais. Union des Syndicats de l'Electricite, Paris. Vol. 1 No. 1 (Jan. 6 1917)-. Periodical. French (summaries and/or abstracts in English). mo (11 issues per year). 729.68F France; 930.00F EEC countries excpet France; 950.00 other. Revue Generale Electricite SA, 48 rue de la Procession, 75724 Paris Cedex 15 France. **Tel** 011 33 1 44496000. **ED** Jacques Toulemonde. **CODEN** RGELAC. **[CCC].** Index available. cum. index. **Bk Rev. Ad Acc.** ctrl circ. Documents available from Article Express International, Ask*IEEE, CASDDS. ***Formed by the union of*** *Revue Electrique* ***and*** *Lumiere Electrique.*
Ind/Abst Alum. Ind. Abstr.; Bioeng. Abstr.; Chem. Abstr.; Coal Abstr.; Ei Page One; Energy Res. Abstr.; Eng. Index Annu.; F&S Index Plus Text, Int. [Select. Cov.]; INSPEC (1968-); Int. Aerosp. Abstr.; Met. Abstr.; PROMT; Saf. Health Work; Surf. Treat. Technol. Abstr.

NE
REVUE INTERNATIONALE DE L'ECLAIRAGE. English (French, German and Spanish). qt. Fl72.00 Netherlands; Fl87.00 North America; Fl74.00 other. Stichting Promethus, PO Box 721, 5600 AS Eindhoven Netherlands. **Tel** 3140 755252, FAX 3140 756406, telex 35000 PHTCNL. Index available. cum. index. **Bk Rev. Pr Rev. Circ:** 1,500.
Desc: Articles on lighting design and lighting projects.

GW
REVUE SIEMENS. (1929)-. Periodical. French. Four times a year. $50.00. Siemens AG ZWD V Verlag, Naegelsbachstrasse 26, D 91052 Erlangen Germany. **Tel** 011 49 9131 723004, FAX 011 49 9131 725022. **(Subscription address:** VCH Publishers Inc., 303 Northwest 12th Avenue, Journals Department, Deerfield FL 33442.**)** **LC** WMLC L 82/366.

FR/1148-2893
REVUE TECHNIQUE - GEC ALSTHOM. (REVUE TECHNIQUE.). (1990)-. Periodical. French. ir. GEC Alsthom, 38 Avenue Kleber, 75795 Paris Cedex 16 France. **Tel** 011 33 1 47552000. **UDC** 62.002. ***Continues*** *Revue Alsthom (Paris), 0992-3829.*

FR/0035-4279
REVUE TECHNIQUE THOMSON-CSF. [Rev. tech. - Thomson-CSF]. **Main/Corp** Thomson-CSF. Vol. 1, (March 1969)-. Periodical. French (summaries and/or abstracts in English and German). Four times a year. 734.57F France; 1050.00F others. Thomson CSF France, CDX 67, 92045 Paris LA Defense France. **Tel** 011 33 1 49078515. **(Subscription address:** Centrale des Revues, 11 rue Gossin, 92543 Montrouge Cedex France.**)** **LC** TK7800; .A52. **CODEN** RTTCBG. **[CCC].** Documents available from Article Express International, Ask*IEEE, CASDDS. ***Supersedes*** *Annales de Radioelectricite; Revue Technique de la Compagnie Francais Thomson Houston-Hotchkiss Brandt.*
Ind/Abst ACM Guide Comput. Lit.; Bioeng. Abstr.; Ceram. Abstr. (19??-); Chem. Abstr.; Comput. Rev.; Ei Page One; Energy Res. Abstr.; Eng. Index Annu.; INSPEC (Sept. 1969-); Int. Aerosp. Abstr.; Math. Rev.

US/0163-9218
RLE PROGRESS REPORT. [RLE prog. rep.]. **Main/Corp** Massachusetts Institute of Technology. Research Laboratory of Electronics. **VFOAT** Progress Report. **VAT** Research Laboratory of Electronics Progress Report. No. 115, (1975)-. Periodical. English. an. Free. Massachusetts Institute of Technology (MIT) / Research Laboratory of Electronics, Communications Office, Room 36-412, Cambridge MA 02139. **Tel** (617)253-2566, FAX (617)258-7864. **ED** Barbara Passero. **LC** TK7800; .M37A. **DD** 621.381/05. Index available. **Circ:** 1,300. ***Continues** Massachusetts Institute of Technology. Research Laboratory of Electronics. Quarterly Progress Report.*
Desc: Describes research programs at RLE during each calendar year. A bibliography of RLE publications and papers presented during the year is included in the report.
Ind/Abst Soc. Plann. Policy Dev. Abstr.

US/1055-9450
ROBERTSON'S CURRENT COMPETITION. [Robertson's curr. compet.]. **VFOAT** Current Competition. Vol. 1, No. 3 (Nov. 1990)-. Periodical. English. mo. $260.00. Robertsons Current Competition, 129 Upper Creek Road, Stockton NJ 08559. **Tel** (201)996-6554, FAX (908)996-3280. **ED** Hope. E. Robertson. **DD** 333. **Circ:** 500. ***Continues** Current Competition, 1054-0989.*
Desc: Tracks opportunity and trends in competition in the electric utility industry.

US
RURALITE. Vol. 21, No. 1 (Jan. 1974)-. Periodical. English. Twelve times a year. $5.00. Ruralite Services Inc, Box 557, Forest Grove OR 97116. **Tel** (503)357-2105. ***Continues** Northwest Ruralite.*

US/0148-3501
RUSHLIGHT (VERNON), THE. (THE RUSHLIGHT.). **Added/Corp** Rushlight Club. (Nov. 1934)-. Periodical. English. Four times a year. $22.50 Comes with Rushlight Club membership. Rushlight Club Inc., 720 Hartranft Avenue, Fort Washington PA 19034. **ED** Marianne Nolan. **LC** TP746; .R86. **DD** 621.32/3/05. Index available. **Circ:** 600 (ctrl).
Desc: Contains articles dealing with early forms of artificial lighting up to and including the development of the electric lamp bulb.

●US/1068-3712
RUSSIAN ELECTRICAL ENGINEERING. [Russ. electr. eng.]. Vol. 64, No. 1 (1993)-. Periodical. English (translations available in Russian). mo. $930.00. Allerton Press, Inc., 150 Fifth Avenue, New York NY 10011. **Tel** (212)924-3950, FAX (212)463-9684, telex 427441 ALPRES. **LC** TK4; .S64. **DD** 621. **CODEN** RELEEG. **[CCC].** Documents available from Ask*IEEE. ***Continues** Soviet Electrical Engineering, 0038-5379.*
Ind/Abst Bioeng. Abstr.; Eng. Index Annu.; INSPEC; Int. Aerosp. Abstr.

UK
SAFETY AND EMC. Newsletter. English. Six times a year. £95.00. ERA Technology Ltd., Cleeve Road, Leatherhead Surrey KT22 7SA England. **Tel** 011 44 372 374151, FAX 011 44 372 374496, telex 264045. **ED** Natalie J. Wood.
Desc: Safety and Electromagnetic Compatibility (EMC) - a newsletter for designers and suppliers of electrical and electronic products; covers new regulations and gives practical details needed to improve market acceptance of products.

FI/0036-2670
SAHKO TELE. **Added/Corp** Sahkoinsinooriliitto (Finland). **VFOAT** Sahko. Vol. 63, 6 (1990)-. Periodical. Finnish (English). mo. Fmk515.00. Sahko Electricity and Electronics, Pohjoinen Rautatiekatu 17A1, SF-00100 Helsinki Finland. ***Continues** Sahko, 0036-2670.*

II
SAKTI VANI. **VFOAT** Shakti Vani. Periodical. Multiple languages (English and Hindi). 0.99 single issue. Som Gupta, Shati Bhawan 14 Ashok Marg, Lucknow India. **LC** TK104.U8; S23.

US/0163-3627
SAMS AUTO RADIO SERVICE DATA. **Main/Corp** Howard W. Sams and Co. **Added/Corp** Howard W. Sams & Co. Auto Radio Service Data. Vol. 267 (Oct. 1978)-. English. Howard Sams & Company, Inc., 2647 Waterfront Parkway E Drive, Indianapolis IN 46214. **Tel** (800)428-7267, (317)298-5400. **LC** TK6570.A8; S29. **DD** 629.2/77. **Bk Rev. Ad Acc.** ***Continues** Sams Photofact Auto Radio Series.*
Desc: Full service documentation for repair of auto radios.

XR
SBORNIK PEDAGOGICKE FAKULTY V PLZNI. ELEKTRONIKA. **VFOAT** Elektronika. (1989)-. Periodical. Czech (summaries and/or abstracts in German and Russian). Statni Pedagogicke Nakladatelstvi, Ostrovni 30, 113 01 Prague 1 Czech Republic. **Tel** (2)203787, FAX (2)293883. **LC** TK7815; .S29.

US/0018-9227
SCANFAX. (SCANFAX: OFFICIAL PUBLICATION OF THE CHICAGO [SECTION], INSTITUTE OF ELECTRICAL & ELECTRONICS ENGINEERS.). **Added/Corp** Institute of Electrical and Electronics Engineers. Chicago Section. (19??)-. Newsletter. English. mo. $3.00. Institution of Electrical Engineers / IEE, Michael Faraday House, Six Hills Way, Stevenage Herts SG1 2AY UK. **Tel** 011 44 438 313311, FAX 011 44 438 742840, telex 825578 IEESTV G. **(Subscription address:** IEE / UK, Publications Sales Department, PO Box 96, Stevenage, Herts, SG1 2SD England.**)** **ED** H. R. Hofmann. **Ad Acc. Circ:** 6,000 (ctrl).
Desc: Newsletter to IEEE members in the Chicago area.

SZ
SCHWEIZERISCHER ELECTROTECHNISCHER VEREIN. Multiple languages (French and German). da. Jean Frey Druck, Postfach 299, CH-8021 Zurich, Switzerland. **Tel** 011 41 1 2078919.

US/0036-8695
SCIENTIA ELECTRICA. ***Ceased.*** [Sci. electr.]. Vol. 1 (1953)-Vol. 36, No. 4 (1990). Periodical. English (French and German; summaries and/or abstracts in French, German and English). qt. Birkhaeuser Verlag Ag, Klosterberg 23, PO Box 133, CH-4010 Basel Switzerland. **Tel** 011 41 61 2717400, FAX 011 41 0 61 2717666, telex 963475 birk ch. **(Subscription address:** Switzerland/ PO Box 133, Elisabethenstr 19, CH-4010 Basel**)** **LC** TK1.A1; S3. **CODEN** SCELAT. **[CCC].** cum. index. Documents available from Article Express International, Ask*IEEE.
Ind/Abst Bioeng. Abstr.; Ei Page One; Eng. Index Annu.; INSPEC (1968-); Pollut. Abstr. Indexes.

US/0885-5005
SCREEN IMAGING TECHNOLOGY FOR ELECTRONICS. ***Ceased.*** (SCREEN IMAGING TECHNOLOGY FOR ELECTRONICS : SITE.). [Screen imaging technol. electron.]. **VFOAT** SITE; SITE Magazine. Vol. 1, No. 1 (Nov. 1985)-(1988). Periodical. English. qt. Signs of the Times Publishing Company, 407 Gilbert Avenue, Cincinnati OH 45202. **Tel** (513)421-2050, (800)925-1110, FAX (513)421-5144. **DD** 686. **[CCC].**

BE
SECTION : CONSTRUCTION ELECTRIQUE. **Main/Corp** Brussels. Centre de Recherches Scientifiques et Techniques de l'industrie des Fabrications Metalliques. French. Rue des Drapiers 21, Bruxelles Belgium. **LC** TK2; .B76A. **DD** 621.31/042/08.

UK/0307-7780
SECURITECH. [Securitech]. **VFOAT** International Guide to Security Equipment. (1972)-. English (French, German, Spanish and Arabic). an. £59.00 UK; $100.00 other. Argus Press Group, Queensway House, 2 Queensway Redhill, Surrey RH1 1QS England. **Tel** 011 44 737 768611, 011 44 737 761685, FAX 011 44 737 760510, telex 948669 TOPJNL G.

US/0276-5535
SELECTED ELECTRONIC AND ASSOCIATED PRODUCTS, INCLUDING TELEPHONE AND TELEGRAPH APPARATUS. (CURRENT INDUSTRIAL REPORTS. MA-36N, SELECTED ELECTRONIC AND ASSOCIATED PRODUCTS, INCLUDING TELEPHONE AND TELEGRAPH APPARATUS / U.S. DEPARTMENT OF COMMERCE, BUREAU OF THE CENSUS.). [Sel. electron. assoc. prod., incl. teleph. telegr. appar.]. Government Publication. English. an. $2.00. US Department of Commerce / Bureau of the Census, Data User Services Division, Customer Services, Washington DC 20233-0800. **Tel** (301)763-4100. **(Subscription address:** Superintendent of Documents, US Government Printing Office, Washington DC 20402.**)** **LC** HD9696.A3; U598. **DD** 338.4/762138/0973.
Desc: Presents timely data on the production, inventories, and orders of approximately 5,000 products, which represents 40 percent of all US manufacturing.

IT
SELEZIONE DI ELETTRONICA. (19??)-. Italian. Eleven times a year. L90000 Italy; L180000 other. Gruppo Editoriale JCE SRL, Via Ferri 6, 20092 Cinisello B Milan Italy. **Tel** 011 39 2 660251, FAX 011 39 2 66025343.

US/0146-4264
SEMI DIRECTORY. ***Title Change.*** **Main/Corp** Semiconductor Equipment and Materials Institute. **VAT** Semiconductor Equipment and Materials Institute Directory. Directory. English. sa. Semiconductor Equipment, 805 East Middlefield, Mountain View CA 94043-4080. **Tel** (415)964-5111, FAX (415)967-5375, telex 856-777 SEMI-MNTV. **LC** TK7805; .S44A. Index available. **Circ:** 4,500. ***Continued by** SEMI Membership Directory (SEMI Conductor Equipment and Materials Institute).*
Desc: Listing of semiconductor equipment and materials international (SEMI) corporate, business affiliate and individual members. Includes product index, geographical index, government development agencies index and industry consultants listing.

US
SEMICONDUCTOR CURRENTS. English. Twelve times a year. $450.00. Semiconductor Currents, PO Box 7000051, San Jose CA 95170. **ED** Sten Dymlinz (editor's address: 930 Brookgrove Lane, Cuperstino, CA 95129-4668; telephone: (408)996-9764). ctrl circ.

US
SEMICONDUCTOR DATA UPDATE. ***Ceased.*** (19??)-(1992). English. qt. Motorola Semiconductor Product, PO Box 20912, Phoenix AZ 85036. **Tel** (602)994-6561.

US/0092-6302
SEMICONDUCTOR HEAT SINK, SOCKET & ASSOCIATED HARDWARE D.A.T.A. BOOK. **Main/Corp** Derivation and Tabulation Associates, Inc. **VAT** Semiconductor Heat Sink, Socket and Associated Hardware Derivation and Tabulation Associates Book. English. an. $24.00. 32 Lincoln Avenue, Orange NJ 07050. **LC** TK7872.H4; D4A. **DD** 621.3815/2.

US/0730-1014
SEMICONDUCTOR INDUSTRY AND BUSINESS SURVEY. (SEMICONDUCTOR INDUSTRY AND BUSINESS SURVEY : SIBS.). [Semicond. ind. bus. surv.]. **VFOAT** SIBS. (19??)-. Periodical. English. Eighteen times a year (Every 3rd Monday). $495.00 (US & Canada); $795.00 (other). HTE Research Inc., 400 Oyster Point Boulevard, Suite 220, San Francisco CA 94080. **Tel** (415)871-4377, FAX (415)871-0513. available on an online database (files 16,636/Full-Text) from DIALOG.
Ind/Abst PROMT [Full Txt.]; PTS Newsl. Database [Full Txt.].

US/0163-3767
SEMICONDUCTOR INTERNATIONAL. [Semicond. int.]. Vol. 1 (Nov./Dec. 1978)-. Periodical. English. Thirteen times a year. $85.00 US; $124.00 Canada; $115.00 Mexico; $145.00 (surface mail) other. Cahners Publishing Company, 249 West 17th Street, New York NY 10011. **Tel** (212)645-0067, FAX (212)242-6987. **(Subscription address:** Cahners Publishing Company / Colorado, Paid Subscription Service Center, PO Box 7610, Highlands Ranch CO 80126-7610.**)** **ED** Don Swanson. **LC** TK7871.85; .S464. **DD** 621.3815/2/05. **CODEN** SITLDD. **[CCC]. Bk Rev. Ad Acc. Circ:** 35,927 (ctrl). available on microfilm and microfiche from University Microfilms International (UMI). Documents available from Article Express International, Ask*IEEE, CASDDS.
Desc: Features articles on a range of topics including wafer fabrication, circuit and mask design, wafer processing, assembly and testing. Also covered are equipment trends, chemicals/materials, assembly techniques, QC/AQ and testing, industry news and forecasts.
Ind/Abst Bioeng. Abstr.; Chem. Abstr.; Ei Page One; Eng. Index Annu.; F&S Index Plus Text, Int. [Select. Cov.]; Infomat Int. Bus.; INSPEC (May 1982-); PROMT.

US/0091-391X
SEMICONDUCTOR SILICON. [Semicond. silicon]. **Added/Corp** Electrochemical Society. Electrochemical Society. Electronics Division. Electrochemical Society. Electrothermics and Metallurgy Division. (1969)-. English. Electrochemical Society, 10 South Main Street, Pennington NJ 08534. **Tel** (609)737-1902. **LC** TK7871.85; .I584. **DD** 621.3815/2.

JA
SEMICONDUCTOR TECHNIQUE. (19??)-. Periodical. Japanese. mo. $162.00. **(Subscription address:** Maruzen Company Ltd., PO Box 5050, Import & Export Department, Tokyo 100 31 Japan.**)**

US/0080-8784
SEMICONDUCTORS AND SEMIMETALS. [Semicond. semimet.]. (1966)-. Monographic series. English. ir. Price varies per volume. Academic Press, Inc., 6277 Sea Harbor Drive, Orlando FL 32887. **Tel** (800)543-9534, (407)345-4100, FAX (407)363-9661. **ED** R. K. Willardson and A. C. Beer. **LC** QC610.9; .S48. **DD** 621.3815/2. **[CCC].** Documents available from The Genuine Article, Ask*IEEE, CASDDS.
Ind/Abst Chem. Abstr.; Ei Page One; INSPEC; Res. Alert [Full Cov.]; Sci. Cit. Index; SCISEARCH.

US/8756-4017
SENSOR TECHNOLOGY. [Sens. technol.]. **Added/Corp** Technical Insights, Inc. Vol. 1, No. 1 (Mar. 1985)-. Periodical. English. mo. $565.00 North America; $625.00 other. Technical Insights Inc., PO Box 1304, Fort Lee NJ 07024-9967. **Tel** (201)568-4744, FAX (201)568-8247, telex 425900 SWIFT UI. **ED** Hal Hellman, Richard Consolas and Joseph Constance. **LC** WMLC 93/4231. **DD** 681. **[CCC].** available on an online database (file 636/Full-Text) from DIALOG.
Desc: Monthly update service following sensors and their array of growing uses in industry.
Ind/Abst Abstr. BioCommer. (-199?); NEXIS; PTS Newsl. Database [Full Txt.].

SZ/0924-4247
SENSORS AND ACTUATORS. A, PHYSICAL. [Sens. actuators. A Phys.]. **VFOAT** Physical. Vol. A21, No. 1-3 (Feb. 1990)-. Periodical. English. Eighteen times a year (6 volumes). 1920.00F; 3705.00F combined subscription with Sensors and Actuators B. Elsevier Sequoia SA, PO Box 564, CH-1001 Lausanne 1 Switzerland. **Tel** 011 41 21 3207381. **ED** S. Middelhoek. **LC** TK7881.2; .S463. **DD** 621.381/54. **CODEN** SAAPEB. **[CCC]. Ad Acc, Adv Mgr:** Ms. W van Cattenburch (Amsterdam). available on microfilm and microfiche from University Microfilms International (UMI). Documents available from Article Express International, The Genuine Article, Ask*IEEE, CASDDS. ***Continues in part*** *Sensors and Actuators, 0250-6874.*
Desc: Devoted for disseminating information on all aspects of research and development of solid-state devices for transducing physical signals.
Ind/Abst Chem. Abstr.; Curr. Contents Eng. Tech. Appl. Sci.; Ei Page One; Eng. Mater. Abstr.; Eng. Index Annu.; INSPEC (Feb. 1990-); Met. Abstr.; Res. Alert [Full Cov.]; Sci. Cit. Index; SCISEARCH.

SZ/0925-4005
SENSORS AND ACTUATORS. B, CHEMICAL. [Sens. actuators. B Chem.]. Vol. B1, Nos. 1-6 (Jan. 1990)-. English. Twenty-one times a year (7 volumes). 2240.00F; 3705.00F combined subscription with Sensors and Actuators A. Elsevier Sequoia SA, PO Box 564, CH-1001 Lausanne 1 Switzerland. **Tel** 011 41 21 3207381. **ED** K. Cammann. **LC** TK7881.2; .S464. **DD** 681.2. **CODEN** SABCEB. **[CCC]. Ad Acc, Adv Mgr:** Ms. W van Cattenburch (Amsterdam). available on microfilm and microfiche from University Microfilms International (UMI). Documents available from Article Express International, The Genuine Article, Ask*IEEE, CASDDS. ***Continues in part*** *Sensors and Actuators, 0250-6874.*
Desc: Devoted to disseminating information on all aspects of research and development of sensor elements transforming and transducing chemical signals into information about the chemical composition of the sample analysed.
Ind/Abst Chem. Abstr.; Curr. Contents Eng. Tech. Appl. Sci.; Eng. Index Annu.; INSPEC (Jan. 1990-); Res. Alert [Full Cov.]; Sci. Cit. Index; SCISEARCH.

US/1046-1965
SERVICE NEWS (YARMOUTH, ME.). See Computers-Computer Industry and Industry Directories.

JA/0286-3383
SHIZUOKA DAIGAKU DENSHI KOGAKU KENKYUJO KENKYU HOKOKU. [Shizuoka Daigaku Denshi KÂogaku Kenkyujo kenkyu hokoku]. **Main/Corp** Shizuoka Daigaku. Denshi Kogaku Kenkyujo. **Added/Corp** Shizuoka Daigaku. Denshi Kogaku Kenkyujo. Bulletin of the Research Institute of Electronics, Shizuoka University. **VFOAT** Bulletin of the Research Institute of Electronics, Shizuoka University. (1966)-. Academic Scholarly Publication. Multiple languages. Shizuoka Daigaku Denshi Kogaku Kenkyujo, (Research Inst. of Electronics, Shizuoka University), 5-1, Johoku 3 Chome, Hamamatsushi, Shizuokaken 432 Japan. **LC** TK7800; .S485a. **CODEN** SDDHDM. Documents available from CASDDS.
Ind/Abst Chem. Abstr.

GW/0173-1726
SIEMENS COMPONENTS. DEUTSCHE AUSGABE. [Siemens compon., Dtsch. Ausg.]. (1980)-. Periodical. German. Six times a year. $52.00. Siemens AG ZWD V Verlag, Naegelsbachstrasse 26, D 91052 Erlangen Germany. **Tel** 011 49 9131 723004, FAX 011 49 9131 725022. **(Subscription address:** VCH Publishers Inc., 303 Northwest 12th Avenue, Journals Department, Deerfield FL 33442.) **UDC** 621.382. ***Continues*** *Bauteilereport, 0341-6550.*

GW/0173-1734
SIEMENS COMPONENTS. ENGLISH AUSGABE. (SIEMENS COMPONENTS.). [Siemens compon., Engl. Ausg.]. **Added/Corp** Siemens Aktiengesellschaft. (1980)-. Periodical. English. bm. $52.00. Siemens AG ZWD V Verlag, Naegelsbachstrasse 26, D 91052 Erlangen Germany. **Tel** 011 49 9131 723004, FAX 011 49 9131 725022. **(Subscription address:** VCH Publishers Inc., 303 Northwest 12th Avenue, Journals Department, Deerfield FL 33442.) **CODEN** SICOD5. **[CCC].** Documents available from Article Express International, Ask*IEEE.
Ind/Abst Bioeng. Abstr.; Ei Page One; Eng. Index Annu.; INSPEC (1980-).

GW/0302-2528
SIEMENS REVIEW. [Siemens rev.]. **Added/Corp** Siemens Aktiengesellschaft. Siemens Schuckertwerke. (1930)-. Academic Scholarly Publication. English. bm. $74.00. Siemens AG ZWD V Verlag, Naegelsbachstrasse 26, D 91052 Erlangen Germany. **Tel** 011 49 9131 723004, FAX 011 49 9131 725022. **(Subscription address:** VCH Publishers Inc., 303 Northwest 12th Avenue, Journals Department, Deerfield FL 33442.) **LC** TK3; .S733. **DD** 621.305. **CODEN** SZTEA6. **[CCC].** cum. index. **Bk Rev. Ad Acc. Pr Rev.** Documents available from Article Express International, The Genuine Article, Ask*IEEE, Documents on Demand. ***Continues*** *Siemens-Schuckert.*
Desc: Covers microelectronics, information technology, factor automation, power plant design and construction, as well as medical engineering.
Ind/Abst Alum. Ind. Abstr.; Coal Abstr.; Curr. Contents Eng. Tech. Appl. Sci.; EMBASE; Energy Inf. Abstr.; Eng. Mater. Abstr.; Eng. Index Annu.; Environ. Abstr.; Ergon. Abstr.; Infomat Int. Bus.; INSPEC (1968-); Int. Aerosp. Abstr.; Met. Abstr.; Res. Alert [Select. Cov.]; Soc. Sci. Cit. Index [Select. Cov.].

GW/0302-251X
SIEMENS ZEITSCHRIFT. [Siemens-Z.]. **Added/Corp** Siemens & Halske. Siemens-Schuckertwerke. (19??)-. Periodical. German. bm. $74.00. Siemens AG ZWD V Verlag, Naegelsbachstrasse 26, D 91052 Erlangen Germany. **Tel** 011 49 9131 723004, FAX 011 49 9131 725022. **(Subscription address:** VCH Publishers Inc., 303 Northwest 12th Avenue, Journals Department, Deerfield FL 33442.) **LC** TK3; .S734. **DD** 621.305. **CODEN** SIEZAB. Documents available from CASDDS.
Ind/Abst Chem. Abstr. (1921-1979); Coal Abstr.; EMBASE; Energy Res. Abstr.; Saf. Health Work.

US
SIERRA SOURCEBOOK : ELECTRONICS INDUSTRY MARKET DATA. VFOAT Electronics Industry Market Data. English. an. $50.00. Sierra Economic Services, 800 Welch Road, Palo Alto CA 94304. **LC** Z5836; .S56. **DD** 016.3384/7/62130973.

NE/0165-1684
SIGNAL PROCESSING. (SIGNAL PROCESSING : THE OFFICIAL PUBLICATION OF THE EUROPEAN ASSOCIATION FOR SIGNAL PROCESSING (EURASIP).). [Signal process.]. **Added/Corp** European Association for Signal Processing. (Jan. 1979)-. Academic Scholarly Publication. English. Twenty-one times a year (6 vols.). Fl2625.00; Fl3128.00 combined subscription with Signal Processing: Image Communication. Elsevier Science Publishers BV, PO Box 211, 1000 AE Amsterdam Netherlands. **Tel** 011 31 20 5803642, FAX 011 31 20 5862696, telex 15682. **ED** Murat Kunt. **LC** TK5102.5; .S54. **DD** 621.38. **CODEN** SPRODR. **[CCC]. Bk Rev. Ad Acc. Pr Rev.** available on microfilm and microfiche from University Microfilms International (UMI). Documents available from Article Express International, The Genuine Article, Ask*IEEE.
Desc: Incorporates all aspects of the field's theory and practice both analogue and digital. Featuring original research, tutorial and review articles as well as accounts of practical developments, the journal acts as a vehicle for the rapid dissemination of knowledge and experience to engineers and scientists active in the field.
Ind/Abst Abstr. Hum. Comput. Interact.; ACM Guide Comput. Lit.; Acoust. Abstr. (Jan. 1979-); Bioeng. Abstr.; Comput. Inf. Syst. Abstr. J. [Full Cov.]; Comput. Rev. (Jan. 1979-); Curr. Contents Eng. Tech. Appl. Sci.; Ei Page One; Elect. Comm. Abstr.; Eng. Index Annu.; GeoRef; INSPEC (Jan. 1979-); Int. Aerosp. Abstr.; Math. Rev. (?-199?); Mech. Eng. Abstr.; Pollut. Abstr. Indexes; Res. Alert [Select. Cov.]; Zentralbl. Math. Ihre Grenzgeb.

NE/0923-5965
SIGNAL PROCESSING. IMAGE COMMUNICATION. [Signal process., Image commun.]. **Added/Corp** European Association for Signal Processing. **VFOAT** Image Communication. Vol. 1 No. 1 (June 1989)-. English. Six times a year (1 volume). Fl575.00; Fl3128.00 combined subscription with Signal Processing. Elsevier Science Publishers BV, PO Box 211, 1000 AE Amsterdam Netherlands. **Tel** 011 31 20 5803642, FAX 011 31 20 5862696, telex 15682. **ED** L Chiariglione. **CODEN** SPICEF. **[CCC].** Index available. **Bk Rev. Ad Acc. Pr Rev.** available on microfilm and microfiche from University Microfilms International (UMI). Documents available from Article Express International, Ask*IEEE.
Desc: Design, implementation and use of image transmission, storage and display systems.
Ind/Abst Comput. Inf. Syst. Abstr. J. [Full Cov.]; Elect. Comm. Abstr.; Eng. Index Annu.; INSPEC (1989-); Mech. Eng. Abstr.

AT/1030-2662
SILICON CHIP. [Silicon chip]. (1987)-. Periodical. English. mo. 46.00Aus$ Australia; 72.00Aus$ (surface mail), 132.00Aus$ (air mail) other. Silicon Chip Publ. Pty Limited, PO Box 139, Collaroy NSW 2097 Australia. **Tel** 011 61 02 9795644, FAX 011 61 02 9796503. **DD** 621.3805.

US/1055-209X
SINE (HESPERIA, CALIF.). (SINE : SERVICE INFORMATION NEWS AND ELECTRONICS.). **VAT** Service Information News and Electronics. (1991)-. Periodical. English. mo. $28.00.

IT
SISTEMA ITALIA. (19??)-. Italian. wk. L200000 Italy; L260000 other. Edisi Spa, Via Listz 21, 00144 Rome Italy. **Tel** 011 39 6 5999442. ***Continues*** *Giornale dell ICE.*

●US/1076-366X
SMART ELECTRONICS. [Smart electron.]. Vol. 1, No. 1 (Dec. 1993/Jan. 1994)-. Periodical. English. Six times a year. $14.95. McMullen Publishing Inc, 2145 West La Palma Avenue, PO Box 70015, Anaheim CA 92801-1785. **Tel** (714)572-2255, FAX (714)572-1864. **DD** 621.

●UK
SMART MATERIALS AND STRUCTURES. Vol. 1 (1992)-. English. qt. £110.00 UK; $220.00 US, Canada and Mexico. Institute of Physics, Techno House, Redcliffe Way, Bristol BS1 6NX England. **Tel** 011 44 272 297481, FAX 011 44 272 294318, telex 449149 INSTP G. **(Subscription address:** American Institute of Physics, Publishing Sales, 500 Sunnyside Blvd., Woodbury NY 11797.) **ED** Richard O. Claus, Gareth J. Knowles and Vigay K. Varadan. Index available in last issue of volume--attached. available on microfiche.
Desc: Provides a much needed forum for the communication of high quality research in this highly interdisciplinary major growth market. Smart materials will essentially be those incorporating integrated distributed sensors measuring a range of parameters. These can be connected to active components, actuators, to alter the configuration of the structure in response to the sensing system.

UK
SMRE DIGEST : ELECTRICAL HAZARDS. VFOAT SMRE Digest; Electrical Hazards. Periodical. English.

US/0890-7900
SMT TRENDS. [SMTrends]. **Added/Corp** Market Intelligence Research Company. **VFOAT** SMT Trends; S.M.T. Trends. **VAT** Surface Mount Technology Trends. (198?)-. Periodical. English. Twelve times a year. $325.00 North America; $345.00 other. Vital Information Publications, 321 Carrera Drive, Mill Valley CA 94941. **Tel** (415)389-8671, (415)345-7018, FAX (415)389-8671, (415)345-7018. **ED** Sarah Collings. **DD** 621. **Bk Rev**, (Qty: 4/year). **Ad Acc.** available on an online database from NEWSNET; and Predicasts, Inc.
Desc: Surface mount technology, advanced packaging, circuit board assembly, electronic components and materials, inspection and test, markets and applications.

UK/0038-1101
SOLID-STATE ELECTRONICS. [Solid-state electron.]. **VFOAT** Solid State Electronics. Vol. 1 (Mar. 1960)-. Periodical. English. mo. $1140.00 The Americas; £765.00 other. Pergamon Press, An Imprint of Elsevier Science Ltd., The Boulevard, Langford Lane, Kidlington, Oxford OX5 1GB United Kingdom. **Tel** 011 44 865 843000, 011 44 865 843699, FAX 011 44 865 843010. **(Subscription address:** Elsevier Science Ltd. Oxford Fulfillment Centre, PO Box 800, Kidlington, Oxford OX5 1DX United Kingdom.) **ED** Sorab K. Ghandhi, F.M. Klaassen, S.J. Pearton. **LC** TK7872.S4; S546. **DD** 621.3815/2/05. **CODEN** SSELA5. **[CCC]. Pr Rev.** available on microfilm from Microfilms International Marketing Corp.; available on microfilm and microfiche from University Microfilms International (UMI); available on microfiche from the publisher. Documents available from Article Express International, The Genuine Article, Ask*IEEE, CASDDS. ***Continued in part by*** *Applied Superconductivity, 0964-1807.*
Desc: Brings together in one publication papers reporting original work in the following areas: 1) applications of solid-state physics in such fields as transistor technology; 2) applications of computer and numerical methods to the modeling and simulation of solid-state devices; 3) physics and design of ultra-small (submicron) microelectronic devices (VLSI).
Ind/Abst Acoust. Abstr.; Appl. Sci. Technol. Index (1991-); Bioeng. Abstr.; Chem. Abstr.; Chem. Titles; Civ. Struct. Eng. Abstr.; Comput. Inf. Syst. Abstr. J. [Full Cov.]; Curr. Contents Eng. Tech. Appl. Sci.; Curr. Contents Phys. Chem. Earth Sci.; Curr. Technol. Index; Ei Page One; Elect. Comm. Abstr.; Eng. Index Annu.; INSPEC (1968-); Int. Aerosp. Abstr.; Manuf. Process Eng. Abstr.; Mater. Sci. Eng. Abstr.; Mech. Eng. Abstr.; Res. Alert [Full Cov.]; Sci. Cit. Index; SCISEARCH; Soc. Sci. Cit. Index [Select. Cov.]; Solid State Supercond. Abstr.

US/0038-111X
SOLID STATE TECHNOLOGY. [Solid state technol.]. Vol. 11, No. 1 (Jan. 1968)-. Periodical. English. Twelve times a year. $152.00 US; $202.00 other. PennWell Publishing Company, 1421 South Sheridan, PO Box 1260, Tulsa OK 74101. **Tel** (918)835-3161, (800)331-4463, FAX (918)831-9497. **(Subscription address:** Solid State Technology, Publishing Services, PO Box 3689, Tulsa OK 74101.) **ED** S. Marshall. **LC** TK7872.S4; S44. **DD** 621.381/05. **CODEN** SSTEAP. **[CCC]. Bk Rev. Ad Acc. Pr Rev. Circ:** 35,000 (ctrl). available on microfilm and microfiche from University Microfilms International (UMI); available on an online database (file 648/Full-Text) from DIALOG. Documents available from Article Express International, The Genuine Article, Ask*IEEE, CASDDS. ***Continues*** *Semiconductor Products and Solid State Technology, 0096-3631.*
Desc: Coverage of technology used in integrated circuit, thin film microelectronics and microstructure manufacturing.
Ind/Abst Abstr. Graphic Arts Tech. Found. (1984); Alum. Ind. Abstr.; Appl. Sci. Technol. Index; Bioeng. Abstr.; Ceram. Abstr.; Chem. Abstr.; Curr. Contents Eng. Tech. Appl. Sci.; Curr. Titles Electrochem.; Ei Page One; Eng. Mater. Abstr.; Eng. Index Annu.; F&S Index Plus Text, Int. [Select. Cov.]; Infomat Int. Bus.; INSPEC (1968-); Met.

Abstr.; PROMT; Res. Alert [Full Cov.]; Sci. Cit. Index; SCISEARCH; Trade Ind. ASAP [Full Txt.]; Trade Ind. Index [Full Txt.].

●US
SOLID STATE TECHNOLOGY ... BUYING GUIDE. (1992)-. English. an. $99.00 US; $110.00 other. PennWell Publishing Company, 1421 South Sheridan, PO Box 1260, Tulsa OK 74101. **Tel** (918)835-3161, (800)331-4463, FAX (918)831-9497. **(Subscription address:** PennWell Books, PO Box 21288, Tulsa OK 74121.**)** **LC** TK7870.3; .S65. **DD** 621.381/029/4. ***Continues*** *Solid State Technology ... Processing & Production Buyers Guide.*
Desc: Complete reference on materials, equipment and services used in the manufacture and processing of solid state devices and circuits.

US/0038-3309
SOUTH DAKOTA HIGH LINER. ***Title Change.*** **Added/Corp** South Dakota Rural Electric Association. (19??)-(19??). Periodical. English. mo. South Dakota Rural Electric Association, PO Box 1138, Pierre SD 57501. **Tel** (605)224-8823, FAX (605)224-4430. ***Continued by*** *South Dakota High Liner Magazine, 1067-4977.*

US/1062-5798
SOUTHEAST POWER REPORT. [Southeast power rep.]. (19??)-. Newsletter. English. bw. $825.00 US and Canada; $875.00 other. McGraw Hill Publishing Company, Inc., 1221 Avenue of the Americas, New York NY 10020. **Tel** (212)512-6410, (800)525-5003, FAX (212)512-6111. **DD** 333.

US/0145-8426
SOUTHERN ELECTRICAL BUYERS' GUIDE. **VFOAT** Electrical Buyers' Guide. Consumer Publication. English. sa. Rickard Publishing Company, 20 North Wacker Drive, Chicago IL 60606. **LC** HD9697.A3; U57. **DD** 381/.45/621302575.

US/1041-2379
SOUTHWEST TECHNOLOGY REPORT. [Southwest technol. rep.]. (19??)-. Periodical. English. sm. $69.00. C / S Communications Incorporated, PO Box 23899, Tempe AZ 85285. **Tel** (602)345-1118, FAX (602)345-1119. **ED** Walter J. Schuch. **DD** 338. Index available.

US/0038-5379
SOVIET ELECTRICAL ENGINEERING. ***Title Change.*** [Sov. electr. engin.]. (19??)-(1993). Periodical. English (translations available in Russian). mo. Allerton Press, Inc., 150 Fifth Avenue, New York NY 10011. **Tel** (212)924-3950, FAX (212)463-9684, telex 427441 ALPRES. **LC** TK4. **CODEN** SOEEAO. **[CCC].** Documents available from Article Express International, Ask*IEEE. ***Continued by*** *Russian Electrical Engineering.*
Ind/Abst Bioeng. Abstr.; Ei Page One; Eng. Index Annu.; INSPEC (1975-); Int. Aerosp. Abstr.; Pig News Inf.

US/8756-6648
SOVIET JOURNAL OF COMMUNICATIONS TECHNOLOGY & ELECTRONICS. ***Title Change.*** [Sov. j. commun. technol. electron.]. **VFOAT** Soviet Journal of Communications Technology and Electronics; Radiotekhnika I Elektronika. Vol. 30 No. 1 (Jan. 1985)-(19??). Periodical. English (translations available in Russian). Sixteen times a year. John Wiley & Sons, Inc., 605 Third Avenue, New York NY 10158-0012. **Tel** (212)850-6000, (212)850-6645, FAX (212)850-6088, telex 12-7063. **(Subscription address:** John Wiley & Sons / England, Baffins Lane, Chichester, West Sussex PO19 1UD England.**)** **ED** Reuben Glass. **LC** TK7800; .R413. **DD** 621.381/05. **[CCC].** available on microfilm and microfiche from University Microfilms International (UMI). Documents available from Article Express International, Ask*IEEE. ***Continues*** *Radiotekhnika i Elektronika. English. Radio Engineering and Electronic Physics, 0033-7889.* ***Continued by*** *Journal of Communications Technology and Electronics, 1064-2269.*
Desc: Devoted to the theory and physical fundamentals of communications and electronics engineering, the journal offers original papers from a foremost research journal of the Soviet Academy of Sciences. Featured are papers in circuit theory, solid state theory, electrodynamics, wave propagation, applied mathematics, communications theory, antennas and wave guides, signal processing, and devices.
Ind/Abst Acoust. Abstr.; Bioeng. Abstr.; Ei Page One; Eng. Index Annu.; INSPEC (1985-); Int. Aerosp. Abstr.; Math. Rev. (?-1992); Pollut. Abstr. Indexes.

US/0049-1748
SOVIET JOURNAL OF QUANTUM ELECTRONICS. ***Title Change.*** [Sov. j. quantum electron.]. **Added/Corp** American Institute of Physics. Vol. 1 (July/Aug. 1971)-(1993). Periodical. English (Russian). mo. American Institute of Physics, 500 Sunnyside Boulevard, Woodbury NY 11797-2999. **Tel** (516)576-2200, FAX (516)349-7669, telex 960983. **(Subscription address:** UK/ Institute of Physics, Techno House, Redcliffe Way, Bristol BS1 6NX England**)** **LC** TK8300; .S6813. **DD** 537.5/05. **CODEN** SJQEAF. **[CCC].** available on microfilm. Documents available from Article Express International, Ask*IEEE, CASDDS. ***Continued by*** *Quantum Electronics.*
Ind/Abst Acoust. Abstr.; Bioeng. Abstr.; Ceram. Abstr. (19??-19??); Chem. Abstr.; Curr. Phys. Index; Ei Page One; Energy Res. Abstr. (Feb. 1973-); Eng. Index Annu.; INSPEC (July/Aug. 1971-); Int. Aerosp. Abstr.; SPIN (1971-).

US/0363-8529
SOVIET MICROELECTRONICS. ***Title Change.*** [Sov. microelectron.]. **Added/Corp** Consultants Bureau. (19??)-(19??). Periodical. English (translations available in Russian). Six times a year. Plenum Press, 233 Spring Street, New York NY 10013-1578. **Tel** (212)620-8000, (800)221-9369, FAX (212)463-0742, (212)807-1047, telex 23/421139. **ED** K A Valiev. **LC** TK7874; .M478. **DD** 621.381/7/05. **CODEN** SOMIDB. **[CCC].** Index available. available on microfilm and microfiche from University Microfilms International (UMI). Documents available from Article Express International, The Genuine Article, Ask*IEEE. ***Continues*** *Microelectronics, 0098-6658.* ***Continued by*** *Russian Microelectronics.*
Desc: This journal contains articles on new advances in the solution of fundamental problems of microelectronics scientists. Discusses new physical principles, materials and methods for creating components especially in large systems.
Ind/Abst Acoust. Abstr.; Bioeng. Abstr.; Curr. Contents Eng. Tech. Appl. Sci.; Ei Page One; Eng. Index Annu.; INSPEC (May-June 1976-); Pollut. Abstr. Indexes; Res. Alert [Full Cov.]; Sci. Cit. Index (19??-19??); SCISEARCH.

US/1068-557X
SPEC NEWSLETTER. [SPEC newsl.]. **Added/Corp** Standard Performance Evaluation Corporation. **VFOAT** Standard Performance Evaluation Corporation Newsletter. (198?)-. Periodical. English. Four times a year (Mar., June, Sept., Dec.). $550.00. SPEC / NCGA, 2722 Merrilee Drive, Suite 200, Fairfax VA 22031. **Tel** (703)698-9600, FAX (703)560-2752. **CODEN** SPEWEL. **Circ:** 300.

US/1059-3772
SPECIALTY REFERENCES. APPLICATION NOTES. [Spec. ref., Appl. notes]. **Added/Corp** D.A.T.A. Business Publishing. **VFOAT** Application Notes. (1990)-. English. an. $95.00. DATA Business Publishing, PO Box 6510, 15 Inverness Way East, Englewood CO 80155. **Tel** (800)447-4666, (303)799-0381, FAX (303)799-4082. **LC** TK7874; .S72. **DD** 621.3815/05. ***Continues*** *Application Notes. Discrete Semiconductors, Integrated Circuits, 1048-2776.*
Desc: Information on integrated circuits and semiconductors.

UK
SPON'S MECHANICAL ELECTRICAL SERVICES PRICE BOOK. **See** Physics-Analytic and Experimental Mechanics.

GW/0931-7260
SPRINGER SERIES IN ELECTRONICS AND PHOTONICS. [Springer ser. electron. photonics]. Vol. 22 (1986)-. Academic Scholarly Publication. English. ir. Price varies per volume. Springer-Verlag GmbH & Company KG, Heidelberger Platz 3, D 14197 Berlin Germany. **Tel** 011 49 30 8207223, FAX 011 49 30 8214091, telex 183 319 SPBLN D. **(Subscription address:** Springer Verlag New York Inc. / for North America, 44 Hartz Way, Secaucus NJ 07096.**)** **CODEN** SSEPEL. Documents available from CASDDS. ***Continues*** *Springer Series in Electrophysics, 0172-5734.*
Ind/Abst Bioeng. Abstr. (1986-); Chem. Abstr. (1986-).

US
STANDARD HANDBOOK FOR ELECTRICAL ENGINEERS. 1st Edition (1908)-. English. ir. $110.50. McGraw Hill Publishing Company, Inc., 1221 Avenue of the Americas, New York NY 10020. **Tel** (212)512-6410, (800)525-5003, FAX (212)512-6111. **(Subscription address:** Glencoe Division, PO Box 543, Blacklick OH 43004.**)** **LC** TK151; .S8. **DD** 621.3.

FR
STATISTIQUES ELECTRICITE. **Main/Corp** Electricite de France. French. Direction des Affaires Exterieures et de la Cooperation, 68 rue du FG Saint Honore, Paris 75008 France. **LC** HD9685.F8; E54D. **DD** 363.6/2/0944.

NO
STATOIL MAGAZINE. **Added/Corp** Norske Statsoljeselskap. Public Affairs Dept. **VFOAT** Statoil. (19??)-. English. qt. Norske Statsoljeselskap, PO Box 300, N-4001, Stavanger Norway.
Ind/Abst Fluid Abstr., Civil Eng.; Fluid Abstr. Proc. Eng.; FLUIDEX (19??-).

US/0162-2927
STATUS OF ELECTRIC POWER IN THE MISSOURI RIVER BASIN. **Main/Corp** Missouri River Basin Commission. 1976-. English. an. Missouri River Basin Commission, 10050 Regency Circle/Suite 403, Omaha NE 68114. **LC** TK23.4; .U54A. **DD** 333.7.

US/0195-9190
STATUS (SCOTTSDALE). (STATUS; A REPORT ON THE INTEGRATED CIRCUIT INDUSTRY.). **Main/Corp** Integrated Circuit Engineering Corporation. (19??)-. English. an (Jan.). $595.00. Integrated Circuit Engineering Corporation, 15022 North 75th Street, Scottsdale AZ 85260. **Tel** (602)998-9780, FAX (602)948-1925. **ED** William McClean. **LC** HD9696 .I58; I58a. **DD** 338.4/762138173/05. Index available. **Bk Rev. Circ:** 1,000 (ctrl).
Desc: A report on the integrated circuit industry with over 300 charts and figures, also with an expanded appendix.

US
STEREO REVIEWS TAPE RECORDING BUYERS' GUIDE. **See** Sound Recordings and Systems.

UK
STUDENT'S QUARTERLY JOURNAL. **VFOAT** SQJ. Vol. 1 (1930)-. Periodical. English. qt.

US/1050-3943
STUDIES OF HIGH TEMPERATURE SUPERCONDUCTORS. (STUDIES OF HIGH TEMPERATURE SUPERCONDUCTORS : ADVANCES IN RESEARCH AND APPLICATIONS.). [Stud. high temp. supercond.]. Vol. 1 (1989)-. Academic Scholarly Publication. English. ir. Price varies per volume. Nova Science Publishers Inc., 6080 Jericho Turnpike, Suite 207, Commack NY 11725-2808. **Tel** (516)499-3103, (516)499-3106, FAX (516)499-3146. **DD** 537. **CODEN** STSUEB. Documents available from CASDDS.
Ind/Abst Chem. Abstr.

JA
SUMITOMO ELECTRIC TECHNICAL REVIEW. Periodical. English (summaries and/or abstracts in French, German and Spanish). an. Sumitomo Electric Industries Ltd, 15 Kitahama 5-chome Higashi-ku, Osaka 541 Japan. **LC** TK1.A1; S9. **DD** 621.3/05. **CODEN** SETRAY. Documents available from Ask*IEEE.
Ind/Abst INSPEC (Nov. 1970-).

JA
SUMMARIES OF REPORTS OF THE ELECTROTECHNICAL LABORATORY. **Main/Corp** Kogyo Gijutsuin (Japan). Denshi Gijutsu Sogo Kenkyugo. No. 24- 1969-. English. an. Kogyo gijutsuin Denshi Gijutsu Sogo Kenkyujo, (Electrotechnical Lab., Agency of Industrial Science & Technology), 1-4, Umezono 1 Chome, Tsukubashi, Ibarakiken 305, Japan. **LC** TK1; .D45A. ***Continues*** *Denki Shikenjo (Japan). Summaries of Reports of the Electrotechnical Laboratory.*

●CN/0825-6667
SUMMARY OF ECONOMIC AND LOAD FORECASTS. **See** Public Administration-Public Utilities.

US
SUNTESTER BULLETIN. ***Ceased.*** No. 1- 19 -Ceased June (1990). Bulletin. English. mo. Sun Electric Company, Sun Test Department, One Sun Parkway, Crystal Lake IL 60014. **Tel** (815)459-7700.

UK
SUPERCONDUCTIVITY ABSTRACTS. ***Suspended.*** (19??)-Suspended. English. mo. DM750.00 (one year), DM1425.00 (two year) Germany; $405.00 (one year), $769.50 (two year) other. Pergamon Press, An Imprint of Elsevier Science Ltd., The Boulevard, Langford Lane, Kidlington, Oxford OX5 1GB United Kingdom. **Tel** 011 44 865 843000, 011 44 865 843699, FAX 011 44 865 843010. **(Subscription address:** US/ 395 Saw Mill River Road, Elmsford, NY 10523; Can/ 150 Consumers Road/Suite 104, Willowdale Ontario M2J 1P9; Aus-NZ/ POB 544, Potts Point NSW 2011**)**

US/0896-3401
SUPERCONDUCTIVITY FLASH REPORT. [Supercond. flash rep.]. **VFOAT** SPR. Vol. 1, No. 1 (Sept. 14, 1987)-. Periodical. English. Twenty-four times a year. $345.00 (individual), $295.00 (institutions & schools). Flash Report Publishers, 212 West Superior, Suite 656, Chicago IL 60610. **Tel** (312)944-5115. **DD** 537.

●US/1054-2698
SUPERCONDUCTIVITY REVIEW. [Supercond. rev.]. Vol. 1, No. 1 (1992)-. Periodical. English. qt. $271.00 (academic institutions), $423.00 (corporate institutions). Gordon & Breach Science Publishers, Inc., PO Box 786, Cooper Station, New York NY 10276. **Tel** (212)206-8900, FAX (212)645-2459. **(Subscription address:** International Publishers Distributor at one of the following addresses: 820 Town Center Drive, Langhorne, PA 19047; or PO Box 90, Reading Berkshire RG1 8JL UK; or Kent Ridge PO Box 1180, Singapore 9111, Republic of Singapore**)** **LC** QC611.9; .S856. **DD** 537.6/23. **CODEN** SPCREU. **[CCC].**

US/0893-5297
SUPERCONDUCTORS UPDATE. ***Ceased.*** [Supercond. update]. Jan./March (1987)-Ceased Dec. (1989). Periodical. English. bw. Fachinformationszentrum

Karlsruhe, Physics & Math, D 76344 Eggenstein Germany. **Tel** 011 49 7247 808149. **ED** David Weisgerber. **LC** Z7144.S8; S86; QC612.S8. **DD** 016.5376/23. **CODEN** SUUPED. Index available.
Desc: Provides relevant information drawn from current literature, including journal articles, patents, technical papers and reports.

US
SUPERCURRENTS. ***Ceased.*** **VFOAT** Super Currents. (Jan. 1988)-Vol. 11. Periodical. English. qt. Supercurrents, PO Box 889, Belmont CA 94002. **Tel** (415)595-3808. **LC** QC611.9; .S87. **DD** 537.6/23.
Ind/Abst Ceram. Abstr. (19??-).

US/0893-3588
SURFACE MOUNT TECHNOLOGY. [Surf. mount technol.]. (1986)-. Periodical. English. bm. $60.00 (one year), $84.00 (two year), $97.00 (three year) US; $48.00 (one year), $83.00 (two year), $108.00 (three year) other. IHS Publishing Group, 17730 West Peterson Road, Libertyville IL 60048. **Tel** (708)362-8711, FAX (708)362-3484. **ED** Tom Williams. **DD** 621. **CODEN** SMTEEL. **[CCC].** Index available. **Ad Acc, Adv Mgr:** Paula Solomini. **Pr Rev. Circ:** 55,000 (ctrl). available on microfilm. Documents available from Article Express International, Ask*IEEE.
Desc: Covers surface mount technology in its application to circuit boards and other electrical products. New product reports are also included.
Ind/Abst Ei Page One; Eng. Index Annu.; INSPEC (1986-).

UK
SURFACE MOUNT TECHNOLOGY. ***Title Change.*** (19??)-(19??). Academic Scholarly Publication. English. bm. Elsevier Science Publishers Ltd, Crown House, Linton Road, Barking Essex IG11 8JU England. **Tel** 011 44 81 5947272, FAX 081-594-5942, telex 896950. ***Continued by*** *Surface Mount International.*

NE/0167-5729
SURFACE SCIENCE REPORTS. [Surf. sci. rep.]. Vol. 1, No. 1 (June 1981)-. Academic Scholarly Publication. English. Twenty-four times a year (3 volumes). FI1224.00; FI16834.00 combined subscription with Surface Science and Applied Surface Science. Elsevier Science Publishers BV, PO Box 211, 1000 AE Amsterdam Netherlands. **Tel** 011 31 20 5803642, FAX 011 31 20 5862696, telex 15682. **ED** W.H. Weinberg. **LC** QC173.4.S94; S9644. **DD** 530.4/17/05. **CODEN** SSREDI. **[CCC]. Pr Rev.** available on microfilm and microfiche from University Microfilms International (UMI). Documents available from Article Express International, The Genuine Article, Ask*IEEE, CASDDS.
Desc: Contains invited review papers on the properties of surfaces and interfaces of metals, semiconductors and insulators.
Ind/Abst Alum. Ind. Abstr.; Chem. Abstr.; Curr. Contents Phys. Chem. Earth Sci.; Ei Page One; Elect. Comm. Abstr.; Eng. Mater. Abstr.; Eng. Index Annu.; Index Sci. Rev. [Full Cov.]; INSPEC (June 1981-); Met. Abstr.; Phys. Briefs; Res. Alert [Full Cov.]; Sci. Cit. Index; SCISEARCH.

RU/0039-7067
SVETOTEKHNIKA (1955). (SVETOTEKHNIKA.). [Svetotehnika]. **Added/Corp** Soviet Union. Ministerstvo Elektrotekhnicheskoi Promyshlennosti. (1955)-. Academic Scholarly Publication. Russian. mo. $79.95. **(Subscription address:** East View Publications Inc., 3020 Harbor Lane North, Suite 110, Minneapolis MN 55447.**) CODEN** SVETAG. Index available in last issue of volume--attached. Documents available from Article Express International, Ask*IEEE, CASDDS. ***Continues*** *Svetotekhnika.*
Ind/Abst Bioeng. Abstr.; Chem. Abstr.; Ei Page One; Energy Res. Abstr.; Eng. Index Annu.; INSPEC (1968-); Saf. Health Work.

SW/0283-8060
SWEDISH DEFENCE MATERIEL ADMINISTRATION QUALIFIED PRODUCT LIST OF ELECTRONIC COMPONENTS : SE-MIL-QPL. English and Swedish. an. Kr800.00. FMV Telelab, Box 13400, S-580 13 Linkoping Sweden. **Tel** 46 13 243000, FAX 46 13 278342, telex 19061 ESCYI S. **ED** Sune Rosenberg. **Circ:** 500 (ctrl).
Desc: Electronic components listed to type an manufactured after qualification for use in Swedish defense equipment.

US/1056-5647
SWEET'S CATALOG FILE. PRODUCTS FOR ENGINEERING AND RETROFIT, ELECTRICAL AND RELATED PRODUCTS. ***Title Change.*** [Sweet's cat. file, Prod. eng. retrofit electr. relat. prod.]. **Added/Corp** McGraw-Hill Information Systems Company. Sweet's Division. **VFOAT** Products for Engineering and Retrofit, Electrical and Related Products. (1984)-(19??). Catalog. English. an. McGraw Hill Publishing Company, Inc., 1221 Avenue of the Americas, New York NY 10020. **Tel** (212)512-6410, (800)525-5003, FAX (212)512-6111. **LC** TK455; .S79. **DD** 621.3/029/473. ctrl circ. available in microform. ***Continues*** *Sweet's Catalog File: Products for Engineering, Electrical and Related Products, 0160-5666.* ***Continued by*** *Sweet's Electrical Engineering & Retrofit Catalog File, 1056-5426.*

US/1056-5426
SWEET'S ELECTRICAL ENGINEERING & REPORT CATALOG FILE. [Sweet's electr. eng. retrofit cat. file]. **Added/Corp** McGraw-Hill, Inc. Sweet's Group. **VFOAT** Sweet's Electrical Engineering and Retrofit Catalog File; Electrical Engineering & Retrofit; Electrical Engineering and Retrofit; Sweet's Catalog File. Electrical Engineering & Rretrofit. Catalog. English. McGraw Hill Publishing Company, Inc., 1221 Avenue of the Americas, New York NY 10020. **Tel** (212)512-6410, (800)525-5003, FAX (212)512-6111. **LC** TK455; .S79. **DD** 621.3/029/4. ***Continues*** *Sweet's Catalog File. Products for Engineering and Retrofit, Electrical and Related Products, 1056-5647.*

US/0275-4932
SWITCHGEAR, SWITCHBOARD APPARATUS, RELAYS, AND INDUSTRIAL CONTROLS. (CURRENT INDUSTRIAL REPORTS. MA-36A, SWITCHGEAR, SWITCHBOARD APPARATUS, RELAYS, AND INDUSTRIAL CONTROLS / U.S. DEPARTMENT OF COMMERCE, BUREAU OF THE CENSUS.). Began in 1971. Government Publication. English. an. $1.00. US Department of Commerce / Bureau of the Census, Data User Services Division, Customer Services, Washington DC 20233-0800. **Tel** (301)763-4100. **(Subscription address:** Superintendent of Documents, US Government Printing Office, Washington DC 20402.**) LC** HD9697.S853; U518. **DD** 338.4/7621317/0973021.
Desc: Presents timely data on the production, inventories, and orders of approximately 5,000 products, which represents 40 percent of all US manufacturing.

US
SYMPOSIUM RECORD / IEEE ... INTERNATIONAL SYMPOSIUM ON ELECTROMAGNETIC COMPATIBILITY. **Added/Corp** Institute of Electrical and Electronics Engineers. IEEE Electromagnetic Compatibility Society. **VFOAT** Electromagnetic Compatibility; IEEE ... Electromagnetic Compatibility. (1985)-. English. an. Institute of Electrical and Electronics Engineers / IEEE, 445 Hoes Lane, Piscataway NJ 08855. **Tel** (908)981-0060. ***Continues*** *International Symposium on Electromagnetic Compatibility. International Symposium on Electromagnetic Compatibility : [Papers].*

US/0272-2917
SYRACUSE NEWS. ***Title Change.*** **Added/Corp** General Electric Company. (19??)-(199?)-. Periodical. English. bw. General Electric Company, 120 Erie Boulevard, Schenectady NY 12305. **Tel** (502)685-6200. ***Continued by*** *Aerospace News (General Electric Company).*

US/0147-6068
SYSTEMS ENGINEERING FOR POWER. **Main/Corp** United States. Division of Electric Energy Systems. Systems Management & Structuring. May 1976-. English. an. National Technical Information Service - NTIS, Room 2027S, 5285 Port Royal Road, Springfield VA 22161. **Tel** (703)487-4630, (703)487-4660, (703)487-4650, FAX (703)321-8547, telex 89-9405. **LC** TK23; .U53A. **DD** 621.31/0973.

US/0093-5379
T.E.L. THE ELECTRIC LETTER. ***Ceased.*** (TEL, THE ELECTRIC LETTER.). [T.E.L. Electr. lett.]. **VFOAT** Electric Letter. (1972)-(19??). Periodical. English. bw. DSM Letter, 111 Presidential Blvd., Suite 127, Bala Cynwyd PA 19004. **Tel** (610)667-2160, FAX (610)667-5593. **ED** John Maxwell. **Ad Acc. Circ:** 400 (ctrl).
Desc: Electric utility marketing and communication.

KO
TAEHAN CHONGI HYOPHOE CHI. **VFOAT** Journal of the Korea Electric Association. Periodical. Korean. mo. Free. Taehan Chongi Hakhoe, 11-4 Supyo-dong, Chung-ku Seoul Korea. **Tel** (02)274-1661/5, K23493, telex KEAYJ. **ED** Kwang-Surk Kim. **LC** TK4; .T254. **Circ:** 7,700.

CH/0257-8166
TAIWAN ELECTRONICS INDUSTRY. [Taiwan electron. ind.]. (1981)-. Periodical. English. mo. $100.00 North & South America, Europe, Africa; $84.00 other. United Pacific International, PO Box 81-417, Taipei Taiwan. **Tel** 011 886 2 7150751. **UDC** 621.38. ***Continues*** *Taiwan Computer.*

US/0092-3680
TECHNICAL DIGEST - I.E.E.E. VEHICULAR TECHNOLOGY ANNUAL CONFERENCE. **See** Transportation-Automobiles.

US/0163-1918
TECHNICAL DIGEST / INTERNATIONAL ELECTRON DEVICES MEETING. [Tech. dig., Int. Electron Devices Meet.]. **Main/Conf** International Electron Devices Meeting. **Added/Corp** IEEE Group on Electron Devices. IEEE Electrical Devices Society. **VFOAT** I.E.D.M. Technical Digest; IEDM Technical Digest. (19??)-. Academic Scholarly Publication. English. an. IEEE, Institution of Electrical and Electronics Engineers, Inc., 345 East 47th Street, New York NY 10017-2394. **Tel** (908)981-1393, FAX (908)981-9667. **(Subscription address:** IEEE / Institute of Electrical and Electronics Engineers, 445 Hoes Lane, PO Box 1331, Piscataway NJ 08855-1331.**) LC** TK7801; .I53. **DD** 621.381/028. **CODEN** TDIMD5. **[CCC].** Documents available from Article Express International, Ask*IEEE, CASDDS. ***Continues*** *International Electron Devices Meeting.*
Ind/Abst Bioeng. Abstr.; Chem. Abstr. (1973-1981); Ei Page One; Eng. Index Annu.; Index IEEE Publ.; INSPEC.

US/0083-8837
TECHNICAL PAPERS. **Main/Corp** Western Electronic Show and Convention. **Added/Corp** Institute of Radio Engineers. Institute of Radio Engineers. Los Angeles Section. Institute of Electrical and Electronics Engineers. Los Angeles Section. Western Electronic Show and Convention. WESCON Convention Record. (1957)-. Periodical. English. ir. Western Periodicals Company, 424 East Main Street, Ventura CA 93001. **Tel** (805)641-2665, FAX (805)643-4854. **LC** TK7800; .W4. **DD** 621.38108. **[CCC].**

US
TECHNICAL REPORT - TEXAS. UNIVERSITY AT AUSTIN. LABORATORIES FOR ELECTRONICS AND RELATED SCIENCE RESEARCH. ***Title Change.*** **Main/Corp** Texas. University at Austin. Laboratories for Electronics and Related Science Research. Monographic series. English. **LC** TK7803; .T4. **DD** 621.381. ***Continues*** *Technical Report / University of Texas at Austin. Electronics Research Center.* ***Continued by*** *Technical Report (University of Texas at Austin).*

CN/0711-4613
TECHNICAL REPORT - UNIVERSITY OF WATERLOO. DEPARTMENT OF ELECTRICAL ENGINEERING. (TECHNICAL REPORT ...). [Tech. rep. - Univ. Waterloo, Dep. Electr. Eng.]. No. 80/1-. English. University of Waterloo Department of Electrical Engineering, Waterloo Ontario N2L 3G1 Canada. **Tel** (519)885-1211, telex 069-55259. **DD** 621.3.
Desc: In addition to undergraduate course notes, the department publishes research reports in computers, communications, control, microelectronics, energy systems.

FR/0994-7590
TECHNICAL REVIEW / GEC ALSTHOM. **Added/Corp** GEC Alsthom. **VFOAT** GEC Alsthom Technical Review. No. 1 (1990)-. English. Four times a year. 320.00F. GEC Alsthom, 38 Avenue Kleber, 75795 Paris Cedex 16 France. **Tel** 011 33 1 47552000. **ED** A.J. Walkden. **CODEN** TREVE9. Index available (Bound in third issue). **Circ:** 12,000 (ctrl). Documents available from Article Express International, Ask*IEEE. ***Continues*** *GEC Review, 0267-9337.*
Ind/Abst Ei Page One; Eng. Index Annu.; INSPEC (Jan. 1990-).

II/0255-9609
TECHNICAL REVIEW - IETE. (IETE TECHNICAL REVIEW.). [Tech. rev. - IETE]. **Added/Corp** Institution of Electronics and Telecommunication Engineers (India). **VFOAT** I.E.T.E. Technical Review. Vol. 1, No. 1 (Jan. 1984)-. Periodical. English. mo. Institution of Electronics and Telecommunication Engineers, 2 Institutional Area, Lodi Road, New Delhi 110003 India. **Tel** 617282, 618529. **(Subscription address:** Prints India, 11 Darya Ganj, New Delhi, 110002 India, (Phone: 011 91 11 3268645)**) LC** TK5101.A1; I355. **DD** 621.38/05. Documents available from Ask*IEEE. ***Separated from*** *Journal of the Institution of Electronics and Telecommunication Engineers.*
Ind/Abst INSPEC (Jan. 1984-).

US
TECHNICIAN ASSOCIATION NEWS. English. mo. $20.00 US; $50.00 others. Electronics Technicians Association, 604 North Jackson Street, Greencastle IN 46135. **Tel** (317)653-5541. **ED** Dick Glass. **Bk Rev. Ad Acc. Circ:** 2,000.

FR/0399-4112
TECHNIQUES DE L'INGENIEUR. ELECTROTECHNIQUE. [Tech. ing., Electrotech.]. **VFOAT** Electrotechnique. 1951-. Academic Scholarly Publication. French. qt. $219.00 North America; 1,315F other. Editions Techniques, 141 rue de Javel, 75747 Paris Cedex 15 France. **Tel** 011 33 1 45589100. **CODEN** TINED7. Documents available from CASDDS.
Ind/Abst Chem. Abstr.

FR
TECHNIQUES DE L'INGENIEUR / INFORMATIQUE HA. French. Editions Techniques, 141 rue de Javel, 75747 Paris Cedex 15 France. **Tel** 011 33 1 45589100.

IT/0390-6698
TECNOLOGIA ELETTRICHE. INDUSTRIA ITALIANA ELETTROTECNICA ED ELETTRONICA. [Tecnol. eletr., Ind. ital. elettrotec. elettron.]. (1974)-. Periodical. Italian (English). Eleven times a year. L85000.00 Italy; L160000.00 other. Stammer Spa, Via della Liberazione 1, 20068 Peschiera Borromeo, Italy. **Tel** 011 39 2 55302606, FAX 011 39 2 55302700, telex 321083. **ED** Girolamo Bellina. **UDC** 621.3. **CODEN** TEELDN. **Bk Rev. Ad Acc. Pr Rev. Circ:** 7,400 (ctrl). Documents available from Ask*IEEE.
Desc: Information on products, general management, marketing, and technology in the electrical sector.
Ind/Abst INSPEC.

●US/1067-3806
TED : THE ELECTRICAL DISTRIBUTORS MAGAZINE. Added/Corp National Association of Electrical Distributors (U.S.). **VFOAT** Electrical Distributors Magazine. Vol. 29, No. 7 (July 1992)-. Periodical. English. mo. The Association, 45 Danbury Road, Wilton CT 06897-0857. **LC** TK1; .E277. ***Continues*** *Electrical Distributor, 0422-8707.*

UN/0204-3599
TEHNICESKAJA ELEKTRODINAMIKA. (TEKHNICHESKAIA ELEKTRODINAMIKA.). [Teh. elektrodin.]. Periodical. Russian (table of contents in English). bm. 7.00rub USSR; $1.00 US. Izdatelstvo Naukova Dumka / Ukrainian Academy of Sciences, Vladimirskaia Ulitsa 54, 252601 Kiev Ukraine. **Tel** 225-63-66, telex 131376. **ED** A K Shidlovsky and G G Schastlivy. **LC** TK4; .T37. **CODEN** TEKEDW. Index available. **Bk Rev. Ad Acc.** ctrl circ. Documents available from Ask*IEEE.
Ind/Abst INSPEC (Jan.-Feb. 1980-); Int. Aerosp. Abstr.

NO/0085-7130
TELEKTRONIKK. [Telektronikk]. **Added/Corp** Norway. Telegrafstyret. (1959)-. Periodical. Norwegian. Four times a year. Kr100.00. Teledirektoratet, Postboks 83, N 2007 Kjeller Norway. **Tel** 011 47 2 6809883. **ED** Ola Espvik. **LC** TK6001; .T44. **CODEN** TKTKAW. available on microfilm from University Microfilms International (UMI). Documents available from Ask*IEEE. ***Supersedes*** *Tekniske Meddelelser fra Telegrafverket.*
Ind/Abst INSPEC (1968-).

US/0040-2621
TELEMETRY JOURNAL. [Telem. j.]. V. 1- Apr./May 1966-. Periodical. English. bm. $15.00. Value Engineering Publications, Inc., 647 North Sepulveda Blvd., Bel Air LA 90049. **LC** TK399; .T34. **DD** 621.37/9.
Ind/Abst Int. Aerosp. Abstr.

US/0040-263X
TELEPHONE ENGINEER & MANAGEMENT. ***Title Change.*** **See** Communication-Telecommunications.

US/0040-263X
TELEPHONE ENGINEER & MANAGEMENT. ***Title Change.*** **VAT** Telephone Engineer and Management. Vol. 1 (Jan. 1909)-(1994). Periodical. English. sm. Advanstar Communications Inc., 131 West First Street, Duluth MN 55802. **Tel** (218)723-9477, (800)346-0085. **LC** TK1; .T33. **DD** 621.38505. **[CCC].** available on microfilm and microfiche from University Microfilms International (UMI); available on an online database (files 16,648/Full-Text) from DIALOG. Documents available from UMI Article Clearinghouse, Ask*IEEE. ***Absorbed*** *Western Telephone Journal.* ***Continued by*** *America's Network, 1075-5292.*
Ind/Abst ABI/INFORM Glob. Ed.; ABI Inform Ondisc (Sept. 1978-); Acad. Search (July 1993-Feb. 1994); Bus. Index (1985-); Ei Page One; F&S Index Plus Text, Int. [Full Txt.] [Select. Cov.]; Gen. BusinessFile (1985-); Gen. Period. Index (1985-); INFO-SOUTH Abstr.; INSPEC (1968-); Mag. Search; PROMT [Full Txt.]; Trade Ind. Index; Vocat. Search (July 1993-).

DK/0492-6110
TELETEKNIK (ENGLISH EDITION). (TELETEKNIK.). [Teletek.]. **Added/Corp** Denmark. Generaldirektoratet for Post- og Telegrafvaesenet. (1957)-. Periodical. English. sa. Free. Teleteknik, Telegade 2, DK-2630 Taastrup Denmark. **Tel** 011 45 2 528022, FAX 011 45 2 527080, telex 22383. **LC** TK5101.A1; T4713. **CODEN** TLKKAS. Documents available from Article Express International, Ask*IEEE.
Ind/Abst Ei Page One; Eng. Index Annu. [Select. Cov.]; INSPEC (1968-).

US/0497-1515
TELEVISION DIGEST WITH CONSUMER ELECTRONICS (1984). See Communication-Broadcasting.

US/0735-567X
TELEVISION EQUIPMENT SPECIFICATION SERVICE. (TESS : TELEVISION EQUIPMENT SPECIFICATION SERVICE.). [Telev. equip. specif. serv.]. **VFOAT** T.E.S.S. English. ir. Knowledge Industry Publications Inc, 701 Westchester Avenue, White Plains NY 10604. **Tel** (914)328-9157, (800)800-5474, FAX (914)328-9093.

UK
TELEVISION; SERVICING, CONSTRUCTION, COLOUR, DEVELOPMENTS. Vol. 21, No. 241 (Oct. 1970)-. English. $49.80 US and Canada; $39.14 UK and Eire; $46.21 other. IPC Magazines Ltd., Perrymount Road, Haywards Heath, West Sussex RH16 3DH England. **Tel** 011 44 444 440421. Documents available from Ask*IEEE.
Ind/Abst INSPEC (Aug. 1971-).

US/0744-1657
TEST & MEASUREMENT WORLD. [Test meas. world]. **VFOAT** Test and Measurement World. Vol. 1, No. 1 (Fall 1981)-. Periodical. English. Thirteen times a year. $65.00 US; $96.00 Canada; $90.00 Mexico; $120.00 (surface mail) other. Cahners Publishing Company, 249 West 17th Street, New York NY 10011. **Tel** (212)645-0067, FAX (212)242-6987. **(Subscription address:** Cahners Publishing Company / Colorado, Paid Subscription Service Center, PO Box 7610, Highlands Ranch CO 80126-7610.**) ED** Charles Masi. **LC** TK7869; .T47. **DD** 621.3815/48/05. **CODEN** TMWOD8. **[CCC].** Index available. cum. index. **Bk Rev. Ad Acc. Pr Rev. Circ:** 73,000 (ctrl). available on microfilm from University Microfilms International (UMI). Documents available from Article Express International, Ask*IEEE. ***Absorbed*** *Electronics Test, 0164-9620.*
Desc: Serves the technical and product information needs of managers and engineers who purchase and use test, measurement and inspection equipment for electronics and electro-optics applications.
Ind/Abst Ei Page One; Eng. Index Annu.; INSPEC (Nov. 1984-).

US/0195-6825
TEXT OF "A" PAPERS FROM THE WINTER MEETING - IEEE POWER ENGINEERING SOCIETY. Main/Corp IEEE Power Engineering Society. **VFOAT** IEEE Power Engineering Society Winter Meeting. 1976-. English. an. IEEE, Institution of Electrical and Electronics Engineers, Inc., 345 East 47th Street, New York NY 10017-2394. **Tel** (908)981-1393, FAX (908)981-9667. **(Subscription address:** IEEE Service Center, 445 Hoes Lane, Piscataway NJ 08854; telephone: (201)981-1393**) LC** TK5; .I25B. **DD** 621.31/05. ***Continues*** *Conference Papers from the Winter Meeting.*
Desc: Contains the full text of all the papers published in abstract "A" form in PA&S.
Ind/Abst Index IEEE Publ.

UK
THESAURUS. Added/Corp INSPEC (Information Service) Institution of Electrical Engineers. **VFOAT** INSPEC Thesaurus. (1991)-. English. be. $85.00. IEEE, Institution of Electrical and Electronics Engineers, Inc., 345 East 47th Street, New York NY 10017-2394. **Tel** (908)981-1393, FAX (908)981-9667. **LC** Z695.1.P5; I57. **DD** 025.4/953. ***Continues*** *INSPEC Thesaurus.*

SZ/0040-6090
THIN SOLID FILMS. [Thin solid films]. Vol. 1 (July 1967)-. Periodical. English (French and German). Thirty-six times a year (18 vols.). 7020.00F. Elsevier Sequoia SA, PO Box 564, CH-1001 Lausanne 1 Switzerland. **Tel** 011 41 21 3207381. **ED** J.E. Greene. **LC** TK7871.15.F5; T45. **DD** 082 0 621.381/71. **CODEN** THSFAP. **[CCC]. Ad Acc, Adv Mgr:** Ms. W van Cattenburch (Amsterdam). **Pr Rev.** available on microfilm and microfiche from University Microfilms International (UMI). Documents available from Article Express International, The Genuine Article, Ask*IEEE, CASDDS.
Desc: Concerned with all aspects of the science and technology of thin solid films, including industrial applications and reports of original work. All papers will be refereed by a panel of acknowledged international experts.
Ind/Abst Acoust. Abstr.; Alum. Ind. Abstr.; Bioeng. Abstr.; Ceram. Abstr.; Chem. Abstr.; Chem. Titles; Civ. Struct. Eng. Abstr.; Comput. Inf. Syst. Abstr. J. [Full Cov.]; Curr. Contents Eng. Tech. Appl. Sci.; Curr. Contents Phys. Chem. Earth Sci.; Ei Page One; Elect. Comm. Abstr.; Energy Res. Abstr.; Eng. Mater. Abstr.; Eng. Index Annu.; INSPEC (May 1969-); Int. Aerosp. Abstr.; Manuf. Process Eng. Abstr.; Mass Spect. Bull.; Mater. Sci. Eng. Abstr.; Mech. Eng. Abstr.; Met. Abstr.; Phys. Briefs; Pollut. Abstr. Indexes; Res. Alert [Full Cov.]; Sci. Cit. Index; SCISEARCH; Solid State Supercond. Abstr.; Surf. Treat. Technol. Abstr.

US/0730-4838
THYRISTOR DISCONTINUED DEVICES D.A.T.A BOOK. ***Ceased.*** (THYRISTOR DISCONTINUED DEVICES.). [Thyristor discontin. devices]. **VAT** Thyristor Discontinued Devices Derivation and Tabulation Associates Book. Ed. 11, Oct. (1980 Through Sept. 1981)-Ceased with 19th Ed. English. an. DATA Business Publishing, PO Box 6510, 15 Inverness Way East, Englewood CO 80155. **Tel** (800)447-4666, (303)799-0381, FAX (303)799-4082. **ED** Steven d'Adolf. **LC** TK7871.99.T5; D46A. **DD** 621.2815/287/0216. ***Continues*** *Discontinued Thyristor D.A.T.A. Book, 0279-9449.*
Desc: Contains specifications on 33,600 devices no longer in production from 89 manufacturers.

US/0092-7228
THYRISTORS, RECTIFIERS, AND DIACS. Main/Corp RCA Corporation. Solid State Division. 1973- Ed. English. an. $2.00. RCA Corporation, Box 3200, Somerville NJ 08876. **Tel** (609)734-3222. **LC** TK7871.85; .R18A. **DD** 621.3815/28.

CH
TIEN HSIN CHI SHU (JEN MIN YU TIEN CHU PAN SHE). (TIEN HSIN CHI SHU.). **VFOAT** Dianxin Jishu. Periodical. Chinese. NT$0.22. Pei-Ching Pao Kan Fa Hsing Chu, Beijing, People's Republic of China. **Tel** 483531. **LC** TK5101.A1; T52. **DD** 621.38.

HK
TIEN SHENG CHIEH. VFOAT Electronic Sound. 1- July 1977-. Chinese (English). $3.00 each issue. Tien Sheng Chieh Kung SSU, 1001 Hung Kei Mansion, 5-8 Queen Victoria Street, Hsiang-Kang Hong Kong. **LC** TK7881.4; .T5. **DD** 621.389/3/05.

US/1052-2433
TODAY IN MISSISSIPPI. Added/Corp Electric Power Associations of Mississippi. Vol. 43, No. 6 (Aug. 1990)-. Periodical. English. mo. $2.50. Electric Power Associations of Mississippi, PO Box 7897, Jackson MS 39284. **Tel** (601)922-2341. **ED** Janna Avalon. **Bk Rev. Ad Acc. Circ:** 13500 (ctrl). ***Continues*** *Mississippi EPA News, 0026-6175.*

KO
TONGNYOK CHAWON YONGU. VFOAT Energy and Resources Research. Periodical. Korean (summaries and/or abstracts in English). Choson Taehakkyo Tongnyok Chawon Yonguso, 17 Pullo-dong Tong-ku, Kwangju-si Korea. **LC** TK4; .T65.

JA
TOSHIBA'S SELECTED PAPERS ON SCIENCE & TECHNOLOGY / TOSHIBA. Added/Corp Toshiba, Kabushiki Kaisha. Vol. 1, No. 1 (1989)-. Periodical. English. sa. **LC** TK105; .T63. **DD** 621.3/05. **CODEN** TSPTEV. ***Continues*** *Toshiba Review. International Edition.*
Ind/Abst Ceram. Abstr. (19??-).

US/0091-9519
TRADE DIRECTORY, MEMBERSHIP LIST - ELECTRONIC INDUSTRIES ASSOCIATION. (TRADE DIRECTORY, MEMBERSHIP LIST.). **Main/Corp** Electronic Industries Association. **VFOAT** Trade Directory and Membership List. (19??)-. Directory. English. an. $85.00 members; $200.00 nonmembers. Electronic Industries Association, 2001 Pennsylvania Avenue Northwest, Washington DC 20006. **Tel** (202)457-4900, telex 710-822-0148 EIA WSH. **ED** Carol S. Cedrone. **LC** TK7800; .E4383. **DD** 338.4/7/62138106273. ctrl circ. ***Continues*** *Electronic Industries Association. Membership List.*
Desc: Listing of association member companies showing corporate and division locations, phone number, trade names and EIA divisional assignments. Also included are product categories and geographic locations.

CH
TRADE WINNERS CONSUMERS ELECTRONICS. VFOAT Shiao Fei Dian Chih Shuan Chou Kan. English. bw (26 issues). $80.00. Trade Winners, 11 Floor 3 190 Section 2 Keelung Road, Taipei Taiwan. **Tel** 011 886 2 7333988.

CN/0576-5161
TRANSACTIONS - ENGINEERING AND OPERATING DIVISION. CANADIAN ELECTRICAL ASSOCIATION. (TRANSACTIONS - CANADIAN ELECTRICAL ASSOCIATION. ENGINEERING AND OPERATION DIVISION.). [Trans. - Eng. Oper. Div., Can. Electr. Assoc.]. **Main/Corp** Canadian Electrical Association. Engineering and Operating Division. **VAT** Transactions - CEA Engineering and Operating Division. (1962)-. Proceedings. English. an. Canadian Electrical Association, 1 Westmount Square, Suite 1600, Montreal Quebec H3Z 2P9 Canada. **Tel** (514)937-6181, FAX (514)937-6498. **DD** 621.3/06/271. **CODEN** CEAEAU. Index available. **Circ:** 150. Documents available from Article Express International.
Desc: Contains selected papers presented at various technical meetings during the year.
Ind/Abst Bioeng. Abstr.; Ei Page One; Eng. Index Annu.

SA/0038-2221
TRANSACTIONS - THE SOUTH AFRICAN INSTITUTE OF ELECTRICAL ENGINEERS. [Trans. S. Afr. Inst. Electr. Eng.]. **Main/Corp** South African Institute of Electrical Engineers. **Added/Corp** South African Institute of Electrical Engineers. Handelinge -Suid-Afrikaanse Instituut van Elektriese Ingenieurs. South African Institute of Electrical Engineers. Transaksies van die South African Institute of Electrical Engineers. South African Institute of Electrical Engineers. Transaksies -Suid-Afrikaanse Instituut van Elektriese Ingenieurs. **VFOAT** Handelinge - Die

Suid-Afrikaanse Instituut van Elektriese Ingenieurs; Transactions of the South African Institute of Electrical Engineers; Transaksies van die South African Institute of Electrical Engineers; Transaksies - Die Suid-Afrikaanse Instituut van Elektriese Ingenieurs. Vol. 1 (Nov. 1909)-. Periodical. English (Afrikaans). Three times a year. R110.00. Phase Four Pty Ltd., PO Box 784279, Sandton 2146 South Africa. **Tel** 011 27 11 4444566. **LC** TK1; .S65. **DD** 621.3/05. **CODEN** TSAEA9.

US/0744-0650
TRANSFORMERS. (CURRENT INDUSTRIAL REPORTS. MA36G, TRANSFORMERS / U.S. DEPARTMENT OF COMMERCE, BUREAU OF THE CENSUS.). [Transformers]. Began in 1979. Government Publication. English. an. $1.25. US Department of Commerce / Bureau of the Census, Data User Services Division, Customer Services, Washington DC 20233-0800. **Tel** (301)763-4100. **(Subscription address:** Superintendent of Documents, US Government Printing Office, Washington DC 20402.**)** **LC** HD9697.T693; U534. **DD** 338.4/7621314/0973082.
Desc: Presents timely data on the production, inventories, and orders of approximately 5,000 products, which represents 40 percent of all US manufacturing.

US
TRANSISTOR D.A.T.A. BOOK. Main/Corp Derivation and Tabulation Associates, Inc. **Added/Corp** Derivation and Tabulation Associates, Inc. D.A.T.A.'s Transistor Characteristics Tabulation. (1956)-. Periodical. English. sa. DATA Business Publishing, PO Box 6510, 15 Inverness Way East, Englewood CO 80155. **Tel** (800)447-4666, (303)799-0381, FAX (303)799-4082.

US/0730-4846
TRANSISTOR DISCONTINUED DEVICES D.A.T.A. BOOK. ***Ceased.*** [Transistor discontin. devices D.A.T.A. book]. **VFOAT** Transistor Discontinued Devices Data Book. **VAT** Transistor Discontinued Devices Derivation and Tabulation Associated Book. Ed. 16, Sept. (1980)-Ceased with 24th Ed. English. an. DATA Business Publishing, PO Box 6510, 15 Inverness Way East, Englewood CO 80155. **Tel** (800)447-4666, (303)799-0381, FAX (303)799-4082. **ED** Steven d'Adolf. **LC** TK7871.9; .D38. **DD** 612.3815/28/0216. ***Continues*** *Discontinued Transistor D.A.T.A. Book, 0271-0722.*
Desc: Contains specifications on 17,500 devices no longer in production from 194 manufacturers.

US
TRANSISTOR SUBSTITUTION HANDBOOK. Main/Corp Howard W. Sams & Co. 1st- Ed.; 1961-. English. Howard Sams and Company Inc, 4300 West 62nd Street, Indianapolis IN 46268. **Tel** (317)298-5400, (800)428-3602. **ED** Howard W Sams. **LC** TK7872.T73; S23. **DD** 621.38151.

US/0041-1280
TRANSMISSION & DISTRIBUTION. (TRANSMISSION AND DISTRIBUTION : T & D.). [Transm. distrib.]. **VFOAT** Transmission & Distribution; T & D; T and D. **VAT** Transmission and Distribution. Vol. 8, No. 10 (Oct. 1956)-. Periodical. English. mo. $34.12 US; $60.00 other. Intertec Publishing Corporation, 9800 Metcalf, Overland Park KS 66212. **Tel** (913)341-1300. **(Subscription address:** Intertec Publishing Corporation, PO Box 2901, Overland Park KS 66282.**)** **ED** Elgin Enabnit. **LC** TJ1; .P773. **DD** 338. **CODEN** TRDIAT. **[CCC]. Bk Rev. Ad Acc. Circ:** 32,416 (ctrl). available on microfilm and microfiche from University Microfilms International (UMI); available on an online database (file 15/Full-Text) from DIALOG. Documents available from Ask*IEEE, UMI Article Clearinghouse, Documents on Demand. ***Continues*** *Power Equipment.*
Desc: Serves field of electric power transmission and distribution metering, electric utilities, industrial plants, government installations and related areas.
Ind/Abst ABI/INFORM Glob. Ed.; ABI Inform Ondisc (July 1988-); Coal Abstr.; Energy Inf. Abstr.; Environ. Abstr.; INSPEC (1968-); UMI ABI/Inform--Bus. Period. Ondisc (Jul. 1988-) [Full Txt.].

US/1050-8686
TRANSMISSION & DISTRIBUTION INTERNATIONAL. [Transm. distrib. int.]. **VFOAT** Transmission and Distribution International. Vol. 1, No. 1 (June 1990)-. Periodical. English. qt. $51.76. Intertec Publishing Corporation, 9800 Metcalf, Overland Park KS 66212. **Tel** (913)341-1300. **(Subscription address:** Intertec Publishing Corporation, PO Box 2901, Overland Park KS 66282.**)** **LC** TK3001; .T62. **DD** 621.319. **CODEN** TDINE9. ctrl circ. Documents available from Ask*IEEE.
Desc: Targeted toward power delivery professionals in the global transmission and distribution segment of the electric utility industry.
Ind/Abst INSPEC (June 1990-).

US/0737-5743
TRANSMISSION/DISTRIBUTION HEALTH & SAFETY REPORT. ***Title Change.*** (TRANSMISSION/DISTRIBUTION HEALTH & SAFETY REPORT.). [Transm./distrib. health saf. rep.]. **VFOAT** Transmission/Distribution Health and Safety Report; T.D.H.S. Report; TDHS Report. **VAT** Transmission, Distribution Health & Safety Report. Vol. 1, No. 4 (Apr. 1983)-(19??). Periodical. English. mo (except July and December). Transmission/Distribution Health & Safety Report, PO Box 14501 University Station, Minneapolis MN 55414. **Tel** (612)623-4646. **ED** Robert S Banks. **Circ:** 200 (ctrl). ***Continues*** *T&D Health and Safety Report, 0736-5047.* ***Continued by*** *EMF Health and Saety Diges, 1062-5526.*
Desc: Electrical health safety bioeffects research regulatory developments elf electric and/or magnetic fields abstracts calendar bibliography.

US
TUBE SUBSTITUTION HANDBOOK. Main/Corp Howard W. Sams & Co. V. 1- 1960-. English. an. Howard Sams & Company, Inc., 2647 Waterfront Parkway E Drive, Indianapolis IN 46214. **Tel** (800)428-7267, (317)298-5400. **ED** John Obst. **LC** TK6565.V3. **DD** 621.38151. **Bk Rev. Ad Acc.** ctrl circ.
Desc: Contains over 6,000 receiving tube direct substitutes, 300 industrial, 600 communications and 4,000 picture tube substitutes included with pinouts.

US/0892-7278
TWICE. (TWICE : THIS WEEK IN CONSUMER ELECTRONICS.). [TWICE]. **VFOAT** This Week in Consumer Electronics. (198?)-. Periodical. English. Twenty-eight times a year. $90.00 US; $154.00 Canada; $144.00 Mexico; $205.00 (surface mail) other. Cahners Publishing Company, 249 West 17th Street, New York NY 10011. **Tel** (212)645-0067, FAX (212)242-6987. **(Subscription address:** Cahners Publishing Company / Colorado, Paid Subscription Service Center, PO Box 7610, Highlands Ranch CO 80126-7610.**)** **DD** 338. **[CCC].**
Desc: Covers sales, merchandising, marketing and manufacturing news of the consumer electronics and major appliance industries. Types of products covered include VCRs, TV sets, audio systems, car stereos, telephones, blank audio tape, security devices, home office equipment, audio and video accessories and major appliances. Coverage includes industry news, sales statistics, financial news, new product introductions, and personnel news.
Ind/Abst Infomat Int. Bus.; Mark. Advert. Ref. Serv.

UK
UK ELECTRICITY / ELECTRICITY ASSOCIATION. See Public Administration-Public Utilities.

US/0892-4023
UNMANNED SYSTEMS. Added/Corp Association for Unmanned Vehicle Systems. Vol. 1, No. 1 (Summer 1982)-. Periodical. English. Four times a year. $40.00 (individuals); $100.00 (institutions). Association of Unmanned Vehicle Systems, 1735 North Lynn Street, Suite 950, Arlington DC 22209. **Tel** (703)524-6646-. **DD** 629. **CODEN** UNSYE3. Documents available from Ask*IEEE. ***Continues*** *UVS Magazine.*
Ind/Abst INSPEC (1986-).

IT
VIDEO MAGAZINE. V. 1, No. 1, (Sept. 1981)-. Periodical. Italian (Italian). mo. 27.000. **LC** TK9960; .V536. **DD** 621.388/332/05.

US/0740-4247
VIDEO MARKETING SURVEYS AND FORECASTS. [Video mark. surv. forecasts]. Vol. 1, No. 1 (Sept. 1983)-. Periodical. English. mo. $4,500.00. Video Marketing / U.S., 1680 Vine Street/Suite 820, Hollywood CA 90028. **Tel** (310)462-6350. **ED** Steve Rosen. **LC** HD9696.T463; U695. **DD** 381/.45621388332. **[CCC].** cum. index.
Desc: Provides between 300 and 400 capsule market surveys and forecasts in the form of charts, graphs, tables, lists and diagrams. Areas of coverage include home video, cable TV, computers, computer software, video games, satellites, broadcasting, motion pictures and consumer electronics.

US/0887-3836
VIDEO REGISTER AND TELECONFERENCING RESOURCES DIRECTORY, THE. ***Ceased.*** 9th Ed. (1987)-12th Ed. Directory. English. an. Knowledge Industry Publications Inc, 701 Westchester Avenue, White Plains NY 10604. **Tel** (914)328-9157, (800)800-5474, FAX (914)328-9093. **LC** TK6655.V5; V5374. **DD** 338.4/7/77859. ***Formed by the union of*** *Teleconferencing Resources Directory, 0739-2966* ***and*** *Video Register, 0190-3705.*

US/0736-2587
VIDEO TEST ANNUAL AND BUYER'S GUIDE. Periodical. English. an. $3.95. Video Magazine, 460 West 34th Street, New York NY 10001. **LC** TK6650; .V49. **DD** 621.388/3/0294. ***Continues*** *Video. Buyer's Guide, 0731-0846.*

FR
VIE ELECTRIQUE SODEL. French. bm. 50.00F France; 60.00F other. Sodel Redaction, 336-340 rue Saint Honore, 75001 Paris France. **Tel** 011 33 1 42603180.

HU/0042-6210
VILLAMOSSAG. ***Title Change.*** [Villamossag]. **Added/Corp** Magyar Elektrotechnikai Egyesulet. (1953)-. Academic Scholarly Publication. Hungarian (summaries and/or abstracts in English, German and Russian). mo. Akademiai Kiado, Publishing House of the Hungarian Academy of Sciences, Prielle Kornelia u. 19-35, H-1117 Budapest Hungary. **Tel** 011 36 1 1811991, FAX 011 36 1 1811991, telex 22-6228 AKNYO H. **(Subscription address:** Kultura, Hungarian Foreign Trading Company, PO Box 149, H-1389 Budapest Hungary**)** **LC** TK4; .V5. **CODEN** VLMSAG. Index available. cum. index. **Bk Rev. Ad Acc. Circ:** 2,800 (ctrl). Documents available from Ask*IEEE. ***Merged into*** *Elektrotechnika, 0367-0708.*
Desc: Covers the basic service and immediate developing problems of the electrical power and strong power manufacturing industries. Regular articles on illumination engineering.
Ind/Abst INSPEC (Nov.-Dec. 1968-).

CN/0712-7170
VISPAC NEWSLETTER. [VISPAC newsl.]. **VAT** Videotex Information Service Providers Association of Canada Newsletter. Jan. 1980-. Newsletter. English. Videotex Information Service Providers Association of Canada, Suite 901, 130 Alberta Street, Ottawa Ontario K1P 5G4, Canada. **DD** 621.38/0414.

●US/1063-9667
VLSI DESIGN. (VLSI DESIGN : PROCEEDINGS / THE ... INTERNATIONAL CONFERENCE ON VLSI DESIGN.). [VLSI des.]. **VAT** Very Large Scale Integration Design. (1992)-. Proceedings. English. IEEE Computer Society, 10662 Los Vaqueros Circle, PO Box 3014, Los Alamitos CA 90720-1264. **Tel** (714)821-8380, (800)272-6657, FAX (714)821-4641. **DD** 004. ***Continues*** *VLSI Design, 1063-9667.*

LV
VOPROSY ELEKTRODINAMIKI I MEKHANIKI SPLOSHNYKH SRED. See Physics-Magnetism.

US
WAFERNEWS CONFIDENTIAL. (Aug. 1994)-. Newsletter. English. Twenty-four times a year. $350.00 (one year), $525.00 (two year),US and Canada; $375.00 other. PennWell Publishing Company, Ten Tara Boulevard 5th Floor, Nashua NH 03062-2801. **Tel** (603)891-0123, (603)891-9177, FAX (603)891-0624, (603)891-0574. available via electronic mail ($49.00).
Desc: Provides semiconductor equipment industry executives with information of developments and trends, industry news and market insights about fab equipment companies and the products and services they offer from around the world.

US/0732-5045
WASHINGTON STATE MONTHLY ELECTRICAL STATUS REPORT. [Wash. State mon. electr. status rep.]. Periodical. English. mo. Washington State Energy Office, Library, 809 Legion Way SE, Olympia WA 98504-1211.

US/1044-6036
WESCON CONFERENCE RECORD (1979). (WESCON ... CONFERENCE RECORD.). [WESCON conf. rec.]. **VAT** Western Electronic Show and Convention ... Conference Record. Vol. 23 (1979)-. English. an. Western Periodicals Company, 424 East Main Street, Ventura CA 93001. **Tel** (805)641-2665, FAX (805)643-4854. **DD** 621. **CODEN** WCREDI. **Bk Rev.** ctrl circ. Documents available from Article Express International, Ask*IEEE. ***Continues*** *WESCON Technical Papers, 0083-8837.*
Ind/Abst Bioeng. Abstr. (19??-); Ei Page One (19??-); Eng. Index Annu. (19??-); INSPEC (19??-).

UK
WHAT'S NEW IN ELECTRONICS. English. mo. £65.00 UK and Northern Ireland; $155.00 other. Morgan Grampian, 40 Beresford Street Woolwich, London SE18 6BQ England. **Tel** 011 44 81 855 7777, FAX 011 44 81 855 5548, telex 896238. available in microform from University Microfilms International (UMI).

UK
WHAT'S NEW IN ELECTRONICS EUROPE. English. bm. £60.00 UK and Northern Ireland; $120.00 other. Morgan Grampian, 40 Beresford Street Woolwich, London SE18 6BQ England. **Tel** 011 44 81 855 7777, FAX 011 44 81 855 5548, telex 896238.

AT
WHAT'S NEW IN SOLID STATE. English. ir. Amalgamated Wireless Australia, Rydalmere New South Wales Australia.

UK
WHO'S WHO AND GUIDE TO THE ELECTRICAL INDUSTRY. See Biographies.

US/1057-6304
WHO'S WHO BUYERS GUIDE TO ELECTRONIC SOURCES (MIDWESTERN ED.). ***Title Change.*** (WHO'S WHO BUYERS GUIDE TO ELECTRONIC SOURCES.). [Who's who buyers guide electron. sources]. **Added/Corp** Harris Publishing Co. (1992)-(1992). English. Harris Publishing Company, 2057-2 Aurora Road, Twinsburg OH 44087. **Tel** (800)888-5900, (216)425-9000, FAX (216)425-7150, telex 510 601 1740. **LC** HD9696.A3; U646. **DD** 338.4/7621381/02577. ***Continues*** *Who's Who in Electronics Sources (Midwestern ed.), 1053-6124.* ***Continued by*** *Who's Who Electronics Buyers Guide (Midwestern Ed.), 1066-7601.*

US/1057-6347
WHO'S WHO BUYERS GUIDE TO ELECTRONIC SOURCES (NORTHEASTERN ED.). ***Title Change.*** (WHO'S WHO BUYERS GUIDE TO ELECTRONIC SOURCES.). [Who's who buy. guide electron. sources]. **Added/Corp** Harris Publishing Co. **VFOAT** Who's Who Buyers Guide. (1992)-(1992). English. Harris Publishing Company, 2057-2 Aurora Road, Twinsburg OH 44087. **Tel** (800)888-5900, (216)425-9000, FAX (216)425-7150, telex 510 601 1740. **LC** HD9696.A3; U647. **DD** 338.4/7621381/02574. ***Continues*** *Who's Who in Electronics Sources (Northeastern Ed.), 1053-6132.* ***Continued by*** *Who's Who Electronics Buyers Guide (Northeastern Ed.), 1066-761X.*

US/1057-6339
WHO'S WHO BUYERS GUIDE TO ELECTRONIC SOURCES (SOUTHEASTERN ED.). ***Title Change.*** (WHO'S WHO BUYERS GUIDE TO ELECTRONIC SOURCES.). [Who's who buy. guide electron. sources]. **Added/Corp** Harris Publishing Co. **VFOAT** Who's Who Buyers Guide. (1992)-(1992). English. Harris Publishing Company, 2057-2 Aurora Road, Twinsburg OH 44087. **Tel** (800)888-5900, (216)425-9000, FAX (216)425-7150, telex 510 601 1740. **LC** HD9696.A3; U644a. **DD** 338.4/7621381/02574. ***Continues*** *Who's Who in Electronics Sources (Southeastern Ed.), 1053-6140.* ***Continued by*** *Who's Who Electronics Buyers Guide (Southeastern Ed.), 1066-7628.*

US/1057-6320
WHO'S WHO BUYERS GUIDE TO ELECTRONIC SOURCES (SOUTHWESTERN ED.). ***Title Change.*** (WHO'S WHO BUYERS GUIDE TO ELECTRONICS SOURCES.). [Who's who buy. guide electron. sources]. **Added/Corp** Harris Publishing Co. **VFOAT** Who's Who Buyers Guide. (1992)-(1992). English. Harris Publishing Company, 2057-2 Aurora Road, Twinsburg OH 44087. **Tel** (800)888-5900, (216)425-9000, FAX (216)425-7150, telex 510 601 1740. **LC** HD9696.A3; U6483. **DD** 338.4/7621381/02579. ***Continues*** *Who's Who in Electronics Sources (Southwestern Ed.), 1053-6159.* ***Continued by*** *Who's Who Electronics Buyers Guides (Southwestern Ed.), 1066-7644.*

●US/1066-7601
WHO'S WHO ELECTRONICS BUYERS GUIDE (MIDWESTERN ED.). (WHO'S WHO ELECTRONICS BUYERS GUIDE.). [Who's who electron. buy. guide]. **Added/Corp** Harris Publishing Co. (1993)-. Consumer Publication. English. an. $49.50 per region. Harris Publishing Company, 2057-2 Aurora Road, Twinsburg OH 44087. **Tel** (800)888-5900, (216)425-9000, FAX (216)425-7150, telex 510 601 1740. **LC** HD9696.A3; U646. **DD** 338.4/7621381/02577. available on CD-ROM and diskette. ***Continues*** *Who's Who Buyers Guide to Electronic Sources (Midwestern Ed.), 1057-6304.*
Desc: Lists approximately 12,500 electronics manufacturers as well as 8,500 distributors and representatives in each of five regional/national editions.

●US/1066-761X
WHO'S WHO ELECTRONICS BUYERS GUIDE (NORTHEASTERN ED.). (WHO'S WHO ELECTRONICS BUYERS GUIDE.). [Who's who electron. buy. guide]. **Added/Corp** Harris Publishing Co. (1993)-. Consumer Publication. English. an. $49.50 per region. Harris Publishing Company, 2057-2 Aurora Road, Twinsburg OH 44087. **Tel** (800)888-5900, (216)425-9000, FAX (216)425-7150, telex 510 601 1740. **LC** HD9696.A3; U647. **DD** 338.4/7621381/02574. available on CD-ROM and diskette. ***Continues*** *Who's Who Buyers Guide to Electronic Sources (Northeastern Ed.), 1057-6347.*
Desc: Lists approximately 12,500 electronics manufacturers as well as 8,500 distributors and representatives in each of five regional/national editions.

●US/1066-7628
WHO'S WHO ELECTRONICS BUYERS GUIDE (SOUTHEASTERN ED.). (WHO'S WHO ELECTRONICS BUYERS GUIDE.). [Who's who electron. buy. guide]. **Added/Corp** Harris Publishing Co. (1993)-. Consumer Publication. English. an. $49.50 per region. Harris Publishing Company, 2057-2 Aurora Road, Twinsburg OH 44087. **Tel** (800)888-5900, (216)425-9000, FAX (216)425-7150, telex 510 601 1740. **LC** HD9696.A3; U644a. **DD** 338.4/7621381/02574. available on CD-ROM and diskette. ***Continues*** *Who's Who Buyers Guide to Electronic Sources (Southeastern Ed.), 1057-6339.*
Desc: Lists approximately 12,500 electronics manufacturers as well as 8,500 distributors and representatives in each of five regional/national editions.

●US/1066-7644
WHO'S WHO ELECTRONICS BUYERS GUIDE (SOUTHWESTERN ED.). (WHO'S WHO ELECTRONICS BUYERS GUIDE.). [Who's who electron. buy. guide]. **Added/Corp** Harris Publishing Co. (1993)-. Consumer Publication. English. an. $49.50 per region. Harris Publishing Company, 2057-2 Aurora Road, Twinsburg OH 44087. **Tel** (800)888-5900, (216)425-9000, FAX (216)425-7150, telex 510 601 1740. **LC** HD9696.A3; U6483. **DD** 338.4/7621381/02579. available on CD-ROM and diskette. ***Continues*** *Who's Who Buyers Guide to Electronic Sources (Southwestern Ed.), 1057-6320.*
Desc: Lists approximately 12,500 electronics manufacturers as well as 8,500 distributors and representatives in each of five regional/national editions.

UK/0043-6011
WIRE INDUSTRY. [Wire ind.]. (1934)-. Academic Scholarly Publication. English (French, German and Italian). mo (plus one annual copy of "Wire Industry Yearbook"). £57.00 UK and Ireland; £84.00 (airmail) Europe; £92.00 (airmail) other. Publex International Ltd., 110 Station Road East, Oxted Surrey RH8 0QA England. **Tel** 011 44 883 717755, FAX 011 44 883 714554, telex 95359 PUBLEX G. **ED** G. J. Bullock. **CODEN** WIRIAZ. Index available (included in Dec. issue). cum. index. **Bk Rev. Ad Acc. Circ:** 5,600. Documents available from Article Express International, CASDDS.
Desc: News and technical papers on production of wire, power cables, telecom cables, wire products.
Ind/Abst Alum. Ind. Abstr.; Bioeng. Abstr.; Chem. Abstr.; Curr. Technol. Index; Ei Page One; EMBASE; Eng. Mater. Abstr.; Eng. Index Annu.; Met. Abstr.

GW/0043-6046
WIRE WORLD INTERNATIONAL. ***Title Change.*** [Wire world int.]. Academic Scholarly Publication. English. bm. Vogel Verlag, Postfach 6740, D-97064 Wuerzburg Germany. **Tel** 011 49 931 4182145, 011 49 931 4182483, FAX 011 49 931 4182670, telex 841 680131. **ED** Hasso Reschenberg. **CODEN** WWINAZ. **[CCC]. Bk Rev. Ad Acc. Circ:** 5,000 (ctrl). Documents available from Article Express International, Ask*IEEE, CASDDS. ***Absorbed*** *Wire Production.* ***Continued by*** *Wireworld.*
Desc: Production and processing of wire and cables.
Ind/Abst Alum. Ind. Abstr.; Bioeng. Abstr.; Chem. Abstr.; Ei Page One; EMBASE; Eng. Mater. Abstr.; Eng. Index Annu. [Select. Cov.]; INSPEC (July-Aug. 1971-); Met. Abstr.; Pollut. Abstr. Indexes.

NE/1022-0038
WIRELESS NETWORKS. (19??)-. English. Four times a year. 176.50F (includes distribution costs). Baltzer Science Publishers BV, Asterweg 1A, 1031 HL Amsterdam Netherlands. **Tel** 011 31 20 6370061, FAX 011 31 20 6323651.

US/0741-8221
WIRING DEVICES AND SUPPLIES. (CURRENT INDUSTRIAL REPORTS. MA-36K, WIRING DEVICES AND SUPPLIES.). Began with 1965. Government Publication. English. an. $1.25. US Department of Commerce / Bureau of the Census, Data User Services Division, Customer Services, Washington DC 20233-0800. **Tel** (301)763-4100. **(Subscription address:** Superintendent of Documents, US Government Printing Office, Washington DC 20402.) **LC** HD9697.S853; U52. **DD** 380.1/45621381537/0973. ***Continues*** *Current Industrial Reports. M36K, Wiring Devices and Supplies.*
Desc: Presents timely data on the production, inventories, and orders of approximately 5,000 products, which represents 40 percent of all US manufacturing.

US
WISCONSIN REC NEWS. See Economics-Cooperatives.

GW/0373-9953
WISSENSCHAFTLICHE ZEITSCHRIFT DER ELEKTROTECHNIK. [Wiss. Z. Elektrotech.]. **VFOAT** WZE; W.Z.E. Vol. 1 (1963)-. German (English and Russian). sa. Deut Post Zeitungsvertriebsamt, Berlin Germany. **(Subscription address:** Technische Universitat Dresden Abt Wissenschaftliche Publikationer, Mommsenstr 13, Dresden 8027 Germany**) LC** TK3; .W5. **DD** 621.3/05. **CODEN** WZEKAR. Documents available from Ask*IEEE.
Ind/Abst INSPEC (1968-).

UK/0951-5747
WORLD ELECTRONICS COMPANIES FILE. [World electron. co. file]. (1987)-. English. mo. $738.00 The Americas; £495.00 other. Elsevier Advanced Technology, An Imprint of Elsevier Science Ltd., The Boulevard, Langford Lane, Kidlington, Oxford OX5 1GB United Kingdom. **Tel** 011 44 865 843000, 011 44 865 843699, FAX 011 44 865 843010. **(Subscription address:** Elsevier Science Ltd. Oxford Fulfillment Centre, PO Box 800, Kidlington, Oxford OX5 1DX United Kingdom.**)** ***Continues*** *File - Mackintosh European Electronics Companies, 0142-9671.*

UK
WORLD ELECTRONICS COMPANIES FILE 1990/91. English. BEP Data Services, Chiltern House, 146 Midland Road, Luton LU2 0BL England. **Tel** (0582) 421981, FAX 0582 29691, telex 827648. **LC** HD9696.A2. **DD** 338.4/7621381.

US
WORLD POWER SYSTEMS INTELLIGENCE. (19??)-. Bulletin. English. Twenty-four times a year. $445.00. Forecast International / DMS Inc., 22 Commerce Road, Newtown CT 06470. **Tel** (203)426-0800, FAX (203)426-1964, telex 467615.

US
WORLDRADIO, INC. See Communication-Telecommunications.

CH
WU HSIEN TIEN. VFOAT Wuxiandian. Periodical. Chinese. NT$0.25. Science Press, 16 Donghuangchenggen North Street, Beijing 100707, People's Republic of China. **Tel** 011 86 1 4019821, 011 86 1 4010642, FAX 011 86 1 4012180, 011 86 1 4019810, telex 210147. **LC** TK6540; .W88. **DD** 384.5.

CH
WU HSIEN TIEN YUEH KAN. VFOAT Radiotronics. Vol. 1- July; 1973 Year 9 Month-. Periodical. Chinese (Chinese). $26.00. The Radiotronics Publishers, 1A Min Street, 9/F Kowloon Hong Kong. **LC** TK7800; .W8.

US/0043-9770
WYOMING RURAL ELECTRIC NEWS. Added/Corp Wyoming Rural Electric Association. Riverton Valley Electric Association (Wyo.). (19??)-. English. mo. $3.50. Wyoming Rural Electric Association, 340 West B Street/Suite 101, Casper WY 82601. **Tel** (307)234-6152.

US
YEAR BOOK - ASSOCIATION OF IRON AND STEEL ENGINEERS. Main/Corp Association of Iron and Steel Engineers. **VFOAT** Iron and Steel Engineers Year Book; AISE Year Book; Yearly Proceedings - Association of Iron and Steel Engineers. **VAT** Yearbook - Association of Iron and Steel Engineers. (1974)-. English. an (May). $63.60 (members), $79.50 (non-members) Pennsylvania; $60.00 (members), $75.00 (non-members) others. Association of Iron and Steel Engineers, Three Gateway Centre, Suite 2350, Pittsburgh PA 15222. **Tel** (412)281-6323, FAX (412)281-4657. **ED** Dennis J. Fuga. Index available (bound in last issue). **Circ:** 1,000 (ctrl). ***Continues*** *Association of Iron and Steel Engineers. Yearly Proceedings -Association of Iron and Steel Engineers.*
Desc: Information relating to the design, construction, operation and maintenance of iron and steel producing facilities and related equipment. This magazine also contains all feature editorial material from issues of the Iron and Steel Engineer.

US
YEARBOOK AND DIRECTORY / SEMICONDUCTOR INDUSTRY ASSOCIATION. Main/Corp Semiconductor Industry Association. **VFOAT** SIA Yearbook and Directory. (19??)-. English. be (once every two years). $95.00 nonmembers; $75.00 members. Semiconductor Industry Association, 4300 Stevens Creek Boulevard 271, San Jose CA 95129. **Tel** (408)246-2711. **ED** Jeanne Alford.
Desc: A comprehensive overview of the US semiconductor industry and a directory providing detailed information about firms manufacturing semiconductors in the United States.

UK/0954-0180
YEARBOOK OF WORLD ELECTRONICS DATA ... VOL. 1, WEST EUROPE. VFOAT West Europe. (19??)-. English. an. £555.00. Elsevier Advanced Technology, An Imprint of Elsevier Science Ltd., The Boulevard, Langford Lane, Kidlington, Oxford OX5 1GB United Kingdom. **Tel** 011 44 865 843000, 011 44 865 843699, FAX 011 44 865 843010. **LC** HD9696.A3; E858. **DD** 338.4/7/621381094. ***Continues*** *Mackintosh Yearbook of West European Electronics Data, 0306-5774.*

UK/0954-0172
YEARBOOK OF WORLD ELECTRONICS DATA ... VOL. 2, AMERICA, JAPAN & ASIA PACIFIC. [Yearb. world electron. data, 2 Am. Jpn. Asia Pac.]. **VFOAT** America, Japan & Asia Pacific; America, Japan and Asia Pacific. 7th Ed. (1990)-. English. an. $1330.00. Elsevier Advanced Technology, An Imprint of Elsevier Science Ltd., The Boulevard, Langford Lane, Kidlington, Oxford OX5 1GB United Kingdom. **Tel** 011 44 865 843000, 011 44 865 843699, FAX 011 44 865 843010.

Engineering —Hydraulic Engineering

LC HD9696.A1; Y4. **DD** 338.4/7621381/05. *Continues Mackintosh Yearbook Electronics Data. Vol. 2, America, Japan, Asia-Pacific.*

US/0098-5910
YEARBOOK - SOCIETY OF WIRELESS PIONEERS. (YEAR BOOK.). **Main/Corp** Society of Wireless Pioneers. English. an. Society of Wireless Pioneers Inc, PO Box 530, Santa Rosa CA 95402. **LC** VK397; .S62A. **DD** 384.5/2/09.

JA/0513-6342
YUASA JIHO / YUASA DENCHI KABUSHIKI KAISHA. [Yuasa jiho]. **VFOAT** Yuasa-Jiho; Technical Review. (1928)-. Academic Scholarly Publication. Japanese (English). sa. Free. Yuasa Battery Company Ltd, 6-6 Josai-cho, Takatsuki-shi Osaka-fu 569 Japan. **Tel** (0726)75-5503, telex 5336-559 YUASA J. **ED** Kazuo Okada. **CODEN** YUJIAX. cum. index. **Circ**: 4,000 (ctrl). Documents available from CASDDS.
Desc: Lead-acid battery, NI-CD battery, NA/S battery, NI/ZN battery, thermal battery, ZN/AIR battery, LI battery, fuel cell, silver oxide battery, sea water battery, charger, power supply system, ups.
Ind/Abst Chem. Abstr.

XO
ZBORNIK VEDECKYCH PRAC ELEKTROTECHNICKEJ FAKULTY SVST BRATISLAVA. Periodical. Slovak (summaries and/or abstracts in English and Russian). Alfa / Slovakia, Hurbanovo Nam 3, 815 89 Bratislava Slovakia. **Tel** 7 331-441, **FAX** 7 594-43. **LC** TK4; .Z43.

CC/0258-8013
ZHONGGUO DIANJI GONGCHENG XUEBAO. (CHUNG-KUO TIEN CHI KUNG CHENG HSUEH PAO / CHUNG-KUO TIEN CHI KUNG CHENG HSUEH HUI.). [Zhongguo dianji gongcheng xuebao]. **Added/Corp** Chung-Kuo Tien Chi Kung Cheng Hsueh Hui (Peking, China). **VFOAT** Proceedings of the CSEE; Proceedings of the Chinese Society of Electrical Engineering. (Feb. 1985)-. Periodical. Chinese (summaries and/or abstracts in English). bm. $37.10. **(Subscription address:** China National Publishers, Import & Export, 16 Gongti East Road Chaoyang Dist., Beijing 10074 China.) **LC** TK4; .C5. **DD** 621.3/05. **CODEN** ZDGXER. Documents available from Article Express International, Ask*IEEE. *Continues Tien Chi Kung Cheng Hsueh Pao.*
Ind/Abst Eng. Index Annu.; INSPEC (1987-).

HYDRAULIC ENGINEERING

US/0099-1856
ACTIVE NAMES OF BUREAU PROJECTS AND MAJOR STRUCTURES. *Title Change.* **Main/Corp** Engineering and Research Center (U.S.). English. US Department of the Interior / US Geological Survey, Books and Open-File Reports Section, Box 25425, Federal Center, Denver CO 80225-0425. **LC** TS556; .U53A. **DD** 627/.8/0973. *Continued by Active Names of Bureau Projects and Major Structures (Engineering and Research Center (U.S.).*

HU
ADVANCED PLANNING / VIZITERV, INSTITUTE FOR HYDRAULIC PLANNING. **Added/Corp** VIZITERV (Firm). (19??)-. Periodical. English. **LC** TC465.5; .A64. **DD** 628.1/05.

UK
ADVANCES IN UNDERWATER TECHNOLOGY, OCEAN SCIENCE, AND OFFSHORE ENGINEERING / SOCIETY FOR UNDERWATER TECHNOLOGY. **Added/Corp** Society for Underwater Technology. (1986)-. Monographic series. English. ir. Price varies per volume. Graham & Trotman Ltd, Sterling House, 66 Wilson Road, London SW1V 1DE England. **Tel** 44 71 8211123. *Continues Advances in Underwater Technology and Offshore Engineering.*
Desc: Information on marine sciences and ocean engineering.

US/0565-0585
ANNUAL OPERATING PLAN, WESTERN DIVISION, MISSOURI RIVER BASIN. (ANNUAL OPERATION PLAN, WESTERN DIVISION, PICK-SLOAN MISSOURI BASIN PROGRAM.). **Main/Corp** United States. Bureau of Reclamation. English. an. Bureau of Reclamation, PO Box 25007, Denver CO 80225. **Tel** (303)234-3000. **LC** TC425.M7; U53B. **DD** 333.9/162.
Desc: Each volume includes projected outlook for the following year.

US/0198-1994
ANNUAL PROGRESS REPORT - WATER MANAGEMENT RESEARCH PROJECT. See Water Resources.

US
ANNUAL PROJECT HISTORY : MANN CREEK PROJECT. **Main/Corp** United States. Bureau of Reclamation. **Added/Corp** Central Snake Projects Office. (1966)-. Periodical. English.

US/0278-1484
ANNUAL REPORT - ARKANSAS-WHITE-RED BASINS INTER-AGENCY COMMITTEE. (ANNUAL REPORT, ARKANSAS-WHITE-RED BASINS INTER-AGENCY COMMITTEE FOR THE YEAR ...). **Main/Corp** Arkansas-White-Red Basins Inter-Agency Committee. July 1, 1958-June 30, 1959-. English. an. Southwestern Division, Corps of Engineers, Dallas TX 75235. **Tel** (501)378-5551. **LC** TC423.9; .A8A. **DD** 353.9/382325/0976. *Continues Report of the Arkansas-White-Red Basins Inter-Agency Committee.*

AT/0728-7879
ANNUAL REPORT - ENGINEERING AND WATER SUPPLY DEPARTMENT ADELAIDE. (19??)-. English.
Ind/Abst AESIS Q.

UK
ANNUAL REPORT / HYDRAULICS RESEARCH STATION. **Added/Corp** Hydraulics Research Station (Great Britain). (1977)-. English. an. £6.80. Her Majesty's Stationery Office, 51 Nine Elms Lane, London SW8 5DR England. **Tel** 011 44 71 873 8459, 011 44 71 873 8499, **FAX** 011 44 71 873 8499, 011 44 71 873 8456, telex 297138. **(Subscription address:** PO Box 276, Public Centre, London SW8 5DT England) **LC** TC1; .W2a. **DD** 627/.05. *Continues Hydraulics Research Station (Great Britain). Hydraulics Research.*
Ind/Abst Irr. Drain. Abstr.

US/0162-0320
ANNUAL REPORT - LOWER COLORADO RIVER AUTHORITY. **Main/Corp** Lower Colorado River Authority. English. an. Lower Colorado River Authority, PO Box 220, Austin TX 78767. **LC** TC425.C6; L67A. **DD** 353.9/764/008232.

TZ/0496-831X
ANNUAL REPORT OF THE WATER DEVELOPMENT AND IRRIGATION DIVISION (DAR ES SALAAM). (ANNUAL REPORT OF THE WATER DEVELOPMENT AND IRRIGATION DIVISION.). **Main/Corp** Tanganyika. Water Development and Irrigation Division. **VFOAT** Annual Report - Water Development and Irrigation Division. Periodical. English. Government Printer / Tanzania, PO Box 2483, Dar es Salaam Tanzania. **LC** TD319.T3; A3. **DD** 627; 628.1. *Continues Annual Report of the Department of Water Development and Irrigation.*

US/0363-8383
ANNUAL REPORT. OPERATION OF THE COLORADO RIVER BASIN. PROJECTED OPERATIONS. (ANNUAL REPORT. OPERATION OF THE COLORADO RIVER BASIN ... PROJECTED OPERATIONS / BUREAU OF RECLAMATION.). **Main/Corp** United States. Bureau of Reclamation. **VFOAT** Operation of the Colorado River Basin ... Projected Operations. Government Publication. English. an. US Department of the Interior Bureau of Reclamation, 1849 C Street NW, Room 7654, Washington DC 20240. **Tel** (202)208-4157, **FAX** (202)343-3484. **LC** TC425.C6; U53A. **DD** 333.9/102/097913. available on microfiche (Vols. for (1985-) distributed to depository libraries).

US/0066-4189
ANNUAL REVIEW OF FLUID MECHANICS. [Annu. rev. fluid mech.]. Vol. 1 (1969)-. English. an (January). $47.00 us; $52.00 other. Annual Reviews Inc., 4139 El Camino Way, PO Box 10139, Palo Alto CA 94303-0139. **Tel** (415)493-4400, (800)523-8635, **FAX** (415)855-9815. **ED** Milton Van Dyke and John L. Lumley. **LC** QC145; .A57. **DD** 532/.005. **CODEN** ARVFA3. **[CCC].** Index available. cum. index. **Pr Rev.** ctrl circ. available on microfilm and microfiche from University Microfilms International (UMI). Documents available from Article Express International, The Genuine Article, BIOSIS Document Express, Ask*IEEE, CASDDS.
Desc: Comprehensive, thorough coverage of latest advances in fluid mechanics, written by acknowledged experts in the field. Extensive literature citations included.
Ind/Abst Abstr. Bull. Inst. Pap. Sci. Tech.; Bioeng. Abstr.; Biol. Abstr.; Chem. Abstr.; Curr. Contents Eng. Tech. Appl. Sci.; Ei Page One; Eng. Index Annu.; Fluid Abstr., Civil Eng.; Fluid Abstr. Proc. Eng.; FLUIDEX (1973-); GeoRef; Index Vet. Aerosp. Abstr.; Life Sci. Collect.; Res. Alert [Full Cov.]; Sci. Cit. Index; SCISEARCH; Zentralbl. Math. Ihre Grenzgeb.

NE/0006-6994
APPLIED SCIENTIFIC RESEARCH. See Engineering-Mechanical Engineering and Machinery.

UK/0263-5534
AQUALINE ABSTRACTS. See Engineering-Abstracting, Bibliographies and Statistics.

PL/0004-0789
ARCHIWUM HYDROTECHNIKI. [Arch. hydrotech.]. **Added/Corp** Polska Akademia Nauk. Instytut Budownictwa Wodnego. Vol. 1 (1954)-. Periodical. Polish (English; summaries and/or abstracts in French and Russian; table of contents in French and Russian). qt. $64.00. **(Subscription address:** ARS Polona, PO Box 1001, 00068 Warsaw Poland.) **LC** TC1; .A7. **CODEN** AHDRAF.
Ind/Abst Fluid Abstr., Civil Eng.; Fluid Abstr. Proc. Eng.; FLUIDEX (1973-); GeoRef; Life Sci. Collect.

GW/0436-1199
BERICHT - MAX-PLANCK-INSTITUT FUER STROMUNGSFORSCHUNG. [Ber. Max-Planck-Inst. Stroemungsforsch.]. **Main/Corp** Max-Planck-Institut fur Stromungsforschung. (19??)-. Monographic series. Multiple languages. Max Planck Institut fuer Stroemung-Forschung, Bottingerstrasse 6/8, D 37073 Goettingen Germany. **CODEN** MPSBBR. Documents available from Ask*IEEE, CASDDS.
Ind/Abst Chem. Abstr.; INSPEC.

II/0006-0461
BHAGIRATH. [Bhagirath]. **Added/Corp** India. Ministry of Irrigation and Power. India. Central Water and Power Commission. Vol. 1 (June 1954)-. Periodical. English. Twelve times a year. Rs96.00 (one year); Rs186.00 (two years): Rs270.00 (three years). Ministry of Information and Broadcasting, Government of India, Patiala House, New Delhi 110 001 India. **Tel** 387983. **LC** TC903; .B5. available on microfilm.
Ind/Abst Indian Geosci. Abstr.

PL/0239-622X
BIBLIOGRAFIA GOSPODARKI I INZYNIERII WODNEJ. See Water Resources.

IT/0006-1042
BIBLIOGRAFIA ITALIANA DI IDRAULICA. *Ceased.* **Added/Corp** Universit·a di Padova. Istituto di Idraulica. Centro di Documentazione Idraulica. **VFOAT** Hydraulic Italian Bibliography. Vol. 1 (Jan./March 1950)-(19??). Periodical. Italian. bm. Universita di Padova, Istituto di Idraulica, Giovanni Poleni, Via L Loredan 20, 35131 Padova Italy. **Tel** 049-831441. **Bk Rev. Circ**: 300.
Desc: Abstracts in Italian of the most relevant books and papers published in Italy. Title translations in English.
Ind/Abst Int. Civil Eng. Abstr.; Soft. Abstr. Eng.

US
BIENNIAL REPORT - NORTH DAKOTA. STATE WATER CONSERVATION COMMISSION. See Water Resources.

BL/0374-6658
BOLETIM TECNICO - DEPARTAMENTO NACIONAL DE OBRAS CONTRA AS SECAS. (BOLETIM TECNICO.). [Bol. tec. dep. nac. obras contra secas]. Vol. 28, No. 1 (Jan./June 1970)-. Bulletin. Portuguese. sa. Banco do Brasil SA, Carteira de Cambio Agencia de Itabuna, 45600 Itabuna Bahia Brazil. **LC** TC841; .A32. **DD** 631.5/87/0981. *Continues Boletim (Brazil. Departamento Nacional de Obras Contra As Secas).*

AG/0325-8106
BOLETIN INFORMATIVO (ARGENTINA.) DEPARTAMENTO GENERAL DE IRRIGACION. (BOLETIN INFORMATIVO.). Periodical. Spanish.

FR
BULLETIN DE DOCUMENTATION - ASSOCIATION TECHNIQUE DE L'INDUSTRIE DES LIANTS HYDRAULIQUES. **Added/Corp** Association Technique de l'Industrie des Liants Hydrauliques. Centre de Documentation. Vol. 1, No. 1 & 2 (1988)-. Bulletin. French. ir (10 issues per year). 1500F France; 1800F other. Association Technique de l'Industrie des Liants Hydrauliques (ATILH), 8 rue Villiot, 75012 Paris France. **Tel** 011 33 1 43460070, **FAX** 43.44.78.11, telex 240 020 F. Index available. *Continues Bulletin Analytique (Association Technique de l'Industrie des Liants Hydrauliques).*

FR/0013-449X
BULLETIN DE LA DIRECTION DES ETUDES ET RECHERCHES. SERIE A. NUCLEAIRE, HYDRAULIQUE, THERMIQUE. [Bull. Dir. etud. rech. - Electr. Fr., Ser. A Nucl. hydraul. therm.]. **VFOAT** Nucleaire, Hydraulique, Thermique. No. 1 (1967)-. Academic Scholarly Publication. French (summaries and/or abstracts in English). qt. Free. Electricite France Direction Etudes, 2 rue Louis Murat, 75784 Paris Cedex 08 France. **Tel** 011 33 1 40423126, telex 40.42.31.26 MME FIEVEZ. **ED** ISRAEL. **CODEN** EFDNAX. **Circ**: 1,600 (ctrl). Documents available from Article Express International, Ask*IEEE,

CASDDS. ***Supersedes*** *Bulletin du Centre de Recherchees et d'Essais de Chatou.*
Ind/Abst Chem. Abstr.; Coal Abstr.; Energy Res. Abstr. (Oct. 1976-); Eng. Index Annu.; Fluid Abstr., Civil Eng.; Fluid Abstr. Proc. Eng.; FLUIDEX (1973-); GeoRef; INSPEC (1969-); Int. Civil Eng. Abstr.

UV/0379-3478
BULLETIN DE LIAISON DU COMITE INTERAFRICAIN D'ETUDES HYDRAULIQUES. [Bull. liaison com. interafr. etud. hydraul.]. Bulletin. French. qt. $20.00 Africa; $25.00 other. Boite Postale 369, Ougadougou Burkina Faso. **Tel** 33 34 76, telex 5277 BF. **CODEN** LBISDN. **Ad Acc.**
Ind/Abst GeoRef.

BE/0374-1001
BULLETIN OF THE PERMANENT INTERNATIONAL ASSOCIATION OF NAVIGATION CONGRESSES. [Bull. Perm. Int. Assoc. Navig. Congr.]. **Added/Corp** Permanent International Association of Navigation Congresses. Permanent International Commission of Navigation Congresses. **VFOAT** Bulletin de l'Association Internationale Permanente des Congres de Navigation. 1st Year, No. 1 (Jan. 1926)-. Bulletin. English (French). Four times a year. $320.00 corporate membership; $55.00 individual membership. PIANC / Permanent International Association of Navigation Congresses, 20 Massachussetts Avenue NW, Washington DC 20314. **LC** TC1; .P4. **CODEN** BPANAL.
Ind/Abst Aquat. Sci. Fish. Abstr. (Computer File); Bioeng. Abstr.; BMT Abstr.; Fluid Abstr., Civil Eng.; Fluid Abstr. Proc. Eng.; FLUIDEX (1973-); GeoRef; Life Sci. Collect.

US/0892-3515
CANAL HISTORY AND TECHNOLOGY PROCEEDINGS. [Canal hist. technol. proc.]. **Added/Corp** Center for Canal History and Technology (Easton, Pa.). Vol. 5 (March 22, 1986)-. Academic Scholarly Publication. English. an. $18.00. Center for Canal History and Technology, PO Box 877, Easton PA 18042. **Tel** (215)250-6700. **ED** Lance E. Metz. **LC** HE395.A1; C36a. **DD** 386/.4/09. cum. index. **Circ:** 500. ***Continues*** *Proceedings of the Canal History and Technology Symposium, 0730-5281.*
Desc: An annual scholarly journal devoted to topics of transportation and industrial history relating to towpath canals, anthracite coal mining, and iron and steel production.

US
CERCULAR / COASTAL ENGINEERING RESEARCH CENTER, THE. **Added/Corp** Coastal Engineering Research Center (U.S.). Vol. CERC-84-1 (May 1984)-. Periodical. English. Four times a year. Free. US Department of the Army Waterways Experiment Station, 3909 Halls Ferry Road, PO Box 631, Vicksburg MS 39180. **Tel** (601)634-2012. ***Continues*** *Quarterly CERCular Information Bulletin.*
Ind/Abst Meteorol. Geoastrophys. Abstr. (199?-).

CC/0890-5487
CHINA OCEAN ENGINEERING. [China ocean eng.]. **Added/Corp** Chinese Ocean Engineering Society. (198?)-. Periodical. English. qt. $260.00. China Ocean Press, 1 Fuxingmenwai Street, Beijing 100860 China. **Tel** 011 86 1 8532211 ext. 5913. **LC** TC1501; .C45. **DD** 620/.4162. available on microfilm and microfiche from University Microfilms International (UMI). Documents available from Article Express International, Petroleum Abstracts Document Delivery Service.
Desc: Concerned with all engineering aspects involved in the exploration and utilization of ocean resources, such as offshore engineering, dive and salvage, utilization of marine energy resources and underwater technology.
Ind/Abst Aquat. Sci. Fish. Abstr. (Computer File); Coal Abstr.; Ecol. Abstr.; Eng. Index Annu.; Fluid Abstr., Civil Eng.; Fluid Abstr. Proc. Eng.; FLUIDEX; Geogr. Abstr. Phys. Geogr.; Geogr. Abstr. Human Geogr.; Geol. Abstr.; Int. Civil Eng. Abstr.; Ocean. Abstr.; Pet. Abstr.; Soft. Abstr. Eng.

JA
CHOSETSU KOHO NIIGATA. **Main/Corp** Japan. Daiichi Kowan Kensetsukyoku. Niigata Chosa Sekkei Jimusho. **VFOAT** Niigata. No. 1, (March 1978)-. Japanese. Unyusho Daiichi Kowan Kensetsukyoku Niigata Chosa Sekkei Jimusho, Hakusanura 1-chome, Niigata 951 Japan. **LC** TC306.N53; J36a.

CU/1013-9850
CIENCIA Y TECNICA EN LA AGRICULTURA. RIEGO Y DRENAJE. [Cienc. tec. agric., Riego drenaje]. **VFOAT** Riego y Drenaje. Vol. 1, No. 1 (Jan. 1979)-. Periodical. Spanish (summaries and/or abstracts in English; table of contents in English). sa. Ediciones Cubanas, Obispo 527, Altos ESQ Bernaza, CP 10100 Havana Cuba. **Tel** 011 632980, 631942, FAX 011 631011, telex 512337, 6540. **CODEN** CARDEK. Documents available from BIOSIS Document Express.
Ind/Abst Agric. Eng. Abstr. (1991-); Biol. Abstr. (1986-); Field Crop Abstr.; Hortic. Abstr.; Potato Abstr.; Soils Fert.

NE
CIVIELE TECHNIEK. **See** Engineering.

JA/0578-5634
COASTAL ENGINEERING IN JAPAN. [Coast. eng. Jpn.]. **Added/Corp** Doboku Gakkai. Doboku Gakkai. Kaigan Kogaku Iinkai. Kaigan Kogaku Koenkai. Vol 1. (1958)-. Periodical. English. sa. $172.00. Doboku Gakkai Kaigan Kogaku Iinkai, (Committee on Coastal Engineering, Japan Society of Civil Engineers), Yotsuya 1 Chome, Shinjukuku, Tokyoto 160 Japan. **(Subscription address:** Maruzen Company Ltd., PO Box 5050, Import & Export Department, Tokyo 100 31 Japan.**)** **LC** TC330; .D6. **DD** 627. **CODEN** CENJA8. Documents available from Article Express International.
Ind/Abst Aquat. Sci. Fish. Abstr. (Computer File); Bioeng. Abstr.; Ei Page One; Eng. Index Annu.; Fluid Abstr., Civil Eng.; Fluid Abstr. Proc. Eng.; FLUIDEX (1973-); Int. Civil Eng. Abstr.; Life Sci. Collect.

US/0360-6864
COLUMBIA RIVER WATER MANAGEMENT REPORT. **Main/Corp** Columbia River Water Management Group. English. an. Columbia River Water Management, Corps of Engineers, 210 Custom House, Portland OR 97209. **LC** TC425.C7; C64A. **DD** 333.9/1/0409797.

NE/0169-6548
COMMUNICATIONS ON HYDRAULIC AND GEOTECHNICAL ENGINEERING. (1986)-. Monographic series. English. te. Price varis per volume. Delft University Press, Stevinweg 1, 2628 CN Delft The Netherlands. **Tel** 011 31 15 783254. **UDC** 626.
Ind/Abst Fluid Abstr., Civil Eng.; Fluid Abstr. Proc. Eng.; FLUIDEX (19??-).

CN/1182-6436
COMPLEXE NBR. [Complexe NBR]. **Added/Corp** Hydro-Quebec. **VAT** Complexe Nottaway-Broadback-Rupert. No 1 (Sept. 1990)-. Periodical. French. **DD** 333.91/4/09714.

UK/0045-7930
COMPUTERS & FLUIDS. [Comput. fluids]. **VFOAT** Computers and Fluids. Vol. 1 (Jan. 1973)-. Periodical. English. Eight times a year. $954.00 The Americas; £640.00 other. Pergamon Press, An Imprint of Elsevier Science Ltd., The Boulevard, Langford Lane, Kidlington, Oxford OX5 1GB United Kingdom. **Tel** 011 44 865 843000, 011 44 865 843699, FAX 011 44 865 843010. **(Subscription address:** Elsevier Science Ltd. Oxford Fulfillment Centre, PO Box 800, Kidlington, Oxford OX5 1DX United Kingdom.**)** **ED** Stanley G. Rubin and Matin Bloom. **LC** TA357; .C59. **DD** 532/.05/02854. **CODEN** CPFLBI. **[CCC]. Pr Rev.** available on microfilm and microfiche from University Microfilms International (UMI). Documents available from Article Express International, The Genuine Article, Ask*IEEE, CASDDS.
Desc: Hydrodynamics, high-speed gas dynamics, turbulence, multiphase flow, rheology, kinetic theory and flows coupled to chemical reactions, radiation and electromagnetics are all of interest - provided that computer technique plays a significant part in the associated studies or design methodology. The development of numerical methods relevant to fluid flow computations and novel applications to flow systems are also of interest.
Ind/Abst Abstr. Bull. Inst. Pap. Sci. Tech.; ACM Guide Comput. Lit.; Bioeng. Abstr.; Chem. Abstr.; Compumath Citation Index [Full Cov.]; Comput. Abstr.; Comput. Rev.; Curr. Contents Eng. Tech. Appl. Sci.; Ei Page One; Eng. Index Annu.; Fluid Abstr., Civil Eng.; Fluid Abstr. Proc. Eng.; FLUIDEX (1973-); HTFS Dig.; INSPEC (Jan. 1973-); Int. Aerosp. Abstr.; Int. Civil Eng. Abstr.; Math. Rev.; Pollut. Abstr. Indexes; Proc. Chem. Eng.; Res. Alert [Full Cov.]; Sci. Cit. Index; SCISEARCH; Soft. Abstr. Eng.; Theoret. Chem. Eng.; Zentralbl. Math. Ihre Grenzgeb.

US/0499-0021
CONFERENCE WITH THE DIRECTORS OF THE NATIONAL RECLAMATION ASSOCIATION. (CONFERENCE WITH THE DIRECTORS OF THE NATIONAL RECLAMATION ASSOCIATION. MEMORANDUM OF THE CHAIRMAN TO THE MEMBERS OF THE COMMITTEE ON INTERIOR AND INSULAR AFFAIRS, UNITED STATES SENATE.). **Main/Corp** United States. Congress. Senate. Committee on Interior and Insular Affairs. **Added/Corp** National Reclamation Association. (1957)-. Government Publication. English. ir. Superintendent of Documents, US Government Printing Office, Washington DC 20402. **Tel** (202)275-3328, FAX (202)786-2377. **LC** HD1720; .A3. **DD** 333.

•US/1069-2657
CORPS REPORT, THE. [Corps rep.]. **Added/Corp** Pasha Publications (Firm). Vol. 1, No. 1 (Apr. 30, 1993)-. Periodical. English. bw (25 issues). $349.00 US; $364.00 other. Pasha Publications Inc., 1616 North Fort Myer Drive, Suite 1000, Arlington VA 22209. **Tel** (800)424-2908, (703)528-1244, FAX (703)528-3742, (703)528-1253. **DD** 627.

JA/0011-5347
DAI DAMU / LARGE DAMS. **VFOAT** Large Dams. (19??)-. Periodical. Japanese (Japanese). qt. Nihon Dai Damu Kaigi, 4-2 Uchisaiwai-cho 1 Chiyoda-ku, Tokyo-to Japan. **Tel** (03)508-1626, telex 24137. **ED** Shigeru Ichiura. **LC** TC558.J3; D28. Index available. cum. index. **Ad Acc. Circ:** 1,600 (ctrl).
Desc: Planning, design and operation of dams.

UK/0958-9341
DAM ENGINEERING. Vol. 1, Issue 1 (Jan. 1990)-. English. qt. £153.00 UK; $263.44 US. Reed Business Publishing Group / England, Quadrant House, Quadrant Sutton Surrey, SM2 5AS England. **Tel** 011 44 81 652-3500.
Ind/Abst Geotech. Abstr. (19??-).

US/0591-0722
DAMS WITHIN JURISDICTION OF THE STATE OF CALIFORNIA. **Main/Corp** California. Dept. of Water Resources. English. $3.00. PO Box 388, Sacramento CA 95802. **LC** TC557.C2; C34A. **DD** 627/.8/09794.

DK/0109-5110
DANISH HYDRAULICS. [Dan. hydr.]. **Added/Corp** Dansk Hydraulisk Institut. No. 1 (Apr. 1981)-. Periodical. English. sa. Free. Danish Hydraulics, Agern Allee 5, DK-2970 Horsholm Denmark. **Tel** 45 45 769555, FAX 45 45 762567, telex 37402 DHI CPH DK.
Desc: A journal of the Danish Hydraulic Institute. It is distributed free of charge to research institutes, public authorities, international organizations, and private companies.
Ind/Abst Fluid Abstr., Civil Eng.; Fluid Abstr. Proc. Eng.; FLUIDEX (1981-).

II
DETAILED ESTIMATES OF IRRIGATION, ELECTRICITY AND PUBLIC WORKS FOR ... . **See** Engineering-Electricity, Electrical Engineering, Electronics.

II/0570-0345
DETAILED IRRIGATION BUDGET. **See** Public Administration-Public Finance and Taxation.

II
DETAILED IRRIGATION BUDGET FOR THE YEAR ... - TAMIL NADU (INDIA). **Main/Corp** Tamil Nadu (India). Periodical. English. an.

UK/0486-0837
DEVELOPMENT STUDIES. **See** Agriculture-Crop Production and Soil.

UK
DEVELOPMENTS IN FLOW MEASUREMENT. 1-. Academic Scholarly Publication. English. Elsevier Science Publishing Company Inc, Madison Square Station, PO Box 882, New York NY 10159-0882. **Tel** (212)633-3950, FAX (212)633-3990. **LC** TA357; .D49. **DD** 532/.053/05.

FR
DOSSIERS TECHNIQUES PAUL HUET / HYDRAULIQUE PNEUMATIQUE. (19??)-. French. ir. 683.81F France; 820.00F other. Editions Techniques Paul Huet, 185 rue Gallieni, 92100 Boulogne, Billancourt, France. **Tel** 011 33 1 46046633.

US
DREDGING RESEARCH. **Added/Corp** U.S. Army Engineer Waterways Experiment Station. Vol. DRP-88-1 (Aug. 1988)-. Periodical. English. ir. free. US Department of the Army Waterways Experiment Station, 3909 Halls Ferry Road, PO Box 631, Vicksburg MS 39180. **Tel** (601)634-2012.
Ind/Abst Meteorol. Geoastrophys. Abstr. (199?-).

CN/0701-0222
EFFLUENT. **Added/Corp** Association Quebecoise des Techniques de l'Eau. Vol. 1 (April 1976)-. Periodical. French. Three times a year. 75.00Can$ (individuals); 450.00Can$ (institutions) Comes with Association Quebecoise des Techniques de l Eau. Association Quebecoise des Techniques de l'Eau, 407 Boul St Laurent Bur 500, Montreal Quebec H2Y 2Y5 Canada. **Tel** (514)874-3700. **DD** 628.1/06/2714. **Circ:** 1,800.
Desc: Information on AQTE'S activities.

US
ELIZABETH RIVER TUNNEL SYSTEM, NORFOLK, VIRGINIA, CONSULTING ENGINEERS ... ANNUAL REPORT. **Main/Corp** Parsons, Brinckerhoff, Quade & Douglas. **Added/Corp** Virginia. Dept. of Highways and Transportation. English. **LC** TA820.V8; P37a. **DD** 353.97550086/4.

US
ENCYCLOPEDIA OF FLUID POWER STANDARDS. VOL. A : COMMUNICATIONS, INCLUDING GRAPHIC SYMBOLS AND METRIC UNITS. **Main/Corp** National Fluid Power Association. (19??)-. English. $30.00. National Fluid Power

Association, 3333 North Mayfair Road, Milwaukee WI 53222. **Tel** (414)778-3369, FAX (414)778-3361, telex 704557.

US
ENCYCLOPEDIA OF FLUID POWER STANDARDS. VOL. B : PRESSURE RATING. **Main/Corp** National Fluid Power Association. (19??)-. English. $25.00. National Fluid Power Association, 3333 North Mayfair Road, Milwaukee WI 53222. **Tel** (414)778-3369, FAX (414)778-3361, telex 704557.

US
ENCYCLOPEDIA OF FLUID POWER STANDARDS. VOL. C : PUMPS, MOTORS, POWER UNITS & RESERVOIRS. **Main/Corp** National Fluid Power Association. (19??)-. English. $30.00. National Fluid Power Association, 3333 North Mayfair Road, Milwaukee WI 53222. **Tel** (414)778-3369, FAX (414)778-3361, telex 704557.

US
ENCYCLOPEDIA OF FLUID POWER STANDARDS. VOL. D : FILTRATION AND CONTAMINATION. **Main/Corp** National Fluid Power Association. (19??)-. English. $45.00. National Fluid Power Association, 3333 North Mayfair Road, Milwaukee WI 53222. **Tel** (414)778-3369, FAX (414)778-3361, telex 704557.

US
ENCYCLOPEDIA OF FLUID POWER STANDARDS. VOL. E : CONDUCTORS AND ASSOCIATED PRODUCTS. **Main/Corp** National Fluid Power Association. (19??)-. English. $25.00. National Fluid Power Association, 3333 North Mayfair Road, Milwaukee WI 53222. **Tel** (414)778-3369, FAX (414)778-3361, telex 704557.

US
ENCYCLOPEDIA OF FLUID POWER STANDARDS. VOL. F : CONTROL PRODUCTS/PNEUMATIC SYSTEMS. **Main/Corp** National Fluid Power Association. (19??)-. English. $75.00. National Fluid Power Association, 3333 North Mayfair Road, Milwaukee WI 53222. **Tel** (414)778-3369, FAX (414)778-3361, telex 704557.

US
ENCYCLOPEDIA OF FLUID POWER STANDARDS. VOL. G : CYLINDERS AND ACCUMULATORS. **Main/Corp** National Fluid Power Association. (19??)-. English. $75.00. National Fluid Power Association, 3333 North Mayfair Road, Milwaukee WI 53222. **Tel** (414)778-3369, FAX (414)778-3361, telex 704557.

US
ENCYCLOPEDIA OF FLUID POWER STANDARDS. VOL. I : TESTING. **Main/Corp** National Fluid Power Association. (19??)-. English. $50.00. National Fluid Power Association, 3333 North Mayfair Road, Milwaukee WI 53222. **Tel** (414)778-3369, FAX (414)778-3361, telex 704557.

US
ENCYCLOPEDIA OF FLUID POWER STANDARDS. VOL. J : BIBLIOGRAPHIES. **See** Engineering-Abstracting, Bibliographies and Statistics.

UK/8756-6796
ENGINEERING APPLICATIONS OF COMPUTATIONAL HYDRAULICS. [Eng. appl. comput. hydraul.]. Vol. 1-. Monographic series. English. Price varies per volume. Longman Group Ltd., Fourth Avenue, Longman House, Harlow Essex CM19 5SR England. **Tel** 011 44 279 429655, FAX 011 44 279 431059, telex 81259. **(Subscription address:** PO Box 1584, Birmingham, AL 35201) **LC** TC163; .E5. **DD** 627/.05.

UK
ENGINEERING SCIENCES DATA UNIT : SUBSERIES FLUID MECHANICS INTERNAL FLOW. (19??)-. English. ir. $4900.00. ESDU International Ltd., 27 Corsham Street, London N1 6UA England. **Tel** 011 44 71 4905151, telex 266168 ENDASAG.

GW/0937-8243
EUROPEAN JOURNAL FOR FLUID POWER, OIL-HYDRAULICS AND PNEUMATICS. (19??)-. English. sa. DM54.00 Germany; DM64.00 other. Vereinigte Fachverlage, Postfach 4068, D 55030 Mainz Germany. **Tel** 011 49 6131 992150.

GW/0723-4864
EXPERIMENTS IN FLUIDS. [Exp. fluids]. Vol. 1, No. 1 (1983)-. Academic Scholarly Publication. English. Twelve times a year. DM1130.00. Springer-Verlag GmbH & Company KG, Heidelberger Platz 3, D 14197 Berlin Germany. **Tel** 011 49 30 8207223, FAX 011 49 30 8214091, telex 183 319 SPBLN D. **(Subscription address:** Springer Verlag New York Inc. / for North America, 44 Hartz Way, Secaucus NJ 07096.) **ED** R J Adrian, W Merzkirch, and J H Whitelaw. **CODEN** EXFLDU. **[CCC]. Pr Rev.** available on microfilm and microfiche from University Microfilms International (UMI). Documents available from Article Express International, The Genuine Article, CASDDS.
Desc: Contains articles on a wide range of applications including aerodynamics, hydrodynamics, basic fluid dynamics, convective heat transfer, combustion, chemical, biological, and geophysical flows, and turbo-machinery.
Ind/Abst Appl. Mech. Rev.; Chem. Abstr. (1983-); Coal Abstr.; Curr. Contents Eng. Tech. Appl. Sci.; Ei Page One; Eng. Index Annu.; Fluid Abstr., Civil Eng.; Fluid Abstr. Proc. Eng.; FLUIDEX (1983-); HTFS Dig.; Int. Aerosp. Abstr. (1983-); Res. Alert [Full Cov.]; Sci. Cit. Index; SCISEARCH.

IT/0254-5284
FAO IRRIGATION AND DRAINAGE PAPER. [FAO irrig. drain. pap.]. **Added/Corp** Food and Agriculture Organization of the United Nations. **VFOAT** F.A.O. Irrigation and Drainage Paper. (1977)-. Academic Scholarly Publication. English. ir. Price varies per volume. Food and Agriculture Organization (FAO) / Italy, GIPC166 via Terme di Caracalla, 00100 Rome Italy. **Tel** 011 39 6 522 52925, FAX 011 39 6 522 55784. **(Subscription address:** UNIPUB, 4611 F Assembly Drive, Lanham MD 20706.) ***Continues** Irrigation and Drainage Paper.*
Ind/Abst Agric. Eng. Abstr. (1991-); EMBASE; World Agric. Econ.

US/0149-6662
FINANCIAL REPORT - STATE OF NEVADA, DIVISION OF COLORADO RIVER RESOURCES. **Main/Corp** Nevada. Division of Colorado River Resources. English. Department of Conservation and Natural Resources / Nevada, 4220 Maryland Parkway, Las Vegas NV 89109. **LC** TC424.N3; N48A. **DD** 353.9/793/008232. ***Continues** Report of Colorado River Commission of Nevada.*

UK/0196-6375
FINITE ELEMENTS IN FLUIDS. [Finite elem. fluids]. Vol. 1 (1975)-. English. **LC** QA911; .F444. **DD** 532/.05.
Ind/Abst Zentralbl. Math. Ihre Grenzgeb.

US/0098-5384
FLOW, ITS MEASUREMENT AND CONTROL IN SCIENCE AND INDUSTRY. **Main/Conf** Symposium on Flow, its Measurement and Control in Science and Industry. V. 1- 1974-. English. Instrument Society of America, 67 Alexander Drive, Research Triangle NC 27709. **Tel** (919)549-8411, FAX (919)549-8288, telex 802 540. **LC** TA357; .S89A. **DD** 620.1/064.
Desc: Describes recent advances, spotlights achievements of accuracy, and probes new and difficult problems of flow measurement. These proceedings contain approximately 100 papers.

UK/0955-5986
FLOW MEASUREMENT AND INSTRUMENTATION. (FLOW MEASUREMENT AND INSTRUMENTATION : FMI.). [Flow meas. instrum.]. **VFOAT** FMI. Vol. 1, No. 1 (Oct. 1989)-. Periodical. English. qt. $291.00 The Americas; £195.00 other. Butterworth Heinemann Publishers, Linacre House, Jordan Hill, Oxford OX2 8DP England. **Tel** 011 44 865 310366. **(Subscription address:** Elsevier Science Ltd. Oxford Fulfillment Centre, PO Box 800, Kidlington, Oxford OX5 1DX United Kingdom.) **LC** TA357.5.M43; F56. **DD** 681/.2. **CODEN** FMEIEJ. **[CCC].** available on microfilm and microfiche from University Microfilms International (UMI). Documents available from Article Express International, Ask*IEEE.
Ind/Abst Ei Page One; Eng. Index Annu.; Fluid Abstr., Civil Eng.; Fluid Abstr. Proc. Eng.; FLUIDEX; HTFS Dig.; INSPEC (Oct. 1989-).

GW/0015-461X
FLUID. (1968)-. Periodical. German. mo. DM158.00 Germany; DM170.00 other. Verlag Moderne Industrie, Justus von Liebigstrasse 1, D 86899 Landsberg Lech Germany. **Tel** 011 49 8191 125453. **UDC** 621.51/.54. **CODEN** 621.8.032/.033.

UK/0962-7162
FLUID ABSTRACTS. PROCESS ENGINEERING. **See** Engineering-Abstracting, Bibliographies and Statistics.

IT/0374-3225
FLUID APPARECCHIATURE IDRAULICHE E PNEUMATICHE. [Fluid Apparecch. Idraul. Pneum.]. (1970)-. Periodical. Italian. mo. L86000.00 (one year), L162000.00 (two year) Italy; L136000.00 (one year), L262000.00 (two year) other. Via Mecenate 89, 20138 Milan Italy. **Tel** 011 39 2 580841. **CODEN** FAIPB7FAIPB7. ***Continues** Apparecchiature Idrauliche e Pneumatische, 0003-6676.*
Ind/Abst Fluid Abstr., Civil Eng.; Fluid Abstr. Proc. Eng.; FLUIDEX (19??-).

NE/0926-5112
FLUID MECHANICS AND ITS APPLICATIONS. [Fluid mech. appl.]. (1990)-. Monographic series. English. ir. Price varies. Kluwer Academic Publishers, Postbus 322, 3300 AH Dordrecht, The Netherlands. **Tel** 011 (31) 78 524400, FAX 011 31 78 183273, telex 20083. **UDC** 532.
Ind/Abst Zentralbl. Math. Ihre Grenzgeb.

US/0069-6099
FLUID MECHANICS PAPERS. **Main/Corp** Colorado. State University, Fort Collins. No. 1 (1964)-. Monographic series. English. ir. Price varies per volume. Colorado State University, Fort Collins CO 80521. **Tel** (303)491-8652. **DD** 531.

US/0096-0764
FLUID MECHANICS : SOVIET RESEARCH. ***Title Change.*** [Fluid mech. Sov. res.]. Vol. 1 (Jan./Feb. 1972)-(19??). Periodical. English. bm. John Wiley & Sons, Inc., 605 Third Avenue, New York NY 10158-0012. **Tel** (212)850-6000, (212)850-6645, FAX (212)850-6088, telex 12-7063. **(Subscription address:** John Wiley & Sons / England, Baffins Lane, Chichester, West Sussex PO19 1UD England.) **ED** Novak Zuber, Ivan Catton, and M S Plesset. **LC** QC145.2; .F55. **DD** 532/.005. **CODEN** FMSVAM. **[CCC]. Ad Acc. Circ:** 400. available on microfilm and microfiche from University Microfilms International (UMI). Documents available from Article Express International, Ask*IEEE, CASDDS.
***Continued by** Fluid Mechanics Research.*
Desc: Publishes translations of theoretical and research papers from a wide range of Soviet periodicals on flow of compressible and incompressible fluids, two-phase vapor-liquid flow, slurry flow and fluidization, turbulence, boundary layers, wakes, channel and nozzle flow.
Ind/Abst Acoust. Abstr.; Bioeng. Abstr.; Chem. Abstr.; Coal Abstr.; Ei Page One; Energy Res. Abstr. (Feb. 1974-); Eng. Index Annu.; Fluid Abstr., Civil Eng.; Fluid Abstr. Proc. Eng.; FLUIDEX (1973-); GeoRef; HTFS Dig.; INIS Atomindex [Micro.]; INSPEC (Jan./Feb. 1972-); Int. Aerosp. Abstr.; Math. Rev.; Pollut. Abstr. Indexes; SPIN (1980-); Zentralbl. Math. Ihre Grenzgeb.

UK/0015-4644
FLUID POWER ABSTRACTS. ***Title Change.*** **Added/Corp** BHRA (Association). (1970)-(19??). English. bm. BHR Group Ltd Brit Hydrom. Research, Cranfield, Bedford MK43 0AJ England. **Tel** 011 44 243 750422, FAX 011 44 243 750074, telex 825059. **ED** J D Hone. **LC** TJ840; .F567. **DD** 621.2/05. Index available. **Bk Rev. Ad Acc. Circ:** 250. available on an online database. ***Merged with** Fluid Flow Measurements Abstracts, 0305-9235; Fluid Sealing Abstracts, 0015-4660; Pipelines Abstracts, 0265-3990; Pumps and Other Fluids Machinery Abstracts, 0302-2870; Solid-Liquid Flow Abstracts, 0038-1063; Computer-Aided Process Control Abstracts, 0955-4319* **and** *Mixing and Separation Technology Abstracts, 0955-7059* **to form** *Fluid Abstracts. Process Engineering, 0962-7162.*
Desc: Oil hydraulic and pneumatic power transmission and control, fluidics, applications of fluid power, design, manufacture and performance of components and systems.

US/0428-7738
FLUID POWER HANDBOOK & DIRECTORY. (FLUID POWER HANDBOOK & DIRECTORY / COMPILED BY THE EDITORS OF HYDRAULICS & PNEUMATICS.). [Fluid power handb. dir.]. **VFOAT** Fluid Power Handbook and Directory. (1964/65)-. English. be (every two years). $80.00 US and Canada; $85.00 Mexico; $90.00 other. Penton Publishing, 1100 Superior Avenue, Cleveland OH 44114-2543. **Tel** (216)696-7000, FAX (216)696-0836. **(Subscription address:** Penton Publishing, PO Box 96732, Chicago IL 60693.) **LC** TJ950; .F5. **DD** 621. available on microfilm from University Microfilms International (UMI). ***Continues** Fluid Power Directory, 0895-6375.*

UK/0015-4652
FLUID POWER INTERNATIONAL. (1935)-. Periodical. English. mo. Morgan Grampian, 40 Beresford Street Woolwich, London SE18 6BQ England. **Tel** 011 44 81 855 7777, FAX 011 44 81 855 5548, telex 896238. **ED** C Robinson. **DD** 621.2621.5. Documents available from Ask*IEEE.
Ind/Abst INSPEC (July/Aug. 1974-).

US/1062-6018
FLUID POWER SERVICE CENTER. [Fluid power serv. cent.]. **VFOAT** Mobile Industrial Fluid Power Service Center. Vol. 1, No. 1 (Fall 1991)-. Periodical. English. Four times a year. $15.00 US; $20.00 Canada; $25.00 Mexico; $30.00 other. Penton Publishing, 1100 Superior Avenue, Cleveland OH 44114-2543. **Tel** (216)696-7000, FAX (216)696-0836. **(Subscription address:** Penton Publishing, PO Box 96732, Chicago IL 60693.) **DD** 620.

UK/0015-4660
FLUID SEALING ABSTRACTS. ***Title Change.*** **Added/Corp** BHRA (Association). (1970)-(19??). English. qt. BHR Group Ltd Brit Hydrom. Research, Cranfield, Bedford MK43 0AJ England. **Tel** 011

44 243 750422, FAX 011 44 243 750074, telex 825059. **ED** N G Guy. **LC** TJ246; .C87. **DD** 621.8/85/05. Index available. cum. index. **Bk Rev. Circ:** 290. ***Continues*** *Current Information on Fluid Sealing.* ***Merged with*** *Fluid Flow Measurements Abstracts, 0305-9235; Fluid Power Abstracts, 0015-4644; Pipelines Abstracts, 0265-3990; Pumps and Other Fluids Machinery Abstracts, 0302-2870; Solid-Liquid Flow Abstracts, 0038-1063; Computer-Aided Process Control Abstracts, 0955-4319* ***and*** *Mixing and Separation Technology Abstracts, 0955-7059* ***to form*** *Fluid Abstracts. Process Engineering, 0962-7162.*
Desc: Covers all types of rotary, reciprocating and other dynamic types of seals, static seals (e.g., gaskets, O-rings, molded seals, packings), and sealants, seal materials, and general design problems, applications, and testing.

UK
FLUIDEX [ONLINE DATABASE]. See Engineering-Abstracting, Bibliographies and Statistics.

SP/0211-1136
FLUIDOS. (1972)-. Periodical. Spanish. mo (10 issues per year). $92.00. Publica SA, Ecuador 75 Entresuelo, 08029 Barcelona Spain. **Tel** 011 34 3 3215046, 4391027. **UDC** 532.

TU
GENEL YAYIN - TURKEY. TOPRASKU GENEL MUDURLUGU. See Agriculture-Crop Production and Soil.

US/0502-1456
GROUND-WATER LEVELS IN THE UNITED STATES : NORTHEASTERN STATES. Main/Corp United States. Geological Survey. (1957)-. English. Superintendent of Documents, US Government Printing Office, Washington DC 20402. **Tel** (202)275-3328, FAX (202)786-2377. **LC** TC801; .U2. ***Supersedes in part*** *Water Levels and Artesian Pressure in Observation Wells in the United States.*

IT/1120-5377
GT. Il GIORNALE DEL TERMOIDRAULICO. VFOAT Giornale del Termoidraulico. (1988)-. Periodical. Italian. mo. L40000 Italy; L85000 Europe; L120000 other. Tecniche Nuove SPA, Via Ciro Menotti 14, 20129 Milan Italy. **Tel** 011 39 2 75701, FAX 011 39 2 7610351, telex 334647 TECHS I. **UDC** 696.

UK
GUIDANCE ON DESIGN CONSTRUCTION OF OFFSHORE INSTALLATIONS AMENDMENT SERVICE. (19??)-. English. ir. £2.00 (latest edition). Her Majesty's Stationery Office, 51 Nine Elms Lane, London SW8 5DR England. **Tel** 011 44 71 873 8459, 011 44 71 873 8499, FAX 011 44 71 873 8499, 011 44 71 873 8456, telex 297138. **(Subscription address:** Her Majesty's Stationery Office, PO Box 276, Publications Centre, London SW8 5DT England.**)**

JA
GUIDE. Main/Corp Kowan Gijutsu Kenkyujo. (19??)-. Periodical. English. Kowan Gijutsu Kenkyujo, 1-1 Nagase 3-chome, Yokosuka-shi, Kanagawa-ken 239 Japan. **LC** TC158; .K65a. **DD** 627/.2/07205213.

US
GULF OF MEXICO UPDATE : OUTER CONTINENTAL SHELF OIL & GAS ACTIVITIES. Main/Corp Outer Continental Shelf Oil and Gas Information Program (U.S.). **VFOAT** Outer Continental Shelf Oil & Gas Activities; Outer Continental Shelf Oil and Gas Activities. (July 1986/April 1988)-. English. OCS Information Program, Offshore Information and Publications, Minerals Management Service, 1951 Kidwell Drive, MS 642/Suite 601, Vienna VA 22180. **LC** HD9567.A13; O93a. **DD** 338.2/728/097605. ***Continues*** *Gulf of Mexico Summary Report/Index.*

HU/0018-1323
HIDROLOGIAI KOZLONY. See Earth Sciences-Hydrology.

RM/0439-0962
HIDROTEHNICA. [Hidrotehnica]. **Added/Corp** Romania. Departamentul Imbunatatirilor Funciare si Gospodaririi Apelor. Consiliul National al Apelor (Romania) Consiliul National al Inginerilor si Tehnicienilor din Republica Socialista Romania. Vol. 15 (Jan. 1970)-. Academic Scholarly Publication. Romanian (summaries and/or abstracts in English, French, German and Russian). mo. DM314.00. **(Subscription address:** Kubon & Sagner, ABT Zeitschriftenimport, D 80328 Munich Germany.**) CODEN** HIDTA3. Documents available from CASDDS. ***Continues*** *Hidrotehnica, Gospod-Arirea Apelor, Meteorologia, 0018-134X.*
Ind/Abst Ceram. Abstr.; Chem. Abstr.; Int. Aerosp. Abstr.; Meteorol. Geoastrophys. Abstr.

CH
HO HAI KUNG CHENG. VFOAT Journal of Harbor and River Eng. Periodical. Chinese (Chinese). Department of Harbour and River Engineering, Provincial College of Marine Science and Technology, PO Box 7-49, Keelung Taiwan. **LC** TC1; .H6.

FR/0018-6368
HOUILLE BLANCHE, LA. [Houille blanche]. **Added/Corp** Association pour la Diffusion de la Documentation Hydraulique. Societe Hydrotechnique de France. No. 1-38 (1902)-(1939); New Series, No. 1 (1946)-. Academic Scholarly Publication. French (French, German and Spanish; summaries and/or abstracts in English, German and Spanish). Eight times a year. 734.57F France; 920.00 EEC countries except France; 940.00F other. Revue Generale Electricite SA, 48 rue de la Procession, 75724 Paris Cedex 15 France. **Tel** 011 33 1 44496000. **ED** M. Jean Valembois. **LC** TC1; .H68. **CODEN** HOBLAB. **[CCC].** Index available in last issue of volume--attached. cum. index. **Bk Rev. Ad Acc. Circ:** 3,000 (ctrl). Documents available from Article Express International, Ask*IEEE.
Desc: Includes documents and books from research organizations and congresses. Also water problems, fluid mechanics, hydraulic theory and its applications, river and maritime engineering works, water resources and their management.
Ind/Abst Acoust. Abstr.; AGRICOLA; Appl. Mech. Rev.; Aquat. Sci. Fish. Abstr. (Computer File); Bioeng. Abstr.; Ei Page One; EMBASE; Energy Res. Abstr.; Eng. Index Annu.; Fluid Abstr., Civil Eng.; Fluid Abstr. Proc. Eng.; FLUIDEX (1972-); GeoRef; INSPEC (1968-1986); Int. Aerosp. Abstr.; Int. Civil Eng. Abstr.; Meteorol. Geoastrophys. Abstr.; Pollut. Abstr. Indexes; Soft. Abstr. Eng.

US/0094-1832
HYDRAULIC RESEARCH IN THE UNITED STATES AND CANADA. Main/Corp United States. National Bureau of Standards. 1972-. English. US Department of Commerce / National Bureau of Standards / Maryland, Gaithersburg MD 20899. **LC** TC158; .U5. **DD** 627/.07/2073. ***Continues*** *Hydraulic Research in the United States.*

US/0730-9678
HYDRAULICS AND HYDROLOGY SERIES. [Hydraul. hydrol. ser.]. **VFOAT** Hydrology and Hydraulics. Monographic series. English. ir. Price varies per volume. Utah Water Research Laboratory, Utah State University, Logan UT 84322-8200. **Tel** (801)750-3200, FAX (801)750-3663, telex 3729283. Index available.
Ind/Abst GeoRef.

US/0018-814X
HYDRAULICS & PNEUMATICS. [Hydraul. pneum.]. **VFOAT** Hydraulics and Pneumatics. **VAT** Hydraulics and Pneumatics. Vol. 13, No. 6 (June 1960)-. Academic Scholarly Publication. English. Twelve times a year. $50.00 US; $65.00 Canada; $75.00 Mexico; $85.00 other. Penton Publishing, 1100 Superior Avenue, Cleveland OH 44114-2543. **Tel** (216)696-7000, FAX (216)696-0836. **(Subscription address:** Penton Publishing, PO Box 96732, Chicago IL 60693.**) LC** TC1; .A5. **CODEN** HYDPAZ. **[CCC].** ctrl circ. available on microfilm and microfiche from University Microfilms International (UMI); available on an online database (file 648/Full-Text) from DIALOG. Documents available from Article Express International, Ask*IEEE. ***Continues*** *Applied Hydraulics & Pneumatics, 0361-0136.*
Desc: Point of contact between maker and user.
Ind/Abst Acoust. Abstr.; Agric. Eng. Abstr.; Appl. Sci. Technol. Index; Bus. ASAP (1990-) [Full Txt.]; Bus. Index (1985-); Coal Abstr.; Ei Page One; EMBASE; Energy Res. Abstr.; Eng. Index Annu.; Fluid Abstr., Civil Eng. (March 1969-); Fluid Abstr. Proc. Eng.; FLUIDEX (199?-); Gen. BusinessFile (1985-); Gen. Period. Index (1985-); INIS Atomindex [Micro.]; INSPEC (March 1969-); Int. Aerosp. Abstr.; Pollut. Abstr. Indexes; Shock Vibr. Dig.; Trade Ind. ASAP [Full Txt.]; Trade Ind. Index (1981-) [Full Txt.].

US/0069-6102
HYDRAULICS PAPERS. No. 1- 1966-. Monographic series. English. Price varies per volume. Colorado State University, Fort Collins CO 80521. **Tel** (303)491-8652.

FR
HYDRO PLUS. Hydro Plus, 2 rue Henri Barbusse, 13421 Marseille Cedex France.

US/0884-0385
HYDRO REVIEW. [Hydro rev.]. **VFOAT** Hydro-Review of . Vol. 1, No. 1 (Spring 1982)-. Periodical. English. Eight times a year. $56.00 US; $68.00 other. HCI Publications, 410 Archibald Street, Kansas City MO 64111. **Tel** (816)931-1311. **LC** WMLC 93/1511. **DD** 338. Documents available from Documents on Demand.
Ind/Abst Energy Inf. Abstr.; Environ. Abstr.; Fluid Abstr., Civil Eng.; Fluid Abstr. Proc. Eng.; FLUIDEX (199?-).

US/0162-8402
HYDROGEN PROGRESS. *Ceased.* [Hydrog. prog.]. ( )-(1984). Periodical. English. qt. Hydrogen Energy Corporation, 6030 Connecticut Avenue, Kansas City MO 64120. **Tel** (816)241-8980.
Ind/Abst Coal Abstr.; Energy Res. Abstr. (Nov. 1977-).

US/0147-3697
HYDROLOGIC REPORT (LOS ANGELES). See Water Resources.

US/0018-8220
HYDROTECHNICAL CONSTRUCTION. [Hydrotech. constr.]. **Added/Corp** Consultants Bureau. American Society of Civil Engineers. No. 1 (Jan. 1967)-. Academic Scholarly Publication. English (Russian). mo. $945.00 US; $1105.00 other. Consultants Bureau, A Division of Plenum Publishing Corporation, 233 Spring Street, New York NY 10013. **Tel** (212)620-8000, (212)620-8466, FAX (212)463-0742, telex 23/421139. **ED** N. A. Lopatin. **LC** TC1; .G513. **CODEN** HYCOAR. **[CCC].** Index available. available on microfilm and microfiche from University Microfilms International (UMI). Documents available from Article Express International, Ask*IEEE.
Ind/Abst Bioeng. Abstr.; Ei Page One; EMBASE; Eng. Index Annu.; Fluid Abstr., Civil Eng.; Fluid Abstr. Proc. Eng.; FLUIDEX; GeoRef; INIS Atomindex [Micro.]; INSPEC (April 1981-); Int. Civil Eng. Abstr.; Soft. Abstr. Eng.

II/0300-2810
I.C.I.D. BULLETIN. (ICID BULLETIN / INTERNATIONAL COMMISSION ON IRRIGATION AND DRAINAGE.). [ICID bull.]. **Added/Corp** International Commission on Irrigation and Drainage. **VFOAT** I.C.I.D. Bulletin. **VAT** International Commission on Irrigation and Drainage Bulletin. (Jan. 1969)-. Bulletin. English (French). sa. $30.00. International Commission on Irrigation and Drainage, 48 Nyaya Marg Chanakyapuri, New Delhi 110021 India. **Tel** 011 91 11 3016837, telex 031-65920 ICID IN. **(Subscription address:** Prints India, 11 Darya Ganj, New Delhi, 110002 India, (Phone: 011 91 11 3268645)**) LC** TC801; .I5322. **DD** 333.91/3/05. **CODEN** IIDBAS. **Bk Rev. Ad Acc. Circ:** 3,500. Documents available from Article Express International. ***Continues*** *International Commission on Irrigation and Drainage. Annual Bulletin.*
Ind/Abst AGRICOLA; Agric. Eng. Abstr. (1991-); AQUAREF; Bioeng. Abstr.; Ei Page One; Eng. Index Annu.; Helminthol. Abstr. (1991-); Irr. Drain. Abstr.; Protozoolog. Abstr.; SEA Abstr.

NE
IAHR BULLETIN. VFOAT AIRH Bulletin. **VAT** International Association for Hydraulic Research Bulletin. Vol. 1, No. 1 (1984)-. Bulletin. English (summaries and/or abstracts in French). ir (five times a year). Fl50.00 Netherlands. International Association for Hydraulic Research, PO Box 177, 2600 MH Delft The Netherlands. **Tel** 011 31 15 569353, FAX 011 31 15 619674, telex 38176. **Ad Acc. Circ:** 3,000 (ctrl).
Desc: Contains summaries of papers published in the Journal of Hydraulic Research, reports on meetings, letters from the president, a conference calendar and new membership announcements.
Ind/Abst Fluid Abstr., Civil Eng.; Fluid Abstr. Proc. Eng.; FLUIDEX.

II
ICID TECHNICAL MEMOIRS. Main/Corp International Commission on Irrigation and Drainage. **VFOAT** Technical Memoirs. No. 1 (1972)-. English. International Commission on Irrigation and Drainage, 48 Nyaya Marg Chanakyapuri, New Delhi 110021 India. **Tel** 011 91 11 3016837, telex 031-65920 ICID IN. **LC** TC801; .I5325. **DD** 627/.52/05.

IT/0390-6655
IDROTECNICA. L'ACQUA NELL'AGRICOLTURA NELL'IGIENE NELL'INDUSTRIA. (IDROTECNICA.). [Idrotec. acqua agric. ig. ind.]. **Added/Corp** Associazione Idrotecnica Italiana. (Jan./Feb. 1974)-. Periodical. Italian. bm. L120000. Maggiolo Editore, Casella Postale 290, 47037 Rimini Italy. **Tel** 011 39 541 626760. **LC** TC1; .I33. **DD** 627/.05. **CODEN** IDTEDH. cum. index. ***Supersedes*** *Acqua Nell'Agricoltura, Nell'Igiene, e Nell'Industria.*
Ind/Abst AGRICOLA; Fluid Abstr., Civil Eng.; Fluid Abstr. Proc. Eng.; FLUIDEX (1974-1990); GeoRef.

US/0364-9059
IEEE JOURNAL OF OCEANIC ENGINEERING. [IEEE j. oceanic eng.]. **Added/Corp** IEEE Council on Oceanic Engineering. Oceanic Engineering Society (U.S.). **VFOAT** Journal of Oceanic Engineering. **VAT** Institute of Electrical and Electronics Engineers Journal of Oceanic Engineering. Vol. OE-1 (Sept. 1976)-. Academic Scholarly Publication. English. qt. $115.00. IEEE, Institution of Electrical and Electronics Engineers, Inc., 345 East 47th Street, New York NY 10017-2394. **Tel** (908)981-1393, FAX (908)981-9667. **(Subscription address:** IEEE / Institute of Electrical and Electronics Engineers, 445 Hoes Lane, PO Box 1331, Piscataway NJ 08855-1331.**) LC** TC1501; .I35. **DD** 620/.4162/05. **CODEN** IJOEDY. **[CCC]. Pr Rev.** available on microfilm and microfiche. Documents available from Article Express International, The Genuine Article, Ask*IEEE, CASDDS, Petroleum Abstracts Document Delivery Service, Documents on Demand.
Desc: Covers the application of electrical and electronics engineering to the oceanic environment.
Ind/Abst Acoust. Abstr.; Appl. Sci. Technol. Index; Aquat. Sci. Fish. Abstr. (Computer File); Bioeng. Abstr.; Chem. Abstr. (1976-1982); Curr. Contents Eng. Tech.

Appl. Sci.; Ei Page One; Eng. Index Annu.; Environ. Abstr.; GeoRef; Index IEEE Publ.; INSPEC (Sept. 1976-); Int. Aerosp. Abstr.; Ocean. Abstr.; Life Sci. Collect.; Pet. Abstr.; Pollut. Abstr. Indexes; Res. Alert [Full Cov.]; Sci. Cit. Index; SCISEARCH.

CE
IIMI CASE STUDY. **Added/Corp** International Irrigation Management Institute. No. 1 (1987)-. Monographic series. English.
Ind/Abst Soils Fert.; World Agric. Econ.

US/0092-2366
INDIANA WATERSHED PROGRESS. **Main/Corp** United States. Soil Conservation Service. English. Soil Conservation Service / Indiana, Atkinson Square West/Suite 2200, 5610 Crawfordsville Road, Indianapolis IN 46244. **LC** TC424.I6; U56A. **DD** 333.9/1/009772.

CU/0253-0678
INGENIERIA HIDRAULICA (LA HABANA). (INGENIERIA HIDRAULICA / PUBLICACION DEL INSTITUTO SUPERIOR POLITECNICO JOSE ANTONIO ECHEVERRIA.). [Ing. hidraul.]. 1-. Periodical. Spanish (summaries and/or abstracts in English). Three times a year. $19.00 US. Ediciones Cubanas, Obispo 527, Altos ESQ Bernaza, CP 10100 Havana Cuba. **Tel** 011 632980, 631942, FAX 011 631011, telex 512337, 6540. **Bk Rev**. **Ad Acc**. **Circ:** 20,000. ***Continues*** *Ciencias Tecnicas. Ingenieria Hidraulica.*
Desc: Covers hydraulics, superficial and subterranean hydrology, and the design and construction of dams and hydraulic structures.
Ind/Abst GeoRef.

UK/0271-2091
INTERNATIONAL JOURNAL FOR NUMERICAL METHODS IN FLUIDS. [Int. j. numer. methods fluids]. Vol. 1, No. 1 (Jan./March 1981)-. Periodical. English. Twenty-four times a year. $1,395.00. John Wiley & Sons Ltd., Baffins Lane, Chichester West Sussex PO19 1UD England. **Tel** 0243 779777, FAX 0243 776128 BTG:JWP001, telex 86290 WIBOOKG. **(Subscription address:** John Wiley / Philadelphia, PO Box 7247, Philadelphia PA 19170.**) ED** C. Taylor and P. M. Gresho. **LC** QA901; .I52. **DD** 532/.005. **CODEN** IJNFDW. **[CCC]**. **Bk Rev**. **Ad Acc**. **Pr Rev**. **Circ:** 950. available on microfilm and microfiche from University Microfilms International (UMI). Documents available from Article Express International, The Genuine Article, Ask*IEEE.
Desc: Disseminates information for engineers and scientists relating to the development and refinement of computer-based numerical techniques for solving problems in fluids.
Ind/Abst Abstr. Bull. Inst. Pap. Sci. Tech.; Acoust. Abstr.; Appl. Mech. Rev.; Bioeng. Abstr.; BMT Abstr.; Civ. Struct. Eng. Abstr.; Compumath Citation Index [Full Cov.]; Curr. Contents Eng. Tech. Appl. Sci.; Ei Page One (1984); Eng. Index Annu.; Environ. Eng. Abstr.; Fluid Abstr., Civil Eng.; Fluid Abstr. Proc. Eng.; FLUIDEX (1981-); Geogr. Abstr. Phys. Geogr.; Geol. Abstr.; GeoRef; HTFS Dig.; INSPEC (Feb. 1984-); Int. Aerosp. Abstr.; Int. Civil Eng. Abstr.; Mater. Sci. Eng. Abstr.; Math. Rev.; Mech. Eng. Abstr.; Pollut. Abstr. Indexes; Res. Alert [Full Cov.]; SCISEARCH; Shock Vibr. Dig.; Soft. Abstr. Eng.; Zentralbl. Math. Ihre Grenzgeb.

US/0893-3960
INTERNATIONAL JOURNAL OF ENGINEERING FLUID MECHANICS. ***Ceased.*** [Int. j. eng. fluid mech.]. Vol. 1 No. 1 (Spring 1988)-(Dec. 1992). Periodical. English. qt. Gulf Publishing Company / Texas, PO Box 2608, Houston TX 77252. **Tel** (800)231-6275, (713)529-4301, FAX (713)520-4433. **ED** Nicholas P Cheremisinoff. **LC** TA357; .I5695. **DD** 620.1/06. **CODEN** IJEME9. **[CCC]**. **Pr Rev**. Documents available from Article Express International, The Genuine Article, Ask*IEEE.
Desc: This journal is intended to provide a vehicle for the international engineering and scientific communities to exchange ideas, report research advances, review and challenge existing theories, and critique new concepts and experimental methods with the overall intent of advancing flow engineering practices.
Ind/Abst Abstr. Bull. Inst. Pap. Sci. Tech.; Curr. Contents Eng. Tech. Appl. Sci.; Ei Page One; Eng. Index Annu.; Fluid Abstr., Civil Eng.; Fluid Abstr. Proc. Eng.; FLUIDEX; HTFS Dig.; INSPEC (Fall 1988-); Res. Alert [Select. Cov.]; SCISEARCH.

UK/0267-1085
INTERNATIONAL UNDERWATER SYSTEMS DESIGN. (INTERNATIONAL UNDERWATER SYSTEMS DESIGN : IUSD.). [Int. underw. syst. des.]. **VFOAT** Underwater Systems Design; IUSD; I.U.S.D. Vol. 1, No. 1 (Feb. 1979)-. Periodical. English. Seven times a year. $159.00 North America; £56.00 UK; £78.00 others. A. P. Publications Ltd, 377 Saint Johns Street, London EC1V 4LD England. **Tel** 011 44 71 837 5921, FAX 011 44 71 837 1197, telex 8955107. **ED** E. Patterson. **LC** TC1501; .I57. **DD** 627/.7/005. Index available. cum. index. **Ad Acc**, **Adv Mgr:** T. Barrett, **Tel** 0926 641640. **Circ:** 10,000 (ctrl).
Desc: Designed as an information science on all aspects of underwater engineering and operations. Subjects cover diving, navigation electrics, TV systems and pipeline inspection.
Ind/Abst Aquat. Sci. Fish. Abstr. (Computer File); BMT Abstr.; Fluid Abstr., Civil Eng.; Fluid Abstr. Proc. Eng.; FLUIDEX; Ocean. Abstr.; Life Sci. Collect.

UK/0306-400X
INTERNATIONAL WATER POWER & DAM CONSTRUCTION. [Int. water power dam constr.]. **VFOAT** Water Power & Dam Construction . **VAT** International Water Power and Dam Construction. Vol. 27 (Jan. 1975)-. Periodical. English. mo. $185.00. Reed Business Publishing Group / England, Quadrant House, Quadrant Sutton Surrey, SM2 5AS England. **Tel** 011 44 81 652-3500. **LC** TK1081; .W3. **DD** 621.312/134/05. **CODEN** IWPCDM. **[CCC]**. available on microfilm and microfiche from University Microfilms International (UMI). Documents available from Article Express International, Ask*IEEE, Documents on Demand. ***Continues*** *Water Power, 0043-1338.*
Ind/Abst Abstr. J. Earthq. Eng. (?-?); AQUAREF (19??-); Aquat. Sci. Fish. Abstr. (Computer File) (19??-); Bioeng. Abstr. (19??-); Civ. Struct. Eng. Abstr. (19??-); Ei Page One (19??-); Energy Inf. Abstr. (19??-); Energy Res. Abstr. (Nov. 1975-); Eng. Index Annu. (19??-); Environ. Abstr. (19??-); Environ. Eng. Abstr. (19??-); Fluid Abstr., Civil Eng. (19??-); Fluid Abstr. Proc. Eng. (19??-); FLUIDEX (1975-); GeoRef (19??-); Geotech. Abstr. (19??-); INSPEC (Feb. 1975-); Int. Civil Eng. Abstr. (19??-); Mech. Eng. Abstr. (19??-); Mintec, Min. Technol. Abstr. (19??-); Life Sci. Collect. (19??-); Pollut. Abstr. Indexes (19??-); Soft. Abstr. Eng. (19??-).

UK
INTERNATIONAL WATER POWER & DAM CONSTRUCTION HANDBOOK. **VFOAT** International Water Power and Dam Construction Handbook; Water Power and Dam Construction Handbook; Water Power & Dam Construction Handbook; Handbook. (1987)-. English. an. Included in subscription for International Water Power and Dam Construction ($185.00). Reed Business Publishing / West Sussex, England, Perrymount Road, Haywards Heath, West Sussex RH16 3DH England. **Tel** 011 44 81 6523500. **LC** TK1081; .I634. **DD** 621.31/2134/05.

IS/0376-5083
IRRICAB. ***Suspended.*** **See** Agriculture-Crop Production and Soil.

UK/0306-7327
IRRIGATION AND DRAINAGE ABSTRACTS / COMMONWEALTH AGRICULTURAL BUREAUX. **See** Engineering-Abstracting, Bibliographies and Statistics.

NE/0168-6291
IRRIGATION AND DRAINAGE SYSTEMS. [Irrig. drain. syst.]. Vol. 1, No. 1 (1986)-. English. qt. $375.00. Kluwer Academic Publishers, Postbus 322, 3300 AH Dordrecht, The Netherlands. **Tel** 011 (31) 78 524400, FAX 011 31 78 183273, telex 20083. **ED** Marinus Bos. **CODEN** IDRSEG. **[CCC]**. **Pr Rev**. **Acid Free**. available on microfilm and microfiche from University Microfilms International (UMI). Documents available from BIOSIS Document Express.
Desc: Offers an outlet for the rapid publication of general research and review articles and short communications on: the influence of the water supply method, design criteria off of systems and the possible re-use of drainage water, the efficiency of irrigation water use, the management of irrigation/drainage schemes and of water users' organizations, the adaptation of irrigation/drainage schemes so as to avoid water related diseases such as malaria, schistosmiasis, and so forth, the influence of irrigation and drainage on the ecosystem, e.g. flora, fauna, water quality, a history of the profession, with appropriate lessons, and planning of and construction methods for channels and related structures.
Ind/Abst AGRICOLA [Full Cov.]; Agric. Eng. Abstr. (1991-); Biol. Abstr. (1990-); Environ. Period. Bibliogr.; Field Crop Abstr.; Fish Rev. (Jan. 1989-July 1992); Fluid Abstr., Civil Eng.; Fluid Abstr. Proc. Eng.; FLUIDEX; Geogr. Abstr. Phys. Geogr. (1990-?); Geogr. Abstr. Human Geogr.; Int. Dev. Abstr.; Irr. Drain. Abstr.; Rice Abstr.; Rural Dev. Abstr.; Soils Fert.; Wildl. Rev. (Jan. 1989-July 1992); World Agric. Econ.

II/0367-9993
IRRIGATION AND POWER. (IRRIGATION & POWER : THE JOURNAL OF THE CENTRAL BOARD OF IRRIGATION & POWER.). [Irrig. power]. **Added/Corp** India. Central Board of Irrigation and Power. **VFOAT** Irrigation and Power. Vol. 8, No. 1 (Jan. 1951)-. Periodical. English (Hindi). Four times a year (Jan., Apr., July, Oct.). Rs200.00. Central Board of Irrigation Power, Maalcha Marg Chanakyapuri, New Delhi 110021 India. **(Subscription address:** Prints House, 11 Darya Ganj, New Delhi 110002 India, telephone: 011 91 11 3268645**) CODEN** IRPWAA. **Bk Rev**. **Ad Acc**. **Circ:** 4,000 (ctrl). Documents available from Article Express International. ***Continues*** *Journal / Central Board of Irrigation.*
Ind/Abst AGRICOLA; Bioeng. Abstr.; Ei Page One; Energy Res. Abstr. (Jan. 1971-); Eng. Index Annu.; Fluid Abstr., Civil Eng.; Fluid Abstr. Proc. Eng.; FLUIDEX (1973-); GeoRef; Indian Geosci. Abstr.; Rice Abstr.; Soils Fert.

US
IRRIGATION ENGINEERING. (19??)-. English. sa (Jul. and Dec.). $44.00 (nonmember), $28.00 (member). American Society of Agricultural Engineers, Department 2510, 2950 Niles Road, St. Joseph MI 49085-9659. **Tel** (616)429-0300, FAX (616)429-3852. Index available (free on request).
Desc: A section of Transactions of the ASAE. Includes over 30 technical articles on drip, surface, sprinkler, trickle and other irrigation methods and practices.

US/0047-1518
IRRIGATION JOURNAL. **See** Agriculture-Agricultural Equipment.

IS/0304-3606
IRRINEWS. **See** Agriculture-Crop Production and Soil.

RU
ISSLEDOVANIIA PO PODZEMNOI GIDROMEKHANIKE. **See** Engineering-Mines and Mining Engineering.

NE
JAARBERICHT / RIJKSWATERSTAAT. **Main/Corp** Netherlands. Rijkswaterstaat. (1982)-. Dutch. an. Rijkswaterstaat, Postbus 20906 Netherlands. **LC** TC477; .N45a.

GW/0340-4838
JAHRBUCH DER HAFENBAUTECHNISCHEN GESELLSCHAFT. **Main/Corp** Hafenbautechnische Gesellschaft (Germany). (19??)-. Monographic series. German. ir. Price varies per volume. Schiffahrts Verlag Hansa, Schroedter & Co., Postfach 520365, D 22605 Hamburg Germany. **Tel** 011 49 40 8228070. **LC** TC203; .H3. **DD** 627.2.

●US/1051-3248
JOURNAL OF ENERGETICS AND FLUIDS ENGINEERING. ***Suspended.*** (1992)-Suspended (1993). Periodical. English. bm. $485.00 US; $560.00 other. John Wiley & Sons, Inc., 605 Third Avenue, New York NY 10158-0012. **Tel** (212)850-6000, (212)850-6645, FAX (212)850-6088, telex 12-7063. **(Subscription address:** John Wiley & Sons / England, Baffins Lane, Chichester, West Sussex PO19 1UD England.**) ED** Novak Zuber. available on microfilm and microfiche from University Microfilms International (UMI). ***Continues*** *Soviet Journal of Applied Physics, 0890-2747.*
Desc: This journal is a translation of the engineering periodical The Bulletin of the Siberian Department of the Soviet Academy of Sciences. Publishes research reports that concentrate on heat transfer, heat engineering, fluid mechanics, and its application in transport processes, as well as high-temperature plasma physics and its applications to coatings technology.
Ind/Abst Appl. Mech. Rev.

●US/1065-3090
JOURNAL OF FLOW VISUALIZATION AND IMAGE PROCESSING. (1993)-. Periodical. English. Four times a year. $145.00. Begell House Inc., PO Box 1109, Pearl River NY 10965. **Tel** (212)725-1999. **[CCC]**.

US/8755-8564
JOURNAL OF FLUID CONTROL, THE. [J. fluid control]. **VFOAT** Fluid Control. Vol. 15, No. 1 (March 1983)-. Periodical. English. qt. $145.00 US; $162.00 other. Delbridge Publishing Co., PO Box 160817, Cupertino CA 95016. **Tel** (408)446-3131, FAX (408)446-3131. **ED** David H Tarumoto. **LC** TJ840; .F587. **DD** 629.8/042. **[CCC]**. Index available. cum. index. **Bk Rev**. **Ad Acc**. **Pr Rev**. **Circ:** 700. Documents available from Article Express International, Ask*IEEE. ***Continues*** *Fluidics Quarterly, 0015-4687.*
Desc: Technical papers on state-of-the-art in fluid control, hydraulics and pneumatics, instrumentation and fluidics.
Ind/Abst Appl. Mech. Rev.; Ei Page One; Eng. Index Annu. (1983-); Fluid Abstr., Civil Eng.; Fluid Abstr. Proc. Eng.; FLUIDEX (1983-1990); INSPEC (March 1983-).

UK/0022-1120
JOURNAL OF FLUID MECHANICS. [J. fluid mech.]. Vol. 1 (May 1956)-. Academic Scholarly Publication. English. Twenty-four times a year. $1265.00 US, Canada & Mexico; £696.00 other. Cambridge University Press, The Edinburgh Building, Shaftesbury Road, Cambridge CB2 2RU United Kingdom. **Tel** 011 44 223 312393, FAX 011 44 223 325959. **(Subscription address:** Cambridge University Press / North America, 110 Midland Avenue, Port Chester NY 10573.**) ED** G. K. Batchelor. **LC** QA901; .J87. **DD** 532.505. **CODEN** JFLSA7. cum. index. **Bk Rev**. **Pr Rev**. available on microfilm and microfiche from University Microfilms International (UMI). Documents available from Article Express International, The Genuine Article, BIOSIS Document Express, Ask*IEEE, Petroleum Abstracts Document Delivery Service, CASDDS.
Desc: Covers theoretical, numerical and experimental investigations of all aspects of the mechanics of fluids. Contains papers on both the fundamental aspects of fluid

Engineering — Hydraulic Engineering

mechanics and their applications to other fields such as aeronautics, astrophysics, chemical and mechanical engineering, hydraulics, meteorology, oceanography, acoustics and combustion. In addition to original research, the journal includes reviews of relevant books and films which cast additional light on these subjects. Of interest to those working with developments in fluid mechanics.
Ind/Abst Abstr. Bull. Inst. Pap. Sci. Tech.; Acoust. Abstr.; Appl. Sci. Technol. Index; Aquat. Sci. Fish. Abstr. (Computer File); Bioeng. Abstr.; Biol. Abstr.; BMT Abstr.; Chem. Abstr.; Curr. Contents Eng. Tech. Appl. Sci.; Curr. Contents Phys. Chem. Earth Sci.; Curr. Technol. Index; Ecol. Abstr. (?-?); Ei Page One; Eng. Index Annu.; Fluid Abstr., Civil Eng.; Fluid Abstr. Proc. Eng.; FLUIDEX (1973-); Geogr. Abstr. Phys. Geogr.; Geol. Abstr.; HTFS Dig.; INSPEC (1968-); Int. Aerosp. Abstr.; Math. Rev.; Meteorol. Geoastrophys. Abstr. (-199?); Ocean. Abstr.; Life Sci. Collect.; Pet. Abstr.; Pollut. Abstr. Indexes; Res. Alert [Full Cov.]; Sci. Cit. Index; SCISEARCH; Zentralbl. Math. Ihre Grenzgeb.

UK/0889-9746
JOURNAL OF FLUIDS AND STRUCTURES.
[J. fluids struct.]. **VFOAT** Journal of Fluid Structures. Vol. 1, No. 1 (Jan. 1987)-. Academic Scholarly Publication. English. Eight times a year. $450.00. Academic Press Ltd., A Division of Harcourt Brace & Company Ltd., 24-28 Oval Road, London NW1 7DX England. **Tel** 071 267 4466, **FAX** 071 482 2293, 071 485 4752, telex 25775 ACPRES G. **(Subscription address:** Harcourt Brace & Company, Ltd., Foots Cray, High Street, Sidcup Kent DA14 5HP England.**) ED** M. P. Paidoussis. **LC** TA357; .J667. **DD** 620.1/06. **[CCC].** Documents available from The Genuine Article.
Desc: Publishes original full-length papers and brief communications on any aspect of fluid-structure interaction and on the dynamics of systems related to such interactions: on the fundamental mechanisms, as well as on specific applications, analytical, experimental, or computational. The journal serves as a focal point of contact and exchange for the many kinds of specialists and practitioners concerned with fundamental and applied aspects of flow-induced excitation mechanisms, solid-fluid interactions, response of mechanical, civil, marine, and physiological structures to flow and flow-acoustic excitation, aeroelasticity, and other relevant aeronautical applications. Review articles, editorials, and letters are also accepted.
Ind/Abst BMT Abstr.; Curr. Contents Eng. Tech. Appl. Sci.; Fluid Abstr., Civil Eng.; Fluid Abstr. Proc. Eng.; FLUIDEX; HTFS Dig.; Res. Alert [Full Cov.]; SCISEARCH; Zentralbl. Math. Ihre Grenzgeb.

US/0098-2202
JOURNAL OF FLUIDS ENGINEERING.
(TRANSACTIONS OF THE ASME. JOURNAL OF FLUIDS ENGINEERING.). [J. fluids eng.]. Vol. 95, No. 1 (March 1973)-. Periodical. English. qt. $150.00 (nonmember), $40.00 (member) US and Canada. American Society of Mechanical Engineers, 22 Law Drive, Fairfield NJ 07007. **Tel** (201)882-1167, (212)705-7722 (editorial). **ED** Cornelia Monahan. **LC** TA357; .T69. **DD** 620.1/06/05. **CODEN** JFEGA4. **[CCC]. Bk Rev. Ad Acc. Pr Rev. Circ:** 1,825. available on microfilm and microfiche from University Microfilms International (UMI). Documents available from Article Express International, The Genuine Article, Ask*IEEE, CASDDS. **Continues in part** Transactions of the ASME. Series D, Journal of Basic Engineering, 0021-9223.
Desc: Fluid mechanics engineering, design of fluid machines and structures, multiphase and cavitating flows, fluid systems, fluid mechanics of medicine and human biology, and fluid transients.
Ind/Abst Abstr. Bull. Inst. Pap. Sci. Tech.; Appl. Sci. Technol. Index; Bioeng. Abstr.; BMT Abstr.; Chem. Abstr.; Civ. Struct. Eng. Abstr.; Coal Abstr.; Comput. Inf. Syst. Abstr. J. [Full Cov.]; Ei Page One; Elect. Comm. Abstr.; Energy Res. Abstr. (Jan. 1975-); Eng. Index Annu.; Environ. Eng. Abstr.; Expand. Acad. Index (1992-); Fluid Abstr., Civil Eng.; Fluid Abstr. Proc. Eng.; FLUIDEX (1978-); HTFS Dig.; INIS Atomindex [Micro.]; INSPEC (1973-); Int. Aerosp. Abstr. (1991-); Int. Build. Serv. Abstr.; Lit. Pat. Abstr.; Oilfield Chem. (1973-); Lit. Abstr., Catal. Catal.; Lit. Abstr., Health Environ.; Lit. Abstr., Pet. Refin. Petrochem.; Lit. Abstr., Pet. Substit.; Lit. Abstr., Transp. Storage; Mater. Sci. Eng. Abstr.; Mech. Eng. Abstr.; Proc. Chem. Eng.; Res. Alert [Full Cov.]; Sci. Cit. Index; SCISEARCH; Solid State Supercond. Abstr.; Theoret. Chem. Eng.

US/0733-9429
JOURNAL OF HYDRAULIC ENGINEERING (NEW YORK, N.Y.).
(JOURNAL OF HYDRAULIC ENGINEERING.). [J. hydraul. eng.]. **Added/Corp** American Society of Civil Engineers. American Society of Civil Engineers. Hydraulics Division. **VFOAT** Hydraulic Engineering; A.S.C.E. Hydraulic Engineering; ASCE Hydraulic Engineering. Vol. 109, No. 1 (Jan. 1983)-. Academic Scholarly Publication. English. mo. $234.00 (nonmember) US; $260.00 (nonmember) other. American Society of Civil Engineers / ASCE, 345 East 47th Street, New York NY 10017-2398. **Tel** (212)705-7179, **FAX** (212)705-7300, telex 422847 ASCE UI. **(Subscription address:** American Society of Civil Engineers, Publisher Fulfillment Agency, Box 828, Somerset NJ 08875.**) LC** TC1; .A39. **DD** 627/.05. **CODEN** JHEND8. **[CCC].** Index available. cum. index. **Circ:** 4,900. available on microfilm and microfiche from University Microfilms International (UMI); available on CD-ROM from American Society of Civil Engineers. Documents available from Article Express International, The Genuine Article, Petroleum Abstracts Document Delivery Service. **Continues** Journal of the Hydraulics Division, 0044-796X.
Desc: Journal covers hydraulics, hydrology, hydraulic engineering and water resources. Topics include reservoir systems, flood control, wastewater discharge, hydrometeorology and urban hydrology.
Ind/Abst Abstr. J. Earthq. Eng.; Appl. Sci. Technol. Index; AQUAREF; ASCE Annu. Comb. Index (1983-); ASCE Publ. Inf. (1983-); BMT Abstr.; Coal Abstr.; Curr. Contents Eng. Tech. Appl. Sci.; Ecol. Abstr. (?-?); Ei Page One; EMBASE; Energy Res. Abstr. (Jan.1983-); Eng. Index Annu.; Expand. Acad. Index (1992-); Fish Rev. (Jan. 1989-July 1992); Fluid Abstr., Civil Eng.; Fluid Abstr. Proc. Eng.; FLUIDEX (1983-); GeoRef; Geotech. Abstr.; Highw. Res. Abstr.; INIS Atomindex [Micro.]; Int. Civil Eng. Abstr.; Irr. Drain. Abstr.; Ocean. Abstr.; Life Sci. Collect.; Pet. Abstr.; Res. Alert [Full Cov.]; Sci. Cit. Index; SCISEARCH; Soft. Abstr. Eng.; Soils Fert.; Trans. Am. Soc. Civ. Eng. (1983-); Wildl. Rev. (Jan. 1989-July 1992).

US/1051-2705
JOURNAL OF HYDRAULIC ENGINEERING (WASHINGTON, D.C.).
Ceased. (JOURNAL OF HYDRAULIC ENGINEERING.). (1991)-Vol. 1, No. 4 (1993). English. qt. Taylor & Francis Ltd., Rankine Road, Basingstoke Hampshire, RG24 8PR United Kingdom. **Tel** 011 44 256 840366, **FAX** 011 44 256 479438, telex 858540. **(Subscription address:** Taylor & Francis Inc., 1900 Frost Road, Suite 101, Bristol PA 19007-1598.**) ED** Jin Yan (editor's address: China Water Resources and Electric Power Press, Erligou, Beijing 100044, China).
Desc: Provides up-to-date information on various aspects of hydraulic engineering research, particularly in China, and will facilitate mutual understanding and international discussion and cooperation in the worldwide circle of hydraulic engineering and its related fields. As a result of support from China Water Resources and Electric Power Press, the journal will now be published in English.
Ind/Abst Aquat. Sci. Fish. Abstr. (Computer File); Energy Inf. Abstr.; Ocean. Abstr.; Pollut. Abstr. Indexes; Soils Fert.

NE/0022-1686
JOURNAL OF HYDRAULIC RESEARCH.
(JOURNAL OF HYDRAULIC RESEARCH. JOURNAL DE RECHERCHES HYDRAULIQUES.). [J. hydraul. res.]. **Added/Corp** International Association for Hydraulic Research. **VFOAT** Journal de Recherches Hydrauliques; Journal of the I.A.H.R.; Journal de l'A.I.R.H. Vol. 2 (1964)-. Periodical. English (French). Six times a year. Fl550.00. International Association for Hydraulic Research, PO Box 177, 2600 MH Delft The Netherlands. **Tel** 011 31 15 569353, **FAX** 011 31 15 619674, telex 38176. **ED** P. Novak. **CODEN** JHYRAF. Index available. cum. index. **Bk Rev. Ad Acc. Pr Rev. Circ:** 3,000 (ctrl) available in microform. Documents available from Article Express International, The Genuine Article. **Continues** Hydraulic Research.
Desc: Scientific papers on hydraulic engineering.
Ind/Abst AQUAREF; Bioeng. Abstr.; Civ. Struct. Eng. Abstr.; Comput. Inf. Syst. Abstr. J. [Full Cov.]; Curr. Contents Eng. Tech. Appl. Sci.; Ei Page One; Eng. Index Annu.; Environ. Eng. Abstr.; Fluid Abstr., Civil Eng.; Fluid Abstr. Proc. Eng.; FLUIDEX (1973-); Geogr. Abstr. Phys. Geogr.; Geol. Abstr.; GeoRef; Mater. Sci. Eng. Abstr.; Mech. Eng. Abstr.; Ocean. Abstr.; Life Sci. Collect.; Res. Alert [Full Cov.]; Sci. Cit. Index; SCISEARCH.

CC/1001-6058
JOURNAL OF HYDRODYNAMICS.
[J. Hydrodynam.]. (1989)-. Periodical. Chinese. qt. $120.00. China Ocean Press, 1 Fuxingmenwai Street, Beijing 100860 China. **Tel** 011 86 1 8532211 ext. 5913. **DD** 532.5. Documents available from Article Express International.
Ind/Abst Ei Page One; Eng. Index Annu.; Math. Rev.; Zentralbl. Math. Ihre Grenzgeb.

JA
JOURNAL OF HYDROSCIENCE AND HYDRAULIC ENGINEERING / COMMITTEE ON HYDRAULICS, JAPAN SOCIETY OF CIVIL ENGINEERS.
Added/Corp Dobuku Gakkai. Suiri Iinkai. **VFOAT** Hydroscience and Hydraulic Engineering. Vol. 1, No. 1 (Apr. 1983)-. Periodical. English. sa. $64.00. Doboku Gakkai Suiri Iinkai, (Committee on Hydraulics, Japan Soc. of Civil Engineers), Yotsuya 1 Chome, Shinjukuku, Tokyoto 160 Japan. **(Subscription address:** Maruzen Company Ltd., PO Box 5050, Import & Export Department, Tokyo 100 31 Japan.**)** Documents available from Article Express International.
Ind/Abst Ei Page One; Eng. Index Annu.; Fluid Abstr., Civil Eng.; Fluid Abstr. Proc. Eng.; FLUIDEX; GeoRef; Soils Fert.

US/0733-9437
JOURNAL OF IRRIGATION AND DRAINAGE ENGINEERING.
[J. irrig. drain. eng.]. **Added/Corp** American Society of Civil Engineers. American Society of Civil Engineers. Irrigation and Drainage Division. **VFOAT** Irrigation and Drainage Engineering; A.S.C.E. Irrigation and Drainage Engineering; ASCE Irrigation and Drainage Engineering. **VAT** American Society of Civil Engineers Irrigation and Drainage Engineering. Vol. 109, No. 1 (March 1983)-. Academic Scholarly Publication. English. bm. $157.00 (nonmember) US; $171.00 (nonmember) other. American Society of Civil Engineers / ASCE, 345 East 47th Street, New York NY 10017-2398. **Tel** (212)705-7179, **FAX** (212)705-7300, telex 422847 ASCE UI. **(Subscription address:** American Society of Civil Engineers, Publisher Fulfillment Agency, Box 828, Somerset NJ 08875.**) LC** TC801; .A4. **DD** 627/.52/05. **CODEN** JIDEDH. **[CCC].** Index available. cum. index. **Pr Rev. Circ:** 2,200. available on microfilm and microfiche from University Microfilms International (UMI); available on CD-ROM from American Society of Civil Engineers. Documents available from Article Express International, The Genuine Article, Documents on Demand. **Continues** Journal of the Irrigation and Drainage Division, 0044-7978.
Desc: All methods of irrigation, drainage and related water management are discussed, including water quality, weather modification and project formulation.
Ind/Abst AGRICOLA [Full Cov.]; Agric. Eng. Abstr. (1991-); Appl. Sci. Technol. Index; AQUAREF; ASCE Annu. Comb. Index (1983-); ASCE Publ. Inf. (1983-); Curr. Contents, Agric. Biol. Environ. Sci.; Curr. Contents Eng. Tech. Appl. Sci.; Ei Page One; EMBASE; Eng. Index Annu.; Environ. Abstr.; Expand. Acad. Index (1992-); Field Crop Abstr.; Fluid Abstr., Civil Eng.; Fluid Abstr. Proc. Eng.; FLUIDEX (1983-); Geogr. Abstr. Phys. Geogr. (?-?); Geogr. Abstr. Human Geogr. (?-?); GeoRef; Geotech. Abstr.; Int. Abstr. Oper. Res. [Select. Cov.]; Int. Civil Eng. Abstr.; Int. Dev. Abstr. (?-?); Irr. Drain. Abstr.; Maize Abstr.; Nematol. Abstr.; Life Sci. Collect.; Res. Alert [Full Cov.]; Rev. Agric. Entomol.; Rice Abstr.; Sci. Cit. Index; SCISEARCH; Soc. Sci. Cit. Index [Select. Cov.]; Soft. Abstr. Eng.; Soils Fert. (1983-); Trans. Am. Soc. Civ. Eng. (1983-); World Agric. Econ.

JA/0287-8607
JOURNAL OF IRRIGATION ENGINEERING AND RURAL PLANNING.
See Agriculture-Crop Production and Soil.

NE/0377-0257
JOURNAL OF NON-NEWTONIAN FLUID MECHANICS.
[J. non-Newton. fluid mech.]. Vol. 1 (Jan. 1976)-. Academic Scholarly Publication. English. Eighteen times a year (6 volumes). Fl2880.00. Elsevier Science Publishers BV, PO Box 211, 1000 AE Amsterdam Netherlands. **Tel** 011 31 20 5803642, **FAX** 011 31 20 5862696, telex 15682. **ED** K Walters. **LC** QA901; .J88. **DD** 532/.005. **CODEN** JNFMDI. **[CCC]. Pr Rev.** available on microfilm and microfiche from University Microfilms International (UMI). Documents available from Article Express International, The Genuine Article, Ask*IEEE, Petroleum Abstracts Document Delivery Service, CASDDS.
Desc: A journal for those working on basic rheological science and applications.
Ind/Abst Bioeng. Abstr.; Chem. Abstr.; Curr. Contents Eng. Tech. Appl. Sci.; Curr. Contents Phys. Chem. Earth Sci.; Ei Page One; Eng. Mater. Abstr.; Eng. Index Annu.; Fluid Abstr., Civil Eng.; Fluid Abstr. Proc. Eng.; FLUIDEX (1976-); GeoRef; HTFS Dig.; INSPEC (Jan. 1976-); Int. Aerosp. Abstr. (1983-); Pet. Abstr.; Polymer Contents; Proc. Chem. Eng.; Res. Alert [Full Cov.]; Sci. Cit. Index; SCISEARCH; Theoret. Chem. Eng.; Zentralbl. Math. Ihre Grenzgeb.

US/0892-7219
JOURNAL OF OFFSHORE MECHANICS AND ARCTIC ENGINEERING.
(TRANSACTIONS OF THE ASME. JOURNAL OF OFFSHORE MECHANICS.). [J. offshore mech. Arct. eng.]. **VFOAT** Offshore Mechanics and Arctic Engineering. Vol. 109, No. 1 (Feb. 1987)-. Academic Scholarly Publication. English. qt. $130.00 (nonmember), $40.00 (member) US and Canada. American Society of Mechanical Engineers, 22 Law Drive, Fairfield NJ 07007. **Tel** (201)882-1167, (212)705-7722 (editorial). **LC** TC1665; .T73. **DD** 627/.98/05. **[CCC].** available on microfilm and microfiche from University Microfilms International (UMI). Documents available from Article Express International, Ask*IEEE, Petroleum Abstracts Document Delivery Service, CASDDS. **Continues in part** Transactions of the ASME. Journal of Energy Resources Technology, 0195-0738.
Ind/Abst Alum. Ind. Abstr. (1987-); Appl. Sci. Technol. Index (1987-); Chem. Abstr. (1987-); Coal Abstr. (1987-); Ei Page One (1987-); EMBASE (1987-); Eng. Index Annu.; Expand. Acad. Index (1992-); Fluid Abstr., Civil Eng.; Fluid Abstr. Proc. Eng.; FLUIDEX (1987-); Geotech. Abstr.; INSPEC (1987-); Int. Aerosp. Abstr. (1987-); Met. Abstr. (1987-); Ocean. Abstr.; Life Sci. Collect. (1987-); Pet. Abstr.; Shock Vibr. Dig.

II
JOURNAL OF THE INSTITUTION OF ENGINEERS (INDIA). MARINE ENGINEERING DIVISION.
Added/Corp Institution of Engineers (India). Marine Engineering Division. **VFOAT** Marine Engineering Division; IE (I) Journal-MA. (19??)-. Periodical. English. Twice a year. $4.00. Institution of Engineers India, 8 Gokhale Road, Calcutta 700020 India. **Tel** 011 91 33 288311, telex 21 7885 IEIC IN. **LC** VM595; .J68. **DD** 623.8/05. **Continues** Journal of the Institution of Engineers (India), 0368-2498.

US/0733-950X
JOURNAL OF WATERWAY, PORT, COASTAL, AND OCEAN ENGINEERING. [J. waterw. port coast. ocean eng.]. **Added/Corp** American Society of Civil Engineers. American Society of Civil Engineers. Waterway, Port, Coastal and Ocean Division. **VFOAT** ASCE Waterway, Port, Coastal and Ocean Engineering. Vol. 109, No. 1 (Feb. 1983)-. Periodical. English. bm. $117.00 (nonmember) US; $129.00 (nonmember) other. American Society of Civil Engineers / ASCE, 345 East 47th Street, New York NY 10017-2398. **Tel** (212)705-7179, FAX (212)705-7300, telex 422847 ASCE UI. **(Subscription address:** American Society of Civil Engineers, Publisher Fulfillment Agency, Box 828, Somerset NJ 08875.**) LC** TC1; .A4. **DD** 627/.05. **CODEN** JWPED5. **[CCC].** Index available. cum. index. **Bk Rev. Ad Acc. Circ:** 4,400 (ctrl). available on microfilm and microfiche from University Microfilms International (UMI); available on CD-ROM from American Society of Civil Engineers. Documents available from Article Express International, The Genuine Article, Petroleum Abstracts Document Delivery Service, Documents on Demand. ***Continues*** *Journal of the Waterway, Port, Coastal, and Ocean Division, 0148-9895.*
Desc: Covers all phases of engineering concerning ports, harbors, offshore facilities, and all other natural and man-made marine formations and structures.
Ind/Abst Abstr. J. Earthq. Eng.; Appl. Sci. Technol. Index; AQUAREF; Aquat. Sci. Fish. Abstr. (Computer File); ASCE Annu. Comb. Index (1983-); ASCE Publ. Inf. (1983-); BMT Abstr.; Coal Abstr.; Curr. Contents Eng. Tech. Appl. Sci.; Ei Page One; Energy Inf. Abstr.; Eng. Index Annu.; Environ. Abstr.; Expand. Acad. Index (1992-); Fluid Abstr., Civil Eng.; Fluid Abstr. Proc. Eng.; FLUIDEX (1983-); Geogr. Abstr. Phys. Geogr. (?-?); GeoRef; Geotech. Abstr.; Int. Civil Eng. Abstr.; J. Plan. Lit.; Ocean. Abstr.; Life Sci. Collect.; Pet. Abstr.; Res. Alert [Full Cov.]; Sci. Cit. Index; SCISEARCH; Trans. Am. Soc. Civ. Eng. (1983-).

JA/0454-1545
KOGYO YOSUI. See Water Resources.

JA
KOWAN GIJUTSU KENKYUJO KOENKAI KOEN SHU. Main/Corp Unyusho Kowan Gijutsu Kenkyujo (Japan). (19??)-. Proceedings. Japanese. an. Unyusho Kowan Gijutsu Kenkyujo, (Port and Harbor Research Institute, Ministry of Transport), 1-1 Yokosukashi Nagase 3-chome, Kanagawaken 239 Japan. **LC** TC203; .K675.

GW/0452-7739
KUESTE. (DIE KUESTE; ARCHIV FUER FORSCHUNG UND TECHNIK AN DER NORD- UND OSTSEE.). [Kueste]. **Added/Corp** Kuestenausschuss Nord- und Ostsee. Vol. 1 (March 1952)-. Periodical. German (summaries and/or abstracts in English). Twice a year. DM45.00. Westholsteinische Verlagsanst Boyens & Co., Postfach 1880, D 25738 Heidelberg Germany. **Tel** 011 49 481 68860. **LC** TC203; .K8. **CODEN** KUSTAP. **Circ:** 700.
Desc: All new knowledge about technical news in order to secure the German coast.
Ind/Abst Ecol. Abstr.; Ei Page One; Fluid Abstr., Civil Eng.; Fluid Abstr. Proc. Eng.; FLUIDEX (1973-1989); Geogr. Abstr. Phys. Geogr.; Geogr. Abstr. Human Geogr.; GeoRef.

NE/0023-7604
LAND & WATER INTERNATIONAL. [Land & water int.]. **VFOAT** Land and Water International; Land + Water International. No. 1 (June 1966)-. Periodical. English (summaries and/or abstracts in French, German and Spanish). Four times a year. Free on request. Netherlands Engineering Consultants, PO Box 90413, 2509 LK The Hague Netherlands. **Tel** 011 31 070 3821545, FAX 011 31 070 3477053, telex 32095 NDECO NL. **ED** Anja Nijenkamp. **LC** TC1; .L26. Index available. **Bk Rev. Circ:** 4,300 (ctrl).
Desc: Review on hydraulic engineering, environmental control and rural development.
Ind/Abst Fluid Abstr., Civil Eng.; Fluid Abstr. Proc. Eng.; FLUIDEX (1973-).

BE/0377-8312
LECTURE SERIES - VON KARMAN INSTITUTE FOR FLUID DYNAMICS. [Lect. ser., Von Karman Inst. Fluid Dyn.]. **Main/Corp** Von Karman Institute for Fluid Dynamics. (19??)-. Monographic series. English. ir. Price varies per volume. Von Karman Institute for Fluid Dynamics, Chaussee de Waterloo 72, 1640 Saint Genese Belgium. **CODEN** LSVDDQ.

TZ/0377-113X
MAJI REVIEW. V. 1- July 1974-. Periodical. English. Ministry of Water Development and Power, PO Box 9291, Dar Es Salaam Tanzania. **LC** TC519.T3; M34. **DD** 333.9/1/009678. **CODEN** MAREDU.
Ind/Abst GeoRef.

RU
MATERIALY. Main/Corp Leningrad. Institut Vodnogo Transporta. Gidrotekhnicheskaia Laboratoriia. (19??)-. Russian. 0.85rub each issue. Transport / St Petersburg, Leningradskoe Otdelenie 190121, Ulitsa Dekabristov 33, St. Petersburg Russia. **LC** HE675; .L38 subser.

PL
MATERIAY BADAWCZE. SERIA: INZYNIERIA WODNA. VFOAT Inzynieria Wodna. No. 1 (1974)-. Monographic series. Polish. ir. Price varies per volume. Instytut Meteorologii i Gospodarki Wodnej, Ul Podlesna 61, 01-673 Warszawa Poland. **Tel** 34-16-51 W 307, telex 814331. **ED** Stefan Reichhart. **Ad Acc. Circ:** 218 (ctrl).
Ind/Abst GeoRef.

GW/0025-8644
MEERESTECHNIK. (MEERESTECHNIK. MARINE TECHNOLOGY.). [Meerestechnik]. **Added/Corp** Verein Deutscher Ingenieure. Deutsches Komitee fuer Meeresforschung und Meerestechnik. **VFOAT** Marine Technology; MT. Vol. 1 (May 1970)-. Periodical. English (German). bm. $75.00. VDI Verlag GmbH, Postfach 101054, D 40001 Dusseldorf Germany. **Tel** 011 49 211 6188313, FAX 011 49 211 6188133. **(Subscription address:** Fulfillment Office, PO Box 1831, Birmingham, AL 35201**) ED** Margarete Pauls. **LC** TC1501; .M4. **CODEN** MRTKA4. **Ad Acc.** Documents available from Article Express International, Ask*IEEE, Petroleum Abstracts Document Delivery Service.
Desc: Covers a wide spectrum of scientific themes, dealing with such topics as raw materials from the sea, hydraulic engineering at sea, and keeping the sea clean.
Ind/Abst Aquat. Sci. Fish. Abstr. (Computer File); Bioeng. Abstr.; Ei Page One; Energy Res. Abstr.; Eng. Index Annu.; Fluid Abstr., Civil Eng.; Fluid Abstr. Proc. Eng.; FLUIDEX (1973-1990); GeoRef; INSPEC (May 1970-); Int. Civil Eng. Abstr.; Pet. Abstr. (1973-); Soft. Abstr. Eng.

RU/0235-2524
MELIORATSIIA I VODNOE KHOZIAISTVO (MOSCOW, R.S.F.S.R.). (MELIORATSIIA I VODNOE KHOZIAISTVO.). **Added/Corp** Soviet Union. Ministerstvo Melioratsii i Vodnogo Khoziaistva. Gosudarstvennyi Agropromyshlennyi Komitet SSSR. Vol. 1 (1988)-. Periodical. Russian (table of contents in English). Six times a year. $89.95. Agropromizdat, Sadovo-Spasskaia, 18, 107807 Moscow Russia. **(Subscription address:** East View Publications Inc., 3020 Harbor Lane North, Suite 110, Minneapolis MN 55447.**) CODEN** MVKHEG. ***Continues*** *Gidrotekhnika i Melioratsiia, 0016-9722.*
Ind/Abst Agric. Eng. Abstr.

US/0148-3811
MID-PACIFIC REGION REPORT. [Mid-pac. reg. rep.]. **Main/Corp** United States. Bureau of Reclamation. 1974-. English. US Bureau of Reclamation Water Operation & Maintenance Branch, D-430/18th and C Streets NW, Washington DC 20240. **LC** TC423.8; .U54A. **DD** 333.9/102/0979.

US/0193-5992
MISCELLANEOUS REPORT - U.S. ARMY, CORPS OF ENGINEERS, COASTAL ENGINEERING RESEARCH CENTER. (MISCELLANEOUS REPORT - COASTAL ENGINEERING RESEARCH CENTER.). [Misc. rep. - U. S. Army, Corps Eng., Coast. Eng. Res. Cent.]. **Main/Corp** Coastal Engineering Research Center (U.S.). **VAT** Miscellaneous Report - United States Army, Corps of Engineers, Coastal Engineering Research Center. No. 1, 1976-. Monographic series. English. Price varies per volume. National Technical Information Service - NTIS, Room 2027S, 5285 Port Royal Road, Springfield VA 22161. **Tel** (703)487-4630, (703)487-4660, (703)487-4650, FAX (703)321-8547, telex 89-9405. ***Continues*** *Coastal Engineering Research Center (U.S.). Miscellaneous Paper, 0565-1611.*
Ind/Abst GeoRef; Ocean. Abstr.

US/0161-4118
MISSOURI RIVER BASIN, STATE AND FEDERAL WATER AND RELATED LAND RESOURCE PROGRAMS. Main/Corp United States. Missouri River Basin Commission. English. an. Missouri River Basin Commission, 10050 Regency Circle/Suite 403, Omaha NE 68114. **LC** TC225.M67; U54A. **DD** 333.9/1/00978.

GW/0343-1223
MITTEILUNGEN - LEICHTWEISS-INSTITUT FUER WASSERBAU DER TECHNISCHEN UNIVERSITAT BRAUNSCHWEIG. [Mitt. - Leichtweiss-Inst. Wasserb. Tech. Univ. Braunsch.]. **Main/Corp** Technische Universitat Carolo-Wilhelmina. Leichtweiss-Institut fur Wasserbau. Periodical. German. **LC** TC1; .T37A. ***Continues*** *Technische Universitat Carlo-Wilhelmina. Leichtweiss-Institut fur Wasserbau und Grundbau. Mitteilungen.*
Ind/Abst Alum. Ind. Abstr.; Ecol. Abstr. (?-?); Geogr. Abstr. Phys. Geogr.; GeoRef; Met. Abstr.

GW/0572-5801
MITTEILUNGSBLATT DER BUNDESANSTALT FUER WASSERBAU. Added/Corp Bundesanstalt fuer Wasserbau (Germany : West). (1953)-. Periodical. German (summaries and/or abstracts in English; table of contents in English and German). ir. DM10.88 (per copy). Bundesanstalt fuer Wasserbau, Kussmaulstrasse 17, D 76187 Karlsruhe 21 Germany. **Tel** 011 49 721 75011. **LC** WMLC L 83/1810.

JA/0387-5504
NAVAL ARCHITECTURE AND OCEAN ENGINEERING. See Naval Science, Navigation.

JA/0387-5016
NIHON KIKAI GAKKAI RONBUNSHU. B. (NIHON KIKAIGAKKAI ROMBUNSHU. B-HEN. TRANSACTIONS OF THE JAPAN SOCIETY OF MECHANICAL ENGINEERS. SERIES B.). [Nihon Kikai Gakkai ronbunshu, B]. **Main/Corp** Nihon Kikaigakkai. **Added/Corp** Nihon Kikai Gakkai. Transactions of the Japan Society of Mechanical Engineers. Series B. **VFOAT** Transactions of the Japan Society of Mechanical Engineers. Series B. Vol. 45, No. 389 (1979)-. Academic Scholarly Publication. Japanese. mo. $775.00. Nihon Kikaigakkai, 4-9 Yoyogi 2-chome, Shibuya-ku 151, Tokyo Japan. **(Subscription address:** Japan Publications Trading Company, Ltd., PO Box 5030, Tokyo International, Tokyo 100-31 Japan.**) LC** TA357; .N53a. **CODEN** NKGBDD. **[CCC].** Documents available from Article Express International, CASDDS. ***Supersedes in part*** *Nihon Kikai Gakkai. Nihon Kikaigakkai Rombunshu.*
Ind/Abst Chem. Abstr.; Coal Abstr.; Ei Page One; Eng. Index Annu.; Fluid Abstr., Civil Eng.; Fluid Abstr. Proc. Eng.; FLUIDEX (1979-); Int. Aerosp. Abstr.

JA
NIKKIREN KAIYO SHIRYO INDEKKUSU. Main/Corp Nihon Kikai Kogyo Rengokai. **VFOAT** Kaiyo Shiryo Indekkusu. No. 1- 1973-. Multiple languages (Japanese and English). Nihon Kikai Kogyo Rengokai, (Japan Machinery Federation), 5-8 Shiba Koen 3-chome, Minatoku Tokyoto 105 Japan. **LC** Z5853.O6; N53A; TC1645.

CN/0846-0795
NOUVELLES HYDRO, PROJETS D'EQUIPEMENT EN BASSE-COTE-NORD. (HYDRO NEWS, LOWER NORTH SHORE INSTALLATIONS PROJECTS.). [Nouv. hydro proj. equip. Basse-Cote-Nord]. **Added/Corp** Hydro-Quebec. Vol. 1, No. 1 (1990)-. Periodical. English (French). Hydro-Quebec, 14E Etage, 75 Ouest Boul Dorchester, Montreal Quebec H2Z 1A4 Canada. **DD** 333.91/4/097141705.

RU
NOVOSTI TEKHNICHESKOI LITERATURY. STROITELSTVO I ARKHITEKTURA. RAZDEL SERIIA XII: VODOKHOZIAISTVENNOE STROITELSTVO. Added/Corp Moscow. Tsentralnyi Institut Nauchnoi Informatsii po Stroitelstvu i Arkhitekture. Tsentralnaia Nauchno-Issledovatelskaia Biblioteka po Stroitelstvu i Arkhitekture. Informatsionno-Bibliograficheskii Otdel. **VFOAT** Stroitel'stvo I Arkhitektura. Razdel A. Vodokhoziaistvennoe Stroitelstvo; Vodokhoziaistvennoe Stroitelstvo. (1974)-. Periodical. Multiple languages (Russian and Multiple languages). mo. Informatsii po Stroitelstvu I Arkhitekture, A-47 Ulitsa Gorkogo Dom 38, Moscow 125047 Russia. **LC** Z5853.S22; N6; TC405. ***Continues*** *Novosti Tekhnicheskoi Literatury. Stroitelstvo I Arkhitektura. Razdel A. Seriia VII: Vodokhoziiaistvennoe Stroitelstvo.*

GW/0341-2660
O + I.E. UND P, OLHYDRAULIK UND PNEUMATIK. VFOAT O und P; Olhydraulik und Pneumatik. Vol. 20 (1976)-. Academic Scholarly Publication. English (German; summaries and/or abstracts in German). mo (11 issues). DM212.00. Vereinigte Fachverlag, Postfach 4068, D 55030 Mainz Germany. **Tel** 011 49 6131 992150. **[CCC].** Documents available from Ask*IEEE. ***Continues*** *Oelhydraulik und Pneumatik, 0029-8697.*
Ind/Abst EMBASE; Fluid Abstr., Civil Eng.; Fluid Abstr. Proc. Eng.; FLUIDEX (19??-); INSPEC (1968-).

US/0029-8018
OCEAN ENGINEERING. [Ocean eng.]. Vol. 1 (July 1968)-. Academic Scholarly Publication. English. Eight times a year. $664.00 The Americas; £445.00 other. Pergamon Press, An Imprint of Elsevier Science Ltd., The Boulevard, Langford Lane, Kidlington, Oxford OX5 1GB United Kingdom. **Tel** 011 44 865 843000, 011 44 865 843699, FAX 011 44 865 843010. **(Subscription address:** Elsevier Science Ltd. Oxford Fulfillment Centre, PO Box 800, Kidlington, Oxford OX5 1DX United Kingdom.**) ED** Michael E. McCormick. **LC** TC1501; .O25. **DD** 620. **CODEN** OCENBQ. **[CCC]. Pr Rev.** available on microfilm from Microfilms International Marketing Corp.; available on microfilm and microfiche from University Microfilms International (UMI). Documents available from Article Express International, The Genuine Article,

Ask*IEEE, Petroleum Abstracts Document Delivery Service, CASDDS, Documents on Demand.
Ind/Abst Acoust. Abstr.; Alum. Ind. Abstr.; Am. Bibliogr. Slavic East Europ. Stud. (19??-19??); Appl. Sci. Technol. Index; AQUAREF; Aquat. Sci. Fish. Abstr. (Computer File); Bioeng. Abstr.; BMT Abstr.; Chem. Abstr.; Curr. Contents Eng. Tech. Appl. Sci.; Curr. Technol. Index; Ei Page One; EMBASE; Energy Inf. Abstr.; Energy Res. Abstr.; Eng. Index Annu.; Environ. Abstr.; Environ. Period. Bibliogr.; Fluid Abstr., Civil Eng.; Fluid Abstr. Proc. Eng.; FLUIDEX (1973-); GeoRef; INSPEC (April 1971-); Int. Aerosp. Abstr.; Int. Civil Eng. Abstr.; Mar. Sci. Contents Tables; Met. Abstr.; Ocean. Abstr.; Life Sci. Collect.; Pet. Abstr.; Pollut. Abstr. Indexes; Res. Alert [Full Cov.]; Sci. Cit. Index; SCISEARCH; Shock Vibr. Dig.; Soft. Abstr. Eng.

US/0078-3137
OCEAN ENGINEERING INFORMATION SERIES. (1969)-. English. ir. Ocean Engineering Info Service 92037.

US/0146-9126
OCEAN RESOURCES ENGINEERING. [Ocean resour. eng.]. Periodical. English. qt. $5.00. Ocean Resources Engineering, PO Box 1589, Dallas TX 75221. **LC** TC1501; .O256. **DD** 620/.416/2. ***Continues*** *Ocean Engineering, 0147-3522.*
Ind/Abst Aquat. Sci. Fish. Abstr. (Computer File); Life Sci. Collect.

AU/0029-9588
OESTERREICHISCHE WASSERWIRTSCHAFT. [Oesterr. Wasserwirtsch.]. **Added/Corp** Austria. Bundesministerium fuer Land- und Forstwirtschaft. Austria. Bundesministerium fuer Bauten und Technik. Osterreichischer Wasserwirtschaftsverband. (1949)-. Academic Scholarly Publication. German. Twelve times a year. $171.00. Springer-Verlag Wien, Sachsenplatz 4 6, PO Box 89, A-1201 Vienna Austria. **Tel** 011 43 1 3302415. **(Subscription address:** Springer Verlag New York Inc. / for North America, 44 Hartz Way, Secaucus NJ 07096.) **ED** W. Biffl, S. Radler and H. Supersperg. **CODEN** OSWAAI. **[CCC]. Bk Rev.** Documents available from BIOSIS Document Express, CASDDS.
Desc: Covers all scientific, technical, legal and economic questions of water resources. Original articles report on such topics as sediment usage, dike and canal construction and waste water handling. Hydrobiology and water chemistry are also covered.
Ind/Abst AGRICOLA; Biol. Abstr.; Chem. Abstr.; EMBASE; Fluid Abstr., Civil Eng.; Fluid Abstr. Proc. Eng.; FLUIDEX (1973-); GeoRef; Int. Civil Eng. Abstr.; Soft. Abstr. Eng.; Vitis Vitic. Enol. Abstr.

UK/0956-6732
OFFSHORE BUSINESS. [Offshore bus.]. (198?)-. Monographic series. English. Four times a year. £390.00 England; £460.00 other. Smith Rea Energy Analysts Ltd, Hunstead House, Nickle Chartham, Canterbury Kent CT4 7PL England. **Tel** (0227)738844, FAX (0227)738866. **ED** George Robinson. Documents available from BLDSC.
Desc: Book series with 46 titles to date.

UK/0305-876X
OFFSHORE ENGINEER. [Offshore eng.]. (1975)-. Periodical. English. Twelve times a year. £53.00 UK; £76.00 other. Thomas Telford Ltd, Thomas Telford House, 1 Heron Quay, London E14 9XF England. **Tel** 011 44 71 987 6999, FAX 011 44 71 538 4101, telex 298105. **ED** David Morgan. **LC** TC1501; .O44. **DD** 338.2/7/280941. **[CCC].** Index available (free). **Ad Acc. Circ:** 21,000. Documents available from Petroleum Abstracts Document Delivery Service. ***Absorbed*** *Northern Offshore.*
Desc: In-depth coverage of North Sea activity; news, comments, and incisive technical reporting on other major offshore activity areas, worldwide.
Ind/Abst Aquat. Sci. Fish. Abstr. (Computer File); BMT Abstr.; Coal Abstr.; Curr. Technol. Index; EMBASE; Fluid Abstr., Civil Eng.; Fluid Abstr. Proc. Eng.; FLUIDEX (1975-); GeoRef; Ocean. Abstr.; Life Sci. Collect.; Pet. Abstr.; Selec. Coop. Index Manage. Period.

UK
OFFSHORE GEODETIC ARCHIVE. (19??)-. Periodical. English. an. £216.00 (includes updates). Ordnance Survey, c/o N. Robinson, Cntl & Info #C552 Romsey Road, Southampton S09 4DH England. **Tel** 011 44 0703 792635.

UK
OFFSHORE INSTALLATIONS : GUIDANCE ON LIFE SAVING APPLIANCE. (19??)-. English. ir. £40.00. Health & Safety Executive, Room 414 St Hughs House Stanley, Btle Merseyside L20 3QY England. **Tel** 011 44 51 951 4000, FAX 011 44 51 922 5394, telex 628235.

US
OFFSHORE SCIENTIFIC & TECHNICAL PUBLICATIONS. VFOAT Offshore Scientific and Technical Publications. Periodical. English. qt. Free. Minerals Management Service Dept Inter, 381 Elden Street/Suite 1400, Herndon VA 22070-4817. **Tel** (703)285-2604. **LC** Z6972; .O34; TN871.3. **DD** 016.622/33819. Index available. **Circ:** 5,700.

NE/0168-5295
ONDERHOUD WATERGANGEN / CENTRAAL BUREAU VOOR DE STATISTIEK, AFDELING NATUURLIJK MILIEU. VFOAT Maintenance of Water-Courses. Dutch (summaries and/or abstracts in English). ir. Fl25.00. Centraal Bureau voor de Statistiek, AFD ALG Zaken, Postbus 959, 2270 AZ Voorburg Netherlands. **Tel** 011 31 70 3373800, FAX 011 31 038 7429, telex 32692 CBS NL. **LC** TC477; .O53.

NE
ORCHIDEEN. Ned Orchideen Vereniging, Reggestraat 31, 7555 KK Heneglo Netherlands.

MY
PENYATA TAHUNAN BAHAGIAN PARIT DAN TALIAIR, KEMENTERIAN PERTANIAN MALAYSIA BAGI TAHUN ... . Main/Corp Malaysia. Bahagian Parit Dan Taliair. **VFOAT** Annual Report of the Drainage and Irrigation Division for the Year ... . 1654-. English (Malay). an. $10.00. Unit Penerbitan Kementerian Pertanian, JL Swettenham, Kuala Lumpur Malaysia. **LC** TC913.M32; M34A. **DD** 333.91/315/09595. ***Continues*** *Penyata Tahunan Bahagian Parit dan Taliair, Kementerian pertanian dan Perikanan Malaysia.*

II
PERFORMANCE BUDGET - ORISSA, INDIA. IRRIGATION AND POWER DEPT. Main/Corp Orissa, India. Irrigation and Power Dept. English. **LC** TC904.O7; O75A. **DD** 354/.54/13008242.

LV/0130-8246
POLIMERY V MELIORACII I VODNOM HOZJAJSTVE. (POLIMERY V MELIORATSII I VODNOM KHOZIAISTVE.). [Polim. melior. vodn. hoz.]. **Added/Corp** Latvijas Hidrotehnikas un MeliorÅacijas Zinatniski Petnieciskais Instituts. Vol. 1 (1974)-. Academic Scholarly Publication. Russian. Latviiskii Nauchno-Issledovania In-t Gidrotekhniki I Melioratsii, Ulitsa Revoliutsiias 43, Elegava Russia. **LC** TC1; .P58. **CODEN** PMVKDF. Documents available from CASDDS.
Desc: Information on drainage, water-supply, and plastics used in hydraulic engineering.
Ind/Abst Chem. Abstr. (1974-1980).

US/0274-9556
PRESSURE. *Ceased.* Periodical. English. bm. Fluid Power Society, 25875 Jefferson, St Clair Shores MI 48081. **Tel** (313)774-8180.

NE/0074-1477
PROCEEDINGS. Main/Corp International Association for Hydraulic Research. **Added/Corp** American Society of Civil Engineers. Hydraulics Division. International Association for Hydraulic Research. Internationaler Verband fuer wasserbauliches Versuchwesen. Association Internationale de Recherches Hydrauliques. International Association for Hydraulic Research. International Association for Hydraulic Research. Bericht uber die Tagung. International Association for Hydraulic Research. **VFOAT** Report of the Meeting.; Rapport sur la Reunion.; IAHR Proceedings. (1937)-. Proceedings. English (French). be. Fl300.00. International Association for Hydraulic Research, PO Box 177, 2600 MH Delft The Netherlands. **Tel** 011 31 15 569353, FAX 011 31 15 619674, telex 38176.

US/0732-2607
PROCEEDINGS - INTERNATIONAL SYMPOSIUM ON URBAN HYDROLOGY, HYDRAULICS, AND SEDIMENT CONTROL (1981). (PROCEEDINGS ... INTERNATIONAL SYMPOSIUM ON URBAN HYDROLOGY, HYDRAULICS, AND SEDIMENT CONTROL.). [Proc. - Int. Symp. Urban Hydrol. Hydraul. Sediment Control]. **Added/Corp** University of Kentucky. Office of Engineering Services. University of Kentucky. College of Engineering. (1981)-. Proceedings. English. an. $22.50. University of Kentucky Office of Engineering Services, College of Engineering, 226 Anderson Hall, Lexington KY 40506-0046. **Tel** (606)257-3343, FAX (606)257-3342. **ED** R William de Vore. **LC** TC401; .I6135a. **DD** 628/.21. **Circ:** 150 (ctrl). ***Continues*** *International Symposium on Urban Storm Runoff. Proceedings.*
Desc: A collection of papers presented during the annual conferences. Topics include computer security, LLTV intrusion detection, security robots, antiterrorism technology, and more.
Ind/Abst GeoRef.

US/0099-409X
PROCEEDINGS, INTERNATIONAL WATER CONFERENCE, ENGINEERS SOCIETY OF WESTERN PENNSYLVANIA. [Proc., Int. Water Conf., Eng. Soc. West. Pa.]. **VFOAT** Proceedings, Annual Water Conference, Engineers Society of Western Pennsylvania. (1940)-. Academic Scholarly Publication. English. an. **CODEN** PWWPAY. Documents available from CASDDS.
Ind/Abst Chem. Abstr.

US
PROCEEDINGS - NORTHEAST WATER RESOURCE RESEARCH DIRECTORS' MEETING. Main/Conf Northeast Water Resource Research Directors' Meeting. Proceedings. English. an. Pennsylvania State University / Air & Water, 226 Fenske Laboratory, University Park PA 16802. **Tel** (814)865-1415. **LC** TC401. **DD** 333.9/1/0072073.

US/0748-7533
PROCEEDINGS OF THE ... ANNUAL DREDGING SEMINAR. [Proc. annu. Dredg. Semin.]. **Main/Conf** Dredging Seminar. **VFOAT** Proceedings of the ... Dredging Seminar. Proceedings. English. an. $8.00. Marine Information Service, Sea Grant College Program, Texas A&M University, College Station TX 77843. **Tel** (409)845-7524. **LC** TC187; .D74A. **DD** 627/.73/05. ***Continues*** *Proceedings of the Dredging Seminar, 0278-8802.*

UK
PROCEEDINGS OF THE FLUID POWER SYMPOSIUM. (19??)-. Proceedings. English. ir (every 2-3 years). $145.00. BHR Group Ltd Brit Hydrom. Research, Cranfield, Bedford MK43 0AJ England. **Tel** 011 44 243 750422, FAX 011 44 243 750074, telex 825059.

US
PROCEEDINGS OF THE ... HYDRAULICS CONFERENCE / IOWA INSTITUTE OF HYDRAULIC RESEARCH. Main/Conf Hydraulics Conference (Iowa Institute of Hydraulic Research). Began with 4th (June 12-15, 1949)-. Proceedings. English. te. John Wiley & Sons, Inc., 605 Third Avenue, New York NY 10158-0012. **Tel** (212)850-6000, (212)850-6645, FAX (212)850-6088, telex 12-7063. **(Subscription address:** John Wiley & Sons / England, Baffins Lane, Chichester, West Sussex PO19 1UD England.) ***Continues*** *Proceedings of Hydraulics Conference).*

●UK/0965-0946
PROCEEDINGS OF THE INSTITUTION OF CIVIL ENGINEERS. WATER, MARITIME AND ENERGY. Added/Corp Institution of Civil Engineers (Great Britain). **VFOAT** Water, Maritime and Energy. Vol. 96, Issue 1 (Mar. 1992)-. Proceedings. English. Four times a year (Mar., June, Sept., Dec.). £73.00 UK; £84.00 others. Thomas Telford Ltd, Thomas Telford House, 1 Heron Quay, London E14 9XF England. **Tel** 011 44 71 987 6999, FAX 011 44 71 538 4101, telex 298105. **CODEN** PICWEV. Documents available from Article Express International, The Genuine Article. ***Continues in part*** *Institution of Civil Engineers (Great Britain)., 0307-8353; Proceedings - Institution of Civil Engineers. Part 1, Design and Construction, 0307-8361; Institution of Civil Engineers (Great Britain)., 0263-788X; Proceedings - Institution of Civil Engineers. Part 2, Research and Theory* ***and*** *Municipal Engineer (Institution of Civil Engineers (Great Britain)).*
Desc: Covers fluid mechanics, hydraulic and river engineering, and power mechanics.
Ind/Abst Curr. Contents Eng. Tech. Appl. Sci.; Eng. Index Annu.; Fluid Abstr., Civil Eng.; Fluid Abstr. Proc. Eng.; FLUIDEX (19??-); Int. Civil Eng. Abstr.; Res. Alert [Full Cov.]; Sci. Cit. Index; SCISEARCH; Soc. Sci. Cit. Index [Select. Cov.].

US
PROCEEDINGS OF THE ... INTERNATIONAL CONFERENCE ON OFFSHORE MECHANICS AND ARCTIC ENGINEERING / ORGANIZED BY OMAE CONFERENCE COMMITTEE AND ASME OFFSHORE MECHANICS AND ARCTIC ENGINEERING DIVISION. Added/Corp American Society of Mechanical Engineers. Offshore Mechanics and Arctic Engineering Division. **VFOAT** OMAE. 7th (1988)-. Proceedings. English. ir. $92.50. American Society of Mechanical Engineers, 22 Law Drive, Fairfield NJ 07007. **Tel** (201)882-1167, (212)705-7722 (editorial). **LC** TC1505; .I585a. **DD** 627/.98. ***Continues*** *International Offshore Mechanics and Arctic Engineering Symposium. Proceeding of the ... International Offshore Mechanics and Arctic Engineering Symposium.*
Ind/Abst Civ. Struct. Eng. Abstr.; Comput. Inf. Syst. Abstr. J. [Full Cov.]; Environ. Eng. Abstr.; Manuf. Process Eng. Abstr.; Mater. Sci. Eng. Abstr.; Mech. Eng. Abstr.; Solid State Supercond. Abstr.

US/0739-5825
PROCEEDINGS OF THE INTERNATIONAL TECHNICAL CONFERENCE ON SLURRY TRANSPORTATION. *Title Change.* (PROCEEDINGS OF THE ... INTERNATIONAL TECHNICAL CONFERENCE ON SLURRY

TRANSPORTATION / SLURRY TRANSPORT ASSOCIATION.). [Proc. Int. Tech. Conf. Slurry Transp.]. **Main/Conf** International Technical Conference on Slurry Transportation. **Added/Corp** Slurry Transport Association. Battelle Memorial Institute. United States. Energy Research and Development Administration. Electric Power Research Institute. **VFOAT** Proceedings of the ... International Technical Conference on Slurry Transportation. (1976)-(1984). Proceedings. English. an. **LC** TJ898; .I582a. **DD** 621.8/67. **CODEN** PTCTDU. Documents available from Article Express International. ***Continued by*** *Proceedings of the ... International Conference on Slurry Technology.*
Ind/Abst Bioeng. Abstr.; Ei Page One; Eng. Index Annu.

US/0160-8428
PROCEEDINGS OF THE NATIONAL CONFERENCE ON FLUID POWER. [Proc. Natl. Conf. Fluid Power]. **Main/Conf** National Conference on Fluid Power. **Added/Corp** Illinois Institute of Technology. Graduate School. IIT Research Institute. Illinois Institute of Technology. National Fluid Power Association. Fluid Power Society. Vol. 18 (1964)-. Proceedings. English. be. $60.00 US; $75.00 other. National Fluid Power Association, 3333 North Mayfair Road, Milwaukee WI 53222. **Tel** (414)778-3369, FAX (414)778-3361, telex 704557. **LC** TC5; .N25. **DD** 621.206373. **CODEN** PCFPAD. Index available. cum. index. **Pr Rev. Circ:** 600. Documents available from Article Express International, Ask*IEEE. ***Continues*** *National Conference on Industrial Hydraulics. Proceedings.*
Desc: Emphasizes research, development, and applications related to fluid power.
Ind/Abst Bioeng. Abstr.; Ei Page One; Energy Res. Abstr. (Dec. 1979-); Eng. Index Annu.; INSPEC.

US/0160-3663
PROCEEDINGS - OFFSHORE TECHNOLOGY CONFERENCE. [Proc., Offshore Technol. Conf.]. **Main/Conf** Offshore Technology Conference. (1975)-. Academic Scholarly Publication. English. an. $58.00. Offshore Technology Conference, PO Box 833836, Richardson TX 75083-3836. **Tel** (214)361-6604. **LC** TC1505; .O352a. **DD** 620/.416/2. **CODEN** OSTCBA. Documents available from Article Express International, CASDDS. ***Continues*** *Preprints - Offshore Technology Conference, 0160-8339.*
Ind/Abst Aquat. Sci. Fish. Abstr. (Computer File); Bioeng. Abstr.; Chem. Abstr. (1969-1983); Ei Page One; Energy Res. Abstr. (Oct. 1978-); Eng. Index Annu.; GeoRef; Lit. Pat. Abstr., Oilfield Chem. (1979-); Lit. Abstr., Catal. Catal.; Lit. Abstr., Health Environ.; Lit. Abstr., Pet. Refin. Petrochem.; Lit. Abstr., Pet. Substit.; Lit. Abstr., Transp. Storage; Ocean. Abstr.

II
PROCEEDINGS / RESEARCH AND DEVELOPMENT SESSION (INDIA). **Main/Corp** India. Central Board of Irrigation and Power. Research and Development Session. Proceedings. English. ir. **LC** TC903; .A25 subser; TC5. **DD** 333.91/3/0954; 627/.05. ***Continues*** *India. Proceedings of the Annual Research Session.*

DK/0301-7176
PROGRESS REPORT - INSTITUTE OF HYDRODYNAMICS AND HYDRAULIC ENGINEERING (LYNGBY). (PROGRESS REPORT.). [Prog. rep. - Inst. Hydrodyn. & Hydraul. Eng.]. **Main/Corp** Danmark Tekniske Hjskoles. Institute of Hydrodynamics and Hydraulic Engineering. No. 24 (1971)-. Academic Scholarly Publication. English. ir (2 to 3 per year). Free on request. Technical University of Denmark, Library ISVA, Building 115, DK-2800 Lyngby Denmark. **Tel** 45 42 88 48 29, FAX 45 45 93 28 60. **CODEN** PRIEE2. Index available. **Circ:** 300. Documents available from Article Express International. ***Supersedes*** *Danmark Tekniske Hjskoles. Coastal Engineering Laboratory, Copenhagen, Denmark. Basic Research - Progress Report.*
Desc: Short articles on ongoing research in hydraulic engineering, hydrology, offshore engineering, sediment transport, harbor engineering, and wave mechanics.
Ind/Abst Ei Page One; Eng. Index Annu.; Life Sci. Collect.

US
PROGRESS REPORT OF THE MONTANA STATE WATER PLAN. **Main/Corp** Montana. Water Resources Division. **VFOAT** Montana's Water Planning Program Progress Report. English. be. Montana Water Resources Division, Sam W Mitchell Building, Helena MT 59601. **LC** TC424.M9; M68A. **DD** 333.9/1/009786.

US/0361-2651
PROJECTS RECOMMENDED FOR DEAUTHORIZATION, ANNUAL REPORT. (PROJECTS RECOMMENDED FOR DEAUTHORIZATION ... ANNUAL REPORT : COMMUNICATION FROM THE DEPUTY ASSISTANT SECRETARY OF THE ARMY (CIVIL WORKS) ...). **Main/Corp** United States. Office of the Assistant Secretary of the Army (Civil Works). Began with 1st, 1975. English. an. Image Southwest, 517 Main Street, Texarkana TX 75501. **Tel** (903)793-5528, FAX (903)794-0080. **LC** TC423; .U52A. **DD** 333.9/1/00973. available on microfiche (Vols. for (June 19, 1985-) distributed to depository libraries).

AG
PUBLICACAO. SERIE 2-M. RELATORIO DOS SERVICOS EXECUTADOS. **Main/Corp** Brazil. Servico de Piscicultura. Periodical. English. Documents available from BIOSIS Document Express.
Ind/Abst Biol. Abstr.

IT
RAPPORTI E STUDI / ISTITUTO VENETO DI SCIENZE, LETTERE ED ARTI, COMMISSIONE DI STUDIO DEI PROVVEDIMENTI PER LA CONSERVAZIONE E DIFESA DELLA LAGUNA E DELLA CITTA DI VENEZIA. **Added/Corp** Commissione di Studio dei Provvedimenti per la Conservazione e Difesa Della Laguna e Della Citta di Venezia. Vol. 2 (1963)-. Italian (summaries and/or abstracts in English). ir. **LC** TC80.V4; R37. **DD** 627/.0945/31. ***Continues*** *Rapporti Preliminari.*

SP/0213-3660
REIGOS Y DRENAJES XXI. [Riegos dren. XXI]. **VFOAT** Riegos y Drenajes; Riegos y Drenajes 21. **VAT** Riegos y Drenajes Veintiuno. (1985)-. Periodical. Spanish. Six times a year. $93.00. Elsevier Prensa SA, Avenida Paral Lel 180, 08015 Barcelona Spain. **Tel** 011 34 3 3255350, FAX 011 34 3 4252880. **Ad Acc.** Full Page (B&W) 125000ptas. Half Page (B&W) 95000ptas. Full Page (Color) 145000ptas. Half Page (Color) 105000ptas. **Circ:** 3,500.
Desc: Contains information on watering systems, drainage, soils, greenhouses and intensive farming.
Ind/Abst Agric. Eng. Abstr.; Soils Fert.

BL
RELATORIO SINTETICO SOBRE O PROGRAMA DE IRRIGACAO DO NORDESTE. **Main/Corp** Brazil. Superintendencia do Desenvolvimento do Nordeste. (19??)-. Portuguese. **LC** HD1741.B8; B73A.

UK/0958-1278
REPORT / HYDRAULICS RESEARCH STATION. [Rep. - Hydraul. Res. Stn.]. **Added/Corp** Hydraulics Research Station (Great Britain). No. 1 (Feb. 1975)-. Monographic series. English. ir. Price varies per volume. HR Wallingford Ltd., Howbery Park, Wallingford Oxfordshire OX10 8BA UK. **Tel** 011 44 491 835381, FAX 011 44 491 826703, telex 848552 HRSWAL G.
Ind/Abst Life Sci. Collect.

RH
REPORT OF THE SECRETARY FOR WATER DEVELOPMENT (RHODESIA). **See** Water Resources.

US
ROTARY RIGS ACTUALLY MAKING HOLE IN THE US & CANADA. English. Fifty-two times a year (Monday). $75.00. International Association of Drilling Contractors, PO Box 4287, Houston TX 77084. **Tel** (713)578-7171.

UK/0893-4665
ROV REVIEW. [ROV rev.]. Vol. 1 (1985)-. English. be (Nov.-Dec.). £75.00. Oilfield Publications Ltd., PO Box 11, Ledbury Hereford HR8 1BN England. **DD** 620.

US
SAN JOAQUIN VALLEY POST-PROJECT ECONOMIC IMPACT / DEPARTMENT OF WATER RESOURCES, SAN JOAQUIN DISTRICT. English. an. California Department of Water Resources, Box 388, Sacramento CA 95802. **Tel** (916)445-3553. **LC** HD1740.S2795; S26. **DD** 330.9794/8/005.

US
SAWMILL HYDROSTATION REDEVELOPMENT ... ANNUAL REPORT. **VFOAT** Small Scale Hydroelectric Power Demonstration Project. English. an. National Technical Information Service - NTIS, Room 2027S, 5285 Port Royal Road, Springfield VA 22161. **Tel** (703)487-4630, (703)487-4660, (703)487-4650, FAX (703)321-8547, telex 89-9405. **LC** TK1424.N4; S28. **DD** 621.31/2134/09742.

US/0090-6808
SELECTED IRRIGATION RETURN FLOW QUALITY ABSTRACTS. 1st- 1968/69-. English. an. $2.75. Environmental Protection Agency / Washington, 401 M Street SW, Washington DC 20460. **Tel** (202)382-2090. **LC** TC809; .S45. **DD** 016.6317.

JA
SHIKENJO NENPO. **Main/Corp** Mizushigen Kaihatsu Kodan. Shikenjo. (19??)-. Periodical. Japanese. Mizushigen Kaihatsu Kodan Shikenjo, (Lab., Water Resources Development Public Corporation), 936 Jinde Urawashi Saitamaken 336 Japan. **LC** TC401; .M59a.

CC/0256-3118
SHP NEWS. **VFOAT** Small Hydro Power News; Asia-Pacific Regional Network for Small Hydro Power News. (1984)-. English. qt.
Ind/Abst Fluid Abstr., Civil Eng.; Fluid Abstr. Proc. Eng.; FLUIDEX (19??-).

CH
SHUI LI SHUI TIEN CHI SHU. **VFOAT** Shuili Shuidian Jishu; Water Resources and Hydropower Engineering. Periodical. Chinese. NT$0.35. Pei-Ching Pao Kan Fa Hsing Chu, Beijing, People's Republic of China. **Tel** 483531. **LC** TC501; .S57. **DD** 621.2/0422/0951.

CC/0559-9350
SHUILI XUEBAO. (SHUI LI HSUEH PAO.). [Shuili xuebao]. **Added/Corp** Chung-Kuo Shui li Hsueh Hui. **VFOAT** Shuili Xuebao; Journal of Hydraulic Engineering. (19??)-. Periodical. Chinese (summaries and/or abstracts in English). mo. $64.44. Chung-Kuo Kuo Chi Shu Tien, PO Box 2820, Beijing, China. **(Subscription address:** China International Book Trading Corporation, PO Box 399, Library Service Department, Beijing 100044 People's Republic of China.) **LC** TC1; .S583. **DD** 627/.05.
Ind/Abst Ei Page One; Fluid Abstr., Civil Eng.; Fluid Abstr. Proc. Eng.; FLUIDEX (19??-); GeoRef.

US/0882-7427
SPECIAL REPORT IN APPLIED MARINE SCIENCE AND OCEAN ENGINEERING. [Spec. rep. appl. mar. sci. ocean eng.]. **Main/Corp** Virginia Institute of Marine Science. Monographic series. English. ir. Price varies per volume. Virginia Institute of Marine Science, Gloucester Point VA 23062. **Tel** (804)642-7116. **DD** 627. **CODEN** SEVSDG. ctrl circ.
Ind/Abst GeoRef.

UK/0266-2205
SUBSEA ENGINEERING NEWS. [Subsea eng. news]. (1984)-. Periodical. English. Two issues per month. £210.00 UK; £215.00 Europe; £230.00 other. Knighton Enterprises Ltd, 2 Marlborough Street, Faringdon Oxon SN7 7JP England. **Tel** 011 44 367 242525, FAX 011 44 367 241125, telex 449703. **ED** Steve Sasanow. **DD** 665.54405. **Bk Rev. Ad Acc.** ***Continues*** *Oil & Gas Pipeline News, 0262-7906.*
Desc: Technical background and market information on subsea and floating production systems, underwater engineering and pipelines.

JA
SUIRI KOENKAI KOENSHU. **Added/Corp** Doboku Gakkai. Suiri Iinkai. (19??)-. Periodical. Japanese. Doboku Gakkai, (Japan Soc. of Civil Engineers), Yotsuya 1-chome, Shinjuku-ku, Tokyo 160 Japan. **LC** TC5; .S86a.

US/0160-7499
TECHNICAL CONFERENCE PROCEEDINGS / IRRIGATION ASSOCIATION. (TECHNICAL CONFERENCE PROCEEDINGS.). [Tech. conf. proc. - Irrig. Assoc.]. **Main/Corp** Irrigation Association. **Added/Corp** Irrigation Association. Annual Technical Conference Proceedings. **VFOAT** Annual Technical Conference Proceedings. (1977)-. Academic Scholarly Publication. English. an. $20.00. Irrigation Association, 1911 North Fort Myer Drive, Suite 1009, Arlington VA 22209-1630. **Tel** (703)524-1200, FAX (703)524-9544. **LC** S612.2; .S67a. **DD** 631.5/87/05. **CODEN** TCPADV. **Ad Acc, Adv Mgr:** Ryan Eliades. Documents available from Article Express International, CASDDS. ***Continues*** *Technical Conference Proceedings - Sprinkler Irrigation Association, 0364-5576.*
Desc: This book is a complication of presentation given during the Technical Sessions at our yearly Trade Show.
Ind/Abst AGRICOLA [Select. Cov.]; Bioeng. Abstr.; Chem. Abstr.; Ei Page One; Eng. Index Annu.

PH
TECHNICAL PAPER / NATIONAL HYDRAULIC RESEARCH CENTER. **Added/Corp** National Hydraulic Research Center. No. 1 (Jan. 1980)-. English.

US/0545-3038
TECHNICAL REPORT (NEW MEXICO. STATE ENGINEER OFFICE). (TECHNICAL REPORT - NEW MEXICO STATE ENGINEER.). [Tech. rep. - N. M. State Eng.]. No. 1-. Monographic series. English. ir. Price varies per volume. **LC** TC424.N6; A3. **DD** 628.1.
Ind/Abst GeoRef.

US/0555-8026
TECHNICAL REPORT - PURDUE UNIVERSITY, WATER RESOURCES RESEARCH CENTER. **See** Water Resources.

US/0500-473X
TECHNICAL REPORT - U. S. WATERWAYS EXPERIMENT STATION, VICKSBURG, MISS. **Main/Corp** Waterways Experiment Station (U.S.). English. U S Waterways Experiment Station, PO Box 631, Vicksburg MI 39180. **LC** TC7. **DD** 627.072.

TU
TEKNIK BULTEN. **Main/Corp** Insaat Muhendisleri Odas. Periodical. Turkish (summaries and/or abstracts in English, French and German). Selanik Cad 19/1, Yenisehir-Ankara Turkey. **LC** TC1; .I66.

NE/0376-6411
TERRA ET AQUA. [Terra aqua]. No. 3/4 (1973)-. Periodical. English (French). Three times a year. Free. International Association of Dredging Companies, PO Box 80521, NL 2508 GM Hague The Netherlands. **Tel** 011 31 70 3523334, FAX 011 31 70 3512654, telex 31102 NL. **ED** Marsha Cohen. **LC** TC187; .T47. **DD** 627/.73. Index Bound in First Issue. **Bk Rev**, (Qty: 6/yr). **Circ:** 4000 (ctrl). Documents available from Documents on Demand. ***Continues*** *Terra.*
Desc: International journal on dredging, public works, ports and waterways development. Public domain publication.
Ind/Abst Coal Abstr.; Environ. Abstr.; Fish Rev.; Fluid Abstr., Civil Eng.; Fluid Abstr. Proc. Eng.; FLUIDEX (1973-); Geogr. Abstr. Phys. Geogr.; Geogr. Abstr. Human Geogr. (?-?); Geol. Abstr.; Int. Dev. Abstr. (?-?); Wildl. Rev.

JA
TOKYO-TO SUIBO KEIKAKU. **Main/Corp** Tokyo. Kensetsukyoku. Kasenbu. Bosaika. Japanese. Tokyo-to Kensetsukyoku Kasenbu Bosaika, 5-1 Marunouch 3-chome, Chiyoda-ku 100 Tokyo Japan. **LC** TC505.5.T64; T6A.

FR
TRADUCTIONS. French. ir. 1264.76F France; 1500.00F EEC; 1700.00F other. Association Technique de l'Industrie des Liants Hydrauliques (ATILH), 8 rue Villiot, 75012 Paris France. **Tel** 011 33 1 43460070, FAX 43.44.78.11, telex 240 020 F.
Ind/Abst SPORT Discus.

II/0589-3127
TRANSACTIONS - CONGRESS ON IRRIGATION AND DRAINAGE. **Main/Conf** Congress on Irrigation and Drainage. **Added/Corp** International Commission on Irrigation and Drainage. **VFOAT** Compte Rendu - Congres des Irrigations et du Drainage. (1951)-. Multiple languages (English and French; summaries and/or abstracts in English and French). ir. International Commission on Irrigation and Drainage, 48 Nyaya Marg Chanakyapuri, New Delhi 110021 India. **Tel** 011 91 11 3016837, telex 031-65920 ICID IN. **(Subscription address:** Prints India, 11 Darya Ganj, New Delhi 110002 India.**)** **LC** TC801; .C57. **DD** 627.

US/0254-0703
TRANSACTIONS ... CONGRESS ON LARGE DAMS. [C. r. - Comm. int. grands barrages, Congr. int. grands barrages]. **Main/Conf** International Congress on Large Dams. **VFOAT** Compte Rendu ... Congres des Grands Barrages; Actas y Memorias ... Congreso de Grandes Presas; Gesamtbericht ... Talsperrenkongress. Began with 1st, in 1933. English (French, German and Spanish). te. **CODEN** TICDDH.

CH/0253-3804
TU MU SHUI LI. **See** Engineering-Civil Engineering.

NE
VERLAG / DIENST WEG- EN WATERBOUWKUNDE. **Main/Corp** Netherlands. Fijkswaterstaat. Dienst Weg- en Waterbouwkunde. **VFOAT** Jaarverslag. Dutch. an. Ministerie van Verkeer en Waterstaat Rijkswaterstaat Dienst Weg- en Waterbouwkunde, 2600 GA Delft, Postbus 5044, Van der Burghweg Netherlands. **Tel** 015-569307. **LC** PAR.

HU/0042-7616
VIZUGYI KOZLEMENYEK. [Vizugyi kozl.]. **VFOAT** Voprosy Gidrotekhiki; Hydraulic Engineering; Revue d'Hydraulique; Wasserbauliche Mitteilungen; Hydraulic Proeedings. (1911)-. Academic Scholarly Publication. Hungarian. qt. Lapkiado Vallalat, Lenin Korut 9-11, 1073 Budapest 7, Hungary. **Tel** 222-408. **LC** GB726.H8. **CODEN** VIKOA7. Documents available from Article Express International.
Ind/Abst AGRICOLA; Bioeng. Abstr.; Coal Abstr.; Ei Page One; EMBASE; Eng. Index Annu.; Fluid Abstr., Civil Eng.; Fluid Abstr. Proc. Eng.; FLUIDEX (1973-); GeoRef; Soils Fert.

UN/0320-8702
VOPROSY GIDRODINAMIKI I TEPLOOBMENA V KRIOGENNYH SISTEMAH. (VOPROSY GIDRODINAMIKI I TEPLOOBMENA V KRIOGENNYKH SISTEMAKH.). **Main/Corp** Fizyko-Tekhnichnyi Instytut Nyzkykh Temperatur (Akademiia Nauk Ukrainskoi RSR). Began in 1970. Academic Scholarly Publication. Russian. 0.85rub single issue. **LC** TP480; .A38B. **CODEN** VGTSDJ. Documents available from CASDDS.
Ind/Abst Chem. Abstr.

SZ/0377-905X
WASSER, ENERGIE, LUFT. [Wasser, Energ., Luft]. **VFOAT** Eau, Energie, Air. (Jan. 1976)-. Periodical. German (French). Seven times a year. 120.00F Switzerland; 140.00F other. Schweizerischer Wasserwirtschaftsverband, Schaftsverband Ruetistr 3A, CH-5401 Baden Switzerland. **Tel** 011 41 56 225069. **ED** G Weber. **LC** TC1; .S4. **Circ:** 3,000. ***Continues*** *Wasser- und Energiewirtschaft, 0043-096X.*
Ind/Abst Int. Civil Eng. Abstr.; Soft. Abstr. Eng.

GW/0043-0986
WASSERWIRTSCHAFT-WASSERTECHNIK (BERLIN, DDR). (WASSERWIRTSCHAFT-WASSERTECHNIK.). [Wasserwirtsch.-Wassertech.]. **Added/Corp** Kammer der Technik. Vol. 1 (July 1951)-. Academic Scholarly Publication. German. ir. DM123.20, $89.17 Germany; DM142.00, $102.78 other. Verlag Fuer Bauwesen GmbH, AM Friedrichshain 22, D-10407 Berlin Germany. **Tel** 011 49 30 4287241. **LC** TC1; .W277. **CODEN** WSWSAO. Documents available from CASDDS.
Ind/Abst Chem. Abstr. (19??-); EMBASE (19??-); Fluid Abstr., Civil Eng. (19??-); Fluid Abstr. Proc. Eng. (19??-); FLUIDEX (1973-); GeoRef (19??-); Int. Civil Eng. Abstr. (19??-); Soft. Abstr. Eng. (19??-).

US
WATER ACTIVITIES TRADE REPORT. English. bw. $100.00. American Water Foundation, 1616 17th Street, Suite 376, Denver CO 80202. **Tel** (303)628-5516, FAX (303)628-5469. **ED** Michael R Vaughan. **Circ:** 100 (ctrl).
Desc: An important AWF service to manufacturers, consulting engineering firms, construction companies and others with an interest in international developments in irrigation and drainage, water supply or hydropower. Provides timely coverage of upcoming projects.

US/0273-2238
WATER ENGINEERING & MANAGEMENT. [Water eng. manage.]. **VFOAT** Water Engineering and Management; Water/Engineering & Management. Vol. 128, No. 1 (Jan. 1981)-. Academic Scholarly Publication. English. mo. $25.00 (one year), $40.00 (two year), $60.00 (three year) US; $45.00 (one year $60.00 (two year), $75.00 (three year) other. Scranton Gillette Communications Inc., 380 East Northwest Highway, Des Plaines IL 60016-2282. **Tel** (708)298-6622, FAX (708)390-0408. **ED** Ian Lisk. **LC** TD1; .W36. **DD** 628/.05. **CODEN** WENMD2. **[CCC]. Ad Acc. Pr Rev. Circ:** 32,125 (ctrl). available on microfilm and microfiche from University Microfilms International (UMI). Documents available from Article Express International, The Genuine Article, UMI Article Clearinghouse, CASDDS, Documents on Demand. ***Formed by the union of*** *Water & Sewage Works, 0043-1125* ***and*** *Water & Wastes Engineering, 0043-115X.*
Ind/Abst ABI/INFORM Glob. Ed.; ABI Inform Ondisc (Jan. 1988-); Abstr. Bull. Inst. Pap. Sci. Tech.; Appl. Sci. Technol. Index; AQUAREF; Aquat. Sci. Fish. Abstr. (Computer File); Bioeng. Abstr.; Chem. Abstr.; Curr. Contents, Agric. Biol. Environ. Sci.; Curr. Contents Eng. Tech. Appl. Sci.; Ei Page One; EMBASE; Energy Inf. Abstr.; Energy Res. Abstr. (April 1982-); Eng. Index Annu.; Environ. Abstr.; F&S Index Plus Text, Int. [Select. Cov.]; Fluid Abstr., Civil Eng.; Fluid Abstr. Proc. Eng.; FLUIDEX (1981-); GeoRef; Int. Civil Eng. Abstr.; Life Sci. Collect.; Pollut. Abstr. Indexes; Proc. Chem. Eng.; PROMT; Protozoolog. Abstr.; Res. Alert [Full Cov.]; Sci. Cit. Index; SCISEARCH; Soc. Sci. Cit. Index [Select. Cov.]; Theoret. Chem. Eng.; UMI ABI/Inform--Bus. Period. Ondisc (Jan. 1988-) [Full Txt.].

US/1055-0348
WAVES (SPRING VALLEY, CALIF.). ***Title Change.*** (WAVES.). [Waves]. Vol. 10, No. 4 (Jan./Feb. 1991)-(19??). Periodical. English. bm. Windate Enterprises Inc, PO Box 368, Spring Valley CA 92077. **Tel** (619)660-0402, FAX (619)660-0408. **ED** Deam Given. **DD** 623. **CODEN** WAVEEP. **Bk Rev. Ad Acc. Circ:** 5,000 (ctrl). ***Continues*** *Subnotes, 0889-7166.* ***Continued by*** *Underwater News and Technology, 1069-6547.*
Desc: International ocean technology news magazine. ROVs, salvage, diving instrumentation, oil exploration, military applications, submersibles.

PH
WORKING PAPER (INTERNATIONAL FOOD POLICY RESEARCH INSTITUTE). (WORKING PAPER - INTERNATIONAL FOOD POLICY RESEARCH INSTITUTE (PHILIPPINES).). No. 1-. Monographic series. English. Price varies per volume.

PL
ZESZYT NAUKOWY. BUDOWNICTWO WODNE I INZYNIERIA SANITARNA. **Added/Corp** Politechnika Krakowska. **VFOAT** Budownictwo Wodne i Inzynieria Sanitarna. Part 19 (1972)-. Monographic series. Polish (summaries and/or abstracts in English and Russian). mo. Price varies per volume. **(Subscription address:** ARS Polona, PO Box 1001, 00068 Warsaw Poland.**)** **LC** TC1.B83. ***Continues*** *Zeszyt Naukowy (Politechnika Krakowska). Budownictwo Wodne.*

INDUSTRIAL ENGINEERING AND DESIGN

GW/0340-3386
3 R, ROHRE, ROHRLEITUNGSBAU, ROHRLEITUNGSTRANSPORT. (3 I.E. DREI R, ROHRE, ROHRLEITUNGSBAU, ROHRLEITUNGSTRANSPORT.). [3 R, Rohre, Rohrleitungsbau, Rohrleitungstransp.]. **VFOAT** 3 [i.e. Drei] R International; Rohre, Rohrleitungsbau, Rohrleitungstransport. (1974)-. Academic Scholarly Publication. German (summaries and/or abstracts in English and French). Ten times a year. DM333.00. Vulkan-Verlag, Dr. W. Classen, Postfach 103962, D 45039 Essen 1 Germany. **Tel** 011 49 201 8200214, telex 8579008. **ED** D. Schmidt. **LC** TS280; .R565. **CODEN** RRRIDC. **[CCC].** Index available. cum. index. **Bk Rev. Ad Acc. Circ:** 2,800. Documents available from CASDDS. ***Continues*** *Rohre, Rohrleitungsbau, Rohrleitungstransport.*
Desc: Covers materials and manufacturing pipes, design laying operations of pipelines and industrial piping systems, testing and control devices. Processes quality assurance and valves.
Ind/Abst Alum. Ind. Abstr.; Chem. Abstr.; Coal Abstr.; Energy Res. Abstr. (Aug. 1976-); Fluid Abstr., Civil Eng.; Fluid Abstr. Proc. Eng.; FLUIDEX (1974-1989); Met. Abstr.

UK/0263-6174
ADSORPTION SCIENCE & TECHNOLOGY. **See** Engineering-Chemical Engineering.

US/0272-4790
ADVANCES IN DRYING. ***Ceased.*** [Adv. dry.]. Vol. 1 (1980)-Vol. 5 (199?). Academic Scholarly Publication. English. ir. Taylor & Francis Ltd., Rankine Road, Basingstoke Hampshire, RG24 8PR United Kingdom. **Tel** 011 44 256 840366, FAX 011 44 256 479438, telex 858540. **(Subscription address:** Taylor & Francis Inc., 1900 Frost Road, Suite 101, Bristol PA 19007-1598.**)** **LC** TP363; .A29. **CODEN** ADDRDO. **[CCC].** Documents available from CASDDS.
Desc: An authoritative book series, innovative, applied and industrial developments in the art, science, and technology of drying.
Ind/Abst Chem. Abstr.; Ei Page One.

FR/0294-1228
ANNALES FRANCAISES DES MICROTECHNIQUES ET DE CHRONOMETRIE. **See** Physics.

CN/0701-5151
ANNUAL REPORT / ALBERTA RESEARCH COUNCIL. [Annu. rep. - Alta. Res. Counc.]. **Main/Corp** Alberta Research Council. **VAT** Annual Report - Alberta Research. Began in 1972. English. an. Free. Alberta Research Council, PO Box 8330 Postal Station F, Edmonton Alberta T6H 5X2 Canada. **Tel** (403)432-8122. **ED** Elizabeth Page. **LC** Q21; .R4. **CODEN** AALRA6. **Circ:** 5,000. ***Continues*** *Research Council of Alberta. Annual Report, 0080-1526.*
Desc: Review of research and development programs in energy, agriculture, advanced technologies, industrial engineering and environment.
Ind/Abst GeoRef.

AT
ANNUAL REPORT / DIVISION OF MATERIALS SCIENCE AND TECHNOLOGY, CSIRO AUSTRALIA. **See** Engineering-Materials Engineering and Mechanics.

UA
ANNUAL REPORT / INDUSTRIAL TECHNOLOGY APPLICATION PROGRAM. **Main/Corp** Industrial Technology Application Program (Egypt). 1983-. English. an. Engineering & Industrial Development Center, 203 Pyramids Road Giza, PO Box 2267, Cairo Egypt. **LC** HC830.Z9; I525A. **DD** 354.620082.

US/0149-3965
ANNUAL REPORT - UNITED TECHNOLOGIES. **Main/Corp** United Technologies Corporation. 1975-. English. an. United Technologies Corporation, PO Box 981, South Windsor CT 06074. **Tel** (203)282-4200. **LC** HD9680.U54; U548. **DD** 338.7/68. ***Supersedes*** *United Aircraft Corporation. Annual Report to Stockholders.*

JA/0570-4480
ANZEN KOGAKU. [Anzen kogaku]. **Added/Corp** Anzen Kogaku Kyokai (Japan). **VFOAT** Journal of Japan Society for Safety Engineering. (1962)-. Academic Scholarly Publication. Japanese (summaries and/or abstracts in English). bm. $174.00. Anzen Kogaku Kyokai, (Japan Society for Safety Engineering), Daiwa Ginko Biru, 3F, 4-47, Onoecho, Nakaku, Yokohamashi, Kanagawaken 231 Japan. **(Subscription address:** Japan Publications Trading Company, Ltd., PO Box 5030,

Tokyo International, Tokyo 100-31 Japan.) **LC** IN PROCESS; T55; .K52. **CODEN** ANKOBG. Documents available from CASDDS.
Ind/Abst Chem. Abstr.; Coal Abstr.

UK/0003-682X
APPLIED ACOUSTICS. (APPLIED ACOUSTICS. ACOUSTIQUE APPLIQUE. ANGEWANDTE AKUSTIK.). [Appl. acoust.]. **VFOAT** Acoustique Applique; Angewandte Akustik. Vol. 1 (Jan. 1968)-. Academic Scholarly Publication. English (French and German). Twelve times a year. $798.00 The Americas; £535.00 other. Elsevier Applied Science, An Imprint of Elsevier Science Ltd., The Boulevard, Langford Lane, Kidlington, Oxford OX5 1GB United Kingdom. **Tel** 011 44 865 843000, 011 44 865 843699, FAX 011 44 865 843010. **(Subscription address:** Elsevier Science Ltd. Oxford Fulfillment Centre, PO Box 800, Kidlington, Oxford OX5 1DX United Kingdom.**)** **ED** Peter Lord, Theodore J. Schultz and Z. Maekawa. **LC** TA365; .A6. **DD** 620.2/05. **CODEN** AACOBL. **[CCC].** Index available in last issue of volume--attached. **Bk Rev. Ad Acc. Pr Rev. Circ:** 800. available on microfilm and microfiche from University Microfilms International (UMI). Documents available from Article Express International, The Genuine Article, Ask*IEEE, Documents on Demand.
Desc: Concerned with the application of acoustic principles to design problems and materials used in their solution. Relevant to buildings, industrial equipment, transport, environmental health, etc.
Ind/Abst Acoust. Abstr. (1973-); Agric. Eng. Abstr.; Bioeng. Abstr.; BMT Abstr. (-199?); Coal Abstr.; Curr. Contents Eng. Tech. Appl. Sci.; Ei Page One; EMBASE; Eng. Index Annu.; Environ. Abstr.; Fluid Abstr., Civil Eng.; Fluid Abstr. Proc. Eng.; FLUIDEX (1973-); INSPEC (July 1969-); Int. Aerosp. Abstr.; Res. Alert [Select. Cov.]; Saf. Health Work; SCISEARCH; Shock Vibr. Dig.

US/1042-0959
APPLIED THERMAL SCIENCES. ***Ceased.*** [Appli. therm. sci.]. **VFOAT** Promyshlennaia Teplotekhnika. Vol. 1, No. 1 (Jan./Feb. 1988)-Vol. 2, No. 4 (19??). Periodical. English. bm. John Wiley & Sons, Inc., 605 Third Avenue, New York NY 10158-0012. **Tel** (212)850-6000, (212)850-6645, FAX (212)850-6088, telex 12-7063. **(Subscription address:** John Wiley & Sons / England, Baffins Lane, Chichester, West Sussex PO19 1UD England.**)** **ED** Novak Zuber. **LC** TJ260; .P766. **DD** 621.402. available on microfilm and microfiche from University Microfilms International (UMI). Documents available from Article Express International.
Desc: This journal is a translation of the Soviet publication Promyshlennaya Teplotekhnika (Industrial Thermal Engineering). It offers a combination of theoretical papers, articles dealing with engineering design, research and data on new processes and devices, and in-depth descriptions of actual industrial experience in applied thermal sciences, energy conservation and fluid mechanics.
Ind/Abst Eng. Index Annu.

FR/0294-8567
ARCHITECTURE INTERIEURE-C.R.E.E. **See** Architecture.

SP/0213-3113
AUTOMATICA E INSTRUMENTACION. **See** Computers-Automation.

NZ/0110-6295
AUTOMATION AND CONTROL. **See** Computers-Automation.

US/0360-8352
COMPUTERS & INDUSTRIAL ENGINEERING. [Comput. ind. eng.]. **VAT** Computers and Industrial Engineering. (1976)-. Periodical. English. Eight times a year. $963.00 The Americas; £646.00 other. Pergamon Press, An Imprint of Elsevier Science Ltd., The Boulevard, Langford Lane, Kidlington, Oxford OX5 1GB United Kingdom. **Tel** 011 44 865 843000, 011 44 865 843699, FAX 011 44 865 843010. **(Subscription address:** Elsevier Science Ltd. Oxford Fulfillment Centre, PO Box 800, Kidlington, Oxford OX5 1DX United Kingdom.**)** **ED** G. E. Whitehouse, Hamed Kamal Eldin, and Yasser Hosni. **LC** T57.5; .C637. **DD** 658.5/0028/54. **CODEN** CINDDL. **[CCC]. Pr Rev.** available on microfilm and microfiche from University Microfilms International (UMI). Documents available from Article Express International, The Genuine Article, Ask*IEEE, UMI Article Clearinghouse.
Desc: Covers computerized industrial engineering applications, methodology for developing viable computer solutions to industrial engineering problems, as well as the implementation of different industrial engineering techniques on computers.
Ind/Abst ABI/INFORM Glob. Ed.; ABI Inform Ondisc (1976-); ACM Guide Comput. Lit.; Bioeng. Abstr.; BMT Abstr. (?-199?); Compumath Citation Index [Full Cov.]; Comput. Abstr.; Comput. Rev. (1976-); Cumul. Index Nurs. Allied Health Lit.; Curr. Contents Eng. Tech. Appl. Sci.; Ei Page One; Eng. Index Annu.; Ergon. Abstr.; Fluid Abstr., Civil Eng.; Fluid Abstr. Proc. Eng.; FLUIDEX; Gen. BusinessFile (1992-); Inf. Sci. Abstr.; INSPEC (1978-); Oper. Res./Manag. Sci.; Pollut. Abstr. Indexes; Res. Alert [Full Cov.]; Robotics Abstr.; SCISEARCH; Soc. Sci. Cit. Index [Select. Cov.].

US
CONFERENCE RECORD - INDUSTRIAL & COMMERCIAL POWER SYSTEM TECHNICAL CONFERENCE. **Main/Conf** Industrial & Commercial Power System Technical Conference. **VFOAT** IEEE Industrial and Commercial Power Systems. 1977-. English. ir. IEEE, Institution of Electrical and Electronics Engineers, Inc., 345 East 47th Street, New York NY 10017-2394. **Tel** (908)981-1393, FAX (908)981-9667. **(Subscription address:** IEEE Service Center, 445 Hoes Lane, Piscataway, NJ 08854; telephone: (201)981-1393**)** **LC** TK3001; .I47. **DD** 621.31. ***Continues*** *IEEE Conference Record of Industrial & Commercial Power Systems Technical Conference.*
Ind/Abst Energy Res. Abstr. (Dec. 1979-); Index IEEE Publ.

US/0892-5046
CONSULTING-SPECIFYING ENGINEER. [Consult.-specif. eng.]. **VFOAT** Consulting Specifying Engineer. Vol. 1, No. 1 (Jan. 1987)-. Trade Publication. English. mo (13 issues per year). $75.00 US; $118.00 Canada; $110.00 Mexico; $145.00 (surface mail) other. Cahners Publishing Company, 249 West 17th Street, New York NY 10011. **Tel** (212)645-0067, FAX (212)242-6987. **(Subscription address:** Cahners Publishing Company / Colorado, Paid Subscription Service Center, PO Box 7610, Highlands Ranch CO 80126-7610.**)** **ED** Robert L. Oliverson. **LC** TA1; .C777. **DD** 620. **[CCC].** Index available. cum. index. **Bk Rev. Ad Acc. Circ:** 50,000 (ctrl). available on microfilm and microfiche from University Microfilms International (UMI). Documents available from UMI Article Clearinghouse. ***Formed by the union of*** *Consulting Engineer, 0010-7107* ***and*** *Specifying Engineer, 0164-5242.*
Desc: Written for engineering professionals who design, specify and select mechanical-electrical/electronic equipment for the commercial, industrial, institutional, new and retrofit building construction industry. Essential integrated engineering concepts centered around HVAC, electrical distribution, plumbing, life safety, and building control systems are covered.
Ind/Abst ABI/INFORM Glob. Ed.; ABI Inform Ondisc (March 1988-); Appl. Sci. Technol. Index; Constr. Index; Ei Page One; F&S Index Plus Text, Int. [Select. Cov.]; INIS Atomindex [Micro.]; PROMT.

XR
CZECHOSLOVAK INDUSTRIAL DESIGN. (1968)-. Periodical. English. sa. **(Subscription address:** Artia Pegas Press Ltd., Palac Metro Narodni Trida 25, 11210 Prague 1 Czech Republic.**)** **DD** 745. **Bk Rev. Circ:** 2,000.
Desc: Problems of the development and application of industrial design.

US/0418-7679
DESIGN IN STEEL. **See** Metals and Metallurgy.

FR
DESIGN INDUSTRIE. **VFOAT** Esthetique Industrielle, Nouvelle Serie. 75- Nov./Dec. 1965-. Periodical. French. ***Continues*** *Esthetique Industrielle.*

UK/0011-9245
DESIGN (LONDON). ***Ceased.*** (DESIGN.). [Design]. No. 1 (Jan. 1949)-. Periodical. English. mo. Design Council, 28 Haymarket, London SW1Y 4SU England. **Tel** 011 44 71 839 8000, FAX 011 44 71 925 2130, telex 8812963. **ED** Steve Braidwood. **LC** TA175; .D38. **DD** 745.4305. Index available. **Bk Rev. Ad Acc. Circ:** 15,000. available on microfilm and microfiche from University Microfilms International (UMI). Documents available from The Genuine Article.
Desc: Covers all aspects of modern industrial design, with regular design surveys of industries. The best work from design practices and a review of new products worldwide.
Ind/Abst Archit. Period. Index (1977-); Art Index; ARTbibliogr. Mod.; Arts Humanit. Citation Index [Full Cov.]; Avery Index Archit. Period. Suppl. Colum. Univ. (1990-); Ceram. Abstr.; Curr. Technol. Index; Ergon. Abstr.; Int. Civil Eng. Abstr.; Manage. Market. Abstr.; Print. Abstr.; Res. Alert [Full Cov.]; Saf. Health Work; Soft. Abstr. Eng.; Tech. Educ. Train. Abstr.

US/0011-9407
DESIGN NEWS. [Des. news]. Vol. 1 (Nov. 1946)-. Periodical. English. sm (24 issues). $95.00 US; $150.00 Canada; $140.00 Mexico; $180.00 (surface mail) other. Cahners Publishing Company, 249 West 17th Street, New York NY 10011. **Tel** (212)645-0067, FAX (212)242-6987. **(Subscription address:** Cahners Publishing Company / Colorado, Paid Subscription Service Center, PO Box 7610, Highlands Ranch CO 80126-7610.**)** **LC** TA175; .D4. **CODEN** DIGNAO. **[CCC].** Documents available from Article Express International, Ask*IEEE, UMI Article Clearinghouse.
Desc: An engineering news and applications magazine. Features application stories on the latest technologies. Written for design engineers and managers in the original equipment market, it showcases innovative materials, components and subsystems that improve products in such fields as aerospace, appliances, autos, computers, defense, machine tools, medical equipment, and telecommunications.
Ind/Abst Acad. Search (July 1993-); Alum. Ind. Abstr.; Appl. Sci. Technol. Index (1959-); Bioeng. Abstr.; Ei Page One; Energy Inf. Abstr.; Eng. Index Annu. [Select. Cov.]; Expand. Acad. Index (1992-); Gen. Period. Index (1985-); INFO-SOUTH Abstr.; INSPEC (1970-1986); Mag. Index Plus (1989-); Mag. Search; Met. Abstr. (1970-1986); Newsp. Period. Abstr. (1988-); Shock Vibr. Dig.; Mag. Index (1981-); Trade Ind. Index (1970-1986); Vocat. Search (July 1993-).

JA/0385-3462
DESIGN NEWS. **VFOAT** Dezain Joho. Periodical. Japanese. bm. $135.00. Nihon Sangyo Dezain Shinkokai, c/o Sekai Boeki Senta Building ku 105, Tokyo Japan. **Tel** (03)435-5633 OR (03)435-5634, FAX (03)432-7346. **LC** TS171.A1; D473. Index available. **Ad Acc. Circ:** 3,500.
Desc: Introduces such case histories and tasks as design development, design methodology, design promotion, design information index, etc.
Ind/Abst Acoust. Abstr.; Appl. Sci. Technol. Index; Bus. Index (1985-); Ceram. Abstr.; F&S Index Plus Text, Int. [Select. Cov.]; Gen. BusinessFile (1985-); PROMT.

US
DESIGN NEWS SPECIFIER'S ANNUAL DIRECTORY. V. 1- 1970-. Directory. English. an. Rogers Publishing Company, 270 St Paul Street, Denver CO 80206. **LC** TA175; .D39. **DD** 621.8/15/02573.

US/1046-980X
DESIGN PROCESSES NEWSLETTER. [Des. process. newsl.]. **Added/Corp** Illinois Institute of Technology. Design Processes Laboratory. **VFOAT** Design Processes. (198?)-. Newsletter. English. Six times a year. $15.00. Design Processes Lab IIT, 10 West 35th Street, Chicago IL 60616. **Tel** (312)808-5308 or (312)808-5300, FAX (312)808-5338. **ED** Kuihsiang Chen. **DD** 620. **Circ:** 2,500.

UK
DESIGN PRODUCTS & APPLICATIONS. **VFOAT** Design Products and Applications. (19??)-. Periodical. English. mo. £55.00 UK; £75.00 Europe; £100.00 other. IML Group, Blair House, 184-186 High Street, Tonbridge Kent, TN9 1BQ England. **Tel** 011 44 732 359990, FAX 011 44 732 770049. **ED** Bob Brooks. **LC** Discard. Index available. **Bk Rev. Ad Acc, Adv Mgr:** Andrew Quenault. **Circ:** 36,110 (ctrl).
Desc: Product and application stories for design engineers.
Ind/Abst Fluid Abstr., Civil Eng.; Fluid Abstr. Proc. Eng.; FLUIDEX.

US/0011-9415
DESIGN QUARTERLY (MINNEAPOLIS, MINN.). **See** Architecture.

UK/0142-694X
DESIGN STUDIES. [Des. stud.]. **Added/Corp** Design Research Society. Vol. 1, No. 1 (July 1979)-. Periodical. English. qt. $343.00 The Americas; £230.00 other. Butterworth Heinemann Publishers, Linacre House, Jordan Hill, Oxford OX2 8DP England. **Tel** 011 44 865 310366. **(Subscription address:** Elsevier Science Ltd. Oxford Fulfillment Centre, PO Box 800, Kidlington, Oxford OX5 1DX United Kingdom.**)** **ED** Nigel Cross (editor's address: The Open University, Milton Keynes United Kingdom). **LC** NA2750; .D416. **DD** 745.2/05. **CODEN** DSSTD5. **[CCC].** Index available. **Bk Rev. Ad Acc.** available on microfilm and microfiche from University Microfilms International (UMI). Documents available from Article Express International.
Desc: Articles on all aspects of design - its nature and effectiveness. Covers its roles in industry and society which develop from comparisons of its applications in all areas, including architecture, engineering, planning and industrial design.
Ind/Abst Archit. Period. Index (1979-); ARTbibliogr. Mod.; ARTbibliogr. Curr. Titles; Avery Index Archit. Period. Suppl. Colum. Univ. (1990-); Bioeng. Abstr.; Comput. Rev.; Educ. Technol. Abstr.; Ei Page One; Eng. Index Annu.; Ergon. Abstr.; HILITES; J. Plan. Lit.; Stud. Women Abstr.; Tech. Educ. Train. Abstr.

US/1066-7504
DESIGN TECHNOLOGIES. ***Ceased.*** [Des. technol.]. (Oct. 1992)-(Feb. 1994). Periodical. English. mo. Cardiff Publishing Company, 6300 South Syracuse Way, Suite 650, Englewood CO 80111. **Tel** (303)220-0600, telex 450726. **(Subscription address:** PO Box 1077, Skokie, IL 60076, Tel. (708)647-1200**)** **DD** 620. ***Continues*** *Design Management, 1042-8534.*

GW
DESIGNERS DIGEST MAGAZINE. **See** The Arts-Graphic Arts.

US/0163-6669
DESIGNFAX. Vol. 1 (April 1979)-. Periodical. English. mo. $54.00 US; $85.00 Canada and Mexico; $155.00 other. Huebcore Communications Inc., 1355 Mendiota Heights, Suite 210, Mendiota Heights MN 55120. **Tel** (612)686-0303. **ED** David T Curry. **[CCC]. Ad Acc. Circ:** 110,047 (ctrl).
Desc: Serves the design engineering function in the original equipment market (OEM).
Ind/Abst Ei Page One.

US/0897-0432
DIRECTORY OF INDUSTRIAL DESIGNERS. [Dir. ind. des.]. **Main/Corp** Industrial Designers Society of America. (198?)-. Directory. English. an. $85.00. Industrial Designers Society of America, 1142 Walker Road, Suites E & F, Great Falls VA 22066. **Tel** (703)759-0100, FAX (703)759-7679. **LC** TS171.A1; I49315. **DD** 745.2/025/73. ***Continues*** *Membership Directory / Industrial Designers Society of America, 0741-2916.*

UK/0013-7898
ENGINEERING DESIGNER. [Eng. des.]. **Added/Corp** Institution of Engineering Designers. (1950)-. Periodical. English (French). Six times a year (Jan., Mar., May, July, Sept., Nov.). £25.00 UK & Eire; $68.00 US & Canada; £32.50 other. Institution of Engineering Designers, Courtleigh Westbury Leigh, Westbury Wilts BA13 3TA England. **Tel** 011 44 373 822801, FAX 011 44 373 858085. **ED** M.J. Osborne. **CODEN** ENDSA2. Index available. **Bk Rev. Ad Acc. Circ:** 7,000 (ctrl). Documents available from Ask*IEEE. ***Absorbed*** *Drawing Office Announcer.*
Desc: News, views, and features of interest to engineering designers. Related to innovation, education, and new technologies.
Ind/Abst Curr. Technol. Index; Fluid Abstr., Civil Eng.; Fluid Abstr. Proc. Eng.; FLUIDEX (1973-); INSPEC (Jan./Feb. 1989-)(Jan.-Feb. 1989-); Surf. Treat. Technol. Abstr.

US/0013-7944
ENGINEERING FRACTURE MECHANICS. See Engineering-Materials Engineering and Mechanics.

UK/0261-2097
EUREKA (BECKENHAM). (EUREKA.). [Eureka]. **VFOAT** Eureka Transfers Technology. (1980)-. Periodical. English. mo. £60.00 UK; £95.00 other. Findlay Publications Ltd, Franks Hall, Horton Kirby, Kent DA4 9LL England. **Tel** 011 44 (0322)222222, FAX 011 44 (0322)289577. **ED** Kevin O'Toole. **CODEN** ERKAEF. **Bk Rev. Ad Acc. Circ:** 26,780 (ctrl). Documents available from Ask*IEEE. ***Absorbed*** *Engineering Materials and Design, 0308-6917.*
Desc: Covers new products, materials and applications for OEM design engineers in the field of machinery, consumer products, and other mechanical/electrical equipment.
Ind/Abst Fluid Abstr., Civil Eng.; Fluid Abstr. Proc. Eng.; FLUIDEX (19??-); INSPEC (1989-).

US
FINANCIAL TIMES INDUSTRIAL COMPANIES. VOLUME III, ENGINEERING. **VFOAT** Industrial Companies. Volume III, Engineering. (1988)-. an. £95.00. Longman Group Ltd., Fourth Avenue, Longman House, Harlow Essex CM19 5SR England. **Tel** 011 44 279 429655, FAX 011 44 279 431059, telex 81259. **(Subscription address:** Fourth Avenue, Harlow Essex CM19 5AA England) **LC** TA12; .F55. ***Continues in part*** *Financial Times Industrial Companies Year Book.*

FI/0358-8904
FORM FUNCTION FINLAND. **Added/Corp** Suomen Taideteollisuusyhdistys. **VFOAT** Form Function. (1980)-. Periodical. English. qt. Fmk150.00 Finland; Fmk200.00 other. The Finnish Society of Crafts and Design, Fabianinkatu 10, 00130 Helsinki 13 Finland. **Tel** 011 358 0 171621, FAX 011 358 0 651449. **(Subscription address:** Art Consulting: Scandanavia, 25777 Punto de Vista Drive, Calabass CA 91302-2155.) **ED** Tapio Pertainen & Iiisa Aula. **LC** NK1471.F5; F67. **DD** 745.4/497897/05. Index available (one year or two years; bound in one issue). cum. index. **Bk Rev**, (Qty: 10). **Ad Acc. Circ:** 5,000 (ctrl).
Desc: FFF is a quarterly magazine in English on design, art, architecture and visual culture in its broadest sense. Covers the environment, lifestyle, and quality of life.
Ind/Abst ARTbibliogr. Mod. (1984-).

GW/0015-7678
FORM (SEEHEIM-JUGENHEIM, WEST GERMANY). (FORM.). Vol. 1 (1957)-. Periodical. German. qt (Mar., June, Sep., Dec.). DM85.00. Verlag Form GmbH, Ernsthoferstrasse 12, D 64342 Seeheim Jugen Germany. **Tel** 011 49 6257 81395. **ED** Karlheinz Krug. **LC** TS149; .F6. **Bk Rev. Ad Acc. Circ:** 11,400.
Ind/Abst ARTbibliogr. Mod.

US
FORMING AND FABRICATING. English. Nine times a year. $75.00 US; $80.00 Canada and Mexico (companies and company libraries); $90.00 (sea mail), $170.00 (air mail) other. Society of Manufacturing Engineers, One SME Drive, PO Box 930, Member's Records Dept., Dearborn MI 48121-0930. **Tel** (313)271-1500, FAX (313)271-2861, telex 297742 SME UR (VIA RCA).

GW/0340-8302
FORTSCHRITTLICHE BETRIEBSEHRUNG UND INDUSTRIAL ENGINEERING. [Fortschrittl. Betriebsf. Ind. Eng.]. **Added/Corp** Verband fuer Arbeitsstudien. Vol. 24 (Feb. 1975)-. Periodical. German. Six times a year. DM120.75. Beuth Verlag GmbH, Burggrafenstrasse 6, D-10787 Berlin Germany. **Tel** 011 49 30 260112573. **LC** HD28; .A733. **[CCC].** Documents available from UMI Article Clearinghouse. ***Formed by the union of*** *Industrial Engineering* ***and*** *Fortschrittliche Betriebsfuehrung.*
Ind/Abst ABI/INFORM Glob. Ed.; ABI Inform Ondisc (Feb. 1981-); Selec. Coop. Index Manage. Period.

NO
HANVERK & INDUSTRI : ORGAN FOR NORSKE HANDVERKER OG INDUSTRIBEDRIFTERS FORBUND. **VFOAT** Handverk og Industri. Vol. 50, 7-8 (July/Aug. 1968)-. Periodical. Norwegian. mo. ***Continues*** *Norges Haandverk.*

SZ
HOCHPARTERRE. German. mo. Hochparterre AG, Industriestrasse 57, 8157 Glattbrugg Switzerland.

●US/0894-5373
I.D. **VFOAT** ID; International Design; I.D. Magazine. Vol. 38 No. 1 (Jan./Feb. 1992)-. Periodical. English. bm (7 issues). $55.00 (one year), $90.00 (two year) US; $65.00 (one year) $110.00 (two year) Canada; $80.00 (one year), $140.00 (two year), other. International Design, 440 Park Avenue South, Floor 14, New York NY 10016. **Tel** (212)447-1400, (212)447-5231. **(Subscription address:** CDS / SIFD Agency Control, 1901 Bell Avenue, Des Moines IA 50315.) ***Continues*** *International Design, 0894-5373.*

US/0894-5373
ID (NEW YORK, N.Y. : 1984). ***Title Change.*** (ID.). [ID]. **VFOAT** Industrial Design. Vol. 31 (Sept./Oct. 1984)-Vol. 36 (Nov./Dec. 19??). Periodical. English. bm. Design Publications Inc., 110 Higgins Hall, 200 Willoughby, Brooklyn NY 11205. **Tel** (718)399-6090. **LC** TS1; .I515. **DD** 745.2/05. available on microfilm and microfiche from University Microfilms International (UMI). Documents available from UMI Article Clearinghouse. ***Continues*** *Industrial Design (New York, N.Y. : 1983), 0883-8267.* ***Continued by*** *International Design.*
Ind/Abst Appl. Sci. Technol. Index (Sept./Oct. 1984-); Art Index (Sept./Oct. 1984-); Avery Index Archit. Period. Suppl. Colum. Univ. (Sept./Oct. 1984-199?); Expand. Acad. Index (1992-); Newsp. Period. Abstr. (1992-).

US/0277-173X
IDSA PAPERS. (IDSA PAPERS / INDUSTRIAL DESIGNERS SOCIETY OF AMERICA.). [IDSA papers]. **VFOAT** I.D.S.A. Papers. **VAT** Industrial Designers Society of America Papers. Vol. 1 (1981)-. Periodical. English. an. Free to members, $20.00 nonmembers. Industrial Designers Society of America, 1142 Walker Road, Suites E & F, Great Falls VA 22066. **Tel** (703)759-0100, FAX (703)759-7679. **LC** TS171.A1; I36. **DD** 745.2/05.

US/0740-817X
IIE TRANSACTIONS. [IIE trans.]. **Added/Corp** Institute of Industrial Engineers (1981-). **VFOAT** I.I.E. Transactions; Transactions. **VAT** Institute of Industrial Engineers Transactions. Vol. 14, No. 1 (March 1982)-. Periodical. English. bm. $150.00 (institutions), $105.00 (individuals) US; $165.00 (institutions), $115.00 (individuals) other. Institute of Industrial Engineers, 25 Technology Park-Atlanta, Norcross GA 30092. **Tel** (404)449-0460, FAX (404)263-8532. **ED** Allen Soyster. **LC** T55.4; .A5. **DD** 620/.005. **CODEN** IIETDM. **[CCC]. Pr Rev. Circ:** 2,600. available on microfilm and microfiche from University Microfilms International (UMI). Documents available from Article Express International, The Genuine Article, UMI Article Clearinghouse, Ask*IEEE, Documents on Demand. ***Continues*** *American Institute of Industrial Engineers. AIIE Transactions, 0569-5554.*
Desc: Covers research and development in industrial engineering. For the international community of industrial and systems engineers.
Ind/Abst ABI/INFORM Glob. Ed.; ABI Inform Ondisc (March 1982-); Bioeng. Abstr.; Coal Abstr.; Curr. Contents Eng. Tech. Appl. Sci.; Ei Page One; Energy Inf. Abstr.; Eng. Index Annu.; Environ. Abstr.; Ergon. Abstr.; Expand. Acad. Index (1992-); Gen. BusinessFile (1992-); INSPEC (March 1982-); Int. Abstr. Oper. Res. [Full Cov.]; Manage. Contents (1982-); Math. Rev.; Oper. Res./Manag. Sci.; Qual. Control Appl. Stat.; Res. Alert [Full Cov.]; Sci. Cit. Index; SCISEARCH; Ship Abstr.; Soc. Sci. Cit. Index [Select. Cov.]; UMI ABI/Inform--Bus. Period. Ondisc (Dec. 1987-) [Full Txt.].

IT
INDESIGN. **VFOAT** In Design. Periodical. English (Italian). bm. Stammer Spa, Via della Liberazione 1, 20068 Peschiera Borromeo, Italy. **Tel** 011 39 2 55302606, FAX 011 39 2 55302700, telex 321083.

US/0888-5885
INDUSTRIAL & ENGINEERING CHEMISTRY RESEARCH. See Engineering-Chemical Engineering.

US/0446-0375
INDUSTRIAL DESIGN IN AMERICA. Vol. 1 (1949/50)-. English. **DD** 745.

JA
INDUSTRIAL DESIGN: JOURNAL OF JAPAN INDUSTRIAL DESIGNERS ASSOCIATION. ***Ceased.*** (19??)-(19??). Japanese. bm. Nihon Indasutoriaru Deazina Kyokai, (Japan Industrial Designers Assoc.), Sekai Boeki Senta Biru Bekkan 4F, 4-1, Hamamatsucho 2 Chome, Minatoku, Tokyoto 105 Japan. **(Subscription address:** Kyowa Book Company Inc., 1-38 Kanda Jinbo-Cho, Chiyoda-Ku, Tokyo 101, Japan (Phone: 03-3293-0727))

US
INDUSTRIAL ENGINEERING. Vol. 1 (1978)-. Monographic series. English. ir. Price varies per volume. Marcel Dekker Inc., 270 Madison Avenue, New York NY 10016. **Tel** (212)696-9000, (800)228-1160, FAX (212)685-4540, telex 421419. **(Subscription address:** Marcel Dekker Inc, PO Box 5017, Monticello NY 12701.) **CODEN** ILENDP. Documents available from Ask*IEEE.
Desc: Each title covers a different aspect of industrial engineering. Topics include quality control and materials handling.
Ind/Abst Anbar Account. Finan. Abstr. [Full Txt.]; Anbar Mark. Distr. Abstr. [Full Txt.]; Anbar Top Manage. Abstr. [Full Txt.]; Bus. Index (1989-); Bus. Source (Jan. 1993-); Gen. BusinessFile (1989-); INSPEC; Manage. Bibliogr. Rev.; Oper. Prod. Manage. Abstr. [Full Txt.]; Oper. Res./Manag. Sci.; Person. Train. Abstr. [Full Txt.]; Qual. Control Appl. Stat.; Vocat. Search (July 1993-); Women Manage. Rev. [Full Txt.]; Work Relat. Abstr. (-19??).

BE
INDUSTRIAL ENGINEERING NEWS. (EUROPEAN EDITION). English. $70.00. Pan European Publishing Company, rue Verte 216, 1210 Brussels 21 Belgium. **Tel** 011 32 2 2420611. ***Continues*** *International Equipment News.*

US/0019-8234
INDUSTRIAL ENGINEERING (NORCROSS, GA.). (INDUSTRIAL ENGINEERING.). [Ind. eng.]. **Added/Corp** Institute of Industrial Engineers. **VFOAT** IE. Vol. 13, No. 10 (Oct. 1981)-. Academic Scholarly Publication. English. mo. $49.00 US; $70.00 other. Institute of Industrial Engineers, 25 Technology Park-Atlanta, Norcross GA 30092. **Tel** (404)449-0460, FAX (404)263-8532. **ED** Richard Green. **LC** T55.4; .I2. **DD** 670.5. **CODEN** IDLEB9. **[CCC]. Bk Rev. Pr Rev. Circ:** 48,000. available on microfilm and microfiche from University Microfilms International (UMI). Documents available from Article Express International, The Genuine Article, UMI Article Clearinghouse, Ask*IEEE. ***Continues*** *Industrial Engineering (American Institute of Industrial Engineers), 0019-8234.*
Desc: Articles cover material handling, robotics, computers, energy management, quality control, production and inventory control, engineering economics, worker motivation, management strategies, office systems, and factory automation.
Ind/Abst ABI/INFORM Glob. Ed.; ABI Inform Ondisc (Oct. 1981-); Acad. Search (July 1993-); Appl. Sci. Technol. Index; Bioeng. Abstr.; Bus. ASAP (1990-) [Full Txt.]; Comput. ASAP [Full Txt.]; Comput. Database [Full Txt.]; Comput. Lit. Index; Comput. Rev.; Curr. Contents Eng. Tech. Appl. Sci.; Ei Page One; EMBASE; Eng. Index Annu.; Ergon. Abstr.; Expand. Acad. Index (1992-); Gen. Period. Index (1985-); Health Plan. Adminis.; INSPEC (Oct. 1981-); Int. Abstr. Oper. Res. [Select. Cov.]; Leadscan; Mag. Search; Manage. Contents; Math. Rev.; Res. Alert [Select. Cov.]; Saf. Health Work; SCISEARCH; Soc. Sci. Cit. Index [Select. Cov.]; Text. Technol. Dig.; Trade Ind. ASAP [Full Txt.]; Trade Ind. Index [Full Txt.]; UMI ABI/Inform--Bus. Period. Ondisc (Dec. 1987-) [Full Txt.].

●US/0019-8285
INDUSTRIAL EQUIPMENT NEWS (NEW YORK). (INDUSTRIAL EQUIPMENT NEWS.). [Ind. equip. news]. **VFOAT** IEN. Vol. 1, (Feb. 1933)-. Periodical. English. ir. $35.00 US; $50.00 Canada; $85.00 other. Thomas Publishing Company, One Penn Plaza, 250 West 34th Street, New York NY 10119. **Tel** (210)290-7277. **ED** Mark Devlin. **LC** TJ1; .I43. **DD** 621.8/05. **Ad Acc. Circ:** 210,000 (ctrl).
Desc: This a decision making process reaching over 71,000 manufacturing locations every month. Includes information and applications for their products.

Ind/Abst Fluid Abstr., Civil Eng.; Fluid Abstr. Proc. Eng.; FLUIDEX (1973-); Trade Ind. Index (1981-?); World Ceram. Abstr.

NZ
INDUSTRIAL PROCESS RESEARCH AND DEVELOPMENT DIVISIONAL ANNUAL REPORT / INDUSTRIAL PROCESSING DIVISION, DEPARTMENT OF SCIENTIFIC AND INDUSTRIAL RESEARCH, NEW ZEALAND. **Main/Corp** New Zealand. Industrial Processing Division. English. an. **LC** T55.778; .N49A. **DD** 670/.9931.

US/0731-2334
INNOVATION (MCLEAN, VA.). (INNOVATION : THE JOURNAL OF THE INDUSTRIAL DESIGNERS SOCIETY OF AMERICA.). [Innovation]. **Added/Corp** Industrial Designers Society of America. Vol. 1, No. 1 (Jan. 1982)-. Periodical. English. qt. $65.00. Industrial Designers Society of America, 1142 Walker Road, Suites E & F, Great Falls VA 22066. **Tel** (703)759-0100, FAX (703)759-7679. **ED** Kristina Goodrich. **LC** TS171.A1; I54. **DD** 745.2/05. **Bk Rev. Ad Acc. Circ:** 2,600.
Desc: Viewpoints, research reports, case studies and how-to articles on design practice, theory, history processes, manufacturing materials and processes and design manufacturing.

US/1055-7288
INTERNATIONAL INDUSTRIAL ENGINEERING CONFERENCE PROCEEDINGS. [Int. Ind. Eng. Conf. proc.]. (19??)-. Proceedings. English. an. $82.00. Institute of Industrial Engineers, 25 Technology Park-Atlanta, Norcross GA 30092. **Tel** (404)449-0460, FAX (404)263-8532. **DD** 670. **CODEN** IIEPEB.

US
INTERNATIONAL INDUSTRIAL ENGINEERING CONFERENCE PROCEEDINGS. **Added/Corp** Institute of Industrial Engineers (1981-). **VFOAT** International Industrial Engineering Conference & Societies' Manufacturing and Productivity Symposium Proceedings. (1988)-. Periodical. English. an. $75.00. Institute of Industrial Engineers, 25 Technology Park-Atlanta, Norcross GA 30092. **Tel** (404)449-0460, FAX (404)263-8532. **CODEN** IIEPEB. ***Continues*** *World Productivity Forum & International Industrial Engineering Conference. World Productivity Forum & ... International Industrial Engineering Conference, 0893-0309.*

●US/1072-4761
INTERNATIONAL JOURNAL OF INDUSTRIAL ENGINEERING. (1993)-. Periodical. English. Four times a year. $95.00. University of Cincinnati / Department of Industrial Engineering, Cincinnati OH 45221. **Tel** (513)556-2652.

NE/0169-8141
INTERNATIONAL JOURNAL OF INDUSTRIAL ERGONOMICS. [Int. j. ind. ergon.]. **VFOAT** IE; Industrial Ergonomics. Vol. 1, No. 1 (Aug. 1986)-. Academic Scholarly Publication. English. Twelve times a year (2 vols.). Fl900.00. Elsevier Science Publishers BV, PO Box 211, 1000 AE Amsterdam Netherlands. **Tel** 011 31 20 5803642, FAX 011 31 20 5862696, telex 15682. **LC** TA166; .I57. **NLM** W1; IN769B. **[CCC].** available on microfilm and microfiche from University Microfilms International (UMI). Documents available from Article Express International.
Desc: Covers all aspects of industrial and occupational ergonomics. Includes such topics as human productivity, work-station design, methods engineering, musculoskeletal injuries, design of tools, machines, controls and displays, safety, physical/mental stress and fatigue, modelling of the human body and human response behaviour, environmental stresses, etc.
Ind/Abst Abstr. Hum. Comput. Interact.; Agric. Eng. Abstr. (1991-); Dairy Sci. Abstr.; Ei Page One; Eng. Index Annu. [Select. Cov.]; Ergon. Abstr.; Health Saf. Sci. Abstr.; Risk Abstr.

II/0253-4754
INTERNATIONAL JOURNAL OF STRUCTURES. [Int. j. struct.]. Vol. 1, No. 1 (Jan.-Mar. 1981)-. Periodical. English. sa. $65.00. **(Subscription address:** Prints India, 11 Darya Ganj, New Delhi 110002 India.**) CODEN** IJOSD8.

UK/0952-4649
JOURNAL OF DESIGN HISTORY. [J. des. his.]. **Added/Corp** Design History Society. **VFOAT** Design History. Vol. 1, No. 1 (1988)-. Periodical. English. qt. £62.00 UK and Europe; $115.00 other. Oxford University Press, Walton Street, Oxford OX2 6DP England. **Tel** 011 44 865 56767, FAX 011 44 865 267773, telex 837330 OXPRES G. **(Subscription address:** Oxford University Press / USA, Journals Marketing Department, Oxford University Press, 2001 Evans Road, Cary NC 27513.**) ED** Christopher Bailey, Charlotte Benton, Colin Chant, Annie Coombes, Anthony Coulson, Clive Dilnot, Tony Evora, Pat Kirkham, Pauline Madge, Tim Putnam, Penny Sparke, and Jonathan Woodham. **LC** NK1175; .J68. **DD** 745.4/4/05. **[CCC]. Bk Rev. Ad Acc.** available on microfilm and microfiche from University Microfilms International (UMI).
Desc: New research in design development and current issues of interest. Promotion of links with other disciplines and exploration of material culture, such as anthropology, architectural history, business history, cultural studies, design management studies, economic and social history, history of science and technology and sociology.
Ind/Abst Am. Hist. Life (1988-); ARTbibliogr. Mod.; Avery Index Archit. Period. Suppl. Colum. Univ. (1990-); BHA : Biblio. Hist. Art.

UK/0954-4828
JOURNAL OF ENGINEERING DESIGN. [J. eng. des.]. **VFOAT** Engineering Design. Vol. 1, No. 1 (1990)-. Periodical. English. qt. £172.00. Carfax Publishing Company, PO Box 25 Abingdon, Oxfordshire OX14 3UE England. **Tel** 011 44 235 555335, FAX (0279)31067, telex 817484. **(Subscription address:** US and Canada/ PO Box 2025, Dunnellon, FL 34430-2025; telephone:(904)489-6996) **ED** Derek Sheldon. **LC** TA174; .J68. **CODEN** JEDSEW. **[CCC].** Index available. cum. index. **Ad Acc.** available on microfiche. Documents available from Ask*IEEE.
Desc: Embraces both industrial and engineering design research activities across the major disciplines of engineering.
Ind/Abst Alum. Ind. Abstr.; INSPEC (1990-); Met. Abstr.

UK/0950-4230
JOURNAL OF LOSS PREVENTION IN THE PROCESS INDUSTRIES. [J. loss prev. process ind.]. Vol. 1, No. 1 (Jan. 1988)-. Periodical. English. Six times a year. $492.00 The Americas; £330.00 other. Butterworth Heinemann Publishers, Linacre House, Jordan Hill, Oxford OX2 8DP England. **Tel** 011 44 865 310366. **(Subscription address:** Elsevier Science Ltd. Oxford Fulfillment Centre, PO Box 800, Kidlington, Oxford OX5 1DX United Kingdom.**) ED** P. F. Nolan (editor's address: Department of Chemical Engineering, South Bank Polytechnic, Borough Road, London SE1 OAA, UK), S. S. Grossel, and T. Hirano. **LC** TP149; .J65. **DD** 660.2/804. **[CCC].** Index available. **Bk Rev. Ad Acc. Pr Rev. Circ:** 350 (ctrl). available on microfilm and microfiche from University Microfilms International (UMI). Documents available from The Genuine Article.
Desc: Covers all areas of process plant safety, from scientific and technical aspects of initial plant design and layout to choice of safe materials. The journal will bring together the different techniques which go to make a safe process plant. It will provide a forum for the exchange of new ideas and to learn the lessons of the past.
Ind/Abst Chem. Hazards Ind.; Curr. Contents Eng. Tech. Appl. Sci.; Lab. Hazards Bull.; Res. Alert [Full Cov.]; SCISEARCH.

US/1048-9002
JOURNAL OF VIBRATION AND ACOUSTICS. **See** Physics-Sound.

UK/0950-4842
KEY ABSTRACTS. ROBOTICS & CONTROL. **See** Computers-Abstracting, Bibliographies and Statistics.

CN/0068-8665
LLOYD'S CANADIAN ENGINEERING & INDUSTRIAL YEAR BOOK. (1961)-. English. an (Nov.). 30.00Can$ Canada; 50.00Can$ US; 60.00Can$ others. Sentinel Business Publications, 7575 Trans Canada Highway, Suite 500, St. Laurent Quebec H4T 1V6 Canada. **Tel** (514)333-1116, FAX (514)631-8858. **ED** Carole Clifford. **DD** 338.4/7/6218. **Ad Acc. Circ:** 9,000 (ctrl). ***Continues*** *Lloyd's Canadian Engineering & Machinery Year Book, 0456-3859.*
Desc: A directory of product listing and suppliers to the engineering and general manufacturing markets.

US
MATERIAL ENGINEERING. (MATERIALS SELECTOR ISSUE.). **VFOAT** Materials in Design Engineering. 52, No. 60 (Nov. 1960)-. Periodical. English. an. $50.00. Penton Publishing, 1100 Superior Avenue, Cleveland OH 44114-2543. **Tel** (216)696-7000, FAX (216)696-0836. **(Subscription address:** Penton Publishing, PO Box 96732, Chicago IL 60693.**)** Index available (free).

UK/0264-1275
MATERIALS & DESIGN. **See** Engineering-Materials Engineering and Mechanics.

US/0025-5319
MATERIALS ENGINEERING. ***Ceased.*** **See** Engineering-Materials Engineering and Mechanics.

UK
OPERATIONS & PRODUCTION MANAGEMENT ABSTRACTS. **See** Engineering-Abstracting, Bibliographies and Statistics.

IT/0391-7487
OTTAGONO. ***Title Change.*** **See** Interior Design.

JA
PACKAGING DESIGN IN JAPAN. **See** Packaging.

US/1069-367X
PROCEEDINGS - IIE INTEGRATED SYSTEMS CONFERENCE. (PROCEEDINGS / IIE INTEGRATED SYSTEMS CONFERENCE & SOCIETY FOR INTEGRATED MANUFACTURING CONFERENCE.). [Proc. - IIE Integr. Syst. Conf.]. **Added/Corp** Institute of Industrial Engineers (1981-) Society for Integrated Manufacturing. Conference. (1989)-. Proceedings. English. ir. $9.95. Institute of Industrial Engineers, 25 Technology Park-Atlanta, Norcross GA 30092. **Tel** (404)449-0460, FAX (404)263-8532. **LC** T55.45; .F34a. **DD** 670.42. ***Continues*** *IIE Integrated Systems Conference. IEE Integrated Systems Conference Proceedings, 0895-2280.*

US
PROCEEDINGS OF THE ANNUAL INDUSTRIAL ENGINEERING CONFERENCE. **Main/Conf** Industrial Engineering Conference. (1970)-. English. an. $80.00. Institute of Industrial Engineers, 25 Technology Park-Atlanta, Norcross GA 30092. **Tel** (404)449-0460, FAX (404)263-8532. ***Supersedes*** *Proceedings of the Annual Industrial Engineering Conference.*

US/1058-546X
PRODUCT & PROCESS INNOVATION. [Prod. process innov.]. **VFOAT** Product and Process Innovation. Vol. 1, No. 1 (Jan./Feb. 1991)-. Periodical. English. bm. Product & Process Innovation, 210 South Street, Boston MA 02111. **LC** HD45; .P758. **DD** 658.5/14/05.

SP/0213-1315
REVISTA INTERNACIONAL DE METODOS NUMERICOS PARA CALCULO Y DISENO EN INGENIERIA. **VFOAT** Metodos Numericos para Calculo y Diseno en Ingenieria. (198?)-. Periodical. Spanish. qt. $150.00. Univ Politecnica Cataluna, Apartado de Correos 30250, 08034 Barcelona Spain. **Tel** 011 34 3 4016200.
Ind/Abst Math. Rev. (1987-).

CU
REVISTA INVESTIGACION OPERACIONAL. **VFOAT** Investigacion Operacional. Spanish. Ediciones Cubanas, Obispo 527, Altos ESQ Bernaza, CP 10100 Havana Cuba. **Tel** 011 632980, 631942, FAX 011 631011, telex 512337, 6540.
Ind/Abst Int. Abstr. Oper. Res. [Select. Cov.].

US
RITTENHOUSE : JOURNAL OF THE AMERICAN SCIENTIFIC INSTRUMENT ENTERPRISE. **VFOAT** Journal of the American Scientific Instrument Enterprise. Vol. 1, No. 1 (Nov. 1986)-. Periodical. English. Four times a year. $25.00 US; $30.00 other. Rittenhouse, PO Box 151, Hastings on Hudson NY 10706. **Tel** (914)478-2594, FAX (914)478-5473. **ED** D J Warner. **LC** Q184; .R58. **DD** 681/.75. **Bk Rev,** (Qty: 4).

KO
SANOP DIJAIN. **Added/Corp** Hanguk Dijain Pojang Sento. **VFOAT** Industrial Design. (1983)-. Periodical. Korean. bm. W18,000. Hanguk Tijain Pojang Sento, 128-8 Yongon-dong Chongno-ku, Seoul Korea. **LC** TS171.A1; T54. ***Continues*** *Dijain, Pojang.*

US/0094-825X
SWEET'S INDUSTRIAL CONSTRUCTION & RENOVATION FILE WITH PLANT ENGINEERING EXTENSION MARKET LIST. **See** Building and Construction.

US/0092-8763
SWEET'S PLANT ENGINEERING EXTENSION INDUSTRIAL CONSTRUCTION AND RENOVATION FILE. **VFOAT** Plant Engineering Extension Industrial Construction and Renovation File. 1974-. English. McGraw Hill Publishing Company, Inc., 1221 Avenue of the Americas, New York NY 10020. **Tel** (212)512-6410, (800)525-5003, FAX (212)512-6111. **LC** TA215; .S8. **DD** 338.4/7/67028. ***Continues*** *Plant Engineering Catalog File.*

KO
TAEHAN SANOP KONGHAKHOE CHI. **Main/Corp** Taehan Sanop Konghakhoe. **VFOAT** Journal of the Korean Institute of Industrial Engineers. (19??)-. Periodical. English (Korean). W3,000. San 1-181 Chongyangni-dong Tongdaemun-ku, Seoul South Korea. **LC** T55.4; .T33A.
Ind/Abst Int. Abstr. Oper. Res. [Select. Cov.].

US
TECHNICAL DIGEST. **Main/Corp** Society of Manufacturing Engineers. **Added/Corp** Society of Manufacturing Engineers. **VFOAT** SME Technical Digest. (1969)-. Periodical. English. qt. $26.00 (non-members), $18.00 (members SME). Society of Manufacturing Engineers, One SME Drive, PO Box 930, Member's Records Dept., Dearborn MI 48121-0930. **Tel** (313)271-1500, FAX (313)271-2861, telex 297742 SME

UR (VIA RCA). Each issue contains an index to its own contents (no volume index)--loose. ***Continues*** *ASTME Technical Digest.*
Desc: Abstracts of all technical papers and articles published throughout the year.
Ind/Abst Fluid Abstr., Civil Eng.; Fluid Abstr. Proc. Eng.; FLUIDEX (1973-).

UK/0261-0345
TRANSACTIONS OF DIESEL ENGINEERS & USERS ASSOCIATION. [Trans. Diesel Eng. Users Assoc.]. **VFOAT** Transactions of Diesel Engineers and Users Association. (19??)-. Periodical. English. bm. $153.00. Mechanical Engineering Publications, PO Box 24, Northgate Avenue, Bury St. Edmunds, Suffolk IP32 6BW England. **Tel** 011 44 284 763277, telex 817376. **(Subscription address:** Mechanical Engineering Publications / Western Hemisphere Subscriptions, Subscription Office, PO Box 361, Birmingham AL 35201-0361.**)** **[CCC].** Documents available from Article Express International.
Ind/Abst Acoust. Abstr.; BMT Abstr. (?-199?); Ei Page One; Eng. Index Annu.

US
TRANSACTIONS OF THE AMERICAN ASSOCIATION OF COST ENGINEERS. ***Title Change.*** **Main/Corp** American Association of Cost Engineers. Meeting. **VFOAT** AACE Transactions. 34th (June 24-27, 1990)-(1992). English. American Association of Cost Engineers, PO Box 1557, Morgantown WV 26507. **Tel** (304)296-8444, (800)858-2678, FAX (304)291-5728, telex 887612 AACE MORG UD. **LC** HD47; .A197. **DD** 658.15/52/05. ***Continues*** *American Association of Cost Engineers. Meeting. Annual Meeting of the American Association of Cost Engineers, 1050-1592.* ***Continued by*** *AACE International. Meeting. Transactions of AACE International, 1074-7397.*

MATERIALS ENGINEERING AND MECHANICS

JA/0924-3046
ADVANCED COMPOSITE MATERIALS : THE OFFICIAL JOURNAL OF THE JAPAN SOCIETY OF COMPOSITE MATERIALS. **Added/Corp** Nihon Fukugo Zairyo Gakkai. Vol. 1, No. 1 (1991)-. Periodical. English. qt. DM340.00. **(Subscription address:** VSP International Science Publishers, PO Box 346, 3700 AH Zeist Netherlands.**)** **ED** H. Miyairi. **Ad Acc. Pr Rev.** Documents available from The Genuine Article, Ask*IEEE. ***Continues*** *Transactions of the Japan Society for Composite Materials, 0385-2571.*
Desc: Presents articles on scientific and technological progress in the field of composite materials and their structures. Topics of interest are physical, chemical and other properties of advanced composites as well as their constituent materials.
Ind/Abst INSPEC (1991-); Res. Alert [Full Cov.].

US/0895-0407
ADVANCED COMPOSITES. ***Ceased.*** [Adv. compos.]. Vol. 1, No. 1 (May/June 1986)-(Mar./Apr. 1994). Periodical. English. bm. Advanstar Communications Inc., 131 West First Street, Duluth MN 55802. **Tel** (218)723-9477, (800)346-0085. **LC** TA418.9.C6; A267. **DD** 620.1/18.

UK/0963-6935
ADVANCED COMPOSITES LETTERS. (19??)-. English. bm (6 issues). £135.00 Europe; $225.00 North and South America; £140.00 other. Woodhead Publishing, Abington Hall, Abington Cambridge CB1 6AH England. **(Subscription address:** Turpin Distribution Services Limited, Blackhorse Road, Letchworth, Hertfordshire SG6 1HN, United Kingdom.**)** **Ad Acc.** Documents available from The Genuine Article.
Desc: Fibre reinforced materials play a central role in engineering materials development. This journal disseminates the newly acquired knowledge that advances the understanding of these materials by the rapid publication of high quality refereed papers.
Ind/Abst Res. Alert.

US
ADVANCED ENGINEERING MATERIALS RESEARCH PROFILE DIRECTORY. (19??)-. Directory. English. ir. $195.00. Materials Research Society, 9800 McKnight Road, Suite 327, Pittsburgh PA 15237-6006. **Tel** (412)367-3003, FAX (412)367-4373.

US/0882-7958
ADVANCED MATERIALS & PROCESSES. [Adv. mater. process.]. **Added/Corp** American Society for Metals. ASM International. **VFOAT** Advanced Materials and Processes. Vol. 1, No. 1 (Sept. 1985)-. Periodical. English. Twelve times a year. $140.00 US; $165.00 other. American Society for Metals International, c/o Deborah Barthelmes, Materials Park OH 44073-0002. **Tel** (216)338-5151, FAX (216)338-4634, telex 980-619. **(Subscription address:** ASM International, Materials Information, Materials Park OH 44073.**)** **LC** TA401; .A296. **DD** 620.1/1. **CODEN** AMAPEXAMPPE6. **[CCC].** available on microfilm and microfiche from University Microfilms International (UMI). Documents available from Article Express International, The Genuine Article, Ask*IEEE, CASDDS. ***Absorbed*** *Metal Progress, 0026-0665; Guide to Engineered Materials, 1040-1202; ASM News, 0044-7889.*
Ind/Abst Alum. Ind. Abstr.; Appl. Sci. Technol. Index; Art Archaeol. Tech. Abstr.; Ceram. Abstr.; Chem. Abstr.; Curr. Contents Eng. Tech. Appl. Sci.; Ei Page One; Eng. Mater. Abstr.; Eng. Index Annu.; Expand. Acad. Index (1992-); Fluid Abstr., Civil Eng.; Fluid Abstr. Proc. Eng.; FLUIDEX (199?-); INIS Atomindex [Micro.]; INSPEC (Aug. 1987-); Int. Aerosp. Abstr. (1991-); Leadscan; Met. Abstr.; Res. Alert [Full Cov.]; SCISEARCH; Soc. Sci. Cit. Index [Select. Cov.].

FR
ADVANCED MATERIALS & TECHNOLOGY. English (French and German). mo. 1125.00F. Sirpe, 76 Rue de Rivoli, 75004 Paris France. **Tel** 011 33 1 42785220.

US/0734-7146
ADVANCED MATERIALS (METUCHEN, N.J.). (ADVANCED MATERIALS.). (1979)-. Periodical. English. Twenty-three times a year. $238.00. Advanced Materials, PO Box 6249, Hilton Head SC 29938. **Tel** (803)842-4940. **ED** Philip West. **DD** 620. **Bk Rev**, (Qty: 12-15). **Circ:** 5,000.
Desc: Newsletter covering high-performance materials. Emphasis is on emerging technologies - metals, composites, ceramics, polymers, elastomers, adhesives and testing.
Ind/Abst Curr. Contents Phys. Chem. Earth Sci.; Eng. Mater. Abstr.; SCISEARCH.

US/0935-9648
ADVANCED MATERIALS (WEINHEIM). (ADVANCED MATERIALS.). [Adv. mat.]. Vol. 1 (1989)-. Academic Scholarly Publication. English. mo. $395.00 (surface mail from Florida), $415.00 (air mail from Germany). VCH Gesellschaft GmbH, Postfach 101161, D 69451 Weinheim Germany. **Tel** 011 49 6201 606459, FAX 011 49 6201 606184. **(Subscription address:** VCH Publishers Inc., 303 Northwest 12th Avenue, Journals Department, Deerfield FL 33442.**)** **LC** TA401; .A29. **DD** 620.1/1/05. **CODEN** ADVMEW. **[CCC].** Documents available from Article Express International, The Genuine Article, Ask*IEEE, CASDDS.
Ind/Abst Chem. Abstr. (1990-); Curr. Contents Phys. Chem. Earth Sci.; Ei Page One; Eng. Index Annu.; INSPEC (1989-); Res. Alert [Full Cov.]; Soc. Sci. Cit. Index [Select. Cov.].

US
ADVANCED METALLIZATION FOR ULSI APPLICATIONS. (19??)-. Monographic series. English. an. Materials Research Society, 9800 McKnight Road, Suite 327, Pittsburgh PA 15237-6006. **Tel** (412)367-3003, FAX (412)367-4373.

NE/0929-1881
ADVANCED PERFORMANCE MATERIALS. qt. $358.00. Kluwer Academic Publishers, Postbus 322, 3300 AH Dordrecht, The Netherlands. **Tel** 011 (31) 78 524400, FAX 011 31 78 183273, telex 20083.

SW/0272-0434
ADVANCES IN THE MECHANICS AND PHYSICS OF SURFACES. [Adv. mech. phys. surf.]. Vol. 1 (1981)-. Academic Scholarly Publication. English. an. Price varies. Harwood Academic Publishers / New York, PO Box 786, Cooper Station, New York NY 10276. **Tel** (212)206-8900, (201)643-7500. **ED** R. M. Latanison and T. E. Fischer. **LC** TA418.7; .A46. **DD** 620.1/1292. **CODEN** AMPSDE. Documents available from Ask*IEEE, CASDDS.
Ind/Abst Chem. Abstr.; INSPEC.

UK/0955-8209
ALUMINIUM TODAY. [Alum. today]. (198?)-. Periodical. English. qt. £128.20 UK; £138.20, $214.20. Argus Press Group, Queensway House, 2 Queensway Redhill, Surrey RH1 1QS England. **Tel** 011 44 737 768611, 011 44 737 761685, FAX 011 44 737 760510, telex 948669 TOPJNL G. **CODEN** ALTOEG. available on an online database (file 16/Full-Text) from DIALOG. Documents available from Article Express International.
Desc: Provides information for all involved in the manufacture and processing of aluminum and its alloys.
Ind/Abst Ei Page One; Eng. Index Annu. [Select. Cov.]; F&S Index Plus Text, Int. [Full Txt.] [Select. Cov.].

US/0192-2998
ANNUAL BOOK OF ASTM STANDARDS. [Annu. book ASTM stand.]. **Main/Corp** American Society for Testing and Materials. **VFOAT** Annual Book of A.S.T.M. Standards; Annual A.S.T.M. Standards; Annual ASTM Standards. **VAT** Annual Book of American Society for Testing and Materials Standards. (1970)-. Periodical. English. ir (68 issues per year). $4300.00 (non-members), $4100.00 (members). American Society for Testing and Materials, 1916 Race Street, Philadelphia PA 19103. **Tel** (215)299-5585, FAX (215)299-9679, telex 710 670 1037. **LC** TA401; .A653. **DD** 620.1/1/0218. **CODEN** ABASCV. **[CCC].** Index available. cum. index. available on microfiche; available on microfilm. Documents available from Article Express International, BIOSIS Document Express, CASDDS. ***Continues*** *Book of ASTM Standards, 0195-783X.*
Desc: A publication of voluntary consensus standards covering a broad spectrum of technological applications. Standards produced through the consensus process assure an equal representation from a cross-current of industrial, academic, and governmental interests.
Ind/Abst Art Archaeol. Tech. Abstr.; Biodeter. Abstr. (1991-); Bioeng. Abstr.; Biol. Abstr.; Chem. Abstr.; Coal Abstr.; Ei Page One; Eng. Index Annu.; For. Prod. Abstr.; For. Abstr.; GeoRef; Text. Technol. Dig.

AT
ANNUAL REPORT / DIVISION OF MATERIALS SCIENCE AND TECHNOLOGY, CSIRO AUSTRALIA. **Main/Corp** Institute of Industrial Technologies (Commonwealth Scientific and Industrial Research Organization (Australia)). Division of Materials Science and Technology. (1988)-. Periodical. English. CSIRO Publications, PO Box 89, 314 Albert Street, East Melborne Victoria 3002 Australia. **Tel** 011 61 3 4187333, 4187217, FAX 011 61 3 4190459, telex AA 30236. **LC** TJ1075.A2; I58a. **DD** 620.1/1/072094. ***Formed by the union of*** *Institute of Physical Sciences (Commonwealth Scientific and Industrial Research Organization (Australia)). Division of Materials Science.; Research Report, 0725-3575* ***and*** *Commonwealth Scientific and Industrial Research Organization (Australia). Division of Chemical Physics.;* ***Continues*** *_tBiennial report.*

US/0198-9677
ANNUAL REPORT / POLYMER SCIENCE AND STANDARDS DIVISION. [Annu. rep. - Polym. Sci. Stand. Div.]. **Main/Corp** Center for Materials Science (National Measurement Laboratory). Polymer Science and Standards Division. **Added/Corp** United States. National Bureau of Standards. (19??)-. English. an. United States Department of Commerce National Bureau of Standards, Polymers Building 224/A305, Washington DC 20234. **LC** TA455.P58; U54a. **DD** 620.1/92/05.

US/0084-6600
ANNUAL REVIEW OF MATERIALS SCIENCE. [Annu. rev. mater. sci.]. Vol. 1 (1971)-. English. an (August). $75.00 US; $80.00 other. Annual Reviews Inc., 4139 El Camino Way, PO Box 10139, Palo Alto CA 94303-0139. **Tel** (415)493-4400, (800)523-8635, FAX (415)855-9815. **ED** Robert A. Huggins. **LC** TA401; .A7. **DD** 620.1/1/05. **CODEN** ARMSCX. **[CCC].** Index available. cum. index. **Pr Rev.** ctrl circ. available on microfilm and microfiche from University Microfilms International (UMI). Documents available from Article Express International, The Genuine Article, Ask*IEEE, CASDDS, Documents on Demand.
Desc: Comprehensive, thorough coverage of latest advances in materials science, written by acknowledged experts in the field. Extensive literature citations included.
Ind/Abst Bioeng. Abstr.; Ceram. Abstr. (19??-); Chem. Abstr.; Curr. Contents Phys. Chem. Earth Sci.; Ei Page One; Energy Inf. Abstr.; Energy Res. Abstr. (Feb. 1972-); Eng. Index Annu.; Environ. Abstr.; GeoRef; Index Sci. Rev. [Full Cov.]; INSPEC; Leadscan; Polymer Contents; Res. Alert [Full Cov.]; Sci. Cit. Index; SCISEARCH.

UK/0003-5599
ANTI-CORROSION METHODS AND MATERIALS. **See** Engineering-Chemical Engineering.

NE/0929-189X
APPLIED COMPOSITE MATERIALS. bm. $406.00. Kluwer Academic Publishers, Postbus 322, 3300 AH Dordrecht, The Netherlands. **Tel** 011 (31) 78 524400, FAX 011 31 78 183273, telex 20083.

PL/0138-032X
ARCHIWUM NAUKI O MATERIAACH. (ARCHIWUM NAUKI O MATERIAACH / POLSKA AKADEMIA NAUK, KOMITET NAUKI O MATERIAACH.). [Arch. nauki mater.]. **Added/Corp** Polska Akademia Nauk. Komitet Nauki o Materiaach. Vol. 1, No. 1/2 (1980)-. Academic Scholarly Publication. Polish (summaries and/or abstracts in English and Russian). qt. $47.00. **(Subscription address:** ARS Polona, PO Box 1001, 00068 Warsaw Poland.**)** **LC** TA401; .A75. **CODEN** ANAMDU. Documents available from Article Express International, Ask*IEEE, CASDDS.
Ind/Abst Alum. Ind. Abstr.; Chem. Abstr.; Eng. Mater. Abstr.; Eng. Index Annu. [Select. Cov.]; INSPEC (1983-); Int. Aerosp. Abstr. (1991-); Met. Abstr.

US
ASTM DIRECTORY. **Main/Corp** American Society for Testing and Materials. (19??)-. English. ir. American Society for Testing and Materials, 1916 Race Street, Philadelphia PA 19103. **Tel** (215)299-5585, FAX (215)299-9679, telex 710 670 1037.

US/0066-0558
ASTM SPECIAL TECHNICAL PUBLICATION. [ASTM spec. tech. publ.]. **Added/Corp** American Society for Testing and Materials. **VFOAT** Special Technical Publication. **VAT** American

Society for Testing and Materials Special Technical Publication. No. 305 (1961)-. Academic Scholarly Publication. English. ir. Price varies per volume. American Society for Testing and Materials, 1916 Race Street, Philadelphia PA 19103. **Tel** (215)299-5585, FAX (215)299-9679, telex 710 670 1037. **LC** UNC. **DD** 620. **CODEN** ASTTA8. **[CCC].** Documents available from Article Express International, Ask*IEEE, CASDDS. ***Continues*** *Special Technical Publication (American Society for Testing Materials), 0066-0558.*
Ind/Abst Bioeng. Abstr.; BMT Abstr. (-199?); Ceram. Abstr.; Chem. Abstr. (1969-); Civ. Struct. Eng. Abstr.; Coal Abstr.; Ei Page One; Elect. Comm. Abstr.; Energy Res. Abstr.; Eng. Index Annu.; GeoRef; Highw. Res. Abstr.; INSPEC; Mater. Sci. Eng. Abstr.

US
ASTM STANDARDS INTERNATIONAL. (19??)-. English. ir. Free on request. American Society for Testing and Materials, 1916 Race Street, Philadelphia PA 19103. **Tel** (215)299-5585, FAX (215)299-9679, telex 710 670 1037.

US/0090-8045
ASTM YEAR BOOK. Main/Corp American Society for Testing and Materials. **VAT** American Society for Testing and Materials Yearbook. (1947)-. English. an. American Society for Testing and Materials, 1916 Race Street, Philadelphia PA 19103. **Tel** (215)299-5585, FAX (215)299-9679, telex 710 670 1037. **DD** 620.1. ***Continues*** *Year Book.*

AT/0004-833X
AUSTRALASIAN CORROSION ENGINEERING. ***Ceased.*** **See** Engineering-Chemical Engineering.

AT/0818-9110
AUSTRALIAN GEOMECHANICS. (19??)-. English. sa (June, Dec.). 30.00NZ$. Institution of Engineers Australia, 11 National Circuit, Barton ACT 2600 Australia. **Tel** 011 61 62 706555. ***Continues*** *Australian Geomechanics News, 0725-1009.*

US/0738-0305
BIBLIOGRAPHY OF SOVIET LASER DEVELOPMENTS. See Engineering-Electricity, Electrical Engineering, Electronics.

UK/0007-0599
BRITISH CORROSION JOURNAL. See Engineering-Chemical Engineering.

UK/0007-1137
BRITISH JOURNAL OF NON-DESTRUCTIVE TESTING. ***Title Change.*** [Br. j. non-destr. test.]. **Added/Corp** Non-Destructive Testing Society of Great Britain. British Institute of Non-destructive Testing. Vol. 1 (July 1959)-(1993). Academic Scholarly Publication. English. mo. British Institute of Non-Destructive Testing, 1 Spencer Parade, Northampton NN1 5AA England. **Tel** 0604 30124, FAX 0604 231489. **ED** F.W. Beaumont. **LC** TA417.2; .B7. **CODEN** BJNTAS. Index available. cum. index. **Bk Rev. Ad Acc. Pr Rev. Circ:** 2,950 (ctrl). available on microfilm from University Microfilms International (UMI). Documents available from Article Express International, The Genuine Article, Ask*IEEE, CASDDS. ***Absorbed*** *Condition Monitoring and Diagnostic Technology, 0957-7661.* ***Merged with*** *European Journal of Non-Destructive Testing* ***to form*** *Insight (Northampton, England).*
Desc: Research practice and application of all methods of non-destructive testing.
Ind/Abst Acoust. Abstr. (?-?); Alum. Ind. Abstr. (?-?); Bioeng. Abstr. (?-?); Chem. Abstr. (?-?); Curr. Contents Eng. Tech. Appl. Sci. (?-?); Curr. Technol. Index (?-?); Ei Page One (?-?); Eng. Mater. Abstr. (?-?); Eng. Index Annu. (?-?); Fluid Abstr., Civil Eng. (?-?); Fluid Abstr. Proc. Eng. (?-?); FLUIDEX (?-?); INSPEC (Dec. 1968-); Met. Abstr. (?-?); Pollut. Abstr. Indexes (?-?); Res. Alert (?-?) [Full Cov.].

RM
BULETIN STIINTIFIC. CHEMISTRY AND MATERIALS SCIENCE / IPB. See Chemistry.

CN/1187-6859
BULLETIN - CANADIAN ASSOCIATION FOR COMPOSITE STRUCTURES AND MATERIALS. (BULLETIN / CANADIAN ASSOCIATION FOR COMPOSITE STRUCTURES AND MATERIALS.). [Bull. - Can. Assoc. Compos. Struct. Mater.]. **Added/Corp** Canadian Association for Composite Structures and Materials. **VFOAT** Bulletin. **VAT** Bulletin - Association Canadienne Pour les Structures et Materiaux Composites. Vol. 4, No. 1 (Feb. 1991)-. Bulletin. English (French). Four times a year (Mar., June, Sept., Dec.). 20.00Can$. Canadian Association for Composite Structured & Materials, 1455 Re Maisonne Boulevard, West H929, Montreal QUE H3G 1M8 Canada. **Tel** (514)848-8746 3494. **DD** 620.1/18/06071. ***Continues*** *Canadian Association for Composite Structures and Materials (Newsletter)., 1184-0854.*

US/0146-4434
CA SELECTS: CORROSION. See Chemistry-Abstracting, Bibliographies and Statistics.

CN/0318-0859
CANADIAN PROCESS EQUIPMENT & CONTROL NEWS. VFOAT Process Equipment & Control News. Vol. 1 (Feb. 1973)-. Periodical. English. bm. 36.00Can$ (one year), 60.00Can$ (two year) Canada; 48.00Can$ (one year), 84.00Can$ (two year) US. Canadian Process Equipment, 343 Eglinton Avenue East, Toronto Ontario M4P AL7 Canada. **Tel** (416)481-6483, FAX (416)481-6436. ctrl circ.
Desc: Serves the process and related industries; presents information on new products and applications.

US/1043-8033
CHINESE JOURNAL OF ENGINEERING THERMOPHYSICS. [Chin. j. eng. thermophys.]. **VFOAT** Engineering Thermophysics. Vol. 1, No. 1 (1989)-. Periodical. English. qt. $295.00. Allerton Press, Inc., 150 Fifth Avenue, New York NY 10011. **Tel** (212)924-3950, FAX (212)463-9684, telex 427441 ALPRES. **LC** QC310.15; .C48. **DD** 621.402/1. **[CCC].**
Ind/Abst Fluid Abstr., Civil Eng.; Fluid Abstr. Proc. Eng.; FLUIDEX (19??-).

SZ/0590-8450
COATING. See Engineering-Chemical Engineering.

UK/0263-8223
COMPOSITE STRUCTURES. [Compos. struct.]. Vol. 1, No. 1 (1983)-. Academic Scholarly Publication. English. Twelve times a year. $1788.00 The Americas; £1200.00 other. Elsevier Applied Science, An Imprint of Elsevier Science Ltd., The Boulevard, Langford Lane, Kidlington, Oxford OX5 1GB United Kingdom. **Tel** 011 44 865 843000, 011 44 865 843699, FAX 011 44 865 843010. **(Subscription address:** Elsevier Science Ltd. Oxford Fulfillment Centre, PO Box 800, Kidlington, Oxford OX5 1DX United Kingdom.**) ED** I. H. Marshall. **CODEN** COMSE2. **[CCC]. Bk Rev. Ad Acc. Pr Rev.** available on microfilm and microfiche from University Microfilms International (UMI). Documents available from Article Express International, The Genuine Article, Ask*IEEE.
Desc: Publishes papers which contribute to knowledge in the use of composite materials in engineering structures.
Ind/Abst Civ. Struct. Eng. Abstr.; Curr. Contents Eng. Tech. Appl. Sci.; Ei Page One; Eng. Index Annu.; Fluid Abstr., Civil Eng.; Fluid Abstr. Proc. Eng.; FLUIDEX; INSPEC (1985-); Int. Aerosp. Abstr. (1984-); Mater. Sci. Eng. Abstr.; Mech. Eng. Abstr.; Polymer Contents; Res. Alert [Full Cov.]; SCISEARCH.

UK/0010-4361
COMPOSITES. [Composites]. Vol. 1 (Sept. 1969)-. Academic Scholarly Publication. English (summaries and/or abstracts in French and German). Twelve times a year. $731.00 (regular subscription), $924.00 (combination subscription with Composites Manufacturing) The Americas; £490.00 (regular subscription), £620.00 (combination subscription with Composites Manufacturing) other. Butterworth Heinemann Publishers, Linacre House, Jordan Hill, Oxford OX2 8DP England. **Tel** 011 44 865 310366. **(Subscription address:** Elsevier Science Ltd. Oxford Fulfillment Centre, PO Box 800, Kidlington, Oxford OX5 1DX United Kingdom.**) ED** John Herriot. **LC** TA418.9.C6; C63. **DD** 620.1/1. **CODEN** CPSOAN. **[CCC].** Index available. cum. index. **Bk Rev. Ad Acc. Pr Rev.** available on microfilm and microfiche from University Microfilms International (UMI). Documents available from Article Express International, The Genuine Article, Ask*IEEE, CASDDS.
Desc: Reports advances in polymer-matrix composites reinforced with glass or high-modulus fibres such as carbon, aramid or boron, cement-matric composites reinforced with steel, glass or polymer fibres, metal and ceramic-matrix composites reinforced with fibres or whiskers of refractories such as silicon carbide or aluminum oxide and organic composites such as wood.
Ind/Abst Alum. Ind. Abstr.; Bioeng. Abstr.; Ceram. Abstr.; Chem. Abstr.; Coal Abstr.; Curr. Contents Eng. Tech. Appl. Sci.; Curr. Technol. Index; Ei Page One; Eng. Mater. Abstr.; Eng. Index Annu.; INSPEC (Dec. 1971-); Int. Aerosp. Abstr.; J. Ferrocement; Met. Abstr.; Polymer Contents; RAPRA Abstr.; Res. Alert [Full Cov.]; Sci. Cit. Index; SCISEARCH; Text. Technol. Dig.; World Text. Abstr.

US/0961-9526
COMPOSITES ENGINEERING. [Compos. eng.]. Vol. 1, No. 1 (1991)-. Periodical. English. mo. $917.00 The Americas; £615.00 other. Pergamon Press, An Imprint of Elsevier Science Ltd., The Boulevard, Langford Lane, Kidlington, Oxford OX5 1GB United Kingdom. **Tel** 011 44 865 843000, 011 44 865 843699, FAX 011 44 865 843010. **(Subscription address:** Elsevier Science Ltd. Oxford Fulfillment Centre, PO Box 800, Kidlington, Oxford OX5 1DX United Kingdom.**) ED** David Hui. **LC** TA418.9.C6; C6319. **DD** 620.1/18. **CODEN** CMENEZ. **[CCC].** available on microfilm and microfiche from University Microfilms International (UMI). Documents available from Article Express International, The Genuine Article, Ask*IEEE.
Desc: Serves as a forum for the publication of original papers in the broad area of composite materials and engineering structures.
Ind/Abst Curr. Contents Eng. Tech. Appl. Sci.; Ei Page One; Eng. Index Annu.; INSPEC (1991-); Int. Aerosp. Abstr.; RAPRA Abstr.; Res. Alert [Full Cov.].

UK/0956-7143
COMPOSITES MANUFACTURING. Vol. 1, No. 1 (March 1990)-. Periodical. English. qt. $291.00 (regular subscription), $924.00 (combination subscription with Composites) The Americas; £195.00 (regular subscription), £620.00 (combination subscription with Composites) other. Butterworth Heinemann Publishers, Linacre House, Jordan Hill, Oxford OX2 8DP England. **Tel** 011 44 865 310366. **(Subscription address:** Elsevier Science Ltd. Oxford Fulfillment Centre, PO Box 800, Kidlington, Oxford OX5 1DX United Kingdom.**) CODEN** CMAUE2. **[CCC].** available on microfilm and microfiche from University Microfilms International (UMI). Documents available from The Genuine Article.
Ind/Abst Int. Aerosp. Abstr.; Res. Alert [Full Cov.].

UK/0266-3538
COMPOSITES SCIENCE AND TECHNOLOGY. [Compos. sci. technol.]. Vol. 22, No. 1 (1985)-. Academic Scholarly Publication. English. Twelve times a year. $1403.00 The Americas; £941.00 other. Elsevier Applied Science, An Imprint of Elsevier Science Ltd., The Boulevard, Langford Lane, Kidlington, Oxford OX5 1GB United Kingdom. **Tel** 011 44 865 843000, 011 44 865 843699, FAX 011 44 865 843010. **(Subscription address:** Elsevier Science Ltd. Oxford Fulfillment Centre, PO Box 800, Kidlington, Oxford OX5 1DX United Kingdom.**) ED** Bryan Harris and Tsu-Wei Chou. **LC** TA418.9.C6; F5. **DD** 620.1/18. **CODEN** CSTCEH. **[CCC]. Bk Rev. Ad Acc. Pr Rev.** available on microfilm and microfiche from University Microfilms International (UMI). Documents available from Article Express International, The Genuine Article, Ask*IEEE, CASDDS. ***Continues*** *Fibre Science and Technology, 0015-0568.*
Desc: Publishes refereed original articles, occasional review papers, and letters, on all aspects of the fundamental and applied science of engineering composites.
Ind/Abst Abstr. Bull. Inst. Pap. Sci. Tech.; Acoust. Abstr.; Ceram. Abstr. (19??-); Chem. Abstr. (1985-); Civ. Struct. Eng. Abstr.; Curr. Contents Eng. Tech. Appl. Sci.; Ei Page One; Eng. Mater. Abstr.; Eng. Index Annu.; INSPEC (1988-); Int. Aerosp. Abstr.; Manuf. Process Eng. Abstr.; Mater. Sci. Eng. Abstr.; Mech. Eng. Abstr.; Polymer Contents; Res. Alert [Full Cov.]; Sci. Cit. Index; SCISEARCH; Solid State Supercond. Abstr.; Text. Technol. Dig.

●NE/0927-0256
COMPUTATIONAL MATERIALS SCIENCE. Vol. 1, No. 1 (Oct. 1992)-. Academic Scholarly Publication. English. Eight times a year (2 volumes). Fl850.00. Elsevier Science Publishers BV, PO Box 211, 1000 AE Amsterdam Netherlands. **Tel** 011 31 20 5803642, FAX 011 31 20 5862696, telex 15682. **ED** U. Landman, R.M. Nieminen. **LC** TA401; .C656. **CODEN** CMMSEM. **[CCC].** Documents available from Ask*IEEE, CASDDS.
Desc: Aims to enhance the communication between experimental materials research and computational work on both existing and new advanced materials and their applications.
Ind/Abst Alum. Ind. Abstr.; Chem. Abstr.; Eng. Mater. Abstr.; INSPEC; Met. Abstr.

PO/0870-1164
CORROSAO E PROTECCAO DE MATERIALS. [Corros. prot. mater.]. **VFOAT** Revista de Corrosao e Proteccao de Materiais. (1982)-. Academic Scholarly Publication. Portuguese. ir. Laboratorio Nacional de Engenharia e Tecnologia Industrial, Civil Avenda de Brasil 101, 1799 Lisbon Codex Portugal. **Tel** 011 351 1 8821317. **LC** TA418.74; .C584. **DD** 620.1/1223/05. **CODEN** CPMAEN. Documents available from CASDDS.
Ind/Abst Chem. Abstr. (1984-); Corros. Abstr. (199?-); Eng. Mater. Abstr.

US/0010-9339
CORROSION ABSTRACTS. See Engineering-Abstracting, Bibliographies and Statistics.

SA/0377-8711
CORROSION & COATINGS SOUTH AFRICA. See Engineering-Chemical Engineering.

AT/0155-6002
CORROSION AUSTRALASIA. See Engineering-Chemical Engineering.

US/0010-9312
CORROSION (HOUSTON, TEX.). See Engineering-Chemical Engineering.

UK/0010-9371
CORROSION PREVENTION AND CONTROL. See Engineering-Chemical Engineering.

US/0364-3301
CORROSION PREVENTION/INHIBITION DIGEST. See Engineering-Chemical Engineering.

UK/0010-938X
CORROSION SCIENCE. See Engineering-Chemical Engineering.

SP/0045-8678
CORROSION Y PROTECCION. *Title Change.* See Engineering-Chemical Engineering.

GW/0723-7901
DHF. DEUTSCHE HEBE- UND FORDERTECHNIK. [DHF, Dtsch. Hebe-Ford.tech.]. **VFOAT** German Material Handling Magazine (1980); Manutention dans l'Industrie Allemande (1980); Deutsche Hebe- und Fordertechnik (1980). (1980)-. Periodical. Multiple languages. ir. DM178.20. AGT Verlag Thum GmbH, Postfach 109, Teinacherstr 34, D 71601 714 Ludwigsburg 10 Germany. **Tel** 011 49 7141 223156. **UDC** 621.86. ***Continues*** *Deutsche Hebe- und Fordertechnik, 0012-0278.*

US/0012-253X
DIE CASTING ENGINEER. [Die cast. eng.]. **Added/Corp** Society of Die Casting Engineers. North American Die Casting Association. Vol. 1 (March 1957)-. Periodical. English. bm (6 issues). $52.00 North America; $65.00 other. North American Die Casting Association, 9701 West Higgins Road, Suite 880, Rosemont IL 60018. **Tel** (708)292-3600. **LC** TS239; .D53. **DD** 671.2/5. **CODEN** DICEAB. available on microfilm and microfiche from University Microfilms International (UMI). Documents available from Article Express International, The Genuine Article, CASDDS.
Ind/Abst Bioeng. Abstr.; Chem. Abstr.; Curr. Contents Eng. Tech. Appl. Sci.; Ei Page One; Eng. Index Annu. [Select. Cov.]; Leadscan; Met. Abstr.; Res. Alert [Select. Cov.]; SCISEARCH.

UK
ENCYCLOPEDIA OF MATERIALS SCIENCE AND ENGINEERING. *Ceased.* (1986)-(19??). English. Massachusetts Institute of Technology (MIT) Press, 55 Hayward Street, Cambridge MA 02142-1399. **Tel** (617)253-2889, (617)625-8481, FAX (617)258-6779. Index available. cum. index.

US/0951-9998
ENGINEERED MATERIALS ABSTRACTS. See Engineering-Abstracting, Bibliographies and Statistics.

US/0013-7944
ENGINEERING FRACTURE MECHANICS. [Eng. fract. mech.]. Vol. 1, No. 1 (June 1968)-. Periodical. English. Eighteen times a year. $2124.00 The Americas; £1425.00 other. Pergamon Press, An Imprint of Elsevier Science Ltd., The Boulevard, Langford Lane, Kidlington, Oxford OX5 1GB United Kingdom. **Tel** 011 44 865 843000, 011 44 865 843699, FAX 011 44 865 843010. **(Subscription address:** Elsevier Science Ltd. Oxford Fulfillment Centre, PO Box 800, Kidlington, Oxford OX5 1DX United Kingdom.**) ED** Harold Liebowitz. **LC** TA409; .E5. **DD** 620.1 126. **CODEN** EFMEAH. **[CCC]. Pr Rev.** available on microfilm and microfiche from University Microfilms International (UMI). Documents available from Article Express International, The Genuine Article, Ask*IEEE, CASDDS.
Desc: Designed to be of broad interest and use to both the researcher and practitioner of fracture mechanics in academic, governmental and industrial fields of endeavour.
Ind/Abst Alum. Ind. Abstr.; Appl. Mech. Rev.; Bioeng. Abstr.; Ceram. Abstr.; Chem. Abstr. (1968-1986); Civ. Struct. Eng. Abstr.; Comput. Inf. Syst. Abstr. J. [Full Cov.]; Curr. Contents Eng. Tech. Appl. Sci.; Ei Page One; Elect. Comm. Abstr.; Eng. Mater. Abstr.; Eng. Index Annu.; Health Saf. Sci. Abstr.; INIS Atomindex [Micro.]; INSPEC (1968-); Int. Aerosp. Abstr.; Linguist. Lang. Behav. Abstr.; Manuf. Process Eng. Abstr.; Mater. Sci. Eng. Abstr.; Math. Rev.; Mech. Eng. Abstr.; Met. Abstr.; Pollut. Abstr. Indexes; Res. Alert [Full Cov.]; Sci. Cit. Index; SCISEARCH; Soc. Plann. Policy Dev. Abstr.; Solid State Supercond. Abstr.

US
EPD CONGRESS. (19??)-. Proceedings. English. an. Minerals, Metals and Materials Society, 420 Commonwealth Drive, Warrendale PA 15086-7514. **Tel** (412)776-9000 ext. 236, (800)759-4867, FAX (412)776-3770.

UK/0261-2097
EUREKA (BECKENHAM). See Engineering-Industrial Engineering and Design.

GW/0946-0470
EUROMATERIALS. (199?)-. English. qt (4 issues). $99.00. VCH Gesellschaft GmbH, Postfach 101161, D 69451 Weinheim Germany. **Tel** 011 49 6201 606459, FAX 011 49 6201 606184. **(Subscription address:** VCH Publishers Inc., 303 Northwest 12th Avenue, Journals Department, Deerfield FL 33442.**)**

US/0014-505X
EXPLOSIVES AND PYROTECHNICS. See Engineering-Chemical Engineering.

UK/0952-3960
EXPLOSIVES ENGINEERING. See Engineering-Chemical Engineering.

US/1048-5090
EXTENDED ABSTRACTS / MATERIALS RESEARCH SOCIETY. [Ext. abstr. - Mater. Res. Soc.]. **Added/Corp** Materials Research Society. EA-1 (1984)-. Monographic series. English. ir. Price varies per volume. Materials Research Society, 9800 McKnight Road, Suite 327, Pittsburgh PA 15237-6006. **Tel** (412)367-3003, FAX (412)367-4373. **DD** 620. **CODEN** MRSEEJ.
Ind/Abst Ceram. Abstr. (19??-).

UK/8756-758X
FATIGUE & FRACTURE OF ENGINEERING MATERIALS & STRUCTURES. [Fatigue fract. eng. mater. struct.]. **VFOAT** Fatigue and Fracture of Engineering Materials and Structures. Vol. 8, No. 1 (1985)-. Periodical. English. Twelve times a year. £520.00. Fatigue and Fracture of Engineering Materials and Structures, University of Sheffield, Faculty of Engineering, Sheffield S1 3JD England. **Tel** 011 44 742 768555. **ED** K.J. Miller. **LC** TA418.38; .F374. **DD** 620.1/123/05. **CODEN** FFESEY. **[CCC]. Bk Rev. Ad Acc. Pr Rev.** available on microfilm and microfiche from University Microfilms International (UMI). Documents available from Article Express International, The Genuine Article, Ask*IEEE. ***Continues*** *Fatigue of Engineering Materials and Structures, 0160-4112.*
Desc: Devoted to research in the fatigue and fracture behavior of engineering materials and structures, and draws together papers on the science, technology and engineering relevant to the understanding and control of the fatigue-fracture problem. Focuses attention on the interdisciplinary approach to the study of all forms of fracture processes, concentrating on engineering applications and design, mathematics, metallurgy, materials science, computer science, physics and chemistry.
Ind/Abst Appl. Mech. Rev.; Curr. Contents Eng. Tech. Appl. Sci.; Ei Page One; Eng. Mater. Abstr.; Eng. Index Annu.; Highw. Res. Abstr.; INSPEC (1985-); Int. Aerosp. Abstr.; Res. Alert [Full Cov.]; SCISEARCH.

SA/0014-6552
FEM. FACTORY EQUIPMENT & MATERIALS. [FEM, Fact. equipm. mater.]. **VFOAT** Factory Equipment Materials. (1968)-. Periodical. English. Twelve times a year. R100,00 South Africa & Namibia & Homelands; R160,00 others. National Publishing Pty Ltd, 155 2nd Avenue Kenilworth 7700, PO Box 2271, Clareinch 7740 South Africa. **Tel** (021)61-1140, FAX (021)611389, telex 9555542+. **DD** 658.7.

US
FIVE-YEAR INDEX TO ASTM TECHNICAL PAPERS AND REPORTS. **Main/Corp** American Society for Testing and Materials. (1955)-. Periodical. English. ir (every five years). $20.00 (latest index). American Society for Testing and Materials, 1916 Race Street, Philadelphia PA 19103. **Tel** (215)299-5585, FAX (215)299-9679, telex 710 670 1037. **LC** TA401; .A514. **DD** 620.11082. Index available.

FR/0985-0503
FRANCE COMPOSITES. (1988)-. French (English and German). 220.00F France; 210.00F other. CEPP, 1 Place d'Estienne d'Orves, 75000 Paris France. **Tel** (1)42 80 67 62, FAX (1)42 82 99 30. **LC** TA418.9.C6; F74. **DD** 620.1/18/0944. Index available. cum. index. **Ad Acc. Pr Rev.** ctrl circ.
Desc: The whole market of composites in France and articles on evolution of composites technology.

CC/1000-3851
FUHE CAILIAO XUEBAO. (FU HO TSAI LIAO HSUEH PAO / ACTA MATERIAE COMPOSITAE SINICA.). [Fuhe cailiao xuebao]. **VFOAT** Acta Materiae Compositae Sinica. (198?)-. Periodical. Chinese. qt. Ko Hsueh chu pan she, Pei-ching China. **CODEN** FCXUEC. Documents available from CASDDS.
Ind/Abst Chem. Abstr. (1985-); Int. Aerosp. Abstr.

JA
FUSHOKU BOSHOKU BUMON IINKAI KENKYU SHUKAI SHIRYO. [Fushoku Boshoku Bumon Iinkai kenkyu shukai shiryo]. **Main/Corp** Nihon Zairyo Gakkai. Fushoku Boshoku Bumon Iinkai. **VFOAT** Kenkyu Shukai Shiryo; Memoirs of Technical Meeting of Corrosion Engineering Division, the Society of Materials Science, Japan. (19??)-. Japanese (summaries and/or abstracts in English). Nihon Zairyo Gakkai Fushoku Boshoku Bumon Iiankai, 1-101 Yoshido Izumidono-cho, Sakyo-ku Kyoto-shi 606 Japan. **CODEN** FBBSDO. Documents available from CASDDS.
Ind/Abst Chem. Abstr.

JA
FUSHOKU BOSHOKU BUMON IINKAI SHIRYO. [Fushoku Boshoku Bumon Iinkai shiryo]. **Main/Corp** Nihon Zairyo Gakkai. Fushoku Boshoku Bumon Iinkai. **VFOAT** Fushoku Boshoku Bumon-Iinkai Shiryo; Proceedings Corrosion Engineering Division, the Society of Materials Science, Japan. (19??)-. Japanese. Nihon Zairyo Gakkai Fushoku Boshoku Bumon Iiankai, 1-101 Yoshido Izumidono-cho, Sakyo-ku Kyoto-shi 606 Japan. **CODEN** FBBGDM. Documents available from CASDDS.
Ind/Abst Chem. Abstr.

JA/0387-0936
GOSEI JUSHI. Added/Corp Nihon Gosei Jushi Gijutsu Kyokai. **VFOAT** Plastics. (1947)-. Periodical. Japanese. mo. Nihon Gosei Jushi Gijutsu Kyokai. Documents available from CASDDS.
Ind/Abst Chem. Abstr.

UK/0018-1544
HIGH TEMPERATURES - HIGH PRESSURES. See Physics-Heat.

UK/0265-0584
INDUSTRIAL CORROSION. [Ind. corros.]. (1982)-. Periodical. English. Six times a year (Jan., Mar., May, July, Sept., Nov.). £38.00 UK & EIRE; £50.00 other. Impact Publications / England, Media House, 55 Old Road, Leighton, Beds LU7 7RB England. **Tel** 011 44 525 370013, FAX 011 44 525 382487. **ED** Janer Brennan. **DD** 620.11223. **Bk Rev**, (Qty: 1). **Ad Acc, Adv Mgr:** Paul Green. **Circ:** 1,750 (ctrl). ***Continues*** *Bulletin - Institution of Corrosion Science and Technology, 0260-4477.*

US/1045-1889
INNOVATIONS IN POLYMER/ENGINEERING PLASTICS. [Innov. polym./eng. plast.]. **VFOAT** Innovations in Polymers Engineering Plastics. (1989)-. Periodical. English. mo. $375.00. Technical Insights Inc., PO Box 1304, Fort Lee NJ 07024-9967. **Tel** (201)568-4744, FAX (201)568-8247, telex 425900 SWIFT UI. **DD** 620.

●UK/1354-2575
INSIGHT (NORTHAMPTON). (INSIGHT : NON-DESTRUCTIVE TESTING AND CONDITION MONITORING.). **Added/Corp** British Institute of Non-Destructive Testing. Vol. 36, No. 4 (Apr. 1994)-. Periodical. English. mo. $185.00 US; £80.00 UK; £105.00 other. British Institute of Non-Destructive Testing, 1 Spencer Parade, Northampton NN1 5AA England. **Tel** 0604 30124, FAX 0604 231489. **ED** F.W. Beaumont. **LC** TA417.2; .B7. **DD** 620.1127. **CODEN** ITMOEN. Index available. cum. index. **Bk Rev. Ad Acc. Circ:** 2,950 (ctrl). available on microfilm. Documents available from Article Express International, The Genuine Article, Ask*IEEE, CASDDS. ***Formed by the union of*** *European Journal of Non-Destructive Testing* ***and*** *British Journal of Non-Destructive Testing, 0007-1137.*

UK/0142-1123
INTERNATIONAL JOURNAL OF FATIGUE. [Int. j. fatigue]. Vol. 1, No. 1 (Jan. 1979)-. Academic Scholarly Publication. English. Eight times a year. $492.00 The Americas; £330.00 other. Butterworth Heinemann Publishers, Linacre House, Jordan Hill, Oxford OX2 8DP England. **Tel** 011 44 865 310366. **(Subscription address:** Elsevier Science Ltd. Oxford Fulfillment Centre, PO Box 800, Kidlington, Oxford OX5 1DX United Kingdom.**) ED** Guy Kitteringham. **LC** TA418.38; .I53. **DD** 620.1/123/05. **CODEN** IJFADB. **[CCC].** Index available. **Bk Rev. Ad Acc. Pr Rev. Circ:** 1,000. available on microfilm and microfiche from University Microfilms International (UMI). Documents available from Article Express International, The Genuine Article, Ask*IEEE, CASDDS.
Desc: Covers fundamental aspects of the fatigue of materials and the relevance of fatigue to engineering and design. Includes original research papers, reviews, conference reports and news stories.
Ind/Abst Abstr. J. Earthq. Eng. (?-?); Acoust. Abstr.; Agric. Eng. Abstr.; Alum. Ind. Abstr.; Appl. Mech. Rev.; Bioeng. Abstr.; Chem. Abstr.; Curr. Contents Eng. Tech. Appl. Sci.; Ei Page One; Energy Res. Abstr. (Nov. 1979-); Eng. Mater. Abstr.; Eng. Index Annu.; INSPEC (Jan. 1980-); Int. Aerosp. Abstr.; Leadscan; Met. Abstr.; Pollut. Abstr. Indexes; Res. Alert [Full Cov.]; Sci. Cit. Index; SCISEARCH; Shock Vibr. Dig.

NE/0376-9429
INTERNATIONAL JOURNAL OF FRACTURE. [Int. j. fract.]. Vol. 9 (March 1973)-. Periodical. English. sm. $3,276.00. Kluwer Academic Publishers, Postbus 322, 3300 AH Dordrecht, The Netherlands. **Tel** 011 (31) 78 524400, FAX 011 31 78 183273, telex 20083. **ED** M. L. Williams. **LC** TA409; .I5. **DD** 620.1/126/05. **CODEN** IJFRAP. **[CCC]. Ad Acc. Pr Rev. Acid Free. Circ:** 1,100 (ctrl). available on microfilm and microfiche from University Microfilms International (UMI). Documents available from Article Express International, The Genuine Article, Ask*IEEE, CASDDS. ***Continues*** *International Journal of Fracture Mechanics, 0020-7268.*
Desc: An outlet for original theoretical or experimental contributions which provide a better understanding of the mechanisms that cause micro and macro fracture in all materials, and their engineering manifestations and significance.
Ind/Abst Abstr. J. Earthq. Eng. (?-?); Acoust. Abstr.; Alum. Ind. Abstr.; Appl. Mech. Rev.; Bioeng. Abstr.; Ceram. Abstr.; Chem. Abstr.; Curr. Contents Eng. Tech. Appl. Sci.; Ei Page One; Eng. Mater. Abstr.; Eng. Index Annu.; INSPEC (March 1973-); Int. Aerosp. Abstr.; Math.

Rev.; Met. Abstr.; Pollut. Abstr. Indexes; Res. Alert [Full Cov.]; Sci. Cit. Index; SCISEARCH; Soc. Sci. Cit. Index [Select. Cov.].

UK/0734-743X
INTERNATIONAL JOURNAL OF IMPACT ENGINEERING. [Int. j. impact eng.]. Vol. 1, No. 1 (1983)-. Periodical. English. Seven times a year. $872.00 The Americas; £585.00 other. Pergamon Press, An Imprint of Elsevier Science Ltd., The Boulevard, Langford Lane, Kidlington, Oxford OX5 1GB United Kingdom. **Tel** 011 44 865 843000, 011 44 865 843699, FAX 011 44 865 843010. **(Subscription address:** Elsevier Science Ltd. Oxford Fulfillment Centre, PO Box 800, Kidlington, Oxford OX5 1DX United Kingdom.**) ED** Norman Jones. **LC** TA354; .I56. **DD** 620.1/054. **CODEN** IJIED4. **[CCC]. Pr Rev.** available on microfilm and microfiche from University Microfilms International (UMI). Documents available from Article Express International, The Genuine Article, Ask*IEEE, Documents on Demand.
Desc: Provides a focal point for the currently diffused literature on the many aspects of impact engineering.
Ind/Abst Abstr. J. Earthq. Eng.; Acoust. Abstr.; Alum. Ind. Abstr.; Appl. Mech. Rev.; Curr. Contents Eng. Tech. Appl. Sci.; Ei Page One; Eng. Mater. Abstr.; Eng. Index Annu.; Environ. Abstr.; INSPEC (1987-); Int. Aerosp. Abstr. (1984-); Int. Civil Eng. Abstr.; Met. Abstr.; Res. Alert [Full Cov.]; SCISEARCH; Shock Vibr. Dig.; Soft. Abstr. Eng.; Surf. Treat. Technol. Abstr.

UK/0141-5530
INTERNATIONAL JOURNAL OF MATERIALS IN ENGINEERING APPLICATIONS. ***Title Change.*** [Int. j. mater. eng. appl.]. Vol. (1978)-. Academic Scholarly Publication. English. qt. Scientific and Technical Press, Chilberton House, Doods Road, Reigate Surrey England. **LC** TA401; .I79. **DD** 620.1/1. **CODEN** IMEADR. available on microfilm from University Microfilms International (UMI). Documents available from CASDDS. ***Continued by*** *Materials in Engineering, 0261-3069.*
Ind/Abst Chem. Abstr.; Ei Page One.

US/0749-6419
INTERNATIONAL JOURNAL OF PLASTICITY. [Int. j. plast.]. Vol. 1, No. 1 (1985)-. Academic Scholarly Publication. English. Eight times a year. $686.00 The Americas; £460.00 other. Pergamon Press, An Imprint of Elsevier Science Ltd., The Boulevard, Langford Lane, Kidlington, Oxford OX5 1GB United Kingdom. **Tel** 011 44 865 843000, 011 44 865 843699, FAX 011 44 865 843010. **(Subscription address:** Elsevier Science Ltd. Oxford Fulfillment Centre, PO Box 800, Kidlington, Oxford OX5 1DX United Kingdom.**) ED** A. S. Khan, J. F. Bell and N. Christescu. **LC** TA418.14; .I55. **DD** 620.1/1233/05. **CODEN** IJPLER. **[CCC]. Pr Rev.** available on microfilm and microfiche from University Microfilms International (UMI). Documents available from Article Express International, The Genuine Article, Ask*IEEE, CASDDS.
Desc: Strives to report original research in a wide spectrum of plasticity related topics including plasticity of single crystals and polycrystalline metallic solids, rock and soil plasticity, post-yield fracture mechanics, and plasticity of composite materials, polymers and ceramics.
Ind/Abst Appl. Mech. Rev.; Chem. Abstr.; Civ. Struct. Eng. Abstr.; Curr. Contents Eng. Tech. Appl. Sci.; Ei Page One; Eng. Mater. Abstr.; Eng. Index Annu.; INSPEC (1985-); Int. Aerosp. Abstr.; Manuf. Process Eng. Abstr.; Mech. Eng. Abstr.; Res. Alert [Full Cov.]; Sci. Cit. Index; SCISEARCH; Solid State Supercond. Abstr.; Zentralbl. Math. Ihre Grenzgeb.

US/0020-7683
INTERNATIONAL JOURNAL OF SOLIDS AND STRUCTURES. See Engineering-Civil Engineering.

US/0891-0138
INTERNATIONAL SAMPE SYMPOSIUM AND EXHIBITION. (INTERNATIONAL SAMPE SYMPOSIUM AND EXHIBITION : [PROCEEDINGS] / SOCIETY FOR THE ADVANCEMENT OF MATERIAL AND PROCESS ENGINEERING.). [Int. SAMPE Symp. Exhib.]. **Added/Corp** Society for the Advancement of Material and Process Engineering. **VAT** International Society for the Advancement of Material and Process Engineering Symposium and Exhibition. 31st (1986)-. Monographic series. English. ir. Price varies per volume. Society for the Advancement of Material & Process Engineering, 1161 Parkview Drive, PO Box 2459, Covina CA 91724. **Tel** (818)331-0616 Ext 611, FAX (818)332-8929, telex 510/600 4889. **LC** TA401.3; .I585a. **DD** 620.1/1. **CODEN** ISSEEG. **[CCC].** Documents available from Article Express International, CASDDS. ***Continues*** *Society for the Advancement of Material and Process Engineering. National SAMPE Symposium and Exhibition, 0147-9598.*
Ind/Abst Chem. Abstr. (1986-); Ei Page One; Eng. Index Annu.

US/0892-2624
INTERNATIONAL SAMPE TECHNICAL CONFERENCE SERIES. [Int. SAMPE tech. conf. ser.]. **Added/Corp** Society for the Advancement of Material and Process Engineering. **VAT** International Society for the Advancement of Material and Process Engineering Technical Conference Series. Vol. 18 (1986)-. Monographic series. English. ir. Price varies per volume. Society for the Advancement of Material & Process Engineering, 1161 Parkview Drive, PO Box 2459, Covina CA 91724. **Tel** (818)331-0616 Ext 611, FAX (818)332-8929, telex 510/600 4889. **LC** UNC. **DD** 620. **CODEN** ISTCEF. Documents available from CASDDS. ***Continues*** *National SAMPE Technical Conference Series, 0147-9601.*
Ind/Abst Chem. Abstr.

RU
ITOGI NAUKI I TEKHNIKI: KORROZIIA I ZASHCHITA OT KORROZII. See Engineering-Chemical Engineering.

US/1066-2375
JMR ABSTRACTS. ***Title Change.*** **See** Engineering-Abstracting, Bibliographies and Statistics.

US/0021-9983
JOURNAL OF COMPOSITE MATERIALS. [J. compos. mater.]. **Added/Corp** Washington University (Saint Louis, Mo.) Monsanto Company. **VFOAT** JCM. Vol. 1 (Jan. 1967)-. Periodical. English. Eighteen times a year. $855.00 (one year), $1,700.00 (two year), $2,545.00 (three year). Technomic Publishing Company, Inc., 851 New Holland Avenue, Box 3535, Lancaster PA 17604. **Tel** (717)291-5609, (800)233-9936, FAX (717)295-4538. **ED** H. Thomas Hahn. **LC** TA418.9.C6; J6. **DD** 620.1/1/05. **CODEN** JCOMBI. **[CCC].** cum. index. **Pr Rev. Circ:** 1,250. available on microfilm and microfiche from University Microfilms International (UMI). Documents available from Article Express International, The Genuine Article, Ask*IEEE, CASDDS.
Desc: Features original studies from international material scientists with an emphasis on practical applications without compromise in technical integrity. Both phenomenological and mechanistic approaches and their interrelations are featured. Fatigue, fracture, structural reliability, and design criteria are given special attention.
Ind/Abst Abstr. Bull. Inst. Pap. Sci. Tech.; Abstr. J. Earthq. Eng. (?-?); Alum. Ind. Abstr.; Appl. Sci. Technol. Index; Bioeng. Abstr.; Ceram. Abstr.; Chem. Abstr.; Civ. Struct. Eng. Abstr.; Curr. Contents Eng. Tech. Appl. Sci.; Ei Page One; Elect. Comm. Abstr.; Eng. Mater. Abstr.; Eng. Index Annu.; INIS Atomindex [Micro.]; INSPEC (July 1970-); Int. Aerosp. Abstr.; J. Ferrocement; Manuf. Process Eng. Abstr.; Mater. Sci. Eng. Abstr.; Mech. Eng. Abstr.; Met. Abstr.; Polymer Contents; Res. Alert [Full Cov.]; Sci. Cit. Index; SCISEARCH; Solid State Supercond. Abstr.; Text. Technol. Dig.

US/0884-6804
JOURNAL OF COMPOSITES TECHNOLOGY & RESEARCH. [J. compos. technol. res.]. **Added/Corp** American Society for Testing and Materials. **VFOAT** Journal of Composites Technology and Research; ASTM Journal of Composites Technology & Research. Vol. 7, No. 1 (Spring 1985)-. Academic Scholarly Publication. English. qt (4 issues). $129.00 North America; $142.00 other (non-member). American Society for Testing and Materials, 1916 Race Street, Philadelphia PA 19103. **Tel** (215)299-5585, FAX (215)299-9679, telex 710 670 1037. **DD** 620. **CODEN** JCTRER. **[CCC]. Pr Rev.** available on microfilm from University Microfilms International (UMI). Documents available from Article Express International, The Genuine Article, Ask*IEEE, CASDDS. ***Continues*** *Composites Technology Review, 0733-9011.*
Ind/Abst Acoust. Abstr.; Alum. Ind. Abstr.; Bioeng. Abstr.; Ceram. Abstr.; Chem. Abstr. (1985-); Curr. Contents Eng. Tech. Appl. Sci.; Ei Page One; Eng. Index Annu.; INSPEC (1985-); Int. Aerosp. Abstr.; Met. Abstr.; Res. Alert [Full Cov.]; SCISEARCH; Shock Vibr. Dig.

US/0094-4289
JOURNAL OF ENGINEERING MATERIALS AND TECHNOLOGY. See Engineering-Mechanical Engineering and Machinery.

US/0738-7989
JOURNAL OF MATERIALS EDUCATION, THE. [J. mater. educ.]. **VFOAT** J.M.E.; JME. Vol. 5, No. 1 (1983)-. Academic Scholarly Publication. English (Japanese). Six times a year. $245.00 (one year), $398.00 (two years). Pennsylvania State University / Journal of Materials Education, 106 Materials Research Lab, University Park PA 16802. **Tel** (814)865-1643, FAX (814)863-7040. **ED** Robert Berretini. **CODEN** JMEDDD. Index available in last issue of volume--attached. cum. index. **Bk Rev,** (Qty: 12). **Pr Rev. Circ:** 300. Documents available from CASDDS. ***Continues*** *Journal of Educational Modules for Materials Science and Engineering, 0197-3940.*
Desc: A journal-textbook hybrid of peer-reviewed instructional modules in materials science and engineering.
Ind/Abst Art Archaeol. Tech. Abstr. (1983-); Chem. Abstr. (1983-).

US/0931-7058
JOURNAL OF MATERIALS ENGINEERING. ***Title Change.*** (JOURNAL OF MATERIALS ENGINEERING / ASM INTERNATIONAL.). [J. mater. eng.]. **Added/Corp** ASM International. (1987)-(199?). Academic Scholarly Publication. English. qt. American Society for Metals International, c/o Deborah Barthelmes, Materials Park OH 44073-0002. **Tel** (216)338-5151, FAX (216)338-4634, telex 980-619. **ED** John R Ogren. **LC** TA401; .J675. **DD** 620.1/1. **CODEN** JMAEEV. **[CCC].** available on microfilm and microfiche from University Microfilms International (UMI). Documents available from Article Express International, Ask*IEEE, CASDDS. ***Continues*** *Journal of Materials for Energy Systems, 0162-9719.* ***Merged with*** *Journal of Heat Treating, 0190-9177* ***and*** *Journal of Materials Shaping Technology, 0931-704X* ***to form*** *Journal of Materials Engineering and Performance, 1059-9495.*
Desc: Publishes reviews and archival data from international sources on the preparation and properties of engineered materials, focusing on the performance of advanced materials including, ceramics, polymers, composites, rapidly solidified materials, and amorphous materials.
Ind/Abst Abstr. Bull. Inst. Pap. Sci. Tech.; Alum. Ind. Abstr. (1987-); Bioeng. Abstr. (1987-); Ceram. Abstr. (19??-); Chem. Abstr. (1987-); Coal Abstr. (1987-); Curr. Titles Electrochem.; Ei Page One (1987-); Energy Res. Abstr. (1987-); Eng. Index Annu.; Fluid Abstr., Civil Eng.; Fluid Abstr. Proc. Eng.; FLUIDEX (1987-); INSPEC (1988-); Int. Aerosp. Abstr. (1987-); Met. Abstr. (1987-); Risk Abstr.; SCISEARCH.

NE/0924-0136
JOURNAL OF MATERIALS PROCESSING TECHNOLOGY. [J. mater. process. technol.]. **VFOAT** Materials Processing Technology. Vol. 21 No. 1 (Jan. 1990)-. Periodical. English. Thirty-two times a year (8 volumes). 2440.00F. Elsevier Sequoia SA, PO Box 564, CH-1001 Lausanne 1 Switzerland. **Tel** 011 41 21 3207381. **CODEN** JMPTEF. **[CCC].** available on microfilm and microfiche from University Microfilms International (UMI). Documents available from Article Express International, The Genuine Article, Ask*IEEE. ***Continues*** *Journal of Mechanical Working Technology, 0378-3804.*
Ind/Abst Ceram. Abstr. (19??-); Civ. Struct. Eng. Abstr.; Comput. Inf. Syst. Abstr. J. [Full Cov.]; Curr. Contents Eng. Tech. Appl. Sci.; Ei Page One; Eng. Index Annu.; Environ. Eng. Abstr.; Fluid Abstr., Civil Eng.; Fluid Abstr. Proc. Eng.; FLUIDEX (19??-); INSPEC (1990-); Manuf. Process Eng. Abstr.; Mater. Sci. Eng. Abstr.; Mech. Eng. Abstr.; Res. Alert [Full Cov.]; SCISEARCH; Solid State Supercond. Abstr.

US/0884-2914
JOURNAL OF MATERIALS RESEARCH. [J. mater. res.]. **Added/Corp** Materials Research Society. American Institute of Physics. **VFOAT** Materials Research. Vol. 1, No. 1 (Jan./Feb. 1986)-. Academic Scholarly Publication. English. mo. $475.00 US; $505.00 (surface mail), $560.00 (airmail) other. Materials Research Society, 9800 McKnight Road, Suite 327, Pittsburgh PA 15237-6006. **Tel** (412)367-3003, FAX (412)367-4373. **(Subscription address:** Kinokuniya Company Ltd., 38-1 Sakuragaoka 5, chome Setagaya-ku, Tokyo 156 Japan.**) ED** Walter L. Brown. **LC** TA404.2; .J68. **DD** 620.1/1/05. **CODEN** JMREEE. **[CCC].** Index available. cum. index. **Bk Rev. Ad Acc. Pr Rev. Circ:** 9,500 (ctrl). available on microfilm and microfiche from University Microfilms International (UMI). Documents available from Article Express International, The Genuine Article, Ask*IEEE, CASDDS.
Desc: Publishes archival papers, commentaries and reviews, and rapid communications. Addresses topics on materials characterization, processing, and synthesis.
Ind/Abst Ceram. Abstr.; Chem. Abstr. (1986-); Chem. Titles; Corros. Abstr. (199?-); Curr. Contents Eng. Tech. Appl. Sci.; Curr. Contents Phys. Chem. Earth Sci.; Curr. Phys. Index; Ei Page One; Eng. Mater. Abstr.; Eng. Index Annu.; Gas Abstr.; Geol. Abstr.; GeoRef; INIS Atomindex [Micro.]; INSPEC (Jan./Feb. 1986-); Int. Aerosp. Abstr.; MRS Bull.; Res. Alert [Full Cov.]; Sci. Cit. Index; SCISEARCH.

UK/0261-8028
JOURNAL OF MATERIALS SCIENCE LETTERS. [J. mater. sci. lett.]. Vol. 1, No. 1 (Jan. 1982)-. Academic Scholarly Publication. English. sm. $3395.00 (includes Journal of Materials Science) US and Canada; £1995.00 (includes Journal of Materials Science) European Community; £2150.00 (includes Journal of Materials Science) other. Chapman & Hall, 2-6 Boundary Row, London SE1 8HN England. **Tel** 011 44 71 865 0066, FAX 011 44 71 522 9623, telex 290164 Chapmag. **(Subscription address:** Chapman & Hall, Cheriton House, North Way, Andover, Hampshire, SP10 5BE England.**) ED** W Bonfield. **LC** TA401; .J6715. **DD** 620.1/1/05. **CODEN** JMSLD5. **[CCC]. Ad Acc. Pr Rev.** available on microfilm and microfiche from University Microfilms International (UMI). Documents available from Article Express International, The Genuine Article, Ask*IEEE, CASDDS. ***Continues in part*** *Journal of Materials Science, 0022-2461.*
Desc: Leading source of primary communications on the structure and properties of engineering materials.
Ind/Abst Alum. Ind. Abstr.; Appl. Mech. Rev.; Bioeng. Abstr.; Ceram. Abstr.; Chem. Abstr.; Chem. Titles; Coal Abstr.; Curr. Biotechnol.; Curr. Contents Eng. Tech. Appl. Sci.; Curr. Contents Phys. Chem. Earth Sci.; Curr. Titles Electrochem.; Ei Page One; Energy Res. Abstr. (May 1982-); Eng. Mater. Abstr.; Eng. Index Annu.; INSPEC (Jan. 1982-); Int. Aerosp. Abstr.; Leadscan; Met. Abstr.;

Polymer Contents; Res. Alert [Full Cov.]; Sci. Cit. Index; SCISEARCH; World Ceram. Abstr.; World Surf. Coat. Abstr.

●US/1064-7562
JOURNAL OF MATERIALS SYNTHESIS AND PROCESSING. [J. mater. synth. process.]. Vol. 1, No. 1 (Jan. 1993)-. Periodical. English. Six times a year. $195.00 institutions, $75.00 individuals US; $230.00 institutions, $90.00 individuals other. Plenum Press, 233 Spring Street, New York NY 10013-1578. **Tel** (212)620-8000, (800)221-9369, FAX (212)463-0742, (212)807-1047, telex 23/421139. **DD** 620. **CODEN** JMSPEI.

US/0195-9298
JOURNAL OF NONDESTRUCTIVE EVALUATION. [J. nondestr. eval.]. Vol. 1 (Mar. 1980)-. Periodical. English. Four times a year. $250.00 US; $295.00 other. Plenum Press, 233 Spring Street, New York NY 10013-1578. **Tel** (212)620-8000, (800)221-9369, FAX (212)463-0742, (212)807-1047, telex 23/421139. **ED** R. Bruce Thompson. **LC** TA417.2; .J68. **DD** 621.1/127/05. **CODEN** JNOED5. **[CCC].** Index available. available on microfilm and microfiche from University Microfilms International (UMI). Documents available from Article Express International, Ask*IEEE.
Desc: Interdisciplinary journal concerned with non-destructive evaluation of structural components. It provides a forum for the broad range of scientific and engineering activities involved in developing a quantitative non-destructive evaluation and capability.
Ind/Abst Abstr. Bull. Inst. Pap. Sci. Tech.; Acoust. Abstr.; Alum. Ind. Abstr.; Bioeng. Abstr.; Ceram. Abstr.; Ei Page One; Energy Res. Abstr. (Dec. 1981-); Eng. Mater. Abstr.; Eng. Index Annu.; Gas Abstr.; INSPEC (March 1980-); Int. Aerosp. Abstr.; Met. Abstr.; Pollut. Abstr. Indexes.

IS/0334-6447
JOURNAL OF POLYMER ENGINEERING. [J. polym. eng.]. Vol. 5, No. 1 (Jan. 1985)-. Academic Scholarly Publication. English. Four times a year. $220.00. Freund Publishing House Ltd, PO Box 35010, 61 Nachmani Street, Tel Aviv 61350 Israel. **Tel** 011 972 3 5662925, FAX 011 972 3 5605335. **(Subscription address:** Freund Publishing House Ltd., Suite 500 Chesham House, 150 Regent Street, London W1R 5FA England.**) ED** M. Narkis, R.E. Cohen, A. Siegmann, J.M. Vergnaud. **CODEN** JPOEEK. Index available. **Bk Rev. Ad Acc. Pr Rev. Circ:** 200. Documents available from Article Express International, The Genuine Article, CASDDS. ***Continues*** *Polymer Engineering Reviews, 0250-8079.*
Desc: A coverage of basic research and innovation in polymer processing, characteristics and properties of fabricated products including composites and applications.
Ind/Abst Chem. Abstr. (1985-); Ei Page One; Eng. Index Annu.; Res. Alert [Full Cov.]; SCISEARCH.

US/0731-6844
JOURNAL OF REINFORCED PLASTICS AND COMPOSITES. [J. reinf. plast. compos.]. **VFOAT** JRPC; J.R.P.C. Vol. 1, No. 1 (Jan. 1982)-. Academic Scholarly Publication. English. mo. $725.00 (one year), $1440.00 (two year), $2155.00 (three year). Technomic Publishing Company, Inc., 851 New Holland Avenue, Box 3535, Lancaster PA 17604. **Tel** (717)291-5609, (800)233-9936, FAX (717)295-4538. **ED** George S. Springer. **LC** TA455.P55; J68. **DD** 620.1/923. **CODEN** JRPCDW. **[CCC].** cum. index. **Pr Rev. Circ:** 400. available on microfilm from University Microfilms International (UMI). Documents available from Article Express International, The Genuine Article, Ask*IEEE, CASDDS.
Desc: Presents research studies on a broad range of today's reinforced plastics and composites. Special editorial emphasis is placed on environmental effects of composites and on non-destructive evaluation and failure of composites. Provides a forum for reporting new and significant advances in the field.
Ind/Abst Alum. Ind. Abstr.; Chem. Abstr.; Civ. Struct. Eng. Abstr.; Curr. Contents Eng. Tech. Appl. Sci.; Ei Page One; Eng. Mater. Abstr.; Eng. Index Annu.; INIS Atomindex [Micro.]; INSPEC (Oct. 1983-); Int. Aerosp. Abstr.; Mater. Sci. Eng. Abstr.; Mech. Eng. Abstr.; Met. Abstr.; Polymer Contents; Res. Alert [Full Cov.]; SCISEARCH; Solid State Supercond. Abstr.

US/0896-1107
JOURNAL OF SUPERCONDUCTIVITY. **See** Engineering-Electricity, Electrical Engineering, Electronics.

UK/0022-5096
JOURNAL OF THE MECHANICS AND PHYSICS OF SOLIDS. [J. mech. phys. solids]. Vol. 1 (Oct. 1952)-. Periodical. English. mo. $1416.00 The Americas; £950.00 other. Pergamon Press, An Imprint of Elsevier Science Ltd., The Boulevard, Langford Lane, Kidlington, Oxford OX5 1GB United Kingdom. **Tel** 011 44 865 843000, 011 44 865 843699, FAX 011 44 865 843010. **(Subscription address:** Elsevier Science Ltd. Oxford Fulfillment Centre, PO Box 800, Kidlington, Oxford OX5 1DX United Kingdom.**) ED** L.B. Freund, J.R. Willis. **LC** TA350; .J68. **CODEN** JMPSA8. **[CCC]. Pr Rev.** available on microfilm and microfiche from University Microfilms International (UMI). Documents available from Article Express International, The Genuine Article, Ask*IEEE, CASDDS.
Desc: Covers all aspects of the fundamental physics and chemistry of the solid state. Emphasis is placed upon experimental and theoretical work which elucidates the basic properties of and processes in condensed systems.
Ind/Abst Agric. Eng. Abstr.; Alum. Ind. Abstr.; Appl. Mech. Rev.; Appl. Sci. Technol. Index (1991-); Bioeng. Abstr.; Ceram. Abstr. (19??-); Chem. Abstr. (1952-1984); Curr. Contents Eng. Tech. Appl. Sci.; Ei Page One; Eng. Mater. Abstr.; Eng. Index Annu. [Select. Cov.]; INIS Atomindex [Micro.]; INSPEC (1968-); Int. Aerosp. Abstr.; Math. Rev.; Met. Abstr.; Res. Alert [Full Cov.]; Sci. Cit. Index; SCISEARCH; Zentralbl. Math. Ihre Grenzgeb.

US/0887-0586
JOURNAL OF WAVE-MATERIAL INTERACTION. [J. wave-mater. interact.]. **VFOAT** Journal of Wave Material Interaction. Vol. 1, No. 1 (Jan. 1986)-. Periodical. English. Four times a year. $130.00 (institutions), $40.00d (individuals) US; $155.00 (institutions), $65.00 (individuals) other. V.K. Varadan Department of Engineering Science, 149 Hammond Building, Pennsylvania State University, University Park PA 16802. **Tel** (814)865-2481, (814)865-0663. **ED** Vijay K Varadan and Vasundara V Varadan. **DD** 620. ctrl circ.

●JA
JSME INTERNATIONAL JOURNAL. SERIES A, MECHANICS AND MATERIAL ENGINEERING. **Added/Corp** Nihon Kikai Gakkai. **VFOAT** Mechanics and Material Engineering. Vol. 36, No. 1 (Jan. 1993)-. Periodical. English. qt. $150.00. Nihon Kikai Gakkai, (Japan Society of Mechanical Engineers), 4-9, Yoyogi 2 Chome, Shibuyaku, Tokyoto 151 Japan. **(Subscription address:** Maruzen Company Ltd., PO Box 5050, Import & Export Department, Tokyo 100 31 Japan.**) LC** TJ1; .J75. **DD** 620.1/12. **CODEN** JJMMEQ. Documents available from Article Express International, The Genuine Article. ***Continues*** *JSME International Journal. Series I, Solid Mechanics, Strength of Materials, 0914-8809.*
Ind/Abst Chem. Abstr.; Civ. Struct. Eng. Abstr.; Comput. Inf. Syst. Abstr. J.; Curr. Contents Eng. Tech. Appl. Sci.; Ei Page One; Elect. Comm. Abstr.; Eng. Index Annu.; Fluid Abstr., Civil Eng.; Fluid Abstr. Proc. Eng.; FLUIDEX; INSPEC; Manuf. Process Eng. Abstr.; Mater. Sci. Eng. Abstr.; Mech. Eng. Abstr.; Res. Alert; Sci. Cit. Index; SCISEARCH; Solid State Supercond. Abstr.

UK/0950-4753
KEY ABSTRACTS. ADVANCED MATERIALS. **See** Engineering-Abstracting, Bibliographies and Statistics.

SZ/1013-9826
KEY ENGINEERING MATERIALS. [Key eng. mater.]. Vol. 9 (1986)-. Periodical. English. mo. $926.00. Trans Tech Publications Ltd., Hardstr. 13, CH-4714 Aedermannsdorf Switzerland. **Tel** 011 41 62 741379, FAX 011 41 12 72 10 58. **LC** TA401; .M42. **DD** 620.1/1/05. **CODEN** KEMAEY. Documents available from Article Express International, Ask*IEEE. ***Continues*** *Mechanical and Corrosion Properties. A, Key Engineering Materials, 0252-1059.*
Ind/Abst Ei Page One; Eng. Index Annu.; INSPEC (1986-).

JA/0914-3793
KYUSHU DAIGAKU KINO BUSSHITSU KAGAKU KENKYUJO HOKOKU. **Added/Corp** Kyushu Daigaku. Kino Busshitsu Kagaku Kenkyujo. **VFOAT** Kino Busshitsu Kagaku Kenkyujo Hokoku; Reports of Institute of Advanced Material Study, Kyushu University. (1987)-. Periodical. Japanese (English). Kyushu Daigaku Kino Busshitsu Kagaku Kenkyujo, (Inst. of Advanced Material Study, Kyushu University), 6-1, Kasuga Koen, Kasugashi, Fukuokaken 816 Japan. **LC** QD130; .K98.
Ind/Abst Int. Aerosp. Abstr.

US
MATERIAL ENGINEERING. **See** Engineering-Industrial Engineering and Design.

US/0025-5262
MATERIAL HANDLING ENGINEERING. [Mater. handl. eng.]. Vol. 14 (Oct. 1958)-. Periodical. English. Thirteen times a year (includes MHE Handbook Directory). $50.00 US; $65.00 Canada; $75.00 Mexico; $90.00 other. Penton Publishing, 1100 Superior Avenue, Cleveland OH 44114-2543. **Tel** (216)696-7000, FAX (216)696-0836. **(Subscription address:** Penton Publishing, PO Box 96732, Chicago IL 60693.**) CODEN** MHENA4. **[CCC].** Documents available from UMI Article Clearinghouse, Ask*IEEE. ***Continues*** *Flow.*
Desc: Edited for the executive responsible for the material handling function in manufacturing or distribution. Articles describe the application of material handling products and systems as a means of increasing productivity, cutting operating costs, improving safety and facilitating materials requirement planning and inventory control.
Ind/Abst ABI/INFORM Glob. Ed.; ABI Inform Ondisc (March 1985-); Appl. Sci. Technol. Index; Ei Page One; Energy Inf. Abstr.; Energy Res. Abstr.; F&S Index Plus Text, Int. [Select. Cov.]; INSPEC (Feb. 1969-); Int. Packag. Abstr.; Pollut. Abstr. Indexes; PROMT; Text. Technol. Dig.; Trade Ind. ASAP [Full Txt.]; Trade Ind. Index [Full Txt.]; UMI ABI/Inform--Bus. Period. Ondisc (Dec. 1987-) [Full Txt.].

US/0025-5262
MATERIAL HANDLING ENGINEERING. HANDBOOK DIRECTORY. (Oct. 1945)-. Periodical. English. an (May). $50.00. Penton Publishing, 1100 Superior Avenue, Cleveland OH 44114-2543. **Tel** (216)696-7000, FAX (216)696-0836. **(Subscription address:** Penton Publishing, PO Box 96732, Chicago IL 60693.**) [CCC].** available on microfilm and microfiche from University Microfilms International (UMI).
Ind/Abst Ei Page One; UMI ABI/Inform--Bus. Period. Ondisc (Dec. 1987-) [Full Txt.].

US/0195-2366
MATERIAL HANDLING PRODUCT NEWS. [Mater. handl. prod. news]. Vol. 1 (Sept. 1979)-. Periodical. English. mo. $25.00 US, Canada & Mexico; $48.00 (surface mail), $73.00 (airmail) other. Cahners Publishing Company, 249 West 17th Street, New York NY 10011. **Tel** (212)645-0067, FAX (212)242-6987. **(Subscription address:** Gordon Publications, Inc., Paid Circulation Department, 301 Gibralter Drive, Box 650, Morris Plains NJ 07950-0650.**) DD** 658.
Desc: Edited for the engineer and manager involved in the operation, design and maintenance of material handling equipment, systems and related services in industry warehousing and other facilities using material handling equipment.

BU/0204-7535
MATERIALOZNANIE I TEKNOLOGIYA. **See** Metals and Metallurgy.

GW/0025-5300
MATERIALPRUFUNG. (MATERIALPRUFUNG. MATERIALS TESTING. MATERIAUX ESSAIS ET RECHERCHES.). [Materialprufung]. **Added/Corp** Deutscher Verband fuer Materialprufung. **VFOAT** Materials Testing; Materiaux Essais et Recherches. Vol. 1 (Jan. 1959)-. Academic Scholarly Publication. German (English and French). Nine times a year. DM405.00. Carl Hanser Verlag, Postfach 860420, D 81631 Munich Germany. **Tel** 011 49 89 998300, FAX 011 49 89 984809. **LC** TA401; .M35. **CODEN** MTPRAJ. **[CCC]. Ad Acc.** Documents available from Article Express International, Ask*IEEE, CASDDS.
Desc: The only journal on the international market that deals with the whole field of materials testing. Contains research reports, test methods, testing equipment, discussions of standardization of terms and expressions used in materials testing and materials technology.
Ind/Abst Alum. Ind. Abstr.; Bioeng. Abstr.; Chem. Abstr.; Coal Abstr.; Ei Page One; Energy Res. Abstr.; Eng. Mater. Abstr. (1973-); Eng. Index Annu.; Fluid Abstr., Civil Eng.; Fluid Abstr. Proc. Eng.; FLUIDEX (1973-1990);; INSPEC (Dec. 1968-); Int. Aerosp. Abstr.; Int. Civil Eng. Abstr.; Met. Abstr.; Soft. Abstr. Eng.; World Alum. Abstr.

UK/0264-1275
MATERIALS & DESIGN. [Mater. des.]. **VFOAT** Materials and Design. Vol. 3, No. 4 (Aug. 1982)-. Academic Scholarly Publication. English. bm. $321.00 The Americas; £215.00 other. Butterworth Heinemann Publishers, Linacre House, Jordan Hill, Oxford OX2 8DP England. **Tel** 011 44 865 310366. **(Subscription address:** Elsevier Science Ltd. Oxford Fulfillment Centre, PO Box 800, Kidlington, Oxford OX5 1DX United Kingdom.**) ED** L. Bovey. **LC** TA401; .M355. **DD** 620.1/1. **CODEN** MADSD2. **[CCC].** Index available. **Bk Rev. Circ:** 700. available on microfilm and microfiche from University Microfilms International (UMI). Documents available from Article Express International, The Genuine Article, CASDDS. ***Continues*** *Materials in Engineering, 0261-3069.*
Desc: Aims to help practicing engineers to appreciate both the properties of modern materials in fields that may not be their immediate concern and the importance of design.
Ind/Abst Abstr. Bull. Inst. Pap. Sci. Tech.; Alum. Ind. Abstr.; Ceram. Abstr.; Chem. Abstr.; Civ. Struct. Eng. Abstr.; Comput. Inf. Syst. Abstr. J. [Full Cov.]; Ei Page One; Eng. Mater. Abstr.; Eng. Index Annu.; Fluid Abstr., Civil Eng.; Fluid Abstr. Proc. Eng.; FLUIDEX; Manuf. Process Eng. Abstr.; Mater. Sci. Eng. Abstr.; Mech. Eng. Abstr.; Met. Abstr.; Res. Alert [Full Cov.]; Solid State Supercond. Abstr.; World Ceram. Abstr.

US/0887-1949
MATERIALS AND PROCESSING REPORT. ***Title Change.*** (MATERIALS AND PROCESSING REPORT : MPR.). [Mater. process. rep.]. **Added/Corp** Massachusetts Institute of Technology. Materials Processing Center. **VFOAT** MPR. Vol. 1, No. 1 (April 1986)-(199?). Academic Scholarly Publication. English. mo. Elsevier Science Publishing Company Inc, Madison Square Station, PO Box 882, New York NY 10159-0882. **Tel** (212)633-3950, FAX (212)633-3990. **DD** 620. **[CCC].** ***Continued by*** *Materials Technology, 1066-7857.*
Desc: An international technical bulletin covering physics and mechanics of electromagnetic phenomena in devices, materials, instruments, and mechanics. It offers

a unique review of the most important current research developments at corporate, federal government, and academic laboratories worldwide.

UK/0960-3409
MATERIALS AT HIGH TEMPERATURES. [Mater. high temp.]. Vol. 9, No. 1 (Feb. 1991)-. Academic Scholarly Publication. English. qt. $492.00 The Americas; £330.00 other. Butterworth Heinemann Publishers, Linacre House, Jordan Hill, Oxford OX2 8DP England. **Tel** 011 44 865 310366. **(Subscription address:** Elsevier Science Ltd. Oxford Fulfillment Centre, PO Box 800, Kidlington, Oxford OX5 1DX United Kingdom.**) LC** TA418.26; .H54. **DD** 620.1/1217. **CODEN** MHTEEM. **[CCC].** available on microfilm and microfiche from University Microfilms International (UMI). Documents available from Article Express International, The Genuine Article, Ask*IEEE, CASDDS. ***Continues*** *High Temperature Technology, 0261-9180.*
Ind/Abst Alum. Ind. Abstr.; Ceram. Abstr. (199?-); Chem. Abstr. (Feb. 1991-); Civ. Struct. Eng. Abstr.; Coal Abstr. (Feb. 1991-); Curr. Contents Eng. Tech. Appl. Sci.; Ei Page One; Energy Inf. Abstr.; Eng. Index Annu.; Environ. Eng. Abstr.; INSPEC (Feb. 1991-); Manuf. Process Eng. Abstr.; Mater. Sci. Eng. Abstr.; Mech. Eng. Abstr.; Met. Abstr.; Res. Alert [Full Cov.]; SCISEARCH; Solid State Supercond. Abstr.; World Ceram. Abstr.

IT
MATERIALS ENGINEERING. Italian. Three times a year. Enrico Mucchi Editore SRL, Via Emilia Est 1527, 41100 Modena Italy. **Tel** 011 39 59 374094, FAX 059/374096.
Ind/Abst Ceram. Abstr. (19??-).

US/0025-5319
MATERIALS ENGINEERING. ***Ceased.*** [Mater. eng.]. **VFOAT** ME. Vol. 65, No. 4 (Apr. 1967)-(Dec. 1992). Academic Scholarly Publication. English. mo. Materials Engineering, 1100 Superior Avenue, Cleveland OH 44114. **Tel** (216)696-7000, FAX (216)696-0177. **ED** Clifford Lewis. **LC** TN1; .M34. **DD** 620.1/1/05. **CODEN** MAENBO. **[CCC]. Bk Rev. Ad Acc. Circ:** 61,100 (ctrl). available on microfilm from University Microfilms International (UMI); available on microfiche. Documents available from Article Express International, CASDDS, Documents on Demand. ***Continues*** *Materials in Design Engineering.*
Desc: Discusses the fall range of engineered materials: composites, metals, plastics, adhesives, elactomers, coatings, ceramics and processing/testing technology.
Ind/Abst Alum. Ind. Abstr.; Appl. Sci. Technol. Index; Art Archaeol. Tech. Abstr.; Bioeng. Abstr.; Ceram. Abstr.; Chem. Abstr.; Chem. Ind. Notes (?-1992); Ei Page One; EMBASE; Energy Inf. Abstr.; Eng. Mater. Abstr.; Eng. Index Annu.; Environ. Abstr.; F&S Index Plus Text, Int. [Select. Cov.]; INIS Atomindex [Micro.]; Int. Packag. Abstr.; Leadscan; Met. Abstr.; PROMT; Text. Technol. Dig.; Trade Ind. ASAP [Full Txt.]; Trade Ind. Index [Full Txt.].

IT/1120-7302
MATERIALS ENGINEERING MODENA. [Mater. eng.Modena]. (1990)-. Periodical. English. Three times a year. L200000 (Italy); L220000 (other). Enrico Mucchi Editore SRL, Via Emilia Est 1527, 41100 Modena Italy. **Tel** 011 39 59 374094, FAX 059/374096. **UDC** 62. Documents available from CASDDS.
Ind/Abst Chem. Abstr.

US/0025-5327
MATERIALS EVALUATION. [Mater. eval.]. **Added/Corp** American Society for Nondestructive Testing. Society for Non-destructive Testing. Vol. 22, No. 1 (Jan. 1964)-. Periodical. English. mo. $95.00 North America; $165.00 other. American Society for Nondestructive Testing, 1711 Arlingate Lane, PO Box 28518, Columbus OH 43228. **Tel** (614)274-6003, (800)222-2768, FAX (614)274-6899. **ED** Patrick O Moore. **DD** 621. **CODEN** MAEVAD. **[CCC].** Index available. cum. index. **Bk Rev. Ad Acc. Pr Rev. Circ:** 11,000 (ctrl). available on microfilm and microfiche from University Microfilms International (UMI). Documents available from Article Express International, The Genuine Article, Ask*IEEE, Petroleum Abstracts Document Delivery Service, CASDDS. ***Continues*** *Nondestructive Testing, 0096-7955.*
Desc: A professional engineering association dedicated to advancing industrial inspection techniques such as x-ray, ultrasound, infrared, etc. Publishes technical and nontechnical information and articles.
Ind/Abst Abstr. Bull. Inst. Pap. Sci. Tech.; Acoust. Abstr.; Appl. Mech. Rev.; Appl. Sci. Technol. Index; Art Archaeol. Tech. Abstr.; Ceram. Abstr.; Chem. Abstr.; Curr. Contents Eng. Tech. Appl. Sci.; Ei Page One; Eng. Mater. Abstr.; Eng. Index Annu.; Highw. Res. Abstr.; INSPEC (1968-); Int. Aerosp. Abstr.; Leadscan; Pet. Abstr.; Res. Alert [Full Cov.]; SCISEARCH.

US
MATERIALS HANDBOOK. (1929)-. English. ir. $74.50. McGraw Hill Publishing Company, Inc., 1221 Avenue of the Americas, New York NY 10020. **Tel** (212)512-6410, (800)525-5003, FAX (212)512-6111. **LC** TA403; .B75. Each issue contains an index to its own contents (no volume index)--loose.

US
MATERIALS INFORMATION ENGINEERED MATERIALS SEARCH-IN-PRINT SERIES. (19??)-. English. $95.00 (member), $105.00 (nonmember) North America. American Society for Metals International, c/o Deborah Barthelmes, Materials Park OH 44073-0002. **Tel** (216)338-5151, FAX (216)338-4634, telex 980-619. **(Subscription address:** ASM International, Materials Information, Materials Park OH 44073.**) Bk Rev.** available on diskette.
Desc: Contains 80 computer generated bibliographies compiled from Engineered Materials Abstracts database. Each reference gives title, author, source, language, and abstracts the cited article.

NE/0167-577X
MATERIALS LETTERS. [Mater. lett.]. **Added/Corp** Materials Research Society. Vol. 1, No. 1 (June 1982)-. Academic Scholarly Publication. English. Eighteen times a year (3 volumes). Fl1350.00. Elsevier Science Publishers BV, PO Box 211, 1000 AE Amsterdam Netherlands. **Tel** 011 31 20 5803642, FAX 011 31 20 5862696, telex 15682. **ED** J.H. Wernick, A.F.W. Willoughby. **LC** TA401; .M37. **DD** 620.1/1/05. **CODEN** MLETDJ. **[CCC]. Pr Rev.** available on microfilm and microfiche from University Microfilms International (UMI). Documents available from Article Express International, The Genuine Article, Ask*IEEE, CASDDS.
Desc: Devoted to the science and technology of materials.
Ind/Abst Alum. Ind. Abstr.; Ceram. Abstr.; Chem. Abstr.; Chem. Titles; Civ. Struct. Eng. Abstr.; Curr. Contents Phys. Chem. Earth Sci.; Ei Page One; Elect. Comm. Abstr.; Eng. Mater. Abstr.; Eng. Index Annu.; INSPEC (June 1982-); Int. Aerosp. Abstr. (1983-); Manuf. Process Eng. Abstr.; Mater. Sci. Eng. Abstr.; Mech. Eng. Abstr.; Met. Abstr.; Pollut. Abstr. Indexes; Res. Alert [Full Cov.]; Sci. Cit. Index; SCISEARCH; Solid State Supercond. Abstr.

US/0094-1492
MATERIALS PERFORMANCE. [Mater. perform.]. **Added/Corp** National Association of Corrosion Engineers. **VFOAT** MP. Vol. 13, No. 1 (Jan. 1974)-. Periodical. English. mo. Free to NACE members; $85.00 nonmembers mainland US; $100.00 nonmembers other. National Association of Corrosion Engineers, 1440 South Creek Drive, Houston TX 77084. **Tel** (713)492-0535, FAX (713)492-8254, telex 792310 NACE HOU. **(Subscription address:** National Association of Corrosion Engineers, PO Box 218340, Houston, TX 77084**) ED** LC Rowe. **LC** TA462; .M373. **DD** 620.1/6/2305. **CODEN** MTPFBI. **[CCC].** Index available. cum. index. **Bk Rev. Ad Acc. Pr Rev. Circ:** 15,500 (ctrl). available on microfilm and microfiche from University Microfilms International (UMI). Documents available from Article Express International, The Genuine Article, Ask*IEEE, Petroleum Abstracts Document Delivery Service, CASDDS. ***Continues*** *Materials Protection and Performance, 0025-5378.*
Desc: Official journal of NACW edited for the corrosion engineer, scientist, technician, and others involved in combating corrosion problems in practical situations.
Ind/Abst Abstr. Bull. Inst. Pap. Sci. Tech.; Alum. Ind. Abstr.; Appl. Sci. Technol. Index; Art Archaeol. Tech. Abstr.; Bioeng. Abstr.; BMT Abstr.; Ceram. Abstr.; Chem. Abstr.; Coal Abstr.; Corros. Abstr.; Curr. Contents Eng. Tech. Appl. Sci.; Curr. Titles Electrochem.; Ei Page One; EMBASE; Eng. Mater. Abstr.; Eng. Index Annu.; Fluid Abstr., Civil Eng.; Fluid Abstr. Proc. Eng.; FLUIDEX (1974-); Gas Abstr.; Highw. Res. Abstr.; HTFS Dig.; INSPEC (Jan. 1984-Dec. 1988); Leadscan; Lit. Pat. Abstr., Oilfield Chem. (1962-); Lit. Abstr., Catal. Catal.; Lit. Abstr., Health Environ.; Lit. Abstr., Pet. Refin. Petrochem.; Lit. Abstr., Pet. Substit.; Lit. Abstr., Transp. Storage; Met. Abstr.; Life Sci. Collect.; Pet. Abstr.; Res. Alert [Full Cov.]; Risk Abstr.; SCISEARCH; Soc. Sci. Cit. Index [Select. Cov.]; Surf. Treat. Technol. Abstr.; World Surf. Coat. Abstr.

US/0148-0529
MATERIALS PERFORMANCE : CORROSION ENGINEERING BUYER'S GUIDE. ***Title Change.*** **See** Engineering-Chemical Engineering.

NE/0167-790X
MATERIALS PROCESSING, THEORY AND PRACTICES. [Mater. process. theory pract.]. Vol. 1 (1980)-. Monographic series. English. Elsevier Science Publishers BV, PO Box 211, 1000 AE Amsterdam Netherlands. **Tel** 011 31 20 5803642, FAX 011 31 20 5862696, telex 15682. **CODEN** MPTPD8. Documents available from CASDDS.
Ind/Abst Chem. Abstr.

UK/0956-2982
MATERIALS RECLAMATION HANDBOOK. [Mater. reclam. handb.]. (1990)-. English. an. Emap Vision, 19 Scarbrook Road, Croydon CR9 1QH England. **Tel** 01-760 9690, FAX 01-681 1672, telex 946665. ***Continues*** *Materials Reclamation Weekly ... Directory and Handbook, 0267-1581.*

US/0025-5408
MATERIALS RESEARCH BULLETIN. [Mater. res. bull.]. Vol. 1 (Sept. 1966)-. Periodical. English (French and German; summaries and/or abstracts in French, German and English). mo. $753.00 The Americas; £505.00 other. Pergamon Press, An Imprint of Elsevier Science Ltd., The Boulevard, Langford Lane, Kidlington, Oxford OX5 1GB United Kingdom. **Tel** 011 44 865 843000, 011 44 865 843699, FAX 011 44 865 843010. **(Subscription address:** Elsevier Science Ltd. Oxford Fulfillment Centre, PO Box 800, Kidlington, Oxford OX5 1DX United Kingdom.**) ED** Heinz K. Henisch. **LC** TA404.2; .M36. **DD** 620.1/1. **CODEN** MRBUAC. **[CCC]. Pr Rev.** available on microfilm and microfiche from University Microfilms International (UMI). Documents available from Article Express International, The Genuine Article, Ask*IEEE, CASDDS, Documents on Demand.
Desc: International rapid publication journal reporting research on crystal growth, materials preparation and characterization.
Ind/Abst Alum. Ind. Abstr.; Bioeng. Abstr.; Ceram. Abstr.; Chem. Abstr.; Chem. Titles; Curr. Contents Phys. Chem. Earth Sci.; Curr. Titles Electrochem.; Ei Page One; Energy Inf. Abstr.; Energy Res. Abstr.; Eng. Mater. Abstr.; Eng. Index Annu.; Environ. Abstr.; GeoRef; INSPEC (1968-); Int. Aerosp. Abstr.; Leadscan; Met. Abstr.; Pollut. Abstr. Indexes; Res. Alert [Full Cov.]; Sci. Cit. Index; SCISEARCH.

SZ/0921-5093
MATERIALS SCIENCE & ENGINEERING. A, STRUCTURAL MATERIALS : PROPERTIES, MICROSTRUCTURE AND PROCESSING. [Mater. sci. eng. A Struct. mater. : prop. microstruct. process.]. **VFOAT** Structural Materials : Properties, Microstructure and Processing; Materials Science and Engineering. A, Structural Materials Properties, Microstructure and Processing; Materials Science & Engineering A. Vol. 101 (May 1988)-. Academic Scholarly Publication. English. Forty-eight times a year (18 volumes). 5440.00F; 8190.00F combined subscription with Materials Science and Engineering B and C, and Materials Science and Engineering Reports; 5850.00F combined subscription with Reports. Elsevier Sequoia SA, PO Box 564, CH-1001 Lausanne 1 Switzerland. **Tel** 011 41 21 3207381. **ED** H. Herman. **LC** TA401; .M382. **DD** 620.1/105. **CODEN** MSAPE3. **[CCC]. Ad Acc, Adv Mgr:** Ms. W van Cattenburch (Amsterdam). **Pr Rev.** available on microfilm and microfiche from University Microfilms International (UMI). Documents available from Article Express International, The Genuine Article, Ask*IEEE, CASDDS, Documents on Demand. ***Continues in part*** *Materials Science and Engineering, 0025-5416.*
Desc: Provides an international medium for the publication of theoretical and experimental studies and reviews of the properties and behavior of a wide range of materials, related both to their structure and to their engineering application.
Ind/Abst Alum. Ind. Abstr.; Bioeng. Abstr.; Ceram. Abstr. (19??-); Chem. Abstr.; Civ. Struct. Eng. Abstr.; Ei Page One; Elect. Comm. Abstr.; EMBASE; Energy Inf. Abstr.; Energy Res. Abstr.; Eng. Index Annu.; Environ. Abstr.; Fluid Abstr., Civil Eng.; Fluid Abstr. Proc. Eng.; FLUIDEX (19??-); GeoRef; INSPEC (May 1988-); Int. Aerosp. Abstr.; Leadscan; Manuf. Process Eng. Abstr.; Mater. Sci. Eng. Abstr.; Mech. Eng. Abstr.; Met. Abstr.; Phys. Briefs; Pollut. Abstr. Indexes; Res. Alert [Full Cov.]; Sci. Cit. Index; SCISEARCH.

US/1063-732X
MATERIALS SCIENCE AND ENGINEERING ABSTRACTS. ***Ceased.*** **See** Engineering-Abstracting, Bibliographies and Statistics.

SZ/0921-5107
MATERIALS SCIENCE & ENGINEERING. B, SOLID-STATE MATERIALS FOR ADVANCED TECHNOLOGY. **VFOAT** Solid-State Materials for Advanced Technology; Solid State Materials for Advanced Technology; Materials Science and Engineering. Solid-State Materials Advanced Technology; Materials Science and Engineering B. Vol B1, No. 1 (Aug. 1988)-. Periodical. English. Twenty-one times a year (7 vols.). 2380.00F; 8190.00F combined subscription with Materials Science and Engineering A & C and Materials Science and Engineering Reports; 2925.00F combined subscription with Reports. Elsevier Sequoia SA, PO Box 564, CH-1001 Lausanne 1 Switzerland. **Tel** 011 41 21 3207381. **ED** M. Balkanski, H. Kamimura and S. Mahajan. **LC** TA401; .M383. **DD** 620.1/105. **CODEN** MSBTEK. **[CCC]. Pr Rev.** available on microfilm and microfiche from University Microfilms International (UMI). Documents available from Article Express International, The Genuine Article, Ask*IEEE, CASDDS. ***Continues in part*** *Materials Science and Engineering, 0025-5416.*
Desc: Addresses the interfacial overlap between the disciplines of materials science and engineering, solid-state physics, solid-state chemistry, and solid-state electronics. It will also publish papers pertaining to the electronic, ionic, magnetic, and optical properties of materials.
Ind/Abst Ceram. Abstr. (19??-); Chem. Abstr.; Civ. Struct. Eng. Abstr.; Ei Page One; Elect. Comm. Abstr.; Eng. Index Annu.; Environ. Eng. Abstr.; Fluid Abstr., Civil Eng.; Fluid Abstr. Proc. Eng.; FLUIDEX (19??-); INSPEC (Aug. 1988-); Manuf. Process Eng. Abstr.; Mater. Sci. Eng. Abstr.; Mech. Eng. Abstr.; Met. Abstr.; Phys. Briefs; Res. Alert [Full Cov.]; Sci. Cit. Index; SCISEARCH.

UK/0267-0836
MATERIALS SCIENCE AND TECHNOLOGY. (MATERIALS SCIENCE AND TECHNOLOGY : MST : A PUBLICATION OF THE INSTITUTE OF METALS.). [Mater. sci. technol.]. **Added/Corp** Institute of Metals. **VFOAT** MST. Vol. 1, No. 1 (Jan. 1985)-. Academic Scholarly Publication. English. mo. £484.00 EEC; £556.60 other. The Institute of Materials, 1 Carlton House Terrace, London SW1Y 5DB England. **Tel** 011 44 71 839 4071, FAX (071)839 2078. **LC** TA401; .M3844. **DD** 620.1/1/05. **CODEN** MSCTEP. **Pr Rev.** available on microfilm and microfiche from University Microfilms International (UMI). Documents available from Article Express International, The Genuine Article, Ask*IEEE, CASDDS. ***Formed by the union of*** *Metals Technology, 0307-1693* ***and*** *Metal Science, 0306-3453.*
Desc: Designed for those concerned with the production, fabrication, structure and properties, and application of structural and electronic engineering materials and their future development.
Ind/Abst Appl. Sci. Technol. Index; Art Archaeol. Tech. Abstr.; Ceram. Abstr.; Chem. Abstr. (1985-); Civ. Struct. Eng. Abstr.; Coal Abstr.; Comput. Inf. Syst. Abstr. J. [Full Cov.]; Curr. Contents Eng. Tech. Appl. Sci.; Curr. Technol. Index; Curr. Titles Electrochem.; Ei Page One; Elect. Comm. Abstr.; Eng. Index Annu.; Environ. Eng. Abstr.; INSPEC (1985-); Int. Aerosp. Abstr.; Leadscan; Manuf. Process Eng. Abstr.; Mater. Sci. Eng. Abstr.; Mech. Eng. Abstr.; Res. Alert [Full Cov.]; Sci. Cit. Index; SCISEARCH; Soc. Sci. Cit. Index [Select. Cov.]; Solid State Supercond. Abstr.

SZ/0255-5476
MATERIALS SCIENCE FORUM. [Mater. sci. forum]. Vol. 1 (1984)-. Academic Scholarly Publication. English. Thirty times a year. $2190.00. Trans Tech Publications Ltd., Hardstr. 13, CH-4714 Aedermannsdorf Switzerland. **Tel** 011 41 62 741379, FAX 011 41 12 72 10 58. **ED** G. E. Murch. **LC** TA401.3; .M3793. **DD** 620.1/1/05. **CODEN** MSFOEP. Index available. cum. index. **Circ:** 600. Documents available from Ask*IEEE, CASDDS. ***Continues*** *Diffusion and Defect Monograph Series, 0250-9776;* ***Absorbed*** *Crystal Properties and Preparation, 1013-5049.*
Desc: Presents basic materials science research.
Ind/Abst Ceram. Abstr.; Chem. Abstr. (1984-); Ei Page One; INSPEC (1984-).

●US/1068-820X
MATERIALS SCIENCE (NEW YORK, N.Y.). (MATERIALS SCIENCES.). [Mater. sci.]. **Added/Corp** Consultants Bureau. Vol. 29, No. 1 (Jan.-Feb. 1993)-. Periodical. English (translations available in Russian). Six times a year. $1145.00 US; $1340.00 other. Consultants Bureau, A Division of Plenum Publishing Corporation, 233 Spring Street, New York NY 10013. **Tel** (212)620-8000, (212)620-8466, FAX (212)463-0742, telex 23/421139. **LC** TA401; .S654. **DD** 620. **CODEN** MSCIEQ. ***Continues*** *Soviet Materials Science, 0038-5565.*

NE/0920-2307
MATERIALS SCIENCE REPORTS. ***Title Change.*** [Mater. sci. rep.]. Vol. 1, No. 1 (Sept. 1986)-Vol. 9, No. 7/8 (Mar. 1993). Academic Scholarly Publication. English. Sixteen times a year (2 vols.). Elsevier Science Publishers BV, PO Box 211, 1000 AE Amsterdam Netherlands. **Tel** 011 31 20 5803642, FAX 011 31 20 5862696, telex 15682. **ED** S.S. Lau and F.W. Saris. **LC** TA401; .M3846. **DD** 620.1/1. **CODEN** MSREEL. **[CCC].** available on microfilm and microfiche from University Microfilms International (UMI). Documents available from Article Express International, The Genuine Article, Ask*IEEE, CASDDS. ***Continued by*** *Materials Science & Engineering. R, Reports, 0927-796X.*
Desc: Serves the materials science community in two ways. It provides a general background of materials science and presents specialized reviews on current and significant developments in the field.
Ind/Abst Ceram. Abstr.; Chem. Abstr. (1986-); Curr. Contents Phys. Chem. Earth Sci.; Ei Page One; Eng. Mater. Abstr.; Eng. Index Annu.; INSPEC (Sept. 1986-); Res. Alert [Full Cov.]; Sci. Cit. Index (19??-19??); SCISEARCH.

US/0198-7798
MATERIALS SCIENCES PROGRAMS. (MATERIALS SCIENCES PROGRAMS / OFFICE OF BASIC ENERGY SCIENCES.). [Mater. sci. programs]. Began with 1976. English. an. National Technical Information Service - NTIS, Room 2027S, 5285 Port Royal Road, Springfield VA 22161. **Tel** (703)487-4630, (703)487-4660, (703)487-4650, FAX (703)321-8547, telex 89-9405. **LC** TA404.2; .U56A. **DD** 620.1/1/072.

US/0272-4170
MATERIALS TECHNOLOGY (COLUMBUS). (MATERIALS TECHNOLOGY.). [Mater. technol.]. Spring 1980-. Periodical. English. $2.50 each copy. General Electric Company, 120 Erie Boulevard, Schenectady NY 12305. **Tel** (502)685-6200. **LC** TA401; .M385. **DD** 620.1/1/05.

●US/1066-7857
MATERIALS TECHNOLOGY (NEW YORK, N.Y.). (MATERIALS TECHNOLOGY.). [Mater. technol.]. **VFOAT** Mat Tech. (1993)-. Academic Scholarly Publication. English. Twelve times a year (1 volume). $475.00 US; $510.00 (includes SAL delivery) other. Elsevier Science Publishing Company Inc, Madison Square Station, PO Box 882, New York NY 10159-0882. **Tel** (212)633-3950, FAX (212)633-3990. **ED** Renee G Ford. **DD** 620. **[CCC].** ***Continues*** *Materials and Processing Report, 0887-1949.*
Desc: Dedicated to facilitating technology transfer through succinct, accurate, and up-to-the-minute reporting of developments worldwide in the synthesis and processing of advanced materials and their applications.

●UK/0967-8638
MATERIALS WORLD : THE JOURNAL OF THE INSTITUTE OF MATERIALS. **Added/Corp** Institute of Materials (London, England). **VFOAT** Journal of the Institute of Materials. Vol. 1, No. 1 (Jan. 1993)-. Academic Scholarly Publication. English. mo. £149.00 EEC; £171.35 other. The Institute of Materials, 1 Carlton House Terrace, London SW1Y 5DB England. **Tel** 011 44 71 839 4071, FAX (071)839 2078. **LC** TN1; .M3737. **CODEN** MORLEE. Documents available from CASDDS. ***Formed by the union of*** *Metals and Materials (London, England : 1985), 0266-7185; Plastics and Rubber International, 0309-4561* ***and*** *British Ceramic, Transactions and Journal, 0266-7606.*
Ind/Abst Chem. Abstr.; Soc. Sci. Cit. Index [Select. Cov.].

GW/0933-5137
MATERIALWISSENSCHAFT UND WERKSTOFFTECHNIK. [Mater.wiss. Werkst.tech.]. **Added/Corp** Dechema. Deutsche Gesellschaft fur Metallkunde. Verein Deutscher Eisenhuttenleute. Vol. 19 No. 1, (Jan. 1988)-. Periodical. German (English). mo. $680.00. VCH Gesellschaft GmbH, Postfach 101161, D 69451 Weinheim Germany. **Tel** 011 49 6201 606459, FAX 011 49 6201 606184. **(Subscription address:** VCH Publishers Inc., 303 Northwest 12th Avenue, Journals Department, Deerfield FL 33442.**) ED** E Broszeit and H Speckhardt. **LC** TA401; .Z38. **DD** 620.1/1. **CODEN** MATWER. **[CCC]. Pr Rev.** Documents available from Article Express International, The Genuine Article, Ask*IEEE, CASDDS. ***Continues*** *Zeitschrift fur Werkstofftechnik, 0049-8688.*
Ind/Abst Chem. Abstr.; Curr. Contents Eng. Tech. Appl. Sci.; Ei Page One; Eng. Index Annu.; INSPEC (Jan. 1988-); Res. Alert [Full Cov.]; SCISEARCH.

PL
MATERIALY OGNIOTRWALE. Polish. bm. **(Subscription address:** ARS Polona, PO Box 1001, 00068 Warsaw Poland.**)** Documents available from CASDDS.
Ind/Abst Chem. Abstr.

JA/0915-3594
MATERIARU RAIFU. **VFOAT** Materials Life. (1989)-. Periodical. Multiple languages. **DD** 620.1. Documents available from CASDDS.
Ind/Abst Chem. Abstr.

FR/0032-6895
MATERIAUX ET TECHNIQUES. [Mater. tech.]. (19??)-. Academic Scholarly Publication. French (English). bm. 810.00F France; 1100.00F other. Sirpe, 76 Rue de Rivoli, 75004 Paris France. **Tel** 011 33 1 42785220. **ED** Roger Drouhin. **LC** TA401; .M386. **CODEN** MATCBW. **[CCC].** Index available. cum. index. **Bk Rev. Ad Acc. Circ:** 3,500 (ctrl). Documents available from Article Express International, CASDDS.
Desc: Covers traditional and new materials in industry (steel, aluminum, composites and ceramics) and technologies for their transformation and work (sintering, bonding, corrosion, etc.).
Ind/Abst Alum. Ind. Abstr.; Art Archaeol. Tech. Abstr.; Bioeng. Abstr.; Chem. Abstr.; Coal Abstr.; Ei Page One; Elect. Comm. Abstr.; Energy Res. Abstr. (Aug. 1972-); Eng. Mater. Abstr.; Eng. Index Annu.; Environ. Eng. Abstr.; Int. Aerosp. Abstr.; Manuf. Process Eng. Abstr.; Mater. Sci. Eng. Abstr.; Mech. Eng. Abstr.; Met. Abstr.; Point Repere (1979-1980); Solid State Supercond. Abstr.

US
MD. **Added/Corp** American Society of Mechanical Engineers. Materials Division. (19??)-. Monographic series. English. ASME United Engineering Center, 345 East 47th Street, New York NY 10017. **CODEN** AMEMD9. Documents available from CASDDS.
Ind/Abst Chem. Abstr.; Civ. Struct. Eng. Abstr.; Manuf. Process Eng. Abstr.; Mater. Sci. Eng. Abstr.; Mech. Eng. Abstr.; Solid State Supercond. Abstr.

NE/0924-2147
MECHANICS ANALYSIS. ***Ceased.*** [Mech., Anal.]. (1972)-(19??). Monographic series. English. ir. Kluwer Academic Publishers, Postbus 322, 3300 AH Dordrecht, The Netherlands. **Tel** 011 (31) 78 524400, FAX 011 31 78 183273, telex 20083. **UDC** 531.
Ind/Abst Zentralbl. Math. Ihre Grenzgeb. (?-?).

NE
MECHANICS, DYNAMICAL SYSTEMS. (1985)-. Monographic series. English. Price varies per volume. Martinus Nijhoff Publishers, Subsidiary of Kluwer Academic Publishers, Koraalrood 50, 2718 SC Zoetermeer Netherlands. **Tel** 011 31 79 684400. ***Continues*** *Monographs and Textbooks on Mechanics of Solids and Fluids. Mechanics, Dynamical Systems, 0169-667X.*
Ind/Abst Math. Rev. (1988-); Zentralbl. Math. Ihre Grenzgeb.

US/0191-5665
MECHANICS OF COMPOSITE MATERIALS. [Mech. compos. mater.]. Vol. 15 (Jan./Feb. 1979)-. Academic Scholarly Publication. English (Russian). bm (6 issues). $1035.00 US; $1210.00 other. Consultants Bureau, A Division of Plenum Publishing Corporation, 233 Spring Street, New York NY 10013. **Tel** (212)620-8000, (212)620-8466, FAX (212)463-0742, telex 23/421139. **ED** V. P. Tamuzh. **LC** TA455.P58; M413. **DD** 620.1/18. **CODEN** MCMAD7. **[CCC].** Index available. **Pr Rev.** available on microfilm and microfiche from University Microfilms International (UMI). Documents available from The Genuine Article, Ask*IEEE, CASDDS. ***Continues*** *Polymer Mechanics, 0032-390X.*
Ind/Abst Appl. Mech. Rev.; Chem. Abstr.; Curr. Contents Eng. Tech. Appl. Sci.; Eng. Mater. Abstr.; Fluid Abstr., Civil Eng.; Fluid Abstr. Proc. Eng.; FLUIDEX (1979-); INSPEC (Jan./Feb. 1979-); Int. Aerosp. Abstr.; Pollut. Abstr. Indexes; Polymer Contents; Res. Alert [Select. Cov.]; SCISEARCH.

UK/1075-9417
MECHANICS OF COMPOSITE MATERIALS AND STRUCTURE. English. qt. $195.00. John Wiley & Sons Ltd., Baffins Lane, Chichester West Sussex PO19 1UD England. **Tel** 0243 779777, FAX 0243 776128 BTG:JWP001, telex 86290 WIBOOKG. **(Subscription address:** John Wiley / Philadelphia, PO Box 7247, Philadelphia PA 19170.**) ED** J.N. Reddy.

UK/0959-5864
MECHANICS OF CREEP BRITTLE MATERIALS. (1989)-. Academic Scholarly Publication. English. Elsevier Science Publishers Ltd, Crown House, Linton Road, Barking Essex IG11 8JU England. **Tel** 011 44 81 5947272, FAX 081-594-5942, telex 896950.
Ind/Abst Ceram. Abstr. (19??-).

NE
MECHANICS OF ELASTIC AND INELASTIC SOLIDS. ***Ceased.*** (19??)-(19??). Monographic series. English. ir. Kluwer Academic Publishers, Postbus 322, 3300 AH Dordrecht, The Netherlands. **Tel** 011 (31) 78 524400, FAX 011 31 78 183273, telex 20083.
Ind/Abst Math. Rev. (?-?); Zentralbl. Math. Ihre Grenzgeb. (?-?).

NE
MECHANICS OF ELASTIC STABILITY. ***Ceased.*** **VFOAT** Monographs and Textbooks on Mechanics of Solids and Fluids. Mechanics of Elastic Stability. (1974)-(19??). Monographic series. English. ir. Kluwer Academic Publishers, Postbus 322, 3300 AH Dordrecht, The Netherlands. **Tel** 011 (31) 78 524400, FAX 011 31 78 183273, telex 20083.
Ind/Abst Zentralbl. Math. Ihre Grenzgeb. (?-?).

NE/0167-6636
MECHANICS OF MATERIALS. (MECHANICS OF MATERIALS : AN INTERNATIONAL JOURNAL.). [Mech. mater.]. Vol. 1, No. 1 (Jan. 1982)-. Academic Scholarly Publication. English. Twelve times a year (3 volumes). Fl1350.00. Elsevier Science Publishers BV, PO Box 211, 1000 AE Amsterdam Netherlands. **Tel** 011 31 20 5803642, FAX 011 31 20 5862696, telex 15682. **ED** S Nemat-Nasser and Johannes Weertman. **LC** TA405; .M52. **DD** 620.1/1/05. **CODEN** MSMSD3. **[CCC]. Pr Rev.** available on microfilm and microfiche from University Microfilms International (UMI). Documents available from Article Express International, The Genuine Article, Ask*IEEE, CASDDS.
Desc: Provides a forum for original scientific research on the flow, fracture, and general constitutive behaviour of geophysical, geotechnical, and technological materials, with balanced coverage of theoretical, experimental, and field investigations.
Ind/Abst Alum. Ind. Abstr.; Bioeng. Abstr.; Ceram. Abstr. (19??-); Chem. Abstr.; Civ. Struct. Eng. Abstr.; Curr. Contents Eng. Tech. Appl. Sci.; Ei Page One; Eng. Mater. Abstr.; Eng. Index Annu.; Geotech. Abstr.; INSPEC (Jan. 1982-); Int. Aerosp. Abstr.; Mech. Eng. Abstr.; Met. Abstr.; Pollut. Abstr. Indexes; Res. Alert [Full Cov.]; SCISEARCH; Solid State Supercond. Abstr.

US/0890-5452
MECHANICS OF STRUCTURES AND MACHINES. [Mechan. struct. mach.]. Vol. 15, No. 1 (March 1987)-. Periodical. English. qt. $650.00 US; $664.00 other. Marcel Dekker Inc., 270 Madison Avenue, New York NY 10016. **Tel** (212)696-9000, (800)228-1160, FAX (212)685-4540, telex 421419. **(Subscription address:** Marcel Dekker Inc, PO Box 5017, Monticello NY 12701.**) ED** E. J. Haug. **LC** TA645; .J65. **DD** 624.1/7. **CODEN** MSMAEI. **[CCC]. Pr Rev.** Documents available from Article Express International, The Genuine Article, Ask*IEEE. ***Continues*** *Journal of Structural Mechanics, 0360-1218.*
Desc: Emphasizing contemporary research of immediate and potential application to aerospace, automotive, civil and mechanical engineering, marine, and related

structures. Expands its scope to present in-depth articles on new and challenging technical problems in important areas such as space structures, robotics, buildings, and bridges. This authoritative journal also explores technical areas of interest, including high-speed computing, numerical methods, variational methods, stability, fatigue and fracture mechanics, limit analysis, and plasticity.
Ind/Abst Abstr. J. Earthq. Eng.; Bioeng. Abstr. (1987-); Curr. Contents Eng. Tech. Appl. Sci.; Ei Page One; Energy Res. Abstr. (1987-); Eng. Index Annu.; INSPEC (1987-); Int. Aerosp. Abstr. (1987-19??); J. Ferrocement; Math. Rev. (1987-); Life Sci. Collect. (1987-); Res. Alert [Full Cov.]; Sci. Cit. Index (1987-); SCISEARCH; Shock Vibr. Dig.

PL/0137-5067
MECHANIKA I KOMPUTER / POLSKA AKADEMIA NAUK, INSTYTUT PODSTAWOWYCH PROBLEMOW TECHNIKI. **Added/Corp** Instytut Podstawowych Problemow Techniki (Polska Akademia Nauk). (19??)-. Periodical. Polish (summaries and/or abstracts in English and Russian). **LC** QA801; .M35. **DD** 531.
Ind/Abst Zentralbl. Math. Ihre Grenzgeb.

LV/0203-1272
MEHANIKA KOMPOZITNYH MATERIALOV. (MEKHANIKA KOMPOZITNYKH MATERIALOV.). [Meh. kompoz. mater.]. **Added/Corp** Latvijas PSR Zinatnu Akademija. (Jan./Feb. 1979)-. Academic Scholarly Publication. Russian. Six times a year. $179.95. **(Subscription address:** East View Publications Inc., 3020 Harbor Lane North, Suite 110, Minneapolis MN 55447.) **LC** TA455.P58; M4. **CODEN** MKMADT. **[CCC].** Documents available from Article Express International, Ask*IEEE, CASDDS. ***Continues*** *Mekhanika Polimerov.*
Ind/Abst Chem. Abstr.; Ei Page One; Eng. Index Annu.; INSPEC (Jan./Feb. 1979-); Int. Aerosp. Abstr.

II/0970-423X
METALS MATERIALS AND PROCESSES. [Met. Mater. Process.]. (1989)-. Periodical. English. qt. $125.00. Meshap Science Publishers, Bombay India. **(Subscription address:** Prints India, 11 Darya Ganj, New Delhi 110002 India.) **UDC** 620.1. Documents available from CASDDS.
Ind/Abst Chem. Abstr.

UK
MODELLING & SIMULATION IN MATERIALS SCIENCE AND ENGINEERING. (19??)-. English. qt. $272.00. Institute of Physics, Techno House, Redcliffe Way, Bristol BS1 6NX England. **Tel** 011 44 272 297481, FAX 011 44 272 294318, telex 449149 INSTP G. **(Subscription address:** American Institute of Physics, Publishing Sales, 500 Sunnyside Blvd., Woodbury NY 11797.) **ED** M I Baskes.
Desc: Covers the whole range of methods and application in materials science and engineering. Aims to serve the emerging multidisciplinary materials community through original contributions to modelling methods and applications.

US
MODERN PLASTICS INTERNATIONAL ENCYCLOPEDIA. (19??)-. Periodical. English. ir. $84.11 Canada; $10.00 Mexico; $90.00 other. McGraw Hill Publishing Company, Inc., 1221 Avenue of the Americas, New York NY 10020. **Tel** (212)512-6410, (800)525-5003, FAX (212)512-6111. **(Subscription address:** Modern Plastics International, Box 605, Hightstown NJ 08520.)

US/0883-7694
MRS BULLETIN. (MRS BULLETIN / MATERIALS RESEARCH SOCIETY.). [MRS bull.]. **Added/Corp** Materials Research Society. **VAT** Materials Research Society Bulletin. (19??)-. Abstracting/Indexing Service. English. mo. $120.00 US; $175.00 other. Materials Research Society, 9800 McKnight Road, Suite 327, Pittsburgh PA 15237-6006. **Tel** (412)367-3003, FAX (412)367-4373. **(Subscription address:** Kinokuniya Company Ltd., 38-1 Sakuragaoka 5, chome Setagaya-ku, Tokyo 156 Japan.) **ED** Gail A. Oare. **LC** TA401; .M78; WMLC 93/1272. **DD** 620. **CODEN** MRSBEA. **[CCC]. Bk Rev. Ad Acc. Circ:** 9,500 (ctrl). available on microfilm and microfiche from University Microfilms International (UMI). Documents available from The Genuine Article, Ask*IEEE, CASDDS. ***Absorbed*** *JMR Abstracts, 1066-2375.*
Desc: Covers multilayers, high temperature superconductors, materials for magnetic and optical data storage, materials for vacuum, materials science of fine particles, etc. Publishes overviews encapsulating the current status and trends in materials research, written in a format understandable to the nonspecialist.
Ind/Abst Ceram. Abstr. (19??-); Chem. Abstr. (1986-); Curr. Contents Phys. Chem. Earth Sci.; Ei Page One; INSPEC (July 1989-); Int. Aerosp. Abstr.; Res. Alert [Full Cov.]; SCISEARCH.

●US/0965-9773
NANOSTRUCTURED MATERIALS. [Nanostruct. mater.]. **VFOAT** NSM. Vol. 1, No. 1 (Jan/Feb 1992)-. Periodical. English. Eight times a year. $460.00 The Americas; £309.00 other. Pergamon Press, An Imprint of Elsevier Science Ltd., The Boulevard, Langford Lane, Kidlington, Oxford OX5 1GB United Kingdom. **Tel** 011 44 865 843000, 011 44 865 843699, FAX 011 44 865 843010. **(Subscription address:** Elsevier Science Ltd. Oxford Fulfillment Centre, PO Box 800, Kidlington, Oxford OX5 1DX United Kingdom.) **ED** B.H. Kear, R.W. Siegel, T. Tsakalakos. **LC** T174.7; .N36. **DD** 620.1/1299. **CODEN** NMAEE7. **[CCC].** Documents available from The Genuine Article, Ask*IEEE.
Desc: Strives to provide a broad interdisciplinary forum for the effective dissemination of scientific and technical information on the synthesis, processing, theory, computational modeling, structure, properties, performance and applications of nanostructured materials.
Ind/Abst Appl. Mech. Rev.; Ceram. Abstr. (19??-); INSPEC (1992-); Res. Alert [Full Cov.].

US
NATIONAL MECHANICAL CONTRACTOR ESTIMATOR. (19??)-. English. $180.00. Harrison Publishing House, PO Box 29, Quincy MA 02269. **Tel** (617)773-1870, FAX (603)444-0826.

UK/0265-3443
NEW MATERIALS/JAPAN. [New mater./Jpn.]. **VFOAT** Gijutsu Joho; New Materials, Japan. (1984)-. Academic Scholarly Publication. English. Twelve times a year. $470.00 The Americas; £315.00 other. Elsevier Advanced Technology, An Imprint of Elsevier Science Ltd., The Boulevard, Langford Lane, Kidlington, Oxford OX5 1GB United Kingdom. **Tel** 011 44 865 843000, 011 44 865 843699, FAX 011 44 865 843010. **(Subscription address:** Elsevier Science Ltd. Oxford Fulfillment Centre, PO Box 800, Kidlington, Oxford OX5 1DX United Kingdom.) **ED** N. Brooks. **CODEN** NMJAE6. **[CCC].** available on an online database from DIALOG. Documents available from Article Express International, CASDDS.
Desc: A specific response to the need for informed and objective news and analysis of developments in Japan in the field of new materials.
Ind/Abst Chem. Abstr.; Chem. Ind. Notes; Ei Page One; Eng. Mater. Abstr.; Eng. Index Annu.; Nonwovens Abstr.; PTS Newsl. Database [Full Txt.].

NE/0952-6196
NEW MATERIALS KOREA. **VFOAT** New Materials/Korea. Vol. 1, No. 1 (Oct. 1987)-. Periodical. English. mo. Newmedia International Japan, AV Infanta Carlota 123 5 A, 08029 Barcelona Spain. **Tel** 011 34 3 4195690, FAX 414 42 13. available on an online database (file 636/Full-Text) from DIALOG.

JA/0385-2563
NIHON FUKUGO ZAIRYO GAKKAI SHI. [Nihon Fukugo Zairyo Gakkaishi]. **Added/Corp** Nihon FukugÂo ZairyÂo Gakkai. **VFOAT** Journal of the Japan Society for Composite Materials. (1975)-. Academic Scholarly Publication. Japanese (summaries and/or abstracts in English). bm. $182.00. Nihon Fudugo Zairyo Gakkai, c/o Gakkai Senta Building, 4-16 Yakoi 2, Bunkyo-ku Tokyo-to Japan. **(Subscription address:** Kyowa Book Company Inc., 1 38 Kanda Jinbocho Chiyoda-ku, Tokyo 101 Japan.) **LC** TA418.9.C6; N53. **CODEN** NFZGDK. Documents available from CASDDS. ***Continues*** *Fukugo Zairyo Kenkyu.*
Ind/Abst Alum. Ind. Abstr.; Chem. Abstr.; Int. Aerosp. Abstr.; Met. Abstr.

JA/0386-3638
NIKKEI MEKANIKARU. [Nikkei mekanikaru]. **VFOAT** Nikkei Mechanical. (1977)-. Periodical. Japanese. bw. $405.00. **(Subscription address:** Maruzen Company Ltd., PO Box 5050, Import & Export Department, Tokyo 100 31 Japan.) **DD** 620. ***Continues*** *Nikkei Mashinari.*

JA
NON DESTRUCTIVE TESTING JOURNAL, JAPAN : NDTJ, THE. **VFOAT** NDTJ; N.D.T.J. Vol. 1, No. 1 (Feb. 1983)-. Periodical. English. qt. $90.00 (sea mail), $106.00 (air mail). Energiteknik Inc, c/o Japan Technical Services, Corration SIC 3F Ohkura Building, 4-10 Shiba-Daimon 1 chome, Minato-ku Tokyo 105 Japan. **LC** TA417.2; .N656. **DD** 620.1/127/05.

US
NTIS ALERT. MATERIALS SCIENCES. **Added/Corp** United States. National Technical Information Service. (19??)-. Periodical. English. Twenty-four times a year. $155.00 US; $220.00 other. National Technical Information Service - NTIS, Room 2027S, 5285 Port Royal Road, Springfield VA 22161. **Tel** (703)487-4630, (703)487-4660, (703)487-4650, FAX (703)321-8547, telex 89-9405. Index available.

●SZ
OBERFLACEHEN WERKSTOFFE / SURFACES MATERIAUX. **VFOAT** Surfaces Materiaux. (1993)-. German. Eleven times a year. 87.00F Switzerland; 98.00F Europe; 120.00F other. Handelszeitung Fachverlag AG, Seestrasse 37, CH 8027 Zurich Switzerland. **Tel** 011 41 1 2883545. ***Continues*** *Oberflaeche.*

UK
PERFORMANCE MATERIALS TECHNOLOGY. ***Ceased.*** (19??)-(April 1994). English. mo. World Business Publications Ltd., 960 High Road, Britannia 4th Floor, London N12 9RY England. **Tel** 11 44 81 446 5141, FAX 11 44 81 446 3659, telex 9419208.

US/0195-1920
PHALANX (ALEXANDRIA). (PHALANX.). (19??)-. Periodical. English. qt. $30.00. Military Operations Research Society, 101 South Whiting Street/Room 202, Alexandria VA 22304. **Tel** (703)751-7290. **ED** John K. Walker. **Bk Rev. Circ:** 8,500 (ctrl). available on microfilm from University Microfilms International (UMI).
Desc: Articles by practitioners, users, and sponsors of military operations research and applications of techniques and computer modeling.

AT
PLASTIC NEWS INTERNATIONAL. English. Eleven times a year (Except Jan.). 55.00Aus$ Australia; 65.00Aus$ New Zealand; $65.00 US. The Editors Desk Pty.Ltd., PO Box 546, Mt Eliza VIC 3930 Australia. **Tel** 011 61 3 7752139, FAX 011 61 3 7876105. **ED** John McGough. **Bk Rev. Ad Acc. Circ:** 2,700 (ctrl).

UK/0959-8111
PLASTICS, RUBBER AND COMPOSITES PROCESSING AND APPLICATIONS. **See** Plastics.

SA/0032-2660
PLASTICS SOUTHERN AFRICA. (PLASTICS SOUTHERN AFRICA : OFFICIAL JOURNAL OF THE PLASTICS INSTITUTE OF SOUTHERN AFRICA [AND] OFFICIAL JOURNAL OF SAMPLAS.). [Plast. south. Afr.]. **Added/Corp** Plastics Institute of Southern Africa. SAMPLAS. **VFOAT** Plastics. (1971)-. Periodical. English. Eleven times a year. R102.60 South Africa; R120.00 APU countries; R140.00 other. George Warman Publications Pty, PO Box 704, Cape Town 8000 South Africa. **Tel** 011 27 21 245320, FAX 011 27 21 261332, telex 5-21849. **CODEN** PSAFD5. **Bk Rev. Ad Acc. Circ:** 2,000 (ctrl).

US/0079-2357
PLENUM PRESS HANDBOOKS OF HIGH-TEMPERATURE MATERIALS. **See** Metals and Metallurgy.

RU
PRIKLADNYE PROBLEMY PROCHNOSTI I PLASTICHNOSTI. **Added/Corp** Gorkovskii Gosudarstvennyi Universitet Imeni N.I Lobachevskogo. (19??)-. Periodical. Russian. Three times a year. 1.60rub each issue. Gorky GSP-1000, Prospect Gagarina 23 Korpus 6, NII Mekhaniki Pri GGU, Nizhni Novgorod Russia. **Tel** 56-41-61. **ED** Ugodchikov Andrei Grigoriyevich. **LC** TA405; .P73. **Ad Acc. Circ:** 1,000 (ctrl).
Desc: Presents the analysis results for applied problems in the mechanics of deformable bodies. The design and optimization aspects of deformable bodies under force, thermal and electromagnetic loads are treated.
Ind/Abst Math. Rev.

US/0066-538X
PROCEEDINGS OF THE ... ANNUAL APPALACHIAN UNDERGROUND CORROSION SHORT COURSE. **See** Engineering-Chemical Engineering.

US/0074-4123
PROCEEDINGS OF THE INTERNATIONAL CONGRESS ON METALLIC CORROSION. **See** Engineering-Chemical Engineering.

UK/0079-6425
PROGRESS IN MATERIALS SCIENCE. [Prog. mater. sci.]. Vol. 9, No. 1 (1961)-. Monographic series. English. Five times a year. $522.00 The Americas; £350.00 other. Pergamon Press, An Imprint of Elsevier Science Ltd., The Boulevard, Langford Lane, Kidlington, Oxford OX5 1GB United Kingdom. **Tel** 011 44 865 843000, 011 44 865 843699, FAX 011 44 865 843010. **(Subscription address:** Elsevier Science Ltd. Oxford Fulfillment Centre, PO Box 800, Kidlington, Oxford OX5 1DX United Kingdom.) **ED** J. W. Christian and T. B. Massalski. **LC** QC1; .P884. **CODEN** PRMSAQ. **[CCC]. Pr Rev.** available on microfilm and microfiche from University Microfilms International (UMI). Documents available from Article Express International, The Genuine Article, Ask*IEEE, CASDDS, Documents on Demand. ***Continues*** *Progress in Metal Physics.*
Desc: Publishes authoritative reviews of recent advances in the science of materials, with emphasis on its fundamental aspects, including thermodynamics, the atomistic and electronic nature of solids and the use of materials in engineering.
Ind/Abst Alum. Ind. Abstr.; Bioeng. Abstr.; Ceram. Abstr.; Chem. Abstr.; Curr. Contents Eng. Tech. Appl. Sci.; Ei Page One; Energy Inf. Abstr.; Eng. Mater. Abstr.; Eng. Index Annu.; Environ. Abstr.; GeoRef; Index Sci.

Rev. [Full Cov.]; INSPEC (1975-); Int. Aerosp. Abstr. (1984-); Met. Abstr.; Res. Alert [Full Cov.]; Sci. Cit. Index; SCISEARCH.

IT/0393-3245
QUADERNI PIGNONE. (1965)-. English. Nuovo Pignone, Industrie Meccaniche e Fonderia SpA, 2 via F Matteucci, PO Box 414, 50100 Florence Italy. Documents available from Article Express International.
Ind/Abst Ei Page One; Eng. Index Annu.; FLUIDEX (1973-).

US/0889-3144
RAPRA REVIEW REPORTS. Vol. 1, No. 1 (1987)-. Academic Scholarly Publication. English. mo (12 issues). £420.00 UK; $750.00 US; £470.00 other. RAPRA Technology Ltd., Shawbury Shrewsbury, Shropshire SY4 4NR England. **Tel** 011 44 939 250383, FAX 011 44 939 251118, telex 35134 RAPRA G. **LC** TA455.P58; R35. **DD** 620.1/92/05. **[CCC].** available on microfilm and microfiche from University Microfilms International (UMI). Documents available from CASDDS.
Desc: Publishes three commissioned reports on areas of advanced and engineering materials technology which are of topical significance. Each report is supported by a comprehensive bibliography, with a summary of each title, taken from the RAPRA Abstracts database.
Ind/Abst Chem. Abstr.

JA /0916-6521
REPORT OF MATERIALS SCIENCE AND TECHNOLOGY. **Added/Corp** Waseda Daigaku. Kagami Memorials Laboratory for Materials Science and Technology. No. 40 (1989)-. Academic Scholarly Publication. English. Kagami Memorial Laboratory for Materials, Waseda University, 8-26 Nishiwaseda, 2 Chome, Shinjuku-ku tokyo 169 Japan. Documents available from CASDDS. ***Continues*** *Report of the Castings Research Laboratory, 0511-1927.*
Ind/Abst Chem. Abstr.

JA/0385-3799
REPORT OF THE RESEARCH LABORATORY OF ENGINEERING MATERIALS (TOKYO). (REPORT OF THE RESEARCH LABORATORY OF ENGINEERING MATERIALS.). [Rep. Res. Lab. Eng. Mater. (Tokyo)]. **Main/Corp** Tokyo Koyo Daigaku. Kogyo Zairyo Kenkyujo. No. 1- 1976-. Academic Scholarly Publication. English. O-Okayama Meguro-ku, Tokyo Japan. **LC** TA401; .T64A. **DD** 620.1/12/05. **CODEN** RRLTDF. Documents available from Ask*IEEE, CASDDS. ***Supersedes in part*** *Bulletin of the Tokyo Institute of Technology, 0366-3736.*
Ind/Abst Alum. Ind. Abstr.; Ceram. Abstr.; Chem. Abstr.; Ei Page One; INSPEC (1983-); Int. Aerosp. Abstr.; Met. Abstr.

JA/0373-8868
RESEARCH AND DEVELOPMENT : R & D. [Res. dev.]. **Added/Corp** Kobe Seiko. **VFOAT** R & D; R&D; R and D; Kobe Seiko Giho; Kobe Steel Engineering Reports. (1968)-. Academic Scholarly Publication. Japanese (summaries and/or abstracts in English). qt. Kobe Steel Ltd, 3-18 Wakinohamacho, 1-Chome Chuoku, Kobe 651 Hyogo Japan. **CODEN** RDKSB9. Documents available from Article Express International, CASDDS. ***Continues*** *Kobe Seiko Giho.*
Ind/Abst Alum. Ind. Abstr.; Bioeng. Abstr.; Chem. Abstr.; Coal Abstr.; Ei Page One; Eng. Index Annu.; Int. Aerosp. Abstr.; Met. Abstr.

CN/0318-3122
S. M. STUDY. (STUDY - SOLID MECHANICS DIVISION, UNIVERSITY OF WATERLOO.). [S. M. study]. **VFOAT** S M Study; Study Series. Began publication in 1969. Monographic series. English. be. Price varies per volume. Solid Mechanics Division, University of Waterloo, Waterloo Ontario Canada. **Tel** (519)885-1211. **DD** 620.1/5.
Ind/Abst GeoRef.

XR/0139-7575
SBORNIK VYSOKE SKOLY CHEMICKO-TECHNOLOGICKE V PRAZE. FIZIKA MATERIALU A MERICI TECHNIKA. SBORNIK PRAZHSKOGO KHIMIKO-TECHNOLOGICHESKOGO INSTITUTA. FIZIKA MATERIALOV I IZMERITELNAIA TEKHNIKA. SCIENTIFIC PAPERS OF THE PRAGUE INSTITUTE OF CHEMICAL TECHNOLOGY. MATERIAL SCIENCE AND MEASUREMENT TECHNIQUE. **Main/Corp** Vysoka Skola Chemicko-Technologicka v Praze. **Added/Corp** Vysoka Skola Chemicko-Technologicka v Praze. Sbornik Prazhskogo Khimiko-Technologicheskogo Instituta. Fizika Materialov i Izmeritelnaia Tekhnika. Vysoka Skola Chemicko-Technologicka v Praze. Scientific Papers of the Prague Institute of Chemical Technology. Material Science and Measurement Technique. **VFOAT** Fizika Materialu a Merici Technika; Sbornik Prazhskogo Khimiko-Technologicheskogo Instituta. Fizika Materialov i Izmeritelnaia Tekhnika; Scientific Papers of the Prague Institute of Chemical Technology. Material Science and Measurement Technique. (1975)-. Periodical. Czech (German and Russian; summaries and/or abstracts in English). Statni Pedagogicke Nakladatelstvi, Ostrovni 30, 113 01 Prague 1 Czech Republic. **Tel** (2)203787, FAX (2)293883. **LC** TA401; .P644a. **CODEN** PFMMDT. Documents available from CASDDS.
Ind/Abst Chem. Abstr.

IS/0792-1233
SCIENCE AND ENGINEERING OF COMPOSITE MATERIALS. [Sci. eng. compos. mater.]. (1988)-. Periodical. English. $200.00. Freund Publishing House Ltd, PO Box 35010, 61 Nachmani Street, Tel Aviv 61350 Israel. **Tel** 011 972 3 5662925, FAX 011 972 3 5605335. **(Subscription address:** Freund Publishing House Ltd., Suite 500 Chesham House, 150 Regent Street, London W1R 5FA England.**)** **ED** M. Narkis, A.H. Cardon, A.T. DiBenedetto, L. Nicolais. **UDC** 62. Documents available from The Genuine Article. ***Continues*** *Composite Materials Science, 0334-181X.*
Ind/Abst Res. Alert [Full Cov.].

JA
SEMICONDUCTOR WORLD. (19??)-. Periodical. Japanese. mo. $253.00. **(Subscription address:** Maruzen Company Ltd., PO Box 5050, Import & Export Department, Tokyo 100 31 Japan.**)** **ED** Masaaki Usui. **LC** TK7871.85; S469. Index available. cum. index. **Bk Rev. Ad Acc. Circ:** 10,000 (ctrl).
Desc: This provides readers with information about semiconductors in general and covers all necessary data in businesses.

US/0038-5565
SOVIET MATERIALS SCIENCE. ***Title Change.*** [Sov. mater. sci.]. **Added/Corp** Consultants Bureau. Vol. 1- (Jan./Feb. 1965)-(199?). Periodical. English (Russian). bm. Plenum Press, 233 Spring Street, New York NY 10013-1578. **Tel** (212)620-8000, (800)221-9369, FAX (212)463-0742, (212)807-1047, telex 23/421139. **ED** V V Panasyuk. **LC** TA401; .S654. **CODEN** SOMSA4. **[CCC].** Index available. **Pr Rev.** available on microfilm and microfiche from University Microfilms International (UMI). Documents available from Article Express International, The Genuine Article, Ask*IEEE. ***Continued by*** *Materials Sciences.*
Desc: This journal reports on current engineering materials and researches such problems as corrosion, cracking, fatigue and fracture, friction and lubrication. It also explores methods of metallic and polymer materials.
Ind/Abst Acoust. Abstr.; Alum. Ind. Abstr.; Appl. Mech. Rev.; Bioeng. Abstr.; Ei Page One; Eng. Mater. Abstr.; Eng. Index Annu.; Fluid Abstr., Civil Eng.; Fluid Abstr. Proc. Eng.; FLUIDEX (1973-); INSPEC (Jan./Feb. 1968-); Int. Aerosp. Abstr.; Met. Abstr.; Pollut. Abstr. Indexes; Res. Alert [Full Cov.].

GW
SPRINGER SERIES IN MATERIALS SCIENCE. **VFOAT** Materials Science. Vol. 1 (1986)-. Academic Scholarly Publication. English. Price varies per volume. Springer-Verlag GmbH & Company KG, Heidelberger Platz 3, D 14197 Berlin Germany. **Tel** 011 49 30 8207223, FAX 011 49 30 8214091, telex 183 319 SPBLN D. **(Subscription address:** Springer Verlag New York Inc. / for North America, 44 Hartz Way, Secaucus NJ 07096.**)** Documents available from CASDDS.
Ind/Abst Chem. Abstr.

US/0740-2961
STANDARDS INFOBRIEFS. **Added/Corp** American Society for Testing and Materials. **VFOAT** ASTM Standards Infobriefs; A.S.T.M. Standards Infobriefs. Vol. 1, No. 1 (1st Quarter 1982)-. Periodical. English. qt (4 issues). $15.00 North America; $17.00 other (non-member). American Society for Testing and Materials, 1916 Race Street, Philadelphia PA 19103. **Tel** (215)299-5585, FAX (215)299-9679, telex 710 670 1037.

GW/0941-388X
STEEL & MATERIALS TECHNOLOGY. **See** Metals and Metallurgy.

GW/0585-427X
STROMUNGSMECHANIK UND STROMUNGSMASCHINEN. [Stromungsmech. Stromungsmasch.]. (1962)-. Periodical. German. G Braun Verlag, Postfach 1709, D 76006 Karlsruhe Germany. **Tel** 011 49 721 165392. **CODEN** SMSMC4. Documents available from Article Express International.
Ind/Abst Bioeng. Abstr.; Ei Page One; Eng. Index Annu.; Fluid Abstr., Civil Eng.; Fluid Abstr. Proc. Eng.; FLUIDEX (1973-).

US/0893-5297
SUPERCONDUCTORS UPDATE. ***Ceased.*** **See** Engineering-Electricity, Electrical Engineering, Electronics.

SZ/0257-8972
SURFACE & COATINGS TECHNOLOGY. [Surf. coat. technol.]. **VFOAT** Surface and Coatings Technology. Vol. 27, No. 1 (Jan. 1986)-. Academic Scholarly Publication. English. Twenty-four times a year (8 vols.). 3200.00F. Elsevier Sequoia SA, PO Box 564, CH-1001 Lausanne 1 Switzerland. **Tel** 011 41 21 3207381. **ED** A. Matthews and B. D. Sartwell. **LC** TS670.A1; E43. **DD** 671.7/3. **CODEN** SCTEEJ. **[CCC].** **Ad Acc, Adv Mgr:** Ms. W van Cattenburch (Amsterdam). **Pr Rev.** available on microfilm and microfiche from University Microfilms International (UMI). Documents available from Article Express International, The Genuine Article, Ask*IEEE, CASDDS. ***Continues*** *Surface Technology, 0376-4583.*
Desc: Principal forum for the interchange of information on the science, technology and applications of thin and thick coatings and modified surfaces which alter the properties of materials.
Ind/Abst Abstr. Bull. Inst. Pap. Sci. Tech.; Chem. Abstr. (1986-); Chem. Titles; Civ. Struct. Eng. Abstr.; Curr. Contents Eng. Tech. Appl. Sci.; Curr. Titles Electrochem.; Ei Page One; Elect. Comm. Abstr.; Eng. Mater. Abstr.; Eng. Index Annu.; Fluid Abstr., Civil Eng.; Fluid Abstr. Proc. Eng.; FLUIDEX (19??-); INSPEC (1986-); Manuf. Process Eng. Abstr.; Mater. Sci. Eng. Abstr.; Mech. Eng. Abstr.; Met. Abstr.; Phys. Briefs; Res. Alert [Full Cov.]; Sci. Cit. Index; SCISEARCH; Solid State Supercond. Abstr.; Surf. Treat. Technol. Abstr.

SZ/0251-169X
SWISS PLASTICS. [Swiss Plast.]. (1979)-. Periodical. Multiple languages (English). Twelve times a year. 100.00F Switzerland; 120.00FEurope; 200.00F other. Verlag Dr Felix Wuest AG, Seestrasse 5/Postfach, CH-8700 Kuesnacht Switzerland. **Tel** 011 41 1 9110055, FAX (01)9106080, telex 825705. **UDC** 678.

US/0733-1924
TRENIE I IZNOS. ***Title Change.*** (SOVIET JOURNAL OF FRICTION AND WEAR.). [Sov. j. frict. wear]. Vol. 1, No. 1 (1981)-(1993). Periodical. English (Russian). bm. Allerton Press, Inc., 150 Fifth Avenue, New York NY 10011. **Tel** (212)924-3950, FAX (212)463-9684, telex 427441 ALPRES. **LC** TA418.72; .T7334. **DD** 621.8/9/05. **CODEN** SJFWDH. **[CCC].** Documents available from Ask*IEEE. ***Continued by*** *Journal of Friction and Wear.*
Ind/Abst INSPEC (1985-).

UK/0301-679X
TRIBOLOGY INTERNATIONAL. [Tribol. int.]. (Feb. 1974)-. Periodical. English. Eight times a year. $440.00 The Americas; £295.00 other. Butterworth Heinemann Publishers, Linacre House, Jordan Hill, Oxford OX2 8DP England. **Tel** 011 44 865 310366. **(Subscription address:** Elsevier Science Ltd. Oxford Fulfillment Centre, PO Box 800, Kidlington, Oxford OX5 1DX United Kingdom.**)** **ED** Nicholas Pinfield. **LC** TJ1075.A2; T75. **DD** 621.8/9/05. **CODEN** TRBIBK. **[CCC].** Index available. **Bk Rev. Ad Acc. Pr Rev. Circ:** 1,000. available on microfilm and microfiche from University Microfilms International (UMI). Documents available from Article Express International, The Genuine Article, Ask*IEEE, CASDDS. ***Continues*** *Tribology, 0041-2678.*
Desc: A multidisciplinary journal specifically designed to inform mechanical and lubrication engineers, designers, research and development engineers, managers and others of the latest knowledge available on all subjects related to materials, equipment and components which move, and to enable this information to be used to minimize the cost of moving parts.
Ind/Abst Acoust. Abstr.; Agric. Eng. Abstr. (1991-); Alum. Ind. Abstr.; Bioeng. Abstr.; Chem. Abstr.; Curr. Contents Eng. Tech. Appl. Sci.; Curr. Technol. Index; Ei Page One; EMBASE; Eng. Mater. Abstr.; Eng. Index Annu.; Fluid Abstr., Civil Eng.; Fluid Abstr. Proc. Eng.; FLUIDEX (1974-); INSPEC (Feb. 1974-); Lit. Pat. Abstr., Oilfield Chem. (1972-); Lit. Abstr., Catal. Catal.; Lit. Abstr., Health Environ.; Lit. Abstr., Pet. Refin. Petrochem.; Lit. Abstr., Pet. Substit.; Lit. Abstr., Transp. Storage; Met. Abstr.; Res. Alert [Full Cov.]; Shock Vibr. Dig.; Soils Fert.

●BW
VESCI AKADEMII NAVUK BELARUSI. SERYA FIZIKA-ENERGETYCNYH NAVUK. (VESTSI AKADEMII NAVUK BELARUSI. SERYIA FIZIKA-ENERHETYCHNYKH NAVUK). **Added/Corp** Akademiia Navuk Belarusi. **VFOAT** Seryia Fizika-Enerhetychnykh Navuk. No. 1 (1992)-. Academic Scholarly Publication. Byelorussian. qt. Nauka i Tekhnika / Byelarus, Science & Technology Publishing House, Ulitsa Zhodinskaya 18, 220067 Minsk Byelarus. **Tel** 0172 63-76-18. **(Subscription address:** Victor Kamkin, 4956 Boiling Brook Parkway, Rockville MD 20852.**)** **CODEN** VAFNET. Documents available from CASDDS. ***Continues*** *Vestsi Akademii Navuk BSSR. Seryia Fizika-Enerhetychnykh Navuk, 0374-4760.*
Ind/Abst Chem. Abstr.; Energy Res. Abstr.

MECHANICAL ENGINEERING AND MACHINERY

US/0277-1659
A-E-C AUTOMATION NEWSLETTER. **See** Architecture.

NE/0165-5108
AANDRIJFTECHNIEK. [Aandrijftechniek]. (1978)-. Periodical. Dutch. Eleven times a year. Price

varies. Misset Uitgeverij BV, Postbus 9000, 6800 DA Arnhem Netherlands. **Tel** 011 31 85 209911. **UDC** 621.85.

SZ/1013-3119
ABB REVIEW. [ABB rev.]. **VAT** ASEA Brown Boveri Review. Vol. 1 (1988)-. Periodical. English (French, German, Italian, Spanish and Swedish). ir (10 issues). 110.00F. ABB Corporate Communications Ltd., Ruetistrasse 6, CH-5401 Baden Switzerland. **Tel** 011 41 56 754836, FAX 011 41 56 212274. **CODEN** ABBREZ. Documents available from Article Express International, Ask*IEEE, Documents on Demand. ***Continues*** *Brown Boveri Mitteilungen, 0007-2486.*
Desc: Focuses on efficient production, transmission, distribution and utilization of electric energy, e.g. in industry and public transport. Also robotics and factory automation, environmental technology.
Ind/Abst BMT Abstr. (1988-); Ei Page One; Energy Inf. Abstr.; Eng. Index Annu.; Environ. Abstr.; INSPEC (1988-); Shock Vibr. Dig. (1988-).

US/0195-0932
ABRASIVE ENGINEERING SOCIETY MAGAZINE. ***Title Change.*** [Abras. Eng. Soc. mag.]. **Main/Corp** Abrasive Engineering Society. **VFOAT** AES Magazine. (March 1978)-(19??). Periodical. English. qt. Meadowlark Technical Services, 108 Elliot Drive, Butler PA 16001. **Tel** (412)282-6210. available on an online database (33) from DIALOG. Documents available from Article Express International. ***Continues*** *Abrasive Technology Magazine.* ***Continued by*** *Abrasives.*
Ind/Abst Alum. Ind. Abstr.; Ei Page One; Eng. Index Annu.; Met. Abstr.

US
ABRASIVES. (19??)-. English. ir (four to six issues per year). $30.00. Meadowlark Technical Services, 108 Elliot Drive, Butler PA 16001. **Tel** (412)282-6210. ***Continues*** *Abrasive Engineering Society Magazine.*

US
ACTA AUTOMATICA SINICA / INSTRUMENT SOCIETY OF AMERICA. **Added/Corp** Instrument Society of America. **VFOAT** Tzu Tung Hua Hsueh Pao. (19??)-. Academic Scholarly Publication. English. bm. $13.86. Science Press, 16 Donghuangchenggen North Street, Beijing 100707, People's Republic of China. **Tel** 011 86 1 4019821, 011 86 1 4010642, FAX 011 86 1 4012180, 011 86 1 4019810, telex 210147. **Ad Acc. Circ:** 11,000.
Ind/Abst Math. Rev.; Zentralbl. Math. Ihre Grenzgeb.

AU/0001-5970
ACTA MECHANICA. [Acta mech.]. Vol. 1 (1965)-. Periodical. English (German; summaries and/or abstracts in German and English). Twenty-four times a year. DM2580.00. Springer-Verlag Wien, Sachsenplatz 4 6, PO Box 89, A-1201 Vienna Austria. **Tel** 011 43 1 3302415. **(Subscription address:** Springer Verlag New York Inc. / for North America, 44 Hartz Way, Secaucus NJ 07096.**)** **ED** S Leibovich, H Troger, G J Weng, F Ziegler, and J Zierep. **LC** TA349; .A3. **CODEN** AMHCAP. **[CCC]. Pr Rev.** available on microfilm from University Microfilms International (UMI). Documents available from Article Express International, The Genuine Article, Ask*IEEE. ***Supersedes*** *Osterreichisches Ingenieur-Archiv.*
Desc: Emphasizes original analytical and experimental contributions of interest and importance to research workers and theoretical engineers.
Ind/Abst Acoust. Abstr.; Bioeng. Abstr.; Curr. Contents Eng. Tech. Appl. Sci.; Ei Page One; Energy Res. Abstr. (May 1973-); Eng. Index Annu.; Fluid Abstr., Civil Eng.; Fluid Abstr. Proc. Eng.; FLUIDEX; GeoRef; INSPEC (1968-); Int. Aerosp. Abstr.; Math. Rev.; Res. Alert [Full Cov.]; Sci. Cit. Index; SCISEARCH; Stat. Theory Method Abstr. (1967); Zentralbl. Math. Ihre Grenzgeb.

FI/0001-687X
ACTA POLYTECHNICA SCANDINAVICA. MECHANICAL ENGINEERING SERIES. [Acta polytech. Scand., Mech. eng. ser.]. **Added/Corp** Scandinavian Council for Applied Research. Teknillisten Tietteiden Akatemia. **VFOAT** Mechanical Engineering Series. No. 1 (1958)-. Monographic series. English. ir. Price varies per volume. The Finnish Academy of Technology, Tekniikantie 12, Fin 02150 Espoo Finland. **Tel** 011 358 0 4554565, FAX 011 358 0 6945041. **ED** Matti Ranta. **LC** TJ7; .A25. **DD** 621.082. **CODEN** APMNA2. Index available. **Circ:** 600. available on microfilm from University Microfilms International (UMI). Documents available from Article Express International, The Genuine Article, Ask*IEEE. ***Continues*** *Acta Polytechnica. Mechanical Engineering Series.*
Desc: Scientific research report series consisting of monographs.
Ind/Abst Bioeng. Abstr.; Curr. Contents Eng. Tech. Appl. Sci.; Ei Page One; Energy Res. Abstr.; Eng. Index Annu.; INSPEC (1980-); Int. Aerosp. Abstr.; Leadscan; Res. Alert [Select. Cov.]; SCISEARCH; Zentralbl. Math. Ihre Grenzgeb.

US/0065-2156
ADVANCES IN APPLIED MECHANICS. [Adv. appl. mech.]. Vol. 1 (1948)-. Monographic series. English. ir. $125.00 (Vol. 31). Academic Press, Inc., 6277 Sea Harbor Drive, Orlando FL 32887. **Tel** (800)543-9534, (407)345-4100, FAX (407)363-9661. **ED** John Hutchingson and Theodore Wu. **LC** TA350; .A4. **DD** 620.1. **CODEN** AAMCAY. **[CCC].** Documents available from Article Express International, The Genuine Article, Ask*IEEE, CASDDS.
Ind/Abst Bioeng. Abstr.; Chem. Abstr. (1948-1982); Ei Page One; Eng. Index Annu.; Index Sci. Rev. [Full Cov.]; INSPEC; Math. Rev.; Life Sci. Collect.; Res. Alert [Full Cov.]; SCISEARCH; Zentralbl. Math. Ihre Grenzgeb.

NE/0921-2647
ADVANCES IN HUMAN FACTORS / ERGONOMICS. [Adv. human factors/ergon.]. **VAT** Advances in Human Factors Ergonomics. Vol. 1 (1984)-. Monographic series. English. ir. Price varies per volume. Elsevier Science Publishing Company Inc, Madison Square Station, PO Box 882, New York NY 10159-0882. **Tel** (212)633-3950, FAX (212)633-3990. **(Subscription address:** Elsevier Science Inc. / New York Books, 655 Avenue of the Americas, New York NY 10010.**)** **LC** TA166; .A38. **DD** 620.8/2. **NLM** W1; AD636F. **Pr Rev.**
Desc: Information on human engineering and man-machine systems.

FR/0761-2494
ADVANCES IN MODELLING & SIMULATION. **VFOAT** Advances in Modelling and Simulation. (1984)-. Periodical. English. an. $78.50. JAI Press Inc., 55 Old Post Road, Suite 2, PO Box 1678, Greenwich CT 06836-1678. **Tel** (203)661-7602, FAX (203)661-0792. **UDC** 658.5:681.3.

US/0164-0917
AEE DIRECTORY OF ENERGY PROFESSIONALS, THE. (THE AEE DIRECTORY OF ENERGY PROFESSIONALS / ASSOCIATION OF ENERGY ENGINEERS.). [AEE dir. energy prof.]. **Main/Corp** Association of Energy Engineers. **VFOAT** Directory of Energy Professionals; A.E.E. Directory of Energy Professionals. **VAT** Association of Energy Engineers Directory of Energy Professionals. 1979-1980-. Directory. English. an. Fairmont Press, 700 Indian Trail, Lilburn GA 30247. **Tel** (404)925-9388, FAX (404)381-9865. **LC** TJ163.165; .A84A. **DD** 621.042/025/73.

US/1071-6947
AES (SERIES). **See** Energy.

US/0572-502X
AGMA DIRECTORY. **Main/Corp** American Gear Manufacturers Association. **VAT** American Gear Manufacturers Association Directory. Directory. English. American Gear Manufactures Association Directory, 1330 Massachusetts Avenue NW, Washington DC 20005. **LC** TJ184; .A532A. **DD** 338.4/7/62183302573.

●GW/0943-4569
ALLIANZ REPORT. (1993)-. German (English, French, Italian and Dutch). Six times a year (Feb., Apr., June, Aug., Oct., Dec.). DM159.00 (without binder), DM177.00 (with binder) Germany; DM189.00 (without binder), DM207.00 (with binder) others. Allianz Techische Information, Postfach 440124, W-80790 Munich F R Germany. **Tel** 011 49 89 38002386, FAX 011 49 89 38003737, telex 841 523011. cum. index. **Bk Rev. Circ:** 6,000 (ctrl).

NE
ALURAMA. ***Ceased.*** **See** Architecture.

IT
AM : AUTO MOTORI. Italian. mo. L58000. Giorgio Mondadori Intl, Via A Ponti 10, 20143 Milan Italy. **Tel** 011 39 2 891661.

US/0160-8835
AMD (NEW YORK, N.Y.). (AMD.). [AMD]. **Main/Corp** American Society of Mechanical Engineers. Applied Mechanics Division. **VFOAT** A.M.D. **VAT** Applied Mechanics Division. (19??)-. Academic Scholarly Publication. English. ir. Price varies per volume. American Society of Mechanical Engineers, 22 Law Drive, Fairfield NJ 07007. **Tel** (201)882-1167, (212)705-7722 (editorial). **CODEN** AMDVAS. Documents available from Article Express International, CASDDS.
Ind/Abst Bioeng. Abstr.; Chem. Abstr. (-1984); Ei Page One; Eng. Index Annu.; Math. Rev.

US/1041-7958
AMERICAN MACHINIST (1988). (AMERICAN MACHINIST.). [Am. mach.]. **VFOAT** AM. Vol. 132, No. 8 (Aug. 1988)-. Periodical. English. Twelve times a year. $65.00 US; $80.00 Canada; $90.00 Mexico; $100.00 other. Penton Publishing, 1100 Superior Avenue, Cleveland OH 44114-2543. **Tel** (216)696-7000, FAX (216)696-0836. **LC** TJ1; .A5. **DD** 671/.05. **[CCC].** available on microfilm and microfiche from University Microfilms International (UMI); available on an online database (file 648/Full-Text) from DIALOG. Documents available from Article Express International. ***Continues*** *American Machinist & Automated Manufacturing, 0886-0335.* ***Continued in part by*** *Metalworking Distributor, 1051-1407.*
Ind/Abst Appl. Sci. Technol. Index; Ei Page One; Eng. Index Annu.; F&S Index Plus Text, Int. [Select. Cov.]; Fluid Abstr., Civil Eng.; Fluid Abstr. Proc. Eng.; FLUIDEX (199?-); Leadscan; Met. Abstr.; PROMT; Trade Ind. ASAP [Full Txt.]; Trade Ind. Index [Full Txt.].

RM
ANALELE UNIVERSITATII DIN GALATI. FASCICULA X. Bulletin. Romanian (English and French). an. Price varies. Redactia Analelor, 6200 Galati, Str Domneasca Nr. 47 Romania. **Tel** 40 93 413602, FAX 40 93 412328.

RM
ANALELE UNIVERSITATII. FASCICULA V. Bulletin. Romanian (English and French). an. Price varies. Redactia Analelor, 6200 Galati, Str Domneasca Nr. 47 Romania. **Tel** 40 93 413602, FAX 40 93 412328.

II
ANNUAL REPORT AND ACCOUNTS - BHARAT PUMPS & COMPRESSORS LIMITED. **Main/Corp** Bharat Pumps & Compressors Limited. Hindi (English). an. Bharat Pumps & Compressors Ltd, Naini, Allahabad India. **Tel** 7412-15, telex 0540-232. **LC** HD9705.I44; B46A. **DD** 354/.54/008242. **Circ:** 2,000 (ctrl).
Desc: Report includes director's report, particulars of employees, balance sheet, profit and loss account and auditor's report.

GW
ANTRIEBSTECHNIK HANDBUCH. (19??)-. German. Twelve times a year (12 issues per year and 1 handbook). DM192.00. Vereinigte Fachverlage, Postfach 4068, D 55030 Mainz Germany. **Tel** 011 49 6131 992150. **LC** TJ1051; .A57.

●US/1068-7181
APPLIED ENERGY. (APPLIED ENERGY. RUSSIAN JOURNAL OF FUEL, POWER, AND HEAT SYSTEMS.). **VFOAT** Russian Journal of Fuel, Power, and Heat Systems. (1993)-. Periodical. English (Russian). bm. $925.00 (Vol. 33, 1995). Allerton Press, Inc., 150 Fifth Avenue, New York NY 10011. **Tel** (212)924-3950, FAX (212)463-9684, telex 427441 ALPRES. **[CCC].** Documents available from Documents on Demand. ***Continues*** *Power Engineering (Russian Academy of Sciences).*
Desc: English translation of Rossiiskaya Akademiya Nauk. Izvestiya. Energetika.
Ind/Abst Coal Abstr.; Energy Inf. Abstr.; Energy Res. Abstr.; Environ. Abstr.

HK/0253-4827
APPLIED MATHEMATICS AND MECHANICS. **See** Mathematics.

US/0003-6900
APPLIED MECHANICS REVIEWS. **See** Engineering-Abstracting, Bibliographies and Statistics.

NE/0003-6994
APPLIED SCIENTIFIC RESEARCH. [Appl. sci. res.]. **Added/Corp** Nederlandse Centrale Organisatie voor Toegepast-Natuurwetenschappelijk Onderzoek. Vol. 16 (1966)-. English. Eight times a year (2 vols.). $976.00. Kluwer Academic Publishers, Postbus 322, 3300 AH Dordrecht, The Netherlands. **Tel** 011 (31) 78 524400, FAX 011 31 78 183273, telex 20083. **ED** F.T.M. Nieuwstadt. **LC** TA349; .A68. **DD** 621/.05. **CODEN** ASRHAU. **[CCC]. Pr Rev. Acid Free.** available on microfilm and microfiche from University Microfilms International (UMI). Documents available from Article Express International, The Genuine Article, Ask*IEEE, CASDDS. ***Formed by the union of*** *Applied Scientific Research. Mechanics, Heat, Mathematical Methods, 0365-7132* ***and*** *Applied Scientific Research. Electrophysics, Acoustics, Optics Mathematical Methods, 0365-7140.*
Desc: Emphasizes thermal, mechanical and electromagnetic phenomena in continua; includes the following topics: continuum mechanics, elasticity, plasticity and rheology, fluid dynamics, electromagnetic fields and waves, acoustics and elastodynamics, magnetohydrodynamics and electrohydrodynamics, heat and mass transfer, biological transport phenomena and membrane physics.
Ind/Abst Alum. Ind. Abstr.; Bioeng. Abstr.; Chem. Abstr.; Coal Abstr.; Curr. Contents Eng. Tech. Appl. Sci.; Ei Page One; Energy Res. Abstr.; Eng. Mater. Abstr. (-1989); Eng. Index Annu.; Fluid Abstr., Civil Eng.; Fluid Abstr. Proc. Eng.; FLUIDEX (1973-); GeoRef; INSPEC (1968-); Int. Aerosp. Abstr.; Math. Rev.; Met. Abstr.; Life Sci. Collect.; Proc. Chem. Eng.; Res. Alert [Full Cov.]; Sci. Cit. Index; SCISEARCH; Theoret. Chem. Eng.; Zentralbl. Math. Ihre Grenzgeb.

US/0939-1533
ARCHIVE OF APPLIED MECHANICS (1991). (ARCHIVE OF APPLIED MECHANICS.). [Arch. appl. mech.]. **VFOAT** Applied Mechanics; Ingenieur-Archiv. Vol. 61, No. 1 (1991)-. Periodical. English (German). Eight times a year. $553.00. Springer-Verlag GmbH & Company KG, Heidelberger Platz 3, D 14197 Berlin Germany. **Tel** 011 49 30 8207223, FAX 011 49 30 8214091, telex 183 319 SPBLN D. **(Subscription address:** Springer Verlag New York Inc. / for North America, 44 Hartz Way, Secaucus NJ 07096.**)** **LC** TA349; .A72. **DD** 620.1/005. **CODEN** AAMEEA. Documents available from Article Express International, The Genuine Article, Ask*IEEE. ***Continues*** *Ingenieur-Archiv, 0020-1154.*

Ind/Abst Curr. Contents Eng. Tech. Appl. Sci.; Eng. Index Annu.; INSPEC (Jan. 1991-); Int. Aerosp. Abstr. (1991-); Leadscan; Res. Alert [Full Cov.]; Sci. Cit. Index; SCISEARCH; Zentralbl. Math. Ihre Grenzgeb.

GW
ARCHIVES OF APPLIED MECHANICS. (19??)-. English (German). Eight times a year. DM636.00 Germany; $355.00 (add $34.00 for postage) US. Springer-Verlag GmbH & Company KG, Heidelberger Platz 3, D 14197 Berlin Germany. **Tel** 011 49 30 8207223, FAX 011 49 30 8214091, telex 183 319 SPBLN D. **(Subscription address:** Springer Verlag New York Inc. / for North America, 44 Hartz Way, Secaucus NJ 07096.) ***Continues*** *Ingenieur Archiv.*

PL/0373-2029
ARCHIVES OF MECHANICS. (ARCHIVES OF MECHANICS. ARCHIWUM MECHANIKI STOSOWANEJ.). [Arch. mech.]. **Added/Corp** Instytut Podstawowych Problemow Techniki (Polska Akademia Nauk). **VFOAT** Archiwum Mechaniki Stosowanej. Vol. 23 (1971)-. Periodical. English (summaries and/or abstracts in Polish and Russian). bm. $168.00. **(Subscription address:** ARS Polona, PO Box 1001, 00068 Warsaw Poland.) **LC** TA350; .A73. **DD** 620.1/005. **CODEN** AVMHBR. Documents available from Ask*IEEE, CASDDS. ***Continues*** *Archiwum Mechaniki Stosowanej.*
Ind/Abst Acoust. Abstr.; Ceram. Abstr.; Chem. Abstr.; GeoRef; INSPEC (1973-); Int. Aerosp. Abstr. (1991-); Math. Rev.; Proc. Chem. Eng.; Theoret. Chem. Eng.; Zentralbl. Math. Ihre Grenzgeb.

PL/0208-4198
ARCHIVUM COMBUSTIONIS. **See** Physics-Heat.

PL/0004-0738
ARCHIWUM BUDOWY MASZYN. (ARCHIWUM BUDOWY MASZYN. ARCHIVE OF MECHANICAL ENGINEERING.). [Arch. bud. masz.]. **Added/Corp** Polska Akadmia Nauk. Komitet Budowy Maszyn. **VFOAT** Archive of Mechanical Engineering. (1954)-. Periodical. Polish (English; summaries and/or abstracts in Russian and English; table of contents in Russian). qt. Price on Request. **(Subscription address:** ARS Polona, PO Box 1001, 00068 Warsaw Poland.) cum. index.
Ind/Abst Alum. Ind. Abstr.; Ceram. Abstr.; Ei Page One; Eng. Mater. Abstr.; Int. Aerosp. Abstr.; Met. Abstr.

PL/0208-418X
ARCHIWUM TERMODYNAMIKI. **See** Physics-Heat.

HK/1015-5023
ASIAMAC JOURNAL. [Asiamac j.]. (1989)-. Periodical. English. qt. $34.00 Asia (except Hong Kong); $38.00 other. Adsale Publishing Company, 14/F Devon House Taikoo Place, 979 King's Road, Quarry Bay, Hong Kong. **Tel** 011 852 811 8897, FAX 011 852 516 5119. **Ad Acc. Circ:** 15,000 (ctrl).

US/0517-5321
ASME BOILER AND PRESSURE VESSEL CODE. [ASME boil. press. vessel code]. **Main/Corp** American Society of Mechanical Engineers. Boiler and Pressure Vessel Committee. **VFOAT** Boiler and Pressure Vessel Code. (19??)-. English. ir (every 3 years with 7 updates). $5,253.00. American Society of Mechanical Engineers, 22 Law Drive, Fairfield NJ 07007. **Tel** (201)882-1167, (212)705-7722 (editorial). **CODEN** ABPVAB. **Bk Rev. Ad Acc.**
Desc: Safety codes for engineers.

US
ASME CHEMICAL PLANT & PETROLEUM REFINERY PIPING. (19??)-. English. ir (every 3 years). $189.00. American Society of Mechanical Engineers, 22 Law Drive, Fairfield NJ 07007. **Tel** (201)882-1167, (212)705-7722 (editorial).

US
ASME GUIDE FOR GAS TRANSMISSION AND DISTRIBUTION PIPING SYSTEMS. **Main/Corp** American Society of Mechanical Engineers. **Added/Corp** United States. Department of Transportation. **VFOAT** Guide for Gas Transmission and Distribution Piping Systems. (1970)-. English. ir. $94.00 per copy. American Society of Mechanical Engineers, 22 Law Drive, Fairfield NJ 07007. **Tel** (201)882-1167, (212)705-7722 (editorial).

US/0279-9316
ASME NEWS (1981). (ASME NEWS.). [ASME news]. **Main/Corp** American Society of Mechanical Engineers. **VAT** American Society of Mechanical Engineers News (1981). Vol. 1, No. 1 (April 1981)-. Periodical. English. Twelve times a year. Comes with American Society of Mechancial Engineers membership. American Society of Mechanical Engineers, 22 Law Drive, Fairfield NJ 07007. **Tel** (201)882-1167, (212)705-7722 (editorial). **ED** Jay O'Leary. **DD** 621. **Ad Acc. Circ:** 120,000 (ctrl).
Desc: Newspaper of the American Society of Mechanical Engineers.

US/1050-8171
ASSEMBLY (CAROL STREAM, ILL.). (ASSEMBLY.). [Assembly]. Vol. 33, No. 7 (July 1990)-. Periodical. English. Nine times a year. $60.00. Chilton Company, 201 King of Prussia Road, Radnor PA 19089. **Tel** (610)964-4122, (800)695-1214, FAX (610)964-4978, telex 6851035 CHILTON UW. **LC** TJ1320; .A75. **DD** 670.42. **CODEN** ASMYEQ. available on microfilm and microfiche from University Microfilms International (UMI). Documents available from Article Express International. ***Continues*** *Assembly Engineering, 0004-5063.*
Ind/Abst Ei Page One; Eng. Index Annu.; Trade Ind. ASAP [Full Txt.]; Trade Ind. Index [Full Txt.].

US/0066-8702
ASSEMBLY ENGINEERING MASTER CATALOG. ***Ceased.*** (19??)-(19??). Catalog. English. an. Chilton, 825 7th Avenue, New York NY 10019. **Tel** (212)887-8560. **LC** TJ1320; .H5. **DD** 338.4/7/62188025. ***Continues*** *Assembly Directory & Handbook.*

AT/0004-9719
AUSTRALIAN MACHINERY AND PRODUCTION ENGINEERING. Academic Scholarly Publication. English. mo (except December). 44.00Aus$ Australia; 100.00Aus$ other. Business Press International Australia, 162 Goulburn Street, Darlinghurst New South Wales 2010 Australia. **Tel** (02)266-9711, FAX (02)267-1223, telex AA121117. **ED** Andrew Nicholls. **LC** TS155.A1; A85. **CODEN** AMPDAY. **Bk Rev. Ad Acc. Circ:** 5,030 (ctrl). Documents available from Article Express International, CASDDS. ***Continues*** *Australian Machinery.*
Desc: New products, techniques and technology for the metalworking industry, and news.
Ind/Abst Chem. Abstr.; Ei Page One; Eng. Index Annu.; Surf. Treat. Technol. Abstr.

US/0890-9121
AUTO GALLERY. [Auto gallery]. Vol. 1, No. 1 (Jan. 1987)-. Periodical. English. mo. $60.00 US; $85.00 Canada and Mexico. Auto Gallery Publishing Company, PO Box 640, Holmes PA 19043. **DD** 629.

US/0005-1071
AUTOMATIC MACHINING. [Autom. mach.]. (Sept. 1955)-. Periodical. English. mo. $30.00. Automatic Machining, 100 Seneca Avenue, Rochester NY 14621-2392. **Tel** (716)338-1522. **ED** Donald E. Wood. **LC** TJ1180.A1; S37. **DD** 621.88205. **CODEN** AUMAAW. **Bk Rev. Ad Acc. Circ:** 16,000 (ctrl). Documents available from Ask*IEEE. ***Continues*** *Screw Machine Engineering.*
Desc: Coverage of news, new products and techniques in high production metal turning and cold forming plants.
Ind/Abst INSPEC (Dec. 1971-1985).

FR/0296-1598
AUTOMATIQUE-PRODUCTIQUE INFORMATIQUE INDUSTRIELLE. (RAIRO. AUTOMATIQUE-PRODUCTIQUE INFORMATIQUE INDUSTRIELLE.). [Autom.-prod. inform. ind.]. **Added/Corp** Centre National de la Recherche Scientifique (France). **VFOAT** Automatique-Productique Informatique Industrielle; RAIRO. Automatic Control Production System; Automatique Productique Informatique Industrielle; Automatic Control Production System; APII. Vol. 19, No. 1 (1985)-. Academic Scholarly Publication. English (French). bm. 980.00F (France); 1290.00F (other). Editions Hermes, 14 rue Lantiez, 75017 Paris France. **Tel** 11 33 1 42294466. **LC** QA267.5.S4; R43. **DD** 003. **CODEN** RAPIEK. **[CCC].** Documents available from Article Express International, The Genuine Article, Ask*IEEE. ***Continues*** *RAIRO: Automatique, 0399-0524.*
Ind/Abst Compumath Citation Index [Full Cov.]; Curr. Contents Phys. Chem. Earth Sci.; Ei Page One; EMBASE; Energy Res. Abstr. (Feb. 1983-); Eng. Index Annu.; INSPEC (1985-); Math. Rev. (1985-); Res. Alert [Full Cov.].

GW
AUTOMATISIERUNGSTECHNIK - AT. **Added/Corp** VDI/VDE-Gesellschaft Mess- und Regelungstechnik. Normenarbeitsgemeinschaft fuer Mess- und Regeltechnik in der Chemischen Industrie. **VFOAT** AT. Vol. 33 (Jan. 1985)-. Periodical. German (summaries and/or abstracts in English). Twenty-four times a year. DM438.00. R Oldenbourg Verlag, Postfach 801360, D 81613 Munich Germany. **Tel** 011 49 89 450190, FAX 011 49 89 45019305. **LC** TJ212; .R4. **DD** 629.8/05. Documents available from Ask*IEEE. ***Continues*** *Regulungstechnik, 0340-434X.*
Ind/Abst Coal Abstr.; INSPEC (Jan. 1985-); Zentralbl. Math. Ihre Grenzgeb.

GW/0178-2320
AUTOMATISIERUNGSTECHNISCHE PRAXIS : ATP. **Added/Corp** VDI/VDE-Gesellschaft Mess- und Regelungstechnik. Normenarbeitsgemeinschaft fuer Mess- und Regeltechnik in der Chemischen Industrie. **VFOAT** ATP. Vol. 27, No. 1 (Jan. 1985)-. Periodical. German. mo. DM158.00. R Oldenbourg Verlag, Postfach 801360, D 81613 Munich Germany. **Tel** 011 49 89 450190, FAX 011 49 89 45019305. **LC** TJ212; .R42. **DD** 629.8/05. **[CCC].** Documents available from Ask*IEEE. ***Continues*** *Regelungstechnische Praxis, 0340-4730;* ***Absorbed*** *Messen, Steuern, Regeln, 0026-0347.*
Desc: Reports on automation technology in introductory and overview articles, theoretical articles and exchange of ideas between the researcher and the operator. Also prints resumes of original research and will supply full text on request.
Ind/Abst Ei Page One; INSPEC (Jan. 1985-).

SP
AUTOMATIZACION INTEGRADA Y REVISTA DE ROBOTICA. ***Title Change.*** (19??)-(19??). Spanish. Ten times a year. Pulsar SA, Gran Via Corts Catalanes 322 324, 08004 Barcelona Spain. **Tel** 011 34 3 4254544. ***Absorbed by*** *Novamaquina 2000, 0210-0118.*

HU/0133-1620
AUTOMATIZALAS. **See** Computers-Automation.

IT/0392-8829
AUTOMAZIONE OGGI. [Autom. oggi]. (1983)-. Periodical. Italian. mo (11 issues per year). L72600 Italy; L145200 other. Gruppo Editoriale Jackson Spa, Via Gorki 69, 20092 Cinisello Balsamo Italy. **Tel** 011 39 2 66034401. **UDC** 681.326.

US/0098-2571
AUTOMOTIVE ENGINEERING. [Automot. eng.]. **Added/Corp** Society of Automotive Engineers. Vol. 80, No. 11 (Nov. 1972)-. Periodical. English. mo. $72.00 North America; $126.00 other. Society of Automotive Engineers, 400 Commonwealth Drive, Warrendale PA 15096. **Tel** (412)776-4841, (412)772-7106, FAX (412)776-5760. **ED** Daniel J. Holt. **LC** TL1; .S5. **DD** 629.2/3/05. **CODEN** AUEGBB. **[CCC]. Bk Rev. Ad Acc. Circ:** 67,000 (ctrl). available on microfilm and microfiche from University Microfilms International (UMI); available on an online database (file 648/Full-Text) from DIALOG. Documents available from Article Express International, Ask*IEEE, UMI Article Clearinghouse. ***Continues*** *SAE Journal of Automotive Engineering, 0097-711X.*
Desc: Articles on materials, electronics, computer-aided design and manufacturing, as well as interviews with industry leaders and the 'International Viewpoints' and 'Washington Report' columns make this publication 'must reading' for anyone interested in vehicle technology.
Ind/Abst Acad. Ind. [Computer File] (1989-); Acoust. Abstr.; Agric. Eng. Abstr.; Alum. Ind. Abstr.; Appl. Sci. Technol. Index; Bioeng. Abstr.; Bus. ASAP (1990-) [Full Txt.]; Bus. Index (1989-); Coal Abstr.; Ei Page One; Energy Res. Abstr. (Nov. 1972-); Eng. Mater. Abstr.; Eng. Index Annu.; Ergon. Abstr.; Expand. Acad. Index (1989-); F&S Index Plus Text, Int. [Select. Cov.]; Fluid Abstr., Civil Eng.; Fluid Abstr. Proc. Eng.; FLUIDEX (1973-); Gen. BusinessFile (1989-); INIS Atomindex [Micro.]; INSPEC (May 1978-); Int. Aerosp. Abstr.; Leadscan; Leis. Recreat. Tour. Abstr.; Lit. Pat. Abstr., Oilfield Chem. (1971-1989); Lit. Abstr., Catal. Catal.; Lit. Abstr., Health Environ.; Lit. Abstr., Pet. Refin. Petrochem.; Lit. Abstr., Pet. Substit.; Lit. Abstr., Transp. Storage; Met. Abstr.; Newsp. Period. Abstr. (1989-); PROMT; Rural Dev. Abstr.; Shock Vibr. Dig.; Trade Ind. ASAP [Full Txt.]; Trade Ind. Index [Full Txt.]; World Agric. Econ.

IT/1121-3450
AUTOTECNICA LOCATE TRIULZI. (AUTOTECNICA.). [AutotecnicaLocate Triulzi]. (1982)-. Periodical. Italian. mo (11 issues per year). L65000 Italy; L130000 other. Nuova Publimilano Srl, Via Molise 3, 20085 Locate Triulzi Italy. **Tel** 011 39 2 9077366. **UDC** 629.113.

RU/0005-2310
AVTOMATIKA I TELEMEHANIKA. (AVTOMATIKA I TELEMEKHANIKA : ORGAN KOMISSII AVTOMATIKI I TELEMEKHANIKI.). [Avtom. telemeh.]. **Added/Corp** Akademiia Nauk SSSR. Komissiia Avtomatiki i Telemekhaniki. Akademiia Nauk SSSR. Komissiia Telemekhaniki i Avtomatiki. Akademiia nauk SSSR. Komitet Telemekhaniki i Avtomatiki. Institut Avtomatiki i Telemekhaniki (Soviet Union) Akademiia nauk SSSR. (1936)-. Academic Scholarly Publication. Russian (summaries and/or abstracts in English; table of contents in English). mo. $346.00. Izdatelstvo Nauka / Akademiia Nauk, Publishing House of the Russian Academy of Sciences, Leninskii Porspekt 14, 117901 Moscow Russia. **Tel** 011 95 954-21-53, FAX 011 95 938-21-44, telex 411964. **(Subscription address:** East View Publications Inc., 3020 Harbor Lane North, Suite 110, Minneapolis MN 55447.) **LC** TJ212; .A9. **CODEN** AVTEAI. **[CCC].** cum. index. **Bk Rev. Ad Acc.** Documents available from Article Express International, Ask*IEEE, CASDDS.
Ind/Abst Chem. Abstr. (-1980); Eng. Index Annu.; INSPEC (1968-); Int. Aerosp. Abstr.; Math. Rev.

RU
AVTOMATIKA I TELEMEKHANIKA. **Added/Corp** Omsk, Siberia. Institut Inzhenerov Zheleznodorozhnogo Transporta. Vol. 1 (1970)-. Russian. $315.00 domestic airmail; $338.00 international airmail. **(Subscription address:** Victor Kamkin, 4956 Boiling Brook Parkway, Rockville MD 20852.) **LC** TJ212; .A922. Documents available from Ask*IEEE.
Ind/Abst INSPEC (1968-); Math. Rev.; Stat. Theory Method Abstr. (1987); Zentralbl. Math. Ihre Grenzgeb.

FR/0757-1631
AXES SCHILTIGHEIM. [Axes Schiltigheim]. **VFOAT** Axes Robotique Automatique (Schiltigheim); Axes Robotique (Schiltigheim). (1983)-. Periodical. French. mo (except Aug. and Oct.). 636.63F France; 840.00F other. Axes Communication, 29 rue Violet, 75015 Paris France. **Tel** 011 33 1 45791051. **UDC** 007.52.

GW/0522-0629
BALL AND ROLLER BEARING ENGINEERING. [Ball roller bear. eng.]. (1963)-. Periodical. English (German, French, Italian, Spanish and Portuguese). ir. Free. FAG Kugelfischer, Postfach 1260, D-8720 Schweinfurt 1 Germany. **Tel** 011 49 9721 9110, telex 96-5934. **LC** TJ1071; .B15. **CODEN** BRBEAD. Index available. cum. index. **Circ:** 90,000 (ctrl). Documents available from Article Express International.
Desc: Reference publication about the state of the art in Rolling Bearing Technology.
Ind/Abst Bioeng. Abstr.; Ei Page One; Eng. Index Annu.; Fluid Abstr., Civil Eng.; Fluid Abstr. Proc. Eng.; FLUIDEX (1973-); Int. Aerosp. Abstr.

UK/0308-1664
BALL BEARING JOURNAL (LUTON). ***Ceased.*** (THE BALL BEARING JOURNAL.). [Ball bear. j.]. Vol. 1 (1926)-No. 241 (1993). Periodical. English. sa. SKF Ltd, Luton, Bedfordshire LU3 1JF England. **LC** TJ1071; .B17. **DD** 621.822. Documents available from Article Express International.
Ind/Abst Acoust. Abstr.; Curr. Technol. Index; Eng. Index Annu.; Fluid Abstr., Civil Eng.; Fluid Abstr. Proc. Eng.; FLUIDEX (1973-1989); Shock Vibr. Dig.

UK/0951-6859
BENCHMARK OBAN. (BENCHMARK / SCOTLAND.). [BenchmarkOban]. (1987)-. Periodical. English. qt (Mar., June, Sept., Dec.). £75.00. National Agency for Finite Element Methods and Standards, E Kilbride, Glasgow G75 0QU Scotland. **Tel** 011 44 41 3552 72639, FAX 011 44 41 3552 72749. **ED** G Leckie and E R Robertson (Editor's Address: Nafems, Nel Technology Park, East Kilbride, Glasgow, Scotland; Editor's Telephone: 011 44 41 3552 25688). **DD** 620.001515353. **Ad Acc, Adv Mgr:** Anne Creechan. **Circ:** 4,000 (ctrl). ***Continues** NAFEMS Newsletter.*
Desc: Official newsletter of NAFEMS containing technical papers, etc.

PL/0300-2438
BIULETYN PRZEMYSKOWEGO INSTYTUTE AUTOMATYKI I POMIAROW. (BIULETYN.). **Main/Corp** Przemysowy Instytut Automatyki i Pomiarow. **Added/Corp** Zjednoczenie Przemysu Automatyki i Aparatury Pomiarowej MERA. (19??)-. Polish. bm. $75.00. **(Subscription address:** ARS Polona, PO Box 1001, 00068 Warsaw Poland.**) LC** TJ212; .P79.

UK/0307-1219
BRITISH COMBUSTION. V. 1- Spring 1975-. Periodical. English. qt. £2.50. Oil Firing Publications, The Fernery Market Place, Midhurst GU29 9DP England. **LC** TJ254.5; .B74. **DD** 621.4/023/05.

UK/0007-1137
BRITISH JOURNAL OF NON-DESTRUCTIVE TESTING. ***Title Change.*** **See** Engineering-Materials Engineering and Mechanics.

RM/1012-3202
BULETINUL INSTITUTULUI POLITEHNIC BUCURESTI. SERIA ENERGETICA. [Bul. Inst. politeh. Bucur., Ser. Energ.]. **Added/Corp** Institutul Politehnic Bucuresti. **VFOAT** Seria Energetica. (1984/1985)-. Romanian (English). an. DM164.00. **(Subscription address:** Kubon & Sagner, ABT Zeitschriftenimport, D 80328 Munich Germany.**) LC** TJ163.13; .B84. **DD** 621/.05. **CODEN** BBENEF. Documents available from Ask*IEEE. ***Continues** Buletinul Institutului Politehnic "Gheorghe Gheorghiu-Dej" Bucuresti. Seria Energetica, 0256-7938.*
Ind/Abst Ceram. Abstr. (19??-); Ei Page One; INSPEC (1985-); Math. Rev.

RM
BULETINUL STIINTIFIC SI TEHNIC AL INSTITUTULUI POLITEHNIC "TRAIAN VUIA" TIMISOARA. SERIA MECANICA. **Added/Corp** Institutul Politehnic "Traian Vuia" Timisoara. **VFOAT** Buletinul Stiintific Si Tehnic Al Institutului Politehnic Traian Vuia Timisoara. Mecanica; Seria Mecanica. (19??)-. Periodical. English (French, German and Romanian). **(Subscription address:** Ilexim Press Department, PO Box 1, 136-1-137, Bucharest, Romania.**) LC** TJ4; .B847.

JA/0374-2725
BULLETIN OF MECHANICAL ENGINEERING LABORATORY. [Bull. Mech. Eng. Lab.]. **Main/Corp** Kikai Gijutsu Kenkyujo. No. 1-. Bulletin. English. Mechanical Engineering Laboratory, 12 1 4 Chome Suginami ku, Tokyo Japan. **Tel** 0298-54-2501. **LC** TJ1; .K54A. **DD** 621/.08. **CODEN** BMEGAX. Documents available from The Genuine Article, Ask*IEEE. ***Continues** Kikai Shikenjo, Tokyo. Bulletin.*
Ind/Abst Alum. Ind. Abstr.; Ei Page One; Fluid Abstr., Civil Eng.; Fluid Abstr. Proc. Eng.; FLUIDEX; INSPEC (1972-); Met. Abstr.; Res. Alert [Select. Cov.].

US/0888-6911
BULLETIN OF THE INTERNATIONAL CENTRE FOR HEAT AND MASS TRANSFER. ***Ceased.*** [Bull. Int. Centre Heat Mass Transf.]. Ceased (Jan. 1991). Bulletin. English. an. Taylor & Francis Ltd., Rankine Road, Basingstoke Hampshire, RG24 8PR United Kingdom. **Tel** 011 44 256 840366, FAX 011 44 256 479438, telex 858540. **(Subscription address:** Taylor & Francis Inc., 1900 Frost Road, Suite 101, Bristol PA 19007-1598.**) ED** Naim Afgan. **LC** QC319.8; .B84. **DD** 536/.2/005. **CODEN** BICHTE4. **[CCC].** Index available. **Bk Rev. Ad Acc. Circ:** 250. available on microfilm and microfiche from University Microfilms International (UMI).
Desc: Presents the latest developments in heat and mass transfer research from laboratories around the world. Reports are written by authorities representing various countries, and are carefully selected by the Executive Committee of the Centre for inclusion. As a special feature, the Bulletin provides abstracts of papers presented at numerous seminars and schools organized by the Centre each year.
Ind/Abst Abstr. Bull. Inst. Pap. Sci. Tech.

FR
BULLETIN SIGNALETIQUE. 890. **Added/Corp** Centre National de la Recherche Scientifique (France). Centre de Documentation Scientifique et Technique. Vol. 35 (1974)-. Bulletin. French. mo. 370.00F. Centre National de la Recherche Scientifique, Informascience, 26 rue Boyer, 75971 Paris France. **Tel** 61.41.11.05, telex CNRSDOC 220880 F. **LC** Z7913; .B84; TJ2. **DD** 016.6. ***Continues** Bulletin Signaletique. 890: Industries Mecaniques, Genie Civil, Transports, Techniques Aerospatiales.*

FR/0223-4246
BULLETIN SIGNALETIQUE. 891: INDUSTRIES MECANIQUES. **Added/Corp** Centre National de la Recherche Scientifique (France). Centre de Documentation Scientifique et Technique. (198?)-. Bulletin. French. mo. Centre National de la Recherche Scientifique, Informascience, 26 rue Boyer, 75971 Paris France. **Tel** 61.41.11.05, telex CNRSDOC 220880 F. **LC** Z5853.M2; B87; TJ145. **DD** 016.62138.

US/0736-7112
BUYERS GUIDE - NATIONAL TOOLING & MACHINING ASSOCIATION. **See** Business-Purchasing.

CN/0008-4379
CANADIAN MACHINERY AND METALWORKING. [Can. mach. metalwork.]. (July 1960)-. Periodical. English. Eleven times a year. 36.00Can$ Canada; 78.00Can$ other. MacLean Hunter Ltd. Business Publishers / Canada, Box 9100, Station A, Toronto ONT M5W 1A5 Canada. **Tel** (416)946-8420, (800)567-0444. **(Subscription address:** Indas, 35 Riviera Drive, Building 17, Markham Ontario L3R 8N4 Canada.**) ED** Nick Hancock. **LC** TJ1; .C37. **DD** 621.8/05. **CODEN** CMCHA3. **[CCC]. Bk Rev. Ad Acc. Circ:** 16,000 (ctrl). available on microfilm and microfiche from University Microfilms International (UMI); available on an online database (file 648/Full-Text) from DIALOG. Documents available from Article Express International, CASDDS. ***Continues** Canadian Machinery.*
Desc: Magazine for metalworking production, engineering and purchasing people; a complete source for machine tooling, components and supplies. An integral part of buying decisions across Canada.
Ind/Abst Chem. Abstr.; Ei Page One; Eng. Index Annu.; F&S Index Plus Text, Int. [Select. Cov.]; PROMT; Trade Ind. ASAP [Full Txt.]; Trade Ind. Index [Full Txt.].

CN/0824-7382
CANADIAN REPRO-DRAFT MAGAZINE. [Can. repro-draft mag.]. **VFOAT** Repro-Draft. Vol. 1/2 (Dec./Jan. 1984)-. Periodical. English. bm. $12.00. TSD Publications, Unit 15, 1121 Bellamy Road, Scarborough Ontario M1H 3B9. **DD** 681/.6/05.

SP/0008-5677
CANTERAS Y EXPLOTACIONES. [Canteras explot.]. (1967)-. Periodical. Spanish. mo. 10700ptas Spain; 12000ptas other Europe; 12500ptas other. Pedeca, Maria Auxiliadora 5, 28040 Madrid Spain. **Tel** 011 34 1 4508837. **ED** Ricardo J Hernandez. **UDC** 622. **[CCC]. Bk Rev. Ad Acc, Adv Mgr:** Magdaleno Romo. **Circ:** 8500.
Desc: Publication about machinery for mining, quarries, cement and hydraulic works.

US/0163-0679
CEM, CHILTON'S CONTROL EQUIPMENT MASTER. **VFOAT** Chilton's Control Equipment Master. English. an. $45.00. CEM Chilton's Control Equipment Master, Chilton Company, Chilton Way, Radnor PA 19089. **Tel** (215)964-4000, (800)695-1214, FAX (215)964-4273, telex 6851035 CHILTON UW. **LC** TA165; .C17.

FR/0399-0001
CETIM INFORMATIONS. [CETIM inf.]. **VFOAT** Informations - CETIM; Centre Technique des Industries Mecaniques Informations. (1967)-. Periodical. French (English). Six times a year. 278.16F France; 410.00F other. CETIM, Service Diffusion BP 67, 60304 Senlis France. **Tel** 011 33 44 583266. **UDC** 66/68.
Desc: Market reports on world fertilizer industry.

CC
CHI CHUNG YUN SHU CHI HSIEH / TI 1 CHI HSIEH KUNG YEH PU CHI CHUNG YUN SHU CHI HSIEH YEN CHIU SO. **Added/Corp** Ti 1 Chi Hsieh Kung Yeh pu Chi Chung Yun Shu Chi Hsieh Yen Chiu so (China). (19??)-. Periodical. Chinese. bm. **LC** TJ1350.A1; C48. **DD** 622/.6/05.

US/1000-9345
CHI HSIEH KUNG CHENG HSUEH PAO. (CHINESE JOURNAL OF MECHANICAL ENGINEERING.). **Added/Corp** Chung-kuo Chi Hsieh Kung Cheng Hsueh Hui (Peking, China). **VFOAT** Chi Hsieh Kung Cheng Hsueh Pao. Vol. 1, No. 1 (May 1988)-. Periodical. English. qt. $120.00. American Society of Mechanical Engineers, 22 Law Drive, Fairfield NJ 07007. **Tel** (201)882-1167, (212)705-7722 (editorial). **LC** TJ1; .C52. **DD** 621. **CODEN** CJMEER. **[CCC].** available on microfilm and microfiche from University Microfilms International (UMI). Documents available from Article Express International.
Ind/Abst Eng. Index Annu.; Fluid Abstr., Civil Eng.; Fluid Abstr. Proc. Eng.; FLUIDEX (-1991).

CC/0577-6686
CHI HSIEH KUNG CHENG HSUEH PAO. **Added/Corp** Chung-kuo Chi Hsieh Kung Cheng Hsueh Hui (Peking, China). **VFOAT** Chinese Journal of Mechanical Engineering. (1953)-. Periodical. Chinese (summaries and/or abstracts in English, German and Russian). qt. $33.60. **(Subscription address:** China International Book Trading Corporation, PO Box 399, Library Service Department, Beijing 100044 People's Republic of China.**) LC** TJ4; .C48. **DD** 621.8/05.
Ind/Abst Met. Abstr.; World Alum. Abstr.

CH
CHIEH NENG CHI SHU / CHUNG-KUO KO HSUEH CHI SHU CHING PAO YEN CHIU SO CHUNG-CHING FEN SO. Periodical. Chinese. NT$0.65. Hsin Hua Shu Tien / Chung-ching China, Chung-ching fa Hsing so, People's Republic of China. **LC** TJ163.3; .C43. **DD** 333.7/1616.

CH
CHUNG-HUA MIN KUO CHI CHI SHE PEI HSUAN LU. **Added/Corp** Chin Shu Kung Yeh Fa Chan Chung Hsin. **VFOAT** Chi Chi She Pei Hsuan Lu; Taiwan Machinery and Equipment Classified Catalog File, Republic of China. (1977)-. Periodical. Chinese (English). ir. $40.00. US International Marketing Company, 17057 Bellflower Boulevard, PO Box 428, Bellflower CA 90706. **Tel** (310)925-2918. **ED** R.M. Heaton. **LC** TJ1175; .C482. **DD** 621.8/029/451249. **Bk Rev. Ad Acc. Circ:** 2,000 (ctrl).
Desc: Full color magazine illustrating and describing machinery available from Taiwan.

CH
CHUNG-HUA MIN KUO CHI CHI YU TIEN KUNG CHI TSAI NIEN CHIEN. **VFOAT** R.O.C. Machinery & Electrical Apparatus Industry Year Book. Multiple languages (Chinese and English). an. $40.00. World Enterprise, 247 San Ming Road Section 3, Taichung Taiwan. **LC** HD9705.T3; C47.

SZ/0007-8506
CIRP ANNALS. (CIRP ANNALS ... MANUFACTURING TECHNOLOGY.). [CIRP ann.]. **Added/Corp** International Institution for Production Engineering Research. **VFOAT** C.I.R.P. Annals ... Manufacturing Technology; Berichte der Internationalen Forschungsgemeinschaft fur Mechanische Produktionstechnik; Annals of the International Institution for Production Engineering Research; Annales du College International pour l'Etude Scientifique des Techniques de Production m,ecanique; Annals of the CIRP; CIRP. Vol. 24, No. 1 (1975)-. English (French and German). Twice a year (July and December). 325.00F Switzerland, 390.00F other, Surface Mail; 390.00F other, Airmail. Hallwag AG, Nordring 4, CH-3001 Bern Switzerland. **Tel** 011 41 31 3323131, FAX 031/414133, telex 912661 HAWA CH. **LC** T175; .I55. **DD** 670/.5. **[CCC]. Bk Rev. Ad Acc.** available on microfilm. Documents available from Article Express International, Ask*IEEE. ***Continues** CIRP, 0373-7284.*
Desc: These are papers submitted by the members of the International Institution for Production Engineering Research.
Ind/Abst Alum. Ind. Abstr.; Bioeng. Abstr.; Civ. Struct. Eng. Abstr.; Comput. Inf. Syst. Abstr. J. [Full Cov.]; Ei Page One; Elect. Comm. Abstr.; Eng. Index Annu.; Environ. Eng. Abstr.; INSPEC; Manuf. Process Eng. Abstr.; Mater. Sci. Eng. Abstr.; Mech. Eng. Abstr.; Met. Abstr.; Solid State Supercond. Abstr.; World Alum. Abstr.

US/0739-036X
CLOSED LOOP (MINNEAPOLIS, MINN.). (CLOSED LOOP.). [Closed loop]. **Added/Corp** MTS Systems Corporation. (19??)-. Periodical. English. ir. Free. MTS Systems Corporation, PO Box 24012, Minneapolis MN 55424. **Tel** (612)937-4000.
Ind/Abst Alum. Ind. Abstr.; Met. Abstr.

US/0884-7339
COGENERATION. ***Title Change.*** [Cogeneration]. Vol. 1, No. 1 (Mar. 1984)-(Jan./Feb. 1993). Periodical. English. bm. Pequot Publishing Inc., PO Box 447, Southport CT 06490. **Tel** (203)259-1812. **LC** TK1041; .C62. **DD** 621.1/9/05. Documents available from Ask*IEEE. ***Continues in part*** *Gas Turbine World & Cogeneration, 0746-4134.* ***Continued by*** *Private Power Executive, 1075-0592.*
Ind/Abst Coal Abstr.; INSPEC (March 1984-).

US/1040-2756
COMBUSTION (NEW YORK, N.Y. : 1989). (COMBUSTION.). [Combustion]. (1989)-. Monographic series. English. ir. Price varies per volume. Taylor & Francis Ltd., Rankine Road, Basingstoke Hampshire, RG24 8PR United Kingdom. **Tel** 011 44 256 840366, FAX 011 44 256 479438, telex 858540. **(Subscription address:** Taylor & Francis Inc., 1900 Frost Road, Suite 101, Bristol PA 19007-1598.**) ED** Norman Chigier. **DD** 541.
Desc: Advances in research on combustion processes.
Ind/Abst Ei Page One.

US/0148-6594
COMPANIES HOLDING BOILER AND PRESSURE VESSEL CERTIFICATES OF AUTHORIZATION FOR USE OF CODE SYMBOL STAMPS. **Main/Corp** American Society of Mechanical Engineers. Boiler and Pressure Vessel Committee. (19??)-. English. Three times a year. $75.00. American Society of Mechanical Engineers, 22 Law Drive, Fairfield NJ 07007. **Tel** (201)882-1167, (212)705-7722 (editorial). **LC** TS283; .A654a. **DD** 338.7/68/176. **Bk Rev. Ad Acc.**

GW/0178-7675
COMPUTATIONAL MECHANICS. Vol. 1, No. 1 (1986)-. Academic Scholarly Publication. English. Twelve times a year. DM1824.00. Springer-Verlag GmbH & Company KG, Heidelberger Platz 3, D 14197 Berlin Germany. **Tel** 011 49 30 8207223, FAX 011 49 30 8214091, telex 183 319 SPBLN D. **(Subscription address:** Springer Verlag New York Inc. / for North America, 44 Hartz Way, Secaucus NJ 07096.**) ED** Satya N Atluri and Genki Yagawa. **[CCC].** available on microfilm and microfiche from University Microfilms International (UMI). Documents available from Article Express International.
Desc: Reports original research of scholarly value of reasonable permanence in those areas of mechanics, mathematics and numerical methods in the practice of modern engineering.
Ind/Abst Appl. Mech. Rev.; Ei Page One; Eng. Mater. Abstr.; Eng. Index Annu.; Zentralbl. Math. Ihre Grenzgeb.

SZ/0927-7951
COMPUTATIONAL MECHANICS ADVANCES. Volume 1 (1993)-. English. Four times a year (1 volume). 455.00F; 5220.00F combined subscription with Computer Methods in Applied Mechanics and Engineering. Elsevier Sequoia SA, PO Box 564, CH-1001 Lausanne 1 Switzerland. **Tel** 011 41 21 3207381. **[CCC].**

UK/0268-8050
CONDITION MONITOR. [Cond. monit.]. (1986)-. Periodical. English. Twelve times a year. $337.00 The Americas; £226.00 other. Elsevier Advanced Technology, An Imprint of Elsevier Science Ltd., The Boulevard, Langford Lane, Kidlington, Oxford OX5 1GB United Kingdom. **Tel** 011 44 865 843000, 011 44 865 843699, FAX 011 44 865 843010. **(Subscription address:** Elsevier Science Ltd. Oxford Fulfillment Centre, PO Box 800, Kidlington, Oxford OX5 1DX United Kingdom.**) [CCC].**
Desc: Newsletter covering all aspects of machine maintenance.

US
CONFERENCE PUBLICATIONS OF THE INSTITUTE OF MECHANICAL ENGINEERS. (19??)-. English. ir. Society of Automotive Engineers, 400 Commonwealth Drive, Warrendale PA 15096. **Tel** (412)776-4841, (412)772-7106, FAX (412)776-5760. **(Subscription address:** SAE, Department L1094P, Pittsburgh, PA 15264**)**

NE/0010-6658
CONSTRUCTEUR. [Constructeur]. (Jan. 1962)-. Periodical. Dutch. mo. Fl216.52 Netherlands; Fl294.52 other. Samson Bedrijfsinformatie, Postbus 4, 2400 HA Alphen Rij Netherlands. **Tel** 011 31 1 72066633. **(Subscription address:** Intermedia BV, Postbus 4, 2400 MA Alphen Rijn Netherlands.**)** ***Absorbed*** *Constructiematerialen, 0589-4719.*
Ind/Abst Saf. Health Work.

RM/0573-7419
CONSTRUCTIA DE MASINI. [Constr. mas.]. **Added/Corp** Romania. Ministerul Metalurgiei si Constructiilor de Masini. Consiliul National al Inginerilor si Tehnicienilor din Republica Socialista Romania. Vol. 15, No. 4 (1963)-. Academic Scholarly Publication. Romanian (summaries and/or abstracts in English, French, German and Russian). mo. DM327.00. **(Subscription address:** Kubon & Sagner, ABT Zeitschriftenimport, D 80328 Munich Germany.**) CODEN** CMASAQ. Documents available from CASDDS. ***Continues in part*** *Metalurgia si Constructia de Masini.*
Desc: Technical and scientifical publication concerned with machine constructions matters.
Ind/Abst Ceram. Abstr.; Chem. Abstr.; Energy Res. Abstr.; Eng. Mater. Abstr.; Saf. Health Work.

GW/0935-1175
CONTINUUM MECHANICS AND THERMODYNAMICS. [Contin. mech. thermodyn.]. Vol. 1 (1989)-. Academic Scholarly Publication. English. Four times a year (Jan., Apr., July, Oct.). DM598.00. Springer-Verlag GmbH & Company KG, Heidelberger Platz 3, D 14197 Berlin Germany. **Tel** 011 49 30 8207223, FAX 011 49 30 8214091, telex 183 319 SPBLN D. **(Subscription address:** Springer Verlag New York Inc. / for North America, 44 Hartz Way, Secaucus NJ 07096.**) ED** K Huttler and I Mueller. **CODEN** CMETEJ. **[CCC].** available on microfilm and microfiche from University Microfilms International (UMI). Documents available from The Genuine Article, Ask*IEEE, CASDDS.
Desc: Reports on recent developments in continuum mechanics, thermodynamics and material science.
Ind/Abst Chem. Abstr. (1989-); Curr. Contents Eng. Tech. Appl. Sci.; INSPEC (1989-); Math. Rev.; Res. Alert [Full Cov.]; SCISEARCH.

UK/0010-8022
CONTROL & INSTRUMENTATION. **See** Computers-Automation.

SZ
CONTROL REVUE. (19??)-. Periodical. German. Four times a year. 75.00F Switzerland; 85.00F other. AGIFA Verlag AG, Bruggacherstrasse 26, CH 8117 Faellanden Switzerland. **Tel** 011 41 1 8256464. **LC** TJ212; .C67. **CODEN** CREWET.
Ind/Abst Fluid Abstr., Civil Eng.; Fluid Abstr. Proc. Eng.; FLUIDEX.

IT
CONTROLLI NUMERICI MACCHINE A CN ROBOT INDUSTRIALI. Periodical. English. bm. $23.76. Tecniche Nuove SRL, Via Moscova 46-9, 20121 Milan Italy. **Tel** 02/6590351, FAX 02/6571058, telex 334647 TECHS I. ***Continues*** *Controlli Numerici e Macchine, 0010-8081.*

IT/0254-1971
COURSES AND LECTURES / INTERNATIONAL CENTRE FOR MECHANICAL SCIENCES. [Courses lect. - Int. Cent. Mech. Sci.]. **Added/Corp** International Centre for Mechanical Sciences. (19??)-. Monographic series. English. ir. Price varies per volume. Springer-Verlag Wien, Sachsenplatz 4 6, PO Box 89, A-1201 Vienna Austria. **Tel** 011 43 1 3302415. **(Subscription address:** Springer Verlag New York Inc. / for North America, 44 Hartz Way, Secaucus NJ 07096.**) CODEN** CICMDR. **[CCC].** Documents available from Article Express International, Ask*IEEE.
Ind/Abst Ei Page One; Eng. Index Annu.; GeoRef; INSPEC.

UK/0307-0018
CRANES TODAY. [Cranes today]. (1972)-. Periodical. English (table of contents in French, German and Italian). Eleven times a year. $140.00 US and Canada; £60.00 UK. Wilmington Publishing Ltd., PO Box 200, Field End Road, Ruislip Middx HA4 OSY England. **Tel** 011 44 81 841 3970, FAX 011 44 81 841 9676. **DD** 338.

US/1052-0139
CRYOGAS INTERNATIONAL. [CryoGas int.]. Vol. 28, No. 7 (Aug./Sept. 1990)-. Periodical. English. Ten times a year (June/July and Aug./Sept. issues combined). $150.00 US, $180.00 other (surface mail); $200.00 airmail. J. R. Campbell and Associates Inc., 5 Militia Drive, Lexington MA 02173. **Tel** (617)862-0624, FAX (617)863-9411. **ED** Linda Grant. **LC** HD9660.G37; C79. **DD** 338.4/7621564/05. **Ad Acc, Adv Mgr:** Lori Frieling. **Circ:** 500. ***Continues*** *Cryogenic Information Report, 0011-2259.*
Desc: Reports advances in technology, market development and new products for the industrial gases and cryogenic equipment industries. Each issue contains articles about new gas plants, mergers and acquisitions, contract awards, organizational changes, financial results and industry statistics. Special sections feature new technology, international patent applications and US patent awards. Applications, market reports, and new products and services are highlighted. Feature articles cover topical issues and include interviews of industry executives.

FR
CT DEC INFORMATION. 250.00F France; 350.00F other. Centre Technique Industrie, du Decoltage BP 65, 74301 Cluses Cedex France. cum. index.
Desc: Technical articles on machining processes, heat and surface treatment, materials, quality, robotics and metrology.

US
CTI JOURNAL. English. sa. $10.00. Cooling Tower Institute, PO Box 73383, Houston TX 77273. **Tel** (713)583-4087, FAX (713)537-1721. **ED** Roy Maze, Robert C Monroe, and Dorothy Garrison. Index available. cum. index. **Ad Acc. Circ:** 6,000 (ctrl). ***Continues*** *Journal of the Cooling Tower Institute, 0273-3250.*
Desc: Devoted solely to the subject of cooling towers and their operations. For professionals responsible for the construction specifications, testing, maintenance, and operation of cooling towers.

US/0884-6324
DES (NORWALK, CONN. 1984). (DES.). [DES]. **VFOAT** Diesel Equipment Superintendent. Vol. 62, No. 8 (1984)-. Periodical. English. mo. $35.00. Business Journals Inc, PO Box 5550, Norwalk CT 06856. **Tel** (203)853-6015, FAX (203)852-8175, telex 353706. **LC** TJ795.A1; D5. **DD** 629.2/24/05. ***Continues*** *Diesel Equipment Superintendent (Norwalk, Conn.), 0731-0803.*

UN/0130-3066
DETALI MASIN (KIEV). (DETALI MASHIN.). [Detali mas.]. (1970)-. Academic Scholarly Publication. Russian. wk. $112.00 domestic airmail; $282.00 international airmail. **(Subscription address:** Victor Kamkin, 4956 Boiling Brook Parkway, Rockville MD 20852.**) CODEN** DMASD6. Documents available from CASDDS. ***Continues*** *Detali Mashin I Podemno-Transportnye Mashiny, 0418-7822.*
Ind/Abst Chem. Abstr.; Int. Aerosp. Abstr.

UK
DIAL ENGINEERING SALES CONTACTS. English. an. £198.00. Dial Industry Publications, Windsor Court, East Grinstead House, East Grinstead West Sussex, RH19 1XA England. **Tel** (0342)326972, FAX (0342)315130, telex 95127 INFSERG. **ED** D Lammin. **Ad Acc. Circ:** 3,000.
Desc: Details on 23,000 companies in the engineering industry with full contact information.

US
DIEMAKING STAMPING & EDMING. ***Title Change.*** (19??)-(19??). English. Six times a year. Eagle Publications / Circulation Department, 42400 Nine Mile Road, Suite B, Novi MI 48050. **Tel** (313)347-3490. ***Continues*** *EDM Digest, 0199-3550.* ***Continued by*** *American Tooldie & Stamping News.*

US/0278-5994
DIESEL & GAS TURBINE WORLDWIDE. [Diesel gas turbine worldw.]. **VFOAT** Diesel and Gas Turbine Worldwide. (19??)-. Periodical. English. Ten times a year. $55.00 (surface mail); $120.00 (airmail). Diesel & Gas Turbine Publishers, 13555 Bishops Court, Brookfield WI 53005. **Tel** (414)784-9177, (800)558-4322, FAX (414)784-8133, telex 275398 DIESL UR. **ED** Joseph Kane. **LC** TJ795.A1; D38. **DD** 621.43/6/05. **Ad Acc. Circ:** 20,000 (ctrl). Documents available from Article Express International, Ask*IEEE. ***Continues*** *Diesel & Gas Turbine Progress Worldwide, 0149-4465.*
Desc: Up-to-date reporting on design, manufacturing, marketing, application, operation and maintenance of diesel and gas engines and gas turbine engines and their driver equipment and control.
Ind/Abst BMT Abstr.; Coal Abstr.; Eng. Index Annu. [Select. Cov.]; Gas Abstr.; INSPEC (July/Aug. 1983-).

●US/1070-4884
DIESEL & GAS TURBINE WORLDWIDE CATALOG (1992). (DIESEL & GAS TURBINE WORLDWIDE CATALOG.). [Diesel gas turbine worldw. cat.]. **VFOAT** Diesel and Gas Turbine Worldwide Catalog. Vol. 57 (1992)-. Catalog. English. an. $75.00. Diesel & Gas Turbine Publishers, 13555 Bishops Court, Brookfield WI 53005. **Tel** (414)784-9177, (800)558-4322, FAX (414)784-8133, telex 275398 DIESL UR. **LC** TJ795.A1; D45. **DD** 621. ***Continues*** *Diesel & Gas Turbine Catalog, 1064-2366.*

US
DIESEL ENGINEERING HANDBOOK. (1925)-. Periodical. English. ir. $34.00. Business Journals Inc, PO Box 5550, Norwalk CT 06856. **Tel** (203)853-6015, FAX (203)852-8175, telex 353706. **ED** Julius Kuttner and L H Morrison. **LC** TJ795.A1; D47. **DD** 621.436.

US/1040-8878
DIESEL PROGRESS ENGINES & DRIVES. [Diesel prog. engines drives]. **VFOAT** Diesel Progress Engines and Drives. Vol. 54, No. 9 (Sept. 1988)-. Periodical. English. mo. $60.00. Diesel & Gas Turbine Publishers, 13555 Bishops Court, Brookfield WI 53005. **Tel** (414)784-9177, (800)558-4322, FAX (414)784-8133, telex 275398 DIESL UR. **LC** TJ795; .D48. **DD** 621.43/6. available on microfilm and microfiche from University Microfilms International (UMI); available on an online database (file 648/Full-Text) from DIALOG.

Documents available from Article Express International, Documents on Demand. ***Continues*** *Diesel Progress North American, 0744-0073.*
Ind/Abst Alum. Ind. Abstr. (Sept. 1988-); Bus. ASAP (1990-) [Full Txt.]; Bus. Index (1990-); Energy Res. Abstr. (Sept. 1988-); Eng. Index Annu. [Select. Cov.]; Environ. Abstr. (Sept. 1988-?); F&S Index Plus Text, Int. [Select. Cov.]; Gen. BusinessFile (1990-); Gen. Period. Index (1990-); Mag. Search; Met. Abstr. (Sept. 1988-); PROMT; Trade Ind. ASAP [Full Txt.]; Trade Ind. Index (Sept. 1988-) [Full Txt.]; Vocat. Search (Jan. 1993-).

US/1056-7038
DIGITAL MEDIA. [Digit. media]. Vol. 1, No. 1 (June 1991)-. Periodical. English. mo. $395.00 US; $413.00 other. Seybold Publications Inc., 428 West Baltimore Pike, PO Box 644, Media PA 19063. **Tel** (610)565-2480, (800)325-3830, FAX (610)565-4659, or 3261, telex 4991494. **DD** 621. **CODEN** DMEDEG. **[CCC].** available on an online database (file 675/Full-Text) from DIALOG.
Ind/Abst Comput. ASAP [Full Txt.]; Comput. Database [Full Txt.].

US/0898-901X
DIGITAL TECHNICAL JOURNAL. (DIGITAL TECHNICAL JOURNAL OF DIGITAL EQUIPMENT CORPORATION.). [Digit. tech. j.]. **Added/Corp** Digital Equipment Corporation. **VFOAT** Digital Technical Journal. No. 1 (Aug. 1985)-. Periodical. English. qt. $40.00. Digital Equipment Corporation, 30 Porter Road, LJO2 D10, Littleton MA 01460. **Tel** (508)493-2894, (508)486-6111. **ED** Jane C. Blake. **LC** QA76.8.D43; D55. **DD** 621. Documents available from Ask*IEEE.
Ind/Abst INSPEC (Feb. 1988-).

RU
DINAMIKA I TOCHNOST FUNKTSIONIROVANIA TEPLOMEKHANICHESKIKH SISTEM. **Added/Corp** Tulskii Politekhnicheskii Institut. (19??)-. Russian. 0.90rub single issue. **LC** TJ260; .D54.

US/0145-3866
DIRECTORY - NATIONAL FLUID POWER ASSOCIATION. **Main/Corp** National Fluid Power Association. (19??)-. English. an. $150.00, $15.00 (members). National Fluid Power Association, 3333 North Mayfair Road, Milwaukee WI 53222. **Tel** (414)778-3369, FAX (414)778-3361, telex 704557. **ED** Carrie Tatman Schwartz. **LC** TJ843; .N36a. **DD** 621.2/06/273. **Circ:** 2,000 (ctrl).
Desc: Complete list of 190 fluid power manufacturers who are members of the National Fluid Power Association. Includes company name, address, telephone, telex, key personnel and products manufactured for each manufacturing plant of the member company, with NFPA bylaws, dues schedule, and annual report.

PK/0376-8473
DIRECTORY OF ENGINEERING UNITS IN PAKISTAN. 1974-. Directory. English. Rs150.00. Development Institute of Pakistan, Mohammadi House, I I Chundrigar Road, Karachi Pakistan. **LC** TJ104.5; .D57. **DD** 338.4/7/6210255491.

US/0360-8794
DIRECTORY OF MEMBERS, OFFICERS, COMMITTEES - AMERICAN VACUUM SOCIETY. **Main/Corp** American Vacuum Society. Directory. English. an. American Vacuum Society, 335 East 45th Street, New York NY 10017. **LC** TJ940; .A7A. **DD** 621.5/5/06273. ctrl circ.

US/0273-1525
DIRECTORY OF SOLAR ENERGY RESEARCH ACTIVITIES IN THE UNITED STATES. **See** Energy.

US/1048-373X
DIRECTORY OF WIRE COMPANIES OF NORTH AMERICA. [Dir. wire companies North Am.]. (19??)-. English. an. $95.00 US; $100.70 Connecticut; $150.00 others. Business Information Services, 7 Hampden Road, Stafford Springs CT 06076. **Tel** (203)684-5877, FAX (203)684-9158. **ED** Richard Callahan and Susan Janssen. **LC** PAR. **DD** 621. **Ad Acc, Adv Mgr:** Cliff Crawford, **Tel** (203)684-5877.
Desc: Compilation of profiles such as history of products, addresses, principal personnel and geographical listing about wire companies in North America, Canada and Mexico.

AT
DIVISIONAL REPORT - CSIRO DIVISION OF MECHANICAL ENGINEERING OF THE INSTITUTE OF INDUSTRIAL TECHNOLOGY. **Main/Corp** Commonwealth Scientific and Industrial Research Organization (Australia). Division of Mechanical Engineering. (June 1979)-. English. CSIRO Publications, PO Box 89, 314 Albert Street, East Melborne Victoria 3002 Australia. **Tel** 011 61 3 4187333, 4187217, FAX 011 61 3 4190459, telex AA 30236. ***Continues*** *Commonwealth Scientific and Industrial Research Organization (Australia). Division of Mechanical Engineering. Report on Research.*

GW
DOMA INFORMATIONSDIENST : FEINBEARBEITUNG. German. mo. Fachinformationszent Technik, Ostbahnhofstrasse 13, D 60314 Frankfurt Germany. **Tel** 011 49 69 4308234, 011 49 69 4308254.

GW
DOMA INFORMATIONSDIENST : NEUE WERKSTOFFE FUER DEN MASCHINEN UND ANLAGENBAU. German. mo. DM400.00. Fachinformationszent Technik, Ostbahnhofstrasse 13, D 60314 Frankfurt Germany. **Tel** 011 49 69 4308234, 011 49 69 4308254.

FR
DOSSIERS TECHNIQUES PAUL HUET / MECANIQUE. (19??)-. Periodical. French. ir. 840.64F France; 997.00F other. Editions Techniques Paul Huet, 185 rue Gallieni, 92100 Boulogne, Billancourt, France. **Tel** 011 33 1 46046633.

FR
DOSSIERS TECHNIQUES PAUL HUET / TRANSMISSION MECANIQUE. (19??)-. Periodical. French. ir. 758.01F France; 900.00F other. Editions Techniques Paul Huet, 185 rue Gallieni, 92100 Boulogne, Billancourt, France. **Tel** 011 33 1 46046633.

US/0925-4668
DYNAMICS AND CONTROL. [Dyn. control]. Vol. 1, No. 1 (Mar. 1991)-. Periodical. English. qt. $486.00. Kluwer Academic Publishers / Massachusetts, PO Box 358, Accord Station, Hingham MA 02018. **Tel** (617)871-6600. **ED** J.M. Skowronski, M. J. Corless, H. Flashner. **CODEN** DYCOEL. **[CCC]. Pr Rev. Acid Free.** available on microfilm and microfiche from University Microfilms International (UMI). Documents available from Article Express International, Ask*IEEE.
Desc: Devoted to the control of dynamic systems. Promotes the use of advanced dynamics in developing control methods. Papers are published in both theory and applications. Topics of interest include control of nonlinear systems, uncertain systems and systems with conflict. Applications covering mechanical, manufacturing, aerospace, and electrical engineering are of interest, as well as applications from other branches of applied science.
Ind/Abst ACM Guide Comput. Lit.; Comput. Rev.; Eng. Index Annu.; Inf. Sci. Abstr.; INSPEC (Mar. 1991-); Int. Aerosp. Abstr.; Zentralbl. Math. Ihre Grenzgeb.

US/0070-8550
ECONOMIC HANDBOOK OF THE MACHINE TOOL INDUSTRY. **Added/Corp** National Machine Tool Builders' Association. (1969)-. English. an (September). $105.00 US and Canada, $115.00 other (postage included). Association for Manufacturing Technology, 7901 West Park Drive, McLean VA 22101. **Tel** (703)827-5260, FAX (703)827-5263. **LC** HD9703.U48; E36. **DD** 338.4/7/6219020973.
Ind/Abst Predicasts Forecasts; Stat. Ref. Index.

US/0013-6158
ELEVATOR WORLD. [Elevator world]. (19??)-. Periodical. English. mo. $52.00 (1 year), $92.00 (2 year), $132.00 (3 year) US and possessions; $90.00 (1 year), $160.00 (2 year), $230.00 (3 year) other. Elevator World, 354 Morgan Avenue, Mobile AL 36606. **Tel** (205)479-4514, FAX (205)479-7043, telex 782 722 ELE WORLD. **ED** William C Sturgeon. **LC** TJ1370; .E43. **DD** 338.7/621877/025. Index available. **Bk Rev. Ad Acc, Adv Mgr:** Patricia Cartee, **Tel** (205)479-4514. **Circ:** 6,000.
Desc: The international communications network for industries transporting through compactly engineered systems on cables or rails.
Ind/Abst CIS Abstr.; Ei Page One; Saf. Health Work.

US
ELEVATOR WORLD SOURCE, THE. (1984)-. English. an. $35.00. Elevator World, 354 Morgan Avenue, Mobile AL 36606. **Tel** (205)479-4514, FAX (205)479-7043, telex 782 722 ELE WORLD. **LC** HD9715.9.E43; E45. **DD** 338.7/621877/025.

XR/0375-8842
ENERGETIKA. (ENERGETIKA; ODBORNY CASOPIS PRO ELEKTRARENSTVI, TEPLARENSTVI A POUZITI ENERGIE.). [Energetika]. **Added/Corp** Czechoslovakia. Federalni Ministerstvo Paliv a Energetiky. Czechoslovakia. Ministerstvo Energetiky. (1951)-. Periodical. Czech (summaries and/or abstracts in English and German). mo (12 issues). $88.70. **(Subscription address:** Artia Pegas Press Ltd., Palac Metro Narodni Trida 25, 11210 Prague 1 Czech Republic.) **LC** TJ4; .E53. **DD** 0421-1774; 621.3. **CODEN** EGKAA2. Documents available from Ask*IEEE.
Ind/Abst Ceram. Abstr.; Coal Abstr.; INSPEC (1968-); Saf. Health Work.

YU
ENERGETSKI BILANS SFR JUGOSLAVIJE. **VFOAT** Savezni Zavod Za Statistiku; Overall Energy for SFR of Yugoslavia; Energetski Bilans. 1981-. Serbo-Croatian (Roman) (Russian and English). an. Savezni Zavod za Statistiku, Kneza Milosa 20, Belgrad Yugoslavia. **LC** TJ163.25.Y8; E53.

GW/0013-7359
ENERGIE (MUNCHEN). (ENERGIE; KOHLE, TREIBSTOFFE, GAS, STROM, WASSERKRAFT.). [Energie]. Vol. 1 (Nov. 1949)-. Academic Scholarly Publication. German. mo. DM220.00. Energiewirtschaft Technik Verlagsges GmbH, Oberrather Str. 2, D 40472 Duesseldorf Germany. **Tel** 011 49 211 658070, FAX 011 49 211 652129, telex 841/8587177. **(Subscription address:** Presse Marketing Service, Postfach 290180, D 47261 Duisburg Germany) **LC** TJ3; .E54. **CODEN** ENERA4. **[CCC].** Documents available from Ask*IEEE, CASDDS.
Ind/Abst Chem. Abstr.; Coal Abstr.; EMBASE; Energy Res. Abstr.; INSPEC (June 1969-); Int. Aerosp. Abstr.

NE/0165-2117
ENERGIESPECTRUM. [Energiespectrum]. V. 1- ; Jan. 1977-. Academic Scholarly Publication. Dutch. Fl48.60. Energieonderzoek Centrum Nederland, Scheveningseweg 112, Den Haag Netherlands. **LC** TJ163.2; .E436. **CODEN** NRGSDB. Documents available from Ask*IEEE, CASDDS. ***Supersedes*** *Atoomenergie en Haar Toepassingen.*
Ind/Abst Chem. Abstr.; Coal Abstr.; EMBASE; INSPEC (Jan. 1977-).

RU
ENERGOEXPORT. (1976)-. Periodical. English (English). ir. $209.95. V/O Energomachexport, 1/4 Deguninskaya U1, 127486 Moscow Russia. **(Subscription address:** East View Publications Inc., 3020 Harbor Lane North, Suite 110, Minneapolis MN 55447.) **LC** HD9695.R9; E53. **DD** 338.4/76218/0947.

US/0161-6048
ENERGY TECHNOLOGY. ***Ceased.*** [Energy technol.]. **Main/Conf** Energy Technology Conference (1974-) (Washington, D.C.). (1974)-?. Academic Scholarly Publication. English. an. Government Institutes Inc., 4 Research Place, Suite 200, Rockville MD 20850. **Tel** (301)921-2300, 921-2355, FAX (301)251-0638. **LC** TJ163.7; .E562A. **DD** 621.042/05. **CODEN** ENTED9. Documents available from Article Express International, CASDDS, Documents on Demand.
Desc: Contains the proceedings of the annual Energy Technology Conference and Exposition. At the conference, leading energy experts present practical ideas and recent developments in the energy conservation. Topics discussed include cogeneration; new building equipment; natural gas deregulation; developments in photovoltaics; wood as a fuel; and energy management systems - plus much more.
Ind/Abst Bioeng. Abstr. (?-?); Chem. Abstr. (?-?); Coal Abstr. (?-?); Ei Page One (?-?); Energy Inf. Abstr. (?-?); Energy Res. Abstr. (Jan. 1980-); Eng. Index Annu.; Environ. Abstr.; GeoRef (?-?); INIS Atomindex [Micro.].

US/1056-4063
ENGINE POWER PERSPECTIVE. ***Title Change.*** [Engine power perspect.]. (July 1988)-(1992). Periodical. English. Twelve times a year. Power Systems Research, 1301 Corporate Center, Suite 113, Eagan MN 55121. **Tel** (612)454-0144, FAX (612)454-0760, telex 291139. **DD** 338. **Circ:** 200. ***Continues*** *Diesel Power Perspective, 0743-0787.* ***Continued by*** *Power Products Business, 1056-4063.*

US/0891-9976
ENGINEERED SYSTEMS. [Eng. syst.]. Vol. 1, No. 1 (May 1984)-. Trade Publication. English. Nine times a year. $39.00 US; $51.00 other. Business News Publishing Company, 755 West Big Beaver Road, Suite 1000, Troy MI 48084. **Tel** (810)362-3700, FAX (810)362-0317, telex 230295. **ED** Robert L Schwed, Gordon D Duffy, and Matthew McCann. **LC** TH7121; .E54. **DD** 697/.005. **CODEN** ENSYEV. **Bk Rev. Ad Acc. Circ:** 57,515 (ctrl). available on microfilm from University Microfilms International (UMI).
Desc: Serves the nonresidential HVAC/R industry. Readers are consulting engineers/architects, mechanical engineers/building operators, design-build contractors.

US/0489-5606
ENGINEERING KNOW-HOW IN ENGINE DESIGN. Pt. 1- 1953-. English. an. Society of Automotive Engineers, 400 Commonwealth Drive, Warrendale PA 15096. **Tel** (412)776-4841, (412)772-7106, FAX (412)776-5760. **LC** TJ751; .S65A. **DD** 621.4.

FR/0765-006X
ENTRAINEMENTS & SYSTEMES. [Entrain. syst.]. **VFOAT** Entrainements et Systemes. (1984)-. Periodical. French. Eight times a year. 320.00F France; 398.00F other. SOPROGE SA, 7 Ter Cour des Petites Ecuries, 75010 Paris France. **Tel** 011 33 1 42471205, FAX 011 33 1 47703394. **UDC** 621.8. Index available. **Ad**

Acc. Circ: 5,000. available with charts; available with illustrations. ***Continues*** *Revue Generale des Transmissions, 0048-8100.*

CN/0710-2720
EQUIPMENT JOURNAL. [Equip. j.]. (19??)-. Trade Publication. English. Seventeen times a year (every third Thursday). 18.00Can$ Canada; 25.00Can$ US; 32.00Can$ other. Pace Publishing Ltd, 150 Lakeshore Road West, Suite 36 Mississauga, Ontario L5H 3R2 Canada. **Tel** (905)274-4883, FAX (905)274-8686. **ED** Gordon Froggatt. **DD** 381/.456218. **Bk Rev**, (Qty: 17). **Ad Acc**, **Adv Mgr:** Jon Baker, **Tel** (416)274-4883. **Circ:** 18,000 (ctrl).
Desc: Serves construction industry and natural resource producers. Advertising medium for buying or selling of new and used equipment.

PL/0137-4990
ERGONOMIA WROCAW. [Ergonomia Wroc.]. (1978)-. Periodical. Polish. sa. **UDC** 331.015.11.
Ind/Abst Ergon. Abstr.

AT/1033-1875
ERGONOMICS AUSTRALIA. [Ergon. Aust.]. (1987)-. Periodical. English. bm. **DD** 620.8205. ***Continues*** *Ergonomics Australasia, 0814-5261.*
Ind/Abst Ergon. Abstr.

UK/0268-5639
ERGONOMIST. [Ergonomist]. (1976)-. Periodical. English. mo.
Ind/Abst Ergon. Abstr.; HILITES.

CN
ESTIMATES. PART III, ENERGY, MINES AND RESOURCES CANADA, MINERALS AND EARTH SCIENCES PROGRAM. **Main/Corp** Canada. **VFOAT** Budget des Depenses. Partie III, Energie, Mines et Ressources Canada, Plan de Depenses du Programme des Mineraux et des Sciences de la Terre. (19??)-. English (French). $9.00 Canada; $10.00 other. Canada Communication Group Publishers, Order Processing, Ottawa Ontario K1A 0S9 Canada. **Tel** (819)956-4800, (819)956-4802. **LC** TJ163.25.C3; C3a. **DD** 354.710082/327.

GW/0013-2845
ETR. **See** Transportation-Railroads.

UK
EUROPEAN DESIGN DIRECTORY. 1974-. Directory. English. an. £42.00. Engineering Materials and Design, 33-40 Bowling Green Lane, London EC1R 0NE England. **Tel** (01)661-3174. **ED** R Narraway. **LC** TA402.5.E85; E9. **DD** 338.4/7/620002541. **Ad Acc.** ctrl circ.
Desc: Covers technical features, new products, data, technology transfer, manufacturing technique and news relating to product, machine and equipment design.

BE/0777-2734
EUROPEAN JOURNAL OF MECHANICAL ENGINEERING. [Eur. j. mech. eng.]. **VFOAT** Revue Europeenne de Mechanique; Europees Tijdschrift voor Mechanica; European Journal Revue M Tijdschrift. Vol. 34, No. 1 (June 1989)-. Periodical. English (French and Dutch; summaries and/or abstracts in English, French and Dutch). qt (1 volume). 3500.00F Belgium; 4250.00F other. BSME / Belgian Society of Mechanical Engineers, rue des Drapiers 21, Brussels Belgium. **Tel** 32 2 5118286, FAX 32 2 5121748. **ED** Francois Crepain. **UDC** 621. Index available. cum. index. **Bk Rev**. **Ad Acc.** Full Page (Color) 20000F. Half Page (Color) 10500F. **Circ:** 2,500 (ctrl). Documents available from Article Express International. ***Continues*** *Revue-M. Mecanique, 0035-3612.*
Desc: Contains original contributions and information of interest to mechanical engineers.
Ind/Abst Ei Page One (19??-); Eng. Index Annu. (19??-).

UK/0966-002X
EUROPEAN MACHINING. (EUROPEAN MACHINING.). [Eur. mach.]. (1989)-. Periodical. English. qt. £33.00 UK; £38.00 (surface), £44.00 (air mail) other. Turret Group, 177 Hagden Lane, Watford Herts WD1 8LN United Kingdom. **Tel** 011 44 923 228577, FAX 011 44 923 221346. **DD** 338.476218094.

UK/0967-9650
EUROPEAN SURFACE TREATMENT. [Eur. surf. treat.]. (1991)-. Periodical. English. qt. £41.00 UK; £48.00 (surface), £55.00 (air mail) other. Turret Group, 177 Hagden Lane, Watford Herts WD1 8LN United Kingdom. **Tel** 011 44 923 228577, FAX 011 44 923 221346. **DD** 667.9.

CN/0383-3445
EVALUATION REPORT - PRAIRIE AGRICULTURAL MACHINERY INSTITUTE. (EVALUATION REPORT.). [Eval. rep. - Prairie Agric. Mach. Inst.]. **Added/Corp** Prairie Agricultural Machinery Institute (Canada). **VFOAT** Machinery Institute Evaluation Report; PAMI Evaluation Report. (1981)-. Periodical. English. Thirty times a year. 10.00Can$ Alberta, Manitoba and Saskatchewan; 20.00Can$ other Canada; 25.00Can$ other. Prairie Agricultural Machinery institute, PO Box 1900, Humboldt Saskatchewan S0K 2A0 Canada. **Tel** (306)682-2555, FAX (306)682-5080. **DD** 631.3. ***Continues*** *PAMI Evaluation Report., 0383-3445.*

US/0732-8818
EXPERIMENTAL TECHNIQUES (WESTPORT, CONN.). (EXPERIMENTAL TECHNIQUES.). [Exp. tech.]. **Added/Corp** Society for Experimental Mechanics. Society for Experimental Stress Analysis. (1976)-. Periodical. English. bm (Feb., Apr., June, Aug., Oct., Dec.). $88.00 (also comes in combination with Experimental Mechanics or membership). Society for Experimental Mechanics, 7 School Street, Bethel CT 06801-1405. **Tel** (203)790-6373, FAX (203)790-4472. **ED** Doris Thackrey. **LC** TA410; .E9. **DD** 620.1/1/0287. **CODEN** EXPTD2. **[CCC].** Index available. cum. index. **Bk Rev**. **Ad Acc.** **Pr Rev.** **Circ:** 4,380 (ctrl). available on microfilm and microfiche from University Microfilms International (UMI). Documents available from Article Express International, Ask*IEEE.
Desc: Contains practical articles in the field of experimental mechanics.
Ind/Abst Abstr. Bull. Inst. Paper Chem.; Abstr. Bull. Inst. Pap. Sci. Tech.; Acoust. Abstr.; Alum. Ind. Abstr.; Appl. Sci. Technol. Index; Ei Page One; Eng. Index Annu.; INIS Atomindex [Micro.]; INSPEC (Jan. 1983-); Int. Aerosp. Abstr. (1983-); Met. Abstr.; Shock Vibr. Dig.; World Alum. Abstr.

NE/0168-3527
FABRIEKEN VAN MACHINES EN APPARATEN VOOR HOUT- EN MEUBELINDUSTRIE, TEXTIEL- EN KLEDINGINDUSTRIE, WASSERIJEN EN CHEMISCHE REINIGING, LEDER- EN LEDERVERWERKENDE INDUSTRIE, PAPIER- EN GRAFISCHE INDUSTRIE / CENTRAAL BUREAU VOOR DE STATISTIEK, HOOFDAFDELING STATISTIEKEN VAN INDUSTRIE EN BOUWNIJVERHEID. **VFOAT** Manufacture of Wood Working Machinery, Textile Machinery, Commercial Laundry Machines, Dry Cleaning and Pressing Machines, Leather Working Machinery, Paper Industry and Printing Trade Machinery. 1981-. Dutch (summaries and/or abstracts in English). an. Fl7.00. Centraal Bureau voor de Statistiek, AFD ALG Zaken, Postbus 959, 2270 AZ Voorburg Netherlands. **Tel** 011 31 70 3373800, FAX 011 31 038 7429, telex 32692 CBS NL. **LC** HD9705.N2; N47E. ***Continues*** *Produktiestatistieken: Fabrieken van Machines en Apparaten Voor de Hout- en Meubelindustrie, de Textiel- en Kledingindustrie, de Wasserijen en Chemische Reiniging, de Leder-, en Lederverwerkende Industrie en Grafische Industrie.*

US/0746-2441
FASTENER TECHNOLOGY INTERNATIONAL. [Fasten. technol. int.]. **VFOAT** Fastener Technology. Vol. 6, No. 4 (Aug. 1983)-. Periodical. English. bm. $35.00 US and Canada; $68.00 other. Initial Publications, 3869 Darrow Road, Suite 101, Stow OH 44224. **Tel** (216)686-9544, FAX (216)686-9563. **ED** Thomas Dreher. **LC** TJ1320; .F25. **DD** 621.8/8/05. **Ad Acc.** **Circ:** 13,000 (ctrl). ***Continues*** *Fastener Technology, 0272-7331.*
Desc: Reports on business and technical development in the fastener and cold heading industry. Contents include feature articles on fastener topics and company profiles as well as departments on new equipment, technological innovations, new products, new literature, patents, fastener design and fastener use. There is also a section on distributor topics.

GW/0015-024X
FERTIGUNGSTECHNIK UND BETRIEB. ***Title Change.*** [Fert.tech. Betr.]. Vol. 9 (1959)-Oct. (1992). Academic Scholarly Publication. German (Russian and English). mo. Verlag Technik GmbH Berlin, AM Friedrichshain 22, D 10407 Berlin Germany. **Tel** 011 49 30 428700. **CODEN** FTGBAJ. Index available. **Bk Rev**. **Ad Acc.** **Circ:** 7,300 (ctrl). Documents available from Ask*IEEE, CASDDS. ***Formed by the union of*** *Fertigungstechnik, 0367-3251* ***and*** *Industriebetrieb, 0443-0239.* ***Continued by*** *Fabrik.*
Desc: Scientific-technical practice-aligned journal on problems of typical machine building.
Ind/Abst Alum. Ind. Abstr.; Chem. Abstr. (1959-1985); Eng. Mater. Abstr.; INSPEC (1968-); Met. Abstr.; Saf. Health Work; Stat. Theory Method Abstr. (1967); Surf. Treat. Technol. Abstr.

FR/0249-6704
FILS, TUBES, BANDES, PROFILES. **VFOAT** Fils, Tubes, Bandes et Profiles. (1967)-. Periodical. French. Six times a year. 298.73F France; 400.00F other. Group Cepp Editions Ampere, 25 rue Dagomo, 75012 Paris France. **Tel** 011 33 1 43473020, FAX 011 33 1 43473080. **UDC** 62-41. **CODEN** 62-462. **[CCC].**

US/0091-7699
FINAL CONTROL ELEMENTS; PROCEEDINGS. **Main/Conf** ISA Final Control Elements Symposium. 1st- 1970-. Proceedings. English. Instrument Society of America, 67 Alexander Drive, Research Triangle NC 27709. **Tel** (919)549-8411, FAX (919)549-8288, telex 802 540. **LC** TJ223.V3; I18A. **DD** 621.8/4.

RU/0015-3214
FIZIKA I KHIMIIA OBRABOTKI MATERIALOV. [Fiz. him. obrab. mater.]. **Added/Corp** Akademiia Nauk SSSR. Otdelenie Fiziko-Khimii i Tekhnologii Neorganicheskikh Materialov. (Jan./Feb. 1967)-. Academic Scholarly Publication. Russian. Six times a year. $142.00. Izdatelstvo Nauka / Akademiia Nauk, Publishing House of the Russian Academy of Sciences, Leninskii Porspekt 14, 117901 Moscow Russia. **Tel** 011 95 954-21-53, FAX 011 95 938-21-44, telex 411964. **(Subscription address:** East View Publications Inc., 3020 Harbor Lane North, Suite 110, Minneapolis MN 55447.**)** **LC** TA401; .F55. **DD** 620.1. **CODEN** FKOMAT. Documents available from Article Express International, Ask*IEEE, CASDDS.
Ind/Abst Alum. Ind. Abstr.; Chem. Abstr.; Ei Page One; Energy Res. Abstr.; Eng. Index Annu.; INSPEC (Jan./Feb. 1972-); Int. Aerosp. Abstr.; Met. Abstr.

GW/0015-461X
FLUID. **See** Engineering-Hydraulic Engineering.

●US/1064-2277
FLUID MECHANICS RESEARCH. [Fluid mech. res.]. (1992)-. Academic Scholarly Publication. English (translations available in Russian). bm. $988.00 US; $1,058.00 Canada and Mexico; $1,080.50 other. Scripta Technica, A Subsidiary of John Wiley & Sons, Inc., 7961 Eastern Avenue, Silver Spring MD 20910. **Tel** (301)588-0484, FAX (301)588-5278. **(Subscription address:** John Wiley / Philadelphia, PO Box 7247, Philadelphia PA 19170.**)** **ED** Novak Zuber, Ivan Catton and M. S. Plesset. **LC** QC145.2; .F55. **DD** 532/.005. Documents available from Article Express International, Ask*IEEE, CASDDS. ***Continues*** *Fluid Mechanics: Soviet Research, 0096-0764.*
Desc: Publishes translations of the theoretical and research papers from a wide range of leading Russian and Ukranian periodicals.
Ind/Abst Bioeng. Abstr.; Chem. Abstr.; Coal Abstr.; Ei Page One; Energy Res. Abstr.; Eng. Index Annu.; Fluid Abstr., Civil Eng.; Fluid Abstr. Proc. Eng.; FLUIDEX; GeoRef; INSPEC (1972-); Int. Aerosp. Abstr.; Math. Rev.; Nucl. Sci. Abstr.; Pollut. Abstr. Indexes; Sel. Water Resour. Abstr.; SPIN.

GW/0373-6482
FOERDERN UND HEBEN. [Foerd. Heben]. **Added/Corp** VDI/AWF-Fachgruppe Foerderwesen (Germany). **VFOAT** F + H; F und H. (April 1951)-. Periodical. German (summaries and/or abstracts in English, French and Spanish). mo (11 issues). DM218.00. Vereinigte Fachverlage, Postfach 4068, D 55030 Mainz Germany. **Tel** 011 49 6131 992150. **ED** Reiner Wesselowski. **LC** TJ1350.A1; F6. **CODEN** FOHBAN. **[CCC].** Index available. cum. index. **Bk Rev**. **Ad Acc.** **Circ:** 12,000 (ctrl). Documents available from Ask*IEEE.
Ind/Abst Alum. Ind. Abstr.; Coal Abstr.; Energy Res. Abstr.; Eng. Mater. Abstr.; Fluid Abstr., Civil Eng.; Fluid Abstr. Proc. Eng.; FLUIDEX (1973-); INSPEC (Nov. 1971-); Met. Abstr.; Pollut. Abstr. Indexes; Saf. Health Work.

US
GAS TURBINE FORECAST. (19??)-. English. Twelve times a year. $1490.00. Forecast International / DMS Inc., 22 Commerce Road, Newtown CT 06470. **Tel** (203)426-0800, FAX (203)426-1964, telex 467615. available on CD-ROM ($1695.00).

US/0747-7988
GAS TURBINE WORLD (1984). (GAS TURBINE WORLD.). [Gas turbine world]. Vol. 14, No. 1 (Jan./Feb. 1984)-. Periodical. English. Six times a year (Feb., Apr., June, Aug., Oct., Dec.). $75.00. Pequot Publishing Inc., PO Box 447, Southport CT 06490. **Tel** (203)259-1812. **LC** TJ778; .G2613. **DD** 621.43/3/05. **Ad Acc.** ctrl circ. Documents available from Ask*IEEE. ***Continues in part*** *Gas Turbine World & Cogeneration, 0746-4134.*
Ind/Abst Coal Abstr.; INSPEC (Mar./April 1984-).

US/0883-458X
GAS TURBINE WORLD HANDBOOK. [Gas turbine world handb.]. **VFOAT** GTW Handbook. Began in 1976-77. English. an. $60.00. Pequot Publishing Inc., PO Box 447, Southport CT 06490. **Tel** (203)259-1812. **LC** TJ778; .G2615. **DD** 621.43/3/05. **Ad Acc.** ctrl circ.

US/0743-6858
GEAR TECHNOLOGY. [Gear technol.]. Vol. 1, No. 1 (June/July 1984)-. Periodical. English. bm. $40.00 (1 year), $73.00 (2 year) US; $50.00 (1 year), $90.00 (2 year) Canada; $55.00 (1 year), $100.00 (2 year) other. Randall Publishing Inc, 1425 Lunt Avenue, Elk Grove Village IL 60007. **Tel** (708)437-6604, FAX (708)437-6618. **ED** Peg Carmack Short. **LC** IN PROCESS. **DD** 621. **CODEN** GEATEL. cum. index. **Ad Acc.** **Pr Rev.** **Circ:** 1,500 (ctrl). Documents available from Article Express International.
Desc: An educational journal for people involved in the design, manufacture, testing and processing of gears.

Our editorial content deals with specific problems and new technology.
Ind/Abst Ei Page One; Eng. Index Annu.

IT
GENTE MOTORI. mo. L050400.00 Italy; L100000.00 other. Rusconi Editore Spa, Servicio Abbonements, V Le Sarca 235, 20126 Milan Italy. **Tel** 011 39 2 66192634.

HU/0231-0686
GEPESZETI SZAKIRODALMI TAJEKOZTATO. (1983)-. Periodical. Hungarian. mo. 8.900ft. Orszagos Muszaki Informacios Kozpont es Konyvtar (O.M.I.K.K.), National Technical Information Centre and Library Museum, u 17, PO Box 12, 1428 Budapest, Hungary. **Tel** (361)118-1994, FAX (361)138-2414, telex 22-4944 OMIKK H. **(Subscription address:** OMIKK Budapest, POB 12, H-1428 Hungary) **ED** Imre Kuruc. **UDC** 016. **Circ:** 150.
Desc: Articles on machinery.

HU/0231-0694
GEPGYARTASTECHNOLOGIAI ES SZERSZAMGEPIPARI SZAKIRODALMI TAJEKOZTATO. (1983)-. Periodical. Hungarian. mo. 9.900. Orszagos Muszaki Informacios Kozpont es Konyvtar (O.M.I.K.K.), National Technical Information Centre and Library Museum, u 17, PO Box 12, 1428 Budapest, Hungary. **Tel** (361)118-1994, FAX (361)138-2414, telex 22-4944 OMIKK H. **(Subscription address:** OMIKK Budapest, POB 12, H-1428 Hungary) **ED** Denes Bernad. **UDC** 016. **Circ:** 120.
Desc: Information on mechanical engineering.

IT/0017-0240
GIORNALE DELL' OFFICINA. [G. off.]. (1956)-. Periodical. Italian. bm. L7000 Italy; L100000 other. Editoriale Tecnica Macchine, Via Ugo Lenzi 1, 40122 Bologna Italy. **Tel** 011 39 51 523183. **UDC** 62. **Bk Rev. Ad Acc. Pr Rev.** ctrl circ.
Desc: Information magazine for mechanical industry managers and engineers. Firm management and organization, economics, trade, and product news.

CN/0384-0077
GUIDE DE LOCATION (MONTREAL). (GUIDE DE LOCATION.). V. 1- 1973-. French. an. Hexa Inc., Bureau 203, 6481 Rue St. Hubert, Montreal Quebec H2A 2M8 Canada. **DD** 381/.45/6218.

CC/1000-4084
GUTI RUNHUA. (KU TI JUN HUA / JOURNAL OF SOLID LUBRICATION / [KU TI JUN HUA PIEN CHI PU].). [Guti runhua]. **Added/Corp** Chung-kuo ko Hsueh Yuan. Lan-Chou hua Hsueh wu li yen Chiu so. **VFOAT** Journal of Solid Lubrication. (198?)-. Periodical. Chinese. qt. Chung-kuo ko Hsueh Yuan, Lan-chou hua Hsueh wu li yen Chiu so,, Lan-chou China. **CODEN** GURUEH. Documents available from CASDDS.
Ind/Abst Chem. Abstr.

UK
HANDLING EQUIPMENT DIRECTORY. Directory. English. an. £22.00 UK; $40.00 US; £24.00 other. Lincoln Publications, 28 Centre Point House, St Giles Street, London WC2H 8LW England. **Tel** 071-240 5562, FAX 071-497 2811. **ED** R Feather. **Ad Acc.**
Desc: A-Z listing of manufacturers and suppliers involved in the handling industry, with their products classified into close on 1,400 categories.

KO
HANGUK KIGYE KONGGU. **VFOAT** Korea Machinery & Tools; Kigye Konggu. Periodical. Korean (Korean). mo. Hanguk Kigye Konggusang Yonhaphoe, 250-1 Changsa-dong Chongno-ku, Seoul 110 Korea. **LC** HD9705.K6; H34.

KO
HANGUK KIGYE YONGUSO SOBO. **VFOAT** Bulletin of Korea Institute of Machinery & Metals. Periodical. Korean (summaries and/or abstracts in English). sa. Korea Institute of Machinery & Metals, 223-13 Guro-dong, Guro-gu Seoul Korea. **LC** TJ4; .H36.

UK
HEALTH AND SAFETY EXECUTIVE GUIDANCE NOTES. PLANT AND MACHINERY. See Public Health and Safety.

●US/1063-1313
HEAT TRANSFER RECENT CONTENTS. [Heat transf. recent contents]. **Added/Corp** American Society of Mechanical Engineers. Vol. 1, No. 1 (July-Aug. 1992)-. Periodical. English. Six times a year. $36.00 (non-members), $24.00 (members of the American Society of Mechanical Engineers). American Society of Mechanical Engineers, 22 Law Drive, Fairfield NJ 07007. **Tel** (201)882-1167, (212)705-7722 (editorial). **DD** 621.
Desc: Delivers a listing of the tables of contents for the world's most important heat transfer research journals. Its 12-16 easy-to-scan pages give readers a quick, concise source to literally hundreds of articles that are published monthly in dozens of journals worldwide.

GW/0017-9442
HEBEZEUGE UND FORDERMITTEL. [Hebezeuge Forderm.]. (1961)-. Periodical. German (summaries and/or abstracts in English and Russian). mo (10 issues per year). DM138.50 Germany; DM168.00 other. Verlag Technik GmbH Berlin, AM Friedrichshain 22, D 10407 Berlin Germany. **Tel** 011 49 30 428700. **UDC** 621.86.

UN/0451-8306
HIMICESKOE MASINOSTROENIE (KIEV). See Engineering-Chemical Engineering.

US/0744-6640
HOME SHOP MACHINIST, THE. Vol. 1, No. 1 (Jan./Feb. 1982)-. Periodical. English. bm. $22.50 US; $41.00 Canada; $57.50 other. Home Shop Machinist Inc, PO Box 1810, Traverse City MI 49685. **Tel** (616)941-7160. **ED** J D Rice. **LC** TT205.A1; H65. **DD** 684/.09/05. **Bk Rev. Ad Acc. Circ:** 15,500 (ctrl). available on microfilm and microfiche from University Microfilms International (UMI).
Desc: Drawings and articles for the machinist in home or work.

US/0737-6316
HUTTON CONSTRUCTION CATALOG : MECHANICAL PRODUCTS. **VFOAT** M.P.C.; Mechanical Products; Yellow Book for Engineers and Mechanical Contractors; MPC. Catalog. English. an. Free to US; $150.00 (surface mail), $200.00 (airmail) other. Hutton Publishing Company Inc, 4300 West 62nd Street, Indianapolis IN 46268. **Tel** (516)935-2740. **ED** Harley Macomber. **LC** TH6010; .M2. **DD** 683. **Ad Acc. Circ:** 16,000 (ctrl). ***Continues** Mechanical Products Catalog.*
Desc: Serves the needs of over 16,000 mechanical consulting engineers, large P.H.C. contractors concerned with industrial and commercial construction.

US/0073-4209
HYDROELECTRIC POWER RESOURCES OF THE UNITED STATES, DEVELOPED AND UNDEVELOPED. [Hydroelectr. power resour. U. S. dev. undev.]. Began with 1953. Government Publication. English. ir (quadrennial). US Department of Energy, 1000 Independence Avenue SW, Washington DC 20585. **Tel** (202)586-5000, FAX (202)586-4073. **LC** TJ23; .A33. **DD** 621.312134.

US/1053-7198
I.B.I. GUIDE. (IBI GUIDE.). [I.B.I. guide]. **Added/Corp** Interchange, Inc. International Bearing Interchange. **VFOAT** I.B.I. Guide; I.B.I. Guide Bearings; IBI Guide Bearings; I.B.I. Bearings. **VAT** International Bearing Interchange Guide. (19??)-. English. be. $235.00 US; $237.00 Canada; $251.00 Mexico; $262.00 Central and South America, Europe, Scandinavia, Turkey, and Greece; $270.00 Australia, New Zealand, and New Guinea; $292.00 other. Interchange Inc, PO Box 16244, St Louis Park MN 55416. **Tel** (612)929-6669, (800)669-6208, FAX (612)929-0395. **LC** TJ1061; .I58. **DD** 338.4/7/621822025. available on diskette.
Desc: A cross-reference technical guide book.

US/0748-5824
I.D.B.I. GUIDE, INTERNATIONAL DRIVE BELT INTERCHANGE. [I.D.B.I. guide, int. drive belt interchange]. **Added/Corp** Interchange, inc. **VFOAT** IDBI Guide, International Drive Belt Interchange; International Drive Belt Interchange; IDBI Guide, Drive Belts; IDBI, Drive Belts; I.D.B.I. Guide, Drive Belts; I.D.B.I., Drive Belts. (1979)-. English. be. $188.00 US; $182.00 Canada; $196.00 Mexico; $201.00 Central America and South America; $205.00 Australia and New Zealand; $200.00 Europe; $222.00 other. Interchange Inc, PO Box 16244, St Louis Park MN 55416. **Tel** (612)929-6669, (800)669-6208, FAX (612)929-0395. **LC** TJ1100; .I14. **DD** 621.8/52/0216. available on diskette.
Desc: A cross-reference technical guide book.

US/0748-7665
I.S.I. GUIDE, INTERNATIONAL SEAL INTERCHANGE. [I.S.I. guide]. **Added/Corp** Interchange, inc. **VFOAT** ISI Guide, International Seal Interchange; International Seal Interchange; ISI Guide, Seals; ISI Seals; I.S.I. Guide, Seals; I.S.I. Seals; I.S.I. Guide. (19??)-. English. be. $180.00 US; $184.00 Canada; $196.00 Mexico; $201.00 Central America and South America; $205.00 Australia and New Zealand; $200.00 Europe; $222.00 other. Interchange Inc, PO Box 16244, St Louis Park MN 55416. **Tel** (612)929-6669, (800)669-6208, FAX (612)929-0395. **LC** TJ246; .I18. **DD** 621.8/85/05. available on diskette.
Desc: A cross-reference technical guide book.

UK/1046-6606
IACM BULLETIN OF THE INTERNATIONAL ASSOCIATION FOR COMPUTATIONAL MECHANICS. (IACM BULLETIN.). [IACM bull. Int. Assoc. Comput. Mech.]. **VFOAT** I A C M Bulletin. **VAT** International Association for Computational Mechanics Bulletin. Vol. 1, No. 1 (Jan. 1985)-. Bulletin. English. qt. Free with membership. **DD** 531. **CODEN** IABLEU.

UK/0019-8145
IDR. INDUSTRIAL DIAMOND REVIEW. (INDUSTRIAL DIAMOND REVIEW.). [IDR. Ind. diamond rev.]. **VFOAT** IDR; I.D.R.; Industrial Diamond Abstracts; Industrial Diamond Review IDR. (1940)-. Academic Scholarly Publication. English. bm (6 issues). Free on request. Kenion Advertising, Charters Sunninghill, Ascot Berkshire SL5 9PX United Kingdom. **ED** P.A. Daniel. **LC** TJ1193; .I524. **DD** 621.9/2. **CODEN** INDRA9. Index available. cum. index. **Bk Rev. Ad Acc. Circ:** 12,000. available on microfilm and microfiche from University Microfilms International (UMI). Documents available from Article Express International. ***Absorbed** Bibliography of Industrial Diamond Applications.*
Desc: Diamond and CBN tools are used in metalworking, civil engineering, mining, and in the glass, ceramics, and electronics industries. IDR looks at new applications in all these industries.
Ind/Abst Bioeng. Abstr.; Curr. Technol. Index; Ei Page One; EMBASE; Eng. Mater. Abstr.; Eng. Index Annu. [Select. Cov.]; Geol. Abstr.; Pollut. Abstr. Indexes; Surf. Treat. Technol. Abstr.; World Ceram. Abstr.

UK/0019-8277
IEN. INDUSTRIAL EQUIPMENT NEWS (SUTTON). See Economics-Industry and Production.

SP/0210-1777
IMHE. INFORMACION DE MAQUINAS-HERRAMIENTA, EQUIPOS Y ACCESORIOS. [IMHE, Inf. maquinas-herram., equipos accesorios]. **VFOAT** Informacion de Maquinas-Herramienta, Equipos y Accesorios. (1974)-. Periodical. Spanish. mo. 7000.00ptas Spain; $120.00 US; 9000.00ptas other. Ediciones Tecnicas Izaro, Mazustegui 21, 48006 Bilbao Spain. **Tel** 011 34 94 415-9022. **UDC** 68.

US/0884-2264
IMPACT COMPRESSORS. ***Title Change.*** [Impact compress.]. (19??)-(199?). Periodical. English. mo. Impact Publications, PO Box 3113, Ketchum ID 83340. **Tel** (208)726-2133, FAX (208)726-2115. **DD** 621. ***Continued by** Impact Compressor/Turbine News & Patents, 1060-538X.*

US/0887-5081
IMPACT PUMP NEWS. ***Title Change.*** [Impact pump news]. (198?)-(1991). Periodical. English. mo. Impact Publications, PO Box 3113, Ketchum ID 83340. **Tel** (208)726-2133, FAX (208)726-2115. **DD** 621. ***Continues** Pump News, 0194-8377. **Continued by** Impact Pump News & Patents, 1056-1536.*

US/1056-1536
IMPACT PUMP NEWS & PATENTS. [Impact Pump News & Pat.]. **VFOAT** Impact Pump News and Patents. Vol. 16, No. 5 (Jan. 1991)-. Periodical. English. Ten times a year (June/July and Aug/Sept. issues combined). $100.00 US; $120.00 other. Impact Publications, PO Box 3113, Ketchum ID 83340. **Tel** (208)726-2133, FAX (208)726-2115. **ED** Mary Jo Helmeke. **DD** 621. Index available (published separately). **Bk Rev. Ad Acc. Circ:** 100 (ctrl). ***Continues** Impact Pump News, 0887-5081.*
Desc: Regular features include new product announcements, patent information, and up-to-date industry news and information on current books, brochures, software, seminars and meetings.

US/0899-031X
IMPACT PUMPS. [Impact pumps]. Vol. 14, No. 8 (April 1988)-. Periodical. English. mo. $75.00. Impact Publications, PO Box 3113, Ketchum ID 83340. **Tel** (208)726-2133, FAX (208)726-2115. **DD** 621. ***Continues** Impact Pumps/Compressors, 0883-7627.*

US/1056-1544
IMPACT VALVE NEWS & PATENTS. [Impact valve news pat.]. **VFOAT** Impact Valve News and Patent. (1991)-. Periodical. English. Ten times a year. $150.00 US; $170.00 other. Impact Publications, PO Box 3113, Ketchum ID 83340. **Tel** (208)726-2133, FAX (208)726-2115. **ED** Mary Jo Helmeke. **DD** 621. Index available (published separately). **Bk Rev. Ad Acc. Circ:** 65 (ctrl).

US/0883-7619
IMPACT VALVES. [Impact valves]. **VFOAT** Valves. Periodical. English. mo. $125.00. Impact Publications, PO Box 3113, Ketchum ID 83340. **Tel** (208)726-2133, FAX (208)726-2115. **DD** 621.

IT/0393-1331
INDUSTRIA MECCANICA, L'. [Ind. mecc.]. (1919)-. Periodical. Italian. mo (11 issues). L120000 Italy; L190000 other. Delar, Via Lorenteggio 35, 20146 Milan Italy. **Tel** 011 39 2 4238975. **UDC** 621.

US/8756-2375
INDUSTRIAL & MARINE GAS TURBINE ENGINES. [Ind. mar. gas turbine engines]. **VFOAT** Industrial and Marine Gas Turbine Engines; GTW Engines. 1st Ed. (1982-83)-. English. Pequot Publishing Inc., PO Box 447, Southport CT 06490. **Tel** (203)259-1812. **LC** TJ778; .I53. **DD** 621.43/3.

NE
INFORMATICA I. KWADRAAT WERKTUIGBOUW. Dutch. mo. Ingenieurspers BV, Postbus 456 Netherlands. **Tel** 011 31 08340 5570.

NE/0923-0408
INFORMATION AND DECISION TECHNOLOGIES (AMSTERDAM). ***Ceased.*** (INFORMATION AND DECISION TECHNOLOGIES.). [Inf. decis. technol.]. Vol. 14 No. 1 (1988)-Vol. 19. Academic Scholarly Publication. English. Six times a year (1 volume). Elsevier Science Publishers BV, PO Box 211, 1000 AE Amsterdam Netherlands. **Tel** 011 31 20 5803642, FAX 011 31 20 5862696, telex 15682. **LC** QA402; .L357. **DD** 003/.71/05. **[CCC].** available on microfilm and microfiche from University Microfilms International (UMI). Documents available from Article Express International, The Genuine Article, Ask*IEEE. ***Continues*** *Large Scale Systems in Information and Decision Technologies, 0167-420X.*
Ind/Abst Compumath Citation Index [Full Cov.]; Comput. Inf. Syst. Abstr. J. [Full Cov.]; Curr. Contents Eng. Tech. Appl. Sci.; Ei Page One; Eng. Index Annu.; Hum. Resour. Abstr.; INSPEC (1988-); Int. Abstr. Oper. Res. [Select. Cov.]; Manuf. Process Eng. Abstr.; Math. Rev.; Mech. Eng. Abstr.; Res. Alert [Full Cov.]; Sci. Cit. Index; SCISEARCH; Soc. Sci. Cit. Index [Select. Cov.].

GW
INFORMATION PUMPEN UND VERDICHTER. **Added/Corp** Kombinat Pumpen und Verdichter, VEB. (1982)-. Periodical. German (summaries and/or abstracts in English, French and Russian). Veb Kombinat Pumpen Und Verdichter, O-4020 Halle (Saale) Germany. **LC** TJ899; .P85. **DD** 621.6. ***Continues*** *Pumpen- und Verdichterinformationen.*
Ind/Abst Fluid Abstr., Civil Eng.; Fluid Abstr. Proc. Eng.; FLUIDEX (1982-1990).

UK/0957-6061
INTEGRATED MANUFACTURING SYSTEMS. (INTEGRATED MANUFACTURING SYSTEMS : IMS.). [Integr. manuf. syst.]. **VFOAT** IMS; IMS Magazine. Vol. 1 No. 1 (Jan. 1990)-. Periodical. English. Five times a year. $669.00. MCB University Press, 60 62 Toller Lane, Bradford West Yorkshire BD8 9BX England. **Tel** 011 44 274 499821, FAX 011 44 274 547143, telex 51317 MCBUNI G. **(Subscription address:** MCB University Press / US and Canada Subscriptions, PO Box 10812, Birmingham AL 35201-0812.**) ED** David Bennett. **LC** TS155.6; .I553. **DD** 670/.285. **CODEN** IMSYEY. **[CCC]. Bk Rev. Ad Acc.** Documents available from UMI Article Clearinghouse, Ask*IEEE. ***Continues*** *FMS Magazine, 0263-9777.*
Desc: Editorial aim is to cover subjects related to the integration of the manufacturing, design and marketing functions, including simultaneous engineering, design for manufacture, materials handling, cellular manufacture, local area networks, automation, simulation and other elements of CIM. It will feature organisational topics, such as planning and scheduling, JIT and group technology.
Ind/Abst ABI/INFORM Glob. Ed.; INSPEC (Jan. 1990-).

US/0278-9302
INTERNAL COMBUSTION ENGINES. (CURRENT INDUSTRIAL REPORTS. MA-35L, INTERNAL COMBUSTION ENGINES / U.S. DEPARTMENT OF COMMERCE, BUREAU OF THE CENSUS.). [Intern. combust. engines]. Began with 1943 issue. Government Publication. English. an. $1.25. US Department of Commerce, 14th Street & Constitution Avenue NW, Washington DC 20230. **Tel** (202)482-2000, FAX (202)482-3772. **LC** TJ751; .I49. **DD** 338.4/762143/0973.
Desc: Presents timely data on the production, inventories, and orders of approximately 5,000 products, which represents 40 percent of all US manufacturing.

●US/1063-7095
INTERNATIONAL APPLIED MECHANICS. [Int. appl. mech.]. **Added/Corp** Consultants Bureau. **VFOAT** Prikladnaia Mekhanika; Prikladnaya Mekhanika. (July 1992)-. Academic Scholarly Publication. English (translations available in Russian). mo. $1295.00 US; $1515.00 other. Consultants Bureau, A Division of Plenum Publishing Corporation, 233 Spring Street, New York NY 10013. **Tel** (212)620-8000, (212)620-8466, FAX (212)463-0742, telex 23/421139. **LC** TA349; .P6852. **DD** 620.1/005. **CODEN** IAMEEU. **[CCC].** Documents available from Article Express International, The Genuine Article, Ask*IEEE, CASDDS. ***Continues*** *Soviet Applied Mechanics, 0038-5298.*
Ind/Abst Appl. Mech. Rev.; Bioeng. Abstr.; Chem. Abstr.; Coal Abstr.; Curr. Contents Eng. Tech. Appl. Sci.; Ei Page One; Eng. Index Annu.; INSPEC; Int. Aerosp. Abstr.; Math. Rev.; Res. Alert [Full Cov.].

UK
INTERNATIONAL CRYOGENICS ENGINEERING CONFERENCE. (19??)-. Monographic series. English. ir. Price varies per volume. Butterworth Heinemann Publishers, Linacre House, Jordan Hill, Oxford OX2 8DP England. **Tel** 011 44 865 310366.

US/0886-9367
INTERNATIONAL JOURNAL OF ANALYTICAL AND EXPERIMENTAL MODAL ANALYSIS, THE. ***Title Change.*** [Int. j. anal. exp. modal anal.]. **Added/Corp** Society for Experimental Mechanics (U.S.). **VFOAT** IJMA. Vol. 1 No. 1 (Jan. 1986)-Vol. 7 No. 4 (Oct. 1992). Periodical. English. qt. Society for Experimental Mechanics, 7 School Street, Bethel CT 06801-1405. **Tel** (203)790-6373, FAX (203)790-4472. **ED** Leanne D Mitchell. **LC** TA654.15; .I56. **DD** 620.1/04. **CODEN** IJAAEL. **[CCC].** Index available. cum. index. **Pr Rev. Circ:** 750 (ctrl). available on microfilm from University Microfilms International (UMI). Documents available from Article Express International. ***Continued by*** *Modal Analysis, 1066-0763.*
Desc: Publishes original papers in vibrations and dynamics-modal analysis.
Ind/Abst Acoust. Abstr.; Civ. Struct. Eng. Abstr.; Comput. Inf. Syst. Abstr. J. [Full Cov.]; Ei Page One; Eng. Index Annu.; Mech. Eng. Abstr.; Shock Vibr. Dig.

●UK/1061-8562
INTERNATIONAL JOURNAL OF COMPUTATIONAL FLUID DYNAMICS. (1992)-. Periodical. English. Four times a year. $356.00. Gordon & Breach Science Publishers, PO Box 90, Reading RG1 8JL England. **Tel** 011 44 734 560080, FAX 011 44 734 568211.

US/0142-727X
INTERNATIONAL JOURNAL OF HEAT AND FLUID FLOW, THE. [Int. j. heat fluid flow]. Vol. 1 (March 1979)-. Academic Scholarly Publication. English. Six times a year. $490.00 US; $560.00 other. Butterworth Heinemann / Woburn, MA, 225 Wildwood Avenue, Unit B, Woburn MA 01801. **Tel** (800)366-2665, FAX (617)928-2620, telex 880052. **(Subscription address:** Elsevier Science Inc. / New York Books, 655 Avenue of the Americas, New York NY 10010.**) ED** B W Martin and F W Schmidt. **LC** TJ260; .I58. **DD** 621.402/05. **CODEN** IJHFD2. **[CCC].** Index available. **Ad Acc. Pr Rev.** available on microfilm and microfiche from University Microfilms International (UMI). Documents available from Article Express International, The Genuine Article, Ask*IEEE, CASDDS. ***Continues*** *Heat and Fluid Flow, 0046-7138.*
Desc: Provides a medium through which academic and industrial researchers and designers can communicate results, review progress and identify requirements for further work in this increasingly significant field.
Ind/Abst Bioeng. Abstr.; Chem. Abstr.; Civ. Struct. Eng. Abstr.; Coal Abstr.; Comput. Inf. Syst. Abstr. J. [Full Cov.]; Curr. Contents Eng. Tech. Appl. Sci.; Ei Page One; Energy Res. Abstr. (July 1979-); Eng. Index Annu.; Environ. Eng. Abstr.; Fluid Abstr., Civil Eng.; Fluid Abstr. Proc. Eng.; FLUIDEX (1979-); HTFS Dig.; INSPEC (Sept. 1990-); Int. Build. Serv. Abstr.; Mater. Sci. Eng. Abstr.; Mech. Eng. Abstr.; Pollut. Abstr. Indexes; Proc. Chem. Eng.; Res. Alert [Full Cov.]; SCISEARCH; Solid State Supercond. Abstr.; Theoret. Chem. Eng.

US/0890-6955
INTERNATIONAL JOURNAL OF MACHINE TOOLS & MANUFACTURE. [Int. j. mach. tools manuf.]. Vol. 27, No. 1 (1985)-. Periodical. English. Twelve times a year. $1066.00 The Americas; £715.00 other. Pergamon Press, An Imprint of Elsevier Science Ltd., The Boulevard, Langford Lane, Kidlington, Oxford OX5 1GB United Kingdom. **Tel** 011 44 865 843000, 011 44 865 843699, FAX 011 44 865 843010. **(Subscription address:** Elsevier Science Ltd. Oxford Fulfillment Centre, PO Box 800, Kidlington, Oxford OX5 1DX United Kingdom.**) ED** R. Davies and T. A. Dean. **LC** TJ1180.A1; I5. **DD** 621.9/02. **CODEN** IMTME3. **[CCC]. Pr Rev.** available on microfilm and microfiche from University Microfilms International (UMI). Documents available from Article Express International, The Genuine Article. ***Continues*** *International Journal of Machine Tool Design & Research, 0020-7357.*
Ind/Abst Bioeng. Abstr. (1987-); Civ. Struct. Eng. Abstr.; Comput. Inf. Syst. Abstr. J. [Full Cov.]; Curr. Contents Eng. Tech. Appl. Sci.; Curr. Technol. Index; Ei Page One (1987-); Eng. Index Annu.; Manuf. Process Eng. Abstr.; Mater. Sci. Eng. Abstr.; Mech. Eng. Abstr.; Pollut. Abstr. Indexes (1987-); Res. Alert [Select. Cov.]; SCISEARCH; Shock Vibr. Dig.; Solid State Supercond. Abstr.

UK/0020-7373
INTERNATIONAL JOURNAL OF MAN-MACHINE STUDIES. ***Title Change.*** **See** Computers-Cybernetics.

UK/0306-4190
INTERNATIONAL JOURNAL OF MECHANICAL ENGINEERING EDUCATION, THE. [Int. j. mech. eng. educ.]. **Added/Corp** Institution of Mechanical Engineers (Great Britain) University of Manchester. Institute of Science and Technology. Vol. 1 (Nov. 1973)-. Periodical. English. Four times a year. £88.00 UK; £164.00 (surface mail); £176.00 (airmail). Ellis Horwood Ltd, Market Cross House, Cooper Street, Chichester West Sussex PO19 1EB England. **Tel** (0243)789942, telex 86516 ELWOOD G. **ED** J. Parker, C. M. Leech and S. S. Gill. **LC** TJ1; .I585. **DD** 621/.07/11. **[CCC]. Bk Rev. Ad Acc. Circ:** 460. available on microfilm and microfiche from University Microfilms International (UMI). Documents available from Article Express International. ***Supersedes*** *Bulletin of Mechanical Engineering Education.*
Desc: Discusses the practice and requirements of the academic and industrial training of mechanical engineers; and what subjects can and should be included in mechanical engineering courses.
Ind/Abst Curr. Technol. Index; Educ. Technol. Abstr.; Ei Page One; Eng. Index Annu.; Fluid Abstr., Civil Eng.; Fluid Abstr. Proc. Eng.; FLUIDEX (1973-); Tech. Educ. Train. Abstr.

UK/0020-7403
INTERNATIONAL JOURNAL OF MECHANICAL SCIENCES. [Int. j. mech. sci.]. Vol. 1 (Jan. 1960)-. Periodical. English. mo. $880.00 The Americas; £590.00 other. Pergamon Press, An Imprint of Elsevier Science Ltd., The Boulevard, Langford Lane, Kidlington, Oxford OX5 1GB United Kingdom. **Tel** 011 44 865 843000, 011 44 865 843699, FAX 011 44 865 843010. **(Subscription address:** Elsevier Science Ltd. Oxford Fulfillment Centre, PO Box 800, Kidlington, Oxford OX5 1DX United Kingdom.**) ED** S. R. Reid. **LC** TJ1; .I59. **DD** 621/.05. **CODEN** IMSCAW. **[CCC]. Pr Rev.** available on microfilm from Microfilms International Marketing Corp.; available on microfilm and microfiche from University Microfilms International (UMI). Documents available from Article Express International, The Genuine Article, Ask*IEEE, CASDDS, Documents on Demand.
Ind/Abst Abstr. J. Earthq. Eng. (?-?); Acoust. Abstr.; Alum. Ind. Abstr.; Bioeng. Abstr.; Chem. Abstr.; Curr. Contents Eng. Tech. Appl. Sci.; Curr. Technol. Index; Ei Page One; Energy Inf. Abstr.; Energy Res. Abstr. (Jan. 1972-); Eng. Index Annu.; Environ. Abstr.; Fluid Abstr., Civil Eng.; Fluid Abstr. Proc. Eng.; FLUIDEX (1973-); INSPEC (1968-); Int. Aerosp. Abstr.; J. Ferrocement; Met. Abstr.; Res. Alert [Full Cov.]; Sci. Cit. Index; SCISEARCH; Shock Vibr. Dig.; Zentralbl. Math. Ihre Grenzgeb.

UK/0308-0161
INTERNATIONAL JOURNAL OF PRESSURE VESSELS AND PIPING, THE. [Int. j. press. vessels piping]. **VFOAT** Pressure Vessels and Piping. Vol. 1, No. 1 (Jan. 1973)-. Academic Scholarly Publication. English. Twelve times a year. $1602.00 The Americas; £1075.00 other. Elsevier Applied Science, An Imprint of Elsevier Science Ltd., The Boulevard, Langford Lane, Kidlington, Oxford OX5 1GB United Kingdom. **Tel** 011 44 865 843000, 011 44 865 843699, FAX 011 44 865 843010. **(Subscription address:** Elsevier Science Ltd. Oxford Fulfillment Centre, PO Box 800, Kidlington, Oxford OX5 1DX United Kingdom.**) ED** R. W. Nichols. **LC** TS283; .I58. **DD** 681/.76. **CODEN** PRVPAS. **[CCC]. Bk Rev. Ad Acc. Pr Rev.** available on microfilm and microfiche from University Microfilms International (UMI). Documents available from Article Express International, The Genuine Article, Ask*IEEE, Petroleum Abstracts Document Delivery Service, CASDDS. ***Absorbed*** *Res Mechanica, 0143-0084.*
Desc: Presents and discusses current developments in all aspects of the various technologies associated with the design, materials, manufacture, inspection, operation and maintenance of pressure vessels and similar components, and of related topics as applied to gas containers and pipelines.
Ind/Abst Abstr. J. Earthq. Eng. (?-?); Alum. Ind. Abstr.; Bioeng. Abstr.; Chem. Abstr.; Civ. Struct. Eng. Abstr.; Comput. Inf. Syst. Abstr. J. [Full Cov.]; Curr. Contents Eng. Tech. Appl. Sci.; Ei Page One; Energy Res. Abstr. (Sept. 1974-); Eng. Mater. Abstr.; Eng. Index Annu.; Environ. Eng. Abstr.; Fluid Abstr., Civil Eng.; Fluid Abstr. Proc. Eng.; FLUIDEX (1973-); INSPEC (1991-); Manuf. Process Eng. Abstr.; Mater. Sci. Eng. Abstr.; Mech. Eng. Abstr.; Met. Abstr.; Pet. Abstr.; Proc. Chem. Eng.; Res. Alert [Select. Cov.]; SCISEARCH; Solid State Supercond. Abstr.; Theoret. Chem. Eng.

US/0020-7683
INTERNATIONAL JOURNAL OF SOLIDS AND STRUCTURES. **See** Engineering-Civil Engineering.

UK/0020-7721
INTERNATIONAL JOURNAL OF SYSTEMS SCIENCE. [Int. j. syst. sci.]. **VFOAT** Systems Science. (July 1970)-. Academic Scholarly Publication. English. mo. £732.00 UK; $1207.00 other. Taylor & Francis Ltd., Rankine Road, Basingstoke Hampshire, RG24 8PR United Kingdom. **Tel** 011 44 256 840366, FAX 011 44 256 479438, telex 858540. **(Subscription address:** Taylor & Francis Inc., 1900 Frost Road, Suite 101, Bristol PA 19007-1598.**) ED** B. Porter (editor's address: Department of Aeronautical and Mechanical Engineering, University of Salford, Salford M5 4WT United Kingdom). **LC** QA402; .I55. **DD** 001.6/1/05. **NLM** W1 IN791M. **CODEN** IJSYA9. **[CCC]. Pr Rev.** available on microfilm from University Microfilms International (UMI). Documents available from Article Express International, The Genuine Article, BIOSIS Document Express, Ask*IEEE.
Desc: Original contributions are published on the theory and practice of mathematical modelling, simulation, optimization and control in relation to biological, economic, environmental, industrial and transportation systems. The mathematical techniques of systems science are also covered, such as block-pulse and Walsh

functions, shifted Legendre approximations, estimation algorithms, functional space analysis, matrix continued fractions, and dynamic and quadratic programming.
Ind/Abst Bioeng. Abstr.; Biol. Abstr.; Biostatistica; Compumath Citation Index [Full Cov.]; Curr. Contents Eng. Tech. Appl. Sci.; Ei Page One; Electron. Commun. Abstr. J.; EMBASE; Eng. Index Annu.; Inf. Sci. Abstr. (?-?); INSPEC (July 1971-); Int. Aerosp. Abstr.; Int. Labour Doc.; ISMEC Bull.; Math. Rev.; Oper. Res./Manag. Sci.; Life Sci. Collect.; Pollut. Abstr. Indexes; Qual. Control Appl. Stat.; Res. Alert [Full Cov.]; Saf. Sci. Abstr. J.; SCISEARCH; Soc. Sci. Cit. Index [Select. Cov.]; Wildl. Rev.; Zentralbl. Math. Ihre Grenzgeb.

AT
INTERNATIONAL LABORATORY ACCREDITATION CONFERENCE DIRECTORY. Directory. English. ir. 40.00Aus$ Australia; 50.00Aus$ other. National Association of Testing Authorities, 7 Leeds Street, Phodes NSW 2138 Australia. **Tel** 011 61 02 7368222, FAX 011 61 2 7435311, telex 26738. **Circ:** 100.

UK/0269-5839
INTERNATIONAL REVIEWS OF ERGONOMICS. ***Ceased.*** Vol. 1 (1987)-Ceased Vol. 3. English. an. Taylor & Francis Ltd., Rankine Road, Basingstoke Hampshire, RG24 8PR United Kingdom. **Tel** 011 44 256 840366, FAX 011 44 256 479438, telex 858540. **(Subscription address:** Taylor & Francis Inc., 1900 Frost Road, Suite 101, Bristol PA 19007-1598.**) ED** David J Oborne (editor's address: Department of Psychology, University College of Swansea, Swansea SA2 8PP UK). **LC** TA166; .I565. **DD** 620.8/2. **NLM** W1; IN835DI. **[CCC].**
Desc: Publishes comprehensive reviews in a variety of ergonomic topics. The journal includes papers submitted by internationally reknowned authors, who cover a wide range of disciplines, which provide informed and authoritative discussions on areas of current interest. Academics and practitioners alike will find it an invaluable source of information and knowledge.

US/1051-1067
INTERNATIONAL SAMPE ELECTRONICS CONFERENCE. (INTERNATIONAL SAMPE ELECTRONICS CONFERENCE : [PROCEEDINGS].). [Int. SAMPE Electron. Conf.]. **Main/Conf** International SAMPE Electronics Conference. **Added/Corp** Society for the Advancement of Material and Process Engineering. (June 23/25, 1987)-. Academic Scholarly Publication. English. an. Society Advancement Material and Process Engineering, PO Box 2459, Covina CA 91722. **Tel** (818)331-0616, FAX (818)332-8929, telex 510/600 4889. **LC** TK7871; .I577a. **DD** 621. **CODEN** ISECE8. Documents available from Article Express International, CASDDS.
Ind/Abst Chem. Abstr.; Ei Page One; Eng. Index Annu.

US
IRON-MEN ALBUM MAGAZNE. Vol. 1 (1946)-. Periodical. English. bm. $13.50 (one year), $25.50 (two year) US; $16.50 (one year), $31.50 (two year) other. Stemgas Publishing Company, PO Box 328, Lancaster PA 17608. **Tel** (717)392-0733. **Bk Rev. Ad Acc. Circ:** 7,500.
Desc: All about steam traction engines.

US/0896-7113
ISMEC, MECHANICAL ENGINEERING ABSTRACTS. ***Title Change.*** **See** Engineering-Abstracting, Bibliographies and Statistics.

AU
ISR, INTERNATIONLE BERG- UND SEILBAHNRUNDSCHAU. INTERNATIONAL AERIAL TRAMWAY REVIEW. **VFOAT** Internationle Berg- und Seilbahnrundschau; International Aerial Tramway Review. (19??)-. Periodical. German (English, French and German). Eight times a year. S899.09 Austria; S1089.00 others. Bohmann Druck und Verlag Ges MBH, Leberstrasse 122, A-1110 Vienna Austria. **Tel** 011 43 1 74095174, FAX 011 43 1 741595-183, telex 132312. **ED** Gerda Stockhammer. **LC** TJ1385; .I53a. **DD** 621.8/68/05. **Ad Acc. Circ:** 3,000 (ctrl). ***Continues*** *Internationale Berg- Und Seilbahn-Rundschau.*
Desc: News and information on cable car techniques, slope grooming and artificial snowmaking.

RU
ISSLEDOVANIE, KONSTRUIROVANIE I RASCHET REZBOVYKH SOEDINENII. **Added/Corp** Ulianovskii Politekhnicheskii Institut. Vol. 1 (1973)-. Russian. 0.50 rub (single issue). Privolzhskoe Knizhnoe Izdatelstvo, Ulitsa Goncharova 52, Ulianovsk Russia. **LC** TJ1338; .I87.

RU/0202-7623
ITOGI NAUKI I TEKHNIKI. REZANIE METALLOV, STANKI I INSTRUMENTY. **Added/Corp** Vsesoiuznyi Institut Nauchnoi i Tekhnicheskoi Informatsii (Soviet Union). **VFOAT** Rezanie Metallov, Stanki I Instrumenty; Itogi Nauki I Tekhniki: Seriia Rezanie Metallov, Stanki I Instrumenty. (1970)-. Periodical. Russian. an. $11.00. **(Subscription address:** Victor Kamkin, 4956 Boiling Brook Parkway, Rockville MD 20852.**) LC** TJ1180; .I86. **CODEN** ITRIEU.

RU
ITOGI NAUKI I TEKHNIKI: VOPROSY TEKHNICHESKOGO PROGRESSA I ORGANIZATSII PROIZVODSTVA V MASHINOSTROENII. **Added/Corp** Vsesoiuznyi Institut Nauchnoi i Tekhnicheskoi Informatsii (Soviet Union). **VFOAT** Voprosy Tehknicheskogo Progressa I Organizatsii Proizvodstva V Mashinostroenii; Itogi Nauki I Tekhniki: Seriia Voprosy Tekhnicheskogo Progressa I Organizatsii Proizvodstva v Mashinostroenii. Vol. 1 (1978)-. Periodical. Russian. 1.60rub. VINITI - Vsesoiuznyi Institut Nauchno-Tekhnicheskoi Informatsii, All-Union Scientific and Technical Information Institute, Baltiiskaia Ulitsa 14, 125219 Moscow Russia. **Tel** 238-46-00, FAX 9430060, telex 411160. **LC** TJ4; .I87. **CODEN** ITVMES.

RU/0202-781X
ITOGI NAUKII TEKHNIKI SERIIA MEKHANIKA ZHIDKOSTEI I GAZA. **Added/Corp** Vsesoiuznyi Institut Nauchnoi i Tekhnicheskoi Informatsii (Soviet Union). **VFOAT** Seriia Mekhanika Zhidkosti i Gaza; Mekhanika Zhidkosti i Gaza; Itogi Nauki i Tekhniki. Mekhanika Zhidkosti i Gaza. (1981)-. Russian. VINITI - Vsesoiuznyi Institut Nauchno-Tekhnicheskoi Informatsii, All-Union Scientific and Technical Information Institute, Baltiiskaia Ulitsa 14, 125219 Moscow Russia. **Tel** 238-46-00, FAX 9430060, telex 411160. **(Subscription address:** Victor Kamkin, 4956 Boiling Brook Parkway, Rockville MD 20852.**)** ***Continues*** *Itogi Nauki i Tekhniki. Mekhanika Zhidkosti i Gaza.*

●RU
IZVESTIIA AKADEMII NAUK. MEKHANIKA ZHIDKOSTI I GAZA / ROSSIISKAIA AKADEMIIA NAUK. **Added/Corp** Rossiiskaia Akademiia Nauk. **VFOAT** Mekhanika Zhidkosti i Gaza; Izvestiia Rossiiskoi Akademii Nauk. Mekhanika Zhidkosti i Gaza. (Jan./Febr. 1992)-. Academic Scholarly Publication. Russian (table of contents in English). Six times a year. $179.95. Izdatelstvo Nauka / Akademiia Nauk, Publishing House of the Russian Academy of Sciences, Leninskii Porspekt 14, 117901 Moscow Russia. **Tel** 011 95 954-21-53, FAX 011 95 938-21-44, telex 411964. **(Subscription address:** East View Publications Inc., 3020 Harbor Lane North, Suite 110, Minneapolis MN 55447.**) CODEN** IANGE7. ***Continues*** *Izvestiia Akademii Nauk SSSR. Mekhanika Zhidkosti i Gaza.*

RU/0572-3299
IZVESTIIA : MEKHANIKA TVERDOGO TELA. **Main/Corp** Akademiia Nauk SSSR. **VFOAT** Mekhanika Tverdogo Tela. (1966)-. Academic Scholarly Publication. Russian. Six times a year. $189.95. Izdatelstvo Nauka / Akademiia Nauk, Publishing House of the Russian Academy of Sciences, Leninskii Porspekt 14, 117901 Moscow Russia. **Tel** 011 95 954-21-53, FAX 011 95 938-21-44, telex 411964. **(Subscription address:** East View Publications Inc., 3020 Harbor Lane North, Suite 110, Minneapolis MN 55447.**)** Documents available from Ask*IEEE. ***Continues*** *Inzhenernyi Zhurnal.*
Ind/Abst GeoRef; INSPEC (1972-).

AI/0002-3051
IZVESTIJA AKADEMII NAUK ARMJANSKOJ SSR. MEHANIKA. (IZVESTIIA AKADEMII NAUK ARMIANSKOI SSR. MEKHANIKA). [Izv. Akad. Arm. SSR, Meh.]. **Main/Corp** Haykakan SSH Gitutyunneri Akademia. **Added/Corp** Haykakan SSR Gitutyunneri Akademia. Haykakan SSH Gitutyunneri Akademia. **VFOAT** Mekhanika; Haykakan SSR Gitutyunneri Akademiayi Teghekagir. Mekhanika; Haykakan SSH Gitutyunneri Akademiayi Teghekagir. Mekhanika. Vol. 19 (1966)-. Academic Scholarly Publication. Russian (summaries and/or abstracts in Armenian and English; table of contents in Armenian). bm. Akademiia Nauk Armianskoi / Armenian Academy of Sciences, Prospekt Marshala Bagramyana 24, 375019 Yerevan Armenia. **Tel** 52 45 80, telex 243344. **LC** WMLC L 83/5081. **CODEN** IAMHAZ. Documents available from CASDDS. ***Continues in part*** *Izvestiia Akademii nauk Armianskoi SSR. Seriia fiziko-Matematicheskikh Nauk.*
Ind/Abst Alum. Ind. Abstr.; Chem. Abstr. (-1975); Int. Aerosp. Abstr.; Math. Rev.; Met. Abstr.

BU/0068-3892
IZVESTIJA NA INSTITUT PO TEHNICESKA MEHANIKA. (IZVESTIIA.). [Izv. Inst. Teh. Meh.]. **Main/Corp** Bulgarska Akademiia Na Naukite Naukite, Sofia. Institut Po Tekhnicheska Mekhanika. (1964)-. Periodical. Bulgarian (summaries and/or abstracts in English, French, German and Russian). 1 rue Tzar Assen, Sofia Bulgaria. **DD** 621.
Ind/Abst Int. Aerosp. Abstr.

RU/0536-1044
IZVESTIJA VYSSIH UCEBNYH ZAVEDENIJ. MASINOSTROENIE. (IZVESTIIA VYSSHIKH UCHEBNYKH ZAVEDENII. MASHINOSTROENIE / MINISTERSTVO VYSSHEGO OBRAZOVANIIA SSSR.). [Izv. vyss. ucebn. zaved., Masinostr.]. **Added/Corp** Soviet Union. Ministerstvo Vysshego Obrazovaniia. Soviet Union. Ministerstvo Vysshego i Srednego Spetsialnogo Obrazovaniia. Soviet Union. Gosudarstvennyi Komitet po Narodnomu Obrazovaniiu. **VFOAT** Mashinostroenie. (1958)-. Periodical. Russian. mo. $189.95. **(Subscription address:** East View Publications Inc., 3020 Harbor Lane North, Suite 110, Minneapolis MN 55447.**) LC** TJ4; .R77. **CODEN** IVUSAH. Documents available from CASDDS. ***Continues in part*** *Nauchnye Doklady Vysshei Shkoly. Mashinostroenie i Priborostroenie.*
Ind/Abst Chem. Abstr.

JA
JAPANESE JOURNAL OF ADVANCED AUTOMATION TECHNOLOGY. (19??)-. Periodical. English. bm. ¥72000. **(Subscription address:** Maruzen Company Ltd., PO Box 5050, Import & Export Department, Tokyo 100 31 Japan.**)**

US/1045-7828
JAPANESE JOURNAL OF TRIBOLOGY. [Jpn. j. tribol.]. **Added/Corp** Nihon Junkatsu Gakkai. **VFOAT** Tribology. Vol. 34, No. 1 (1989)-. Periodical. English. mo. $590.00. Allerton Press, Inc., 150 Fifth Avenue, New York NY 10011. **Tel** (212)924-3950, FAX (212)463-9684, telex 427441 ALPRES. **(Subscription address:** Japan Publications Trading Company, Ltd., PO Box 5030, Tokyo International, Tokyo 100-31 Japan.**) ED** Kyosuke Ono. **LC** TJ1075.A2; J66. **DD** 621.8/9. **[CCC].** ***Continues*** *Journal of JSLE, 0389-5483.*
Desc: Publication of the Japanese Society of Tribologists. Includes information on tribological surfaces, contact problems, fluid lubrication and wear.
Ind/Abst Fluid Abstr., Civil Eng.; Fluid Abstr. Proc. Eng.; FLUIDEX (19??-); Lit. Pat. Abstr., Oilfield Chem. (1989-); Lit. Abstr., Catal. Catal.; Lit. Abstr., Health Environ.; Lit. Abstr., Pet. Refin. Petrochem.; Lit. Abstr., Pet. Substit.; Lit. Abstr., Transp. Storage.

JA
JAPANESE MACHINE TOOL ... GUIDE. **VFOAT** Japanese Machine Tool. '81-'82-. English. $50.00. News Digest Publishing Company Ltd., 3-5-3 Uchiyama, Chikusa-ku Nagoya 464 Japan. **Tel** 052 732 2455, telex J5954 NEWSDIGT. **LC** TJ1185; .J37. **DD** 621.9/02/029452.

HU/0021-5511
JARMUVEK, MEZOGAZDASAGI GEPEK. **Added/Corp** Gepipari Tudomanyos Egyesulet. (Jan. 1954)-. Periodical. Hungarian. mo. **LC** TJ1; .J3.
Ind/Abst Agric. Eng. Abstr.; Field Crop Abstr.; Hortic. Abstr.; Postharvest News Inf.; Rev. Agric. Entomol.; Seed Abstr.; Soils Fert.; Wheat Barley Trit. Abstr.

JA
JIDOKA GIJUTSU: MECHANICAL AUTOMATION. Japanese. mo. $212.50. Kogyo Chsakai, (Kogyo Chosakai Publishing Co., Ltd.), 14-7, Hongo 2 Chome, Bunkyoku, Tokyoto 113 Japan. **(Subscription address:** Kyowa Book Company Inc., 1-38 Kanda Jinbo-Cho, Chiyoda-Ku, Tokyo 101, Japan (Phone: 03-3293-0727)**)**

CC/0254-6051
JINSHU RECHULI. **See** Metals and Metallurgy.

US/0021-8936
JOURNAL OF APPLIED MECHANICS. [J. appl. mech.]. **Added/Corp** American Society of Mechanical Engineers. Applied Mechanics Division. Vol. 2, No. 1 (March 1935)-. Academic Scholarly Publication. English. qt. $165.00 (nonmember), $40.00 (member) US and Canada. American Society of Mechanical Engineers, 22 Law Drive, Fairfield NJ 07007. **Tel** (201)882-1167, (212)705-7722 (editorial). **LC** TA1; .J6. **DD** 620. **CODEN** JAMCAV. **[CCC].** available on microfilm and microfiche from University Microfilms International (UMI). Documents available from Article Express International, The Genuine Article, Ask*IEEE, CASDDS. ***Continues*** *Applied Mechanics.*
Ind/Abst Abstr. Bull. Inst. Pap. Sci. Tech.; Abstr. J. Earthq. Eng.; Acoust. Abstr.; Alum. Ind. Abstr.; Appl. Sci. Technol. Index; Bioeng. Abstr.; Chem. Abstr.; Coal Abstr.; Curr. Contents Eng. Tech. Appl. Sci.; Ei Page One; Eng. Mater. Abstr.; Eng. Index Annu.; Expand. Acad. Index (1992-); Fluid Abstr., Civil Eng.; Fluid Abstr. Proc. Eng.; FLUIDEX (1978-); GeoRef; HTFS Dig.; INSPEC (1968-); Int. Aerosp. Abstr. (1991-); Int. Civil Eng. Abstr.; J. Ferrocement; Math. Rev.; Met. Abstr.; Res. Alert; Sci. Cit. Index; SCISEARCH; Shock Vibr. Dig.; Soft. Abstr. Eng.; Surf. Treat. Technol. Abstr.; World Ceram. Abstr.; Zentralbl. Math. Ihre Grenzgeb.

US/0021-8944
JOURNAL OF APPLIED MECHANICS AND TECHNICAL PHYSICS. [J. appl. mech. tech. phys.]. **Added/Corp** Consultants Bureau. Vol. 6 (Jan. 1965)-. Periodical. English (Russian). bm (6 issues). $1265.00 US; $1480.00 other. Consultants Bureau, A Division of Plenum Publishing Corporation, 233 Spring Street, New York NY 10013. **Tel** (212)620-8000, (212)620-8466, FAX (212)463-0742, telex 23/421139. **ED** B. A. Lugovtsov. **LC** QC1; .P1513. **CODEN** JMPYAQ. **[CCC].** Index available. available on microfilm and microfiche from University Microfilms International (UMI). Documents available from Article Express International,

Ask*IEEE, CASDDS.
Desc: Covers topics such as hypersonic flow, boundary layer theory, plasma physics, shock waves, detonation fronts, theory of combustion, heat and mass transfer, and thermophysical properties.
Ind/Abst Acoust. Abstr.; Appl. Mech. Rev.; Chem. Abstr.; Ei Page One; Eng. Index Annu.; Fluid Abstr., Civil Eng.; Fluid Abstr. Proc. Eng.; FLUIDEX (1973-); INIS Atomindex [Micro.]; INSPEC (1968-); Int. Aerosp. Abstr.; Math. Rev.; Pollut. Abstr. Indexes.

●US
JOURNAL OF DYNAMIC AND CONTROL SYSTEMS.
(1994)-. Periodical. English. Four times a year. $145.00 US; $170.00 other. Plenum Press, 233 Spring Street, New York NY 10013-1578. **Tel** (212)620-8000, (800)221-9369, FAX (212)463-0742, (212)807-1047, telex 23/421139.

US/0733-9402
JOURNAL OF ENERGY ENGINEERING.
[J. energy eng.]. **Added/Corp** American Society of Civil Engineers. Energy Division. **VFOAT** Energy Engineering. Vol. 109, No. 1 (Mar. 1983)-. Academic Scholarly Publication. English. Three times a year. $84.00 (nonmember) US; $90.00 (nonmember) other. American Society of Civil Engineers / ASCE, 345 East 47th Street, New York NY 10017-2398. **Tel** (212)705-7179, FAX (212)705-7300, telex 422847 ASCE UI. **(Subscription address:** American Society of Civil Engineers, Publisher Fulfillment Agency, Box 828, Somerset NJ 08875.**) LC** TJ1; .A65. **DD** 621.042/05. **CODEN** JLEED9. **[CCC].** Index available. cum. index. **Bk Rev. Ad Acc. Circ:** 5,200 (ctrl). available on microfilm and microfiche from University Microfilms International (UMI); available on CD-ROM from American Society of Civil Engineers. Documents available from Article Express International, The Genuine Article, CASDDS. ***Continues** Journal of the Energy Division, 0190-8294.*
Desc: Covers all areas of energy and sources, including electric, fossil power, nuclear power, radioactive waste, hydropower and nonconventional sources.
Ind/Abst Abstr. J. Earthq. Eng.; Appl. Sci. Technol. Index; AQUAREF; ASCE Annu. Comb. Index (1983-); ASCE Publ. Inf. (1983-); Chem. Abstr. (1983-); Coal Abstr.; Curr. Contents Clin. Med.; Ei Page One; EMBASE; Energy Res. Abstr. (March 1983-); Eng. Index Annu.; Expand. Acad. Index (1992-); Fluid Abstr., Civil Eng.; Fluid Abstr. Proc. Eng.; FLUIDEX (1983-); Geogr. Abstr. Human Geogr. (?-?); GeoRef; Geotech. Abstr.; INIS Atomindex [Micro.]; Int. Civil Eng. Abstr.; J. Plan. Lit.; Life Sci. Collect.; Pollut. Abstr. Indexes; Res. Alert [Select. Cov.]; Sci. Cit. Index; SCISEARCH; Trans. Am. Soc. Civ. Eng. (1983-).

US/0742-4795
JOURNAL OF ENGINEERING FOR GAS TURBINES AND POWER.
(TRANSACTIONS OF THE ASME. JOURNAL OF ENGINEERING FOR GAS TURBINES AND POWER.). [J. eng. gas turbine power]. Vol. 106, No. 1 (Jan. 1984)-. Academic Scholarly Publication. English. qt. $150.00 (nonmember), $40.00 (member) US and Canada. American Society of Mechanical Engineers, 22 Law Drive, Fairfield NJ 07007. **Tel** (201)882-1167, (212)705-7722 (editorial). **LC** TJ1; .A712. **DD** 621/.05. **CODEN** JETPEZ. **[CCC].** available on microfilm and microfiche from University Microfilms International (UMI). Documents available from Article Express International, The Genuine Article, Ask*IEEE, CASDDS. ***Continues** Journal of Engineering for Power, 0022-0825.* ***Continued in part by** Transactions of the ASME. Journal of Turbomachinery, 0889-504X.*
Ind/Abst Acoust. Abstr.; Alum. Ind. Abstr.; Appl. Sci. Technol. Index; Chem. Abstr. (1984-); Coal Abstr.; Curr. Contents Eng. Tech. Appl. Sci.; Ei Page One; EMBASE; Energy Inf. Abstr.; Energy Res. Abstr. (Jan. 1984-); Eng. Mater. Abstr.; Eng. Index Annu.; Expand. Acad. Index (1992-); Fluid Abstr., Civil Eng.; Fluid Abstr. Proc. Eng.; FLUIDEX; HTFS Dig.; INSPEC (Jan. 1984-); Int. Aerosp. Abstr. (19??-19??); Lit. Pat. Abstr., Oilfield Chem. (1960-); Lit. Abstr., Catal. Catal.; Lit. Abstr., Health Environ.; Lit. Abstr., Pet. Refin. Petrochem.; Lit. Abstr., Pet. Substit.; Lit. Abstr., Transp. Storage; Met. Abstr.; Res. Alert [Full Cov.]; Sci. Cit. Index; SCISEARCH; Shock Vibr. Dig.

US/0094-4289
JOURNAL OF ENGINEERING MATERIALS AND TECHNOLOGY.
(TRANSACTIONS OF THE ASME. JOURNAL OF ENGINEERING MATERIALS AND TECHNOLOGY.). [J. eng. mater. technol.]. Vol. 95, No. 1 (Jan. 1973)-. Periodical. English. qt. $140.00 (nonmember), $40.00 (member) US and Canada. American Society of Mechanical Engineers, 22 Law Drive, Fairfield NJ 07007. **Tel** (201)882-1167, (212)705-7722 (editorial). **ED** Cornelia Monahan. **LC** TA1; .J62. **DD** 620.1/1/05. **CODEN** JEMTA8. **[CCC]. Bk Rev. Ad Acc. Pr Rev. Circ:** 1,638. available on microfilm and microfiche from University Microfilms International (UMI). Documents available from Article Express International, The Genuine Article, Ask*IEEE, CASDDS. ***Continues in part** Transactions of the ASME. Series D, Journal of Basic Engineering, 0021-9223.*
Desc: Biomedical materials, composites, environmental effects, effects of fabrication procedures, structure property relationships, friction and wear, metals and alloys, and test procedures.
Ind/Abst Abstr. Bull. Inst. Pap. Sci. Tech.; Abstr. J. Earthq. Eng.; Alum. Ind. Abstr.; Appl. Sci. Technol. Index; ASCE Annu. Comb. Index (19??-19??); ASCE Publ. Inf. (19??-19??); Bioeng. Abstr.; Chem. Abstr.; Coal Abstr.; Curr. Contents Eng. Tech. Appl. Sci.; Ei Page One; Energy Res. Abstr. (1975-); Eng. Mater. Abstr.; Eng. Index Annu.; Expand. Acad. Index (1992-); Fluid Abstr., Civil Eng.; Fluid Abstr. Proc. Eng.; FLUIDEX (1978-); INIS Atomindex [Micro.]; INSPEC (1973-); Int. Aerosp. Abstr. (1991-); J. Ferrocement; Met. Abstr.; Res. Alert [Full Cov.]; Sci. Cit. Index; SCISEARCH; Trans. Am. Soc. Civ. Eng.

US/0733-9399
JOURNAL OF ENGINEERING MECHANICS.
(JOURNAL OF ENGINEERING MECHANICS / AMERICAN SOCIETY OF CIVIL ENGINEERS.). [J. eng. mech.]. **Added/Corp** American Society of Civil Engineers. **VFOAT** ASCE Engineering Mechanics; A.S.C.E. Engineering Mechanics. Vol. 109, No. 1 (Feb. 1983)-. Periodical. English. mo. $284.00 (nonmember) US; $319.00 (nonmember) other. American Society of Civil Engineers / ASCE, 345 East 47th Street, New York NY 10017-2398. **Tel** (212)705-7179, FAX (212)705-7300, telex 422847 ASCE UI. **(Subscription address:** American Society of Civil Engineers, Publisher Fulfillment Agency, Box 828, Somerset NJ 08875.**) LC** TA1; .A5233. **DD** 620.1/005. **CODEN** JENMDT. **[CCC].** Index available. cum. index. **Pr Rev. Circ:** 3,450. available on microfilm and microfiche from University Microfilms International (UMI); available on CD-ROM from American Society of Civil Engineers. Documents available from Article Express International, The Genuine Article, Petroleum Abstracts Document Delivery Service. ***Continues** Journal of the Engineering Mechanics Division, 0044-7951.*
Desc: Research presented on solid, structural and fluid mechanics. Behavior of structures under impulsive loading such as blast, earthquake and periodic forces is also examined.
Ind/Abst Abstr. Bull. Inst. Pap. Sci. Tech.; Abstr. J. Earthq. Eng. (1983-); Acoust. Abstr.; Appl. Sci. Technol. Index; Aquat. Sci. Fish. Abstr. (Computer File); ASCE Annu. Comb. Index (1983-); ASCE Publ. Inf. (1983-); BMT Abstr. (-199?); Curr. Contents Eng. Tech. Appl. Sci.; Ei Page One; Energy Inf. Abstr.; Eng. Index Annu.; Expand. Acad. Index (1992-); Fluid Abstr., Civil Eng.; Fluid Abstr. Proc. Eng.; FLUIDEX (1983-); Geogr. Abstr. Phys. Geogr. (?-?); GeoRef; Geotech. Abstr.; Highw. Res. Abstr.; Int. Aerosp. Abstr.; Int. Civil Eng. Abstr.; J. Ferrocement; Ocean. Abstr.; Life Sci. Collect.; Pet. Abstr. (1983-); Res. Alert [Full Cov.]; Sci. Cit. Index; SCISEARCH; Shock Vibr. Dig.; Soft. Abstr. Eng.; Trans. Am. Soc. Civ. Eng. (1983-).

US/1052-6188
JOURNAL OF MACHINERY MANUFACTURE AND RELIABILITY.
(PROBLEMY MASHINOSSTROENIIA I NADEZHNOSTI MASHIN.). [J. mach. manuf. reliab.]. **VFOAT** Journal of Machinery Manufacture and Reliability. (1990)-. Periodical. English (Russian). bm. $880.00. Allerton Press, Inc., 150 Fifth Avenue, New York NY 10011. **Tel** (212)924-3950, FAX (212)463-9684, telex 427441 ALPRES. **LC** TJ1; .M328. **DD** 621. **[CCC]. *Continues*** *Mashinovedenie. English. Soviet Machine Science, 0739-8999.*

●US/1059-9495
JOURNAL OF MATERIALS ENGINEERING AND PERFORMANCE.
[J. mater. eng. perform.]. **Added/Corp** ASM International. **VFOAT** JMEP. Vol. 1, No. 1 (Feb. 1992)-. Periodical. English. bm (6 issues). $430.00 (nonmember), $50.00 (ASM member). American Society for Metals International, c/o Deborah Barthelmes, Materials Park OH 44073-0002. **Tel** (216)338-5151, FAX (216)338-4634, telex 980-619. **(Subscription address:** ASM International, Materials Information, Materials Park OH 44073.**) LC** TA401; .J674. **DD** 620.1/1/05. **CODEN** JMEPEG. **[CCC]. Pr Rev.** Documents available from Article Express International, The Genuine Article. ***Formed by the union of** Journal of Materials Shaping Technology, 0931-704X; Journal of Heat Treating, 0190-9177* ***and** Journal of Materials Engineering, 0931-7058.*
Ind/Abst Appl. Sci. Technol. Index; Curr. Contents Eng. Tech. Appl. Sci.; Ei Page One; Eng. Index Annu.; Res. Alert [Full Cov.].

US/1050-0472
JOURNAL OF MECHICAL DESIGN (1990).
(JOURNAL OF MECHANICAL DESIGN.). [J. mech. des.]. **Added/Corp** American Society of Mechanical Engineers. **VFOAT** Transactions of the ASME. Journal of Mechanical Design. Vol. 112, No. 1 (March 1990)-. Periodical. English. qt. $150.00 (nonmember), $40.00 (member) US and Canada. American Society of Mechanical Engineers, 22 Law Drive, Fairfield NJ 07007. **Tel** (201)882-1167, (212)705-7722 (editorial). **DD** 620. **CODEN** JMDEEC. available on microfilm and microfiche from University Microfilms International (UMI). Documents available from The Genuine Article, Ask*IEEE. ***Continues** Journal of Mechanisms, Transmissions, and Automation in Design, 0738-0666.*
Ind/Abst Curr. Contents Eng. Tech. Appl. Sci.; Expand. Acad. Index (1992-); Fluid Abstr., Civil Eng.; Fluid Abstr. Proc. Eng.; FLUIDEX (19??-); INSPEC (June 1990-); Res. Alert [Select. Cov.]; SCISEARCH; Shock Vibr. Dig.

UK/0960-1317
JOURNAL OF MICROMECHANICS AND MICROENGINEERING : STRUCTURES, DEVICES, AND SYSTEMS.
See Engineering-Electricity, Electrical Engineering, Electronics.

II/0449-5721
JOURNAL OF PLANT AND MACHINERY.
Periodical. English. T S Krishna Rao Company, 2235 B G Battaram 1, Thanjavur India. **LC** TS191; .J68. **DD** 621.9/005.

SZ/0378-7753
JOURNAL OF POWER SOURCES.
[J. power sources]. Vol. 1 (July 1976)-. Academic Scholarly Publication. English (French and German). Twelve times a year (6 volumes). 2400.00F. Elsevier Sequoia SA, PO Box 564, CH-1001 Lausanne 1 Switzerland. **Tel** 011 41 21 3207381. **ED** C.K. Dyer, P.T. Moseley, D.A.J. Rand. **LC** TJ163.2; .J69. **DD** 621. **CODEN** JPSODZ. **[CCC]. Pr Rev.** available on microfilm and microfiche from University Microfilms International (UMI). Documents available from Article Express International, The Genuine Article, Ask*IEEE, CASDDS.
Desc: Interdisciplinary forum on all aspects of the science, technology and commercialization of primary/secondary batteries and fuel cells, as well as on their application in important and emerging markets.
Ind/Abst Alum. Ind. Abstr.; Bioeng. Abstr.; Chem. Abstr.; Chem. Titles; Comput. Inf. Syst. Abstr. J. [Full Cov.]; Curr. Contents Eng. Tech. Appl. Sci.; Curr. Contents Phys. Chem. Earth Sci.; Curr. Titles Electrochem.; Ei Page One; Elect. Comm. Abstr.; Energy Inf. Abstr.; Energy Res. Abstr. (Feb. 1977-); Eng. Mater. Abstr.; Eng. Index Annu.; Environ. Eng. Abstr.; Health Saf. Sci. Abstr.; INSPEC (July 1976-); Int. Aerosp. Abstr.; Leadscan; Manuf. Process Eng. Abstr.; Mater. Sci. Eng. Abstr.; Mech. Eng. Abstr.; Met. Abstr.; Pollut. Abstr. Indexes; Res. Alert [Full Cov.]; Risk Abstr.; Sci. Cit. Index; SCISEARCH; Solid State Supercond. Abstr.

US/0094-9930
JOURNAL OF PRESSURE VESSEL TECHNOLOGY.
[J. press. vessel technol.]. **Added/Corp** American Society of Mechanical Engineers. Vol. 96, No. 1 (Feb. 1974)-. Periodical. English. Four times a year. $145.00 (non-member), $40.00 (member) US and Canada. American Society of Mechanical Engineers, 22 Law Drive, Fairfield NJ 07007. **Tel** (201)882-1167, (212)705-7722 (editorial). **ED** G. E. O. Widera. **LC** TS283; .T73. **DD** 681/.76041. **CODEN** JPVTAS. **[CCC]. Bk Rev. Ad Acc. Pr Rev.** available on microfilm and microfiche from University Microfilms International (UMI). Documents available from Article Express International, The Genuine Article, Ask*IEEE, Petroleum Abstracts Document Delivery Service, CASDDS.
Desc: Covers the technologies associated with the design, analysis, material testing, fabrication, examination, operation, maintenance and inspection of pressure vessels, piping and related components.
Ind/Abst Abstr. J. Earthq. Eng.; Acoust. Abstr.; Alum. Ind. Abstr.; Appl. Sci. Technol. Index; Bibliogr. Mission. (1978-); Bioeng. Abstr.; Chem. Abstr.; Coal Abstr.; Curr. Contents Eng. Tech. Appl. Sci.; Ei Page One; Energy Res. Abstr. (Feb. 1983-); Eng. Mater. Abstr.; Eng. Index Annu.; Expand. Acad. Index (1992-); Fluid Abstr., Civil Eng.; Fluid Abstr. Proc. Eng.; FLUIDEX (1978-); GeoRef; HTFS Dig.; INIS Atomindex [Micro.]; INSPEC (Feb. 1974-); Int. Aerosp. Abstr. (1984-); Met. Abstr.; Pet. Abstr.; Pollut. Abstr. Indexes; Res. Alert [Full Cov.]; Sci. Cit. Index; SCISEARCH; Shock Vibr. Dig.

UK/0309-3247
JOURNAL OF STRAIN ANALYSIS FOR ENGINEERING DESIGN, THE.
[J. strain anal. eng. des.]. Vol. 11, No. 1 (Jan. 1976)-. Academic Scholarly Publication. English. qt. $264.00. Mechanical Engineering Publications, PO Box 24, Northgate Avenue, Bury St. Edmunds, Suffolk IP32 6BW England. **Tel** 011 44 284 763277, telex 817376. **(Subscription address:** Mechanical Engineering Publications / Western Hemisphere Subscriptions, Subscription Office, PO Box 361, Birmingham AL 35201-0361.**) ED** R. Fidler. **LC** TA404.8; .J6. **DD** 624.1/76/05. **CODEN** JSADDZ. **[CCC].** Index available. **Bk Rev. Ad Acc. Pr Rev. Circ:** 700. available on microfilm and microfiche from University Microfilms International (UMI). Documents available from Article Express International, The Genuine Article, Ask*IEEE, CASDDS. ***Continues** Journal of Strain Analysis, 0022-4758.*
Desc: Covers a range of activities including mathematical and numerical analysis, experimental methods of strain measurement and experimental investigations of stress and strain in specific applications.
Ind/Abst Alum. Ind. Abstr.; Bioeng. Abstr.; Chem. Abstr. (1976-1983); Coal Abstr.; Curr. Contents Eng. Tech. Appl. Sci.; Ei Page One; Energy Res. Abstr. (Jan. 1983-); Eng. Mater. Abstr.; Eng. Index Annu.; Fluid Abstr., Civil Eng.; Fluid Abstr. Proc. Eng.; FLUIDEX (1976-); INSPEC (Oct. 1979-); Int. Aerosp. Abstr.; Met. Abstr.; Pollut. Abstr. Indexes; Res. Alert [Full Cov.]; Sci. Cit. Index; SCISEARCH.

II/0020-3408
JOURNAL OF THE INSTITUTION OF ENGINEERS (INDIA). MECHANICAL ENGINEERING DIVISION. (JOURNAL OF THE INSTITUTION OF ENGINEERS (INDIA). MECHANICAL ENGINEERING.). [J. Inst. Eng., India, Mech. eng. div.]. **Main/Corp** Institution of Engineers (India). Mechanical Engineering Division. **Added/Corp** Institution of Engineers (India). Mechanical Engineering Division. **VFOAT** Mechanical Engineering Division; IE (I) Journal-ME. Vol. 41, Pt. ME 1 (July 1961)-. Periodical. English. Four times a year. $18.00. Institution of Engineers India, 8 Gokhale Road, Calcutta 700020 India. **Tel** 011 91 33 288311, telex 21 7885 IEIC IN. **ED** D. K. Ghosh, P. P. Sinha and R. Sridharan. **LC** TJ1; .J66. **DD** 621/.05. **CODEN** JEMDAS. **Ad Acc. Circ:** 15,000 (ctrl). Documents available from Article Express International, Ask*IEEE. ***Continues in part*** *Journal of the Institution of Engineers (India), 0368-2498.*
Desc: Contains original research papers on control stability of mechanical systems, fluid mechanics and machinery, machine dynamics, lubrication and noise, solid mechanics materials and technology.
Ind/Abst Bioeng. Abstr.; Coal Abstr.; Ei Page One; Energy Res. Abstr. (July 1974-); Eng. Index Annu.; Fluid Abstr., Civil Eng.; Fluid Abstr. Proc. Eng.; FLUIDEX (1973-); INSPEC (Nov. 1968-); Int. Aerosp. Abstr.

UK/0334-8938
JOURNAL OF THE MECHANICAL BEHAVIOR OF MATERIALS. Vol. 1 No. 1-4 (1988)-. Academic Scholarly Publication. English. ir. $200.00. Freund Publishing House Ltd, PO Box 35010, 61 Nachmani Street, Tel Aviv 61350 Israel. **Tel** 011 972 3 5662925, FAX 011 972 3 5605335. **(Subscription address:** Freund Publishing House Ltd., Suite 500 Chesham House, 150 Regent Street, London W1R 5FA England.) **ED** B.Z. Weiss, E.C. Aifantis. **LC** TA417.6; .R48. **DD** 620.1/123/05. **CODEN** JMBMEQ. Documents available from CASDDS. ***Continues*** *Reviews on the Deformation Behavior of Materials.*
Ind/Abst Chem. Abstr.; Int. Aerosp. Abstr.

II/0253-7265
JOURNAL OF THERMAL ENGINEERING, THE. [J. therm. eng.]. Vol. 1, No. 1 (Jan.-March 1980)-. Academic Scholarly Publication. English. qt. $30.00 libraries and reader organizations, $15.00 personal use. Indian Institute of Technology / Department of Mechanical Engineering, Indian Institute of Technology, New Delhi 110016 India. **LC** TJ260; .J59. **DD** 621.402/05. **CODEN** JTENDO. Documents available from CASDDS.
Ind/Abst Alum. Ind. Abstr.; Chem. Abstr.; Eng. Mater. Abstr.; Met. Abstr.

UK/0149-5739
JOURNAL OF THERMAL STRESSES. [J. therm. stress.]. Vol. 1 (July 1978)-. Periodical. English. bm. £279.00 UK; $460.00 other. Taylor & Francis Ltd., Rankine Road, Basingstoke Hampshire, RG24 8PR United Kingdom. **Tel** 011 44 256 840366, FAX 011 44 256 479438, telex 858540. **(Subscription address:** Taylor & Francis Inc., 1900 Frost Road, Suite 101, Bristol PA 19007-1598.) **ED** Richard B. Hetnarski (editor's address: Department of Mechanical Engineering, Rochester Institute of Technology, Rochester, NY 14623). **LC** TA418.58; .J68. **DD** 620.1/121/05. **CODEN** JTSTDA. **[CCC].** Index available. **Bk Rev. Ad Acc. Pr Rev. Circ:** 400. available on microfilm and microfiche from University Microfilms International (UMI). Documents available from Article Express International, The Genuine Article, Ask*IEEE.
Desc: Publishes applications of thermal stresses. Intended as a forum for those engaged in analytic as well as experimental research, it includes mathematical papers and practical applications-related articles. Emphasis is placed on following new developments in thermoelasticity, thermoplasticity, and theory and applications of thermal stresses.
Ind/Abst Alum. Ind. Abstr.; Bioeng. Abstr.; Civ. Struct. Eng. Abstr.; Curr. Contents Eng. Tech. Appl. Sci.; Ei Page One; Elect. Comm. Abstr.; Eng. Mater. Abstr.; Eng. Index Annu.; INSPEC (July 1978-); Int. Aerosp. Abstr.; Manuf. Process Eng. Abstr.; Mater. Sci. Eng. Abstr.; Math. Rev.; Mech. Eng. Abstr.; Met. Abstr.; Res. Alert [Full Cov.]; SCISEARCH; Solid State Supercond. Abstr.; World Alum. Abstr.

US/0742-4787
JOURNAL OF TRIBOLOGY. [J. tribol.]. **Added/Corp** American Society of Mechanical Engineers. Vol. 106, No. 1 (Jan. 1984)-. Academic Scholarly Publication. English. qt. $150.00 (nonmember), $40.00 (member) US and Canada. American Society of Mechanical Engineers, 22 Law Drive, Fairfield NJ 07007. **Tel** (201)882-1167, (212)705-7722 (editorial). **LC** TJ1075.A2; J68. **DD** 621.8/9/05. **CODEN** JOTRE9. **[CCC].** available on microfilm and microfiche from University Microfilms International (UMI). Documents available from Article Express International, The Genuine Article, Ask*IEEE, CASDDS. ***Continues*** *Journal of Lubrication Technology, 0022-2305.*
Ind/Abst Acoust. Abstr.; Appl. Sci. Technol. Index; Bioeng. Abstr.; Chem. Abstr. (1984-); Curr. Contents Eng. Tech. Appl. Sci.; Ei Page One; Eng. Mater. Abstr.; Eng. Index Annu.; Expand. Acad. Index (1992-); Fluid Abstr., Civil Eng.; Fluid Abstr. Proc. Eng.; FLUIDEX (1984-); INIS Atomindex [Micro.]; INSPEC (April 1984-); Int. Aerosp. Abstr.; Lit. Pat. Abstr., Oilfield Chem. (1967-); Lit. Abstr., Catal. Catal.; Lit. Abstr., Health Environ.; Lit. Abstr., Pet. Refin. Petrochem.; Lit. Abstr., Pet. Substit.; Lit. Abstr., Transp. Storage; Res. Alert [Full Cov.]; Sci. Cit. Index; SCISEARCH; Shock Vibr. Dig.

US/0889-504X
JOURNAL OF TURBOMACHINERY. (TRANSACTIONS OF THE ASME. JOURNAL OF TURBOMACHINERY.). [J. turbomach.]. Vol. 108, No. 1 (July 1986)-. Periodical. English. qt. $150.00 (nonmember), $40.00 (member) US and Canada. American Society of Mechanical Engineers, 22 Law Drive, Fairfield NJ 07007. **Tel** (201)882-1167, (212)705-7722 (editorial). **LC** TJ267; .T68. **DD** 621. **[CCC]. Pr Rev.** Documents available from Article Express International, The Genuine Article, Ask*IEEE. ***Continues in part*** *Transactions of the ASME. Journal of Engineering for Gas Turbines and Power, 0742-4795.*
Ind/Abst Coal Abstr.; Curr. Contents Eng. Tech. Appl. Sci.; Ei Page One; Eng. Index Annu.; Expand. Acad. Index (1992-); Fluid Abstr., Civil Eng.; Fluid Abstr. Proc. Eng.; FLUIDEX; INSPEC (Oct. 1986-); Int. Aerosp. Abstr. (19??-19??); Res. Alert [Full Cov.]; SCISEARCH; Shock Vibr. Dig.

FR
JOURNAL ROBOTIQUE INFORMATIQUE INDUSTRIELLE, LE. French. Saincy Communication, 15 rue d'Hauteville, 75010 Paris France. **Tel** 011 33 1 482240240. ***Continues*** *Le Journal Robotique, 0764-5171.*

US/0892-9661
JPL PUBLICATION. See Aeronautics, Astronautics.

JA/0914-8817
JSME INTERNATIONAL JOURNAL. SERIES 2, FLUIDS ENGINEERING, HEAT TRANSFER, POWER, COMBUSTION, THERMOPHYSICAL PROPERTIES. ***Title Change.*** (JSME INTERNATIONAL JOURNAL. SERIES II, FLUIDS ENGINEERING, HEAT TRANSFER, POWER, COMBUSTION, THERMOPHYSICAL PROPERTIES.). [JSME int. j., Ser. 2 Fluids eng. heat transf. power combust. thermophys. prop.]. **Added/Corp** Nihon Kikai Gakkai. **VFOAT** Fluids Engineering, Heat Transfer, Power, Combustion, Thermophysical Properties. Vol. 31, No. 1 (Feb. 1988)-Vol. 35, No. 4 (1992). Periodical. English. mo (12 issues). Japan Society of Mechanical Engineers, Sanshin Hokusei Building / 4-9 Yoyogi, Shibuya-ku, Tokyo 151 Japan. **LC** TJ1; .J752. **DD** 621.4/005. **CODEN** JSFPET. **[CCC]. Pr Rev.** Documents available from Article Express International, The Genuine Article, Ask*IEEE, CASDDS. ***Continues in part*** *JSME International Journal, 0913-185X.* ***Continued by*** *JSME International Journal. Series B, Fluids and Thermal Engineering.*
Desc: Source for Japanese and worldwide engineering research. It includes both original, refereed research papers and review articles. Areas discussed include new materials, energy, mechatronics and bioengineering, though all fields of mechanical engineering are represented.
Ind/Abst Chem. Abstr.; Comput. Inf. Syst. Abstr. J. [Full Cov.]; Curr. Contents Eng. Tech. Appl. Sci.; Ei Page One; Elect. Comm. Abstr.; Eng. Index Annu.; Environ. Eng. Abstr.; Fluid Abstr., Civil Eng.; Fluid Abstr. Proc. Eng.; FLUIDEX; HTFS Dig.; INSPEC (Feb. 1988-); Int. Aerosp. Abstr.; Mater. Sci. Eng. Abstr.; Mech. Eng. Abstr.; Res. Alert [Full Cov.]; Sci. Cit. Index (19??-19??); SCISEARCH; Solid State Supercond. Abstr.

JA/0914-8825
JSME INTERNATIONAL JOURNAL. SERIES 3, VIBRATION, CONTROL ENGINEERING, ENGINEERING FOR INDUSTRY. ***Title Change.*** (JSME INTERNATIONAL JOURNAL. SERIES III, VIBRATION, CONTROL ENGINEERING, ENGINEERING FOR INDUSTRY.). [JSME int. j., Ser. 3 Vib. control eng. eng. ind.]. **Added/Corp** Nihon Kikai Gakkai. **VFOAT** Vibration, Control Engineering, Engineering for Industry. Vol. 31, No. 1 (Mar. 1988)-Vol. 35, No. 4 (Dec. 1992). Periodical. English. mo (12 issues). Japan Society of Mechanical Engineers, Sanshin Hokusei Building / 4-9 Yoyogi, Shibuya-ku, Tokyo 151 Japan. **LC** TJ1; .J753. **DD** 620.1. **[CCC]. Pr Rev.** Documents available from Article Express International, The Genuine Article, Ask*IEEE. ***Continues in part*** *JSME International Journal, 0913-185X.* ***Continued by*** *JSME International Journal. Series C, Dynamics, Control, Robotics, Design and Manufacturing.*
Desc: Source for Japanese and worldwide engineering research. It includes both original, refereed research papers and review articles. Areas discussed include new materials, energy, mechatronics and bioengineering, though all fields of mechanical engineering are represented.
Ind/Abst Curr. Contents Eng. Tech. Appl. Sci.; Ei Page One; Eng. Index Annu.; Fluid Abstr., Civil Eng.; Fluid Abstr. Proc. Eng.; FLUIDEX; INSPEC (March 1988-); Int. Aerosp. Abstr.; Res. Alert [Full Cov.]; Sci. Cit. Index (19??-19??); SCISEARCH.

JA
JSME INTERNATIONAL JOURNAL. SERIES B, FLUIDS AND THERMAL ENGINEERING. **Added/Corp** Nihon Kikai Gakkai. **VFOAT** Fluids and Thermal Engineering. Vol. 36, No. 1 (Feb. 1993)-. Academic Scholarly Publication. English. Four times a year. $150.00. Japan Society of Mechanical Engineers, Sanshin Hokusei Building / 4-9 Yoyogi, Shibuya-ku, Tokyo 151 Japan. **(Subscription address:** Maruzen Company Ltd., PO Box 5050, Import & Export Department, Tokyo 100 31 Japan.) **LC** IN PROCESS. **CODEN** JIJEEE. Documents available from CASDDS. ***Continues*** *JSME International Journal. Series II, Fluids Engineering, Heat Transfer, Power, Combustion, Thermophysical Properties, 0914-8817.*
Ind/Abst Chem. Abstr.; Sci. Cit. Index.

JA
JSME INTERNATIONAL JOURNAL. SERIES C, DYNAMICS, CONTROL, ROBOTICS, DESIGN AND MANUFACTURING. **Added/Corp** Nihon Kikai Gakkai. **VFOAT** Dynamics, Control, Robotics, Design and Manufacturing. Vol. 36, No. 1 (Mar. 1993)-. Periodical. English. Four times a year. $150.00. Japan Society of Mechanical Engineers, Sanshin Hokusei Building / 4-9 Yoyogi, Shibuya-ku, Tokyo 151 Japan. **(Subscription address:** Maruzen Company Ltd., PO Box 5050, Import & Export Department, Tokyo 100 31 Japan.) **LC** TJ1; .J753. **DD** 620.1. **CODEN** JCDMEY. ***Continues*** *JSME International Journal. Series III, Vibration, Control Engineering, Engineering for Industry, 0914-8825.*
Ind/Abst Sci. Cit. Index.

JA/0914-8809
JSME INTERNATIONAL JOURNAL. SERIES I, SOLID MECHANICS, STRENGTH OF MATERIALS. ***Title Change.*** **Added/Corp** Nihon Kikai Gakkai. **VFOAT** Solid Mechanics, Strength of Materials. Vol. 31, No. 1 (Jan. 1988)-Vol. 35, No. 4 (Oct. 1992). Periodical. English. mo (12 issues). Japan Society of Mechanical Engineers, Sanshin Hokusei Building / 4-9 Yoyogi, Shibuya-ku, Tokyo 151 Japan. **LC** TJ1; .J75. **DD** 620.1/12. **CODEN** JSSMEH. **[CCC]. Pr Rev.** Documents available from Article Express International, The Genuine Article, Ask*IEEE, CASDDS. ***Continues in part*** *JSME International Journal, 0913-185X.* ***Continued by*** *JSME International Journal. Series A, Mechanics and Material Engineering.*
Desc: Source for Japanese and worldwide engineering research. It includes both original, refereed research papers and review articles. Areas discussed include new materials, energy, mechatronics and bioengineering, though all fields of mechanical engineering are represented.
Ind/Abst Chem. Abstr.; Civ. Struct. Eng. Abstr.; Comput. Inf. Syst. Abstr. J. [Full Cov.]; Curr. Contents Eng. Tech. Appl. Sci.; Ei Page One; Elect. Comm. Abstr.; Eng. Index Annu.; Fluid Abstr., Civil Eng.; Fluid Abstr. Proc. Eng.; FLUIDEX; INSPEC (Jan. 1988-); Manuf. Process Eng. Abstr.; Mater. Sci. Eng. Abstr.; Mech. Eng. Abstr.; Res. Alert [Full Cov.]; Sci. Cit. Index (19??-19??); SCISEARCH; Solid State Supercond. Abstr.

JA
KENKYU SEIKA NENPO. **Main/Corp** Shin-Energi Sogo Kaihatsu Kiko (Japan). (19??)-. Japanese. an. Shin-Energi Sogo Kaihatsu Kiko, 1-ban 1-go Higashiikebukuro 3-chome Toshima-ku, Tokyo-to Japan. **LC** TJ163.13; .S48a.

JA/0451-9396
KIKAI GIJUTSU. [Kikai gijutsu]. **VFOAT** Kikai Gijutsu Mechanical Engineering. (1953)-. Academic Scholarly Publication. Japanese. Fourteen times a year. $368.00. Nikkan Kogyo Shinbunsha, (Nikkan Kogyo Shinbun, Ltd.), 8-10, Kudan Kita 1 Chome, Chiyodaku, Tokyoto 102, Japan. **(Subscription address:** Kyowa Book Company Inc., 1 38 Kanda Jinbocho Chiyoda-ku, Tokyo 101 Japan.) **CODEN** KIGIAI. Documents available from CASDDS.
Ind/Abst Chem. Abstr.

JA/0387-1045
KIKAI SEKKEI. [Kikai sekkei]. **VFOAT** Machine Design (Tokyo. 1959). (1959)-. Periodical. Japanese. mo. $320.00. **(Subscription address:** Maruzen Company Ltd., PO Box 5050, Import & Export Department, Tokyo 100 31 Japan.) **DD** 621. ***Continues*** *Shin Kikai, 0387-0979.*

JA/0387-1053
KIKAI TO KOGU. [Kikai to kogu]. **VFOAT** Tool Engineer. (1957)-. Academic Scholarly Publication. Japanese. mo. $209.50. Kogyo Chosakai, (Kogyo Chosakai Publishing Co., Ltd.), 14-7, Hongo 2 Chome, Bunkyoku, Tokyoto 113, Japan. **(Subscription address:** Maruzen Company Ltd., PO Box 5050, Import & Export Department, Tokyo 100 31 Japan.) **ED** Yoshimoto. **CODEN** KITKAL. **Ad Acc. Circ:** 32,000 (ctrl). Documents available from CASDDS.
Desc: Introduces the latest report in the field of manufacturing techniques.
Ind/Abst Chem. Abstr.

GW/0341-6615
KONSTRUIEREN + GIESSEN. [Konstr. + giess.]. **Added/Corp** Zentrale fuer Gussverwendung (Dusseldorf, Germany). **VFOAT** Konstruieren und Giessen. (19??)-. Academic Scholarly Publication. German. Four times a year. Zentrale fuer Gussverwendung, ZGV Sohnstr 70, D 40237 Dusseldorf Germany. **Tel** 011 49 211 68710. **LC** TJ230; .K6727. **DD** 621.8/05. **CODEN** KOGIDT. Documents available from CASDDS.
Ind/Abst Alum. Ind. Abstr.; Chem. Abstr.; Ei Page One; EMBASE; Eng. Mater. Abstr.; Met. Abstr.

UN
KONSTRUIROVANIE I TEKHNOLOGIIA PROIZVODSTVA SELSKOKHOZIAISTVENNYKH MASHIN. Vol. 3- 1973-. Russian. 0.79rub. Tekhnika, Pushkinskaia 28, Kiev Ukraine. **Tel** 282243. **LC** TJ1480.A1; K65. ***Continues*** *Konstruirovanie I Proizvodstvo Selskokhoziaistvennykh Mashin.*

GW/0720-5953
KONSTRUKTION (1981). (KONSTRUKTION : ORGAN DER VDI GESELLSCHAFT KONSTRUKTION UND ENTWICKLUNG.). [Konstruktion]. **Added/Corp** VDI-Gesellschaft Konstruktion und Entwicklung. Year No. 1 (Jan. 1981)-. Periodical. German. Twelve times a year. DM524.00. Springer-Verlag GmbH & Company KG, Heidelberger Platz 3, D 14197 Berlin Germany. **Tel** 011 49 30 8207223, FAX 011 49 30 8214091, telex 183 319 SPBLN D. **(Subscription address:** Springer Verlag New York Inc. / for North America, 44 Hartz Way, Secaucus NJ 07096.**)** **ED** W Beitz and B Kuffer. **CODEN** KMAGAA. **[CCC].** available on microfilm from University Microfilms International (UMI). Documents available from Article Express International. ***Continues*** *Konstruktion Im Maschinen-Apparate- und Geratebau, 0023-3625.*
Desc: Focuses on problems between concept and realization in machines, apparatuses and instrumentation. Also included are new product reports, labor and standard updates, material selection and wave technology.
Ind/Abst Acoust. Abstr.; Bioeng. Abstr.; Ei Page One; Energy Res. Abstr. (Jan. 1981-); Eng. Index Annu.; Fluid Abstr., Civil Eng.; Fluid Abstr. Proc. Eng.; FLUIDEX (1981-).

GW/0937-4167
KONSTRUKTIONSPRAXIS. [Konstruktionspraxis]. (1990)-. Periodical. German. Twelve times a year. DM220.00 Germany; DM230.00 other. Vogel Verlag, Postfach 6740, D-97064 Wuerzburg Germany. **Tel** 011 49 931 4182145, 011 49 931 4182483, FAX 011 49 931 4182670, telex 841 680131. **UDC** 62. ***Continues*** *Techno-Tip, 0341-5570.*

CC
KU TI LI HSUEH HSUEH PAO. **VFOAT** Acta Mechanica Solida Sinica; Guti Lixue Xuebao. Periodical. Chinese (summaries and/or abstracts in English). qt. Guozi Shudian, PO Box 399, Chegongzhuang Xilu 35, Beijing, People's Republic of China. **Tel** 1 8414284, FAX 1 8412023, telex 22496. **LC** TA349; .K8. **DD** 620.1/05. **CODEN** KTLPD8. Documents available from Article Express International, Ask*IEEE.
Ind/Abst Bioeng. Abstr.; Ei Page One; Eng. Index Annu.; INSPEC (1980-); Int. Aerosp. Abstr.

US/0458-5526
L. RAY BUCKENDALE LECTURE. **Added/Corp** Society of Automotive Engineers. No. 1 (1954)-. English. an (Mar.). Society of Automotive Engineers, 400 Commonwealth Drive, Warrendale PA 15096. **Tel** (412)776-4841, (412)772-7106, FAX (412)776-5760. **(Subscription address:** SAE / Society of Automotive Engineers, Department L1094P, Pittsburgh PA 15264.**)**

FR
LETTRE DE L'AUTOMATIQUE, LA. (19??)-. Periodical. French. Four times a year. 391.77F France. Cal Automatique Ensmp, 35 rue St. Honore, 77305 Fontainebleau Cedex France. **Tel** 011 33 1 64224821.

CN/1186-6152
LIST OF CSA CERTIFIED ELEVATOR EQUIPMENT. [List CSA certif. elev. equip.]. **Main/Corp** Canadian Standards Association. **Added/Corp** Canadian Standards Association. Certification and Testing Division. **VFOAT** List of Canadian Standards Association Certified Elevator Equipment. (1990)-. English. Free. Canadian Standards Association, 178 Rexdale Boulevard, Rexdale Ontario M9W 1R3 Canada. **Tel** (416)747-4000, (416)747-4044, telex 06-989344. **DD** 621.8/77.
Desc: Covers elevators and the elevator industry.

US
LOCATOR. **VFOAT** MDNIS Locator. V. 1- Sept. 1969-. English. mo. $15.00. Machinery Information System Inc., 1110 Spring Street, Silver Spring MD 20910. **Tel** (301)585-9498. **ED** Rick Shontz. **LC** TJ1040; .L63. **DD** 338.4/7/621802573. **Ad Acc. Circ:** 77,000 (ctrl).
Desc: A publication listing classified ads of used metal working equipment available for sale from equipment dealers inventories.

US/0740-3712
LOCATOR OF USED MACHINERY & EQUIPMENT. **VFOAT** Locator of Used Machinery and Equipment; Locator. (19??)-. Periodical. English. Twelve times a year. $38.00 US, Canada and Mexico; $40.00 others. Machinery Information System Inc., 1110 Spring Street, Silver Spring MD 20910. **Tel** (301)585-9498. **ED** Rick Shontz. Index available (bound in issue). **Ad Acc, Adv Mgr:** Bill Wood. **Circ:** 83,000 (ctrl).
Desc: It's the industry sourcebook for machinery, parts, plant services and supplies.

UK
LOGISTICS TODAY. English. qt. Institute of Materials Management, Cranfield Institute of Technology, Cranfield MK43 0AL England. Documents available from Ask*IEEE.
Ind/Abst INSPEC (Jan. 1985-).

US/0024-7154
LUBRICATION ENGINEERING. [Lubr. eng.]. **Added/Corp** American Society of Lubrication Engineers. Society of Tribologists and Lubrication Engineers. Vol. 1 (June 1945)-. Academic Scholarly Publication. English. mo. $61.00 (one year), $106.00 (two years) US; $90.00 (one year), $149.00 (two years) other. Society of Tribologists and Lubrication Engineers, 840 Busse Highway, Park Ridge IL 60068. **Tel** (708)825-5536, FAX (708)825-1456. **ED** Jeanie S. McCoy and Karen J. Vanderheyden. **LC** TJ1075.A2; L83. **DD** 621.8905. **CODEN** LUENAG. **[CCC].** Index available. cum. index. **Bk Rev. Ad Acc. Pr Rev. Circ:** 6,000 (ctrl). available on microfilm and microfiche from University Microfilms International (UMI). Documents available from Article Express International, The Genuine Article, CASDDS.
Desc: Edited for major industries and provides heavy coverage in manufacturing industries, particularly metalworking. News articles and technical papers keep the readership up-to-date on developments in the lubrication industry. Technical papers cover: lubrication in practice, research, design and development.
Ind/Abst Acoust. Abstr.; Alum. Ind. Abstr.; Appl. Sci. Technol. Index; Bioeng. Abstr.; Ceram. Abstr.; Chem. Abstr.; Coal Abstr.; Curr. Contents Eng. Tech. Appl. Sci.; Ei Page One; EMBASE; Eng. Mater. Abstr.; Eng. Index Annu.; Fluid Abstr., Civil Eng.; Fluid Abstr. Proc. Eng.; FLUIDEX (1973-); Int. Aerosp. Abstr.; Lit. Pat. Abstr., Oilfield Chem. (1954-); Lit. Abstr., Catal. Catal.; Lit. Abstr., Health Environ.; Lit. Abstr., Pet. Refin. Petrochem.; Lit. Abstr., Pet. Substit.; Lit. Abstr., Transp. Storage; Met. Abstr.; Res. Alert [Full Cov.]; SCISEARCH; Shock Vibr. Dig.; Surf. Treat. Technol. Abstr.

US/0024-7146
LUBRICATION (NEW YORK, N.Y. : 1911). (LUBRICATION.). [Lubrication]. Vol. 1; Aug. 1911-. Periodical. English. Three times a year. Texaco Inc, 135 East 42nd Street, New York NY 10017. **LC** TJ1075.A2; L8. **DD** 621.8/9. **CODEN** LUBRAD. cum. index. available on microfilm and microfiche from University Microfilms International (UMI). Documents available from Article Express International, CASDDS.
Ind/Abst Chem. Abstr.; Ei Page One; Eng. Index Annu.; Fluid Abstr., Civil Eng.; Fluid Abstr. Proc. Eng.; FLUIDEX (1973-); Int. Aerosp. Abstr.; Lit. Pat. Abstr., Oilfield Chem. (1966-); Lit. Abstr., Catal. Catal.; Lit. Abstr., Health Environ.; Lit. Abstr., Pet. Refin. Petrochem.; Lit. Abstr., Pet. Substit.; Lit. Abstr., Transp. Storage; Surf. Treat. Technol. Abstr.

IT/0024-8959
MACCHINE. (19??)-. Italian. Nine times a year. L90000 Italy; L120000 other. Editoriale Tecnica Macchine, Via Ugo Lenzi 1, 40122 Bologna Italy. **Tel** 011 39 51 523183. **Bk Rev. Ad Acc. Pr Rev.** ctrl circ.
Desc: Technical review of the mechanical engineering industry. Workshop and engineering techniques, metrology, tooling, production and organization.

US
MACHINE AND TOOL DIRECTORY. V. 1- 1952-. Directory. English. an. $30.00. Hitchcock Publishing Company, 191 South Gary Avenue, Carol Stream IL 60188. **Tel** (708)665-1000. **(Subscription address:** Fulfillment Office, PO Box C-409, Birmingham, AL 35283-0409**)** **ED** Ray Spiotta. **LC** TJ1180.A1; M26. **DD** 621.9/02/02573. **Ad Acc. Circ:** 40,000 (ctrl).
Desc: Alpha listing of machine tools and related products listing manufacturers of same. Also addresses of manufacturer's and metalworking handbook.

II/0541-6388
MACHINE BUILDING INDUSTRY. [Mach. build. ind.]. Academic Scholarly Publication. English. mo. Chary Publications, 14 Sidh Prasad Ghatkopar Mahul Road, Tilak Nagar PO 89, Bombay India. **Tel** 5518254. **LC** TJ1; .M14. **CODEN** MBUIAR. Documents available from CASDDS.
Ind/Abst Chem. Abstr.

US/0024-9114
MACHINE DESIGN. [Mach. des.]. Vol. 1 (Sept. 1929)-. Periodical. English. Twenty-three times a year. $100.00 US; $140.00 Canada; $150.00 Mexico; $160.00 other. Penton Publishing, 1100 Superior Avenue, Cleveland OH 44114-2543. **Tel** (216)696-7000, FAX (216)696-0836. **(Subscription address:** Penton Publishing, PO Box 96732, Chicago IL 60693.**)** **ED** Ronald Khol. **LC** TJ1; .M15. **DD** 621.8/15/05. **CODEN** MADEAP. **[CCC]. Ad Acc. Circ:** 170,000 (ctrl). available on microfilm and microfiche from University Microfilms International (UMI); available on an online database from DIALOG. Documents available from Article Express International, UMI Article Clearinghouse, Ask*IEEE, CASDDS. ***Absorbed*** *Penton's Controls & Systems, 1061-0235.*
Desc: Provides technical articles, how-to information, technical news, personal and professional guidance, and new product and process information for the design engineer.
Ind/Abst ABI/INFORM Glob. Ed.; ABI Inform Ondisc (April 1988-); Abstr. Bull. Inst. Pap. Sci. Tech.; Acad. Search (July 1993-); Acoust. Abstr.; Alum. Ind. Abstr.; Appl. Sci. Technol. Index; Bioeng. Abstr.; Bus. Index (1985-); Ceram. Abstr.; Chem. Abstr.; Coal Abstr.; Ei Page One; EMBASE; Eng. Mater. Abstr.; Eng. Index Annu.; Ergon. Abstr.; F&S Index Plus Text, Int. [Select. Cov.]; Fluid Abstr., Civil Eng.; Fluid Abstr. Proc. Eng.; FLUIDEX (1973-); Foods Adlibra; Gen. BusinessFile (1985-); Gen. Period. Index (1985-); Highw. Res. Abstr.; HTFS Dig.; INSPEC (Oct. 1977-); Int. Aerosp. Abstr.; Met. Abstr.; PROMT; Robotics Abstr.; Saf. Health Work; Shock Vibr. Dig.; Trade Ind. ASAP [Full Txt.]; Trade Ind. Index (1981-) [Full Txt.]; UMI ABI/Inform--Bus. Period. Ondisc (Apr. 1988-) [Full Txt.]; Vocat. Search (July 1993-).

FR/0024-9149
MACHINE OUTIL. [Mach. outil]. (1971)-. Periodical. French. Ten times a year. Sofetec, 20 rue de la Saussiere, F 92100 Boulogne France. **Tel** 011 33 1 48250328, FAX 011 33 1 4825 0313, telex 206 848F. **ED** Eleonore Robert and Jaeky Ledref. **LC** TJ1180; .M23. **DD** 621.9/02/05. **Bk Rev. Ad Acc. Circ:** 12,000. ***Continues*** *Machine-Outil Francaise.*
Desc: Manufacturing facts about metalworking.
Ind/Abst Saf. Health Work.

US/0939-7418
MACHINE VIBRATION. English. qt. £144.00. Springer-Verlag New York Inc., 175 5th Avenue, New York NY 10010. **Tel** (212)460-1500, telex 232 235 SPB UR. **(Subscription address:** Springer Verlag New York Inc. / for North America, 44 Hartz Way, Secaucus NJ 07096.**)** **ED** D.G. Gorman. **[CCC].**
Desc: Experimental and analytical studies of vibration from machinery. Along with examples of industrial applications of vibration analysis and control, techniques for its abatement, health monitoring, and plant installation are also presented.

CN/0319-3977
MACHINERIE LOURDE. (MACHINERIE LOURDE. HEAVY EQUIPMENT MAGAZINE.). **Added/Corp** Association des Proprietaires de Machinerie Lourde du Quebec. **VFOAT** Heavy Equipment Magazine. Vol. 5, No. 7 (Sept. 1975)-. French. Six times a year. Free on request. Machinerie Lourde, 365 Normand Street 220, Ste Jn Richelieu J3A 1T6 Canada. **Tel** (514)348-7318. **DD** 629.22/5/05. ***Continues*** *Travaux Mecanises du Quebec, 0319-3969.*

CN/0831-8603
MACHINERY & EQUIPMENT MRO. (MACHINERY & EQUIPMENT MRO : MAINTENANCE REPAIR OVERHAUL.). [Mach. equip. MRO]. **VAT** Machinery and Equipment Maintenance Repair Overhaul. Vol. 1, No. 1 (Nov./Dec. 1985)-. Periodical. English. bm. 42.00Can$ (one year), 78.00Can$ (two year), 99.00Can$ (three year) Canada; 68.00Can$ US; 99.00Can$ other. Southam Information and Technology Group Inc., 1450 Don Mills Road, Don Mills Ontario M3B 2X7 Canada. **Tel** (416)445-6641, (800)668-2374, FAX (416)442-2261. **DD** 620/.0046/05.

US/0091-8377
MACHINERY & EQUIPMENT PRICING GUIDE. 1972/73-. English. an. $19.95. Construction Publishing Company / New York, 2 Park Avenue, New York NY 10016. **LC** HD9705.U6; M32. **DD** 338.4/3621/8.

UK/0024-919X
MACHINERY AND PRODUCTION ENGINEERING. [Mach. prod. eng.]. Vol. 107, No. 2747; (July 1965)-. Periodical. English. sm. £85.00 UK, £130.00 other. Findlay Publications Ltd, Franks Hall, Horton Kirby, Kent DA4 9LL England. **Tel** 011 44 (0322)222222, FAX 011 44 (0322)289577. **ED** Chris Powley. **LC** TJ1; .M17. **CODEN** MPREAU. **[CCC]. Bk Rev. Ad Acc. Circ:** 15,000 (ctrl). available on microfilm and microfiche from University Microfilms International (UMI). Documents available from Article Express International, Ask*IEEE. ***Continues*** *Machinery (London, England).*
Desc: While machine tools are the cornerstone, all aspects of production engineering from planning to dispatch, and from production techniques to support services are covered.
Ind/Abst Alum. Ind. Abstr.; Bioeng. Abstr.; Curr. Technol. Index; Ei Page One; Eng. Index Annu.; Fluid Abstr., Civil Eng.; Fluid Abstr. Proc. Eng.; FLUIDEX (1973-); INSPEC (1968-); Int. Aerosp. Abstr.; Leadscan; Met. Abstr.; Pollut. Abstr. Indexes; Saf. Health Work; World Text. Abstr.

UK
MACHINERY BUYERS GUIDE. See Business-Purchasing.

UK
MACHINERY CLASSIFIED. English. wk. £60.00 UK; £85.00 other. Findlay Publications Ltd, Franks Hall, Horton Kirby, Kent DA4 9LL England. **Tel** 011 44 (0322)222222, FAX 011 44 (0322)289577.

CN/0835-0132
MACHINERY INDUSTRIES, EXCEPT ELECTRICAL MACHINERY (1986). (MACHINERY INDUSTRIES, EXCEPT ELECTRICAL MACHINERY / STATISTICS CANADA, INDUSTRY DIVISION, CENSUS OF MANUFACTURES SECTION.). [Mach. ind. elect. mach.]. **Added/Corp** Statistics Canada. Census of Manufactures Section. Statistics Canada. Industry Division. **VFOAT** Industries de la Machineries [i.e. Machinerie], Sauf Electriques. (1985)-. English (French). an. 38.00Can$ Canada; $46.00 US; $54.00 other. Statistics Canada, Publications Sales & Services, Main Building Room 1710, Ottawa Ontario K1A 0T6 Canada. **Tel** (613)951-5078, (800)267-6677, FAX (613)951-1584, telex 053-3585. **LC** HD9705.C2; M3. **DD** 338.4/76313/097105. ***Formed by the union of*** *Agricultural Implement Industry (Statistics Canada : Final)., 0527-4753; Other Machinery and Equipment Industries., 0831-4217; Commercial Refrigeration and Air Conditioning Equipment Manufacturers (Final)., 0527-4931* ***and*** *Office, Store and Business Machine Industries., 0829-8688.*
Desc: Annual census of manufacturers.

UK/0024-9211
MACHINERY MARKET. [Mach. mark.]. **VFOAT** Machinery Market and the Machinery and Engineering Materials Gazette. (1879)-. Periodical. English. wk. £55.00 UK; £70.00 other. Machinery Market, 6 Blyth Road, Bromley Kent BR1 3RX England. **Tel** 011 44 81 460 4224, FAX 081 290 1668. ***Continues*** *Machinery and Engineering Materials Gazette.*
Desc: Commercial news and new developments in machine tools, general plant and machinery. Supplement of advertisements for sale, wanted, and auction.

US
MACHINERY'S HANDBOOK. 1st Edition (1914)-. English. ir (Publishes every four to five years). Price varies. Industrial Press Inc., 200 Madison Avenue, New York NY 10016. **Tel** (212)889-6330.

FR/0047-536X
MACHINES PRODUCTION PARIS. (MACHINES PRODUCTION.). (1971)-. Periodical. French. Twenty-five times a year. 812.93F France; 1100.00F other. Sofetec, 20 rue de la Saussiere, F 92100 Boulogne France. **Tel** 011 33 1 48250328, FAX 011 33 1 4825 0313, telex 206 848F. **ED** Jean Cyssau. **UDC** 62. cum. index. **Ad Acc. Circ:** 20,000 (ctrl).
Desc: Metalworking tools, machine tools and machinery.

RU
MACHINOEXPORT. Added/Corp Vneshtorgreklama, V/O. (1976)-. English. sa. Soviet Export Magazine Korp, 2 31 Ul Kahovka, 113461 Moscow Russia. **LC** TJ85; .M24. **DD** 681/.76.

YU
MAG. Main/Corp Zdruzeno Preduzece Masinogradnja. V. 1- Feb. 1972-. Serbo-Croatian (Roman) (summaries and/or abstracts in English). Economska Politika, Trg Marksa i Engelsa 7, 11000 Belgrad Yugoslavia. **LC** TJ4; .Z38A.

CN/0227-6062
MARKET (TORONTO). (MARKET.). [Market]. Vol. 1, No. 1 (Dec. 1979)-. Periodical. English. mo (12 issues). 25.00Can$ Canada; 35.00Can$ other. Market / Canada, PO Box 5355 Terminal A, Toronto Ontario M5W 1N6 Canada. **DD** 621.9/005.

CN/0319-2709
MART (MONTREAL). (LE MART.). Vol. 3, No. 4 (May 1973)-. Periodical. French. mo. $19.35. Communications Vero Inc, 1600 Henri Bourassa Boulevard, Montreal Quebec H3M 3E2 Canada. **Tel** (514)332-8376, FAX (541)332-2666. **ED** Camil Chartrand. **DD** 380.1/45/62180971. **Bk Rev. Ad Acc. Circ:** 9,214 (ctrl). ***Continues*** *Centre d'Equipement et Machinerie, 0319-2717.*

GW/0340-5737
MASCHINE, DIE. [Maschine]. (Nov 1948)-. Periodical. German. mo. DM123.70. AGT Verlag Thum GmbH, Postfach 109, Teinacherstr 34, D 71601 714 Ludwigsburg 10 Germany. **Tel** 011 49 7141 223156. **LC** TJ3; .M22. **Bk Rev. Ad Acc. Circ:** 10,000 (ctrl).
Desc: Covers the production and operation of machine tools for casting and manufacturing processes. It introduces new developments from the fields of assembly, operations and material movement as well as automation in manufacturing.
Ind/Abst Energy Res. Abstr. (May 1979-); Fluid Abstr., Civil Eng.; Fluid Abstr. Proc. Eng.; FLUIDEX (199?-).

GW
MASCHINE DOKUMENTATION, DIE. German. A G T Verlag Thum GMBH, Postfach 109, D 71601 Ludwigsburg Germany. **Tel** 011 49 7141 223156. **LC** TJ3; .M225.

GR
MASCHINEN-INDUSTRIE IM DEUTSCHEN REICH, DIE. (1937)-. German. Verlag Hoppenstedt & Company, Postfach 100139, D 64201 Darmstadt Germany. **Tel** 011 49 6151 380436.

GW/0025-4517
MASCHINEN SCHADEN, DER. [Maschinenschaden]. (1924)-. Periodical. German. bm. DM162.00 (with binder), DM143.00 (without binder) Germany; DM170.00 (with binder), DM149.50 (without binder) other. Allianz Techische Information, Postfach 440124, W-80790 Munich F R Germany. **Tel** 011 49 89 38002386, FAX 011 49 89 38003737, telex 841 523011. **LC** TJ3; .M27.
Ind/Abst Corros. Abstr. (199?-); Leadscan.

SZ
MASCHINENBAU. Added/Corp Schweizerischer Verband Diplomierter Mechanikermeister. (19??)-. Periodical. German. mo (11 issues). 60.00F. Olympia Verlag AG, Spindelstr 2 Postfach, 8021 Zurich Switzerland. **Tel** 011 41 1 2429545, FAX 011 41 1 2419458, telex 812 648. **ED** Ch C Schlumpf. **LC** TJ3; .M277. **Bk Rev. Ad Acc. Circ:** 12,000.
Desc: Covers machine industries, handling technique, measurements and control engineering, process engineering, machine tools and controls, transport, handling, and fair reports.

SZ/0025-4495
MASCHINENBAUTECHNIK. ***Ceased.*** [Maschinenbautechnik]. Vol. 1- ; (April 1952)-Ceased (1991). Periodical. German. mo. Deutscher Judo Verband, Redaktion Ippon Segewaldweg 40, D 12557 Berlin Germany. **Tel** 011 49 711 210770, telex 051 678. **LC** TJ3; .M287. **CODEN** MTECAL. Documents available from Article Express International.
Ind/Abst Acoust. Abstr.; Bioeng. Abstr.; Ei Page One; EMBASE; Eng. Index Annu. [Select. Cov.]; Fluid Abstr., Civil Eng.; Fluid Abstr. Proc. Eng.; FLUIDEX (1973-); Saf. Health Work; Shock Vibr. Dig.

GW/0025-4517
MASCHINENSCHADEN, DER. ***Title Change.*** [Maschinenschaden]. (19??)-(1993). Academic Scholarly Publication. German (French, Dutch and Italian; summaries and/or abstracts in English, French, Dutch and Italian). Six times a year. Allianz Techische Information, Postfach 440124, W-80790 Munich F R Germany. **Tel** 011 49 89 38002386, FAX 011 49 89 38003737, telex 841 523011. **ED** Theo J. M. Zimmer. **CODEN** MSCNA3. Index available. cum. index. **Bk Rev. Circ:** 8,500 (ctrl). Documents available from Article Express International, Ask*IEEE, CASDDS. ***Continued by*** *Allianz Report, 0943-4569.*
Desc: Covers machinery damage.
Ind/Abst Alum. Ind. Abstr.; Bioeng. Abstr.; Chem. Abstr.; Coal Abstr.; Ei Page One; EMBASE; Energy Res. Abstr. (Sept. 1971-); Eng. Mater. Abstr.; Eng. Index Annu.; Fluid Abstr., Civil Eng.; Fluid Abstr. Proc. Eng.; FLUIDEX (19??-); INSPEC (1968-); Met. Abstr.; Saf. Health Work.

AU/0025-4533
MASCHINENWELT ELEKTROTECHNIK. ***Ceased.*** [Maschinenwelt, Elektrotech.]. Vol. 1 (May 1948)-(1994). Academic Scholarly Publication. German. mo. Reinhold Schmidt Verlag, Kastanienweg 9, A 2362 Biedermannsdorf Austria.
Ind/Abst EMBASE; Saf. Health Work.

BU/0025-455X
MASHINOSTROENE. [Mashinostroene]. (1960)-. Academic Scholarly Publication. Bulgarian (table of contents in English, German and Russian). mo. $58.00. **(Subscription address:** Hemus Foreign Trade Organization, 6 Tzar Osvoboditel Boulevard, 1000 Sofia Bulgaria.**) CODEN** MASFAZ. Index available in last issue of volume--attached. Documents available from CASDDS. ***Continues*** *Tezhka Promishlenost.*
Ind/Abst Acoust. Abstr.; Alum. Ind. Abstr.; Chem. Abstr. (1960-1983); Energy Res. Abstr. (April 1972-); Eng. Mater. Abstr.; Met. Abstr.

UK
MATERIAL MATTERS. ***Title Change.*** (19??)-(19??). Periodical. English. mo. Institute of Mechanical Engineers, 3 Birdcage Walk, London WS1H 9JN England. **Tel** 011 44 71 799 1808. ***Continued by*** *Engineering Materials.*

UK/0025-5351
MATERIALS HANDLING NEWS. [Mater. hand. news]. No. 1- 1956-. Periodical. English. mo. Reed Business Publishing / West Sussex, England, Perrymount Road, Haywards Heath, West Sussex RH16 3DH England. **Tel** 011 44 81 6523500. available on microfilm and microfiche from University Microfilms International (UMI). ***Absorbed*** *Mechanical Handling International.*
Ind/Abst Anbar Account. Finan. Abstr. [Full Txt.]; Anbar Mark. Distr. Abstr. [Full Txt.]; Anbar Top Manage. Abstr. [Full Txt.]; Curr. Technol. Index; Energy Inf. Abstr.; Ergon. Abstr. (?-?); Infomat Int. Bus.; Int. Packag. Abstr.; Manage. Market. Abstr.; Manage. Bibliogr. Rev.; Oper. Prod. Manage. Abstr. [Full Txt.]; Person. Train. Abstr. [Full Txt.]; Saf. Health Work; Women Manage. Rev. [Full Txt.]; World Ceram. Abstr.; World Text. Abstr.

UK/0020-2940
MEASUREMENT AND CONTROL. [Meas. & control]. **Added/Corp** Institute of Measurement and Control. Institute of Measurement and Control. Transactions. **VFOAT** Measurement + Control. Vol. 1 (Jan. 1968)-. Academic Scholarly Publication. English. mo. £91.00 UK, £119.00 other. Institute of Measurement and Control, 87 Gower Street, London WC1E 6AA England. **Tel** 011 44 71 387 4949, FAX 011 44 71 388 8431, telex 946797 PRONTO G. **LC** TJ212; .M372. **CODEN** MEACBX. Documents available from Article Express International, Ask*IEEE, CASDDS. ***Continues*** *Transactions - Society of Instrument Technology, 0959-3659.* ***Continued in part by*** *Transactions of the Institute of Measurement and Control, 0142-3312.*
Ind/Abst Bioeng. Abstr.; Chem. Abstr.; Curr. Biotechnol.; Curr. Technol. Index; Ei Page One; EMBASE; Eng. Index Annu.; Environ. Eng. Abstr.; Fluid Abstr., Civil Eng.; Fluid Abstr. Proc. Eng.; FLUIDEX (1973-); Gas Abstr.; HTFS Dig.; INSPEC (1968-); Int. Aerosp. Abstr.; Manuf. Process Eng. Abstr.; Pap. Board Abstr.; Proc. Chem. Eng.; Theoret. Chem. Eng.; World Text. Abstr.

US/0543-1972
MEASUREMENT TECHNIQUES. [Meas. tech.]. **Added/Corp** Soviet Union. Komitet Standartov, Mer i Izmeritelnykh Priborov. Instrument Society of America. Consultants Bureau. Consultants Bureau Enterprises. **VFOAT** Izmeritelnaya Tekhnika. (1958)-. Periodical. English (Russian). mo. $1295.00 US; $1515.00 other. Consultants Bureau, A Division of Plenum Publishing Corporation, 233 Spring Street, New York NY 10013. **Tel** (212)620-8000, (212)620-8466, FAX (212)463-0742, telex 23/421139. **ED** V. I. Pustovoit. **LC** TJ1313; .I923. **DD** 620.78. **CODEN** MSTCAL. **[CCC].** Index available. **Pr Rev.** available on microfilm and microfiche from University Microfilms International (UMI). Documents available from Article Express International, The Genuine Article, Ask*IEEE, CASDDS.
Desc: This journal covers topics such as general problems of metrology, mechanical thermotechnical, electrical and high and ultra high frequency measurements.
Ind/Abst Appl. Mech. Rev.; Bioeng. Abstr.; Chem. Abstr.; Ei Page One; Eng. Index Annu.; Fluid Abstr., Civil Eng.; Fluid Abstr. Proc. Eng.; FLUIDEX (1973-); INSPEC (June 1967-); Int. Aerosp. Abstr.; Pollut. Abstr. Indexes; Res. Alert [Full Cov.]; Sci. Cit. Index; SCISEARCH; Soc. Sci. Cit. Index [Select. Cov.].

●FR
MECANIQUE INDUSTRIELLE ET MATERIAUX : REVUE DU GAMI. **Added/Corp** GAMI (Association). Vol. 46, No 1 (Mar. 1993)-. Periodical. French (English). Five times a year. 636.36F France; 700.00F European Union; 830.00F other. VB Promotion, 15 Rue du 19 Janvier, 92380 Garches France. **Tel** 011 33 1 47014474. **LC** IN PROCESS. ***Continues*** *Mecanique, Materiaux, Electricite, 0025-6439.*

FR/0025-6439
MECANIQUE, MATERIAUX, ELECTRICITE. ***Title Change.*** [Mec., mater., electr.]. **Added/Corp** GAMI (Association). Vol. 53, No. 244 (April 1970)-(199?). Academic Scholarly Publication. French. ir. VB Promotion, 15 Rue du 19 Janvier, 92380 Garches France. **Tel** 011 33 1 47014474. **LC** TJ2; .M43. **CODEN** MMXEA5. **Ad Acc. Circ:** 3,000. Documents available from Article Express International, CASDDS. ***Continues*** *Mechanique, Electricite.* ***Continued by*** *Mecanique Industrielle et Materiaux.*
Desc: New techniques in industry. Includes information about materials, production, automation, CAD, CAD-CAM, artificial intelligence, vibrations, structures, composites, welding, bonding, lasers, mechanics, and machine tools.
Ind/Abst Alum. Ind. Abstr.; Bioeng. Abstr.; Chem. Abstr. (1970-1983); Coal Abstr.; Ei Page One; EMBASE; Energy Res. Abstr. (Jan. 1971-); Eng. Mater. Abstr.; Eng. Index Annu.; Fluid Abstr., Civil Eng.; Fluid Abstr. Proc. Eng.; FLUIDEX (1974-1990); Math. Rev.; Met. Abstr.; Saf. Health Work.

IT/1121-2047
MECCANICA OGGI. [Mecc. oggi]. (1989)-. Periodical. Multiple languages. mo (11 issues). L59400.00 Italy; L118800.00 other. Gruppo Editoriale Jackson Spa, Via Gorki 69, 20092 Cinisello Balsamo Italy. **Tel** 011 39 2 66034401. **UDC** 531. ***Absorbed*** *Meccanica Italiana, 0391-6618.*

●US/1063-7311
MECHANICAL ENGINEERING ABSTRACTS. **See** Engineering-Abstracting, Bibliographies and Statistics.

II/0379-5527
MECHANICAL ENGINEERING BULLETIN. [Mech. eng. bull.]. **Added/Corp** Central Mechanical Engineering Research Institute. Vol. 1 (Feb. 1970)-. Academic Scholarly Publication. English. qt. $15.00. Central Mechanical Engineering Research Institute, Durgapur 713209 India. **Tel** 2261-2264. **(Subscription address:** Prints India, 11 Darya Ganj, New Delhi, 110002 India, (Phone: 011 91 11 3268645)**) ED** B K Sinha and D Roy. **LC** TJ1; .M414. **DD** 621.05.

CODEN MEGBBQ. Index available. cum. index. **Bk Rev. Circ:** 600. available in microform from University Microfilms International (UMI). Documents available from Article Express International, Ask*IEEE, CASDDS.
Ind/Abst Bioeng. Abstr.; Chem. Abstr. (1970-1982); Coal Abstr.; Ei Page One; Eng. Index Annu.; Fluid Abstr., Civil Eng.; Fluid Abstr. Proc. Eng.; FLUIDEX (1973-); INSPEC (Dec. 1979-).

US
MECHANICAL ENGINEERING DEPARTMENT, RESEARCH ENGINEERING DIVISION ACTIVITIES HIGHLIGHTS REPORT. Main/Corp Lawrence Livermore Laboratory. Mechanical Engineering Dept. Research Engineering Division. Government Publication. English. US Department of Energy, 1000 Independence Avenue SW, Washington DC 20585. **Tel** (202)586-5000, FAX (202)586-4073.

US/0899-3858
MECHANICAL ENGINEERING (MARCEL DEKKER, INC.). (MECHANICAL ENGINEERING.). [Mech. eng.]. (1978)-. Monographic series. English. Price varies per volume. Marcel Dekker Inc., 270 Madison Avenue, New York NY 10016. **Tel** (212)696-9000, (800)228-1160, FAX (212)685-4540, telex 421419. **(Subscription address:** Marcel Dekker Inc, PO Box 5017, Monticello NY 12701.) **LC** UNC. **DD** 621. Documents available from Ask*IEEE.
Desc: Covers topics such as lubrication fundamentals, industrial noise control, and solar engineering for domestic buildings.
Ind/Abst INSPEC.

US/0025-6501
MECHANICAL ENGINEERING (NEW YORK, N.Y. 1919). (MECHANICAL ENGINEERING : THE JOURNAL OF THE AMERICAN SOCIETY OF MECHANICAL ENGINEERS.). [Mech. eng.]. **Added/Corp** American Society of Mechanical Engineers. Vol. 41 (Jan. 1919)-. Academic Scholarly Publication. English. Twelve times a year. $24.00 (members), $54.00 (nonmembers) US and Canada. American Society of Mechanical Engineers, 22 Law Drive, Fairfield NJ 07007. **Tel** (201)882-1167, (212)705-7722 (editorial). **ED** Charles Beardsley. **LC** TJ1; .A72. **CODEN** MEENAH. **[CCC]. Bk Rev. Ad Acc. Circ:** 80,095. available on microfilm and microfiche from University Microfilms International (UMI). Documents available from Article Express International, The Genuine Article, UMI Article Clearinghouse, Ask*IEEE, Petroleum Abstracts Document Delivery Service, CASDDS. ***Continues*** *American Society of Mechanical Engineers. Journal of the American Society of Mechanical Engineers, 0095-909X;* ***Absorbed*** *Computers in Mechanical Engineering, 0745-9726.*
Desc: Manufacturing processes, engineering materials, research and technology, industrial production, job related design problems and instrumentation.
Ind/Abst ABI/INFORM Glob. Ed.; ABI Inform Ondisc (Jan. 1988-); Abstr. Bull. Inst. Pap. Sci. Tech.; Acad. Search (July 1993-); Acoust. Abstr.; Alum. Ind. Abstr.; Appl. Sci. Technol. Index; Art Archaeol. Tech. Abstr.; Bioeng. Abstr.; BMT Abstr. (-199?); Ceram. Abstr.; Chem. Abstr. (1919-1983); Coal Abstr.; Curr. Contents Eng. Tech. Appl. Sci.; Ei Page One; EMBASE; Energy Inf. Abstr.; Energy Res. Abstr.; Eng. Mater. Abstr.; Eng. Index Annu.; Expand. Acad. Index (1992-); F&S Index Plus Text, Int. [Select. Cov.]; Fluid Abstr., Civil Eng.; Fluid Abstr. Proc. Eng.; FLUIDEX (1973-); Highw. Res. Abstr.; HTFS Dig.; INSPEC (1968-); Int. Aerosp. Abstr.; Lit. Pat. Abstr., Oilfield Chem. (1954-1990); Lit. Abstr., Catal. Catal.; Lit. Abstr., Health Environ.; Lit. Abstr., Pet. Refin. Petrochem.; Lit. Abstr., Pet. Substit.; Lit. Abstr., Transp. Storage; Mag. Search; Met. Abstr.; Newsp. Period. Abstr. (1988-); NEXIS (1982-); Life Sci. Collect.; Pet. Abstr.; PROMT; Res. Alert [Select. Cov.]; Saf. Health Work; SCISEARCH; Shock Vibr. Dig.; Soc. Sci. Cit. Index [Select. Cov.]; SportSearch; Surf. Treat. Technol. Abstr.; Text. Technol. Dig.; Trade Ind. ASAP [Full Txt.]; Trade Ind. Index [Full Txt.]; UMI ABI/Inform--Bus. Period. Ondisc (Jan. 1988-) [Full Txt.]; Zentralbl. Math. Ihre Grenzgeb.

US/0025-651X
MECHANICAL ENGINEERING NEWS (FAYETTEVILLE, ARK.). (MECHANICAL ENGINEERING NEWS.). [Mech. eng. news]. **Added/Corp** American Society for Engineering Education. Mechanical Engineering Division. Vol. 1 (1964)-. Periodical. English. Three times a year. $9.00 (departmental & individuals); $15.00 (institutions); $25.00 (others). Mechanical Engineering Division of the American Society for Engineering Education, PO Box 690668, Stockton CA 95269-0668. **Tel** (209)946-3083, (209)951-8130, FAX (209)951-8130. **ED** John R. O'Dell (phone: (209)951-8217). **LC** TJ1; .M436. **DD** 621/.05. **CODEN** MEENBI. **Bk Rev. Ad Acc.** Full Page (B&W) $225.00. Half Page (B&W) $125.00. **Circ:** 1,100 (ctrl). Documents available from Article Express International.
Desc: Publishes papers concerning such topics as mechanical systems, engineering reviews, engineering systems, sounds and vibrations. Also reports nationwide university departmental news.

Ind/Abst Abstr. Bull. Inst. Pap. Sci. Tech.; Bioeng. Abstr.; Ei Page One; Eng. Index Annu.; Fluid Abstr., Civil Eng.; Fluid Abstr. Proc. Eng.; FLUIDEX (1973-).

UK/0954-6529
MECHANICAL INCORPORATED ENGINEER. [Mech. inc. eng.]. **Added/Corp** Institution of Mechanical Incorporated Engineers. Vol. 1, No. 1 (Oct. 1988)-. Periodical. English. bm. $83.00 US and Canada; £30.00 UK and Eire; £42.00 other. The Institution of Mechanical Incorporated Engineers, 3 Birdcage Walk, Westminster London, SW1H 9JN England. **Tel** 44 71 7991808. **ED** Rebecca Booth. **LC** TA1; .M514. **DD** 620/.005. **Bk Rev,** (Qty: Varies). **Ad Acc, Adv Mgr:** Sydney Jary Ltd., **Tel** 44 272 741640. **Circ:** 8,000 (ctrl). Documents available from Ask*IEEE. ***Formed by the union of*** *General Engineer, 0308-650X* ***and*** *Mechanical Engineering Technology, 0261-7188.*
Ind/Abst Ei Page One; INSPEC (1988-).

UK/0888-3270
MECHANICAL SYSTEMS AND SIGNAL PROCESSING. [Mech. syst. signal process.]. Vol. 1, No. 1 (Jan. 1987)-. Academic Scholarly Publication. English. bm (6 issues). $350.00. Academic Press Ltd., A Division of Harcourt Brace & Company Ltd., 24-28 Oval Road, London NW1 7DX England. **Tel** 071 267 4466, FAX 071 482 2293, 071 485 4752, telex 25775 ACPRES G. **(Subscription address:** Harcourt Brace & Company, Ltd., Foots Cray, High Street, Sidcup Kent DA14 5HP England.) **ED** Simon G. Braun. **LC** TA654; .M38. **DD** 621. **[CCC]. Pr Rev.** Documents available from The Genuine Article, Ask*IEEE.
Desc: Strives to publish refereed papers of the highest quality reflecting the activities and interests of workers in academic and industrial research and development.
Ind/Abst Acoust. Abstr.; Comput. Rev.; Curr. Contents Eng. Tech. Appl. Sci.; INSPEC (May 1991-); Res. Alert [Select. Cov.]; SCISEARCH; Shock Vibr. Dig.; Zentralbl. Math. Ihre Grenzgeb.

US/0890-5452
MECHANICS OF STRUCTURES AND MACHINES. **See** Engineering-Materials Engineering and Mechanics.

US/0076-5783
MECHANICS (URBANA). (MECHANICS.). [Mechanics]. **Added/Corp** American Academy of Mechanics. American Society of Mechanical Engineers. Vol. 1 (Jan. 1972)-. Periodical. English. Ten times a year. $48.00. American Academy of Mechanics, 9500 Gilman Drive, La Jolla CA 92093. **Tel** (619)534-2036, FAX (619)534-7078. **LC** TA349; .M4272. ***Supersedes*** *Mechanics.*

PL/0025-6552
MECHANIK. [Mechanik]. **Added/Corp** Stowarzyszenie In'Zynierow i Technikow Mechanikow Polskich. (1920)-. Academic Scholarly Publication. Polish (table of contents in Russian, English and German). mo. $96.00. **(Subscription address:** ARS Polona, PO Box 1001, 00068 Warsaw Poland.) **CODEN** MCNKA5. Documents available from Article Express International, CASDDS.
Ind/Abst Bioeng. Abstr.; Ceram. Abstr.; Chem. Abstr.; Ei Page One; Eng. Index Annu.; Saf. Health Work; Surf. Treat. Technol. Abstr.

PL
MECHANIKA I BUDOWNICTWO. VFOAT Mechanics and Building Engineering. No. 1- 1974-. Polish (summaries and/or abstracts in English and Russian). 14.00 each issue. Akademii Rolniczo-Technicznej W Olsztynie, Ksiegarnia Akademicka, Olsztyn Poland. **LC** TJ4; .M4277.

UK/0094-114X
MECHANISM AND MACHINE THEORY. [Mech. mach. theory]. **Added/Corp** International Federation for the Theory of Machines and Mechanisms. Vol. 7, No. 1 (Spring 1972)-. Periodical. English. Eight times a year. $969.00 The Americas; £650.00 other. Pergamon Press, An Imprint of Elsevier Science Ltd., The Boulevard, Langford Lane, Kidlington, Oxford OX5 1GB United Kingdom. **Tel** 011 44 865 843000, 011 44 865 843699, FAX 011 44 865 843010. **(Subscription address:** Elsevier Science Ltd. Oxford Fulfillment Centre, PO Box 800, Kidlington, Oxford OX5 1DX United Kingdom.) **ED** T. E. Shoup. **LC** TJ1; .J63. **DD** 621.8/11/05. **CODEN** MHMTAS. **[CCC]. Pr Rev.** available on microfilm and microfiche from University Microfilms International (UMI). Documents available from Article Express International, The Genuine Article, Ask*IEEE. ***Continues*** *Journal of Mechanisms.*
Ind/Abst Appl. Mech. Rev.; Bioeng. Abstr.; Civ. Struct. Eng. Abstr.; Coal Abstr.; Comput. Inf. Syst. Abstr. J. [Full Cov.]; Curr. Contents Eng. Tech. Appl. Sci.; Curr. Technol. Index; Ei Page One; Elect. Comm. Abstr.; Eng. Index Annu.; Environ. Eng. Abstr.; INSPEC (Spring 1972-); Int. Aerosp. Abstr.; Manuf. Process Eng. Abstr.; Mater. Sci. Eng. Abstr.; Mech. Eng. Abstr.; Pollut. Abstr. Indexes; Res. Alert [Full Cov.]; Sci. Cit. Index; SCISEARCH; Shock Vibr. Dig.

RU
MEKHANIKA. Added/Corp Kuibushevskii Politekhnicheskii Institut. Vol. 1 (1969)-. Periodical. Russian. 1.00rub. Ministerstvo Vysshego I Srednego Spetsialnogo Obrazovaniia / Kuibyshev, Ulitsa Galaktionovskaia 141, Kuibyshev Russia. **LC** TA349; .M48.
Ind/Abst Zentralbl. Math. Ihre Grenzgeb.

UN
METALLOREZHUSCHIE STANKI. Russian. 0.75rub. Tekhnika, Pushkinskaia 28, Kiev Ukraine. **Tel** 282243. **LC** TJ1180; .M45.

US
METALWORKING MACHINERY / U.S. DEPARTMENT OF COMMERCE, BUREAU OF THE CENSUS. Government Publication. English. qt (summary issue). $5.50; $1.00 (single issue), $1.75 (Summary Issue) US; $6.90; $1.25 (single issue), $2.19 (Summary Issue) other. US Department of Commerce / Bureau of the Census, Data User Services Division, Customer Services, Washington DC 20233-0800. **Tel** (301)763-4100. **(Subscription address:** Superintendent of Documents, US Government Printing Office, Washington DC 20402.) **UDC** 621.7-1/-9.
Desc: Presents tables and statistics, based on a survey of manufacturers, on total production, value, shipment, and consumption of products manufactured by industries in the United States.

NE/0168-342X
METTALBEWERKINGSMACHINE - INDUSTRIE EN MACHINEGEREEDSCHAPPENFABRIEK EN / CENTRAAL BUREAU VOOR DE STATISTIED, HOOFDAFDELING STATISTIEKEN VAN INDUSTRIE EN BOUWNIFVERHEID. VFOAT Manufacture of Metal Working Machinery and Interchangeable Machine Tools. 1981-. Dutch (summaries and/or abstracts in English). an. Fl9.00. Centraal Bureau voor de Statistiek, AFD ALG Zaken, Postbus 959, 2270 AZ Voorburg Netherlands. **Tel** 011 31 70 3373800, FAX 011 31 038 7429, telex 32692 CBS NL. **LC** HD9705.N2; N47G. ***Continues*** *Netherlands. Centraal Bureau voor de Statistiek. Metaalbewerkingsmachine- Industrie en Machinegereedschappenfabrieken Produktiestatistieken.*

●US/1066-0763
MODAL ANALYSIS. (MODAL ANALYSIS : THE INTERNATIONAL JOURNAL OF ANALYTICAL AND EXPERIMENTAL MODAL ANALYSIS.). [Modal anal.]. **Added/Corp** Society for Experimental Mechanics (U.S.). Vol. 8, No. 1 (Jan. 1993)-. Periodical. English. qt (Jan., Apr., July, Oct.). $75.00 (one year), $140.00 (two year). Society for Experimental Mechanics, 7 School Street, Bethel CT 06801-1405. **Tel** (203)790-6373, FAX (203)790-4472. **LC** TA654.15; .I56. **DD** 620. **CODEN** MNALEO. Documents available from Article Express International. ***Continues*** *International Journal of Analytical and Experimental Modal Analysis, 0886-9367.*
Desc: Information on modal analysis.
Ind/Abst Appl. Mech. Rev.; Eng. Index Annu.; Int. Aerosp. Abstr.

FR/0761-2516
MODELLING, SIMULATION & CONTROL. B. (MODELLING, SIMULATION & CONTROL. B, MECHANICAL & THERMAL ENGINEERING, MATERIALS & RESOURCES, CHEMISTRY.). [Model. simul. control, B]. **Added/Corp** Association for the Advancement of Modelling and Simulation Techniques in Enterprises. **VFOAT** Mechanical & Thermal Engineering, Materials & Resources, Chemistry; Mechanical and Thermal Engineering, Materials & Resources, Chemistry. (1984)-. Periodical. English. **CODEN** MSCBE5. Documents available from Article Express International, Ask*IEEE. ***Continues*** *Modelling, Simulation & Control, 0242-9985.*
Ind/Abst Ei Page One; Eng. Index Annu. [Select. Cov.]; INSPEC (1989-).

US/0026-8003
MODERN MACHINE SHOP. [Mod. mach. shop]. Vol. 1 (June 1928)-. Periodical. English. mo. $120.00 airmail; $30.00 (surface mail) North America; $60.00 (surface mail) other. Gardner Publications Inc, 6600 Clough Pike, Cincinnati OH 45244. **Tel** (513)231-8020, (513)231-2818, telex 214132. **ED** Kenneth M Gettelman. **LC** TJ1; .M77. **DD** 621.7505. **CODEN** MMASAY. **[CCC]. Bk Rev. Ad Acc. Circ:** 106,000 (ctrl). available on microfilm and microfiche from University Microfilms International (UMI); available on an online database (file 648/Full-Text) from DIALOG. Documents available from Ask*IEEE.
Desc: Geared toward general management, production executives and engineering professionals in metal-working plants of all sizes, plus responsible individuals in plants whose end product is not primarily metal products but who conduct various metal-working operations.
Ind/Abst Alum. Ind. Abstr.; Appl. Sci. Technol. Index; Bus. ASAP (1990-) [Full Txt.]; Bus. Index (1985-); Ei Page One; Eng. Mater. Abstr.; Gen. BusinessFile (1985-); Gen. Period. Index (1985-); INSPEC (Jan. 1977-); Mag. Search; Met. Abstr.; Pollut. Abstr. Indexes; Trade Ind. Index (1981-) [Full Txt.].

US
MODERN MACHINE SHOP NC/CIM GUIDEBOOK. **VFOAT** Modern Machine Shop Numerical Control/Computer-Integrated Manufacturing. 1987-. English. an. Gardner Publications Inc, 6600 Clough Pike, Cincinnati OH 45244. **Tel** (513)231-8020, (513)231-2818, telex 214132. ***Continues*** *Modern Machine Shop NC/CAM Guidebook, 0148-5776.*

IT
MONITOR. **See** Building and Construction.

US/1053-4644
MOTION CONTROL. [Motion control]. Vol. 1, No. 1 (Sept./Oct. 1990)-. Periodical. English. qt. $30.00 US and Canada; $50.00 other. Instrument Society of America, 67 Alexander Drive, Research Triangle NC 27709. **Tel** (919)549-8411, FAX (919)549-8288, telex 802 540. **LC** TJ214.5; .M68. **DD** 629.8/323. **[CCC].**

IT
MOTOTECNICA. (19??)-. Italian. mo (11 issues). L70000 Italy; L140000 other. Nuovi Periodici Milanesi Srl, Via Molise 3, 20085 Locate Triulzi Italy. **Tel** 011 39 2 90780478.

GW/0024-8525
MTZ. MOTORTECHNISCHE ZEITSCHRIFT. [MTZ. Motortech. Z.]. **Added/Corp** Reichsgruppe Industrie. Wirtschaftsgruppe Maschinenbau. Fachgruppe Verbrennungsmotoren. **VFOAT** Motortechnische Zeitschrift. (1940)-. Academic Scholarly Publication. German (summaries and/or abstracts in English). Twelve times a year. DM277.20 Germany; DM286.20 other. Franckhsche Verlagshandlung Kosmos Verlag, Postfach 106011, D-70049 Stuttgart Germany. **Tel** 011 49 711 2191332. **LC** TJ751; .M13. **CODEN** MOTZAS. **[CCC].** Documents available from Article Express International, CASDDS.
Ind/Abst Bioeng. Abstr.; Chem. Abstr.; Coal Abstr.; Ei Page One; EMBASE; Energy Res. Abstr.; Eng. Index Annu.; Fluid Abstr., Civil Eng.; Fluid Abstr. Proc. Eng.; FLUIDEX (1973-); Int. Aerosp. Abstr.; Shock Vibr. Dig.

BL
MUNDO MECANICO. ***Suspended.*** Vol. 1 (July 1976)-(19??). Periodical. Portuguese. mo. $85.00. M Gruenwald, Caixa Postal 30.556, Sao Paulo 01000 Brazil. **Tel** 280-9411, telex 1130410. **LC** TJ4; .M75. Index available. **Ad Acc. Circ:** 29,000.

UN
NADEZHNOST I DOLGOVECHNOST MASHIN I SOORUZHENII / AKADEMIIA NAUK UKRAINSKOI SSR, INSTITUT PROBLEM PROCHNOSTI. Vol. 1-. Periodical. Russian. 1.30rub. Izdatelstvo Naukova Dumka / Ukrainian Academy of Sciences, Vladimirskaia Ulitsa 54, 252601 Kiev Ukraine. **Tel** 225-63-66, telex 131376. **LC** TJ153; .N235.

AT/0311-8185
NATA DIRECTORY SYDNEY. [NATA dir.Syd.]. **VFOAT** National Association of Testing Authorities Directory (Sydney). (1974)-. Periodical. English. an. $110.00 members; $140.00 nonmembers. National Association of Testing Authorities, 7 Leeds Street, Phodes NSW 2138 Australia. **Tel** 011 61 02 7368222, FAX 011 61 2 7435311, telex 26738. **ED** Paul Davies. **DD** 542.106294. **Ad Acc. Circ:** 5,500 (ctrl). ***Continues*** *NATA Index (Sydney), 0311-9920.*

AT/0311-662X
NATA NEWS SYDNEY. [NATA news.Syd.]. **VFOAT** National Association of Testing Authorities News. (1974)-. Periodical. English. Four times a year. Free on request. National Association of Testing Authorities, 7 Leeds Street, Phodes NSW 2138 Australia. **Tel** 011 61 02 7368222, FAX 011 61 2 7435311, telex 26738. **ED** Paul Davies. **DD** 620.1120994. **Ad Acc. Circ:** 5,500 (ctrl).

GW
NC PRAXIS. **VFOAT** N.C. Praxis. Periodical. German. sa. 20.00 Single Issue. Verlag Wolfgana Dummer & Company, KG Justus-Von-Lie-Str 1, Landsberg Germany. **LC** TJ1189; .N366. **DD** 621.9/023/05.

US/0271-1079
NC SHOPOWNER. ***Suspended.*** [NC shopown.]. **VAT** Numerical Control Shop Owner; NC Shop Owner. Vol. 1, No. 1 (Nov. 1980)-Suspended Dec. 1984. Periodical. English. mo. $30.00 US and Canada, $40.00 other. McGraw Hill Publishing Company, Inc., 1221 Avenue of the Americas, New York NY 10020. **Tel** (212)512-6410, (800)525-5003, FAX (212)512-6111. **LC** TJ1189; .N37. **DD** 621.9/023/05. **[CCC].** available on microfilm from University Microfilms International (UMI).

CC
NEI JAN CHI KUNG CHENG. **Added/Corp** Chung-Kuo Nei Jan Chi Hsueh Hui. **VFOAT** Chinese Internal Combustion Engine Engineering. (19??)-. Periodical. Chinese (summaries and/or abstracts in English). qt. Science Press, 16 Donghuangchenggen North Street, Beijing 100707, People's Republic of China. **Tel** 011 86 1 4019821, 011 86 1 4010642, FAX 011 86 1 4012180, 011 86 1 4019810, telex 210147. **LC** TJ751; .N45 . **DD** 621.43/05.
Ind/Abst Fluid Abstr., Civil Eng.; Fluid Abstr. Proc. Eng.; FLUIDEX.

CC/1000-0925
NEIRANJI GONGCHENG. **VFOAT** Chinese Internal Combustion Engine Engineering. (1979)-. Periodical. Chinese. qt. $1.50 (per issue). **(Subscription address:** China International Book Trading Corporation, PO Box 399, Library Service Department, Beijing 100044 People's Republic of China.**)** **DD** 621.43.
Ind/Abst Ei Page One; Fluid Abstr., Civil Eng.; Fluid Abstr. Proc. Eng.; FLUIDEX (19??-).

GW
NEUSEELAND: ENERGIEWIRTSCHAFT. **Main/Corp** Bundesstelle fur Aussenhandelsinformation (Germany). German. DM2.00. Bundesstelle fuer Aussenhandelsinformation, Agrippastr 87 93, D 50676 Cologne Germany. **Tel** 011 49 221 2057316, FAX 011 49 221 2057212. **LC** TJ163.25.N4.

US/0028-4963
NEW EQUIPMENT DIGEST. **VFOAT** NED. (1936)-. Periodical. English. Twelve times a year. $50.00 US; $75.00 Canada; $85.00 Mexico; $95.00 other. Penton Publishing, 1100 Superior Avenue, Cleveland OH 44114-2543. **Tel** (216)696-7000, FAX (216)696-0836. **(Subscription address:** Penton Publishing, PO Box 96732, Chicago IL 60693.**)** **ED** Robert King. **LC** TJ1; .N4. **DD** 621.905. **[CCC]. Bk Rev. Ad Acc. Circ:** 205,000 (ctrl). available on microfilm and microfiche from University Microfilms International (UMI).
Desc: Provides description of new and/or improved industrial products, materials, components, equipment, and services. Books and catalogs are also reviewed.

JA/0387-4168
NIHON GASU TABIN GAKKAI SHI. **VFOAT** Journal of the Gas Turbine Society of Japan. Japanese. Nihon Gasu Tabin Gakkai, c/o Dai 3 Koshin Building 5-13, Nishi Shinjuku Shinjuku-ku, Tokyo 160 Japan. **LC** TJ778; .N55.

JA/0387-5008
NIHON KIKAI GAKKAI RONBUNSHU. A. (NIHON KIKAIGAKKAI ROMBUNSHU. A-HEN. TRANSACTIONS OF THE JAPAN SOCIETY OF MECHANICAL ENGINEERS. SERIES A.). [Nihon Kikai Gakkai ronbunshu, A]. **Main/Corp** Nihon Kikai Gakkai. **Added/Corp** Nihon Kikai Gakkai. Transactions of the Japan Society of Mechanical Engineers. Series A. **VFOAT** Transactions of the Japan Society of Mechanical Engineers. Series A. Vol. 45 , No. 389 (1979)-. Academic Scholarly Publication. Japanese. mo. $524.00. Nihon Kikaigakkai, 4-9 Yoyogi 2-chome, Shibuya-ku 151, Tokyo Japan. **(Subscription address:** Japan Publications Trading Company, Ltd., PO Box 5030, Tokyo International, Tokyo 100-31 Japan.**)** **LC** TA401; .N53a. **CODEN** NKGADA. **[CCC].** Documents available from Article Express International, CASDDS. ***Continues in part*** *Nihon Kikaigakkai Rombunshu. B-Hen; Nihon Kikaigakkai Rombunshu. C-Hen; Nihon Kikaigakkai. Transactions.*
Ind/Abst Abstr. J. Earthq. Eng.; Chem. Abstr.; Ei Page One; Eng. Index Annu.; Int. Aerosp. Abstr.

JA/0387-5024
NIHON KIKAI GAKKAI RONBUNSHU. C. (NIHON KIKAIGAKKAI ROMBUNSHU. C-HEN. TRANSACTIONS OF THE JAPAN SOCIETY OF MECHANICAL ENGINEERS. SERIES C.). [Nihon Kikai Gakkai ronbunshu, C]. **Main/Corp** Nihon Kikai Gakkai. **Added/Corp** Nihon Kikai Gakkai. Transactions of the Japan Society of Mechanical Engineers. Series C. **VFOAT** Transactions of the Japan Society of Mechanical Engineers. Series C. Vol. 45, No. 389-391 (1979)-. Academic Scholarly Publication. Japanese. mo. $607.00. Nihon Kikaigakkai, 4-9 Yoyogi 2-chome, Shibuya-ku 151, Tokyo Japan. **(Subscription address:** Japan Publications Trading Company, Ltd., PO Box 5030, Tokyo International, Tokyo 100-31 Japan.**)** **LC** TJ4; .N527. **CODEN** NKCHDB. **[CCC].** Documents available from Article Express International, CASDDS. ***Supersedes in part*** *Nihon Kikai Gakkai. Nihon Kikaigakkai Rombunshu.*
Ind/Abst Abstr. J. Earthq. Eng.; Chem. Abstr.; Ei Page One; Eng. Index Annu.; Fluid Abstr., Civil Eng.; Fluid Abstr. Proc. Eng.; FLUIDEX (1979-).

JA/0549-4974
NINGEN KOGAKU. [Ningen kogaku]. **VFOAT** Japanese Journal of Ergonomics; Nihon Ningen Kogakkaishi. (1965)-. Periodical. Multiple languages. bm. $120.00. Nihon Ningen Kogakkai, (Japan Ergonomics Research Soc.), c/o Nihon Daigaku Igakubu, Eiseigaku Kyoshitsu, 30-1, Oyaguchi Kamicho, Itabashiku, Tokyoto 173, Japan. **(Subscription address:** Kyowa Book Company Inc., 1 38 Kanda Jinbocho Chiyoda-ku, Tokyo 101 Japan.**)** **DD** 620.8. Documents available from Ask*IEEE.
Ind/Abst Ergon. Abstr.; INSPEC (Dec. 1984-).

US/0027-6782
NLGI SPOKESMAN. [NLGI spokesman]. **Main/Corp** National Lubricating Grease Institute. **Added/Corp** National Lubricating Grease Institute. Spokesman. **VAT** National Lubricating Grease Institute Spokesman. Vol. 17, No. 4 (July 1953)-. Periodical. English. Twelve times a year. $20.00 (surface mail); $86.00 (airmail); $53.00 (one year) annual meetings papers. National Lubricating Grease Institute, 4635 Wyandotte Street, Kansas City MO 64112. **Tel** (816)931-9480, FAX (816)753-5026. **ED** Duane J. Fike. **LC** TJ1077.A1; N2. **DD** 621.8905. **CODEN** NLGIA4. **[CCC].** Index available. cum. index. **Bk Rev. Ad Acc. Circ:** 2,500 (ctrl). available on microfilm and microfiche from University Microfilms International (UMI). Documents available from Article Express International, CASDDS. ***Continues*** *Institute Spokesman.*
Desc: An technical journal edited for manufacturers, users and suppliers of lubricating grease. This content is approximately 50% scientific or technical , and deals with grease manufacture, new developments, application, and environmental issues.
Ind/Abst Bioeng. Abstr.; Chem. Abstr.; Ei Page One; Eng. Index Annu.; Fluid Abstr., Civil Eng.; Fluid Abstr. Proc. Eng.; FLUIDEX (1973-); Lit. Pat. Abstr., Oilfield Chem. (1954-); Lit. Abstr., Catal. Catal.; Lit. Abstr., Health Environ.; Lit. Abstr., Pet. Refin. Petrochem.; Lit. Abstr., Pet. Substit.; Lit. Abstr., Transp. Storage.

US/1058-9759
NONDESTRUCTIVE TESTING AND EVALUATION. [Nondestr. test. eval.]. Vol. 5, No. 1 (Dec. 1989)-. Periodical. English. ir (6 per volume). $678.00 (university and hospital libraries) $1058.00 other. Gordon & Breach Science Publishers, Inc., PO Box 786, Cooper Station, New York NY 10276. **Tel** (212)206-8900, FAX (212)645-2459. **LC** TA417.2; N675. **DD** 620.1/127/05. **CODEN** NTEVEPNTCODES. **[CCC].** Documents available from Article Express International, Ask*IEEE. ***Continues*** *Nondestructive Testing Communications, 0278-0895.*
Ind/Abst Ei Page One; Eng. Index Annu.; INSPEC (1990-).

NE/0167-5931
NORTH-HOLLAND SERIES IN APPLIED MATHEMATICS AND MECHANICS. [North-Holl. ser. appl. math. mech.]. **VFOAT** North Holland Series in Applied Mathematics and Mechanics. Vol. 1 (1967)-. Monographic series. English. ir. Price varies per volume. North-Holland Publishing Company, PO Box 211, Amsterdam The Netherlands. Documents available from Ask*IEEE.
Ind/Abst GeoRef; INSPEC; Zentralbl. Math. Ihre Grenzgeb.

SP/0210-0118
NOVAMAQUINA 2000. ***Suspended.*** [Novamaquina 2000]. **VFOAT** Novamaquina Dos Mil. (1975)-(1993). Periodical. Spanish. Ten times a year. 8500.00ptas. Pulsar SA, Gran Via Corts Catalanes 322 324, 08004 Barcelona Spain. **Tel** 011 34 3 4254544. **UDC** 621. ***Absorbed*** *Automatizacion Integrada Revista de Robotica.*

IT
NT, TECNICA & TECNOLOGIA / AMMA. **Added/Corp** AMMA (Association). **VFOAT** NT, Tecnica e Tecnologia; NT; Tecnica & Tecnologia; Tecnica e Tecnologia. **VAT** Notiziario Tecnico, Tecnica e Tecnologia. Vol. 10, No. 1 (Jan./Feb. 1988)-. Periodical. Italian (summaries and/or abstracts in English). bm (6 issues). L60000.00 Italy; L70000.00 other. Samma Srl, Redazione Tecnica Tecnologia, Via Vela 17, 10128 Turin Italy. **Tel** 011 39 11 5718412, 011 39 11 5718378, FAX 011 39 11 5718361. **LC** TJ4; .N78. **DD** 621/.05. Index available. **Ad Acc.** ctrl circ. ***Continues*** *Notiziario Tecnico (AMMA (Association)), 0392-4521.*
Desc: Covers mechanical and production engineering.

US/0275-3340
NTDPMA BUYERS GUIDE, THE. ***Title Change.*** **See** Business-Purchasing.

US
NTIS ALERT. COMBUSTION, ENGINES & PROPELLANTS. **Added/Corp** United States. National Technical Information Service. (19??)-. Periodical. English. Twenty-four times a year. $160.00 US; $225.00 other. National Technical Information Service - NTIS, Room 2027S, 5285 Port Royal Road, Springfield VA 22161. **Tel** (703)487-4630, (703)487-4660, (703)487-4650, FAX (703)321-8547, telex 89-9405.

US/1040-7782
NUMERICAL HEAT TRANSFER. PART A, APPLICATIONS. **See** Physics-Heat.

US/1040-7790
NUMERICAL HEAT TRANSFER. PART B, FUNDAMENTALS. **See** Physics-Heat.

AT/1031-4555
OLDE MACHINERY MART. (1985)-. Periodical. English. Six times a year (Feb., Apr., June, Aug., Oct., Dec.). 27.00Aus$. Olde Machinery Mart, Box 1200, Caboolture Queensland 4510 Australia. **Tel** 011 61 74 952233. **ED** Ian Stewart. Index available. **Bk Rev. Ad Acc. Circ:** 2,500.
Desc: For restorers and enthusiasts of all types of old machinery and early Australian mechanical endeavours.

IT
ORGANI DI TRASMISSIONE. Periodical. Italian. mo. L50000 Italy; L150000 US. Tecniche Nuove

SPA, Via Ciro Menotti 14, 20129 Milan Italy. **Tel** 011 39 2 75701, FAX 011 39 2 7610351, telex 334647 TECHS I. **LC** TJ204; .O73. **Bk Rev. Ad Acc. Circ:** 4,356.

JA/0473-5587
OTOMESHON. **VFOAT** Automation. (19??)-. Periodical. Japanese. mo. $250.00. **(Subscription address:** Maruzen Company Ltd., PO Box 5050, Import & Export Department, Tokyo 100 31 Japan.**)**

US/0402-1215
PAPERS - AMERICAN SOCIETY OF MECHANICAL ENGINEERS. [Papers-Am. Soc. Mech. Eng.]. **Main/Corp** American Society of Mechanical Engineers. (1949)-. Monographic series. English. ir. Price varies. American Society of Mechanical Engineers, 22 Law Drive, Fairfield NJ 07007. **Tel** (201)882-1167, (212)705-7722 (editorial). **DD** 621. **[CCC].** Documents available from Article Express International.
Ind/Abst Coal Abstr.; Ei Page One; Energy Res. Abstr. (Apr. 1976-); Eng. Index Annu.

CN/0710-362X
PEM : PLANT ENGINEERING AND MAINTENANCE. [PEM, Plant eng. maint.]. **VFOAT** Plant Engineering and Maintenance. **VAT** Plant Engineering and Maintenance (1981). Vol. 4, Issue 5 (Sept. 1981)-. Periodical. English. Five times a year (Feb., Apr., June, Sept., Nov./Dec.). 32.00Can$ Canada; 64.00Can$ US; 96.00Can$ other. Clifford Elliot & Associates Ltd, PO Box 358, Oakville Ontario L6J 5A2 Canada. **Tel** (905)842-2884, FAX (905)842-8226. **ED** R. Robb. **DD** 658.2/05. **Ad Acc, Adv Mgr:** Julie Clifford. **Circ:** 21,000 (ctrl). Documents available from UMI Article Clearinghouse. ***Continues*** *Maintenance Engineering/Management., 0227-664X.* ***Continued in part by*** *Industrial Literature Guide, 0826-2934.*
Desc: Technical, problem-solving approach keeps readers in touch with new management thinking, production developments, engineering and maintenance programs, material handling ideas, computer-based operating and maintenance programs, the plant programs, the plant energy scene, facilities maintenance, fluid handling, mechanical power transmission, pollution and environmental controls, supervisory skills, controls and instrumentation, safety, labour/management relations and more.
Ind/Abst ABI/INFORM Glob. Ed.; ABI Inform Ondisc (Feb. 1988-); Fluid Abstr., Civil Eng.; Fluid Abstr. Proc. Eng.; FLUIDEX (1981-); Int. Build. Serv. Abstr.; World Surf. Coat. Abstr.; World Text. Abstr.

HU/0324-6051
PERIODICA POLYTECHNICA : MECHANICAL ENGINEERING. MASHINOSTROENIE. [Period. polytech., Mech. eng. - Masinostr.]. **Added/Corp** Budapesti Muszaki Egyetem. **VFOAT** Mechanical Engineering; Mashinostroenie. Vol. 13 (1969)-. Periodical. English (German and Russian). qt. $12.00. **(Subscription address:** Kultura, PO Box 149, H 1389 Budapest 62 Hungary.**) LC** TA4; .P38. **CODEN** PPMMBT. **[CCC].** Documents available from Article Express International. ***Continues*** *Periodica Polytechnica : Engineering; Maschinen- und Bauwesen.*
Ind/Abst Alum. Ind. Abstr. (19??-); Bioeng. Abstr. (19??-); Ei Page One (19??-); Eng. Mater. Abstr. (19??-); Eng. Index Annu. (19??-) [Select. Cov.]; Fluid Abstr., Civil Eng. (19??-); Fluid Abstr. Proc. Eng. (19??-); FLUIDEX (1973-); Int. Aerosp. Abstr. (19??-); Math. Rev. (19??-); Met. Abstr. (19??-).

US/0032-0145
PIPE LINE INDUSTRY (HOUSTON, TEX.). (PIPE LINE INDUSTRY.). [Pipe line ind.]. Vol. 1 (July 1954)-. Periodical. English. mo. $22.00 US, Canada and Latin America; $26.00 other. Gulf Publishing Company / Texas, PO Box 2608, Houston TX 77252. **Tel** (800)231-6275, (713)529-4301, FAX (713)520-4433. **ED** William R Quarles. **LC** TJ930; .P5. **DD** 621.867205. **[CCC].** Index available. **Bk Rev. Ad Acc. Circ:** 26,538 (ctrl). available on microfilm and microfiche from University Microfilms International (UMI); available on an online database (file 648/Full-Text) from DIALOG. Documents available from Article Express International, Petroleum Abstracts Document Delivery Service, Documents on Demand.
Desc: Targets the design, engineering, construction, operation, maintenance and management of gas transmission and distribution systems as well as pipeline systems for crude oil products, water and slurries.
Ind/Abst Alum. Ind. Abstr.; Appl. Sci. Technol. Index; Bioeng. Abstr.; Coal Abstr.; Corros. Abstr.; Curr. Titles Electrochem.; Ei Page One; Energy Inf. Abstr.; Energy Res. Abstr. (Oct. 1974-); Eng. Mater. Abstr.; Eng. Index Annu.; Environ. Abstr.; F&S Index Plus Text, Int. [Select. Cov.]; Gas Abstr.; Lit. Pat. Abstr., Oilfield Chem. (1972-); Lit. Abstr., Catal. Catal.; Lit. Abstr., Health Environ.; Lit. Abstr., Pet. Refin. Petrochem.; Lit. Abstr., Pet. Substit.; Lit. Abstr., Transp. Storage; Met. Abstr.; Life Sci. Collect.; Pet. Abstr.; Predicasts Forecasts; Trade Ind. ASAP [Full Txt.]; Trade Ind. Index [Full Txt.]; World Alum. Abstr.

US/0896-1069
PIPELINE & UTILITIES CONSTRUCTION. [Pipeline util. constr.]. **VFOAT** Pipeline and Utilities Construction; Pipeline and Underground Utilities Construction. Vol. 40, No. 7 (June 15, 1985)-. Periodical. English. mo. $50.00 US; $70.00 (surface mail), $120.00 (air mail). Oildom Publ Company, PO Box 219368, Houston TX 77218. **Tel** (713)558-6930, FAX (713)558-7029, telex 203218 ACTH UR. **LC** TJ930; .P548. **DD** 628.1/5. **[CCC].** available on an online database (file 16/Full-Text) from DIALOG. ***Continues*** *Pipeline and Underground Utilities Construction, 0032-0196.*
Ind/Abst F&S Index Plus Text, Int. [Full Txt.] [Select. Cov.]; Gas Abstr.; PROMT [Full Txt.].

UK/0265-3990
PIPELINES ABSTRACTS : BHRA ABSTRACTS JOURNAL. ***Title Change.*** **Added/Corp** BHRA (Association). (19??)-(19??). English. bm. Learned Information Ltd., Woodside Hinksey Hill, Oxford OX1 5AU England. **Tel** 44 865 730275, FAX 44 865 736354, telex 23667. **LC** TJ930; .P569. **DD** 621.8/672. Index available. cum. index. **Bk Rev. Circ:** 250. ***Merged with*** *Fluid Flow Measurements Abstracts, 0305-9235; Fluid Power Abstracts, 0015-4644; Fluid Sealing Abstracts, 0015-4660; Pumps and Other Fluids Machinery Abstracts, 0302-2870; Solid-liquid Flow Abstracts, 0038-1063; Computer-aided Process Control Abstracts, 0955-4319* ***and*** *Mixing and Separation Technology Abstracts, 0955-7059* ***to form*** *Fluid Abstracts. Process Engineering, 0962-7162.*
Desc: Covers all aspects of the planning, design, construction and use of piplines for transport of gases, liquids, and solids; includes pipe protection and leakage testing.

JA
PIPING AND PROCESS MACHINERY. (19??)-. Periodical. Japanese. mo. $140.00. **(Subscription address:** Maruzen Company Ltd., PO Box 5050, Import & Export Department, Tokyo 100 31 Japan.**)**

UK/0032-0838
PLANT ENGINEER, THE. [Plant eng.]. **Added/Corp** Institution of Plant Engineers (Great Britain). (1964)-. Periodical. English. Six times a year (Feb., Apr., June, Aug., Oct., Dec.). £22.00 UK; £30.00 other. Institution of Plant Engineers, 77 Great Peter Street, London SW1P 2EZ England. **Tel** 011 44 71 233 2855, FAX 011 44 71 233 2604. **LC** TJ164; .I643. **CODEN** PLEGAA. **Bk Rev. Ad Acc. Circ:** 7,000 (ctrl). Documents available from Ask*IEEE. ***Continues*** *Institution of Plant Engineers (Great Britain). Journal.*
Desc: Covers all aspects of engineering and maintenance of mobile and static plant, equipment, buildings and services.
Ind/Abst Alum. Ind. Abstr.; CIS Abstr.; Curr. Technol. Index; Eng. Mater. Abstr.; INSPEC (July 1971-); Met. Abstr.; Saf. Health Work; World Alum. Abstr.

US/0199-8013
PLANT SERVICES. [Plant serv.]. (Mar. 1980)-. Periodical. English. Twelve times a year. $60.00 US; $95.00 (surface mail), $195.00 (airmail) other; $15.00 (single issue). Putnam Publishing Company, 301 East Erie Street, Chicago IL 60611. **Tel** (312)644-2020, FAX (312)644-1131. **LC** TS184; .P59. **DD** 658.2/005. **[CCC].** available on microfilm and microfiche from University Microfilms International (UMI).

NE/0032-4108
POLYTECHNISCH TIJDSCHRIFT. WERKTUIGBOUW. (PT. WERKTUIGBOUW.). [Polytech. tijdschr., Werktuigb.]. **Added/Corp** Nederlandse Ingenieursvereniging. **VFOAT** Werktuigbouw. **VAT** Polytechnisch Tijdschrift. Werktuigbouw. (1966)-. Academic Scholarly Publication. Dutch. Twelve times a year. Fl165.00. Ten Hagen and Stam BV, Postbus 34, 2501 AG The Hague Netherlands. **Tel** 011 31 70 3569100. **CODEN** PTWTAP. Documents available from Ask*IEEE, CASDDS. ***Continues*** *Polytechnisch Tijdschrift, Editie A.*
Ind/Abst Chem. Abstr.; EMBASE; INSPEC (Jan. 1982-).

II/0032-5953
POWER ENGINEER (BOMBAY). (POWER ENGINEER.). V. 1- 1951-. Periodical. English. qt. Society of Power Engineers, 34 Sant Taukaram Road, Bombay 400009 India. **LC** TJ1; .P756.

US/0032-5961
POWER ENGINEERING (BARRINGTON, ILL.). (POWER ENGINEERING.). [Power eng.]. Vol. 54, No. 5 (May 1950)-. Academic Scholarly Publication. English. Twelve times a year. $55.00 US; $60.00 Canada and Mexico; $150.00 other. PennWell Publishing Company, 1421 South Sheridan, PO Box 1260, Tulsa OK 74101. **Tel** (918)835-3161, (800)331-4463, FAX (918)831-9497. **(Subscription address:** Power Engineering, Publishing Services, PO Box 1440, Tulsa OK 74101.**) ED** Robert Smock. **LC** TJ1; .P77. **DD** 621/.05. **CODEN** POENAI. **[CCC].** Index available in last issue of volume--attached. **Ad Acc. Pr Rev. Circ:** 53,000 (ctrl). available on microfilm and microfiche from University Microfilms International (UMI). Documents available from Article Express International, Ask*IEEE, CASDDS, Documents on Demand. ***Continues*** *Power Generation, 0097-2843.*
Desc: Serves electric utilities, independent power producers and the manufacturing industries that generate steam and electricity for power, as well as the consulting/constructor firms building power plants.
Ind/Abst Appl. Sci. Technol. Index; Bioeng. Abstr.; Ceram. Abstr.; Chem. Abstr. (1950-1984); Coal Abstr.; Ei Page One; EMBASE; Energy Inf. Abstr.; Energy Res. Abstr.; Eng. Index Annu.; Environ. Abstr.; F&S Index Plus Text, Int. [Select. Cov.]; INSPEC (April 1970-); Int. Aerosp. Abstr.; PROMT; Soc. Sci. Cit. Index [Select. Cov.]; Trade Ind. ASAP [Full Txt.]; Trade Ind. Index [Full Txt.]; UMI ABI/Inform--Bus. Period. Ondisc (Jun. 1988-) [Full Txt.].

US/0160-5216
POWER ENGINEERING (NEW YORK). ***Title Change.*** (POWER ENGINEERING.). [Power engin.]. **Main/Corp** Akademiia Nauk SSSR. **VFOAT** Soviet Power Engineering. (19??)-(1993). Academic Scholarly Publication. English (Russian). bm. Allerton Press, Inc., 150 Fifth Avenue, New York NY 10011. **Tel** (212)924-3950, FAX (212)463-9684, telex 427441 ALPRES. **LC** TJ4; .A584. **DD** 621.4/005. **CODEN** POENDL. **[CCC].** Documents available from Article Express International, The Genuine Article, Ask*IEEE, CASDDS. ***Continued by*** *Power Engineering (Russian Academy of Sciences).*
Ind/Abst Bioeng. Abstr.; Chem. Abstr.; Coal Abstr.; Curr. Contents, Agric. Biol. Environ. Sci.; Ei Page One; Energy Inf. Abstr.; Energy Res. Abstr. (Aug. 1979-); Eng. Index Annu.; Health Saf. Sci. Abstr.; INSPEC (1974-); Res. Alert [Select. Cov.]; SCISEARCH.

US
POWER ENGINEERING (RUSSIAN ACADEMY OF SCIENCES). ***Title Change.*** (1993)-(199?). English. Six times a year. Allerton Press, Inc., 150 Fifth Avenue, New York NY 10011. **Tel** (212)924-3950, FAX (212)463-9684, telex 427441 ALPRES. ***Continues*** *Power Engineering (USSR Academy of Sciences).* ***Continued by*** *Applied Energy : Russian Journal of Fuel Power and Heat Systems, 1068-7181.*

AT/0817-6043
POWER EQUIPMENT AUSTRALASIA. [Power equip. Australas.]. (1985)-. Periodical. English. Six times a year (Jan., Mar., May, July, Sept., Nov.). 24.00Aus$ Australia; 32.00Aus$ New Zealand; 42.00Aus$ other. Glenvale Publications, PO Box 347, Glen Waverely, 3150 Australia. **Tel** 11 61 3 5442233, FAX 11 61 3 5431150. **ED** Steve Symmons. **DD** 338.4762190099. **Bk Rev. Ad Acc. Circ:** 8,700. ***Continues*** *Power Equipment Australia, 0817-6035.*
Desc: Specialized information on power tools and equipment.

UK/0950-1487
POWER INTERNATIONAL. [Power int.]. Vol. 32, No. 373 (Jan. 1986)-. Periodical. English. mo. £150.00 (1 year), £240.00 (2 year) UK and Europe; $300.00 (1 year), $440.00 (2 year) (surface mail), $320.00 (1 year), $480.00 (2 year) (air mail) other. Uplands Press Ltd, 28 Centre Point House, St Giles High Street, London WC2H 8LW England. **Tel** 011 44 71 2405562, FAX 011 44 71 4972811, telex 261177. **ED** Richard Jorro. **LC** TJ840; .H95. **DD** 621.2/05. **CODEN** PIHEE2. **[CCC].** Index available. **Bk Rev. Ad Acc. Circ:** 5,900 (ctrl). Documents available from Ask*IEEE. ***Continues*** *Hydraulic Pneumatic Mechanical Power Drives, Transmissions and Controls, 0306-4069.*
Desc: Developments, application of oil-hydraulics, pneumatics, mechanical and electronic power transmission and controls.
Ind/Abst BMT Abstr. (-199?); Curr. Technol. Index; Fluid Abstr., Civil Eng.; Fluid Abstr. Proc. Eng.; FLUIDEX; INSPEC (1986-).

US/1056-4063
POWER PRODUCTS BUSINESS. English. Twelve times a year. $365.00. Power Systems Research, 1301 Corporate Center, Suite 113, Eagan MN 55121. **Tel** (612)454-0144, FAX (612)454-0760, telex 291139. **ED** Gordon Gilbert. **Circ:** 150 (ctrl).

US/0032-6070
POWER TRANSMISSION DESIGN. [Power transm. des.]. Vol. 1, No. 1 (Jan. 1959)-. Periodical. English. Twelve times a year. $50.00 US; $70.00 Canada; $75.00 Mexico; $85.00 other. Penton Publishing, 1100 Superior Avenue, Cleveland OH 44114-2543. **Tel** (216)696-7000, FAX (216)696-0836. **(Subscription address:** Penton Publishing, PO Box 96732, Chicago IL 60693.**) ED** Phil Kingsley. **LC** TJ1045; .P58. **CODEN** PWTDAH. **[CCC]. Bk Rev. Ad Acc. Circ:** 52,000 (ctrl). available on microfilm and microfiche from University Microfilms International (UMI); available on an online database (file 648/Full-Text) from DIALOG. Documents available from Article Express International, Ask*IEEE.
Desc: Magazine of industrial motion and control covering adjustable-speed drives, clutches, brakes, gear, couplings, bearings, belts, chains, controls, sensors, and related products.
Ind/Abst Bioeng. Abstr.; Ei Page One; Energy Res. Abstr. (Oct. 1976-); Eng. Index Annu.; INSPEC (Jan. 1982-); Shock Vibr. Dig.

US/1070-1702
POWER TRANSMISSION DESIGN ... GUIDE TO PT PRODUCTS. [Power transm. des. guide PT prod.]. **VFOAT** Guide to PT Products; Guide to Power Transmission Products. (1991)-. English. an. $30.00 US; $35.00 Canada; $40.00 Mexico; $45.00 other. Penton Publishing, 1100 Superior Avenue, Cleveland OH 44114-2543. **Tel** (216)696-7000, FAX (216)696-0836. **(Subscription address:** Penton Publishing, PO Box 96732, Chicago IL 60693.**) LC** TJ1045; .P6. **DD** 621.8/2/05. ***Continues*** *Power Transmission Design Handbook, 0146-9134.*

PL/0079-3205
PRACE INSTYTUTU MASZYN PRZEPYWOWYCH. (PRACE INSTYTUTU MASZYN PRZEPYWOWYCH. TRANSACTIONS OF THE INSTITUTE OF FLUID-FLOW MACHINERY.). [Pr. Inst. Masz. Przepyw.]. **Main/Corp** Polska Akademia Nauk. Instytut Maszyn Przepywowych. **Added/Corp** Polska Akademia Nauk. Instytut Maszyn Przepywowych. Transactions of the Institute of Fluid-Flow Machinery. **VFOAT** Transactions of the Institute of Fluid-Flow Machinery. (1960)-. Academic Scholarly Publication. Polish (summaries and/or abstracts in English and Russian; table of contents in Russian). Z30.00. Panstwowe Wydawn Naukowe, Miodowa 10, PO Box 391, 00251 Warsaw Poland. **ED** K Steller. **LC** TJ4; .P63. **DD** 621.2/6/05. **CODEN** PIMZAI. **Circ:** 400. Documents available from Article Express International, CASDDS.
Desc: Theoretical and experimental investigations of all aspects of the mechanics and thermodynamics of fluid-flow with special reference to fluid-flow machinery.
Ind/Abst Bioeng. Abstr.; Chem. Abstr. (1960-1983); Ei Page One; Energy Res. Abstr.; Eng. Index Annu.; Int. Aerosp. Abstr.; Math. Rev.

PL
PRACE NAUKOWE INSTYTUTU MATEMATYKI POLITECHNIKI WROCAWSKIEJ. **See** Mathematics.

PL/0137-2335
PRACE NAUKOWE - POLITECHNIKA WARSZAWSKA. MECHANIKA. (PRACE NAUKOWE. MECHANIKA.). [Pr. nauk. - Politech. Warsz., Mech.]. **VFOAT** Mechanika. No. 1- 1968-. Monographic series. Polish (summaries and/or abstracts in French and Russian). Price varies per volume. **LC** TA349; .W315. **CODEN** PWPMAO. Documents available from Article Express International.
Ind/Abst Bioeng. Abstr.; Ei Page One; Eng. Index Annu.; Int. Aerosp. Abstr.

US/0141-6359
PRECISION ENGINEERING. [Precis. eng.]. **Added/Corp** American Society for Precision Engineering. Vol. 1 (Jan. 1979)-. Academic Scholarly Publication. English. qt (January, April, July and October). $385.00 US; $425.00 other. Butterworth Heinemann / Woburn, MA, 225 Wildwood Avenue, Unit B, Woburn MA 01801. **Tel** (800)366-2665, FAX (617)928-2620, telex 880052. **(Subscription address:** Elsevier Science Inc. / New York Books, 655 Avenue of the Americas, New York NY 10010.**) ED** Steve Bailey. **LC** TS500; .P65. **DD** 620/.0045. **CODEN** PREGDL. **[CCC].** Index available. **Bk Rev. Ad Acc. Pr Rev. Circ:** 500. available on microfilm and microfiche from University Microfilms International (UMI). Documents available from Article Express International, CASDDS.
Desc: A international journal devoted to the latest advances in ultra-high precision engineering and metrology. Its scope covers the whole interdisciplinary range of the many techniques and disciplines necessary for today's precision engineer.
Ind/Abst Alum. Ind. Abstr.; Bioeng. Abstr.; Chem. Abstr. (1979-1983); Ei Page One; Eng. Mater. Abstr.; Eng. Index Annu.; Fluid Abstr., Civil Eng.; Fluid Abstr. Proc. Eng.; FLUIDEX (1973-); Met. Abstr.; Pollut. Abstr. Indexes; SCISEARCH.

UK/0264-4703
PRECISION TOOLMAKER. Added/Corp Gauge and Tool Makers' Association. National Society of Master Patternmakers. **VFOAT** Toolmaker. Vol. 1, No. 1 (March 1983)-. Periodical. English. bm. £68.00 UK; £94.00, $173.00 other. Argus Press Group, Queensway House, 2 Queensway Redhill, Surrey RH1 1QS England. **Tel** 011 44 737 768611, 011 44 737 761685, FAX 011 44 737 760510, telex 948669 TOPJNL G. available on an online database (file 16/Full-Text) from DIALOG. ***Absorbed*** *Tooling and Machining.*
Desc: Devoted to the design, manufacture and application of precision tooling.
Ind/Abst F&S Index Plus Text, Int. [Full Txt.] [Select. Cov.]; PROMT [Full Txt.].

RU
PRIKLADNAIA MEKHANIKA. Main/Corp Leningrad. Universitet. Matematiko-Mekhanicheskii Fakultet. **VFOAT** Applied Mechanics. Vol. 1 (1974)-. Russian. mo. $159.95. Izdatelstvo Naukova Dumka / Ukrainian Academy of Sciences, Vladimirskaia Ulitsa 54, 252601 Kiev Ukraine. **Tel** 225-63-66, telex 131376. **(Subscription address:** East View Publications Inc., 3020 Harbor Lane North, Suite 110, Minneapolis MN 55447.**) LC** TA349; .L45a. Index available. **Bk Rev.**
Ind/Abst Acoust. Abstr.; Zentralbl. Math. Ihre Grenzgeb.

RU/0032-8235
PRIKLADNAJA MATEMATIKA I MEHANIKA. (PRIKLADNAIA MATEMATIKA I MEKHANIKA. NOVAIA SERIIA.). [Prikl. mat. meh.]. **Added/Corp** Leningradskoe Mekhanicheskoe NIT Obshchestvo. Akademiia Nauk SSSR. Gruppa Tekhnicheskoi Mekhaniki. Institut Mekhaniki (Akademiia Nauk SSSR) Akademiia Nauk SSSR. Otdelenie Tekhnicheskikh Nauk. **VFOAT** Applied Mathematics and Mechanics; Zhurnal Prikladnoi Matematiki i Mekhaniki. Vol. 1 (1933)-. Academic Scholarly Publication. Russian (English; summaries and/or abstracts in English, French and German; table of contents in French and German). bm. $211.00. Izdatelstvo Nauka / Akademiia Nauk, Publishing House of the Russian Academy of Sciences, Leninskii Porspekt 14, 117901 Moscow Russia. **Tel** 011 95 954-21-53, FAX 011 95 938-21-44, telex 411964. **(Subscription address:** East View Publications Inc., 3020 Harbor Lane North, Suite 110, Minneapolis MN 55447.**) LC** QA801; .P7. **CODEN** PMAMAF. **[CCC].** Index available. cum. index. **Circ:** 3,015. available on microfilm. Documents available from Article Express International, Ask*IEEE, CASDDS. ***Continues*** *Vestnik Mekhaniki i Prikladnoi Matematiki.*
Ind/Abst Chem. Abstr. (1933-1980); Eng. Index Annu.; INSPEC (1968-); Int. Aerosp. Abstr. (19??-19??); Math. Rev.; Zentralbl. Math. Ihre Grenzgeb.

UN/0032-8243
PRIKLADNAJA MEHANIKA (KIEV). (PRIKLADNAIA MEKHANIKA.). [Prikl. meh.]. Vol. 1, (1965)-. Periodical. Russian. mo. $236.00 domestic airmail; $246.00 international airmail. **(Subscription address:** Victor Kamkin, 4956 Boiling Brook Parkway, Rockville MD 20852.**) LC** TA349; .P685. **CODEN** PKMKAL. Documents available from Article Express International, Ask*IEEE, CASDDS. ***Supersedes*** *Prykladna Mekhanika.*
Ind/Abst Chem. Abstr. (1965-1983); Coal Abstr.; Energy Res. Abstr. (Oct. 1976-); Eng. Index Annu.; GeoRef; INSPEC (Dec. 1971-); Int. Aerosp. Abstr.; Math. Rev.; Zentralbl. Math. Ihre Grenzgeb.

UK/0266-8920
PROBABILISTIC ENGINEERING MECHANICS. [Prob. eng. mech.]. Vol. 1, No. 1 (March 1986)-. Academic Scholarly Publication. English. qt. $313.00 The Americas; £210.00 other. Elsevier Applied Science, An Imprint of Elsevier Science Ltd., The Boulevard, Langford Lane, Kidlington, Oxford OX5 1GB United Kingdom. **Tel** 011 44 865 843000, 011 44 865 843699, FAX 011 44 865 843010. **(Subscription address:** Elsevier Science Ltd. Oxford Fulfillment Centre, PO Box 800, Kidlington, Oxford OX5 1DX United Kingdom.**) ED** M. Shinozuka and P. D. Spanos. **LC** TA340; .P73. **DD** 620/.0072. **CODEN** PEMEEX. **[CCC]. Bk Rev. Ad Acc.** Documents available from Article Express International.
Desc: A major forum for scholarly work dealing primarily with probabilistic and statistical approaches to contemporary solid and fluid mechanics.
Ind/Abst Abstr. J. Earthq. Eng.; Eng. Index Annu.; Fluid Abstr., Civil Eng.; Fluid Abstr. Proc. Eng.; FLUIDEX; Int. Civil Eng. Abstr.; Soft. Abstr. Eng.

RU/0235-7119
PROBLEMY MASHINOSTROENIIA I NADEZHNOSTI MASHIN / AKADEMIIA NAUK SSSR. Added/Corp Akademiia Nauk SSSR. Rossiiskaia Akademiia Nauk. No. 1 (Jan./Feb. 1990)-. Academic Scholarly Publication. Russian. Six times a year. $79.95. Izdatelstvo Nauka / Akademiia Nauk, Publishing House of the Russian Academy of Sciences, Leninskii Porspekt 14, 117901 Moscow Russia. **Tel** 011 95 954-21-53, FAX 011 95 938-21-44, telex 411964. **LC** TJ4; .P725. **CODEN** PMNMEG. Documents available from CASDDS. ***Continues*** *Mashinovedenie.*
Ind/Abst Chem. Abstr.

UN/0131-2928
PROBLEMY MASINOSTROENIJA. (PROBLEMY MASHINOSTROENIIA.). [Probl. masinostr.]. **Added/Corp** Akademiia Nauk URSR, Kiev. Instytut Problem Mashynobudovannia. Vol. 1 (1975)-. Academic Scholarly Publication. Russian. 0.82rub each issue. Izdatelstvo Naukova Dumka / Ukrainian Academy of Sciences, Vladimirskaia Ulitsa 54, 252601 Kiev Ukraine. **Tel** 225-63-66, telex 131376. **LC** TJ241; .P76. **CODEN** PRMSDT. Documents available from CASDDS.
Ind/Abst Chem. Abstr.; Int. Aerosp. Abstr.

MX/0254-4679
PROCEEDINGS / EUROPEAN CONFERENCE ON SOIL MECHANICS AND FOUNDATION ENGINEERING. [Proc. - Eur. Conf. Soil Mech. Found. Eng.]. **Added/Corp** International Society for Soil Mechanics and Foundation Engineers. **VFOAT** Comptes Rendus; Proceedings of the ... European Conference on Soil Mechanics and Foundation Engineers. (19??)-. English (French and Spanish). ir. $55.00. Soc Mexic de Mecanica Suelos, Valle de Bravo 19 Tlalpan, 14340 Mexico DF Mexico. **Tel** 52 5 677 3730. **CODEN** ESMFA9.
Ind/Abst Soils Fert.

US/0097-2126
PROCEEDINGS OF THE AMERICAN POWER CONFERENCE. [Proc. Am. Power Conf.]. **Main/Conf** American Power Conference. **Added/Corp** Illinois Institute of Technology. (1952)-. Academic Scholarly Publication. English. an (Oct.). $150.00. American Power Conference, Illinois Institute of Technology, Eng One Building, Room 218, Chicago IL 60616. **Tel** (312)567-3406. **LC** TJ5; .A55. **DD** 621/.05. **CODEN** PAPWA2. **[CCC].** Documents available from Article Express International, Ask*IEEE, CASDDS. ***Continues*** *Midwest Power Conference. Proceedings of the Midwest Power Conference.*
Ind/Abst Bioeng. Abstr.; Chem. Abstr.; Coal Abstr.; Ei Page One; Energy Res. Abstr. (June 1980-); Eng. Index Annu.; INSPEC.

US/0097-059X
PROCEEDINGS OF THE HEAT TRANSFER AND FLUID MECHANICS INSTITUTE. [Proc. Heat Transfer Fluid Mech. Inst.]. **Main/Corp** Heat Transfer and Fluid Mechanics Institute. (1960)-. Proceedings. English. be. $40.00. Department for Mechanical Engineering, California State University, 6000 J Street, Sacramento CA 95819. **Tel** (916)278-6624, FAX (916)278-5949. **ED** Fred Reardon. **CODEN** PHTFAK. **Circ:** 250. Documents available from Article Express International, CASDDS. ***Continues*** *Preprints of Papers - Heat Transfer and Fluid Mechanics Institute, 0096-2155.*
Desc: Contains papers presented at the meetings of the Heat Transfer and Fluid Mechanics Institute. Covers vortex shedding and pressure oscillations propulsion systems, pulsating flow in a pump-turbine, atomization in high speeds flows, viscous flow heating of liquids, and dryout of capillary grooves in heat pumps and more.
Ind/Abst Chem. Abstr.; Eng. Index Annu.

•US/1071-1813
PROCEEDINGS OF THE HUMAN FACTORS AND ERGONOMICS SOCIETY ... ANNUAL MEETING. [Proc. Hum. Factors Ergon. Soc. Annu. Meet.]. **Main/Corp** Human Factors and Ergonomics Society. Meeting. (1993)-. Proceedings. English. an. $65.00. Human Factors and Ergonomics Society, PO Box 1369, Journals Department, Santa Monica CA 90406-1369. **Tel** (310)394-1811, (310)394-9793, FAX (310)394-2410. **LC** TA166; .H82a. **DD** 620. **NLM** W1; HU447G. ***Continues*** *Human Factors Society. Proceedings of the Human Factors Society Annual Meeting, 0163-5182.*

US/0163-5182
PROCEEDINGS OF THE HUMAN FACTORS SOCIETY ANNUAL MEETING. ***Title Change.*** [Proc. Hum. Factors Soc. annu. meet.]. **Main/Corp** Human Factors Society. (1974)-(1992). English. Human Factors and Ergonomics Society, PO Box 1369, Journals Department, Santa Monica CA 90406-1369. **Tel** (310)394-1811, (310)394-9793, FAX (310)394-2410. **LC** TA166; .H82a. **DD** 620.8/2/05. **NLM** W1; PR585RV. **CODEN** PHFSDQ. **[CCC].** available on microfilm from University Microfilms International (UMI). Documents available from Article Express International. ***Continues*** *Proceedings of the Annual Meeting of the Human Factors Society, 0363-9797.* ***Continued by*** *Human Factors and Ergonomics Society. Meeting. Proceedings of the Human Factors and Ergonomics Society ... Annual Meeting, 1071-1813.*
Desc: Contains hundreds of papers each year describing current research in the field of ergonomics.
Ind/Abst Eng. Index Annu.

GW
PROCEEDINGS OF THE IFAC WORLD CONGRESS. Main/Corp International Federation of Automatic Control. (19??)-. Proceedings. English. Instrument Society of America, 67 Alexander Drive, Research Triangle NC 27709. **Tel** (919)549-8411, FAX (919)549-8288, telex 802 540. **LC** TJ212; .I537. **DD** 629.8. ***Continues*** *International Federation of Automatic Control. Automatic and Remote Control; Proceedings of the Congress.*

II/0589-3143
PROCEEDINGS OF THE INDIAN SOCIETY OF THEORETICAL AND APPLIED MECHANICS. Main/Conf Congress on Theoretical and Applied Mechanics. **Added/Corp** Indian Institute of Technology, Kharagpur, India. Indian Society of Theoretical and Applied Mechanics. (1955)-. Proceedings. English. an. $25.00. Indian Society of Theoretical and Applied Mechanics, Kharagpur, India. **(Subscription address:** Prints India, 11 Darya Ganj, New Delhi 110002 India.**) LC** TA349; .C6.

UK/0020-3483
PROCEEDINGS OF THE INSTITUTION OF MECHANICAL ENGINEERS. Main/Corp Institution of Mechanical Engineers (Great Britain). Vol. 192, (1978)-. Proceedings. English. qt. $2,329.00 (parts A through J). Mechanical Engineering Publications, PO Box 24, Northgate Avenue, Bury St. Edmunds, Suffolk IP32 6BW England. **Tel** 011 44 284 763277, telex 817376. **(Subscription address:** Mechanical Engineering Publications / Western Hemisphere Subscriptions,

Subscription Office, PO Box 361, Birmingham AL 35201-0361.) **[CCC].** available on microfilm and microfiche from University Microfilms International (UMI). ***Continues*** *Proceedings - Institution of Mechanical Engineers, London.*

UK/0957-6509
PROCEEDINGS OF THE INSTITUTION OF MECHANICAL ENGINEERS. PART A, JOURNAL OF POWER AND ENERGY. **Added/Corp** Institution of Mechanical Engineers (Great Britain). **VFOAT** Journal of Power and Energy. Vol. 204, No. A1 (1990)-. Proceedings. English. qt. $289.00. Mechanical Engineering Publications, PO Box 24, Northgate Avenue, Bury St. Edmunds, Suffolk IP32 6BW England. **Tel** 011 44 284 763277, telex 817376. **(Subscription address:** Mechanical Engineering Publications / Western Hemisphere Subscriptions, Subscription Office, PO Box 361, Birmingham AL 35201-0361.) **CODEN** PMAEET. **[CCC].** available on microfilm and microfiche from University Microfilms International (UMI). Documents available from Article Express International, Ask*IEEE. ***Continues*** *Proceedings of the Institution of Mechanical Engineers. Part A, Journal of Power Engineering, 0954-4046.*
Ind/Abst Appl. Sci. Technol. Index; Eng. Index Annu.; Fluid Abstr., Civil Eng.; Fluid Abstr. Proc. Eng.; FLUIDEX (19??-); INSPEC (1990-); Lit. Pat. Abstr., Oilfield Chem. (1969-1971, 1975-1991); Lit. Abstr., Catal. Catal.; Lit. Abstr., Health Environ.; Lit. Abstr., Pet. Refin. Petrochem.; Lit. Abstr., Pet. Substit.; Lit. Abstr., Transp. Storage; Soc. Sci. Cit. Index [Select. Cov.]; World Ceram. Abstr.

UK/0954-4054
PROCEEDINGS OF THE INSTITUTION OF MECHANICAL ENGINEERS. PART B, JOURNAL OF ENGINEERING MANUFACTURE. [Proc. Inst. Mech. Eng., B J. eng. manuf.]. **VFOAT** Journal of Engineering Manufacture. Vol. 203, No. B1 (1989)-. Proceedings. English. bm. $385.00. Mechanical Engineering Publications, PO Box 24, Northgate Avenue, Bury St. Edmunds, Suffolk IP32 6BW England. **Tel** 011 44 284 763277, telex 817376. **(Subscription address:** Mechanical Engineering Publications / Western Hemisphere Subscriptions, Subscription Office, PO Box 361, Birmingham AL 35201-0361.) **ED** A N Bramley. **LC** TJ1; .P862. **DD** 670.42/05. **CODEN** PIBMEU. **[CCC].** available on microfilm and microfiche from University Microfilms International (UMI). Documents available from Article Express International, The Genuine Article, Ask*IEEE. ***Continues*** *Proceedings of the Institution of Mechanical Engineers. Part B, Management and Engineering Manufacture, 0263-7146.*
Desc: Provides a focus for manufacturing developments by publishing papers covering scientific, technical and managerial aspects of original research, development work and good practice in manufacturing.
Ind/Abst Appl. Sci. Technol. Index; BMT Abstr.; Curr. Contents Eng. Tech. Appl. Sci.; Eng. Index Annu.; Fluid Abstr., Civil Eng.; Fluid Abstr. Proc. Eng.; FLUIDEX (19??-); INSPEC (1989-); Res. Alert [Select. Cov.]; SCISEARCH.

UK/0954-4062
PROCEEDINGS OF THE INSTITUTION OF MECHANICAL ENGINEERS. PART C, JOURNAL OF MECHANICAL ENGINEERING SCIENCE. [Proc. Inst. Mech. Eng. C J. mech. eng. sci.]. **VFOAT** Journal of Mechanical Engineering Science. Vol. 203, No. C1 (1989)-. Proceedings. English. bm. $385.00. Mechanical Engineering Publications, PO Box 24, Northgate Avenue, Bury St. Edmunds, Suffolk IP32 6BW England. **Tel** 011 44 284 763277, telex 817376. **(Subscription address:** Mechanical Engineering Publications / Western Hemisphere Subscriptions, Subscription Office, PO Box 361, Birmingham AL 35201-0361.) **ED** R C Baker. **[CCC].** **Circ:** 1,200. available on microfilm and microfiche from University Microfilms International (UMI). Documents available from Article Express International, The Genuine Article, Ask*IEEE. ***Continues*** *Proceedings of the Institution of Mechanical Engineers. Part C, Mechanical Engineering Science, 0263-7154.*
Desc: Publishes papers which present engineering science solutions to well-defined industrial problems. Offers the practising engineer an improved approach to the design, development and materials aspects of industrial processes and products.
Ind/Abst Appl. Sci. Technol. Index; BMT Abstr.; Civ. Struct. Eng. Abstr.; Curr. Contents Eng. Tech. Appl. Sci.; Eng. Index Annu.; Fluid Abstr., Civil Eng.; Fluid Abstr. Proc. Eng.; FLUIDEX (19??-); INSPEC (1989-); Int. Aerosp. Abstr.; Res. Alert [Full Cov.]; Sci. Cit. Index; SCISEARCH.

UK/0954-4070
PROCEEDINGS OF THE INSTITUTION OF MECHANICAL ENGINEERS. PART D, JOURNAL OF AUTOMOBILE ENGINEERING. **VFOAT** Journal of Automobile Engineering; Proceedings IMECHE. Part D, Journal of Automobile Engineering. Vol. 203, No. D1 (1989)-. Proceedings. English. qt. $289.00. Mechanical Engineering Publications, PO Box 24, Northgate Avenue, Bury St. Edmunds, Suffolk IP32 6BW England. **Tel** 011 44 284 763277, telex 817376. **(Subscription address:** Mechanical Engineering Publications / Western Hemisphere Subscriptions, Subscription Office, PO Box 361, Birmingham AL 35201-0361.) **ED** M Lewis. **LC** TJ1; .P863. **DD** 629.2. **[CCC].** available on microfilm and microfiche from University Microfilms International (UMI). Documents available from Article Express International, Ask*IEEE. ***Continues in part*** *Proceedings of the Institution of Mechanical Engineers. Part D, Transport Engineering, 0265-1904.*
Desc: Papers are concerned with research, design, development, production, operation, servicing and repair of cars, commercial vehicles, public service vehicles, off-highway vehicles and industrial and agricultural tractors.
Ind/Abst Appl. Sci. Technol. Index; BMT Abstr.; Eng. Index Annu.; Fluid Abstr., Civil Eng.; Fluid Abstr. Proc. Eng.; FLUIDEX; Highw. Res. Abstr.; HTFS Dig.; INSPEC (1989-).

UK/0954-4089
PROCEEDINGS OF THE INSTITUTION OF MECHANICAL ENGINEERS. PART E, JOURNAL OF PROCESS MECHANICAL ENGINEERING. [Proc. Inst. Mech. Eng., E J. process mech. eng.]. **VFOAT** Journal of Process Mechanical Engineering. Vol. 203, No. E1 (1989)-. Proceedings. English. Twice a year (January and July). $169.00. Mechanical Engineering Publications, PO Box 24, Northgate Avenue, Bury St. Edmunds, Suffolk IP32 6BW England. **Tel** 011 44 284 763277, telex 817376. **(Subscription address:** Mechanical Engineering Publications / Western Hemisphere Subscriptions, Subscription Office, PO Box 361, Birmingham AL 35201-0361.) **ED** G Thompson. **LC** TS176; .P7286. **DD** 621/.05. **[CCC].** available on microfilm from University Microfilms International (UMI). Documents available from Article Express International, Ask*IEEE.
Desc: Publishes high-quality papers which are of interest to the mechanical engineering discipline embracing health and safety, research and development, design, management, intallation, operation, maintenance and decomissioning.
Ind/Abst Appl. Sci. Technol. Index; Eng. Index Annu.; Fluid Abstr., Civil Eng.; Fluid Abstr. Proc. Eng.; FLUIDEX (19??-); INSPEC (1989-).

UK/0954-4097
PROCEEDINGS OF THE INSTITUTION OF MECHANICAL ENGINEERS. PART F, JOURNAL OF RAIL AND RAPID TRANSIT. [Proc. Inst. Mech. Eng., F J. rail rapid transit]. **Added/Corp** Institution of Mechanical Engineers (Great Britain). **VFOAT** Journal of Rail and Rapid Transit. Vol. 203, No. F1 (1989)-. Proceedings. English. Twice a year (March and September). $169.00. Mechanical Engineering Publications, PO Box 24, Northgate Avenue, Bury St. Edmunds, Suffolk IP32 6BW England. **Tel** 011 44 284 763277, telex 817376. **(Subscription address:** Mechanical Engineering Publications / Western Hemisphere Subscriptions, Subscription Office, PO Box 361, Birmingham AL 35201-0361.) **ED** D J W Souch. **LC** TF1; .P76. **DD** 625.1/005. **CODEN** PMFTEV. **[CCC].** available on microfilm and microfiche from University Microfilms International (UMI). Documents available from Article Express International, Ask*IEEE. ***Continues in part*** *Proceedings of the Institution of Mechanical Engineers. Part D, Transport Engineering, 0265-1904.*
Desc: Covers railway and rapid transit systems and rolling stock.
Ind/Abst Appl. Sci. Technol. Index (1991-); Eng. Index Annu.; INSPEC (1989-).

UK/0954-4100
PROCEEDINGS OF THE INSTITUTION OF MECHANICAL ENGINEERS. PART G, JOURNAL OF AEROSPACE ENGINEERING. **See** Aeronautics, Astronautics.

UK/0959-6518
PROCEEDINGS OF THE INSTITUTION OF MECHANICAL ENGINEERS. PART I, JOURNAL OF SYSTEMS & CONTROL ENGINEERING. **Added/Corp** Institution of Mechanical Engineers (Great Britain). **VFOAT** Journal of Systems and Control Engineering. Vol. 205, No. 1 (1991)-. Proceedings. English. qt. $289.00. Mechanical Engineering Publications, PO Box 24, Northgate Avenue, Bury St. Edmunds, Suffolk IP32 6BW England. **Tel** 011 44 284 763277, telex 817376. **(Subscription address:** Mechanical Engineering Publications / Western Hemisphere Subscriptions, Subscription Office, PO Box 361, Birmingham AL 35201-0361.) **ED** C R Burrows, R Whalley. **LC** TJ5; .P77. **DD** 621.3. **CODEN** PMJEE6. Index available. cum. index. **Bk Rev.** **Pr Rev.** available on microfilm and microfiche from University Microfilms International (UMI). Documents available from Ask*IEEE.
Desc: Provides a unifying framework for a wide range of engineering disciplines and industrial applications. Carries details of forthcoming meetings, a diary of events, and reviews of new books.
Ind/Abst INSPEC (1991-).

●UK/1350-6501
PROCEEDINGS OF THE INSTITUTION OF MECHANICAL ENGINEERS. PART J, JOURNAL OF ENGINEERING TRIBOLOGY. **Added/Corp** Institution of Mechanical Engineers (Great Britain). **VFOAT** Journal of Engineering Tribology; JET. Vol. 208, No. J1 (1994)-. Periodical. English. qt. $289.00. Mechanical Engineering Publications, PO Box 24, Northgate Avenue, Bury St. Edmunds, Suffolk IP32 6BW England. **Tel** 011 44 284 763277, telex 817376. **(Subscription address:** Mechanical Engineering Publications / Western Hemisphere Subscriptions, Subscription Office, PO Box 361, Birmingham AL 35201-0361.) **LC** TJ1075.A2; P76. **CODEN** PEJTET.

US/0036-1313
PROCEEDINGS, OF THE SOCIETY FOR EXPERIMENTAL STRESS ANALYSIS. **Main/Conf** Society for Experimental Stress Analysis. (1943)-. Proceedings. English. an. $100.00. Society for Experimental Mechanics, 7 School Street, Bethel CT 06801-1405. **Tel** (203)790-6373, FAX (203)790-4472. **ED** Meg E. Yergin. Index available. cum. index. **Circ:** 1,000 (ctrl). available on microfilm from University Microfilms International (UMI). ***Continues*** *Eastern Photoelasticity Conference. Proceedings.*
Desc: Original material relevant to experimental solid mechanics.

US
PROCEEDINGS OF THE ... U.S. NATIONAL CONGRESS OF APPLIED MECHANICS. **Main/Conf** U.S. National Congress of Applied Mechanics Mechanics. **Added/Corp** American Society of Mechanical Engineers. U.S. National Committee on Theoretical and Applied Mechanics. **VFOAT** Proceedings of the ... US National Congress of Applied Mechanics. 1st (1951)-. Proceedings. English. Twelve times a year. $92.00. American Society of Mechanical Engineers, 22 Law Drive, Fairfield NJ 07007. **Tel** (201)882-1167, (212)705-7722 (editorial). **LC** TA5; .U52. **DD** 620.1/05.

US/0032-9819
PRODUCTION. [Production]. Vol. 32, No. 2 (Aug. 1953)-. Periodical. English. mo. $144.00 (airmail); $36.00 (US, Canada & Mexico), $72.00 (other) surface mail. Gardner Publications Inc, 6600 Clough Pike, Cincinnati OH 45244. **Tel** (513)231-8020, (513)231-2818, telex 214132. **ED** Robert F Huber. **LC** TJ1180.A1; P7. **DD** 621.9/005. **CODEN** PDTNAG. **[CCC].** **Bk Rev.** **Ad Acc.** **Circ:** 75,000 (ctrl). available on microfilm and microfiche from University Microfilms International (UMI). Documents available from Ask*IEEE, UMI Article Clearinghouse. ***Continues*** *Production Engineering & Management.*
Desc: For key decisionmakers in the metalworking industries. Purpose is to help manufacturing managers and engineering executives interpret, evaluate and implement new technologies, methods and equipment into workable long-term manufacturing strategies.
Ind/Abst ABI/INFORM Glob. Ed.; ABI Inform Ondisc (Aug. 1976-); Acad. Search (Jan. 1993-); Bus. ASAP (1990-) [Full Txt.]; Bus. Index (1985-); F&S Index Plus Text, Int. [Select. Cov.]; Gen. BusinessFile (1985-); Gen. Period. Index (1985-); INSPEC (March 1985-); Mag. Search; Manage. Contents; Oper. Res./Manag. Sci.; PROMT; Qual. Control Appl. Stat.; Robotics Abstr.; Stat. Ref. Index; Trade Ind. ASAP [Full Txt.]; Trade Ind. Index [Full Txt.]; UMI ABI/Inform--Bus. Period. Ondisc (Dec. 1987-) [Full Txt.]; Vocat. Search (Jan. 1993-).

GW
PRODUZIERENDES GEWERBE. REIHE 6.1, BESCHAFTIGUNG, UMSATZ, INVESTITIONEN UND KOSTENSTRUKTUR DER UNTERNEHMEN IN DER ENERGIE UND WASSERVERSORGUNG / HERAUSGEBER STATISTISCHES BUNDESAMT. **Added/Corp** Germany (West). Statistisches Bundesamt. **VFOAT** Beschaftigung, Umsatz, Investitionen und Kostenstruktur der Unternehmen in der Energie- und Wasserversorgung; Facgserue 4. (198?)-. Dutch. an. DM13.00. Metzler Poeschel Verlag Veroeffen, Statist Bundesamt Kernerstr 43, D 70182 Stuttgart Germany. **Tel** 011 49 7071 935350. **(Subscription address:** Metzler Poeschel H Leins GmbH, Postfach 1152, D 72125 Kusterdingen Germany.) **LC** TJ163.25.G3; G49b. ***Continues*** *Germany (West). Statistisches Bundesamt. Produzierendes Gewerbe. Reihe 6.1: Beschaftigung, Umsatz und Unvestitionen der Unternehmen in der Energie- und Wasserversorgung.*

GW
PRODUZIERENDES GEWERBE. REIHE 6.3: KOSTENSTRUKTUR DER UNTERNEHMEN IN DER ENERGIE- UND WASSERVERSORGUNG. ***Suspended.*** **Main/Corp** Germany (West). Statistisches Bundesamt. **Added/Corp** Germany (West). Statistisches Bundesamt. Kostenstruktur der Unternehmen in der Energie- und Wasserversorgung. (1975)-Suspended. German. Metzler

Poeschel Verlag Veroeffen, Statist Bundesamt Kernerstr 43, D 70182 Stuttgart Germany. **Tel** 011 49 7071 935350. **LC** TJ163.25.G3; G49c. ***Continues*** *Unternehmen und Arbeitsstatten. Reihe 1: die Kostenstruktur in der Wirtschaft. I. Industrie und Energiewirtschaft.*

UK/0953-6639
PROFESSIONAL ENGINEERING. [Prof. eng.]. **Added/Corp** Institution of Mechanical Engineers (Great Britain). Vol. 1, No. 1 (May 1988)-. Periodical. English. Twenty-two times a year (twice monthly except once in Jan. and Aug.). $237.00. Mechanical Engineering Publications, PO Box 24, Northgate Avenue, Bury St. Edmunds, Suffolk IP32 6BW England. **Tel** 011 44 284 763277, telex 817376. **(Subscription address:** Mechanical Engineering Publications / Western Hemisphere Subscriptions, Subscription Office, PO Box 361, Birmingham AL 35201-0361.**) LC** TJ1; .I526. **CODEN** PFLEEZ. **[CCC].** Index available. **Bk Rev. Ad Acc. Circ:** 56,000 (ctrl). available on microfilm and microfiche from University Microfilms International (UMI). ***Continues*** *Chartered Mechanical Engineer (London, England : 1977), 0306-9532;* ***Absorbed*** *Engineering News.*
Desc: A multidisciplinary journal which keeps the profession informed of developments in areas as diverse as business and market strategy, control engineering and instrumentation, systems analysis, computing and information systems, human relations, product liability, continuing education and training, factory system economics, financial justification, business systems and strategic planning.
Ind/Abst BMT Abstr. (?-199?); Fluid Abstr., Civil Eng.; Fluid Abstr. Proc. Eng.; FLUIDEX; HTFS Dig.; Leadscan; Manage. Market. Abstr.; Shock Vibr. Dig.

IT/1120-8368
PROFESSIONAL PULIZIE. ***Ceased.*** [Prof. pulizi]. (1991)-(Dec. 1992). Periodical. Italian. Five times a year. Morgan Edizioni Ecniche, Piazzale Archinto 9, 20159 Milan Italy. **Tel** (039)02-48010095, FAX 48010011. **UDC** 648.02. **Bk Rev. Ad Acc. Circ:** 9,000 (ctrl).
Desc: Machines and products for industrial cleaning.

UK/0360-1285
PROGRESS IN ENERGY AND COMBUSTION SCIENCE. **See** Energy.

SP/0214-3135
PROMECANICA BARCELONA.
[Promecanica Barc.]. (1988)-. Periodical. English. Four times a year. 3.500ptas Spain; $47.00 other. Elsevier Prensa SA, Avenida Paral Lel 180, 08015 Barcelona Spain. **Tel** 011 34 3 3255350, FAX 011 34 3 4252880. **UDC** 62.
Desc: An international magazine of machines, tools, mechanical procedures, accessories, products and equipment.

UN/0204-3602
PROMYSLENNAJA TEPLOTEHNIKA.
(PROMYSHLENNAIA TEPLOTEKHNIKA.). [Prom. teploteh.]. **Added/Corp** Akademiia Nauk Ukrainskoi RSR. Viddilennia Fizyko-Tekhnichnykh Problem Energetyky. Vol. 1 (Sept./Oct. 1979)-. Academic Scholarly Publication. Russian (summaries and/or abstracts in English). Six times a year. $161.00. Izdatelstvo Naukova Dumka / Ukrainian Academy of Sciences, Vladimirskaia Ulitsa 54, 252601 Kiev Ukraine. **Tel** 225-63-66, telex 131376. **(Subscription address:** East View Publications Inc., 3020 Harbor Lane North, Suite 110, Minneapolis MN 55447.**) LC** TJ260; .P765. **CODEN** PRTLD9. Documents available from CASDDS.
Desc: Information on heat engineering.
Ind/Abst Chem. Abstr.; Coal Abstr.; Energy Res. Abstr. (Jan. 1982-); Int. Aerosp. Abstr.

SP/0213-6171
PROYECTO 2000. ***Suspended.*** [Proy. 2000]. **VFOAT** Proyecto Dos Mil. (1984)-(1994). Periodical. Spanish. bm. 7500.00ptas Spain. Pulsar SA, Gran Via Corts Catalanes 322 324, 08004 Barcelona Spain. **Tel** 011 34 3 4254544. **UDC** 621.
Ind/Abst LABORDOC.

PL/0033-2259
PRZEGLAD MECHANICZNY. [Przegl. mech.]. **Added/Corp** Stowarzyszenie Inzynierow i Technikow Mechanikow Polskich. **VFOAT** PM. (1935)-. Periodical. Polish (table of contents in English, French and Russian). sm. Price on Request. **(Subscription address:** ARS Polona, PO Box 1001, 00068 Warsaw Poland.**) LC** TJ4; .P75. **CODEN** PPRMDM. Documents available from Article Express International.
Ind/Abst Bioeng. Abstr.; Ceram. Abstr.; Coal Abstr.; Ei Page One; Eng. Index Annu.; Fluid Abstr., Civil Eng.; Fluid Abstr. Proc. Eng.; FLUIDEX (1973-); Saf. Health Work; Surf. Treat. Technol. Abstr.

US/1045-3962
PT DISTRIBUTOR, THE. [PT distrib.]. (198?)-. Periodical. English. Four times a year. $20.00 US; $25.00 Canada; $30.00 Mexico; $35.00 other. Penton Publishing, 1100 Superior Avenue, Cleveland OH 44114-2543. **Tel** (216)696-7000, FAX (216)696-0836. **(Subscription address:** Penton Publishing, PO Box 96732, Chicago IL 60693.**) DD** 621. **CODEN** PTDIE3. **[CCC].** available in microform from University Microfilms International (UMI).

US/0276-2544
PUMPS AND COMPRESSORS. (CURRENT INDUSTRIAL REPORTS. MA-35P, PUMPS AND COMPRESSORS / U.S. DEPARTMENT OF COMMERCE, BUREAU OF THE CENSUS.). [Pumps compress.]. Government Publication. English. an. $1.25. US Department of Commerce, 14th Street & Constitution Avenue NW, Washington DC 20230. **Tel** (202)482-2000, FAX (202)482-3772. **LC** HD9705.5.P853; U636. **DD** 338.4/76215/0973.
Desc: Presents timely data on the production, inventories, and orders of approximately 5,000 products, which represents 40 percent of all US manufacturing.

UK/0302-2870
PUMPS AND OTHER FLUIDS MACHINERY ABSTRACTS. ***Title Change.*** **VFOAT** Pumps Abstracts. (Jan./Feb. 1971)-(19??). English. bm. BHR Group Ltd Brit Hydrom. Research, Cranfield, Bedford MK43 0AJ England. **Tel** 011 44 243 750422, FAX 011 44 243 750074, telex 825059. **LC** TJ900; .P86. **DD** 621.2/52/08. Index available. cum. index. **Bk Rev. Circ:** 250. ***Merged with*** *Fluid Flow Measurements Abstracts, 0305-9235; Fluid Power Abstracts, 0015-4644; Fluid Sealing Abstracts, 0015-4660; Pipelines Abstracts, 0265-3990; Solid-Liquid Flow Abstracts, 0038-1063; Computer-Aided Process Control Abstracts, 0955-4319* ***and*** *Mixing and Separation Technology Abstracts, 0955-7059* ***to form*** *Fluid Abstracts. Process Engineering, 0962-7162.*
Desc: Covers new research and developments relating to industrial pumps and pumping systems, and allied fluids handling machinery such as fans, compressors, and hydraulic turbines.

●US/1065-108X
PUMPS AND SYSTEMS. [Pumps syst.]. **VFOAT** Pumps and Systems Magazine. Vol. 1, No. 1 (Jan. 1993)-. Periodical. English. ir (13 issues). Free to qualified industrial pump users; $60.00 US; $75.00 Canada and Mexico; $195.00 other. AES Marketing Inc., 123 North College Avenue, Suite 260, Fort Collins CO 80524. **Tel** (303)221-2006. **DD** 621.

US/0277-027X
PVP - AMERICAN SOCIETY OF MECHANICAL ENGINEERS. PRESSURE VESSELS AND PIPING DIVISION. (PVP / SPONSORED BY THE PRESSURE VESSELS AND PIPING DIVISION, ASME.). [PVP - Am. Soc. Mech. Eng., Press. Vessels Pip. Div.]. **Added/Corp** American Society of Mechanical Engineers. Pressure Vessels and Piping Division. (19??)-. Academic Scholarly Publication. English. ir. Price varies. American Society of Mechanical Engineers, 22 Law Drive, Fairfield NJ 07007. **Tel** (201)882-1167, (212)705-7722 (editorial). **CODEN** APVPDMAMPPD5. **[CCC].** Documents available from Article Express International, CASDDS.
Ind/Abst Bioeng. Abstr.; Chem. Abstr. (1979-1981); Ei Page One; Eng. Index Annu.

UK/0033-5614
QUARTERLY JOURNAL OF MECHANICS AND APPLIED MATHEMATICS, THE. [Q. j. mech. appl. math.]. Vol. 1 (March 1948)-. Periodical. English. qt. £125.00 UK and Europe; $225.00 other. Oxford University Press, Walton Street, Oxford OX2 6DP England. **Tel** 011 44 865 56767, FAX 011 44 865 267773, telex 837330 OXPRES G. **(Subscription address:** Oxford University Press / USA, Journals Marketing Department, Oxford University Press, 2001 Evans Road, Cary NC 27513.**) ED** A. H. England, L. M. Hocking and R. Shail. **LC** QA1; .Q16. **DD** 510.5. **CODEN** QJMMAV. **[CCC].** Index available. **Ad Acc. Pr Rev. Circ:** 1,100. available on microfilm and microfiche from University Microfilms International (UMI). Documents available from Article Express International, The Genuine Article, Ask*IEEE, CASDDS.
Desc: Original articles in the general field of mechanics, particularly theoretical mechanics (including all branches of the mechanics of fluids and solids), classical electromagnetism, nonlinear dynamics and combined fields such as magnetohydro-numerical methods.
Ind/Abst Acoust. Abstr.; Bioeng. Abstr.; Chem. Abstr.; Compumath Citation Index [Full Cov.]; Curr. Contents Eng. Tech. Appl. Sci.; Curr. Contents Phys. Chem. Earth Sci.; Ei Page One; Eng. Index Annu.; Fluid Abstr., Civil Eng.; Fluid Abstr. Proc. Eng.; FLUIDEX (1973-); HTFS Dig.; INSPEC (Feb. 1971-); Int. Aerosp. Abstr. (19??-19??); Math. Rev.; Res. Alert [Full Cov.]; Sci. Cit. Index; SCISEARCH; World Ceram. Abstr.; Zentralbl. Math. Ihre Grenzgeb.

FR/0373-6601
R.F.M., REVUE FRANCAISE DE MECANIQUE. [RFM. Rev. fr. mec.]. **VFOAT** R.F.M.; Revue Francaise de Mecanique. No. 1 (1962)-. Periodical. French (English). qt. 680.00F (France), 1120.00F (other) non-members; 560.00F (Societe Francaise Mecaniciens members); 340.00F (SFM & or GAMAC France members). Societe Francaise des Mecaniciens, 39 41 rue Louis Blanc, 92400 Courbevoie France. **Tel** 11 33 1 47176489, FAX (1)45 63 59 86, telex 280 900 FEDEMEC. Index available. cum. index. **Circ:** 800 (ctrl). Documents available from Article Express International. ***Formed by the union of*** *S.F.M., Bulletin de la Societe Francaise de Mecaniciens* ***and*** *Analyse des Contraintes.*
Desc: Publishes the results of group study examinations of documents pertaining to scientific and technical topics of mechanical equipment.
Ind/Abst Alum. Ind. Abstr.; Energy Res. Abstr. (Feb. 1976-); Eng. Index Annu.; Int. Aerosp. Abstr.; Met. Abstr.

●US/1061-835X
RANDOM & COMPUTATIONAL DYNAMICS. [Random comput. dyn.]. **VFOAT** Random and Computational Dynamics. Vol. 1, No. 1 (1992)-. Periodical. English. Four times a year. $250.00 US; $264.00 other. Marcel Dekker Inc., 270 Madison Avenue, New York NY 10016. **Tel** (212)696-9000, (800)228-1160, FAX (212)685-4540, telex 421419. **(Subscription address:** Marcel Dekker Inc, PO Box 5017, Monticello NY 12701.**) LC** IN PROCESS; QA614.8; .R36. **DD** 510. **CODEN** RCDYEM.
Desc: Focuses on applied problems in dynamical systems. It will provide a large audience of applied researchers with a home for their works, and enable an even larger audience of academic and industrial scientists working in dynamical systems to find a source to consult and interact with for their own applied problems.
Ind/Abst Math. Rev.

ML
RAPPORT D'ACTIVITIE / CENTRE REGIONAL D'ENERGIE SOLAIRE.
Main/Corp Centre Regional d'Energie Solaire (Bamako, Mali). French. an. Centre Regional d'Energie Solaire, BP 1872, Bamako Mali. **LC** TJ811.5.M35; C45A.

RU
RASCHET PROSTRANSTVENNYKH KONSTRUKTSII; SBORNIK STATEI.
(1950)-. Periodical. Russian. **ED** Editor: 1950- A.A. Umanskii.

US/0272-3506
RECOMMENDED RULES FOR CARE OF POWER BOILERS. [Recomm. rules care power boil.]. **Main/Corp** American Society of Mechanical Engineers. Subgroup on Care of Power Boilers. **VFOAT** ASME Boiler and Pressure Vessel Code, Section VII. English. ASME United Engineering Center, 345 East 47th Street, New York NY 10017. **LC** TJ289; .A6. **DD** 621.1/94/05. ***Continues*** *Suggested Rules for Care of Power Boilers.*

US
RECOMMENDED RULES FOR THE CARE AND OPERATION OF HEATING BOILERS. **Main/Corp** American Society of Mechanical Engineers. Subgroup on Care and Operation of Heating Boilers. 19 -. English. The American Society of Mechanical Engineers, United Engineering Center, 345 East 47th Street, New York NY 10017. **LC** TH7470; .A53. **DD** 621.1/84.

RU/0034-2599
REFERATIVNYJ ZURNAL - VSESOJUZNYJ INSTITUT NAUCNOJ I TEHNICESKOJ INFORMACII. TEHNOLOGIJA MASINOSTROENIJA.
(REFERATIVNYI ZHURNAL : TEKHNOLOGIIA MASHINOSTROENIIA.). [Ref. z. - Vses. inst. naucn. teh. inf., Tehnol. masinostr.]. **Added/Corp** Vsesoiuznyi Institut Nauchnoi Tekhnicheskoi Informatsii (Soviet Union) Institut Nauchnoi Informatsii (Akademiia Nauk SSSR). **VFOAT** Tekhnologiia Mashinostroeniia. (Jan. 1963)-. Abstracting/Indexing Service. Russian. mo. $599.95. VINITI - Vsesoyuznyi Institut Nauchno-Tekhnicheskoi Informatsii, All-Union Scientific and Technical Information Institute, Baltiiskaia Ulitsa 14, 125219 Moscow Russia. **Tel** 238-46-00, FAX 9430060, telex 411160. **(Subscription address:** East View Publications Inc., 3020 Harbor Lane North, Suite 110, Minneapolis MN 55447.**) CODEN** RZTMBK. Documents available from CASDDS. ***Supersedes in part*** *Referativnyi Zhurnal: Mashinostroeniia.*
Ind/Abst Chem. Abstr.

RU/0034-2483
REFERATIVNYJ ZURNAL - VSESOUZNYJ INSTITUT NAUCNOJ I TEHNICESKOJ INFORMACII. MEHANIKA. (REFERATIVNYI ZHURNAL. 16, MEKHANIKA.). [Ref. z. - Vses. inst. naucn. teh. inf., Meh.]. **Added/Corp** Vsesoiuznyi Institut Nauchnoi i Tekhnicheskoi Informatsii (Soviet Union). **VFOAT** Mekhanika. Vol. 1 (1982)-. Abstracting/Indexing Service. Russian (table of contents in English). mo. $599.95. VINITI - Vsesoyuznyi Institut Nauchno-Tekhnicheskoi Informatsii, All-Union Scientific and Technical Information Institute, Baltiiskaia Ulitsa 14, 125219 Moscow Russia. **Tel** 238-46-00, FAX 9430060, telex 411160. **(Subscription address:** East View Publications Inc., 3020 Harbor Lane North, Suite 110, Minneapolis MN 55447.**) LC** QC1; .A41963. Index Available published separately, bound from publisher, free-automatically sent. ***Continues*** *Referativnyi Zhurnal. Mekhanika, 0034-2483.*

GW/0340-3955
REGELUNGSTECHNIK (DUSSELDORF, GERMANY). (REGELUNGSTECHNIK / INFORMATIONSDIENST, VDI.). German. mo. DM980.00. VDI Verlag GmbH, Postfach 101054, D 40001 Dusseldorf Germany. **Tel** 011 49 211 6188313, FAX 011 49 211 6188133. **(Subscription address:** Fulfillment Office, PO Box 1831, Birmingham, AL 35201) **LC** TJ212; .R414. **DD** 629.8/05.

US/1058-2088
REGIONAL INDUSTRIAL BUYING GUIDE. UPSTATE NEW YORK. Added/Corp Thomas Regional Directory Co. **VFOAT** Upstate New York; Upstate New York Regional Industrial Buying Guide. Edition 9 (1991)-. Consumer Publication. English. Thomas Regional Directory Company Inc, 330 West 34th Street, New York NY 10001. ***Continues*** *Regional Industrial Buying Guide. Western/Central New York.*

UK
RENEWABLE ENERGY BULLETIN. A. ***Title Change.*** Vol. 7, No. 1A (Jan./Feb. 1980)-(19??). Periodical. English. bm. Multi Science Publishing Company Ltd., 107 High Street, Brentwood, Essex CM14 4RX England. **Tel** 011 44 277 224632, FAX 011 44 277 223453, telex 89-8452. **LC** Z5853.P83; R463; TJ808. Index available. available on microfiche. ***Continues in part*** *Renewable Energy Bulletin, 0306-364X.* ***Merged with*** *Renewable Energy Bulletin. Part B.* ***to form*** *Renewable Energy Bulletin.*
Desc: Offers abstracts of papers from a wide range of sources on the various aspects of solar energy, including wind energy.

UK
RENEWABLE ENERGY BULLETIN. B. ***Title Change.*** Vol. 7, No. 1B (Jan./Feb. 1980)-(19??). Periodical. English. bm. Multi Science Publishing Company Ltd., 107 High Street, Brentwood, Essex CM14 4RX England. **Tel** 011 44 277 224632, FAX 011 44 277 223453, telex 89-8452. **LC** Z5853.P83; R464; TJ808. Index available. available on microfiche. ***Continues in part*** *Renewable Energy Bulletin, 0306-364X.* ***Merged with*** *Renewable Energy Bulletin. Part A.* ***to form*** *Renewable Energy Bulletin.*
Desc: Offers abstracts on the geothermal, hydro, tidal and ocean, biomass, waste conversion and hydrogen topics.

US/0484-4041
RENTAL RATE BLUE BOOK. Added/Corp Pacific Appraisal Company. National Research Division. **VFOAT** Rental Rate Blue Book for Construction Equipment. (1962/63)-. English. ir. $447.75. K III Press Inc., 424 West 33rd Street, New York NY 10001. **Tel** (212)714-3100, (800)221-5488. **LC** TA213; .R4. **DD** 690.

US/0569-8243
REPORT ON DIESEL AND GAS ENGINES POWER COSTS. Main/Corp American Society of Mechanical Engineers. English. The American Society of Mechanical Engineers, United Engineering Center, 345 East 47th Street, New York NY 10017. **LC** TJ164; .A52. **DD** 338.4/562/1312133. ***Supersedes*** *Report on Oil and Gas Engine Power Costs.*

JA/0916-2879
REPORTS OF THE INSTITUTE OF FLUID SCIENCE, TOHOKU UNIVERSITY. [Rep. Inst. Fluid Sci., Tohoku Univ.]. **Added/Corp** Tohoku Daigaku. Ryutai Kagaku Kenkyujo. **VFOAT** Tohoku Daigaku Kenkyujo Hokoku. Kogaku. Vol. 1, No. 1 (1990)-. Periodical. English. ir (approximately 2 per year). Institute of Fluid Science, Tohoku University, Katahira 2 Chome, Sendaishi Miyagiken 980 Japan. **Tel** 011 81 22 227-6200 ext. 2430. **ED** S. Kamiyama. **LC** TA357; .R45. **DD** 620.1/06. **CODEN** RIFUES. cum. index. **Circ:** 1,300 (ctrl). Documents available from Ask*IEEE. ***Continues*** *Reports of the Institute of High Speed Mechanics, Tohoku University, 0370-5315.*
Ind/Abst INSPEC (1990-).

SP/0212-3754
REVISTA DE ROBOTICA. ***Title Change.*** [Rev. rob.]. (1982)-(1993). Periodical. Spanish. Ten times a year. Pulsar SA, Gran Via Corts Catalanes 322 324, 08004 Barcelona Spain. **Tel** 011 34 3 4254544. **UDC** 621-52. ***Continued by*** *Automatizacion Integrada y Revista de Robotica.*

SW
REVUE DES ROULEMENTS, LA. Added/Corp SKF (Firm). (19??)-. French. ir. Aktiebolaget Svenska Kullagerfabriken, S-415 50, Goteburg Sweden. **LC** TJ1071; .R47. **DD** 621.8/22/05.

FR/0181-0529
REVUE FRANCAISE DE GEOTECHNIQUE. See Earth Sciences-Geology.

FR/0035-3159
REVUE GENERALE DE THERMIQUE. [Rev. gen. therm.]. Vol. 1, No. 1 (Jan. 1962)-. Academic Scholarly Publication. French (English). mo. 2840.00F France; 3400F other. Edicion Europeenes Thermique et Industrie, 3 rue Henry Heine, 75016 Paris France. **Tel** 011 33 1 44304176. **CODEN** RGTHA7. **[CCC]. Bk Rev. Pr Rev. Circ:** 1,200. Documents available from Article Express International, The Genuine Article, Ask*IEEE, CASDDS. ***Formed by the union of*** *Chaleur et Industrie and Flamme et Thermique.*
Desc: Specializes in the questions connected with fuels and various kinds of energy, thermodynamics and thermic equipment; pollution at least.
Ind/Abst Alum. Ind. Abstr.; Bioeng. Abstr.; Ceram. Abstr. (19??-); Chem. Abstr.; Coal Abstr.; Curr. Contents Eng. Tech. Appl. Sci.; Ei Page One; Energy Res. Abstr.; Eng. Mater. Abstr.; Eng. Index Annu.; Fluid Abstr., Civil Eng.; Fluid Abstr. Proc. Eng.; FLUIDEX (1973-); Gas Abstr. (?-?); HTFS Dig.; INSPEC (May 1970-); Int. Aerosp. Abstr.; Int. Build. Serv. Abstr.; Met. Abstr.; Proc. Chem. Eng.; Res. Alert [Full Cov.]; Saf. Health Work; Theoret. Chem. Eng.

RM
REVUE ROUMAINE DE MECANIQUE APPLIQUE. (199?)-. Multiple languages (English, French, Spanish, German and Russian). $150.00. **(Subscription address:** Rompresfilatelia, PO Box 12 201, Bucharest Romania.) ***Continues*** *Revue Roumaine des Sciences Techniques Serie de Mecanique Applique, 0035-4074.*
Desc: Information on applied mechanics.

RM/0035-4074
REVUE ROUMAINE DES SCIENCES TECHNIQUES. SERIE DE MECANIQUE APPLIQUEE. ***Title Change.*** **Added/Corp** Academia Republicii Populare Romine. Institutul de Mecanica Aplicata. "Traian Vuia". **VFOAT** Serie de Mecanique Appliquee. Vol. 1 (1956)-(19??). Periodical. Multiple languages (French, English, German, Russian and Spanish). bm. **(Subscription address:** Rompresfilatelia, PO Box 12 201, Bucharest Romania.) **LC** TA349; .A234. Documents available from Ask*IEEE. ***Supersedes in part*** *Revue des Sciences Techniques* ***and*** *Academia Republicii Populare Romine. Science dans la Republique Populaire Roumaine.* ***Continued by*** *Revue Roumaine de Mecanique Applique.*
Desc: Publishes studies on applied mechanics.
Ind/Abst Acoust. Abstr.; Appl. Mech. Rev.; Ei Page One; Eng. Mater. Abstr.; GeoRef; INSPEC (1968-); Int. Aerosp. Abstr.; Math. Rev.; Zentralbl. Math. Ihre Grenzgeb.

IT/0035-6301
RIVISTA DI MECCANICA. [Riv. mec.]. (19??)-. Periodical. Italian. bw. L132000.00 Italy; L250000.00 other. Etas SRL, Via Mecenate 89, 20138 Milan Italy. **Tel** 011 39 2 580841. **CODEN** RVMCAS. **Ad Acc.**
Desc: Articles by technicians and managers from Italian mechanical industry update readers on research, industry and manufacturing plans, and new frontiers in automation. Includes relevant articles from non-Italian periodicals.
Ind/Abst CIS Abstr.; Fluid Abstr., Civil Eng.; Fluid Abstr. Proc. Eng.; FLUIDEX (1973-); Saf. Health Work.

US/0730-0891
ROCKY MOUNTAIN ENERGY DIRECTORY. See Energy.

RM
ROMANIAN ENGINEERING. Added/Corp Camera de Comert a Republicii Socialiste Romania. No. 1 (1966)-. Periodical. English. ir. DM212.00. **(Subscription address:** Kubon & Sagner, ABT Zeitschriftenimport, D 80328 Munich Germany.) **LC** TJ1; .R6.
Desc: Papers in the field of technique, industry, cooperation, and foreign trade.

●US/1068-798X
RUSSIAN ENGINEERING RESEARCH. Vol. 12, No. 1 (1992)-. Periodical. English (translations available in Russian). Twelve times a year. $915.00 US and Canada; $650.00 UK; $990.00 other. Allerton Press, Inc., 150 Fifth Avenue, New York NY 10011. **Tel** (212)924-3950, FAX (212)463-9684, telex 427441 ALPRES. **LC** TJ1; .S67. **DD** 621/.05. **[CCC].** ***Continues*** *Soviet Engineering Research, 0144-6622.*
Ind/Abst Fluid Abstr., Civil Eng.; Fluid Abstr. Proc. Eng.; FLUIDEX (19??-).

●RU/1061-7566
RUSSIAN JOURNAL OF COMPUTATIONAL MECHANICS. [Russ. j. comput. mech.]. **VFOAT** A.RJCM. (1992)-. Periodical. English. qt. $340.00 US; $380.00 Canada and Mexico; $395.00 other. John Wiley & Sons Ltd., Baffins Lane, Chichester West Sussex PO19 1UD England. **Tel** 0243 779777, FAX 0243 776128 BTG:JWP001, telex 86290 WIBOOKG. **(Subscription address:** John Wiley / Philadelphia, PO Box 7247, Philadelphia PA 19170.) **ED** Academician O. M. Belotserkovskii. **LC** IN PROCESS. **DD** 530. **CODEN** RJCMEU.
Desc: Provides a forum for rapid publication of original scientific works in the field of computational mechanics and its applications.

●US/1068-3720
RUSSIAN JOURNAL OF HEAVY MACHINERY. [Russ. j. heavy mach.]. No. 1 (1993)-. Periodical. English (translations available in Russian). mo. $925.00. Allerton Press, Inc., 150 Fifth Avenue, New York NY 10011. **Tel** (212)924-3950, FAX (212)463-9684, telex 427441 ALPRES. **LC** TJ163.9; .S68. **DD** 621. **[CCC].** ***Continues*** *Tiazheloe Mashinostroenie (Moscow, Russia : 1990). English. Soviet Journal of Heavy Machinery, 1052-6196.*

●US/1061-8309
RUSSIAN JOURNAL OF NONDESTRUCTIVE TESTING. Added/Corp Consultants Bureau. (Sept. 1992)-. Academic Scholarly Publication. English (translations available in Russian). mo. $1430.00 US; $1675.00 other. Consultants Bureau, A Division of Plenum Publishing Corporation, 233 Spring Street, New York NY 10013. **Tel** (212)620-8000, (212)620-8466, FAX (212)463-0742, telex 23/421139. **LC** TA417.2; .S65. **DD** 620. **CODEN** RJNTE4. **[CCC].** Documents available from Article Express International, The Genuine Article, Ask*IEEE, CASDDS. ***Continues*** *Soviet Journal of Nondestructive Testing, 0038-5492.*
Ind/Abst Appl. Mech. Rev. (1992-); Bioeng. Abstr. (1992-); Chem. Abstr. (1992-); Ei Page One (1992-); Energy Res. Abstr. (1992-); Eng. Index Annu.; INSPEC (1992-); Int. Aerosp. Abstr. (1992-); Met. Abstr. (1992-); Pollut. Abstr. Indexes (1992-); Res. Alert [Full Cov.].

US/0148-7191
SAE TECHNICAL PAPER SERIES. [SAE tech. pap. ser.]. **Added/Corp** Society of Automotive Engineers. **VAT** Society of Automotive Engineers Technical Paper Series. (197?)-. Monographic series. English. an. $895.00. Society of Automotive Engineers, 400 Commonwealth Drive, Warrendale PA 15096. **Tel** (412)776-4841, (412)772-7106, FAX (412)776-5760. **DD** 629. **CODEN** STPSDN. **[CCC].** Documents available from Article Express International. ***Continues*** *Society of Automotive Engineers. Society of Automotive Engineers Technical Paper Series, 0740-6975.*
Ind/Abst Agric. Eng. Abstr.; Bioeng. Abstr.; Ei Page One; Eng. Index Annu.; Hortic. Abstr.; Lit. Pat. Abstr., Oilfield Chem.; Lit. Abstr., Catal. Catal.; Lit. Abstr., Health Environ.; Lit. Abstr., Pet. Refin. Petrochem.; Lit. Abstr., Pet. Substit.; Lit. Abstr., Transp. Storage; Postharvest News Inf.

JA
SANSHAIN KEIKAKU NYUSU. Added/Corp Kogyo Gijutsuin (Japan). Sanshain Keikaku Suishin Hombu. (19??)-. Periodical. Japanese. ¥500. Kogyo Gijutsuin, (Agency of Industrial Science and Technology), 3-1 Kasumigaseki 1 chome, Chiyodaku Tokyoto 100 Japan. **LC** TJ163.13; .S25.

XR
SBORNIK VEDECKYCH PRACI VYSOKE SKOLY BANSKE V OSTRAVE. RADA STROJNICKA. VFOAT Rada Strojni; Doklady Ostravskogo Gorno- Metallurgicheskogo Instituta. Seriia Mashinostroitelnaia; Transactions of the Institute of Mining and Metallurgy Ostrava. Engineering Series; Rada Strojni a Elektrotechnicaa. Vol. 12, No. 1 (1966)-. Czech (summaries and/or abstracts in English, German and Russian). an. Ustredni Knihovna Studijno Informa Nal Centrum, Vysoke Skoly Banske, Studeniska Ul 1770, Ostrava-Poruba Czech Republic. **LC** TJ4. ***Continues in part*** *Sbornik Vedeckych Praci.*
Ind/Abst MINPROC; Mintec, Min. Technol. Abstr.

PL
SERIA MONOGRAFIE - POLITECHNIKA WROCAWSKA, INSTYTUT CYBERNETYKI TECHNICZNEJ. Main/Corp Politechnika Wrocawska. Instytut Cybernetyki Technicznej. **VFOAT** Monografie - Politechnika Wrocawska, Instytut Cybernetyki Technicznej. Monographic series. Polish (summaries and/or abstracts in English and Russian). Price varies per volume. **(Subscription address:** ARS Polona, PO Box 1001, 00068 Warsaw Poland.) **LC** TJ212; .B74 subser.

PL/0324-9611
SERIA STUDIA I MATERIAY - POLITECHNIKA WROCAWSKA, INSTYTUT MATEMATYKI. See Mathematics.

SI
SERIES IN THEORETICAL AND APPLIED MECHANICS. Vol. 1 (1985)-. Monographic series. English. Price varies per volume. World Scientific Publishing Company, PO Box 128, Farrer Road, Singapore 9128 Singapore. **Tel** 011 65 3825663, FAX 011 65 3825919, telex RS 28561 WSPC.
Ind/Abst Math. Rev.; Zentralbl. Math. Ihre Grenzgeb.

US/0583-1024
SHOCK AND VIBRATION DIGEST, THE. See Engineering-Abstracting, Bibliographies and Statistics.

US/0583-1032
SHOCK AND VIBRATION MONOGRAPH SERIES. Added/Corp Shock and Vibration Information Center. No. 1 (1968)-. Monographic series. English. ir. Price varies per volume. Shock & Vibration Information Center, Washington DC. **ED** Gordon Showalter. **Circ:** 1,500 (ctrl).
Desc: State of the art books on specific topics of interest to the shock and vibration community.

CN/0381-8667
SHOP (DON MILLS). ***Ceased.*** (SHOP.). (1???)-(Aug. 1993). Periodical. English. Twelve times a year. Pace Publishing Ltd, 150 Lakeshore Road West, Suite 36 Mississauga, Ontario L5H 3R2 Canada. **Tel** (905)274-4883, FAX (905)274-8686. **ED** Gordon Froggatt. **Ad Acc, Adv Mgr:** M. C. Figurel, **Tel** 274-4883. **Circ:** 18,000 (ctrl).
Desc: Provides its readers with up-to-date information on the used machinery industry. It also carries writeups on new and improved industrial products. Readership is composed of buying influences in all types of plants.

CN/0317-7130
SM PAPER. (PAPER - SOLID MECHANICS DIVISION, UNIVERSITY OF WATERLOO.). **VFOAT** SM Paper. **VAT** Solid Mechanics Paper. Began with: No. 101? Jan. 1972. Monographic series. English. Price varies per volume. Solid Mechanics Division University of Waterloo, Waterloo Ontario N2L 3G1 Canada. **Tel** (519)885-1211 ext. 3351. **DD** 620.1/05. ***Continues*** *Report (University of Waterloo. Solid Mechanics Division: 1969), 0317-7122.*

CN/0317-7114
SM REPORT (BLUE SERIES). (REPORT - SOLID MECHANICS DIVISION, UNIVERSITY OF WATERLOO.). **VFOAT** S M Report. No. 15- ; Jan. 1972-. Monographic series. English. Price varies per volume. Solid Mechanics Division University of Waterloo, Waterloo Ontario N2L 3G1 Canada. **Tel** (519)885-1211 ext. 3351. **DD** 620.1/05. ***Continues*** *Technical Report (University of Waterloo. Solid Mechanics Division), 0317-7106.*

US
SMALL AIR COOLED ENGINES SERVICE MANUAL. **Added/Corp** Intertec Publishing Corporation. Technical Publications Division. **VFOAT** Small Air-cooled Engines; Small Engines. **VAT** Small Air Cooled Engines; Small Air-cooled Engines Service Manual. 13th Ed. (1981)-. Periodical. English. ir. Intertec Publishing Corporation, 9800 Metcalf, Overland Park KS 66212. **Tel** (913)341-1300. **(Subscription address:** Intertec Publishing Corporation, PO Box 2901, Overland Park KS 66282.**)** **LC** TJ766.7; .S63. **DD** 621.43.

US/0038-0741
SOIL MECHANICS AND FOUNDATION ENGINEERING. [Soil mech. found. eng.]. **Added/Corp** Consultants Bureau. Consultants Bureau Enterprises. Vol. 1 (Jan./Feb. 1964)-. Academic Scholarly Publication. English (Russian; translations available in Russian). Six times a year. $1145.00 US; $1340.00 other. Consultants Bureau, A Division of Plenum Publishing Corporation, 233 Spring Street, New York NY 10013. **Tel** (212)620-8000, (212)620-8466, FAX (212)463-0742, telex 23/421139. **ED** A. Kh Slavorosov. **LC** TA710.A1; O813. **CODEN** SMFEAF. **[CCC].** Index available. available on microfilm and microfiche from University Microfilms International (UMI). Documents available from Article Express International, CASDDS.
Desc: This journal provides the western grower with a look at Soviet advances in heavy construction techniques. Provides general rules for soil analysis and foundation design.
Ind/Abst Appl. Mech. Rev.; Bioeng. Abstr.; Chem. Abstr.; Ei Page One; Eng. Index Annu.; GeoRef; Geotech. Abstr.; J. Plan. Lit.; Pollut. Abstr. Indexes; Soils Fert.

NE/0925-0042
SOLID MECHANICS AND ITS APPLICATIONS. [Solid mech. appl.]. (1990)-. Monographic series. English. ir. Price varies per volume. Kluwer Academic Publishers, Postbus 322, 3300 AH Dordrecht, The Netherlands. **Tel** 011 (31) 78 524400, FAX 011 31 78 183273, telex 20083. **(Subscription address:** Kluwer Academic Publishers / US Subscriptions, PO Box 253, Accord Station, Hingham MA 02018.**)** **UDC** 531.
Ind/Abst Zentralbl. Math. Ihre Grenzgeb.

SA/0036-0848
SOUTH AFRICAN MACHINE TOOL REVIEW. [S. Afr. Mach. Tool Rev.]. (1968)-. Periodical. English. Twelve times a year. R102.60 South Africa; R120.00 APU countries; R140.00 other. George Warman Publications Pty, PO Box 704, Cape Town 8000 South Africa. **Tel** 011 27 21 245320, FAX 011 27 21 261332, telex 5-21849. **DD** 621.902. **Ad Acc. Circ:** 4,500 (ctrl).

SA/0038-2442
SOUTH AFRICAN MECHANICAL ENGINEER, THE. [S. Afr. mech. eng.]. **Added/Corp** South African Institution of Mechanical Engineers. (1955)-. Periodical. English. mo (11 issues per year). R160.00 South Africa; R190.00 other. Promech Publishing, PO Box 85502, Emmaretia 2029, South Africa. **Tel** 011 27 11 8884047. **LC** TJ1; .S58. **CODEN** SAMEAY. ***Continues*** *South African Institution of Mechanical Engineers Journal -South African Institution of Mechanical Engineers.*

US/0038-5298
SOVIET APPLIED MECHANICS. ***Title Change.*** [Sov. appl. mech.]. Periodical. English (translations available in Russian). mo. Plenum Press, 233 Spring Street, New York NY 10013-1578. **Tel** (212)620-8000, (800)221-9369, FAX (212)463-0742, (212)807-1047, telex 23/421139. **ED** A N Guz'. **LC** TA349. **DD** 620.1/005. **CODEN** SOAMBT. **[CCC].** Index available. **Pr Rev.** available on microfilm and microfiche from University Microfilms International (UMI). Documents available from Article Express International, Ask*IEEE, CASDDS. ***Continued by*** *International Applied Mechanics.*
Desc: Areas of interest include non-linear oscillations, stress concentrations around openings and thermal stresses. Deals with practical problems encountered by mechanical engineers working in aviation, shipbuilding, turbo machinery and construction industries.
Ind/Abst Appl. Mech. Rev.; Bioeng. Abstr.; Chem. Abstr.; Coal Abstr.; Ei Page One; Eng. Index Annu.; INSPEC (Jan. 1971-); Int. Aerosp. Abstr.; Math. Rev.; Sci. Cit. Index (19??-19??); SCISEARCH; Zentralbl. Math. Ihre Grenzgeb.

UK
SOVIET INVENTIONS ILLUSTRATED. SECTIONS P, Q: GENERAL/MECHANICAL. **VFOAT** General/Mechanical. (Jan. 12, 1977)-. Periodical. English. ir. price varies per volume. Derwent Publications Ltd., Derwent House 14, Great Queen Street, London WC2B 5DF England. **Tel** 011 44 71 3442800. ***Continues*** *Soviet Inventions Illustrated. Part II: Mechanical & General.*
Desc: Abstracts of soviet patent and author's certificates.

US/1052-6196
SOVIET JOURNAL OF HEAVY MACHINERY. ***Title Change.*** (TIAZHELOE MASHIOSTROENIE.). [Sov. j. heavy mach.]. **VFOAT** Tyazheloe Mashinostroenie. (1990)-(199?). Periodical. English (translations available in Russian). bm. Allerton Press, Inc., 150 Fifth Avenue, New York NY 10011. **Tel** (212)924-3950, FAX (212)463-9684, telex 427441 ALPRES. **LC** TJ163.9; .S68. **DD** 621. **[CCC].** ***Continues*** *Soviet Energy Technology, 0734-1024.* ***Continued by*** *Russian Journal of Heavy Machinery.*

NE
SOVIET JOURNAL ON STRUCTURAL MECHANICS AND DESIGN OF STRUCTURES. **See** Engineering-Civil Engineering.

US/0888-689X
SOVIET MATERIALS SCIENCE REVIEWS. ***Ceased.*** [Sov. mater. sci. rev.]. Periodical. English. Four times a year. Taylor & Francis Ltd., Rankine Road, Basingstoke Hampshire, RG24 8PR United Kingdom. **Tel** 011 44 256 840366, FAX 011 44 256 479438, telex 858540. **(Subscription address:** Taylor & Francis Inc., 1900 Frost Road, Suite 101, Bristol PA 19007-1598.**)** **ED** Vladimir Zilberstein. **CODEN** SMSREL. **[CCC].** Index available. **Bk Rev. Ad Acc. Circ:** 150. available on microfilm from University Microfilms International (UMI).
Desc: Covering advances in materials science spanning metallurgy, properties, and composite materials. The scope of this publication also includes production methods for materials and final products, as well as authoritative contributions treating special materials such as refactories, ceramics, and high-alloy steels.

SZ/0275-7893
SOVIET TECHNOLOGY REVIEWS. SECTION A, ENERGY REVIEWS. ***Ceased.*** **See** Energy.

IT
SPECIALISTA. (19??)-. Italian. Eleven times a year. L50000 Italy; L100000 other. Ansid Editoriale Srl, Viale Monte Ceneri 58, 20155 Milan Italy. **Tel** 011 39 2 39215800.

●US/1068-8005
ST. PETERSBURG UNIVERSITY MECHANICS BULLETIN. **Added/Corp** Sankt-Peterburgskii Universitet. **VFOAT** Saint Petersburg University Mechanics Bulletin; Vestnik Sankt-Peterburgskogo universiteta. Mekhanika. No. 1 (1992)-. Bulletin. English. Four times a year. $520.00. Allerton Press, Inc., 150 Fifth Avenue, New York NY 10011. **Tel** (212)924-3950, FAX (212)463-9684, telex 427441 ALPRES. **[CCC].** ***Continues*** *Leningrad University Mechanics Bulletin, 0883-623X.*

US/1051-2136
STAFDA ... DIRECTORY. **See** Economics-Industry and Production.

NE/0168-3578
STOOMKETEK- EN KRACHTWERKTUIGENINDUSTRIE / CENTRAAL BUREAU VOOR DE STATISTITEK, HOOFDAFDELING STATISTIEKEN VAN INDUSTRIE EN BOUWNIFVERHEID. **VFOAT** Manufacture of Steamboilers, Engines, and Turbines. 1981-. Dutch (summaries and/or abstracts in English). an. Fl8.00. Centraal Bureau voor de Statistiek, AFD ALG Zaken, Postbus 959, 2270 AZ Voorburg Netherlands. **Tel** 011 31 70 3373800, FAX 011 31 038 7429, telex 32692 CBS NL. **LC** HD9529.B6; N416. ***Continues*** *Netherlands. Centraal Bureau Voor de Statistiek. Produktiestatistieken: Stoomketel- en Krachtwerktuigenindustrie.*

UK/0039-2103
STRAIN. [Strain]. **Added/Corp** British Society for Strain Measurement. Vol. 1 (Jan. 1965)-. Periodical. English. Four times a year (Feb., May, Aug., Nov.). £55.00 UK; £64.00 other. British Society for Strain Measurement / Department of Civil Engineering, University of Surrey, Guildford GU2 5XH England. **Tel** 011 44 483 509214, FAX 011 44 483 300803. **ED** R. Royles and G. Buckley. **CODEN** STRNBG. Index Available in first issue of next volume--loose--separately paged. cum. index. **Bk Rev. Ad Acc. Circ:** 1,850 (ctrl). Documents available from Article Express International, Ask*IEEE.
Desc: Strain and stress measurement and analysis using strain gauges, transducers and other engineering measurements to assist product design evaluation and test.
Ind/Abst Alum. Ind. Abstr.; Appl. Mech. Rev.; Bioeng. Abstr.; Curr. Technol. Index; Ei Page One; Eng. Mater. Abstr.; Eng. Index Annu.; Highw. Res. Abstr.; INSPEC (1968-); Int. Aerosp. Abstr.; Met. Abstr.; Life Sci. Collect.; World Ceram. Abstr.

US/0039-2316
STRENGTH OF MATERIALS. [Strength mater.]. **Added/Corp** Consultants Bureau. (July 1969)-. Periodical. English (translations available in Russian). mo. $1430.00 US; $1675.00 other. Consultants Bureau, A Division of Plenum Publishing Corporation, 233 Spring Street, New York NY 10013. **Tel** (212)620-8000, (212)620-8466, FAX (212)463-0742, telex 23/421139. **ED** V. T. Troshchenko. **LC** TA405; .P752. **DD** 620. **CODEN** SMTLB5. **[CCC].** Index available. available on microfilm and microfiche from University Microfilms International (UMI). Documents available from Ask*IEEE, CASDDS.
Ind/Abst Appl. Mech. Rev.; Ceram. Abstr. (19??-); Chem. Abstr.; INSPEC (Jan. 1972-); Int. Aerosp. Abstr.; Pollut. Abstr. Indexes.

XR
STROJIRENSKA VYROBA. Czech. mo. Artiia Foreign Trade Corp, Ve Smeckach 30 111 27, Prague 1 Czech Republic. **Tel** 011 42 2 246041.
Ind/Abst Fluid Abstr., Civil Eng.; Fluid Abstr. Proc. Eng.; FLUIDEX.

XR/0039-2464
STROJIRENSTVI. [Strojirenstvi]. Began 1951. Academic Scholarly Publication. Czech (summaries and/or abstracts in English and Russian). mo. **(Subscription address:** Artia Pegas Press Ltd., Palac Metro Narodni Trida 25, 11210 Prague 1 Czech Republic.**)** **CODEN** STRJA3. Documents available from CASDDS.
Ind/Abst Alum. Ind. Abstr.; Chem. Abstr.; Eng. Mater. Abstr.; Met. Abstr.; Saf. Health Work.

GW/0934-4373
STRUCTURAL OPTIMIZATION. [Struct. optim.]. Vol. 1, No. 1 (1989)-. Periodical. English. Eight times a year. DM796.00. Springer-Verlag GmbH & Company KG, Heidelberger Platz 3, D 14197 Berlin Germany. **Tel** 011 49 30 8207223, FAX 011 49 30 8214091, telex 183 319 SPBLN D. **(Subscription address:** Springer Verlag New York Inc. / for North America, 44 Hartz Way, Secaucus NJ 07096.**)** **ED** G Rozvany. **LC** TA658.8; .S77. **DD** 620/.0042. **CODEN** SOPTEQ. **[CCC].** available in microform from University Microfilms International (UMI). Documents available from The Genuine Article, Ask*IEEE.
Desc: Deals with the optimal design of all systems that consist, at least partially, of solids and are subject to stresses and/or deformations.
Ind/Abst Curr. Contents Eng. Tech. Appl. Sci.; INSPEC (Mar. 1990-); Res. Alert [Select. Cov.].

US
STUDIES IN APPLIED MECHANICS. Vol. 1 (1979)-. Monographic series. English. ir. Price varies per volume. Elsevier Science Publishing Company Inc, Madison Square Station, PO Box 882, New York NY 10159-0882. **Tel** (212)633-3950, FAX (212)633-3990.
Ind/Abst Zentralbl. Math. Ihre Grenzgeb.

SZ
SULZER TECHNICAL REVIEW (1985). (SULZER TECHNICAL REVIEW.). Vol. 67 (1985)-. Academic Scholarly Publication. English. bm. 60.00F Switzerland; 72.00F other. Swiss Book Center / Schweizer Buchzentrum, Postfach 522, CH 4600 Olten 1 Switzerland. **Tel** 011 41 62 476161. Documents available from Article Express International, Ask*IEEE, CASDDS. ***Absorbed*** *Sulzer Technical Review, Escher Wyss News.*
Ind/Abst Abstr. Bull. Inst. Pap. Sci. Tech.; Chem. Abstr.; Chem. Hazards Ind.; Curr. Biotechnol.; Dairy Sci. Abstr.; Ei Page One; Energy Inf. Abstr.; Eng. Index Annu.; Fluid Abstr., Civil Eng.; Fluid Abstr. Proc. Eng.; FLUIDEX; INSPEC (1969-); Int. Build. Serv. Abstr.; Lab. Hazards Bull.; Pap. Board Abstr.; Proc. Chem. Eng.; Text. Technol. Dig.; Theoret. Chem. Eng.

US/0039-615X
SURPLUS RECORD, THE. (19??)-. Periodical. English. Twelve times a year. $30.00 US; $35.00 Canada and Mexico; $75.00 other. Surplus Record Subscriptions, 20 North Wacker Drive, Chicago IL 60606. **Tel**

(312)372-9077, FAX (312)372-6537, telex 270-119. **LC** TJ1; .S875. **DD** 681/.76/029473. **Ad Acc. Adv Mgr Tel** (312)372-9077. **Circ:** 120,000 (ctrl). ***Continues*** *Surplus Record and Index.*
Desc: Exclusively devoted to advertising surplus capital equipment.

US/0894-9859
SYSTEMS PRACTICE. See Computers-Computer Systems.

US/0073-5264
T.& A.M. REPORT. [T.A.M. rep.]. **Added/Corp** University of Illinois at Urbana-Champaign. Dept. of Theoretical and Applied Mechanics. **VFOAT** T & AM Report. **VAT** Theoretical and Applied Mechanics Report. No. 1 (1946)-. Monographic series. English. ir. Price varies per volume. University of Illinois / Engineering, 208 Engineering Hall, Urbana IL 61801. **Tel** (217)333-1510. **DD** 530; 620. **CODEN** ITAMCN. Documents available from Article Express International.
Ind/Abst Bioeng. Abstr.; Ei Page One; Eng. Index Annu.

•CH
TAI-WAN PAO CHUANG CHI HSIEH PIEN LAN. See Packaging.

US/0191-0841
TECHNICAL PAPER - SOCIETY OF MANUFACTURING ENGINEERS. EE. [Tech. pap. - Soc. Manuf. Eng.]. **Main/Corp** Society of Manufacturing Engineers. Academic Scholarly Publication. English. $625.00. Society of Manufacturing Engineers, One SME Drive, PO Box 930, Member's Records Dept., Dearborn MI 48121-0930. **Tel** (313)271-1500, FAX (313)271-2861, telex 297742 SME UR (VIA RCA). **CODEN** STPEDF. Documents available from Article Express International, CASDDS.
Desc: Conference papers on new research and applications in manufacturing technology. Over 700 papers yearly on a variety of topics.
Ind/Abst Bioeng. Abstr.; Chem. Abstr. (1976-1977); Ei Page One; Eng. Index Annu.

CN/0082-5182
TECHNICAL PUBLICATION SERIES - DEPARTMENT OF MECHANICAL ENGINEERING, UNIVERSITY OF TORONTO. Main/Corp University of Toronto. Dept. of Mechanical Engineering. Began publication in 1962?. Monographic series. English. Price varies per volume. University of Toronto Department of Mechanical Engineering, Front Campus, Toronto Ontario M5S 7A6 Canada. **DD** 621. **CODEN** TMEPAK. Documents available from Article Express International.
Ind/Abst Ei Page One; Eng. Index Annu.

XR/0231-5297
TECHNICKE PRIUCKY (STATNI VYZKUMNY USTAV PRO STAVBU STROJU). (TECHNICKE PRIUCKY.). [Tech. priucky - Statni vyzk. ust. stavbu stroju Praha-Bechovice]. Began in 1975. Academic Scholarly Publication. Czech. ir. Price varies per volume. Atatni Vyzkumny Ustav Pro Stavbu Stroju, Prague Bechovice Czech Republic. **Tel** 743051-9, telex 121 333 INSBC. **CODEN** TSSPDX. **Bk Rev. Circ:** 1,000 (ctrl). Documents available from CASDDS.
Desc: Covers practical problems of structures, machine parts, flow mechanics, thermomechanics, measuring techniques and drying. Includes picture documentation, tables, diagrams and charts. Intended for use by factories and other establishments in Czechoslovakia.
Ind/Abst Chem. Abstr. (1975-1983).

XR
TECHNICKY SBORNIK - VYZKUMNY USTAV CKD. Main/Corp Vyzkumny Ustav Ckd. Czech (summaries and/or abstracts in German, Russian and English). Vu-Ckd, Na Harfe 7, Prague Czech Republic. **LC** TJ4; .V96A.

GR/0251-0316
TECHNIKA CHRONIKA EPISTEMONIKE EKDOSE T.E.E. EPISTEMONIKE PERIOCHE B. Added/Corp Technikon Epimeleterion Hellados. **VFOAT** Technika Chronika Epistemonike Ekdose TEE. Epistemonike Perioche B; Technika Chronika Scientific Journal of the Technical Chamber of Greece. Section B. (198?)-. Periodical. Greek, Modern (English and French). qt. Technical Chamber of Greece, rue Karageorgi Servias 4, Athens 125 Greece. **Tel** (01)32 54 590-9, telex TEEGR 218374. **LC** IN PROCESS. ***Continues in part*** *Technika Chronika. Genike Ekdosis.*

FR/0997-9565
TECHNOLOGIES MECANIQUES SENLIS. (TECHNOLOGIES MECANIQUES.). (1989)-. Periodical. French. mo (11 issues). 868.00F. CETIM, Service Diffusion BP 67, 60304 Senlis France. **Tel** 011 33 44 583266. **UDC** 621 (443.5). Index available. cum. index. **Circ:** 500. ***Continues*** *Bulletin de la Construction Mecanique (Senlis), 0396-1370.*

IT/0391-1683
TECNOLOGIE MECCANICHE. [Tecnol. mecc.]. (1970)-. Periodical. Italian (English). mo. L100000.00 Italy; L180000.00 other. Stammer Spa, Via della Liberazione 1, 20068 Peschiera Borromeo, Italy. **Tel** 011 39 2 55302606, FAX 011 39 2 55302700, telex 321083. **ED** Girolamo Bellina. **UDC** 62. **CODEN** TEMED8. **Bk Rev. Ad Acc. Pr Rev. Circ:** 15,100 (ctrl).
Desc: High technology in tool machines, production, marketing, general management, and financial trends in the field.

BW/0137-0235
TEORETICESKAJA I PRIKLADNAJA MEHANIKA (MINSK). (TEORETICHESKAIA I PRIKLADNAIA MEKHANIKA.). [Teor. prikl. meh.]. **Added/Corp** Belaruski Palitekhnichny Instytut. (1975)-. Periodical. Russian. **LC** QA801; .T424. **CODEN** TPRMDW. Documents available from CASDDS.
Ind/Abst Chem. Abstr. (1975-1981); Int. Aerosp. Abstr.; Math. Rev.

RU
TEORIIA MASHIN METALLURGICHESKOGO I GORNOGO OBORUDOVANIIA. Added/Corp Sverdlovsk, Russia. Uralskii Politekhnicheskii Institut. (19??)-. Academic Scholarly Publication. Russian. an. 1.50rub each issue. Ministerstvo Vysshego I Srednego Spetsialnogo, 620002 Sverdlovsk, Upi Im S M Kirova, Redaktsionno-Izdatelskii Otdel, Sverdlovsk Russia. **Tel** 44 86 94. **ED** V I Sokolovsky. **LC** TN675.5; .T47. **CODEN** TMMODQ. **Ad Acc.** ctrl circ. available on diskette. Documents available from CASDDS.
Desc: Contains research works in the field of plastic forming technology and machines.
Ind/Abst Chem. Abstr.

RU/0040-3636
TEPLOENERGETIKA (MOSKVA, 1954). (TEPLOENERGETIKA.). [Teploenergetika]. **Added/Corp** Akademiia Nauk SSSR. Soviet Union. Ministerstvo Elekrostantsii. Soviet Union. Ministerstvo Tiazhelogo Mashinostroeniia. Soviet Union. Gosudarstvennyi Komitet Po Koordinatsii Nauchno-Issledovatelskikh Rabot. Nauchno-Tekhnicheskoe Obshchestvo Energeticheskoi Promyshlennosti (Soviet Union) Soviet Union. Gosudarstvennyi Komitet Po Nauke i Tekhnike. Nauchno-Tekhnicheskoe Obshchestvo Energetiki i Ektroteknicheskoi Promyshlennosti (Soviet Union). Tsentralnoe Pravlenie. (1954)-. Periodical. Russian (summaries and/or abstracts in English). mo. $249.95. MAIK Nauka / Interperiodica, Ulitsa Profsoyuznaya 90, Moscow 117864 Russia. **(Subscription address:** East View Publications Inc., 3020 Harbor Lane North, Suite 110, Minneapolis MN 55447.) **LC** TJ4; .T43. **CODEN** TPLOA5. **[CCC]. Bk Rev. Circ:** 9,800. Documents available from Article Express International, Ask*IEEE, CASDDS.
Ind/Abst Alum. Ind. Abstr.; Bioeng. Abstr.; Chem. Abstr.; Coal Abstr.; Ei Page One; Energy Res. Abstr.; Eng. Mater. Abstr.; Eng. Index Annu.; INSPEC (April 1969-); Int. Aerosp. Abstr.; Met. Abstr.; World Alum. Abstr.

US/1053-9328
TEST INDUSTRY REPORTER, THE. [Test ind. report.]. Vol. 1, No. 1 (Oct. 1990)-. Periodical. English. mo. $120.00. ADS Associates, PO Box 1179, Webster MA 01570. **DD** 621.
Desc: Dedicated to covering the electronics test industry for design, test and marketing. This newsletter is a practical source of information for design engineering managers, test engineering managers, design engineers, test engineers, and sales and marketing managers.

US/0193-4120
TEST (OAKHURST, N.J.). (TEST : ENGINEERING AND MANAGEMENT.). [Test]. **VFOAT** Test Engineering and Management; Test Engineering & Management; Test Engineering. Vol. 9, No. 2 (Feb. 1963)-. Periodical. English. Six times a year (Feb., Apr., June, Aug., Oct., Dec.). $35.00 North America; $45.00 other; $69.00 airmail. Mattingley Publishing Company Inc., 3756 Grand Avenue, Suite 205, Oakland CA 94610. **Tel** (510)839-0909, FAX (510)839-2950. **ED** Eve Mattingley-Hannigan. **LC** TA171; .T47. **DD** 620/.0044. **Bk Rev. Ad Acc. Circ:** 10,475 (ctrl). Documents available from Article Express International. ***Continues*** *Test Engineering (Oakhurst, N.J.), 0097-3882.*
Desc: A forum for the exchange of ideas and information among reliability/qualification-testing professionals; technically by-lined articles by those working hands-on in the field.
Ind/Abst Ei Page One; Eng. Index Annu. [Select. Cov.]; Ref. Sources; Shock Vibr. Dig.

JA
THEORETICAL AND APPLIED MECHANICS. Main/Corp Japan National Congress for Applied Mechanics. **Added/Corp** Japan National Committee for Theoretical and Applied Mechanics. (1971)-. Monographic series. English. ir. Price varies per volume. University of Tokyo Press, 7 3 1 Hongo Bunkyo-ku, Tokyo 113 Japan. **Tel** 011 81 3 3811 0964. **(Subscription address:** Columbia University Press, 136 South Broadway, Irvington NY 10533, telephone: (914)591-9370) **LC** TA350; .J35. **DD** 620.1. Documents available from Article Express International. ***Continues*** *Japan National Congress for Applied Mechanics. Proceedings.*
Ind/Abst Ei Page One; Eng. Index Annu.; Zentralbl. Math. Ihre Grenzgeb.

RU
TIAZHELOE MASHINOSTROENIE (MOSCOW, R.S.F.S.R. : 1990). (TIAZHELOE MASHINOSTROENIE : TM.). **Added/Corp** Soviet Union. Ministerstvo Tiazhelogo Mashinostroeniia. Vsesoiuznoe Nauchno-Tekhnicheskoe Obshchestvo Mashinostroitelei. **VFOAT** TM. Vol. 1 (1990)-. Academic Scholarly Publication. Russian. mo. $109.95. **(Subscription address:** East View Publications Inc., 3020 Harbor Lane North, Suite 110, Minneapolis MN 55447.) **LC** TJ4; .E57. **CODEN** TYMAEZ. Documents available from CASDDS. ***Continues*** *Energomashinostroenie, 0131-1336.*
Ind/Abst Chem. Abstr.; Fluid Abstr., Civil Eng.; Fluid Abstr. Proc. Eng.; FLUIDEX (19??-).

NE/0921-4348
TIJDSCHRIFT VOOR ERGONOMIE. [Tijdschr. ergon.]. (1981)-. Periodical. Dutch. bm. Fl68.87 Europe; Fl73.00 other. Ned Ver Voor Ergonomie, W G Plein 564, 1054 SJ Amsterdam Netherlands. **Tel** 011 31 20 6180930. **UDC** 331.101.1. ***Continues*** *Ergonomie, 0921-4402.*
Ind/Abst Ergon. Abstr.

AT/1033-1069
TODAY'S MOTOR. [Today's motor]. (1988)-. Periodical. English. Six times a year (Feb., Apr., June, Aug., Oct., Dec.). 25.00Aus$ one year; 50.00Aus$ two year; 75.00Aus$ three year. Direct Specialist Publishing, PO Box 6337, Toowoomba Qld 4350 Australia. **Tel** 011 61 76 333262, FAX 011 61 76 333285. **ED** Peter Buffey. **DD** 629.22205. Index available. **Bk Rev**, (Qty: varies). **Ad Acc. Circ:** 10,000 (ctrl).
Desc: Contains articles on motoring.

II/0377-9408
TOOL & ALLOY STEELS. [Tool alloy steels]. **Added/Corp** Alloy Steel Producers' Association of India. **VAT** Tool and Alloy Steels. (196?)-. Academic Scholarly Publication. English. mo. $75.00. Alloy Steel Producer Association of India, 322 Hind Rajasthan Building, Dadar Bombay 40014 India. **Tel** 448364. **(Subscription address:** Prints India, 11 Darya Ganj, New Delhi 110002 India.) **ED** D M Lakhiani. **CODEN** TASTDL. **Bk Rev. Ad Acc. Circ:** 6,000. Documents available from CASDDS.
Desc: Steel manufacturing, application and treatment (mechanical engineering).
Ind/Abst Alum. Ind. Abstr.; Chem. Abstr.; Met. Abstr.

US/0040-9243
TOOLING & PRODUCTION. [Tool. prod.]. **VFOAT** Tooling and Production. (1960)-. Academic Scholarly Publication. English. Twelve times a year. $90.00 US; $125.00 Canada & Mexico; $195.00 others. Huebcore Communications Inc., 1355 Mendiota Heights, Suite 210, Mendiota Heights MN 55120. **Tel** (612)686-0303. **(Subscription address:** Huebcore Communications Inc., 29100 Aurora Road, Suite 200, Solon OH 44139.) **CODEN** TOPRAR. **[CCC].** available on an online database (file 648/Full-Text) from DIALOG. Documents available from Article Express International, Ask*IEEE, CASDDS. ***Continues*** *Tooling and Production Magazine.*
Ind/Abst Alum. Ind. Abstr.; Appl. Sci. Technol. Index; Bus. ASAP (1990-) [Full Txt.]; Bus. Index (1985-); Chem. Abstr.; Ei Page One; Eng. Index Annu.; F&S Index Plus Text, Int. [Select. Cov.]; Gen. BusinessFile (1985-); INSPEC (July 1971-); Met. Abstr.; Pollut. Abstr. Indexes; PROMT; Trade Ind. ASAP [Full Txt.]; Trade Ind. Index (1981-) [Full Txt.].

JA/0915-1168
TORAIBOROJISUTO. Added/Corp Nihon Junkatsu Gakkai. **VFOAT** Journal of Japanese Society of Tribologists. (1989)-. Periodical. Japanese. mo. $397.50. Japanese Society of Tribologists, Kikaishingko Kaikan, Rm. 407-2, 5-8 Shibakoen, 3-chome Minato-ku, Tokyo 105 Japan. **Tel** 03-3434-1926, FAX 03-3434-3556. **(Subscription address:** Japan Publications Trading Company, Ltd., PO Box 5030, Tokyo International, Tokyo 100-31 Japan.) **LC** TJ1075.A2; J86. **CODEN** TORAEO. Documents available from The Genuine Article, CASDDS. ***Continues*** *Junkatsu, 0449-4156.*
Ind/Abst Ceram. Abstr. (19??-); Chem. Abstr.; Ei Page One; Res. Alert [Full Cov.]; SCISEARCH; Soc. Sci. Cit. Index [Select. Cov.].

US/0097-6822
TRANSACTIONS OF THE AMERICAN SOCIETY OF MECHANICAL ENGINEERS. [Trans. Am. Soc. Mech. Eng.]. **Main/Corp** American Society of Mechanical Engineers. **VFOAT** ASME Transactions. Vol. 1 (1880)-. English. an. $2,150.00 (non-members), $680.00 (members) US & Canada. American Society of Mechanical Engineers, 22 Law Drive, Fairfield NJ 07007. **Tel** (201)882-1167, (212)705-7722 (editorial). **LC** TJ1; .A7. **DD** 621/.05. **[CCC].** available on microfilm from University Microfilms International (UMI). ***Absorbed*** *American Society of Mechanical Engineers. Record and Index.*
Ind/Abst AESIS Q.; Shock Vibr. Dig.

CN/0315-8977
TRANSACTIONS OF THE CANADIAN SOCIETY FOR MECHANICAL ENGINEERING. [Trans. Can. Soc. Mech. Eng.]. **Added/Corp** Canadian Society for Mechanical Engineering. **VFOAT** Transactions de la Societe Canadienne de Genie Mecanique. Vol. 1 (March 1972)-. Periodical. English (French). qt. 75.00Can$. Canadian Society Mechanical Engineers, Dept. Mechanical Engineering, University of Alberta, Room 4-9 Mec.E. Bldg., Edmonton, Alberta, T6G 2G8 Canada. **Tel** (403)492-0416, FAX (403)492-2200. **ED** Tom Forest. **LC** TJ1; .T69. **DD** 621/.05. **CODEN** TCMEAP. **Pr Rev. Circ:** 325 (ctrl). Documents available from Article Express International, The Genuine Article.
Desc: Contains original reference and archival papers in mechanical engineering and related fields.
Ind/Abst Curr. Contents Eng. Tech. Appl. Sci.; Ei Page One; Eng. Index Annu.; Fluid Abstr., Civil Eng.; Fluid Abstr. Proc. Eng.; FLUIDEX (1973-); Int. Aerosp. Abstr.; Nucl. Sci. Abstr.; Res. Alert [Select. Cov.].

UK/0142-3312
TRANSACTIONS OF THE INSTITUTE OF MEASUREMENT AND CONTROL. [Trans. Inst. Meas. Control]. **Main/Corp** Institute of Measurement and Control. Vol. 1 (Jan./March 1979)-. Academic Scholarly Publication. English. qt. £149.00 Europe; £175.00 other. Institute of Measurement and Control, 87 Gower Street, London WC1E 6AA England. **Tel** 011 44 71 387 4949, FAX 011 44 71 388 8431, telex 946797 PRONTO G. **LC** TJ212; .I489a. **DD** 681/.2/05. **CODEN** TICODG. Documents available from Article Express International, Ask*IEEE, CASDDS.
Ind/Abst Bioeng. Abstr.; Chem. Abstr.; Curr. Biotechnol.; Curr. Technol. Index; Ei Page One; EMBASE; Eng. Index Annu.; Fluid Abstr., Civil Eng.; Fluid Abstr. Proc. Eng.; FLUIDEX (1979-); INSPEC (Jan./March 1979-); Proc. Chem. Eng.; Theoret. Chem. Eng.

AT/0727-7369
TRANSACTIONS OF THE INSTITUTION OF ENGINEERS, AUSTRALIA. MECHANICAL ENGINEERING. [Trans. Inst. Eng., Aust., Mech. eng.]. **Added/Corp** Institution of Engineers, Australia. **VFOAT** Transactions of Mechanical Engineering. Vol. ME 4 (Nov. 1979)-. Periodical. English. qt. 70.00Aus$. Engineers Australia Pty Ltd, 2 Ernest Street, Crows Nest Centre, Crows Nest New South Wales 2065, Australia. **Tel** 011 61 2 438-1533, FAX 011 61 2 438-5934, telex 27640. **LC** TJ1; .M47. **DD** 621/.05. **CODEN** TEAMD6. **Circ:** 12,000 (ctrl). Documents available from Article Express International, Ask*IEEE. ***Continues*** *Mechanical Engineering Transactions.*
Desc: Learned papers covering all aspects of mechanical engineering.
Ind/Abst Ei Page One; Eng. Index Annu.; Fluid Abstr., Civil Eng.; Fluid Abstr. Proc. Eng.; FLUIDEX (1979-); INSPEC (Nov. 1979-); Pollut. Abstr. Indexes; Robotics Abstr.

RU
TRUDY TSNIITMASH. **Main/Corp** Tsentralnyi Nauchno-Issledovatelskii Institut Tekhnologii I Mashinostroeniia. **VAT** Trudy Tsentralnogo Nauchno-Isseldovatelskogo Institut Tekhnologii Mashinostroeniia. (19??)-. Academic Scholarly Publication. Russian. 1.80rub each issue. **LC** T4; .M6. **CODEN** TTTMAX. Documents available from CASDDS. ***Continues*** *TSentralnyi Nauchno-Issledovatelskii Institut Tekhnologii i Mashinostroeniia. (Soviet Union) [Trudy].*
Ind/Abst Chem. Abstr. (?-1976).

US
TURBOMACHINERY DIGEST. English. Six times a year. $260.00 US; $280.00 other. Concepts ETI Inc, PO Box 643, Norwich VT 05055. **Tel** (802)296-2321, FAX (802)296-2325. **Bk Rev.** ctrl circ. ***Continues*** *Turbomachinery Design Digest.*
Desc: Limited to reviews and listings of turbomachinery related material only.

US/0149-4147
TURBOMACHINERY INTERNATIONAL. [Turbomach. int.]. **VAT** Turbo Machinery International. Vol. 18, No. 5 (Sept./Oct. 1977)-. Periodical. English. Seven times a year. $49.00 (one year), $75.00 (two year). Business Journals Inc, PO Box 5550, Norwalk CT 06856. **Tel** (203)853-6015, FAX (203)852-8175, telex 353706. **ED** Martin Autuori. **LC** TJ266; .S28. **DD** 621.4/06/05. **CODEN** TUINDP. **Ad Acc. Circ:** 10,540. available on microfilm and microfiche from University Microfilms International (UMI). Documents available from Article Express International. ***Continues*** *Sawyer's Gas Turbine International, 0163-7134.*
Desc: Published for key management and engineering personnel in turbomachinery-using industries. Covers all important developments in the field, both business and technical.
Ind/Abst Acoust. Abstr.; Bioeng. Abstr.; Coal Abstr.; Ei Page One; Electron. Commun. Abstr. J.; Energy Res. Abstr. (April 1978-);; Eng. Index Annu. [Select. Cov.]; Fluid Abstr., Civil Eng.; Fluid Abstr. Proc. Eng.; FLUIDEX (1977-); Gas Abstr.; Int. Aerosp. Abstr.; ISMEC Bull.; Pollut. Abstr. Indexes; Saf. Sci. Abstr. J.; Shock Vibr. Dig.

US/0748-0903
TURBOMACHINERY INTERNATIONAL HANDBOOK. [Turbomach. int. handb.]. (1981/1982)-. English. an. $50.00. Business Journals Inc, PO Box 5550, Norwalk CT 06856. **Tel** (203)853-6015, FAX (203)852-8175, telex 353706. **LC** TJ266; .T876. **DD** 621.406. **Ad Acc.** available in microform. ***Continues*** *Turbomachinery International Workbook.*

GW/0300-3167
UMFORMTECHNIK. [Umformtechnik]. (1967)-. Periodical. German. bm. DM114.00. Meisenbach GmbH, Postfach 2069, D 96011 Bamberg Germany. **Tel** 011 49 951 861135.
Ind/Abst Alum. Ind. Abstr.; Eng. Mater. Abstr.; Met. Abstr.

US/1045-3954
USED EQUIPMENT DIRECTORY. [Used equip. dir.]. **VFOAT** UED. (19??)-. Periodical. English. Twelve times a year. $45.00 (first class), $30.00 (third class) US; $65.00 (first class) Canada; $100.00 (airmail) other. Penton Publishing, 1100 Superior Avenue, Cleveland OH 44114-2543. **Tel** (216)696-7000, FAX (216)696-0836. **(Subscription address:** Penton Publishing, PO Box 96732, Chicago IL 60693.**)** **DD** 338. **[CCC].**

US/1051-8045
USSR JOURNAL OF THEORETICAL AND APPLIED MECHANICS. ***Ceased.*** Vol. 1 (1990)-(1992). Academic Scholarly Publication. English. qt. Elsevier Science Publishing Company Inc, Madison Square Station, PO Box 882, New York NY 10159-0882. **Tel** (212)633-3950, FAX (212)633-3990. **ED** V M Fomin. **LC** TA349; .R87. **DD** 620.1/005.
Desc: Publishes the latest research in mechanics currently underway at the major institutions in the USSR. This journal covers essential advances in theoretical, analytical, experimental and applied mechanics, and also includes articles on: mathematical modeling in mechanics, aerodynamics, physical mechanics and gas dynamics.
Ind/Abst Int. Aerosp. Abstr. (19??-1992).

IT/0392-6567
UTENSIL. [Utensil]. (1979)-. Academic Scholarly Publication. English. ir. L90000, $62.00 Italy; L120000, $83.24 other. Editoriale Tecnica Macchine, Via Ugo Lenzi 1, 40122 Bologna Italy. **Tel** 011 39 51 523183. **CODEN** UTEND9. **Bk Rev. Ad Acc. Pr Rev.** Documents available from CASDDS.
Desc: Review of technology and marketing for the industry: it deals with field of the tools trade. Mechanical and manually operated tools, accessories, abrasives, equipment, gauges and products for mechanical works.
Ind/Abst Alum. Ind. Abstr. (19??-); Chem. Abstr. (1979-1985); Ei Page One (19??-); Met. Abstr. (19??-).

●US/0737-5727
VALVE BUYERS HANDBOOK. **VFOAT** Valve Buyers Hand Book. (1993)-. English. Lyons Publishing Company / St. Louis, MO, 7535 Harlan Walk, St. Louis MO 63123.

GW/0042-1766
VDI-Z. (VDI-Z : ZEITSCHRIFT DES VEREINS DEUTSCHER INGENIEURE FUER MASCHINENBAU UND METALLBEARBEITUNG.). [VDI-Z]. **Added/Corp** Verein Deutscher Ingenieure. **VFOAT** V.D.I.-Z. **VAT** Verein Deutscher Ingenieure-Zeitschrift. (1969)-. Academic Scholarly Publication. German. Eleven times a year. DM329.00 Germany; DM365.00 other. VDI Verlag GmbH, Postfach 101054, D 40001 Dusseldorf Germany. **Tel** 011 49 211 6188313, FAX 011 49 211 6188133. **LC** TA3; .V5. **DD** 621/.05. **CODEN** VZGTAJVDIZAT. **[CCC]. Ad Acc.** Documents available from Article Express International, Ask*IEEE, CASDDS. ***Continues*** *VDI-Zeitschrift.*
Desc: Contains papers on subjects pertinent to mechanical technology and related fields, annual surveys of selected tools, and much more.
Ind/Abst Alum. Ind. Abstr.; Bioeng. Abstr.; Ceram. Abstr.; Chem. Abstr.; Ei Page One; EMBASE; Energy Res. Abstr. (Oct. 1976-); Eng. Index Annu.; Fluid Abstr., Civil Eng.; Fluid Abstr. Proc. Eng.; FLUIDEX (1973-); INSPEC (1969-); Int. Aerosp. Abstr.; Met. Abstr.; Saf. Health Work; Shock Vibr. Dig.

NE/0042-3114
VEHICLE SYSTEM DYNAMICS. [Veh. syst. dyn.]. **Added/Corp** International Association for Vehicle System Dynamics. Vol. 1 (May 1972)-. Periodical. English (French and German; summaries and/or abstracts in French and German). Ten times a year. Fl950.00. Swets & Zeitlinger BV, Heereweg 347B PO Box 825, 2160 SZ Lisse Holland. **Tel** 011 31 2521 35111, FAX 02521-15888, telex 41325. **(Subscription address:** Swets Publishing Service, PO Box 825, 2160 SZ Lisse The Netherlands**)** **ED** Dr P Lugner, Prof J Karl Hedrick. **LC** TL243; .V35. **DD** 629.2/31. **CODEN** VSDYA4. **[CCC]. Bk Rev. Ad Acc. Pr Rev. Circ:** 800. Documents available from Article Express International, The Genuine Article, Ask*IEEE.
Desc: Provides a source of information for the vehicle engineer and the applied scientist. Emphasizes the theoretical background of research and development problems of all kinds of ground based vehicles.
Ind/Abst Agric. Eng. Abstr. (1991-); Bioeng. Abstr.; Civ. Struct. Eng. Abstr.; Curr. Contents Eng. Tech. Appl. Sci.; Ei Page One; Eng. Index Annu.; Fluid Abstr., Civil Eng.; Fluid Abstr. Proc. Eng.; FLUIDEX (1973-1989); Highw. Res. Abstr.; INSPEC (May 1972-); Mech. Eng. Abstr.; Pollut. Abstr. Indexes; Res. Alert [Select. Cov.].

DK
VEJVISER FOR MASKININDUSTRIEN. Vol. 1 (1950)-. Danish. an. **ED** G F Kentorp. **LC** TJ4; .V285.

US
VENTURE / AMERICAN NATURAL RESOURCES SYSTEM. Periodical. English. qt. ANR, One Woodward Avenue, Detroit MI 48226. **LC** TJ163.13.

SW/0042-4056
VERKSTADERNA. [Verkstaderna]. (1905)-. Periodical. Swedish. Sixteen times a year. Kr475.00. Verkstaderna, Box 5510, S-11485 Stockholm Sweden. **Tel** 468 782 0800, telex 17045 SWEMET S. **ED** PerHenrik Angstrom. **LC** TJ4; .S952. **CODEN** VSTDAL. Index available. **Bk Rev. Ad Acc. Circ:** 17,000 (ctrl). Documents available from Ask*IEEE.
Desc: The Swedish Engineering Employers Association's official organ; much of content is devoted to technical matters and production economy.
Ind/Abst Energy Res. Abstr. (Oct. 1979-); INSPEC (1968-); Saf. Health Work (19??-).

US/0883-623X
VESTNIK LENINGRADSKOGO UNIVERSITETA. MATEMATIKA, MEKHANIKA, ASTRONOMIIA. ***Title Change.*** (LENINGRAD UNIVERSITY MECHANICS BULLETIN.). (1984)-(199?). Bulletin. English (Russian). qt. Allerton Press, Inc., 150 Fifth Avenue, New York NY 10011. **Tel** (212)924-3950, FAX (212)463-9684, telex 427441 ALPRES. **LC** QA801; .V44. **DD** 531. **UDC** 51; 531; 52. **[CCC].** ***Continued by*** *St. Petersburg University Mechanics Bulletin.*
Ind/Abst Zentralbl. Math. Ihre Grenzgeb.

RU/0579-9368
VESTNIK MOSKOVSKOGO UNIVERSITETA SERIIA I, MATEMATIKA, MEKHANIKA. See Mathematics.

US/1045-1498
VOICE TECHNOLOGY NEWS. [Voice tech. news]. Vol. 1, No. 1 (Aug. 15, 1989)-. Periodical. English. bw (25 issues). $497.00 US; $530.00 other. Phillips Business Information, Inc., 1201 Seven Locks Road, Potomac MD 20854. **Tel** (301)424-3338, (800)777-5006, FAX (301)309-3847. **DD** 621. **[CCC].** available on an online database (file 636/Full-Text) from DIALOG.
Ind/Abst PTS Newsl. Database [Full Txt.].

RU/0130-0415
VOPROSY TEORII SISTEM AVTOMATICESKOGO UPRAVLENIJA. (VOPROSY TEORII SISTEM AVTOMATICHESKOGO UPRAVLENIIA.). [Vopr. teor. sist. avtom. upr.]. **Added/Corp** Russian S.F.S.R. Ministerstvo Vysshego i Srednego Spetsialnogo Obrazovaniia. **VFOAT** Automatic Control System Theory Problems. Vyp. 6. Vol. 1 (1974)-. Russian. 1.00rub (single issue). St Petersburg State University / Izdatelstvo Leningradskogo Universiteta, Universitetskaia Nab 7/9, 199034 St Petersburg Russia. **Tel** 011 95 218-97-88, FAX 011 95 218-51-52, telex 121481. **ED** Y Bortsov. **LC** TJ212; .V66. **CODEN** VTSUD9. **Ad Acc. Circ:** 1,500. Documents available from CASDDS.
Desc: Deals with the problems of the automated management systems theory, investigates new methods, mathematical apparatus, algorithms and gives new results of researches in the field.
Ind/Abst Chem. Abstr. (1974-1980); Int. Aerosp. Abstr.; Math. Rev.; Zentralbl. Math. Ihre Grenzgeb.

IT/0391-3155
VUOTO, SCIENZA E TECNOLOGIA. [Vuoto Sci. tecnol.]. **Added/Corp** Associazione Italiana del Vuoto. (19??)-. Periodical. Italian. Four times a year (Jan., Apr., June, Sept.). L75000.00 Italy; L85000.00 others. Patron Editore, Via Badini 12, 40050 Quarto Inf. Bologna Italy. **Tel** 011 39 51 767003, FAX 011 39 51 768252. **LC** TJ940; .V86. **CODEN** VSTCBJ. Documents available from Ask*IEEE.
Ind/Abst Ei Page One; INSPEC (1985-).

GW/0042-9929
WARME- UND STOFFUBERTRAGUNG. ***Title Change.*** [Warme- Stoffubertrag.]. **VFOAT** Thermo- and Fluid Dynamics. (1968)-(1995). Periodical. English (German). Eight times a year. Springer-Verlag GmbH & Company KG, Heidelberger Platz 3, D 14197 Berlin Germany. **Tel** 011 49 30 8207223, FAX 011 49 30 8214091, telex 183 319 SPBLN D. **(Subscription address:** Springer Verlag New York Inc. / for North America, 44 Hartz Way, Secaucus NJ 07096.**)** **ED** E.R.G. Eckert, P. Grassman, U. Grigull and F. Mayinger. **LC** TJ260; .W22. **DD** 621.402/1/05. **CODEN** WASBBW. **[CCC]. Pr Rev.** available on microfilm and microfiche from University Microfilms International (UMI). Documents available from Article Express International, The Genuine

Article, Ask*IEEE, CASDDS. ***Continued by*** *Heat and Mass Transfer.*
Desc: Serves in the circulation of new developments in the field of basic research of heat and mass transfer phenomena, as well as related material properties and their measurements.
Ind/Abst Bibliogr. Mission. (1973-); Bioeng. Abstr.; Chem. Abstr.; Curr. Contents Eng. Tech. Appl. Sci.; Ei Page One; Energy Res. Abstr.; Eng. Index Annu.; Fluid Abstr., Civil Eng.; Fluid Abstr. Proc. Eng.; FLUIDEX (1973-); HTFS Dig.; INSPEC (1968-); Int. Aerosp. Abstr.; Nucl. Sci. Abstr.; Proc. Chem. Eng.; Res. Alert [Full Cov.]; Sci. Cit. Index; SCISEARCH; Theoret. Chem. Eng.

SZ/0043-1648
WEAR. (WEAR. AN INTERNATIONAL JOURNAL ON THE SCIENCE AND TECHNOLOGY OF FRICTION, LUBRICATION AND WEAR.). [Wear]. **VFOAT** Usure; Verschleiss. Vol. 1 (Aug. 1957)-. Periodical. English. Twenty times a year (10 vols.). 4050.00F. Elsevier Sequoia SA, PO Box 564, CH-1001 Lausanne 1 Switzerland. **Tel** 011 41 21 3207381. **ED** Duncan Dowson. **LC** TA401; .W4. **DD** 620.16. **CODEN** WEARAH. **[CCC].** cum. index. **Ad Acc, Adv Mgr:** Ms. W van Cattenburch (Amsterdam). **Pr Rev.** available on microfilm and microfiche from University Microfilms International (UMI). Documents available from Article Express International, The Genuine Article, Ask*IEEE, CASDDS.
Desc: This international journal is dedicated to the rapid publication of papers on the subject of wear, together with papers in related fields such as friction and lubrication.
Ind/Abst Acoust. Abstr.; Alum. Ind. Abstr.; Appl. Mech. Rev.; Bioeng. Abstr.; Chem. Abstr.; Civ. Struct. Eng. Abstr.; Coal Abstr.; Curr. Technol. Index; Ei Page One; Elect. Comm. Abstr.; Eng. Mater. Abstr.; Eng. Index Annu.; Fluid Abstr., Civil Eng.; Fluid Abstr. Proc. Eng.; FLUIDEX (1973-); Highw. Res. Abstr.; INSPEC (Aug. 1971-); Int. Aerosp. Abstr.; Lit. Pat. Abstr., Oilfield Chem. (1960-); Lit. Abstr., Catal. Catal.; Lit. Abstr., Health Environ.; Lit. Abstr., Pet. Refin. Petrochem.; Lit. Abstr., Pet. Substit.; Lit. Abstr., Transp. Storage; Manuf. Process Eng. Abstr.; Mater. Sci. Eng. Abstr.; Mech. Eng. Abstr.; Met. Abstr.; Res. Alert [Full Cov.]; Sci. Cit. Index; SCISEARCH; Solid State Supercond. Abstr.

US/0192-4990
WEAR OF MATERIALS. [Wear mater.]. **Main/Corp** American Society of Mechanical Engineers. (1977)-. Academic Scholarly Publication. English. ir (every 2 years). $143.50. American Society of Mechanical Engineers, 22 Law Drive, Fairfield NJ 07007. **Tel** (201)882-1167, (212)705-7722 (editorial). **LC** TA418.4; .A45a. **DD** 620.1/1292. **CODEN** WMATDE. **[CCC].** Documents available from Article Express International, CASDDS.
Ind/Abst Chem. Abstr.; Ei Page One; Eng. Index Annu.

GW/0043-2792
WERKSTATT UND BETRIEB. [Werkstatt betr.]. Vol. 79. No. 1 (Apr. 1946)-. Academic Scholarly Publication. English. Ten times a year. DM155.00. Carl Hanser Verlag, Postfach 860420, D 81631 Munich Germany. **Tel** 011 49 89 998300, FAX 011 49 89 984809. **CODEN** WKUBA9. **[CCC].** Documents available from Article Express International, Ask*IEEE, CASDDS. ***Continues in part*** *Fertigungstechnik.*
Desc: Fundamental essays and test reports of which the core is on manufacturing operations and production devices (such as machine tools, tools and instruments, machine components).
Ind/Abst Alum. Ind. Abstr.; Bioeng. Abstr.; Chem. Abstr. (-1988); CIS Abstr.; Ei Page One; EMBASE; Energy Res. Abstr. (Jan. 1971-); Eng. Mater. Abstr.; Eng. Index Annu.; INSPEC (1968-); Met. Abstr.; Saf. Health Work; World Alum. Abstr.

US/0732-8540
WESTERN MACHINERY AND STEEL WORLD. BUYERS GUIDE. [West. mach. steel world., Buy. guide]. **VFOAT** Western Machinery ... Buyers Guide. Vol. 66 (1976)-. Consumer Publication. English. an. $27.50. Cardinal Publishing Company, 1098 Harrison Street, San Francisco CA 94103. **LC** HD9703.U52; A178. **DD** 621.9/02/029478. ***Continues*** *Western Machinery and Steel World. Buyers Directory, 0732-8559.*

GW
WHO MAKES MACHINERY AND PLANT. ***Title Change.*** **Added/Corp** Verband Deutscher Maschinen- und Anlagenbau. (198?)-(1992). English. Verlag Hoppenstedt GmbH, Postfach 10 01 39, D 64201 Darmstadt Germany. **Tel** 0045 6151 380 0, FAX 0045 6151 380 360. **LC** TJ1170; .W43. **DD** 621.8/0294. ***Continues*** *Who Makes Machinery?.* ***Continued by*** *Who Makes Machinery in Germany.*

●GW
WHO MAKES MACHINERY IN GERMANY. **Added/Corp** Verband Deutscher Maschinen- und Anlagenbau. 55th Ed. (1993)-. English. an (February). DM45.00. Verlag Hoppenstedt GmbH, Postfach 10 01 39, D 64201 Darmstadt Germany. **Tel** 0045 6151 380 0, FAX 0045 6151 380 360. **LC** TJ1170; .W43. **DD** 621.8/029/443. **Bk Rev**, (Qty: 15). **Ad Acc, Adv Mgr:** Thomas Wengenroth. Full Page (B&W) DM4375.00. Half Page (B&W) DM2215.00. **Acid Free. Circ:** 40,700 (ctrl). ***Continues*** *Who Makes Machinery and Plant.*

Desc: Reference for specialized sources and procurement guide for machines, plants, systems and computers, devices, precision tools, fittings, machine parts and ancillary equipment.

UK
WORKSHOP YEARBOOK AND PRODUCTION ENGINEERING MANUAL, THE. (1945)-. English. Paul Elek Ltd, 54 58 Caledonian Road, London N1 9RN England. ***Continues*** *Machine Shop Yearbook and Production Engineer's Manual.*

US/1053-5802
WORLD COGENERATION. [World cogener.]. (1989)-. Periodical. English. Four times a year. $35.00 US; $50.00 Canada; $75.00 others. Flanagan Group Inc., 8454 118th Street, Kew Gardens NY 11415. **Tel** (718)847-0230. **ED** Jim Watts. **DD** 621. **Bk Rev. Ad Acc. Pr Rev. Circ:** 21,000 (ctrl).
Ind/Abst F&S Index Plus Text, Int. [Full Txt.] [Select. Cov.].

US/0744-8643
WORLD OF PUMPS. (WORLD OF PUMPS : NEWS FOR THE SPECIFIERS, USERS, DISTRIBUTORS, AND MAKERS OF PUMPS AND RELATED EQUIPMENT.). Periodical. English. mo. $5.00. Banner News Service, PO Box 9887, Seattle WA 98109-0368. **Tel** (206)284-6176. ***Continues*** *World of Pumps Monthly, 0194-6722.*

UK/0262-1762
WORLD PUMPS. [World pumps]. **Added/Corp** European Committee of Pump Manufactures. No. 1 (1982)-. Academic Scholarly Publication. English (summaries and/or abstracts in French and German). Twelve times a year. $155.00 The Americas; £104.00 other. Elsevier Advanced Technology, An Imprint of Elsevier Science Ltd., The Boulevard, Langford Lane, Kidlington, Oxford OX5 1GB United Kingdom. **Tel** 011 44 865 843000, 011 44 865 843699, FAX 011 44 865 843010. **(Subscription address:** Elsevier Science Ltd. Oxford Fulfillment Centre, PO Box 800, Kidlington, Oxford OX5 1DX United Kingdom.**) ED** Christopher Dickenson. **LC** TJ899; .W67. **DD** 621.6. **CODEN** WOPUD4. **[CCC]. Bk Rev. Ad Acc. Circ:** 6,200 (ctrl). available on microfilm and microfiche from University Microfilms International (UMI). Documents available from Article Express International. ***Continues*** *Pumps and Their Applications, 0141-4283.*
Desc: Official journal of 12 country "Europump". Covers selection, application, installation, operation, maintenance of pumps and arcillary equipment.
Ind/Abst Alum. Ind. Abstr.; Bioeng. Abstr.; BMT Abstr. (-199?); Coal Abstr.; Curr. Technol. Index (1982-); Ei Page One; EMBASE; Eng. Mater. Abstr. (-19??); Eng. Index Annu.; Fluid Abstr., Civil Eng.; Fluid Abstr. Proc. Eng.; FLUIDEX (1982-); Met. Abstr.

GW/0340-4544
WT. WERKSTATTSTECHNIK. (WT : ORGAN DER VDI-GESELLSCHAFT PRODUKTIONSTECHNIK (ADB).). [WT, Werkstattstech.]. **Added/Corp** VDI-Gesellschaft Produktionstechnik (ADB). **VFOAT** Werkstattstechnik. (Apr. 1969)-. Periodical. German. Twelve times a year. DM324.00. Springer-Verlag GmbH & Company KG, Heidelberger Platz 3, D 14197 Berlin Germany. **Tel** 011 49 30 8207223, FAX 011 49 30 8214091, telex 183 319 SPBLN D. **(Subscription address:** Springer Verlag New York Inc. / for North America, 44 Hartz Way, Secaucus NJ 07096.**) ED** H J Warnecke. **LC** TJ3; .W43. **DD** 621/.05. **[CCC]. Bk Rev.** available on microfilm from University Microfilms International (UMI). Documents available from The Genuine Article. ***Continues*** *Werkstattstechnik (Berlin, Germany : 1959).*
Desc: Specialists from industry and research report on problems and solutions from all areas of industrial manufacturing, including processes, start-up and planning. Contains notes on new products, updating and new machinery.
Ind/Abst Alum. Ind. Abstr.; Energy Res. Abstr.; Met. Abstr.; Res. Alert [Full Cov.]; Saf. Health Work.

KO
YUNHWAL KWALLI. **VFOAT** Lubrication Management. Periodical. Korean (Korean). bm. Hanguk Yuryu Sihon Komsaso, 587-10 Sinsa-dong Kangnam-ku, Seoul 135-00 Korea. **LC** TJ1075.A2; Y86.

PL/0137-5474
ZAGADNIENIA EKSPLOATACJI MASZYN. [Zagadn. eksploat. masz.]. **Added/Corp** Polska Akademia Nauk. Komitet Budowy Maszyn. (1973)-. Polish (summaries and/or abstracts in English and Russian). qt. $50.00. **(Subscription address:** ARS Polona, PO Box 1001, 00068 Warsaw Poland.**) LC** TJ4; .Z32.
Ind/Abst Energy Res. Abstr. (Dec. 1979-).

CI
ZBORNIK RADOVA. **Main/Corp** Zagreb. Univerzitet. Fakultet Strojarstva I Brodogradnje. 1- 1970-. Serbo-Croatian (Roman) (summaries and/or abstracts in English). Ure Salaja 7, Zagreb Croatia. **LC** TJ4; .Z33.

JA
ZENKOKU KIKAI KOJO MEIBO. **Added/Corp** Japan. Tsusho Sangyosho. Chosa Tokeibu. (19??)-. Japanese. be. Tsusho Sangyo Chosakai, (Research Institute on International Trade and Industry), Kobikikan Ginza Biru, 8-9 Ginza 2 chome Chuoku, Tokyoto 104 Japan. **LC** TJ1170; .Z45.

GW
ZENTRALBLATT FUER MECHANIK. Vol. 1 (1933)-. Periodical. English (German). Thirty-one times a year. DM7,998.00. Springer-Verlag GmbH & Company KG, Heidelberger Platz 3, D 14197 Berlin Germany. **Tel** 011 49 30 8207223, FAX 011 49 30 8214091, telex 183 319 SPBLN D. **(Subscription address:** Springer Verlag New York Inc. / for North America, 44 Hartz Way, Secaucus NJ 07096.**) LC** Z7144.M4; Z6. **DD** 621.05. ***Supersedes in part*** *Zentralblatt fur Mathematik und Ihre Grenzgebiete, 0044-4235.*

CH/0257-9731
ZHONGGUO JIXIE GONGCHENG XUEKAN. (CHUNG-KUO CHI HSIEH KUNG CHENG HSUEH KAN.). [Zhongguo jixie gongcheng xuekan]. **Added/Corp** Chung-kuo Chi Hsieh Kung Cheng Hsueh Hui (Taipei, Taiwan). Chung-kuo Chi Hsieh Kung Cheng Hsueh Hui (Taipei, Taiwan). Journal of the Chinese Society of Mechanical Engineers. **VFOAT** Journal of CSME; Journal of the Chinese Society of Mechanical Engineers. (19??)-. Periodical. Chinese (English; table of contents in English). bm. $18.12. Chinese Society of Mechanical Engineers, 44 Lane 204, Sung-Kiang Rd., Taipei Taiwan. **(Subscription address:** China International Book Trading Corporation, PO Box 399, Library Service Department, Beijing 100044 People's Republic of China.**) CODEN** CCHPEK. Documents available from Article Express International, Ask*IEEE.
Ind/Abst Eng. Index Annu.; INSPEC (April 1984-); Int. Aerosp. Abstr.

GW/0932-0482
ZWF CIM. (ZEITSCHRIFT FUER WIRTSCHAFTLICHE FERTIGUNG UND AUTOMATISIERUNG.). [ZWF CIM]. **Added/Corp** Gesellschaft fuer Informatik. Fachgruppe Rechnerunterstutzes Entwerfen und Konstruieren. **VFOAT** ZWFCIM; ZWF CIM; ZWF. Vol. 81, No. 1 (Jan. 1986)-. Academic Scholarly Publication. German. Ten times a year. DM224.00. Carl Hanser Verlag, Postfach 860420, D 81631 Munich Germany. **Tel** 011 49 89 998300, FAX 011 49 89 984809. **ED** H.C. Gunter Spur. **LC** IN PROCESS. **CODEN** ZZWAEM. Index available. **Bk Rev. Ad Acc. Circ:** 5,043 (ctrl). Documents available from Ask*IEEE, CASDDS. ***Continues*** *Zeitschrift fuer Wirtschaftliche Fertigung, 0044-3743.*
Desc: Focuses on production planning and factory equipment, material flow automation, thermal treatment and hardening technology.
Ind/Abst Chem. Abstr. (1874-1985),(1986-); CIS Abstr. (1986-); Energy Res. Abstr. (Jan. 1971-);; INSPEC (1987-); Saf. Health Work.

MINES AND MINING ENGINEERING

IO
ABSTRAK MINYAK DAN GAS BUMI DALAM NEGERI. **VFOAT** Abstrak Guntingan Berita Minyak Dan Gas Bumi Di Indonesia. Indonesian. Cipulir Kebayoran Lama, PO Box 89 JKT, Jakarta Indonesia. **LC** TN860; .A19.

XR/0365-1398
ACTA MONTANA. [Acta montana]. **Added/Corp** Ceskoslovenska Akademie Ved. Hornicky Ustav. (1970)-. Czech (summaries and/or abstracts in English, German and Russian). **LC** TN275.A1; A25. **CODEN** ACMTCX. Documents available from CASDDS. ***Continues*** *Zpravy Hornickeho Ustavu CSAV.*
Ind/Abst Chem. Abstr.

AG/0326-6672
ACTIVIDAD MINERA. [Act. min.]. (1983)-. Periodical. Spanish. mo. 86.000. Minera Piedra Libre Srl, Bolivar 187, P4 B, 1066 Buenos Aires Argentina. **Tel** 30 6138. **ED** Horacio H Piccinini and Mario de Pablos. **UDC** 622. **Ad Acc. Circ:** 1,500 (ctrl).
Desc: Journal for information relating to mining and energy.

MR
ACTIVITIES / BUREAU DE RECHERCHES ET DE PARTICIPATIONS MINIERES. **Main/Corp** Maktab Al-Abhath Wa-Al-Musahamat Al-Madiniyah (Rabat, Morocco). **VFOAT** Nashat an Sanat ... . Arabic (French). **LC** TN119.M6; B8. **DD** 338.2/0964. ***Continues*** *Bureau de Recherches et de Participations Minieres.*

FR/0994-0235
AFRICA ENERGY & MINING. See Energy.

JA/0389-8040
AKITA DAIGAKU KOZAN GAKUBU KENKYU HOKOKU. [Akita Daigaku Kozan Gakubu kenkyu hokoku]. **VFOAT** Scientific and Technical Reports of the Mining College, Akita University. Academic Scholarly Publication. English (Japanese). Akita Daigaku

Engineering —Mines and Mining Engineering

Kozan Gakubu, 1-ban 1-go Tegata Gakuen-Machi Akita, Akita-shi 010 Japan. **LC** TN4; .A39. **CODEN** KHADD3. Documents available from CASDDS.
Ind/Abst Chem. Abstr.

US/1061-9585
ALABAMA INDUSTRIAL DIRECTORY.
[Ala. ind. dir.]. **Added/Corp** Alabama Development Office. (1991)-. Directory. English. be. $55.00. Alabama Development Office, 401 Adams Avenue, State Capitol, Attention: Ms. Miller, Montgomery AL 36130. **Tel** (205)242-0400, FAX (205)242-0486. **ED** Thomas W. McGuire, Jr. **LC** T12; .A42. **DD** 338/.0025/761. Index available. **Circ:** 5,000 (ctrl). **Continues** Alabama Mining and Manufacturing Directory, 1051-5240.

US/0191-1589
ALI-ABA COURSE OF STUDY. LEGAL ISSUES IN THE COAL INDUSTRY : MATERIALS. See Law.

US/0891-6209
AMC JOURNAL.
[AMC j.]. Sept. (1986)-. Academic Scholarly Publication. English. mo. $36.00 (one year), $72.00 (two year). American Mining Congress, 1920 N Street NW/Suite 300, Washington DC 20036. **Tel** (202)861-2800. **ED** James Beizer. **LC** TN5; .A7. **DD** 338.2/05. Index available. **Bk Rev**. **Ad Acc**. **Circ:** 12,000. available in microform from University Microfilms International (UMI). Documents available from Article Express International, Documents on Demand.
Continues American Mining Congress Journal, 0277-8688.
Desc: Current concise coverage of news and developments vital to the mining industry.
Ind/Abst Appl. Sci. Technol. Index; EMBASE; Energy Inf. Abstr.; Eng. Index Annu. [Select. Cov.]; Environ. Abstr.; GeoRef; Leadscan.

US/0894-2706
AMERICAN GOLD NEWS & WESTERN PROSPECTOR. Suspended. See Earth Sciences-Mineralogy.

US
AMERICAN LAW OF MINING. See Law.

CN/0840-8610
AMERICAN MINES HANDBOOK.
[Am. mines handb.]. **Added/Corp** Northern Miner Press. (1989)-. English. an. 46.00Can$ Canada; 47.00Can$ other. Southam Information and Technology Group Inc., 1450 Don Mills Road, Don Mills Ontario M3B 2X7 Canada. **Tel** (416)445-6641, (800)668-2374, FAX (416)442-2261. **LC** PAR. **DD** 338.7/622/02573.

US/0276-4547
AMERICAN MINING CONGRESS LEGISLATIVE BULLETIN.
[Am. Min. Congr. legis. bull.]. **Main/Corp** American Mining Congress. Bulletin. ir. American Mining Congress, 1920 N Street NW/Suite 300, Washington DC 20036. **Tel** (202)861-2800.

AT
AMIRA ... ANNUAL REPORT / AUSTRALIAN MINERAL INDUSTRIES RESEARCH ASSOCIATION LIMITED.
Main/Corp Australian Mineral Industries Research Association. **VFOAT** A.M.I.R.A. ... Annual Report. (19??)-. English. an. Australian Mineral Industries Research Association Ltd, 11th Floor/63 Exhibition Street, Melbourne Victoria 30002 Australia. **LC** TN201; .A93a. **DD** 553/.072094.
Ind/Abst AESIS Q.

AT/1033-2774
AMREP RESOURCE POLITICS.
[AMREP resour. polit.]. (1989)-. Periodical. English. mo. AMREP Resource Politics, Mining Resource Politics, PO Box 131, Aldgate 5154 Australia. **Tel** (08)339 2960. **DD** 338.270994. **Continues** AMREP Database Bulletin, 0816-942X.
Desc: Newsletter containing information on mining.
Ind/Abst AESIS Q.

BE/0003-4290
ANNALES DES MINES DE BELGIQUE.
Ceased. (ANNALES DES MINES DE BELGIQUE; ANNALEN DER MIJNEN VAN BELGIE.). [Ann. mines belg.]. **Added/Corp** Belgium. Administration des Mines. **VFOAT** Annalen der Mijnen van Belgie. (1896)-(19??). Academic Scholarly Publication. French. mo. Institut National Indust Extractiv, rue du Chera 200, B-4000 Liege Belgium. **Tel** 041 527150. **LC** TN2; .A64. **CODEN** ANMBAK. **Bk Rev**. **Ad Acc**. **Circ:** 500 (ctrl). Documents available from Article Express International, CASDDS.
Desc: Studies and research in the areas of mines, energy, new materials, biotechnology, plastics, security, environment and aid to industries.
Ind/Abst Bioeng. Abstr.; Chem. Abstr.; Coal Abstr.; Ei Page One; EMBASE; Energy Res. Abstr. (June 1980-); Eng. Index Annu.; MINPROC; Mintec, Min. Technol. Abstr.; Saf. Health Work.

FR/1140-7123
ANNUAIRE DE L'ADMINISTRATION DES DIRECTIONS REGIONALES DE L'INDUSTRIE ET DE LA RECHERCHE.
(1986)-. French. an. 337.90F France; 369.00F other. Editions Eska, 27 rue Dunois, 75013 Paris France. **Tel** 011 33 1 44068042. **UDC** 058.7. Index available. cum. index. **Ad Acc**. **Circ:** 10,000 (ctrl).
Desc: Overview of business and administration offices of mines and mining engineering.

FR
ANNUAIRE DE L'ADMINISTRATION DES MINES.
French. an. 4 rue Las Cases, 75700 Paris France. **LC** HD9506.F7; A52. **DD** 338.2/025/44.
Continues Annuaire de l'Administration et du Corps des Mines.

FR
ANNUAIRE MINEMET.
Main/Corp Minemet. (1977)-. French. an. Societe Minemet Direction Market, 33 Avenue du Maine, 75755 Paris Cedex 15 France. **LC** HD9506.A1; M544A. **DD** 338.2/02/12. **Continues** Minemet. Annuaire.

AT
ANNUAL MAGAZINE / WESTERN AUSTRALIAN SCHOOL OF MINES.
Main/Corp Western Australian School of Mines. (19??)-. English. **LC** WMLC 93/863.
Ind/Abst AESIS Q.

US/0270-7837
ANNUAL MEETING OF THE MINNESOTA SECTION, AIME AND ANNUAL MINING SYMPOSIUM.
(ANNUAL MEETING OF THE MINNESOTA SECTION, AIME AND ... ANNUAL MINING SYMPOSIUM : [PROCEEDINGS]). [Annu. meet. Minn. Sect., AIME annu. Min. Symp.]. **Main/Conf** American Institute of Mining, Metallurgical, and Petroleum Engineers. **VAT** Annual Meeting of the Minnesota Section, American Institute of Mining, Metallurgical and Petroleum Engineers and Annual Mining Symposium. (1974)-. English. an. **CODEN** PMMAD8. Documents available from CASDDS.
Continues American Institute of Mining, Metallurgical, and Petroleum Engineers. Minnesota Section. Meeting. Annual Meeting and ... Mining Symposium.
Ind/Abst Chem. Abstr.

US
ANNUAL REPORT AND DIRECTORY OF MINES / STATE OF WEST VIRGINIA, DIVISION OF ENERGY, HEALTH SAFETY AND TRAINING, MINES AND MINERALS.
Main/Corp West Virginia. Division Energy. Health, Safety and Training (Section). **Added/Corp** West Virginia. Division of Energy. Mines and Minerals (Section). **VFOAT** Directory of Mines. (1989)-. Directory. English. West Virginia Department of Mines, Charleston WV 25305. **Tel** (304)348-3500. **Continues** West Virginia. Division of Mines and Minerals. Annual Report and Directory of Mines.

AT/0067-1762
ANNUAL REPORT / AUSTRALIAN COAL INDUSTRY RESEARCH LABORATORIES.
Main/Corp Australian Coal Industry Research Laboratories. (19??)-. English. an. Australian Coal Industry Research Laboratories, PO Box 83, 22-30 Delhi Road, North Ryde NSW 2113 Australia. **Tel** 011 61 2 8873777. **LC** TN811.A8; A83a. **DD** 662.6/2/072094.

SA
ANNUAL REPORT - BANTU MINING CORPORATION.
Main/Corp Bantu Mining Corporation. **Added/Corp** Bantu Mining Corporation. Jaarverslag - Bantoemynboukorporasie. **VFOAT** Jaarverslag - Bantoemynboukorporasie. (19??)-. Multiple languages (Afrikaans and English). an. Bantu Mining Corporation, Poynton Centre West Wing, 1029 Church Street, Pretoria South Africa. **LC** HD9506.S74; B33a. **DD** 338.7/62/20968.

CN/1181-9294
ANNUAL REPORT / BRITISH COLUMBIA ACID MINE DRAINAGE TASK FORCE.
[Annu. rep. - B.C. Acid Mine Drain. Task Force]. **Main/Corp** British Columbia Acid Mine Drainage Task Force. (1989/1990)-. English. **DD** 622/.5/09711.

SA/0379-4520
ANNUAL REPORT / CHAMBER OF MINES OF SOUTH AFRICA.
[Annu. rep. - Chamb. Mines S. Afr.]. **Main/Corp** Chamber of Mines of South Africa. (1967-1992). English. Chamber of Mines of South Africa, 5 Holland Street, Johannesburg 2001 South Africa. **Tel** (011)838-8211, FAX (011)934-3804. **LC** HD9506.A1; S6. **DD** 354/.68/008238. **Continues** Transvaal and Orange Free State Chamber of Mines.; Annual Report. **Continued in part by** Chamber of Mines of South Africa.; Presidential Address.
Ind/Abst AESIS Q.

RH
ANNUAL REPORT / CHAMBRE OF MINES, ZIMBABWE.
Main/Corp Chamber of Mines (Zimbabwe). **VFOAT** Report. English. Stewart House, 4 Central Avenue, PO Box 712, Harare Zimbabwe. **Tel** 702843, telex 262712W. **Continues** Report / Chamber of Mines, Zimbabwe.

SA
ANNUAL REPORT / COUNCIL FOR MINERAL TECHNOLOGY.
Main/Corp Council for Mineral Technology (South Africa). **VAT** Council for Mineral Technology Annual Report. (1981)-. English (Afrikaans). an. Free. Mintek, Private Bag X3015, Randburg 2125 South Africa. **Tel** 011 27 11 7933511, FAX 011 27 11 7932413, telex 4-24867. **ED** H W Glen. **Circ:** 1,700 (ctrl). **Continues** Annual Report / National Institute for Metallurgy.
Desc: Report of the activities of the Council for Mineral Technology for the calendar year.
Ind/Abst AESIS Q.

AT
ANNUAL REPORT / DEPARTMENT OF MANUFACTURING AND INDUSTRY DEVELOPMENT, VICTORIA, AUSTRALIA.
Main/Corp Victoria. Dept. of Manufacturing and Industry Development. **VFOAT** DMID Annual Report. (1991)-. English. **LC** QE347; .A21. **Continues** Annual Report.

AT/0725-9727
ANNUAL REPORT - DEPARTMENT OF MINES AND ENERGY, NORTHERN TERRITORY.
[Annu. rep. - Dep. Mines Energy, North. Territ.]. (1979)-. English. an. **DD** 354.94290682327.
Ind/Abst AESIS Q.

CL
ANNUAL REPORT / ENAMI, EMPRESA NACIONAL DE MINERIA.
Main/Corp Empresa Nacional de Mineria. English. Mac-Iver 459, PO Box 100-D, Santiago Chile.

AT
ANNUAL REPORT FOR THE YEAR ENDING JUNE 30TH ... .
Main/Corp New South Wales. Dept. of Mineral Resources. **VFOAT** A Year of Achievement. (19??)-. English. Australian Bureau of Statistics, PO Box 10, Belconnen Australian Capital Territory, 2616 Australia. **Tel** 011 61 6 2527911, FAX 011 61 6 2516009. **Continues** New South Wales. Dept. of Mineral Resources and Development. Annual Report.
Ind/Abst AESIS Q.

CN/0382-0734
ANNUAL REPORT - HOLLINGER MINES LIMITED.
Main/Corp Hollinger Mines Limited. **VFOAT** Rapport Annuel - Hollinger Mines Limited. 1968-. Periodical. Multiple languages. an. Hollinger Mines Limited, Suite 601, Commerce Court East, PO Box 221, Commerce Court Postal Station M5L 1E8. **Supersedes** Hollinger Consolidated Gold Mines Limited. Annual Report.

UK
ANNUAL REPORT / IEA COAL RESEARCH.
Main/Corp IEA Coal Research. (198?)-. Corporate Report. English. an. Free. IEA Coal Research, 10-18 Putney Hill, Gemini House, London SW15 6AA England. **Tel** 011 41 81 780 2111, FAX 011 41 81 780 1746, telex 917624. **LC** TN799.9; .I18a. **DD** 553.2/4/072041. Documents available from FAXON Xpress. **Continues** IEA Coal Research. Report.
Ind/Abst AESIS Q.

US/0093-2396
ANNUAL REPORT - INTERIM COMPLIANCE PANEL (WASHINGTON). See Law.

CN/0837-6786
ANNUAL REPORT - MANITOBA NATURAL RESOURCES.
(ANNUAL REPORT.). [Annu. rep. - Manit. Nat. Resour.]. **Main/Corp** Manitoba. Manitoba Natural Resources. (1983/1984)-. English. Department of Natural Resources / Manitoba Canada, Box 22, 1495 St James Street, Winnipeg Manitoba R3H 0W9 Canada. **Tel** (204)945-6786. **LC** TN27.M5; M36a. **DD** 354.71270082/32. **Continues** Annual Report, Year Ending March 31st ...., 0711-8260.

SA/0250-2348
ANNUAL REPORT / NATIONAL INSTITUTE FOR COAL RESEARCH.
Main/Corp National Institute for Coal Research (South Africa). **VFOAT** Jaarverslag. 1983-. Periodical. Afrikaans (English). an. Free. Division for Energy Technology, CSIR, PO Box 217, Pretoria 0001 South Africa. **Tel** (012)342-1020, FAX 342-1020, telex 3-20430. **LC** TP325; .N28A. **DD** 662.6/2/072068. **Circ:** 1,000 (ctrl).
Desc: Information on coal technology, chemistry, physics and analysis of coal, conversion, preparation and utilization.

AT/1034-7380
ANNUAL REPORT - QUEENSLAND. DEPARTMENT OF RESOURCE INDUSTRIES. (ANNUAL REPORT.). [Annu. rep. - Qld., Dep. Resour. Ind.]. (1990)-. English. an. **DD** 354.9430082382. ***Continues*** *Annual Report - Queensland Department of Mines, 1034-6791.*
Ind/Abst AESIS Q.

MY
ANNUAL REPORT / SEATRAD CENTRE. **Main/Corp** SEATRAD Centre. (19??)-. English. **LC** TN476.I5; S42a. **DD** 354.1/82382.
Ind/Abst AESIS Q.

AT/0813-2127
ANNUAL REPORT - SOUTH AUSTRALIAN CHAMBER OF MINES INCORPORATED. (1980)-. English. an.
Ind/Abst AESIS Q.

RH
ANNUAL REPORT (UNIVERSITY OF ZIMBABWE. INSTITUTE OF MINING RESEARCH). (ANNUAL REPORT / INSTITUTE OF MINING RESEARCH, UNIVERSITY OF ZIMBABWE.). **Added/Corp** University of Zimbabwe. Institute of Mining Research. (Jan. 1981)-. English. an. University of Zimbabwe / Department of Law, PO Box MP 167, Mount Pleasant, Harare Zimbabwe. **Tel** 011 263 0 303211 ext. 1813, FAX 011 263 4 303273. **LC** TN119.R45; A56. **DD** 622/.096891. ***Continues*** *Annual Report / University of Rhodesia. Institute of Mining Research.*

GW/0003-5238
ANSCHNITT, DER. [Anschnitt]. **Added/Corp** Vereiningung der Feunde von Kunst und Kultur im Bergbau. (Nov. 1949)-. German. **[CCC].**
Ind/Abst BHA : Biblio. Hist. Art; GeoRef.

US
ANTIMONY IN ... . **See** Engineering-Abstracting, Bibliographies and Statistics.

CL/0066-5096
ANUARIO DE LA MINERIA DE CHILE / MINISTERIO DE ECONOMIA, SERVICO NACIONAL DE GEOLOGIA Y MINERIA. Spanish. an. $8.00 US. Servicio Nacional de Geologia y Mineria, Casilla 10465, Santiago Chile. **Tel** 375050. **ED** Juan Williams. **LC** HD9506.C5; A58. **DD** 338.2/0983. **Circ:** 1,000.
Desc: Statistics of the mining production of Chile.
Ind/Abst Coal Abstr.

CL
ANUARIO ESTADISTICO DE LA SIDERURGIA Y MINERIA DEL HIERRO DE AMERICA LATINA / INSTITUTO LATINOAMERICANO DEL FIERRO Y EL ACERO. **See** Engineering-Abstracting, Bibliographies and Statistics.

US/0741-0603
APPLICATION OF COMPUTERS AND OPERATIONS RESEARCH IN THE MINERAL INDUSTRY / SPONSORED BY COLORADO SCHOOL OF MINES. **See** Earth Sciences-Mineralogy.

PL/0860-7001
ARCHIVES OF MINING SCIENCES. [Arch. Min. Sci.]. **VFOAT** Archiwum Gornictwa. (1987)-. Periodical. Polish. qt. **UDC** 622. Documents available from CASDDS. ***Continues*** *Archiwum Gornictwa, 0004-0754.*
Ind/Abst Chem. Abstr.

PL/0004-0754
ARCHIWUM GORNICTWA. (ARCHIWUM GORNICTWA / POLSKA AKADEMIA NAUK, KOMITET GORNICTWA.). [Arch. gor.]. **Added/Corp** Polska Akademia Nauk. Komitet Gornictwa. **VFOAT** Archives of Mining Sciences. Vol 1, Part. 1 (1956)-. Academic Scholarly Publication. Polish (English; summaries and/or abstracts in Russian; table of contents in Russian). qt. $60.00. **(Subscription address:** ARS Polona, PO Box 1001, 00068 Warsaw Poland.**)** **LC** TN4; .A63. **CODEN** AGORAT. Index Available, published separately, free-automatically sent. Documents available from Article Express International, CASDDS. ***Continues in part*** *Archiwum Gornictwa I Hutnictwa.*
Ind/Abst Bioeng. Abstr.; Chem. Abstr. (1956-1986); Coal Abstr.; Ei Page One; Eng. Index Annu.; GeoRef; Mintec, Min. Technol. Abstr.

US/1045-4802
ARIZONA GEOLOGY. **See** Earth Sciences-Geology.

NO
ARSBERETNING - OLJEDIREKTORATET. **Main/Corp** Norway. Oljedirektoratet. 1973-. Norwegian (English). PO Box 600, 4000 Stavanger Norway. **LC** TN874.N8; N67A.

US
ASBESTOS. Periodical. English. an. US Department of the Interior / Bureau of Mines, Publications Department, PO Box 18070, Cochrans Mill Road, Pittsburgh PA 15236. **Tel** (412)892-6400.

US/0886-3148
ASH AT WORK. [Ash work]. **Added/Corp** National Ash Association. (19??)-. Periodical. English. Twelve times a year. $220.00 membership. American Coal Ash Association, 1913 I Street NW, 6th Floor, Washington DC 20006. **Tel** (202)659-2303. **DD** 338.
Ind/Abst Coal Abstr.

CN/0840-6693
ATLANTIC MINING JOURNAL. [Atl. min. j.]. Vol. 1, No. 1 (July 1988)-. Periodical. English. ir. 18.00Can$. Atlantic Mining Journal, 2099 Gottingen Street, Halifax NS B3K 3B2 Canada. **ED** Ken Patridge. **DD** 338.2/09715. **Ad Acc.** ctrl circ.
Desc: Tabloid covering mining activity in Atlantic Canada.

CN
AU NORD DU 60E : MINES ET MINERAUX, ACTIVITE. **Main/Corp** Canada. Northern Natural Resources and Environment Branch. Mining Section. 1972-. French. an. Information Canada, 171 Slater Street, Ottawa Ontario K1A 0S9 Canada. **Tel** (819)997-1095. **LC** TN27.N72; C26A. **DD** 338.2/09719/1. ***Continues*** *Mines et Mineraux: Activite.*

GW/0004-783X
AUFBEREITUNGS-TECHNIK. [Aufbereit. Tech.]. (1960)-. Periodical. German (French and English). mo. DM276.00 Germany; DM316.00 other. Bauverlag GmbH, Postfach 1460, D 65173 Wiesbaden Germany. **Tel** 011 49 6123 7000, FAX 011 49 6123 700122. **ED** Rolf Kohling and Otto M Heintz. **CODEN** AUFTAK. **[CCC].** Index available. **Bk Rev. Ad Acc. Circ:** 4,000. Documents available from Article Express International, CASDDS.
Desc: Journal for preparation and processing.
Ind/Abst Alum. Ind. Abstr.; Bioeng. Abstr.; Chem. Abstr.; Coal Abstr.; Ei Page One; EMBASE; Energy Res. Abstr. (Jan. 1972-); Eng. Mater. Abstr.; Eng. Index Annu.; F&S Index Plus Text, Int. [Select. Cov.]; Fluid Abstr., Civil Eng.; Fluid Abstr. Proc. Eng.; FLUIDEX (1973-); GeoRef; Leadscan; Met. Abstr.; MINPROC; Mintec, Min. Technol. Abstr.; Proc. Chem. Eng.; Saf. Health Work; Theoret. Chem. Eng.

AU/1034-6775
AUSIMM BULLETIN / THE AUSTRALASIAN INSTITUTE OF MINING AND METALLURGY, THE. **Added/Corp** Australasian Institute of Mining and Metallurgy. **VFOAT** Bulletin. **VAT** Australasian Institute of Mining and Metallurgy Bulletin. No. 1 (March 1990)-. Academic Scholarly Publication. English. Six times a year. 120.00Aus$ (surface mail), 200.00Aus$ (airmail). Australasian Institute of Mining and Metallurgy, PO Box 122, Parkville Victoria 3052 Australia. **Tel** 011 61 3 3473166, FAX 011 61 3 3478525, telex 33552. **LC** TN121; .A67. **DD** 622/.05. **CODEN** AIBUEP. Documents available from Article Express International, CASDDS. ***Continues in part*** *AusIMM Bulletin and Proceedings, 0818-3848.*
Ind/Abst AESIS Q.; Bioeng. Abstr.; Chem. Abstr.; Eng. Index Annu. [Select. Cov.]; GeoRef.

AT/1034-6783
AUSIMM PROCEEDINGS. **Added/Corp** Australasian Institute of Mining and Metallurgy. **VFOAT** Proceedings. **VAT** Australasian Institute of Mining and Metallurgy Proceedings. Vol. 295, No. 1 (May 1990)-. Proceedings. English. Three times a year. Australasian Institute of Mining and Metallurgy, PO Box 122, Parkville Victoria 3052 Australia. **Tel** 011 61 3 3473166, FAX 011 61 3 3478525, telex 33552. **LC** TN1; .A78. **DD** 622/.05. Documents available from Article Express International. ***Continues in part*** *AusIMM Bulletin and Proceedings, 0818-3848.*
Ind/Abst AESIS Q.; Eng. Index Annu. [Select. Cov.].

AT
AUSTRALIAN COAL JOURNAL. ***Ceased.*** (19??)-(June 1994). English. Four times a year (Mar., June, Sept., Dec.). Australian Coal Industry Research Laboratories, PO Box 83, 22-30 Delhi Road, North Ryde NSW 2113 Australia. **Tel** 011 61 2 8873777.
Desc: Regular updates on research results and research commercialisation and much more of topical interest to the coal industry.

AT/0727-419X
AUSTRALIAN JOURNAL OF COAL MINING TECHNOLOGY AND RESEARCH, THE. ***Title Change.*** [Aust. j. coal min. technol. res.]. **Added/Corp** University of New South Wales. School of Mining Engineering. No. 1 (1982)-(1992). Periodical. English. Australian Coal Industry Research Laboratories, PO Box 83, 22-30 Delhi Road, North Ryde NSW 2113 Australia. **Tel** 011 61 2 8873777. ***Continued by*** *Australian Coal Journal.*

AT/0817-9646
AUSTRALIAN JOURNAL OF MINING. [Aust. j. min.]. **VFOAT** AJM. (1986)-. Periodical. English. mo (published Feb. through Dec. with Yearbook published in Jan.). 135.00Aus$. GMC Studio Pty Ltd., 394A Victoria Street, Richmond North 3121 Australia. **Tel** 011 61 3 4295599. **DD** 622.0994.
Ind/Abst AESIS Q.

AT
AUSTRALIAN MINER, THE. 1979. Periodical. English. bw. $107.72. Asher Joel Media Group, PO Box 3780, 120 Clarence Street, Sydney New South Wales 2001 Australia. **Tel** 02 20249. **ED** John Vanos. **LC** TN121; .A77. **DD** 622/.0994. **Ad Acc. Circ:** 5,176.
Desc: Contains the latest on government resources, policy exploration reports, new equipment and mining methods, people in the news, overseas resources news.
Ind/Abst Energy Res. Abstr. (July 1982-).

AT/0819-6508
AUSTRALIAN MINERALOGIST. ***Ceased.*** Vol. 2, No. 1 (July 1987)-Vol. 6, No. 2. Periodical. English. qt. Gemcraft, 291-295 Wattletree Road, East Malvern Victoria 3145 Australia. **Tel** 03-5091181.
Ind/Abst AESIS Q.

AT/0004-976X
AUSTRALIAN MINING. [Aust. min.]. Vol. 58, No. 1 (Jan. 15, 1966)-. Periodical. English. Eleven times a year. 77.00Aus$ Australia; 104.00Aus$ New Zealand, Papua New Guinea; 109.00Aus$ Malaysia, Indonesia, Fiji; 110.00Aus$ Japan, India, Hong Kong; 124.00Aus$ US, Canada, Lebanon; 134.00Aus$ Europe, Africa, former USSR. Thomson Publications / Australia, 47 Chippen Street, Chippendale New South Wales, 2008 Australia. **Tel** 011 61 2 6992411, FAX 011 61 2 698 3920, telex 122226. **(Subscription address:** Thomson Publications Australia, PO Box 815, Strawberry Hills, New South Wales, 2012 Australia.**)** **ED** Lou Caruana. **LC** TP1; .C36. **DD** 669/.0994. **CODEN** AUMNA3. Index available. **Bk Rev. Ad Acc. Circ:** 7,040 (ctrl). available on microfilm and microfiche from University Microfilms International (UMI). Documents available from Article Express International, Documents on Demand. ***Continues*** *Mining & Chemical Engineering Review.*
Ind/Abst AESIS Q.; Alum. Ind. Abstr.; Bioeng. Abstr.; Coal Abstr.; Ei Page One; Energy Res. Abstr.; Eng. Mater. Abstr.; Eng. Index Annu.; Environ. Abstr.; GeoRef; Met. Abstr.; Mintec, Min. Technol. Abstr.

AT/0812-857X
AUSTRALIAN MINING AND PETROLEUM LAW ASSOCIATION YEARBOOK. **See** Law.

AT
AUSTRALIAN MINING'S PRODUCT REGISTER. ***Ceased.*** **VFOAT** Product Register; Australian Mining Product Register. (1988)-(1993-1994) Edition. English. an. Thomson Publications / Australia, 47 Chippen Street, Chippendale New South Wales, 2008 Australia. **Tel** 011 61 2 6992411, FAX 011 61 2 698 3920, telex 122226. **(Subscription address:** Thomson Publications Australia, PO Box 815, Strawberry Hills, New South Wales, 2012 Australia.**)** **LC** HD9506.A7; A97. **DD** 622/.029/494.

AT
AUSTRALIA'S MINING MONTHLY. (1984)-. Trade Publication. English. mo. 44.00Aus$ Australia; 72.00Aus$ New Zealand, Papua, New Guinea, Southeast Asia, Japan; 84.00Aus$ other. Australia's Mining Monthly, PO Box 78, Leederville WA 6007 Australia. **Tel** 011 61 09 3821800, FAX 011 61 9 3811848. **ED** Darrel E Cake. **Bk Rev. Ad Acc. Circ:** 7,480 (ctrl). ***Continues*** *Mining Monthly, 0725-9131.*
Desc: High technology trade, technical, and professional magazine directed at a readership associated with all sectors of mining (gold and base metals) and the petroleum and gas industry.
Ind/Abst Coal Abstr.

CN/0838-5998
B.C. MINERAL STATISTICS ANNUAL SUMMARY TABLES. (B.C. MINERAL STATISTICS ANNUAL SUMMARY TABLES / PREPARED BY MINERAL STATISTICS SECTION, MINERAL POLICY & EVALUATION BRANCH, MINERAL RESOURCES DIVISION.). [B.C. miner. stat. annu. summ. tables]. **Added/Corp** British Columbia. Ministry of Energy, Mines and Petroleum Resources. British Columbia. Mineral Statistics Section. **VFOAT** British Columbia Mineral Statistics Annual Summary Tables. (1985)-. English. Ministry of Energy, Mines and Petroleum Resources, Petroleum Resources Division, Energy Resources Division, Victoria British Columbia Canada. **LC** HD9506.C23; B627. **DD** 338.2/09711/021. ***Separated from*** *British Columbia. Mineral Resources Division.; Summary of Operations, 0825-6896.*

BL
BAHIA, ANUARIO DA MINERACAO. Yearly V. 1-1977-. Portuguese. Secretaria das Minas e Energia Coordenacao da Producao Mineral, Centro Administrativo da Bahia, Av Luiz Viana Filho S/N, 40.000 Salvador Brazil. **LC** HD9506.B73; B313.

BL
BAHIA, BOLETIM INFORMATIVO SETOR MINERAL. **Main/Corp** Bahia, Brazil (State). Coordenacao da Producao Mineral. Yearly V. 7- (No. 70-); Nov. 1978-. Bulletin. Portuguese. Secretaria des Minas e Energia Mineral, Av Luiz Viana Filho S/No, 40.000 Salvador Brazil. **LC** TN42.B3; I582. ***Continues*** *Inventario dos Recursos Minerais do Estado da Bahia: Periodico.*

HU/0375-9504
BANYASZATI ES KOHASZATI LAPOK. OENTOEDE. (BANYASZATI ES KOHASZATI LAPOK. OENTOEDE : AZ ORSZAGOS MAGYAR BANYASZATI ES KOHASZATI EGYESUELET LAPJA.). [Banyasz. kohasz. lapok. Oentoede]. **Added/Corp** Orszagos Magyar Banyaszati es Kohaszati Egyesuelet. (1968)-. Academic Scholarly Publication. Hungarian (summaries and/or abstracts in English, German and Russian). mo. **(Subscription address:** Kultura, PO Box 149, H 1389 Budapest 62 Hungary.**)** Documents available from CASDDS. ***Continues*** *Oentoede.*
Ind/Abst Alum. Ind. Abstr.; Art Archaeol. Tech. Abstr.; Chem. Abstr.; Eng. Mater. Abstr.; Met. Abstr.

HU/0572-6034
BANYASZATI ES KOHASZATI LOPOK. KOOLAJ ES FOLDGAZ. (KOOLAJ ES FOLDGAZ.). [Banyasz. kohasz. lapok, Koolaj foldgaz]. **Added/Corp** Orszagos Magyar Banyaszati es Kohaszati Egyesuelet. Muszaki es Termeszettudomanyi Egyesuletek Szovetsege. (19??)-. Academic Scholarly Publication. Hungarian. mo. Akademiai Kiado, Publishing House of the Hungarian Academy of Sciences, Prielle Kornelia u. 19-35, H-1117 Budapest Hungary. **Tel** 011 36 1 1811991, FAX 011 36 1 1811991, telex 22-6228 AKNYO H. **LC** TN860; .K64. **CODEN** BKKFAC. Documents available from Petroleum Abstracts Document Delivery Service, CASDDS. ***Continues in part*** *Banyaszati es Kohaszati Lapok. Banyaszat, Koolaj es Foldgaz, Kohaszat, Onetoede.*
Ind/Abst Chem. Abstr.; Coal Abstr.; Gas Abstr.; Pet. Abstr.

HU/0231-0651
BANYASZATI SZAKIRODALMI TAJEKOZTATO. (1983)-. Periodical. Hungarian. bm. 8.600. Orszagos Muszaki Informacios Kozpont es Konyvtar (O.M.I.K.K.), National Technical Information Centre and Library Museum, u 17, PO Box 12, 1428 Budapest, Hungary. **Tel** (361)118-1994, FAX (361)138-2414, telex 22-4944 OMIKK H. **(Subscription address:** OMIKK Budapest, POB 12, H-1428 Hungary**)** **ED** Denes Panto. **UDC** 016. **Circ:** 80.
Desc: Articles on mines and mining engineering.

UK
BCRA QUARTERLY : A REVIEW OF PUBLISHED LITERATURE ON COAL, COKA AND ALLIED TOPICS. **See** Engineering-Abstracting, Bibliographies and Statistics.

DK/0107-3117
BERETNING FOR PERIODEN ... / FRA FLLESRADET VEDRRENDE MINERALSKE RASTOFFER I GRNLAND. **Main/Corp** Denmark. Fllesradet Vedrrende Mineralske Rastoffer I Grnland. Danish. an. Rastofforvaltningen for Grnland, Hausergade 3, 1128 Kbenhavn K Denmark. **LC** TN125.5; .D46A.

GW/0342-5681
BERGBAU (HATTINGEN). (BERGBAU.). [Bergbau]. **Added/Corp** Ring Deutscher Bergingenieure. (1949)-. Periodical. German. mo. DM101.40. Bertelsmann Fachzeitschriften GmbH, Carl-Bertelsmann Strasse 270, D-33311 Frankfurt Germany. **Tel** 011 49 5241 802199. **(Subscription address:** Translibris GmbH, PO Box 301373, D 50783 Cologne Germany**)** **ED** Aribert Langer. **LC** TN3; .B435. **Bk Rev. Ad Acc. Circ:** 11,000 (ctrl).
Desc: The official organ of Ring Deutscher Bergingenieure RDB Essen.
Ind/Abst Coal Abstr.; Energy Res. Abstr. (May 1978-); GeoRef; Saf. Health Work.

GW
BERGBAU UND VERARBEITENDES GEWERBE. **Main/Corp** Niedersachsisches Landesverwaltungsamt. (19??)-. Periodical. German. DM13.20. Niedersachsisches Landesverwaltungsamt, Postfach 107, 3000 Hannover Germany. **Tel** (0511)108-9466. **LC** HD9506.G23; S397a. **DD** 338.4/7/000943. **Bk Rev. Circ:** 270.
Desc: Different publications according to different inquiries: orders, output, staff, enterprises, turnover, investments available for districts or Federal State of Lower Saxony.

SW/0284-0448
BERGSMANNEN. **Added/Corp** Nordiska Stalforbundet. **VFOAT** Bergsmannen Med Jernkontorets Annaler; Jernkontorets Annaler. Vol. 1 (1987)-. Periodical. Swedish (English). bm. Kr220.00 US. Bergsmannen Med Jernkontorets Annaler, PO Box 5, S-151 21 Sodertalje Sweden. **Tel** 011 46 8 55061690, FAX 011 46 8 55085600. **ED** Anders Almgren. **LC** PAR. **Bk Rev**, (Qty: 6/yr). **Ad Acc**, **Adv Mgr:** L. Eck. **Circ:** 4500 (ctrl). ***Continues*** *Jernkontoret (Sweden). JKA, Jernkontorets Annaler, 0280-4239.*
Ind/Abst Ei Page One.

RU/0409-2961
BEZOPASNOST TRUDA V PROMYSHLENNOSTI. [Bezop. truda prom.]. (1957)-. Academic Scholarly Publication. Russian. mo. $75.00. **(Subscription address:** Victor Kamkin, 4956 Boiling Brook Parkway, Rockville MD 20852.**)** **CODEN** BZTPAM. Index available in last issue of volume--attached. Documents available from CASDDS.
Desc: A mass scientific-production journal of the Committee on Safe Conduction of Operations in Industry and Mining Supervision under the Council of Ministers.
Ind/Abst Chem. Abstr.; Coal Abstr.; Saf. Health Work.

US/0006-4149
BLACK DIAMOND, THE. ***Suspended.*** [Black diam.]. Vol. 1, No. 1 (Aug. 1885)-(19??). Periodical. English. bm. $12.00. Black Diamond, 343 South Dearborn Street, Chicago IL 60604. **Tel** (312)922-8031. **LC** TN1; .B6. **DD** 338.
Ind/Abst Coal Abstr.

PO/0006-5935
BOLETIM DE MINAS. [Bol. minas]. **Added/Corp** Portugal. Direccao-Geral de Minas e Servicos Geologicos. (19??)-. Bulletin. Portuguese (summaries and/or abstracts in English and French). qt. Direccao-Geral de Geologia e Minas, Rua Antonio Enes 7, 1097 Lisbon Codex, Portugal. **LC** TN83; .B65. **CODEN** PBMIBL.
Ind/Abst PAIS Int. Print.

CL/0577-7933
BOLETIN DE ESTADISTICA MINERA. **See** Engineering-Abstracting, Bibliographies and Statistics.

CK/0120-9523
BOLETIN DE MINAS Y ENERGIA. [Bol. minas energ.]. **Added/Corp** Colombia. Ministerio de Minas y Energia. Vol. 1 (Jan. 1977)-. Periodical. Spanish. qt. Fondo Rotativo Dane, Apartado 80043, Bogota Colombia. **Tel** 011 57 1 2221750. **LC** TN4; .B62. ***Supersedes*** *Boletin de Minas; Boletin de Petroleos.*
Ind/Abst GeoRef.

UK
BQSF REVIEW. ***Ceased.*** **Main/Corp** British Quarrying & Slag Federation. **Added/Corp** British Quarrying & Slag Federation. Review. Vol. 9 (April 1978)-?. Periodical. English. qt. British Quarrying & Slag Federation, 14 Waterloo Place, London SW1Y 4AR England. **LC** TN950.A1; B74a. **DD** 338.2/75/0941. ***Continues*** *British Quarrying & Slag Federation. Technical Review.*

CN/0846-0051
BRITISH COLUMBIA MINERAL EXPLORATION REVIEW. [B.C. miner. explor. rev.]. 1985-. English. an. Free. British Columbia Ministry of Energy, Mines and Petroleum Resources, Parliament Buildings, Victoria British Columbia V8V 1X4 Canada. **Tel** (604)387-5538. **LC** TN27.B9; B69. **DD** 333.8/5/09711. ***Continues*** *British Columbia Exploration Review.*
Desc: Reviews mineral exploration activity in British Columbia. Includes details on exploratory trenching and drilling.

US
BROMINE. **Added/Corp** United States. Bureau of Mines. **VFOAT** Annual Report. Bromine. (1990)-. Government Publication. English. US Department of the Interior / Bureau of Mines, 810 7th Street NW, Room 604, Washington DC 20241. **Tel** (202)501-9300. ***Continues*** *Minerals Yearbook. Bromine.*

US
BROMINE IN ... . **See** Earth Sciences-Abstracting, Bibliographies and Statistics.

US/0008-1000
BULLETIN / CALIFORNIA DIVISION OF MINES AND GEOLOGY. [Bull. - Calif., Div. Mines Geol.]. Bulletin. English. ir. Price varies per volume. California Division of Mines and Geology, PO Box 2980, Sacramento CA 95812. **Tel** (916)445-0514. **LC** TN24.C2; A3. **DD** 551. **CODEN** CDMBA6. ***Continues*** *Bulletin (California. Division of Mines).*
Ind/Abst GeoRef.

US/0082-9129
BULLETIN / DEPARTMENT OF THE INTERIOR, BUREAU OF MINES. [Bull., U.S. Dept. Inter. Bur. Mines]. No. 1 (1910)-. Bulletin. English. ir. Price varies per volume. Superintendent of Documents, US Government Printing Office, Washington DC 20402. **Tel** (202)275-3328, FAX (202)786-2377. **LC** TN23; .U4. **DD** 622. **CODEN** XBMBAJ. cum. index. Documents available from Article Express International, CASDDS.
Ind/Abst AESIS Q.; Ceram. Abstr.; Chem. Abstr. (1910-1980); Ei Page One; Eng. Index Annu.; GeoRef.

US/0097-191X
BULLETIN - NEVADA BUREAU OF MINES AND GEOLOGY. **See** Earth Sciences-Geology.

US/0096-4581
BULLETIN - NEW MEXICO BUREAU OF MINES & MINERAL RESOURCES. [Bull. - N. M. Bur. Mines Miner. Resour.]. **Main/Corp** New Mexico. Bureau of Mines and Mineral Resources. **Added/Corp** New Mexico. Bureau of Mines and Mineral Resources. **VAT** Bulletin - New Mexico Bureau of Mines and Mineral Resources. (1928)-. Academic Scholarly Publication. English. ir. Price varies per volume. New Mexico Bureau of Mines, Campus Station, Socorro NM 87801. **Tel** (505)835-5410, FAX (505)835-6333. **ED** J. Zibek. **LC** TN24.N6; A232. **DD** 622.0711789. **CODEN** NEXBAJ. **Bk Rev. Ad Acc.** ctrl circ. Documents available from CASDDS. ***Continues*** *Bulletin (New Mexico. Mineral Resources Survey).*
Desc: Geology, mineral resources, energy resources, and metallurgy pertaining fully or in part to the state of New Mexico.
Ind/Abst Ceram. Abstr.; Chem. Abstr.; GeoRef.

US/0582-5083
BULLETIN OF SELENIUM-TELLURIUM, THE. **Added/Corp** Selenium-Tellurium Development Association (Darien, Conn.). **VFOAT** The Bulletin of Selenium-Tellurium Development Association, Inc. (19??)-. Bulletin. English. Selenium-Tellurium Development Association, PO Box 3096, Darien CT 06820.
Ind/Abst AESIS Q.

MY
BULLETIN OF STATISTICS RELATING TO THE MINING INDUSTRY OF MALAYSIA. ***Title Change.*** **See** Engineering-Abstracting, Bibliographies and Statistics.

TU
BULLETIN OF THE MINERAL RESEARCH AND EXPLORATION. **Added/Corp** Turkey. Maden Tetkik ve Arama Genel Mudurlugu. No. 101/102 (October 1983-April 1984)-. Bulletin. English (French and German). sa. $30.00. Maden Tetkik Ve Arama Enstitus, Genel Mudurlugu, Ankara Turkey. **LC** HD9506.A1; A62. **DD** 333.8/5/09561. ***Continues*** *Bulletin of the Mineral Research and Exploration Institute of Turkey.*
Ind/Abst Geogr. Abstr. Phys. Geogr.

UK/0031-3637
BULLETIN OF THE PEAK DISTRICT MINES HISTORICAL SOCIETY. (BULLETIN.). [Bull. Peak Dist. Mines Hist. Soc.]. **Main/Corp** Peak District Mines Historical Society. (1959)-. Bulletin. English. **LC** TN58.D4; P4.
Ind/Abst Geogr. Abstr. Human Geogr.

MR
BUREAU DE RECHERCHES ET DE PARTICIPATIONS MINIERES : RAPPORT. ***Title Change.*** **See** Earth Sciences-Meteorology.

US/1066-5544
BUREAU OF MINES INFORMATION CIRCULAR. (INFORMATION CIRCULAR.). [Bur. Mines inf. circ.]. **Added/Corp** United States. Bureau of Mines. **VFOAT** I.C.; IC. (1925)-. Monographic series. English. ir. Price varies per volume. US Department of the Interior / Bureau of Mines, 810 7th Street NW, Room 604, Washington DC 20241. **Tel** (202)501-9300. **ED** J.N. Walker. **LC** TN295; .U4. **DD** 622.06173. **CODEN** XIMIAL. Index available. cum. index. **Circ:** 2,000 (ctrl). available on microfiche (from National Technical Information Service). Documents available from Article Express International, CASDDS.
Desc: Surveys of mineral resources and related mining and operating activities, compilations of statistical and economic data on minerals, summaries of technical meetings and symposia.
Ind/Abst Bioeng. Abstr.; Chem. Abstr.; Coal Abstr.; Ei Page One; Eng. Index Annu.; GeoRef.

US/0737-626X
BUREAU OF MINES RESEARCH. [Bur. Mines res.]. **Added/Corp** United States. Bureau of Mines. **VFOAT** Research; U.S. Bureau of Mines Research. (1971)-. Government Publication. English. ir. US Department of the Interior / Bureau of Mines, 810 7th Street NW, Room 604, Washington DC 20241. **Tel** (202)501-9300. **(Subscription address:** Superintendent of Documents, US Government Printing Office, Washington DC 20402.**)** **ED** Jerald Pederson. **DD** 622/.07/2073; 622. **CODEN** BMREDR. ***Continues*** *United States. Bureau of Mines. Research Summaries.*
Desc: Highlights such topics as cyanide heap leaching and the environmental issues associated with the "gold rush of the 1980's", mine fire warning systems, automation in mining, land use restraints on federal lands, and international coal production costs and competitiveness.
Ind/Abst GeoRef.

US/0362-725X
BUREAU OF MINES TECHNICAL PROGRESS REPORT. [Bur. Mines tech. prog. rep.]. **Added/Corp** United States. Bureau of Mines. (Mar. 1968)-. Monographic series. English. ir. Price varies per volume. Superintendent of Documents, US Government Printing Office, Washington DC 20402. **Tel** (202)275-3328, FAX (202)786-2377. **DD** I 28.26/6. **CODEN** XMTPB4. Documents available from Article Express International, CASDDS.
Ind/Abst Bioeng. Abstr.; Ceram. Abstr. (19??-); Chem. Abstr. (1968-1983); Coal Abstr.; Ei Page One; Eng. Index Annu.; GeoRef.

JA
BUTSURI TANKO CHOSA KENKYU ICHIRAN. **Added/Corp** Chishitsu Chosajo (Japan). **VFOAT** Survey List of Geophysical Prospecting. No. 1 (1948/1952)-. Japanese. Kogyo Gijutsuin Chishitsu Chosajo, (Geological Survey of Japan, Agency of Industrial Science & Technology), 1-3, Higashi 1 Chome, Tsukubashi, Ibarakiken 305 Japan. **(Subscription address:** Japan Publications Trading Company, Ltd., PO Box 5030, Tokyo International, Tokyo 100-31 Japan.**) LC** TN105; .B88.

II/0303-8556
C. E. G. BULLETIN. [CEG bull.]. **Main/Corp** Osmania University, Hyderabad, India. Centre of Exploration Geophysics. **VAT** Centre of Exploration Geophysics Bulletin. Bulletin. English. Osmania University / Centre of Exploration, Geophysics Council Scientific Ind Res, Hyderabad India. **LC** TN269; .O8A. **DD** 622/.15/05.
Ind/Abst GeoRef.

CN/0701-0710
C I M REPORTER. [C I M report.]. **Main/Corp** Canadian Institute of Mining and Metallurgy. (1???)-. Periodical. English. ir. free on request. Canadian Institute of Mining, Metallurgy and Petroleum, 3400 de Maisonneuve Boulevard West, Xerox Tower, Suite 1210, Montreal, Quebec H3Z 3B8 Canada. **Tel** (514)939-2710, FAX (514)939-2714, telex 055-62344. **ED** P. Michaud. **DD** 338.2/0971. **Bk Rev**. **Ad Acc. Circ:** 6,200 (ctrl).
Desc: Newspaper published in conjunction with major mining meetings focuses on current and technological news of interest to the minerals industry.
Ind/Abst Coal Abstr.; MINPROC; Mintec, Min. Technol. Abstr.

CN/0228-1821
C R S PERSPECTIVES. [CRS perspect.]. **Main/Corp** Queen's University (Kingston, Ont.). Centre for Resource Studies. **VAT** Centre for Resource Studies Perspectives. No. 1 (April 1978)-. Periodical. English. Six times a year. 30.00Can$. Centre for Resource Studies, Queen's University, Kingston Ontario K7L 3N6 Canada. **Tel** (613)545-2553, FAX (613)545-6651. **ED** Moira Jackson. **DD** 338.2/0971. Index available. cum. index. **Ad Acc. Circ:** 1,800.
Desc: Newsletter distributed to CRS mailing list.

US/0008-1299
CALIFORNIA MINING JOURNAL. ***Title Change.*** [Calif. min. j.]. (1931)-(1993). Periodical. English. mo. California Mining Journal, PO Box 2260, 9032 Soquel Drive, Aptos CA 95001. **Tel** (408)662-2899, FAX (408)662-3014. **ED** Kenneth L. Harn. Index available. **Ad Acc, Adv Mgr:** D.Craig. **Circ:** 40,000. ***Continued by*** *International California Mining Journal.*
Desc: A publication for miners, prospectors, precious metals investors and companies of all sizes involved in the mining industry.
Ind/Abst Calif. Period. Index (19??-); Calif. Period. Microfi. (19??-); GeoRef.

CN/0380-7797
CANADA'S MINERAL PRODUCTION, PRELIMINARY ESTIMATES. [Can. miner. prod., Prelim. estim.]. **Main/Corp** Statistics Canada. Manufacturing and Primary Industries Division. **Added/Corp** Canada. Dominion Bureau of Statistics. Canada. Dominion Bureau of Statistics. Industry Division. Canada. Dominion Bureau of Statistics. Manufacturing and Primary Industries Division. Statistics Canada. Manufacturing and Primary Industries Division. Statistics Canada. Census of Manufactures Section. **VFOAT** Production Minerale du Canada, Calcul Preliminaire. (1964)-. English (French). an. 24.00Can$ Canada; $29.00 US; $34.00 other. Statistics Canada, Publications Sales & Services, Main Building Room 1710, Ottawa Ontario K1A 0T6 Canada. **Tel** (613)951-5078, (800)267-6677, FAX (613)951-1584, telex 053-3585. **DD** 338.2/0971. ***Continues*** *Preliminary Estimates of Canada's Mineral Production., 0380-7800.*
Desc: Presents statistics on the number of mines or plants, average number of employees, salaries and wages, costs of fuel and electricity, costs of materials and gross selling value of products, with comparative totals for earlier years with breakdown by province. Further detail is given on fuel by kind and electricity used, quantity and cost, and various products shipped, with selling value.

●CN
CANADIAN DIRECTORY OF EFFICIENCY AND ALTERNATIVE ENERGY TECHNOLOGIES. **Added/Corp** Canada. Energy, Mines and Resources Canada. Canada. External Affairs and International Trade Canada. **VFOAT** Repertoire Canadien des Technologies de l'Efficacite Energetique et des Energies de Remplacement. (1991/1992)-. Directory. English. Energy Publications / Canada, c/o Canada Communications Group, Ottawa Ontario K1A 0S9 Canada.

CN/0068-9270
CANADIAN MINERALS YEARBOOK. **See** Earth Sciences-Mineralogy.

CN/0068-9289
CANADIAN MINES HANDBOOK. [Can. mines handb.]. **Added/Corp** Northern Miner Press. (1931)-. English. an. 50.95Can$. Southam Information and Technology Group Inc., 1450 Don Mills Road, Don Mills Ontario M3B 2X7 Canada. **Tel** (416)445-6641, (800)668-2374, FAX (416)442-2261. **ED** C D Gardiner. **LC** HG5159.M4; C3. **DD** 338.2065. **Bk Rev. Ad Acc. Circ:** 15,000.
Desc: Directory of Canadian mining companies.
Ind/Abst F&S Index Plus Text, Int. [Select. Cov.]; GeoRef.

CN/0823-5716
CANADIAN MINES, PERSPECTIVE. (CANADIAN MINES.). [Can. mines perspect.]. **Added/Corp** Canada. Minerals. **VFOAT** Mines au Canada. (1979)-. English (French). 19.95Can$. Canada Communication Group Publishers, Order Processing, Ottawa Ontario K1A 0S9 Canada. **Tel** (819)956-4800, (819)956-4802. **LC** HD9506.C2; C29. **DD** 338.2/74/0971. ***Absorbed*** *Mine Reserves and Currently Promising Deposits, 0848-4732.*

CN/0008-4492
CANADIAN MINING JOURNAL. [Can. min. j.]. Vol. 28, No.3 (March 1907)-. Periodical. English. Six times a year. 24.50Can$ (one year), 33.00Can$ (two year), 40.00Can$ (three year) Canada & US; 43.00Can$ other. Southam Information and Technology Group Inc., 1450 Don Mills Road, Don Mills Ontario M3B 2X7 Canada. **Tel** (416)445-6641, (800)668-2374, FAX (416)442-2261. **ED** Jane Werniuk. **CODEN** CAMJA9. **[CCC]**. Index available. cum. index. **Bk Rev. Ad Acc. Circ:** 10,470 (ctrl). available on microfilm from Micromedia Limited; available on microfilm and microfiche from University Microfilms International (UMI); available on an online database (file 16/Full-Text) from DIALOG. Documents available from Article Express International, The Genuine Article, Petroleum Abstracts Document Delivery Service, CASDDS, Documents on Demand. ***Continues*** *Canadian Mining Review, 0381-6877.*
Desc: An independent publication serving Canada's mining industry from exploration to the production, smelting and refining of minerals.
Ind/Abst ASTIS Curr. Aware. Bull. (1978-); AESIS Q.; AQUAREF; ASTIS Bibliogr. (1978-); Bioeng. Abstr.; Ceram. Abstr. (1978-); Chem. Abstr. (1907-1983); Coal Abstr.; Curr. Contents Eng. Tech. Appl. Sci.; Ei Page One; EMBASE; Energy Inf. Abstr.; Energy Res. Abstr.; Eng. Index Annu.; Environ. Abstr.; GeoRef; Leadscan; MINPROC; Mintec, Min. Technol. Abstr.; Pet. Abstr. (1978-); PROMT [Full Txt.]; Res. Alert [Select. Cov.]; Saf. Health Work; SCISEARCH.

CN/1184-9738
CANADIAN MINING LIFE & EXPLORATION NEWS. [Can. min. life explor. news]. **VFOAT** Mining Life. Issue No. 28 (Dec. 1990/Jan. 1991)-. Periodical. English. mo. $21.00 per year. Directories North Publications, 35 Birch Street North, Timmins Ontario P4N 6C8 Canada. **DD** 338.2. ***Continues*** *Ontario-Quebec Mining Life and Exploration News., 0841-2898.*

CN
CANADIAN MINING SOURCEBOOK. an. 72.50Can$ Canada; 89.00Can$ other. Southam Information and Technology Group Inc., 1450 Don Mills Road, Don Mills Ontario M3B 2X7 Canada. **Tel** (416)445-6641, (800)668-2374, FAX (416)442-2261.

CN/1185-0183
CARIBOO MINER. (THE CARIBOO MINER / CMA.). [Cariboo min.]. **Added/Corp** Cariboo Mining Association. Vol. 1, No. 1 (June 1, 1990)-. Periodical. English. ir. Free to members. Cariboo Mining Association, PO Box 4699, Quesnel, British Columbia V2J 3J9 Canada. **DD** 338.2/741/097117505.

AT
CENSUS OF MINING ESTABLISHMENTS: INDUSTRY CONCENTRATION STATISTICS, AUSTRALIA. **See** Engineering-Abstracting, Bibliographies and Statistics.

RH/0009-1162
CHAMBER OF MINES JOURNAL. (THE CHAMBER OF MINES JOURNAL : CMJ.). [Chamb. Mines j.]. **VFOAT** CMJ. Vol. 1 (May 1959)-?. Periodical. English. mo. $100.00. Modus Publications Ltd, PO Box 66070, KOPJE, Harare Zimbabwe. **Tel** 738722, FAX 707130, telex 26334. **ED** Shaun Orange. **LC** TN119.R6; C5. **CODEN** CHMJBP. **Bk Rev. Ad Acc. Circ:** 1,200 (ctrl). ***Continues*** *Gold Output;* ***Absorbed*** *Rhodesian Mining and Engineering.* ***Continued in part by*** *Mining and Engineering, 0254-0304.*
Desc: Mining industry in Africa.
Ind/Abst GeoRef; MINPROC; Mintec, Min. Technol. Abstr.

SA
CHAMBER OF MINES' NEWSLETTER. **See** Earth Sciences-Mineralogy.

HK/0258-3062
CHINA COAL INDUSTRY YEARBOOK. [China coal ind. yearb.]. **VFOAT** Chung-kuo Mei Tan Kung Yeh Nien Chien. 1982-. English. an. HK$300.00 Denmark; $50.00 US. Economic Information & Agency, 342 Hennessy Road, 10-16th Floor, Hong Kong Hong Kong. **Tel** 011 852 5 738217, telex 60647 EICC HX. **ED** Ye Qing. **LC** TN809.C47; C487. **DD** 338.2/724/0951. **Ad Acc. Circ:** 1,500 (ctrl).
Desc: Past, present and future development of China's coal industry with statistics support.

JA
CHISHITSU KAISEKI IINKAI HOKOKUSHO. **Main/Corp** Kinzoku Kogyo Jigyodan. Chishitsu Kaiseki Iinkai. (19??)-. Periodical. Japanese. Kinzoku Kogyo Jigyodan Shigen Joho Senta, (Mineral Resources Information Centre, Metal Mining Agency of Japan), 25-5 Toranomon 1 chome, Minatoku Tokyoto 105 Japan. **LC** TN260; .K56a.

KO
CHONGUK CHUNGSO KWANGGONGOP TONGGYE CHOSA POGOSO. **VFOAT** Survey Report on Small and Medium Industry in Mining and Manufacturing. 1979-. English (Korean). Chungso Kiop Chinhung Kongdan, 1-1040 Youido-dong Yongdungpo-ku, Seoul 150 Korea. **LC** HD9736.ZK65; C48.

FR/0182-564X
CHRONIQUE DE LA RECHERCHE MINIERE. **See** Earth Sciences-Geology.

CN/0317-0926
CIM BULLETIN. [CIM bull.]. **Added/Corp** Canadian Institute of Mining and Metallurgy. **VFOAT** Canadian Mining and Metallurgical Bulletin. Vol. 61, No. 669 (Jan. 1968)-. Bulletin. English (summaries and/or abstracts in French). Ten times a year. 135.00Can$ Canada; $150.00 other. Canadian Institute of Mining, Metallurgy and Petroleum, 3400 de Maisonneuve Boulevard West, Xerox Tower, Suite 1210, Montreal, Quebec H3Z 3B8 Canada. **Tel** (514)939-2710, FAX (514)939-2714, telex 055-62344. **ED** P. Michaud. **LC** TN1; .C23. **DD** 669/.00971. **CODEN** CIBUBA. **Bk Rev. Ad Acc. Pr Rev. Circ:** 11,000 (ctrl). available on microfilm and microfiche from University Microfilms International (UMI). Documents available from Article Express International, The Genuine Article, Ask*IEEE, CASDDS, Documents on Demand. ***Continues*** *Canadian Mining and Metallurgical Bulletin, 0008-4484.*
Desc: Devoted to geology, mining engineering and metallurgy read by 11,000 men and women who have the power to make major changes to their companies to reduce cost, improve productivity through technological exchange and upgrade worker participation. It carries well-researched articles and is highly regarded by decision-makers and scientists.
Ind/Abst ASTIS Curr. Aware. Bull. (1978-); AESIS Q.; Alum. Ind. Abstr.; Appl. Sci. Technol. Index; AQUAREF; ASTIS Bibliogr. (1978-); Ceram. Abstr. (1973-); Chem. Abstr.; Coal Abstr.; Curr. Biotechnol.; Curr. Contents Eng. Tech. Appl. Sci.; Ei Page One; EMBASE; Energy Res. Abstr. (Oct. 1976-); Eng. Mater. Abstr.; Eng. Index Annu.; Environ. Abstr.; Fluid Abstr., Civil Eng.; Fluid Abstr. Proc. Eng.; FLUIDEX (1973-1989); GeoRef; INIS Atomindex [Micro.]; INSPEC (1986-); Leadscan; Met. Abstr.; MINPROC; Mintec, Min. Technol. Abstr.; Life Sci. Collect.; Proc. Chem. Eng.; Res. Alert [Full Cov.]; Saf. Health Work; Sci. Cit. Index; SCISEARCH; Soc. Sci. Cit. Index [Select. Cov.]; Theoret. Chem. Eng.

CN/0068-9009
CIM DIRECTORY. [CIM dir.]. **Main/Corp** Canadian Institute of Mining, Metallurgy and Petroleum. **VAT** Canadian Institute of Mining, Metallurgy and Petroleum Directory. 24th Ed. (1990)-. Directory. English. an (Sept.). 90.00Can$. Canadian Institute of Mining, Metallurgy and Petroleum, 3400 de Maisonneuve Boulevard West, Xerox Tower, Suite 1210, Montreal, Quebec H3Z 3B8 Canada. **Tel** (514)939-2710, FAX (514)939-2714, telex 055-62344. **DD** 338.2/025/71. ***Continues*** *Canadian Institute of Mining and Metallurgy. The CIM Directory., 0068-9009.*

US/0073-506X
CIRCULAR - ILLINOIS STATE GEOLOGICAL SURVEY. (CIRCULAR / STATE OF ILLINOIS, DEPT. OF REGISTRATION AND EDUCATION, DIVISION OF THE STATE GEOLOGICAL SURVEY.). [Circ. - Ill. State Geol. Survey]. **Added/Corp** Illinois State Geological Survey. No. 22 (1938)-. Monographic series. English. ir. Price varies per volume. Illinois Geological Survey, Natural Resources Building, Urbana IL 61801. **DD** 557. Documents available from BIOSIS Document Express. ***Continues*** *Information*

Circular (Illinois State Geological Survey).
Ind/Abst Biol. Abstr.; Ceram. Abstr.; Coal Abstr.; GeoRef.

US/0069-4592
CLAY RESOURCES BULLETIN. [Clay resour. bull.]. Began in 1967. Bulletin. English. Price varies per volume. Louisiana Geological Survey, Department of Conservation, Baton Rouge LA. **LC** TN941; .C56. **DD** 553. **CODEN** LGCRAM.
Ind/Abst GeoRef.

US
CMRI QUARTERLY REVIEW. English. qt. $36.00. California Mining Research Institute, 10240 San Pablo, El Cerrito CA 94530.
Desc: Index keys to unpublished mining engineer's inspection reports of mining prospects and mines with maps and assays - US and non-US.

UK
CO-OPERATORS' YEAR BOOK. (19??)-. English. mo. $265.00. **ED** D Gump and Harry Baisden.
Desc: Monitors utility stock piles and burns on a plant-by-plant basis, presents consumption reports and predicts when new coal-fired plants will come online.

US/0197-6354
COAL AGE LIBRARY OF OPERATING HANDBOOKS. [Coal age libr. oper. handb.]. V. 1-. Monographic series. English. Price varies per volume. Coal Age Mining Informational Services, McGraw Hill, 1221 Avenue of the Americas, New York NY 10020. **Tel** (212)512-2000, (800)525-5003, FAX (212)512-6111.

CN/0380-6847
COAL AND COKE STATISTICS. See Engineering-Abstracting, Bibliographies and Statistics.

II/0376-7493
COAL & MINING REVIEW. VAT Coal and Mining Review. English. Rs2.00. 2/1 A Keyatola Road, 29 Calcutta India. **LC** TN809.I4; C62. **DD** 338.2/0954.

US/1040-7820
COAL (CHICAGO, ILL. : 1988). (COAL.). [Coal]. Vol. 25, No. 2 (Feb. 1988)-Vol. 26, No. 12 (Dec. 1989); Vol. 95, No. 1 (Jan. 1990)-. Periodical. English. mo. $31.25 (one year), $56.25 (two year), $75.00 (three year) US & Canada; $50.00 (one year), $87.50 (two year), $118.75 (three year) other. MacLean Hunter Publishing Corporation / Chicago, IL, 29 North Wacker Drive, Chicago IL 60606-3298. **Tel** (312)726-2802, FAX (312)726-3091. **ED** Paul Merritt. **LC** TN799.9; .C59. **DD** 622/.334. **CODEN** COALEN. **[CCC].** Index available. **Bk Rev. Ad Acc. Circ:** 30,000 (ctrl). available on microfilm and microfiche from University Microfilms International (UMI). Documents available from CASDDS. ***Formed by the union of*** *Coal Mining (Chicago, Ill.), 0749-1948* ***and*** *Coal Age, 0009-9910.*
Ind/Abst AESIS Q.; Appl. Sci. Technol. Index; Bus. Period. Index; Chem. Abstr.; Chem. Ind. Notes; Ei Page One; Energy Inf. Abstr.; GeoRef; INIS Atomindex [Micro.]; Mag. Search; Trade Ind. Index; Vocat. Search (July 1993-).

US/0160-5941
COAL (DENVER). (COAL.). **Main/Corp** Colorado. Division of Mines. **VFOAT** Colorado Coal Mine Inspection. 1972-. English. an. $1.00 per copy. Colorado Division of Mines, 1313 Sherman Street, St Centennial, Denver CO 80203. **LC** TN805.C6; A2. **DD** 553/.24/09788. ***Continues*** *Coal, 0160-5941.*
Ind/Abst Bus. Index (1988-); Bus. Period. Index; F&S Index Plus Text, Int. [Select. Cov.]; Gas Abstr.; Gen. BusinessFile (1988-); Gen. Period. Index (1988-); Wilson Bus. Abstr.

CN/0821-7068
COAL FOCUS / THE COAL ASSOCIATION OF CANADA. [Coal focus]. **Added/Corp** Coal Association of Canada. Issue No. 59 (Jan./Feb. 1983)-. Periodical. English. mo. Free. Coal Association of Canada, 205 9th Avenue SE/Suite 502, Calgary Alberta T2G 0R3 Canada. **Tel** (403)262-1544, FAX (403)265-7604, telex 03-827596. **ED** Jim Wood. **DD** 338.2/724/0971. **CODEN** COFOEN. **Ad Acc. Circ:** 700 (ctrl). ***Continues*** *Coal Canada Focus, 0821-705X.*
Desc: Focuses on international and domestic events as they relate to the Canadian coal industry.

AT/0815-6883
COAL JOURNAL. [Coal j.]. **VFOAT** Australia's Journal of Coal Mining Technology and Research. (1984)-. Periodical. English. qt. **DD** 622.334072094. ***Continues*** *Australian Journal of Coal Mining Technology and Research, 0727-419X.*
Ind/Abst AESIS Q.

US
COAL LAW & REGULATION / [PATRICK C. MCGINLEY, DONALD VISH, EDITORS]. ***Ceased.*** **See** Law.

US/1045-6430
COAL MINE DIRECTORY, UNITED STATES AND CANADA. [Coal mine dir. U. S. Can.]. **VFOAT** Coal Mine Directory. (19??)-. Periodical. English. an. $126.00 US & Canada; $143.00 other. MacLean Hunter Publishing Corporation / Chicago, IL, 29 North Wacker Drive, Chicago IL 60606-3298. **Tel** (312)726-2802, FAX (312)726-3091. **LC** TN805.A4; C78. **DD** 622.33. ***Continues*** *Coal Mine Directory.*

UK
COAL MINES - (GREAT BRITAIN). **Main/Corp** Great Britain. Health and Safety Executive. English. an. £1.50. Health & Safety Executive, Room 414 St Hughs House Stanley, Btle Merseyside L20 3QY England. **Tel** 011 44 51 951 4000, FAX 011 44 51 922 5394, telex 628235. **LC** TN295; .G572P. **DD** 363.1/19622334/0941.

US/0190-7867
COAL MINING AND QUARRYING. **Added/Corp** Virginia. Division of Mines and Quarries. Vol. 13 (Oct. 1975)-. Periodical. English. ir. Free on request. Division of Mines & Quarries, 219 Wood Avenue, Department of Labor Industries, Big Stone Gap VA 24219. **LC** TN805.V8; C62. **DD** 622/.334/09755. ***Continues*** *Monthly Review of Coal Mining and Quarrying.*

US/0748-1993
COAL MINING TECHNOLOGY, ECONOMICS, AND POLICY. (COAL MINING TECHNOLOGY, ECONOMICS, AND POLICY : SESSION PAPERS FROM THE AMERICAN MINING CONGRESS INTERNATIONAL COAL SHOW.). [Coal min. technol. econ. policy]. **Main/Conf** International Coal Show. **Added/Corp** American Mining Congress. **VFOAT** Session Papers from the American Mining Congress International Coal Show. (1984)-?. English. ir. American Mining Congress, 1920 N Street NW/Suite 300, Washington DC 20036. **Tel** (202)861-2800. **LC** TN799.9; .I57a. **DD** 622/.334/05. ***Formed by the union of*** *International Coal Show. Session Papers, 0749-6338* ***and*** *Coal Technology. Coal Convention.* ***Continued in part by*** *AMC MINExpo International.*

US/0734-7243
COAL PLANNER. (COAL PLANNER / DATA RESOURCES, INC.). [Coal plann.]. Periodical. English. DRI McGraw Hill, 24 Hartwell Avenue, Lexington MA 02173. **Tel** (617)863-5100. **LC** HD9541; .C6. **DD** 333.8/22/0973.

US/0734-9343
COAL PREPARATION (NEW YORK, N.Y.). (COAL PREPARATION.). [Coal prep.]. Vol. 1, No. 1 (March 1984)-. Academic Scholarly Publication. English. Four times a year. $1188.00. Gordon & Breach Science Publishers, Inc., PO Box 786, Cooper Station, New York NY 10276. **Tel** (212)206-8900, FAX (212)645-2459. **ED** J. S. Laskowski. **LC** TN816.A1; C62. **DD** 662.6/2. **CODEN** COAPDY. **[CCC].** Index available. **Bk Rev. Ad Acc.** Documents available from Article Express International, CASDDS.
Desc: Publishes original research papers, short communications, review articles, book reviews and symposium announcements on all aspects of coal preparation.
Ind/Abst Chem. Abstr. (1984-); Coal Abstr.; Ei Page One; Eng. Index Annu.

US/0147-1708
COAL PROCESSING TECHNOLOGY. [Coal process. technol.]. **Added/Corp** American Institute of Chemical Engineers. Vol. 1 (1974)-. Academic Scholarly Publication. English. American Institute of Chemical Engineers, 345 East 47th Street, New York NY 10017. **Tel** (212)705-7663, (212)705-7703, FAX (212)705-8400. **CODEN** CPRTD2. Documents available from Article Express International, CASDDS.
Ind/Abst Bioeng. Abstr.; Chem. Abstr.; Coal Abstr.; Ei Page One; Eng. Index Annu.

US/0736-4504
COAL PRODUCTION. (COAL PRODUCTION / ENERGY INFORMATION ADMINISTRATION, OFFICE OF COAL, NUCLEAR, ELECTRIC, AND ALTERNATE FUELS, U.S. DEPARTMENT OF ENERGY.). [Coal prod.]. **Added/Corp** United States. Office of Coal, Nuclear, Electric, and Alternate Fuels. (19??)-. English. an. $7.50. National Energy Information Center, Energy Information Administration, Forrestal Building, Room 1F-048, Washington DC 20585. **Tel** (202)586-8800. **LC** TN805.A3; C62. **DD** 338.2/724/0973. ***Continues*** *Bituminous Coal and Lignite Production and Mine Operations;* ***Absorbed*** *Coal-- Pennsylvania Anthracite.*
Desc: U.S. coal production and related data are reported for the current year with similar data for the previous year given for comparison. Among the items covered are prices, production, employment, productivity, stocks, and recoverable reserves. Also included are a glossary of coal terms used, a map of the coal producing districts, and form EIA-7A with instructions.
Ind/Abst Energy Inf. Abstr.; Predicasts Forecasts.

US/0191-4103
COAL REVIEW (LEXINGTON). (COAL REVIEW.). **Main/Corp** Data Resources, Inc. **VFOAT** Coal Review Update; Data Resources Coal Review. Vol. 1 (Nov. 1978)-. English. qt (Mar., June, Sept., Dec.). pric varies per volume. DRI McGraw Hill, 24 Hartwell Avenue, Lexington MA 02173. **Tel** (617)863-5100. **(Subscription address:** Data Resources, PO Box 5 0210, Woburn MA 01815.) **LC** HD9541; .D37a. **DD** 338.2/7/20973.

NE/0167-9449
COAL SCIENCE AND TECHNOLOGY. [Coal sci. technol.]. Vol. 1 (1981)-. Academic Scholarly Publication. English. ir. Price varies per volume. Elsevier Science Publishers BV, PO Box 211, 1000 AE Amsterdam Netherlands. **Tel** 011 31 20 5803642, FAX 011 31 20 5862696, telex 15682. **CODEN** CSTYEF. Documents available from CASDDS.
Ind/Abst Chem. Abstr. (1985-); GeoRef.

US/0149-578X
COAL WEEK. [Coal week]. Vol. 1 (March 31, 1975)-. Newsletter. English. wk. $950.00 US and Canada; $984.00 other. McGraw Hill Publishing Company, Inc., 1221 Avenue of the Americas, New York NY 10020. **Tel** (212)512-6410, (800)525-5003, FAX (212)512-6111. **(Subscription address:** McGraw Hill Management Information Center, 1221 Avenue of the Americas, 36th Floor, New York NY 10020.) **DD** 662. available on an online database (file 624/Full-Text) from DIALOG. ***Absorbed*** *Mine Regulation & Productivity Report, 0277-8696.*
Ind/Abst Coal Abstr.; NEXIS (Jan. 5, 1981-); Trade Ind. Index.

UK
COALTRANS INTERNATIONAL. Vol. 1, Issue 1 (June 1986)-. Trade Publication. English. Six times a year (Feb., Apr., June, Aug., Oct., Dec.). £64.00 Europe; £70.00 others. CoalTrans Publishing Ltd, 42 Rutherwyke Epsom, Surrey KT17 2NB England. **Tel** 011 44 81 786 8202, FAX 011 44 81 786 8175. **ED** Norman Penwarden. **Bk Rev**, (Qty: 16). **Ad Acc. Pr Rev. Circ:** 4,728 (ctrl). Documents available from BLDSC.

UK/0269-381X
COALTRANS WORCESTER PARK. See Energy.

GW/0937-9258
COKEMAKING INTERNATIONAL. [Cokemak. int.]. (1990)-. Periodical. English. sa. DM71.00. Verlag Stahleisen mbH, Postfach 105164, D 40042 Duesseldorf Germany. **Tel** 011 49 211 67070. **UDC** 66/68. **Ad Acc. Circ:** 1,100.
Desc: Covers the whole field of cokemaking technology from raw material issues extending over all process engineering correlations of cokemaking process.

UK/0010-1281
COLLIERY GUARDIAN. [Colliery guard.]. (1942)-. Periodical. English. bm. $193.40 (surface mail) US. Argus Press Group, Queensway House, 2 Queensway Redhill, Surrey RH1 1QS England. **Tel** 011 44 737 768611, 011 44 737 761685, FAX 011 44 737 760510, telex 948669 TOPJNL G. **(Subscription address:** FMJ International Publications Ltd., Queensway House, 2 Queensway Redhill, Surrey RH1 1QS England.) **ED** Keith Whitworth. **LC** TN800; .C68. **CODEN** CLGUAL. **Ad Acc.** available on microfilm and microfiche from University Microfilms International (UMI). Documents available from Article Express International, CASDDS. ***Absorbed in part*** *Steel & Coal;* ***Absorbed*** *Coal International, 0264-9799.*
Desc: Articles on the enormous technological advances in the coal industry.
Ind/Abst Bioeng. Abstr.; Chem. Abstr.; Coal Abstr.; Curr. Technol. Index; Ei Page One; EMBASE; Energy Res. Abstr. (June 1980-); Eng. Index Annu. [Select. Cov.]; GeoRef; MINPROC; Mintec, Min. Technol. Abstr.; Saf. Health Work; Trade Ind. Index.

US/0163-9153
COLORADO SCHOOL OF MINES QUARTERLY. ***Title Change.*** [Colo. Sch. Mines q.]. **Added/Corp** Colorado School of Mines. **VFOAT** Quarterly of the Colorado School of Mines. Began with Vol. 73, No. 3 (197?)-(19??). Academic Scholarly Publication. English. qt. CMS Press, Colorado School of Mines, Golden CO 80401. **Tel** (303)273-3326, FAX (303)273-3310. **LC** TN210; .C68. **DD** 622/.05. **CODEN** CSMQDN. **[CCC]. Pr Rev. Circ:** 950 (ctrl). Documents available from Article Express International, Ask*IEEE, Petroleum Abstracts Document Delivery Service, CASDDS, Documents on Demand. ***Continues*** *Quarterly of the Colorado School of Mines, 0010-1753.* ***Continued by*** *Colorado School of Mines Quarterly Review of Engineering, Science, Education and Reserach, 1068-2937.*
Desc: Refereed scholarly journal dealing with all aspects of mineral engineering and earth science. Research results must be documented.
Ind/Abst AESIS Q.; Bioeng. Abstr.; Ceram. Abstr.; Chem. Abstr. (1978-1985); Coal Abstr.; Ei Page One; Energy Inf. Abstr.; Energy Res. Abstr. (Dec. 1979-); Eng. Index Annu.; Environ. Abstr.; Gas Abstr.; GeoRef; INIS Atomindex [Micro.]; INSPEC (1978-); MINPROC; Mintec, Min. Technol. Abstr.; Pet. Abstr.; SCISEARCH.

●US/1068-2937
COLORADO SCHOOL OF MINES QUARTERLY REVIEW OF ENGINEERING, SCIENCE, EDUCATION AND RESEARCH. [Colo. Sch. Mines q. rev. eng. sci. educ. res.]. **Added/Corp** Colorado School of Mines.

VFOAT Quarterly Review of Engineering, Science, Education and Research; Quarterly Review; CSM Quarterly Review of Engineering, Science, Education and Research. Vol. 92, No. 1 (Winter 1992)-. Academic Scholarly Publication. English. qt (Jan., Apr., Jul., Oct.). $60.00. CMS Press, Colorado School of Mines, Golden CO 80401. **Tel** (303)273-3326, FAX (303)273-3310. **LC** TN210; .C68. **DD** 622. **CODEN** CSEREL. Documents available from CASDDS, Documents on Demand. ***Continues*** *Colorado School of Mines Quarterly, 0163-9153.*
Ind/Abst Bioeng. Abstr. (1992-); Chem. Abstr. (1992-); Coal Abstr. (1992-); Energy Inf. Abstr. (1992-); Energy Res. Abstr. (1992-); Environ. Abstr. (1992-); GeoRef (1992-); MINPROC (1992-); Mintec, Min. Technol. Abstr. (1992-).

AT
COMMON CAUSE. See Economics-Labor.

US/1068-4425
COMPUTERS & MINING. [Comput. min.]. **Added/Corp** Gibbs Associates. **VFOAT** Computers and Mining. Vol. 1, No. 1 (Sept. 1985)-. Periodical. English. mo. $90.00 US; $115.00 other. Gibbs Associates, PO Box 706, Boulder CO 80306. **Tel** (303)444-6032, FAX (303)444-6032, telex 6502845832 MCI. **ED** Betty L. Gibbs. **DD** 622. **Bk Rev**, (Qty: varies). **Ad Acc. Circ:** 200.
Desc: Provides a forum for information transfer for mining and related computer applications. Includes articles on current topics as well as information about software and hardware applicable in earth science companies.
Ind/Abst AESIS Q.

AT/0728-7178
CONFERENCE SERIES - AUSTRALASIAN INSTITUTE OF MINING AND METALLURGY. (CONFERENCE SERIES.). [Conf. ser. - Aust. Inst. Min. Metall.]. **Main/Corp** Australasian Institute of Mining and Metallurgy. (1972)-. Academic Scholarly Publication. English. an. 120.00Aus$ (nonmembers), 80.00Aus$ (members). Australasian Institute of Mining and Metallurgy, PO Box 122, Parkville Victoria 3052 Australia. **Tel** 011 61 3 3473166, FAX 011 61 3 3478525, telex 33552. **LC** UNC. **CODEN** CSAMDJ. Documents available from Article Express International, CASDDS.
Ind/Abst Chem. Abstr. (1972-1983); Ei Page One; Eng. Index Annu.; GeoRef.

US
COPPER INDUSTRY ANNUAL SUPPLEMENT / U.S. DEPARTMENT OF THE INTERIOR, BUREAU OF MINES. See Engineering-Abstracting, Bibliographies and Statistics.

CN
CORPORATE EXPLORATION STRATEGIES. English. ir. $7,500. Metals Economics Group, 1718 Argyle Street, #300 Halifax Nova Scotia, B3J 3C4 Canada. **Tel** (902)429-2880, FAX (902)429-6593, telex 0636700485.

MX/0187-8565
CRM, BOLETIN DE INFORMACION : ORGANO DE COMUNICACION INTERNO. [Bol. inf. - Cons. Recur. Miner.]. **Main/Corp** Consejo de Recursos Minerales (Mexico). **VAT** Consejo de Recursos Minerales, Boletin de Informacion. Periodical. Spanish. Consejo de Recursos Minerales, Ninos Heroes No L39, Mexico-7 DF Mexico.
Ind/Abst GeoRef.

KO/0379-7511
DAIHAN GWANSANHAG HOI JI. (TAEHAN KWANGSAN HAKHOE CHI.). [Daihan gwansanhag hoi ji]. **Main/Corp** Taehan Kwangsan Hakhoe. **VFOAT** Journal of the Korean Institute of Mineral and Mining Engineers. Academic Scholarly Publication. English (Korean). Korean Institute of Mineral and Mining Engineers, Room 603/Korean Science and Technology Center Building, San 76-561 Yeoksam-dong, Kangnam-ku, Seoul South Korea. **LC** TN4. **CODEN** TKHCBH. Documents available from CASDDS.
Ind/Abst Chem. Abstr.; Coal Abstr.; GeoRef.

UK
DIAMOND RESEARCH. **Main/Corp** Industrial Diamond Information Bureau, London. (1964)-. Periodical. English. **LC** TJ1193; .I5.
Ind/Abst Ceram. Abstr. (19??-).

RU
DINAMIKA I PROCHNOST GORNYKH MASHIN. **Added/Corp** Instytut Heotekhnichnoi Mekhaniky (Akademiia Nauk Ukrainskoi RSR). (1973)-. Russian. 0.77rub (single issue). Izdatelstvo Naukova Dumka / Ukrainian Academy of Sciences, Vladimirskaia Ulitsa 54, 252601 Kiev Ukraine. **Tel** 225-63-66, telex 131376. **LC** TN345; .D57.

CK
DIRECTORIO MINERO NACIONAL. (19??)-. Spanish. Ministerio de Minas y Energia, Ave el Dorado-Can-A A, 80319 Oficina No 417, Bogota de Colombia. **LC** TN45; .D57.

AT
DIRECTORS' REPORT - AUSTRALIAN MINES AND METALS ASSOCIATION. (DIRECTORS' REPORT - AUSTRALIAN MINES AND METALS ASSOCIATION, TO BE PRESENTED AT THE ANNUAL MEETING OF THE ASSOCIATION.). **Main/Corp** Australian Mines and Metals Association. **VFOAT** Directors' Report to be Presented at the Annual Meeting. Periodical. English.
Ind/Abst AESIS Q.

US/0273-0553
DIRECTORY OF ACTIVE MINES IN ARIZONA. [Dir. act. mines Ariz.]. Directory. English. Arizona Department of Mineral Resources, Mineral Building Fairgrounds, Phoenix AZ 85007. **Tel** (602)255-3791.
Desc: Listing of all the mines that were active in Arizona in a given year. Names, addresses and telephone numbers are provided along with commodities produced and number of employees.

US/0417-612X
DIRECTORY OF MINE SUPPLY HOUSES, DISTRIBUTORS AND SALES AGENTS. **VFOAT** Mine Supply House Directory. 1961-. Directory. English. $20.00. McGraw Hill Publishing Company, Inc., 1221 Avenue of the Americas, New York NY 10020. **Tel** (212)512-6410, (800)525-5003, FAX (212)512-6111.

CN/0383-1779
DIRECTORY OF MINES PERSONNEL. ***Title Change.*** **VFOAT** Directory of Mining Companies and Personnel. 1965-. Directory. English. Alberta & Northwest Chamber of Mines & Resources, 9915 108 St Petroleum Plaza, Edmonton Alberta Canada. **DD** 338.2/025/719. ***Supersedes*** *Mining Companies and Personnel, 0383-1760.* ***Continued by*** *Directory of Companies & Personnel, 0383-1787.*

US/0884-917X
DIRECTORY OF MINING PROGRAMS. [Dir. min. programs]. Directory. English. an. $75.00, $110.00 (including diskette). Gibbs Associates, PO Box 706, Boulder CO 80306. **Tel** (303)444-6032, FAX (303)444-6032, telex 6502845832 MCI. **ED** Betty L Gibbs. **LC** TN1; .D57. **DD** 622/.028/553. Index available. **Ad Acc. Circ:** 550. available on diskette.
Desc: Compilation of mining software covering all phases of mining applications.

UK
DIRECTORY OF QUARRIES AND PITS. Directory. English. Quarry Managers Journal Ltd, 7 Regent Street, Nottingham NG1 5BY England. **Tel** 011 44 602 411315. **LC** TN12; .D643. **DD** 338.2/7/502542. ***Continues*** *Directory of Quarries, Clayworks, Sand and Gravel Pits, etc.*

UN/0321-1363
DONBAS : LITERATURNO-KHUDOZHNII TA HROMADS'KO-POLITYCHNYI ZHURNAL SPILKY PYSMENNYKIV UKRAINY. **Added/Corp** Spilka Pysmennykiv Ukrainy. **VFOAT** Donbass. (19??)-. Periodical. Ukrainian (Russian). bm. $14.50. **(Subscription address:** Victor Kamkin, 4956 Boiling Brook Parkway, Rockville MD 20852.**)** **LC** AP50; .D67. ***Continues*** *Donbass.*
Ind/Abst MLA Int. Bibl. Books Artic. Mod. Lang. Lit.

CN/0714-4865
DOSSIER - INSTITUTE DE RECHERCHE EN EXPLORATION MINERALE. (DOSSIER ...). [Doss. - Inst. rech. explor. miner.]. Vol. 1 (1976)-. Monographic series. French. Price varies per volume. Institut de Recherche en Exploration Minerale, CP 6079 Succursale A, Montreal Quebec H3C 3A7 Canada. **DD** 622/.1/09714.

US
E & MJ INTERNATIONAL DIRECTORY OF MINING. **VFOAT** E & MJ; E. and M.J. International Directory of Mining; E. and M.J.; E&MJ. **VAT** E&MJ International Directory of Mining; Engineering and Mining Journal International Directory of Mining. (1981)-. Directory. English. an. $126.00 US & Canada; $143.00 other. MacLean Hunter Publishing Corporation / Chicago, IL, 29 North Wacker Drive, Chicago IL 60606-3298. **Tel** (312)726-2802, FAX (312)726-3091. **LC** HD9506.A1; E22. **DD** 338.7/622/025. **Bk Rev. Ad Acc. Circ:** 2,500 (ctrl). ***Continues*** *E/MJ International Directory of Mining and Mineral Processing Operations.*

US/0149-5275
E/MJ INTERNATIONAL DIRECTORY MINING ACTIVITY DIGEST. [E/MJ intern. dir, Min. act. dig.]. **VFOAT** E/MJ Mining Activity Digest; Mining Activity Digest. (1967)-. Periodical. English. mo. MacLean Hunter Publishing Corporation / Chicago, IL, 29 North Wacker Drive, Chicago IL 60606-3298. **Tel** (312)726-2802, FAX (312)726-3091. **Circ:** 1,000.
Desc: Worldwide mining and mineral update.
Ind/Abst GeoRef; NEXIS (May 1982-).

US/0732-2763
E/MJ LIBRARY OF OPERATING HANDBOOKS. [E/MJ libr. oper. handb.]. **VAT** Engineering and Mining Journal Library of Operating Handbooks. Vol. 1 (1977)-. Monographic series. English. ir. Price varies per volume. McGraw Hill Publishing Company, Inc., 1221 Avenue of the Americas, New York NY 10020. **Tel** (212)512-6410, (800)525-5003, FAX (212)512-6111. **(Subscription address:** McGraw Hill Book Company, Princeton Road, Hightstown NJ 08520.**)** **LC** UNC.

RU
EKONOMIKA UGOLNOI PROMYSHLENNOSTI. **Added/Corp** Tsentralnyi Nauchno-Issledovatelskii Institut Ekonomiki i Nauchno-tekhnicheskoi Informatsii Ugolnoi Promyshlennosti. Tsentralnaia Nauchno-Tekhnicheskaia Biblioteka Ugolnoi Promyshlennosti. (19??)-. Russian. Tsentr GSP-2 PL Nogina D 2/5 Tsentral Naia Nauchno-Tekhnicheskaia Biblioteka Ugolnoi Promyshlennosti, Moscow Russia. **LC** Z6738.C6; E38.

EC
ENCUESTA ANUAL DE MANUFACTURA Y MINERIA / REPUBLICA DEL ECUADOR, INSTITUTO NACIONAL DE ESTADISTICA Y CENSOS. **Added/Corp** Instituto Nacional de Estadistica y Censos (Ecuador). (1976)-. Statistical Publication. Spanish. an. $27.50 (1986 vol. 1), $12.50 (1986 vol. 2). Instituto Nacional de Estadistica y Censos, Avda 10 de Agosto 229, Quito Ecuador. **Tel** 51.95.97/51.93.20, telex 21421 INFEC ED. **LC** HD9734.E3; I57a. **DD** 338.4/5/0009866. ***Continues*** *Encuesta de Manufactura y Mineria.*

US/0095-8948
ENGINEERING AND MINING JOURNAL (1926). (ENGINEERING AND MINING JOURNAL.). [Eng. min. j.]. **VFOAT** Engineering & Mining Journal; Engineering/Mining Journal; E/MJ; E&MJ. **VAT** E and MJ. Engineering and Mining Journal. Vol. 122, No. 1 (July 3, 1926)-. Academic Scholarly Publication. English. mo. $60.00 (one year), $97.50 (two year), $120.00 (three year) US & Canada; $90.00 (one year), $142.50 (two year), $195.00 (three year) other. MacLean Hunter Publishing Corporation / Chicago, IL, 29 North Wacker Drive, Chicago IL 60606-3298. **Tel** (312)726-2802, FAX (312)726-3091. **LC** TA1; .E56. **DD** 622. **CODEN** ENMJAK. **[CCC]. Ad Acc. Pr Rev.** available on microfilm and microfiche from University Microfilms International (UMI); available on an online database (file 648/Full-Text) from DIALOG. Documents available from Article Express International, The Genuine Article, CASDDS, Documents on Demand. ***Continues*** *Engineering and Mining Journal-Press, 0095-9731;* ***Absorbed*** *International Mining.*
Ind/Abst Acad. Search (July 1993-); AESIS Q.; Alum. Ind. Abstr.; Appl. Sci. Technol. Index; Bioeng. Abstr.; Bus. Index (1985-1986); Ceram. Abstr. (19??-); Chem. Abstr.; Coal Abstr.; Curr. Contents Eng. Tech. Appl. Sci.; Ei Page One; EMBASE; Energy Inf. Abstr.; Energy Res. Abstr.; Eng. Index Annu.; Environ. Abstr.; F&S Index Plus Text, Int. [Select. Cov.]; Fluid Abstr., Civil Eng.; Fluid Abstr. Proc. Eng.; FLUIDEX (Jan. 1981-); Gen. BusinessFile (1985-1986); Gen. Period. Index (1988-); GeoRef; INFO-SOUTH Abstr.; Leadscan; Mag. Search; Met. Abstr.; MINPROC; Mintec, Min. Technol. Abstr.; NEXIS (Jan. 1981-); Predicasts Forecasts; Res. Alert [Full Cov.]; Soc. Sci. Cit. Index [Select. Cov.]; Soils Fert.; Stat. Ref. Index; Trade Ind. ASAP [Full Txt.]; Trade Ind. Index (1981-) [Full Txt.]; Vocat. Search (July 1993-).

UK
ENGINEERING GEOLOGY SPECIAL PUBLICATION / GEOLOGICAL SOCIETY OF LONDON. (1985)-. Monographic series. English. Price varies per volume.

AO/0301-6552
ESTATISTICA DA ACTIVIDADE MINEIRA NO ESTADO DE ANGOLA. See Engineering-Abstracting, Bibliographies and Statistics.

CN
ESTIMATES. PART III, ENERGY, MINES AND RESOURCES CANADA. ***Title Change.*** **Main/Corp** Canada. **VFOAT** Budget des Depenses. Partie III, Energie, Mines et Ressources Canada. (19??)-(1993/1994). English (French). Canada Communication Group Publishers, Order Processing, Ottawa Ontario K1A 0S9 Canada. **Tel** (819)956-4800, (819)956-4802. **LC** TJ163.25.C3; C3b. **DD** 354.710082/38. ***Continued by*** *Canada. Estimates. Part III, Natural Resources Canada.*

FR
ETUDES DES GITES MINERAUX DE LA FRANCE. **Main/Corp** France. Service des Topographics Souterraines. French. **LC** TN71; .A3.

●UK/0964-1823
EXPLORATION AND MINING GEOLOGY : JOURNAL OF THE GEOLOGICAL SOCIETY OF CIM. **Added/Corp** Geological Society of CIM. Vol. 1, No. 1 (Jan. 1992)-. Periodical.

English. qt. $190.00 The Americas; £128.00 other. Pergamon Press, An Imprint of Elsevier Science Ltd., The Boulevard, Langford Lane, Kidlington, Oxford OX5 1GB United Kingdom. **Tel** 011 44 865 843000, 011 44 865 843699, FAX 011 44 865 843010. **(Subscription address:** Elsevier Science Ltd. Oxford Fulfillment Centre, PO Box 800, Kidlington, Oxford OX5 1DX United Kingdom.**) ED** J. F. Davies, H. L. Gibson, and R. E. Whitehead. **DD** 622. **CODEN** EMGEE6. **[CCC]. Pr Rev.**
Desc: An international publication dealing with mineral deposits, mining geology, geochemistry, geophysics, geomathematics and directly related environmental and earth sciences studies. The journal aims to publish research investigations, whether laboratory or exclusively field-derived, which represent significant contributions to mineral deposits studies and exploration and mining geology.

CN/0823-2059
EXPLORATION IN BRITISH COLUMBIA. ***Title Change.*** [Explor. B.C.]. (1975)-. English. an. British Columbia Ministry of Energy, Mines and Petroleum Resources, Parliament Buildings, Victoria British Columbia V8V 1X4 Canada. **ED** John M Newell. **LC** TN270; .E944. **DD** 622/.1/09711. **Circ:** 400. ***Continues in part*** *Geology, Exploration and Mining in British Columbia, 0085-1027.* ***Continued by*** *Assessment Report Summary of Exploration in British Columbia, 0825-0278.*
Desc: Contains an overview of mineral exploration activity, descriptions of selected mineral properties, and summaries of industry assessment work reports in computerized format.

US
EZSEARCH-MINING. English. qt. $65.00 North America; $75.00 other. Gibbs Associates, PO Box 706, Boulder CO 80306. **Tel** (303)444-6032, FAX (303)444-6032, telex 6502845832 MCI. **ED** Betty L Gibbs. **Circ:** 70 (ctrl). available on diskette.
Desc: Diskette containing list of earth science software. Search program provided.

US
FACTS ABOUT COAL. 1982-. English. an. $10.00. National Coal Association, 1130 17th Street Northwest, Washington DC 20036. **Tel** (202)463-2640. **ED** Tom Johnson. **Ad Acc.** ***Continues*** *Coal Facts.*
Desc: Contains a wealth of current information covering six major areas - the history of coal in America, coal resources, production, labor, transporation and utilization. Also contains graphs, maps and tables with the latest government and coal industry figures presented in an easy-to-read and understandable format.

CN/0316-2281
FACTS AND FIGURES : MINING IN CANADA. **VFOAT** Mining in Canada. 1967-. English. an. Mining Association of Canada, 350 Sparks Street/Suite 705, Ottawa Ontario K1R 7S8 Canada. **Tel** (613)233-9391, telex 053-3732. **LC** HD9506.C2; F33. **DD** 338.2/0971.

US/0192-3862
FEDERAL COAL MANAGEMENT REPORT. (FEDERAL COAL MANAGEMENT REPORT : ANNUAL REPORT OF THE SECRETARY OF THE INTERIOR UNDER SECTION 8 OF THE FEDERAL COAL LEASING AMENDMENTS ACT OF 1976 (P.L. 94 377).). Began with 1977/78. Government Publication. English. an. Department of the Interior, 1849 C Street Northwest, Washington DC 20240. **Tel** (202)343-3171, FAX (202)208-5048. **LC** TN805; .A3915A. **DD** 333.8/22/0973. available on microfiche (Vols. for (1981-) distributed to depository libraries). ***Continues*** *Annual Report on Coal.*

US
FIELDSTON COAL TRANSPORTATION MANUAL. **See** Energy.

UK/0141-3244
FINANCIAL TIMES MINING INTERNATIONAL YEAR BOOK. **VFOAT** Mining Year Book; Mining. (1983)-. English. an. $238.00. Longman Group Ltd., Fourth Avenue, Longman House, Harlow Essex CM19 5SR England. **Tel** 011 44 279 429655, FAX 011 44 279 431059, telex 81259. **(Subscription address:** US & Canada: Gale Research Inc., 835 Penobscot Building, Detroit, MI 48226**) LC** TN13; .M7. **DD** 338.7/622/025. **[CCC].** ***Continues*** *Mining International Year Book.*
Desc: Provides narrative, production and financial details of 819 major companies involved in the mining, production and distribution of metals, minerals and precious stones throughout the world.

RU/0015-3273
FIZIKO-TEKHNICHESKIE PROBLEMY RAZRABOTKI POLEZNYKH ISKOPAEMYKH. [Fiz.-teh. probl. razrab. polezn. iskop.]. **Added/Corp** Akademiia Nauk SSSR. Sibirskoe Otdelenie. (1965)-. Academic Scholarly Publication. Russian. Six times a year. $143.00. **(Subscription address:** East View Publications Inc., 3020 Harbor Lane North, Suite 110, Minneapolis MN 55447.**) CODEN** FTRIAR. Documents available from Article Express International, CASDDS.
Ind/Abst Alum. Ind. Abstr.; Chem. Abstr.; Coal Abstr.; Ei Page One; Eng. Mater. Abstr.; Eng. Index Annu.; Met. Abstr.

FR/0046-4481
FORAGES. (1958)-. Periodical. French. qt. 151.77F France; 200.00F other. AEMS-IFP, 1-4 Avenue Bois Preau, 92502 Rueil Malmaison France. **Tel** 011 33 1 47526148. **UDC** 550. **[CCC].**

GW/0071-9390
FREIBERGER FORSCHUNGSHEFTE. REIHE A. (FREIBERGER FORSCHUNGSHEFTE. A.). [Freib. forsch.h. A]. **Added/Corp** Bergakademie Freiberg. (1951)-. Monographic series. German. ir. Price varies per volume. Deutscher Verlag Grundstoffind, Karl Heine Strasse 27, D 04211 Leipzig Germany. **Tel** 011 49 341 4081011. **LC** TN7; .F7. **CODEN** FFRAA7. **Circ:** 350. Documents available from Article Express International, CASDDS.
Desc: Contains research material, reports, lecture transcripts and dissertations on specific themes taken from all areas of mines and mining engineering, industrial health and safety, chemical engineering, mechanical engineering and machinery ecology.
Ind/Abst Bioeng. Abstr.; Chem. Abstr.; Coal Abstr.; Ei Page One; Eng. Index Annu.; Geogr. Abstr. Phys. Geogr.; GeoRef.

GW/0071-9412
FREIBERGER FORSCHUNGSHEFTE. REIHE D. (FREIBERGER FORSCHUNGSHEFTE. D.). [Freib. Forsch. h., D]. **Added/Corp** Bergakademie Freiberg. Vol. 1 (1952)-. Monographic series. German (English and Russian). ir. Price varies per volume. Deutscher Verlag fuer Grundstoffindustrie GmbH, Postfach 16, Karl-Heine-Str. 27B, D 04211 Leipzig, Germany. **Tel** 011 49 341 490570, FAX 011 49 341 4012571. **LC** CB478; .F7. **Circ:** 300.
Desc: Contains research material, reports, lecture transcripts and dissertations on specific themes of enterprise management, mining and commercial law and the history of mining science.
Ind/Abst GeoRef; Zentralbl. Math. Ihre Grenzgeb.

US
FROTH FLOTATION. **Added/Corp** United States. Bureau of Mines. (19??)-. English. an. US Department of the Interior / Bureau of Mines, Publications Department, PO Box 18070, Cochrans Mill Road, Pittsburgh PA 15236. **Tel** (412)892-6400.

US/0884-3759
FUEL SCIENCE & TECHNOLOGY INTERNATIONAL. **See** Energy.

US
GALLIUM IN ... . **See** Metals and Metallurgy-Abstracting, Bibliographies and Statistics.

CN/0824-9210
GENERAL INDEX TO PUBLISHED REPORTS, MINERAL RESOURCES GROUP. [Gen. index publ. rep., Miner Resour. Group]. **Main/Corp** Ontario Geological Survey. Geoscience Data Centre. **Added/Corp** Ontario. Ministry of Natural Resources. **VFOAT** General Index. Vol. 8 (1975)-. English. ir. Ministry of Natural Resources / Ontario, Whitney Block, Parliament Buildings, Toronto Ontario M7A 1W3 Canada. **LC** Z6739.C32; O66a; TN27.O4. **DD** 016.553/09713. ***Continues*** *Ontario. Dept. of Mines. General Index.*

US/0885-6362
GEOBYTE. ***Ceased.*** [Geobyte]. **Added/Corp** American Association of Petroleum Geologists. Vol. 1, No. 1 (Winter 1985)-(Dec. 1992). Periodical. English. bm. American Association of Petroleum Geologists, PO Box 979, Tulsa OK 74101-0979. **Tel** (918)584-2555, FAX (918)584-0469, telex 49-9432. **ED** Ken Milam. **DD** 622. **[CCC]. Ad Acc. Circ:** 5,000 (ctrl). available on microfilm and microfiche from University Microfilms International (UMI). Documents available from Petroleum Abstracts Document Delivery Service.
Desc: Computer applications to the exploration industry. Covers the geological, geophysical, and engineering industries.
Ind/Abst AESIS Q.; GeoRef; Pet. Abstr.

AT/0369-6715
GEOLOGICAL SURVEY OF NEW SOUTH WALES, MINERAL INDUSTRY OF NEW SOUTH WALES. (THE MINERAL INDUSTRY OF NEW SOUTH WALES.). [Geol. Surv. N.S.W., miner. ind. N.S.W]. Monographic series. English. Price varies per volume. Geological Survey of New South Wales, Department of Mineral Resources, 8-18 Bent Street, Sydney New South Wales 2000 Australia. **LC** TN122.N5; A52. **DD** 338.2/09944. **CODEN** NWMGA3.
Ind/Abst AESIS Q.; GeoRef.

AT/0371-7240
GEOLOGICAL SURVEY REPORT. TASMANIA. [Geol. Surv. Rep., Tasman.]. **VFOAT** Tasmania, Department of Mines, Geological Survey Report. (1910)-. English. ir. Government Printing Tasmania, 188 Collins Street, Hobart Tasmania Australia. **CODEN** TGSRBLTGSRA.
Ind/Abst AESIS Q.

XO/0016-7738
GEOLOGICKY ZBORNIK / GEOLOGICA CARPATHICA. **See** Earth Sciences-Geology.

NE/0016-7746
GEOLOGIE EN MIJNBOUW. **See** Earth Sciences-Geology.

UN/0135-2164
GEOLOGIIA I GEOKHIMIIA GORIUCHIKH ISKOPAEMYKH (KIEV, UKRAINE : 1974). (GEOLOGIIA I GEOKHIMIIA GORIUCHIKH ISKOPAEMYKH / AKADEMIIA NAUK UKRAINSKOI SSR, INSTITUT GEOLOGII I GEOKHIMII GORIUCHIKH ISKOPAEMYKH.). **Added/Corp** Instytut Heolohii i Heokhimii Horiuchykh Kopalyn (Akademiia Nauk Ukrainskoi RSR). (1974)-. Russian. ir. Izdatelstvo Naukova Dumka / Ukrainian Academy of Sciences, Vladimirskaia Ulitsa 54, 252601 Kiev Ukraine. **Tel** 225-63-66, telex 131376. **LC** TN260; .G46. Documents available from CASDDS. ***Continues*** *Heolohiia i Heokhimiia Horiuchykh Kopalyn.*
Ind/Abst Chem. Abstr.

RU/0016-7770
GEOLOGIJA RUDNYH MESTOROZDENIJ. (GEOLOGIIA RUDNYKH MESTOROZHDENII.). [Geol. rudn. mestorozd.]. **Added/Corp** Akademiia Nauk SSSR. (1959)-. Academic Scholarly Publication. Russian. bm. $144.00. Izdatelstvo Nauka / Akademiia Nauk, Publishing House of the Russian Academy of Sciences, Leninskii Porspekt 14, 117901 Moscow Russia. **Tel** 011 95 954-21-53, FAX 011 95 938-21-44, telex 411964. **(Subscription address:** East View Publications Inc., 3020 Harbor Lane North, Suite 110, Minneapolis MN 55447.**) CODEN** GRMAA9. **[CCC].** Index available. **Bk Rev. Ad Acc.** Documents available from CASDDS.
Ind/Abst Chem. Abstr.; GeoRef.

MX/0185-1314
GEOMIMET. [Geomimet]. **Added/Corp** Asociacion de Ingenieros de Minas, Metalurgistas y Geologos de Mexico. (1973)-. Periodical. Spanish. bm. $45,000 Mexico, free to members. Asociacion de Ingenieros Minas, Jaime Torres Bodet No. 176, CP06400 Mexico DF Mexico. **Tel** 011 52 5 5471094, 011 52 5 5471473. **LC** TN4; .M468. **DD** 553/.0972. **CODEN** GEOMDZ. cum. index. **Ad Acc. Circ:** 10,000. Documents available from CASDDS. ***Continues*** *Mineria y Metalurgia (Asociacion de Ingenieros de Minas, Metalurgistas y Geologos de Mexico).*
Ind/Abst Chem. Abstr.; Coal Abstr.; GeoRef.

CN/0374-3268
GEOS. **See** Environmental Issues-Conservation and Natural Resources.

●UK/0960-3182
GEOTECHNICAL AND GEOLOGICAL ENGINEERING. (1992)-. English. qt. $280.00 US and Canada; £160.00 Europe; £175.00 other. Chapman & Hall, 2-6 Boundary Row, London SE1 8HN England. **Tel** 011 44 71 865 0066, FAX 011 44 71 522 9623, telex 290164 Chapmag. **(Subscription address:** Chapman & Hall, Cheriton House, North Way, Andover, Hampshire, SP10 5BE England.**) ED** D. G. Toll, J. M. Kemeny. available on microfilm from University Microfilms International (UMI). ***Continues*** *International Journal of Mining & Geological Engineering.*
Desc: Emphasizes the practical aspects of geotechnical engineering and engineering geology. Publishes papers on theoretical and experimental advances in soil and rock mechanics.
Ind/Abst AESIS Q.

GW
GLUCKAUF (ESSEN). (GLUCKAUF; ZEITSCHRIFT FUER TECHNIK UND WIRTSCHAFT DES BERGBAUS.). [Gluckauf]. Vol. 106, (1970)-. Academic Scholarly Publication. German. Twenty-four times a year. $293.99 Germany; $361.84 Europe;. Verlag Glueckauf GmbH, Postfach 185619, D-45206 Essen Germany. **Tel** 011 49 2054 924200, 011 49 2054 924201, 011 49 2054 924202, telex 08579545. **(Subscription address:** 303 NW 12th Avenue, Deerfield Beach FL 33442; telephone: (305)428-5566**)** Documents available from Article Express International, CASDDS. ***Continues*** *Gluckauf.*
Ind/Abst AESIS Q.; Chem. Abstr.; Ei Page One; Eng. Index Annu.; GeoRef.

GW/0017-1387
GLUCKAUF-FORSCHUNGSHEFTE. [Gluckauf-Forschungsh.]. Vol. 26 (Feb. 1965)-. Periodical. German (summaries and/or abstracts in English and French). qt. DM391.00. Verlag Glueckauf GmbH, Postfach 185619, D-45206 Essen Germany. **Tel** 011 49 2054 924200, 011 49 2054 924201, 011 49 2054 924202, telex 08579545. **CODEN** GKRFAA. **[CCC].** Documents available from Article Express International, CASDDS. ***Continues*** *Bergbau-Archiv.*
Ind/Abst Chem. Abstr.; Ei Page One; EMBASE; Eng. Index Annu.; GeoRef; Saf. Health Work.

GW
GLUCKAUF MINING REPORTER. 1982/83-. Periodical. English. sa. Verlag Glueckauf GmbH, Postfach 185619, D-45206 Essen Germany. **Tel** 011 49 2054 924200, 011 49 2054 924201, 011 49 2054 924202, telex 08579545. ***Continues** Mining Reporter.*
Ind/Abst AESIS Q.

GW/0174-1799
GLUCKAUF. WITH ENGLISH TRANSLATION (ESSEN). (GLUCKAUF.). [Gluckauf, Engl. transl. (Essen)]. **VFOAT** Gluckauf and Translation; Gluckauf + Translation; Translation Gluckauf. (1978)-. Periodical. German (English and German). Twenty-four times a year. $280.00. Verlag Glueckauf GmbH, Postfach 185619, D-45206 Essen Germany. **Tel** 011 49 2054 924200, 011 49 2054 924201, 011 49 2054 924202, telex 08579545. **LC** TN3; .G54. **DD** 622/.05. **[CCC].** Documents available from Article Express International.
Ind/Abst Ei Page One; Eng. Index Annu.

BU
GODISHNIK NA MINNO-GEOLOZHKIIA UNIVERSITET, SOFIIA / ANNUAL OF THE MINE AND GEOLOGY UNIVERSITY, SOFIA. See Earth Sciences-Geology.

UK
GOLD. Added/Corp Consolidated Gold Fields Limited. Gold Fields Mineral Services Ltd. (19??)-. English. an. $95.00. Gold Fields Mineral Service Ltd., Greencoat House, Francis Street, London SW1P 1DH United Kingdom. **Tel** 011 44 71 828 8040. **LC** HG293; .C65a. **DD** 338.2/741/05.
Ind/Abst AESIS Q.

US
GOLD / BUREAU OF MINES, U.S. DEPARTMENT OF THE INTERIOR. 1978-. English. mo. Free. US Department of the Interior / Bureau of Mines, Publications Department, PO Box 18070, Cochrans Mill Road, Pittsburgh PA 15236. **Tel** (412)892-6400.

US/1058-6164
GOLD NEWS (WASHINGTON, D.C.). See Earth Sciences-Mineralogy.

US/0745-6344
GOLD PROSPECTOR. (GOLD PROSPECTOR : OFFICIAL PUBLICATION FOR MEMBERS OF THE GOLD PROSPECTORS ASSOCIATION.). [Gold prospect.]. **Added/Corp** Gold Prospectors Association of America. **VFOAT** Gold Prospectors News; Gold Prospector Magazine. (19??)-. Periodical. English. bm. $20.00. Gold Prospector Association of America, 43445 Business Park Drive, # 113, Tenecula CA 92590. **Tel** (619)699-4749. **DD** 622.

PL/0138-0990
GORNICTWO. [Gornictwo]. **Added/Corp** Akademia Gorniczo-Hutnicza im. S. Staszica w Krakowie. (1977)-. Academic Scholarly Publication. Polish (summaries and/or abstracts in English and Russian). qt. Z15.00 single issue. **LC** TN4; .G77. **CODEN** GORNDL. Documents available from CASDDS.
Ind/Abst Chem. Abstr.; Coal Abstr.; GeoRef.

US
GOWER FEDERAL SERVICE: MINING. See Law.

US/0731-4094
GRANITE & MARBLE DIRECTORY ... / AMERICAN MONUMENT ASSOCIATION. VFOAT Granite and Marble Directory. Directory. English. American Monument Association, 933 High Street / Suite 220, Worthington OH 43085-4046. **Tel** (614)885-2713. **LC** TN970; .G69. **DD** 338.2/752/02573.

UK/0964-9107
GREENHOUSE GASES BULLETIN. ***Ceased.*** **Added/Corp** IEA Greenhouse Gas R & D Programme. IEA Coal Research. (1992)-(Jan. 1994). Bulletin. English. IEA Greenhouse Gas Research & Development Program, Cre Stoke Orchard Cheltenham, Glos GLS2 4R2 England. **Tel** 011 44 81 7802111.

UK/0072-8713
GUIDE TO THE COALFIELDS. (19??)-. Periodical. English. an. £97.60 UK; $163.00 other. Argus Press Group, Queensway House, 2 Queensway Redhill, Surrey RH1 1QS England. **Tel** 011 44 737 768611, 011 44 737 761685, FAX 011 44 737 760510, telex 948669 TOPJNL G. **ED** R. Sansom. **Ad Acc.**
Desc: Lists deep and surface coal mines located in the UK, and a classified list of suppliers. All information related to coal production.

AT/0726-1519
HANDBOOK (SOUTH AUSTRALIA. DEPT. OF MINES AND ENERGY). (HANDBOOK / DEPARTMENT OF MINES AND ENERGY, SOUTH AUSTRALIA.). [Handb. - Dep. Mines Energy]. No. 1, 1961-. Monographic series. English. Price varies per volume. Department of Mines and Energy, Australia 5063 Australia. **Tel** (08)274 7500. **CODEN** HSAME7. Documents available from BIOSIS Document Express.
Ind/Abst AESIS Q.; Biol. Abstr. (-1984).

US
HELIUM RESOURCES OF THE UNITED STATES. English. be. US Department of the Interior / Bureau of Mines, Publications Department, PO Box 18070, Cochrans Mill Road, Pittsburgh PA 15236. **Tel** (412)892-6400. **LC** TN295; .U4 subser; TN883. **DD** 622 S.

CC
HO-PEI MEI TAN. VFOAT Hebei Meitan. Began in 1978. Periodical. Chinese. qt. RMBY1.40. Post Office, Ho-Pei, People's Republic of China. **LC** TN809.C48; H663. **DD** 622/.334/095115.

UK/0019-0020
IMM ABSTRACTS. See Metals and Metallurgy.

US/0192-4680
IMMR (INSTITUTE FOR MINING AND MINERALS RESEARCH, UNIVERSITY OF KENTUCKY). (IMMR.). [IMMR]. **Main/Corp** University of Kentucky. Institute for Mining and Minerals Research. (19??)-. Academic Scholarly Publication. English. **CODEN** UKIIDJ. Documents available from CASDDS.
Ind/Abst Bioeng. Abstr.; Chem. Abstr.

US/0146-2520
IN SITU. See Earth Sciences-Mineralogy.

●US
INDIAN MINERAL RESOURCE HORIZONS / BIA DIVISION OF ENERGY AND MINERAL RESOURCES. Added/Corp United States. Bureau of Indian Affairs. Division of Energy and Mineral Resources. Vol. 1, No. 1 (May 1992)-. Periodical. English. sa.

II/0019-5936
INDIAN MINERALS. [Indian miner.]. **Added/Corp** Geological Survey of India. Mineral Information Bureau. Geological Survey of India. Vol. 1, No. 1 (Jan. 1947)-. Periodical. English. qt. $80.00. **(Subscription address:** Prints India, 11 Darya Ganj, New Delhi 110002 India.) **LC** TN4; .I55. **DD** 553/.0954. **CODEN** INMIAR. cum. index. Documents available from Article Express International, CASDDS.
Ind/Abst Ceram. Abstr.; Chem. Abstr.; Coal Abstr.; Ei Page One; Eng. Index Annu.; Geogr. Abstr. Phys. Geogr.; GeoRef; Indian Geosci. Abstr.

II/0445-7897
INDIAN MINERALS YEARBOOK. [Indian miner. yearb.]. **Added/Corp** Indian Bureau of Mines. (1959)-. English. an. Price varies. Indian Bureau of Mines, Nagpur, India. **(Subscription address:** Prints India, 11 Darya Ganj, New Delhi 110002 India.) **CODEN** IMYBAP. ***Continues** Mineral Production in India.*

II/0019-5944
INDIAN MINING & ENGINEERING JOURNAL, THE. [Indian min. eng. j.]. **Added/Corp** Mining Engineers Association of India. **VFOAT** Indian Mining and Engineering Journal. (1962)-. Periodical. English. mo. $40.00. IME Publications, Esperanga Ground Floor, Colaba Causeway Bombay India. **Tel** 2021665/2022357. **(Subscription address:** Prints India, 11 Darya Ganj, New Delhi 110002 India.) **ED** J F De Souza. **Bk Rev. Ad Acc. Circ:** 3,000 (ctrl). ***Continues** Mineral Markets.*
Ind/Abst Coal Abstr.; Energy Res. Abstr. (May 1972-); Indian Geosci. Abstr.; MINPROC; Mintec, Min. Technol. Abstr.

US/0898-5308
INDICATOR (SAINT PAUL, MINN. 1985). (INDICATOR.). [Indicator]. **Added/Corp** Minnesota Mining and Manufacturing Company. Vol. 1, No. 1 (March 1985)-. Periodical. English. sm. Minnesota Mining Manufacturing Charpenier, 555 2 Street, St Paul MN 55101. **DD** 616. **NLM** W1; JO67BP v.3 no. 5 etc. ***Continues** Infection Control Rounds, 0272-1619.*
Ind/Abst Hospit. Health Admin. Index (Mar. 1985-).

SP/0210-2307
INDUSTRIA MINERA. (INDUSTRIA MINERA : BOLETIN DE INFORMACION DEL CONSEJO SUPERIOR DE COLLGIOS DE INGENIEROS DE MINAS DE ESPANO.). [Ind. min.]. **Added/Corp** Consejo Superior de Colegios de Ingenieros de Minas de Espana. (19??)-. Academic Scholarly Publication. Spanish. Six times a year. Price varies. Consejo Superior de Colegios de Ingenieros de Minas, Rios Rosas 19 BIS, 28003 Madrid Spain. **Tel** 011 34 1 4414611. **CODEN** INMIDU. **[CCC].** Documents available from CASDDS.
Ind/Abst Chem. Abstr.; GeoRef.

US/1066-5544
INFORMATION CIRCULAR - UNITED STATES. BUREAU OF MINES. (INFORMATION CIRCULAR / BUREAU OF MINES.). [Inf. circ. - U.S., Bur. Mines]. **Added/Corp** United States. Bureau of Mines. **VFOAT** IC; Bureau of Mines Information Circular. (19??)-. Monographic series. English. Price varies per volume. US Department of the Interior / Bureau of Mines, Publications Department, PO Box 18070, Cochrans Mill Road, Pittsburgh PA 15236. **Tel** (412)892-6400. **DD** 622.
Ind/Abst AESIS Q.; Ceram. Abstr. (19??-).

UK/0371-7453
INSTITUTION OF MINING AND METALLURGY. TRANSACTIONS. SECTION B : APPLIED EARTH SCIENCES. (TRANSACTIONS. SECTION B, APPLIED EARTH SCIENCE / INSTITUTION OF MINING & METALLURGY.). [Inst. Min. Metall., Trans., B]. **Added/Corp** Institution of Mining and Metallurgy (Great Britain). **VFOAT** Transactions of the Institution of Mining and Metallurgy. Section B, Applied Earth Science; Applied Earth Science. Vol. 75, (Feb. 1966)-. Periodical. English. Three times a year (Mar., July, Nov.). £60.00. Institution of Mining and Metallurgy, 44 Portland Place, London W1N 4BR England. **Tel** 011 44 71 580-3802, FAX 011 44 71 436-5388, telex 261410. **LC** TN260; .T73. **DD** 622/.05. **CODEN** TIAEA7. **[CCC]. Bk Rev. Circ:** 3,300. Documents available from Article Express International, The Genuine Article, Petroleum Abstracts Document Delivery Service, CASDDS. ***Continues in part** Transactions of the Institution of Mining and Metallurgy, 0371-7836.* ***Continued in part by** IMM Bulletin.*
Desc: Contains technical papers, review papers and technical notes.
Ind/Abst AESIS Q.; Alum. Ind. Abstr.; Bioeng. Abstr.; Chem. Abstr.; Coal Abstr.; Curr. Contents Phys. Chem. Earth Sci.; Curr. Technol. Index; Ei Page One; Energy Inf. Abstr.; Energy Res. Abstr.; Eng. Index Annu.; GeoRef; Leadscan; Met. Abstr.; MINPROC; Mintec, Min. Technol. Abstr.; Life Sci. Collect.; Pet. Abstr.; Res. Alert [Full Cov.]; Sci. Cit. Index; SCISEARCH.

US/0361-3070
INSTRUMENTATION IN THE MINING AND METALLURGY INDUSTRIES. [Instrum. min. metall. ind.]. **Added/Corp** Instrument Society of America. Mining and Metallurgy Group. Vol. 1 (1973)-. English. ir. $25.00 (latest issue). Instrument Society of America, 67 Alexander Drive, Research Triangle NC 27709. **Tel** (919)549-8411, FAX (919)549-8288, telex 802 540. **LC** TN153; .I47. **DD** 669/.0028. **CODEN** IMIDBK. **[CCC].** Documents available from Article Express International, Ask*IEEE, CASDDS.
Desc: Proceedings of the annual symposium for the Mining and Metallurgy Industries Division of the Instrument Society of America.
Ind/Abst Bioeng. Abstr.; Chem. Abstr.; Coal Abstr.; Ei Page One; Eng. Index Annu.; INIS Atomindex [Micro.]; INSPEC.

●US
INTERNATIONAL CALIFORNIA MINING JOURNAL. Vol. 63, No. 5 (Jan. 1994)-. Periodical. English. mo. $21.95. California Mining Journal, PO Box 2260, 9032 Soquel Drive, Aptos CA 95001. **Tel** (408)662-2899, FAX (408)662-3014. **ED** Kenneth L. Harn. **LC** TN1; .I5. Index available. **Ad Acc, Adv Mgr:** D.Craig. **Circ:** 40,000. ***Continues** California Mining Journal, 0008-1299.*
Desc: A publication for miners, prospectors, precious metals investors and companies of all sizes involved in the mining industry.
Ind/Abst Calif. Period. Index.

BE
INTERNATIONAL COAL LETTER. (19??)-. English (German). Twenty-six times a year. 20500.00F. International Coal Letter, Rue Capouillet 19 21 Box 1, 1060 Brussels Belgium. **Tel** 011 32 2 536 86 11. **ED** Peter E. Doerell. **Bk Rev.** ctrl circ. ***Continues** World Coal Letter.*
Desc: Newsletter on coal in energy policy, market trends, research, development and demonstration, environment and transport.

US/0534-8145
INTERNATIONAL COAL PREPARATION CONGRESS. [Int. Coal Prep. Congr.]. **Main/Conf** International Coal Preparation Congress. 2nd (Sept. 1954)-. Academic Scholarly Publication. English. Australian National Committee for the International Coal Preparation Congress, GPO Box 908, Brisbane Queensland 4001 Australia. **Tel** 011 61 7 221 8366. **CODEN** ICPCDI. Documents available from CASDDS.
Ind/Abst Chem. Abstr.

NE/0301-7516
INTERNATIONAL JOURNAL OF MINERAL PROCESSING. [Int. j. miner. process.]. Vol. 1 (March 1974)-. Academic Scholarly Publication. English. Twelve times a year (3 vols.). Fl1275.00. Elsevier Science Publishers BV, PO Box 211, 1000 AE Amsterdam Netherlands. **Tel** 011 31 20 5803642, FAX 011 31 20 5862696, telex 15682. **ED** J Cases and D W Fuerstenau. **LC** TN500; .I49. **DD** 622.7/05. **CODEN** IJMPBL. **[CCC]. Pr Rev.** available on microfilm and microfiche from University Microfilms International (UMI). Documents available from Article Express International, The Genuine Article, CASDDS, Documents on Demand.

Desc: Covers all aspects of solid-mineral materials such as metallic and non-metallic ores, coals and other solid sources of secondary materials, etc.
Ind/Abst AESIS Q.; Alum. Ind. Abstr.; Bioeng. Abstr.; Ceram. Abstr.; Chem. Abstr.; Chem. Titles; Coal Abstr.; Comput. Inf. Syst. Abstr. J. [Full Cov.]; Curr. Contents Eng. Tech. Appl. Sci.; Ei Page One; Energy Inf. Abstr.; Energy Res. Abstr. (July 1976-); Eng. Mater. Abstr.; Eng. Index Annu.; Environ. Abstr.; Fluid Abstr., Civil Eng.; Fluid Abstr. Proc. Eng.; FLUIDEX (1974-); GeoRef; Indian Geosci. Abstr.; Leadscan; Manuf. Process Eng. Abstr.; Mater. Sci. Eng. Abstr.; Mech. Eng. Abstr.; Met. Abstr.; MINPROC; Life Sci. Collect.; Res. Alert [Full Cov.]; Sci. Cit. Index; SCISEARCH; Soils Fert.; Solid State Supercond. Abstr.; World Ceram. Abstr.

UK/0269-0136
INTERNATIONAL JOURNAL OF MINING AND GEOLOGICAL ENGINEERING. ***Title Change.*** **VFOAT** Mining and Geological Engineering. Vol. 4, No. 1 (March 1986)-?. Periodical. English. qt. Chapman & Hall, 2-6 Boundary Row, London SE1 8HN England. **Tel** 011 44 71 865 0066, FAX 011 44 71 522 9623, telex 290164 Chapmag. **(Subscription address:** International Thomson, Publishing Services Ltd., North Way, Andover Hampshire SP10 5BE United Kingdom; telephone: (0264)332424**) ED** I W Farmer, USA; S S Peng, USA. **[CCC].** Index available. **Ad Acc. Pr Rev. Circ:** 300. available on microfilm from University Microfilms International (UMI). ***Continues*** *International Journal of Mining Engineering, 0263-4546.* ***Continued by*** *Geotechnical and Geological Engineering.*
Desc: Covers all aspects of mining and geological engineering.
Ind/Abst Coal Abstr. (1986-); GeoRef; Geotech. Abstr.

US/0888-7462
INTERNATIONAL JOURNAL OF POWDER METALLURGY (PRINCETON, N.J.). **See** Metals and Metallurgy.

UK/0148-9062
INTERNATIONAL JOURNAL OF ROCK MECHANICS AND MINING SCIENCES & GEOMECHANICS ABSTRACTS. [Int. j. rock mech. min. sci. geomech. abstr.]. **VFOAT** International Journal of Rock Mechanics and Mining Sciences and Geomechanics Abstracts. **VAT** International Journal of Rock Mechanics and Mining Sciences and Geomechanics Abstracts. Vol. 10, No. 2 (Mar. 1973)-. English. Eight times a year. $976.00 The Americas; £655.00 other. Pergamon Press, An Imprint of Elsevier Science Ltd., The Boulevard, Langford Lane, Kidlington, Oxford OX5 1GB United Kingdom. **Tel** 011 44 865 843000, 011 44 865 843699, FAX 011 44 865 843010. **(Subscription address:** Elsevier Science Ltd. Oxford Fulfillment Centre, PO Box 800, Kidlington, Oxford OX5 1DX United Kingdom.**) ED** J. Hudson. **LC** TA706; .I45. **DD** 624/.1513/05. **CODEN** IRMGBG. **[CCC]. Pr Rev.** available on microfilm and microfiche from University Microfilms International (UMI). Documents available from Article Express International, The Genuine Article, Ask*IEEE. ***Formed by the union of*** *Geomechanics Abstracts* ***and*** *International Journal of Rock Mechanics and Mining Sciences, 0020-7624.*
Ind/Abst Appl. Mech. Rev.; Aqualine Abstr.; Bioeng. Abstr.; Coal Abstr.; Curr. Contents Eng. Tech. Appl. Sci.; Ei Page One; EMBASE; Energy Res. Abstr. (April 1976-); Eng. Index Annu.; GeoRef; Highw. Res. Abstr.; INIS Atomindex [Micro.]; INSPEC (Jan. 1974-); Int. Civil Eng. Abstr.; Leadscan; MINPROC; Mintec, Min. Technol. Abstr.; Res. Alert [Full Cov.]; Sci. Cit. Index; SCISEARCH.

US
INTERNATIONAL JOURNAL OF SURFACE MINING & RECLAMATION. **VFOAT** IJSM. Vol. 4, No. 1 (1990)-. Periodical. English. qt. Fl165.00. AA Balkema, Box 1675, 3000 BR Rotterdam Netherlands. **Tel** 011 31 10 4145822, FAX 011 31 10 4135947, telex 41605. ***Continues*** *International Journal of Surface Mining.*

US/0732-9911
INTERNATIONAL LAND RIG DRILLING REPORT, THE. [Int. land rig drill. rep.]. Periodical. English. mo. $650.00. Petroconsultants Inc, PO Box 740619, Houston TX 77274. **Tel** (713)995-1764, FAX (713)995-8593, telex 4620521. **LC** TN871.2; .I583. **DD** 622/.338.

UK/0269-378X
INTERNATIONAL MINING. ***Title Change.*** [Int. min.]. (1984)-(19??). Periodical. English. mo. Quarto International Ltd., 4 Brandon Road, London N7 9TR England. **Tel** 011 44 71 609-2177, FAX 011 44 71 609-4985. ***Absorbed by*** *Engineering and Mining Journal, 0095-8948.*

UK
INTERNATIONAL MINING REVIEW. (19??)-. Periodical. English. mo. $395.00 US; £260.00 other. David Williamson Association Ltd, 78 Old Broad Street, London EC2M 1QP England. **Tel** 011 44 71 628 3989, FAX 011 44 71 920 0563.
Desc: Covers metal markets statistics; guest article from mining company executive; world metal and mining company news; advice for mining equity investors; editor's article on financial or political events affecting metals and mining markets.

US
IODINE. **See** Earth Sciences-Mineralogy.

RU
ISPOLZOVANIE NEORGANICHESKIKH RESURSOV OKEANICHESKOI VODY. **Added/Corp** Institut Khimii (Akademia Nauk SSSR. Dalnevostochnyi Nauchnyi Tsentr) Mezhduvedomstvennyi Sovet po Koordinatsii Nauchnykh Issledovanii po Estestvennym i Ovshchestvennym Naukam (Soviet Union). **VFOAT** Utilization of Sea Water Inorganic Components. Vol. 1 (1975)-. Periodical. Russian (summaries and/or abstracts in English). 0.88rub single issue. Dalnevostocknyi Nauch, Leninskaia 50, Vladivostock Russia. **LC** TN264; .I86.

RU
ISSLEDOVANIIA PO PODZEMNOI GIDROMEKHANIKE. Vol. 1 (1976)-. Periodical. Russian. 1.05rub. **LC** TN871; .I79.

RU
ITOGI NAUKI I TEKHNIKI: GORNOE I NEFTEPROMYSLOVOE MASHINOSTROENIE. **Added/Corp** Vsesoiuznyi Institut Nauchnoi i Teknicheskoi Informatsii (Soviet Union). **VFOAT** Gornoe I Neftepromyslovoe Mashinostroenie; Itogi Nauki I Tekhniki: Seriia Gornoe I Neftepromyslovoe Mashinostroenie. Vol. 2, (1969)-. Russian. 1.00rub (single issue). VINITI - Vsesoyuznyi Institut Nauchno-Tekhnicheskoi Informatsii, All-Union Scientific and Technical Information Institute, Baltiiskaia Ulitsa 14, 125219 Moscow Russia. **Tel** 238-46-00, FAX 9430060, telex 411160. **(Subscription address:** V/O Mezhdunarodnaya Kniga, 113095 Dimitrova Ul 39, Moscow USSR**) LC** TN345; .I82. ***Continues*** *Itogi Nauki I Tekhniki: Gornye Mashiny.*

RU
ITOGI NAUKI I TEKHNIKI : RAZRABOTKA MESTOROZHDENII TVERDYKH POLEZNYKH ISKOPAEMYKH. **Added/Corp** Vsesoiuznyi Institut Nauchnoi i Tekhnicheskoi Informatsii (Soviet Union). **VFOAT** Itogi Nauki I Tekhniki: Seriia Razrabotka Mestorozhdenii Tverdykh Poleznykh Iskopaemykh; Razrabotka Mestorozhdenii Tverdykh Poleznykh Iskopaemykh. Vol. 14 (1976)-. Academic Scholarly Publication. Russian. 6.00rub. VINITI - Vsesoyuznyi Institut Nauchno-Tekhnicheskoi Informatsii, All-Union Scientific and Technical Information Institute, Baltiiskaia Ulitsa 14, 125219 Moscow Russia. **Tel** 238-46-00, FAX 9430060, telex 411160. **(Subscription address:** V/O Mezhdunarodnaya Kniga, 113095 Dimitrova Ul 39, Moscow USSR**) LC** TN275.A1; I86. **CODEN** ITRIDT. Documents available from CASDDS. ***Continues*** *Itogi Nauki I Tekhniki : Tekhnologiia Razrabotki Tverdykh Poleznykh Iskopaemykh.*
Ind/Abst Chem. Abstr.; Coal Abstr.

US/0360-036X
ITOGI, SUMMARIES OF SCIENTIFIC PROGRESS : DEVELOPMENT OF OIL AND GAS DEPOSITS. **See** Petroleum and Natural Gas.

RU/0536-1028
IZVESTIJA VYSSIH UCEBNYH ZAVEDENIJ. GORNYJ ZURNAL. (IZVESTIIA VYSSHIKH UCHEBNYKH ZAVEDENII. GORNYI ZHURNAL.). [Izv. vyss. ucebn. zaved., Gorn. z.]. **Added/Corp** Sverdlovskii Gornyi Institut im. V.V. Vakhrusheva. **VFOAT** Gornyi Zhurnal; Izvestiia Vysshikh Uchebnykh Zavedenii Ministerstva Vysshego Obrazovaniia SSSR. Gornyi Zhurnal; Izvestiia Vysshikh Uchebnykh Zavedenii Ministerstva Vysshego i Srednego Spetsialnogo Obrazovaniia SSSR. (1958)-. Periodical. Russian. mo. **(Subscription address:** Victor Kamkin, 4956 Boiling Brook Parkway, Rockville, MD 20852**) CODEN** IVUOA5. Documents available from Ask*IEEE, CASDDS. ***Absorbed*** *Soviet Union. Ministerstvo Vysshego Obrazovaniia. Nauchnye Doklady Vysshei Shkoly. Gornoe Delo.*
Ind/Abst Chem. Abstr.; Coal Abstr.; INSPEC (1968-); MINPROC; Mintec, Min. Technol. Abstr.; Saf. Health Work.

AT/0075-3777
JOBSON'S MINING YEAR BOOK. **VFOAT** Jobson's Investment Digest Mining Year Book. (1957)-. English. an. 275.00Aus$. Riddell Information Services Pty Limited, PO Box 3942, Sydney New South Wales, 2001 Australia. **Tel** 11 61 23682100, FAX 11 61 23682150, telex 126736. **ED** Bernadette McBride. **LC** HG5899.M4; J6. **DD** 338.2. **Bk Rev. Ad Acc, Adv Mgr:** Chris Peuegrinetti, **Tel** 001 02 368 2299. **Circ:** 6,600 (ctrl). ***Continues*** *Jobson's Who's Who in Australian Mining & Oil.*
Desc: Directory of mining and petroleum companies in Australia and New Zealand plus extensive articles and features relating to both industries.

US/0276-9719
JOHANNESBURG QUARTERLY GOLD STOCK REPORT. [Johannesbg. q. gold stock rep.]. English. qt. Johannesburg Publications USA Inc, 503 Sharpsburg Circle, Birmingham AL 35213. **LC** HD9536.S6; J63. **DD** 338.2/741/0968.

KO/0253-3863
JOSA NYENGU BOGO - JANWEN GAIBAR NYENGUSO. (CHOSA YONGU POGO - CHAWON KAEBAL YONGUSO.). [Josa nyengu bobo - Janwen gaibar nyenguso]. **Main/Corp** Chawon Kaebal Yonguso. **VFOAT** Report on Geoscience and Mineral Resources. V. 1-. Academic Scholarly Publication. Korean (summaries and/or abstracts in English). sa. **LC** TN106.5. **CODEN** JYBODD. Documents available from CASDDS.
Ind/Abst Chem. Abstr. (1977-1980).

UK/0308-3845
JOURNAL - CAMBORNE SCHOOL OF MINES. [J. - Camborne Sch. Mines]. **Main/Corp** Camborne School of Mines. **VFOAT** Camborne School of Mines Journal; CSM Journal. (1972)-. Academic Scholarly Publication. English. an. £5.00 UK; £6.05 other. Camborne School of Mines, Pool Redruth, Cornwall TR15 3SE England. **Tel** 011 44 209 714866, FAX 011 44 209 716977, telex 45315 CHASM G. **ED** R. Pascoe. **CODEN** CSMJD2. Index available. **Ad Acc. Circ:** 5,000 (ctrl). Documents available from CASDDS.
Ind/Abst Chem. Abstr. (1972-1982); Coal Abstr.; GeoRef.

JA
JOURNAL - MINING AND METALLURGICAL INSTITUTE OF JAPAN. **See** Metals and Metallurgy.

NE/0375-6742
JOURNAL OF GEOCHEMICAL EXPLORATION. [J. geochem. explor.]. **Added/Corp** Association of Exploration Geochemists. Vol. 1 (July 1972)-. Academic Scholarly Publication. English. Nine times a year (3 volumes). Fl1425.00. Elsevier Science Publishers BV, PO Box 211, 1000 AE Amsterdam Netherlands. **Tel** 011 31 20 5803642, FAX 011 31 20 5862696, telex 15682. **ED** E M Cameron. **LC** TN270.A1; J68. **DD** 622/.1. **CODEN** JGCEAT. **[CCC]. Pr Rev.** available on microfilm and microfiche from University Microfilms International (UMI). Documents available from Article Express International, The Genuine Article, Petroleum Abstracts Document Delivery Service, CASDDS.
Desc: Covers all aspects of the application of geochemistry to the search for mineral deposits, including petroleum.
Ind/Abst AESIS Q.; Bioeng. Abstr.; Chem. Abstr.; Chem. Titles; Curr. Contents Phys. Chem. Earth Sci.; Ecol. Abstr. (?-?); Ei Page One; Energy Res. Abstr. (Oct. 1974-); Eng. Index Annu.; Fluid Abstr., Civil Eng.; Fluid Abstr. Proc. Eng.; FLUIDEX (1973-); Geogr. Abstr. Phys. Geogr.; Geogr. Abstr. Human Geogr.; Geol. Abstr.; GeoRef; Indian Geosci. Abstr.; Life Sci. Collect.; Pet. Abstr.; Res. Alert [Full Cov.]; Sci. Cit. Index; SCISEARCH; Soils Fert.

UK
JOURNAL OF LEEDS UNIVERSITY MINING SOCIETY, THE. **VFOAT** Leeds University Mining Society Journal. Vol. 1 (1922)-. English. an. **LC** TN1; .L44. **DD** 622/.05.

US/0892-9017
JOURNAL OF MINERAL LAW & POLICY. ***Title Change.*** **See** Law.

II/0022-2755
JOURNAL OF MINES, METALS & FUELS. [J. mines met. fuels]. Vol. 7, No. 2 (Feb. 1959)-. Academic Scholarly Publication. English. Twelve times a year. $48.00. Books & Journals Private Ltd, 6-2 Madan Street, Calcutta 72 India. **Tel** 011 91 33 271711, 011 91 33 275867, FAX 011 91 33 24829737, telex 021-4427 ITOP IN, 021-4513 ITO IN. **ED** P. K. Menon and A. K. Ghose. **CODEN** JMMFAM. **Bk Rev. Ad Acc. Circ:** 2,500 (ctrl). Documents available from Article Express International, CASDDS. ***Continues*** *Indian Mining Journal.*
Desc: Devoted to all aspects technical, engineering, commerical and administrative of mining, geology, metallurgy and fuel technology.
Ind/Abst Bioeng. Abstr.; Chem. Abstr.; Coal Abstr.; Ei Page One; EMBASE; Energy Res. Abstr.; Eng. Index Annu.; GeoRef; Indian Geosci. Abstr.; MINPROC; Mintec, Min. Technol. Abstr.; Saf. Health Work.

NR/0022-2763
JOURNAL OF MINING AND GEOLOGY. [J. mining geol.]. **Added/Corp** Nigerian Mining, Geological and Metallurgical Society. (1966)-. Academic Scholarly Publication. English. Twice a year. University of Ife / Department of Geology, Ile-Ife Nigeria. **LC** TN275.A1; J68. **DD** 550/.5. **CODEN** JMIGA5. **[CCC].** Documents available from CASDDS. ***Continues*** *Nigerian Mining, Geological and Metallurgical Society. Journal.*
Ind/Abst Chem. Abstr.; Energy Res. Abstr. (July 1976-); GeoRef.

●II
JOURNAL OF MINING RESEARCH. **Added/Corp** Central Mining Research Station (Dhanbad, India). **VFOAT** JMR. Vol. 1, No. 1 (Apr.-June 1992)-. Periodical. English. qt. $120.00. Central Mining Research Station, Dhanbad, Bihar, India. **(Subscription address:** Prints India, 11 Darya Ganj, New Delhi, 110002 India, (Phone: 011 91 11 3268645)).

●US/1062-7391
JOURNAL OF MINING SCIENCE. **Added/Corp** Consultants Bureau. (1992)-. Periodical. English (translations available in Russian). bm (6 issues). $1195.00 US; $1400.00 other. Consultants Bureau, A Division of Plenum Publishing Corporation, 233 Spring Street, New York NY 10013. **Tel** (212)620-8000, (212)620-8466, FAX (212)463-0742, telex 23/421139. **[CCC]**. Documents available from Article Express International. ***Continues** Soviet Mining Science, 0038-5581.*
Ind/Abst Coal Abstr.; Ei Page One; Energy Res. Abstr.; Eng. Index Annu.; GeoRef; MINPROC; Mintec, Min. Technol. Abstr.

SA/0020-2983
JOURNAL OF THE INSTITUTE OF MINE SURVEYORS OF SOUTH AFRICA. [J. Inst. Mine Surv. S. Afr.]. **Added/Corp** Institute of Mine Surveyors of South Africa. **VFOAT** Institute of Mine Surveyors of South Africa Journal; Joernaal van die Instituut von Mynopmeters van Suid-Afrika. (1951)-. Periodical. English. Three times a year. R24.00. Institute of Mine Surveyors of South Africa, PO Box 27943, 18A Gill Street, Yeoville 2143, South Africa. **Tel** 11 27 11 4873511. **(Subscription address:** University of Utah Libraries, Serials Order-ESS, Salt Lake City UT 841112; Serials Department, New Mexico Institute of Mining and Technology, Socorro 87801 New Mexico**) ED** A W Harris. **CODEN** JMSVAW. Index available. **Bk Rev. Ad Acc. Circ:** 700 (ctrl). Documents available from Article Express International.
Desc: Ideas in the areas of mine survey and valuation.
Ind/Abst Bioeng. Abstr.; Coal Abstr.; Ei Page One; Energy Res. Abstr. (July 1978-); Eng. Index Annu.

II/0257-442X
JOURNAL OF THE INSTITUTION OF ENGINEERS (INDIA). MINING ENGINEERING. **Added/Corp** Institution of Engineers (India). Mining Engineering. Institution of Engineers (India). Mining Engineering Division. **VFOAT** Journal of the Institution of Engineers (India). Mining Engineering Division; Mining Engineering; Mining Engineering Division; IE (I) Journal-ME. Vol. 65, Pt. MI 1 (Nov. 1984)-. Periodical. English. Twice a year. $4.00. Institution of Engineers India, 8 Gokhale Road, Calcutta 700020 India. **Tel** 011 91 33 288311, telex 21 7885 IEIC IN. **LC** TN1; .J69. **DD** 622/.05. ***Continues in part** Journal of the Institution of Engineers (India). Mining and Metallurgy Division, 0020-3394.*
Ind/Abst Indian Geosci. Abstr.

SA
JOURNAL OF THE MINE MEDICAL OFFICERS' ASSOCIATION OF SOUTH AFRICA. **Added/Corp** Mine Medical Officers' Association of South Africa. Vol. 63, No. 433 (Apr. 1987)-. Periodical. English. **NLM** W1; JO941L. ***Continues** Proceedings of the Mine Medical Officers' Association of S. A., 0026-4490.*
Ind/Abst Trop. Dis. Bull.

SA/0368-3206
JOURNAL OF THE MINE VENTILATION SOCIETY OF SOUTH AFRICA. [J. Mine Vent. Soc. S. Afr.]. Vol.10 (Jan. 1957)-. Periodical. English. Twelve times a year. R200.64 South Africa; R440.00 (surface mail), R610.00 (airmail) other. Mine Ventilation Society of South Africa, PO Box 93480, 2143 Yeoville South Africa. **Tel** 27 21 8322177. **ED** R E Gunderson. **CODEN** JMVSA4. Index available. **Ad Acc.** ctrl circ. Documents available from Article Express International. ***Continues** Mine Ventilation Society of South Africa. Monthly Bulletin -Mine Ventilation Society of South Africa,.*
Ind/Abst Bioeng. Abstr.; Coal Abstr.; Ei Page One; Energy Res. Abstr. (July 1976-); Eng. Index Annu.; Fluid Abstr., Civil Eng.; Fluid Abstr. Proc. Eng.; FLUIDEX (1973-); Mintec, Min. Technol. Abstr.; Saf. Health Work; Stat. Theory Method Abstr. (1968).

SA/0038-223X
JOURNAL OF THE SOUTH AFRICAN INSTITUTE OF MINING & METALLURGY. [J. S. Afr. Inst. Min. Metall.]. **Main/Corp** South African Institute of Mining and Metallurgy. **Added/Corp** South African Institute of Mining and Metallurgy. Joernaal van die Suid-Afrikaanse Instituut vir Mynbon & Metallurgie. **VFOAT** Joernaal van die Suid-Afrikaanse Instituut vir Mynbon & Metallurgie. Vol.57 (1956)-. Academic Scholarly Publication. English. mo. $120.00. South African Institute of Mining and Metallurgy, 11-13 MacLaren Street/13th Floor, Cape Towers, Johannesburg 2001 South Africa, P.O.Box 61127 Marshalltown 2107. **Tel** 011 27 834 1273 7, FAX 011 27 838 5923, telex 4-86431. **(Subscription address:** PO Box 61127, Marshalltown 2107 South Africa**) CODEN** JSAMAP. **[CCC]**. Index available. **Bk Rev. Ad Acc. Pr Rev. Circ:** 2,800 (ctrl). available on microfilm and microfiche from University Microfilms International (UMI). Documents available from Article Express International, The Genuine Article, CASDDS. ***Continues** Journal of the Chemical, Metallurgical and Mining Society of South Africa, 0368-1661 .*
Desc: Major function is the publication of technical papers and notes related to research, development and practice in the mining and metallurgical industries.
Ind/Abst AESIS Q.; Alum. Ind. Abstr.; Anal. Abstr.; Bioeng. Abstr.; Ceram. Abstr.; Chem. Abstr.; CIS Abstr.; Civ. Struct. Eng. Abstr.; Coal Abstr.; Comput. Inf. Syst. Abstr. J. [Full Cov.]; Curr. Contents Eng. Tech. Appl. Sci.; Ei Page One; Energy Res. Abstr.; Eng. Mater. Abstr.; Eng. Index Annu.; GeoRef; Highw. Res. Abstr.; Leadscan; Manuf. Process Eng. Abstr.; Mater. Sci. Eng. Abstr.; Met. Abstr.; MINPROC; Mintec, Min. Technol. Abstr.; Nucl. Sci. Abstr.; Proc. Chem. Eng.; Res. Alert [Full Cov.]; Saf. Health Work; SCISEARCH; Sel. Water Resour. Abstr.; Solid State Supercond. Abstr.; Stat. Theory Method Abstr. (1968); Theoret. Chem. Eng.; World Alum. Abstr.

JA
KAIGAI SHRIYO RISUTO. Periodical. Multiple languages (English, French, German, Italian, Japanese and Spanish). Kinzoku Kogyo Jigyodan, (Metal Mining Agency), 24-14 Toranomon 1 chome, Minatoku Tokyoto 105 Japan. **LC** Z6737; .K34; HD9506.A1.

US
KEYSTONE COAL INDUSTRY MANUAL. (1969)-. Periodical. English. an. $196.00 US & Canada; $236.00 other. MacLean Hunter Publishing Corporation / Chicago, IL, 29 North Wacker Drive, Chicago IL 60606-3298. **Tel** (312)726-2802, FAX (312)726-3091. **(Subscription address:** Mining Information Services, PO Box 6500, Chicago IL 60680.**) LC** TN805.A4; K4. **DD** 388.2/7/20973; 338.2. **Ad Acc. Circ:** 4,500. ***Continues** Keystone Coal Buyers Manual, 0450-1772.*
Desc: Coal reference in US and Canada.

US/0149-5801
KEYSTONE NEWS BULLETIN. ***Ceased.*** [Keyst. news bull.]. (19??)-(Dec. 1993). Bulletin. English. mo. MacLean Hunter Publishing Corporation / Chicago, IL, 29 North Wacker Drive, Chicago IL 60606-3298. **Tel** (312)726-2802, FAX (312)726-3091. **LC** HD9541; .K45. **DD** 338.2/7/20973. ***Continues** Keystone Coal Buyers Manual.*
Desc: Newsletter updates.
Ind/Abst Coal Abstr.; Energy Res. Abstr. (April 1980-); NEXIS (May 1982-).

US/1047-4269
KING'S COAL EXPORT REPORT. (KING'S COAL EXPORT REPORT : A WEEKLY SUPPLEMENT TO KING'S COALSTATS DATABASE SERVICE.). [King's coal export rep.]. **VFOAT** Coal Export Report. Issue No. 712 (June 19, 1989)-. Periodical. English. wk. $575.00. King Publishing Company, PO Box 52210, Knoxville TN 37950. **Tel** (615)584-6294, FAX (615)558-6101, telex 705286. **DD** 382. available on diskette (King's Coalstats. Coal Export Report). ***Continues** King's Coal Export Week, 0749-0658.*

US/1050-172X
KING'S COALSTATS. COAL EXPORT REPORT. (KING'S COALSTATS. COAL EXPORT REPORT [COMPUTER FILE].). [King's coalstats, Coal export rep.]. **Added/Corp** King Publishing Company. **VFOAT** Coal Export Report. (198?)-. English. mo. $1450.00. King Publishing Company, PO Box 52210, Knoxville TN 37950. **Tel** (615)584-6294, FAX (615)558-6101, telex 705286. **DD** 382. ***Continues in part** King's Coalstats, 0896-3843.*
Desc: Available in dBase III+, LOTUS 123, ASCII and King's Software on 5 1/4" and 3 1/2" diskettes.

US/1050-1665
KING'S COALSTATS. COAL PRODUCTION REPORT. (KING'S COALSTATS. COAL PRODUCTION REPORT [COMPUTER FILE].). [King's coalstats, Coal prod. rep.]. **Added/Corp** King Publishing Company. **VFOAT** Coal Production Report. 4th Quarter (1989)-. English. qt. King Publishing Company, PO Box 52210, Knoxville TN 37950. **Tel** (615)584-6294, FAX (615)558-6101, telex 705286. **DD** 338. ***Continues in part** King's Coalstats, 0896-3843.*
Desc: Available in dBase III+, LOTUS 123, ASCII, and King's Software on 5 1/4" and 3 1/2" diskettes.

US/1050-1525
KING'S COALSTATS. ELECTRIC UTILITIES REPORT. (KING'S COALSTATS. ELECTRIC UTILITIES REPORT [COMPUTER FILE].). [King's coalstats, Electr. util. rep.]. **Added/Corp** King Publishing Company. **VFOAT** Electric Utilities Report. (198?)-. English. mo. $1300.00. King Publishing Company, PO Box 52210, Knoxville TN 37950. **Tel** (615)584-6294, FAX (615)558-6101, telex 705286. **DD** 338. ***Continues in part** King's Coalstats, 0896-3843.*
Desc: Available in dBase III+, LOTUS 123, ASCII, and King's Software on both 5 1/4" and 3 1/2" diskettes.

US/1050-1649
KING'S COALSTATS. FOB MINE PRICES. (KING'S COALSTATS. FOB MINE PRICES [COMPUTER FILE].). [King's coalstats, FOB mine prices]. **Added/Corp** King Publishing Company. **VFOAT** FOB Mine Prices. (198?)-. English. mo. King Publishing Company, PO Box 52210, Knoxville TN 37950. **Tel** (615)584-6294, FAX (615)558-6101, telex 705286. **DD** 338. available in print (As: King's Coalstats. Monthly Coal Guide. Mine Price Report.). ***Continues in part** King's Coalstats, 0896-3843.*
Desc: Available in dBase III+, LOTUS 123, ASCII, and King's Software on both 5 1/4" and 3 1/2" diskettes.

US/1050-1703
KING'S COALSTATS. INTERNATIONAL COAL TRADE. (KING'S COALSTATS. INTERNATIONAL COAL TRADE [COMPUTER FILE].). [King's coalstats, Int. coal trade]. **Added/Corp** King's Publishing Company. **VFOAT** International Coal Trade. (198?)-. English. mo. King Publishing Company, PO Box 52210, Knoxville TN 37950. **Tel** (615)584-6294, FAX (615)558-6101, telex 705286. **DD** 382. ***Continues in part** King's Coalstats, 0896-3843.*
Desc: Available in dBase III+, LOTUS 123, ASCII, and King's Software on 5 1/4" and 3 1/2" diskettes.

US/1050-1533
KING'S COALSTATS. MONTHLY COAL GUIDE. [King's coalstats, Mon. coal guide]. **VFOAT** Monthly Coal Guide; King's Monthly Coal Guide; King's Coalstats. (Nov. 1989)-. English. mo. King Publishing Company, PO Box 52210, Knoxville TN 37950. **Tel** (615)584-6294, FAX (615)558-6101, telex 705286. **DD** 338. ***Continues in part** King's Coalstats, 0896-3843.*

US/1050-1495
KING'S COALSTATS. MONTHLY COAL GUIDE. ELECTRIC UTILITIES REPORT. [King's coalstats, Mon. coal guide, Electr. util. rep.]. **VFOAT** Monthly Coal Guide. Electric Utilities Report; King's Coalstats. English. mo. King Publishing Company, PO Box 52210, Knoxville TN 37950. **Tel** (615)584-6294, FAX (615)558-6101, telex 705286. **DD** 338. ***Continues in part** King's Coalstats, 0896-3843.*

US/1050-1509
KING'S COALSTATS. MONTHLY COAL GUIDE. MINE PRICE REPORT. [King's coalstats, Mon. coal guide, Mine price rep.]. **VFOAT** Monthly Coal Guide; Mine Price Report; King's Coalstats. (Aug./Sept. 1989)-. English. mo. $750.00. King Publishing Company, PO Box 52210, Knoxville TN 37950. **Tel** (615)584-6294, FAX (615)558-6101, telex 705286. **DD** 338. available on CD-ROM (King's Coalstats. [Computer File] FOB Mine Prices). ***Continues in part** King's Coalstats, 0896-3843.*

US/1050-1517
KING'S COALSTATS. MONTHLY COAL GUIDE. MINE PRODUCTION REPORT. [King's coalstats, Mon. coal guide, Mine prod. rep.]. **Added/Corp** King's Energy Information Systems. **VFOAT** Monthly Coal Guide. Mine Production Report; Mine-by-Mine Production King's Coalstats. (3rd Qtr. 1989)-. English. mo. $750. King Publishing Company, PO Box 52210, Knoxville TN 37950. **Tel** (615)584-6294, FAX (615)558-6101, telex 705286. **DD** 338. available on diskette (King's Coalstats. Coal Product Report). ***Continues in part** King's Coalstats, 0896-3843.*

US/1050-1711
KING'S COALSTATS. PETROLEUM COKE EXPORT REPORT. (KING'S COALSTATS. PETROLEUM COKE EXPORT REPORT [COMPUTER FILE].). [King's coalstats, Pet. coke export rep.]. **Added/Corp** King Publishing Company. **VFOAT** Petroleum Coke Export Report. (198?)-. English. mo. $1440.00 US; $1460.00 other. King Publishing Company, PO Box 52210, Knoxville TN 37950. **Tel** (615)584-6294, FAX (615)558-6101, telex 705286. **DD** 382. ***Continues in part** King's Coalstats, 0896-3843.*
Desc: Available in dBase III+, LOTUS 123, ASCII, and King's Software on both 5 1/4" and 3 1/2" diskettes.

US/0749-9043
KING'S INTERNATIONAL COAL TRADE & WORLD COAL STATISTICS. [King's int. coal trade world coal stat.]. **Added/Corp** King Publishing Company. **VFOAT** King's International Coal Trade and World Coal Statistics; International Coal Trade & World Coal Statistics; International Coal Trade and World Coal Statistics; International Coal Trade. (Sept. 28, 1984)-. Periodical. English. Fifty times a year. $890.00 (one year); $1,520.00 (two years). King Publishing Company, PO Box 52210, Knoxville TN 37950. **Tel** (615)584-6294, FAX (615)558-6101, telex 705286. **DD** 382. ctrl circ. available on diskette. Documents available from Documents on Demand. ***Continues in part** King's Coalstats, 0896-3843.*
Ind/Abst Energy Inf. Abstr.; Environ. Abstr.

US/1047-4285
KING'S PETROLEUM COKE REPORT. [King's pet. coke rep.]. **VFOAT** Petroleum Coke Report. (June 1988)-. Periodical. English. mo. King Publishing

Company, PO Box 52210, Knoxville TN 37950. **Tel** (615)584-6294, FAX (615)558-6101, telex 705286. **DD** 382. ***Continues in part*** *King's Coalstats, 0896-3843.*

JA/0368-6450
KOGYO KAYAKU. [Kogyo kayaku]. **Added/Corp** Kogyo Kayaku Kyokai. **VFOAT** Journal of the Industrial Explosives Society of Japan; Explosion and Explosives. (1939)-. Periodical. Japanese (summaries and/or abstracts in English). bm. $152.00. **(Subscription address:** Kyowa Book Company Inc., 1-38 Kanda Jinbo-Cho, Chiyoda-Ku Tokyo 101, Japan**) CODEN** KOKYBR. Documents available from Article Express International, CASDDS.
Ind/Abst Chem. Abstr.; Coal Abstr.; Ei Page One; Eng. Index Annu.

GW/0342-0809
KOMPASS (BOCHUM), DER. **See** Insurance.

RU
KOMPLEKSNOE ISPOLZOVANIE MINERALNOGO SYRIA. [Kompleksn. ispolz. miner. syrja]. **Added/Corp** Qazaq SSR Ghylym Akademiiasy. (1978)-. Academic Scholarly Publication. Russian. mo. $71.00. **(Subscription address:** Victor Kamkin, 4956 Boiling Brook Parkway, Rockville MD 20852.**) LC** TN265; .K65. **CODEN** KIMSDD. Documents available from CASDDS.
Ind/Abst Chem. Abstr.; Coal Abstr.

JA/0287-9840
KOZAN. [Kozan]. **VFOAT** Bulletin of Japan Mining Industry Association. (1948)-. Academic Scholarly Publication. Japanese. mo. $99.50. Nihon Kogyo Kyokai, (Japan Mining Industry Assoc.), 3-6, Uchisaiwaicho 1 Chome, Chiyodaku, Tokyoto 100, Japan. **(Subscription address:** Maruzen Company Ltd., PO Box 5050, Import & Export Department, Tokyo 100 31 Japan.**) ED** Ichiro Kaneoka. **CODEN** KOZADW. **Circ:** 1,200 (ctrl). Documents available from CASDDS.
Desc: Technique of mining or refinement, and a tendency of production are introduced.
Ind/Abst Chem. Abstr.

CH/0300-3760
KUANG YE JI SHU. (KUANG YEH CHI SHU.). **Added/Corp** Ching Chi Pu Lien Ho Kuang Yeh Yen Chiu So. Ching Chi Pu Kuang Yeh Yen Chiu Fu Wu Tsu. Chung-Kuo Kuang Yeh Kung Cheng Hsueh Hui. **VFOAT** Mining Technical Digest. (1963)-. Periodical. Chinese. mo. Ching Chi Pu Lien Ho Kuang Yeh Yen Chiu So, Taipei Taiwan. **CODEN** KYCSA4. Documents available from CASDDS.
Ind/Abst Chem. Abstr.

CC/0253-6099
KUANGYE GONGCHENG. (KUANG YEH KUNG CHENG.). [Kuangye gongcheng]. **VFOAT** Mining and Metallurgical Engineering. 1981, 1-. Academic Scholarly Publication. Chinese (summaries and/or abstracts in English). qt. $100.00. Kuang Yeh Kung Cheng Pien Chi Pu, PO Box 67, Chang-Sha Hunan, People's Republic of China. **Tel** 82826, telex 6386. **ED** Li Yihong. **LC** TN4; .K83 . **DD** 622/.05. **CODEN** KUGODL. Index available. **Bk Rev. Ad Acc. Circ:** 2,500. Documents available from CASDDS.
Desc: Mining, mineral processing, metallurgy and metal materials processing are mainly included.
Ind/Abst Chem. Abstr.; Ei Page One.

KO
KWANGSAN CHIJIL. **Added/Corp** Taehan Kwangsan Chijil Hakhoe. Taehan Kwangsan Chijil Hakhoe. Journal. **VFOAT** Journal of the Korean Institute of Mining Geology. (19??)-. Periodical. Korean (summaries and/or abstracts in English). Taihan Kwangsan Chijie Hakhoe, c/o Yonsei University, 134 Sinchon-dong, Seoul South Korea. **LC** TN260; .K87.
Ind/Abst Coal Abstr.

JA
KYUSHU SEKITAN KOKUSU TOKEI NENKAN. **Added/Corp** Japan. Fukuoka Tsusho Sangyokyoku. Sekitanbu. Nihon Sekitan Kyokai. Kyushu Shibu. **VFOAT** Kyushu Sekitan Tokei Nenkan. (1962)-. Periodical. Japanese. Nihon Sekitan Kyokai Kyushu Shibu, c/o Nihon Kanko Building, 1-20 Tenjin 3-chome Chuo-ku, Fukuoka 810 Japan. **LC** HD9556.J32; K936. ***Continues*** *Kyushu Sekitan Tokei Nenkan.*

UK/0267-5099
LATIN AMERICAN MINING LETTER. [Lat. Am. min. lett.]. **VFOAT** LAML. (Jan. 1982)-. Periodical. English (Spanish). Two issues per month. £396.00. MIIDA Limited, PO Box 2137, London NW10 6TN England. **Tel** 011/44/81/9617487. **ED** M. Wood. **Bk Rev. Ad Acc.**
Desc: Provides a comprehensive and up-to-date news coverage of the region's mining industry as well as providing Latin American readers with a convenient terminal markets perspective.

US
LEAD / U.S. DEPARTMENT OF THE INTERIOR, BUREAU OF MINES. **See** Metals and Metallurgy.

US/1051-533X
LEGAL QUARTERLY DIGEST OF MINE SAFETY AND HEALTH DECISIONS. **See** Law.

US/0024-4902
LITHOLOGY AND MINERAL RESOURCES. [Lithol. miner. resour.]. **Added/Corp** Consultants Bureau. (1966)-. Periodical. English (Russian). bm (6 issues). $1275.00 US; $1480.00 other. Consultants Bureau, A Division of Plenum Publishing Corporation, 233 Spring Street, New York NY 10013. **Tel** (212)620-8000, (212)620-8466, FAX (212)463-0742, telex 23/421139. **ED** V. N. Kholodov. **LC** TN1; .L5413. **CODEN** LTMRAR. **[CCC].** Index available. available on microfilm and microfiche from University Microfilms International (UMI). Documents available from Article Express International.
Desc: Publishes articles on the latest developments in geology, mineralogy, lithogenesis, prospecting, mining science and rock mechanics.
Ind/Abst AESIS Q.; Alum. Ind. Abstr.; Coal Abstr.; Ei Page One; Eng. Mater. Abstr.; Eng. Index Annu.; GeoRef; Met. Abstr.

RU/0024-497X
LITOLOGIA I POLEZNYE ISKOPAEMYE. (LITOLOGIIA I POLEZNYE ISKOPAEMYE.). [Litol. polezn. iskop.]. **Added/Corp** Akademiia Nauk SSSR. Gosudarstvennyi Geologicheskii Komitet SSSR. Soviet Union. Ministerstvo Geologii. **VFOAT** Lithology and Mineral Resources. (1963)-. Academic Scholarly Publication. Russian. Six times a year. $142.00. Izdatelstvo Nauka / Akademiia Nauk, Publishing House of the Russian Academy of Sciences, Leninskii Porspekt 14, 117901 Moscow Russia. **Tel** 011 95 954-21-53, FAX 011 95 938-21-44, telex 411964. **(Subscription address:** East View Publications Inc., 3020 Harbor Lane North, Suite 110, Minneapolis MN 55447.**) CODEN** LPIKAQ. Documents available from CASDDS.
Ind/Abst Chem. Abstr.; Coal Abstr.; GeoRef.

US/0362-1553
M.I.R.L. REPORT. [M. I. R. L. rep.]. **Added/Corp** University of Alaska, Fairbanks. Mineral Industry Research Laboratory. University of Alaska (College). Mineral Industry Research Laboratory. **VFOAT** MIRL. **VAT** Mineral Industry Research Laboratory Report. (19??)-. Academic Scholarly Publication. English. ir. Price varies per volume. Mineral Industry Research Lab, University of Alaska, Fairbanks AK 99775. **Tel** (907)474-7135. **ED** P.D. Rao. **LC** TN24.A4; A65. **DD** 553/.09798. **CODEN** AMIRB8. Documents available from CASDDS.
Ind/Abst ASTIS Curr. Aware. Bull. (1978-); ASTIS Bibliogr. (1978-); Chem. Abstr.; GeoRef.

CH/0377-1571
M.R.S.O. REPORT. (MRSO REPORT.). [MRSO rep.]. **Main/Corp** Kung Yeh Chi Shu Yen Chiu Yuan. Kuang Yeh Yen Chiu So. **VAT** Mining Research and Science Organization Report. (19??)-. Chinese (Chinese). Mining Research and Service Organization, Taipei, Taiwan. **LC** TN102.5; .A25a. ***Continues*** *Ching chi pu Lien ho.Kuang yeh yen Chiu so. MRSO Report, 0377-1571.*
Ind/Abst GeoRef.

CG/0250-538X
MAADINI. [Maadini]. 1974-. Academic Scholarly Publication. French. Division des Relations Publiques de la Gecamines, B P 450, Lumbashi Congo Zaire. **LC** TN119.Z3; M3. **DD** 553/.09675/1. **CODEN** MAADDA. Documents available from CASDDS.
Ind/Abst Chem. Abstr. (1974-1981).

MY
MAJALLAH PERANGKAAN BERKENAAN PERUSAHAAN PERLOMBONGAN MALAYSIA. **Main/Corp** Malaysia. Kementerian Perusahaan Utama. (1970)-. Multiple languages (English and Malay). Jalan Gurney, Kuala Lumpur, Mines Department, Selangor Malaysia. **Tel** 2929797. **LC** HD9506.M36; M35A. **DD** 338.2/09595. ***Continues*** *Bulletin of Statistics Relating to the Mining Industry of Malaysia.*

AT/0158-6335
MAJOR MANUFACTURING AND MINING INVESTMENT PROJECTS. **See** Manufacturing.

US/0149-0397
MARINE MINING. ***Title Change.*** [Mar. min.]. Vol. 1 (1977)-. Academic Scholarly Publication. English. qt. Taylor & Francis Ltd., Rankine Road, Basingstoke Hampshire, RG24 8PR United Kingdom. **Tel** 011 44 256 840366, FAX 011 44 256 479438, telex 858540. **(Subscription address:** Taylor & Francis Inc., 1900 Frost Road, Suite 101, Bristol PA 19007-1598.**) ED** J Robert Moore (editor's address: Department of Marine Studies, The University of Texas, Austin TX 78712-1162). **LC** TN291.5; .M35. **DD** 622/.29. **CODEN** MARMDK. **[CCC]. Bk Rev. Ad Acc. Pr Rev. Circ:** 600 (ctrl). available on microfilm and microfiche from University Microfilms International (UMI). Documents available from Article Express International, The Genuine Article, BIOSIS Document Express, Petroleum Abstracts Document Delivery Service, CASDDS, Documents on Demand. ***Continued by*** *Marine Georesources & Geotechnology.*
Desc: Provides scientists and engineers with current research studies on marine minerals exploration and marine mining in general, recovery and processing of ore, seafloor mineral surveys and assessment, manganese nodules, analytical techniques related to marine mining, shipboard mining systems, and seafloor lodes and placers.
Ind/Abst Appl. Mech. Rev.; Aquat. Sci. Fish. Abstr. (Computer File); Bioeng. Abstr.; Biol. Abstr.; Chem. Abstr.; Curr. Aware. Biol. Sci., CABS; Curr. Contents Eng. Tech. Appl. Sci.; Curr. Contents Phys. Chem. Earth Sci.; Ecol. Abstr.; Ei Page One; Eng. Index Annu.; Environ. Abstr.; Fluid Abstr., Civil Eng.; Fluid Abstr. Proc. Eng.; FLUIDEX (1977-); Geogr. Abstr. Phys. Geogr.; Geogr. Abstr. Human Geogr.; Geol. Abstr.; GeoRef; Health Saf. Sci. Abstr.; Mater. Sci. Eng. Abstr.; MINPROC; Mintec, Min. Technol. Abstr.; Ocean. Abstr.; Life Sci. Collect.; Pet. Abstr.; Pollut. Abstr. Indexes; Res. Alert [Full Cov.]; Sci. Cit. Index (19??-19??); SCISEARCH; Solid State Supercond. Abstr.

GW/0174-1357
MARKSCHEIDEWESEN, DAS. (MARKSCHEIDEWESEN.). [Markscheidewesen]. **Added/Corp** Deutscher Markscheider-Verein. (1979)-. Academic Scholarly Publication. German. Four times a year. DM108.00. Verlag Glueckauf GmbH, Postfach 185619, D-45206 Essen Germany. **Tel** 011 49 2054 924200, 011 49 2054 924201, 011 49 2054 924202, telex 08579545. **LC** TN273; .M5. ***Continues*** *Mitteilungen aus dem Markscheidewesen.*
Ind/Abst Coal Abstr.; EMBASE; Energy Res. Abstr. (Aug. 1982-); GeoRef.

BW/0134-9570
MASINY I TEHNOLOGIJA TORFJANOGO PROIZVODSTVA. (MASHINY I TEKHNOLOGIIA TORFIANOGO PROIZVODSTVA.). [Mas. tehnol. torf. proizvod.]. **Added/Corp** Belaruski Palitekhnichny Instytut. Vol. 4 (19??)-. Academic Scholarly Publication. Russian. 1.73rub (single issue). Izdatelstvo Vysheishaia Shkola, Masherova 11, 220048 Minsk Byelarus. **Tel** 0172 23-54-15, FAX 0172 23-54-15. **LC** TN837; .T34. **CODEN** MTTPD2. Documents available from CASDDS. ***Continues*** *Tekhnologiia Torfianogo Proizvodstva i Torfianye Mashiny.*
Ind/Abst Chem. Abstr. (?-1976).

PL/0208-7448
MECHANIZACJA I AUTOMATYZACJA GORNICTWA. [Mech. autom. gorn.]. **Added/Corp** Zakady Konstrukcyjno-Mechanizacyjne Przemysu Weglowego. Osrodek Badawczo-Rozwojowy Systemow Mechanizacji Elektroniki i Automatyki Gorniczej. (1972)-. Polish (summaries and/or abstracts in English and Russian). mo. Price on Request. **(Subscription address:** ARS Polona, PO Box 1001, 00068 Warsaw Poland.**) LC** TN345; .M34.
Ind/Abst Coal Abstr.

CC/0253-2336
MEITAN KEXUE JISHU. (MEI TAN KO HSUEH CHI SHU.). [Meitan kexue jishu]. **VFOAT** Coal Science and Technology. (19??)-. Academic Scholarly Publication. Chinese (summaries and/or abstracts in English). mo. $49.56. **(Subscription address:** China International Book Trading Corporation, PO Box 399, Library Service Department, Beijing 100044 People's Republic of China.**) ED** Jiang Guangxi. **LC** TN4; .M3 . **DD** 622/.334/05. **CODEN** CSTPDL. **Ad Acc. Circ:** 20,000. Documents available from CASDDS.
Desc: To propagate technical policies of Chinese coal industry, spread the latest technological informations domestic and abroad, report advanced experiences and results in coal production, etc.
Ind/Abst Chem. Abstr.; Coal Abstr.; Ei Page One; GeoRef.

US/0077-1120
MEMOIR (MONTANA BUREAU OF MINES AND GEOLOGY). (MEMOIR / STATE OF MONTANA, BUREAU OF MINES AND GEOLOGY.). [Mem. State Mont. Bur. Mines Geol.]. **Added/Corp** Montana Bureau of Mines and Geology. (1931)-. Monographic series. English. ir. Price varies per volume. Montana Bureau of Mines and Geology, Montana College of Mineral Science, Butte MT 59701. **Tel** (406)496-4174, FAX (406)496-4133. **CODEN** MBGMA3. Index Available Published separately--free--upon request. Documents available from CASDDS. ***Continues*** *Memoir (Montana. State Bureau of Mines and Metallurgy).*
Ind/Abst Chem. Abstr.; GeoRef.

US/0548-5975
MEMOIR - NEW MEXICO BUREAU OF MINES & MINERAL RESOURCES. [Mem. N. M. Bur. Mines Miner. Resour.]. **Main/Corp** New Mexico. Bureau of Mines and Mineral Resources. **Added/Corp** New Mexico. Bureau of Mines and Mineral Resources. **VFOAT** Memoir - State Bureau of Mines and Mineral Resources. **VAT** Memoir - New Mexico Bureau of Mines and Mineral Resources. (1956)-. Monographic series. English. ir. Price varies per volume. New Mexico Bureau of Mines, Campus Station, Socorro NM 87801. **Tel** (505)835-5410, FAX (505)835-6333. **ED** J. Zibek. **CODEN** NMMMAJ. **Bk Rev. Ad Acc.** ctrl circ.

Engineering — Mines and Mining Engineering

Documents available from CASDDS.
Desc: Geology, mineral resources, energy resources, and metallurgy pertaining fully or in part to the state of New Mexico.
Ind/Abst Ceram. Abstr.; Chem. Abstr.; GeoRef.

SP
MEMORIA GENERAL - INSTITUTO GEOLOGICO Y MINERO DE ESPANA.
See Earth Sciences-Geology.

CK
MEMORIAS AL CONGRESO NACIONAL / REPUBLICA DE COLOMBIA, MINISTERIO DE MINAS Y ENERGIA.
Main/Corp Colombia. Ministerio de Minas y Energia. (1991)-. Spanish. Ministerio de Minas y Energia, Ave el Dorado-Can-A A, 80319 Oficina No 417, Bogota de Colombia.

US
MERCURY IN ... .
English. an. US Department of the Interior / Bureau of Mines, Publications Department, PO Box 18070, Cochrans Mill Road, Pittsburgh PA 15236. **Tel** (412)892-6400.

US/0364-7919
MERCURY (UNITED STATES. BUREAU OF MINES).
See Metals and Metallurgy-Abstracting, Bibliographies and Statistics.

US
METAL INDUSTRY INDICATORS / BUREAU OF MINES.
Added/Corp United States. Bureau of Mines. **VFOAT** Bureau of Mines Metal Industry Indicators. (July 1991)-. Government Publication. English. mo. US Department of the Interior / Bureau of Mines, 810 7th Street NW, Room 604, Washington DC 20241. **Tel** (202)501-9300.

CN/0824-7471
METAL TRENDS.
See Economics-Industry and Production.

UK
METALS & MINERALS ANNUAL REVIEW.
VFOAT Metals and Minerals Annual Review. (1990)-. English. an. £63.00 UK; £78.00, $140.00 other (Comes with Mining Annual Review). Mining Journal Ltd., 60 Worship Street, London EC2A 2HD England. **Tel** 011 44 071 377 2020, FAX 071 247 4100, telex 8952809 MINING G. **ED** David Bird, Tony Brewis, John Chadwick, Des Clifford, Elizabeth Dougherty, Roger Ellis, Alan Kennedy, Richard Morgan, Geoff Pearse, Nathalie Rosin, John Spooner and Michael West. **Continues** Mining Annual Review, 0076-8995.
Desc: Statistical information on the application of minerals and metals.
Ind/Abst F&S Index Plus Text, Int. [Select. Cov.]; PROMT.

CN/0847-0197
METALS ECONOMICS GROUP STRATEGIC REPORT.
English. bm. $975.00. Metals Economics Group, 1718 Argyle Street, #300 Halifax Nova Scotia, B3J 3C4 Canada. **Tel** (902)429-2880, FAX (902)429-6593, telex 0636700485. **Continues** Mine Development Bimonthly.

SZ
MINARIA HELVETICA.
(1981)-. Periodical. French (German). Prof S Graeser, Naturhistorisches Museum, Augustinergasse 2, CH-4001 Basel Switzerland. **LC** TN91; .M56. **DD** 553/.09494.

UK/0369-1632
MINE AND QUARRY.
[Mine quarry]. **Added/Corp** Minerals Engineering Society. **VFOAT** Mine & Quarry. (April 1972)-. Academic Scholarly Publication. English. Ten times a year. £55.00 UK; £75.00 Europe; £100.00 other. IML Group, Blair House, 184-186 High Street, Tonbridge Kent, TN9 1BQ England. **Tel** 011 44 732 359990, FAX 011 44 732 770049. **ED** Tim Fryer. **DD** 622/.05. **CODEN** MQRYAT. **Bk Rev**. **Ad Acc**, **Adv Mgr:** Graeme Mercantile. **Circ:** 4,000 (ctrl). Documents available from Article Express International, CASDDS.
Supersedes Mining and Minerals Engineering.
Desc: Aims to give mine and quarry managers and their advisors essential information on equipment, methods etc., to enable greater production at optimum cost.
Ind/Abst AESIS Q.; Chem. Abstr. (1972-1983); Coal Abstr.; Curr. Technol. Index; Ei Page One; EMBASE; Energy Res. Abstr. (June 1975-); Eng. Index Annu. [Select. Cov.]; Fluid Abstr., Civil Eng.; Fluid Abstr. Proc. Eng.; FLUIDEX (1973-); GeoRef; MINPROC; Mintec, Min. Technol. Abstr.; Saf. Health Work.

AT/0085-3453
MINE AND QUARRY MECHANISATION.
Ceased. [Mine quarry mech.]. (1960)-Ceased 1985-86. English. an. Magazine Associates Pty Ltd, PO Box 5, Hamilton New South Wales 2303 Australia. **Tel** 049-69-3328. **ED** Max T Fiddler. **Ad Acc.** **Circ:** 1,500 (ctrl).
Desc: Technical and review articles relating to mining and quarrying mechanisation throughout the world emphasis on Australian mines and quarries. Special section on new products. Press releases welcome.
Ind/Abst MINPROC (?-?); Mintec, Min. Technol. Abstr. (?-?).

AT/1031-8380
MINE LIFE.
[Mine life]. (1988)-. Periodical. English. Three times a year. Free. Chamber of Mines and Energy of Western Australia, 12 St Georges Terrace/7th Floor, Perth Western Australia 6000 Australia. **Tel** 09 325 2955, FAX 09 221 3701. **DD** 622.09941.

US
MINE PRODUCTION OF SILVER IN ... / THE SILVER INSTITUTE.
Added/Corp Silver Institute. **VFOAT** Mine Production of Silver. (19??)-. English. Silver Institute, 1112 16th Street NW, Suite 240, Washington DC 20036. **Tel** (202)835-0185, FAX (202)783-2127, telex 904233 DAV INC WSH. **LC** HD9536.A1; M55. **DD** 338.2/7421/021.
Ind/Abst F&S Index Plus Text, Int. [Select. Cov.]; Predicasts Forecasts.

US/1040-8223
MINE REGULATION REPORTER. See Law.

BL/0100-6908
MINERACAO METALURGIA (1968).
See Metals and Metallurgy.

US
MINERAL & ENERGY INFORMATION SOURCES.
VFOAT Mineral and Energy Information Sources. 1984/85-. English. $10.00. Mineral Information Institute, 1125 17th Street, PO Box 2070, Denver CO 80202. **Tel** (303)297-3226. **Bk Rev. Circ:** 8,000.
Continues Mineral Information Sources.
Desc: Lists hundreds of low cost or free films, video tapes, and printed materials on mineral and energy related subjects. Contains brief descriptions of available items and information on where they can be obtained.

US/0160-5151
MINERAL COMMODITY SUMMARIES.
See Engineering-Abstracting, Bibliographies and Statistics.

US/0160-3779
MINERAL ECONOMICS ABSTRACTS.
Added/Corp Atlantis Energy & Mineral Economic Services. Mineral Economics Consultants, Inc. Vol. 1 (Jan. 1978)-. Periodical. English (French). mo. $250.00. Atlantis Inc, 20 Juniper Place, Wilton CT 06897. **LC** HD9506.A1; M55. **DD** 016.3382.

US/0544-2486
MINERAL EXPLORATION, MINING, AND PROCESSING PATENTS.
(1967)-. English. an. Society for Mining, Metallurgy and Exploration Inc, 8307 Shaffer Parkway, Littleton CO 80162. **Tel** (303)973-9550, FAX (303)973-3845, telex 881988. **(Subscription address:** Society Mining Metallurgy & Exploration, PO Box 625002, Littleton CO 80162.) **LC** TN257; .M5. **DD** 669/.0027/2; 622; 669.
Continues Mineral Processing Patents Issued During ..., 0733-8333.

AT/0313-6086
MINERAL INDUSTRY QUARTERLY.
(MINERAL INDUSTRY QUARTERLY / S.A. DEPARTMENT OF MINES.). [Miner. ind. q.]. No. 1 (Quarter ending Jan. 31, 1976)-. Periodical. English. qt. Department of Mines and Energy, Australia 5063 Australia. **Tel** (08)274 7500. **LC** TN122.S7; M56.
Ind/Abst Energy Res. Abstr. (Sept. 1982-); GeoRef.

CN/0707-3623
MINERAL INDUSTRY REPORT. NORTHWEST TERRITORIES.
See Economics-Industry and Production.

US/0886-0564
MINERAL INDUSTRY SURVEYS.
(MINERAL INDUSTRY SURVEYS / U.S. DEPARTMENT OF THE INTERIOR, BUREAU OF MINES.). [Miner. ind. surv.]. English. ir. Free. US Department of the Interior / Bureau of Mines, Publications Department, PO Box 18070, Cochrans Mill Road, Pittsburgh PA 15236. **Tel** (412)892-6400. **DD** 338.2/05.

US
MINERAL INDUSTRY SURVEYS. CADMIUM.
VFOAT Cadmium. English. qt. US Department of the Interior / Bureau of Mines, Publications Department, PO Box 18070, Cochrans Mill Road, Pittsburgh PA 15236. **Tel** (412)892-6400.
Desc: Timely statistical and economic data on cadmium.

US/0739-2125
MINERAL INDUSTRY SURVEYS. GRAPHITE, NATURAL IN ... . [Graph., nat.].
English. an. Free. US Department of the Interior / Bureau of Mines, Publications Department, PO Box 18070, Cochrans Mill Road, Pittsburgh PA 15236. **Tel** (412)892-6400. **ED** Harold A Taylor Jr. **LC** TN845; .G62. **DD** 338.2/752/0973. **CODEN:** 900. **Continues** Natural Graphite in ... (Washington D.C. : 1980).
Desc: Graphite statistics and industry news.

AT/0725-6221
MINERAL INFORMATION SERIES ADELAIDE.
(1977)-. Periodical. English. mo.
Ind/Abst AESIS Q.

US/0749-9876
MINERAL INFORMATION SOURCES. See
Earth Sciences.

US/0897-6694
MINERAL LAW NEWSLETTER. See Law.

US/0889-6925
MINERAL MATTERS.
[Miner. matters]. **Added/Corp** Southern Illinois University at Carbondale. Coal Extraction and Utilization Research Center. (19??)-. Periodical. English. Twice a year (Apr. & Oct.). Free. Coal Extraction and Utilization Research Center, Southern Illinois University at Carbondale, Carbondale IL 62901-4623. **Tel** (618)536-5521, FAX (618)453-7346. **ED** Donna C. Davin. **DD** 553. **Circ:** 3,000.
Desc: Update of coal and coal-related research projects being done at Southern Illinois University at Carbondale.
Ind/Abst Coal Abstr.

CN/0713-7044
MINERAL POLICY SECTOR INTERNAL REPORT.
[Miner. Policy Sect. intern. rep.]. **VAT** Internal Report - Mineral Policy Sector. Energy, Mines and Resources Canada. Monographic series. English. Price varies per volume. Energy Mines and Resources Canada, 580 Booth Street, Ottawa Ontario K1A 0E4 Canada.
Ind/Abst GeoRef.

UK/0882-7508
MINERAL PROCESSING AND EXTRACTIVE METALLURGY REVIEW.
(MINERAL PROCESSING AND EXTRACTIVE METALLURGY REVIEW.). [Miner. process. extr. metall. rev.]. Vol. 2, No. 1 and 2 (Oct. 1985)-. Academic Scholarly Publication. English. qt. $746.00 (university and hospital libraries); $1164.00 other. Gordon & Breach Science Publishers, PO Box 90, Reading RG1 8JL England. **Tel** 011 44 734 560080, FAX 011 44 734 568211. **LC** TN496; .M56. **DD** 622/.7. **CODEN** MPERE8. **[CCC].** **Bk Rev**. **Ad Acc**. Documents available from Article Express International, CASDDS. **Continues** Mineral Processing and Technology Review, 0735-9632.
Ind/Abst Chem. Abstr. (-1987); Ei Page One; Eng. Index Annu.

AT/0727-9272
MINERAL PRODUCTION, NEW SOUTH WALES.
[Miner. prod., N. S. W.]. (1978)-. Periodical. English. qt. **DD** 338.209944.
Ind/Abst AESIS Q.

AT/0077-8737
MINERAL RESOURCES.
[Miner. resour.]. No. 1 (1898)-. Academic Scholarly Publication. English. Price varies per volume. Geological Survey of New South Wales, Department of Mineral Resources, 8-18 Bent Street, Sydney New South Wales 2000 Australia. **CODEN** MRWGDA. Documents available from CASDDS.
Ind/Abst AESIS Q.; Chem. Abstr.; GeoRef.

TH/0082-8114
MINERAL RESOURCES DEVELOPMENT SERIES.
[Miner. resour. dev. ser.]. **Added/Corp** United Nations. Economic Commission for Asia and the Far East. United Nations. Economic and Social Commission for Asia and the Pacific. (1952)-. Government Publication. English. ir. Price varies per volume. United Nations Publications, 2 United Nations Plaza, Room DC2 0853, Department 007C, New York NY 10017. **Tel** (212)963-8303, (800)253-9646. **LC** TN1.A1; U53. **DD** 338.2. **CODEN** UNEMAT.
Ind/Abst GeoRef; Indian Geosci. Abstr.

AT/1031-556X
MINERALS AND ENERGY RESEARCH NEWS.
(1988)-. Periodical. English. sa. **Continues** Mining and Petroleum Research News, 0811-5443.
Ind/Abst AESIS Q.

AT
MINERALS AND MINERAL DEVELOPMENT, WESTERN AUSTRALIA.
VFOAT Minerals and Mineral Development. English. an. Department of Resources Development, PO Box 7234, Cloisters Square, Perth Western Australia 6850 Australia. **Tel** 011 61 9 3275555. **LC** TN122.W5; M552. **DD** 338.2/09941.

UK/0892-6875
MINERALS ENGINEERING.
[Miner. eng.]. Vol. 1, No. 1 (1988)-. Academic Scholarly Publication. English. mo. $552.00 The Americas; £370.00 other. Pergamon Press, An Imprint of Elsevier Science Ltd., The Boulevard, Langford Lane, Kidlington, Oxford OX5 1GB United Kingdom. **Tel** 011 44 865 843000, 011 44 865 843699, FAX 011 44 865 843010. **(Subscription address:** Elsevier Science Ltd. Oxford Fulfillment Centre, PO Box 800, Kidlington, Oxford OX5 1DX United Kingdom.) **ED** Barry A. Wills (editor's address: Camborne School of Mines, Pool, Redruth, Cornwall TR15 3SE

United Kingdom). **LC** TN1; .M52318. **DD** 669/.005. **CODEN** MENGEB. **[CCC]**. Index available. **Bk Rev. Ad Acc. Pr Rev. Circ:** 1,250. available on microfilm and microfiche from University Microfilms International (UMI). Documents available from Article Express International, The Genuine Article, CASDDS.
Desc: Provides rapid publication of topical papers featuring practical developments in the allied fields of mineral processing and extractive metallurgy. Wide range coverage of both research and practical (operating) topics.
Ind/Abst AESIS Q.; Biodeter. Abstr. (1991-); Chem. Abstr. (1988-); Comput. Inf. Syst. Abstr. J. [Full Cov.]; Curr. Contents Eng. Tech. Appl. Sci.; Ei Page One; Eng. Index Annu.; Manuf. Process Eng. Abstr.; Mater. Sci. Eng. Abstr.; Mech. Eng. Abstr.; Met. Abstr.; Res. Alert [Full Cov.]; SCISEARCH; Solid State Supercond. Abstr.

AT
MINERALS GAZETTE. [Miner. gaz.]. (1991)-. English. Eleven times a year. 85.00Aus$ Australia; 110.00Aus$ Papua New Guinea, New Zealand, & Asia; 135.00Aus$ others. Resource Information Unit, 100 Ahy Street Suite 8 10, R Louthean, Subiaco WA 6008 Australia. **Tel** 011 61 9 3823955. ***Continues*** *Metals Gazette, 1032-3821.*
Ind/Abst AESIS Q.

UK/0265-3923
MINERALS HANDBOOK (LONDON, ENGLAND). (MINERALS HANDBOOK.). (1982/83)-. English. be. $150.00 US and Canada; £65.00 other (two years). Globe Book Services Ltd, Stockton H SE, 1 Melbourne Place, London WC2B 4LF England. **Tel** 011 44 71 836 6633.

AT
MINERALS QUARTERLY. English. qt. Department of Resource Industries, GPO Box 194/61, Mary Street, Brisbane Queensland 4001 Australia. **Tel** 011 61 7 2371435, FAX 011 61 7 2297770.

AT
MINERALS RESEARCH IN CSIRO. **Added/Corp** Commonwealth Scientific and Industrial Research Organization (Australia). (Nov. 1972)-. Periodical. English. ir. Free on request. CSIRO Publications, PO Box 89, 314 Albert Street, East Melborne Victoria 3002 Australia. **Tel** 011 61 3 4187333, 4187217, FAX 011 61 3 4190459, telex AA 30236.
Ind/Abst AESIS Q.

CU/0253-5653
MINERIA EN CUBA, LA. [Min. Cuba]. V. 1-July/Sept. 1975-. Academic Scholarly Publication. Spanish (summaries and/or abstracts in English and Russian). qt. $21.00. Ediciones Cubanas, Obispo 527, Altos ESQ Bernaza, CP 10100 Havana Cuba. **Tel** 011 632980, 631942, FAX 011 631011, telex 512337, 6540. **CODEN** MICUDP. **Circ:** 10,000 (ctrl). Documents available from CASDDS.
Desc: Publishes papers by Cuban and foreign authors on geology, geophysics, mining, and metallurgy. materials related to these sciences.
Ind/Abst Chem. Abstr.; GeoRef.

US/0890-6157
MINER'S NEWS. [Min. news]. Vol. 1, Issue 1 (June 1986)-. Periodical. English. Six times a year (Feb., Apr., June, Aug., Oct., Dec.). $25.00. Miners News, PO Box 5694, Boise ID 83706. **Tel** (800) 624-7212 (208)375-3680, FAX (208)375-0975. **ED** Shirley White. **DD** 622. **Bk Rev**, (Qty: 10). **Ad Acc, Adv Mgr:** Arnie Weber. **Circ:** 7,000 (ctrl).

FR/0994-2556
MINES & CARRIERES. [Mines carr.]. **Added/Corp** Societe de l'Industrie Minerale (France). **VFOAT** Industrie Minerales, Industrie Minerale; Mines & Carrieres, Industrie Minerale. **VAT** Mines et carri-eres. Vol. 70, No. 1560 (Aug./Sept. 1988)-. Academic Scholarly Publication. French. mo. 700.00F France; 935.00F other. Societe de l'industrie Minerale, 41-47 rue de Grange Aux Belles, 75010 Paris France. **Tel** 011 33 1 42020792. **CODEN** MICAEY. Documents available from Article Express International, CASDDS. ***Continues*** *Industrie Minerale, Mines et Carrieres, 0296-2918.*
Ind/Abst Chem. Abstr.; Ei Page One; Eng. Index Annu. [Select. Cov.].

AT/1034-8794
MINES AND ENERGY REVIEW. Added/Corp South Australia. Dept. of Mines and Energy. **VFOAT** Mines and Energy Review. No. 157-(1990)-. English. Department of Mines and Energy, Australia 5063 Australia. **Tel** (08)274 7500. ***Continues*** *Mineral Resources Review.*
Ind/Abst AESIS Q.

CN/1184-6518
MINES AND MINERALS INFORMATION CIRCULAR. [Mines Miner. inf. circ.]. **Added/Corp** Ontario. Mines and Minerals Division. Ontario. Ministry of Northern Development and Mines. **VFOAT** Information Circular. No. 1 (1990)-. Monographic series. English. Price varies per volume. **DD** 338.2/09713/05.

CN/0068-7863
MINES BRANCH MONOGRAPH (OTTAWA). ***Title Change.*** (MONOGRAPH - MINES BRANCH.). [Mines Branch monogr.]. **Main/Corp** Canada. Mines Branch. **VAT** Mines Br. Monograph; Mines Br. Mono. (19??)-(19??). Monographic series. English. ***Continued by*** *Monograph (Canada Centre for Mineral and Energy Technology), 0821-8234.*
Ind/Abst Lit. Pat. Abstr., Oilfield Chem. (1976-1990); Lit. Abstr., Catal. Catal. (1976-1990); Lit. Abstr., Health Environ. (1976-1990); Lit. Abstr., Pet. Refin. Petrochem. (1976-1990); Lit. Abstr., Pet. Substit. (1976-1990); Lit. Abstr., Transp. Storage (1976-1990).

CN
MINES DE CHARBON. See Engineering-Abstracting, Bibliographies and Statistics.

US/0197-9965
MINES DIRECTORY. [Mines dir.]. Directory. English. Eight times a year. $30.00 US and Canada. Colorado School Mines Alumni Association, PO Box 1410, Golden CO 80402. **Tel** (303)273-3291, FAX (303)273-3165. **ED** Ellen E Glover. **LC** TN210.C7; M55. **DD** 553/.025/78. Index available. **Bk Rev. Ad Acc. Circ:** 6,000.
Desc: Publishes articles on mineral policy, political and world issues, business, and technological developments affecting the nation's basic industries. Emphasis on alumni affairs.

US/0096-4859
MINES MAGAZINE. See Earth Sciences-Mineralogy.

CN/0317-9524
MINES (TORONTO). (LES MINES.). 1973-. French. an. Association Miniere Du Canada, 20, Rue Toronto, Toronto Ontario M5C 2C2. **DD** 338.2/0971. ***Continues*** *Industrie Miniere, 0317-9516.*

II
MINETECH. (19??)-. Periodical. English. qt.
Ind/Abst Indian Geosci. Abstr.

AT/0812-0293
MINFO. [Minfo]. (1983)-. Periodical. English. qt. Free on request. Publications Officer, Department of Minerals and Energy, PO Box 536, St. Leonards NSW 2065 Australia. **Tel** 61 2 9018888, FAX 61 2 9018246. **DD** 338.209944.
Ind/Abst AESIS Q.

RH/0254-0304
MINING AND ENGINEERING. [Min. eng.]. Vol. 45, No. 1 (Jan. 1980)-. Periodical. English. mo. Thomson Publications Zimbabwe Pvt Ltd, PO Box 1683, Harare Zimbabwe. **LC** TN1; .M58. **DD** 622/.05. ***Continues in part*** *Chamber of Mines Journal.*
Ind/Abst For. Abstr.; GeoRef; Soils Fert.

CN/0825-219X
MINING AND MINERAL PROCESSING OPERATIONS IN CANADA. [Min. miner. process. oper. Can.]. **Added/Corp** Canada. Minerals. (1980)-. English. ir. Canada Communication Group Publishers, Order Processing, Ottawa Ontario K1A 0S9 Canada. **Tel** (819)956-4800, (819)956-4802. **LC** TN26; .M52. **DD** 622/.7/02571. ***Formed by the union of*** *Metallurgical Works in Canada: Nonferrous and Precious Metals, 0076-6704; Metallurgical Works in Canada: Primary Iron and Steel, 0076-6712* ***and*** *Metal and Industrial Mineral Mines and Processing Plants in Canada, 0319-5406.*

US/0748-2027
MINING AND PUBLIC LANDS REPORT. [Min. public lands rep.]. **VFOAT** M.P.L. Report; MPL Report. Vol. 2, Issue 6 (June 1984)-. Periodical. English. mo. $400.00. Congressional Resources, PO Box 45, Mt. Vernon VA 22121. **LC** KF5601.A3; M56. **DD** 346.7304/5. ***Continues*** *Update (Mt. Vernon, VA.).*

UK/0076-8995
MINING ANNUAL REVIEW. ***Title Change.*** [Min. annu. rev.]. (1964)-(19??). English. an. Mining Journal Ltd., 60 Worship Street, London EC2A 2HD England. **Tel** 011 44 071 377 2020, FAX 071 247 4100, telex 8952809 MINING G. **ED** Michael West. **LC** HD9506.U6; M52. **DD** 338.2/0973. Index available. **Ad Acc. Circ:** 11,000. ***Continues*** *Mining Journal. Annual Review Number.* ***Continued by*** *Metals & Minerals Annual Review.*
Desc: Review of international minerals industry. Articles on each of 60 metals/minerals in each of 125 countries. Includes comprehensive index and buyers guide.
Ind/Abst AESIS Q.; Coal Abstr.; F&S Index Plus Text, Int. [Select. Cov.]; GeoRef; Leadscan; MINPROC; Mintec, Min. Technol. Abstr.; NEXIS (1981-); PROMT.

US/1055-9957
MINING BUSINESS DIGEST. [Mining bus. dig.]. Vol. 5, No. 5 (May 1991)-. Periodical. English. mo. $170.00 (one year), $310.00 (two years) US; $195.00 (one year), $360.00 (two years) Canada and Mexico; $220.00 (one year), $410.00 (two years) other. Lumac Marketing Services, Inc., 11 Robin Crest Lane, Littleton CO 80123. **Tel** (303)798-9365, FAX (303)798-6654. **ED** Frank L Ludeman. **LC** HD9506.U6; M524. **DD** 338.2/0973/05. ***Continues*** *Western Minerals Activity Report, 0896-8527.*

UK
MINING DATABASE. ***Title Change.*** (19??)-(1994). English. qt. Mining Journal Ltd., 60 Worship Street, London EC2A 2HD England. **Tel** 011 44 071 377 2020, FAX 071 247 4100, telex 8952809 MINING G. **ED** Richard Morgan. ***Continued by*** *Metallica 2000.*
Desc: Self-contained computerized database of precious metal mines and companies.

UK/0307-9066
MINING DEPARTMENT MAGAZINE. [Min. Dep. mag. - Univ. Nott.]. **Main/Corp** Nottingham, Eng. University. Dept. of Mining Engineering. **Added/Corp** University of Nottingham. Dept. of Mining Engineering. (1948)-. Periodical. English. an. £5.50. Mining Engineering Department, University of Nottingham, Nottingham England. **Tel** 011 44 602 484848, FAX 011 44 602 421681. **ED** B. Denby, S.F.Smith. **Ad Acc. Circ:** 1,500.
Desc: The magazine covers all aspects of mining engineering with technical papers submitted by leading authorities in rock mechanics, ventilation surveying and mineral processing.
Ind/Abst GeoRef.

UK/0262-7965
MINING DIRECTORY, THE. 4th ed. (1988)-. Directory. English. Associated Book Publishers / 11 New Fetter Lane, London EC4P 4EE England. ***Continues*** *Mines and Mining Equipment and Service Companies World Wide.*

UK/0026-5179
MINING ENGINEER (LONDON). (THE MINING ENGINEER.). [Min. eng.]. **Added/Corp** Institution of Mining Engineers (Great Britain). Vol. 1 (1960)-. Periodical. English. Twelve times a year. £70.00 UK; £73.50 Europe; £83.50 other. Institution of Mining Engineer, Danum House South Parade, Doncaster DN1 2DY England. **Tel** 011 44 302 320486, FAX 011 44 302 340554. **(Subscription address:** TG Scott Subscriber Services, 6 Bourne Enterprise Centre, Kent TN15 8DG United Kingdom.) **ED** W. J. W. Bourne. **LC** TN1; .I67. **CODEN** MNEGAP. Index available. cum. index. **Bk Rev. Ad Acc. Circ:** 4,000. Documents available from Article Express International. ***Continues*** *Institution of Mining Engineers (Great Britain). Transactions of the Institution of Mining Engineers, 0371-9634.*
Desc: Scientific and technical papers, articles, personal notes, branch news, industrial news, mining matters, and more.
Ind/Abst Bioeng. Abstr.; Coal Abstr.; Curr. Technol. Index; Ei Page One; Energy Res. Abstr. (June 1980-); Eng. Mater. Abstr.; Eng. Index Annu.; GeoRef; Highw. Res. Abstr.; MINPROC; Mintec, Min. Technol. Abstr.; Saf. Health Work.

US/0026-5187
MINING ENGINEERING. [Min. eng.]. **Added/Corp** Society of Mining Engineers of AIME. American Institute of Mining and Metallurgical Engineers. Mining Branch. American Institute of Mining and Metallurgical Engineers. American Institute of Mining, Metallurgical, and Petroleum Engineers. Vol. 1 (Jan. 1949)-. Periodical. English. Twelve times a year. $100.00 Europe; $124.00 others. Society for Mining, Metallurgy and Exploration Inc, 8307 Shaffer Parkway, Littleton CO 80162. **Tel** (303)973-9550, FAX (303)973-3845, telex 881988. **(Subscription address:** Society Mining Metallurgy & Exploration, PO Box 625002, Littleton CO 80162.) **ED** Tim O'Neil. **LC** TN1; .A5258. **CODEN** MIENAB. **Bk Rev. Ad Acc. Circ:** 26,000. available on microfilm and microfiche from University Microfilms International (UMI). Documents available from Article Express International, Petroleum Abstracts Document Delivery Service, CASDDS. ***Formed by the union of*** *Mining Technology (York, Pa.), 0097-2045; Coal Technology (York, Pa.), 0095-8786* ***and*** *Mining and Metallurgy (New York, N.Y. : 1920), 0096-7289.*
Desc: Publishes the latest technical information related to the overall business of finding, mining and processing metallic and nonmetallic ores and coal.
Ind/Abst AESIS Q.; Alum. Ind. Abstr.; Appl. Sci. Technol. Index; Bioeng. Abstr.; Chem. Abstr.; CIS Abstr.; Coal Abstr.; Ei Page One; Elect. Comm. Abstr.; Energy Inf. Abstr.; Energy Res. Abstr. (April 1974-); Eng. Index Annu.; Environ. Eng. Abstr.; GeoRef; INIS Atomindex [Micro.]; Manuf. Process Eng. Abstr.; Mech. Eng. Abstr.; Met. Abstr.; MINPROC; Mintec, Min. Technol. Abstr.; Pet. Abstr.; Ref. Sources; Saf. Health Work; Sel. Water Resour. Abstr.; Soils Fert.; Solid State Supercond. Abstr.; Stat. Theory Method Abstr. (1972).

CN
MINING EXPLAINED. an. 25.00Can$. Southam Information and Technology Group Inc., 1450 Don Mills Road, Don Mills Ontario M3B 2X7 Canada. **Tel** (416)445-6641, (800)668-2374, FAX (416)442-2261.

CN/0318-1766
MINING EXPLORATION AND DEVELOPMENT REVIEW, BRITISH COLUMBIA AND YUKON TERRITORY. [Min. explor. dev. rev., B.C. Yukon Territ.]. **Added/Corp** British Columbia & Yukon Chamber of Mines. (1974)-.

English. an (May). $10.90 US & Canada; $12.14 others. British Columbia & Yukon Chamber of Mines, 840 West Hastings Street, Vancouver British Columbia V6C 1C8 Canada. **Tel** (604)681-5328. **ED** John Doyle. **LC** TN26; .M53. **DD** 622/.0971. **Bk Rev. Ad Acc. Circ:** 1,500. ***Formed by the union of*** *Mining Exploration Review, British Columbia-Yukon, 0318-1774 (OCoLC) 1794417* ***and*** *Mining Development Review, 0318-1782.*
Desc: Summary of the mineral exploration and development that took place in British Columbia and the Yukon Territory during the preceding year.
Ind/Abst GeoRef.

RH
MINING IN ZIMBABWE. 16th Ed. (1980)-. English. an. 37.40Zin$ Zimbabwe; 38.10Zin$ Africa; 39.00Zin$ other. Thomson Publications Zimbabwe PVT Ltd., Box 1683, Harare Zimbabwe. **Tel** 011 263 4 736835, FAX 011 263 4 706055. **LC** TN119.R4; M59. **DD** 338.2/096891. ***Continues*** *Mining in Zimbabwe, Rhodesia.*

CN
MINING INDUSTRY OF BRITISH COLUMBIA AND THE YUKON, THE. **Added/Corp** British Columbia Hydro and Power Authority. Industrial Development Department. 1st Ed. (1964)-. Periodical. English. British Columbia Hydro and Power Authority, 970 Burrard Street, Vancouver British Columbia V6Z 1Y3 Canada. **LC** HD9506.C23; B7. **DD** 338.2/09711.

UK
MINING JOURNAL GOLD SERVICE. English. £210.00, $375.00 (Includes International Gold Mining Newsletter and International Quarterly). Mining Journal Ltd., 60 Worship Street, London EC2A 2HD England. **Tel** 011 44 071 377 2020, FAX 071 247 4100, telex 8952809 MINING G.

UK/0026-5225
MINING JOURNAL (LONDON. 1908). (MINING JOURNAL.). [Min. j.]. (Feb. 8, 1908)-. Periodical. English. wk. £190.00 UK; $455.00, £255.00 (airmail) other (journal is only available as part of a combined package including the Mining Magazine, the Mining Annual Review, and the Metals & Minerals Annual Review). Mining Journal Ltd., 60 Worship Street, London EC2A 2HD England. **Tel** 011 44 071 377 2020, FAX 071 247 4100, telex 8952809 MINING G. **(Subscription address:** Mining Journal Ltd., PO Box 10 Edenbridge, Kent TN8 5NE England.**) ED** Chris Hinde, Roger Ellis, Nathalie Rosin and Andrew Shaw. **LC** TN1; .M65. **CODEN** MJOLAS. **[CCC].** Index available. cum. index. **Bk Rev. Ad Acc. Circ:** 7,000. available on microfilm and microfiche from University Microfilms International (UMI). ***Continues*** *Mining Journal, Railway and Commercial Gazette.*
Desc: Serves the field of mining including exploration, development, milling, melting, refining or other processing of metals and nonmetallics, and the mining, preparation and primary distribution of coal. Also served are mining and mineral processing consulting companies, government departments, engineering schools, colleges, financial firms and libraries.
Ind/Abst AESIS Q.; Coal Abstr.; Eng. Mater. Abstr.; F&S Index Plus Text, Int. [Select. Cov.]; Infomat Int. Bus.; NEXIS (Jan. 2, 1981-); PROMT.

US/0276-9786
MINING MACHINERY AND MINERAL PROCESSING EQUIPMENT. (CURRENT INDUSTRIAL REPORTS. MA-35F, MINING MACHINERY AND MINERAL PROCESSING EQUIPMENT / U.S. DEPARTMENT OF COMMERCE, BUREAU OF THE CENSUS.). [Min. mach. miner. process. equip.]. 1979-. Government Publication. English. an. $1.25. US Department of Commerce / Bureau of the Census, Data User Services Division, Customer Services, Washington DC 20233-0800. **Tel** (301)763-4100. **(Subscription address:** Superintendent of Documents, US Government Printing Office, Washington DC 20402.**) LC** HD9506.U6; M54. **DD** 338.4/7622/0973. ***Continues*** *Mining Machinery and Equipment.*
Desc: Presents timely data on the production, inventories, and orders of approximately 5,000 products, which represents 40 percent of all US manufacturing.

UK/0308-6631
MINING MAGAZINE (LONDON). (THE MINING MAGAZINE.). [Min. mag.]. V. 1 (Sept. 1909)-. Periodical. English. mo. £30.00 UK; $85.00, £47.00 other. Mining Journal Ltd., 60 Worship Street, London EC2A 2HD England. **Tel** 011 44 071 377 2020, FAX 071 247 4100, telex 8952809 MINING G. **ED** Tony Brewis and Alan Kennedy. **LC** TN1; .M653. **CODEN** MMALAD. **[CCC].** Index available. cum. index. **Bk Rev. Ad Acc. Circ:** 13,500 (ctrl). available on microfilm and microfiche from University Microfilms International (UMI); available on an online database (file 648/Full-Text) from DIALOG. Documents available from Article Express International, CASDDS.
Desc: Technical articles on mining activities world-wide; equipment news; mining company news. Activities in over 100 countries covered.
Ind/Abst AESIS Q.; Alum. Ind. Abstr.; Bioeng. Abstr.; Chem. Abstr.; Coal Abstr.; Curr. Technol. Index; Ei Page One; Energy Res. Abstr. (June 1980-); Eng. Mater. Abstr.; Eng. Index Annu.; F&S Index Plus Text, Int. [Select. Cov.]; Fluid Abstr., Civil Eng.; Fluid Abstr. Proc. Eng.; FLUIDEX (1973-); GeoRef; Highw. Res. Abstr.; Leadscan; Met. Abstr.; MINPROC; Mintec, Min. Technol. Abstr.; NEXIS (Jan. 1981-); Predicasts Forecasts; Trade Ind. ASAP [Full Txt.]; Trade Ind. Index [Full Txt.]; World Ceram. Abstr.

US
MINING MIRROR. Periodical. English. mo. $8.50 US; K20.00 Zambia. Zambia Consolidated Copper Mines, PO Box 71605 Kalewa Road, Ndola Zambia. **Tel** 02-640133/640142, telex ZA 51370/51380. **ED** D C Simukonda. **LC** MICROFILM 05516; TN; TN119.Z34. **Bk Rev. Ad Acc. Circ:** 50,000 (ctrl).
Desc: Caters for mine employees at all levels and has a wide readership overseas particularly in Zambia missions abroad. Covers social and industrial news from the mining community and other towns.

●AT/1320-3770
MINING QUARTERLY. Vol. 1, No. 1 (1993)-. English. qt. 1200.00Aus$. Australian Mineral Economics Pty Ltd., GPO Box 3602, Sydney NSW 2001 Australia. **Tel** 011 61 2 2622264.
Desc: Gives industry highlights, production statistics and more.

US/0026-5241
MINING RECORD (1968), THE. (THE MINING RECORD.). [Min. rec.]. Vol. 79, No. 13 (April 4, 1968)-. Newspaper. English. wk. $39.00 (US); $65.00 (Canada & Mexico); $82.00 (other). The Mining Record Company, PO Box 37510, Denver CO 80237. **Tel** (303)770-6791, FAX (303)770-6796. **ED** Don E. Howell. **DD** 338. **Ad Acc. Circ:** 6,700 (ctrl). available on microfilm. ***Continues*** *Mining and Natural Resources Record, 0270-5818.*
Desc: Directed to mining and allied industries; covers exploration and development, production, milling and smelting, government reports, company profiles and stock prices.

US/0197-906X
MINING RESEARCH REVIEW. [Min. res. rev.]. **Main/Corp** United States. Bureau of Mines. 1970-. Government Publication. English. an. US Department of the Interior / Bureau of Mines, 810 7th Street NW, Room 604, Washington DC 20241. **Tel** (202)501-9300. **LC** TN23; .U48A. **DD** 622/.05.

AT/0314-4607
MINING REVIEW CANBERRA 1977. [Min. rev.Canb. 1977]. (1977)-. Periodical. English. Six times a year. Free upon request. Australian Mining Industry Council, PO Box 363, Dickson ACT 2602 Australia. **Tel** 11 61 6 2793600, FAX 11 61 6 2793699, telex 62285. **ED** Peter Waterman. **DD** 338.20994. cum. index. **Circ:** 5,000 (ctrl). ***Continues*** *Newsletter - Australian Mining Industry Council, 0314-4593.*
Ind/Abst APAIS, Aust. Public Aff. Inf. Ser. (1986-).

CN/0711-3277
MINING REVIEW (NORTH VANCOUVER). (MINING REVIEW.). [Min. rev.]. **Added/Corp** British Columbia & Yukon Chamber of Mines. (Jan./Feb. 1981)-. Periodical. English. bm (6 issues). 32.95Can$ (1 year), 48.95Can$ (2 year) Canada; 37.95Can$ other. Naylor Communications / Vancouver, 124 West 8th Street, North Vancouver BC V7M 3H2, Canada. **Tel** (604)985-8711, FAX (604)985-7399. **ED** John Doyle. **DD** 622/.1/0971. Index available. **Ad Acc. Circ:** 3,800 (ctrl). ***Continues*** *British Columbia & Yukon Chamber of Mines. Chamber Reports, 0702-7419;* ***Absorbed*** *British Columbia & Yukon Chamber of Mines. Directory of Equipment, Supply and Service Members, 0318-482X.*
Desc: Deals with issues of relevance to the mineral exploration industry.
Ind/Abst AESIS Q.; APAIS, Aust. Public Aff. Inf. Ser.; Coal Abstr.; GeoRef.

CN/0840-6723
MINING SOURCE BOOK. [Min. source book]. **VFOAT** Canadian Mining Journal ... Mining Source Book; CMJ's Mining Source Book; Canadian Mining Journal's Mining Sourcebook; Canadian Mining Source Book. 98th Edition (1989)-. English. an. 76.00Can$ Canada; 92.50Can$ other. Southam Information and Technology Group Inc., 1450 Don Mills Road, Don Mills Ontario M3B 2X7 Canada. **Tel** (416)445-6641, (800)668-2374, FAX (416)442-2261. **LC** TN26; .C29. **DD** 622/.025/71. ***Continues*** *Canadian Mining Journal. Reference Manual and Buyer's Guide, 0315-9140.*

CN
MINING STATISTICS : NORTH OF 60. See Engineering-Abstracting, Bibliographies and Statistics.

SA/0026-5268
MINING SURVEY (JOHANNESBURG). (MINING SURVEY.). [Min. surv.]. English (Afrikaans). Three times a year. Free. Transvaal Orange Free State, Chamber Mines 5 Holland Street, Johannesburg South Africa. **Tel** 011 27 11 8388211, telex 4-87057. **ED** Barbara Zatlokal. **LC** HD9506.S7; M57. **DD** 338.2/0968. **Bk Rev. Circ:** 40,000.
Desc: Publication which represents the South African mining industry, promoting various aspects of its activities, including mine conditions, mineral profiles and book reviews.
Ind/Abst AESIS Q.; Coal Abstr.; Ecol. Abstr.; Geogr. Abstr. Human Geogr.; GeoRef; Int. Dev. Abstr.; Saf. Health Work.

AT
MINING TASMANIA. See Engineering-Abstracting, Bibliographies and Statistics.

UK/0026-5276
MINING TECHNOLOGY (MANCHESTER). (MINING TECHNOLOGY.). [Min. technol.]. **Added/Corp** Association of Mining Electrical and Mechanical Engineers. Vol. 51 (May 1969)-. Periodical. English. Ten times a year. £45.00 UK; £65.00 (surface mail), £75.00 (airmail) other. Marylebone Press Ltd, Lloyds House, 18 Lloyd Street, Manchester M2 5WA England. **Tel** 011 44 61 832 6541, FAX 011 44 61 832 8129, telex 669362. **ED** Earnest Rhodes. **LC** TN1; .A7. **DD** 622/.05. **CODEN** MNGTB7. Index available. cum. index. **Bk Rev. Ad Acc. Circ:** 5,000. Documents available from Article Express International, Ask*IEEE, Documents on Demand. ***Continues*** *Mining Electrical & Mechanical Engineer, 0374-373X.*
Ind/Abst Alum. Ind. Abstr.; Bioeng. Abstr.; CIS Abstr.; Coal Abstr.; Curr. Technol. Index; Ei Page One; EMBASE; Energy Inf. Abstr.; Energy Res. Abstr. (June 1980-); Eng. Mater. Abstr.; Eng. Index Annu.; Environ. Abstr.; INSPEC (May 1969-); Met. Abstr.; Mintec, Min. Technol. Abstr.; Saf. Health Work; World Alum. Abstr.

CN/0317-9508
MINING (TORONTO). (MINING.). 1968-. Periodical. English. an. Mining Association of Canada, 350 Sparks Street/Suite 705, Ottawa Ontario K1R 7S8 Canada. **Tel** (613)233-9391, telex 053-3732. **DD** 338.2/0971. ***Continues*** *What the Mining Industry Means to Canada.*

AT
MINING, WESTERN AUSTRALIA / AUSTRALIAN BUREAU OF STATISTICS, WESTERN AUSTRALIAN OFFICE. See Engineering-Abstracting, Bibliographies and Statistics.

US/1047-7551
MINING WORLD NEWS. [Min. world news]. (1989)-. Periodical. English. Six times a year. $44.00 US; $49.00 Canada; $64.00 other. Mining International, 90 West Grove Street #200, Reno NV 89509. **Tel** (702)827-1115, FAX (702)827-1292. **ED** Dorothy Kosich (editor's phone: (702)827-2262). **DD** 338. **Ad Acc. Circ:** 30,000.

US
MINOR NONMETALS. **Added/Corp** United States. Bureau of Mines. (19??)-. English. an. US Department of the Interior / Bureau of Mines, Publications Department, PO Box 18070, Cochrans Mill Road, Pittsburgh PA 15236. **Tel** (412)892-6400.

UK/0951-0680
MINOR ORES AND MINERALS. July 1986-. English. be. $200.00. Drewry Shipping Consultants Ltd, 11 Heron Quay, London E14 4JF England. **Tel** 011 44 71 5380191, FAX 01-987-9396, telex 21167 HPDLDG.

CN/0828-8461
MINPROC : MINERAL PROCESSING ABSTRACTS. ***Ceased.*** **See** Engineering-Abstracting, Bibliographies and Statistics.

CN/0823-0773
MINTEC : MINING TECHNOLOGY ABSTRACTS. ***Ceased.*** **See** Engineering-Abstracting, Bibliographies and Statistics.

SA/1012-5299
MINTEK BULLETIN. [Mintek bull.]. (1988)-. Periodical. Multiple languages. mo. Council for Mineral Technology, Private Bag X3015, Randburg 2125 South Africa. **Tel** 011 27 11 7933511.
Ind/Abst AESIS Q.

US/0091-052X
MISSOURI MINERAL NEWS. ***Title Change.*** **See** Earth Sciences-Mineralogy.

US
MISSOURI'S ABANDONED MINED LANDS ... ANNUAL REPORT. **Main/Corp** Missouri. Abandoned Mine Land Section. **VFOAT** Annual Report of the Abandoned Mind Land Section. 1985-. English. an. Department of Natural Resources / Missouri, PO Box 176, Jefferson City MO 65102. **LC** TD195.C58; M56A. **DD** 333.8. ***Continues*** *Annual Report of the Abandoned Mine Land Section.*

II/0378-6366
MMR, MINERALS & METALS REVIEW. **See** Metals and Metallurgy.

CN/0821-8234
MONOGRAPH - CANMET. (MONOGRAPH / ENERGY, MINES AND RESOURCES CANADA, CANMET, CANADA CENTRE FOR MINERAL AND ENERGY TECHNOLOGY.). [Monogr. - CANMET]. **Added/Corp** Canada Centre for Mineral and Energy Technology. (197?)-. Monographic series. English. Price varies per volume. ***Continues*** *Canada. Mines Branch. Monograph - Mines Branch, 0068-7863.*
Ind/Abst GeoRef.

AT
MONOGRAPH SERIES. **Main/Corp** Australasian Institute of Mining and Metallurgy. Monographic series. English. ir. Price varies per volume. Australian Institute of Mining & Metallurgy, PO Box 122, Parkville Victoria 3052 Australia. **Tel** 03 347 3166, FAX 03 347 8525. **Bk Rev**, (Qty: 4). Documents available from FAXON Xpress, BLDSC.

US
MONTANA MINING DIRECTORY. **Added/Corp** Montana Bureau of Mines and Geology. Montana College of Mineral Science and Technology. **VFOAT** Mining Directory. (1989-1990)-. English. an. Montana Bureau of Mines and Geology, Montana College of Mineral Science, Butte MT 59701. **Tel** (406)496-4174, FAX (406)496-4133. **LC** TN12; .M7. **DD** 338.2/025/786. ***Continues*** *Directory of Montana Mining Enterprises for ..., 0741-4544.*

US/0275-9438
MOUNTAIN STATES MINING SURVEY. **See** Earth Sciences-Mineralogy.

US
MRCR, MINING RESEARCH CONTRACT REVIEW. **VFOAT** Mining Research Contract Review. English. sa. Bureau of Mines, Denver Mining Research Center, Office of Environmental Activities, Building 20, Denver Federal Center, Denver CO 80225.

US
NATIONAL STONE ASSOCIATION BUYER'S GUIDE. English. an. National Stone Association, 1415 Elliot Place NW, Washington DC 20007. **Tel** (202)342-1100, FAX (202)342-0702. **ED** Frank Atlee. **Ad Acc. Circ:** 2,000 (ctrl).
Desc: List of member companies and equipment services.

US/0470-3219
NATIONAL STRIPPER WELL SURVEY. **Added/Corp** Interstate Oil Compact Commission. National Stripper Well Association. (19??)-. English. an. $3.00. Interstate Oil Compact Commission, PO Box 53127, Oklahoma City OK 73152. **Tel** (405)525-3556. **LC** TN872; .A317. **DD** 338.3/7/282.

KZ
NAUCHNYE TRUDY. **Main/Corp** Vsesoiuznyi Nauchno-Issledovatelskii I Proektno-Konstruktorskii Ugolnyi Institut. (19??)-. Russian. 1.54rub. 55 Bulvar Mira, 74-A Karaganda, Kazakhstan. **LC** TN802; .K3. ***Continues*** *Nauchnye Trudy / Karaganda. Nauchno-Issledovatelskii Ugolnyi Institut.*

RU
NEFTEPROMYSLOVOE DELO: BURENIE NEFTIANYKH I GAZOVYKH I SKVAZHIN, DOBYCHA NEFTI. **Added/Corp** Kuibyshevskii Politekhnicheskii Institut Imeni V.V. Kuibysheva. (1973)-. Periodical. Russian. 1.20rub. Ministerstvo Vysshego I Srednego Spetsialnogo Obrazovaniia / Kuibyshev, Ulitsa Galaktionovskaia 141, Kuibyshev Russia. **LC** TN860; .N454.

GW/0047-9403
NEUE BERGBAUTECHNIK. ***Title Change.*** [Neue Bergbautech.]. **Added/Corp** Kammer der Technik. Fachverband Bergbau. Bergakademie Freiberg. Montanwissenschaftliche Gesellschaft der DDR. (1971)-(Vol. 22, 1993). Periodical. German (summaries and/or abstracts in English and Russian; table of contents in English and Russian). mo. Deutscher Verlag Grundstoffind, Karl Heine Strasse 27, D 04211 Leipzig Germany. **Tel** 011 49 341 4081011. **LC** TN3; .N38. **CODEN** NEBBAB. Documents available from Article Express International, CASDDS. ***Formed by the union of*** *Bergbautechnik* ***and*** *Bergakademie.* ***Merged into*** *Die Braunkohle.*
Ind/Abst Alum. Ind. Abstr.; Bioeng. Abstr.; Chem. Abstr.; Coal Abstr.; Ei Page One; EMBASE; Eng. Mater. Abstr.; Eng. Index Annu.; GeoRef; Met. Abstr.; Saf. Health Work.

US
NEW PUBLICATIONS OF THE BUREAU OF MINES. **Main/Corp** United States. Bureau of Mines. (198?)-. Periodical. English. bm. Free on request. US Bureau of Mines, 810 Seventh Street NW, MS 9800, Washington DC 20241. **Tel** (202)501-9559. ***Continues*** *United States. Bureau of Mines. New Publications.*

US/0364-1376
NEW PUBLICATIONS (UNITED STATES. BUREAU OF MINES). (NEW PUBLICATIONS / BUREAU OF MINES.). [New publ. - Bur. Mines]. **Added/Corp** United States. Bureau of Mines. **VFOAT** New Publications of the Bureau of Mines. Vol. 1 (Oct. 1910)-. Government Publication. English. bm. Free on request. US Department of the Interior / Bureau of Mines, Publications Department, PO Box 18070, Cochrans Mill Road, Pittsburgh PA 15236. **Tel** (412)892-6400. **ED** Shelby Palya. **Circ:** 10,000 (ctrl). Documents available from Documents on Demand.
Desc: Lists and abstracts all Bureau of Mines publications issued in the month specified. Includes information on ordering copies.

Ind/Abst Am. Stat. Index; Anal. Abstr.; Energy Res. Abstr. (Dec. 1980-); MINPROC; Mintec, Min. Technol. Abstr.

AT/1030-4851
NEW SOUTH WALES COAL INDUSTRY PROFILE. [N.S.W. coal ind. profile]. (1984)-. English. be. **DD** 622.33309944.
Ind/Abst AESIS Q.

AT/0727-5757
NEW SOUTH WALES MINERAL INDUSTRY REVIEW. [N. S. W. miner. ind. rev.]. (1980)-. English. an. **DD** 338.209944.
Ind/Abst AESIS Q.

AT/0813-1767
NEWSLETTER - AUSTRALIAN COAL ASSOCIATION. [Newsl. - Aust. Coal Assoc.]. **Added/Corp** Australian Coal Association. (1984)-. Periodical. English. bm. **DD** 338.27240994. ***Continues*** *Newsletter - New South Wales Coal Association, 0813-1120.*
Ind/Abst AESIS Q.

CN/0590-580X
NORTH OF 60. MINES AND MINERALS ACTIVITIES. (MINES AND MINERALS ACTIVITIES.). [North 60, Mines miner. act.]. **VAT** Mines and Minerals North of 60. Activities. 1971-. English. an. Free. Department of Indian and Northern Affairs, 400 Laurier Avenue West/Room 630, Ottawa Ontario K1A 0H4 Canada. **LC** TN27.Y6; C35A. **DD** 338.2/09719/1.
Ind/Abst GeoRef.

US/1060-8036
NORTHEAST & MIDWEST MINING DIRECTORY. [Northeast midwest min. dir.]. **VFOAT** Northeast and Midwest Mining Directory. (1991)-. Directory. English. $23.95. The Northeast & Midwest Mining Directory, PO Box 5694, Boise ID 83705. **DD** 622.

CN/0029-3164
NORTHERN MINER, THE. [North. miner]. (1915)-. Periodical. English. wk. 74.90Can$ (2nd class mail), 130.54Can$ (1rst class mail) Canada; 70.00Can$ (2nd class mail), 122.00Can$ (1rst class mail) US; 80.00Can$ other. Southam Information and Technology Group Inc., 1450 Don Mills Road, Don Mills Ontario M3B 2X7 Canada. **Tel** (416)445-6641, (800)668-2374, FAX (416)442-2261. **ED** James S Borland. **LC** HD9506.C2; N6. **DD** 338.205. Index available. **Bk Rev. Ad Acc. Circ:** 28,000. available in microform; available on microfilm; available on an online database (file 16/Full-Text) from DIALOG. Documents available from Documents on Demand.
Ind/Abst Can. Period. Index (19??-); Coal Abstr.; Energy Inf. Abstr.; Environ. Abstr.; F&S Index Plus Text, Int. [Select. Cov.]; GeoRef; MINPROC; Mintec, Min. Technol. Abstr.; PROMT [Full Txt.].

CN/0830-9396
NORTHERN MINER MAGAZINE, THE. ***Ceased.*** [North. min. mag.]. **VFOAT** Northern Miner. Vol. 1, No. 1 (Jan. 1986)-(May 1993). Periodical. English. mo. Southam Information and Technology Group Inc., 1450 Don Mills Road, Don Mills Ontario M3B 2X7 Canada. **Tel** (416)445-6641, (800)668-2374, FAX (416)442-2261. **DD** 338.2/0971.
Ind/Abst Can. Period. Index (19??-).

RU
OBOGASHCHENIE RUD CHERNYKH METALLOV. **Added/Corp** Russia (1923- U.S.S.R.). Ministerstvo Chernoi Metallurgii. Nauchno-Issledovatelskii i Proektnyi Institut po Obogashcheniiu i Aglomeratsii Rud Chernykh Metallov "Mekhanobrchermet.". No. 1 (1972)-. Academic Scholarly Publication. Russian. 1.46rub each issue. Izdatelstvo Metallurgiia, 2-i Obydenskii Per.14, G-34, Moscow Russia. **LC** TN500; .O253. **CODEN** ORCMAF. Documents available from CASDDS.
Ind/Abst Chem. Abstr. (?-1981).

UK
OCCASIONAL PAPERS OF THE INSTITUTION OF MINING AND METALLURGY. **Added/Corp** Institution of Mining and Metallurgy (Great Britain). (1982)-. Monographic series. English. Price varies per volume. Institution of Mining and Metallurgy, 44 Portland Place, London W1N 4BR England. **Tel** 011 44 71 580-3802, FAX 011 44 71 436-5388, telex 261410.
Ind/Abst AESIS Q.

US/0030-1736
OKLAHOMA GEOLOGY NOTES. **See** Earth Sciences-Mineralogy.

UK
ON-SHORE WEEKLY. English. wk. £450.00 UK; $775.00 other. Girozentrale Gilbert Eliott, Salisburg House, London Wall EC2M 5SB England. **Tel** 011 44 71 628 6782, FAX 011 44 71 628 3500. **ED** John Hartley and Ken White. Index available. cum. index. **Ad Acc. Pr Rev.** available on diskette.
Desc: Onshore drilling information in new Europe.

JA/0369-7665
ONSEN KOGAKKAI SHI. [Onsen Kogakkai-shi]. **Added/Corp** Onsen Kogakkai (Japan). **VFOAT** Onsen Kogakkaishi; Journal of the Society of Engineers for Mineral Springs, Japan. (1963)-. Academic Scholarly Publication. Japanese. tq. $41.40 (US, Canada, Central America, West Indies); $43.60 (Europe, Africa, South America, USSR, Middle & Near East); $39.20 (Asia, Australia, New Zealand). **(Subscription address:** Japan Publications Trading Company, Ltd., PO Box 5030, Tokyo International, Tokyo 100-31 Japan.**)** **CODEN** ONKOBY. Documents available from CASDDS.
Ind/Abst Chem. Abstr. (?-1987).

US
OPEN-FILE REPORT - BUREAU OF MINES. **Main/Corp** United States. Bureau of Mines. No. 1 (1962)-. Monographic series. English. Price varies per volume. US Department of the Interior / Bureau of Mines, 810 7th Street NW, Room 604, Washington DC 20241. **Tel** (202)501-9300.
Ind/Abst Aquat. Sci. Fish. Abstr. (Computer File).

US/0731-5066
OPEN FILE REPORT (SOCORRO, N.M.). (OPEN FILE REPORT.). [Open file rep.]. **Main/Corp** New Mexico. Bureau of Mines and Mineral Resources. 1-. Monographic series. English. Price varies per volume.
Ind/Abst GeoRef.

SA
P. R. D. SERIES. English. Chamber of Mines of South Africa, 5 Holland Street, Johannesburg 2001 South Africa. **Tel** (011)838-8211, FAX (011)934-3804. **LC** TN119.S7; C45. **DD** 622/.08. ***Continues*** *P. R. D. Series.*

AG
PANORAMA MINERO. (19??)-. Periodical. Spanish. Sucre 1333 (3. D), Buenos Aires Argentina. **LC** TN4; .P34.
Ind/Abst Ceram. Abstr. (19??-).

CN/0225-6592
PANORAMA - NORANDA (ENGLISH ED.). (PANORAMA : A PUBLICATION SERVING THE EMPLOYEES OF THE NORANDA GROUP AND AFFILIATED COMPANIES.). [Panorama - Noranda]. V. 12, No. 2 (Feb. 1970)-. Periodical. English. mo. Free to employees and retired personnel. Noranda Mines, PO Box 45 Commerce Court West, Toronto Ontario M5L 1C2 Canada. **DD** 338.7/622/0971. ***Continues in part*** *Panorama (Noranda Mines Limited). English & French, 0225-6592.*

SA
PAPERS AND DISCUSSIONS - ASSOCIATION OF MINE MANAGERS OF SOUTH AFRICA. **Main/Corp** Association of Mine Managers of South Africa. Periodical. English. Three times a year. Rs80.00. Chamber of Mines of South Africa, 5 Holland Street, Johannesburg 2001 South Africa. **Tel** (011)838-8211, FAX (011)934-3804. **ED** A T Fredericks. **LC** TN4. **DD** 622.062682. Index available. **Ad Acc. Pr Rev. Circ:** 2,000 (ctrl).
Desc: Technical papers on mining techniques, solving of problems, new mining methods, use of latest technology, all aspects of mining.

FR/0761-182X
PASCAL FOLIO. F41, GISEMENTS METALLIQUES ET NON METALLIQUES, ECONOMIE MINIERE. ***Title Change.*** **VFOAT** Pascal Folio. F41, Metallic and Non-Metallic Deposits, Mineral Economics; Gisements Metalliques et Non Metalliques, Economie Miniere; Metallic and Non-Metallic Deposits, Mineral Economics. (1984)-?. Periodical. French (English). mo. Institut de l'Information Scientique et Technique (INIST), 2 Allee du Parc de Brabois, 54514 Vandoeuvre Nancy Cedex France. **Tel** 011 33 83 504600, FAX 011 33 83 504650. ***Continues*** *Bulletin Signaletique. 221, Gisements Metalliques et Non Metalliques, Economie Miniere.* ***Continued by*** *Gisements Metalliques et Non-Metalliques. F41.*

IE
PEAT ABSTRACTS. **Added/Corp** Bord na Mona. (1946-). Oifig Ealadhanta. (19??)-. English. tq (3 issues). $25.00 US. Peat Abstracts, Bord na Mona, Research & Development Department, Newbridge Co Kildare Ireland. **Tel** 011 353 45 33106. **ED** Tony McKenna. **LC** Z6915; .P43. **DD** 016.6314. **Circ:** 400 (ctrl).
Desc: Abstracts world literature on peat for fuel and horticulture and general peatland development.
Ind/Abst Coal Abstr.

US
PERLITE. **See** Engineering-Abstracting, Bibliographies and Statistics.

AT/0310-4184
PEX. **See** Petroleum and Natural Gas.

US/0032-0293
PIT & QUARRY. [Pit quarry]. **VAT** Pit and Quarry. (1916)-. Academic Scholarly Publication. English. mo. $38.00 US and possessions; $50.00 Canada; $75.00

other. Advanstar Communications Inc., 131 West First Street, Duluth MN 55802. **Tel** (218)723-9477, (800)346-0085. **ED** Don Michard. **LC** TN1; .P65. **DD** 622/.31/05. **CODEN** PIQUAN. **[CCC]. Circ:** 20,892. available on microfilm and microfiche from University Microfilms International (UMI). Documents available from Article Express International, CASDDS. ***Absorbed*** *Cement-Mill & Quarry, 0095-9952.* ***Continued in part by*** *Modern Concrete, 0026-7619.*
Desc: Serves the informational needs of those who specify and/or buy equipment, supplies and services for the mining, quarrying and processing of non-metallic minerals.
Ind/Abst Bioeng. Abstr.; Bus. Index (1985-); Chem. Abstr.; Coal Abstr.; Concr. Abstr.; Ei Page One; EMBASE; Eng. Index Annu. [Select. Cov.]; F&S Index Plus Text, Int. [Select. Cov.]; Gen. BusinessFile (1985-); Gen. Period. Index (1985-); GeoRef; Mag. Search; MINPROC; Mintec, Min. Technol. Abstr.; PROMT; Saf. Health Work; Stat. Ref. Index; Trade Ind. Index; Vocat. Search (July 1993-).

US/0732-4898
PIT & QUARRY DIRECTORY OF THE U.S. NONMETALLIC MINING INDUSTRIES. [Pit quarry dir. U. S. nonmet. min. ind.]. **VFOAT** Pit and Quarry Directory of the U.S. Nonmetallic Mining Industries; Pit and Quarry Directory, Nonmetallic Minerals Industries; Pit and Quarry Directory; Pit & Quarry Directory, Nonmetallic Minerals Industries; Pit & Quarry Directory. 1982 Ed.-. Directory. English. $175.00. Pit and Quarry Publications Inc, 205 West Wacker Drive, Chicago IL 60606. **LC** TN12; .P5. **DD** 553.6/025/73. ***Continues*** *Pit and Quarry Directory of the Nonmetallic Minerals Industries.*

US/0146-1893
PIT & QUARRY HANDBOOK AND BUYERS GUIDE FOR THE NONMETALLIC MINERALS INDUSTRIES. **VFOAT** Pit and Quarry Handbook. **VAT** Pit and Quarry Handbook and Buyers Guide for the Nonmetallic Minerals Industries. 53rd- Ed.; 1960-. Consumer Publication. English. an. $50.00. Pit and Quarry Publications Inc, 205 West Wacker Drive, Chicago IL 60606. **LC** TN277; .P52. **DD** 622. Documents available from Article Express International. ***Continues*** *Pit and Quarry Handbook of the Nonmetallic Minerals Industry.*
Ind/Abst Ei Page One; Eng. Index Annu.

RU
PLANIROVANIE, TSENOOBRAZOVANIE I KHOZRASCHET V UGOLNOI PROMYSHLENNOSTI. **Added/Corp** Tsentralnyi Nauchno-Issledovatelskii Institut Ekonomiki i Nauchno-Tekhnicheskoi Informatsii Ugolnoi Promyshlennosti. No. 1 (1978)-. Periodical. Russian. 0.97rub single issue. Ministerstvo Ugolnoi Promyshl, Tsneiugol Moskva K-12, Pr Sapunova D 13/15, Moscow Russia. **LC** HD9540.1; P56.

US
PLATINUM-GROUP METALS IN ... . See Metals and Metallurgy-Abstracting, Bibliographies and Statistics.

US/8756-6257
POPULAR MINING. **VFOAT** Popular Mining Magazine. (19??)-. Periodical. English. bm. $18.00 (1 year), $33.00 (2 year), $46.00 (3 year) US; $24.00 (1 year), $45.00 (2 year), $64.00 (3 year) Canada; $33.00 (1 year), $63.00 (2 year), $91.00 (3 year) other. Popular Mining, 4460 West Reno Avenue #D, Las Vegas NV 89118. **Tel** (702)362-1511, FAX (702)367-9623. **ED** Nancy Glenn. (index published separately). cum. index. **Bk Rev**, (Qty: 4). **Ad Acc. Circ:** 20,000 (ctrl).

GW/0934-7348
POWDER HANDLING & PROCESSING. **VFOAT** Powder Handling and Processing. Vol. 1, No. 1 (Mar. 1989)-. Periodical. English. qt. $196.00. Trans Tech Publications Ltd., Hardstr. 13, CH-4714 Aedermannsdorf Switzerland. **Tel** 011 41 62 741379, FAX 011 41 12 72 10 58. **ED** R. H. Wohlbier. **LC** TS180; .P68. Index available. **Bk Rev. Ad Acc. Circ:** 10,000 (ctrl).
Ind/Abst Fluid Abstr., Civil Eng.; Fluid Abstr. Proc. Eng.; FLUIDEX (19??-); Foods Adlibra.

US/0146-7204
POWELL GOLD INDUSTRY GUIDE AND INTERNATIONAL MINING ANALYST, THE. [Powell gold ind. guide int. min. anal.]. **Added/Corp** Reserve Research, ltd. **VFOAT** Powell International Mining Analyst. (1976)-. Periodical. English. qt. $120.00. Reserve Research Ltd, C/O L.M. Powell, 622 Congress Street, PO Box 4135 Station A, Portland ME 04101. **Tel** (207)774-4971. **ED** Larson M Powell. **LC** HD9536.A1; P68. **DD** 338.2/7/4105. ***Continues*** *Powell Monetary Analyst, 0146-7190.*
Desc: Review of outlook for gold, silver, aluminum, copper and platinum plus descriptions and financial statistics on 100 mining companies in the US and abroad.

PL
PRACE - AKADEMIA GORNICZO-HUTNICZA W KRAKOWIE. INSTYTUT GORNICTWA PODZIEMNEGO. **Main/Corp** Akademia Gorniczo-Hutnicza w Krakowie. Instytut Gornictwa Podziemnego. Polish (summaries and/or abstracts in English and Russian). Z20.00 each issue. Akademia Gorniczo-Hutnicza w Krakowie, Instytut Mechaniki i Wibroakustyki, Al Mickiewicza 30, Krakow Poland. **LC** TN4; .K7 subser.

PL
PRACE - KRAKOW. AKADEMIA GORNICZO-HUTNICZA. INSTYTUT PODSTAW BUDOWY MASZY. **Main/Corp** Instytut Podstaw Budowy Maszyn (Akademia Gorniczo-Hutnicza Im. S. Staszica W Krakowie) Maszyn. Polish (summaries and/or abstracts in English and Russian). Z12.00 each issue. Panstwowe Wydawn Naukowe, Miodowa 10, PO Box 391, 00251 Warsaw Poland. **LC** TN343; .E64 subser.

PL/0324-9689
PRACE NAUKOWE INSTYTUTU GORNICTWA POLITECHNIKI WROCAWSKIEJ. MONOGRAFIE. (MONOGRAFIE.). [Pr. nauk. Inst. Gorn. Politech. Wroc., Monogr.]. **Main/Corp** Politechnika Wrocawska. Instytut Gornictwa. **VFOAT** Seria Monografie. No. 1- 1973-. Polish (summaries and/or abstracts in English and Russian). Z18.00 single issue. Wojewodzka Ksiegarnia Techniczna, Ul Swidnicka 8, 50-064 Warsaw Poland. **LC** TN275.A1; B7 subser.
Ind/Abst Coal Abstr.; GeoRef.

US
PREPRINT FROM THE BUREAU OF MINES MINERALS YEARBOOK. **Main/Corp** United States. Bureau of Mines. 1934-. Periodical. English. an. US Department of the Interior / Bureau of Mines, Publications Department, PO Box 18070, Cochrans Mill Road, Pittsburgh PA 15236. **Tel** (412)892-6400.

US
PREPRINTS OF THE SOCIETY OF MINING ENGINEERS OF THE AIME ANNUAL MEETING. (19??)-. Proceedings. English. ir. $5.00. Society for Mining, Metallurgy and Exploration Inc, 8307 Shaffer Parkway, Littleton CO 80162. **Tel** (303)973-9550, FAX (303)973-3845, telex 881988. **(Subscription address:** Society Mining Metallurgy & Exploration, PO Box 625002, Littleton CO 80162.**)**

SA
PRESIDENTIAL ADDRESS / CHAMBER OF MINES OF SOUTH AFRICA. **Main/Corp** Chamber of Mines of South Africa. (1991)-. English. Chamber of Mines of South Africa, 5 Holland Street, Johannesburg 2001 South Africa. **Tel** (011)838-8211, FAX (011)934-3804. **LC** HD9536.S6; C5p. ***Separated from*** *Annual Report.*

US
PRIMARY COPPER INDUSTRY OF ARIZONA IN ... / ARIZONA DEPT. OF MINERAL RESOURCES, THE. 1975-1976-. English. an. **ED** Michael N Greeley. **LC** HD9539.C5; A75. **DD** 338.2/743/0979105. **Circ:** 350. ***Continues*** *Profile of Arizona's Primary Copper Industry.*
Desc: Statistical information on the copper industry in a given year in Arizona.

US/0278-0739
PRINCIPLES AND PRESENTATION. MINING. [Princ. present., Min.]. **Added/Corp** Peat, Marwick, Mitchell & Co. **VFOAT** Mining. (19??)-. English. an. $20.00. Peat Marwick Mitchell & Company / New York, 345 Park Avenue, New York NY 10154. **Tel** (212)758-9700. **LC** HD9506.U6; P73. **DD** 657/.86203/05.

RU
PROBLEMY OBOGASHCHENIIA TVERDYKH GOEIUCHIKH ISKOPAEMYKH. **Main/Corp** Nauchno-Issledovatelskii i Proektno-Konstruktorskii Institut Obogashcheniia Tverdykh Goriuchikh Iskopaemykh. Vol. 1, (1971)-. Russian. **LC** TN816.A1; N38a. **CODEN** TIOTAK. Documents available from CASDDS.
Ind/Abst Chem. Abstr.

UK/0700-5741
PROCEEDINGS - COMMONWEALTH MINING AND METALLURGICAL CONGRESS. [Proc. - Commonw. Min. Metall. Congr.]. **Main/Corp** Commonwealth Mining and Metallurgical Congress. 6th- 1957-. Academic Scholarly Publication. English. ir. Institution of Mining and Metallurgy, 44 Portland Place, London W1N 4BR England. **Tel** 011 44 71 580-3802, FAX 011 44 71 436-5388, telex 261410. **CODEN** CMLPB5. Documents available from CASDDS. ***Continues*** *Empire Mining and Metallurgical Congress. Proceedings, 0700-5733.*
Ind/Abst Chem. Abstr. (1957-1978); GeoRef.

US
PROCEEDINGS ... CONFERENCE ON GROUND CONTROL IN MINING. **Added/Corp** West Virginia University. Dept. of Mining Engineering. **VFOAT** Proceedings of the ... Annual Conference on Ground Control in Mining. 1st (1981)-. Proceedings. English. an. Department of Mining Engineering, College of Mineral and Energy Resources, West Virginia University, PO Box 6070, Morgantown WV 26506. **Tel** (304)293-7680, FAX (304)293-5708. **ED** Syd S. Peng and Prof. Charles T. Holland. Index available (author index). **Bk Rev. Circ:** 500.
Desc: Selected papers on thruss and roof bolting, longwall mining, coal pillar and bump, design and measurement, geological and stress effects, and surface subsidence.

CN/0711-6039
PROCEEDINGS (QUEEN'S UNIVERSITY (KINGSTON, ONT.). CENTRE FOR RESOURCE STUDIES). (PROCEEDINGS / CENTRE FOR RESOURCE STUDIES, QUEEN'S UNIVERSITY.). [Proc. - Cent. Resour. Stud., Queen's Univ.]. **Added/Corp** Queen's University (Kingston, Ont.). Centre for Resource Studies. (1978)-. Monographic series. English. ir. Price varies per volume. Centre for Resource Studies, Queen's University, Kingston Ontario K7L 3N6 Canada. **Tel** (613)545-2553, FAX (613)545-6651. **LC** UNC. **DD** 338.2/0971.
Ind/Abst AESIS Q.

UK
PRODUCTIVITY AND PRODUCTION BULLETIN. See Economics-Industry and Production.

US/0735-8148
PRODUCTIVITY REPORT FOR ALL PRODUCERS BY CONTROLLING COMPANY. (PRODUCTIVITY REPORT ... DATA & PREV 12 MONTHS ... FOR ALL PRODUCERS BY CONTROLLING COMPANY.). [Prod. rep. all prod. control. co.]. **Added/Corp** Coal Marketronix. **VFOAT** Productivity Report; Productivity Report ... Data and Previous Twelve Months. (19??)-. English. qt. $545.00 US; $585.00 other. Pasha Publications Inc., 1616 North Fort Myer Drive, Suite 1000, Arlington VA 22209. **Tel** (800)424-2908, (703)528-1244, FAX (703)528-3742, (703)528-1253. ***Continues in part*** *Coal Outlook's Productivity Report, 0272-0523.*
Desc: Gives you the productivity for each mine and past performance data for that mine.

US/0735-8172
PRODUCTIVITY REPORT FOR ALL PRODUCERS BY STATE, COUNTY, & TYPE MINING. (PRODUCTIVITY REPORT ... DATA & PREV 12 MONTHS ... FOR ALL PRODUCERS BY STATE, COUNTY & TYPE MINING.). [Prod. rep. all prod. state cty. type min.]. **Added/Corp** Coal Marketronix. **VFOAT** All Producers by State, County, and Type Mining; Productivity Report; Productivity Report ... Data and Previous Twelve Months. (19??)-. English. qt. $545.00 US; $585.00 other. Pasha Publications Inc., 1616 North Fort Myer Drive, Suite 1000, Arlington VA 22209. **Tel** (800)424-2908, (703)528-1244, FAX (703)528-3742, (703)528-1253. ***Continues in part*** *Coal Outlook's Productivity Report, 0272-0523.*

US
PROGRAM UPDATE ... AS OF DECEMBER 31 ... / CLEAN COAL TECHNOLOGY DEMONSTRATION PROGRAM. See Earth Sciences-Mineralogy.

AT/1033-5196
PROSPECT PERTH. (PROSPECT.). [Prospect Perth]. (1988)-. Periodical. English. qt. 12.00Aus$. Department of Resources Development, PO Box 7234, Cloisters Square, Perth Western Australia 6850 Australia. **Tel** 011 61 9 3275555. **DD** 338.09941. ***Continues*** *Prospect Western Australia, 1033-5188.*
Ind/Abst AESIS Q.

CN/0843-6819
PROSPECT (VANCOUVER). (PROSPECT / PLACER DOME.). [Prospect]. **Added/Corp** Placer Dome Inc. Vol. 1, No. 1 (1989)-. Periodical. English (French). qt ((Mar., June, Sept., and Dec.)). Free upon request. Placer Dome Inc, Corporate Communications Dept, 1600-1055 Dunsmuir St, Vancouver, BC V7X 1P1 Canada. **ED** Hugh Leggatt (phone:(604)661-1554). **DD** 338.2/741/05. **Circ:** 7,000.
Desc: For employees and friends of Placer-Dome Inc.. Features articles on company-related mining and metals topics, plus news items about operating gold and copper mines.

UK/0141-3376
PROSPECTING IN AREAS OF GLACIATED TERRAIN. **VFOAT** Prospecting in Areas of Glacial Terrain. Began with issue for: 1973. Academic Scholarly Publication. English. be. Institution of

Mining and Metallurgy, 44 Portland Place, London W1N 4BR England. **Tel** 011 44 71 580-3802, FAX 011 44 71 436-5388, telex 261410. **LC** TN270.A1; P8. **DD** 622/.1. **CODEN** PGTPDC. **Ad Acc.** Documents available from CASDDS.
Desc: Deals with recent developments in technology for all types of prospecting in glaciated terrain and put forward new concepts of mineral exploration in these areas.
Ind/Abst Chem. Abstr.

CN/1181-6414
PROSPECTOR : EXPLORATION AND INVESTMENT BULLETIN, THE. [Prospect., Explor. investm. bull.]. (July/Aug. 1990)-. Periodical. English. Six times a year (Feb., Apr., June, Aug., Oct., Dec.). 20.00Can$ Canada; 25.00Can$ US; 30.00Can$ other. KW Publishing Ltd, 1268 West Pender Street, Vancouver British Columbia V6E 2Z8 Canada. **Tel** (604)688-2271, FAX (604)688-2038. **ED** Kevin Barker. **DD** 338.2/05. **Ad Acc, Adv Mgr:** Barry McNeil, **Tel** (604)688-2271. ctrl circ. ***Continues** North West Prospector., 0824-6149.*
Desc: Mining and investment newspaper. Features indepth coverage of Canadian and US mining interests at home and abroad. Each issue also features information on industry suppliers and contractors.

PL/0033-216X
PRZEGLAD GORNICZY. [Prz. gor.]. (1946)-. Academic Scholarly Publication. Polish. mo. $99.00. **(Subscription address:** ARS Polona, PO Box 1001, 00068 Warsaw Poland.) **LC** TN4; .P85. **CODEN** PRGOAI. Documents available from Article Express International, CASDDS.
Ind/Abst Bioeng. Abstr.; Chem. Abstr.; Coal Abstr.; Ei Page One; Eng. Index Annu.; GeoRef; MINPROC; Mintec, Min. Technol. Abstr.; Saf. Health Work.

AT
PUBLICATIONS INDEX / THE AUSTRALASIAN INSTITUTE OF MINING AND METALLURGY ; PRODUCED BY AUSTRALIAN MINERAL FOUNDATION. **Main/Corp** Australasian Institute of Mining and Metallurgy. **Added/Corp** Australian Mineral Foundation. **VFOAT** Australasian Institute of Mining and Metallurgy Publications Index; AusIMM Index. (19??)-. English. Australasian Institute of Mining and Metallurgy, PO Box 122, Parkville Victoria 3052 Australia. **Tel** 011 61 3 3473166, FAX 011 61 3 3478525, telex 33552. **LC** Z6739.A9; A98a; TN121. **DD** 016.622.
Ind/Abst AESIS Q.

FR/0766-7159
PUBLICATIONS TECHNIQUES DES CHARBONNAGES DE FRANCE. [Publ. tech. Charbon. Fr.]. **VFOAT** Publications Techniques. Periodical. French (summaries and/or abstracts in English, German and Russian). 9 Avenue Percier, 75008 Paris France. **LC** TN71; .P83. **DD** 622/.334/0944.
Ind/Abst Coal Abstr.; Saf. Health Work.

UK/0950-9526
QUARRY MANAGEMENT. [Quarry manag.]. Vol. 11, No. 1 (Jan. 1984)-. Academic Scholarly Publication. English. mo. £66.00 (airmail), £33.00 (surface mail). Quarry Managers Journal Ltd, 7 Regent Street, Nottingham NG1 5BY England. **Tel** 011 44 602 411315. **LC** TN950.A1; Q37. **DD** 622/.31/068. Documents available from Article Express International. ***Continues** Quarry Management and Products, 0305-9421.*
Ind/Abst AESIS Q.; Bioeng. Abstr.; Coal Abstr. (1984-); Curr. Technol. Index; Ei Page One; EMBASE; Eng. Index Annu. [Select. Cov.]; Fluid Abstr., Civil Eng.; Fluid Abstr. Proc. Eng.; FLUIDEX (1984-1990); GeoRef (1984-); MINPROC; Mintec, Min. Technol. Abstr.

AT
QUARTERLY MINERAL STATISTICS. **Added/Corp** Australian Bureau of Agricultural and Resource Economics. **VFOAT** Mineral Statistics. (June 1989)-. Periodical. English. qt. $48.00. ABARE / Australian Bureau of Agriculture and Resource Economics, GPO Box 1563, Canberra ACT 2601 Australia. **Tel** 011 61 6 2722000, FAX 011 61 6 272 2001. ***Formed by the union of** Metal Ore and Concentrate Prices; Australian Mineral Industry : Quarterly Summary Statistics; Base Metal Statistics; Mineral Sands Statistics; Australian Mineral Industry Quarterly, 0155-9419 **and** Major Energy Statistics.*
Ind/Abst AESIS Q.

US
QUARTZ CRYSTAL. See Engineering-Abstracting, Bibliographies and Statistics.

AT/0033-6149
QUEENSLAND GOVERNMENT MINING JOURNAL. [Queensl. gov. min. j.]. **Added/Corp** Queensland. Dept. of Mines. Vol. 1, No. 1 (June 1900)-. Periodical. English. mo. 90.00Aus$, Australia; 123.00Aus$, New Zealand and PNG; 130.00Aus$, Indonesia; 139.00Aus$, India and Japan; 150.00Aus$, US; 156.00Aus$ other. Department of Resource Industries, GPO Box 194/61, Mary Street, Brisbane Queensland 4001 Australia. **Tel** 011 61 7 2371435, FAX 011 61 7 2297770. **ED** Mike Holliday. **LC** TN1; .Q8. **CODEN** QGMJAZ. Index available. cum. index. **Ad Acc. Circ:** 1,200. available in microform (back issues); available on microfiche.
Desc: Provides a record of mining industry developments of Queensland geology. Publishes scientific and technical information of assistance to mining and mineral exploration enterprises.
Ind/Abst AESIS Q.; Coal Abstr.; Geol. Abstr.; GeoRef; Mintec, Min. Technol. Abstr.

AT
QUEST INFORMATION. English. Four times a year (Mar., June, Sept., Dec.). 67.00Aus$ Australia; 91.00Aus$ others. Department of Resource Industries, GPO Box 194/61, Mary Street, Brisbane Queensland 4001 Australia. **Tel** 011 61 7 2371435, FAX 011 61 7 2297770.

US/1057-4921
RANDOL BUYER'S GUIDE. [Randol buy. guide]. **Added/Corp** Randol International Ltd. **VFOAT** Buyer's Guide. (1991)-. English. Randol International Ltd., 21578 Mountsfield Drive, Golden CO 80401. **Tel** (303)526-1626, FAX (303)526-1650. **LC** TN347; .R18. **DD** 622/.029/4. ***Continues in part** Randol Gold Mining Directory.*

US/1054-027X
RANDOL MINING DIRECTORY. [Randol min. dir.]. **Added/Corp** Randol International Ltd. **VFOAT** Mining Directory. (19??)-. Directory. English. be. $120.00 US and Canada; $135.00 other. Randol International Ltd., 21578 Mountsfield Drive, Golden CO 80401. **Tel** (303)526-1626, FAX (303)526-1650. **LC** TN23; R245. **DD** 338.2/025/73. **Bk Rev**, (Qty: 200). **Ad Acc, Adv Mgr Tel** (303)278-9199. **Circ:** 3500 (ctrl).

BE
RAPPORT. **Main/Corp** Institut National des Industries Extractives. (19??)-. French (Dutch). an. Free. Institut Scientifique de Service Public, 200 rue du Chera, B-4000 Liege Belgium. **Tel** 32 41 527150, FAX 32 41 524665. **LC** TN2; .I55a. **DD** 669/.005. Index available. **Circ:** 4,000 (ctrl).

FR
RAPPORT D'ACTIVITE / CHARBONNAGES DE FRANCE. **Main/Corp** Charbonnages de France. French. an. **LC** HD9552.1; .C54. **DD** 338.7/622334/0944. ***Continues** Charbonnages de France. Rapport de Gestion.*

IV
RAPPORT PROVISOIRE SUR LES ACTIVITES DU SECTEUR. **Main/Corp** Ivory Coast. Direction des Mines et de la Geologie. French. Direction des Mines et de la Geologie, BP 1368, Abidjan Ivory Coast. **LC** TN119.I9; I93A.

RU/0034-026X
RAZVEDKA I OKHRANA NEDR. **Added/Corp** Soviet Union. Ministerstvo Geologii i Okhrany Nedr. Gosudarstvennyi Geologicheskii Komitet SSSR. Soviet Union. Ministerstvo Geologii. Profsoiuz Rabochikh Geologorazvedochnykh Rabot. Tsentralnyi Komitet. No. 3 (1953)-. Academic Scholarly Publication. Russian. mo. $99.00. **(Subscription address:** Victor Kamkin, 4956 Boiling Brook Parkway, Rockville MD 20852.) **CODEN** RZONAV. **[CCC].** Documents available from Article Express International, CASDDS. ***Continues** Razvedka Nedr.*
Ind/Abst Bioeng. Abstr.; Chem. Abstr.; Coal Abstr.; Ei Page One; Eng. Index Annu.; GeoRef; Int. Aerosp. Abstr.

PE/1010-0962
RE METALLICA, DE. See Metals and Metallurgy.

FR
REALITES INDUSTRIELLES. **VFOAT** Annales des Mines. (Juil.-Aout 1989)-. Periodical. French (summaries and/or abstracts in English, German, Russian and Spanish). bm. 660.00F. AGPAU, Les Editions ESKA, 27 rue Dunois, Paris 75013, France. **Tel** (1)45 83 62 02, FAX (1)44 24 06 94. **LC** TN2; .A62. **DD** 338.2. **CODEN** REAIE7. Index available. **Bk Rev. Ad Acc. Pr Rev. Circ:** 4,000 to 20,000 (ctrl). ***Continues** Annales des Mines, 0003-4282.*
Desc: Most recent features about mines and mining engineering.
Ind/Abst PAIS Int. Print.

CN/0832-0322
RECORDER. ***Ceased.*** (RECORDER. CANADIAN SOCIETY OF EXPLORATION GEOPHYSICIST.). [Recorder]. (Jan. 1975)-(199?). Periodical. English. mo. Canadian Society of Exploration Geophysicist, 206 SW 7th Avenue, Room 501, Calgary Alta T2P 0W7 Canada. **DD** 622/.15/06071.

US/0080-049X
REFRACTORY MATERIALS. (REFRACTORY MATERIALS : A SERIES OF MONOGRAPHS.). [Refract. mater.]. (19??)-. Monographic series. English. ir. Price varies per volume. Academic Press, Inc., 6277 Sea Harbor Drive, Orlando FL 32887. **Tel** (800)543-9534, (407)345-4100, FAX (407)363-9661. **ED** Louis E. Toth.

AT
REGISTER OF AUSTRALIAN MINING. **VFOAT** RAM; R.A.M. (1980)-. English. an. 269.00Aus$; 293.00Aus$ other. Resource Info Unit, c/o R Louthean, PO Box 452, Subiaco WA 6008 Australia. **Tel** 011 61 9 3823955, FAX (09)388 1025. **ED** R Louthean and D Macdonald. **Bk Rev. Ad Acc. Circ:** 3,500. ***Continues** Australian Mines Handbook.*
Desc: Comprehensive coverage of Australian mineral and oil and gas deposits. Details ownership, administration, geology, reserves, production status and relevant comments.

AT/0816-9411
REPORT - COAL CORPORATION OF VICTORIA. [Rep. - Coal Corp. Vic.]. (1985)-. English. an. **DD** 338. 76626209945.
Ind/Abst AESIS Q.

AT/0084-7100
REPORT / DEPARTMENT OF RESOURCES AND ENERGY, BUREAU OF MINERAL RESOURCES, GEOLOGY AND GEOPHYSICS. See Earth Sciences-Geology.

AT/0155-1531
REPORT - DIRECTOR OF MINES (HOBART). (REPORT FOR THE YEAR ENDED ... / DIRECTOR OF MINES.). [Rep. - Dir. Mines]. **Main/Corp** Tasmania. Dept. of Mines. **VFOAT** Report for ... . English. an. T J Hughes, Government Printer, Hobart Tasmania Australia. **LC** TN122.T3; A25. **DD** 354.9460082/38/06. **CODEN** TGSRAK. ***Continues** Tasmania. Dept. of Mines. Report of the Director of Mines.*
Ind/Abst GeoRef.

US
REPORT FOR CALENDAR YEAR ... / CHIEF MINE INSPECTOR, DEPARTMENT OF MINES. **Main/Corp** Oklahoma. Dept. of Mines. English. an. Free. Oklahoma Department of Mines, 4040 North Lincoln Boulevard/Suite 107, Oklahoma City OK 73105. **Tel** (405)521-3859. **LC** TN24.O5; O38A. **DD** 353.97660082/382/06. **Circ:** 800 (ctrl). ***Continues** Oklahoma. Dept. of Mines. Annual Report, 0732-1090.*

RH
REPORT / INSTITUTE OF MINING RESEARCH, UNIVERSITY OF ZIMBABWE. **Added/Corp** University of Zimbabwe. Institute of Mining Research. (1981)-. Monographic series. English. Price varies per volume. **LC** UNC. **CODEN** RUZRDW. ***Continues** University of Rhodesia. Institute of Mining Research. Report.*
Ind/Abst AESIS Q.

AT/0312-6358
REPORT - JOINT COAL BOARD. **Main/Corp** Joint Coal Board (Australia and New South Wales). (1948)-. Periodical. English. an. 10.00Aus$ Australia; 13.00Aus$ other. Joint Coal Board, GPO Box 3842, Sydney New South Wales 2001 Australia. **Tel** 011 61 2 248 9666. **LC** HD9558.A8; A36; J905; .L3 subser. **DD** 338.2/7/20994.

US/0095-5264
REPORT / NEVADA BUREAU OF MINES AND GEOLOGY. See Earth Sciences-Geology.

CN/1184-8006
REPORT OF ACTIVITIES - MINERALS DIVISION (WINNIPEG). See Earth Sciences-Geology.

US/0099-4227
REPORT OF INVESTIGATION - NORTH DAKOTA GEOLOGICAL SURVEY. See Earth Sciences-Geology.

US/1066-5552
REPORT OF INVESTIGATIONS - UNITED STATES. BUREAU OF MINES. (REPORT OF INVESTIGATIONS / BUREAU OF MINES.). [Rep. investig. - U.S., Bur. Mines]. **Added/Corp** United States. Bureau of Mines. **VFOAT** RI. (19??)-. Monographic series. English. Price varies per volume. US Department of the Interior / Bureau of Mines, Publications Department, PO Box 18070, Cochrans Mill Road, Pittsburgh PA 15236. **Tel** (412)892-6400. **DD** 622.
Ind/Abst AESIS Q.; Aquat. Sci. Fish. Abstr. (Computer File); Ceram. Abstr. (19??-).

US/1066-5552
REPORT OF INVESTIGATIONS - UNITED STATES. BUREAU OF MINES. (REPORT OF INVESTIGATIONS.). [Rep. invest. - U.S., Bur. Mines]. **Added/Corp** United States. Bureau of Mines. **VFOAT** Monthly Reports of Investigations; RI; Bureau of Mines Report of Investigations. (1919)-. Monographic series. English. ir. Price varies per volume. US Department of the Interior / Bureau of Mines, 810 7th Street NW, Room 604, Washington DC 20241. **Tel** (202)501-9300. **LC** TN23; .U43. **DD** 622.06173. **CODEN** XBMIA6. **Circ:** 3,000.

Engineering —Mines and Mining Engineering

Documents available from Article Express International, Ask*IEEE, CASDDS. **Desc:** Presents results of research and investigations conducted by the US Bureau of Mines at its research centers.
Ind/Abst Bioeng. Abstr.; Chem. Abstr.; Coal Abstr.; Ei Page One; Eng. Index Annu.; GeoRef; INSPEC.

AT
REPORT OF THE DIRECTOR OF MINES (HOBART. 1940). (REPORT OF THE DIRECTOR OF MINES.). **Main/Corp** Tasmania. Dept. of Mines. **VFOAT** Director of Mines Report for the Year. (1940)-. English. *Continues* Tasmania. Dept of Mines. Report of the Secretary for Mines.
Ind/Abst AESIS Q.

II
REPORT ON ANDHRA PRADESH MINING CORPORATION. See Economics-Industry and Production.

CN
REPORT ON THE ADMINISTRATION OF THE EMERGENCY GOLD MINING ASSISTANCE ACT. Main/Corp Canada. Department of Mines and Technical Surveys. Periodical. English. an. Queen's Printer, 506 Government Street, Victoria British Columbia V8V 4R6 Canada. **Tel** 387-1901. **LC** HD9536.C2; A37. **DD** 338.2741. *Continues* Canada. Mines, Forests and Scientific Services Branch. Report on the Administration of the Emergency Gold Mining Assistance Act.

MY
REPORT - STATES OF MALAYA CHAMBER OF MINES. COUNCIL.
Main/Corp States of Malaya Chamber of Mines. Council. English. States of Malaya Chamber of Mines Council, 130 Jalan Belfield, Ipoh Malaysia. **LC** HD9506.M36; S8B. **DD** 338.2/09595/1.

SA
REPORT / UNIVERSITY OF THE WITWATERSRAND, BUREAU FOR MINERALS STUDIES. Added/Corp University of the Witwatersrand. Bureau for Minerals Studies. No. 1 (June 1977)-. Monographic series. English. Price varies per volume. Bureau for Minerals Studies, 1 Jan Smuts Avenue, Johannesburg 2001 South Africa.
Ind/Abst GeoRef.

UK
REPORTS OF H.M. INSPECTORS OF MINES AND QUARRIES UNDER THE MINES AND QUARRIES ACT 1954 : SOUTH WALES DISTRICT. *Ceased.*
Main/Corp Great Britain. Mines and Quarries Inspectorate. (19??)-?. English. Her Majesty's Stationery Office, 51 Nine Elms Lane, London SW8 5DR England. **Tel** 011 44 71 873 8459, 011 44 71 873 8499, FAX 011 44 71 873 8499, 011 44 71 873 8456, telex 297138. **(Subscription address:** PO Box 276, Public Centre, London SW8 5DT England) **LC** TN295; .G572f. **DD** 614.8/52.

UK
REPORTS OF H. M. INSPECTORS OF MINES AND QUARRIES UNDER THE MINES AND QUARRIES ACT 1954 : THE NORTH OF ENGLAND DISTRICT.
Main/Corp Great Britain. Mines and Quarries Inspectorate. **VAT** Reports of Her Majesty's Inspectors of Mines and Quarries and the Mines and Quarries Act 1954: the North of England District. English. £0.85. **LC** TN295; .G572G. **DD** 622.8/094286.

US/0083-260X
RESEARCH AND DEVELOPMENT REPORT - OFFICE OF COAL RESEARCH, DEPARTMENT OF THE INTERIOR. (RESEARCH AND DEVELOPMENT REPORT.). [Res. dev. rep. - Off. Coal Res. Dep. Inter.]. **VFOAT** R & D Report; Office of Coal Research R & D Report; Coal Research and Development Report; R & D Report - Office of Coal Research; OCR Report; OCR Research and Development Report; OCR R & D Report; R and D Report. No. 1-. Monographic series. English. Price varies per volume. US Department of the Interior / Office of Coal Research, 2401 East Street NW, Washington DC 20241. **LC** TN805; .A395. **DD** 553.2/4. **CODEN** XCRDAN. Documents available from CASDDS.
Ind/Abst Chem. Abstr.; GeoRef.

CN/0714-4857
RESEARCH NOTE - MINERAL EXPLORATION RESEARCH INSTITUTE (1977). (RESEARCH NOTE ...). [Res. note - Miner. Explor. Res. Inst.]. 77/2-. English (French). ir (10 per year). 15.00Can$ Canada. Mineral Exploration Research Institute, PO Box 6079 Station A, Montreal Quebec H3C 3A7 Canada. **Tel** (514)340-4991, telex 05-24146. **DD** 622/.1/09714. **CODEN** RNMIDR. Index available. cum.

index. **Circ:** 500. *Continues* Research Paper (Mineral Exploration Research Institute), 0714-4830.
Ind/Abst GeoRef.

AT/1033-3908
RESEARCH REPORT - CSIRO DIVISION OF MINERAL AND PROCESS ENGINEERING. (RESEARCH REPORT.). [Res. rep. - CSIRO Div. Miner. Process Eng.]. (1988)-. English. be. CSIRO Publications, PO Box 89, 314 Albert Street, East Melborne Victoria 3002 Australia. **Tel** 011 61 3 4187333, 4187217, FAX 011 61 3 4190459, telex AA 30236. **DD** 622.072094. *Continues* Research Report - CSIRO Division of Mineral Engineering, 1034-750X.
Ind/Abst AESIS Q.

AT
RESEARCH REVIEW / ACIRL COAL RESEARCH. Main/Corp Australian Coal Industry Research Laboratories. (19??)-. English. an (Sept.). 45.00Aus$. Australian Coal Industry Research Laboratories, PO Box 83, 22-30 Delhi Road, North Ryde NSW 2113 Australia. **Tel** 011 61 2 8873777. **LC** TP326.A8; A97a.
Ind/Abst AESIS Q.

SA
REVIEW / CHAMBER OF MINES OF SOUTH AFRICA. See Earth Sciences-Mineralogy.

BL
REVISTA ESCOLA DE MINAS : REM.
VFOAT REM; R.E.M. V. 35, No. 3 (April 1982)-. Periodical. Portuguese. qt. $15.00. Revista da Escola de Minas, Praca Tiradentes 20, 35400 Ouro Preto, Minas Gerais Brazil. **LC** TN4; .R52. **DD** 553/.0981. *Continues* Revista de Escola de Minas.

RM
REVISTA MINELOR. Added/Corp Romania. Departamentul Minelor. Vol. 41 No. 7 (1990)-. Periodical. Romanian (summaries and/or abstracts in English, French, German and Russian). Four times a year. DM290.00. **(Subscription address:** Kubon & Sagner, ABT Zeitschriftenimport, D 80328 Munich Germany.) **CODEN** REVMEM. Documents available from CASDDS. *Continues* Mine, Petrol, Gaze.
Ind/Abst Chem. Abstr.

FR
REVUE DU GAZ DANS LA CONSTRUCTION. (19??)-. Periodical. French. qt. **LC** TN880.A1; R47.

US
RHENIUM. English. an. US Department of the Interior / Bureau of Mines, Publications Department, PO Box 18070, Cochrans Mill Road, Pittsburgh PA 15236. **Tel** (412)892-6400.

SP/0378-3316
ROCAS Y MINERALES. [Rocas miner.]. **VFOAT** Revista de Tecnicas y Procesos de Minas y Canteras. (1972)-. Periodical. Spanish. mo. $30.00 Spain; $46.00 Europe; $57.00 other. Editorial Rocas y Minerales, Arturo Soria 166, 28043 Madrid, Spain. **Tel** 011 34 1 4151804, FAX 011 34 1 4151661. **ED** Laureano Fueyo. **UDC** 622. **Bk Rev. Ad Acc. Pr Rev.**
Desc: Main theme is mining, quarrying and public works machinery and techniques.

BL
ROCHAS DE QUALIDADE. (19??)-. Periodical. Portuguese. bm. CR4.00. EMC, Av Prestes Maia 241 - 350 Andar Conjunto 3520, Sao Paulo CEP 01032 Brazil. **Tel** 011 227 8360 228 9290, FAX 011 227 8360 229 7370. **ED** Emanuel Mateus de Castro. **LC** TN950.A1; R6. **Ad Acc. Circ:** 1,200 (ctrl). **Desc:** Of interest to those working with ornamental stones.

AU/0723-2632
ROCK MECHANICS AND ROCK ENGINEERING. [Rock mech. rock eng.]. Vol. 16, No. 1 (Feb. 1983)-. Periodical. English. Four times a year. $197.00. Springer-Verlag Wien, Sachsenplatz 4 6, PO Box 89, A-1201 Vienna Austria. **Tel** 011 43 1 3302415. **(Subscription address:** Springer Verlag New York Inc. / for North America, 44 Hartz Way, Secaucus NJ 07096.) **ED** K. Kovari. **LC** TA710.A1; R599. **DD** 264.1/5132/05. **CODEN** RMREDX. **[CCC].** available on microfilm and microfiche from University Microfilms International (UMI). Documents available from Article Express International, The Genuine Article, Ask*IEEE. *Continues* Rock Mechanics, 0035-7448.
Desc: Covers the experimental and theoretical aspects of rock mechanics including laboratory and field testing, methods of computation and field observation of structural behavior.
Ind/Abst Appl. Mech. Rev.; Curr. Contents Eng. Tech. Appl. Sci.; Eng. Index Annu.; GeoRef; Geotech. Abstr.; INSPEC (Feb. 1983-); Int. Civil Eng. Abstr.; Res. Alert [Full Cov.]; Sci. Cit. Index; SCISEARCH; Soft. Abstr. Eng.

US/0747-3605
ROCK PRODUCTS (1964). (ROCK PRODUCTS.). [Rock prod.]. Vol. 67, No. 7 (July 1964)-. Academic Scholarly Publication. English. mo. $31.25 (one

year), $56.25 (two year), $75.00 (three year) US & Canada; $50.00 (one year), $87.50 (two year), $118.75 (three year) other. MacLean Hunter Publishing Corporation / Chicago, IL, 29 North Wacker Drive, Chicago IL 60606-3298. **Tel** (312)726-2802, FAX (312)726-3091. **LC** TN950; .A3. **CODEN** ROPRA5. available on an online database (file 648/Full-Text) from DIALOG. Documents available from Article Express International, CASDDS. *Continues* Rock Products Mining & Processing.
Ind/Abst AESIS Q.; Appl. Sci. Technol. Index; Bioeng. Abstr.; Bus. Period. Index; Ceram. Abstr. (199?-); Chem. Abstr.; Coal Abstr.; Concr. Abstr.; Ei Page One; EMBASE; Eng. Index Annu. [Select. Cov.]; F&S Index Plus Text, Int. [Select. Cov.]; GeoRef; MINPROC; Mintec, Min. Technol. Abstr.; Predicasts Forecasts.

US/0886-0912
ROCKY MOUNTAIN PAY DIRT. VFOAT Pay Dirt. No. 73 (Oct. 1985)-. Periodical. English. mo. $25.00 (one year), $45.00 (two year). Copper Queen Publishing Company, Inc., PO Drawer 48, Bisbee AZ 85603. **Tel** (602)432-2244. **ED** William C. Epler. **Bk Rev. Ad Acc. Circ:** 4,200 (ctrl). *Formed by the union of* Intermountain Pay Dirt, 0199-5952 *and* Big Sky Pay Dirt, 0273-799X.
Desc: Contains information on all facets of the mining industry and the people who maintain its viability.

CS/0483-5093
RUDY. *Title Change.* (RUDY : ODBORNY CASOPIS RUDNEHO HORNICTVI.). [Rudy]. **Added/Corp** Czechoslovakia. Ministerstvo Hutniho Prumyslu a Rudnych Dolu. (Feb. 1953)-(19??). Academic Scholarly Publication. Czech (table of contents in English, French, German and Russian). mo. **(Subscription address:** Artia Pegas Press Ltd., Palac Metro Narodni Trida 25, 11210 Prague 1 Czech Republic.) **LC** TN4; .R845. **CODEN** RUDYA8. Documents available from CASDDS. *Separated from* Uhli a Rudy. *Merged with* Uhli (Prague, Czechoslovakia : 1959) *to form* Uhli, Rudy.
Ind/Abst Alum. Ind. Abstr.; Chem. Abstr.; Eng. Mater. Abstr.; GeoRef; Met. Abstr.

UK
SAML: SOUTH-EAST ASIA MINING LETTER. English. sm (24 issues). £396.00. Francophone Business Publishing, 28 Barclay Road, London SW6 1EH England. **Tel** 011 44 71 7367604.

CN/1182-9125
SASKATCHEWAN HORIZONTAL WELL SUMMARY. [Sask. horiz. well summ.]. **Added/Corp** Saskatchewan. Petroleum and Natural Gas. (July 1990)-. Periodical. English. mo. **DD** 622/.3382.

XR/0474-8476
SBORNIK VEDECKYCH PRACI. VYSOKA SKOLA BANSKA, OSTRAVA. RADA HORNICKO-GEOLOGICKA. See Earth Sciences-Geology.

GW/0720-1877
SCHRIFTENREIHE DER GDMB GESELLSCHAFT DEUTSCHER METALLHUTTEN- UND BERGLEUTE.
See Metals and Metallurgy.

MY/0126-9860
SEATRAD BULLETIN. Added/Corp SEATRAD Centre. **VAT** Southeast Asia Tin Research and Development Bulletin. (19??)-. Bulletin. English. qt. **LC** TN470; .S43. **DD** 669/.6/05.
Ind/Abst AESIS Q.

US
SECONDARY RECOVERY AND PRESSURE MAINTENANCE OPERATIONS IN LOUISIANA. Main/Corp Louisiana. Office of Conservation. 1976-. English. an. $8.00. Office of Conservation, State Land and Natural Resources Building, PO Box 44275 Capitol Station, Baton Rouge LA 70804. **LC** TN872.L8; A33. **DD** 622/.3382. *Continues* Secondary Recovery and Pressure Maintenance Operations in Louisiana.

US/0148-3285
SECONDARY RECOVERY REPORT.
[Second. recovery rep.]. No. 1-. English. Geological Survey Division, Box 30028, R Thomas Segal, Lansing MI 48909. **LC** TN871; .S417. **DD** 622/.33/82. **CODEN** SMGPDM.
Ind/Abst GeoRef.

CN/0848-5704
SECURITE ET CONTROLE DES EXPLOSIFS AU CANADA. [Secur. Controle explos. Can.]. **Main/Corp** Canada. Direction des Explosifs. **VFOAT** Explosives Safety and Control in Canada. French (English). Energie Mines et Resources, 580 Booth Street, Ottawa Ontario K1A 0E4 Canada. **DD** 354.710075/05. *Continues* Rapport de la Direction des Explosifs. Canada. Direction des Explosifs, 0710-7196; *Absorbed* Explosives Safety and Control in Canada. Canada Direction des Explosifs.

JA
SEIMITSU CHOSA HOKOKUSHO. HIDA CHIIKI. 1980-. Japanese. Kinzoku Kogyo Jigyodan, (Metal Mining Agency), 24-14 Toranomon 1 chome, Minatoku Tokyoto 105 Japan. **LC** TN106.H53; S44.

JA
SEIMITSU CHOSA HOKOKUSHO: JOZANKEI CHIIKI. Main/Corp Kinzoku Kogyo Jigyodan. (1973)-. Periodical. Japanese. sa. Kinzoku Kogyo Jigyodan, (Metal Mining Agency), 24-14 Toranomon 1 chome, Minatoku Tokyoto 105 Japan. **LC** TN106.J68; K45a.

JA
SEIMITSU CHOSA HOKOKUSHO. NISHIKIGAWA CHIIKI. 1981-. Japanese. Kinzoku Kogyo Jigyodan, (Metal Mining Agency), 24-14 Toranomon 1 chome, Minatoku Tokyoto 105 Japan. **LC** TN106.N57; S45.

JA
SEKITAN KENKYU SHIRYO SOSHO. Japanese. an. Free. Kyushu Daigaku Sekitan Kenkyu Shiry Senta, 10-ban 1-go Hakozaki 6-chome Higashi-ku, Fukuoka-shi Japan. **Tel** (092)641-1101. **LC** HD9556.J32; F847. **Circ:** 300 (ctrl).
Desc: Contains primary and secondary historical documents on the coal mining industry and related industries.

JA
SEKIYU KOGYO GIJUTSU KOZA: KISOHEN. Main/Corp Sekiyu Kogyo Gijutsu Koza. **Added/Corp** Seikiyu Kaihatsu Kodan. Japanese. ¥2000. c/o Dai Juqomiri Building, 16 Shiba Nishikubo, Akefunecho Minato-ku Japan. **LC** TN860; .S39A.

RU
SHAKHTNYI I KARERNYI TRANSPORT. No. 1 (1974)-. Russian. 1.49rub (single issue). Izdatelstvo Nedra, 3 Pl Belorusskogo Vakzala, 125047 Moscow Russia. **Tel** 250-52-55. **LC** TN331; .S483. Index available. cum. index. **Bk Rev. Ad Acc.** ctrl circ.

JA/0916-1740
SHIGEN TO SOZAI. Added/Corp Shigen Sozai Gakkai. **VFOAT** Journal of the Mining and Materials Processing Institute of Japan; Shigen Sozai Gakkai Shi. (1989)-. Academic Scholarly Publication. Japanese (summaries and/or abstracts in English). Twelve times a year. $306.00. **(Subscription address:** Maruzen Company Ltd., PO Box 5050, Import & Export Department, Tokyo 100 31 Japan.**)** **LC** TN275.A1; N55. **CODEN** SHSOEB. Documents available from Article Express International, CASDDS. ***Continues** Nihon Kogyokai Shi, 0369-4194.*
Ind/Abst Chem. Abstr.; Ei Page One; Eng. Index Annu.; GeoRef.

CC
SHIH YU TI CHIU WU LI KAN TAN. VFOAT Oil Geophysical Prospecting. (1981)-. Periodical. Chinese (summaries and/or abstracts in English; table of contents in English). Six times a year. $46.70. Science Press, 16 Donghuangchenggen North Street, Beijing 100707, People's Republic of China. **Tel** 011 86 1 4019821, 011 86 1 4010642, FAX 011 86 1 4012180, 011 86 1 4019810, telex 210147. **(Subscription address:** China International Book Trading Corporation, PO Box 399, Library Service Department, Beijing 100044 People's Republic of China.**)** **LC** TN270.A1; S48. **DD** 622/.15/05.
Ind/Abst GeoRef.

US/0037-6329
SKILLINGS' MINING REVIEW. [Skillings' min. rev.]. **VFOAT** Mining Review. (1912)-. Periodical. English. wk. $30.00 (one year), $58.00 (two year), $85.00 (three year). Skillings Mining Review, 130 West Superior, First Bank Place, Suite 728, Duluth MN 55802-2083. **Tel** (218)722-2310, FAX (218)722-0134. **ED** David N. Skillings Jr. **LC** TN1; .S6. Index available. **Bk Rev. Ad Acc. Pr Rev. Circ:** 3,000 (ctrl).
Ind/Abst Coal Abstr.; Eng. Mater. Abstr.; F&S Index Plus Text, Int. [Select. Cov.]; Geogr. Abstr. Human Geogr.; GeoRef; MINPROC; Mintec, Min. Technol. Abstr.; PROMT.

SA
SOUTH AFRICAN MINING WORLD. (19??)-. English. mo. R39.30 South Africa; R65.00 other. Phase Four Pty Ltd., PO Box 784279, Sandton 2146 South Africa. **Tel** 011 27 11 4444566.

AT
SOUTH AUSTRALIAN MAJOR MANUFACTURING, MINING AND DEVELOPMENT PROJECTS. See Manufacturing.

US/1060-8044
SOUTHEASTERN STATES MINING DIRECTORY. [Southeast. states min. dir.]. (1991)-. Directory. English. $23.95. Southeastern States Mining Directory, PO Box 5694, Boise ID 83705. **DD** 622.

●US/1056-8638
SOUTHEASTERN STATES MINING DIRECTORY. [Southeast. states min. dir.]. (1992)-. Directory. English. ir. $19.95. Graphic One, Inc., PO Box 5694, Boise ID 83705. **LC** TN12; .S67. **DD** 338.2/02575.

US/0886-0920
SOUTHWESTERN PAY DIRT. VFOAT Pay Dirt. No. 556 (Oct. 1985)-. Periodical. English. Twelve times a year. $25.00 (one year); $45.00 (two years); $60.00 (three years). Copper Queen Publishing Company, Inc., PO Drawer 48, Bisbee AZ 85603. **Tel** (602)432-2244. **ED** William C. Epler. **Bk Rev. Ad Acc. Circ:** 4,500 (ctrl). ***Formed by the union of** Arizona Pay Dirt **and** New Mexico Pay Dirt, 0199-5960.*
Desc: Includes up-to-date information on all facets of the mining industry and the people who maintain its viability.

US/0038-5581
SOVIET MINING SCIENCE. ***Title Change.*** [Sov. min. sci.]. **Added/Corp** Consultants Bureau. Consultants Bureau Enterprises. Vol. 1 (Jan./Feb. 1965)-(1992). Periodical. English (Russian; translations available in Russian). bm. Plenum Press, 233 Spring Street, New York NY 10013-1578. **Tel** (212)620-8000, (800)221-9369, FAX (212)463-0742, (212)807-1047, telex 23/421139. **ED** E I Shemyakin. **LC** TN4; .S784. **CODEN** SMNSAT. **[CCC].** Index available. available on microfilm and microfiche from University Microfilms International (UMI). Documents available from Article Express International, The Genuine Article, CASDDS. ***Continued by** Fiziko-Tekhnicheskie Problemy Razrabotki Poleznykh Iskopaemykh. English. Journal of Mining Science, 1062-7391.*
Desc: This journal documents the combined efforts of scientists and engineers in the solution of the many problems connected with the mining of minerals.
Ind/Abst Bioeng. Abstr.; Chem. Abstr.; Coal Abstr.; Curr. Contents Eng. Tech. Appl. Sci.; Ei Page One; Energy Res. Abstr. (June 1975-); Eng. Index Annu.; GeoRef; MINPROC; Mintec, Min. Technol. Abstr.; Res. Alert [Full Cov.].

AT/0726-1527
SPECIAL PUBLICATION / DEPARTMENT OF MINES AND ENERGY. [Spec. publ. - Dep. Mines Energy]. **Added/Corp** South Australia. Dept. of Mines and Energy. No. 1, (1982)-. Monographic series. English. Price varies per volume. **CODEN** SPSEE3. Documents available from BIOSIS Document Express.
Ind/Abst AESIS Q.; Biol. Abstr.

JM
SPECIAL PUBLICATION - MINES & GEOLOGY DIVISION. Main/Corp Jamaica. Mines and Geology Division. No.1-. Monographic series. English. Price varies per volume. Mines and Geology Division, PO Box 189, Hope Gardens 6, Kingston Jamaica. **CODEN** PJMGD5.
Ind/Abst GeoRef.

US/0731-762X
SPECIAL PUBLICATION - UNITED STATES. BUREAU OF MINES. (SPECIAL PUBLICATION / BUREAU OF MINES.). [Spec. pub. - U.S., Bur. Mines]. **Added/Corp** United States. Bureau of Mines. (19??)-. Monographic series. English. ir. Price varies per volume. Superintendent of Documents, US Government Printing Office, Washington DC 20402. **Tel** (202)275-3328, FAX (202)786-2377. **DD** 622.
Ind/Abst Ceram. Abstr. (19??-); Coal Abstr.; GeoRef.

US
SPECIAL STUDY / UTAH GEOLOGICAL SURVEY. See Earth Sciences-Geology.

CN/0826-6166
SPECIAL VOLUME (CANADIAN INSTITUTE OF MINING AND METALLURGY : 1982). (SPECIAL VOLUME.). [Spec. vol. - Can. Inst. Min. Metall.]. **Added/Corp** Canadian Institute of Mining and Metallurgy. (1982)-. Monographic series. English. ir. Price varies per volume. Canadian Institute of Mining, Metallurgy and Petroleum, 3400 de Maisonneuve Boulevard West, Xerox Tower, Suite 1210, Montreal, Quebec H3Z 3B8 Canada. **Tel** (514)939-2710, FAX (514)939-2714, telex 055-62344. **LC** UNC. **DD** 338.2/0971. ***Continues** CIM Special Volume, 0713-7672.*

CN/0707-2767
STATISTICAL REVIEW OF COAL IN CANADA. See Engineering-Abstracting, Bibliographies and Statistics.

AT
STATISTICAL SUMMARY / DEPARTMENT OF MINES, WESTERN AUSTRALIA. ***Title Change.*** **Main/Corp** Western Australia. Dept. of Mines. **Added/Corp** Western Australia. Dept. of Mines. (19??)-?. Statistical Publication. English. an. Australia Department of Mines, 427-431 Spencer Street, West Melbourne 3003 Australia. **LC** TN122.W5; S73. **DD** 338.2/09941/021. ***Merged with** Annual Review **and** Annual Report **to form** Department of Mines Western Australia in ... .*

II
STATISTICS OF MINES IN INDIA: COAL. Main/Corp India (Republic). Directorate-General of Mines Safety. (1966)-. English. an. Price varies. Controller of Publications / Civil Lines, Government of India, Civil Lines, New Delhi 110054 India. **Tel** 3015984, telex 3166415. **(Subscription address:** Prints India, 11 Darya Ganj, New Delhi, 110002 India, (Phone: 011 91 11 3268645)**)** ***Continues** Statistics of Mines in India: Coal.*

II
STATISTICS OF MINES IN INDIA: NON-COAL. Main/Corp India (Republic). Directorate-General of Mines Safety. (1966)-. English. an. Price varies. Controller of Publications / Civil Lines, Government of India, Civil Lines, New Delhi 110054 India. **Tel** 3015984, telex 3166415. **(Subscription address:** Prints India, 11 Darya Ganj, New Delhi, 110002 India, (Phone: 011 91 11 3268645)**)** ***Continues** Statistics of Mines in India: Non-Coal.*

BE
STATISTIQUES: HOUILLE, COKES, AGGLOMERES, METALLURGIE, CARRIERES. STATISTIEKEN: STEENKOLEN, COKES, AGGLOMERATEN, METAALNIJVERHEID, GROVEN. See Engineering-Abstracting, Bibliographies and Statistics.

US/0735-8253
STEAM COAL WATCH. (STEAM COAL WATCH / PRODUCED SOLELY BY COAL OUTLOOK.). (Aug. 1982)-. English. mo. $325.00. Resource Data International Inc., PO Box 106, Boulder CO 80306. **Tel** (303)444-7788.
Desc: Monitors utility stockpiles & burn on a plant by plant basis, consumption reports and predicts when new coal-fired plants are coming online.

GW/0039-1018
STEINBRUCH UND SANDGRUBE (1952). (STEINBRUCH UND SANDGRUBE.). [Steinbruch Sandgrube]. (1952)-. Periodical. German. Twelve times a year. DM72.00 Germany; DM80.00 other. Verlagsgesellschaft Grutter, Lagenfeld Strasse 8, 3003 Ronnenberg 3 Germany. **Tel** 011 49 511 4609300. **LC** TN950; .A38.
Ind/Abst GeoRef.

AU
STEIRISCHE BEITRAGE ZUR ROHSTOFF- UND ENERGIEFORSCHUNG. No. 1 (March 1982)-. German. an. Free. Amt der Steiermarkischen Landesregierung, Praesidialabteilung, Referat Statistik, Burgring 4, A-8010 Graz, Austria. **ED** Dietmar Kellermann. **LC** TN65.2.S78; S74. **DD** 553/.09436. **Circ:** 500.
Desc: The journal's intention is to circulate results of research projects which have been subsidized by public means to potential users.

US/8750-9210
STONE REVIEW. (STONE REVIEW / NATIONAL STONE ASSOCIATION.). [Stone rev.]. **Added/Corp** National Stone Association (U.S.). Vol. 1 No. 1 (Feb. 1985)-. Periodical. English. bm. $48.00. Stone Review, National Stone Association, 1415 Elliot Place NW, Washington DC 20007-2599. **Tel** (202)342-1100, (800) 342-1415, FAX (202)342-0702. **ED** Frank E Atlee. **DD** 338. **Ad Acc. Circ:** 3,000 (ctrl). ***Continues** Stone News, 0270-1723.*
Desc: Provides a communication forum for the stone industry and facilitates exchange of information on industry technology, trends, developments and concerns.

US/1052-6994
STONE WORLD. [Stone world]. (1984)-. Trade Publication. English. mo. $62.00. Business News Publishing Company, 755 West Big Beaver Road, Suite 1000, Troy MI 48084. **Tel** (810)362-3700, FAX (810)362-0317, telex 230295. **DD** 338.
Desc: Provide in-depth coverage of the international stone industry from quarrying and fabrication to installation, maintenance and restoration.
Ind/Abst Constr. Index.

JA/0371-408X
SUIYOKAI SHI. [Suiyokai-shi]. **Added/Corp** Suiyokai. **VFOAT** Suiyokwai-Shi; Journal of Mining and Metallurgy, Kyoto; Transactions of the Mining and Metallurgical Alumni Association; Transactions of the Mining and Metallurgical Association. (1907)-. Academic Scholarly Publication. Japanese (summaries and/or abstracts in English). tq. Suiyokai, (Mining & Metallurgical Assoc.), c/o Kyoto Daigaku Kogakubu, Yoshida Honcho, Sakyoku, Kyotoshi, Kyotofu 606, Japan. **LC** TN4; .S89. **CODEN** SUIYAA. Documents available from CASDDS.
Ind/Abst Alum. Ind. Abstr.; Chem. Abstr.; Coal Abstr.; Met. Abstr.

CN/0825-6896
SUMMARY OF OPERATIONS / MINERAL RESOURCES DIVISION. [Summ. oper. - Miner. Resour. Div.]. **Main/Corp** British Columbia. Mineral Resources Division. (1981)-?. English. an. 10.00Can$.

Ministry of Energy, Mines and Petroleum Resources, Petroleum Resources Division, Energy Resources Division, Victoria British Columbia Canada. **LC** TN27.B9; B67a. **DD** 354.7110082/327. ***Continues*** *Summary of Operations / Mineral Resources Branch, 0825-6446.* ***Continued in part by*** *B.C. Mineral Statistics Annual Summary Tables, 0838-5998.*
Desc: A compilation of information that details the activities of the Petroleum Resources Division and the petroleum industry.

US/0731-3497
SUMMER MINING INDUSTRY SURVEY. [Summer min. ind. surv.]. **VFOAT** Survey; Summer Mining Industry. English. an. Mountain States Employers Council, 1790 Logan Street, PO Box 539, Denver CO 80201. **LC** HD8039.M5982; U68. **DD** 331.2/822/0978.

CN/0833-9600
SURVEY OF MINES AND ENERGY RESOURCES. [Surv. mines energy resour.]. **VFOAT** Financial Post Survey of Mines and Energy Resources; Mines and Energy Resources. 59th (1985)-. English. an. 98.95Can$. Financial Post DataGroup, 333 King Street East, Toronto Ontario M5A 4N2 Canada. **Tel** (800)661-7678, FAX (416)350-6501. **DD** 338.7/622/02571. ***Continues*** *Financial Post Survey of Mines and Energy Resources, 0227-1656.*
Desc: Provides a comprehensive review of the mining, petroleum and energy industries for all publicly-owned Canadian companies.

SW
SVENSK BERGS- & BRUKSTIDNING. **VAT** Svensk Bergs- Och Brukstidning. Began in 1922. Periodical. Swedish. ir. Svensk Bergs Och Brukstiding, Kungsbroplan 1, Stockholm K Sweden. **LC** TN4; .S895.

US
TAXATION OF MINING OPERATIONS. **See** Public Administration-Public Finance and Taxation.

GW/0340-5060
TECHNISCHE BERICHTE - THYSSEN. ***Ceased.*** **See** Metals and Metallurgy.

US/0196-0792
TECHNOLOGY NEWS - UNITED STATES. BUREAU OF MINES. (TECHNOLOGY NEWS / FROM THE BUREAU OF MINES, UNITED STATES DEPARTMENT OF THE INTERIOR.). [Technol. news - U.S., Bur. Mines]. **Added/Corp** United States. Bureau of Mines. (1974)-. Government Publication. English. US Department of the Interior / Bureau of Mines, 810 7th Street NW, Room 604, Washington DC 20241. **Tel** (202)501-9300. **DD** 622.
Ind/Abst AESIS Q.

UK/0040-795X
TIN INTERNATIONAL. [Tin int.]. (Jan. 1964)-. Periodical. English. mo. £120.00. MIIDA Limited, PO Box 2137, London NW10 6TN England. **Tel** 011/44/81/9617487. **LC** TN793.A1; T43. **Bk Rev. Ad Acc. Circ:** 7,200. available on microfilm from University Microfilms International (UMI); available on an online database (file 648/Full-Text) from DIALOG. ***Continues*** *Tin (London, England);* ***Absorbed*** *Tin-Printer and Box Maker.*
Desc: Tin mining, commodity markets, tin smelting, tinplate, can making, solders, tin chemicals, statistics, developing world economics.
Ind/Abst Alum. Ind. Abstr.; Curr. Technol. Index; GeoRef; Int. Packag. Abstr.; Met. Abstr.

US/0886-1331
TIN (WASHINGTON, D.C. ANNUAL). (TIN.). [Tin]. **Added/Corp** United States. Bureau of Mines. Division of Nonferrous Metals. **VFOAT** Tin in ... . English. an. Free. US Department of the Interior / Bureau of Mines, Publications Department, PO Box 18070, Cochrans Mill Road, Pittsburgh PA 15236. **Tel** (412)892-6400. **DD** 338.

GW/0722-9488
TIZ. ***Title Change.*** [TIZ]. **VFOAT** TIZ Fachberichte Rohstoff Engineering. Vol. 104, No. 4 (April 1980)-(1992). Academic Scholarly Publication. German (English). mo. Sprechsaal Publishing Group, PO Box 2962, D-96418 Coburg Germany. **Tel** 011 49 9561 742810, FAX 011 49 9561 90009, telex 179561817. **ED** Christoph Muller and Ulrich Haese. **CODEN** TTZED8. Index available. **Bk Rev. Ad Acc. Circ:** 8,400 (ctrl). Documents available from Ask*IEEE, CASDDS. ***Continues*** *TIZ: Tonindustrie Zeitung, 0170-0146.* ***Continued by*** *TIZ International Powder & Bulk Magazine.*
Desc: Magazine concerning cement and gypsum technology, minerals engineering, mining and preparation, chemical plants and proccessing, and bulk solids handling.
Ind/Abst Ceram. Abstr.; Chem. Abstr.; EMBASE; GeoRef; INSPEC (April 1991-).

GW
TIZ INTERNATIONAL POWDER & BULK MAGAZINE. ***Title Change.*** (19??)-(19??). German. mo. Sprechsaal Publishing Group, PO Box 2962, D-96418 Coburg Germany. **Tel** 011 49 9561 742810, FAX 011 49 9561 90009, telex 179561817. **(Subscription address:** Domhardt Pressevertrieb, Naegleinsgasse 2, D-96450 Coburg, Germany (011 49 9561 742810)) ***Continues*** *TIZ, 0722-9488.* ***Continued by*** *TIZ Pulver + Schuettgut Magazin.*

GW/0942-8194
TIZ PULVER + SCHUETTGUT MAGAZIN. (199?)-. German. mo (12 issues). DM415.00 Germany; DM535.00 other. Sprechsaal Publishing Group, PO Box 2962, D-96418 Coburg Germany. **Tel** 011 49 9561 742810, FAX 011 49 9561 90009, telex 179561817. **(Subscription address:** Domhardt Pressevertrieb, Naegleinsgasse 2, D 96450 Coburg Germany.) ***Continues*** *TIZ International Powder & Bulk Magazine, 0937-7271.*

KO
TONGNYOK CHAWON. **See** Energy.

CN
TRANSACTIONS - CANADIAN INSTITUTE OF MINING AND METALLURGY. **Main/Corp** Canadian Institute of Mining and Metallurgy. V. 1- 1898-. Monographic series. English. an. Price varies per volume. Can Inst Mining and Metallurgy, 3400 Maisonneuve Boulevard West/Suite 1210, Montreal Quebec H3Z 3B8 Canada. **Tel** (514)939-2710. **LC** TN1.
Desc: Vols. for 1918- include the Transactions of the Mining Society of Nova Scotia.

US
TRANSACTIONS OF SOCIETY FOR MINING, METALLURGY, AND EXPLORATION, INC. **Added/Corp** Society for Mining, Metallurgy, and Exploration (U.S.) American Institute of Mining, Metallurgical, and Petroleum Engineers. **VFOAT** Mining; Transactions. Vol. 286 (1989)-. Academic Scholarly Publication. English. Society of Mining Engineers, PO Box 625002, Littleton CO 80162-5002. **Tel** (303)973-9550, FAX (303)973-3845, telex 881988. **LC** TN1; .A5. **CODEN** TMEIE3. Documents available from CASDDS. ***Continues*** *Transactions of Society of Mining Engineers, Inc.*
Ind/Abst Chem. Abstr.

UK/0371-7844
TRANSACTIONS. SECTION A, MINING INDUSTRY / INSTITUTION OF MINING & METALLURGY. [Inst. Min. Metall., Trans., sect. A: Min. ind.]. **Added/Corp** Institution of Mining and Metallurgy (Great Britain). **VFOAT** Transactions of the Institution of Mining and Metallurgy. Section A, Mining industry; Mining Industry. Vol. 75, (Jan. 1966)-. Periodical. English. Four times a year (Jan., Apr., July, Oct.). £60.00. Institution of Mining and Metallurgy, 44 Portland Place, London W1N 4BR England. **Tel** 011 44 71 580-3802, FAX 011 44 71 436-5388, telex 261410. **ED** M. J. Jones. **LC** TN1; .T73. **DD** 622/.05. **CODEN** TIMNAQ. **[CCC]. Bk Rev. Ad Acc. Circ:** 3,200 (ctrl). Documents available from Article Express International, The Genuine Article. ***Continues in part*** *Transactions of the Institution of Mining and Metallurgy, 0371-7836.* ***Continued in part by*** *IMM Bulletin, 0308-9789.*
Desc: These are technical notes, meetings, reports, and papers on science and technology. It includes other articles on the mining industry, mineral processing and earth science.
Ind/Abst AESIS Q.; Alum. Ind. Abstr.; Bioeng. Abstr.; Coal Abstr.; Curr. Contents Eng. Tech. Appl. Sci.; Curr. Technol. Index; Ei Page One; Energy Inf. Abstr.; Energy Res. Abstr. (Dec. 1974-); Eng. Index Annu.; Ergon. Abstr.; Geogr. Abstr. Phys. Geogr.; Geogr. Abstr. Human Geogr.; GeoRef; Leadscan; Met. Abstr.; MINPROC; Mintec, Min. Technol. Abstr.; Res. Alert [Full Cov.].

UK
TRENDS IN PRODUCTION OF LEAD AND ZINC. (1990)-. English. £30.00 UK; $50.00 US. International Lead and Zinc Study Group, Metro House, 58 St. James Street, London SW1A 1LD England. **Tel** 011 44 71 4999373, FAX 011 44 71 4933725, telex 299819 ILZSG G.
Desc: Reviews the development of world mine and metal production of lead and zinc since 1960 and the principal factors which have influenced their rates growth. Changes in the relative importance of main producing areas and individual countries are examined together with the proportion of world supply provided by newly industrialising and developing countries.

UK/0143-3911
TUNNELLING. (TUNNELLING : PROCEEDINGS OF THE INTERNATIONAL SYMPOSIUM.). [Tunnelling]. 1st (1976)-. Proceedings. English. ir. Institution of Mining and Metallurgy, 44 Portland Place, London W1N 4BR England. **Tel** 011 44 71 580-3802, FAX 011 44 71 436-5388, telex 261410. **ED** M J Jones. **LC** TA800; .T7897. **DD** 624.1/93/05. **Circ:** 650.
Desc: Proceedings of papers presented at international conferences held at three years intervals on tunnelling.
Ind/Abst GeoRef.

US
U.S. COAL MINE PRODUCTION BY SEAM. **Added/Corp** McGraw-Hill Mining Publications. Mining Informational Services. (1975)-. English. ir. $77.00. McGraw Hill Publishing Company, Inc., 1221 Avenue of the Americas, New York NY 10020. **Tel** (212)512-6410, (800)525-5003, FAX (212)512-6111. **(Subscription address:** McGraw Hill, 1221 Avenue of the Americas, 41st Floor, New York NY 10020.) **Circ:** 2,000.
Desc: Coal production by seam.

RU/0041-5790
UGOL. [Ugol]. **Added/Corp** Nauchno-Tekhnicheskoe Gornoe Obshchestvo. Tsentralnoe Upravlenie. Soviet Union. Obedinenie Gosudarstvennoi Kammenougolnoi Promyshlennosti Uglia i Vostuglia. Soviet Union. Ministerstvo Ugolnoi Promyshlennosti. Soviet Union. Gosudarstvennyi Nauchno-Tekhnicheskii Komitet. (1925)-. Academic Scholarly Publication. Russian. ir. $139.95. Izdatelstvo Nedra, 3 Pl Belorusskogo Vakzala, 125047 Moscow Russia. **Tel** 250-52-55. **(Subscription address:** East View Publications Inc., 3020 Harbor Lane North, Suite 110, Minneapolis MN 55447.) **CODEN** UGOLAR. **[CCC].** Index available. **Bk Rev. Ad Acc.** Documents available from Article Express International, CASDDS. ***Continues*** *Ugol i Zhelezo.*
Ind/Abst Bioeng. Abstr.; Chem. Abstr.; CIS Abstr.; Coal Abstr.; Ei Page One; Energy Res. Abstr. (June 1980-); Eng. Index Annu.; GeoRef; MINPROC; Saf. Health Work.

XR/0041-5812
UHLI, RUDY. ***Title Change.*** **Added/Corp** Zamestnavatelsky Svaz Dulniho a Naftoveho Prumyslu. (1992)-(1994). Periodical. Czech (Slovak; summaries and/or abstracts in English, French, German and Russian). **(Subscription address:** Artia Pegas Press Ltd., Palac Metro Narodni Trida 25, 11210 Prague 1 Czech Republic.) **CODEN** UHRUEC. ***Formed by the union of*** *Uhli (Prague, Czechoslovakia : 1959)* ***and*** *Rudy.* ***Merged with*** *Geologicky Pruzkum, 0016-772X* ***to form*** *Uhli-Rudy Geologicky Pruzkum, 1210-7697.*

US
UNITED STATES COAL PRODUCTION BY COMPANY. English. an. $40.00. McGraw Hill Publishing Company, Inc., 1221 Avenue of the Americas, New York NY 10020. **Tel** (212)512-6410, (800)525-5003, FAX (212)512-6111. **Circ:** 2,000.
Desc: Coal producers, 100,000 tons or more.

US
URANIUM INDUSTRY ANNUAL. **Added/Corp** United States. Office of Coal, Nuclear, Electric, and Alternate Fuels. (1984)-. English. an. $11.00 US. National Energy Information Center, Energy Information Administration, Forrestal Building, Room 1F-048, Washington DC 20585. **Tel** (202)586-8800. **LC** HD9539.U72; U58. **DD** 338.2/74932/0973021. ***Formed by the union of*** *Survey of U.S. Uranium Exploration Activity, 0743-6068* ***and*** *Survey of United States Uranium Marketing Activity, 0364-8672.*
Desc: A statistical profile of the U.S. uranium industry is presented in this report, based on data obtained from the domestic industry concerning the status of major industry activities as of December 31, 1985.
Ind/Abst Predicasts Forecasts (19??-).

US/0742-8502
URANIUM MILL TAILINGS MANAGEMENT. (URANIUM MILL TAILINGS MANAGEMENT : PROCEEDINGS OF A SYMPOSIUM ... / ORGANIZED BY THE GEOTECHNICAL ENGINEERING PROGRAM, CIVIL ENGINEERING DEPARTMENT, COLORADO STATE UNIVERSITY.). [Uranium mill tailings manage.]. 1st (Nov. 20, 21, 1978)-. Proceedings. English. an. Colorado State University, Fort Collins CO 80521. **Tel** (303)491-8652. **LC** TD899.U73; U74. **DD** 622/.34932.
Ind/Abst GeoRef.

US
VANADIUM / U.S. DEPARTMENT OF THE INTERIOR, BUREAU OF MINES. **See** Economics-Industry and Production.

GW
VERWALTUNGSBERICHT DES BEZIRKS CLAUSTHAL-ZELLERFELD DER BERGBAU-BERUFSGENOSSENSCHAFT. **Main/Corp** Bergbau-Berufsgenossenschaft. Bezirksverwaltung Clausthal-Zellerfeld. German. Bezirksverwaltung Clausthal-Zellerfeld der Bergbau-Berufsgenossenschaft, Berliner Strasse 2, 3392 Clausthal-Zellerfeld Germany. **LC** TN3; .B44143.

RU/0042-4633
VESTNIK MASINOSTROENIJA. (VESTNIK MASHINOSTROENIIA.). [Vestn. maŝinostr.]. **Added/Corp** Soviet Union. Ministerstvo Stroitelnogo i Dorozhnogo Mashinostroeniia. Soviet Union. Ministerstvo Sudostroitelnoi Promyshlennosti. Soviet Union. Ministerstvo Transportnogo Mashinostroeniia. Soviet Union. Ministerstvo Tiazhelogo Mashinostroeniia. Vol. 1 (Nov. 1921)-. Academic Scholarly Publication. Russian. mo. $129.95. **(Subscription address:** East View Publications Inc., 3020 Harbor Lane North, Suite 110, Minneapolis MN 55447.) **[CCC].** Documents available from Ask*IEEE, CASDDS. ***Continues*** *Tiazheloe Mashinostroenie.*

Ind/Abst Acoust. Abstr.; BMT Abstr.; Chem. Abstr.; Fluid Abstr., Civil Eng.; Fluid Abstr. Proc. Eng.; FLUIDEX (?-19??); INSPEC (1969-); Surf. Treat. Technol. Abstr.

US/0733-0545
WEEKLY COAL PRODUCTION. [Wkly. coal prod.]. **Added/Corp** United States. Energy Information Administration. United States. Office of Coal, Nuclear, Electric, and Alternate Fuels. **VFOAT** W.C.P.; WCP. (19??)-. Academic Scholarly Publication. English. wk. $77.00 US; $96.25 other. National Energy Information Center, Energy Information Administration, Forrestal Building, Room 1F-048, Washington DC 20585. **Tel** (202)586-8800. **CODEN** WCOPD2. Documents available from CASDDS. ***Continues** Weekly Coal Report, 0191-4367.*
Desc: Provides information on coal supply and demand, including production, consumption, prices, stocks, and exports. Gives data on United States production of bituminous, lignite, and anthracite coals.
Ind/Abst Chem. Abstr. (1982-1984).

US
WEST VIRGINIA COAL BELL. VFOAT Coal Bell. Began in Jan. 1981. Periodical. English. mo. Free. West Virginia Surface Mining & Reclamation Association, 1624 Kanawha Boulevard East, Charleston WV 25311. **Tel** (304)346-5318. **ED** Daniel Miller. **Ad Acc.**
Desc: News and editorial material relating to the coal industry, with emphasis on West Virginia.

US/0091-5513
WEST VIRGINIA COAL FACTS. [W. V. coal facts]. **Added/Corp** West Virginia Coal Association. (1971)-. English. an. $10.00. West Virginia Coal Association, 1301 Laidley Tower, Charleston WV 25301. **Tel** (304)342-4153. **LC** HD9547.W39; W48. **DD** 338.2/7/209754.

US/0743-5282
WEST VIRGINIA MINING DIRECTORY. [W. Va. min. dir.]. **VFOAT** Mining Directory. 1983 Ed.-. Directory. English. an. $29.95. Coal & Gas Computer Services Inc, PO Box 989, Blackburg VA 24061. **LC** HD9506.U63; W45. **DD** 338.7/622334/025754.

US/0162-9026
WESTERN MINING DIRECTORY. [West. min. dir.]. Vol. 1 (1978)-. Directory. English. an. $49.00. Howell Publishing Co., PO Box 37510, Denver CO 80237. **Tel** (303)770-6794, FAX (303)770-6796. **ED** Don E Howell. **LC** TN12; .W49. **DD** 338.2/025/78. **Bk Rev. Ad Acc. Circ:** 8,000.
Desc: Lists mines and mining companies in the western United States geographically and alphabetically. Equipment suppliers listed alphabetically by company and product.
Ind/Abst GeoRef.

AT/0159-1878
WHO'S DRILLING. See Petroleum and Natural Gas.

AT/0817-6353
WHO'S PEGGING. See Petroleum and Natural Gas.

CN/0226-7616
WORKING PAPER (QUEEN'S UNIVERSITY (KINGSTON, ONT.). CENTRE FOR RESOURCE STUDIES). (WORKING PAPER / CENTRE FOR RESOURCE STUDIES.). [Cent. Resour. Stud. work. pap.]. **Added/Corp** Queen's University (Kingston, Ont.). Centre for Resource Studies. **VFOAT** Centre for Resource Studies Working Paper. **VAT** Working Paper - Centre for Resource Studies. No. 1 (1977)-. Monographic series. English. ir. Price varies per volume. Centre for Resource Studies, Queen's University, Kingston Ontario K7L 3N6 Canada. **Tel** (613)545-2553, FAX (613)545-6651. **LC** UNC. **DD** 338.2/0971.
Desc: Working papers are usually the result of CRS-sponsored research.
Ind/Abst AESIS Q.

●UK/0968-3224
WORLD COAL DORKING. [World CoalDorking]. (1992)-. Periodical. English. mo. Tradeship Publications Limited, Old Kings Head Court, High Street, Dorking, Surrey RH4 1AR England. **Tel** 011 44 306 740363, 011 44 306 740383, FAX 011 44 306 740660, telex 94016994 CEMT. **ED** David Hargreaves, Catherine Read & Andrew Gaved.
Desc: Contains news, developments and corporate activity within the international coal industry.

US/1045-0343
WORLD DREDGING, MINING & CONSTRUCTION. [World dredg. min. constr.]. **VFOAT** World Dredging. Vol. 24, No. 7, (June/July 1988)-. Academic Scholarly Publication. English. mo. $28.00 (one year); $48.00 (two year); $62.00 (three year). Wodcon Association, PO Box 17479, Irvin CA 92713. **Tel** (714)553-0836. **DD** 622. Documents available from Article Express International. ***Continues** World Dredging & Marine Construction, 0043-8405.*
Ind/Abst AQUAREF; Aquat. Sci. Fish. Abstr. (Computer File); Bioeng. Abstr.; Ei Page One; EMBASE; Eng. Index Annu.; Fluid Abstr., Civil Eng.; Fluid Abstr. Proc. Eng.; FLUIDEX (1988-); Mintec, Min. Technol. Abstr.; Life Sci. Collect.

US
WORLD MINE PRODUCTION OF GOLD. Added/Corp Gold Institute. (19??)-. English. Gold Institute, 1112 16th Street Northwest, Suite 240, Washington DC 20036. **Tel** (202)835-0185, FAX (202)835-0155, telex 904233 DAV INC WSH. **LC** HD9536.A1; W67. **DD** 338.2/741/021.
Ind/Abst F&S Index Plus Text, Int. [Select. Cov.]; Predicasts Forecasts.

US/0746-729X
WORLD MINING EQUIPMENT. [World min. equip.]. Vol. 7, No. 11 (Nov. 1983)-. Academic Scholarly Publication. English. mo. $208.00 US, Canada & South America. Metal Bulletin PLC, PO Box 28E, Worcester Park, Surrey KT4 7HX England. **Tel** 011 44 71 827 9977, FAX 011 44 81 337 8943. **LC** TN345; .W69. **DD** 622/.028. **[CCC].** available on microfilm and microfiche from University Microfilms International (UMI). ***Formed by the union of** World Mining (San Francisco, Calif. : 1974), 0043-8707; World Coal, 0361-7483 **and** Mining Equipment International, 0192-902X.*
Ind/Abst Acad. Search (Jan. 1994-); AESIS Q.; Bus. Index (1985-); Bus. Period. Index; Coal Abstr.; EMBASE; Energy Res. Abstr. (Nov. 1983-); F&S Index Plus Text, Int. [Select. Cov.]; Fluid Abstr., Civil Eng.; Fluid Abstr. Proc. Eng.; FLUIDEX (1983-); Gen. BusinessFile (1985-); Gen. Period. Index (1985-); INFO-SOUTH Abstr.; Mag. Search; MINPROC; Mintec, Min. Technol. Abstr.; PROMT; Trade Ind. Index; Vocat. Search (Jan. 1993-).

UK
WORLD TUNNELLING & SUBSURFACE EXCAVATION. English. Ten times a year. £35.00 UK; £42.00, $75.00 other. Mining Journal Ltd., 60 Worship Street, London EC2A 2HD England. **Tel** 011 44 071 377 2020, FAX 071 247 4100, telex 8952809 MINING G. available on an online database (file 648/Full-Text) from DIALOG.

US/0511-0289
WYOMING DIRECTORY OF MANUFACTURING AND MINING. See Manufacturing.

RU/0514-1958
ZAKONOMERNOSTI RAZMESENIA POLEZNYH ISKOPAEMYH. See Earth Sciences-Mineralogy.

ZA
ZAMBIA MINING YEAR BOOK. (19??)-. English. Copper Industry Service Bureau, PO Box 2100, Kitwe Zambia. **LC** TN119.Z34; Z35. **DD** 338.2/09689/4.

XO
ZBORNIK SLOVENSKEHO BANSKEHO MUZEA. Began with Vol. for 1967. Periodical. Slovak (summaries and/or abstracts in German and Russian). 30.00. **LC** TN95.Y8; Z26.

PL/0372-9508
ZESZYTY NAUKOWE POLITECHNIKI SLASKIEJ. GORNICTWO. [Zesz. nauk., Politech. Sl., Gor.]. **Added/Corp** Politechnika Slaska im. W. Pstrowskiego. **VFOAT** Gornictwo; Zeszyty Naukowe. Gornictwo. (1956)-. Academic Scholarly Publication. Polish (summaries and/or abstracts in English, French, German and Russian). **LC** TN4; .G6. **CODEN** ZNSGAY. Documents available from CASDDS.
Ind/Abst Chem. Abstr.; Coal Abstr.; Energy Res. Abstr. (Oct. 1982-).

CH/0253-4347
ZHONGNAN KUANGYE XUEYUAN XUEBAO. (CHUNG-NAN KUANG YEH HSUEH YUAN HSUEH PAO.). [Zhongnan kuangye xueyuan xuebao]. **VFOAT** Journal of Central-South Institute of Mining and Metallurgy. Academic Scholarly Publication. Chinese (summaries and/or abstracts in English). bm. $18.00. Science Press, 16 Donghuangchenggen North Street, Beijing 100707, People's Republic of China. **Tel** 011 86 1 4019821, 011 86 1 4010642, FAX 011 86 1 4012180, 011 86 1 4019810, telex 210147. **ED** Zuo Tieyong. **LC** TN4; .C48. **DD** 622/.05. **CODEN** CKYPDO. **Ad Acc.** ctrl circ. Documents available from Article Express International, CASDDS.
Desc: Publishes articles on geology, mining, mineral engineering, nonferrous metallurgy, materials science and engineering, mechanical engineering, engineering of automatic control, computer science, chemistry, mathematics and physics.
Ind/Abst Alum. Ind. Abstr.; Bioeng. Abstr.; Chem. Abstr.; Ei Page One; Eng. Index Annu.; GeoRef.

AT/0158-7765
ZINC TODAY. [Zinc today]. (1969)-. Periodical. English. qt. **DD** 673.52.
Ind/Abst AESIS Q.

NUCLEAR ENGINEERING

FR
ACTIVITES SCIENTIFIQUES ET TECHNIQUES - COMMISSARIAT A L'ENERGIE ATOMIQUE. Main/Corp France. Commissariat a l'Energie Atomique. French. $384.00. New York Yomiuri Express, 500 5th Avenue/Suite 1927, New York NY 10110. **Tel** (212)661-5977. **LC** QC770; .F73A. **DD** 539.7/05.

US
ADVANCED TWO-PHASE FLOW INSTRUMENTATION PROGRAM QUARTERLY PROGRESS REPORT FOR ... . English. qt. GPO Sales Program, Division of Technical Information and Document Control, US Nuclear Regulatory Commission, Washington DC 20555.

US/0065-2989
ADVANCES IN NUCLEAR SCIENCE AND TECHNOLOGY. [Adv. nucl. sci. technol.]. Vol. 1 (1962)-. Monographic series. English. ir. Price varies per volume. Plenum Press, 233 Spring Street, New York NY 10013-1578. **Tel** (212)620-8000, (800)221-9369, FAX (212)463-0742, (212)807-1047, telex 23/421139. **LC** TK9001; .A3. **DD** 621.48058. **NLM** W1 AD685. **CODEN** ANUTAC. **[CCC].** Documents available from Article Express International, Ask*IEEE, CASDDS.
Ind/Abst Bioeng. Abstr.; Chem. Abstr.; Ei Page One; Energy Res. Abstr.; Eng. Index Annu.; INIS Atomindex [Micro.]; INSPEC.

US/1044-9876
AGENDA OF REGULATIONS. [Agenda regul.]. **Main/Corp** U.S. Nuclear Regulatory Commission. **VFOAT** U.S. Nuclear Regulatory Commission's Agenda of Regulations. (1989)-. English. an. $65.00. Nuclear Licensing Reports, PO Box 10866, Rockville MD 20850-0866. **Tel** (301)424-4132, FAX (301)762-2663. **ED** Joseph M. Felton. **LC** PAR. **DD** 621. Index available. cum. index. ctrl circ.
Desc: Contains all regulations proposed or under consideration by the NRC including an abstract of the rule the staff contact and the expected completion date.

US/0190-9673
ALI-ABA COURSE OF STUDY. ATOMIC ENERGY LICENSING AND REGULATION : MATERIALS. See Law.

UK/0306-4549
ANNALS OF NUCLEAR ENERGY. [Ann. nucl. energy]. Vol. 2 (Jan. 1975)-. Periodical. English. mo. $857.00 The Americas; £575.00 other. Pergamon Press, An Imprint of Elsevier Science Ltd., The Boulevard, Langford Lane, Kidlington, Oxford OX5 1GB United Kingdom. **Tel** 011 44 865 843000, 011 44 865 843699, FAX 011 44 865 843010. **(Subscription address:** Elsevier Science Ltd. Oxford Fulfillment Centre, PO Box 800, Kidlington, Oxford OX5 1DX United Kingdom.) **ED** L. E. Weaver and M. M. R. Williams. **LC** TK9001; .A55. **DD** 621.48/05. **NLM** W1 AN6153. **CODEN** ANENDJ. **[CCC]. Pr Rev.** available on microfilm from Microfilms International Marketing Corp.; available on microfilm and microfiche from University Microfilms International (UMI). Documents available from Article Express International, The Genuine Article, Ask*IEEE, CASDDS, Documents on Demand. ***Continues** Annals of Nuclear Science and Engineering, 0302-2927.*
Desc: Provides an international medium for the communication of original research, ideas and developments in all areas of the field of nuclear energy.
Ind/Abst Bioeng. Abstr.; Chem. Abstr.; Chem. Titles; Civ. Struct. Eng. Abstr.; Coal Abstr.; Comput. Inf. Syst. Abstr. J. [Full Cov.]; Curr. Contents Eng. Tech. Appl. Sci.; Curr. Technol. Index; Ei Page One; EMBASE; Energy Inf. Abstr.; Energy Res. Abstr. (Oct. 1975-); Eng. Index Annu.; Environ. Abstr.; Environ. Eng. Abstr.; Environ. Period. Bibliogr.; Health Saf. Sci. Abstr.; HTFS Dig.; INIS Atomindex [Micro.]; INSPEC (Jan. 1975-); Math. Rev.; Mech. Eng. Abstr.; Pollut. Abstr. Indexes; Res. Alert [Full Cov.]; Sci. Cit. Index; SCISEARCH; Soc. Sci. Cit. Index [Select. Cov.].

CN/0227-0129
ANNUAL CONFERENCE. CONFERENCE SUMMARIES - CANADIAN NUCLEAR SOCIETY. (CONFERENCE SUMMARIES / CANADIAN NUCLEAR SOCIETY, ANNUAL CONFERENCE.). [Annu. conf., Conf. summ. - Can. Nucl. Soc.]. **Main/Corp** Canadian Nuclear Society. Conference. **VFOAT** Summaries for Annual Conference of Canadian Nuclear Society; Sommaries de la Conference; Sommaires du Congres. **VAT** Congres Annuel. Sommaires du Congres - Societe Nucleaire Canadienne (1983). (1981)-. English. ir. 10.00Can$ Canada; $15.00 others. Canadian Nuclear Association, 144 Front Street West, Suite 725, Toronto Ontario M5J 2L7 Canada. **Tel** (416)977-6152, (416)977-7620, FAX (416)979-8356, telex 06-23741. **LC** TK9006; .C35a. **DD** 621.48/305. **Circ:** 400. Documents available from Article Express International. ***Continues***

Canadian Nuclear Society. Conference. Transactions, 0226-7470.
Ind/Abst Bioeng. Abstr.; Ei Page One; Eng. Index Annu.

CN/0227-1907
ANNUAL CONFERENCE. PROCEEDINGS - CANADIAN NUCLEAR SOCIETY. (PROCEEDINGS, ... ANNUAL CONFERENCE.). [Annu. conf., Proc. - Can. Nucl. Soc.]. **Main/Corp** Canadian Nuclear Society. Conference. **VFOAT** Comptes Rendus, ... Congres Annuel. 2nd (1981)-. Academic Scholarly Publication. English (summaries and/or abstracts in French). an. 65.00Can$ (members), 75.00Can$ (nonmembers). Canadian Nuclear Association, 144 Front Street West, Suite 725, Toronto Ontario M5J 2L7 Canada. **Tel** (416)977-6152, (416)977-7620, FAX (416)979-8356, telex 06-23741. **LC** TK9006. **DD** 621.48. **CODEN** CCSCDZ. **Circ:** 150. Documents available from Ask*IEEE, CASDDS. ***Continues** Canadian Nuclear Society. Conference. Comptes Rendus, Congres Annuel, 0227-7153.*
Desc: Full text of technical papers presented at Canadian Nuclear Society Annual Conference.
Ind/Abst Chem. Abstr.; INSPEC.

CN/0706-1293
ANNUAL INTERNATIONAL CONFERENCE / CANADIAN NUCLEAR ASSOCIATION. [Annu. int. conf. - Can. Nucl. Assoc.]. **Main/Corp** Canadian Nuclear Association. International Conference. **VFOAT** Congres International Annuel. (1973)-. Academic Scholarly Publication. English (French). an. 80.00Can$ (members), 90.00Can$ (nonmembers). Canadian Nuclear Association, 144 Front Street West, Suite 725, Toronto Ontario M5J 2L7 Canada. **Tel** (416)977-6152, (416)977-7620, FAX (416)979-8356, telex 06-23741. **LC** TK9026; .C35a. **DD** 621.48/05. **CODEN** PNICDZ. **Circ:** 150. Documents available from Article Express International, CASDDS. ***Continues** Canadian Nuclear Association. Conference. Proceedings of the Annual Conference, 0317-168X.*
Desc: Full text of papers presented at the Canadian Nuclear Association annual conference.
Ind/Abst Chem. Abstr. (1961-1981); Eng. Index Annu.

AT
ANNUAL REPORT / AUSTRALIAN NUCLEAR SCIENCE AND TECHNOLOGY ORGANISATION. **Main/Corp** Australian Nuclear Science and Technology Organisation. **Added/Corp** Australian Atomic Energy Commission. **VFOAT** Implementing Strategies for Change. (1986/87)-. English. an. Australian Nuclear Science and Technology Organisation, Private Bag 1, Menai NSW 2234 Australia. **Tel** FAX 011 61 2 5439274. **LC** HD9698.A8; A3. **DD** 333.792/4/072094. ***Continues** Annual Report - Australian Atomic Energy Commission, 0519-4849.*

US/0363-7956
ANNUAL REPORT / U.S. NUCLEAR REGULATORY COMMISSION. ***Suspended.*** [Annu. rep. - U.S. Nucl. Regul. Comm.]. **Main/Corp** U.S. Nuclear Regulatory Commission. **VAT** Annual Report - United States Nuclear Regulatory Commission. (1975)-(19??). English. an. Superintendent of Documents, US Government Printing Office, Washington DC 20402. **Tel** (202)275-3328, FAX (202)786-2377. **LC** TK9152; .U55a. **DD** 621.48/35. ***Continues** United States. Atomic Energy Commission. Annual Report to Congress, 0082-8815.*

LU
ANNUAL STATUS REPORT. THERMONUCLEAR FUSION TECHNOLOGY / COMMISSION OF THE EUROPEAN COMMUNITIES. **Added/Corp** Commission of the European Communities. Joint Research Centre. Commission of the European Communities. Joint Research Centre. Multiannual Programme of the Joint Research Centre, 1980-1983. **VFOAT** Thermonuclear Fusion Technology. (19??)-. English. an. **LC** TK9204; .A56. **DD** 621.48/4.

US/0091-875X
ANNUAL SUMMARY REPORT. PROGRESS AND PLANS - AMES LABORATORY, U.S.A.E.C. (ANNUAL SUMMARY REPORT : PROGRESS AND PLANS). **Main/Corp** Ames Laboratory. **VAT** Annual Summary Report. Progress and Plans - Ames Laboratory, United States Atomic Energy Commission. English. an. $3.00. National Technical Information Service - NTIS, Room 2027S, 5285 Port Royal Road, Springfield VA 22161. **Tel** (703)487-4630, (703)487-4660, (703)487-4650, FAX (703)321-8547, telex 89-9405. **LC** Z5160; .U552A. **DD** 621.48/1.

US/0737-6812
ANS NEWS. [ANS news]. **Added/Corp** American Nuclear Society. **VFOAT** A.N.S. news. (198?)-. Periodical. English. Twelve times a year. $90.00. American Nuclear Society, PO Box 97781, Chicago IL 60678-7781. **Tel** (708)352-6611, FAX (708)579-8314.

SW
ANSLAGSFRAMSTALLNING FOR BUDGETARET. **Main/Corp** Sweden. Statens Karnkraftinspektion. Swedish. Statens Karnkraftinspektion, Box 27 106, 102 52 Stockholm Sweden. **LC** TK9089; .S94A.

AT/1030-7745
ANSTO/E. **See** Science and Technology.

PH/0115-3757
ATOMEDIA, PHILIPPINES. [Atomedia Philipp.]. **Added/Corp** Philippine Atomic Energy Commission. Vol. 1 (1975)-. English. Philippine Atomic Energy Commission, Don Mariano Marcos Avenue, Quezon City Philippines. **LC** TK9113.P6; A86. **DD** 333.7.
Ind/Abst Energy Res. Abstr. (Jan. 1982-).

●US/1063-4258
ATOMIC ENERGY (NEW YORK, N.Y.). (ATOMIC ENERGY.). [At. energy]. **Added/Corp** Consultants Bureau. **VFOAT** Atomnaia Energiia; Atomnaya Energiya. (1992)-. Academic Scholarly Publication. English (translations available in Russian). mo. $1295.00 US; $1515.00 other. Consultants Bureau, A Division of Plenum Publishing Corporation, 233 Spring Street, New York NY 10013. **Tel** (212)620-8000, (212)620-8466, FAX (212)463-0742, telex 23/421139. **LC** QC770; .A843. **DD** 539. **CODEN** AENYEZ. **[CCC].** Documents available from CASDDS, Documents on Demand. ***Continues** Atomnaia Energiia. English. Soviet Atomic Energy, 0038-531X.*
Ind/Abst Appl. Mech. Rev.; Bioeng. Abstr.; Chem. Abstr.; Energy Inf. Abstr.; Environ. Abstr.; Pollut. Abstr. Indexes; Sci. Cit. Index; Soc. Sci. Cit. Index [Select. Cov.].

US
ATOMIC ENERGY NEWSLETTER. Began with issue for Mar. 1, 1949. Newsletter. English. wk. $495.00 US; $618.00 (surface mail), $725.00 (airmail) other. Congressional Information Bureau, 3030 Clarendon Boulevard, Suite 202, Arlington VA 22201. **Tel** (703)516-4801. **ED** Elizabeth Wright. **LC** TK9001; .A785. **DD** 621.48/05. **Bk Rev.**
Desc: United States and international nuclear power news since 1955. Includes inside information on NRC, Congress, the courts, industry and utilities. Free introductory issue available.

RU
ATOMNO-VODORODNAIA ENERGETIKA I TEKHNOLOGIIA. [At-vodorodnaja energ. tehnol.]. **VFOAT** Nuclear-Hydrogen Energy and Technology. (1978)-. Academic Scholarly Publication. Russian (summaries and/or abstracts in English). an. 3.00rub. Atomizdat, Ulitsa Zhdanova 5, 103031 Moscow K-31 Russia. **LC** TK1078; .A72. **CODEN** AVETDP. Documents available from CASDDS.
Ind/Abst Chem. Abstr.; Energy Res. Abstr. (Jan. 1982-); Int. Aerosp. Abstr.

RU
ATOMNYE ELEKTRICHESKIE STANTSII. (1977)-. Periodical. Russian. **LC** TK1078; .A73. **CODEN** AESTDA. Documents available from CASDDS.
Ind/Abst Chem. Abstr.

IT/0004-7171
ATOMO E INDUSTRIA. ***Ceased.*** Vol. 1 (1957)-(Jan. 1988). Periodical. Italian. Ed Atomoc Ind Srl, Via Paisiello 26128, 00198 Rome Italy.

JA
ATOMS IN JAPAN. **See** Energy.

GW/0365-8414
ATOMWIRTSCHAFT, ATOMTECHNIK. [Atomwirtsch., atomtech.]. Year 10- Jan. 1965-. Academic Scholarly Publication. German (summaries and/or abstracts in English and French). mo. DM198.00 Germany; DM186.00 US. Handelsblatt GmbH, Postfach 102716, D-40018 Duesseldorf Germany. **Tel** 011 49 211 8871730. **LC** TK9001; .A97. **CODEN** AWAKAG. **[CCC].** Index available. cum. index. **Bk Rev. Ad Acc. Pr Rev.** ctrl circ. available on microfilm and microfiche from University Microfilms International (UMI). Documents available from Article Express International, The Genuine Article, Ask*IEEE, CASDDS, Documents on Demand. ***Continues** Atomwirtschaft.*
Desc: All items of the peaceful uses of nuclear energy.
Ind/Abst Art Archaeol. Tech. Abstr.; Bioeng. Abstr.; Chem. Abstr.; Coal Abstr.; Curr. Contents Eng. Tech. Appl. Sci.; Ei Page One; EMBASE; Energy Res. Abstr.; Eng. Index Annu.; Environ. Abstr.; GeoRef; INSPEC (Jan. 1969-); Res. Alert [Full Cov.]; Sci. Cit. Index; SCISEARCH; Soc. Sci. Cit. Index [Select. Cov.].

UN/0005-111X
AVTOMATICESKAJA SVARKA (KIEV). **See** Engineering-Electricity, Electrical Engineering, Electronics.

JA/0387-6144
BULLETIN OF THE RESEARCH LABORATORY FOR NUCLEAR REACTORS. [Bull. Res. Lab. Nucl. React.]. (1976)-. Periodical. English. an. Tokyo Institute of Technology / Nuclear Research, Research Laboratory for Nuclear Reactors, Tokyo 152 Japan. **DD** 621.48. Documents available from Ask*IEEE, CASDDS.
Ind/Abst Chem. Abstr.; INSPEC (1976-).

US/0078-2610
BUYER'S GUIDE (HINSDALE, ILL.). (NUCLEAR NEWS BUYERS GUIDE.). **Added/Corp** American Nuclear Society. **VFOAT** Nuclear News Buyer's Guide. (1969)-. Consumer Publication. English. an. $70.00. American Nuclear Society, PO Box 97781, Chicago IL 60678-7781. **Tel** (708)352-6611, FAX (708)579-8314. **ED** Jon Payne. **LC** TK9012; .N82. **DD** 338.4/7/62148025. **Ad Acc. Circ:** 16,000.
Desc: An alphabetical listing of nuclear products, materials and services, with the companies that supply these items. About 500 product categories are included. Over 2,000 suppliers listed.

FR/1157-741X
CHOCS (VILLENEUVE-SAINT-GEORGES). (CHOCS : REVUE SCIENTIFIQUE ET TECHNIQUE DE LA DIRECTION DES APPLICATIONS MILITAIRES.). **Added/Corp** France. Commissariat a l'Energie Atomique. Direction des Applications Militaires. **VFOAT** Revue Scientifique et Technique de la Direction des Applications Militaires. No. 1 (Feb. 1991)-. Periodical. French (summaries and/or abstracts in English). sa. Commissariat a l'Energie Atomique, Centre d'Etudes de Limeil-Valenton, 94195 Billeneuve-Saint Georges Cedex France. **Tel** 45 95 61 46. **ED** Alain Gourod. **LC** TK9001; .C56. **DD** 621.48/0944.
Ind/Abst Int. Aerosp. Abstr.

US/0272-6777
COMPANIES HOLDING NUCLEAR CERTIFICATES OF AUTHORIZATION. [Co. hold. nucl. certif. auth.]. **Main/Corp** American Society of Mechanical Engineers. (19??)-. English. bm. $65.00. American Society of Mechanical Engineers, 22 Law Drive, Fairfield NJ 07007. **Tel** (201)882-1167, (212)705-7722 (editorial). **LC** TK9012; .A43a. **DD** 621.48/025/73. **Bk Rev. Ad Acc.**
Desc: Companies holding nuclear certificates of ASME and physical list.

US/0254-3427
CSNI REPORT. [CSNI rep.]. **VFOAT** C.S.N.I Report. **VAT** Committee on the Safety of Nuclear Installations Report. Academic Scholarly Publication. English. Price varies per volume. GPO Sales Program, Division of Technical Information and Document Control, US Nuclear Regulatory Commission, Washington DC 20555. **CODEN** CSRPDB. Documents available from CASDDS.
Ind/Abst Chem. Abstr.

JA
DONEN. **Main/Corp** Doryokuro Kakunenryo Kaihatsu Jigyodan. Periodical. Japanese. Doryokuro Kakunenryo Kaihatsu Jigyodan, (Power Reactor & Nuclear Fuel Development Corp.), 9-13, Akasaka 1 Chome, Minatoku, Tokyoto 107 Japan. **LC** TK9202; .D67B.

US
EDDY-CURRENT INSPECTION FOR STEAM GENERATOR TUBING PROGRAM ANNUAL PROGRESS REPORT FOR PERIOD ENDING ... / OAK RIDGE NATIONAL LABORATORY, METALS AND CERAMICS DIVISION. English. an. GPO Sales Program, Division of Technical Information and Document Control, US Nuclear Regulatory Commission, Washington DC 20555. available on microfiche (Vols. for 1981- distributed to depository libraries).

US/0739-5159
ELECTRICAL OVERSTRESS/ELECTROSTATIC DISCHARGE SYMPOSIUM PROCEEDINGS. [Electr. Overstress/Electrost. Disch. Symp. proc.]. **Main/Conf** Electrical Overstress/Electrostatic Discharge Symposium. **VFOAT** E.S.D./E.D.S. Symposium Proceedings; ESD/EOS Symposium Proceedings. EOS-1 (1979)-. Proceedings. English. an. $25.00 (members), $40.00 (nonmembers). EOS / ESD Association Inc, 200 Liberty Plaza, Rome NY 13440. **Tel** (315)339-6937. **LC** TK7869; .E39A. **DD** 621.381. **CODEN** EOEPD8. Documents available from Article Express International.
Desc: Covers a wide range of topics on the EOS/ESD field. Range from factory issues and materials evaluation through modeling, design, failure analysis, etc.
Ind/Abst Bioeng. Abstr.; Ei Page One; Eng. Index Annu.

BL/0100-3593
ENERGIA NUCLEAR E AGRICULTURA. [Energ. nucl. agric.]. **Added/Corp** Universidade de Sao Paulo. Centro de Energia Nuclear na Agricultura. (Jan./June 1979)-. Academic Scholarly Publication. Portuguese (English; summaries and/or abstracts in English). sa. $10.00. Centro de Energia Nuclear Na Agricultura, Caixa Postal 96, 13.400 Piracicaba, Sao Paulo Brazil. **Tel** (0194)335122, telex (019)1097 CENA. **ED** Frederico W Wiendl. **CODEN** ENAGDM. Index

available. **Bk Rev.** **Ad Acc.** **Circ:** 500. Documents available from BIOSIS Document Express, CASDDS. ***Continues*** *Boletim Cientifico (Universidade de Sao Paulo. Centro de Energia Nuclear na Agricultura), 0100-2384.*
Ind/Abst Agrindex; Biol. Abstr.; Chem. Abstr.; Energy Res. Abstr. (Oct. 1979-).

SP/0013-7324
ENERGIA NUCLEAR (MADRID).
Suspended. (ENERGIA NUCLEAR.). [Energ. nucl.]. Vol. 1- (No. 1- Jan./March 1957)-Suspended with Vol. 6 (1985). Academic Scholarly Publication. Spanish. qt. Centro Nacl Energia Nuclear, Ciudad Universitaria, Madrid 3 Spain. **LC** TK9001; .E48. **CODEN** ENNCA4. **[CCC].** cum. index. Documents available from Ask*IEEE, CASDDS.
Ind/Abst Chem. Abstr. (1957-1985); INSPEC (Jan./Feb. 1972-).

IT/0013-7332
ENERGIA NUCLEARE (MILANO).
(ENERGIA NUCLEARE.). [Energ. nucl.]. **Added/Corp** Centro informazioni Studi Esperienze, Milan. Yearly Vol. 1 (Nov. 15, 1951)-. Academic Scholarly Publication. Italian. Three times a year. L40000 Italy; L50000 other. ENEA, V le Regina Margherita 125, 00198 Rome Italy. **Tel** 011 39 6 85281, . **CODEN** ENNLAV. Documents available from Article Express International, Ask*IEEE, CASDDS.
Ind/Abst Chem. Abstr.; Ei Page One; EMBASE; Energy Res. Abstr.; Eng. Mater. Abstr.; Eng. Index Annu.; INSPEC (1969-1973); Int. Aerosp. Abstr.; Saf. Health Work.

IT
ENERGIA NUCLEARE (ROME, ITALY).
(ENERGIA NUCLEARE.). (Dec. 1984)-. Academic Scholarly Publication. Italian (English). ir. ENEA, V le Regina Margherita 125, 00198 Rome Italy. **Tel** 011 39 6 85281, . **LC** QC770; .E53. **DD** 621.48/05. **CODEN** ENNUES. Documents available from CASDDS.
Ind/Abst Chem. Abstr. (1985-).

US/1056-9030
ENFORCEMENT ACTIONS.
(ENFORCEMENT ACTIONS : SIGNIFICANT ACTIONS RESOLVED.). [Enforc. actions]. **Main/Corp** U.S. Nuclear Regulatory Commission. Office of Enforcement. **VFOAT** Significant Actions Resolved. Periodical. English. qt. $22.00 US; $27.50 other. Nuclear Regulatory Commission, 1717 H Street NW, Washington DC 20555. **Tel** (301)492-7000. **DD** 353. ***Continues*** *Enforcement Actions, 1056-9030.*

SZ/0379-4229
EUROPEAN APPLIED RESEARCH REPORTS. NUCLEAR SCIENCE AND TECHNOLOGY SECTION.
[Eur. appl. res. rep., Nucl. sci. technol.]. **Added/Corp** Commission of the European Communities. Directorate-General for Scientific and Technical Information and Information Management. Vol. 1, No. 1 (1979)-. Academic Scholarly Publication. English. $1865.00 (academic institutions), $2909.00 (corporate institutions). Harwood Academic Publishers, PO Box 90, Reading RG1 8JL England. **Tel** 011 44 734 560080. **(Subscription address:** International Publishers Distributor at one of the following addresses: 820 Town Center Drive, Langhorne, PA 19047; or PO Box 90, Reading Berkshire RG1 8JL UK; or Kent Ridge PO Box 1180, Singapore 9111, Republic of Singapore**)** **ED** Edward Phillips. **LC** TK9001; .E85. **DD** 621.48/05. **CODEN** EARRDF. **[CCC].** Index available. **Bk Rev.** **Ad Acc.** **Pr Rev.** Documents available from Article Express International, Ask*IEEE, CASDDS.
Desc: Publishes papers covering all applied research areas in nuclear science and technology which have been sponsored by or published in collaboration with the commission of the European Communities.
Ind/Abst Alum. Ind. Abstr.; Bioeng. Abstr.; Chem. Abstr.; Ei Page One; EMBASE; Eng. Index Annu.; INSPEC (1979-); Met. Abstr.

AT/0725-783X
FLINDERS UNIVERSITY OF SOUTH AUSTRALIA. INSTITUTE FOR ATOMIC STUDIES, FIAS-R.
(FIAS-R / FLINDERS UNIVERSITY OF SOUTH AUSTRALIA, INSTITUTE FOR ATOMIC STUDIES, SCHOOL OF PHYSICAL SCIENCES.). **Added/Corp** Flinders University of South Australia. Institute for Atomic Studies. (Mar. 1976)-. Periodical. English. Flinders University, South Australia Crnle, Bedford Park South Australia 5042 Australia. **Tel** 2752459. **CODEN** FUSFDX. Documents available from CASDDS.
Ind/Abst Chem. Abstr.

US/0163-3856
FUSION ENERGY UPDATE.
Ceased. (July 1977)-Ceased (Dec. 1986). Periodical. English. mo. National Technical Information Service - NTIS, Room 2027S, 5285 Port Royal Road, Springfield VA 22161. **Tel** (703)487-4630, (703)487-4660, (703)487-4650, FAX (703)321-8547, telex 89-9405. **LC** TK9204; .F88. **DD** 621.48/4.

NE/0920-3796
FUSION ENGINEERING AND DESIGN.
Vol. 5, No. 1 (April 1987)-. Periodical. English. Sixteen times a year (4 volumes). 2120.00F. Elsevier Sequoia SA, PO Box 564, CH-1001 Lausanne 1 Switzerland. **Tel** 011 41 21 3207381. **ED** Robert W. Conn, G. Casini, P. Konarek, G.L. Kulcinski, A. Miyahara and K. Tomabechi. **[CCC].** **Pr Rev.** available on microfilm and microfiche from University Microfilms International (UMI). Documents available from Article Express International, The Genuine Article, Ask*IEEE, CASDDS. ***Continues*** *Nuclear Engineering and Design/Fusion.*
Desc: The journal accepts papers of a theoretical, analytical, methods, related, and experimental nature in fusion technology, particularly dealing with structural mechanics, heat transfer, thermal hydraulics, materials behaviour, vacuum technology, mechanical design and reactor safety.
Ind/Abst Chem. Abstr.; Curr. Contents Eng. Tech. Appl. Sci.; Ei Page One; Energy Inf. Abstr.; Eng. Index Annu.; INSPEC (April 1987-); Res. Alert [Full Cov.]; Risk Abstr.; Sci. Cit. Index; SCISEARCH.

US/0276-2919
FUSION POWER REPORT.
See Energy.

US/0748-1896
FUSION TECHNOLOGY.
(FUSION TECHNOLOGY : A JOURNAL OF THE AMERICAN NUCLEAR SOCIETY AND THE EUROPEAN NUCLEAR SOCIETY.). [Fus. technol.]. **Added/Corp** American Nuclear Society. European Nuclear Society. Vol. 6, No. 1 (July 1984)-. Periodical. English. ir (8 issues). $560.00 (includes 3 additional supplements). American Nuclear Society, PO Box 97781, Chicago IL 60678-7781. **Tel** (708)352-6611, FAX (708)579-8314. **LC** TK9204; .N82. **DD** 621.48/4/05. **CODEN** FUSTE8. **Pr Rev.** Documents available from Article Express International, The Genuine Article, Ask*IEEE, CASDDS. ***Continues*** *Nuclear Technology/Fusion, 0272-3921.*
Ind/Abst Appl. Sci. Technol. Index; Bioeng. Abstr.; Chem. Abstr. (1984-); Chem. Titles; Curr. Contents Eng. Tech. Appl. Sci.; Ei Page One; Energy Inf. Abstr.; Eng. Mater. Abstr.; Eng. Index Annu.; HTFS Dig.; INIS Atomindex [Micro.]; INSPEC (July 1984-); Int. Aerosp. Abstr. (1984-); Mech. Eng. Abstr.; Res. Alert [Full Cov.]; Sci. Cit. Index; SCISEARCH.

JA
GENKEN KENKYU SEIKA SHOROK SHU.
Main/Corp Nihon Genshiryoku Kinkyujo. **VFOAT** Jaeri Reports Abstracts. Japanese (Japanese). Nihon Genshiryoku Kenkyujo, Ibaraki-ken 319-11 Japan. **LC** QC770; .N53A.

JA
GENSHIRYOKU ANZEN IINKAI GEPPO.
Main/Corp Japan. Genshiryoku Anzen Iinkai. **VFOAT** Nuclear Safety Commission Monthly Report. Japanese (Japanese). $110.00. Kagaku Gijutsucho Genshiryoku Anzenkyoku Anzenka Genshiryoku Anzen Chosashitsu, 2-1 Kasumigaseki, Chiyoda-ku 100, Tokyo Japan. **LC** TK9152; .J34A.
Ind/Abst Energy Res. Abstr. (Jan. 1981-).

JA
GENSHIRYOKU KISEI KANKEI HOREISHU / KAGAKU GIJUTSUCHO GENSHIRYOKU ANZENKYOKU KANSHU.
Added/Corp Japan. Kagaku Gijutsucho. Genshiryoku Anzenkyoku. Japanese. ¥3100. Taisei Shuppansha, 1-7-11 Hanegi 1, Setagaya-ku, Tokyo-to Japan. **LC** LAW.

JA/0433-4035
GENSHIRYOKU KOGYO.
Added/Corp Nikkan Kogyo Shinbunsha. **VFOAT** Nuclear Engineering. (1955)-. Periodical. Japanese (summaries and/or abstracts in English). mo. $276.00. Nikkan Kogyo Shinbusha, 8-10 Kudan Kita 1 Chiyoda-ku, Tokyo-to 102 Japan. **(Subscription address:** Kyowa Book Co., Inc., 1-38 Kanda Jinbo-Cho Chiyoda-Ku, Tokyo 101, Japan**)** **CODEN** GKOGAM. Documents available from CASDDS.
Ind/Abst Chem. Abstr.

US/0162-7899
GROUNDSWELL.
Ceased. [Groundswell]. Vol. 1 (Sept. 15 1978)-(Oct. 19??). Periodical. English. bm. Nuclear Info and Resource Svc, 1424 16th Street NW/Suite 601, Washington DC 20036. **Tel** (202)328-0002. **ED** Michael Mariotte. **DD** 363. **Bk Rev.** **Circ:** 900.
Desc: Covers the nuclear power industry, the courts, congress, the NRC and anti-nuclear power activism. In-depth treatment of major nuclear power issues.
Ind/Abst Altern. Press Index (-1992).

FR
GUIDE INTERNATIONAL DE L'ENERGIE NUCLEAIRE.
VFOAT International Nuclear Energy Guide; Nuclear Guide; Guide Nucleaire. Began in 1978. French (English). an. 605.00F France; 110.00F US. Societe des Editions Technip, 27 rue Ginoux, 75737 Paris Cedex 15 France. **Tel** 011 33 1 45771108, telex 200 375 F EDITECP. **LC** TK9071; .G85. **DD** 621.48/0944. ***Continues*** *Guide International de l'Energie Atomique.*
Desc: This yearbook analyses the companies and bodies working in the nuclear field and gives the latest technological developments in this branch.

KO
HANGUK ENOJI YONGUSO HWIBO.
VFOAT K.A.E.R.I. Journal; KAERI Journal. V. 1- (July, 1981)-. Periodical. Korean. sa. Korea Advanced Energy Research Institute, 150 Dukjin-dong Yusoung-ku, Daejon 302-353 Republic of Korea. **Tel** (042)820-2000, FAX (042)820-2702, telex KAERI K45553. **ED** Han Pil-Soon. **LC** TK1364.K6; H36.

CC/0258-0926
HEDONGLI GONGCHENG.
[Hedongli gongcheng]. **VFOAT** Nuclear Power Engineering. (1980)-. Periodical. Chinese. bm. Zhongguo Hexuehui, Beijing, People's Republic of China. **UDC** 623. Documents available from CASDDS.
Ind/Abst Chem. Abstr.

CH/0253-3219
HEJISHU.
(HO CHI SHU.). [Hejishu]. **VFOAT** Nuclear Techniques. Academic Scholarly Publication. Chinese (Chinese). bm. NT$57.60 (surface mail). Science Press, 16 Donghuangchenggen North Street, Beijing 100707, People's Republic of China. **Tel** 011 86 1 4019821, 011 86 1 4010642, FAX 011 86 1 4012180, 011 86 1 4019810, telex 210147. **LC** TK9001; .H58. **CODEN** NUTEDL. Documents available from Ask*IEEE, CASDDS.
Ind/Abst Art Archaeol. Tech. Abstr.; Chem. Abstr.; INSPEC (Feb. 1981-).

US
HIGH-TEMPERATURE GAS-COOLED REACTOR SAFETY STUDIES FOR THE DIVISION OF ACCIDENT EVALUATION QUARTERLY PROGRESS REPORT.
Apr. 1-June 30, 1982-. Periodical. English. qt. Government Printing Office Sales Program, Division of Technical Information and Document Control, US Nuclear Regulatory Commission, Washington DC 20555. available on microfiche (Vols. for Oct. 1-Dec. 31, 1982- distributed to depository libraries). ***Continues*** *High-Temperature Gas-Cooled Reactor Safety Studies for the Division of Reactor Safety Research Quarterly Progress Report.*

JA/0914-899X
HITACHI CABLE REVIEW.
[Hitachi Cable rev.]. **VFOAT** Technical Journal of Hitachi Cable, Ltd. (1982)-. Periodical. English. an. Free. Hitachi Cable Review, Engineering Department, 1-2 Marunouchi 2-chome, Chiyoda-ku Tokyo 100 Japan. **Tel** 011 81 3 2161611. **ED** Takashi Yagi. **DD** 621.319.

CC
HO KO HSUEH YU KUNG CHENG.
Added/Corp Chung-kuo ho Hsueh Hui. **VFOAT** Chinese Journal of Nuclear Science and Engineering. (19??)-. Periodical. Chinese (summaries and/or abstracts in English). qt. Pei-Ching Pao Kan Fa Hsing Chu, Beijing, People's Republic of China. **Tel** 483531. **LC** TK9001; .H6. **DD** 621.48/05.
Ind/Abst HTFS Dig.

CH
HO NENG I CHI TSU NIEN TU KUNG TSO PAO KAO.
Main/Corp Ho Neng yen Chiu So. Ho Neng i Chi Tsu. Periodical. Chinese (summaries and/or abstracts in English). an. **LC** TK9178; .H6A. **DD** 621.48/3.

BU/0204-6989
IADERNAIA ENERGIIA / BOLGARSKAIA AKADEMIIA NAUK.
Added/Corp Institut za Iadreni Izsledvaniia i Iadrena Energetika (Bulgarska Akademiia na Naukite). **VFOAT** Nuclear Energy. (1985)-. Academic Scholarly Publication. Russian (summaries and/or abstracts in English; table of contents in English and Russian). bm. 1.35lv. Bulgarska Akademiia na Naukite, 7 Noemvri 1, Sofia Bulgaria. **ED** V. Khristov. **CODEN** YAENEN. Documents available from Ask*IEEE, CASDDS. ***Continues*** *IAdrena Energiia.*
Ind/Abst Ceram. Abstr.; Chem. Abstr.; INSPEC (1981-); Int. Aerosp. Abstr.

US/0018-9499
IEEE TRANSACTIONS ON NUCLEAR SCIENCE.
[IEEE trans. nucl. sci.]. **Added/Corp** Institute of Electrical and Electronics Engineers. Professional Technical Group on Nuclear Science. Institute of Electrical and Electronics Engineers. Nuclear Science Group. IEEE Nuclear Science Group. IEEE Nuclear and Plasma Sciences Society. **VFOAT** Transactions on Nuclear Science; Nuclear Science. Vol. NS-10, No. 1 (Jan. 1963)-. Periodical. English. bm. $200.00. IEEE, Institution of Electrical and Electronics Engineers, Inc., 345 East 47th Street, New York NY 10017-2394. **Tel** (908)981-1393, FAX (908)981-9667. **(Subscription address:** IEEE / Institute of Electrical and Electronics Engineers, 445 Hoes Lane, PO Box 1331, Piscataway NJ 08855-1331.**)** **LC** TK9001; .I2. **CODEN** IETNAE. **[CCC].** cum. index. **Pr Rev.** Documents available from Article Express International, The Genuine Article, Ask*IEEE, CASDDS, Documents on Demand. ***Continues*** *IRE Transactions on Nuclear Science, 0096-2015.*
Desc: Covers all aspects of the theory and application of nuclear science and engineering, including instrumentation, high energy physics, reactor controls,

and radiation effects.
Ind/Abst Acoust. Abstr.; Bioeng. Abstr.; Ceram. Abstr.; Chem. Abstr.; Coal Abstr.; Curr. Contents Eng. Tech. Appl. Sci.; Curr. Contents Phys. Chem. Earth Sci.; Ei Page One; EMBASE; Energy Inf. Abstr.; Energy Res. Abstr.; Eng. Index Annu.; Environ. Abstr.; Expand. Acad. Index (1992-); Index IEEE Publ.; INIS Atomindex [Micro.]; INSPEC (1968-); Int. Aerosp. Abstr.; Life Sci. Collect.; Res. Alert [Full Cov.]; Sci. Cit. Index; SCISEARCH.

II/0970-2210
IGCAR. [IGCAR]. **Added/Corp** Indira Gandhi Centre for Atomic Research. India. Dept. of Atomic Energy. (19??)-. Monographic series. English. **CODEN** IGCAEA. Documents available from CASDDS. ***Continues*** *RRC, 0970-2202.*
Ind/Abst Chem. Abstr.

US/0742-5821
INTERNATIONAL DIRECTORY OF NUCLEAR UTILITIES. [Int. dir. nucl. util.]. **Added/Corp** Lotte, Ltd. (1984)-. Directory. English. an. $235.00. Nuexco, 1515 Arapahoe, 3 Park Central, Suite 900, Denver CO 80202. **Tel** (303)899-4500, telex 450202. **ED** Crolyn B. McCants. **LC** TK9012; .I57. **DD** 621.48/3/025. **Circ:** 300.
Desc: International listings of all nuclear utilities. Includes utility address, phone number, key personnel, type and location of generating facilities.

IS
INTERNATIONAL JOURNAL OF RADIATION ENGINEERING. V. 1- July 1971-. Periodical. English. mo. $25.00. Jacob Slonim Publishing Ltd, PO BOX 35, Tel Aviv Israel.
Ind/Abst Energy Res. Abstr. (April 1975-).

GW
IRS-SCHRIFTTUM. **Main/Corp** Institut fur Reaktorsicherheit der Technischen Uberwachungs-Verein. **VAT** Institut fur Reaktorsicherheit Schrifttum. German. Glockengasse 2, W-5000 Koln 1 Germany. **LC** Z5160; .I32A; TK9152.

GW/0720-9207
JAHRESTAGUNG KERNTECHNIK. (TAGUNGSBERICHT / JAHRESTAGUNG KERNTECHNIK.). [Jahrestag. Kerntech.]. **Main/Conf** Jahrestagung Kerntechnik. **Added/Corp** Kerntechnische Gesellschaft (Bonn, Germany) Deutsches Atomforum. (1980)-. Academic Scholarly Publication. German. an. DM80.00. Inforum Verlags und Verwaltungs GmbH, Heussallee 10, 53113 Bonn Germany. **Tel** (0)228/507-223, FAX (0)228/502-219, telex 88 69 44 4 DATF D. **(Subscription address:** Inforum GmBH, z.Jd.Frau Tapsoba, Postfach 120611, 53048 Bonn Germany.**)** **LC** TK9006; .J33a. **DD** 621.48/05. **CODEN** TJKEDX. Index available. **Bk Rev. Circ:** 1,250. Documents available from Article Express International, Ask*IEEE, CASDDS. ***Continues*** *Reaktortagung.*
Desc: The publication covers the recent progress in the peaceful use of nuclear technology.
Ind/Abst Bioeng. Abstr.; Chem. Abstr.; Ei Page One; Eng. Index Annu.; INSPEC.

US/0893-6188
JNMM : JOURNAL OF THE INSTITUTE OF NUCLEAR MATERIALS MANAGEMENT. [JNMM]. **VFOAT** Journal of the Institute of Nuclear Materials Management. Vol. 15, No. 1 (Oct. 1986)-. Academic Scholarly Publication. English. qt. $75.00 US; $100.00 other. Institute of Nuclear Materials Management, 60 Revere Drive/Suite 500, Northbrook IL 60062. **Tel** (312)480-9573, FAX (312)480-9282, telex 910-220-5870. **ED** Greg Schultz. **LC** TK9185.A1; N83. **DD** 604. Index available. **Bk Rev. Ad Acc. Circ:** 7,500 (ctrl). Documents available from Article Express International, Ask*IEEE, CASDDS. ***Continues in part*** *Nuclear Materials Management, 0362-0034.*
Desc: Publishes volumes consisting of issues and proceedings of the institute's annual meetings. Material includes concerns for nuclear materials management, safeguards, waste management, transportation, physical protection and measurements.
Ind/Abst Bioeng. Abstr. (1986-); Chem. Abstr. (1986-); Ei Page One (1986-); EMBASE (1986-); Energy Res. Abstr. (1986-); Eng. Index Annu.; INSPEC (1986-).

US/0164-0313
JOURNAL OF FUSION ENERGY. **See** Energy.

NE/0022-3115
JOURNAL OF NUCLEAR MATERIALS. [J. nucl. mater.]. **VFOAT** Journal des Materiaux Nucleaires. Vol. 1 (April 1959)-. Academic Scholarly Publication. English (French and German). Thirty-three times a year (11 volumes). FI6061.00. Elsevier Science Publishers BV, PO Box 211, 1000 AE Amsterdam Netherlands. **Tel** 011 31 20 5803642, FAX 011 31 20 5862696, telex 15682. **ED** L.K. Mansur, H. Kleykamp, S. Ishino, G. Saada, L.O. Werme. **LC** TK9185.A1; J6. **DD** 621.4833. **CODEN** JNUMAM. **[CCC].** Index available. cum. index. **Bk Rev. Pr Rev. Circ:** 900 (ctrl). available on microfilm and microfiche from University Microfilms International (UMI). Documents available from Article Express International, The Genuine Article, Ask*IEEE, CASDDS.
Desc: Publishes papers in the entire field of materials for nuclear science and technology and irradiation effects in solids.
Ind/Abst Alum. Ind. Abstr.; Appl. Mech. Rev.; Bioeng. Abstr.; Ceram. Abstr.; Chem. Abstr.; Chem. Titles; Curr. Contents Eng. Tech. Appl. Sci.; Curr. Contents Phys. Chem. Earth Sci.; Ei Page One; Energy Inf. Abstr.; Energy Res. Abstr.; Eng. Mater. Abstr.; Eng. Index Annu.; INSPEC (1968-); Int. Aerosp. Abstr.; Leadscan; Met. Abstr.; Phys. Briefs; Pollut. Abstr. Indexes; Res. Alert [Full Cov.]; Sci. Cit. Index; SCISEARCH.

JA/0022-3131
JOURNAL OF NUCLEAR SCIENCE AND TECHNOLOGY. [J. nucl. sci. technol.]. **Added/Corp** Nihon Genshiryoku Gakkai. **VFOAT** Nihon Genshiryoku Gakkai Obum Rombun Shi. Vol. 1 (April 1964)-. Academic Scholarly Publication. English. mo. $210.00. Nihon Genshiryoku Gakkai, (Atomic Energy Soc. of Japan), Nihon Genshiryoku Kenkyujo, 1-13, Shinbashi 1 Chome, Minatoku, Tokyoto 105, Japan. **(Subscription address:** Maruzen Company Ltd., PO Box 5050, Import & Export Department, Tokyo 100 31 Japan.**)** **CODEN** JNSTAX. **[CCC]. Pr Rev.** Documents available from Article Express International, The Genuine Article, Ask*IEEE, CASDDS, Documents on Demand.
Ind/Abst Alum. Ind. Abstr.; Bioeng. Abstr.; Chem. Abstr.; Chem. Titles (1973-); Civ. Struct. Eng. Abstr.; Comput. Inf. Syst. Abstr. J. [Full Cov.]; Curr. Contents Eng. Tech. Appl. Sci.; Ei Page One; Elect. Comm. Abstr.; EMBASE; Energy Res. Abstr.; Eng. Mater. Abstr.; Eng. Index Annu.; Environ. Abstr.; Environ. Eng. Abstr.; Fluid Abstr., Civil Eng.; Fluid Abstr. Proc. Eng.; FLUIDEX (1973-1990); HTFS Dig.; INSPEC (1968-); Int. Aerosp. Abstr.; Manuf. Process Eng. Abstr.; Mater. Sci. Eng. Abstr.; Math. Rev.; Mech. Eng. Abstr.; Met. Abstr.; Nucl. Sci. Abstr.; Pollut. Abstr. Indexes; Res. Alert [Full Cov.]; Sci. Cit. Index; SCISEARCH; Solid State Supercond. Abstr.

JA
KAIROSHITSU GIHO - TOKYO DAIGAKU GENSHIKAKU KENKYUJO KAIROSHITSU. **Main/Corp** Tokyo Daigaku. Genshikaku Kenkyujo. Kairoshitsu. **Added/Corp** Tokyo Daigaku. Genshikaku Kenkyujo. Kairoshitsu. Technical Report of Electronis Shop, Institute for Nuclear Study, University of Tokyo. **VFOAT** Technical Report of Electronics Shop, Institute of Nuclear Study, University of Tokyo. (19??)-. Academic Scholarly Publication. Japanese (summaries and/or abstracts in English). **LC** TK7868.P8; T6a. Documents available from CASDDS.
Ind/Abst Chem. Abstr.

GW/0932-3902
KERNTECHNIK (1987). (KERNTECHNIK.). [Kerntechnik]. Vol. 50, No. 1 (March/April 1987)-. Periodical. English (German). Four times a year. DM498.00. Carl Hanser Verlag, Postfach 860420, D 81631 Munich Germany. **Tel** 011 49 89 998300, FAX 011 49 89 984809. **ED** Alfred Kraut. **LC** TK9001; .A867. **DD** 621.48/05. **CODEN** KERNEU. **[CCC].** Index available. **Bk Rev. Ad Acc. Pr Rev. Circ:** 2,000. Documents available from Article Express International, The Genuine Article, Ask*IEEE, CASDDS. ***Continues*** *Atomkernenergie/Kerntechnik, 0171-5747;* ***Absorbed*** *Kernergie, 0023-0642.*
Desc: Independent journal for nuclear engineering, energy systems and radiation.
Ind/Abst Chem. Abstr.; Curr. Contents Eng. Tech. Appl. Sci.; Ei Page One; Eng. Index Annu.; HTFS Dig.; INSPEC (1987-); Res. Alert [Full Cov.]; Sci. Cit. Index; SCISEARCH; Soc. Sci. Cit. Index [Select. Cov.].

US/0278-3487
LICENSED OPERATING REACTORS, STATUS SUMMARY REPORT. [Licens. oper. react., status summ. rep.]. **Added/Corp** U.S. Nuclear Regulatory Commission. U.S. Nuclear Regulatory Commission. Office of Management and Program Analysis. U.S. Nuclear Regulatory Commission. Office of Resource Management. U.S. Nuclear Regulatory Commission. Office of Information and Resources Management. U.S. Nuclear Regulatory Commission. Division of Computer and Telecommunications Services. **VFOAT** Gray Book; Gray Book. (198?)-. Government Publication. English. mo. $85.00 domestic; $106.25 other. Superintendent of Documents, US Government Printing Office, Washington DC 20402. **Tel** (202)275-3328, FAX (202)786-2377. **LC** TK1343; .U56b. **DD** 621.31/25/0973. Documents available from Documents on Demand. ***Continues*** *Operating Units Status Report, Licensed Operating Reactors, 0193-7219.*
Desc: Also referred to as the "Gray Book," this monthly publication provides data on the operation of nuclear units as timely and accurately as possible. Contains three sections: highlights and statistics for commercial operating units, detailed information on each unit, and an appendix for miscellaneous information such as spent fuel storage capabilities.
Ind/Abst Am. Stat. Index.

US
LONG-RANGE RESEARCH PLAN. **Main/Corp** U.S. Nuclear Regulatory Commission. Office of Nuclear Regulatory Research. FY 1984/FY 1988-. English. an. NRC/GPO Sales Program, US Nuclear Regulatory Commission, Washington DC 20555. ***Continues*** *Long Range Research Plan.*

US/0742-4582
MONTHLY REPORT ON THE NUCLEAR FUEL MARKET. ***Title Change.*** (MONTHLY REPORT ON THE NUCLEAR FUEL MARKET / NUEXCO.). [M. rep. nucl. fuel mark.]. **Added/Corp** Nuexco (Firm). (1983)-(1993). Periodical. English. mo. Nuexco, 1515 Arapahoe, 3 Park Central, Suite 900, Denver CO 80202. **Tel** (303)899-4500, telex 450202. **ED** R. Wesley Miller. Index available. **Circ:** 300. ***Continues*** *Monthly Report on the Uranium Market.* ***Continued by*** *Nuexco Review, 1074-8695.*
Desc: International uranium and enrichment market information; supply/demand prices and transactions. Detailed articles on uranium production, nuclear power, legal and legislation issues. An annual review is included.

US
MULTIROD BURST TEST PROGRAM PROGRESS REPORT FOR ... - U.S. NUCLEAR REGULATORY COMMISSION, OFFICE OF NUCLEAR REGULATORY RESEARCH. English. National Technical Information Service - NTIS, Room 2027S, 5285 Port Royal Road, Springfield VA 22161. **Tel** (703)487-4630, (703)487-4660, (703)487-4650, FAX (703)321-8547, telex 89-9405.

FR
NEWSLETTER - OECD NUCLEAR ENERGY AGENCY. **Main/Corp** OECD Nuclear Energy Agency. **Added/Corp** Centre d'Etudes Nucleaires de Saclay. (Mar. 1973)-. Multiple languages (English and French). ir. OECD Publications and Information Center, 2 rue Andre-Pascal, 75775 Paris Cedex 16 France. **Tel** 011 33 1 45248167, US:(202)785-6323, FAX 011 33 1 45248500 OR 45248176, telex 620 160 OCDE. **LC** TK2965; .O74a. **DD** 621.312. ***Continues*** *Newsletter - European Nuclear Agency of the OECD.*

CN/0383-8536
NUCLEAR CANADA YEARBOOK. **See** Energy.

UK/0262-5091
NUCLEAR ENGINEER, THE. [Nucl. eng.]. V. 21, No. 3- May/June 1980-. Academic Scholarly Publication. English. bm. £70.00. Institution of Nuclear Engineers, 1 Penerley Road, London SE6 2LQ England. **Tel** FAX 081-695-6409. **ED** S M Blackburn. **LC** TK9001; .N73. **DD** 621.48/05. **CODEN** NUEND7. **[CCC]. Bk Rev. Ad Acc. Circ:** 2,000 (ctrl). available on microfilm and microfiche from University Microfilms International (UMI). Documents available from Article Express International, Ask*IEEE, CASDDS. ***Continues*** *Journal of the Institution of Nuclear Engineers, 0368-2595.*
Desc: The journal covers all aspects of nuclear power generation, research, marine propulsion, health and environmental topics as well as general industrial uses and applications.
Ind/Abst Bioeng. Abstr.; Chem. Abstr.; Civ. Struct. Eng. Abstr.; Comput. Inf. Syst. Abstr. J. [Full Cov.]; Curr. Technol. Index; Ei Page One; EMBASE; Energy Res. Abstr. (Jan. 1981-); Eng. Index Annu.; Environ. Eng. Abstr.; INSPEC (May/June 1980-); Mater. Sci. Eng. Abstr.; Mech. Eng. Abstr.

NE/0029-5493
NUCLEAR ENGINEERING AND DESIGN. (NUCLEAR ENGINEERING AND DESIGN : AN INTERNATIONAL JOURNAL DEVOTED TO THE THERMAL, MECHANICAL AND STRUCTURAL PROBLEMS OF NUCLEAR ENERGY.). [Nucl. eng. des.]. **Added/Corp** North-Holland Publishing Company. Vol. 3, (Jan. 1966)-. Academic Scholarly Publication. English (French and German). Twenty-four times a year (8 vols.). 4240.00F; 5880.00F combined subscription with Fusion Engineering and Design. Elsevier Sequoia SA, PO Box 564, CH-1001 Lausanne 1 Switzerland. **Tel** 011 41 21 3207381. **ED** K. Kussmaul. **CODEN** NEDEAU. **[CCC].** available on microfilm and microfiche from University Microfilms International (UMI). Documents available from Article Express International, The Genuine Article, Ask*IEEE, CASDDS, Documents on Demand. ***Continues*** *Structural Engineering.* ***Continued in part by*** *Nuclear Engineering and Design/Fusion.*
Desc: Devoted to the thermal, mechanical and structural problems associated with nuclear energy, comprising topics of civil, mechanical and chemical engineering, applied nuclear physics and health physics.
Ind/Abst Abstr. J. Earthq. Eng.; Acoust. Abstr.; Appl. Mech. Rev.; Bioeng. Abstr.; Ceram. Abstr.; Chem. Abstr.; Curr. Contents Eng. Tech. Appl. Sci.; Ei Page One; Energy Inf. Abstr.; Energy Res. Abstr.; Eng. Mater. Abstr.; Eng. Index Annu.; Environ. Abstr.; Fluid Abstr., Civil Eng.; Fluid Abstr. Proc. Eng.; FLUIDEX (1973-); GeoRef; HTFS Dig.; INIS Atomindex INIS Atomindeks; INSPEC (July 1968-1983); Int. Aerosp. Abstr.; Leadscan; Phys. Briefs; Pollut. Abstr. Indexes; Res. Alert [Full Cov.]; Risk Abstr.; Sci. Cit. Index; SCISEARCH; Shock Vibr. Dig.; Soc. Sci. Cit. Index [Select. Cov.].

US/8755-9145
NUCLEAR ENGINEERING ENROLLMENTS AND DEGREES. [Nucl. eng. enroll. degrees]. English. an. National Technical Information Service - NTIS, Room 2027S, 5285 Port Royal Road, Springfield VA 22161. **Tel** (703)487-4630,

(703)487-4660, (703)487-4650, FAX (703)321-8547, telex 89-9405. **LC** TK9166; .N79. available on microfiche (Vols. for 1976, 1982- distributed to depository libraries).

UK/0029-5507
NUCLEAR ENGINEERING INTERNATIONAL. [Nucl. eng. int.]. Vol. 13, No. 150 (Nov. 1968)-. Academic Scholarly Publication. English (summaries and/or abstracts in French and German). Twelve times a year. $180.00. Reed Business Publishing / West Sussex, England, Perrymount Road, Haywards Heath, West Sussex RH16 3DH England. **Tel** 011 44 81 6523500. **LC** TK9001; .N75. **DD** 621.48/05. **CODEN** NEINBF. **[CCC]. Pr Rev.** available on microfilm and microfiche from University Microfilms International (UMI). Documents available from Article Express International, The Genuine Article, Ask*IEEE, CASDDS, Documents on Demand. ***Continues*** *Nuclear Engineering (London, England).*
Ind/Abst AESIS Q.; Alum. Ind. Abstr.; Appl. Sci. Technol. Index (-1990); Bioeng. Abstr.; Ceram. Abstr.; Chem. Abstr. (1968-1983); Coal Abstr.; Curr. Contents Eng. Tech. Appl. Sci.; Curr. Technol. Index; Ei Page One; EMBASE; Energy Inf. Abstr.; Energy Res. Abstr.; Eng. Mater. Abstr.; Eng. Index Annu. [Select. Cov.]; Environ. Abstr.; Fluid Abstr., Civil Eng.; Fluid Abstr. Proc. Eng.; FLUIDEX (1973-); Health Saf. Sci. Abstr.; HTFS Dig.; INSPEC (1968-); Leadscan; Met. Abstr.; Pollut. Abstr. Indexes; Res. Alert [Select. Cov.]; Risk Abstr.; SCISEARCH.

SZ/1016-5975
NUCLEAR EUROPE WORLDSCAN. (NUCLEAR EUROPE WORLDSCAN : JOURNAL OF ENS.). [Nucl. Eur. worldscan]. **Added/Corp** European Nuclear Society. **VFOAT** Journal of ENS. No. 1/2 (Jan./Feb. 1990)-. Academic Scholarly Publication. English. mo. 160.00F Europe; 230.00F other. Nuclear Europe Worldscan, c/o ENS Secretariat, PO Box 5032, CH-3001 Berne Switzerland. **Tel** 011 44 31 3206111, FAX 011 41 31 3824466, telex 912 110 ATAG CH. **ED** Peter Holt. **LC** TX9001; .N758. **DD** 621.48/3. **Bk Rev. Ad Acc, Adv Mgr:** A. Hunter. **Circ:** 23,500. Documents available from Ask*IEEE, CASDDS. ***Continues*** *Nuclear Europe, 0254-8348.*
Ind/Abst Chem. Abstr.; HTFS Dig.; INSPEC (Jan./Feb. 1990-).

II/0029-5523
NUCLEAR INDIA. [Nucl. India]. **Added/Corp** India. Dept. of Atomic Energy. (Sept. 1962)-. Periodical. English. ir. Department of Atomic Energy Publ Off, Apollo Pier Road, Bombay 1 India. **LC** TK9103; .A3. **NLM** W1 NU122C.
Ind/Abst Art Archaeol. Tech. Abstr.; Energy Res. Abstr.; Indian Geosci. Abstr.; SEA Abstr.

US
NUCLEAR INDUSTRY. Dec. 1953-. Periodical. English. mo. US Council Energy Awareness, 1776 I Street NW/Suite 400, Washington DC 20006. **Tel** (202)293-0770.

US/0564-9099
NUCLEAR INDUSTRY, THE. [Nucl. ind.]. **Main/Corp** United States. Energy Research and Development Administration. Office of Industry Relations. Government Publication. English. an. US Department of Energy, 1000 Independence Avenue SW, Washington DC 20585. **Tel** (202)586-5000, FAX (202)586-4073. **LC** TK9023; .A35. **DD** 338.4/7/621480973. ***Continues*** *Nuclear Industry, 0564-9099.*

US/0893-3774
NUCLEAR LICENSING REPORTS. [Nucl. licens. rep.]. **Added/Corp** U.S. Nuclear Regulatory Commission. Vol. 1, No. 1 (May 1987)-. Periodical. English. mo. $275.00 (one year), $495.00 (two year), $660.00 (three year) US; $280.00 (one year), $505.00 (two year), $675.00 (three year) Canada; $295.00 (one year), $535.00 (two year), $720.00 (three year) other. Nuclear Licensing Reports, PO Box 10866, Rockville MD 20850-0866. **Tel** (301)424-4132, FAX (301)762-2663. **ED** Robert F Brennan. **DD** 351.
Desc: Provides radioactive material licensees of the U.S. nuclear regulatory commission and agreement states with the latest information on regulations and policies affecting them.

US/0029-5574
NUCLEAR NEWS (HINSDALE). (NUCLEAR NEWS.). [Nucl. news]. **Added/Corp** American Nuclear Society. Vol. 1 (July 1959)-. Academic Scholarly Publication. English. mo. $206.00 (includes 3 special issues and Buyer's Guide). American Nuclear Society, PO Box 97781, Chicago IL 60678-7781. **Tel** (708)352-6611, FAX (708)579-8314. **ED** Jon Payne. **LC** QC770; .N75. **CODEN** NUNWA8. **[CCC]. Bk Rev. Ad Acc. Circ:** 18,000. Documents available from Ask*IEEE, CASDDS.
Desc: Newsmagazine for nuclear industry.
Ind/Abst Alum. Ind. Abstr.; Appl. Sci. Technol. Index (1991-); Chem. Abstr.; EMBASE; INSPEC (March 1970-); Met. Abstr.; NEXIS (1982-).

CN/0713-0597
NUCLEAR NOTES (TORONTO). (NUCLEAR NOTES : A PERIODIC INFORMATION SERVICE FOR MEMBERS OF THE CANADIAN NUCLEAR ASSOCIATION.). [Nucl. notes]. **Added/Corp** Canadian Nuclear Association. (197?)-. Periodical. English. bm. Canadian Nuclear Association, 144 Front Street West, Suite 725, Toronto Ontario M5J 2L7 Canada. **Tel** (416)977-6152, (416)977-7620, FAX (416)979-8356, telex 06-23741. **DD** 016.33379/24.

US/1054-9447
NUCLEAR PLANT MAINTENANCE NEWSLETTER. [Nucl. plant maint. newsl.]. **Added/Corp** Equipment Engineering and Sales, Inc. (Apr. 1989)-. Newsletter. English. mo. $220.00. Equipment Engineering & Sales Inc., 799 Roosevelt Road Building 6, Suite 208, Glen Ellyn IL 60137. **Tel** (708)858-6161, FAX (708)858-8787. **ED** Newal K. Agnihotri. **DD** 621. **[CCC]. Circ:** 200. ***Continues*** *Equipment Maintenance & Qualification Newsletter, 0892-6948.*
Desc: Serves the international nuclear power industry with updates on maintenance of electrical and mechanical equipment.

US/0198-6465
NUCLEAR POWER PLANT OPERATING EXPERIENCE ... ANNUAL REPORT. [Nucl. power plant oper. exp., annu. rep.]. English. an. NRC/GPO Sales Program, US Nuclear Regulatory Commission, Washington DC 20555. **LC** TK1343; .U56C. **DD** 363.6/2. available on microfiche (Vols. for 1980- distributed to depository libraries).

US/0735-2492
NUCLEAR REACTOR SAFETY. [Nucl. rect. safety]. **Added/Corp** United States. Dept. of Energy. Technical Information Center. (1982)-. Government Publication. English. Twelve times a year. $165.00 US; $330.00 other. US Department of Energy, 1000 Independence Avenue SW, Washington DC 20585. **Tel** (202)586-5000, FAX (202)586-4073. **(Subscription address:** National Technical Information Service, 5285 Port Royal Road, Springfield, VA 22161**)**

US/0896-5153
NUCLEAR REACTORS AND TECHNOLOGY. ***Ceased.*** (NUCLEAR REACTORS AND TECHNOLOGY : CURRENT ABSTRACTS / U.S. DEPARTMENT OF ENERGY ; PREPARED FOR OFFICE OF NUCLEAR ENERGY ; PREPARED BY OFFICE OF SCIENTIFIC AND TECHNICAL INFORMATION.). [Nucl. react. technol.]. **Added/Corp** United States. Dept. of Energy. Office of Scientific and Technical Information. United States. Office of the Assistant Secretary for Nuclear Energy. **VFOAT** NRT. Vol. 88, No. 1 (Jan. 1988)-(Jan. 1994). Government Publication. English. mo. US Department of Energy, 1000 Independence Avenue SW, Washington DC 20585. **Tel** (202)586-5000, FAX (202)586-4073. **(Subscription address:** National Technical Information Service, 5285 Port Royal Road, Springfield, VA 22161**) LC** TK9001; .N784. **DD** 621.48/05.

US/0029-5604
NUCLEAR SAFETY. [Nucl. saf.]. **Added/Corp** United States. Dept. of Energy. Office of Scientific and Technical Information. United States. Dept. of Energy. Nuclear Safety Information Center. U.S. Atomic Energy Commission. Oak Ridge National Laboratory. U.S. Nuclear Regulatory Commission. United States. Dept. of Energy. Technical Information Center. (Sept. 1959)-. Academic Scholarly Publication. English. qt. $14.00 domestic; $17.50 other. Superintendent of Documents, US Government Printing Office, Washington DC 20402. **Tel** (202)275-3328, FAX (202)786-2377. **ED** Ernest G. Silver. **LC** TK9152; .N8. **DD** 621.48/35. **NLM** W1 NU127. **CODEN** NUSAAZ. Index available. cum. index. **Bk Rev. Pr Rev. Circ:** 3,000. available on microfilm and microfiche from University Microfilms International (UMI). Documents available from Article Express International, The Genuine Article, BIOSIS Document Express, Ask*IEEE, CASDDS, Documents on Demand.
Desc: Provides concise and authoritative evaluation of scientific and technological developments relating to nuclear safety as they emerge from atomic research and development programs.
Ind/Abst Appl. Sci. Technol. Index; Biol. Abstr.; Chem. Abstr.; Curr. Contents Eng. Tech. Appl. Sci.; Ei Page One; EMBASE; Energy Inf. Abstr.; Energy Res. Abstr.; Eng. Index Annu. [Select. Cov.]; Environ. Abstr.; Environ. Period. Bibliogr. (?-?); Fluid Abstr., Civil Eng.; Fluid Abstr. Proc. Eng.; FLUIDEX (1973-); Geogr. Abstr. Phys. Geogr.; Health Saf. Sci. Abstr.; HTFS Dig.; INSPEC (March-April 1981-); Leadscan; Pollut. Abstr. Indexes; Res. Alert [Full Cov.]; Risk Abstr.; Sci. Cit. Index; SCISEARCH; Soc. Sci. Cit. Index [Select. Cov.].

US/0029-5639
NUCLEAR SCIENCE AND ENGINEERING. [Nucl. sci. eng.]. **Added/Corp** American Nuclear Society. Vol. 1, No. 1 (March 1956)-. Academic Scholarly Publication. English. ir (9 issues). $430.00. American Nuclear Society, PO Box 97781, Chicago IL 60678-7781. **Tel** (708)352-6611, FAX (708)579-8314. **ED** John Kallfelz. **LC** QC770; .N8. **DD** 539.7605. **CODEN** NSENAO. **[CCC]. Bk Rev. Pr Rev. Circ:** 1,400. available on microfiche (from the American Nuclear Society). Documents available from Article Express International, The Genuine Article, Ask*IEEE, CASDDS, Documents on Demand.
Desc: Articles on research and development related to peaceful use of nuclear energy, radiation, and alternative energy sources.
Ind/Abst Alum. Ind. Abstr.; Bioeng. Abstr.; Ceram. Abstr.; Chem. Abstr.; Comput. Abstr.; Curr. Contents Eng. Tech. Appl. Sci.; Ei Page One; Elect. Comm. Abstr.; EMBASE; Energy Inf. Abstr.; Energy Res. Abstr.; Eng. Mater. Abstr.; Eng. Index Annu.; Environ. Abstr.; Health Saf. Sci. Abstr.; HTFS Dig.; INSPEC (1968-); Int. Aerosp. Abstr.; Leadscan; Manuf. Process Eng. Abstr.; Mater. Sci. Eng. Abstr.; Mech. Eng. Abstr.; Met. Abstr.; Pollut. Abstr. Indexes; Res. Alert [Full Cov.]; Sci. Cit. Index; SCISEARCH; Solid State Supercond. Abstr.

US
NUCLEAR SCIENCE SERIES, REPORT. **Main/Corp** National Research Council. Committee on Nuclear Science. English. ir. National Research Council, 2101 Constitution Avenue, Washington DC 20418.

CN/0838-3871
NUCLEAR SECTOR FOCUS. **See** Energy.

AT/0815-0249
NUCLEAR SPECTRUM. ***Ceased.*** [Nucl. spectr.]. **Added/Corp** Australian Atomic Energy Commission. Vol. 1, No. 1 (March 1985)-(19??). Periodical. English. an. Lucas Heights Research Laboratory, Private Mail Bag, Sutherland New South Wales, 2232 Australia. **Tel telex** 79020273. **ED** Andrew Best. **LC** QC792.78.A8; N83. **DD** 621.48/0994. **CODEN** NUSPEG. **Circ:** 5,000. Documents available from Ask*IEEE. ***Continues*** *Atomic Energy in Australia, 0004-7090.*
Desc: Promotes a better understanding of nuclear science and technology. Informs the community of nuclear developments.
Ind/Abst Ei Page One; INSPEC (1985-199?).

US/0029-5655
NUCLEAR STANDARDS NEWS. (19??)-. English. Twelve times a year. $255.00. American Nuclear Society, PO Box 97781, Chicago IL 60678-7781. **Tel** (708)352-6611, FAX (708)579-8314.

US/0029-5450
NUCLEAR TECHNOLOGY. [Nucl. technol.]. **Added/Corp** American Nuclear Society. Vol. 10 (Jan. 1971)-. Academic Scholarly Publication. English. mo. $455.00. American Nuclear Society, PO Box 97781, Chicago IL 60678-7781. **Tel** (708)352-6611, FAX (708)579-8314. **ED** Paul Vlajcic. **LC** TK9001; .N72. **DD** 621.48/05. **CODEN** NUTYBB. **[CCC]. Pr Rev.** Documents available from Article Express International, The Genuine Article, BIOSIS Document Express, Ask*IEEE, CASDDS, Documents on Demand. ***Continues*** *Nuclear Applications & Technology, 0550-3043.*
Desc: Devoted to applications of technology and know-how in the nuclear field. It is read by nuclear scientists, and engineers located at reactor and accelerator sites, colleges, medical institutions, private and governmental agencies and laboratories. Articles cover the entire spectrum of activities in the nuclear industry.
Ind/Abst Alum. Ind. Abstr. (1971-); Appl. Sci. Technol. Index (1971-); Bioeng. Abstr. (1971-); Biol. Abstr. (1971-); Chem. Abstr. (1971-); Chem. Titles; Coal Abstr. (1971-); Comput. Inf. Syst. Abstr. J. [Full Cov.]; Curr. Contents Eng. Tech. Appl. Sci.; Ei Page One (1971-); EMBASE (1971-); Energy Res. Abstr. (Jan. 1971-); Eng. Mater. Abstr.; Eng. Index Annu.; Environ. Abstr. (1971-); HTFS Dig.; INSPEC (Feb. 1971-); Int. Aerosp. Abstr. (1971-); Leadscan; Mech. Eng. Abstr.; Met. Abstr. (1971-); Res. Alert [Full Cov.]; Risk Abstr.; Sci. Cit. Index; SCISEARCH; Soc. Sci. Cit. Index [Select. Cov.].

US/0149-3574
NUCLEARFUEL. [Nuclearfuel]. (19??)-. Newsletter. English. Twenty-six times a year. $1595.00 US and Canada; $1690.00 other. McGraw Hill Publishing Company, Inc., 1221 Avenue of the Americas, New York NY 10020. **Tel** (212)512-6410, (800)525-5003, FAX (212)512-6111. **LC** TK9360; .N86. **DD** 338.4/7/6214833505. available on an online database from DIALOG.
Ind/Abst NEXIS (Jan. 5, 1981-).

XR/0302-8542
NUCLEON. **Added/Corp** Ustav Jaderneho Vyzkumu Rez. (1991)-. Periodical. English. Nuclear Research Institute, 250 67 Rez Near Prague, Czech Republic. **LC** TK9001; .N85.

CL/0716-0054
NUCLEOTECNICA. (NUCLEOTECNICA : ORGANO DE DIFUSION DE LA COMISION CHILENA DE ENERGIA NUCLEAR.). [Nucleotecnica]. **Added/Corp** Comision Chilena de Energia Nuclear. Vol. 1, No. 1 (Jan. 1981)-. Academic Scholarly Publication. Spanish (English). sa. Free on request. Comis Chilena Energia Nuclear, Amunategui 95, Casilla 188-D, Santiago Chile. **Tel** 011 56 2 6990070, FAX 011 56 2 713121, telex 340465. **LC** TK9001; .N83. **DD** 333.79/24/0983. **CODEN** NUCLEQ. Index available. **Bk Rev**, (Qty: 2). **Circ:** 2,000 (ctrl). available on CD-ROM. Documents available from CASDDS.
Desc: Reports on experimental work on nuclear science, technology and medicine.
Ind/Abst Chem. Abstr. (1985-).

•US/1074-8695
NUEXCO REVIEW. [Nuexco rev.]. **Added/Corp** Nuexco (Firm). (Apr. 1993)-. Periodical. English. mo. Nuexco, 1515 Arapahoe, 3 Park Central, Suite 900, Denver CO 80202. **Tel** (303)899-4500, telex 450202. **DD** 332. ***Continues*** *Monthly Report on the Nuclear Fuel Market, 0742-8695.*

GW
NUKEM MARKET REPORT ON THE NUCLEAR FUEL CYCLE. mo. DM4000.00 companies, financial institutions, and government agents in nuclear fuel business; DM1100.00 other. NUKEM GmbH, D-63754 Alzenau, Germany. **Tel** 011 49 6023 5000, FAX 011 49 6023 500214, telex 4188233.

PL/0029-5922
NUKLEONIKA. [Nukleonika]. **Added/Corp** Polska Akademia Nauk. Komitet do Spraw Pokojowego Wykorzystania Energii Jadrowej. Resortowy Osrodek Informacji Naukowej, Technicznej i Ekonomicznej Energetyki i Energii Atomowej (Warsaw, Poland). Vol. 1 (1956)-. Academic Scholarly Publication. English (Polish and Russian). qt. Price on request. **(Subscription address:** ARS Polona, PO Box 1001, 00068 Warsaw Poland.**) LC** TK9001; .N86. **NLM** W1 NU19. **CODEN** NUKLAS. Index Available in first issue of next volume--loose--separately paged. Documents available from Ask*IEEE, CASDDS.
Ind/Abst Alum. Ind. Abstr.; Chem. Abstr.; Coal Abstr.; Energy Res. Abstr.; INSPEC (1968-); Int. Aerosp. Abstr.; Met. Abstr.; Saf. Health Work; SCISEARCH.

US/0278-1670
NUREG/CR (UNITED STATES. NUCLEAR REGULATORY COMMISSION). (NUREG/CR.). [NUREG/CR]. **Main/Corp** U.S. Nuclear Regulatory Commission. (197?)-. Academic Scholarly Publication. English. Nuclear Regulatory Commission, 1717 H Street NW, Washington DC 20555. **Tel** (301)492-7000. **CODEN** USNCDE. Documents available from CASDDS.
Ind/Abst Chem. Abstr. (?-1983)(19??-); GeoRef.

AU
OPERATING EXPERIENCE WITH NUCLEAR POWER STATIONS IN MEMBER STATES. **Main/Corp** International Atomic Energy Agency. (1970)-. English. an. S2240.00 (latest edition). International Atomic Energy Agency / IAEA, Wagramerstrasse 5, PO Box 100, A-1400 Vienna Austria. **Tel** 011 43 1 2360 ext. 2530, FAX 011 43 1 234564. **(Subscription address:** UNIPUB, 4611 F Assembly Drive, Lanham MD 20706.**) LC** TK1078; .I57a. **DD** 333.7.
Desc: Annual report on operating experience with nuclear power stations in member states. It is a direct output from the Agency's Power-Reactor Information System and contains data on electricity production, overall plant operating performance and plant outage information.

AU/0074-1876
PANEL PROCEEDINGS SERIES - INTERNATIONAL ATOMIC ENERGY AGENCY. **See** Energy.

US
PHYSICAL PROTECTION OF NUCLEAR FACILITIES, QUARTERLY PROGRESS REPORT / SANDIA LABORATORIES ; PREPARED FOR DIVISION OF SAFEGUARDS, FUEL CYCLE AND ENVIRONMENTAL RESEARCH, OFFICE OF NUCLEAR REGULATORY RESEARCH, U.S. NUCLEAR REGULATORY COMMISSION. **Added/Corp** U.S. Nuclear Regulatory Commission. Office of Nuclear Regulatory Research. Division of Facility Operations. Safeguards Branch. Sandia National Laboratories. U.S. Nuclear Regulatory Commission. Division of Safeguards, Fuel Cycle, and Environmental Research. Sandia Laboratories. (19??)-. Periodical. English. qt. National Technical Information Service - NTIS, Room 2027S, 5285 Port Royal Road, Springfield VA 22161. **Tel** (703)487-4630, (703)487-4660, (703)487-4650, FAX (703)321-8547, telex 89-9405.

US
POWER REACTOR CONFERENCE PROCEEDINGS. **Main/Corp** Florida. University, Gainesville. Engineering and Industrial Experiment Station. 1st (1955)-. Proceedings. English. Florida Engineering and Industrial Experiment Station, University of Florida, College of Engineering, Gainesville FL 32601. **LC** TA1; .F62. **DD** 621.48.

US/0741-1359
POWER REACTOR EVENTS. ***Suspended.*** (POWER REACTOR EVENTS / UNITED STATES NUCLEAR REGULATORY COMMISSION.). [Power react.events]. Vol. 1, No. 1 (Mar. 1979)-Suspended. Periodical. English. bm. $20.00 US; $25.00 other. Nuclear Regulatory Commission, 1717 H Street NW, Washington DC 20555. **Tel** (301)492-7000. **LC** TK1343; .P68. **DD** 363.1/79. ***Continues*** *Current Events. Power Reactors, 0145-1111.*
Desc: A newsletter that compiles operating experience information about commercial nuclear powerplants. Includes summaries of noteworthy events and listings/abstracts of United States NRC and other documents that discuss safety- related or possible generic issues.

US
PROCEEDINGS, ANNUAL MEETING, INSTITUTE OF NUCLEAR MATERIALS MANAGEMENT. **Main/Corp** Institute of Nuclear Materials Management. **VFOAT** INMM Proceedings. (19??)-. Proceedings. English. an. $65.00. Institute of Nuclear Materials Management, 60 Revere Drive/Suite 500, Northbrook IL 60062. **Tel** (312)480-9573, FAX (312)480-9282, telex 910-220-5870. **ED** C E Pietri. Index available. **Circ:** 2,500 (ctrl).
Desc: Publishes volumes consisting of issues and proceedings of the Institute's annual meetings. Material includes concerns for nuclear materials management; safeguards; waste management; transportation; physical protection and measurements.

UK/0149-1970
PROGRESS IN NUCLEAR ENERGY (NEW SERIES). (PROGRESS IN NUCLEAR ENERGY.). [Prog. nucl. energy]. Vol. 1, (1977)-. Academic Scholarly Publication. English. Four times a year. $418.00 The Americas; £280.00 other. Pergamon Press, An Imprint of Elsevier Science Ltd., The Boulevard, Langford Lane, Kidlington, Oxford OX5 1GB United Kingdom. **Tel** 011 44 865 843000, 011 44 865 843699, FAX 011 44 865 843010. **(Subscription address:** Elsevier Science Ltd. Oxford Fulfillment Centre, PO Box 800, Kidlington, Oxford OX5 1DX United Kingdom.**) ED** T.D. Beynon, D.J. Dudziak. **LC** TK9001; .P73. **DD** 621.48/05. **CODEN** PNENDE. **[CCC].** Index available. cum. index. **Ad Acc.** ctrl circ. available on microfilm and microfiche from University Microfilms International (UMI); and Pergamon Press. Documents available from The Genuine Article, Ask*IEEE, CASDDS, Documents on Demand. ***Formed by the union of*** *Physics and Mathematics, 0555-4055; Reactors (London, England); Process Chemistry, 0079-6514; Technology, Engineering, and Safety, 0079-6522; Metallurgy and Fuels, 0555-408X; Biological Sciences, 0555-4098; Medical Sciences (London, England), 0555-4101; Economics of Nuclear Power, Including Administration and Law, 0555-411X; Analytical Chemistry (Oxford, England), 0079-6530; Law and Administration, 0079-6549; Plasma Physics and Termonuclear Research, 0555-4136* ***and*** *Health Physics (New York, N.Y. : 1959), 0079-6557.*
Desc: An international review journal covering all aspects of nuclear science and engineering. In keeping with the maturity of nuclear power, articles on safety, siting and environmental problems are most welcome and also those associated with economics and fuel management. However, basic physics and engineering will remain an important aspect of the editorial publishing policy.
Ind/Abst Chem. Abstr.; Curr. Contents Eng. Tech. Appl. Sci.; Energy Inf. Abstr.; Energy Res. Abstr. (Feb. 1978-); Environ. Abstr.; Environ. Period. Bibliogr. (?-?); Index Sci. Rev. [Full Cov.]; INSPEC (1977-); Res. Alert [Full Cov.]; Risk Abstr.; Sci. Cit. Index; SCISEARCH; Soc. Sci. Cit. Index [Select. Cov.].

US
PROPERTIES OF RADIOACTIVE WASTES AND WASTE CONTAINERS, STATUS REPORT / NUCLEAR WASTE MANAGEMENT DIVISION, DEPARTMENT OF NUCLEAR ENERGY, BROOKHAVEN NATIONAL LABORATORY. English. an. GPO Sales Program, Division of Technical Information and Document Control, US Nuclear Regulatory Commission, Washington DC 20555.

US/0740-0640
RADIATION PROTECTION MANAGEMENT. **See** Industrial Health and Safety.

RU/0137-0057
RADIATSIONNAIA BEZOPASNOST I ZASHCHITA AES. [Radioc. bezop. zasc. AES]. **VAT** Radiatsionnaia Bezopasnost i Zashchita Atomnykh Elektrostantsii. (1974)-. Academic Scholarly Publication. Russian. 2.28rub (single issue). **LC** TK1078; .R318. **CODEN** RBZADI. Documents available from CASDDS. ***Supersedes*** *Voprosy Fiziki Zashchity Reaktorov.*
Ind/Abst Chem. Abstr.

US
REGULATORY AND TECHNICAL REPORTS (ABSTRACT INDEX JOURNAL). **Main/Corp** U.S. Nuclear Regulatory Commission. Regulatory Publications Branch. (198?)-. Government Publication. English. qt. $7.50 US; $9.40 other. Superintendent of Documents, US Government Printing Office, Washington DC 20402. **Tel** (202)275-3328, FAX (202)786-2377. ***Continues*** *U.S. Nuclear Regulatory Commission. Policy and Publications Management Branch. Regulatory and Technical Reports.*
Desc: A compilation, cumulated annually, of regulatory and technical reports and conference proceedings issued by the United States Nuclear Regulatory Commission staff and contractors.

US
REGULATORY GUIDE / U.S. NUCLEAR REGULATORY COMMISSION, OFFICE OF STANDARDS DEVELOPMENT. **See** Industrial Health and Safety.

BL
RELATORIO ANUAL - COMISSAO NACIONAL DE ENERGIA NUCLEAR. **Main/Corp** Brazil. Comissao Nacional de Energia Nuclear. Portuguese. an. Ministerio das Minas E Energia Nuclear, Bel Horizonte Brazil. **LC** TK9041; .B7A. **DD** 333.7.

AG
RELATORIO TECNICO ANUAL DE ... / COMISSAO NACIONAL DE ENERGIA NUCLEAR, INSTITUTO DE ENGENHARIA NUCLEAR. **Main/Corp** Instituto de Engenharia Nuclear. Portuguese. an. Instituto de Engenharia, CP 2186, 20001 Rio de Janeiro RJ Brazil. **LC** TK9041; .I57. **DD** 621.48/05.

US/0748-4151
REPORT TO CONGRESS ON ABNORMAL OCCURRENCES. [Rep. Congr. abnorm. occur.]. **Added/Corp** U.S. Nuclear Regulatory Commission. Office of Management and Program Analysis. U.S. Nuclear Regulatory Commission. Office of Management Information and Program Control. U.S. Nuclear Regulatory Commission. Office for Analysis and Evaluation of Operational Data. (1975)-. Government Publication. English. qt. $7.00 US; $8.75 other. Superintendent of Documents, US Government Printing Office, Washington DC 20402. **Tel** (202)275-3328, FAX (202)786-2377. **LC** TK9152; .R46. **DD** 363.1/79. available on microfiche (from NRC/GPO Sales Program).
Desc: Reports abnormal occurrences, an unscheduled incident or event which the NRC determined significant from the standpoint of public health and safety, involving facilities and activities regulated by the NRC and those regulated by the agreement States.

US/0193-1970
REVIEW AND EVALUATION OF THE NUCLEAR REGULATORY COMMISSION SAFETY RESEARCH PROGRAM. (REVIEW AND EVALUATION OF THE NUCLEAR REGULATORY COMMISSION SAFETY RESEARCH PROGRAM FOR FISCAL YEAR ...). **Main/Corp** U.S. Nuclear Regulatory Commission. Advisory Committee on Reactor Safeguards. (19??)-. English. an. GPO Sales Program, Division of Technical Information and Document Control, US Nuclear Regulatory Commission, Washington DC 20555. **LC** HD9698.U5; U54a. **DD** 621.48/35/0973. available on microfiche.

AG/0326-7873
REVISTA ARGENTINA NUCLEAR. Vol. 1, No. 1 (March/April 1986)-. Periodical. Spanish. Six times a year. $70.00. Editorial Nueva Ciencia SRL, Presidente Peron, 1410 Piso 10, 1307 Buenos Aires Argentina. **Tel** 011 54 1 404110. **LC** TK1359.A7; R48. **DD** 333.79/24/0981.

FR/0335-5004
REVUE GENERAL NUCLEAIRE. **See** Energy.

US/0038-531X
SOVIET ATOMIC ENERGY. ***Title Change.*** [Sov. at. energy]. Vol. 13, No. 6 (Nov. 1963)-(1992). Academic Scholarly Publication. English (Russian). mo. Plenum Press, 233 Spring Street, New York NY 10013-1578. **Tel** (212)620-8000, (800)221-9369, FAX (212)463-0742, (212)807-1047, telex 23/421139. **ED** N N Ponomarev-Stepnoi. **LC** QC770; .A843. **CODEN** SATEAZ. **[CCC].** Index available. **Pr Rev.** available in microform from University Microfilms International (UMI). Documents available from Article Express International, The Genuine Article, Ask*IEEE, CASDDS. ***Continues*** *Soviet Journal of Atomic Energy.* ***Continued by*** *Atomic Energy.*
Desc: This journal is devoted to peacetime uses of atomic energy. Covers radioactive waste disposal, radiation monitoring and safety and utilization of radioactive isotopes in industry.
Ind/Abst Appl. Mech. Rev.; Bioeng. Abstr.; Chem. Abstr.; Curr. Contents Eng. Tech. Appl. Sci.; Ei Page One; EMBASE; Eng. Index Annu.; HTFS Dig. (19??-1992); INSPEC (Jan. 1972-); Pollut. Abstr. Indexes; Res. Alert [Full Cov.]; Sci. Cit. Index (19??-19??); SCISEARCH.

UK/0039-8047
SYSTEMS TECHNOLOGY. [Syst. technol.]. V. 1- June 1967-. Periodical. English. qt. Free. Plessey Telecommunications Ltd, Edge Lane, Liverpool L7 9NW England. **LC** TK7800; .S95. **CODEN** SYTEAX. Documents available from Article Express International,

Ask*IEEE. ***Supersedes*** *Plessey Communication Journal.* **Ind/Abst** Bioeng. Abstr.; Ei Page One; Eng. Index Annu.; INSPEC (Aug. 1968-); Int. Aerosp. Abstr.

CH/1017-0529
TAI-DIAN HENENG YUEKAN. (TAI TIEN HO NENG YUEH KAN.). [Tai-dian heneng yuekan]. **Added/Corp** Tai-wan Tien li Kung ssu. Vol. 1 (Jan. 1983)-. Academic Scholarly Publication. Chinese. mo. Tai-Wan Tien Li Kung SSU, 242 Lo-SSU-Fu Lu, Taipei Taiwan. **LC** TK9001; .T34. **DD** 621.48/05. **CODEN** TTHKE5. Documents available from CASDDS.
Ind/Abst Chem. Abstr. (1986-).

GW
TATIGKEITSBERICHT - INSTITUT FUR REAKTORSICHERHEIT DER TECHNISCHEN UBERWACHUNGS-VEREINE. **Main/Corp** Institut fur Reaktorsicherheit der Technischen Uberwachungs-Vereine. German. Glockengasse 2, W-5000 Koln 1 Germany. **LC** TK9152; .I46A.

FR/0765-0019
TRAITEMENT DU SIGNAL. **Added/Corp** GRETSI (Organization). Vol. 1, No 1 (Oct./Dec. 1984)-. Periodical. French. Six times a year (two special issues per year). 300.00F (students), 770.00F Europe; 930.00F other. Dunod Gauthier Villars, 15 rue Gossin, 92543 Montrouge cedex France. **Tel** 011 33 1 46 56 52 66, FAX 011 33 1 46 57 40 69. **(Subscription address:** Centrale des Revues, 11 rue Gossin, 92543 Montrouge Cedex France.**)** **LC** TK5102.5; .T64. **DD** 621.38/043. Documents available from Ask*IEEE.
Ind/Abst INSPEC (Oct./Dec. 1984-); Math. Rev. (1984); Zentralbl. Math. Ihre Grenzgeb.

US/0003-018X
TRANSACTIONS OF THE AMERICAN NUCLEAR SOCIETY. [Trans. Am. Nucl. Soc.]. **Added/Corp** European Nuclear Society. American Nuclear Society. **VFOAT** Transactions. Vol. 1, No. 1 (June 1958)-. Monographic series. English. Three times a year (2 issues plus 1 supplement). $350.00. American Nuclear Society, PO Box 97781, Chicago IL 60678-7781. **Tel** (708)352-6611, FAX (708)579-8314. **LC** QC770; .A47. **DD** 539.7/06/273. **CODEN** TANSAO. Documents available from Article Express International, BIOSIS Document Express, Ask*IEEE, CASDDS, Documents on Demand.
Ind/Abst Alum. Ind. Abstr.; Bioeng. Abstr.; Biol. Abstr. (1968-); Ceram. Abstr. (19??-); Chem. Abstr.; Coal Abstr.; Ei Page One; Energy Inf. Abstr.; Energy Res. Abstr.; Eng. Mater. Abstr.; Eng. Index Annu.; Environ. Abstr.; HTFS Dig.; INSPEC (1968-); Int. Aerosp. Abstr.; Met. Abstr.

US/0193-8657
U.S. CENTRAL STATION NUCLEAR ELECTRIC GENERATING UNITS, SIGNIFICANT MILESTONES. [U. S. cent. stn. nucl. electr. gener. units: signif. milest.]. **Added/Corp** United States. Dept. of Energy. Division of Nuclear Power Development. United States. Dept. of Energy. Office of Nuclear Energy Programs. United States. Office of the Assistant Secretary for Nuclear Energy. United States. Office of Nuclear Reactor Programs. (19??)-. English. qt. $6.00. National Technical Information Service - NTIS, Room 2027S, 5285 Port Royal Road, Springfield VA 22161. **Tel** (703)487-4630, (703)487-4660, (703)487-4650, FAX (703)321-8547, telex 89-9405. **LC** TK1343; .U5a. **DD** 338.4/76213125/0973.

GW
UBERSETZUNGEN, KERNTECHNISCHE REGELN. **Main/Corp** Gesellschaft fuer Reaktorsicherheit. (1972)-. Government Publication. German. an. Price varies. Kerntechnischer Ausschub Geschaftsstelle / KTA, Seesebestrasse 9, 38239 Salzgitter Germany. **Tel** 05341 2 25 0, FAX 05341 2 25 2 25. **LC** TK9152; .I46b. Index available. cum. index. **Bk Rev**, (Qty: 1). **Pr Rev. Acid Free. Circ:** 500. available on diskette from the publisher. ***Continues*** *Institut fuer Reaktorsicherheit der Technischen Uberwachungs-Vereine. Ubersetzungen, Kerntechnische Regeln.*
Desc: News and information of nuclear safety standards.

UK
UKAEA LIST OF PUBLICATIONS. CUMULATION. **Main/Corp** United Kingdom Atomic Energy Authority. No. 32 (Jan./Dec. 1987)-. Periodical. English. an. **LC** Z7144.N8; U45A; QC792. **DD** 016.62148. ***Continues*** *UKAEA List of Publications Available to the Public.*

US/0731-3225
UPDATE (ATLANTA, GA.). (UPDATE : A BIMONTHLY REVIEW OF THE NUCLEAR INDUSTRY / NUCLEAR ASSURANCE CORPORATION.). [Update]. **Added/Corp** Nuclear Assurance Corporation. Nuclear Assurance Corporation. Resource Analysis Division. Nuclear Assurance Corporation. **VFOAT** NAC Update. Issue 1 (Aug. 1980)-. Periodical. English. bm. $250.00. Nuclear Assurance Corporation, 6251 Crooked Creek Road, Norcross GA 30092. **Tel** (404)447-1144. **LC** TK1078; .U68. **DD** 338.4/7621483/0212. ***Continues*** *Nuclear Industry Status, 0092-9751* ***and*** *Nuclear Fuel Status and Forecast, 0092-993X.*

US/0741-9244
UPDATE - UNITED STATES. OFFICE OF CONVERTER REACTOR DEVELOPMENT. (UPDATE.). **VFOAT** Nuclear Power Program Information and Data. English. National Technical Information Service - NTIS, Room 2027S, 5285 Port Royal Road, Springfield VA 22161. **Tel** (703)487-4630, (703)487-4660, (703)487-4650, FAX (703)321-8547, telex 89-9405. **LC** TK9023; .U62. **DD** 363.6/2/0973. available on microfiche.

US
WATER REACTOR SAFETY RESEARCH DIVISION QUARTERLY PROGRESS REPORT / DEPARTMENT OF NUCLEAR ENERGY, BROOKHAVEN NATIONAL LABORATORY. **VFOAT** Water Reactor Safety Research Programs Quarterly Report. English. qt. GPO Sales Program, Division of Technical Information and Document Control, US Nuclear Regulatory Commission, Washington DC 20555. ***Continues in part*** *Reactor Safety Research Programs, Quarterly Progress Report (Brookhaven National Laboratory, Dept. of Nuclear Energy).*

US/1056-9065
WEEKLY INFORMATION REPORT - U.S. NUCLEAR REGULATORY COMMISSION. (WEEKLY INFORMATION REPORT / OFFICE OF THE EDO.). [Wkly. inf. rep. - U. S. Nucl. Regul. Comm.]. **Added/Corp** U.S. Nuclear Regulatory Commission. Office of the Executive Director for Operations. U.S. Nuclear Regulatory Commission. (19??)-. Government Publication. English. wk. $135.00 US; $168.75 other. Superintendent of Documents, US Government Printing Office, Washington DC 20402. **Tel** (202)275-3328, FAX (202)786-2377. **DD** 353.
Desc: Summarizes items of interest and actions taken by the NRC's Offices, items approved by the Commission, a status report of Freedom of Information Act request, a list of Request for Proposals issued, contracts awarded and closed out, and a status report from the Three Mile Island Program Office.

KO
WONJARYOK ANJON CHONGBO. Periodical. Korean. Hanguk Wonjaryok Yonguso, PO Box 7 Chongyangni, Seoul South Korea. **LC** TK9152; .W66. ctrl circ.

KO
WONJARYOK SANOP. Periodical. Korean. sm. Hanguk Wonjaryok Sanop Hoeui, 5 2-ka Namdaemun-No, Chung-ku, Seoul South Korea. **LC** TK9001; .W66.

UK
WORLD NUCLEAR INDUSTRY HANDBOOK. **VFOAT** Nuclear Engineering International World Nuclear Industry Handbook. (1987)-. English. an. $200.00. Reed Business Publishing Group / England, Quadrant House, Quadrant Sutton Surrey, SM2 5AS England. **Tel** 011 44 81 652-3500. **LC** TK9001; .W68. **DD** 621.48/025. **CODEN** WNIHEQ.

CC/1000-6931
YUANZINENG KEXUE JISHU. (YUAN TZU NENG KO HSUEH CHI SHU.). [Yuanzineng kexue jishu]. **VFOAT** Yuanzineng Kexue Jishu; Atomic Energy Science and Technology. (19??)-. Periodical. Chinese (summaries and/or abstracts in English). bm. Zhongguo Yuanzineng Kexue Yanjiuyuan, Chinese Science Academy of Nuclear Energy, 43 Fucheng Lu, Beijing 100037, People's Republic of China. **Tel** 8417733. **ED** S. Zuxun. **LC** QC791.9; .Y83. **DD** 338.79/24/05. **CODEN** YKJIEZ. Documents available from CASDDS, BLDSC, CASDDS.
Ind/Abst Chem. Abstr.

ENVIRONMENTAL ISSUES

IT/0393-3369
AB (BRESCIA). (AB : ATLANTE BRESCIANO.). [AB]. **VFOAT** Atlante Bresciano. Vol. 1, No. 1 (1984)-. Periodical. Italian. qt. L60000 Italy; L90000 other. Grafo Edizioni, Via A Bassi 10, 25123 Brescia Italy. **Tel** 39 30 393221, FAX 39 30 307397. Index available. **Bk Rev. Ad Acc, Adv Mgr:** Matteo Monzagnoli. **Circ:** 5,000.

US
ACCESS EPA. **Main/Corp** United States. Environmental Protection Agency. **Added/Corp** United States. Environmental Protection Agency. Information Access Branch. (1991)-. English. an (Dec.). $34.00 North America; $58.00 others. National Technical Information Service - NTIS, Room 2027S, 5285 Port Royal Road, Springfield VA 22161. **Tel** (703)487-4630, (703)487-4660, (703)487-4650, FAX (703)321-8547, telex 89-9405. **LC** Z675.E75; U55a. **DD** 027.6/9.

IT/0391-5557
ACQUA ARIA (1977). (ACQUA ARIA.). [Acqua aria]. (1977)-. Academic Scholarly Publication. Italian. Ten times a year. L110000 Italy; L160000 EEC countries; L250000 other. Arti Poligrafiche Europee SAS, Via Casella 16, 20156 Milan Italy. **Tel** 011 39 02 330221, FAX 011 39 02 394341, telex 326544 ANTO I. **CODEN** AQARDW. Documents available from CASDDS. ***Continues*** *Ecologia Acqua e Aria Suolo.*
Ind/Abst Chem. Abstr.; Coal Abstr.; Curr. Biotechnol.

US/0092-9891
ACTIVE RESEARCH TASKS REPORT (CINCINNATI). (ACTIVE RESEARCH TASKS REPORT.). [Act. res. tasks rep.]. **Main/Corp** National Environmental Research Center, Cincinnati. English. National Environmental Research Center, Cincinnati OH 45268. **LC** TD169; .N38A. **DD** 363.6.

US/1040-4309
ADVANCES IN ENVIRONMENT, BEHAVIOR, AND DESIGN. [Adv. environ. behav. des.]. **Added/Corp** Environmental Design Research Association. **VFOAT** Environment, Behavior, and Design. Vol. 1 (1987)-. Monographic series. English. ir. Price varies per volume. Plenum Press, 233 Spring Street, New York NY 10013-1578. **Tel** (212)620-8000, (800)221-9369, FAX (212)463-0742, (212)807-1047, telex 23/421139. **ED** Ervin H. Zube and Gary T. Moore. **LC** TA166; .A36. **DD** 620.8/2/05.

AT/0725-6272
AES WORKING PAPER. (1978)-. English. ir.
Ind/Abst AESIS Q.

SG/1010-5522
AFRICAN ENVIRONMENT. [Afr. environ.]. **Added/Corp** Environment Training Programme. International African Institute. Vol. 1, No. 2 (April 1975)-. Periodical. English. Four times a year. $54.00. Enda T M, B P 3370, Dakar Senegal Africa. **Tel** 011 221 220942. **ED** Jacques Bugincourt. **LC** QH194; .A327. **DD** 301.31/096. **Bk Rev.** Documents available from Documents on Demand. ***Supersedes*** *Environment in Africa.*
Ind/Abst AGRICOLA [Select. Cov.]; Environ. Abstr.; Environ. Period. Bibliogr.; For. Abstr.; Irr. Drain. Abstr.; Leis. Recreat. Tour. Abstr.; Nematol. Abstr.; Rev. Agric. Entomol.; Rural Dev. Abstr.; World Agric. Econ.

•US/1066-3053
AFROTECH ENVIRONMENTALIST. (AFROTECH ENVIRONMENTALIST / GLOBAL ENVIRONMENTAL FORUM.). [Afrotech environ.]. **Added/Corp** Global Environmental Forum. Vol. 1, Issue 1 (Jan./Feb. 1993)-. Periodical. English. bm. $10.00. Global Environmental Forum, PO box 4028, Logan UT 84321. **DD** 363.

CH/1000-0267
AGRO-ENVIRONMENTAL PROTECTION. **See** Agriculture.

HK
AIR QUALITY IN HONG KONG. **Added/Corp** Hong Kong. Environmental Protection Agency. (19??)-. English. ir. HK$36.00. Hong Kong Government Information Service, Beaconsfield House, 4 Queens Road, Hong Kong Hong Kong. **Tel** 011 852 8428801 4, telex 61190 HKGIS. **LC** TD883.7.H6; A7. **DD** 363.73/92/095125.

US/0002-2608
AIR/WATER POLLUTION REPORT. [Air-water pollut. rep.]. (1963)-. Periodical. English. wk. $595.00. Business Publishers Inc., 951 Pershing Drive, Silver Spring MD 20910-4464. **Tel** (301)587-6300, (800)274-0122, FAX (301)585-9075. **ED** Caroline Long. **CODEN** AWPREE. **[CCC].** available on an online database from DIALOG; available on microfilm and microfiche from University Microfilms International (UMI). ***Absorbed*** *Air and Water News, 0002-2187; State Environment Report, 1054-2604.*
Desc: Coverage of environmental legislation, regulations and litigation from the nation's capital, plus special reports on state and local activities, pollution control industry news, and research and development throughout the world.
Ind/Abst BioBusiness (1991-); PTS Newsl. Database [Full Txt.].

CN/1185-0388
ALERT (CALGARY). (ALERT.). [Alert]. **Main/Corp** Alberta Environmental Research Trust. (Spring Issue 1990)-. Periodical. English. **DD** 363.7/007207123.

CN/0002-6638
ALTERNATIVES (PETERBOROUGH). (ALTERNATIVES.). [Alternatives]. **Added/Corp** Trent University. Vol. 1, No. 1 (Summer 1971)-. Periodical. English (French). qt. 21.96Can$ (individual), 43.93Can$ (institution) Canada; 27.50Can$ (individual), 55.00Can$ (institution) other. University of Waterloo Alternatives, c/o Faculty Environmental Study, Waterloo Ontario N2L 3G1 Canada. **Tel** (519)885-1211 ext 6783, FAX

(519)746-0292. **ED** Professor Robert Gibson. **LC** HC79.E5; A45. **DD** 301.31/05. **NLM** W1 AL987K. Index available. cum. index. **Bk Rev**, (Qty: 40). **Ad Acc, Adv Mgr:** M Ruby, **Tel** (519)888-4545. **Pr Rev. Circ:** 4,000. available on microfilm from Information Access Company; and Micromedia Limited; available on microfilm and microfiche from University Microfilms International (UMI). Documents available from The Genuine Article, Documents on Demand. ***Absorbed** Conserver Society Notes, 0709-5791.*
Desc: Relies on a network of scholars and grassroots activists to provide a unique perspective on Canadian and international environmental issues. Feature length articles are accompanied by news reports, book reviews and a provocative opinion column.
Ind/Abst Altern. Press Index; AQUAREF; Can. Index (?-?); Can. Period. Index; Curr. Index J. Educ.; Environ. Abstr.; Environ. Period. Bibliogr.; INIS Atomindex [Micro.]; J. Plan. Lit.; Peace Res. Abstr. J. (1983-1987); Res. Alert [Select. Cov.]; Soc. Sci. Cit. Index [Select. Cov.]; Soils Fert.; U.S. Polit. Sci. Doc.; World Agric. Econ.

IT/0393-0521
AMBIENTE RISORSE SALUTE. [Ambiente risorse salute]. (1982)-. Periodical. Italian. Eleven times a year. L90000. Centro Studi L' Uomo Ambiente, Via Delle Palme 113, 35137 Padoua Italy. **Tel** 11 39 49 8759622, FAX 11 39 49 657264. **UDC** 159.922.2. cum. index. **Bk Rev. Ad Acc. Circ:** 5,000 (ctrl).
Desc: Environmental sciences and technologies, and environmental legislation.

SW/0044-7447
AMBIO. [Ambio]. **Added/Corp** Kungl. Svenska Vetenskapsakademien. Vol. 1, No. 1 (Feb. 1972)-. Periodical. English (English). Eight times a year. $61.00 (individual); $170.00 (institution). Royal Swedish Academy of Sciences, Publications Department, Box 50005, S-104 05 Stockholm Sweden. **Tel** 011 46 8 150430, FAX 011 46 8 155670, telex 17073 ROYACOD S. **(Subscription address:** AMBIO, PO Box 1897, Lawrence KS 66044-8897.**) ED** Arno Rosemarin (editor's address: Royal Swedish Academy of Science, Box 50005, S-104 Stockholm Sweden). **LC** QH540; .A52. **DD** 301.31/05. **NLM** W1 AM103K. **CODEN** AMBOCX. **[CCC]. Ad Acc. Pr Rev. Acid Free.** available on microfilm and microfiche from University Microfilms International (UMI). Documents available from Article Express International, The Genuine Article, BIOSIS Document Express, CASDDS, Documents on Demand.
Desc: Publishes recent work in the interrelated fields of environmental management, technology and the natural sciences. It presents professional news of high scientific standards in a form that is comprehensible and instructive not only to environmental specialists, but also to scientists in other fields, students, politicians, professional planners and interested laymen.
Ind/Abst Agrofor. Abstr. (19??-19??); Appl. Soc. Sci. Index Abstr.; AQUAREF; Biodeter. Abstr.; Bioeng. Abstr.; Biol. Agric. Index; Biol. Abstr.; Biol. Dig.; Chem. Abstr.; Coal Abstr.; Curr. Aware. Biol. Sci., CABS; Curr. Contents, Agric. Biol. Environ. Sci.; Curr. Contents Eng. Tech. Appl. Sci.; Curr. Lit. Sci. Sci.; Curr. Ref. Fish Res.; Dairy Sci. Abstr.; Ecol. Abstr.; Ecology Abstr.; Ei Page One; EMBASE; Energy Inf. Abstr.; Energy Res. Abstr. (Jan. 1974-); Eng. Index Annu.; Entomol. Abstr.; Environ. Abstr.; Environ. Period. Bibliogr.; Fish Rev.; Food Sci. Technol. Abstr.; For. Prod. Abstr. (19??-19??); For. Abstr.; Geogr. Abstr. Phys. Geogr.; Geogr. Abstr. Human Geogr.; Geol. Abstr.; GeoRef; Health Saf. Sci. Abstr.; Index Vet.; INIS Atomindex [Micro.]; Int. Aerosp. Abstr.; Int. Dev. Abstr.; Irr. Drain. Abstr.; Leadscan; Middle East Abstr. Index; Nutr. Abstr. Rev., Ser. B, Live Feeds and Feed.; Ocean. Abstr.; Life Sci. Collect.; Plant Genet. Resour. Abstr.; Pollut. Abstr. Indexes; Protozoolog. Abstr.; Res. Alert [Full Cov.]; Rev. Agric. Entomol.; Rev. Med. Vet. Entomol.; Rev. Plant Pathol.; Rice Abstr.; Risk Abstr.; Saf. Health Work; Sage Fam. Stud. Abstr. (?-?); Sage Public Adm. Abstr. (?-?); Sage Urban Stud. Abstr; Sci. Cit. Index; SCISEARCH; Soc. Sci. Cit. Index [Select. Cov.]; Soils Fert.; Vet. Bull.; Trop. Dis. Bull.; Vitis Vitic. Enol. Abstr.; Wildl. Rev.; World Agric. Econ.

US/0195-4180
AMCA NEWSLETTER. Main/Corp American Mosquito Control Association. **Added/Corp** American Mosquito Control Association. Newsletter. **VAT** American Mosquito Control Association Newsletter. (June 1975)-. Newsletter. English. Four times a year. $50.00 (individuals), $85.00 (institutions) Comes with American Mosquito Control Association membership. American Mosquito Control Association, PO Box 5416, Lake Charles LA 70606-5416. **Tel** (318)474-2723, FAX (318)439-8615, (318)478-9434.

US/1051-2306
AMERICAN ENVIRONMENTAL LABORATORY. [Am. environ. lab.]. **Added/Corp** International Scientific Communications, Inc. **VFOAT** Environmental Laboratory. Vol. 1, No. 1 (1989)-. Periodical. English. Six times a year. $144.00. International Scientific Communications Inc, PO Box 870, 30 Controls Drive, Shelton CT 06484-0870. **Tel** (203)926-9300, FAX (203)926-9310, telex 964292. **LC** TD178.8.U5; A43. **DD** 620. **CODEN** AELAEL. Documents available from Documents on Demand.
Ind/Abst BioBusiness (1990-); Environ. Abstr.

US/0270-0697
ANALYTICAL STUDIES FOR THE U.S. ENVIRONMENTAL PROTECTION AGENCY. [Anal. stud. U.S. Environ. Prot. Agency]. **VAT** Analytical Studies for the United States Environmental Protection Agency. V. 1-. Monographic series. English. Price varies per volume. Printing and Publishing Office, Washington DC 20418.

US
ANNUAL AGENCY PLAN. Main/Corp Washington (State). Dept. of Ecology. (1990)-. English. **LC** TD171.3.W2; W38a. ***Continues** Washington (State). Dept. of Ecology. Ecology's Annual Program Plan.*

US
ANNUAL ENVIRONMENTAL MONITORING REPORT. MOUND FACILITY. Main/Corp Mound Facility. (1977)-. Government Publication. English. an. US Department of Energy, 1000 Independence Avenue SW, Washington DC 20585. **Tel** (202)586-5000, FAX (202)586-4073. ***Continues** Mound Laboratory. Annual Environmental Monitoring Report.*

US/0742-8022
ANNUAL EVALUATION - NEW MEXICO. ENVIRONMENTAL IMPROVEMENT DIVISION. (ANNUAL EVALUATION / STATE OF NEW MEXICO, HEALTH AND ENVIRONMENT DEPARTMENT, ENVIRONMENTAL IMPROVEMENT DIVISION.). [Annu. eval. - N.M., Environ. Improv. Div.]. **Main/Corp** New Mexico. Environmental Improvement Division. **VFOAT** E.I.D. Annual Evaluation; EIC annual Evaluation. English. an. New Mexico Environmental Improvement Division, PO Box 968, Santa Fe NM 87503. **LC** TD171.3.N49; N46A. **DD** 363.7/009789.

UK/0141-2604
ANNUAL LIST OF PUBLICATIONS - DEPARTMENT OF THE ENVIRONMENT. DEPARTMENT OF TRANSPORT. LIBRARY SERVICES. (ANNUAL LIST OF PUBLICATIONS - GREAT BRITAIN. DEPT. OF THE ENVIRONMENT. LIBRARY SERVICES.). [Annu. list publ. - Dep. Environ. Dep. Transp. Libr. Serv.]. **Main/Corp** Great Britain. Dept. of the Environment. Library Services. 1976-. English. an. £5.00. Department of the Environment and Transport, Government Building Block, 3 1 Spur 2 RMI, Limegreen Eastcote HA4 8ISEE. **Tel** 011 44 81 4295170. **ED** J M Stannard. **LC** Z5861; .G7A; TA170. **DD** 016.30131/0941. **[CCC].** Index available. **Circ:** 2,300. ***Continues** DOE Annual List of Publications, 0305-2474.*
Desc: Concerned with social and environmental planning, roads, traffic and transport, countryside recreation, housing, local government, water supply, waste disposal, pollution and conservation.

CN/0383-3739
ANNUAL REPORT - ALBERTA ENVIRONMENT. [Annu. rep. - Alta. Environ.]. **Main/Corp** Alberta. Alberta Environment. 1971-. English. an. Alberta Environment, 9th Floor, 9915 108 Street, S Tower, Edmonton Alberta T5K 2C9 Canada. **Tel** (403)427-8636. **LC** HC117.A6; A52A. **DD** 354/.7123/0077.

CN/1181-8336
ANNUAL REPORT - BRITISH COLUMBIA. MINISTRY OF ENVIRONMENT (1989). (ANNUAL REPORT / PROVINCE OF BRITISH COLUMBIA, MINISTRY OF ENVIRONMENT AND PARKS.). [Annu. rep. - B.C., Minist. Environ.]. **Main/Corp** British Columbia. Ministry of Environment. (1988/1989)-. English. Ministry of Parks, Public Information, 3rd Floor/4000 Seymour Place, Victoria British Columbia V8V 1X5 Canada. **Tel** (604)387-4609, FAX (604)387-5757. **LC** TD171.5.C2; B74a. **DD** 354.7110682/32/05. ***Continues in part** British Columbia. Ministry of Environment and Parks. Annual Report, 0838-1933.*

CN/1185-9660
ANNUAL REPORT - CANADIAN COUNCIL OF MINISTERS OF THE ENVIRONMENT. (ANNUAL REPORT.). [Annu. rep. - Can. Counc. Minist. Environ.]. **Main/Corp** Canadian Council of Ministers of the Environment. **VFOAT** Rapport Annuel; National Contaminated Sites Remediation Program. **VAT** Rapport Annuel - Conseil Canadien des Ministres de l'Environnement. (1991)-. English (French). **DD** 363.7/0971.

UK
ANNUAL REPORT - CENTRE FOR ENVIRONMENTAL STUDIES. Main/Corp Centre For Environmental Studies (Great Britain). Periodical. English. an. Centre for Environmental Studies, 62 Chandos Place, London WC2N 4HH England.

US/0092-7937
ANNUAL REPORT - CITIZENS ADVISORY COUNCIL (HARRISBURG). (ANNUAL REPORT.). **Main/Corp** Pennsylvania. Citizens' Advisory Council. 1st- 1971/72-. English. an. Free. Citizens Advisory Council, Department of Environmental Resources, Commonwealth of Pennsylvania, PO Box 2357, Harrisburg PA 17120. **Tel** (717)787-4527. **ED** Mark M McClellan. **LC** HC107.P43; E56A. **DD** 301.31/09748. **Circ:** 500 (ctrl).
Desc: Summarizes the council's activities during its 14th year of existence. Reflects actions of the council relative to the major environmental problems and issues falling within the review of its mandate.

UK
ANNUAL REPORT - DEPARTMENT OF THE ENVIRONMENT (NORTHERN IRELAND). Main/Corp Northern Ireland. Dept. of the Environment. 1974/75-. English. an. £55.00. **LC** HC257.I65; N525A. **DD** 354/.416/0077.

CN/0711-1320
ANNUAL REPORT - ENVIRONMENT CANADA (1980). (ANNUAL REPORT.). **Main/Corp** Canada. Environment Canada. **VFOAT** Rapport Annuel. (1980)-. English (French). an. Free. Information Directorate, Department of the Environment, Ottawa Ontario K1A 0H3 Canada. **Tel** (613)998-9622. **LC** HC120.E5; C29a. **DD** 354.710082/32/06. ***Continues in part** Canada. Fisheries and Environment Canada. Annual Report, 0706-2583.*

AT/0310-4796
ANNUAL REPORT - ENVIRONMENT PROTECTION AUTHORITY MELBOURNE. [Annu. rep. - Environ. Prot. Auth. Melb.]. (1972)-. Periodical. English. an. **DD** 354.9450068715.
Ind/Abst AESIS Q.

US/0091-9837
ANNUAL REPORT - ENVIRONMENTAL DEFENSE FUND. (ANNUAL REPORT.). **Main/Corp** Environmental Defense Fund. English. an. Environmental Defense Fund, 257 Park Avenue South/Floor 16, New York NY 10010. **Tel** (212)505-2100. **LC** HC110.E5; E4984A. **DD** 301.31/0973.

US/0091-0457
ANNUAL REPORT - ENVIRONMENTAL QUALITY COUNCIL. (ANNUAL REPORT.). **Main/Corp** Montana Environmental Quality Council. 1st- 1971/72-. English. an. Montana Environmental Quality Control, State Capital, Helena MT 59601. **LC** GF504.M9; M63A. **DD** 301.31/09786.

US
ANNUAL REPORT / ILLINOIS ENVIRONMENTAL FACILITIES FINANCING AUTHORITY. Main/Corp Illinois Environmental Facilities Financing Authority. English. an. **LC** HC107.I33; E55A. **DD** 353.97730082/322/06.

US/0090-8967
ANNUAL REPORT - ILLINOIS INSTITUTE FOR ENVIRONMENTAL QUALITY. (ANNUAL REPORT.). [Annu. rep. - Ill. Inst. Environ. Qual.]. **Main/Corp** Illinois Institute for Environmental Quality. (19??)-. English. an. Illinois Institute for Environmental Quality, 309 West Washington, Chicago IL 60606. **LC** TD171.3.I45; I45a. **DD** 333.7/2/09773.

US/0364-3964
ANNUAL REPORT - INDUSTRIAL ENVIRONMENTAL RESEARCH LABORATORY. (ANNUAL REPORT / INDUSTRIAL ENVIRONMENTAL RESEARCH LABORATORY (RESEARCH PARK).). Began with 1975. English. an. Technical Information Service, Mail Drop 64, Industrial Environmental Research Laboratory, Environmental Protection Agency, Research Triangle Park NC 27711. **LC** TD157.5; .I48A. **DD** 628.5. ***Continues** Annual Report (National Environmental Research Center) Research Triangle Park, N.C. (Control Systems Laboratory), 0161-5165.*

CN/0845-9606
ANNUAL REPORT - MANITOBA ENVIRONMENT AND WORKPLACE SAFETY AND HEALTH. ***Title Change.*** (ANNUAL REPORT.). [Annu. rep. - Manit. Environ. Workplace Saf. Health]. **Main/Corp** Manitoba. Manitoba Environment and Workplace Safety and Health. **VFOAT** Rapport Annuel. **VAT** Rapport Annuel - Environnement et Securite et Hygiene du Travail Manitoba. 1983/84-. English (French). **LC** HC117.M3; M228a. **DD** 354.71270082/321/06. ***Absorbed by** Annual Report of the Environmental Management Division Year Ending March 31, 0711-8252; Annual Report of the Workplace Safety and Health Division, 0845-017X.*

CN/0380-9803
ANNUAL REPORT - MANITOBA ENVIRONMENTAL COUNCIL. Main/Corp Manitoba. Environmental Council. 1- 1972/73-. English.

an. Free. Manitoba Environmental Council, Box 139, 139 Tuxedo Avenue, Winnipeg Manitoba R3N OH6 Canada. **LC** TD171.5.C2; M36A. **DD** 354/.7127/008232.

US
ANNUAL REPORT - NATIONAL ADVISORY ENVIRONMENTAL HEALTH SCIENCES COUNCIL, NATIONAL INSTITUTES OF HEALTH. **Main/Corp** National Advisory Environmental Health Sciences Council. English. an. National Advisory, Environmental Health Sciences Council, National Institutes of Health, 9000 Rockville Pike, Bethesda MD 20014.

US
ANNUAL REPORT / NATIONAL INSTITUTE FOR GLOBAL ENVIRONMENTAL CHANGE. **Main/Corp** National Institute for Global Environmental Change. **Added/Corp** United States. Dept. of Energy. **VFOAT** Annual Report to the U.S. Dept. of Energy. (1991)-. English. National Institute for Global Environmental Change, 1477 Drew Avenue, Suite 104, University of California, Davis CA 95616.

US/0361-9087
ANNUAL REPORT OF THE EASTERN ENVIRONMENTAL RADIATION FACILITY, U. S. ENVIRONMENTAL PROTECTION AGENCY. **Main/Corp** Eastern Environmental Radiation Facility (U.S.). **VAT** Annual Report of the Eastern Environmental Radiation Facility, United States Environmental Protection Agency. English. an. Eastern Environmental Radiation Facility, PO Box 244012, Montgomery AL 36124-4012. **LC** TD196.R3; E18A. **DD** 353/.007/7.

US
ANNUAL REPORT / OHIO ENVIRONMENTAL PROTECTION AGENCY. **Main/Corp** Ohio EPA. (1975)-. English. an. Free. Ohio Environmental Protection Agency, Box 1049, Columbus OH 43266-0149. **Tel** (614)466-8508. **ED** Allan Franks. **LC** TD171.3.O35; O36A. **DD** 353.97710082/321/06. **Circ:** 1,000.
Desc: Information about pollution control programs in the state of Ohio, including air and water pollution and waste disposal/management.

US/0094-1697
ANNUAL REPORT ON THE QUALITY OF THE ENVIRONMENT (ST. PAUL). (ANNUAL REPORT ON THE QUALITY OF THE ENVIRONMENT.). **Main/Corp** Minnesota. Governor. **VFOAT** Report On the Quality of the Environment. No. 1 (1974)-. English. an. Centennial Office Building, St Paul MN 55155. **LC** GF504.M6; M55A. **DD** 301.31/09776.

CN
ANNUAL REPORT - PRINCE EDWARD ISLAND. ENVIRONMENTAL CONTROL COMMISSION. **Main/Corp** Prince Edward Island. Environmental Control Commission. 1971/72-. English. an. **LC** TD27.P7; P75A. **DD** 354/.717/008232.

US/0191-4049
ANNUAL REPORT - VIRGINIA ENVIRONMENTAL ENDOWMENT. **Main/Corp** Virginia Environmental Endowment. 1977-. English. an. Free. Virginia Environmental Endowment, PO Box 790, Richmond VA 23206-0790. **Tel** (804)644-5000. **LC** TD171.3.V8; V57A. **DD** 333.7. **Circ:** 5,000 (ctrl).

AT
ANNUAL REPORTS / ENVIRONMENTAL PROTECTION AUTHORITY AND CONSERVATION AND ENVIRONMENT COUNCIL. **Main/Corp** Western Australia. Environmental Protection Authority. **Added/Corp** Western Australia. Conservation and Environment Council. **VFOAT** Annual Report. (19??)-. English. **LC** TD171.5.A83; W47a. **DD** 354.9410082/321/06. ***Continues*** *Western Australia. Environmental Protection Authority. Environmental Protection Authority Annual Report Incorporating Conservation & Environment Council Annual Report.*
Ind/Abst AESIS Q.

US
API ABSTRACTS. HEALTH & ENVIRONMENT. ***Title Change.*** **See** Environmental Issues-Abstracting, Bibliographies and Statistics.

●NE/0926-3373
APPLIED CATALYSIS. B : ENVIRONMENTAL. **VFOAT** Environmental. Vol. 1 No. 1 (Feb. 1992)-. Academic Scholarly Publication. English. Eight times a year (2 vols.). Fl950.00; Fl6225.00 combination subscription with Applied Catalysis A. Elsevier Science Publishers BV, PO Box 211, 1000 AE Amsterdam Netherlands. **Tel** 011 31 20 5803642, FAX 011 31 20 5862696, telex 15682. **ED** B. Delmon. **LC** QD505; .A662. **CODEN** ACBEE3. **[CCC].** Documents available from Article Express International, The Genuine Article, CASDDS. ***Continues in part*** *Applied Catalysis, 0166-9834.*
Desc: Publishes papers on all environmental aspects of applied catalysis. Provides news and views relevant to environmental catalysis, together with meeting reports, project summaries, book reviews, and a calendar of forthcoming events.
Ind/Abst Chem. Abstr.; Curr. Contents Eng. Tech. Appl. Sci.; Curr. Contents Phys. Chem. Earth Sci.; Eng. Index Annu.; Lit. Pat. Abstr., Oilfield Chem. (1992-); Lit. Abstr., Catal. Catal.; Lit. Abstr., Health Environ.; Lit. Abstr., Pet. Refin. Petrochem.; Lit. Abstr., Pet. Substit.; Lit. Abstr., Transp. Storage; Res. Alert [Full Cov.]; Sci. Cit. Index; Soc. Sci. Cit. Index [Select. Cov.].

FI/0787-0396
ARCHIVES OF COMPLEX ENVIRONMENTAL STUDIES : ACES. **VFOAT** ACES. Vol. 1, No. 1 (Dec. 1989)-. Periodical. English. Three times a year (Approx. 3-4 times per year). $191.00 (individuals); $320.00 (institution). ACES Publishing Ltd, PO Box 114, SF-33101 Tampere Finland. **Tel** 011/358/31/633207. **ED** Olavi Manninen. **LC** RA565.A1; A73. **DD** 616.9/8/005. **NLM** W1; AR451ZE. **Bk Rev. Ad Acc. Pr Rev.** ctrl circ.
Desc: Complex interactions between and combined effects of various physical, chemical, psycho-social, biological and organization environmental factors are the main interest of the periodical. So far the periodical distributes information about research, applications and methods that are suited for the study of complex environmental regulations and planning, and which specially deal with environment and work based loading factors.
Ind/Abst Ergon. Abstr.

US/0090-4341
ARCHIVES OF ENVIRONMENTAL CONTAMINATION AND TOXICOLOGY. [Arch. environ. contam. toxicol.]. **VFOAT** Environmental Contamination and Toxicology. Vol. 1 (1973)-. Periodical. English. Eight times a year. $478.00. Springer-Verlag New York Inc., 175 5th Avenue, New York NY 10010. **Tel** (212)460-1500, telex 232 235 SPB UR. **(Subscription address:** Springer Verlag New York Inc. / for North America, 44 Hartz Way, Secaucus NJ 07096.**) ED** A Benevue and M C Bowman. **LC** QH545.P4; A7. **DD** 615.9. **NLM** W1 AR454R. **CODEN** AECTCV. **[CCC]. Pr Rev.** available on microfilm and microfiche from University Microfilms International (UMI). Documents available from The Genuine Article, CASDDS, Documents on Demand.
Desc: Covers original experimental and theoretical research pertaining to environmental contamination and toxicology.
Ind/Abst AGRICOLA [Select. Cov.]; AQUAREF; BioBusiness; Biodeter. Abstr. (1991-); Chem. Abstr.; Chem. Hazards Ind.; Chem. Titles; Coal Abstr.; CSA Neuro. Abstr. (?-?); Curr. Contents, Agric. Biol. Environ. Sci.; Curr. Contents Life Sci.; Curr. Ref. Fish Res.; Dairy Sci. Abstr.; Ecol. Abstr. (?-?); Ecology Abstr.; EMBASE; Energy Inf. Abstr.; Energy Res. Abstr. (Dec. 1978-); Entomol. Abstr.; Environ. Abstr.; Environ. Period. Bibliogr.; Fish Rev.; Food Sci. Technol. Abstr.; For. Prod. Abstr. (19??-19??); For. Abstr.; GeoRef; Health Saf. Sci. Abstr.; Health Plan. Adminis.; Helminthol. Abstr. (19??-19??); Index Med.; Int. Aerosp. Abstr.; Irr. Drain. Abstr.; Key Word Index Wildl. Res.; Lab. Hazards Bull.; Leadscan; Microbiol. Abstr. Sect. A; Microbiol. Abstr. Sect. C; Nutr. Abstr. Rev., Ser. B, Live Feeds and Feed.; Nutr. Abstr. Rev., Ser. A, Hum. Exp.; Nutr. Res. Newsl.; Ocean. Abstr.; Life Sci. Collect.; PESTDOC; Phys. Briefs; Pollut. Abstr. Indexes; Postharvest News Inf.; Res. Alert [Full Cov.]; Rev. Agric. Entomol.; Rev. Med. Vet. Entomol.; Rev. Med. Vet. Mycology; Rice Abstr.; Sci. Cit. Index; SCISEARCH; Soils Fert.; Toxicol. Abstr.; Weed Abstr.; Wildl. Rev.

PL/0324-8461
ARCHIWUM OCHRONY SRODOWISKA. [Arch. ochr. sr.]. **Added/Corp** Zakad Ochrony Srodowiska Regionow Przemysowych (Polska Akademia Nauk). **VFOAT** Arkhiv Po Okhrane Sredy; Archives of Environmental Protection. (1975)-. Academic Scholarly Publication. Polish (summaries and/or abstracts in English, French and Russian). qt. Price on request. **(Subscription address:** ARS Polona, PO Box 1001, 00068 Warsaw Poland.**) LC** TD169; .A73. **CODEN** AOSRD6. Documents available from CASDDS. ***Continues*** *Biuletyn (Zakad Ochrony Srodowiska Regionow Przemysowych (Polska Akademia Nauk)), 0324-847X.*
Ind/Abst Chem. Abstr. (Oct. 1982-); Coal Abstr.; Energy Res. Abstr.

UK/0953-0428
AREE. ANNUAL REVIEW OF ENVIRONMENTAL EDUCATION. (AREE.). [AREE., Annu. rev. environ. educ.]. **VFOAT** Annual Review of Environmental Education. (1987)-. Academic Scholarly Publication. English. an. £10.00. Council for Environmental Education, University of Reading, London Road, Reading RG1 5AQ England. **Tel** 0734 756061, FAX 0734 756264. **ED** Steve Sterling. **DD** 333.707041. **Bk Rev**, (Qty: 4). **Ad Acc. Pr Rev. Circ:** 1,000. available on microfiche from ERIC. Documents available from BLDSC. ***Continues*** *R.E.E.D. Review of Environmental Education Developments, 0307-1626.*
Desc: Reports, evaluates, encourages and guides progress in environmental education, providing information on important initiatives in the UK and comparative international developments. Emphasis is on current thinking and developments rather than practice and methodology.
Ind/Abst Br. Educ. Index.

US/1049-9342
ARIZONA ENVIRONMENTAL LAW LETTER. **See** Law.

PH/0116-2993
ASIAN ENVIRONMENT. [Asian environ.]. (19??)-. Academic Scholarly Publication. English. qt. $30.00 (one year), $55.00 (two year), $70.00 (three year). Ear Quad, PO Box 90, MCC Makati Philippines. **Tel** 8160672/8195909. **CODEN** ASENEL. Index available. cum. index. **Bk Rev. Ad Acc.** ctrl circ. Documents available from CASDDS.
Ind/Abst Biodeter. Abstr. (1991-); Chem. Abstr. (1985-); Ecol. Abstr.; Environ. Period. Bibliogr.; Field Crop Abstr.; Fluid Abstr., Civil Eng.; Fluid Abstr. Proc. Eng.; FLUIDEX (199?-); Geogr. Abstr. Phys. Geogr.; Geogr. Abstr. Human Geogr.; Hum. Rights Intern. Rep.; Int. Dev. Abstr.; Life Sci. Collect.; Pollut. Abstr. Indexes; Seed Abstr.; Soils Fert.; Weed Abstr.; Wheat Barley Trit. Abstr.

MY/0127-7170
ASIAN-PACIFIC ENVIRONMENT. ***Suspended.*** **Added/Corp** Sahabat Alam Malaysia. **VFOAT** APEN. (1983)-Vol. 7 No. 1 (19??). Periodical. English. Eight times a year. $24.00 (two year). APPEN, 19 Kelawai Road, 10250 Penang Malaysia. **Tel** 011 60 4 375705 376930.
Ind/Abst Altern. Press Index (199?-).

UK/0957-1272
ATMOSPHERIC ENVIRONMENT. PART B, URBAN ATMOSPHERE. ***Title Change.*** [Atmos. environ., B. Urban atmos.]. **VFOAT** Urban Atmosphere. Vol. 24B, No. 1 (1990)-Vol. 27B, No. 4 (Dec. 1993). Academic Scholarly Publication. English. Three times a year. Pergamon Press, An Imprint of Elsevier Science Ltd., The Boulevard, Langford Lane, Kidlington, Oxford OX5 1GB United Kingdom. **Tel** 011 44 865 843000, 011 44 865 843699, FAX 011 44 865 843010. **ED** R. D. Bornstein. **LC** TD881; .A82. **DD** 628.5/3. **CODEN** AEBAE5. available on microfilm and microfiche from University Microfilms International (UMI). Documents available from The Genuine Article, BIOSIS Document Express, Ask*IEEE, CASDDS. ***Continues in part*** *Atmospheric Environment, 0004-6981.* ***Merged with*** *Atmospheric Environment. Part A, General Topics, 0960-1686* ***to form*** *Atmospheric Environment (Oxford, England : 1994).*
Desc: Articles will include issues on field studies, data analysis, models and reviews of urbanization on the atmosphere.
Ind/Abst Air Pollut. Titles; Anal. Abstr.; Appl. Sci. Technol. Index; Aqualine Abstr.; Aquat. Sci. Fish. Abstr. (Computer File); Biol. Abstr. (1990-); Chem. Abstr.; Curr. Aware. Biol. Sci., CABS; Curr. Contents, Agric. Biol. Environ. Sci.; Curr. Contents Phys. Chem. Earth Sci.; Ei Page One; EMBASE; Environ. Period. Bibliogr.; Fluid Abstr., Civil Eng.; Fluid Abstr. Proc. Eng.; FLUIDEX; Geogr. Abstr. Human Geogr.; GeoRef; INSPEC (1990-); Lit. Pat. Abstr., Oilfield Chem. (1990-); Lit. Abstr., Catal. Catal.; Lit. Abstr., Health Environ.; Lit. Abstr., Pet. Refin. Petrochem.; Lit. Abstr., Pet. Substit.; Lit. Abstr., Transp. Storage; Res. Alert [Full Cov.]; Sci. Cit. Index; SCISEARCH; Soc. Sci. Cit. Index [Select. Cov.]; Soils Fert.

●US/1065-0385
$AVE OUR PLANET. **VFOAT** Save Our Planet. (1992)-. Periodical. English. mo. $18.00. Kelly Green Productions, PO Box 2835, Kensington MD 20891.

US/0092-5756
BIBLIOGRAPHY OF NOISE, A. ***Ceased.*** 1965/70-Ceased ?. Bibliography. English. ir. Whitston Publishing Company Inc, PO Box 958, Troy NY 12181. **Tel** (518)283-4363. **ED** Irving Stephens. **LC** Z5862.2.N6; B55. **DD** 016.6202/3. **NLM** ZWA 776 F645B. **Bk Rev. Ad Acc. Circ:** 200 (ctrl).
Desc: International listing of all material published on the physical and social effects of noise.

UK/0951-0621
BIODETERIORATION ABSTRACTS. **See** Environmental Issues-Abstracting, Bibliographies and Statistics.

GR/1012-2516
BIONEWS ATHENS. [Bionews Athens]. (1987)-. Periodical. English. Biopolitics International Organisation, c/o Dr Agni Vlavianos-Arvanitis, 10 Tim Vassou Street, GR 115 21 Athens Greece. **Tel** 643.2419, FAX 643.4093. **ED** Dr. Agni Vlavianos-Arvanitis.

GR/1012-2532
BIOPOLITICS ATHENS. [Biopolitics Athens]. **VFOAT** Proceedings - International Conference on Biopolitics. (1988)-. Periodical. English. $15.00. Biopolitics International Organisation, c/o Dr Agni Vlavianos-Arvanitis, 10 Tim Vassou Street, GR 115 21 Athens Greece. **Tel** 643.2419, FAX 643.4093. **ED** Dr Agni

Vlavianos-Arvanitis. **Circ:** 1,500.
Desc: Covers subject areas with emphasis on the relationship between humans and their environment.

US/1049-8893
BNA'S NATIONAL ENVIRONMENT WATCH. ***Ceased.*** (BNA'S NATIONAL ENVIRONMENT WATCH / THE BUREAU OF NATIONAL AFFAIRS, INC.). [BNA's natl. environ. watch]. **Added/Corp** Bureau of National Affairs. **VFOAT** National Environment Watch. **VAT** Bureau of National Affairs's National Environment Watch. Vol. 1, No. 1 (Apr. 16, 1990)-(Dec. 1993). Periodical. English. wk. Bureau of National Affairs Inc., 9435 Key West Avenue, Rockville MD 20850. **Tel** (800)372-1033, (301)258-1033, FAX (301)948-5823. **DD** 344. **[CCC].**

●US/1065-8076
BNA'S STATE ENVIRONMENT & SAFETY REGULATORY MONITORING REPORT. **Added/Corp** Bureau of National Affairs (Washington, D.C.). **VFOAT** BNA's State Environment and Safety Regulatory Monitoring Report; State Environment and Safety Regulatory Monitoring Report; State Environment & Safety Regulatory Monitoring Report. **VAT** Bureau of National Affairs' State Environment and Safety Regulatory Monitoring Report. (1993)-. Periodical. English. bw. $895.00. Bureau of National Affairs Inc., 9435 Key West Avenue, Rockville MD 20850. **Tel** (800)372-1033, (301)258-1033, FAX (301)948-5823. **[CCC].**

NE/0925-1650
BODEM ALPHEN AAN DEN RIJN. (BODEM.). (1991)-. English. qt (Mar., June, Sept., Dec.). Fl89.50. Samsom, H D Tjeenk Willink, Antwoordnummer 10153, 2400 VB Alphen Aan de Rijn, Netherlands. **Tel** 011 31 1720668223.

SZ
BRUNDTLAND BULLETIN / THE CENTRE FOR OUR COMMON FUTURE. **Added/Corp** Centre for Our Common Future. (198?)-. Bulletin. English. qt. $60.00. Centre for Our Common Future, Palais Wilson, 52 Rue de Paquis, 1201 Geneva Switzerland. **Tel** 011 41 22 732 7117. **ED** Anja Halle. **LC** HC79.E5; B8. Index available. cum. index. ctrl circ.
Desc: Information on the environment and development.

UK/0306-8307
BULLETIN / BRITISH ECOLOGICAL SOCIETY. [Bull. - Br. Ecol. Soc.]. **Added/Corp** British Ecological Society. (June 1970)-. Bulletin. English. qt. Expediters of the Printed Word, 515 Madison Avenue, New York NY 10022. **Tel** 01-686-2599.

CN/1183-4528
BULLETIN / CANADIAN ENVIRONMENTAL NETWORK. [Bull. - Can. Environ. Netw.]. **Added/Corp** Reseau Canadien de l'Environnement. Vol. 2, No. 1 (Jan./Feb. 1991)-. Bulletin. French (English). bm. Free for members. Reseau Canadien de L'Environnement, CP 1289, Succ. B, Ottawa Ontario K1P 5R3 Canada. **DD** 333.7. ***Continues*** *Environmental News (Ottawa, Ont.).*

CN/1183-4528
BULLETIN / CANADIAN ENVIRONMENTAL NETWORK. [Bull. - Can. Environ. Netw.]. **Added/Corp** Canadian Environmental Network. **VAT** Canadian Environmental Network Bulletin. Vol. 2, No. 1 (Jan./Feb. 1991)-. Bulletin. English (French). Five times a year. 25.00Can$ (individuals), 40.00Can$ (institutions). Canadian Environmental Network, PO Box 1289, Station B, Ottawa Ontario K1P 5R3 Canada. **Tel** (613)563-2078, FAX (613)563-7236. **DD** 333.7. ***Continues*** *Environmental News (Ottawa, Ont.).*
Desc: Forum for environmental groups across Canada to share views and keep up to date on national environmental caucases, consultations involving public interest groups, and major environmental activities.

FR/0980-949X
BULLETIN DE DOCUMENTATION / MINISTERE DE L'ENVIRONNEMENT. **Added/Corp** France. Ministere de l'Environnement. (19??)-. Periodical. French. Five times a year. 210.00F France; 275.00F other. Documentation Francaise, 29 Quai Voltaire, 75344 Paris Cedex 7 France. **Tel** 011 33 1 40157000, FAX 011 33 1 40157230, telex 204 826 DOCFRAN. **(Subscription address:** Documentation Francaise, 124 rue Henri Barbusse, 93308 Aubervilliers Cedex France.**)** **LC** Z5863.P6; B84; HC280.E5. **DD** 016.3637/0944/05. ***Continues*** *Bulletin de Documentation (France. Secretariat d'Etat Aupres du Premier Ministre Charge de l'Enviornnement et de la Qualite de la Vie).*

CN/0227-3462
BULLETIN - ENVIRONMENT COUNCIL OF ALBERTA. [Bull. - Environ. Counc. Alta.]. **Main/Corp** Environment Council of Alberta. No. 1-. Bulletin. English. Environment Council of Alberta, 2100 College Plaza Tower 3, 8215 112th Street, Edmonton Alberta T6G 2M4 Canada. **DD** 363.7/0097123.

AT/1030-0120
BULLETIN - ENVIRONMENTAL PROTECTION AUTHORITY, WESTERN AUSTRALIA. [Bull. - Environ. Prot. Auth. West. Aust.]. (1987)-. Monographic series. English. ir. Price varies per volume. **DD** 333.7209941. ***Continues*** *Bulletin - Department of Conservation and Environment, Western Australia, 0156-2983.*
Ind/Abst AESIS Q.

UK/0268-7402
BULLETIN - UK CENTRE FOR ECONOMIC AND ENVIRONMENTAL DEVELOPMENT. **See** Economics.

US/1052-7206
BUSINESS AND THE ENVIRONMENT. [Bus. environ.]. **Added/Corp** Cutter Information Corp. Vol. 1, No. 1 (1 Sept. 1990)-. Periodical. English. Twelve times a year. $197.00 (university), $497.00 (other) US; $237.00*(university), $597.00 (other) other. Cutter Information Corporation, 37 Broadway, Arlington MA 02174-5539. **Tel** (617)648-8700, (800)964-5118, FAX (617)648-8707, (617)648-1950, telex 650 100 9891. **DD** 363. **[CCC].** available on an online database (file 636/Full-Text) from DIALOG.
Ind/Abst PTS Newsl. Database [Full Txt.].

US
BUYER'S GUIDE TO ENVIRONMENTAL MEDIA. (BUYER'S GUIDE TO ENVIRONMENTAL MEDIA; A DIRECTORY OF BOOKS, MAGAZINES, FILMS, AND INFORMATION SOURCES.). **Added/Corp** Environmental Information Center. **VFOAT** Energy. No. 1 (1973)-. Directory. English. Environmental Information Center / New York, 292 Madison Avenue, New York NY 10017. **Tel** (212)685-0845. **DD** 301.3.

US/1073-5852
BUZZWORM'S EARTH JOURNAL. ***Ceased.*** **VFOAT** Earth Journal. (1993)-Ceased with Vol. 5 (199?). English. bm. Buzzworm Inc., 2305 Canyon Boulevard, Suite 206, Boulder CO 80302. **Tel** (800)825-0061, (303)442-1969. ***Continues*** *Buzzworm, 0898-2996.*
Desc: An environmental guide and annual reference source that covers major eco-issues, film, music, green business, new products and eco-travel, plus offers valuable eco-tips, original surveys and more.
Ind/Abst Mag. Artic. Summar. Elite (Nov. 1993-Feb. 1994).

US/0148-0324
CALIFORNIA ENVIRONMENTAL DIRECTORY. Ed. 2 (1977)-. Directory. English. ir. $40.00, $25.00 (public, academic and governmental libraries). California Institute of Public Affairs, PO Box 189040, Claremont College, Sacramento CA 95818. **Tel** (916)442-2472. **ED** Thaddeus C Trzyna. **LC** HC107.C23; E556. **DD** 301.31/09794. ***Supersedes*** *California Environment Yearbook & Directory, 0092-1343.*
Desc: Describes more than 1,000 agencies and citizens' groups. User's guide identifies groups interested in 40 broad subject categories.

US/0895-2299
CALIFORNIA ENVIRONMENTAL INSIDER. [Calif. environ. insid.]. **VFOAT** CEI. Vol. 1, No. 1 (June 5, 1987)-. Periodical. English. Twenty-four times a year. $295.00. California Envrl Insider, PO Box 10106, San Rafael CA 94912. **Tel** (415)456-8411, FAX (415)456-1314. **ED** Roger W. Pearson (phone: (415)647-8633). **DD** 363. Index available (Quarterly).
Desc: Provides comprehensive coverage of California air and water quality. Hazardous and solid waste and toxic materials issues.

US/0739-8042
CALIFORNIA TODAY. (CALIFORNIA TODAY PLANNING & CONSERVATION LEAGUE.). **Added/Corp** Planning & Conservation League (Calif.). (19??)-. Periodical. English. Six times a year (Jan. Mar., May, July, Sept., Nov.). $33.00. Planning and Conservation League, 926 J Street, Auite 612, Sacramento CA 95814. **Tel** (916)444-8726, FAX (916)448-1789.

CN/0711-6659
CANADIAN ACOUSTICS. [Can. acoust.]. **Added/Corp** Canadian Acoustical Association. **VFOAT** Acoustique Canadienne. Vol. 10, No. 1 (Jan. 1982)-. Periodical. English (French). qt. 20.00Can$ Canada; 25.00Can$ US; 35.00Can$ other. Canadian Acoustical Association, 2410 Old Pheasant Road, Mississauga, Ontario L5A 2S1, Canada. **Tel** (905)949-2164. **ED** R Hetu and M Hodgson. **DD** 363.7/4/05. **CODEN** CAACDX. **Bk Rev. Ad Acc. Pr Rev. Circ:** 500. Documents available from Ask*IEEE. ***Continues*** *Acoustics and Noise Control in Canada, 0229-2238.*
Desc: Contains refereed papers and news on regarding sound and noise, especially in Canada.
Ind/Abst Acoust. Abstr.; Ind. Hyg. Dig. (19??-); INSPEC (Jan. 1982-); Shock Vibr. Dig.

CN/1187-1202
CANADIAN ENVIRONMENTAL DIRECTORY. [Can. environ. dir.]. (1991)-. Directory. English. $160.00 per vol. Canadian Almanac and Directory Publishing Co., 2775 Matheson Boulevard East, Mississauga Ontario L4W 9Z9 Canada. **Tel** (905)238-6074. **DD** 363.7/002571.

CN
CANADIAN ENVIRONMENTAL PROTECTION. (19??)-. English. Nine times a year (Jan./Feb., July,/Aug., & Nov./Dec. issues combined). 39.00Can$ Canada; 45.00Can$ US; 75.00Can$ other. Baum Publications Ltd., 1625 Ingleton Avenue, Burnaby British Columbia V5C 4L8 Canada. **Tel** (604)291-9900, FAX (604)291-1906. **ED** Dan Kennedy. **Ad Acc, Adv Mgr:** Ian Stuart, **Tel** (604)291-9900. ctrl circ.

CN/1181-795X
CANADIAN ENVIRONMENTAL REGULATION & COMPLIANCE NEWS. [Can. environ. reg. compliance news]. **VAT** Canadian Environmental Regulation and Compliance News. Vol. 1, No. 1 (Sept. 90)-. Periodical. English. mo. 297.00Can$ Canada; $317.00 other. Templegate Information Service, 131 Bloor Street West, Suite 200 - 206, Toronto Ontario M5S 9Z9 Canada. **Tel** (416)873-6424. **DD** 344.71/046/05.
Desc: Information on environmental law, policy and the general environment.

CN/0316-0343
CANADIAN PLAINS BULLETIN. **See** History(General)-History of North, South, and Central America.

US/0884-7452
CAS BIOTECH UPDATES. ENVIRONMENTAL BIOTECHNOLOGY. **See** Medical Science and Technology-Biotechnology.

BE
CATALYST FOR ENVIRONMENTAL CONTROL STATIONARY SOURCES. English. ir. Strategic Analysis Europe, Avenue Louise 66, 1050 Brussels Belgium.

US/0275-827X
CENTRAL NEW YORK ENVIRONMENT. [Cent. N.Y. environ.]. **VFOAT** Environment. (June/July 1975)-. Newspaper. English. Six times a year. $9.00 US; $14.00 Canada; $19.00 other. Central New York Environment, 658 West Onondaga Street, Syracuse NY 13204. **Tel** (315)437-6481. **ED** Lee Gechas (editor's phone: (315)446-5319). **Ad Acc, Adv Mgr:** Walt Aikman.

CN/1182-7955
CHAIRMAN'S UPDATE / PREMIER'S ROUND TABLE ON ENVIRONMENT AND ECONOMY. [Chairm. update - Prem. Round Table Environ. Econ.]. **Main/Corp** New Brunswick. Premier's Round Table on Environment and Economy. (June 1990)-. Periodical. English. **DD** 333.7/09715/1.

US/0738-7776
CHEMECOLOGY. [Chemecology]. **Added/Corp** Chemical Manufacturers Association (U.S.) Manufacturing Chemists' Association (U.S.). **VFOAT** Chem Ecology. (1972)-. Periodical. English. Ten times a year. Free. Chemical Manufacturers Association, 2501 M Street Northwest, Washington DC 20037. **Tel** (202)887-1100. **ED** Keith C. Skillman. **CODEN** CHMCE7. **Circ:** 24,000 (ctrl). Documents available from Documents on Demand. ***Continues*** *Currents/Pilot.*
Desc: Environmental topics including hazardous waste, clean air and water; health and safety issues.
Ind/Abst Biol. Dig.; Curr. Index J. Educ.; Environ. Abstr.; Environ. Period. Bibliogr.; Ind. Hyg. Dig.

US/1054-5131
CHEMICAL PACKAGING REVIEW, THE. [Chem. packag. rev.]. Vol. 1 No. 1 (May/June 1990)-. Periodical. English. Six times a year (Jan. Mar., May, July, Sept., Nov.). $195.00 US; $203.88 Canada; $204.06 Mexico; $213.06 Europe; $217.56 Asia & Africa; $218.10 other. Packaging Research International Incorporated, PO Box 3144, West Chester PA 19381. **Tel** (215)436-8292, FAX (215)436-9422. **ED** Vincent Vitallo. **LC** TP201; .C515. **DD** 660. Index Available Received separately--bound from publisher (Bound in Vol. 4 No. 1 (May 30, 1993)-). cum. index. **Bk Rev. Ad Acc. Circ:** 7,800 (ctrl).

UK/0954-2299
CHEMICAL SPECIATION AND BIOAVAILABILITY. [Chem. speciat. bioavailab.]. Vol. 1, No. 1 (Mar. 1989)-. Academic Scholarly Publication. English. qt. £98.00 (institution), £43.00 (individual) UK; $196.00 (institution), $86.00*(individual). Science and Technology Letters, PO Box 81, Northwood, Middlesex, HA6 3DN UK. **Tel** 11 44 9238 23586, FAX 11 44 9238 25066. **LC** TD196.C45; C484. **DD** 628.5/2. **CODEN** CHSBEY. **[CCC].** Index available. cum. index. **Bk Rev. Ad Acc. Circ:** 500. Documents available from BIOSIS Document Express, CASDDS.
Desc: Presents papers which explore the chemical, physical, biological and ecological aspects of chemical species in the environment, together with process chemistry.
Ind/Abst Biodeter. Abstr. (1991-); Biol. Abstr. (1991-); Chem. Abstr.; Curr. Contents, Agric. Biol. Environ. Sci.; Soils Fert.; Weed Abstr.

Environmental Issues

US/1056-8948
CHICAGO ENVIRONMENT, THE. [Chic. environ.]. **Added/Corp** South Chicago Legal Clinic. Vol. 1, No. 1 (Summer 1991)-. Periodical. English. qt. Free. South Chicago Legal Clinic, 2938 East 91st Street, Chicago IL 60617. **DD** 333.

●UK
CLEAN AIR AND ENVIRONMENTAL PROTECTION. Added/Corp National Society for Clean Air and Environmental Protection. **VFOAT** Clean Air. Vol.22 No.1 (1992)-. Periodical. English. *Continues Clean Air.*

US
CLEAN AIR NEWSLETTER. (July 1991)-. Newsletter. English. bm. Free. Illinois Environmental Protection Agency, 2200 Churchill Road, Springfield IL 62706.
Desc: Keeps you informed as to the current status of the implementation of the Clean Air Act Ammendments (CAAA) and related air issues.

US
CLEARING. English (summaries and/or abstracts in Spanish). Five times a year (Jan., Mar., May, Sept., Nov.). $15.00 (individuals); $25.00 (institutions). Environmental Education Project, 19600 South Molalla Avenue, Orgeon City OR 97045. **Tel** (503)229-4721. **ED** Lawrence J. Beutler, (editor's address: P. O. Box 5176, Oregon City, OR 97045, phone: (503)656-0155). **Circ:** 2,000.

US/1066-5404
CLEARINGHOUSE BULLETIN / CARRYING CAPACITY NETWORK. [Clgh. bull. - Carr. Capacity Netw.]. **Added/Corp** Carrying Capacity Network. (1991)-. Periodical. English. mo. $85.00 (institutions), $20.00 (individuals). Carrying Capacity Network, 1325 G Street Northwest, Suite 1003, Washington DC 20005-3104. **Tel** (202)879-3044, FAX (202)879-3019. **ED** David E. Durham. **DD** 363.
Desc: Provides information on a variety of organizations concerned with sustainability issues. Includes a review of environmental legislation, and news with analysis from a carrying capacity perspective.

US/0271-4094
CODE OF FEDERAL REGULATIONS. 40, PROTECTION OF ENVIRONMENT. [Code Fed. regul., 40. Prot. environ.]. **Added/Corp** United States. Office of the Federal Register. **VFOAT** Protection of Environment; CFR. N40, Protection of Environment. **VAT** Code of Federal Regulations. Forty. Protection of Environment. (1971)-. English. an. $765.00. Regulations Management Corporation, 1505 Arlington Road, Bloomington IN 47404. **Tel** (812)333-7347. **NLM** KF 70.A3 C668.
Desc: Special edition of the Federal Register, containing a codification of documents.

FR/0397-6416
CODE PERMANENT ENVIRONNEMENT ET NUISANCES. [Code perm. environ. nuis.]. (1973)-. French. ir. 1140.00F. Editions Legislatives et Admin, 80 82 Avenue de la Marne, 92546 Montrouge Cedex France. **Tel** 011 33 1 40926868. **UDC** 628.5.
Desc: Focuses on the affects of industry, commerce, and various forms of pollution on the environment.

FR/0184-7473
COMBAT NATURE PERIGUEUX. (1974)-. Periodical. French. qt. 170.00F. Fedn Natl Def de l'Environment, BP 3046, 24003 Perigneux, Cedex France. **Tel** 33 53 082901, FAX 33 53 095252. **ED** Alain de Lwarte. **UDC** 502.7. **Bk Rev,** (Qty: 4). **Ad Acc, Adv Mgr:** same as editor. **Circ:** 12,000 (ctrl). *Formed by the union of Maisons et Paysages (Panazol), 0184-7481 and Mieux Vivre (Paris. 1973), 0184-749X.*
Desc: Review about environmental protection associations and about ecological action.

US/1052-6331
COMMON SENSE ON ENERGY AND OUR ENVIRONMENT. See Energy.

US/0192-270X
COMPREHENSIVE ENVIRONMENT, HEALTH, AND SAFETY PROGRAM REPORT. See Public Health and Safety.

FR/0250-4499
CONNECT: UNESCO-UNEP ENVIRONMENTAL EDUCATION NEWSLETTER. Added/Corp Unesco. United Nations Environment Programme. Vol. 1 Jan. (1976)-. Newsletter. English (French, Spanish, Russian, Arabic, Hindi and Chinese). qt. free. UNESCO / France, 31 rue Francois Bonvin, 75732 Paris Cedex 15 France. **Tel** 011 33 1 45684564, 011 33 1 45684565, FAX 011 33 1 42733007, telex 204461 Paris. **Circ:** 20,000. *Continues Connexion.*
Desc: The official newsletter of the UNESCO-UNEP International Environmental Education Programme.
Ind/Abst Mag. Artic. Summar. Elite (July 1994-).

US/1040-9203
CONNECTICUT ENVIRONMENT. *Ceased.* Ceased June 1991. English. mo. Connecticut Department of Environmental Protection, 165 Capitol Avenue, Room 115, Hartford CT 06106. **Tel** (203)566-2110, FAX (203)566-7932. *Continues Citizens Bulletin, 0889-3527.*

US
CONNECTICUT ENVIRONMENT REVIEW : THE ANNUAL REPORT OF THE COUNCIL ON ENVIRONMENTAL QUALITY. Main/Corp Connecticut. Council on Environmental Quality. English. an. State Office Building, Hartford CT 06115. **LC** TD171.3.C6; C65A. **DD** 363.7/056/09746. *Continues Annual Report on the Status of Connecticut's Environment.*

●US/1064-2382
CONNECTICUT ENVIRONMENTAL COMPLIANCE UPDATE. See Law.

US/0010-6259
CONNECTICUT WOODLANDS. Added/Corp Connecticut Forest and Park Association. Vol. 1, No. 1 (Feb. 1936)-. Periodical. English. qt. $10.00 US; $13.50 other. Connecticut Forest and Park Association, Middlefield, 16 Meriden Road, Rockfall CT 06481-2961. **Tel** (203)346-2372, FAX (203)347-7463. **ED** John E. Hibbard and Linda Rapp. Index available (by special request). **Ad Acc. Circ:** 3,000 (ctrl).
Desc: Agriculture, land use, hiking, conservation, forestry, environment, and water quality, etc., are some of the topics covered.

SA/0258-3313
CONSERVA. Added/Corp South Africa. Dept. of Environment Affairs. Vol. 1, No. 1 (April 1986)-. Periodical. Afrikaans (English). bm. Free on request. Department of Environmental Affairs / South Africa, Private Bag X 447, Pretoria 0001 South Africa. **Tel** 012 319 3441. **LC** S934.S6; C64. **DD** 333.95/16/0968. *Continues Omgewing RSA.*
Desc: Focuses on environmental issues.

●UK/0967-0661
CONTROL ENGINEERING PRACTICE. Added/Corp International Federation of Automatic Control. Vol. 1, No. 1 (Feb. 1993)-. Periodical. English. mo. £686.00 The Americas; £460.00 other. Pergamon Press, An Imprint of Elsevier Science Ltd., The Boulevard, Langford Lane, Kidlington, Oxford OX5 1GB United Kingdom. **Tel** 011 44 865 843000, 011 44 865 843699, FAX 011 44 865 843010. **(Subscription address:** Elsevier Science Ltd. Oxford Fulfillment Centre, PO Box 800, Kidlington, Oxford OX5 1DX United Kingdom.**) LC** TJ212; .C62. **DD** 629.8. **CODEN** COEPEL. **[CCC].**

US/1055-7865
CORPORATE ENVIRONMENTAL OFFICER MAGAZINE. (1991)-. Periodical. English. bm. $19.50. Environmental Publications Inc, 1400 Front Avenue, PO Box 4357, Lutherville MD 21093. **Tel** (301)828-6618. **LC** TD897.7; .A84. **DD** 658.4/08. **Ind/Abst** Ind. Hyg. Dig. (19??-).

UK
CREATIVE CONSERVATION. *Ceased.* **See** Environmental Issues-Conservation and Natural Resources.

US/1040-838X
CRITICAL REVIEWS IN ENVIRONMENTAL CONTROL. *Title Change.* [Crit. rev. environ. control]. **VFOAT** CRC Critical Reviews in Environmental Control. **VAT** Chemical Rubber Company Critical Reviews in Environmental Control. Vol. 10, Issue 2 (1980)-Vol. 22, Issues 3,4 (1992). Academic Scholarly Publication. English. Four times a year. CRC Press Inc., 2000 Corporate Boulevard Northwest, Boca Raton FL 33431. **Tel** (407)994-0555, (800)272-7737, FAX (407)998-9784, telex 568689. **LC** TD172; .C5. **DD** 363.7/005. **CODEN** CCECAU. **[CCC].** Documents available from The Genuine Article, CASDDS, Documents on Demand. *Continues CRC Critical Reviews in Environmental Control, 0007-8999. Continued by Critical Reviews in Environmental Science and Technology, 1064-3389.*
Desc: Cognizant of the literature and developments in their fields, recognized experts review and place these concepts and methodologies in perspective in relation to environment.
Ind/Abst AGRICOLA (19??-19??) [Select. Cov.]; Appl. Sci. Technol. Index (19??-19??); Biodeter. Abstr. (1991-19??); Chem. Abstr. (19??-19??); Curr. Aware. Biol. Sci., CABS (19??-19??); Curr. Contents, Agric. Biol. Environ. Sci. (19??-19??); EMBASE (19??-19??); Energy Inf. Abstr. (19??-19??); Environ. Abstr. (19??-19??); Fish Rev. (Jan. 1989-July 1992); GeoRef (19??-19??); Index Vet. (19??-19??); Irr. Drain. Abstr. (19??-19??); J. Plan. Lit. (19??-19??); Life Sci. Collect. (19??-19??); Res. Alert (19??-19??) [Full Cov.]; Sci. Cit. Index (19??-19??); SCISEARCH (19??-19??); Soc. Sci. Cit. Index (19??-19??) [Select. Cov.]; Vet. Bull. (19??-19??); Wildl. Rev. (Jan. 1989-July 1992).

●US/1064-3389
CRITICAL REVIEWS IN ENVIRONMENTAL SCIENCE AND TECHNOLOGY. (1993)-. Academic Scholarly Publication. English. qt. $285.00 institution. CRC Press Inc., 2000 Corporate Boulevard Northwest, Boca Raton FL 33431. **Tel** (407)994-0555, (800)272-7737, FAX (407)998-9784, telex 568689. **(Subscription address:** CRC Press Inc., PO Box 750, Pearl River NY 10965.**) ED** Terry J. Logan. **NLM** W1; CR216ZBDM. Documents available from CASDDS, Documents on Demand. *Continues Critical Reviews in Environmental Control, 1040-838X.*
Desc: This is the complex and dynamic interaction of diverse scientific disciplines, including earth and agricultural sciences, chemistry, biology, medicine, and engineering, and the development of new disciplines like environmental toxicology and risk assessment.
Ind/Abst Appl. Sci. Technol. Index; Chem. Abstr.; EMBASE; Energy Inf. Abstr.; Environ. Abstr.; GeoRef; Life Sci. Collect.; Sci. Cit. Index.

US
DEQ FLASH RULES. LEVEL THREE. English. Twelve times a year. $200.00 (Level One); $400.00 (Level Two); $500.00 (Level Three. Environmental Compliance Reporter, 3154-B College Drive, Suite 522, Baton Rouge LA 70808. **Tel** (504)383-3937.

IS/0011-9172
DESALINATION AND RECYCLING ABSTRACTS. *Ceased.* **See** Environmental Issues-Abstracting, Bibliographies and Statistics.

US
DETAILED TECHNICAL PLAN FOR THE GREAT LAKES ENVIRONMENTAL RESEARCH LABORATORY. Main/Corp Great Lakes Environmental Research Laboratory. **VFOAT** Detailed Technical Plan for GLERL. English. an.

NE/0167-8892
DEVELOPMENTS IN ENVIRONMENTAL MODELLING. [Dev. environ. model.]. Academic Scholarly Publication. English. Price varies per volume. Elsevier Science Publishers BV, PO Box 211, 1000 AE Amsterdam Netherlands. **Tel** 011 31 20 5803642, FAX 011 31 20 5862696, telex 15682. **CODEN** DEMODW. Documents available from Ask*IEEE, CASDDS.
Ind/Abst Chem. Abstr.; GeoRef; INSPEC.

NE/0165-2214
DEVELOPMENTS IN TOXICOLOGY AND ENVIRONMENTAL SCIENCE. See Medical Science and Technology-Toxicology.

UK
DIA YEARBOOK. Main/Corp Design and Industries Association (Great Britain). **VAT** Design and Industries Association Yearbook. (19??)-. English. an (Aug.). £6.50 UK; £11.50 other. Design & Industries Association, 17 Lawn Crescent, Kew Gardens, Surrey TW9 3NR England. **Tel** 011 44 81 940 4925. **LC** T177.G7; D47a. **DD** 745.2/06/241.

US
DIGEST OF ENVIRONMENTAL LAW. See Law.

CN/0704-1497
DIRECTORY OF CANADIAN ENVIRONMENTAL EXPERTS. *Title Change.* (DIRECTORY OF CANADIAN ENVIRONMENTAL EXPERTS / ENVIRONMENT CANADA). [Dir. Can. environ. experts]. **Added/Corp** Canada Institute for Scientific and Technical Information. Canada. Environment Canada. **VFOAT** Repertoire des Specialistes Canadiens de l'Environnement. (1978)-(1984). Directory. English (French). be. Statistics Canada, Publications Sales & Services, Main Building Room 1710, Ottawa Ontario K1A 0T6 Canada. **Tel** (613)951-5078, (800)267-6677, FAX (613)951-1584, telex 053-3585. **LC** TD182; .D57. **DD** 363.7/0025/71. *Continued by Canadian Sources of Environmental Information, 0832-9176.*

US/0882-6048
DIRECTORY OF CONSULTANTS IN ENVIRONMENTAL SCIENCE, THE. [Dir. consult. environ. sci.]. **VFOAT** Directory of Consultants in Environmental Science (and Agriculture). (1985)-. Directory. English. ir. **(Subscription address:** Research Publications Inc. / Microfilm, 12 Lunar Drive Drawer AB, Woodbridge CT 06525.**) LC** TD169.6; .D5693. **DD** 363.7/0025/7.

US
DIRECTORY OF ENVIRONMENTAL CONSULTANTS. (1972)-. Directory. English. an. $4.00. Directory Press, PO Box 8002, St Louis MO 63108. **LC** TD12; .D55. **DD** 301.31/025.

●US/1053-7880
DIRECTORY OF ENVIRONMENTAL GROUPS IN THE NEWLY INDEPENDENT STATES AND BALTIC NATIONS, THE. [Dir. environ. groups newly indep. states Balt. nations.]. (1992)-. Directory. English. $25.00. Kompass Resources International, 1635 17th Street Northwest, Suite 22, Washington DC 20009. **LC** GE20; .D57. **DD** 363.7/0025/47.

US/1040-1555
DIRECTORY OF NATIONAL ENVIRONMENTAL ORGANIZATIONS. [Dir. natl. environ. organ.]. **Added/Corp** U.S. Environmental Directories. (1984)-. English. ir (Publishes every 2 or 3 years). $54.00 (latest edition). US Environmental Directories, PO Box 65156, St Paul MN 55165. **Tel** (612)331-6050. **ED** John Brainard and Roger McGrath. **DD** 333.
Desc: Directory of national environmental organizations including contacts and synopsis of activities. Includes a subject index.

US
DIRECTORY OF ORGANIZATIONS CONCERNED WITH ENVIRONMENTAL RESEARCH. ***Title Change.*** **Added/Corp** New York State University College, Fredonia. Lake Erie Environmental Studies. 1970-?. Directory. English. Lake Erie Environmental Studies, State University College, Fredonia NY 14063. **ED** Wendall A Mordy and Phyllis A Sholtys. **DD** 574; 628. ***Continued by*** *World Directory of Environmental Research Centers.*

●II
DOWN TO EARTH : SCIENCE AND ENVIRONMENT FORTNIGHTLY.
Added/Corp Society for Environmental Communications. **VFOAT** Science and Environment Fortnightly. Vol. 1, No. 1 (May 31, 1992)-. Periodical. English. Twenty-six times a year. $100.00. Society for Environmental Communications, New Delhi, India. **(Subscription address:** Prints India, 11 Darya Ganj, New Delhi 110002 India.**)** **LC** IN PROCESS.

US/1064-3958
DUKE ENVIRONMENTAL LAW & POLICY FORUM. **See** Law.

CN/0708-7292
E A UPDATE SUMMARY. **Main/Corp** Ontario. Environmental Approvals Branch. Jan. 1979-. English. an. Environmental Approvals Branch, 135 Saint Clair Avenue West, Toronto Ontario M4V 1P5 Canada.

US/1046-8021
E (NORWALK, CONN.). (E : THE ENVIRONMENTAL MAGAZINE.). [E]. **Added/Corp** Earth Action Network. **VFOAT** E Magazine. Vol. 1, No. 1 (Jan./Feb. 1990)-. Periodical. English. bm (Jan., Mar., May, July, Sept., Nov.). $20.00 US; $25.00 Canada; $30.00 other. Earth Action Network Inc, PO Box 5098, Westport CT 06881. **Tel** (203)854-5559, FAX (203)866-0602. **(Subscription address:** Kable Publishers Aide, 308 East Hitt Street, Subscription Department, Mt. Morris IL 61054-1473.**)** **ED** Elissa Wolfson. **LC** TD171.7; .E13. **DD** 363.7. Index available. **Bk Rev**, (Qty: varies). **Ad Acc**, **Adv Mgr:** Alyssa Burger. **Circ:** 75,000. Documents available from UMI Article Clearinghouse, Documents on Demand.
Desc: A clearinghouse of information, news and commentary on environmental issues and concerns. Written for the general reader but also in sufficient depth to involve the dedicated environmentalist.
Ind/Abst Abr. Read. Guide Period. Lit.; Access (1991-?); Altern. Press Index (199?-); Environ. Abstr.; Environ. Period. Bibliogr.; Gen. Period. Index (1992-); Geogr. Abstr. Human Geogr.; Mag. Artic. Summar. Elite (July 1994-); Mag. Index Plus (1992-); Newsp. Period. Abstr. (1992-); Read. Guide Period. Lit.

US
E.P.A.'S IRIS CHEMICAL INFORMATION DATABASE [COMPUTER FILE]. **Added/Corp** United States. Environmental Protection Agency. **VFOAT** Environmental Protection Agency's Integrated Risk Information System Chemical Information Database; EPA's IRIS Chemical Information Database; IRIS Chemical Information Database; IRIS; EPA's IRIS. (19??)-. English. qt. $410.00. Lewis Publishing Inc., 2000 Corporate Boulevard Northwest, Boca Raton FL 33431. **Tel** (313)475-8619, telex 949478. **ED** Lawrence Keith. **LC** RA1211. ctrl circ.
Desc: Features comprehensive information about 500 hazardous regulated and unregulated substances. Gives extensive textual and numberic information complete with EPA contacts and full references.

US/1055-8411
EARTH FIRST! (1991). (EARTH FIRST! : THE RADICAL ENVIRONMENTAL JOURNAL.). [Earth first]. Vol. 11, No. 3 (Feb. 2, 1991)-. Periodical. English. Eight times a year (Feb., Mar., May, June, Aug., Sept., Nov., Dec.). $25.00. Earth First, PO Box 1415, Eugene OR 97440. **Tel** (503)741-9191, FAX (503)741-9192. **ED** Kimberly, Dawn & Craig Benneville, Jim Flynn, John Green. **DD** 363. **Bk Rev**, (Qty: 8). **Ad Acc. Circ:** 7,000. available on microfilm from University Microfilms International (UMI). Documents available from Documents on Demand. ***Continues*** *First Earth! Journal, 1055-8845.*
Desc: A radical uncompromising voice for wilderness preservation and biological diversity.
Ind/Abst Environ. Abstr.

US/1041-0406
EARTH ISLAND JOURNAL. [Earth Isl. j.]. **Added/Corp** Earth Island Institute. (198?)-. Periodical. English. Four times a year. Free with membership: $25.00 US; $39.00 other. Earth Island Institute, 300 Broadway/Suite 28, San Francisco CA 94133. **Tel** (415)788-3666, FAX (415)788-7324, telex 6502829302 MCI OW. **ED** Gar Smith, Justin Lowe, John Sterling. **LC** WMLC 93/1289. **DD** 333. Index available (published separately). **Bk Rev**. **Ad Acc**, **Adv Mgr:** Justin Lowe. **Circ:** 20,000. available on microfilm from University Microfilms International (UMI). Documents available from The Genuine Article, UMI Article Clearinghouse, Documents on Demand.
Desc: Contains international environmental news, and environmental success stories from around the world.
Ind/Abst Altern. Press Index (199?-); Environ. Abstr.; Environ. Period. Bibliogr.; Expand. Acad. Index (1992-); Newsp. Period. Abstr. (1992-); Res. Alert [Select. Cov.]; Soc. Sci. Cit. Index [Select. Cov.].

US/1059-6488
EARTH JOURNAL (BOULDER, COLO.). ***Title Change.*** (EARTH JOURNAL: ENVIRONMENTAL ALMANAC AND RESOURCE DIRECTORY.). [Earth j.]. (1992)-(19??). Directory. English. an. Buzzworm Inc., 2305 Canyon Boulevard, Suite 206, Boulder CO 80302. **Tel** (800)825-0061, (303)442-1969. **LC** GE1; .E19. **DD** 363.7. ***Continues*** *Buzzworm.* ***Continued by*** *Buzzworm's Earth Journal, 1073-5852.*
Desc: An environmental guide and annual reference source that covers major eco-issues, film, music, green business, new products and eco-travel, plus offers valuable eco-tips, original surveys and more.

US
EARTH NOTES. **Added/Corp** United States. Environmental Protection Agency. Communications, Education, and Public Affairs. (Fall 1991)-. Periodical. English. qt. Free on request. US Environmental Protection Agency, 401 M Street SW, Washington DC 20460. **Tel** (202)755-9163.

US/1066-9175
EARTH SUMMIT UPDATE. [Earth Summit update]. **Added/Corp** Environmental and Energy Study Institute. No. 1 (July 1991)-. Periodical. English. ir. $10.00. Environmental and Energy Study Institute, 122 C Street Northwest, Suite 700, Washington DC 20001. **Tel** (202)628-1400, FAX (202)628-1825. **DD** 333.

CN/1181-7828
EARTHKEEPER MAGAZINE. [Earthkeep. mag.]. Vol. 1, Issue 1 (Sept./Oct. 1990)-. Periodical. English. bm (Jan., Mar., May, July, Sept., Nov.). 22.43Can$ Canada; 30.00Can$ other. Earthkeeper Inc, PO Box 60, Lindsay Ontario K9V 4R8 Canada. **Tel** (705)878-7003, FAX (705)878-1715. **ED** Norman Wagner. **DD** 363.7/0525/09713. Index available. cum. index. **Bk Rev**, (Qty: 20). **Ad Acc**, **Adv Mgr:** M. Johnson. **Circ:** 18,000.
Desc: Earthkeeper is the Canadian environmental voice. Attempts to bridge the gap between the scientific community and the average individual and provides the consumer with good information. Earthkeeper also deals with news items that are not covered by mainstream media, and provides high school educators with information they can use.
Ind/Abst Can. Period. Index (Vol. 1, Issue 1 Sept./Oct. 1990-).

UK/0968-4425
EARTHLINES. (19??)-. Newsletter. English. Council for Environmental Education, University of Reading, London Road, Reading RG1 5AQ England. **Tel** 0734 756061, FAX 0734 756264. **ED** Margaret Feneley.
Desc: Newsletter of the Youth and Environment Network.

US/0270-398X
EARTHSPEAK. ***Suspended.*** Vol. 1 (Spring 1980)-?. Periodical. English. qt. $14.00. Agnew Tech-Tran, PO Box 789, Woodland Hills CA 91365.

US/0890-1201
EARTHWATCH OREGON. (EARTHWATCH OREGON: NEWS REPORT OF THE OREGON ENVIRONMENTAL COUNCIL.). **Added/Corp** Oregon Environmental Council. (1972)-. Periodical. English. qt (Mar., June, Sept., Dec.). $30.00 individuals; $40.00 libraries. Oregon Environmental Council, 027 SW Arthur Street, Portland OR 97201. **Tel** (503)222-1963, FAX (503)222-1405. **ED** Jane Haley. **DD** 333. **Circ:** 1,600 (ctrl). ***Continues*** *Newsletter (Oregon Environmental Council).*

US
EARTHWISE. (EARTHWISE : ENVIRONMENTAL LEARNING SERIES.). English. Four times a year. $27.95. WP Press, PO Box 65768, Tuscon AZ 85728. **Tel** (602)544-0455. **ED** Joanne Metcalfe Pifer.
Desc: Series of books designed for students in grades 5 to 8. Its objective is to develop a better understanding of the global environment in young people's minds.

US
EARTHWORD. (1990)-. English. qt. $20.00 US; $27.00 Canada & Mexico; $30.00 Pan American Nations; $34.00 Europe; $42.00 Asia, Africa & India. EOS Institute, 580 Broadway, Suite 200, Laguna Beach CA 92651. **Tel** (714)497-1896, FAX (714)494-7861. **ED** Lynne Bayless. **Bk Rev**, (Qty: 3). **Ad Acc. Circ:** 5,000.
Desc: Provides problem-solving information on topically focused environmental issues.

US
EAST END ENVIRONMENT. Periodical. English.

UK
EC ENVIRONMENTAL POLICY MONITOR. English. qt. £500.00. Environmental Policy Consultants, 6 Donaldson Road, London NW6 6NB England. **Tel** 011 44 71 3727122.

SA/0250-9989
ECOFORUM ENGLISH EDITION. (1976)-. Periodical. English (French, Spanish and Arabic). bm. $30.00. Environment Liaison Centre International, PO Box 72461, Nairobi Kenya. **Tel** 011 254 2 562015, FAX 011 254 2 562175, telex 23240 ELC KE.
Ind/Abst Hum. Rights Intern. Rep.

US
ECOL NEWS. **Main/Corp** Environmental Conservation Library of Minnesota. **VFOAT** E C O L News. (Sept. 1972)-. Periodical. English. Minneapolis Public Library, 300 Nicollet Mall, Minneapolis MN 55401. **Tel** (612)372-6570.
Desc: One long essay in each issue, plus a list of new environmental books.

US/0889-6151
ECONOCAST. (ECONOCAST / M.G. LEWIS ECONOMETRICS.). [Econocast]. (1984)-. Periodical. English. qt. $300.00. Fishkind & Associates, 12424 Research Parkway, Orlando FL 32826. **Tel** (407)382-3256. **DD** 330.

IT/0012-9836
ECONOMIA MONTANA ROMA. **See** Environmental Issues-Ecology.

BL/0104-0030
ECORIO. (1991)-. Portuguese. mo. Tricontinental Editora Ltda, 54 Avenue Pres. Antonio Carlos, 20020 Centro, Rio de Janeiro RJ Brazil. **Tel** 021-533-0269.

CN/1181-9707
ECOSOURCE. ***Ceased.*** **VFOAT** Eco Source. (1990)-(19??). English. bm. EcoSource Inc, Box 1270, Guelph Ontario N1H 6N6 Canada. **Tel** (519)763-7555, FAX (519)763-7094. **ED** Tony Leighton.
Desc: International executive digest on the environment whose content is gleaned from more than 50 newspapers and 130 periodicals from around the world.
Ind/Abst PTS Newsl. Database [Full Txt.].

US/1065-1993
EH & S DIGEST. ***Ceased.*** (EH & S DIGEST : ENVIRONMENTAL, HEALTH, AND SAFETY.). [EH S dig.]. **Added/Corp** Warren, Gorham & Lamont, Inc. **VFOAT** EH&S Digest; EH and S Digest. **VAT** Environmental, Health and Safety Digest; Environmental, Health & Safety Digest. (1992)-Vol. 2, No. 1 (June 1993). Periodical. English. mo. Warren Gorham & Lamont Inc., Park Square Building, 31 St. James Avenue, Boston MA 02116-4112. **Tel** (617)423-2020, (800)950-1207, FAX (617)423-2026. **DD** 363.
Ind/Abst Ind. Hyg. Dig. (19??-); Pollut. Abstr. Indexes.

US/1056-7585
EIKENBURG & STILES' TEXAS ENVIRONMENTAL LAW LETTER. ***Title Change.*** **See** Law.

US/0364-1074
EIS. (EIS. DIGESTS OF ENVIRONMENTAL IMPACT STATEMENTS.). [EIS]. **Added/Corp** Herner and Company. **VFOAT** Digests of Environmental Impact Statements. **VAT** Environmental Impact Statements. Vol. 3, No. 7 (July 1979)-. Periodical. English. bm (plus annual index). $560.00 US; $615.00 other. Cambridge Scientific Abstracts, 7200 Wisconsin Avenue, #601, Bethesda MD 20814-4823. **Tel** (301)961-6750, (800)843-7751, FAX (301)961-6720. **ED** Roberta Gorinson. **DD** 333. **NLM** ZWA 670 E105. **CODEN** EEISDZ. Index available. cum. index. available on microfiche; available on magnetic tape; available via Internet (to the current year's abstracts and five-year backfiles) from Cambridge Scientific Abstracts. ***Continues*** *EIS, 0364-1074.*
Desc: Covers all environmental impact statements issued by US federal government, including areas of defense, energy policy, hazardous substances, land use, manufacturing, parks, roads and railroads, urban renewal, flood control, waterways, and waste disposal.
Ind/Abst Coal Abstr.; Energy Res. Abstr. (July 1979-); INIS Atomindex [Micro.].

US/0190-0250
EIS CUMULATIVE. **Added/Corp** Herner and Company. **VFOAT** EIS. **VAT** Environmental Impact Statements Cumulative. (1977)-. English. an. $375.00 US; $415.00 other. Cambridge Scientific Abstracts, 7200 Wisconsin Avenue, #601, Bethesda MD 20814-4823. **Tel** (301)961-6750, (800)843-7751, FAX (301)961-6720. **LC** TD194.6; .E18. **DD** 333.7. available on magnetic tape.

●US/1076-7975
ELECTRONIC GREEN JOURNAL. (ELECTRONIC GREEN JOURNAL [COMPUTER FILE].). [Electron. green j.]. **Added/Corp** University of Idaho. Library. Vol. 1, No. 1 (June 1994)-. Periodical. English. ir. $40.00 (institution) US. University of Idaho Library, Mary Bolin, Moscow ID 83843. **Tel** (208)885-7737. **DD** 025. **Bk Rev. Ad Acc, Adv Mgr:** Katie Manjotich, **Tel** (510)841-9975. **Pr Rev.** Documents available from Documents on Demand. ***Continues*** *Green Library Journal (Berkeley, Calif. : 1992), 1059-0838.*
Desc: Information about conservation, environmental protection, natural resource management, ecologically balanced regional development in libraries, publishing industries and information sciences.
Ind/Abst Curr. Index J. Educ.; Environ. Abstr.

●US/1066-0348
EMERGENCY SERVICES SOURCEBOOK. **See** Public Health and Safety.

US/0145-9236
ENDANGERED SPECIES TECHNICAL BULLETIN. (ENDANGERED SPECIES TECHNICAL BULLETIN / DEPARTMENT OF THE INTERIOR, U.S. FISH AND WILDLIFE SERVICE, ENDANGERED SPECIES PROGRAM.). [Endanger. species tech. bull.]. **Added/Corp** Endangered Species Program (U.S.) U.S. Fish and Wildlife Service. Vol. 1, No. 1 (July 1976)-. Bulletin. English. mo. Endangered Species Update, School of Natural Resources, University of Michigan, Ann Arbor MI 48109-1115. **Tel** (313)763-3243.
Ind/Abst AGRICOLA [Select. Cov.].

US/0147-8850
ENERGY AND ENVIRONMENT ANNUAL REPORT. **See** Energy.

US
ENERGY, POWER, AND ENVIRONMENT. **See** Energy.

TH/0125-1783
ENFO. [Enfo]. (1978)-. Periodical. English. Four times a year. $130.00 US, Canada, Europe, Australia, Japan, New Zealand & Middle East; $75.00 others (institutions) $80.00 US, Canada, Europe, Australia, Japan, New Zealand & Middle East; $50.00 others (individuals). Asian Institute of Technology / Regional Energy Resources Information Center / RERIC, PO Box 2754, 10501 Bangkok, Thailand. **Tel** 011 66 2 516-0110-29, 011 66 2 516-0130-44, FAX 011 66 2 516-2126. **DD** _a628.

US/0276-9956
ENFO. [ENFO]. **Added/Corp** Florida Conservation Foundation. Environmental Information Center. (1974)-. Periodical. English. Five times a year. $25.00 organizational membership, $50.00 contributing membership, $100.00 supporting membership. Environmental Information Center / Florida, 1251-B Miller Avenue, Winter Park FL 32789. **Tel** (407)644-5377. **ED** Gerald Grow. **Bk Rev. Ad Acc. Circ:** 1,200. ***Continues*** *Enfo Newsletter.*
Desc: Environmental studies and issues affecting Florida.
Ind/Abst Trop. Dis. Bull.

GW/0724-6870
ENTSORGUNGSPRAXIS. [Entsorgungspraxis]. (1983)-. Trade Publication. German. mo (10 issues per year). DM105.00. Bertelsmann Fachzeitschriften, Carl Bertelsmann Str 270, D-33311 Frankfurt Germany. **Tel** 011 49 5241 802199. **(Subscription address:** Translibris GmbH, PO Box 301373, D 50783 Cologne Germany.**) ED** Renak Wedig and Rainer Surig. **UDC** 628.3/.6. **Circ:** 10,250.
Desc: Trade journal dealing with environmental technology in industry and in local authorities. It provides information about the latest developments in environmental technology in the refuse industry, air purification, waste water technology and noise prevention.

US/1059-390X
ENVIROBUSINESS REPORT. (ENVIROBUSINESS REPORT : EBR.). [EnviroBus. rep.]. **VFOAT** EBR. (1991)-. Periodical. English. mo. $192.00. ZM Investment Research, Inc., 550 North Brand Boulevard, Suite 700, Glendale CA 91203. **DD** 338.

US
ENVIROFAX. (19??)-. English. wk (faxed every Friday). $187.50. Business Publishers Inc., 951 Pershing Drive, Silver Spring MD 20910-4464. **Tel** (301)587-6300, (800)274-0122, FAX (301)585-9075.

CN/0847-4524
ENVIROLINE (CALGARY). (ENVIROLINE.). [EnviroLine]. **VFOAT** Enviro Line. Vol. 1, No. 1 (Dec. 4, 1989)-. Periodical. English. ir. $395.00. Ross Marketing Services, 650 1040 7 Avenue Southwest, Calgary Alberta T2P 3G9 Canada. **Tel** (403)263-3272, FAX (403)263-3280. **ED** Nicola Ross. **DD** 363.7/00971/05. **Bk Rev**, (Qty: 50). ctrl circ.
Desc: Covers environmental trends, technology and regulatory matters covering vehicle maintenance and refueling.

US/1072-2416
ENVIROLINE (FINDLAY, OHIO). (ENVIROLINE.). [EnviroLine]. **Added/Corp** Environmental Development Corporation. Vol. 1, No. 1 (Jan.-Mar. 1991)-. Periodical. English. bm. $139.00 (1 year), $249.00 (2 year). Environmental Development Corporation, PO Box 854, Findlay OH 45839. **Tel** (419)422-1200, FAX (419)422-1832. **ED** David M. Augenstein. **DD** 363. **Bk Rev**, (Qty: 2). **Circ:** 500.
Desc: Environmental issues in vehicle maintenance and refueling operations.

UK/0962-4740
ENVIRONEWS SHREWSBURY. (ENVIRONEWS.). [EnviroNewsShrewsbury]. (1991)-. English. bm (6 issues). £150.00 UK; $270.00 US; £160.00 other. RAPRA Technology Ltd., Shawbury Shrewsbury, Shropshire SY4 4NR England. **Tel** 011 44 939 250383, FAX 011 44 939 251118, telex 35134 RAPRA G. **DD** 333.72.

US/0093-3287
ENVIRONMENT ABSTRACTS. **See** Environmental Issues-Abstracting, Bibliographies and Statistics.

US/0000-1198
ENVIRONMENT ABSTRACTS ANNUAL. **See** Environmental Issues-Abstracting, Bibliographies and Statistics.

●US/1066-954X
ENVIRONMENT & DEVELOPMENT / APA, AMERICAN PLANNING ASSOCIATION. [Environ. dev.]. **Added/Corp** American Planning Association. **VFOAT** Environment and Development. (Jan. 1992)-. Periodical. English. mo. $50.00 US; $60.00 other. American Planning Association, 1313 East 60th Street, Chicago IL 60637. **Tel** (312)955-9100, FAX (312)955-8312. **LC** HC110.E5; E484. **DD** 363.7/00973/05.

UK/0956-2478
ENVIRONMENT AND URBANIZATION. **Added/Corp** International Institute for Environment and Development. Human Settlements Programme. Vol. 1, No. 1 (April 1989)-. Periodical. English. sa (April and October). $15.00 Africa, Asia, Latin America and Caribbean; $31.00 other. Human Settlements Programme, IIED, 3 Endsleigh Street, London WC1H 0DD England. **Tel** 11 44 71 388 2117, FAX 11 44 71 388 2826, telex 261681. **LC** HT243.D44; E58. **DD** 307.76/09172/405. **CODEN** ENUREK.
Ind/Abst Geogr. Abstr. Human Geogr.; Int. Bibliogr. Sociol.; Int. Dev. Abstr.; PAIS Int. Print (1991-); Soc. Plann. Policy Dev. Abstr.; Soc. Sci. Cit. Index [Full Cov.].

UK
ENVIRONMENT BRAZIL. English. ir. $190.00 UK and Europe; $225.00 other. Environment Brazil, 40 Daws Hill Lane, High Wycombe HP11 1PU England.

UK/0959-7042
ENVIRONMENT BUSINESS. (19??)-. Periodical. English. Twenty-four times a year. £237.00 UK and EEC countries; £267.00 other. Information for Industry Ltd, 18-20 Ridgway, London SW19 4QN England. **Tel** 011 44 081 944 2930, FAX 011 44 081 944 1982. **ED** Ian Grant (phone: (081)877-9130). **LC** TD194; .E57. **DD** 363.73/1. **CODEN** ENVBEB. Index available. **Bk Rev. Ad Acc, Adv Mgr:** Steven Voss, **Tel** (081)877-9130. ***Absorbed*** *PM Environmental Newsletter, 0951-9424.*
Desc: An incorporating PM environmental newsletter and greengauge.

●US/1064-7422
ENVIRONMENT CONNECTIONS. **Added/Corp** Earth Information Center. (1992)-. Periodical. English. bm. $20.00. Environmental Connections, PO Box 387, Springfield IL 62705.

US/1058-3955
ENVIRONMENT DAILY (ARLINGTON, VA.). ***Ceased.*** (ENVIRONMENT DAILY.). [Environ. dly.]. (1991)-(19??). Periodical. English. da. Bureau of National Affairs Inc., 9435 Key West Avenue, Rockville MD 20850. **Tel** (800)372-1033, (301)258-1033, FAX (301)948-5823. **DD** 363.

UK/0951-5100
ENVIRONMENT DIGEST. [Environ. dig.]. (1987)-. Periodical. English. mo. £19.00 (individual), £38.00 (institution) UK; £24.00 (individual), £43.00 (institution) other. Environment Digest, 11 21 Struton Street, Cambridge CB1 2SN England. **Tel** 011 44 223 568017. **DD** 016.3337.

●UK
ENVIRONMENT ENCYCLOPEDIA AND DIRECTORY, THE. **See** Encyclopedias and General Reference Books.

US/0090-0486
ENVIRONMENT FILM REVIEW. ***Ceased.*** (THE ENVIRONMENT FILM REVIEW.). **Added/Corp** Environment Information Center. Film Reference Dept. (19??)-(19??). English. an. The Environment Film Review, 124 East 39th Street, New York NY 10016. **LC** GF1; .E55. **DD** 301.31/05. **NLM** Z 5322.E2 E59.

US/0272-9008
ENVIRONMENT (GUILFORD). (ENVIRONMENT.). [Environment]. **VFOAT** Annual Editions: Environment. 2nd Ed. (1980/81)-. Periodical. English. an. $10.95. Dushkin Publishing Group Inc., Sluice Dock, Guilford CT 06437. **Tel** (203)453-4351, (800)243-6532, FAX (203)453-6000. **ED** John L. Allen. **LC** TD172; .R42. **DD** 304.2. ***Continues*** *Readings in Environment, 0196-4542.*
Desc: An updated collection of public press articles covering current issues in environment. Includes a glossary of terms and a section on sources of environmental information.
Ind/Abst Appl. Soc. Sci. Index Abstr.; Environ. Period. Bibliogr.; Geogr. Abstr. Human Geogr.; Ref. Upd. Deluxe Ed.

US/1050-3285
ENVIRONMENT HAWAII. [Environ. Hawaii]. (1990)-. Periodical. English. mo. $50.00 (institution), $25.00 (individual). Environment Hawaii Publishing, 733 Bishop Street, Suite 170-51, Honolulu HI 96813. **DD** 363.

UK/0964-5322
ENVIRONMENT INFORMATION BULLETIN. [Environ. inf. bull.]. (1991)-. Periodical. English. mo. £95.00 UK; £105.00 other. Eclipse Publications Ltd, 18 20 Highbury Place, London N5 1QP England. **Tel** 011 44 71 354 5858. **DD** 332.720941.

AT/1030-1429
ENVIRONMENT INSTITUTE OF AUSTRALIA NEWSLETTER. [Newsl. Environ. Inst. of Aust.]. (1987)-. Newsletter. English. Four times a year (Mar., June, Sept., Dec.). 45.00Aus$. Environment Institute of Australia, Private Bag 6, Deakin ACT 2600 Australia. **Tel** 011 61 6 2854234. **ED** Iveta Mylchveest. **DD** 363.705. **Bk Rev. Ad Acc.**

UK/0160-4120
ENVIRONMENT INTERNATIONAL. [Environ. int.]. Vol. 1, No. 1.2 (1979)-. Academic Scholarly Publication. English. bm. $589.00 The Americas; £395.00 other. Pergamon Press, An Imprint of Elsevier Science Ltd., The Boulevard, Langford Lane, Kidlington, Oxford OX5 1GB United Kingdom. **Tel** 011 44 865 843000, 011 44 865 843699, FAX 011 44 865 843010. **(Subscription address:** Elsevier Science Ltd. Oxford Fulfillment Centre, PO Box 800, Kidlington, Oxford OX5 1DX United Kingdom.**) ED** Alan Mogsissi and Barbara Moghissi. **LC** TD169; .E54. **DD** 363.7/005. **NLM** W1 EN98NV. **CODEN** ENVIDV. **[CCC]. Bk Rev. Ad Acc. Pr Rev.** available on microfilm and microfiche from University Microfilms International (UMI). Documents available from Article Express International, The Genuine Article, BIOSIS Document Express, CASDDS, Documents on Demand.
Desc: A multi-disciplinary forum for the publication of original environmental literature. Vital data, causes of pollution, and methods for protection are all featured, covering the entire field of environmental protection.
Ind/Abst Aqualine Abstr.; AQUAREF; Biodeter. Abstr. (19??-19??); Bioeng. Abstr.; Biol. Abstr.; Chem. Abstr.; Coal Abstr.; Crop Physiol. Abstr.; Curr. Aware. Biol. Sci., CABS; Curr. Contents, Agric. Biol. Environ. Sci.; Ecol. Abstr.; Ecology Abstr.; Ei Page One; EMBASE; Energy Inf. Abstr.; Energy Res. Abstr. (Oct. 1978-); Eng. Index Annu. [Select. Cov.]; Environ. Abstr.; Environ. Period. Bibliogr.; Fish Rev.; Geogr. Abstr. Phys. Geogr.; Geogr. Abstr. Human Geogr.; Geol. Abstr.; GeoRef; Grasslands For. Abstr.; Health Saf. Sci. Abstr.; INIS Atomindex [Micro.]; Int. Dev. Abstr.; Meteorol. Geoastrophys. Abstr.; Life Sci. Collect.; Pollut. Abstr. Indexes; Res. Alert [Select. Cov.]; Rev. Agric. Entomol.; Rev. Med. Vet. Entomol.; Risk Abstr.; SCISEARCH; Soc. Sci. Cit. Index [Select. Cov.]; Soils Fert.; Weed Abstr.; Wildl. Rev.

US/1049-7404
ENVIRONMENT LIBRARY. (ENVIRONMENT LIBRARY [COMPUTER FILE].). [Environ. libr.]. **Added/Corp** OCLC. (1989)-. English. an. $300.00 OCLC members, $675.00 multi-users, $450.00 all others US; $350.00 OCLC members; $675.00 multi-users; $450.00 all others - other. Silverplatter Information Inc., 100 River Ridge Drive, Norwood MA 02062. **Tel** (800)343-0064, (617)769-2599, FAX (617)235-1715. **DD** 550. ***Continues*** *Environment (Dublin, Ohio), 0897-1382.*
Desc: Contains over 300,000 citations to materials on the environment and related subjects.

UK
ENVIRONMENT MATTERS. **Added/Corp** World Petrochemicals Analysis Limited. (Sept. 1989)-. Periodical. English. mo. £315.00 UK; £345.00 other. Infonet Publications Ltd., 67 Chancery Lane, London WC21 1AF United Kingdom. **ED** Simon Geschwindt. **LC**

TD896; .E58. **DD** 263.72/8.
Desc: Independent newsletter examining the environmental challenges faced by producers and users of chemicals.

UK/0966-9272
ENVIRONMENT MATTERS (INTERNATIONAL). [Environ. matters int.]. **VFOAT** Environment Matters. (1989)-. English. mo. £315.00 UK; £345.00 other. Infonet Publications Ltd., 67 Chancery Lane, London WC21 1AF United Kingdom.
Desc: Independent newsletter examining the environmental challenges faced by producers and users of chemicals.

US/0013-919X
ENVIRONMENT MONTHLY, THE. June 1969-. Periodical. English. mo. $35.00. Environment League Inc., 284 Alexander Avenue, Bronx NY 10454. **NLM** W1 EN98P. available on microfilm from University Microfilms International (UMI).

US/0364-1317
ENVIRONMENT NEWS (BOSTON). ***Ceased.*** (ENVIRONMENT NEWS / UNITED STATES ENVIRONMENTAL PROTECTION AGENCY, REGION I, OFFICE OF PUBLIC AWARENESS.). Periodical. English. mo. Enviromental Protection Agency, JFK Federal Building, Road 2203, Boston MA 02203.

US
ENVIRONMENT NEWS DIGEST. (19??)-. English. ir (seasonally when funds are available). $5.00. Environment News Digest, PO Box 1581, Leesburg VA 22075. **Tel** (202)347-0020.

PL/0324-8828
ENVIRONMENT PROTECTION ENGINEERING. [Environ. prot. eng.]. Vol. 1-(1975)-. Academic Scholarly Publication. English (Polish and Russian). qt. $108.00. Technical University of Wroclaw, Wybrzeze Wyspianskiego 27, 50-370 Wroclaw Poland. **Tel** 20-36-39, telex 0712254 PWRPL. **(Subscription address:** ARS Polona, Krakowskie Przedmiescie 7, 00-068 Warszawa Poland**) ED** Tomasz Z Winnicki, Alicja Mika and Lucjan Pawlowski. **LC** TD169; .E56. **DD** 628.5/05. **CODEN** EPEND9. **[CCC]. Bk Rev. Ad Acc. Circ:** 300 (ctrl). Documents available from CASDDS, Documents on Demand.
Desc: Covers water purification, wastewater treatment, emission abatement, dedusting processes, systems of air and water pollution control, ecological problems and environmental economy.
Ind/Abst Chem. Abstr.; Coal Abstr.; Ei Page One; EMBASE; Environ. Abstr.; GeoRef; Pollut. Abstr. Indexes.

US/0013-9203
ENVIRONMENT REPORT. Vol. 1 (May 7, 1970)-. Periodical. English. sm. $650.00 (one year), $1,150.00 (two years). Trends Publishing Inc., 1079 National Press Building, Washington DC 20045. **Tel** (202)393-0031, FAX (202)393-1732. **ED** A Kranish. **Bk Rev.** available on microfilm and microfiche from University Microfilms International (UMI).
Desc: General environmental topics - water pollution, air pollution, pesticides etc. Also book reports and upcoming items of interests.

US
ENVIRONMENT REPORTER. CURRENT DEVELOPMENTS. Added/Corp Bureau of National Affairs (Washington, D.C.). Vol. 1 (May 1970)-. English. wk. $1157.00. Bureau of National Affairs Inc., 9435 Key West Avenue, Rockville MD 20850. **Tel** (800)372-1033, (301)258-1033, FAX (301)948-5823.

US
ENVIRONMENT REPORTER. DECISIONS. Added/Corp Bureau of National Affairs (Washington, D.C.). Vol. 1, (19??)-. English. Forty-eight times a year. $1,213.00. Bureau of National Affairs Inc., 9435 Key West Avenue, Rockville MD 20850. **Tel** (800)372-1033, (301)258-1033, FAX (301)948-5823. **(Subscription address:** Telephone: Fax (301)948-5823**)**

UK/0965-3813
ENVIRONMENT RISK. ***Title Change.*** (Jan. 1992)-(199?). Periodical. English. mo. Euromoney Publications PLC, Nestor House, Playhouse Yard, London EC4Z 5EX England. **Tel** 011 44 71 779 8888, FAX 011 44 71 779 8617, telex 290700 EUROMON G. Documents available from UMI Article Clearinghouse. ***Merged into*** *International Corporate Law.*
Desc: First international business magazine to approach environmental issues from the perspective of multinational companies, and their need to manage environmental opportunities and risk. An essential source of information for senior company executives, directors and managers responsible for environmental policy and management, as well as bankers, insurers, fund managers, accountants, management and environmental consultants, lawyers and regulators worldwide.
Ind/Abst ABI/INFORM Glob. Ed.

UK/0965-0482
ENVIRONMENT, TECHNOLOGY AND INDUSTRY. ***Ceased.*** [Environ. technol. ind.]. (1992)-(Sept. 1992). Academic Scholarly Publication. English. mo. Elsevier Science Publishers Ltd, Crown House, Linton Road, Barking Essex IG11 8JU England. **Tel** 011 44 81 5947272, FAX 081-594-5942, telex 896950. **DD** 628.5. ***Continues*** *Environment and Industry Digest Newsletter, 0958-2126.*

US/1054-7517
ENVIRONMENT TODAY. [Environ. today]. (1990)-. Periodical. English. mo. $56.00 (one year), $82.00 (two year) US; $76.00 (one year), $110.00 (two year) Canada; $125.00 (one year), $185.00 (two year) other. Enterprise Communications Inc, 2425 Torreya Drive, Tallahassee FL 32303. **Tel** (703)448-0322. **DD** 363. **CODEN** ENTYE2. **Ad Acc. Circ:** 54,000 (ctrl). available on microfilm and microfiche from University Microfilms International (UMI); available on an online database (file 15/Full-Text) from DIALOG.
Desc: News tabloid covering the pollution control industry, and environmental protection.
Ind/Abst BioBusiness (1991-).

CN/0701-9637
ENVIRONMENT VIEWS. [Environ. views]. **Added/Corp** Alberta. Alberta Environment. Vol. 1 (Apr./May 1978)-. Periodical. English. bm. Alberta Environment, 9th Floor, 9915 108 Street, S Tower, Edmonton Alberta T5K 2C9 Canada. **Tel** (403)427-8636. **ED** Mary Helen Vicars. **Bk Rev. Circ:** 10,500. available on microfiche. Documents available from Documents on Demand. ***Supersedes*** *Environment News, 0701-6840.*
Ind/Abst AQUAREF; Can. Period. Index (Dec. 1990-); Energy Inf. Abstr.; Environ. Abstr.; Environ. Period. Bibliogr.

US/1063-5955
ENVIRONMENT WATCH. EAST EUROPE, RUSSIA & EURASIA. ***Title Change.*** (ENVIRONMENT WATCH. EAST EUROPE, RUSSIA & EURASIA : NEWS & ANALYSIS FOR BUSINESS AND POLICY PROFESSIONALS FROM CUTTER INFORMATION CORP.). [Environ. watch, East Eur. Russ. Eurasia]. **Added/Corp** Cutter Information Corp. **VFOAT** East Europe, Russia & Eurasia; East Europe, Russia and Eurasia. Vol. 1, No. 1 (June 1992)-(199?). Periodical. English. mo. Cutter Information Corporation, 37 Broadway, Arlington MA 02174-5539. **Tel** (617)648-8700, (800)964-5118, FAX (617)648-8707, (617)648-1950, telex 650 100 9891. **DD** 333. available on an online database (file 636/Full-Text) from DIALOG. ***Merged into*** *East West Executive Guide, 1067-635X.*

US/1041-8105
ENVIRONMENT WEEK. (ENVIRONMENT WEEK / BY THE EDITORS OF THE ENERGY DAILY AND NEW TECHNOLOGY WEEK.). [Environ. week]. Vol. 1, No. 1 (Dec. 8, 1988)-. Periodical. English. wk (50 issues). $790.00. King Publishing Group, 627 National Press Building, Washington DC 20045. **Tel** (202)638-4260, FAX (202)662-9744. **ED** Dennis Wamstead. **LC** TD171; .E555. **DD** 363.7/005. **[CCC].** available on an online database (files 16,636/Full-Text) from DIALOG; and NEWSNET.
Desc: Coverage of environmental issues including the green house effect, acid rain, nuclear and hazardous waste disposal.
Ind/Abst PROMT [Full Txt.]; PTS Newsl. Database [Full Txt.].

US/0013-922X
ENVIRONMENTAL ACTION (WASHINGTON, D.C.). (ENVIRONMENTAL ACTION.). [Environ. action]. **Added/Corp** Environmental Action (Association). **VFOAT** Environmental Action Magzaine. Vol. 1 (Feb. 19, 1970)-. Periodical. English. qt (4 issues). $40.00 (institution), $25.00 (individual). Environmental Action, 6930 Carroll Avenue, Suite 600, Takoma Park MD 20912. **Tel** (301)891-1100, FAX (301)891-2218. **ED** Barbara Ruben and David Lapp. **LC** HC110.E5; E496. **DD** 301.31/0973. **CODEN** ENACDA. **[CCC].** Index available. **Bk Rev**, (Qty: 8). **Ad Acc, Adv Mgr:** Jim Pierce, **Tel** (301)891-1100. **Circ:** 14,000. available on microfilm and microfiche from University Microfilms International (UMI); available on CD-ROM. Documents available from UMI Article Clearinghouse, Documents on Demand. ***Absorbed*** *Rodale's Environment Action Bulletin, 0048-850X* ***and*** *Re:Sources.*
Desc: News journal on environmental issues, including toxics, energy, nuclear weapons, pollution, politics, agriculture, urban, transportation, etc.
Ind/Abst Acad. Abstr. Full Text Elite (July 1990-); Acad. Abstr. (July 1990-); Acad. Search (July 1990-); Altern. Press Index; BioBusiness (1990-); Biol. Dig.; Coal Abstr.; Environ. Abstr.; Environ. Period. Bibliogr.; Expand. Acad. Index (1992-); Gen. Period. Index (1992-); Gen. Sci. Source (Jul. 1990-); INFO-SOUTH Abstr.; INIS Atomindex [Micro.]; Mag. Artic. Summar. Elite (July 1990-); Mag. Artic. Summar. Select (July 1990-); Mag. Artic. Summar. CD-ROM (July 1990-); Mag. Search; Newsp. Period. Abstr. (1992-); PAIS Int. Print (1991-); Urban Aff. Abstr.

US
ENVIRONMENTAL AND ENERGY STUDY SPECIAL REPORTS. English. Thirty-five times a year. $200.00. Environmental and Energy Study Institute, 122 C Street Northwest, Suite 700, Washington DC 20001. **Tel** (202)628-1400, FAX (202)628-1825. **UDC** 32.
Desc: A series of fact sheets, legislative updates and issue reports. Offers timely and in-depth coverage of acid rain, ground water, global warming, hazardous waste and broad range of environmental and energy issues.

UK
ENVIRONMENTAL AND HEALTH CONTROLS ON LEAD. (June 1989)-. English. £20.00 UK; $30.00 US. International Lead and Zinc Study Group, Metro House, 58 St. James Street, London SW1A 1LD England. **Tel** 011 44 71 4999373, FAX 011 44 71 4933725, telex 299819 ILZSG G.
Desc: Review of current and proposed regulation controlling lead in works, lead in the atmosphere and lead in water in 25 countries.

NE/0924-6460
ENVIRONMENTAL AND RESOURCE ECONOMICS. Added/Corp European Association of Environmental and Resource Economists. **VFOAT** Environmental and Resource Economics. Vol. 1, No. 1 (1991)-. Periodical. English. Eight times a year. $758.00. Kluwer Academic Publishers, Postbus 322, 3300 AH Dordrecht, The Netherlands. **Tel** 011 (31) 78 524400, FAX 011 31 78 183273, telex 20083. **ED** J B Opschoor. **LC** HC79.E5; E576. **CODEN** ERECEP. **[CCC]. Pr Rev.** available on microfilm and microfiche from University Microfilms International (UMI). Documents available from Documents on Demand.
Desc: Covers the applications of economic theory and methods to environmental issues that require rational economic analysis. Focus is on environmental problems of broad international dimensions. The publication of empirical and policy-oriented research receives high priority in the journal, which thus functions as a platform for the critical discussion of the economic impact of environmental policy, the environmental consequences of economic activities, and incentive systems for improved environmental protection.
Ind/Abst Curr. Aware. Biol. Sci., CABS; Econ. Lit. Index; Environ. Abstr. (July 29, 1992-); Environ. Period. Bibliogr.; Geogr. Abstr. Human Geogr.

US/1044-033X
ENVIRONMENTAL AND URBAN ISSUES. **See** Housing and Urban Development.

US/0748-1527
ENVIRONMENTAL ASSESSMENT OF THE ALASKAN CONTINENTAL SHELF. ANNUAL REPORTS OF PRINCIPAL INVESTIGATORS FOR THE YEAR ENDING ... . [Environ. assess. Alsk. contin. shelf, Annu. rep. princ. invest.]. **VFOAT** Annual Reports of Principal Investigators for the Year Ending .... Began with 1976. English. an. National Oceanic and Atmospheric Administration / Juneau, PO Box 1808, Juneau AK 99802. **LC** TD194.6; .E5825. **DD** 333.91/8. available on microfiche (Vols. for (1980, V. 7-) distributed to depository libraries).

US/0891-1053
ENVIRONMENTAL ASSESSMENT OF THE ALASKAN CONTINENTAL SHELF. FINAL REPORTS OF PRINCIPAL INVESTIGATORS. PHYSICAL SCIENCE STUDIES. ***Title Change.*** [Environ. assess. Alsk. cont. shelf, Final rep. princ. invest., Phys. sci.

stud.]. **Added/Corp** Outer Continental Shelf Environmental Assessment Program. United States. Bureau of Land Management. **VFOAT** Final Reports of Principal Investigators. Physical Science Studies; Physical Science Studies; OCS Physical Science Studies. Vol. 1, (1979)-(19??). English. National Oceanic and Atmospheric Administration / Juneau, PO Box 1808, Juneau AK 99802. **DD** 333. ***Merged with*** *Environmental Assessment of the Alaskan Continental Shelf. Final Reports of Principal Investigators. Biological Studies* ***to form*** *Environmental Assessment of the Alaskan Continental Shelf. Final Reports of Principal Investigators.*
Ind/Abst GeoRef.

NE/0378-1909
ENVIRONMENTAL BIOLOGY OF FISHES. **See** Fish and Fisheries.

●US/1062-3957
ENVIRONMENTAL BUILDING NEWS : A NEWSLETTER ON ENVIRONMENTALLY SUSTAINABLE DESIGN & CONSTRUCTION. **See** Building and Construction.

US/1045-8611
ENVIRONMENTAL BUSINESS JOURNAL. (ENVIRONMENTAL BUSINESS JOURNAL : STRATEGIC INFORMATION FOR A CHANGING INDUSTRY.). [Environ. bus. j.]. **Added/Corp** Environmental Business Publishing Inc. Environmental Business International Inc. (Oct. 1988)-. Periodical. English. mo. $395.00 North America; $445.00 other. Enviroquest Business International, PO Box 371769, San Diego CA 92137. **Tel** (619)295-7685, FAX (619)295-5743. **ED** Grant Ferrir. **LC** HD9718.U6; E55. **DD** 338.4/76285/05. **CODEN** EBUJEE. Index available.

cum. index. available on an online database (files 16,636/Full-Text) from DIALOG.
Desc: Provides a strategic overview of the environmental industry.
Ind/Abst BioBusiness (1989-); PROMT [Full Txt.]; PTS Newsl. Database [Full Txt.].

●US/1072-1835
ENVIRONMENTAL CAREER DIRECTORY. [Environ. career dir.]. 1st Ed. (1993)-. Directory. English. be. $29.95 (hardcover), $17.95 (softcover). Gale Research Inc., 835 Penobscot Building, Detroit MI 48226. **Tel** (800)877-GALE, (313)961-2242, FAX (313)961-6083, telex TWX 810-221-7086. **DD** 333.
Desc: From forestry and fish and wildlife management to soil and water conservation, this directory will guide you to practical information on finding a job in the industry.

●US/1065-8548
ENVIRONMENTAL CHANGE. (ENVIRONMENTAL CHANGE : EC.). **VFOAT** EC. (1993)-. Periodical. English. qt. Gordon & Breach Science Publishers, Inc., PO Box 786, Cooper Station, New York NY 10276. **Tel** (212)206-8900, FAX (212)645-2459. **(Subscription address:** International Publishers Distributor at one of the following addresses: 820 Town Center Drive, Langhorne, PA 19047; or PO Box 90, Reading Berkshire RG1 8JL UK; or Kent Ridge PO Box 1180, Singapore 9111, Republic of Singapore**)**

US/1072-1029
ENVIRONMENTAL COMMUNICATOR. [Environ. commun.]. **Added/Corp** North American Association for Environmental Education. (19??)-. Periodical. English. bm. $20.00. North American Association for Environmental Education, PO Box 400, Troy OH 45373. **Tel** (513)676-2514, FAX (513)335-5623. **DD** 333.

US/1061-155X
ENVIRONMENTAL CONTRACT OPPORTUNITY REPORT, THE. [Environ. contract oppor. rep.]. (1991)-. Periodical. English. Fifty-two times a year. $347.00 (one year), $684.00 (two years). United Communications Group, 11300 Rockville Pike, Suite 1100, Rockville MD 20852. **Tel** (301)816-8950 ext. 223, FAX (301)816-8945. **DD** 338.

US/0013-9238
ENVIRONMENTAL CONTROL NEWS FOR SOUTHERN INDUSTRY. Added/Corp Ramcon, inc. **VFOAT** Southern Pollution Control Newsletter; Environmental Control News. (1971)-. Periodical. English. mo. $29.95 US; $32.00 others. Williams and Associates, 751 East Brookhaven Circle, Memphis TN 38117. **Tel** (901)685-2077, FAX (901)452-3525. **ED** E. F. Williams. **Bk Rev. Ad Acc. Circ:** 300 (ctrl). available on microfilm and microfiche from University Microfilms International (UMI).
Desc: Industrial pollution control newsletter reporting regulatory, legislative, and technical developments plus activities of environmentalists within the South.

US/0192-8856
ENVIRONMENTAL CONTROL TECHNOLOGY ACTIVITIES OF THE DEPARTMENT OF ENERGY. (1976/77)-. English. an. $6.25. National Technical Information Service - NTIS, Room 2027S, 5285 Port Royal Road, Springfield VA 22161. **Tel** (703)487-4630, (703)487-4660, (703)487-4650, FAX (703)321-8547, telex 89-9405. **LC** HC110.E5; E4983. **DD** 301.31/0973.

US
ENVIRONMENTAL DEVELOPMENT PLAN. BIOMASS ENERGY SYSTEMS. Main/Corp United States. Dept. of Energy. Office of Energy Technology. **VFOAT** Biomass Energy Systems. 1979-. English. US Department of Energy Office of Energy Technology, 1000 Independence Avenue SW, Washington DC 20585. ***Continues*** *Environmental Development Plan. Fuels from Biomass.*

US
ENVIRONMENTAL DEVELOPMENT PLAN. URANIUM MINING, MILLING, AND CONVERSION. Main/Corp United States. Dept. of Energy. Office of the Assistant Secretary for Environment. **VFOAT** Uranium Mining, Milling, and Conversion. Government Publication. English. US Department of Energy, 1000 Independence Avenue SW, Washington DC 20585. **Tel** (202)586-5000, FAX (202)586-4073.

CN/1183-6466
ENVIRONMENTAL DIGEST. [Environ. dig.]. Vol. 1, No. 1 (Jan. 1991)-. Periodical. English. mo. $24.00 + 7% G.S.T. per year. Rob Alden, PO Box 1874, Main Post Office, Edmonton Alberta T5J 2P2 Canada. **DD** 363.7/00971.

UK/0267-310X
ENVIRONMENTAL DIGEST FOR WALES / WELSH OFFICE / CRYNHOAD O YSTADEGAU'R AMGYLCHEDD / Y SWYDDFA GYMREIG. Added/Corp Great Britain. Welsh Office. **VFOAT** Crynhoad o Ystadegau'r Amgylchedd. No. 1 (1984)-. Periodical. English (Welsh). Welsh Office Publications Unit, Crown Building, Cathay's Park, Cardiff CF1 3NQ Wales. **Tel** 011 44 222 825111. **LC** TD171.5.G72; W34. **DD** 363.7/009429.

●US/1062-4961
ENVIRONMENTAL DISCOVERY. (1992)-. Periodical. English. qt. $20.00. Environmental Discovery Publishing, PO Box 20025, Spokane WA 99204-0025.

UK/0144-9281
ENVIRONMENTAL EDUCATION AND INFORMATION. [Environ. educ. inf.]. **Added/Corp** Institution of Environmental Sciences. Vol. 1, No. 1 (Jan./Mar. 1981)-. Periodical. English. qt. £21.00 UK; £30.00 other Europe; £29.00 other. Environmental Education and Information, Newton Building, University of Salford, Salford M5 4WT England. **Tel** 011 44 61 745 5221, FAX 011 44 61 745 5999, telex 668680. **ED** M Pugh Thomas. Index available. cum. index. **Bk Rev**, (Qty: 35). **Ad Acc. Pr Rev. Circ:** 500.
Desc: For the study of the environment, with the aim of encouraging knowledge, understanding, awareness and protection of the global environment.
Ind/Abst Br. Educ. Index; Curr. Index J. Educ.; Ecol. Abstr.; Environ. Period. Bibliogr.; Geogr. Abstr. Phys. Geogr.; Geogr. Abstr. Human Geogr.; Int. Dev. Abstr.

●UK/1350-4622
ENVIRONMENTAL EDUCATION RESEARCH. Vol. 1 (1995)-. English. Three times a year. £98.00. Carfax Publishing Company, PO Box 25 Abingdon, Oxfordshire OX14 3UE England. **Tel** 011 44 235 555335, FAX (0279)31067, telex 817484. **ED** Chris Oulton.
Desc: Focuses on international, analytical, and theory-based approaches to environmental education and its applications and implementation.

●US/1072-5083
ENVIRONMENTAL ENCYCLOPEDIA. (1993)-. English. $195.00. Gale Research Inc., 835 Penobscot Building, Detroit MI 48226. **Tel** (800)877-GALE, (313)961-2242, FAX (313)961-6083, telex TWX 810-221-7086. **ED** William P. Cunningham, Terence Ball, Terence H. Cooper, Eville Gorham, Malcolm T. Hepworth and Alfred A. Marcus.
Desc: Presents a comprehensive, multidisciplinary approach to the study of the environment. Consists of over 1,300 signed articles and term definitions.

US/1063-7346
ENVIRONMENTAL ENGINEERING ABSTRACTS. ***Ceased.*** **See** Environmental Issues-Abstracting, Bibliographies and Statistics.

●US/1056-7054
ENVIRONMENTAL ENGINEERING (NEW YORK, N.Y.). (ENVIRONMENTAL ENGINEERING.). (1993)-. Periodical. English. qt. $110.00. Executive Enterprises, 22 West 21st Street, New York NY 10010-6990. **Tel** (800)332-8804, FAX (212)645-8689.

US/0163-4275
ENVIRONMENTAL ETHICS. [Environ. ethics]. **Added/Corp** John Muir Institute for Environmental Studies. University of New Mexico. Environmental Philosophy, Inc. University of Georgia. Vol. 1, No. 1 (Spring 1979)-. Academic Scholarly Publication. English. qt (Feb., May, Aug., Nov.). $40.00 (institutions); $20.00 (individuals). Environmental Ethics, Department of Philosophy, PO Box 13496, Denton TX 76203. **Tel** (817)565-2727, FAX (817)565-4448. **ED** Eugene C. Hargrove. **LC** GF80; .E58. **DD** 304.2/05. **CODEN** ENETDD. Index available. cum. index. **Bk Rev. Ad Acc, Adv Mgr:** Jan Dickson. **Pr Rev. Acid Free. Circ:** 1,900. available on microfilm and microfiche from University Microfilms International (UMI). Documents available from The Genuine Article, BIOSIS Document Express, UMI Article Clearinghouse, Documents on Demand.
Desc: An interdisciplinary journal dedicated to the philosophical aspects of environmental problems.
Ind/Abst Acad. Ind. [Computer File] (1992-); Acad. Search (Jan. 1994-); AGRICOLA [Select. Cov.]; Biol. Abstr.; Curr. Contents Soc. Behav. Sci.; Curr. Index J. Educ.; EMBASE; Energy Res. Abstr. (Apr. 1980-); Environ. Abstr.; Environ. Period. Bibliogr. (1990-); Expand. Acad. Index (1989-); Gen. Sci. Index (1992-); Gen. Sci. Source (Jul. 1993-); Health Saf. Sci. Abstr.; Humanit. Index; Humanit. Source (Jul. 1993-); INFO-SOUTH Abstr.; Int. Dev. Abstr.; Int. Bibliogr. Rezen. Wissen. Lit.; Int. Bibliogr. Zeitschriftenliteratur Allen Gebieten Wissens; J. Plan. Lit.; Mag. Search; Newsp. Period. Abstr. (1991-); Life Sci. Collect.; Philos. Index; Pollut. Abstr. Indexes; Ref. Z.; Relig. Theol. Abstr.; Res. Alert [Full Cov.]; Soc. Plann. Policy Dev. Abstr.; Soc. Sci. Cit. Index [Full Cov.]; Sociol. Abstr.; SportSearch; Wildl. Rev.

●US/1067-7208
ENVIRONMENTAL EXECUTIVE DIRECTORY. [Environ. exec. dir.]. **Added/Corp** Public Affairs Group, Inc. (1993)-. Directory. English. an. $165.00. Carroll Publishing Company, 1058 Thomas Jefferson Street Northwest, Washington DC 20007-3832. **Tel** (202)333-8620, FAX (202)337-7020. **LC** TD169.6; .E588. **DD** 333.
Desc: Provides direct access to key decision makers in every facet of the environmental field. Coverage includes nearly 10,000 environmental executives in more than 5,000 corporations and organizations. Each entry includes name, title, address, phone number, and useful background data on the company or organization.

US/1054-8017
ENVIRONMENTAL FINANCE (NEW YORK, N.Y.). ***Ceased.*** (ENVIRONMENTAL FINANCE.). [Environ. finance]. Vol. 1, No. 1 (Spring 1991)-(June 1992). Periodical. English. qt. Executive Enterprises, 22 West 21st Street, New York NY 10010-6990. **Tel** (800)332-8804, FAX (212)645-8689. **DD** 363. **[CCC].** available on microfilm and microfiche from University Microfilms International (UMI).

UK/0269-4042
ENVIRONMENTAL GEOCHEMISTRY AND HEALTH. [Environ. geochem. health]. Vol. 7, No. 1 (March 1985)-. Academic Scholarly Publication. English. qt. £106.00 (institution), £43.40 (individual) UK; $212.00 (institution), $86.80 (individual) US. Chapman & Hall, 2-6 Boundary Row, London SE1 8HN England. **Tel** 011 44 71 865 0066, FAX 011 44 71 522 9623, telex 290164 Chapmag. **(Subscription address:** International Thomson Publishing Svcs. Ltd., Subscription Department North Way Andover, Hampshire SP10 5BE England.**) ED** Brien E. Davies. **LC** TD195.M5. **DD** 333.73. **NLM** W1; EN981R. **CODEN** EGHEE3. **[CCC]. Bk Rev. Ad Acc. Circ:** 1,000. Documents available from The Genuine Article, BIOSIS Document Express, CASDDS, Documents on Demand. ***Continues*** *Minerals and the Environment, 0142-7245.*
Ind/Abst Biol. Abstr. (1985-); Chem. Abstr. (1985-); Coal Abstr. (1985-); Curr. Aware. Biol. Sci., CABS; Curr. Contents, Agric. Biol. Environ. Sci.; Curr. Contents Eng. Tech. Appl. Sci.; Ecol. Abstr.; EMBASE (1985-); Energy Res. Abstr. (1985-); Environ. Abstr. (1985-); Field Crop Abstr.; Food Sci. Technol. Abstr.; Geogr. Abstr. Phys. Geogr.; Geogr. Abstr. Human Geogr.; Geol. Abstr.; GeoRef (1985-); Health Saf. Sci. Abstr.; Int. Dev. Abstr.; Leadscan; MINPROC (1985-); Mintec, Min. Technol. Abstr. (1985-); Life Sci. Collect. (1985-); Pollut. Abstr. Indexes (1985-); Res. Alert [Select. Cov.]; Rev. Agric. Entomol.; SCISEARCH; Soils Fert.

US
ENVIRONMENTAL GEOSCIENCES. (19??)-. Academic Scholarly Publication. English. sa. $75.00 (institution), $50.00 (individual) US; $85.00 (institution), $60.00 (individual) other. Blackwell Scientific Publishers, 238 Main Street, Cambridge MA 02142. **Tel** (617)547-7110, (800)835-6770, FAX (617)547-0789.

DK/1011-4173
ENVIRONMENTAL HEALTH (COPENHAGEN). (ENVIRONMENTAL HEALTH SERIES.). [Environ. health]. **Added/Corp** World Health Organization. Regional Office for Europe. **VFOAT** Environmental Health; EH. Vol. 1 (1985)-. Monographic series. English. **NLM** W1; EN984AG.
Ind/Abst Trop. Dis. Bull.

AT/0818-5670
ENVIRONMENTAL HEALTH REVIEW, AUSTRALIA : THE OFFICIAL JOURNAL OF THE AUSTRALIAN INSTITUTE OF ENVIRONMENTAL HEALTH. Added/Corp Australian Institute of Environmental Health. (1986)-. Periodical. English. Four times a year (Feb., May, Aug., Oct.). 28.00Aus$ Australia & New Zealand; $35.00 other. Australian Institute Environmental Health, PO Box 26, Torrens ACT 2607 Australia. **Tel** 011 61 6 2853119, FAX 011 61 06 2854634. **ED** Adrain O'Loughlin, (phone: (06) 285 3119). **NLM** W1; EN984ACL. **Ad Acc, Adv Mgr:** Neil Wilson, **Tel** 02 319 3933. **Circ:** 2,800 (ctrl). ***Continues*** *Australian Health Surveyor.*

UK
ENVIRONMENTAL IMPACT. English. mo (July-Aug. usually combined). £308.70 UK; £335.00 other. Industry & Environment Association, 77 Temple Sheen Road, East Sheen, London SW14 7RS England. **Tel** 011 44 81 876-3367, FAX 011 44 81 876 1674. **ED** P. Shimell. **Bk Rev. Ad Acc.**
Desc: Covering auditing, conservation, toxicology, pollution, and general environmental topics.

US/0195-9255
ENVIRONMENTAL IMPACT ASSESSMENT REVIEW. [Environ. impact. asses. rev.]. **VFOAT** EIA Review. Vol. 1 (March 1980)-. Academic Scholarly Publication. English. Six times a year (1 volume). $263.00 US; $303.00 other. Elsevier Science Publishing Company Inc, Madison Square Station, PO Box 882, New York NY 10159-0882. **Tel** (212)633-3950, FAX (212)633-3990. **ED** Lawrence E Susskind and Teresa Hill. **LC** TD194.6; .E593. **DD** 333.7/1/0973. **NLM** W1 EN984Q. **CODEN** EIARDK. **[CCC].** available on microfilm and microfiche from University Microfilms International (UMI). Documents available from The Genuine Article, Documents on Demand.
Ind/Abst AgBiotech News Inf.; Coal Abstr.; Ecol. Abstr. (?-?); Ei Page One; EMBASE; Energy Inf. Abstr.; Energy Res. Abstr. (Dec. 1980-); Environ. Abstr.; Environ. Period. Bibliogr.; Fish Rev.; For. Abstr.; Geogr. Abstr. Human

Geogr.; INIS Atomindex [Micro.]; Int. Dev. Abstr.; J. Plan. Lit.; Leis. Recreat. Tour. Abstr.; Pollut. Abstr. Indexes; Ref. Z.; Res. Alert [Select. Cov.]; Rural Dev. Abstr.; Soc. Sci. Cit. Index [Select. Cov.]; World Agric. Econ.

US/0148-8317
ENVIRONMENTAL IMPACT NEWS. [Environ. imp. news]. Vol. 1 (Jan. 1975)-. Periodical. English. mo. $35.00. Technomic Publishing Company, Inc., 851 New Holland Avenue, Box 3535, Lancaster PA 17604. **Tel** (717)291-5609, (800)233-9936, FAX (717)295-4538.
Ind/Abst Energy Res. Abstr. (Oct. 1976-).

US/1061-9755
ENVIRONMENTAL INDEX, THE. ***Ceased.*** [Environ. index]. **Added/Corp** University Microfilms International. 1st Quarter (1992)-(1992). English. qt. University Microfilms International, 300 North Zeeb Road, Ann Arbor MI 48106-1346. **Tel** (313)761-4700, (800)521-0600 Exts. 2490, 2491, FAX (313)973-1540. **DD** 363.

UK
ENVIRONMENTAL INTERPRETATION : THE BULLETIN OF THE CENTRE FOR ENVIRONMENTAL INTERPRETATION. **Added/Corp** Manchester Polytechnic. Centre for Environmental Interpretation. **VFOAT** CEI Environmental Interpretation. (Oct. 1988)-. Bulletin. English. Three times a year. £12.50 England; £15.00 others. Manchester Metropolitan University, Old Hall Lane, Manchester M14 6HR England. **Tel** 011 44 61 247 2000. **(Subscription address:** Manchester Polytechnic, St. Augustine's, Lower Chatham Street, Manchester, M15 6BY England, telephone: 061-247-1067**)** ***Continues** Interpretation (Manchester, England).*
Desc: Essential reading if you are concerned with visitor management. Lively and easy to read and keep you up-to-date with original research, case studies and new perspectives, with the practical details you need to put ideas into action.
Ind/Abst Leis. Recreat. Tour. Abstr.

UK
ENVIRONMENTAL ISSUES NEWSLETTER. (19??)-. Newsletter. English. Twelve times a year. £395.00. Leatherhead Food Research Association, Randalls Road, Leatherhead Surrey KT22 7RY United Kingdom. **Tel** 011 44 372 376761, FAX 011 44 372 386228, telex 929846.

●US/1061-3935
ENVIRONMENTAL ISSUES REPORT. [Environ. issues rep.]. (1992)-. Periodical. English. sm. $295.00. Capitol Reports, 921 11th Street, Suite 701, Sacramento CA 95814-2814. **DD** 351. ***Continues** Toxics News, 0748-4747.*

US/1043-2698
ENVIRONMENTAL LIABILITY REPORT, THE. ***Ceased.*** [Environ. liabil. rep.]. Vol. 1, No. 1 (July 1988)-. Periodical. English. mo. Donley Technology, PO Box 335, Garrisonville VA 22463-0335. **Tel** (703)659-1954. **ED** Veronica Deschambault. **DD** 346. **Bk Rev. Ad Acc.** ctrl circ.
Desc: Helps real estate buyers, sellers, lenders, and environmental consultants identify and limit environmental liabilities. Each issue addresses topics such as state and federal environmental cleanup responsibility legislation and litigation.

UK
ENVIRONMENTAL MANAGEMENT. (19??)-. Periodical. English. qt. £212.65. Croner Publ Ltd, Croner House, London Road, Kingston upon Thames, Surrey KT2 6SR England. **Tel** 011 44 81 5473333, FAX 081 547-2637.

UK/0956-6163
ENVIRONMENTAL MANAGEMENT AND HEALTH. (1990)-. Periodical. English. qt. $929.00. MCB University Press, 60 62 Toller Lane, Bradford West Yorkshire BD8 9BX England. **Tel** 011 44 274 499821, FAX 011 44 274 547143, telex 51317 MCBUNI G. **(Subscription address:** MCB University Press / US and Canada Subscriptions, PO Box 10812, Birmingham AL 35201-0812.**) ED** Professor J. Rose. **LC** RA565.A1; E586. **DD** 363.7. **NLM** W1; EN984UF. **CODEN** EMHEEB. Documents available from UMI Article Clearinghouse.
Desc: Provides an international assessment of the current situation in the environment and remedies needed to attain an improvement of man's health by sensible means, regardless of political factors or vested interests. The aim of the journal is to examine in a deep and objective manner, the various environmental factors and their impact on human health.
Ind/Abst ABI/INFORM Glob. Ed.; Biodeter. Abstr. (1991-); Environ. Period. Bibliogr.

US/0364-152X
ENVIRONMENTAL MANAGEMENT (NEW YORK). (ENVIRONMENTAL MANAGEMENT.). [Environ. manage.]. Vol. 1 (1976)-. Academic Scholarly Publication. English. Six times a year. $282.00. Springer-Verlag New York Inc., 175 5th Avenue, New York NY 10010. **Tel** (212)460-1500, telex 232 235 SPB UR. **(Subscription address:** Springer Verlag New York Inc. / for North America, 44 Hartz Way, Secaucus NJ 07096.**) ED** D Alexander. **LC** TD169; .E6. **DD** 363.6. **NLM** W1 EN984U. **CODEN** EMNGDC. **[CCC]. Pr Rev.** available on microfilm and microfiche from University Microfilms International (UMI). Documents available from Article Express International, The Genuine Article, BIOSIS Document Express, CASDDS, Documents on Demand. ***Continues** Environmental Auditor, 0933-0437.*
Desc: Presents complementary and contradictory ideas within the format of a single, international publication. Covers a broad spectrum of conservation, preservation, reclamation, and utilization, the journal publishes material dealing with ecological modeling, resource management, energy hazard response, environmental monitoring, and hazardous substances.
Ind/Abst AGRICOLA [Select. Cov.]; Agrofor. Abstr.; AQUAREF; Biodeter. Abstr.; Bioeng. Abstr.; Biol. Abstr. (1986-); Chem. Abstr.; Coal Abstr.; Curr. Contents, Agric. Biol. Environ. Sci.; Curr. Ref. Fish Res.; Ecol. Abstr.; Ecology Abstr.; Ei Page One; EMBASE; Energy Inf. Abstr.; Energy Res. Abstr. (June 1978-); Eng. Index Annu.; Environ. Abstr.; Field Crop Abstr.; Fish Rev.; For. Prod. Abstr. (19??-19??); For. Abstr.; Geogr. Abstr. Phys. Geogr.; Geogr. Abstr. Human Geogr.; Geol. Abstr.; GeoRef; INIS Atomindex [Micro.]; Int. Aerosp. Abstr.; Int. Dev. Abstr.; Irr. Drain. Abstr.; Key Word Index Wildl. Res.; Leis. Recreat. Tour. Abstr.; Ocean. Abstr.; Life Sci. Collect.; Pollut. Abstr. Indexes; Res. Alert [Full Cov.]; Rev. Plant Pathol.; Rural Dev. Abstr.; Sci. Cit. Index; SCISEARCH; Soc. Sci. Cit. Index [Select. Cov.]; Soils Fert.; SportSearch; Weed Abstr.; Wildl. Rev.; World Agric. Econ.

US/0893-3413
ENVIRONMENTAL MANAGEMENT NEWS. ***Title Change.*** [Environ. manage. news]. Vol. 1, No. 1 (Jan./Feb. 1986)-(July 1990). Periodical. English. mo. Stevens Publishing Corporation, 225 North New Road, Waco TX 76702-2604. **Tel** (800)727-7573, (817)776-9000. **DD** 344. **CODEN** EMNEE7. **[CCC]. *Continued by*** *Environmental Protection News, 1050-7124.*
Ind/Abst BioBusiness; Ind. Hyg. Dig. (19??-19??).

US
ENVIRONMENTAL MANAGEMENT / PA. **See** Environmental Issues-Pollution and Waste Management.

AT
ENVIRONMENTAL MANAGER. (19??)-. English. Forty-eight times a year. 395.00Aus$. Newsletter Information Service, PO Box 693, Manly New South Wales 2095 Australia. **Tel** 011 61 2 9777500.

JA/0287-0517
ENVIRONMENTAL MEDICINE : ANNUAL REPORT OF THE RESEARCH INSTITUTE OF ENVIRONMENTAL MEDICINE, NAGOYA UNIVERSITY. **See** Medical Science and Technology.

NE/0167-6369
ENVIRONMENTAL MONITORING AND ASSESSMENT. [Environ. monit. assess.]. Vol. 1, No. 1 (April 1981)-. Academic Scholarly Publication. English. Fifteen times a year (Fifteen times per year). $1,580.00. Kluwer Academic Publishers, Postbus 322, 3300 AH Dordrecht, The Netherlands. **Tel** 011 (31) 78 524400, FAX 011 31 78 183273, telex 20083. **ED** G Bruce Wiersma. **LC** TD169; .E617. **DD** 363.7/063. **NLM** W1; EN9844M. **CODEN** EMASDH. **[CCC]. Bk Rev. Ad Acc. Pr Rev. Acid Free. Circ:** 550. available on microfilm and microfiche from University Microfilms International (UMI). Documents available from The Genuine Article, BIOSIS Document Express, Ask*IEEE, CASDDS, Documents on Demand.
Desc: Devoted to progress in pollution monitoring. The journal emphasizes technical development and data arising from environmental monitoring and assessment, the use of scientific principles in the design of monitoring systems at the local, regional and global scales, and the use of monitoring data in assessing pollution risks to mankind and the environment. The journal covers a wide range of pollutants and examines monitoring systems designed to estimate exposure both at the individual and population levels.
Ind/Abst Air Pollut. Titles; Art Archaeol. Tech. Abstr.; Biodeter. Abstr. (1991-); Biol. Abstr.; Chem. Abstr.; Curr. Aware. Biol. Sci., CABS; Curr. Contents, Agric. Biol. Environ. Sci.; Ecol. Abstr.; EMBASE; Energy Inf. Abstr.; Environ. Abstr.; Environ. Period. Bibliogr. (1981-); Fish Rev. (1981-); Food Sci. Technol. Abstr.; For. Abstr.; Geogr. Abstr. Phys. Geogr. (1983-); Geogr. Abstr. Human Geogr.; GeoRef; Health Saf. Sci. Abstr.; Index Vet.; INSPEC (1981-); Int. Aerosp. Abstr. (1983-); Int. Dev. Abstr.; Irr. Drain. Abstr.; Key Word Index Wildl. Res.; Meteorol. Geoastrophys. Abstr. (199?-); Ocean. Abstr.; Life Sci. Collect.; Pollut. Abstr. Indexes; Res. Alert [Select. Cov.]; Rev. Agric. Entomol.; Rev. Med. Vet. Entomol.; Sage Race Relat. Abstr.; Sage Urban Stud. Abstr; SCISEARCH; Soc. Sci. Cit. Index [Select. Cov.]; Soils Fert.; Vet. Bull.; Wildl. Rev. (1981-).

US
ENVIRONMENTAL MONITORING AND ECOLOGICAL STUDIES PROGRAM. **Main/Corp** Northern States Power Company. Engineering Vice Presidential Staff Dept. **VFOAT** Annual Report of the Environmental Monitoring and Ecological Studies Program. (1970)-. Periodical. English. **LC** TD877.5; .N66. **DD** 628; 628.5.

US/0148-6004
ENVIRONMENTAL MONITORING AT MAJOR U.S. ENERGY RESEARCH & DEVELOPMENT ADMINISTRATION CONTRACTOR SITES. [Environ. monit. major U. S. Energy Res. & Dev. Adm. contract. sites]. **Main/Corp** United States. Energy Research and Development Administration. Division of Safety, Standards, & Compliance. **VAT** Environmental Monitoring of Major United States Energy Research and Development Administrator Contractor Sites. English. an. $18.75. National Technical Information Service - NTIS, Room 2027S, 5285 Port Royal Road, Springfield VA 22161. **Tel** (703)487-4630, (703)487-4660, (703)487-4650, FAX (703)321-8547, telex 89-9405. **LC** TD195.E4; U527A. **DD** 363.6.

US
ENVIRONMENTAL MONITORING REPORT, UNITED STATES DEPARTMENT OF ENERGY, PADUCAH GASEOUS DIFFUSION PLANT. **See** Energy.

KO
ENVIRONMENTAL MUTAGENS AND CARCINOGENS. (HANGUK HWANGYONGSONG TOLYON PYONI, PALAMWON HAKHOE CHI.). [Environ. mutagens carcinog.]. **Added/Corp** Hanguk Hwangyongsong Tolyon Pyoni, Palamwon Hakhoe. **VFOAT** Environmental Mutagens and Carcinogens. (1981)-. Periodical. Korean (English). **NLM** W1; HA524BW. **CODEN** EMCAE8. Documents available from BIOSIS Document Express, CASDDS.
Ind/Abst Biol. Abstr.; Chem. Abstr.

US
ENVIRONMENTAL NEWSLINE. English. $206.70 Kentucky Residents (includes 6% sales tax); $195.00 other. Kentucky Chamber of Commerce, Box 817, 464 Chenault Road, Frankfort KY 40602. **Tel** (502)695-4700, FAX (502)695-6824.

US/0899-9511
ENVIRONMENTAL OUTLOOK (SEATTLE, WASH.). (ENVIRONMENTAL OUTLOOK.). [Environ. outlook]. **Added/Corp** University of Washington. Institute for Environmental Studies. Vol. 1 (Mar. 1973)-. Periodical. English. Ten times a year. Free to US & Canada; $15.00 others. Institute of Environmental Studies, University of Washington FM 12, Seattle WA 98195. **Tel** (206)743-1812. **DD** 333.

US/0145-3815
ENVIRONMENTAL PERIODICALS BIBLIOGRAPHY. **See** Environmental Issues-Abstracting, Bibliographies and Statistics.

US/1053-1440
ENVIRONMENTAL PERIODICALS BIBLIOGRAPHY ON CD-ROM. **See** Environmental Issues-Abstracting, Bibliographies and Statistics.

UK/0961-9356
ENVIRONMENTAL POLICY AND PRACTICE. [Environ. policy pract.]. (1991)-. Periodical. English. qt (4 issues). £22.00 (individuals), £66.00 (organizations) UK; £32.00 (individuals), £76.00 (organizations) other. EPP Publications, 52 Kings Road, Richmond TW10 6RP, United Kingdom. **Tel** 011 44 81 948 7165, FAX 011 44 81 747 9663. **DD** _a363.7.

IS/0792-0032
ENVIRONMENTAL POLICY REVIEW. **Added/Corp** Merkaz Le-heker Beri. Ha-M. u-Mizrah Eropah a. Sh. Marg'ori Meirok. Vol. 1, No. 1 (June 1987)-. Periodical. English. Twice a year. $15.00. Soviet and East European Resource Center, FAC-Social Sciences, Mount Scopus, Jerusalem 91905 Israel. **Tel** (011)972 2 883180, FAX (011)972 2 322545, telex 26458. **ED** Dr. Zeev Wolfson. **LC** HC340.E5; E58. **DD** 363.7/056/0947. **CODEN** EPRFEH. **Bk Rev.** ctrl circ.
Desc: Articles on ecological problems and policy changes in the USSR and Eastern Europe.
Ind/Abst PAIS Int. Print (1991-).

●UK/0964-4016
ENVIRONMENTAL POLITICS. (1992)-. Periodical. English. qt. $140.00. Frank Cass & Company Ltd, Newbury House, 890-900 Eastern Avenue, Newbury Park, Ilford, Essex IG2 7HH United Kingdom. **Tel** 011 44 81 599 8866, FAX 011 44 81 599 0984, telex 897719. **LC** JA75.8; .E58. **Ad Acc, Adv Mgr:** Anne Kidson.
Desc: Concerned with three particular aspects of the study of environmental politics, with a focus on the industrialized countries. Firstly, it will examine the evolution of environmental movements and parties. Secondly, it will provide an analysis of the making and implementation of public policy in the area of the environment at international, national and local levels. Thirdly, it will carry comment on ideas, from both a 'deep'

and 'shallow' perspective, generated by the various environmental movements and organizations, and by individual theorists.

US/0191-5398
ENVIRONMENTAL PROFESSIONAL, THE. (THE ENVIRONMENTAL PROFESSIONAL : THE OFFICIAL JOURNAL OF THE NATIONAL ASSOCIATION OF ENVIRONMENTAL PROFESSIONALS (NAEP).). [Environ. prof.]. **Added/Corp** National Association of Environmental Professionals. (1979)-. Academic Scholarly Publication. English. qt. $130.00 (institution), $75.00 (individuals). Blackwell Scientific Publishers, 238 Main Street, Cambridge MA 02142. **Tel** (617)547-7110, (800)835-6770, FAX (617)547-0789. **LC** WMLC 93/1314. **CODEN** EPROD9. **[CCC]**. Index available. cum. index. **Bk Rev. Ad Acc. Pr Rev. Circ:** 2,300 (ctrl). available on microfilm from University Microfilms International (UMI). Documents available from BIOSIS Document Express, Documents on Demand.
Desc: Publishes multidisciplinary studies designed for professionals in diverse practice settings faced with developing imaginative approaches to the solution of environmental problems.
Ind/Abst Biol. Abstr.; Coal Abstr.; Energy Inf. Abstr.; Energy Res. Abstr. (Jan. 1981-); Environ. Abstr.; Environ. Period. Bibliogr.; Fish Rev. (Jan. 1989-July 1992); GeoRef; Health Saf. Sci. Abstr.; INIS Atomindex [Micro.]; Middle East Abstr. Index; Life Sci. Collect.; Pollut. Abstr. Indexes; Wildl. Rev. (Jan. 1989-July 1992).

US/0099-2275
ENVIRONMENTAL PROGRAM ADMINISTRATORS. Main/Corp United States. Environmental Protection Agency. Office of Regional and Intergovernmental Operations. English. an. Environmental Protection Agency / Regional and Intergovernmental Operations, 401 M Street SW, Washington DC 20460. **LC** TD12; .U54A. **DD** 353.008/232.

US/1057-171X
ENVIRONMENTAL PROTECTION NEWS. (ENVIRONMENTAL PROTECTION NEWS.). [Environ. prot. news]. **VFOAT** Environmental Protection Week. (1990)-. Periodical. English. sm. $283.50 US; $299.50 Canada; $297.50 Mexico; $317.50 other. Stevens Publishing Corporation, 225 North New Road, Waco TX 76702-2604. **Tel** (800)727-7573, (817)776-9000. **(Subscription address:** Stevens Publishing Corp., PO Box 2573, Waco TX 76702.**)** **DD** 344. **CODEN** EPRNE7. ***Continues** Environmental Protection Week, 1050-7124.*
Ind/Abst BioBusiness; Ind. Hyg. Dig. (199?-).

UK
ENVIRONMENTAL PROTECTION SURVEY. Periodical. English. £2.00. 30 Calderwood Street, London SE18 6QH England. **LC** TD169; .E64. **DD** 363.6.

UK/0966-4904
ENVIRONMENTAL PROTECTION TECHNOLOGY. [Environ. prot. technol.]. (198?)-. Periodical. English. mo. £254.00 UK; $445.00 US. World Business Publications Ltd., 960 High Road, Britannia 4th Floor, London N12 9RY England. **Tel** 11 44 81 446 5141, FAX 11 44 81 446 3659, telex 9419208. **DD** 363.7.

US/1057-4298
ENVIRONMENTAL PROTECTION (WACO, TEX.). (ENVIRONMENTAL PROTECTION.). [Environ. prot.]. (199?)-. Periodical. English. mo. $84.00 US; $106.00 Canada; $102.00 Mexico; $114.00 other. Stevens Publishing Corporation, 225 North New Road, Waco TX 76702-2604. **Tel** (800)727-7573, (817)776-9000. **LC** TD169; .E63. **DD** 363. **CODEN** ENPRET. Documents available from Documents on Demand.
Ind/Abst Environ. Abstr. (Sept. 13, 1991-); Risk Abstr.

US/1050-7124
ENVIRONMENTAL PROTECTION WEEK. ***Title Change.*** [Environmental prot. week]. (19??)-(19??). Periodical. English. wk. Stevens Publishing Corporation, 225 North New Road, Waco TX 76702-2604. **Tel** (800)727-7573, (817)776-9000. **DD** 344. **CODEN** EPWEE5. ***Continues** Environmental Management News, 0893-3413.* ***Continued by** Environmental Protection News, 1057-171X.*
Desc: Provides accurate and authoritative information in regard to the subject matter covered.
Ind/Abst BioBusiness (1990-); Ind. Hyg. Dig. (19??-19??).

GW/0300-824X
ENVIRONMENTAL QUALITY AND SAFETY. [Environ. qual. saf.]. **VFOAT** EQS, Environmental Quality and Safety: Chemistry, Toxicology and Technology. V. 1 (1972)-. Academic Scholarly Publication. Multiple languages (English, French and German). Georg Thieme Verlag Stuttgart, Postfach 301120, D 70451 Stuttgart Germany. **Tel** 011 49 711 89310, FAX 011 49 711 8931298, telex 7 252 275 GTVD. **(Subscription address:** Thieme Medical Publishers Inc., 381 Park Avenue South, New York NY 10016.**)** **LC** QH545.A1. **DD** 615.9/02/05. **NLM** W1 EN984XK. **CODEN** EQSFAP. Documents available from BIOSIS Document Express, CASDDS.
Ind/Abst AGRICOLA; Biol. Abstr. (1972-1976); Chem. Abstr.; Health Plan. Adminis.; Life Sci. Collect.; Weed Abstr.

US
ENVIRONMENTAL QUALITY SERIES. No. 1-. Monographic series. English. ir. Price varies per volume. Institute of Government & Public Affairs, University of California, Los Angeles CA 90024.

US/0095-2044
ENVIRONMENTAL QUALITY (WASHINGTON). (ENVIRONMENTAL QUALITY : THE ... ANNUAL REPORT OF THE COUNCIL ON ENVIRONMENTAL QUALITY.). [Environ. qual.]. English. an. Council on Environmental Quality, 722 Jackson Place NW, Washington DC 20006. **Tel** (202)395-5700. **LC** TD169; .U53A. **DD** 301.31. **NLM** W2 A C93E. available on microfilm from University Microfilms International (UMI).
Ind/Abst Energy Res. Abstr. (June 1980-); Life Sci. Collect.; Pollut. Abstr. Indexes.

US
ENVIRONMENTAL REGISTER. English. Twenty-four times a year. $145.00. Environmental Compliance Reporter, 3154-B College Drive, Suite 522, Baton Rouge LA 70808. **Tel** (504)383-3937.

US/1055-7598
ENVIRONMENTAL REGULATION. (1991)-. Periodical. English. qt. $110.00. Executive Enterprises, 22 West 21st Street, New York NY 10010-6990. **Tel** (800)332-8804, FAX (212)645-8689.

●US/1071-538X
ENVIRONMENTAL REMEDIATION TECHNOLOGY. [Environ. remediat. technol.]. Vol. 1, No. 1 (1993)-. Periodical. English. bw (26 issues). $390.00. Business Publishers Inc., 951 Pershing Drive, Silver Spring MD 20910-4464. **Tel** (301)587-6300, (800)274-0122, FAX (301)585-9075. **DD** 628.

AT/0314-9781
ENVIRONMENTAL REPORT CLAYTON. (1977)-. English. ir.
Ind/Abst Int. Dev. Abstr.

US
ENVIRONMENTAL REPORTER. **Added/Corp** Harvard University. Cabot House. Environmental Coalition. Harvard University. Environmental Action Committee. Vol. 1, No. 1 (Fall 1991)-. Periodical. English. qt.

SW
ENVIRONMENTAL RESEARCH. English. an. **LC** QH540; .E57. **DD** 333.7/2/0720485.
Ind/Abst Toxicol. Abstr.

AT/0156-6245
ENVIRONMENTAL RESEARCH BULLETIN. [Environ. res. bull.]. (1977)-. Monographic series. English. ir. Price varies per volume. **DD** _a301.310994.
Ind/Abst AESIS Q.

US/0013-9351
ENVIRONMENTAL RESEARCH (NEW YORK, N.Y.). (ENVIRONMENTAL RESEARCH.). [Environ. res.]. Vol. 1 (June 1967)-. Academic Scholarly Publication. English. Eight times a year. $825.00 US and Canada; $935.00 other. Academic Press, Inc., 6277 Sea Harbor Drive, Orlando FL 32887. **Tel** (800)543-9534, (407)345-4100, FAX (407)363-9661. **ED** Philip J. Landrigan and Irving J. Selikoff. **LC** RA565; .E53. **DD** 616. **NLM** W1 EN985J. **CODEN** ENVRAL. **[CCC]**. Index available. **Bk Rev. Pr Rev.** Documents available from The Genuine Article, BIOSIS Document Express, CASDDS, Documents on Demand.
Desc: Features original research on the health effects of environmental factors. Focuses on environmental components that contribute to pathological conditions. Presents recent findings in specific as well as broad problems of environmental biology and medicine.
Ind/Abst AGRICOLA [Select. Cov.]; Air Pollut. Titles; Appl. Sci. Technol. Index; AQUAREF; Biol. Abstr.; Chem. Abstr.; Coal Abstr.; CSA Neuro. Abstr. (?-?); Curr. Aware. Biol. Sci., CABS; Curr. Contents, Agric. Biol. Environ. Sci.; Curr. Contents Life Sci.; Dairy Sci. Abstr.; EMBASE; Energy Res. Abstr.; Environ. Abstr.; Fish Rev. (Jan. 1989-July 1992); Gas Abstr.; GeoRef; Health Saf. Sci. Abstr.; Health Plan. Adminis.; Index Med.; Index Vet.; Ind. Hyg. Dig. (19??-19??); INIS Atomindex [Micro.]; Int. Aerosp. Abstr.; Int. Exec.; Leadscan; Lit. Pat. Abstr., Oilfield Chem. (1972-); Lit. Abstr., Catal. Catal.; Lit. Abstr., Health Environ.; Lit. Abstr., Pet. Refin. Petrochem.; Lit. Abstr., Pet. Substit.; Lit. Abstr., Transp. Storage; Meteorol. Geoastrophys. Abstr.; Middle East Abstr. Index; Nutr. Abstr. Rev., Ser. B, Live Feeds and Feed.; Nutr. Abstr. Rev., Ser. A, Hum. Exp.; Nutr. Res. Newsl.; Life Sci. Collect.; Pollut. Abstr. Indexes; Poult. Abstr.; Protozoolog. Abstr.; Ref. Upd. Deluxe Ed.; Res. Alert [Full Cov.]; Rice Abstr.; Saf. Health Work; Sci. Cit. Index; SCISEARCH; Soc. Sci. Cit. Index [Select. Cov.]; Vet. Bull.; Wildl. Rev. (Jan. 1989-July 1992).

AT/0156-7268
ENVIRONMENTAL RESEARCH NOTE. [Environ. res. note]. (1977)-. Monographic series. English. ir. Price varies per volume. **DD** 301.310994.
Ind/Abst AESIS Q.

US/1062-0834
ENVIRONMENTAL RISK WATCH. ***Ceased.*** [Environ. risk watch]. **Added/Corp** Ebasco Environmental. (Nov. 1991)-Vol. 2, No. 25 (Dec. 1993). Periodical. English. bw. ERW, c/o Ebasco Environmental, 10900 NE 8th Street, Bellevue WA 98004-4405. **DD** 333.

●US/1065-6588
ENVIRONMENTAL SATELLITE DATA RESEARCH. (1992)-. Periodical. English. mo. $240.00. Heckman Research, PO Box 1161, Clarksville MD 21029.

CN/0835-605X
ENVIRONMENTAL SCIENCE & ENGINEERING (AURORA). **See** Engineering.

US
ENVIRONMENTAL SCIENCE AND POLLUTION SERIES. Monographic series. English. ir. Price varies per volume. Marcel Dekker Inc., 270 Madison Avenue, New York NY 10016. **Tel** (212)696-9000, (800)228-1160, FAX (212)685-4540, telex 421419. **(Subscription address:** Marcel Dekker Inc, PO Box 5017, Monticello NY 12701.**)** **ED** Walter R. Niessen.
Desc: Topics covered have included polymer degradation, unit processes in drinking water, and nitrogen fertilization in the environment.

US/0013-936X
ENVIRONMENTAL SCIENCE & TECHNOLOGY. [Environ. sci. technol.]. **Added/Corp** American Chemical Society. **VFOAT** Environmental Science and Technology; ES&T. Vol. 12 (Jan. 1978)-. Academic Scholarly Publication. English. ir (13 issues). $585.00 (institution) US. American Chemical Society, 1155 Sixteenth Street Northwest, Washington DC 20036. **Tel** (800)333-9511, (800)227-5558, (614)447-3776, FAX (202)833-7736. **(Subscription address:** American Chemical Society / Ohio, Department L 0011, Columbus OH 43268-0011.**)** **ED** William H. Glaze. **LC** TD180; .E5. **DD** 628/.5/05. **NLM** W1 EN985S. **CODEN** ESTHAG. **[CCC]**. Index available (free). **Bk Rev. Ad Acc, Adv Mgr Tel** (203)256-8211. **Pr Rev. Acid Free. Circ:** 12,000 (ctrl). available on microfilm and microfiche from University Microfilms International (UMI). Documents available from Article Express International, BIOSIS Document Express, Ask*IEEE, UMI Article Clearinghouse, CASDDS, Petroleum Abstracts Document Delivery Service, Documents on Demand. ***Continues** Environmental Science & Technology, 0013-936X.*
Desc: Serves environmental engineers and scientists with legislative action, emerging technology, industrial activity, contributed technical articles, news, new products and new literature sections and a reader service department.
Ind/Abst Abstr. Bull. Inst. Pap. Sci. Tech.; Abstr. Graphic Arts Tech. Found. (1984); Acad. Search (July 1993-); AGRICOLA [Select. Cov.]; Anal. Abstr.; Appl. Sci. Technol. Index; AQUAREF; Art Archaeol. Tech. Abstr.; Biodeter. Abstr.; Bioeng. Abstr.; Biol. Abstr.; Ceram. Abstr.; Chem. Abstr.; Chem. Hazards Ind.; Chem. Ind. Notes; Crop Physiol. Abstr.; Curr. Biotechnol.; Curr. Ref. Fish Res.; Dairy Sci. Abstr.; Ei Page One; EMBASE; Energy Inf. Abstr. (0147-6521); Energy Res. Abstr.; Eng. Index Annu. [Select. Cov.]; Environ. Abstr.; Environ. Period. Bibliogr. (?-?); Field Crop Abstr.; Fish Rev.; Food Sci. Technol. Abstr.; For. Abstr.; Gas Abstr.; Gen. Sci. Index; Gen. Sci. Source (Jul. 1993-); Geogr. Abstr. Human Geogr.; Geol. Abstr.; GeoRef; Grasslands For. Abstr.; Health Saf. Sci. Abstr.; Index Vet.; Ind. Hyg. Dig.; INFO-SOUTH Abstr.; INSPEC (June 1979-); Int. Aerosp. Abstr.; Key Word Index Wildl. Res.; Lab. Hazards Bull.; Leadscan; Lit. Pat. Abstr., Oilfield Chem. (1972-); Lit. Abstr., Catal. Catal.; Lit. Abstr., Health Environ.; Lit. Abstr., Pet. Refin. Petrochem.; Lit. Abstr., Pet. Substit.; Lit. Abstr., Transp. Storage; Mag. Search; Mass Spect. Bull.; Met. Abstr.; Meteorol. Geoastrophys. Abstr.; Middle East Abstr. Index; MINPROC; Mintec, Min. Technol. Abstr.; Newsp. Period. Abstr. (1992-); Nutr. Res. Newsl.; Pet. Abstr.; Plant Grow. Reg. Abstr.; PROMT; Rev. Plant Pathol.; Saf. Health Work; Soc. Sci. Cit. Index [Select. Cov.]; Soils Fert.; Weed Abstr.; Wheat Barley Trit. Abstr.; Wildl. Rev.; World Surf. Coat. Abstr.

US/0013-936X
ENVIRONMENTAL SCIENCE & TECHNOLOGY MICROFORM. [Environ. sci. technol.]. **Added/Corp** American Chemical Society. **VFOAT** ES&T, Environmental Science & Technology. **VAT** Environmental Science and Technology. Vol. 1, No. 1 (Jan. 1967)-. Periodical. English. Thirteen times a year. $585.00 (institution) US. American Chemical Society, 1155 Sixteenth Street Northwest, Washington DC 20036. **Tel** (800)333-9511, (800)227-5558, (614)447-3776, FAX (202)833-7736. **(Subscription address:** American Chemical Society / Ohio, Department L 0011, Columbus OH 43268-0011.**)** **CODEN** ESTHAG. **[CCC]**. available in

print.
Desc: Information on pollution, sanitary chemistry and environmental engineering.

US/0194-0287
ENVIRONMENTAL SCIENCE AND TECHNOLOGY (NEW YORK). (ENVIRONMENTAL SCIENCE AND TECHNOLOGY.). [Environ. sci. technol.]. (19??)-. Monographic series. English. ir. Price varies per volume. John Wiley & Sons, Inc., 605 Third Avenue, New York NY 10158-0012. **Tel** (212)850-6000, (212)850-6645, FAX (212)850-6088, telex 12-7063. **(Subscription address:** John Wiley & Sons / England, Baffins Lane, Chichester, West Sussex PO19 1UD England.**)** Documents available from The Genuine Article.
Ind/Abst Acad. Ind. [Computer File] (1992-); Air Pollut. Titles; Appl. Sci. Technol. Index; BioBusiness; Biodeter. Abstr. (19??-19??); Biol. Dig.; Chem. Ind. Notes; Chem. Titles; Coal Abstr.; Curr. Aware. Biol. Sci., CABS; Curr. Contents, Agric. Biol. Environ. Sci.; Curr. Contents Eng. Tech. Appl. Sci.; Ecol. Abstr.; Environ. Period. Bibliogr.; Expand. Acad. Index (1992-); F&S Index Plus Text, Int. [Select. Cov.]; Foods Adlibra; For. Prod. Abstr. (1991-); Gen. Sci. Index; Geogr. Abstr. Phys. Geogr.; Int. Aerosp. Abstr.; Int. Dev. Abstr.; Irr. Drain. Abstr.; J. Plan. Lit.; PESTDOC; Pollut. Abstr. Indexes; Res. Alert [Full Cov.]; Rev. Agric. Entomol.; Rev. Med. Vet. Entomol.; Risk Abstr.; Sci. Cit. Index; SCISEARCH; Trade Ind. Index.

US
ENVIRONMENTAL SCIENCE AND TECHNOLOGY SERIES. V. 1-. Monographic series. English. ir. Price varies per volume. Marcel Dekker Inc., 270 Madison Avenue, New York NY 10016. **Tel** (212)696-9000, (800)228-1160, FAX (212)685-4540, telex 421419. **(Subscription address:** Marcel Dekker Inc, PO Box 5017, Monticello NY 12701.**) ED** J. Carrell Morris.
Desc: This is an ongoing series each title in the series has a different subject.
Ind/Abst Int. Aerosp. Abstr.

JA
ENVIRONMENTAL SCIENCE, HOKKAIDO : JOURNAL OF THE GRADUATE SCHOOL OF ENVIRONMENTAL SCIENCE, HOKKAIDO UNIVERSITY, SAPPORO. Vol. 8, No. 1 (June 1985)-. Periodical. English. Publishing Committee of the Graduate School of Environmental Science, Hokkaido University, Sapporo 060 Japan. **LC** TD169; .K36. **DD** 363.7/005. ***Continues*** *Kankyo Kagaku, 0386-8788.*
Ind/Abst Geogr. Abstr. Phys. Geogr.; Geogr. Abstr. Human Geogr.; Int. Dev. Abstr.

US/0090-0427
ENVIRONMENTAL SCIENCE RESEARCH. [Environ. sci. res.]. (1972)-. Monographic series. English. ir. Price varies per volume. Plenum Press, 233 Spring Street, New York NY 10013-1578. **Tel** (212)620-8000, (800)221-9369, FAX (212)463-0742, (212)807-1047, telex 23/421139. **LC** UNC. **NLM** W1 EN986F. **CODEN** EVSRBT. Documents available from BIOSIS Document Express, CASDDS.
Ind/Abst AGRICOLA; Biol. Abstr. (1975-); Chem. Abstr.; GeoRef.

●US/1071-8923
ENVIRONMENTAL SCIENCE REVIEW. (1994)-. Periodical. English. bm. Gordon & Breach Science Publishers, Inc., PO Box 786, Cooper Station, New York NY 10276. **Tel** (212)206-8900, FAX (212)645-2459. **(Subscription address:** International Publishers Distributor at one of the following addresses: 820 Town Center Drive, Langhorne, PA 19047; or PO Box 90, Reading Berkshire RG1 8JL UK; or Kent Ridge PO Box 1180, Singapore 9111, Republic of Singapore**)**

US
ENVIRONMENTAL SCIENCES. AN INTERNATIONAL JOURNAL ON ENVIRONMENTAL PHYSIOLOGY AND TOXICOLOGY. (19??)-. Periodical. English. qt. $180.00. **(Subscription address:** Maruzen Company Ltd., PO Box 5050, Import & Export Department, Tokyo 100 31 Japan.**)**

UK/0266-9838
ENVIRONMENTAL SOFTWARE. [Environ. softw.]. **Added/Corp** Computational Mechanics Institute (Southampton, England) AeroVironment Inc. Vol. 1, No. 1 (June 1986)-. Academic Scholarly Publication. English. Four times a year. $373.00 The Americas; £250.00 other. Elsevier Applied Science, An Imprint of Elsevier Science Ltd., The Boulevard, Langford Lane, Kidlington, Oxford OX5 1GB United Kingdom. **Tel** 011 44 865 843000, 011 44 865 843699, FAX 011 44 865 843010. **(Subscription address:** Elsevier Science Ltd. Oxford Fulfillment Centre, PO Box 800, Kidlington, Oxford OX5 1DX United Kingdom.**) ED** P. Zanetti. **LC** TD169; .E647. **DD** 363.7/0028/5. **CODEN** ENSOEZ. **[CCC]. Bk Rev. Ad Acc.** Documents available from Ask*IEEE, Documents on Demand.
Ind/Abst Air Pollut. Titles; Comput. Lit. Index; Curr. Aware. Biol. Sci., CABS; Ei Page One; Environ. Abstr. (Oct. 1, 1990-); Environ. Period. Bibliogr.; Fluid Abstr., Civil Eng.; Fluid Abstr. Proc. Eng.; FLUIDEX; INSPEC (1986); Int. Civil Eng. Abstr.; Pollut. Abstr. Indexes; Soft. Abstr. Eng.

US/1043-9056
ENVIRONMENTAL SOFTWARE DIRECTORY. [Environ. softw. dir.]. (1989)-. English. an. $69.00. Donley Technology, PO Box 335, Garrisonville VA 22463-0335. **Tel** (703)659-1954. **ED** Elizabeth Donley. **LC** TD173.5; .E59. **DD** 628/.0285/536. **Ad Acc, Adv Mgr:** Veronica Deschambault, **Tel** (703)659-1954.
Desc: A reference book on government and commercial databases, on-line systems, and software packages for the environmental field. Describes over 500 systems, listing a description, hardware and software requirements, point of contact, and cost. Indexed by software name, distributor, computer system and key words.

US/1043-2884
ENVIRONMENTAL SOFTWARE REPORT. [Environ. softw. rep.]. Vol. 1, No. 1 (April 1988)-. Periodical. English. Eight times a year. $95.00. Donley Technology, PO Box 335, Garrisonville VA 22463-0335. **Tel** (703)659-1954. **ED** Veronica Deschambault. **DD** 005. **Bk Rev**, (Qty: 6). **Ad Acc.** ctrl circ.
Desc: Examines software packages, databases, an on-line systems for the environmental field. It covers both government and commercial systems and includes system reviews, industry news, and events.

US/0013-9386
ENVIRONMENTAL SPECTRUM. Periodical. English. bm. Free. Rutgers University / Cook College, PO Box 231, New Brunswick NJ 08903. **Tel** (201)932-9408, (201)932-9461. **ED** Joseph J Soporowski. **Bk Rev. Circ:** 7,000 (ctrl).
Desc: Current information for the continuing education of those involved or interested in the environmental sciences.
Ind/Abst Pollut. Abstr. Indexes.

CN/0706-1072
ENVIRONMENTAL STUDIES. Added/Corp Canada. Indian and Northern Affairs Canada. No. 5 (1978)-. Monographic series. English. Price varies per volume. **CODEN** ESCID5. ***Continues*** *Environmental Studies (Canada. Indian and Northern Affairs).*
Ind/Abst Ecol. Abstr.; Geogr. Abstr. Human Geogr.; Soils Fert.

US
ENVIRONMENTAL SURVEILLANCE AT LOS ALAMOS DURING ... / ENVIRONMENTAL SURVEILLANCE GROUP. English. an. Los Alamos Scientific Laboratory, PO Box 1663, Los Alamos NM 87645.

UK/0959-3330
ENVIRONMENTAL TECHNOLOGY. Vol. 11, No. 1 (Jan. 1990)-. Academic Scholarly Publication. English (French and German). mo. $375.00. Selper Limited, 79 Rusthall Avenue, Chiswick, London W4 1BN England. **Tel** 011 44 81 995 4053, FAX 011 44 81 9954160. **LC** TD1; .E565. **DD** 628/.05. **CODEN** ENVTEV. **Ad Acc. Pr Rev.** Documents available from The Genuine Article, CASDDS. ***Continues*** *Environmental Technology Letters, 0143-2060 (DLC) 84640643.*
Desc: Publication of technological manuscripts in the field of applied environmental studies, including environmental biotechnology, environmental and sanitary engineering, industrial waste treatment and hazardous waste disposal, air and water pollution control, solid waste management, industrial hygiene and associated technologies.
Ind/Abst AgBiotech News Inf.; Biodeter. Abstr. (1991-); Chem. Abstr.; Curr. Aware. Biol. Sci., CABS; Curr. Contents, Agric. Biol. Environ. Sci.; EMBASE; Environ. Period. Bibliogr.; Field Crop Abstr.; Food Sci. Technol. Abstr.; For. Abstr.; Grasslands For. Abstr.; Leadscan; Maize Abstr.; Res. Alert [Full Cov.]; Sci. Cit. Index; SCISEARCH; Seed Abstr.; Soils Fert.; Weed Abstr.; Wheat Barley Trit. Abstr.

US
ENVIRONMENTAL TECHNOLOGY AND PRODUCT PROFILES. English. ir (15-20 new profiles each quarter). $2,500.00. National Environmental Technology Applications Corporation, 615 William Pitt Way, Pittsburgh PA 15238. **Tel** (412)826-5511, FAX (412)826-3360. **(Subscription address:** Subscription Office, PO Box 1831, Birmingham, AL 35201-1831, USA, Telephone: (800)633-4931, (205)995-1567, Fax: (205)995-1588**)**
Desc: Contains summary descriptions of a wide variety of innovative environmental technologies and products.

●US/1068-7432
ENVIRONMENTAL TESTING & ANALYSIS. [Environ. test. anal.]. **VFOAT** Environmental Testing and Analysis. (1992)-. Periodical. English. bm (6 issues). $40.00 (non-qualified readers), free (qualified readers). Target Group, 1907 West Burbank Boulevard, Burbank CA 91506. **Tel** (818)842-4777, FAX (818)842-0578. **ED** Susan Hale Abbot (editor's telephone: (508)448-2061). **DD** 363. **CODEN** ETANEI. **Ad Acc. Circ:** 20,013 (ctrl).
Desc: Providing information to environmental testing and analytical professionals working in the laboratory, manufacturing facility, government labs, etc.. or in the field.
Ind/Abst Ind. Hyg. Dig. (19??-19??).

UK/1046-5294
ENVIRONMENTAL TOPICS. VFOAT Environmental Studies. (1990)-. Monographic series. English. ir. Price varies per volume. Gordon & Breach Science Publishers, PO Box 90, Reading RG1 8JL England. **Tel** 011 44 734 560080, FAX 011 44 734 568211. **(Subscription address:** International Publishers Distributor at one of the following addresses: 820 Town Center Drive, Langhorne, PA 19047; or PO Box 90, Reading Berkshire RG1 8JL UK; or Kent Ridge PO Box 1180, Singapore 9111, Republic of Singapore**)**

US/1061-7787
ENVIRONMENTAL TOXICOLOGY NEWSLETTER. / COOPERATIVE EXTENSION, UNIVERSITY OF CALIFORNIA. [Environ. toxicol. newsl.]. **Added/Corp** University of California (System). Cooperative Extension. **VAT** y. Vol. 1 No. 1 (Nov. 14, 1980)-. Newsletter. English. ir. $6.00. Regents University of California, 6701 San Pablo Avenue, K. Varcoe, Oakland CA 94608. **Tel** (909)787-5241, FAX (909)787-7251. **DD** 363.

●US/1065-3570
ENVIRONMENTAL TRADE EVENT PREVIEW. [Environ. trade event preview.]. Vol. 1, No. 1 (Sept. 1992)-. Periodical. English. mo. $495.00. The Yorklyn Press, PO Box 343, Arlington MA 02174. **DD** 363.

AT/1034-9731
ENVIRONMENTAL UPDATE MELBOURNE. (ENVIRONMENTAL UPDATE.). [Environ. updat. Melb.]. (1990)-. Periodical. English. mo. 395.00Aus$ Australia; 418.00Aus$ New Zealand, Papua New Guinea; 422.00Aus$ Indonesia, Malaysia, Singapore; 426.00Aus$ Japan, India; 432.00Aus$ US & Canada; 436.00Aus$ Europe. International Public Relations Pty Ltd., 33 Walsh Street, West Melbourne Victoria 3003 Australia. **Tel** 011 61 03 329 9333, FAX 011 61 03 329 7996. **DD** 333.720994.

US
ENVIRONMENTAL UPDATE / NEBRASKA DEPARTMENT OF ENVIRONMENTAL CONTROL. Added/Corp Nebraska. Dept. of Environmental Control. (198?)-. Periodical. English. qt. Nebraska Department of Environmental Control, PO Box 94877, State House Station, Lincoln NE 68509-4877. **LC** TD171.3.N2; E58. **DD** 363.7/009782. Documents available from Documents on Demand.
Ind/Abst Environ. Abstr.

●US/1064-816X
ENVIRONMENTAL UPDATE (NEW YORK, N.Y.). (ENVIRONMENTAL UPDATE.). [Environ. update]. Vol. 1, No. 1 (July 1992)-. Periodical. English. qt. Mark & Murase, 399 Park Avenue, New York NY 10022-4689. **DD** 344.

●UK/0963-2719
ENVIRONMENTAL VALUES. Vol. 1, No. 1 (Spring 1992)-. Periodical. English. Four times a year. $110.00 (institutions), $60.00 (individuals). The White Horse Press, 10 High Street, Knapwell, Cambridge CB3 8NR England. **Tel** 011 44 9 547527. **CODEN** ENVLE7. Documents available from Documents on Demand.
Ind/Abst Arts Humanit. Citation Index [Select. Cov.]; Econ. Lit. Index; Environ. Abstr. (July 2, 1992-); Environ. Period. Bibliogr.; Soc. Sci. Cit. Index [Full Cov.].

●US/1063-116X
ENVIRONMENTAL VIEWPOINTS. (ENVIRONMENTAL VIEWPOINTS : SELECTED ESSAYS AND EXCERPTS ON ISSUES IN ENVIRONMENTAL PROTECTION.). [Environ. viewp.]. Vol. 1 (1992)-. English. $49.95. Gale Research Inc., 835 Penobscot Building, Detroit MI 48226. **Tel** (800)877-GALE, (313)961-2242, FAX (313)961-6083, telex TWX 810-221-7086. **LC** TD169; .E656. **DD** 363.7/005.

●UK/1180-4009
ENVIRONMETRICS (LONDON, ONT.). (ENVIRONMETRICS.). [Environmetrics]. Vol.1 (1992)-. Periodical. English. Four times a year (Jan., Apr., July, Oct.). $395.00. John Wiley & Sons Ltd., Baffins Lane, Chichester West Sussex PO19 1UD England. **Tel** 0243 779777, FAX 0243 776128 BTG:JWP001, telex 86290 WIBOOKG. **(Subscription address:** John Wiley / Philadelphia, PO Box 7247, Philadelphia PA 19170.**) ED** A. H. El-Shaarawi and I. B. MacNeill. **LC** GE45.S73; E58. **DD** 628/.01/5195. **CODEN** ENVCEE. available on microfilm and microfiche from University Microfilms International (UMI). Documents available from The Genuine Article.

Desc: A multidisciplinary journal concerned with the development and application of statistical methodology in environmental sciences. The scope covers a wide range of methodological topics including sampling design, statistical modelling, methods of data analysis and interpretation, statistical quality control, risk assessment, time series methods, multivariate analysis, and other statistical methods.
Ind/Abst Curr. Aware. Biol. Sci., CABS; Curr. Index Stat.; Environ. Period. Bibliogr. (?-?); Res. Alert [Select. Cov.]; SCISEARCH; Soc. Sci. Cit. Index [Select. Cov.].

BE
ENVIRONNEMENT. French. Six times a year. 950F Belgium; 1620F other. Centre Info Sur Environnement, R de la Regence 36, 4000 Liege Belgium. **Tel** 02/539-09.78, FAX 02/539-09.21. **ED** Jean Lue Rolaus. **Bk Rev**. **Ad Acc**. ctrl circ.
Desc: Contains information about a subject and some news about the environment in the Walloon Region.

FR
ENVIRONNEMENT ACTUALITE.
Suspended. (19??)-(1994). French. mo. 100.00F. Tresor Public, 14 Bd de General Leclerc, 92524 Neuilly Seine Cedex France. **Tel** 011 33 1 47581212.

FR/0986-2943
ENVIRONNEMENT & TECHNIQUE.
VFOAT ID Environnement et Technique; Environnement et Technique. (1987)-. Periodical. French. ir (10 issues). 550.00F France; 760.00F other. Set, 7 Chemin de Gordes, 38100 Grenoble France. **Tel** 011 33 76 432864. **UDC** 628.54. ***Continues*** *Infodechets, 0751-1957.*

CN/0711-5806
ENVIRONNEMENT PLUS. [Environ. plus]. **VFOAT** Revue Environnement Plus. Summer 1981. Periodical. French. qt. $1.50 per number, $6.00 per issue. Environnement Plus, 57-B Bellevue, Drummondville Quebec J2B 6V1 Canada. **DD** 574.5/09714.

●CN/1192-4578
ENVIRONNEMENT (QUEBEC).
(ENVIRONNEMENT : SOMMAIRE DE LA DOCUMENTATION COURANTE.). [Environnement]. **Added/Corp** Quebec (Province). Ministere de l'Environnement. Centre de Documentation et de Renseignements. Vol. 13, No 1 (Jan. 1993)-. Periodical. French. Ten times a year. 99.00Can$. Les Publications du Quebec, CP 1190, Outremont Quebec H2V 4S7 Canada. **Tel** (514)948-1222, (800)463-2100, FAX (514)278-3030. **DD** 016.3337.

US/1053-8852
ENVIRONTECH (OAKLAND GARDENS, N.Y.). (ENVIRONTECH : ENVIRONMENTAL CONSERVATION AND RESTORATION TECHNOLOGY.). [Environtech]. Vol. 1, No. 1 (Nov. 1990)-. Periodical. English. mo. $297.00 (one year), $544.00 (two year) North America; $337.00 (one year), $624.00 (two year) other. High Tech Resources International, PO Box 310, Oakland Gardens NY 11364. **Tel** (718)279-4871, FAX (718)225-6071. **ED** Barbara Consola (editor's phone: (718)279-4871). **DD** 363. Index available. cum. index.
Desc: The newsletter of environmental conservation and restoration technology. A resource for anyone engaged in developing or applying technological solutions to environmental and energy problems. Focuses on technology transfer from university, government, and industrial laboratories to end-users.

CN/1183-420X
ENVIROSOURCE (HULL. ED. FRANCAISE). (REPERTOIRE DES FONDS DE RENSEIGNEMENTS.). [Envirosource]. **Main/Corp** Canada. Environnement Canada. **VFOAT** Envirosource. (1991)-. French. be. **DD** 354.710082/32/025.

US/0272-1120
ENVIROSOUTH. ***Suspended.*** [Envirosouth]. **VFOAT** Environmental Periscope; South's Environmental Quarterly. Vol. 1 (Spring 1977)-?. Periodical. English. qt. $20.00. Envirosouth, Box 11468, Montgomery AL 36111. **Tel** (205)277-7050. **LC** QH104.5.S59; E58. **DD** 333.95/0975. **Ad Acc.**

US/1040-1725
ENVIRONMENTAL HOTLINE. [Environ. hotline]. (1988)-. Periodical. English. mo. $48.00. Deuel & Associates Environmentals, Inc., 7208 Jefferson Street NE, 7208 Jefferson Street NE, Albuquerque Albuquerque NM NM 87109 87109. **Tel** (505)345-8732, , FAX , , telex , . **DD** 363. ***Continues*** *Hazardous Waste Hotline (Albuquerque, N.M.), 0889-096X.*

US
EOHSI INFOLETTER. English. bm. $19.00 non-profit organizations; $30.00 (except non-profit organizations) US; $40.00 (except non-profit organizations) other. Resource Center of EOHSI, Frelinghuysen Road, Piscataway NJ 08854. **Tel** (908)932-0110. **ED** Patricia Yelavich. **Pr Rev. Circ:** 300.
Desc: Environmental and occupational health briefs.

US
EPA ADMINISTRATIVE LAW REPORTER. **See** Law-Environmental Law.

US
EPA CITIZEN'S BULLETIN. **Added/Corp** Environmental Protection Agency. (1971)-. Bulletin. English. mo. $5.00. Connecticut Department of Environmental Protection, 165 Capitol Avenue, Room 115, Hartford CT 06106. **Tel** (203)566-2110, FAX (203)566-7932. **ED** Robert Paier. **Circ:** 7,000.
Desc: Wide range of articles on Connecticut's natural resources, beauty and issues of environmental concern; regular contributions by authorities and experts in their fields.

US/0145-1189
EPA JOURNAL. [EPA j.]. **Added/Corp** United States. Environmental Protection Agency. United States. Environmental Protection Agency. Office of Public Awareness. United States. Environmental Protection Agency. Office of Public Affairs. United States. Environmental Protection Agency. Office of Communications and Public Affairs. **VFOAT** Environmental Protection Agency journal. **VAT** Environmental Protection Agency Journal. Vol. 1, No. 1 (Jan. 1975)-. Government Publication. English. qt. $7.50 domestic; $9.40 other. Superintendent of Documents, US Government Printing Office, Washington DC 20402. **Tel** (202)275-3328, FAX (202)786-2377. **LC** TD169; .U54a. **DD** 363.6. **CODEN** EPAJDB. available on microfilm and microfiche from University Microfilms International (UMI). Documents available from UMI Article Clearinghouse.
Desc: Provides brief, authoritative, and well-written articles on a broad range of environmental issues affecting the United States. Each issue focuses on a particular theme, such as Earth Day, garbage disposal, the greenhouse effect, or the marine environment. Typically runs forty four to fifty six pages and includes fifteen to sixteen articles ranging from two to six pages in length, accompanied by black and white photographs.
Ind/Abst Abstr. Bull. Inst. Pap. Sci. Tech.; Acad. Abstr. Full Text Elite (July 1993-) [Full Txt.]; Acad. Abstr. (July 1993-); Acad. Ind. [Computer File] (1992-); Acad. Search (July 1993-); AGRICOLA [Select. Cov.]; BioBusiness; Biol. Dig.; Coal Abstr.; Curr. Index J. Educ.; EMBASE; Environ. Period. Bibliogr.; Expand. Acad. Index (1989-); Foods Adlibra; Gen. Sci. Index; Gen. Sci. Source (Jul. 1993-) [Full Txt.]; GeoRef; Health Source (July 1993-) [Full Txt.]; Humanit. Source (Jul. 1993-) [Full Txt.]; INFO-SOUTH Abstr.; J. Plan. Lit.; Mag. Artic. Summar. Elite (July 1993-) [Full Txt.]; Mag. Artic. Summar. Select [Full Txt.]; Mag. Artic. Summar. CD-ROM (July 1993-); Mag. Search; Newsp. Period. Abstr. (1988-); PAIS Int. Print; Pollut. Abstr. Indexes; Risk Abstr.; Soc. Sci. Source (Jul. 1993-) [Full Txt.]; Urban Aff. Abstr.

AT/1035-0233
EPA REVIEW. **VFOAT** Environmental Protection Authority. (1990)-. Periodical. English. tq. ***Continues*** *EPA News, 0729-1981.*

●US/1065-920X
EPA WATCH. [EPA watch]. **Added/Corp** American Policy Center (Chantilly, Va.). **VAT** Environmental Protection Agency Watch. (1992)-. Periodical. English. sm. $165.00. DeWeese Company, 14140L Parke Long Court, Chantilly VA 22021. **Tel** (703)968-9768, FAX (703)968-9771. **ED** Bonner R. Cohen. **DD** 363. **Bk Rev**, (Qty: 2). **Circ:** 1,200 (ctrl).
Desc: Survey of environmental regulatory activities undertaken by the EPA, the Department of Interior, OSHA, the White House, the US Congress, and federal, state, and local agencies.

GW
ERGEBNISSE DER AEROLOGISCHEN UND BODENNAHEN OZONMESSUNGEN. **See** Earth Sciences-Meteorology.

FR/0293-082X
ESF COMMUNICATIONS. **Added/Corp** European Science Foundation. (Nov. 1981)-. Periodical. English. European Science Foundation, 1 Quai Lezay-Marnesia, 67080 Strasbourg France. **Tel** 88353063, FAX 88370532. Documents available from Documents on Demand.
Ind/Abst Environ. Abstr.

BE/0778-7928
EUROPE ENVIRONMENT. [Eur. environ.]. **Added/Corp** Europe Information Service. (19??)-. Periodical. English (French and Swedish). bw (22 issues per year). 21100.00F Belgium; (add 1000.00F postage) Europe; (add 1400.00F postage) North Africa, Israel, and Turkey; (add 1600.00F postage) North, South, and Central America; (add 1900.00F postage) Asia; (add 2100.00F postage) Australia. Europe Information Service, rue de Geneve 6, 1140 Brussels Belgium. **Tel** 011 32 2 242 6020, FAX 011 32 2 242 9549. **CODEN** EENVDZ. **Bk Rev**. available on an online database (file 636/Full-Text) from DIALOG.
Desc: Information on environmental policy.
Ind/Abst Chem. Bus. Bull.; Chem. Bus. NewsBase (1988-); Chem. Bus. Update.

UK/0272-4626
EUROPEAN APPLIED RESEARCH REPORTS. ENVIRONMENT AND NATURAL RESOURCES SECTION.
Ceased. [Eur. appl. res. rep., Environ. nat. resour. sect.]. Vol. 1, No. 1 (Nov. 1980)-Ceased Vol. 2. Academic Scholarly Publication. English. ir. Harwood Academic Publishers / New York, PO Box 786, Cooper Station, New York NY 10276. **Tel** (212)206-8900, (201)643-7500. **(Subscription address:** International Publishers Distributor at one of the following addresses: 820 Town Center Drive, Langhorne, PA 19047; or PO Box 90, Reading Berkshire RG1 8JL UK; or Kent Ridge PO Box 1180, Singapore 9111, Republic of Singapore) **ED** Edward Phillips. **LC** TD1; .E93. **DD** 628.5/05. **CODEN** EAPRD5. Index available. **Bk Rev**. **Ad Acc**. **Pr Rev**. Documents available from Article Express International, CASDDS.
Desc: Publishes refereed papers covering all applied research areas in environmental and natural resources which have been sponsored by or published in collaboration with the commissions of the European communities.
Ind/Abst Bioeng. Abstr.; Chem. Abstr.; Ei Page One; Eng. Index Annu.; Soils Fert.

●US/1060-3573
EUROPEAN ENVIRONMENTAL BUSINESS NEWS, THE. (1992)-. Periodical. English. bm. Centurion, 189 Bedford Street, Lexington MA 02173.

UK
EUROPEAN ENVIRONMENTAL YEARBOOK. English (Italian). ir (Every three years). £63.15 UK; £66.17 others. DocTer International UK, Hyde Park House, Manfred Road, London SW15 2RS England. **Tel** 081 877-1080, FAX 081 874-2150. Index available. **Bk Rev**. **Ad Acc**. **Circ:** 3,000 (ctrl).
Desc: Presents an up-to-date summary of information on Nature and Country Planning in the twelve member states of the European Economic Community

●FR/1164-5563
EUROPEAN JOURNAL OF SOIL BIOLOGY. **See** Agriculture-Crop Production and Soil.

LU/1017-5849
EUROSTAT. RAPID REPORTS. ENVIRONMENT. [EUROSTAT, Rapid rep., Environ.]. **VFOAT** Rapid Reports. Environment. (1991)-. Periodical. English. ir. ECU 206.00 (complete set). Office for Official Publications of the European Communities, 2 Rue Mercier, 2985 Luxembourg Luxembourg. **Tel** 011 352 499281, FAX 011 352 488573. **UDC** 502. **CODEN** CE.

US/0749-3940
EVERYONE'S BACKYARD. (EVERYONE'S BACKYARD / CITIZEN'S CLEARINGHOUSE FOR HAZARDOUS WASTES, INC.). [Everyone's backyard]. **Added/Corp** Citizen's Clearinghouse for Hazardous Wastes (Arlington, Va.). **VFOAT** Everyone's Back Yard. Vol. 1, No. 1 (Fall 1982)-. Periodical. English. Six times a year (Jan., Mar., May, July, Sept., Nov.). $35.00 (individuals) libraries; $100.00 (corporate). Citizen's Clearinghouse for Hazardous Waste, PO Box 6806, Falls Church VA 22040. **Tel** (703)237-2249. **ED** Kim Guenther. **DD** 363. Index available. cum. index. **Bk Rev**. **Ad Acc**. **Circ:** 7,500 (ctrl). ***Continues*** *Action Bulletin.*
Desc: Looks at controversial hazardous waste issues, in depth, from a grassroots perspective.
Ind/Abst Environ. Period. Bibliogr.

NE/0300-5194
EXCERPTA MEDICA. SECTION 46. ENVIRONMENTAL HEALTH AND POLLUTION CONTROL. **See** Medical Science and Technology-Abstracting, Bibliographies and Statistics.

CL
EXECUTIVE NOTES ON ENVIRONMENT AND DEVELOPMENT : INFORMATION BULLETIN PREPARED JOINTLY BY THE ENVIRONMENT AND HUMAN SETTLEMENTS DIVISION AND THE INFORMATION SERVICE OF THE ECONOMIC COMMISSION FOR LATIN AMERICA AND THE CARIBBEAN, ECLAC. **See** Economics.

IT
FINMECCANICA AMBIENTE. (19??)-. Italian. mo. Free on request. Redazione Finmeccanica Ambiente SRA Manazza, Vle Pilsudski 92, 00197 Rome Italy. **Tel** 011 39 6 80902331. Index available. cum. index. **Circ:** 6,500 (ctrl).
Desc: A monthly environmental publication discussing the most important environmental subjects in Italy, in the European Economics Community, and in the world; also covers Italian and EEC legislation.

US/0193-3558
FISH KILLS CAUSED BY POLLUTION IN ... (1975). See Fish and Fisheries.

US
FLORIDA CHAMBERS ENVIRONMENTAL NETWORK. ***Ceased.*** English. Florida Chamber of Commerce, PO Box 11309, Tallahassee FL 32302. **Tel** 800/940-3034, FAX (904)425-1260.

US/0894-9743
FLORIDA ENVIRONMENTS. [Fla. environ.]. (198?)-. Periodical. English. mo. $18.95 (one year), $34.00 (two year), $57.00 (three year) Florida; $17.88 (one year), $32.08 (two year), $53.77 (three year) other. Florida Environments Publishing Inc., 4010-B Newberry Road, Gainesville FL 32607. **Tel** (904)373-1401, FAX (904)373-1405. **ED** David Newport. **Bk Rev. Ad Acc, Adv Mgr:** M Hutchens. **Circ:** 10,000 (ctrl).

US/0897-4624
FLORIDA JOURNAL OF ENVIRONMENTAL HEALTH. [Fla. j. environ. health]. **Added/Corp** Florida Environmental Health Association. **VFOAT** FJEH. Issue No. 122 (Jan. 1988)-. Periodical. English. qt (Feb., June, Aug., Nov.). $15.00 US; $20.00 other. Florida Journal of Environmental Health, 3211 Affirmed Ct., Tallahassee FL 32308. **Tel** (904)488-3370, FAX (904)921-0298. **ED** Julia M. Winter. **DD** 362. **NLM** W1; FL79R. **Ad Acc.** ***Continues*** *Sanichat, 0162-3990.*

US/0015-4172
FLORIDA NATURALIST, THE. See Animal Welfare.

US/1062-3086
FOCUS ON GLOBAL CHANGE. ***Ceased.*** (FOCUS ON GLOBAL CHANGE [COMPUTER FILE].). [Focus glob. change]. **Added/Corp** Institute for Scientific Information. Vol. 1, No. 1 (Mar. 5, 1990)-No. 7 (April 1993). Periodical. English. bw. Institute for Scientific Information, 3501 Market Street, Philadelphia PA 19104. **Tel** (215)386-0100, (800)523-1850, FAX (215)386-6362, telex 84-5305. **(Subscription address:** Institute for Scientific Information, PO Box 71416, Chicago, IL 60694**)** **DD** 016.
Desc: Available on 3 1/2" or 5 1/4" diskettes in DOS or MAC formats. System requirements: NEC 9800 series, IBM PC or compatible computer, 640K RAM, DOS 3.1 or higher, hard disk, floppy disk drive. Apple MAC, 1M RAM, System 6.0.2 or higher, hard disk, floppy disk drive.

US/1062-7472
FOCUS (WASHINGTON, D.C. 1991). (FOCUS / CARRYING CAPACITY NETWORK.). [Focus]. **Added/Corp** Carrying Capacity Network. (1991)-. Periodical. English. Four times a year (Seasonally with volume changes every winter). $20.00. Carrying Capacity Network, 1325 G Street Northwest, Suite 1003, Washington DC 20005-3104. **Tel** (202)879-3044, FAX (202)879-3019. **ED** Monique Miller and David Durham. **LC** HC79.E5; F6. **DD** 363.7/005. Index available. **Circ:** 5,000. Documents available from Documents on Demand.
Desc: Contains selected essays which provide perspectives on current carrying capacity issues, interviews with personalities in the field, and a point-counterpoint debate on a carrying capacity topic.
Ind/Abst Environ. Abstr. (July 20, 1992-).

GW
FORSCHUNG UND VEROFFENTLICHUNGEN DES INTERNATIONALEN INSTITUTS FUR UMWELT UND GESELLSCHAFT. German. **LC** HC79.E5; F63. **DD** 333.7/06/01.

●SZ/1018-4619
FRESENIUS ENVIRONMENTAL BULLETIN. **VFOAT** FEB. Vol. 1, No. 1 (Jan. 15, 1992)-. Academic Scholarly Publication. English. mo. 325.90F Switzerland; 342.00F other. Birkhaeuser Verlag Ag, Klosterberg 23, PO Box 133, CH-4010 Basel Switzerland. **Tel** 011 41 61 2717400, FAX 011 41 0 61 2717666, telex 963475 birk ch. **(Subscription address:** Birkhauser Verlag AG, PO Box 151, CH 4106 Therwil Switzerland; Phone: 011 41 61 7217740**)** **ED** F. Korte. **NLM** W1; FR839K. **CODEN** FENBEL. Documents available from CASDDS.
Desc: Journal for rapid communication, which receives the latest information available in the field in a condensed form. The journal covers the following areas: natural and synthetic chemical products and their effects on life in soil, water and air, biotic and abiotic cicles, case studies, biomonitoring, natural sources of physical agents and emissions, epidemiology, bioaccumulation, bioavailability, indoor pollution, ecotoxicology and general contamination and pollution.
Ind/Abst Chem. Abstr.; Curr. Aware. Biol. Sci., CABS; Pollut. Abstr. Indexes.

●US/1059-0919
GALE ENVIRONMENTAL SOURCEBOOK. [Gale environ. sourceb.]. **Added/Corp** Gale Research Inc. 1st Ed. (1992)-. English. be. $80.00. Gale Research Inc., 835 Penobscot Building, Detroit MI 48226. **Tel** (800)877-GALE, (313)961-2242, FAX (313)961-6083, telex TWX 810-221-7086. **LC** GE20; .G35. **DD** 363.7/0025/73. available on magnetic tape; available on diskette.
Desc: Provides up-to-date information on organizations, agencies, programs and publications involved in all aspects of the environment, including advocacy, education, policy, enforcement and more.

UK/0962-9327
GC/MS UPDATE. PART A ENVIRONMENTAL. [GC/MS update, Part A, Environ.]. (1991)-. English. Six times a year (Feb., Apr., June, Aug., Oct., Dec.). $310.00. HD Science LImited, 4A Bessell Lane Stapleford, Nottingham NG9 7BX England. **Tel** 011 44 602 491704, FAX 011 44 602 491703. **ED** Steve Down. **DD** 016.5430896. Index available. cum. index. **Bk Rev**, (Qty: 25). **Ad Acc.** ctrl circ. available on a computer list.

US
GEOCHEMISTRY AND THE ENVIRONMENT. [Geochem. environ.]. V. 1-. English. National Academy of Sciences, 2101 Constitution Avenue NW, Washington DC 20418. **Tel** (202)334-2525, FAX (202)334-2926. **NLM** QU130 .G341 1972.
Ind/Abst GeoRef.

AT
GEODATE. See Geography.

RU/0131-1697
GIGIENICESKIE ASPEKTY OHRANY OKRUZAJUSCEJ SREDY. (GIGIENICHESKIE ASPEKTY OKHRANY OKRUZHAIUSHCHIE SREDY.). [Gig. aspekty ohr. okruzajuscej sredy]. **Added/Corp** Institut Obshchei i Kommunalnoi Gigieny Imeni A.N. Sysina. (1974)-. Academic Scholarly Publication. Russian. **CODEN** GAOSDP. Documents available from CASDDS.
Ind/Abst Chem. Abstr. (-1977).

AT/1038-8451
GLOBAL AGENDA. ***Ceased.*** (19??)-(19??). English. Six times a year. Ideas Centre Bulletin, PO Box A100, Sydney S NSW 2000 Australia. **Tel** 011 61 02 281 8099, FAX 011 61 02 281 9639. **ED** Kristina Sturm. **Circ:** 600.
Desc: Contains summaries of articles containing the most important and new issues of environment and development appearing in a wide range of magazines.

US/0278-9132
GLOBAL ATMOSPHERIC BACKGROUND MONITORING FOR SELECTED ENVIRONMENTAL PARAMETERS BAPMON DATA FOR ... . **VAT** Global Atmospheric Background Monitoring for Selected Environmental Parameters. Background Air Pollution Monitoring Network Data. 1978-. English. an. National Climate Data Center, Federal Building, Asheville NC 28801-2696. **Tel** (704)259-0682, FAX (704)259-0876, telex 6502643731. **LC** QC976.T8; N37A. **DD** 628.5/3/028. ***Continues*** *Global Monitoring of the Environment for Selected Atmospheric Constituents, 0270-0018.*

●US/1068-0586
GLOBAL CITY REVIEW. See Literary and Political Reviews.

UK/0959-3780
GLOBAL ENVIRONMENTAL CHANGE. (GLOBAL ENVIRONMENTAL CHANGE : HUMAN AND POLICY DIMENSIONS.). [Glob. environ. change]. **Added/Corp** United Nations University. Vol. 1, No. 1 (Dec. 1990)-. Periodical. English. Five times a year. $246.00 The Americas; £165.00 other. Butterworth Heinemann Publishers, Linacre House, Jordan Hill, Oxford OX2 8DP England. **Tel** 011 44 865 310366. **(Subscription address:** Elsevier Science Ltd. Oxford Fulfillment Centre, PO Box 800, Kidlington, Oxford OX5 1DX United Kingdom.**)** **LC** HC79.E5; G593. **DD** 363.7/005. **[CCC].** available in microform from University Microfilms International (UMI). Documents available from The Genuine Article.
Ind/Abst Environ. Period. Bibliogr.; Geogr. Abstr. Phys. Geogr.; Geogr. Abstr. Human Geogr.; Int. Dev. Abstr.; Pollut. Abstr. Indexes; Res. Alert; SCISEARCH; Soc. Sci. Cit. Index [Select. Cov.]; Soils Fert.

AT
GOULD LEAGUER, THE. ***Suspended.*** **VFOAT** New South Wales Gould Leaguer. V. 1, No. 1 Feb. 1969-Suspended Vol. 4, No. 5 Oct. 1991. Periodical. English. ir. 4.00Aus$. Gould League of New South Wales, Mary Street, Beecroft New South Wales 2119 Australia. **Tel** 484 6235. **(Subscription address:** PO Box 150, Beecroft New South Wales 2119 Australia**)** **Circ:** 70,000 (ctrl).
Desc: Environmental education resource materials for teachers and pupils, interdisciplinary approaches are largely adopted in published materials.

US
GOVERNOR'S REPORT ON ENVIRONMENTAL QUALITY, THE. **Main/Corp** Minnesota. Governor. **Added/Corp** Minnesota State Planning Agency. (1979)-. English. an. Minnesota State Planning Agency, 300 Centennial Office Building, St Paul MN 55155-1600. **LC** GF504.M6; M55a. **DD** 333.7/2/09776. ***Continues*** *Minnesota. Governor. Annual Report on the Quality of the Environment, 0094-1697.*

US
GRANT$ FOR ENVIRONMENTAL PROTECTION AND ANIMAL WELFARE. See Philanthropy.

US/0748-9544
GREAT LAKES REPORTER, THE. ***Ceased.*** [Great Lakes rep.]. **Added/Corp** Center for The Great Lakes (Chicago, Ill.). Vol. 1, No. 1 (June/July 1984)-(April 1993). Periodical. English. bm. Center for Great Lakes Studies, 35 East Wacker Drive, Suite 1870, Chicago IL 60601. **Tel** (312)263-0785. **ED** Paul Botts. **DD** 333. cum. index. **Circ:** 5,000 (ctrl). available on an online database from Internet. Documents available from Documents on Demand.
Desc: Binational magazine of news and analysis.
Ind/Abst Can. Period. Index (Jan./Feb. 1990-); Environ. Abstr.

US
GREAT LAKES UNITED, THE. **Added/Corp** Great Lakes United (Organization). Vol. 1, No. 1 (Apr. 1986)-. Periodical. English. qt (June, Sept., Dec., March). $100.00 institutions, $20.00 individuals. Great Lakes United, 1300 Elmwood Ave/Cassety Hall, Buffalo NY 14222. **Tel** (716)886-0142, FAX (716)886-0303. **ED** Bruce Kershner. **Circ:** 8,000 (ctrl).
Desc: Newsletter highlighting key environmental issues around the Great Lakes, from a grass roots/citizen viewpoint.

●US/1064-8852
GREEN ALTERNATIVES FOR HEALTH AND THE ENVIRONMENT. [Green altern. health environ.]. **VFOAT** Green Alternatives. Vol. 2, No. 3 (Nov./Dec. 1992)-. Periodical. English. Six times a year. $19.95. Green Keeping Inc., PO Box 28, Annandale-on-Hudson NY 12504. **Tel** (914)876-6525. **LC** IN PROCESS. **DD** 304. ***Continues*** *Green-Keeping, 1058-594X.*

●US/1062-9211
GREEN BOOK. NEW YORK/NEW JERSEY, THE. (THE GREEN BOOK. NEW YORK/NEW JERSEY: ENVIRONMENTAL RESOURCE DIRECTORY.). **VFOAT** Environmental Resource Directory. (1992)-. Directory. English. $89.95. The Green Book, 100 Burtt Road, Corporation Center, Suite 123, Andover MA 01810. **Tel** (508)474-5000.

●US/1062-4589
GREEN BOOK REPORT, THE. [Green book rep.]. (1992)-. Periodical. English. wk. $1,195.00. Green Book Report, 100 Burtt Road, Corporate Place, Andover MA 01810. **Tel** (800)527-2204, (508)474-5054. **ED** Christopher McIntosh. **DD** 363. **Ad Acc, Adv Mgr:** Chris McIntosh, **Tel** (617)935-4800. ctrl circ.
Desc: This publication offers a complete, up-to-date listings of local, state, federal and private environmental projects in the Northeast and Florida every week.

●US/1055-6893
GREEN BOOK (WOBURN, MASS.), THE. (THE GREEN BOOK: ENVIRONMENTAL RESOURCE DIRECTORY, NEW ENGLAND.). [Green book, N. Engl.]. **VFOAT** Environmental Resource Directory; Green Book-New England, the Environmental Resource Directory. (1992)-. Directory. English. an. $89.95. The Green Book, 100 Burtt Road, Corporation Center, Suite 123, Andover MA 01810. **Tel** (508)474-5000. **LC** HD9718.U63; A114. **DD** 363.7/0029/474.

●US/1056-490X
GREEN BUSINESS LETTER, THE. [GreenBusiness lett.]. **VFOAT** Green Business Letter. (June 1991)-. Periodical. English. Twelve times a year. $127.00. Tilden Press Inc., 1519 Connecticut Avenue Northwest, Washington DC 20036. **Tel** (202)332-1700, FAX (202)332-3028. **ED** Joel Makower. **DD** 658. **[CCC].** Index available. cum. index. **Bk Rev.** Documents available from Documents on Demand.
Desc: The hands-on journal for environmentally conscious companies.
Ind/Abst Environ. Abstr.

US/1049-2747
GREEN CONSUMER LETTER, THE. ***Ceased.*** [Green consum. lett.]. (Apr. 1990)-(Jan. 1994). Periodical. English. Twelve times a year. Tilden Press Inc., 1519 Connecticut Avenue Northwest, Washington

DC 20036. **Tel** (202)332-1700, FAX (202)332-3028. **LC** IN PROCESS. **DD** 640. **CODEN** GCLEEH. **[CCC].**
Ind/Abst Foods Adlibra (1990-).

UK/0960-8796
GREEN ENGINEERING. ***Ceased.*** [Green eng.]. (1991)-(1994). Periodical. English. mo. Mechanical Engineering Publications, PO Box 24, Northgate Avenue, Bury St. Edmunds, Suffolk IP32 6BW England. **Tel** 011 44 284 763277, telex 817376. **DD** 620.
Desc: Abstracts over 500 sources focusing on environmental issues for the engineering profession.

●US/1055-9396
GREEN INDEX. (GREEN INDEX: A STATE-BY-STATE GUIDE TO THE NATION'S ENVIRONMENTAL HEALTH.). [Green index]. **Added/Corp** Institute for Southern Studies. (1991/1992)-. English. ir. Island Press, 1718 Connecticut Avenue Northwest, Suite 300, Washington DC 20009. **Tel** (202)232-7933. **(Subscription address:** Island Press, PO Box 7, Covelo CA 95428.) **LC** GE150; .G74. **DD** 363.7/02/0973.

US/0888-3408
GREEN LANDS. [Green lands]. Vol. 9, No. 4 (Winter 1979/80)-. Periodical. English. qt. Free. West Virginia Surface Mining & Reclamation Association, 1624 Kanawha Boulevard East, Charleston WV 25311. **Tel** (304)346-5318. **DD** 628. **CODEN** GRLAE8. Documents available from Documents on Demand. ***Continues*** *Green Lands Quarterly, 0271-0110.*
Ind/Abst Environ. Abstr.

US/1059-0838
GREEN LIBRARY JOURNAL (BERKELEY, CALIF. 1992). ***Title Change.*** (GREEN LIBRARY JOURNAL: ENVIRONMENTAL TOPICS IN THE INFORMATION WORLD.). [Green Libr. j.]. **Added/Corp** Green Library. University of Idaho. (1992)-(199?). Periodical. English. Three times a year. Green Library Inc., PO Box 11284, Berkeley CA 94701. **Tel** (510)841-9975, FAX (510)841-9996. **ED** Maria Jankowska (Editor's telephone: (208)885-6260). **LC** GE30; G74. **DD** 025.06/3637. **Bk Rev. Ad Acc, Adv Mgr:** Katie Manjotich, **Tel** (510)841-9975. **Pr Rev. Circ:** 600. Documents available from Documents on Demand. ***Continues*** *Green Library Journal, 1059-0838.* ***Continued by*** *Electronic Green Journal, 1076-7975.*
Desc: Information about conservation, environmental protection, natural resource management, ecologically balanced regional development in libraries, publishing industries and information sciences.
Ind/Abst Curr. Index J. Educ.; Environ. Abstr.

US/0883-5462
GREEN MAGAZINE. (198?)-. Periodical. English. mo. Richard and Carol Hain, Rural Route 1, Bee NE 68314.
Ind/Abst Ecol. Abstr.; Geogr. Abstr. Phys. Geogr.; Geogr. Abstr. Human Geogr.; Int. Dev. Abstr.

US/1052-1755
GREEN MARKETALERT. ***Ceased.*** [Green marketalert]. **VFOAT** Green Market Alert; Marketalert; Market Alert. (Oct. 1990)-(May 1994). Periodical. English. mo. MarketAlert Publications, 345 Wood Creek Road, Bethlehem CT 06751. **LC** HF5413; .G73. **DD** 363. available on an online database (files 16,570,636/Full-Text) from DIALOG.
Ind/Abst Mark. Advert. Ref. Serv. [Full Txt.]; PROMT [Full Txt.]; PTS Newsl. Database [Full Txt.].

UK/0953-3028
GREEN TEACHER (BRITISH EDITION). [Green teach.]. (1986)-. Periodical. English. bm (6 issues). £30.00 Australia; £16.00 other. Green Teacher Cooperative Ltd, The Old Station, Machynlleth SY20 8BL Wales. **Tel** 011 44 0654 702141. **(Subscription address:** Australia: PO Box 1042, Vindsor VIC 3181 Australia;) **Acid Free. Circ:** 2,000. Documents available from Documents on Demand.
Desc: Environmental issues publication for teachers.
Ind/Abst Environ. Abstr.

CN/1192-1285
GREEN TEACHER (TORONTO). (GREEN TEACHER.). [Green teach.]. (Feb. 1991)-. Periodical. English. Five times a year (Feb., Apr., June, Oct., Dec.). 25.23Can$ (one year), 46.73Can$ (two year); $27.00Can$ (one year), $50.00 (two year) other. Green Teacher c/o Tim Grant, 95 Robert Street, Toronto, Ontario M5S 2K5 Canada. **Tel** (416)960-1244, FAX (416)925-3474. **ED** Tim Grant and Gail Littlejohn. **DD** 333.7/2/07071. **Bk Rev. Ad Acc. Circ:** 4,000.

US/1053-6418
GREEN2000 (WEST CHESTER, PA.). ***Title Change.*** (GREEN2000.). [Green2000]. **VFOAT** Green 2000; Green Two Thousand. Vol. 1, No. 1 (Oct. 31, 1990)-(1992). Periodical. English. mo. Packaging Strategies, 122 South Church Street, West Chester PA 19382. **Tel** (215)436-4220, FAX (215)436-6277, telex 757674. **ED** Ben Miyares. **DD** 363. **CODEN** GREEEJ. ***Continued by*** *GreenPackaging 2000, 1068-4271.*
Desc: Covers news and analyzes legislative issues, technology developments, and how companies are adjusting to environmental packaging strategies for the '90s and beyond.
Ind/Abst Foods Adlibra (1990-).

UK
GREENER MANAGEMENT INTERNATIONAL. (19??)-. English. qt (Jan., April, July and Oct.). $250.00 US; £150.00 UK. Interleaf Productions Limited, Exchange Works, Sidney Street, Sheffield S1 3QF England. **Tel** 011 44 742 739721. **ED** Board. Index available. **Bk Rev. Ad Acc. Acid Free. Circ:** 300 (ctrl).
Desc: Journal of corporate environmental strategy and practice.

●US/1068-4271
GREENPACKAGING 2000. See Packaging.

UK/0962-9467
GREENPEACE BUSINESS. [Greenp. bus.]. (1991)-. Periodical. English. bm (Feb., Apr., June, Aug., Oct., Dec.). £90.00. Greenpeace Business Ltd., Canonbury Villas, London N1 2PN England. **Tel** 011 44 71 8545100, FAX 011 44 71 3594372. **ED** Steve Warshal. **DD** 333.7. **Bk Rev. Pr Rev. Circ:** 600. ***Continues*** *City Line (London), 0962-7944.*

US/0899-0190
GREENPEACE (WASHINGTON, D.C.). (GREENPEACE.). [Greenpeace]. **Added/Corp** Greenpeace USA. **VFOAT** Greenpeace Quarterly; Greenpeace Magazine. Vol. 12, No. 1 (Jan./Mar. 1987)-Vol. 15, No. 6 (Nov./Dec. 1990); (Jan./Feb. 1991)-. Periodical. English. qt. $30.00 (minimum requested donation). Greenpeace / Washington DC, 1436 U Street Northwest, Washington DC 20009. **Tel** (202)462-1177. **ED** David Zuckerman. **LC** QH75.A1; G74. **DD** 333.7/2/05. ***Continues*** *Greenpeace Examiner (Washington, D.C.).*
Desc: Newsletter covering conservation and other environmental issues.

GW/0721-1694
GSF-BERICHT. [GSF-Ber.]. (1985)-. Academic Scholarly Publication. German. **NLM** W1; G626PC. **CODEN** GSFBEM. Documents available from CASDDS. ***Formed by the union of*** *GSF-Bericht A; GSF-Bericht AF; GSF-Bericht AO; GSF-Bericht B; GSF-Bericht BC; GSF-Bericht BT; GSF-Bericht H; GSF-Bericht M; GSF-Bericht MD* ***and*** *Gesellschaft fuer Strahlen- und Umweltforschung. GSF-Bericht S.*
Ind/Abst Chem. Abstr. (1985-); GeoRef.

CN/1183-4803
GUIDE DE L'ENVIRONNEMENT. [Guide environ.]. Vol. 1 (April 1991)-. French. 9.95Can$. Guide de l'Environment, 6024 Avenue de l'Esplanade, Montreal Quebec H2T 3A3. **DD** 363.7/005.

NE
HANDHAVING. (19??)-. Dutch. bm (6 issues). Fl30.00 (latest issue). Min V Rom AFD DVEB KMR F17, Postbus 20951, 2500 EZ Den Haag Netherlands. **Tel** 011 31 070 3264201.

CN/1183-0077
HARMONY (OTTAWA). (HARMONY / HARMONY FOUNDATION OF CANADA.). [Harmony]. **Added/Corp** Harmony Foundation of Canada. (Summer 1990)-. Periodical. English. qt. $20.00 per year. Harmony Foundation of Canada, PO Box 4016, Station C, Ottawa, Ontario K1Y 4P2 Canada. **DD** 363.7/00971/05.

US/0730-5427
HAZARD ASSESSMENT OF CHEMICALS. Vol. 1 (1981)-. Academic Scholarly Publication. English. ir. Price varies per volume. Academic Press, Inc., 6277 Sea Harbor Drive, Orlando FL 32887. **Tel** (800)543-9534, (407)345-4100, FAX (407)363-9661. **LC** QH545.A1. **DD** 363.7/384. **NLM** W1; HA984L. **CODEN** HACCDU. Documents available from BIOSIS Document Express, CASDDS.
Ind/Abst Biol. Abstr. (1986-); Chem. Abstr.; Ei Page One.

US/1076-8920
HAZARDOUS SUBSTANCES & PUBLIC HEALTH. (HAZARDOUS SUBSTANCES & PUBLIC HEALTH : A PUBLICATION OF THE AGENCY FOR TOXIC SUBSTANCES AND DISEASE REGISTRY.). [Hazard. subst. public health]. **Added/Corp** United States. Agency for Toxic Substances and Disease Registry. **VFOAT** Hazardous Substances and Public Health; ATSDR. Vol. 1 No. 1 (Nov. 1990)-. Periodical. English. Five times a year. Free. US Department of Health and Human Services, 1600 Clifton Road, MS E41, Atlanta GA 30333. **Tel** (404)639-0938, FAX (404)639-0943. **DD** 363. Documents available from Documents on Demand.
Ind/Abst Environ. Abstr.; Ind. Hyg. Dig. (19??-19??).

UK
HEALTH, SAFETY AND ENVIRONMENT BULLETIN. See Public Health and Safety.

US/0199-6894
HOOSIER CONSERVATION. See Environmental Issues-Ecology.

CC/0253-9705
HUANJING BAOHU (BEIJING). See Environmental Issues-Pollution and Waste Management.

CC/0254-6108
HUANJING HUAXUE. (HUAN CHING HUA HSUEH.). [Huanjing huaxue]. **Added/Corp** Chung-Kuo ko Hsueh Yuan. Huan Ching Hua Hsueh Yen Chiu so. Chung-Kuo Huan Ching ko Hsueh Hsueh Hui. Huan Ching Hua Hsueh Chuan Yeh Wei Yuan Hui. **VFOAT** Environmental Chemistry; Huanjing Huaxue. (1982)-. Periodical. Chinese (summaries and/or abstracts in English). bm. $94.00. Science Press, 16 Donghuangchenggen North Street, Beijing 100707, People's Republic of China. **Tel** 011 86 1 4019821, 011 86 1 4010642, FAX 011 86 1 4012180, 011 86 1 4019810, telex 210147. **LC** QD1; .H8. **DD** 540. **Ad Acc. Pr Rev. Circ:** 21,200. Documents available from CASDDS, CASDDS.
Ind/Abst Chem. Abstr.

CC/0250-3301
HUANJING KEXUE. (HUAN CHING KO HSUEH. HUANJING KEXUE.). [Huanjing kexue]. **Added/Corp** Chung-Kuo Ko Hsueh Yuan. Huan Ching Ko Hsueh Wei Yuan Hui. **VFOAT** Huanjing Kexue; Journal of Environment Science. (19??)-. Academic Scholarly Publication. Chinese. Six times a year. $79.20. Chinese Academy of Sciences, Environmental Science Committee, Science Press, 16 Donghuangchenggen North Street, Beijing 100707, People's Republic of China. **Tel** 011 86 1 4019821, FAX 011 86 4012180, telex 210147. **ED** Wu Lin. **LC** TD4; .H78. **NLM** W1; HU6429V. **CODEN** HCKHDV. **Pr Rev.** Documents available from BIOSIS Document Express, CASDDS.
Ind/Abst Biol. Abstr. (1987-); Chem. Abstr.; Ei Page One; GeoRef.

CC/0253-2468
HUANJING KEXUE XUEBAO. See Engineering.

US/0888-661X
HUDSON VALLEY GREEN TIMES. (HUDSON VALLEY GREEN TIMES / HUDSON VALLEY GRASS ROOTS AND ENVIRONMENTAL NETWORK.). [Hudson Vall. green times]. **Added/Corp** Hudson Valley Grass Roots Energy and Environmental Network. **VFOAT** Green; Green Times. (19??)-. Periodical. English. Four times a year (Within the seasons). $15.00. Hudson Valley Green, PO Box 208, Red Hook NY 12571. **Tel** (914)758-4484. **DD** 333. **Bk Rev**, (Qty: 2-4). **Ad Acc. Circ:** 10,000.
Desc: An newsletter of people coming together bringing their thoughts, talents, energy, and skills into preserving the Hudson Valley region.

JA/0385-9290
HYOGO-KEN KOGAI KENKYUJO KENKYU HOKOKU. See Environmental Issues-Pollution and Waste Management.

●US/1073-0478
ILLAHEE (SEATTLE, WASH.). (ILLAHEE : JOURNAL FOR THE NORTHWEST ENVIRONMENT.). [Illahee]. **Added/Corp** University of Washington. Institute for Environmental Studies. (1994)-. Periodical. English. qt. $40.00 (institutions); $25.00 (individuals). Institute for Environmental Studies, University of Washington, Seattle WA 98195. **Tel** (206)543-2100. **ED** Dr. James Karr and Ellen Chu. **LC** TD181.N93; N67. **DD** 363.7/009795. **CODEN** ILLHE9. Index available. cum. index. **Bk Rev. Ad Acc, Adv Mgr:** Ellen Chu, **Tel** (206)543-1812. **Circ:** 500. Documents available from The Genuine Article, BIOSIS Document Express. ***Continues*** *Northwest Environmental Journal, 0749-7962.*
Desc: Contains research and policy analyses about the environmental problems and challenges facing Northwestern America:
Ind/Abst Biol. Abstr.

●US/1059-5074
ILLINOIS ENVIRONMENTAL LAW LETTER. See Law.

●US
IMAGES OF A CHANGING PLANET COMPUTER FILE. (1992)-. Periodical. English.

US/0734-9165
IMPACT ASSESSMENT BULLETIN. [Impact assess. bull.]. **Added/Corp** International Association for Impact Assessment. Vol. 1, No. 2 (Winter 1982)-. Bulletin. English. qt. $65.00. International Association of Impact Assessment, PO Box 70, Belhaven NC 27810. **Tel** (919)964-2338, FAX (919)964-2340. **ED** Dr. Tom Roper (editor's address: Roger-Hulman Institute of Technology, 5500 Wabash Avenue, Terre Haute, IN 47803). **LC** T174.5; .I18. **DD** 333.7/1/05. **Bk Rev**, (Qty: 12-15/yr). **Circ:** 850. ***Continues*** *IAIA Bulletin.*
Desc: Publication of short articles, professional experience, reviews, and news, and professional opportunities.

IT
IMPRESA AMBIENTE, L'. (19??)-. Periodical. Italian. mo (10 issues). L99000 Italy; L300000 other. SEME 24 Ore, Via Parabiago 19, 20151 Milan Italy. **Tel** 011 39 2 3103295. **LC** GE170; .I47. **DD** 363.7/00945.

II/0367-827X
INDIAN JOURNAL OF ENVIRONMENTAL HEALTH. [Indian j. environ. health]. **Added/Corp** Central Public Health Engineering Research Institute (India). Vol. 13, No. 3 (July 1971)-. Academic Scholarly Publication. English. qt. $25.00. National Environmental Engineering Research Institute, Nehru Marg, Nagpur 440 020 India. **Tel** 26071, telex 0715-0233. **(Subscription address:** Prints India, 11 Darya Ganj, New Delhi 110002 India.**) ED** P Khanna. **LC** RA565.A1; E56. **DD** 628/.05. **NLM** W1 IN208N. **CODEN** IJEHBP. Index available. **Bk Rev. Ad Acc. Circ:** 1,600. Documents available from Article Express International, BIOSIS Document Express, CASDDS. ***Continues*** *Environmental Health.*
Desc: Covers all aspects of environmental engineering and sciences including air, water, wastewater, industrial and solid wastes, ecology, ecosystems and instrumentation.
Ind/Abst Agric. Eng. Abstr. (1991-); Biodeter. Abstr. (1991-); Bioeng. Abstr.; Biol. Abstr.; Chem. Abstr.; Chem. Hazards Ind.; Coal Abstr.; Curr. Biotechnol.; Ei Page One; EMBASE; Eng. Index Annu.; Environ. Period. Bibliogr. (?-?); Lab. Hazards Bull.; Sug. Indus. Abstr.

II/0253-7141
INDIAN JOURNAL OF ENVIRONMENTAL PROTECTION. [Indian j. environ. prot.]. **VFOAT** Journal of Environmental Protection. Vol. 1, No. 1 (Jan. 1981)-. Academic Scholarly Publication. English. mo. $250.00. Kalpana Corporation, PO Box 5, Varanasi 221010 India. **(Subscription address:** Prints India, 11 Darya Ganj, New Delhi 110002 India.**) ED** Surendra Kumar. **LC** TD171.5.I4; I53. **DD** 363.7/00954. **NLM** W1; IN208NR. **CODEN** IJEPDH. **[CCC].** Index available. cum. index. **Bk Rev. Ad Acc. Circ:** 3,000 (ctrl). Documents available from CASDDS, Documents on Demand.
Desc: Articles related to all aspects of environmental pollution control.
Ind/Abst Chem. Abstr.; Coal Abstr.; EMBASE; Energy Inf. Abstr.; Environ. Abstr.; Int. Aerosp. Abstr.; Life Sci. Collect.; Pollut. Abstr. Indexes; Soils Fert.

US/1053-6183
INDIANA ENVIRONMENTAL LAW LETTER. ***Title Change.*** **See** Law.

US/1055-5242
INDOOR AIR BULLETIN. (1991)- Vol. 3 No. 3 Mar. 1993)-. Periodical. English. mo. $195.00. Indoor Air Information Service, Inc., PO Box 8446, Santa Cruz CA 95061. **Tel** (408)426-6624, FAX (408)426-6522. **ED** Hal Levin. Index available. cum. index. **Bk Rev**, (Qty: unlimited). **Pr Rev. Circ:** 500 (ctrl).
Desc: Focuses on all aspects of indoor air quality important to occupational health, comfort and productivity.

●US/1062-0621
INDOOR AIR QUALITY DIRECTORY, THE. [Indoor air qual. dir.]. **Added/Corp** IAQ Publications, Inc. (1993)-. English. an. $125.00. IAQ Publications, Inc., 2 Wisconsin Circle, Suite 430, Chevy Chase MD 20815. **Tel** (800)394-0115, (301)913-0115. **LC** HD9718.5.A573; U55. **DD** 338.7/613637392. ***Absorbed*** *The Radon Directory.*

●SZ/1016-4901
INDOOR ENVIRONMENT : THE JOURNAL OF INDOOR AIR INTERNATIONAL. **Added/Corp** International Association for Indoor Air Quality. (1992)-. Periodical. English. bm. $325.00. S. Karger AG, Allschwilerstrasse 10, PO Box - Postfach - Case Postale, CH-4009 Basel Switzerland. **Tel** 011 41 61 306-1111, FAX 011 41 61 306-1234, telex CH 962 652. **ED** J.A. Hoskins. **NLM** W1; IN358N. **CODEN** IENVEC. **[CCC].** Documents available from CASDDS.
Desc: Focuses on original reports pertaining to the quality of the indoor environment at home and in the workplace. Featured are papers on engineering aspects, as well as topics in toxicology and chemistry. Enquiries into the sources of contamination include studies on bacteria and volatile substances from internal sources and on external emissions such as those from industrial plants, radon, vehicle exhaust and pollens.
Ind/Abst Chem. Abstr.; Pollut. Abstr. Indexes; Ref. Upd. Deluxe Ed.; Risk Abstr.

●US
INDUSTRIAL & ENVIRONMENTAL CRISIS QUARTERLY. **Added/Corp** Bucknell University. Dept. of Management. Industrial Crisis Institute (New York, N.Y.). **VFOAT** Industrial and Environmental Crisis Quarterly. Vol. 7, No. 1 (1993)-. Periodical. English. qt. **LC** HD49; .I52. ***Continues*** *Industrial Crisis Quarterly, 0921-8106.*
Desc: Information on crisis management in the natural environment and in the workplace.

AT/0725-6558
INFORMATION BULLETIN. P & R. [Inf. Bull., P R]. (1979)-. English. tw. **DD** 333.7209945.
Ind/Abst AESIS Q.

●US/1057-8293
INFORMATION PLEASE ENVIRONMENTAL ALMANAC, THE. (THE ... INFORMATION PLEASE ENVIRONMENTAL ALMANAC / COMPILED BY WORLD RESOURCES INSTITUTE.). **Added/Corp** World Resources Institute. **VFOAT** Environmental Almanac. (1992)-. English. an. $9.95. Houghton Mifflin Company, Wayside Road, Burlington MA 01803. **Tel** (800)225-3362, (617)272-1500. **LC** TD176.4; .I54. **DD** 363.7/005.

IT
INFORMAZIONI SANITAIRE EUROPEE. Italian. Twelve times a year. 300000ptas. Di Renzo, Viale Manzoni 59, 00185 Rome Italy. **Tel** 011 39 6 77209020, FAX 011 39 6 70474067.

IT
INFORMAZIONI SANITARIE. Italian. Twenty-four times a year. 360000ptas. Di Renzo, Viale Manzoni 59, 00185 Rome Italy. **Tel** 011 39 6 77209020, FAX 011 39 6 70474067. ctrl circ.

BO
INFORME R. **Added/Corp** Centro de Documentacion e Informacion--Bolivia. (198?)-. Periodical. Spanish. Twenty-three times a year. $60.00 US & Canada; $100.00 others. Cedoin, Casilla 11595, La Paz Bolivia. **Tel** 011 591 2 372940. **ED** Sara Monroy Pascoe.
Desc: Contains information of summaries and analysis on the economy, environment and politics.

US/0360-4985
INFORUM: ENVIRONMENTAL REPORT DATA SYSTEM. **Added/Corp** National Environmental Studies Project. **VFOAT** Environmental Report Data System. Vol. 1 (Aug. 1975)-. English. ir. $300.00. 1747 Pennsylvania Avenue NW, Suite 1150, Washington DC 20006. **LC** TD195.E4; I54. **DD** 016.3337.

US/0270-8965
INSIDE E.P.A. WEEKLY REPORT. (INSIDE E.P.A. WEEKLY REPORT; AN EXCLUSIVE REPORT ON THE ENVIRONMENTAL PROTECTION AGENCY.). [Inside E.P.A. wkly. rep.]. **VFOAT** Inside E.P.A. **VAT** Inside Environmental Protection Agency Weekly Report. (1980)-. Periodical. English. wk. $860.00. Inside Washington Publishers, PO Box 7167, Benjamin Franklin Station, Washington DC 20044. **Tel** (703)416-8500, (800)424-9068. **ED** Julie Edelson. **DD** 353.
Desc: Coverage of environmental policy and regulation.

US
INSTRUMENTATION FOR ENVIRONMENTAL MONITORING. **Main/Corp** Lawrence Berkeley Laboratory. Environmental Instrumentation Group. **Added/Corp** National Science Foundation (U.S.). Research Applied to National Needs Program United States. Energy Research and Development Administration. Division of Biomedical and Environmental Research. Vol. 1 (May 1972)-. Periodical. English. ir. Lawrence Berkeley Laboratory, University of California, Berkeley CA 94720. **Tel** (415)486-4000.

UK/0962-1113
INTEGRATED ENVIRONMENTAL MANAGEMENT. [Integr. environ. manag.]. (1991)-. Academic Scholarly Publication. English. Ten times a year. £225.00. Blackwell Scientific Publications Ltd, Marston Book Services, PO Box 87, Oxford OX2 ODT UK. **Tel** 011 44 865 791155, FAX 011 44 865 791927, telex 837 515 MARDIS G. **DD** 363.728.

US/0105-175X
INTER-NOISE. (INTER-NOISE; PROCEEDINGS.). **Main/Conf** International Conference on Noise Control Engineering. **Added/Corp** Institute of Noise Control Engineering. Danmarks Tekniske Hjskole. Laboratoriet for Akustik. Acoustical Society of America. (1972)-. Proceedings. English. an. $125.00. Institute of Noise Control Engineering, PO Box 3206, Arlington Branch, Poughkeepsie NY 12603. **Tel** (914)462-4006. **LC** TD891; .I56a. **DD** 620.2/3. **CODEN** PICEDA.
Ind/Abst Bioeng. Abstr.

CN/1188-3146
INTERACTIONS (TILLSONBURG). (INTERACTIONS.). [Interactions]. **Added/Corp** Ontario Society for Environmental Education. Environmental Science Teachers' Association of Ontario. (1988)-. Periodical. English. Five times a year. $35.00. Ontario Society for Environmental Education, 54 Blackfoot Place, Woodstock Ontario N4T 1E6 Canada. **Tel** (519)537-2347. **ED** Bill Thompson (eidtor's phone: (519)539-8413). **DD** 333.7/071/0713. **Ad Acc.** ***Continues*** *Bulletin (Environmental Science Teachers' Association of Ontario).*
Desc: An educational journal on environmental topics to provide information to keep people current in the field. There are some teaching ideas to help educators present material to classes.

US/0270-2584
INTERNATIONAL CONFERENCE ON ENVIRONMENTAL PROBLEMS OF THE EXTRACTIVE INDUSTRIES. [Int. Conf. Environ. Probl. Extr. Ind.]. Academic Scholarly Publication. English. ir. Wright Company, 1436 Adirondack Trail, Dayton OH 45409. **CODEN** ICEIDF. Documents available from CASDDS.
Ind/Abst Chem. Abstr.

UK/0141-4836
INTERNATIONAL ENVIRONMENT & SAFETY. [Int. environ. saf.]. **VAT** International Environment and Safety. (1978)-. Academic Scholarly Publication. English. Four times a year. $120.00 US and Canada; £70.00 other. International Labmate Limited, Newgate Sandpit Lane, St. Albans Herts, AL4 0BS England. **Tel** 011 44 727 858840, FAX 011 44 727 41694. **ED** M. H. Pattison. **CODEN** IESAD7. **Bk Rev. Ad Acc. Circ:** 13,000 (ctrl). Documents available from CASDDS.
Desc: News and information for environmental health and safety officers.
Ind/Abst Chem. Abstr. (1978-1985).

UK/0963-7362
INTERNATIONAL ENVIRONMENTAL TECHNOLOGY. [Int. environ. technol.]. (1991)-. Periodical. English. bm. £15.00 UK; £20.00 Europe; £35.00 others. International Labmate Limited, Newgate Sandpit Lane, St. Albans Herts, AL4 0BS England. **Tel** 011 44 727 858840, FAX 011 44 727 41694. **DD** 628.5.
Desc: Covers news and the responsibility for environmental control, monitoring, and clean up.

AT/1035-8544
INTERNATIONAL ENVIRONMENTAL UPDATE. [Int. environ. update]. (1990)-. Periodical. English. mo. 300.00Aus$ Australia; 305.00Aus$ New Zealand, Papua New Guinea; 310.00Aus$ Indonesia, Malaysia, Singapore, 315.00Aus$ Japan, India; 320.00Aus$ US & Canada; 325.00Aus$ Europe. International Public Relations Pty Ltd., 33 Walsh Street, West Melbourne Victoria 3003 Australia. **Tel** 011 61 03 329 9333, FAX 011 61 03 329 7996. **DD** 363.7005.

US/1054-853X
INTERNATIONAL JOURNAL OF ENERGY, ENVIRONMENT, ECONOMICS. **See** Energy.

SZ/0957-4352
INTERNATIONAL JOURNAL OF ENVIRONMENT AND POLLUTION. **Added/Corp** European Centre for Pollution Research. Vol. 1, Nos. 1/2 (1991)-. Academic Scholarly Publication. English. Four times a year. £135.00 UK; $185.00 North America; DM340.00 other. Inderscience Enterprises Ltd, World Trade Center Building, 110 Avenue Louis Casai, Case Postale 306, CH-1215 Geneva-Aeroport Switzerland. **Tel** 011 41 22 7383437, FAX 011 41 22 7910885, telex 28 99 50. **LC** TD1; .I573. **CODEN** IJVLEN. Documents available from Article Express International, CASDDS, Documents on Demand.
Desc: Journal of environmental pollution, policy, science and technology.
Ind/Abst Chem. Abstr.; Eng. Index Annu.; Environ. Abstr.; Environ. Period. Bibliogr.

UK/0960-3123
INTERNATIONAL JOURNAL OF ENVIRONMENTAL HEALTH RESEARCH. [Int. j. environ. health res.]. Vol. 1, No. 1 (Mar. 1991)-. Periodical. English. qt. $245.00 US and Canada; £140.00 Europe; £145.00 other. Chapman & Hall, 2-6 Boundary Row, London SE1 8HN England. **Tel** 011 44 71 865 0066, FAX 011 44 71 522 9623, telex 290164 Chapmag. **(Subscription address:** Chapman & Hall, Cheriton House, North Way, Andover, Hampshire, SP10 5BE England.**) ED** Paul Smith, Michael Jackson, Joan Rose, Ron Pickett, Ahmad Gaber. **LC** RA566.27; .I57. **NLM** W1; IN766GP. **CODEN** IJEREO. Documents available from ADONIS.
Desc: Devoted to the rapid publication of research papers on all aspects of the interaction between the environment and human health. The range of topics that is covered is broadly divided into three areas: the natural environment and health, the built environment and health, and communicable diseases.
Ind/Abst ADONIS; Food Sci. Technol. Abstr.; Geogr. Abstr. Human Geogr.; Soc. Sci. Cit. Index [Select. Cov.].

US/0020-7233
INTERNATIONAL JOURNAL OF ENVIRONMENTAL STUDIES, THE. [Int. j. environ. stud.]. **VFOAT** Environmental Studies; Environmental Science and Technology. Vol. 1 (Oct. 1970)-. Academic Scholarly Publication. English. ir. Gordon & Breach Science Publishers, PO Box 90, Reading RG1 8JL England. **Tel** 011 44 734 560080, FAX 011 44 734 568211. **(Subscription address:** Gordon & Breach Science Publishers / US, 820 Town Center Drive, Langhorne PA 19047.**) LC** HC79.E5; I55. **DD** 301.3/1/05. **NLM** W1 IN766H. **CODEN** IJEVAW. **[CCC].** Documents available from BIOSIS Document Express, UMI Article Clearinghouse, CASDDS.
Ind/Abst ABI Inform Ondisc (July 1972-July 1973);

AGRICOLA; Agric. Eng. Abstr.; AQUAREF; Biocont. News Inf.; Biodeter. Abstr.; Biol. Abstr. (-1984); Chem. Abstr.; Coal Abstr.; Curr. Aware. Biol. Sci., CABS; EMBASE; Energy Res. Abstr. (Sept. 1971-); Environ. Period. Bibliogr.; For. Prod. Abstr. (1991-); For. Abstr.; GeoRef; Grasslands For. Abstr.; Highw. Res. Abstr.; Int. Aerosp. Abstr.; Irr. Drain. Abstr.; J. Plan. Lit.; Leadscan; Lit. Pat. Abstr., Oilfield Chem. (1975-1985); Lit. Abstr., Catal. Catal.; Lit. Abstr., Health Environ.; Lit. Abstr., Pet. Refin. Petrochem.; Lit. Abstr., Pet. Substit.; Lit. Abstr., Transp. Storage; Maize Abstr.; Ornamental Hort. (1991-); Life Sci. Collect.; PESTDOC; Pollut. Abstr. Indexes; Rev. Agric. Entomol.; Rice Abstr.; Soils Fert.; Trop. Dis. Bull.; Wheat Barley Trit. Abstr.; World Agric. Econ.

US/0020-7233
INTERNATIONAL JOURNAL OF ENVIRONMENTAL STUDIES. SECTION B, ENVIRONMENTAL SCIENCE AND TECHNOLOGY, THE. **VFOAT** Environmental Science and Technology. Vol. 25, No. 1/2 (1985)-. Periodical. English. qt. £212.00. Gordon & Breach Science Publishers, Inc., PO Box 786, Cooper Station, New York NY 10276. **Tel** (212)206-8900, FAX (212)645-2459. **(Subscription address:** International Publishers Distributor at one of the following addresses: 820 Town Center Drive, Langhorne, PA 19047; or PO Box 90, Reading Berkshire RG1 8JL UK; or Kent Ridge PO Box 1180, Singapore 9111, Republic of Singapore) **[CCC].** ***Continues in part*** *International Journal of Environmental Studies, 0020-7233.*
Ind/Abst Field Crop Abstr.; Fish Rev. (19??-199?); Helminthol. Abstr. (1991-); Irr. Drain. Abstr.; Leis. Recreat. Tour. Abstr.; Lit. Pat. Abstr., Oilfield Chem. (1985-1989); Lit. Abstr., Catal. Catal.; Lit. Abstr., Health Environ.; Lit. Abstr., Pet. Refin. Petrochem.; Lit. Abstr., Pet. Substit.; Lit. Abstr., Transp. Storage; Soils Fert.

●US/1062-6832
INTERNATIONAL JOURNAL OF ENVIRONMENTALLY CONSCIOUS MANUFACTURING. **See** Manufacturing.

●US/1077-3525
INTERNATIONAL JOURNAL OF OCCUPATIONAL AND ENVIRONMENT HEALTH. (1995)-. English. qt. $70.00 (individual), $90.00 (institutional) US & Possessions; $80.00 (individual), $100.00 (institutional) Other. Hanley & Belfus Inc., 210 South 13th Street, Philadelphia PA 19107. **Tel** (215)546-7293, FAX (215)790-9330.

NE/1037-0544
INTERNATIONAL JOURNAL OF SALT LAKE RESEARCH. **See** Science and Technology.

US/8755-5328
INTERNATIONAL PERSPECTIVES IN PUBLIC HEALTH. **See** Public Health and Safety.

US/1059-4078
INVIRONMENT (BUFFALO GROVE, ILL.). (INVIRONMENT : THE NEWSLETTER OF BUILDING MANAGEMENT AND INDOOR AIR QUALITY.). [Invironment]. Vol. 1, No. 1 (Spring 1991)-. Newsletter. English. Four times a year (Jan., Apr., July, Oct.). $95.00. Invironment, One Pierce Place, Suite 245 C, Itasca IL 60143. **Tel** (800)262-6722 (708)250-5770, FAX (708)250-5771. **ED** George Benda and Gail Melson. **DD** 658. **Bk Rev**, (Qty: 4). **Pr Rev.**

IS/0334-3804
ISRAEL ENVIRONMENT BULLETIN. [Isr. environ. bull.]. **Added/Corp** Israel. Sherut Li-Shemirat Ekhut Ha-Sevivah. Vol. 1 (March 1974)-. Periodical. English. Four times a year. Free. Ministry of the Environment / Israel, POB 6234, Jerusalem 91061 Israel. **Tel** 011 972 2 701606, FAX 011 972 2 385038, telex 25629 ENVIR IL. **ED** Shoshana Gabbay. **Bk Rev. Circ:** 2,000. Documents available from Documents on Demand.
Desc: Survey of environmental protection activities in Israel including air and water quality, noise, environmental education, legislation, energy, environmental impact statements and cleanliness.
Ind/Abst Energy Inf. Abstr.; Environ. Abstr.

RU
ISSLEDOVANIE EKOSISTEMY BALTIISKOGO MORIA / GOSUDARSTVENNYI KOMITET SSSR PO GIDROMETEOROLOGII I KONTROLIU PRIRODNOI SREDY; AGENSTVO PO ZASHCHITE OKRUZHAIUSHCHEI SREDY SHVETSII.
Added/Corp Gosudarstvennyi Komitet SSSR po Gidrometeorologii i Kontroliu Prirodnoi Sredy. Sweden. Statens Naturvardsverk. (1981)-. Periodical. Russian. Gidrometeoizdat, Vasilevskii Ostrov, 3, V-53, 199053 St.Petersburg, Russia. **CODEN** IEBMER. Documents available from CASDDS.
Ind/Abst Chem. Abstr.

●UK/1350-7583
ISSUES IN ENVIRONMENTAL SCIENCE AND TECHNOLOGY. **See** Science and Technology.

UK
ISSUES PAPER / INTERNATIONAL INSTITUTE FOR ENVIRONMENT AND DEVELOPMENT, DRYLAND NETWORKS PROGRAMME. **Added/Corp** Dryland Networks Programme. **VFOAT** Dryland Networks Programme Issues Paper. Paper No. 15 (1990)-. Monographic series. English. Price varies per volume. International Institute for Environment and Development, #13 Endsleigh Street, London WC1 H 0DD England. **Tel** 011 44 71 3882117. **LC** S612; .D79. ***Continues*** *Issues Paper (Drylands Programme).*
Ind/Abst Agrofor. Abstr.; For. Abstr.; Soils Fert.

GW/0179-3462
IWL UMWELTBRIEF. **See** Environmental Issues-Conservation and Natural Resources.

SZ
JAHRBUCH FUR UMWELTSCHUTZ. 1973-. German. Keller and Company, Baselstrasse 11, CH-6002 Luzern Switzerland. **Tel** 041 281111, FAX 041 222253. **LC** TD169; .J33.

US/1052-1062
JOURNAL OF CLEAN TECHNOLOGY AND ENVIRONMENTAL SCIENCES. [J. clean technol. environ. sci.]. **Added/Corp** International Association for Clean Technology. **VFOAT** JCTES. (Jan. 1991)-. Periodical. English. Four times a year. $120.00. Princeton Scientific Publishing Company Inc., PO Box 2155, Princeton NJ 08543. **Tel** (609)683-4750, FAX (609)683-0838. **ED** M A Mehlman. **LC** TD194; .J68. **DD** 363.72/8. **[CCC]. Bk Rev. Ad Acc, Adv Mgr:** MA Mehlman. **Pr Rev. Circ:** , . Documents available from The Genuine Article.
Desc: The purpose is to promote the research and application of clean technologies and methodologies. Topics include policy and management issues pertaining to clean technology, the economics of clean technology; the elimination or prevention of occupational hazards; engineering controls and industrial hygiene studies; environmental technologies; ecology, and environmental sciences.
Ind/Abst Res. Alert [Select. Cov.]; SCISEARCH.

●US/1070-4965
JOURNAL OF ENVIRONMENT & DEVELOPMENT, THE. **See** Economics.

US/0095-8964
JOURNAL OF ENVIRONMENTAL EDUCATION, THE. [J. environ. educ.]. Vol. 2, No. 3 (Spring 1971)-. Periodical. English. qt. $35.00 (individual), $68.00 (institutional), add $12.00 (foreign postage). Heldref Publications, 1319 Eighteenth Street Northwest, Washington DC 20036-1802. **Tel** (202)296-6267, (800)365-9753, FAX (202)296-5149. **ED** Alan W Ewert, John C Miles, and John R Paulk. **LC** S946; .E54. **DD** 333.7/2/07. **CODEN** JEVEB9. **[CCC].** available on microfilm and microfiche from University Microfilms International (UMI). Documents available from BIOSIS Document Express, Documents on Demand. ***Continues*** *Environmental Education (Madison, Wis.), 0013-9254.*
Desc: A vital research journal for everyone teaching about the environment. Each issue features case studies of relevant projects, evaluation of new research, and discussion of public policy and philosophy in the area of environmental education. An excellent resource for department chairpersons and directors of programs in outdoor education.
Ind/Abst Biol. Abstr.; Contents Pages Educ.; Curr. Index J. Educ.; Ecology Abstr.; Educ. Index; EMBASE (1989/90-); Environ. Abstr.; Environ. Period. Bibliogr.; Health Saf. Sci. Abstr.; J. Plan. Lit.; Leis. Recreat. Tour. Abstr.; Middle East Abstr. Index; Life Sci. Collect.; Pollut. Abstr. Indexes; Psychol. Abstr. (1983-); PsycINFO; PsycLit; West. Hist. Q.

US/0022-0892
JOURNAL OF ENVIRONMENTAL HEALTH. [J. environ. health]. **Added/Corp** National Environmental Health Association. National Association of Sanitarians. Vol. 26, No. 2 (Sept./Oct. 1963)-. Academic Scholarly Publication. English. Ten times a year (Jan./Feb., & July/Aug. issues combined). $75.00 US & Canada; $100.00 other. National Environmental Health Association, 720 South Colorado Boulevard, Suite 970, Denver CO 80222-1904. **Tel** (303)756-9090, FAX (303)691-9490. **ED** Simonne Gallaty. **DD** 614. **NLM** W1 JO644B. **CODEN** JEVHAH. **Ad Acc, Adv Mgr:** Scott Houston, **Tel** (303)756-9090. **Pr Rev. Circ:** 20,000. available on microfilm and microfiche from University Microfilms International (UMI); available on CD-ROM from EBSCO Publishing - Birmingham. Documents available from UMI Article Clearinghouse, CASDDS, Documents on Demand. ***Continues*** *Sanitarian's Journal of Environmental Health, 0092-6957.*
Desc: Professional articles on all aspects of environmental health and protection. Provides current information on employment and educational opportunities in environmental health. Useful for environmental health and environmental protection professionals.
Ind/Abst Acad. Search (July 1993-); AGRICOLA; Appl. Sci. Technol. Index; Biol. Abstr.; Chem. Abstr.; Coal Abstr.; Curr. Aware. Biol. Sci., CABS; Curr. Contents, Agric. Biol. Environ. Sci.; Curr. Index J. Educ.; Dairy Sci. Abstr.; Ecol. Abstr. (?-?); EMBASE; Energy Inf. Abstr.; Environ. Abstr.; Environ. Period. Bibliogr.; Expand. Acad. Index (1989-); Gen. Sci. Index; Gen. Sci. Source (Jul. 1993-); Geogr. Abstr. Human Geogr. (?-?); Health Saf. Sci. Abstr.; Health Source (Jul. 1993-); Hospit. Health Admin. Index (1963-1990); Index Vet.; INFO-SOUTH Abstr.; INIS Atomindex [Micro.]; Leadscan; Mag. Search; Newsp. Period. Abstr. (1991-); Nutr. Abstr. Rev., Ser. B, Live Feeds and Feed.; Nutr. Abstr. Rev., Ser. A, Hum. Exp.; Life Sci. Collect.; Pollut. Abstr. Indexes; Poult. Abstr.; Protozoolog. Abstr.; Res. Alert [Select. Cov.]; Rev. Agric. Entomol.; Rev. Med. Vet. Entomol.; Risk Abstr.; Saf. Health Work; SCISEARCH; Soc. Sci. Cit. Index; Weed Abstr.

UK/0301-4797
JOURNAL OF ENVIRONMENTAL MANAGEMENT. [J. environ. manage.]. Vol. 1 (Jan. 1973)-. Academic Scholarly Publication. English. mo. $495.00. Academic Press Ltd., A Division of Harcourt Brace & Company Ltd., 24-28 Oval Road, London NW1 7DX England. **Tel** 071 267 4466, FAX 071 482 2293, 071 485 4752, telex 25775 ACPRES G. **(Subscription address:** Harcourt Brace & Company, Ltd., Foots Cray, High Street, Sidcup Kent DA14 5HP England.) **ED** J. N. R. Jeffers. **LC** HC79.E5. **DD** 301.31. **NLM** W1 JO644BD. **CODEN** JEVMAW. **[CCC]. Pr Rev.** Documents available from The Genuine Article, BIOSIS Document Express, Documents on Demand.
Desc: Publishes papers on all aspects of management and use of the environment, both natural and man-made. As governments and the general public become more keenly aware of the critical issues arising from man's use of his environment, the journal aims to provide a forum for the discussion of environmental problems around the world and for the presentation of management results. Aimed not only at the environmental manager, but at everyone concerned with the wise use of environmental resources. The journal tries particularly to publish examples of the use of modern mathematical and computer techniques and encourages contributions from the developing countries in the Third World.
Ind/Abst AgBiotech News Inf.; AGRICOLA; Agrofor. Abstr. (1991-); AQUAREF; Biodeter. Abstr.; Biol. Abstr.; Br. Humanit. Index; Coal Abstr.; Curr. Contents, Agric. Biol. Environ. Sci.; Curr. Contents Soc. Behav. Sci.; Curr. Ref. Fish Res.; Ecol. Abstr.; Ecology Abstr.; EMBASE; Energy Res. Abstr. (Aug. 1976-); Environ. Abstr.; Environ. Period. Bibliogr.; Field Crop Abstr.; Fish Rev.; For. Prod. Abstr.; For. Abstr.; Geogr. Abstr. Phys. Geogr.; Geogr. Abstr. Human Geogr.; Grasslands For. Abstr.; Health Saf. Sci. Abstr.; Hortic. Abstr.; Int. Abstr. Oper. Res. [Select. Cov.]; Int. Bibliogr. Sociol.; Int. Dev. Abstr.; J. Plan. Lit.; Key Word Index Wildl. Res.; Leis. Recreat. Tour. Abstr.; Middle East Abstr. Index; Ocean. Abstr.; Life Sci. Collect.; Pig News Inf.; Pollut. Abstr. Indexes; Res. Alert [Full Cov.]; Rev. Agric. Entomol.; Rev. Med. Vet. Entomol.; Rev. Plant Pathol.; Risk Abstr.; Rural Dev. Abstr.; Sci. Cit. Index; SCISEARCH; Soc. Sci. Cit. Index [Full Cov.]; Soils Fert.; SportSearch; Wildl. Rev.; World Agric. Econ.

●US/1064-7546
JOURNAL OF ENVIRONMENTAL POLYMER DEGRADATION. **See** Chemistry.

UK/0272-4944
JOURNAL OF ENVIRONMENTAL PSYCHOLOGY. **See** Psychology.

US/1055-7547
JOURNAL OF ENVIRONMENTAL QUALITY MANAGEMENT. (1991)-. Periodical. English. qt. $110.00. Executive Enterprises, 22 West 21st Street, New York NY 10010-6990. **Tel** (800)332-8804, FAX (212)645-8689.

US/1055-7563
JOURNAL OF ENVIRONMENTAL QUALITY (NEW YORK, N.Y.). (JOURNAL OF ENVIRONMENTAL QUALITY.). (1991)-. Periodical. English. qt. $110.00. Executive Enterprises, 22 West 21st Street, New York NY 10010-6990. **Tel** (800)332-8804, FAX (212)645-8689.
Ind/Abst Appl. Sci. Technol. Index; Geogr. Abstr. Human Geogr.

US/1055-758X
JOURNAL OF ENVIRONMENTAL REGULATION. [J. environ. regul.]. **VFOAT** Environmental Regulations. Vol. 1, No. 1 (Autumn 1991)-. Periodical. English. qt. $159.00 US & Canada; $209.00 other. John Wiley & Sons, Inc., 605 Third Avenue, New York NY 10158-0012. **Tel** (212)850-6000, (212)850-6645, FAX (212)850-6088, telex 12-7063. **(Subscription address:** John Wiley & Sons Inc / New Jersey, PO Box 2575, Secaucus NJ 07096-2575.) **LC** IN PROCESS. **DD** 344. **[CCC].**
Desc: Written for environmental managers, engineers, consultants, attorneys and corporate executives, this publication provides a detailed overview of all major

environmental legislation. Contains explanations of existing regulations, updates on proposed legislation, and advice on planning for and implementing new regulations.

US/0360-1226
JOURNAL OF ENVIRONMENTAL SCIENCE AND HEALTH. PART A, ENVIRONMENTAL SCIENCE AND ENGINEERING. [J. environ. sci. health, Part A, Environ. sci. eng.]. **VFOAT** Environmental Science and Engineering. (1976)-. Academic Scholarly Publication. English. Ten times a year. $825.00 US; $860.00 other; $1,495.00 US; $1,558.00 other (combined with parts B & C). Marcel Dekker Inc., 270 Madison Avenue, New York NY 10016. **Tel** (212)696-9000, (800)228-1160, FAX (212)685-4540, telex 421419. **(Subscription address:** Marcel Dekker Inc, PO Box 5017, Monticello NY 12701.) **ED** James W. Robinson, James R. Brock and Joe E. Ledbetter. **LC** TD1; .J665. **DD** 620.8/5. **NLM** W1 JO644BH. **CODEN** JESEDU. **[CCC]. Bk Rev. Ad Acc. Pr Rev.** available on microfiche. Documents available from Article Express International, The Genuine Article, BIOSIS Document Express, CASDDS, Documents on Demand. ***Supersedes in part*** *Environmental Letters, 0013-9300.*
Desc: Articles range from notes to completed studies in this comprehensive journal that provides an international forum for the rapid publication of essential information - including the latest engineering innovations, effects of pollutants on health, control systems, laws, and projections - pertinent to environmental problems whether in the air, water, or soil. This timely journal offers answers to serious contemporary environmental issues.
Ind/Abst AgBiotech News Inf.; AGRICOLA [Select. Cov.]; Air Pollut. Titles; Anal. Abstr.; AQUAREF; Biodeter. Abstr. (19??-19??); Biol. Abstr.; Chem. Abstr.; Chem. Hazards Ind.; Chem. Titles; Coal Abstr.; Curr. Biotechnol.; Curr. Contents, Agric. Biol. Environ. Sci.; Dairy Sci. Abstr.; Ecol. Abstr. (?-?); Ecology Abstr.; Ei Page One; EMBASE; Energy Res. Abstr. (Aug. 1976-); Eng. Index Annu.; Environ. Abstr.; Environ. Period. Bibliogr.; Fish Rev.; Geogr. Abstr. Phys. Geogr. (?-?); GeoRef; Health Saf. Sci. Abstr.; Index Med.; Index Vet.; INIS Atomindex [Micro.]; Irr. Drain. Abstr.; Lab. Hazards Bull.; Leadscan; Nutr. Abstr. Rev., Ser. B, Live Feeds and Feed.; Nutr. Abstr. Rev., Ser. A, Hum. Exp.; Phys. Briefs; Pollut. Abstr. Indexes; Ref. Upd. Deluxe Ed.; Res. Alert [Full Cov.]; Rev. Agric. Entomol.; Rev. Med. Vet. Entomol.; Rev. Plant Pathol.; Sci. Cit. Index; SCISEARCH; Soc. Sci. Cit. Index [Select. Cov.]; Soils Fert.; Vet. Bull.; Wildl. Rev.

US/0360-1234
JOURNAL OF ENVIRONMENTAL SCIENCE AND HEALTH. PART B, PESTICIDES, FOOD CONTAMINANTS, AND AGRICULTURAL WASTES. [J. environ. sci. health, Part B, Pestic. food contam. agric. wastes]. **VFOAT** Pesticides, Food Contaminants, and Agricultural Wastes. (1976)-. Academic Scholarly Publication. English. bm. $550.00 US; $571.00 other; $1,495.00 US; $1,558.00 other (combination of Parts A, B, and C). Marcel Dekker Inc., 270 Madison Avenue, New York NY 10016. **Tel** (212)696-9000, (800)228-1160, FAX (212)685-4540, telex 421419. **(Subscription address:** Marcel Dekker Inc, PO Box 5017, Monticello NY 12701.) **ED** Shahamat U. Khan. **LC** QH545.A1; J68. **DD** 574.2/4. **NLM** W1 JO644BI. **CODEN** JPFCD2. **[CCC]. Bk Rev. Ad Acc. Pr Rev.** available on microfiche. Documents available from Article Express International, The Genuine Article, BIOSIS Document Express, CASDDS, Documents on Demand. ***Supersedes in part*** *Environmental Letters, 0013-9300.*
Desc: This journal provides an outlet for original research reports on analytical techniques or improvements on existing methods applicable to residues of pesticides, food contaminants (natural and additive), and other chemical contaminants, and their metabolites in the ecosphere. 'Pesticides, Food Contaminants, and Agricultural Wastes' offers original factual reports on the persistence, binding, translocation, chemical and biodegradation, and metabolic fate of these chemicals; their effectual contamination of the biosphere; methods of detoxification; and their toxicological considerations and consequences. The journal also encompasses the developments in integrated methods of pest control and various aspects of agricultural wastes.
Ind/Abst AGRICOLA [Full Cov.]; Agric. Eng. Abstr. (1991-); Anal. Abstr.; AQUAREF; BioBusiness; Bioeng. Abstr.; Biol. Abstr.; Chem. Abstr.; Chem. Hazards Ind.; Chem. Titles; Coal Abstr.; Crop Physiol. Abstr.; CSA Neuro. Abstr. (?-?); Curr. Aware. Biol. Sci., CABS; Curr. Contents, Agric. Biol. Environ. Sci.; Dairy Sci. Abstr.; Ecol. Abstr.; Ecology Abstr.; Ei Page One; EMBASE; Energy Res. Abstr. (Aug. 1976-); Eng. Index Annu.; Environ. Abstr.; Environ. Period. Bibliogr.; Field Crop Abstr.; Fish Rev.; Food Sci. Technol. Abstr.; For. Abstr.; Geogr. Abstr. Phys. Geogr.; Health Saf. Sci. Abstr.; Helminthol. Abstr. (1991-); Hortic. Abstr.; Index Med.; Index Vet.; INIS Atomindex [Micro.]; Irr. Drain. Abstr.; Lab. Hazards Bull.; Leadscan; Maize Abstr.; Nematol. Abstr.; Nutr. Abstr. Rev., Ser. A, Hum. Exp.; Life Sci. Collect.; PESTDOC; Pig News Inf.; Plant Grow. Reg. Abstr.; Pollut. Abstr. Indexes; Postharvest News Inf.; Protozoolog. Abstr.; Ref. Upd. Deluxe Ed.; Res. Alert [Full Cov.]; Rev. Med. Vet. Entomol.; Rev. Med. Vet. Mycology; Rev. Plant Pathol.; Rice Abstr.; Sci. Cit. Index; SCISEARCH; Soils Fert.; Vet. Bull.; Weed Abstr.; Wheat Barley Trit. Abstr.; Wildl. Rev.

JA/0915-6194
JOURNAL OF ENVIRONMENTAL SCIENCE LABORATORY. [J. Environ. Sci. Lab.]. **VFOAT** Senshu Daigaku Hokkaido Tanki Daigaku Kankyo Kagaku Kenkyujo Hokoku. (1989)-. Periodical. English. an. **DD** 500 600.
Ind/Abst Soils Fert.

●US/1065-7568
JOURNAL OF ENVIRONMENTAL STATISTICS. (1993)-. Periodical. English. Four times a year. $140.00. Van Nostrand Reinhold Company Inc., 115 5th Avenue, New York NY 10003. **Tel** (212)254-3232, FAX (212)673-1239, telex 272562.

US/0047-2433
JOURNAL OF ENVIRONMENTAL SYSTEMS. [J. environ. syst.]. **VFOAT** Environmental Systems. Vol. 1 (March 1971)-. Periodical. English. qt. $118.00. Baywood Publishing Company Inc., 26 Austin Avenue, PO Box 337, Amityville NY 11701. **Tel** (516)691-1270, (800)638-7819, FAX (516)691-1770. **ED** Paul R Decicco. **LC** TD1; .J67. **DD** 620.8. **CODEN** JEVSBH. **Pr Rev.** Documents available from Article Express International, The Genuine Article, BIOSIS Document Express, Documents on Demand.
Desc: Addressed to the professional concerned with management of our environment offering solutions to problems relating to system complexes.
Ind/Abst AGRICOLA; AQUAREF; Bioeng. Abstr.; Biol. Abstr.; Crim. Justice Abstr. (-199?); Curr. Contents Soc. Behav. Sci.; Ei Page One; EMBASE; Eng. Index Annu.; Environ. Abstr.; Environ. Period. Bibliogr.; Health Saf. Sci. Abstr.; Highw. Res. Abstr.; J. Plan. Lit.; Life Sci. Collect.; Pollut. Abstr. Indexes; Res. Alert [Full Cov.]; Risk Abstr.; Sage Urban Stud. Abstr; Soc. Sci. Cit. Index [Full Cov.]; SportSearch; Wildl. Rev.

US/1053-4245
JOURNAL OF EXPOSURE ANALYSIS AND ENVIRONMENTAL EPIDEMIOLOGY. [J. expo. anal. environ. epidemiol.]. **Added/Corp** International Society of Exposure Analysis. Vol. 1, No. 1 (Jan. 1991)-. Academic Scholarly Publication. English. Four times a year. $180.00. Princeton Scientific Publishing Company Inc., PO Box 2155, Princeton NJ 08543. **Tel** (609)683-4750, FAX (609)683-0838. **ED** Edo Pellizzari. **LC** RA565.A1; J673. **DD** 615.9/02/05. **NLM** W1; JO644YK. **CODEN** JEAEE9. **[CCC]. Bk Rev. Ad Acc, Adv Mgr:** M A Mehlman. **Pr Rev. Acid Free. Circ:** 600. Documents available from The Genuine Article, CASDDS.
Desc: Welcomes manuscripts dealing with measurements, modeling, instrumentation, questionnaires; studies on chemical, biological, and physical principles required to analyze human exposure from single, and multiple media and routes, and epidemiological investigations.
Ind/Abst Chem. Abstr.; Curr. Aware. Biol. Sci., CABS; Curr. Contents, Agric. Biol. Environ. Sci.; Index Med. (1991-); Res. Alert [Select. Cov.]; Soc. Sci. Cit. Index [Select. Cov.].

●SZ/1061-026X
JOURNAL OF MARINE ENVIRONMENTAL ENGINEERING. [J. marine environ. eng.]. **VFOAT** Marine Environmental Engineering. Vol. 1, No. 1 (1993)-. Periodical. English. Four times a year. $258.00 (academic institutions), $402.00 (corporate institutions). Gordon & Breach Science Publishers, PO Box 90, Reading RG1 8JL England. **Tel** 011 44 734 560080, FAX 011 44 734 568211. **(Subscription address:** International Publishers Distributor at one of the following addresses: 820 Town Center Drive, Langhorne, PA 19047; or PO Box 90, Reading Berkshire RG1 8JL UK; or Kent Ridge PO Box 1180, Singapore 9111, Republic of Singapore) **DD** 628. **CODEN** JMEEEH. **[CCC].**
Desc: Covers the issues that confront engineers and scientists seeking solutions to environmental problems in ocean and estuary waters, and inland seas.

US/1055-7555
JOURNAL OF QUALITY ENVIRONMENTAL MANAGEMENT. (1991)-. Periodical. English. qt. $110.00. Executive Enterprises, 22 West 21st Street, New York NY 10010-6990. **Tel** (800)332-8804, FAX (212)645-8689.

US/1052-2883
JOURNAL OF THE IES. [J. IES]. **Added/Corp** Institute of Environmental Sciences. **VAT** Journal of the Institute of Environmental Sciences. Vol. 33, No. 1 (Jan./Feb. 1990)-. Academic Scholarly Publication. English. Six times a year (Jan., Mar., May, July, Sept., Nov.). $35.00 US & US possessions; $70.00 others surface mail; $130.00 airmail. Institute of Environment Science, 940 East NorthWest Highway, Mt Prospect IL 60056. **Tel** (312)255-1561, FAX 312-255-1699. **ED** Janet Ehmann. **LC** TA1; .J637. **DD** 628. **NLM** W1; JO93BH. **CODEN** JOIEEH. **[CCC].** Index available. cum. index. **Bk Rev. Ad Acc. Pr Rev. Circ:** 5,000. available on microfilm and microfiche from University Microfilms International (UMI). Documents available from Article Express International, The Genuine Article, Ask*IEEE, CASDDS, Documents on Demand. ***Continues*** *Journal of Environmental Sciences, 0022-0906.*
Desc: Technical articles and reports on the researching, simulating, testing and teaching of environmental sciences and technologies.
Ind/Abst Appl. Sci. Technol. Index (Jan./Feb. 1990-); Chem. Abstr. (Jan./Feb. 1990-); Coal Abstr.; Curr. Contents Eng. Tech. Appl. Sci.; Ei Page One; EMBASE (Jan./Feb. 1990-); Energy Inf. Abstr.; Energy Res. Abstr.; Eng. Index Annu.; Eng. Index Energy Abstr.; Environ. Abstr.; GeoRef; INIS Atomindex [Micro.]; INSPEC; Int. Aerosp. Abstr.; Ref. Sources; Res. Alert [Select. Cov.]; Risk Abstr.; SCISEARCH; Sel. Water Resour. Abstr.; Shock Vibr. Dig.

II/0251-110X
JOURNAL OF THE INSTITUTION OF ENGINEERS (INDIA). PART EN CALCUTTA, ENVIRONMENTAL ENGINEERING DIVISION, THE. [J. Inst. Eng., India, Environ. eng. div.]. **Main/Corp** Institution of Engineers (India). Environmental Engineering Division. Vol. 56, No. 2 (Feb. 1976)-. Periodical. English. Twice a year. Rs60.00 India; $8.00 US. Institution of Engineers India, 8 Gokhale Road, Calcutta 700020 India. **Tel** 011 91 33 288311, telex 21 7885 IEIC IN. **ED** D. K. Ghosh, P. P. Sinha and R. Sridharan. **LC** TD1; .J68. **DD** 620.6254. **NLM** W1 JO931Q. **CODEN** JEEEDS. **Ad Acc. Circ:** 6,000 (ctrl). Documents available from Article Express International. ***Continues*** *Journal of the Institution of Engineers (India). Part PH, 0020-3416.*
Desc: Contains original research papers on environmental engineering subjects.
Ind/Abst Bioeng. Abstr.; Coal Abstr.; Ei Page One; Energy Res. Abstr. (Feb. 1977-); Eng. Index Annu.; GeoRef.

JA
JUMIN KATSUDO. No. 1- 1972-. Periodical. Japanese. ir. ¥250 single issue. Shinseikatsu Undo Kyokai, 1-3 Hibiya Koen Chiyoda-ku, Tokyo Japan. **LC** HC465.E5; J84. ***Supersedes*** *Shinseikatsu Tokushin.*

JA/0910-5158
KAGOSHIMA-KEN KANKYO SENTA SHOHO. [Kagoshima-ken Kankyo Senta shoho]. **Added/Corp** Kagoshima-Ken Kankyo Senta. **VFOAT** Annual Report of Kagoshima Prefectural Institute of Environmental Science. (1985)-. Japanese. an. Kagoshimaken Kankyo Senta, (Kagoshima Prefectural Inst. of Environmental Science), 18, Jonancho, Kagoshimashi, Kagoshimaken 892 Japan. **CODEN** KKSSEO. Documents available from CASDDS.
Ind/Abst Chem. Abstr.

JA/0389-9365
KANAGAWA-KEN KOGAI SENTA KENKYU HOKOKU. (KENKYU HOKOKU / KANAGAWA-KEN KOGAI SENTA.). [Kanagawa-ken Kogai Senta kenkyu hokoku]. **Added/Corp** Kanagawa-Ken Kogai Senta. **VFOAT** Bulletin of Kanagawa Prefectural Environmental Center. (19??)-. Japanese. Kanagawa-ken Kogai Senta, 1-81-1 Futamatagawa, Asahi-ku, Yokohama 241 Japan. **CODEN** KHKSEV. Documents available from CASDDS.
Ind/Abst Chem. Abstr.

JA/0910-0865
KANKYO HENIGEN KENKYU. [Kankyo henigen kenkyu]. **Added/Corp** Nihon Kankyo Henigen Gakkai. **VFOAT** Environmental Mutagen Research Communications. (1978)-. Periodical. Japanese. sa. Nihon Kankyo Henigen Gakkai, (Environmental Mutagen Soc. of Japan), Kokuritsu Idengaku Kenkyujo, 1111, Yata, Mishimashi, Shizuokaken 411 Japan. **NLM** W1; KA46M. **CODEN** KHKEEN. Documents available from CASDDS.
Ind/Abst Chem. Abstr.

JA/0285-5895
KANKYO KAGAKU SOGO KENKYUJO NENPO. [Kankyo Kagaku Sogo Kenkyujo nenpo]. **Added/Corp** Kankyo Kagaku Sogo Kenkyujo (Japan). **VFOAT** Bulletin of the Interdisciplinary Research Institute of Environmental Sciences. (1974)-. Japanese. Kankyo Kagaku Sogo Kenkyujo, (Interdisciplinary Research Inst. of Environmental Science), 540, Higashiyanagicho, Shichihonmatsu Nishi Iru, Itsutsuji Doori, Kamigyoku, Kyotoshi, Kyotofu 602 Japan. **CODEN** KASND6. Documents available from CASDDS.
Ind/Abst Chem. Abstr.

HU
KORNYEZETSTATISZTIKAI ADATGYUJTEMENY. **Main/Corp** Hungary. Kozponti Statisztikai Hivatal Kommunalis es Igazgatasi Szolgaltatasok Statisztikai Osztalaya. Hungarian (English and Russian). bm. 250.00ft. Statisztikai Kiado Vallalat, PO Box 99, H-1033 Budapest 3 Hungary. **Tel** 803-311, telex 22-6699-SKV-H. **LC** TD171.5.H9; H85A. **Circ:** 5,000.
Desc: Covers the quality of the earth, soil, waters, forests, biosphere and air in Hungary, the protection of the environment.

JA/0389-5041
KYOTO-FU EISEI KENKYUJO NENPO. **See** Public Health and Safety.

Environmental Issues

UK/0967-0513
LAND CONTAMINATION & RECLAMATION. [Land contam. reclam.]. **VFOAT** Land Contamination and Reclamation. (1993)-. Periodical. English. qt (4 issues). £35.00 (individuals), £69.00 (organizations) UK; £45.00 (individuals), £79.00 (organizations) other. EPP Publications, 52 Kings Road, Richmond TW10 6RP, United Kingdom. **Tel** 011 44 81 948 7165, FAX 011 44 81 747 9663. **DD** 333.7153.

CN/0710-6920
LAST GASP. (LAST GASP : NEWSLETTER OF THE ENVIRONMENTAL WORKING GROUP.). [Last gasp!]. **VFOAT** Etouffes. No. 1 (May 22, 1981)-. Newsletter. English (French). Free. Environmental Working Group, PO Box 2150 Station B, Place du Portage, Hull Quebec J8X 3Z4 Canada. **DD** 620.8/5/09714221. ctrl circ. **Absorbed** Etouffee, 0710-6939.

US/0740-5820
LATHAM LETTER, THE. [Latham lett.]. **Added/Corp** Latham Foundation. Vol. 1, No. 1 (Fall 1980)-. Periodical. English. qt $12.00 US; $17.00 Canada; $24.00 other. The Latham Foundation, Latham Plaza, Clement and Schiller, Alameda CA 94501. **Tel** (415)521-0920. **ED** Hugh H. Tebault. **Bk Rev**. **Circ**: 2,500.
Desc: Perspectives on humane and related environmental issues.

CN/1188-3022
LET'S TALK GREEN. [Let's talk green]. **Added/Corp** Canada. Environmental Protection Directorate. **VFOAT** Parlons Vert. Vol. 1, No. 1 (Nov. 1991)-. Periodical. English (French). qt. **DD** 363.7/005.

CN/1188-3022
LET'S TALK GREEN. (PARLONS VERT.). [Let's talk green]. **Added/Corp** Canada. Direction Generale de la Protection de l'Environnement. **VFOAT** Let's Talk Green. Vol. 1, No 1 (Nov. 1991)-. Periodical. French (English). qt. **DD** 363.7/005.

CN/0848-8754
LINKS - ENVIRONMENTAL EDUCATORS' PROVINCIAL SPECIALIST ASSOCIATION. (LINKS.). [Links - Environ. Educ. Prov. Spec. Assoc.]. **Added/Corp** Environmental Educators' Provincial Specialist Association. (Sept. 1987)-. Periodical. English. qt. Limited free distribution. Environmental Outdoor Ed Association, 2235 Burrard Street, Vancouver British Columbia V6J 3H9 Canada. **DD** 574.5/071/0711. **Continues** Bare Links., 0827-6730.

●UK
LOCAL ENVIRONMENT JOURNAL, THE. (1994)-. Periodical. English. Three times a year (Feb., Jun., Oct.). £68.00 Europe; £70.00 Other (Institutions). Longman Group Ltd., Fourth Avenue, Longman House, Harlow Essex CM19 5SR England. **Tel** 011 44 279 429655, FAX 011 44 279 431059, telex 81259.

UK/0264-5904
LONDON ENVIRONMENTAL BULLETIN. [Lond. environ. bull.]. (1983)-. English. qt. **DD** 333.7209421.
Ind/Abst Ecol. Abstr.; Geogr. Abstr. Phys. Geogr.; Geogr. Abstr. Human Geogr.

US/0195-1955
LONE STAR SIERRAN. **Added/Corp** Texas Sierra Club. Sierra Club. Lone Star Chapter. Vol. 1 (1966)-. Periodical. English. bm. $5.00. Lone Star Sierran, PO Box 1931, Austin TX 78767. **Tel** (512)477-1729, FAX (512)477-8526. **ED** Jackie McFadden (editor's address: 1104 Nueces Street, Suite 2, Austin, TX 78701; phone: (512)474-5270). **Bk Rev** (Qty: 1). **Ad Acc**. **Circ**: 20,000.
Desc: Information concerning state environmental issues and club announcements, such as outings and meetings, as well as legislative action alerts.

US/1055-257X
LOUISIANA INDUSTRY ENVIRONMENTAL ALERT. [La. Ind. Environ. Alert]. **VFOAT** Environmental Alert. (1985)- Vol. 8 (Jan. 1993)-. Periodical. English. Thirteen times a year. $275.00. Environmental Compliance Reporter, 3154-B College Drive, Suite 522, Baton Rouge LA 70808. **Tel** (504)383-3937. **DD** 363. available on an online database (files 16,636/Full-Text) from DIALOG.
Desc: Articles on environmental issues
Ind/Abst PROMT [Full Txt.]; PTS Newsl. Database [Full Txt.].

NE
LUCHT EN OMGEVING. Dutch. bm. Samson Bedrijfsinformatie, Postbus 4, 2400 HA Alphen Rij Netherlands. **Tel** 011 31 1 72066633.

US/0744-5288
MACKINAC, THE. (THE MACKINAC / MICHIGAN'S SIERRA CLUB CHAPTER.). **Added/Corp** Sierra Club. Mackinac Chapter. (19??)-. Periodical. English. qt (Jan, Apr, July, Oct). $4.00 (non-members); $1.00 (members). Mackinac Sierrra Club Chapter, 115 W Allegan, Suite 10-B, Lansing MI 48933. **Tel** (517)484-2372. **Ad Acc**.

US/0025-0783
MAINE TIMES. See Newspapers.

UK
MANAGING THE ENVIRONMENT. English. an. £295.00; $450.00 US. Business International Ltd, 40 Duke Street, Sales Dept, Helena C, London W1A 1DW England. **Tel** 011 44 71 493 6711.
Desc: This report analyses how companies in Europe are responding to the environmental challenge. The report offers a unique combination of policy analysis and management briefings, illustrated by company case studies. The report draws on the experience and expertise of some of Europe's leading companies, and draws out general lessons (often in checklist form) for the way ahead.

UK
MANUAL OF ENVIRONMENTAL POLICY: THE EC & BRITAIN. (19??)-. Periodical. English. sa. £87.00 Europe; £94.00 Other (Institutions). Longman Group Ltd., Fourth Avenue, Longman House, Harlow Essex CM19 5SR England. **Tel** 011 44 279 429655, FAX 011 44 279 431059, telex 81259.

US/1063-7354
MANUFACTURING AND PROCESS ENGINEERING ABSTRACTS. Ceased. See Environmental Issues-Abstracting, Bibliographies and Statistics.

GR
MAP TECHNICAL REPORTS SERIES / MEDITERRANEAN ACTION PLAN, MED POL, UNITED NATIONS ENVIRONMENT PROGRAMME. **VFOAT** Mediterranean Action Plan Technical Reports Seroes. Monographic series. English (Spanish and French). Price varies per volume.

UK/0141-1136
MARINE ENVIRONMENTAL RESEARCH. [Mar. environ. res.]. Vol. 1, No. 1 (July 1978)-. Academic Scholarly Publication. English. Eight times a year. $604.00 The Americas; £405.00 other. Elsevier Applied Science, An Imprint of Elsevier Science Ltd., The Boulevard, Langford Lane, Kidlington, Oxford OX5 1GB United Kingdom. **Tel** 011 44 865 843000, 011 44 865 843699, FAX 011 44 865 843010. **(Subscription address**: Elsevier Science Ltd. Oxford Fulfillment Centre, PO Box 800, Kidlington, Oxford OX5 1DX United Kingdom.) **ED** G. Roesijadi and R. B. Spies. **LC** QH545.W3; M35. **DD** 574.5/2636/05. **CODEN** MERSDW. **[CCC]**. **Bk Rev**. **Ad Acc**. **Pr Rev**. available on microfilm and microfiche from University Microfilms International (UMI). Documents available from Article Express International, The Genuine Article, BIOSIS Document Express, Petroleum Abstracts Document Delivery Service, CASDDS, Documents on Demand.
Desc: A scientific journal concerned specifically with the natural and man-made influences on a resource which is becoming ever more valuable. Provides a forum for discussion of relevant research on all aspects of the marine environment in the fields of biology, chemistry, oceanography, pollution and particular marine monitoring methods.
Ind/Abst AQUAREF; Aquat. Sci. Fish. Abstr. (Computer File); Bioeng. Abstr.; Biol. Abstr.; Chem. Abstr.; Curr. Aware. Biol. Sci.; CABS; Curr. Contents; Agric. Biol. Environ. Sci.; Curr. Ref. Fish Res.; Ecol. Abstr.; Ecology Abstr.; Ei Page One; EMBASE; Energy Inf. Abstr.; Eng. Index Annu.; Environ. Abstr.; Environ. Period. Bibliogr.; Fish Rev. (19??-199?); Food Sci. Technol. Abstr.; Geogr. Abstr. Phys. Geogr. (?-?); Geogr. Abstr. Human Geogr. (?-?); Geol. Abstr.; GeoRef; Index Vet.; Leadscan; Lit. Pat. Abstr., Oilfield Chem. (1979-); Lit. Abstr., Catal. Catal.; Lit. Abstr., Health Environ.; Lit. Abstr., Pet. Refin. Petrochem.; Lit. Abstr., Pet. Substit.; Lit. Abstr., Transp. Storage; Mar. Sci. Contents Tables; Nematol. Abstr.; Ocean. Abstr.; Oncog. Growth Factors Abstr.; Life Sci. Collect.; Pet. Abstr.; Pollut. Abstr. Indexes; Res. Alert [Full Cov.]; Rev. Agric. Entomol.; Rev. Med. Vet. Entomol.; Risk Abstr.; Sci. Cit. Index; SCISEARCH; Toxicol. Abstr. (19??-).

US
MASSACHUSETTS ENVIRONMANAGEMENT REPORT. English. mo. $295.00 (one year); $553.00 (two year). Massachusetts Environment Report, PO Box 1450, Cambridge MA 02238. **Tel** (617)497-6330, FAX (617)547-6158.

●GW
MATERIALIEN / LANDESUMWELTAMT. See Environmental Issues-Pollution and Waste Management.

UK/0145-5729
MAZINGIRA (EDICION EN ESPANOL). Title Change. (MAZINGIRA.). (1977)-(19??). Periodical. Spanish. qt. Tycooly International Publishing, 6 Crofton Terrace, Dun Laoghaire Dublin Ireland. **Merged into** Ecologist.

UK/0145-5710
MAZINGIRA (EDITION FRANCAISE). Title Change. (MAZINGIRA.). (1977)-(19??). Periodical. French. qt. Tycooly International Publishing, 6 Crofton Terrace, Dun Laoghaire Dublin Ireland. **Merged into** Ecologist.

●GW
MERKBLATTER / LANDESUMWELTAMT. See Environmental Issues-Pollution and Waste Management.

●US/1075-9034
MEXICAN ENVIRONMENTAL BUSINESS. See Business.

US/0747-735X
MICHIGAN ENVIRONMENTAL REPORT:. [Mich. environ. rep.]. **Added/Corp** Michigan Environmental Council. (198?)-. Periodical. English. Six times a year (Feb., Apr., June, Aug., Oct., Dec). $55.00. Michigan Environmental Council, 115 Allegan, Suite 10B, Lansing MI 48933. **Tel** (517)487-9539. **ED** Sharon Riggle. **DD** 333. Index available. cum. index. **Circ**: 500.
Desc: This gives you in-depth coverage on vital and timely environmental issues facing our state.

NE/0927-6513
MICROPOROUS MATERIALS. See Chemistry.

NE
MILIEU. (19??)-. Periodical. Dutch. Six times a year. Fl142.50 (institution) Netherlands; Fl143.50 other. Uitgeverij Boom, Postbus 400, 7940 AK Meppel Netherlands. **Tel** 011 31 20 5220 57012, FAX 011 31 20 5220 54452, telex 42829.

NE/0924-6282
MILIEU MAGAZINE ALPHEN AAN DEN RIJN. Title Change. (MILIEU MAGAZINE.). [Milieu mag. Alphen Rijn]. (1990)-(1994). Periodical. Dutch. mo. Samson HD Tjeenk Willink, Antwoordnummer 10153, 2400 VB Alphen Rijn Netherlands. **Tel** 011 31 1720676223, FAX 31-20-6383871. **(Subscription address**: Samsom H.D. Tjeenk Willink bv, Postbus 4, 2400 AH Alphen aan den Rijn Holland) **ED** Michiel van Kleef. **UDC** 502. **Bk Rev**. **Ad Acc**. **Circ**: 12,000. **Continues** Nieuwe Beta, 0168-1036. **Continued by** Milieustrategie.
Desc: Aims at being the main forum of discussion between government and private sector concerning environmental policy.

NE
MILIEUMARKT. Uitgeverij Johan Janssen BV, Postbus 240, 5060 AE Oisterwijk Netherlands. **Tel** 011 31 4242 16923.

●NE/0929-791X
MILIEUSTRATEGIE ALPHEN AAN DEN RIJN. 1994. (MILIEUSTRATEGIE.). (1994)-. Periodical. Dutch. Twelve times a year. Fl155.66 Netherlands; Fl165.00 Belgium; Fl232.50 other. Samson HD Tjeenk Willink, Antwoordnummer 10153, 2400 VB Alphen Rijn Netherlands. **Tel** 011 31 1720676223, FAX 31-20-6383871. **Continues** Milieu Magazine., 0924-6282.

NO
MILJSTATISTIKK. Main/Corp Norway. Statistisk Sentralbyra. **VFOAT** Environmental Statistics. 1976-. Norwegian (summaries and/or abstracts in English). **LC** HC365; .N596A.

NE
MISSETS MILIEU MAGAZINE. Misset Uitgeverij BV, Postbus 9000, 6800 DA Arnhem Netherlands. **Tel** 011 31 85 209911.

US
MISSOURI'S ENVIRONMENT. V.1- 1975-. Periodical. English. mo. Department of Natural Resources / Missouri, PO Box 176, Jefferson City MO 65102.

UK/0273-2939
MONOGRAPHS IN TOXICOLOGY : ENVIRONMENTAL AND SAFETY ASPECTS. See Medical Science and Technology-Toxicology.

US/1060-488X
MORRISON ENVIRONMENTAL DIRECTORY. See Engineering.

US/0091-3669
MOSQUITO SYSTEMATICS. [Mosq. syst.]. **Added/Corp** American Mosquito Control Association. North Carolina State University. Dept. of Entomology. Vol. 4 (March 1972)-. Periodical. English. Three times a year (Mar., July, Nov.). $25.00 (individuals), $50.00 (institutions). American Mosquito Control Association, PO Box 5416, Lake Charles LA 70606-5416. **Tel** (318)477-2723, FAX (318)439-8615, (318)478-9434. **ED** Lewis T. Neilsen. **LC** QL536; .M695. **DD** 595.7/71. **CODEN** MSQSAK. **[CCC]**. **Bk Rev**. **Ad Acc**. **Pr Rev**. **Circ**: 400. Documents available from BIOSIS Document Express. **Continues** Mosquito Systematics Newsletter,

0091-3677.
Desc: Devoted to the improvement and support of mosquito taxonomy as a vital service to sound mosquito control activities.
Ind/Abst AGRICOLA [Full Cov.]; Biol. Abstr.; Protozoolog. Abstr.; Rev. Med. Vet. Entomol.

US/1058-1332
MUNICIPAL ENVIRONMENTAL JOURNAL. (1991)-. English. qt. $168.00. Executive Enterprises, 22 West 21st Street, New York NY 10010-6990. **Tel** (800)332-8804, FAX (212)645-8689.

●US
NATIONAL ECONOMIC, SOCIAL, & ENVIRONMENTAL DATA BANK [COMPUTER FILE] : NESE DB / U.S. DEPT. OF COMMERCE. **Added/Corp** United States. Dept. of Commerce. United States. Dept. of Commerce. Office of Business Analysis. **VFOAT** National Economic, Social, and Environmental Data Bank; NESE DB; NESEDB. (Apr. 1992)-. Periodical. English. qt. $360.00 US; $720.00 other. National Technical Information Service - NTIS, Room 2027S, 5285 Port Royal Road, Springfield VA 22161. **Tel** (703)487-4630, (703)487-4660, (703)487-4650, FAX (703)321-8547, telex 89-9405. **LC** HC101.

US/1067-2583
NATIONAL ENVIRONMENTAL JOURNAL, THE. (THE NATIONAL ENVIRONMENTAL JOURNAL : TNEJ.). [Natl. environ. j.]. **VFOAT** TNEJ. Vol. 1, No. 1, (Jan./Feb. 1991)-. Periodical. English. bm. Free to qualified subscribers; $38.00 US; $45.00 Canada and Mexico; $90.00 (airmail) other. Campbell Publishing Inc., 5636 Whiteville Road, Suite A2, Columbus GA 31904. **Tel** (706)324-6746, FAX (706)324-1177. **ED** Paul Cheremisinoff. **DD** 333. **Ad Acc, Adv Mgr:** C.B. Campbell. **Pr Rev. Circ:** 90,000 (ctrl). Documents available from Documents on Demand.
Ind/Abst Environ. Abstr.

US/1054-3287
NATIONAL ENVIRONMENTAL SCORECARD, THE. (THE ... NATIONAL ENVIRONMENTAL SCORECARD / LEAGUE OF CONSERVATION VOTERS.). [Natl. environ. scorec.]. **Added/Corp** League of Conservation Voters. (198?)-. English. an. Free to colleges & students; $6.00 others. League of Conservation Voters, 1707 L Street Northwest, Suite 550, Washington DC 20036. **Tel** (202)785-8683. **LC** HC110.E5; N356. **DD** 333.7/0973/05.
Desc: Rates members of Congress on environmental voting records.

CN/1188-0945
NATIONAL ROUND TABLE REVIEW. (LA REVUE DE LA TABLE RONDE NATIONALE.). [Natl. round table rev.]. **Main/Corp** Table Ronde Nationale Sur l'Environnement et l'Economie (Canada). **VFOAT** The National Round Table Review. (Summer 1991)-. Periodical. French (English). qt. **DD** 333.7.

AU/0028-0607
NATUR UND LAND. [Nat. Land]. Periodical. German. bm. S150.00 Austria; $15.00 US; S180.00 other. Osterreichischer Naturschutzbund, PO Box 910, A-6040 Innsbruck Austria. Index available. **Bk Rev. Ad Acc. Circ:** 3,000.
Desc: Nature protection, environmental protection and ecology.

IT
NATURA E MONTAGNA. **See** Earth Sciences.

NE/0921-030X
NATURAL HAZARDS (DORDRECHT). (NATURAL HAZARDS.). [Nat. hazards]. **Added/Corp** International Society for the Prevention and Mitigation of Natural Hazards. Vol. 1, No. 1 (1988)-. Periodical. English. bm. $598.00. Kluwer Academic Publishers, Postbus 322, 3300 AH Dordrecht, The Netherlands. **Tel** 011 (31) 78 524400, FAX 011 31 78 183273, telex 20083. **ED** M.I. El-Sabh, G. Schneider, and Y. Tsuchiya. **LC** GB5000; .N39. **DD** 363.3/4. **CODEN** NAHZEL. **[CCC]. Pr Rev.** available on microfilm and microfiche from University Microfilms International (UMI). Documents available from Ask*IEEE.
Desc: Devoted to original research work on the physical aspects of the natural hazards, the statistics of forecasting catastrophic events, risk assessment, and the nature of precursors of natural and/or technological hazards. Hazards of interest to the journal are included in the following sections: general, atmospheric, climatological, oceanographic, storm surges, tsunamis, floods, snow, avalanches, landslides, erosion, earthquakes, volcanoes, man-made, technological, and risk assessment.
Ind/Abst Abstr. J. Earthq. Eng.; Curr. Aware. Biol. Sci., CABS; Ecol. Abstr. (1988-?); Geogr. Abstr. Phys. Geogr.; Geogr. Abstr. Human Geogr.; Geol. Abstr. (1988-); GeoRef; INSPEC (1988-); Int. Dev. Abstr.; J. Plan. Lit.; Risk Abstr. (1988-).

FR
NATURE AND ENVIRONMENT SERIES. No. 1 (1968)-. Monographic series. English. ir. Price varies per volume. Council of Europe / Group Pact ED, Pharmacopoeia BP 907, 67029 Strasbourg Cedex 01 France. **Tel** 011 33 88 412036, FAX 011 33 88 41277181, telex 880388. **(Subscription address:** Manhattan Publishing Company, PO Box 650, Croton-on-Hudson NY 10520**)**
Ind/Abst For. Abstr.; Rev. Agric. Entomol.; Soils Fert.

FR
NATURELLEMENT : JOURNAL DU MOUVEMENT NATIONAL DE LUTTE POUR L'ENVIRONNEMENT. French. Five times a year. 65.00F. Mouvement National de Lutte pour l'Environnement, BP 79, 93505 Pantin Cedex France. **Tel** 011 33 1 48460414.
Desc: Speaks about the great questions raised by international environmental reports on the different actions of the organizations affiliated with the MNLE in France.

NE/0925-1049
NEDERLANDSE MILIEULITERATUUR. [Ned. milieulit.]. (1990)-. Periodical. Dutch. bm. Fl348.00. Koninklijke Vermande, Postbus 20, 8200 AA Lelystad Netherlands. **Tel** 011 31 3200 22944. **UDC** 504.

US/8756-0356
NEHW HEALTH WATCH. **See** Medical Science and Technology-Nursing.

US/0198-8476
NEW ENGLAND ENVIRONMENTAL NETWORK NEWS. ***Title Change.*** (NEW ENGLAND ENVIRONMENTAL NETWORK NEWS / LINCOLN FILENE CENTER FOR CITIZENSHIP AND PUBLIC AFFAIRS.). [New Engl. environ. netw. news]. **Added/Corp** Lincoln Filene Center for Citizenship and Public Affairs. New England Environmental Network. (1979)-Vol. 11, No. 1 (Winter 1992). Periodical. English. qt. New England Environmental Network, Lincoln Filene Center, Turts University, Medford MA 02155. **Tel** (617)381-3451, FAX (617)381-3401. **ED** Nancy Anderson. **Bk Rev. Circ:** 4,000. ***Continued by*** *Environmental News (Medford, Mass.).*
Desc: Environmental news emphasizing action that can be taken by individuals, groups, agencies, and businesses.

SA/1016-9075
NEW GROUND. **Added/Corp** Environmental and Development Agency (South Africa). Vol. 1, No. 1 (Sept. 1990)-. Periodical. English. Four times a year. R13.50 Africa. EDA Publishing, PO Box 322, Newtown 2113 South Africa. **Tel** 011 27 11 8341905, FAX 011 27 11 8360188. **ED** Dick Doete. **LC** IN PROCESS. cum. index. **Bk Rev. Ad Acc, Adv Mgr:** L. De Bruyn. **Circ:** 5,500.

US
NEW HAMPSHIRE ENVIRONMENTAL MONITOR. (19??)-. English. Twelve times a year. $94.00. Putney Press, PO Box 935, Brattleboro VT 05302. **Tel** (802)257-7505, FAX (802)254-7630. ***Continues*** *New Hampshire Monitor.*

US/1055-2588
NEW JERSEY INDUSTRY ENVIRONMENTAL ALERT. [N. J. Ind. Environ. Alert]. **VFOAT** Environmental Alert. (1990)- Vol. 6 (Aug. 1992)-. Periodical. English. Twenty-two times a year. $295.00. Environmental Compliance Reporter, 3154-B College Drive, Suite 522, Baton Rouge LA 70808. **Tel** (504)383-3937. **DD** 363. available on an online database (files 16,636/Full-Text) from DIALOG.
Desc: Included all articles on issues. It also includes the "Environmental Register."
Ind/Abst PROMT [Full Txt.]; PTS Newsl. Database [Full Txt.].

US/0273-6438
NEW YORK ENVIRONMENTAL NEWS : NYEN. [New York environ. news]. **Added/Corp** State University of New York. Institute on the Environment. State University of New York. Atmospheric Sciences Research Center. **VFOAT** NYEN. (1974)-. Periodical. English. sm (except Aug.). Free. NYEN New York Environmental News, Atmospheric Sciences Research Center Suny-Albany, Albany NY 12222. **LC** TD171.3.N5; N9. **DD** 363.7/009747.

US/0048-0053
NEW YORK STATE ENVIRONMENT. ***Suspended.*** [N.Y. State environ.]. **VFOAT** NYS Environment. Vol. 1 (July 1971)-(19??). Periodical. English. ir. Free. Department of Environmental Conservation / New York, 50 Wolf Road, Room 604, Albany NY 12233. **Tel** (518)457-2344, FAX (518)457-6996. **ED** Mary Kadlecek. **Circ:** 45,000.
Desc: Descriptions and discussions of ongoing programs for New York's natural resources, focusing on water, air, solid, and hazardous waste, fish and wildlife, lands and forests enforcement.

NZ/0112-0212
NEW ZEALAND JOURNAL OF ENVIRONMENTAL HEALTH. **See** Public Health and Safety.

US/1052-2239
NEWS OF THE EARTH. (NEWS OF THE EARTH [COMPUTER FILE].). [News earth]. (1990)-. Periodical. English. da. Free. John B. Harlan, PO Box 693, South Bend IN 46624-0693. **DD** 909. ***Formed by the union of*** *JBH News, 1048-7999* ***and*** *JBH Online, 0896-8241.*
Desc: Available from BITNET/CSNet and INTERNET.

UK/0960-9199
NEWSHEET - COUNCIL FOR ENVIRONMENTAL EDUCATION. (NEWSHEET.). [Newsh. - Counc. Environ. Educ.]. (1974)-. Newsletter. English. Ten times a year. £8.00. Council for Environmental Education, University of Reading, London Road, Reading RG1 5AQ England. **Tel** 0734 756061, FAX 0734 756264. **ED** Fiona Bradley. **Bk Rev**, (Qty: 150). **Circ:** 18,000.
Desc: Notices of new publications and reports of developments in environmental education.

UK/0264-5807
NEWSLETTER OF THE SOCIETY FOR ENVIRONMENTAL THERAPY. [Newsl. Soc. Environ. Ther.]. Began with: Vol. 1, No. 1 (Sept. 1981). Newsletter. English. qt. **NLM** W1; NE998WK.

NE/0924-4301
NIEUWSBRIEF MILIEUTECHNOLOGIE. [Nieuwsbr. milieutechnol.]. (1989)-. Periodical. Dutch. Twenty times a year. Fl295.00. Stichting Nationaal Milieucent, Zaagmolenlaan 4 Postbus 217, 3440 AE Woerden Netherlands. **Tel** 011 31 3480 32900. **UDC** 504 :66/68.

JA/0389-0805
NIHON KANKYO EISEI SENTA SHOHO. [Nihon Kankyo Eisei Senta shoho]. **Added/Corp** Nihon Kankyo Eisei Senta. **VFOAT** Bulletin of Japan Environmental Sanitation Center. (1973)-. Academic Scholarly Publication. Japanese. **CODEN** NKESDK. Documents available from CASDDS.
Ind/Abst Chem. Abstr.

JA/0286-438X
NINGEN TO KANKYO. [Ningen to kankyo]. **Added/Corp** Kankyo Kagaku Sogo Kenkyukai (Japan). **VFOAT** Man and Environment. (1974)-. Academic Scholarly Publication. Japanese. sa. Nihon Kankyo Gakkai, (Japan Assoc. on the Environmental Studies), Tokyo Noko Daigaku Nogakubu, 5-8, Saiwaicho 3 Chome, Fuchushi, Tokyoto 183, Japan. **CODEN** NKANDJ. Documents available from CASDDS.
Ind/Abst Chem. Abstr.

UK/0957-4565
NOISE & VIBRATION WORLDWIDE. [Noise vib. worldw.]. **VFOAT** Noise and Vibration Worldwide. Vol. 20 No. 10 (Nov. 1989)-. Periodical. English. Eleven times a year (1 volume). $176.00. IOP Publishing Limited, Unit 1 & 2, Audie House 260 Field End Road, Ruislip Middlesex HA4 9LG England. **Tel** 011 44 81 8684499. **LC** TD891; .N65. **DD** 620.2. **CODEN** NVWOE6. **[CCC].** available on microfilm and microfiche from University Microfilms International (UMI). Documents available from Article Express International, Ask*IEEE. ***Continues*** *Noise & Vibration Control Worldwide, 0143-6481.*
Desc: Devoted to the engineering discipline of noise control and vibration reduction. Deals with cause and effects, measurement, desirable levels, methods of control at source, confinement, insulation, and international law.
Ind/Abst Ei Page One; Eng. Index Annu. [Select. Cov.]; Fluid Abstr., Civil Eng.; Fluid Abstr. Proc. Eng.; FLUIDEX (19??-); INSPEC (Nov. 1989-); Leadscan; Pollut. Abstr. Indexes; Shock Vibr. Dig.

US/0736-2935
NOISE-CON PROCEEDINGS. (NOISE-CON PROCEEDINGS / NATIONAL CONFERENCE ON NOISE CONTROL ENGINEERING.). [NOISE-CON proc.]. **Main/Conf** National Conference on Noise Control Engineering. **Added/Corp** Institute of Noise Control Engineering. United States. National Bureau of Standards. North Carolina State University. Center for Acoustical Studies. Massachusetts Institute of Technology. Dept. of Mechanical Engineering. Massachusetts Institute of Technology. Dept. of Aeronautics and Astronautics. **VFOAT** Noise CON Proceedings; Proceedings of Noise-CON. (1973)-. Proceedings. English. be. $95.00 US; $120.00 others. Institute of Noise Control Engineering, PO Box 3206, Arlington Branch, Poughkeepsie NY 12603. **Tel** (914)462-4006. **(Subscription address:** Noise Control Foundation, PO Box 2469, Arlington Branch, Poughkeepsie NY 12603.**) LC** TD891; .N34a. **DD** 620.2/3/05. Documents available from Article Express International.
Ind/Abst Acoust. Abstr.; Bioeng. Abstr.; Ei Page One; Eng. Index Annu.

US/0736-2501
NOISE CONTROL ENGINEERING JOURNAL. [Noise control eng. j.]. **Added/Corp** Institute of Noise Control Engineering. Acoustical Society of America. Vol. 19, No. 2 (Sept./Oct. 1982)-. Academic Scholarly Publication. English. Six times a year (Jan.,

Mar., May, July, Sept., Nov.). $60.00. Institute of Noise Control Engineering, PO Box 3206, Arlington Branch, Poughkeepsie NY 12603. **Tel** (914)462-4006. **ED** M. Crocker. **LC** TD891; .N655. **DD** 620.2/3/05. **CODEN** NCEJD5. **[CCC]. Bk Rev. Ad Acc. Pr Rev. Circ:** 2,500. available on microfilm from University Microfilms International (UMI). Documents available from Article Express International, The Genuine Article, Ask*IEEE, Documents on Demand. ***Continues*** *Noise Control Engineering, 0093-9978.*
Desc: Technical articles on noise control, including aircraft noise, surface transportation noise and industrial noise control.
Ind/Abst Acoust. Abstr. (1983-); Appl. Sci. Technol. Index; BMT Abstr. (-19??); Curr. Contents Eng. Tech. Appl. Sci.; Ei Page One; EMBASE; Eng. Index Annu.; Environ. Abstr.; Fluid Abstr., Civil Eng.; Fluid Abstr. Proc. Eng.; FLUIDEX; Health Saf. Sci. Abstr.; INSPEC (Nov./Dec. 1982-); Int. Aerosp. Abstr.; Pollut. Abstr. Indexes; Res. Alert [Select. Cov.]; SCISEARCH; Shock Vibr. Dig.; Soc. Sci. Cit. Index [Select. Cov.].

US/0146-4809
NOISE NEWS. ***Title Change.*** **Added/Corp** Institute of Noise Control Engineering. Noise Control Foundation. Acoustical Society of America. (1971)-(199?). Periodical. English. bm. Institute of Noise Control Engineering, PO Box 3206, Arlington Branch, Poughkeepsie NY 12603. **Tel** (914)462-4006. **ED** G Maling. **Bk Rev. Circ:** 1,500. ***Merged with*** *Newsletter of the International Institute of Noise Control Engineering* ***to form*** *Noise News, 0146-4809.*
Desc: Information on technical meetings, government reports, book reviews and other news items.

US/0733-172X
NOISE POLLUTION PUBLICATIONS ABSTRACTS. [Noise pollut. publ. abstr.]. Vol. 1, No. 1 (Jan. 1981)-. Periodical. English. mo. $150.00. Noise Pollution Publication Abstracts, 12614 East Park Street, Cerritos CA 90701. **Tel** (310)926-3955. **ED** Richard L King. cum. index. **Bk Rev. Ad Acc.** ctrl circ.
Desc: Abstracts of world's English language literature about all aspects of noise pollution.

US/1043-5565
NOISE REGULATION REPORT. [Noise regul. rep.]. Vol. 15, No. 10 (Oct. 7, 1988)-. Periodical. English. bw (26 issues). $455.00. Business Publishers Inc., 951 Pershing Drive, Silver Spring MD 20910-4464. **Tel** (301)587-6300, (800)274-0122, FAX (301)585-9075. **LC** KF3813.A73; B87. **DD** 344.73/04638/05; 347.304463805. **[CCC].** ***Formed by the union of*** *Noise Regulation Reporter, 0148-7957* ***and*** *Noise Control Report, 0146-4817.*
Desc: Tight enforcement is just one of the many issues facing noise control professionals today. Whether you're one of the regulators or one of the regulated, there's too much happening to rely on just the newspaper. Each issue provides you with vital information.

US/0749-7962
NORTHWEST ENVIRONMENTAL JOURNAL, THE. ***Title Change.*** (THE NORTHWEST ENVIRONMENTAL JOURNAL / INSTITUTE FOR ENVIRONMENTAL STUDIES, UNIVERSITY OF WASHINGTON.). [Northwest environ. j.]. **Added/Corp** University of Washington. Institute for Environmental Studies. Vol. 1, No. 1 (Autumn 1984)-(1993). Periodical. English. Four times a year. Institute for Environmental Studies, University of Washington, Seattle WA 98195. **Tel** (206)543-2100. **ED** Dr. James Karr and Ellen Chu. **LC** TD181.N93; N67. **DD** 363.7/009795. **CODEN** NENJEV. Index available. cum. index. **Bk Rev. Ad Acc, Adv Mgr:** Ellen Chu, **Tel** (206)543-1812. **Pr Rev. Circ:** 500. Documents available from The Genuine Article, BIOSIS Document Express. ***Continued by*** *Illahee, 1073-0478.*
Desc: Contains research and policy analyses about the environmental problems and challenges facing Northwestern America:
Ind/Abst Biocont. News Inf. (?-?); Biol. Abstr. (1986-); Curr. Aware. Biol. Sci., CABS (?-?); Curr. Contents, Agric. Biol. Environ. Sci. (?-?); Ecol. Abstr. (?-?); Environ. Period. Bibliogr. (?-?); For. Abstr. (?-?); Geogr. Abstr. Human Geogr. (?-?); Res. Alert (?-?) [Select. Cov.]; Rev. Agric. Entomol. (?-?); SCISEARCH (?-?).

UK/0140-6787
NSCA MEMBERS' HANDBOOK. [NSCA memb. handb.]. **Main/Corp** National Society for Clean Air. **Added/Corp** National Society for Clean Air. Members' Handbook. **VAT** National Society for Clean Air Members' Handbook. (1977/1978)-. English. an. £7.60. National Society for Clean Air, 136 North Street, Brighton East Sussex BN1 1RG England. **Tel** 011 44 273 326313. **ED** Loveday Murley. **NLM** W1 NA735K. **Ad Acc. Circ:** 2,000. ***Continues in part*** *Year Book - National Society for Clean Air.*
Desc: Guide to the society, smoke control areas, trade directory and buyers' guide, consultants films, and directories of organizations in Great Britain and overseas.

UK/0144-7785
NVB. NOISE & VIBRATION BULLETIN. [NVB, Noise vib. bull.]. **VFOAT** Noise & Vibration Bulletin. **VAT** NVB. Noise and Vibration Bulletin. (Jan. 1971)-. Periodical. English. mo. £99.00 UK and Europe; £105.00 (add £15.00 airmail) other. Multi Science Publishing Company Ltd., 107 High Street, Brentwood, Essex CM14 4RX England. **Tel** 011 44 277 224632, FAX 011 44 277 223453, telex 89-8452. **NLM** ZWD 735 N107. **Bk Rev. Ad Acc.** ***Supersedes*** *Noise & Vibration Bulletin.*
Desc: Reports on all aspects of this wide-ranging topic. Carries at least one major piece of research as a full length paper, plus summaries of many recently published papers from the world's periodical literature, conference reports, plus items from the lay and technical press, and more.

US/1070-7336
NYCAP NEWS. (NYCAP NEWS / NEW YORK COALITION FOR ALTERNATIVES TO PESTICIDES.). [NYCAP news]. **Added/Corp** New York Coalition for Alternatives to Pesticides. **VFOAT** New York Coalition for Alternatives to Pesticides News. Vol. 1, No. 2 (Winter 1990)-. Periodical. English. Four times a year. $15.00 (individuals), $25.00 (institutions organizations & professional), $50.00 (business) Comes with New York Coalition for Alternatives to Pesticides membership. New York Coalition for Alternatives to Pesticides, 33 Central Avenue, Albany NY 12210. **Tel** (518)426-8246. **ED** Tracy Frisch. **DD** 363. **Bk Rev. Circ:** 6,500. ***Continues*** *NYCAP Newsletter.*
Desc: News and information on pesticides, environment and occupational health.

AT/1034-1412
OCCASIONAL PAPER - CENTRE FOR ENVIRONMENTAL STUDIES, UNIVERSITY OF TASMANIA. (OCCASIONAL PAPER.). [Occas. pap. - Cent. Environ. Stud. Univ. Tasman.]. (1989)-. Monographic series. English. ir. Price varies per volume. **DD** 333.709946. ***Continues*** *Environmental Studies Occasional Paper (Hobart. 1981), 0810-4395.*
Ind/Abst AESIS Q.

CN/0317-8641
OCCASIONAL PAPER - FACULTY OF ENVIRONMENTAL STUDIES. UNIVERSITY OF WATERLOO. (OCCASIONAL PAPER - UNIVERSITY OF WATERLOO, FACULTY OF ENVIRONMENTAL STUDIES.). **Main/Corp** University of Waterloo. Faculty of Environmental Studies. No. 4- Nov. 1972-. Monographic series. English. Price varies per volume. University of Waterloo Faculty of Environmental Studies, Waterloo Ontario N2L 3G1 Canada. **DD** 301.31. **CODEN** WEOPAD. Documents available from BIOSIS Document Express. ***Continues*** *University of Waterloo. Division of Environmental Studies. Occasional Paper, 0317-8633.*
Ind/Abst Biol. Abstr.

SA
OCCASIONAL PAPER - JOHANNESBURG. UNIVERSITY OF THE WITWATERSRAND. DEPT. OF GEOGRAPHY AND ENVIRONMENTAL STUDIES. **Main/Corp** Johannesburg. University of the Witwatersrand. Dept. of Geography and Environmental Studies. **VFOAT** Environmental Studies. No. 1-. Monographic series. English. Price varies per volume. **CODEN** PWGEDQ.
Ind/Abst GeoRef.

UK/0957-0985
OCCASIONAL PAPER / WYE COLLEGE, UNIVERSITY OF LONDON, DEPARTMENT OF AGRICULTURE, HORTICULTURE AND THE ENVIRONMENT. **See** Agriculture.

GW
OEKO TEST. **See** Consumer Interests.

US
OFFICE OF AIR AND WATER PROGRAMS PUBLICATION. **Main/Corp** United States. Environmental Protection Agency. Office of Air and Water Programs. English. National Technical Information Service - NTIS, Room 2027S, 5285 Port Royal Road, Springfield VA 22161. **Tel** (703)487-4630, (703)487-4660, (703)487-4650, FAX (703)321-8547, telex 89-9405. **LC** TD883.2; .A33. **DD** 363.6. ***Continues*** *Publication APTD.*

US
OFFICE OF ENVIRONMENT STATEMENT OF PROGRAMS. **Main/Corp** United States. Dept. of Energy. Office of the Assistant Secretary for Environment. 1978/79-. Government Publication. English. an. US Department of Energy, 1000 Independence Avenue SW, Washington DC 20585. **Tel** (202)586-5000, FAX (202)586-4073.

US/1054-8718
OH! ZONE. ***Ceased.*** [Oh! zone]. **Added/Corp** Marquette Institute for the Environment. **VFOAT** Ozone. Vol. 1, No. 1 (Feb. 1991)-(199?). Periodical. English. mo. Marquette Institute for the Environment, 420 East Hewitt Drive, Marquette MI 49855-3714. **DD** 363.
Desc: For ages 12-adult. For youth of art, news, and opinion. Non-commercial, non-profit, not politically motivated.

US
OHIO INDUSTRY ENVIRONMENTAL ADVISOR. English. Twenty-two times a year. $295.00. Environmental Compliance Reporter, 3154-B College Drive, Suite 522, Baton Rouge LA 70808. **Tel** (504)383-3937. available on an online database (files 16,636/Full-Text) from DIALOG.

JA/0285-5801
OSAKA SHIRITSU KANKYO KAGAKY KENKYUJO HOKOKU. CHOSA KENKYU NENPO. **See** Public Health and Safety.

US
OUR EARTH. **See** Encyclopedias and General Reference Books.

JA/0917-8260
OZONEWS IN JAPAN. [Ozonews Jpn.]. (1991)-. Periodical. Japanese. qt. Nihon Ozon Kyokai, Japan Ozone Association, Zosu Sokushin Senta 3-4, Akasaka 2-chome, Minato-ku Tokyo 107 Japan.

CN/0840-8114
PATHWAYS (HAMILTON). (PATHWAYS : THE ONTARIO JOURNAL OF OUTDOOR EDUCATION.). [Pathways]. **Added/Corp** Council of Outdoor Educators of Ontario. Vol. 1, No. 1 Jan. (1989)-. Periodical. English. Six times a year. 38.00Can$. Council of Outdoor Educators of Ontario, 1220 Sheppard Aveune East, Willowdale, Ontario M2K 2X1 Canada. **Tel** (416)495-4264, FAX (416)495-4310. **ED** Bob Henderson. **DD** 371.3/8. **Bk Rev**, (Qty: 6). **Ad Acc. Circ:** 600. ***Continues*** *Anee, 0711-351X.*

US
PATHWAYS TO OUTDOOR COMMUNICATION : OFFICIAL PUBLICATION OF THE NEW YORK STATE OUTDOOR EDUCATION ASSOCIATION. **Added/Corp** New York State Outdoor Education Association. Vol. 1, No. 1 (Fall 1991)-. Periodical. English. sa. NYSOEA Pathways, c/o Pocono Envrionmental Educational Center, Road 2, Box 1010, Dingmass Ferry PA 18328. ***Formed by the union of*** *Outdoor Communicator* ***and*** *Outdoor Path.*
Ind/Abst Curr. Index J. Educ.

CN/1181-9391
PEACE AND ENVIRONMENT NEWS. (PEACE AND ENVIRONMENT NEWS / OTTAWA PEACE AND ENVIRONMENT RESOURCE CENTRE.). [Peace environ. news]. **Added/Corp** Ottawa Peace and Environment Resource Centre. Vol. 5, No. 9 (Nov. 1990)-. Periodical. English. mo. Limited free distribution. Ottawa Peace and Environment Resource Centre, PO Box 4075, Station E, Ottawa, Ontario K1S 5B1 Canada. **DD** 327.1/72/05. ***Continues*** *Ottawa Peace Calendar, Peace and Environment News., 1184-6011.*

US
PENNSYLVANIA INDUSTRY ENVIRONMENTAL ADVISOR. Vol. 2 (Apr. 1992)-. English. Twelve times a year. $255.00. Environmental Compliance Reporter, 3154-B College Drive, Suite 522, Baton Rouge LA 70808. **Tel** (504)383-3937. available on an online database (files 16,636/Full-Text) from DIALOG.

CN/1189-0347
PEOPLE OF ACTION. (PEOPLE OF ACTION : ENVIRONMENTAL PARTNERS FUND BULLETIN.). [People action]. **Main/Corp** Environmental Partners Fund (Canada). **VFOAT** Gens d'Action. Vol. 1, No. 1 (Sept. 1991)-. Bulletin. English (French). **DD** 333.7.

UK
PERSPECTIVES : INTERNATIONAL INSTITUTE FOR ENVIRONMENT & DEVELOPMENT. English. Free. International Institute for Environment and Development, #13 Endsleigh Street, London WC1 H ODD England. **Tel** 011 44 71 3882117.

UK/0967-6597
PESTICIDES NEWS. [Pestic. news]. (1988)-. Periodical. English. qt. £65.00 (Corporate), £32.00 (non-profit), £15.00 (student, low income individuals). Pesticides Trust, Eurolink Centre, 49 Effra Road, London SW2 1BZ England. **Tel** 011 44 71 2748895, FAX 11 44 71 2749084. **DD** 632.9505.

US/1056-7399
PHLI ENVIRONMENTAL LIFE LETTER, THE. [PHLI environ. life lett.]. **Added/Corp** Parsons Holder Lifestyle Institute. **VFOAT** Environmental Life Letter. **VAT** Parsons Holder Lifestyle Institute Environmental Life Letter. No. 1 (Summer 1991)-. Periodical. English. qt. $11.00. Barry G Parsons and Judy Holder, PO Box 10979, Daytona Beach FL 32120. **DD** 333.

Environmental Issues

CN/1183-6040
PLANET TODAY. (THE PLANET TODAY.). [Planet today]. Vol. 1, No. 31 (Jan. 1990)-. Periodical. English. mo. 18.00Can$ Canada; 21.40Can$ other. Sinclair Stevens, Suite 15, 250 Harry Walker Parkway, Newmarket Ontario L3Y 8E2 Canada. **Tel** (416)727-2300, FAX (416)853-3754. **DD** 333.7/2/.05. **ED** Luane Macrae. **Bk Rev**. **Ad Acc**. **Circ:** 285,000. available on diskette. *Continues The Planet This Week., 0847-8023.*

FR
POLLUTION DE L'EAU DE L'AIR ET DU SOL DECHETS BRUIT, E36. See Environmental Issues-Pollution and Waste Management.

●US/1056-1102
PRACTICAL ENVIRONMENTAL REGULATION. (1993)-. Periodical. English. qt. $110.00. Executive Enterprises, 22 West 21st Street, New York NY 10010-6990. **Tel** (800)332-8804, FAX (212)645-8689.

CN/0317-6282
PRAIRIE FORUM. See History(General)-History of North, South, and Central America.

US/1052-6102
PROCEEDINGS / A & WMA ANNUAL MEETING. [Proc. - Air Waste Manage. Assoc., Meet.]. **Main/Corp** Air & Waste Management Association. Meeting. (June 25-30, 1989)-. Academic Scholarly Publication. English. an. $1800.00 (non-members); $1200.00 (members). Air & Waste Management Association, PO Box 2861, Pittsburgh PA 15230. **Tel** (412)232-3444. **LC** RA565.A2; 457a. **DD** 615.9/02. **CODEN** PAMEE5. Documents available from CASDDS. *Continues APCA (Association : U.S.). Meeting. Proceedings, 1052-8598.*
Ind/Abst Chem. Abstr. (1989).

US/0090-0729
PROCEEDINGS / INSTITUTE OF ENVIRONMENTAL SCIENCES. See Engineering.

US/0078-1703
PROCEEDINGS OF THE ... ANNUAL MEETING OF THE NORTHEASTERN WEED SCIENCE SOCIETY. [Proc. annu. meet. Northeast. Weed Sci. Soc.]. **Main/Corp** Northeastern Weed Science Society (U.S.). Meeting. **VFOAT** Proceedings of the Northeastern Weed Science Society. 25th (1971)-. Academic Scholarly Publication. English. an. $25.00 US and Canada; $30.00 others. Northeastern Weed Science Society, PO Box 4, Geneva NY 14456. **DD** 632. **CODEN** PNWSBF. Documents available from BIOSIS Document Express, CASDDS. *Continues Proceedings of the ... Annual Meeting, 0096-7068.*
Ind/Abst AGRICOLA [Select. Cov.]; Biol. Abstr.; Chem. Abstr.; PESTDOC (-1988).

US
PROCEEDINGS OF THE SECTION ON STATISTICS AND THE ENVIRONMENT / AMERICAN STATISTICAL ASSOCIATION. **Main/Corp** American Statistical Association. Section on Statistics and the Environment. (1991)-. Statistical Publication. English. $41.00. American Statistical Association, 1429 Duke Street, Alexandria VA 22314. **Tel** (703)684-1221, (202)393-3253, FAX (703)684-2037 (orders). **LC** TD169; .A443.
Ind/Abst Curr. Index Stat. (199?-).

●US/1066-3711
PROCEEDINGS OF THE THEMATIC CONFERENCE ON REMOTE SENSING FOR MARINE AND COASTAL ENVIRONMENTS. (PROCEEDINGS OF THE ... THEMATIC CONFERENCE ON REMOTE SENSING FOR MARINE AND COASTAL ENVIRONMENTS.). [Proc. Themat. Conf. Remote Sens. Mar. Coast. Environ.]. **Added/Corp** Environmental Research Institute of Michigan. (1993)-. Proceedings. English. be. $125.00. Environmental Research Institute of Michigan, PO Box 134001, Ann Arbor MI 48103. **LC** GC10.4.R4; T46. **DD** 621.

UK/0957-5820
PROCESS SAFETY AND ENVIRONMENTAL PROTECTION. (PROCESS SAFETY AND ENVIRONMENTAL PROTECTION : TRANSACTIONS OF THE INSTITUTIONS OF CHEMICAL ENGINEERS, PART B.). [Process saf. environ prot.]. **Added/Corp** Institution of Chemical Engineers (Great Britain). **VFOAT** Transactions of the Institution of Chemical Engineers, Part B. Vol. 68, No. B1 (Feb. 1990)-. Academic Scholarly Publication. English. qt. £149.00 UK; $2494.00 other; £499.00 UK, $847.00 other (combined subscription to all 4 titles to journals of "The Institution of Chemical Engineers."). Taylor & Francis Ltd., Rankine Road, Basingstoke Hampshire, RG24 8PR United Kingdom. **Tel** 011 44 256 840366, FAX 011 44 256 479438, telex 858540. **(Subscription address:** Taylor & Francis Inc., 1900 Frost Road, Suite 101, Bristol PA 19007-1598.) **ED** G. F. Hewitt, R. C. Clayton, M. L. Brown, R. F. Griffiths and S. M. Richardson. **LC** TP149; .P72. **DD** 660/.2804. **CODEN** PSEPEM. **[CCC]**. available on microfilm and microfiche from University Microfilms International (UMI). Documents available from Article Express International, The Genuine Article, CASDDS.
Desc: A learned journal in the increasingly significant safety and environmental fields. Focuses on research, development and practical engineering solutions to topical problems. Topics covered include clean process and minimum waste technology, solid waste management, water and waste water treatment, air pollution, atmospheric dispersion, safety, industrial hygiene, dust explosions, hazardous reactions, hazard and risk analysis and noise.
Ind/Abst Chem. Abstr.; Curr. Contents Eng. Tech. Appl. Sci.; Eng. Index Annu.; Fluid Abstr., Civil Eng.; Fluid Abstr. Proc. Eng.; FLUIDEX (19??-); Res. Alert [Select. Cov.]; Soc. Sci. Cit. Index [Select. Cov.].

UK/0309-1333
PROGRESS IN PHYSICAL GEOGRAPHY. See Geography.

US
PROTECT. English. bm. $50.00. Tennessee Environmental Council, 1700 Hayes Street, Suite 101, Nashville TN 37203-2921. *Continues Tennessee Environmental Report.*

CN/1188-0368
PROVING GROUND : ENVIRONMENTAL RESEARCH & TECHNOLOGY DEVELOPMENT, THE. See Science and Technology.

AT/0159-8430
PUBLICATION - ENVIRONMENT PROTECTION AUTHORITY OF VICTORIA. [Publ. - Environ. Prot. Auth. Vic.]. (1980)-. English. ir. **DD** 333.7209945. *Continues Report - Environment Protection Authority (Melbourne), 0155-5227.*
Ind/Abst AESIS Q.

US
PUBLICATIONS - NATIONAL ENVIRONMENTAL RESEARCH CENTER. **Main/Corp** National Environmental Research Center, (Corvallis Or.). (19??)-. Government Publication. English. ir. Superintendent of Documents, US Government Printing Office, Washington DC 20402. **Tel** (202)275-3328, FAX (202)786-2377. **LC** Z5862; .N39a. **DD** 016.6285.

US
PUGET SOUND UPDATE : ... ANNUAL REPORT OF THE PUGET SOUND AMBIENT MONITORING PROGRAM. See Water Resources.

Il/0303-139X
QIYYUM. (KIYUM.). [Qiyyum]. Vol. 1- Sept. 1971-. English (Hebrew). Rehov Ha-Universitah 26, Ramat Aviv, Tel Aviv Israel. **LC** TD883.7.I75; K56.

US
QUARTERLY SUMMARY - UNITED STATES. SOUTHEAST ENVIRONMENTAL RESEARCH LABORATORY, ATHENS, GA. **Main/Corp** United States. Southeast Environmental Research Laboratory, Athens, Ga. **VFOAT** Southeast Environmental Research Laboratory Quarterly Summary. Periodical. English. qt. US Environmental Protection Agency / Georgia, Southeast Environmental Research Laboratory, College Station Road, Athens GA 30601.

SP/0212-0054
QUERCUS. [Quercus]. (1981)-. Periodical. Spanish. mo. 4800ptas (institutions), 3900ptas (individuals) Spain; 6240ptas (institutions), 5070ptas (individuals) other. Editorial Quercus, Calle la Pedriza 1, 28002 Madrid Spain. **Tel** 011 34 1 4134075. **(Subscription address:** Libreria Linneo Camino, Hormigueras 122 Planta 5P1, 28031 Madrid Spain.) **UDC** 502.

●US/1076-2833
QUINTESSENCE (CHICAGO, ILL.). See Medical Science and Technology-Abstracting, Bibliographies and Statistics.

US
RAINFOREST ACTION NETWORK ALERT & WORLD RAINFOREST REPORT. English. mo. $25.00. Rainforest Action Network, 450 Sansome St, San Francisco CA 94111. **Tel** (415)398-4404, FAX (414)398-2732. **ED** Jim Rendon. **Bk Rev**, (Qty: varies): **Circ:** 30,000 (ctrl).
Desc: Promotes the issues surrounding the causes of rainforest destruction.

PL/0209-3871
RAPORT O STANIE, ZAGROZENIU I OCHRONIE SRODOWISKA ... . Added/Corp Poland. Gowny Urzad Statystyczny. (1990)-. Polish. *Continues Ochrona Srodowiska, 0209-3871.*

US
RCRA LAND DISPOSAL RESTRICTIONS : A GUIDE TO COMPLIANCE / COMPILED AND PUBLISHED BY MCCOY AND ASSOCIATES, THE. Added/Corp McCoy & Associates. **VAT** Resource Conservation and Recovery Act Land Disposal Restrictions. (1987)-. English. an. $70.00 (US & Canada); $76.99 (Pan-American nations);$85.81 (other). McCoy and Associates Inc, 13701 West Jewell Avenue, Suite 252, Lakewood CO 80228. **Tel** (303)987-0333, FAX (303) 989-7917. **LC** KF3946; .R38. **DD** 344.730462/05; 347.30446205.

US
RCRA REGULATIONS AND KEYWORD INDEX. Added/Corp McCoy Engineering. **VFOAT** Resource Conservation and Recovery Act Regulations and Keyword Index; Regulations and Keyword Index. (19??)-. Academic Scholarly Publication. English. an. $125.00 US; $158.00 other. Elsevier Science Publishing Company Inc, Madison Square Station, PO Box 882, New York NY 10159-0882. **Tel** (212)633-3950, FAX (212)633-3990. **LC** KF3946.A3697; R37. **DD** 344.73/04622; 347.3044622.

GW/0174-1446
RECYCLING. [Recycling]. (1980)-. Periodical. German. sa. DM24.30 Germany; DM30.00 other. Handelsblatt GmbH, Postfach 102716, D-40018 Duesseldorf Germany. **Tel** 011 49 211 8871730. **UDC** 339.375. **[CCC]**. *Continues Der Schrottbetrieb, 0174-1438.*

US/1053-0525
RECYCLING RELATED NEWSLETTERS, PUBLICATIONS, PERIODICALS, ETC. : AN UPDATING REFERENCE. [Recycl. relat. newsl. publ. period. etc.]. **VFOAT** Recycling Related. Vol. 1:1 (1990)-. English. be. $7.50 US; $11.50 other. Continnuus / Houston, PO Box 570213, Houston TX 77257. **Tel** (713)867-3438. **ED** A C Doyle. **DD** 363. **Circ:** 1500.
Desc: A reference on publications related to recycling.

US
REGFILE-SYSTEM. English. $3504.00. Regfiles Inc., PO Box 14289, Tallahassee FL 32317. **Tel** (904)878-1285.

US
REGFILE SYSTEM SERVICE FOR WMD. English. $3288.00. Regfiles Inc., PO Box 14289, Tallahassee FL 32317. **Tel** (904)878-1285.

CN/0256-3231
REGLEMENTATION POUR LE TRANSPORT DES MARCHANDISES DANGEREUSES. (REGLEMENTATION POUR LE TRANSPORT DES MARCHANDISES DANGEREUSES. IATA.). **Main/Corp** Association Du Transport Aerien International. **VFOAT** IATA Reglementation Pour Le Transport Des Marchandises Dangereuses. **VAT** Reglementation International Air Transport Association Pour Le Transport Des Marchandises Dangereuses. (Jan. 1983)-. French. an (September). $73.00. International Air Transport Association / Montreal, 2000 Peel Street, Room 3050, Montreal Quebec H3A 2R4 Canada. **Tel** (514)844-6311 ext. 232, FAX (514)844-5286, telex 05-267627. **DD** 363.1/77. **Ad Acc**. *Continues Association Du Transport Aerien International. Reglementation IATA Pour Le Transport Des Articles Dangereux.*

UK
REGULATIONS IN THE AREAS OF TRANSPORT, LABELLING, CLASSIFICATION AND STORAGE, AFFECTING THE RECYCLING OF LEAD. See Metals and Metallurgy.

US/1055-4122
REGULATORY COMPLIANCE UPDATE. (REGULATORY COMPLIANCE UPDATE : OFFICIAL NEWSLETTER OF THE NATIONAL REGISTRY OF ENVIRONMENTAL PROFESSIONALS.). [Regul. compliance update]. Added/Corp National Registry of Environmental Professionals (U.S.). **VFOAT** RCU. Vol. 1, No. 1 (Mar. 1991)-. Newsletter. English. mo. $195.00. Newton and Associates, PO Box 831441, Stone Mountain GA 30083-0025. **DD** 344.

US/1051-5658
REMEDIATION (NEW YORK, N.Y.). (REMEDIATION : THE JOURNAL OF ENVIRONMENTAL CLEANUP COSTS, TECHNOLOGIES & TECHNIQUES.). [Remediation]. Vol. 1, No. 1 (Winter 1990/91)-. Periodical. English. qt. $159.00 US & Canada; $209.00 other. John Wiley &

Sons, Inc., 605 Third Avenue, New York NY 10158-0012. **Tel** (212)850-6000, (212)850-6645, FAX (212)850-6088, telex 12-7063. **(Subscription address:** John Wiley & Sons Inc / New Jersey, PO Box 2575, Secaucus NJ 07096-2575.) **LC** TD1; .R46. **DD** 628. **[CCC].** available on microfilm and microfiche from University Microfilms International (UMI).
Desc: Focuses on environmental remediation techniques and technologies at both superfund and non-superfund sites--if and how they work, what the advantages and disadvantages are, how close they come to achieving the desired state and federal "standards", and the costs involved.
Ind/Abst Food Sci. Technol. Abstr.

PE/0252-7987
REPINDEX : INDICE COMPUTARIZADO DE LA RED PANAMERICANA DE INFORMACION Y DOCUMENTACION EN INGENIERIA SANITARIA Y CIENCIAS DEL AMBIENTE (REPIDISCA). ***Ceased.*** **Added/Corp** Red Panamericana de Informacion y Documentacion en Ingenieria Sanitaria y Ciencias del Ambiente. Centro Panamericano de Ingenieria Sanitaria y Ciencias del Ambiente. (198?)-(19??). Periodical. Spanish. qt. **NLM** ZWA 30; R425.

CN/0707-9079
REPORT - ALBERTA ENVIRONMENT. RESEARCH SECRETARIAT. (REPORT.). 1978/1-. Monographic series. English. Price varies per volume. Alberta Environment, 9th Floor, 9915 108 Street, S Tower, Edmonton Alberta T5K 2C9 Canada. **Tel** (403)427-8636. **DD** 363.7'0097123.

US
REPORT (BUSINESS INTELLIGENCE PROGRAM). **Added/Corp** Business Intelligence Program (SRI International). (1984)-. Monographic series. English. Price varies per volume. SRI, 333 Ravenswood Avenue, Menlo Park CA 94025. **LC** HC101; .S77. **DD** 330. ***Continues*** *Research Report (Business Intelligence Program (SRI International)), 0149-2098.*

AT
REPORT - DEPARTMENT OF THE ENVIRONMENT AND CONSERVATION. **Main/Corp** Australia. Dept. of the Environment and Conservation. 1972/74-. English. $2.25. Canberra Department of Environment and Conservation, PO Box 1875, Canberra City Australian Capital Territory 2001 Australia. **LC** J905; .L3 subser; HC610.E5. **DD** 328.94/0 S; 354/.94/008232.

AT/0312-567X
REPORT - DIVISION OF ENVIRONMENTAL MECHANICS. CSIRO (CANBERRA). (REPORT FOR ... / ENVIRONMENTAL MECANICS, CSIRO.). [Rep., Div. Environ. Mech. CSIRO (Canb.)]. **Main/Corp** Commonwealth Scientific and Industrial Research Organization (Australia). Division of Environmental Mechanics. (1971/1972)-. English. be. CSIRO Publications, PO Box 89, 314 Albert Street, East Melborne Victoria 3002 Australia. **Tel** 011 61 3 4187333, 4187217, FAX 011 61 3 4190459, telex AA 30236. **LC** Z5863.P7; A87a; TD170. **DD** 016.628/5.

UK
REPORT (INSTITUTE OF GEOLOGICAL SCIENCES (GREAT BRITAIN). ENVIRONMENTAL PROTECTION UNIT). **See** Environmental Issues-Pollution and Waste Management.

US/0092-0770
REPORT OF PROGRESS BY THE ILLINOIS ENVIRONMENTAL PROTECTION AGENCY. (REPORT OF PROGRESS.). **Main/Corp** Illinois Environmental Protection Agency. **VFOAT** Our Shared Environment. English. an. Illinois Environmental Protection Agency, 2200 Churchill Road, Springfield IL 62706. **LC** TD171.3.I45; I43A. **DD** 353.9/773/0084.

UK/0072-7008
REPORT OF THE COUNCIL / NATURAL ENVIRONMENT RESEARCH COUNCIL. [Rep. Counc. ... - Nat. Environ. Res. Counc.]. **Main/Corp** Great Britain. Natural Environment Research Council. (1966)-. English. an. Her Majesty's Stationery Office, 51 Nine Elms Lane, London SW8 5DR England. **Tel** 011 44 71 873 8459, 011 44 71 873 8499, FAX 011 44 71 873 8499, 011 44 71 873 8456, telex 297138. **(Subscription address:** PO Box 276, Public Centre, London SW8 5DT England**)** **LC** WMLC L 82/143. **DD** 301.3. **NLM** W2 FA1 N5R. **CODEN** NERRB4.
Ind/Abst GeoRef; Ocean. Abstr.

US/0270-9376
REPORT OF THE PROCEEDINGS - NATIONAL CENTER FOR A BARRIER FREE ENVIRONMENT, A. **Main/Corp** National Center for a Barrier Free Environment. Proceedings. English. National Center for a Barrier Free Environment, Suite 1006, 1140 Conn. Avenue, Washington DC 20024.

CN/1191-0305
REPORT ON ENVIRONMENTAL RESEARCH, TECHNOLOGY DEVELOPMENT AND AWARENESS ACTIVITIES. [Rep. environ. res. technol. dev. aware. act.]. **Main/Corp** Ontario. Ministry of the Environment. Research and Technology Branch. (1991)-. English. **DD** 363.7.

US/0277-2868
REPORT TO THE CONGRESS ON OCEAN POLLUTION AND OFFSHORE DEVELOPMENT. **See** Earth Sciences-Oceanography.

US/0148-0596
REPORT TO THE PRESIDENT AND TO THE COUNCIL ON ENVIRONMENTAL QUALITY. **Main/Corp** United States. Citizens' Advisory Committee on Environmental Quality. 1973-. English. an. Citizens' Advisory Committee on Environmental Quality, 1700 Pennsylvania Avenue NW, Washington DC 20006. ***Continues*** *Annual Report to the President and to the Council on Environmental Quality.*

SW
RESEARCH ACTIVITY CATALOGUE. **Main/Corp** Sweden. Statens Naturvardsverk. English. Swedish National Environmental Protection Board, PO Box 1302, Information Section, Solna S17125 Sweden. **Tel** (468)799-1000, FAX (468)984513, telex 11131 ENVIRONS. **LC** TD883.7.S9; S93A.

US
RESEARCH REPORTING SERIES. 9, MISCELLANEOUS REPORTS. **Added/Corp** United States. Environmental Protection Agency. Office of Research and Development. **VFOAT** Miscellaneous Reports. (19??)-. Monographic series. English.
Ind/Abst Ocean. Abstr.

UK
RESEARCH SERIES (CENTRE FOR ENVIRONMENTAL STUDIES (GREAT BRITAIN)). (RESEARCH SERIES / CENTRE FOR ENVIRONMENTAL STUDIES.). **VFOAT** CES Research Series. (1977)-. Monographic series. English. Price varies per volume. Centre for Environmental Studies, 62 Chandos Place, London WC2N 4HH England. ***Continues*** *CES Research Paper.*

IS/0048-7554
REVIEWS ON ENVIRONMENTAL HEALTH. [Rev. environ. health]. Vol. 1 (1972)-. Academic Scholarly Publication. English. ir. $220.00. Freund Publishing House Ltd, PO Box 35010, 61 Nachmani Street, Tel Aviv 61350 Israel. **Tel** 011 972 3 5662925, FAX 011 972 3 5605335. **(Subscription address:** Freund Publishing House Ltd., Suite 500 Chesham House, 150 Regent Street, London W1R 5FA England.**)** **ED** S. Samueloff. **LC** RA565.A1; R47. **DD** 614.7/05. **NLM** W1 RE257CH. **CODEN** REVHA3. Documents available from CASDDS.
Ind/Abst Air Pollut. Titles; Chem. Abstr.; Ecol. Abstr.; EMBASE; Energy Res. Abstr. (Sept. 1974-); Geogr. Abstr. Human Geogr.; Index Med.; Int. Dev. Abstr.; Life Sci. Collect.; Trop. Dis. Bull.

FR/0250-4219
RISCPT BULLETIN. [RISCPT bull.]. **VFOAT** Registre International des Substances Chimiques Potentiellement Toxiques Bulletin. (1978)-. Periodical. French. sa. $25.00. United Nations Environment Program, 16 Avenue Jean Trembley, 1209 Geneva Switzerland. **Tel** 011 41 22 7988400. **UDC** 54.

CN/1186-0308
ROUND TABLE NEWS. **See** Economics.

US/0160-8290
SAFETY AND ENVIRONMENTAL PROTECTION DIVISION PROGRESS REPORT. **Main/Corp** United States. Brookhaven National Laboratory, Upton, N.Y. Safety and Environmental Protection Division. English. an. $4.50. National Technical Information Service - NTIS, Room 2027S, 5285 Port Royal Road, Springfield VA 22161. **Tel** (703)487-4630, (703)487-4660, (703)487-4650, FAX (703)321-8547, telex 89-9405. **LC** TD196.R3; U52A. **DD** 628.5.

UK/0938-5215
SAFETY, ENVIRONMENTAL PROTECTION, AND ANALYSIS. (19??)-. English. mo (12 issues). £121.00 EC; $220.00 US; £121.00 other. Royal Society of Chemistry, Thomas Graham House, Science Park, Cambridge CB4 4WF England. **Tel** 011 44 223 420066, FAX 011 44 223 423429, telex 818293 ROYAL. **(Subscription address:** Turpin Distribution Services Limited, Blackhorse Road, Letchworth, Hertfordshire SG6 1HN, United Kingdom.**)**
Desc: Contains abstracts for scientists and technologists working in the safety and environmental areas. Emphasis is on the role of analytical methods in these fields and in the chemical process industries generally.

JN/0285-5380
SANGYO TO KANKYO. **See** Environmental Issues-Pollution and Waste Management.

US
SAVE THE PLANET ... [COMPUTER FILE]. **Added/Corp** Save the Planet Software (Firm). (1991)-. English.

GW
SCHRIFTTUMSUBERSICHT LARMMINDERUNG. **See** Environmental Issues-Abstracting, Bibliographies and Statistics.

NE/0048-9697
SCIENCE OF THE TOTAL ENVIRONMENT, THE. [Sci. total environ.]. Vol. 1 (May 1972)-. Academic Scholarly Publication. English (French and German). Forty-eight times a year (16 volumes). Fl4800.00. Elsevier Science Publishers BV, PO Box 211, 1000 AE Amsterdam Netherlands. **Tel** 011 31 20 5803642, FAX 011 31 20 5862696, telex 15682. **ED** Eric I Hamilton, M Benarie, and J O Nriagu. **LC** RA565; .S365. **DD** 614.7/05. **NLM** W1 SC751N. **CODEN** STENDLSTEVA8. **[CCC].** Index available. **Bk Rev. Ad Acc. Pr Rev.** available on microfilm and microfiche from University Microfilms International (UMI). Documents available from The Genuine Article, BIOSIS Document Express, CASDDS, Documents on Demand.
Desc: An international medium for the publication of research into those changes in the environment caused by man's activities. Specifically, it is concerned with the changes in the natural level and distribution of chemical elements and compounds which may affect the well-being of the living world, and ultimately harm man himself.
Ind/Abst AQUAREF; Aquat. Sci. Fish. Abstr. (Computer File); Art Archaeol. Tech. Abstr.; Biodeter. Abstr. (1991-); Biol. Abstr.; Chem. Abstr.; Chem. Titles; Coal Abstr.; Cot. Trop. Fibr. Abstr. Bibliogr.; CSA Neuro. Abstr. (?-?); Curr. Aware. Biol. Sci., CABS; Curr. Biotechnol.; Curr. Contents, Agric. Biol. Environ. Sci.; Curr. Ref. Fish Res.; Dairy Sci. Abstr.; Ecol. Abstr.; Ecology Abstr.; Ei Page One; EMBASE; Energy Inf. Abstr.; Environ. Abstr.; Environ. Period. Bibliogr.; Fish Rev.; Food Sci. Technol. Abstr.; For. Abstr.; Geogr. Abstr. Phys. Geogr.; Geogr. Abstr. Human Geogr.; Geol. Abstr.; GeoRef; Grasslands For. Abstr.; Health Saf. Sci. Abstr.; Helminthol. Abstr. (19??-19??); Hortic. Abstr.; Index Med.; Index Vet.; Int. Aerosp. Abstr.; Int. Dev. Abstr.; Key Word Index Wildl. Res.; Environ.; Maize Abstr.; Middle East Abstr. Index; Nutr. Abstr. Rev., Ser. B, Live Feeds and Feed.; Nutr. Abstr. Rev., Ser. A, Hum. Exp.; Ocean. Abstr.; PESTDOC; Plant Grow. Reg. Abstr.; Pollut. Abstr. Indexes; Potato Abstr.; Res. Alert [Full Cov.]; Rev. Agric. Entomol.; Rev. Med. Vet. Entomol.; Rev. Med. Vet. Mycology; Rice Abstr.; Risk Abstr.; Sci. Cit. Index; SCISEARCH; Soc. Sci. Cit. Index [Select. Cov.]; Soils Fert.; Soyabean Abstr.; Vet. Bull.; Toxicol. Abstr.; Weed Abstr.; Wildl. Rev.

US/0146-7956
SCIENTIFIC AND TECHNICAL PUBLICATIONS OF THE ENVIRONMENTAL RESEARCH LABORATORIES. English. an. National Oceanic and Atmospheric Administration NOAA, 325 Broadway, Boulder CO 80303. **Tel** (303)497-3173. **LC** Z6685; .E57A; QC861.2. **DD** 016.5515. ***Continues*** *Scientific and Technical Publications of The ESSA Research Laboratories, 0566-6767.*

US/0275-7389
SCOPE MISCELLANEOUS PUBLICATION. [SCOPE misc. publ.]. **Main/Corp** International Council of Scientific Unions. Scientific Committee on Problems of the Environment. **VAT** Scientific Committee on Problems of the Environment Miscellaneous Publication. No. 1-. Monographic series. English. Price varies per volume. Scope Secretariat, 51 Boulevard de Montmorency, Paris 75016 France.

US
SCRAP TIRE NEWS. (19??)-. English. mo. $108.00 US Government; $118.00 other. Recycling Research Institute, 133 Mountain Road, PO Box 714, Suffield CT 06078. **Tel** (203)668-5422. **ED** Mary B. Sikora. Index available. cum. index. **Ad Acc, Adv Mgr:** Mike Sikora.
Desc: Dedicated to providing information on the recycling, recovery and disposal of used tires.

US
SCRAP TIRE USERS DIRECTORY. (19??)-. Directory. English. an. $45.00. Recycling Research Institute, 133 Mountain Road, PO Box 714, Suffield CT 06078. **Tel** (203)668-5422. **ED** Mary Sikora. **Ad Acc, Adv Mgr:** Mike Sikora, **Tel** (703)280-9112.
Desc: Reference manual for the tire recycling industry.

JA
SEIKATSU TO KANKYO. **Added/Corp** Nihon Kankyo Eisei Senta. Japan. Koseisho. Kankyo Eiseikyoku. Vol. 17, No. 8 (Aug. 1972)-. Periodical. Japanese. mo. Japan Environmental Sanitation Center, Kawasaki Japan. **NLM** W1 SE251T. **CODEN** STKADC. Documents available from CASDDS.
Ind/Abst Chem. Abstr.

Environmental Issues

CC/1000-3975
SHANGHAI HUANJING KEXUE. **VFOAT** Shanghai Environmental Sciences. (1982)-. Academic Scholarly Publication. Chinese (table of contents in English). mo. RMBY12.00. Shanghai Huanjing Baohu Ju, (Shanghai Environmental Protection Bureau), Shanghai Huanjing Kexue Zazhishe, 508 Qinzhou Lu, Shanghai 200233, People's Republic of China. **Tel** 021-4365379. **(Subscription address:** China International Book Trading Corporation, PO Box 399, Library Service Department, Beijing 100044 People's Republic of China.**)** **ED** Chen Jiangtao. **DD** 620.8. Documents available from BLDSC, CASDDS.
Ind/Abst Chem. Abstr.

AT/0314-3155
SIMPLY LIVING. [Simply Living]. (1976)-. Periodical. English. Four times a year. 32.00Aus$ Australia; 36.00Aus$ Asia; 34.00Aus$ Papua New Guinea; 40.00Aus$ other. Otter Publications Pty Ltd., 78 Renwick Street, Redfern NSW 2016, Australia. **Tel** 011 61 2 3101433. **DD** 301.220994.
Ind/Abst Altern. Press Index (199?-).

US/0741-5761
SOCIAL IMPACT ASSESSMENT. See Sociology.

●US/1062-9599
SOCIETY AND NATURE. [Soc. nat.]. **VFOAT** Koinonia Kai Physe. Vol. 1, No. 1 (May-Aug. 1992)-. Periodical. English. Three times a year. $50.00 (one year), $95.00 (two years), $140.00 (three years). Aigis Publications Ltd., PO Box 637, Littleton CO 80160-0637. **Tel** (303)730-6232, FAX (303)798-6568. **ED** Takis Fotopoulos, (editor's address: 1449 West Littleton Boulevard, Suite 200, Littleton, CO 80120). **LC** IN PROCESS. **[CCC].** **Bk Rev**, (Qty: varies). **Ad Acc**, **Adv Mgr:** Pavlos, **Tel** (303)730-6232. **Circ:** 1,000.
Desc: An international journal of social and political ecology which provides a comprehensive forum for dialogue between social ecologists, ecosocialists, radical greens, feminists, and activists in the land-based and indigenous movements.

US/0094-2871
STATE AIR POLLUTION IMPLEMENTATION PLAN PROGRESS REPORT. **Main/Corp** United States. Environmental Protection Agency. Office of Air and Water Programs. Jan./June 1973-. English. sa. US Environmental Protection Agency / Office of Air Quality and Planning, 401 M Street SW, Washington DC 20460. **LC** TD883.2; .U54C. **DD** 363.6.

IT
STATISTICHE AMBIENTALI. (1984)-. Italian. Istituto Nazionale Statistica, GBP SEZ4 Via Cesare Balbo 16, 00184 Rome Italy. **Tel** 011 39 6 46735118. **LC** TD171.5.I8; S7.

US/0094-3142
SUMMARIES OF FOREIGN GOVERNMENT ENVIRONMENTAL REPORTS. **VFOAT** Foreign Documents Announcements. Periodical. English. mo. $35.00 US; $45.00 other. Environmental Protection Agency / Washington, 401 M Street SW, Washington DC 20460. **Tel** (202)382-2090. **LC** TD172; .S77. **DD** 363.6.

CN/0707-9796
SURVEILLANCE REPORT. [Surveill. rep.]. **VFOAT** Rapport de Surveillance; Rapport de Surveillance (Ed. Anglaise et Francaise); Report EPS 5; Rapport EPS 5; Surveillance Report - Environmental Protection Service. Academic Scholarly Publication. Multiple languages. ir. Price varies per volume. Environment Canada / Emergencies Science Division, Ottawa Ontario K1A 0H3 Canada. **Tel** (819)998-9622. **DD** 363.70 0971. Documents available from CASDDS.
Ind/Abst Chem. Abstr.

US/0038-1810
SV. SOUND AND VIBRATION. See Physics-Sound.

FR/0295-5873
SYSTEMES SOLAIRES. See Energy.

US/1042-3168
TENNESSEE ENVIRONMENTAL LAW LETTER. See Law.

US/0892-5925
TENNESSEE ENVIRONMENTAL REPORT. (TENNESSEE ENVIRONMENTAL REPORT : A PUBLICATION OF THE TENNESSEE ENVIRONMENTAL COUNCIL.). [Tenn. environ. rep.]. Periodical. English. mo. $20.00 individuals, $35.00 institutions. Tennessee Environmental Council, 1700 Hayes Street, Suite 101, Nashville TN 37203-2921. **DD** 363.

US/1050-6403
TEXAS ENVIRONMENT. *Suspended.* [Tex. environ.]. **VFOAT** Texas Environment Magazine. Vol. 1, No. 1 (Aug. 1990)-Vol. 1 No. 9. Periodical. English. mo. $30.00. GrassRoots Resources Inc., PO Box 27303, Austin TX 78755-2303. **DD** 363.

II/0970-860X
THIRD WORLD SCIENCE & ENVIRONMENT PERSPECTIVES. See Science and Technology.

UY
TIERRA AMIGA. **Added/Corp** Amigos de la Tierra Uruguay. Red de Ecologia Social. Amigos de la Tierra America Latina y el Caribe. Vol. 1, No. 1 (Spring 1991)-. Periodical. Spanish (Portuguese). qt. Amigos de la Tierra de America Latina y el Caribe, Avda. Millan 4113, 12900 Montevideo Uruguay. **Tel** 35-62-65, FAX 38-16-40. **LC** TD171.5.L29; T54. **DD** 363.7/0098.

II/0970-9703
TISGLOW NEW DELHI. [TISGLOW New Delhi]. **VFOAT** Teri Information Service on Global Warming. (1990)-. Periodical. English. sa. $25.00. Tata Energy Research Institute, 9 Jor Bagh Publications Unit, New Delhi 110 003 India. **Tel** 011 91 11 4623983, FAX 011 91 11 4621770, telex 31-6159 TERI IN. **(Subscription address:** Prints India, 11 Darya Ganj, New Delhi 110002 India.**) DD** 620.9.
Ind/Abst Energy Inf. Abstr.

AT/1034-5337
TODAY MONA VALE. *Ceased.* (TODAY.). (1990)-Vol. 2 No. 2 (19??). English. Six times a year. ASM Group, PO Box 341, 1 Bungan Lane, Mona Vale New South Wales 2103 Australia. **Tel** 011 61 2 9971188, FAX 011 61 2 9132342.

SW
TOMORROW : THE GLOBAL ENVIRONMENT MAGAZINE. Vol. 1, No. 1 (1991)-. Periodical. English. qt. Tomorrow Magzn & Media Prod AB, Kungsgatan 27, 111 56 Stockholm Sweden. **Tel** 011 46 8 243480.
Ind/Abst Environ. Period. Bibliogr.; Geogr. Abstr. Human Geogr.

NE/0166-2082
TOPICS IN ENVIRONMENTAL HEALTH. See Public Health and Safety.

US/0172-6048
TOPICS IN ENVIRONMENTAL PHYSIOLOGY AND MEDICINE. (1974)-. Monographic series. English. ir. Price varies per volume. Springer-Verlag New York Inc., 175 5th Avenue, New York NY 10010. **Tel** (212)460-1500, telex 232 235 SPB UR. **(Subscription address:** Springer Verlag New York Inc. / for North America, 44 Hartz Way, Secaucus NJ 07096.**)**
Desc: Contains articles on man and animal and health and the environment.

US/1055-7571
TOTAL QUALITY ENVIRONMENTAL MANAGEMENT. [Total qual. environ. manage.]. Vol. 1, No. 1 (Autumn 1991)-. Periodical. English. qt. $159.00 US & Canada; $209.00 other. John Wiley & Sons, Inc., 605 Third Avenue, New York NY 10158-0012. **Tel** (212)850-6000, (212)850-6645, FAX (212)850-6088, telex 12-7063. **(Subscription address:** John Wiley & Sons Inc / New Jersey, PO Box 2575, Secaucus NJ 07096-2575.**) LC** TD194; .T68. **DD** 658.4/08. **[CCC].** available on an online database (file 15/Full-Text) from DIALOG.
Desc: Covers the growing application of total quality management to environmental programs. Shows how to apply TQM into environmental practice and turn pollution prevention into profit. Includes case studies of award-winning programs.
Ind/Abst Pollut. Abstr. Indexes; Risk Abstr.

CN
TOXIC REAL ESTATE MANUAL. an. 147.00Can$. Southam Information and Technology Group Inc., 1450 Don Mills Road, Don Mills Ontario M3B 2X7 Canada. **Tel** (416)445-6641, (800)668-2374, FAX (416)442-2261.

US
TOXICS PROGRAM COMMENTARY. FLORIDA. English. ir (Includes 1 loose-leaf sub service in binder + minimum of 4 updates per year.). $205.00. Specialty Technical Publishers Inc, #306-267 West Esplande, North Vancouver BC V7M 1A5 Canada. **Tel** (604)983-3434, FAX (604)983-3445. ctrl circ.

CN
TOXICS PROGRAM COMMENTARY. ILLINOIS. English. ir (Includes 1 loose-leaf sub service in binder + minimum of 4 updates per year.). $205.00. Specialty Technical Publishers Inc, #306-267 West Esplande, North Vancouver BC V7M 1A5 Canada. **Tel** (604)983-3434, FAX (604)983-3445. ctrl circ.

CN
TOXICS PROGRAM COMMENTARY. MASSACHUSETTS. English. ir (Includes 1 loose-leaf sub service in binder + minimum of 4 updates per year.). $205.00. Specialty Technical Publishers Inc, #306-267 West Esplande, North Vancouver BC V7M 1A5 Canada. **Tel** (604)983-3434, FAX (604)983-3445. ctrl circ.

CN
TOXICS PROGRAM COMMENTARY. NEW JERSEY. English. ir (Includes 1 loose-leaf sub service in binder + minimum of 4 updates per year.). $205.00. Specialty Technical Publishers Inc, #306-267 West Esplande, North Vancouver BC V7M 1A5 Canada. **Tel** (604)983-3434, FAX (604)983-3445. ctrl circ.

CN
TOXICS PROGRAM COMMENTARY. NEW YORK. English. ir (Includes 1 loose-leaf sub service in binder + minimum of 4 updates per year.). $205.00. Specialty Technical Publishers Inc, #306-267 West Esplande, North Vancouver BC V7M 1A5 Canada. **Tel** (604)983-3434, FAX (604)983-3445.

CN
TOXICS PROGRAM COMMENTARY. OHIO. English. ir (Includes 1 loose-leaf sub service in binder + minimum of 4 updates per year.). $205.00. Specialty Technical Publishers Inc, #306-267 West Esplande, North Vancouver BC V7M 1A5 Canada. **Tel** (604)983-3434, FAX (604)983-3445. ctrl circ.

CN
TOXICS PROGRAM COMMENTARY. PENNSYLVANIA. English. ir (Includes 1 loose-leaf sub service in binder + minimum of 4 updates per year.). $205.00. Specialty Technical Publishers Inc, #306-267 West Esplande, North Vancouver BC V7M 1A5 Canada. **Tel** (604)983-3434, FAX (604)983-3445. ctrl circ.

CN
TOXICS PROGRAM COMMENTARY. TEXAS. English. ir (Includes 1 loose-leaf sub service in binder + minimum of 4 updates per year.). $205.00. Specialty Technical Publishers Inc, #306-267 West Esplande, North Vancouver BC V7M 1A5 Canada. **Tel** (604)983-3434, FAX (604)983-3445. ctrl circ.

CN
TOXICS PROGRAM MATRIX. English. Specialty Technical Publishers Inc, #306-267 West Esplande, North Vancouver BC V7M 1A5 Canada. **Tel** (604)983-3434, FAX (604)983-3445.

CN
TOXICS PROGRAM MATRIX. MASSACHUSETTS. English. ir (2 updates per year). $35.00. Specialty Technical Publishers Inc, #306-267 West Esplande, North Vancouver BC V7M 1A5 Canada. **Tel** (604)983-3434, FAX (604)983-3445. ctrl circ.

CN
TOXICS PROGRAM MATRIX. NEW YORK. (19??)-. English. ir (2 updates per year). $35.00. Specialty Technical Publishers Inc, #306-267 West Esplande, North Vancouver BC V7M 1A5 Canada. **Tel** (604)983-3434, FAX (604)983-3445. ctrl circ.

US
TOXICS PROGRAM MATRIX. TEXAS. (19??)-. English. ir (2 updates per year). $35.00. Specialty Technical Publishers Inc, #306-267 West Esplande, North Vancouver BC V7M 1A5 Canada. **Tel** (604)983-3434, FAX (604)983-3445. ctrl circ.

NZ/0114-1562
TRANSACTIONS OF THE INSTITUTION OF PROFESSIONAL ENGINEERS NEW ZEALAND. GENERAL SECTION. **VFOAT** Institution of Professional Engineers New Zealand Transactions. (1988)-. English. **UDC** 620.005.
Ind/Abst Concr. Abstr.; Ei Page One.

US/0161-5645
U.S. ENVIRONMENTAL PROTECTION AGENCY LIBRARY SYSTEM BOOK CATALOG. See Library and Information Sciences.

NE
UITVOERINGSPROGRAMMA BELEIDSPLAN MILIEUHYGIENE. Dutch. **LC** RA566.5.N4; U38.

GW/0173-363X
UMWELTMAGAZIN WURZBURG. (1980)-. Periodical. German. mo. DM138.00 Germany; DM148.00 other. Vogel Verlag, Postfach 6740, D-97064 Wuerzburg Germany. **Tel** 011 49 931 4182145, 011 49 931 4182483, FAX 011 49 931 4182670, telex 841 680131. **UDC** 628. **CODEN** 658.

TH
UNEP, ASIA-PACIFIC REPORT. **Added/Corp** UNEP Regional Office for Asia and the Pacific. **VFOAT** UNEP Asia Pacific Report; Asia-Pacific Report. (19??)-. English. **LC** TD171.5.A78; U53. **DD** 363.7/0095. *Continues UNEP-Asia Report.*

Environmental Issues —Abstracting, Bibliographies and Statistics

GW
UNSERE UMWELT. Periodical. German. ir. DM16.00. Almanach Verlags Gesellschaft, Landsgraf Philipps Anlage 52, 61 Darmstadt Germany. **LC** TD169; .U55. **DD** 628.5/05.

CN/0715-3392
UPDATE / INTERPRETATION CANADA. See Education.

CN/1185-3999
UPDATE / SASKATCHEWAN ROUND TABLE ON ENVIRONMENT AND ECONOMY. [Update - Sask. Round Table Environ. Econ.]. **Main/Corp** Saskatchewan Round Table on Environment and Economy. Issue 1 (May 1991)-. Periodical. English. qt. **DD** 333.7/2/09712405.

US/0417-1233
URBAN ENVIRONMENT STUDY; PUBLICATION. Main/Corp Detroit. Metropolitan Area Regional Planning Commission. Began with No. 1, 1953. Periodical. English.

GW
UWD UMWELTSCHUTZDIENST. German. DM219.00 (add DM48.00 postage). ESV - Verlag GmbH, Postfach 320424, W-4000 Duesseldorf 30 Germany.
 Desc: Information on environmental politics, energy and raw materials and load and provision.

SW/0042-1995
VA-NYTT. (VA NYTT : LITTERATUROVERSIKT OM MILJOVARD.). [Va-nytt]. (1966)-. Periodical. Swedish. Six times a year (Feb., Apr., June, Aug., Oct., Dec.). Kr770.00. Byggdok, Haelsingegatan 47, S 113 31 Stockholm Sweden. **Tel** 011 46 8 340170, FAX 011 46 8 324859. **ED** Gerard Lingre. **Bk Rev**. available on an online database from the publisher, the publisher.
 Desc: A journal on international interest in environmental protection technology.

US
VERMONT ENIIVRONMENTAL MONITOR. (19??)-. English. Twelve times a year. $79.00. Putney Press, PO Box 935, Brattleboro VT 05302. **Tel** (802)257-7505, FAX (802)254-7630. Index available. cum. index. **Continues** Vermont Monitor.

US
VERMONT ENVIRONMENTAL REPORT. English. ir. Vermont Natural Resources Council, 9 Bailey Avenue, Montpelier VT 05602. **Tel** (802)223-2328. Documents available from Documents on Demand.
 Ind/Abst Environ. Abstr.

US/1050-6861
VERMONT MONITOR. Title Change. (VERMONT MONITOR : A REPORT ON THE ENVIRONMENT, LAND USE & SOLID WASTE.). [Vt. monit.]. (1990)-(19??). Periodical. English. mo. Putney Press, PO Box 935, Brattleboro VT 05302. **Tel** (802)257-7505, FAX (802)254-7630. **DD** 363. **Continued by** Vermont Environmental Monitor.

GW/0175-4211
WABOLU-HEFTE. (WABOLU HEFTE / INSTITUT FUER WASSER-, BODEN- UND LUFTHYGIENE DES BUNDESGESUNDHEITSAMTES.). [WaBoLu-Hefte]. **Added/Corp** Institut fur Wasser-, Boden- und Lufthygiene des Bundesgesundheitsamtes (Germany). **VAT** Institut fur Wasser-, Boden- und Lufthygiene des Bundesgesundheitsamtes Hefte. (1984)-. Academic Scholarly Publication. German (summaries and/or abstracts in English). Documents available from CASDDS. **Continues** WaBoLu Berichte, 0172-7702.
 Ind/Abst Chem. Abstr.

JA/0915-3179
WAKAYAMA-KEN EISEI KOGAI KENKYU SENTA NENPO. Added/Corp Wakayama-Ken Eisei Kogai Kenkyu Senta. **VFOAT** Annual Report of Wakayama Prefectural Research Center of Environment and Public Health. (198?)-. Academic Scholarly Publication. Japanese. Wakayamaken Eisei Kogai Kenkyu Senta, (Wakayama Prefectural Research Center of Environment & Public Health), 3-45, Sunayama Minami 3 Chome, Wakayamashi, Wakayamaken 640, Japan. **CODEN** WEKNEP. Documents available from CASDDS. **Continues** Wakayama-Ken Eisei Kenkyujo Nenpo.
 Ind/Abst Chem. Abstr. (1984-).

US/0899-1405
WARY CANARY, THE. (1987)-. Periodical. English. qt. $30.00 (institutions), $20.00 (individuals). The Wary Canary, PO Box 2204, Fort Collins CO 80522. **Tel** (303)224-0083. **DD** 616. Documents available from Documents on Demand.
 Ind/Abst Environ. Abstr.

GW
WASSER, LUFT UND BODEN. HANDBUCH UMWELTTECHNIK. VFOAT Handbuch Umwelttechnik; WLB-Handbuch Umwelttechnik. (1990)-. German. Vereinigte Fachverlage, Postfach 4068, D 55000 Mainz Germany. **Tel** 011 49 6131 992150. **LC** TD3; .W37. **DD** 628/.0943. **Continues** Wasser, Luft und Betrieb. WLB-Handbuch Umwelttechnik.

US/0112-398X
WASTELINES. [Wastelines]. (1979)-. Periodical. English. qt. $15.00 non-profit organizations; $20.00 government, $25.00 business. Environment Action, 6930 Carroll Avenue, Suite 600, Takoma Park MD 20912. **Tel** (301)891-1100. **DD** 628.445.

UK/0956-0157
WATER & ENVIRONMENT INTERNATIONAL. See Water Resources.

●UK/0968-3321
WATER & ENVIRONMENT MANAGEMENT. See Water Resources.

US/0043-1273
WATER NEWSLETTER. See Water Resources.

US/1055-0852
WHO IS WHO (WAYNESVILLE, N.C.). (WHO IS WHO : PEOPLE, PROJECTS, ORGANIZATIONS IN SERVICE TO THE EARTH.). (1991)-. Periodical. English. $16.95. Visionlink, 185 Shelton Cove Road, Waynesville NC 28786.

US/1055-1166
WILD EARTH. [Wild earth]. **Added/Corp** Wild Earth Association. Vol. 1, No. 1, (Spring 1991)-. Periodical. English. qt. $25.00. Cenozoic Society Inc., PO Box 455, Richmond VT 05477. **Tel** (802)434-4077. **ED** Dave Foreman and John Davis. **LC** QH75.A1; W553. **DD** 333. **CODEN** WIEAEI. [CCC]. **Bk Rev**, (Qty: 6-10). **Ad Acc**, **Adv Mgr:** Tom Butler. **Pr Rev. Circ:** 3,000. Documents available from Documents on Demand.
 Desc: Serving the biocentric grassroots elements within the conservation movement, advocating the restoration and protection of all natural elements of biodiversity. Publishes wilderness proposals throughout the continent, provide a voice for regional and wilderness groups and defend wilderness both as concept and place.
 Ind/Abst Environ. Abstr.

UK/0954-6324
WILDFOWL (SLIMBRIDGE). See Zoology-Ornithology.

US/1044-2618
WILDLIFE REHABILITATION TODAY. See Animal Welfare.

US/0887-8927
WISCONSIN ARBORIST, THE. See Forestry.

US/1047-4633
WOMBLE, CARLYLE, SANDRIDGE & RICE'S NORTH CAROLINA ENVIRONMENTAL LAW LETTER. See Law.

US
WOODLANDS FORUM, THE. Added/Corp Center for Global Studies. (1984)-. Periodical. English. ir (2 or 3 times a year). Free. Center for Global Studies, 4800 Research Forest Drive, The Woodlands TX 77381. **Tel** (713)363-7913, FAX (713)363-7924. **ED** Deborah Myers, (phone: (713)363-7930). **Circ:** 6,000 (ctrl).

US/0094-4742
WORLD ENVIRONMENTAL DIRECTORY. Vol. 1 (Summer 1974)-. English. ir. $233.00. Business Publishers Inc., 951 Pershing Drive, Silver Spring MD 20910-4464. **Tel** (301)587-6300, (800)274-0122, FAX (301)585-9075. **ED** Beverly Gough. **LC** TD12; .W65. **DD** 363.6. **NLM** WA 22 W9273.
 Desc: Contains the name of key people and organizations you need to contact in the environmental field, over 40,000 listings, with names, addresses, phone numbers, products, services, branches, and specialities.

GW/0933-9027
ZEITSCHRIFT FUER ANGEWANDTE UMWELTFORSCHUNG. German. qt. DM169.00 Europe; DM189.00 other. Verlagsgesellschaft Analytica, Postfach 1133, W-5880 Luenscheid Germany. **Tel** 011 49 02351 52245.

JA/0385-1028
ZENKOKU KOGAIKEN KAISHI. [Zenkoku Kogaiken kaishi]. **Added/Corp** Zenkoku Kogaiken (Japan) Zenkoku Kogaiken (Japan). Kyogikai Henshu linkai. **VFOAT** Journal of Environmental Laboratories Association. (1976)-. Academic Scholarly Publication. Japanese. sa. Zenkoku Kogaiken Kaishi Jimukyoku, (Environmental Laboratories Assoc.), 1-244, Kogaiken 9 Chome, Minatoku, Tokyo 107, Japan. **CODEN** ZKKADQ. Documents available from CASDDS.
 Ind/Abst Chem. Abstr.

CC/1000-6923
ZHONGGUO HUANJING KEXUE. (CHUNG-KUO HUAN CHING KO HSUEH.). [Zhongguo huanjing kexue]. **Added/Corp** Chung-Kuo Huan Ching Ko Hsueh Hsueh Hui. **VFOAT** Zhongguo Huanjing Kexue; Environmental Sciences in China. (1981)-. Academic Scholarly Publication. Chinese (table of contents in English). qt. Chinese Society for Environmental Sciences, No. 115, Xizhimennei Nanxiaojie, Beijing 100035 People's Republic of China. **Tel** 6066498, FAX 6020031. **LC** TD4; .C46. **DD** 620.8/05. **NLM** W1; CH988BD. **Pr Rev.** Documents available from BLDSC, CASDDS.
 Ind/Abst Chem. Abstr.

ABSTRACTING, BIBLIOGRAPHIES AND STATISTICS

US/0002-2497
AIR POLLUTION TITLES. Ceased. Added/Corp Pennsylvania State University. Center for Air Environment Studies. (1965)-(Dec. 1994). Abstracting/Indexing Service. English. bm. Environment Resources Research Institute, Center for Air Environment Studies, Information Services, 226 Fenske Laboratory, Pennsylvania State University, University Park PA 16802. **Tel** (814)865-1415, FAX (814)863-1696. **ED** Elizabeth J. Carroll. **LC** Z5862.2.A4; A43; TD883. **DD** 016.3636. Index available. **Circ:** 70. available on microfilm from University Microfilms International (UMI).
 Desc: Survey of current air pollution literature, listing titles on air environment, effects of air pollution on plants and people, control of air pollution, monitoring and analysis of air pollution.

US
AIR QUALITY DATA - STATISTICS. Main/Corp United States. Environmental Protection Agency. National Air Data Branch. (19??)-. Periodical. English. qt. National Technical Information Service - NTIS, Room 2027S, 5285 Port Royal Road, Springfield VA 22161. **Tel** (703)487-4630, (703)487-4600, (703)487-4650, FAX (703)321-8547, telex 89-9405. **LC** TD883.2; .U54f. **DD** 363.6. **Continues** Air Quality Data from the National Air Surveillance Networks and Contributing State and Local Networks.

NE
ALGEMENE MILIEUSTATISTIEK / CENTRAAL BUREAU VOOR DE STATISTIEK. VFOAT General Environmental Statistics. Dutch (summaries and/or abstracts in English). Centraal Bureau voor de Statistiek, AFD ALG Zaken, Postbus 959, 2270 AZ Voorburg Netherlands. **Tel** 011 31 70 3373800, FAX 011 31 038 7429, telex 32692 CBS NL. **LC** TD171.5.N4; A45.

US
API ABSTRACTS. HEALTH & ENVIRONMENT. Title Change. Added/Corp American Petroleum Institute. Central Abstracting and Indexing Service. **VFOAT** Health and Environment; Health & Environment. (1986-1992). Abstracting/Indexing Service. English. wk. American Petroleum Institute, 275 Seventh Avenue, New York NY 10001. **Tel** (212)366-4040, FAX (212)366-4298. **ED** Monica Pronin (Director). **Continues** Air and Water Conservation. **Continued by** Literature Abstracts. Health & Environment, 1065-0490.

US
BIBLIOGRAPHY OF SMALL WASTEWATER FLOWS. 1979-. Bibliography. English. an. EPA Small Wastewater Flows, Clearinghouse Centennial House, West Virginia University, Morgantown WV 26506. **LC** Z5853.S22; B53; TD741. **DD** 016.6283/6.

UK/0951-0621
BIODETERIORATION ABSTRACTS. [Biodeterior. abstr.]. **Added/Corp** C.A.B. International. Vol. 1, No. 1 (March 1987)-. Abstracting/Indexing Service. English. qt. $223.00. CAB International Centre, Wallingford, Oxon OX10 8DE United Kingdom. **Tel** 44 491 832111, FAX 44 491 833508, telex 847964 (COMAGG G). **ED** V. J. Dring BSc. **NLM** ZWA 671; B615. **CODEN** BABSE8. Index available. cum. index. **Bk Rev**. **Ad Acc**. available on magnetic tape and CD-ROM; available on an online database from Tsukuba Daigaku; CAN/OLE; STN International; JICST; DATA-STAR; DIMDI; ESA-IRS; BRS; and DIALOG. **Separated from** International Biodeterioration, 0265-3036.
 Desc: Biodeterioration of materials of economic importance by living organisms; biodegradation of waste materials to less objectionable, more easily disposable or higher-value products by living organisms.
 Ind/Abst Biocont. News Inf. (19??-19??); Rev. Agric. Entomol.; Sug. Indus. Abstr.

UK/0951-1542
CONTAMINATION CONTROL ABSTRACTS. [Contam. control abstr.]. (?986)-. Abstracting/Indexing Service. English. Four times a year (Mar., June, Sept., Dec.). £90.00. University of Technology PSTIS Subscriptions, c/o R. W. Newbold, Department of Chemical Engineering, Loughborough LE11 3TU England. **Tel** 011 44 509 222528, telex 34319. **ED** R. W. Newbold. **DD** 016.6200028. Index available. cum. index. **Bk Rev**. **Ad Acc. Circ:** 100.
 Desc: Abstracting journal dealing with clean room technology, contamination control, and ultrapure manufacturing.

UK/0955-6648
CURRENT ADVANCES IN ECOLOGICAL & ENVIRONMENTAL SCIENCES. [Curr. adv. ecol. environ. sci.]. **VFOAT** Current Advances in Ecological and Environmental Sciences; Ecological & Environmental Sciences. Vol. 15, No. 1 (Jan. 1989)-. Abstracting/Indexing Service. English. mo. $1088.00 The Americas; £730.00 other. Elsevier Geo Abstracts, An Imprint of Elsevier Science Ltd., The Boulevard, Langford Lane, Kidlington, Oxford OX5 1GB United Kingdom. **Tel** 011 44 865 843000, 011 44 865 843699, FAX 011 44 865 843010. **(Subscription address:** Elsevier Science Ltd. Oxford Fulfillment Centre, PO Box 800, Kidlington, Oxford OX5 1DX United Kingdom.**) ED** Harry Smith (editor's address: Department of Botany, University of Leicester, University Road, Leicester LE1 7QQ UK) and Peter N Campbell (editor's address: Department of Biochemistry, University College, London WC1E 6BT UK). **LC** QH540; .C87. **DD** 016.5745. **NLM** Z 5322.E2; C976. available on microfiche; available on diskette. ***Continues*** *Current Advances in Ecological Sciences, 0306-3291.*
Desc: A current literature searching service which now has extended coverage of papers on pollution and environmental processes relevant to ecology, new sections to cover the 'up-and-coming' areas of behavioral and evolutionary ecology, and a 'functional' approach to the subject.
Ind/Abst Health Saf. Sci. Abstr.

IS/0011-9172
DESALINATION AND RECYCLING ABSTRACTS. ***Ceased.*** **Added/Corp** Merkaz le-medatehnologi u-madai (Israel). Vol. 20, No. 1 (Jan. 1985)-(Jan. 1986). Abstracting/Indexing Service. English. qt. National Center for Scientific and Technological Information, PO Box 20125, Tel Aviv 61201 Israel. **Tel** 03-5612676, FAX 03-5614619, telex 03-2332 IL. **LC** TD478; .D43. **DD** 628.1/67/05. ***Continues*** *Desalination Abstracts, 0011-9202.*

US/1055-8411
EARTH FIRST! (1991). **See** Environmental Issues.

UK/0305-196X
ECOLOGICAL ABSTRACTS. (1974)-. Abstracting/Indexing Service. English. Twelve times a year (1 index). $984.00 The Americas; £660.00 other. Elsevier Geo Abstracts, An Imprint of Elsevier Science Ltd., The Boulevard, Langford Lane, Kidlington, Oxford OX5 1GB United Kingdom. **Tel** 011 44 865 843000, 011 44 865 843699, FAX 011 44 865 843010. **(Subscription address:** Elsevier Science Ltd. Oxford Fulfillment Centre, PO Box 800, Kidlington, Oxford OX5 1DX United Kingdom.**) ED** P. J. Jarvis. **LC** QH540; .E27. **DD** 574.5/05. **[CCC].** Index available, published separately, free-automatically sent. **Circ:** 600. available on microfilm and microfiche from University Microfilms International (UMI).
Desc: Gives comprehensive coverage of recent literature for ecologists working in marine, freshwater and terrestrial environments.
Ind/Abst Field Crop Abstr.; Fish Rev.; For. Prod. Abstr.; For. Abstr.; Grasslands For. Abstr.; Wildl. Rev.

US/0143-3296
ECOLOGY ABSTRACTS. [Ecol. abstr.]. **Added/Corp** Information Retrieval Limited. Cambridge Scientific Abstracts, Inc. Vol. 6 (Jan. 1980)-. Abstracting/Indexing Service. English. mo (includes annual index). $865.00 US; $985.00 other. Cambridge Scientific Abstracts, 7200 Wisconsin Avenue, #601, Bethesda MD 20814-4823. **Tel** (301)961-6750, (800)843-7751, FAX (301)961-6720. **ED** Robert Hilton. **LC** QH540; .A66. **DD** 574.5. Index available. cum. index. available on CD-ROM (Pollution/Toxicology CD-ROM) from Cambridge Scientific Abstracts; available on microfiche; available on an online database; available on magnetic tape; available via Internet (to the current year's abstracts and five-year backfiles) from Cambridge Scientific Abstracts. ***Continues*** *Applied Ecology Abstracts, 0305-3040.*
Desc: Focuses on how organisms of all kinds interact with their environments and with other organisms. Included are relevant papers on evolutionary biology, economics and systems analysis as they relate to ecosystems or the environment. With coverage ranging from habitats to food chains, from erosion to land reclamation, this journal provides an important cross-section of current findings in target research areas.

US/1076-6464
ENVIRO/ENERGYLINE ABSTRACTS PLUS. ***Title Change.*** (ENVIRO/ENERGYLINE ABSTRACTS PLUS COMPUTER FILE.). [Env./energyline abstr. plus]. **Added/Corp** Bowker Electronic Publishing. (Spring 1991)-(1993). Abstracting/Indexing Service. English. qt. R R Bowker, A Reed Reference Publishing Company, Part of Reed International PLC, PO Box 31, 121 Chanlon Drive, New Providence NJ 07974. **Tel** (908)464-6800, (800)521-8110, FAX (908)665-6688, telex 138-755. **LC** QH540; QH540; .E58. **DD** 363. ***Continued by*** *Environment Abstracts.*
Desc: Featuring complete Environment Abstracts, Energy Information Abstracts and the back files of Acid Rain Abstracts. Delivers up to 240,000 citations for critical, current data on topics ranging from global warming to nuclear fusion. Updated quarterly.

US/0093-3287
ENVIRONMENT ABSTRACTS. [Environ. abstr.]. **Added/Corp** Environment Information Center. EIC Intelligence Inc. Vol. 4 (Jan. 1974)-. Abstracting/Indexing Service. English. mo (except bimonthly May/June and Nov./Dec.). $1,070.00. Congressional Information Service Inc, 4520 East-West Highway, Suite 800, Bethesda MD 20814-3389. **Tel** (800)638-8380, (301)654-1550, FAX (301)654-4033, telex 292386 CIS UR. **ED** Leigh C Yuster, David Packer, Tim Wahrer, Sue Himmelstein, and Mindy Fleisher. **LC** GF1; .E553. **DD** 016.30131. **NLM** Z 5322.E2 E61. **[CCC].** Index available (contains indexes). cum. index. available on CD-ROM; available on microfiche; available on an online database from ESA-ISA; DATA-STAR; ORBIT; and DIALOG. ***Continues*** *Environment Information Access, 0013-9181;* ***Absorbed*** *Acid Rain Abstracts.*
Desc: Contains abstracts and indexes to worldwide environmental literature, covering the latest information on hazardous waste, acid rain, government policy, and more.
Ind/Abst Fish Rev. (Jan. 1989-19??); Mag. Index (?-?); Wildl. Rev. (Jan. 1989-19??).

US/0000-1198
ENVIRONMENT ABSTRACTS ANNUAL. [Environ. abstr. annu.]. **Added/Corp** Environment Information Center. EIC Intelligence Inc. Bowker A&I Publishing. Vol. 10, No. 1-12 (1980)-. Abstracting/Indexing Service. English. an. $495.00 (2 volume set). Congressional Information Service Inc, 4520 East-West Highway, Suite 800, Bethesda MD 20814-3389. **Tel** (800)638-8380, (301)654-1550, FAX (301)654-4033, telex 292386 CIS UR. **DD** 016. **NLM** Z 5322.E2; E57. **[CCC].** Index available. cum. index. available on microfiche; available on CD-ROM from R.R. Bowker; available on an online database from ESA-ISA; DATA-STAR; ORBIT; and DIALOG. ***Absorbed*** *Environment Index, 0090-791X* ***and*** *Acid Raid Abstracts Annual, 0000-1228.*
Desc: Abstracts and indexed information from scientific, technical and business journals, conference and symposium proceedings, newsletters, and academic, corporate, and government reports. Addresses the impact of humankind and technology on the environment, with attention to air, water, and noise pollution, solid and toxic wastes, radiological contamination, toxicological effects, control technologies, resource management, population, endangered species, and geophysical and climatic change.

●US
ENVIRONMENT ABSTRACTS [COMPUTER FILE]. **Added/Corp** Congressional Information Service. **VFOAT** Environment Abstracts on CD-ROM; Environment Abstracts Plus. (Spring 1994)-. Abstracting/Indexing Service. English. qt. $1,295.00. Congressional Information Service Inc, 4520 East-West Highway, Suite 800, Bethesda MD 20814-3389. **Tel** (800)638-8380, (301)654-1550, FAX (301)654-4033, telex 292386 CIS UR. **LC** GF1; .E554. available in print. ***Continues*** *Enviro/Energyline Abstracts Plus, 1076-6464.*
Desc: Delivers more than 200,000 records for critical, current data on topics ranging from global warming to nuclear fusion.

US/1063-7346
ENVIRONMENTAL ENGINEERING ABSTRACTS. ***Ceased.*** [Environ. eng. abstr.]. **Added/Corp** Cambridge Scientific Abstracts, Inc. Engineering Information, Inc. Vol. 1, No. 1 (1993)-(1995). Abstracting/Indexing Service. English. mo. Cambridge Scientific Abstracts, 7200 Wisconsin Avenue, #601, Bethesda MD 20814-4823. **Tel** (301)961-6750, (800)843-7751, FAX (301)961-6720. **DD** 628. available on magnetic tape.
Desc: Published in collabortion with Engineering Information Inc., this journal focuses on environmental engineering, a relatively new field addressing pollution and other environmental impact resulting from industrial development and population growth. Topics covered include technological and engineering aspects of air and water quality, environmental safety, and alternate energy sources.

US/0145-3815
ENVIRONMENTAL PERIODICALS BIBLIOGRAPHY. [Environ. period. bibliogr.]. **Added/Corp** International Academy at Santa Barbara. Environmental Studies Institute. Vol. 2 (Feb. 1973)-. Abstracting/Indexing Service. English. bm. International Academy at Santa Barbara, 800 Garden Street, Suite D, Santa Barbara CA 93101. **Tel** (805)965-5010, FAX (805)965-6071. **(Subscription address:** CD-ROM/ National Information Services Corporation, Suite 6, Wyman Towers, 3100 St. Paul Street, Baltimore, MD 21218; telephone: (301)243-0797**) ED** Miriam Flacks. **LC** Z5863.E57; E58; TD145. **DD** 363.6. **NLM** ZWA 30 E63. Index available. **Circ:** 1,000. available in microform; available on an online database; available on CD-ROM from National Information Service Corporation (NISC). ***Continues*** *Environmental Periodicals, 0046-2306.*
Desc: Tables of contents reproduced from periodicals on all facets of environment, 25,000-plus articles per year.

US/1053-1440
ENVIRONMENTAL PERIODICALS BIBLIOGRAPHY ON CD-ROM. (ENVIRONMENTAL PERIODICALS BIBLIOGRAPHY ON CD-ROM. COMPUTER FILE.). [Environ. period. bibliogr.]. **Added/Corp** International Academy at Santa Barbara. Environmental Studies Institute. National Information Services Corporation. (1990)-. Bibliography. English. sa. Rates are based on customer's library budget. International Academy at Santa Barbara, 800 Garden Street, Suite D, Santa Barbara CA 93101. **Tel** (805)965-5010, FAX (805)965-6071. **DD** 363.
Desc: Intended for the new or experienced CD-ROM user who needs basic or sophisticated search access, queries, and database analysis.

CN/0709-8847
ENVIRONNEMENT (MONTREAL). (L'ENVIRONNEMENT.). [Environnement]. **Added/Corp** Societe pour Vaincre la Pollution. Vol. 6, No. 3 (May 1979)-. Abstracting/Indexing Service. French. ir. 10.00Can$. Society Pour Vaincre la Pollution, PO Box 65 Place d'Armes, Montreal Quebec H2Y 3E9 Canada. **Tel** (514)844-5477. **DD** 301.31/0971. **Circ:** 5,000. ***Continues*** *Journal l'Environnement, 0382-7828.*
Desc: Environmental research that seeks to inform and involve the public.

US/0196-0091
EPA PUBLICATIONS BIBLIOGRAPHY. (EPA PUBLICATIONS BIBLIOGRAPHY / SPONSORED BY LIBRARY SYSTEMS BRANCH, U.S. ENVIRONMENTAL PROTECTION AGENCY IN COOPERATION WITH EPA OFFICES OF AIR AND WASTE MANAGEMENT ... [ET AL.].). [EPA publ. bibliogr.]. **Added/Corp** United States. Environmental Protection Agency. Library Systems Branch. United States. Environmental Protection Agency. Office of Air and Waste Management. United States. Environmental Protection Agency. Library Systems Staff. United States. National Technical Information Service. Center for Environmental Research Information (U.S.). **VFOAT** Environmental Protection Agency Publications Bibliography. (Oct./Dec. 1977)-. Bibliography. English. qt. $145.00 US; $290.00 other. US Environmental Protection Agency, 401 M Street SW, Washington DC 20460. **Tel** (202)755-9163. **(Subscription address:** National Technical Information Service, 5285 Port Royal Road, Springfield, VA 22161**) LC** Z5863.P7; U58a; TD170. **DD** 016.3637. **NLM** ZWA 670 U576E. cum. index. Documents available from Documents on Demand. ***Continues*** *EPA Reports Bibliography, 0196-0083.*
Ind/Abst Abstr. Bull. Inst. Pap. Sci. Tech.; Am. Stat. Index.

JA
KAGAKU GIJUTSU BUNKEN SOKUHO: KANKYO KOGAI HEN. **Added/Corp** Nihon Kagaku Gijutsu Joho Senta. **VFOAT** Current Bibliography on Science and Technology Environmental Pollution. Vol. 1 April (1975)-. Multiple languages (English, French, German, Japanese and Russian). mo. ¥36000. Nihon Kagaku Gijutsu Joho Senta, (Japan Information Center of Science & Technology), 5-2, Nagatacho 2 Chome, Chiyodaku, Tokyoto 100 Japan. **LC** Z5862; .K28; TD174. **NLM** ZWA 670 K16. ***Supersedes*** *Kankyo Kogai Bunken Shu, 0302-0274.*

SZ
KEY-WORD-INDEX OF WILDLIFE RESEARCH. **Added/Corp** Schweizerische Dokumentationsstelle fur Wildforschung. **VAT** Keyword Index of Wildlife Research. Vol. 1 (1974)-. Abstracting/Indexing Service. English (German). an. 70.00F Switzerland. Swiss Wildlife Information Service, University of Zurich, Strickhofstrasse 39, CH-8057 Zurich Switzerland. **Tel** 01 362 77 28. **ED** Ch Mosler. **Circ:** 500.
Desc: Indexes international publications in wildlife biology and management; copying service.

●US/1065-0490
LITERATURE ABSTRACTS. HEALTH & ENVIRONMENT. (LITERATURE ABSTRACTS. HEALTH & ENVIRONMENT / CENTRAL ABSTRACTING & INFORMATION SERVICES, AMERICAN PETROLEUM INSTITUTE.). [Lit. abstr., Health environ.]. **Added/Corp** American Petroleum Institute. Central Abstracting & Information Services. **VFOAT** Health & Environment; Health and Environment; Health and Environment/Literature; American Petroleum Institute Literature Abstracts. Health & Environment; Health & Environment/Literature. Vol. 39, No. 5 (Feb. 3, 1992)-. Abstracting/Indexing Service. English. wk. American Petroleum Institute, 275 Seventh Avenue, New York NY 10001. **Tel** (212)366-4040, FAX (212)366-4298. **DD** 616. Index available. cum. index. ctrl circ. available on an online database (as APILIT) from DIALOG; (as APILIT) STN International (Math) Database; and (as APILIT) ORBIT. ***Continues*** *API Abstracts. Health & Environment.*

US/1063-7354
MANUFACTURING AND PROCESS ENGINEERING ABSTRACTS. ***Ceased.*** [Manuf. process eng. abstr.]. **Added/Corp** Cambridge Scientific Abstracts, Inc. Engineering Information, Inc. Vol. 1, No. 1 (1993)-(1995). Abstracting/Indexing Service. English. mo. Cambridge Scientific Abstracts, 7200

Wisconsin Avenue, #601, Bethesda MD 20814-4823. **Tel** (301)961-6750, (800)843-7751, FAX (301)961-6720. **DD** 670. available on magnetic tape. Documents available.
Desc: Addresses the growing changes of pollution arising from industrial development and population growth. Professionals in this field need access to current, comprehensive, information on pollution control and waste treatment.

US/0278-1328
NATIONAL PARK STATISTICAL ABSTRACT. (NATIONAL PARK STATISTICAL ABSTRACT / NATIONAL PARK SERVICE.). 1978-. Statistical Publication. English. an. Chief Statistical Section, Branch of Science, Denver Service Center, National Park Service, PO Box 25287, Denver CO 80225. **Tel** (303)969-2060. **LC** SB482; .A1948. **DD** 333.78/0973. **Circ:** 2,500 (ctrl). available on microfiche (Vols. for (1984-) distributed to depository libraries). ***Continues*** *Statistical Abstract (United States. National Park Service).*
Desc: Contains information on public use of national park service administered areas, overnight stays, back country use, urban and rural park use, and list of units in N.P.S.

PL/0032-2830
POLISH ECOLOGICAL BIBLIOGRAPHY. [Pol. ecol. bibliogr.]. 1959-. Bibliography. English (translations available in Polish). **(Subscription address:** ARS Polona, PO Box 1001, 00068 Warsaw Poland.**)** **CODEN** PECBA4. ***Continues*** *Polish Bibliography of Selected Ecological Problems.*

US/0191-1724
POLLUTION ABSTRACTS. ANNUAL INDEX. (197?)-. English. an. $435.00 US; $495.00 other (index only). Cambridge Scientific Abstracts, 7200 Wisconsin Avenue, #601, Bethesda MD 20814-4823. **Tel** (301)961-6750, (800)843-7751, FAX (301)961-6720. **ED** Roberta Gorinson. available via Internet (to the current year's abstracts and five-year backfiles) from Cambridge Scientific Abstracts.
Desc: Abstracts of journal articles dealing with air, marine and fresh water pollution. Sewage and water treatment waste management, land pollution, toxicology. Noise and radiation effect on man.

US/0032-3624
POLLUTION ABSTRACTS WITH INDEXES. (POLLUTION ABSTRACTS.). [Pollut. abstr. indexes]. Vol. 1 (May 1970)-. Abstracting/Indexing Service. English. mo. $895.00 US, $995.00 other (includes annual index). Cambridge Scientific Abstracts, 7200 Wisconsin Avenue, #601, Bethesda MD 20814-4823. **Tel** (301)961-6750, (800)843-7751, FAX (301)961-6720. **ED** Roberta Gorinson. **LC** TD172; .P65. **DD** 628/.5/08. **NLM** ZWA 754 P777. **CODEN** PLNAB4. Index available. cum. index. **Bk Rev.** available on an online database from Pollution and Toxicology Database; available on CD-ROM; available on magnetic tape; available via Internet (to the current year's abstracts and five-year backfiles) from Cambridge Scientific Abstracts. Documents available from Petroleum Abstracts Document Delivery Service.
Desc: Provides fast access to the environmental information necessary to resolve day-to-day problems, ensure ongoing compliance and handle emergency situations more effectively. Combines information on scientific research and government policies in all forms of pollution including air, water, land and noise pollution as well as waste management.
Ind/Abst Pet. Abstr.

US/0190-7670
SANITARY LANDFILLS. (SANITARY LANDFILLS; A BIBLIOGRAPHY.). June 1972/Feb. 1977-. Government Publication. English. US Department of the Interior / Water Resources Scientific Information Center, Washington DC 20240. **NLM** ZWA 780 S227. ***Continues*** *Sanitary Landfills, 0190-7670.*
Desc: Produced from the information base comprising the Selected water resources abstracts (SWRA).

GW
SCHRIFTTUMSUBERSICHT LARMMINDERUNG. **Added/Corp** Verein Deutscher Ingenieure. Fachdokumentation Larmminderung. (19??)-. Periodical. German. mo. DM72.00. VDI Verlag / Vertrieb Zeitschriften, Postfach 10 10 54, 4001 Dusseldorf 1 Germany. **Tel** 02 11 61 88 313, FAX 02 11 61 88 133, telex 8 587743. **LC** Z5862.2.N6; S37.

CN/0383-5898
STATISTICS - ONTARIO MINISTRY OF NATURAL RESOURCES. (STATISTICS - MINISTRY OF NATURAL RESOURCES.). [Stat. - Ont. Minist. Nat. Resour.]. **Main/Corp** Ontario. Ministry of Natural Resources. 1973-. English. an. 2.00Can$. Ministry of Natural Resources / Ontario, Whitney Block, Parliament Buildings, Toronto Ontario M7A 1W3 Canada. **LC** QH77.C2; O57A. **DD** 354/.713/008232. **Circ:** 1,500 (ctrl).
Desc: A statistical supplement to the annual report of the Ontario Ministry of Natural Resources.

UK
WASTE DISPOSAL STATISTICS BASED ON ESTIMATES. **Main/Corp** Society of County Treasurers. English. Society of County Treasurers, County Hall, Truro TR1 3BD England. **LC** TD793.7; .S63A. **DD** 363.6.

UK
WASTE DISPOSAL STATISTICS ... ESTIMATES / CIPFA, STATISTICAL INFORMATION SERVICE. Statistical Publication. English. £5.00. Chartered Institute of Public Finance and Accountancy, 2 3 Robert Street, London WC2N 6BH England. **Tel** 011 44 1 895 8823. **LC** TD793.7; .S63A. **DD** 363.7/28/0942. ***Continues*** *Waste Disposal Statistics Based on Estimates.*

US/0043-5511
WILDLIFE REVIEW (FORT COLLINS). (WILDLIFE REVIEW.). **Added/Corp** U.S. Fish and Wildlife Service. Colorado State University. United States. Bureau of Biological Survey. Patuxent Wildlife Research Center. (Sept. 1935)-. Abstracting/Indexing Service. English. bm. $30.00 domestic; $37.50 other. US Fish and Wildlife Service, 1201 Oak Ridge Drive, Suite 200, Fort Collins CO 80525-5589. **Tel** (303)223-9709. **LC** SK351; .W58. **DD** 016.799; 016.33378. **NLM** Z 7993 W673. cum. index. **Circ:** 22,000. available on microfilm and microfiche from University Microfilms International (UMI); available on CD-ROM from National Information Service Corporation (NISC). Documents available from BIOSIS Document Express.
Desc: Contains citations to current wildlife/natural resource literature. Citations are taken selectively from over 1080 journals and periodicals. Reference to more than 500 books and symposia proceedings concerning wildlife and natural resources is included annually. All citations are comprehensively cross-referenced in appended indices.
Ind/Abst Biol. Abstr.; Key Word Index Wildl. Res.

CONSERVATION AND NATURAL RESOURCES

●US/1059-5112
A TO Z. (A TO Z, THE NEW JERSEY STATE AQUARIUM AT CAMDEN, THE PHILADELPHIA ZOO.). [A z]. **Added/Corp** Philadelphia Zoological Garden. Zoological Society of Philadelphia. New Jersey State Aquarium at Camden. **VAT** Aquarium to Zoo. Vol. 1, No. 1 (Winter 1992)-. Periodical. English. Four times a year. $30.00 Comes with Philadelphia Zoo membership. Philadelphia Zoo, PO Box 41877 271, Philadelphia PA 19101. **Tel** (215)243-1100 ext. 254. **DD** 590. ***Continues*** *Zoo One, 0745-1555.*
Desc: The official publication of the New Jersey State Aquarium at Camden and the Philadelphia Zoo. Activities and events, stories about different animals and programs at the two facilities.

US/1061-9135
AAZPA ANNUAL REPORT ON CONSERVATION AND SCIENCE. [AAZPA annu. rep. conserv. sci.]. **Added/Corp** American Association of Zoological Parks and Aquariums. **VFOAT** Annual Report on Conservation and Science. (1990/91)-. Periodical. English. AAZPA Conservation Center, 7970-D Old Georgetown Road, Bethesda MD 20814-2493. **DD** 590.

CN/1188-0392
ACAP NEWS. [ACAP news]. **Main/Corp** Atlantic Coastal Action Program (Canada). **VAT** Atlantic Coastal Action Program News. No. 1 (Autumn 1991)-. Periodical. English. qt. **DD** 333.91.

US/0364-4693
ACCIDENT CONTROL REPORT. **Main/Corp** United States. Fish and Wildlife Service. Office of Safety. Government Publication. English. US Department of the Interior / Fish & Wildlife Service, 1849 C Street NW, Room 3256, Washington DC 20240. **Tel** (202)208-4717, FAX (202)208-4473. **LC** SK361; .U62A. **DD** 639/.9/0973.

SW/0281-5087
ACID RAIN. **Main/Corp** Swedish Society for the Conservation of Nature. English.
Ind/Abst Int. Exec.

US/0194-1488
ADMINISTRATION OF THE MARINE MAMMAL PROTECTION ACT OF 1972. (UNITED STATES. FISH AND WILDLIFE SERVICE). (ADMINISTRATION OF THE MARINE MAMMAL PROTECTION ACT OF 1972.). **VAT** Administration of the Marine Mammal Protection Act of Nineteen Hundred and Seventy-Two. Began with 1972/73. Government Publication. English. an. US Department of Interior, Division of Federal Aid, Washington DC 70240. **LC** QL713.2; .U5A. **DD** 353.008/232. available on microfiche (Vols. for (1984-) distributed to depository libraries).
Desc: The responsibility of the Department encompasses the protection of polar bear, sea otter, marine otter, walrus, manatees and dugong.

US/0192-558X
ADVANCES IN THE ECONOMICS OF ENERGY AND RESOURCES. **See** Energy.

CN/0225-6533
ADVENTURING IN CONSERVATION. [Advent. conserv.]. **Added/Corp** Manitoba Forestry Association. Issue No. 1 (Apr. 1978)-. Periodical. English. sa. Free. Manitoba Forestry Association, 900 Corydon Avenue, Winnipeg Manitoba R3M 0Y4 Canada. **Tel** (204)453-3182. **ED** Dianne J. Beaven. **DD** 333.75/06/07127. **Ad Acc. Circ:** 1,000 (ctrl).
Desc: Information on association programs, president's report, executive director's report, list of members, editorials on forestry- and conservation-related matters.

SA/0002-0273
AFRICAN WILDLIFE. [Afr. wildl.]. **Added/Corp** Wildlife Society of Southern Africa. Wild Life Protection Society of South Africa. Wild Life Protection and Conservation Society of South Africa. Vol. 1 (1946)-. Periodical. English (Afrikaans and English). Six times a year. $77.20. Wildlife Society Southern Africa, P.O.Box 44189 Linden 2104, South Africa. **Tel** 011 27 41 29606. **CODEN** AFWLAA. available on microfilm and microfiche from University Microfilms International (UMI). Documents available from BIOSIS Document Express, Documents on Demand.
Ind/Abst Bibliogr. Mission. (1985-); Biol. Abstr.; Ecol. Abstr.; Energy Inf. Abstr.; Environ. Abstr.; Environ. Period. Bibliogr.; Fish Rev. (Jan. 1989-July 1992); Geogr. Abstr. Human Geogr.; Int. Dev. Abstr.; Wildl. Rev. (Jan. 1989-July 1992).

KE/0002-0281
AFRICANA. ***Suspended.*** **See** Zoology.

AT/1032-9722
AGRICULTURE & RESOURCES QUARTERLY. ***Title Change.*** **See** Agriculture.

PL
AIR CONSERVATION. **Added/Corp** National Center for Scientific, Technical and Economic Information. Foreign Scientific Publications Dept. United States. Environmental Protection Agency. National Science Foundation (U.S.) Centralny Instytut Informcji Naukowo-Techniznej i Ekonomicznej Zakad Wspopracy z Zagramica w Zakresie Pismiennicwa Naukowego. Metallurgic Engineers and Technicians Association. Periodical. English (Polish). National Technical Information Service - NTIS, Room 2027S, 5285 Port Royal Road, Springfield VA 22161. **Tel** (703)487-4630, (703)487-4660, (703)487-4650, FAX (703)321-8547, telex 89-9405. **LC** TD881; .O2613. **DD** 614.7/1/05.

JA/0913-9907
AKITA DAIGAKU KOZAN GAKUBU SHIGEN CHIGAKU KENKYU SHISETSU HOKOKU. **Added/Corp** Akita Daigaku. Shigen Chigaku Kenkyu Shisetsu. **VFOAT** Shigen Chigaku Kenkyu Shisetsu Hokoku; Report of the Research Institute of Natural Resources, Mining College, Akita University. (1987)-. Academic Scholarly Publication. Japanese (summaries and/or abstracts in English). **LC** HC461; .A687. **CODEN** SCKHEH. Documents available from CASDDS. ***Continues*** *Akita Daigaku Kozan Gakubu Chika Shigen Kenkyu Shisetsu Hokoku, 0385-6879.*
Ind/Abst Chem. Abstr.

JO
AL-RIM. **VFOAT** Al-Reem; Reem. Periodical. Arabic (summaries and/or abstracts in English). qt. 3.00JD Jordan; $12.00 US. Al-Jamiyah Al Malakiayah, Li-Himayat Al-Tabiah S B 6354, Amman Al-Urdun Jordan. **Tel** 811689. **ED** Kamel Abu Jaber. **LC** S934.J6; R56. Index available. cum. index. **Ad Acc. Circ:** 4,500.
Desc: Covers environmental and nature conservation in addition to the establishment and management of nature reserves in Jordan.

US/0002-4171
ALABAMA CONSERVATION. [Ala. conserv.]. **Added/Corp** Alabama. Dept. of Conservation and Natural Resources. Alabama. Dept. of Conservation. Vol. 1, No. 1-8 (Nov. 1940)-. Periodical. English. Four times a year (Feb., May, July, Sept.). $8.00 (one year); $14.00 (two years); $20.00 (three years). Alabama Conservation, 64 North Union Street, Montgomery AL 36107. **Tel** (205)242-3151, (800)262-3151. **ED** Bettina Wood. **LC** SH11.A6; A4. **DD** 333. **CODEN** ALCNAQ. **Circ:** 12,000. ***Continues*** *Alabama Game and Fish News.*
Desc: Magazine promotes the wide use of Alabama's natural resources.
Ind/Abst Fish Rev.; Wildl. Rev.

US/0734-4155
ALASKA OCSEAP NEWSLETTER. ***Ceased.*** [Alsk. OCSEAP newsl.]. **VFOAT** Alaska O.C.S.E.A.P. Newsletter. **VAT** Alaska Outer Continental Shelf Environmental Assessment Program Newsletter. (1980)-?. Newsletter. English. National Oceanic and

Environmental Issues — Conservation and Natural Resources

Atmospheric Administration / Juneau, PO Box 1808, Juneau AK 99802. *Continues in part* Alaska Field Office Newsletter, 0734-4163.

US/0164-9558
ALASKA'S RESOURCES. V. 19, No. 9- Sept. 1978-. Periodical. English. qt. Department of Natural Resources / Alaska, PO Box 80007, 794 University Avenue, Fairbanks AK 99709. **Tel** (907)474-7147. **LC** HC107.A45; A5982. **DD** 353.97980082/32/06. *Continues* Alaska Land Lines, 0002-4511.

CN/0835-5851
ALCES. [Alces]. **Added/Corp** Lakehead University. School of Forestry. **VFOAT** Alces. Subject and Author Index. Vol. 17 (1981)-. English (summaries and/or abstracts in French). an (Spring). $17.00 per issue. Lakehead University / Bookstore, Oliver Road, Thunder Bay Ontario P7B 5E1 Canada. **Tel** (807)343-8110 ext. 8130. **DD** 636.2/94. Documents available from Documents on Demand. *Continues* North American Moose Conference and Workshop. Proceedings, 0836-8716.
 Ind/Abst Environ. Abstr.; For. Abstr.; Nutr. Abstr. Rev., Ser. B, Live Feeds and Feed.

FR/0044-7463
AMENAGEMENT ET NATURE. **Added/Corp** Association pour les Espaces Naturels. (1965)-. French. Four times a year (Mar., June, Sept., Dec.). 200.00F France; 235.00F other. Amenagement et Nature, 21 rue du Conseiller Collignon, 75116 Paris France. **Tel** 33-1-4520-1500, FAX 45204536. **ED** Rolaud Bechmann.
 Bk Rev, (Qty: 6). **Ad Acc. Circ:** 4,000 (ctrl).
 Desc: This magazine is on the preservation, conservation, landscape, management of land, national parks, ecological planning, and natural resources.
 Ind/Abst GeoRef; Key Word Index Wildl. Res.; Life Sci. Collect.; Point Repere (1983-).

US/0888-899X
AMERICAN RIVERS. (AMERICAN RIVERS / AMERICAN RIVERS CONSERVATION COUNCIL.). [Am. rivers]. **Added/Corp** American Rivers Conservation Council. (19??)-. Periodical. English. Four times a year (Mar., June, Sept., Dec.). $20.00 Comes with American Rivers membership. American Rivers, 801 Pennsylvania Avenue, Suite 400, Washington DC 20003. **Tel** (202)547-6900. **LC** WMLC L 83/9327. **DD** 333.
 Desc: Covers river legislation and other legal developments.

●US
AMERICAN SPIRIT / TAKE PRIDE IN AMERICA. **Main/Corp** Take Pride in America. (1992)-. Periodical. English. qt. Take Pride in America, Box USA, Washington DC 20240. *Continues* Take Pride in America.; National Campaign News.

US/1050-4036
AMERICAN TRAPPER. (AMERICAN TRAPPER : OFFICIAL PUBLICATION OF THE NATIONAL TRAPPERS ASSOCIATION.). [Am. trapp.]. (19??)-. Periodical. English. bm. $6.00 junior; $12.00 (one year), $38.00 (two year), $55.00 (three year) individuals; $20.00 libraries. National Trappers Association, PO Box 3667, Bloomington IL 61702. **Tel** (309)829-2422, FAX (309)829-7615. **ED** Tom Krause (307)856-3830. **DD** 639. **Ad Acc. Circ:** 17,000 (ctrl). *Continues* Voice of the Trapper, 0194-6927.

US
AMERICAN WILDLIFE REGION SERIES. *Ceased.* Vol. 1 (1965)-?. Monographic series. English. ir. Naturegraph Publishing Inc, PO Box 1075, Happy Camp CA 96309.

US/0276-7201
AMICUS JOURNAL, THE. [Amic. j.]. **Added/Corp** Natural Resources Defense Council. Vol. 2, No. 1 (Summer 1980)-. Periodical. English. qt. $10.00 (one year), $18.00 (two year), $23.00 (three year). Natural Defense Resources Council, 40 West 20th Street, 11th Floor, New York NY 10011. **Tel** (212)727-2700. **ED** Peter Borrelli. **LC** S930; .A65. **DD** 333.95/16/0973. Index available. cum. index. **Bk Rev. Circ:** 110,000. available on microfilm and microfiche from University Microfilms International (UMI). Documents available from UMI Article Clearinghouse, Documents on Demand. *Continues* Amicus, 0192-5776; *Absorbed* Newsline (Natural Resources Defense Council).
 Desc: A journal of thought and opinion on environmental affairs, particularly those relating to policies of national and international significance.
 Ind/Abst Altern. Press Index; Environ. Abstr.; Environ. Period. Bibliogr.; Expand. Acad. Index (1992-); Index Period. Artic. Relat. Law; J. Plan. Lit.; Newsp. Period. Abstr. (1992-); PAIS Int. Print (1991-); Urban Aff. Abstr.; Wildl. Rev.

GR/0302-1033
ANNALES MUSEI GOULANDRIS. *See* Natural History.

US/0095-6643
ANNUAL AUDIT - ARIZONA STATE PARKS BOARD. *See* Business-Accounting.

US/0731-0226
ANNUAL FINANCIAL REPORT OF THE TEXAS PARKS & WILDLIFE DEPARTMENT. (ANNUAL FINANCIAL REPORT OF THE TEXAS PARKS & WILDLIFE DEPARTMENT FOR THE FISCAL YEAR ... .). **Main/Corp** Texas. Parks and Wildlife Dept. (1979/1980)-. English. an. Texas Parks & Wildlife, 4200 Smith School Road, Austin TX 78744. **Tel** (512)707-0032. **LC** SB482.T4; T47a. **DD** 353.97640072/2368632. *Continues* Annual Report of the Texas Parks & Wildlife Department for the Fiscal Year ... .

US
ANNUAL PERFORMANCE REPORT OF SURVEY-INVENTORY ACTIVITIES / ALASKA DEPARTMENT OF FISH AND GAME, DIVISION OF WILDLIFE CONSERVATION. **Main/Corp** Alaska. Division of Wildlife Conservation. **VFOAT** Annual Performance Report of Survey Inventory Activities; Federal Aid in Wildlife Restoration. (19??)-. English. ADF&G, Wildlife Conservation, PO Box 22526, Juneau AK 99802. **LC** SK367; .A65b. **DD** 353.9/798/00823305. *Continues* Alaska. Division of Game.; Annual Report of Survey-Inventory Activities, 0362-6962.

US/0148-2521
ANNUAL PRESERVATION PROGRAM, THE. (THE ANNUAL PRESERVATION PROGRAM - INDIANA. DIVISION OF MUSEUMS AND MEMORIALS.). **Main/Corp** Indiana. Division of Museums and Memorials. **VFOAT** Indiana's Historic Preservation Plan. English. an. Indiana Geological Survey, 611 North Walnut Grove, Bloomington IN 47405. **Tel** (812)885-9350. **LC** F527; .I53A. **DD** 069/.53/09772.

US/0731-874X
ANNUAL PROCEEDINGS. WATER SYMPOSIUM / ARIZONA WATER SYMPOSIUM. *See* Water Resources.

US/8755-4690
ANNUAL PROGRESS REPORT, CHILKAT RIVER COOPERATIVE BALD EAGLE STUDY. *See* Zoology.

AT
ANNUAL REPORT. **Main/Corp** Australian Conservation Foundation. (1968)-. English. an. 30.00Aus$ (membership fee). Australian Conservation Foundation, 340 Gore Street, Fitzroy Victoria 3065 Australia. **Tel** 011 61 3 4161455, FAX 011 61 3 4160767. **LC** QH77.A8; A87a. **DD** 333.7/2/06294. **Circ:** 15,000 (ctrl).
 Desc: Report of the activities of the Australian Conservation Foundation under the headings forestry, land management, employment, education, etc.

US/0095-2206
ANNUAL REPORT - ARKANSAS ENVIRONMENTAL PRESERVATION COMMISSION. **Main/Corp** Arkansas. Environmental Preservation Commission. (1973)-. English. an. Arkansas Department of Planning, 400 Train Station Square, Victory at Markham, Little Rock AK 72201. **LC** QH76.5.A8; A73a. **DD** 333.7/2/09767.

AT
ANNUAL REPORT / DEPARTMENT OF CONSERVATION AND LAND MANAGEMENT. **Main/Corp** Western Australia. Dept. of Conservation and Land Management. 22nd March 1985-. English. an. Free. Department of Conservation and Land Management, PO Box 104, Corp Relations Division, Como WA 6152 Australia. **Tel** 011 61 09 3670333. **LC** QH77.A8; W465A. **DD** 354.9410082/32/06.
 Desc: A summary of the department's work for the previous year.

US
ANNUAL REPORT - DEPARTMENT OF ENVIRONMENTAL CONSERVATION. **Main/Corp** New York (State). Dept. of Environmental Conservation. **Added/Corp** New York (State). Dept. of Environmental Conservation. State of New York's Environment. New York (State). Dept. of Environmental Conservation. New York State Environment. **VFOAT** State of New York's Environment. (19??)-. English. an. Department of Environmental Conservation / New York, 50 Wolf Road, Room 604, Albany NY 12233. **Tel** (518)457-2344, FAX (518)457-6996. **ED** Mary Kadlecek. **LC** TD171.3.N5; N47a. **DD** 353.9/747/008232. **Circ:** 5,000.
 Desc: Contains programs in natural resources, includes statistical tables.

AT
ANNUAL REPORT / DEPARTMENT OF RESOURCES DEVELOPMENT. **Main/Corp** Western Australia. Dept. of Resources Development. (19??)-. English. an. Department of Resources Development, SGIO Atrium, 170 St. George's Terr, Perth WA 6000 Australia. **Tel** 011 61 9 3275555, FAX 011 61 9 3275500. **LC** HC607.W47; W474b. **DD** 354.9410082/32/06.

AT/0156-0204
ANNUAL REPORT - EARTH RESOURCES FOUNDATION. UNIVERSITY OF SYDNEY. (1977)-. English. an.
 Ind/Abst AESIS Q.

CN
ANNUAL REPORT FOR THE PERIOD ... / QUEEN'S UNIVERSITY, CENTRE FOR RESOURCE STUDIES. **Main/Corp** Queen's University (Kingston, Ont.). Centre for Resource Studies. (19??)-. English. Centre for Resource Studies, Queen's University, Kingston Ontario K7L 3N6 Canada. **Tel** (613)545-2553, FAX (613)545-6651.
 Ind/Abst AESIS Q.

AT
ANNUAL REPORT FOR YEAR ENDING 30 JUNE ... CONSERVATION COMMISSION OF THE NORTHERN TERRITORY. **Main/Corp** Conservation Commission of the Northern Territory. 1st (1980)-. English. an. Free. Conservation Commission of the Northern Territory, Gap Road, PO Box 1046, Alice Springs Northern Territory 0871 Australia. **Tel** (089)508-211, FAX (089)52-5390, telex AAS1191. **LC** QH197; .N67A. **DD** 354.94290082/32/06. **Circ:** 250 (ctrl). *Continues* Northern Territory. Territory Parks and Wildlife Commission. Annual Report for the Year Ended 30th June ... .

US
ANNUAL REPORT - HERITAGE CONSERVATION AND RECREATION SERVICE, MID-CONTINENT REGION. **Main/Corp** United States. Heritage Conservation and Recreation Service. Mid-Continent Region. 1977/78-. Government Publication. English. an. US Department of the Interior / Heritage Conservation & Recreation Service, Washington DC 20240. **LC** GV191.42.N75; U53A. **DD** 790/.0978. *Continues* Annual Report - U.S. Department of the Interior, Bureau of Outdoor Recreation, Mid-Continent Region, 0098-1060.

AT/0158-7404
ANNUAL REPORT / INSTITUTE OF BIOLOGICAL RESOURCES. **Main/Corp** Institute of Biological Resources (Australia). (1980)-. English. CSIRO Publications, PO Box 89, 314 Albert Street, East Melborne Victoria 3002 Australia. **Tel** 011 61 3 4187333, 4187217, FAX 011 61 3 4190459, telex AA 30236. **LC** QH197; .C64a. **DD** 574.6/0994.

US/0733-2017
ANNUAL REPORT - MISSISSIPPI. DEPT. OF WILDLIFE CONSERVATION. (ANNUAL REPORT / MISSISSIPPI DEPARTMENT OF WILDLIFE CONSERVATION.). [Annu. rep. - Miss. Dept. Wildl. Conserv.]. **Main/Corp** Mississippi. Dept. of Wildlife Conservation. 1979-80-. English. an. Mississippi Department of Wildlife, PO Box 451, Jackson MS 39205. **LC** QL84.22.M7; M57A. **DD** 353.97620082/32.

ZA
ANNUAL REPORT - NATIONAL PARKS AND WILDLIFE SERVICE (ZAMBIA). **Main/Corp** Zambia. National Parks and Wildlife Service. 1974-. English. 30. **LC** SB484.Z33; Z35A. **DD** 354/.689/4008232. *Supersedes in part* Zambia. Dept. of Wildlife, Fisheries and National Parks. Annual Report.

CN
ANNUAL REPORT OF THE DEPARTMENT OF NATURAL RESOURCES (REGINA). (ANNUAL REPORT OF THE DEPARTMENT OF NATURAL RESOURCES.). **Main/Corp** Saskatchewan. Department of Natural Resources. **VFOAT** Annual Report - Saskatchewan Department of Natural Resources. (1949/50)-. Periodical. English. Department of Natural Resources / Saskatchewan Canada, Regina Saskatchewan S4P 3GH Canada. **LC** HC117.S3; A28. **DD** 333.72. *Continues* Annual Report of the Department of Natural Resources and Industrial Development of the Province of Saskatchewan.

US/0442-7637
ANNUAL REPORT OF THE DIVISION OF FISH AND GAME, INDIANA DEPARTMENT OF CONSERVATION. **Main/Corp** Indiana. Division of Fish and Game. Periodical. English. Indiana Department of Conservation, Division of Fish and Game, Indianapolis IN 46204. **LC** SH11.I64; A3. **DD** 333.7.

US/0495-2928
ANNUAL REPORT OF THE WILDLIFE DIVISION, PARKS AND WILDLIFE DEPARTMENT. **Main/Corp** Texas. Wildlife Division. **Added/Corp** Texas. Game and Fish

Commission. Annual Report of the Game and Fish Commission, State of Texas, 1962/63. (1962/63)-. English. an. Texas Parks & Wildlife, 4200 Smith School Road, Austin TX 78744. **Tel** (512)707-0032. **LC** SH11.T4; A37. **DD** 333.9. ***Continues*** *Annual Report of the Game and Fish Commission, State of Texas.*

CN/0848-5844
ANNUAL REPORT - PRINCE EDWARD ISLAND. DEPT. OF THE ENVIRONMENT (1989). (ANNUAL REPORT / PRINCE EDWARD ISLAND, DEPARTMENT OF THE ENVIRONMENT.). [Annu. rep. - P.E.I., Dep. Environ.]. **Main/Corp** Prince Edward Island. Dept. of the Environment. (1990)-. English. **DD** 354.71706823/2/05. ***Separated from*** *Prince Edward Island. Dept. of Community and Cultural Affairs. Annual Report of the Prince Edward Island Department of Community and Cultural Affairs for the Year Ending December 31., 0827-987X.*

CN/0711-2815
ANNUAL REPORT / RECREATION, PARKS AND WILDLIFE FOUNDATION. **See** Public Administration-Parks and Recreation.

US/0486-5561
ANNUAL REPORT - RESOURCES FOR THE FUTURE. [Annu. rep., Resour. Future]. **Main/Corp** Resources for the Future. **VFOAT** RF Annual Report; RFF Annual Report. (1954)-. English. an. Free. Resources for the Future, 1616 P Street Northwest, Washington DC 20036. **Tel** (202)328-5025. **ED** Kent A Price. **LC** HC103.7; .R4. **DD** 333/.005. **CODEN** RSFRAH. **Bk Rev. Circ:** 20,000.
Desc: Covers public policy issues concerning natural resources, energy, and environmental quality.
Ind/Abst GeoRef.

US/0364-1619
ANNUAL REPORT - SOUTH CAROLINA LAND RESOURCES CONSERVATION COMMISSION. **Main/Corp** South Carolina. Land Resources Conservation Commission. **VFOAT** Report of the State Land Resources Conservation Commission. 1971/72-. English. an. PO Box 11708, 1400 Lady Street, Columbia SC 29211. **LC** S916.S75; L35A. **DD** 353.9/757/008232.

AT/0155-8072
ANNUAL REPORT / THE GREAT BARRIER REEF MARINE PARK AUTHORITY. **Main/Corp** Great Barrier Reef Marine Park Authority. (1982/1983)-. Government Publication. English. an. Great Barrier Reef Marine Park Authority, PO Box 1379, Townsville Queensland 4810 Australia. **LC** J905; .L3 subser.; QH91.75.A8. **DD** 082. ***Continues*** *Great Barrier Reef Marine Park Authority. Research Report.*
Ind/Abst AESIS Q.

US/0362-6997
ANNUAL REPORT - UNITED STATES DEPARTMENT OF THE INTERIOR, BUREAU OF SPORT FISHERIES AND WILDLIFE, FISH AND WILDLIFE SERVICE. (ANNUAL REPORT, NEW MEXICO DISTRICT.). **Main/Corp** United States. Division of Wildlife Services. **Added/Corp** New Mexico State University. New Mexico. Dept. of Agriculture. (19??)-. English. an. US Department of Interior / Division of Wildlife Services, 10304 Candelaria NE, Albuquerque NM 87112. **LC** SK427; .U54a. **DD** 353.9/789/008232.

US
ANNUAL REPORT / WEST VIRGINIA DEPARTMENT OF NATURAL RESOURCES. **Main/Corp** West Virginia. Dept. of Natural Resources. English. an. Department of Natural Resources / West Virginia, State Capitol, Charleston WV 25305. **Tel** (304)558-9152. **LC** HC107.W5; W29A. **DD** 353.97540082/32/06.

UK
ANNUAL REVIEW FOR ... / THE GAME CONSERVANCY. **Main/Corp** Game Conservancy (Great Britain). 1971-1972; No. 5 (1973)-. English. an. **LC** SK505; .G35A. **DD** 639.9/782942. ***Continues*** *Game Conservancy (Great Britain). Annual Review.*

US/0003-6641
APPALACHIAN TRAILWAY NEWS. **See** Recreation, Leisure-Outdoor Life.

US/0190-3322
APPALACHIAN VOICE, THE. Periodical. English. mo. Free. AFL-CIO Appalachian Council, 901 Stanley Building, Charleston WV 25301.

US/0271-0331
AQUATIC SERIES. [Aquat. ser.]. No. 8 (Jan. 1974)-. Monographic series. English. Price varies per volume. Missouri Department of Conservation, 2901 North Ten Mile Drive, Jefferson City MO 65101. ***Continues*** *D-J Series, 0737-5107.*
Ind/Abst GeoRef.

●CN/1188-553X
AQUATIC SURVIVAL. **See** Fish and Fisheries.

GW/0003-9306
ARCHIV FUER NATURSCHUTZ UND LANDSCHAFTSFORSCHUNG. [Arch. Naturschutz Landschaftsforsch.]. **Added/Corp** Deutsche Akademie der Landwirtschaftswissenschaften zu Berlin Deutsche Akademie der Landwirtschaftswissenschaften zu Berlin. (1961)-. Periodical. German (summaries and/or abstracts in English and Russian; table of contents in English and Russian). qt. $151.00 (academic institutions), $236.00 (corporate institutions). Harwood Academic Publishers, PO Box 90, Reading RG1 8JL England. **Tel** 011 44 734 560080. **(Subscription address:** International Publishers Distributor at one of the following addresses: 820 Town Center Drive, Langhorne, PA 19047; or PO Box 90, Reading Berkshire RG1 8JL UK; or Kent Ridge PO Box 1180, Singapore 9111, Republic of Singapore) **CODEN** ARNLBG. **[CCC].** Documents available from CASDDS.
Ind/Abst Chem. Abstr. (1961-1982); EMBASE; For. Prod. Abstr.; For. Abstr.; Hortic. Abstr.; INIS Atomindex [Micro.]; Irr. Drain. Abstr.; Leis. Recreat. Tour. Abstr.; Nutr. Abstr. Rev., Ser. B, Live Feeds and Feed.; Ornamental Hort. (1991-); Life Sci. Collect.; Rural Dev. Abstr.; Soils Fert.; World Agric. Econ.

US/0044-8788
AREAS OF CONCERN. Periodical. English. mo. Areas of Concern, PO Box 47, Bryn Mawr PA 19010. **Tel** (215)527-1129. available in microform from Xerox; available on microfilm from University Microfilms International (UMI).

US/0277-9455
ARID LANDS NEWSLETTER. [Arid lands newsl.]. **Added/Corp** University of Arizona. Office of Arid Lands Studies. (1975)-. Newsletter. English. Twice a year. Free. University of Arizona / Arid Lands, Office of Arid Lands Studies, 845 North Park Avenue, Tucson AZ 85719. **Tel** (602)621-1955. **CODEN** ALABDH. ***Continues*** *University of Arizona. Arid/Semi-Arid Natural Resources Program. Newsletter.*
Ind/Abst AGRICOLA [Select. Cov.]; Environ. Period. Bibliogr.; Fish Rev. (Jan. 1989-July 1992); GeoRef; Hortic. Abstr.; Nutr. Abstr. Rev., Ser. A, Hum. Exp.; Rural Dev. Abstr.; Soils Fert.; Wildl. Rev. (Jan. 1989-July 1992); World Agric. Econ.

US/0745-0834
ARIZONA WILDLIFE NEWS. (ARIZONA WILDLIFE NEWS : OFFICIAL PUBLICATION OF THE ARIZONA WILDLIFE FEDERATION / ARIZONA WILDLIFE FEDERATION.). **Added/Corp** Arizona Wildlife Federation. **VFOAT** Wildlife News; AWN. (19??)-. Periodical. English. Twelve times a year. $25.00 Comes with Arizona Wildlife Federation membership. Arizona Wildlife Federation, 644 North Country Club Drive, Suite E, Mesa AZ 85201. **Tel** (602)644-0077.

US/0882-5572
ARIZONA WILDLIFE VIEWS. (ARIZONA WILDLIFE VIEWS : THE NEWSPAPER OF THE ARIZONA GAME AND FISH DEPARTMENT.). **Added/Corp** Arizona. Game and Fish Dept. **VFOAT** Wildlife Views. (19??)-. Periodical. English. mo. $6.50. Arizona Game & Fish Department, 2221 West Greenway Road, Phoenix AZ 85023. **Tel** (602)942-3000 ext.217. **ED** Charone Monday. **LC** SK51; .A33. **DD** 799/.09791. **Circ:** 20,000 (ctrl). ***Continues*** *Wildlife Views, 0043-5538.*

CN/0849-1410
ARK (TORONTO). (THE ARK / THE NATURE CONSERVANCY OF CANADA.). [Ark]. **Added/Corp** Nature Conservancy of Canada. (Winter 1989/1990)-. Periodical. English. sa. Nature Conservancy of Canada, 794A Broadview Avenue, Toronto, Ontario M4K 2P7 Canada. **DD** 333.95/16/0971. ***Continues*** *Newsletter (Nature Conservancy of Canada)., 0836-706X.*

US
ARKANSAS PRESERVATION. English. Four times a year (Seasonally). $15.00 (members) local organization; $20.00 (regular); $250.00 (businesses), includes Historic Preservation Alliance of Arkansas membership. Historic Preservation Alliance of Arkansas, PO Box 305, Little Rock AR 72203. **Tel** (501)372-4757. **ED** Jamye Landis. **Ad Acc. Circ:** 1,100.
Desc: Provides statewide news on developments in historic preservation, technical articles and other miscellaneous regular features.

●US/1063-0953
ARKANSAS WILDLIFE. [Ark. wildl.]. **Added/Corp** Arkansas Game & Fish Commission. Vol. 23, Issue 1 (Spring 1992)-. Periodical. English. Five times a year (Mar., June, July, Oct., Dec.). $10.00. Arkansas Game and Fish Commission, Game & Fish Building, No 2 Natural Resources Drive, Little Rock AR 72205. **Tel** (501)223-6300, (800)364-4163, FAX (501)223-6447. **ED** Keith Sutton, (phone: (501)223-6406). **LC** SK371; .A55. **DD** 639. **Bk Rev**, (Qty: varies). **Circ:** 40,000. ***Continues*** *Arkansas Game and Fish, 0004-1807.*

CN/1188-2891
ARNEWS ANNUAL REPORT. **See** Forestry.

MY/0128-0538
ASIAN WETLAND NEWS. **Added/Corp** Asian Wetland Bureau. No. 1 (Jan. 1988)-. Periodical. English. sa. Free (Malaysia); $10.00 (individual), $20.00 (institution) other. Asian Wetland Bureau / Institute of Advanced Studies, University of Malaysia, 59100 Kuala Lumpur Malaysia. **Tel** 03 75 66624.
Ind/Abst Fish Rev. (Jan. 1989-July 1992); Wildl. Rev. (Jan. 1989-July 1992).

US/0004-6809
ATLANTIC NATURALIST. (ATLANTIC NATURALIST / AUDUBON SOCIETY OF THE DISTRICT OF COLUMBIA.). [Atl. nat.]. **Added/Corp** Audubon Society of the District of Columbia. Audubon Naturalist Society of the Central Atlantic States. (1950)-. English. an. Audubon Naturalist Society of the Central Atlantic States, 8940 Jones Mill Road, Chevy Chase MD 20815. **Tel** (301)652-9188, FAX (301)951-7179. **DD** 500. ***Continues*** *Wood Thrush.*
Ind/Abst Biol. Dig.; Fish Rev. (Jan. 1989-July 1992); Wildl. Rev. (Jan. 1989-July 1992).

US
ATTRACT WILDLIFE, IMPROVE OUR ENVIRONMENT. **Main/Corp** Kester's Wild Game Food Nurseries. (19??)-. Periodical. English.

US/0093-6596
AUDIT REPORT - STATE OF NEVADA. DEPARTMENT OF CONSERVATION AND NATIONAL RESOURCES. DIVISION OF STATE PARKS. ***Title Change.*** (DIVISION OF STATE PARKS AUDIT REPORT.). **Main/Corp** Nevada. Legislative Counsel Bureau. English. an. Nevada Legislative Counsel Bureau / Carson City, Legislative Building, Carson City NV 89701. **LC** SB482.N3; N46A. **DD** 353.9/793/0086305. ***Continued by*** *State of Nevada, Department of Conservation and Natural Resources, Division of State Parks Audit Report.*

US/0097-7136
AUDUBON. [Audubon]. **Added/Corp** National Audubon Society. **VFOAT** Audubon Magazine. Vol. 63, No. 4, (July/Aug. 1961)-. Periodical. English. bm. Free to members; $20.00 membership. National Audubon Society, 700 Broadway, New York NY 10003. **Tel** (212)979-3117. **(Subscription address:** Neodata / Colorado, PO Box 2606, Boulder Boulder CO 80322.) **ED** Les Line, Gary Soucie, Kathleen Fitzpatrick, Mary McCarthy, Catherine Dold. **LC** QL671; .A82. **DD** 596.0973. **CODEN** AUDUAD. **Circ:** 425,000. available on microfilm and microfiche from University Microfilms International (UMI); available on an online database (file 647/Full-Text) from DIALOG. Documents available from BIOSIS Document Express, UMI Article Clearinghouse, Documents on Demand, Magazine Collection. ***Continues*** *Audubon Magazine, 0004-7694.*
Desc: Illustrated articles on nature and wildlife. Reports on environmental problems. Features on fascinating people and wilderness preservation.
Ind/Abst Acad. Abstr. Full Text Elite (Jan. 1984-); Acad. Abstr. (Jan. 1984-); Acad. Ind. [Computer File] (1984-); Acad. Search (Jan. 1984-); AQUAREF; Biol. Abstr.; Biol. Dig.; Book Rev. Index; Ecol. Abstr. (?-?); Energy Inf. Abstr.; Environ. Abstr.; Environ. Period. Bibliogr.; Expand. Acad. Index (1984-); Garden Lit. (1992-); Gen. Period. Index (1985-); Gen. Sci. Index; INFO-SOUTH Abstr.; Key Word Index Wildl. Res.; Mag. Artic. Summar. Elite (Jan. 1984-); Mag. Artic. Summar. Select (Jan. 1984-); Mag. Artic. Summar. CD-ROM (Jan. 1984-); Mag. Express (1986-) [Full Txt.]; Mag. Index Plus (1989-); Mag. Index Sel. Microfiche (1986-) [Full Txt.]; Mag. Index. Sel. (1986-); Mag. Search; Mid. Search (Jan. 1984-); Newsp. Period. Abstr. (1988-); Read. Guide Abstr. Select Ed.; Read. Guide Period. Lit.; Resource/One Ondisc; Mag. Index (1977-); TOM Gen. Index (1985-) [Full Txt.]; Vocat. Search (Jan. 1984-).

US/0898-915X
AUDUBON ACTIVIST. **See** Environmental Issues-Ecology.

US/0571-8805
AUDUBON CONSERVATION REPORT. No. 1-. Monographic series. English. ir. Price varies per volume. National Audubon Society, 700 Broadway, New York NY 10003. **Tel** (212)979-3117.

AT
AUSTRALIAN DEER. **Added/Corp** Australian Deer Association. (19??)-. Periodical. English. bm (6 issues). 40.00Aus$. Australian Deer Association, PO Box 363, Launceston 7250 Tasmania Australia. **Tel** 011 61 003 340114. Index available. cum. index. **Bk Rev. Ad Acc. Circ:** 5,500 (ctrl).
Ind/Abst Fish Rev.; Key Word Index Wildl. Res.; Wildl. Rev.

US/0567-2856
AVICULTURAL BULLETIN. **See** Zoology-Ornithology.

CN/0228-8842
B.C. NATURALIST. [B.C. nat.]. **Added/Corp** Federation of British Columbia Naturalists. **VAT** British Columbia Naturalist. Vol. 18, No. 1 (Spring 1980)-. Periodical. English. Six times a year (Feb., Apr., June,

Aug., Oct., Dec.). 15.00Can$. Federation of British Columbia Naturalists, 321-1367 West Broadway, Vancouver British Columbia V6H 4A9 Canada. **Tel** (604)737-6057, FAX (604)738-7175. **ED** Jude Grass (editor's address: #103-7065 Stride Ave, Burnaby BC V3N 1T3 Canada; editor's phone: (604)520-3706). **DD** 333.95/16/09711. **Bk Rev. Ad Acc. Circ:** 8,000 (ctrl). ***Continues** Newsletter (Federation of British Columbia Naturalists), 0046-3566.*
Desc: A publication mailed directly to our members and others to keep them informed and advised of conservation, nature and the outdoors in British Columbia.
Ind/Abst Fish Rev. (Jan. 1989-July 1992); Wildl. Rev. (Jan. 1989-July 1992).

US/1049-3972
BACK FORTY (ALEXANDRIA, VA.), THE. (THE BACK FORTY : THE NEWSLETTER OF LAND CONSERVATION LAW.). [Back Forty]. **Added/Corp** Land Conservation Law Institute. (1990)-. Newsletter. English. Six times a year. $110.00 (one year), $195.00 (two year). Hastings College of Law, 200 McAllister Street, San Francisco CA 94102. **Tel** (415)565-4816, (415)565-4738, FAX (415)565-4814. **DD** 344.

FI/0357-2994
BALTIC SEA ENVIRONMENT PROCEEDINGS. **See** Earth Sciences-Oceanography.

US/1049-0043
BATS (AUSTIN, TEX.). (BATS.). [Bats]. **Added/Corp** Bat Conservation International, Inc. (1983)-. Periodical. English. qt. $25.00 (included in regular membership dues). Bat Conservation International Inc, PO Box 1626033, Austin TX 78716. **Tel** (512)327-9721. **LC** QL737.C5; B36. **DD** 599.4.
Ind/Abst Fish Rev. (Jan. 1989-July 1992); Wildl. Rev. (Jan. 1989-July 1992).

UK/0265-3656
BBC WILDLIFE. [BBC wildl.]. **VFOAT** B.B.C. Wildlife; BBC Wildlife Magazine; B.B.C. Wildlife Magazine. Vol. 1, No. 1 (Nov. 1983)-. Periodical. English. mo. $35.00 (one year), $60.00 (two year) US and Canada; £21.50 UK and Ireland; £23.00 other. Wildlife Publications Ltd, PO Box 168, Tunbridge Wells, Kent TN2 3UX England. **Tel** 44 892 511678. Documents available from Documents on Demand. ***Continues** Wildlife (London, England).*
Ind/Abst Biol. Dig.; Curr. Aware. Biol. Sci., CABS; Ecol. Abstr.; Environ. Abstr.; Environ. Period. Bibliogr.; Geogr. Abstr. Human Geogr.; Int. Dev. Abstr.; Key Word Index Wildl. Res.

AT/0313-7872
BEACH CONSERVATION. ***Ceased.*** [Beach conserv.]. (1970)-Vol. 69 (1993). Periodical. English. qt. Beach Protection Authority of Queensland, GPO Box 2595, Brisbane Queensland, 4000 Australia. **Tel** 11 61 7 2277111. **DD** 333.91709943. **Circ:** 5000 (ctrl).
Desc: Technical articles and news items dealing with protection of beaches against erosion in Queensland, Australia.

US/0885-615X
BEAR NEWS. [Bear news]. **Added/Corp** Great Bear Foundation. (19??)-. Periodical. English. ir (3-4 issues). $15.00. Great Bear Foundation, PO Box 2699, Missoula MT 59806. **Tel** (406)721-3009. **ED** Lance Olsen. **DD** 639. **Bk Rev. Circ:** 3,600. Documents available from Documents on Demand.
Desc: Covers conservation of bear habitats around the world.
Ind/Abst Environ. Abstr.

GW/0340-3750
BERICHT - NATURFORSCHENDE GESELLSCHAFT BAMBERG. (BERICHT / NATURFORSCHENDE GESELLSCHAFT BAMBERG.). [Ber. - Naturforsch. Ges. Bamb.]. **Main/Corp** Naturforschende Gesellschaft Bamberg. Vol. 30, (1947)-. Periodical. German. Naturforschende Gesellschaft Bamberg, Bergstrasse 14, W-8602 Viereth Germany. ***Continues** Bericht der Naturforschende Gesellschaft in Bamberg.*
Ind/Abst GeoRef.

US
BIENNIAL REPORT / IOWA PRESERVES BOARD. **See** Natural History.

US/0085-297X
BIENNIAL REPORT - MAINE, SOIL AND WATER CONSERVATION COMMISSION. **Main/Corp** Maine. Soil and Water Conservation Commission. Periodical. English. be. Maine Soil and Water Conservation Commission, Augusta ME 04330. **LC** S624.M2; M36A. **DD** 353.9/741/008232.

US/0090-8177
BIENNIAL REPORT - MINNESOTA DEPARTMENT OF NATURAL RESOURCES. (BIENNIAL REPORT.). **Main/Corp** Minnesota. Dept. of Natural Resources. English. be. Department of Natural Resources / Minnesota, 350 Centennial Building, St Paul MN 55155. **LC** HC107.M6; A33. **DD** 353.9/776/008232. ***Continues** Minnesota. Dept. of Conservation. Biennial Report.*

US
BIENNIAL REPORT / STATE OF CALIFORNIA, CALIFORNIA COASTAL COMMISSION. **Main/Corp** California Coastal Commission. (1978)-. English. be. California Coastal Commission, 631 Howard Street/4th Floor, San Francisco CA 94105. **Tel** (415)543-8555. **LC** HT393.C3; C318a. **DD** 353.97940082/326.

US
BIENNIAL REPORT - STATE OF WISCONSIN, CONSERVATION WORK PROJECTS BOARD. **Main/Corp** Wisconsin. Conservation Work Projects Board. 1977/79-. English. be. Conservation Work Projects Board, Box 7773, Madison WI 53707. **LC** S916.W6; C66A. **DD** 333.7/2/09775.

UK/0960-3115
BIODIVERSITY AND CONSERVATION. (1992)-. Periodical. English. ir (9 issues). $365.00 US and Canada; £215.00 Europe; £235.00 other. Chapman & Hall, 2-6 Boundary Row, London SE1 8HN England. **Tel** 011 44 71 865 0066, FAX 011 44 71 522 9623, telex 290164 Chapmag. **(Subscription address:** Chapman & Hall, Cheriton House, North Way, Andover, Hampshire, SP10 5BE England.**) ED** Alan T. Bull (International Institute of Biotechnology, University of Kent, UK). Documents available from The Genuine Article, ADONIS.
Desc: Devoted to the publication of papers on biological diversity in all its aspects, its description, analysis and conservation, and its controlled and rational use by man. Deals with the practicalities of conservation management, economic, social and political issues and case studies. Provides a forum for examining the conflicts between sustainable development and human dependence on biodiversity, especially in such fields as agriculture, environmental management and biotechnology.
Ind/Abst ADONIS; Curr. Aware. Biol. Sci., CABS; Curr. Contents, Agric. Biol. Environ. Sci.; Res. Alert [Select. Cov.]; Soc. Sci. Cit. Index [Select. Cov.].

NE/0168-2563
BIOGEOCHEMISTRY. [Biogeochemistry]. Vol. 1, No. 1 (1984)-. Academic Scholarly Publication. English. mo. $1,132.00. Kluwer Academic Publishers, Postbus 322, 3300 AH Dordrecht, The Netherlands. **Tel** 011 (31) 78 524400, FAX 011 31 78 183273, telex 20083. **ED** Robert W Howarth. **CODEN** BIOGEP. **[CCC]. Ad Acc. Pr Rev. Acid Free.** available on microfilm and microfiche from University Microfilms International (UMI). Documents available from The Genuine Article, BIOSIS Document Express, CASDDS.
Desc: Publishes original papers on biotic controls on the chemistry of the environment, or with the geochemical control of the structure and functions of ecosystems. Cycles are considered, either of individual elements or of specific classes of natural or anthropogenic compounds in ecosystems. Particular emphasis is placed on the interactions of element cycles. Global aspects of biogeochemistry are covered in the form of work on the global carbon and sulfur cycles, for instance, and studies on both natural and artificial ecosystems are published when they contribute to a general understanding of biogeochemistry.
Ind/Abst AGRICOLA [Select. Cov.]; Biol. Abstr. (1986-); Chem. Abstr. (1984-); Curr. Aware. Biol. Sci., CABS; Curr. Contents, Agric. Biol. Environ. Sci.; Ecol. Abstr. (1984-); For. Abstr.; Geogr. Abstr. Phys. Geogr.; Geol. Abstr.; GeoRef; Irr. Drain. Abstr.; Res. Alert [Full Cov.]; Sci. Cit. Index; SCISEARCH; Soils Fert.

UK/0006-3207
BIOLOGICAL CONSERVATION. [Biol. conserv.]. Vol. 1, No. 1 (Oct. 1988)-. Academic Scholarly Publication. English (French). Twelve times a year. $894.00 The Americas; £600.00 other. Elsevier Applied Science, An Imprint of Elsevier Science Ltd., The Boulevard, Langford Lane, Kidlington, Oxford OX5 1GB United Kingdom. **Tel** 011 44 865 843000, 011 44 865 843699, FAX 011 44 865 843010. **(Subscription address:** Elsevier Science Ltd. Oxford Fulfillment Centre, PO Box 800, Kidlington, Oxford OX5 1DX United Kingdom.**) ED** Eric Duffey. **LC** S900; .B5. **DD** 333.7/2/05. **NLM** W1 BI74. **CODEN** BICOBK. **[CCC]. Bk Rev. Ad Acc. Pr Rev.** available on microfilm and microfiche from University Microfilms International (UMI). Documents available from The Genuine Article, BIOSIS Document Express, Documents on Demand.
Desc: Original papers dealing with the preservation of wildlife and the conservation or wise use of biological and allied natural resources. It is concerned with plants and animals and their habitats in a changing and increasingly man-dominated biosphere in fresh and salt waters as well as on land and in the atmosphere.
Ind/Abst AGRICOLA [Select. Cov.]; AQUAREF; Biocont. News Inf.; Biol. Agric. Index; Biol. Abstr.; Coal Abstr.; Curr. Aware. Biol. Sci., CABS; Curr. Contents, Agric. Biol. Environ. Sci.; Curr. Geogr. Publ. (199?-); Curr. Ref. Fish Res.; Ecol. Abstr.; Ecology Abstr.; EMBASE; Energy Inf. Abstr.; Energy Res. Abstr. (June 1980-); Entomol. Abstr.; Environ. Abstr.; Environ. Period. Bibliogr.; Field Crop Abstr.; For. Prod. Abstr.; For. Abstr.; Geogr. Abstr. Phys. Geogr.; Geogr. Abstr. Human Geogr.; GeoRef; Grasslands For. Abstr.; Index Vet.; Int. Aerosp. Abstr.; Int. Dev. Abstr.; Key Word Index Wildl. Res.; Leis. Recreat. Tour. Abstr.; Life Sci. Collect.; Plant Breed. Abstr.; Plant Genet. Resour. Abstr.; Res. Alert [Full Cov.]; Rev. Agric. Entomol.; Rev. Med. Vet. Entomol.; Sci. Cit. Index; SCISEARCH; Seed Abstr.; Soc. Sci. Cit. Index [Select. Cov.]; Vet. Bull.; Wildl. Rev.

US/0895-1926
BIOLOGICAL REPORT (WASHINGTON, D.C.). **See** Biology.

CN/0824-1600
BIOSPHERE (OTTAWA). (BIOSPHERE.). [Biosphere]. **Added/Corp** Federation Canadienne de la Faune. Vol. 1, No. 1 (Jan./Feb. 1985)-. Periodical. French. bm (6 issues). 25.00Can$ Canada; 33.00Can$ other. Canadian Wildlife Federation, 2740 Queensview Drive, Ottawa Ontario K2B 1A2 Canada. **Tel** (800)563-9453, (613)721-2286. **DD** 333.95/05. Index available. cum. index. **Circ:** 30,000.
Ind/Abst Can. Period. Index (19??-); Point Repere.

●US/1061-5466
BIRDS OF NORTH AMERICA, THE. **See** Zoology-Ornithology.

ZA/0045-219X
BLACK LECHWE. Periodical. English. K6.00 (surface mial); K0.21 (airmail) US and Australasia; K0.19 (airmail) Europe; K0.18 (airmail) South Africa. Black Lechwe, Wildlife Conservation Society of Zambia. **LC** S964.Z35; B55. **DD** 639/.9/096894.
Ind/Abst Fish Rev.; Wildl. Rev.

AT
BOARD OF ENVIRONMENTAL STUDIES RESEARCH PAPER. **Added/Corp** University of Newcastle. Board of Environmental Studies. **VFOAT** Research Paper. (1973)-. Monographic series. English. ir. Price varies per volume. University of Newcastle / Board of Environmental Studies, Newcastle New South Wales 2308 Australia.

AT/0159-6586
BOGONG. [Bogong]. (1980)-. Periodical. English. qt (Mar., June, Sept., Dec.). 15.00Aus$ individuals; 20.00Aus$ institutions. Environment Centre, PO Box 1875, Canberra CT ACT, 2001 Australia. **Tel** 062-473064. **ED** Kerrie Tucker. **DD** 304.20994. Index available. cum. index. **Bk Rev**, (Qty: 16). **Ad Acc. Circ:** 500.
Ind/Abst Altern. Press Index (199?-).

BL/0585-8658
BOLETIM DE RECURSOS NATURAIS. [Bol. rec. nat.]. Bulletin. Portuguese. Sudene DRN, 10 Andar Av Dantas Barreto, Recife Brazil. **LC** HC187.5; .B58. **DD** 333.7/0981. **CODEN** SUDBAI. ***Continues** Sudene: Boletin de Recursos Naturais.*
Ind/Abst GeoRef.

BL
BOLETIM FBCN. **VFOAT** Boletim F.B.C.N. Began with V. for 1977. Bulletin. Portuguese. an. Cr$10.00 Brazil; $30.00 other. Fundacao Brasileira Para a Conservacao da Natureza, rua Miranda Valverde 103, Botafogo 22.281, Rio de Janeiro RJ Brazil. **Tel** (021)266-5008, telex 2137984 FBCN BR. **LC** QH77.B7; F8. **DD** 333.95/16/0981. **Ad Acc. Circ:** 3,500 (ctrl). ***Continues** Boletim Informativo (Fundacao Brasileira Para A Conservacao da Natureza).*

SA/0256-9175
BONTEBOK. [Bontebok]. **Added/Corp** Cape of Good Hope (South Africa). Cape Dept. of Nature and Environmental Conservation. (19??)-. English. ir. Free. Department of Nature and Environmental Conservation, Private Bag X9086, Cape Town, 8000 South Africa. **Tel** 011 27 21 4834227. **LC** QH77; .S62; B66. **DD** 639.9/0968. ***Continues** Cape of Good Hope (South Africa). Dep. of Nature Conservation. Investigational Report, 0528-0397.*
Ind/Abst Life Sci. Collect.

UK
BOTANIC GARDENS CONSERVATION NEWS : MAGAZINE OF THE IUCN BOTANIC GARDENS CONSERVATION SECRETARIAT. **VFOAT** BGC News; Botanic Garden Conservation News. Vol. 1, No. 1 (Dec. 1987)-. Periodical. English. sa. IUCN Botanic Gardens Conservation, 199 Kew Road Descanso House, Richmond Sur TW9 3BW England.

US/0899-2681
BOUNDARY WATERS JOURNAL, THE. [Bound. Waters j.]. (198?)-. Periodical. English. Four times a year (Mar., June, Sept., Dec.). $13.00 (one year); $24.00 (two years); $34.00 (three years). Boundary Waters Journal, 9396 Rocky Ledge Road, Ely MN 55731. **Tel** (218)365-6184. **ED** Stuart Osthoff. **DD** 917. Index available. cum. index. **Bk Rev. Ad Acc, Adv Mgr:** L. Antonson, **Tel** (218)365-6184. **Circ:** 24,000.
Desc: This journal contains 12 in-depth articles for everyone who wants to learn more about Boundary Waters Canoe Area Wilderness. Topics includes wilderness, canoe routes, camping, fishing, resort/cabin vacations, hiking, hunting, photography, cross country

skiing, wildlife, conservation and resource management, equipment field test reviews, outdoor cooking, area history, regional lifestyles and personalities, fictional essays plus many other special features.

UK
BRITISH WILDLIFE. **See** Recreation, Leisure-Outdoor Life.

US/0889-6445
BUGLE. (BUGLE : THE QUARTERLY JOURNAL OF THE ROCKY MOUNTAIN ELK FOUNDATION.). [Bugle]. **Added/Corp** Rocky Mountain Elk Foundation. (19??)-. Periodical. English. qt. $25.00. Rocky Mountain Elk Foundation, PO Box 8249, Missoula MT 59807. **Tel** (406)523-4572, FAX (406)549-4325. **ED** Lance Schelvan. Index available. **Bk Rev. Ad Acc, Adv Mgr:** Kathy Jackson, **Tel** (406)523-4595. **Circ:** 150,000 (ctrl).
Desc: Wildlife photography, essays on hunting ethics, and hunting stories.

US
BULLETIN / COLLEGE OF FORESTRY, WILDLIFE AND RANGE SCIENCES. No. 8 (April 1976)-. Bulletin. English. ir. Price varies per volume. University of Idaho College of Forestry, Wildlife, and Range Sciences, Moscow ID 83843. **Tel** (208)885-7952. **ED** George Savage. **Pr Rev. Circ:** 1,000-3,000. ***Continues** Bulletin (University of Idaho. Forest, Wildlife and Range Experiment Station).*
Desc: Results of research in fisheries, wildlife, forestry, forest products, range science, wildland recreation management and tourism.
Ind/Abst Biol. Dig.

US/0073-4586
BULLETIN - FOREST, WILDLIFE AND RANGE EXPERIMENT STATION. [Bull. - For. Wildl. Range Exp. Sta.]. **Main/Corp** Idaho. University. Forest, Wildlife, and Range Experiment Station, Moscow. **Added/Corp** Intermountain Forest and Range Experiment Station (U.S.). (1955)-. Monographic series. English. ir. Price varies per volume. University of Idaho Forest Wildlife and Range Experiment Station, Moscow ID 83843. **Tel** (208)885-6674. **ED** George H. Savage. **LC** SD12; .I218. **Circ:** 1,500.
Desc: Nonscheduled research reports by scientist of the University of Idaho Forest, Wildlife and Range Experimental Station.
Ind/Abst For. Prod. Abstr.; For. Abstr.

NE/0074-6444
BULLETIN - INTERNATIONAL INSTITUTE FOR LAND RECLAMATION AND IMPROVEMENT. [Bull. - Int. Inst. Land Reclam. Improv.]. **Main/Corp** International Institute for Land Reclamation and Improvement. (1958)-. Monographic series. English. ir. Price varies per volume. International Institute for Land Reclamation and Improvement, PO Box 45, 6700 AA Wageningen Netherlands. **Tel** 011 31 837019100, FAX 11524, telex 75230 NL. **DD** 627. **CODEN** BILRA5.
Ind/Abst GeoRef; Soils Fert.

AT/0157-308X
BULLETIN OF THE AUSTRALIAN LITTORAL SOCIETY. [Bull. Aust. Littoral Soc.]. (1978)-. Periodical. English. Six times a year (five or six issues per year). 30.00Aus$ (institutions), 25.00Aus$ (individuals) Comes with Australian Littoral Society membership. Australian Littoral Society, PO Box 49, Moorooka Queensland 4105 Australia. **Tel** 011 61 07 848 5235, FAX 011 61 07 892 5814. **ED** D. Tarte. **DD** 333.91706294. Index available. **Bk Rev**, (Qty: 2-3). **Circ:** 750. Documents available from the publisher.
Desc: Journal of the Australian Littoral Society, for those concerned about life in Australia's rivers, coastal waters, and coral reefs.

UK
BULLETIN OF THE INTERNATIONAL COUNCIL FOR BIRD PRESERVATION. **Main/Corp** International Council for Bird Preservation. No. 8 (1962)-. Bulletin. English. an. $35.00. International Council for Bird Preservation, 32 Cambridge Road, Girton Cambridge CB3 0PJ England. **Tel** 011 44 223 277318, FAX 011 44 223 277200. **ED** T Urquhart. **Circ:** 4,000 (ctrl). ***Continues** Bulletin of the International Committee for Bird Preservation.*
Desc: Report on annual activity to further cause of world bird conservation, including education, research and field projects.

US/0740-3771
BULLETIN / PACIFIC SEABIRD GROUP. **See** Zoology-Ornithology.

CN/0823-5392
BULLETIN - SOTRAC. (BULLETIN : ORGANE D'INFORMATION SOTRAC.). [Bull. - SOTRAC]. **VAT** Bulletin - Societe des Travaux de Correction du Complexe la Grande. V. 1, No 1 (Feb. 1979)-. Bulletin. English (French and Cree). ir. SOTRAC, 8th Floor/800 Maisonneuve Boulevard East, Montreal Quebec H2L 4M8 Canada. **DD** 333.7/2/06071417.

US
BULLETIN - STATE OF ALASKA, ALASKA OIL AND GAS CONSERVATION COMMISSION. **Main/Corp** Alaska Oil and Gas Conservation Commission. (1979)-. Periodical. English. Twelve times a year. Free on request. Alaska Oil & Gas Conservation Commission, 3001 Porcupine Drive, Anchorage AK 99501. **Tel** (907)279-1433, FAX (907)276-7542. **Pr Rev. Circ:** 300. available on microfiche. ***Continues** Bulletin - State of Alaska, Division of Oil and Gas Conservation.*
Desc: Synopsis of conservation rulings issued, lists of drilling permits and information on recently completed wells, summaries of petroleum production and water injection operations.

US/1044-4823
BULLETIN - UNIVERSITY OF CALIFORNIA (SYSTEM). DIVISION OF AGRICULTURE AND NATURAL RESOURCES. **See** Agriculture.

US/0506-7510
BULLETIN - VERMONT FISH AND GAME DEPARTMENT. **Main/Corp** Vermont. Fish and Game Department. **VFOAT** Vermont Fish and Game Department Bulletin. (196?)-. Bulletin. English. Price varies per volume. Vermont Fish and Wildlife Department, 103 South Main, Building 10-S, Waterbury VT 05671. **Tel** (802)244-7331. **DD** 333.7. ***Continues** Wildlife Bulletin.*

US/0271-8545
BULLETIN - WASHINGTON DEPARTMENT OF NATURAL RESOURCES, DIVISION OF GEOLOGY AND EARTH RESOURCES. **See** Earth Sciences-Geology.

US
BULLETIN - WEST VIRGINIA DEPARTMENT OF NATURAL RESOURCES, WILDLIFE RESOURCES DIVISION. **Main/Corp** West Virginia. Wildlife Resources Division. Bulletin. English. Price varies per volume. West Virginia Wildlife Resources Division, 1800 Washington Street East, Charleston WV 25305. ***Continues** Bulletin - West Virginia Department of Natural Resources, Division of Game and Fish.*

US/0898-2996
BUZZWORM (BOULDER, COLO.). ***Title Change.*** (BUZZWORM.). [Buzzworm]. **VFOAT** Buzzworm, the Environmental Journal. Vol. 1, No. 1 (Summer 1988)-(1993. Periodical. English. bm. Buzzworm Inc., 2305 Canyon Boulevard, Suite 206, Boulder CO 80302. **Tel** (800)825-0061, (303)442-1969. **(Subscription address:** PO Box 6853, Syracuse, NY 13217-7930) **ED** Joseph E Daniel and Elizabeth Darby Junkin. **LC** QH75.A1; B89. **DD** 333.95/16. Index available. **Bk Rev. Ad Acc. Circ:** 50,000. available on microfilm and microfiche from University Microfilms International (UMI). Documents available from UMI Article Clearinghouse, Documents on Demand. ***Continued by** Earth Journal, 1059-6488.*
Desc: Environmental magazine that presents an independent look at conservation.
Ind/Abst Abr. Read. Guide Period. Lit. (1991-); Acad. Abstr. Full Text Elite (Jan. 1992-Oct. 1993); Acad. Abstr. (Jan. 1992-Oct. 1993); Acad. Search (Jan. 1992-Oct. 1993); Curr. Index J. Educ.; Energy Inf. Abstr.; Environ. Abstr.; Environ. Period. Bibliogr.; Garden Lit. (1992-); Gen. Period. Index (1989-); Health Source (Jan. 1992-); INFO-SOUTH Abstr.; Mag. Artic. Summar. Elite (Jan. 1992-Oct. 1993); Mag. Artic. Summar. Select (Jan. 1992-); Mag. Artic. Summar. CD-ROM (Jan. 1992-Oct. 1993); Mag. Index Plus (1989-); Mag. Index. Sel. (1989-); Mag. Search; Mid. Search (Jan. 1992-); Newsp. Period. Abstr. (1988-); Prim. Search (Jan. 1992-); Read. Guide Abstr. Select Ed.; Read. Guide Period. Lit. (1991-); Mag. Index (1989-); TOM Gen. Index (1989-) [Full Txt.].

NE
CADDET NEWSLETTER. **See** Energy.

US/0008-1078
CALIFORNIA FISH AND GAME. [Calif. fish game]. **Added/Corp** California. Dept. of Fish and Game. California. Fish and Game Commission. California. Division of Fish and Game. Vol. 1 (Oct. 1914)-. Periodical. English. Four times a year. $10.00. California Department of Fish and Game, 1416 9th Street, Sacramento CA 95814. **Tel** (916)653-7664. **ED** Dr. Loft. **LC** SK373; .C3. **DD** 799. **CODEN** CAFGAX. Index available. **Bk Rev**, (Qty: 2-6). **Pr Rev. Circ:** 2,000 (ctrl). available on microfilm and microfiche from University Microfilms International (UMI). Documents available from The Genuine Article, BIOSIS Document Express, Documents on Demand.
Desc: Presents results of scientific investigations as they relate to management programs and the conservation of California natural resources.
Ind/Abst Aquat. Sci. Fish. Abstr. (Computer File); Biol. Abstr.; Calif. Period. Index; Calif. Period. Microfi. (19??-); Curr. Aware. Biol. Sci., CABS; Curr. Contents, Agric. Biol. Environ. Sci.; Curr. Ref. Fish Res.; Ecol. Abstr. (?-?); Ecology Abstr.; Electron. Commun. Abstr. J.; Energy Inf. Abstr.; Environ. Abstr.; Environ. Period. Bibliogr.; For. Abstr.; Index Vet.; ISMEC Bull.; Key Word Index Wildl. Res.; Leis. Recreat. Tour. Abstr.; Nutr. Abstr. Rev., Ser. B, Live Feeds and Feed.; Nutr. Abstr. Rev., Ser. A, Hum. Exp.; Ocean. Abstr.; Life Sci. Collect.; Pollut. Abstr. Indexes; Protozoolog. Abstr.; Res. Alert [Select. Cov.]; Rev. Agric. Entomol.; Rev. Med. Vet. Entomol.; Saf. Sci. Abstr. J.; SCISEARCH; Sel. Water Resour. Abstr.; Vet. Bull.; Wildl. Rev.

CN/0822-2320
CANADIAN WILDLIFE ADMINISTRATION. [Can. wildl. adm.]. Periodical. English (French). Canadian Wildlife Service Publications, Environment Canada, Ottawa Ontario K1A 0E7 Canada. **Tel** (819)997-1095, FAX (819)997-0547. **DD** 333.95/0971.
Ind/Abst Soc. Plann. Policy Dev. Abstr.; Sociol. Abstr. (?-?).

US
CARDINAL NEWS, THE. **See** Zoology.

CN/0712-2055
CARIBOU NEWS. (CARIBOU NEWS / TUTUK TUSARATSAIT.). [Caribou news]. **VFOAT** Tutuk Tusaratsait. **VAT** Tutuk Tusaratsait (1981). (1981)-. Periodical. English (Eskimo; summaries and/or abstracts in Cree). Six times a year. 21.30Can$ Canada; 27.30Can$ others. Nortext Information Design Ltd., 16 Concourse Gate, Suite 200, Nepean Ontario K2E 7S8 Canada. **Tel** (613)727-5466. **DD** 639.9/797357. ***Continues** Keewatin Caribou, 0712-2047.*

SZ
CAT NEWS. (19??)-. English. sa. $30.00. International Union for the Conservation of Nature & Natural Resources / IUCN, SSC Cat Specialist Group, World Conservation Centre, CH 1172 Bougy Switzerland. **Tel** 011 44 21 8086012, FAX 011 41 21 8086012. **ED** Peter Jackson. **Bk Rev. Circ:** 500.
Desc: Reports on the states and conservation of wild cats, principally from the Cat Specialist Groups of the World Conservation Union.

CN/1180-3223
CCI NEWSLETTER OTTAWA. (CCI NEWSLETTER.). [CCI newsl. Ott.]. **VFOAT** Bulletin de l'ICC; Canadian Conservation Institute Newsletter (Ottawa). (1992)-. Newsletter. Multiple languages. sa. Canadian Conservation Institute, National Museums of Canada, Ottawa Ontario K1A 0M8 Canada. **Tel** (613)998-3721. **DD** 363.6. ***Continues** Newsletter - Canadian Conservation Institute (1987), 1193-4816.*
Ind/Abst Museum Abstr.

CN/0714-6221
CCI NOTES. [CCI notes]. **Added/Corp** Canadian Conservation Institute. **VFOAT** Notes de l'ICC. **VAT** Canadian Conservation Institute Notes. (Mar. 1991)-. English. **DD** 069/.53/05. ***Continues** ICC Notes., 0714-6221.*

AT/0312-1372
CHAIN-REACTION (CARLTON, VIC.). (CHAIN-REACTION.). [Chain react.]. **Added/Corp** Friends of the Earth Australia. **VFOAT** Chain Reaction. (1975)-. Periodical. English. qt. 12.00Aus$ (1 year), 23.00Aus$ (2 year) student rate. Chain Reaction Cooperative Ltd, PO Box 45, OConnor ACT, 2601 Australia. **Tel** 11 61 6 2480289, FAX 011-61-8-2938535. **ED** Clare Henderson and Larry O'Loughlin. Index available. **Bk Rev. Ad Acc. Circ:** 4,000. ***Continues** Bulletin (Greenpeace Pacific), 0312-1364.*
Desc: Covers environmental issues, social issues, news and views not published by the main stream media.
Ind/Abst Altern. Press Index (199?-).

KO
CHAYON POHO. **Added/Corp** Chayon Poho Chungang Hyobuihoe (Korea). **VFOAT** The Conservation of Nature; Conservation of Nature. (19??)-. Periodical. Korean (Korean). bm. **LC** QH77.K6; C475.

KO
CHAYON POJON. **VFOAT** Nature Conservation. Periodical. English (Korean). qt. Hanguk Chayon Pojon Hyophoe, San 1 Chongnyangni-dong Tongdaemun-ku, Seoul 131 Korea. **LC** QH77.K6; C484.

KO
CHAYON POJON YONGU POGOSO. **VFOAT** Bulletin of the Korean Association for Conservation of Nature. (1979)-. Periodical. Korean (summaries and/or abstracts in English). Korean Association for Conservation of Nature, Hanguk Chayon Pojon Hyophoe, San 1 Chongnyangni-dong, Seoul 131 Korea. **LC** QH77.K6; C485.

PL/0009-6172
CHROMNY PRZYRODE OJCZYSTA. [Chronmy przyr. ojcysta]. **Added/Corp** Poland. Panstwowa Rada Ochrony Przyrody. Vol. 1 (Sept. 1945)-. Periodical. Polish (summaries and/or abstracts in English). bm. $39.00. **(Subscription address:** ARS Polona, PO Box 1001, 00068 Warsaw Poland.) **CODEN** CPZOAO.
Ind/Abst Fish Rev.; Wildl. Rev.

US
CIRCULAR (NEW YORK STATE MUSEUM : 1981). (CIRCULAR.). No. 49 (Dec. 1981)-. Monographic series. English. ir. Price varies per volume. New York State Museum, 3140 Cultural Education Center, Albany NY 12230. **Tel** (518)474-3505. Documents available from BIOSIS Document Express. ***Continues*** *Circular (New York State Museum and Science Service).*
Ind/Abst Biol. Abstr.; GeoRef.

US/0529-9268
CLEAN WATERS FOR OHIO. Periodical. English.
Ind/Abst Field Crop Abstr.; Grasslands For. Abstr.; Plant Breed. Abstr.; Protozoolog. Abstr.; Rev. Med. Vet. Mycology; Rev. Plant Pathol.; Weed Abstr.

CN
CLI REPORT. Main/Corp Canada Land Inventory. English. Information Canada, 171 Slater Street, Ottawa Ontario K1A 0S9 Canada. **Tel** (819)997-1095. **LC** HD107; .C3. **DD** 333.7/0971. ***Continues*** *Canada Land Inventory. Report, 0068-7693.*

US/0194-5742
COAST WATCH. See Earth Sciences-Oceanography.

US/0892-0753
COASTAL MANAGEMENT. [Coast. manage.]. Vol. 15, No. 1 (1987)-. Periodical. English. Four times a year. £99.00 UK; $163.00 other. Taylor & Francis Ltd., Rankine Road, Basingstoke Hampshire, RG24 8PR United Kingdom. **Tel** 011 44 256 840366, FAX 011 44 256 479438, telex 858540. **(Subscription address:** Taylor & Francis Inc., 1900 Frost Road, Suite 101, Bristol PA 19007-1598.**) ED** Marc J. Hershman (editor's address: School of Marine Affairs, University of Washington (HF-05), Seattle WA 98195). **DD** 309. **CODEN** CMANEF. **[CCC]. Bk Rev. Ad Acc. Pr Rev. Circ:** 800 (ctrl). available on microfilm and microfiche from University Microfilms International (UMI). Documents available from Article Express International, The Genuine Article, Petroleum Abstracts Document Delivery Service, Documents on Demand. ***Continues*** *Coastal Zone Management Journal, 0090-8339.*
Desc: Explores the technical, legal, political and social issues surrounding the managerial responsibilities of our valuable and unique coastal resources and environments. Presents timely information on management tools and techniques as well as recent findings from research and analysis that bear directly on management and policy. Serves as a forum for the exchange of ideas among professionals involved in the advancement of coastal management programs in developed and developing countries. An essential source of information to experts in the environmental sciences , engineering, law and resource planning.
Ind/Abst AQUAREF; Aquat. Sci. Fish. Abstr. (Computer File); Bioeng. Abstr. (1987-); Can. Environ. (1987-); Coal Abstr. (1987-); Curr. Aware. Biol. Sci., CABS; Curr. Contents, Agric. Biol. Environ. Sci.; Ecology Abstr.; Ei Page One (1987-); Electron. Commun. Abstr. J. (1987-); Energy Inf. Abstr. (1987-); Eng. Index Annu.; Environ. Abstr. (1987-); Environ. Period. Bibliogr.; Fish Rev.; Fluid Abstr., Civil Eng.; Fluid Abstr. Proc. Eng.; FLUIDEX; Geogr. Abstr. Phys. Geogr. (?-?); Geogr. Abstr. Human Geogr.; Geol. Abstr.; GeoRef (1987-); Index Period. Artic. Relat. Law (1987-19??);; Int. Aerosp. Abstr. (1987-); Int. Dev. Abstr.; ISMEC Bull. (1987-); Ocean. Abstr. (1987-); Oceanic Abstr. Indexes (1987-); PAIS Bull. (1987-); PAIS Int. Print (1991-); Life Sci. Collect. (1987-); Pet. Abstr. (1987-); Pollut. Abstr. Indexes (1987-); Public Aff. Inf. Serv. Bull. (1987-); Res. Alert [Select. Cov.]; Saf. Sci. Abstr. J. (1987-); SCISEARCH; Sel. Water Resour. Abstr. (1987-); Soc. Sci. Cit. Index [Select. Cov.]; Wildl. Rev.

US/0271-5376
COASTAL RESEARCH. See Earth Sciences.

US
CODE OF FEDERAL REGULATIONS. 10, ENERGY. See Energy.

US/0891-3463
COLORADO ENVIRONMENTAL REPORT, THE. (THE COLORADO ENVIRONMENTAL REPORT : THE VOICE OF COLORADO'S ENVIRONMENTAL COMMUNITY.). [Colo. environ. rep.]. **Added/Corp** Colorado Environmental Coalition. (Jan./Feb. 1986)-. Periodical. English. Six times a year. $30.00 membership. Colorado Environmental Coalition, 777 Grant Street / Suite 606, Denver CO 80203. **Tel** (303)837-8701. **ED** Elizabeth Otto. **DD** 333. **Bk Rev. Ad Acc. Circ:** 1,800.
Desc: Environmental articles, primarily about Colorado issues.

US/0010-1699
COLORADO OUTDOORS. [Colo. outdoors]. **Added/Corp** Colorado. Game and Fish Dept. Colorado. Game, Fish, and Parks Dept. Colorado. Division of Game, Fish, and Parks. Colorado. Division of Wildlife. **VFOAT** Outdoors. (1959)-. Periodical. English. Six times a year (Jan., Mar., May, July, Sept., Nov.). Free, Colorado schools and libraries; $8.50 other. Division of Wildlife, 6060 Broadway, Denver CO 80216. **Tel** (303)291-7469, FAX (303)298-1120. **ED** Russell C. Bromby (phone: (303)291-7286). **LC** SK351; .C66. **DD** 799/.09788; 333.7. Index Available Received separately--bound from publisher (Nov/Dec bound issues). **Bk Rev**, (Qty: 2-3). **Circ:** 48,000 (ctrl). Documents available from Documents on Demand. ***Continues*** *Colorado Outdoors Magazine.*
Desc: Presents articles on the conservation of animals, fish, soil and forests, with coverage of camping, hunting, fishing and related outdoor activities in Colorado.
Ind/Abst Energy Inf. Abstr.; Environ. Abstr.; Key Word Index Wildl. Res.; West. Hist. Q.; Wildl. Rev.

UK/0010-3381
COMMONWEALTH FORESTRY REVIEW, THE. See Forestry-Lumber and Wood.

US/0198-9103
COMPENDIUM NEWSLETTER, THE.
Added/Corp Ecology Center of Southern California. (197?)-. Periodical. English. bm (Jan., Mar., May., July, Sept., Nov.). $20.00. Educational Communications, PO Box 351419, Los Angeles CA 90035-9119. **Tel** (310)559-9160. **ED** Nancy Pearlman. **Bk Rev. Ad Acc. Circ:** 700. available on diskette.
Desc: A newsletter featuring topical summaries of key environmental problems and solutions with listings for TV and radio series, regional, national and international events, materials, action ideas and more.

CN/0701-0400
CONNECTIONS (EDMONTON). (CONNECTIONS.). [Connections]. **Added/Corp** Alberta Teachers' Association. Environmental and Outdoor Education Council. Vol. 1, No. 2 (Oct. 1976)-. Periodical. English. qt. Free to members of the Environmental and Outdoor Education Council. Alberta Teachers Association, 11010-142 Street, Barnett House, Edmonton Alberta T5N 2R1 Canada. **Tel** (403)453-2411. **DD** 333.7/2/07. ***Continues*** *Ondinnonk, 0701-0397.*
Ind/Abst Can. Educ. Index.

CN/0714-8550
CONNECTIONS JOURNAL. *Title Change.* [Connect. j.]. Vol. 2, No. 1 (Spring 1982). Periodical. English. ir. Alberta Teachers Association, 11010-142 Street, Barnett House, Edmonton Alberta T5N 2R1 Canada. **Tel** (403)453-2411. **DD** 333.7/2/07. ctrl circ. ***Continues*** *Connections, 0701-0400.* ***Continued by*** *Connections (Alberta Teachers' Association. Environmental and Outdoor Education Council), 0824-2704.*

CN/0702-732X
CONSERVATION. Vol. 1 (March 1977)-. Periodical. English. qt. Free. Department of Land & Forest, Box 68, Truro Nova Scotia B2N 5B8 Canada. **Tel** (902)424-5444.

CN/1183-773X
CONSERVATION AUTHORITY DIRECTORY. (CONSERVATION AUTHORITY DIRECTORY / COMPILED BY THE LANDS AND WATERS POLICY BRANCH OF THE MINISTRY OF NATURAL RESOURCES.). [Conserv. auth. dir.]. **Main/Corp** Ontario. Lands and Waters Policy Branch. (1991)-. Directory. English. **DD** 352.94. ***Continues*** *Conservation Authority Directory.*

US/0888-8892
CONSERVATION BIOLOGY. [Conserv. biol.]. Vol. 1, No. 1 (May 1987)-. Academic Scholarly Publication. English (summaries and/or abstracts in Spanish). bm. $210.00 (institution), $120.00 (individual) US; $240.00'(institution), $150.00 (individual) other. Blackwell Scientific Publishers, 238 Main Street, Cambridge MA 02142. **Tel** (617)547-7110, (800)835-6770, FAX (617)547-0789. **ED** David Ehrenfeld. **LC** QH75.A1; C665. **DD** 639. **CODEN** CBIOEF. **[CCC]. Bk Rev. Ad Acc. Pr Rev. Circ:** 3,000 (ctrl). available on microfilm and microfiche from University Microfilms International (UMI). Documents available from The Genuine Article, BIOSIS Document Express, Documents on Demand.
Desc: Presents articles on current research, scientific thought, and management problems related to natural resource conservation and development, wildlife management and the extinction crisis.
Ind/Abst Anim. Breed. Abstr.; Biol. Abstr. (1987-); Curr. Aware. Biol. Sci., CABS; Curr. Contents, Agric. Biol. Environ. Sci.; Curr. Geogr. Publ. (199?-); Ecol. Abstr.; Ecology Abstr.; Entomol. Abstr.; Environ. Abstr.; Environ. Period. Bibliogr.; Fish Rev.; Geogr. Abstr. Human Geogr.; Grasslands For. Abstr.; Int. Dev. Abstr.; Key Word Index Wildl. Res.; Protozoolog. Abstr.; Res. Alert [Select. Cov.]; Rev. Agric. Entomol.; SCISEARCH; Soc. Sci. Cit. Index [Select. Cov.]; Wildl. Rev.

CN/0381-4610
CONSERVATION COMMENT. Jan. 1970-. Periodical. English. mo. Development & Extension, Box 11, 139 Tuxedo Boulevard, Winnipeg Manitoba Canada. ***Supersedes*** *Conservation Newsletter, 0381-4629.*

US/0589-4468
CONSERVATION COURT DIGEST, THE. Vol. 1 Jan. 1967. Periodical. English. mo. Juridical Digests Institute, 1860 Broadway/Suite 1401, New York NY 10023.
Desc: A monthly summary of the reported and published state and federal court opinions concerning conservation, natural resources, fishlife, plantlife, wildlife, minerals, forests, soil, and water.

US/0069-911X
CONSERVATION DIRECTORY. [Conserv. dir.]. **Added/Corp** National Wildlife Federation. (1956)-. English. an. $24.85. National Wildlife Federation / Virginia, 8925 Leesburg Pike, Vienna VA 22184. **Tel** (703)790-4000, (800)822-9919, FAX (703)442-7332. **ED** Rue Gordon. **LC** S920; .C64. **DD** 333.9/5/02573. **Ad Acc. Circ:** 8,000 (ctrl). ***Supersedes*** *Directory of Organizations and Officials Concerned with the Protection of Wildlife and other Natural Resources.*
Desc: Extensive listing of government agencies and private organizations in US and Canada concerned with conservation and natural resource management.

IT
CONSERVATION GUIDES. (19??)-. English. ir. Food and Agriculture Organization (FAO) / Italy, GIPC166 via Terme di Caracalla, 00100 Rome Italy. **Tel** 011 39 6 522 52925, FAX 011 39 6 522 55784. **(Subscription address:** UNIPUB, 4611 F Assembly Drive, Lanham MD 20706.**)**

US/0094-1670
CONSERVATION IN KANSAS. Main/Corp Kansas. State Conservation Commission. (1972)-. Government Publication. English. ir. Free on request. Kansas State Conservation Commission, 109 Southwest Ninth Street, Suite 500, Topeka KS 66612. **Tel** (913)296-3600. **ED** Lola Warner. **LC** S916.K2; S7a. **DD** 333.7/2/09781. **Circ:** 600. ***Continues*** *Soil Conservation in Kansas.*

US/0069-9128
CONSERVATION NOTE (WASHINGTON). (CONSERVATION NOTE.). **Added/Corp** United States. Fish and Wildlife Service. Office of Information. Vol. 1 (1959)-. Monographic series. English. ir. Price varies per volume. Superintendent of Documents, US Government Printing Office, Washington DC 20402. **Tel** (202)275-3328, FAX (202)786-2377. **LC** S964.U6; A3. **DD** 574.

UK
CONSERVATION NOW. English. bm. £9.90 UK; £19.80 other. Community Service Publ Ltd, 61-B High Street, Ascot Berks SL5 7HR England. **Tel** 011 44 344-23242.
Ind/Abst Biodeter. Abstr. (1991-).

II/0376-7965
CONSERVATION OF CULTURAL PROPERTY IN INDIA. Main/Corp Indian Association for the Study of Conservation of Cultural Property. English. Rs15.00. Indian Association for the Study of Conservation of Cultural Property, c/o National Museum, Janapath New Delhi 11 India. **LC** N9051; .I53A. **DD** 915.4.
Ind/Abst Art Archaeol. Tech. Abstr.

US/0565-2421
CONSERVATION RESEARCH REPORT. [Conserv. res. rep.]. Began with No. 1, Aug. 1965. Monographic series. English. ir. Price varies per volume. US Department of Agriculture, 14th Street and Independence Avenue SW, Washington DC 20250. **Tel** (202)720-5457. **LC** S950; .U55. **CODEN** XDCRAV. Documents available from BIOSIS Document Express, CASDDS.
Ind/Abst Biol. Abstr.; Chem. Abstr. (1965-1980).

US/0362-0328
CONSERVATION (SACRAMENTO). (CONSERVATION, A REPORT OF THE DEPT. OF CONSERVATION.). **Main/Corp** California. Dept. of Conservation. (19??)-. English. Sacramento Department of Conservation, 1416 Ninth Street/Room 1535, Sacramento CA 95814. **LC** S916.C2; D46a. **DD** 353.9/794/008232.

US/0010-650X
CONSERVATIONIST, THE. [Conservationist]. **Added/Corp** New York (State). Dept. of Environmental Conservation. New York (State). Conservation Dept. Vol. 14 No. 5 (Apr/May 1960)-. Periodical. English. bm. $7.00 primary and secondary schools in New York State; $10.00 US. The Conservationist, PO Box 1500, Latham NY 12110. **Tel** (518)457-6668. **(Subscription address:** CDS Agency Hard Copy, PO Box 4966, Des Moines, IA 50340**) ED** John Dupont. **LC** QH76.5.N7; C66. **DD** 500.9/747/05. **CODEN** CNSVAU. Index available. **Bk Rev. Ad Acc. Circ:** 175,000 (ctrl). available on microfilm and microfiche from University Microfilms International (UMI). Documents available from UMI Article Clearinghouse, Documents on Demand. ***Continues*** *New York State Conservationist, 0097-3319.*
Desc: Covers hunting and fishing, the management of both game and non-game species, outdoor education and matters of environmental concern to residents of New York.
Ind/Abst Acad. Abstr. Full Text Elite (Sept. 1984-) [Full Txt.]; Acad. Abstr. (Sept. 1984-); Acad. Search (Sept. 1984-); Biol. Dig.; Curr. Index J. Educ.; Environ. Abstr.; Environ. Period. Bibliogr.; Fish Rev.; Gen. Period. Index (1985-); Gen. Sci. Index; Gen. Sci. Source (Jan. 1988-)

[Full Txt.]; GeoRef; INFO-SOUTH Abstr.; Mag. Artic. Summar. Elite (Sept. 1984-) [Full Txt.]; Mag. Artic. Summar. Select (Sept. 1984-) [Full Txt.]; Mag. Artic. Summar. CD-ROM (Sept. 1984-); Mag. Express (1988-) [Full Txt.]; Mag. Index Plus (1989-); Mag. Index. Sel. (1986-); Mag. Search; Newsp. Period. Abstr. (1988-); Life Sci. Collect.; Read. Guide Abstr. Select Ed.; Read. Guide Period. Lit.; Resource/One Ondisc; Mag. Index (1977-); Vocat. Search (Sept. 1984-) [Full Txt.]; West. Hist. Q.; Wildl. Rev.

CN/0319-4914
CONSERVATIONIST (SUDBURY). (THE CONSERVATIONIST.). V. 1- June 1965-. Periodical. English. bm. Nickel District Conservation Authority, 295 Willow Street, Sudbury Ontario Canada.

US
CONSULTANT, THE. **See** Forestry.

US/0097-0832
CONTRIBUTION - UNIVERSITY OF MARYLAND, NATURAL RESOURCES INSTITUTE. **Main/Corp** Maryland. University. Natural Resources Institute. Monographic series. English. Price varies per volume. University of Maryland Natural Resources Institute, Solomon MD 20688. **Tel** (301)326-4281. **LC** QH301; .C5. **DD** 574.92/1/4708. ctrl circ. ***Continues*** *Chesapeake Biological Laboratory. Contribution.*

US/0193-6999
CONVENTION ON INTERNATIONAL TRADE IN ENDANGERED SPECIES OF WILD FAUNA AND FLORA. English. an. Federal Wildlife Permit Office, US Fish and Wildlife Service, 18th and C Street NW/Suite 314AR, Washington DC 20250-0001. **LC** QL81.5; .U54A. **DD** 338.4/7639. available on microfiche (Vols. for (1984-) distributed to depository libraries).

US/0363-8170
COORDINATION DIRECTORY OF STATE AND FEDERAL AGENCY WATER AND LAND RESOURCES OFFICIALS. Directory. English. Missouri River Basin Commission, 10050 Regency Circle/Suite 403, Omaha NE 68114. **LC** HD1694; .A114. **DD** 333.9/1/002573.

FR
COURRIER DE LA NATURE, LE. Periodical. French (summaries and/or abstracts in English). bm. 149.00F. Societe Natl Protection Nature, 57 rue Cuvier BP 405, 75221 Paris Cedex 05 France. **Tel** 011 33 1 47073195. **ED** Christian Jouanin (editor's address: 57 rue Cuvier BP405, 75005 Paris France). **LC** QH75.A1. Index available. **Bk Rev. Ad Acc. Circ:** 10,000 (ctrl).
Desc: Magazine on nature and protection and natural history ecology in France and the world.

CN/0706-1811
COURTAGE IMMOBILIER, LE. [Courtage immobil.]. **Added/Corp** Quebec (Province). Service du Courtage Immobliier. (1???)-. Periodical. French (English). ir. Free. Service Courtage Immobilier du Quebec, 220 Grande Allee East, Suite 910, Quebec Quebec G1R 2J1 Canada. **Tel** (418)643-4597. **DD** 333.33/09714.

UK
CREATIVE CONSERVATION. ***Ceased.*** (19??)-(19??). English. qt. More Graphics Ltd, #2 McKay Trading Est, Kensal Road, London W10 5BN England. **Tel** 011 44 81 968 8228.

AT
CSIRO RANGELANDS RESEARCH. **Added/Corp** Commonwealth Scientific and Industrial Research Organization (Australia). Rangelands Research Group. **VFOAT** C.S.I.R.O. Rangelands Research; Rangelands Research. (19??)-. English. an. CSIRO / Division of Wildlife and Ecology, PO Box 84, Lyneham ACT 2602 Australia. **Tel** FAX 011 61 62 413343. **LC** SF85.4.A8; C74. **DD** 636/.01/0994.

US
CULTURAL RESOURCE SERIES. **VFOAT** Cultural Resources Series Monograph. No. 1-. Monographic series. English. Price varies per volume. US Department of the Interior Bureau of Land Management / Salt Lake City, Utah State Office, PO Box 45155, Salt Lake City UT 84145. **Tel** (801)539-4010, FAX (801)539-4183.

US
CULTURAL RESOURCE SERIES (UNITED STATES. BUREAU OF LAND MANAGEMENT. NEVADA STATE OFFICE. (CULTURAL RESOURCE SERIES / BUREAU OF LAND MANAGEMENT.). **VFOAT** Cultural Resource Series Monograph. No. 1-. Monographic series. English. ir. Price varies per volume. BLM, Nevada State Office, 300 Booth Street, Reno NV 89509.

US/0271-633X
CULTURAL RESOURCES SERIES (DENVER). (CULTURAL RESOURCES SERIES.). [Cult. resour. ser.]. Began with No. 1. Monographic series. English. ir. Price varies per volume. US Department of the Interior Bureau of Land Management / Lakewood, Colorado State Office, 2850 Youngfield Street, Lakewood CO 80215. **Tel** (303)239-3701, FAX (303)239-3933.

US
CURRENT FEDERAL AID RESEARCH REPORT. WILDLIFE. **VFOAT** Wildlife. English. an. US Fish and Wildlife Service, Divison of Federal Aid, 18th and C Streets NW, Washington DC 20240. **ED** C Phillip Agee and Claude E Stephens.

US/0748-1616
CURRENT PUBLICATIONS FROM THE FOREST, WILDLIFE AND RANGE EXPERIMENT STATION. **See** Forestry.

US
DATELINE : NRPA. Periodical. English. bm. Natl Recreation and Park Assn, 3101 Park Center Drive/12th Floor, Alexandria VA 22302. **Tel** (703)820-4940.

GW/0170-608X
DATEN UND DOKUMENTE ZUM UMWELTSCHUTZ. ***Ceased.*** [Daten Dok. Umweltschutz]. **Added/Corp** Universitat Hohenheim. Dokumentationsstelle. **VFOAT** Data and Documents about Environment Protection. (1972)-(Dec. 1987). Academic Scholarly Publication. German (English). ir. Verlag Eugen Ulmer, Postfach 700561, D 70574 Stuttgart Germany. **Tel** 011 49 711 4507108, FAX 011 49 711 4507120, telex 7-23634. **CODEN** DDUMDP. Documents available from CASDDS.
Ind/Abst Chem. Abstr. (1972-1983).

US/0162-6337
DEFENDERS. [Defenders]. **Added/Corp** Defenders of Wildlife. Vol. 50, No. 4, (1975)-. Periodical. English. bm. $20.00 (membership) US; $22.00 other. Defenders of Wildlife, 1244 19th Street NW, Washington DC 20036. **Tel** (202)659-9510. **ED** James G Deane. **LC** S960; .D43. **DD** 333.95/16/0973. **Bk Rev. Ad Acc. Circ:** 80,000. available on microfilm and microfiche from University Microfilms International (UMI). Documents available from Documents on Demand. ***Continues*** *Defenders of Wildlife, 0162-6329; Defenders of Wildlife News.*
Desc: Membership magazine with provocative, informative coverage of major wildlife conservation issues in the United States and abroad; high-quality color, black and white photography and art.
Ind/Abst Biol. Dig.; Environ. Abstr.; Environ. Period. Bibliogr.; Fish Rev.; Wildl. Rev.

GW/0045-9852
DELAWARE CONSERVATIONIST. ***Title Change.*** [Del. conserv.]. **Added/Corp** Delaware. Dept. of Natural Resources and Environmental Control. Delaware Board of Game and Fish Commissioners. Vol. 1; Winter (1956/57)-(19??). Periodical. English. qt. Department of Natural Resources and Environmental Control / Delaware, PO Box 1401, Dover DE 19903. **Tel** (302)739-4403, FAX (302)739-6242. **ED** Sharon H Fitzgerald. **DD** 333.7. **Bk Rev. Circ:** 15,000. Documents available from Documents on Demand. ***Continued by*** *Outdoor Delaware, 1068-3240.*
Desc: Educating the public about natural resources such as wildlife and state parks and about the environmental concerns of Delaware.
Ind/Abst Energy Inf. Abstr.; Environ. Abstr.; Fish Rev.; Wildl. Rev.

US
DEPARTMENT OF NATURAL RESOURCES GEOLOGICAL SURVEY GUIDEBOOK. (DEPARTMENT OF NATURAL RESOURCES GEOLOGICAL SURVEY GUIDEBOOK (INDIANA).). **Main/Corp** Indiana. Geological Survey. No. 11 (1965)-. Monographic series. English. Price varies per volume. Indiana Geological Survey, 611 North Walnut Grove, Bloomington IN 47405. **Tel** (812)885-9350. **LC** QE1; .I45. **DD** 550.793. ***Continues*** *Field Conference Guidebook.*

US
DEPARTMENT OF NATURAL RESOURCES GEOLOGICAL SURVEY SPECIAL REPORT. **VFOAT** Geological Survey Special Report; Special Report. No. 3-. English. ir. Indiana Geological Survey, 611 North Walnut Grove, Bloomington IN 47405. **Tel** (812)885-9350. ***Continues*** *Special Report (Indiana. Geological Survey).*

US/0270-1111
DIRECTORY OF ENVIRONMENTAL ORGANIZATIONS (LOS ANGELES). **See** Environmental Issues-Ecology.

US/1040-1555
DIRECTORY OF NATIONAL ENVIRONMENTAL ORGANIZATIONS. **See** Environmental Issues.

CN/0319-8480
DISCOVERY (VANCOUVER. 1972). ***Title Change.*** (DISCOVERY.). **VFOAT** V.N.H.S. Discovery. 1970-1972; New Ser., V. 1- (No. 154-): Mar./May 1972-. Periodical. English. qt. Vancouver Natural History Society, PO Box 3021, Vancouver British Columbia V6B 3X5 Canada. **Tel** (604)736-9471. **Bk Rev. Ad Acc. Circ:** 1,500. ***Continues*** *Vancouver Natural History Society. Bulletin.* ***Continued by*** *Newsletter - Vancouver Natural History Society, 0382-0211.*
Desc: Natural history, conservation, mammalogy, ornithology, marine biology, entomology, botany, geology, flora, fauna, wildlife, ecosystems, astronomy, general interest.

US
DIVISION OF FISH AND GAME. (DIVISION OF FISH AND GAME - (RHODE ISLAND).). **Main/Corp** Rhode Island. Division of Fish and Game. **VFOAT** Report - Division of Fish and Game; Report - Office of Fish and Game. (1935)-. Periodical. English. Department of Natural Resources / Rhode Island, Division of Fish and Wildlife, Providence RI 02903. **LC** SH11; .R42. **DD** 639.061745. ***Supersedes*** *Annual Report of the Commissioners of Inland Fisheries Made to the General Assembly.*

AT/0812-2237
DIVISION OF WILDLIFE AND RANGELANDS RESEARCH TECHNICAL PAPER. [Div. Wildl. Rangel. Res. tech. pap.]. **Added/Corp** Commonwealth Scientific and Industrial Research Organization (Australia). Division of Wildlife and Rangelands Research. No. 35 (1984)-. Monographic series. English. ir. Price varies per volume. CSIRO Publications, PO Box 89, 314 Albert Street, East Melborne Victoria 3002 Australia. **Tel** 011 61 3 4187333, 4187217, FAX 011 61 3 4190459, telex AA 30236. **CODEN** DWRPEH. Documents available from BIOSIS Document Express. ***Continues*** *Division of Wildlife Research Technical Paper, 0069-763X.*
Ind/Abst Biol. Abstr. (1984-).

US/0276-0231
DIVISION REPORT / COLORADO DIVISION OF WILDLIFE. [Div. rep. - Colo., Div. Wildl.]. **Main/Corp** Colorado. Division of Wildlife. Began with: No. 1, published in 1974. Monographic series. English. ir. Price varies per volume. Colorado Division of Wildlife, 6060 Broadway, Denver CO 80216. **ED** Nancy McEwen. **Circ:** 600.
Desc: Deals with wildlife and fisheries management.

PH
DNR PERFORMANCE REPORT. **Main/Corp** Philippines. Dept. of Natural Resources. **Added/Corp** Philippines. Dept. of Natural Resources. Department of Natural Resources Performance Report. **VFOAT** Department of Natural Resources Performance Report. (19??)-. English. **LC** HC453.5; .P44a. **DD** 354/.599/008232.

CN/0824-3689
DOCUMENTATION DU MINISTERE DE L'ENERGIE ET DES RESSOURCES, REPERTOIRE. **See** Economics-Economic History, Conditions.

GW/0026-6957
DOKUMENTATION FUER UMWELTSCHUTZ UND LANDESPFLEGE. ***Title Change.*** **Added/Corp** Bundesanstalt fur Vegetationskunde, Naturschutz und Landschaftspflege. Vol. 11, No. 1 (1971)-. Periodical. German. qt. W Kohlhammer Verlag GmbH, Postfach 800430, D 70549 Stuttgart Germany. **Tel** 011 49 711 78631, FAX 011 49 711 7863263, telex 7-255820. **ED** Rainer Flueck. **[CCC]. Bk Rev.** ***Continues*** *Mitteilungen zur Landschaftspflege.* ***Continued by*** *Dokumentation Natur und Landschaft, 0936-0948.*
Desc: Articles on conservation of the land.
Ind/Abst For. Prod. Abstr.; For. Abstr.

GW/0936-0948
DOKUMENTATION NATUR UND LANDSCHAFT. [Dok. Nat. Landsch.]. **Added/Corp** Bundesforschungsanstalt feur Naturschutz und Landschaftsokologie. (1989)-. Periodical. German. qt. DM79.00. W Kohlhammer Verlag GmbH, Postfach 800430, D 70549 Stuttgart Germany. **Tel** 011 49 711 78631, FAX 011 49 711 7863263, telex 7-255820. ***Continues*** *Dokumentation fuer Umweltschutz und Landespflege, 0026-6957.*

US/0012-6950
DUCKS UNLIMITED. [Ducks unltd.]. **Added/Corp** Ducks Unlimited. **VFOAT** Ducks Unlimited Magazine. Vol. 1 (1938)-. Periodical. English. Six times a year (Jan., Mar., May, July, Sept., Nov.). $20.00. Ducks Unlimited Incorporated, 1 Waterfowl Way, Memphis TN 38120. **Tel** (901)758-3825. **ED** Lee D. Salber. **DD** 639. **Bk Rev. Ad Acc. Circ:** 600,000 (ctrl).
Desc: Features focus on wetland habitat conservation, wildlife management and conservation activities.
Ind/Abst AQUAREF.

US/0278-0909
DUPAGE CONSERVATIONIST, THE. (THE DUPAGE CONSERVATIONIST : THE FOREST PRESERVE DISTRICT QUARTERLY.). **Added/Corp** DuPage County (Ill.). Forest Preserve District. (19??)-. Periodical. English. Four times a year. Free DuPage

County, $5.00 other. Forest Preserve District of DuPage City, PO Box 2339, 185 Spring Avenue, Glen Ellyn IL 60138. **Tel** (708)790-4900 Ext. 316. **ED** Sandy Rodman. **LC** Discard. **Circ:** 22,000.
Desc: Includes original articles, artwork and photographs of the natural areas' wildlife, historical features, environmental education and recreation opportunities found in DuPage County forest preserves.

UK/0142-2324
EARTH SCIENCE CONSERVATION. [Earth sci. conserv.]. **Added/Corp** Nature Conservancy Council (Great Britain) Nature Conservancy Council (Great Britain). Geology and Physiography Section. Nature Conservancy Council (Great Britain). Geological Conservation Review Unit. No. 15 (Oct. 1978)-. Periodical. English. sa (published April and September). £16.50 (institutions), £5.50 (individuals) UK; £22.00 (institutions), £10.00 (individuals) other. English Nature, Northminster House / Department EN5, Peterborough PE1 1UA England. **Tel** 011 44 733 340345. **ED** Mike Harley. **Circ:** 1,200. ***Continues*** *Information Circular - Geology and Physiography Section, Nature Conservancy Council.*
Ind/Abst GeoRef.

US/1060-5053
EARTH WORK. **Added/Corp** Student Conservation Association (U.S.). Vol. 1, No. 1 (Feb. 1991)-. Periodical. English. Eleven times a year. $29.95 (one year), $45.00 (two years), $19.95 (six months) US; $35.95 (one year), $53.00 (two Years), $23.95 (six months) other. Student Conservation Association, PO Box 550, Charlestown NH 03603. **Tel** (603)543-1700, FAX (603)543-1828. **ED** Joan Moody (Edotor's Address: 1800 North Kent Street, Suite 1260. Arlington, VA 22209). **DD** 331. **Ad Acc, Adv Mgr:** Devi Cannon, **Tel** (703)524-2441. **Circ:** 7,000. ***Absorbed*** *Job-Scan, 1048-7883.*
Desc: Career magazine for environmental professionals, students, and job seekers. Contains the nation's most up-to-date listing of environmental/natural resources job opening.

US/0732-684X
EARTHCARE NORTHWEST. (EARTHCARE NORTHWEST. SEATTLE AUDUBON SOCIETY.). [Earthcare Northwest]. **Added/Corp** Seattle Audubon Society. **VFOAT** Earth Care Northwest. Vol. 22, No. 1 (Sept. 1981)-. Periodical. English. Nine times a year. $15.00. Seattle Audubon Society, 8028 35th Avenue Northeast, Seattle WA 98115. **Tel** (206)523-4483. **ED** Robert Ashbaugh. **DD** 363. **Bk Rev**, (Qty: 4). **Ad Acc. Pr Rev. Circ:** 5,500 (ctrl). ***Continues*** *Seattle Audubon Notes.*
Desc: Conservation and Environment news local, regional, and national activities. Field trips and tours Natural History, features reviews as appropriate.

US/0895-6928
ECB NEWSLETTER. [ECB newsl.]. **VAT** Environmental Conservation Board Newsletter. Newsletter. English. mo. Environmental Conservation Board, 4615 Forbes Avenue, Pittsburgh PA 15213. **DD** 686.
Ind/Abst Graph. Arts Bull. Inst. Pap. Sci. Technol. (May 1989).

CN/0833-448X
ECO ALERT / CONSERVATION COUNCIL. [Eco alert]. **Added/Corp** Conservation Council of New Brunswick. Vol. 17, No. 1 (Winter 1986)-. Periodical. English. bm. 25.00Can$. Conservation Council of New Brunswick, 180 St. John Street, Fredericton New Brunswick E3B 4A9 Canada. **Tel** (506)458-8747. **ED** Mark Lutes. **DD** 333.7/2/060715. **Bk Rev. Circ:** 500 (ctrl). ***Continues*** *Conservation, 0227-8642.*
Desc: The newsletter of the Conservation Council of New Brunswick, A charitable environmental organization. It contains articles on environmental issues and conservation society news.

CN/1183-2355
ECODECISION (MONTREAL). (ECODECISION). [Ecodecision]. **Added/Corp** Societe Environnement et Politiques. **VFOAT** Ecodecision. (1991)-. Periodical. French (English). qt (Jan., Apr., July, Oct.). 93.46Can$ (institution), 55.14Can$ (individual). Ecodecision, Suite 924, 276 West St. Jacques Street, Montreal Quebec H2Y 1N3 Canada. **Tel** (514)284-3043. **DD** 333.7/2/05. **Ad Acc.**
Desc: Forum for critical environmental analysis and debate. Its purpose is to interpret the sciences to enable sustainable environmental responses, policies, decisions and actions by our readers, the decision-makers.

CN/1183-2355
ECODECISION (MONTREAL). (ECODECISION.). [Ecodecision]. **Added/Corp** Environment and Policy Society. **VFOAT** Ecodecision. (1991)-. Periodical. English (French). qt (July, Oct., Jan., Apr.). 59.00Can$ (one year), 99.00Can$ (two year) (individuals), 100.00Can$ (one year), 160.00 (two year), (institutions). Ecodecision, Suite 924, 276 West St. Jacques Street, Montreal Quebec H2Y 1N3 Canada. **Tel** (514)284-3043. **DD** 333.7/2/05.
Ind/Abst Can. Period. Index (19??-); Environ. Period. Bibliogr.

BO
ECOLOGIA EN BOLIVIA : REVISTA DEL INSTITUTO DE ECOLOGIA. **See** Environmental Issues-Ecology.

US/0885-7237
ECONEWS (ARCATA, CALIF.). (ECONEWS : NEWSLETTER OF THE NORTHCOAST ENVIRONMENTAL CENTER.). **Added/Corp** Northcoast Environmental Center. (19??)-. Newsletter. English. Eleven times a year (Jan./Feb. issues combined). $20.00. Northcoast Environmental Center, 879 Ninth Street, Arcata CA 95521. **Tel** (707)822-6918, FAX (707)822-0827. **ED** Sid Darmmitz. **DD** 363. **Bk Rev**, (Qty: 11). **Ad Acc, Adv Mgr:** Joanie, **Tel** (707)822-6918.
Desc: Environmental news and opinion for the temperate rainforest region of the west.

US/8755-7053
ECONOMIC IMPACT ANALYSIS PROGRAM, THE ANNUAL REPORT. (ECONOMIC IMPACT ANALYSIS PROGRAM, THE ... ANNUAL REPORT / REPORT OF ILLINOIS, INSTITUTE OF NATURAL RESOURCES.). [Econ. impact anal. program annu. rep.]. English. an. Illinois Institute of Natural Resources, 325 West Adams Street/Room 300, Springfield IL 62706. **Tel** (217)784-5470. **ED** Niels Herlevsen. **LC** TD194.6; .E26. **DD** 330.9773/043. ***Continues*** *Economic Impact Studies, the ... Year in Review / Illinois Institute of Natural Resources, 8755-7045.*

US/0424-3110
ECONOMICS OF MARINE RESOURCES. English. University of Rhode Island Department of Resource Economics, Kingston RI 01881. **DD** 639.

UK/0143-9073
ECOS. **Added/Corp** British Association of Nature Conservationists. **VFOAT** Ecos. (19??)-. Periodical. English. Four times a year (Feb., May, Aug., Nov.). £30.00 UK; £35.00 other. British Association of Nature Conservationists, Nature Conservation Bur, 36 King Fisher Court, Hambridge Road, Newbury Berks RG14 5SJ England. **Tel** 011 44 0635550380. **ED** Rick Minter. **Bk Rev. Ad Acc, Adv Mgr:** Rick Minter, **Tel** 0242 579059. **Circ:** 1,000. Documents available from Documents on Demand.
Ind/Abst Curr. Aware. Biol. Sci., CABS; Curr. Geogr. Publ. (199?-); Environ. Abstr.; Environ. Period. Bibliogr.

UK/0143-9073
ECOS BRITISH ASSOCIATION OF NATURE CONSERVATIONISTS. [ECOSBr. Assoc. Nat. Conserv.]. **VFOAT** Journal of BANC. (1980)-. Periodical. English. qt. Packard Publishing Ltd, 16 Lynch Down Funtingdon, Chichester West Sussex PO18 9LR, UK. **DD** 639.905.
Ind/Abst Leis. Recreat. Tour. Abstr.

●US/1071-8478
ECOS (LEXINGTON, KY.). (ECOS : THE ENVIRONMENTAL COMMUNIQUE OF THE STATES.). [Ecos]. **Added/Corp** Centers for Health and Environment (Lexington, Ky.). Vol. 1, No. 1 (Sept./Oct. 1993)-. Periodical. English. bm (6 issues). $69.99 state officials and non-profit organizations; $99.99 other. Council of State Governments, PO Box 11910, Iron Works Pike, Lexington KY 40578-1910. **Tel** (800)800-1910, (606)231-1850. **(Subscription address:** Council of State Governments, PO Box 2167, Lexington, KY 40595) **DD** 333.

US/0364-3840
ECP REPORT. **See** Energy.

US/0163-2566
EDF LETTER. **Main/Corp** Environmental Defense Fund, Inc. **VFOAT** Environmental Defense Fund Newsletter. **VAT** Environmental Defense Fund Letter. (1971)-. Periodical. English. bm. $20.00. Environmental Defense Fund, 257 Park Avenue South/Floor 16, New York NY 10010. **Tel** (212)505-2100. **ED** Norma H. Watson. **Circ:** 50,000. Documents available from The Genuine Article.
Desc: Reports EDF efforts to protect human health and natural resources form environmental damage by promoting environmentally sound, economically feasible, technically possible and publicly acceptable solutions.
Ind/Abst Res. Alert [Select. Cov.]; Soc. Sci. Cit. Index [Select. Cov.].

US/0589-4476
EDUCATION : KEY TO CONSERVATION. **Added/Corp** Conservation Education Association. **VFOAT** Key to Conservation. No. 1 (1965)-. Monographic series. English. Price varies per volume. Conservation Education Association / Danville, 19-17 North Jackson Street, Danville IL 61832. **LC** S946; .C58. **DD** 333.7.

RU
EKHO. : EKOLOGIIA, KHOZIAISTVO, OKRUZHAIUSHCHAIA SREDA. **VFOAT** Ekologiia, Khoziaistvo, Okruzhaiushchaia Sreda. (1990)-. Russian.

US/0193-4651
ELEMENTS (WASHINGTON), THE. (THE ELEMENTS.). Oct. 1974-. Periodical. English. mo. $25.00. Public Resource Center, 1747 Connecticut Avenue NW, Washington DC 20009. **LC** HD9502.A1; E43. **DD** 333.7/05. available on microfilm and microfiche from University Microfilms International (UMI).

US/0013-6069
ELEPAIO. [Elepaio]. **Added/Corp** Hawaii Audubon Society. Vol. 1, (1939)-. Periodical. English. Twelve times a year. $10.00 (surface mail), $16.00 (airmail) US; $17.00 Canada; $16.00 Mexico; $18.00 (surface mail), $28.00 (airmail) others. Hawaii Audubon Society, 212 Merchant Street, Suite 320, Honolulu HI 96813. **Tel** (808)528-1432. **DD** 598. Index available (index published separately). cum. index. **Bk Rev. Circ:** 2,400 (ctrl). Documents available from BIOSIS Document Express.
Desc: Disseminates information to encourage the preservation and appreciation of Hawaii's Native Wildlife in Hawaii and the Tropical Pacific.
Ind/Abst Biol. Abstr.; Wildl. Rev.

US
EMAP MONITOR / ENVIRONMENTAL MONITORING AND ASSESSMENT PROGRAM. **Main/Corp** Environmental Monitoring and Assessment Program. **Added/Corp** United States. Environmental Protection Agency. Office of Research and Development. **VFOAT** EPA EMAP Monitor. (Jan 1991)-. English. US Environmental Protection Agency/Region 1, Office of Research and Development, Boston MA 02203. **LC** WMLC 91/672.

II/0970-1753
ENCOLOGY. **See** Environmental Issues-Ecology.

US
ENDANGERED SPECIES UPDATE. **Added/Corp** University of Michigan. School of Natural Resources. Vol. 4, No. 9 & 10 (July/Aug. 1987)-. Periodical. English. mo. $18.00 students and senior citizens, $23.00 other. Endangered Species Update, School of Natural Resources, University of Michigan, Ann Arbor MI 48109-1115. **Tel** (313)763-3243. **ED** Lynn Gooch. **CODEN** ESUPEF. **Bk Rev**, (Qty: 10). **Circ:** 1,100. Documents available from Documents on Demand. ***Continues*** *Endangered Species Technical Bulletin Reprint.*
Desc: A forum for the exchange of ideas and information on endangered species protection.
Ind/Abst Environ. Abstr.; Environ. Period. Bibliogr.; Expand. Acad. Index (1992-); Garden Lit. (1992-).

US/0162-9131
ENERGY USER NEWS. **See** Energy.

FR/1143-4627
ENTENTE EUROPEENNE POUR L'ENVIRONNEMENT PARIS. ***Ceased.*** (ENTENTE EUROPEENNE POUR L'ENVIRONNEMENT.). (1989)-(1993). Periodical. French. bm. Entente Eur Pour l'Env, 233 Bd St Germain Bouchardeau, 75007 Paris France. **Tel** 011 33 1 40 638436. **UDC** 502.

●US
ENVIRONMENT ABSTRACTS [COMPUTER FILE]. **See** Environmental Issues-Abstracting, Bibliographies and Statistics.

UK/0958-2126
ENVIRONMENT & INDUSTRY DIGEST. ***Title Change.*** [Environ. ind. dig.]. **VFOAT** Environment and Industry Digest. (1990)-(199?). Academic Scholarly Publication. English. mo (1 volume). Elsevier Science Publishers Ltd, Crown House, Linton Road, Barking Essex IG11 8JU England. **Tel** 011 44 81 5947272, FAX 081-594-5942, telex 896950. **ED** John O'Hara. **DD** 628.5. **[CCC]. Bk Rev. Circ:** 75. ***Continued by*** *Environment Technology & Industry.*

AT/0727-5366
ENVIRONMENT VICTORIA. [Environ. Vic.]. **VFOAT** C.C.V. Newsletter. (1981)-. Periodical. English. Three times a year. 32.00Aus$. Conservation Council of Victoria, 247 Flinders Lane, Environment Center, Melbourne VIC 3000 Australia. **Tel** 03 654-4833, FAX 03 650-5684. **ED** Geoffrey Heard. **DD** 333.72060945. ctrl circ. ***Continues*** *Newsletter - Conservation Council of Victoria, 0155-4123.*

US
ENVIRONMENTAL AND RESOURCE ASSESSMENT PROGRAM; PROGRAM SUMMARY. **Main/Corp** United States. Dept. of Energy. Division of Solar Energy. 1976/77-. English. an. US Department of Energy Office of Energy Technology, 1000 Independence Avenue SW, Washington DC 20585.

US/0742-6062
ENVIRONMENTAL AUDIT ADVISER. [Environ. audit advis.]. Vol. 1, No. 1 (June 1984)-. Periodical. English. mo. $144.00. John Wiley & Sons, Inc., 605 Third Avenue, New York NY 10158-0012. **Tel** (212)850-6000, (212)850-6645, FAX (212)850-6088,

telex 12-7063. **(Subscription address:** John Wiley / Philadelphia, PO Box 7247, Philadelphia PA 19170.**) DD** 333. **[CCC].**

SZ/0376-8929
ENVIRONMENTAL CONSERVATION. [Environ. conserv.]. Vol. 1 (Spring 1974)-. Academic Scholarly Publication. English. qt (1 volume). Fl404.00. Elsevier Science Publishers BV, PO Box 211, 1000 AE Amsterdam Netherlands. **Tel** 011 31 20 5803642, FAX 011 31 20 5862696, telex 15682. **ED** Nicholas Polunin. **LC** TD169; .E58. **DD** 363.6. **CODEN** EVCNA4. **[CCC]. Pr Rev.** available on microfilm and microfiche from University Microfilms International (UMI). Documents available from Article Express International, The Genuine Article, BIOSIS Document Express, CASDDS, Documents on Demand.
Desc: Devoted to maintaining global viability through exposing and countering environmental deterioration resulting from human population pressure and unwise technology.
Ind/Abst AGRICOLA; AQUAREF; Biocont. News Inf.; Biodeter. Abstr.; Biol. Abstr.; Biol. Dig.; Chem. Abstr.; Coal Abstr.; Curr. Contents, Agric. Biol. Environ. Sci.; Curr. Ref. Fish Res.; Ecol. Abstr.; Ecology Abstr.; Ei Page One; EMBASE; Energy Res. Abstr. (July 1975-); Eng. Index Annu. [Select. Cov.]; Environ. Abstr.; Environ. Period. Bibliogr.; Fish Rev.; For. Prod. Abstr.; For. Abstr.; Geogr. Abstr. Phys. Geogr.; Geogr. Abstr. Human Geogr.; GeoRef; Grasslands For. Abstr.; Health Saf. Sci. Abstr.; Index Vet.; Indian Geosci. Abstr.; Int. Aerosp. Abstr.; Int. Dev. Abstr.; Irr. Drain. Abstr.; Key Word Index Wildl. Res.; Leis. Recreat. Tour. Abstr.; Meteorol. Geoastrophys. Abstr.; Middle East Abstr. Index; Ocean. Abstr.; Life Sci. Collect.; Pollut. Abstr. Indexes; Protozoolog. Abstr.; Res. Alert [Full Cov.]; Rev. Agric. Entomol.; Rev. Med. Vet. Entomol.; Rural Dev. Abstr.; Sci. Cit. Index; SCISEARCH; Soc. Sci. Cit. Index [Select. Cov.]; Soils Fert.; Weed Abstr.; World Agric. Econ.

RU/0234-7059
ENVIRONMENTAL MANAGEMENT ABSTRACTS. Added/Corp Vsesoiuznyi Institut Nauchnoi i Tekhnicheskoi Informatsii (Soviet Union). **VFOAT** EMA. (1986)-. English. bm. VINITI - Vsesoiuznyi Institut Nauchno-Tekhnicheskoi Informatsii, All-Union Scientific and Technical Information Institute, Baltiiskaia Ulitsa 14, 125219 Moscow Russia. **Tel** 238-46-00, FAX 9430060, telex 411160. **LC** QH75.A1; E6. **DD** 333.7/2/05.
Desc: English translation of abstracts of articles and books published in the USSR, other CMEA countries, and Yugoslavia.

US/0736-9603
ENVIRONMENTAL OPPORTUNITIES. (ENVIRONMENTAL OPPORTUNITIES / SPONSORED BY ENVIRONMENTAL STUDIES DEPARTMENT, ANTIOCH/NEW ENGLAND GRADUATE SCHOOL.). [Environ. oppor.]. **Added/Corp** Antioch/New England Graduate School. Environmental Studies Dept. (March 1982)-. Periodical. English. mo. $47.00 (one year), $75.00 (two years). Environmental Opportunities, PO Box 788, Walpole NH 03608. **Tel** (603)756-4553, FAX (603)756-4553. **ED** Sanford Berry. **Circ:** 3,500. ***Continues*** *Environmental Opportunities/Northeast.*
Desc: Contains current environmental job openings.

US/1017-4648
ENVIRONMENTAL STRATEGY & PLANNING : BULLETIN OF THE COMMISSION ON ENVIRONMENTAL STRATEGY AND PLANNING OF THE WORLD CONSERVATION UNION. Added/Corp International Union for Conservation of Nature and Natural Resources. Commission on Environmental Strategy and Planning. **VFOAT** Environmental Strategy and Planning. (1991)-. Bulletin. English. qt. $20.00 (general), Free to members. Commission on Environmental Strategy and Planning of the World Conservation Union, PO Box 189040, Sacramento CA 95818.

US/1049-8877
ENVIRONMENTAL WATCH (CHICAGO, ILL.). ***Ceased.*** **See** Real Estate.

UK/0251-1088
ENVIRONMENTALIST, THE. [Environmentalist]. Vol. 1, No. 1 (Spring 1981)-. Academic Scholarly Publication. English. qt. £121.00 (institution), £67.00 (individual) UK; $242.00 (institution), $134.00 (individual) US. Chapman & Hall, 2-6 Boundary Row, London SE1 8HN England. **Tel** 011 44 71 865 0066, FAX 011 44 71 522 9623, telex 290164 Chapmag. **(Subscription address:** International Thomson Publishing Svcs. Ltd., Subscription Department North Way Andover, Hampshire SP10 5BE England.**) ED** John F. Potter. **[CCC]. Bk Rev. Ad Acc. Pr Rev. Circ:** 1,000. Documents available from Documents on Demand.
Desc: Concerned with environmental awareness, the journal publishes authoritative papers on global actions, case studies, research, global news and comments, plus major review papers and IUCN supplements.
Ind/Abst Curr. Aware. Biol. Sci., CABS; Curr. Index J. Educ.; Curr. Ref. Fish Res.; Ecol. Abstr.; Ecology Abstr.; EMBASE; Energy Inf. Abstr.; Environ. Abstr.; Environ. Period. Bibliogr.; Geogr. Abstr. Phys. Geogr.; Geogr. Abstr. Human Geogr.; Int. Dev. Abstr.; Int. Labour Doc.; J. Plan. Lit.; Leis. Recreat. Tour. Abstr.; PAIS Int. Print (1991-?); Life Sci. Collect.; Pollut. Abstr. Indexes; Risk Abstr.

FR
ENVIRONNEMENT : BULLETIN DE DOCUMENTATION, L'. Bulletin. French. Documentation Francaise, 29 Quai Voltaire, 75344 Paris Cedex 7 France. **Tel** 011 33 1 40157000, FAX 011 33 1 40157230, telex 204 826 DOCFRAN. **LC** Z5863.P7; E56; TD170. **DD** 016.30131.

US/0161-8490
EPA ACTIVITIES UNDER THE RESOURCE CONSERVATION AND RECOVERY ACT OF 1976. Main/Corp United States. Environmental Protection Agency. **VFOAT** Annual Report to the President and the Congress. **VAT** Environmental Protection Agency Activities Under the Resource Conservation and Recovery Act of Nineteen Hundred and Seventy-Six. 1976/77-. English. an. US Environmental Protection Agency, 401 M Street SW, Washington DC 20460. **Tel** (202)755-9163. **LC** HC110.E5; U55A. **DD** 301.31/0973.

US/8755-2000
ERIGENIA. See Biology-Botany.

CN
ESTIMATES. PART III, ENVIRONMENT CANADA, PARKS CANADA PROGRAM. Main/Corp Canada. **VFOAT** Budget des Depenses. Partie III, Environnement Canada, Programme Parcs Canada. (19??)-. English (French). $6.00 Canada; $7.20 other. Canada Communication Group Publishers, Order Processing, Ottawa Ontario K1A 0S9 Canada. **Tel** (819)956-4800, (819)956-4802. **LC** SB484.C2; C23a. **DD** 354.710086/32.

●CN
ESTIMATES. PART III, NATURAL RESOURCES CANADA. Main/Corp Canada. **VFOAT** Budget des Depenses. Partie III, Ressources Naturelles Canada. (1994/1995)-. English (French). Canada Communication Group Publishers, Order Processing, Ottawa Ontario K1A 0S9 Canada. **Tel** (819)956-4800, (819)956-4802. **LC** TJ163.25.C3; C3b. **DD** 354.710082/38. ***Continues*** *Canada. Estimates. Part III, Energy, Mines and Resources Canada.*

CN/1195-5015
EUSKARIEN (QUEBEC). (L'EUSKARIEN.). [Euskarien]. **Added/Corp** Societe Provancher d'Histoire Naturelle du Canada. Vol. 1, No. 1 (1979)-. Periodical. French. sa. 15.00Can$. Societe Provancher Histoire Naturelle au Canada, 9141 Avenue du Zoo, Charlesbourg Quebec G1G4G4 Canada. **Tel** (418)843-6416. **DD** 508.714/05. **Circ:** 1,500.

KE/0259-2940
EVALUATION REPORT : REPORT OF THE EXECUTIVE DIRECTOR. [Eval. rep. - U. N. Environ. Programme]. **Main/Corp** United Nations Environment Programme. (1985)-. Government Publication. English. ir. Free. United Nations Publications, 2 United Nations Plaza, Room DC2 0853, Department 007C, New York NY 10017. **Tel** (212)963-8303, (800)253-9646. **LC** HC79.E5; U46d. **DD** 341.7/62/05.

US/1046-1485
EXCHANGE (ALEXANDRIA, VA.). (EXCHANGE : JOURNAL OF THE LAND TRUST ALLIANCE.). [Exchange]. **Added/Corp** Land Trust Exchange (U.S.) Land Trust Alliance. Vol. 7, No. 4 (Fall 1988)-. Periodical. English. qt. $35.00. Land Trust Alliance, 1319 F Street NW Suite 501, Washington DC 20004. **Tel** (202)638-4725, FAX (202)638-4730. **ED** Karen Deans. **DD** 333. ctrl circ. ***Continues*** *Land Trusts' Exchange, 0885-4106.*
Desc: Professional journal for land trusts.

US/0736-5470
EYAS, THE. ***Ceased.*** (THE EYAS : A NEWSLETTER FROM THE NATIONAL WILDLIFE FEDERATION'S RAPTOR INFORMATION CENTER.). [Eyas]. **Added/Corp** Raptor Information Center (Washington, D.C.). Vol. I, No. 1 (fall 1977)-Ceased 1991. Newsletter. English. tq. National Wildlife Federation / Washington, 1400 16th Street Northwest, Washington DC 20036. **Tel** (800)432-6564, (202)797-6800.

IT
FAO CONSERVATION GUIDE. Added/Corp Food and Agriculture Organization of the United Nations. **VFOAT** F.A.O. Conservation Guide. (1976)-. Monographic series. English. ir. Price varies per volume. Food and Agriculture Organization (FAO) / Italy, GIPC166 via Terme di Caracalla, 00100 Rome Italy. **Tel** 011 39 6 522 52925, FAX 011 39 6 522 55784.
Ind/Abst Agrofor. Abstr.; For. Prod. Abstr.; For. Abstr.

US
FEDERAL AID IN SPORT FISH AND WILDLIFE RESTORATION PROGRAMS. ***Title Change.*** **Added/Corp** U.S. Fish and Wildlife Service. U.S. Fish and Wildlife Service. Division of Federal Aid. (1990)-(199?). Government Publication. English. US Department of Interior, Division of Federal Aid, Washington DC 70240. **LC** SK361; .W5. **DD** 799; 333.78*. ***Continues*** *Federal Aid in Fish and Wildlife Restoration, 0092-9697.* ***Split into*** *Federal Aid in Sport Fish Restoration Program* ***and*** *Federal Aid in Wildlife Restoration Program.*

US
FEDERAL AID IN SPORT FISH RESTORATION PROGRAM : PROJECT REPORTS. Added/Corp U.S. Fish and Wildlife Service. Division of Federal Aid. (199?)-. Government Publication. English. ir. US Department of Interior, Division of Federal Aid, Washington DC 70240. **LC** SK361; .W5. **DD** 799; 333.78*. ***Continues in part*** *Federal Aid in Sport Fish and Wildlife Restoration Programs.*

US
FEDERAL AID IN WILDLIFE RESTORATION PROGRAM : PROJECT REPORTS. Added/Corp U.S. Fish and Wildlife Service. Division of Federal Aid. (199?)-. Government Publication. English. ir. US Department of Interior, Division of Federal Aid, Washington DC 70240. **LC** IN PROCESS. ***Continues in part*** *Federal Aid in Sport Fish and Wildlife Restoration Programs.*

UK
FEDERAL ENVIRONMENTAL REGULATIONS. (19??)-. English. ir. $165.00. Butterworth Heinemann Publishers, Linacre House, Jordan Hill, Oxford OX2 8DP England. **Tel** 011 44 865 310366.

US
FEDERAL RECREATION FEE REPORT TO CONGRESS : INCLUDING FEDERAL RECREATION VISITATION AND FEE DATA WITH STATE PARK INFORMATION SUPPLEMENT. See Recreation, Leisure.

●US/1071-3239
FISH AND WILDLIFE INFORMATION EXCHANGE NEWSLETTER. (FISH AND WILDLIFE INFORMATION EXCHANGE NEWSLETTER / DEPARTMENT OF FISHERIES AND WILDLIFE, VIRGINIA TECH.). [Fish Wildl. Inf. Exch. newsl.]. **Added/Corp** Virginia Polytechnic Institute and State University. Fish and Wildlife Information Exchange. Virginia Polytechnic Institute and State University. Dept. of Fisheries and Wildlife Sciences. **VFOAT** FWIE Newsletter. Vol. 1, No. 1 (Spring 1992)-. Newsletter. English. qt. $22.50. Virginia Tech / Department of Fish & Wildlife Science, 2206 South Main, Suite B, Blackburg VA 24060. **Tel** (703)231-7348, FAX (703)231-7019. **ED** Karen Reay. **DD** 333. **Circ:** 80.

US/0899-451X
FISH AND WILDLIFE LEAFLET. [Fish wildl. leafl.]. (1984)-. Monographic series. English. ir. Price varies per volume. Office of Biological Services, Fish & Wildlife Service, Department of the Interior, Washington DC 20240. **DD** 639. **CODEN** XFWLAP. Documents available from BIOSIS Document Express. ***Continues*** *Wildlife Leaflet, 0084-0165.*
Ind/Abst AGRICOLA; Biol. Abstr. (1985-).

US
FISH AND WILDLIFE NEWS. Nov. 1973-. Periodical. English. bm. Free. Office of Current Information Public Affairs, US Fish and Wildlife Service, Department of the Interior, Washington DC 20240. **Tel** (202)208-5634, FAX (202)208-5850. **ED** Patricia W Fisher. **Circ:** 11,000.
Desc: Issues of interest to Fish and Wildlife Services employees and retirees.

US/1040-2411
FISH AND WILDLIFE RESEARCH. [Fish wildl. res.]. **Added/Corp** U.S. Fish and Wildlife Service. Vol. 1 (1986)-. Monographic series. English. Price varies per volume. US Geological Survey / Denver, PO Box 25286, Denver CO 80225. **Tel** (303)493-8401. **DD** 639. **Circ:** 1,200 (ctrl). available in microform (from US Department of Commerce, National Technical Information Service). Documents available from BIOSIS Document Express. ***Formed by the union of*** *Research Report (U.S. Fish and Wildlife Service : 1976)* ***and*** *Wildlife Research Report (U.S. Fish and Wildlife Service), 0149-1849.*
Desc: Scientific and technical reports; original research of scholarly quality; interpretive literature reviews or theoretical presentations.
Ind/Abst Aquat. Sci. Fish. Abstr. (Computer File); Biol. Abstr. (1986-); Ecol. Abstr. (1986-); Fish Rev. (19??-199?); Wildl. Rev.

US/0899-3505
FISH AND WILDLIFE TECHNICAL REPORT. See Fish and Fisheries.

US/0891-7523
FISHERIES AND WILDLIFE RESEARCH AND DEVELOPMENT. See Fish and Fisheries.

CN/0707-2783
FISHERIES POLLUTION REPORT (LETHBRIDGE). See Fish and Fisheries.

AT/1035-4549
FISHERIES RESEARCH REPORT (PERTH). (FISHERIES RESEARCH REPORT.). [Fish. res. rep.]. **Added/Corp** Western Australia. Fisheries Dept. No. 83 (1990)-. Monographic series. English. **CODEN** FRREE5. Documents available from BIOSIS Document Express. ***Continues*** *Fisheries Report (Perth, W.A.).*
Ind/Abst Biol. Abstr. (1990-).

US/0426-5750
FLORIDA GARDENER, THE. **See** Gardening and Horticulture.

US
FLORIDA PRESERVATION NEWS. **Added/Corp** Florida Trust for Historic Preservation. Florida. Bureau of Historic Preservation. **VFOAT** Preservation News; FPN. Vol. 1, No. 1(1985)-. Periodical. English. bm. Florida Trust for Historic Preservation, PO Box 11206, Tallahassee FL 32302. **Tel** (904)487-2333.

US/0015-4369
FLORIDA WILDLIFE. **Added/Corp** Florida. Game and Fresh Water Fish Commission. Vol. 1 (June 1947)-. Periodical. English. bm. $10.00. Florida Wildlife, 620 South Meridian Street, Tallahassee FL 32399. **Tel** (904)488-5564. **ED** Andrea H. Bloont. **LC** SK1; .F65. **DD** 333.9/5. **Bk Rev. Circ:** 30,000 (ctrl). ***Supersedes*** *Florida Game and Fish.*
Desc: Wildlife conservation, hunting, fishing, photography, appreciation of natural resources, state of Florida wildlife magazine.
Ind/Abst Fish Rev.; Wildl. Rev.

US/0273-009X
FOCUS ON RENEWABLE NATURAL RESOURCES. [Focus renew. nat. resour.]. **Added/Corp** University of Idaho. Forest, Wildlife, and Range Experiment Station. **VFOAT** Focus. Vol. 2, No. 1 (197?)-. English. an. Free. University of Idaho College of Forestry, Wildlife, and Range Sciences, Moscow ID 83843. **Tel** (208)885-7952. **ED** Diane Noel. **Circ:** 3,500. ***Continues*** *Focus on Natural Renewable Resources, 0741-6717.*
Desc: Yearly review of research in renewable natural resources by scientists at the University of Idaho.
Ind/Abst AGRICOLA [Full Cov.]; Environ. Period. Bibliogr.

US/1046-7009
FOREST & CONSERVATION HISTORY. **See** Forestry.

CN/0380-321X
FORET CONSERVATION. **See** Forestry.

GW/0342-202X
FORUM, STADTE, HYGIENE. [Forum staedte-hyg.]. **Added/Corp** Russelsheimer Arbeitskreis Hygiene des Abwassers. Technische Universitat Hannover. Institut fuer Siedlungswasserwirtschaft. Arbeitsgemeinschaft Giessener Universitatsintitute fuer Abfallwirtschaft. Vol. 28 (Jan. 1977)-. Academic Scholarly Publication. German (summaries and/or abstracts in English). bm (6 issues). DM198.90 Germany; DM209.70 other. Patzer Verlag, Postfach 330460, D 14174 Berlin Germany. **Tel** 011 49 30 8959030. **ED** K. H. Knoll and Bernhard Patzer. **LC** TD3; .F67. **NLM** W1 FO958I. **CODEN** FSHYDL. Index available. **Bk Rev. Ad Acc. Circ:** 1,000. Documents available from CASDDS. ***Continues*** *Forum Umwelt-Hygiene, 0340-2290.*
Ind/Abst Biodeter. Abstr.; Chem. Abstr.; Curr. Biotechnol.; EMBASE; Energy Res. Abstr. (Nov. 1978-); GeoRef; Helminthol. Abstr.; Index Vet.

GW/0340-7705
FORUM WARE. [Forum Ware]. (1976)-. Periodical. German. an. S500.00 Austria; S550.00 other. Inst Warenwirtschaft Technolog, Augasse 2-6, a 1090 Vienna, Austria. **Tel** 4313 1336 4806, FAX 4313 1336 706. **UDC** 620.2. **Bk Rev**, (Qty: 20). **Ad Acc, Adv Mgr:** I. Wagner. **Circ:** 1,000. ***Continues*** *DGWT-Informationen, 0340-7713.*

CN/0822-7284
FRANC-NORD. ***Title Change.*** [Franc-Nord]. **Added/Corp** Union Quebecoise pour la Conservation de la Nature. Vol. 1 (Winter 1984)-(19??). Periodical. French. ir. Franc Vert, 690 Grand Allee Est/4e Etage, Quebec, Quebec G1R 2K5 Canada. **Tel** (418)648-2104. **DD** 333.7/09714. ***Continued by*** *Franc-Vert.*
Ind/Abst Point Repere (1991-).

CN
FRANC-VERT. French. Six times a year. 21.00Can$ Canada; 22.00Can$ other. Franc Vert, 690 Grand Allee Est/4e Etage, Quebec, Quebec G1R 2K5 Canada. **Tel** (418)648-2104. ***Continues*** *Franc-Nord, 0822-7284.*
Ind/Abst Can. Period. Index (19??-).

US/0016-1284
FRIEND O'WILDLIFE. **Added/Corp** North Carolina Wildlife Federation. (19??)-. Periodical. English. Six times a year. $5.00. North Carolina Wildlife Confederation, 1024 Washington Street, Raleigh NC 27605. **Tel** (919)833-1923.

US/1054-1829
FRIENDS OF THE EARTH. **See** Environmental Issues-Ecology.

US/0749-2804
FROM THE STATE CAPITALS. PARKS AND RECREATION TRENDS, (NEW HAVEN, CONN.). ***Title Change.*** **See** Public Administration-Parks and Recreation.

US
FWS. **See** Forestry.

US
FY ... ANNUAL REPORT / ALABAMA DEPARTMENT OF CONSERVATION AND NATURAL RESOURCES. **Main/Corp** Alabama. Dept. of Conservation and Natural Resources. English. an. Department of Conservation and Natural Resources / Alabama, 64 North Union Street, Montgomery AL 36130. **LC** HC107.A4; A35. **DD** 353.97610082/32/06. ***Continues*** *Alabama. Dept. of Department of Conservation and Natural Resources, 0093-755X.*

US
GAME BIRD BULLETIN. **Added/Corp** Pennsylvania Game Bird Breeders Association. (19??)-. Bulletin. English. bm. $25.00. Astrographics, 346 Center Street, Millersburg PA 17061. **Tel** (610)689-5388. **ED** Debra B. Trace (editor's address: RD 2, Box 544, Douglasville, PA 19518). Index available. cum. index. **Bk Rev. Ad Acc. Circ:** 450.
Desc: For game bird breeders and hunting preserve operators. Articles on disease, propagation, management, legislation, technology, research; original articles, reprints, columns.

US/1044-3061
GARBAGE (BROOKLYN, NEW YORK, N.Y.). ***Ceased.*** (GARBAGE : THE PRACTICAL JOURNAL FOR THE ENVIRONMENT.). [Garbage]. **VFOAT** Garbage. Vol. 1, No. 1 (Sept./Oct. 1989)-(Fall 1994). Periodical. English. qt. Dovetale Publishers, 2 Main Street, Gloucester MA 01930. **Tel** (508)283-3200, (508)281-8803, FAX (508)283-4629. **(Subscription address:** Neodata / Colorado, PO Box 2606, Boulder Boulder CO 80322.**) ED** Patricia Poore. **LC** TD785; .G37. **DD** 363.72/8/0973. **CODEN** GARBEO. **Bk Rev. Ad Acc. Circ:** 100,000. Documents available from The Genuine Article, UMI Article Clearinghouse, Documents on Demand.
Desc: An independent environmental journal. Must-read for environmental planners, the industry, media and concerned public. Solid, unbiased, science-based information on environmental technologies, ongoing debates and controversies, and market realities.
Ind/Abst Acad. Search (July 1993-); Curr. Index J. Educ.; Environ. Abstr.; Environ. Period. Bibliogr.; Expand. Acad. Index (1992-); Foods Adlibra; Garden Lit. (1992-); Gen. Period. Index (1992-); Gen. Sci. Index (1992-); Gen. Sci. Source (Jul. 1993-); Index Inf.; INFO-SOUTH Abstr.; Mag. Artic. Summar. Elite (July 1993-); Mag. Index Plus (1992-); Mag. Search; Newsp. Period. Abstr. (1992-); Read. Guide Period. Lit.; Res. Alert [Select. Cov.]; Soc. Sci. Cit. Index [Select. Cov.].

US/0732-4715
GEORGE WRIGHT FORUM, THE. [George Wright forum]. **Added/Corp** George Wright Society. **VFOAT** Forum. (19??)-. Periodical. English. qt (Mar., June, Sept., Dec.). $35.00. George Wright Society, PO Box 65, Hancock MI 49930-0065. **Tel** (906)487-9722. **ED** David Harmon. **LC** SB482.A4; G46. **DD** 333.78/16/0973. Index available. cum. index. **Bk Rev**, (Qty: 1-2). **Circ:** 1,200 (ctrl).

US/0164-8608
GEORGIA WILDLIFE. **Added/Corp** Georgia Wildlife Federation. National Wildlife Federation. Vol. 1 (Oct. 1978)-. Periodical. English. qt (Jan., May, Aug., Nov.). $16.00 (one year), $30.00 (two year). Georgia Wildlife Federation, 1930 Iris Drive/#G, Conyers GA 30207-5046. **Tel** (404)929-3350, FAX (404)929-3534. **ED** James R. Wilson. **Bk Rev. Circ:** 10,000 (ctrl).

CN/0374-3268
GEOS. [Geos]. Summer 1972-. Periodical. Multiple languages. qt. Free. Canada Department of Energy, Mines and Resources, Communications Branch/8th Floor, 580 Booth Street, Ottawa Ontario K1A 0E4 Canada. **Tel** (613)995-5030, FAX (613)996-9094. **ED** Primrose Ketchum. **LC** TN1; .G43. **DD** 333.7. **CODEN** GEOSCI. Index available. cum. index. **Circ:** 15,000. Documents available from Ask*IEEE, Petroleum Abstracts Document Delivery Service.
Ind/Abst ASTIS Curr. Aware. Bull. (1978-); AQUAREF; ASTIS Bibliogr. (1978-); Can. Period. Index; Coal Abstr.; Ecol. Abstr.; Energy Res. Abstr. (Jan. 1981-); Geogr. Abstr. Phys. Geogr.; Geogr. Abstr. Human Geogr.; Geol. Abstr.; INIS Atomindex [Micro.]; INSPEC (Summer 1972-); Environ.; Mintec, Min. Technol. Abstr.; Life Sci. Collect.; Pet. Abstr.; Soils Fert.

US/0892-1776
GILDEA REVIEW. (GILDEA REVIEW : A NEWSLETTER OF THE GILDEA RESOURCE CENTER.). [Gildea rev.]. Vol. 1, No. 1 (Fall 1986)-. Newsletter. English. qt. $25.00. Gildea Resource Center, Community Environmental Council Inc, 930 Miramonte Drive, Santa Barbara CA 93109. **DD** 333. ***Continues*** *Gildea Resource Center Newsletter, 8756-8802.*

SW/0284-6578
GOTEBORG STUDIES IN CONSERVATION. [Goteb. stud. conserv.]. (1988)-. Monographic series. English (Swedish). ir. Price varies per volume. Acta Universitatis Gothoburgensis, PO Box 5096, S-402 22 Goteborg Sweden. **Tel** 011 46 31 7731000. **(Subscription address:** Acta Universitatis Gothoburgensis, Box 5096, B-402, Goteborg, Sweden.**) ED** Jan Rosvall. **UDC** 71.

US
GRASSROOTS / VIRGINIA DEPARTMENT OF CONSERVATION AND RECREATION, DIVISION OF SOIL AND WATER CONSERVATION. **Added/Corp** Virginia. Division of Soil and Water Conservation. Vol. 22, No. 3 (1991)-. Periodical. English. qt. ***Continues*** *Soil & Water Grassroots.*

SA
GREAT OUTDOORS. **See** Recreation, Leisure-Outdoor Life.

US/1058-594X
GREEN-KEEPING (ANNANDALE-ON-HUDSON, N.Y.). ***Ceased.*** (GREEN-KEEPING.). [Green-keeping]. (Mar./Apr. 1991)-(199?). Periodical. English. bm. Greenkeeping, Box 28, Annandale NY 12504. **DD** 304.

CN/1185-0957
GREEN LIVING. [Green living]. Vol. 1, No. 1 (June/July 1990)-. Periodical. English. Six times a year. Free. Green Living Publishing, 80 Mavety Street, Toronto, Ontario M6P 2L6 Canada. **Tel** (416)769-4167. **DD** 363.7/009713/54105.

US/0836-5040
GREENPEACE (CANADA ED.). (GREENPEACE.). [Greenpeace]. **Added/Corp** Greenpeace USA. Greenpeace Foundation. **VFOAT** Greenpeace Quarterly. Vol. 12 No. 1 (Jan./Mar 1987)-. Periodical. English. qt. $36.84 Canada; $20.00 other. Greenpeace / Washington DC, 1436 U Street Northwest, Washington DC 20009. **Tel** (202)462-1177. **ED** Andre Carothers. **DD** 333.95/16/0601. **Circ:** 2,000,000. Documents available from UMI Article Clearinghouse, Documents on Demand. ***Continues*** *Greenpeace Examiner (Vancouver, B.C.), 0828-7988.*
Ind/Abst Altern. Press Index; Environ. Abstr.; Environ. Period. Bibliogr. (?-?); Expand. Acad. Index (1992-); Newsp. Period. Abstr. (1992-).

AT/1034-5876
GREENWEEK. [Greenweek]. (1989)-. Periodical. English. wk (Fri.). 790.00Aus$. Greenweek, PO Box 1982, Southport QLD 4215 Australia. **Tel** 011 60 75 328333, FAX 011 60 75 918206. **ED** Julia Holland. **DD** 333.720994. **Bk Rev.** ctrl circ. available on an online database.
Desc: This publication provides information on governmental action concerning environmental issues, energy reports, consumer surveys, and news from international environmental agencies.

US/0196-5395
GUIDES TO FOREST AND CONSERVATION HISTORY OF NORTH AMERICA. **Added/Corp** Forest History Society. No. 1, (1976)-. Monographic series. English. ir. Price varies per volume. Forest History Society, 701 Vickers Avenue, Durham NC 27701. **Tel** (919)682-9319. **ED** Alice E. Ingerson. **LC** UNC.

US/0739-2052
HABITAT (FALMOUTH, ME.). (HABITAT : JOURNAL OF THE MAINE AUDUBON SOCIETY.). **Added/Corp** Maine Audubon Society. Vol. 1, No. 1 (Oct./Nov. 1983)-. Periodical. English. qt. comes with membership. Maine Audubon Society, 118 Old Route One, Falmouth ME 04105. **Tel** (207)781-2330. **DD** 363. Index available. cum. index. **Bk Rev. Ad Acc. Circ:** 7,500.
Desc: Environmental issues and natural history of Maine.

UK/0028-9043
HABITAT (LONDON). (HABITAT.). [Habitat]. **Added/Corp** Council for Nature. Council for Environmental Conservation (Great Britain). Vol. 1 (Feb. 1965)-. Periodical. English. Ten times a year. £13.50 UK; £17.50 other. Environment Council, 21 Elizabeth Street, London SWIW 9RP England. **Tel** 011 44 71 8248411. **ED** Susan Joy. **Bk Rev. Ad Acc. Circ:** 1,700. ***Continues*** *News for Naturalists, 0545-8250.*
Desc: Provides news and information on a wide range of environmental issues plus book reviews, future events and job vacancies.

AT/0310-2939
HABITAT (MELBOURNE). (HABITAT.). [Habitat]. **Added/Corp** Australian Conservation Foundation. **VFOAT** Habitat Australia. No. 1 (June

1973)-. Periodical. English. Four times a year (Feb., May, Aug., Nov.). 41.00Aus$ Australia; 58.00Aus$ others; 36.00Aus$ Australia, 55.00Aus$ others (individuals), 50.00Aus$ Australia, 69.00Aus$ others schools, communities & government departments, 200.00Aus$ Australia, 219.00Aus$ others corporate & association Comes with Australian Conservation Foundation membership. Australian Conservation Foundation, 340 Gore Street, Fitzroy Victoria 3065 Australia. **Tel** 011 61 3 4161455, FAX 011 61 3 4160767. **ED** Anatoly Sawenko. **LC** QH77.A8; H3. **DD** 333.7/2/0994. Index available. **Bk Rev**. **Ad Acc**. **Circ:** 19,000.
Desc: Features articles and picture essays on a range of topics of interest to those concerned with the environment, conservation and peace.
Ind/Abst APAIS, Aust. Public Aff. Inf. Ser. (1974-); Fish Rev.; J. Plan. Lit.; Wildl. Rev.

US
HAWK MOUNTAIN NEWS. **Added/Corp** Hawk Mountain Sanctuary Association. (April 1978)-. English. Twice a year. $20.00. Hawk Mountain Sanctuary Association, Route 2, Kempton PA 19529. **Tel** (215)756-6961. ***Continues*** *Newsletter (Hawk Mountain Sanctuary Association).*
Ind/Abst Fish Rev.; Wildl. Rev.

FI/0782-2790
HELSINGIN YLIOPISTON YMPARISTONSUOJELUN LAITOKSEN JULKAISUJA. [Hels. yliop. ymp. suoj. laitok. julk.]. **VFOAT** Publikationer Fran Institutionen for Miljovard vid Helsingfors Universitet; Publications of the Department of Environmental Conservation of the University of Helsinki. (1985)-. Monographic series. Multiple languages. ir. **UDC** 502. ***Continues*** *Helsingin Yliopiston Ymparistonsuojelun Laitoksen Monistejulkaisu, 0357-9565.*
Ind/Abst For. Abstr.; Nematol. Abstr.; Soils Fert.

UK/0261-1988
HERITAGE OUTLOOK. ***Title Change.*** **See** Architecture.

UK/0269-8498
HERPETOFAUNA NEWS. **See** Zoology.

US/0191-5657
HIGH COUNTRY NEWS. [High ctry. news]. **VFOAT** Mountain West's High Country News. Vol. 2, No. 5 (Jan. 30, 1970)-. Newspaper. English. bw (only 1 issue in January and July). $28.00 (one year), $49.00 (two years), $69.00 (three years) public libraries, school libraries (public and private) and individuals; $38.00 (one year), $67.00 (two years), $97.00 (three years) other. High Country News, Box 1090, Paonia CO 81428. **Tel** (303)527-4898. **ED** Betsy Marston. **[CCC]**. Index available. cum. index. **Bk Rev**. **Ad Acc**. **Circ:** 9,000 (ctrl). available on microfiche; available on microfilm. Documents available from Documents on Demand. ***Continues*** *Camping News Weekly;* ***Absorbed*** *Western Colorado Report.*
Desc: Covers environmental and natural resource issues in the inter-mountain West.
Ind/Abst Coal Abstr.; Energy Inf. Abstr.; Environ. Abstr.; Environ. Period. Bibliogr.

MW
HIGHLIGHTS. **See** Agriculture.

US/0018-4780
HOOSIER OUTDOORS. **See** Recreation, Leisure-Outdoor Life.

US
HORIZONS (SAN ANTONIO, TEX.). (HORIZONS / TEXAS NATURE CONSERVANCY.). **Added/Corp** Texas Nature Conservancy. (19??)-. Periodical. English. qt. The Texas Nature Conservancy, PO Box 1440, San Antonio TX 78295-1440.

JA/0385-9290
HYOGO-KEN KOGAI KENKYUJO KENKYU HOKOKU. **See** Environmental Issues-Pollution and Waste Management.

US/0277-1330
ICBP TECHNICAL PUBLICATION. (TECHNICAL PUBLICATION / INTERNATIONAL COUNCIL FOR BIRD PRESERVATION.). [Tech. publ. - Int. Counc. Bird Preserv.]. **Added/Corp** International Council for Bird Preservation. No. 1 (1981)-. Monographic series. English. ir. Price varies per volume. International Council for Bird Preservation, 32 Cambridge Road, Girton Cambridge CB3 0PJ England. **Tel** 011 44 223 277318, FAX 011 44 223 277200. **DD** 363.

CL/0073-4675
IDESIA. **See** Agriculture.

UK/0536-1737
IIC NEWS. **VAT** International Institute for Conservation News. Vol. 1 (Jan. 1960)-. Periodical. English. qt. International Institute for Conservation of Historic and Artistic Works / England, 6 Buckingham Street, London WC2N 6BA England. **Tel** 011 44 71 839 5975. ***Continues*** *IIC Notes d'Actualite. News Letter.*

●US/1058-9309
ILLINOIS STEWARD, THE. [Ill. steward]. **Added/Corp** Illinois Stewardship Committee. Vol. 1, No. 1 (Winter 1992)-. Periodical. English. qt (4 issues). $10.00. Illinois Stewardship Committee, 1102 South Goodwin Avenue, Urbana IL 61801. **Tel** (217)244-6254. **ED** Mike Bolin. **LC** S932.I3; I55. **DD** 333.95/16/09773. ctrl circ.
Desc: Explores issues of stewardship pertaining to Illinois' natural resources and natural heritage.

US/0019-2317
ILLINOIS WILDLIFE. **Added/Corp** Illinois Federation of Sportsmen's Clubs. Illinois Wildlife Federation. Vol. 1 (Nov. 1945)-. Periodical. English. bm (6 issues). $12.00 US; $14.00 Canada; $15.00 other. Illinois Wildlife Federation, 123 South Chicago, Rossville IL 60963. **Tel** (217)748-6365. **ED** Tom Mills. **Bk Rev**, (Qty: 4). **Ad Acc**. **Circ:** 10,500 (ctrl).
Desc: Covers conservation and environmental interests.
Ind/Abst Biol. Dig.

US
INFO. (INFO / HCRS, U.S. DEPARTMENT OF THE INTERIOR, HERITAGE CONSERVATION AND RECREATION SERVICE.). **VFOAT** HCRS Info. Periodical. English. mo. Heritage Conservation and Recreation Service, US Department of the Interior, 550 G Street NW, Washington DC 20243.

US/0275-522X
INFORM REPORTS. (INFORM REPORTS.). [Inf. rep.]. **Added/Corp** INFORM, Inc. **VFOAT** I.N.F.O.R.M. Reports. Vol. 1, No. 1 (Jan./Feb. 1981)-. Periodical. English. Four times a year. $35.00. Inform / New York, 381 Park Avenue South, Suite 1201, New York NY 10016. **Tel** (212)689-4040. **ED** Perrin Stryker. **Circ:** 2,000 (ctrl). Documents available from Documents on Demand.
Desc: Reports on research studies that identify practical actions for the protecting and conservation of natural resources, including disposal of hazardous wastes, irrigation, industrial safety and water pollution.
Ind/Abst Environ. Abstr.

US/0470-3847
INFORMATION BULLETIN - THE NATURE CONSERVANCY. **Main/Corp** Nature Conservancy. (19??)-. Bulletin. English. Price varies per volume. The Nature Conservancy, 1815 North Lynn Street, Arlington VA 22209. **Tel** (703)841-5300. **DD** 333.7.

US/0198-8735
INFORMATION SERIES - COLORADO WATER RESOURCES RESEARCH INSTITUTE. (INFORMATION SERIES / COLORADO WATER RESOURCES RESEARCH INSTITUTE.). **Added/Corp** Colorado Water Resources Research Institute. No. 25 (Jan. 1978)-. Monographic series. English. ir. Colorado State University / Environmental Resources, Environmental Resources Center, Ft. Collins CO 80521. **CODEN** ISCIDF. ***Continues*** *Information Series (Colorado State University. Environmental Resources Center), 0147-5061.*
Ind/Abst Chem. Abstr.

JA
INOCHI ARU CHIKYU. **Added/Corp** Japan. Kankyocho. Somuka. Issue No. 1 (1973)-. Periodical. Japanese. ¥1500. Gyosei Corporation Ltd., 4-2 Nishi Goken-cho, Shinjuku-Ku Tokyo 162 Japan. **Tel** 33269-4145, FAX 33268-2315. **LC** HC79.E5; I515.

UK
INTELCOL NEWSLETTER. Newsletter. English. INTERCOL Institute Ecology, University of Georgia, Athens GA 30602.

US/8756-6281
INTERACTION (WASHINGTON, D.C. : 1981). (INTERACTION : NEWSLETTER OF THE GLOBAL TOMORROW COALITION.). [Interaction]. Vol. 1, No. 1 (Nov./Dec. 1981)-. Newsletter. English. qt. $50.00. Global Tomorrow Coalition, 1325 G Street NW, Washington DC 20005. **Tel** (202)879-3040. **ED** Philip C Ritterbush. **LC** HC79.E5; I519. **DD** 302/.05. **Bk Rev**. **Circ:** 8,000.
Desc: Reviews US role in addressing world environment, population, and resource problems.

US
INTERNATIONAL ASSOCIATION OF MILK FOOD AND ENVIRONMENTAL SANITARIANS 3A SANITARY STANDARDS. **See** Food and Food Industry.

●US/1051-4201
INTERNATIONAL BIBLIOGRAPHY OF WILDLAND FIRE. **See** Fire Prevention.

US/1041-4665
INTERNATIONAL ENVIRONMENTAL AFFAIRS. [Int. environ. aff.]. **VFOAT** IEA. Vol. 1, No. 1 (Winter 1989)-. Periodical. English. Four times a year. $85.00 (institutions), $50.00 (individuals) US; $95.00 (institutions), $60.00 (individuals) other. University Press of New England, 23 South Main Street, Hanover NH 03755. **Tel** (800)421-1561, (603)643-7110, FAX (603)643-1540. **ED** Konrad von Moltke. **LC** WMLC 93/305; HC79.E5; I58. **DD** 363. **[CCC]**. Index available. cum. index. **Bk Rev**. **Circ:** 400. Documents available from The Genuine Article, Documents on Demand.
Desc: Contains three articles, a commentary, a document reprint, two institutional profiles, and ten book reviews of various lengths. Subjects include: European air pollution control; Central America; the US national acid precipitation program, etc.
Ind/Abst Air Pollut. Titles; Curr. Index J. Educ.; Environ. Abstr.; Environ. Period. Bibliogr.; Fish Rev. (Jan. 1989-July 1992); Geogr. Abstr. Human Geogr.; Int. Dev. Abstr.; Int. Polit. Sci. Abstr.; PAIS Int. Print (1991-); Res. Alert [Select. Cov.]; Soc. Sci. Cit. Index [Select. Cov.]; Wildl. Rev. (Jan. 1989-July 1992).

US/0890-0698
INTERNATIONAL GAME WARDEN, THE. [Int. game ward.]. (August 1984)-. Periodical. English. qt. $14.00 US; $17.00 Canada; $26.00 other. The International Game Warden, PO Box 595, Edwardsville IL 62025. **ED** D. Hastings (Editors Phone: (407)723-2968). **DD** 333.

US/0020-7233
INTERNATIONAL JOURNAL OF ENVIRONMENTAL STUDIES. SECTION A, ENVIRONMENTAL STUDIES, THE. **VFOAT** Environmental Studies. Vol. 24, No. 1 (1985)-. Periodical. English. qt. £212.00. Gordon & Breach Science Publishers, Inc., PO Box 786, Cooper Station, New York NY 10276. **Tel** (212)206-8900, FAX (212)645-2459. **(Subscription address:** International Publishers Distributor at one of the following addresses: 820 Town Center Drive, Langhorne, PA 19047; or PO Box 90, Reading Berkshire RG1 8JL UK; or Kent Ridge PO Box 1180, Singapore 9111, Republic of Singapore**)** **NLM** W1; IN766HE. **[CCC]**. Documents available from Article Express International. ***Continues in part*** *International Journal of Environmental Studies, 0020-7233.*
Ind/Abst Ecol. Abstr. (?-?); Ei Page One; Eng. Index Annu.; Fish Rev. (19??-199?); Helminthol. Abstr. (1991-); Int. Dev. Abstr. (?-?); Key Word Index Wildl. Res.; Leis. Recreat. Tour. Abstr.; Lit. Pat. Abstr., Oilfield Chem. (1985-1989); Lit. Abstr., Catal. Catal.; Lit. Abstr., Health Environ.; Lit. Abstr., Pet. Refin. Petrochem.; Lit. Abstr., Pet. Substit.; Lit. Abstr., Transp. Storage; Rural Dev. Abstr.; Wildl. Rev. (19??-199?).

US/0020-9112
INTERNATIONAL WILDLIFE. [Int. wildl.]. **Added/Corp** National Wildlife Federation. Canadian Wildlife Federation. Vol. 1, No. 1 (Jan./Feb. 1971)-. Periodical. English. bm (6 issues). $16.00. National Wildlife Federation / Virginia, 8925 Leesburg Pike, Vienna VA 22184. **Tel** (703)790-4000, (800)822-9919, FAX (703)442-7332. **ED** Jonathan Fisher. **LC** QL81.5; .I56. **DD** 333.95/05. **CODEN** INWLAI. **Circ:** 650,000 (ctrl). available on microfilm and microfiche from University Microfilms International (UMI); available on CD-ROM. Documents available from BIOSIS Document Express, UMI Article Clearinghouse, Documents on Demand. ***Absorbed in part*** *Conservation News, 0010-647X.*
Desc: A journal of the remote corners of the earth. Includes photographs, and fascinating facts. Conservation magazine of nature and the environment.
Ind/Abst Acad. Abstr. Full Text Elite (Jan. 1989-); Acad. Abstr. (Jan. 1989-); Acad. Ind. [Computer File] (1984-); Acad. Search (Jan. 1984-); Biol. Abstr.; Biol. Dig.; Can. Period. Index (19??-); Child. Mag. Guide; Curr. Aware. Biol. Sci., CABS; Energy Inf. Abstr.; Environ. Abstr.; Environ. Period. Bibliogr.; Expand. Acad. Index (1984-); Gen. Period. Index (1985-); Gen. Sci. Index; Index Sci. Rev.; INFO-SOUTH Abstr.; Mag. Artic. Summar. Elite (Jan. 1984-); Mag. Artic. Summar. Select (Jan. 1989-); Mag. Artic. Summar. CD-ROM (Jan. 1989-); Mag. Index Plus (1989-); Mag. Search; Mid. Search (Jan. 1989-); Newsp. Period. Abstr. (1988-); Prim. Search (Jan. 1989-); Read. Guide Abstr. Select Ed.; Read. Guide Period. Lit.; Mag. Index (1977-); Vocat. Search (Jan. 1984-).

US/0548-3549
INVENTORY SERIES - STATE OF NEVADA, DEPARTMENT OF CONSERVATION AND NATURAL RESOURCES. **Main/Corp** Nevada. Department of Conservation and Natural Resources. **Added/Corp** United States. Water Resources Council. United States. Office of Water Resources Research. **VFOAT** Water and Land Resources Plan for Nevada. No. 1 (July 1967)-. Monographic series. English. ir. Price varies per volume. Department of Conservation and Natural Resources / Nevada, 4220 Maryland Parkway, Las Vegas NV 89109. **DD** 333.7.

US/0021-0471
IOWA CONSERVATIONIST. **Added/Corp** Iowa State Conservation Commission. Iowa Conservation Commission. Iowa. Dept. of Natural Resources. Vol. 1 (Feb. 1942)-. Periodical. English. mo. $9.97. Department of Natural Resources / Iowa, 900 East Grand, Wallace State Building, Des Moines IA 50319. **Tel** (515)281-3887. **ED** Julie Sparks. Index available. **Bk Rev**. **Circ:** 60,000 (ctrl). Documents available from BIOSIS Document Express.

Desc: Articles on Iowa's natural resources, including recreation, management, issues and general information.
Ind/Abst Biol. Abstr.; Wildl. Rev.

RU/0202-7321
ITOGI NAUKI I TEHNIKI - VSESOUZNYJ INSTITUT NAUCNOJ I TEHNICESKOJ INFORMACII. SERIA OHRANA PRIRODY I VOSPROIZVODSTVO PRIRODNYH RESURSOV. (ITOGI NAUKI I TEKHNIKI. SERIIA OKHRANA PRIRODY I VOSPROIZVODSTVO PRIRODNYKH RESURSOV.). [Itogi nauki teh. - Vses. inst. naucn. teh. inf., Ser. Ohr. prir. vosproizvod. prir. resur.]. **Added/Corp** Vsesoiuznyi Institut Nauchnoi I Tekhnicheskoi Informatsii (Soviet Union). **VFOAT** Seriia Okhrana Prirody I Vosproizvodstvo Prirodnykh Resursov; Okhrana Prirody I Vosproizvodstvo Prirodnykh Resursov; Itogi Nauki I Tekhniki: Okhrana Prirody I Vosproizvodstvo Prirodnykh Resursov. Vol.1 (1978)-. Monographic series. Russian. mo. Price varies per volume. VINITI - Vsesoyuznyi Institut Nauchno-Tekhnicheskoi Informatsii, All-Union Scientific and Technical Information Institute, Baltiiskaia Ulitsa 14, 125219 Moscow Russia. **Tel** 238-46-00, FAX 9430060, telex 411160. **(Subscription address:** Victor Kamkin, 4956 Boiling Brook Parkway, Rockville MD 20852.) **LC** QH75; .I85. ***Continues*** *Itogi Nauki. Okhrana Prirody I Vosproizvodstvo Prirodnykh Resursov, 0202-7321.*
Ind/Abst Coal Abstr.

SZ/0020-9058
IUCN BULLETIN. [IUCN bull.]. **Main/Corp** International Union for Conservation of Nature and Natural Resources. **VAT** International Union for Conservation of Nature and Natural Resources Bulletin. Vol. 1 (Aug. 1961)-. Bulletin. English. qt. $55.00. International Union for Conservation of Nature and Natural Resources, rue Mauverney 28, CH1196 Gland Switzerland. **Tel** 011 41 22 647181, FAX 011 41 22 642926, telex 419605. **ED** Robert Lamb. **LC** QH75.A1; I62a. **DD** 333.9/5/05. **Bk Rev. Circ:** 9,000 (ctrl). Documents available from Documents on Demand. ***Supersedes*** *Bulletin - International Union for Conservation of Nature and Natural Resources.*
Desc: International perspective on problems facing today's conservation achievers and modern methodologies for implementing the world conservation strategy with emphasis on the work of International Union for Conservation of Nature.
Ind/Abst Energy Inf. Abstr.; Environ. Abstr.; Key Word Index Wildl. Res.; Life Sci. Collect.

SZ
IUCN MONOGRAPH. **Main/Corp** International Union for Conservation of Nature and Natural Resources. No. 1- 1971-. Monographic series. English. Price varies per volume. International Union for Conservation of Nature and Natural Resources, rue Mauverney 28, CH1196 Gland Switzerland. **Tel** 011 41 22 647181, FAX 011 41 22 642926, telex 419605.

SZ
IUCN OCCASIONAL PAPER. **Main/Corp** International Union for Conservation of Nature and Natural Resources. No. 1- June 1971-. Monographic series. English. Price varies per volume. International Union for Conservation of Nature and Natural Resources, rue Mauverney 28, CH1196 Gland Switzerland. **Tel** 011 41 22 647181, FAX 011 41 22 642926, telex 419605.
Ind/Abst Fish Rev.; Life Sci. Collect.; Wildl. Rev.

SZ/0074-9273
IUCN PUBLICATIONS NEW SERIES. **Main/Corp** International Union for Conservation of Nature and Natural Resources. **VFOAT** UICN - Publications Nouvelle Serie. No. 1- 1963-. Monographic series. Multiple languages (English and French). Price varies per volume. International Union for Conservation of Nature and Natural Resources, rue Mauverney 28, CH1196 Gland Switzerland. **Tel** 011 41 22 647181, FAX 011 41 22 642926, telex 419605. **DD** 333.7.
Ind/Abst Life Sci. Collect.

SZ/0591-2741
IUCN PUBLICATIONS NEW SERIES. SUPPLEMENTARY PAPER. **Main/Corp** International Union for Conservation of Nature and Natural Resources. No. 1 (1964)-. Monographic series. English (French). mo. Price varies per volume. UNIPUB, 4611-F Assembly Drive, Lanham MD 20706-4391. **Tel** (800)274-4888, FAX (301)459-0056, telex 28787 GATT CH.

SZ
IUCN YEARBOOK. **Main/Corp** International Union for Conservation of Nature and Natural Resources. **VFOAT** Yearbook - International Union for Conservation of Nature and Natural Resources. 1970-. English (English and French). International Union for Conservation of Nature and Natural Resources, rue Mauverney 28, CH1196 Gland Switzerland. **Tel** 011 41 22 647181, FAX 011 41 22 642926, telex 419605. **DD** 333.7. ***Continues*** *Annual Report - International Union for Conservation of Nature and Natural Resources, 0074-9265.*

GW/0179-3462
IWL UMWELTBRIEF. (19??)-. German. mo. DM307.30. Deutscher Wirtschaftsdienst GmbH, Marienburgerstrasse 22, D 50968 Cologne Germany. **Tel** 011 49 221 376950.

INT/1016-1317
IWRB NEWS. [IWRB news]. **VFOAT** International Waterfowl and Wetlands Research Bureau News. (1989)-. Periodical. English. sa. £10.00. International Waterfowl & Wetlands Research Bureau, New Grounds, Slimbridge GL2 7BX England. **Tel** 011 44 453 890624.

BE
JACHT EN NATUURBEHEER. **See** Recreation, Leisure-Outdoor Life.

GW/0171-4694
JAHRBUCH DES VEREINS ZUM SCHUTZ DER BERGWELT. [Jahrb. Ver. Schutz Bergwelt]. **Main/Corp** Verein zum Schutz der Bergwelt. 42.- Yearly volume; 1977-. German. an. DM35.00 Germany; $20.00 US. Verein Zum Schutz der Bergwelt 22, Germany. **Tel** 089 4171114. **LC** QH77.A46; V47A. **DD** 333.9/5/094947. Index available. cum. index. **Bk Rev. Ad Acc. Circ:** 5,000 (ctrl). ***Continues*** *Verein zum Schutze der Alpenflanzen und Tiere. Jahrbuch.*
Ind/Abst GeoRef; Key Word Index Wildl. Res.

GW
JAHRESBERICHT - BUNDESVERBAND DER DEUTSCHEN GAS- UND WASSERWIRTSCHAFT. **Main/Corp** Bunderverband der Deutschen Gas- und Wasserwirtschaft. (19??)-. German. **LC** TA73; .B86a. **DD** 363.6/3/0943.

CH
JEN YU TI. **VFOAT** Man and Land; Man and Land Monthly. (1984)-. Periodical. Chinese. mo. $500.00. Jen Yu Ti Tsa Chih She 1 Tun Hua S Road, Taipei Taiwan. **LC** HD936; .J46. **DD** 333.73. ***Continues*** *Tu Ti Kai Ko.*

US
JOB SEEKER. **See** Occupations and Careers.

UK/0264-6811
JOURNAL OF ENERGY & NATURAL RESOURCES LAW. **See** Law.

II/0970-5945
JOURNAL OF NATURE CONSERVATION. **See** Environmental Issues-Ecology.

US/0022-4561
JOURNAL OF SOIL AND WATER CONSERVATION. [J. soil water conserv.]. **Added/Corp** Soil Conservation Society of America. **VFOAT** Journal of Soil & Water Conservation. Vol. 1; (July 1946)-. Academic Scholarly Publication. English. bm. $42.00 (one year), $81.00 (two year), US and Canada; $54.00 (one year), $99.00 (two year), other. Journal of Soil and Water Conservation, 7515 Northeast Ankeny Road, Ankeny IA 50021. **Tel** (515)289-2331, FAX (515)289-1227. **ED** Max Schnepf. **LC** S622; .S5. **DD** 631.4/5/05. **CODEN** JSWCA3. Index available. cum. index. **Bk Rev. Ad Acc. Pr Rev. Acid Free. Circ:** 13,000 (ctrl). available on microfilm and microfiche from University Microfilms International (UMI). Documents available from The Genuine Article, BIOSIS Document Express, UMI Article Clearinghouse, CASDDS, Documents on Demand. ***Absorbed*** *Soil Conservation Society of America. News, Notes and Activities.*
Desc: A forum for the discussion of land and water resources management.
Ind/Abst AGRICOLA [Select. Cov.]; Agric. Eng. Abstr. (1991-); Agrofor. Abstr.; AQUAREF; Aquat. Sci. Fish. Abstr. (Computer File); Biogr. Index; Biol. Agric. Index; Biol. Abstr.; Biol. Dig.; Chem. Abstr.; Coal Abstr.; Cot. Trop. Fibr. Abstr. Bibliogr.; Curr. Aware. Biol. Sci., CABS; Curr. Contents, Agric. Biol. Environ. Sci.; Ecol. Abstr.; Ecology Abstr.; EMBASE; Energy Inf. Abstr.; Environ. Abstr.; Environ. Period. Bibliogr.; Expand. Acad. Index (1992-); Field Crop Abstr.; Fish Rev.; For. Abstr.; Geogr. Abstr. Phys. Geogr.; Geogr. Abstr. Human Geogr.; Geol. Abstr.; Grasslands For. Abstr.; Health Saf. Sci. Abstr.; Int. Dev. Abstr.; Irr. Drain. Abstr.; Maize Abstr.; Newsp. Period. Abstr. (1992-); Ocean. Abstr.; Life Sci. Collect.; Plant Breed. Abstr.; Pollut. Abstr. Indexes; Res. Alert [Full Cov.]; Rev. Agric. Entomol.; Risk Abstr.; Rural Dev. Abstr.; Sci. Cit. Index; SCISEARCH; Seed Abstr.; Soc. Sci. Cit. Index [Select. Cov.]; Soils Fert.; Sorghum Mill. Abstr.; Soyabean Abstr.; Urban Aff. Abstr.; Weed Abstr.; World Agric. Econ.

II/0022-457X
JOURNAL OF SOIL AND WATER CONSERVATION IN INDIA. [J. soil water conserv. India]. **Added/Corp** Soil Conservation Society in India. Vol. 1 (Oct. 1952)-. Periodical. English. qt. $30.00. India Soil Conservation Society, Hazari Bagh, Bihar India. **(Subscription address:** Prints India, 11 Darya Ganj, New Delhi 110002 India.) **LC** S954.I5; J65. **CODEN** JSWIAL. Documents available from CASDDS.
Ind/Abst AGRICOLA; Chem. Abstr. (1952-1978); GeoRef.

US/1047-3289
JOURNAL OF THE AIR & WASTE MANAGEMENT ASSOCIATION. ***Title Change.*** [J. Air Waste Manage. Assoc.]. **Added/Corp** Air & Waste Management Association. **VFOAT** Journal of the Air and Waste Management Association. Vol. 40 No. 1 (Jan. 1990)-Vol. 42 No. 12 (Dec. 1992). Periodical. English. mo. Air & Waste Management Association, PO Box 2861, Pittsburgh PA 15230. **Tel** (412)232-3444. **LC** TD883; .A48. **DD** 628.5/3/05. **NLM** W1; JO907EH. **CODEN** JAWAEB. **Pr Rev.** available on microfilm and microfiche from University Microfilms International (UMI). Documents available from Article Express International, The Genuine Article, BIOSIS Document Express, Ask*IEEE, CASDDS, Documents on Demand. ***Continues*** *JAPCA, 0894-0630.* ***Continued by*** *Air & Waste.*
Ind/Abst Abstr. Bull. Inst. Paper Chem. (1990-); Abstr. Bull. Inst. Pap. Sci. Tech.; AGRICOLA [Select. Cov.]; Air Pollut. Titles; Appl. Sci. Technol. Index (1990-); Bibliogr. Agric. (1990-); BioBusiness (1990-); Biol. Abstr.; Chem. Abstr. (1990-); Coal Abstr. (1990-); Crop Physiol. Abstr.; Curr. Aware. Biol. Sci., CABS; Curr. Contents, Agric. Biol. Environ. Sci.; Curr. Contents Eng. Tech. Appl. Sci.; Ecol. Abstr.; Ei Page One; EMBASE; Energy Inf. Abstr. (1990-); Energy Res. Abstr. (1990-); Eng. Index Annu. [Select. Cov.]; Environ. Abstr. (1990-); Environ. Period. Bibliogr.; Field Crop Abstr.; Fluid Abstr., Civil Eng.; Fluid Abstr. Proc. Eng.; FLUIDEX (199?-); For. Prod. Abstr. (1991-); For. Abstr.; Geogr. Abstr. Phys. Geogr.; Geogr. Abstr. Human Geogr.; Health Saf. Sci. Abstr.; Health Plan. Adminis.; Highw. Res. Abstr.; Index Med. (1990-); INIS Atomindex [Micro.]; INSPEC (1990-); Int. Aerosp. Abstr. (1990-); J. Plan. Lit.; Leadscan; Lit. Pat. Abstr., Oilfield Chem. (1989-); Lit. Abstr., Catal. Catal.; Lit. Abstr., Health Environ.; Lit. Abstr., Pet. Refin. Petrochem.; Lit. Abstr., Pet. Substit.; Lit. Abstr., Transp. Storage; Maize Abstr.; Pollut. Abstr. Indexes; Res. Alert [Full Cov.]; Risk Abstr.; Sci. Cit. Index; SCISEARCH; Soc. Sci. Cit. Index [Select. Cov.]; Soils Fert.

CN/0833-0018
JOURNAL OF WILD CULTURE, THE. [J. wild cult.]. **Added/Corp** Society for the Preservation of Wild Culture. Vol. 1, No. 1 (1987)-. Periodical. English. qt. $15.00 Canada; $17.00 US. Society for the Preservation of Wild Culture, PO Box 1127, Station A, Toronto, Ontario M5W 1G6 Canada. **DD** 051.
Ind/Abst Can. Period. Index (1989-).

US/0022-541X
JOURNAL OF WILDLIFE MANAGEMENT, THE. [J. wildl. manage.]. **Added/Corp** Wildlife Society. Vol. 1 (July 1937)-. Academic Scholarly Publication. English. Four times a year. $110.00 US, Canada, and Mexico; $120.00 other (includes Wildlife Monographs and also comes with Wildlife Society Bulletin). Wildlife Society, 5410 Grosvenor Lane, Bethesda MD 20814. **Tel** (301)897-9770, FAX (301)530-2471. **LC** SK351; .J68. **DD** 799; 333*. **CODEN** JWMAA9. Index available (bound in last issue). cum. index. **Pr Rev.** available on microfilm and microfiche from University Microfilms International (UMI). Documents available from The Genuine Article, BIOSIS Document Express, UMI Article Clearinghouse, CASDDS, Documents on Demand.
Desc: Disseminate scientific research and management information relating to all phases of wildlife science and management.
Ind/Abst ASTIS Curr. Aware. Bull. (1978-); Acad. Abstr. Full Text Elite (July 1990-); Acad. Abstr. (July 1990-); Acad. Ind. [Computer File] (1992-); Acad. Search (July 1990-); AGRICOLA [Select. Cov.]; Agrofor. Abstr. (19??-19??); Anim. Behav. Abstr.; AQUAREF; ASTIS Bibliogr. (1978-); Biol. Agric. Index; Biol. Abstr.; Chem. Abstr.; Curr. Aware. Biol. Sci., CABS; Curr. Contents, Agric. Biol. Environ. Sci.; Curr. Ref. Fish Res.; Ecol. Abstr.; Ecology Abstr.; EMBASE; Environ. Abstr.; Environ. Period. Bibliogr.; Expand. Acad. Index (1989-); Fish Rev.; For. Abstr.; Gen. Sci. Index; Geogr. Abstr. Phys. Geogr.; Grasslands For. Abstr.; INFO-SOUTH Abstr.; Key Word Index Wildl. Res.; Leadscan; Mag. Artic. Summar. Elite (July 1990-); Mag. Artic. Summar. Select (July 1990-); Mag. Artic. Summar. CD-ROM (July 1990-); Mag. Search; Middle East Abstr. Index; Newsp. Period. Abstr. (1991-); Nutr. Abstr. Rev., Ser. B, Live Feeds and Feed.; Life Sci. Collect.; Pollut. Abstr. Indexes; Poult. Abstr.; Res. Alert [Full Cov.]; Rev. Med. Vet. Entomol.; Sci. Cit. Index; SCISEARCH; Wildl. Rev.

●US/1071-2232
JOURNAL OF WILDLIFE REHABILITATION. (JOURNAL OF WILDLIFE REHABILITATION : A PUBLICATION OF THE INTERNATIONAL WILDLIFE REHABILITATION COUNCIL.). [J. wildl. rehabil.]. **Added/Corp** International Wildlife Rehabilitation Council. Vol. 16, No. 1 (Spring 1993)-. Periodical. English. Four times a year. $38.00. International Wildlife Rehabilitation Council, 4437 Central Place, Suite B4, Suisun CA 94585. **Tel** (707)864-1761, FAX (707)864-3107. **ED** Jan White. **LC** SF996.45; .J69. **DD** 639.9/6/05. cum. index. **Bk Rev. Ad Acc. Circ:** 1,500 (ctrl). ***Continues*** *Wildlife Journal, 0893-6560.*
Desc: Reviewed journal of wildlife rehabilitation. Includes information on natural history, rescue, care, treatment, and post-release follow-up.
Ind/Abst Fish Rev.; Wildl. Rev.

Environmental Issues —Conservation and Natural Resources

UK
JOURNAL - WORLD PHEASANT ASSOCIATION. Main/Corp World Pheasant Association. **VFOAT** WPA Journal; W.P.A. Journal. (1976)-. Periodical. English. an. £10.00. World Pheasant Association, PO Box 5, Lower Busildon, Reading RG8 9PF England. **Tel** 0734-845140. **ED** Nigella Hilgarth. **Bk Rev. Ad Acc. Circ:** 800 (ctrl).
Ind/Abst Anim. Breed. Abstr.; Fish Rev. (19?-); Index Vet.; Key Word Index Wildl. Res.; Poult. Abstr.; Wildl. Rev. (19??-).

JA
KAGAKU GIJUTSUCHO SHIGEN CHOSAJO KIHO. / THE QUARTERLY REPORT OF [THE] NATIONAL INSTITUTE OF RESOURCES. Main/Corp Shigen Chosajo. **Added/Corp** Kagaku Gijutsucho Shigen Chosajo (Japan). Quarterly Report of the National Institute of Resources. **VFOAT** The Quarterly Report of the National Institute of Resources. Vol. 1 (1976)-. Periodical. Japanese. qt. Gaimusho / Ajiakyoku, 2-1 Kasumigaseki 2-chome, Chiyoda-ku 100 Tokyo Japan. **LC** HC462.5; .S5c.

JA
KAIHATSU TO KOGAI. (March 1978)-. Japanese. ¥800. Orijin Shuppan Senta, c/o Meja Kagurazaka, 16 Iwatocho, Shinjuku-ku Tokyo 162 Japan. **LC** HC465.E5; K33.

JA/0388-9459
KANKYO GIJUTSU. [Kankyo gijutsu]. **Added/Corp** Kankyo Gijutsu Kenkyukai (Japan). **VFOAT** Environmental Conservation Engineering. (1972)-. Periodical. Japanese. mo. $166.00. Kankyo Gijutsu Kenkyukai, Kyoni Bldg, 1-14-25 Kyomachibori, Nishi-ku, Osaka 550 Japan. **(Subscription address:** Kyowa Book Co., Inc., 1 38 Kanda Jinbocho Chiyoda Ku, Tokyo 101 Japan, Tel. 81 3 3293 0727) **CODEN** KAGIDX. **[CCC]**. Documents available from CASDDS.
Ind/Abst Chem. Abstr.

US/0898-6975
KANSAS WILDLIFE & PARKS. [Kans. wildl. parks]. **Added/Corp** Kansas. Dept. of Wildlife and Parks. **VFOAT** Kansas Wildlife and Parks. Vol. 45, No. 2 (March/April 1988)-. Periodical. English. bm (6 issues). $8.00 (one year), $15.00 (two year), $21.00 (three year). INF Education Division of the Kansas Department of Wildlife and Parks, 512 Southeast 25th Avenue, Pratt KS 67124-8174. **Tel** (316)672-5911. **ED** Mike Miller. **LC** SK397; .K36. **DD** 639.9/09781. **CODEN** KWPAE5. **Bk Rev. Circ:** 30,000. *Continues* Kansas Wildlife, 0279-9030.
Desc: Descriptions of Kansas wild creatures and places, outdoor activities, and resource management. How-to articles on hunting, fishing, photography, camping, and parks.
Ind/Abst Fish Rev.; Wildl. Rev.

IS/0302-6566
KARKA (TEL AVIV). (KARKA.). **VFOAT** Land. No. 2- Spring 1972-. English (English). PO Box 4083, Tel Aviv Israel. **LC** HD951.P3; A152. **DD** 333.7/07/205694.

US/0023-0235
KENTUCKY HAPPY HUNTING GROUND. *Title Change.* See Recreation, Leisure-Outdoor Life.

US/0892-1350
KENTUCKY PARKS. Ceased. [Ky. parks]. **VFOAT** Kentucky Parks Magazine. (1985)-(1987). Periodical. English. qt. Kentucky Parks, Circulation, Department of Parks, 10th Floor/Capital Plaza Tower, Frankfort KY 40601. **DD** 363.

SZ
KEY-WORD-INDEX OF WILDLIFE RESEARCH. See Environmental Issues-Abstracting, Bibliographies and Statistics.

US/1050-821X
KIND NEWS JR. (KIND NEWS JR. / KIDS IN NATURE'S DEFENSE CLUB.). [KIND news jr.]. **Added/Corp** Kids in Nature's Defense Club. **VFOAT** KIND News Junior. (Sept. 1983)-. Periodical. English. Five times a year. $25.00 US; $37.00 other. National Association for the Advancement of Humane Education, PO Box 362, East Haddam CT 06423. **Tel** (203)434-8666. **DD** 051.

KO/0023-4036
KOREAN NATURE. Added/Corp Choson Chayon Poho Hyophoe. No. 1 (1965)-. Periodical. English. qt. Association for Nature Conservation of the Democratic Peoples Republic of China, Pyongyang North Korea. **LC** QH77.K6; K65. **DD** 333.7/2/095193. available with charts; available with illustrations.

KO
KUNGNIP KONGWON. Added/Corp Hanguk Kungnip Kongwon Hyophoe. **VFOAT** National Parks. (19??)-. Periodical. English (Korean). qt. Hanguk Kungnip Kongwon Hyophoe, 105-67 Kongduk-dong, Mapo-ku, Seoul South Korea. **LC** DS902.15; .K86.

US
LAND & NATURAL RESOURCES DIVISION JOURNAL. VFOAT Land and Natural Resources Division Journal. Vol. 3, No. 10 (Oct. 1965)-. Periodical. English. bm. Free. US Department of Justice, 10th Street & Constitution Avenue NW, Washington DC 20530. **Tel** (202)514-2000, FAX (202)633-4371. cum. index. *Continues* Lands Division Journal.

US/0192-9453
LAND AND WATER (FORT DODGE). (LAND AND WATER.). [Land water]. **Added/Corp** Land Improvement Contractors of America. (1976)-. Periodical. English. Six times a year. $14.40. Land and Water Magazine, PO Box 1197, Fort Dodge IA 50501. **Tel** (515)576-3191, FAX (515)576-2606. **ED** Teresa Doyle. **DD** 333. **CODEN** LAWAEX. **Ad Acc, Adv Mgr:** Amy Dencklau. Full Page (B&W) $1800.00. Half Page (B&W) $1050.00. **Circ:** 20,000. Documents available from Documents on Demand. *Continues* Land and Water Development.
Desc: Edited for those individuals involved in natural resource management and restoration. Contains case histories and applied technologies of the newest advances.
Ind/Abst AGRICOLA; BioBusiness (1990-); Energy Inf. Abstr.; Environ. Abstr.

US/0272-6068
LAND AND WATER REPORT. Main/Corp Illinois. Dept. of Conservation. 1979-. English. an. Illinois Department of Conservation, 524 South Second Street, Springfield IL 62706. **Tel** (217)782-7454. **LC** S916; .I3; I42A. **DD** 333.7/2/09773. *Continues* Land and Water Acreage-Facilities, 0094-1867.

UK/0898-5812
LAND DEGRADATION AND REHABILITATION. See Agriculture-Crop Production and Soil.

US/0890-7625
LAND LETTER (WASHINGTON, D.C.). (LAND LETTER : THE NEWSLETTER FOR LAND CONSERVATION PROFESSIONALS.). [Land lett.]. (19??)-. Newsletter. English. Thirty-four times a year. Conservation Fund, 1800 North Kent Street Suite 1120, Arlington VA 22209. **Tel** (703)525-6300. **DD** 333.

US/0275-6161
LAND RESOURCES LABORATORY SERIES. [Land resour. lab. ser.]. **Added/Corp** University of Texas at Austin. Bureau of Economic Geology. (19??)-. English. ir. Bureau of Economic Geology, University of Texas, University Station Box X, Austin TX 78713-7508. **Tel** (512)471-1534, 471-7721, FAX (512)471-0140.
Ind/Abst GeoRef.

AT
LAND RESOURCES MANAGEMENT : DIVISIONAL REPORT FROM THE CSIRO DIVISION OF LAND RESOURCES MANAGEMENT / CSIRO, DIVISION OF LAND RESOURCES MANAGEMENT, PERTH, WESTERN AUSTRALIA. Added/Corp Commonwealth Scientific and Industrial Research Organization (Australia). Division of Land Resources Management. (19??)-. English. CSIRO Publications, PO Box 89, 314 Albert Street, East Melborne Victoria 3002 Australia. **Tel** 011 61 3 4187333, 4187217, FAX 011 61 3 4190459, telex AA 30236. **LC** S934.A8; L36. **DD** 333.7/15/0994.
Ind/Abst AGRICOLA.

SA
LAND UPDATE : A PUBLICATION OF THE NATIONAL LAND COMMITTEE. Added/Corp National Land Committee (South Africa). (19??)-. Periodical. English. Ten times a year. R20.00 South Africa; R35.00 other. National Land Committee, PO Box 16858, Doornfontein 2028, South Africa. **Tel** 011 27 11 8321123. **LC** WMLC 93/3985.
Ind/Abst Hum. Rights Intern. Rep.

AT/0815-4465
LANDSCOPE. Vol. 1, (June 1985)-. Periodical. English. Four times a year (Jan., Apr., Aug., Dec.). 20.00Aus$ Australia; 30.00Aus$ other. Department of Conservation and Land Management, PO Box 104, Corp Relations Division, Como WA 6152 Australia. **Tel** 011 61 09 3670333. **ED** David Gough (phone: (09)3898644). **LC** S934.A8; L38. Index available. cum. index. **Bk Rev**, (Qty: 4). **Ad Acc. Circ:** 14,000. Formed by the union of *S.W.A.N.S.* and *Forest Focus.*
Desc: A magazine dealing with conservation, national papers, forests and wildlife.
Ind/Abst Fish Rev.; Wildl. Rev.

US/0738-1492
LEADER / NATIONAL WILDLIFE FEDERATION, THE. [Leader]. **Added/Corp** National Wildlife Federation. (19??)-. Periodical. English. mo. Free (to affiliate leaders). National Wildlife Federation / Washington, 1400 16th Street Northwest, Washington DC 20036. **Tel** (800)432-6564, (202)797-6800. **DD** 333.

US/1064-0185
LEAF (FORT COLLINS, COLO.), THE. (THE LEAF : NEWSLETTER OF THE INTERNATIONAL WILDERNESS LEADERSHIP (WILD) FOUNDATION.). [Leaf]. **Added/Corp** International Wilderness Leadership Foundation. No. 1 (1988)-. Newsletter. English. Three times a year. $20.00; $38.95 (including For the Conservation of the Earth). International Wilderness Leadership Fund, 211 West Magnolia, Fort Collins CO 80521. **Tel** (303)498-0303, FAX (303)498-0403, telex 9103506369. **LC** QH75.A1; L39. **DD** 333.78/2/05. **Pr Rev.**

CN/1186-7035
LEMOYNE-TILLY LIGNE A 735 KV. [Lemoyne-Tilly ligne 735 kV]. **Added/Corp** Hydro-Quebec. **VAT** Lemoyne-Tilly ligne a Sept Cent Trente Cinq Kilovolts. No 1 (Feb. 1991)-. Periodical. French. Hydro-Quebec, 14E Etage, 75 Ouest Boul Dorchester, Montreal Quebec H2Z 1A4 Canada. **DD** 333.79.

NE/0024-1520
LEVENDE NATUUR, DE. [Levende nat.]. (1987)-. Periodical. Dutch (summaries and/or abstracts in English). bm. F57.50. Natuurmonumenten, Noordereinde 60, 1243 JJS Graveland Netherlands. **Tel** 011 31 35 559914, FAX 011 31 35 63174. Index available (Index in each November edition). cum. index. **Bk Rev**, (Qty: 6).

●CN/1188-8539
LIAISON / CONSEIL REGIONAL DE L'ENVIRONNEMENT CHAUDIERE-APPALACHES. [Liaison - Cons. reg. environ. Chaudiere-Appalach.]. **Added/Corp** Conseil Regional de l'Environnement Chaudiere-Appalaches. **VFOAT** Bulletin d'Information. (May 1992)-. Periodical. French. sa. Limited free distribution. Conseil Regional de l'Environnement Chaudiere-Appalaches, CP 276, Montmagny Quebec G5V 3S6 Canada. **DD** 363.7/009714/7.

AT
LIFESTYLES SEASON. See New Age Publications.

PH
LIKAS-YAMAN. Main/Conf Natural Resources Management Forum. (1978)-. Periodical. English. Ministry of Natural Resources, Visayes Avenue Diliman, Quezon City Metro Manila Philippines. **LC** WMLC L 83/604.
Ind/Abst Philip. Sci. Technol. Abstr.

CE/0024-6514
LORIS. V. 1- Nov. 1936-. Periodical. English. sa. $4.00. 3, Ceylon Chaitiya Road, Ft Colombo 1 SRI Landa Ceylon. **Tel** 25248, FAX 941-580721, telex 22933 METALIX CE. **ED** Sirancee Gunawardena. **LC** SK1; .L6. **DD** 799; 333.78. Index available. **Ad Acc. Circ:** 2,000.
Ind/Abst Fish Rev.; Key Word Index Wildl. Res.

US/0024-6778
LOUISIANA CONSERVATIONIST (1948). (LOUISIANA CONSERVATIONIST.). **Added/Corp** Louisiana Wild Life and Fisheries Commission Louisiana. Wildlife and Fisheries Dept. Vol. 1 (Sept. 1948)-. Periodical. English. Six times a year. $8.00. Louisiana Wildlife & Fisheries Commission, PO Box 98000, Baton Rouge LA 70898-9000. **Tel** (504)765-2918. *Supersedes Louisiana Game, Fur and Fish.*
Ind/Abst Biol. Dig.; Life Sci. Collect. (1985-).

US/0738-8098
LOUISIANA OUT-OF-DOORS. See Recreation, Leisure-Outdoor Life.

FI/0355-3728
LOUNAIS-HAMEEN LUONTO. Main/Corp Lounais-Hameen Luonnonsuojeluyhdistys. Periodical. Finnish (German). Lounais-Hameen, Luonnonsuojeluyhdistys, SF-30101 Forssa Finland. **LC** QH77.F55; L67. **DD** 333.95/094897/3.

SA
MADOQUA. Periodical. English. ir. R25.00. Nature Conservation Director, P Bag, 13306 Windhoek 9100 Namibia South West Africa. **Tel** 061/63131, FAX 061/63195, telex 509083180. **ED** C J Brown. Index available. **Pr Rev. Circ:** 600 (ctrl). *Formed by the union of Madoqua Series I and Madoqua Series II.*
Desc: Journal of arid zone biology and nature conservation research. Contributions are submitted to two expert referees.
Ind/Abst Anim. Breed. Abstr.; Fish Rev.; Key Word Index Wildl. Res.; Wildl. Rev.

US/0148-0359
MAINE DIRECTORY OF NATURAL RESOURCE ORGANIZATIONS. 1977-. Directory. English. an. State Planning Office / Maine, 189 State Street, Augusta ME 04333. **LC** HC107.M2; M362. **DD** 333.

US/0898-7742
MAINE ENVIRONMENT. (MAINE ENVIRONMENT : BULLETIN OF THE NATURAL RESOURCES COUNCIL OF MAINE.). [Me. environ.]. **Added/Corp** Natural Resources Council of Maine.

(19??)-. Bulletin. English. Ten times a year (June/July & Aug./Sept. issues combined). $28.00 (Comes with Natural Resources Council of Maine membership). Natural Resources Council of Maine, 271 State Street, Augusta ME 04330. **Tel** (207)622-3101. **DD** 363.

US/0095-1676
MANAGEMENT SERIES (INDIANAPOLIS). (MANAGEMENT SERIES.). **Added/Corp** Indiana. Division of Fish and Wildlife. No. 1 (1974)-. Monographic series. English. Division of Fish & Wildlife, 697 State Office Building, Indianapolis IN 46204. **LC** SK351; .M25. **DD** 639.9.

AT
MANAGEMENT SUMMARY (PERTH, W.A.). (MANAGEMENT SUMMARY.). **Added/Corp** Western Australia. Land Information System Support Centre. (19??)-. English. Government of Western Australia / Land Information System Support Centre, Perth 6000 WA Australia. **LC** HD1039.W47; M36. **DD** 333.73/13/09941.

US/0025-4924
MASSACHUSETTS WILDLIFE. **Added/Corp** Massachusetts. Division of Fisheries and Game. (19??)-. Periodical. English. qt. $6.00 US; $9.00 other. Massachusetts Division of Fisheries and Wildlife, Field Headquarters, Westboro MA 01581. **Tel** (800)289-4778, (508)792-7270. **ED** Peter G. Mirick. **LC** SK407; .M37. **DD** 333.9/5/09744. **Bk Rev. Circ:** 23,000 (ctrl).
Desc: Covers all topics relating to fish and wildlife resources in Massachusetts, including management programs, life histories, ecological issues, hunting, fishing, nongame wildlife, outdoor photography, etc.

CN/0711-1754
MEDWAY VALLEY NEWS (1978). (THE MEDWAY VALLEY NEWS.). [Medway Val. news]. (Fall/Winter 1978)-. Periodical. English. sa. $6.00 North America; $7.00 other. Medway Valley News, PO Box 111, Arva Ontario N0M 1C0 Canada. **ED** Stevenson Winder, Alice Gibb. **DD** 333.95/16/0971325. Index available. **Bk Rev. Ad Acc. Circ:** 350. ***Continues** Hoot (London, Ont.), 0822-4781.*
Desc: Offers a variety of social activities in every season: hikes, car tours, Heritage Holidays, and essays on culture and the natural world around us, heritage education and recreation. Also includes Ecological philosophy, Heritage Updates, etc.

US/0271-5082
MEMBERSHIP DIRECTORY AND CERTIFICATION REGISTRY. **Main/Corp** Wildlife Society. (19??)-. Directory. English. an. $3.00 nonmembers. Wildlife Society, 5410 Grosvenor Lane, Bethesda MD 20814. **Tel** (301)897-9770, FAX (301)530-2471.

US
METROPARKS EMERALD NECKLACE. **See** Recreation, Leisure-Outdoor Life.

US/0275-8180
MICHIGAN NATURAL RESOURCES MAGAZINE, THE. [Mich. nat. resour. mag.]. **Added/Corp** Michigan. Dept. of Natural Resources. (1977)-. Periodical. English. Five times a year. $11.50 US; $19.50 other. Michigan Natural Resources, 30600 Telegraph Road, Suite 1386, Bingham Farm MI 48025. **Tel** (517)373-9267. **(Subscription address:** Michigan Natural Resources, PO Box 7355, Red Oak IA 51591-0355.**)** **ED** Norris R. McDowell. **LC** SK351; .M47. **DD** 639.9/09774. Index available. cum. index. **Circ:** 120,000 (ctrl). ***Continues** Michigan Natural Resources, 0026-2358.*
Ind/Abst AGRICOLA.

US/0026-2382
MICHIGAN OUT-OF-DOORS. [Mich. out-of-doors]. **Added/Corp** Michigan United Conservation Clubs. Michigan Wildlife Federation. **VAT** Michigan Out of Doors. (1950)-. Periodical. English. Twelve times a year. $25.00 (one year), 440.00 (two years). Michigan United Conservation Clubs, PO Box 30235, Lansing MI 48909. **Tel** (517)371-1041, FAX (517)371-1505. **ED** Ken Lowe. **Bk Rev**, (Qty: 12). **Ad Acc**, **Adv Mgr:** Bill Donahue. **Circ:** 115,000.
Desc: Covers Michigan and Great Lakes area outdoor recreation, conservation and environmental issues.

CN
MIGRATORY BIRDS CONVENTION ACT AND MIGRATORY BIRD REGULATIONS. **Main/Corp** Canada. English (French). an. Canadian Wildlife Service Publications, Environment Canada, Ottawa Ontario K1A 0E7 Canada. **Tel** (819)997-1095, FAX (819)997-0547. ***Continues** Migratory Birds Convention Act and Regulations There Under.*
Desc: Lists all regulations pertaining to the hunting of migratory game birds in Canada during the most recent hunting season. It includes a complete summary of hunting zones, dates and bag limits for each provinces and territory.

NE
MILIEU AANSPRAKELIJKHEID. **VFOAT** Environmental Liability Law Quarterly; Tijdschrift voor Milieu-Aansprakelijkheid. Dutch. qt. Koninklijke Vermande, Postbus 20, 8200 AA Lelystad Netherlands. **Tel** 011 31 3200 22944.

CN/0380-2760
MILIEU (SAINTE-FOY). ***Suspended.*** (MILIEU.). [Milieu]. **Added/Corp** Centre de Recherches Forestieres des Laurentides. Canada. Service de la Gestion de l'Environnement. No 1 (Jan. 1972)-(1993). Periodical. French. ir.
Ind/Abst Can. Period. Index (19??-); For. Abstr.; Environ. (1983-); Leis. Recreat. Tour. Abstr.; Point Repere.

US
MINERAL RESOURCES DEVELOPMENT SERIES. **Main/Corp** United Nations. Economic Commission for Asia and The Far East. (1952)-. Government Publication. English. ir. United Nations Publications, 2 United Nations Plaza, Room DC2 0853, Department 007C, New York NY 10017. **Tel** (212)963-8303, (800)253-9646.
Desc: Proceedings and reports dealing with mineral resources in the ESCAP area.

US
MINERAL REVENUES : THE ... REPORT ON RECEIPTS FROM FEDERAL AND INDIAN LEASES. **Main/Corp** Royalty Management Program (U.S.). **VFOAT** Report on Receipts from Federal and Indian Leases. (1982)-. Government Publication. English. an. US Department of the Interior / Mineral Data Analysis, Washington DC 20240. **Tel** (202)634-1001. **LC** HD242; .R69A. **DD** 333.33/9.

US/0196-593X
MINNESOTA VOLUNTEER, THE. **Added/Corp** Minnesota. Dept. of Natural Resources. (1971)-. Periodical. English. ir. must order direct. The Minnesota Volunteer, Department of Natural Resources, Box 46, 500 Lafayette Road, St Paul MN 55155. **Tel** (612)296-3336. **ED** Robert Kraske. **LC** S916.M6; A3. **DD** 639/.9/09776. **Bk Rev. Circ:** 100,000. ***Continues** Conservation Volunteer.*
Desc: Information and education service to the people of Minnesota. Mission is the management and preservation of the state's natural resources - forests, minerals, water, state parks and trails, waterways, fish and wildlife.

US/1040-0680
MINNESOTA WILDLIFE REPORT. [Minn. wildl. rep.]. **Added/Corp** Minnesota. Dept. of Natural Resources. (1985)-. Monographic series. English. ir. Price varies per volume. Department of Natural Resources / Minnesota, 350 Centennial Building, St Paul MN 55155. **DD** 639. **CODEN** MWREEF. Documents available from BIOSIS Document Express. ***Continues** Wildlife Research Quarterly / Minnesota Department of Natural Resources, Division of Fish and Wildlife, Section of Wildlife, 0736-0843.*
Ind/Abst Biol. Abstr. (1987-); Fish Rev. (Jan. 1989-July 1992); Wildl. Rev. (Jan. 1989-July 1992).

US
MINUTES OF THE MEETING - NORTHEASTERN RESOURCES COMMITTEE. **Main/Corp** Northeastern Resources Committee. **VFOAT** Minutes of the Meeting of the Northeastern Resources Committee. Periodical. English. qt.

US/0026-6515
MISSOURI CONSERVATIONIST. **Added/Corp** Missouri. Conservation Commission. Missouri. Dept. of Conservation. **VFOAT** Conservationist. Vol. 1, (July 1938)-. Periodical. English. mo. Free, Missouri residents; $5.00 other. Missouri Conservation Commission, Box 180, Jefferson City MO 65101. **Tel** (314)751-4115. **ED** Kathy Love. **LC** SK351; .M55. **DD** 799. Index available. **Circ:** 400,000.
Desc: Adult information in forestry, fisheries and wildlife conservation.
Ind/Abst Fish Rev.; Ozark Period. Index; Wildl. Rev.

US
MISSOURI RESOURCE REVIEW. **Added/Corp** Missouri. Dept. of Natural Resources. Missouri. Dept. of Natural Resources. Office of Public Affairs. Missouri. Dept. of Natural Resources. Public Information Office. **VFOAT** Resource Review. (1982)-. Periodical. English. qt. Department of Natural Resources / Missouri, PO Box 176, Jefferson City MO 65102. **LC** TD171.3.M8; M57. **DD** 333.7/16/09778.
Ind/Abst Energy Inf. Abstr.

US
MISSOURI WILDLIFE. **See** Environmental Issues-Ecology.

CN/1187-5666
MODIFICATION DE LA LIGNE RIVIERE-DU-LOUP-SAINT-CLEMENT. [Modif. ligne Riviere-du-Loup-St.-Clement]. **Added/Corp** Hydro-Quebec. No 1 (Oct. 1991)-. Periodical. French. Hydro-Quebec, 14E Etage, 75 Ouest Boul Dorchester, Montreal Quebec H2Z 1A4 Canada. **DD** 333.79.

US/0746-9896
MONTANA WILDLIFE (BOZEMAN, MONT.). (MONTANA WILDLIFE / MONTANA WILDLIFE FEDERATION.). **Added/Corp** Montana Wildlife Federation. (19??)-. Periodical. English. bm. $10.00. Montana Wildlife Federation, PO Box 3526, Bozeman MT 59772. **Tel** (406)587-1713.

NO/0802-4618
N & M. NATUR OG MILJ. [N M, Nat. milj̈]. **VFOAT** Natur og Milj̈. (1989)-. Periodical. Norwegian. bm (6 issues). Kr340.00, $61.00. Scandinavian University Press, PO Box 2959 Toeyen, N 0608 Oslo 6 Norway. **Tel** 011 47 2 2575400, FAX 011 47 2 2575353, telex 71896 UROR N. **(Subscription address:** Scandinavian University Press, 200 Meacham Ave., Elmont NY 11003.**)** **ED** Ragnhild Sved. **DD** 363.7. **Bk Rev. Ad Acc. Circ:** 40,000. ***Continues in part** Norsk Natur, 0549-687X **and** Milj Magasinet, 0332-6179.*
Desc: A politically independent and critical journal on nature, resources and the environment.

AT/0729-8226
NATIONAL CONSERVATION STRATEGY FOR AUSTRALIA. NCSA NEWSLETTER. [Natl. conserv. strategy Aust., NCSA newsl.]. **VFOAT** NCSA Newsletter. (1981)-. English. ir. **DD** 333.7206094.
Ind/Abst AESIS Q.

US
NATIONAL DIRECTORY OF COUNTY PARK AGENCIES. **Added/Corp** National Recreation and Park Association. National Society for Park Resources (U.S.). (1982)-. Directory. English. Dr D M Knudson, Department of Forestry and Natural Resources, Purdue University, West Lafayette IN 47907.

US/0049-044X
NATIONAL NEWS REPORT. ***Ceased.*** **Added/Corp** Sierra Club. (1969)-(19??). Periodical. English. Twenty-seven times a year (published weekly when Congress in session). Sierra, 730 Polk Street, San Francisco CA 94109. **Tel** (415)923-5656. **ED** Anthony Antico. Index available (free). **Circ:** 5,000.
Desc: Keeps readers informed about developments in environmental politics on national issues before Congress, administrative agencies, and the courts.

US
NATIONAL PARK SERVICE INTERPRETIVE SERIES. HISTORY. **Added/Corp** United States. National Park Service. **VFOAT** History; Interpretive Series. History. No. 1 (1942)-. Government Publication. English. ir. Price varies per volume. Superintendent of Documents, US Government Printing Office, Washington DC 20402. **Tel** (202)275-3328, FAX (202)786-2377. **LC** E160; .U6185. **DD** 917.3.

US/0278-1328
NATIONAL PARK STATISTICAL ABSTRACT. **See** Environmental Issues-Abstracting, Bibliographies and Statistics.

JA
NATIONAL PARKS. **See** Public Administration-Parks and Recreation.

JA
NATIONAL PARKS JAPAN. (19??)-. Periodical. Japanese. mo. $78.00. **(Subscription address:** Maruzen Company Ltd., PO Box 5050, Import & Export Department, Tokyo 100 31 Japan.**)**

AT/0047-9012
NATIONAL PARKS JOURNAL. English. Six times a year (Feb., Apr., June, Aug., Oct., Dec.). $50.00. National Parks Association of New South Wales Inc., PO Box A96, Sydney South 2000 Australia. **Tel** 011 61 2 2647994, FAX 011 61 2 2647160. **ED** Kathy Fook. Index available. **Bk Rev**, (Qty: 12). **Ad Acc. Circ:** 8,000 (ctrl).
Desc: Information on national parks and nature conservation, and the growth and management of national parks in New South Wales.
Ind/Abst APAIS, Aust. Public Aff. Inf. Ser.; Environ. Period. Bibliogr.

US/0276-8186
NATIONAL PARKS (WASHINGTON, D.C.). **See** Public Administration-Parks and Recreation.

US/0028-0402
NATIONAL WILDLIFE. [Natl. wildl.]. **Added/Corp** National Wildlife Federation. **VFOAT** Wildlife. Vol. 1, No. 1 (Dec. 1962-Jan. 1963)-. Periodical. English. bm (6 issues). $16.00. National Wildlife Federation / Virginia, 8925 Leesburg Pike, Vienna VA 22184. **Tel** (703)790-4000, (800)822-9919, FAX (703)442-7332. **ED** Mark Wexler. **LC** S964.U6; N35. **Circ:** 950,000 (ctrl). available on microfilm and microfiche from University Microfilms International (UMI); available on CD-ROM. Documents available from BIOSIS Document Express, UMI Article Clearinghouse, Documents on Demand. ***Absorbed in part** Conservation News, 0010-647X.*
Desc: Treatment of America's wild creatures and places

through full-color photo galleries, natural history features, outdoor adventure articles and news items of ecological concern. Conservation-minded magazine of nature and the environment.
Ind/Abst ASTIS Curr. Aware. Bull. (1978-); Abr. Read. Guide Period. Lit.; Acad. Abstr. Full Text Elite (Jan. 1984-); Acad. Abstr. (Jan. 1984-); Acad. Ind. [Computer File] (1984-); Acad. Search (Jan. 1984-); AQUAREF; ASTIS Bibliogr. (1978-); Biogr. Index; Biol. Abstr.; Biol. Dig.; Child. Mag. Guide (1981-); Curr. Aware. Biol. Sci., CABS; Curr. Index J. Educ.; Environ. Abstr.; Environ. Period. Bibliogr.; Expand. Acad. Index (1984-); Gen. Period. Index (1985-); Gen. Sci. Index; Index Sci. Rev.; INFO-SOUTH Abstr.; Mag. Artic. Summar. Elite (Jan. 1984-); Mag. Artic. Summar. Select (Jan. 1984-); Mag. Artic. Summar. CD-ROM (Jan. 1984-); Mag. Index Plus (1989-); Mag. Index. Sel. (1986-); Mag. Search; Mid. Search (Jan. 1984-); Newsp. Period. Abstr. (1986-); Prim. Search (Jan. 1984-); Read. Guide Abstr. Select Ed.; Read. Guide Period. Lit.; Soc. Sci. Index; Mag. Index (1977-); TOM Gen. Index (1985-); Vocat. Search (Jan. 1984-).

US
NATIONAL WILDLIFE REFUGES.
Main/Corp United States. Bureau of Sport Fisheries and Wildlife. (1965)-. Government Publication. English. US Department of the Interior / Bureau of Sport Fisheries and Wildlife, Washington DC 20241. **LC** S914; .A3. **DD** 333.9; 639; 639/.9/08S.

GW
NATUR. (19??)-. Periodical. German. mo. DM81.60 Germany; DM96.00 other. Ringier Verlag GmbH, Gustav Heinemann Ring 212, D 81739 Munich Germany. **Tel** 011 49 89 638180. **LC** QH5; .N19. **DD** 574/.05.

GW/0028-0615
NATUR UND LANDSCHAFT (STUTTGART). See Natural History.

US/0885-8608
NATURAL AREAS JOURNAL. [Nat. areas j.]. **Added/Corp** Natural Areas Association (U.S.). Vol. 2, No. 1 (Jan. 1982)-. Periodical. English. qt (Jan., Apr., July, Oct.). $25.00 (individuals), $50.00 (libraries), $100.00 (insstitutions). The Natural Areas Association, 108 Fox Street, Mukwonago WI 53149. **Tel** (415)363-5500. **ED** Don Leopold (editor's address: State University of New York, College Environment Science & Forestry, Syracuse NY 13210; editor's phone: (315)470-6784). **LC** QH76; .J68. **DD** 333.78/2/0973. **CODEN** NAJOEW. Index available. **Bk Rev**, (Qty: 6-16). **Pr Rev. Circ:** 2,400. Documents available from The Genuine Article, BIOSIS Document Express. ***Continues*** *Journal of the Natural Areas Association, 0899-0107.*
Desc: Research and management activities on nature preserves, natural areas, parks and endangered species; land preservation techniques.
Ind/Abst Biol. Abstr. (1984-); Curr. Aware. Biol. Sci., CABS; Curr. Contents, Agric. Biol. Environ. Sci.; Ecology Abstr.; Entomol. Abstr.; Environ. Period. Bibliogr.; Fish Rev.; Garden Lit. (1992-); Leis. Recreat. Tour. Abstr.; PAIS Bull. (1986-); PAIS Int. Print (1991-); Res. Alert [Select. Cov.]; Rev. Agric. Entomol.; Wildl. Rev.; World Agric. Econ.

US/0890-8575
NATURAL RESOURCE MODELING.
Added/Corp Rocky Mountain Mathematics Consortium. Vol. 1, No. 1 (Fall 1986)-. Periodical. English. Four times a year (Jan., Apr., July, Oct.). $190.00. Arizona State University / Rocky Mountain Mathematics Consortium, Department of Mathematics, Box 871904, Tempe AZ 85287-1904. **Tel** (602)965-3788. **LC** WMLC 93/1868. **DD** 510. **CODEN** NRMOEU.
Ind/Abst Ecol. Abstr.; Econ. Lit. Index (199?-); Environ. Period. Bibliogr.; Fish Rev. (Jan. 1989-July 1992); Geogr. Abstr. Human Geogr.; J. Econ. Lit. (1989-); Math. Rev. (1987-); Wildl. Rev. (Jan. 1989-July 1992).

GW/0340-2797
NATURAL RESOURCES AND DEVELOPMENT. [Nat. resour. dev.]. V. 1-. Periodical. English. sa. Institute for Scientific Co-Operation, Landhausstrasse 18, W-7400 Tubingen Germany. **Tel** 07071/5066. **LC** HC55; .N33. **DD** 333/.005. **CODEN** NREDEP.
Ind/Abst AESIS Q.; GeoRef; Potato Abstr.

US/0163-1438
NATURAL RESOURCES & EARTH SCIENCES. ***Ceased.*** [Nat. resour. earth sci.]. **VAT** Natural Resources and Earth Sciences. (Jan. 3, 1977)-(Jan. 1992). Periodical. English. wk (with annual subject index). National Technical Information Service - NTIS, Room 2027S, 5285 Port Royal Road, Springfield VA 22161. **Tel** (703)487-4630, (703)487-4660, (703)487-4650, FAX (703)321-8547, telex 89-9405. ***Continues*** *Natural Resources (United States. National Technical Information Service), 0364-4979.*

US/0251-723X
NATURAL RESOURCES & ENERGY. [Nat. resour. energy]. **Added/Corp** United Nations. Natural Resources and Energy Division. Centre for Natural Resources, Energy, and Transport (United Nations). **VFOAT** Natural Resources and Energy Newsletter. **VAT** Natural Resources and Energy. (1978)-. Periodical. English. bm. Free on request. United Nations Secretariat, Division of Natural Resources and Energy, New York NY 10017. **LC** TJ163.13; .N37. **DD** 662.6.
Ind/Abst Coal Abstr.; GeoRef.

US/0882-3812
NATURAL RESOURCES & ENVIRONMENT. See Law-Environmental Law.

US/1043-7460
NATURAL RESOURCES (COLLEGE PARK, MD.). (NATURAL RESOURCES [COMPUTER FILE].). [Nat. resour.]. **Added/Corp** National Information Services Corporation. (1989)-. English. sa. $681.00 US; $695.00 other. **DD** 363.

US/0890-5673
NATURAL RESOURCES COMPUTER NEWSLETTER. (NATURAL RESOURCES COMPUTER NEWSLETTER: NARCON.). [Nat. resour. comput. newsl.]. **VFOAT** Narcon. Vol. 1, Issue 1 (July/Aug. 1986)-. Periodical. English. Nine times a year. $98.00 US; $104.00 Canada; $114.00 other. Michaelsons Micro Magic, PO Box 7332, Fredericksburg VA 22404. **Tel** (703)775-3059. **ED** Nancy Michaelsen. **DD** 333. Index available. cum. index. **Ad Acc. Circ:** 1,000 (ctrl).
Desc: Provides articles about computer uses in all natural resource disciplines: forestry, fisheries, wildlife, etc.

NE/0165-0203
NATURAL RESOURCES FORUM. [Nat. resour. forum]. **Added/Corp** Centre for Natural Resources, Energy, and Transportation (United Nations). Vol. 1 (Oct. 1976)-. Academic Scholarly Publication. English. qt. $276.00 The Americas; £185.00 other. Butterworth Heinemann Publishers, Linacre House, Jordan Hill, Oxford OX2 8DP England. **Tel** 011 44 865 310366. **(Subscription address:** Elsevier Science Ltd. Oxford Fulfillment Centre, PO Box 800, Kidlington, Oxford OX5 1DX United Kingdom.**)** **ED** Raymond Knowles. **LC** HC55; .N35. **DD** 333.7/05. **CODEN** NRFODS. **[CCC]. Bk Rev**. **Ad Acc. Pr Rev. Circ:** 1,000 (ctrl). available on microfilm and microfiche from University Microfilms International (UMI). Documents available from Article Express International, The Genuine Article, Ask*IEEE, UMI Article Clearinghouse, CASDDS, Documents on Demand.
Desc: Devoted to the study of the economic, scientific, technological and policy aspects of energy, mineral and water resources development.
Ind/Abst AESIS Q.; AGRICOLA [Select. Cov.]; Bioeng. Abstr.; Chem. Abstr.; Coal Abstr.; Curr. Contents Soc. Behav. Sci.; Ei Page One; Eng. Index Annu.; Environ. Abstr.; Environ. Period. Bibliogr.; For. Prod. Abstr. (1991-); For. Abstr.; Geogr. Abstr. Human Geogr.; GeoRef; INSPEC (Oct. 1983-); Int. Bibliogr. Sociol.; Int. Dev. Abstr.; Int. Labour Doc.; Irr. Drain. Abstr.; MINPROC; Mintec, Min. Technol. Abstr.; Newsp. Period. Abstr. (1992-); Life Sci. Collect.; Res. Alert [Full Cov.]; Rural Dev. Abstr.; Soc. Plann. Policy Dev. Abstr.; Soc. Sci. Cit. Index [Full Cov.]; Sociol. Abstr. (?-?); Soils Fert.; World Agric. Econ.

NE/0167-4110
NATURAL RESOURCES FORUM LIBRARY. [Nat. resour. forum libr.]. V. 1-. Academic Scholarly Publication. English. Price varies per volume. D. Reidel Publishing Company, PO Box 17, 3300 AA Dordrecht The Netherlands. **Tel** 011 31 78 334210, FAX (31) 78 183273, telex 29245 KAPGNL. **ED** Raymond Knowles. **CODEN** NRFLDJ. **Bk Rev. Ad Acc.** Documents available from Petroleum Abstracts Document Delivery Service, CASDDS.
Desc: Current problems and issues associated with the economic, scientific, technological and policy aspects of energy and mineral and water resources development.
Ind/Abst Chem. Abstr.; Pet. Abstr.

US/0748-481X
NATURAL RESOURCES INFORMATION DIRECTORY FOR THE STATE OF CONNECTICUT AND LIST OF PUBLICATIONS FOR THE CONNECTICUT GEOLOGICAL AND NATURAL HISTORY SURVEY. (NATURAL RESOURCES INFORMATION DIRECTORY FOR THE STATE OF CONNECTICUT AND LIST OF PUBLICATIONS FOR THE CONNECTICUT GEOLOGICAL AND NATURAL HISTORY SURVEY / STATE OF CONNECTICUT, DEPARTMENT OF ENVIRONMENTAL PROTECTION, THE NATURAL RESOURCES CENTER AND STATE GEOLOGICAL AND NATURAL HISTORY SURVEY.). **VFOAT** Natural Resources Information Directory and List of Publications; List of Publications for the Connecticut Geological and Natural History Survey; Natural Resources Information Directory & List of Publications. Directory. English. an. **LC** HC107.C8; N382. **DD** 333.7/09746. ***Formed by the union of*** *List of Publications* ***and*** *Natural Resources Information Directory for the State of Connecticut, 0748-481X.*

US/1053-1394
NATURAL RESOURCES METABASE. (NATURAL RESOURCES METABASE [COMPUTER FILE].). **Added/Corp** National Information Services Corporation. (1991)-. Periodical. English. an. $681.00 US; $695.00 other. National Information Services Corp, 3100 St Paul Street, Wyman Towers, Suite 6, Baltimore MD 21218. **Tel** (410)243-0797, FAX (410)243-0982. ***Continues*** *Natural Resources (College Park, Md.), 1043-7460.*
Desc: System requirements: CD-ROM drive with MS-DOS extensions, IBM compatible computer, 512K RAM.

US/0090-9483
NATURAL RESOURCES, SCIENCE AND TECHNOLOGY NEWSLETTER. No. 19/20-June 1971-. Newsletter. English. United Nations Economic Commission for Africa, PO Box 3001, Addis Ababa Ethiopia. **Tel** (212)754-8302, telex 21029 VNECA ET. **LC** HC502.5; .N3. **DD** 333. ***Continues*** *Natural Resources Newsletter.*

US/1050-1932
NATURAL RESOURCES TAX REVIEW, THE. [Nat. resour. tax rev.]. **Added/Corp** Tax Analysts (Firm : U.S.). Vol. 1, No. 1 (Mar./Apr. 1988)-. Periodical. English. mo. $349.00. Tax Analysts, 6830 North Fairfax Drive, Arlington VA 22213. **Tel** (703)533-4400, (800)955-3444. **LC** KF6495.M5; A136. **DD** 343. **[CCC].**
Ind/Abst Fed. Tax Artic.

US/1010-397X
NATURAL RESOURCES/WATER SERIES. [Nat. resour./water ser.]. **Added/Corp** United Nations. Dept. of Economic and Social Affairs. United Nations. Dept. of Technical Cooperation for Development. **VFOAT** Natural Resources Water Series. No. 1 (1975)-. Government Publication. English. ir. United Nations Publications, 2 United Nations Plaza, Room DC2 0853, Department 007C, New York NY 10017. **Tel** (212)963-8303, (800)253-9646. **LC** JX1977; .A2 subser. **DD** 300/.8 S; 333.9/1.
Ind/Abst GeoRef.

●US/1060-9938
NATURALIST (DANVILLE, VT.), THE. (THE NATURALIST.). Spring (1992)-. Periodical. English. qt. $8.00. Kevin Wisner, PO Box 272, Danville VT 05828. **DD** 363. ***Continues*** *Eco-ideas, 1055-6117.*

US/0888-6547
NATURALIST REVIEW. ***Ceased.*** (NATURALIST REVIEW : A PUBLICATION OF THE AUDUBON NATURALIST SOCIETY OF THE CENTRAL ATLANTIC STATES.). [Nat. rev.]. **Added/Corp** Audubon Naturalist Society of the Central Atlantic States. (Feb. 1986)-(1992). Periodical. English. qt. Audubon Naturalist Society of the Central Atlantic States, 8940 Jones Mill Road, Chevy Chase MD 20815. **Tel** (301)652-9188, FAX (301)951-7179. **ED** Kathryn Rushing and Judith Nierman. **DD** 500. **Bk Rev. Ad Acc.** ctrl circ.
Desc: Features reviews of new natural history titles by scientists and naturalists from all over the world. Reviews cover children's and adult's books on birds, wildlife, plants, travel, photography, classics, conservation and more; includes bibliographies and feature articles.

CN/1185-8877
NATURE ALERT. [Nat. alert]. **Added/Corp** Canadian Nature Federation. Vol. 1, No. 1 (Oct. 1991)-. Periodical. English. bm. Free to members of the Canadian Nature Federation. Canadian Nature Federation, 1 Nicholas Street, Suite 520, Ottowa Ontario K1N 7B7 Canada. **Tel** (613)562-3447, (800)267-4088. **DD** 333.7/2/0971.
Ind/Abst Acad. Abstr. (Jan. 1992-); Acad. Search (Jan. 1992-); Gen. Sci. Source (Jan. 1992-); Mag. Artic. Summar. Elite (Jan. 1992-); Mag. Artic. Summar. CD-ROM (Jan. 1992-).

FR
NATURE AND ENVIRONMENT SERIES. See Environmental Issues.

FR/0028-0844
NATURE AND RESOURCES. [Nat. resour.]. **Added/Corp** Unesco. **VFOAT** Nature & Resources. Vol. 1, (June 1965)-. Academic Scholarly Publication. English. qt. £68.00 (institutions), £32.00 (individuals). Parthenon Publishing, Casterton Hall Carnforth, Lancashire LA6 2LA England. **Tel** 011 44 5242 72084, FAX 44-5242-71587. **LC** GB651; .N3. **CODEN** NAREB5. Documents available from The Genuine Article.
Desc: Concerned with scientific research in environmental resources and conservation of nature; emphasizes current symposia and conferences, and contains specific discussions of water resources and ecology.
Ind/Abst AESIS Q.; AGRICOLA [Select. Cov.]; AQUAREF; Curr. Lit. Sci. Sci.; Ecol. Abstr.; EMBASE; Energy Res. Abstr. (Sept. 1977-); Environ. Period. Bibliogr.; Geol. Abstr.; Grasslands For. Abstr.; Life Sci. Collect.; Pollut. Abstr. Indexes; Res. Alert [Select. Cov.]; SCISEARCH; Soc. Sci. Cit. Index [Select. Cov.]; Soils Fert.; Wildl. Rev.

CN/0374-9894
NATURE CANADA. [Nat. Can.]. **Added/Corp** Canadian Nature Federation. Vol. 1, (Jan./March 1972)-. Periodical. English. qt. 25.00Can$ (institution), 30.00Can$ (individual) Canada; 35.00Can$ (institution),

40.00Can$ (individual) other. Canadian Nature Federation, 1 Nicholas Street, Suite 520, Ottowa Ontario K1N 7B7 Canada. **Tel** (613)562-3447, (800)267-4088. **ED** Barbara Stevenson. **LC** WMLC 93/1897. **DD** 508.71/05. **CODEN** NTCNBM. Index available. **Bk Rev**. **Ad Acc**. **Circ:** 20,000 (ctrl). available on microfilm and microfiche from University Microfilms International (UMI). Documents available from BIOSIS Document Express, UMI Article Clearinghouse. ***Supersedes*** *Canadian Audubon, 0008-2929.*
Desc: Canada's national nature magazine focuses on the amazing diversity of this country's wildlife and wilderness areas. Through the words and images of leading nature writers, photographers and artists, each colorful issue investigates the most interesting aspects of the natural world around us, from butterflies to beluga whales, from wildflowers to Halley's Comet.
Ind/Abst ASTIS Curr. Aware. Bull. (1978-); Acad. Abstr. Full Text Elite (Jan. 1992-); Acad. Abstr. (Jan. 1992-); Acad. Search (Jan. 1992-); AQUAREF; ASTIS Bibliogr. (1978-); Biol. Abstr.; Biol. Dig.; Can. Index (?-?); Can. Period. Index; Child. Mag. Guide (1981-); Environ. Period. Bibliogr.; Gen. Period. Index (1985-); Gen. Sci. Source (Jan. 1992-); INFO-SOUTH Abstr.; Key Word Index Wildl. Res.; Environ.; Mag. Artic. Summar. Elite (Jan. 1992-); Mag. Artic. Summar. Select (Jan. 1992-); Mag. Artic. Summar. CD-ROM (Jan. 1992-); Mag. Index Plus (1989-); Mag. Search; Mid. Search (Jan. 1992-); Newsp. Period. Abstr. (1988-); Peace Res. Abstr. J. (1974-1975); Mag. Index (1983-); TOM Gen. Index (1989-).

US
NATURE CENTER NEWS. Main/Corp Kalamazoo Nature Center. No. 1- Mar. 1963-. Periodical. English. mo. $5.00. Kalamazoo Nature Center, 7000 North Westnedge Avenue, Kalamazoo MI 49007. **Tel** (616)381-1574. **ED** Laura Evers. **Circ:** 4,300.
Desc: Promotion of nature center programs, articles on natural history and environmental topics.

US
NATURE CONSERVANCY MAGAZINE. Added/Corp Nature Conservancy (U.S.). **VFOAT** Nature Conservancy. Vol. 37, No. 4 (Aug./Oct. 1987)-. Periodical. English. bm. comes with membership. Nature Conservancy, 1815 North Lynn street, Arlington VA 22209. **Tel** (703)841-5300. **ED** Sue E. Dodge. **LC** QH76; .N33a. **DD** 333.9516/0973. **Circ:** 500,000. Documents available from Documents on Demand. ***Continues*** *Nature Conservancy News, 0028-0852.*
Desc: A report on the Nature Conservancy's efforts to protect natural lands and the rare and endangered species that they shelter.
Ind/Abst Curr. Aware. Biol. Sci., CABS; Environ. Abstr.; Environ. Period. Bibliogr.

UK/0304-2995
NATURE ET RESSOURCES. [Nat. ressour.]. (1965)-. Periodical. French. qt. 98.00F (institutions), 45.00F (individuals) US. Parthenon Publishing, Casterton Hall Carnforth, Lancashire LA6 2LA England. **Tel** 011 44 5242 72084, FAX 44-5242-71587. **UDC** 339.5. ***Continues*** *Zone Aride, 1014-5265.*

US/0888-4862
NATURE FRIEND MAGAZINE. [Nat. friend mag.]. **VFOAT** Nature Friend. Issue No. 1 (Jan. 1984)-. Periodical. English. mo. $22.00 US; $25.00 Canada; $30.00 other. Nature Friend Magazine, PO Box 73, Goshen IN 46527-0073. **Tel** (219)534-2245, FAX (219)534-2333. **ED** Stanley Brubaker. **Circ:** 10,000.

US/1068-0969
NATURE OF ILLINOIS, THE. [Nature Ill.]. **Added/Corp** Society for the Illinois Scientific Surveys. Nature of Illinois Foundation. Vol. 1, No. 1 (Summer 1986)-. Periodical. English. qt. $25.00. Nature of Illinois Foundation, 208 South Lasalle, Suite 666, Chicago IL 60604. **Tel** (312)201-0650. **DD** 508.

SW/1101-3192
NATURMILJON I SIFFROR. VFOAT Natural Environment in Figures. Swedish. SCB Statistiska Centralbyran, 11581 Stockholm Sweden. ***Continues*** *Naturmiljon.*

FR/0250-7072
NATUROPA (ENGLISH EDITION). (NATUROPA.). [Naturopa]. **Added/Corp** European Information Centre for Nature Conservation. Documentation and Information Centre for the Environment and Nature. Centre Naturopa. Council of Europe. No. 20 (1974)-. Periodical. French (English, German, Italian, Spanish and Portuguese). Three times a year. Free on request. Council of Europe / Group Pact ED, Pharmacopoeia BP 907, 67029 Strasbourg Cedex 01 France. **Tel** 011 33 88 412036, FAX 011 33 88 41277181, telex 880388. **ED** Hayo H. Hoekstra. **LC** QH77.E9; N37. **DD** 333.7/2/05. **Circ:** 21,000 (ctrl). Documents available from Documents on Demand. ***Continues*** *Nature in Focus.*
Desc: Devoted to exotic and endangered wildlife, the plight of the world's oceans, the impact of tourism on the environment, the need for implementing environmental education programs, and the effect of European land use policies on plant and animal life. Also includes information on recent activities of the Council of Europe related to the environment.

Ind/Abst Biol. Dig.; Ecol. Abstr. (?-?); EMBASE; Environ. Abstr.; Environ. Period. Bibliogr.; Fish Rev.; Key Word Index Wildl. Res.; Wildl. Rev.

NE
NATUURBEHOUD. Dutch. qt. Fl35.00. Natuurmonumenten, Noordereinde 60, 1243 JJS Graveland Netherlands. **Tel** 011 31 35 559914, FAX 011 31 35 63174.

RU
NAUCHNYE OSNOVY OKHRANY PRIRODY. SBORNIK STATEI. VFOAT Scientific Elements of Nature Conservation. No. 1- 1971-. Periodical. Russian (summaries and/or abstracts in English). **LC** QH81.

US
NEBRASKA RESOURCES. Added/Corp Nebraska. Soil and Water Conservation Commission. Nebraska Natural Resources Commission. No. 1 (Fall 1970)-. Periodical. English. qt. Free on request. Nebraska Natural Resources Commission, PO Box 94876, Cent. Mall South, Lincoln NE 68509. **Tel** (402)471-2081. **Bk Rev**. **Circ:** 1,500.

US/0028-1964
NEBRASKALAND. **See** Recreation, Leisure.

US/0277-4690
NEW ENGLAND CONSERVATIONIST, THE. [New Engl. conserv.]. V. 1- Jan./Feb. 1979-. Periodical. English. bm. $4.00 US; $5.00 other. The New England Conservationist, 12 Main Street, Newport ME 04953.

NE/0169-4286
NEW FORESTS. **See** Forestry.

US/0028-5889
NEW JERSEY OUTDOORS. Added/Corp New Jersey. Division of Fish, Game and Shellfisheries. Vol. 1 (Jan./Feb. 1974)-. Periodical. English. Four times a year. $15.00 (one year), $26.00 (two year). New Jersey Outdoors, CN 402, Trenton NJ 08625. **Tel** (609)292-2477. **ED** Steve Perrone. **LC** SK1; .N452. **DD** 639.9/09749. cum. index. **Bk Rev**. **Circ:** 60,000 (ctrl). ***Supersedes*** *New Jersey Outdoors, 0028-5889.*
Desc: Dedicated to the wise management and conservation of our natural resources and to foster a greater appreciation of the outdoors.

US/0028-6338
NEW MEXICO WILDLIFE. [N. M. wildl.]. **Added/Corp** New Mexico. Dept. of Game and Fish. Public Affairs Division. New Mexico. Dept. of Game and Fish. Information and Education Section. New Mexico. Dept. of Game and Fish. Information and Education Division. (1960)-. Periodical. English. bm. $10.00 (one year), $18.00 (two year). New Mexico Game & Fish Department, State Capital, Villagra Building, Santa Fe NM 87503. **Tel** (505)827-7841. **ED** Jeffery L. Pederson. **LC** SK427; .N4. **DD** 333.95/9/09789. **CODEN** NMWIAN. Index available. cum. index. **Bk Rev**. **Circ:** 8,500 (ctrl). available on microfilm from University Microfilms International (UMI). Documents available from BIOSIS Document Express, BIOSIS Document Express.
Desc: Wildlife, conservation, game and fish features.
Ind/Abst Biol. Abstr.; Fish Rev.; Wildl. Rev.

US/0745-8835
NEW YORK STATE CONSERVATION COUNCIL COMMENTS. (NEW YORK STATE CONSERVATION COUNCIL COMMENTS / NYSCC, NEW YORK STATE CONSERVATION COUNCIL INC.). **Added/Corp** New York State Conservation Council. **VFOAT** Conservation Council Comments. (19??)-. Periodical. English. Ten times a year (Not published in January or July). $5.00. New York State Conservation Council, 8 East Main Street, Ilion NY 13357-1899. **Tel** (315)894-3302, FAX (315)894-2893. **ED** William R. Hilts, 5115 Baer Road, Sanborn, NY 14132; Telephone: (716)731-9984. **Ad Acc**. **Circ:** 2,700.
Desc: Concerned with all phases of the outdoor field including conservation education, hunting, fishing, trapping, water pollution, air pollution, forest management, gun safety, archery, legislation, etc.

US
NEWS / CONSERVATION EDUCATION ASSOCIATION. Added/Corp Conservation Education Association. **VFOAT** CEA News. Vol. 34, No. 2 (Winter 1987/88)-. Periodical. English. qt. Conservation Education Association / Green Bay, c/o Dennis Bryan Secretary/Treasurer, University of Wisconsin-Green Bay, Green Bay WI 54301. **Tel** (414)465-2397. ***Continues*** *Newsletter, 0010-6461.*

US/0744-3366
NEWS - FLORIDA ASSOCIATION OF SOIL AND WATER CONSERVATION DISTRICT SUPERVISORS. (NEWS / FLORIDA ASSOCIATION OF SOIL AND WATER CONSERVATION DISTRICT SUPERVISORS.). **Added/Corp** Florida Association of Soil and Water Conservation District Supervisors. Florida. Dept. of Agriculture and Consumer Services. (19??)-. Periodical. English. qt. Free on request. Florida Association Conservation District, PO Box 1269, Gainesville FL 32602. **Tel** (904)376-1990. **Circ:** 1,000 (ctrl).

CN/0705-0216
NEWSLETTER. [Newsl. - Sierra Club Alta.]. No. 6 (Aug. 1977)-. Newsletter. English. qt. Free to members. Sierra Club of Alberta, Box 4520 Station C, Calgary Alberta T2T 5N3 Canada. **Tel** (403)244-4487, FAX (403)244-2340. **DD** 333.7/2/0607123. **Ad Acc**. **Circ:** 600 (ctrl). ***Continues*** *Occasional Newsletter (Sierra Club of Alberta), 0713-6013.*

US/0517-4856
NEWSLETTER - AMERICAN SHORE AND BEACH PRESERVATION ASSOCIATION. [Newsl. - Am. Shore Beach Preserv. Assoc.]. **Main/Corp** American Shore and Beach Preservation Association. (1960)-. Periodical. English. Four times a year (Mar., June, Sept., Dec.). $40.00 US, Canada, Puerto Rico & Mexico; $52.00 other Comes with American Shore & Beach Preservation Association membership. American Shore & Beach Preservation Association, 3000 Citrus Circle, Suite 230, Walnut Creek CA 94598. **Tel** (415)944-5411. **Ad Acc**. **Circ:** 4,000 (ctrl). Documents available from Documents on Demand.
Desc: Newsletter covering the up-keep on the beaches across the nation. Dedicated to the preservation and development of shores and beaches.
Ind/Abst Environ. Abstr.

CN/0318-5133
NEWSLETTER - CANADIAN SOCIETY OF ENVIRONMENTAL BIOLOGISTS. [Newsl. - Can. Soc. Environ. Biol.]. **Main/Corp** Canadian Society of Environmental Biologists. **VFOAT** Bulletin. Vol. 29 (1972)-. Newsletter. English (summaries and/or abstracts in French). qt. 23.36Can$ Canada; 35.00Can$ other. Canadian Society Environmental Biologists, Box 962 Station F, Toronto Ontario M4Y 2N9 Canada. **Tel** (403)483-3499, FAX (403)483-1574. **ED** Katrina Hodgson (editor's phone: (403)481-1253). **DD** 574.5/06/271. **Bk Rev**, (Qty: 14). **Ad Acc**. **Circ:** 500 (ctrl).
Desc: Environmental management and research news.
Ind/Abst AQUAREF.

US
NEWSLETTER - LAKE GEORGE PARK COMMISSION. Main/Corp Lake George Park Commission. Newsletter. English. Lake George Park Commission, Lake George NY 12845.

NP
NEWSLETTER - NEPAL NATURE CONSERVATION SOCIETY. Main/Corp Nepal Nature Conservation Society. Newsletter. English. Nepal Nature Conservation Society, PO Box 229, Kathmandu Nepal. **LC** QH77.N35; N46A. **DD** 333.9/5/095496.

NZ/0111-686X
NEWSLETTER - NEW ZEALAND. NATURE CONSERVATION COUNCIL. Main/Corp Nature Conservation Council (N.Z.). No. 1- Oct. 1972-. Newsletter. English. qt. Free. New Zealand Nature Conservation Council, PO Box 12-200 Thorndon, Wellington New Zealand. **Tel** 710-726. **ED** Pam Crisp. **LC** QH77.N45; N48A. **DD** 333.7/2/09931. **Bk Rev**. **Ad Acc**. **Circ:** 2,500 (ctrl).
Desc: Covers a range of topics of conservation interest in New Zealand, including protection of natural features, rare and endangered species, environmental education and some overseas items.

US/0890-8842
NEWSLETTER / TENNESSEE CITIZENS FOR WILDERNESS PLANNING. [Newsl. - Tenn. Citiz. Wilderness Plan.]. **Added/Corp** Tennessee Citizens for Wilderness Planning. (19??)-. Newsletter. English. Eight times a year. comes with membership. Tennessee Citizens for Wilderness Planning (TCWP) Inc., 219 East Vanderbilt Drive, Oak Ridge TN 37830. **Tel** (615)483-8055. **ED** Liane B. Russell. **DD** 333. **Circ:** 525.

US
NEWSLETTER - THE NATURE CONSERVANCY (U.S.). IOWA CHAPTER. Main/Corp The Nature Conservancy (U.S.). Iowa Chapter. Vol. 1 (1965)-. Newsletter. English. qt.

US/0886-6619
NJ AUDUBON. [NJ Audubon]. **Added/Corp** New Jersey Audubon Society. **VFOAT** N.J. Audubon; NJAS; N.J.A.S.; New Jersey Audubon Magazine. **VAT** New Jersey Audubon. Vol. 4 (Mar./Apr. 1978)-. Periodical. English. qt. $25.00 US; $30.00 other. New Jersey Audubon Society, 790 Ewing Avenue, PO Box 125, Franklin Lakes NJ 07417. **Tel** (201)891-1211. **ED** Pete Dunne, Cape May Bird Observatory, PO Box 3, Cape May Point, NJ, Tel. (609)884-2736. **DD** 639. **Bk Rev**. **Ad Acc**. **Circ:** 8,500. ***Continues*** *New Jersey Audubon.*
Desc: A general-interest magazine which includes analyses of conservation issues, news from our nature centers, and details about our activities and programs. "Records or New Jersey Birds", a separate magazine, contains reports of bird sightings and reserach bring

conducted by New Jersey Audubon Society.
Ind/Abst AGRICOLA; Biol. Dig.; Fish Rev. (19??-199?); Wildl. Rev. (19??-199?).

●US/0961-1444
NONRENEWABLE RESOURCES.
Added/Corp International Association for Mathematical Geology. Vol. 1, No. 1 (Spring 1992)-. Periodical. English. qt (4 issues). $218.00 US; $238.00 other. Oxford University Press / New York, 200 Madison Avenue, New York NY 10016. **Tel** (212)679-7300, (919)677-0977, (800)451-7556, (800)445-9714, FAX (919)677-1303. **(Subscription address:** Oxford University Press / USA, Journals Marketing Department, Oxford University Press, 2001 Evans Road, Cary NC 27513.**) LC** TN1; .N75. **DD** 553/.05. **[CCC]. Ad Acc. Acid Free.** available on microfilm and microfiche from University Microfilms International (UMI).
Desc: Directed towards natural resource economists, corporate energy and mineral management personnel, economic geologists, exploration geologists, and others dealing with risk analysis or cost/benefit studies on natural resources.
Ind/Abst Eng. Mater. Abstr.; Environ. Period. Bibliogr.; GeoRef; Met. Abstr.

US/0029-2958
NORTH WOODS CALL, THE. **See** Recreation, Leisure-Outdoor Life.

US/1070-812X
NORTHBOUND (EAGLE RIVER, WIS.). (NORTHBOUND.). [Northbound]. **Added/Corp** Trees for Tomorrow Resources Education Center. Trees for Tomorrow Natural Resources Education Center. (19??)-. Periodical. English. Four times a year. $15.00 (regular); $3.00 (schools). Trees for Tomorrow, PO Box 609, Eagle River WI 54521. **Tel** (715)479-6456. **ED** Martha J. Enlinger. **DD** 333. **Circ:** 2,500 (ctrl). ***Continues** Tree Tips (1982).*
Desc: A forum for natural resource issues and education. These issues have focus on rivers, acid rain, endangered species, and wetlands.

US
NORTHEAST WILDLIFE. **Added/Corp** Wildlife Society. Northeast Section. **VFOAT** Transactions of the Northeast Section, the Wildlife Society. Vol. 49 (1992)-. English. University of Massachusetts / Department of Forestry and Wildlife, Holdsworth Hall, Amherst MA 01003. **LC** SK351; .W64a. ***Continues** Transactions of the Northeast Section of the Wildlife Society, 1043-2973.*

CN/0380-5522
NORTHERN PERSPECTIVES. [North. perspect.]. **Added/Corp** Canadian Arctic Resources Committee. Northern Perspectives. Vol. 1 (Jan. 1973)-. Periodical. English (summaries and/or abstracts in French). ir. comes with membership. Canadian Arctic Resources Committee, 1 Nicholas Street Suite 412, Ottawa ONT K1N 7B7 Canada. **Tel** (613)241-7379, FAX (613)236-7379. **ED** Alan Saunders. **CODEN** NPEREJ. **Circ:** 16,000 (ctrl).
Desc: Analysis of resource development, economic, social, and political issues in Canada's North and the circumpolar Arctic.
Ind/Abst ASTIS Curr. Aware. Bull. (1978-); ASTIS Bibliogr. (1978-).

CN/1183-5869
NORTHERN VOICE. [North. voice]. **Added/Corp** Northern Foundation (Ottawa, Ont.). No. 1 (Spring 1991)-. Periodical. English. $25.00 per year. Northern Foundation, PO Box 115, Station B, Ottawa Ontario K1P 6C3 Canada. **DD** 971/.005. ***Continues** Continuing Crisis (Ottawa, Ont.), 0843-638X.*

US/0885-5870
NORTHWEST ENERGY NEWS. [Northwest energy news]. **Added/Corp** Northwest Power Planning Council (U.S.). **VFOAT** Energy News. Vol. 1, No. 1 (March 1982)-. English. Six times a year. Free. Northwest Power Planning Council, 851 Southwest 6th, Suite 1100, Portland OR 97204. **Tel** (503)222-5161, FAX (503)222-9246. **ED** Carlotta Collette. **LC** TK23.7; .N67. **DD** 363.6/2/09795. **Circ:** 22,000. Documents available from Documents on Demand.
Desc: Public information vehicle for Pacific Northwest on electric energy conservation, power planning and fish and wildlife mitigation efforts.
Ind/Abst Energy Inf. Abstr.; Environ. Abstr.

BE
NOTICIAS DE GALAPAGOS. [Not. Galapagos]. No. 1 (July 1963)-. Periodical. English (French and Spanish). Twice a year. $25.00 Comes with Charles Darwin Foundation membership. Charles Darwin Foundation, 100 North Washington Street, Suite 311, Falls Church VA 22046. **Tel** (703)538-6833. **LC** QH123; .N66. **CODEN** NOGAB2. Documents available from BIOSIS Document Express.
Ind/Abst Biol. Abstr. (-1988); Fish Rev. (Jan. 1989-July 1992); Wildl. Rev. (Jan. 1989-July 1992).

US/0736-1394
NOTIFICATIONS / HCRS INFORMATION EXCHANGE. [Notif. - HCRS Inf. Exch.]. **Main/Corp** Heritage Conservation and Recreation Service. **Added/Corp** United States. Heritage Conservation and Recreation Service. Park and Recreation Technical Services. HCRS Information Exchange. (19??)-. English. The HCRS Information Exchange, 440 G Street NW, Washington DC 20243. ***Continues** Technical Assistance Notifications, 0736-1386.*

US/0196-2493
NRDC WORLD ENVIRONMENT ALERT.
Main/Corp Natural Resources Defense Council. International Project. **VAT** Natural Resources Defense Council World Environment Alert. Periodical. English. International Project Natural Resources Defense Council Inc, 1350 New York Avenue NW/Suite 300, Washington DC 20005.

MW
NYALA / NATIONAL FAUNA PRESERVATION SOCIETY OF MALAWI.
Began in 1975. English. sa. K4.00 Malawi; $6.00 US. National Fauna Preservation Society of Malawi, PO Box 1429, Blantyre Malawi. **ED** C O Dudley. **Bk Rev. Ad Acc.**
Ind/Abst Fish Rev.; Wildl. Rev.

CN/0576-6370
OCCASIONAL PAPER - CANADIAN WILDLIFE SERVICE. [Occas. pap., Can. Wildl. Serv.]. **VFOAT** Occasional Paper Series; Occasional Papers. No. 1; 1957-. Monographic series. English (French). Price varies per volume. Information Canada, 171 Slater Street, Ottawa Ontario K1A 0S9 Canada. **Tel** (819)997-1095. **CODEN** CWOPAL. **Circ:** 1,100 (ctrl). available on microfiche. Documents available from BIOSIS Document Express.
Ind/Abst ASTIS Curr. Aware. Bull. (1978-); ASTIS Bibliogr. (1978-); Biol. Abstr.; Ecol. Abstr. (?-?); Fish Rev.; Key Word Index Wildl. Res.; Wildl. Rev.

AT/0810-5766
OCCASIONAL PAPER SERIES - FISHERIES AND WILDLIFE DIVISION, MINISTRY FOR CONSERVATION.
(OCCASIONAL PAPER SERIES / MINISTRY FOR CONSERVATION, FISHERIES AND WILDLIFE DIVISION.). [Occas. pap. ser. - Fish. Wildl. Div. Minist. Conserv.]. **Added/Corp** Victoria. Fisheries and Wildlife Division. (1983)-. Monographic series. English. ir. Price varies per volume. Ministry for Conservation, Fisheries and Wildlife Division, Box 41, East Melbourne Victoria 3002 Australia. **CODEN** OPFCEO. Documents available from BIOSIS Document Express.
Ind/Abst Biol. Abstr. (1989-).

XR
OCHRANA ROSTLIN. **See** Biology-Botany.

US/0085-4468
OHIO FISH AND WILDLIFE REPORT.
[Ohio fish wildlife rep.]. No. 1 (1971)-. Monographic series. English. ir. Price varies per volume. Ohio Division of Wildlife, c/o Ken Laub, 1840 Belcher Drive, Columbus OH 43224-1329. **Tel** (614)265-6558. **ED** Kenneth W Laub. **CODEN** OFWRBD. **Pr Rev. Circ:** 1,200 (ctrl). Documents available from BIOSIS Document Express. ***Supersedes** Ohio Game Monographs, 0078-4036; Ohio Fish Monographs, 0078-4028.*
Desc: Reports of fish and wildlife research and management.
Ind/Abst Biol. Abstr.; Life Sci. Collect.; Wildl. Rev. (19??-199?).

US
OHIO WOODLANDS. **See** Forestry.

CN/0383-6479
ONTARIO CONSERVATION NEWS.
Added/Corp Conservation Council of Ontario. (1975)-. Periodical. English. qt. 25.00Can$ (individuals), 100.00Can$ (institutions). Conservation Council Ontario, 489 College Street/Suite 506, Toronto Ontario M6G 1A5 Canada. **Tel** (416)969-9637, FAX (416)960-8053. **ED** Paul Grunthal. **DD** 333.7/2/062713. Index available ((Annual Index published starting 1991)). **Bk Rev**, (Qty: 16-20). **Circ:** 1,000. ***Continues** Conservation News, 0317-5839.*
Desc: Conservation news and issues; for example, forestry, acid rain, waste management, environmental assessment, Great Lakes, etc.

CN/0078-4834
ONTARIO FIELD BIOLOGIST, THE.
***Ceased.* See** Biology.

UK
OPEN SPACE (OPEN SPACES SOCIETY, GREAT BRITAIN). (OPEN SPACE.). **Added/Corp** Open Spaces Society (Great Britain). Vol. 21, No. 5 (Autumn Journal 1982)-. Periodical. English. Three times a year (Mar., June, Sept.). £15.00. Common Open Spaces, 25A Bell Street, Henley on Thames, Oxon RG9 2BA England. **Tel** 011 44 491 573535. **ED** Kate Ashbrook. **Bk Rev**, (Qty: 30). **Ad Acc, Adv Mgr:** Nicole Bentham. **Circ:** 2,500 (ctrl). ***Continues** Journal (Commons, Open Spaces and Footpaths Preservation Society).*
Desc: Covers campaigns to create and conserve common land, village greens, open spaces and rights of public access, in England and Wales.

US/0094-7113
OREGON WILDLIFE. **Added/Corp** Oregon. Dept. of Fish and Wildlife. Oregon. Wildlife Commission. Vol. 29 (1974)-. Periodical. English. Six times a year. Free. Oregon Department of Fish & Wildlife, PO Box 59, 2501 Southwest 1st Street, Portland OR 97201. **Tel** (503)229-5400. **ED** Jim Gladson and Pat Wray. **LC** SK119; .O74. **DD** 799/.09795. Index available. **Circ:** 42,000 (ctrl). ***Continues** Oregon State Game Commission Bulletin; **Absorbed** Biennial Report. Oregon. Dept. of Fish and Wildlife.*
Ind/Abst Biol. Dig.; Wildl. Rev.

UK/0030-6053
ORYX. (ORYX : THE JOURNAL OF THE FAUNA PRESERVATION SOCIETY.). [Oryx]. **Added/Corp** Fauna Preservation Society (Great Britain) Fauna and Flora Preservation Society (Great Britain). (Oct. 1950)-. Academic Scholarly Publication. English. Four times a year. $135.00 US & Canada; £79.00 Europe; £87.00 other. Blackwell Scientific Publications Ltd, Marston Book Services, PO Box 87, Oxford OX2 ODT UK. **Tel** 011 44 865 791155, FAX 011 44 865 791927, telex 837 515 MARDIS G. **ED** Dr. Jacqui Morris. **LC** QL81.5; .O79. **CODEN** ORYXAM. **[CCC].** Index available (bound in last issue). **Bk Rev. Ad Acc. Pr Rev. Circ:** 5,000 (ctrl). available on microfilm and microfiche from University Microfilms International (UMI). Documents available from BIOSIS Document Express, Documents on Demand. ***Continues** Society for the Preservation of the Fauna of the Empire (Great Britain). Journal of the Society for the Preservation of the Fauna of the Empire.*
Desc: For the latest research, news and views in international wildlife conservation.
Ind/Abst AQUAREF; Biol. Abstr.; Biol. Dig.; Curr. Aware. Biol. Sci., CABS; Ecol. Abstr.; Ecology Abstr.; Environ. Abstr.; Environ. Period. Bibliogr.; Geogr. Abstr. Phys. Geogr.; Int. Dev. Abstr.; Key Word Index Wildl. Res.; Wildl. Rev.

US
OUR LAND. Vol. 1, No. 1 (Spring 1989)-. English. qt. $25.00. Our Land Magazine, 530 Park Avenue, Idaho Falls ID 83402. **Tel** (208)523-5000. **ED** Steve Janes.
Desc: Conservative environmental journal.

GW/1068-3240
OUTDOOR DELAWARE. [Outdoor Del.].
Added/Corp Delaware. Dept. of Natural Resources and Environmental Control. (19??)-. Periodical. English. qt. **DD** 333. ***Continues** Delaware Conservationist, 0045-9852.*
Desc: Covers the conservation or wildlife and natural resources.

US/0279-9065
OUTDOOR NEWS (OKLAHOMA CITY, OKLA.). (OUTDOOR NEWS / OKLAHOMA WILDLIFE FEDERATION.). [Outdoor news]. **Added/Corp** Oklahoma Wildlife Federation. (19??)-. Periodical. English. mo. $20.00. Outdoor News, 3900 North Santa Fe Avenue, Oklahoma City OK 73118. **Tel** (405)524-7009, FAX (405)521-9270. **ED** Margaret Ruff. **DD** 639. **Ad Acc, Adv Mgr:** Randy Goodman, **Tel** (405)733-3050. **Circ:** 14,500.
Desc: Articles on conservation issues, hunting and fishing in Oklahoma. 20-page monthly tabloid newspaper designed to inform readers of issues relating to wildlife and habitat. Includes pollution, legislative updates, hunting/fishing stories, and habitat protection initiatives.

US/0030-7106
OUTDOOR OKLAHOMA. **See** Recreation, Leisure-Outdoor Life.

US
OUTDOORS WEST. **See** Recreation, Leisure-Outdoor Life.

AT/0728-7275
OWNER BUILDER MAGAZINE. **See** Building and Construction.

●AT/1038-2097
PACIFIC CONSERVATION BIOLOGY. Vol. 1, No. 1 (June 1993)-. English. Four times a year (Mar., June, Sept., Dec.). 58.00Aus$ (individuals), 175.00Aus$ (institutions) Australia & New Zealand; 81.00Aus$ (individuals), 218.00Aus$ (institutions) others. Surrey Beatty & Sons Pty Ltd, 43 Rickard Road, Chipping Norton NSW 2170 Australia. **Tel** (02)602-3888, FAX (02)821-1253. **Bk Rev. Ad Acc.**
Desc: This journal is devoted to conservation and land management in the Pacific region.

NZ/0113-0846
PACIFIC WORLD. **Added/Corp** Pacific Institute of Resource Management. Vol. 1, No. 1 (Nov./Dec. 1986)-. Periodical. English. Four times a year (Feb., May, Aug., Nov.). 20.00NZ$ New Zealand; 24.00NZ$ Australia & South Pacific; 24.00NZ$ other. Pacific Institute Resource Management, PO Box 10-123, Terrace Wellington New Zealand. **Tel** 011 64 04 4738312, FAX 011 64 4 4726374. **ED** George Porter. **Bk Rev**, (Qty: 4). **Circ:** 500.
Desc: Covers issues of global ecology sustainability and social inclusiveness, reform of economic and political system and the work movement of non-government organizations.

US/0460-6590
PAMPHLET - MAINE DEPARTMENT OF INLAND FISHERIES AND GAME, INFORMATION AND EDUCATION DIVISION. **Main/Corp** Maine. Department of Inland Fisheries and Game. Information and Education Division. No. 1 (1954)-. Monographic series. English. Price varies per volume. Maine Department of Inland Fisheries and Game, Information and Education Division, Augusta ME 04333. **DD** 333.7.

US
PANORAMA / GEORGIA CONSERVANCY. **Added/Corp** Georgia Conservancy. Vol. 17, No. 2 (Mar./Apr. 1988)-. Newsletter. English. bm. (Comes with Georgia Conservancy membership). Georgia Conservancy, 3110 Maple Street, Suite 407, Atlanta GA 30305. **Tel** (404)262-1967. ***Continues*** *Georgia Conservancy Newsletter.*

FR
PARCS DEPARTEMENTAUX DE L'EQUIPEMENT, LES. **Added/Corp** France. Direction des Routes et de la Circulation Routiere. (19??)-. French. 244 Boulevard Saint-Germain VIIE, 75775 Paris Cedex 16 France. **LC** HE363.F6; P37.

FR/0982-6246
PARCS PARIS. 1987. (PARCS.). (1987)-. Periodical. French. Three times a year. 150.00F. Fed Parcs Naturels de France, 4 rue de Stockholm, 75008 Paris France. **Tel** 33 1 42949084. **UDC** 502.72. cum. index. **Circ:** 5,000. ***Continues*** *Nouvelles Breves - Parcs Naturels Regionaux, 1144-2050.*

US/0735-9462
PARK SCIENCE. (PARK SCIENCE / NATIONAL PARK SERVICE, U.S. DEPARTMENT OF THE INTERIOR.). [Park sci.]. **Added/Corp** United States. National Park Service. Vol. 2, No. 1 (Fall 1981)-. Periodical. English. Four times a year. National Park Services, 3200 Jefferson, Corvallis OR 97331. **Tel** (503)757-4321, (503)757-4579. ***Continues*** *Pacific Park Science, 0736-8631.*

UK/0960-233X
PARKS NEWBURY. (PARKS.). [Parks Newbury]. (1990)-. Periodical. English (Spanish and French). Three times a year. £25.20. Parks, 36 Kingfisher Crthambridge Road, Newbury RG14 5SJ United Kingdom. **DD** 719.3. **Bk Rev. Circ:** 2,000. ***Continues*** *Parques.*
Desc: News information and feature articles on the management of protected areas. It is aimed at managers dealing with practical issues.
Ind/Abst Curr. Aware. Biol. Sci., CABS.

AT
PARKWATCH. English. qt. 18.00Aus$. Victorian National Parks Association, Box 785F GPO, Melbourne 3001 Australia. **Tel** 011 61 3 6508296, FAX 011 61 3 6505684. **ED** Barbara Vaughan. **Bk Rev. Ad Acc. Circ:** 3,500. ***Continues*** *Victorian National Parks Association Journal.*

US
PEREGRINE FUND NEWSLETTER, THE. **Main/Corp** Peregrine Fund (U.S.). **Added/Corp** Cornell University. Laboratory of Ornithology. **VFOAT** Newsletter. No. 1 (Aug. 1973)-. Newsletter. English. Twice a year (Mar., Dec.). $25.00. Peregrine Fund, 5666 West Flying Hawk Lane, Boise ID 83709. **Tel** (208)362-3716. **ED** Wm. A. Burnham Ph.D. **Circ:** 6,000 (ctrl).
Desc: News and information of birds of prey conservation programs.

BL/0103-7641
PERFIL DO ESTADO DA BAHIA : ESTATISTICAS SELECIONADAS / GOVERNO DO ESTADO DA BAHIA, SECRETARIA DO PLANEJAMENTO, CIENCIA E TECNOLOGIA, CENTRO DE ESTATISTICA E INFORMACOES, CEI. **Added/Corp** Bahia (Brazil : State). Centro de Estatistica E Informacoes. (June 1991)-. Portuguese. **LC** HC188.B3; P46. **DD** 330.981/42/0021.

CN/0847-9607
PITCH-IN NEWS. [Pitch-in news]. (1988)-. Periodical. English. qt. Outdoors Unlittered, 200-1676 Martin Drive, White Rock British Columbia V4A 6E7 Canada. **Tel** (604)538-0577, FAX (604)538-3497. **DD** 363.7/28. **Circ:** 25,000 (ctrl). ***Continues*** *Newslitter (British Columbia Ed.), 0383-915X; Newslitter (Alberta Edition), 0383-9168.*
Desc: Newsletter for Outdoors Unlittered in British Columbia, Alberta and Ontario.

US/0270-739X
PITTMAN-ROBERTSON GAME MANAGEMENT TECHNICAL SERIES. [Pittman-Robertson game manage. tech. ser.]. **Added/Corp** Kentucky. Dept. of Fish and Wildlife Resources. United States. Bureau of Sport Fisheries and Wildlife. (19??)-. Monographic series. English. ir. Price varies per volume. Kentucky Department of Fish & Wildlife Resources, 1 Game Farm Road, Frankfort KY 40601. **Tel** (502)564-4336, FAX (502)564-6508. **LC** SK361; .P57. **DD** 639/.0973.

US/0556-3968
PLANNING AND RESOURCE DEVELOPMENT SERIES. **Added/Corp** Holdsworth Natural Resources Center. University of Massachusetts, Amherst. Cooperative Extension Service. (19??)-. Monographic series. English. Price varies per volume. Holdsworth & Assoc, 625 E Seegers Road, Des Plaines IL 60018. **DD** 338.1.

US/0470-3855
POLICY BULLETIN - THE NATURE CONSERVANCY. **Main/Corp** Nature Conservancy. (19??)-. Bulletin. English. The Nature Conservancy, 1815 North Lynn Street, Arlington VA 22209. **Tel** (703)841-5300. **DD** 333.7.

US/0478-1392
PRESERVATION PROGRESS (CHARLESTON). **See** Architecture.

US
PRESIDENT'S ... ENVIRONMENT AND CONSERVATION CHALLENGE AWARDS, THE. **Added/Corp** Council on Environmental Quality (U.S.). (1991)-. English. Council on Environmental Quality, 722 Jackson Place NW, Washington DC 20006. **Tel** (202)395-5700.

US/0898-6207
PRIMATE CONSERVATION. (PRIMATE CONSERVATION : THE NEWSLETTER AND JOURNAL OF THE IUCN/SSC PRIMATE SPECIALIST GROUP.). [Primate conserv.]. **Added/Corp** IUCN/SSC Primate Specialist Group. World Wildlife Fund (U.S.). Primate Program. No. 5 (Jan. 1985)-. Newsletter. English. an. $15.00. Conservation International, 1015 18th Street NW, Suite 1000, Washington DC 20036. **Tel** (202)429-5660, FAX (202)887-5188. **ED** Wiliam R. Konstant. **LC** QL737.P9; P6724. **DD** 333.95/9. ctrl circ. ***Continues*** *IUCN/SSC Primate Specialist Group Newsletter, 1043-8521.*

US/0278-4750
PROBLEMY OSVOENIIA PUSTYN. (PROBLEMS OF DESERT DEVELOPMENT.). [Probl. desert dev.]. No. 1 (1980)-. English (Russian). Six times a year. $800.00. Allerton Press, Inc., 150 Fifth Avenue, New York NY 10011. **Tel** (212)924-3950, FAX (212)463-9684, telex 427441 ALPRES. **LC** GB611; .P736. **DD** 333.73. **CODEN** PDEDDG. **[CCC].** Documents available from BIOSIS Document Express.
Ind/Abst AGRICOLA [Full Cov.]; Agric. Eng. Abstr. (1991-); Agrofor. Abstr. (1991-); Biol. Abstr. (-1983); Crop Physiol. Abstr.; Field Crop Abstr.; Fish Rev. (Jan. 1989-July 1992); For. Abstr.; GeoRef; Grasslands For. Abstr.; Hortic. Abstr.; Irr. Drain. Abstr.; Leis. Recreat. Tour. Abstr.; Maize Abstr.; Nematol. Abstr.; Rev. Agric. Entomol.; Rice Abstr.; Soils Fert.; Sorghum Mill. Abstr.; Wheat Barley Trit. Abstr.; Wildl. Rev. (Jan. 1989-July 1992); World Agric. Econ.

UK/0308-4167
PROCEEDINGS OF SYMPOSIUM ... OF THE ASSOCIATION OF BRITISH WILD ANIMAL KEEPERS. **Main/Corp** Association of British Wild Animal Keepers. Proceedings. English. an. Association of British Wild Animal Keepers, 12 Tackley Road, Eastville, Bristol BS5 6UQ England. **Tel** 011 44 272 515950.

US/0748-7576
PROCEEDINGS OF THE ANNUAL NACD CONVENTION. (PROCEEDINGS OF THE ... ANNUAL NACD CONVENTION / NATIONAL ASSOCIATION OF CONSERVATION DISTRICTS.). **Main/Corp** NACD Convention. **VFOAT** Proceedings of the ... Annual N.A.C.D. Convention. Proceedings. English. an. $8.00. **LC** S622; .N27. **DD** 333.7/2/06073. ***Continues*** *National Association of Conservation Districts. Proceedings of the Annual Convention.*

US/0883-542X
PROCEEDINGS OF THE ANNUAL TECHNICAL SYMPOSIUM - WILD GOOSE ASSOCIATION. TECHNICAL SYMPOSIUM. (PROCEEDINGS OF THE ... ANNUAL TECHNICAL SYMPOSIUM / THE WILD GOOSE ASSOCIATION.). [Proc. Annu. Tech. Symp. - Wild Goose Assoc., Tech. Symp.]. **Main/Corp** Wild Goose Association. Technical Symposium. Proceedings. English. an. Wild Goose Association, PO Box 556, Bedford MA 01730. **LC** VK560; .W48B. **DD** 623.89/32.

US/0161-3332
PROCEEDINGS OF THE CONVENTION - INTERNATIONAL ASSOCIATION OF FISH AND WILDLIFE AGENCIES. [Proc. conv. - Int. Assoc. Fish Wildl. Agencies]. **Main/Corp** International Association of Fish and Wildlife Agencies. 67th (1977)-. Proceedings. English. an (Sept.). $20.00 Comes with International Association of Fisheries & Wildlife Agencies Membership. International Association of Fish and Wildlife Agencies, 444 North Capitol Street Northwest, Suite 534, Washington DC 20001. **Tel** (202)624-7890, FAX (202)624-7891. **ED** Jack H. Berryman and Kenneth J. Sabol. **LC** SK352; .C66. **DD** 639. Index available. **Circ:** 700. ***Continues*** *Convention of the International Association of Fish and Wildlife Agencies, 0163-8653.*
Desc: News and information on the proceedings of wildlife and fisheries management.
Ind/Abst AGRICOLA.

US/0198-6600
PROCEEDINGS OF THE WESTERN ASSOCIATION OF FISH AND WILDLIFE AGENCIES AND THE WESTERN DIVISION AMERICAN FISHERIES ASSOCIATION. (PROCEEDINGS OF THE WESTERN ASSOCIATION OF FISH AND WILDLIFE AGENCIES AND THE WESTERN DIVISION, AMERICAN FISHERIES SOCIETY.). [Proc. West. Assoc. Fish Wildl. Agencies West. Div. Am. Fish. Assoc.]. **Main/Corp** Western Association of Fish and Wildlife Agencies (U.S.). **Added/Corp** Western Association of Fish and Wildlife Agencies. Western Proceedings. American Fisheries Society. Western Division. Proceedings of the Western Association of Fish and Wildlife Agencies and the Western Division, American Fisheries Association. **VFOAT** Western Proceedings. 57th (1977)-. Proceedings. English. an. $10.00. Western Association of Fish and Wildlife Agencies, 600 Walnut Street, PO Box 25, Boise ID 83707. **Tel** (916)445-7613. **ED** Sandra Wolfe. **LC** SK351; .W55. **DD** 333.95/40978. ctrl circ. ***Continues*** *Proceedings of the Annual Conference of Western Association of State Game and Fish Commissioners, 0085-8102.*
Desc: Copies of papers presented at annual meeting.
Ind/Abst Fish Rev. (19??-199?); Wildl. Rev. (19??-199?).

US
PROGRESS REPORT OF CONSERVATION ACTIVITIES. **Main/Corp** United States. Soil Conservation Service. **VFOAT** Conservation Activities. English. an. USDA Soil Conservation Service / South Dakota, Huron SD 57350. **LC** S624.S58; U55A. **DD** 333.76/16/09783.

US/0732-0264
PUBLIC LAND LAW REVIEW, THE. **See** Law.

US/0270-8094
PUBLIC LANDS NEWS. [Public lands news]. Vol. 1 (1976)-. Periodical. English. Twenty-four times a year (Except the last two weeks in Aug. and Dec.). $207.00 one year; $373.00 two years; $559.00 three years. Resources Publishing Company, 1010 Vermont Avenue Northwest, Suite 708, Washington DC 20005. **Tel** (202)638-7529, FAX (202)393-2075. **ED** James Coffin.
Desc: The in-depth reporting on legislative and administrative changes that is affecting the natural resources on the public lands. Others articles may be included are energy development, timber harvesting, range management and planning.
Ind/Abst GeoRef.

US/0093-3074
PUBLIC USE OF THE NATIONAL PARKS SYSTEMS (WASHINGTON). (PUBLIC USE OF THE NATIONAL PARK SYSTEM; FISCAL YEAR REPORT.). **Main/Corp** United States. National Park Service. 1972/73-. English. an. US National Park Service, 18th & C Streets NW, Washington DC 20007. **LC** SB482; .A195A. **DD** 333.7/8/0973. ***Continues in part*** *Public Use of the Natural Parks.*

CN/0713-6986
PUBLICATIONS LIST - MANITOBA. DEPARTMENT OF NATURAL RESOURCES. (PUBLICATIONS LIST.). [Publ. list - Manit. Dep. Nat. Resour.]. **Main/Corp** Manitoba. Dept. of Natural Resources. Summer 1980-. Periodical. English. Department of Natural Resources / Manitoba Canada, Box 22, 1495 St James Street, Winnipeg Manitoba R3H 0W9 Canada. **Tel** (204)945-6786. **DD** 016.3337/097127. ***Continues*** *Manitoba. Dept. of Northern Affairs. Publications List, 0708-1839.*

●US/1072-3129
QUAD REPORT, THE. (1992)-. English. mo. $395.00 without updates; $590.00 with updates. Consumer Energy Council of the American Research Foundation, 2000 L Street Northwest, Suite 802, Washington DC 20036. **Tel** (202)659-0404, FAX (202)659-0407. **ED** Kennedy Maize.
Desc: Articles deal with energy efficiency and its relation to other environmental issues. Also provides news of events concerning energy efficiency.

CN/0705-6923
QUEBEC VERT. **Added/Corp** Federation Interdisciplinaire de l'Horticulture Ornementale du Quebec. Vol. 1 (May 1978)-. Newsletter. French. Twelve times a year. 32.89Can$ regular; 28.56Can$ student. Editions Versicolores Inc., 1320 Boulevard Saint-Joseph, A Marchand Quebec, G2K 1G2 Quebec, Canada. **Tel**

Environmental Issues —Conservation and Natural Resources

(418)628-8690, (800)463-1576, FAX (418)628-0524. **ED** Rolf Bramann. **DD** 635/.05. Index available (free). **Bk Rev. Ad Acc. Circ:** 250 (ctrl). *Supersedes Fleuriste du Quebec, 0380-3163.*
Desc: Newsletter of the Green Party. Devoted to the protection of the environment and fighting the nuclear threat (nuclear power and nuclear weapons).

CN/0712-4600
RAPPORT ANNUEL / COMMISSION DE PROTECTION DU TERRITOIRE AGRICOLE DU QUEBEC. [Rapp. annu. - Comm. prot. territ. agric. Que.]. **Main/Corp** Commission de Protection du Territoire Agricole du Quebec. French. an. Editeur Officiel du Quebec, 1283 Boul Charest Ouest, Quebec Quebec G1N 2C9 Canada. **LC** HD319.Q3; C65A. **DD** 354.7140082/326.

CN/0228-9113
RAPPORT ANNUEL - MINISTERE DE L'ENERGIE ET DES RESSOURCES (QUEBEC). (RAPPORT ANNUEL / MINISTERE DE L'ENERGIE ET DES RESSOURCES.). [Rapp. annu. - Minist. energ. ressour.]. **Main/Corp** Quebec (Province). Ministere de l'Energie et des Ressources. (1980)-. French. an. Price varies. Les Publications du Quebec, CP 1190, Outremont Quebec H2V 4S7 Canada. **Tel** (514)948-1222, (800)463-2100, FAX (514)278-3030. **LC** HD9502.C33; Q444a. **DD** 354.7140082/3. *Continues Quebec (Province). Ministere des Richesses Naturelles. Rapport Annuel, 0703-0940; Quebec (Province). Ministere des Terres et Forets. Rapport Annuel, 0703-4938.*

CN
RAPPORT ANNUEL - QUEBEC (PROVINCE). DEPT. OF NATURAL RESOURCES. **Main/Corp** Quebec (Province). Dept. of Natural Resources. Periodical. French. an. Department of Natural Resources / Quebec Canada, 1640 Boul del Entente, Quebec Quebec G1S 4N6 Canada. **LC** HC117.Q4; A26. **DD** 354/.714/008232.

US/1048-8030
RAPTOR REPORT. See Zoology-Ornithology.

SW/0349-6287
RAW MATERIALS REPORT. [Raw mater. rep.]. **Added/Corp** Raw Materials Group. Vol. 1, No. 1 (Autumn 1981)-. Periodical. English. qt. $150.00 (individuals), $75.00 (institutions). Raw Materials Report, PO Box 90103, S 120 21 Stockholm Sweden. **Tel** 011 46 8 6427577, FAX 011 46 8 6401187. **ED** Olle af Geijerstam. **LC** HF1051; .R36. **DD** 333.7/05. Index available. cum. index. **Bk Rev. Ad Acc. Pr Rev. Circ:** 1,000. available on microfilm and microfiche from University Microfilms International (UMI).
Desc: Political economy of natural resources, mainly metallic minerals. Focusing on problems of ownership, control and Third World mineral policies.
Ind/Abst Altern. Press Index; Alum. Ind. Abstr.; Eng. Mater. Abstr.; Geogr. Abstr. Human Geogr.; GeoRef; Int. Dev. Abstr.; Met. Abstr.; PAIS Int. Print; Rural Dev. Abstr.

US
REGION II REPORT. **Main/Corp** United States. Environmental Protection Agency. Region II. Periodical. English. Environmental Protection Agency / New York, 26 Federal Plaza, New York NY 10007.

US/1055-9922
REMOTE SENSING OF EARTH RESOURCES (ALBUQUERQUE, N.M.), THE. *Ceased.* See Physics.

US/0738-6532
RENEWABLE RESOURCES JOURNAL. [Renew. resour. j.]. **Added/Corp** Renewable Natural Resources Foundation (U.S.). Vol. 1, No. 2 & 3 (Fall 1982 & Winter 1983)-. Periodical. English. qt. $19.00 (individuals), $36.00 (institutions). Renewable Natural Resource Foundation, 5430 Grosvenor Lane/Suite 220, Bethesda MD 20814. **Tel** (301)493-9101. **ED** Robert D. Day and Watson Fenimore. **DD** 363. **CODEN** RRJOEP. *Continues Resources Evaluation Journal, 0734-2098.*
Desc: Academic-style articles and reports of activities of member groups.
Ind/Abst BioBusiness (1990-); Curr. Aware. Biol. Sci., CABS; Environ. Period. Bibliogr.; Fish Rev.; GeoRef; J. Plan. Lit.; Pollut. Abstr. Indexes; Wildl. Rev.

CN
REPERTOIRE DES PUBLICATIONS. **Main/Corp** Quebec (Province). Dept. of Natural Resources. French. Department of Natural Resources / Quebec Canada, 1640 Boul del Entente, Quebec Quebec G1S 4N6 Canada. **LC** Z7761.N3; Q42A. **DD** 016.55714.

KE
REPORT. **Main/Corp** Kenya National Park's Trustees. (1950)-. English. Kenya National Parks Trustees, Nairobi Kenya Africa. **LC** SB484.; .K424. **DD** 916.76.

US/0274-502X
REPORT - AUDUBON SOCIETY OF RHODE ISLAND. **Main/Corp** Audubon Society of Rhode Island. **VFOAT** Audubon Society of Rhode Island Report. (19??)-. Periodical. English. Six times a year (Jan., Mar., May, July, Sept., Nov.). $10.00. Audubon Society of Rhode Island, 12 Sanderson Road, Smithfield RI 02917. **Tel** (401)949-5454, FAX (401)949-5788. **ED** Deborah Poor. **Bk Rev,** (Qty: 2). **Ad Acc. Circ:** 4,500 (ctrl).
Desc: Birdlife, bird records, natural history, environmental issues in Rhode Island. Refuge programs and events for members and general public. Society affairs.

AT
REPORT - DEPARTMENT OF THE ENVIRONMENT AND CONSERVATION. See Environmental Issues.

US
REPORT - ILLINOIS NATURE PRESERVES COMMISSION. **Main/Corp** Illinois Nature Preserves Commission. 1977-78-. English. be. Illinois Nature Preserve Commission, 524 South 2nd Street, Springfield IL 62706. **LC** QH76.5.I5; A3. **DD** 353.97730082/32. *Continues Two-Year Report (Illinois Nature Preserve Commission).*
Desc: Description and status of Illinois nature preserves system.

AT
REPORT - NATIONAL PARKS AUTHORITY OF W.A. **Main/Corp** Western Australia. National Parks Authority. **VFOAT** Annual Report - National Parks Authority, Western Australia. 1976/77-. English. **LC** SB484.A9; A34. **DD** 354/.941/008232.

US/0147-3263
REPORT OF ACCOMPLISHMENTS, RHODE ISLAND. See Agriculture.

US
REPORT OF INVESTIGATIONS (WASHINGTON STATE). DIVISION OF GEOLOGY AND EARTH RESOURCES. See Earth Sciences-Geology.

NZ
REPORT OF THE NATURE CONSERVATION COUNCIL FOR THE YEAR ENDED 31 MARCH ... . **Main/Corp** Nature Conservation Council (N.Z.). English. an. **LC** QH77.N45; N36A. **DD** 354.9310082/32.

UK
REPORT OF THE NATURE RESERVES COMMITTEE. **Main/Corp** Northern Ireland. Nature Reserves Committee. English. **LC** QH77.N58; N67A. **DD** 354/.416/008232.

RH
REPORT OF THE SECRETARY FOR LANDS - RHODESIA, SOUTHERN. **Main/Corp** Rhodesia, Southern. Ministry of Lands. 1968-. English. Salisbury Ministry of Lands, Publications Office, POB 8062 Causeway, Harare Zimbabwe. **LC** HD989.R45; A35. **DD** 333.7/09689/1. *Supersedes in part Rhodesia, Southern. Report of the Secretary for Mines and Lands.*

AT
REPORT ON ACTIVITIES / DEPARTMENT OF RESOURCES DEVELOPMENT, GOVERNMENT OF WESTERN AUSTRALIA. **Main/Corp** Western Australia. Dept. of Resources Development. (19??)-. English. an. **LC** HC607.W47; W474a. **DD** 354.9410082/3/06.

AT
REPORT - VICTORIA, AUSTRALIA. NATIONAL PARKS ADVISORY COMMITTEE. **Main/Corp** Victoria, Australia. National Parks Advisory Committee. English. Melbourne Government Printer, 232 Victoria Parade, East Melbourne 3002 Australia. **Tel** 03 628 5777, FAX 03 628 5631. **LC** SB484.A9; V47A. **DD** 354/.94/00863.

AT/1032-0407
REPORT - WOOD UTILISATION RESEARCH CENTRE, DEPARTMENT OF CONSERVATION AND LAND MANAGEMENT. See Forestry-Lumber and Wood.

US/0486-5553
REPRINT - RESOURCES FOR THE FUTURE. **Main/Corp** Resources for the Future, Inc. **VFOAT** R.F.F. Reprint. No. 1- 1958?-. Monographic series. English. qt. Price varies per volume. 1616 P Street NW, Washington DC 20036. **Tel** (202)328-5000. **DD** 333.7. Index available. **Circ:** 18,000 (ctrl).

US
RESEARCH ACCOMPLISHMENTS - WILDLIFE RESEARCH CENTER (DENVER). (RESEARCH ACCOMPLISHMENTS - WILDLIFE RESEARCH CENTER.). **Main/Corp** Wildlife Research Center, Denver. Periodical. English. US Fish & Wildlife Service, Denver Wildlife Research Center, Denver CO 80225. **DD** 333.7. *Continues Research Accomplishments - Wildlife Research Laboratory, 0502-5699.*

US/0500-2230
RESEARCH AND DEVELOPMENT PROGRESS REPORT / OFFICE OF SALINE WATER. [Res. dev. prog. rep. - U. S., Off. Saline Water]. **VFOAT** Saline Water Research and Development Progress Report; Saline Water Conversion Progress Report. No. 1 (1954)-. Government Publication. English. US Department of the Interior, Washington DC 20241. **DD** 551. **CODEN** XISWAP. Documents available from CASDDS.
Desc: No. 47-A new progress for the production of fresh water from sea water, by Hans Svanoe (and others).
Ind/Abst Chem. Abstr. (1954-1973).

UK/0952-4738
RESEARCH & SURVEY IN NATURE CONSERVATION. [Res. surv. nat. conserv.]. **VFOAT** Research and Survey in Nature Conservation; Research and Survey in Nature Conservation Series. (1985)-. English. ir.
Ind/Abst Agrofor. Abstr.; For. Abstr.; Grasslands For. Abstr.; Weed Abstr.

AT/1032-8106
RESEARCH BULLETIN - DEPARTMENT OF CONSERVATION AND LAND MANAGEMENT WESTERN AUSTRALIA. (RESEARCH BULLETIN.). [Res. bull. - Dep. Conserv. Land Manage. West. Aust.]. **Added/Corp** Western Australia. Dept. of Conservation and Land Management. Vol. 2 (Nov. 1988)-. Bulletin. English. Price varies per volume. Department of Conservation and Land Management, PO Box 104, Corp Relations Division, Como WA 6152 Australia. **Tel** 011 61 09 3670333. Documents available from BIOSIS Document Express. *Continues Bulletin (Western Australia. Dept. of Conservation and Land Management), 0816-9675.*
Ind/Abst Biol. Abstr. (1988-); Ecol. Abstr.

US
RESEARCH BULLETIN - PENNSYLVANIA GAME COMMISSION. **Main/Corp** Pennsylvania. Game Commission. No. 2 (1939)-. Bulletin. English. Price varies per volume. Pennsylvania Game Commission, 2001 Elmerton Avenue, Harrisburg PA 17110-9797. **Tel** (717)787-3745, FAX (717)772-0542. **LC** SK441; .A38. **DD** 799.09748. *Continues Research Bulletin - Board of Game Commissioners, Commonwealth of Pennsylvania.*

US/0192-8376
RESEARCH OUTLOOK / UNITED STATES ENVIRONMENTAL PROTECTION AGENCY, RESEARCH AND DEVELOPMENT. Began with 3rd (1978). English. an. US Environmental Protection Agency, 401 M Street SW, Washington DC 20460. **Tel** (202)755-9163. **LC** TD178.6; .U54A. **DD** 363.7/00973. **NLM** W2 A E43R. *Continues Environmental Research Outlook, 0147-4456.*

TZ
RESEARCH PAPER (CHUO KIKUU CHA DAR ES SALAAM. BUREAU OF RESOURCE ASSESSMENT AND LAND USE PLANNING). *Title Change.* (RESEARCH PAPER - BUREAU OF RESOURCE ASSESSMENT AND LAND USE PLANNING, THE UNIVERSITY OF DAR ES SALAAM.). **Main/Corp** University of Dar es Salaam. Bureau of Resource Assessment and Land Use Planning. **VFOAT** Bralup Research Paper. No. 12- 1970-. Periodical. English. ir. Studies in Adult Education, PO Box 20679, Institute of Adult Education, Dar es Salaam Tanzania. **Tel** 011 255 51 25211. **LC** HD107. *Continues Research Paper - dar es Salaam University College Bureau of Resource Assessment and Land Use Planning. Continued by Research Paper (Chuo Kikuu Cha Dar Es Salaam. Institute of Resource Assessment).*
Ind/Abst GeoRef.

US/0079-063X
RESEARCH PUBLICATION. [Res. publ. - Inst. Res. Land Water Resour. Pa. State Univ.]. **Main/Corp** Pennsylvania State University. Institute of Research on Land and Water Resources. No. 50 (July 1967)-. Monographic series. English. ir. Price varies per volume. Penn State University Environmental Resources Research Institute, University Park PA 16802. **DD** 333.7. **CODEN** RPILDU. *Formed by the union of Water Resources Research Publication and Research Report - Institute for Research on Land and Water Resources.*
Ind/Abst EMBASE; GeoRef.

US/0501-7467
RESEARCH REPORT - UNITED STATES DEPARTMENT OF THE INTERIOR, BUREAU OF RECLAMATION. (RESEARCH REPORT - BUREAU OF RECLAMATION.). [Res. rep. - U. S. Dep. Inter., Bur. Reclam.]. **Main/Corp** United States. Bureau of Reclamation. **Added/Corp** United States. Bureau of Reclamation. **VFOAT** Research Report. No. 1 (1963)-. Monographic series. English. ir. Price varies per volume. Bureau of Reclamation, PO Box 25007, Denver CO 80225. **Tel** (303)234-3000. **LC** TC801; .U12. **DD** 627/.5/08. **CODEN** RRBRDR.
Ind/Abst GeoRef.

US/0084-0556
RESEARCH REPORT - WISCONSIN. DEPT. OF NATURAL RESOURCES. (RESEARCH REPORT - DEPARTMENT OF NATURAL RESOURCES.). [Res. rep. - Wis., Dep. Nat. Resour.]. **Main/Corp** Wisconsin. Dept. of Natural Resources. Monographic series. English. ir. Price varies per volume. Department of Natural Resources / Wisconsin, Bureau of Research, PO Box 7921, Madison WI 53707. **Tel** (608)266-2121. **ED** Betty Les and Stefanie Brouwer. **LC** S916.W6; A32. **DD** 333. **Pr Rev. Circ:** 500 (ctrl). ***Continues** Research Report - Research and Planning Division.*
Desc: Presents results of studies conducted by research scientists in the Wisconsin Department of Natural Resources. Topics include: fisheries, wildlife ecology, water resources management, and environmental pollution.
Ind/Abst GeoRef; Life Sci. Collect.

UK/0143-0386
RESEARCH REPORTS DIGEST / NATURE CONSERVANCY COUNCIL. **Added/Corp** Nature Conservancy Council (Great Britain). Information & Library Services. (197?)-. English.

US/0887-7130
RESOURCE BULLETIN NC. (RESOURCE BULLETIN NC / UNITED STATES DEPARTMENT OF AGRICULTURE, FOREST SERVICE, NORTH CENTRAL FOREST EXPERIMENT STATION.). [Resour. bull. NC]. **VAT** Resource Bulletin North Central. No. 56 (1981)-. Bulletin. English. Price varies per volume. US Department of Agriculture / North Central Forest Experiment Station, St. Paul MN. **DD** 338. ***Continues** USDA Forest Service Resource Bulletin NC, 0363-6097.*
Ind/Abst For. Prod. Abstr.; For. Abstr.; Life Sci. Collect.

US/0887-4832
RESOURCE BULLETIN SO. **See** Forestry.

UK/0142-2391
RESOURCE MANAGEMENT AND OPTIMIZATION. [Resour. manage. optim.]. Vol. 1, No. 1 (Feb. 1980)-. Academic Scholarly Publication. English. Four times a year. $508.00 (university and hospital libraries), $792.00 other. Harwood Academic Publishers, PO Box 90, Reading RG1 8JL England. **Tel** 011 44 734 560080. **ED** William B. Morgan. **LC** HC10; .R327. **DD** 333.7/05. **CODEN** RMOPDH. **[CCC].** Index available. **Bk Rev. Ad Acc.** Documents available from Article Express International, BIOSIS Document Express, Ask*IEEE, Documents on Demand.
Desc: Interdisciplinary and international exchanges of knowledge concerning resource management.
Ind/Abst AGRICOLA [Select. Cov.]; Agrofor. Abstr.; Bioeng. Abstr.; Biol. Abstr.; Ei Page One; EMBASE; Eng. Index Annu.; Environ. Abstr.; Environ. Period. Bibliogr.; Field Crop Abstr.; Fish Rev. (Jan. 1989-July 1992); For. Prod. Abstr.; For. Abstr.; Grasslands For. Abstr.; INSPEC (1980-); Int. Dev. Abstr. (?-?); Life Sci. Collect.; Soils Fert.; Wildl. Rev. (Jan. 1989-July 1992).

CN
RESOURCE MANAGEMENT REPORT. **Main/Corp** Ontario. Fish and Wildlife Branch. (19??)-. English. **LC** SK471.O5; O57a. **DD** 639/.9/09713.

US/0163-4801
RESOURCE PUBLICATION - U.S. FISH AND WILDLIFE SERVICE. (RESOURCE PUBLICATION / UNITED STATES DEPARTMENT OF THE INTERIOR, FISH AND WILDLIFE SERVICE.). (1975)-. Monographic series. English. ir. Price varies per volume. Fish and Wildlife Service, Office of Information Transfer, 1025 Pennock Place/Suite 212, Fort Collins CO 80524. **Tel** (303)493-8401. **LC** S914; .A3. **DD** 639/.9/08. **CODEN** RPFWDE. Index available. cum. index. **Pr Rev. Circ:** 3,000 (ctrl). available in microform (from U.S. Department of Commerce, National Technical Information Services). ***Continues** Resource Publication (United States. Bureau of Sport Fisheries and Wildlife), 0565-0720.*
Desc: Semitechnical or instructional materials, lengthy reports, or material that requires numerous half-tone or color illustrations. Typical products are guides, handbooks, bibliographies, manuals, historical reports, popular articles, and proceedings of non-technical workshops or conferences.
Ind/Abst Ecol. Abstr.; Fish Rev. (19??-199?); Geogr. Abstr. Phys. Geogr.; Key Word Index Wildl. Res.; Wildl. Rev. (19??-199?).

US/0548-0825
RESOURCE REPORT / UNIVERSITY OF NEBRASKA CONSERVATION AND SURVEY DIVISION. **Added/Corp** University of Nebraska--Lincoln. Conservation and Survey Division. No. 1, (Feb. 1968)-. Monographic series. English. ir. Price varies per volume. University of Nebraska - Lincoln, 901 North 17th Street, 113 Nebraska Hall, Lincoln NE 80517. **Tel** (402)472-3471. **ED** Charles Flowerday.
Desc: Earth Science topics about Nebraska.

US/8755-1918
RESOURCE REVIEW (ANCHORAGE, ALASKA). (RESOURCE REVIEW / RESOURCE DEVELOPMENT COUNCIL FOR ALASKA INC.). [Resour. rev.]. Periodical. English. mo. $50.00. Resource Development Council for Alaska, Box 100516, Anchorage AK 99510. **Tel** (907)276-0700. **ED** Carl Portman. **DD** 338. **Ad Acc. Circ:** 2,000.
Desc: Reviews resource development projects in Alaska or roadblocks for development of such projects.
Ind/Abst GeoRef.

KE
RESOURCES. **Added/Corp** Kenya Energy and Environment Organizations. Vol. 1 No. 1 (June 1989)-. Periodical. English. Three times a year. $27.00 Europe; $30.00 US; $25.00 others. Kengo, PO Box 48197, Nairobi Kenya. **Tel** 011 254 2 749747 748281. **LC** HC865.Z65; R47. **DD** 333.7/096762/05.
Ind/Abst Agrofor. Abstr.; For. Prod. Abstr. (1991-); For. Abstr.; Hortic. Abstr.; Seed Abstr.; Weed Abstr.

NE/0921-3449
RESOURCES, CONSERVATION AND RECYCLING. [Resour. conserv. recycl.]. Vol. 1, No. 1 (Mar. 1988)-. Academic Scholarly Publication. English. Twelve times a year (3 volumes). Fl1464.00. Elsevier Science Publishers BV, PO Box 211, 1000 AE Amsterdam Netherlands. **Tel** 011 31 20 5803642, FAX 011 31 20 5862696, telex 15682. **LC** TD794.5; .R4587. **DD** 363.72/82/05. **CODEN** RCREEW. **[CCC]. Pr Rev.** available on microfilm and microfiche from University Microfilms International (UMI). Documents available from Article Express International, The Genuine Article, BIOSIS Document Express, CASDDS. ***Formed by the union of** Resources and Conservation, 0166-3097 **and** Conservation & Recycling, 0361-3658.*
Ind/Abst AgBiotech News Inf.; Biodeter. Abstr. (19??-19??); Biol. Abstr.; Chem. Abstr.; Curr. Aware. Biol. Sci., CABS; Curr. Contents, Agric. Biol. Environ. Sci.; Curr. Contents Eng. Tech. Appl. Sci.; Dairy Sci. Abstr.; EMBASE; Energy Inf. Abstr.; Eng. Index Annu.; Environ. Period. Bibliogr.; Food Sci. Technol. Abstr.; Gas Abstr.; Geogr. Abstr. Human Geogr. (1988-); Geol. Abstr.; Grasslands For. Abstr.; Health Saf. Sci. Abstr.; Int. Dev. Abstr.; Int. Packag. Abstr.; Leadscan; Pap. Board Abstr.; Pig News Inf.; Pollut. Abstr. Indexes; Res. Alert [Select. Cov.]; Soils Fert.; Soyabean Abstr.; Sug. Indus. Abstr.; Weed Abstr.

UK/0301-4207
RESOURCES POLICY. [Resour. policy]. Vol. 1 (Sept. 1974)-. Periodical. English. qt. $358.00 The Americas; £240.00 other. Butterworth Heinemann Publishers, Linacre House, Jordan Hill, Oxford OX2 8DP England. **Tel** 011 44 865 310366. **(Subscription address:** Elsevier Science Ltd. Oxford Fulfillment Centre, PO Box 800, Kidlington, Oxford OX5 1DX United Kingdom.) **ED** Roderick G. Eggert. **LC** TN1; .R38. **DD** 333.8/05. **CODEN** RSPCAM. **[CCC].** Index available. **Bk Rev. Ad Acc. Pr Rev. Circ:** 3,500 (ctrl). available on microfilm and microfiche from University Microfilms International (UMI). Documents available from Article Express International, The Genuine Article, CASDDS.
Desc: Provides a forum which brings together the different disciplines involved in the study of raw materials, policy and planning. It serves an international readership drawn from academic, government, industrial and commercial quarters.
Ind/Abst AESIS Q.; Alum. Ind. Abstr.; Bioeng. Abstr.; Chem. Abstr.; Coal Abstr.; Contents Recent Econ. J.; Curr. Contents Soc. Behav. Sci.; Econ. Lit. Index; Ei Page One; EMBASE; Energy Inf. Abstr.; Energy Res. Abstr. (Aug. 1976-); Eng. Mater. Abstr.; Eng. Index Annu.; Gas Abstr.; Geogr. Abstr. Human Geogr.; Geol. Abstr.; GeoRef; Int. Bibliogr. Sociol.; Int. Dev. Abstr.; J. Plan. Lit.; Leadscan; Met. Abstr.; PAIS Int. Print; Life Sci. Collect.; Res. Alert [Full Cov.]; Soc. Sci. Cit. Index [Full Cov.]; World Ceram. Abstr.

US/0048-7376
RESOURCES (WASHINGTON, D.C. 1959). (RESOURCES.). [Resources]. **Added/Corp** Resources for the Future. No. 1 (May 1959)-. Periodical. English. qt. Free. Resources for the Future, 1616 P Street Northwest, Washington DC 20036. **Tel** (202)328-5025. **ED** Jo Hinkel and Kent A. Price. **LC** WMLC L 83/1757. **NLM** W1 RE247. **Bk Rev. Circ:** 25,000. available on microfilm and microfiche from University Microfilms International (UMI). Documents available from Documents on Demand.
Desc: Succinct timely articles on RFF work in progress and analysis of world developments in natural resources, food and agriculture policy, energy, and the quality of the environment.
Ind/Abst Abstr. Bull. Inst. Pap. Sci. Tech.; Energy Inf. Abstr.; Energy Res. Abstr. (Sept. 1975-); Environ. Abstr.; Environ. Period. Bibliogr.; F&S Index Plus Text, Int. [Select. Cov.]; Index Free Period.; J. Plan. Lit.; PAIS Int. Print; Pollut. Abstr. Indexes; Risk Abstr.

US/0733-0707
RESTORATION & MANAGEMENT NOTES. (RESTORATION & MANAGEMENT NOTES / THE UNIVERSITY OF WISCONSIN-MADISON ARBORETUM.). [Restor. manage. notes]. **Added/Corp** University of Wisconsin--Madison. Arboretum. Society for Ecological Restoration and Management. Society for Ecological Restoration. **VFOAT** Restoration and Management Notes. Vol. 1, No. 1 (June 1981)-. Periodical. English. sa. $56.00 (one year), $110.00 (two year), $163.00 (three year), institution; $21.00 (one year), $42.00 (two year), $63.00 (three year), individuals. University of Wisconsin Press, Journal Division, 114 North Murray Street, Madison WI 53715. **Tel** (608)262-4952, FAX (608)262-8909. **ED** William R. Jordan III. **LC** QH76; .R47. **DD** 333.7/2/0973. **[CCC]. Bk Rev. Ad Acc. Circ:** 1,400. available on microfilm from University Microfilms International (UMI).
Desc: A forum for the exchange of news, views, and information among ecologists, land reclamationists, managers of parks, preserves and rights- of-way, naturalists, engineers, landscape architects and others committed to the restoration and wise stewardship of plant and animal communities. Contains timely feature articles and current notes.
Ind/Abst Environ. Period. Bibliogr.; Fish Rev.; Garden Lit. (1992-); J. Plan. Lit.; Wildl. Rev.

NZ/0114-7366
REVIEW (NEW ZEALAND MOUNTAIN LANDS INSTITUTE). [Rev. - N.Z. Mount. Lands. Inst.]. **Added/Corp** New Zealand Mountain Lands Institute. **VFOAT** Journal of the New Zealand Mountain Lands Institute. 46 (Dec. 1989)-. Periodical. English. Lincoln College, Box 56, Canterbury New Zealand. **Tel** 03-252811, FAX 643 252944. ***Continues** Review (Tussock Grasslands and Mountain Lands Institute), 0577-9898.*

UK
REVIEW : THE QUARTERLY JOURNAL OF RENEWABLE ENERGY. **See** Energy.

FR/0249-7395
REVUE D'ECOLOGIE. **See** Environmental Issues-Ecology.

BL/0101-7616
ROESSLERIA. [Roessleria]. V. 1-. Periodical. Portuguese. sa. Instituto de Pesquisas de Recursos Naturais Renovaeis, rua Goncalves Dias 570, Porto Alegre 90000 Brazil. **Tel** (0512)33 56 87, telex MAEE BR 0511211. **ED** Jane M de O Vasconcellos. **LC** QH77.B7; R63. Index available. **Bk Rev. Circ:** 600 (ctrl).
Ind/Abst AGRICOLA.

UK
RSPB BIRD LIFE. **See** Zoology-Ornithology.

UK
RSPB CONSERVATION REVIEW. No. 1 (1987)-. English. an. £5.00. Royal Society for the Protection of Birds, The Lodge, Sandy Bedfordshire SG19 2DL England.

II
SANCTUARY ASIA. **VFOAT** Sanctuary. Vol. 1 (Oct./Dec. 1981)-. Periodical. English. qt. Rs50.00. Madhu Sahgal Sanctuary Magazine, 7 Union Co-Op Insurance Building, Sir P M Road, Bombay 400 001 India. **Tel** 230061-230081. **ED** Bittu Sahgal. **LC** QL300; .S26. **DD** 591.95. **Bk Rev. Ad Acc. Circ:** 27,000.
Desc: Conservation and natural resources; zoology; vertebrate and invertebrate.
Ind/Abst Fish Rev. (19??-199?); Wildl. Rev. (19??-199?).

US/0272-8966
SANCTUARY (LINCOLN, MASS.). **See** Natural History.

CN/1185-4839
SASKATCHEWAN GAME MANAGEMENT. **See** Recreation, Leisure-Outdoor Life.

CN/1186-8090
SASKATCHEWAN STATE OF THE ENVIRONMENT REPORT. [Sask. state environ. rep.]. **Added/Corp** Saskatchewan. Saskatchewan Environment and Public Safety. (June 1991)-. English. Saskatchewan Environment and Public Safety, 1855 Victoria Avenue/5th Floor, Regina Saskatchewan 54P 3V5 Canada. **DD** 333.7/2/097124.

CN/0713-5866
SAVE THE BULKLEY NEWSLETTER. [Save Bulkley newsl.]. Vol. 1, No. 1 (Nov. 1979)-. Newsletter. English. ir. Free to Members. Save the Bulkley, Box 2781, Smithers British Columbia V0J 2N0 Canada. **DD** 333.91/6216/097112.

NE/0925-1413
SCAN (WAGENINGEN). (SCAN.). [Scan]. **Added/Corp** Staring Centrum, Instituut voor Onderzoek van het Landelijk Gebied. No. 1 (1990)-. English. **Ind/Abst** Rice Abstr.; Soils Fert.

GW
SCHRIFTENREIHE FUER LANDSCHAFTSPFLEGE UND NATURSCHUTZ. **Added/Corp** Bundesanstalt fuer Vegetationskunde, Naturschutz und Landschaftspflege. No. 1 (1966)-. Monographic series. German. Price varies per volume. **LC** QH77.G3; S35. **DD** 333.7,2.

SZ
SCHWEIZER NATURSCHUTZ = PROTECTION DE LA NATURE. **Added/Corp** Schweizerischer Bund fur Naturschutz. **VFOAT** Protection de la Nature. No. 1 (Feb. 1935)-. Periodical. German (French). Eight times a year. 46.00F. Swiss League Protect of Nature, CP 73 Wartenbergstrasse 22, CH-4020 Basel Switzerland. **Tel** 011 41 61 427442. ***Continues*** *Schweizerische Blatter fur Naturschutz.*

CN/1011-1603
SEA WIND. (SEA WIND : BULLETIN OF THE INTERNATIONAL MARINELIFE ALLIANCE.). [Sea wind]. **Added/Corp** International Marinelife Alliance. (Jan./Mar. 1987)-. Bulletin. English (French and Spanish; summaries and/or abstracts in French). Four times a year. $50.00. Ocean Voice International, 2883 Otterson Drive, Ottawa Ontrio K1V 7B2 Canada. **Tel** (613)990-8819, FAX (613)521-4205. **ED** Don McAllister. **DD** 551.46/005. Index available. **Bk Rev. Circ:** 500.
Desc: Shares fisherpeople and scientific knowledge about sea life, conservation and equitable sustainable marine harvesting.

US/8755-4682
SEICHE, THE. [Seiche]. **Added/Corp** Minnesota Marine Advisory Service. Lake Superior Basin Studies Center. University of Minnesota. Minnesota Sea Grant Extension Program. VOL. 1 (Fall 1976)-. Newsletter. English. sa. Free on request. Minnesota Sea Grant, 208 Washburn Hall, University of Minnesota Duluth, Duluth MN 55812. **Tel** (218)726-8106. **ED** Alice Tibbetts. **DD** 574. **Circ:** 3,200.
Desc: Newsletter covering research and extension activities related to fisheries, water policy, biotechnology, aquaculture, Great Lakes economics, tourism, water quality and environmental issues.

●JA/0916-9997
SHIGEN TO TANKYO. **Added/Corp** Shigen Kankyo Gijutsu Sogo Kenkyujo (Japan). **VFOAT** Journal of NIRE; Journal of National Institute for Resources and Environment. (May 1992)-. Periodical. Japanese (summaries and/or abstracts in English). qt. National Institute Research Environment, 16 3 Onogawa, Tsukuba Shi Ibaraki 30 Japan. **Tel** 011 81 298 588113, 011 81 298 588114. **LC** GE1; .S47. ***Continues*** *Kogai Shigen Kenkyojo Hijo.*

JA
SHIZEN HOGO KOZA JISSHI HOKOKUSHO. **Main/Corp** Shizen Hogo Koza. Issue No. 1 (1972)-. Japanese. Nature Conservation Society of Japan, Toranomon Denki Building/4F, 2-8-1 Toranomon Minato-ku, Tokyo 105 Japan. **LC** QH77.J3; S536A.

UK
SHOOTING & CONSERVATION. **VFOAT** Shooting and Conservation. Autumn 1981-. Periodical. English. qt. ***Continues*** *WAGBI.*

US/0037-4237
SHORE AND BEACH. (SHORE & BEACH JOURNAL.). [Shore beach]. **Added/Corp** American Shore and Beach Preservation Association. **VFOAT** Shore and Beach. Vol. 1 (Apr. 1933)-. Periodical. English. Four times a year (Jan., Apr., July, Oct.). $40.00 US, Canada, Puerto Rico & Mexico; $52.00 other Comes with American Shore & Beach Preservation Association membership. American Shore & Beach Preservation Association, 3000 Citrus Circle, Suite 230, Walnut Creek CA 94598. **Tel** (415)944-5411. **ED** Robert L. Wiegel. **LC** TC330.A1; A5. **DD** 627/.58/05. **CODEN** SHBEAS. cum. index. **Ad Acc. Circ:** 1,000 (ctrl). Documents available from Article Express International, Documents on Demand.
Desc: A non-profit organization researching the up keep of the beaches across the nation. Dedicated to the preservation and development of shores and beaches.
Ind/Abst AQUAREF; Aquat. Sci. Fish. Abstr. (Computer File); Bioeng. Abstr.; Curr. Geogr. Publ. (199?-); Ei Page One; Eng. Index Annu.; Environ. Abstr.; Environ. Period. Bibliogr.; Fluid Abstr., Civil Eng.; Fluid Abstr. Proc. Eng.; FLUIDEX (1973-); GeoRef; J. Plan. Lit.

JA
SHOSHIGEN/SHOENERUGI GIJUTSU KOGAI BOSHI GIJUTSU RISUTO. Began in 1948. Japanese. Chusho Kigyo Joho Senta, Sankaido Building, 9-13 Akasaka 1-chome, Minato-ku 107 Tokyo Japan. **LC** TD170.94.J3; S47.

CC
SHUI TU PAO CHIH TUNG PAO. **VFOAT** Bulletin of Soil and Water Conservation. (19??)-. Periodical. Chinese. bm. Post Office / China, People's Republic of China. **LC** S622; .S43. **DD** 631.4/05.

US/0161-7362
SIERRA. [Sierra]. **Added/Corp** Sierra Club. Vol. 62, No. 8 (Oct. 1977)-. Periodical. English. Six times a year. $15.00 US; $20.00 other; $4.00 single issue; comes also with Sierra Club membership. Sierra, 730 Polk Street, San Francisco CA 94109. **Tel** (415)923-5656. **(Subscription address:** Neodata, PO Box 2606, Boulder, CO 80322**) ED** Jonathan F. King. **LC** F868.S5; S5. **DD** 910/.5. Index available. **Bk Rev. Ad Acc. Circ:** 445,000. available on microfilm and microfiche from University Microfilms International (UMI); available on CD-ROM; available on diskette. Documents available from UMI Article Clearinghouse, Documents on Demand, Magazine Collection. ***Continues*** *Sierra Club Bulletin, 0037-4725.*
Desc: Features color photography, articles on conservation, energy, outdoor recreation adventures, reports from Washington, regional reports, book reviews, Sierra Club Outings' schedule and much more pertaining to the environment.
Ind/Abst Acad. Abstr. Full Text Elite (March 1984-) [Full Txt.]; Acad. Abstr. (Mar. 1984-); Acad. Ind. [Computer File] (1986-); Acad. Search (Mar. 1984-); AQUAREF; Biol. Dig.; Book Rev. Index; Coal Abstr.; Energy Inf. Abstr.; Energy Res. Abstr. (Oct. 1977-); Environ. Abstr.; Environ. Period. Bibliogr.; Expand. Acad. Index (1986-); Gen. Period. Index (1986-); Gen. Sci. Index; Gen. Sci. Source (Jan. 1988-) [Full Txt.]; GeoRef; Guide Soc. Sci. Relig.; Health Source (Mar. 1984-); INFO-SOUTH Abstr.; Mag. Artic. Summar. Elite (Mar. 1984-) [Full Txt.]; Mag. Artic. Summar. Select (March 1984-) [Full Txt.]; Mag. Artic. Summar. CD-ROM (March 1984-); Mag. Express (1988-) [Full Txt.]; Mag. Index Plus (1989-); Mag. Index Sel. Microfiche (1986-) [Full Txt.]; Mag. Index. Sel. (1986-); Mag. Search; Mid. Search (Mar. 1984-) [Full Txt.]; Newsp. Period. Abstr. (1988-); Read. Guide Abstr. Select Ed.; Read. Guide Period. Lit.; Resource/One Ondisc; Mag. Index (1977-); TOM Gen. Index [Full Txt.]; Vocat. Search (Mar. 1984-) [Full Txt.]; West. Hist. Q.

US/8750-5681
SIERRA CLUB YODELER. Periodical. English. mo. Sierra Club Yodeler, San Francisco Bay Chapter of the Sierra Club, 6014 College Avenue, Oakland CA 94618. **DD** 363. ***Continues*** *Yodeler, 0162-3915.*

BL
SOBREVIVENCIA. No. 1- Sept. 1973-. Periodical. Portuguese. sa. Free. Associacao Gaucha de Protecao Ao Ambiente Natural, Caixa 1996, Porto Alegre Brazil. **Tel** (0512)287352. **ED** Jose Celso A Marques. **LC** QH75.A1; S65. **Ad Acc. Circ:** 2,500 (ctrl).
Desc: Newsletter dealing with top environmental issues in Brazil and throughout the world.

US/0894-1920
SOCIETY & NATURAL RESOURCES. [Soc. nat. resour.]. **VFOAT** Society and Natural Resources. Vol. 1, No. 1 (1988)-. Periodical. English. bm (6 issues). £109.00 UK; $180.00 other. Taylor & Francis Ltd., Rankine Road, Basingstoke Hampshire, RG24 8PR United Kingdom. **Tel** 011 44 256 840366, FAX 011 44 256 479438, telex 858540. **(Subscription address:** Taylor & Francis Inc., 1900 Frost Road, Suite 101, Bristol PA 19007-1598.**) ED** Donald R. Field and Rabel J. Burdge. **LC** HC10; .S625. **DD** 304.2. **CODEN** SNREEI. **[CCC]. Pr Rev.** available on microfilm from University Microfilms International (UMI). Documents available from The Genuine Article, BIOSIS Document Express, Documents on Demand.
Desc: This journal will bring order to the literature on social science research on leisure and recreation. This will help identify future needs and will provide knowledge about natural resource management issues on biological and physical changes resulting from acid rain, biological and genetic diversity in worldwide agriculture, and water resource degradation.
Ind/Abst AGRICOLA [Full Cov.]; Biol. Abstr.; Curr. Contents Soc. Behav. Sci.; Ecol. Abstr.; Ecology Abstr.; Environ. Abstr.; Environ. Period. Bibliogr.; Fish Rev. (Jan. 1989-July 1992); For. Prod. Abstr. (1991-); For. Abstr.; Geogr. Abstr. Human Geogr.; Int. Dev. Abstr.; Leis. Recreat. Tour. Abstr.; Res. Alert [Full Cov.]; Rev. Agric. Entomol.; Risk Abstr.; Rural Dev. Abstr.; Soc. Plann. Policy Dev. Abstr.; Soc. Sci. Cit. Index [Full Cov.]; Soils Fert.; Wildl. Rev. (Jan. 1989-July 1992); World Agric. Econ.

US/0889-2415
SOCM SENTINEL, THE. [SOCM sentinel]. **Added/Corp** Save Our Cumberland Mountains (U.S.). **VAT** Save Our Cumberland Mountains Sentinel. (19??)-. Periodical. English. mo (ten issues per year). comes with membership. Save Our Cumberland Mountains, PO Box 479, Lake City TN 37769. **Tel** (615)426-9455. **DD** 363. **Circ:** 800 (ctrl).
Desc: Describes efforts made by membership to maintain decent quality of life in face of development plans for stripped coal, oil, gas extraction, toxic waste burial, and other land uses inconsistent with residents' intentions.

AT/0810-1434
SOFT TECHNOLOGY. **See** Energy.

CN/0709-504X
SOL (WINNIPEG). **See** Energy.

SA/0379-4369
SOUTH AFRICAN JOURNAL OF WILDLIFE RESEARCH. [S. Afr. j. wildl. res.]. **Added/Corp** Southern African Wildlife Management Association. Foundation for Education, Science, and Technology (South Africa). Bureau for Scientific Publications. **VFOAT** Suid Afrikaanse Tydskrif vir Natuurnavorsing; Wildlife Research; Natuurnavorsing. Vol. 6 (1976)-. Periodical. English (summaries and/or abstracts in Afrikaans). qt. R87.00 South Africa; R90.00 other. Foundation for Education Science & Technology, PO Box 1758, Pretoria 0001 South Africa. **Tel** 011 27 12 3226404, FAX 011 27 12 3207803. **ED** N. Fairall. **LC** SK575.S5; S69a. **CODEN** SAJRDR. **[CCC]. Bk Rev. Pr Rev. Circ:** 850. Documents available from The Genuine Article, BIOSIS Document Express. ***Continues*** *Southern African Wildlife Management Association. Journal of the Southern African Wildlife Management Association.*
Desc: Original research articles on conservation of wildlife by improving knowledge of their physiology and habits.
Ind/Abst Abstr. Anthropol. (19??-); Anim. Behav. Abstr.; Biol. Abstr.; Curr. Aware. Biol. Sci., CABS; Curr. Contents, Agric. Biol. Environ. Sci.; Curr. Ref. Fish Res.; Ecol. Abstr.; Ecology Abstr.; Fish Rev.; For. Abstr.; Geogr. Abstr. Phys. Geogr. (?-?); Geogr. Abstr. Human Geogr.; Grasslands For. Abstr.; Helminthol. Abstr.; Index Vet.; Int. Dev. Abstr.; Key Word Index Wildl. Res.; Life Sci. Collect.; Poult. Abstr.; Res. Alert [Full Cov.]; Rev. Med. Vet. Entomol.; Sci. Cit. Index; SCISEARCH; Seed Abstr.; Soils Fert.; Vet. Bull.; Wildl. Rev.

US/0887-9249
SOUTH CAROLINA OUT-OF-DOORS. [S.C. out doors]. **Added/Corp** South Carolina Wildlife Federation. (19??)-. Periodical. English. Twelve times a year. $25.00 Comes with South Carolina Wildlife Federation membership. South Carolina Wildlife Federation, 715 Woodrow Street, Columbia SC 29205. **Tel** (803)771-4417, FAX (803)771-6120. **ED** Liz Lucas Lee. **DD** 796. **Bk Rev**, (Qty: 2). **Ad Acc. Circ:** 7,000.

US/0038-3198
SOUTH CAROLINA WILDLIFE. **Added/Corp** South Carolina. Wildlife and Marine Resources Dept. South Carolina. Wildlife Resources Dept. Vol. 1 (Winter 1954)-. Periodical. English. bm. $10.00 US; $14.00 other. South Carolina Wildlife, PO Box 167, Columbia SC 29202. **Tel** (803)734-3944. **ED** John E. Davis. **LC** SK1; .S53. **DD** 500.9/.757. **Bk Rev. Circ:** 63,000.
Desc: Dedicated to the education of our people in conservation, protection, and restoration of wildlife and natural resources.

US/0038-3279
SOUTH DAKOTA CONSERVATION DIGEST. Periodical. English. bm. $5.00. South Dakota Game, Fish and Parks Department, 523 East Capitol Avenue, Pierre SD 57501. **Tel** (605)773-3361. **Bk Rev. Circ:** 17,000 (ctrl).
Desc: Articles on game, fish and parks in South Dakota.

AT
SPECIAL PUBLICATION / AUSTRALIAN NATIONAL PARKS AND WILDLIFE SERVICE. **Added/Corp** Australian National Parks and Wildlife Service. 1 (1979)-. Monographic series. English. ir. Price varies per volume. Australian National Parks and Wildlife Service, PO Box 636, Canberra City Australian Capital Territory 2061 Australia. **LC** UNC.

US/0085-0640
SPECIAL PUBLICATION - FLORIDA. BUREAU OF GEOLOGY. **See** Earth Sciences-Geology.

US/0084-8875
SPECIAL REPORT / COLORADO DIVISION OF WILDLIFE. [Spec. rep., Colo. Div. Wildl.]. **Main/Corp** Colorado. Division of Wildlife. **Added/Corp** Colorado. Division of Wildlife. No. 29 (March 1973)-. Monographic series. English. Price varies per volume. **DD** 639. **CODEN** CWSPA7. Documents available from BIOSIS Document Express, CASDDS. ***Continues*** *Colorado Division of Game, Fish and Parks. Special Report.*
Ind/Abst Biol. Abstr.; Chem. Abstr.; Fish Rev.; Key Word Index Wildl. Res.; Wildl. Rev.

US/1016-927X
SPECIES (BROOKFIELD). (SPECIES : NEWSLETTER OF THE SSC.). **Added/Corp** International Union for Conservation of Nature and Natural Resources. Species Survival Commission. **VFOAT** Newsletter of the Species Survival Commission. (Jan. 1986)-. Newsletter. English. Twice a year (June and Dec.). Free to members of the Species Survival Commission; $18.00 other. Species Survival Commission, c/o Chicago Zoological Society, Brookfield IL 60513. **Tel** (708)485-0263 ext 304, FAX (708)485-3532. **ED** Timothy Sullivan (editor's telephone:

Environmental Issues — Conservation and Natural Resources

(708)485-0263 ext.304). **Bk Rev**, (Qty: 5-8). **Circ:** 1000 (ctrl). *Continues Species Survival Commission Newsletter, 1010-1667.*
Desc: Provides leadership for conservation efforts to specific plant and animal groups and contributes technical and scientific counsel to biodiversity conservation projects throughout the world.

US/0172-6161
SPRINGER SERIES ON ENVIRONMENTAL MANAGEMENT. Vol. 1 (1979)-. Monographic series. English. ir. Price varies per volume. Springer-Verlag New York Inc., 175 5th Avenue, New York NY 10010. **Tel** (212)460-1500, telex 232 235 SPB UR. **(Subscription address:** Springer Verlag New York Inc. / for North America, 44 Hartz Way, Secaucus NJ 07096.)
Desc: The study of fisheries, natural waters, and landscape ecology.

US
STATE BAR SECTION REPORT. NATURAL RESOURCES. Main/Corp State Bar of Texas. English. State Bar of Texas, PO Box 12487, Capitol Station, Austin TX 78711. **Tel** (512)463-1411. **LC** KFT1643.A15; S7. **DD** 346.76404/4.

US/0147-7617
STATE OF MONTANA DEPARTMENT OF NATURAL RESOURCES AND CONSERVATION : REPORT ON EXAMINATION OF FINANCIAL STATEMENT. Main/Corp Montana. Office of the Legislative Auditor. English. an. Montana Office of the Legislative Auditor, State Capitol, Helena MT 59601. **LC** HC107.M9; M52A. **DD** 353.9/786/008232.

US
STATE OF NEVADA, DEPARTMENT OF CONSERVATION AND NATURAL RESOURCES, DIVISION OF STATE PARKS AUDIT REPORT. See Public Administration.

US
STATE OF TEXAS/ENVIRONMENTAL PROTECTION AGENCY AGREEMENT FOR FISCAL YEAR ..., THE. English. an. **LC** HC107.T43; E55. **DD** 353.97640082/321/05.

US
STATE PROGRAM OVERVIEWS / U.S. DEPARTMENT OF THE INTERIOR, NATIONAL PARK SERVICE, DIVISION OF STATE PLANS AND GRANTS. English. an. National Park Service, Room 5103/1100 L Street NW, Washington DC 20240. **LC** E151; .S74. **DD** 363.6/9/0973.

US
STATE RESOURCE CONSERVATION AND RECOVERY ACTIVITIES. Main/Corp United States. Office of Solid Waste. State Programs and Resource Recovery Division. English. an. Environmental Protection Agency / Office of Water and Waste Management, Office of Water and Waste Management, 401 M Street SW, Washington DC 20460.

US
STATEWIDE COMPREHENSIVE PLAN FOR FISH AND WILDLIFE ON THE NATIONAL FORESTS IN THE STATE OF OREGON, A. Main/Corp Oregon. Dept. of Fish and Wildlife. English. an. Oregon Department of Fish and Wildlife, PO Box 59, Portland OR 97207. **Tel** (503)229-5400.

US/0073-4594
STATION NOTE - UNIVERSITY OF IDAHO FOREST, WILDLIFE AND RANGE EXPERIMENT STATION. Main/Corp University of Idaho. Forest, Wildlife, and Range Experiment Station. No. 1-. Monographic series. English. ir. Price varies per volume. University of Idaho College of Forestry, Wildlife, and Range Sciences, Moscow ID 83843. **Tel** (208)885-7952. **ED** George H Savage. **Pr Rev. Circ:** 1,000.
Desc: Results of research in fisheries, wildlife, forestry, forest products, range science, wildland recreation management.
Ind/Abst AGRICOLA [Full Cov.]; For. Abstr.

US/0273-1916
STATISTICAL REPORT - STATE OF ALASKA, ALASKA OIL AND GAS CONSERVATION COMMISSION. (STATISTICAL REPORT / STATE OF ALASKA, ALASKA OIL AND GAS CONSERVATION COMMISSION.). **Added/Corp** Alaska Oil and Gas Conservation Commission. (1978)-. Statistical Publication. English. $10.00. Alaska Oil & Gas Conservation Commission, 3001 Porcupine Drive, Anchorage AK 99501. **Tel** (907)279-1433, FAX (907)276-7542. **LC** TN872.A7; A43a. **DD** 333.8/2316/09798. **Pr Rev. Circ:** 500. available on microfiche. *Continues Statistical Report (Alaska. Division of Oil and Gas Conservation), 1059-2261.*

CN/0383-5898
STATISTICS - ONTARIO MINISTRY OF NATURAL RESOURCES. See Environmental Issues-Abstracting, Bibliographies and Statistics.

AU
STEIRISCHE BEITRAGE ZUR ROHSTOFF- UND ENERGIEFORSCHUNG. See Engineering-Mines and Mining Engineering.

GW
STUDIEN ZUM INTERNATIONALEN ROHSTOFFRECHT. See Law.

NZ/0113-0994
STUDIES IN RESOURCE MANAGEMENT. [Stud. resour. manag.]. (1986)-. Monographic series. English. ir. varies. Royal New Zealand Institute of Horticulture, PO Box 12, Lincoln College, Canterbury New Zealand. **Tel** 011 03 252811 ext 788. **DD** 333.709931. **Bk Rev. Circ:** 300. available in print.
Desc: A variety of volumes focusing on issues in resource management, and environmental policy.

UK
STUDY REPORT / INTERNATIONAL COUNCIL FOR BIRD PRESERVATION. See Zoology-Ornithology.

CN/0840-4666
SUSTAINABLE DEVELOPMENT. Ceased. (SUSTAINABLE DEVELOPMENT : A CONSERVATION AND PROTECTION NEWSLETTER.). [Sustain. dev.]. Vol. 9, No. 2, Aug. (1988)-?. Newsletter. English (French). Three times a year. Canadian Wildlife Service Publications, Environment Canada, Ottawa Ontario K1A 0E7 Canada. **Tel** (819)997-1095, FAX (819)997-0547. **(Subscription address:** Sustainable Development Branch, c/o E Neville Ward, Environment Canada, Ottawa Ontario K1A 0H3 Canada) **ED** E Neville Ward. **DD** 333/.00971. **Pr Rev. Circ:** 10,000. *Continues Land (Ottawa, Ont.), 0707-9850.*
Desc: A newsletter devoted to articles on all aspects of sustainable development and the environment.

SW/0039-6974
SVERIGES NATUR. [Sver. nat.]. 1943-. Periodical. Swedish. ir. Kr46.00. SNF Etc, Kungsholms Strand 125 112, 34 Stockholm Sweden. **LC** QH169; .S96. **CODEN** SVNAA4. Documents available from BIOSIS Document Express.
Ind/Abst Biol. Abstr.; Fish Rev.; Wildl. Rev.

CH
TA TZU JAN (TAIPEI, TAIWAN). (TA TZU JAN.). **VFOAT** Nature. V. 72- (Oct. 25, 1983)-. Periodical. Chinese. qt. NT$360.00. Li Ming Shu Pao She, Taipei Taiwan. **LC** QH77.T28; T3. **DD** 333.7/2/0951249.

US/0894-833X
TALKING LEAVES (WARRENVILLE, ILL.). (TALKING LEAVES : A SEASONAL JOURNAL OF THE INSTITUTE FOR EARTH EDUCATION.). **Added/Corp** Institute for Earth Education. (19??)-. Periodical. English. qt. $25.00 individual; $35.00 institution (comes with membership to Institute for Earth Education). Institute for Earth Education, Cedar Grove, Greenville WV 24945. **Tel** (304)832-6404. **ED** Laurie Farber. **DD** 363. **Bk Rev**, (Qty: 4-8).
Desc: Official international journal of the Institute of Earth Education. Its purpose is to provide ongoing clarification of the Institute's goals and methods, to serve as a vehicle for announcing programs and events, and to share ideas and insights with the Institute's worldwide network of members and representatives.

CN/0706-4152
TECHNICAL BULLETIN - CANADIAN CONSERVATION INSTITUTE. [Tech. bull. - Can. Conserv. Inst.]. **VFOAT** Bulletin Technique. **VAT** Fiche Technique - Institut Canadien de Conservation; Bulletin Technique - Institut Canadien de Conservation. (Edition Anglaise et Francaise). 1 (1975)-. Bulletin. English (summaries and/or abstracts in French). ir. Price varies per volume. Canadian Conservation Institute, National Museums of Canada, Ottawa Ontario K1A 0M8 Canada. **Tel** (613)998-3721. **LC** AM145; .T43.
Ind/Abst Art Archaeol. Tech. Abstr.

US/0886-0882
TECHNICAL BULLETIN - NATIONAL COUNCIL OF THE PAPER INDUSTRY FOR AIR AND STREAM IMPROVEMENT (U.S.). (1981). See Paper and Pulp Industry.

US
TECHNICAL BULLETIN - SOUTH DAKOTA DEPARTMENT OF GAME, FISH AND PARKS. Main/Corp South Dakota. Dept. of Game, Fish, and Parks. **VFOAT** Bulletin - South Dakota Department of Game, Fish and Parks. No. 1-1952-. Bulletin. English. Price varies per volume. South Dakota Game, Fish and Parks Department, 523 East Capitol Avenue, Pierre SD 57501. **Tel** (605)773-3361.

US/0084-0564
TECHNICAL BULLETIN - WISCONSIN DEPARTMENT OF NATURAL RESOURCES. [Tech. bull. - Wis. Dep. Nat. Resour.]. No. 39, (1968)-. Bulletin. English. ir. Price varies per volume. Department of Natural Resources / Wisconsin, Bureau of Research, PO Box 7921, Madison WI 53707. **Tel** (608)266-2121. **ED** Betty Les and Stefanie Brouwer. **LC** SK463; .A27. **CODEN** WDNTAD. **Pr Rev. Circ:** 1,500 (ctrl). Documents available from BIOSIS Document Express. *Continues Technical Bulletin - Wisconsin Conservation Department, 0097-1340.*
Desc: Presents comprehensive results of studies conducted by research scientists in the Wisconsin Department of Natural Resources. Topics include: fisheries, wildlife ecology, water resources, and environmental pollution.
Ind/Abst Biol. Abstr.; Ecol. Abstr. (?-?); Fish Rev.; GeoRef; Key Word Index Wildl. Res.; Life Sci. Collect.; Wildl. Rev.

US/0096-5197
TECHNICAL PUBLICATION (UTAH. DEPT. OF NATURAL RESOURCES). (TECHNICAL PUBLICATION / STATE OF UTAH, DEPT. OF NATURAL RESOURCES.). [Tech. publ. - State Utah Dep. Nat. Resour.]. No. 18 (1968)-. Monographic series. English. Price varies per volume. Department of Natural Resources / Utah, 1636 West North Temple, Suite 316, Salt Lake City UT 84116. **Tel** (801)538-7200, FAX (801)538-7315. **LC** TA7; .U77. **DD** 620/.005. **CODEN** UDNTAP. Documents available from CASDDS. *Continues Technical Publication (Utah. State Engineer's Office).*
Ind/Abst Chem. Abstr.; GeoRef.

US
TECHNICAL REPORT - COASTAL STUDIES INSTITUTE, CENTER FOR WETLAND RESOURCES, LOUISIANA STATE UNIVERSITY. Main/Corp Louisiana State University, Baton Rouge. Coastal Studies Institute. No. ; 197 -. Monographic series. English. Price varies per volume. Louisiana State University / Coastal Studies Institute, Baton Rouge LA 70803. *Continues Technical Report - Coastal Studies Institute, Louisiana State University.*

AT/0729-9990
TECHNICAL REPORT (CONSERVATION COMMISSION OF THE NORTHERN TERRITORY). (TECHNICAL REPORT - CONSERVATION COMMISSION OF THE NORTHERN TERRITORY (AUSTRALIA).). Monographic series. English. ir. Price varies per volume. Conservation Commission of the Northern Territory, Gap Road, PO Box 1046, Alice Springs Northern Territory 0871 Australia. **Tel** (089)508-211, FAX (089)52-5390, telex AAS1191. **Circ:** 400 (ctrl).

US
TECHNICAL REPORT (COOPERATIVE NATIONAL PARK RESOURCES STUDIES UNIT (DAVIS, CALIF.)). (TECHNICAL REPORT / COOPERATIVE NATIONAL PARK RESOURCES STUDIES UNIT, UNIVERSITY OF CALIFORNIA, WESTERN REGION, NATIONAL PARK SERVICE, DEPARTMENT OF THE INTERIOR.). No. 1-. Monographic series. English. Price varies per volume. University of California, Western Region National Park Service, Department of the Interior, Davis CA 95616.

US
TECHNICAL REPORT (COOPERATIVE NATIONAL PARK RESOURCES STUDIES UNIT (TUCSON, ARIZ.)). (TECHNICAL REPORT / COOPERATIVE NATIONAL PARK RESOURCES STUDIES UNIT, UNIVERSITY OF ARIZONA.). No. 1-. Monographic series. English. Price varies per volume. Cooperative National Park Resources, Park Resources Studies Unit, University of Arizona, 125 Biological Sciences, East Building #43, Tucson AZ 85721.

US
TECHNICAL REPORT - COOPERATIVE NATIONAL PARK RESOURCES STUDIES UNIT, UNIVERSITY OF HAWAII AT MANOA. Main/Corp Cooperative National Park Resources Studies Unit, University of Hawaii. **Added/Corp** United States. National Park Service. University of Hawaii at Manoa. (197?)-. Monographic series. English. ir. Price varies per volume. CNPRSU, University of Hawaii at Manoa, Department of Botany, Honolulu HI 96822. **Tel** (808)948-8218. **ED** Clifford W. Smith. **Circ:** 200 (ctrl).
Desc: Research results and management recommendations concerning national parks in Hawaii, Guam and Saipan.

AT/0810-5774
TECHNICAL REPORT SERIES / ARTHUR RYLAH INSTITUTE FOR ENVIRONMENTAL RESEARCH. [Tech. rep. ser. - Arthur Rylah Inst. Environ. Res.]. **Added/Corp** Arthur Rylah Institute for Environmental Research. (1982)-. Monographic series. English.
Ind/Abst Fish Rev. (Jan. 1989-July 1992); Wildl. Rev. (Jan. 1989-July 1992).

US
TECHNICAL REPORT / SOUTH CAROLINA MARINE RESOURCES CENTER. **Added/Corp** South Carolina. Marine Resources Division. **VFOAT** Technical Report Series (South Carolina Marine Resources Center). (19??)-. Monographic series. English. ir. Price varies per volume. South Carolina Wildlife and Marine Resources Department, Charleston SC 29412.
Ind/Abst Fish Rev.; Life Sci. Collect.; Wildl. Rev.

AT/0816-6757
TECHNICAL REPORT (WESTERN AUSTRALIA. DEPT. OF CONSERVATION AND LAND MANAGEMENT). (TECHNICAL REPORT / DEPARTMENT OF CONSERVATION AND LAND MANAGEMENT.). [Tech. rep. - Dep. Conserv. Land Manage. W.A.]. **Added/Corp** Western Australia. Dept. of Conservation and Land Management. No. 1 (Nov. 1985)-. Monographic series. English. ir. Price varies per volume. **LC** UNC. **CODEN** TRWME4. Documents available from BIOSIS Document Express.
Ind/Abst Biol. Abstr. (1986-); Fish Rev. (19??-199?); Wildl. Rev. (19??-199?).

US/0040-3202
TENNESSEE CONSERVATIONIST, THE. [Tenn. conserv.]. **Added/Corp** Tennessee. Wildlife Resources Agency. Tennessee. Dept. of Conservation. Tennessee. State Game and Fish Commission. (194?)-. Periodical. English. Six times a year (Jan., Mar., May, Jun., Sep., Nov.). $10.00 (one year); $17.00 (two year); $25.00 (three year); $14.50 other, (one year). Tennessee Conservationist, Department of Conservation, C/O V. Marks, Nashville TN 37243-0440. **Tel** (615)742-6743. **ED** Valary Marks (editor's address: Department of Enviroment and Conservation, Nashville, TN 37243-0440 phone: (615)532-0060). **DD** 639. **Circ:** 16,000 (ctrl). Documents available from Documents on Demand. ***Continues*** *Tennessee Wildlife and Conservationist.*
Desc: Features articles on Tennessee's history, natural resources, recreation, environmental protection activities, community life and more.
Ind/Abst Environ. Abstr.

US/0190-2377
TENNESSEE OUT OF DOORS. **Added/Corp** Tennessee Conservation League. **VFOAT** Out of Doors. **VAT** Tennessee Out-of-Doors. (19??)-. Periodical. English. Six times a year. $10.00 Comes with Tennessee Conservation League membership. Tennessee Conservation League, 1720 West End Avenue, Suite 308, Nashville TN 37203.

US/0886-1269
TENNESSEE WILDLIFE (NASHVILLE, TENN. 1977). (TENNESSEE WILDLIFE.). [Tenn. wildl.]. Vol. 1, No. 1 (July/Aug. 1977)-. Periodical. English. bm. $9.00. Tennessee Wildlife Resources Agency, Publications Division, Ellington Agricultural Center, PO Box 40747, Nashville TN 37204. **Tel** (615)741-1486. **LC** SK449; .T45. **DD** 639.9/09768.
Ind/Abst Energy Res. Abstr. (Aug. 1978-); Fish Rev.; Wildl. Rev.

CN/0823-9843
THAMES RIVER REVIEW. (THAMES RIVER REVIEW : NEWSLETTER OF THE LOWER THAMES VALLEY CONSERVATION AUTHORITY.). [Thames River rev.]. **Added/Corp** Lower Thames Valley Conservation Authority. Vol. 1 No. 1 (Jan. 1978)-. Newsletter. English. bm. Free. Lower Thames Valley Conservation Authority, 41 Fourth Street, Chatham Ontario N7M 2G3. **DD** 333.91/621/0971333. ctrl circ. ***Continues*** *LTVCA (Lower Thames Valley Conservation Authority), 0823-9835.*

CN/0841-7563
TIDES OF CHANGE. [Tides change]. **Added/Corp** Atlantic Environmental Network. **VFOAT** Marees Changeantes. Vol. 1, No. 1 (March 1988)-. Periodical. English (French). qt. 20.00Can$. Atlantic Environmental Network, 180 St. John Street, Fredericton NB E3B 4A9 Canada. **DD** 333.7/09715.

TH
TIGERPAPER. **Added/Corp** Food and Agriculture Organization of the United Nations. Regional Office for Asia and the Far East. **VFOAT** Tiger Paper. (1976)-. Periodical. English. qt (Mar., June, Sept., Dec.). $12.00. FAO Regional Office for Asia & the Pacific, Phra Atit Road, Maliwan Mansion, Bangkok 10200 Thailand. **Tel** 011 66 2 281-7844, FAX 011 66 2 2800445, telex 82815 FOODAG. **ED** J. S. Naewboonnien. **LC** QL84.5.A1; T53. **DD** 639.9/095. **Bk Rev. Circ:** 2,000.
Desc: News bulletin dedicated to the exchange of information relating to wildlife and national parks management for the Asia-Pacific region.
Ind/Abst Agrofor. Abstr.; Fish Rev.; For. Abstr.; Index Vet.; Key Word Index Wildl. Res.; Leis. Recreat. Tour. Abstr.; Vet. Bull.; Wildl. Rev.; World Agric. Econ.

SA/0256-6095
TOKTOKKIE AFRIKAANSE ED. [Toktokkie Afr. ed.]. (1980)-. Periodical. Afrikaans. bm. R39.00. Wildlife Society Southern Africa, P.O.Box 44189 Linden 2104, South Africa. **Tel** 011 27 41 29606. **UDC** 57. ***Continues*** *Toktokkie (Bilingual ed.), 0256-8926.*

US
TOPICAL BRIEFS, FISH AND WILDLIFE RESOURCES AND ELECTRIC POWER GENERATION / BIOLOGICAL SERVICES PROGRAM. **Added/Corp** Biological Services Program (U.S.) National Power Plant Team. **VFOAT** Fish and Wildlife Resources and Electric Power Generation. No. 1 (March 1977)-. Monographic series. English. ir. free on request. US Fish & Wildlife Service, Route 3, Box 44, Kearneysville WV 25430. **Tel** (304)725-2061. **LC** UNC. **Circ:** 1,000.
Desc: Effects of air pollution and acid rain on fish, wildlife, and their habitats.

US/0040-9723
TOTEM (OLYMPIA). (TOTEM.). [Totem]. **Added/Corp** Washington (State). Dept. of Natural Resources. Vol. 1 (1958)-. Periodical. English. Six times a year. Free. Washington Department of Natural Resources, Public Affairs Office, Cherberg Building, Olympia WA 98504. **Tel** (206)753-5330. **ED** Julianne G. Crane. **DD** 333.7. **Circ:** 12,000.
Desc: Explains various aspects of the department's programs to interested people outside the agency.
Ind/Abst GeoRef.

US/0738-8810
TRACKS (LANSING, MICH.). (TRACKS.). **Added/Corp** Michigan United Conservation Clubs. (19??)-. Periodical. English. mo (9 issues Sept.-May). $5.00. Michigan United Conservation Clubs, PO Box 30235, Lansing MI 48909. **Tel** (517)371-1041, FAX (517)371-1505. **ED** Christie Bleck. **Circ:** 90,500.
Desc: A conservation reader for elementary school children which features stories about animals and wildlife management.

UK/0267-4297
TRAFFIC BULLETIN - WILDLIFE TRADE MONITORING UNIT. [Traffic bull. - Wildl. Trade Monit. Unit]. (1981)-. Periodical. English. Three times a year. Free. Traffic International, World Conservation Monitoring Centre, 219C Huntingdon Road, Cambridge CB3 0DL United Kingdom. **Tel** 011 44 223 277427, FAX 011 44 0223 277237, telex 817036. **ED** Jorgen Thomsen and Kim Lochen. **DD** 382.45574. Index available. **Pr Rev. Circ:** 3,000. ***Continues*** *TRAFFIC International Bulletin, 0144-0896.*
Desc: Devoted to wildlife trade issues, covering all aspects of trade in wild animals, plants and derived products.

US/0739-0971
TRANET. (TRANET / TRANSNATIONAL NETWORK FOR APPROPRIATE/ALTERNATIVE TECHNOLOGIES.). [Tranet]. **VFOAT** Transnational Network for Appropriate/Alternative Technologies; T.R.A.N.E.T. (1976)-. English. bm. $150.00 institutions; $30.00 individuals. TRANET, Box 567, Rangeley ME 04970. **Tel** (205)864-2252. **ED** William N. Ellis. **Bk Rev. Circ:** 1500 (ctrl). ***Formed by the union of*** *Rain, 0739-621X.*
Desc: A non-profit, transnational network of, by and for people and organizations that are changing the world by changing their lifestyles, helping one another become self-reliant, and are adopting appropriate techniques.

US/0418-7598
TRANSACTIONS - DESERT BIGHORN COUNCIL. **Main/Corp** Desert Bighorn Council. **VFOAT** Desert Bighorn Council Transactions. (1962)-. English. an (Published in May). $21.00 nonmembers & institutions; $20.00 members. Desert Bighorn Council, 1500 North Decatur Boulevard, Las Vegas NV 89108. **Tel** (702)646-3401. **ED** Paul R. Krausman. **LC** SK305.M6; D4. **DD** 591. Index available (published separately). cum. index. ***Continues*** *Desert Bighorn Council. Meeting. Annual Meeting.*
Desc: Established to promote the advancement of knowledge concerning the Desert Bighorn Sheep and their long-range welfare.
Ind/Abst AGRICOLA; Key Word Index Wildl. Res.

US/0078-1355
TRANSACTIONS OF THE ... NORTH AMERICAN WILDLIFE AND NATURAL RESOURCES CONFERENCE. [Trans. North Am. Wildl. Nat. Resour. Conf.]. **Main/Conf** North American Wildlife and Natural Resources Conference. **Added/Corp** Wildlife Management Institute. **VFOAT** Transactions--North American Wildlife and Natural Resources Conference. (Mar. 7, 8, and 9, 1960)-. English. an. $35.00. Wildlife Management Institute, 1101 14th Street NW/Suite 801, Washington DC 20005. **Tel** (202)371-1808, FAX (202)408-5059. **LC** SK351; .N872. **CODEN** NAWTA6. **Circ:** 1,000. Documents available from BIOSIS Document Express. ***Continues*** *Transactions of the North American Wildlife Conference, 0097-6830.*
Desc: Conference proceedings containing 65-75 papers covering wildlife management, environmental problems, forestry, land management, resource planning and resource economics.
Ind/Abst AGRICOLA [Select. Cov.]; Biol. Abstr.; Fish Rev.; Key Word Index Wildl. Res.; Life Sci. Collect.; Wildl. Rev.

US/0893-214X
TRANSACTIONS OF THE WESTERN SECTION OF THE WILDLIFE SOCIETY. [Trans. west. Sect. Wildl. Soc.]. **Added/Corp** Wildlife Society. Western Section. Vol. 22 (1986)-. English. an. $15.00. Wildlife Society Western Section, PO Box 21368, Oakland CA 94620. **Tel** (707)576-2275. **ED** Eric Loft. **LC** SK373; .C28. **DD** 333.95/16/0978. **CODEN** TWSSE3. **Pr Rev.** ***Continues*** *Cal-Neva Wildlife, 0095-3601.*
Ind/Abst AGRICOLA [Select. Cov.]; Fish Rev.; Key Word Index Wildl. Res.; Wildl. Rev.

AT/0814-4680
TREES AND NATURAL RESOURCES. [Trees nat. resour.]. Vol. 27, No. 1 (March 1985)-. Periodical. English. qt. 20.00Aus$ Australia; 25.00Aus$ other. Natural Resources Conservation League of Victoria, PO Box 105, Springvale 3171 Australia. **Tel** (03)547-8791. **ED** Les G Schultz, Felicity Anderson. **LC** S934.A8; V5. Index available. **Bk Rev. Ad Acc. Circ:** 5,500 (ctrl). Documents available from BIOSIS Document Express. ***Continues*** *Trees and Victoria's Resources.*
Ind/Abst APAIS, Aust. Public Aff. Inf. Ser.; Biol. Abstr. (1985-); Irr. Drain. Abstr.; Soils Fert.

AT/1032-6111
TREESPEAK ADELAIDE. [Tresspeak Adel.]. (198?)-. Periodical. English. Six times a year (Jan., Mar., May, July, Sept., Nov.). 20.00Aus$. Greening Australia SA Inc., GPO Box 9868, Adelaide SA 5001 Australia. **Tel** 011 61 8 2078757, FAX 011 61 8 2078755. **ED** Malcolm Campbell. **DD** 333.720994. **Ad Acc. Circ:** 7,000 (ctrl).

●US/0854-1566
TROPICAL BIODIVERSITY. **Added/Corp** Yayasan Bina Sains Hayati Indonesia. Vol. 1, No. 1 (Sept. 1992)-. English. qt. Indonesian Foundation for the Advancement of Biological Sciences, 158 Louis Lane, Davis CA 95616. **LC** IN PROCESS; QH75.A1; T76.
Desc: Covers biological diversity conservation and wildlife conservation.

US
TROPICUS. Vol. 1 (Fall 1987)-. Periodical. English. qt. $15.00. Conservation International, 1015 18th Street NW, Suite 1000, Washington DC 20036. **Tel** (202)429-5660, FAX (202)887-5188.
Desc: Covers the Conservation International group's causes and activities.

AT
TRUST NEWS. **Main/Corp** National Trust of Australia (Victoria). **Added/Corp** National Trust of Australia (Victoria) Trust. **VFOAT** Trust. (19??)-. English. bm. 32.00Aus$. Trust News Australia, 4 Parliament Place, East Melbourne Victoria 3002 Australia. **Tel** (03)654-4711, FAX (03)650-5397. **ED** Pamela Wells. **LC** DU200; .N37a. **DD** 363.6/9/060945. Index available. **Bk Rev. Ad Acc. Circ:** 17,000 (ctrl).
Desc: Articles relevant to the preservation of Australia's heritage of buildings, conservation areas and significant trees.

US/1058-7381
TUEBOR TERRA. ***Ceased.*** (TUEBOR TERRA : DEFENDING MICHIGAN'S ENVIRONMENT.). [Tuebor terra]. **Added/Corp** Michigan United Conservation Clubs. Vol. 1, No. 1 (May/June 1990)-(1993). Periodical. English. bm. Michigan United Conservation Clubs, PO Box 30235, Lansing MI 48909. **Tel** (517)371-1041, FAX (517)371-1505. **DD** 333.

US/0047-8733
TUESDAY LETTER. **Added/Corp** National Association of Conservation Districts. (19??)-. Periodical. English. Forty-Four times a year. $35.00 (basic member); $60.00 (contributing member). NACD, Box 855, League City TX 77573. **Tel** (713)332-3402. **ED** Ronald G. Francis. **Bk Rev. Ad Acc. Circ:** 25,000.
Desc: Publication distributed to conservation district with interest to the conservation practices in the community.

CC
TZU JAN TZU YUAN HSUEH PAO / CHUNG-KUO TZU JAN TZU YUAN YEN CHIU HUI PIEN CHI. **Added/Corp** Chung-Kuo Tzu Jan Tzu Yuan Yen Chiu Hui. **VFOAT** Journal of Natural Resources. (1986)-. Periodical. Chinese (summaries and/or abstracts in English). qt. **LC** HC427.5; .T98.
Ind/Abst For. Abstr.

US/0270-8655
U.S. DEPARTMENT OF THE INTERIOR NATIONAL PARK SERVICE TRANSACTIONS AND PROCEEDINGS SERIES. (TRANSACTIONS AND PROCEEDINGS SERIES - NATIONAL PARK SERVICE.). [U.S. Dep. Inter. Natl. Park Serv. trans. proc. ser.]. **Main/Corp** United States. National Park Service. **VFOAT** Proceedings and Transactions Series. No. 2-. Proceedings. English. Price varies per volume. USNPS Natural History Division, Washington DC 20005. ***Continues*** *National Park Service Symposium Series.*
Ind/Abst GeoRef.

KE/1014-949X
UNEP ENVIRONMENTAL MANAGEMENT GUIDELINES. [UNEP environ. manag. guidel.]. **Added/Corp** United Nations Environment Programme. **VFOAT** U.N.E.P. Environmental Management Guidelines; Environmental Management Guidelines. **VAT** United Nations Environment Programme Environmental Management Guidelines. No. 1 (1982)-. Monographic series. English. ir. Price varies per volume. Pergamon Press, An Imprint of Elsevier Science Ltd., The Boulevard, Langford Lane, Kidlington, Oxford OX5 1GB United Kingdom. **Tel** 011 44 865 843000, 011 44 865 843699, FAX 011 44 865 843010.
Ind/Abst Agrofor. Abstr.

SZ
UNITED NATIONS LIST OF NATIONAL PARKS AND PROTECTED AREAS. **Added/Corp** International Union for Conservation of Nature and Natural Resources. IUCN Commission on National Parks and Protected Areas. **VFOAT** Liste des Nations Unies des Parcs Nationaux et des Aires Protegees; United Nations List. (1982)-. English (French). an. International Union for Conservation of Nature and Natural Resources, rue Mauverney 28, CH1196 Gland Switzerland. **Tel** 011 41 22 647181, FAX 011 41 22 642926, telex 419605. ***Continues*** *United Nations List of National Parks and Equivalent Reserves.*

GW
UNSER WALD : ZEITSCRIFT DER SCHUTZGEMEINSCHAFT DEUTSCHER WALD. **See** Forestry.

US/0882-584X
URBAN WILDLIFE MANAGER'S NOTEBOOK. **Added/Corp** National Institute for Urban Wildlife (U.S.). (198?)-. English. qt. Free to members. National Institute for Urban Wildlife, 10921 Trotting Ridge Way, Columbia MD 21044. **Tel** (301)596-3311. **ED** Louise E. Dove. **DD** 333. **Bk Rev. Circ:** 1,000 (ctrl).
Desc: Series of informational leaflets that suggests practical, scientific methods for those who wish to attract desirable wildlife species into backyards and urban open spaces.
Ind/Abst Wildl. Rev.

US/0882-5858
URBAN WILDLIFE NEWS. **See** Environmental Issues-Ecology.

US
URSUS. **See** Environmental Issues-Ecology.

US/0147-2380
UTAH BLACK BEAR HARVEST. **Main/Corp** Utah. Division of Wildlife Resources. **VFOAT** Utah Black Bear Harvest Report. English. Department of Natural Resources / Utah, 1636 West North Temple, Suite 316, Salt Lake City UT 84116. **Tel** (801)538-7200, FAX (801)538-7315. **LC** SK453; .A25 subser; SK295. **DD** 333.9/5 S; 799.2/77/4446.

GW/0342-684X
VEROFFENTLICHUNGEN FUER NATURSCHUTZ UND LANDSCHAFTSPFLEGE IN BADEN-WURTTEMBERG. **See** Natural History.

SP/0210-3605
VIDA SILVESTRE. [Vida silv.]. **Added/Corp** Instituto Nacional para la Conservacion de la Naturaleza. (1972)-. Periodical. Spanish. sa. 1500ptas Spain; 2400ptas other. Instituto Nacional Para La Conservacion de la Naturaleza, Gran V S Francisco 35 41, 28005 Madrid Spain. **LC** QL84.4.S7; V5.
Ind/Abst Fish Rev.; Wildl. Rev.

US/0042-6792
VIRGINIA WILDLIFE. **Added/Corp** Virginia Commission of Game and Inland Fisheries. Virginia Wildlife Federation. Vol. 1 (Sept. 1937)-. Periodical. English. mo. $10.00 (one year), $24.00 (three years). Commission of Game & Inland Fisheries, PO Box 11104, Richmond VA 23230. **Tel** (804)367-1000. **ED** Virginia Shepherd, 4010 W Broad St, Richmond, VA 23220-1104 (804)367-1000. **LC** SK137; .V5. Index available. **Circ:** 55,000.
Desc: State-supported publication designed to educate the public on the hunting and fishing opportunities in the state of the conservation of the state's natural resources.
Ind/Abst Biol. Dig.; Fish Rev. (Jan. 1989-July 1992); Wildl. Rev. (Jan. 1989-July 1992).

GW/0042-7993
VOGELWELT, DIE. **See** Zoology-Ornithology.

US/0898-6193
VOICE OF WALDEN, THE. (THE VOICE OF WALDEN : WALDEN FOREVER WILD NEWSLETTER.). [Voice Walden]. No. 9 (Fall 1985)-. Newsletter. English. sa. Walden Forever Wild, Box 275, Concord MA 01742. **DD** 363. ***Continues*** *Newsletter (Walden Forever Wild Committee (Concord, Mass.)).*

RU/0206-4731
VOPROSY EKOLOGII I OKHRANY PRIPRODY. **Added/Corp** Russian S.F.S.R. Ministerstvo Vysshego i Srednego Spetsialnogo Obrazovaniia. Leningradskii Gosudarstvennyi Universitet Imeni A.A. Zhdanova. (1981)-. Russian. ir. St Petersburg State University / Izdatelstvo Leningradskogo Universiteta, Universitetskaia Nab 7/9, 199034 St Petersburg Russia. **Tel** 011 95 218-97-88, FAX 011 95 218-51-52, telex 121481.
Ind/Abst Nematol. Abstr.

US/0744-1266
WALLEYE. **See** Recreation, Leisure-Outdoor Life.

SA
WARDEN'S ... ANNUAL REPORT ON THE RONDEVLEI BIRD SANCTUARY FOR THE YEAR ... / RONDEVLEI BIRD SANCTUARY, THE. **Main/Corp** Rondevlei Bird Sanctuary. English (Afrikaans). an. Free on request. Western Cape Regional Services Council, PO Box 1073, Cape Town 8000 South Africa. **Tel** (021)242200 SA, FAX (021)241595, telex (021)52 1495. **ED** C H Langley. **LC** QL692.S6; R66A. **DD** 598.29687. **Circ:** 1,000 (ctrl). ***Continues*** *Annual Report on the Rondevlei Bird Sanctuary by the Warden.*

US
WASHINGTON COASTAL CURRENTS. **Added/Corp** Washington (State). Dept. of Ecology. Vol. 6, No. 9 (June 1982)-. Periodical. English. ir. Free. Washington Coastal Currents, Washington State Department of Ecology, Olympia WA 98504. **Tel** (206)459-6288, (206)459-6356. **ED** Mikel C. McCormick. Index available. **Bk Rev. Circ:** 3,000 (ctrl). ***Continues*** *Shoreline/Coastal Zone Management, 0739-7933.*
Desc: Management of shorelines and coastal zone of Washington state, environmental protection.

JA
WATASHITACHI NO SHIZEN. NATURE. **Added/Corp** Nihon Chorui Hogo Remmei. **VFOAT** Nature. (19??)-. Periodical. Japanese (Japanese). mo. ¥170. Nihon Chorui Hogo Remmei, c/o Yamashina Chorui Kenkyujo, 8-20 Nampeidaimachi, Shibuya-ku 150, Tokyo Japan. **LC** QL691.J4; W37.

US/0271-8049
WATER AND LAND RESOURCE ACCOMPLISHMENTS. FEDERAL RECLAMATION PROJECTS, SUMMARY REPORT. [Water land resour. accomp., Fed. reclam. proj. summ. rep.]. **Main/Corp** United States. Dept. of the Interior. Water and Power Resources Service. 1978-. Government Publication. English. an. US Department of the Interior Bureau of Reclamation, 1849 C Street NW, Room 7654, Washington DC 20240. **Tel** (202)208-4157, FAX (202)343-3484. **LC** HD1720. **DD** 333.91/00973. ***Continues*** *Summary Report. Federal Reclamation Projects, Water & Land Resource Accomplishment, 0161-2379.*

US/0739-0327
WATERFOWLER'S WORLD. Periodical. English. bm. $12.00. Waterfowl Publications Ltd Inc, PO Box 38613, Germantown TN 38138.

CN/1188-360X
WATERSHED SENTINEL, THE. [Watershed sentin.]. **Added/Corp** Friends of Cortes Island. (Jan. 1991)-. Periodical. English. Six times a year. $12.00. Watershed Sentinel, Box 25, Whaletown British Columbia V0P 1Z0 Canada. **Tel** (604)935-6992. **DD** 333.7/2/09711105.

US/0279-0580
WEST VIRGINIA HILLS & STREAMS. (WEST VIRGINIA HILLS & STREAMS : OFFICIAL PUBLICATION OF WEST VIRGINIA HILLS & STREAMS, INC.). **VAT** West Virginia Hills and Streams. Periodical. English. bm. $5.00. West Virginia Hills & Streams Inc, PO Box 66, Renwick WV 24966. **Tel** (304)497-2788. **ED** Robert Harvey. **Bk Rev. Ad Acc. Circ:** 1,000 (ctrl).
Desc: Covers field and Stream conservation activities. Also contains short fiction or drama relating to West Virginia or Appalachia. Also contains a "how to", and "back then" section.

US/0276-3834
WEST VIRGINIA WILDLIFE RESEARCH. **VAT** West Va. Wildl. Res. English. an. Division of Wildlife Resources West Virginia, Department of Natural Resources, Operations Center, PO Box 67, Elkins WV 26241. **LC** SK461; .W48. **DD** 639.9/09754.

CN/0836-446X
WESTERN CANADA OUTDOORS (ALBERTA EDITION). (WESTERN CANADA OUTDOORS.). [West. Can. outdoors]. Vol. 1, No. 1 (March/April 1977)-. Periodical. English. bm. $6.50. McIntosh Publications Co Ltd, Box 430, North Battleford 291 2Y5 Canada. **Tel** (306)445-7477, FAX (306)445-1977. **ED** Stan Nowakowski. **DD** 799/.097123. **Bk Rev. Ad Acc. Circ:** 42,000 (ctrl). ***Continues in part*** *Western Canada Outdoors, 0703-8399.*
Desc: Policy statements on wildlife, habitat, fish and development of water quality. Trying to improve the quality for outdoor recreation.

CN/0836-4451
WESTERN CANADA OUTDOORS (SASKATCHEWAN EDITION). (WESTERN CANADA OUTDOORS.). [West. Can. outdoors]. Vol. 1, No. 2 (March/April 1977)-. Periodical. English. bm. $6.50. McIntosh Publications Co Ltd, Box 430, North Battleford 291 2Y5 Canada. **Tel** (306)445-7477, FAX (306)445-1977. **ED** Stan Nowakowski. **DD** 799/.097124. **Bk Rev. Ad Acc. Circ:** 42,000 (ctrl). ***Continues in part*** *Western Canada Outdoors, 0703-8399.*
Desc: Policy statements on wildlife, habitat, fish and development of water quality. Trying to improve the quality for outdoor recreation.

US/1065-0806
WESTERN RESOURCES WRAP-UP. ***Ceased.*** [West. resour. wrap-up]. **VFOAT** Western Resources Wrap Up; WRW. (19??)-(June 1994). Periodical. English. Fifty-two times a year. Western Resources Wrap-Up, 123 6th Street SE, Washington DC 20003. **Tel** (202)546-1350, FAX (202)546-1228. **ED** Helene C. Monberg. **DD** 333. **Circ:** 240.

US/0363-6690
WESTERN WILDLANDS. ***Suspended.*** [West. wildlands]. **Added/Corp** Montana Forest and Conservation Experiment Station. Vol. 1 (1974)-Suspended (Fall 1992). Periodical. English. qt. University of Montana School of Forestry, Missoula MT 59812. **Tel** (406)243-6655. **ED** Jennifer O'Loughlin. **LC** QH76.5.M9; W47. **DD** 333.9/5/05; 333. Index available. **Bk Rev. Circ:** 1,500.
Desc: Features articles on natural resource management, including forestry, wildlife, range recreation, soils and air and water quality.
Ind/Abst Environ. Period. Bibliogr.; Fish Rev.; GeoRef; Key Word Index Wildl. Res.; Leis. Recreat. Tour. Abstr.; West. Hist. Q.; Wildl. Rev.

US/0277-5212
WETLANDS (WILMINGTON, N.C.). (WETLANDS : THE JOURNAL OF THE SOCIETY OF THE WETLANDS SCIENTISTS.). **Added/Corp** Society of Wetland Scientists (U.S.). (Sept. 1981)-. Periodical. English. qt. $100.00 library, $200.00 other. Society of Wetland Scientists. **(Subscription address:** Wetlands, PO box 1897, Lawrence KS 66044-8897.**) ED** Doug Wilcox. **LC** QH75.A1; W47. **DD** 333.91/8/0973. **CODEN** WETLEU. **Pr Rev. Acid Free. Circ:** 2,500 (ctrl). Documents available from The Genuine Article, BIOSIS Document Express.
Desc: An international journal concerned with all aspects of wetlands biology, ecology, hydrology, water chemistry, soil and sediment characteristics, management, and laws and regulations. The goal of the journal is to centralize the publication of pioneering wetlands work that is currently spread among a myriad of other journals.
Ind/Abst Biol. Abstr. (1985-); Curr. Aware. Biol. Sci., CABS; Curr. Contents, Agric. Biol. Environ. Sci.; Ecology Abstr.; Entomol. Abstr.; Fish Rev.; GeoRef; Ocean. Abstr.; Pollut. Abstr. Indexes; Res. Alert [Select. Cov.]; Soils Fert.; Wildl. Rev.

US/0273-4419
WHALEWATCHER. **See** Zoology.

CN/0049-7592
WHOOPER, THE. ***Title Change.*** Vol. 1 (June 1968)-. Periodical. English. mo. Saskatchewan Wildlife Federation, PO Box 1327, Moose Jaw Saskatchewan S6H 4R3 Canada. **DD** 639.9/097124. ***Merged with*** *Defending All Outdoors, 0045-9836* ***to form*** *Western Canada Outdoors, 0703-8399.*

UK
WILD CAT. **Added/Corp** Cat Survival Trust. Vol.1 (Oct. 1977)-. Periodical. English. Wild Cat - Cat Survival Trust, 4 Ninnings Lane, Rabley Heath, Welwyn Herts AL6 9TD England. **ED** Peter Watkiss and Angela Watkiss.

US
WILD OREGON. **Added/Corp** Oregon Wilderness Coalition. (19??)-. Periodical. English. qt. $25.00 (one year); $45.00 (two year), $60.00 (three year). Oregon Natural Resource Council, 1161 Lincoln Street, Eugene OR 97401. **Tel** (503)344-0675.

AT
WILDERNESS. (19??)-. English. Six times a year. 25.00Aus$ (concession or senior), 36.00Aus$ (regular), 42.00Aus$ (household), 60.00Aus$ (organization),

1,000.00Aus$ (life) Comes with Wilderness Society membership. Wilderness Society - Australia, 130 Davey Street, hobart Tasmania 7000 Australia. **Tel** 011 61 2349366, FAX 011 61 2235112. **ED** Melissa Swanson (editor's address: 1A James Lane, Sydney New South Wales, 2000 Australia, phone: 011 61 02 267 2098). **Ad Acc. Circ:** 15,000 (ctrl). ***Continues*** *Wilderness News.*
Desc: Information on protecting, preserving and promoting the wilderness.

CN/0830-8284
WILDERNESS ALBERTA. ***Title Change.*** [Wilderness Alta.]. **Added/Corp** Alberta Wilderness Association. **VFOAT** Alberta Wilderness Association Newsletter. Vol. 15, No. 3 (Fall 1985)-(1993). Periodical. English. qt. Alberta Wilderness Association, PO Box 6398 Station D, Calgary Alberta T2P 2E1 Canada. **Tel** (403)283-2025. **ED** Jane Kennedy. **DD** 333.78/097123. **Bk Rev. Ad Acc. Circ:** 2,500 (ctrl). ***Continues*** *Alberta Wilderness Association Newsletter, 0708-7128.* ***Continued by*** *Wild Lands Advocate, 1192-6287.*
Desc: Describes progress in conservation of wilderness, wild rivers and parks in Alberta and activities of Alberta Wilderness Association. Aimed at protection of wilderness areas.

US/0194-3030
WILDERNESS RECORD. (WILDERNESS RECORD : PROCEEDINGS OF THE CALIFORNIA WILDERNESS COALITION.). **Added/Corp** California Wilderness Coalition. (197?)-. Proceedings. English. mo. $20.00 (Comes with membership to California Wilderness Coalition). California Wilderness Coalition, 2655 Portage Bay East, Suite 5, Davis CA 95616. **Tel** (916)758-0380. **ED** Lucy Rosenau. Index available. cum. index. **Bk Rev,** (Qty: 12). **Ad Acc. Circ:** 2,000 (ctrl).
Desc: Provides information on nature conservation and wilderness areas.

CN/0828-9654
WILDERNESS TRAILS 'N' TALES. See Recreation, Leisure-Outdoor Life.

US/0736-6477
WILDERNESS (WASHINGTON, D.C.). (WILDERNESS.). [Wilderness]. **Added/Corp** Wilderness Society. Vol. 46, No. 158 (Fall 1982)-. Periodical. English. qt (Mar., June, Sept., Dec.). $20.00 (includes Wilderness Society Membership). The Wilderness Society, 900 17th Street Northwest, Washington DC 20006. **Tel** (202)833-2300 or, 429-2627. **ED** T. H. Watkins. **LC** QH1; .L93. **DD** 333.95/16/0973. **Bk Rev. Ad Acc. Circ:** 350,000 (ctrl). available on microfilm and microfiche from University Microfilms International (UMI). Documents available from BIOSIS Document Express, UMI Article Clearinghouse, Documents on Demand. ***Continues*** *Living Wilderness, 0024-5305.*
Desc: A conservation organization whose primary purpose is the preservation and proper management of all federal lands including national parks and forests, wilderness, wild and scenic rivers, bureau of land management lands and national wildlife refuges. Includes Wilderness Society membership.
Ind/Abst Acad. Abstr. Full Text Elite (March 1984-) [Full Txt.]; Acad. Abstr. (March 1984-); Acad. Ind. [Computer File] (1984-); Acad. Search (Mar. 1984-); Biol. Abstr.; Book Rev. Index; Coal Abstr.; Environ. Abstr.; Environ. Period. Bibliogr.; Expand. Acad. Index (1984-); Gen. Period. Index (1985-); Gen. Sci. Index; INFO-SOUTH Abstr.; Mag. Artic. Summar. Elite (March 1984-) [Full Txt.]; Mag. Artic. Summar. Select (March 1984-); Mag. Artic. Summar. CD-ROM (March 1984-); Mag. Index Plus (1989-); Mag. Index. Sel. (1986-); Mag. Search; Mid. Search (Mar. 1984-); Newsp. Period. Abstr. (1988-); Read. Guide Abstr. Select Ed.; Read. Guide Period. Lit.; Mag. Index (Fall 1982-); Vocat. Search (Mar. 1984-).

CN/0842-5132
WILDFLOWER. [Wildflower]. Vol. 1, No. 1 (Winter 1985)-. Periodical. English. qt. 20.00Can$ (one year), 35.00Can$ (two year) North America; 25.00Can$ (one year), 45.00Can$ (two year) other. Wildflower, 75 Ternhill Cr, North York Ontario M3C 2E4 Canada. **Tel** (416)449-7907. **ED** James Hodgins (editor's address: 90 Wolfrey Avenue, Toronto Ontario M4K 1K8 Canada). **DD** 635.9/676/05. Index available. cum. index. **Bk Rev. Ad Acc. Circ:** 3,000.
Desc: Devoted exclusively to wild flora. Contains a variety of articles of interest to both the expert and the novice. Book reviews, plant sources, coming events and information of interest to wildflower enthusiasts are also featured.
Ind/Abst Garden Lit. (1992-).

CN/0316-3350
WILDLAND NEWS. V. 1- Sept. 1968-. Periodical. English. ir. Algonquin Wildlands League, 47 Colborne Street/308, Toronto Ontario M5E 1E3 Canada.

US/0499-4175
WILDLIFE ABSTRACTS. Added/Corp U.S. Fish and Wildlife Service. United States. Bureau of Sport Fisheries and Wildlife. (1951)-. Government Publication. English. ir. Superintendent of Documents, US Government Printing Office, Washington DC 20402. **Tel** (202)275-3328, FAX (202)786-2377. **DD** 016.33372.

US/1046-6479
WILDLIFE & FISH WORLDWIDE. VOLUME 1. ***Title Change.*** (WILDLIFE & FISH WORLDWIDE. VOLUME 1 [COMPUTER FILE].). [Wildl. fish worldw., Vol. 1]. **Added/Corp** National Information Services Corporation. U.S. Fish and Wildlife Service. **VFOAT** Wildlife and Fish Worldwide. Volume 1. (1990)-(199?). English. sa. National Information Services Corp, 3100 St Paul Street, Wyman Towers, Suite 6, Baltimore MD 21218. **Tel** (410)243-0797, FAX (410)243-0982. **DD** 639. ***Split into*** *Wildlife Review & Fisheries Review, 1070-499X; Wildlife Worldwide, 1070-5007* ***and*** *Fisheries Worldwide.*
Desc: Wildlife coverage ranges from studies of species to specific habitat types, hunting, economics, wildlife behavior, management techniques, diseases, and parasites. Fish coverage includes culture and propagation, limnology and oceanography, genetics and behavior, natural history, parasites, disease, and general research and management topics.

AT/0043-5481
WILDLIFE AUSTRALIA. Added/Corp Wildlife Preservation Society of Queensland. **VFOAT** Wildlife in Australia. Vol. 20, No. 2 (June 1983)-. Periodical. English. qt. 20.00Aus$ Australia; 40.00Aus$ other. Wildlife Preservation Society of Queensland, 160 Edward Street, Level 4, Brisbane Queensland 4000 Australia. **Tel** 011 7 2210194, FAX 011 61 7 2210701. **ED** Anthony Brown. **LC** QL338; .W58. **DD** 591.994. **Bk Rev. Ad Acc. Circ:** 10,000. ***Continues*** *Wildlife in Australia.*
Desc: Articles on Australian and natural environments. For schools and universities. Scientific accuracy combined with informal style. Entertaining, informative, visually appealing.
Ind/Abst Key Word Index Wildl. Res.

CN/0827-2409
WILDLIFE COLLECTABLES JOURNAL, THE. [Wildl. collect. j.]. Vol. 1, No. 1 (Apr. 15, 1984)-. Periodical. English. mo. 24.00Can$ Canada; $30.00 other. Wildlife Collectables Journal, c/o Insight Publications, Box 130, Durham Ontario N0G 1R0 Canada. **Tel** (519)369-5155. **DD** 704.9/432. **Bk Rev. Ad Acc.** ctrl circ.
Desc: The Canadian wildlife art market and the programs and strategies of Canada's conservation groups are featured. The emphasis is on limited edition art forms.

US/1048-4949
WILDLIFE CONSERVATION. [Wildl. conserv.]. **Added/Corp** New York Zoological Society. Vol. 93, No. 1 (Jan./Feb. 1990)-. Periodical. English. bm (6 issues). $14.98. New York Zoological Society, New York Zoological Park, Bronx NY 10460. **Tel** (212)220-5121. **(Subscription address:** Neodata / Colorado, PO Box 2606, Boulder Boulder CO 80322.**) LC** QL1; .N5. **DD** 639.9/05. **CODEN** WICOEG. available on microfiche from University Microfilms International (UMI). ***Continues*** *Animal Kingdom, 0003-3537.*
Desc: Takes you on an exciting adventure exploring Earth's wild things, beauty, diversity, and problems. Covers timely, sensitive matters with photography and award-winning articles.
Ind/Abst Acad. Search (July 1993-); Biol. Dig.; Environ. Period. Bibliogr.; Gen. Sci. Index (1992-); Gen. Sci. Source (Jul. 1993-); INFO-SOUTH Abstr.; Mag. Search; Wildl. Rev. (199?-).

US/0891-2734
WILDLIFE CONSERVATION REPORT. [Wildl. conserv. rep.]. **Added/Corp** Wildlife Information Center, Inc. No. 1 (Nov. 1986)-. Monographic series. English. Free. **DD** 333.
Ind/Abst Fish Rev. (Jan. 1989-July 1992); Wildl. Rev. (Jan. 1989-July 1992).

US/0886-3458
WILDLIFE HARVEST. See Recreation, Leisure-Outdoor Life.

US/0043-549X
WILDLIFE IN NORTH CAROLINA. Added/Corp North Carolina Wildlife Resources Commission. North Carolina. Dept. of Conservation and Development. Division of Game and Inland Fisheries. Vol. 10 (May 1946)-. Periodical. English. Twelve times a year. $7.50 (one year); $20.00 (three years). Wildlife in North Carolina, 512 North Salisbury Street, Raleigh NC 27604-1188. **Tel** (919)662-4377. **ED** Jim Dean. **LC** SK351; .W68. **Bk Rev. Circ:** 80,000. ***Continues*** *North Carolina Wildlife Conservation.*
Desc: Articles on wildlife, the outdoors, hunting, fishing and conservation.
Ind/Abst Fish Rev.; Wildl. Rev.

US/0893-6560
WILDLIFE JOURNAL. ***Title Change.*** (WILDLIFE JOURNAL : JOURNAL OF THE INTERNATIONAL WILDLIFE REHABILITATION COUNCIL.). [Wildl. j.]. **Added/Corp** International Wildlife Rehabilitation Council. Wildlife Rehabilitation Council. **VFOAT** IWRC Journal. (19??)-(199?). Periodical. English. Four times a year. International Wildlife Rehabilitation Council, 4437 Central Place, Suite B4, Suisun CA 94585. **Tel** (707)864-1761, FAX (707)864-3107. **ED** Jan White. **DD** 639. **CODEN** WJOUEX. cum. index. **Bk Rev,** (Qty: 1). **Ad Acc. Pr Rev. Circ:** 1,500 (ctrl). ***Continued by*** *Journal of Wildlife Rehabilitation, 1071-2232.*

Desc: Reviewed journal of wildlife rehabilitation. Includes information on natural history, rescue, care, treatment, and post-release follow-up.
Ind/Abst Fish Rev.; Wildl. Rev.

US/0148-9461
WILDLIFE MANAGEMENT LEAFLET. (1960)-. Monographic series. English. Price varies per volume. California Department of Fish and Game, 1416 9th Street, Sacramento CA 95814. **Tel** (916)653-7664.

US
WILDLIFE NEWS / AFRICAN WILDLIFE LEADERSHIP FOUNDATION. Added/Corp African Wildlife Leadership Foundation. Vol. 12 (Spring 1977)-. Periodical. English. Three times a year. $15.00. African Wildlife Leader Foundation, 1717 Massachusetts NW, Washington DC 20036. ***Continues*** *News (African Wildlife Leadership Foundation).*

US/0511-9480
WILDLIFE PAMPHLET (PROVIDENCE). (WILDLIFE PAMPHLET.). **Added/Corp** Rhode Island. Division of Fish and Game. Pamphlet Rhode Island. Division of Fish and Game. Pittman-Robertson Pamphlet Rhode Island. Division of Fish and Wildlife. Rhode Island. Division of Conservation. Rhode Island. Division of Fish and Game. (1940)-. Monographic series. English. ir. Price varies per volume. Department of Natural Resources / Rhode Island, Division of Fish and Wildlife, Providence RI 02903. **DD** 333.7.

US/0734-5518
WILDLIFE POPULATIONS AND RESEARCH UNIT PROJECT DESCRIPTIONS. (WILDLIFE POPULATIONS AND RESEARCH UNIT PROJECT DESCRIPTIONS / MINNESOTA DEPARTMENT OF NATURAL RESOURCES, DIVISION OF FISH AND WILDLIFE, SECTION OF WILDLIFE.). [Wildl. popul. res. unit proj. descr.]. **VFOAT** Project Descriptions; Wildlife Project Descriptions. 1981-. English. be. Department of Natural Resources / Minnesota, 350 Centennial Building, St Paul MN 55155. **LC** SK411; .W54. **DD** 639.9/09776.

US
WILDLIFE PRESERVATION TRUST ... ANNUAL REPORT. Main/Corp Jersey Wildlife Preservation Trust. 1981-. English. an. Free with $25.00 membership. Wildlife Preservation Trust International, 34th Street and Girard Avenue, Philadelphia PA 19104. **Tel** (215)222-3636. **ED** William R Konstant. **Circ:** 5,000 (ctrl).

NZ
WILDLIFE PUBLICATION (WELLINGTON). (WILDLIFE PUBLICATION.). No. 1- 1949-. Monographic series. English. Price varies per volume. New Zealand Department of Internal Affairs, Government Printer, Wellington New Zealand. **LC** SK577. **DD** 799.

US
WILDLIFE REHABILITATION. Main/Corp National Wildlife Rehabilitators' Association (U.S.). Symposium. **Added/Corp** National Wildlife Rehabilitators' Association (U.S.). Vol. 3 (1984)-. Periodical. English. an. $27.50. National Wildlife Rehabilitation Association, 14 North Seventh Avenue, St. Cloud MN 56303. **Tel** (612)257-4086. ***Continues*** *Wildlife Rehabilitation.*
Ind/Abst Rev. Med. Vet. Entomol.

US/0361-1256
WILDLIFE RESEARCH. Main/Corp Minnesota. Section of Wildlife. Periodical. English. qt. Department of Natural Resources / Minnesota, 350 Centennial Building, St Paul MN 55155. **LC** SK411; .M55A. **DD** 639/.9/09776. ***Continues*** *Game Research Project.*
Ind/Abst Curr. Contents, Agric. Biol. Environ. Sci.; Field Crop Abstr.

US/0277-4070
WILDLIFE RESEARCH REPORT (DENVER, COLO.). (WILDLIFE RESEARCH REPORT.). [Wildl. res. rep.]. Began in 1980. English. Colorado Division of Wildlife, 6060 Broadway, Denver CO 80216. **LC** SK375; .W54. **DD** 639.9/09788. ***Continues*** *Game Research Report, 0531-1330.*

●US/1070-499X
WILDLIFE REVIEW & FISHERIES REVIEW. (WILDLIFE REVIEW & FISHERIES REVIEW [COMPUTER FILE].). [Wildl. rev. fish. rev.]. **Added/Corp** National Information Services Corporation. U.S. Fish and Wildlife Service. **VFOAT** Wildlife Review and Fisheries Review. (July 1992)-. Periodical. English. sa. $695.00. National Information Services Corp, 3100 St Paul Street, Wyman Towers, Suite 6, Baltimore MD 21218. **Tel** (410)243-0797, FAX (410)243-0982. **DD** 639. ***Continues in part*** *Wildlife & Fish Worldwide. Volume 1, 1046-6479.*

US/0043-5511
WILDLIFE REVIEW (FORT COLLINS). See Environmental Issues-Abstracting, Bibliographies and Statistics.

US/0091-7648
WILDLIFE SOCIETY BULLETIN. [Wildl. Soc. bull.]. **Main/Corp** Wildlife Society. **Added/Corp** Wildlife Society. Bulletin. Vol. 1 (Spring 1973)-. Periodical. English. Four times a year. $85.00 North America; $90.00 other (comes also with Journal of Wildlife Management and Wildlife Monographs). Wildlife Society, 5410 Grosvenor Lane, Bethesda MD 20814. **Tel** (301)897-9770, FAX (301)530-2471. **ED** Fred S. Guthery. **LC** SK351; .W62a. **DD** 639/.9/05. **CODEN** WLSBA6. **Pr Rev. Acid Free. Circ:** 6,000 (ctrl). Documents available from The Genuine Article, BIOSIS Document Express, UMI Article Clearinghouse. ***Supersedes** Wildlife Society News, 0043-552X.*
Desc: Contains original papers relating to all phases of wildlife management and conservation.
Ind/Abst AGRICOLA [Select. Cov.]; AQUAREF; Biol. Abstr.; Curr. Contents, Agric. Biol. Environ. Sci.; Dairy Sci. Abstr.; Ecol. Abstr.; EMBASE; Environ. Period. Bibliogr.; Expand. Acad. Index (1992-); Field Crop Abstr.; Fish Rev.; For. Abstr.; Geogr. Abstr. Phys. Geogr. (?-?); Geogr. Abstr. Human Geogr. (?-?); Grasslands For. Abstr.; Hortic. Abstr.; Index Vet.; Int. Dev. Abstr.; Key Word Index Wildl. Res.; Leis. Recreat. Tour. Abstr.; Newsp. Period. Abstr. (1989-); Ornamental Hort. (1991-); Res. Alert [Full Cov.]; Sci. Cit. Index; SCISEARCH; Soc. Sci. Cit. Index [Select. Cov.]; Vet. Bull.; Wildl. Rev.

US
WILDLIFE TECHNICAL BULLETIN.
Added/Corp Alaska. Dept. of Fish and Game. No. 7 (1984)-. Monographic series. English. Alaska Department of Fish and Game, PO Box 3-2000, Juneau AK 99802. **Tel** (907)465-4100, (907)465-4286. **LC** SK367; .G35. ***Continues** Game Technical Bulletin.*

●US/1070-5007
WILDLIFE WORLDWIDE. (WILDLIFE WORLDWIDE [COMPUTER FILE].). [Wildl. worldw.]. **Added/Corp** National Information Services Corporation. (July 1992)-. English. sa. $695.00. National Information Services Corp, 3100 St Paul Street, Wyman Towers, Suite 6, Baltimore MD 21218. **Tel** (410)243-0797, FAX (410)243-0982. **DD** 639. ***Continues in part** Wildlife & Fish Worldwide. Volume 1, 1046-6479.*

US/0164-3649
WISCONSERVATION. **VAT** Wisconsin Conservation. 1973. Periodical. English. mo. $3.00. Wisconsin Wildlife Federation, Tranquil Acres, Reeseville WI 53579. **Tel** (414)297-3131. **ED** Robert A Lachmund. **Bk Rev. Ad Acc. Circ:** 6,000 (ctrl).
Desc: Articles on legislation on state and national levels pertaining to conservation, conservation education, hunting, fishing, trapping, and other out of doors activities.

US/0736-2277
WISCONSIN NATURAL RESOURCES.
[Wis. nat. resour.]. **Added/Corp** Wisconsin. Dept. of Natural Resources. (Jan./Feb. 1977)-. Periodical. English. bm. $6.97 US; $9.97 Canada. Wisconsin Natural Resources, PO Box 7921, Madison WI 53707. **Tel** (800)678-9472, (800)444-5470. **(Subscription address:** Wisconsin Natural Resources, PO Box 7191, Madison WI 53707.**)** **ED** David L. Sperling. **LC** HC107.W6; A42. **DD** 333.7/16/09775. **Circ:** 80,000 (ctrl). ***Continues** Wisconsin Natural Resources Bulletin, 0147-7595.*
Desc: Wisconsin's natural resources and examinations of current environmental issues.
Ind/Abst Fish Rev.; GeoRef; Wildl. Rev.

US
WISCONSIN OUTDOORS AND CONSERVATION NEWS. ***Title Change.* See** Recreation, Leisure-Outdoor Life.

US/0030-7157
WONDERFUL WEST VIRGINIA.
Added/Corp West Virginia. Dept. of Natural Resources. Vol. 33, No. 11, Jan. (1970)-. Periodical. English. Twelve times a year. $12.00. Department of Natural Resources / West Virginia, State Capitol, Charleston WV 25305. **Tel** (304)558-9152. **ED** Nancy Clark. **LC** SK461; .A33. **DD** 333.7/09754. **Circ:** 60,000 (ctrl). ***Continues** Outdoor West Virginia.*
Desc: Articles about natural resources, parks and the natural and cultural heritage of West Virginia. Includes wildlife and scenic photographs.

US
WOODLAND DUNES DUNESLETTER.
Added/Corp Woodland Dunes Nature Center (Manitowoc, Wis.). **VFOAT** Dunesletter. (197?)-. Periodical. English. Four times a year (Mar., June, Sept., Dec.). $10.00 Comes with Woodland Dunes Nature Center membership. Woodland Dunes Nature Center, PO Box 2108, Manitowac WI 54221. **Tel** (414)793-4007.

CN/0229-7183
WORKING FOR WILDLIFE. (WORKING FOR WILDLIFE / WORLD WILDLIFE FUND CANADA.). [Work. wildl.]. **Added/Corp** World Wildlife Fund (Canada). Vol. 1, No. 1 (Feb./Mar. 1980)-. Periodical. English. Four times a year. 26.20Can$. World Wildlife Fund / Canada, 90 Eglinton Avenue East, Suite 504, Totonto Ontario M4P 2Z7 Canada. **Tel** (416)489-8800, (800)267-2632, FAX (416)489-3611. **ED** Pegi Dover and Carol Miller. **DD** 333.95/16/0601. **Bk Rev. Circ:** 50,000 (ctrl). ***Formed by the union of** World Wildlife Fund (Canada). (Newsletter), 0710-135X **and** Panada Club News, 0710-8133.*
Desc: Conservation work, including wildlife, wilderness, rainforest, and toxicology.

US
WORKING PAPER / UNIVERSITY OF MINNESOTA, CENTER FOR NATURAL RESOURCE POLICY AND MANAGEMENT STUDIES. **Added/Corp** University of Minnesota. Center for Natural Resource Policy and Management Studies. **VFOAT** Working Paper Series. No. 1 (1984)-. Monographic series. English.
Ind/Abst For. Abstr.

CN/1182-4506
WORKPLAN (TORONTO). (WORKPLAN.). [Workplan]. **Main/Corp** Ontario. Northwestern Ontario Forest Technology Development Unit. (1991)-. English. **DD** 354.7130082/338042.

UK
WORLD BIRDWATCH : THE NEWSLETTER OF THE INTERNATIONAL COUNCIL FOR BIRD PRESERVATION. (19??)-. Newsletter. English. qt. £25.00. Birdlife International, Wellbrook Court, Girton Road, Cambridge CB3 0NA England. **Tel** 011 44 223 277318, FAX 011 44 223277200. **ED** G.L.M. Green. **Bk Rev**, (Qty: varies). **Ad Acc, Adv Mgr:** Leslie Stanton, **Tel** same as publisher. **Circ:** 6,000.
Desc: News and articles on bird conservation.

US/0092-0908
WORLD DIRECTORY OF ENVIRONMENTAL ORGANIZATIONS.
[World dir. environ. organ.]. **Added/Corp** Sierra Club. International Union for Conservation of Nature and Natural Resources. California Institute of Public Affairs. **VFOAT** Annuaire Mondial des Organismes de l'Environnement. (1973)-. Multiple languages (English and French). $27.44. Europa Publications Ltd, 18 Bedford Square, London WC1B 3JN England. **Tel** 011 44 71 5808236, telex 21540 EUROPA G. **LC** S920; .W67. **DD** 333.

US/1042-8011
WORLD RESOURCE REVIEW. [World resour. rev.]. **Added/Corp** Institute for World Resource Research. (1990)-. Periodical. English. qt. $72.00 (individuals), $143.00 (institutions) North America; (add $24.60 airmail postage) other. SUPCON International, One Heritage Plaza, Woodridge IL 60517. **Tel** (708)910-1551, FAX (708)910-1561. **ED** Sinyan Shen. **LC** HC10; .W826. **DD** 333.7/05. **CODEN** WRRVE5. Index available. cum. index. **Bk Rev. Ad Acc. Pr Rev. Circ:** 2,000. available in microform.
Desc: Oriented towards policy makers and persons in business and government who have an interest in the technical expert's analysis of the impacts of technology and resource management.

US/0887-0403
WORLD RESOURCES. (WORLD RESOURCES : A REPORT BY THE WORLD RESOURCES INSTITUTE AND THE INTERNATIONAL INSTITUTE FOR ENVIRONMENT AND DEVELOPMENT.). [World res.]. 1986-. English (Chinese). an. $50.00. Marketing Manager, World Resources Institute, 1750 New York Avenue NW, Washington DC 20006. **Tel** (202)393-4055, telex 904059 WSH. **ED** Kathleen Courrier. **LC** HC10; .W827. **DD** 333.7/05. **CODEN** WORSE9. Index available. **Bk Rev. Circ:** 20,000. Documents available from BIOSIS Document Express.
Desc: An assessment of the resource base that supports the global economy, produced jointly by the World Resources Institute and the International Institute for Environment and Development. The wealth of facts and data makes it an indispensable one-stop desk-top reference for policy-makers, journalists, scholars and activists with an interest in the global prospect.
Ind/Abst Biol. Abstr. (1986-).

US/0270-8019
WORLDWATCH PAPER. [Worldwatch paper]. **Added/Corp** Worldwatch Institute. (1975)-. Monographic series. English. ir (published 6-8 times per year). Price varies per volume (comes with Worldwatch Library membership). Worldwatch Institute, 1776 Massachusetts Avenue Northwest, Washington DC 20036. **Tel** (202)452-1999, (800)825-0061. **(Subscription address:** Worldwatch Institute, 1776 Massechusets Avenue Northwest, Washington DC 20036.**)** **CODEN** WOPADC. Documents available from BIOSIS Document Express.
Ind/Abst AgBiotech News Inf.; Biol. Abstr.; For. Prod. Abstr.; Geogr. Abstr. Phys. Geogr.; Geogr. Abstr. Human Geogr.; Int. Dev. Abstr.; Popul. Index (?-?); Rural Dev. Abstr.; World Agric. Econ.

SZ/0254-3893
WWF NEWS. (WWF NEWS : THE INTERNATIONAL NEWSPAPER OF WWF, WORLD WIDE FUND FOR NATURE.). [WWF news]. **Added/Corp** World Wildlife Fund. World Wide Fund for Nature. (19??)-. Periodical. English. bm. $21.00. WWF International, Avenue Dumont Blanc, CH 1196 Gland Switzerland. **Tel** 41 22 364 9552, FAX 41 22 364 5358. **ED** Lesa Griffith. Index available. cum. index. **Bk Rev**, (Qty: 12). **Circ:** 21,000 (ctrl). Documents available from Documents on Demand. ***Continues** World wildlife News.*
Desc: Provides conservation news on WWF fieldwork and policy.
Ind/Abst Environ. Abstr.

US/0043-9819
WYOMING WILDLIFE. [Wyo. wildl.].
Added/Corp Wyoming. Game and Fish Dept. Wyoming. Game and Fish Commission. **VFOAT** Wyoming Wildlife. Vol. 4, No. 2/3 (Feb./Mar. 1939)-. Periodical. English. Twelve times a year. Free to Wyoming schools, colleges, and public libraries; $10.00 others. Wyoming Game & Fish Commission, 5400 Bishop Boulevard, Cheyenne WY 82006. **Tel** (307)777-4535, (800)548-9453, FAX (307)777-4610. **ED** Chris Madson. **CODEN** WYWLA. Index available. cum. index. **Circ:** 34,000. Documents available from BIOSIS Document Express. ***Continues** Wyoming Wild Life Magazine.*
Desc: Wildlife, conservation, hunting, and fishing.
Ind/Abst Biol. Abstr.; Wildl. Rev.

US/0192-4621
YEAR-END REPORT - HERITAGE CONSERVATION AND RECREATION SERVICE. **Main/Corp** United States. Heritage Conservation and Recreation Service. 1978-. Government Publication. English. an. US Department of the Interior / Heritage Conservation & Recreation Service, Washington DC 20240. **LC** E151; .U53A. **DD** 353.008/5.

SZ
YEARBOOK / WWF, WORLD WILDLIFE FUND. **Main/Corp** World Wildlife Fund. **VFOAT** WWF Yearbook. **VAT** World Wildlife Fund Yearbook. Began with: 1979-80. English. an. WWF International, Avenue Dumont Blanc, CH 1196 Gland Switzerland. **Tel** 41 22 364 9552, FAX 41 22 364 5358. ***Continues** World Wildlife Yearbook.*

US/0276-9271
YOUTH CONSERVATION CORPS. (YOUTH CONSERVATION CORPS : YEARBOOK / UNITED STATES YOUTH CONSERVATION CORPS.). [Youth Conserv. Corps]. 1979-. English. an. Division of State Parks, Capital Complex, Carson City NV 89710. **LC** S932.N4; Y33. **DD** 333.78/3/09793. ***Continues** YCC Program, 0276-9263.*

US/0190-8367
YOUTH CONSERVATION CORPS PROGRAM. **Main/Corp** United States. Youth Conservation Corps. **VFOAT** Annual Report: Youth Conservation Corps Programs. English. an. National Park Service, Room 5103/1100 L Street NW, Washington DC 20240. **LC** S914; .Y68A. **DD** 353.008/232. ***Continues** Youth Conservation Corps Pilot Program, 0094-503X.*

ECOLOGY

SP/0210-9506
ACTA BOTANICA MALACITANA. See Biology-Botany.

FR/1146-609X
ACTA OECOLOGICA (MONTROUGE).
(ACTA OECOLOGICA.). [Acta oecol.]. **Added/Corp** Institut National de la Recherche Agronomique (France) O.R.S.T.O.M. (Agency : France). Vol. 11, No. 1 (1990)-. Academic Scholarly Publication. English (French). Six times a year. 1100.00F (institutions), 550.00 (individual) France; 1400.00F (institutions), 825.00F (individuals) other. Gauthier-Villars, 15 rue Gossin, 92543 Montrouge Cedex France. **Tel** 33 1 40 92 65 00, FAX 33 1 40 92 65 97. **(Subscription address:** Centrale des Revues, 11 rue Gossin, 92543 Montrouge Cedex France.**)** **ED** R. Barbault. **LC** QH540; .A22. **DD** 574.5/05. **CODEN** ACOEEY. **[CCC].** Documents available from The Genuine Article, BIOSIS Document Express, CASDDS. ***Formed by the union of** Acta Oecologica. Oecologia Generalis, 0243-766X; Acta Oecologica. Oecologia Applicata, 0243-7678 **and** Acta Oecologica. Oecologia Plantarum, 0243-7651.*
Desc: Concerned with ecology; provides rapid publication of research and review articles. Specific research areas covered include: behavioural ecology, genetical ecology, population biology, community ecology, and the functioning of natural and man-modified ecosystems.
Ind/Abst Biocont. News Inf. (1991-); Biol. Abstr. (1991-); Chem. Abstr.; Crop Physiol. Abstr.; Curr. Aware. Biol. Sci., CABS; Curr. Contents; Ecol. Abstr.; Ecology Abstr.; Entomol. Abstr.; Field Crop Abstr.; Fish Rev. (Jan. 1989-July 1992); Geogr. Abstr. Phys. Geogr.; Grasslands For. Abstr.; Helminthol. Abstr. (1991-); Hortic. Abstr.; Irr. Drain. Abstr.; Res. Alert; Rev. Agric. Entomol.; Rev. Plant Pathol.; Sci. Cit. Index; SCISEARCH; Seed Abstr.; Soils Fert.; Weed Abstr.; Wildl. Rev. (Jan. 1989-July 1992).

UK/0065-2504
ADVANCES IN ECOLOGICAL RESEARCH. [Adv. ecol. res.]. Vol. 1 (1962)-. Monographic series. English. ir. Price varies per volume. Academic Press Ltd., A Division of Harcourt Brace &

Company Ltd., 24-28 Oval Road, London NW1 7DX England. **Tel** 071 267 4466, FAX 071 482 2293, 071 485 4752, telex 25775 ACPRES G. **(Subscription address:** Academic Press Inc., PO Box 620000, Orlando FL 32891-8340.**) ED** J. B. Cragg. **LC** QH540; .A23. **DD** 574.5082. **NLM** W1 AD55. **CODEN** AELRAY. **Pr Rev.** Documents available from The Genuine Article, BIOSIS Document Express, CASDDS.
Ind/Abst Biol. Agric. Index; Biol. Abstr.; Chem. Abstr.; Curr. Aware. Biol. Sci., CABS; Fish Rev. (Jan. 1989-July 1992); For. Abstr.; Index Sci. Rev. [Full Cov.]; Life Sci. Collect.; Pollut. Abstr. Indexes; Res. Alert [Full Cov.]; Rev. Agric. Entomol.; Sci. Cit. Index; SCISEARCH; Seed Abstr.; Soils Fert.; Wildl. Rev. (Jan. 1989-July 1992).

US/0147-4863
ADVANCES IN MICROBIAL ECOLOGY. [Adv. microb. ecol.]. Vol. 1 (1977)-. Academic Scholarly Publication. English. ir. Price varies per volume. Plenum Press, 233 Spring Street, New York NY 10013-1578. **Tel** (212)620-8000, (800)221-9369, FAX (212)463-0742, (212)807-1047, telex 23/421139. **ED** Gwynfryn Jones. **LC** QR100; .A36. **DD** 576/.15. **NLM** W1 AD68M. **CODEN** AMIED5. **Pr Rev.** Documents available from The Genuine Article, CASDDS.
Ind/Abst AGRICOLA [Select. Cov.]; Biocont. News Inf.; Biodeter. Abstr.; Chem. Abstr.; For. Prod. Abstr.; Index Sci. Rev. [Full Cov.]; Index Vet.; Nutr. Abstr. Rev., Ser. B, Live Feeds and Feed.; Nutr. Abstr. Rev., Ser. A, Hum. Exp.; Life Sci. Collect.; Res. Alert [Full Cov.]; Sci. Cit. Index; SCISEARCH; Vet. Bull.

SG/1010-5522
AFRICAN ENVIRONMENT. See Environmental Issues.

UK/0141-6707
AFRICAN JOURNAL OF ECOLOGY. [Afr. j. ecol.]. **Added/Corp** East African Wild Life Society. Vol. 17 (March 1979)-. Academic Scholarly Publication. English. qt (4 issues). $284.00 US & Canada; £166.00 Europe; £183.00 other. Blackwell Scientific Publications Ltd, Marston Book Services, PO Box 87, Oxford OX2 ODT UK. **Tel** 011 44 865 791155, FAX 011 44 865 791927, telex 837 515 MARDIS G. **ED** S. K. Eltringham and F. I. B. Kayanja. **LC** QL337.E25; E3. **DD** 599/.005. **CODEN** AJOEDE. **[CCC]. Bk Rev. Ad Acc. Pr Rev. Circ:** 12,000. available on microfilm and microfiche from University Microfilms International (UMI). Documents available from The Genuine Article, BIOSIS Document Express. ***Continues** East African Wildlife Journal.*
Desc: Ecology of African animals, populations, behaviour, breeding, etc.
Ind/Abst Abstr. Anthropol.; Anim. Breed. Abstr.; Biol. Abstr.; Curr. Aware. Biol. Sci., CABS; Curr. Contents, Agric. Biol. Environ. Sci.; Curr. Ref. Fish Res.; Dairy Sci. Abstr.; Ecol. Abstr.; Ecology Abstr.; Environ. Period. Bibliogr.; Field Crop Abstr.; Fish Rev.; For. Prod. Abstr.; For. Abstr.; Geogr. Abstr. Phys. Geogr.; Grasslands For. Abstr.; Index Vet.; Int. Dev. Abstr.; Key Word Index Wildl. Res.; Nutr. Abstr. Rev., Ser. B, Live Feeds and Feed.; Nutr. Abstr. Rev., Ser. A, Hum. Exp.; Life Sci. Collect.; Plant Breed. Abstr.; Plant Genet. Resour. Abstr.; Protozoolog. Abstr.; Res. Alert [Full Cov.]; Rev. Agric. Entomol.; Sci. Cit. Index; SCISEARCH; Seed Abstr.; Soils Fert.; Vet. Bull.; Wildl. Rev.

NE/0167-4366
AGROFORESTRY SYSTEMS. [Agrofor. syst.]. **Added/Corp** International Council for Research in Agroforestry. Vol. 1, No. 1 (1982)-. Periodical. English. mo. $1,128.00. Kluwer Academic Publishers, Postbus 322, 3300 AH Dordrecht, The Netherlands. **Tel** 011 (31) 78 524400, FAX 011 31 78 183273, telex 20083. **ED** H J von Maydell. **CODEN** AGSYE6. **[CCC]. Bk Rev. Ad Acc. Pr Rev. Acid Free. Circ:** 500. available on microfilm and microfiche from University Microfilms International (UMI). Documents available from The Genuine Article, BIOSIS Document Express, Documents on Demand.
Desc: An international, multidisciplinary journal which provides a rapid publication outlet for all types of research concerned with the various aspects of agroforestry systems and for critical reviews on all sustainable land management systems which combine agriculture, animal husbandry, and trees on the same unit of land.
Ind/Abst Agrofor. Abstr. (19??-19??); Biol. Abstr.; Curr. Aware. Biol. Sci., CABS; Curr. Contents, Agric. Biol. Environ. Sci.; Ecol. Abstr.; Environ. Abstr.; Environ. Period. Bibliogr.; Field Crop Abstr.; Fish Rev. (Jan. 1989-July 1992); For. Prod. Abstr. (1991-); For. Abstr.; Geogr. Abstr. Phys. Geogr.; Geogr. Abstr. Human Geogr.; Grasslands For. Abstr.; Hortic. Abstr.; Int. Dev. Abstr.; Int. Labour Doc.; Irr. Drain. Abstr.; Maize Abstr. (1990-); Plant Breed. Abstr.; Plant Genet. Resour. Abstr.; Potato Abstr.; Res. Alert [Select. Cov.]; Rice Abstr.; Rural Dev. Abstr.; SCISEARCH; Seed Abstr.; Soc. Sci. Cit. Index [Select. Cov.]; Soils Fert.; Soyabean Abstr.; Weed Abstr.; Wheat Barley Trit. Abstr.; Wildl. Rev. (Jan. 1989-July 1992); World Agric. Econ.

IT
AIRONE JUNIOR. (19??)-. Italian. mo. L48000 Italy; L78000 other. Giorgio Mondadori Intl, Via A Ponti 10, 20143 Milan Italy. **Tel** 011 39 2 891661.

SJ
AL-BIAH / TUSDIRUHA AMANAT AL-LAJNAH AL-QAWMIYAH LIL-BIAH, AL-MAJLIS AL-QAWMI LIL-BUHUTH. V. 1, No. 1, (Jan. 1980)-. Periodical. Arabic. qt. Amanat Al-Lajnah Al-Qawmiyah Lil-Biiah, Al-Majlis Al-Qawmi Lil-Buhuth S B 2404, Al-Khartum Sudan. **LC** QH195.S9; B5.

CN/0835-5851
ALCES. See Environmental Issues-Conservation and Natural Resources.

IT/0392-5722
ALTROCONSUMO. [Altroconsumo]. (1974)-. Periodical. Italian. mo (11 issues). L42700.00 Italy; L59500.00 other. Editoriale Altroconsumo, Cas Postale 10608, 20110 Milan Italy. **Tel** 011 39 2 66720401. **UDC** 33.123.4.

IT
AMBIENTE. Italian. mo. L100.000 Italy; L120.00 other. Ceep, Via S Francesco DA Paola 17, 10123 Turin Italy. **Tel** 06-6781713, FAX 06-6781667. Index available. **Bk Rev. Ad Acc. Circ:** 15,000 (ctrl).
Desc: Editorials, articles, notes on local nes, reviews, and legislative surveys.

IT
AMBIENTE SALUTE TERRITORIO. Italian. Three times a year. L50000.00. Liviana Medicina SRL, Via A de Gasperi 55, 80133 Naples Italy. **Tel** 011 39 81 5524733, FAX 011 39 81 5518295. **Bk Rev,** (Qty: 12). **Ad Acc, Adv Mgr:** Guido Gnocchi. **Circ:** 4,000 (ctrl).

SP/0213-4004
ANALES DE BIOLOGIA. SECCION BIOLOGIA AMBIENTAL. [An. biol., Secc. biol. ambient.]. **Added/Corp** Universidad de Murcia. Facultad de Biologia. **VFOAT** Seccion Biologia Ambiental; Biologia Ambiental; Anales de Biologia. Biologia Ambiental. (1985)-. Periodical. Spanish. an. 2000ptas. University of Murcia Secretariado Publicaciones, Apartado 4021, 30380 Murcia Spain. **Tel** 011 34 68 363013, 011 34 68 363014. **LC** QH540; .A525. **DD** 574/.5/05. **CODEN** ABSAEZ. Documents available from BIOSIS Document Express.
Ind/Abst Biol. Abstr. (-1988); Entomol. Abstr.

FR/1142-2998
ANNALES SCIENTIFIQUES DE L'UNIVERSITE DE FRANCHE-COMTE. BIOLOGIE-ECOLOGIE. See Biology.

US/0066-4162
ANNUAL REVIEW OF ECOLOGY AND SYSTEMATICS. [Ann. rev. ecolog. syst.]. Vol. 1 (1970)-. English. an (November). $47.00 US; $52.00 other. Annual Reviews Inc., 4139 El Camino Way, PO Box 10139, Palo Alto CA 94303-0139. **Tel** (415)493-4400, (800)523-8635, FAX (415)855-9815. **ED** Daphne Gail Fautin. **LC** QH540; .A53. **DD** 574.5/05. **NLM** W1 AN77K. **CODEN** ARECBC. **[CCC].** Index available. cum. index. **Pr Rev.** ctrl circ. available on microfilm and microfiche from University Microfilms International (UMI). Documents available from The Genuine Article, BIOSIS Document Express, CASDDS.
Desc: Comprehensive, thorough coverage of latest advances in ecology and systematics, written by acknowledged experts in the field. Extensive literature citations included.
Ind/Abst AGRICOLA [Select. Cov.]; Anim. Breed. Abstr.; Biol. Agric. Index; Biol. Abstr.; Chem. Abstr. (1970-1982); Curr. Aware. Biol. Sci., CABS; Curr. Contents, Agric. Biol. Environ. Sci.; Ecology Abstr.; Field Crop Abstr.; Fish Rev. (19??-199?); For. Prod. Abstr.; For. Abstr.; Grasslands For. Abstr.; Helminthol. Abstr.; Index Sci. Rev. [Full Cov.]; Key Word Index Wildl. Res.; Life Sci. Collect.; Plant Breed. Abstr.; Protozoolog. Abstr.; Res. Alert [Full Cov.]; Rev. Agric. Entomol.; Rev. Med. Vet. Entomol.; Sci. Cit. Index; SCISEARCH; Soils Fert.; Wildl. Rev. (19??-199?).

US/0892-7936
ANTHROZOOS. See Zoology.

US/0893-7702
AQUAPHYTE. See Biology-Botany.

UK/1052-7613
AQUATIC CONSERVATION. (AQUATIC CONSERVATION : MARINE AND FRESHWATER ECOSYSTEMS.). [Aquat. conserv.]. **VFOAT** Aquatic Conservation, Marine and Freshwater Ecosystems. (1991)-. Periodical. English. qt. $225.00. John Wiley & Sons Ltd., Baffins Lane, Chichester West Sussex PO19 1UD England. **Tel** 0243 779777, FAX 0243 776128 BTG:JWP001, telex 86290 WIBOOKG. **(Subscription address:** John Wiley / Philadelphia, PO Box 7247, Philadelphia PA 19170.**) ED** Philip J. Boon and Roger Mitchell. **LC** QH541.5.W3; A67. **DD** 333.95/216/05. **CODEN** AQCOEY. available on microfilm and microfiche from University Microfilms International (UMI). Documents available from The Genuine Article.
Desc: Original papers that relate to freshwater, brackish or marine habitats and encouraging work that spans these ecosystems. Provides forum in which all aspects of the conservation of aquatic biological resources can be presented and discussed, enabling greater cooperation and efficiency in solving problems in aquatic resource conservation.
Ind/Abst Curr. Aware. Biol. Sci., CABS; Ecol. Abstr.; Environ. Period. Bibliogr. (?-?); Geogr. Abstr. Phys. Geogr.; Geogr. Abstr. Human Geogr.; Res. Alert [Full Cov.]; SCISEARCH.

UK/0953-4466
AQUATIC ENVIRONMENT PROTECTION : ANALYTICAL METHODS. [Aquat. environ. prot. anal. methods]. Monographic series. English. Price varies per volume. Ministry of Agriculture Fisheries & Food, Directorate of Fisheries Research, Lowestoft Suffolk NR33 0HT England.

US/0734-1687
AQUATIC TOXICOLOGY SERIES. [Aquat. toxicol. series.]. Vol. 1 (1982)-. Monographic series. English. ir. Price varies per volume. Raven Press, 1185 Avenue of the Americas, 37th Floor, New York NY 10036. **Tel** (212)930-9500, (212)930-9604, FAX (212)869-3495, (212)302-8507, telex 640073. **ED** Lavern J. Weber. **CODEN** ATOXD5. Documents available from BIOSIS Document Express.
Ind/Abst Biol. Abstr.; Mar. Sci. Contents Tables.

MY/0128-0538
ASIAN WETLAND NEWS. See Environmental Issues-Conservation and Natural Resources.

US/0898-915X
AUDUBON ACTIVIST. [Audubon act.]. **Added/Corp** National Audubon Society. **VFOAT** Activist. Vol. 1 No. 1 (Sept. 1986)-. Periodical. English. bm. Free to members; $20.00 membership. National Audubon Society, 700 Broadway, New York NY 10003. **Tel** (212)979-3117. **ED** Fred Baumgarten, (212)546-9197. **DD** 363. **Circ:** 20,000. ***Continues** NAS.*

PL/0137-3668
AURA. [Aura]. (1973)-. Periodical. Polish. mo. $39.00. **(Subscription address:** ARS Polona, PO Box 1001, 00068 Warsaw Poland.**) UDC** 502.5.

AT/0307-692X
AUSTRALIAN JOURNAL OF ECOLOGY. [Aust. j. ecol.]. **Added/Corp** Ecological Society of Australia. (Jan. 1976)-. Academic Scholarly Publication. English. Four times a year. 320.00Aus$ Australia; $362.00 other. Blackwell Scientific Publications Australia, 54 University Street, PO Box 378, Carlton Victoria 3053 Australia. **Tel** 011 61 3 3470300, FAX 011 61 3 3475001, telex 10716421. **(Subscription address:** UK/ Marston Book Services, PO Box 87, Oxford UK; US/ 3 Cambridge Center, Suite 208, Cambridge MA 02142; Germany/ Meinekestrasse 4, D-1000 Berlin 15 Germany; France/ Arnette, 2 rue Casimir Delavigne, 75006 Paris France; Austria/ Blackwell MZV, Medizinische Zeitschriftenverlags Gesellschaft, Feldgasse 13, A-1238 Vienna Austria**) ED** M. Bull, D. O'Dowd and P. Fairweather. **LC** QH197; .A78. **DD** 574.5/05. **CODEN** AJECDQ. **[CCC].** Index available in last issue of volume--attached. **Bk Rev. Pr Rev. Circ:** 1,000. available on microfilm and microfiche from University Microfilms International (UMI). Documents available from The Genuine Article, BIOSIS Document Express, CASDDS.
Desc: Devoted to reports of ecological research and critical reviews of methodology based on work of Australasian origin. Much of the material has a strong theoretical base and is therefore of relevance to workers in other geographical areas.
Ind/Abst Abstr. Anthropol.; AGRICOLA [Select. Cov.]; Biodeter. Abstr.; Biol. Abstr.; Chem. Abstr. (1976-1985); Curr. Aware. Biol. Sci., CABS; Curr. Contents, Agric. Biol. Environ. Sci.; Curr. Ref. Fish Res.; Ecol. Abstr.; Ecology Abstr.; Entomol. Abstr.; Environ. Period. Bibliogr.; Field Crop Abstr.; For. Prod. Abstr.; For. Abstr.; Geogr. Abstr. Phys. Geogr. (?-?); Geol. Abstr.; Grasslands For. Abstr.; Key Word Index Wildl. Res.; Life Sci. Collect.; Plant Genet. Resour. Abstr.; Protozoolog. Abstr.; Res. Alert [Full Cov.]; Rice Abstr.; Sci. Cit. Index; SCISEARCH; Soc. Sci. Cit. Index [Select. Cov.]; Soils Fert.

AT/0814-0626
AUSTRALIAN JOURNAL OF ENVIRONMENTAL EDUCATION. See Education.

US/1045-2249
BEHAVIORAL ECOLOGY. (BEHAVIORAL ECOLOGY : OFFICIAL JOURNAL OF THE INTERNATIONAL SOCIETY FOR BEHAVIORAL ECOLOGY.). [Behav. ecol.]. **Added/Corp** International Society for Behavioral Ecology. Vol. 1, No. 1 (Summer 1990)-. Periodical. English. qt (4 issues). $153.00 US; $175.00 other. Oxford University Press / New York, 200 Madison Avenue, New York NY 10016. **Tel** (212)679-7300, (919)677-0977, (800)451-7556, (800)445-9714, FAX (919)677-1303. **(Subscription address:** Oxford University Press / USA, Journals Marketing Department, Oxford University Press, 2001 Evans Road, Cary NC 27513.**) LC** QL750; .B534. **DD** 591.51/05. **CODEN** BEECE3. **[CCC]. Ad Acc. Acid Free.** available on microfilm and microfiche from University Microfilms International (UMI). Documents available from The Genuine Article, BIOSIS Document Express.

Desc: Covering both empirical and theoretical work, the taxonomic scope of this journal is very wide, with articles covering the range from simple invertebrates to man. Areas of research covered include foraging, anti-predator, mating and parental care strategies, habitat selection, dispersal and migration, sexual selection, cooperation and conflict, communication, spacing and group behavior, and social organization.
Ind/Abst Anim. Behav. Abstr.; Biol. Abstr. (1990-); Curr. Aware. Biol. Sci., CABS; Curr. Contents, Agric. Biol. Environ. Sci.; Ecol. Abstr.; Ecology Abstr.; Res. Alert [Select. Cov.]; SCISEARCH; Zool. Rec.

GW/0340-5443
BEHAVIORAL ECOLOGY AND SOCIOBIOLOGY. [Behav. ecol. sociobiol.]. Vol. 1 (1976)-. Periodical. English. Twelve times a year. DM1718.00. Springer-Verlag GmbH & Company KG, Heidelberger Platz 3, D 14197 Berlin Germany. **Tel** 011 49 30 8207223, FAX 011 49 30 8214091, telex 183 319 SPBLN D. **(Subscription address:** Springer Verlag New York Inc. / for North America, 44 Hartz Way, Secaucus NJ 07096.**) ED** J Alcock, J W Bradbury, R H Crozier and P Marler. **LC** QL750; .B533. **DD** 591.5/05. **NLM** W1 BE13C. **CODEN** BESOD6. **[CCC]. Pr Rev.** available on microfilm and microfiche from University Microfilms International (UMI). Documents available from The Genuine Article.
Desc: Publishes original contributions and short communications dealing with quantitative studies and the experimental analysis of animal behaviour.
Ind/Abst Abstr. Anthropol.; AGRICOLA [Select. Cov.]; Anim. Breed. Abstr.; Biocont. News Inf.; Curr. Aware. Biol. Sci., CABS; Curr. Contents, Agric. Biol. Environ. Sci.; Curr. Ref. Fish Res.; Ecol. Abstr.; Ecology Abstr.; Entomol. Abstr.; Environ. Period. Bibliogr.; Geogr. Abstr. Phys. Geogr.; Helminthol. Abstr. (19??-19??); Key Word Index Wildl. Res.; Nutr. Abstr. Rev., Ser. B, Live Feeds and Feed.; Life Sci. Collect.; Phys. Briefs; Postharvest News Inf.; Protozoolog. Abstr.; Psychol. Abstr. (1982-); PsycINFO; PsycLit; Res. Alert [Full Cov.]; Rev. Agric. Entomol.; Rev. Med. Vet. Entomol.; Sci. Cit. Index; SCISEARCH; Soc. Sci. Cit. Index [Select. Cov.]; Wildl. Rev.

US/0095-4640
BENCHMARK PAPERS IN ECOLOGY. [Benchmark pap. ec.]. Vol. 1 (1974)-. Monographic series. English. ir. Price varies per volume. Van Nostrand Reinhold Company Inc., 115 5th Avenue, New York NY 10003. **Tel** (212)254-3232, FAX (212)673-1239, telex 272562. **(Subscription address:** Van Nostrand Reinhold, 7625 Empire Drive, Florence, KY 41042, telephone: (800)842-3636**) ED** F. B. Golley. **NLM** W1 BE515E. **CODEN** BPECDB. Documents available from BIOSIS Document Express.
Ind/Abst Biol. Abstr. (-1983).

CN/0715-4259
BETWEEN THE ISSUES. [Between issues]. **Added/Corp** Ecology Action Centre. (1980)-. Periodical. English. qt. 40.00Can$. Ecology Action Centre, 3115 Veith Street 3rd Floor, Halifax Nova Scotia B3K 3G9 Canada. **Tel** (902)454-7828. **DD** 304.2/0971.

GW/0067-8244
BIBLIOTH·EQUE ARCTIQUE ET ANTARCTIQUE. 1 (1960)-. Monographic series. French. ir. Walter de Gruyter Inc., PO Box 303421, D 10728 Berlin Germany. **Tel** 011 49 30 260050, FAX 011 49 30 26005251. **DD** 998; 999.

UK/0305-1978
BIOCHEMICAL SYSTEMATICS AND ECOLOGY. See Biology-Biochemistry.

NE/0168-2563
BIOGEOCHEMISTRY. See Environmental Issues-Conservation and Natural Resources.

RU
BIOGEOTSENOLOGIIA. Added/Corp Gosudarstvennaia Publichnaia Nauchno-Tekhnicheskaia Biblioteka (Akademiia Nauk SSSR). (1973)-. Academic Scholarly Publication. Multiple languages (Russian and Multiple languages). mo. 0.19rub (single issue). Izdatelstvo Nauka / Akademiia Nauk, Publishing House of the Russian Academy of Sciences, Leninskii Porspekt 14, 117901 Moscow Russia. **Tel** 011 95 954-21-53, FAX 011 95 938-21-44, telex 411964. **LC** Z5322.E2; B55; QH540.

RU
BIOKHIMICHESKAIA EKOLOGIIA I MEDITSINA. See Medical Science and Technology.

DK
BIOLOGISKE MILJUNDERSGELSER I NORDGRNLAND. See Biology.

FR
BIOMETRIE ET ECOLOGIE. Main/Corp Societe Francaise de Biometrie. No. 1, (1978)-. Periodical. French (summaries and/or abstracts in English).

GW/0935-7092
BIOORGANIC MARINE CHEMISTRY. [Bioorg. mar. chem.]. **VFOAT** Bio-Organic Marine Chemistry. Vol. 1 (1987)-. Monographic series. English. ir. Price varies per volume. Springer-Verlag GmbH & Company KG, Heidelberger Platz 3, D 14197 Berlin Germany. **Tel** 011 49 30 8207223, FAX 011 49 30 8214091, telex 183 319 SPBLN D. **(Subscription address:** Springer Verlag New York Inc. / for North America, 44 Hartz Way, Secaucus NJ 07096.**) ED** Paul J. Scheuer. **LC** QH541.5.S3; B575. **DD** 574.5/2636. **NLM** W1; BI876KH. **CODEN** BMACE5. Documents available from BIOSIS Document Express, CASDDS. ***Continues** Marine Natural Products, 0163-8572.*
Desc: Series covering marine ecology, natural products and bioorganic chemistry.
Ind/Abst Biol. Abstr. (1987-); Chem. Abstr.

FR/0395-7217
BULLETIN D'ECOLOGIE. [Bull. ecol.]. **Added/Corp** Societe d'Ecologie. Vol. 4 (1973)-. Bulletin. French. qt. 520.00F institutions, 425.00F individuals, EEC; 540.00F institutions, 500.00F individuals, other. Societe d'Ecologie, 57 rue Cuvier, 75231 Paris Cedex 05 France. **Tel** 011 33 1 3365432. **CODEN** BUECDC. Documents available from BIOSIS Document Express.
Ind/Abst Biocont. News Inf.; Biol. Abstr.; For. Abstr.; GeoRef; Grasslands For. Abstr.; Irr. Drain. Abstr.; Life Sci. Collect.; Protozoolog. Abstr.; Rev. Med. Vet. Entomol.; Soils Fert.

●US
BULLETIN OF TALL TIMBERS RESEARCH, INC. See Forestry.

US/0012-9623
BULLETIN OF THE ECOLOGICAL SOCIETY OF AMERICA. [Bull. Ecol. Soc. Am.]. **Added/Corp** Ecological Society of America. Vol. 1 (1917)-. Periodical. English. qt (Mar., June, Sept. and Dec.). $25.00 (institutions) US; $35.00 (institutions) other. Ecological Society of America, Center for Environmental Studies, Arizona State University, Tempe AZ 85287-3211. **Tel** (602)965-3000, FAX (602)965-8087. **DD** 574. **NLM** W1 BU846F. **CODEN** BECLAG. available on microfilm and microfiche from University Microfilms International (UMI). Documents available from BIOSIS Document Express. ***Absorbed** Ecological Society of America. Directory of Members. **Continued in part by** Ecological Society of America. Directory.*
Ind/Abst Biol. Abstr.; Curr. Aware. Biol. Sci., CABS; Ecol. Abstr. (?-?); Fish Rev.; Life Sci. Collect.; Wildl. Rev.

US/0146-6429
BULLETIN OF THE SOCIETY OF VECTOR ECOLOGISTS. (BULLETIN OF THE SOCIETY FOR VECTOR ECOLOGY.). [Bull. Soc. Vector Ecol.]. **Added/Corp** Society for Vector Ecology. (198?)-. English. Twice a year (June & Dec.). $45.00 Comes with Society for Vector Ecology membership. Society for Vector Ecology, PO Box 87, Santa Ana CA 92702. **Tel** (714)971-2421, FAX (714)971-3940. **ED** Marc J. Klowden Ph.D (editor's address: Division of Entomology, University of Idaho, Moscow, ID 83844-2339, phone: (208)885-7546). **LC** RA639; .S63a. **DD** 614.4/3/05. **NLM** W1; BU889EG. **CODEN** BSVEEM. **Bk Rev. Ad Acc, Adv Mgr:** H. B. Munn, **Tel** (209)295-3540. **Pr Rev. Circ:** 850. Documents available from BIOSIS Document Express. ***Continues** Society of Vector Ecologists. Bulletin of the Society of Vector Ecologists, 0146-6429.*
Ind/Abst Biocont. News Inf.; Biol. Abstr.; Ecology Abstr.; Rev. Med. Vet. Entomol.; Rice Abstr.; Trop. Dis. Bull.

US/0040-9618
BULLETIN OF THE TORREY BOTANICAL CLUB, THE. See Biology-Botany.

FR/0759-2310
CAHIERS - ASSOCIATION INTERNATIONALE DES ENTRETIENS ECOLOGIQUES. (1984)-. Periodical. French. qt. 125.00F France; 135.00F other. AIDEC, BP 108, 21003 Dijon Cedex France. **UDC** 502.7:719. ***Continues** Cahiers Trimestriels.*

US/0889-7344
CAMPUS ECOLOGIST, THE. [Campus ecol.]. Vol. 1, No. 1 (Winter 1983)-. Periodical. English. Four times a year. $12.00. Campus Ecologist Newsletter, PO Box 9597, Fort Collins CO 80525. **Tel** (303)493-3239. **ED** James H Banning. **DD** 378. **Bk Rev. Circ:** 300.
Desc: A newsletter for the exchange of information, ideas and resources about college students and their environment.

US/0008-4271
CANADIAN JOURNAL OF SOIL SCIENCE. See Earth Sciences-Geology.

US/1045-5752
CAPITALISM, NATURE, SOCIALISM. [Capital. nat. social.]. **VFOAT** CNS. No. 1 Fall (1988)-. Periodical. English. Six times a year. $65.00 (institutions); $80.00 others. Guilford Publications Inc., 72 Spring Street, New York NY 10012. **Tel** (212)431-9800, (800)365-7006, FAX (212)966-6708. **(Subscription address:** Turpin Distribution Services Limited, Blackhorse Road, Letchworth, Hertfordshire SG6 1HN, United Kingdom.**) ED** James O'Connor. **LC** HD75.6; .C36. **DD** 304.2/05. **CODEN** CNSOED. **[CCC]. Ad Acc. Pr Rev.** available on microfilm and microfiche from University Microfilms International (UMI).
Desc: Explores such topics as historical ecology, marxism and ecology, sustainable development, philosophy of nature, political economy of ecology, socialist eco-feminism, environmentalism and the state and ecological racism.
Ind/Abst Abstr. Anthropol. (19??-); Altern. Press Index (199?-); Environ. Period. Bibliogr.; Left Index.

US/0008-7475
CASTANEA. See Biology-Botany.

●US
CATALOG OF TRAINING / FISH AND WILDLIFE SERVICE, U.S. DEPARTMENT OF THE INTERIOR. Main/Corp U.S. Fish and Wildlife Service. **Added/Corp** U.S. Fish and Wildlife Service. Office of Training and Education. (1992)-. Catalog. English. US Department of the Interior / Fish and Wildlife Service, Virginia, Office of Training and Education, 4401 North Fairfax Drive, Room 741, Arlington VA 22203.

RU/0203-2198
CHELOVEK I STIKHIIA. VFOAT ChIS. (19??)-. Russian. ir. Gidrometeoizdat, Vasilevskii Ostrov, 3, V-53, 199053 St.Petersburg, Russia. **LC** Q162; .C453.

US/0275-7540
CHEMISTRY IN ECOLOGY. [Chem. ecol.]. **VFOAT** Chemistry and Ecology. Vol. 1, No. 1 (Feb. 1982)-. Academic Scholarly Publication. English. qt. $798.00 (academic institutions), $1244.00 (corporate institutions). Gordon & Breach Science Publishers, Inc., PO Box 786, Cooper Station, New York NY 10276. **Tel** (212)206-8900, FAX (212)645-2459. **(Subscription address:** International Publishers Distributor at one of the following addresses: 820 Town Center Drive, Langhorne, PA 19047; or PO Box 90, Reading Berkshire RG1 8JL UK; or Kent Ridge PO Box 1180, Singapore 9111, Republic of Singapore**) LC** QH545.A1; C48. **DD** 574.5/222. **NLM** W1 CH36S. **CODEN** CHECDY. **[CCC].** Documents available from CASDDS.
Ind/Abst Chem. Abstr.; Ecology Abstr.; Irr. Drain. Abstr.; Life Sci. Collect.; Pollut. Abstr. Indexes; Protozoolog. Abstr.

PO/0870-1695
CIENCIA BIOLOGICA. B, ECOLOGIA E SISTEMATICA. [Cienc. biol., B Ecol. sist.]. **VFOAT** Ciencia Biologica. Ecologia e Sistematica; Ciencia Biologica. Ecology and Systematics. (1972)-. Periodical. Multiple languages. sa. $10.00. Universidade de Coimbra, 3049 Coimbra Codex Portugal. **UDC** 591.
Ind/Abst For. Abstr.; Protozoolog. Abstr.

CR
CIENCIAS AMBIENTALES. Vol. 1 (July/Dec. 1980)-. Periodical. Spanish. sa.
Ind/Abst Agrofor. Abstr.; For. Prod. Abstr.

US/0733-9569
COASTAL AND ESTUARINE SCIENCES. [Coast. estuar. sci.]. **Added/Corp** American Geophysical Union. (1981)-. Monographic series. English. ir. Price varies per volume. American Geophysical Union, 2000 Florida Avenue Northwest, Washington DC 20009. **Tel** (202)462-6903, (800)966-2481, FAX (202)328-0566. **LC** UNC. **CODEN** CESCEG. **[CCC].** Documents available from BIOSIS Document Express, Ask*IEEE.
Ind/Abst Biol. Abstr. (1986-); INSPEC.

IT/0393-9154
COENOSES. [Coenoses]. Vol. 1, No. 1 (Spring 1986)-. Periodical. English. Three times a year. $75.00. CETA Ctr Ecologia Teorica Applicata, Via Vittorio Veneto 19, 34170 Gorizia Italy. **Tel** 011 39 481 536466, FAX 011 39 481 536470. **CODEN** COESEU. Documents available from BIOSIS Document Express.
Ind/Abst Biol. Abstr.; Ecology Abstr.

FR/0335-7473
COLLECTION D'ECOLOGIE. Vol. 1 (1973)-. Monographic series. French. ir. Price varies per volume. Scientific & Medical Publishers of France, 100 East 42nd Street, Suite 1002, New York NY 10017-5613. **Tel** (212)983-6278.
Ind/Abst Math. Rev.

II/0379-0436
COMPARATIVE PHYSIOLOGY AND ECOLOGY. See Biology-Physiology.

US/0198-9103
COMPENDIUM NEWSLETTER, THE. See Environmental Issues-Conservation and Natural Resources.

US/0888-8892
CONSERVATION BIOLOGY. See Environmental Issues-Conservation and Natural Resources.

CN/0829-240X
CONTRETEMPS (MONTREAL). (CONTRETEMPS.). [Contretemps]. **Added/Corp** Cooperative d'Information et de Recherche Ecologiste du Quebec. Vol. 1, No. 1 (May 1984)-. Periodical. French. qt

(Feb., May, Aug., Nov.). 10.00Can$ (individuals), 20.00Can$ (institutions) Canada; 13.20Can$ (individuals), 23.20Can$ (institutions) US; 22.80Can$ (individuals), 32.80Can$ (institutions) other. Cooperative d'Information et de Recherche Ecologiste du Quebec, Contretemps, CP 1047 Succursale C, Montreal Quebec H2L 4V3 Canada. **Tel** (514)277-8874. **DD** 304.2/09714. **Bk Rev. Ad Acc, Adv Mgr:** S. McKay.
Ind/Abst AQUAREF; Point Repere.

CN/0707-8935
CORRESPONDANCES (SILLERY). (CORRESPONDANCES.). No. 1 Nov. 1978-. Periodical. French. $3.00 per no. Conseil International d'Education Mesologique du Pays de Langue Francaise, CP 91, Sillery Quebec G1T 2P7 Canada. **DD** 574.5/07.

UK/0011-023X
COUNTRY-SIDE. [Ctr.-side]. (1905)-. Periodical. English. bm. $35.00. British Naturalists Association, 23 Oak Hill Close, Woodford Green Essex, IG8 9HP England. **Tel** 011 44 933 314672. **(Subscription address:** British Naturalists Association, 48 Russell Way, Higham Ferrers, Northants, NN9 8EJ England**) Bk Rev. Ad Acc. Pr Rev. Circ:** 15,000 (ctrl).
Desc: Articles on natural history and environment conservation.

AT/0727-9620
CUNNINGHAMIA : ECOLOGICAL CONTRIBUTIONS FROM THE NATIONAL HERBARIUM OF NEW SOUTH WALES. **See** Biology-Botany.

UK/0955-6648
CURRENT ADVANCES IN ECOLOGICAL & ENVIRONMENTAL SCIENCES. **See** Environmental Issues-Abstracting, Bibliographies and Statistics.

II/0378-7540
CURRENT TRENDS IN LIFE SCIENCES. **See** Biology-Botany.

IT/0392-8950
D.A. DIFESA AMBIENTALE. ***Ceased.*** (DIFESA AMBIENTALE : D.A.). [D.A., Dif. ambientale]. **Added/Corp** Centro Informazioni Studi Ambientali (Italy). **VFOAT** D.A. (19??)-(Dec. 1992). Academic Scholarly Publication. Italian. mo. Editoriale PEG Spa, Via Fratelli Bressan 2, 20126 Milan Italy. **Tel** 011 39 2 2579841, FAX 011 39 2 255-2779, telex 323088 PEGMOS I. **CODEN** DADID9. Documents available from CASDDS.
Ind/Abst Chem. Abstr. (1983-).

DK/0374-7344
DANISH REVIEW OF GAME BIOLOGY. **See** Zoology.

IT
DELTAMBIENTE. ***Suspended.*** (19??)-Vol.1, No. 1. Italian. bm (6 issues). Deltambiente, Via Asmara 21, 00198 Rome Italy.

NE/0166-2287
DEVELOPMENTS IN AGRICULTURAL AND MANAGED FOREST ECOLOGY. [Dev. agric. managed-for. ecol.]. V. 1-. Monographic series. English. ir. Price varies per volume. Elsevier Science Publishers BV, PO Box 211, 1000 AE Amsterdam Netherlands. **Tel** 011 31 20 5803642, FAX 011 31 20 5862696, telex 15682. **CODEN** DAMED8. Documents available from BIOSIS Document Express, CASDDS.
Ind/Abst AGRICOLA [Full Cov.]; Biol. Abstr. (1988-); Chem. Abstr. (1975-1981); Life Sci. Collect.

US
DIRECTORY / ECOLOGICAL SOCIETY OF AMERICA. **Main/Corp** Ecological Society of America. (198?)-. Directory. English. an. $10.00. Ecological Society of America, Center for Environmental Studies, Arizona State University, Tempe AZ 85287-3211. **Tel** (602)965-3000, FAX (602)965-8087. **NLM** QH 35; E19d. ***Separated from*** *Bulletin of the Ecological Society of America.*

US/0270-1111
DIRECTORY OF ENVIRONMENTAL ORGANIZATIONS (LOS ANGELES). (DIRECTORY OF ENVIRONMENTAL ORGANIZATIONS.). [Dir. environ. organ.]. **Added/Corp** Educational Communications, Inc. (1980)-. English. an. $30.00. Educational Communications, PO Box 351419, Los Angeles CA 90035-9119. **Tel** (310)559-9160. **ED** Nancy Pearlman. **LC** GE1; .D57. **DD** 363.7/0025/7949. **Bk Rev. Ad Acc.** available on diskette (Appleworks database); available on labels. ***Continues*** *Environmental Organizations Directory (Los Angeles, Calif.).*
Desc: Publication listing organizations concerned about the environment. Emphasis on Los Angeles and Orange counties, California and state and national plus international groups; 4,000 names with addresses and telephone numbers.

US/0093-5816
DIRECTORY OF PUBLISHED PROCEEDINGS. SERIES PCE : POLLUTION CONTROL/ECOLOGY. **See** Environmental Issues-Pollution and Waste Management.

FR/0335-5330
DOCUMENTS DE CARTOGRAPHIE ECOLOGIQUE. [Doc. cartogr. ecol.]. **Added/Corp** Universite Scientifique et Medicale de Grenoble. Laboratoire de Biologie Vegetale. Vol. 11 (1973)-. Monographic series. Multiple languages (French and German; summaries and/or abstracts in English and Italian). ir. Price varies per volume. ADR Biologie Veg Bibliotheque, BP 68, 38402 St Martin D Heres France. **LC** QK297; .D6. **DD** 574.5/05. **CODEN** DCAEDU. Documents available from BIOSIS Document Express. ***Continues*** *Documents pour la Carte de la Vegetation des Alpes.*
Ind/Abst Biol. Abstr.; Ecol. Abstr. (?-?); Geogr. Abstr. Phys. Geogr. (?-?); Geogr. Abstr. Human Geogr. (?-?).

IT
DOSSIER AMBIENTE. Associazione Ambiente Lavoro, Viale Marelli 497, 20099 Sesto San Giovanni Italy.

US/1054-0067
EARTH CARE ANNUAL. [Earth care annu.]. **Added/Corp** National Wildlife Federation. (1990)-. English. an. $22.45. National Wildlife Federation / Washington, 1400 16th Street Northwest, Washington DC 20036. **Tel** (800)432-6564, (202)797-6800. **LC** IN PROCESS. **DD** 363.

●US/1062-9076
EARTH FORUM. (1992)-. Periodical. English. mo. $36.00. Focused Communications Corp., 3100 West Alabama, Suite 227, Houston TX 77098.

IT
ECO E NOTIZIARIO DELL ECOLOGIA. ***Suspended.*** (19??)-(Dec. 1993). Italian. qt. L90000.00 (one year); L170000.00 (two year) Italy; L150000.00 (one year); L280000.00 (two year) other. Nuova Ecoedizini Srl, Viale Piave 62 64, 25123 Brescia Italy. **Tel** 011 39 30 364690. **Bk Rev. Ad Acc.**

US
ECO FORUM : NEWSLETTER OF THE SOUTH DAKOTA RESOURCES COALITION. **Added/Corp** South Dakota Resources Coalition. (197?)-. Newsletter. English. bm. $10.00. South Dakota Resources Coalition, PO Box 7020, Brookings SD 57007. **Tel** (605)692-6026, (605)688-6172. **ED** Luanne Napton.

US
ECO LOGIC. (19??)-. Periodical. English. Ten times a year (July/Aug. & Nov./Dec. issues combined). $10.00. Tri City Ecology Center, PO Box 674, Fremont CA 95437. **Tel** (415)797-2755. **ED** Donna Olsen (editor's address: 37890 Aita Drive, Freemont, CA 94536). **Bk Rev**, (Qty: 2). **Circ:** 310.
Desc: Focus mainly on the Bay area - especially Freemont, Netwark and Union City. Most issues contains information on recycling, wetlands, open space preservation, local nature activities and children's projects.

IT
ECO MODEL. Italian. mo (except Aug.). L90000.00 Italy; L100000.00 other Europe; L130000.00 other. Eco Model Redazione, Via Medesano 36, 40023 Castelgeulfo BO Italy. **Tel** 011 39 542 53118.

●DK/0906-7590
ECOGRAPHY. **Added/Corp** Nordic Society Oikos. Vol. 15 No. 1 (Jan. 1992)-. Periodical. English. qt. kr810.00 US, Canada and Japan; kr770.00 other. Munksgaard International Publishers Ltd, PO Box 2148, DK-1016 Copenhagen K Denmark. **Tel** 011 45 33 12 70 30, FAX 011 45 33 12 93 87, telex 19431 MUNKS DK. **LC** QH84.1; .H64. **DD** 574.5/2621/05. **CODEN** ECOGEG. **[CCC].** Documents available from The Genuine Article. ***Continues*** *Holarctic Ecology, 0105-9327.*
Ind/Abst AGRICOLA; Curr. Aware. Biol. Sci., CABS; Curr. Contents, Agric. Biol. Environ. Sci.; Environ. Period. Bibliogr.; Res. Alert [Full Cov.]; Sci. Cit. Index; SCISEARCH.

IT
ECOLE. (19??)-. Italian. Five times a year. L45000.00 Italy; L90000.00 other. Schole, Via S Francesco d'Assissi 3, 10122 Turin Italy. **Tel** 011 39 11 545567. **ED** Andrea Rosso and Mario Salamone. **Bk Rev. Ad Acc. Circ:** 1500.
Desc: Information on ecology, education on environmental issues, news, philosophy, economy and history.

AG/0327-5477
ECOLOGIA AUSTRAL. Periodical. Spanish. sa. $15.00 Argentina; $20.00 other. **(Subscription address:** Department of Ecologia, Facultad de Agronomia, Universidad de Buenos Aires, Av. San Martin 4453, (1417) Buenos Aires, Argentina**) ED** Martin Oesterheld, Jorge Rabinovich. **UDC** 574.

BO
ECOLOGIA EN BOLIVIA : REVISTA DEL INSTITUTO DE ECOLOGIA. No. 1 (Feb. 1982)-. Periodical. Spanish. Comite de Redaccion, Instituto de Ecologia, Casilla 20127, La Paz Bolivia.

SP/0214-0896
ECOLOGIA (MADRID). (ECOLOGIA.). [Ecologia]. **Added/Corp** Instituto Nacional para la Conservacion de la Naturaleza. (1987)-. Periodical. Spanish (summaries and/or abstracts in English). an. 1100ptas Spain; 1500ptas other. Instituto Nacional Para La Conservacion de la Naturaleza, Gran V S Francisco 35 41, 28005 Madrid Spain. **LC** QH171; .E36. **DD** 574.5/0946/05. **CODEN** ECOLEV. ***Continues*** *Boletin de la Estacion Central de Ecologia, 0210-2536.*
Ind/Abst Ecol. Abstr.; Field Crop Abstr.; For. Abstr.; GeoRef; Rev. Plant Pathol.; Soils Fert.

FR/0153-8756
ECOLOGIA MEDITERRANEA. (ECOLOGIA MEDITERRANEA : REVUE D'ECOLOGIE TERRESTRE ET LIMNIQUE.). [Ecol. Mediterr.]. **Added/Corp** Universite de Droit, d'Economie et des Sciences d'Aix-Marseille. Vol. 1 (1975)-. Monographic series. French (Italian, Spanish, English and German). ir (2-3 issues per volume). Price varies per volume. Ecologia Mediterranea, Boite 461, Fac St Jerome, 13397 Marseille Cedex 13 France. **Tel** 011 33 91 288535, 011 33 91 288534, FAX 011 33 91 288668. **ED** P. Quezel and R. Loisel. **CODEN** EMEDDQ. **Bk Rev.** Documents available from BIOSIS Document Express.
Ind/Abst Biol. Abstr.; GeoRef.

UK/0305-196X
ECOLOGICAL ABSTRACTS. **See** Environmental Issues-Abstracting, Bibliographies and Statistics.

US/1051-0761
ECOLOGICAL APPLICATIONS. (ECOLOGICAL APPLICATIONS : A PUBLICATION OF THE ECOLOGICAL SOCIETY OF AMERICA.). [Ecol. appl.]. **Added/Corp** Ecological Society of America. Vol. 1, No. 1 (Feb. 1991)-. Periodical. English. qt. $290.00 (US), $335.00 (other) (combined subscription with Ecological Applications/Ecology). Ecological Society of America, Center for Environmental Studies, Arizona State University, Tempe AZ 85287-3211. **Tel** (602)965-3000, FAX (602)965-8087. **LC** QH540; .E273. **DD** 574.5/05. **CODEN** ECAPE7. **Ad Acc. Acid Free.** available on microfilm and microfiche from University Microfilms International (UMI). Documents available from The Genuine Article, BIOSIS Document Express.
Desc: The scope is broad, including global change and biogeochemistry, conservation biology, ecotoxicology and pollution ecology, fisheries and wildlife ecology, forestry, agroecosystems, range management, soils, hydrology and groundwater, landscape ecology, and epidemiology.
Ind/Abst AGRICOLA [Select. Cov.]; Biol. Abstr.; Curr. Aware. Biol. Sci., CABS; Curr. Contents, Agric. Biol. Environ. Sci.; Ecol. Abstr.; Ecology Abstr.; Environ. Period. Bibliogr.; For. Abstr.; Gen. Sci. Index; Geogr. Abstr. Human Geogr.; Res. Alert [Full Cov.]; Risk Abstr.; Sci. Cit. Index; SCISEARCH; Soc. Sci. Cit. Index [Select. Cov.]; Zool. Rec.

SW/0346-6868
ECOLOGICAL BULLETINS. [Ecol. bull.]. **Added/Corp** Statens Naturvetenskapliga Forskningsrad (Sweden). (1975)-. Monographic series. English. ir. Price varies per volume. Munksgaard International Publishers Ltd, PO Box 2148, DK-1016 Copenhagen K Denmark. **Tel** 011 45 33 12 70 30, FAX 011 45 33 12 93 87, telex 19431 MUNKS DK. **ED** Peho H. Buckell. **NLM** W1 EC911. **CODEN** ECBUDQ. Documents available from CASDDS. ***Continues*** *Bulletins from the Ecological Research Committee - N.F.R., 0587-1433.*
Ind/Abst AGRICOLA [Select. Cov.]; Biocont. News Inf.; Chem. Abstr.; Coal Abstr.; Ecol. Abstr. (?-?); EMBASE; Energy Res. Abstr. (March 1979-); Environ. Period. Bibliogr. (?-?); For. Prod. Abstr.; For. Abstr.; Geogr. Abstr. Phys. Geogr. (?-?); Irr. Drain. Abstr.; Life Sci. Collect.; Soils Fert.

NE/0921-8009
ECOLOGICAL ECONOMICS. (ECOLOGICAL ECONOMICS : THE JOURNAL OF THE INTERNATIONAL SOCIETY FOR ECOLOGICAL ECONOMICS.). [Ecol. econ.]. **Added/Corp** International Society for Ecological Economics. **VFOAT** Journal of the International Society for Ecological Economics. Vol. 1, No. 1 (Feb. 1989)-. Academic Scholarly Publication. English. Twelve times a year (4 vols.). Fl1224.00. Elsevier Science Publishers BV, PO Box 211, 1000 AE Amsterdam Netherlands. **Tel** 011 31 20 5803642, FAX 011 31 20 5862696, telex 15682. **LC** HC79.E5; E18. **DD** 333. **CODEN** ECECEM. **[CCC].** available on microfilm and microfiche from University Microfilms International (UMI). Documents available from The Genuine Article, Documents on Demand.
Ind/Abst Biodeter. Abstr. (1991-); Curr. Aware. Biol. Sci., CABS; Ecol. Abstr.; Environ. Abstr.; Environ. Period. Bibliogr.; Geogr. Abstr. Human Geogr.; GeoRef; Int. Bibliogr. Sociol.; Int. Dev. Abstr.; Res. Alert [Select. Cov.]; Rural Dev. Abstr.; Sage Urban Stud. Abstr; Soc. Sci. Cit. Index [Select. Cov.].

●NE/0925-8574
ECOLOGICAL ENGINEERING. See Engineering.

UK/0307-6946
ECOLOGICAL ENTOMOLOGY. See Zoology-Entomology.

CN/0823-406X
ECOLOGICAL LAND CLASSIFICATION SERIES. (ECOLOGICAL LAND CLASSIFICATION SERIES / LANDS DIRECTORATE, ENVIRONMENT CANADA.). [Ecol. land classif. ser.]. **Added/Corp** Canada. Lands Directorate. **VFOAT** Serie de la Classification Ecologique de Territoire. No. 1 (1977)-. Monographic series. English (French). ir. Free on request. Environment Canada / Emergencies Science Division, Ottawa Ontario K1A 0H3 Canada. **Tel** (819)998-9622.
Ind/Abst ASTIS Curr. Aware. Bull. (1978-); ASTIS Bibliogr. (1978-); Fish Rev. (Jan. 1989-July 1992); Wildl. Rev. (Jan. 1989-July 1992).

NE/0304-3800
ECOLOGICAL MODELLING. [Ecol. modell.]. Vol. 1 (May 1975)-. Academic Scholarly Publication. English. Twenty-one times a year (7 vols.). Fl2380.00. Elsevier Science Publishers BV, PO Box 211, 1000 AE Amsterdam Netherlands. **Tel** 011 31 20 5803642, FAX 011 31 20 5862696, telex 15682. **ED** S E Jorgensen. **LC** QH541.15.M3; E27. **DD** 574.5/01/84. **CODEN** ECMODT. **[CCC]. Pr Rev.** available on microfilm and microfiche from University Microfilms International (UMI). Documents available from The Genuine Article, BIOSIS Document Express, CASDDS, Documents on Demand.
Desc: Concerned with the use of mathematical models and systems analysis for the description of ecosystems and for the control of environmental pollution and resource development.
Ind/Abst AGRICOLA; AQUAREF; Biocont. News Inf. (1991-); Biol. Abstr.; Biostatistica (19??-19??); Chem. Abstr.; Coal Abstr.; Crop Physiol. Abstr.; Curr. Contents, Agric. Biol. Environ. Sci.; Curr. Ref. Fish Res.; Ecol. Abstr.; Ecology Abstr.; EMBASE; Energy Inf. Abstr.; Energy Res. Abstr. (Sept. 1978-); Entomol. Abstr.; Environ. Abstr.; Environ. Period. Bibliogr.; Field Crop Abstr.; Fish Rev.; For. Prod. Abstr.; For. Abstr.; Geogr. Abstr. Phys. Geogr.; Geogr. Abstr. Human Geogr. (?-?); GeoRef; Grasslands For. Abstr.; Health Saf. Sci. Abstr.; Hortic. Abstr.; Int. Dev. Abstr. (?-?); Irr. Drain. Abstr.; Key Word Index Wildl. Res.; Microbiol. Abstr. Sect. C; Nematol. Abstr.; Nutr. Abstr. Rev., Ser. B, Live Feeds and Feed.; Life Sci. Collect.; Pollut. Abstr. Indexes; Postharvest News Inf.; Potato Abstr.; Protozoolog. Abstr.; Res. Alert [Full Cov.]; Rev. Agric. Entomol.; Rev. Med. Vet. Entomol.; Risk Abstr.; Sci. Cit. Index; SCISEARCH; Seed Abstr.; Soc. Sci. Cit. Index [Select. Cov.]; Soils Fert.; Soyabean Abstr.; Weed Abstr.; Wheat Barley Trit. Abstr.; Wildl. Rev.; World Agric. Econ.

US/0012-9615
ECOLOGICAL MONOGRAPHS. [Ecol. monogr.]. **Added/Corp** Ecological Society of America. Vol. 1 (Jan. 1931)-. Monographic series. English. qt (Feb., May, Aug., Nov.). $50.00 US; $60.00 other. Ecological Society of America, Center for Environmental Studies, Arizona State University, Tempe AZ 85287-3211. **Tel** (602)965-3000, FAX (602)965-8087. **ED** Lee Miller. **LC** QH540; .E28. **DD** 574.5/05. **NLM** W1 EC912. **CODEN** ECMOAQ. Index available. cum. index. **Ad Acc. Pr Rev. Acid Free.** available on microfilm and microfiche from University Microfilms International (UMI). Documents available from The Genuine Article, BIOSIS Document Express, UMI Article Clearinghouse, CASDDS, Documents on Demand.
Desc: Provides one of the major avenues of communication between scientists studying the relationships between diverse organisms and their past, present, and future environments.
Ind/Abst Acad. Ind. [Computer File] (1992-); Acad. Search (Jan. 1994-); AGRICOLA [Select. Cov.]; Biocont. News Inf. (1991-); Biol. Agric. Index; Biol. Abstr.; Chem. Abstr. (1931-1985); Curr. Aware. Biol. Sci., CABS; Curr. Contents Clin. Med.; Curr. Ref. Fish Res.; Ecol. Abstr.; Ecology Abstr.; EMBASE; Energy Inf. Abstr.; Energy Res. Abstr.; Environ. Abstr.; Environ. Period. Bibliogr.; Expand. Acad. Index (1989-); Field Crop Abstr.; For. Prod. Abstr.; For. Abstr.; Gen. Sci. Index; Gen. Sci. Source (Jul. 1993-); GeoRef; Grasslands For. Abstr.; Index Vet.; INFO-SOUTH Abstr.; INIS Atomindex [Micro.]; Meteorol. Geoastrophys. Abstr.; Nematol. Abstr.; Newsp. Period. Abstr. (1991-); Nutr. Abstr. Rev., Ser. B, Live Feeds and Feed.; Nutr. Abstr. Rev., Ser. A, Hum. Exp.; Life Sci. Collect.; Plant Breed. Abstr.; Protozoolog. Abstr.; Res. Alert [Full Cov.]; Rev. Med. Vet. Entomol.; Sci. Cit. Index (19??-19??); SCISEARCH; Seed Abstr.; Soils Fert.; Weed Abstr.; Wildl. Rev.

US/1040-7413
ECOLOGICAL PSYCHOLOGY. See Psychology.

JA/0912-3814
ECOLOGICAL RESEARCH. [Ecol. res.]. **Added/Corp** Nihon Seitai Gakkai. Vol. 1, No. 1 (April 1986)-. Academic Scholarly Publication. English. Three times a year. 224.00Aus$ Australia; ¥15700 Japan; $157.00 other. Blackwell Scientific Publications Australia, 54 University Street, PO Box 378, Carlton Victoria 3053 Australia. **Tel** 011 61 3 3470300, FAX 011 61 3 3475001, telex 10716421. **LC** QH540; .E275. **DD** 574.5/05. **CODEN** ECRSEX. **[CCC].** Documents available from The Genuine Article, BIOSIS Document Express, CASDDS. ***Continues in part*** *Nihon Seitai Gakkai Shi, 0021-5007.*
Ind/Abst Anim. Breed. Abstr.; Biocont. News Inf. (1991-); Biol. Abstr. (1987-); Chem. Abstr. (1986-); Crop Physiol. Abstr.; Curr. Aware. Biol. Sci., CABS; Curr. Contents, Agric. Biol. Environ. Sci.; Ecol. Abstr.; Ecology Abstr.; Fish Rev. (Jan. 1989-July 1992); For. Abstr.; Geogr. Abstr. Phys. Geogr.; Grasslands For. Abstr.; Postharvest News Inf.; Res. Alert [Select. Cov.]; Rev. Agric. Entomol.; Sci. Cit. Index; SCISEARCH; Soils Fert.; Weed Abstr.; Wheat Barley Trit. Abstr.; Wildl. Rev. (Jan. 1989-July 1992).

US/1052-2468
ECOLOGICAL RESEARCH SERIES. [Ecol. res. ser.]. **Added/Corp** United States. Environmental Protection Agency. Office of Research and Development. United States. Environmental Protection Agency. Office of Research and Monitoring. (1972)-. Monographic series. English. **DD** 574.
Ind/Abst Aquat. Sci. Fish. Abstr. (Computer File); Ocean. Abstr.; Life Sci. Collect.

AT
ECOLOGICAL SOCIETY OF AUSTRALIA BULLETIN. Bulletin. English. qt. 20.00Aus$. Ecological Society of Australia, Box 1564 Canberra, Australian Capital Territory, 2601 Australia. **ED** Dr. Ray Wills. **Bk Rev**, (Qty: 6). **Ad Acc. Circ:** 800.

GW/0070-8356
ECOLOGICAL STUDIES. (ECOLOGICAL STUDIES : ANALYSIS AND SYNTHESIS.). [Ecol. stud.]. Vol. 1 (1970)-. Monographic series. English. ir. Price varies per volume. Springer-Verlag GmbH & Company KG, Heidelberger Platz 3, D 14197 Berlin Germany. **Tel** 011 49 30 8207223, FAX 011 49 30 8214091, telex 183 319 SPBLN D. **(Subscription address:** Springer Verlag New York Inc. / for North America, 44 Hartz Way, Secaucus NJ 07096.) **ED** W.D. Billings, F. Golley, O.L. Lange, J.S. Olsen, H.A. Mooney, H. Remmert. **LC** UNC. **DD** 574. **NLM** W1 EC912K. **CODEN** ESASAM. Documents available from BIOSIS Document Express, CASDDS.
Ind/Abst AGRICOLA [Select. Cov.]; Biol. Abstr.; Chem. Abstr.; GeoRef; Life Sci. Collect.; Soils Fert.

FR
ECOLOGIE. French. Ecologie, 12 rue Neuve du Patis, BP 59, 45200 Montargis France.

UK/0261-3131
ECOLOGIST (1979). (THE ECOLOGIST.). [Ecologist]. **Added/Corp** Wadebridge Ecological Centre. Vol. 9 No. 3 (May 1979)-. Academic Scholarly Publication. English. bm (Feb., Arp., June, Aug., Oct., Dec.). $21.00 (individuals), $45.00 (institutions). Ecosystems Ltd, 29A High Street, New Malden Surrey KT3 4BY England. **Tel** 011 44 403 782644, FAX 011 44 81 9429385. **(Subscription address:** Massachusetts Institute of Technology Press, 55 Hayward Street, Cambridge MA 02142.) **ED** E. Goldsmith, N. Hildyard, P. Bunyard and P. McCully. **LC** QH540; .E297. **DD** 304.2/05. **CODEN** ECLGEZ. Index available. **Bk Rev. Ad Acc. Circ:** 5,000 (ctrl). available on microfilm and microfiche from University Microfilms International (UMI). Documents available from BIOSIS Document Express, UMI Article Clearinghouse, Documents on Demand. ***Absorbed*** *Mazingira.;* ***Formed by the union of*** *English Ed., 0250-6858* ***and*** *Ecologist Quarterly, 0142-0399 New Ecologist, 0141-6952.*
Desc: Considers articles on environmental and social issues.
Ind/Abst Acad. Search (July 1993-); AGRICOLA; Agrofor. Abstr. (1991-); Altern. Press Index (199?-); Biol. Abstr.; Biol. Dig.; Curr. Technol. Index; Ecol. Abstr.; EMBASE; Energy Inf. Abstr.; Environ. Abstr.; Environ. Period. Bibliogr.; Expand. Acad. Index (1989-); Field Crop Abstr.; Fish Rev.; For. Prod. Abstr. (1991-); For. Abstr.; Gen. Sci. Index; Gen. Sci. Source (July 1993-); Geogr. Abstr. Phys. Geogr.; Geogr. Abstr. Human Geogr.; Grasslands For. Abstr.; Index Sci. Rev.; Index Vet.; INFO-SOUTH Abstr.; Int. Dev. Abstr.; Int. Labour Doc.; Leis. Recreat. Tour. Abstr.; Mag. Search; Middle East Abstr. Index; Newsp. Period. Abstr. (1991-); PAIS Int. Print; Peace Res. Abstr. J. (1970-1973); Life Sci. Collect.; Pollut. Abstr. Indexes; Rev. Plant Pathol.; Rural Dev. Abstr.; Soils Fert.; Vet. Bull.; Wildl. Rev.; World Agric. Econ.

US/0143-3296
ECOLOGY ABSTRACTS. See Environmental Issues-Abstracting, Bibliographies and Statistics.

GW
ECOLOGY AND FARMING : INTERNATIONAL IFOAM MAGAZINE. See Agriculture.

NE
ECOLOGY, ECONOMY & ENVIRONMENT. **VFOAT** Ecology, Economy and Environment; ECEE; EE&E. Vol. 1 (1991)-. Monographic series. English. ir. Price varies per volume. Kluwer Academic Publishers, Postbus 322, 3300 AH Dordrecht, The Netherlands. **Tel** 011 (31) 78 524400, FAX 011 31 78 183273, telex 20083.
Ind/Abst AGRICOLA.

US/0361-2600
ECOLOGY (HOUSTON). (ECOLOGY.). Periodical. English. wk. $135.00. Sheffer Company, PO Box 19247, Houston TX 77024. **LC** QH540; .S64. **DD** 333.7/2/05. ***Continues*** *Special Report Ecology.*

US
ECOLOGY INTERNATIONAL. **Added/Corp** International Association for Ecology. **VFOAT** Ecology International Bulletin. No. 17 (1989)-. Periodical. English. ir. Intecol Institute of Ecology, University of Georgia, Athens GA 30602. **Tel** (404)542-2968. **LC** IN PROCESS. ***Continues*** *International Association for Ecology. INTECOL Bulletin, 1012-9162.*

US/0012-9658
ECOLOGY (TEMPE). (ECOLOGY.). [Ecology]. **Added/Corp** Ecological Society of America. Vol. 1 (Jan. 1920)-. Periodical. English. Eight times a year. $290.00 US; $335.00 other (combined subscription with Ecology/Ecological Applications). Ecological Society of America, Center for Environmental Studies, Arizona State University, Tempe AZ 85287-3211. **Tel** (602)965-3000, FAX (602)965-8087. **ED** Lee Miller. **LC** QH540; .E3. **NLM** W1 EC914. **CODEN** ECOLAR. Index available. cum. index. **Bk Rev. Ad Acc. Pr Rev. Acid Free.** available on microfilm and microfiche from University Microfilms International (UMI). Documents available from The Genuine Article, BIOSIS Document Express, UMI Article Clearinghouse, CASDDS. ***Supersedes*** *Plant World, 0096-8307.*
Desc: Publishes research papers dealing with all aspects of ecology, as well as discussions and essays that develop ecological theory.
Ind/Abst Acad. Abstr. Full Text Elite (July 1990-); Acad. Abstr. (July 1990-); Acad. Ind. [Computer File] (1992-); Acad. Search (July 1990-); AGRICOLA [Select. Cov.]; Agrofor. Abstr.; AQUAREF; Biocont. News Inf. (19??-19??); Biol. Agric. Index; Biol. Abstr.; Book Rev. Index; Chem. Abstr.; Curr. Contents, Agric. Biol. Environ. Sci.; Ecology Abstr.; EMBASE; Energy Inf. Abstr.; Energy Res. Abstr.; Entomol. Abstr.; Environ. Period. Bibliogr.; Expand. Acad. Index (1989-); Fish Rev.; For. Prod. Abstr.; For. Abstr.; Gen. Sci. Index; Gen. Sci. Source (Jul. 1990-); GeoRef; Helminthol. Abstr. (1991-); INFO-SOUTH Abstr.; INIS Atomindex [Micro.]; Int. Aerosp. Abstr.; J. Plan. Lit.; Key Word Index Wildl. Res.; Mag. Search; Meteorol. Geoastrophys. Abstr.; Nematol. Abstr.; Newsp. Period. Abstr. (1990-); Nutr. Abstr. Rev., Ser. B, Live Feeds and Feed.; Ocean. Abstr.; Life Sci. Collect.; Plant Breed. Abstr.; Plant Genet. Resour. Abstr.; Postharvest News Inf.; Ref. Upd. Deluxe Ed.; Res. Alert [Full Cov.]; Rev. Agric. Entomol.; Rev. Med. Vet. Entomol.; Rev. Plant Pathol.; Sci. Cit. Index; SCISEARCH; Seed Abstr.; Soc. Sci. Cit. Index [Select. Cov.]; Soils Fert.; Weed Abstr.; Wildl. Rev.

US/0098-6615
ECOLOGY USA (HOUSTON). (ECOLOGY USA.). **VAT** Ecology United States of America. (19??)-. Periodical. English. bw. $104.50 (North America); $122.00 (other) airmail. CJE Associates, 237 Gretna Green Court, Alexandria VA 22304-5602. **Tel** (703)823-0662. **ED** Elaine Eiserer. **LC** QH104; .E3. **DD** 574.5/0973. **[CCC].**
Desc: Covers global warming, acid rain, endangered species, wetlands, water resources, wildlife, forests and parks, agriculture, grants and contracts, upcoming events, publications and state news.
Ind/Abst Irr. Drain. Abstr.

IT
ECONOMIA E AMBIENTE. (19??)-. Italian. Four times a year. L44000.00 Italy; L80000.00. Economia E Ambiente, Via Pratale 64 CP 272, 56100 Pisa Italy. **Tel** 011 39 50 571198. **ED** Romano Molesti, Ilya Prigogine, Barry Commoner and G Roegen.

IT/0012-9836
ECONOMIA MONTANA ROMA. (ECONOMIA MONTANA). [Econ. mont.Roma]. (1969)-. Periodical. Italian (summaries and/or abstracts in English). bm. L80000 Italy; L90000 other. Agrifutura Editrice, Casella Postale 5101, 00153 Rome Italy. **Tel** 011 39 6 540-3224, FAX 011 39 6 70 30 00 38. **ED** Via M. Musco. **UDC** 338.43.01 631.95. Index available. **Ad Acc. Adv Mgr:** Flaminio Laureri, **Tel** 06 54 03 224. **Circ:** 12,000. ***Continues*** *Economia Montana.*
Desc: Technical and cultural articles on ecology and environment, landscape and forestry subjects.
Ind/Abst Rev. Agric. Entomol.

US/0147-6513
ECOTOXICOLOGY AND ENVIRONMENTAL SAFETY. [Ecotoxicol. environ. saf.]. **Added/Corp** International Academy of Environmental Safety. International Society of Ecotoxicology and Environmental Safety. Vol. 1 (June 1977)-. Academic Scholarly Publication. English. Nine times a year. $439.00 US and Canada; $539.00 other. Academic Press, Inc., 6277 Sea Harbor Drive, Orlando FL 32887. **Tel** (800)543-9534, (407)345-4100, FAX (407)363-9661. **ED** Frederick Coulston and Friedhelm Korte. **LC** QH545.A1; E29. **DD** 574.5/2. **NLM** W1 EC94. **CODEN** EESADV. **[CCC]. Pr Rev.** Documents available

from The Genuine Article, BIOSIS Document Express, CASDDS, Documents on Demand.
Desc: Publishes studies that examine the biologic and toxic effects of natural or synthetic chemical pollutants on animal, plant, or microbial ecosystems, and their routes into the affected organisms.
Ind/Abst AGRICOLA [Select. Cov.]; Biodeter. Abstr. (19??-19??); Biol. Abstr. (1984-); Chem. Abstr.; Chem. Titles; Coal Abstr.; CSA Neuro. Abstr. (?-?); Curr. Aware. Biol. Sci., CABS; Curr. Contents, Agric. Biol. Environ. Sci.; Curr. Contents Life Sci.; Curr. Ref. Fish Res.; Dairy Sci. Abstr.; Ecol. Abstr.; Ecology Abstr.; EMBASE; Energy Res. Abstr. (Aug. 1979-); Environ. Abstr.; Fish Rev.; Food Sci. Technol. Abstr.; Geogr. Abstr. Phys. Geogr.; Geogr. Abstr. Human Geogr. (?-?); Hortic. Abstr.; Index Med. (1977-); Index Vet.; INIS Atomindex [Micro.]; Int. Aerosp. Abstr.; Leadscan; Maize Abstr.; Microbiol. Abstr. Sect. C; Nematol. Abstr.; Life Sci. Collect.; Pollut. Abstr. Indexes; Res. Alert [Full Cov.]; Rev. Agric. Entomol.; Rev. Med. Vet. Entomol.; Rice Abstr.; Sci. Cit. Index; SCISEARCH; Soils Fert.; Soyabean Abstr.; Vet. Bull.; Toxicol. Abstr.; Weed Abstr.; Wildl. Rev.

●UK/0963-9292
ECOTOXICOLOGY LONDON. [EcotoxicologyLond.]. (1992)-. Periodical. English. Six times a year. $285.00 US and Canada; £165.00 Europe; £180.00 other. Chapman & Hall, 2-6 Boundary Row, London SE1 8HN England. **Tel** 011 44 71 865 0066, FAX 011 44 71 522 9623, telex 290164 Chapmag. **(Subscription address:** Chapman & Hall, Cheriton House, North Way, Andover, Hampshire, SP10 5BE England.**) ED** David Peakall, Lee Shugart. **DD** 363.73. Documents available from ADONIS.
Desc: Devoted to the publication of fundamental research in ecotoxicology. Papers published will be aimed at understanding the mechanisms and processes whereby chemicals exert their effects on ecosystems, and the impact of the chemicals at the population or community level.
Ind/Abst ADONIS; Curr. Aware. Biol. Sci., CABS.

VE/1012-1692
ECOTROPICOS : REVISTA DE LA SOCIEDAD VENEZOLANA DE ECOLOGIA. Vol. 1, No. 1 (1988)-. Periodical. Spanish (English). Sociedad Venezolana De Gecologia, Apartado Postal 47543, Caracas 1041-A Venezuela.
Ind/Abst Ecol. Abstr.; Geogr. Abstr. Phys. Geogr.

ER/0868-5894
EESTI TEADUSTE AKADEEMIA TOIMETISED. OKOLOOGIA. Added/Corp Eesti Teaduste Akadeemia. **VFOAT** Okoloogia; Ekologiia; Ecology; Izvestiia Akademii Nauk Estonii. Ekologiia; Proceedings of the Estonian Academy of Sciences. Ecology; Eesti TA Toimetised. Okoloogia; Izvestiia AN Estonii. Ekologiia. (1991)-. Periodical. English (summaries and/or abstracts in Estonian and Russian). qt. $132.95. Kirjastus Perioodika, Pk 107, Parnu Mnt 8, Tallinn EE0090 Estonia. **Tel** 0142 441 262, FAX 0142 442 484. **(Subscription address:** East View Publications Inc., 3020 Harbor Lane North, Suite 110, Minneapolis MN 55447.**) LC** QH540; .E37.

XO
EKOLOGIA BRATISLAVA / ECOLOGY BRATISLAVA. VFOAT Ecology Bratislava. (199?)-. Periodical. English (summaries and/or abstracts in Slovak; table of contents in Slovak). qt. Slovenska Akademia Vied / Slovak Academy of Sciences, PO Box 57, 81005 Bratislava Slovakia. **Tel** 011 42 7 3782715, 011 42 7 3782925, FAX 011 42 7 496849, telex 93261. **LC** QH540; .E43. ***Continues** Ekologia CSFR.*

XO/0862-9129
EKOLOGIA CSFR / ECOLOGY CSFR. *Title Change.* VFOAT Ecology (CSFR). Vol. 10, No. 1 (1991)-(1992). Periodical. English (summaries and/or abstracts in Czech; table of contents in Czech). qt. Slovenska Akademia Vied / Slovak Academy of Sciences, PO Box 57, 81005 Bratislava Slovakia. **Tel** 011 42 7 3782715, 011 42 7 3782925, FAX 011 42 7 496849, telex 93261. **LC** WMLC 93/2909; QH540; .E43. **CODEN** EKCSEE. Documents available from The Genuine Article. ***Continues** Ekologia (CSSR). **Continued by** Ekologia Bratislava.*
Ind/Abst Curr. Aware. Biol. Sci., CABS (?-?); Curr. Contents, Agric. Biol. Environ. Sci. (?-?); Ecol. Abstr. (?-?); Geogr. Abstr. Phys. Geogr. (?-?); Geogr. Abstr. Human Geogr. (?-?); Res. Alert (?-?) [Select. Cov.]; SCISEARCH (?-?); Soc. Sci. Cit. Index (?-?) [Select. Cov.].

PL/0420-9036
EKOLOGIA POLSKA (1970). (EKOLOGIA POLSKA. POLISH JOURNAL OF ECOLOGY.). [Ekol. pol.]. **Added/Corp** Instytut Ekologii (Polska Akademia Nauk). **VFOAT** Polish Journal of Ecology. Vol. 18 (1970)-. Periodical. English (summaries and/or abstracts in Polish). qt. $70.00. **(Subscription address:** ARS Polona, PO Box 1001, 00068 Warsaw Poland.**) LC** QH162; .E38. **DD** 574.5/05. **NLM** W1 EK27D. **CODEN** ELPLBS. Documents available from BIOSIS Document Express, CASDDS. ***Continues** Ekologia Polska. Seria A.*
Ind/Abst AGRICOLA; Biol. Abstr.; Chem. Abstr.; Coal Abstr.; Curr. Ref. Fish Res.; Ecol. Abstr.; Ecology Abstr.; EMBASE; Field Crop Abstr.; Fish Rev.; For. Prod. Abstr.; For. Abstr.; Geogr. Abstr. Phys. Geogr.; Geol. Abstr.; GeoRef; Grasslands For. Abstr.; Hortic. Abstr.; Key Word Index Wildl. Res.; Life Sci. Collect.; Plant Breed. Abstr.; Pollut. Abstr. Indexes; Protozoolog. Abstr.; Rev. Agric. Entomol.; Soils Fert.; Weed Abstr.; Wheat Barley Trit. Abstr.; Wildl. Rev.

BU/0204-7675
EKOLOGIA (SOFIA). (EKOLOGIIA.). [Ekologia]. **Added/Corp** Bulgarska Akademiia na Naukite. **VFOAT** Ecology. (1975)-. Bulgarian (summaries and/or abstracts in English, German and Russian). ir. Price varies. Izdatelstvo na Bulgarskata Akademiia Na Naukite, 6 Rouski Boulevard, Sofia Bulgaria. **Tel** FAX 80 13 41, telex 22267 HEMKIK. **LC** QH540; .E43. **NLM** W1 EK27HC. **CODEN** EKOLDI. Documents available from BIOSIS Document Express, CASDDS.
Ind/Abst AGRICOLA; Biol. Abstr.; Chem. Abstr.; For. Abstr.

RU/0134-4978
EKOLOGIIA I ZASHCHITA LESA : MEZHVUZOVSKII SBORNIK NAUCHNYKH TRUDOV / LENINGRADSKAIA LESOTEKHNICHESKAIA AKADEMIIA IMENI S.M. KIROVA. [Ekol. zasc. lesa]. **Added/Corp** Leningradskaia Lesotekhnicheskaia Akademiia Imeni S.M. Kirova. (19??)-. Academic Scholarly Publication. Russian. **CODEN** EZLEDJ. Documents available from CASDDS.
Ind/Abst Abstr. Bull. Inst. Pap. Sci. Tech.; Chem. Abstr.

UN
EKOLOGIIA MORIA / AKADEMIIA NAUK UKRAINSKOI SSR, INSTITUT BIOLOGII IUZHNYKH MOREI IM. A.O. KOVALEVSKOGO. See Biology-Marine Biology.

RU/0367-0597
EKOLOGIJA. (EKOLOGIIA.). [Ekologija]. **Added/Corp** Akademiia Nauk SSSR. (1970)-. Academic Scholarly Publication. Russian. bm. $136.00. **(Subscription address:** East View Publications Inc., 3020 Harbor Lane North, Suite 110, Minneapolis MN 55447.**) LC** QH540; .E44. **DD** 574.5/05. **NLM** W1 EK27H. **CODEN** EKIAAK. available on microfilm from University Microfilms International (UMI). Documents available from BIOSIS Document Express, CASDDS.
Ind/Abst Biol. Abstr.; Chem. Abstr.; GeoRef; Plant Breed. Abstr.; Rev. Med. Vet. Entomol.

YU/0531-9110
EKOLOGIJA. VFOAT Acta Biologica Iugoslavica. Ekologija. Vol. 1 (1966)-. Periodical. Serbo-Croatian (Roman) (German, French and Russian). sa. Unija Bioloskih Nauchih, Drustava Jugoslavie Beograd ZM, 1108 Nemanjina 6 Yugoslavia. **LC** QH540.

LI/0235-7224
EKOLOGIJA / LIETUVOS MOKSLU AKADEMIJA / EKOLOGIIA / LITOVSKAIA AKADEMIIA NAUK / ECOLOGY / THE LITHUANIAN ACADEMY OF SCIENCES. Added/Corp Lietuvos Mokslu Akademija. Prezidiumas. Botanikos Institutas (Lietuvos Mokslu Akademija) Zoologijos ir Parazitologijos Institutas (Lietuvos Mokslu Akademija) Ekologijos Institutas (Lietuvos Mokslu Akademija). **VFOAT** Ekologiia; Ecology; Lietuvos Mokslu Akademija, Ekologija. No. 1 (1990)-. Periodical. Russian (English and Lithuanian). qt. Ekologija, A Gostaitp 12, 2600 Vilnius Lithuania. **LC** IN PROCESS. **CODEN** EKOLEJ. ***Continues in part** Lietuvos TSR Mokslu Akademijos Darbai. Serija C, 0131-3851.*

●US/1066-0348
EMERGENCY SERVICES SOURCEBOOK. See Public Health and Safety.

II/0970-1753
ENCOLOGY. [Encology (Bombay)]. Vol. 1, No. 1 (June 1986)-. Periodical. English. mo. **LC** TD187.5.I4; E53. **DD** 363.7/00954.
Ind/Abst Coal Abstr.

CN/0833-8000
ENJEU - ENJEU ET ENVIRONNEMENT JEUNESSE. (L'ENJEU.). [Enjeu - Enjeu environ. jeun.]. **Added/Corp** Enjeu et Environnement Jeunesse. Vol. 5, No. 5 (Sept. 1985)-. Periodical. French. qt. 18.69Can$ (institution), 14.02Can$ (individual). Environnement Jeunesse, 4545 Avenue Pierre Coub/CP 1000, Montreal Quebec H1V 3R2 Canada. **Tel** (514)252-3016. **DD** 363.7/058/060714. ***Continues** Journal L'Enjeu., 0712-2128.*

US/0013-9165
ENVIRONMENT AND BEHAVIOR. [Environ. behav.]. **VFOAT** EB. Environment and Behavior. Vol. 1 (June 1969)-. Periodical. English. bm (Jan., Mar., May, July, Sept., Nov.). $204.00. SAGE Periodical Press, 2455 Teller Road, Thousand Oaks CA 91320. **Tel** (805)499-0721, FAX (805)499-0871, telex 100799. **ED** Robert B. Bechtel (University of Arizona). **LC** HM206; .E5. **DD** 301.3. **NLM** W1 EN98NK. **CODEN** EVBHAF. **[CCC]. Pr Rev. Acid Free.** available on microfilm and microfiche from University Microfilms International (UMI). Documents available from The Genuine Article, UMI Article Clearinghouse, Documents on Demand.
Desc: Reports rigorous experimental and theoretical work on the study, design and control of the physical environment and its interaction with human behavioral systems.
Ind/Abst Acad. Search (Jan. 1994-); AGRICOLA [Select. Cov.]; Appl. Soc. Sci. Index Abstr.; AQUAREF; Avery Index Archit. Period. Suppl. Colum. Univ. (19??-199?); Crim. Justice Abstr.; Curr. Contents Soc. Behav. Sci.; Curr. Geogr. Publ. (199?-); Curr. Index J. Educ.; Educ. Adm. Abstr.; EMBASE; Energy Inf. Abstr.; Energy Res. Abstr. (Dec. 1978-); Environ. Abstr.; Environ. Period. Bibliogr.; Expand. Acad. Index (1989-); Gen. Sci. Source (Jul. 1993-); Geogr. Abstr. Phys. Geogr. (?-?); Geogr. Abstr. Human Geogr.; High. Educ. Abstr. (1975-19??); INFO-SOUTH Abstr.; INIS Atomindex [Micro.]; Int. Bibliogr. Sociol.; Int. Civil Eng. Abstr.; J. Plan. Lit.; Mag. Search; Middle East Abstr. Index; Newsp. Period. Abstr. (1991-); Life Sci. Collect.; Pollut. Abstr. Indexes; Psychol. Abstr. (1969-); PsycINFO; PsycLit; PsycScan: Appl. Psych.; Res. Alert [Full Cov.]; Res. High. Educ. Abstr.; Sage Fam. Stud. Abstr.; Sage Urban Stud. Abstr; Soc. Plann. Policy Dev. Abstr.; Soc. Sci. Source (Jul. 1993-); Soc. Sci. Cit. Index [Full Cov.]; Soc. Sci. Index; Soc. Sci. Index Fulltext (Nov. 1988-) [Full Txt.]; Sociol. Abstr.; SportSearch; Urban Aff. Abstr.; Work Relat. Abstr.

US/0013-9157
ENVIRONMENT (ST. LOUIS). (ENVIRONMENT [MICROFORM].). **Added/Corp** Helen Dwight Reid Educational Foundation. Committee for Environmental Information (Saint Louis, Mo.) Scientists' Institute for Public Information. Vol. 11 No. 1 (Jan./Feb. 1969)-. Periodical. English. Heldref Publications, 1319 Eighteenth Street Northwest, Washington DC 20036-1802. **Tel** (202)296-6267, (800)365-9753, FAX (202)296-5149. **[CCC]. *Continues** Scientist and Citizen.*

●UK/1352-8505
ENVIRONMENTAL AND ECOLOGICAL STATISTICS. (1994)-. Periodical. English. Four times a year. $139.00 US and Canada; £90.00 Europe; £99.00 Other. Chapman & Hall, 2-6 Boundary Row, London SE1 8HN England. **Tel** 011 44 71 865 0066, FAX 011 44 71 522 9623, telex 290164 Chapmag. **(Subscription address:** Chapman & Hall, Cheriton House, North Way, Andover, Hampshire, SP10 5BE England.**)**

UK/0144-9281
ENVIRONMENTAL EDUCATION AND INFORMATION. See Environmental Issues.

US
ENVIRONMENTAL MONITORING AND ECOLOGICAL STUDIES PROGRAM. See Environmental Issues.

US/0736-9603
ENVIRONMENTAL OPPORTUNITIES. See Environmental Issues-Conservation and Natural Resources.

IT
ENVIRONMENTAL RESEARCH NEWSLETTER. (19??)-. Newsletter. English. sa. Free on request. Institute Environment, Dr. G Rossi, Joint Research Center, 21020 Ispra Va Italy. **Tel** 011 39 332 789724.
Desc: Progress of the research and regulatory actions of the commission of the European Communities in the field of the protection of the environment.

●CN/1181-8700
ENVIRONMENTAL REVIEWS. [Environ. rev.]. **Added/Corp** National Research Council Canada. **VFOAT** Dossiers Environnement. Vol. 1, No. 1 (1993)-. Periodical. English. qt (4 issues). 163.00Can$ (institution), 57.00Can$ (individual) Canada; $163.00 (institution), $63.00 (individual) other. National Research Council of Canada, Receiver General for Canada, Ottawa Ontario K1A 0R6 Canada. **Tel** (613)993-0362, FAX (613)952-7656. **ED** Thomas C. Hutchinson. **Ad Acc, Adv Mgr:** Bob Barrette, **Tel** (613)993-9085.
Desc: Emphasizes the effects on, and responses of, both natural and man-made ecosystems to anthropogenic stress. More specific areas to be covered will include climate change, forest management and harvesting impacts, forest decline, air pollution, ozone, acid rain, pesticide use and effects, lake acidification, marine pollution, ecology of oil spills, toxic chemicals in aquatic and terrestial food chains, heavy metals in the environment, ecological impacts of dams, and much more.

IT/0394-0276
ETA VERDE, L'. (1974)-. Periodical. Italian (English). bm. L25000.00 Italy; L35000.00 other. Giardini Editori Stampatori, Via Santa Bibbiana 28, 56127 Pisa Italy. **Tel** 011 39 50 934242. **UDC** 577.4. **Circ:** 6,000.
Desc: Cultural publication about ecological information and activities within the area of permanent training.

IT/0394-9370
ETHOLOGY, ECOLOGY & EVOLUTION. **See** Zoology.

UK/0269-7653
EVOLUTIONARY ECOLOGY. [Evol. ecol.]. Vol. 1, No. 1 (Jan. 1987)-. Periodical. English. bm. $399.00 US and Canada; £235.00 Europe; £250.00 other. Chapman & Hall, 2-6 Boundary Row, London SE1 8HN England. **Tel** 011 44 71 865 0066, FAX 011 44 71 522 9623, telex 290164 Chapmag. **(Subscription address:** Chapman & Hall, Cheriton House, North Way, Andover, Hampshire, SP10 5BE England.**) ED** M. Rosenzweig. **CODEN** EVECEJ. **[CCC].** Index available. **Ad Acc. Pr Rev. Circ:** 500. available on microfilm from University Microfilms International (UMI). Documents available from The Genuine Article, BIOSIS Document Express.
Desc: A journal of basic concepts at the interface of evolution and ecology. Publishes theoretical and empirical papers of original research, and includes genetic, behavioural, paleobiological, physiological, population-level and community studies, regardless of the taxon or biome from which they are drawn.
Ind/Abst Anim. Breed. Abstr.; Biol. Abstr. (1987-); Chemorecept. Abstr.; Curr. Aware. Biol. Sci., CABS; Curr. Contents, Agric. Biol. Environ. Sci.; Ecol. Abstr.; Ecology Abstr.; Entomol. Abstr.; Environ. Period. Bibliogr.; Fish Rev.; Helminthol. Abstr. (1991-); Hortic. Abstr.; Key Word Index Wildl. Res.; Ornamental Hort. (1991-); Plant Breed. Abstr.; Protozoolog. Abstr.; Res. Alert [Select. Cov.]; Rev. Agric. Entomol.; SCISEARCH; Weed Abstr.; Wildl. Rev.

GW/0932-2205
EXCELLENCE IN ECOLOGY. [Excell. ecol.]. **Added/Corp** Ecology Institute. (1987)-. Monographic series. English. an. Price varies per volume. Inter-Research Science Publishing, Nordbuente 23, D 21385 Oldendorf Germany. **Tel** 011 49 4132 7127, FAX 011 49 4123 8883. **ED** O. Kinne. Documents available from BIOSIS Document Express.
Desc: Features books in the fields of marine, terrestrial or limnetic ecology.
Ind/Abst Biol. Abstr.; Curr. Aware. Biol. Sci., CABS.

IT
FAO ENVIRONMENT AND ENERGY PAPER. **See** Agriculture.

NE/0168-6496
FEMS MICROBIOLOGY, ECOLOGY. **See** Biology-Microbiology.

NE/0378-1097
FEMS MICROBIOLOGY LETTERS. **See** Biology-Microbiology.

FI/0783-4365
FINNISH GAME RESEARCH. [Finn. game res.]. **Added/Corp** Riista-ja Kalatalouden Tutkimuslaitos (Finland). Riistantutkimusosasto. (1988)-. Academic Scholarly Publication. English. ir. Finnish Game and Fisheries Research Institute / Game Division, PO Box 202, FIN-00151 Helsinki Finland. **ED** Harto Linden. **LC** SK1; .S912. **CODEN** FGREEU. **Pr Rev. Circ:** 700. Documents available from BIOSIS Document Express. ***Continues** Riistatieteellisia Julkaisuja, 0015-2447.*
Ind/Abst Biol. Abstr.; Fish Rev.; Key Word Index Wildl. Res.; Wildl. Rev.

GW/0367-2530
FLORA. MORPHOLOGIE, GEOBOTANIK, OKOLOGIE. **VFOAT** Morphologie, Geobotanik, Okologie. Vol. 180 No. 1/2 (1988)-. Periodical. English (French and German). Four times a year. DM604.00 Germany; DM612.00 other. Gustav Fischer Verlag Jena, Postfach 100537, D 07705 Jena Germany. **Tel** 011 49 3641 27332, FAX 011 49 3641 626500. **(Subscription address:** VCH Publishers Inc., 303 Northwest 12th Avenue, Journals Department, Deerfield FL 33442.**) ED** Prof D H Heusel. **[CCC].** Index available. **Bk Rev. Ad Acc. Circ:** 620. Documents available from The Genuine Article. ***Continues** Flora. Morphologie, Geobotanik, Oekophysiologie, 0300-2691.*
Desc: Open to papers on experimental ecology, which deals with the functions of plant communities in relation to their existence in particular habitats.
Ind/Abst AGRICOLA; Ecol. Abstr.; For. Prod. Abstr. (1991-); Res. Alert [Full Cov.]; Sci. Cit. Index; SCISEARCH.

DK/0015-3818
FLORA OG FAUNA. **See** Zoology.

FR
FRANCE ECOPECHE. French. Ouest France, 10 rue du Breil, 35051 Rennes Cedex France. **Tel** 011 33 99 326357, FAX 011 33 99 326025. ***Continues** France Peche; Ecopeche.*

UK/0046-5070
FRESHWATER BIOLOGY. **See** Biology.

US/1054-1829
FRIENDS OF THE EARTH. [Friends earth]. **Added/Corp** Friends of the Earth. Vol. 20 No. 4 (Oct. 1990)-. Periodical. English. Four times a year. $25.00 Comes with Friends of the Earth membership. Friends of the Earth, 1025 Vermont Avenue, Suite 300, Washington DC 20005. **Tel** (202)783-7400. **LC** QH540; .N6. **DD** 333. Documents available from Documents on Demand. ***Continues** Not Man Apart, 0194-1062.*
Ind/Abst Altern. Press Index (199?-); Environ. Abstr.

UK/0269-8463
FUNCTIONAL ECOLOGY. [Funct. ecol.]. **Added/Corp** British Ecological Society. Vol. 1, No. 1 (1987)-. Academic Scholarly Publication. English. bm (6 issues). $335.00 US & Canada; £197.00 Europe; £216.00 other. Blackwell Scientific Publications Ltd, Marston Book Services, PO Box 87, Oxford OX2 ODT UK. **Tel** 011 44 865 791155, FAX 011 44 865 791927, telex 837 515 MARDIS G. **LC** QH540; .F85. **DD** 574.5/05. **CODEN** FECOE5. **[CCC].** Documents available from The Genuine Article, BIOSIS Document Express.
Ind/Abst AgBiotech News Inf.; AGRICOLA [Select. Cov.]; Anim. Breed. Abstr.; Biocont. News Inf. (19??-19??); Biol. Abstr. (1987-); Crop Physiol. Abstr.; Curr. Aware. Biol. Sci., CABS; Curr. Contents, Agric. Biol. Environ. Sci.; Ecol. Abstr.; Ecology Abstr.; Entomol. Abstr.; Environ. Period. Bibliogr.; Field Crop Abstr.; Fish Rev.; For. Abstr.; Geogr. Abstr. Phys. Geogr. (?-?); Geol. Abstr.; Grasslands For. Abstr.; Int. Dev. Abstr. (?-?); Irr. Drain. Abstr.; Maize Abstr.; Ornamental Hort.; Plant Breed. Abstr.; Plant Genet. Resour. Abstr.; Postharvest News Inf.; Res. Alert [Select. Cov.]; Rev. Agric. Entomol.; Rev. Med. Vet. Entomol.; SCISEARCH; Seed Abstr.; Soils Fert.; Weed Abstr.; Wheat Barley Trit. Abstr.; Wildl. Rev.

IT
FUTURO SOSTENIBILE. **VFOAT** Sustainable Future. (1990)-. Periodical. Italian (summaries and/or abstracts in English). Three times a year. Centro Futuro Sostenibile, Via Giulio Cesare 49, 00192 Rome Italy. **Tel** 011 39 6 3215491.

BE/0379-0452
GEO-ECO-TROP. [Geo-Eco-Trop]. **Added/Corp** Centre International de Semiologie (Universite Nationale du Zaire, Campus de Lubumbashi). Vol. 1 (Jan. 1977)-. Academic Scholarly Publication. French (English). an. $45.00. Geo-Eco-Trop, 36 Bois de Mariomont, B 4804 Jalhay Belgium. **Tel** 11 32 87222538. **ED** S. Alexandre. **CODEN** GETRD7. cum. index. Documents available from CASDDS.
Desc: Information on ecology and geography.
Ind/Abst Chem. Abstr. (1977-1981); Ecol. Abstr.; Field Crop Abstr.; For. Prod. Abstr.; For. Abstr.; Geogr. Abstr. Phys. Geogr.; Geogr. Abstr. Human Geogr. (?-?); Geol. Abstr.; Potato Abstr.; Rev. Agric. Entomol.; Soils Fert.

GW/0940-6581
GEOBOTANISCHE KOLLOQUIEN. **VFOAT** Geobot. Kolloq. Vol. 7 (June/July 1991)-. German (summaries and/or abstracts in English). an. DM15.00. Geobotanik Im Fachbereich Biologie der J W Goethe-Universitat, Sissmayerstr 70, Postfach 11 19 32, 6000 Frankfurt 11 Germany. **Tel** 69 798 4739, FAX 69 798 4822. **ED** R Wittig. **Ad Acc, Adv Mgr:** Dr. Ballach, **Tel** 69 798 4757. **Pr Rev.** ***Continues** Dusseldorfer Geobotanische Kolloquien, 0176-0769.*
Desc: Original and reviewed papers on the field of ecology (particular of plants), vegetation science, biological conservation, and related subjects.

GW/0940-6581
GEOBOTANISCHE KOLLOQUIEN. German (summaries and/or abstracts in English). an. DM15.00. Geobotanik Im Fachbereich Biologie der J W Goethe-Universitat, Sissmayerstr 70, Postfach 11 19 32, 6000 Frankfurt 11 Germany. **Tel** 69 798 4739, FAX 69 798 4822. **ED** R Wittig. **Ad Acc, Adv Mgr:** Dr. Ballach, **Tel** 69 798 4757. **Pr Rev.**
Desc: Original and reviewed papers on the field of ecology (particular of plants), vegetation science, biological conservation, and related subjects.

GW/0170-3250
GEOECOLOGICAL RESEARCH. [Geoecol. res.]. (1972)-. Monographic series. English. ir. Price varies per volume. Franz Steiner Verlag GmbH, Postfach 101061, D 70009 Stuttgart Germany. **Tel** 011 49 0711 2582372, FAX 011 49 0711 2582290, telex 723636 daz d. **ED** Ulrich Schweinfurth, H. Flohn, J.J. Stephan, Tilmann Liess. **UDC** 581.5/.9 :911.2.
Ind/Abst Geogr. Abstr. Human Geogr.

FR/0761-9243
GIBIER, FAUNE SAUVAGE. [Gibier faune sauvage]. 1984, No. 1-. Periodical. French (English). qt. 235.00F France; 280.00F other. Office National de la Chasse, 85 Bis Avenue de Wagram, 75017 Paris France. **Tel** (1)42 27 81 75, FAX (1)47 63 79 13. **ED** G Pringalle. **LC** QL1; .G53. **CODEN** GFSAER. Index available. cum. index. **Bk Rev. Circ:** 1,000. Documents available from BIOSIS Document Express. ***Continues in part** Bulletin Mensuel (France. Office National de la Chasse).*
Desc: Scientific articles on the ecology of game or wildlife species, their habitats and ethology.
Ind/Abst Biol. Abstr.; Fish Rev.; For. Abstr.; Index Vet.; Key Word Index Wildl. Res.; Poult. Abstr.; Vet. Bull.; Wildl. Rev.

IT
GIORNALE DELLA NATURA. L55.000 Italy; $55.00 other. Federico Ceratti Editore, C Postale 1, Via XXV Aprile 11, 20060 Vignate Milan Italy. **Tel** 011 39 2 9560530.
Desc: "Olistic" way of living, day-by-day ecological behaviors, suggestions for a new culture in balance with nature.

UK/0960-7447
GLOBAL ECOLOGY AND BIOGEOGRAPHY LETTERS. Vol. 1, No. 1 (Jan. 1991)-. Academic Scholarly Publication. English. bm (6 issues). Comes with Journal of Biogeography. Blackwell Scientific Publications Ltd, Marston Book Services, PO Box 87, Oxford OX2 ODT UK. **Tel** 011 44 865 791155, FAX 011 44 865 791927, telex 837 515 MARDIS G. **LC** QH84; .G58. **DD** 574.9/05. **CODEN** GEBLE2. Documents available from The Genuine Article, Documents on Demand.
Ind/Abst Curr. Aware. Biol. Sci., CABS; Curr. Contents, Agric. Biol. Environ. Sci.; Curr. Geogr. Publ. (199?-); Ecol. Abstr.; Environ. Abstr.; Environ. Period. Bibliogr.; Geogr. Abstr. Human Geogr.; Int. Dev. Abstr.; Res. Alert [Full Cov.]; Sci. Cit. Index; SCISEARCH.

US/1049-9083
GLOBAL ENVIRONMENTAL CHANGE REPORT. (GLOBAL ENVIRONMENTAL CHANGE REPORT : POLICY, SCIENCE, AND INDUSTRY NEWS WORLDWIDE FROM CUTTER INFORMATION CORP.). [Glob. environ. change rep.]. **Added/Corp** Cutter Information Corp. **VFOAT** GECR. Vol. 1, No. 1 (Dec. 8, 1989)-. Periodical. English. sm. $257.00 (university), $457.00 (other) US, Canada, & Mexico. Cutter Information Corporation, 37 Broadway, Arlington MA 02174-5539. **Tel** (617)648-8700, (800)964-5118, FAX (617)648-8707, (617)648-1950, telex 650 100 9891. **DD** 363. **[CCC].** available on an online database (file 636/Full-Text) from DIALOG.
Ind/Abst Abstr. Bull. Inst. Pap. Sci. Tech.; PTS Newsl. Database [Full Txt.].

US/1062-5356
GREAT LAKES WETLANDS. [Great Lakes wetl.]. **Added/Corp** Tip of the Mitt Watershed Council. Vol. 1 No. 1 (Winter 1989)- Vol. 4 (Jan. 1993-94)-. Periodical. English. Four times a year (Mar., June, Sept., Dec.). $15.00. Tip of the Mitt Watershed Council, PO Box 300, Conway MI 49722. **Tel** (616)347-1181, FAX (616)347-5928. **ED** Wil Cwikiel. **DD** 574. Index available (publish separately). cum. index. **Bk Rev. Circ:** 500.
Desc: "Great Lakes Wetlands" is an informative quarterly newsletter that deals with specific policy and scientific issues related to wetland protection and management in the Great Lakes Basin.

IT/0111-4506
GREENPEACE NEWS. (19??)-. Italian. Six times a year. L35000. Associazione Greenpeace, Via Gelsomini 28, 00153 Rome Italy. **Tel** 011 39 6 5782484, 011 39 6 5780479. **Circ:** 60,000 (ctrl).

II/0970-2903
HIMALAYAN JOURNAL OF ENVIRONMENT AND ZOOLOGY. [Him. j. env. zool.]. **Added/Corp** Indian Academy of Environmental Sciences. (198?)-. Periodical. English. sa. $50.00. Indian Academy of Environmental Sciences, Hardwar, India. **(Subscription address:** Prints India, 11 Darya Ganj, New Delhi 110002 India.**) LC** IN PROCESS.

US/0199-6894
HOOSIER CONSERVATION. **Added/Corp** Indiana Conservation Council. Indiana Wildlife Federation. (19??)-. Periodical. English. bm. $20.00. Indiana Wildlife Federation, 301 East Carmel Drive, Suite G 200, Carmel IN 46032. **Tel** (800)347-3445. **ED** Sharon Wiggins, phone: (317)296-3779). **Ad Acc.** ctrl circ.

US/0018-7178
HUMAN ECOLOGY FORUM. [Human ecol. forum]. **Added/Corp** New York State College of Human Ecology. (1970/71)-. Periodical. English. Three times a year. $22.00. Cornell University / Department of Human Ecology, 1150 Comstock Hall, Ithaca NY 14853. **Tel** (607)255-1574. **ED** James Titus. **LC** HM206; .H8. **DD** 301.3/1/05. Index available. cum. index. **Circ:** 5,000. available on microfilm and microfiche from University Microfilms International (UMI). Documents available from UMI Article Clearinghouse.
Desc: Research reports of the College of Human Ecology; commentaries on critical social problems by faculty and outside experts; summaries of public policy studies.
Ind/Abst Acad. Abstr. Full Text Elite (Jan. 1992-); Acad. Abstr. (Jan. 1992-); Acad. Search (Jan. 1992-); AGRICOLA [Select. Cov.]; Energy Res. Abstr. (Aug. 1978-); Environ. Period. Bibliogr.; Expand. Acad. Index (1989-); Gen. Sci. Source (Jan. 1992-); INFO-SOUTH Abstr.; J. Plan. Lit.; Mag. Search; Newsp. Period. Abstr. (1991-); PAIS Int. Print; Soc. Sci. Source (Jan. 1992-); Soc. Sci. Index; Soc. Sci. Index Fulltext (1988-) [Full Txt.].

US/0300-7839
HUMAN ECOLOGY (NEW YORK, N.Y.). (HUMAN ECOLOGY.). [Hum. ecol.]. Vol. 1 (March 1972)-. Periodical. English. Four times a year. $260.00 institutions, $55.00 individuals US; $305.00 institutions, $64.00 individuals other. Plenum Press, 233 Spring Street, New York NY 10013-1578. **Tel** (212)620-8000, (800)221-9369, FAX (212)463-0742, (212)807-1047, telex 23/421139. **ED** Susan H. Lees and Daniel G. Bates. **LC** GF1; .H84. **DD** 301.31/05. **NLM** W1 HU446DE.

CODEN HMECAJ. **[CCC]**. Index available. **Pr Rev.** available on microfilm and microfiche from University Microfilms International (UMI). Documents available from Article Express International, The Genuine Article, BIOSIS Document Express, UMI Article Clearinghouse, Documents on Demand.
Desc: Provides a forum for papers concerned with the varied systems of interaction between people and their environment.
Ind/Abst Abstr. Anthropol.; Acad. Search (July 1993-); AGRICOLA [Select. Cov.]; Agrofor. Abstr. (19??-19??); Anthropol. Index; Anthropol. Lit.; Bioeng. Abstr.; Biol. Abstr.; Curr. Aware. Biol. Sci., CABS; Curr. Contents Soc. Behav. Sci.; Dairy Sci. Abstr.; Ecol. Abstr.; Ecology Abstr.; Ei Page One; EMBASE; Energy Inf. Abstr.; Energy Res. Abstr. (April 1976-); Eng. Index Annu.; Environ. Abstr.; Environ. Period. Bibliogr.; Expand. Acad. Index (1988-); Fish Rev.; For. Abstr.; Gen. Sci. Source (Jul. 1993-); Geogr. Abstr. Human Geogr.; Hum. Resour. Abstr. (?-?); INFO-SOUTH Abstr.; Int. Dev. Abstr.; J. Plan. Lit.; Mag. Search; Maize Abstr.; Middle East Abstr. Index; Newsp. Period. Abstr. (1991-); Peace Res. Abstr. J. (1976-1984); Life Sci. Collect.; Pollut. Abstr. Indexes; Res. Alert [Full Cov.]; Rev. Agric. Entomol.; Rural Dev. Abstr.; Sage Fam. Stud. Abstr.; Soc. Plann. Policy Dev. Abstr.; Soc. Sci. Source (Jul. 1993-); Soc. Sci. Cit. Index [Full Cov.]; Soc. Sci. Index; Soc. Sci. Index Fulltext (June 1988-) [Full Txt.]; Sociol. Abstr.; Stud. Women Abstr.; Wildl. Rev.; Women Stud. Abstr.; World Agric. Econ.

NE/0165-1404
HYDROBIOLOGICAL BULLETIN. ***Title Change.*** **See** Biology.

CN/0823-5724
IDEES ET PRATIQUES ALTERNATIVES. ***Ceased.*** [Idees prat. altern.]. **VFOAT** Alternatives. Vol. 1, No. 1 (Fall 1983). Ceased (1986). Periodical. French. qt. Productions Reseau, CP67 Succ Rosemont, Montreal Quebec H1X 3B6 Canada. **Tel** (514)739-4440. **DD** 304.2/8/05.
Ind/Abst Point Repere (19??-19??).

II/0304-5250
INDIAN JOURNAL OF ECOLOGY. [Indian j. ecol.]. **Added/Corp** Indian Ecological Society. Vol. 1 (July 1974)-. Academic Scholarly Publication. English. sa. $25.00. Indian Ecological Society, Punjab Agricultural University, Ladhiana India. **(Subscription address:** Prints India, 11 Darya Ganj, New Delhi 110002 India.**)** **LC** QH183; .I53. **CODEN** IJECDC. Documents available from BIOSIS Document Express, CASDDS, Documents on Demand.
Ind/Abst AGRICOLA; Biocont. News Inf.; Biodeter. Abstr.; Biol. Abstr.; Chem. Abstr.; Cot. Trop. Fibr. Abstr. Bibliogr.; Crop Physiol. Abstr.; Ecology Abstr.; EMBASE; Environ. Abstr.; Environ. Period. Bibliogr. (?-?); Field Crop Abstr.; Fish Rev.; Microbiol. Abstr. Sect. A; Microbiol. Abstr. Sect. C; Life Sci. Collect.; Plant Grow. Reg. Abstr.; Pollut. Abstr. Indexes; Potato Abstr.; Rice Abstr.; Soils Fert.; Sorghum Mill. Abstr.; Wildl. Rev.

IT/0393-0793
INFORMATORE DEL RECUPERO, L'. [Inf. recupero]. (1979)-. Periodical. Italian. Eleven times a year. L50000 Italy; L60000 other. Cofiri SRL, Via Guicciardini 5, 20129 Milan, Italy. **Tel** 011 39 2 783362. **UDC** 62.002.82.

RU
INFORMATSIONNYE MATERIALY INSTITUTA EKOLOGII RASTENII I ZHIVOTNYKH. **Main/Corp** Institut Ekologii Rastenii i Zhivothykh (Akademiia Nauk SSSR). Vol. 1 (1974)-. Russian. 0.20rub (single issue). K-49 Pervomaiskaia 91, Sverdlovsk, Russia. **LC** QH540; .A45a.

US/1012-6880
INTECOL NEWSLETTER. [INTECOL newsl.]. (1970)-. Periodical. English. bm (6 issues). $40.00 (institutions & libraries), $15.00 (students & developing countries), $25.00 regular membership in INTECOL. Savannah River Ecology Lab, Drawer E, Aiken SC 29802. **Tel** (803)725-2472, FAX (803)725-3309.
Desc: Publication of INTECOL, an international non-governmental professional organization that represents ecologists worldwide.

UK
INTERIM REPORT / JOS PLATEAU ENVIRONMENTAL RESOURCES DEVELOPMENT PROGRAMME.
Added/Corp Jos Plateau Environmental Resources Development Programme. (19??)-. Monographic series. English. ***Continues*** *Report (Jos Plateau Environmental Resources Development Programme).*
Ind/Abst Agrofor. Abstr.; For. Abstr.

US/1041-4665
INTERNATIONAL ENVIRONMENTAL AFFAIRS. **See** Environmental Issues-Conservation and Natural Resources.

II/0377-015X
INTERNATIONAL JOURNAL OF ECOLOGY AND ENVIRONMENTAL SCIENCES. [Int. j. ecol. environ. sci.]. Vol. 1 (Aug. 1974)-. Periodical. English. Three times a year. $60.00. International Scientific Publishers, 50-B Pocket C, Siddhartha Extension, New Delhi 110014 India. **Tel** 632169. **(Subscription address:** Prints India, 11 Darya Ganj, New Delhi 110002 India.**)** **ED** P S Ramakrishnan, Brij Gopal. **LC** QH540; .I6. **DD** 574.5/05. **CODEN** IJESDQ. **[CCC]**. Index available. cum. index. **Bk Rev. Ad Acc. Circ:** 600. Documents available from BIOSIS Document Express, CASDDS.
Desc: Publishes original research and review papers in all fields of pure and applied ecology (plant, animal and human ecology) and environmental sciences (including environmental pollution, conservation, and resource management).
Ind/Abst AGRICOLA; Agrofor. Abstr. (1991-); Biol. Abstr.; Chem. Abstr.; Crop Physiol. Abstr.; Ecol. Abstr.; EMBASE; For. Abstr.; Geogr. Abstr. Human Geogr.; Grasslands For. Abstr.; Hortic. Abstr.; Index Vet.; Int. Dev. Abstr.; Ornamental Hort. (1991-); Life Sci. Collect.; Rev. Plant Pathol.; Seed Abstr.; Soils Fert.; Weed Abstr.; Wheat Barley Trit. Abstr.

US/0020-7233
INTERNATIONAL JOURNAL OF ENVIRONMENTAL STUDIES. SECTION A, ENVIRONMENTAL STUDIES, THE. **See** Environmental Issues-Conservation and Natural Resources.

UK/1350-4509
INTERNATIONAL JOURNAL OF SUSTAINABLE DEVELOPMENT AND WORLD ECOLOGY, THE. (19??)-. English. qt. £75.00 (institutional), £35.00 (individual). Parthenon Publishing, Casterton Hall Carnforth, Lancashire LA6 2LA England. **Tel** 011 44 5242 72084, FAX 44-5242-71587.

US/0896-5781
INTERNATIONAL PERMACULTURE SPECIES YEARBOOK, THE. ***Title Change.*** [Int. permac. species yearb.]. **VFOAT** Tipsy. (1986)-?. English. an. Yankee Permaculture, c/o Betsy Keenan, PO Box 264, Maloy IA 50852. **DD** 632. **Bk Rev. Ad Acc. Circ:** 1,000. ***Continues*** *International Permaculture Seed Yearbook.* ***Continued by*** *International Permaculture Solutions Journal, 1046-8366.*

US
ISLE / INTERDISCIPLINAREY STUDIES IN LITERATURE AND ENVIRONMENT. Periodical. English. sa. $25.00 institutions, $10.00 individuals. Indiana University of Pennsylvania / English Department, 110 Leonard Hall, Indiana PA 15705. **Tel** (412)357-6486, FAX (412)357-3056. **ED** Patrick D. Murphy.
Desc: Encourages essays exploring such topics as ecological literary/performance criticism, environmental arts and nature philosophies in popular culture.

UK/0957-7238
ITE RESEARCH PUBLICATION. [ITE res. publ.]. **VFOAT** Institute of Terrestrial Ecology Research Publication. (198?)-. Monographic series. English. **DD** 574.5264.
Ind/Abst Rev. Plant Pathol.

UK/0263-8614
ITE SYMPOSIUM. [ITE symp.]. **Added/Corp** Institute of Terrestrial Ecology. **VFOAT** I.T.E. Symposium. **VAT** Institute of Terrestrial Ecology Symposium. No. 1 (1981)-. Monographic series. English. ir. Price varies per volume. Institute of Terrestrial Ecology, Merlewood Research Station, Grange Over Sands, Aumbria LAU 6JU United Kingdom. ***Continues*** *Monks Wood Symposium, 0077-0426.*
Ind/Abst AGRICOLA [Select. Cov.]; Agrofor. Abstr.

UK/0021-8790
JOURNAL OF ANIMAL ECOLOGY, THE. **See** Zoology.

UK/0021-8901
JOURNAL OF APPLIED ECOLOGY, THE. [J. appl. ecol.]. **Added/Corp** British Ecological Society. Vol. 1 (May 1964)-. Academic Scholarly Publication. English. qt (4 issues). $335.00 US & Canada; £197.00 Europe; £216.00 other. Blackwell Scientific Publications Ltd, Marston Book Services, PO Box 87, Oxford OX2 ODT UK. **Tel** 011 44 865 791155, FAX 011 44 865 791927, telex 837 515 MARDIS G. **ED** W. Block and J. Miles. **LC** S3; .J86. **NLM** W1 JO541F. **CODEN** JAPEAI. **[CCC]**. Index available (bound in last issue). **Bk Rev. Ad Acc. Pr Rev. Circ:** 3,400. available on microfilm and microfiche from University Microfilms International (UMI). Documents available from The Genuine Article, BIOSIS Document Express, CASDDS, Documents on Demand.
Desc: Original research on most aspects of applied ecology.
Ind/Abst AGRICOLA; Agrofor. Abstr. (1991-); AQUAREF; Biocont. News Inf. (1991-); Biodeter. Abstr.; Biol. Agric. Index; Biol. Abstr.; Biostatistica (19??-19??); Chem. Abstr.; Coal Abstr.; Curr. Contents, Agric. Biol. Environ. Sci.; Curr. Geogr. Publ. (199?-); Ecol. Abstr.; Ecology Abstr.; EMBASE; Energy Res. Abstr.; Entomol. Abstr.; Environ. Abstr.; Environ. Period. Bibliogr.; Field Crop Abstr.; Fish Rev.; For. Prod. Abstr.; For. Abstr.; Fresh. Aqua. Contents Tables; Geogr. Abstr. Phys. Geogr.; Geogr. Abstr. Human Geogr.; Grasslands For. Abstr.; Helminthol. Abstr. (1991-); Hortic. Abstr.; Int. Dev. Abstr. (?-?); Irr. Drain. Abstr.; Leis. Recreat. Tour. Abstr.; Nematol. Abstr.; Nutr. Abstr. Rev., Ser. B, Live Feeds and Feed.; Nutr. Abstr. Rev., Ser. A, Hum. Exp.; Ornamental Hort.; Life Sci. Collect.; PESTDOC; Plant Breed. Abstr.; Plant Genet. Resour. Abstr.; Plant Grow. Reg. Abstr.; Pollut. Abstr. Indexes; Protozoolog. Abstr.; Res. Alert [Full Cov.]; Rev. Agric. Entomol.; Rev. Med. Vet. Entomol.; Rev. Plant Pathol.; Rice Abstr.; Rural Dev. Abstr.; Sci. Cit. Index; SCISEARCH; Seed Abstr.; Soils Fert.; Sorghum Mill. Abstr.; Weed Abstr.; Wildl. Rev.; World Agric. Econ.

US/0098-0331
JOURNAL OF CHEMICAL ECOLOGY. [J. chem. ecol.]. **Added/Corp** International Society of Chemical Ecology. Vol. 1 (Jan. 1975)-. Academic Scholarly Publication. English. Twelve times a year. $695.00 institutions, $152.00 individuals US; $815.00 institutions, $178.00 individuals other. Plenum Press, 233 Spring Street, New York NY 10013-1578. **Tel** (212)620-8000, (800)221-9369, FAX (212)463-0742, (212)807-1047, telex 23/421139. **ED** Robert M. Silverstein and John B. Simeone. **LC** QD1; .J926. **DD** 574.5/01/54. **NLM** W1 JO58P. **CODEN** JCECD8. **[CCC]**. Index available. **Pr Rev.** available on microfilm and microfiche from University Microfilms International (UMI). Documents available from The Genuine Article, BIOSIS Document Express, CASDDS, Documents on Demand.
Desc: This journal is devoted to the promoting and understanding of the function and significance of natural chemicals that mediate interactions within and between organisms.
Ind/Abst Abstr. Bull. Inst. Pap. Sci. Tech.; AGRICOLA [Select. Cov.]; Anim. Behav. Abstr.; Anim. Breed. Abstr.; Biocont. News Inf. (19??-19??); Biodeter. Abstr. (19??-19??); Biol. Abstr.; Chem. Abstr.; Chem. Titles; Chemorecept. Abstr.; Cot. Trop. Fibr. Abstr. Bibliogr.; Crop Physiol. Abstr.; CSA Neuro. Abstr. (?-?); Curr. Aware. Biol. Sci., CABS; Curr. Contents, Agric. Biol. Environ. Sci.; Curr. Ref. Fish Res.; Ecology Abstr.; Energy Inf. Abstr.; Energy Res. Abstr. (Oct. 1975-); Entomol. Abstr.; Environ. Abstr.; Field Crop Abstr.; Fish Rev.; For. Prod. Abstr. (19??-19??); For. Abstr.; Grasslands For. Abstr.; Helminthol. Abstr.; Hortic. Abstr.; Index Vet.; INIS Atomindex [Micro.]; Irr. Drain. Abstr.; Key Word Index Wildl. Res.; Maize Abstr.; Microbiol. Abstr. Sect. C; Nematol. Abstr.; Nutr. Abstr. Rev., Ser. B, Live Feeds and Feed.; Ornamental Hort. (19??-19??); Life Sci. Collect.; PESTDOC; Plant Breed. Abstr.; Plant Genet. Resour. Abstr.; Plant Grow. Reg. Abstr.; Postharvest News Inf.; Potato Abstr.; Protozoolog. Abstr.; Res. Alert [Full Cov.]; Rev. Agric. Entomol.; Rev. Med. Vet. Entomol.; Rev. Plant Pathol.; Rice Abstr.; Sci. Cit. Index; SCISEARCH; Seed Abstr.; Small Anim. Abstr. Bibliogr.; Soils Fert.; Soyabean Abstr.; Vet. Bull.; Weed Abstr.; Wheat Barley Trit. Abstr.; Wildl. Rev.

II/0970-9037
JOURNAL OF ECOBIOLOGY. [J. Ecobiol.]. Vol. 1, No. 1 (Mar. 1989)-. Periodical. English. qt. $110.00. Palani Paramount Publications, 69D, Anna Nagar, Palani 624502, India. **(Subscription address:** Prints India, 11 Darya Ganj, New Delhi, 110002 India, (Phone: 011 91 11 3268645)**)** **LC** QH183; .J67. **DD** 574.5/05. **CODEN** JECBEA.
Ind/Abst Agrofor. Abstr.; Curr. Aware. Biol. Sci., CABS; Ecology Abstr.; Entomol. Abstr.; Helminthol. Abstr. (1991-); Pollut. Abstr. Indexes; Rev. Agric. Entomol.

US/0047-2425
JOURNAL OF ENVIRONMENTAL QUALITY. [J. environ. qual.]. **Added/Corp** American Society of Agronomy. Crop Science Society of America. Soil Science Society of America. **VFOAT** Environmental Quality. Vol. 1 (Jan./March 1972)-. Periodical. English. bm (6 issues). $108.00 US; $120.00 other. American Society of Agronomy, 677 South Segoe Road, Madison WI 53711. **Tel** (608)273-8080, FAX (608)273-2021. **LC** S1; .J78. **DD** 631. **NLM** W1 JO644BG. **CODEN** JEVQAA. Index available (bound in last issue). **Pr Rev.** available on microfilm and microfiche from University Microfilms International (UMI). Documents available from Article Express International, The Genuine Article, BIOSIS Document Express, CASDDS, Documents on Demand.
Desc: Brings together reviews and technical reports concerned with protection and improvement of environmental quality in natural and agricultural systems.
Ind/Abst AgBiotech News Inf.; AGRICOLA [Select. Cov.]; Agric. Eng. Abstr.; AQUAREF; BioBusiness; Biodeter. Abstr. (19??-19??); Biol. Agric. Index; Biol. Abstr.; Biol. Dig.; Chem. Abstr.; Chem. Titles; Coal Abstr.; Cot. Trop. Fibr. Abstr. Bibliogr.; Crop Physiol. Abstr.; Curr. Contents, Agric. Biol. Environ. Sci.; Curr. Ref. Fish Res.; Dairy Sci. Abstr.; Ecol. Abstr.; Ecology Abstr.; Ei Page One; EMBASE; Energy Res. Abstr. (Jan. 1973-); Eng. Index Annu.; Environ. Abstr.; Environ. Period. Bibliogr.; Field Crop Abstr.; Fish Rev.; Food Sci. Technol. Abstr.; For. Prod. Abstr.; For. Abstr.; Geogr. Abstr. Phys. Geogr.; Geol. Abstr.; Grasslands For. Abstr.; Health Saf. Sci. Abstr.; Hortic. Abstr.; INIS Atomindex [Micro.]; Int. Aerosp. Abstr.; Irr. Drain. Abstr.; J. Plan. Lit.; Leadscan; Leis. Recreat. Tour. Abstr.; Microbiol. Abstr. Sect. A; Nematol. Abstr.; Nutr. Abstr. Rev., Ser. B, Live Feeds and Feed.; Life Sci. Collect.; PESTDOC; Plant Breed. Abstr.; Plant

Genet. Resour. Abstr.; Pollut. Abstr. Indexes; Potato Abstr.; Protozoolog. Abstr.; Res. Alert [Full Cov.]; Rev. Agric. Entomol.; Rev. Med. Vet. Mycology; Rev. Plant Pathol.; Rice Abstr.; Risk Abstr. (19??-19??); Rural Dev. Abstr.; Sci. Cit. Index; SCISEARCH; Seed Abstr.; Soils Fert.; Sorghum Mill. Abstr.; Soyabean Abstr.; Weed Abstr.; Wildl. Rev.; World Agric. Econ.

US/0270-5060
JOURNAL OF FRESHWATER ECOLOGY. [J. freshw. ecol.]. Vol. 1, No. 1 (March 1981)-. Academic Scholarly Publication. English. qt (Mar., June, Sept., Dec.). $56.00 (institutions), $36.00 (individuals) US; $66.00 (institutions), $46.00 (individuals) other. Oikos Publishers Inc, PO Box 2558, La Crosse WI 54601. **Tel** (608)526-9577. **ED** Joseph Kawatski. **LC** PAR. **CODEN** JFREDW. **Pr Rev. Circ:** 600 (ctrl). Documents available from The Genuine Article, BIOSIS Document Express, CASDDS, Documents on Demand.
Desc: A vehicle for dissemination of current limnological information; original ecological studies, observations, surveys, and techniques.
Ind/Abst Aquat. Sci. Fish. Abstr. (Computer File); Biol. Abstr.; Chem. Abstr.; Curr. Aware. Biol. Sci., CABS; Curr. Contents, Agric. Biol. Environ. Sci.; Curr. Ref. Fish Res.; Ecology Abstr.; Environ. Abstr.; Environ. Period. Bibliogr.; Fish Rev.; Pollut. Abstr. Indexes; Protozoolog. Abstr.; Res. Alert [Full Cov.]; Rev. Med. Vet. Entomol.; Sci. Cit. Index; SCISEARCH; Soils Fert.

II
JOURNAL OF HIMALAYAN STUDIES & REGIONAL DEVELOPMENT. Added/Corp Garhwal University. Institute of Himalayan Studies and Regional Development. Vol. 2 (1978)-. Periodical. English. an. Price varies. Dr Jagdish Kaur, Managing Editor, Tourism Recreation Research, Centre for Tourism Research, A-965/6 Indira Nagar India. **(Subscription address:** Prints India, 11 Darya Ganj, New Delhi 110002 India.**) ED** Tej Vir Singh. **LC** DS485.H6; H546. **DD** 954/.005. **Bk Rev. Ad Acc. Circ:** 500. ***Continues*** *Himalaya.*
Desc: Himalayan ecology, development planning, tourism, forestry, mountain problems, and solution finding research, anthropology and socio-cultural problems of the Himalayan regions, Garhwal Himalaya in particular.

II/0970-9274
JOURNAL OF HUMAN ECOLOGY (DELHI). (JOURNAL OF HUMAN ECOLOGY.). [J. hum. ecol.]. Vol. 1, No. 1 (Jan. 1990)-. Periodical. English. tq. $60.00. Kamla-Raj Enterprises, New Delhi, India. **(Subscription address:** Prints India, 11 Darya Ganj, New Delhi, 110002 India, (Phone: 011 91 11 3268645)**) LC** GF661; .J68. **DD** 363.7/00954. **CODEN** JHECEA.

KO/1012-0408
JOURNAL OF KOREAN APPLIED ECOLOGY. [J. Kor. appl. ecol.]. (1987)-. Periodical. English. an.
Ind/Abst For. Abstr.

II/0970-5945
JOURNAL OF NATURE CONSERVATION. [J. Nat. Conserv.]. (1989)-. Periodical. English. sa. **UDC** 339.5.
Ind/Abst Ecology Abstr.

US/0887-3593
JOURNAL OF THE NORTH AMERICAN BENTHOLOGICAL SOCIETY. [J. North Am. Benthol. Soc.]. **Added/Corp** North American Benthological Society. Vol. 5, No. 1 (March 1986)-. Periodical. English. qt. $60.00. North American Benthological Society. **(Subscription address:** Journal of the North American Benthological Society, PO Box 1897, Lawrence KS 66044-8897.**) ED** Rosemary Mackay. **LC** QL141; .F73. **DD** 592.092/9/05. **CODEN** JNASEC. Index available. cum. index. **Bk Rev. Pr Rev. Circ:** 1,100. Documents available from The Genuine Article, BIOSIS Document Express. ***Continues*** *Freshwater Invertebrate Biology, 0738-2189.*
Desc: Publishes articles on benthic communities and their role in aquatic ecosystems.
Ind/Abst Aquat. Sci. Fish. Abstr. (Computer File); Biocont. News Inf. (1991-); Biol. Abstr. (1986-); Curr. Aware. Biol. Sci., CABS; Curr. Contents, Agric. Biol. Environ. Sci.; Ecology Abstr.; Entomol. Abstr.; Fish Rev.; For. Abstr.; Fresh. Aqua. Contents Tables; Microbiol. Abstr. Sect. C; Nematol. Abstr.; Res. Alert [Select. Cov.]; Rev. Med. Vet. Entomol.; SCISEARCH; Soils Fert.

UK/0266-4674
JOURNAL OF TROPICAL ECOLOGY. [J. trop. ecol.]. **Added/Corp** International Association for Ecology. Vol. 1, Pt. 1 (Feb. 1985)-. Academic Scholarly Publication. English. qt (4 issues). $176.00 US, Canada and Mexico; £96.00 other. Cambridge University Press, The Edinburgh Building, Shaftesbury Road, Cambridge CB2 2RU United Kingdom. **Tel** 011 44 223 312393, FAX 011 44 223 325959. **(Subscription address:** Cambridge University Press / North America, 110 Midland Avenue, Port Chester NY 10573.**) ED** Adrian G. Marshall. **LC** IN PROCESS. **CODEN** JTECEQ. **[CCC]. Bk Rev. Pr Rev.** available on microfilm from University Microfilms International (UMI). Documents available from The Genuine Article, BIOSIS Document Express.
Desc: Publishes papers in the important and rapidly growing field of the ecology of tropical regions arising either from original research, experimental or descriptive, or forming significant reviews. Short communications and notes are also published.
Ind/Abst Abstr. Anthropol.; AGRICOLA [Select. Cov.]; Agrofor. Abstr.; Biocont. News Inf.; Biol. Abstr. (1986-); Crop Physiol. Abstr.; Curr. Aware. Biol. Sci., CABS; Curr. Contents, Agric. Biol. Environ. Sci.; Ecol. Abstr.; Ecology Abstr.; Entomol. Abstr.; Fish Rev.; For. Abstr.; Geogr. Abstr. Phys. Geogr.; Geogr. Abstr. Human Geogr. (?-?); Irr. Drain. Abstr.; Plant Breed. Abstr.; Plant Genet. Resour. Abstr.; Res. Alert [Select. Cov.]; Rev. Agric. Entomol.; Rev. Med. Vet. Entomol.; Rice Abstr.; SCISEARCH; Seed Abstr.; Soils Fert.; Weed Abstr.

HU/0231-0716
KORNYEZETVEDELMI SZAKIRODALMI TAJEKOZTATO. (1983)-. Periodical. Hungarian. bm. 3.900ft. Orszagos Muszaki Informacios Kozpont es Konyvtar (O.M.I.K.K.), National Technical Information Centre and Library Museum, u 17, PO Box 12, 1428 Budapest, Hungary. **Tel** (361)118-1994, FAX (361)138-2414, telex 22-4944 OMIKK H. **(Subscription address:** OMIKK Budapest, POB 12, 1428 Hungary**) ED** Istvan Polay. **UDC** 016. Index available. cum. index. **Bk Rev. Ad Acc. Circ:** 260 (ctrl).
Desc: Information on environmental protection and control of waste materials.

CN/0702-9861
LAND MANAGEMENT REPORT. See Forestry.

NE/0921-2973
LANDSCAPE ECOLOGY. [Landsc. ecol.]. Vol. 1, No. 1 (July 1987)-. English. Six times a year. Fl350.00. SPB Academic Publishing, PO Box 97747, 2509 GC The Hague Netherlands. **Tel** 011 31 70 3280616, 011 31 70 3250616. **ED** Frank B. Golley. **LC** QH75.A1; L36. **CODEN** LAECEH. **Ad Acc. Pr Rev.** Documents available from The Genuine Article, BIOSIS Document Express.
Desc: Deals with the biological, abiotic and anthropogenic aspects and scales as well as biogeography, global change, land-use and planning, nature management and environmental conservation. Provided that they refer to the level-of-integration of the landscape, rather than to the ecosystem or species.
Ind/Abst Biol. Abstr. (1987-); Curr. Aware. Biol. Sci., CABS; Curr. Contents, Agric. Biol. Environ. Sci.; Ecol. Abstr.; Ecology Abstr.; Fish Rev.; Geogr. Abstr. Phys. Geogr.; Geogr. Abstr. Human Geogr.; Res. Alert [Select. Cov.]; Wildl. Rev.

US/1064-0185
LEAF (FORT COLLINS, COLO.), THE. See Environmental Issues-Conservation and Natural Resources.

GW/0303-4283
LEBEN UND UMWELT. See Biology.

US
LIFEFORCE ECOLOGY NEWS. Added/Corp Lifeforce (Organization). Vol. 1, No. 1 (Spring 1991)-. Periodical. English.

IT
LOMBARDIA VERDE. (19??)-. Italian. bm (6 issues). L27000. La Tipografica Varese, Via Tonale 49, 21100 Varese Italy. **Tel** 011 39 332 332160.

US/0195-1955
LONE STAR SIERRAN. See Environmental Issues.

GW
MANNHEIMER GEOGRAPHISCHE ARBEITEN. See Geography.

GW/0173-9565
MARINE ECOLOGY (BERLIN, WEST). (MARINE ECOLOGY.). [Mar. ecol.]. Vol. 1, No. 1 (1980)-. Academic Scholarly Publication. English. Four times a year. DM564.00 Europe; DM560.00 other. Blackwell Wissenschafts-Verlag, Kurfuerstendamm 57, D 10707 Berlin Germany. **Tel** 011 49 30 32790623, 011 49 30 32790624, FAX 011 49 30 327 90610. **ED** Jorg Ott, Rupert Riedl. **CODEN** MAECDR. **[CCC].** Index available. cum. index. **Bk Rev. Ad Acc. Pr Rev. Circ:** 2,500. Documents available from The Genuine Article, BIOSIS Document Express, CASDDS, Documents on Demand.
Desc: Continues the reports of the Stazione Zoologica di Napoui and is of interest to marine biologists, ecologists, geologists, and oceanographers.
Ind/Abst Biol. Abstr.; Chem. Abstr.; Curr. Aware. Biol. Sci., CABS; Curr. Contents, Agric. Biol. Environ. Sci.; Ecol. Abstr.; Ecology Abstr.; Energy Inf. Abstr.; Environ. Abstr.; Environ. Period. Bibliogr.; Geogr. Abstr. Phys. Geogr.; Health Saf. Sci. Abstr.; Mar. Sci. Contents Tables; Life Sci. Collect.; Pollut. Abstr. Indexes; Res. Alert [Full Cov.]; Sci. Cit. Index; SCISEARCH.

GW/0171-8630
MARINE ECOLOGY. PROGRESS SERIES (HALSTENBEK). (MARINE ECOLOGY PROGRESS SERIES.). [Mar. ecol. Prog. ser.]. Vol. 1 (July 30, 1979)-. Academic Scholarly Publication. English. ir. DM4120.00 Germany; DM4250.00 other. Inter-Research Science Publishing, Nordbuente 23, D 21385 Oldendorf Germany. **Tel** 011 49 4132 7127, FAX 011 49 4123 8883. **ED** O. Kinne. **LC** QH541.5.S3; M26. **DD** 574.5/2636. **CODEN** MESEDT. **[CCC].** Index available. cum. index. **Ad Acc. Pr Rev.** ctrl circ. Documents available from The Genuine Article, BIOSIS Document Express, CASDDS.
Desc: Research and review papers in the fields of basic and applied marine ecology.
Ind/Abst Anim. Behav. Abstr.; Aquat. Sci. Fish. Abstr. (Computer File); Biol. Abstr.; Chem. Abstr.; Curr. Aware. Biol. Sci., CABS; Curr. Contents, Agric. Biol. Environ. Sci.; Curr. Ref. Fish Res.; Ecol. Abstr.; Ecology Abstr.; Fish Rev.; For. Abstr.; Geogr. Abstr. Phys. Geogr.; GeoRef; Leadscan; Mar. Sci. Contents Tables; Microbiol. Abstr. Sect. B; Microbiol. Abstr. Sect. C; Nematol. Abstr.; Ocean. Abstr.; Life Sci. Collect.; Pollut. Abstr. Indexes; Res. Alert [Full Cov.]; Risk Abstr.; Sci. Cit. Index; SCISEARCH; Wildl. Rev.

IT
METAFORA VERDE. (19??)-. Italian. bm (6 issues). L150000. Metafora, V Matilde di Canossa 34, 00162 Rome Italy. **Tel** 011 39 6 44237895.

US/0095-3628
MICROBIAL ECOLOGY. [Microb. ecol.]. Vol. 1 (1974)-. Periodical. English. Six times a year. $263.00. Springer-Verlag New York Inc., 175 5th Avenue, New York NY 10010. **Tel** (212)460-1500, telex 232 235 SPB UR. **(Subscription address:** Springer Verlag New York Inc. / for North America, 44 Hartz Way, Secaucus NJ 07096.**) ED** M Fletcher. **LC** QR100; .M5. **DD** 576/.15/05. **NLM** W1 MI263. **CODEN** MCBEBU. **[CCC]. Pr Rev.** available on microfilm and microfiche from University Microfilms International (UMI). Documents available from The Genuine Article, BIOSIS Document Express, CASDDS, Documents on Demand.
Desc: Publishes an issue devoted to a single subject; topics of past special issues have included in-depth studies of pathogens and current trends in biotechnology.
Ind/Abst AgBiotech News Inf.; AGRICOLA [Select. Cov.]; AQUAREF; Aquat. Sci. Fish. Abstr. (Computer File); Biodeter. Abstr. (19??-19??); Biol. Abstr.; Chem. Abstr.; Coal Abstr.; Curr. Contents, Agric. Biol. Environ. Sci.; Ecology Abstr.; EMBASE; Energy Inf. Abstr.; Energy Res. Abstr. (Sept. 1978-); Environ. Abstr.; For. Abstr.; GeoRef; Index Vet.; Microbiol. Abstr. Sect. B; Microbiol. Abstr. Sect. A; Microbiol. Abstr. Sect. C; Nematol. Abstr.; Nutr. Abstr. Rev., Ser. B, Live Feeds and Feed.; Life Sci. Collect.; Pollut. Abstr. Indexes; Protozoolog. Abstr.; Ref. Upd. Deluxe Ed.; Res. Alert [Full Cov.]; Rev. Agric. Entomol.; Rev. Plant Pathol.; Rice Abstr.; Sci. Cit. Index; SCISEARCH; Sel. Water Resour. Abstr.; Soils Fert.; Weed Abstr.; Wheat Barley Trit. Abstr.

JA/0385-3381
MIE DAIGAKU KANKYO KAGAKU KENKYU KIYO. Main/Corp Mie Daigaku. Kankyo Kagaku Sogo Kenkyushitsu. **Added/Corp** Mie Daigaku. Mie Daigaku. Kankyo Kagaku Sogo Kenkyushitsu. Report of Environmental Science of Mie University. Mie Daigaku. Report of Environmental Science of Mie University. **VFOAT** Report of Environmental Science of Mie University. (1976)-. English (Japanese). Mie Daigaku Kankyo Kagaku Sogo Kenkyushitsu, (Administration of Mie University), 1515, Kamihamacho, Tsushi, Mieken 514 Japan. **LC** TD187.5.J32; M536a. **CODEN** MKKKDF. Documents available from CASDDS.
Ind/Abst Chem. Abstr.; Irr. Drain. Abstr.

US/0026-5675
MINNESOTA SCIENCE. See Agriculture.

US
MISSOURI WILDLIFE. Main/Corp Conservation Federation of Missouri. **Added/Corp** National Wildlife Federation. English. bm. $6.00 US; $15.00 other. Conservation Federation of Missouri, 728 West Main Street, Jefferson City MO 65101. **Tel** (314)634-2322. **ED** Charles Davidson. **Bk Rev. Ad Acc. Circ:** 35,000 (ctrl).
Desc: Covers the wildlife and ecology of Missouri including articles on fishing, bird watching and conservation.

GW/0171-2446
MITTEILUNGEN DER VERSUCHSANSTALT FUER PILZANBAU DER LANDWIRTSCHAFTSKAMMER RHEINLAND, KREFELD-GROSSHUTTENHOF. See Forestry.

●UK/0962-1083
MOLECULAR ECOLOGY. [Mol. ecol.]. Vol. 1, No. 1 (May 1992)-. Academic Scholarly Publication. English. qt (4 issues). $460.00 (institutions), $68.00 (individuals) US & Canada; £270.00 (institutions), £125.00 (individuals) Europe; £297.00 (institutions), £44.00 (individuals) other. Blackwell Scientific Publications Ltd, Marston Book Services, PO Box 87, Oxford OX2 ODT UK. **Tel** 011 44 865 791155, FAX 011 44 865 791927, telex 837 515 MARDIS G. **LC** QH541.15.M63; .M64. **DD** 574.5/05. **NLM** W1; MO196DR. **CODEN** MOECEO. **[CCC].** Documents

available from CASDDS.
Ind/Abst AGRICOLA; Chem. Abstr.; Curr. Aware. Biol. Sci., CABS; Sci. Cit. Index.

AT/0818-8238
MULGA RESEARCH CENTRE JOURNAL. See Aeronautics, Astronautics-Abstracting, Bibliographies and Statistics.

GW/0258-1256
NATO ASI SERIES. SERIES G, ECOLOGICAL SCIENCES. [NATO ASI ser., Ser. G: Ecol. sci.]. **VFOAT** N.A.T.O. A.S.I. Series. Series G, Ecological Sciences; Ecological Sciences. **VAT** North Atlantic Treaty Organization Advanced Study Institutes. Series G. Ecological Sciences. Academic Scholarly Publication. English. Price varies per volume. Springer-Verlag GmbH & Company KG, Heidelberger Platz 3, D 14197 Berlin Germany. **Tel** 011 49 30 8207223, FAX 011 49 30 8214091, telex 183 319 SPBLN D. **(Subscription address:** Springer Verlag New York Inc. / for North America, 44 Hartz Way, Secaucus NJ 07096.**) DD** 574.5/05. **CODEN** NASGEJ. Documents available from CASDDS.
Ind/Abst AGRICOLA [Select. Cov.]; Chem. Abstr. (1984-).

US/0197-4475
NATO CONFERENCE SERIES. I. ECOLOGY. [NATO conf. ser., I., Ecol.]. **Main/Corp** North Atlantic Treaty Organization. Scientific Affairs Division. **VFOAT** Ecology. **VAT** North Atlantic Treaty Organization Conference Series. One. Ecology. (197?)-. Academic Scholarly Publication. English. ir. Price varies per volume. North Atlantic Treaty Organization / NATO Scientific Affairs Division, B 1110 Brussels Belgium. **CODEN** NCSEDQ. Documents available from CASDDS.
Ind/Abst Chem. Abstr.

AU/0028-0607
NATUR UND LAND. See Environmental Issues.

US
NATURAL CONNECTION, THE. English. bm. $64.95 (one year), $89.95 (two year), $114.95 (three year). Natural Connection Publishers, PO Box 8233, North Brattleboro VT 05304. **Tel** (802)365-7188.
Desc: Published for entrepreneurs in the eco-industry. Includes articles on building customer traffic, sales, industry updates, marketing and eco-industry entrepreneurs. Lists sources of eco-friendly inventory.

JA/0915-9444
NATURAL HISTORY RESEARCH. **Added/Corp** Chiba Kenritsu Chuo Hakubutsukan. No. 1 (Mar. 25, 1990)-. Periodical. English (summaries and/or abstracts in Japanese). Natural History Museum and Institute, Editorial Board, Chiba, 955-2 Aoba-cho, Chiba 280 Japan.
Ind/Abst Curr. Aware. Biol. Sci., CABS; Ecol. Abstr.; Geogr. Abstr. Human Geogr.

US
NATURAL IMAGE, THE. See Photography and Video.

●US/1060-9938
NATURALIST (DANVILLE, VT.), THE. See Environmental Issues-Conservation and Natural Resources.

CN/0028-0798
NATURALISTE CANADIEN, LE. ***Ceased.*** [Nat. can.]. **Added/Corp** Societe Linneenne de Quebec. Universite Laval. Vol. 1 (Dec. 1868)- Vol. 118 No. 1 (Apr. 1993). Academic Scholarly Publication. French (English; summaries and/or abstracts in English). Four times a year. Presses de l'Universite Laval, CP 2447 Avenue de la Medicine, Saint Foy Quebec G1K 7P4 Canada. **Tel** (418)656-5106, (418)656-2590. **ED** Pierre Morisset. **LC** QH3; .N22. Index available. cum. index. **Bk Rev. Circ:** 800. available on microfilm and microfiche from University Microfilms International (UMI). Documents available from BIOSIS Document Express, CASDDS.
Desc: Presents papers in French and English based on original research in aquatic and terrestrial ecology; systematics of plants and animals; and agricultural, forest and aquatic resources.
Ind/Abst AGRICOLA; AQUAREF; Biocont. News Inf. (19??-19??); Biol. Abstr.; Chem. Abstr.; Ecol. Abstr.; Ecology Abstr.; Fish Rev.; For. Abstr.; Geogr. Abstr. Phys. Geogr.; Geogr. Abstr. Human Geogr.; GeoRef; Hortic. Abstr.; Int. Dev. Abstr.; Environ.; Ocean. Abstr.; Point Repere (1983-); Potato Abstr.; Rev. Med. Vet. Entomol.; Rev. Plant Pathol.; Soils Fert.; Weed Abstr.; Wildl. Rev.

US/0028-0860
NATURE STUDY - AMERICAN NATURE STUDY SOCIETY. (NATURE STUDY.). [Nat. study - Am. Nat. Study Soc.]. **Added/Corp** American Nature Study Society. Vol. 19 (Mar. 1965)-. Periodical. English. qt. comes with membership. American Nature Study Society, 5881 Cold Brook Road, Homer NY 13077. **Tel** (607)749-3655. available on microfilm and microfiche from University Microfilms International (UMI). ***Continues*** *American Nature Study Society. ANSS News.*
Ind/Abst Curr. Index J. Educ.

UK/0951-5305
NERC NEWS / NATURAL ENVIRONMENT RESEARCH COUNCIL. **Added/Corp** Natural Environment Research Council (Great Britain). No. 1 (Mar. 1987)-. Periodical. English. qt. Free on request. Natural Environment Research Council, Polaris House, North Star Avenue, Swindon Wilts SN5 8AF United Kingdom. **Tel** 011 44 793 411750. **LC** QH1; .G74. **DD** 574.5/072041. ***Continues*** *Natural Environment Research Council (Great Britain). NERC Newsjournal, 0305-8336.*
Ind/Abst Curr. Aware. Biol. Sci., CABS; Fluid Abstr., Civil Eng.; Fluid Abstr. Proc. Eng.; FLUIDEX (19??-); GeoRef; Meteorol. Geoastrophys. Abstr. (199?-).

●NE
NETHERLANDS JOURNAL OF AQUATIC ECOLOGY : JOURNAL OF THE NETHERLANDS SOCIETY OF AQUATIC ECOLOGY. See Biology-Marine Biology.

CN/0384-9147
NEW DIRECTIONS (VANCOUVER). (NEW DIRECTIONS.). No. 15 (Sept. 1976)-. Periodical. English. mo. 25.00Can$ Canada; 35.00Can$ other. New Directions, PO Box 34279, Station D, Vancouver BC V6N 1H2 Canada. **Tel** (604)438-3149, FAX (604)438-3149. **DD** 301.3/1/05. ***Continues*** *New Age Community, 0384-9139.*

US/0198-8476
NEW ENGLAND ENVIRONMENTAL NETWORK NEWS. ***Title Change.*** See Environmental Issues.

NZ/0110-6465
NEW ZEALAND JOURNAL OF ECOLOGY. [N.Z. j. ecol.]. **Added/Corp** New Zealand Ecological Society. Vol. 1 (1978)-. Academic Scholarly Publication. English. sa. 80.00NZ$. New Zealand Ecological Society, PO Box 25178, Christchurch New Zealand. **Tel** 011 64 3 3517099, FAX 011 64 63 505623. **ED** G.L. Rapson. **LC** QH540; .N43. **DD** 574.5/05. **CODEN** NZJED6. Index available. cum. index. **Bk Rev. Pr Rev. Circ:** 750. Documents available from The Genuine Article, The Genuine Article, CASDDS. ***Supersedes*** *Proceedings - New Zealand Ecological Society, 0077-9946.*
Desc: Covers all aspects of Ecology. New Zealand ecology.
Ind/Abst Chem. Abstr.; Curr. Aware. Biol. Sci., CABS; Curr. Contents, Agric. Biol. Environ. Sci.; Curr. Ref. Fish Res.; Ecol. Abstr.; Ecology Abstr.; EMBASE; For. Abstr.; Geogr. Abstr. Phys. Geogr.; Geogr. Abstr. Human Geogr. (?-?); Grasslands For. Abstr.; Key Word Index Wildl. Res.; Nutr. Abstr. Rev., Ser. B, Live Feeds and Feed.; Life Sci. Collect.; Res. Alert [Full Cov.]; Sci. Cit. Index; SCISEARCH; Soils Fert.; Weed Abstr.; Wildl. Rev.

CN/0715-3368
NEWSLETTER / NATIONAL SURVIVAL INSTITUTE. [Newsl. - Natl. Surviv. Inst.]. **Added/Corp** National Survival Institute. **VFOAT** NSI Newsletter. **VAT** National Survival Institute Newsletter. (197?)-. Newsletter. English. National Survival Institute, 229 College Street, Toronto Ontario M5T 1R4 Canada. **DD** 304.2/0971.

US/0090-4864
NFEC DIRECTORY OF ENVIRONMENTAL INFORMATION SOURCES. (DIRECTORY OF ENVIRONMENTAL INFORMATION SOURCES.). **Added/Corp** National Foundation for Environmental Control. **VAT** National Foundation for Environmental Control Directory of Environmental Information Sources. 2d Ed. (1972)-. Directory. English. ir. $78.00 US; $94.00 other. Government Institutes Inc., 4 Research Place, Suite 200, Rockville MD 20850. **Tel** (301)921-2300, 921-2355, FAX (301)251-0638. **LC** HC110.E5; A7. **DD** 301.3/1/0973. **NLM** WA 22 AA1 D2. ***Continues*** *Annual Directory of Environmental Information Sources.*
Desc: Details federal information sources; primary state environmental contracts; environmental publications; trade and membership organizations and current databases. Includes hotline numbers.

JA/0021-5007
NIHON SEITAI GAKKAI SHI. [Nihon Seitai Gakkaishi]. **Added/Corp** Nihon Seitai Gakkai. **VFOAT** Japanese Journal of Ecology. (1954)-. Academic Scholarly Publication. Japanese (English). Three times a year. $126.00. **(Subscription address:** Maruzen Company Ltd., PO Box 5050, Import & Export Department, Tokyo 100 31 Japan.**) LC** QH540; .N53 . **CODEN** NSGSAF. Documents available from BIOSIS Document Express, CASDDS. ***Continues*** *Shokubutsu Seitai Gakkai Ho.* ***Continued in part by*** *Ecological Research, 0912-3814.*
Ind/Abst Biol. Abstr.; Chem. Abstr. (-1986); Crop Physiol. Abstr.; Ecology Abstr.; GeoRef; Life Sci. Collect.

US/0360-2842
NOAA DATA REPORT MESA. **Main/Corp** United States. Marine Ecosystems Analysis Program Office. **VAT** National Oceanic and Atmospheric Administration Data Report Marine Ecosystems Analysis. No. 1- 1975-. English. National Oceanic and Atmospheric Administration NOAA, 325 Broadway, Boulder CO 80303. **Tel** (303)497-3173. **LC** QH541.5.S3; U55A. **DD** 574.5/2636/05.
Ind/Abst Aquat. Sci. Fish. Abstr. (Computer File).

IT
NOI E L'AMBIENTE. (19??)-. Periodical. Italian. Four times a year. Free on request. Assn Ambiente Prov Modena, Via Giardini 474, 41100 Modena, Italy. **Tel** 011 39 59 209111.

CN/0380-5522
NORTHERN PERSPECTIVES. See Environmental Issues-Conservation and Natural Resources.

IT
NOTIZIARIO DELL'ECOLOGIA, IL. No. 1 (May 1983)-. Academic Scholarly Publication. Italian. mo. Ecoedizioni Cooperativa Srl, Vilae Piave 62-64, 25123 Brescia Italy. **Tel** 011 39 30 364690. **CODEN** NOECDY. Documents available from CASDDS.
Ind/Abst Chem. Abstr. (1983-1986).

IT
NOTIZIARIO GENERALE SEZIONE AMBIENTE. Agenzia Naz Stampa Assn, Soc Coop Arl, Via della Dataria 94, 000187 Rome Italy.

IT
NUOVA ECOLOGIA, LA. (19??)-. Italian. mo. L67000 Italy; L101800 other. Arnoldo Mondadori Editore, UFF Cont Abbonamenti, 20090 Segrate MI Italy. **Tel** 011 39 2 75422015, telex 320457 MONDMI I.

US/0749-2421
OCCASIONAL PAPERS (UNIVERSITY OF NEW MEXICO. MUSEUM OF SOUTHWESTERN BIOLOGY). (OCCASIONAL PAPERS / THE MUSEUM OF SOUTHWESTERN BIOLOGY.). [Occas. pap. - Mus. Southwest. Biol.]. **Added/Corp** University of New Mexico. Museum of Southwestern Biology. No. 1 (June 17, 1983)-. Monographic series. English. ir. Price varies per volume. University of New Mexico - Museum, Department of Biology, Albuquerque NM 87131. **Tel** (505)277-8601 Ext 3700. **ED** James S. Findley, Terry L. Yates, Norman J. Scott, Rayann E. Robino, Robert Miles Sullivan. **DD** 574. **Pr Rev. Circ:** 1,500.
Desc: This is a peer-reviewed series in the general area of ecology and evolutionary biology. Emphasis is on southwestern studies although any regional, laboratory, or theoretical investigations are considered.

GW/0029-8549
OECOLOGIA. [Oecologia]. Vol. 1 (April 1968)-. Periodical. English (French and German; summaries and/or abstracts in French and German). Sixteen times a year. DM3800.00. Springer-Verlag GmbH & Company KG, Heidelberger Platz 3, D 14197 Berlin Germany. **Tel** 011 49 30 8207223, FAX 011 49 30 8214091, telex 183 319 SPBLN D. **(Subscription address:** Springer Verlag New York Inc. / for North America, 44 Hartz Way, Secaucus NJ 07096.**) ED** H Remmert and E D Schulze. **LC** QH540; .O3. **DD** 591.5. **NLM** W1 OE28. **CODEN** OECOBX. **[CCC]. Pr Rev.** available on microfilm and microfiche from University Microfilms International (UMI). Documents available from The Genuine Article, BIOSIS Document Express, Documents on Demand. ***Supersedes in part*** *Zeitschrift fur Morphologie und Okologie der Tiere.*
Desc: Presents articles on developments in research on the functional relationships between plant and animal organisms and their environment.
Ind/Abst AGRICOLA [Select. Cov.]; Agrofor. Abstr. (1991-); Anim. Behav. Abstr.; AQUAREF; Aquat. Sci. Fish. Abstr. (Computer File); Biocont. News Inf. (19??-19??); Biol. Abstr.; Can. Environ.; Coal Abstr.; Crop Physiol. Abstr.; Curr. Aware. Biol. Sci., CABS; Curr. Contents, Agric. Biol. Environ. Sci.; Curr. Ref. Fish Res.; Ecol. Abstr.; Ecology Abstr.; EMBASE; Energy Inf. Abstr.; Energy Res. Abstr.; Entomol. Abstr.; Environ. Abstr.; Field Crop Abstr.; Fish Rev.; For. Abstr.; Geogr. Abstr. Phys. Geogr.; GeoRef; Grasslands For. Abstr.; Helminthol. Abstr. (19??-19??); Hortic. Abstr.; Index Vet.; Irr. Drain. Abstr.; Key Word Index Wildl. Res.; Maize Abstr.; Microbiol. Abstr. Sect. C; Nematol. Abstr.; Nucl. Sci. Abstr.; Nutr. Abstr. Rev., Ser. B, Live Feeds and Feed.; Nutr. Abstr. Rev., Ser. A, Hum. Exp.; Ocean. Abstr.; Ornamental Hort. (1991-); Life Sci. Collect.; Plant Breed. Abstr.; Pollut. Abstr. Indexes; Protozoolog. Abstr.; Res. Alert [Full Cov.]; Rev. Agric. Entomol.; Rev. Med. Vet. Entomol.; Rev. Plant Pathol.; Risk Abstr.; Sci. Cit. Index; SCISEARCH; Seed Abstr.; Soils Fert.; Soyabean Abstr.; Vitis Vitic. Enol. Abstr.; Weed Abstr.; Wheat Barley Trit. Abstr.; Wildl. Rev.

SP/0210-9352
OECOLOGIA AQUATICA. [Oecol. aquat.]. No. 1 (June 1973)-. Periodical. Spanish (English). an. 2000ptas Spain; $20.00 US. Departament D'Ecologia, Facultat de Biologia, Universidat de Barcelona, Avenida Diagonal 645, Barcelona 08028 Espana. **Tel** 93.3308851. **ED** Narcis Prat. **LC** QH171; .O34. **DD** 574.5/263/05. Index available. cum. index. **Ad Acc. Circ:** 600.
Desc: Scientific journal publishing papers on aquatic ecology, limnology and biological oceanography, mainly

Environmental Issues —Ecology

by the members of the Ecology Department of the University of Barcelona.
Ind/Abst Aquat. Sci. Fish. Abstr. (Computer File); Curr. Aware. Biol. Sci., CABS; GeoRef.

DK/0030-1299
OIKOS. [Oikos]. **Added/Corp** Nordic Society Oikos. Vol. 1, No. 1 (1949)-. Academic Scholarly Publication. English (French and German; summaries and/or abstracts in Russian). Nine times a year. kr2630.00 US, Canada and Japan; kr2580.00 other. Munksgaard International Publishers Ltd, PO Box 2148, DK-1016 Copenhagen K Denmark. **Tel** 011 45 33 12 70 30, FAX 011 45 33 12 93 87, telex 19431 MUNKS DK. **ED** Per Brinck. **LC** QH540; .O35. **CODEN** OIKSAA. **[CCC].** Index available. **Bk Rev. Ad Acc. Pr Rev. Circ:** 1,000 (ctrl). Documents available from The Genuine Article, BIOSIS Document Express, CASDDS, Documents on Demand.
Desc: Journal presents original work in all aspects of ecology.
Ind/Abst ASTIS Curr. Aware. Bull. (1978-); AGRICOLA; Agrofor. Abstr.; Anim. Behav. Abstr.; AQUAREF; ASTIS Bibliogr. (1978-); Biocont. News Inf. (19??-19??); Biodeter. Abstr.; Biol. Abstr.; Chem. Abstr.; Crop Physiol. Abstr.; Curr. Aware. Biol. Sci., CABS; Curr. Contents, Agric. Biol. Environ. Sci.; Curr. Ref. Fish Res.; Ecol. Abstr.; Ecology Abstr.; EMBASE; Energy Inf. Abstr.; Energy Res. Abstr.; Entomol. Abstr.; Environ. Abstr.; Environ. Period. Bibliogr.; Field Crop Abstr.; Fish Rev.; For. Abstr.; Fresh. Aqua. Contents Tables; Geogr. Abstr. Phys. Geogr. (?-?); GeoRef; Irr. Drain. Abstr.; Key Word Index Wildl. Res.; Leadscan; Microbiol. Abstr. Sect. C; Nutr. Abstr. Rev., Ser. B, Live Feeds and Feed.; Life Sci. Collect.; Plant Breed. Abstr.; Plant Genet. Resour. Abstr.; Res. Alert [Full Cov.]; Sci. Cit. Index; SCISEARCH; Soils Fert.; Weed Abstr.; Wildl. Rev.

IT
OIKOS : RIVISTA QUADRIMESTRALE PER UNA ECOLOGIA DELLE IDEE.
Suspended. (1990)-Suspended with 3 (1991). Periodical. Italian. tq. Pier Luigi Lubrina Editore, V Le Vittorio Emuanuele 19, 24100 Bergamo Italy. **Tel** 011 39 35 223050. **LC** B4; .O35. **DD** 105.

US
ONE PEACEFUL WORLD. English. qt. $30.00. One Peaceful World, Box 10, Becket MA 01223. **Tel** (413)623-5742, FAX (413)623-8827. **ED** Alex Jack. **Bk Rev. Ad Acc. Circ:** 5,000.
Desc: Newsletter on international macrobiotics and personal and planetary health. Network and Friendship Society.

DK/0078-5326
OPHELIA. See Biology-Marine Biology.

US/0883-6809
OUT OF DOORS (PIERRE, S.D.). See Recreation, Leisure-Outdoor Life.

PL/0867-6550
PARKI NARODOWE. [Parki Nar.]. (1991)-. Periodical. Polish. qt. $14.00. **(Subscription address:** ARS Polona, PO Box 1001, 00068 Warsaw Poland.**)** UDC 502.6.

●UK/0968-1655
PEOPLE & THE PLANET / IPPF, UNFPA, IUCN. See Population Studies.

NE/0300-3604
PHOTOSYNTHETICA. See Biology-Biochemistry.

JA/0370-9612
PHYSIOLOGY AND ECOLOGY JAPAN. (1964)-. Periodical. English. Seiri Seitai Kankokai, (Physiology & Ecology Japan Editorial Office), Kyoto Daigaku Rigakubu Dobutsugaku, Kyoshitsu, Kitashirakawa, Sakyoku, Kyotoshi, Kyotofu 606, Japan. **LC** QH188; .P48. **DD** 574.5/0952. **CODEN** PEJAE6.
Ind/Abst Anim. Breed. Abstr.; Ecol. Abstr.; Helminthol. Abstr. (1991-); Index Vet.; Life Sci. Collect.; Protozoolog. Abstr.; Rev. Med. Vet. Mycology.

US/0031-9430
PHYTOLOGIA. See Biology-Botany.

CN/0225-7114
PICA. See Natural History.

SP/0373-2568
PIRINEOS. (PIRINEOS : PUBLICACION DE LA ESTACION DE ESTUDIOS PIRENAICOS.). [Pirineos]. **Added/Corp** Instituto de Estudios Pirenaicos (Spain) Estacion de Estudios Pirenaicos (Zaragoza, Spain) Instituto Pirenaico de Ecologia. Vol. 1, No. 1 (January/June 1945)-. Spanish (English and French). ir. Consejo Superior Investigacion Cientificas (CSIC), Vitruvio 8, 28006 Madrid Spain. **Tel** 011 34 1 5612833, FAX 011 34 1 4113077, telex 42182. **CODEN** PRNOAJ. **[CCC].**
Ind/Abst Am. Hist. Life (1955-1972); Ecol. Abstr.; For. Abstr.; Geogr. Abstr. Phys. Geogr.; Geogr. Abstr. Human Geogr.; Geol. Abstr.; GeoRef; Key Word Index Wildl. Res.; Soils Fert.

CN/1189-0355
POINT SUR LES PROJETS DU SAINT-MAURICE, LE. [Point proj. St.-Maurice]. **Added/Corp** Hydro-Quebec. Bulletin No 1 (Oct. 1991)-. Periodical. French. Hydro-Quebec, 14E Etage, 75 Ouest Boul Dorchester, Montreal Quebec H2Z 1A4 Canada. **DD** 333.91.

PL/0324-8763
POLISH ECOLOGICAL STUDIES. [Pol. ecol. stud.]. Vol. 1; (1975)-. Periodical. English (summaries and/or abstracts in Polish). qt. $60.00. VCH Publishers Inc, 220 East 23rd Street, New York NY 10010. **Tel** (212)683-8333, , FAX (212)481-0897. **(Subscription address:** VCH Publishers Inc., 303 Northwest 12th Avenue, Journals Department, Deerfield FL 33442.**)** LC QH540. **DD** 574.5/05. **CODEN** PECTDR. **[CCC].** Documents available from BIOSIS Document Express, CASDDS.
Ind/Abst AGRICOLA; Biol. Abstr.; Chem. Abstr.; Ecol. Abstr.; Ecology Abstr.; EMBASE; Fish Rev.; Geogr. Abstr. Phys. Geogr. (?-?); Geogr. Abstr. Human Geogr. (?-?); GeoRef; Key Word Index Wildl. Res.; Rev. Agric. Entomol.; Soils Fert.; Weed Abstr.; Wildl. Rev.

TK/0032-9428
PROBLEMY OSVOENIIA PUSTYN. See Agriculture.

US/0564-7207
PROCEEDINGS - TALL TIMBERS CONFERENCE ON ECOLOGICAL ANIMAL CONTROL BY HABITAT MANAGEMENT. See Pest Control.

US
PROCEEDINGS / TALL TIMBERS FIRE ECOLOGY CONFERENCE. **Added/Corp** Tall Timbers Research Station. Tall Timbers Association (U.S.). (1991)-. Proceedings. English. Tall Timbers Research Station, Route 1 Box 678, Tallahassee FL 32312. **Tel** (904)893-4153. **Continues** Proceedings...Tall Timbers Ecology and Management Conference.

IT/1120-1681
PROTEC. (1986)-. Periodical. Italian. Nine times a year. L76000.00 Italy; L136000.00 other. Publi & Consult Spa, Via Tagliamento 29 2, 00198 Rome Italy. **Tel** 011 39 6 8546754. UDC 614.

IT
PROTECTA-PROTEZIONE CIVILE ECOLOGIA AMBIENTE. (19??)-. Italian. ir. L130000.00. Gruppo Edit Sedifim, Circonv Trionfale 145, 00195 Rome Italy. **Tel** 011 39 6 39734535.

SZ
PROTECTION DE L'ENVIRONNEMENT SUISSE. French. qt. Free. BUWAL, Bibliothek W+L, Postfach 5662, 3001 Bern Switzerland.

US/0737-6960
RADWASTE NEWS. Ceased. See Environmental Issues-Pollution and Waste Management.

US
RAINFOREST ACTION NETWORK ALERT & WORLD RAINFOREST REPORT. See Environmental Issues.

SW/0348-422X
RAPPORT / SVERIGES LANTBRUKSUNIVERSITET, INSTITUTIONEN FOR EKOLOGI OCH MILJOVARD. See Forestry.

II
RECENT RESEARCHES IN ECOLOGY, ENVIRONMENT, AND POLLUTION. (1988)-. Monographic series. English. Price varies per volume. Today and Tomorrow's Printers and Publishers, 24-B/5 Desh Bandhu Gupta Road, Karol Bagh, New Delhi 110 005 India. **Tel** 91 11 5721928, 5721928, 5727770, FAX 9111-7210073 (TTPP).
Desc: Research scientists, industrial technologists, and professional specialists in environmental pollution monitoring and control present their findings in their own areas of specialization.

FR/1156-962X
RECYCLAGE RECUPERATION PARIS. (RECYCLAGE RECUPERATION.). (1990)-. Periodical. French. wk. 650.00F France; 900.00F other. Bureau d'Info Professionnelles, 142 rue Montmartre, 75073 Paris Cedex 02 France. **Tel** 011 33 1 40268321, FAX 011 33 1 40399752, telex 220528 BIP. **ED** Claude Platier. UDC 62. **Bk Rev. Ad Acc. Circ:** 3,275 (ctrl).

US/0736-1890
RECYCLING UPDATE. English. ir. $7.95 US; $9.95 Canada; $11.95 other. Update Publicare Company, c/o Prosperity and Profits Unlimited, Box 570213, Houston TX 77257-0213. **Tel** (713)923-7929. **ED** A C Doyle. **Circ:** 4,500.
Desc: A newsletter that lists publications, conventions, products and other information.

UK/0961-6071
REPORT / IGER. See Agriculture.

DK/0107-7430
REPORT OF THE MARINE POLLUTION LABORATORY. [Rep. Mar. Pollut. Lab.] (1982)-. Monographic series. English. **DD** 363.739 4.
Ind/Abst Ocean. Abstr.

JA/0034-5466
RESEARCHES ON POPULATION ECOLOGY. **Added/Corp** Society of Population Ecology. Kyoto. University. Entomological Laboratory. Japanese Society of Population Ecology. VFOAT Kotai-Gunseigaku No Kenkyu; Kotaigun Seitaigaku No Kenkyu. Vol. 1 (March 1952)-. Periodical. English (summaries and/or abstracts in Japanese). sa. $154.00. Kotaigun Seitai Gakkai, (Soc. of Population Ecology), Ogawa Higashi Iru, Shimodachuri Doori, Kamigyoku, Kyotoshi, Kyotofu 602, Japan. **(Subscription address:** Maruzen Company Ltd., PO Box 5050, Import & Export Department, Tokyo 100 31 Japan.**) CODEN** KOGSBN. **Pr Rev.** Documents available from The Genuine Article, BIOSIS Document Express.
Ind/Abst Biocont. News Inf. (1991-); Biol. Abstr.; Curr. Aware. Biol. Sci., CABS; Curr. Contents, Agric. Biol. Environ. Sci.; Ecol. Abstr.; Ecology Abstr.; Environ. Period. Bibliogr.; Fish Rev.; For. Abstr.; Maize Abstr.; Nematol. Abstr.; Life Sci. Collect.; Postharvest News Inf.; Res. Alert [Full Cov.]; Rev. Agric. Entomol.; Rev. Med. Vet. Entomol.; Rev. Plant Pathol.; Rice Abstr.; Sci. Cit. Index; SCISEARCH; Seed Abstr.; Wildl. Rev.

●US/1061-2971
RESTORATIVE ECOLOGY. [Restor. ecol.]. **Added/Corp** Society for Ecological Restoration. Vol. 1, No. 1 (Mar. 1993)-. Academic Scholarly Publication. English. Four times a year. $135.00 (institution), $75.00 (individual) US;`$155.00 (institution), $95.00 (individual) other. Blackwell Scientific Publishers, 238 Main Street, Cambridge MA 02142. **Tel** (617)547-7110, (800)835-6770, FAX (617)547-0789. **LC** IN PROCESS. **DD** 333. **[CCC].**

FR/0249-7395
REVUE D'ECOLOGIE. (REVUE D'ECOLOGIE : LA TERRE ET LA VIE.). [Rev. d'ecol.]. **Added/Corp** Societe Nationale de Protection de la Nature et d'Acclimatation de France. VFOAT Terre et la Vie. (1982)-. Periodical. French (English; summaries and/or abstracts in English, French and German; table of contents in English). qt. Societe Nationale de Protection de la Nature et d'Acclimation de France, 57 rue Cuvier, BP 405, 75221 Paris Cedex 05 France. **LC** QH5401; .T4. Documents available from The Genuine Article.
Continues Revue d'Ecologie Appliquee a la Protection de la Nature, 0249-7395.
Ind/Abst Curr. Aware. Biol. Sci., CABS; Curr. Contents, Agric. Biol. Environ. Sci.; Ecol. Abstr.; Geogr. Abstr. Phys. Geogr.; Life Sci. Collect.; Protozoolog. Abstr.; Res. Alert [Full Cov.]; Sci. Cit. Index; SCISEARCH; Soc. Sci. Cit. Index [Select. Cov.].

SP/1130-958X
RFE. REVISTA FORESTAL ESPANOLA. See Forestry.

IT
RIFIUTI OGGI. Gaia Srl, Via Sebino 11, 00199 Rome Italy.

BL/0101-7616
ROESSLERIA. See Environmental Issues-Conservation and Natural Resources.

●US/1067-4136
RUSSIAN JOURNAL OF ECOLOGY. [Russ. j. ecol.]. **Added/Corp** Consultants Bureau. (1993)-. Academic Scholarly Publication. English (translations available in Russian). bm. $940.00 US; $1105.00 other. MAIK Nauka / Interperiodica, Ulitsa Profsoyuznaya 90, Moscow 117864 Russia. **LC** QH540; .E4413. **DD** 574.5/05. **CODEN** RJOEEW. **[CCC].** Documents available from BIOSIS Document Express, CASDDS, Documents on Demand. **Continues** Soviet Journal of Ecology, 0096-7807.
Ind/Abst Biol. Abstr.; Chem. Abstr.; Coal Abstr.; Energy Inf. Abstr.; Energy Res. Abstr.; Environ. Abstr.; GeoRef; Life Sci. Collect.; Pollut. Abstr. Indexes.

II/0254-0568
SCIENTIFIC REVIEWS ON ARID ZONE RESEARCH. [Sci. rev. arid zone res.]. Vol. 1 (1982)-. English (French and English). An Rs300.00 India; $60.00 other. Arid Zone Research Association India, Jodhpur 342 003, Rajasthan India. Tel telex 218 CAZRI_IN_JU. **(Subscription address:** Prints India, 11 Darya Ganj, New Delhi 110002 India.**) ED** H. S. Mann, J. L. Cloudsley Thompson and Pawan Kumar. **LC** QH541.5.A74; S33. **DD** 551.4. Index available. cum. index. **Ad Acc. Circ:** 500.
Desc: Original work and review articles covering biology,

technology, sociology, land utilisation and environmental resource use planning.
Ind/Abst AGRICOLA; Int. Dev. Abstr.

UK/0271-972X
SCOPE (CHICHESTER). (SCOPE REPORT.). [Scope]. **Added/Corp** International Council of Scientific Unions. Scientific Committee on Problems of the Environment. **VFOAT** SCOPE; SCOPE Reports. **VAT** Scientific Committee on Problems of the Environment Report. Vol. 1 (1971)-. Academic Scholarly Publication. English. ir. Price varies per volume. John Wiley & Sons Ltd., Baffins Lane, Chichester West Sussex PO19 1UD England. **Tel** 0243 779777, FAX 0243 776128 BTG:JWP001, telex 86290 WIBOOKG. **LC** UNC. **CODEN** SCORDW. Documents available from CASDDS.
Ind/Abst Chem. Abstr.; GeoRef.

FR/1147-7806
SECHERESSE MONTROUGE. See Earth Sciences.

JA/0386-8141
SEITAI KAGAKU. [Seitai kagaku]. **VFOAT** Ecological Chemistry. (1978)-. Periodical. Japanese (table of contents in English). qt. ¥5600. Orpes Srl, Viale Marche 40, 20159 Milan Italy. **Tel** 011 39 2 688-0641, FAX 011 39 2 607-1001. **CODEN** SKGKDR. Documents available from CASDDS.
Ind/Abst Chem. Abstr.

CC/1000-0933
SHENG TAI HSUEH PAO. Added/Corp Chung-Kuo Sheng Tai Hsueh Hsueh Hui. **VFOAT** Acta Ecologica Sinica. (19??)-. Periodical. Chinese (summaries and/or abstracts in English). qt. $28.76. **(Subscription address:** China International Book Trading Corporation, PO Box 399, Library Service Department, Beijing 100044 People's Republic of China.) **LC** QH540; .S53. **DD** 574.5/05.
Ind/Abst Biocont. News Inf.; Soils Fert.

CC
SHENG TAI HSUEH TSA CHIH / CHUNG-KUO SHENG TAI HSUEH HSUEH HUI CHU PAN. Added/Corp Chung-kuo Sheng tai Hsueh Hsueh hui. **VFOAT** Journal of Ecology. (Feb. 1982)-. Periodical. Chinese (summaries and/or abstracts in English). bm. **LC** QH540; .S533. **DD** 574.5/05.
Ind/Abst Biocont. News Inf.; Biodeter. Abstr.; Crop Physiol. Abstr.; Sorghum Mill. Abstr.

CH/1000-4890
SHENGTAIXUE ZAZHI. VFOAT Journal of Ecology. (1982)-. Periodical. Chinese. bm. **DD** 574.5.
Ind/Abst Agric. Eng. Abstr.; Biocont. News Inf.; Soyabean Abstr.

IT
SNOP DEGLI AMBIENTI. (19??)-. Italian. Snop Degli Ambienti, Via Ciamician 2, 40127 Bologna Italy.

CN/0712-3361
SOURCE (RIMOUSKI, QUEBEC). (LA SOURCE.). [Source]. Vol. 1, No 1 (1977)-. Periodical. French. mo. Free. Conseil Regional De l'Environnement De l'Est Du Quebec, CP 1119, Rimouski Quebec G5L 1A8. **DD** 363.7/006/07147.

US/0096-7807
SOVIET JOURNAL OF ECOLOGY, THE. ***Title Change.*** [Sov. j. ecol.]. Vol. 2 (Jan./Feb. 1971)-(199?). Periodical. English (Russian). Six times a year. Plenum Press, 233 Spring Street, New York NY 10013-1578. **Tel** (212)620-8000, (800)221-9369, FAX (212)463-0742, (212)807-1047, telex 23/421139. **ED** L F Semerikov. **LC** QH540. **DD** 574.5/05. **NLM** W1 SO996L. **CODEN** SJECAH. **[CCC].** Index available. **Pr Rev.** available on microfilm and microfiche from University Microfilms International (UMI). Documents available from BIOSIS Document Express, CASDDS. ***Continues*** *Ecology, 0094-6621.* ***Continued by*** *Russian Journal of Ecology.*
Desc: This journal offers full detailed plans of the state of the Soviet ecological studies devoting special attention to applied ecological investigations such as the ecology of crop plants and domestic animals.
Ind/Abst AGRICOLA [Select. Cov.]; Biocont. News Inf.; Biol. Abstr. (-1984); Chem. Abstr.; Coal Abstr.; Curr. Aware. Biol. Sci., CABS; Curr. Contents, Agric. Biol. Environ. Sci.; Curr. Ref. Fish Res.; Ecol. Abstr. (?-?); EMBASE; Energy Res. Abstr. (May 1981-); Field Crop Abstr.; Fish Rev.; For. Abstr.; GeoRef; Grasslands For. Abstr.; Health Saf. Sci. Abstr.; Irr. Drain. Abstr.; Key Word Index Wildl. Res.; Nutr. Abstr. Rev., Ser. B, Live Feeds and Feed.; Ornamental Hort.; Life Sci. Collect.; Plant Genet. Resour. Abstr.; Pollut. Abstr. Indexes; Rev. Agric. Entomol.; Rev. Med. Vet. Entomol.; Rev. Plant Pathol.; Seed Abstr.; Soils Fert.; Wheat Barley Trit. Abstr.; Wildl. Rev.

BM/1012-0335
SPECIAL PUBLICATION / BERMUDA BIOLOGICAL STATION FOR RESEARCH, INC. [Spec. publ. - Bermuda Biol. Stn. Res.]. 1969-. Monographic series. English. Price varies per volume. **CODEN** BMBSBL. Documents available from BIOSIS Document Express.
Ind/Abst Biol. Abstr. (-1984); GeoRef.

UK/0262-7027
SPECIAL PUBLICATION ... OF THE BRITISH ECOLOGICAL SOCIETY,. [Spec. publ. Br. Ecol. Soc.]. **Added/Corp** British Ecological Society. **VFOAT** Special Publications Series of the British Ecological Society. No. 1 (1982)-. Monographic series. English. ir. Price varies per volume. Mosby Year Book Inc., 11830 Westline Industrial Drive, St Louis MO 63146. **Tel** (800)325-4177, (314)872-8370, FAX (314)432-1380, telex 44-2402. **LC** UNC.
Ind/Abst AGRICOLA [Select. Cov.].

US/0192-5563
SPECIAL PUBLICATION SERIES - PYMATUNING LABORATORY OF ECOLOGY, UNIVERSITY OF PITTSBURGH. (SPECIAL PUBLICATION SERIES - PYMATUNING LABORATORY OF ECOLOGY.). V. 5-. Monographic series. English. ir. Price varies per volume. Pymatuning Laboratory of Ecology, University of Pittsburgh, Route 1/Box 7, Linesville PA 16424. **Tel** (814)683-5813. **LC** QH540; .P95. **DD** 574.5. **Bk Rev.** ***Continues*** *Special Publication -Pymatuning Laboratory of Ecology.*

CN/1185-5762
STATE OF THE ENVIRONMENT, REPORT FOR MANITOBA. [State environ. rep. Manit.]. **Main/Corp** Manitoba. Manitoba Environment. (1991)-. English. **LC** IN PROCESS. **DD** 333.7/2/09712705.

US/0886-070X
STATISTICAL ECOLOGY SERIES. [Stat. ecol. ser.]. **Added/Corp** International Statistical Ecology Program. **VFOAT** Statistical Ecology. Vol. 4, (1979)-. Statistical Publication. English. ir. Price varies per volume. International Co-Operative Publishing House, PO Box 245, Burtonsville MD 20730. **Tel** (301)384-2627. **LC** UNC. **DD** 574.
Ind/Abst Math. Rev.

CN/0383-9990
STUDENT DISCUSSION PAPER. Main/Corp York University (Toronto, Ont.). Faculty of Environmental Studies. No. 1- Nov. 1975-. Monographic series. English. Price varies per volume. Faculty of Environmental Studies Resources Centre, York University, 4700 Keele Street, Downsview Ontario M3J 1P3 Canada. **DD** 301.31.

IT
STUDI PER L'ECOLOGIA DEL QUATERNARIO : PERIODICO DEL CENTRO STUDI PER L'ECOLOGIA QUATERNARIO. Added/Corp Centro Studi per l'Ecologia del Quaternario (Florence, Italy). No. 1 (1979)-. Italian. an. L50000. Professor E Borzati, Ist Antrop V Proconsolo 12, 50122 Florence Italy. **Tel** 011 39 55 239028.
Ind/Abst Anthropol. Lit.

SP/0211-4623
STUDIA OECOLOGICA. Added/Corp Universidad de Salamanca. **VFOAT** Studia Oecologica. (198?)-. Periodical. Spanish (summaries and/or abstracts in English). an. 300ptas. Ediciones Universidad de Salamanca, Apartado Postal 325, 37080 Salamanca Spain. **Tel** 011 34 23 294598, FAX 011 34 23 263046. **LC** QH171; .S88. **DD** 574.5/0946/05.
Ind/Abst Agrofor. Abstr.; For. Abstr.; Irr. Drain. Abstr.

NE/0166-1116
STUDIES IN ENVIRONMENTAL SCIENCE (AMSTERDAM). (STUDIES IN ENVIRONMENTAL SCIENCE.). [Stud. environ. sci.]. Vol. 1 (1978)-. Academic Scholarly Publication. English. ir. Price varies per volume. Elsevier Science Publishers BV, PO Box 211, 1000 AE Amsterdam Netherlands. **Tel** 011 31 20 5803642, FAX 011 31 20 5862696, telex 15682. **(Subscription address:** Elsevier Science Inc. / New York Books, 655 Avenue of the Americas, New York NY 10010.) **CODEN** SENSDA. **[CCC].** Documents available from BIOSIS Document Express, CASDDS.
Ind/Abst AGRICOLA [Select. Cov.]; Bioeng. Abstr.; Biol. Abstr. (1986-); Chem. Abstr.; Ei Page One.

LH
STUDIES ON TROPICAL ANDEAN ECOSYSTEMS. VFOAT Estudios de Ecosistemas Tropandinos. Vol. 1 (1983)-. Monographic series. Spanish.
Ind/Abst Soils Fert.

RU
SVET. Added/Corp Goskompriroda SSSR. (1991)-. Periodical. Russian. mo. $89.95. Izdatelstvo Ekologiia, Ulitsa Marshala Rybalko 8 Russia, 123436 Moscow Russia. **(Subscription address:** East View Publications Inc., 3020 Harbor Lane North, Suite 110, Minneapolis MN 55447.) **LC** QH45.5; .P74. ***Continues*** *Priroda i Chelovek.*

UK/0068-1954
SYMPOSIUM OF THE BRITISH ECOLOGICAL SOCIETY, THE. [Symp. Br. Ecol. Soc.]. **Main/Corp** British Ecological Society. Symposium. **VFOAT** Symposium. No. 1 (Apr. 1959)-. Monographic series. English. ir. Price varies per volume. Blackwell Scientific Publications Ltd, Marston Book Services, PO Box 87, Oxford OX2 ODT UK. **Tel** 011 44 865 791155, FAX 011 44 865 791927, telex 837 515 MARDIS G. **LC** QK911.B7; A35. **DD** 581.5/05. **NLM** W1 BR381. **CODEN** BESSAF. Documents available from BIOSIS Document Express, CASDDS.
Ind/Abst AGRICOLA [Full Cov.]; Biol. Abstr.; Chem. Abstr.; GeoRef; Wildl. Rev.

US/0892-6476
TALON (AURORA, COLO.). See Zoology.

IT
TERRA. Patron Editore, Via Badini 12, 40050 Quarto Inf. Bologna Italy. **Tel** 011 39 51 767003, FAX 011 39 51 768252.

FR/0040-3865
TERRE ET LA VIE, LA. Added/Corp Societe Nationale d'Acclimatation et de Protection de la Nature. Societe Nationale d'Acclimatation et de Protection de la Nature. Bulletin. Vol. 1 (1854)- Vol. 118 (1971); Vol. 26 (1972)-. Periodical. French. qt. cum. index. ***Supersedes*** *Revue d'Histoire Naturelle.*
Ind/Abst Ecology Abstr.

IT
TERRITORIO E AMBIENTE. (19??)-. Italian. Forty-eight times a year. Adn Kronos Servizi Srl, Relaz Comm V Ripetta 22, 00186 Rome Italy. **Tel** 011 39 6 3222482.

US/1065-366X
TIGHTWAD GAZETTE. See Home Economics.

UK
TRACE SUBSTANCES IN ENVIRONMENTAL HEALTH. English. an. Science Reviews Ltd, 18 Oaklands Gate, Northwood Middlesex, HA6 3AA England. **Tel** 011 44 923 823586.

UK/0361-5162
TRACE SUBSTANCES IN ENVIRONMENTAL HEALTH. (TRACE SUBSTANCES IN ENVIRONMENTAL HEALTH; PROCEEDINGS OF THE UNIVERSITY OF MISSOURI'S ANNUAL CONFERENCE ON TRACE SUBSTANCES IN ENVIRONMENTAL HEALTH.). [Trace subst. environ. health]. **Added/Corp** University of Missouri. Environmental Health Center. University of Missouri. Extension Division. University of Missouri--Columbia. Environmental Trace Substances Center. University of Missouri--Columbia. Extension Division. (1968)-. Proceedings. English. an. $60.00. Science Reviews Ltd, 18 Oaklands Gate, Northwood Middlesex, HA6 3AA England. **Tel** 011 44 923 823586. **LC** RA565.A1; U54. **DD** 614.8/3. **NLM** W3 C936. **CODEN** PUMTAG. Documents available from Article Express International, BIOSIS Document Express, CASDDS. ***Continues*** *Conference on Trace Substances in Environmental Health. Proceedings.*
Ind/Abst AGRICOLA [Select. Cov.]; Bioeng. Abstr.; Biol. Abstr.; Chem. Abstr.; Coal Abstr.; Ei Page One; Eng. Index Annu.; GeoRef.

FR
TRAVAUX DE LA STATION MARINE DE VILLEFRANCHE-SUR-MER. See Zoology.

UK/0169-5347
TRENDS IN ECOLOGY & EVOLUTION (AMSTERDAM). (TRENDS IN ECOLOGY & EVOLUTION.). [Trends ecol. & evol.]. **VFOAT** Trends in Ecology and Evolution; Ecology & Evolution; Ecology and Evolution; TREE. Vol. 1, No. 1 (July 1986)-. Academic Scholarly Publication. English. mo. $514.00 The Americas; £345.00 other. Elsevier Trends Journals, An Imprint of Elsevier Science Ltd., The Boulevard, Langford Lane, Kidlington, Oxford OX5 1GB United Kingdom. **Tel** 011 44 865 843000, 011 44 865 843699, FAX 011 44 865 843010. **(Subscription address:** Elsevier Science Ltd. Oxford Fulfillment Centre, PO Box 800, Kidlington, Oxford OX5 1DX United Kingdom.) **ED** Andrew Sugden. **LC** QH540; .T67. **DD** 574.5. **NLM** W1; TR3408. **CODEN** TREEEQ. **[CCC].** **Pr Rev.** available on microfilm and microfiche from University Microfilms International (UMI). Documents available from The Genuine Article, BIOSIS Document Express, CASDDS.
Desc: Contains reviews, commentaries, discussions and letters in all areas of ecology and evolutionary science, thus serving as a source of information for researchers, lecturers, teachers, field workers and students.
Ind/Abst AgBiotech News Inf.; Anim. Behav. Abstr.; Anim. Breed. Abstr.; Biocont. News Inf.; Biol. Abstr. (1986-); Chem. Abstr. (1986-); Curr. Aware. Biol. Sci., CABS; Curr. Contents, Agric. Biol. Environ. Sci.; Ecol. Abstr.; Ecology Abstr.; Entomol. Abstr.; Environ. Period. Bibliogr.; Fish Rev.; For. Abstr.; Geogr. Abstr. Phys. Geogr. (?-?); Geogr. Abstr. Human Geogr.; Geol. Abstr.; GeoRef; Index Vet.; Int. Dev. Abstr.; Key Word Index Wildl. Res.; Leis. Recreat. Tour. Abstr.; Plant Breed. Abstr.; Plant Genet. Resour. Abstr.; Protozoolog. Abstr.; Ref. Upd. Deluxe Ed.; Res. Alert [Full Cov.]; Rev. Agric.

Entomol.; Rev. Med. Vet. Entomol.; Sci. Cit. Index; SCISEARCH; Seed Abstr.; Soc. Sci. Cit. Index [Select. Cov.]; Weed Abstr.; Wildl. Rev.

NE
TROPENBOS SCIENTIFIC SERIES. **Added/Corp** Tropenbos Programme. (1987)-. Monographic series. English. Price varies per volume.

II/0564-3295
TROPICAL ECOLOGY. [Trop. ecol.]. **Added/Corp** International Society for Tropical Ecology. Vol. 2 (1961)-. Academic Scholarly Publication. English (French, Portuguese and Spanish). Twice a year (June and December). $60.00. International Society for Tropical Ecology, Banaras Hindu University, Department of Botany, Varanasi 221005 India. **Tel** 11 91 542 312989, FAX 011 91 542 312059, telex 0545-304 BHU IN. **(Subscription address:** Prints India, 11 Darya Ganj, New Delhi 110002 India.**)** **ED** J S Singh and K P Singh. **LC** QH540; .T7. **DD** 574.5/2623/05. **CODEN** ISTEBI. Index available (Bound in next issue). **Bk Rev**, (Qty: 8-15). **Ad Acc. Circ:** 600. Documents available from BIOSIS Document Express, CASDDS. ***Continues*** *Bulletin of the International Society for Tropical Ecology.*
Desc: Plant and animal ecology of all tropical regions in widest sense.
Ind/Abst AGRICOLA; Agrofor. Abstr. (1991-); Biocont. News Inf. (1991-); Biodeter. Abstr. (1991-); Biol. Abstr.; Chem. Abstr.; Curr. Aware. Biol. Sci., CABS; Ecology Abstr.; EMBASE; Entomol. Abstr.; Environ. Period. Bibliogr.; Fish Rev. (Jan. 1989-July 1992); For. Abstr.; Grasslands For. Abstr.; Helminthol. Abstr. (1991-); Hortic. Abstr.; Irr. Drain. Abstr.; Life Sci. Collect.; Protozoolog. Abstr.; Rev. Agric. Entomol.; Rev. Med. Vet. Entomol.; Rice Abstr.; Soils Fert.; Weed Abstr.; Wildl. Rev. (Jan. 1989-July 1992).

CN/0832-6193
TRUMPETER (VICTORIA). (THE TRUMPETER.). [Trumpeter]. Vol. 1, No. 1 (Fall 1983)-. Academic Scholarly Publication. English. Four times a year. $25.00 (individuals), $50.00 (institutions). Lightstar Press, PO Box 5853, Station B, Victoria BC V8R 6S8 Canada. **Tel** (604)598-7004, FAX (604)595-8265. **ED** Alan Drengson. **DD** 304.2/01. **CODEN** TRUMES. Index available. cum. index. **Bk Rev**, (Qty: 6-10). **Circ:** 700-800.
Desc: Dedicated to exploration of and contributions to a new ecological consciousness and sensibilities, and to the practice of forms of life imbued with esocophy (ecological wisdom and harmony). Thematic, with article from both scholarly and non-scholarly sources. Also contains poetry, art, film and book reviews.
Ind/Abst Environ. Period. Bibliogr.

GW/0772-494X
TUEXEMIA. (1981)-. Academic Scholarly Publication. German (English). an. Floristisch-Soziologische Arbeitsgemeinschaft eV, Wilhelm-Weber-Str 2, W-3400 Goettingen Germany. **Tel** 0551 395700, FAX 0551 398449. **ED** Hartmut Dierschke. **Bk Rev**, (Qty: 30-40). **Acid Free. Circ:** 1,600 (ctrl). Documents available from FAXON Xpress.
Desc: Articles in vegetation science, ecology, and nature conservation.

US/0082-6782
TULANE STUDIES IN ZOOLOGY AND BOTANY. **See** Zoology.

US/0882-5858
URBAN WILDLIFE NEWS. [Urban wildl. news]. **Added/Corp** National Institute for Urban Wildlife. (U.S.). (19??)-. Periodical. English. Four times a year. $25.00 membership. National Institute for Urban Wildlife, 10921 Trotting Ridge Way, Columbia MD 21044. **Tel** (301)596-3311. **ED** Louise E Dove. **DD** 333. **Bk Rev. Circ:** 1,000 (ctrl).
Desc: Serves as a clearinghouse for current urban wildlife research activities. It also, coordinates recent information on nongame and urban wildlife management, and lists publications and meetings of interest to conservationists.

US
URSUS. **Added/Corp** Cornell University. Vol. 1, No. 1 (Spring 1991)-. English. Cornell University Press, 124 Roberts Place, Ithaca NY 14853. **Tel** (607)277-2338.

IT
VERDE AMBIENTE. (19??)-. Italian. bm (6 issues). L50000 Italy; L80000 other. Editoriale Verde Ambiente, Cso Vittorio Emanuele 251, 00186 Rome Italy. **Tel** 011 39 6 68300856.

IT
VERDEDOMANI. Italian. mo. L60000 Italy; L140000 other. Toscana Verde, Via Manzoni 21, 50121 Florence Italy. **Tel** 011 39 55 2479228. ***Continues*** *Toscanaverde.*

CN/0828-6841
VERDURE (VALLEYFIELD). (VERDURE. JOURNAL INTERNE DE CRIVERT GROUPE ECOLOGIQUE DE VALLEYFIELD.). **Added/Corp** Crivert (Organisation). **VFOAT** Journal Interne de Crivert. (March 1984)-. Periodical. French. Six times a year. Crivert Groupe Ecologique, 28 Saint-Paul, Valleyfield QUE J6S 4A8 Canada. **DD** 574.5/06/071432.

GW/0171-1113
VERHANDLUNGEN / GESELLSCHAFT FUER OKOLOGIE. [Verh. - Ges. Okol.]. **Main/Corp** Gesellschaft fur Okologie (Germany). **VFOAT** Verhandlungen der Gesellschaft fur Okologie; Okologie. (19??)-. German (summaries and/or abstracts in English). an. **LC** QH540; .G47a. **DD** 574.5/05. **CODEN** VGOEDK. Documents available from BIOSIS Document Express, CASDDS.
Ind/Abst Biol. Abstr. (1987-); Chem. Abstr.; Crop Physiol. Abstr.; Ecol. Abstr.; Field Crop Abstr.; For. Abstr.; Geogr. Abstr. Phys. Geogr.; Geogr. Abstr. Human Geogr.; Hortic. Abstr.; Nematol. Abstr.; Ornamental Hort. (1991-); Rev. Agric. Entomol.; World Agric. Econ.

FR/0240-8759
VIE ET MILIEU (1980). (VIE ET MILIEU / LABORATOIRE ARAGO, UNIVERSITE P. ET M. CURIE.). [Vie milieu]. **Added/Corp** Laboratoire Arago (Banyuls-Sur-Mer, France). Vol. 30, No. 1 (March 1980)-. Academic Scholarly Publication. French (English). qt (Mar., June, Sept., Dec.). 660.00F France; 870.00F other. Laboratoire Arago, Univ Cure CNRS UA 117, 66650 Banyuls Sur Mer France. **Tel** 011 33 68 88 00 40, FAX 011 33 68 88 16 99, telex 505020F. **ED** Nicole Coineau. **CODEN** VIMID2. Index available (Publishes in Dec. issue). cum. index. **Bk Rev**, (Qty: 3-4/yr). **Pr Rev. Circ:** 900 (ctrl). Documents available from BIOSIS Document Express. ***Formed by the union of*** *Vie et Milieu. Serie AB, Biologie Marine et Oceanographie, 0506-8916* ***and*** *Vie et Milieu. Serie C, Biologie Terrestre, 0506-8932.*
Desc: Journal of ecology in marine terrestrial and lagoonar environments: oceanography, ecology, biology, microbiology, zoology, sedimentology, systematics, biogeography, invertebrates, vertebrates, and botanics.
Ind/Abst Anim. Behav. Abstr.; Aquat. Sci. Fish. Abstr. (Computer File); Biol. Abstr.; Curr. Contents, Agric. Biol. Environ. Sci.; Ecol. Abstr.; Ecology Abstr.; EMBASE; Entomol. Abstr.; Fish Rev.; Geogr. Abstr. Phys. Geogr.; Helminthol. Abstr.; Mar. Sci. Contents Tables; Nematol. Abstr.; Ocean. Abstr.; Life Sci. Collect.; Rev. Agric. Entomol.; Rev. Med. Vet. Entomol.; Zool. Rec.; Wildl. Rev.

MY
WALLACEANA. [Wallaceana]. **Added/Corp** Universiti Malaya. Universiti Malaya. Dept. of Zoology. Universiti Malaya. Division of Ecology. International Society for Tropical Ecology. No. 1 (Aug. 1973)-. Periodical. English. qt. 24.00Mal$ (individuals), 40.00Mal$ (institutions) South East Asia; 40.00Mal$ (individuals), 60.00Mal$ (institutions) other. University of Malaysia / Institute of Advanced Studies, A C Wallaceana, 59100 Kuala Lumpur Malaysia. **Tel** 03 555 466 ext 369. **ED** Dr. Phang S. Moi. **CODEN** WALLEU. **Bk Rev**, (Qty: 4). **Ad Acc. Circ:** 200 subscribers, 1500 readership (ctrl). Documents available from Documents on Demand.
Desc: A global newsletter, serving as a forum for the presentation and discussion of information related to tropical ecology.
Ind/Abst Agrofor. Abstr.; Environ. Abstr.

US
WASHINGTON COASTAL CURRENTS. **See** Environmental Issues-Conservation and Natural Resources.

NE/0923-4861
WETLANDS ECOLOGY AND MANAGEMENT. [Wetlands ecol. manag.]. Vol. 1, No. 1 (Jan. 1989)-. Periodical. English. qt. Fl255.00. SPB Academic Publishing, PO Box 97747, 2509 GC The Hague Netherlands. **Tel** 011 31 70 3280616, 011 31 70 3250616. **CODEN** WEMAEU.
Desc: Papers on fundamental and applied aspects of wetland of freshwater, brackishwater or marine origin. Emphasis will be placed on papers presenting results of original research, but reviews of recent developments in the field of wetlands ecology and management will also be published.
Ind/Abst Curr. Aware. Biol. Sci., CABS; Geogr. Abstr. Phys. Geogr.

US
WETLANDS RESEARCH UPDATE. **Added/Corp** Wetlands Research Program (U.S.) Corvallis Environmental Research Laboratory. (1991)-. English. EPA Environmental Research Lab, Kristina Miller, Wetlands Team, 200 SE 35th Street, Corvallis OR 97333.

PL/0013-2969
WIADOMOSCI EKOLOGICZNE. [Wiad. ekol.]. **Added/Corp** Polska Akademia Nauk. Komitet Ekologii. Vol. 16 (1970)-. Periodical. Polish (English; summaries and/or abstracts in English; table of contents in English). qt. $36.00. **(Subscription address:** ARS Polona, PO Box 1001, 00068 Warsaw Poland.**)** **CODEN** WEKLAF. Documents available from BIOSIS Document Express. ***Continues*** *Ekologia Polska. Seria B. Referaty, Dyskusje, 0424-7205.*
Ind/Abst Biol. Abstr.

US/0084-0122
WILDLIFE BEHAVIOR AND ECOLOGY SERIES. (1972)-. Monographic series. English. ir. Price varies per volume. University of Chicago Press / Book Department, 11030 South Langley Avenue, Chicago IL 60628. **Tel** (800)621-2736, (312)568-1550, FAX (312)753-0811, telex 23933.

JA
YOKOHAMA KOKURITSU DAIGAKU KANKYO KAGAKU KENKYU SENTA KIYO BULLETIN: INSTITUTE OF ENVIRONMENTAL SCIENCE AND TECHNOLOGY, YOKOHAMA NATIONAL UNIVERSITY. **See** Environmental Issues-Pollution and Waste Management.

POLLUTION AND WASTE MANAGEMENT

US/0740-9923
305(B) TECHNICAL REPORT FOR OKLAHOMA. (305(B) TECHNICAL REPORT FOR OKLAHOMA / PREPARED BY THE OKLAHOMA STATE DEPARTMENT OF HEALTH ; COORDINATED BY THE POLLUTION CONTROL COORDINATING BOARD.). **Added/Corp** Oklahoma. State Dept. of Health. Oklahoma. Pollution Control Coordinating Board. **VFOAT** Three Hundred Five (B) Technical Report for Oklahoma. (19??)-. English. be. 1000 Northeast 10th, Oklahoma City OK 73152. **LC** TD224.O5; A57. **DD** 363.7/3942/09766.

AT
AAPMA RULES FOR SAFE TRANSPORT HANDLING & STORAGE OF DANGEROUS SUBSTANCES & OILS PORT AREAS. English. ir (updated periodically). 85.00Aus$. Association of Australian Port Marine Authorities, PO Box 590 / Grosvenor Place, Sydney 2000 Australia. **Tel** 011 61 2 2477581, FAX 011 61 2 2477585.

US/0093-1616
ABATEMENT AND POLLUTION CONTROL TRAINING AND EDUCATIONAL PROGRAMS PRESENTED BY THE UNITED STATES ENVIRONMENTAL PROTECTION AGENCY. (ABATEMENT AND POLLUTION CONTROL TRAINING AND EDUCATIONAL PROGRAMS.). **Main/Corp** United States. Environmental Protection Agency. Office of Education and Manpower Planning. English. be. $23.00. Environmental Protection Agency / Office of Education and Manpower, 401 M Street, Washington DC 20460. **Tel** FAX (703)321-8547, telex 89-9405. **(Subscription telephone:** (703)487-4650**)** **LC** TD171; .U56A. **DD** 628.5/0973.

US/1051-4856
ABERDEEN'S PARKING AREA MAINTENANCE & INTERNATIONAL SWEEPER. ***Title Change.*** **VFOAT** Parking Area Maintenance and International Sweeper; Parking Area Maintenance & International Sweeper; Aberdeen's Parking Area Maintenance and International Sweeper. (1990)-?. Periodical. English. bm. Aberdeen Group, 426 South Westgate, Addison IL 60101. **Tel** (312)543-0870, FAX (708)543-3112. ***Continued by*** *Aberdeen's Pavement Maintenance, 1051-4848; Aberdeen's Pavement Maintenance Trader, 1053-2870.*

GW
ABFALLWIRTSCHAFT IN FORSCHUNG UND PRAXIS. (1976)-. Monographic series. German. Erich Schmidt Verlag GmbH, Postfach 304240, D 10724 Berlin Germany. **Tel** 011 49 30 25008525. Documents available from CASDDS.
Ind/Abst Chem. Abstr.

AU/0379-6914
ABSTRACTS - SYMPOSIUM ON RECENT ADVANCES IN THE ANALYTICAL CHEMISTRY OF POLLUTANTS. **See** Chemistry-Analytical Chemistry.

GW/0932-3708
ABWASSERTECHNIK 1983. [Abwassertechnik1983]. **VFOAT** Awt. Abwassertechnik; Abwassertechnik, Abfalltechnik + Recycling. (1983)-. Trade Publication. German. bm (6 issues). DM147.00 Germany; DM171.00 other. Bauverlag GmbH, Postfach 1460, D 65173 Wiesbaden Germany. **Tel** 011 49 6123 7000, FAX 011 49 6123 700122. **UDC** 628.3. ***Continues*** *Abwassertechnik und Abfalltechnik, 0342-4022.*
Desc: Publication of interest to those involved in the waste water removal industry.

SW/0282-0196
ACID MAGAZINE. Added/Corp Sweden. Statens Naturvardsverk. (Spring 1984)-. Periodical. English. Twice a year. Free. Swedish National Environmental Protection Board, PO Box 1302, Information Section, Solna S17125 Sweden. **Tel** (468)799-1000, FAX (468)984513, telex 11131 ENVIRONS. **ED** Peter Hanneberg. **Circ:** 12,000. Documents available from Documents on Demand.
Desc: Dissemination of news and news on air pollution and the acidification of the environment. It is intended to enable readers in other countries to keep abreast of developments in Sweden in the way of research and measures for dealing with these problems.
Ind/Abst AESIS Q.; Coal Abstr.; Energy Inf. Abstr.; Environ. Abstr.; GeoRef.

SW/0281-5087
ACID NEWS STOCKHOLM. [Acid news Stockh.]. (1982)-. Periodical. Swedish. ir. Swedish NGO Secretary on Acid Rain, Box 245 S 401, 24 Goteborg Sweden. **Tel** 011 46 31 153955. **UDC** 502. Documents available from Documents on Demand.
Ind/Abst Energy Inf. Abstr.; Environ. Abstr.

US/0741-5230
ACID PRECIPITATION. [Acid precip.]. **Added/Corp** United States. Dept. of Energy. Technical Information Center. DOE/APC-83/1 (Oct. 30, 1983)-. Government Publication. English. mo. $160.00 US; $320.00 other. US Department of Energy, 1000 Independence Avenue SW, Washington DC 20585. **Tel** (202)586-5000, FAX (202)586-4073. **(Subscription address:** National Technical Information Service, 5285 Port Royal Road, Springfield, VA 22161**) ED** Polly Blackburn.

US/0740-2252
ACID PRECIPITATION DIGEST. *Ceased.* [Acid precip. dig.]. Vol. 1, No. 1 (Jan. 1983)-Ceased June (1993). English. bm. Center for Environmental Information, 50 West Main St., Rochester NY 14614. **Tel** (716)262-2870. **ED** Robert W Pratt (editor's address: RD #1, Box 185, Valley Falls, NY 12185; (518)753-7838)).
Desc: Provides timely access to technical and general information related to acidic deposition and transboundary air pollution. Aims to encourage communication across various disciplines and among interested parties at the state, national, and international levels.

US/0883-3435
ACID RAIN ESSENTIALS. [Acid rain essent.]. **Added/Corp** Technical & Management Services. Vol. 1, No. 1 (Sept./Oct. 1984)-. Periodical. English. bm. $232.00 US; $240.00 other. Acid-Rain-Essentials, PO Box 1325, Ellicott City MD 21043-1325. **DD** 363.

CN/0824-5096
ACID RAIN NOTES. (ACID RAIN NOTES / DISTRICT MUNICIPALITY OF MUSKOKA.). [Acid rain notes]. Vol. 1, No. 1 (Sept. 1982)-. English. an. Free. District Municipality of Muskoka, 10 Pine Street, PO Box 1720, Bracebridge Ontario P0B 1C0 Canada. **DD** 363.7/392/0971316.

CN/0824-880X
ACIDIC PRECIPITATION IN ONTARIO STUDY. [Acid. precip. Ont. study]. (1981)-. Monographic series. English. ir. **DD** 354.7130082324. Documents available from CASDDS.
Ind/Abst Chem. Abstr.

UK/1012-4411
ACOPS YEARBOOK / ADVISORY COMMITTEE ON POLLUTION OF THE SEA, LONDON. *Ceased.* [Yearb. - ACOPS]. **VAT** Advisory Committee on Pollution of the Sea Yearbook. (1983)-(19??). English. an. Pergamon Press, An Imprint of Elsevier Science Ltd., The Boulevard, Langford Lane, Kidlington, Oxford OX5 1GB United Kingdom. **Tel** 011 44 865 843000, 011 44 865 843699, FAX 011 44 865 843010. **(Subscription address:** US/ 395 Saw Mill River Road, Elmsford, NY 10523; Can/ 150 Consumers Road/Suite 104, Willowdale Ontario M2J 1P9; Aus-NZ/ POB 544, Potts Point NSW 2011**) LC** GC1080; .A36. **DD** 363.7/394.

US/0065-2563
ADVANCES IN ENVIRONMENTAL SCIENCE AND TECHNOLOGY. [Adv. environ. sci. tech.]. Vol. 2 (1971)-. Monographic series. English. ir. Price varies per volume. John Wiley & Sons Inc / New Jersey, 1 Wiley Drive, Somerset NJ 08875. **Tel** (800)225-5945, (908)469-4400. **(Subscription address:** John Wiley & Sons / England, Baffins Lane, Chichester, West Sussex PO19 1UD England.**) LC** TD180; .A38. **DD** 628/.05. **NLM** W1 AD552T. **CODEN** AESTC9. Documents available from BIOSIS Document Express, Ask*IEEE, CASDDS. ***Continues** Advances in Environmental Sciences, 0095-4535.*
Ind/Abst AGRICOLA [Select. Cov.]; Aquat. Sci. Fish. Abstr. (Computer File); Biol. Agric. Index; Biol. Abstr.; Chem. Abstr. (1971-1986)(199?-); Energy Res. Abstr. (Dec. 1979-); INSPEC; Life Sci. Collect.; Pollut. Abstr. Indexes.

JA
AICHI-KEN KOGAI CHOSA SENTA SHOHO. Main/Corp Aichi-ken Kogai Chosa Senta. **VFOAT** Bulletin of the Aichi Environmental Research Center. No. 1- 1973-. Academic Scholarly Publication. Japanese. Aichi-Ken Kogai Chosa Senta, 7-ban 6-go Aza Nagare Tsujicho, Nagoya Japan. **LC** TD178.7.J3; A36A. **CODEN** AKCSD3. Documents available from CASDDS.
Ind/Abst Chem. Abstr.

●US
AIR & WASTE : JOURNAL OF THE AIR & WASTE MANAGEMENT ASSOCIATION. Added/Corp Air & Waste Management Association. **VFOAT** Journal of the Air & Waste Management Association; Air and Waste. Vol. 43, No. 1 (Jan. 1993)-. Academic Scholarly Publication. English. mo. $90.00 (non-profit institutions), $200.00 (general). Air & Waste Management Association, PO Box 2861, Pittsburgh PA 15230. **Tel** (412)232-3444. **LC** TD881; .J18. **CODEN** AIWAE2. Documents available from BIOSIS Document Express, CASDDS, Documents on Demand. ***Continues** Journal of the Air & Waste Management Association, 1047-3289.*
Ind/Abst Appl. Sci. Technol. Index; BioBusiness; Biol. Abstr.; Chem. Abstr.; Coal Abstr.; Energy Inf. Abstr.; Energy Res. Abstr.; Environ. Abstr.; Index Med.; Int. Aerosp. Abstr.

US/0890-0396
AIR & WATER POLLUTION CONTROL. [Air water pollut. control]. **Added/Corp** Bureau of National Affairs (Washington, D.C.). **VFOAT** Air and Water Pollution Control. Vol. 1, No. 1 (Oct. 8, 1986)-. Periodical. English. bw. $315.00 (newsletter only). Bureau of National Affairs Inc., 9435 Key West Avenue, Rockville MD 20850. **Tel** (800)372-1033, (301)258-1033, FAX (301)948-5823. **(Subscription address:** 9435 Key West Avenue, Rockville MD 20850; telephone: FAX (301)948-5823**) ED** Eileen Z Joseph. **LC** KF3786.A3; A37. **DD** 344.73/04634/05; 347.304463405. **CODEN** AWPCE3. **[CCC].** ***Formed by the union of** Air Pollution Control (Washington, D.C.), 0196-7150 **and** Water Pollution Control (Washington, D.C. : 1979), 0194-0147.*
Desc: A review of developments in pollution laws, regulations, and trends in government and trends.

US/1058-6628
AIR POLLUTION CONSULTANT, THE. (THE AIR POLLUTION CONSULTANT : A BIMONTHLY PUBLICATION OF MCCOY AND ASSOCIATES, INC.). [Air pollut. consult.]. **Added/Corp** McCoy & Associates. Vol. 1, Issue 1 (Sept./Oct. 1991)-. Academic Scholarly Publication. English. Seven times a year (1 volume). $550.00 US; $624.00 other. Elsevier Science Publishing Company Inc, Madison Square Station, PO Box 882, New York NY 10159-0882. **Tel** (212)633-3950, FAX (212)633-3990. **LC** TD883.2; .A634. **DD** 363.73/92/0973. **[CCC].**

US/0161-3901
AIR POLLUTION CONTROL. [Air pollut. control]. Vol. 1 (1971)-. Academic Scholarly Publication. English. ir. $79.00 (latest volume). John Wiley & Sons, Inc., 605 Third Avenue, New York NY 10158-0012. **Tel** (212)850-6000, (212)850-6645, FAX (212)850-6088, telex 12-7063. **(Subscription address:** John Wiley & Sons / England, Baffins Lane, Chichester, West Sussex PO19 1UD England.**) CODEN** APLCCY. Documents available from CASDDS.
Ind/Abst Chem. Abstr.

CN
AIR POLLUTION CONTROL HANDBOOK. an. 199.00Can$ Canada; 199.00Can$ other. Southam Information and Technology Group Inc., 1450 Don Mills Road, Don Mills Ontario M3B 2X7 Canada. **Tel** (416)445-6641, (800)668-2374, FAX (416)442-2261.

US/0002-2497
AIR POLLUTION TITLES. *Ceased.* See Environmental Issues-Abstracting, Bibliographies and Statistics.

US/0094-5293
AIR QUALITY ABSTRACTS. Added/Corp Pollution Abstracts Inc. (19??)-. English. $75.00. Pollution Abstracts Inc, PO Box 2369, La Jolla CA 92037. **LC** TD883; .A573. **DD** 363.6.

US
AIR QUALITY CONTROL DIGEST. Periodical. English. bm. $93.00 US; $100.00 Canada; $121.00 other. University of Digest Services, 5844 Little Pine Lane, Rochester MI 48064. **Tel** (313)651-2528. **ED** Arthur D Even.
Desc: Includes three sections: (1) sources/treatment of pollution; (2) effects/avoidance of pollution; (3) general sections subdivided as applicable.

US/8755-6243
AIR QUALITY CONTROL FOR ARIZONA. [Air qual. control Ariz.]. English. an. Arizona Department of Health Services, 1740 West Adams Street, Phoenix AZ 85007. **Tel** (602)542-1025, FAX (602)642-1062. **LC** TD883.5.A6; A37. **DD** 363.7/3926/09791.

US/0093-8165
AIR QUALITY DATA. Main/Corp United States. Environmental Protection Agency. Office of Air Quality Planning and Standards. English. an. Air Pollution Technical Information Center, US Environmental Protection Agency, Office of Air Quality and Planning, Durham NC 27711. **LC** TD883.2; .U54B. **DD** 363.6. ***Continues** Air Quality Data.*

US
AIR QUALITY DATA - STATISTICS. See Environmental Issues-Abstracting, Bibliographies and Statistics.

US/0361-5650
AIR QUALITY IN MINNESOTA. Main/Corp Minnesota Pollution Control Agency. Air Quality Division. Technical Services Section. (1973)-. English. an. Air Quality in Minnesota, 1935 West County Road B-2, Roseville MN 55113. **LC** TD883.5.M5; M58a. **DD** 363.6.

SZ/1013-5480
AIR QUALITY IN SELECTED URBAN AREAS. (AIR QUALITY IN SELECTED URBAN AREAS / PREPARED IN COOPERATION WITH THE WHO COLLABORATING CENTER ON ENVIRONMENTAL POLLUTION CONTROL AND UNITED STATES ENVIRONMENTAL PROTECTION AGENCY.). [Air qual. sel. urban areas]. **Added/Corp** United States. Environmental Protection Agency. World Health Organization. WHO Collaborating Centre on Environmental Pollution Control. Global Environmental Monitoring System. Began with (1973/74)-. English. be. World Health Organization, Distribution and Sales, 20 Avenue Appia, CH-1211 Geneva 27 Switzerland. **Tel** 011 41 22 7912111, FAX 011 41 22 7880401. **LC** TD890; .A374. **DD** 363.7/3922/091732. **NLM** W1; W15E no.76 etc.

US/0568-3653
AIR QUALITY MONOGRAPHS. Added/Corp American Petroleum Institute. American Petroleum Inatitute. Division of Environmental Affairs. (1969)-. Monographic series. English. ir. Price varies per volume. American Petroleum Institute / Washington DC, 1220 L Street Northwest, Washington DC 20005. **Tel** (202)682-8378. **(Subscription address:** 1970 Chain Bridge Road, McLean, VA 22109-6000**)**

CN/0713-9330
AIR QUALITY, NORTHWESTERN ONTARIO : ANNUAL REPORT ... . [Air qual., Northwest. Ont., Annu. rep.]. 1980-. English. an. Ministry of the Environment / Toronto, 135 St Clair Avenue West, 7th Floor, Toronto Ontario M4V 1P5 Canada. **Tel** (416)965-7117. **DD** 363.7/3922/0971311. ***Formed by the union of** Air Quality, Atikokan, Kenora, Red Rock, 0713-1941; Air Quality, Balmerton, 0704-3279; Air Quality, Dryden, 0704-3309; Air Quality, Fort Frances, 0704-3287; Air Quality, Marathon, 0704-3317 **and** Air Quality, 0704-3252.*

US
AIR QUALITY WEEK. English. Fifty times a year (Fri. each week). $227.00. Hall Publishing Co., 4418 McArthur Boulevard, Washington DC 20007. **Tel** (800)486-8201, FAX (202)298-8210. **ED** George Spencer.

US/0094-8160
AIR RESEARCH SUMMARY. Main/Corp Oregon. State University. Corvallis. Air Resources Center. **VFOAT** Air: Air Research Summary. 1971-. English. be. **LC** TD883.15; .O7A. **DD** 363.6.

US/1048-4485
AIR TOXICS REPORT. *Ceased.* [Air toxics rep.]. **Added/Corp** Business Publishers. Vol. 1, No. 1 (Sept. 1988)-(Apr. 1993). Periodical. English. mo. Business Publishers Inc., 951 Pershing Drive, Silver Spring MD 20910-4464. **Tel** (301)587-6300, (800)274-0122, FAX (301)585-9075. **DD** 363. **NLM** W1; AI723K. **[CCC].**
Desc: Features news and analysis to help you better deal with changes in air pollution regulation. Also identifies for you consulting contracts and research grants, new detection and protection equipment, successful air toxics reduction programs, and emergency preparedness training courses.
Ind/Abst PTS Newsl. Database [Full Txt.].

US
AIR WAVES. V. 1- Aug. 1979-. Periodical. English. mo. National Commission for Air Quality, 499 South Capitol Street Southwest 2nd Floor, Washington DC 20003.

MY/0126-7280
ALAM SEKITAR. V. 1- July/Aug. 1976-. Periodical. English (Malay). qt. 6.40Mal$. Alam Sekitar, PO Box 382, Jalan Sultan, 46740, Petaling Jaya Selangor Malaysia. **Tel** 03-7757767, FAX 03-7754039. **ED** N Nithiyananthan. **LC** TD171.5.M4; A4. **DD** 363.7/009595. **Bk Rev. Ad Acc. Circ:** 800.
Desc: Independent environmental magazine discussing Malaysian. Issues especially from a citizen perspective.

Environmental Issues — Pollution and Waste Management

CN/1182-2376
ALBERTA WASTE MATERIALS EXCHANGE. (ALBERTA WASTE MATERIALS EXCHANGE : [BULLETIN].). [Alta. Waste Mater. Exch.]. **Added/Corp** Alberta Waste Materials Exchange. (1985)-. Periodical. English. bm. 35.00Can$. Research Council of Alberta, 303A Provincial Building, Red Deer Alberta T4N6K8 Canada. **Tel** (403)450-5111, (403)450-5408, FAX (403)450-5477. **DD** 363.72/8/097123.

NE
ALGEMENE MILIEUSTATISTIEK / CENTRAAL BUREAU VOOR DE STATISTIEK. See Environmental Issues-Abstracting, Bibliographies and Statistics.

GW
ALTANLAGEN-REPORT. German. an. Unweltbundesamt, Bismarckplatz 1, W-1000 Berlin 33 Germany. **LC** TD897.8.G3; A45. **DD** 363.7/3922/0943.

US
AMERICAN RECYCLING MARKET ... DIRECTORY/REFERENCE MANUAL : ARM. **VFOAT** American Recycling Market Directory Reference Manual; ARM. **VAT** American Recycling Market. 6th (1990)-. English. $125.00. Recoup Publishing, PO Box 577, Ogdensburg NY 13669. **LC** HD9975.U5; R4. **Continues** Recoup's American Recycling Market, 0885-2537.

GW/0179-7247
ANALYSES OF HAZARDOUS SUBSTANCES IN BIOLOGICAL MATERIALS. (ANALYSES OF HAZARDOUS SUBSTANCES IN BIOLOGICAL MATERIALS / EDITED BY ... WORKING GROUP "ANALYTICAL CHEMISTRY", COMMISSION FOR THE INVESTIGATION OF HEALTH HAZARDS OF CHEMICAL COMPOUNDS IN THE WORK AREA.). [Anal. hazard. subst. biol. mater.]. **Added/Corp** Deutsche Forschungsgemeinschaft. Arbeitsgruppe Analytische Chemie. Vol. 1 (1985)-. English. VCH Publishers Inc, 220 East 23rd Street, New York NY 10010. **Tel** (212)683-8333, , FAX (212)481-0897. **(Subscription address:** VCH Publishers Inc., 303 Northwest 12th Avenue, Journals Department, Deerfield FL 33442.) **LC** RA1229.4; .A5. **DD** 615.9/02/05. **CODEN** AHSMEB. Documents available from BIOSIS Document Express, CASDDS.
Ind/Abst Biol. Abstr.; Chem. Abstr.

CN/0388-557X
ANNUAIRE. QUALITE DES EAUX. See Water Resources.

US
ANNUAL PROGRESS REPORT OF THE NEW YORK STATE NEWSPAPER RECYCLING TASK FORCE MONITORING COMMITTEE / PREPARED BY NEW YORK NEWSPAPER PUBLISHERS ASSOCIATION, NEW YORK PRESS ASSOCIATION, NEW YORK STATE DEPARTMENT OF ECONOMIC DEVELOPMENT, NEW YORK STATE DEPARTMENT OF ENVIRONMENTAL CONSERVATION. **Added/Corp** New York Newspaper Publishers Association. New York Press Association. New York (State). Dept. of Economic Development. New York (State). Dept. of Environmental Conservation. (June 1991)-. English. Department of Environmental Conservation / New York, 50 Wolf Road, Room 604, Albany NY 12233. **Tel** (518)457-2344, FAX (518)457-6996.

CN/0842-3733
ANNUAL PROGRESS REPORT TO THE INTERNATIONAL JOINT COMMISSION FROM THE INTERNATIONAL REFERENCE GROUP ON GREAT LAKES POLLUTION FROM LAND USE ACTIVITIES (PLUARG). [Annu. rep. Intern. Jt. Comm. Int. Ref. Group Gt. Lakes Pollut. Land Use Act. PLUARG]. **Main/Corp** International Reference Group on Great Lakes Pollution from Land Use Activities. 1975-. English. an. International Joint Commission, 100 Oellette Avenue, Windsor Ont N9A 6T3 Canada. **Tel** (313)226-2170. **LC** TD223.3; .I44B. **DD** 363.6/1. available on microfiche (Vols. for (1975-) distributed to depository libraries). **Continues** Progress Report to the Great Lakes Water Quality Board.

UK/0144-9370
ANNUAL REPORT AND ACCOUNTS - WATER RESEARCH CENTRE. **Title Change.** [Annu. rep. acc. - Water Res. Cent.]. **Main/Corp** Water Research Centre. (1978/79)-(1984). English. an. Water Research Centre, WRC PLC Frankland Road, Blagrove Swindon SN5 8YF England. **Tel** 011 44 793 511711, FAX 011 44 793 511712, telex 449541. **NLM** W1 WA692AB. **Continues** Annual Report - Water Research Centre, 0143-2443. **Continued by** Annual Review.

ANNUAL REPORT AND AUDITED FINANCIAL STATEMENTS / NORTHEAST MARYLAND WASTE DISPOSAL AUTHORITY. **Main/Corp** Northeast Maryland Waste Disposal Authority. English. an. Northeast Maryland Waste Disposal Authority, 25 S Charles Street/Apt 2105, Baltimore MD 21201-3330. **LC** HD4484.M3; N67A. **DD** 352.6/3/097527.

US/0090-5429
ANNUAL REPORT - BUREAU OF POLLUTION CONTROL. STATE OF NEW JERSEY. DEPARTMENT OF ENVIRONMENTAL PROTECTION. (ANNUAL REPORT.). [Annu. rep. - Bur. Air Pollut. Control, State N. J., Dept. Environ. Prot.]. **Main/Corp** New Jersey. Bureau of Air Pollution Control. English. an. New Jersey Bureau of Air Pollution Control, Trenton NJ 08625. **LC** TD883.5.N5; A3. **DD** 353.9/749/008232.

US
ANNUAL REPORT / IOWA DEPARTMENT OF WATER, AIR, AND WASTE MANAGEMENT. **Main/Corp** Iowa. Dept. of Water, Air, and Waste Management. 1982/83-. English. an. Iowa Department of Water Air and Waste Management, Henry A Wallace Building, 900 East Grand Avenue, Des Moines IA 50319. **LC** TD171.3.I8; I7A. **DD** 353.7770082/32. **Continues** Iowa Environmental Quality Commission. Annual Report.

CN/0845-9606
ANNUAL REPORT - MANITOBA ENVIRONMENT AND WORKPLACE SAFETY AND HEALTH. **Title Change.** See Environmental Issues.

US/0193-158X
ANNUAL REPORT - MISSISSIPPI AIR AND WATER POLLUTION CONTROL COMMISSION. **Main/Corp** Mississippi. Air & Water Pollution Control Commission. English. an. Mississippi Air and Water Pollution Control Commission, PO Box 827, Jackson MS 39205. **LC** TD171.3.M7; M57A. **DD** 614.7/09762.

US
ANNUAL REPORT - NATIONAL CENTER FOR RESOURCE RECOVERY. **Main/Corp** National Center for Resource Recovery. English. an. National Center for Resource Recovery, 1211 Connecticut Avenue NW, Washington DC 20036. **Tel** (202)223-6154. **LC** TD794.5; .N372A. **DD** 354.5990083.

US/0093-4135
ANNUAL REPORT ON THE QUALITY OF THE AIR IN WASHINGTON, D.C. **Main/Corp** District of Columbia. Air & Water Monitoring Division. (19??)-. English. an. **LC** TD883.5.D6; D56a. **DD** 363.6.

US/0883-3222
ANNUAL REPORT - OREGON. SOLID WASTE DIVISION. (ANNUAL REPORT / SOLID WASTE DIVISION.). **Main/Corp** Oregon. Solid Waste Division. **VFOAT** Solid Waste Annual Report. English. an. DEQ, 811 SW 6th Avenue, Portland OR 97204-1334. **LC** TD788.4.O7; O73A. **DD** 363.7/28.

US/0272-4529
ANNUAL REPORT, PUBLIC WATER SUPPLIES FOR THE STATE OF OKLAHOMA, NORTHWEST DISTRICT. [Annu. rep. public water supplies State Okla. Northwest Dist.]. **Main/Corp** Oklahoma. State Water Quality Laboratory. **VFOAT** Public Water Supply Report, Northwest District. English. an. State Water Quality Laboratory, 1000 NE 10th, Oklahoma City OK 73152. **LC** TD224.O5; S8A. **DD** 363.6/1.

US/0190-3934
ANNUAL REPORT - STATE ENVIRONMENTAL IMPROVEMENT AUTHORITY. **Title Change.** **Main/Corp** State Environmental Improvement Authority. English. an. State Environmental Improvement Authority, 330 East High Street, Jefferson City MO 65101. **LC** TD171.3.M8; S7A. **DD** 614.7. **Continued by** Annual Report. Missouri. Environmental Improvement and Energy Resources Authority.

JA
ANNUAL REPORT - TOKYO-TO KOGAI KENKYUJO. [Annu. rep. Tokyo Metrop. Res. Inst. Environ. Prot.]. **Main/Corp** Tokyo-To Kogai Kenkyujo. Began in 1970. Academic Scholarly Publication. English. an. Tokyo-To Kogai Kenkyujo, 5 Yurakucho 2-chome Chiyoda-ku, Tokyo Japan. **LC** TD169; .T64A. **DD** 301.31/0952. **CODEN** TKKNDX. Documents available from CASDDS.
Ind/Abst Chem. Abstr.

US/0271-9754
ANNUAL STATUS REPORT ON THE INACTIVE URANIUM MILL TAILINGS SITES REMEDIAL ACTION PROGRAM. [Annu. status rep. inact. uranium mill tailings sites remedial action program]. **Main/Corp** United States. Dept. of Energy. Division of Environmental Control Technology. 1979-. English. an. $9.25. National Technical Information Service - NTIS, Room 2027S, 5285 Port Royal Road, Springfield VA 22161. **Tel** (703)487-4630, (703)487-4660, (703)487-4650, FAX (703)321-8547, telex 89-9405. **LC** TD899.U73; U54A. **DD** 363.7/28.

US/0277-0504
ANNUAL STATUS REPORT ON THE URANIUM MILL TAILINGS REMEDIAL ACTION PROGRAM. English. an. National Technical Information Service - NTIS, Room 2027S, 5285 Port Royal Road, Springfield VA 22161. **Tel** (703)487-4630, (703)487-4660, (703)487-4650, FAX (703)321-8547, telex 89-9405. **LC** TD899.U73; A55.

US
ANNUAL WASTE CONFERENCE PROCEEDINGS : MUNICIPAL AND INDUSTRIAL WASTE. (19??)-. Proceedings. English. an. $35.00. University of Wisconsin Engineering Experiment Station, Madison WI 53706.

JA
AOMORI-KEN KOGAI SENTA SHOHO. [Aomori-ken Kogai Senta shoho]. No. 1- ; 1975-. Academic Scholarly Publication. Japanese. an. 1-131 Oaza Kawaragi Aza Kitanuma, Hachinoe 031 Japan. **LC** TD187.5.J32; A565A. **CODEN** AKSSDF. Documents available from CASDDS.
Ind/Abst Chem. Abstr.

CN/0826-6425
APC (SASKATCHEWAN. AIR POLLUTION CONTROL BRANCH). (APC - AIR POLLUTION CONTROL BRANCH.). [APC, Air Pollut. Control]. **VAT** Air Pollution Control. Monographic series. English. Price varies per volume. Department of the Environment Air Pollution Control Branch, Saskatchewan Power Building, Regina Saskatchewan S4P 0R9 Canada.

US/0094-9191
APCA DIRECTORY AND RESOURCE BOOK. **Main/Corp** Air Pollution Control Association. Directory. English. an. Air Pollution Control Association, PO Box 2861, Pittsburgh PA 15230. **LC** TD882; .A37A. **DD** 363.6. **Ad Acc. Circ:** 9,000 (ctrl). **Continues** APCA Directory.
Desc: A directory of members, annual reports, and produce guide.

US/0253-4525
APPROPRIATE TECHNOLOGY FOR WATER SUPPLY AND SANITATION. [Appropr. technol. water supply sanit.]. **Added/Corp** World Bank. Transportation, Water, and Telecommunications Dept. (1980)-. Monographic series. English. ir. World Bank Publications, 1818 H Street Northwest, Washington DC 20433. **Tel** (202)473-1155, (202)473-1155, FAX (202)522-3224, telex WUI 64145 WORLDBANK. **LC** UNC. **NLM** W1; AP535F.

US/0361-2945
APTD. (PUBLICATION APTD.). [APTD]. **Main/Corp** United States. Environmental Protection Agency. Office of Air Quality Planning and Standards. Academic Scholarly Publication. English. US Environmental Protection Agency / Office of Air Quality and Planning, 401 M Street SW, Washington DC 20460. **LC** TD883.2; .A33. **DD** 628.5/3/0973. **CODEN** XETDAD. Documents available from CASDDS. **Continues** Publication APTD.
Ind/Abst Chem. Abstr.

US
AQMD ADVISOR. (19??)-. English. ir. Free. South Coast Air Quality Management District, 2185 East Copely Drive, Diamond Bar CA 91765. **Tel** (714)396-3720. **Continues** Air Quality Digest.

CN
AQUAREF. See Water Resources-Abstracting, Bibliographies and Statistics.

US/0893-4533
ASBESTOS CONTROL REPORT. **Title Change.** [Asbestos control rep.]. (1987)-(19??). Periodical. English. bw. Business Publishers Inc., 951 Pershing Drive, Silver Spring MD 20910-4464. **Tel** (301)587-6300, (800)274-0122, FAX (301)585-9075. **DD** 363. **[CCC].** available from an online database (file 636/Full-Text) from DIALOG. **Merged into** Asbestos Abatement Report.
Ind/Abst PTS Newsl. Database [Full Txt.].

HK
ASIAN WATER & SEWAGE. [Asian water sew.]. (1984)-. English. qt (Mar., June, Sept., Dec.). $140.00. Toucan Publications PTE Ltd, 322-C King George's Avenue, Singapore 0820. **Tel** 011 65 2997121, FAX 011 65 2997545.

UK/0960-1686
ATMOSPHERIC ENVIRONMENT. PART A, GENERAL TOPICS. ***Title Change.*** [Atmos. environ., A Gen. topics]. **VFOAT** General Topics. Vol. 24A, No. 1 (1990)-Vol. 27A, No. 17/18 (Dec. 1993). Academic Scholarly Publication. English. mo. Pergamon Press, An Imprint of Elsevier Science Ltd., The Boulevard, Langford Lane, Kidlington, Oxford OX5 1GB United Kingdom. **Tel** 011 44 865 843000, 011 44 865 843699, FAX 011 44 865 843010. **ED** P Brimblecombe. **LC** TD881; .A818. **DD** 628.5/3. **CODEN** AEATEN. available on microfiche from the publisher. Documents available from The Genuine Article, BIOSIS Document Express, Ask*IEEE, CASDDS. ***Continues in part*** *Atmospheric Environment, 0004-6981.* ***Merged with*** *Atmospheric Environment. Part B, Urban Atmosphere, 0957-1272* ***to form*** *Atmospheric Environment (Oxford, England : 1994), 1352-2310.*
Ind/Abst Agric. Eng. Abstr. (1991-); Appl. Sci. Technol. Index; Biol. Abstr. (1990-); Chem. Abstr.; Curr. Aware. Biol. Sci., CABS; Curr. Contents, Agric. Biol. Environ. Sci.; Curr. Contents Phys. Chem. Earth Sci.; Ecol. Abstr.; EMBASE; Field Crop Abstr.; Fluid Abstr., Civil Eng.; Fluid Abstr. Proc. Eng.; FLUIDEX; Geogr. Abstr. Human Geogr.; Grasslands For. Abstr.; Hortic. Abstr.; INIS Atomindex [Micro.]; INSPEC (1990-); Leadscan; Lit. Pat. Abstr., Oilfield Chem. (1990-); Lit. Abstr., Catal. Catal.; Lit. Abstr., Health Environ.; Lit. Abstr., Pet. Refin. Petrochem.; Lit. Abstr., Pet. Substit.; Lit. Abstr., Transp. Storage; Res. Alert [Full Cov.]; Rev. Plant Pathol.; Sci. Cit. Index; Soc. Sci. Cit. Index [Select. Cov.]; Soils Fert.

US/1056-5663
ATOMS & WASTE. [Atoms waste]. **Added/Corp** Don't Waste U.S., Inc. **VFOAT** Atoms and Waste. (1991)-. Periodical. English. mo. $35.00 (libraries), $250.00 (industry). Don't Waste U.S., Inc., 2311 15th Street NW, #101, Washington DC 20009. **DD** 333. ***Continues*** *Radwaste Report.*
Ind/Abst Environ. Period. Bibliogr.

AT/1035-0764
AUSTRALIAN TOXIC NETWORK NEWS. (1990)-. Periodical. English. qt. 25.00Aus$. Total Environment Centre, 18 Argyle Street, Sydney New South Wales, 2000 Australia. **Tel** 11 61 2 22478476.

GW
BEITRAEGE ZUR UMWELTGESTALTUNG. **Added/Corp** Fond fuer Umweltstudien. (19??)-. Monographic series. German (English and French). ir. Price varies per volume. Erich Schmidt Verlag GmbH, Postfach 304240, D 10724 Berlin Germany. **Tel** 011 49 30 25008525. **Bk Rev.**
Desc: Studies on environment, pollution, environmental law, and environmental policies.

BE
BELGIUM ENVIRONMENTAL RESEARCH INDEX. Vol. 1-2 (1971)-. Periodical. English. Twice a year. 400F. Bibliotheque Royal Albert, Boulevard de l'Empereur 4, B-1000 Brussels Belgium. **Tel** 011 32 2 5195551.
Ind/Abst Pollut. Abstr. Indexes.

GW/0515-1074
BERICHTE DER ABWASSERTECHNISCHEN VEREINIGUNG. **Main/Corp** Abwassertechnische Vereinigung. (1950)-. German. Documents available from CASDDS.
Ind/Abst Chem. Abstr.

BE/0771-4181
BESWA REVUE. [BESWA-Rev.]. **Added/Corp** Begian Solid Wastes Association. **VFOAT** B.E.S.W.A. Revue. **VAT** Belgian Solid Wastes Association Revue. (19??)-. Academic Scholarly Publication. French (Dutch). sa. 300.00F Belgium; 400.00F other. Belgian Solid Waste Association, JF Kennedylaan 48, B-2630 Aartselaar Belgium. **CODEN** BSWRDV. Documents available from CASDDS.
Ind/Abst Chem. Abstr. (1970-1984).

US/0090-2055
BIBLIOGRAPHY OF WATER QUALITY RESEARCH REPORTS. **See** Water Resources.

US
BIENNIAL REPORT - LAND RECLAMATION COMMISSION. **Main/Corp** Missouri. Land Reclamation Commission. 1st- 1972/73-. English. be. Land Reclamation Commission, PO Box 1368, Jefferson City MO 65101. **LC** TD195.S75; M57A. **DD** 353.9/778/008232.

US
BIENNIAL REPORT OF EXAMINING AND LICENSING BOARDS - MINNESOTA. ENVIRONMENTAL HEALTH SPECIALIST/SANITARIAN ADVISORY COUNCIL. **Main/Corp** Minnesota. Environmental Health Specialist/Sanitarian Advisory Council. English. be. Environmental Health Specialist/Sanitarian Advisory Council, 717 Delaware Street SE, Minneapolis MN 55440. **LC** RA566.4.M6; M56A. **DD** 353.97760077/2.

US/0270-1596
BIENNIAL REPORT PREPARED IN ACCORDANCE WITH THE OZONE PROTECTION PROVISION, SECTION 153 (G), OF THE CLEAN AIR ACT AMENDMENTS OF 1977. (BIENNIAL REPORT PREPARED IN ACCORDANCE WITH THE STRATOSPHERIC OZONE PROTECTION PROVISION, SECTION 153(G), OF THE CLEAN AIR ACT AMENDMENT OF 1977 / FEDERAL AVIATION ADMINISTRATION, HIGH ALTITUDE POLLUTION PROGRAM.). [Bienn. rep. prep. accord. ozone prot. provis., sect. 153 (g), Clean Air Act amend. 1977]. **Main/Corp** High Altitude Pollution Program (U.S.). English. be. National Technical Information Service - NTIS, Room 2027S, 5285 Port Royal Road, Springfield VA 22161. **Tel** (703)487-4630, (703)487-4660, (703)487-4650, FAX (703)321-8547, telex 89-9405. **LC** TD886.7; .U53A. **DD** 353.0082/324.

US/0276-5055
BIOCYCLE. [Biocycle]. Vol. 22, No. 1 (Jan./Feb. 1981)-. Academic Scholarly Publication. English. mo. $63.00 (one year), $103.00 (two year). The JG Press Inc, 419 State Avenue, Emmaus PA 18049. **Tel** (215)967-4135. **ED** Jerome Goldstein. **LC** S661; .C6. **DD** 628.4/458. **CODEN** BCYCDK. **[CCC].** Index available. **Bk Rev. Ad Acc. Pr Rev. Circ:** 13,000. available on microfilm and microfiche from University Microfilms International (UMI); available on an online database (file 15/Full-Text) from DIALOG. Documents available from Article Express International, The Genuine Article, BIOSIS Document Express, UMI Article Clearinghouse, CASDDS, Documents on Demand. ***Continues*** *Compost Science/Land Utilization, 0160-7413.*
Desc: Specializes in new solutions for managing city and industry wastes. Reports (technical and operations) on composting, recycling, and land application.
Ind/Abst Abstr. Bull. Inst. Pap. Sci. Tech.; AgBiotech News Inf.; AGRICOLA [Select. Cov.]; Agric. Eng. Abstr. (1991-); Alum. Ind. Abstr.; Appl. Sci. Technol. Index (1991-); BioBusiness (1989-); Biodeter. Abstr. (19??-19??); Bioeng. Abstr.; Biol. Abstr. (1981-1989); Chem. Abstr.; Coal Abstr.; Curr. Aware. Biol. Sci., CABS; Curr. Contents, Agric. Biol. Environ. Sci.; Curr. Contents Eng. Tech. Appl. Sci.; Dairy Sci. Abstr.; Ei Page One; EMBASE; Energy Inf. Abstr.; Eng. Mater. Abstr.; Eng. Index Annu. [Select. Cov.]; Environ. Abstr.; Environ. Period. Bibliogr.; Expand. Acad. Index (1992-); Field Crop Abstr.; Foods Adlibra; Gas Abstr.; Geogr. Abstr. Human Geogr.; Grasslands For. Abstr.; Health Saf. Sci. Abstr.; Hortic. Abstr.; Met. Abstr.; Newsp. Period. Abstr. (1992-); Life Sci. Collect.; PESTDOC; Pig News Inf.; Pollut. Abstr. Indexes; Protozoolog. Abstr.; Res. Alert [Full Cov.]; Risk Abstr.; Sci. Cit. Index; SCISEARCH; Soc. Sci. Cit. Index [Select. Cov.]; Soils Fert.; Text. Technol. Dig.

NE/0923-9820
BIODEGRADATION (DORDRECHT). (BIODEGRADATION.). [Biodegradation]. Vol. 1, No. (1990)-. Periodical. English. qt. $484.00. Kluwer Academic Publishers, Postbus 322, 3300 AH Dordrecht, The Netherlands. **Tel** 011 (31) 78 524400, FAX 011 31 78 183273, telex 20083. **ED** T Leisinger, W Verstraete, R Hansen, B E Rittman and A Stouthamer. **LC** QR97.X46; B56. **DD** 628.4. **NLM** W1; BI662S. **CODEN** BIODEG. **[CCC].** Index available. cum. index. **Bk Rev. Ad Acc. Pr Rev. Acid Free. Circ:** 200. available on microfilm and microfiche from University Microfilms International (UMI). Documents available from The Genuine Article, CASDDS.
Desc: Publishes papers on all aspects of science pertaining to the detoxification, recycling, amelioration or treatment of waste materials and pollutants by naturally-occuring microbial or associations or recombinant organisms.
Ind/Abst AGRICOLA [Select. Cov.]; Biodeter. Abstr. (1991-); Chem. Abstr.; Curr. Aware. Biol. Sci., CABS; Environ. Period. Bibliogr. (?-?); Res. Alert [Full Cov.]; Weed Abstr.

UK/0960-8524
BIORESOURCE TECHOLOGY. (BIORESOURCE TECHNOLOGY : BIOMASS, BIOENERGY, BIOWASTES, CONVERSION TECHNOLOGIES, BIOTRANSFORMATIONS, PRODUCTION TECHNOLOGIES.). [Bioresour. technol.]. **Added/Corp** Biommass Energy Research Association. Biomass and Biofuels Association (Great Britain). Vol. 35, No. 1 (1991)-. Academic Scholarly Publication. English. Twelve times a year. $1014.00 The Americas; £680.00 other. Elsevier Applied Science, An Imprint of Elsevier Science Ltd., The Boulevard, Langford Lane, Kidlington, Oxford OX5 1GB United Kingdom. **Tel** 011 44 865 843000, 011 44 865 843699, FAX 011 44 865 843010. **(Subscription address:** Elsevier Science Ltd. Oxford Fulfillment Centre, PO Box 800, Kidlington, Oxford OX5 1DX United Kingdom.**)** **ED** R. Bhamidimarri, B. E. Dale, A. G. Hashimoto, P. Hobson. **LC** TP360; .B5957. **DD** 662/.88/05. **CODEN** BIRTEB. **[CCC].** available on microfilm and microfiche from University Microfilms International (UMI). Documents available from Article Express International, The Genuine Article, BIOSIS Document Express, CASDDS, Documents on Demand. ***Formed by the union of*** *Biomass (Barking, London, England), 0144-4565* ***and*** *Biological Wastes, 0269-7483.*
Desc: Aims to advance and disseminate knowledge in all related areas such as biomass, biological waste treatment, bioenergy, biotransformation and bioresource systems analysis, and technologies associated with conversion or production.
Ind/Abst Abstr. Bull. Inst. Pap. Sci. Tech.; AGRICOLA [Select. Cov.]; Agric. Eng. Abstr. (1991-); Biodeter. Abstr. (1991-); Biol. Abstr.; Chem. Abstr.; Civ. Struct. Eng. Abstr.; Curr. Aware. Biol. Sci., CABS; Curr. Contents, Agric. Biol. Environ. Sci.; Ei Page One; EMBASE; Energy Inf. Abstr.; Eng. Index Annu.; Environ. Abstr.; Environ. Eng. Abstr.; Environ. Period. Bibliogr. (?-?); Field Crop Abstr.; Fish Rev. (Jan. 1989-July 1992); Food Sci. Technol. Abstr.; For. Abstr.; Gas Abstr.; Geogr. Abstr. Human Geogr.; Hortic. Abstr.; Int. Dev. Abstr.; Mater. Sci. Eng. Abstr.; Mech. Eng. Abstr.; PESTDOC; Pig News Inf.; Res. Alert [Full Cov.]; Rice Abstr.; Sci. Cit. Index; SCISEARCH; Soc. Sci. Cit. Index [Select. Cov.]; Soils Fert.; Solid State Supercond. Abstr.; Sorghum Mill. Abstr.; Sug. Indus. Abstr.; Wildl. Rev. (Jan. 1989-July 1992).

US/1058-0239
BIOTREATMENT NEWS. **See** Science and Technology.

BL
BOLETIM TECNICO DA SECRETARIA DO SANEAMENTO, HABITACAO E OBRAS. **Main/Corp** Pernambuco, Brazil (State). Secretaria do Saneamento, Habitacao e Obras. (19??)-. Bulletin. Portuguese. Secrataria do Saneamento, Av Cruz Cabuga 1111, Recife Brazil. **LC** TD41.P47; P47a.

US/0008-1620
BULLETIN - CALIFORNIA WATER POLLUTION CONTROL ASSOCIATION. [Bull. - Calif. Water Pollut. Control Assoc.]. **Main/Corp** California Water Pollution Control Association. V. 1- July 1964-. Bulletin. English. qt. $20.00. California Water Pollution Control Association, PO Box 575, Lafayette CA 94549-0575. **Tel** (510)284-1778. **ED** Linda Brewer. **DD** 363. **Bk Rev. Ad Acc. Circ:** 6,000 (ctrl).
Desc: Publication distributed to members, wastewater engineers, operators, designers regulators and academicians.
Ind/Abst Int. Aerosp. Abstr.

FR
BULLETIN DE DOCUMENTATION - MINISTERE DE LA QUALITE DE LA VIE. **Main/Corp** France. Ministere de la Qualite de la Vie. (19??)-. Bulletin. French. Documentation Francaise, 29 Quai Voltaire, 75344 Paris Cedex 7 France. **Tel** 011 33 1 40157000, FAX 011 33 1 40157230, telex 204 826 DOCFRAN. **LC** Z5863.P6; F72a; HC280.E5. **DD** 016.6147.

BE/0524-7802
BULLETIN MENSUEL: POLLUTION ATMOSPHERIC, FUMEE ET SO2. MAANDBERICHT: LUCHTVERONTREINIGING, ROOK EN SO2. **Main/Corp** Brussels. Institut Royal Meteorologique de Belgique. **VFOAT** Maanderbericht: Luchtverontreiniging, Rook en So2. (19??)-. Bulletin. French. mo. 1000.00F. Institut Hygiene en Epidemiologie, Bibliotheek, J Wijtsmanstraat 4, 1050 Bruxelles Belgium. **Tel** 011 32 2 6425111. **DD** 551.5. **Circ:** 200.
Desc: Daily value and monthly average of smoke and SO2 in more than 100 points of measuring in Belgium and Luxembourg.

US/0007-4861
BULLETIN OF ENVIRONMENTAL CONTAMINATION AND TOXICOLOGY. **See** Medical Science and Technology-Toxicology.

FR/0301-3499
BULLETIN SIGNALETIQUE. 885: NUISANCES. **Added/Corp** Centre National de la Recherche Scientifique (France). Centre de Documentation. Vol. 34 (1973)-. Bulletin. French. mo. Centre National de la Recherche Scientifique, Informascience, 26 rue Boyer, 75971 Paris France. **Tel** 61.41.11.05, telex CNRSDOC 220880 F. **LC** Z5853.S22; B84. **DD** 016.6268. ***Continues*** *Bulletin Signaletique. 885: Eau et Assainissement, Pollution Atmospherique.*

●US
C & D DEBRIS RECYCLING. (1994)-. Periodical. English. qt. Free on request. MacLean Hunter Publishing Corporation / Chicago, IL, 29 North Wacker Drive, Chicago IL 60606-3298. **Tel** (312)726-2802, FAX (312)726-3091.

US/0895-5980
CA SELECTS: AIR POLLUTION (BOOKS & REVIEWS). See Chemistry-Abstracting, Bibliographies and Statistics.

US/0160-9041
CA SELECTS: ENVIRONMENTAL POLLUTION. See Chemistry-Abstracting, Bibliographies and Statistics.

GT
CALIDAD DEL AGUA - GUATEMALA. INSTITUTO GEOGRAFICO NACIONAL.
Main/Corp Guatemala. Instituto Geografico Nacional. **VFOAT** Programa de Investigacion de Los Recursos de Agua de la Republica de Guatemala. No. 1-. Spanish. Av Las Americas 5 76 Zona 13, Guatemala Guatemala. **LC** TD231.G8; G82A. **DD** 363.6/1.

US/0008-087X
CALIFORNIA AIR QUALITY DATA.
Main/Corp California. Air Resources Board. Technical Services Division. V. 8 (1976)-. English. an. Air Resources Board, Technical Services Division, PO Box 2815, Sacramento CA 95812. **LC** TD883.5.C2; C32C. **DD** 628. **NLM** W1 CA285K.

CN
CALIFORNIA HAZARDOUS MATERIALS PROGRAM COMMENTARY. English. Four times a year. 205.00Can$. Specialty Technical Publishers Inc, #306-267 West Esplande, North Vancouver BC V7M 1A5 Canada. **Tel** (604)983-3434, FAX (604)983-3445. ctrl circ.

CN
CALIFORNIA HAZARDOUS MATERIALS PROGRAM MATRIX. English. sa. 35.00Can$. Specialty Technical Publishers Inc, #306-267 West Esplande, North Vancouver BC V7M 1A5 Canada. **Tel** (604)983-3434, FAX (604)983-3445. ctrl circ.

CN/0832-9176
CANADIAN SOURCES OF ENVIRONMENTAL INFORMATION.
(CANADIAN SOURCES OF ENVIRONMENTAL INFORMATION / ENVIRONMENT CANADA, DEPARTMENTAL LIBRARY). [Can. sources environ. inf.]. **Added/Corp** Canada. Environment Canada. Library. **VFOAT** Sources Canadiennes d'Information sur l'Environnement. (1986)-. English (French). be. Canada Communication Group Publishers, Order Processing, Ottawa Ontario K1A 0S9 Canada. **Tel** (819)956-4800, (819)956-4802. **LC** TD182; .D57. **DD** 363.7/0072071. ***Continues** Directory of Canadian Environmental Experts, 0704-1497.*

CN
CANADIAN WASTE MATERIALS EXCHANGE BULLETIN. Bulletin. English. Six times a year. 70.00Can$. Ortech International, 2395 Speakman Drive, Mississauga Ontario, L5K 1B3 Canada. **Tel** (416)822-4111, FAX (416)823-1446.

US
CARBON DIOXIDE EFFECTS RESEARCH AND ASSESSMENT PROGRAM. CARBON DIOXIDE RESEARCH PROGRESS REPORT.
Main/Corp United States. Dept. of Energy. Office of Health and Environmental Research. **VFOAT** Carbon Dioxide Effects Research Progress Report. 1978/79-. English. an. National Technical Information Service - NTIS, Room 2027S, 5285 Port Royal Road, Springfield VA 22161. **Tel** (703)487-4630, (703)487-4660, (703)487-4650, FAX (703)321-8547, telex 89-9405.

US/0275-2751
CENTED MONOGRAPH SERIES. [Monogr. - Clark Univ. (Worcester, Mass.), Cent. Technol., Environ., Dev.]. **VFOAT** Center for Technology, Environment, and Development Monograph Series. No. 1-. Monographic series. English. ir. Price varies per volume. Clark University Center for Technology Environment and Development, 950 Main Street, Worcester MA 01610.

NE
CHANGE : ATMOSPHERIC POLLUTION AND CLIMATE CHANGE. English. qt. Free. Min Housing Phys Planning Envr, PO Box 20951, 2500 EZ The Hague Netherlands.

US
CHARACTERISTICS OF WASTES AND SOILS AFFECTING TRANSPORT OF RADIONUCLIDES THROUGH THE SOIL AND THEIR RELATIONSHIP TO WASTE MANAGEMENT. 1979-. English. an. Government Printing Office / Washington, Washington DC 20402. **Tel** (202)783-3238. ***Continues** Characteristics of Wastes and Soils Which Affect Transport of Radionuclides Through the Soil and Their Relationship to Waste Management.*

US/0889-0633
CHEMICAL WASTE LITIGATION REPORTER. See Law-Environmental Law.

UK/0045-6535
CHEMOSPHERE (OXFORD).
(CHEMOSPHERE.). [Chemosphere]. Vol. 1 (Jan. 1972)-. Academic Scholarly Publication. English (French and German). Twenty-four times a year. $1602.00 The Americas; £1075.00 other. Pergamon Press, An Imprint of Elsevier Science Ltd., The Boulevard, Langford Lane, Kidlington, Oxford OX5 1GB United Kingdom. **Tel** 011 44 865 843000, 011 44 865 843699, FAX 011 44 865 843010. **(Subscription address:** Elsevier Science Ltd. Oxford Fulfillment Centre, PO Box 800, Kidlington, Oxford OX5 1DX United Kingdom.) **ED** O. Hutzinger and T. Stephen. **LC** QH540; .C48. **DD** 574.5/05. **NLM** W1 CH38. **CODEN** CMSHAF. **[CCC]**. Index available. **Bk Rev. Ad Acc. Pr Rev.** available on microfilm from University Microfilms International (UMI). Documents available from The Genuine Article, BIOSIS Document Express, CASDDS, Documents on Demand.
Ind/Abst Abstr. Bull. Inst. Pap. Sci. Tech.; AgBiotech News Inf.; AGRICOLA; Anal. Abstr.; Aqualine Abstr.; AQUAREF; Aquat. Sci. Fish. Abstr. (Computer File); Biodeter. Abstr. (19??-19??); Biol. Abstr.; Chem. Abstr.; Chem. Titles; Coal Abstr.; Crop Physiol. Abstr.; Curr. Contents, Agric. Biol. Environ. Sci.; Curr. Ref. Fish Res.; Dairy Sci. Abstr.; Ecology Abstr.; Ei Page One; EMBASE; Energy Inf. Abstr.; Energy Res. Abstr. (June 1980-); Environ. Abstr.; Environ. Period. Bibliogr.; Field Crop Abstr.; Fish Rev.; Food Sci. Technol. Abstr.; For. Prod. Abstr.; For. Abstr.; GeoRef; Grasslands For. Abstr.; Health Saf. Sci. Abstr.; Hortic. Abstr.; Index Vet.; INIS Atomindex [Micro.]; Int. Aerosp. Abstr.; Irr. Drain. Abstr.; Leadscan; Mass Spect. Bull.; Microbiol. Abstr. Sect. B (19??-19??); Microbiol. Abstr. Sect. C; Nutr. Abstr. Rev., Ser. B, Live Feeds and Feed.; Nutr. Abstr. Rev., Ser. A, Hum. Exp.; Ocean. Abstr.; Life Sci. Collect.; PESTDOC; Pollut. Abstr. Indexes; Potato Abstr.; Protozoolog. Abstr.; Res. Alert [Full Cov.]; Rev. Agric. Entomol.; Rev. Med. Vet. Entomol.; Rev. Med. Vet. Mycology; Rev. Plant Pathol.; Rice Abstr.; Risk Abstr.; Sci. Cit. Index; SCISEARCH; Soc. Sci. Cit. Index [Select. Cov.]; Soils Fert.; Soyabean Abstr.; Toxicol. Abstr.; Weed Abstr.; Wheat Barley Trit. Abstr.; Wildl. Rev.

JA
CHIBA-KEN KANKYO HAKUSHO.
Main/Corp Chiba-Ken (Japan). Kankyobu. Vol. 49 (1974)-. Periodical. Japanese. Chiba-ken Kankyobu, 1-1 Ichibacho, Chiba 280 Japan. **LC** TD187.5J32; C53a. ***Continues** Chiba-Ken Kogai Hakusho.*

JA
CHIBA-KEN KOGAI KENKYUJO KENKYU HOKOKU. [Chiba-ken Kogai Kenkyujo kenkyu hokoku]. **Main/Corp** Chiba-Ken Kogai Kenkyujo. **VFOAT** Bulletin of Chiba Prefectural Research Institute for Environmental Pollution. Academic Scholarly Publication. Japanese (summaries and/or abstracts in English). Chibaken Suishitsu Hozen Kenkyujo, (Chiba Prefectural Laboratory of Water Pollution), 5-1 Inagekaigan 3-chome, Mihama-ku, Chiba-shi, Chiba-ken, 261, Japan. **LC** TD187.5.J32; C54A. **CODEN** CKHUDM. Documents available from CASDDS.
Ind/Abst Chem. Abstr. (1972-1980).

UK/0300-5143
CLEAN AIR. [Clean air]. **Added/Corp** National Society for Clean Air. Vol. 1 (Spring 1971)-. Academic Scholarly Publication. English. qt. £22.00. National Society for Clean Air, 136 North Street, Brighton East Sussex BN1 1RG England. **Tel** 011 44 273 26313, FAX 011 44 273 735802. **ED** Loveday Murley. **DD** 628/.53/05. **NLM** W1 CL122K. **CODEN** CLNABV. Index available. **Bk Rev. Ad Acc. Circ:** 2,500. Documents available from BIOSIS Document Express, Ask*IEEE, CASDDS. ***Supersedes** Smokeless Air.*
Desc: Contains feature articles, scientific and technical data, pollution abstracts, industrial news, book reviews, and international news.
Ind/Abst Biol. Abstr.; Chem. Abstr.; Coal Abstr.; Curr. Technol. Index; EMBASE; Environ. Period. Bibliogr.; Health Saf. Sci. Abstr.; INSPEC; Int. Aerosp. Abstr.; Meteorol. Geoastrophys. Abstr.; Pollut. Abstr. Indexes.

AT/0009-8647
CLEAN AIR (HEIDELBERG). (CLEAN AIR.). [Clean air]. **Added/Corp** Clean Air Society of Australia and New Zealand. (1967)-. Periodical. English. qt. 75.00Aus$. Clean Air Society of Australia and New Zealand, PO Box 191, Eastwood New South Wales 2122 Australia. **Tel** 011 61 2 8584663. **CODEN** CLNABV. available on microfilm from University Microfilms International (UMI). Documents available from Article Express International, Ask*IEEE, Documents on Demand.
Ind/Abst Bioeng. Abstr.; Ei Page One; Energy Inf. Abstr.; Eng. Index Annu.; Environ. Abstr.; Environ. Period. Bibliogr.; INSPEC (Nov. 1971-); Int. Exec.; World Ceram. Abstr.

CN/1187-3612
CLEAN CURRENTS / HALIFAX HARBOUR CLEANUP INC. [Clean curr.]. **Main/Corp** Halifax Harbour Cleanup Inc. (N.S.). Vol. 1, No. 1 (Summer 1991)-. Periodical. English. qt. **DD** 628.3/09716/22.

US/0009-8620
CLEAN WATER REPORT. See Water Resources.

US/0092-9433
CLEAN WATER (WASHINGTON). See Water Resources.

US/0747-2218
CLEARWATER NAVIGATOR. **Added/Corp** Hudson River Sloop Clearwater, Inc. (19??)-. Periodical. English. Six times a year (Jan., Mar., May, July, Sept., Nov.). $25.00 (individuals), $35.00 (family), $75.00 (contributing students) Comes with Hudson River Slope Clearwater Inc. Membership). Hudson River Sloop Clearwater, 112 Market Street, Poughkeepsie NY 12601. **Tel** (914)454-7673. **ED** Marguerite Culp and Gary McGivern. **Circ:** 9,000 (ctrl).

FR
COLLECTION ECOLOGIE APPLIQUEE ET SCIENCES DE L'ENVIRONNEMENT.
VFOAT Ecologie Appliquee et Sciences de l'Environnement. (1980)-. Monographic series. French. ir. Price varies per volume.

US/0891-3463
COLORADO ENVIRONMENTAL REPORT, THE. See Environmental Issues-Conservation and Natural Resources.

CN/0709-4191
COMMON SENSE (GALENDA BAY).
Ceased. (COMMON SENSE.). No. 1 (1978)-?. Periodical. English. bm. Kootenay Environmental Institute Ltd., Box 2, Galena Bay, Via Revelstoke, B.C. V0E 1X0. **Tel** (604)358-7764. **DD** 301.31/05.

CN
COMPLETE GUIDE TO HAZARDOUS MATERIALS ENFORCEMENT AND LIABILITY. English. ir (4 to 6 updates per year). $305.00. Specialty Technical Publishers Inc, #306-267 West Esplande, North Vancouver BC V7M 1A5 Canada. **Tel** (604)983-3434, FAX (604)983-3445. ctrl circ.

●US/1065-657X
COMPOST SCIENCE & UTILIZATION.
[Compost sci. util.]. **VFOAT** Compost Science and Utilization. Vol. 1, No. 1 (1993)-. Periodical. English. qt. $125.00 (one year), $215.00 (two year). The JG Press Inc, 419 State Avenue, Emmaus PA 18049. **Tel** (215)967-4135. **LC** TD796.5; .C584. **DD** 631.8/6.
Desc: Reports on theories, research, and applications advancing the utilization of compost.

US/0147-3557
CONNECTICUT AIR QUALITY SUMMARY. **Main/Corp** Connecticut. Dept. of Environmental Protection. English. an. Connecticut Department of Environmental Protection, 165 Capitol Avenue, Room 115, Hartford CT 06106. **Tel** (203)566-2110, FAX (203)566-7932. **LC** TD883.5.C8; C66A. **DD** 363.6.

US/0145-5907
CONNIE DATA SUMMARIES. **Main/Corp** Texas. Air Control Board. English. an. Texas Air Control Board, 8520 Shoal Creek Blvd., Austin TX 78758. **LC** TD883.5.T4; T43C. **DD** 363.6.

US/1070-8057
CONTAINER & PACKAGING RECYCLING UPDATE. [Contain. packag. recycl. update]. **Added/Corp** Container Recycling Institute. **VFOAT** Container and Packaging Recycling Update. (1991)-. Periodical. English. qt (Jan., Apr., July, Oct.). $15.00 individuals; $25.00 government & nonprofit organizations; $35.00 corporate. Container Recycling Institute, 710 G Street Southeast, Washington DC 20003. **Tel** (202)543-9449. **ED** Pat Franklin & Mike Hogan. **DD** 363. **Circ:** 3,000.

CK
CONTAMINACION AMBIENTAL.
Added/Corp Fondo Colombiano de Investigaciones Cientificas y Proyectos Especiales "Francisco Jose de Caldas". Vol. 1, No. 1 (1977)-. Periodical. Spanish. sa. University Pontificia Bolivariana, Centro de Investigacion Desarrollo Integ Cidi, Medellin Colombia. **Tel** 011 57 4 2486892, telex 65047 UPB. **ED** Sol Angel Ardila. **Bk Rev. Ad Acc. Circ:** 1,500 (ctrl).
Desc: Articles on environmental pollution problems and their solutions.

UK/0952-1542
CONTAMINATION CONTROL ABSTRACTS. See Environmental Issues-Abstracting, Bibliographies and Statistics.

BM
CONTRIBUTIONS FROM THE BERMUDA BIOLOGICAL STATION FOR RESEARCH. [Contrib. Bermuda Biol. Stn. Res.]. **Main/Corp** Bermuda Biological Station for Research. (1904)-. English. an. Bermuda Biological Station, 17 Biological Station Lane, Ferry Reach, St. Georges GE01

Environmental Issues — Pollution and Waste Management

Bermuda. **Tel** (809)297-1880, FAX (809)297-8143. **CODEN** CBBRDM. Index available. **Circ:** 150 (ctrl).
Desc: Reprints of papers, monographs and books published on environmental and oceanographic research conducted at the Biostation.

US
CONTROL OF WASTE AND WATER POLLUTION FROM COAL-FIRED POWER PLANTS; B.R & D REPORT.
Added/Corp United States. Industrial Environmental Research Laboratory (Research Triangle Park, N.C.) United States. Environmental Protection Agency. Office of Research and Development. (1978)-. English. an. Environmental Protection Agency / Industrial Environmental Research Laboratory, Office of Research and Development, Office of Energy Minerals and Industry, Springfield VA 22161. **Continues** Control of Waste and Water Pollution from Power Plant Flue Gas Cleaning Systems.

US/0278-2995
CONTROL OF WASTE AND WATER POLLUTION FROM POWER PLANT FLUE GAS CLEANING SYSTEMS. 1976-.
Periodical. English. an. Environmental Protection Agency / Industrial Environmental Research Laboratory, Office of Research and Development, Office of Energy Minerals and Industry, Springfield VA 22161.

UK/0967-2508
CORE. COATINGS, REGULATIONS AND THE ENVIRONMENT. See Paints and Painting-Abstracting, Bibliographies and Statistics.

US/0275-0384
COST OF CLEAN AIR AND CLEAN WATER, THE. [Cost clean air clean water].
Main/Corp United States. Environmental Protection Agency. 1979-. English. an. Environmental Protection Agency / Washington, 401 M Street SW, Washington DC 20460. **Tel** (202)382-2090. **LC** HC110.P55; U55A. **DD** 338.4/336373/0973. **Formed by the union of** Cost of Clean Air **and** Economics of Clean Water.

UK
CRONER'S SUBSTANCES HAZARDOUS TO HEALTH. (19??)-. Periodical. English. qt.
£180.70. Croner Publ Ltd, Croner House, London Road, Kingston upon Thames, Surrey KT2 6SR England. **Tel** 011 44 81 5473333, FAX 081 547-2637.

US
CUMULATIVE INDEX OF THE JOURNAL OF THE AIR POLLUTION CONTROL ASSOCIATION. Main/Corp Air Pollution Control Association. 1951/72-. English. ir (every 5 years). Air & Waste Management Association, PO Box 2861, Pittsburgh PA 15230. **Tel** (412)232-3444. **ED** Harold M Englund.
Desc: Subject and author index to JAPCA–The International Journal of Air Pollution Control and Hazardous Waste Management.

UK/0955-6648
CURRENT ADVANCES IN ECOLOGICAL & ENVIRONMENTAL SCIENCES. See Environmental Issues-Abstracting, Bibliographies and Statistics.

US/0361-3569
DAMMING THE SOLID WASTE STREAM : THE BEGINNING OF SOURCE REDUCTION IN MINNESOTA. Main/Corp
Minnesota. Pollution Control Agency. 1st (1975)-. English. an. Air Quality in Minnesota, 1935 West County Road B-2, Roseville MN 55113. **LC** TD788.4.M5; M56A. **DD** 363.6.

UK
DANGEROUS SUBSTANCES & AMENDMENTS. (19??)-. Periodical. English. bm (6 issues). £209.90. Croner Publ Ltd, Croner House, London Road, Kingston upon Thames, Surrey KT2 6SR England. **Tel** 011 44 81 5473333, FAX 081 547-2637.

GW
DATEN ZUR UMWELT. Main/Corp Statistisches Landesamt Baden-Wurttemberg. (1977)-. Periodical. German. be. Statistisches Landesamt Baden-Wuerttemberg, Postfach 10 60 30, 70049 Stuttgart Germany. **Tel** 011 49 771 6410, FAX 011 49 711 6412440. **LC** HA1320.B2; A32 subser; TD789.G72B3.

US/1052-0635
DEFENSE CLEANUP. [Def. cleanup]. Vol. 1, No. 1 (Aug. 3, 1990)-. Periodical. English. Fifty times a year. $495.00 US; $525.00 other. Pasha Publications Inc., 1616 North Fort Myer Drive, Suite 1000, Arlington VA 22209. **Tel** (800)424-2908, (703)528-1244, FAX (703)528-3742, (703)528-1253. **DD** 353. **[CCC].** available on an online database (file 636/Full-Text) from DIALOG.
Ind/Abst PTS Newsl. Database [Full Txt.].

KE/0379-2455
DESERTIFICATION CONTROL.
(DESERTIFICATION CONTROL BULLETIN / UNITED NATIONS ENVIRONMENT PROGRAMME.). [Desertif. control]. **Added/Corp** United Nations Environment Programme. (1984)-. Periodical. English. sa. Free on request. Desertification Control, UNEP, POB 30552, Nairobi Kenya. **LC** GB611; .U55a. **DD** 333.79. **Continues** Desertification Control, 0379-2455.
Ind/Abst AGRICOLA [Select. Cov.]; Agrofor. Abstr.; GeoRef; PAIS Int. Print.

CC/1000-4742
DIANDU YU HUANBAO. See
Engineering-Electricity, Electrical Engineering, Electronics.

UK
DIGEST OF ENVIRONMENTAL PROTECTION AND WATER STATISTICS / DEPARTMENT OF THE ENVIRONMENT. Added/Corp Great Britain. Dept. of the Environment. No. 6 (1983)-. Her Majesty's Stationery Office, 51 Nine Elms Lane, London SW8 5DR England. **Tel** 011 44 71 873 8459, 011 44 71 873 8499, FAX 011 44 71 873 8499, 011 44 71 873 8456, telex 297138. **(Subscription address:** Her Majesty's Stationery Office, PO Box 276, Publications Centre, London SW8 5DT England.) **LC** TD186.5.G7; D52. **DD** 363.7/3/0941. **Continues** Digest of Environmental Pollution and Water Statistics.
Desc: Information on pollution and environmental protection.

US
DIGESTER, OVER THE SPILLWAY, THE.
Periodical. English. Illinois Environmental Protection Agency, 2200 Churchill Road, Springfield IL 62706. **LC** TD524.I3; D53. **Formed by the union of** Digester, 0362-8795 **and** Over the Spillway.

US/0093-5476
DIRECTORY OF AIR QUALITY MONITORING SITES. Directory. English. Air Pollution Technical Information Center, US Environmental Protection Agency, Office of Air Quality and Planning, Durham NC 27711. **LC** TD883.2; .D56. **DD** 363.6.

CN/1189-3273
DIRECTORY OF CANADIAN MARINE OILSPILL SPECIALISTS. [Dir. Can. mar. oilspill spec.]. **Added/Corp** Environmental Studies Research Funds (Canada) Harper Environmental Services. (1991)-. Directory. English. **DD** 333.8/232/0971.

US
DIRECTORY OF COMPUTER SOFTWARE APPLICATIONS. ENVIRONMENTAL POLLUTION & CONTROL, A. See Computers.

CN/1194-2355
DIRECTORY OF HAZARDOUS WASTE SERVICES. [Dir. hazard. waste serv.]. **Added/Corp** Corpus Information Services. Southam Information & Technology Group. 1st Ed. (1985)-. Directory. English. an. 95.00Can$. Southam Information and Technology Group Inc., 1450 Don Mills Road, Don Mills Ontario M3B 2X7 Canada. **Tel** (416)445-6641, (800)668-2374, FAX (416)442-2261.

US/0093-5816
DIRECTORY OF PUBLISHED PROCEEDINGS. SERIES PCE : POLLUTION CONTROL/ECOLOGY. [Dir. publ. proc., Ser. PCE Pollut. control-ecol.]. Vol. 1 (March 1974)-. Directory. English. an. $150.00. InterDok Corporation, PO Box 326, Harrison NY 10528. **Tel** (914)835-3506, FAX (914)835-6757. **ED** Rose Besada and Carol Hoffman. **LC** Z7916; .D57. **DD** 016.30131. **NLM** W 3.5 D597. cum. index. ctrl circ.
Desc: Provides information on proceedings in the fields of ecology, environment and energy.

US/0197-2731
DIVISION OF ENVIRONMENTAL CONTROL TECHNOLOGY PROGRAM.
[Div. Environ. Control Technol. Program]. Began with 1976/77. English. an. National Technical Information Service - NTIS, Room 2027S, 5285 Port Royal Road, Springfield VA 22161. **Tel** (703)487-4630, (703)487-4660, (703)487-4650, FAX (703)321-8547, telex 89-9405. **LC** TD195.E49; U54B. **DD** 353.0082/321.

●US
DRAFT INTENDED USE PLAN, PROJECT PRIORITY SYSTEM, PROJECT PRIORITY LIST, FEDERAL FISCAL YEAR: NEW YORK STATE REVOLVING FUND FOR WATER POLLUTION CONTROL. Added/Corp New York State Environmental Facilities Corporation. VFOAT NYSWPCRF Intended Use Plan. (1992)-. English. The State of New York, Department of Environmental Conservation, Environmental Facilities Corporation, Box 2328, Grand Central Station NY 10017. **Continues** New York State Water Pollution Control Revolving Fund.

CN/0847-9933
EARTH WORDS (OTTAWA). (EARTH WORDS.). [Earth words]. **Added/Corp** Friends of the Earth (Canada). VFOAT Earthwords. Vol. 1, No. 1 (Feb. 1989)-. Periodical. English. Four times a year. $15.00 (institutions), $10.00 (individuals). Friends of the Earth / Canada, 701 251 Laurier Avenue West, Ottawa, Ontario K1P 5J6 Canada. **Tel** (613)230-3352. **DD** 363.7/384/0971. **Continues in part** Infoetox, 0831-5523.
Ind/Abst Can. Period. Index (19??-).

FR/0755-5016
EAU, L'INDUSTRIE, LES NUISANCES, L'. [Eau, ind., nuis.]. (1982)-. Periodical. French. Nine times a year. 485.00F France; 570.00F other. Pierre Johanet & Fils Editeurs SA, 7 Avenue Fd Roosevelt, 75008 Paris France. **Tel** 33 1 43590887, FAX 33 1 42255947, telex 649712 F. **ED** Pierre Johanet. **CODEN** EINUDQ. Index available. cum. index. **Bk Rev.** **Ad Acc.** **Circ:** 6,500. Documents available from CASDDS. **Continues** Eau et l'Industrie.
Desc: Keeps readers up-to-date on all subjects concerning the different aspects of water processing, purification, sanitation, measurements, regulations, valves, distribution systems, use of wastes, etc.
Ind/Abst Chem. Abstr.; Energy Res. Abstr. (1982-); Fluid Abstr., Civil Eng.; Fluid Abstr. Proc. Eng.; FLUIDEX (19??-); GeoRef.

FR/0247-8277
ECO 3. [Eco 3]. VFOAT Eco Trois; Nuisances et Environnement. No. 96 (Feb. 1981)-. Academic Scholarly Publication. French. mo. 182.00F. Editions de Presse d'Information Economique, 20 rue Richer, 75441 Paris Cedex 09 France. **NLM** W1 EC909D. **Continues** Nuisances & Environnement.
Ind/Abst EMBASE; Energy Res. Abstr. (Feb. 1983-); Environ.

CN/0704-4062
ECO/LOG. CANADIAN POLLUTION LEGISLATION. (1977)-. Periodical. English. mo. 929.00Can$ Canada; 1049.00Can$ other. Southam Information and Technology Group Inc., 1450 Don Mills Road, Don Mills Ontario M3B 2X7 Canada. **Tel** (416)445-6641, (800)668-2374, FAX (416)442-2261. **DD** 344.71046. **Continues** ECO/LOG. Environmental Legislation Information Service, 0704-4054.

CN/0315-0380
ECO/LOG WEEK. (1972)-. Periodical. English. wk. 555.00Can$ Canada; 655.00Can$ other. Southam Information and Technology Group Inc., 1450 Don Mills Road, Don Mills Ontario M3B 2X7 Canada. **Tel** (416)445-6641, (800)668-2374, FAX (416)442-2261. **ED** William M Glenn and Deborah Orchard. Index available. cum. index. **Bk Rev.** ctrl circ.
Desc: Newsletter covering waste management and industrial pollution control technology, Canadian environmental concerns, toxic chemicals, and transportation of dangerous goods.
Ind/Abst PROMT [Full Txt.].

BL
ECOLOGIA E DESENVOLVIMENTO. Vol. 1, No. 1 (1991)-. Periodical. Portuguese.

AT/0311-4546
ECOS. [Ecos]. **Added/Corp** Commonwealth Scientific and Industrial Research Organization (Australia). No. 1 (Aug. 1974)-. Periodical. English. qt. 22.00Aus$ Australia; 40.00Aus$ other. CSIRO Publications, PO Box 89, 314 Albert Street, East Melborne Victoria 3002 Australia. **Tel** 011 61 3 4187333, 4187217, FAX 011 61 3 4190459, telex AA 30236. **[CCC].** **Ad Acc.**
Ind/Abst AESIS Q.; Coal Abstr.; Ecol. Abstr.; Geogr. Abstr. Phys. Geogr. (?-?); Int. Dev. Abstr.

US/0147-6513
ECOTOXICOLOGY AND ENVIRONMENTAL SAFETY. See
Environmental Issues-Ecology.

US/0163-2566
EDF LETTER. See Environmental Issues-Conservation and Natural Resources.

US/1042-251X
EI DIGEST. [EI dig.]. **Added/Corp** Environmental Information Ltd. VAT Environmental Information Digest. (Jan. 1989)-. Academic Scholarly Publication. English. mo. $1250.00 US; $1300.00 other. Environmental Information Ltd, 4801 West 81st Street, Suite 119, Minneapolis MN 55437. **Tel** (612)831-2473, FAX (612)831-6550. **ED** Cary L. Perket. **LC** HD9975.U5; E5. **DD** 338.4/76047/097305. **CODEN** EDIGER. Index available. Documents available from CASDDS.
Ind/Abst Chem. Abstr.

US/1053-475X
EI ENVIRONMENTAL SERVICES DIRECTORY. [EI environ. serv. dir.]. **Added/Corp** Environmental Information Ltd. VFOAT Environmental Services Directory. **VAT** Environmental Information

Environmental Services Directory. (1991)-. Directory. English. an. $395.00. Environmental Information Ltd, 4801 West 81st Street, Suite 119, Minneapolis MN 55437. **Tel** (612)831-2473, FAX (612)831-6550. **ED** Cary L. Perket. **LC** HD9975.U5; I53. **DD** 338.7/6285. **NLM** WA 22; AA1 I42. Index available. ***Continues*** *Industrial & Hazardous Waste Management Firms, 0885-1735.*

GW
ELSNERS HANDBUCH FUER STADTISCHEN INGENIEURBAU. VFOAT Handbuch fuer Stadtischen Ingenieurbau. (1973)-. German. O Elsner Verlagsgesellschaft, Schofferstrasse 15, 6100 Darmstadt Germany. **LC** TD159.A1; E58.

US/0747-8186
EMPLOYMENT OPPORTUNITIES / UNITED STATES ENVIRONMENTAL PROTECTION AGENCY, PERSONNEL MANAGEMENT DIVISION. See Business-Personnel Management.

US/0147-7587
END OF YEAR REPORT. REGIONAL PROGRAM PLANS ASSESSMENT. See Public Administration.

UK
ENDS REPORT. Added/Corp Environmental Data Services, Ltd. **VFOAT** Ends. **VAT** Environmental Data Services Report. (19??)-. Periodical. English. mo. $220.00. Environmental Data Service Ltd, Finsbury Business Centre, 40 Bowling Green Lane, London EC1R One England. **Tel** 011 44 71 278 7624, FAX 011 44 71 415 0106. **ED** Marek Mayer. Index available. **Ad Acc, Adv Mgr:** Gail Davis. **Circ:** 18,000. Documents available from Documents on Demand.
Desc: A wide range of topics including air, land and water pollution; waste management, material recovery and recycling. Also contains company response to environmental pressures.
Ind/Abst Chem. Hazards Ind.; Environ. Abstr.; Infomat Int. Bus.; Lab. Hazards Bull.

SW/1101-7341
ENVIRO. Added/Corp Sweden. Statens Naturvardsverk. No. 11 (Apr. 1991)-. Periodical. English. sa. Free (on request). Swedish National Environmental Protection Board, PO Box 1302, Information Section, Solna S17125 Sweden. **Tel** (468)799-1000, FAX (468)984513, telex 11131 ENVIRONS. **LC** QH545.A17; A25. Documents available from Documents on Demand. ***Continues*** *Acid Enviro.*
Ind/Abst Environ. Abstr.; Environ. Period. Bibliogr.

US/0270-0751
ENVIROLINE USER'S MANUAL. *Ceased.* Ceased (1984). English. EIC/Intelligence Inc, 48 West 38th Street, New York NY 10018. **Tel** (212)944-8500. **Bk Rev.** ctrl circ.
Desc: Manual giving search strategies and keyterm lists to aid in use of Enviroline.

●UK/1352-8882
ENVIRONMENT BUSINESS MAGAZINE. VFOAT EBM. (January 1, 1994)-. Periodical. English. Eight times a year. £47.00 UK; £57.00 other. Information for Industry Ltd, 18-20 Ridgway, London SW19 4QN England. **Tel** 011 44 081 944 2930, FAX 011 44 081 944 1982. **ED** Alastair Baillie. **Photos. Ad Acc, Adv Mgr:** Steven Voss. **Circ:** 7,482 (ctrl).
Desc: Targeted at buyers and specifiers of environmental technology and services in manufacturing and other waste generating business in the United Kingdom.

US/0013-9157
ENVIRONMENT (ST. LOUIS). (ENVIRONMENT.). [Environment]. **Added/Corp** Helen Dwight Reid Educational Foundation. Scientists' Institute for Public Information. Committee for Environmental Information (Saint Louis, Mo.). Vol. 11 (Jan./Feb. 1969)-. Academic Scholarly Publication. English. mo (Combined issues in Jan./Feb. and Jul./Aug.). $35.00 (individual), $70.00 (institution). Heldref Publications, 1319 Eighteenth Street Northwest, Washington DC 20036-1802. **Tel** (202)296-6267, (800)365-9753, FAX (202)296-5149. **LC** UF767; .S33. **DD** 301.31. **CODEN** ENVTAR. **[CCC].** Documents available from The Genuine Article, BIOSIS Document Express, UMI Article Clearinghouse, CASDDS, Documents on Demand, Magazine Collection. ***Continues*** *Scientist and Citizen.*
Desc: Presents objective appraisals of topics in science, policy and the global environment. Contains a variety of readable and authoritative articles on subjects from acid rain to nuclear waste. Regular features include news briefs of current issues, critical reviews of major government and institutional reports, and commentaries that provide differing points of view articles.
Ind/Abst Abr. Read. Guide Period. Lit. [Full Txt.]; Acad. Abstr. Full Text Elite (Oct. 1984-) [Full Txt.]; Acad. Abstr. (Oct. 1984-); Acad. Ind. [Computer File]; Acad. Search (Oct. 1984-); AgBiotech News Inf.; AGRICOLA; Appl. Sci. Technol. Index; AQUAREF; Biol. Agric. Index; Biol. Abstr.; Book Rev. Index; Chem. Abstr.; Coal Abstr.; Curr. Aware. Biol. Sci., CABS; Curr. Index J. Educ.; Ecol. Abstr.; EMBASE; Energy Inf. Abstr.; Energy Res. Abstr.; Environ. Abstr.; Expand. Acad. Index; Fish Rev.; Foods Adlibra; Fut. Surv.; Gen. Period. Index; Gen. Sci. Index; Gen. Sci. Source (Jan. 1988-) [Full Txt.]; GeoRef; Guide Soc. Sci. Relig.; Health Saf. Sci. Abstr.; Health Source (Jan. 1988-) [Full Txt.]; INFO-SOUTH Abstr.; INIS Atomindex [Micro.]; Int. Aerosp. Abstr.; Int. Dev. Abstr.; J. Plan. Lit.; Mag. Artic. Summar. Elite (Oct. 1984-) [Full Txt.]; Mag. Artic. Summar. Select (Oct. 1984-); Mag. Artic. Summar. CD-ROM (Oct. 1984-); Mag. Express; Mag. Index Plus; Mag. Index Sel. Microfiche; Mag. Index. Sel.; Mag. Search; Maize Abstr.; Mid. Search (Jan. 1988-) [Full Txt.]; Newsp. Period. Abstr.; Peace Res. Abstr. J.; Prim. Search (Jan. 1988-); Read. Guide Abstr. Select Ed.; Read. Guide Period. Lit.; Res. Alert; Resource/One Ondisc; Rural Dev. Abstr.; Sage Urban Stud. Abstr; Sci. Cit. Index; SCISEARCH; Soc. Sci. Cit. Index [Select. Cov.]; Mag. Index; TOM Gen. Index; Vocat. Search (Oct. 1984-) [Full Txt.]; West. Hist. Q.; Wildl. Rev.; World Agric. Econ.

CN/0714-9263
ENVIRONMENT UPDATE (CANADA. ENVIRONMENT CANADA). (ENVIRONMENT UPDATE.). [Environ. update]. **VFOAT** Environnement a la Une. Periodical. English (French). bm. Free. Environment Canada / Emergencies Science Division, Ottawa Ontario K1A 0H3 Canada. **Tel** (819)998-9622. **DD** 363.7/00971.
Ind/Abst Abstr. Bull. Inst. Pap. Sci. Tech.; Pollut. Abstr. Indexes.

CN/0835-3778
ENVIRONMENTAL & WASTE MANAGEMENT WORLD. *Ceased.* [Environ. waste manag. world]. **VAT** Environmental and Waste Management World. Vol. 1, No. 1 (June 1987)-(1992). Periodical. English. mo. Specialty Technical Publishers Inc, #306-267 West Esplande, North Vancouver BC V7M 1A5 Canada. **Tel** (604)983-3434, FAX (604)983-3445. **DD** 363.7/005.

US/0197-1956
ENVIRONMENTAL ASSESSMENT. ELECTRIC HYBRID VEHICLE RESEARCH, DEVELOPMENT AND DEMONSTRATION PROGRAM. Main/Corp United States. Dept. of Energy. Office of Conservation and Solar Applications. **VFOAT** Electric Hybrid Vehicle Research, Development and Demonstration Program. English. an. National Technical Information Service - NTIS, Room 2027S, 5285 Port Royal Road, Springfield VA 22161. **Tel** (703)487-4630, (703)487-4660, (703)487-4650, FAX (703)321-8547, telex 89-9405. available on microfiche (from NTIS).

US/0094-7237
ENVIRONMENTAL BIOLOGY. See Biology.

US/1068-4980
ENVIRONMENTAL BUYERS' GUIDE. *Title Change.* (ENVIRONMENTAL BUYERS' GUIDE / AMERICAN CHEMICAL SOCIETY.). [Environ. buy. guide]. **Added/Corp** American Chemical Society. **VFOAT** American Chemical Society Environmental Buyers' Guide. Vol. 1 (1991)-(1993). Consumer Publication. English. ir. ACS, American Chemical Society, 1155 16th Street NW, Washington DC 20036. **LC** TD193; .E55. **DD** 628.5/029/4. ***Absorbed by*** *Environmental Science & Technology (Easton, Pa.), 0013-936x.*

CN
ENVIRONMENTAL COMPLIANCE. A NATIONAL SIMPLIFIED GUIDE. English. $282.00. Specialty Technical Publishers Inc, #306-267 West Esplande, North Vancouver BC V7M 1A5 Canada. **Tel** (604)983-3434, FAX (604)983-3445. ctrl circ.

CN
ENVIRONMENTAL COMPLIANCE CALIFORNIA. INCLUDES UPDATES. English. ir (4 to 6 updates per year). $266.00. Specialty Technical Publishers Inc, #306-267 West Esplande, North Vancouver BC V7M 1A5 Canada. **Tel** (604)983-3434, FAX (604)983-3445. ctrl circ.

US
ENVIRONMENTAL DEVELOPMENT PLAN. BIOMASS ENERGY SYSTEMS. See Environmental Issues.

US
ENVIRONMENTAL DEVELOPMENT PLAN. COAL LIQUEFACTION. Main/Corp United States. Office of the Assistant Secretary for Fossil Energy. **VFOAT** Coal Liquefaction. Aug. 1980-. Government Publication. English. US Department of Energy, 1000 Independence Avenue SW, Washington DC 20585. **Tel** (202)586-5000, FAX (202)586-4073. ***Continues*** *Environmental Development Plan (EDP). Coal Liquefaction Program.*

US
ENVIRONMENTAL DEVELOPMENT PLAN. DECONTAMINATION AND DECOMMISSIONING. Main/Corp United States. Dept. of Energy. Office of the Assistant Secretary for Environment. **VFOAT** Decontamination and Decommissioning. July 1979-. Government Publication. English. US Department of Energy, 1000 Independence Avenue SW, Washington DC 20585. **Tel** (202)586-5000, FAX (202)586-4073. ***Continues*** *Environmental Development Plan (EDP). Decontamination Decommissioning.*

CN/1183-8795
ENVIRONMENTAL DIGEST (OWEN SOUND). (ENVIRONMENTAL DIGEST.). [Environ. dig.]. Vol. 1, No. 1 Feb. 26, (1990)-. Periodical. English. bw (25 issues). 235.00Can$. Sydenham Publishing, 344 23rd Street West, Owen Sound ONT N4K 4G7 Canada. **Tel** (519)371-6289, FAX (519)371-3676. **ED** Stella Coultas. **DD** 363.73/0971/05. **Bk Rev**, (Qty: 5-6).
Desc: Bi-weekly environment news review.

US
ENVIRONMENTAL EFFECTS OF DREDGING : INFORMATION EXCHANGE BULLETIN / U.S. ARMY CORPS OF ENGINEERS, WATERWAYS EXPERIMENT STATION. Vol. D-83-2 (May 1983)-. Bulletin. English. qt. ***Continues*** *Dredged Materials Research : Notes, News, Reviews, etc.*
Ind/Abst Fluid Abstr., Civil Eng.; Fluid Abstr. Proc. Eng.; FLUIDEX (1983-).

US/0732-7188
ENVIRONMENTAL ENGINEERING & POLLUTION CONTROL. (ENVIRONMENTAL ENGINEERING & POLLUTION CONTROL MICROFORM.). [Environ. eng. pollut. control]. **Added/Corp** Comtex Scientific Corporation. **VFOAT** Environmental Engineering and Pollution Control. Vol. 1, No. 1 (1982)-. Monographic series. English. ir. Price varies per volume. Comtex, 850 3rd Avenue, New York NY 10017.

UK/0954-5824
ENVIRONMENTAL ENGINEERING (BURY SAINT EDMUNDS, ENG. : 1988). See Engineering.

●US/1056-7054
ENVIRONMENTAL ENGINEERING (NEW YORK, N.Y.). See Environmental Issues.

US/0735-5394
ENVIRONMENTAL FINANCE. See Public Administration-Public Finance and Taxation.

US/0196-0598
ENVIRONMENTAL HEALTH LETTER. (19??)-. Periodical. English. bw. $312.00. Business Publishers Inc., 951 Pershing Drive, Silver Spring MD 20910-4464. **Tel** (301)587-6300, (800)274-0122, FAX (301)585-9075. **ED** Gershon W. Fishbein. **NLM** W1 EN984. **[CCC]. Bk Rev.**
Desc: News and developments on health and related aspects of pollution control.

US/1053-4180
ENVIRONMENTAL HISTORY REVIEW : EHR. [Environ. hist. rev.]. **VFOAT** EHR. Vol. 14, No. 1-2 (Spring/Summer 1990)-. Periodical. English. qt. $24.00 (individual), $30.00 (institution). New Jersey Institute of Technology, Center for Technology Studies, Newark NJ 07102. **Tel** (201)596-3270. **ED** John Opie and Arlene McKenna. **LC** GF1; .E59. **DD** 304. (Free). cum. index. **Bk Rev. Ad Acc. Pr Rev. Circ:** 600. available on microfilm and microfiche from University Microfilms International (UMI). Documents available from Documents on Demand. ***Continues*** *Environmental Review (Pittsburgh, Pa.), 0147-2496.*
Desc: An international journal that seeks understanding of human ecology through the perspectives of history and the humanities.
Ind/Abst Am. Hist. Life (1976-); Ecol. Abstr.; Environ. Abstr.; Environ. Period. Bibliogr.; Geogr. Abstr. Human Geogr.

US/1051-2837
ENVIRONMENTAL MANAGEMENT (DENVER, COLO.). (ENVIRONMENTAL MANAGEMENT.). [Environ. manage.]. **Added/Corp** Environmental Management Association. (1990)-. Periodical. English. qt. Free (members). Environmental Management Association, 4350 de Paolo Center, Suite C, Glenview IL 60025. **Tel** (708)699-6362. **DD** 363. Documents available from Documents on Demand. ***Continues*** *Professional Sanitation Management, 0033-0191.*
Ind/Abst Environ. Abstr. (Apr. 16, 1991-); Geogr. Abstr. Human Geogr.

US
ENVIRONMENTAL MANAGEMENT / PA. English. mo. $95.00. Hazardous Materials Publishing Company, PO Box 308, Kutztown PA 19530. **Tel** (610)683-7853, FAX (610)683-3171.

US/1043-786X
ENVIRONMENTAL MANAGER. [Environ. manager]. Vol. 1, No. 1 (Aug. 1989)-. Periodical. English. mo. $135.00 US & Canada; $185.00 other. John Wiley & Sons, Inc., 605 Third Avenue, New York NY 10158-0012.

Tel (212)850-6000, (212)850-6645, FAX (212)850-6088, telex 12-7063. **(Subscription address:** John Wiley & Sons Inc / New Jersey, PO Box 2575, Secaucus NJ 07096-2575.**) ED** Jane G. Bensahely. **LC** TD897.5; .E58. **DD** 628/.05. **CODEN** ENVMEA. **[CCC].** Index available. **Ad Acc.** available on microfilm and microfiche from University Microfilms International (UMI). Documents available from Documents on Demand.
Desc: Current environmental news and practical information featuring case studies of solutions to problems such as toxic waste clean ups; coverage of regulation and legislation and new clean up technology and methods.
Ind/Abst BioBusiness (1991-); Environ. Abstr. (Sept. 4, 1990-).

NE/0167-6369
ENVIRONMENTAL MONITORING AND ASSESSMENT. See Environmental Issues.

NZ
ENVIRONMENTAL NEWS. Added/Corp University of Waikato. Environmental Studies Unit. (19??)-. Periodical. English.
Ind/Abst Ind. Hyg. Dig. (19??-19??).

US/0740-5847
ENVIRONMENTAL NOTICE BULLETIN. [Environ. not bull.]. **Added/Corp** New York (State). Dept. of Environmental Conservation. (19??)-. Bulletin. English. wk. $12.00. Environmental Notice Bulletin, Department of Environmental Conservation, Albany NY 12233. **ED** Betty-Jo Daly, NYS DEC, Bureau of Publications, 50 Walf Road, Albany, NY 12233-4500, (518)457-2344. ctrl circ.

US/1051-1229
ENVIRONMENTAL OUTLOOK. VFOAT Environmental Outlook Management Sourcebook. (1991)-. English. an. $20.00. Environmental Publications Inc, 1400 Front Avenue, PO Box 4357, Lutherville MD 21093. **Tel** (301)828-6618.

UK/0269-7491
ENVIRONMENTAL POLLUTION (1987). (ENVIRONMENTAL POLLUTION.). [Environ. pollut.]. Vol. 43, No. 1 (1987)-. Academic Scholarly Publication. English. Twelve times a year. $1349.00 The Americas; £905.00 other. Elsevier Applied Science, An Imprint of Elsevier Science Ltd., The Boulevard, Langford Lane, Kidlington, Oxford OX5 1GB United Kingdom. **Tel** 011 44 865 843000, 011 44 865 843699, FAX 011 44 865 843010. **ED** J. P. Dempster and W. J. Manning. **LC** TD172; .E57. **DD** 363.73/05. **NLM** W1; EN984XFA. **CODEN** ENPOEK. **[CCC]. Bk Rev. Ad Acc. Pr Rev.** available on microfilm and microfiche from University Microfilms International (UMI). Documents available from The Genuine Article, BIOSIS Document Express, Ask*IEEE, CASDDS. ***Formed by the union of*** *Environmental Pollution. Series A, Ecological and Biological, 0143-1471* ***and*** *Environmental Pollution. Series B, Chemical and Physical, 0143-148X.*
Desc: Concerned with the biological effects of pollution and includes research papers on ecological effects on all types of environmental pollution and pollution control.
Ind/Abst AgBiotech News Inf.; AGRICOLA [Select. Cov.]; Agric. Eng. Abstr. (1991-); Biodeter. Abstr. (19??-19??); Biol. Agric. Index; Biol. Abstr. (1987-); Biol. Dig.; Chem. Abstr. (1987-); Chem. Titles; Cot. Trop. Fibr. Abstr. Bibliogr.; Crop Physiol. Abstr.; Curr. Aware. Biol. Sci., CABS; Curr. Contents, Agric. Biol. Environ. Sci.; Curr. Ref. Fish Res.; Ecol. Abstr.; Ecology Abstr.; Ei Page One; EMBASE; Environ. Period. Bibliogr.; Fluid Abstr., Civil Eng.; Fluid Abstr. Proc. Eng.; FLUIDEX (19??-); For. Abstr.; Geogr. Abstr. Phys. Geogr.; Geogr. Abstr. Human Geogr.; Geol. Abstr.; GeoRef; Grasslands For. Abstr.; Health Saf. Sci. Abstr.; Helminthol. Abstr.; Hortic. Abstr.; Index Vet.; INSPEC (1987-); Irr. Drain. Abstr.; J. Plan. Lit.; Key Word Index Wildl. Res.; Leadscan; Lit. Pat. Abstr., Oilfield Chem. (1972-); Lit. Abstr., Catal. Catal.; Lit. Abstr., Health Environ.; Lit. Abstr., Pet. Refin. Petrochem.; Lit. Abstr., Pet. Substit.; Lit. Abstr., Transp. Storage; Maize Abstr.; Middle East Abstr. Index; Nematol. Abstr.; Nutr. Abstr. Rev., Ser. B, Live Feeds and Feed.; Nutr. Abstr. Rev., Ser. A, Hum. Exp.; Ocean. Abstr.; Ornamental Hort.; PESTDOC; Pig News Inf.; Plant Breed. Abstr.; Plant Grow. Reg. Abstr.; Pollut. Abstr. Indexes; Potato Abstr.; Poult. Abstr.; Protozoolog. Abstr.; Res. Alert [Full Cov.]; Rev. Agric. Entomol.; Rev. Med. Vet. Entomol.; Rev. Plant Pathol.; Rice Abstr.; Risk Abstr. (19??-19??); Sci. Cit. Index; SCISEARCH; Seed Abstr.; Soils Fert.; Soyabean Abstr.; SportSearch; Sug. Indus. Abstr.; Vet. Bull.; Trop. Dis. Bull.; Weed Abstr.; Wheat Barley Trit. Abstr.

US/0278-4491
ENVIRONMENTAL PROGRESS. [Environ. prog.]. **Added/Corp** American Institute of Chemical Engineers. Vol. 1, No. 1 (Feb. 1982)-. Academic Scholarly Publication. English. qt (4 issues). $165.00 US; $195.00 other. American Institute of Chemical Engineers, 345 East 47th Street, New York NY 10017. **Tel** (212)705-7663, (212)705-7703, FAX (212)705-8400. **ED** Joan Muraro. **LC** TD1; .E56. **DD** 628.5/46/05. **CODEN** ENVPDI. **[CCC].** Index available. **Bk Rev. Ad Acc. Pr Rev. Circ:** 3,300 (ctrl). available on microfilm and microfiche from University Microfilms International (UMI). Documents available from Article Express International, The Genuine Article, CASDDS, Documents on Demand.
Desc: Reports advances of interest to the chemical and environmental engineer concerning pollution as related to water, atmosphere, liquid and solid wastes.
Ind/Abst Appl. Sci. Technol. Index; Bioeng. Abstr.; Chem. Abstr.; Coal Abstr.; Curr. Aware. Biol. Sci., CABS; Curr. Biotechnol.; Curr. Contents Eng. Tech. Appl. Sci.; Ei Page One; Eng. Index Annu. [Select. Cov.]; Environ. Abstr. (Jan. 2, 1992-); Fish Rev. (Jan. 1989-July 1992); Gas Abstr.; GeoRef; INIS Atomindex [Micro.]; Lit. Pat. Abstr., Oilfield Chem. (1982-); Lit. Abstr., Catal. Catal.; Lit. Abstr., Health Environ.; Lit. Abstr., Pet. Refin. Petrochem.; Lit. Abstr., Pet. Substit.; Lit. Abstr., Transp. Storage; Pollut. Abstr. Indexes; Proc. Chem. Eng.; Res. Alert [Select. Cov.]; SCISEARCH; Soils Fert.; Theoret. Chem. Eng.; Wildl. Rev. (Jan. 1989-July 1992).

US
ENVIRONMENTAL PROTECTION AGENCY PLANNING AND BUDGETING GUIDANCE. Main/Corp United States. Environmental Protection Agency. **VFOAT** Budgeting and Planning Guidance; EPA Policy Guidance. English. an. Environmental Protection Agency / Washington, 401 M Street SW, Washington DC 20460. **Tel** (202)382-2090.

UK/0957-9052
ENVIRONMENTAL PROTECTION BULLETIN. (19??)-. Bulletin. English. bm (6 issues). £130.00 (institutions), £40.00 (universities) UK; £155.00 (institutions), £50.00 (universities) other. Institution of Chemical Engineers, Davis Building, 165-189 Railway Terrace, Rugby Warwickshire CV21 3HQ England. **Tel** 011 44 1788 578214, FAX 011 44 1788 560833, telex 311780. **ED** Delyth Forsdyke. Index available (ú70.00 on computer disk). **Pr Rev.**
Desc: The bulletin contains information on a wide range of topics related to pollution control, waste management and environmental legislation.

NZ/0110-9944
ENVIRONMENTAL RADIOACTIVITY ANNUAL REPORT. [Environ. radioact. annu. rep.]. **Added/Corp** National Radiation Laboratory (New Zealand). (1971)-. English. an (Mar.). 25.00NZ$. National Radiation Laboratory, PO Box 25-099, Christchurch NZ. **Tel** 011 64 3 665059. **LC** TD196.R3; E6. **DD** 363.17/992/0993021. **NLM** W2 KN4 N27F. ***Continues*** *Environmental Radioactivity in New Zealand.*

US/1060-8648
ENVIRONMENTAL SAFETY ALERT. [Environ. saf. alert]. (199?)-. Periodical. English. mo. $132.00. Executive Enterprises, 22 West 21st Street, New York NY 10010-6990. **Tel** (800)332-8804, FAX (212)645-8689. **LC** TD191.5; .S86. **DD** 604.7. **[CCC].** ***Continues*** *Supervisor's Environmental Alert, 1052-1542.*
Desc: Offers plant managers in all types of industries practical interpretations of their responsibilities under EPA, OSHA, and DOT laws and regulations so they can avoid violations and keep their workforce safe. Written in easy to understand language, it provides hand-on advice from experienced practioners.

●US/1077-2537
ENVIRONMENTAL SOLUTIONS. [Environ. solut.]. Vol. 7, No. 6 (June 1994)-. Periodical. English. Twelve times a year. $50.00 US & US Possessions; $75.00 others. Advanstar Communications Inc., 131 West First Street, Duluth MN 55802. **Tel** (218)723-9477, (800)346-0085. **LC** TD1060; .H39. **DD** 628.4/2. ***Continues*** *HazMat World, 0898-5685.*
Desc: Targets individuals who specify and purchase products, systems, equipment and services used for hazardous materials and waste management.

US
ENVIRONMENTAL SURVEILLANCE REPORT FOR THE INEL RADIOACTIVE WASTE MANAGEMENT COMPLEX. VAT Environmental Surveillance Report for the Idaho National Engineering Laboratory Radioactive Waste Management Complex. English. an. National Technical Information Service - NTIS, Room 2027S, 5285 Port Royal Road, Springfield VA 22161. **Tel** (703)487-4630, (703)487-4660, (703)487-4650, FAX (703)321-8547, telex 89-9405.

US/0730-7268
ENVIRONMENTAL TOXICOLOGY AND CHEMISTRY. (ENVIRONMENTAL TOXICOLOGY AND CHEMISTRY / SETAC.). [Environ. toxicol. chem.]. **Added/Corp** SETAC (Society). Vol. 1, No. 1 (1982)-. Academic Scholarly Publication. English. mo. $556.00 The Americas; £374.00 other. Pergamon Press, An Imprint of Elsevier Science Ltd., The Boulevard, Langford Lane, Kidlington, Oxford OX5 1GB United Kingdom. **Tel** 011 44 865 843000, 011 44 865 843699, FAX 011 44 865 843010. **(Subscription address:** Elsevier Science Ltd. Oxford Fulfillment Centre, PO Box 800, Kidlington, Oxford OX5 1DX United Kingdom.**) ED** C. Hebert Ward. **LC** QH545.A1; E594. **DD** 574.2/4. **NLM** W1; EN986KF. **CODEN** ETOCDK. **[CCC]. Pr Rev.** available on microfilm and microfiche from University Microfilms International (UMI). Documents available from Article Express International, The Genuine Article, BIOSIS Document Express, CASDDS, Documents on Demand.
Desc: Provides a forum for professionals in academia, industry, government and other segments of society involved in the use, protection and management of the environment for the enhancement of ecological health and human welfare.
Ind/Abst Abstr. Bull. Inst. Pap. Sci. Tech.; AGRICOLA [Select. Cov.]; Biodeter. Abstr. (19??-19??); Biol. Abstr.; Chem. Abstr.; Chem. Titles; Crop Physiol. Abstr.; Curr. Aware. Biol. Sci., CABS; Curr. Contents, Agric. Biol. Environ. Sci.; Ecol. Abstr. (?-?); Ecology Abstr.; Ei Page One; EMBASE; Eng. Index Annu. [Select. Cov.]; Environ. Abstr. (Dec. 17, 1990-); Environ. Period. Bibliogr.; Fish Rev.; Food Sci. Technol. Abstr.; Genet. Abstr.; GeoRef; Health Saf. Sci. Abstr.; Index Vet.; INIS Atomindex [Micro.]; Irr. Drain. Abstr.; Key Word Index Wildl. Res.; Microbiol. Abstr. Sect. B (19??-19??); Microbiol. Abstr. Sect. A; Microbiol. Abstr. Sect. C; Nematol. Abstr.; Nutr. Abstr. Rev., Ser. B, Live Feeds and Feed.; Life Sci. Collect.; PESTDOC; Pollut. Abstr. Indexes; Poult. Abstr.; Res. Alert [Full Cov.]; Rev. Agric. Entomol.; Rev. Med. Vet. Entomol.; Rice Abstr.; Risk Abstr.; Sci. Cit. Index; SCISEARCH; Seed Abstr.; Soils Fert.; Soyabean Abstr.; Vet. Bull.; Toxicol. Abstr.; Weed Abstr.; Wheat Barley Trit. Abstr.; Wildl. Rev.

US/1061-7787
ENVIRONMENTAL TOXICOLOGY NEWSLETTER. / COOPERATIVE EXTENSION, UNIVERSITY OF CALIFORNIA. See Environmental Issues.

GW/0935-0209
ENVIRONMENTAL TOXIN SERIES. [Environ. toxin ser.]. Vol. 1 (1987)-. Monographic series. English. ir. Price varies per volume. Springer-Verlag GmbH & Company KG, Heidelberger Platz 3, D 14197 Berlin Germany. **Tel** 011 49 30 8207223, FAX 011 49 30 8214091, telex 183 319 SPBLN D. **(Subscription address:** Springer Verlag New York Inc. / for North America, 44 Hartz Way, Secaucus NJ 07096.**) ED** Stephen Safe, O. Hutzinger. **NLM** W1; EN986L. **CODEN** ETSEED. Documents available from BIOSIS Document Express, CASDDS.
Ind/Abst AGRICOLA [Select. Cov.]; Biol. Abstr. (1987-); Chem. Abstr.

US/1049-4715
ENVIRONMENTAL WASTE MANAGEMENT. ***Ceased.*** [Environ. waste manage.]. **Added/Corp** National Association of Hazardous Waste Generators. Vol. 8, No. 4 (Apr. 1990)-Vol. 10 No. 6 (Nov./Dec. 1992). Periodical. English. mo. Hazardous Materials Publishing Company, PO Box 308, Kutztown PA 19530. **Tel** (215)683-6721, FAX (215)683-3171. **LC** TD811.5; .H394. **DD** 628. **CODEN** EWMAEQ. **Ad Acc, Adv Mgr:** Katie Keegan, **Tel** (215)683-5098. **Circ:** 34,000. ***Continues*** *Hazardous Waste Management, 1047-479X.*
Desc: Serves generators and shippers of hazardous materials, chemicals or waste; transporters; federal, state and municipal facilities; hazardous waste treatment, storage and disposal facilities; consulting firms and others allied to the field.
Ind/Abst BioBusiness (1990-); Environ. Period. Bibliogr.

XR
ENVIRONMENTALICA. English (Czech). **LC** QH545.A1; E598. **DD** 574.5/222.
Ind/Abst Ecol. Abstr.

CN/0709-8847
ENVIRONNEMENT (MONTREAL). See Environmental Issues-Abstracting, Bibliographies and Statistics.

US
EPA AND THE ACADEMIC COMMUNITY, PARTNERS IN RESEARCH SOLICITATION FOR GRANT PROPOSALS. Main/Corp United States. Environmental Protection Agency. **VAT** Environmental Protection Agency and the Academic Community, Partners in Research, Solicitation for Grant Proposals. English. Center for Environmental Protection Agency, Cincinnati OH 45268.

US/0732-8257
EPA PROGRAM STATUS REPORT, OIL SHALE. [EPA prog. status rep., oil shale]. **VFOAT** E.P.A. Program Status Report, Oil Shale; Program Status Report, Oil Shale. **VAT** Environmental Protection Agency Program Status Report: Oil Shale. Began with vol. for 1978. English. Environmental Protection Agency / Minerals and Industry, National Technical Information Service, 5285 Port Royal Road, Springfield VA 22161. **Tel** (800)553-6847, (703)487-4812. **LC** TD195.O4; E6. **DD** 363.7/01.

US/0192-5008
EPA PUBLICATIONS. (PUBLICATIONS - A QUARTERLY GUIDE / UNITED STATES ENVIRONMENTAL PROTECTION AGENCY, OFFICE OF FACILITIES AND SUPPORT SERVICES, PRINTING MANAGEMENT.). **Added/Corp** United States. Environmental Protection Agency. Printing Management. (19??)-. Periodical. English. ir. US Environmental Protection Agency / Printing Management, 401 M Street SW, Washington DC 20460. **LC** Z5863.P7; U58b; TD170.

Environmental Issues — Pollution and Waste Management

DD 016.6147/0973. Each issue contains an index to its own contents (no volume index)--loose.
Ind/Abst Fish Rev. (19??-199?); Wildl. Rev.

US
EQB MONITOR. Main/Corp Minnesota. Environmental Quality Board. Vol. 1 (1976)-. Periodical. English. wk. $8.00. Environmental Quality Board, 550 Cedar Street, 100 Capital Square, St. Paul MN 55101. **Tel** (612)296-8542.

US/0149-3094
EQL REPORT. [EQL rep.]. **Main/Corp** California Institute of Technology, Pasadena. Environmental Quality Laboratory. **VAT** Environmental Quality Laboratory Report. Monographic series. English. Price varies per volume. California Institute of Technology, Engineering, and Science, 315 South Hill Avenue, Pasadena CA 91125. **Tel** (818)395-6327. **CODEN** CEQLAT.
Ind/Abst GeoRef.

UK
EUROPEAN AGREEMENT CONCERNING THE INTERNATIONAL CARRIAGE OF DANGEROUS GOODS BY ROAD. (19??)-. English. ir. £26.00. Her Majesty's Stationery Office, 51 Nine Elms Lane, London SW8 5DR England. **Tel** 011 44 71 873 8459, 011 44 71 873 8499, FAX 011 44 71 873 8499, 011 44 71 873 8456, telex 297138. **(Subscription address:** Her Majesty's Stationery Office, PO Box 276, Publications Centre, London SW8 5DT England.**)**

US/0732-8044
FEAT MAGAZINE, THE. VFOAT F.E.A.T. Magazine. **VAT** Flint Environmental Action Team Magazine. Periodical. English. qt. Feat Foundation, 2701 Camden/Suite 5, Flint MI 48507.

US
FEDERAL REGISTER REPRINT FOR HAZARDOUS MATERIALS AND WASTE REGULATION. (19??)-. English. mo. $225.00. Hazardous Materials Publishing Company, PO Box 308, Kutztown PA 19530. **Tel** (215)683-6721, FAX (215)683-3171.

GW/0506-3159
FORTSCHRITT-BERICHTE DER VDI ZEITSCHRIFTEN. REIHE 11, SCHWINGUNGS TECHNIK, LARMBEKAMPFUNG. [Fortschrittber. VDI Z., 11, Schwingungstech. Larmbekampf.]. **VFOAT** Schwingungstechnik, Larmbekampfung; Fortschritte-Berichte der VDI-Zeitschriften. No. 8 (August 1970)-. Monographic series. German. Price varies per volume. VDI Verlag GmbH, Postfach 101054, D 40001 Dusseldorf Germany. **Tel** 011 49 211 6188313, FAX 011 49 211 6188133.
Ind/Abst Int. Aerosp. Abstr.

US/1061-9682
FROM THE STATE CAPITALS. ENVIRONMENTAL REGULATION. [From state cap., Environ. regul.]. **VFOAT** Environmental Regulation. (1991)-. Periodical. English. wk. $211.50 (one year), $378.00 (two year) public and institutional libraries; $235.00 (one year), $420.00 (two year) other. Wakeman Walworth Inc., 300 North Washington Street #204, Alexandria VA 22314. **Tel** (703)549-8606. **DD** 363.
Absorbed From the State Capitals. Waste Disposal and Pollution Control, 0749-2758; From the State Capitals. Water Supply, 0734-1237.

US
FROM THE UNICEF WATERFRONT.
VFOAT Waterfront; UNICEF Waterfront. No. 1 (Aug. 15, 1975)-. English. UNICEF Water and Environmental Sanitation Team (WET), Box 20, New York NY 10163-0020.

JA/0388-6166
FUKUOKA-SHI EISEI SHIKENJO HO. [Fukuoka-shi Eisei Shikenjoho]. **VFOAT** Annual Report of Fukuoka City Hygienic Laboratory. Academic Scholarly Publication. Japanese. an. Fukuoka Inst. of Public Health, 2-5-10 Maizuru Chuo-ku, Fukuoka-shi 810 Japan. **CODEN** FESHDT. Documents available from CASDDS.
Ind/Abst Chem. Abstr.; Food Sci. Technol. Abstr.

US/1044-3061
GARBAGE (BROOKLYN, NEW YORK, N.Y.). Ceased. See Environmental Issues-Conservation and Natural Resources.

CN/0382-6015
GARBAGE COALITION. Title Change. Vol. 1 (May 1973)-?. Periodical. English. bm. Ontario Garbage Coalition, c/o 43 Queen's Park Crescent East, Toronto Ontario M5S 2C3 Canada. **DD** 628.44/09713. **Continued by** Garbage Coalition Bulletin, 0382-6023.

CN/0382-6023
GARBAGE COALITION BULLETIN.
Bulletin. English. bm. Ontario Garbage Coalition, c/o 43 Queen's Park Crescent East, Toronto Ontario M5S 2C3 Canada. **DD** 628.44/09713. **Continues** Garbage Coalition, 0382-6015.

PL/0016-5352
GAZ, WODA I TECHNIKA SANITARNA.
[Gaz, woda tech. sanit.]. **VFOAT** Gaz, Woda, Technika Sanitarna. (1921)-. Academic Scholarly Publication. Polish (summaries and/or abstracts in English, French, Polish and Russian). mo. $72.00. **(Subscription address:** ARS Polona, PO Box 1001, 00068 Warsaw Poland.**) CODEN** GWTSAV. Documents available from CASDDS.
Ind/Abst Chem. Abstr.; Coal Abstr.; EMBASE; Saf. Health Work.

IT/0394-8382
GEA. VFOAT Governo Ed Economia dell'Ambiente; Governo Locale Ed Economia dell'Ambiente. Vol. 1, No. 1 (Sept./Oct. 1986)-. Periodical. Italian. Six times a year. L200000 Italy; L175000 others. Maggioli Editore, Casella Postale 290, 47037 Rimini, Italy. **Tel** 011 39 541 628666, FAX 011 39 541 742217.

JA/0285-6220
GEKKAN HAIKIBUTSU. [Gekkan haikibutsu]. **VFOAT** Haikibutsu. Began in 1975. Academic Scholarly Publication. Japanese. mo. ¥13,000. Nippo K K, Tokyo-to, Chiyoda-ku, Handabashi 4 4 5 Tokyo Japan. **Tel** 03-262-3461. **ED** Kinya Hisatomi. **CODEN** GEHADW. **Ad Acc. Circ:** 150,000 (ctrl). Documents available from CASDDS.
Desc: Waste, garbage, litter, dust, rubbish, trash, refuse, throwing away dirt, incineration, on transportation, by reclamation, by crushing, etc.
Ind/Abst Chem. Abstr.

JA/0021-4639
GESUIDO KYOKAI SHI. Added/Corp Nihon Gesuido Kyokai. **VFOAT** Journal of Japan Sewage Works Association. (June 1964)-. Periodical. Japanese. mo. $222.00. **(Subscription address:** Kyowa Book Company Inc., 1-38 Kanda Jinbo-Cho, Chiyoda-Ku Tokyo 101, Japan**) LC** TD511; .G48. **NLM** W1 GE842. **CODEN** GSKSAQ.

GW/0367-4223
GESUNDE PFLANZEN. [Gesunde Pflanz.]. Vol. 1 (1949)-. Academic Scholarly Publication. German (summaries and/or abstracts in English). Eight times a year. DM198.00. Blackwell Wissenschafts-Verlag, Kurfuerstendamm 57, D 10707 Berlin Germany. **Tel** 011 49 30 32790623, 011 49 30 32790624, FAX 011 49 30 327 90610. **CODEN** GEPFAG. Index available. cum. index. **Bk Rev. Ad Acc. Circ:** 500. Documents available from CASDDS.
Desc: This is a journal for plant protection, and environmental protection.
Ind/Abst AgBiotech News Inf.; AGRICOLA; Agric. Eng. Abstr. (1991-); Agrofor. Abstr. (1991-); Biocont. News Inf. (19??-19??); Biodeter. Abstr.; Chem. Abstr.; Crop Physiol. Abstr.; EMBASE; Field Crop Abstr.; Food Sci. Technol. Abstr.; For. Prod. Abstr.; For. Abstr.; Grasslands For. Abstr.; Hortic. Abstr.; Nematol. Abstr.; Nutr. Abstr. Rev., Ser. A, Hum. Exp.; Ornamental Hort. (19??-19??); PESTDOC; Plant Breed. Abstr.; Plant Grow. Reg. Abstr.; Potato Abstr.; Protozoolog. Abstr.; Rev. Agric. Entomol.; Rev. Med. Vet. Entomol.; Rev. Plant Pathol.; Seed Abstr.; Soils Fert.; Soyabean Abstr.; Vitis Vitic. Enol. Abstr.; Weed Abstr.; Wheat Barley Trit. Abstr.

GW/0932-6200
GI. GESUNDHEITS-INGENIEUR (1985).
(GESUNDHEITS-INGENIEUR : GI.). [GI, Gesundh.-Ing.]. **VFOAT** Gesundheits Ingenieur; GI; Gesundheits-Ingenieur, Haustechnik, Bauphysik, Umwelttechnik. Vol. 106, No. 1 (Feb. 1985)-. Academic Scholarly Publication. German. bm (6 issues). DM224.00. R Oldenbourg Verlag, Postfach 801360, D 81613 Munich Germany. **Tel** 011 49 89 450190, FAX 011 49 89 45019305. **NLM** W1; GE911B. **CODEN** GHBUEG. Documents available from CASDDS. **Continues** Haustechnik, Bauphysik, Umwelttechnik, 0172-8199.
Ind/Abst Chem. Abstr. (1985-); Coal Abstr. (1985-); Energy Res. Abstr. (1985-).

US/1051-6255
GOLOB'S OIL POLLUTION BULLETIN.
(GOLOB'S OIL POLLUTION BULLETIN : THE INTERNATIONAL NEWSLETTER ON OIL POLLUTION, PREVENTION, CONTROL, AND CLEANUP FROM WORLD INFORMATION SYSTEMS AND THE CENTER FOR SHORT-LIVED PHENOMENA.). [Golob's oil pollut. bull.]. **Added/Corp** World Information Systems. Center for Short-Lived Phenomena (Cambridge, Mass.). **VFOAT** Oil Pollution Bulletin. (1989)-. Newsletter. English. bw. $335.00 (US); $375.00 (other). World Information Systems, PO Box 535 Harvard Square, Cambridge MA 02238. **Tel** (617)491-5100, FAX (617)492-3312. **LC** TD427.P4; G62. **DD** 363.73/82/05. **[CCC]**.

US/0742-1230
GREAT LAKES WASTE & POLLUTION REVIEW MAGAZINE. [Great Lakes waste pollut. rev. mag.]. **Added/Corp** Waste Systems Institute of Michigan. **VFOAT** Great Lakes Waste and Pollution Review Magazine; GLWPRM; G.L.W.P.R.M. (198?)-. Periodical. English. bm. $24.00. Waste System Institute of Michigan, 3250 Townsend NE, Grand Rapids MI 49505. **LC** WMLC L 83/1786.

●US/1059-6143
GREEN CAR JOURNAL. See Transportation-Automobiles.

US/1042-5039
GREENHOUSE EFFECT REPORT. Title Change. [Greenh. eff. rep.]. Vol. 1, No. 1 (1989)-(19??). Periodical. English. bw. Business Publishers Inc., 951 Pershing Drive, Silver Spring MD 20910-4464. **Tel** (301)587-6300, (800)274-0122, FAX (301)585-9075. **DD** 363. **[CCC]**. available on an online database (file 636/Full-Text) from DIALOG. **Merged with** Multinational Environmental Outlook, 0899-5079 **to form** World Environment Report (1992).

IT
GREENWATCH : LETTERA CONFIDENZIALE IN DIFESA DI AGRICOLTURA E INDUSTRIA. (19??)-. Italian. sm. L1000000 Italy and CEE countries; L1200000 other. Vita Nova Arl, Via Muzio Scevola 26, 00181 Rome Italy. **Tel** 011 39 6 71543915.

AT/1034-5876
GREENWEEK. See Environmental Issues-Conservation and Natural Resources.

US/0899-3521
GROUNDWATER POLLUTION NEWS. Title Change. [Groundw. pollut. news]. **VFOAT** Ground Water Pollution News. Vol. 1, No. 1 (July 21, 1988)-(1993). Periodical. English. bw. Business Publishers Inc., 951 Pershing Drive, Silver Spring MD 20910-4464. **Tel** (301)587-6300, (800)274-0122, FAX (301)585-9075. **ED** Richard Hagan. **DD** 344. **[CCC]**. **Merged into** Groundwater Monitor, 0882-6188.
Desc: A newsletter on legislation, regulation and litigation concerning groundwater pollution.

CN/1187-2195
GUIDE TO THE HANDLING AND DISPOSAL OF HAZARDOUS SUBSTANCES IN THE SCHOOLS, A.
[Guide handl. dispos. hazard. subst. sch.]. **Added/Corp** Quebec (Province). Ministere de l'Education. Quebec (Province). Ministere de l'Environnement. 2nd Ed. (1991)-. English. Ministere de l'Education, 1035 de la Chev Rotiere, Quebec 10 Quebec Canada. **DD** 363.17/6/09714.

US/1061-043X
GUIDELINE FOR THE PREPARATION OF A HAZARD COMMUNICATION RIGHT-TO-KNOW PROGRAM / PREPARED BY HAZARDOUS COMMUNICATION AND RIGHT-TO-KNOW TASK FORCE, AMERICAN BOILER MANUFACTURERS ASSOCIATION.
[Guidel. prep. hazard commun. right know program]. **Added/Corp** American Boiler Manufacturers' Association. Hazardous Communication and Right-to-Know Task Force. 1st Ed. (1991)-. English. American Boiler Manufacturers Association, 950 North Glebe Road, Suite 160, Arlington VA 22203-1824. **LC** T55.3.H3; G853. **DD** 604.7.

JA/0917-0855
HAIKIBUTSU GAKKAISHI. VFOAT Waste Management Research (Tokyo. 1990). (1990)-. Periodical. Multiple languages. **DD** 628. Documents available from CASDDS.
Ind/Abst Chem. Abstr.

GW/0172-9578
HANDBUCH DER GEFAHRLICHEN GUTER. (1970)-. German. ir. price varies per volume. Springer Verlag New York Inc., PO Box 19386 Books, Newark NJ 07195. **Tel** (201)348-4033.

US/1042-6574
HAZ PACKS. Ceased. [Haz packs]. Vol. 1 (1989)-(Dec. 1994). Periodical. English. mo. Teaberry Associates, 21 Saw Mill Road, RR 21, Hadley NJ 08055. **Tel** (609)983-2619, FAX (609)983-7523. **ED** Jim Mackenzie. **DD** 604. **Ad Acc. Circ:** 10.
Desc: An educational program for emergency response personnel to meet federal and state mandated training requirements for the response to hazardous materials incidents.

US/0742-6410
HAZARD MONTHLY. [Hazard mon.]. **VFOAT** Hazard. Vol. 1 (June 1980)-. Periodical. English. Ten times a year. $39.00 (individuals); $48.00 (organizations) one year; $72.00 (individuals), $90.00 (organizations) two year; $99.00 (individuals), $126.00 (organizations) three year. Research Alternatives, 1401 Rockville Pike, Suite 500, Rockville MD 20850. **Tel** (301)424-2803, FAX (301)738-1026. **ED** K C Chartrand. **Ad Acc. Circ:** 1,400 (ctrl).

US/1044-0631
HAZARDOUS AND INDUSTRIAL WASTE. (HAZARDOUS AND INDUSTRIAL WASTE : PROCEEDINGS OF THE ... MID-ATLANTIC INDUSTRIAL WASTE CONFERENCE.). [Hazard. ind. waste]. **Added/Corp** Hazardous Materials Control Research Institute. **VFOAT** Hazardous and Industrial Wastes. 20th (1988)-. Proceedings. English. an. $85.00 (current issue). Technomic Publishing Company, Inc., 851 New Holland Avenue, Box 3535, Lancaster PA 17604. **Tel** (717)291-5609, (800)233-9936, FAX (717)295-4538. **LC** TD811.5; .M53a. **DD** 628.4/2. **CODEN** HIWAEB. Documents available from Article Express International, CASDDS. ***Continues*** *Mid-Atlantic Industrial Waste Conference. Toxic and Hazardous Waste, 0894-0290.*
Ind/Abst Chem. Abstr.; Ei Page One; Eng. Index Annu.

US/0890-5509
HAZARDOUS & SOLID WASTE MINIMIZATION & RECYCLING REPORT. **Added/Corp** Government Institutes. **VFOAT** Hazardous and Solid Waste Minimization and Recycling Report. (1986)-. Periodical. English. mo. $198.00. Government Institutes Inc., 4 Research Place, Suite 200, Rockville MD 20850. **Tel** (301)921-2300, 921-2355, FAX (301)251-0638. **DD** 363.

US/0163-9099
HAZARDOUS AND TOXIC SUBSTANCES. [Hazard. toxic subst.]. Vol. 1 (1978)-. Academic Scholarly Publication. English. ir. Price varies per volume. Marcel Dekker Inc., 270 Madison Avenue, New York NY 10016. **Tel** (212)696-9000, (800)228-1160, FAX (212)685-4540, telex 421419. **(Subscription address:** Marcel Dekker Inc, PO Box 5017, Monticello NY 12701.) **LC** UNC. **NLM** W1 HA984M. **CODEN** HTSUDP. Documents available from CASDDS.
Desc: Covers the various aspects of environmental pollution and toxicology. Topics include hazardous materials spills, the toxicity of heavy metals in the environment and more.
Ind/Abst Chem. Abstr. (1978-1979).

US
HAZARDOUS LOCATION EQUIPMENT DIRECTORY. **Added/Corp** Underwriters' Laboratories. (197?)-. Directory. English. an (June). $9.00. Underwriters Laboratories Inc., 333 Pfingsten Road, Northbrook IL 60062. **Tel** (708)272-8800 Ext.3542, FAX (708)272-8129, telex 6502543343. ***Continues*** *Hazardous Location Equipment List.*

US/0895-3260
HAZARDOUS MATERIALS CONTROL. [HMCRI's hazard. mat. control]. (1988)-. Periodical. English. bm. $29.00 (one year), $50.00 (two year). Hazardous Materials Control Research Institute, 7237 Hanover Pkwy., Greenbelt MD 20770. **Tel** (301)982-9500, FAX (301)220-3870. **NLM** W1; HM129. **CODEN** HMCOEF. Documents available from CASDDS, Documents on Demand.
Desc: Created to fill a major gap in literature, HMC has quickly become the foremost magazine devoted exclusively to hazardous materials and hazardous waste control.
Ind/Abst Ceram. Abstr.; Chem. Abstr.; Environ. Abstr.; Ind. Hyg. Dig.

US/1061-706X
HAZARDOUS MATERIALS CONTROL BUYER'S GUIDE AND SOURCE BOOK (SILVER SPRING, MD. 1991). (HAZARDOUS MATERIALS CONTROL BUYER'S GUIDE AND SOURCE BOOK.). [Hazard. mater. control buy. guide source book]. **Added/Corp** Hazardous Materials Control Research Institute. **VFOAT** HMC Buyer's Guide and Source Book; Hazardous Materials Control; HMC Buyer's Guide & Source Book. 6th Ed. (1991)-. English. Jackie Thomas, PO Box 2582, Salisbury MD 21802-2582. **LC** TD1040; .H36. **DD** 604.7/025/73. ***Continues*** *Hazardous Materials Control Directory.*

US/0272-9628
HAZARDOUS MATERIALS INTELLIGENCE REPORT. [Hazard. mater. intell. rep.]. **Added/Corp** World Information Systems. (1980)-. Periodical. English. wk. $375.00 (US); $445.00 (other). World Information Systems, PO Box 535 Harvard Square, Cambridge MA 02238. **Tel** (617)491-5100, FAX (617)492-3312. **ED** Richard S Golob. **DD** 363. **[CCC].** Index available. cum. index. **Ad Acc. Circ:** 1,300 (ctrl).
Desc: An international weekly newsletter that focuses on a wide range of hazardous materials and hazardous waste issues.

CN/1193-2074
HAZARDOUS MATERIALS MANAGEMENT. [Hazard. mater. manage.]. (1990)-. Periodical. English. bm. 39.50Can$ (one year), 65.00Can$ (two years) Canada; 59.50Can$ (one year), 85.00Can$ (two years) other. Canadian Hazardous Materials Management, 401 Richmond Street West #139, Toronto Ontario M5V 1X3 Canada. **Tel** (416)348-9922, (416)348-0403, FAX (416)348-9744. **ED** Guy Crittenden. **DD** 363.170971. **Ad Acc, Adv Mgr:** Arnie Gess. **Circ:** 18,000. Documents available from Documents on Demand. ***Continues*** *Hazardous Materials Management Magazine, 0843-9303.*
Desc: Contains Canadian industry an unparalleled information source on hazardous materials and waste management issues. The magazine encompasses all disciplines of environmental engineering including air, water, soil, sludge and solid waste management, with regular features on new regulations, personal protection, emergency response, and safe hazards removal, transport, treatment and disposal.
Ind/Abst Environ. Abstr.

US/0889-3454
HAZARDOUS MATERIALS NEWSLETTER (BARRE, VT.). (HAZARDOUS MATERIALS NEWSLETTER.). [Hazard. mater. newsl.]. (April 1980)-. Newsletter. English. bm (Feb., Apr., June, Aug., Oct., Dec.). $47.00 North America; $50.00 other. Hazardous Materials Newsletter, PO Box 204, Barre VT 05641. **Tel** (802)479-2307. **ED** John R. Cashman. **DD** 363. Index available (published separately). cum. index. **Ad Acc. Circ:** 695.
Desc: Response to and control of hazardous materials/waste incidents; planning, tactics, hazardous materials response teams, fire and chemical control, personal protective equipment, decontamination, evacuation, etc.

US/0197-3177
HAZARDOUS MATERIALS TRANSPORTATION (BOSTON). (HAZARDOUS MATERIALS TRANSPORTATION.). [Hazard. mater. transp.]. (197?)-. Periodical. English. bw (published every other Wednesday). $617.00 North America; $672.00 other. Washington Business Information Inc., 1117 North 19th Street, Suite 200, Arlington VA 22209. **Tel** (703)247-3433, (800)426-0416, FAX (703)247-3421. **ED** Robert Billings. **[CCC].**

UK/0964-962X
HAZARDOUS SUBSTANCES (SUDBURY). (HAZARDOUS SUBSTANCES.). [Hazard. subst. Sudbury]. (1990)-. Periodical. English. mo. £132.00 UK and Northern Ireland; £154.00 other. Monitor Press, Rectory Road, Great Waldingfield, Sudbury Suffolk CO10 0TL United Kingdom. **Tel** 011 44 787 378607. **DD** 363.17.

US/0882-5696
HAZARDOUS WASTE & HAZARDOUS MATERIALS. [Hazard. waste hazard. mater.]. **Added/Corp** Hazardous Materials Control Research Institute. **VFOAT** Hazardous Waste and Hazardous Materials. Vol. 2, No. 1 (Spring 1985)-. Academic Scholarly Publication. English. qt. $166.00. Mary Ann Liebert Inc., 1651 Third Avenue, New York NY 10128. **Tel** (212)289-2300, (800)M-LIEBERT, FAX (212)289-4697. **ED** James Noble. **LC** TD811.5; .H3957. **DD** 628.5. **NLM** W1; HA99M. **CODEN** HWHME2. Documents available from The Genuine Article, BIOSIS Document Express, CASDDS, Documents on Demand. ***Continues*** *Hazardous Waste, 0738-6168.*
Desc: Information on technology, health and environmental effects, and public policy for hazardous waste and related hazardous materials. Published for a professional readership with the aim of bringing together the contributions of several disciplines which support this field of study.
Ind/Abst Appl. Sci. Technol. Index (1991-); Biodeter. Abstr. (1991-); Biol. Abstr. (1988-); Chem. Abstr. (1985-); Chem. Hazards Ind.; Curr. Aware. Biol. Sci., CABS; Curr. Contents, Agric. Biol. Environ. Sci.; Curr. Contents Eng. Tech. Appl. Sci.; EMBASE; Environ. Abstr.; GeoRef; Health Saf. Sci. Abstr.; Ind. Hyg. Dig.; Lab. Hazards Bull.; Pollut. Abstr. Indexes (1985-); Res. Alert [Select. Cov.]; Risk Abstr.; SCISEARCH; Soc. Sci. Cit. Index [Select. Cov.]; Soils Fert.; Weed Abstr.

US/1057-0012
HAZARDOUS WASTE & HAZARDOUS MATERIALS TRANSPORT DIRECTORY, THE. ***Title Change.*** [Hazard. waste hazard. mater. transp. dir.]. **VFOAT** Hazardous Waste and Hazardous Materials Transport Directory. (1992)-(1992). Directory. English. K III Press Inc., 424 West 33rd Street, New York NY 10001. **Tel** (212)714-3100, (800)221-5488. **LC** HD9975.U5; H38. **DD** 363.17/029/473. ***Continued by*** *Hazardous Waste & Materials Management Directory.*

US
HAZARDOUS WASTE & MATERIALS MANAGEMENT DIRECTORY, THE. **VFOAT** Hazardous Waste and Materials Management Directory. (1993)-. Directory. English. an. $157.00 US, Canada, and Mexico; $163.00 other. K III Press Inc., 424 West 33rd Street, New York NY 10001. **Tel** (212)714-3100, (800)221-5488. **LC** HD9975.U5; H38. **DD** 363.17/029/473. ***Continues*** *Hazardous Waste & Hazardous Materials Transport Directory, 1057-0012.*

US/0897-2699
HAZARDOUS WASTE BUSINESS. [Hazard. waste bus.]. **VFOAT** Hazardouswastebusiness. (19??)-. Newsletter. English. bw. $795.00 US and Canada; $820.00 other. McGraw Hill Publishing Company, Inc., 1221 Avenue of the Americas, New York NY 10020. **Tel** (212)512-6410, (800)525-5003, FAX (212)512-6111. **DD** 363. available on an online database (file 624/Full-Text) from DIALOG.

US/1055-5099
HAZARDOUS WASTE CASE LAW UPDATE. [Hazard. waste case law update]. **VFOAT** Hazardous Waste. (1990)-. Periodical. English. mo. $427.00. Spencer-Logan Publications, PO Box 1082, Silver Spring MD 20910-1082. **DD** 344.

US/0738-0232
HAZARDOUS WASTE CONSULTANT, THE. (THE HAZARDOUS WASTE CONSULTANT : A BIMONTHLY PUBLICATION OF MCCOY & ASSOCIATES.). [Hazard. waste consult.]. **Added/Corp** McCoy & Associates. Vol. 1, No. 1 (July 1983)-. Academic Scholarly Publication. English. Seven times a year (1 volume). $620.00 US; $694.00 other. Elsevier Science Publishing Company Inc, Madison Square Station, PO Box 882, New York NY 10159-0882. **Tel** (212)633-3950, FAX (212)633-3990. **ED** Lark H McCoy. **LC** TD811.5; .H396. **DD** 363.7/28. **[CCC].** Index available. cum. index.
Desc: Technical, regulatory and legal issues pertaining to hazardous wastes. The authors are engineers writing for a scientific readership.

US/1044-5080
HAZARDOUS WASTE DRIVER SAFETY MANUAL, THE. [Hazard. waste driv. saf. man.]. **Added/Corp** Chemical Waste Transportation Institute. National Solid Wastes Management Association. (June 1989)-. English. an. National Solid Wastes Management, 1730 Rhode Island Avenue NW/Suite 1000, Washington DC 20036. **Tel** (202)861-0708. **DD** 604.

US/0275-0244
HAZARDOUS WASTE LITIGATION REPORTER. **See** Law-Environmental Law.

US/1055-3495
HAZARDOUS WASTE MANAGEMENT & BUSINESS OPPORTUNITIES NEWSLETTER / CAE CONSULTANTS INC. [Hazard. waste manage. bus. oppor. newsl.]. **Added/Corp** CAE Consultants, Inc. **VFOAT** Hazardous Waste; Hazardous Waste Management and Business Opportunities Newsletter; Hazardous Waste Management & Business Opportunities. (Feb. 15, 1991)-. Newsletter. English. sm. $360.00 (corporations), $120.00 (educational institutions and libraries). Cae Consultants, Inc., 41 Tavers Avenue, Yonkers NY 10705. **DD** 363.

CN/0711-7140
HAZARDOUS WASTE MANAGEMENT HANDBOOK. [Hazard. waste manage. handb.]. **Added/Corp** Corpus Information Services. **VFOAT** Eco/Log Hazardous Waste Management Handbook. (1982)-. English. be. 177.00Can$. Southam Information and Technology Group Inc., 1450 Don Mills Road, Don Mills Ontario M3B 2X7 Canada. **Tel** (416)445-6641, (800)668-2374, FAX (416)442-2261. **ED** Patrick Folkes and Deborah Orchard. **DD** 363.7/28/0971. **Circ:** 1,000.
Desc: Covers hazardous waste management programs, policies, and practices in Canada. Full federal/provincial coverage. Topics include classification, transportation, treatment, disposal, institutional wastes, handling and spill cleanup.

US/0743-7331
HAZARDOUS WASTE MANAGEMENT IN MASSACHUSETTS. English. an. Bureau of Solid Waste Disposal, Massachusetts Department of Environmental Management, Boston MA. **LC** TD811.5; .H3998. **DD** 363.7/28.

US/0275-374X
HAZARDOUS WASTE NEWS. [Hazard. waste news]. Vol. 3, No. 7 (Feb. 16, 1981)-. Periodical. English. wk. $570.00. Business Publishers Inc., 951 Pershing Drive, Silver Spring MD 20910-4464. **Tel** (301)587-6300, (800)274-0122, FAX (301)585-9075. **[CCC].** available on an online database (file 636/Full-Text) from DIALOG. ***Continues in part*** *Hazardous Waste News including Nuclear Waste Bulletin, 0275-374X;* ***Absorbed*** *Hazardous Waste Report.*
Desc: Plugs you into new opportunities for research grants, service contracts, and equipment sales throughout the country.
Ind/Abst PTS Newsl. Database [Full Txt.].

●US/1074-1291
HAZARDOUS WASTE UPDATE SERVICE, THE. (1994)-. Academic Scholarly Publication. English. Twelve times a year (1 volume). $475.00 US; $525.00 other. Elsevier Science Publishing Company Inc, Madison Square Station, PO Box 882, New York NY 10159-0882. **Tel** (212)633-3950, FAX (212)633-3990. ***Continues*** *McCoy's Hazardous Waste Regulatory Update Service.*

US/1054-7142
HAZMAT NEWS. (HAZMAT NEWS : THE AUTHORITATIVE NEWS RESOURCE FOR HAZARDOUS CONTROL AND WASTE MANAGEMENT.). [Hazmat news]. (1990)-. Periodical.

English. sm. $388.50 US; $431.50 Canada; $402.50 Mexico; $422.50 other. Stevens Publishing Corporation, 225 North New Road, Waco TX 76702-2604. **Tel** (800)727-7573, (817)776-9000. **(Subscription address:** Stevens Publishing Corp., PO Box 2573, Waco TX 76702.) **DD** 363.

US
HAZMAT TRANSPORT NEWS. (19??)-. English. bw (26 issues). $429.00. Business Publishers Inc., 951 Pershing Drive, Silver Spring MD 20910-4464. **Tel** (301)587-6300, (800)274-0122, FAX (301)585-9075. available on an online database (file 636/Full-Text) from DIALOG. ***Continues*** *Toxic Materials Transport.*
Ind/Abst PTS Newsl. Database [Full Txt.].

US/0898-5685
HAZMAT WORLD. ***Title Change.*** [HazMat world]. **VFOAT** Haz Mat World; Hazardous Materials World. (Aug. 1988)-Vol. 7, No. 5 (May 1994). Periodical. English. mo. Advanstar Communications Inc., 131 West First Street, Duluth MN 55802. **Tel** (218)723-9477, (800)346-0085. **ED** Jim Bishop. **LC** TD1060; .H39. **DD** 628.4/2. **CODEN** HMWOED. **[CCC]. Bk Rev. Ad Acc. Circ:** 33,400 (ctrl). Documents available from Documents on Demand. ***Continued by*** *Environmental Solutions, 1077-2537.*
Desc: Targets individuals who specify and purchase products, systems, equipment and services used for hazardous materials and waste management.
Ind/Abst BioBusiness (1990-); Environ. Abstr.

US/1051-3221
HAZTECH NEWS. (HAZTECH NEWS: THE NEWSLETTER OF HAZARDOUS WASTE TREATMENT TECHNOLOGY.). [HazTECH news]. (1986)-. Periodical. English. bw (one issue in Dec.). $360.00 US, Canada, and Mexico; $375.00 other. HazTECH News, 14120 Huckleberry Lane, Silver Spring MD 20906. **Tel** (301)871-3289. **DD** 628. **CODEN** HTNEEL.
Desc: Examines the technology from across the country to help you find the systems that are most appropriate to your storage, treatment and disposal requirements. Each issue features articles on a variety of waste technologies, many of which you could utilize.

SZ/0259-7268
HEALTH AND SAFETY GUIDE. (HEALTH AND SAFETY GUIDE / IPCS.). [Health saf. guide]. **Added/Corp** International Program on Chemical Safety. World Health Organization. No. 12 (1988)-. Monographic series. English. ir. Price varies per volume. World Health Organization, Distribution and Sales, 20 Avenue Appia, CH-1211 Geneva 27 Switzerland. **Tel** 011 41 22 7912111, FAX 011 41 22 7880401. **LC** RA1190; .H4. **DD** 615.9/005. **NLM** W1; HE264GG.
Ind/Abst Biodeter. Abstr.

US
HIGH LEVEL RADIOACTIVE WASTE NEWSLETTER / NATIONAL CONFERENCE OF STATE LEGISLATORS. Added/Corp National Conference of State Legislators. (198?)-. Periodical. English. bm (6 issues). Free on request. National Conference of State Legislatures, 1560 Broadway, Suite 700, Denver CO 80202. **Tel** (303)830-2054, FAX (303)863-8003.

JA/0389-0082
HIROSHIMA-KEN KANKYO SENTA KENKYU HOKOKU. [Hiroshima-ken Kankyo Senta kenkyu hokoku]. **VFOAT** Bulletin of Hiroshima Prefectural Research Center for Environmental Sciences. No. 1-. Academic Scholarly Publication. Japanese (summaries and/or abstracts in English). Hiroshima-Ken Kankyo Senta, 6-29 Minamimachi 1-chome, Hiroshima-shi 734 Japan. **LC** TD187.5.J32; H576. **CODEN** HIHODB. Documents available from CASDDS.
Ind/Abst Chem. Abstr.

US
HMC&M, HAZARDOUS MATERIAL CONTROL & MANAGEMENT [COMPUTER FILE] : HMIS, HAZARDOUS MATERIALS INFORMATION SYSTEM. Added/Corp United Sttes. Dept. of Defense. **VFOAT** Hazardous Material Control & Management; HMIS; Hazardous Materials Information System; HMC&M/HMIS CD-ROM System. (19??)-. Periodical. English. qt. US Department of Defense, The Pentagon, Washington DC 20301. **Tel** (703)545-6700.

US
HMC&M [COMPUTER FILE] : HAZARDOUS MATERIAL CONTROL & MANAGEMENT ; HMIS : HAZARDOUS MATERIAL INFORMATION SYSTEM / DEPT. OF DEFENSE. Added/Corp United States. Dept. of Defense. United States. Navy. Supply Corps. Defense General Supply Center (U.S.). **VFOAT** HMC and M; Hazardous Material Control & Management; Hazardous Material Control and Management; HMIS; Hazardous Material Information System. (Aug. 1991)-. Government Publication. English. qt. $155.00 US; $193.75 other. Superintendent of Documents, US Government Printing Office, Washington DC 20402. **Tel** (202)275-3328, FAX (202)786-2377. **ED** Commanding Officer, NCTAMS Lant, 9456 Fourth Avenue, Suite 215, Norfolk, VA 23511-2199; Telephone: (804)445-9192. **LC** T55.3.H3. ctrl circ. ***Continues*** *DoD Hazardous Materials Information System (CD-ROM).*
Desc: System requirements: IBM PC, XT, AT or compatible with 500K; MS-DOS 3.1 or higher; CD-ROM drive; MS-DOS CD-ROM extensions 2.0 or higher capable of reading ISO 9660 format; hard disk; graphics board.

CH
HUAN CHING KO HSUEH TSA CHIH. VFOAT Huan Ching Ko Hsueh; Environmental Sciences. V. 1-. Periodical. Chinese. ir. $160.00. Tung Hai Ta Hsuen Huan Ching Ko Hsuen Yen Chiu Chung Hsin, PO Box 915, Taichung Shih Taiwan. **LC** TD4; .H795. **DD** 620.8/05.
Ind/Abst NAPRALERT.

CC/0253-9705
HUANJING BAOHU (BEIJING). (HUAN CHING PAO HU.). [Huanjing baohu]. **Added/Corp** Pei-Ching Shih Huan Ching Pao Hu Ko Hsueh Yen Chiu So. **VFOAT** Huanjing Baohu. (19??)-. Periodical. Chinese. bm. RMBY0.25. Jogging International, 24 rue du Surmelin, 75020 Paris France. **Tel** 011 33 1 40300046. **LC** TD169; .H83. **DD** 363.7/005. **CODEN** HCPHDM. Documents available from CASDDS.
Ind/Abst Chem. Abstr.

CC/1001-3865
HUANJING WURAN YU FANGZHI. (HUAN CHING WU JAN YU FANG CHIH.). [Huanjing wuran yu fangzhi]. **VFOAT** Environmental Pollution & Control; Environmental Pollution and Control. (197?)-. Periodical. Chinese. bm. Zhejiang Huanjing Baohu Kexue Yanjiusuo / Zhejiang Institute of Environmental Protection, 43 Tianmushan lu, Hangzhou, Zhejiang 310007, People's Republic of China. **Tel** 882847. **ED** W. Shizhen. **CODEN** HWYFEW. Documents available from CASDDS, BLDSC, CASDDS.
Ind/Abst Chem. Abstr.

KO
HWANGYONG KWA KONGHAE. VFOAT The Environment and Pollution; Environment and Pollution. Periodical. Korean (Korean). mo. Hyondae Hwangyong Kwalliso, 991-2 Taerim-dong Yongdungpo-ku, Seoul Korea. **LC** TD172; .H94.
Ind/Abst Energy Res. Abstr. (Oct. 1981-).

KO
HWANGYONG POJON. VFOAT Journal of the Korea Environmental Preservation Association. Periodical. Korean (summaries and/or abstracts in English). Hwangyong Pojon Hyophoe, 111 Sogong-dong Chung-ku, Seoul Korea. **LC** TD187.5.K6; H89 .

KO
HWANGYONG YONGU. Added/Corp Souldae Hwangyong Taehagwon. Wonuhoe. **VFOAT** Environmental Studies. (19??)-. Periodical. English (Korean). an. Not for sale. Soul Taehakkyo Hwangyong, Taehagwon Wonuhoe San 156-1 Sillim-dong, Kwanak-ku Seoul Korea. **LC** HC470.E5; H83.

JA/0385-9290
HYOGO-KEN KOGAI KENKYUJO KENKYU HOKOKU. (HYOGO-KEN KOGAI KENKYUSHO KENKYU HOKOKU. REPORT OF THE ENVIRONMENTAL SCIENCE INSTITUTE OF HYOGO PREFECTURE.). [Hyogo-ken Kogai Kenkyujo kenkyu hokoku]. **Added/Corp** Hyogo-Ken Kogai Kenkyusho. **VFOAT** Report of the Environmental Science Institute of Hyogo Prefecture. (1970)-. Japanese (summaries and/or abstracts in English). **NLM** W1 HY837K. **CODEN** HKKHDJ. Documents available from CASDDS.
Ind/Abst Chem. Abstr.

IT/0394-5871
IA. INGEGNERIA AMBIENTALE. [IA, Ing. ambient.]. (1987)-. Periodical. Italian. Nine times a year. L105000.00 Italy; L200000.00 other. Centro Ingegneria Prot Ambient, Via Andrea Palladio 26, 20135 Milan Italy. **Tel** 011 39 2 58301528, FAX +39 2 58301550. **UDC** 628. Index available. cum. index. **Bk Rev. Ad Acc. Pr Rev. Circ:** 2,000. Documents available from CASDDS. ***Continues*** *Ingegneria Ambientale Inquinamento e Depurazione, 0302-7775.*
Desc: Environmental engineering and sanitary engineering.
Ind/Abst Chem. Abstr.; Pollut. Abstr. Indexes.

CN/0226-2460
IAO INSPECTOR. (THE IAO INSPECTOR.). [IAO insp.]. **Added/Corp** Insurers' Advisory Organization of Canada. Insurer's Advisory Organization of Canada. Loss Control Engineering Dept. **VFOAT** Inspecteur du GTA. **VAT** Insurers' Advisory Organization Inspector; Inspecteur du Groupement Technique des Asseurers du Canada. Vol. 11, No. 2 (Summer 1974)-(19??). Periodical. English (French). qt. Free. Insurers' Advisory Organization of Canada, 180 Dundas Street West, Toronto Ontario M5G 1Z9 Canada. **DD** 628.9/22. ***Continues*** *CUA Inspector, 0821-7149.* ***Continued in part by*** *Inspecteur du GTA. (French).*

JA
IBARAKI-KEN KOGAI GIJUTSU SENTA NEMPO. Main/Corp Ibaraki-Ken Kogai Gijutsu Senta. **Added/Corp** Ibaraki-Ken Kogai Gijutsu Senta. Annual Report of the Environmental Pollution Research Center of Ibaraki-Ken. **VFOAT** Annual Report of the Environmental Pollution Research Center of Ibaraki-Ken. (19??)-. Japanese. an. Ibarakiken Kogai Gijutsu Senta, (Environmental Pollution Research Center of Ibarakiken), 4043-36, Ishikawa 1 Chome, Mitoshi, Ibarakiken 310 Japan. **LC** TD187.5.J32; I36a. **CODEN** IKGNDS. Documents available from CASDDS.
Ind/Abst Chem. Abstr.

JA
IBARAKI-KEN NI OKERU HOSHANO CHOSA. Main/Corp Ibarnki-Ken Kogai Gijutsu Senta. Japanese. Ibaraki-ken Kogai Gijutsu Senta, 4043 Ishikawa 1-chome 310, Mita Japan. **LC** TD196.R3; I2A.

NE/0920-8771
ILEIA NEWSLETTER. **See** Agriculture-Crop Production and Soil.

US
IMPLEMENTATION OF LITTLE BLUE RIVER BASIN WATER QUALITY MANAGEMENT PLAN. Main/Corp Nebraska. Natural Resources Commission. 1976/77-. English. be. Nebraska Natural Resources Commission, PO Box 94876, Cent. Mall South, Lincoln NE 68509. **Tel** (402)471-2081. **LC** TD225.L627; N4A. **DD** 363.7/39456/097823.

US/0190-2458
IN BUSINESS. [In bus.]. (1979)-. Periodical. English. bm. $29.00 (one year), $49.00 (two year). The JG Press Inc, 419 State Avenue, Emmaus PA 18049. **Tel** (215)967-4135. **ED** Jerome Goldstein. **LC** HF5001; .I35. **DD** 658/.022/05. **CODEN** INBSD5. **[CCC].** Index available. **Bk Rev. Ad Acc. Circ:** 65,000. available on microfilm and microfiche from University Microfilms International (UMI). Documents available from UMI Article Clearinghouse, Ask*IEEE, UMI Article Clearinghouse.
Desc: Covers environmental entrepreneuring.
Ind/Abst ABI/INFORM Glob. Ed.; ABI Inform Ondisc (Nov. 1980-Aug. 1981); Bus. Index (1979-?); Environ. Period. Bibliogr.; INSPEC (Sept.-Oct. 1982-); Person. Manage. Abstr.

UK
INDEX OF CURRENT GOVERNMENT AND GOVERNMENTAL-SUPPORTED RESEARCH IN ENVIRONMENTAL POLLUTION IN GREAT BRITAIN. English. Department of the Environment / England, 2 Marsham Street, London SW1P 3EB England. **LC** TD178.7.G7; I52. **DD** 363.6.

II
INDIAN ASSOCIATION FOR WATER POLLUTION CONTROL NEWSLETTER - IAWPC. VFOAT IAWPC Newsletter. Newsletter. English. mo. Indian Association for Water Pollution Control (IAWPC), Nehru Marg C O Neeri, Nagpur 440020 Maharastra India. **LC** TD187.5.I4; I52. **DD** 363.7/394/0954.
Ind/Abst Pollut. Abstr. Indexes.

US/0160-6662
INDIVIDUAL ONSITE WASTEWATER SYSTEMS. [Individ. onsite wastewater syst.]. **Main/Conf** National Conference on Individual Onsite Wastewater Systems. **Added/Corp** National Sanitation Foundation (U.S.) Technology Transfer Program (U.S.). (1974)-. English. an. Ann Arbor Science Publishers Inc, PO Box 1425, Ann Arbor MA 48106. **LC** TD523; .N27a. **DD** 628/.74. **CODEN** IOWSDF. Documents available from CASDDS.
Ind/Abst Chem. Abstr.; GeoRef.

DK/0905-6947
INDOOR AIR. [Indoor air]. **Added/Corp** International Society of Indoor Air Quality and Climate. Vol. 1, No. 1 (Mar. 1991)-. Periodical. English. qt. kr1130.00 US, Canada and Japan; kr1110.00 other. Munksgaard International Publishers Ltd, PO Box 2148, DK-1016 Copenhagen K Denmark. **Tel** 011 45 33 12 70 30, FAX 011 45 33 12 93 87, telex 19431 MUNKS DK. **ED** David Grimsrud. **NLM** W1; IN358D. **CODEN** INAIE5. **Ad Acc. Pr Rev. Circ:** 600.

US/0896-8594
INDOOR POLLUTION NEWS. [Indoor pollut. news]. Vol. 1, No. 1 (Jan. 28, 1988)-. Periodical. English. bw (26 issues). $507.00. Business Publishers Inc., 951 Pershing Drive, Silver Spring MD 20910-4464. **Tel** (301)587-6300, (800)274-0122, FAX (301)585-9075. **ED** Richard Hagan. **DD** 363. **CODEN** IPONE2. **[CCC].**
Desc: Provides information on problems with air quality in buildings (including radon, formaldehyde, solvents and asbestos), and on other pollution, such as lead in pipes and technical developments.
Ind/Abst BioBusiness (1991-).

UK/0961-4710
INDUSTRIAL WASTE MANAGEMENT. [Ind. waste manag.]. (1990)-. Periodical. English. mo. £45.00 UK; £61.00 other. Faversham House Group Ltd, 111 St. James Road, Croydon, Surrey CR9 2TH England. **Tel** 011 44 81 6844082, , FAX 011 44 81 6849729, telex 266332 HET. **DD** 363.728.

US/0046-9262
INDUSTRIAL WASTES. ***Ceased.*** [Ind. wastes]. (1971)-Ceased Vol. 29, No. 6 (Dec. 1983). Periodical. English. bm. Scranton Gillette Communications Inc, 380 NW Highway, Des Plaines IL 60016. **LC** TD896. **DD** 628.4. **CODEN** INWABK. Documents available from CASDDS.
Ind/Abst Appl. Sci. Technol. Index; Bioeng. Abstr.; Chem. Abstr. (1969-1983); Coal Abstr.; EMBASE; Energy Res. Abstr. (Sept 1985); INIS Atomindex [Micro.].

●US/1067-5337
INDUSTRIAL WASTEWATER. **See** Water Resources.

GW/0073-7755
INDUSTRIEABWASSER. (1958)-. Academic Scholarly Publication. German. an. Deutscher Kommunal Verlag, Roseggerstrasse 5 A, Dusseldorf Germany. Documents available from CASDDS.
Ind/Abst Chem. Abstr.

US
INFECTIOUS WASTES NEWS. English. bw. $320.00 (US & Canada); $400.00 (other). National Solid Wastes Management, 1730 Rhode Island Avenue NW/Suite 1000, Washington DC 20036. **Tel** (202)861-0708.
Ind/Abst Pollut. Abstr. Indexes.

FR/0012-9003
INFORMATION EAUX. **See** Water Resources.

IT/0001-4982
INQUINAMENTO. [Inquinamento]. Vol. 12, No. 1 (Mar. 1970)-. Academic Scholarly Publication. Italian (summaries and/or abstracts in English). mo (July/Aug iss. combined). L120000.00 Italy; L180000.00 other. Etas SRL, Via Mecenate 89, 20138 Milan Italy. **Tel** 011 39 2 580841. **LC** TD204; .A23. **CODEN** IQAAAW. Index available (free). **Ad Acc**. Documents available from CASDDS. ***Continues*** *Acqua Industriale Inquinamento, 0567-7149.*
Desc: Reports on new problems and developments in the fields of water, air, soil, garbage, noise and energy pollution. Includes articles on research, technology, products, legislation and the economic aspects of pollution problems and their solution.
Ind/Abst AGRICOLA; Chem. Abstr.; Coal Abstr.; GeoRef; Int. Aerosp. Abstr.

CN/0382-8174
INSIDE CANADA. V. 1- 1970-. English. an. Metroland Printing Publishing & Distributing, 3145 Wolfedale Road, Mississauga, Ontario L5C 3A9 Canada. **Tel** (416)273-5680, FAX (416)273-4991. **ED** B Vass.

CN/0226-2452
INSPECTEUR DE GTA (1975). (L'INSPECTEUR DU GTA.). [Insp. GTA]. **VAT** Inspecteur de Groupement Technique des Assureurs du Canada (1975). Periodical. English (French). qt. Free. Insurers Advisory Organization of Canada, 180 Dundas Street West, Toronto Ontario M5G 1Z9 Canada. **DD** 628.9/22. ***Separated from*** *IAO Inspector, 0226-2460.*

US/1049-1562
INTEGRATED WASTE MANAGEMENT. [Integr. waste manage.]. (January 24, 1990)-. Newsletter. English. bw. $845.00 US and Canada; $870.00 other. McGraw Hill Publishing Company, Inc., 1221 Avenue of the Americas, New York NY 10020. **Tel** (212)512-6410, (800)525-5003, FAX (212)512-6111. **DD** 604. **CODEN** IWMAE2. available on an online database (file 624/Full-Text) from DIALOG. ***Continues*** *Waste-to-Energy Report, 0884-3317.*

US/0161-0120
INTERFACE (SOCIETY FOR ENVIRONMENTAL GEOCHEMISTRY AND HEALTH). (INTERFACE.). [Interface]. Academic Scholarly Publication. English. sa. $25.00. Interface/SEGH, c/o Betsy T Kagey MSPH, Empire State College, 17 South Street, Glens Falls NY 12801. **ED** Betsy T Kagey and Brian Davies. **CODEN** ITFCBH. **Bk Rev. Circ:** 300. Documents available from CASDDS.
Desc: Newsletter servicing the members of the Society for Environmental Geochemistry and Health. Membership news, book reviews, current questions and issues as well as calendar of events of interest to membership.
Ind/Abst Chem. Abstr.; GeoRef.

US/0893-8776
INTERNATIONAL WATER REPORT. [Int. water rep.]. **Added/Corp** Water Information Center, Inc. **VFOAT** WIC International Water Report. (1977). Periodical. English. qt. $37.00 US and Canada; $47.00 other. Water Information Center Inc, 1099 18th Street, Suite 2150, Denver CO 80202. **Tel** (303)391-8799. **ED** Judith Schoeck and Maureen Portland. **DD** 628. **[CCC]**. **Bk Rev**.
Desc: Water supply and treatment, pollution and waste control, legislation, new products, research and developments.

US/0092-9158
INVENTORY OF WASTE WATER PRODUCTION AND WASTE WATER RECLAMATION PRACTICES IN CALIFORNIA. **Main/Corp** California. Dept. of Water Resources. English. an. $1.50. Department of Water Resources / California, PO Box 942836, Sacramento CA 94236-0001. **Tel** (916)445-3553. **LC** TD524.C2; C28A. **DD** 333.9/1/009794.

UK
INVESTIGATION OF AIR POLLUTION; NATIONAL SURVEY, SMOKE AND SULPHUR DIOXIDE, THE. **Main/Corp** Warren Spring Laboratory (Stevenage, England). **Added/Corp** Warren Spring Laboratory (Stevenage, England). National Survey, Smoke and Sulphur Dioxide. **VFOAT** National Survey, Smoke and Sulphur Dioxide. (19??)-. English. Warren Spring Library, PO Box 20, Gunnels Wood Road, Hartfordshire SG1 2BX England. **LC** TD883.7.G7; S825a. **DD** 628.5/3.

US
IOWA AIR QUALITY REPORT UPDATE WITH ... AIR MONITORING DATA. **Added/Corp** Iowa. Environmental Protection Division. (198?)-. English. Program Development Division, Iowa Department of Water Air and Waste Management, Henry A Wallace Building, 900 East Grand Avenue, Des Moines IA 50319. ***Continues*** *Annual Air Quality Report (Des Moines, Iowa), 0882-7796.*

US
IRC BULLETIN / UNITED STATES ENVIRONMENT PROTECTION AGENCY, NATIONAL TRAINING AND OPERATIONAL TECHNOLOGY CENTER. ***Ceased.*** **See** Water Resources.

SZ/0253-4606
IRCWD NEWS. [IRCWD news]. **VFOAT** International Reference Center for Wastes Disposal News. (19??)-. Periodical. English. Free on request. IRCWD International Reference Center for Waste Disposal, Uberlandstr 133, CH 8600 Duebendorf Switzerland. **Tel** 011 41 1 8235286, FAX 011 41 1 8235399, telex 828687. **ED** Brigitte Hauser. **UDC** 551.49.

SZ/0250-4227
IRPTC BULLETIN. [IRPTC bull.]. **Added/Corp** International Register of Potentially Toxic Chemicals (United Nations). **VAT** International Register of Potentially Toxic Chemicals Bulletin. Vol. 1, No. 1 (Jan. 1979)-. Government Publication. English. sa. $20.00. United Nations Publications, 2 United Nations Plaza, Room DC2 0853, Department 007C, New York NY 10017. **Tel** (212)963-8303, (800)253-9646. **NLM** W1; IR578F. cum. index. Documents available from Documents on Demand.
Desc: Provides general information on new or proposed legislation and regulations for the control of chemical materials in environmental situations.
Ind/Abst Chem. Hazards Ind.; Environ. Abstr.; Lab. Hazards Bull.; Life Sci. Collect.; Trop. Dis. Bull.

SW/0347-8696
IVL. B. (INSTITUTET FOR VATTEN- OCH LUFTVARDS FORSKNING. B : IVL : PUBLIKATION.). **VFOAT** IVL. B. Academic Scholarly Publication. Swedish (English). ir. Price varies per volume. IVL Box 21060, 100 31 Stockholm Sweden. **Tel** 08 24 96 80, FAX 08 31 85 16. **CODEN** IVLBDQ. ctrl circ. Documents available from CASDDS.
Ind/Abst Chem. Abstr.

GW
JAHRESBERICHT DER HAUPTABTEILUNG STADTENTWASSERUNG. **Main/Corp** Hamburg. Amt. fur Ingineurwesen 3. Hauptabteilung Stadtentwasser. (19??)-. German. an. **LC** TD574.H35; H35a. **DD** 628/.3/0943.

YU
JAVNI VODOVOD I KANALIZACIJA U NASELJIMA SR SRBIJE. **See** Water Resources.

●II
JOURNAL OF ECOTOXICOLOGY & ENVIRONMENTAL MONITORING : INTERNATIONAL JOURNAL FOR SCIENTIFIC RESEARCH ON TOXICOLOGY AND POLLUTIONS. **VFOAT** Journal of Ecotoxicology and Environmental Monitoring; International Journal for Scientific Research on Toxicology and Pollutions. Vol. 1, No. 1 (Jan. 1991)-. Periodical. English. qt. $110.00. Palani Paramount Publications, 69D, Anna Nagar, Palani 624502, India. **(Subscription address:** Prints India, 11 Darya Ganj, New Delhi 110002 India.**)** **LC** IN PROCESS.
Ind/Abst Pollut. Abstr. Indexes; Risk Abstr.

II/0254-8704
JOURNAL OF ENVIRONMENTAL BIOLOGY. [J. environ. biol.]. **Added/Corp** Academy of Environmental Biology, India. Vol. 1 (1980)-. Academic Scholarly Publication. English. qt. $125.00. Journal of Environmental Biology, 567/5, Civil Lines South, Muzaffarnagar 251 001 India. **Tel** (01312)25306. **(Subscription address:** Prints India, 11 Darya Ganj, New Delhi 110002 India.**)** **ED** R C Dalela. **NLM** W1 JO644AP. **CODEN** JEBIDP. Index available. cum. index. **Bk Rev. Ad Acc. Pr Rev. Circ:** 5,000. Documents available from The Genuine Article, BIOSIS Document Express, CASDDS, Documents on Demand.
Desc: Publishes original research dealing with all aspects of environmental pollution and toxicology.
Ind/Abst Anim. Behav. Abstr.; Biodeter. Abstr. (19??-19??); Biol. Abstr. (1986-); Chem. Abstr.; Crop Physiol. Abstr.; CSA Neuro. Abstr. (?-?); Curr. Aware. Biol. Sci., CABS; Curr. Contents, Agric. Biol. Environ. Sci.; Curr. Ref. Fish Res.; Dairy Sci. Abstr.; Ecol. Abstr.; Ecology Abstr.; EMBASE; Energy Inf. Abstr.; Entomol. Abstr.; Environ. Abstr.; Field Crop Abstr.; Geogr. Abstr. Phys. Geogr.; Geol. Abstr.; Health Saf. Sci. Abstr.; Helminthol. Abstr.; Hortic. Abstr.; Indian Sci. Abstr.; Leadscan; Nematol. Abstr.; Nutr. Abstr. Rev., Ser. B, Live Feeds and Feed.; Life Sci. Collect.; Plant Grow. Reg. Abstr.; Pollut. Abstr. Indexes; Postharvest News Inf.; Res. Alert [Select. Cov.]; Rev. Med. Vet. Entomol.; Rev. Med. Vet. Mycology; SCISEARCH; Seed Abstr.; Soils Fert.; Toxicol. Abstr.; Weed Abstr.

US/0095-0696
JOURNAL OF ENVIRONMENTAL ECONOMICS AND MANAGEMENT. **See** Economics.

US/0733-9372
JOURNAL OF ENVIRONMENTAL ENGINEERING (NEW YORK N.Y.). (JOURNAL OF ENVIRONMENTAL ENGINEERING.). [J. environ. eng.]. **Added/Corp** American Society of Civil Engineers. Environmental Engineering Division. **VFOAT** A.S.C.E. Environmental Engineering; ASCE Environmental Engineering. Vol. 109, No. 1 (Feb. 1983)-. Academic Scholarly Publication. English. mo. $212.00 (nonmember) US; $240.00 (nonmember) other. American Society of Civil Engineers / ASCE, 345 East 47th Street, New York NY 10017-2398. **Tel** (212)705-7179, FAX (212)705-7300, telex 422847 ASCE UI. **(Subscription address:** American Society of Civil Engineers, Publisher Fulfillment Agency, Box 828, Somerset NJ 08875.**)** **LC** TD1; .A32. **DD** 628/.05. **CODEN** JOEEDU. **[CCC]**. Index available. cum. index. **Bk Rev. Ad Acc. Pr Rev. Circ:** 5,200 (ctrl). available on microfilm and microfiche from University Microfilms International (UMI); available on CD-ROM from American Society of Civil Engineers. Documents available from Article Express International, The Genuine Article, CASDDS. ***Continues*** *American Society of Civil Engineers. Environmental Engineering Division. Journal of the Environmental Engineering Division, 0090-3914.*
Desc: Concerned with provision of safe, ample water supply, proper disposal and/or recycling of wastewater and solid wastes and all areas of sanitation and pollution.
Ind/Abst Abstr. Bull. Inst. Pap. Sci. Tech.; Abstr. J. Earthq. Eng.; Acoust. Abstr.; AgBiotech News Inf.; AGRICOLA [Select. Cov.]; Appl. Sci. Technol. Index; AQUAREF; ASCE Annu. Comb. Index (1983-); ASCE Publ. Inf. (1983-); Biodeter. Abstr. (19??-19??); Chem. Abstr. (1983-); Coal Abstr.; Curr. Contents, Agric. Biol. Environ. Sci.; Curr. Contents Eng. Tech. Appl. Sci.; Ecol. Abstr. (?-?); Ei Page One; EMBASE; Energy Res. Abstr. (Feb. 1983-); Eng. Index Annu.; Fish Rev. (Jan. 1989-July 1992); Fluid Abstr., Civil Eng.; Fluid Abstr. Proc. Eng.; FLUIDEX (1983-); GeoRef; Geotech. Abstr.; Health Saf. Sci. Abstr.; Highw. Res. Abstr.; INIS Atomindex [Micro.]; Int. Civil Eng. Abstr.; Life Sci. Collect.; Pollut. Abstr. Indexes; Res. Alert [Full Cov.]; Risk Abstr.; Sci. Cit. Index; SCISEARCH; Soft. Abstr. Eng.; Soils Fert.; Sug. Indus. Abstr.; Trans. Am. Soc. Civ. Eng. (1983-); Weed Abstr.; Wildl. Rev. (Jan. 1989-July 1992).

UK/0265-931X
JOURNAL OF ENVIRONMENTAL RADIOACTIVITY. [J. environ. radioact.]. Vol. 1, No. 1 (1984)-. Academic Scholarly Publication. English. Twelve times a year. $708.00 The Americas; £475.00 other. Elsevier Applied Science, An Imprint of Elsevier Science Ltd., The Boulevard, Langford Lane, Kidlington, Oxford OX5 1GB United Kingdom. **Tel** 011 44 865 843000, 011 44 865 843699, FAX 011 44 865 843010. **(Subscription address:** Elsevier Science Ltd. Oxford Fulfillment Centre, PO Box 800, Kidlington, Oxford OX5 1DX United Kingdom.**)** **ED** M. S. Baxter. **NLM** W1; JO644BGH. **CODEN** JERAEE. **[CCC]**. **Pr Rev.** available on microfilm and microfiche from University Microfilms International (UMI). Documents available from Article Express International, The Genuine Article, BIOSIS Document Express, Ask*IEEE, CASDDS, Documents on Demand.
Desc: Provides a coherent international forum for publication of original research or review papers on any aspect of the occurrence of radioactivity in natural systems.

Ind/Abst Biol. Abstr. (1987-); Chem. Abstr. (1984-); Crop Physiol. Abstr.; Curr. Aware. Biol. Sci., CABS; Curr. Contents, Agric. Biol. Environ. Sci.; Dairy Sci. Abstr.; Ecol. Abstr.; Ei Page One; EMBASE; Eng. Index Annu. [Select. Cov.]; Environ. Abstr.; Environ. Period. Bibliogr.; Field Crop Abstr.; Fish Rev.; Fluid Abstr., Civil Eng.; Fluid Abstr. Proc. Eng.; FLUIDEX (199?-); Food Sci. Technol. Abstr.; Geogr. Abstr. Phys. Geogr.; Geogr. Abstr. Human Geogr.; Geol. Abstr.; GeoRef; Grasslands For. Abstr.; Index Vet.; INSPEC (1986-); Nutr. Abstr. Rev., Ser. B, Live Feeds and Feed.; Nutr. Abstr. Rev., Ser. A, Hum. Exp.; Res. Alert [Select. Cov.]; Rev. Med. Vet. Entomol.; Risk Abstr. (19??-19??); SCISEARCH; Soils Fert.; Vet. Bull.; Wildl. Rev.

US/1059-0501
JOURNAL OF ENVIRONMENTAL SCIENCE AND HEALTH. PART C, ENVIRONMENTAL CARCINOGENESIS & ECOTOXICOLOGY REVIEWS. [Environ. carcinog. ecotoxicol. rev.]. **VFOAT** Environmental Carcinogenesis & Ecotoxicology Reviews; Environmental Carcinogenesis and Ecotoxicology Reviews. Vol. C9, No. 1 (1991)-. Academic Scholarly Publication. English. sa. $295.00 US; $302.00 other; $1,495.00 US; $1,558.00 other (combination of Parts A, B and C). Marcel Dekker Inc., 270 Madison Avenue, New York NY 10016. **Tel** (212)696-9000, (800)228-1160, FAX (212)685-4540, telex 421419. **(Subscription address:** Marcel Dekker Inc, PO Box 5017, Monticello NY 12701.**) LC** RC268.5; .J68. **DD** 616.99/4071/05. **CODEN** JSHREB. Documents available from The Genuine Article, BIOSIS Document Express, CASDDS, Documents on Demand. ***Continues*** *Journal of Environmental Science and Health. Part C, Environmental Carcinogenesis Reviews, 0736-3001.*
Desc: Covers carcinogenesis, pollution, and environmentally induced diseases.
Ind/Abst Air Pollut. Titles; Biol. Abstr.; Chem. Abstr.; Curr. Aware. Biol. Sci., CABS; Curr. Contents, Agric. Biol. Environ. Sci.; Curr. Contents Life Sci.; Ecol. Abstr. (?-?); EMBASE; Energy Res. Abstr. (1991-); Environ. Abstr.; Environ. Period. Bibliogr.; Leadscan; Life Sci. Collect.; Pollut. Abstr. Indexes; Ref. Upd. Deluxe Ed.; Res. Alert [Full Cov.]; Sci. Cit. Index.

CC/1001-0742
JOURNAL OF ENVIRONMENTAL SCIENCES (CHINA). [J. environ. sci. (China)]. **Added/Corp** Chung-kuo Ko Hsueh Yuan. Huan Ching Ko Hsueh Wei Yuan Hui. Vol. 1, No. 1 (1989)-. Periodical. English. qt. Fl386.00. IOS Press, Van Diemenstraat 94, 1013 CN Amsterdam Netherlands. **Tel** 011 31 20 6382189, FAX 011 31 20 620 3419. **LC** TD187.5.C6; J68. **DD** 628.5. **CODEN** JENSEE. Documents available from BIOSIS Document Express, CASDDS, Documents on Demand.
Ind/Abst Biol. Abstr. (1991-); Chem. Abstr.; Environ. Abstr. (Sept. 19, 1991-).

NE/0304-3894
JOURNAL OF HAZARDOUS MATERIALS. [J. hazard. mater.]. Vol. 1 (Sept. 1975)-. Academic Scholarly Publication. English. Fifteen times a year (5 volumes). Fl2200.00. Elsevier Science Publishers BV, PO Box 211, 1000 AE Amsterdam Netherlands. **Tel** 011 31 20 5803642, FAX 011 31 20 5862696, telex 15682. **ED** G.F. Bennett, R.E. Britter. **LC** T55.3.H3; J68. **DD** 614.8/3/05. **CODEN** JHMAD9. **[CCC]. Bk Rev. Ad Acc. Pr Rev.** available on microfilm and microfiche from University Microfilms International (UMI). Documents available from Article Express International, The Genuine Article, BIOSIS Document Express, CASDDS, Documents on Demand.
Desc: Brings together original papers covering all the environmental problems that can arise from the manufacture, use and disposal of potentially hazardous materials.
Ind/Abst Appl. Sci. Technol. Index; AQUAREF; BioBusiness; Bioeng. Abstr.; Biol. Abstr.; Chem. Abstr.; Chem. Hazards Ind.; Coal Abstr.; Curr. Contents Eng. Tech. Appl. Sci.; Ei Page One; EMBASE; Energy Inf. Abstr.; Energy Res. Abstr. (May 1977-); Eng. Index Annu.; Environ. Abstr.; Environ. Period. Bibliogr.; GeoRef; Health Saf. Sci. Abstr.; HTFS Dig.; Lab. Hazards Bull.; Leadscan; Lit. Pat. Abstr., Oilfield Chem. (1993-); Lit. Abstr., Catal. Catal.; Lit. Abstr., Health Environ.; Lit. Abstr., Pet. Refin. Petrochem.; Lit. Abstr., Pet. Substit.; Lit. Abstr., Transp. Storage; Life Sci. Collect.; Pollut. Abstr. Indexes; Proc. Chem. Eng.; Res. Alert [Full Cov.]; Risk Abstr.; Saf. Health Work; Sci. Cit. Index; SCISEARCH; Soc. Sci. Cit. Index [Select. Cov.]; Theoret. Chem. Eng.

II/0970-8480
JOURNAL OF INDIAN ASSOCIATION FOR ENVIRONMENTAL MANAGEMENT. [J. Indian Assoc. Environ. Manag.]. **Added/Corp** Indian Association for Environmental Management. (1989)-. Periodical. English. tq. $25.00. Indian Association for Environmental Management, Nagpur, India. **(Subscription address:** Prints India, 11 Darya Ganj, New Delhi 110002 India.**) CODEN** JIAMER. ***Continues*** *IAWPC Technical Annual, 0970-1621.*

II/0970-2083
JOURNAL OF INDUSTRIAL POLLUTION CONTROL. [J. ind. pollut. control]. Vol. 1, No. 1 (June 1985)-. Periodical. English. sa. $100.00. Environmental Publications / India, Post Box 60, Karad 415 110 India. **(Subscription address:** Prints India, 11 Darya Ganj, New Delhi 110002 India.**) LC** TD896; .J68. **DD** 363.7/31. **NLM** W1; JO705H. **CODEN** JIPCE4. Documents available from CASDDS.
Ind/Abst Chem. Abstr.

UK/0263-0923
JOURNAL OF LOW FREQUENCY NOISE AND VIBRATION. VFOAT Journal of Low Frequency Noise & Vibration. Vol. 1, No. 1 (1982)-. Periodical. English. qt. £98.00 UK; £105.00 (add £12.00 for airmail postage) other. Multi Science Publishing Company Ltd., 107 High Street, Brentwood, Essex CM14 4RX England. **Tel** 011 44 277 224632, FAX 011 44 277 223453, telex 89-8452. **ED** H.G. Leventhall. **[CCC].** available on microfiche. Documents available from Ask*IEEE.
Desc: Covers the considerable and growing interest in the phenomena of low frequency noise and vibration and their powerful effects on man, animals and the environment. Journal spreads across several disciplines; studies and investigations on these topics are to be found at present in the periodical literature of acoustics, geophysics, architecture, civil and mechanical engineering, psychology and zoology.
Ind/Abst INSPEC (1983-); Shock Vibr. Dig.

US/0893-357X
JOURNAL OF PESTICIDE REFORM. See Pest Control.

US/1052-1550
JOURNAL OF POLLUTION PREVENTION. (1990)-. Periodical. English. qt. $137.00 US & Canada; $182.00 other. Executive Enterprises Publications Company Inc, 22 West 21st Street, 10th Floor, PO Box 10088, New York NY 10010-6990. **Tel** (212)645-7880, (800)332-8804, FAX (212)675-4883.
Desc: Covers both source reduction and recycling with case studies, applications of new technologies, processes, substitute materials and recycling programs in use at companies. Columnists cover federal developments and brings you a wide range of proven techniques for ensuring compliance while reducing cost.

US/0745-6999
JOURNAL OF RESOURCE MANAGEMENT AND TECHNOLOGY, THE. [J. resour. manage. technol.]. **Added/Corp** University of Pennsylvania. National Center Chair for Resource Recovery and Management. Vol. 12, No. 1 (Jan. 1983)-. Periodical. English. Four times a year (Mar., June., Sept., Dec.). $60.00 US; $65.00 Hawaii & Alaska & Canada & Mexico & Puerto Rico; $70.00 other. University of Pennsylvania / The Journal of Resource Management and Technology, 220 South 33rd Street, Town Building Room 229, Philadelphia PA 19104. **Tel** (215)898-2771, FAX (215)573-2065. **LC** TD785; .N35a. **DD** 333.7. cum. index (Dec. iss.). **Pr Rev.** Documents available from Documents on Demand. ***Continues*** *NCRR Bulletin, 0099-1821.*
Desc: To contribute significantly to the science, technology, economics, or management of environment, energy and non-fuel resources.
Ind/Abst Environ. Abstr.; Environ. Period. Bibliogr.; Pollut. Abstr. Indexes; Soils Fert.; Urban Aff. Abstr.

●US/1056-2575
JOURNAL OF SOLID WASTE. (1993)-. Periodical. English. qt. $110.00. Executive Enterprises, 22 West 21st Street, New York NY 10010-6990. **Tel** (800)332-8804, FAX (212)645-8689.

US/0096-4255
JOURNAL OF THE MISSOURI WATER AND SEWERAGE CONFERENCE. *Title Change.* Main/Conf Missouri Water and Sewerage Conference. **Added/Corp** Missouri. Division of Health. **VFOAT** Missouri Water & Sewage Conference Journal. Vol. 12 (Jan. 1941)-. Periodical. English. an. Missouri Water and Wastewater Conference, PO Box 774, Jefferson City MO 65102. **Tel** (314)635-3365. **ED** Robert S Miller. **LC** TD1; .M55. Index available. **Ad Acc. Circ:** 1,400. ***Continues*** *Report of the ... Annual Missouri Water and Sewerage Conference.* ***Continued by*** *Missouri Water and Wastewater Conference.*
Desc: Water and wastewater operations.

US
JOURNAL OF THE NEW ENGLAND WATER ENVIRONMENT ASSOCIATION. (19??)-. English. Twice a year (May & Nov.). $10.00. Journal of New England Water Environment Association, 85 Merrimac Street, Boston MA 02114. **Tel** (617)367-8554. ***Continues*** *New England Water Pollution Control Association.*

US/0548-4502
JOURNAL OF THE NEW ENGLAND WATER POLLUTION CONTROL ASSOCIATION. *Title Change.* [J. N. Engl. Water Pollut. Control Assoc.]. **Main/Corp** New England Water Pollution Control Association. (196?)-(19??). Periodical. English. Twice a year (May & Nov.). Journal of New England Water Environment Association, 85 Merrimac Street, Boston MA 02114. **Tel** (617)367-8554. **LC** TD201; .N48a. **DD** 363. **CODEN** NEWJB5. **Ad Acc. Circ:** 2,000. Documents available from Article Express International. ***Continued by*** *Journal of the New England Water Environment Association.*
Desc: Publish technical papers on studies, wastewater treatment technology, operation and maintenance of treatment works, state organization information and items of interest to the environmental field.
Ind/Abst Aquat. Sci. Fish. Abstr. (Computer File); Bioeng. Abstr.; Ei Page One; Eng. Index Annu.

●US/1063-455X
JOURNAL OF WATER CHEMISTRY AND TECHNOLOGY. [J. water chem. technol.]. **Added/Corp** Akademiia nauk SSSR. Akademiia nauk Ukrainskoi RSR. (1992)-. Academic Scholarly Publication. English (translations available in Russian). mo. $975.00. Allerton Press, Inc., 150 Fifth Avenue, New York NY 10011. **Tel** (212)924-3950, FAX (212)463-9684, telex 427441 ALPRES. **LC** TD204; .K46. **DD** 628.3/05. **[CCC].** ***Continues*** *Khimia i Tekhnologiia vody. English. Soviet Journal of Water Chemistry and Technology, 0734-1679.*
Ind/Abst Coal Abstr.; EMBASE; GeoRef.

JA
KAGAKU GIJUTSU BUNKEN SOKUHO: KANKYO KOGAI HEN. See Environmental Issues-Abstracting, Bibliographies and Statistics.

JA
KANAGAWA-KEN KOGAI SENTA NEMPO. [Kanagawa-ken Kogai Senta nenpo]. **Main/Corp** Kanagawa-Ken Kogai Senta. (1968)-. Academic Scholarly Publication. Japanese. an. 87-1 Futamatagawa 1-chome Asahi-ku, Yokohama Japan. **Tel** 045-363-1030. **LC** TD187.5.J32; K366A. **CODEN** KKNPDN. **Circ:** 350. Documents available from CASDDS.
Ind/Abst Chem. Abstr. (1967-1981).

JA
KANAGAWA-KEN TAIKI OSEN CHOSA KENKYU HOKOKU. [Kanagawa-ken taiki osen chosa kenkyu hokoku]. **Added/Corp** Kanagawa-Ken (Japan). Kankyo-Bu. **VFOAT** Taiki Osen Chosa Kenkyu Hokoku; Annual Report on Survey and Research of Air Pollution in Kanagawa Prefecture, Japan. (1957)-. Japanese. an. Kanagawaken Kankyobu, (Environment Div., Kanagawa Prefectural Government), 1, Nihon Odoori, Nakaku,, Yokohamashi, Kanagawaken 231, Japan. **CODEN** KTOHDX. Documents available from CASDDS.
Ind/Abst Chem. Abstr.

JA
KANKYO HAKUSHO. Main/Corp Saitama-Ken (Japan). Kankyobu. Kankyo Kanrika. (19??)-. Japanese. an. ¥500 Japan. Saitama-ken Kankyobu Kankyo, Kanrika 15-1, Takasago 3 Urawa Japan. **LC** TD187.5.J32; S2327. **Circ:** 1,000 (ctrl).

JA
KANKYO HAKUSHO. Main/Corp Nagasaki (Prefecture). (19??)-. Periodical. Japanese. an. Nagasakiken Hoken Kankyobu, (Public Health and Environment Department, Nagasaki Prefectural Government, 2-13 Edomachi Nagasakishi, Nagasakiken 850 Japan. **LC** TD187.5.J32; N326a.

JA
KANKYO HAKUSHO. Main/Corp Miyagi, Japan (Prefecture). Seikatsu Kankyobu. **VFOAT** Mayagi-Ken Kankyo Hakusho. 1977-. Periodical. Japanese. an. Miyagi-ken Seikatsu Kankyobu, 8-1 Honcho 3-chome, Sendai Japan. **LC** TD187.5.J32; M587. ***Continues*** *Kogai Hakusho.*

JA
KANKYO HAKUSHO. Added/Corp Japan. Kankyocho. (1972)-. Periodical. Japanese. an. ¥1,900. Kankyocho, (Environment Agency), Printing Bureau, Ministry of Finance, 2-4 Toranomon 2 chome, Minatoku Tokyoto 105 Japan. **LC** HC465.E5; K37. **NLM** W1 KA47C. ***Continues*** *Kogai Hakusho.*

JA
KANKYO HAKUSHO. Main/Corp Kagoshima, Japan (Prefecture). (1975)-. Periodical. Japanese. an. Kagoshimaken Hoken Kankyobu, (Health and Environment Department, Kagoshima Prefectural Government), 14-50 Yamashitacho 892, Kagoshimashi Kagoshimaken 892 Japan. **LC** TD187.5.J32; K324a.

JA
KANKYO HAKUSHO. Main/Corp Gifu-Ken (Japan). Kankyobu. (19??)-. Japanese. an. Gifu Prefectural Government, Yabuta Gifushi, Gifuken 500 Japan. **LC** TD187.5.J32; G534. ***Continues*** *Kankyo Hakusho.*

JA
KANKYO HAKUSHO. Main/Corp Tochigi, Japan (Prefecture) Eisei Kankyobu. (1974)-. Japanese. 1-20

Environmental Issues — Pollution and Waste Management

Haniwada 1, 320 Utsunomiya Japan. **LC** TD187.5.J32; T536a. *Continues Kogai No Jokyo ni Kansuru Nenji Hokoku.*

JA
KANKYO HAKUSHO. Main/Corp Shiga, Japan. Seikatsu Kankyobu. Kankyo Hozenka. 1975-. Japanese. an. Free. Shiga-ken Kaju Kumiai Rengoki, c/o Shiga-Kencho Nosan-Fukyuka, 1 Kyomachi, 4-chome, Otsu 520 Japan. **Tel** 0775-24-1121, FAX 0775-23-1581. **LC** HC463.S45; S45A. **Circ**: 870 (ctrl). *Continues Kogai Hakusho.*
Desc: A report of Shiga prefecture on the environment.

JA
KANKYO HAKUSHO (AOMORI-KEN, JAPAN). (KANKYO HAKUSHO.). **Added/Corp** Aomori-ken (Japan). (1979)-. Periodical. Japanese. an. Aomoriken Kankyo Hokenbu, (Environmental Health Division, Aomori Prefectural Government), 1-1 Nagashima 1 chome, Aomorishi Aomoriken 030 Japan. **LC** TD187.5.J32; A563a. *Continues Kogai Hakusho (Aomori-Ken, Japan).*

JA
KANKYO HAKUSHO (EHIME-KEN, JAPAN). (KANKYO HAKUSHO.). Japanese. Ehime-ken 4-2 Ichiban-cho 4-chome, Matsuyama-shi 790 Japan. **LC** TD187.5.J3; K36.

JA
KANKYO HAKUSHO (FUKUSHIMA-KEN, JAPAN. KOGAI KISEIKA). (KANKYO HAKUSHO / HENSHU, FUKUSHIMA-KEN HOKEN KANKYOBU KOGAI KISEIKA.). Japanese. an. Sukushima-ken, 2-6 Sugitsumacho, Fukushima-shi 960 Japan. **LC** TD187.5.J32; F855. *Continues Kogai Hakusho (Fukushima-Ken, Japan).*

JA
KANKYO HAKUSHO (SHIZUOKA-KEN, JAPAN). (KANKYO HAKUSHO.). **Added/Corp** Shizuoka-ken (Japan). (1972)-. Japanese. an. Shizuokaken Seikatsu Kankyobu, (Living Environment Division,, Shizuoka Prefectural Government), 9-6 Otemachi, Shizuokashi Shizuokaken 420 Japan. **LC** TD187.5.J32; S475.

JA
KANKYO HOZEN NO GENKYO TO TAISAKU. Main/Corp Oita, Japan (Prefecture) Kankyo Hokenbu. (1977)-. Periodical. Japanese. an. Oita-Ken Kankyo Hokenbu, (Environmental Health Division,, Oita Prefectural Government), 1-1 Otemachi 3-chome, Oitashi, Oitaken 870 Japan. **LC** TD187.5.J32; O434.

US/0279-5078
KANSAS ENVIRONMENT. Summer 1980-. Periodical. English. qt. Kansas Department of Health and Environment, Office of Research and Analysis, 109 Southwest 9th Street, Suite 400A, Topeka KS 66612-2219. **Tel** (913)296-0632. *Continues Waterwatch.*
Desc: News of trends and developments in air pollution, water pollution, solid wast disposal and other environmental health matters.

US/1059-342X
KEEP FLORIDA BEAUTIFUL. [Keep Fla. beautiful]. **VFOAT** Keep Florida Beautiful Magazine. (Fall 1991)-. Periodical. English. qt. $30.00. Keep Florida Beautiful, Inc., 402 West College Avenue, Tallahassee FL 32301. **DD** 363.

JA/0287-5071
KENKYU HOKOKU / KANKYO KAGAKU KENKYUJO. [Kankyo Kagaku Kenkyujo kenkyu hokoku]. **VFOAT** Report of the Environmental Science Research Institute, Kinki University; Kinki Daigaku Kankyo Kagaku Kagakubu, Shinaki Yasunaga Hiro-machi Kure, Hiroshima-ken 737-01 Japan. **CODEN** KKKDE7. Documents available from CASDDS. *Continues Kinki Daigaku Kogai Kagaku Kenkyu Kenkyujo Kenkyu Hokoku (Kinki Daigaku); Kogai Kagaku Kenkyujo Kenkyu Hokoku (Kinki Daigaku).*
Ind/Abst Chem. Abstr.

US
KENTUCKY CONVERSATION NEWS / DIVISION OF CONSERVATION. Periodical. English. bm. Department of Natural Resources / Kentucky, Environmental Protection, 628 Teton Trail, Frankfort KY 40601. **Tel** (502)564-3350.

●US/1069-0212
KEYSTONE WATER QUALITY MANAGER. *See* Water Resources.

US/0734-1679
KHIMIIA I TEKHNOLOGIIA VODY. *Title Change.* (SOVIET JOURNAL OF WATER CHEMISTRY AND TECHNOLOGY). [Sov. j. water chem. technol.]. **Added/Corp** Akademiia nauk SSSR. Akademiia nauk Ukrainskoi RSR. Vol. 3 No. 1 (1982)-(199?)-. Academic Scholarly Publication. English (translations available in Russian). bm. Allerton Press, Inc., 150 Fifth Avenue, New York NY 10011. **Tel** (212)924-3950, FAX (212)463-9684, telex 427441 ALPRES. **LC** TD204; .K46. **DD** 628.3/05. **[CCC].** *Continued by Khimia i Tekhnologiia Vody. English. Journal of Water Chemistry and Technology, 1063-455X.*
Ind/Abst Coal Abstr.; EMBASE; GeoRef.

BU
KHRANITELNA PROMISHLENOST. Added/Corp Bulgaria Komitet po Promishlenostta. (19??)-. Periodical. Bulgarian. mo. Documents available from CASDDS.
Ind/Abst Biodeter. Abstr.; Chem. Abstr.; Dairy Sci. Abstr.; Nutr. Abstr. Rev., Ser. A, Hum. Exp.; PESTDOC; Postharvest News Inf.

JA/0454-9015
KOGAI. [Kogai]. **VFOAT** Pollution Control. (1966)-. Academic Scholarly Publication. Japanese. bm. $84.00. Kogyo Gijutsuin Kogai Shigen Kenkyujo, (National Research Inst. for Pollution & Resources, Agency of Industrial Science & Technology), 16-3, Onogawa, Tsukubashi, Ibarakiken 305 Japan. **(Subscription address:** Maruzen Company Ltd., PO Box 5050, Import & Export Department, Tokyo 100 31 Japan.) **CODEN** KGAIA8. **Ad Acc. Circ**: 6,000 (ctrl). Documents available from CASDDS.
Desc: Introduces research concerning the technique of environmental pollution control.
Ind/Abst Chem. Abstr.; Coal Abstr.; Curr. Biotechnol.

JA
KOGAI KANKEI TOSHO MOKUROKU. TSUIROKU. Main/Corp Zenkoku Shiyu Bukken Saigai Kyosaikai. Bosai Semmon Toshokan. (1969)-. Japanese. 2-4-1 Hirakawacho Chiyoda-ku, Tokyo Japan. **LC** Z5862; .Z452; TD174.
Desc: Information on environmental pollution.

JA
KOGAI KANKEI ZASSHI KIJI SAKUIN. 1973-. Japanese. Osaka Shiritsu Chuo Toshokan, 1 Kita Horie Mikedori 5-chome Nishi-ku, Osaka Japan. **LC** TD172; .K65.

JA
KOGAI KENKYU NEMPO. Main/Corp Tokyo-To Kogat Kenkyujo. (19??)-. Periodical. Japanese. Tokyo Daigaku Shuppankai, Todai Konai Hongo Bunkyo-ku, Tokyo 113 Japan. **LC** TD172; .T63a.

JA
KOGAI NO ARAMASHI. Main/Corp Tokyo. Kogaikyoku. Somubu. Sodanka. Japanese. Tokyo-To Kogaikyoku Somubu Sodanka, 7-1 Yurakucho 1-chome, Chiyoda-ku 100 Tokyo Japan. **LC** TD187.5.J32; T6212.

JA/0368-685X
KOGAI SHIGEN KENKYUJO HOKOKU. [Kogai Shigen Kenkyujo hokoku]. **Added/Corp** Kogai Shigen Kenkyujo. **VFOAT** Report of the National Research Institute for Pollution and Resources. No. 1 (Nov. 1970)-. Japanese. National Research Institute for Pollution and Resources, Kawaguchi Japan. Documents available from CASDDS.
Ind/Abst Chem. Abstr.

JA
KOGAI SHIGENKEN NYUSU. Main/Corp Kogai Shigen Kenkyujo. Japanese. Kogyo Gijutsuin Kogai Shigen Kenkyujo, (National Research Inst. for Pollution & Resources, Agency of Industrial Science & Technology), 16-3, Onogawa, Tsukubashi, Ibarakiken 305 Japan. **LC** TD178.8.J33; K34B.
Ind/Abst Coal Abstr.

JA/0286-0945
KOKKAIDO KOGAI BOSHI KENKYUJO HO. [Hokkaido Kogai Boshi Kenkyujo ho]. **Main/Corp** Hokkaido Kogai Boshi Kenkyujo. **VFOAT** Report of Hokkaido Research Institute for Environmental Pollution. No. 1-; 1975-. Academic Scholarly Publication. Japanese (summaries and/or abstracts in English and Japanese). NISHI, 12-Chome, Kita 19-JO, Kita-KU. **LC** TD172. **CODEN** HKBKDH. Documents available from CASDDS.
Ind/Abst Chem. Abstr.

JA
KOKURITSU KOGAI KENKYUJO KENKYU HOKOKU. [Kokuritsu Kogai Kenkyu kenkyu hokoku]. **VFOAT** Research Report from the National Institute for Environmental Studies. (1978)-. Academic Scholarly Publication. English (Japanese). ir. Price varies per volume. National Institute for Environmental Studies, Tsukuba Yatabe, Ibaraki 300-21 Japan. **CODEN** KKOKDD. Documents available from CASDDS.
Ind/Abst Chem. Abstr.; Irr. Drain. Abstr.; Plant Grow. Reg. Abstr.; Poult. Abstr.

GW/0341-1540
KORRESPONDENZ ABWASSER : KA. [KA, Korresp. Abwasser]. **Added/Corp** Gesellschaft zur Forderung der Abwassertechnik. Abwassertechnische Vereinigung (Germany). **VFOAT** KA. (19??)-. Periodical. German. mo. Korrespondenz Abwasser, Postfach 1160, D 53757 Sankt Augustin Germany. **Tel** 011 49 2241 2320. **LC** TD511; .K67. Documents available from CASDDS.
Ind/Abst Chem. Abstr.; Soils Fert.

JA/0023-5032
KUKI SEIJO. [Kuki seijo]. **Added/Corp** Nihon Kuki Seijo Kyokai. **VFOAT** Journal of Japan Air Cleaning Association. (1964)-. Periodical. Japanese (table of contents in English). Nihon Kuki Seijo Kyokai, Tokyo Japan. **LC** TD881; .K84. **CODEN** KUSEBF. Documents available from CASDDS.
Ind/Abst Chem. Abstr.

CH
KUNG YEH WU JAN FANG CHIH / CHING CHI PU KUNG YEH WU JAN FANG CHIH CHI SHU FU TAO HSIAO TSU PIEN. Added/Corp Ching chi pu Kung yeh wu jan Fang Chih chi shu fu tao Hsiao tsu (China). (1982)-. Periodical. Chinese. Ching Chi Pu Kung Yeh Wu Jan Fang Chih Chi Shu Fu Tao Hsiao, Taipei Taiwan. **LC** TD172; .K87. **DD** 363.7.

US/1040-2381
LAKE AND RESERVOIR MANAGEMENT. [Lake reserv. manage.]. **Added/Corp** North American Lake Management Society. (19??)-. English. Twice a year. $75.00. North American Lake University of Florida, 1 Progress Boulevard, PO Box 27, Alachua FL 32615. **Tel** (904)462-2554, FAX (904)462-2568. **DD** 628. **CODEN** LRMAEY. Documents available from BIOSIS Document Express, Documents on Demand. *Continues Proceedings of the ... Annual Conference / North American Lake Management Society, 0743-8141.*
Ind/Abst Aquat. Sci. Fish. Abstr. (Computer File); Biol. Abstr. (1987-); Ecology Abstr.; Environ. Abstr.; Fish Rev.; For. Abstr.; Index Vet.; Int. Exec.; Pollut. Abstr. Indexes; Rev. Agric. Entomol.; Risk Abstr.; Soils Fert.; Weed Abstr.; Wheat Barley Trit. Abstr.; Wildl. Rev.

US
LAKE ERIE WASTEWATER MANAGEMENT STUDY PUBLIC INFORMATION FACT SHEET. VFOAT Public Information Fact Sheet. Began with unnumbered issues for Oct. 1977. Periodical. English. Department of Defense and Department of the Army, 1776 Niagara Street, Buffalo NY 14207. *Supersedes Lake Erie Water Quality Newsletter.*

US
LAND, AIR & WATER. English. qt (published within the seasons). Free. Kentucky Department of Environmental Protection, 18 Reilly Road, Frankfort KY 40651. **Tel** (502)564-2150, FAX (502)564-4245. Documents available from Documents on Demand.
Ind/Abst Environ. Abstr.

BL
LIMPEZA PUBLICA. Portuguese. Associacao Brasileira de Residuos Solidos e Limpeza Publica, Viaduto Dona Paulina 80-80 Andar, CEP 01361 Sao Paulo Brazil. **LC** TD785; .L55.

GW/0340-4900
LITERATURBERICHTE UEBER WASSER, ABWASSER, LUFT UND FESTE ABFALLSTOFFE. Added/Corp Verein fuer Wasser-, Boden- und Lufthygiene (Germany) Institut fuer Wasser-, Boden- und Lufthygiene, Forschungsstatte fuer Allgemeine Hygiene und Gesundheitstechnik, des Bundesgesungheitsamtes zu Berlin-Dahlem. Vol. 16, (1968)-. German. Six times a year. DM470.00 Germany; DM482.00 other. Gustav Fischer Verlag Stuttgart, Postfach 720143, Wollgrassweg 49, D 70577 Stuttgart Germany. **Tel** 011 49 711 458030, FAX 0711-4580334, telex 2627-7111488. **(Subscription address:** VCH Publishers Inc., 303 Northwest 12th Avenue, Journals Department, Deerfield FL 33442.) **LC** Z6673; .L5; TD1. **NLM** ZWA 675 L776. **[CCC].** *Continues Literaturberichte Uber Wasser, Luft und Boden.*

●US/1065-0490
LITERATURE ABSTRACTS. HEALTH & ENVIRONMENT. *See* Environmental Issues-Abstracting, Bibliographies and Statistics.

SW
LJUSKULTUR. Began publication in 1929. Periodical. Swedish. bm. Kr130.00. Ljuskultur, PO Box 5512, South 114-85 Stockholm Sweden. **Tel** 46-(8)6675834, FAX 46-(8)6673491. **LC** TH7700; .L53. **CODEN** LJUSAY. **Ad Acc.** ctrl circ. Documents available from Ask*IEEE.
Ind/Abst Ergon. Abstr.; INSPEC (1968-); Int. Build. Serv. Abstr.

NE
LUCHTVERONTREINIGING, METINGEN BUITENLUCHT / CENTRAAL BUREAU VOOR DE STATISTIEK, AFDELING MILIEUHYGIENE. Added/Corp Netherlands. Centraal Bureau voor de Statistiek. Afdeling Milieuhygiene. **VFOAT** Air pollution, Monitoring of Ambient Air. (19??)-. Dutch (summaries and/or abstracts

in English). an. Fl21.50. Staatsuitgeverij, Christoffel Plantijnstraat 1, 2515 TZ'S Gravenhage Netherlands. **Tel** 070/78-95-70. **LC** TD883.7.N4; C37.

NE
MAGAZINE RECYCLING BENELUX. Misset Uitgeverij BV, Postbus 9000, 6800 DA Arnhem Netherlands. **Tel** 011 31 85 209911.

US/0147-4596
MAINE WATER QUALITY STATUS. See Water Resources.

US/0025-0929
MAINTENANCE SUPPLIES. [Maint. supplies]. Vol. 6 No. 11 (Nov. 1961)-. Periodical. English. Twelve times a year. $45.00 US and Canada; $80.00 other. PTN Publishing Company, 445 Broad Hollow Road, Melville NY 11747. **Tel** (516)845-2700, FAX (516)845-7109. **ED** Dominic Mariani. **DD** 648. **Bk Rev. Ad Acc. Circ:** 10,000 (ctrl). ***Continues*** *Maintenance-Sanitary Supplies;* ***Absorbed*** *Building Services Contractor, 0007-3644.*
Desc: A magazine for distributors of sanitary supplies and equipment.

US/0737-2957
MANAGING SOLID WASTE IN OREGON. (MANAGING SOLID WASTE IN OREGON : ANNUAL REPORT / SOLID WASTE DIVISION.). **Added/Corp** Oregon. Solid Waste Division. (1980)-. English. an. Free on request. Oregon Department of Environmental Quality, 811 Southwest 6th Avenue, Portland OR 97204. **LC** TD788.4.O7; M36. **DD** 363.7/28.
Desc: Deals with refuse and refuse disposal.

UK/0025-326X
MARINE POLLUTION BULLETIN. [Mar. pollut. bull.]. (June 1968)-. Academic Scholarly Publication. English. Twenty-four times a year. $462.00 (regular subscription), $529.00 (combination subscription with Spill Science & Technology Bulletin) The Americas; £310.00 (regular subscription), £355.00 (combination subscription with Spill Science & Technology Bulletin) other. Pergamon Press, An Imprint of Elsevier Science Ltd., The Boulevard, Langford Lane, Kidlington, Oxford OX5 1GB United Kingdom. **Tel** 011 44 865 843000, 011 44 865 843699, FAX 011 44 865 843010. **(Subscription address:** Elsevier Science Ltd. Oxford Fulfillment Centre, PO Box 800, Kidlington, Oxford OX5 1DX United Kingdom.**) ED** Charles Sheppard. **LC** GC1080; .M35. **NLM** W1 MA654N. **CODEN** MPNBAZ. **[CCC]. Pr Rev.** available on microfilm and microfiche from University Microfilms International (UMI). Documents available from Article Express International, The Genuine Article, BIOSIS Document Express, Ask*IEEE, Petroleum Abstracts Document Delivery Service, CASDDS, Documents on Demand.
Ind/Abst Aqualine Abstr.; AQUAREF; Aquat. Sci. Fish. Abstr. (Computer File); Biodeter. Abstr. (19??-19??); Biol. Abstr.; Chem. Abstr.; Coal Abstr.; CSA Neuro. Abstr. (?-?); Curr. Aware. Biol. Sci., CABS; Curr. Contents, Agric. Biol. Environ. Sci.; Curr. Ref. Fish Res.; Ecol. Abstr.; Ecology Abstr.; Ei Page One; EMBASE; Energy Inf. Abstr.; Energy Res. Abstr. (Jan. 1971-); Eng. Index Annu.; Environ. Abstr.; Environ. Period. Bibliogr.; Fish Rev.; Food Sci. Technol. Abstr.; Geogr. Abstr. Phys. Geogr.; Geogr. Abstr. Human Geogr.; Geol. Abstr.; GeoRef; Health Saf. Sci. Abstr.; Index Vet.; INIS Atomindex [Micro.]; INSPEC (Jan. 1978-); Int. Dev. Abstr.; Key Word Index Wildl. Res.; Leadscan; Leis. Recreat. Tour. Abstr.; Lit. Pat. Abstr., Oilfield Chem. (1972-); Lit. Abstr., Catal. Catal.; Lit. Abstr., Health Environ.; Lit. Abstr., Pet. Refin. Petrochem.; Lit. Abstr., Pet. Substit.; Lit. Abstr., Transp. Storage; Mar. Sci. Contents Tables; Microbiol. Abstr. Sect. C; Ocean. Abstr.; Life Sci. Collect.; PESTDOC; Pet. Abstr.; Pollut. Abstr. Indexes; Res. Alert [Full Cov.]; Rev. Agric. Entomol.; Risk Abstr.; Sci. Cit. Index; SCISEARCH; Soc. Sci. Cit. Index [Select. Cov.]; Vet. Bull.; Toxicol. Abstr.; Wildl. Rev.

UK
MARINE POLLUTION RESEARCH TITLES. Added/Corp Marine Biological Association of the United Kingdom. Marine Pollution Information Centre. (19??)-. English. mo. $185.00 (US), £86.00 (UK) surface mail; $215.00 (US), £103.00 (UK) airmail. Natural Environmental Research Council, Plymouth Marine Laboratory, Citadel Hill, Plymouth PLl 2PB, Devon, England. **Tel** 0752-222772, FAX 0752-670637. **ED** D S Moulder. **LC** Z5862.2.M3; M37; GC1085. **DD** 016.6281/686/162. **Ad Acc. Circ:** 220.
Desc: Marine and estuarine pollution references including detection, analysis, levels, effects, and removal.

●GW
MATERIALIEN / LANDESUMWELTAMT. (1994)-. Monographic series. German. ir. Price varies per volume. Landesumweltamt Nordrhein-Westfalen, (North-Rhine Westphalia State Environment Agency), Wallneyer Strasse 6, 45133 Essen Germany. **Tel** 0049 0207 7995-0, FAX 0049 0207 7995 446, 0049 0207 7995 447. **Ad Acc.**
Desc: Reports on the results of environmental monitoring, and investigations. Covers environmental quality management, environmental engineering, and environmental fees and licenses.

US
MATERIALS RECOVERY AND RECYCLING YEARBOOK : DIRECTORY & GUIDE. Added/Corp Governmental Advisory Associates. (1991)-. Directory. English. be. $250.00 (non-profit and government agencies); $345.00 (private industry). Governmental Advisory Associates, 177 East 87th Street, Suite 506-A, New York NY 10128. **Tel** (212)410-4165, FAX (212)410-6607. **ED** Robert Gould. available on diskette.

UK
MATERIALS RECYCLING WEEKLY. (19??)-. Periodical. English. wk. £54.00 UK; £73.00 Europe; £98.00 other. EMAP Readerlink, Audit House, 260 Field End Road, Ruislip Middlesex HA4 9LT England. **Tel** 011 44 081 868 4499, FAX 011 44 081 429 3117.

PL
MATERIALY BADAWCZE. SERIA: GOSPODARKA WODNA I OCHRONA WOD. See Water Resources.

US/0894-2374
MCGRAW-HILL HAZARDOUS WASTE MONITOR. [McGraw-Hill hazard. waste monit.]. **Added/Corp** McGraw-Hill Book Company. **VFOAT** McGraw Hill Hazardous Waste Monitor; Hazardous Waste Monitor. Vol. 1, No. 3 (1987)-. Periodical. English. qt. McGraw Hill Publishing Company, Inc., 1221 Avenue of the Americas, New York NY 10020. **Tel** (212)512-6410, (800)525-5003, FAX (212)512-6111. **LC** KF3946.A15; M34. **DD** 344.73/04622; 347.3044622. ***Continues*** *McGraw-Hill Hazardous Waste Report, 0891-2491.*

US/0897-3407
MEALEY'S LITIGATION REPORTS. SUPERFUND. See Law-Environmental Law.

●US/1064-1475
MEALEY'S LITIGATION REPORTS. TOXIC TORTS. See Law.

US/1048-4493
MEDICAL WASTE NEWS. See Medical Science and Technology.

●GW
MERKBLATTER / LANDESUMWELTAMT. (1994)-. Periodical. German. ir. Price varies per volume. Landesumweltamt Nordrhein-Westfalen, (North-Rhine Westphalia State Environment Agency), Wallneyer Strasse 6, 45133 Essen Germany. **Tel** 0049 0207 7995-0, FAX 0049 0207 7995 446, 0049 0207 7995 447. **Ad Acc.**
Desc: General technical environmental directions.

UK/0141-075X
METHODS FOR THE EXAMINATION OF WATERS AND ASSOCIATED MATERIALS. [Methods exam. waters assoc. mater.]. (19??)-. Academic Scholarly Publication. English. ir. Price varies per volume. Her Majesty's Stationery Office, 51 Nine Elms Lane, London SW8 5DR England. **Tel** 011 44 71 873 8459, 011 44 71 873 8499, FAX 011 44 71 873 8499, 011 44 71 873 8456, telex 297138. **CODEN** MEWMD5. Documents available from CASDDS. ***Continues*** *Analysis of Raw, Potable and Waste Waters.*
Ind/Abst Chem. Abstr.

US/0275-2840
MICHIGAN ANNUAL AIR QUALITY REPORT. (MICHIGAN ... ANNUAL AIR QUALITY REPORT / MICHIGAN DEPARTMENT OF NATURAL RESOURCES, AIR QUALITY DIVISION.). **VFOAT** Air Quality Report. English. an. Air Quality Division, PO Box 30028, Lansing MI 48909. **Tel** (517)373-7023. **LC** TD883.5.M47; M53. **DD** 363.7/3922/09774.

US/0270-4579
MICHIGAN CRITICAL MATERIALS REGISTER. Main/Corp Michigan. Environmental Protection Bureau. Environmental Services Division. **Added/Corp** Michigan. Environmental Protection Bureau. Environmental Services Division. Critical Materials Register. **VFOAT** Critical Materials Register. (19??)-. English. an. Department of Natural Resources / Michigan, Box 30028, Lansing MI 48909. **Tel** (517)373-1257. **LC** TD224.M5; .M48a. **DD** 363.7/38/09774. ***Continues*** *Critical Materials Register.*

US/0896-4246
MICHIGAN WASTE REPORT. (MICHIGAN WASTE REPORT : SOLID WASTE, HAZARDOUS WASTE, TOXICS.). [Mich. waste rep.]. **Added/Corp** Waste Systems Institute of Michigan. Waste Information & Management Services. Vol. 1, No. 1 (Jan. 1, 1981)-. Periodical. English. Twenty-one times a year (21 regular issues & 3 special directories.). $200.00 (nonprofit organizations), $325.00 other. Waste Information and Management Services, 3250 Townsend North East, Grand Rapids MI 49505. **Tel** (616)363-3262, FAX (616)363-0058.

UK/0140-5098
MIDDLE EAST WATER & SEWAGE. ***Title Change.*** **See** Water Resources.

NE
MILIEU MANAGEMENT. Studiecentrum Bedrijf Overheid, Postbus 828, 5600 AV Eindhoven Netherlands. **Tel** 011 31 40 608888.

CN/0835-1457
MILIEU (OTTAWA). (MILIEU.). [Milieu]. **Added/Corp** Canada. Environment Canada. (19??)-. Periodical. English. Environment Canada / Emergencies Science Division, Ottawa Ontario K1A 0H3 Canada. **Tel** (819)998-9622. **DD** 363.7/00971.
Ind/Abst AQUAREF; Can. Period. Index (19??-); Point Repere.

NE
MILIEUFACETTEN / CBS, CENTRAAL BUREAU VOOR DE STATISTIEK, MILIEUSTATISTIEKEN. VFOAT Facets of the Environment. Dutch. Centraal Bureau voor de Statistiek, AFD ALG Zaken, Postbus 959, 2270 AZ Voorburg Netherlands. **Tel** 011 31 70 3373800, FAX 011 31 038 7429, telex 32692 CBS NL. **LC** LOCTD186.5.N47; M55.

US
MINNESOTA WATER QUALITY WORK PLAN FY ... / MINNESOTA POLLUTION CONTROL AGENCY. Main/Corp Minnesota Pollution Control Agency. 1980-1-. English. an. Air Quality in Minnesota, 1935 West County Road B-2, Roseville MN 55113. **LC** TD224.M6; M53A. **DD** 363.7/39456/09776. ***Continues*** *State of Minnesota Water Quality Work Plan, 0278-0100.*

US
MISSOURI WATER AND WASTEWATER CONFERENCE. See Water Resources.

SW
MONITOR (STOCKHOLM, SWEDEN). (MONITOR.). Swedish. an. Liber Distribution, Prenumberationsorder, Forlagsorder 162 89, Stockholm Sweden. **LC** QH545.A1; M64. **DD** 363.7/3/09485.

US/0732-2801
MONTANA AIR QUALITY DATA AND INFORMATION SUMMARY FOR ... . [Mont. air qual. data inf. summ.]. **Added/Corp** Montana. Air Quality Bureau. **VFOAT** Montana Air Quality Data & Information Summary for ... . (19??)-. English. an. Air Quality Bureau, Department of Health and Environmental Sciences, Helena MT 59620. **Tel** (406)444-3454. **ED** Stan Sternberg and Patricia Davidson. **LC** TD883.5.M6; M64a. **DD** 363.7/3922/09786. **Circ:** 200. ***Continues*** *Annual Air Quality Data Summary for Montana, 0161-1666.*
Desc: Summary of air quality data collected within the state and information on air quality topics.

US/0193-8126
MONTANA ENVIRONMENTAL SCIENCES. English. an. Montana Department of Health & Environmental Sciences, 1400 Broadway, Cogswell Building, Room C108, Helena MT 59620. **Tel** (406)444-2544, FAX (406)444-2606. **LC** TD171.3.M9; M66. **DD** 614.7/09786.

US/0883-4458
MONTANA ... NETWORK REVIEW. English. an. Free. Air Quality Bureau, Department of Health and Environmental Sciences, Helena MT 59620. **Tel** (406)444-3454. **ED** Stan Sternberg. **LC** TD883.5.M6; M67. **DD** 363.7/39263/09786. **Circ:** 200.
Desc: Review of the state's ambient air monitoring network required by the U.S. EPA.

US/1053-7899
MSW MANAGEMENT. (MSW MANAGEMENT : THE JOURNAL FOR MUNICIPAL SOLID WASTE PROFESSIONALS.). [MSW manage.]. **VAT** Municipal Solid Waste Management. Vol. 1, No. 1 (Mar./Apr. 1991)-. Periodical. English. bm. $60.00. Forester Communications, 216 East Gutierrez Street, Santa Barbara CA 93101. **Tel** (213)576-6180. **LC** TD788; .M74. **DD** 628.4/4/068.

GW/0934-3482
MULLMAGAZIN. [Mullmagazin]. (1988)-. Periodical. German (English). Four times a year (Feb., May, Aug., Nov.). DM60.00. Institute fur Okol Recycling, Kurforstenstr 14, D-10785 Berlin F R Germany. **Tel** 011 49 30 2628021, FAX 011 49 30 2650366. **UDC** 628. Index available. cum. index. **Bk Rev**, (Qty: 5). **Ad Acc, Adv Mgr:** Anne Wispler, **Tel** 030 2628027. **Circ:** 2,600.
Desc: Providing information about concepts, policies, research, and technologies of waste prevention, waste minimization and recycling.

CN/0820-4446
MUNICIPAL & INDUSTRIAL WATER & POLLUTION CONTROL. [Munic. ind. water pollut. control]. **VFOAT** Water and Pollution Control. **VAT** Municipal and Industrial Water and Pollution Control. Vol. 123, No. 6 (Nov./Dec. 1985)-. Periodical. English. Seven

Environmental Issues —Pollution and Waste Management

times a year. 70.00Can$ Canada; $70.00 other. Zanny Limited, 11966 Woodbine Avenue, Gormley ONT L0H 1G0 Canada. **Tel** (905)887-4813. **LC** TA1; .M84. **DD** 363.6/1/05. **CODEN** MIWCE4. **Continues** Water & Pollution Control, 0043-1117.
Ind/Abst Abstr. Bull. Inst. Pap. Sci. Tech.

US/0027-3465
MUNICIPAL ENGINEERS JOURNAL, THE. [Munic. eng. j.]. **Added/Corp** Municipal Engineers of the City of New York. Vol. 1 (May 1915)-. Periodical. English. Three times a year. $15.00. Municipal Engineers of the City of New York, 51 Chamber Street, Room 515A, New York NY 10007. **Tel** (212)349-5795. **LC** TD1; .M925. **DD** 628.1/05. **CODEN** MUEJAF. cum. index. Documents available from Article Express International.
Ind/Abst Ei Page One; Eng. Index Annu.; Int. Civil Eng. Abstr.

US
N.C. ... ANNUAL REPORT OF HAZARDOUS WASTE GENERATED, STORED, TREATED OR DISPOSED. **Added/Corp** North Carolina. Solid & Hazardous Waste Management Branch. **VFOAT** NC ... Annual Report of Hazardous Waste Generated, Stored, Treated, or Disposed; Annual Report of Hazardous Waste; North Carolina ... Annual Report of Hazardous Waste. (19??)-. Periodical. English. an. Free on request. North Carolina Division Solid Waste Management, PO Box 27687, Raleigh NC 27611. **Tel** (919)733-2178. **LC** TD811.5; .N14. **DD** 363.7/28. **Bk Rev. Ad Acc. Circ:** 1,000 (ctrl).
Desc: A report of waste, generation and handling.

JA/0387-9070
NAGANO-KEN EISEI KOGAI KENKYUJO KENKYU HOKOKU. See Public Health and Safety.

SZ/1012-8778
NAGRA INFORMIERT. [Nagra Inf.]. **Added/Corp** Nationale Genossenschaft fuer die Lagerung Radioaktiver Abfalle (Switzerland). **VAT** Nationale Genossenschaft fuer die Lagerung Radioaktiver Abfalle Informiert. (1979)-. Academic Scholarly Publication. German. qt. **CODEN** NAINEO. Documents available from CASDDS.
Ind/Abst Chem. Abstr.

CN
NATIONAL AIR POLLUTION SURVEILLANCE. Ceased. Main/Corp Canada. Environmental Protection Service. **Added/Corp** Canada. Air Pollution Control Directorate. **VFOAT** Surveillance Nationale de la Pollution Atmospherique; Extrait Mensuel. (1???)-(19??). Periodical. Multiple languages (English and French). Environment Canada / Emergencies Science Division, Ottawa Ontario K1A 0H3 Canada. **Tel** (819)998-9622.

CN/0381-2995
NATIONAL AIR POLLUTION SURVEILLANCE. ANNUAL SUMMARY. (NATIONAL AIR POLLUTION SURVEILLANCE, ANNUAL SUMMARY / SURVEILLANCE NATIONALE DE LA POLLUTION ATMOSPHERIQUE, SOMMAIRE ANNUEL.). **Added/Corp** Canada. Air Pollution Control Directorate. Canada. Environmental Protection Programs Directorate. Technical Services Branch. Canada. Technology Development and Technical Services Branch. **VFOAT** Surveillance Nationale de la Pollution Atmospherique; Air Surveillance Atmospherique. (1970)-. English (French). an. **LC** TD883.7.C2; N36. **DD** 363.7/3922/0971.

US/0094-8748
NATIONAL EMISSIONS REPORT. **Main/Corp** United States. Environmental Protection Agency. National Air Data Branch. English. National Technical Information Service - NTIS, Room 2027S, 5285 Port Royal Road, Springfield VA 22161. **Tel** (703)487-4630, (703)487-4660, (703)487-4650, FAX (703)321-8547, telex 89-9405. **LC** TD883.2; .U54E. **DD** 363.6.

US/0195-9794
NATIONAL ENVIRONMENTAL IMPACT PROJECTION. [Natl. environ. impact proj.]. No. 1-. Government Publication. English. an. US Department of Energy, 1000 Independence Avenue SW, Washington DC 20585. **Tel** (202)586-5000, FAX (202)586-4073. **NLM** W1 NA405.

US
NATIONAL MARINE POLLUTION PROGRAM. SUMMARY OF FEDERAL PROGRAMS AND PROJECTS, FY ... UPDATE. Title Change. Added/Corp United States. National Ocean Pollution Program Office. **VFOAT** Summary of Federal Programs and Projects, FY Update. (1985)-(199?). English. **LC** GC1080; .N4. **DD** 363.7/394/09162. **Formed by the union of** National Marine Pollution Program. Agency Program Summaries, FY Update **and** National Marine Pollution Program. Catalog of Federal Projects, 0748-5018. **Continued by** Summary of Federal Programs and Projects.

US/0192-0359
NATIONAL UTILITY CONTRACTOR, THE. See Building and Construction.

US/0730-9600
NATO CHALLENGES OF MODERN SOCIETY. [NATO, chall. mod. soc.]. **Added/Corp** North Atlantic Treaty Organization. Committee on the Challenges of Modern Society. **VFOAT** N.A.T.O. Challenges of Modern Society. (1981)-. Academic Scholarly Publication. English. ir. Price varies per volume. North Atlantic Treaty Organization / NATO Scientific Affairs Division, B 1110 Brussels Belgium. **CODEN** NCMSD4. Documents available from Article Express International, Ask*IEEE, CASDDS.
Ind/Abst Bioeng. Abstr.; Chem. Abstr.; Ei Page One; Eng. Index Annu.; INSPEC (1984-).

NE
NATUUR- EN MILIEUVOORLICHTING. Dutch. Stichting Natuur en Milieu, Noordereinde 60, 1243 JJ Graveland Netherlands. **LC** TD169.5.

US
NCASI SPECIAL REPORT. See Paper and Pulp Industry.

US/0738-9477
NECNP NEWSLETTER. [NECNP newsletter]. **Added/Corp** New England Coalition on Nuclear Pollution. **VFOAT** N.E.C.N.P. Newsletter. **VAT** New England Coalition on Nuclear Pollution Newsletter. (Summer 1983)-. Newsletter. English. qt. $15.00. New England Coalition on Nuclear Pollution, Box 637, Brattleboro VT 05301. **Continues** On the Watch.

US/1070-9266
NEW YORK WASTE REPORTER. Ceased. (NEW YORK WASTE REPORTER : NEW YORK'S WASTE MANAGEMENT NEWSLETTER.). [N.Y. waste report.]. **VFOAT** Reporter; New York State's Waste Management Newsletter. Vol. 1, No. 1 (July 1991)-(Sept. 1994). Newsletter. English. Twelve times a year. New York Waste Reporter, PO Box 305, Fredonia NY 14063. **Tel** (716)673-1390, FAX (716)679-1850. **ED** Michael Bobseine. **DD** 363. cum. index (This year only). **Circ:** 500.

US/1042-5160
NEWS & VIEWS (PITTSBURGH, PA.). (NEWS & VIEWS.). [News views]. **Main/Corp** Air and Waste Management Association. **VFOAT** News and Views. (Feb. 1989)-. Periodical. English. bm. Free (members). Air & Waste Management Association, PO Box 2861, Pittsburgh PA 15230. **Tel** (412)232-3444. **DD** 363. **Continues** APCA (Association : U.S.). APCA News, 0746-7249.

CN/1187-3663
NEWS / FEDERAL-PROVINCIAL ENVIRONMENTAL ASSESSMENT REVIEW PANEL, HALIFAX-DARTMOUTH METROLITAN WASTEWATER MANAGEMENT SYSTEM. [News - Fed.-Prov. Environ. Assess. Rev. Panel Halifax-Dartm. Metrop. Wastewater Manage. Syst.$b]. **Main/Corp** Federal-Provincial Environmental Assessement Review Panel, Halifax-Dartmouth Metropolitan Wastewater Management System (Canada). 1st Ed. (1991)-. Periodical. English. **DD** 354.7108.

US
NEWSLETTER - BUREAU OF LABORATORIES. Main/Corp South Carolina. Dept. of Health and Environmental Control. Bureau of Laboratories. 19 -. Newsletter. English. mo. 2600 Bull Street, Columbia SC 29201. **Tel** (803)734-4860, FAX (803)754-5554. Index available. cum. index.

US/1041-701X
NEWSLETTER - PENNSYLVANIA STATE UNIVERSITY. ENVIRONMENTAL RESOURCES RESEARCH INSTITUTE. (NEWSLETTER / ENVIRONMENTAL RESOURCES RESEARCH INSTITUTE, PENNSYLVANIA STATE UNIVERSITY.). [Newsl. - Pa. State Univ., Environ. Resour. Res. Inst.]. **VFOAT** ERRI Newsletter. Vol. 17, No. 3 (Winter 1987)-. Newsletter. English. qt. Penn State University Environmental Resources Research Institute, University Park PA 16802. **DD** 333. **Continues** Newsletter (Pennsylvania State University). Institute for Research on Land and Water Resources), 0020-2614.

CN/0708-918X
NEWSLETTER - PLANETARY ASSOCIATION FOR CLEAN ENERGY. See Energy.

US
NEWSROOM DIRECTORY & GUIDE TO THE ILLINOIS ENVIRONMENTAL PROTECTION AGENCY. See Public Administration.

US/0748-9110
NORTHEAST MONITORING PROGRAM ... ANNUAL REPORT. Added/Corp National Ocean Survey. (1981)-. English. an. National Ocean Service, NOAA Distribution Branch NCG33, Riverdale MD 20737. **Tel** (301)436-6993. **LC** GC1212.A115; N67. **DD** 363.7/394/0974. available on microfiche (Vols. for 1981- distributed to depository libraries).

US
NORTHEAST RECYCLING COUNCIL NEWS. English. Four times a year (Jan., Apr., July, Oct.). $15.00. Northeast Recycling Council, 139 Main Street, Suite 401, Battleboro VT 05301. **Tel** (802)254-3636, (800)800-1910, (606)231-1939, FAX (802)254-5870. **Circ:** 300.

RU
NOVOSTI TEKHNICHESKOI LITERATURY. STROITELSTVO I ARKHITEKTURA. RAZDEL SERIIA X: SANITARNAIA TEKHNIKA, INZHENERNOE OBORUDOVANIE ZDANII. Added/Corp Moscow. Tsentralnyi Institut Nauchnoi Informatsii po Stroitelstvu i Arkhitekture. Tsentralnaia Nauchno-Tekhnicheskaia Biblioteka po Stroitelstvu i Arkhitekture. Informatsionno-Bibliograficheskii Otdel. **VFOAT** Stroitelstvo I Arkhitektura. Seriia X: Sanitarnaia Tekhnika, Inzhenernoe Oborudovanie Zdanii; Sanitarnaia Tekhnika, Inzhenernoe Oborudovanie Zdanii. (1974)-. Multiple languages (Russian and Multiple languages). mo. Informatsii po Stroitelstvu i Arkhitekture, A-47 Ulitsa Gorkogo Dom 38, Moscow 125047 Russia. **LC** Z5853.S22; N673; TD145. **Continues** Novosti Tekhnicheskoi Literatury. Stroitelstvo I Arkhitektura. Razdel A. Seriia XII: Sanitarnaia Tekniika, Inzhemeneo Oborudovsnie Zdanii.

US
NSWMA REPORTS FOR THE WASTE MANAGEMENT INDUSTRY / NATIONAL SOLID WASTES MANAGEMENT ASSOCIATION. VFOAT N.S.W.M.A. Reports for the Waste Management Industry. **VAT** National Solid Wastes Management Association Reports for the Waste Management Industry. Began with: Vol. 12, No. 6 (June 1977). Periodical. English. mo. National Solid Wastes Management Association, Suite 930/1120 Connecticut Avenue NW, Washington DC 20036. **Continues** NSWMA Washington Report.

US
NTIS ALERT. ENVIRONMENTAL POLLUTION & CONTROL. (1992)-. English. Twenty-four times a year. $175.00 US; $245.00 other. National Technical Information Service - NTIS, Room 2027S, 5285 Port Royal Road, Springfield VA 22161. **Tel** (703)487-4630, (703)487-4660, (703)487-4650, FAX (703)321-8547, telex 89-9405. **Continues** Environmental Pollution & Control / NTIS, 0364-4936.

US/1066-016X
NUCLEAR SAFETY & CLEANUP REPORT. Title Change. [Nucl. saf. cleanup rep.]. **Added/Corp** Business Publishers. **VFOAT** Nuclear Safety and Cleanup Report; CIS/Eastern Europe Nuclear Safety & Cleanup Report. (Aug. 1992)-(Aug. 1994). Periodical. English. mo. Business Publishers Inc., 951 Pershing Drive, Silver Spring MD 20910-4464. **Tel** (301)587-6300, (800)274-0122, FAX (301)585-9075. **LC** IN PROCESS. **DD** 363. **Absorbed by** Nuclear Waste News, 0276-2897.

US/0196-772X
NUCLEAR WASTE MANAGEMENT PROGRAM SUMMARY DOCUMENT. [Nucl. waste manage. program summ. doc.]. **Main/Corp** United States. Dept. of Energy. Office of Nuclear Waste Management. English. National Technical Information Service - NTIS, Room 2027S, 5285 Port Royal Road, Springfield VA 22161. **Tel** (703)487-4630, (703)487-4660, (703)487-4650, FAX (703)321-8547, telex 89-9405. **LC** TD898; .U533A. **DD** 363.7/28.

US/0276-2897
NUCLEAR WASTE NEWS (SILVER SPRING, MD.). (NUCLEAR WASTE NEWS.). [Nucl. waste news]. Vol. 1, No. 1 (Feb. 12, 1981)-. Periodical. English. wk. $695.00. Business Publishers Inc., 951 Pershing Drive, Silver Spring MD 20910-4464. **Tel** (301)587-6300, (800)274-0122, FAX (301)585-9075. **[CCC].** available on an online database (file 636/Full-Text) from DIALOG. **Continues in part** Hazardous Waste News, Including Nuclear Waste Bulletin, 0275-374X; **Absorbed** Nuclear Safety & Cleanup, 1066-016X.
Desc: The information source that you can rely on for up to the minute information on radioactive waste management. You're also kept up to date on what other nations are doing in the field. Special sections are devoted to calendar listings of important conferences, publications announcements, and people in the news.
Ind/Abst PTS Newsl. Database [Full Txt.].

CC/1000-0267
NUNG YEH HUAN CHING PAO HU. **Added/Corp** Chung-kuo Nung Yeh Huan Ching Pao hu Hsieh Hui. Nung mu yu Yeh pu Huan Ching Pao hu ko Yen Chien Tse so (China). **VFOAT** Agro-Environmental Protection; Nongye Huanjing Baohu. (19??)-. Periodical. Chinese (summaries and/or abstracts in English; table of contents in English). bm. RMBY9.00. Zhongguo Nongye Shengtai Huanjing Baohu Xiehui, Chinese Society of Agro-Ecological Environment Protection, 31 Kangfu Lu, Nankai Qu, Tianjin 300191 People's Republic of China. **Tel** 361247. **ED** M. Yongbin. **LC** S589.75; .N86. **DD** 363.7/31. **Pr Rev.**
Desc: Covers agricultural pollution and environmental protection.

UK/0959-9134
O.S.B.E.R. OIL SPILL BULLETIN AND ENVIRONMENTAL REVIEW. [O.S.B.E.R., Oil spill bull. environ. rev.]. **VFOAT** Oil Spill Bulletin and Environmental Review. (1990)-. Bulletin. English. Twelve times a year. £75.00 UK; £85.00 Europe; £95.00. Alba International Ltd, Leading Light Building, 142 Sinclair Road, Aberdeen AB1 3PR Scotland. **Tel** 0224 878188, FAX 0224 879781, telex 73337 ALBA G. **ED** John McMurtrie. **Bk Rev**, (Qty: 4). **Ad Acc**, **Adv Mgr:** Frances Johnson, **Tel** 0224 878188 x 32. **Pr Rev. Acid Free. Circ:** 1,000 (ctrl). available in print.

IE/0332-4397
OFFALY RESOURCES FOR ENVIRONMENTAL STUDIES / COUNTY OFFALY VOCATIONAL EDUCATION COMMITTEE. [Offaly resour. environ. stud.]. **VFOAT** Resources for Environmental Studies. 1-. Monographic series. English. Price varies per volume.
Ind/Abst GeoRef.

GW
OFFENTLICHE ABFALLBESEITIGUNG. German. ir. DM7.50. Niedersachsisches Landesverwaltungsamt, Postfach 107, 3000 Hannover Germany. **Tel** (0511)108-9466. **LC** TD789.G42; L686. **DD** 363.7/28/0943. **Bk Rev. Circ:** 400.
Desc: Covers public waste product removal.

US/1054-9277
OFFICIAL GUIDE FOR THE TRANSPORTATION OF HAZARDOUS MATERIALS, THE. [Off. guide transp. hazard. mater.]. **VFOAT** Hazardous Materials; Hazardous Materials Directory. (1989)-. English. an. $157.00 US, Canada & Mexico; $163.00 other. K III Press Inc., 424 West 33rd Street, New York NY 10001. **Tel** (212)714-3100, (800)221-5488. **LC** IN PROCESS. **DD** 363.

JA
OITA-KEN KOGAI EISEI SENTA NENPO. **Main/Corp** Oita-Ken Kogai Eisei Senta. **VFOAT** Annual Report of Institute of Environmental Pollution and Public Health, Oita Prefecture. Japanese (Japanese). an. Oita-Ken Kogai Eisei Senta, Aza Yoshikawara Danchi, Oaza Magari, Oita-shi 870 Japan. **LC** TD187.5.J32; O437.

US/8756-8322
OKLAHOMA'S WATER QUALITY STANDARDS. [Okla. water qual. stand.]. English. Oklahoma Water Resources Board, 2241 NW 40th Street, Oklahoma City OK 73112. **LC** TD224.O5; A3 subser. **DD** 363.7/39462/09766.

CN
ONATRIO RECYCLING RESOURCEBOOK. an. 79.00Can$. Southam Information and Technology Group Inc., 1450 Don Mills Road, Don Mills Ontario M3B 2X7 Canada. **Tel** (416)445-6641, (800)668-2374, FAX (416)442-2261.

CN/0383-6479
ONTARIO CONSERVATION NEWS. **See** Environmental Issues-Conservation and Natural Resources.

CN/0823-6143
ONTARIO RECYCLING UPDATE. ***Title Change.*** [Ont. recycl. update]. **Added/Corp** Recycling Council of Ontario. (1981)-(19??). Periodical. English. bm. Recycling Council of Ontario, 489 College Street, Suite 504, Toronto Ontario M6G 1A5 Canada. **Tel** (416)960-1025. **ED** Jack McGinnis and Pat McFarlane. **DD** 363.7/28. **Bk Rev. Ad Acc. Circ:** 900 (ctrl). ***Continued by*** *RCO Update.*
Desc: Information on recycling, energy-from-waste, composting, etc. especially as applied to municipal solid waste, in Ontario.

US/0887-2104
OPERATIONS FORUM. (OPERATIONS FORUM : A WPCF PUBLICATION FOR WASTEWATER PROFESSIONALS.). [Oper. forum]. **Added/Corp** Water Pollution Control Federation. Vol. 1, No. 1 (July 1984)-. Periodical. English. mo. $79.00 US; $99.00 other. Water Environment Federation, 601 Wythe Street, Alexandria VA 22314-1994. **Tel** (703)684-2400, FAX (703)684-2492. **DD** 628. Index available (free).
Desc: Reports from water and wastewater treatment plants from across the country offering practical and proven solutions to common operations problems.
Ind/Abst Pollut. Abstr. Indexes.

CN/0715-0237
OWMC EXCHANGE, THE. [OWMC exch.]. **Main/Corp** Ontario Waste Management Corporation. **VFOAT** Exchange. **VAT** Ontario Waste Management Corporation Exchange; Exchange (Toronto. 1982). Vol. 1, No. 1 (Summer 1982)-. Periodical. English. qt. Free. Ontario Waste Management Corporation, 2 Bloor Street West/11th Floor, Toronto Ontario M4W 3E2 Canada. **DD** 363.1/76/09713.

US
PACIFIC NORTHWEST REGION ENVIRONMENTAL QUALITY PROFILE / UNITED STATES ENVIRONMENTAL PROTECTION AGENCY, REGION 10. English. an. US Environmental Protection Agency Region 10, 1200 Sixth Avenue, Seattle WA 98101. **LC** TD171.3.N67; P32. **DD** 363.7/02/09795.

US/1072-1223
PAPER RECYCLER. **Added/Corp** Miller Freeman Inc. (19??)-. Newsletter. English. Twelve times a year. $327.00. Miller Freeman Inc., 600 Harrison Street, San Francisco CA 94107. **Tel** (415)905-2337, FAX (415)905-2240, telex 278273.
Desc: Covers and forecasts changes in supply, demand, and price for grades in all five wastepaper categories - old newspapers, old corrugated containers, mixed paper, pulp substitutes, and deinking grades.

CN/0083-8799
PAPERS PRESENTED AT THE ANNUAL CONVENTION. (PAPERS PRESENTED AT THE ANNUAL CONVENTION - WESTERN CANADA WATER AND SEWAGE CONFERENCE.). **Main/Corp** Western Canada Water and Sewage Conference. Periodical. English. **LC** TD201; .W5. **DD** 628; 628/.09712.

II
PARYAVARAN ABSTRACTS. **Added/Corp** Environmental Information System (India). Vol. 1, No. 1 (Dec. 1984)-. Periodical. English. qt. Centre Science & Environment, 807 Vishal Bhawan, 95 Nehru Pl., New Delhi 110019 India. **Tel** 643-3394 or 613-8109. **LC** TD171.5.I4; P37. **DD** 363.7/00954.

CN/0703-7643
PEST MANAGEMENT PAPERS. ***Ceased.*** **Added/Corp** Simon Fraser University. Pestology Centre. No. 1 (1975)-No. 30. Monographic series. English. ir. Simon Fraser University, University Bookstore, Burnaby BC V5A 1S6 Canada. **Tel** (604)291-3224, FAX (604)291-4969.

US
PHOENIX : VOICE OF THE SCRAP RECYCLING INDUSTRY. **Added/Corp** Institute of Scrap Recycling Industries. Vol. 21, No. 3 (Fall 1989)-. Periodical. English. ir. Free. ISRI Institute of the Scrap Recycling Industries Inc, 1325 G Street Northwest, Washington DC 20005. **Tel** (202)737-1770, FAX (202)626-0900. **ED** David Krohne. **Circ:** 45,000. ***Continues*** *Phoenix Quarterly (Washington, D.C.).*

UK/0032-020X
PIPES & PIPELINES INTERNATIONAL (1965). **See** Petroleum and Natural Gas.

US
PLANNED AIR POLLUTION RESEARCH / STATE OF CALIFORNIA, AIR RESOURCES BOARD. **Added/Corp** California. Air Resources Board. (1991)-. English. **LC** TD883.5.C2; L664. ***Continues*** *Research Plan (California. Air Resources Board).*

US/1046-3046
PLASTIC WASTE STRATEGIES. ***Title Change.*** **See** Packaging.

FR/0300-3574
POLLUSTOP. **VFOAT** Pollu Stop. Periodical. French. mo. Editions Edidam, 4, Avenue De La Porte-Villiers, 17 EME Parris France. **LC** HC280.E5; P63. **DD** 301.31/0944.

US/0092-0320
POLLUTING INCIDENTS IN AND AROUND U.S. WATERS. (POLLUTING INCIDENTS IN AND AROUND U.S. WATERS / DEPARTMENT OF TRANSPORTATION, COAST GUARD.). **VAT** Polluting Incidents in and Around United States Waters. English. an. G-WEP-1/73, US Coast Guard, Washington DC 20590. **LC** TD223; .U5A. **DD** 614.7/72/0973. ***Continues*** *Polluting Spills in U.S. Waters.*

UK/0048-4748
POLLUTION. (19??)-. English. Twelve times a year. £82.50 UK; £87.50 other. Springfield Information Services / Petersborough, PO Box 31, Cross Street Court, Peterborough PE1 1SD England. **Tel** 011 44 733 267272.

US/0191-1724
POLLUTION ABSTRACTS. ANNUAL INDEX. **See** Environmental Issues-Abstracting, Bibliographies and Statistics.

US/0032-3624
POLLUTION ABSTRACTS WITH INDEXES. **See** Environmental Issues-Abstracting, Bibliographies and Statistics.

FR
POLLUTION ATMOSPHERIQUE ET NUISANCES / PREFECTURE DE POLICE, LABORATOIRE CENTRAL. **Main/Corp** Paris (France). Prefecture de Police. Laboratoire Central. (1990)-. French. **LC** TD883.7.F7; P37. ***Continues*** *Paris (France). Prefecture de Police. Laboratoire Central. Etudes de Pollution Atmospherique a Paris et dans les Departements Peripheriques.*

FR/0032-3632
POLLUTION ATMOSPHERIQUE (PARIS, FRANCE). (POLLUTION ATMOSPHERIQUE.). [Pollut. atmos.]. **Added/Corp** Centre National de la Recherche Scientifique (France) Association pour la Prevention de la Pollution Atmospherique (France). (1964)-. Academic Scholarly Publication. French. qt. 435.85F France; 440.00F French overseas depts. and territories; 645.00F other. Soc. Revue Pollution Atmospherique, 58 rue du Rocher, 75008 Paris France. **Tel** 011 33 1 42936930. **CODEN** POATBH. Documents available from CASDDS. ***Continues*** *Revue de la Pollution Atmospherique, 0245-9140.*
Ind/Abst Chem. Abstr.; Coal Abstr.; EMBASE; Energy Res. Abstr. (Dec. 1973-); Int. Aerosp. Abstr.; Pollut. Abstr. Indexes; Saf. Health Work.

US/0273-253X
POLLUTION (BOCA RATON). (POLLUTION.). Vol. 1, Article 1-. English. an. Social Issues Resources Series Inc, PO Box 2348, Boca Raton FL 33427. **Tel** (800)327-0513, (407)994-0079. **ED** E C Goldstein. **LC** TD172; .P64. **DD** 363.7/3/05.
Desc: Interdisciplinary resource material consisting of reprinted articles from popular and professional journals, newspapers, magazines and government documents.

US
POLLUTION CONTROL. (19??)-. English. mo. $225.00. Predicasts Inc., A Ziff Communications Company, 11001 Cedar Avenue, Cleveland OH 44106. **Tel** (800)321-6388, (216)795-3000, FAX (216)229-9944, telex 985 604. **(Subscription address:** Information Access Company, PO Box 61000, Department 1851, San Francisco, CA 94161; Phone: (800)321-6388**)**

US/0095-6074
POLLUTION CONTROL JOURNAL. Periodical. English. qt. $4.00. L Thomas, PO Box 533, Denver CO 80202. **LC** TD169; .P6416. **DD** 363.6.

FR
POLLUTION DE L'EAU DE L'AIR ET DU SOL DECHETS BRUIT, E36. French. 1021.00F France; 1055.00F other. CNRS / Institut d'Information Scientifique et Technique, (Centre National de la Recherche Scientifique), 15 Quai Anatole France, Paris 75700 France. **Tel** 011 33 1 47531515, telex 299 356 F.

US/0032-3640
POLLUTION ENGINEERING. [Pollut. eng.]. **VFOAT** Pollution Engineering Yellow Pages. Vol. 1 (Oct./Nov. 1969)-. Academic Scholarly Publication. English. mo (13 issues). $70.00 US; $102.00 Canada; $95.00 Mexico; $130.00 other. Cahners Publishing Company, 249 West 17th Street, New York NY 10011. **Tel** (212)645-0067, FAX (212)242-6987. **(Subscription address:** Cahners Publishing Company / Colorado, Paid Subscription Service Center, PO Box 7610, Highlands Ranch CO 80126-7610.**) ED** Richard A. Young. **LC** TD172; .P66. **DD** 628.5/05. **CODEN** PLENBW. **[CCC].** Index available. cum. index. **Bk Rev. Ad Acc. Circ:** 50,000 (ctrl). available on microfilm and microfiche from University Microfilms International (UMI). Documents available from Article Express International, UMI Article Clearinghouse, Ask*IEEE, CASDDS, Documents on Demand.
Desc: Includes feature articles devoted to practical engineering applications useful for the recognition, measurement, control and disposal of hazardous, solid air, and liquid containments. Every issue also includes case histories, new products and literature, and news to clarify the frequent changes in environmental control policy.
Ind/Abst ABI/INFORM Glob. Ed.; ABI Inform Ondisc (Oct. 1973-Jan. 1976); AGRICOLA; Appl. Sci. Technol. Index; AQUAREF; Bioeng. Abstr.; Ceram. Abstr.; Chem. Abstr.; Coal Abstr.; Curr. Biotechnol.; Ei Page One; EMBASE; Energy Inf. Abstr.; Energy Res. Abstr. (April 1976-); Eng. Index Annu.; Environ. Abstr.; Foods Adlibra; Ind. Hyg. Dig. (19??-19??); INSPEC (Aug. 1973-); Lit. Pat. Abstr., Oilfield Chem. (1972-); Lit. Abstr., Catal. Catal.; Lit. Abstr., Health Environ.; Lit. Abstr., Pet. Refin. Petrochem.; Lit. Abstr., Pet. Substit.; Lit. Abstr., Transp. Storage; Pollut. Abstr. Indexes; Risk Abstr.

US/0148-4435
POLLUTION ENGINEERING AND TECHNOLOGY. [Pollut. eng. technol.]. Vol. 1 (1976)-. Academic Scholarly Publication. English. ir. Price varies per volume. Marcel Dekker Inc., 270 Madison Avenue, New York NY 10016. **Tel** (212)696-9000, (800)228-1160, FAX (212)685-4540, telex 421419. **(Subscription address:** Marcel Dekker Inc, PO Box 5017, Monticello NY 12701.**)** **LC** UNC. **CODEN** PEGTDD. Documents available from Ask*IEEE, CASDDS.
Desc: Presents information on the various aspects of pollution technology and engineering. Topics include wastewater treatment and air pollution.
Ind/Abst Chem. Abstr. (-1985); INSPEC.

US/0032-3659
POLLUTION EQUIPMENT NEWS. (Dec. 1968)-. Periodical. English. Eight times a year. $35.00 (US & Canada); $50.00 (other). Rimbach Publishing Company, 8650 Babcock Boulevard, Pittsburgh PA 15237. **Tel** (412)364-5366. **ED** Richard Rimbach and David Lavender. **LC** TD1; .P64. **DD** 628/.05. **Bk Rev. Ad Acc. Circ:** 91,000 (ctrl).
Desc: Edited for the person responsible for controlling air, water, waste water, and hazardous waste pollution.
Ind/Abst Text. Technol. Dig.

UK
POLLUTION PREVENTION. English. Seven times a year. £55.00 UK; £90.00 other. MacDonald Communications / London, 281 City Road, Rococo House, London EC1V 1LA England. **Tel** 011 44 250-1234 UK, (713)-266-0610 US. **(Subscription address:** 3300 S Gessner, Suite 150, Houston TX 77063**)** **ED** Pamela Wolfe and Brian Dumbleton. **Bk Rev. Ad Acc. Circ:** 16,500 (ctrl).
Desc: Contains industry news, legislation details, product technology information, contracts awarded plus all articles on all news of the environment.

US/1056-4586
POLLUTION PREVENTION ADVISOR. [Pollut. prev. advis.]. **Added/Corp** United States. Dept. of Energy. Office of the Assistant Secretary for Defense Programs. Vol. 1, No. 1 (July 1991)-. Periodical. English. qt. Pollution Prevention Advisor, PO Box 2003, MS 7606, Oak Ridge TN 37831-7606. **DD** 363.

UK/0965-5948
POLLUTION PREVENTION LONDON. [Pollut. prev.Lond.]. (1991)-. Periodical. English. Seven times a year. $125.00. MacDonald Communications / Texas, 3300 South Gessner, Suite 118, Houston TX 77063. **Tel** (713)266-0610, FAX (713)266-6657. **DD** 363.736094.

US/1053-4253
POLLUTION PREVENTION REVIEW. [Pollut. prev. rev.]. **VFOAT** Pollution Prevention. Vol. 1, No. 1 (Winter 1990/91)-. Periodical. English. qt. $159.00 US; $209.00 other. John Wiley & Sons, Inc., 605 Third Avenue, New York NY 10158-0012. **Tel** (212)850-6000, (212)850-6645, FAX (212)850-6088, telex 12-7063. **(Subscription address:** John Wiley & Sons Inc / New Jersey, PO Box 2575, Secaucus NJ 07096-2575.**)** **LC** TD896; .P64. **DD** 363.73/7. **[CCC].** available on microfilm and microfiche from University Microfilms International (UMI).
Ind/Abst Abstr. Bull. Inst. Pap. Sci. Tech.

II/0257-8050
POLLUTION RESEARCH. [Pollut. res.]. **Added/Corp** Indian Association for Pollution Chemists and Biologists. Vol. 1, No. 1 & 2 (1982)-. Periodical. English. qt. $150.00. Indian Association for Pollution Chemists, Karad Maharashtra, India. **(Subscription address:** Prints India, 11 Darya Ganj, New Delhi, 110002 India, (Phone: 011 91 11 3268645)**)** **NLM** W1; PO254T. **CODEN** PORSDX.

US/0090-516X
POLLUTION TECHNOLOGY REVIEW. ***Ceased.*** [Pollut. technol. rev.]. (1973)-Series complete (19??). Monographic series. English. ir. Noyes Data Corporation, 120 Mill Road, Park Ridge NJ 07656. **Tel** (201)391-8484. **ED** J. Paul. **LC** UNC. **CODEN** PTERDY. Index available. Documents available from Article Express International. ***Supersedes*** *Pollution Control Review, 0079-3116.*
Desc: Environmental engineering technology.
Ind/Abst Bioeng. Abstr.; Ei Page One; Eng. Index Annu.; GeoRef.

US
POLTOX [COMPUTER FILE]. **Added/Corp** Cambridge Scientific Abstracts, Inc. **VFOAT** Pol Tox; Compact Cambridge Poltox. (1989)-. Periodical. English. qt. $1295.00 (single user). Silverplatter Information Inc., 100 River Ridge Drive, Norwood MA 02062. **Tel** (800)343-0064, (617)769-2599, FAX (617)235-1715.
Desc: Provides coverage of the last ten years of: Pollution Abstracts; Toxicology Abstracts; The National Library of Medicine's TOXLINE; Ecology Abstracts; Health and Safety Science Abstracts; the Toxicology section of Food Science and Technology Abstracts; and, AFSA Part 3: Aquatic Pollution and Environmental Quality.

CN/0380-7916
PROBE (LONDON). (THE PROBE.). (February 1971)-. Periodical. English. The Pollution Probe Foundation, 12 Madison Avenue, Toronto Ontario M5R 2S1 Canada, London Ontario Canada. **Tel** (416)926-1647. **(Subscription address:** Probe Post, 12 Madison Ave., Toronto Ont M5R 2S1 Canada**)** ***Supersedes*** *Pollution Probe, London, Ont. Newsletter, 0380-7908.*

UN
PROBLEMY KONTROLIA I ZASHCHITA ATMOSFERY OT ZAGRIAZNENIIA. **Added/Corp** Instytut Tekhnichnoi Teplofizyky (Akademiia Nauk Ukrainskoi RSR). (19??)-. Academic Scholarly Publication. Russian. Izdatelstvo Naukova Dumka / Ukrainian Academy of Sciences, Vladimirskaia Ulitsa 54, 252601 Kiev Ukraine. **Tel** 225-63-66, telex 131376. **LC** TD881; .P77. **CODEN** PKZZDW. Documents available from CASDDS.
Ind/Abst Chem. Abstr.

US/0193-9688
PROCEEDINGS, A&WMA ANNUAL MEETING. **Main/Corp** Air & Waste Management Association. (1???)-. Academic Scholarly Publication. English. Documents available from CASDDS.
Ind/Abst Chem. Abstr.

US/0160-6751
PROCEEDINGS AND PAPERS OF THE ANNUAL CONFERENCE OF THE CALIFORNIA MOSQUITO AND VECTOR CONTROL ASSOCIATION. [Proc. pap. annu. conf. Calif. Mosq. Vector Control Assoc., inc.]. **Main/Corp** California Mosquito and Vector Control Association. Vol. 45 (1977)-. Academic Scholarly Publication. English. an. $21.00. California Mosquito Vector Control Association, 197 Otto Circle, Sacramento CA 95822. **Tel** (916)393-7216, FAX (916)393-8624. **ED** John C Combs. **NLM** W1 PR583. **CODEN** PCMVDZPCMUDZ. Index available. **Bk Rev. Ad Acc. Circ:** 600. Documents available from BIOSIS Document Express, CASDDS. ***Continues*** *Proceedings and Papers of the Annual Conference of the California Mosquito Control Association, Inc., 0091-6501.*
Desc: Mosquito research papers presented at the California Mosquito and Vector Control Association, Inc Annual Conference.
Ind/Abst AGRICOLA [Full Cov.]; Biocont. News Inf.; Biol. Abstr. (-1985); Chem. Abstr.; Dairy Sci. Abstr.; Index Vet.; Nematol. Abstr.; Rev. Med. Vet. Entomol.

US/0198-7267
PROCEEDINGS, ANNUAL MEETING - NEW JERSEY MOSQUITO CONTROL ASSOCIATION, INC. [Proc., annu. meet. - N. J. Mosq. Control Assoc.]. **Main/Corp** New Jersey Mosquito Control Association. **Added/Corp** American Mosquito Control Association. Proceedings, Annual Meeting - American Mosquito Control Association. 62nd (1975)-. English. an. Mosquito Research & Control, PO Box 231, Cook College, New Brunswick NJ 08903. **Tel** (201)549-0665. **ED** Henry R. Rupp. **NLM** W1; NE446R. **CODEN** PMNADD. cum. index. **Circ:** 500. ***Continues*** *Proceedings of the Annual Meeting - New Jersey Mosquito Extermination Association, 0096-5596.*
Desc: Papers on mosquito control: pesticides, biological control, environmental management and mosquito borne diseases.
Ind/Abst AGRICOLA.

US/0278-5986
PROCEEDINGS - NORTH AMERICAN MOTOR VEHICLE EMISSIONS CONTROL CONFERENCE. (PROCEEDINGS / SPONSORS, STATE AND TERRITORIAL AIR POLLUTION PROGRAM ADMINISTRATORS, U.S. ENVIRONMENTAL PROTECTION AGENCY.). [Proc.- North Am. Mot. Veh. Control. Conf.]. **Main/Conf** North American Motor Vehicle Emissions Control Conference. **Added/Corp** State and Territorial Air Pollution Program Administrators (U.S.) United States. Environmental Protection Agency. (19??)-. Proceedings. English. an. **LC** TD886.5; .N67a. **DD** 363.7/392.

US/0145-4781
PROCEEDINGS OF NATIONAL WASTE PROCESSING CONFERENCE (1976). (PROCEEDINGS OF THE NATIONAL WASTE PROCESSING CONFERENCE.). [Proc. Natl. Waste Process. Conf.]. **Main/Conf** National Waste Processing Conference. **Added/Corp** American Society of Mechanical Engineers. Solid Waste Processing Division. **VFOAT** Discussions. 7th (1976)-. Academic Scholarly Publication. English. ir. $155.00. American Society of Mechanical Engineers, 22 Law Drive, Fairfield NJ 07007. **Tel** (201)882-1167, (212)705-7722 (editorial). **LC** TD796; .N38a. **DD** 628.4/45/05. **CODEN** PWPCDV. **[CCC].** Documents available from Article Express International, CASDDS. ***Continues*** *Proceedings of ... National Incinerator Conference, 0085-3763.*
Ind/Abst Bioeng. Abstr.; Chem. Abstr.; Ei Page One; Eng. Index Annu.

CN/0833-5192
PROCEEDINGS OF THE ... ANNUAL CONVENTION, INCLUDING THE ... ANNUAL CONVENTION OF THE WESTERN CANADA SECTION, AMERICAN WATER WORKS ASSOCIATION, AND THE ... ANNUAL CONVENTION OF THE WESTERN CANADA POLLUTION CONTROL ASSOCIATION, WATER POLLUTION CONTROL FEDERATION. **See** Water Resources.

CN
PROCEEDINGS OF THE ANNUAL JOINT MEETING OF THE PUBLIC ADVISORY COMMITTEE ON THE ENVIRONMENT AND THE ENVIRONMENT COUNCIL OF ALBERTA. **Main/Corp** Environment Council of Canada. Public Advisory Committee on the Environment. **VFOAT** Proceedings of the ... Annual Joint Meeting with the Environment Council of Alberta. (Nov. 1980)-. Proceedings. English. an. Environment Council of Alberta, 2100 College Plaza Tower 3, 8215 112th Street, Edmonton Alberta T6G 2M4 Canada. **LC** HC117.A6; E6A. **DD** 363.7/0097123. ***Continues*** *Annual Joint Meeting of the Public Advisory Committee and the Environment Council of Alberta.*

US/0160-2950
PROCEEDINGS OF THE ANNUAL NORTHEASTERN FOREST INSECT WORK CONFERENCE. **Main/Conf** Northeastern Forest Insect Work Conference. **Added/Corp** Northeastern Forest Experiment Station (Radnor, Pa.). (1968)-. English. an. Pennsylvania Department of Agriculture, 2301 North Cameron Street, Harrisburg PA 17110. **Tel** (717)772-2853, FAX (717)787-2387.

US/0163-2345
PROCEEDINGS OF THE INDUSTRIAL WASTE, ADVANCED WATER AND SOLID WASTE CONFERENCE. **Main/Conf** Industrial Waste, Advanced Water and Solid Waste Conference. Proceedings. English. **LC** TD896; .I63A. **DD** 628/.4.

US/0073-7682
PROCEEDINGS OF THE INDUSTRIAL WASTE CONFERENCE. [Proc. Ind. Waste Conf.]. 1st (1944)-. Proceedings. English. an (April). $95.00. Lewis Publishing Inc., 2000 Corporate Boulevard Northwest, Boca Raton FL 33431. **Tel** (313)475-8619, telex 949478. **(Subscription address:** CRC Press, Inc., 2000 Corporate Boulevard Northwest, Boca Raton, FL 33431; telephone: (800)272-7737**)** **LC** TP995.A1; I5. **DD** 660.288.
Desc: Contains information on waste products.

BE/0377-7669
PROCEEDINGS OF THE MEETING OF THE EXPERT PANEL ON AIR POLLUTION MODELING. **Main/Corp** North Atlantic Treaty Organization. Expert Panel on Air Pollution Modeling. Proceedings. English. North Atlantic Treaty Organization / NATO Scientific Affairs Division, B 1110 Brussels Belgium. **LC** TD881; .N63A. **DD** 628.5/3/0184.

US/0149-3019
PROCEEDINGS OF THE TECHNICAL PROGRAM - NATIONAL NOISE AND VIBRATION CONTROL CONFERENCE. [Proc. tech. program]. **Main/Conf** National Noise and Vibration Control Conference. **VFOAT** Noisexpo Proceedings. 1973-. Proceedings. English. an. Acoustical Publications, 27101 E Oviatt Rd, PO Box 40416, Bay Village OH 44140. **Tel** (216)835-0101, FAX (216)835-9303. **LC** TD891; .N35A. **DD** 363.6. **NLM** W3 NO372. **CODEN** PTPCDA. Documents available from Article Express International.
Ind/Abst Bioeng. Abstr.; Ei Page One; Eng. Index Annu.

US/0193-1652
PROFILE OF ENVIRONMENTAL QUALITY. REGION 8: COLORADO, MONTANA, NORTH DAKOTA, SOUTH DAKOTA, UTAH, WYOMING. (PROFILE OF ENVIRONMENTAL QUALITY. REGION 8, COLORADO, MONTANA, NORTH DAKOTA, SOUTH DAKOTA, UTAH, WYOMING / UNITED STATES ENVIRONMENTAL PROTECTION AGENCY, REGION 8, OFFICE OF PUBLIC AWARENESS.). **VAT** Profile of Environmental Quality. Region Eight: Colorado, Montana, North Dakota, South Dakota, Utah, Wyoming. Began with 1978. English. US Environmental Protection Agency / Denver, 999 18th Street 1300, Denver CO 80202-2413. **LC** TD181.M54; U54A. **DD** 614.7.0978.

US/0093-8106
PROGRAM AND PROJECT ACCOMPLISHMENTS (NEW ORLEANS). (PROGRAM AND PROJECT ACCOMPLISHMENTS; ANNUAL PROGRESS REPORT.). **Main/Corp** Louisiana. Air Control Commission. English. an. Air Control Commission, PO Box 60630, New Orleans LA 70160. **LC** TD883.5.L8; L67A. **DD** 363.6.

CN/0849-3650
PROGRAM OVERVIEW - WASTEWATER TECHNOLOGY CENTRE, CANADA. (PROGRAM OVERVIEW.). [Program overv. - Wastewater Technol. Cent. Can.]. **Main/Corp** Wastewater Technology Centre (Canada). **VFOAT** Wastewater Technology Centre ... Program Overview. (1989)-. English. Eastman Kodak Company, 343 State Street, Department 412 L, Rochester NY 14650. **Tel** (716)724-4000, (800)242-2424. **DD** 363.72/84/097105. ***Continues*** *Annual Report - Wastewater Technology Centre., 0317-7890.*

US
PROGRAM REQUIREMENTS MEMORANDA FOR FISCAL YEAR ... : MUNICIPAL WASTEWATER TREATMENT WORKS CONSTRUCTION GRANTS PROGRAM / UNITED STATES ENVIRONMENTAL PROTECTION AGENCY, OFFICE OF WATER PROGRAMS OPERATIONS. **Main/Corp** United States. Environmental Protection Agency. Office of Water Program Operations. (19??)-. English. an. United States Environmental Protection Agency / Office of Water Program Operations WH-547, Washington DC 20460.

US/8756-4866
PROGRESS AND CHALLENGE, WASTE-TO-ENERGY PROJECTS. (PROGRESS AND CHALLENGE, WASTE-TO-ENERGY PROJECTS / CALIFORNIA WASTE MANAGEMENT BOARD.). **Main/Corp** California Waste Management Board. **VFOAT** Waste-to-Energy Projects. 1982-. English. an. California Waste Management Board, 1020 Ninth Street/Suite 300, Sacramento CA 95814. **LC** TD796.2; .C35A. **DD** 333.79/38/09794. ***Continues*** *Refuse-to-Energy Projects Report for ..., 8756-4874.*

US/0098-0463
PROGRESS IN AIR POLLUTION CONTROL. **Main/Corp** Wayne Co., Mich. Air Pollution Control Division. (19??)-. English. Wayne County Health Department, Air Pollution Control Division, 1311 East Jefferson, Detroit MI 48207. **LC** TD883.5.M47; W38a. **DD** 363.6. ***Continues*** *Wayne Co., Mich. Air Pollution Control Division. Air Pollution Control Progress Report.*

US/0090-5860
PROGRESS IN HAZARDOUS CHEMICALS HANDLING AND DISPOSAL. **Main/Conf** Symposium on Hazardous Chemicals Handling and Disposal. 3d- 1972-. English. $20.00. Noyes Data Corporation, 120 Mill Road, Park Ridge NJ 07656. **Tel** (201)391-8484. **LC** T55.3.H3; S95. **DD** 660.2/804. **NLM** W3 PR9461. ***Continues*** *Hazardous Chemicals Handling and Disposal.*

US/1061-1452
PROGRESS IN PAPER RECYCLING. **See** Paper and Pulp Industry.

UK/0271-7395
PROGRESS IN RESOURCE MANAGEMENT AND ENVIRONMENTAL PLANNING. [Prog. resour. manage. environ. plann.]. Vol. 1 (1979)-. Monographic series. English. ir. Price varies per volume. John Wiley & Sons Ltd., Baffins Lane, Chichester West Sussex PO19 1UD England. **Tel** 0243 779777, FAX 0243 776128 BTG:JWP001, telex 86290 WIBOOKG. **(Subscription address:** John Wiley & Sons Inc / New Jersey, PO Box 2575, Secaucus NJ 07096-2575.**) ED** T O'Riordan and R C D'Arge. **LC** HN18; .P756. **DD** 361.6/1.

US/0098-7069
PROGRESS IN THE IMPLEMENTATION OF MOTOR VEHICLE EMISSION STANDARDS. (PROGRESS IN THE IMPLEMENTATION OF MOTOR VEHICLE EMISSION STANDARDS : REPORT TO CONGRESS.). **Main/Corp** United States. Environmental Protection Agency. English. US Environmental Protection Agency / Office of Public Affairs, 401 M Street SW, Washington DC 20460. **LC** TD886.5; .U46A. **DD** 363.6.

●CN/1195-6755
PROMOTION DE LA SANTE AU CANADA. (1993)-. Periodical. French. qt. Department National Health and Welfare, Ottowa, Ontario K1A 1B4 Canada. **Tel** (613)954-8842, FAX (613)990-7097. ***Continues*** *Promotion de la Sante, 0833-7608.* **Ind/Abst** Can. Period. Index.

CN/0833-7608
PROMOTION DE LA SANTE (OTTAWA). ***Title Change.*** (PROMOTION DE LA SANTE.). [Promot. sante]. **Added/Corp** Canada. Direction de la Promotion de la Sante. Vol. 24, No. 2 (Autumn 1985)-(1993). Periodical. French. qt. Department National Health and Welfare, Ottowa, Ontario K1A 1B4 Canada. **Tel** (613)954-8842, FAX (613)990-7097. **DD** 613/.07/071. ***Continues*** *Education Sanitaire, 0700-1991.* ***Continued by*** *Promotion de la Sante au Canada, 1195-6755.* **Ind/Abst** Can. Period. Index.

US
PROPERTIES OF RADIOACTIVE WASTES AND WASTE CONTAINERS, PROGRESS REPORT / NUCLEAR WASTE MANAGEMENT RESEARCH GROUP, DEPARTMENT OF NUCLEAR ENERGY, BROOKHAVEN NATIONAL LABORATORY. English. qt. National Technical Information Service - NTIS, Room 2027S, 5285 Port Royal Road, Springfield VA 22161. **Tel** (703)487-4630, (703)487-4660, (703)487-4650, FAX (703)321-8547, telex 89-9405.

US
PROPOSED FISCAL YEAR ... PROGRAM. FINAL ENVIRONMENTAL IMPACT STATEMENT / BONNEVILLE POWER ADMINISTRATION. **Main/Corp** United States. Bonneville Power Administration. **VFOAT** Final Environmental Impact Statement. English. an. National Technical Information Service - NTIS, Room 2027S, 5285 Port Royal Road, Springfield VA 22161. **Tel** (703)487-4630, (703)487-4660, (703)487-4650, FAX (703)321-8547, telex 89-9405. ***Continues*** *United States. Bonneville Power Administration. Final Environmental Statement.*

US
PUBLICATIONS AND FINAL REPORTS ON CONTRACTS AND GRANTS. English. an. US Department of Commerce / National Oceanic & Atmospheric Administration NOAA, 6010 Executive Boulevard, Washington Science Center, Building 5, Rockville MD 20852. **Tel** (202)482-6090, FAX (202)482-3154. available on microfiche (Vols. for (1983-) distributed to depository libraries).

SW/0280-4026
PUBLIKATION / CHALMERS TEKNISKA HOGSKOLA, GOTEBORG, INSTITUTIONEN FOR VATTENFORSORJNINGS- OCH AVLOPPSTEKNIK. [Publ. - Chalmers tek. hogs. Goteb., Inst. vattenforsorjn.-avloppstek.]. 1982-. Academic Scholarly Publication. Swedish. ir. Price varies per volume. Institutionen for Vattenforsorjnings- och Avloppsteknik, Chalmers Tekniska Hogskola 412 96, Goteborg Sweden. **Tel** 46/31/722121, FAX 46/31/189705. **CODEN** PCTHET. Documents available from CASDDS. ***Formed by the union of*** *Publikation A (Chalmers Tekniska Hogskola. Institutionen for Va-Teknik); Publikation B (Chalmers Tekniska Hogskola. Institutionen for Va-Teknik)* ***and*** *Publikation C (Chalmers Tekniska Hogskola. Institutionen for Va-Teknik).* **Ind/Abst** Chem. Abstr.

US/0161-7796
RADIATION PROTECTION ACTIVITIES. **Main/Corp** United States. Environmental Protection Agency. Office of Radiation Programs. 1976-. English. an. Environmental Protection Agency / Office of Radiation Programs, Office of Radiation Programs, 401 M Street SW, Washington DC 20460. **LC** TD196.R3; U53B. **DD** 614.8/39/0973. **NLM** W2 A O35A. ***Continues*** *Radiation Protection.*

US/0891-3013
RADIOACTIVE EXCHANGE, THE. [Radioact. exch.]. Vol. 1, No. 1 (Jan. 1982)-. Periodical. English. Two issues per month (except Aug.). $549.00 US and Canada; $569.00 other. Exchange Publications, 2014 P Street NW, Washington DC 20036. **Tel** (202)296-2814, FAX (202)362-5437. **(Subscription address:** Exchange Publications, PO Box 5757, Washington DC 20016.**) DD** 363.

US
RADIOACTIVE MATERIALS RELEASED FROM NUCLEAR POWER PLANTS ... ANNUAL REPORT. **Added/Corp** Brookhaven National Laboratory. U.S. Nuclear Regulatory Commission. Office of Management and Program Analysis. U.S. Nuclear Regulatory Commission. Office of Management Information and Program Control. U.S. Nuclear Regulatory Commission. Division of Data Automation and Management Information. U.S. Nuclear Regulatory Commission. Division of Budget and Analysis. U.S. Nuclear Regulatory Commission. Office of Administration and Resources Management. U.S. Nuclear Regulatory Commission. Division of Rules and Records. U.S. Nuclear Regulatory Commission. Office of Information and Resources Management. (1974)-. Government Publication. English. an. $16.00. Superintendent of Documents, US Government Printing Office, Washington DC 20402. **Tel** (202)275-3328, FAX (202)786-2377. **LC** TD899.A8; R3. **DD** 363.72/892/0973021. available on microfiche (Vols. for 1980- distributed to depository libraries).

●UK/1065-609X
RADIOACTIVE WASTE MANAGEMENT AND ENVIRONMENTAL RESTORATION. (1993)-. Periodical. English. Four times a year (4 issues per volume). $463.00 university and hospital libraries, $723.00 other. Harwood Academic Publishers, PO Box 90, Reading RG1 8JL England. **Tel** 011 44 734 560080. ***Continues*** *Radioactive Waste Management and the Nuclear Fuel Cycle, 0739-5876.*

SZ/0739-5876
RADIOACTIVE WASTE MANAGEMENT AND THE NUCLEAR FUEL CYCLE. ***Title Change.*** [Radioact. waste manage. nucl. fuel cycle]. Vol. 3, No. 1 (Sept. 1982)-. Academic Scholarly Publication. English. qt. Harwood Academic Publishers, PO Box 90, Reading RG1 8JL England. **Tel** 011 44 734 560080. **(Subscription address:** International Publishers Distributor at one of the following addresses: 820 Town Center Drive, Langhorne, PA 19047; or PO Box 90, Reading Berkshire RG1 8JL UK; or Kent Ridge PO Box 1180, Singapore 9111, Republic of Singapore**) ED** A M Platt and D R Anderson. **LC** TD812; .R33. **DD** 621.48/38/05. **CODEN** RWMCD4. **[CCC]**. Index available. **Bk Rev. Ad Acc. Pr Rev.** Documents available from Article Express International, The Genuine Article, Ask*IEEE, CASDDS, Documents on Demand. ***Continues*** *Radioactive Waste Management (Chur, Switzerland : 1980), 0142-2405.* ***Continued by*** *Radioactive Waste Management and Environmental Restoration.*
Desc: Reports on waste disposal problems derived from nuclear energy production and the use of radio isotope techniques in industrial, scientific and medical fields.
Ind/Abst Bioeng. Abstr.; Chem. Abstr.; Curr. Contents Eng. Tech. Appl. Sci.; Ei Page One; EMBASE; Energy Inf. Abstr.; Energy Res. Abstr. (March 1983-); Eng. Index Annu.; Environ. Abstr.; Environ. Period. Bibliogr.; GeoRef; INSPEC (1982-); Life Sci. Collect.; Res. Alert [Select. Cov.].

SZ/0275-7273
RADIOACTIVE WASTE MANAGEMENT (CHUR, SWITZERLAND : 1981). (RADIOACTIVE WASTE MANAGEMENT.). [Radioact. waste manage.]. (1981)-. Academic Scholarly Publication. English. ir. Price varies per volume. Harwood Academic Publishers, PO Box 90, Reading RG1 8JL England. **Tel** 011 44 734 560080. **(Subscription address:** International Publishers Distributor at one of the following addresses: 820 Town Center Drive, Langhorne, PA 19047; or PO Box 90, Reading Berkshire RG1 8JL UK; or Kent Ridge PO Box 1180, Singapore 9111, Republic of Singapore**) ED** R. D. Anderson. **DD** 604. **CODEN** RAWMDW. **Bk Rev. Ad Acc.** Documents available from Ask*IEEE, CASDDS.
Ind/Abst Chem. Abstr.; INSPEC.

US/0898-8161
RADIOACTIVE WASTE MANAGEMENT HANDBOOK. [Radioact. waste manage. handb.]. Vol. 1, (1989)-. Monographic series. English. ir. Price varies per volume. Harwood Academic Publishers / New York, PO Box 786, Cooper Station, New York NY 10276. **Tel** (212)206-8900, (201)643-7500. **(Subscription address:** International Publishers Distributor at one of the following addresses: 820 Town Center Drive, Langhorne, PA 19047; or PO Box 90, Reading Berkshire RG1 8JL UK; or Kent Ridge PO Box 1180, Singapore 9111, Republic of Singapore**) LC** UNC. **DD** 363. **CODEN** RMHAE6.

US/0275-3707
RADIOACTIVE WASTE MANAGEMENT (OAK RIDGE, TENN.). (RADIOACTIVE WASTE MANAGEMENT.). [Radioact. waste manage.]. **Added/Corp** United States. Dept. of Energy. Technical Information Center. (Jan. 15, 1981)-. Government Publication. English. Twelve times a year. $180.00 US; $360.00 other. US Department of Energy, 1000 Independence Avenue SW, Washington DC 20585. **Tel** (202)586-5000, FAX (202)586-4073. **(Subscription address:** National Technical Information Service, 5285 Port Royal Road, Springfield, VA 22161**)**

US/1054-8815
RADIOLOGICAL INSPECTION REPORTS. [Radiol. insp. rep.]. (Feb. 15, 1991)-. Periodical. English. mo. $4200.00. Family Matters Press, PO Box 5674, Rockville MD 20855. **Tel** (301)309-9329. **DD** 658.

US/0363-9819
RADIOLOGICAL QUALITY OF THE ENVIRONMENT. (RADIOLOGICAL QUALITY OF THE ENVIRONMENT IN THE UNITED STATES.). **Main/Corp** United States. Environmental Protection

Environmental Issues —Pollution and Waste Management

Agency. Office of Radiation Programs. May (1976)-. Periodical. English. an. US Environmental Protection Agency / Office of Radiation Programs, 401 M Street SW, Washington DC 20460. **LC** TD196.R3; U53a. **DD** 614.8/39. **NLM** W1 RA335.

US/0896-7180
RADON NEWS DIGEST. [Radon news dig.]. (1987)-. Periodical. English. Twelve times a year. $150.00. Hoosier Environmental Publications, 801 Congressional Boulevard, Suite 200, Carmel IN 46032. **Tel** (317)843-0804. **ED** Rich Jordan and Scott Abel. **DD** 363. Index available. **Bk Rev. Ad Acc.** ctrl circ.
Desc: Timely information for anyone interested in staying informed on the subject of radon gas. A must for attorneys, health agencies, builders, realtors, and companies with transferees. Also, an excellent source of current and background information on radon gas.

●US/1070-9541
RADWASTE MAGAZINE. Added/Corp American Nuclear Society. (1994)-. Periodical. English. Six times a year. $355.00. American Nuclear Society, PO Box 97781, Chicago IL 60678-7781. **Tel** (708)352-6611, **FAX** (708)579-8314.

US/0737-6960
RADWASTE NEWS. Ceased. [Radwaste news]. Vol. 1, No. 1 (Dec. 20, 1979)-Vol. 10 (1989). Periodical. English. ir (twenty issues per year). Regulatory Science Press, PO Box 7166, Alexandria VA 22307. **Tel** (703)765-3546. **ED** Barbara Moghissi. **LC** TD898; .R35. **DD** 363.7/28. Index available.
Desc: Covers technical, regulatory, legislative, economic and socio-political aspects of radioactive waste. Included are mixed waste, and generation, treatment, transportation and disposal.

FR
RAPPORT ANNUEL - GROUPE INTERMINISTERIEL D'EVALUATION DE L'ENVIRONNEMENT. Main/Corp France. Groupe Interministeriel d'Evaluation de l'Environnement. French. an. Documentation Francaise, 29 Quai Voltaire, 75344 Paris Cedex 7 France. **Tel** 011 33 1 40157000, **FAX** 011 33 1 40157230, telex 204 826 DOCFRAN. **LC** HC280.E5; F734A.

NE/0481-8024
RAT EN MUIS. No. 2, (July, 1961)-. Periodical. Dutch. qt.

CN
RCO UPDATE. (19??)-. English. ir. 100.00Can$ (municipalities with population of less than 20,000); 200.00Can$ (corporations municipalities with population of over 20,000); 75.00Can$ others. Recycling Council of Ontario, 489 College Street, Suite 504, Toronto Ontario M6G 1A5 Canada. **Tel** (416)960-1025. **Continues** Ontario Recycling Update, 0823-6143.

US/1053-7503
RECHARGER (RIVERSIDE, CALIF.). (RECHARGER : SERVING THE CARTRIDGE RECYCLING INDUSTRY.). [Recharger]. (19??)-. Periodical. English. mo. $45.00. Recharger, 3340 Sunrise Suite 101, Las Vegas NV 89101. **Tel** (702)438-5557. **LC** HD9696.C6; R43.

CN/0709-6402
RECOUP. Vol. 1, Mar. 1978-. Periodical. English. mo. $67.32. Recoup Publishing Ltd, PO Box 100, Chesterville Ontario K0C 1H0 Canada. **Tel** (613)448-2383, (800)267-0707. **ED** Thomas J Daigneault. **DD** 338.4/76046. **Bk Rev. Ad Acc.** ctrl circ. **Continued in part by** Recoup's Canadian Recycling Market, 0227-650X.
Desc: Resource recovery news and market trends for recyclable commodities across North America. Industrial and scientific perspectives

CN/0884-4526
RECOUP'S MATERIALS RECYCLING MARKETS. VFOAT Materials Recycling Markets. Vol. 7, No. 8 (Aug. 1984)-. Periodical. English. Twelve times a year. 97.00Can$. Recoup Publishing Ltd, PO Box 100, Chesterville Ontario K0C 1H0 Canada. **Tel** (613)448-2383, (800)267-0707. **ED** Robert E. Boulanger. **DD** 604. **Ad Acc. Circ:** 500 (ctrl). **Continues** Recoup's Recyclable Materials Update, 0824-2569.
Desc: Resource recovery news and market trends for recyclable commodities across Canada.

US/1051-9831
RECYCLED PAPER NEWS. [Recycl. pap. news]. **Added/Corp** Center for Earth Resource Management Applications. Vol. 1, No. 1 (Aug. 1990)-. Periodical. English. Ten times a year (monthly with July/Aug. & Nov./Dec issues combined). $225.00. R P Publications Inc., 6732 Huntsman Boulevard, Springfield VA 22151. **Tel** (703)451-0688. **LC** TS1120.5; .R448. **DD** 676/.142.
Ind/Abst Abstr. Bull. Inst. Pap. Sci. Tech.

CN/1183-8809
RECYCLING CANADA. [Recycl. Can.]. Vol. 1, No. 1 Dec. (1990)-. Periodical. English. mo. 110.00Can$. Sydenham Publishing, 344 23rd Street West, Owen Sound ONT N4K 4G7 Canada. **Tel** (519)371-6289, **FAX** (519)371-3676. **ED** Stella Coultas. **DD** 363.72/82/0971. Index available. **Bk Rev,** (Qty: 5-6).
Desc: Insider's report on waste management for resource recovery.

●US/1064-4938
RECYCLING SOURCEBOOK. [Recycl. sourceb.]. **Added/Corp** Gale Research Inc. (1993)-. English. be. $75.00. Gale Research Inc., 835 Penobscot Building, Detroit MI 48226. **Tel** (800)877-GALE, (313)961-2242, **FAX** (313)961-6083, telex TWX 810-221-7086. **ED** Karen Hill & Thomas J. Cichonski. **LC** TD794.5; R439. **DD** 363.72/82/0973.

●US
RECYCLING TODAY. Vol. 30, No. 11 (Nov. 1992)-. Periodical. English. mo. $30.00 US; $47.00 Canada; $105.00 other. GIE Publishing Company, 4012 Bridge Avenue, Cleveland OH 44113. **Tel** (216)961-4130, (800)456-0707, **FAX** (216)961-0364. **LC** TD794.5; .R4427. **DD** 338.4/76284/4580973. Documents available from Documents on Demand. **Formed by the union of** Recycling Today (Scrap Processing Market Ed.), 1051-1091 **and** Recycling Today (Municipal (Post-Consumer) Market Ed.), 1051-0109.
Ind/Abst Abstr. Bull. Inst. Pap. Sci. Tech.; Environ. Abstr.; PROMT.

US/1051-0109
RECYCLING TODAY (MUNICIPAL (POST-CONSUMER) MARKET ED.). Title Change. (RECYCLING TODAY.). [Recycl. today]. Vol. 28, No. 5 (May 1990)-(1992). Periodical. English. mo. GIE Publishing Company, 4012 Bridge Avenue, Cleveland OH 44113. **Tel** (216)961-4130, (800)456-0707, **FAX** (216)961-0364. **ED** Jeff Solomon-Hess. **LC** TD794.5; .R443. **DD** 363.72/82/0973. **Ad Acc, Adv Mgr:** S France. **Circ:** 14,000. Documents available from Documents on Demand. **Continues in part** Recycling Today, 0887-6649. **Merged with** Recycling Today (Scrap Processing Market Ed.), 1051-1091 **to form** Recycling Today (1992).
Desc: Serves the rapidly emerging post-consumer recycling market segment comprising state, county, federal, municipal, regulatory agencies, recycling centers, waste management, and resource recovery services in North America.
Ind/Abst Alum. Ind. Abstr.; Energy Inf. Abstr.; Environ. Abstr.; Environ. Period. Bibliogr.; Met. Abstr.

US/1051-1091
RECYCLING TODAY (SCRAP PROCESSING MARKET ED.). Title Change. (RECYCLING TODAY.). [Recycl. today]. Vol. 28, No. 5 (May 15, 1990)-(199?). Periodical. English. mo. GIE Publishing Company, 4012 Bridge Avenue, Cleveland OH 44113. **Tel** (216)961-4130, (800)456-0707, **FAX** (216)961-0364. **ED** John Bruening. **DD** 338. **Ad Acc, Adv Mgr:** S France. **Circ:** 12,200. Documents available from Documents on Demand. **Continues** Recycling Today, 0887-6649. **Merged with** Recycling Today (Municipal Post-Consumer Market Ed.), 1051-0109 **to form** Recycling Today (1992).
Desc: Covers recycling of secondary materials in the form of all metallics, waste, paper and textiles. Also includes information on heavy equipment to process above materials.
Ind/Abst Alum. Ind. Abstr.; Appl. Sci. Technol. Index; Energy Inf. Abstr.; Environ. Abstr.; Environ. Period. Bibliogr.; F&S Index Plus Text, Int. [Select. Cov.]; Met. Abstr.

US/0736-1890
RECYCLING UPDATE. See Environmental Issues-Ecology.

US
RECYCLING UPDATE-TELEMARKETING SCRIPT PRESENTATIONS EDITION. (1992)-. English. ir. $7.95 US; $9.95 Canada; $11.95 Other. Prosperity & Profits Unlimited, PO Box 416, Denver CO 80201-0416. **ED** A. Doyle. **Circ:** 4,500.
Desc: Telemarketing presentations for those in the recycling business.

US
REFUSE NEWS. (19??)-. English. mo. $18.00 (one year), $33.00 (two year), $45.00 (three year). K J W B Publications, 440 South Cataract Avenue # F, San Dimas CA 91773. **Tel** (909)599-9710, **FAX** (909)599-0312. **ED** John E. Waddell. **Bk Rev,** (Qty: 6-12). **Ad Acc, Adv Mgr:** Kurt Bullen. **Circ:** 4,790 (ctrl).
Desc: Coverage of the sanitation and recycling industries in the West and Midwest.

US
REGISTERED PROFESSIONAL SANITARIANS ... ROSTER. Jan. 1984-. English. an. Texas Department of Health, 1100 West 49th Street, Austin TX 78756-3180. **Tel** (512)458-7550, **FAX** (512)458-7407. **LC** RA7.6.T4; R44. **DD** 628/.025/764. **Continues** Roster of Registered Professional Sanitarians of the State of Texas.

US/1065-1063
REGULATORY ANALYST. MEDICAL WASTE. Title Change. See Medical Science and Technology.

BL
RELATORIO ANUAL DA DIRETORIA - CETESB. Main/Corp Companhia Estadual de Tecnologia de Saneamento Basico e de Defesa do Meio Ambiente. Portuguese. Av Professor Fredico Hermann Jr, 345 CEP, 05459 Sao Paulo Brazil. **LC** TD171.5.B6; C64A.

BL
RELATORIO DA DIRETORIA - CORSAN. Main/Corp Corsan. Portuguese. Rua Caldas Junio 120 - 17 18, 19 Andares, Porto Alegre Brazil. **LC** TD241.R5; C67A.

BL
RELATORIO DE GESTAO / COMPANHIA DE SANEAMENTO DE MINAS GERAIS. Main/Corp Companhia de Saneamento de Minas Gerais. (19??)-. Periodical. Portuguese. Copasa Mg, rua Sergipe 580, 30.000 Belo Horizonte Brazil. **LC** TD41.M56; C65a. **Continues** Companhia de Saneamento de Minas Gerais. Relatorio - Companhia de Saneamento de Minas Gerais.

US
REMEDIATION REVIEW : A JOURNAL OF HAZARDOUS WASTE MANAGEMENT / NEW YORK STATE DEPARTMENT OF ENVIRONMENTAL CONSERVATION. Added/Corp New York (State). Dept. of Environmental Conservation. New York (State). Office of Environmental Remediation. Vol. 1 (Sept. 1988)-. Periodical. English. qt. Department of Environmental Conservation / New York, 50 Wolf Road, Room 604, Albany NY 12233. **Tel** (518)457-2344, **FAX** (518)457-6996. **LC** IN PROCESS. Documents available from Documents on Demand.
Ind/Abst Environ. Abstr.

US/1050-4885
RENEW AMERICA REPORT, THE. [Renew Am. rep.]. **Added/Corp** Renew America (Organization). (198?)-. Periodical. English. Four times a year. $25.00 Comes with Renew America Project membership. Renew America, 1400 16th Street Northwest, Suite 710, Washington DC 20036. **Tel** (202)232-2252. **DD** 621. **Circ:** 7,000. **Continues** Sun Times, 0278-582X.
Desc: Describe's the group's activities.
Ind/Abst Energy Res. Abstr. (Feb. 1982-).

●CN/1193-2228
REPERTOIRE QUEBECOIS DES RECUPERATEURS ET DES RECYCLEURS, LE. [Repert. que. recuper. recycl.]. **Added/Corp** Quebec (Province). Ministere de l'Environnement. (1992)-. French. **DD** 363.72/82/025714.

UK
REPORT (INSTITUTE OF GEOLOGICAL SCIENCES (GREAT BRITAIN). ENVIRONMENTAL PROTECTION UNIT). (REPORT / ENVIRONMENTAL PROTECTION UNIT, INSTITUTE OF GEOLOGICAL SCIENCES.). Monographic series. English. Price varies per volume. Fluid Processes Research Group, Keyworth Nottingham, NG12 5GG England.
Ind/Abst GeoRef; Life Sci. Collect.

US
REPORT - NEW ENGLAND INTERSTATE WATER POLLUTION CONTROL COMMISSION. Main/Corp New England Interstate Water Pollution Control Commission. English. an. **LC** TD223.15.N4; A3.

US/0093-8947
REPORT NO. TES. Main/Corp United States. Dept. of Transportation. Office of Hazardous Materials. (19??)-. English. US Department of Transportation / Office of Hazardous Materials, Washington DC 20590. **LC** HE199.5.D3; U62a. **DD** 604.7.

US
REPORT OF ACTIVITIES. MINNESOTA ENVIRONMENTAL QUALITY BOARD. Main/Corp Minnesota Environmental Quality Board. English. be. Minnesota Environmental Quality Board, 550 Cedar Street, 100 Capital Square, St. Paul MN 55101. **Tel** (612)296-8542. **LC** TD195.E4; M56A. **DD** 363.6/2.

US/0193-3310
REPORT OF PROGRESS - MERL. Main/Corp Municipal Environmental Research Laboratory. **VAT** Report of Progress - Municipal Environmental Research Laboratory. English. an. Municipal Environmental Research Laboratory, Office of Research and Development, US Environmental Protection Agency, Cincinnati OH 45268. **LC** TD178.8.U53; C565. **DD** 628/.4/072073.

Environmental Issues —Pollution and Waste Management

DK/0107-7430
REPORT OF THE MARINE POLLUTION LABORATORY. See Environmental Issues-Ecology.

US/1043-268X
REPORT ON DEFENSE PLANT WASTES. See Military and Defense.

US/0147-2887
REPORT ON ENVIRONMENTAL RADIATION SURVEILLANCE IN NORTH CAROLINA. (REPORT ON ENVIRONMENTAL RADIATION SURVEILLANCE IN NORTH CAROLINA FOR ... / SUBMITTED TO N.C. RADIATION PROTECTION COMMISSION BY DAYNE H. BROWN, CHIEF, RADIATION PROTECTION SECTION.) **Added/Corp** North Carolina. Radiation Protection Branch. North Carolina. Radiation Protection Section. **VFOAT** Environmental Radiation Surveillance. (19??)-. English. ir. Price varies. State Department of Human Resources / North Carolina, 701 Barbour Street, Raleigh NC 27603. **Tel** (919)733-4283. **LC** TD196.R3; R46. **DD** 363.1/79. **NLM** W2 AN8 D52R. ctrl circ.

US/0163-4755
REPORT TO CONGRESS ON ADMINISTRATION OF OCEAN DUMPING ACTIVITIES. PUBLIC LAW 92-532, MARINE PROTECTION, RESEARCH, AND SANCTUARIES ACT OF 1972. **Main/Corp** United States. Army. Corps of Engineers. 1976-. English. US Department of Defense Department of the Army, The Pentagon, SAPA-CR, Room 3E718, Washington DC 20310. **Tel** (703)695-0363, FAX (703)693-5737. **LC** TD763; .U52A. **DD** 614.7/6.

US/0733-3633
REPORT TO THE COLORADO WATER QUALITY CONTROL COMMISSION. See Water Resources.

US/0277-2868
REPORT TO THE CONGRESS ON OCEAN POLLUTION AND OFFSHORE DEVELOPMENT. See Earth Sciences-Oceanography.

US
REPORT TO THE HONORABLE ... GOVERNOR OF THE STATE OF ALABAMA AND MEMBERS OF THE ALABAMA LEGISLATURE, A. **Main/Corp** Alabama. Water Improvement Commission. **VFOAT** Report of Progress. 1980-. English. an. Public Health Services Building, Montgomery AL 36130. **LC** TD224.A2; A4A. **DD** 353.97610082/325. **Continues** Annual Report of the Alabama Water Improvement Commission.

US
RESEARCH ISSUES AND SUPPORTING RESEARCH OF THE NATIONAL PROGRAM ON CARBON DIOXIDE, ENVIRONMENT AND SOCIETY. Fiscal Year 1980-. English. National Technical Information Service - NTIS, Room 2027S, 5285 Port Royal Road, Springfield VA 22161. **Tel** (703)487-4630, (703)487-4660, (703)487-4650, FAX (703)321-8547, telex 89-9405.

US/0148-5547
RESEARCH PROGRAMS / NATIONAL INSTITUTE OF ENVIRONMENTAL HEALTH SCIENCES. **Main/Corp** National Institute of Environmental Health Sciences. English. National Institute of Environmental Health Sciences, PO Box 12233, Research Triangle Park NC 27711. **Tel** (202)245-6296. **LC** RA566.3; .N37A. **DD** 614.7/07/2073. **NLM** W 20.5 R434.

US/1041-5505
RESEARCH REPORT - HEALTH EFFECTS INSTITUTE. (RESEARCH REPORT / HEI.). [Res. rep. - Health Eff. Inst.]. **Added/Corp** Health Effects Institute. No. 1 (1985)-. Monographic series. English. ir. Price varies per volume. Health Effects Institute, 215 First Street, Cambridge MA 02142. **DD** 363. **NLM** W1; RE234AWCD. Documents available from CASDDS.
Ind/Abst Chem. Abstr.; Health Plan. Adminis.; Index Med. (No. 1, 1985-).

US/0735-3081
RESOURCE RECOVERY REPORT. [Resour. recovery rep.]. **VFOAT** Resource Recovery. (1976)-. Periodical. English. mo. $227.00. Resource Recovery Report, PO Box 3356, Warrenton VA 22186. **Tel** (703)347-4500, FAX (703)349-4540. **ED** Frank McManus (editor's telephone: (202)362-6034). **Circ:** 550.
Desc: Energy and materials recovery from municipal and industrial waste recycling, bioconversion and resource recovery.

US/0744-4710
RESOURCE RECYCLING / NORTH AMERICA'S RECYCLING JOURNAL. (RESOURCE RECYCLING.). [Resour. recycl.]. Vol. 1, No. 1 (March/April 1982)-. Periodical. English. mo. $42.00 (one year), $68.00 (two year), $92.00 (three year) US; $55.00 (one year), $94.00 (two year), $131.00 (three year) other. Resource Recycling, PO Box 10540, Portland OR 97210. **Tel** (503)227-1319, (800)227-1424, FAX (503)227-6135. **ED** Jerry Powell. **LC** TD794.5; .R4585. **DD** 628.4/458/05. **CODEN** REREEC. Index available (bound in Jan. issue). **Bk Rev**, (Qty: 50-60). **Ad Acc**, **Adv Mgr:** Rick Downing, **Tel** (216)255-1454. **Circ:** 16,000. Documents available from Documents on Demand.
Desc: Covers recycling and composting, including technologies, markets, economics and legislation.
Ind/Abst Energy Inf. Abstr.; Environ. Abstr.; Environ. Period. Bibliogr.; PAIS Int. Print; Public Aff. Inf. Serv. Bull.

US/1052-4916
RESOURCE RECYCLING'S BOTTLE/CAN RECYCLING UPDATE. [Resour. recycl. bottle/can recycl. update]. **VFOAT** Bottle Can Recycling Update; Bottle/Can Recycling Update. (Jan. 1990)-. Periodical. English. Twelve times a year. $75.00 (one year), $129.00 (two year) US; $82.00 (one year), $143.00 (two year) other. Resource Recycling, PO Box 10540, Portland OR 97210. **Tel** (503)227-1319, (800)227-1424, FAX (503)227-6135. **ED** Steve Apotheker. **DD** 363. **Bk Rev. Circ:** 2,000.
Desc: Provides extensive data and information on the recovery and utilization of scrap glass bottles, plastic containers and metal cans.

US/1052-4908
RESOURCE RECYCLING'S PLASTICS RECYCLING UPDATE. See Plastics.

US
RESULTS OF RESEARCH RELATED TO STRATOSPHERIC OZONE PROTECTION / PREPARED FOR CONGRESS OF THE UNITED STATES ; PREPARED BY OFFICE OF RESEARCH AND DEVELOPMENT, U.S. ENVIRONMENTAL PROTECTION AGENCY. **Added/Corp** United States. Congress. United States. Environmental Protection Agency. Office of Research and Development. **VFOAT** Research and Development, Results of Research Related to Stratospheric Ozone Protection. (1978)-. English. be. US Environmental Protection Agency / Center for Environmental Research Information, 401 M Street SW, Washington DC 20460. **Continues** Results of Research Related to Stratospheric Ozone Protection, Report to Congress.

US/0048-7457
REUSE/RECYCLE. [Reuse recycle]. Vol. 1 (May 1971)-. Periodical. English. mo. $195.00 (one year), $380.00 (two year), $565.00 (three year). Technomic Publishing Company, Inc., 851 New Holland Avenue, Box 3535, Lancaster PA 17604. **Tel** (717)291-5609, (800)233-9936, FAX (717)295-4538. **[CCC]. Circ:** 100. available on microfilm from University Microfilms International (UMI).
Desc: Provides news and information on important developments in both industrial and municipal recycling. Focuses on large-scale post-consumer, post-commercial, and post-industrial waste recycling. Covers the recycling of a wide range of materials and both waste-to-energy and waste-to-materials processes. Includes new uses and markets for recycled materials, recycling processing, plants, equipment, and case histories of successsful projects and programs in the U.S. and Europe.
Ind/Abst Energy Res. Abstr. (Aug. 1978-).

US/0179-5953
REVIEWS OF ENVIRONMENTAL CONTAMINATION AND TOXICOLOGY. [Rev. environ. contam. toxicol.]. Vol. 98 (1987)-. Academic Scholarly Publication. English. ir. Price varies. Springer-Verlag New York Inc., 175 5th Avenue, New York NY 10010. **Tel** (212)460-1500, telex 232 235 SPB UR. **(Subscription address:** Springer Verlag New York Inc. / for North America, 44 Hartz Way, Secaucus NJ 07096.) **LC** TX501; .R48. **DD** 363.1/92. **NLM** W1; RE257DB. **CODEN** RCTOE4. **[CCC]. Pr Rev.** Documents available from The Genuine Article, BIOSIS Document Express, CASDDS. **Continues** Residue Reviews, 0080-181X.
Ind/Abst AGRICOLA [Select. Cov.]; Biodeter. Abstr. (19??-19??); Biol. Agric. Index (1987-); Biol. Abstr. (1987-); Chem. Abstr. (1987-); Crop Physiol. Abstr.; Dairy Sci. Abstr.; EMBASE; Energy Res. Abstr. (1987-); Fish Rev.; Food Sci. Technol. Abstr.; GeoRef; Index Med. (1987-); Index Sci. Rev. [Full Cov.]; Index Vet.; Nematol. Abstr.; Nutr. Abstr. Rev., Ser. A, Hum. Exp.; Life Sci. Collect. (1987-); PESTDOC (1987-); Plant Grow. Reg. Abstr.; Res. Alert [Full Cov.]; Rev. Agric. Entomol.; Rev. Med. Vet. Entomol.; Rev. Plant Pathol.; Sci. Cit. Index; SCISEARCH; Soils Fert.; Vet. Bull.; Vitis Vitic. Enol. Abstr.; Weed Abstr.

MX/0188-4999
REVISTA INTERNACIONAL DE CONTAMINACION AMBIENTAL. [Rev. int. contam. ambient.]. **VFOAT** International Journal of Environmental Pollution. (1989)-. Periodical. Multiple languages. an. $5.00 Mexico; $7.00 US and Canada; $10.00 other. Universidad Autonoma de Tlaxcala / Contaminacion Ambiental, PO Box 27 069, 06760 Mexico DF Mexico. **Tel** 011 52 5 5505215 Ext. 4391. **DD** 363.739. **Continues** Contaminacion Ambiental - Universidad Autonoma de Tlaxcala, 0187-0238.

US/0742-4426
RIVER QUALITY REPORT. **Added/Corp** Metropolitan Waste Control Commission (Minn.). Quality Control Dept. (1981)-. English. an. Metropolitan Waste Control, 230 East 5th Street/6th Floor, St Paul MN 55101. **Tel** (612)291-6426. **LC** TD225.M6; M47a. **DD** 363.7/3942/0977657. **Continues** Metropolitan Waste Control Comission (Minn.). Quality Control Dept. Water Quality Report of River Water Quality in the Minneapolis-St. Paul Metropolitan Area, 0734-323X.

IT/0394-5391
RS. RIFIUTI SOLIDI. [RS, Rifiuti solidi]. **VFOAT** Rifiuti Solidi. (1987)-. Periodical. Italian (English). bm. L90000.00 Italy; L180000.00 other. Centro Ingegneria Prot Ambient, Via Andrea Palladio 26, 20135 Milan Italy. **Tel** 011 39 2 58301528, FAX +39 2 58301550. Index available. cum. index. **Bk Rev**. **Ad Acc**. **Pr Rev. Circ:** 1,000.
Desc: Covers solid waste treatment, disposal and contaminated soils.

JA
SANGYO KOGAI BOSHI NO GIJUTSU. 1973-. Japanese. Tokyo Toritsu Kogyo Gijutsu Senta, 13-10 Nishigaoka 3 Kita-ku, Tokyo 115 Japan. **LC** TD187.5.J32; T615.

JN/0285-5380
SANGYO TO KANKYO. [Sangyo to kankyo]. **Added/Corp** Tsusan Shiryo Chosakai. (1972)-. Periodical. Japanese. mo. Tsusan Shiryo Chosakai, 5-ban 12-go Fujimicho 2-chome, Chiyoda-ku, Tokyo-to 102 Japan. **CODEN** SAKADF. Documents available from CASDDS.
Ind/Abst Chem. Abstr.

US/0069-6129
SANITARY ENGINEERING PAPERS. No. 1- June 1966-. Monographic series. English. Price varies per volume. Colorado State University, Fort Collins CO 80521. **Tel** (303)491-8652. **ED** D Hendricks. **LC** TD1; .S2. **DD** 628. **Circ:** 50 (ctrl).
Desc: Sanitary engineer thesis and dissertations summary reports.

US/0036-4436
SANITARY MAINTENANCE. (19??)-. Periodical. English. mo. $49.00 (one year), $89.00 (two year) US; $69.00 (one year), $100.00 (one year) (surface mail), $169.00 (1 year), $200.00 (2 year) (air mail) other. Trade Press Publishing Company, 2100 West Florist Avenue, Milwaukee WI 53209. **Tel** (414)228-7701, FAX (414)228-1134. **ED** Ron Gillette. **LC** HD9999.S383; U57. **DD** 338.4/7/6485. Index available. **Bk Rev**. **Ad Acc**. **Circ:** 15,000 (ctrl). available on microfilm from University Microfilms International (UMI).
Desc: Main focus is on sanitary supply distributors. Features include new products, sales techniques, management issues.

US
SAVANNAH RIVER LABORATORY QUARTERLY REPORT, WASTE MANAGEMENT. **Main/Corp** Savannah River Laboratory. **VFOAT** Waste Management. English. qt. Savannah River Laboratory, Aiken SC 29801.

GW/0342-9474
SCHRIFTENREIHE DER LANDESANSTALT FUER IMMISSIONSSCHUTZ DES LANDES NORDRHEIN-WESTFALEN, ESSEN. (SCHRIFTENREIHE DER LANDESANSTALT FUER IMMISSIONSSCHUTZ DES LANDES NORDRHEIN-WESTFALEN.). [Schriftenr. Landesanst. Immiss.schutz Landes Nordrh.-Westf.]. **Added/Corp** Landesanstalt fur Immissionsschutz des Landes Nordrhein-Westfalen. (1977)-. Multiple languages (German and English). **CODEN** SLINDJ. Documents available from CASDDS. **Continues** Schriftenreihe der Landesanstalt fur Immissions- und Bodennutzungeschutz des Landes Nordrhein-Westfalen.
Ind/Abst Chem. Abstr.

GW
SCHRIFTENREIHE DES ISWW KARLSRUHE. See Water Resources.

GW
SCHRIFTENREIHE FUER NATURSCHUTZ UND LANDSCHAFTSPFLEGE. **Added/Corp** Bavaria. Landesamt fuer Umweltschutz. **VFOAT**

Naturschutz und Landschaftspflege; Schriftenreihe Naturschutz und Landschaftspflege. No. 6 (1975)-. Monographic series. German. Price varies per volume.

II/0970-5139
SCIENCE AND ENVIRONMENT. See Science and Technology.

GW/0720-0773
SEAWATER AND DESALTING. ***Ceased.*** Vol. 1-?. English. be. Springer-Verlag GmbH & Company KG, Heidelberger Platz 3, D 14197 Berlin Germany. **Tel** 011 49 30 8207223, FAX 011 49 30 8214091, telex 183 319 SPBLN D. **(Subscription address:** Springer Verlag New York Inc. / for North America, 44 Hartz Way, Secaucus NJ 07096.**) LC** TD478; .S4. **DD** 628.1/67/05.

JA/0385-1907
SEISO GIHO. **Main/Corp** Tokyo. Seisokyoku. **VFOAT** Technical Report - Bureau of Public Cleansing, Tokyo Metropolitan Government. V. 1- ; 1976-. Academic Scholarly Publication. Japanese (Japanese). Tokyo-to Seisokyoku, 5-1 Marunouchi 3-chome Chiyoda-ku 100, Tokyo Japan. **LC** TD785; .T64A. **CODEN** SIGHD4. Documents available from CASDDS.
Ind/Abst Chem. Abstr.

US/0195-7228
SELECTED INDUSTRIAL AIR POLLUTION CONTROL EQUIPMENT. (CURRENT INDUSTRIAL REPORTS. MA-35J, SELECTED INDUSTRIAL AIR POLLUTION CONTROL EQUIPMENT.). Academic Scholarly Publication. English. an. $1.00. US Department of Commerce, 14th Street & Constitution Avenue NW, Washington DC 20230. **Tel** (202)482-2000, FAX (202)482-3772. **LC** HD9718.5.A573; U63. **CODEN** CUSEDV. Documents available from CASDDS.
Desc: Presents timely data on the production, inventories, and orders of approximately 5,000 products, which represents 40 percent of all US manufacturing.
Ind/Abst Chem. Abstr.

US
SEMIANNUAL REPORT - DIVISION OF AIR POLLUTION CONTROL. **Main/Corp** Illinois. Division of Air Pollution Control. (19??)-. English. sa. **LC** TD883.5.I45; I42a. **DD** 363.6.

US/0149-5879
SEWAGE TREATMENT CONSTRUCTION GRANTS MANUAL. ***Ceased.*** ( )-(1989). Periodical. English. mo. Bureau of National Affairs Inc., 9435 Key West Avenue, Rockville MD 20850. **Tel** (800)372-1033, (301)258-1033, FAX (301)948-5823. **(Subscription telephone:** FAX (301)948-5823**) [CCC].**

JA
SHIGA KENRITSU EISEI KANKYO SENTA SHOHO. See Public Health and Safety.

CN
SITE AUDITING. English. ir (4 to 6 times per year). $279.00. Specialty Technical Publishers Inc, #306-267 West Esplande, North Vancouver BC V7M 1A5 Canada. **Tel** (604)983-3434, FAX (604)983-3445. ctrl circ.

US
SITE REGISTER / TOXICS CLEANUP PROGRAM, WASHINGTON STATE DEPARTMENT OF ECOLOGY. **Main/Corp** Washington (State). Toxics Cleanup Program. Issue No. 90-10 (Aug. 28, 1990)-. Periodical. English. **LC** TD1042.W2; W38a. ***Continues*** *Washington (State). Hazardous Waste Investigations and Cleanup Program. Site Register.*

US/0148-4125
SLUDGE. [Sludge]. **VFOAT** Sludge Newsletter. (197?)-. Periodical. English. bw (26 issues). $351.00. Business Publishers Inc., 951 Pershing Drive, Silver Spring MD 20910-4464. **Tel** (301)587-6300, (800)274-0122, FAX (301)585-9075. **ED** Susan Darcey Bartlett. **LC** TD523; .S6. **DD** 628.3/5. **[CCC].** available on an online database (file 636/Full-Text) from DIALOG. Documents available from Documents on Demand.
Desc: A report on pollution control residuals management: generation, collection storage treatment and ultimate disposal. Also covers legislation, research, and product development.
Ind/Abst Energy Inf. Abstr.; Environ. Abstr.; PTS Newsl. Database [Full Txt.].

US/0893-5793
SLUDGE MANAGEMENT SERIES. **Added/Corp** Hazardous Materials Control Research Institute. (197?)-. Monographic series. English. Price varies per volume. Hazard Materials Control Research Institute, 9300 Columbia Boulevard, Silver Spring MD 20910. **LC** UNC. **DD** 604.

US
SMALL FLOWS. **Added/Corp** National Small Flows Clearinghouse. (Oct. 1985)-. Periodical. English. Four times a year. Free on request. National Small Flows Clearinghouse, West Virginia University, PO Box 6064, Morgantown WV 26506. **Tel** (800)624-8301. **ED** Jill A. Ross. cum. index. **Circ:** 38,000 (ctrl). available on an online database.
Desc: Information on wastewater treatment issues and technologies for those working with small communities (engineers, regulators, government officials, etc.).

US/1058-9074
SOLID WASTE & POWER. [Solid waste power]. **VFOAT** Solid Waste and Power. Vol. 1, No. 1, Feb. (1987)-. Academic Scholarly Publication. English. bm. $49.00 US and Canada; $60.00 other. HCI Publications, 410 Archibald Street, Kansas City MO 64111. **Tel** (816)931-1311. **LC** TD796.2; .S65. **DD** 662/.8. **CODEN** SWPOEX. Documents available from CASDDS, Documents on Demand.
Desc: Covers the technical and feature aspects of the waste-to-energy industry. Regular coverage includes industrial, technical and environmental articles.
Ind/Abst Chem. Abstr.; Energy Inf. Abstr.; Environ. Abstr.; Environ. Period. Bibliogr.; Health Saf. Sci. Abstr.

US/1055-1298
SOLID WASTE MANAGEMENT ECONOMICS REPORT : SWMER. [Solid waste manage. econ. rep.]. **Added/Corp** SWMER Communications. **VFOAT** SWMER. (Apr 1991)-. Periodical. English. mo. $370.00. SWMER Communications, PO Box 55098, Tulsa OK 74155-5098. **DD** 363.

US
SOLID WASTE MANAGEMENT NEWSLETTER. ***Ceased.*** Vol. 1, No. 1 Jan.(1977)-Ceased with (1988). Newsletter. English. bm. Garrett Park Press, PO Box 190 F, Garrett Park MD 20896. **Tel** (301)946-2553. ***Continues*** *Air Pollution Notes.*
Desc: Each issues cites around 70 fields or career aids on such subjects as the following: employment trends, free and inexpensive career materials, new reports and new books, fields with jobs, liberal arts education and careers, minority and women's interests, forthcoming meetings and other activities, financial aid, and women and careers.
Ind/Abst Pollut. Abstr. Indexes.

US/0038-1128
SOLID WASTE REPORT. Vol. 1 (Oct. 19, 1970)-. Periodical. English. wk. $525.00. Business Publishers Inc., 951 Pershing Drive, Silver Spring MD 20910-4464. **Tel** (301)587-6300, (800)274-0122, FAX (301)585-9075. **ED** Susan Darcey-Bartlett. **LC** TD795; .S63. **[CCC].** available on an online database (file 636/Full-Text) from DIALOG; and DIALOG.
Desc: Report on solid waste collection, processing, recovery, recycling, and ultimate disposal.
Ind/Abst PTS Newsl. Database [Full Txt.].

US/0892-8436
SOURCE SAMPLING NEWS. ***Ceased.*** [Source sampl. news]. -Ceased with March (1988). Periodical. English. mo. Technomic Publishing Company, Inc., 851 New Holland Avenue, Box 3535, Lancaster PA 17604. **Tel** (717)291-5609, (800)233-9936, FAX (717)295-4538. **ED** Howard F Schiff. **DD** 628. **Circ:** 150. ***Continues*** *Stack Sampling News, 0148-8309.*
Desc: Information for air pollution control professionals on techniques for monitoring, sampling and analysis; on new findings on sources and emissions; on new equipment, instruments and systems.

US
SOURCE (UNITED NATIONS DEVELOPMENT PROGRAMME). ***Ceased.*** (SOURCE / UNDP.). **Added/Corp** United Nations Development Programme. Vol. 1, No. 1 (June 1989)-(199?). Periodical. English. Four times a year. United Nations Development Programme / New York, 1900 One United Nations Plaza, New York NY 10017. **Tel** (212)906-5000, FAX (212)826-2057. **ED** I. Rajeswary. **LC** HC59.8; .S58. **DD** 338.9/1/091724. **Bk Rev. Circ:** 27,000 (ctrl). ***Continues*** *Decade Watch, 1011-2553.*
Desc: Features public information on water and sanitation activities in LDCs.

●US/1065-7975
SOUTH CAROLINA ENVIRONMENTAL COMPLIANCE UPDATE. [S.C. environ. compliance update]. **VFOAT** Environmental Compliance Update. (1992)-. Periodical. English. mo. $137.00. M. Lee Smith Publishers and Printers, 162 4th Avenue North, PO Box 198867, Nashville TN 37219. **Tel** (615)242-7395, (800)274-6774, FAX (615)256-6601. **DD** 363.

US/1044-3479
SOUTH FLORIDA ENVIRONMENTAL READER (ELECTRONIC ED.). (SOUTH FLORIDA ENVIRONMENTAL READER [COMPUTER FILE].). [South Fl. environ. read.]. (1989)-. Periodical. English. bw. Free. South Florida Environmental Reader, PO Box 1041, South Miami FL 33243-1041. **Tel** (305)669-1943. **DD** 333. available in print (as: South Florida Environmental Reader).
Desc: Electronic newsletter distributed over a number of computer networks. Consists of articles about or related to the environment of South Florida, as well as meeting information of the various environmental groups. Mode of access Email on Internet. INTERNET SEER c/o MTHVAX.MIAMI.EDU; UUCP !UUNET!MTHVAX!SFER.

US/1044-3479
SOUTH FLORIDA ENVIRONMENTAL READER (PRINT ED.). (SOUTH FLORIDA ENVIRONMENTAL READER.). [South Fl. environ. read.]. (1989)-. Periodical. English. ir. $15.00. South Florida Environmental Reader, PO Box 1041, South Miami FL 33243-1041. **Tel** (305)669-1943. **ED** Andrew Mossberg. **DD** 333. available via electronic mail (South Florida Environmental Reader [Computer File]).
Desc: Consists of articles about or related to the environment of South Florida, as well as meeting information of the various environmental groups.

US/0892-5739
SOUTHERN WASTE INFORMATION EXCHANGE CATALOG, THE. (THE SOUTHERN WASTE INFORMATION EXCHANGE CATALOG / SWIX.). [South. Waste Inf. Exch. cat.]. **Added/Corp** Southern Waste Information Exchange (Tallahassee, Fla.). **VFOAT** SWIX Catalog; Catalog. (198?)-. Catalog. English. Three times a year (Apr., Aug., Dec.). $15.00. Southern Waste Information Exchange, PO Box 960, Tallahassee FL 32302. **Tel** (904)644-5516, FAX (904)574-6704. **ED** Gene Jones. **DD** 363. Index available. cum. index. **Ad Acc, Adv Mgr:** Gene Jones, **Tel** (800)441-7949. **Circ:** 6,500 (ctrl). available on an online database. ***Continues*** *FLIX Catalog.*

US/8756-7059
SPEER'S DIGEST OF TOXIC SUBSTANCES STATE LAW. See Law-Environmental Law.

US
SPENT FUEL AND RADIOACTIVE WASTE INVENTORIES, PROJECTIONS, AND CHARACTERISTICS. Oct. 1982-. English. an. National Technical Information Service - NTIS, Room 2027S, 5285 Port Royal Road, Springfield VA 22161. **Tel** (703)487-4630, (703)487-4660, (703)487-4650, FAX (703)321-8547, telex 89-9405. available on microfiche (Vols. for 1982- distributed to depository libraries). ***Continues*** *Spent Fuel and Radioactive Waste Inventories and Projections as of ... .*

UK/1353-2561
SPILL SCIENCE AND TECHNOLOGY BULLETIN. (19??)-. Bulletin. English. sa. $63.00 North, Central and South America; £42.00 other. Pergamon Press, An Imprint of Elsevier Science Ltd., The Boulevard, Langford Lane, Kidlington, Oxford OX5 1GB United Kingdom. **Tel** 011 44 865 843000, 011 44 865 843699, FAX 011 44 865 843010. **(Subscription address:** Elsevier Science Ltd. Oxford Fulfillment Centre, PO Box 800, Kidlington, Oxford OX5 1DX United Kingdom.**) ED** F. Rainer Engelhardt. **Photos. Ad Acc. Pr Rev.**
Desc: Covers oil and chemical spill science and technology, focusing on the effects and control of discharges of oil, oil products and other hazardous substances.

●US/1059-423X
STABILIZATION AND SOLIDIFICATION OF HAZARDOUS, RADIOACTIVE, AND MIXED WASTES. [Stab. solidif. hazard. radioact. mix. wastes]. **Added/Corp** American Society for Testing and Materials. (1992)-. English. be. ASTM - American Society fo Testing and Materials, 1916 Race Street, Philadelphia PA 19103. **Tel** (215)299-5585. **DD** 628.

DK
STADS- OG HAVNEINGENIREN. **Added/Corp** Stads- Og Havneingenirforeningen i Danmark. (19??)-. Periodical. Danish. Twelve times a year. kr160.00 Denmark; kr270.00 others. Danish Technical Press, Skelbaekgade 4, DK 1717 Copenhagen 5 Denmark. **Tel** 011 45 31216801. **LC** TD4; .S82.

US/8755-3546
STANDARD METHODS FOR THE EXAMINATION OF WATER AND WASTEWATER. (STANDARD METHODS FOR THE EXAMINATION OF WATER AND WASTEWATER : INCLUDING BOTTOM SEDIMENTS AND SLUDGES / PREPARED AND PUBLISHED JOINTLY BY AMERICAN PUBLIC HEALTH ASSOCIATION, AMERICAN WATER WORKS ASSOCIATION, WATER POLLUTION CONTROL FEDERATION.). [Stand. meth. exam. water wastewater]. **Added/Corp** American Public Health Association. American Water Works Association. Water Pollution Control Federation. **VFOAT** Standard Methods. 11th Ed. (1960)-. English. ir. Price varies per volume. American Public Health Association, 1015 15th Street Northwest, Washington DC 20005. **Tel** (202)789-5666. **ED** Arnold E. Greenburg, Lenore S. Clesceri and Andrew D. Eaton. **LC** QD142; .A5. **DD** 543.3. ***Continues*** *Standard Methods for the Examination of Water, Sewage, and Industrial Wastes.*
Desc: Contains a comprehensive collection of water and wastewater analysis methods.

US
STANDARD TRANSPORTATION COMMODITY CODE. HAZARDOUS MATERIALS OR SUBSTANCES OR HAZARDOUS WASTES. **Added/Corp** Association of American Railroads. (1991)-. English. Association of American Railroads, 50 F Street Northwest, Room 5401, Washington DC 20001. **Tel** (202)639-2550. ***Separated from*** *Standard Transportation Commodity Code. Alphabetical-Numerical, 0160-6875.*

II
STATE OF INDIA'S ENVIRONMENT : A CITIZEN'S REPORT, THE. **Added/Corp** Centre for Science and Environment (New Delhi, India). (1982)-. Monographic series. English. ir. Price varies per volume. Centre Science & Environment, 807 Vishal Bhawan, 95 Nehru Pl., New Delhi 110019 India. **Tel** 643-3394 or 613-8109. **ED** Anil Agrwal and Sunita Narayan. **LC** TD171.5.I4; S73. **DD** 363.7/00954. **Circ:** 6,000.
Desc: Comprehensive study of Indian environment and it's impact on the society.

US
STATE OF WASHINGTON ENVIRONMENTAL RADIATION PROGRAM ... ANNUAL REPORT. **Main/Corp** Washington (State). Environmental Protection Section. **Added/Corp** Washington (State). Office of Radiation Protection. **VFOAT** Environmental Radiation Program ... Annual Report; Report, Environmental Radiation Program. (1984)-. English. **LC** TD196.R3; W37a. **DD** 363.73/8. ***Continues*** *State of Washington Environmental Radiation Program ... Annual Report.*

●US/1070-3217
STATE RECYCLING LAWS UPDATE (QUARTERLY ED.). (STATE RECYCLING LAWS UPDATE.). [State recycl. laws update]. **VFOAT** SRLU Quarterly; SRLU. (1992)-. Periodical. English. Four times a year. $260.00 (corporate), $200.00 (non-profit. Raymond Communications, 6429 Auburn Avenue, Riverdale MD 20737. **Tel** (301)345-4237, FAX (301)345-4768. **ED** Michele Raymond. **DD** 333. **Bk Rev**, (Qty: 2). available on an online database.
Desc: Covers recycling laws relating to business, analysis, and forecasting.

US/0069-8458
STATISTICAL STANDARDS AND STUDIES. **Main/Conf** Conference of European Statisticians. **Added/Corp** United Nations. Statistical Commission and Economic Commission for Europe. (1963)-. Statistical Publication. English. ir. $8.50. United Nations Publications, 2 United Nations Plaza, Room DC2 0853, Department 007C, New York NY 10017. **Tel** (212)963-8303, (800)253-9646. **LC** JX1977; .A2. **DD** 314.
Desc: Statistics of air quality including some methods.

GW/0039-0771
STAUB, REINHALTUNG DER LUFT. [Staub Reinhalt. Luft]. **Added/Corp** Hauptverband der Gewerblichen Berufsgenossenschaften. Staubforschungsinstitut. VDI-Kommission Reinhaltung der Luft. (1966)-. Academic Scholarly Publication. German (summaries and/or abstracts in English and French). Twelve times a year. DM426.00. Springer-Verlag GmbH & Company KG, Heidelberger Platz 3, D 14197 Berlin Germany. **Tel** 011 49 30 8207223, FAX 011 49 30 8214091, telex 183 319 SPBLN D. **(Subscription address:** Springer Verlag New York Inc. / for North America, 44 Hartz Way, Secaucus NJ 07096.**)** **ED** K Grefen and K Justel. **LC** TD881; .S73. **NLM** W1 ST431. **CODEN** STRHAV. **[CCC]**. **Bk Rev**. **Ad Acc**. **Pr Rev**. ctrl circ. available on microfilm and microfiche from University Microfilms International (UMI). Documents available from Article Express International, The Genuine Article, CASDDS, Documents on Demand. ***Continues*** *Staub.*
Desc: Presents information on dust-cleanliness.
Ind/Abst Anal. Abstr.; Bioeng. Abstr.; Chem. Abstr.; Chem. Hazards Ind.; Coal Abstr.; Curr. Contents Eng. Tech. Appl. Sci.; Ei Page One; EMBASE; Energy Inf. Abstr.; Energy Res. Abstr. (March 1973-); Eng. Index Annu.; Environ. Abstr.; Health Saf. Sci. Abstr.; Int. Aerosp. Abstr.; Lab. Hazards Bull.; Lit. Pat. Abstr., Oilfield Chem. (1972-); Lit. Abstr., Catal. Catal.; Lit. Abstr., Health Environ.; Lit. Abstr., Pet. Refin. Petrochem.; Lit. Abstr., Pet. Substit.; Lit. Abstr., Transp. Storage; Nucl. Sci. Abstr.; Pollut. Abstr. Indexes; Proc. Chem. Eng.; Res. Alert [Full Cov.]; Risk Abstr.; Saf. Health Work; Soc. Sci. Cit. Index [Select. Cov.]; Theoret. Chem. Eng.; Trop. Dis. Bull.; World Ceram. Abstr.

CN/1186-8392
STRATEGY REPORT - MANITOBA. WASTE REDUCTION AND PREVENTION BRANCH. (STRATEGY REPORT / WASTE REDUCTION AND PREVENTION.). [Strategy rep. - Manit., Waste Reduct. Prev. Branch]. **Main/Corp** Manitoba. Waste Reduction and Prevention Branch. (1991)-. English. **DD** 354.71270077.

CI/0562-1887
STROJARSTVO. [Strojarstvo]. 1959-. Academic Scholarly Publication. Serbo-Croatian (Roman). bm. Strojarstvo, Berislaviceva 6, 41000 Zagreb Croatia. **CODEN** STJSAO. Documents available from The Genuine Article, CASDDS, Documents on Demand.
Ind/Abst Alum. Ind. Abstr.; BMT Abstr.; Chem. Abstr.; Curr. Contents Eng. Tech. Appl. Sci.; Ei Page One; Energy Inf. Abstr.; Eng. Mater. Abstr.; Environ. Abstr.; Fluid Abstr., Civil Eng.; Fluid Abstr. Proc. Eng.; FLUIDEX (1973-); Met. Abstr.; Pollut. Abstr. Indexes; Res. Alert [Select. Cov.]; World Text. Abstr.

RM/1011-9485
STUDII - INSTITUTUL DE CERCETARI SI PROIECTARI PENTRU GOSPODARIREA APELOR. EPURAREA APELOR. (STUDII DE EPURAREA APELOR.). [Studii - Inst. cercet. proiect. pentru gospod. apelor, Epur. apelor]. **Main/Corp** Institutul de Studii, Cercetari Si Proiectari Pentru Gospodarirea Apelor. (19??)-. Romanian (summaries and/or abstracts in English, French and Russian). **LC** TD511; .I53a. **CODEN** SEAPD4. Documents available from BIOSIS Document Express.
Ind/Abst Biol. Abstr.

JA/0387-2025
SUISHITSU ODAKU KENKYU (TOKYO. 1978). ***Title Change.*** (SUISHITSU ODAKU KENKYU.). [Suishitsu odaku kenkyu]. **Added/Corp** Nihon Suishitsu Odaku Kenkyu Kyokai. **VFOAT** Japan Journal of Water Pollution Research. (1978)-(199?). Academic Scholarly Publication. Japanese (summaries and/or abstracts in English). bm. Kogai Taisaku Gijutsu Doyukai, (Assoc. for Environmental Pollution Control), 1-244, Akasaka 9 Chome, Minatoku, Tokyoto 107, Japan. **LC** TD424.5; .S84. **CODEN** SOKEDN. Documents available from CASDDS. ***Continued by*** *Mizu Kankyo Gakkaishi, 0916-8958.*
Ind/Abst Chem. Abstr.; Curr. Biotechnol.

JA
SUJI DE MIRU KOGAI. **Added/Corp** Tokyo-to Kogai Kenkyujo. (1970)-. Periodical. Japanese. be. Tokyo-to Kogaki Kenkyujo, 7-1 Yurakucho 2 Chiyoda-ku, Tokyo Japan. **LC** TD187.5.J32; T618.

US
SUMMARY OF AIR QUALITY IN CALIFORNIA'S SOUTH COAST AIR BASIN. ***Title Change.*** **Added/Corp** South Coast Air Quality Management District (Calif.). (1982)-(19??). Periodical. English. South Coast Air Quality Management District, 2185 East Copely Drive, Diamond Bar CA 91765. **Tel** (714)396-3720. ***Continues*** *Summary of Air Quality in the South Coast Air Basin of California.* ***Merged with*** *AQMD Advisor.*

US/0892-2985
SUPERFUND. ***Title Change.*** [Superfund]. **VFOAT** Super Fund. (1987)-(19??). Periodical. English. bw (except 1st week in Jan. and 2nd week in July). Pasha Publications Inc., 1616 North Fort Myer Drive, Suite 1000, Arlington VA 22209. **Tel** (800)424-2908, (703)528-1244, FAX (703)528-3742, (703)528-1253. **DD** 363. **[CCC]**. available on an online database (files 636,648/Full-Text) from DIALOG. ***Continued by*** *Superfund Week.*
Desc: Reports on Superfund litigation cases, innovative cleanup methods and costs, cleanup standards and noncompliance penalties.
Ind/Abst PTS Newsl. Database [Full Txt.]; Trade Ind. ASAP [Full Txt.]; Trade Ind. Index [Full Txt.].

US
SUPERFUND WEEK. (19??)-. Periodical. English. Fifty times a year. $495.00 US; $525.00 other. Pasha Publications Inc., 1616 North Fort Myer Drive, Suite 1000, Arlington VA 22209. **Tel** (800)424-2908, (703)528-1244, FAX (703)528-3742, (703)528-1253. ***Continues*** *Superfund.*

SZ/1011-6710
SWISS CONTAMINATION CONTROL. [Swiss contam. control]. (1988)-. Periodical. English (German). Six times a year. 100.00F Switzerland; 120.00F Europe; 200.00F other. Verlag Dr Felix Wuest AG, Seestrasse 5/Postfach, CH-8700 Kuesnacht Switzerland. **Tel** 011 41 1 9110055, FAX (01)9106080, telex 825705.

FR/0397-6513
T.E.C. (PARIS). (TRANSPORT, ENVIRONNEMENT, CIRCULATION / EDITE PAR L'ASSOCIATION POUR LE DEVELOPPEMENT DES TECHNIQUES DE TRANSPORT, D'ENVIRONNEMENT ET DE CIRCULATION.). [T.E.C.]. **Added/Corp** Association pour le Developpement des Techniques de Transport, d'Environnement et de Circulation. **VFOAT** TEC. No. 1 (1973)-. Periodical. French (English, German and Spanish; summaries and/or abstracts in English, French and German). Six times a year. 660.00F France; 750.00F other. Association Pour le Developpement des Techniques de Transport d'Environnement et de Circulation, 38 Avenue Emile Zola, 75015 Paris France. **Tel** 011 33 1 45755611, FAX 011 33 1 45795286. **ED** Andre Imbert. Index Available, published separately, free-automatically sent. **Bk Rev**. **Pr Rev**. Documents available from Ask*IEEE.
Ind/Abst INSPEC (March/April 1983-).

KO
TAEHAN HWANGYONG KONGHAKHOE CHI. **VFOAT** Journal of Korean Society of Environmental Engineers. Periodical. Korean (summaries and/or abstracts in English). Taehan Hwangyong Konghakhoe, 56-3 Supyo-dong, Chung-ku, Seoul South Korea. **LC** TD169; .T33. **DD** 620.8.

CH
TAI-WAN SHUI LI. **VFOAT** Taiwan Water Conservancy. Began with June 1953 issue. Periodical. Chinese (English). qt. NT$240.00 China; $45.00 other. Taiwan Water Conservancy Publishing Commision, 11-4 5th Floor, Tzuen Hsien Street, Taichung Taiwan 40429. **Tel** (04)2260781-3, FAX 04-2202397. **ED** Zu-I Wang, Yuan-chien Lee, Chia-chiang Shih, Yu-li Lin. **LC** TD302.5.A1; T34. **DD** 333.91/16/0951249. Index available. **Bk Rev**. **Ad Acc**. **Circ:** 700 (ctrl).
Desc: Thesis on water conservancy research. Information of experimental survey statistics for planning and design in irrigation and drainage systems.

JA/0386-7064
TAIKI OSEN GAKKAI SHI. [Taiki Osen Gakkaishi]. **VFOAT** Journal of Japan Society of Air Pollution. Began in 1978. Academic Scholarly Publication. Japanese. bm. $116.00. Taiki Osen kenkyu Kyokai, (Japan Soc. of Air Pollution), 29-8, Shinjuku 1 Chome, Shinjukuku, Tokyoto 160, Japan. **(Subscription address:** Kyowa Book Company Inc., 1-38 Kanda Jinbo-Cho, Chiyoda-Ku, Tokyo 101, Japan (Phone: 03-3293-0727)**)** **CODEN** TOSGDC. Documents available from CASDDS. ***Continues*** *Taiki Osen Kenkyu.*
Ind/Abst AGRICOLA; Chem. Abstr.; EMBASE; Hortic. Abstr.; Int. Aerosp. Abstr.; Rice Abstr.; Soils Fert.

JA
TAIKI OSEN JOJI SOKUTEIKYOKU SOKUTEI KEKKA HOKOKU. KEINENPO. Japanese. an. Tokyo-to Kankyo Hozenkyoku Taiki Hozenbu, c/o Yuraku-cho Denki Building 7-1, Yuraku-cho 1 Chiyoda-ku, Tokyo-to 100 Japan. **Circ:** 200 (ctrl).

JA
TAIKI OSEN JOJI SOKUTEIKYOKU SOKUTEI KEKKA HOKOKU. NENPO. Japanese. an. Tokyo-to Kankyo Hozenkyoku Taiki Hozenbu, c/o Yuraku-cho Denki Building 7-1, Yuraku-cho 1 Chiyoda-ku, Tokyo-to 100 Japan. **Circ:** 200 (ctrl).

JA
TAIKI OSEN NYUSU. **VFOAT** Air Pollution News Report. Japanese (Japanese). Taiki Osen Kenkyu Zenkoku Kyogikai, 6-1 Shirokanedai 4-chome Minato-ku, Tokyo 108 Japan. **LC** TD881; .T34. **NLM** W1 TA41R.

CN
TECHNICAL BULLETIN. **Main/Corp** Canada. Inland Waters Directorate. **Added/Corp** Canada. Inland Waters Branch. Canada. Centre for Inland Waters. No. 65 (1974)-. Monographic series. English. ir. Free on request. Environment Canada / Emergencies Science Division, Ottawa Ontario K1A 0H3 Canada. **Tel** (819)998-9622. ***Continues*** *Canada. Inland Waters Branch. Technical Bulletin.*

FR/0299-7258
TECHNIQUES, SCIENCES, METHODES : TSM. **VFOAT** TSM; T.S.M.-L'EAU; T.S.M. (Jan. 1986)-. Academic Scholarly Publication. French (English). mo (July/Aug. issue combined). 455.00F France; 510.00F other. Association Generale des Hygienistes et Techniciens Municipaux, 9 rue de Phalsbourg, 75017 Paris France. **Tel** (1)227-3891, FAX (1)43.80.65.90. **Bk Rev**. **Ad Acc**. **Circ:** 3,500. Documents available from CASDDS, Documents on Demand. ***Continues*** *Techniques et Sciences Municipales, 0151-6973.*
Desc: Technology and science as it applies to cities.
Ind/Abst Chem. Abstr.; Environ. Abstr.; Fluid Abstr., Civil Eng.; Fluid Abstr. Proc. Eng.; FLUIDEX (19??-); Health Saf. Sci. Abstr.; Pollut. Abstr. Indexes.

US/0882-4584
TECHNOLOGY ASSESSMENT AND RESEARCH PROGRAM FOR OFFSHORE MINERALS OPERATIONS. [Technol. Assess. Res. Program offshore miner. oper.]. English. be. Free. Minerals Management Service, 647 National Center, Reston VA 22091. **Tel** (703)648-7752. **ED** John B Gregory and Charles E Smith. **LC** TN264; .T43. **DD** 622/.09162. **Circ:** 2,000.
Desc: Describes the technologies examined to assure safe, pollution free operations. Categories are blowout prevention, structures verification, oil spill containment, cleanup, and engine exhaust emissions control.

RU
TEKHNICHESKIE USLOVIIA NA METODY OPREDELENIIA VREDNYKH VESHCHESTV V VOZDUKHE. **Added/Corp** Nauchno-Issledovatelskii Institut Gigieny Vodnogo Transporta. Problemnaia Komissiia "Nauchnye Osnovy Gigieny Truda i Professionalnoi Patologii." Metodicheskaia Sektsiia po Promyshlenno-Sanitarnoi Khimii. Russia (U.S.S.R.) Glavnaia Gosudarstvennaia Sanitarnaia Inspektsiia SSR. Metodicheskaia Komissiia po Promyshlenno-Sanitarnoi Khimii. Vol. 1 (1960)-.

Environmental Issues —Pollution and Waste Management

Russian. Twelve times a year. $99.95. **(Subscription address:** East View Publications Inc., 3020 Harbor Lane North, Suite 110, Minneapolis MN 55447.**) NLM** W1 TE296K.

US
TELEPHONE DIRECTORY - U.S. ENVIRONMENTAL PROTECTION AGENCY. Main/Corp United States. Environmental Protection Agency. Office of Administration and Resources Management. Directory. English. sa. US Environmental Protection Agency / North Carolina, Office of Administration and Resources Management, Research Triangle Park NC 27711.

US/0271-9371
TOXIC AND HAZARDOUS WASTE DISPOSAL. [Toxic hazard. waste dispos.]. Vol. 1 (1979)-. Academic Scholarly Publication. English. ir. Price varies per volume. Butterworth & Company Ltd. / Canada, 75 Clegg Road, Markham Ontario L6G 1A1 Canada. **Tel** (905)479-2665, (800)668-6481. **ED** Robert B. Pojasek. **CODEN** THWDD8. Documents available from CASDDS.
Ind/Abst AGRICOLA; Chem. Abstr.

US/0276-2242
TOXIC CONTROL. See Medical Science and Technology-Toxicology.

US/0093-5891
TOXIC MATERIALS NEWS. *Title Change.* (Mar. 15, 1974)-(May 1994). Periodical. English. wk (mailed every Wed.). Business Publishers Inc., 951 Pershing Drive, Silver Spring MD 20910-4464. **Tel** (301)587-6300, (800)274-0122, FAX (301)585-9075. **[CCC].** available on an online database (file 636/Full-Text) from DIALOG. *Absorbed by Air Water Pollution Report.*
Desc: Features up to date information on the myriad laws, regulations and court cases that affect your business. You get first hand coverage of such vital issues as: EPA, OHSA Actions; Air/Water Toxics; Chemical Testing; Risk Assessment and many others.
Ind/Abst PTS Newsl. Database [Full Txt.].

US/0275-3766
TOXIC MATERIALS TRANSPORT. *Title Change.* See Transportation.

US
TOXIC TIMES. (1988)-. Periodical. English. qt. $15.00. National Toxics Campaign, 1168 Commonwealth Avenue, Boston MA 02134.

CN/1193-8250
TRANSPORTATION OF DANGEROUS GOODS REGULATIONS. [Transp. danger. goods regul.]. Main/Corp Canada. Added/Corp International Compliance Centre. VFOAT Guide to Canadian Transportation of Dangerous Goods Act and Regulations. (1991)-. English. ir. 130.00Can$. International Compliance Center, 2150 Liberty Drive, Unit 2, Niagara Falls NY 14304. **Tel** (716)283-0002, FAX (716)283-0119. **DD** 343.7109/32/0263.

●US/1061-3595
TRANSPORTING HAZARDOUS MATERIALS. (1992)-. Periodical. English. John Wiley & Sons, Inc., 605 Third Avenue, New York NY 10158-0012. **Tel** (212)850-6000, (212)850-6645, FAX (212)850-6088, telex 12-7063. **(Subscription address:** John Wiley & Sons / England, Baffins Lane, Chichester, West Sussex PO19 1UD England.**)**

BE
TRIBUNE DE L'EAU / MINISTERE DE LA REGION WALLONNE, UNION WALLONNE DES ENTREPRISES, [ET] CEBEDEAU. Added/Corp Wallonia (Belgium) Union Wallonne des Entreprises. Centre Belge d'Etude et de Documentation de l'Eau. Vol. 41 No. 531 (May 1988)-. Academic Scholarly Publication. French. 3900.00F Belgium; 4640.00 other. Cebeboc Sprl, Rue Armand Stevart 2, B-4000 Liege Belgium. **LC** TD202; .C43. **NLM** W1; TR543. **CODEN** TREAEE. Documents available from CASDDS. *Continues Tribune du CEBEDEAU.*
Ind/Abst Chem. Abstr. (1988-).

US
UDS AIR QUALITY CONTROL DIGEST. Ceased. Added/Corp University Digest Services. Vol. 2, No. 7 (July/August 1971)-Ceased Vol. 19, No. 6 (Nov. 1988). Periodical. English. bm. University Digest, 5844 Little Pine Lane, Rochester MI 48064. **Tel** (313)651-2528. **ED** A D Even. *Continues Air Quality Control Digest.*

GW/0041-6355
UMWELT (DUSSELDORF). (UMWELT.). [Umwelt]. Added/Corp Verein Deutscher Ingenieure. (1971)-. Academic Scholarly Publication. German. Eight times a year. DM223.00 Germany; DM250.00 other. VDI Verlag GmbH, Postfach 101054, D 40001 Dusseldorf Germany. **Tel** 011 49 211 6188313, FAX 011 49 211 6188133. **ED** Henzy Hermann Warncke. **LC** TD172; .U46. **NLM** W1 UM16. **CODEN** UMWLDA. **[CCC]. Ad Acc**. Documents available from CASDDS.
Desc: Contains information on such topics as environmental research and planning, waste disposal, noise control, solving problems in industry, landscape and town planning.
Ind/Abst Chem. Abstr.; Coal Abstr.; Ei Page One; EMBASE; Energy Res. Abstr. (Dec. 1974)-; GeoRef.

AU
UMWELTDATEN. Main/Corp Osterreichisches Statistisches Zentralamt. 1978-. Periodical. German. S270.00. **LC** HA1173; .A27 subser; TD186.5.A9 A9.
Desc: Contains data collected by the state, counties and municipalities in Austria including emissions, immissions of poison materials and other direct and indirect sources that have influence on the environment.

GW
UMWELTFORSCHUNGSKATALOG. VFOAT Umplis, Informations und Dokumentations-System zur Umweltplanung; Umwelt. German. sa. Varies. Erich Schmidt Verlag GmbH, Postfach 304240, D 10724 Berlin Germany. **Tel** 011 49 30 25008525. **LC** TD171.5.G3; U46. **DD** 363.7/0072.

GW/0174-3244
UMWELTHYGIENE (ESSEN). (UMWELTHYGIENE : JAHRESBERICHT / MEDIZINISCHES INSTITUT FUER UMWELTHYGIENE.). [Umwelthygiene]. VFOAT Jahresbericht (Medizinisches Institut fur Umwelthygiene (Universitat Dusseldorf). V. 12 (1979)-. Academic Scholarly Publication. German (in). ar. Girardet, Girardetstr 2-38 Postfach 9, 4300 Essen 1 Germany. **NLM** W1; UM17. **CODEN** UMHYD8. Documents available from CASDDS. *Continues Lufthygiene und Silikoseforschung, 0341-2846.*
Ind/Abst Chem. Abstr. (1979-1981); Text. Technol. Dig.

GW/0934-3504
UMWELTWISSENSCHAFTEN UND SCHADSTOFF-FORSCHUNG : ORGAN DER ARBEITSGEMEINSCHAFT UMWELTCHEMIE UND OKOTOXIKOLOGIE DER GESELLSCHAFT DEUTSCHER CHEMIKER. Added/Corp Gesellschaft Deutscher Chemiker. Arbeitsgemeinschaft Umweltchemie und Okotoxikologie. Chemische Gesellschaft der Deutschen Demokratischen Republik. Arbeitsgemeinschaft Umweltchemie und Okotoxikologie. Verband Deutscher Geookologen. VFOAT UWSF-Z Umweltchem. Okotox. (Mar. 1989)-. Academic Scholarly Publication. German (summaries and/or abstracts in English). qt. DM366.00 Germany; DM370.00 other. Ecomed Verlagsgesellschaft GmbH, Postfach 1752, D 86895 Landsberg Germany. **Tel** 011 49 8191 125544, FAX 011 49 8191 125513. **(Subscription address:** ESPR Subscription Service, ecomed publishers, Rudolf-Diesel-Strabe 3, D-86 899 Landsberg, Germany (Tel. 49-8191-125544)**) ED** Otto Hutzinger. **LC** TD172; .U49. **DD** 363.73. **NLM** W1; UM22. **CODEN** USZOE9. Documents available from CASDDS.
Ind/Abst Chem. Abstr.

TH
UNEP-ASIA REPORT. *Title Change.* Added/Corp UNEP Regional Office for Asia and the Pacific. (1977)-?. English. an. UNEP Regional Office for Asia & the Pacific, United Nations Building/10th Floor Rajdamnern Avenue, Bangkok 2 Thailand. **LC** TD171.5; .A78; U53. **DD** 363.7/0095. *Continued by UNEP, Asia-Pacific Report.*

US/0742-8502
URANIUM MILL TAILINGS MANAGEMENT. See Engineering-Mines and Mining Engineering.

US/1056-7135
USER'S GUIDE TO ARTICLE 80, A. See Fire Prevention.

NO/0042-2592
VANN. [Vann]. Added/Corp Norsk Forening for Vassdragspleie og Vannhygiene. Vol. 1 (1966)-. Periodical. Norwegian. ir. Norwegian Water Conservation & Hygiene Association, Kronpinninsensgt 17, Oslo 1 Norway. **LC** TD204; .V34.
Ind/Abst Energy Res. Abstr. (May 1978)-.

NE
VERSLAG ONDERZOEK KWALITEIT OPPERVLAKTEWATER IN ZEELAND. Main/Corp Zealand. Provinciale Waterstaatsdienst. Dutch. an. Rouaansekaai 43, Middelburg Netherlands. **LC** TD278.Z4; Z45A.

GW/0174-1993
VERZEICHNIS DER WISSENSCHAFTLICHEN FILME. TEILVERZEICHNIS B. See Agriculture.

IT
VIA. Vol. 1, No. 1 (March 1987)-. Periodical. Italian (summaries and/or abstracts in English). qt. $55.00. L'Arca Edizioni Spa, Vialle Bianca Maria 11, 20122 Milan Italy. **Tel** 011 39 2 790240.

US/0736-6647
VIRUSES IN WASTE, RENOVATED, AND OTHER WATERS. 1969-. English. an. US Environmental Protection Agency / Center for Environmental Research Information, 401 M Street SW, Washington DC 20460. **NLM** ZQW 80 V821. Each issue contains an index to its own contents (no volume index)--loose.

HU
VIZGAZDALKODAS ES KORNYEZETVEDELEM. See Water Resources.

HU
VIZMINOSEGI ES VIZTECHNOLOGIAI KUTATASI EREDMENYEK. Main/Corp Vizgazdalkodasi Tudomanyos Kutato Intezet Vizminosegi es Viztechnologiai Foosztaly. VFOAT Research in Water Quality and Water Technology. 1958/68-. Hungarian (English). **LC** TD365; .B83A.

RU/0321-4044
VODOSNABZENIE I SANITARNAJA TEHNIKA. (VODOSNABZHENIE I SANITARNAIA TEKHNIKA.). [Vodosnabz. sanit. teh.]. Added/Corp Soviet Union. Gosudarstennyi Komitet po Delam Stroitelstva. (193?)-. Periodical. Russian. mo. $79.95. **(Subscription address:** East View Publications Inc., 3020 Harbor Lane North, Suite 110, Minneapolis MN 55447.**) CODEN** VSTEAO. *Continues Sanitarnaia Tekhnika.*
Ind/Abst Coal Abstr.; Saf. Health Work.

US
VOLUNTEER LAKE MONITORING PROGRAM. English. Illinois Environmental Protection Agency, 2200 Churchill Road, Springfield IL 62706. **LC** TD224.I3; V64. **DD** 363.73/942/09773.

UK
WARMER BULLETIN. Added/Corp Warmer Campaign for Warmth and Energy from Rubbish (Great Britain). VFOAT World Action for Recycling Materials & Energy From Rubbish. (198?)-. Bulletin. English (German). qt (Feb., May, Aug., Nov.). Free. Warmer Campaign, 83 Mount Ephraim, Tunbridge, Wells Kent TN4 8B5 England. **Tel** 011 44 892 24626, FAX 011 44 892 25287. **ED** Maggie Thurgood. **Bk Rev**, (Qty: 12-14/yr). **Acid Free. Circ:** 65,000 (ctrl). Documents available from Documents on Demand.
Desc: Articles and information from around the world on recycling, reuse and energy from waste.
Ind/Abst Energy Inf. Abstr.; Environ. Abstr.; Infomat Int. Bus.

US
WASHINGTON ENVIRONMENTAL QUALITY PROFILE / UNITED STATES, ENVIRONMENTAL PROTECTION AGENCY, REGION). Began with 1977. English. an. US Environmental Protection Agency Region 10, 1200 Sixth Avenue, Seattle WA 98101.

GW/0341-2679
WASSER, LUFT UND BODEN : WLB. VFOAT WLB. (19??)-. Academic Scholarly Publication. German. mo. Vereinigte Fachverlage, Postfach 4068, D 55030 Mainz Germany. **Tel** 011 49 6131 992150. **LC** TD897; .W3. **DD** 628/.05. **CODEN** WWBOE7. **[CCC].** Documents available from CASDDS. *Continues WLB. Wasser, Luft und Betrieb.*
Ind/Abst Chem. Abstr.; GeoRef.

AU/0508-122X
WASSER UND ABWASSER (VIENNA). (WASSER UND ABWASSER.). [Wasser Abwasser]. Added/Corp Bundesanstalt fur Wassergute (Austria) Bundesanstalt fur Wasserbiologie und Abwasserforschung in Wien-Kaisermuhlen (Austria). (1956)-. Academic Scholarly Publication. German. **LC** TD741; .W3. **CODEN** WAABDC. Documents available from CASDDS.
Ind/Abst Chem. Abstr.

GW
WASSERVERSORGUNG UND ABWASSERBESEITIGUNG IN DER WIRTSCHAFT. See Water Resources.

US/0043-1001
WASTE AGE. [Waste age]. Added/Corp National Solid Wastes Management Association. (Apr. 1970)-. Periodical. English. mo. $55.00 US & Canada; $155.00 other. Environmental Industry Association, 4031 Conn Avenue Northwest, Suite 300, Washington DC 20008. **Tel** (202)861-0708 Ext. 369. **(Subscription address:** Waste Age Magazine, PO Box420285, Palm Coast FL 32137.**) ED** Joe Salimando. **DD** 628. Index available. **Bk Rev. Ad Acc. Circ:** 30,000 (ctrl). available on microfilm and microfiche from University Microfilms International (UMI). Documents available from Article Express International, Documents on Demand.
Desc: Reports on all facets of waste management and industry from a variety of perspective; social, political, economical, as well as providing exclusives such as industry product and service guides. Recipients include

private contract firms, governmental entities, consulting engineers, industrial plants, etc.
Ind/Abst Abstr. Bull. Inst. Pap. Sci. Tech. (19??-); Appl. Sci. Technol. Index (19??-); AQUAREF (19??-); Ei Page One (19??-); EMBASE (19??-); Energy Res. Abstr. (Feb. 1975-); Eng. Index Annu. (19??-) [Select. Cov.]; Environ. Abstr. (19??-); Environ. Period. Bibliogr. (19??-); F&S Index Plus Text, Int. (19??-) [Select. Cov.]; Int. Aerosp. Abstr. (19??-); Ocean. Abstr. (19??-); Pollut. Abstr. Indexes (19??-); PROMT (19??-); Risk Abstr. (19??-); Urban Aff. Abstr. (19??-).

US/1042-0614
WASTE AGE'S RECYCLING TIMES. [Waste age's recycl. times]. **Added/Corp** National Solid Wastes Management Association. **VFOAT** Recycling Times. (1989)-. Periodical. English. Twenty-six times a year. $99.00 US & Canada; $215.00 others. Environmental Industry Association, 4031 Conn Avenue Northwest, Suite 300, Washington DC 20008. **Tel** (202)861-0708 Ext. 369. **(Subscription address:** Recycling Times, PO Box 420285, Palm Coast FL 32137.**) ED** Joe Salamando. **DD** 363. **Ad Acc. Circ:** 5,000.
Desc: Covers issues surrounding commercial, industrial, and municipal solid waste recycling.

●UK/0965-4496
WASTE & ENVIRONMENT TODAY. BIBLIOGRAPHIC JOURNAL. Added/Corp Atomic Energy Research Establishment (Harwell, England). Waste Management Information Bureau. **VFOAT** Waste and Environment Today. Bibliographic Journal. Vol. 5, No. 1 (Jan. 1992)-. Periodical. English. mo. £240.00, $422.37 UK; £260.00, $467.67 other. AEA Technology Communication, Dir 11 Charles II Street, London SW1Y 4QP England. **Tel** 011 44 71 3896565. **(Subscription address:** Waste & Environment Today NETC, F6 Culham, Abingdon Oxford OX14 3DB England.**)** ***Continues** Waste Management Today. Bibliographic Journal, 0954-495X.*
Desc: News and bibliographic journal.

●UK/0965-4488
WASTE & ENVIRONMENT TODAY. NEWS JOURNAL. Added/Corp AEA Environment and Energy (Firm). Waste Management Information Bureau. **VFOAT** Waste and Environment Today. News Journal. Vol. 5, No. 1 (Jan. 1992)-. Periodical. English. mo. **LC** TD1; .W27. ***Continues** Waste Management Today. News Journal, 0953-0975.*

CN/1185-4731
WASTE BUSINESS WEST. [Waste bus. west]. Vol. 2, No. 2 (Apr. 1991)-. Periodical. English. Six times a year. 39.50Can$ Canada; $39.50 US; $45.00 other. Waste Business, 85 Somerset Avenue #200, Toronto Ontario M6H 2R3 Canada. **Tel** (416)658-7519, FAX (416)658-9708. **ED** Matthew Keegan. **DD** 363.72/8/09182305. **CODEN** WBWEE3. **Bk Rev. Ad Acc. Circ:** 45,000 (ctrl). Documents available from Documents on Demand. ***Continues** Waste Business International West., 1185-474X.*
Desc: Environmental isues with editorials on hazardous waste, recycling, etc.
Ind/Abst Environ. Abstr.

AT/0311-3558
WASTE DISPOSAL AND WATER MANAGEMENT IN AUSTRALIA. [Waste dispos. water manage. Aust.]. (1974)-. Periodical. English. bm. 38.00Aus$ Australia; 64.00Aus$ other. Editorial Publishing Consultants P L, 29 First Avenue, Klemzig SA 5087, Australia. **Tel** 011 61 8 2615837. **DD** 628.440994.
Ind/Abst AESIS Q.; Biodeter. Abstr.

UK
WASTE DISPOSAL STATISTICS BASED ON ESTIMATES. See Environmental Issues-Abstracting, Bibliographies and Statistics.

UK
WASTE DISPOSAL STATISTICS ... ESTIMATES / CIPFA, STATISTICAL INFORMATION SERVICE. See Environmental Issues-Abstracting, Bibliographies and Statistics.

US/1050-3153
WASTE INFORMATION DIGESTS. (WASTE INFORMATION DIGESTS : WID / ENVIRONMENTAL STUDIES INSTITUTE.). [Waste inf. dig.]. **Added/Corp** International Academy at Santa Barbara. Environmental Studies Institute. **VFOAT** WID. Vol. 1, No. 1 (Jan./Feb. 1990)-. Periodical. English. Eight times a year. $247.00 US; $257.00 (air mail) other. International Academy at Santa Barbara, 800 Garden Street, Suite D, Santa Barbara CA 93101. **Tel** (805)965-5010, FAX (805)965-6071. **DD** 363. **[CCC].** available on an online database (file 636/Full-Text) from DIALOG.
Ind/Abst PTS Newsl. Database [Full Txt.].

UK
WASTE MANAGEMENT. (19??)-. Periodical. English. qt. £195.35. Croner Publ Ltd, Croner House, London Road, Kingston upon Thames, Surrey KT2 6SR England. **Tel** 011 44 81 5473333, FAX 081 547-2637.

US/0275-6196
WASTE MANAGEMENT. (WASTE MANAGEMENT : PROCEEDINGS OF THE SYMPOSIUM ON WASTE MANAGEMENT.). [Waste manage.]. **Added/Corp** University of Arizona. College of Engineering. (1979)-. Academic Scholarly Publication. English. an. **LC** TD898; .S92a. **DD** 363.7/28. **CODEN** PSWMDY. Documents available from CASDDS. ***Continues** Symposium on Waste Management. Waste Management and Fuel Cycles ..., 0733-8783.*
Ind/Abst Bioeng. Abstr.; Chem. Abstr.; Coal Abstr.; GeoRef.

AT
WASTE MANAGEMENT & ENVIRONMENT. English. Twelve times a year. 152.00Aus$ Australia; 180.00Aus$ others. Rala Publications, PO Box 134, 203-205 Darling Street, Balmain NSW 2041 Australia. **Tel** 011 61 2 5551944, FAX 011 61 2 5551496. **ED** Shane Rochfort. **Bk Rev. Ad Acc, Adv Mgr:** D. Williams, **Tel** 02 555 1944. **Circ:** 6,000 (ctrl).

UK/0734-242X
WASTE MANAGEMENT & RESEARCH. (WASTE MANAGEMENT & RESEARCH : THE JOURNAL OF THE INTERNATIONAL SOLID WASTES AND PUBLIC CLEANSING ASSOCIATION, ISWA.). [Waste manage. res.]. **Added/Corp** International Solid Wastes and Public Cleansing Association. **VFOAT** Waste Management and Research. Vol. 1, No. 1 (March 1983)-. Academic Scholarly Publication. English. bm (6 issues). $360.00. Academic Press Ltd., A Division of Harcourt Brace & Company Ltd., 24-28 Oval Road, London NW1 7DX England. **Tel** 071 267 4466, FAX 071 482 2293, 071 485 4752, telex 25775 ACPRES G. **(Subscription address:** Harcourt Brace & Company, Ltd., Foots Cray, High Street, Sidcup Kent DA14 5HP England.**) ED** P. Rushbrook. **LC** TD896; .W35. **DD** 628/.4/05. **CODEN** WMARD8. **[CCC]. Pr Rev.** Documents available from Article Express International, The Genuine Article, BIOSIS Document Express, CASDDS.
Desc: Publishes a broad cross section of researchers and practitioners from academic institutions and government bodies, engineers, regulators, and industry. Publishes papers on all aspects of solid waste management with the main focus on the discussion of solutions to problems that arise primarily from municipal and industrial solid wastes and sludges. In particular, the scope does not include papers on waste water (sewage) collection and treatment. In order to achieve balanced coverage, special attention is given to papers that help to bridge the gap between academic studies and practical operational problems.
Ind/Abst Abstr. AIT Rep. Publ. Energy; Biol. Abstr.; Chem. Abstr.; Curr. Aware. Biol. Sci., CABS; Curr. Contents, Agric. Biol. Environ. Sci.; Curr. Contents Eng. Tech. Appl. Sci.; Ecol. Abstr. (1991-); Ei Page One; EMBASE; Eng. Index Annu.; Environ. Period. Bibliogr.; Fluid Abstr., Civil Eng.; Fluid Abstr. Proc. Eng.; FLUIDEX (199?-); Geogr. Abstr. Phys. Geogr.; Geogr. Abstr. Human Geogr.; Health Saf. Sci. Abstr.; Int. Civil Eng. Abstr.; Int. Dev. Abstr. (1983-); Pollut. Abstr. Indexes; Res. Alert [Select. Cov.]; Risk Abstr.; Soc. Sci. Cit. Index [Select. Cov.]; Soft. Abstr. Eng.

UK
WASTE MANAGEMENT BULLETIN. Bulletin. English. Three times a year.

US/0956-053X
WASTE MANAGEMENT (ELMSFORD). (WASTE MANAGEMENT.). [Waste manag.]. Vol. 9, No. 1 (1989)-. Academic Scholarly Publication. English. Eight times a year. $768.00 The Americas; £515.00 other. Pergamon Press, An Imprint of Elsevier Science Ltd., The Boulevard, Langford Lane, Kidlington, Oxford OX5 1GB United Kingdom. **Tel** 011 44 865 843000, 011 44 865 843699, FAX 011 44 865 843010. **(Subscription address:** Elsevier Science Ltd. Oxford Fulfillment Centre, PO Box 800, Kidlington, Oxford OX5 1DX United Kingdom.**) ED** William Cawley. **LC** TD811.5; .N82. **DD** 628.4/2/05. **CODEN** WAMAE2. **[CCC].** available on microfilm from the publisher; available on microfilm and microfiche from University Microfilms International (UMI). Documents available from Article Express International, BIOSIS Document Express, Ask*IEEE, CASDDS, Documents on Demand. ***Continues** Nuclear and Chemical Waste Management, 0191-815X.*
Ind/Abst AESIS Q.; Appl. Sci. Technol. Index; Bioeng. Abstr.; Biol. Abstr.; Chem. Abstr.; Curr. Aware. Biol. Sci., CABS; Ecol. Abstr.; Ei Page One; EMBASE; Energy Inf. Abstr.; Energy Res. Abstr.; Eng. Index Annu.; Environ. Abstr.; Environ. Period. Bibliogr.; Geogr. Abstr. Phys. Geogr.; GeoRef; INSPEC (1989-); Pollut. Abstr. Indexes; Risk Abstr.; Soils Fert.

●US/1062-7529
WASTE MANAGEMENT NEWS (WACO, TEX.). (WASTE MANAGEMENT NEWS.). [Waste manag. news]. (1992)-. Periodical. English. sm. $367.50 US; $405.50 Canada; $381.50 Mexico; $401.50 other. Stevens Publishing Corporation, 225 North New Road, Waco TX 76702-2604. **Tel** (800)727-7573, (817)776-9000. **DD** 363. ***Continues** Water and Waste News.*

AU
WASTE MANAGEMENT RESEARCH ABSTRACTS : INFORMATION ON RESEARCH IN PROGRESS. Added/Corp International Atomic Energy Agency. (19??)-. Periodical. English (French, Russian and Spanish). an. Free. International Atomic Energy Agency - IAEA, Wagramerstrasse 5, PO Box 100, A-1400 Vienna Austria. **Tel** 011 43 222 2360.
Ind/Abst Energy Res. Abstr. (March 1982-).

US
WASTE MANAGEMENT RESEARCH REPORT. NEWS FROM STATE UNIVERSITY OF NEW YORK AT BUFFALO AND STONY BROOK AND CORNELL UNIVERSITY. Added/Corp College of Environmental Science and Forestry. Vol. 1, No. 1 (Winter 1989)-. English. tq. College of Environmental Science and Forestry, State University of New York, Forestry Drive, Syracuse NY 13210. Documents available from Documents on Demand.
Ind/Abst Environ. Abstr.; Environ. Period. Bibliogr.

US/1064-6140
WASTE MINIMIZATION UPDATE. [Waste minim. update]. **Added/Corp** Local Government Commission (Calif.). Toxics Project. (1988)-. Periodical. English. bm (6 issues). $18.00. Local Government Commission, 909 12th Street, Suite 203, Sacramento CA 95814. **Tel** (916)448-1198. **DD** 363. **Pr Rev. Circ:** 200.

UK/0965-3147
WASTE PLANNING. [Waste plan.]. (1991)-. Periodical. English. qt. £39.00 UK; £44.00 Europe; £54.00 other. Mineral Planning, 2 Greenways Little Fencote, Northallerton DL7 0TS England. **Tel** 44 609 748709, FAX 44 609 748709. **ED** Milford Harrison and Steven Machin. **DD** 363.728. Index available (bound in March). **Bk Rev,** (Qty: no limit). **Ad Acc, Adv Mgr:** Liz Harrison, **Tel** 0609-748709. **Circ:** 1000. ***Continues in part** Mineral Planning, 0267-1409.*
Desc: Reports on legal matters relating to waste handling and disposal; determinations under COPA, Environmental Protection Act, T & CP Act; national and local policies; environmental considerations, publications and waste practice.

US/0889-0072
WASTE RECOVERY REPORT. [Waste recovery rep.]. Vol. 10, No. 1 (Jan. 1985)-. Periodical. English. mo. $50.00 US and Canada; $75.00 other. ICON Information Concepts Inc., 211 South 45th Street, Philadelphia PA 19104. **Tel** (215)349-6500, FAX (215)349-6502. **ED** Alan Krigman. **DD** 604. **Bk Rev,** (Qty: 20-30). **Circ:** 500. ***Continues** Recovery Engineering News.*
Desc: Covers recycling, reuse, reprocessing of waste to derive material and energy value while reducing landfill burden and avoiding toxicity and pollution hazard.

US/0885-0003
WASTE TREATMENT TECHNOLOGY NEWS. [Waste treat. technol. news]. Vol. 1, No. 1 (Sept. 1985)-. Periodical. English. mo. $350.00. Business Communications Inc., 25 Van Zant Street, Suite 13, Norwalk CT 06855. **Tel** (203)853-4266. **DD** 604. **[CCC].** available on an online database (file 636/Full-Text) from DIALOG. Documents available from Documents on Demand.
Ind/Abst Environ. Abstr.; PTS Newsl. Database [Full Txt.].

II
WASTELANDS NEWS : A QQUARTERLY NEWSLETTER OF SOCIETY FOR PROMOTION OF WASTELANDS DEVELOPMENT.
Added/Corp Society for Promotion of Wastelands Development (India). (19??)-. Newsletter. English. qt.
Ind/Abst Curr. Lit. Sci. Sci.

UK/0263-8126
WASTES MANAGEMENT. Added/Corp Institute of Solid Wastes Management. Vol. 72, No. 1 (Jan. 1982)-. Periodical. English. mo. £48.00 UK; £54.00 other. Institute of Wastes Management / England, 9 Saxib Court St. Peters Gardens, Northhampton NN1 1SX England. **Tel** 011 44 604 20426, FAX 011 44 604 21339. **ED** David Loyd. Index available. cum. index. **Bk Rev. Ad Acc, Adv Mgr:** Jennie Harris. **Circ:** 3,000 (ctrl). ***Continues** Solid Wastes, 0306-6509.*
Desc: Covers all aspects of the treatment, collection and disposal of wastes.
Ind/Abst Curr. Technol. Index.

US/1040-8916
WASTETECH NEWS. [WasteTech news]. **VFOAT** Waste Tech News; WTN. Vol. 1, No. 1 (Sept. 6, 1988)-. Periodical. English. Twenty-four times a year. $55.00 US; $75.00 Canada; $150.00 other. WasteTech News, 131 Madison Street, Denver CO 80206. **Tel**

(303)394-2905, FAX (303)394-3011. **ED** Jim Shrine. **DD** 604. **Bk Rev. Ad Acc, Adv Mgr:** James Hatenbower. **Circ:** 15,000.

NE/0049-6979
WATER, AIR, AND SOIL POLLUTION. [Water air soil pollut.]. Vol. 1, No. 1 (Nov. 1971)-. Academic Scholarly Publication. English. Twenty-eight times a year. $3,164.00. Kluwer Academic Publishers, Postbus 322, 3300 AH Dordrecht, The Netherlands. **Tel** 011 (31) 78 524400, FAX 011 31 78 183273, telex 20083. **ED** Billy M McCormac. **LC** TD172; .W36. **DD** 628.5/05. **NLM** W1 WA69D. **CODEN** WAPLAC. **[CCC].** Index available. **Bk Rev. Ad Acc. Pr Rev. Circ:** 1,100. available on microfilm and microfiche from University Microfilms International (UMI). Documents available from Article Express International, The Genuine Article, BIOSIS Document Express, Ask*IEEE, CASDDS, Documents on Demand.
Desc: An interdisciplinary journal for all the physical and biological processes affecting our flora, air, water, and solid earth in relation to environmental pollution. Publishes a wide variety of articles, including those on all aspects of sources, transport, deposition, accumulation, disposition, and mitigation of acid precipitation, atmospheric pollution, heavy metals, water pollution, waste water, wastes, pesticides, soil pollution, sewage sediments and so on; the effects of pollutants on human beings, vegetation, fish, aquatic species, microogorganic
Ind/Abst AGRICOLA; Agrofor. Abstr. (1991-); Air Pollut. Titles; AQUAREF; Aquat. Sci. Fish. Abstr. (Computer File); Art Archaeol. Tech. Abstr.; BioBusiness; Biodeter. Abstr. (1991-); Biol. Abstr.; Chem. Abstr.; Chem. Titles; Coal Abstr.; Crop Physiol. Abstr.; Curr. Aware. Biol. Sci., CABS; Curr. Biotechnol.; Curr. Contents, Agric. Biol. Environ. Sci.; Curr. Ref. Fish Res.; Ecol. Abstr.; Ecology Abstr.; Ei Page One; EMBASE; Energy Res. Abstr. (April 1976-); Eng. Index Annu.; Environ. Abstr.; Environ. Period. Bibliogr.; Field Crop Abstr.; Fish Rev.; Fluid Abstr., Civil Eng.; Fluid Abstr. Proc. Eng.; FLUIDEX (1973-); For. Prod. Abstr. (19??-19??); For. Abstr.; Geogr. Abstr. Phys. Geogr.; Geogr. Abstr. Human Geogr. (?-?); Geol. Abstr.; GeoRef; Grasslands For. Abstr.; Health Saf. Sci. Abstr.; Hortic. Abstr.; Index Vet.; INSPEC (Nov. 1971-); Int. Aerosp. Abstr.; J. Plan. Lit.; Lit. Pat. Abstr., Oilfield Chem. (1975-); Lit. Abstr., Catal. Catal.; Lit. Abstr., Health Environ.; Lit. Abstr., Pet. Refin. Petrochem.; Lit. Abstr., Pet. Substit.; Lit. Abstr., Transp. Storage; Maize Abstr.; Meteorol. Geoastrophys. Abstr.; Microbiol. Abstr. Sect. A; Microbiol. Abstr. Sect. C; Nematol. Abstr.; Nutr. Abstr. Rev., Ser. B, Live Feeds and Feed.; Ocean. Abstr.; Life Sci. Collect.; PESTDOC; Pollut. Abstr. Indexes; Res. Alert [Full Cov.]; Rev. Agric. Entomol.; Rev. Plant Pathol.; Rice Abstr.; Sci. Cit. Index; SCISEARCH; Soc. Sci. Cit. Index [Select. Cov.]; Soils Fert.; Soyabean Abstr.; Toxicol. Abstr.; Weed Abstr.; Wheat Barley Trit. Abstr.; Wildl. Rev.

UK/0951-7359
WATER AND ENVIRONMENTAL MANAGEMENT : JOURNAL OF THE INSTITUTION OF WATER AND ENVIRONMENTAL MANAGEMENT. **Added/Corp** Institution of Water and Environmental Management. **VFOAT** Journal of the Institution of Water and Environmental Management. Vol. 1, No. 1 (Aug. 1987)-. Periodical. English. bm. £107.00. Institution of Water and Environmental Management, 15 John Street, London WC1N 2EB England. **Tel** 011 44 71 831 3110, FAX 011 44 71 405 4967. **LC** TD201; .W29. **DD** 628.1/05. **NLM** W1; WA69E. Index available. **Ad Acc. Pr Rev.** available on microfilm and microfiche from University Microfilms International (UMI). Documents available from Article Express International, The Genuine Article, CASDDS, Documents on Demand. ***Formed by the union of** Water Pollution Control, 0043-129X; Journal of the Institution of Water Engineers and Scientists, 0309-1600* ***and** Public Health Engineer, 0300-5925.*
Desc: Includes information on water, water resources, river management, pollution control, sea defense, and flood alleviation, sewerage, industrial sewage, navigation and more.
Ind/Abst AGRICOLA; Biodeter. Abstr. (1991-); Chem. Abstr.; Curr. Aware. Biol. Sci., CABS; Curr. Contents, Agric. Biol. Environ. Sci.; Curr. Technol. Index; Ecol. Abstr.; Ei Page One; EMBASE; Energy Inf. Abstr.; Eng. Index Annu.; Environ. Abstr.; Environ. Period. Bibliogr.; Fluid Abstr., Civil Eng.; Fluid Abstr. Proc. Eng.; FLUIDEX (199?-); For. Prod. Abstr. (1991-); For. Abstr.; Geogr. Abstr. Phys. Geogr.; Geogr. Abstr. Human Geogr.; GeoRef; Int. Abstr. Oper. Res. [Select. Cov.]; Int. Dev. Abstr.; Irr. Drain. Abstr.; PESTDOC; Res. Alert [Full Cov.]; Rural Dev. Abstr.; Sci. Cit. Index; SCISEARCH; Soc. Sci. Cit. Index [Select. Cov.]; Soils Fert.; Trop. Dis. Bull.; Weed Abstr.

UK/0950-6551
WATER & WASTE TREATMENT (1985). (WATER & WASTE TREATMENT.). [Water waste treat.]. **VFOAT** WWT; Water and Waste Treatment. Vol. 28, No. 3 (March 1985)-. Periodical. English. mo. £43.00 UK; £50.00. Faversham House Group Ltd, Faversham House, 111 Saint James Road, Croydon Surrey CR9 2TH England. **Tel** 011 44 81 684 4082. ***Continues** Water & Waste Treatment Journal (1982).*
Ind/Abst Aquat. Sci. Fish. Abstr. (Computer File); BMT Abstr.; Fluid Abstr., Civil Eng.; Fluid Abstr. Proc. Eng.; FLUIDEX.

US/0043-1141
WATER AND WASTES DIGEST. See Water Resources.

US/0748-2612
WATER & WASTEWATER DIGEST. [Water wastewater dig.]. **VFOAT** Water and Wastewater Digest. Oct. 1981-. Periodical. English. mo. Department of Natural Resources / Missouri, PO Box 176, Jefferson City MO 65102. **ED** James R Yancey and Virginia Ismay. **LC** TD224.M8; M63. **DD** 363.6/1/09778. **Ad Acc. Circ:** 3,500 (ctrl). ***Continues** Missouri Water & Wastewater Digest, 0731-2903.*
Desc: Articles of interest to water and wastewater treatment, plant operators, training course announcements, legislative updates, "practice" problems for operator certification, employment opportunities.

US/1044-9493
WATER ENVIRONMENT & TECHNOLOGY. (WATER ENVIRONMENT & TECHNOLOGY / WATER POLLUTION CONTROL FEDERATION.). [Water environ. technol.]. **Added/Corp** Water Pollution Control Federation. Water Environment Federation. **VFOAT** Water Environment and Technology. Vol. 1, No. 1 (Sept. 1989)-. Academic Scholarly Publication. English. mo. $158.00 US; $205.00 other; (comes also in combination with Water Environment Research). Water Environment Federation, 601 Wythe Street, Alexandria VA 22314-1994. **Tel** (703)684-2400, FAX (703)684-2492. **LC** TD365; .W35. **DD** 628.1/68. **CODEN** WAETEJ. **[CCC]. Ad Acc.** available on microfilm and microfiche from University Microfilms International (UMI). Documents available from Article Express International, BIOSIS Document Express, CASDDS, Documents on Demand. ***Continues in part** Journal (Water Pollution Control Federation), 0043-1303.*
Desc: Mix of technical and nontechnical feature articles.
Ind/Abst Abstr. Bull. Inst. Pap. Sci. Tech.; Anal. Abstr.; Appl. Mech. Rev.; Appl. Sci. Technol. Index; Aquat. Sci. Fish. Abstr. (Computer File); BioBusiness; Biol. Abstr.; Chem. Abstr.; Ei Page One; EMBASE; Eng. Index Annu. [Select. Cov.]; Environ. Abstr.; Environ. Period. Bibliogr.; Geol. Abstr.; GeoRef; Helminthol. Abstr.; Index Med.; Ocean. Abstr.; Pollut. Abstr. Indexes; Risk Abstr.; Soils Fert.; Wildl. Rev. (199?-).

●US/1074-2972
WATER ENVIRONMENT LABORATORY SOLUTIONS. **Added/Corp** Water Environment Federation. (1994)-. Periodical. English. mo. $79.00 US; $99.00. Water Environment Federation, 601 Wythe Street, Alexandria VA 22314-1994. **Tel** (703)684-2400, FAX (703)684-2492. ***Continues** Bench Sheet, 0737-4186.*
Desc: This journal is designed for laboratory professional. Contains articles that discuss new methods and tests to improve operating procedures, current information on accreditation requirements and quality control procedures.

UK
WATER INDUSTRY. UNITED KINGDOM SERVICE AND COSTS ... AND CHARGES FOR SERVICE .... See Water Resources.

AT/0310-0367
WATER (MELBOURNE). (WATER : OFFICIAL JOURNAL OF THE AUSTRALIAN WATER AND WASTEWATER ASSOCIATION.). [Water]. **Added/Corp** Australian Water and Wastewater Association. Vol. 1, No. 1 (Mar. 1974)-. Academic Scholarly Publication. English. bm. 35.00Aus$, $28.02. Australian Water & Wastewater, 4 Pleasant View E A Swintor, Glen Waverly VIC 3150 Australia. **Tel** 011 61 3 560 4752. **CODEN** WTRMDP. Documents available from CASDDS.
Ind/Abst Chem. Abstr. (19??-).

US/0890-4553
WATER POLLUTION CONTROL ASSOCIATION OF PENNSYLVANIA MAGAZINE. ***Title Change.*** [Water Pollut. Control Assoc. Pa. mag.]. **Added/Corp** Water Pollution Control Association of Pennsylvania. Vol. 1, No. 1 (March-April 1968)-(199?). Periodical. English. bm. Pennsylvania Water Environment Association, 251 Baltimore Street, 2nd Floor, Gettysburg PA 17325. **Tel** (717)337-1972, FAX (717)337-3826. **ED** Terry R. Fabian and Lynn L. Hill. **DD** 628. **Ad Acc. *Continued by** Keystone Water Quality Manager, 1069-0212.*
Ind/Abst Pollut. Abstr. Indexes.

US
WATER POLLUTION CONTROL NEWS. (19??)-. Periodical. English. sm. $361.50 US; $375.50 Mexico; $395.50 other. Stevens Publishing Corporation, 225 North New Road, Waco TX 76702-2604. **Tel** (800)727-7573, (817)776-9000. **(Subscription address:** Stevens Publishing Corp., PO Box 2573, Waco TX 76702.) ***Absorbed** Groundwater News.*

US/0091-4541
WATER POLLUTION CONTROL PLAN (SPRINGFIELD). See Water Resources.

VI
WATER POLLUTION REPORT. See Water Resources.

CN/0197-9140
WATER POLLUTION RESEARCH JOURNAL OF CANADA. [Water pollut. res. j. Can.]. **Added/Corp** Canadian Association on Water Pollution Research and Control. Vol. 15, No. 1 (1980)-. Academic Scholarly Publication. English (French; summaries and/or abstracts in French). qt. 150.00Can$ US and Canada; 200.00Can$ other. Canadian Association on Water Quality, P.O.Box 5050, Burlington ONT L7R 4A6 Canada. **Tel** (416)336-4598, FAX (416)336-4858, telex 0618296. **ED** Dr. J.M.Barica and Dr. K.L.Murphy. **LC** TD419.5; .C36. **DD** 363.7/394/0971. **CODEN** WRJCD9. **[CCC]. Pr Rev. Circ:** 400. available on microfilm. Documents available from Article Express International, BIOSIS Document Express, Ask*IEEE, CASDDS. ***Continues** Water Pollution Research in Canada, 0705-288X.*
Desc: Publishes papers on all aspects of water pollution research. Primarily a forum for Canadian examples of original research in that area and closely related science areas.
Ind/Abst AQUAREF; Aquat. Sci. Fish. Abstr. (Computer File); Biodeter. Abstr. (1991-); Biol. Abstr.; Chem. Abstr.; Ei Page One; EMBASE; Eng. Index Annu.; Environ. Period. Bibliogr.; GeoRef; Health Saf. Sci. Abstr.; INSPEC (1981-); Ocean. Abstr.; Pollut. Abstr. Indexes; Rev. Agric. Entomol.; Rev. Plant Pathol.; Soils Fert.; Weed Abstr.

UK
WATER POLLUTION RESEARCH (OXFORD). ***Title Change.*** (WATER POLLUTION RESEARCH; PROCEEDINGS OF THE INTERNATIONAL CONFERENCE.). (1974)-(19??). Proceedings. English. Pergamon Press, An Imprint of Elsevier Science Ltd., The Boulevard, Langford Lane, Kidlington, Oxford OX5 1GB United Kingdom. **Tel** 011 44 865 843000, 011 44 865 843699, FAX 011 44 865 843010. ***Continues** Advances in Water Pollution Research,, 0065-3535.* ***Continued by** Water Pollution Research and Development : Proceedings of a Conference ... /.*

US/0502-0395
WATER POLLUTION SURVEILLANCE SYSTEM : ANNUAL COMPILATION OF DATA. **Main/Corp** United States. Division of Water Supply and Pollution Control. **VFOAT** PHS Water Pollution Surveillance System; Public Health Service Water Pollution Surveillance System. 6th- 1962/63-. Periodical. English. an. US Division of Water Supply and Pollution Control, Washington DC 20017. **LC** GB701. **DD** 614. ***Continues** National Water Quality Network: Annual Compilation of Data.*

US
WATER QUALITY AND POLLUTION CONTROL IN MICHIGAN. **Added/Corp** Michigan. Bureau of Water Management. Michigan. Environmental Protection Bureau. (19??)-. English. an. Department of Natural Resources / Michigan, Box 30028, Lansing MI 48909. **Tel** (517)373-1257. **LC** TD224.M5; W29. **DD** 363.7/394/09774.

US/0745-1512
WATER QUALITY ASSOCIATION NEWSLETTER. (WATER QUALITY ASSOCIATION NEWSLETTER / WATER QUALITY ASSOCIATION.). [Water Qual. Assoc. newsl.]. Newsletter. English. mo. $150.00. Water Quality Association, 4151 Naperville Road, Lisle IL 60532. **Tel** FAX (312)369-1637. **ED** Maribeth Robb and Laura A Stramaglia. **DD** 363. **Circ:** 3,000 (ctrl).

US/0043-1346
WATER QUALITY CONTROL DIGEST. ***Ceased.*** **See** Water Resources.

UK/0892-211X
WATER QUALITY INTERNATIONAL. [Water qual. int.]. **Added/Corp** International Association on Water Pollution Research and Control. **VFOAT** WQI. No. 1 (1987)-. Periodical. English. Four times a year. $135.00 The Americas; £90.00 other. Pergamon Press, An Imprint of Elsevier Science Ltd., The Boulevard, Langford Lane, Kidlington, Oxford OX5 1GB United Kingdom. **Tel** 011 44 865 843000, 011 44 865 843699, FAX 011 44 865 843010. **(Subscription address:** Elsevier Science Ltd. Oxford Fulfillment Centre, PO Box 800, Kidlington, Oxford OX5 1DX United Kingdom.**) ED** Wendy Horobin. **LC** TD365; .I24. **DD** 628.1/62/05. **CODEN** WQINEV. **[CCC].** available on microfilm and microfiche from University Microfilms International (UMI). Documents available from Article Express International. ***Continues** IAWPRC Newsletter, 0256-4513.*
Desc: Aims to provide a digest of the scientific and technical information produced by its many activities, including conferences and expert groups and topics of interest on water pollution control internationally.
Ind/Abst BioBusiness (1987-); Curr. Aware. Biol. Sci.,

Environmental Issues —Pollution and Waste Management

CABS; Ei Page One; Eng. Index Annu. [Select. Cov.]; Fluid Abstr., Civil Eng.; Fluid Abstr. Proc. Eng.; FLUIDEX (19??-); GeoRef; Health Saf. Sci. Abstr.; Pollut. Abstr. Indexes.

US
WATER QUALITY MANAGEMENT PROGRAM SUPPLEMENTAL GUIDANCE FOR FY ... . Main/Corp United States. Environmental Protection Agency. Water Planning Division. 81-. English. an. US Environmental Protection Agency / Office of Water Program Operations, 401 M Street SW, Washington DC 20460. *Continues Supplemental Water Quality Management Program Guidance for FY ... .*

US/0097-7519
WATER QUALITY MONITORING DATA FOR GEORGIA STREAMS. See Water Resources.

US/0275-7249
WATER-RELATED DISEASE OUTBREAKS SURVEILLANCE. ANNUAL SUMMARY. (WATER-RELATED DISEASE OUTBREAKS SURVEILLANCE.). [Water-relat. dis. outbreaks surveill., Annu. summ.]. Annual Summary (1978)-. English. an. Centers for Disease Control, 1600 Clifton Road NE, Atlanta GA 30333. **Tel** (404)639-3311, FAX (404)639-3296. **LC** RC143; .W37. **DD** 614.4. **NLM** W2 A C2FB. available on microfiche (Vols. for (1983) distributed to depository libraries). *Continues in part Foodborne & Waterborne Disease Surveillance, 0737-1241.*

UK/0301-7028
WATER SERVICES. [Water serv.]. Vol. 78, No. 935 (Jan. 1974)-. Periodical. English. mo. £108.00 UK; £119.00, $203.00 other. Argus Press Group, Queensway House, 2 Queensway Redhill, Surrey RH1 1QS England. **Tel** 011 44 737 768611, 011 44 737 761685, FAX 011 44 737 760510, telex 948669 TOPJNL G. **ED** Victor H French. **LC** TD201; .W325. **DD** 628.1/05. **CODEN** WTSVAK. **Bk Rev. Ad Acc. Circ:** 2,500. available on microfilm and microfiche from University Microfilms International (UMI). Documents available from Article Express International, CASDDS. *Continues Water and Water Engineering, 0043-1168.*
Desc: Water supply and treatment, distribution, sewage treatment, effluent reuse, sludge disposal.
Ind/Abst Bioeng. Abstr.; Chem. Abstr.; Coal Abstr.; Curr. Technol. Index; Ei Page One; EMBASE; Eng. Index Annu.; Fluid Abstr., Civil Eng.; Fluid Abstr. Proc. Eng.; FLUIDEX (1974-); Infomat Int. Bus.; Int. Civil Eng. Abstr.; Pollut. Abstr. Indexes; Soft. Abstr. Eng.

UK/0307-1782
WATER SERVICES YEARBOOK. See Water Resources.

SA/0257-8700
WATER SEWAGE & EFFLUENT. See Water Resources.

US/0889-7123
WATER TREATMENT INSTITUTE NEWSLETTER. [Water treat. inst. newsl.]. (198?)-. Newsletter. English. ir. $49.00. Watesco Consultants, 740 Robinwood Drive, Pittsburgh PA 15220. **Tel** (412)343-0184. **DD** 628. Index available (Free on request).

US/0747-9735
WATERWORLD NEWS. Title Change. [Waterworld news]. **Added/Corp** American Water Works Association. **VFOAT** Water World News. Vol. 1, No. 1 (Jan./Feb. 1985)-Vol. 8, No. 6 (Nov/Dec 1992). Periodical. English. bm. American Water Works Association / Colorado, 6666 West Quincy Avenue, Denver CO 80235. **Tel** (303)794-7711, (303)794-7310 (editorial), FAX (303)794-7310 (editorial), (303)795-1989 (marketing). **ED** Deborah Brewer. **LC** TD485; .W38. **DD** 628. **[CCC]. Ad Acc. Circ:** 100,000 (ctrl). Documents available from Documents on Demand. *Continued by WaterWorld Review, 1068-5839.*
Desc: Publishes feature articles on developments in the drinking water, wastewater and industrial water industries. It includes information and descriptions of products and services, industrial conferences, literature information and manufacturers' forums.
Ind/Abst Abstr. Bull. Inst. Pap. Sci. Tech.; Environ. Abstr.; Ind. Hyg. Dig.

US/1047-8957
WEAPONS COMPLEX MONITOR. See Military and Defense.

US/1058-0646
WELL SERVICE MARKET REPORT. [Well serv. mark. rep.]. (May 1991)-. Periodical. English. Twelve times a year. $216.50 Texas; $200.00 US; $250.00 other. RJM Communications, PO Box 6645, Lubbock TX 79493. **Tel** (806)741-1531. **ED** Ricmaro J. Mason (phone: (806)741-1531). **DD** 628.

SZ
WHO IS WHO IN RECYCLING WORLDWIDE / TREND. Added/Corp Trend Associates. **VFOAT** WIW; Trend's Who is Who in Recycling Worldwide. (1991)-. English. Trend Associates, Inc., 1125 NE, 125th Street North, Miami FL 33161. **LC** TD794.5; .W47. **DD** 338.4/736372/820294.

US/1053-1432
WOMEN, WATER AND SANITATION. (WOMEN, WATER AND SANITATION [COMPUTER FILE].). [Women water sanit.]. **Added/Corp** National Information Services Corporation. 1st Edition (1990)-. Periodical. English. ir. $336.00 US; $350.00 others. National Information Services Corp, 3100 St Paul Street, Wyman Towers, Suite 6, Baltimore MD 21218. **Tel** (410)243-0797, FAX (410)243-0982. **DD** 628.
Desc: System requirements: CD-ROM drive with MS-DOS extensions; IBM compatible computer; 512K RAM.

US
WORKING NOTES ON COMMUNITY RIGHT TO KNOW. English. ir. $15.00. Working Group Community Right to Know, 215 Pennsylvania Avenue, RTK/PIRG, Washington DC 20003. **Tel** (202)546-9707. **ED** Paul Orum. Index available (Jan./Feb. 1993 issue). **Circ:** 2,000.
Desc: A right to know about toxics in your area.

UK
WORLD BANK STUDIES IN WATER SUPPLY AND SANITATION. See Water Resources.

●US/0098-8235
WORLD ENVIRONMENT REPORT. Vol. 18, No. 1 (Jan. 7, 1992)-. Periodical. English. bw (26 issues). $494.00. Business Publishers Inc., 951 Pershing Drive, Silver Spring MD 20910-4464. **Tel** (301)587-6300, (800)274-0122, FAX (301)585-9075. **NLM** W1; WO8566. *Formed by the union of Greenhouse Effect Report, 1042-5039 and Multinational Environmental Outlook, 0899-5079.*
Desc: This journal has kept government and business executives informed on how these rules, laws and problems can vary widely from nation to nation. It pays special attention to agreements between nations - such as international protocols to reduce global warming and the efforts to curb the greenhouse effect. Also covers new environmental studies throughout the world.
Ind/Abst PTS Newsl. Database [Full Txt.].

US/1064-8429
WORLD WASTES. Vol. 34, No. 12 (Dec. 1991)-. Periodical. English. Twelve times a year. $48.00. Argus Business, 6151 Powers Ferry Road, Atlanta GA 30339. **Tel** (404)995-2500, (800)233-3359. **(Subscription address:** Sunbelt Fulfillment Services, PO Box 41530, Nashville TN 37204.) **Tel** (301)791; .S665. **DD** 363.7/2/005. **CODEN** WASTEL. **[CCC].** available on an online database (files 15,648/Full-Text) from DIALOG. Documents available from Article Express International. *Continues Management of World Wastes, 0745-6921.*
Ind/Abst BioBusiness (1992-); Ei Page One; Eng. Index Annu. [Select. Cov.]; Environ. Period. Bibliogr.; Gas Abstr.; PROMT; Trade Ind. ASAP [Full Txt.]; Trade Ind. Index [Full Txt.].

UK
WORLD WATER AND ENVIRONMENTAL ENGINEER. See Water Resources.

US/0098-0846
WYOMING STATE PLAN. See Water Resources.

JA
YAMAGUCHI-KEN KOGAI SENTA NENPO. Main/Corp Yamaguchi-ken Kogai Senta. **VFOAT** Annual Report of Yamaguchi Prefectural Environmental Pollution Research Center. Academic Scholarly Publication. Japanese (Publication). Yamaguchi-Ken Kogai Senta, 535 Aza Hiruta, Oaza Asada, Yamaguchi 75 Japan. **LC** TD187.5.J32; Y3794A. **CODEN** YKSNDQ. Documents available from CASDDS.
Ind/Abst Chem. Abstr.

US/0066-068X
YEARBOOK - AMERICAN SOCIETY OF SANITARY ENGINEERING. Main/Corp American Society of Sanitary Engineering. (19??)-. English. an (Apr.). $10.00. American Society of Sanitary Engineering, Po Box 40362, Bay Village OH 44140. **Tel** (216)835-3040. **ED** Gael Dunn. Index available. cum. index. **Ad Acc. Circ:** 2,500.
Desc: Meetings information and other related fields.

US
YEARBOOK - WATER POLLUTION CONTROL FEDERATION. Main/Corp Water Pollution Control Federation. 1960-. English. ir.

JA
YOKOHAMA KOKURITSU DAIGAKU KANKYO KAGAKU KENKYU SENTA KIYO BULLETIN: INSTITUTE OF ENVIRONMENTAL SCIENCE AND TECHNOLOGY, YOKOHAMA NATIONAL UNIVERSITY. Main/Corp Yokohama Kokuritsu Daigaku. Kankyo Kagaku Kenkyu Senta. **Added/Corp** Yokohama Kokuritsu Daigaku. Kankyo Kagaku Kenkyu Senta Bulletin: Institute of Environmental Science and Technology, Yokohama National University. **VFOAT** Bulletin: Institute of Environmental Science and Technology, Yokohama National University. (19??)-. English (German and Japanese). Yokohama National University, 41 Shimizugaoka Minami-ku, Yokohama Japan. **LC** TD172; .Y64a. **CODEN** YKDKDA. Documents available from CASDDS.
Ind/Abst Chem. Abstr.

JA
YOKOHAMA SHIRITSU DAIGAKU SOGO KENKYU. VFOAT Kankyo Kanri No Kenkyu. Vol. 1- (March 2, 1982)-. Japanese. Yokohama Shiritsu Daigaku Kankyo Kanri Keikaku, Kankyukai 22-2 Seto Kanazawa-ku, Yokohama-shi 236 Japan. **LC** TD169; .Y64.

JA/0513-5907
YOSUI TO HAISUI. [Yosui to haisui]. **Added/Corp** Sangyo Yosui Chosakai (Japan). **VFOAT** Journal of Water and Waste; Water and Waste. (1959)-. Academic Scholarly Publication. Japanese. mo. $234.00. Sangyo Yosui Chosakai, (The Industrial Water Inst.), Dai 1 Shiruba Biru, 20-11, Sendagaya 5 Chome, Shibuyaku, Tokyoto 151, Japan. **(Subscription address:** Kyowa Book Company Inc., 1-38 Kanda Jinbo-Cho, Chiyoda-Ku Tokyo 101, Japan) **ED** Fiusako Yamane. **CODEN** YOHASP. **Ad Acc. Circ:** 28,000 (ctrl). Documents available from CASDDS.
Desc: The journal of environmental integrity about water.
Ind/Abst Chem. Abstr.

GW/0174-1098
ZEITSCHRIFT FUER LARMBEKAMPFUNG. [Zeitschr. Larmbekampf.]. **Added/Corp** Deutscher Arbeitsring fuer Larmbekampfung. (1980)-. Periodical. German. Six times a year. DM210.00. Springer-Verlag GmbH & Company KG, Heidelberger Platz 3, D 14197 Berlin Germany. **Tel** 011 49 30 8207223, FAX 011 49 30 8214091, telex 183 319 SPBLN D. **(Subscription address:** Springer Verlag New York Inc. / for North America, 44 Hartz Way, Secaucus NJ 07096.) **ED** G Jansen, M Heckl, G Notbohm, A Schick, and H G Thomassen. **LC** TD891; .K35. **[CCC]. Bk Rev** available on microfilm from University Microfilms International (UMI). *Continues Kampf Dem Larm.*
Desc: Only German language journal for the noise-control field; covers technical aspects of noise as well as legal and organizational areas. Original articles, industry news and new product profiles are offered. Of interest to engineers, medical and legal professionals and architects.
Ind/Abst Acoust. Abstr.; EMBASE.

GW/0044-3727
ZEITSCHRIFT FUER WASSER- UND ABWASSER FORSCHUNG. Title Change. See Earth Sciences-Hydrology.

ETHICS

FR/0241-5089
A.H. AUMONERIES DES HOPITAUX. See Medical Science and Technology.

US/0740-4050
ABA/BNA LAWYERS' MANUAL ON PROFESSIONAL CONDUCT. CURRENT REPORTS. See Law.

CN/0714-8828
ACTUALITE VIE. [Actual. vie]. **Added/Corp** Alliance Pour La Vie. **VFOAT** Actualite Vie-Canada. Vol. 1, No. 1 (Winter 1981)-. Periodical. French. Twelve times a year. 10.00Can$. Alliance for Life, B1-90 Garry Street, Winnipeg Manitoba R3C 4H1 Canada. **Tel** (204)942-4772, FAX (204)943-9283. **ED** Anna Desilets. **DD** 363.4/6/05. **Bk Rev,** (Qty: occasionally). **Circ:** 3,000.
Desc: Promotes the right to life. Discusses fetal development, bioethical questions, discrimination of handicapped, dignity and rights of each person.

US
ADVISORY OPINIONS OF THE STATE OF SOUTH CAROLINA STATE ETHICS COMMISSION. Main/Corp State of South Carolina State Ethics Commission. 1976-1977 Opinions-. English.

Ethics

an. South Carolina Ethics Commission, PO Box 11926, Columbia SC 29211. **Tel** (803)253-4192. **LC** KFS2206; .A557. **DD** 353.9757009/95.

US/0147-4383
AGENCY DIRECTORY - AMERICAN HUMANE. See Sociology-Social Services and Welfare.

FR/0984-4783
AGORA PARIS. 1986. (AGORA.). (1986)-. Periodical. French. qt. 244.86F France; 310.00F other EEC; 370.00F other. Hopital Rothschild, 33 6D De Picpus, 75711 Paris Cedex 12 France. **Tel** 011 33 1 42 78 60 78. **UDC** 61 :30. Index available. cum. index. **Bk Rev**. **Pr Rev**. ctrl circ.

US/1059-4515
AMERICAN CHARACTER, THE. (THE AMERICAN CHARACTER : A COMMENTARY ON DOMESTIC ISSUES FROM THE ETHICS AND PUBLIC POLICY CENTER.). [Amer. character]. **Added/Corp** Ethics and Public Policy Center (Washington, D.C.). No. 1 (Fall 1991)-. Periodical. English. qt. Ethics and Public Policy Center, 1015 15th Street Northwest, Suite 900, Washington DC 20005. **Tel** (202)682-1200. **DD** 170.

US/0732-4928
ANNUAL OF THE SOCIETY OF CHRISTIAN ETHICS, THE. See Religion and Theology.

US
ANNUAL REPORT TO THE GOVERNOR. See Political Science.

US
BETWEEN THE SPECIES : A JOURNAL OF ETHICS. Vol. 1, No. 1 (Winter 1984/85)-. Periodical. English. qt. $25.00, add $15.00 (airmail) postage. Schweitzer Center, PO Box 254, Berkeley CA 94701. **Tel** (510)526-5346. **ED** Steve F Sapontzis and John Stockwell. **Bk Rev**. **Circ:** 400.
Desc: Moral philosophy dealing with ethics and animals.
Ind/Abst AGRICOLA [Select. Cov.]; Philos. Index.

US/0363-0161
BIBLIOGRAPHY OF BIOETHICS. See Medical Science and Technology.

US/0363-9193
BIENNIAL REPORT - STATE OF WISCONSIN ETHICS BOARD. **Main/Corp** Wisconsin. Ethics Board. Periodical. English. be. Ethics Board, 122 West Washington Avenue, Madison WI 53703. **LC** JK6045; .W57A. **DD** 353.9/775/0099.

UK/0269-9702
BIOETHICS. See Medical Science and Technology.

●US/1063-3596
BIOETHICS BULLETIN (WASHINGTON, D.C.). See Law.

●US/1065-7274
BIOETHICS FORUM. [Bioethics forum]. **Added/Corp** Midwest Bioethics Center. (1992)-. Periodical. English. Four times a year. $20.00. Midwest Bioethics Center, 410 Archibald, Suite 200, Kansas City MO 64111. **Tel** (816)756-2713. **ED** Alan S. Lubert. **LC** IN PROCESS. **DD** 174. **Bk Rev**, (Qty: 1-4). **Pr Rev. Circ:** 3,000. Continues Midwest Medical Ethics, 1054-4119.
Desc: Dedicated to a community-based model of bioethics and seeks to publish a variety of essays that strengthen the capacity to think together about moral issues in health care.

US/0886-8913
BIOETHICS LITERATURE REVIEW. [Bioeth. lit. rev.]. Vol. 1, No. 1 (Jan. 1986)-. Periodical. English. mo (12 issues). $65.00 US; $75.00 other. University Publishing Group Inc., 107 East Church Street, Frederick MD 21701-5441. **Tel** (301)694-8531, (800)654-8188. **DD** 174. **NLM** ZW 50; B615H.
Desc: Offers comprehensive and interdisciplinary coverage of biomedical lilterure. Provides complete references for all summaries, including the address of the pricipal author for convenient reprint requests or correspondence.

IT
BIOETICA. (19??)-. Italian. sa. L60000 Italy; L85000 other. Franco Angeli Riviste SRL, Viale Monza 106, 20127 Milan Italy. **Tel** 011 39 2 2827651, 011 39 2 289562.

US
BIOLAW. See Medical Science and Technology.

US/0742-1796
BIOMEDICAL ETHICS REVIEWS. See Medical Science and Technology.

UK
BULLETIN OF MEDICAL ETHICS. No. 53 (1989)-. Periodical. English. Ten times a year. £65.00 UK and Eire; £75.00 other. Professional & Scientific Publishers, Tavistock House, East Tavistock Square, London WC1H 9JR England. **Tel** 011 44 71 387-4499, telex 005311. **NLM** W1; BU803G. Continues Bulletin (Institute of Medical Ethics (Great Britain)).
Desc: Publishes information in the field of healthcare ethics.

US/0277-2027
BUSINESS & PROFESSIONAL ETHICS JOURNAL. See Business.

●UK/0962-8770
BUSINESS ETHICS: A EUROPEAN REVIEW. (1992)-. Academic Scholarly Publication. English. qt. $145.00 North America; £105.00 other. Basil Blackwell Publishers Ltd, 108 Cowley Road, Oxford OX4 1JF England. **Tel** 011 44 865 791100, FAX 011 44 865 791347, telex 837022 OXBOOK G. **(Subscription address:** Blackwell Publishers / UK, Marston Book Services, PO Box 87, Oxford OX2 0DT England.) **[CCC]**. available on microfilm and microfiche from University Microfilms International (UMI).

US/0894-6582
BUSINESS ETHICS (MADISON, WIS.). (BUSINESS ETHICS.). [Bus. ethics]. Vol. 1 No. 1 (July 1987)-. Periodical. English. Four times a year. $25.00 (new subscription), $49.00 (renewal subscription) US; $35.00 (new Subscription), $59.00 (renewal subscription) other. Mavis Publications Inc., 52 South 10th Street, Suite 110, Minneapolis MN 55403. **Tel** (612)962-4700. **ED** Craig Cox. **DD** 174. **Bk Rev**, (Qty: 54). **Ad Acc**, **Adv Mgr:** M Kniaz. **Circ:** 10,000. available in microform from University Microfilms International (UMI).
Desc: Resource for students and professors of business, philosophy, religion and environmental education, practical ideals for working managers on socially responsible marketing, personnel management, recycling, philanthropy, and more. Case studies, resource directory, calendar.
Ind/Abst Altern. Press Index (199?-); Person. Manage. Abstr.

US/1052-150X
BUSINESS ETHICS QUARTERLY. See Business.

US/1064-0223
BUSINESS ETHICS RESOURCE. See Business.

●US/1061-0081
BUSINESS ETHICS REVIEW. [Bus. ethics rev.]. Vol. 1, Issue 1 (Jan./Feb. 1992)-. Periodical. English. Six times a year (Jan., Mar., May, July, Sept., Nov.). $45.00. Bear Publishing, PO Box 3364, Los Angeles CA 90078. **Tel** (818)788-9382. **ED** David Lewis. **DD** 174. cum. index.

●US/0963-1801
CAMBRIDGE QUARTERLY OF HEALTHCARE ETHICS : CQ : THE INTERNATIONAL JOURNAL FOR HEALTHCARE ETHICS COMMITTEES. See Medical Science and Technology.

CN/0824-0663
CHOOSE LIFE (WEYBURN, SASK.). (CHOOSE LIFE.). [Choose life]. **Added/Corp** Weyburn & District Pro-life Society. Saskatchewan Pro-Life Association. (1983)-. Periodical. English. ir. $10.00. Weyburn & District Prolife Society, PO Box 1201, Weyburn Saskatchewan S4H 2L5 Canada. **DD** 363.4/6.

NE/1380-3603
CHRISTIAN BIOETHICS. See Religion and Theology.

NE
CLINICAL MEDICAL ETHICS. Vol. 1 (1991)-. Monographic series. English. ir. Price varies per volume. Kluwer Academic Publishers, Postbus 322, 3300 AH Dordrecht, The Netherlands. **Tel** 011 (31) 78 524400, FAX 011 31 78 183273, telex 20083. **NLM** W1; CL73N.

US/1060-5045
COGEL BLUE BOOK. See Public Administration.

US/1061-8775
CORPORATE CONDUCT QUARTERLY. [Corp. conduct q.]. **Added/Corp** Rutgers University. Forum for Policy Research. **VFOAT** CCQ. (1991)-. Corporate Report. English. qt. $50.00 (institutions), $36.00 (individuals). Rutgers University / Camden, 401 Cooper Street, Camden NJ 08102. **Tel** (609)757-6311, FAX (609)757-6074. **ED** James W. Artz. **LC** HF5387; .C667. **DD** 174/.4/097305. **Bk Rev**. **Ad Acc**. **Circ:** 3,000.

CN/0841-1956
CORPORATE ETHICS MONITOR, THE. See Business.

US/0731-129X
CRIMINAL JUSTICE ETHICS. [Crim. justice ethics]. **Added/Corp** John Jay College of Criminal Justice. Institute for Criminal Justice Ethics. Vol. 1, No. 1 (Winter/Spring 1982)-. Periodical. English. Twice a year. $15.00 (individual), $30.00 (institutional) memberships US; add $5.00 postage other. Institute of Criminal Justice Ethics, John Jay College of Criminal Justice, The City University of New York, 899 Tenth Avenue, New York NY 10019. **Tel** (212)237-8033, FAX (212)237-8901. **LC** HV7231; .C75. **DD** 174/.9364. **Bk Rev**, (Qty: 2-4). **Pr Rev. Circ:** 1,200. available on microfilm and microfiche from University Microfilms International (UMI). Documents available from UMI Article Clearinghouse.
Desc: Interdisciplinary discussions of ethical issues in criminal justice.
Ind/Abst Acad. Abstr. Full Text Elite (Jan. 1992-); Acad. Abstr. (Jan. 1992-); Acad. Search (Jan. 1992-); Crim. Justice Abstr. (19??-); Crim. Justice Period. Index; Crim. Penol. Police Sci. Abstr.; Curr. Law Index (1984-); Expand. Acad. Index (1983-); INFO-SOUTH Abstr.; Leg. Resour. Index (1984-);(1982-); LegalTrac (1983-); Mag. Search; Newsp. Period. Abstr. (1991-); Philos. Index; Soc. Sci. Source (Jan. 1992-); Soc. Sci. Index; Soc. Sci. Index Fulltext (Summer 1988-) [Full Txt.].

US/0748-1187
DEATH STUDIES. See Psychology.

CN/0710-0493
DIG (TORONTO). (DIG : THE HUMANITARIANS' NEWS MAGAZINE.). [Dig]. No. 1 (May/June 1981)-. Periodical. English. ir. $6.00. DIG, PO Box 126 Station L, Toronto Ontario M6E 2W0 Canada. **DD** 179.

US
DIGEST OF ADVISORY OPINIONS.
Main/Corp Hawaii. State Ethics Commission. English. an. State Ethics Commission / Hawaii, 1001 Bishop Street/Pacific Tower 970, PO Box 616, Honolulu HI 96809. **Tel** (808)548-6401. **LC** KFH406.A59; E813. **DD** 353.9969009/95. Index available. **Circ:** 600 (ctrl).
Desc: Opinions and decisions issued by the State Ethics Commission on the application of the ethics code. Printed yearly, the opinions and decisions are written so that the identity of the persons involved are not disclosed.

US
DIRECTORY OF BIOMEDICAL ETHICS ORGANIZATIONS / AHA. See Medical Science and Technology.

US
DISCERNMENT. English. Three times a year. $5.00 one year; $8.00 two years. Center of Applied Christian Ethics, Wheaton College, Wheaton IL 60187. **Tel** (708)752-5886, FAX (708)752-5935. **ED** Dr. Dennis Okholm. **Pr Rev. Circ:** 1,000.

JA
DOTOKU TO KYOIKU. See Education.

JA/0287-2145
ECHOES OF PEACE. [Echoes peace]. VFOAT Quarterly Bulletin of the Niwano Peace Foundation. (1982)-. Periodical. English. qt. **DD** 341.1.
Ind/Abst Hum. Rights Intern. Rep.

BE
ENTREPRISE ET L'HOMME. **Added/Corp** Association des Dirigeants et Cadres Chretiens. **VFOAT** L'Enterprise & l'Homme. (19??)-. Periodical. French. Six times a year (Feb., Apr., June, Sept., Oct., Dec.). $130.00. ADIC Entreprise et l' Homme, Avenue Conrad Adenauer 8, B-1200 Brussels Belgium. **Tel** 11 32 2 7714731, FAX 11 32 2 7724633. Index available in last issue of volume--attached. cum. index. **Bk Rev**, (Qty: 6). **Ad Acc. Circ:** 10,000.
Desc: A review of ethics and Christian reflection about enterprise, industry and general management for business and top-level managers.
Ind/Abst Saf. Health Work.

CN/0840-9935
ETHICA (RIMOUSKI). (ETHICA.). [Ethica]. **Added/Corp** Groupe de Recherche ETHOS. Universite du Quebec -a Rimouski. Vol. 1, No. 1 (Jan. 1989)-. French. sa (Jan., July). 20.09Can$ Canada; 28.04Can$ Institutions; 25.00Can$ other. Groupe de Recherche Ethos, Universite du Quebec a Rimouski, 300 Allee des Ursulines, Rimouski, Quebec G5L 3A1 Canada. **Tel** (418)724-1784, (418)724-1440, (418)724-1440, FAX (418)724-1525. **DD** 170/.5. Continues Universite du Quebec a Rimouski Departement des Sciences Religieuses. Cahiers Ethicologiques de l'U. Q. A. R., 0318-9554.

US
ETHICAL CURRENTS. Center for Bioethics, St Joseph Health System, 440 South Batavia Street, Orange CA 92668.

US/0362-0859
ETHICAL HUMANIST, THE. [Ethical humanist]. V. 21, No. 4- Dec. 1975-. Periodical. English. mo. Ethical Society of Boston, 5 Commonwealth Avenue, Boston MA 02116. **DD** 170. Continues Ethical News, 0363-695X.

US
ETHICAL ISSUES IN MEDICINE. Ceased. Vol. 1, No. 1 (Sept. 1984)-Ceased (1992). Periodical. English. mo. Regents of the University of California at Los Angeles, 405 Hilgard Avenue, Los Angeles CA 90024-1447. **Tel** (310)825-6634. **ED** L S Rothenberg and Judith Ross. Index available. **Circ:** 3,000.

US/1058-6571
ETHICAL MANAGEMENT. [Ethical manage.]. **Added/Corp** Business Strategies (Firm). (1991)-. Periodical. English. Twelve times a year. $99.00 (government, educational, and non-profit); $127.00 (others). Business Strategies, PO Box 19358, Portland OR 97280. **Tel** (503)244-5710. **ED** Kathleen Purdy. **LC** HF5387; .E835. **DD** 174. **Bk Rev**, (Qty: 12).
Desc: To serve as a resource for those who strive to accomplish their goals as well as maintain their ethical values. To provide insight into the ethical dilemmas in everyday decision-making. To serve as an exchange or ideas.

US/0014-1704
ETHICS. [Ethics]. Vol. 48, No. 3 (April 1938)-. Periodical. English. qt (4 issues). $66.00 institution; $30.00 individual; $25.00 APA individual member; $22.00 student US; $76.62 istitutions, $38.10 individuals, $32.75 APA individual member, $29.54 students, Canada; $72.00 institutions, $36.00 individual, $31.00 APA individual members, $28.00 students. University of Chicago Press / Journals Division, PO Box 37005, 5720 South Woodlawn, Chicago IL 60637. **Tel** (312)753-3347, FAX (312)753-0811. **(Subscription telephone:** (312)753-8083**) ED** Gerald Dworkin. **LC** BJ1; .I6. **DD** 170/.5. **[CCC]**. cum. index. **Pr Rev. Acid Free.** available on microfilm and microfiche from University Microfilms International (UMI). Documents available from The Genuine Article, UMI Article Clearinghouse. ***Continues*** *International Journal of Ethics.*
Desc: An interdisciplinary journal devoted to the study of the ideas and principles that form the basis for individual and collective action.
Ind/Abst ABC POL SCI; Acad. Ind. [Computer File] (1992-); Arts Humanit. Citation Index [Full Cov.]; Book Rev. Digest; Book Rev. Index; Crim. Penol. Police Sci. Abstr.; Curr. Contents Arts Humanit.; Expand. Acad. Index (1981-); Index Book Rev. Relig.; Index Period. Artic. Relat. Law; Int. Bibliogr. Sociol.; Int. Polit. Sci. Abstr.; J. Plan. Lit.; Leg. Resour. Index (1980-); LegalTrac (1981-); Newsp. Period. Abstr. (1989-); Philos. Index; Relig. Index One Period.; Res. Alert [Full Cov.]; Soc. Plann. Policy Dev. Abstr.; Soc. Sci. Cit. Index [Full Cov.]; Soc. Sci. Index; Soc. Sci. Index Fulltext (Jan. 1989-) [Full Txt.]; Sociol. Abstr.; U.S. Polit. Sci. Doc.

US/1050-8422
ETHICS & BEHAVIOR. [Ethics behav.]. **VFOAT** Ethics and Behavior. Vol. 1, No. 1 (1991)-. Periodical. English. qt. $170.00 US & Canada; $195.00 other. Lawrence Erlbaum Associates, 365 Broadway, Suite 102, Hillsdale NJ 07642. **Tel** (201)666-4110, (800)926-6579, FAX (201)666-2394. **LC** BJ1725; .E755. **DD** 174/.05. **NLM** W1; ET436.
Ind/Abst Psychoanal. Abstr.; Psychol. Abstr. (1991-); PsycINFO; PsycScan: Appl. Exp. Eng. Psych.; PsycScan: LD/MR; PsycScan: Neuropsych.

US/1068-3526
ETHICS & LOBBYING. (ETHICS & LOBBYING : LEGISLATION & LITIGATION / COGEL, COUNCIL ON GOVERNMENTAL ETHICS LAWS.). [Ethics lobby.]. **Added/Corp** Council on Governmental Ethics Laws. **VFOAT** Ethics and Lobbying. (19??)-. English. ir. $20.00. Council of State Governments, PO Box 11910, Iron Works Pike, Lexington KY 40578-1910. **Tel** (800)800-1910, (606)231-1850. **(Subscription address:** Council of State Governments, PO Box 2167, Lexington, KY 40595**) LC** KF4948.Z95; E86. **DD** 342.73/05; 347.3025.

UK/0266-688X
ETHICS & MEDICINE : A CHRISTIAN PERSPECTIVE ON ISSUES IN BIOETHICS. **See** Medical Science and Technology.

US/1071-3778
ETHICS AND MEDICS. **See** Medical Science and Technology.

US/1065-0113
ETHICS & POLICY. (ETHICS & POLICY / A PUBLICATION OF THE CENTER FOR ETHICS & SOCIAL POLICY OF THE GRADUATE THEOLOGICAL UNION.). [Ethics policy]. **Added/Corp** Graduate Theological Union. Center for Ethics and Social Policy. **VFOAT** Ethics and Policy. (197?)-. Periodical. English. qt. $35.00 (comes with membership). Center for Ethics and Social Policy, 2400 Ridge Road, Berkeley CA 94709. **Tel** (415)848-1674. **ED** Chris Adams. **DD** 170. **Bk Rev**, (Qty: 4). **Circ:** 2,500.

●US/1064-8771
ETHICS & PSYCHOTHERAPY. **Added/Corp** International Society for Ethical Psychotherapy. **VFOAT** Ethics and Psychotherapy. (1992)-. Periodical. English. qt. $40.00 (institutions). International Society for Ethical Psychotherapy, 560 Riverside Drive, #14L, New York NY 10027. **NLM** W1; ET436N.

US/0273-2513
ETHICS (BOCA RATON). (ETHICS.). [Ethics]. Vol. 1, Article 1, (1979)-. English. an. Social Issues Resources Series Inc, PO Box 2348, Boca Raton FL 33427. **Tel** (800)327-0513, (407)994-0079. **ED** Eleanor C Goldstein. **LC** BJ1; .E73. **DD** 170/.5.
Desc: Interdisciplinary resource material consisting of reprinted articles from popular and professional journals, newspapers, magazines and government documents.
Ind/Abst Acad. Abstr. Full Text Elite (Jan. 1992-); Acad. Abstr. (Jan. 1992-); Acad. Search (Jan. 1992-); INFO-SOUTH Abstr.; Mag. Search; Soc. Sci. Source (Jan. 1992-).

US/0897-0106
ETHICS, EASIER SAID THAN DONE. [Ethics easier said than done]. **Added/Corp** Josephson Institute for the Advancement of Ethics. **VFOAT** Easier Said Than Done. Vol. 1, No. 1 (Winter 1988)-. Periodical. English. qt. $52.00 (1 year), $85.00 (2 year), $114.00 (three year) for institutions only. Josephson Institute, 4640 Admiralty Way/Suite 1001, Marina del Rey CA 90292. **Tel** (213)306-1868, FAX (213)827-1864. **ED** Christopher Tyner. **LC** BJ1; .E74. **DD** 170/.5. **Ad Acc. Circ:** 13,000 (ctrl).
Desc: A compendium of articles, stories, excerpts and quotations covering the ethical dimensions of news items, social trends and the nation's professions. It is designed to provide a forum for serious discussion of the ethical issues that shape contemporary American culture.

US/0279-2869
ETHICS IN GOVERNMENT REPORTER. **Added/Corp** Washington Service Bureau, Inc. (1980)-. English. mo. $657.20 Washington, D.C. residents (tax included); $620.00 other. Washington Service Bureau Inc., 655 15th Street Northwest, Suite 270, Washington DC 20005. **Tel** (800)955-5219, (202)508-0600. **[CCC]**. Index available (free).

CN/0824-5622
ETHICS IN-SERVICE. [Ethics in-serv.]. Sept. 1983-. Periodical. English. Five times a year. 18.00Can$. Ethics in Education, c/o Ontario Institute for Studies in Education, 252 Bloor Street West, Toronto Ontario M5S 1V6 Canada. **Tel** (416)923-6641, FAX (416)926-4725, telex 06217720. **ED** Mark Holmes, John R McConnell. **DD** 370.11/4/05. **Bk Rev. Ad Acc. Circ:** 1,900 (ctrl).
Desc: Focuses on issues and topics in moral/values education of interest to the practitioner by presenting alternative perspectives and practices in the field. To help educators examine and improve their own programs and practices in the field.

US/0748-5344
ETHICS RESOURCE CENTER REPORT. [Ethics Resour. Cent. rep.]. Vol. 1, No. 1 (Summer 1984)-. Periodical. English. qt. Free. The Ethics Resource Center Inc, 1025 Connecticut Avenue NW, Suite 1003, Washington DC 20036. **Tel** (202)223-3411. **ED** Robert Biesenbach and Lydia Schindler. **DD** 170. **Bk Rev. Circ:** 10,000.

●US/1064-5438
ETHICS ROUNDTABLE. (1993)-. Periodical. English. sa. $60.00 (institutions). Carol Matseoane, 560 Riverside Drive, #14L, New York NY 10027.

GW/0935-7335
ETHIK IN DER MEDIZIN. [Ethik Med.]. (1989)-. Periodical. Multiple languages. Four times a year. DM118.00. Springer-Verlag GmbH & Company KG, Heidelberger Platz 3, D 14197 Berlin Germany. **Tel** 011 49 30 8207223, FAX 011 49 30 8214091, telex 183 319 SPBLN D. **(Subscription address:** Springer Verlag New York Inc. / for North America, 44 Hartz Way, Secaucus NJ 07096.**) ED** F Anschutz, D Ritschl, and E Seidler. **UDC** 61 :17. **[CCC]**. available in microform.

GW/0937-938X
ETHIK UND SOZIALWISSENSCHAFTEN. **VFOAT** EuS. Vol. 1 (1990)-. Academic Scholarly Publication. German (summaries and/or abstracts in English). Four times a year. DM104.00. Westdeutscher Verlag GMBH, Postfatch 5829, 65048 Wiesbaden, Germany. **Tel** 011 49 611 160230, FAX 011 49 611 160229. **CODEN** ETSOE9. Index available. **Circ:** 500.

US/0895-5026
ETHIKOS. (ETHIKOS : EXAMINING ETHICAL ISSUES IN BUSINESS.). [Ethikos]. Vol. 1, No. 1 (Summer 1987)-. Periodical. English. bm (July, Sept., Nov., Jan., Mar., May). $85.00 (one year), $150.00 (two year) non-profit individuals & institutions; $125.00 (one year), $240.00 (two year) other. Ethikos, 540 East Boston Post Road, Mamaroneck NY 10543. **Tel** (914)381-7475 or, 800 373-7723, FAX (914)381-7478. **ED** Andrew Singer, (phone: (914)381-7475). **LC** K5; .T35. **DD** 174. **[CCC]. Bk Rev**, (Qty: 6/yr).
Desc: Articles on the nature of ethics in the business world.

FR/1151-5422
ETHIQUE. **Added/Corp** Societe Francaise de Reflexion Bioethique. Universite de Rennes. Centre d'Etudes et de Reflexions Bioethiques. Universite Catholique de Louvain (1970-). Centre de Bioethique. No. 1 (Summer 1991)-. Periodical. French. qt. Editions Universitaires Francaises, GROUPE MAME, 13 rue Raymond Losserand, 75014 Paris France. **Tel** 011 33 40 47 8000, FAX 011 33 40 47 6649. **ED** D. Folscheid. **LC** BJ2; .E84. **DD** 174/.9574/05. **NLM** W1; ET439Q.
Desc: Information on bioethics and social ethical issues.

AG
ETICA. Vol. 1 No. 1 (Nov. 7, 1991)-. Periodical. Spanish. Editorial Etica, Periodismo para la Gente S.A., Sarmiento 1889 6o B, Buenos Aires Argentina. **Tel** 46-4408. **ED** Ramon Roque Cuello.

PL/0014-2263
ETYKA. [Etyka]. **Added/Corp** Instytut Filozofii i Socjologii (Polska Akademia Nauk). Vol. 1 (1966)-. Periodical. Polish (summaries and/or abstracts in Russian and English). an. $20.00. **(Subscription address:** ARS Polona, PO Box 1001, 00068 Warsaw Poland.**) LC** BJ8.P6; E8.
Ind/Abst Philos. Index.

UN/0868-5045
ETYKA, ESTETYKA I TEORIIA KULTURY / MINISTERSTVO VYSHCHOI I SEREDNOI SPETSIALNOI OSVITY URSR, KYIVSKYI ORDENA LENINA I ORDENA ZHOVTNEVOI REVOLIUTSII DERZHAVNYI UNIVERSYTET IM. T.H. SHEVCHENKA. **Added/Corp** Kyivskyi Derzhavnyi Universytet Im. T.H. Shevchenka. (1991)-. Ukrainian. ***Continues*** *Etika i Estetika, 0201-8691.*

US/0884-2981
EUTHANASIA REVIEW, THE. ***Ceased.*** [Euthan. rev.]. Vol. 1, No. 1 (Spring 1986)-Ceased Vol. 3. Periodical. English. qt. Human Sciences Press, PO Box 735, 233 Spring Street, New York NY 10013. **Tel** (212)620-8000, FAX (212)807-1047, telex 23421139. **LC** R726; .E7927. **DD** 174/.24. **NLM** W1; EU83YE. **CODEN** EUREEF. **[CCC]**. available on microfilm and microfiche from University Microfilms International (UMI).
Ind/Abst PsycINFO (?-?).

US/0071-3619
FACET BOOKS. SOCIAL ETHICS SERIES. No. 1 (1964)-. English. Fortress Press, 2900 Queen Lane, Philadelphia PA 19129. **Tel** (215)848-6800. **DD** 284.

US
FORMAL ETHICS OPINION / BOARD OF PROFESSIONAL RESPONSIBILITY OF THE SUPREME COURT OF TENNESSEE. **Main/Corp** Board of Professional Responsibility of the Supreme Count of Tennessee. Ethics Committee. English. Board of Professional Responsibility of the Supreme Court of Tennessee, 1101 Kermit Drive/Suite 405, Nashville TN 37217. **LC** KFT76.5.A2; A492. **DD** 174/.3/09768. ***Continues*** *Formal Ethics Opinion.*

US
FORMAL OPINIONS - COMMITTEE ON PROFESSIONAL ETHICS, NEW YORK STATE BAR ASSOCIATION. **See** Law.

US/1041-5548
GEORGETOWN JOURNAL OF LEGAL ETHICS, THE. **See** Law.

US/1059-6224
GUARDIAN (LEXINGTON, KY.), THE. (THE GUARDIAN / COUNCIL ON GOVERNMENTAL ETHICS LAWS.). [Guardian]. **Added/Corp** Council on Governmental Ethics Laws. Council of State Governments. **VFOAT** COGEL Guardian. (19??)-. Periodical. English. bm (6 issues). $60.00; also comes with Council on Governmental Ethics Laws membership. Council of State Governments, PO Box 11910, Iron Works Pike, Lexington KY 40578-1910. **Tel** (800)800-1910, (606)231-1850. **(Subscription address:** Council of State Governments, PO Box 2167, Lexington, KY 40595**) LC** KF4568.A15; G8. **DD** 174/.3/05. ***Continues*** *COGEL Guardian, 1071-6734.*
Desc: Covers political ethics and corruption.

US/0093-0334
HASTINGS CENTER REPORT, THE. **See** Medical Science and Technology.

US
HEALTH CARE ETHICS USA. **See** Medical Science and Technology.

NE/0956-2737
HEC FORUM. **See** Medical Science and Technology-Hospital Administration and Medical Centers.

US/0742-5376
HEMLOCK QUARTERLY. ***Title Change.*** [Hemlock q.]. **Added/Corp** Hemlock (Society). Issue 1 (Oct. 1980)-(199?). Periodical. English. qt (4 issues). National Hemlock Society, PO Box 11830, Eugene OR 97440. **Tel** (503)342-5748. **ED** Kris Larson. **LC** R726; .H43. **DD** 362.1/75. **Bk Rev**, (Qty: 4). **Circ:** 20,000 (ctrl). ***Continued by*** *TimeLines, 1074-1593.*
Desc: Reports on latest developments in voluntary euthanasia, right-to-die, living, wills, etc.
Ind/Abst Hum. Rights Intern. Rep.

US
HIGHER EDUCATION OPPORTUNITIES FOR MINORITIES AND WOMEN ANNOTATED SELECTIONS. See Education-Higher Education.

US/8756-8519
HOSPITAL ETHICS. [Hosp. ethics]. **Added/Corp** American Hospital Association. Vol. 1, No. 1 (Mar./Apr. 1985)-. Periodical. English. bm. $85.00 (AHA members), $135.00 (nonmembers). American Hospital Association, 840 North Lake Shore Drive, Chicago IL 60611. **Tel** (312)280-6000, (800)242-2626. **DD** 174. **NLM** W1; HO774J.
Ind/Abst Health Plan. Adminis.

US/0885-0615
HUMAN RESEARCH REPORT. See Medical Science and Technology.

US/0146-7808
HYPOTHETICAL ADVISORY OPINIONS. Main/Corp Nevada. Ethics Commission. English. Nevada Ethics Commission, Capitol Complex, Carson City NV 89710. **LC** KFN1006; .A82. **DD** 174/.09793.

US/1054-1373
ILLNESS CRISIS & LOSS. [Illn. crises loss]. **VFOAT** Illness, Crises and Loss. (1991)-. Periodical. English. Four times a year (Jan., Apr., July, Oct.). $58.00 (institutions); $36.00 (individuals). Charles Press Publishers, PO Box 15715, Philadelphia PA 19103. **Tel** (215)545-8933, FAX (215)545-8937. **ED** Elizabeth J. Clark. **DD** 152. **NLM** W1; IL735. **Bk Rev**, (Qty: 8). **Ad Acc, Adv Mgr:** C. Drivas, **Tel** (215)925-3995. **Pr Rev. Circ:** 800.
Desc: For health professionals and interested laypeople, focusing on long-term and life-threatening illness, death, and bereavement. Includes essays, research notes, and calendar.

●US/1062-9564
IN/FIRE ETHICS. (IN/FIRE ETHICS: NEWSLETTER OF THE INTERNATIONAL NETWORK OF FEMINISTS INTERESTED IN REPRODUCTIVE HEALTH.). [In/fire ethics]. **Added/Corp** International Network of Feminists Interested in Reproductive Health. **VFOAT** In Fire Ethics; Ethics. (1992)-. Periodical. English. qt. Free. The International Network of Feminists Interested in, Reproductive Health and Ethics, 1436 U Street, Suite 301, Washington DC 20009. **DD** 363.

●US
INDEX TO ... ETHICS ADVISORY OPINIONS. Main/Corp Texas Ethics Commission. (1992)-. English. ir. $55.00. Texas Ethics Commission, PO Box 12070 Capital Station, Austin TX 78711. **Tel** 800 325-8506. **LC** IN PROCESS.

CN/0848-1660
INTEGRITY. [Integrity]. **Added/Corp** Emissary Foundation International. **VFOAT** Integrity International. (1989)-. Periodical. English. qt. Integrity International, PO Box 9, 100 Mile House British Columbia V0K 2E0 Canada. **Tel** (604)395-2026. **DD** 170/.5. ***Continues*** *Integrity International., 0712-7685.*

NE
INTERNATIONAL HUMANIST. See Philosophy.

US/0739-098X
INTERNATIONAL JOURNAL OF APPLIED PHILOSOPHY, THE. [Int. j. appl. philos.]. Vol. 1, No. 3 (Spring 1983)-. Periodical. English. Twice a year. $12.00 institutions; $10.00 individuals. Indian River Community College, 3209 Virginia Avenue, Fort Pierce FL 34981. **Tel** (407)462-4700. **ED** Elliot Cohen. **LC** BJ1; .A66. **DD** 170/.5. **Ad Acc.** ***Continues*** *Applied Philosophy (Fort Pierce, Fla.), 0733-155X.*
Desc: This journal is dedicated to the thesis that philosophy, its theories and methods, can and should be brought to bear upon the clarification and solution of the practical issues of life.
Ind/Abst Philos. Index.

UK/0267-9655
INTERNATIONAL JOURNAL OF MORAL AND SOCIAL STUDIES. ***Ceased.*** **VFOAT** Moral and Social Studies; Moral & Social Studies. Vol. 1, No. 1 (Spring 1986)-(Dec. 1993). Periodical. English. Three times a year (published in spring, summer, and autumn). Journals Ltd, 1 Harewood Row, London NW1 6SE England. **Tel** 865-52736, FAX (1)7246145, telex (1)267967. **ED** S Wolfram. Index available. cum. index. **Bk Rev. Ad Acc. Pr Rev. Circ:** 500.
Desc: Publishes papers of 6,000 words from any relevant discipline. Has a particular interest in work lying between disciplines but also publishes specialised articles in Philosophy, Sociology, Anthropology, Law, History, Politics, etc, provided these are written in clear, concise, untechnical language.
Ind/Abst Abstr. Anthropol.; Hum. Resour. Abstr. (?-?); Philos. Index; Sage Public Adm. Abstr. (?-?); Soc. Plann. Policy Dev. Abstr.; Sociol. Abstr.

US/0193-7758
IRB. Added/Corp Hastings Center. **VAT** Institutional Review Boards. Vol. 1 (Mar. 1979)-. Periodical. English. bm. $40.00 (individuals), $260.00 (institutions). The Hastings Center, 255 Elm Road, Briarcliff Manor NY 10510-9974. **Tel** (914)762-8500, FAX (914)762-2124. **ED** Robert J. Levine. **NLM** W1 I268G. **Circ:** 1,000.
Desc: Directed toward members and institutional review boards who are involved with protocols in human subjects research.
Ind/Abst Index Period. Artic. Relat. Law (19??-); Psychol. Abstr.; PsycINFO; PsycLit.

US/0888-9201
ISSUES (SAINT LOUIS, MO.). (ISSUES : A CRITICAL EXAMINATION OF CONTEMPORARY ETHICAL ISSUES IN HEALTH CARE.). [Issues]. **Added/Corp** Sisters of St. Mary Health Care System (Saint Louis, Mo.). Vol. 1, No. 1 (Summer 1986)-. Periodical. English. Six times a year (Jan., Mar., May, July, Sept., Nov.). $125.00. SSM Healthcare System, 477 North Lindbergh Boulevard, St Louis MO 63141. **Tel** (314)994-7910, FAX (314)994-7900. **ED** Rev. Dennis Bradeur (phone: (314)994-7800). **LC** R724; .I88. **DD** 174. **Circ:** 2,000 (ctrl).

US/1058-112X
JOHNS HOPKINS CENTER FOR ALTERNATIVES TO ANIMAL TESTING : NEWSLETTER, THE. See Medical Science and Technology.

FR/1145-0762
JOURNAL INTERNATIONAL DE BIOETHIQUE. See Biology.

CN/1187-7863
JOURNAL OF AGRICULTURAL & ENVIRONMENTAL ETHICS. [J. agric. environ. ethics]. **Added/Corp** University of Guelph. Vol. 4, No. 1 (1991)-. Periodical. English. sa (Apr. and Oct.). 45.00Can$ Canada; 48.00Can$ other (institution). University of Guelph / Business Office, Room 039, Mackinnon Building, Guelph, Ontario N1G 2W1 Canada. **Tel** (519)824-4120 ext. 6925, FAX (519)837-9953. **DD** 174/.963/05. **CODEN** JAETEC. **[CCC]. Bk Rev. Ad Acc. Pr Rev. Circ:** 200. Documents available from The Genuine Article, BIOSIS Document Express. ***Continues*** *Journal of Agricultural Ethics, 0893-4282.*
Desc: Creates a forum for discussion of moral issues arising from actual or projected social policies in regard to a wide range of questions concerning the responsibilities of agrologists, veterinarians, or food scientists; the use of biotechnology, the safety, availability, and affordability of food.
Ind/Abst AGRICOLA; Biol. Abstr. (1991-); Can. Period. Index (1991-); Curr. Aware. Biol. Sci., CABS; Curr. Contents, Agric. Biol. Environ. Sci.; Nutr. Abstr. Rev., Ser. B, Live Feeds and Feed.; Philos. Index (1991-); Poult. Abstr.; Res. Alert [Select. Cov.]; Rural Dev. Abstr.; World Agric. Econ.

UK/0264-3758
JOURNAL OF APPLIED PHILOSOPHY. See Philosophy.

US/1050-3404
JOURNAL OF BIBLICAL ETHICS IN MEDICINE. [J. Biblic. ethics med.]. **Added/Corp** Forum for Biblical Ethics in Medicine. Vol. 1, No. 1 (Jan. 1987)-. Periodical. English. Four times a year. $18.00. Forum Biblical Ethics in Medicine, PO Box 13231, Florence SC 29504. **Tel** (803)665-6853. **ED** Hilton P. Terrell, MD. **DD** 174. **NLM** W1; JO561G. **Bk Rev**, (Qty: 3/yr). **Pr Rev. Circ:** 1,000 (ctrl).
Desc: Devoted to medical ethics from a biblical perspective.
Ind/Abst Christ. Period. Index (19??-).

NE/0167-4544
JOURNAL OF BUSINESS ETHICS. (JOURNAL OF BUSINESS ETHICS : JBE.). [J. bus. ethics]. **VFOAT** JBE; J.B.E. Vol. 1, No. 1 (Feb. 1982)-. Periodical. English. mo. $724.00. Kluwer Academic Publishers, Postbus 322, 3300 AH Dordrecht, The Netherlands. **Tel** 011 (31) 78 524400, FAX 011 31 78 183273, telex 20083. **ED** Alex C Michalos and Deborah C Poff. **LC** HF5387; .J68. **DD** 174/.4/05. **[CCC]. Bk Rev. Ad Acc. Pr Rev. Acid Free. Circ:** 1,000. available on microfilm and microfiche from University Microfilms International (UMI); available on an online database (files 15,648/Full-Text) from DIALOG. Documents available from The Genuine Article, UMI Article Clearinghouse.
Desc: Original articles from a wide variety of methodological and disciplinary perspectives concerning ethical issues related to business. Speculative philosophy as well as reports of empirical research are both published. All papers published are written in a style that is free of specialist jargon, so the journal is approachable by, and promotes a dialogue between, the various interested groups. Book reviews are a regular feature of the journal.
Ind/Abst ABI/INFORM Glob. Ed.; ABI Inform Ondisc (Nov. 1984-); ABI/INFORM Ondisc: Expr. Ed.; Acad. Ind. [Computer File] (1992-); Acad. Search (July 1993-); Anbar Account. Finan. Abstr. [Full Txt.]; Anbar Mark. Distr. Abstr. [Full Txt.]; Anbar Top Manage. Abstr. [Full Txt.]; Bus. ASAP (1992-) [Full Txt.]; Bus. Index (1985-); Bus. Period. Index; Bus. Source (Jul. 1993-); Commun. Abstr. (?-?); Contents Pages Manage.; Curr. Contents Soc. Behav. Sci.; Expand. Acad. Index (1984-); Gen. BusinessFile (1985-); Gen. Period. Index (1985-); INFO-SOUTH Abstr.; J. Plan. Lit.; Mag. Search; Manage. Market. Abstr.; Manage. Bibliogr. Rev. (1984-); Newsp. Period. Abstr. (1989-); Oper. Prod. Manage. Abstr. [Full Txt.]; PAIS Int. Print (1991-); Person. Train. Abstr. (1986-) [Full Txt.]; Philos. Index; Res. Alert [Full Cov.]; Soc. Sci. Source (Jul. 1993-); Soc. Sci. Cit. Index [Full Cov.]; Soc. Sci. Index; Soc. Sci. Index Fulltext (Sept. 1988-) [Full Txt.]; UMI ABI/Inform--Bus. Period. Ondisc (Nov. 1987-) [Full Txt.]; Wilson Bus. Abstr.; Women Manage. Rev. [Full Txt.]; Work Relat. Abstr.

US/1046-7890
JOURNAL OF CLINICAL ETHICS, THE. [J. clin. ethics]. Vol. 1, No. 1 (Spring 1990)-. Periodical. English. qt (published during the seasons). $115.00 US; $125.00 other. University Publishing Group Inc., 107 East Church Street, Frederick MD 21701-5441. **Tel** (301)694-8531, (800)654-8188. **ED** Edmund G. Howe. **LC** R724; .J68. **DD** 174/.2/05. **NLM** W1; JO588CJK. **CODEN** JCLEEG. **Bk Rev. Pr Rev.**
Desc: Provides a forum for the presentation, discussion and analysis of the practical issues and problems that you face in identifying, analyzing and resolving ethical problems in clinical practice. Bridges the gap between theory and practice. Combines quantitative clinical research with philosophical analysis. The only journal exclusively focused on clinical practice - on action.
Ind/Abst Index Med. (spring 1990-); Soc. Sci. Cit. Index [Full Cov.].

US/0899-7691
JOURNAL OF HUMANISM & ETHICAL RELIGION. [J. humanism ethical relig.]. **Added/Corp** American Ethical Union. National Leaders' Council. **VFOAT** Journal of Humanism and Ethical Religion; Humanism & Ethical Religion. Vol. 1, No. 1 (Fall 1988)-. Periodical. English. an. $8.00 (individuals), $10.00 (institutions). American Ethical Union, 2 West 64th Street, New York NY 10023. **Tel** 212 873-6500. **(Subscription address:** National Leaders Council American Ethical Union-Union of Li 38 Old Center Road, Garden City, NY 11530) **LC** BP605.E84; J68. **DD** 211/.6/05.
Ind/Abst Index Book Rev. Relig.; Relig. Index One Period.

●US/1061-9321
JOURNAL OF INFORMATION ETHICS. [J. infor. ethics]. (1992)-. Periodical. English. sa. $38.00 (US); $44.00 (other). McFarland & Company, PO Box 611, Jefferson NC 28640. **Tel** (919)246-4460, FAX (919)246-5018. **ED** Robert Hauptman. **LC** Z682.35.P75; J68. **DD** 170. **Bk Rev. Ad Acc, Adv Mgr:** Steve Wilson. **Circ:** 200.
Desc: The art of being an honest, moral, good person is explored in this journal for librarians and related professionals. Covers issues all information workers face on a daily basis.

US/0894-8879
JOURNAL OF LAW AND ETHICS IN DENTISTRY. ***Ceased.*** **See** Dentistry.

●US/1073-1105
JOURNAL OF LAW, MEDICINE & ETHICS, THE. See Law.

US/0890-0523
JOURNAL OF MASS MEDIA ETHICS. (JOURNAL OF MASS MEDIA ETHICS : MME.). [J. mass media ethics]. **VFOAT** Mass Media Ethics; MME; JMME. Vol. 1, No. 1 (Fall/Winter 1985/1986)-. Periodical. English. Four times a year. $145.00 US & Canada; $170.00 other. Lawrence Erlbaum Associates, 365 Broadway, Suite 102, Hillsdale NJ 07642. **Tel** (201)666-4110, (800)926-6579, FAX (201)666-2394. **ED** Ralph D Barney, John Jay Black. **LC** P94; .J68. **DD** 175/.1/05. **Bk Rev. Circ:** 400. Documents available from UMI Article Clearinghouse.
Desc: Provides a forum for discussion of mass media ethics philosophies and problems for academics, students, and professionals in all mass media fields.
Ind/Abst Commun. Abstr.; Expand. Acad. Index (1992-); Newsp. Period. Abstr. (1992-).

UK/0306-6800
JOURNAL OF MEDICAL ETHICS. See Medical Science and Technology.

UK/0305-7240
JOURNAL OF MORAL EDUCATION. See Education.

US
JOURNAL OF NURSING ETHICS, THE. ***Suspended.*** **Added/Corp** National Center for Nursing Ethics. Vol. 1 (Fall 1978)-Suspended (199?). Periodical. English. qt. National Center for Nursing Ethics, PO Box 2237, Cincinnati OH 45201.

●UK/0966-7369
JOURNAL OF PENTECOSTAL THEOLOGY. See Religion and Theology-Protestantism.

Ethics

US/0384-9694
JOURNAL OF RELIGIOUS ETHICS, THE. [J. relig. ethics]. **Added/Corp** American Academy of Religion. Harvard Divinity School. Emory University. Rutgers University. University of Tennessee, Knoxville. Vol. 1 (Fall 1973)-. Academic Scholarly Publication. English. sa. $24.00 institutions, $18.00 individuals. Scholars Press / Georgia, PO Box 15399, Atlanta GA 30333-0399. **Tel** (404)636-4757, (404)727-2320, FAX (404)727-2348. **ED** James T. Johnson. **LC** BJ1; J67. **DD** 291.5/05. cum. index. **Bk Rev. Ad Acc. Circ:** 1,000. available on microfilm and microfiche from University Microfilms International (UMI). Documents available from The Genuine Article, UMI Article Clearinghouse.
Desc: Scholarly essays on religious ethics in major world religions.
Ind/Abst Acad. Search (July 1993-); Arts Humanit. Citation Index [Full Cov.]; Curr. Contents Arts Humanit.; Expand. Acad. Index (1989-); Humanit. Index; Humanit. Source (Jul. 1993-); Index Book Rev. Relig.; INFO-SOUTH Abstr.; Mag. Search; Newsp. Period. Abstr. (1991-); Philos. Index; Relig. Index One Period. (1973-); Relig. Theol. Abstr.; Res. Alert [Full Cov.]; Soc. Sci. Cit. Index [Select. Cov.].

US/0145-2797
JRE STUDIES IN RELIGIOUS ETHICS. **VFOAT** Studies in Religious Ethics. **VAT** Journal of Religious Ethics Studies in Religious Ethics. Monographic series. English. Price varies per volume. Scholars Press / Georgia, PO Box 15399, Atlanta GA 30333-0399. **Tel** (404)636-4757, (404)727-2320, FAX (404)727-2348.

US/1054-6863
KENNEDY INSTITUTE OF ETHICS JOURNAL. [Kennedy Inst. Ethics j.]. **Added/Corp** Kennedy Institute of Ethics. Vol. 1, No. 1 (Mar. 1991)-. Periodical. English. Four times a year. $73.00 US; $80.00 Canada and Mexico; $80.30 other. Johns Hopkins University Press, 2715 North Charles Street, Baltimore MD 21218-4319. **Tel** (410)516-6987, FAX (410)516-6968. **ED** Robert Veatch and Renie Schapiro. **LC** QH332; .K46. **DD** 174/.2/05. **NLM** W1; KE645T. **CODEN** KIEJEF. **[CCC].** Documents available from BIOSIS Document Express.
Desc: Featuring opinion and analysis of all aspects of bioethics. Non-sectarian, interdisciplinary journal will help medical professionals, public policy makers, and the general public come to terms with moral issues.
Ind/Abst Biol. Abstr. (1991-); Health Plan. Adminis.; Hospit. Health Admin. Index (Mar. 1991-); PAIS Int. Print.

KO
KUNGMIN YULLI YONGU. Periodical. Korean. **LC** BJ8.K6; K85.

CN/1198-3922
LAST RIGHTS. (1991)-. Periodical. English. qt. Right to Die Society of Canada, PO Box 39018, Victoria BC V8V 4X8 Canada. **Tel** (604)380-1112, FAX (604)386-3800. **ED** John Hofsess.
Desc: Specializes in international coverage of "right to die" issues and original research in methods of self-deliverance.

US/8755-5352
LESBIAN ETHICS. [Lesbian ethics]. Vol. 1, No. 1 (Fall 1984)-. Periodical. English. Twice a year (Publishes two or three times per year). $14.00 (individuals), $18.00 (institutions). Lesbian Ethics, PO Box 4723, Albuquerque NM 87196. **LC** WMLC 93/3305. **DD** 809.

FR/0296-4074
LETTRE D'INFORMATION DU COMITE CONSULTATIF NATIONAL D'ETHIQUE POUR LES SCIENCES DE LA VIE ET DE LA SANTE. **Added/Corp** France. Comite Consultatif National d'Ethique pour les Sciences de la vie et de la Sante. Mission de l'Information et de la Communication de l'INSERM. **VFOAT** Lettre. (198?)-. Periodical. French. Four times a year. Price varies. Documentation Francaise, 29 Quai Voltaire, 75344 Paris Cedex 7 France. **Tel** 011 33 1 40157000, FAX 011 33 1 40157230, telex 204 826 DOCFRAN. **(Subscription address:** Documentation Francaise, 124 rue Henri Barbusse, 93308 Aubervilliers Cedex France.) **NLM** W1; LE889UG.

FR
LETTRE D'INFORMATIONS DU COMITE CONSULTATIF NATIONAL D ETHIQUE. French. Documentation Francaise, 29 Quai Voltaire, 75344 Paris Cedex 7 France. **Tel** 011 33 1 40157000, FAX 011 33 1 40157230, telex 204 826 DOCFRAN.

US/0024-3639
LINACRE QUARTERLY, THE. [Linacre q.]. V. 1-. Dec. 1932-. Periodical. English. qt. $24.00. National Federation of Catholic Physicians Guild, 850 Elm Grove Road, Elm Grove WI 53122. **Tel** (414)784-3435, FAX (414)782-8788. **ED** John Mullooly. **LC** R15; .L58. **NLM** W1 LI623P. Index available. cum. index. **Bk Rev. Circ:** 2500. available on microfilm and microfiche from University Microfilms International (UMI).
Desc: A journal of the philosophy and ethics of medical practice.
Ind/Abst Bibliogr. Mission.; Abr. Cathol. Period. Lit. Index; Cathol. Period. Lit. Index.

US/0896-2154
LIVING WORLD (LOS ANGELES, CALIF.). (LIVING WORLD / INTERNATIONAL LIFE SERVICES, INC.). [Living world]. **Added/Corp** International Life Services, Inc. (Los Angeles, Calif.). **VFOAT** Living World Magazine. (198?)-. Periodical. English. qt. $15.00. International Life Services Inc., 2606 1/2 West 8th Street, Los Angeles CA 90057. **Tel** (213)382-2156, FAX (213)283-4203. **ED** Louise Walsh. **DD** 363. **Bk Rev** (Qty: 4). **Ad Acc, Adv Mgr:** Ruth Phillips. **Circ:** 1,500.
Desc: Deals with topics of current interest and contemporary ethical issues.

CN/0705-6346
LUMIERE ET PAIX. V. 1- Feb. 1977-. Periodical. French. bm. $2.00. Lumiere et Paix, C P 517 Succursale Youville, Montreal Quebec H2P 2W1 Canada. **DD** 174/.2/05. **Supersedes** Bulletin des Infirmieres Catholiques de Canada, 0007-4470.

●SW/1102-769X
LUND STUDIES IN ETHICS AND THEOLOGY. [Lund stud. ethics theol.]. (1992)-. Monographic series. Multiple languages. ir. Price varies per volume. Lund University Press, Box 141, S-22100 Lund Sweden. **Tel** 011 46 46 312000, FAX 011 46 46 305338, telex 33345 EDUCATE S. **ED** G. Bexell. **UDC** 241.

US/0145-9783
MAN AND MEDICINE. [Man med.]. (Autumn 1975)-. Periodical. English. qt $12.00. Michael Meyer/Executive Editor, 650 W 168th Street, New York City NY 10032. **LC** R724; .M17. **DD** 174/.2/05. **NLM** W1 MA566.
Ind/Abst EMBASE; Psychol. Abstr. (1975-).

US/0364-0019
MARCH FOR LIFE PROGRAM/JOURNAL. **Title Change.** [March Life program/j.]. **Added/Corp** March for Life, Inc. **VFOAT** March for Life Program Journal. Jan. 22-23, (1978)-(19??). English. an. PO Box 2950, Washington DC 20013. **LC** HQ767.5.U5; M35. **DD** 323.4/3.097305. **Continues** Marching for Life, 0891-348X. **Continued by** March for Life : [Report], 1069-7098.

RU
MARKSISTSKO-LENINSKAIA ETIKA / AKADEMIIA NAUK SSSR, INSTITUT NAUCHNOI INFORMATSII PO OBSHCHESTVENNYM NAUKAM. **Added/Corp** Institut Nauchnoi Informatsii po Obshchestvennym Naukam (Akademiia Nauk SSSR). (1973)-. Russian. **LC** Z5873; .M27; BJ1390. **DD** 171./7.

US/0886-0653
MEDICAL ETHICS ADVISOR. [Med. ethics advisor]. **Added/Corp** American Health Consultants. Vol. 1, No. 1 (Feb. 1985)-. Periodical. English. mo. $269.00. American Health Consultants, 3525 Piedmont Road, Suite 400, Atlanta GA 30305. **Tel** (800)688-2421, (404)262-7436. **(Subscription address:** American Health Consultants, PO Box 95278, Chicago IL 60694.) **NLM** W1; ME316E. **[CCC].**
Desc: Gain winning formulas to improve quality and dignity of care, ensure wise use of technology, prevent costly lawsuits, avoid disastrous publicity, protect rights of patients, and more.
Ind/Abst Hospit. Manage. Rev. (19??-).

US/0025-7397
MEDICAL-MORAL NEWSLETTER, THE. **See** Medical Science and Technology.

IT/0025-7834
MEDICINA E MORALE. See Medical Science and Technology.

MX/0188-5022
MEDICINA Y ETICA. (MEDICINA Y ETICA : REVISTA INTERNACIONAL DE BIOETICA, DEONTOLOGIA Y ETICA MEDICA.). [Med. etica]. (1990)-. Periodical. Spanish. qt. $75.00 Latin America; $85.00 other. Investigaciones y Estudios Superiores, Escuela Med / Universidad Anahuac, AP 10844, 1000 Mexico DF Mexico. **Tel** 011 52 5 8990000, FAX 011 52 5 892200. **DD** _a174.2.
Desc: Forum for bioethic studies.

US/0163-6480
MORAL EDUCATION FORUM. See Education.

US/0733-2424
MORALITY. Vol. 1, No. 1 (Winter 1982)-. Periodical. English. $2.25 each issue. Carnegie Corporation of New York, 437 Madison Avenue, New York NY 10022. **Tel** (212)371-3200. **LC** HN90.M6; M67. **DD** 373./05.
Desc: Issues for winter 1982-include a year designation in conjunction with the title, e.g. Morality '82.

JA
MORAROJI KENKYU. Added/Corp Moraroji Kenkyujo. **VFOAT** Studies in Moralogy. No. 1 (1973)-. Japanese (summaries and/or abstracts in English). sa. The Institute of Moralogy, Hikarigaoka, Kashiwa Chiba-ken 277 Japan. **Tel** 0471-73-3252, FAX 0471-76-1177, telex 2975406 REITAC J. **LC** BJ8.J3; M67. **Bk Rev. Circ:** 1,000.

US
NATIONAL REPORTER ON LEGAL ETHICS AND PROFESSIONAL RESPONSIBILITY. See Law.

CN/1181-8778
NCBHR COMMUNIQUE. [NCBHR commun.]. **Added/Corp** National Council on Bioethics in Human Research. **VFOAT** NCBHR Communique; National Council on Bioethics in Human Research Communique; Communique CNBRH. Vol. 1, No. 1 (Oct./Nov. 1990)-. Periodical. English (French). Three times a year. Limited free distribution. National Council on Bioethics in Human Research, 74 Stanley Avenue, Ottawa, Ontario K1M 1P4 Canada. **DD** 174/.28/097105.

US/0361-6347
NEW TITLES IN BIOETHICS. See Medical Science and Technology.

NZ/1170-5485
NEWSLETTER - EUBIOS ETHICS INSTITUTE. (NEWSLETTER.). [Newsl - Eubios Ethics Inst.]. (1991)-. Newsletter. English. bm. $20.00. Eubios Ethics Institute, 31 Colwyn Street, Christchurch New Zealand. **(Subscription address:** Eubios Ethics Institute, PO Box 125, Tsukuba Ibaraki 305 Japan) **DD** 174.957405. **Pr Rev.**

US
NEWSLETTER - SOUTH CAROLINA STATE ETHICS COMMISSION. Main/Corp State of South Carolina State Ethics Commission. **VFOAT** Digest of Advisory Opinions. Sept. 1979-. Newsletter. English. qt. Free. South Carolina Ethics Commission, PO Box 11926, Columbia SC 29211. **Tel** (803)253-4192. **ED** Gary R Baker. Index available. **Circ:** 2,000.

US/0883-3648
NOTRE DAME JOURNAL OF LAW, ETHICS & PUBLIC POLICY. See Law.

US/0030-6789
OUR ANIMALS. (OUR ANIMALS : THE JOURNAL OF THE SAN FRANCISCO SOCIETY FOR THE PREVENTION OF CRUELTY TO ANIMALS.). Periodical. English. qt. $15.00. San Francisco Society for the Prevention of Cruelty to Animals, 2500 16th Street, San Francisco CA 94103-6589. **Tel** (415)554-3000. **ED** Richard Avanzino. **Circ:** 32,000 (ctrl).
Desc: News and feature stories about the animals, people and programs of the San Francisco SPCA.

US/0191-4537
PHILOSOPHY & SOCIAL CRITICISM. See Philosophy.

US
PHYSICIAN ASSISTANT NEWSLETTER OF ETHICS. English. Four times a year. $20.00. Physician Assistant Newsletter, PO Box 1034, Glenside PA 19038. Index available (published separately). cum. index. **Ad Acc, Adv Mgr:** Bernard Stuetz, **Tel** (215)884-7972. **Circ:** 2,000 (ctrl).

US
PROCEEDINGS OF THE ... ANNUAL CONFERENCES. See Public Administration.

US
PROCUREMENT ETHICS DESKTOP REFERENCE. See Public Administration.

●US/1063-6579
PROFESSIONAL ETHICS (GAINESVILLE, FLA.). (PROFESSIONAL ETHICS.). [Prof. ethics]. Vol. 1, No. 1 & 2 (Spring/Summer 1992)-. Periodical. English. qt (Mar., June, Sept., Dec.). $50.00. University of Florida / Center for Applied Philosophy, 332 Griffin-Floyd Hall, Gainesville FL 32611. **Tel** (904)392-2084, FAX (904)392-5577. **(Subscription address:** Professional Ethics, PO Box 15017, Gainesville FL 32604.) **ED** Robert J. Baum. **LC** BJ1725; .P75. **DD** 174/.05. **Acid Free.**

US/1042-5675
PROFESSIONAL LAWYER : PL / SPECIAL COORDINATING COMMITTEE ON PROFESSIONALISM, AMERICAN BAR ASSOCIATION CENTER FOR PROFESSIONAL RESPONSIBILITY, THE. See Law.

US/1045-2044
PROJECT BREED DIRECTORY. (PROJECT BREED DIRECTORY : A NATIONWIDE SOURCE BOOK FOR RESCUE AND ADOPTION OF ALL BREEDS OF DOGS.). **VFOAT** Project Breed (Breed Rescue Efforts & Education) Directory. Vol. 1, No. 1

(1989)-. Directory. English. ir. $15.95. Network for ANI-Males & Females Inc, 18707 Curry Powder Lane, Germantown MD 20874. **ED** Shirley Weber. **LC** HV4746; .P76. **DD** 636.7/083.
 Desc: Sources of rescue assistance in the US and Canada for 72 breeds.

US/0360-9006
RECENT ACTIVITIES - HASTINGS CENTER. Main/Corp Hastings Center. (19??)-. English. an. Free upon request. The Hastings Center, 255 Elm Road, Briarcliff Manor NY 10510-9974. **Tel** (914)762-8500, FAX (914)762-2124. **LC** R724; .H27a. **DD** 174/.2/05.

US/0276-055X
RECENT ETHICS OPINIONS. [Recent ethics opin.]. **Main/Corp** American Bar Association. Standing Committee on Ethics and Professional Responsibility. (197?)-. English. ir. $28.00. American Bar Association, 750 North Lake Shore Drive, Chicago IL 60611. **Tel** (312)988-5522, (312)988-5241, FAX (312)988-5528, telex 270593. cum. index.

IT
RENDICONTI (ACCADEMIA NAZIONALE DEI LINCEI. CLASSE DI SCIENZE MORALI, STORICHE E FILOLOGICHE). (RENDICONTI / CLASSE DI SCIENZE MORALI, STORICHE E FILOLOGICHE). **Added/Corp** Accademia Nazionale dei Lincei. Classe di Scienze Morali e Filologiche. (194?)-. Periodical. Italian (French, English, German, Latin and Spanish). qt. L50000 Italy; $46.00 US. Atti Della Accademia Nazionale dei Lincei, Via Della Lungara 10, 00165 Rome Italy. **Tel** 06/680-31. **ED** C F Golisano. **Circ:** 850. **Continues** Rendiconti della Classe di Scienze Morali, Storiche.
 Desc: Publishes only contributions of fellows of the Academy of Lincei or scholars presented by fellows; requires a 200-word abstract.
 Ind/Abst BHA : Biblio. Hist. Art; MLA Int. Bibl. Books Artic. Mod. Lang. Lit.

JA
RINRIGAKU NEMPO. VFOAT Annals of Ethics; Rinrigaku-Nenpo. Japanese. an. ¥1800. Nihon Rinri Gakkai, Waseda Daigakubu Tetsugaku Kenkyushitsu, 1-24-1 Toyama, Shinjuku-ku, Tokyo Japan. **Tel** 03-203-4111. **LC** BJ8.J3; R56. **Circ:** 1,000.

GW
SCHRIFTEN ZUR RECHTSTHEORIE. See Law.

US
SCOPE NOTE / JOSEPH AND ROSE KENNEDY INSTITUTE OF ETHICS, GEORGETOWN UNIVERSITY. See Medical Science and Technology.

US/0890-1570
SECOND OPINION (PARK RIDGE, ILL.). See Medical Science and Technology.

US
SOUNDINGS (NOTRE DAME). See Business.

IT/0081-6736
STUDIA MORALIA. Added/Corp Pontificia Universita Lateranense. Academia Alfonsiana. Institutum Superius Theologiae Moralis. Vol. 1 (1963)-. Periodical. English (French, German and Italian). sa. $38.00. Edacalf Editiones Academiae, CP 2458, 00100 Rome Italy. **Tel** 011 39 6 73158 41. Each issue contains an index to its own contents (no volume index)--loose. **Bk Rev. Circ:** 1,200.
 Desc: Publishes scientific articles on moral theology, issues in different languages.
 Ind/Abst Bibliogr. Mission.

FR/0750-1455
SUPPLEMENT, LE. (LE SUPPLEMENT : REVUE D'ETHIQUE ET THEOLOGIE MORALE.). [Supplement]. Vol. 23, No. 92 (Feb. 1970-. Periodical. French. Four times a year. 65.00F. Editions du Cerf, BP 65, 77932 Perthes Cedex France. **Tel** 011 33 1 44181212.
 (Subscription address: Novalis, PO Box 990, Outremont H2V 4S7 Canada.) **LC** BJ2; .S87. **DD** 170/.5. **Continues** Vie Spirituelle. Supplement.
 Ind/Abst Abr. Cathol. Period. Lit. Index; Cathol. Period. Lit. Index.

US/0275-7656
TANNER LECTURES ON HUMAN VALUES, THE. [Tanner lect. hum. values]. (1980)-. English. an (June). $30.00. University of Utah Press, 101 University Services Building, Salt Lake City UT 84112. **Tel** (801)581-6771. **LC** BD232; .T24. **DD** 170.

US/1052-9314
THEOLOGY & PUBLIC POLICY. See Religion and Theology.

●US/1074-1593
TIMELINES (EUGENE, OR). (TIMELINES.). **VFOAT** Time Lines. (1994)-. English. qt (4 issues). $25.00. National Hemlock Society, PO Box 11830,
Eugene OR 97440. **Tel** (503)342-5748. **ED** Kris Larson. **Bk Rev. Circ:** 20,000 (ctrl). **Continues** Hemlock Quarterly, 0742-5376.
 Desc: Reports on latest developments in voluntary euthanasia, right-to-die, living, wills, etc.
 Ind/Abst Hum. Rights Intern. Rep.

CN/1191-1700
TRENDS AND ALTERNATIVES IN TESTING. (TRENDS AND ALTERNATIVES IN TESTING : THE JOSEPH F. MORGAN RESEARCH FOUNDATION NEWSLETTER.). [Trends altern. test.]. **Added/Corp** Joseph F. Morgan Research Foundation. Vol. No. 1 (Fall/Winter 1991)-. Newsletter. English. qt. Free. Joseph F Morgan Research Foundation, 205-151 Slater Street, Ottawa Ontario K1P 5N1 Canada. **DD** 179.

●US/1062-5364
TRENDS IN HEALTH CARE, LAW & ETHICS. [Trends health care law ethics]. **Added/Corp** Robert Wood Johnson Medical School. **VFOAT** Trends in Health Care, Law and Ethics. Vol. 7, No. 2 (Winter 1992)-. Periodical. English. qt. $50.00 (institutions), $40.00 (individuals) US; $54.00 (institutions), $44.00 (individuals) Canada; $64.00 (institutions), $54.00 (individuals) other. Robert Wood Johnson Medical School, 675 Hoes Lane, Piscataway NJ 08855. **Tel** (800)732-4162, (908)463-4549, FAX (908)463-4569. **ED** Russell McIntyre. **LC** IN PROCESS. **DD** 344. **NLM** W1; TR341CHH. Index available. **Bk Rev**, (Qty: 4-6). **Ad Acc, Adv Mgr:** same as editor. **Circ:** 2,550. **Continues** Info Trends, 1054-629X.
 Ind/Abst Int. Nurs. Index (1992-).

US/0731-2865
UNITED STATES AIR FORCE ACADEMY JOURNAL OF PROFESSIONAL MILITARY ETHICS. See Military and Defense.

UK/0953-8208
UTILITAS. Vol. 1, No. 1 (May 1989)-. Periodical. English. sa (2 issues). £48.00 UK and Europe; $92.00 other. Oxford University Press, Walton Street, Oxford OX2 6DP England. **Tel** 011 44 865 56767, FAX 011 44 865 267773, telex 837330 OXPRES G. **(Subscription address:** Oxford University Press / USA, Journals Marketing Department, Oxford University Press, 2001 Evans Road, Cary NC 27513.) **ED** Fred Rosen. **LC** IN PROCESS. **[CCC].** available on microfilm and microfiche from University Microfilms International (UMI). **Formed by the union of** Mill News Letter, 0026-4253 **and** Bentham Newsletter.
 Ind/Abst Am. Humanit. Index (199?-); Int. Bibliogr. Sociol.

US/0893-4851
VERA LEX. (VERA LEX / NATURAL LAW SOCIETY.). [Vera lex]. **Added/Corp** Natural Law Society. Pace University. Human Studies Dept. Vol. 1, No. 1 (Jan. 1980)-. Academic Scholarly Publication. English (French, Spanish and German). Twice a year. $30.00 institutions, $15.00 individuals. Pace University / Philosophy & Religious Studies, Buchsbaum Faculty Center, Pleasantville NY 10570. **Tel** (914)773-3309, (914)969-1624, FAX (914)773-3541, (914)969-16247. **ED** Virginia Black and Myron Miller. **LC** K26; .E65. **DD** 171. cum. index (every five years). **Bk Rev**, (Qty: 10-12). **Ad Acc. Pr Rev. Circ:** 400.
 Desc: Dialogues on natural law and natural rights; clarifies its supporting ideas with consistency and scholarly integrity. Strengthens the current revival of discussion of morals and law and advances its historical research.

CN/1180-1395
VITAL NEXUS. (THE VITAL NEXUS.). [Vital nexus]. **Added/Corp** Saint Mary's University (Halifax, N.S.). Institute of Human Values. Vol. 1, No. 1 (May 1990)-. English (French). an. 15.00Can$ Canada; $11.91 other. Institute of Human Values, St Mary's University, Halifax, Nova Scotia B3H 3C3 Canada. **Tel** (902)420-5753. **DD** 170/.5.

CN/1185-1988
VITALITE. [Vitalite]. **Added/Corp** Campagne Quebec-vie. Vol. 1, No 1 (Mar 1991)-. Periodical. French. qt. Free for Members. Campagne Quebec-Vie, CP 370, Succursale R, Montreal Quebec H2S 3M2 Canada. **DD** 179/.76/0971405.

US/0898-6606
WATERWHEEL (SILVER SPRING, MD.). See Religion and Theology.

US
WESTERN BIOETHICS NETWORK. No. 6 (Feb. 1987)-. Periodical. English. bm. Janice Hagerlof, 324 Holyoke Street, San Francisco CA 94134. **Continues** California Bioethics Network.

●US/1061-8643
WORKPLACE ISSUES & ANSWERS. **VFOAT** Workplace Issues and Answers; Workplace. (1992)-. Periodical. English. bm. $24.00. Workplace Publications, Inc., PO Box 1129, Durant OK 74702.
GW/0044-2674
ZEITSCHRIFT FUER EVANGELISCHE ETHIK. See Religion and Theology-Protestantism.

ETHNIC INTERESTS

US/0164-5234
20 DE MAYO. See Newspapers.

●US/1074-9144
21ST CENTURY AFRO REVIEW. VFOAT Twenty-First Century Afro Review. (1994)-. Periodical. English. qt. $55.00 (institutions), $32.00 (individuals). IAAS Publications, 7676 New Hampshire Avenue, Suite 306, Langley Park MD 20783. **Tel** (800)858-4227, (301)431-3161, FAX (301)431-2195. **ED** Nikongo BaNikongo. **Continues** 21st Century Policy Review, 1055-3630.
 Desc: Deals primarily with issues of interest to Afro-America, Africa and the Afro-Diaspora.

US/1055-3630
21ST CENTURY POLICY REVIEW. Title Change. [21st century policy rev.]. **Added/Corp** Institute for Afro-American Scholarship. **VFOAT** JAS. Vol. 1, No. 1 (Winter 1992)-(199?). Periodical. English. sa. IAAS Publications, 7676 New Hampshire Avenue, Suite 306, Langley Park MD 20783. **Tel** (800)858-4227, (301)431-3161, FAX (301)431-2195. **DD** 305. **CODEN** CPOREG. **Continued by** 21st Century Afro Review.

US/1070-9401
A. MAGAZINE. (A MAGAZINE : THE ASIAN AMERICAN QUARTERLY.). [A mag.]. **VFOAT** A. Magazine; Asian American Quarterly. Vol. 1, No. 1 (Spring 1991)-. Periodical. English. qt (4 issues). $10.00. The Asian American Quarterly, 296 Elizabeth Street #2F, New York NY 10012. **Tel** (212)505-1416, FAX (212)725-2077. **ED** Jeff Yang. **DD** 051. **Bk Rev**, (Qty: 15). **Ad Acc, Adv Mgr:** Phoebe Eng. **Pr Rev. Acid Free. Circ:** 60,000. available on CD-ROM.
 Desc: Targets Asians in the U.S., supplying the Asian-American perspective on current, national and international events, media, art, politics and fashion. Its readers are English-speaking, professional and educated. Also contains news and reviews.

US
AAH EXAMINER : THE NEWSLETTER OF AFRICAN AMERICANS FOR HUMANISM. See Philosophy.

US/0360-7178
AAMOA REPORTS. See Music.

US/8756-0267
ABBWA JOURNAL. See Literature.

CN/0382-4632
ABEGWEIT REVIEW. (THE ABEGWEIT REVIEW.). **Added/Corp** University of Prince Edward Island. Vol. 1 March (1974)-. Periodical. English (French; summaries and/or abstracts in French). Twice a year (Mar. & Nov.). 16.00Can$. University Prince Edward Island, Prince Edward Island, Charlottetown C1A 4P3 Canada. **Tel** (902)566-0404. **ED** Wendell P. MacIntyre. **DD** 051. **Pr Rev. Circ:** 500 (ctrl).
 Desc: The review focuses on the ethnic groups on Prince Edward Island, in Canada.

US/1046-7041
ABNF JOURNAL, THE. See Medical Science and Technology-Nursing.

AT
ABORIGINAL CHILD AT SCHOOL, THE. See Education-Special Education and Rehabilitation.

AT/0310-723X
ABORIGINAL NEWS (CANBERRA). (ABORIGINAL NEWS.). **Added/Corp** Australia. Dept. of Aboriginal Affairs. (1973)-. Periodical. English. mo. Australian Department of Aboriginal Affairs, M L C Tower/Woden Town Centre, Canberra Australian Capital Territory Australia. **LC** GN665; .A64. **DD** 301.45/19/91094. **Bk Rev. Circ:** 6,000.
 Desc: News about developments in aboriginal affairs, achievements of Australian aboriginal people.

●US/1071-3182
ABYA YALA NEWS. (ABYA YALA NEWS : JOURNAL OF THE SOUTH AND MESO AMERICAN INDIAN INFORMATION CENTER.). [Abya yala news]. **Added/Corp** South and Meso-American Indian Information Center. Vol. 7, No. 1 & 2 (Winter/Spring 1993)-. Periodical. English (Spanish). Four times a year (Seasonally). $15.00 (individuals), $40.00 (institutions). South & Meso-American Indian Information Center, PO Box 28703, Oakland CA 94604. **Tel** (510)834-4263, FAX (510)834-4264. **LC** E59.G6; N48. **DD** 305. **Bk Rev**, (Qty: varies). **Ad Acc, Adv Mgr:** David Techlon. **Circ:** 3,500. **Continues** Newsletter (South and Meso-American Indian Information Center : 1990), 1056-5876.

Ethnic Interests

Desc: Covering news related to Indigenous Peoples in Central and South America from the Indigenous people's perspective. Includes interviews with the leaders, first-hand coverage of Indigenous organizing, human rights reports, calendars of events, as well as, in-depth analysis of key issues facing the Indigenous people.

US/0001-4397
ACADIANA PROFILE. Vol. 1 (Jan./Feb. 1969)-. Periodical. English (French). Four times a year. $9.00. Acadiana Profile, PO Box 52247, Lafayette LA 70505. **Tel** (318)235-7919. **ED** Trent Angers. **LC** F380.F8; A26. **DD** 301.453/716/0763. **Bk Rev. Ad Acc. Circ:** 10,000 (ctrl).
Desc: Feature stories on the Cajun country of South Louisiana.

●US/1064-6981
ACCENT (MARLBORO, MASS.). (ACCENT : A MAGAZINE FOR BANGLADESHIS, INDIANS, PAKISTANIS, AND SRI LANKANS AROUND THE WORLD.). [Accent (Marlboro Mass.)]. Spring (1992)-. Periodical. English. qt. $10.00. Leena Prasad, 100 Granger Boulevard, #205, Marlboro MA 01752-2847. **DD** 305.

CN/0316-4837
ACCESSION LIST - NATIONAL INDIAN BROTHERHOOD, LIBRARY. *Title Change.* **Main/Corp** National Indian Brotherhood of Canada. Library. No. 1- Aug. 1973-. Periodical. English. National Indian Brotherhood, 102 Bank Street, Ottawa Ontario K1P 5N4 Canada. **DD** 016.971/004/97. *Continued by National Indian Brotherhood. Library & Information Services. Weekly Acquisitions.*

CN/0226-7845
ACCORD (CALGARY). (ACCORD : THE VOICE OF SOUTH ASIANS.). [Accord]. **Added/Corp** Council of South Asians. Vol. 3, No. 1 (Jan/Feb 1980)-. Periodical. English. bm. 10.00Can$. Council of South Asians, PO Box 6231 Station D, Calgary Alberta T2P 2C8 Canada. **Tel** (403)245-1730. **ED** S. R. Sreenivasan. **DD** 971/.004914/05. **Bk Rev. Ad Acc. Circ:** 1,000 (ctrl). *Continues Accord (Committee of South Asians), 0226-7845.*
Desc: Intercultural communication, citizenship development, and community service.

US/0749-2642
ADC TIMES. (ADC TIMES : THE NEWSLETTER OF THE AMERICAN-ARAB ANTI-DISCRIMINATION COMMITTEE.). [ADC times]. **Added/Corp** ADC Research Institute. **VAT** American-Arab Anti-Discrimination Committee Times. Vol. 5, No. 1 (Oct. 1984)-. Periodical. English. Ten times a year. $35.00 Comes with American Arab Anti Discrimination Committee membership. American Arab Anti Discrimination Committee, 4201 Connecticut Avenue Northwest, Suite 500, Washington DC 20008. **Tel** (202)244-2990. **DD** 305. **Bk Rev. Ad Acc. Circ:** 15,000 (ctrl). *Continues ADC Reports.*

US/1061-5202
ADL ON THE FRONTLINE. (ADL ON THE FRONTLINE : PUBLISHED BY THE ANTI-DEFAMATION LEAGUE.). [ADL frontline]. **Added/Corp** B'Nai B'Rith. Anti-Defamation League. **VFOAT** Frontline. **VAT** Anti-Defamation League on the Frontline. Vol. 1, No. 1 (Sept. 1991)-. Periodical. English. Ten times a year. $12.00. Anti-Defamation League B'Nai B'Rith, 823 United Nations Plaza, New York NY 10017. **Tel** (212)490-2525. **LC** DS146.U6; A34. **DD** 305.8/00973. *Continues ADL Bulletin, 0001-0936.*

US/0001-9003
ADVOCATE (NEW YORK, N.Y.), THE. *Ceased.* (THE ADVOCATE.). **VFOAT** Irish Advocate. (1893)-(19??). Periodical. English. wk. Irish American Advocate, 15 Park Row, New York NY 10038. **Tel** (212)233-4672. **ED** James N O'Connor. **LC** NEWSPAPER. **Bk Rev. Ad Acc. Circ:** 17,500. available in microform from New York Public Library.
Desc: To aid and promote the social and economic welfare for the Irish-American population throughout the United States.

FR/0291-2708
AFGHAN REALITIES. *See Political Science-Civil Rights.*

IT/0001-9747
AFRICA. **Added/Corp** Associazione fra le Imprese Italiane in Affrica. Istituto Italiano per l'Africa. Vol. 1 (1946)-. Periodical. Italian (English, French and Spanish). Four times a year (Mar., June, Sept., Dec.). L50000 Italy; L60000 others. Instituto Italo-Africano, Via Ulisse Aldrovandi, 16, 00196 Rome Italy. **Tel** 011 39 6 3216712. Index available (Dec. issue). cum. index. available on microfilm.
Ind/Abst MLA Int. Bibl. Books Artic. Mod. Lang. Lit.

SA
AFRICA ENTERPRISE UPDATE. English. mo. $10.00 US, Canada and Africa; 12.50 other. Africa Enterprise, PO Box 647, Pietermaritzburg, 3200 South Africa. **Tel** 0331 56321. **ED** R. Jarvis. **Circ:** 40,000 (ctrl)

●US/1071-8710
AFRICAN-AMERICAN ALMANAC, THE. **Added/Corp** Gale Research Inc. (1993)-. Periodical. English. te. $150.00. Gale Research Inc., 835 Penobscot Building, Detroit MI 48226. **Tel** (800)877-GALE, (313)961-2242, FAX (313)961-6083, telex TWX 810-221-7086. **ED** Kenneth Estell. *Continues Negro Almanac.*
Desc: Comprehensive source to works about the history and culture of blacks in American, Africa and the Western Hemisphere.

●US/1065-0180
AFRICAN-AMERICAN BUSINESS. *See Business.*

US/1057-9001
AFRICAN AMERICAN JOURNAL. (AFRICAN AMERICAN JOURNAL [VIDEORECORDING].). (1991)-. Periodical. English. $95.00. Imagco, PO Box 130378, Houston TX 77219-0378.

US/1050-6071
AFRICAN-AMERICAN JOURNAL OF CHIROPRACTIC. (1991)-. Periodical. English. $5.00 (single isssue). Addison Chiropractic Educational Foundation, 1033 Franklin Road, Suite 11-204, Marietta GA 30067.

CN/0827-8040
AFRICAN LETTER, THE. [Afr. lett.]. (1980)-. Periodical. English. sm. 24.00Can$. The African Letter, 2462 Du Ferin Street, Toronto Ontario M6B 3P7 Canada. **Tel** (416)784-0816. **DD** 960/.005.
Desc: A focus on African affairs.

NR/0002-0087
AFRICAN NOTES. (AFRICAN NOTES : BULLETIN OF THE INSTITUTE OF AFRICAN STUDIES, UNIVERSITY OF IBADAN.). [Afr. notes]. **Added/Corp** University of Ibadan. Institute of African Studies. Vol. 1, No. 1 (Oct. 1963)-. Bulletin. English. ir. N20.00 Nigeria; $15.00 North America; £10.00 other. Institute of African Studies / Nigeria, University of Ibadan, Ibadan Nigeria. **Tel** (022)400550-614. **ED** Dele Layiwola. cum. index. **Bk Rev. Ad Acc. Circ:** 500.
Desc: African agriculture, archaeology, arts, folklore, history, linguistics, literature, traditional medicine, and sociology.
Ind/Abst Am. Hist. Life (1968-); Anthropol. Lit.; Ethnoarts Index; Int. Bibliogr. Sociol.; MLA Int. Bibl. Books Artic. Mod. Lang. Lit.

US
AFRICANA ANNUAL. *See Library and Information Sciences.*

●US/1055-7385
AFRO-AMERICAN HISTORY KIT (7TH GRADE AND ABOVE ED.). *See History(General)-History of North, South, and Central America.*

US/0364-2437
AFRO-AMERICANS IN NEW YORK LIFE AND HISTORY. [Afro-Am. N.Y. life hist.]. **Added/Corp** Afro-American Historical Association of the Niagara Frontier. Vol. 1 (Jan. 1977)-. Periodical. English. sa (Jan., July). $8.00 US; $12.00 other. Afro-Americans in New York Life, Box 1663, Buffalo NY 14216. **ED** Monroe Fordham. **LC** F128.9.N4; A36. **DD** 974.7/004/96073. **Bk Rev.** (Qty: 6 per year). **Ad Acc. Pr Rev. Circ:** 800 (ctrl).
Desc: Interdisciplinary journal on Afro-Americans in New York state life and history.
Ind/Abst Am. Hist. Life (1977-).

●US/1056-8689
AFROCENTRIC SCHOLAR, THE. **Added/Corp** West Virginia University. Center for Black Culture and Research. (1992)-. Periodical. English. Twice a year. $30.00 (individuals); $64.00 (institutions). National Council For Black Studies, 208 Mount Hall, 1050 Carmack Road, Columbus OH 43210. **Tel** (304)293-7029.

●US/1066-3053
AFROTECH ENVIRONMENTALIST. *See Environmental Issues.*

●US/1072-1150
AGENDA, JEWISH EDUCATION. *See Education.*

US
AIM : AMERICAS INTERCULTURAL MAGAZINE. *See Sociology.*

US/0194-2069
AIM FOR RACIAL HARMONY & PEACE. *Title Change. See Sociology.*

CN/0384-8469
AJAKIRI. No. 1 (Jan. 1976)-. Periodical. Estonian (English). ir. 13.00Can$ Canada; 12.00Can$ US. Aja Kiri, 2661 Kingston Road, Scarborough Ontario M1M 1M3 Canada. **Tel** (905)265-2458. **ED** Vello Salo. **DD** 971/.004/94545. Index available. **Bk Rev. Ad Acc. Circ:** 500. available on microfiche.
Desc: Survey of Estonian culture (language, literature, history etc.) in Estonia and abroad.

US/0002-3949
AKWESASNE NOTES. *Suspended. See Sociology-Manners and Customs.*

US/1066-3479
AL-FAJR : JERUSALEM PALESTINIAN WEEKLY. *Suspended.* **VFOAT** Dawn. (1980)-(19??). Periodical. English. wk. $50.00 (individual). Al - Fajr Newspaper, 16 Crowell Street, Hempstead NY 11550. **Tel** (516)485-5736.
Ind/Abst Hum. Rights Intern. Rep.

US/0883-8526
ALASKA NATIVE LANGUAGE CENTER RESEARCH PAPERS. *See Linguistics.*

CN/0829-4135
ALBERTA NATIVE NEWS. [Alta. native news]. Vol. 1, No. 1 (July/Aug. 1984)-. Periodical. English. mo. 42.06Can$ (one year), 74.77Can$ (two years) Canada; 70.00Can$ (one year), 120.00Can$ other. Alberta Native News, Suite 530, 10036 Jasper Avenue, Edmonton Alberta T5J 2W2 Canada. **Tel** (403)421-7966, FAX (403)424-3951. **DD** 971.23/00497/005.

IS/0736-8518
ALEF. [Alef]. **Added/Corp** Chamah (Organization). (198?)-. Periodical. Russian. wk. $55.00. Chamah, 78 Pearl Street, New York NY 10004. **Tel** (212)943-9690. **Ad Acc.**

AT/0727-0046
ALTRO POLO. *See History(General)-History of Europe.*

XR
AMARO LAV. **Added/Corp** Czechoslovakia. Federalni Ministerstvo Prace a Socialnich Veci. Romanska Obcanska Iniciativa. (1991)-. Periodical. Czech (Slovak and Romany). mo. *Continues Lacho Lav, 0862-5476.*

US
AMBASSADOR (WASHINGTON, D.C.). (AMBASSADOR / NATIONAL ITALIAN AMERICAN FOUNDATION.). **Added/Corp** National Italian American Foundation. (19??)-. Periodical. English. Four times a year. $25.00 Comes with National Italian American Foundation membership. National Italian American Foundation, 666 11th Street Northwest, Suite 800, Washington DC 20001. **Tel** (202)683-0220.

US/0044-7471
AMERASIA JOURNAL. [Amerasia j.]. **Added/Corp** University of California, Los Angeles. Asian American Studies Center. Yale Asian American Students Association. Vol. 1 (Mar. 1971)-. Periodical. English. Three times a year (Apr., Aug., Nov.). $24.00 (individuals); $36.00 (institutions). Asian American Studies Center, University of California, 3230 Campbell Hall, Los Angeles CA 90024. **Tel** (310)825-2968, FAX (310)206-9844. **ED** Russell C. Leong, (phone: (310)206-2892) and Glenn Owotsu, (phone: (310)825-3415). **LC** E184.O6; A44. **DD** 917.3/06/9505. **CODEN** AMEJEZ. cum. index. **Bk Rev. Ad Acc, Adv Mgr:** G. Owotsu, **Tel** (310)825-3415. **Pr Rev. Circ:** 1,500. available on microfilm and microfiche from University Microfilms International (UMI). Documents available from The Genuine Article, UMI Article Clearinghouse.
Desc: Interdisciplinary analysis of Asian Americans, social historical, literary aspects; especially race and class, immigration, and community history.
Ind/Abst Acad. Abstr. Full Text Elite (July 1993-); Acad. Abstr. (July 1993-); Acad. Ind. [Computer File] (1992-); Acad. Search (July 1993-); Am. Hist. Life (1971-); Arts Humanit. Citation Index [Full Cov.]; Curr. Contents Arts Humanit.; Curr. Index J. Educ.; Expand. Acad. Index (1992-); Linguist. Lang. Behav. Abstr.; Mag. Artic. Summar. Elite (July 1993-); Mag. Artic. Summar. CD-ROM (July 1993-); Newsp. Period. Abstr. (1992-); Res. Alert [Full Cov.]; Sage Race Relat. Abstr.; Soc. Plann. Policy Dev. Abstr.; Soc. Sci. Cit. Index [Select. Cov.]; Sociol. Abstr.; West. Hist. Q.

US/0279-6201
AMERICA UKRAINIAN CATHOLIC DAILY. (AMERYKA.). [Am. Ukr. Cathol. daily]. **Added/Corp** Providence Association of Ukrainian Catholics in America. **VFOAT** America; Ukrainian Catholic Daily; Ukrainskyi Katolytskyi Shchodennyk; Amerkya Ukrains'kyi Katolyts'kyi Shchodennyk. (1912)-. Newspaper. Ukrainian (English). tw. Ameryka, 817 N Franklin St, Philadelphia PA 19123. **LC** Newspaper. available on microfilm.
Ind/Abst MLA Int. Bibl. Books Artic. Mod. Lang. Lit.

US
AMERICAN INDIAN COLLEGE STUDENTS IN NEW YORK STATE : NEW YORK STATE AMERICAN INDIAN AID FOR POSTSECONDARY EDUCATION. **Added/Corp** University of the State of New York. Native American Indian Education Unit. 1st Annual Report (1989/1990)-. English.

US/0161-6463
AMERICAN INDIAN CULTURE AND RESEARCH JOURNAL. [Am. Indian cult. res. j.]. **Added/Corp** University of California, Los Angeles. American Indian Culture and Research Center. Vol. 1 (1974)-. Periodical. English. Four times a year. $30.00 (institutions), $20.00 (individuals) US; add $5.00 postage other. UCLA American Indian Studies Center, 405 Hilgard Avenue, 3220 Campbell Hall, Los Angeles CA 90024-1548. **Tel** (310)825-7315, FAX (310)206-7060. **ED** Derek Milne (book review editor); telephone: (310)206-7508. **LC** E75; .A5124. **DD** 970/.004/97. Index available ($5.00). **Bk Rev. Ad Acc. Pr Rev. Circ:** 1,000 (ctrl). available on microfilm and microfiche from University Microfilms International (UMI). Documents available from UMI Article Clearinghouse. ***Supersedes*** *American Indian Culture Center. Journal - American Indian Culture Center.*
Desc: Research and scholarship on historical and contemporary topics of concern to American Indians, scholars and professionals who work with American Indian tribes and organizations.
Ind/Abst Abstr. Anthropol.; Am. Hist. Life (1983-); Am. Humanit. Index; Anthropol. Lit.; Arts Humanit. Citation Index [Full Cov.]; Curr. Contents Arts Humanit.; Curr. Geogr. Publ. (199?-); Curr. Index J. Educ.; Ethnoarts Index; Expand. Acad. Index (1992-); Linguist. Lang. Behav. Abstr.; Multicult. Educ. Abstr.; Newsp. Period. Abstr. (1992-); Sage Race Relat. Abstr.; Soc. Plann. Policy Dev. Abstr.; Soc. Sci. Cit. Index [Select. Cov.]; Sociol. Abstr.; Spec. Educ. Needs Abstr.; West. Hist. Q.

US/0145-9910
AMERICAN INDIAN EARLY CHILDHOOD EDUCATION. See Education-Early Childhood and Primary Education.

US/0094-002X
AMERICAN INDIAN LAW REVIEW. See Law.

US
AMERICAN INDIAN MAP BOOK SERIES. **VFOAT** American Indian Map-Book Series. Vol. 1 (1969)-. Monographic series. English. ir. Price varies per volume. Naturegraph Publishing Inc, PO Box 1075, Happy Camp CA 96309. **LC** E75; .A53.

US/0095-182X
AMERICAN INDIAN QUARTERLY. [Am. Indian q.]. **Added/Corp** University of California, Berkeley. Native American Studies. Southwestern American Indian Society (U.S.) Society for American Indian Studies & Research (U.S.). **VFOAT** AIQ, American Indian Quarterly. Vol. 1 (Spring 1974)-. Periodical. English. Four times a year (Jan., Apr., July, Oct.). $25.00 (individuals); $45.00 (institutions). University of Nebraska Press, PO Box 880484, Lincoln NE 68588-0520. **Tel** (402)472-3584, (800)755-1105, FAX (402)472-6214, (800)526-2617. **(Subscription address:** NAS/3415 Dwinelle Hall, Berkeley, CA 94720) **ED** Robert Black (phone: (510)642-6607). **LC** E75; .A547. **DD** 970/.004/97. **CODEN** AIQEW. **Bk Rev. Ad Acc. Pr Rev. Circ:** 650. available on microfilm and microfiche from University Microfilms International (UMI). Documents available from UMI Article Clearinghouse.
Desc: Provides a forum for contemporary scholarship and research in American Indian studies from an interdisciplinary perspective.
Ind/Abst Abstr. Engl. Stud.; Acad. Abstr. Full Text Elite (Jan. 1990-); Acad. Abstr. (Jan. 1990-); Acad. Ind. [Computer File] (1992-); Acad. Search (Jan. 1990-); Am. Hist. Life (1974-); Annu. Bibliogr. Engl. Lang. Lit.; Anthropol. Lit.; ARTbibliogr. Mod.; Book Rev. Index (?-?); Curr. Index J. Educ.; Ethnoarts Index; Expand. Acad. Index (1989-); Humanit. Index; Humanit. Source (Jul. 1990-); INFO-SOUTH Abstr.; Linguist. Lang. Behav. Abstr.; Mag. Search; MLA Int. Bibl. Books Artic. Mod. Lang. Lit.; Newsp. Period. Abstr. (1990-); Sage Race Relat. Abstr.; Soc. Plann. Policy Dev. Abstr.; Sociol. Abstr.; West. Hist. Q.

●US/1058-563X
AMERICAN INDIAN STUDIES. [Am. Indian stud.]. Vol. 1 (1992)-. Monographic series. English. ir. Price varies per volume. Verlag Peter Lang AG, Jupiterstrasse 15, CH-3000 Bern 15 Switzerland. **Tel** 011 41 31 9411122, FAX 011 41 31 321131. **(Subscription address:** Peter Lang Publishing Inc., 62 West 45th Street, 4th Floor, New York NY 10036.) **DD** 970.

US/0002-905X
AMERICAN JEWISH ARCHIVES. [Am. Jew. arch.]. **Added/Corp** Hebrew Union College-Jewish Institute of Religion. American Jewish Archives. Hebrew Union College. Vol. 1 (June 1948)-. Academic Scholarly Publication. English. ir. Price varies. American Jewish Archives, 3101 Clifton Avenue, Cincinnati OH 45220. **Tel** (513)221-1875 ext. 216, FAX (513)221-7812. **ED** Abraham J. Peck and Jacob B. Marcus. **LC** E184.J5; A37. **DD** 296. Index available. cum. index. **Bk Rev. Pr Rev. Circ:** 5,000 (ctrl). available on microfilm and microfiche from University Microfilms International (UMI). Documents available from The Genuine Article.
Desc: Scholarly articles and reviews which detail some significant experience.
Ind/Abst Am. Hist. Life (1954-); Am. Bibliogr. Slavic East Europ. Stud.; Arts Humanit. Citation Index (19??-19??) [Full Cov.]; Curr. Contents Arts Humanit.; Index Book Rev. Relig.; Index Jew. Period.; Middle East Abstr. Index; Relig. Index One Period.; Res. Alert [Full Cov.]; West. Hist. Q.

US/0164-0178
AMERICAN JEWISH HISTORY. [Am. Jew. hist.]. **Added/Corp** American Jewish Historical Society. Vol. 68 (Sept. 1978)-. Periodical. English. Four times a year (Jan., Apr., July, Oct.). $60.00 US; $63.50 Canada and Mexico; $67.00 other. Johns Hopkins University Press, 2715 North Charles Street, Baltimore MD 21218-4319. **Tel** (410)516-6987, FAX (410)516-6968. **(Subscription address:** John Hopkins University Press, Journals Publishing Division, PO Box 19966, Baltimore MD 21211.) **ED** Marc L. Raphael and Jeffrey Gurock. **LC** E184.J5; A5. **DD** 970/.004/924. Index available. cum. index. **Bk Rev. Ad Acc. Circ:** 3,300 (ctrl). available on microfiche. Documents available from The Genuine Article, UMI Article Clearinghouse. ***Continues*** *American Jewish Historical Quarterly, 0002-9068.*
Desc: Contains articles, book reviews, and bibliographies relating to the history of the Jews in the western hemisphere from the period of earliest settlement to the present day.
Ind/Abst Acad. Search (July 1991-); Am. Hist. Life (1954-); Am. Bibliogr. Slavic East Europ. Stud.; Annu. Bibliogr. Engl. Lang. Lit.; Arts Humanit. Citation Index [Full Cov.]; Curr. Contents Arts Humanit.; Expand. Acad. Index (1989-); Film Lit. Index (19??-); Hist. Source (July 1993-); Humanit. Index; Humanit. Source (Jul. 1993-); Index Book Rev. Relig.; Index Jew. Period. (19??-199?); INFO-SOUTH Abstr.; Int. Bibliogr. Sociol.; Mag. Search; Middle East Abstr. Index; Newsp. Period. Abstr. (1990-); Res. Alert [Full Cov.]; U.S. Polit. Sci. Doc. (-199?).

US/1043-7029
AMERRIKUA! (SCHUYLER FALLS, N.Y.). ***Ceased.*** (AMERRIKUA!). [Amerrikua!]. (Winter 1983)-(199?). Periodical. English (Spanish). sa. Amerrikua, c/o Don Papson, PO Box 35, Schuyler Falls NY 12985. **Tel** (518)643-9254. **ED** Don Papson, RR 1, Box 280, Saranac, NY 12981, (518)293-7119. **DD** 909. **Bk Rev**, (Qty: 4-6). **Ad Acc, Adv Mgr:** Donald Papson. **Circ:** 500 (ctrl).
Desc: A cross-cultural review of native and non-native people of the Americas. Seeks to rediscover ancient universal roots and to celebrate the birth of a world civilization based on wisdom and understanding.

FR/0220-4592
AMITIES ACADIENNES. (LES AMITIES ACADIENNES : [REVUE].). [Amities acadiennes]. **Added/Corp** Amities Acadiennes (Association). (1977)-. Periodical. French. Four times a year. 75.00F France; 100.00F others. Les Amities Acadiennes, 17 Quai de Grenelle, 75015 Paris France. **Tel** 011 33 1 45750999. **DD** 305.811/40715.

FR/0399-0443
ANNALES DU CENTRE DE RECHERCHES SUR L'AMERIQUE ANGLOPHONE. See Literature.

US/0740-8536
ANNALS OF THE CHINESE HISTORICAL SOCIETY OF THE PACIFIC NORTHWEST / MEI-KUO HSI PEI HUA JEN LI SHIH HSUEH HUI, THE. [Ann. Chin. Hist. Soc. Pac. Northwest]. **Added/Corp** Chinese Historical Society of the Pacific Northwest. **VFOAT** Mei-kuo hsi pei Hua jen li Shih Hsueh hui Nien kan. (1983)-. Periodical. English (Chinese). an. **LC** F855.2.C5; A56. **DD** 979.5/004951.
Ind/Abst Am. Hist. Life.

US/0360-3687
ANNUAL REPORT - AMERICAN INSTITUTE OF INDIAN STUDIES. **Main/Corp** American Institute of Indian Studies. English. an. AIIS, 1130 E 59th Street, University of Chicago, Chicago IL 60637.

US
ANNUAL REPORT OF INDIAN EDUCATION IN EASTERN OKLAHOMA. See Education.

AT/0812-566X
ANNUAL REPORT / VICTORIAN ETHNIC AFFAIRS COMMISSION. See Public Administration.

AT
ANNUAL REPORT / VICTORIAN MINISTRY OF IMMIGRATION & ETHNIC AFFAIRS. See Emigration and Immigration.

CN/0003-5459
ANTHROPOLOGICA (OTTAWA). See Anthropology.

●US/1067-9464
APA NEWSLETTERS ON THE BLACK EXPERIENCE, COMPUTER USE, FEMINISM, LAW, MEDICINE, TEACHING. See Philosophy.

US/0279-9804
APUNTES (DALLAS, TEX.). See Religion and Theology.

AT
ARCHIVE OF AUSTRALIAN JUDAICA HOLDINGS TO ... . See Genealogy and Heraldry-Archives.

IT/0392-1050
ARCHIVIO PER L'ALTO ADIGE. [Arch. Alto Adige]. **Added/Corp** Istituto di Studi per l'Alto Adige, Florence. (1906)-. Italian (German, French, English and Latin). an. L80000 Italy; L90000 other. Istituto Studi Alto Adige, Via C Battisti 4, 50122 Florence Italy. **Tel** 011 39 55 211355. Index available. **Bk Rev. Circ:** 200.
Desc: Deals with cultural inquiries in the alpine regions. Subjects include linguistics, toponomy, folklore, ethnography.
Ind/Abst BHA : Biblio. Hist. Art; MLA Int. Bibl. Books Artic. Mod. Lang. Lit.

AT/0570-720X
ARCHIVS. See Anthropology.

US/0360-0467
AREITO. [Areito]. Yearly Vol. 1 (April 1974)-. Periodical. Spanish (English). qt. $20.00 (institutions), $12.00 (individuals) US and Puerto Rico; $30.00 (institutions), $18.00 (individuals) other. Areito Inc, PO Box 441803, Miami FL 33144. **Tel** (212)245-8829. **ED** Iraida Lopez-Iniguez. **LC** F1751; .A68. **Bk Rev. Ad Acc. Circ:** 4,000.
Desc: Latin America/Caribbean: socio-political and cultural issues, Hispanic minorities in the US.
Ind/Abst HAPI Hisp. Am. Period. Index (19??-); Index Am. Period. Verse.

US
ARKANSAS STATE PRESS. **VFOAT** State Press. Vol. 19, No. 26 (Apr. 11, l984)-. Newspaper. English. wk. $20.00. Arkansas State Press, PO Box 164 037, Little Rock AR 72216. **Tel** (501)371-9991.

RU/0004-2293
ARMENIA TODAY. **Added/Corp** Armenian Society of Friendship and Cultural Relations with Foreign Countries. (19??)-. Periodical. English.
Ind/Abst Numis. Lit.

US/1070-3969
ASIAN AMERICAN NEWS (HOUSTON, TEX.). (ASIAN AMERICAN NEWS.). [Asian Am. news]. Vol. 1, No. 1, (June 1991)-. Newspaper. English. Twelve times a year. $30.00 one year. NFAAUM, 330 Ellis Street, Room 508, San Francisco CA 94102. **Tel** (415)776-7747, FAX (415)776-1154. **ED** Douglas Franks. **DD** 051. **Bk Rev. Circ:** 2,000 (ctrl).
Desc: News and resources relevant to Asian-American United Methodists and non-Asians interest in Asian constituencies in the churches.

US/1062-1830
ASIAN AMERICAN POLICY REVIEW. [Asian Am. policy rev.]. **Added/Corp** John F. Kennedy School of Government. University of California, Berkeley. Graduate School of Public Policy. (1990)-. Periodical. English. an. $5.00 students, $10.00 individuals, $25.00 institutions. Harvard University / JFK School of Government, 79 JFK Street, Cambridge MA 02138. **Tel** (617)495-1100, FAX (617)495-1972. **ED** Bonaparte Liu, Linda Yuch (617)495-1311. **DD** 327. **Bk Rev**, (Qty: 1-2). **Ad Acc, Adv Mgr:** Grace Kim.

●US/1059-2458
ASIAN AMERICANS INFORMATION DIRECTORY. [Asian Am. inf. dir.]. **Added/Corp** Gale Research Inc. (1992)-. Directory. English. ir. $75.00. Gale Research Inc., 835 Penobscot Building, Detroit MI 48226. **Tel** (800)877-GALE, (313)961-2242, FAX (313)961-6083, telex TWX 810-221-7086. **ED** Charles B. Montney. **LC** E184.O6; A844. **DD** 973/.0495/0025. available on magnetic tape; available on diskette.
Desc: Contains more than 5,200 listings that direct users to organizations, agencies, institutions, programs, services and publications concerned with Asian American life and culture.

US
ASMAT SKETCH BOOK, AN. See Anthropology.

GW/0722-3587
ASSISTENZ. [Assistenz]. (1982)-. Periodical. German. bm. DM198.00. FBO Fachverlag GmbH, Postfach 316, D-76482 Baden-Baden Germany. **Tel** 011 49 7221 271066-68, FAX 07221/33228. **UDC** 651.44. ***Continues*** *Sekretarin, 0170-5377.*

Ethnic Interests

US
ATLANTA DAILY WORLD. Vol. 5, No. 36 (March 18, 1932)-. Newspaper. English. da. $65.00. Atlanta Daily World, 145 Auburn Avenue, Atlanta GA 30335-1201. **Tel** (404)659-1110. **ED** C.A. Scott and Portia Scott (Managing Editor). **LC** Newspaper. **Bk Rev**. **Photos**. **Ad Acc**, **Adv Mgr:** J.R. Simmons. Full Page (B&W) $1,499.40. Half Page (B&W) $749.70. **Pub. Size:** Standard. **Wire Svcs.:** API, UPI, NP. **Circ:** 18,000 (Sun.), 16,000 (weekdays). available on microfilm. *Continues Atlanta World.*

PL/0137-8570
AUSRA. **Added/Corp** Lietuviu VisuomeninÄes Kulturos Draugija (Poland). Centro Valdyba. (19??)-. Periodical. Lithuanian. Twenty-six times a year. z41.00. **(Subscription address:** ARS Polona, PO Box 1001, 00068 Warsaw, Poland) **LC** DK4121.5.L56; A93. **Ind/Abst** Hum. Rights Intern. Rep.

AT/0729-4352
AUSTRALIAN ABORIGINAL STUDIES (CANBERRA, A.C.T. : 1983). See History(General)-History of Australia and Oceania.

AT/0811-2908
AUSTRALIAN ABORIGINES IN THE NEWS. GEOGRAPHIC GUIDE TO HEADINGS AND INDEX TO THE CLIPPINGS. *Ceased.* [Aust. Aborig. news, Geogr. guide head. index clipp.]. **Added/Corp** Australian Institute of Aboriginal Studies. (1981)-(1992). Periodical. English. Twice a year. Australian Institute of Aboriginal and Torres Strait Island Studies, PO Box 553, Canberra ACT 2601 Australia. **Tel** 011 061 6 2461111, FAX 011 061 6 2497310. **DD** 305.89915.

AT/1037-0838
AUSTRALIAN JOURNAL OF JEWISH STUDIES. **Added/Corp** Australian Association for Jewish Studies. **VFOAT** AJJS. Vol. 5, No. 1 (1991)-. Periodical. English. Twice a year (June, Dec.). 40.00Aus$ Australia; 50.00Aus$ others. Australian Association of Jewish Studies, PO Box 255, Camberwell VIC 3124 Australia. **Tel** 011 61 3 4792368, FAX 03 882-0259. **LC** DS135.A88; M46. **DD** 994/.004924/005. **Bk Rev**. **Circ:** 150. *Continues Menorah (Australian Association for Jewish Studies), 0819-9957.*

FR/0764-7573
AWAL. [Awal]. **Added/Corp** Maison des Sciences de l'Homme (Paris, France) Centre d'Etudes et de Recherches Amazigh (France). No. 1 (1985)-. Periodical. French (Berber languages and English; summaries and/or abstracts in Spanish). an. 170.00F France; 190.00F other. Centre d'Etudes et de Recherches Amazigh, 4 rue de Chevreuse, 75006 Paris France. **Tel** 46 33 04 34. **LC** DT193.5.B45; A9. **DD** 305.8/933/005. **Desc:** Publication for those interested in Berbers and their culture. **Ind/Abst** Anthropol. Lit.

US/0749-1816
AWANYU. See Archaeology.

CN/0823-9231
AWASIS (JOURNAL). (AWASIS : THE JOURNAL OF THE INDIAN/NATIVE EDUCATION COUNCIL.). [Awasis]. Vol. 1, No. 1 (Fall 1981)-. English. Free to Members. Indian/Native Education Council, PO Box 1108, Saskatoon Saskatchewan S7K 3N3 Canada. **DD** 371.97/97/07124.

US/0005-2604
AZTLAN. [Aztlan]. **Added/Corp** University of California, Los Angeles. Chicano Studies Center. University of California, Los Angeles. Mexican American Cultural Center. University of California, Los Angeles. Chicano Cultural Center. Vol. 1 (Spring 1970)-. Periodical. English. Twice a year. $15.00 (individuals) $35.00 (institutions) US & Mexico; $25.00 (individuals), $45.00 (institutions) others. Chicano Studies Research Center, UCLA, 405 Hilgard Avenue, Los Angeles CA 90024. **Tel** (310)825-2642. **LC** E184.M5; A98. available on microfilm and microfiche from University Microfilms International (UMI). Documents available from UMI Article Clearinghouse. **Desc:** A multidisciplinary journal devoted to research on the immigration, education, social welfare, history, language, and artistic and cultural expression of the Mexican-origin population. **Ind/Abst** Acad. Ind. [Computer File] (1987-); Acad. Search (Jan. 1992-); Am. Hist. Life (1970-); Chicano Index; Curr. Index J. Educ.; Ethnoarts Index; Expand. Acad. Index (1987-); HAPI Hisp. Am. Period. Index; INFO-SOUTH Abstr.; Linguist. Lang. Behav. Abstr.; MLA Int. Bibl. Books Artic. Mod. Lang. Lit.; Newsp. Period. Abstr. (1991-); PAIS Int. Print (1991-?); Relig. Index One Period. (1982-); Sage Race Relat. Abstr.; Soc. Plann. Policy Dev. Abstr.; Soc. Sci. Source (Jul. 1993-); Soc. Sci. Index; Soc. Sci. Index Fulltext (Fall 1986-) [Full Txt.]; Sociol. Abstr.

CN/0845-4817
BAN VIET (1987). (BAN VIET). **Added/Corp** Vietnamese Association Toronto. **VFOAT** Vietnamese Monthly Magazine. (1987)-. Periodical. Vietnamese (summaries and/or abstracts in English). Twelve times a year. 30.00Can$ (individual), 40.00Can$ (institution), Canada; 50.00Can$ other. Banviet, 1364 Dundas Street West, Toronto ONT M6J 1Y2 Canada. **Tel** (416)536-3611 or 536-3358, FAX (416)536-8364. **ED** Hoang Trong. **DD** 059/.95922. **Ad Acc**, **Adv Mgr:** Nghi Do, **Tel** (416)536-3611. **Circ:** 2,200. *Continues Nguyet San Ban Viet, 0821-7297.*

●US/1062-0486
BANDELE'S ANNUAL VENDOR'S GUIDE TO AFRICAN-AMERICAN EVENTS. **VFOAT** Annual Vendor's Guide to African-American Events. (1992)-. English. $15.00. Bandele Publications, PO Box 21540, Washington DC 20009.

US/0276-7902
BARRIO (WASHINGTON, D.C.), EL. (EL BARRIO.). Vol. 1, No. 1 (Aug. 1981)-. Periodical. Spanish. mo. $5.00. El Barrio Centro de Juventud Latinoamericana, 3045 15th Street NW, Washington DC 20009.

IS/0302-8178
BAY ZIK. See Literature.

CN
BEEDAUDJIMOWIN. (19??)-. Periodical. English. qt. 20.00Can$ (institutions), 10.00Can$ (individuals) Canada; 25.00Can$ (institutions), 15.00Can$ (individuals) other. Native Peoples Research, 512 Lansdowne Avenue, Suite 12, Toronto Ontario M6H 3Y3 Canada. **Tel** (416)534-4811, FAX (416)535-1273. **Bk Rev**. **Ad Acc**. **Circ:** over 15,000. **Desc:** Dedicated to publishing information about the struggles of Indigenous peoples world-wide as a means of educating both Native and non-Native people. Committed to promoting the uniqueness of First Nations people from the perspective of First Nations people.

US/0148-8198
BIENNIAL REPORT - NEVADA INDIAN COMMISSION. **Main/Corp** Nevada. Indian Commission. English. be. Nevada Indian Commission, 1135 Terminal Way, Suite 109, Reno NV 89502. **LC** E78.N4; N39. **DD** 353.9/793/008484. *Continues Nevada Indian Affairs Commission. Report.*

US/0360-7518
BIENNIAL REPORT - OKLAHOMA INDIAN AFFAIRS COMMISSION. **Main/Corp** Oklahoma. Indian Affairs Commission. English. be. Oklahoma Indian Affairs Commission, 4901 North Lincoln Blvd, Oklahoma City OK 73105. **LC** E78.O45; O37A. **DD** 353.9/766/008484.

US
BIRMINGHAM TIMES, THE. (1964)-. Periodical. English. Fifty-two times a year. $25.00. The Birmingham Times, PO Box 10503, 115 West 3rd Avenue, Birmingham AL 35202-0503. **Tel** (205)251-5158, FAX (205)323-2294. **ED** Bernadette Wiggins. **Bk Rev** (Qty: 25 per year). **Ad Acc**, **Adv Mgr:** Comer Allen, **Tel** (205)251-5158. Full Page (B&W) $1,325.52. Half Page (B&W) $662.76. **Pub. Size:** Standard. **Circ:** 16,500. **Desc:** Documents African-American history in Birmingham, Alabama. Welcomes all points of view that have a presence within the Birmingham community.

CN/0503-1036
BJULETEN' - KOMITETU UKRAJINCIV KANADY. See History(General)-History of North, South, and Central America.

US/0882-6595
BLACFAX. [Blacfax]. Vol. 1, No. 1 (Winter 1982)-. Periodical. English. Four times a year. $8.00. Blacfax, 214 West 138th Street, New York NY 10030. **Tel** (212)234-4115. **ED** R. Edward Lee and Janet Hughes. **DD** 305. Index available. **Ad Acc**. **Circ:** 1,500. **Desc:** An account of life in the U.S. for blacks with history and commentary. Each issue generally includes a cartoon, poetry, crosswords, quizzes and biography. **Ind/Abst** Mag. Artic. Summar. Elite (July 1994-).

US/1045-8050
BLACK AMERICANS INFORMATION DIRECTORY. [Black Am. inf. dir.]. **Added/Corp** Gale Research Inc. **VFOAT** BAID. 1st Ed. (1990/1991)-. Directory. English. an. $79.00. Gale Research Inc., 835 Penobscot Building, Detroit MI 48226. **Tel** (800)877-GALE, (313)961-2242, FAX (313)961-6083, telex TWX 810-221-7086. **ED** Wendy S. Van de Sande. **LC** E185.5; .B513. **DD** 973/.0496073/0025. **Desc:** Essential timesaver for black Americans and those seeking information about black American life and culture. Over 5,200 entries provide contact information on a wide range of nonprofit, private, public, educational, and governmental organizations and agencies concerned with black Americans.

US/1055-0976
BLACK AND GAY. (1991)-. English. $12.95. Fondren Enterprises 2000, 216 Avenue T, Pratt City, Birmingham AL 35214.

US/1042-7104
BLACK ARTS ANNUAL. See The Arts-Art.

US/0745-8649
BLACK BEAT. See Music.

US
BLACK BOOKS BULLETIN. WORDS WORK. See Literature.

US
BLACK CAMERA : THE NEWSLETTER OF THE BLACK FILM CENTER / ARCHIVES. See Motion Picture.

●US/1058-5680
BLACK COLLEGES AND UNIVERSITIES LISTING. (BLACK COLLEGES AND UNIVERSITIES LISTING/ MSII ENTERPRISES.). **VFOAT** MSII Enterprises Black Colleges and Universities Listing. (1992)-. English. $6.00. MSII Enterprises, 1004 Rhode Island Avenue NW, Washington DC 20001.

US/0895-1780
BLACK CONGRESSIONAL MONITOR. [Black Congr. monit.]. **VFOAT** BCM. (1987)-. Periodical. English. sm. $39.00 (one year), $74.00 (two year). Len Mor Publications, PO Box 75035, Washington DC 20013. **Tel** (202)488-8879, FAX (202)554-3116. **ED** Lenora Moragne. **DD** 328. **Desc:** Review of legislative initiatives of African Americans in the US Congress; plus information on available grants, contracts, scholarships, and public hearings and meetings.

US/0882-1593
BLACK ELECTED OFFICIALS. See Political Science.

US/0885-9647
BLACK ELEGANCE. See General Interest-General Interest-North America.

US/1043-6677
BLACK ETHNIC COLLECTIBLES. [Black ethn. collect.]. (198?)-. Periodical. English. qt (4 issues). $35.00. Black Ethnic Collectibles, 1401 Asbury Court, Hyattsville MD 20782. **Tel** (301)559-6363. **ED** Jeannette Carson. **DD** 302. **Desc:** Black memorabilia from Aunt Jemima to children's books and art is featured in 45 illustrated pages. Price news, regional activities, conventions, shows, personalities, etc. are covered. There are five to six articles on various collectibles. Each issue opens with a special feature in which a collecting topic is treated in great detail.

US/0279-0718
BLACK FAMILY. [Black fam.]. **VFOAT** Black Family Magazine. Vol. 1, No. 1 (3rd Quarter, 1980)-. Periodical. English. ir. $17.00. Black Family Publications Inc, PO Box 1046, Herndon VA 22070. **Tel** (703)860-3411. **ED** Frank C. Kent. **LC** WMLC 93/238. **Bk Rev**. **Ad Acc**. **Circ:** 250,000 (ctrl). **Desc:** A magazine for the entire black family. Features include health, food, home enhancement ideas, success stories of black Americans, black history features, fiction and nonfiction photo essays, and discussion of current issues facing black families.

US/0045-2165
BLACK GRAPHICS INTERNATIONAL. See The Arts.

US/1055-0550
BLACK HISTORY IS NO MYSTERY. [Black hist. no mystery]. Vol. 1, No. 1 (1991)-. Periodical. English. qt. $15.00. Quest Company, 473 Massachusetts Avenue, Boston MA 02118. **Tel** (617)267-4079. **DD** 305.

●US/1054-8769
BLACK HISTORY MONTHLY (LITTLE ROCK, ARK.). (BLACK HISTORY MONTHLY.). (1992)-. Periodical. English. mo. $1.95 (single issue). Zinse Agginie, POB 1565, Little Rock AR 72203.

US/0742-0277
BLACK ISSUES IN HIGHER EDUCATION. See Education-Higher Education.

US/1049-3298
BLACK LACE. See Homosexuality.

US/0276-3605
BLACK MUSIC RESEARCH JOURNAL. See Music.

US/0740-929X
BLACK NATION, THE. *Suspended.* [Black nation]. Began with issue for summer 1981-Suspended with Vol. 5, No.1. Periodical. English. sa. $10.00. Getting Together Publications, PO Box 29293, Oakland CA 94604. **Tel** (510)652-4327.

US/1063-0473
BLACK PAGES OF AMERICA. **VFOAT** Black Pages of America-Raleigh-Durham Edition. (1991)-. English. Black Pages of America, National Headquarters, 101 North 6th Street, Richmond VA 23219. **DD** 338.

Ethnic Interests

US/1063-0449
BLACK PAGES OF AMERICA (BALTIMORE METROPLITAN ED.). (BLACK PAGES OF AMERICA.). [Black pages Am.]. **VFOAT** Black Pages of America, Baltimore. (1991)-. English. Black Pages of America, National Headquarters, 101 North 6th Street, Richmond VA 23219. **DD** 338.

US/1063-0457
BLACK PAGES OF AMERICA (HAMPTON ROADS METROPOLITAN ED.). (BLACK PAGES OF AMERICA.). [Black pages Am.]. **VFOAT** Black Pages of America, Hampton Roads. (1990/91)-. English. Black Pages of America, National Headquarters, 101 North 6th Street, Richmond VA 23219. **DD** 338.

US/1060-3921
BLACK PAGES OF AMERICA (WASHINGTON, D.C., METROPOLITAN ED.). (BLACK PAGES OF AMERICA.). [Black pages Am.]. **VFOAT** Black Pages of America, Washington. (1991)-. Periodical. English. Black Pages of America, National Headquarters, 101 North 6th Street, Richmond VA 23219. **DD** 338.

US
BLACK POST. (1977)-. Newspaper. English. wk (Published on Fridays) $35.00. SC Black Media Group, PO Box 11128, Columbia SC 29211. **Tel** (803)799-5252, FAX (803)799-7709. **Continues** Sumter Black Post. **Desc:** Publication about Afro-Americans.

US/0882-0643
BLACK RESOURCE GUIDE, THE. [Black resour. guide]. (1981)-. English. an. $69.95. Black Resource Guide Inc, 501 Oneida Place Northwest, Washington DC 20011. **Tel** (202)291-4373. **ED** R. Benjamin Johnson. **LC** E185.5; .B565. **DD** 973/.0496073/0025. Index available. cum. index. **Bk Rev. Circ:** 25,000 (ctrl). available on diskette. **Desc:** Gives immediate access to key blacks in America. This highly acclaimed reference book puts you in touch with politicians, church leaders, lawyers, bankers, colleges, business leaders, public administrators and national associations. Feature listings in over 50 categories.

SA
BLACK REVIEW. Added/Corp Black Community Programmes (Agency). (1972)-. English. an. Black Community Programmes, 86 Beatrice Street, Durban South Africa. **LC** DT763.6; .B45. **DD** 301.45/19/6068.

US/0006-4246
BLACK SCHOLAR, THE. [Black sch.]. **Added/Corp** Black World Foundation (U.S.). Vol. 1 (Nov. 1969)-. Periodical. English. qt (4 issues). $50.00 (institution), $30.00 (individual) US. Black Scholar Press, PO Box 2869, Oakland CA 94609. **Tel** (510)547-6633, FAX (510)547-6679. **ED** Robert Chrisman and Jonina Abron. **LC** E185.5; .B575. **DD** 301.451/96/073. Index available (bound in Sept. issue). **Bk Rev. Ad Acc. Circ:** 9,000 (ctrl). available on microfilm and microfiche from University Microfilms International (UMI). Documents available from The Genuine Article, UMI Article Clearinghouse.
Ind/Abst Abstr. Engl. Stud.; Acad. Abstr. Full Text Elite (July 1990-); Acad. Abstr. (July 1990-); Acad. Ind. [Computer File] (1987-); Acad. Search (July 1990-); Altern. Press Index; Am. Hist. Life (1989-); Annu. Bibliogr. Engl. Lang. Lit.; Book Rev. Index; Chicano Index; Contents Pages Educ.; Curr. Contents Soc. Behav. Sci.; Curr. Index J. Educ.; Expand. Acad. Index (1987-); Guide Soc. Sci. Relig.; INFO-SOUTH Abstr.; Infobank (Jan. 1969-); Left Index; Linguist. Lang. Behav. Abstr.; Mag. Search; Newsp. Period. Abstr. (1988-); PAIS Int. Print (1991-); Res. Alert [Full Cov.]; Sage Race Relat. Abstr.; Soc. Plann. Policy Dev. Abstr.; Soc. Sci. Source (Jul. 1990-); Soc. Sci. Cit. Index [Full Cov.]; Soc. Sci. Index; Soc. Sci. Index Fulltext (July 1988-) [Full Txt.]; Soc. Work Abstr. [Select. Cov.]; Sociol. Abstr.; Women Stud. Abstr.

US/1071-9830
BLACK SECRETS. [Black secrets]. **VFOAT** Secrets. (1990)-. Periodical. English. bm. $10.00 (one year), $19.00 (two year). Sterling Macfadden, 233 Park Avenue South, New York NY 10003. **Tel** (212)979-4800. **DD** 051. **Continues** Secrets, 0037-0649.

US
BLACK SUN (COLUMBIA, S.C. : FLORENCE ED.). (1977)-. Newspaper. English. wk (Thursdays) $25.00. SC Black Media Group, PO Box 11128, Columbia SC 29211. **Tel** (803)799-5252, FAX (803)799-7709. available on microfilm.
Desc: Includes Afro-American interests.

US/1062-3825
BLACK TALENT NEWS. See The Arts-Performing Arts.

US
BLACK VIEW. Title Change. Vol. 1 (Nov. 1973)-(19??)-. Periodical. English. Impact Publications / California, Box 2368, Inglewood CA 90305. **Supersedes** Black View. **Continued by** Umoja Sasa.

US
BLACK VOICE NEWS, THE. Vol. 18, No. 40 (Nov. 1, 1990)-. Newspaper. English. wk. $39.00. Hardy and Cheryl Brown, PO Box 1581, Riverside CA 92502. **Tel** (909)682-6070. **ED** Cheryl Brown. **Bk Rev,** (Qty: 12-25). **Ad Acc. Circ:** 7,500 (ctrl). available on microfilm. **Continues** Voice (Riverside, Calif.).

●US/1049-3271
BLACKFIRE. [Blackfire]. **VFOAT** Black Fire. (1992)-. Periodical. English. bm. $5.95. BLK Publishing Company, PO Box 83912, Los Angeles CA 90083-0912. **Tel** (310)410-0808, FAX (310)410-9250. **ED** Alan Bell. **DD** 051.
Desc: Blackfire is a erotic magazine featuring handsome black men in sizzling photographs and tantalizing fiction.

PL/0006-470X
BLETER FAR GESHIKHTE. [Bl. gesz.]. **Added/Corp** Zydowski Instytut Historyczny w Polsce. **VFOAT** Bleter far Geszichte. (1948)-. Yiddish (summaries and/or abstracts in English, French, Polish and Russian). ir. **LC** DS135.P6; B54.
Ind/Abst Am. Hist. Life (1954-1970,1980-).

BO
BOLETIN CHITAKOLLA : EDICION MENSUAL DEL CENTRO DE FORMACION E INVESTIGACION DE LAS CULTURAS INDIAS. Added/Corp Centro de Formacion e Investigacion de las Culturas Indias (La Paz, Bolivia). (19??)-. Periodical. Spanish. mo.
Ind/Abst Hum. Rights Intern. Rep.

PE
BOLETIN COPAL. Periodical. Spanish. Santa Isabel 180, Lima 18 Peru.

VE
BOLETIN DEL PROGRAMA ARQUEOLOGIA DE RESCATE / CORPOZULIA -UNIVERSIDAD DEL ZULIA, CENTRO DE ESTUDIOS HISTORICOS. See Archaeology.

US/0738-5161
BOYCOTT REPORT. [Boycott rep.]. **Added/Corp** American Jewish Congress. **VFOAT** Developments and Trends Affecting the Arab Boycott. Vol. 1 (Mar. 1977)-. Periodical. English. Nine times a year (three double issues). $40.00. American Jewish Congress, 15 East 84th Street, New York NY 10028. **Tel** (212)879-4500 Ext.200/212, FAX (212)249-3672. **ED** Will Maslow. **DD** 337. **Circ:** 5,000 (ctrl).
Desc: Developments and trends affecting the Arab Boycott of Israel and Arab influence in the USA.

US/0892-6220
BRANCHES (BERKELEY, CALIF.). (BRANCHES.). [Branches]. **Added/Corp** Pacific & Asian American Center for Theology & Strategies (Berkeley, Calif.). Vol. 1, No. 1 (Winter 1979)-. Periodical. English. an. $25.00 Comes with Pacific People. Pacific and Asian American Center for Theology and Strategies, 1798 Scenic Avenue, Berkeley CA 94703. **Tel** (510)849-0653. **LC** BR1; .B83. **DD** 230/.08995073.

US/1065-1462
BROWARD TIMES, THE. (19??)-. Newspaper. English. wk. $35.00. Broward Times, 2001 West Sample Road, Suite 140, Pampano Beach FL 33064. **Tel** (305)968-3656.

US/0045-3285
BUCKEYE REVIEW. (THE BUCKEYE REVIEW.). **VFOAT** Review. (Apr. 1937)-. Newspaper. English. Fifty-two times a year (Fridays). $15.00. Williams Publishing Company, 620 Belmont Avenue, Youngstown OH 44502. **Tel** (216)743-2250. **ED** Crystal Ann Williams. **Bk Rev. Ad Acc. Circ:** 5,000.
Desc: Positive achievements of black Americans and minorities. News that affects the minority communities of Youngstown and Warren, Ohio. Miscellaneous items, beauty, health, sports, etc.

MX
BULLETIN. Title Change. Main/Corp American Society of Mexico (Founded 1942). (1???)-(19??). Bulletin. English. **Continued by** Amistad.

CN/0315-8705
BULLETIN - CANADIAN ETHNIC STUDIES ASSOCIATION. Main/Corp Canadian Ethnic Studies Association. (July 1974)-. Bulletin. English (French). Three times a year. 15.00Can$ (students), 35.00Can$ (individuals), 40.00Can$ (institutions). Canadian Ethnic Studies Association, c/o Centre for Ukrainian Canadian Studies, University of Manitoba, Winnipeg Mani R3T 2N2 Canada. **Tel** (204)474-8906, FAX (204)275-0803. **ED** Helen Ralston. **LC** F1035.A1; C354A. **Circ:** 1,000.
Desc: A newsletter to keep members and subscribers informed. Carries notices of upcoming conferences and meetings. Describes and announces current CESA/SCEE happenings.
Ind/Abst Multicult. Educ. Abstr.; Spec. Educ. Needs Abstr.

US/0577-9065
BULLETIN - CHINESE HISTORICAL SOCIETY OF AMERICA. See History(General)-History of North, South, and Central America.

US/0196-8319
BULLETIN OF THE ARCHAEOLOGICAL SOCIETY OF NEW JERSEY. See Archaeology.

US/0078-432X
BULLETIN OF THE OKLAHOMA ANTHROPOLOGICAL SOCIETY. See Anthropology.

US/0893-8601
BULLETIN / THE JAPANESE AMERICAN LIBRARY. [Bull. - Jpn. Am. Libr.]. **Added/Corp** Japanese American Library. **VFOAT** Japanese American Library Bulletin. Vol. 1, No. 1 (Fall 1986)-. Periodical. English. qt. $15.00 (institutions), $10.00 (individuals). Japanese American Library, PO Box 590598, San Francisco CA 94159-0598. **Tel** (415)567-5006. **ED** Karen Seriguchi. **LC** E184.J3; B94. **DD** 027. **Bk Rev. Circ:** 7,000.
Desc: Summarizes the news articles on Japanese American community in North America.

US/0748-4259
BURRELLE'S BLACK MEDIA DIRECTORY. Title Change. See Communication.

●US
BUSINESS AFFIRMATIVE ACTION DIRECTORY. See Economics-Industry and Production.

US/0095-3083
BUYERS GUIDE TO INDIAN ART. See The Arts-Art.

US/0145-0735
CALIFORNIA INDIAN EDUCATION CENTERS. See Education.

US/0744-8600
CALIFORNIAI MAGYARSAG. [Calif. Magy.]. **VFOAT** California Hungarians. (1922)-. Newspaper. Hungarian (English). wk. $24.00. Californiai Magyarsag, 207 South Western Avenue, Suite 201, Los Angeles CA 90004. **Tel** (310)463-3473, FAX (310)384-7642. **ED** Maria Fenyes. **LC** Newspaper. **DD** 071. **Photos. Ad Acc.** Full Page (B&W) $400.00. Half Page (B&W) $250.00. **Pub. Size:** Tabloid. **Circ:** 7,000.
Desc: Covers news of Hungary, international politics, literature and art, local social and church news.

US/0161-2492
CALLALOO. See Literature.

CN/0712-1016
CALUMET JOURNAL. [Calumet j.]. V. 1, No. 6 (Jan./Feb. 1980)-. Periodical. English. sm. Free. Canadian Council of Christians and Jews, 49 Front Street East, Toronto Ontario M5E 1B3 Canada. **DD** 305.8/00971. **Continues** Calumet, 0228-0353.

SP
CAMPANA. Spanish. Twenty-one times a year. 33000ptas Spain; 55000ptas other. Campana Sa, C Sagasta 30, 28004 Madrid Spain. **Tel** 011 34 1 4488301, 011 34 1 4450107.

CN/0008-3496
CANADIAN ETHNIC STUDIES. [Can. ethn. stud.]. **Added/Corp** University of Calgary. Research Centre for Canadian Ethnic Studies. Canadian Ethnic Studies Association. **VFOAT** Etudes Ethniques du Canada. Vol. 1 (1969)-. Periodical. English (French). Three times a year. 45.00Can$ (individuals), 55.00Can$ (institutions) Comes with Canadian Ethnic Studies Association membership. Canadian Ethnic Studies Association Centre, Ukrainian Canadian Studies, University of Manitoba, Winnipeg MANI R3T 2N2 Canada. **Tel** (204)474-8906, FAX (204)275-0803. **ED** J. Frideres and A. Rasporich. **[CCC].** Index available. cum. index. **Bk Rev. Ad Acc. Adv Mgr Tel** (403)220-7257. **Pr Rev. Circ:** 800. available on microfiche from University Microfilms International (UMI).
Desc: Devoted to the study of ethnicity, immigration, intergroup relations and the history and cultural life of ethnic groups in Canada.
Ind/Abst ASTIS Curr. Aware. Bull. (1978-); Acad. Search (July 1993-); Am. Hist. Life (1976-); Am. Bibliogr. Slavic East Europ. Stud.; Anthropol. Index; ASTIS Bibliogr. (1978-); Can. Index; Can. Period. Index; Humanit. Source (Jul. 1993-); INFO-SOUTH Abstr.; Linguist. Lang. Behav. Abstr.; Mag. Search; MLA Int. Bibl. Books Artic. Mod. Lang. Lit.; PAIS Int. Print (1991-?); Sage Race Relat. Abstr.; Soc. Plann. Policy Dev. Abstr.; Sociol. Abstr.

CN/0008-3941
CANADIAN JEWISH NEWS (TORONTO). (THE CANADIAN JEWISH NEWS.). [Can. Jew. news]. (19??)-. English. Forty-seven times a year. $50.00 US; $60.00 other. Canadian Jewish News, 10 Gateway

Ethnic Interests

Boulevard, Suite 420, Don Mills, Ontario M3C 3A1 Canada. **Tel** (416)422-2331, FAX (416)424-1886. **DD** 971/.004924.

CN/0710-1481
CANADIAN JOURNAL OF NATIVE EDUCATION. See Education.

CN/1182-722X
CANADIAN LINK. *Ceased.* [Can. link]. **Added/Corp** Multicultural Communications Foundation. Vol. 8, No. 3 (July 1990)-(199?). Periodical. English. mo. $15.00 per year. Canadian Link, 414 10136 100 Street, Edmonton Alberta T5J 0P1 Canada. **Tel** (403)425-5465. **DD** 305.8/00971. *Continues The Prairie Link., 0824-2003.*

CN/0707-7300
CANADIAN MULTICULTURAL SCENE. V. 1- July 1978-. Periodical. English. mo. Free. AAP-KI-Mehfil Cultural Society, 201-206 East 6th Avenue, Vancouver BC V5T 1J8 Canada. **DD** 954/.005. ctrl circ.

CN/1180-968X
CANADIAN QUAKER HISTORY JOURNAL. *Ceased.* [Can. Quaker hist. j.]. **Added/Corp** Canadian Friends Historical Association. No. 46 (Winter 1990)-(199?). Periodical. English. sa. Maclean Hunter Canada / Montreal, 1001 bvd. de Maisonneuve W., Montreal, Quebec H3A 3E1 Canada. **Tel** 514-845-5141, FAX 514-845-4302, telex 055-60604. **DD** 289.6/71/09. *Continues Canadian Quaker History Newsletter., 0319-3934.*

US/1049-9954
CAREER FOCUS FOR TODAY'S RISING BLACK PROFESSIONAL. *Title Change.* **See** Occupations and Careers.

US/1049-9946
CAREER FOCUS FOR TODAY'S RISING HISPANIC PROFESSIONAL. *Title Change.* **See** Occupations and Careers.

US
CAREER FOCUS FOR TODAY'S RISING PROFESSIONAL. See Occupations and Careers.

●US/1063-0775
CARIBBEAN DIGEST. [Caribb. dig.]. Vol. 1, No. 1 (Spring 1992)-. Periodical. English. qt. $6.00. Aubrey Duncan, Box 680608, Miami FL 33168. **DD** 305. *Continues CarAm Digest, 1040-4554.*

●VI/1057-2872
CARIBBEAN ETHNOLOGY. (1993)-. Periodical. English. Four times a year. $50.00. Caribbean Anthropological Foundation, Inc., PO Box 1848, Frederiksted, St. Croix VI 00841.

US/0739-1730
CAROLINA INDIAN VOICE, THE. Vol. 1 (Jan. 1973)-. Newspaper. English. wk. $20.00 North Carolina; $25.00 other. Carolina Indian Voice, PO Box 1075, Pembroke NC 28372. **Tel** (903)521-2826. Index available. cum. index. **Ad Acc. Adv Mgr:** Helen Locklear.

US
CAROLINA PEACEMAKER. Vol. 1, No. 1 (Mar. 30, 1967)-. Newspaper. English. wk (52 issues per year). $18.00. Carolina Peacemaker, PO Box 20853, Greensboro NC 27420. **Tel** (910)274-6210, (910)274-7829, FAX (910)273-5103. **ED** John Kilimanjaro & Hal Sieber. **Ad Acc, Adv Mgr:** Tom Price, Jr. **Circ:** 6,500 (ctrl).

US/0749-9213
CARPATHO-RUSYN AMERICAN. [Carpatho-Rusyn Am.]. **Added/Corp** Carpatho-Rusyn Research Center (U.S.). Vol. 1, No. 1 (Spring 1978)-. Periodical. English. qt. $12.00. Carpatho-Rusyn American, 7556 Middle Ridge Road, Madison OH 44057. **Tel** (612)689-1720. **ED** Patricia Krafcik. **LC** E184.U5; C37. **DD** 973/.0491791. Index available. cum. index. **Bk Rev. Circ:** 1,200 (ctrl).
Desc: Covers the national culture of Carpatho-Rusyn people in Europe and America.
Ind/Abst Am. Bibliogr. Slavic East Europ. Stud.

SP/0213-5949
CATALAN REVIEW. [Catalan rev.]. **Added/Corp** North American Catalan Society. Quaderns Crema (Firm). Vol. 1, No. 1 (June 1986)-. Periodical. English (Catalan). sa (Published in June and December.). $30.00. Catalan Review, 9909 Kentsdale Drive, Potomac MD 20854. **Tel** (301)469-5986. **ED** Mercedes V. Tibbits. **LC** DP302.C616; C367. **DD** 946/.7/005. **Bk Rev**. (Qty: 10 to 12). **Pr Rev. Circ:** 500 (ctrl).
Desc: International journal of Catalan culture.

US/1043-1241
CBMR DIGEST. See Music.

US/1061-8783
CBP'S GUIDE TO BLACK CHARLOTTE.
VFOAT Guide to Black Charlotte. (1991)-. Periodical. English. qt. $8.00. CBP's Guide to Black Charlotte, PO Box 36160, Charlotte NC 28236.

US
CHALLENGE / JOURNAL OF RESEARCH ON AFRICAN-AMERICAN MEN. Periodical. English. Twice a year. $10.00. Morehouse Research Institute, 830 Westview Drive SW, Atlanta GA 30314. **Tel** (404)215-2676, FAX (404)222-0422. **Circ:** 1,000.

US/0890-4448
CHEROKEE ONE FEATHER, THE.
Added/Corp Eastern Band of Cherokee Indians. Tribal Council. **VFOAT** One Feather. (1968)-. Newspaper. English (Cherokee). wk (except Christmas and New Year's Day). $20.00. Cherokee One Feather, PO Box 501, Cherokee NC 28719. **Tel** (704)497-5513, FAX (704)497-4810. **ED** Richard L. Welch. **DD** 970.1. **Bk Rev. Ad Acc. Circ:** 2,000 (ctrl).
Desc: North American Indian community news.

US/0745-7014
CHICAGO DEFENDER (1973). See Newspapers.

US/0009-370X
CHICAGO SHIMPO, THE. (19??)-. Newspaper. Japanese (English). One hundred issues per year. $50.00. Chicago Shimpo, 4670 North Manor, Chicago IL 60625. **Tel** (312)478-6170.
Desc: A Japanese-American newspaper.

US
CHICAGO SHORELAND NEWS, THE. See Newspapers.

US/1056-2516
CHICANO DATABASE. (CHICANO DATABASE [COMPUTER FILE].). [Chicano database]. **Added/Corp** University of California, Berkeley. Chicano Studies Library. Publications Unit. Version 1 (1990)-. Periodical. English (Spanish). sa $495.00 (per disc). Chicano Studies Library Publications, University of California, 3404 Dwinelle Hall, Berkeley CA 94720. **Tel** (510)642-3859, FAX (510)642-6456. **ED** Lillian Castillo-Speed. **DD** 305. cum. index. **Circ:** 100.
Desc: Contains 36,000 bibliographic citations about Mexican-Americans in all subject areas. System requirements: IBM PC or compatible with 640K RAM, MS-DOS or PC-DOS 3.1 or higher, hard disk, and CD-ROM drive.

US/1056-2516
CHICANO DATABASE ON CD-ROM.
English (Spanish). (every six months). $495.00 per disc. Chicano Studies Library Publications, University of California, 3404 Dwinelle Hall, Berkeley CA 94720. **Tel** (510)642-3859, FAX (510)642-6456. **ED** Lillian Castillo-Speed. cum. index. **Circ:** 100.
Desc: Contains 36,000 bibliographic citations about Mexican-Americans in all subject areas.

US
CHICANO EDUCATION DIGEST. See Education.

US
CHICANOS IN THESE TIMES. VFOAT Chicanos in the Times. (Jan. 1987)-. Periodical. English. mo. $110.00. ATM Information Services, PO Box 3887, Santa Fe Springs CA 90670. **Tel** (310)948-4547.

US/1051-7642
CHINESE AMERICA, HISTORY AND PERSPECTIVES. [Chin. Am. hist. perspect.]. **Added/Corp** Chinese Historical Society of America. San Francisco State University. Asian American Studies Dept. (1987)-. Periodical. English. an. $17.50. Chinese Historical Society of America, 650 Commercial Street, San Francisco CA 94111. **Tel** (415)391-1188. **ED** H M Lai, Judy Yung, K L McCunn, M Horn, L W McClair. **LC** E184.C5; C475. **DD** 973/.04951/005. **Ad Acc. Circ:** 1,000 (ctrl).
Ind/Abst Acad. Abstr. (July 1993-); Acad. Search (July 1993-); Am. Hist. Life (1987-); Hist. Artic. Summar. Elite (July 1993-); Mag. Artic. Summar. CD-ROM (July 1993-).

US/0895-4690
CHINESE AMERICAN FORUM. See Education.

US/0882-4460
CHOCOLATE SINGLES. [Choc. singles].
VFOAT Chocolate Singles Magazine. (1987?)-. Periodical. English. bm (6 issues). $11.00 US; $25.00 other. Chocolate Singles Enterprises, PO Box 333, Jamaica NY 11413. **Tel** (718)978-4800. **ED** B. Miles and R. Mollo. **DD** 305. **Bk Rev. Ad Acc. Circ:** 110,000 (ctrl).
Desc: Contains lifestyles of today's single black person.

CC
CHUNG YANG MIN TSU HSUEH YUAN HSUEH PAO / ZHONGYANG MINZU XUEYUAN XUEBAO. *Title Change.*
Added/Corp Chung Yang min tsu ta Hsueh (China).

VFOAT Zhongyang Minzu Xueyuan Xuebao; Zhongyan Minzu Xueyuan Xuebao; Journal of the Central Institute for Nationalities. (19??)-(199?). Periodical. Chinese. qt. Science Press, 16 Donghuangchenggen North Street, Beijing 100707, People's Republic of China. **Tel** 011 86 1 4019821, 011 86 1 4010642, FAX 011 86 1 4012180, 011 86 1 4019810, telex 210147. **ED** Luo Am Yuan. **LC** DS730; .C4498. **DD** 951/.004. **Bk Rev. Circ:** 4,500 (ctrl). *Continued by Chung Yang min tsu ta Hsueh Hsueh pao.*

●CC/1000-8667
CHUNG YANG MIN TSU TA HSUEH HSUEH PAO / ZHONGYANG MINZU DAXUE XUEBAO. **Added/Corp** Chung Yang min tsu ta Hsueh (China). **VFOAT** Zhongyang Minzu Daxue Xuebao; Journal of the Central University for Nationalities. (1994)-. Academic Scholarly Publication. Chinese. bm. Science Press, 16 Donghuangchenggen North Street, Beijing 100707, People's Republic of China. **Tel** 011 86 1 4019821, 011 86 1 4010642, FAX 011 86 1 4012180, 011 86 1 4019810, telex 210147. **LC** DS730; .C4498. **DD** 951/.004. *Continues Chung Yang min tsu Hsueh Yuan Hsueh pao.*

CN/0382-8557
CIAO (MONTREAL). (CIAO.). V. 1- Sept. 1970-. Periodical. Multiple languages (English, French and Italian). mo. Ciao Publishing Company, 2125 Jean-Talon East, Montreal Quebec H2E 1V4 Canada.

US/1067-5639
CIRCLE (MINNEAPOLIS, MINN.), THE. (THE CIRCLE : NEWS FROM AN AMERICAN INDIAN PERSPECTIVE.). [Circle]. **Added/Corp** Minneapolis Regional Native American Center. Minneapolis American Indian Center. (197?)-. Periodical. English. mo $16.00 (institutions); $14.00 (individuals). Minneapolis American Indian Center, 1530 East Franklin Avenue, Minneapolis MN 55404. **Tel** (612)874-0713. **LC** E75; .C57. **DD** 970.004/97/005.

US
CODE OF FEDERAL REGULATIONS. 25, INDIANS. VFOAT Indians; CFR. 25, Indians. Government Publication. English. an. 35.00. Superintendent of Documents, US Government Printing Office, Washington DC 20402. **Tel** (202)275-3328, FAX (202)786-2317. **(Subscription address:** U.S. Government Bookstore O'Neil Building 2023 3rd Avenue North, Birmingham, Al 35203) Index available. available on microfiche (Vols. for (1984-) distributed to some depository libraries).
Desc: Special edition of the Federal Register, containing a codification of documents.

US/1059-5007
COLOR (ATLANTA, GA.). (COLOR : THE SOURCE OF INFORMATION FOR PEOPLE OF AFRICAN DESCENT.). [Color]. Vol. 1, No. 1 (1991)-. Periodical. English. mo. Color, PO Box 245, Atlanta GA 30301. **DD** 305.

US
COLUMBUS TIMES, THE. See Newspapers.

PO/0871-178X
COMUNICACOES DO INSTITUTO DE INVESTIGACAO CIENTIFICA TROPICAL, SERIE DE CIENCIAS ETNOLOGICAS E ETNOMUSEOLOGICAS. Portuguese. Instituto de Investigacao Cientifica Tropical, Centro de Documentacao e Informacao, rua Jau 47, 1 300 Lisbon Portugal. **Tel** 645321. **Circ:** 1,000 (ctrl).

US
COMUNICO : THE NATIONAL MAGAZINE FOR MEMBERS OF UNICO.
Added/Corp Unico National. Vol. 47, No. 1 (Oct. 1991)-. Periodical. English. bm. $13.00. Communico Magazine, 72 Burroughs Place, Bloomfield NJ 07033. *Continues CommUnico, 1044-7202.*

AG
COMUNIDAD (ASOCIACION MUTUAL ISRAELITA ARGENTINA). (COMUNIDAD.).
VFOAT Kehlia : Organo de Difusion de la Asociacion Mutual Israelita Argentina. Yearly V. 1, No. 1, (Sept. 1979)-. Spanish (Spanish). $1.000 single issue. Asociacion Mutual Israelita Argentina, Pasteur 633, Buenos Aires Argentina. **LC** DS101; .C634. **DD** 305.8/924/082.

US/0197-1441
COMUNIUNEA ROMANEASCA. See Literature.

CN/0710-0418
CONGRES JUIF CANADIEN RAPPORT INTERIMAIRE. (RAPPORT INTERIMAIRE / CONGRES JUIF CANADIEN). **Added/Corp** Canadian Jewish Congress. **VAT** Rapport Interimaire - Congres Juif Canadien. 1978/79-. French. an. Congres Juif Canadien, 1590 Av Docteur Penfield, Montreal Quebec H3G 1C5 Canada. **Tel** (514)931-7531. **DD** 305.8/924/071.

US/0887-0764
CONGRESS MONTHLY (1985). (CONGRESS MONTHLY.). [Congr. mon.]. **Added/Corp** American Jewish Congress. Vol. 52, No. 2 (Feb./March 1985)-. Periodical. English. Six times a year (Jan., Mar., May, July, Sept., Nov.). $12.50 (one year), $24.00 (two years), $35.00 (three years) US; $15.50 (one year), $30.00 (two years), $44.00 (three years) other. American Jewish Congress, 15 East 84th Street, New York NY 10028. **Tel** (212)879-4500 Ext.200/212, FAX (212)249-3672. **ED** Maier Deshell. **DD** 909. **Bk Rev. Ad Acc. Circ:** 30,000 (ctrl). available on microfilm and microfiche from University Microfilms International (UMI). ***Continues*** *American Jewish Congress Monthly, 0739-1927.*
Desc: Subjects of interest to the Jewish audience.
Ind/Abst Am. Bibliogr. Slavic East Europ. Stud.; Index Jew. Period.; Index Period. Artic. Relat. Law; Middle East Abstr. Index.

CN
CONSTITUTIONALLY SPEAKING. See Law.

●US/1058-1316
CONTEMPORARY BLACK BIOGRAPHY. [Contemp. Black biogr.]. Vol. 1 (1992)-. English. sa. $42.00. Gale Research Inc., 835 Penobscot Building, Detroit MI 48226. **Tel** (800)877-GALE, (313)961-2242, FAX (313)961-6083, telex TWX 810-221-7086. **ED** Barbara Carlisle Bigelow. **LC** E185.96; .C66. **DD** 920/.009296073. available on magnetic tape; available on diskette; available on an online database (File GALBIO in the PEOPLE, ENTERTAINMENT, and SPORTS Libraries) from NEXIS.
Desc: Covers important and influential persons from the international black community. Presents information on contemporary figures from fields such as government, science and technology, medicine, and religion, as well as leaders in sports, entertainment and the arts.

US/0147-1694
CONTEMPORARY JEWRY. [Contemp. Jew.]. **Added/Corp** Association for the Sociological Study of Jewry. Association for the Social Scientific Study of Jewry. **VFOAT** Journal of Sociological Inquiry. Vol. 3, No. 1 (Fall/Winter 1977)-. Academic Scholarly Publication. English. an (Oct.). $18.00. Connecticut College, C/O J. A. Winter, Department Sociology, 270 Mohegan Avenue, New London CT 06320. **Tel** (203)439-2241, FAX (203)439-5332. **ED** Alan Winter. **LC** DS101; .C67. **DD** 305. **[CCC]. Bk Rev**, (Qty: 10-15). **Ad Acc. Pr Rev. Circ:** 350. available on microfilm and microfiche from University Microfilms International (UMI). Documents available. ***Continues*** *Jewish Sociology and Social Research.*
Desc: Facilitates scholarly communication on the character of contemporary Jewish life. Includes articles and research reports as well as discussions of theoretical and methodological issues.
Ind/Abst Am. Hist. Life (1988-); Linguist. Lang. Behav. Abstr.; Soc. Plann. Policy Dev. Abstr.; Sociol. Abstr. [Full Cov.].

US/0069-9624
CONTRIBUTIONS IN AFRO-AMERICAN AND AFRICAN STUDIES. See History(General)-History of Africa.

US/0196-7088
CONTRIBUTIONS IN ETHNIC STUDIES. [Contrib. ethn. stud.]. No. 1 (1980)-. Monographic series. English. ir. Price varies per volume. Greenwood Press Inc., PO Box 5007, Westport CT 06881-5007. **Tel** (203)226-3571, FAX (203)222-1502. **ED** Leonard W. Doob. **Bk Rev. Ad Acc.**

US
CORAJE CHICANO, EL. V. 1- ; April 1979-. Periodical. English (Spanish).

IT
CORPUS ANTIQUITATUM AMERICANENSIUM. ITALIA. VFOAT Italia. Vol. 1, No. 1-. Italian (Italian). **LC** E61; .C76. **DD** 909/.09812/005.

US
COSSMHO REPORTER, THE. Periodical. English. bm. $25.00. COSSMHO, 1015 15th Street NW/Suite 402, Washington DC 20005. **Tel** (202)371-2100. **ED** William A Bogan. **LC** RC451.5.H57; C677. **Ad Acc. Circ:** 1,000.
Desc: Devoted to health and human services research, programs, and information, focused on U.S. Hispanic populations.

US/0011-1422
CRISIS (NEW YORK, N.Y.), THE. (THE CRISIS.). [Crisis]. **Added/Corp** National Association for the Advancement of Colored People. Vol. 1, No. 1 (Nov. 1910)-. Periodical. English. ir (8 issues). $15.00. Crisis Publications Inc., 4805 Mount Hope Drive, Baltimore MD 21215. **Tel** (410)358-8900, (800)781-5058. **ED** Fred Beauford. **LC** E185.5; .C92. **DD** 973/.04/96073. **Bk Rev. Ad Acc. Circ:** 300,000 (ctrl). available on microfilm and microfiche from University Microfilms International (UMI). Documents available from UMI Article Clearinghouse.
Desc: Subject matter includes current events, politics, economic development, sports, corporate America, international news and the arts.
Ind/Abst Acad. Abstr. (July 1993-); Acad. Ind. [Computer File] (1992-); Acad. Search (July 1993-); Am. Hist. Life (1969-); Am. Humanit. Index; Curr. Index J. Educ.; Expand. Acad. Index (1992-); Guide Soc. Sci. Relig.; Mag. Artic. Summar. Elite (July 1993-); Newsp. Period. Abstr. (1992-); PsycINFO (1990-); PsycLit; Soc. Sci. Index.

US
CROSS CURRENTS. See History(General)-History of Asia.

PE
CUADERNOS AFRO-AMERICANOS. Yearly V. 1- 1975-. Spanish. Universidad Central de Venezuela / Urbanizacion los Chaguaramos, Avenida la Colina, Calle Las Cumbres Quinta Quetzalcoat, Caracas Venezuela. **LC** E29.N3; C8. ***Supersedes*** *Afroamerica.*

US/1070-3160
CULTURAL DIVERSITY AT WORK. See Economics-Labor.

US/0740-3291
CULTURAL SURVIVAL QUARTERLY. See Political Science-Civil Rights.

US/0705-8365
CUVANTUL ROMANESC. VFOAT Romanian Voice. Vol. 1, No. 1 (1976)-. Periodical. Romanian (English). mo. $10.00 individuals, $20.00 institutions. Romanian Voice, PO Box 4217 Station D, Hamilton Ontario L8V 4L6 Canada. **LC** Microfilm; 05831 DR; DR 201.

US/0011-6637
DARBININKAS. Added/Corp Amerikos Lietuviu R.k. Svento Juozapo Darbininku Sajunga. Franciscans. **VFOAT** Worker. (1915)-. Newspaper. Lithuanian. wk. $30.00. Darbininkas, 341 Highland Boulevard, Brooklyn NY 11207. **Tel** (718)827-1352. ***Absorbed*** *Amerika (Brooklyn, New York, N.Y.); Lietuviu Zinios.*

US/0271-8561
DATA ON EARNED DEGREES CONFERRED BY INSTITUTIONS OF HIGHER EDUCATION BY RACE, ETHNICITY AND SEX. See Education-Higher Education.

US
DAYBREAK (HIGHLAND (HOWARD COUNTY, MD.)). (DAYBREAK.). Vol. 1, Issue 1 (Autumn 1987)-. Periodical. English. qt. $12.00 US; $15.00 Canada & Mexico; $20.00 other. Daybreak, State University of New York, Box 315, American Studies Department, Williamsville NY 14231. **Tel** (716)645-2546. Documents available from Documents on Demand.
Desc: A modern interpretation of the wisdom of tribal cultures, reflecting native American perspective on current issues and alternative thinking.
Ind/Abst Altern. Press Index (199?-); Environ. Abstr.; Hum. Rights Intern. Rep.

PY
DIALOGO INDIGENA MISIONERO : DIM. Added/Corp Equipo Nacional de Misiones (Catholic Church. Conferencia Episcopal Paraguaya). Servicio de Informacion. **VFOAT** DIM; D.I.M. (19??)-. Periodical. Spanish. qt. Gs2,500 Paraguay; $5.00 US; $8.00 other. Equipo Nacional de Misiones, Alberdi 782, Asuncion Paraguay. **Tel** 021-90920. **Circ:** 1,000.
Desc: Provides information on the present state of Paraguayan Indian societies and of indigenous activity in the country.

US
DIARIO LA PRENSA, EL. (1913)-. Periodical. Spanish. da.

●US/1062-6972
DIASPORA (MAGNOLIA, ARK.). See Literature.

CN
DIEN AN NGI VIET. (1990)-. Periodical. Vietnamese. Dien an Ngi Viet, PO Box 874, Station C, Montreal, Quebec H2L 2L6 Canada. **LC** IN PROCESS. ***Continues*** *Ngi Viet (Montreal, Quebec).*

IS/0070-4903
DINE ISRAEL. See Law-Civil Law.

●US
DIRECTORY OF AFRICAN AND AFRICAN-AMERICAN STUDIES IN THE UNITED STATES. 8th Edition (1993)-. English. ir. $23.00. African Studies Association, Emory University, Credit Union Building, Atlanta GA 30322. **Tel** (404)329-6410, FAX (404)329-6433. **LC** DT19.9.U5; D56. ***Continues*** *Directory of African & Afro-American Studies in the United States.*

US/1055-8519
DIRECTORY OF AMERICAN INDIAN LAW ATTORNEYS. See Law.

US/0161-2298
DIRECTORY OF CONSTITUENT ORGANIZATIONS. Main/Corp National Jewish Community Relations Advisory Council (U.S.). Directory. English. National Jewish Community Relations Advisory Council, 55 West 42nd Street, New York NY 10036. **LC** E184.J5; N593A. **DD** 301.45/19/24073.

US/0271-0277
DIRECTORY OF JEWISH FAMILY & CHILDREN'S AGENCIES. See Sociology-Social Services and Welfare.

US/0364-6955
DIRECTORY OF NATIONAL SOURCES OF DATA ON BLACKS IN HIGHER EDUCATION. See Education-Higher Education.

CN/0227-1109
DIRECTORY OF NATIVE COMMUNITIES AND ORGANIZATIONS IN ONTARIO. [Dir. native communities organ. Ont.]. **VFOAT** Directory, Native Communities and Organizations in Ontario. Began with 1980? issue. Directory. English. $2.50. Native Community Branch, Publications Services Section, 5th Floor/880 Bay Street, Toronto Ontario M7A 1N8 Canada. **LC** E78.O5; D57. **DD** 971.3/00497/0025.

US/0017-6524
DOAR, HA-. See Religion and Theology-Judaism.

US/0884-5611
DOLLARS & SENSE (CHICAGO, ILL.). See Business.

SA
DOREM AFRIKE. VFOAT South Africa; Suid-Afrika. (1-); Sept. 1948-. Yiddish. bm. $8.00. Dorem-Afrikaner Yidisher Kultur-Federatsye, 913 S A Centre, Johannesburg South Africa. **LC** DS101; .D67.

CN/0703-1491
DROCHAID. (AN DROCHAID. THE BRIDGE.). **Added/Corp** Clans and Scottish Societies of Canada. **VFOAT** Bridge. (1976)-. Newsletter. English. Five times a year. 8.00Can$. Clans and Scottish Societies of Canada, 73 Simcoe Street St. Andrew Pres., Toronto Ontario M5J 1W9 Canada. **Tel** (416)234-0062. **DD** 971/.004/9163. ctrl circ.
Desc: A newsletter that is the written communication of the member groups of the Clans and Scottish Societies of Canada.

US/1053-7457
EAE (RENTON, WASH.), THE. ***Title Change.*** (THE EAE : THE ETHNIC-AMERICAN EXPERIENCE MAGAZINE SERVING THE PACIFIC NORTHWEST.). [EAE]. **VFOAT** EAE Magazine. **VAT** Ethnic-American Experience; Ethnic-American Experience Magazine. (1991?)-Vol. 2, No. 4 (Dec. 1992/Feb. 1993). Periodical. English. qt. The EAE, PO Box 1235, Renton WA 98057. **LC** F855; .E2. **DD** 305. ***Continues*** *African-American Experience Magazine, 1050-0812.* ***Continued by*** *Ethnic American Experience, 1069-1170.*

US/0012-9011
EBONY. [Ebony]. Vol. 1, (Nov. 1945)-. Periodical. English. mo. $16.00 (one year), $28.00 (two year), $40.00 (three year). Johnson Publishing Company / Illinois, 820 South Michigan Avenue, Chicago IL 60605. **Tel** (312)322-9200, (800)272-6602. **ED** Herbert Nipson. **LC** AP2; .E165. **DD** 05L. **Ad Acc. Circ:** 1,850,000 (ctrl). available on microfilm and microfiche from University Microfilms International (UMI); available on an online database (file 647/Full-Text) from DIALOG. Documents available from UMI Article Clearinghouse, Magazine Collection.
Desc: Features colorful pictorial articles and exclusive informative stories about Black America's history, goals, aspirations, fashion, food, features and enlightening editorials.
Ind/Abst Abr. Read. Guide Period. Lit.; Acad. Abstr. Full Text Elite (Feb. 1984-) [Full Txt.]; Acad. Abstr. (Feb. 1984-); Acad. Ind. [Computer File] (1984-); Acad. Search (Feb. 1984-); Biogr. Index; Expand. Acad. Index (1984-); Film Lit. Index; Gen. Period. Index (1985-); Health Index (1992-); Health Plan. Adminis.; Health Ref. Cent. (1987-) [Select. Cov.]; INFO-SOUTH Abstr.; Infobank (Jan. 1969-); Mag. Artic. Summar. Elite (Feb. 1984-) [Full Txt.]; Mag. Artic. Summar. Select (Feb. 1984-); Mag. Artic. Summar. CD-ROM (Feb. 1984-); Mag. ASAP Plus [Full Txt.]; Mag. ASAP Sel. [Full Txt.]; Mag. Express (1986-) [Full Txt.]; Mag. Index Plus (1989-); Mag. Index Sel. Microfiche (1986-) [Full Txt.]; Mag. Index. Sel. (1986-); Mag. Search; Med. Rev. Dig.; Mid. Search (Feb. 1984-) [Full Txt.]; Newsp. Period. Abstr. (1986-); Prim. Search (Feb. 1984-); Read. Guide Abstr. Select Ed.; Read. Guide Period. Lit.; Resource/One Ondisc; Mag. Index (1977-?); TOM Gen. Index (1985-) [Full Txt.]; Vocat. Search (Feb. 1984-) [Full Txt.].

US
ECO DE VIRGINIA, EL. Vol. 1, Issue 1 (Jul. 1991)-. Periodical. Spanish (English). wk.

Ethnic Interests

US
ECONOMIC FORUM MINORITY BUSINESS REVIEW. See Business.

SA/0258-7831
EDUCATION. WHITES / REPUBLIC OF SOUTH AFRICA, DEPARTMENT OF STATISTICS. See Education.

BE
EF-AVISEN. Added/Corp Commission of the European Communities. Directorate General of Information. (19??)-. Periodical. Danish. mo. kr95.00. Kommiss Europaeiske Faellesska, PO Box 144 Ostergade 61, DK-1004 Copenhagen K Denmark.

CN/0226-6873
EGALITE (MONCTON). See Political Science.

AT
EL TELEGRAPH. See Newspapers.

US
ELDER VOICES. (1983)-. English. Twelve times a year. Free on request. National Indian Council on Aging, 6400 Uptown Boulevard, Suite 510W, Albuquerque NM 87110. **Formed by the union of** Update (National Indian Council on Aging) **and** Quarterly.

CN/0846-3298
EMBER (MARKHAM). (EMBER.). [Ember]. Vol. 1, No. 1 (Feb./Mar. 1991)-. Periodical. English. bm. Ember Publications, Suite 528, 7305 Woodbine Avenue, Markham Ontario L3R 3V7 Canada. **DD** 305.48/96/9729071.

US/0737-9021
EMIE BULLETIN. See Library and Information Sciences.

UK
EMPOWERING BLACK MANAGERS. See Business-General Management.

US/0161-6536
ENCORE AMERICAN & WORLDWIDE NEWS. [Encore Am. worldw. news]. **VFOAT** Encore American and Worldwide News. Began with issue for Jan. 7, 1975. Periodical. English. mo. $18.00 US; 22.00Can$ Canada. Tanner Publications Company, 2 Penn Plaza, New York NY 10001. **LC** E185.5; .E5. **DD** 909/.0496. available on microfilm and microfiche from University Microfilms International (UMI). **Continues** Encore (New York, N.Y. : 1972), 0046-1954.
Ind/Abst Read. Guide Period. Lit.

US/0071-1039
EQUAL OPPORTUNITY. See Education-Higher Education.

FR/1168-1179
ESPACES LATINO-AMERICAINS. See Political Science.

CN
ESTIMATES. PART III, INDIAN AND NORTHERN AFFAIRS CANADA AND CANADIAN POLAR COMMISSION.
Main/Corp Canada. **Added/Corp** Canada. Indian and Northern Affairs Canada. Canadian Polar Commission. **VFOAT** Budget des Depenses. Partie III, Affaires Indiennes et du Nord Canada et Commission Canadienne des Affaires Polaires. (1992/1993)-. English (French). Canada Communication Group Publishers, Order Processing, Ottawa Ontario K1A 0S9 Canada. **Tel** (819)956-4800, (819)956-4802. **LC** E92; .C213a.
Continues Canada. Estimates. Part III, Indian and Northern Affairs Canada.

PO/0870-8584
ESTUDOS ITALIANOS EM PORTUGAL. See History(General)-History of Europe.

●US/1069-1170
ETHNIC AMERICAN EXPERIENCE. [Ethn. Am. exp.]. **VFOAT** Ethnic-American Experience; EAE. Vol. 3, No. 1 (Mar.-May 1993)-. Periodical. English. qt. $12.00. **LC** F855; .E2. **DD** 305. **Continues** EAE, 1053-7457.

CN/0384-0441
ETHNIC AND CULTURAL DIRECTORY. 1975-. Directory. English. Central Information Service, Suite 609, 42 James Street North, Hamilton Ontario L8R 2K2 Canada. **DD** 917.13/52.

UK/0141-9870
ETHNIC AND RACIAL STUDIES. [Ethn. racial stud.]. **VFOAT** ERS, Ethnic and Racial Studies. Vol. 1 (Jan. 1978)-. Periodical. English. Four times a year. $115.00 (US & Canada); £77.00 (UK); £82.00 (other). Routledge, 11 New Fetter Lane, London EC4P 4EE England. **Tel** 071 583 9855, FAX 071 842 2298. **(Subscription address:** Kinokuniya Company Ltd., 38-1 Sakuragaoka 5, Setagaya-ku, Tokyo 156 Japan.**)** **ED** J Stone. **LC** HT1501; .E73. **DD** 301.45/1/04205. **[CCC]. Bk Rev. Ad Acc. Pr Rev. Circ:** 900. Documents available from The Genuine Article, UMI Article Clearinghouse.
Desc: An international journal of ethnic and race relations, studying minority groups and cultures.
Ind/Abst ABC POL SCI; Abstr. Anthropol.; Acad. Abstr. Full Text Elite (Jan. 1992-); Acad. Abstr. (Jan. 1992-); Acad. Search (Jan. 1992-); Am. Hist. Life (1978-); Appl. Soc. Sci. Index Abstr.; Arts Humanit. Citation Index [Select. Cov.]; Chicano Index; Curr. Contents Soc. Behav. Sci.; Expand. Acad. Index (1989-); Index Islam. Lit.; INFO-SOUTH Abstr.; Int. Bibliogr. Sociol.; Int. Polit. Sci. Abstr.; Mag. Search; Middle East Abstr. Index; Newsp. Period. Abstr. (1991-); Res. Alert [Full Cov.]; Sage Race Relat. Abstr.; Soc. Plann. Policy Dev. Abstr.; Soc. Sci. Source (Jan. 1992-); Soc. Sci. Cit. Index [Full Cov.]; Soc. Sci. Index; Soc. Sci. Index Fulltext (April 1988-) [Full Txt.]; Soc. Work Abstr. [Select. Cov.]; Sociol. Abstr.; Sociol. Educ. Abstr.; SportSearch.

AT
ETHNIC BROADCASTING IN AUSTRALIA. See Communication-Broadcasting.

AT/1035-1094
ETHNIC COMMUNITIES' REFERENCE YEARBOOK. [Ethn. communities' ref. yearb.]. (1990)-. English. an. Ethnic Communities Council, 221 Cope Street, Waterloo 2017 Australia. **Tel** 011 61 2 3190288, FAX 011 61 2 3194229. **ED** Phaedra Johnson. **DD** 362.8405.
Desc: Reference divided into six sections: community groups, educational bodies, the media, government, granti-in-aid workers and ethnic health workers.

CN/0705-3177
ETHNIC DIRECTORY. 1977-. Directory. English. an. Thunder Bay Multicultural Association, 17 North Court Street, Thunder Bay Ontario P7A 4T4 Canada. **Tel** (807)345-0551. **DD** 301.45/1/02571312. **Continues** Thunder Bay Ethnic Groups, 0318-8744.

CN
ETHNIC DIRECTORY OF ALASKA, HAWAII, OREGON AND WASHINGTON. Directory. English. 10.00Can$. Western Publishers, Dr Vladimir Markotic, University of Calgary, Calgary Alberta T2N 1N4 Canada. **Tel** 289-3301. **ED** Vladimir Markotic. **LC** F915.A1; E83. **DD** 301.45/025/79. **Circ:** 300.
Desc: Religious, social, cultural, archives, bookshops, newspapers, embassies, libraries, restaurants, etc.

CN
ETHNIC DIRECTORY OF CALIFORNIA. Directory. English. Western Publishers, Dr Vladimir Markotic, University of Calgary, Calgary Alberta T2N 1N4 Canada. **Tel** 289-3301. **ED** Vladimir Markotic. **LC** F870.A1; E85. **DD** 979.4/05/025. **Circ:** 500.
Desc: Business, churches, archives, libraries, bookshops, clubs, newspapers, publishers, ethnic societies etc.

CN/0703-8348
ETHNIC DIRECTORY OF WINDSOR & ESSEX COUNTY. 1976-. Directory. English. Free. Multicultural Council of Windsor and Essex, 1100 University Avenue West, Windsor Ontario N9A 5S7. **DD** 971.3/31/004. ctrl circ.

US/0278-9078
ETHNIC FORUM. (ETHNIC FORUM : BULLETIN OF ETHNIC STUDIES AND ETHNIC BIBLIOGRAPHY.). [Ethn. forum]. **Added/Corp** Kent State University. Center for the Study of Ethnic Publications. Intercollegiate Academic Council on Ethnic Studies (Ohio). Vol. 1, No. 1 (Dec. 1980)-. Periodical. English. an. $27.00 US; $32.00 other. Kent State University / Library Science, School of Library Science, Kent OH 44242. **Tel** (216)672-2782, FAX (216)672-7965. **ED** Lubomyr R. Wynar. **LC** E184.A1; E82. **DD** 306/.089. **Bk Rev. Ad Acc, Adv Mgr Tel** (216)672-2782. **Circ:** 400.
Desc: Serves as a channel of communication among those interested in the ethnic experience in the U.S. and Canada. Covers ethnic studies, curricula in educational institutions and library services.
Ind/Abst Am. Hist. Life (1980-); Am. Bibliogr. Slavic East Europ. Stud.; Curr. Index J. Educ.

US/0308-6860
ETHNIC GROUPS. Title Change. [Ethn. groups]. Vol. 1 (June 1976)-(1993). Periodical. English. qt. Gordon & Breach Science Publishers, Inc., PO Box 786, Cooper Station, New York NY 10276. **Tel** (212)206-8900, FAX (212)645-2459. **ED** A. La Ruffa. **LC** GN495.4; .E84. **DD** 301.45/1/05. **CODEN** ETGREQ. **[CCC]. Bk Rev. Ad Acc.** Documents available from UMI Article Clearinghouse. **Supersedes** Afro-American Studies. **Continued by** Identities (Yverdon, Switzerland), 1070-289X.
Ind/Abst Abstr. Anthropol. (19??-); Acad. Search (Jan. 1993-Dec. 1993); Am. Hist. Life (1976-1984); Am. Bibliogr. Slavic East Europ. Stud.; Anthropol. Lit.; Expand. Acad. Index (1989-); INFO-SOUTH Abstr.; Int. Bibliogr. Sociol.; Middle East Abstr. Index; Newsp. Period. Abstr. (1991-); Sage Race Relat. Abstr. (1976-); Soc. Plann. Policy Dev. Abstr.; Soc. Sci. Source (Jul. 1993-); Soc. Sci. Index; Soc. Sci. Index Fulltext (1988-) [Full Txt.]; Sociol. Abstr.

US/0738-1719
ETHNIC INFORMATION SOURCES OF THE UNITED STATES. [Ethn. inf. sources U.S.]. (1976)-. Periodical. English. ir. $140.00. Gale Research Inc., 835 Penobscot Building, Detroit MI 48226. **Tel** (800)877-GALE, (313)961-2242, FAX (313)961-6083, telex TWX 810-221-7086. **ED** Paul Wasserman and Alice Kennington. **LC** E184.A1; E835. **DD** 305.8/0025/73.
Desc: A reference guide to many live and print sources of information about ethnic groups in the U.S.

UK
ETHNIC MINORITIES & EMPLOYMENT. See Economics-Labor.

US/0095-0548
ETHNIC MINORITY AFFAIRS DIRECTORY. Directory. English. Washington State Council on Higher Education, 908 East 5th Street, Olympia WA 98504. **LC** L903.W3; E84. **DD** 378.797.

US
ETHNIC NEWS WATCH [COMPUTER FILE]. **VFOAT** Ethnic Newswatch; Ethnic News Watch on CDROM. (19??)-. Periodical. English (Spanish). bm. Softline Information Inc, PO Box 16845, Stamford CT 06905.

●**US**
ETHNIC NEWSWATCH [COMPUTER FILE]. Added/Corp Softline Information, Inc. (1992)-. English. qt. $1923.00. Softline Information, Inc, PO Box 16845, Stamford CT 06905.
Desc: System requirements: IBM PC AT or compatible with at least 512 real memory and one 20MB hard disk, MS-DOS 3.0 or higher and a CD-ROM drive.

US/0736-6086
ETHNIC RACIAL BROTHERHOOD (1982). (ETHNIC RACIAL BROTHERHOOD : A JOINT PERIODICAL PUBLICATION OF THE BLACK EMPLOYEES OF THE LIBRARY OF CONGRESS (BELC) AND THE ETHNIC EMPLOYEES OF THE LIBRARY OF CONGRESS (EELC).). **Added/Corp** Black Employees of the Library of Congress. Ethnic Employees of the Library of Congress. (1982)-(19??). Periodical. English. ir. Library of Congress / Cataloging Distribution Service, Washington DC 20541-5017. **Tel** (800)255-3666, (202)707-6100, FAX (202)707-1334. **LC** Z733.U6; E78. **DD** 027.5/08996073. **Continues** Racial Ethnic Brotherhood, 0736-0215.

US/0893-7362
ETHNIC REPORTER (CLAREMONT, CALIF.), THE. (THE ETHNIC REPORTER / NAES.). **Added/Corp** National Association for Ethnic Studies (U.S.). Vol. 11, No. 1 (Spring 1986)-. Periodical. English. ir. $35.00 (individuals); $100.00 (institutions) Comes with National Association for Ethnics Studies membership. National Association of Ethnic Studies Inc., Arizona State University, Department of English, Tempe AZ 85287. **Tel** (602)965-2197, FAX (602)965-2012. **ED** Gretchen M. Bataille. **DD** 301. cum. index. **Bk Rev. Ad Acc. Circ:** 350 (ctrl). available on microfilm. **Absorbed** Newsletter (National Association for Ethnic Studies (U.S.), 0887-6711.
Desc: Provides news on conferences and research opportunities in ethnic studies.
Ind/Abst Am. Hist. Life (1986-).

CN/0317-3011
ETHNIC SCENE. Aug. 1970-. English. Ethnic Liaison Council, 21 Tyler Place, Weston Ontario M9R 1L8 Canada. **DD** 971/.004.

AT/1035-3682
ETHNIC SCHOOLS IN FOCUS. See Education.

US/0897-4683
ETHNIC WOMAN, THE. [Ethn. woman]. Vol. 1, No. 1 (Dec. 1977)-. Periodical. English. sa (with monthly supplements). $15.00 US; $20.00 other. Ethnic Woman, PO Box 1033, Cooper Station, New York NY 10003. **Tel** (718)655-1657, FAX (718)547-5696. **ED** Thelma Dailey. **DD** 305. **Bk Rev. Circ:** 5,000 (ctrl).
Desc: History of the United States, international articles, result's of South African election (woman's view).

US
ETHNICITY AND PUBLIC POLICY SERIES. Vol. 1-. Monographic series. English. an. Price varies per volume. University of Wisconsin System Institute on Race and Ethnicity, University of Wisconsin-Milwaukee, PO Box 413, Milwaukee WI 53201. **Tel** (414)229-6701. **ED** Winston A Van Horne and Thonas V Tonnesen. **Bk Rev. Circ:** 1,000.
Desc: Contains a compilation of scholarly essays dealing with the ways that racial/ethnic concerns impact on public policy questions, and vice versa.

BE/0014-178X
ETHNIE FRANCAISE : REVUE TRIMESTRIELLE DE LA FONDATION CHARLES PLISNIER, L'. Added/Corp Fondation Charles Plisnier. (1965)-. Periodical. French.

qt. 750F Belgium; 900F other. Foundation Charles Plisnier, 15-17 Place Van Meenen/Bte 3, B-1060 Brussels Belgium. **Tel** 011 32 2 5370449. **ED** Charles Plisnier. ***Continues*** *Bulletin d'Information et de Presse de la Fondation Charles Plisnier, 0771-1484* ***and*** *L'Ethnie Francaise d'Europe.*
Desc: Belgian and French literature.

US/0073-4667
ETHNIES. ***Ceased.*** Monographic series. French (English). ir. Walter de Gruyter Inc. / Hawthorne, 200 Saw Mill River Road, Hawthorne NY 10532. **Tel** (914)747-0110, GERMANY: 011/49/30/260050, FAX (914)747-1326, telex 646677. **(Subscription address:** Germany/ PO Box 110240, 1 Berlin 11**)**

GR
ETHNIKE BIBLIOTHEKE. See Library and Information Sciences.

US/0014-1801
ETHNOHISTORY. (ETHNOHISTORY : THE BULLETIN OF THE OHIO VALLEY HISTORIC INDIAN CONFERENCE.). [Ethnohistory]. **Added/Corp** American Society for Ethnohistory. Vol. 1 (Apr. 1954)-. Bulletin. English. qt (4 issues). $40.00 (institutions), $24.00 (individuals) includes membership in the American Society for Ethnohistory. Duke University Press, PO Box 90660, Durham NC 27708-0660. **Tel** (919)687-3600, (919)688-5134 (orders), FAX (919)688-4574, telex 802829. **ED** Ross Hassig. **LC** E51; .E8. **DD** 970.1. cum. index. **Bk Rev. Ad Acc. Pr Rev. Circ:** 1,200. available on microfilm and microfiche from University Microfilms International (UMI). Documents available from The Genuine Article, UMI Article Clearinghouse.
Desc: Culture history of ethnic peoples, especially North American Indians.
Ind/Abst Abstr. Anthropol.; Acad. Abstr. Full Text Elite (Jan. 1992-); Acad. Abstr. (Jan. 1992-); Acad. Search (Jan. 1992-); Am. Hist. Life (1963-); Am. Bibliogr. Slavic East Europ. Stud.; Anthropol. Lit.; Arts Humanit. Citation Index [Full Cov.]; Curr. Contents Arts Humanit.; Curr. Contents Soc. Behav. Sci.; Curr. Geogr. Publ. (199?-); Ethnoarts Index; Expand. Acad. Index (1989-); Hist. Source (Jan. 1992-); INFO-SOUTH Abstr.; Mag. Search; Middle East Abstr. Index; Newsp. Period. Abstr. (1991-); Res. Alert [Full Cov.]; Soc. Sci. Source (Jan. 1992-); Soc. Sci. Cit. Index [Full Cov.]; Soc. Sci. Index; Soc. Sci. Index Fulltext (Fall 1988-) [Full Txt.].

FR/0046-2616
ETHNOLOGIE FRANCAISE. [Ethnol. fr.]. **Added/Corp** Societe d'Ethnographie Francaise. New Series, Vol. 1 (1971)-. Periodical. French (summaries and/or abstracts in English). qt. $138.00 institutions; $115.00 individuals. Librairie Armand Colin, BP 22, 41354 Vineuil Cedex France. **Tel** 011 33 54 438994. **(Subscription address:** 7A Boulevard de Perolles, CH-1701 Fribourg Switzerland**)** ***Supersedes*** *Arts et Traditions Populaires; Folklore Paysan; Mois d'Ethnographie Francaise. Bulletin de la Societe d'Ethnographie Francaise; Annales. Societe d'Ethnographie Francaise.*
Ind/Abst Anthropol. Lit.; BHA : Biblio. Hist. Art; MLA Int. Bibl. Books Artic. Mod. Lang. Lit.

US/0749-4033
ETHNOMUSICOLOGY AT UCLA. ***Title Change.*** **See** Music.

IT
ETNIE. ***Suspended.*** (19??)-(1991). Periodical. Italian. ir. Etnie, V le Bligny 22, 20136 Milan Italy. **Tel** 011 39 2 58300530. **LC** GN495.4; .E85. **DD** 305.8/005.

CN/0701-1008
ETUDES INUIT. See Anthropology.

AU/0014-2492
EUROPA ETHNICA. [Eur. ethn.]. **Added/Corp** Federal Union of European Nationalities. Vol. 18, No. 1 (1961)-. Periodical. German (English and French). Four times a year. S480.00 Austria; S555.00 other. Wilhelm Braumueller, Servitengasse 5, A 1092 Vienna, Austria. **Tel** 011 43 1 3191482, 3191159. **ED** Wilhelm Braumuller. **Bk Rev. Ad Acc. Circ:** 1,200 (ctrl). ***Absorbed*** *Bulletin of the Federal Union of European Nationalities;* ***Continues*** *Nation und Staat.*
Desc: A quarterly for problems of nationalities with official news of the Federal Union of European Nationalities and the International Institute of Ethnic Groups' Rights and Regionalism.
Ind/Abst Am. Hist. Life (1971-); Int. Bibliogr. Sociol.; PAIS Int. Print; Soc. Plann. Policy Dev. Abstr.

UK/0952-391X
EUROPEAN JOURNAL OF INTERCULTURAL STUDIES. Vol. 1, No. 1 (1990)-. Periodical. English. Three times a year. £60.00 UK, £70.00 other (institutions); £35.00 UK, £40.00 others (individuals). Trentham Books Ltd, Westview House, 734 London Road, Oakhill, Stoke-on-Trent, Staffordshire ST4 5NP England. **Tel** 011 44 782 745567, FAX 011 44 782 745553. **ED** Maurice Blanc, John Eggleston, and Barry Troyna. Index available. **Bk Rev. Ad Acc. Pr Rev. Circ:** 1,000.
Desc: Focus on interaction between majority and minority groups.
Ind/Abst Br. Educ. Index; Soc. Plann. Policy Dev. Abstr.

GW/0238-1486
EUROPEAN REVIEW OF NATIVE AMERICAN STUDIES. (1987)-. Periodical. English. sa (May, Nov.). $25.00. Christian F Feest, Fasanenweg 4A, D 63674 Altenstadt Germany. **Tel** 011 49 69 7982122, 011 49 6047 67566, FAX 011 43 222 5351069. **ED** Christian F. Feest. **LC** WMLC 93/301. **Bk Rev**, (Qty: 20). **Ad Acc. Pr Rev. Circ:** 400. ***Absorbed*** *American Indian Workshop Newsletter.*
Ind/Abst Anthropol. Lit.

IS/0334-4436
EVREI I EVREISKII NAROD. MATERIALY IZ SOVETSKOI PECHATI. ***Ceased.*** **See** Religion and Theology-Judaism.

UK
EXETER HISPANIC TEXTS. Added/Corp University of Exeter. (1972)-. Monographic series. English (Spanish). Price varies per volume. University of Exeter Press, Reed Hall, Streatham Drive, Exeter EX4 4RJ United Kingdom. **Tel** 011 44 392 263202.

US/0730-904X
EXPLORATIONS IN ETHNIC STUDIES. [Explor. ethn. stud.]. **Added/Corp** National Association of Interdisciplinary Ethnic Studies (U.S.) National Association for Interdisciplinary Ethnic Studies (U.S.) National Association for Ethnic Studies (U.S.). Vol. 1, No. 1 (Jan. 1978)-. Periodical. English. sa. $35.00. National Association of Ethnic Studies Inc., Arizona State University, Department of English, Tempe AZ 85287. **Tel** (602)965-2197, FAX (602)965-2012. **ED** Gretchen M. Bataille. **LC** E184.A1; E94. **CODEN** EETSEN. cum. index. **Bk Rev. Ad Acc. Pr Rev. Circ:** 350 (ctrl). available on microfilm. Documents available from UMI Article Clearinghouse.
Desc: An interdisciplinary journal devoted to the study of ethnicity, ethnic groups, intergroup relations, and the cultural life of ethnic minorities. Supplemented by a review issue and biannual newsletter.
Ind/Abst Am. Hist. Life (1978-); Am. Bibliogr. Slavic East Europ. Stud.; Expand. Acad. Index (1992-); MLA Int. Bibl. Books Artic. Mod. Lang. Lit.; Newsp. Period. Abstr. (1992-); Soc. Work Abstr. (Summer 1987-?) [Select. Cov.].

US/0733-3323
EXPLORATIONS IN SIGHTS AND SOUNDS. [Explor. sights sounds]. **Added/Corp** National Association of Interdisciplinary Ethnic Studies (U.S.). No. 1 (Mar. 1981)-. Periodical. English. an. $35.00 (individuals), $100.00 (institutions) Comes with National Association of Ethnic Studies membership. National Association of Ethnic Studies Inc., Arizona State University, Department of English, Tempe AZ 85287. **Tel** (602)965-2197, FAX (602)965-2012. **(Subscription address:** University of Washington, NAES Membership, c/o Johnnella Butler, American Ethnic Studies GN-80, Seattle, WA 98195**) ED** Gretchen M. Bataille. **LC** E184.A1; E96. **DD** 973/.04/005. cum. index. **Bk Rev. Circ:** 300 (ctrl). available on microfilm.
Desc: Publishes reviews of books and non-print media of interest to teachers, students, and scholars in ethnic studies as well as to community organizations.

US/0734-2659
FALL COLLEGE ENROLLMENTS BY RACIAL/ETHNIC CATEGORY. See Education-Higher Education.

●US/1063-4630
FILIPINAS (SAN FRANCISCO, CALIF.). (FILIPINAS.). [Filipinas]. (May 1992)-. Periodical. English. mo. $24.00. Filipinas Publishing Incorporated, 5222 Diamond Heights Boulevard, San Francisco CA 94131. **Tel** (800)654-7777, (415)824-0735, FAX (415)824-3808. **ED** Rene Ciria-Cruz. **LC** WMLC 93/1100. **DD** 051. **Bk Rev. Ad Acc, Adv Mgr:** B.Bitagon.

US/0745-905X
FILIPINO AMERICAN, THE. (Oct. 2-8, 1981)-. Periodical. English. ir. The Filipino American, 2741 Fruitridge Road, Sacramento CA 95820. ***Continues*** *Bataan News, 0199-0535.*

US
FILIPINO-AMERICAN HERALD, THE. Periodical. English. mo. Filipino-American Herald, 508 Maynard Avenue South, Seattle WA 98140.

US
FINNAM NEWSLETTER / FINNISH-AMERICAN HISTORICAL SOCIETY OF THE WEST. Added/Corp Finnish American Historical Society of the West. Vol. 2, No. 1 (Dec. 6, 1965)-Vol. 7, No. 3 (Aug. 1972); New Ser., No. 1 (Jan. 1974)-. Newsletter. English. qt. Free to members; $7.50 membership fee. Finnish-American Historical Society of the West, PO Box 5522, Portland OR 97208. **Tel** (503)654-0448. **ED** Gene A. Knapp. **LC** E184.F5; F44. Index available. **Bk Rev.** ***Continues*** *Newsletter (Finnish American Historical Society of the West).* ***Continued in part by*** *Finnish Emigrant Studies Series.*
Desc: Documents the rich and varied culture of Finnish-Americans who immigrated to America's West.

US/0195-5411
FIRMS IN THE 8(A) BUSINESS DEVELOPMENT PROGRAM. (FIRMS IN THE 8(A) BUSINESS DEVELOPMENT PROGRAM / U.S. SMALL BUSINESS ADMINISTRATION, ASSOCIATE ADMINISTRATOR/OFFICE OF MINORITY SMALL BUSINESS AND CAPITOL OWNERSHIP DEVELOPMENT, PROGRAM PLANNING AND CONTROL STAFF (PPCS).). **VAT** Firms in the Eight(A) Business Development Program. English. Small Business Administration, 1030 15th Street, Washington DC 20417. **Tel** (202)653-6963. **LC** HD2346.U5; U57B. **DD** 338.6/422/02573.

CN
FIRST PERSPECTIVE. English. Twelve times a year. 32.20Can$ (one year); 57.60Can$ (two years). Brokenhead First Nation, General Delivery, Scanterbury R0E 1W0 Canada. **Tel** (204)766-2686, 474-2358, FAX (204)478-9800. **ED** J. Wastasecont (editor's address: 753A St. Mary's Road, Winnipeg, Manitoba R2M 3N6 Canada; telephone: (204)256-8035). **Bk Rev**, (Qty: 24 per year). **Ad Acc. Circ:** 11,000 (ctrl).
Desc: An Aboriginal publication featuring news, analysis, information and data on events pertaining to First Nations of Canada.

US
FLORIDA INDIANS. See History(General)-History of North, South, and Central America.

US/0740-0195
FOCUS - JOINT CENTER FOR POLITICAL STUDIES. (FOCUS.). [Focus - Jt. Cent. Polit. Stud.]. V. 1- Nov. 1972-. Periodical. English. mo. $12.00. Joint Center Political Studies, Washington DC 20004. **Tel** (202)626-3500. **ED** Kevin D Armstrong. **LC** E185.5; .F6. **DD** 301.45/19/6073. **Bk Rev. Circ:** 11,000.
Desc: Articles written by scholars, analysts and others on political and public policy issues of special interest to black Americans.
Ind/Abst PAIS Int. Print (1991-).

HU
FOLKLOR ARCHIVUM. See Folklore.

RM/0015-7902
FORSCHUNGEN ZUR VOLKS- UND LANDESKUNDE. [Forsch. Volks- Landeskd.]. **Added/Corp** Academia Republicii Socialiste Romania. Academia Republicii Populare Romine. Academia Republicii Populare Romine. Sektion fur Gesellschaftswissenschaften--Hermannstadt. Academia de Stiinte Sociale si Politice a Republicii Socialiste Romania. (1959)-. Periodical. German. sa. DM198.00. Editura Academia Republicii Socialiste Romania, Calea Victoriei Nr 125, R-79717 Bucuresti Romania. **Tel** telex 10376 PRSFI R. **(Subscription address:** Kubon & Sagner, ABT Zeitschriftenimport, D 80328 Munich Germany.**)**
Ind/Abst Am. Hist. Life (1985-); BHA : Biblio. Hist. Art.

US/0747-2757
FRANCE AMERIQUE (NEW YORK, N.Y.). See Newspapers.

CN/1183-2487
FRANCOPHONIES D'AMERIQUE. [Francoph. Am.]. No 1 (1991)-. French. 19.95Can$. Francophonies D'Amerique, 603 Rue Cumberland, Ottawa Ontario K1N 6N5 Canada. **DD** 440/.971/05.

CN/0823-6577
FRATERNALLY YOURS. (FRATERNALLY YOURS : OFFICIAL PUBLICATION OF THE NEW FRATERNAL JEWISH ASSOCIATION.). [Fratern. yours]. **VFOAT** Unzere Tetikeyt. Periodical. English (Yiddish). bm. Free to members. Fraternally Yours, c/o New Fraternal Jewish Association, 110 Overbrook Place, Downsview Ontario M3H 4P8 Canada. **DD** 909/.04924/005.

UK
FREE ROMANIAN : ORGAN OF THE WORLD UNION OF FREE ROMANIANS, THE. Added/Corp Uniunea Romanilor Liberi. Vol. 1, No. 1 (May 1985)-. Periodical. English. mo. **LC** DR201; .F73. ***Continues in part*** *Free Romanian Press.*
Ind/Abst Hum. Rights Intern. Rep.

UK
FWZ REVIEW. ***Title Change.*** **See** Women's Interests.

IS/0334-4258
GALED. [Galced]. **Added/Corp** Galed (Society) Universitat Tel-Aviv. Makhon le-Heker ha-Tefutsot. **VFOAT** Gal-ed. (1973)-. Hebrew (summaries and/or abstracts in English). an. Tel Aviv University / Publications, Publications Department, Tel Aviv Israel. **LC** DS135.P6; G34.
Ind/Abst Am. Hist. Life (1973-).

AT
GENERATION : A JOURNAL OF AUSTRALIAN JEWISH LIFE, THOUGHT AND COMMUNITY. (19??)-. Periodical. English. qt. 30.00Aus$ Australia; 50.00Aus$ other. General

Journal Inc., 306 Hawthorn Road Caulfield SO, Victoria 312 Australia. **Tel** 011 61 3 5313508, FAX 011 61 3 5256585. **ED** Mark Baker. **LC** DS135.A88; G46. **DD** 994/.004924.
Ind/Abst Index Jew. Period. (19??-).

US/1054-9226
GENEVA CHRONICLE (BERKELEY, CALIF.). (GENEVA CHRONICLE : A DIGEST & ANALYSIS OF AFRICAN AMERICAN CULTURE & THOUGHT.). (1991)-. Periodical. English. bm. $60.00. Geneva Publishing Co., PO Box 5875, Berkeley CA 94705.

US
GENTE DE AZTLAN, LA. Added/Corp Associated Students of UCLA. Communications Board. **VFOAT** Gente. Vol. 17, No. 1 (Oct. 1986)-. Periodical. English. ir (twice every ten weeks). La Gente de Aztlan, 308 Westwood Plaza, 112D Kerckhoff Hall, Los Angeles CA 90024. **Tel** (310)825-9836. cum. index. **Circ:** 10,000. ***Continues*** *Gente (Los Angeles, Calif. : 1982).*
Desc: Student publication at the University of California, Los Angeles which serves the Native American, Chicano, and Latino communities.

CN/0836-7124
GLASNIK (NORTH BURNABY). See History(General)-History of Europe.

CN/0318-0042
GOLOS INSTYTUTU. (HOLOS INSTITUTU.). V. 1- 1963-. Periodical. Multiple languages (Ukrainian and English). ir. Holos Institutu, 1240 Temperance Street, Sakatoon Saskatchewan S7N 0P1 Canada. **Tel** 653-1944. **ED** Terry Makowsky. **Bk Rev. Circ:** 1,900 (ctrl).
Desc: Cultural, social, religious, activities; events in Moltyca institute, chaplains Ukrainian orthodox religious messages, donation lists and special articles of interest on Ukrainian themes.

US
GRANTS FOR MINORITIES / FOUNDATION CENTER. See Philanthropy.

US/1056-215X
GREEK-AMERICAN REVIEW. [Greek-Am. rev.]. H Nea Yopkh, PO Box 675 Grand Central Station, New York NY 10163. **LC** WMLC 90/0753. **DD** 051. ***Continues*** *He nea Yorke, 0742-4728.*

US/0890-0035
GREEKAMERICAN, THE. [GreekAm.]. **VFOAT** Greek American. (198?)-. Periodical. English. wk. $45.00 one year; $75.00 two years. The GreekAmerican, 25 - 50 Crescent Street, Astoria NY 11102. **Tel** (718)626-7676, FAX (718)626-7830. **ED** Michael Efthimiades. **DD** 051. **Bk Rev. Ad Acc.** ***Continues*** *Weekly Review, Proini, 0888-4900.*

US/0256-9043
GUANGHUA (ZHONG-YINGWEN BAN). (KUANG HUA.). **VFOAT** Sinorama; Sinorama Magazine. Vol. 3, No. 1 (January 1978)-. Periodical. Chinese (English). mo. $32.00 (one year); $55.00 (two year). Kwang Hwa Publishing, 900 North Western Avenue, Suite 101, Los Angeles CA 90029. **Tel** (213)461-4918, FAX (213)461-1769. **Circ:** 9,000 US, 500 Canada. ***Continues*** *Kuang Hua Hua Pao.*

AG
GUIA ANUAL ISRAELITA. See Religion and Theology-Judaism.

AT/0811-6636
GUIDE TO ETHNIC MEDIA IN VICTORIA / VICTORIAN ETHNIC AFFAIRS COMMISSION. Added/Corp Victorian Ethnic Affairs Commission. (19??)-. English. an. Free. Victorian Ethnic Affairs Commission, 232 Victoria Parade, East Melbourne 3002 Australia. **Tel** (03)4126257, FAX (03)4171211. **LC** P94.5.M552; A84. **DD** 001.51/025/945. **Circ:** 3,000.
Desc: Listing on ethnic community media, with contact information, for Victoria, Australia.

US/0272-1066
GUIDE TO JEWISH CHICAGO, AND YEARBOOK. [Guide Jew. Chicago yearb.]. **Main/Corp** American Jewish Congress. 4th- Ed.; 1978-. English. $2.50. American Jewish Congress, 15 East 84th Street, New York NY 10028. **Tel** (212)879-4500 Ext.200/212, FAX (212)249-3672. **LC** F548.9.J5; A46A. **DD** 305.8/924/077311.

US
HAMPTON REVIEW : HR, THE. VFOAT HR. Vol. 14, No. 1 (Fall 1988)-. English. an. Hampton University, Department of History, Philosophy and Religion, Hampton VA 23688. ***Continues*** *Journal of Ethnic Studies.*

CN/0707-574X
HANDBOOK FOR INDIANS IN OTTAWA-HULL, A. VAT South Asians in Canada. Began publication in 1975?. English. an. $1.50. B.P. Mathur, Apartment 2, 349 Booth Street, Ottawa K1R 7K1. **DD** 917.13/84/0025.

US
HARAMBEE. (19??)-. English. Six times a year (Feb., Mar., Apr., May, Sept., Nov.). $15.00. Just Us Books Inc., 301 Main Street, Suite 22-24, Orange NJ 07050. **Tel** (201)676-4345, FAX (201)677-0234. **ED** Constance L. Diggs. **Bk Rev**, (Qty: 1). **Ad Acc, Adv Mgr:** C. Diggs. **Circ:** 4,000.
Desc: African-American news and information.

US/0897-2761
HARVARD BLACKLETTER JOURNAL, THE. See Political Science-Civil Rights.

US/1074-1917
HARVARD JOURNAL OF HISPANIC POLICY. [Harv. j. Hisp. policy]. **VFOAT** Journal of Hispanic Policy. Vol. 6 (1992/1993)-. English. an. $45.00 (institutions), $15.00 (individuals). Hispanic Journal of Hispanic Policy, 79 JFK Street, Cambridge MA 02138. **Tel** (617)495-1311. **LC** E184.S75; J68. **DD** 305. ***Continues*** *Journal of Hispanic Policy, 0892-6115.*

US/8750-913X
HAWAII HERALD (1969). (THE HAWAII HERALD.). Vol. 1, No. 1 (May 16, 1980)-. Newspaper. English. sm. $20.00. The Hawaii Herald, PO Box 17429, Honolulu HI 96817. **Tel** (808)845-2255, FAX (808)847-7215. **ED** Arnold T Hiura. Index available. cum. index. **Bk Rev. Ad Acc. Circ:** 7,500 (ctrl). available on microfiche. ***Continues*** *Hawaii Herald (Honolulu, Hawaii : 1969), 8750-913X.*
Desc: Covers cultural, historical and contemporary issues affecting Japanese Americans in Hawaii.

US/1054-2671
HAYKAKAN ELLOPEYJ : KALIFORNIAHAY ENDARDZAK HERATSUTSAK. VFOAT Armenian Yellow Pages. 1st Ed. (1991)-. Armenian (English). $20.00. Armenian Reference Books Co., PO Box 231, Glendale CA 91209.

BL
HEBRAICA, A. Periodical. Portuguese. mo. Associacao Brasileira A Hebraica de Sao Paulo, rua Alvea Gumaraes 645, CEP 05410 Sao Paulo Brazil. **LC** AP93; .H4. **DD** 305.8/924/08161. ***Continues*** *Hebraica em Revista.*

US/0748-7568
HEJNA. (HEJNA : POLISH AMERICAN CULTURAL ASSOCIATION OF METRO ST. LOUIS NEWSLETTER.). Vol. 1, No. 1 (Nov. 1978)-. Newsletter. English. qt. $6.00. Polish American Cultural Society of Metro St Louis, 12205 Rollingsford Drive, Florissant MO 63033. **Tel** (314)741-2763. **ED** Delphine Z Kaminski. **LC** F474.S29; P694. Index available. **Bk Rev. Ad Acc. Circ:** 1,800.
Desc: Our publication is primarily educational because there is a need for a Polish-American publication. We do print local and national news, and are in seven archives including the Library of Congress.

US
HELLENIC CHRONICLE, THE. (1950)-. Newspaper. English. wk. $20.00 (1 year) $35.00 (2 year) US; $45.00 (1 year), $85.00 (2 year) Canada; $55.00 (1 year), $90.00 (2 year) other. Hellenic Publishing Corporation, 324 Newbury Street, Boston MA 02115. **Tel** (617)262-4500. **LC** Newspaper.

US/0895-0792
HERITAGE (CARSON, CALIF.). (HERITAGE.). Vol. 1, No. 1 (June 1987)-. Periodical. English (Tagalog). qt (March, June, Sept., Dec.). $15.00 (individuals), $20.00 (institutions) US; $21.00 (individuals), $26.00 (institutions) Canada; $31.00 (individuals), $36.00 (institutions) other. Heritage Publishers, PO Box 9160, Long Beach CA 90810-0160. **Tel** (310)635-1087. **ED** Victor P. Gendrano. **DD** 959. **Bk Rev. Ad Acc.** ctrl circ.
Desc: A general interest magazine about Philipine history, culture, customs and traditions. Covers the history and culture of Filipinos and features biographical sketches of successful Filipinos in all fields.
Ind/Abst Acad. Search (July 1993-); Mag. Artic. Summar. Elite (July 1993-).

US/0161-5378
HIGHLANDER (BARRINGTON), THE. (THE HIGHLANDER.). (1963)-. Periodical. English. Seven times a year (bi-monthly with annual directory). $15.50 (one year), $29.50 (two year). Angus J. Ray Publisher, PO Box 397, Barrington IL 60011. **Tel** (312)382-1035, FAX (312)382-0322. **ED** Angus J. Ray. **LC** E184.S3; H5. **DD** 973/.049163/005. Index available. **Bk Rev**, (Qty: 10 per year). **Ad Acc. Circ:** 40,000.
Desc: The journal reports on the activities of the Scottish societies in the US and Canada such as the highland games, piping dancing and other Scottish events. Features on famous Scots, Clans, genealogical information and historical events that have shaped the Scottish heritage.

●US
HILLEL GUIDE TO JEWISH LIFE ON CAMPUS, THE. Added/Corp B'nai B'rith Hillel Foundations. **VFOAT** Jewish Life on Campus. (1991/1992)-. English. ***Continues*** *Jewish Life on Campus.*

US/0018-2168
HISPANIC AMERICAN HISTORICAL REVIEW, THE. See History(General)-History of North, South, and Central America.

US/1046-3933
HISPANIC AMERICAN INFORMATION DIRECTORY. [Hisp. Am. inf. dir.]. **Added/Corp** Gale Research, Inc. **VFOAT** HAID. 1st Ed. (1990/1991)-. Directory. English. be. $85.00. Gale Research Inc., 835 Penobscot Building, Detroit MI 48226. **Tel** (800)877-GALE, (313)961-2242, FAX (313)961-6083, telex TWX 810-221-7086. **ED** Charles B. Montney. **LC** E184.S75; H566. **DD** 973/.0468/0025. Index available. available on magnetic tape; available on diskette.
Desc: Provides complete contact information and additional details on a wide range of organizations, agencies, and programs, including national, state, and local Hispanic associations.

US/1056-7992
HISPANIC AMERICANS (BOULDER, COLO.). (HISPANIC AMERICANS : A STATISTICAL SOURCEBOOK.). [Hisp. Am.]. **Added/Corp** Numbers & Concepts (Firm). (1991)-. Statistical Publication. English. Numbers & Concepts, Suite E4-221, 2525 Arapahoe Avenue, Boulder CO 80302. **LC** E184.S75; H5655. **DD** 305.868/0021. **NLM** E 184.S75; H673.

US/0199-0349
HISPANIC BUSINESS. See Business.

US/0739-9863
HISPANIC JOURNAL OF BEHAVIORAL SCIENCES. [Hisp. j. behav. sci.]. **Added/Corp** Spanish Speaking Mental Health Research Center (U.S.). Vol. 1, No. 1 (March 1979)-. Academic Scholarly Publication. English (Spanish). qt (Feb., May, Aug., Nov.). $262.00. SAGE Periodical Press, 2455 Teller Road, Thousand Oaks CA 91320. **Tel** (805)499-0721, FAX (805)499-0871, telex 100799. **ED** Amado M. Padilla (Stanford University). **LC** RC451.5.H57; H58. **DD** 362.2/08968073. **CODEN** HJBSEZ. Index available. **Bk Rev. Ad Acc. Pr Rev. Acid Free. Circ:** 625. available on microfilm and microfiche from University Microfilms International (UMI). Documents available from The Genuine Article, BIOSIS Document Express, UMI Article Clearinghouse.
Desc: Publishes research articles, case histories, critical reviews and scholarly notes that are of theoretical interest or deal with methodological issues related to Hispanic populations.
Ind/Abst Biol. Abstr. (1987-); Chicano Index; Curr. Contents Soc. Behav. Sci.; Curr. Index J. Educ.; Curr. Lit. Fam. Plan.; Expand. Acad. Index (1992-); HAPI Hisp. Am. Period. Index; High. Educ. Abstr. (1980-); Hum. Resour. Abstr.; Newsp. Period. Abstr. (1992-); Psychol. Abstr. (1979-); PsycINFO; PsycLit; Res. Alert [Full Cov.]; Sage Fam. Stud. Abstr.; Soc. Plann. Policy Dev. Abstr.; Soc. Sci. Cit. Index [Full Cov.]; Soc. Work Abstr. [Select. Cov.]; Spec. Educ. Needs Abstr.

US
HISPANIC LINK. Began publication in Feb 1980. Periodical. English. wk. $96.00. Hispanic Link, 1420 N Street NW, Washington DC 20005. **Tel** (202)234-0280. **ED** Felix Perez. **Bk Rev. Ad Acc. Circ:** 1,100 (ctrl).
Desc: A single, comprehensive source for news and information on what's happening that impacts the lives and opportunities of 20 million US Hispanics.

US
HISPANIC LINK WEEKLY REPORT. Added/Corp Hispanic Link News Service. Vol. 1, No. 1 (Sept. 5 1983)-. Newsletter. English. Fifty times a year. $128.00. Hispanic Link News Service, 1420 North Street Northwest, Washington DC 20005. **Tel** (202)234-0280, FAX (202)234-4090. **ED** Jonathan Higuera. **LC** E184.S75; H53. **Bk Rev**, (Qty: 50). **Ad Acc, Adv Mgr:** Carlos, **Tel** (210)239-0280. **Circ:** 1,100.
Desc: Newsletter that covers hispanic issues nationwide.

●US/1071-4553
HISPANIC MEDIA & MARKET SOURCE. See Business-Marketing.

US/0191-6297
HISPANIC NOTABLES IN THE UNITED STATES OF NORTH AMERICA. Periodical. English (Spanish). an. Saguaro Publications Inc, 13118 Cedarbrook Avenue NE, Albuquerque NM 87111. **LC** E184.S75; H58. **DD** 920/.0092/6873.

US
HISPANIC RESOURCE DIRECTORY. (1988)-. Directory. English. ir (every 2-3 years). $47.50 US; $50.50 Canada. Denali Press, PO Box 021535, Juneau AK 99802. **Tel** (907)586-6014, FAX (907)463-6780. **LC** E184.S75; H584.

US/0892-1369
HISPANIC TIMES MAGAZINE. See Occupations and Careers.

US
HISPANIC TODAY. (198?)-. Periodical. English. mo. $15.00. Hispanic Today, 21757 Devonshire, Suite #3, Chatsworth CA 91311. **Tel** (818) 595-3203.

Ethnic Interests

US/0898-3097
HISPANIC (WASHINGTON, D.C.).
(HISPANIC.). [Hispanic]. (April 1988)-. Periodical. English. mo (11 issues). $18.00. Hispanic Publishing Corporation, 98 San Jacinto Boulevard, Suite 1150, Austin TX 78701. **Tel** (512)476-5599, (800)251-2688. **(Subscription address:** Kable Publishers Aide, 308 East Hitt Street, Subscription Department, Mt. Morris IL 61054-1473.) **ED** Alfredo J. Estrada and Maria Elena Sharpe. **LC** E184.S75; H54. **DD** 973/.0468/005. **Bk Rev**. **Ad Acc**. **Circ:** 150,000. Documents available from UMI Article Clearinghouse.
Desc: Features prominent, interesting Hispanics in the fields of education, business, politics, art, sciences, entertainment, sports, etc.
Ind/Abst Acad. Abstr. Full Text Elite (Jan. 1992-); Acad. Abstr. (Jan. 1992-); Acad. Search (Jan. 1992-); Chicano Index; INFO-SOUTH Abstr.; Mag. Artic. Summar. Elite (Jan. 1992-); Mag. Artic. Summar. CD-ROM (Jan. 1992-); Mag. Index Plus (1989-); Mag. Index. Sel. (1989-); Mag. Search; Newsp. Period. Abstr. (1990-); Mag. Index (1989-); TOM Gen. Index (1989-).

US
HISPANO NEWS, EL. **VFOAT** Hispano. Vol. 20, No. 35 (Jan. 17, 1986)-. Newspaper. Spanish. wk. $10.00 (one year); $18.00 (two years); $26.00 (three years). El Hispano / New Mexico, 900 Park Avenue Southwest, PO Box 986, Albuquerque NM 87102. **Tel** (505)243-6161, **FAX** (505)842-5464, telex 505. **ED** Ramon Huerta, and Francisco Collado (Managing Editor). **Bk Rev.** (Qty: 20). **Photos**. **Ad Acc**, **Adv Mgr:** A. B. Collado. Full Page (B&W) $700.00. Half Page (B&W) $350.00. Full Page (Color) $825.00. Half Page (Color) $475.00. **Pub. Size:** Tabloid. **Circ:** 10,000 (ctrl). available in microform.
Continues Hispano (Albuquerque, N.M. : 1966).

US
HISPANO (SACRAMENTO, CALIF.). See Newspapers.

CN/0837-1342
HOLLANDSE KRANT. (DE HOLLANDSE KRANT.). [Holl. krant]. (1969)-. Newspaper. Dutch. mo. 17.00Can$ US & Canada; 33.00Can$ other. De Hollandse Krant, 12-20505 Fraser Highway, Langley British Columbia, V3A 4G3 Canada. **Tel** (604)530-9446, **FAX** (604)530-9766. **ED** Gerald Bonekamp. **DD** 971.0043931. **Bk Rev**, (Qty: 6). **Ad Acc** **Circ:** 7,400 (ctrl).

VM
HON VIET. **Added/Corp** Oan Sinh-Vien Xa-Hoi Dalat. (19??)-. Periodical. Vietnamese. Twelve times a year. $32.00 US; $55.00 others. Hon Viet Magazine, PO Box 609, Midway City CA 92655. **Tel** (714)265-2665, **FAX** (714)265-2702.

US/1066-6311
HON VIET (GARDEN GROVE, CALIF.). (HON VIET.). [Hon Viet]. **VFOAT** Hon Viet Magazine. (19??)-. Periodical. Vietnamese. mo. $32.00 (one year); $60.00 (two year) US; $55.00 (one year), $105.00 (two year) other. Hon Viet Magazine, PO Box 609, Midway City CA 92655. **Tel** (714)265-2665, **FAX** (714)265-2702. **ED** Kiem Ngor Nguyen. **DD** 059.

US/0018-4721
HOOSHARAR. **Added/Corp** Armenian General Benevolent Union. (19??)-. Periodical. English. mo (except July and Aug.). $10.00. Armenian General Benevolent Union, 585 Saddle River Road, Saddle Brook NJ 07662. **Tel** (201)797-7600, **FAX** (201)797-4883. **ED** Terry Chisholm. **LC** E184.A7; H66. **DD** 973/.0491992/005. **Bk Rev**. **Circ:** 7,500 (ctrl).
Desc: Covers news and features about people and events of interest to those aligned with the Armenian culture around the world.

US/0741-9384
HORA (NEW YORK, N.Y.). See Dance.

CN/0708-580X
HORIZON (MONTREAL. 1979). (HORIZON.). [Horizon]. Vol. 1 (May 28, 1979)-. Periodical. Armenian. wk. 20.00Can$. Horizon / Canada, 3401 Olivar-Asselin, Montreal Quebec H4J 1L5 Canada. **DD** 071/.14/281.

US/0018-599X
HOSPODAR. Began in 1891. Periodical. Czech. mo. Czechoslovak Publishing Company, Box 38, West TX 76691.

US
HOWNIKAN. English. Free to tribal members; $10.00 other. Potawatomi Indians of Oklahoma, 1901 S Gordon Cooper Drive, Shawnee OK 74801. **Tel** (800)657-7334, (405)275-3121.
Desc: The Citizen Band Potawatomi Tribal newspaper.

US/1056-3873
HUA WEN ZA ZHI. (HUA WEN TSA CHIH). [Hua wen za zhi]. **VFOAT** Chinese Journal. (1990)-. Periodical. Chinese. mo. $18.00. Chinese Journal, 620 Kearny Street, San Francisco CA 94108. **DD** 051.

US/0889-2695
HUNGARIAN HERITAGE REVIEW. [Hung. herit. rev.]. **VFOAT** Magyar Oroksegunk. Vol. 14, No. 12 (Dec. 1985)-. Periodical. English. mo. $25.00 US; 25.00Can$ Canada; $35.00 other. Rakoczi Press International Inc, PO Box 2203, Union NJ 07083. **Tel** (201)964-8464. **ED** Paul Pulitzer. **LC** E184.H95; E36. **DD** 973/.0494511/05. **Bk Rev**. **Ad Acc**. ctrl circ. *Continues Eighth Hungarian Tribe.*
Desc: An English language magazine for American and Canadian citizens of Hungarian descent featuring articles on history, culture, customs, folklore, literature, etc.

CN/0046-8452
ICELANDIC CANADIAN. (THE ICELANDIC CANADIAN.). **Added/Corp** Icelandic Canadian Club. (Oct. 1942)-. Academic Scholarly Publication. English. Four times a year. 18.00Can$ (one year), 34.00Can$ (two year). Icelandic Canadian, 1005-880 Arlington Street, Winnipeg Manitoba R3E 3H2 Canada. **Tel** (204)775-2275. **ED** Sigrid Johnson, Dafoe Library, University of Manitoba, R3T 2N2 Canada; (204)474-6345. **Bk Rev**, (Qty: 8-12). **Ad Acc**, **Adv Mgr:** Rosemary Isford, **Tel** (204)284-2169. **Pr Rev**. **Circ:** 1,000.
Desc: Short scholarly articles, editorials and poetry on Icelandic themes: Vikings, immigration, early settlements in North America, heritage, and speeches from major celebrations.
Ind/Abst Am. Hist. Life (1987-); Sage Race Relat. Abstr.

CN
IDEAS. IDEES. **Added/Corp** Canada. Dept. of Indian Affairs and Northern Development. Indian and Eskimo Affairs Program. **VFOAT** Idees. Vol. 2, No. 1 (Mar. 1974)-. Periodical. Multiple languages (English and French).

●**SZ/1070-289X**
IDENTITIES (YVERDON, SWITZERLAND). (IDENTITIES : GLOBAL STUDIES IN CULTURE AND POWER.). [Identities]. Vol. 1, No. 1 (June 1994)-. Periodical. English. qt. Gordon & Breach Science Publishers, PO Box 90, Reading RG1 8JL England. **Tel** 011 44 734 560080, **FAX** 011 44 734 568211. **DD** 301. *Continues Ethnic Groups, 0308-6860.*
Ind/Abst Acad. Search (Jan. 1994-).

US/0749-5951
IMMIGRANT COMMUNITIES & ETHNIC MINORITIES IN THE UNITED STATES & CANADA. [Immigr. communities ethn. minor. U.S. Can.]. **VFOAT** Immigrant Communities and Ethnic Minorities in the United States and Canada. (1984)-. Monographic series. English. ir. Price varies per volume. AMS Press Inc., 56 East 13th Street, New York NY 10003. **Tel** (212)777-4700, **FAX** (212)995-5413, telex 710 581 2302. **ED** James G Chadney. **LC** UNC. **DD** 305.
Desc: Strives to be of value in promoting a deeper understanding of ethnic Americans, ethnic Canadians, and the concept of cultural pluralism.

US/1056-0467
IMMINENCE! (ARLINGTON, VA.). *Ceased.* (IMMINENCE!). [Imminence!]. (1991)-Vol. 2, No. 1 (Sept. 1993). Periodical. English. mo. Glossary Ink, 2329 Kirby Drive, Hillcrest Heights MD 20748. **DD** 305.

US/0090-3930
IMPACT (PHILADELPHIA). (IMPACT.). **Added/Corp** American Negro Commemorative Society. (197?)-. Periodical. English. Ten times a year. 20.00Aus$. American Negro Commemorative Society, Lewis Tower Building, Philadelphia PA 19102. **LC** E185.5; .I45. **DD** 973/.04/96073.

US/0738-9116
IMPARTIAL CITIZEN (SYRACUSE, N.Y. : 1980), THE. (THE IMPARTIAL CITIZEN.). Vol. 1, No. 1 (Sept. 3-9, 1980)-. Newspaper. English. Twenty-four times a year (Wed.). $15.00 (surface mail); $25.00 Canada, $150.00 others (airmail). Impartial Citizen, PO Box 98, Colvin Station, Syracuse NY 13205. **Tel** (315)635-6318, **FAX** (315)638-0778.

GW
IMPULSE (AUGSBURG, GERMANY). (IMPULSE.). **Added/Corp** Arbeitskreis fuer Volksgruppen- und Minderheitenfragen. Sudetendeutsche Landsmannschaft. Bezirksverband Schwaben. (1986)-. Monographic series. German. Price varies per volume. Gruner und Jahr Ag & Co, Abonnenten Service, D 20080 Hamburg Germany. **Tel** 011 49 40 37030.

US/1053-7864
IN PERSPECTIVE OF THE BLACK AMERICAN VETERAN. See Military and Defense.

US/1059-1230
IN YOUR FACE. (IN YOUR FACE : AN OFFICIAL PUBLICATION OF THE CENTER FOR RACIAL EDUCATION.). [In your face]. **Added/Corp** University of California, Berkeley. Center for Racial Education. Vol. 1, Issue 1 (1990)-. Periodical. English. mo. Subscription comes with donation. Center for Racial Education, 312 Eshleman Hall, University of Berkeley, Berkeley CA 94270. **ED** Gina Grega. **LC** PS509.M5; I5. **DD** 810.8/0920693. **Circ:** 150.

IS/0073-5817
INDEX TO ARTICLES ON JEWISH STUDIES. (RESHIMAT MA'AMARIM BE-MADA'E HA-YAHADUT.). [Index artic. Jew. stud.]. **Added/Corp** Bet ha-Sefarim ha-Leumi Veha-Universitai bi-Yerushalayim. **VFOAT** Index of Articles on Jewish Studies; RAMBI; IAJS. (1966)-. Hebrew (English). sa (2 issues). $20.00; Comes also with World Union of Jewish Studies membership. Jewish National and University Library, PO Box 34165, Jerusalem 91341 Israel. **Tel** 011 972 2 585039, 585019, **FAX** 011 972 2 586315, telex 25307. **ED** Bitya Ben Shammai. **Circ:** 2,000 (ctrl).

US/0899-6253
INDEX TO BLACK PERIODICALS. See Ethnic Interests-Abstracting, Bibliographies and Statistics.

II/0376-9747
INDEX TO INDIAN PERIODICAL LITERATURE. English. Indian Documentation Service, Patel Nagar, PO Box 13, Gurgaon 122 001 Haryana India. **Tel** 011 91 2205 Ext.9227 2205. **LC** AI3; .I55. **DD** 016.052.

US/0046-8932
INDIA ABROAD. (1970)-. Newspaper. English. wk. 34.24Can$ (1 year), 63.13Can$ (2 year), 19.26Can$ (6 mos.), 320.00Can$ (lifetime) Canada; $29.00 (1 year), $54.00 (2 year), $16.00 (6 mos.), $290.00 (lifetime) other. India Abroad, PO Box 1051 833 Helena Street, Ft Erie Ont L2A 5N8 Canada. **Tel** (416)740-4153. **ED** Gopal Raju. **Bk Rev**. **Ad Acc**. **Circ:** 50,000. available on microfilm from New York Public Library.
Desc: News and features related to India and Indians living abroad.

II
INDIA MAGAZINE OF HER PEOPLE AND CULTURE, THE. **VFOAT** India Magazine. No. 1 (Dec. 1980)-. Periodical. English. Twelve times a year. $45.00 Pakistan & Burma & Sri Lanka & Bangladesh & Afganistan; $58.00 others. Business India Group of Publishers, Wadia Building, 17 19 Dalal Street, Bombay 400 001 India. **Tel** 011 91 22 274161, 275388, telex 011 3557 BZIN IN. **ED** Malvika Singh. **LC** DS401; .I27466. **DD** 954/.005. **Bk Rev**. **Ad Acc**. **Circ:** 25,000.
Desc: Articulates the strength and diversity of the rich Indian culture. It covers every cultural aspect of life in India.
Ind/Abst Art Archaeol. Tech. Abstr.

US/0046-8967
INDIAN AFFAIRS (NEW YORK). (INDIAN AFFAIRS.). **Added/Corp** Association on American Indian Affairs. (19??)-. Periodical. English. Three times a year. $10.00. Association on American Indian Affairs, 245 Fifth Avenue, Suite 1801, New York NY 10016. **Tel** (212)689-8720, **FAX** (212)685-4692. **ED** Gary Kimble. **Circ:** 40,000 (ctrl). available on microfilm and microfiche from University Microfilms International (UMI).
Desc: Emphasis is on happenings of major significance in current Indian affairs. Self determination, legal defense, education, health, resource utilization, family defense, and foster care are some of the articles listed.

US/1054-1640
INDIAN-AMERICAN (NEW YORK, N.Y.), THE. (THE INDIAN-AMERICAN.). [Indian-Am.]. **VFOAT** Indian American. Vol. 1, No. 1 (Feb. 1991)-. Periodical. English. mo. $2.50 (single issue). The American-Indian, 18 East 16th Street, 6th Floor, New York NY 10003. **LC** WMLC 91/4508. **DD** 305.

US/0896-1972
INDIAN AWARENESS CENTER NEWS LETTER. (INDIAN AWARENESS CENTER NEWS LETTER / FULTON COUNTY HISTORICAL SOCIETY, INC.). [Indian Aware. Cent. news lett.]. **Added/Corp** Indian Awareness Center (Fulton County Historical Society (Ind.) Fulton County Historical Society (Ind.). **VFOAT** Indian Awareness Center Newsletter; Indian Awareness Newsletter. (198?)-. Newsletter. English. mo. $7.50 family membership; $5.00 individual membership. Fulton County Historical Society, 37 East 375 North, Rochester IN 46975. **Tel** (219)223-4436.
Desc: New in current Native American affairs.

US
INDIAN ECONOMIC EMPLOYMENT ASSISTANCE PROGRAM, PROGRESS REPORT. See Sociology-Social Services and Welfare.

US
INDIAN EDUCATION. See Education.

US/0361-1590
INDIAN EDUCATION ACT OF 1972; REPORT OF PROGRESS, THE. See Education.

II/0019-4700
INDIAN EDUCATIONAL REVIEW. See Education.

Ethnic Interests

US/0892-6654
INDIAN HIGHWAYS (TEMPE, ARIZ.).
(INDIAN HIGHWAYS.). Periodical. English. qt. Free. Indian Highways, 708 South Lindon Lane, Tempe AZ 85281. **Tel** (602)968-9354. **ED** Carol L Brookes. Index available. cum. index. **Circ:** 15,000 (ctrl).
Desc: A newsletter which reflects the activities and interests of those involved in native american christian leadership training.

US/0364-8028
INDIAN LEADER, THE. See Education.

CN/0226-9317
INDIAN LIFE MAGAZINE. (INDIAN LIFE.). [Indian life mag.]. **Added/Corp** American Ministries International. **VAT** Indian Life (Winnipeg). Vol. 1 (Nov./Dec. 1979)-. Periodical. English. bm (6 issues). 7.00Can$ (one year), 13.00Can$ (two year), 18.00Can$ (three year) Canada; $7.00 (one year), $13.00 (two year), $18.00 (three year) other. Intertribal Christian Communications, PO Box 3765, Station B, Winnipeg Manitoba R2W 3R6 Canada. **Tel** (204)661-9333, FAX (204)661-3982. **ED** Ed Hughes. **Circ:** 25,000. **Formed by the union of** Indian Christian **and** Indian Life, 0734-9289.
Desc: A news magazine written by Indians for Indians. Features positive news, stories, legends, and other information relevant to native people in Canada and the US; non-denominational in approach.
Ind/Abst Acad. Abstr. (July 1993-); Acad. Search (July 1993-); Mag. Artic. Summar. Elite (July 1993-); Mag. Artic. Summar. CD-ROM (July 1993-).

US/0892-6409
INDIAN MARKET. (INDIAN MARKET / SOUTHWESTERN ASSOCIATION ON INDIAN AFFAIRS.). [Indian mark.]. **Added/Corp** Southwestern Association on Indian Affairs (U.S.) (1986)-. Periodical. English. an (July). $30.00 Comes with Southwestern Association on Indian Affairs membership. Southwestern Association of Indian Affairs, 509 Camino de los Marquez #1, Santa Fe NM 87501. **Tel** (505) 983-5220, FAX (505)983-7674. **ED** Peter Eichstaedt. **DD** 708. Index available ($5.00). **Ad Acc, Adv Mgr:** J. Young. **Circ:** 12,000 (ctrl). **Continues** SWAIA.
Ind/Abst Ethnoarts Index.

MX/0185-6278
INDIAN NEWS OF THE AMERICAS / INTER-AMERICAN INDIAN INSTITUTE.
Added/Corp Inter-American Indian Institute. **VFOAT** Indian News from the Americas. No. 24 (Dec. 1983)-. Periodical. English. qt. Inter-American Indian Institute, Insurgentes sur 1690, Col Florida, 01030 Mexico D. F.,, Mexico.
Ind/Abst Hum. Rights Intern. Rep.

US/0019-6193
INDIAN PROGRESS. Added/Corp Associated Executive Committee of Friends on Indian Affairs. Vol. 1 (1955)-. Periodical. English. Three times a year (Feb., Jun., Oct.). $3.00 (institution); Free on request (individual). Associated Executive Committee of Friends on Indian Affairs, PO Box 1661, Richmond IN 47375. **Tel** (317)962-9169. **ED** Harold V Smuck. **Circ:** 1,800 (ctrl).
Desc: News from the six centers serving local areas. Severely limited general information on matters of concern to Indians.

US/0364-7056
INDIAN SCHOOL JOURNAL. See Education.

US/0046-9076
INDIAN TRADER, THE. See History(General)-History of North, South, and Central America.

US/0091-102X
INDIAN VOICE (SANTA CLARA). See History(General)-History of North, South, and Central America.

US
INDIGENA. No. 1- 1974?-. Periodical. English (Spanish).

SP
INDIGENISMO : BOLETIN DEL SEMINARIO ESPANOL DE ESTUDIOS INDIGENISTAS, INSTITUTO DE COOPERACION IBEROAMERICANA.
Added/Corp Instituto de Cooperacion Iberoamericana (Madrid, Spain) Seminario Espanol de Estudios Indigenistas. (19??)-. Periodical. Spanish.
Ind/Abst Hum. Rights Intern. Rep.

US/1070-1400
INDIGENOUS WOMAN. (INDIGENOUS WOMAN : A PUBLICATION OF THE INDIGENOUS WOMEN'S NETWORK.). [Indig. woman]. **Added/Corp** Indigenous Women's Network. (19??)-. Periodical. English. sa. $10.00. Indigenous Women's Network, PO Box 174, Lake Elmo MN 55042. **Tel** (612)770-3861. **LC** E98.W8; I5. **DD** 305. **Bk Rev. Circ:** 4,000 (ctrl).
Desc: Presents success stories of indigenous women; strives to educate the public about culture and issues affecting native communities

US
INDIGENOUS WORLD. VFOAT Mundo Indigena. No. 1 (Spring 1982)-. Periodical. English (Spanish). qt.
Ind/Abst Hum. Rights Intern. Rep.

AT/0815-6905
INFOCUS NEWS MAGAZINE. [Infocus news mag.]. (1984)-. Periodical. English. bm. 10.00Aus$. Ethnic Communities Council, 221 Cope Street, Waterloo 2017 Australia. **Tel** 011 61 2 3190288, FAX 011 61 2 3194229. **ED** Gosia Dybka. **DD** 305.8009944. **Ad Acc. Circ:** 2,000. **Continues** Newsletter - Ethnic Communities Council of N.S.W., 0157-3942.
Desc: Publication of the Ethnic Communities' Council of New South Wales.

US/0748-6502
INFORMATION BULLETIN (ROMANIAN-AMERICAN HERITAGE CENTER (U.S.). See History(General)-History of North, South, and Central America.

US/0199-7602
INSIDE (PHILADELPHIA, PA.). (INSIDE.). [Inside]. **Added/Corp** Federation of Jewish Agencies of Greater Philadelphia. (Spring 1980)-. Periodical. English. Four times a year. $6.95 (one year), $12.47 (two year). Inside Magazine, 226 South 16th Street, Philadelphia PA 19102. **Tel** (215)893-5710. **Continues** Expo, 0164-6753.

●US/1059-9452
INTERNATIONAL GUIDE TO AFROCENTRIC EVENTS. (INTERNATIONAL GUIDE TO AFROCENTRIC EVENTS: COMPREHENSIVE LISTINGS FOR OVER 150 SOURCES IN THE U.S., AFRICA AND THE CARIBBEAN.). (1992)-. English. $12.95. Osborne Communications, 18565 N.E., 1 Court, Miami FL 33179. **DD** 305.

●US/1059-7808
INTERNATIONAL GUIDE TO AFROCENTRIC MERCHANDISE. (INTERNATIONAL GUIDE TO AFROCENTRIC MERCHANDISE: COMPREHENSIVE LISTINGS FOR OVER 150 SOURCES IN THE U.S., AFRICA AND THE CARIBBEAN.). (1992)-. English. $14.95. Osborne Communications, 18565 N.E., 1 Court, Miami FL 33179. **DD** 305.

●US/1059-9460
INTERNATIONAL GUIDE TO AFROCENTRIC TALENT. (1992)-. English. $10.95. Osborne Communications, 18565 N.E., 1 Court, Miami FL 33179.

●US/1045-8042
INTERNATIONAL JOURNAL OF AFRICAN DANCE. See Dance.

US/1047-5370
INTERRACE (SCHENECTADY, N.Y.). (INTERRACE.). [Interrace]. **VFOAT** Inter Race. Vol. 1, No. 1 (Nov./Dec. 1989)-. Periodical. English. Nine times a year (monthly Nov.-May, Summer, Sept.-Oct.). $24.00 (1 year); $48.00 (2 year) US; $34.00 (1 year), $68.00 (2 year) Canada; $40.00 (1 year), $82.00 (2 year) Pan-American nations; $50.00 (1 year), $100.00 (2 year) other. InterRace Publications, PO Box 12048, Atlanta GA 30355. **Tel** (404)364-9690. **ED** Candace L. Mills. **LC** HQ1031; .I62. **DD** 051. **Bk Rev,** (Qty: 5-9). **Ad Acc, Adv Mgr:** Gabe Grosz. **Circ:** 15,000.
Desc: For interracial couples, families, and biracial people and those that have adopted trans-racially.

US/0146-5562
INTERRACIAL BOOKS FOR CHILDREN BULLETIN. See Children and Youth Interests.

US
INTERRACIAL DIGEST. Added/Corp Council on Interracial Books for Children. (1976)-. Periodical. English. ir. Council on Interracial Books, 1841 Broadway, New York NY 10023. **Tel** (212)757-5339.

CN/0020-9872
INUKTITUT (ENGLISH AND INUIT EDITION). (INUKTITUT.). [Inuktitut]. **Added/Corp** Canada. Dept. of Northern Affairs and National Resources. Canada. Dept. of Indian Affairs and Northern Development. Canada. Indian and Northern Affairs. Canada. Indian and Northern Affairs Canada. Inuit Tapirisat of Canada. **VFOAT** Inuttitun; Inuttituut. **VAT** Inuktitun (1972). (May 1959)-. Periodical. Eskimo (English and French). Four times a year. $30.00. Artic Society of Canada, 170 Laurier Ave. W., Suite 510, Ottawa Ontario K1P 5V5 Canada. **Tel** (613)238-8181, FAX (613)234-1991, telex 0533517. **ED** John Bennett. **LC** E99.E7; I57. **DD** 971/.004971/005. **Bk Rev,** (Qty: 2). **Circ:** 10,000 (ctrl). available on microfilm from Micromedia Limited. **Absorbed** Inuktitut (French and Inuktitut Ed), 0705-8527.
Desc: Inuktitut language development and culture for/about/by Inuit including music and arts.

Ind/Abst ASTIS Curr. Aware. Bull. (1978-); ASTIS Bibliogr. (1978-); Can. Index; Can. Period. Index (19??-); Ethnoarts Index.

CN/0382-8085
INUMMARIT (ESKIMO EDITION).
(INUMMARIT.). **VFOAT** Inumarit. Mar. 1972-. Periodical. Eskimo (French and English). qt. $5.81. Inummarit Cultural Association Territories, Canada. **DD** 970/.004/97.

CN/0832-2007
IRANIYAN (TORONTO). (IRANIYAN / IRANIANS : ETHNIC NEWSPAPER.). [Iraniyan]. **VFOAT** Iranians. (Sept. 1985)-. Newspaper. Persian (English). mo. 75.00Can$ Canada. Iranians Community Newspaper, 39 Kimbercroft Court #507, Scarborough ONT M1S 5B5 Canada. **Tel** (416)297-7680, FAX (416)348-9082. **ED** M. H. Yazdanfar. **DD** 071/.13541. **Bk Rev,** (Qty: 12). **Ad Acc. Circ:** 9,000.
Desc: 60 percent Canadian, 20 percent world, 20 percent home country news and events, including social, economic, cultural, arts and business.

US/0192-1215
IRISH ECHO. 1928. Periodical. English. wk. $15.00. Irish Echo, 309 5th Avenue, New York NY 10016. **Tel** (212)686-1266. **ED** John Thornton. **Bk Rev. Ad Acc. Circ:** 34,500. available on microfilm from New York Public Library.
Desc: Contains news of Ireland and the Irish-American community including sports, the arts, politics and commentary.

US/1063-7532
IRISH EDITION. Vol. 1, No. 1 (March 1981)-. Newspaper. English. mo. $15.00 (one year), $28.00 (two years); $39.00 (three years). Irish Edition, PO Box 44102, Philadelphia PA 19144. **Tel** (215)836-4900, FAX (215)836-1929. **ED** Jane Duffin (Editor-in-Chief) and A. R. Byrne (Managing Editor). **Bk Rev,** (Qty: 50). **Photos. Ad Acc, Adv Mgr:** Mary Kay Cavanaugh. Full Page (B&W) $550.00. Half Page (B&W) $300.00. Full Page (Color) $605.00. Half Page (Color) $330.00. **Pub. Size:** Tabloid. **Pr Rev. Circ:** 15,000.
Desc: News, articles, advertisements of interest to Irish and Irish Americans.

US
IRISH IN AMERICA, THE. (1988)-. English. ir. University of Notre Dame Press, PO Box 635, South Bend IN 46624. **Tel** (219)239-6349, (800)677-3232, FAX (219)239-8148.

US/0895-4534
IRISH VOICE (NEW YORK, N.Y.). See Newspapers.

IS
ISLAMIC CULTURE. 1 (1927)-. Periodical. English. qt. $30.00. Dyal Singh Trust Library, Nisbet Road, Lahore Pakistan. **Tel** 26 86 45. **LC** DS36.85; .I78. **DD** 909/.097/671.
Ind/Abst Am. Hist. Life (1972-1981, 1986-); Middle East Abstr. Index; Middle East J.

US/1041-3839
ISSUES & VIEWS. [Issues views]. **VFOAT** Issues and Views. Vol. 1, No. 1 (Oct. 1985)-. Periodical. English. Four times a year. $5.00 (student); $10.00 (regular). Issues & Views, PO Box 467, New York NY 10025. **Tel** (718)655-7847, FAX (718)655-7847. **ED** Elizabeth Wright. **LC** E185.8; .I88. **DD** 305. **Bk Rev,** (Qty: 4). **Circ:** 5,000.
Desc: Focuses on self-help and business enterprise in the black community. Challenges conventional civil rights approach the social issues.

US/0096-8846
ITALIAN AMERICANA. [Ital. Am.]. Vol. 1 (Autumn 1974)-. Periodical. English. Twice a year. $15.00 (individuals), $22.50 (institutions). Italian Americana, University of Rhode Island, 199 Promenade Street / CCE, Providence RI 02908. **Tel** (401)277-3824. **ED** Carol Bonomo Albright; (phone: (401)277-3890). **LC** E184.I8; I72. **DD** 973/.04/51. **Bk Rev,** (Qty: 25-35/yr). **Ad Acc. Pr Rev. Circ:** 1,000.
Desc: An historical and cultural journal devoted to the Italian experience in America. Articles of award-winning short stories, reviews, poetry and bibliographies.
Ind/Abst Am. Hist. Life (1974-1986,1990-);(1974-); Annu. Bibliogr. Engl. Lang. Lit.; MLA Int. Bibl. Books Artic. Mod. Lang. Lit.; Writ. Am. Hist.

CN/1184-1087
ITALIAN LINK. [Ital. link]. Vol. 1, No. 1 (July 15, 1990)-. Periodical. English (Italian). mo. $12.00. Italian Link, 10010-107 A Avenue, Edmonton, Alberta T5H 4H8 Canada. **DD** 971.23/3400451.

US
ITALIAN TRIBUNE NEWS. See Newspapers.

GW/0938-3611
JAHRESBERICHT / BAYERISCHE STAATSGEMALDESAMMLUNGEN. See Anthropology.

US
JAMES S. COLEMAN AFRICAN STUDIES CENTER NEWSLETTER. **Added/Corp** University of California, Los Angeles. James S. Coleman African Studies Center. **VFOAT** Newsletter; UCLA James S. Coleman African Studies Center Newsletter. (Spring 1989)-. Newsletter. English. sa. UCLA African Studies Center, 405 Hilgard Avenue, 10244 Bunche Hall, Los Angeles CA 90024. **Tel** (310)825-1218. **ED** Mark Lipschutz. ***Continues** African Studies Center Newsletter (University of California, Los Angeles. African Studies Center).*
Desc: Provides articles in African studies, scholarship and grant information, and news for and about the James S Coleman African Studies Center.

US/1059-6208
JASHNVARAH (LOS ANGELES, CALIF.). (JASHNVARAH). [Jashnvarah]. **VFOAT** Festival; Jashnvareh Magazine. No. 1 (Sept. 1991)-. Periodical. English (Persian). mo. $25.00. Photogenic Publishing, PO Box 25913, Los Angeles CA 90025. **DD** 305.

TI
JERUSALEM. **Added/Corp** Palestine Committee for NGOs. (19??)-. Periodical. English. **LC** DS119.7; .J43.
Ind/Abst Hum. Rights Intern. Rep.

US/0021-5996
JET. [Jet]. Vol. 1, (Nov. 1951)-. Periodical. English. wk. $36.00 (one year), $66.00 (two year), $96.00 (three year). Johnson Publishing Company / Illinois, 820 South Michigan Avenue, Chicago IL 60605. **Tel** (312)322-9200, (800)272-6602. **ED** Robert E. Johnson. **LC** E185.5; .J4. **DD** 973/.04/96073. Index available. **Bk Rev. Ad Acc. Circ:** 900,000. available on microfilm and microfiche from University Microfilms International (UMI). Documents available from UMI Article Clearinghouse, Magazine Collection.
Desc: Black news magazine featuring current news in government, business, education, society, medicine, and entertainment.
Ind/Abst Abr. Read. Guide Period. Lit.; Acad. Abstr. Full Text Elite (Jan. 1989-); Acad. Abstr. (Jan. 1989-); Gen. Period. Index (1985-); Infobank (Jan. 1969-); Mag. Artic. Summar. Elite (Jan. 1989-); Mag. Artic. Summar. Select (Jan. 1989-); Mag. Artic. Summar. CD-ROM (Jan. 1989-); Mag. Express (1986-) [Full Txt.]; Mag. Index Plus (1989-); Mag. Index Sel. Microfiche (1986-) [Full Txt.]; Mag. Index. Sel. (1986-); Mag. Search; Mid. Search (Jan. 1989-); Newsp. Period. Abstr. (1986-); Prim. Search (Jan. 1989-); Read. Guide Abstr. Select Ed.; Read. Guide Period. Lit.; Resource/One Ondisc; Mag. Index (1978-); TOM Gen. Index (1985-) [Full Txt.]; Vocat. Search (Jan. 1989-).

US
JEWISH ADVOCATE, THE. **VFOAT** Connecticut Hebrew Record; Springfield Hebrew Record; Springfield Review. Vol. 9, No. 12 (May 28, 1909)-. Newspaper. English. wk (published on Thursday). $26.00 Massachusetts, Maine, New Hampshire, Vermont, Rhode Island, Connecticut; $30.00 US; $43.00 other. Jewish Advocate, 15 School Street, Boston MA 02108. **Tel** (617)367-9100, FAX (617)367-9310. **ED** Robert Israel. **Bk Rev**, (Qty: 12). **Photos. Ad Acc, Adv Mgr:** Eleanor Grosser, **Tel** (617)367-9100 ext. 36. Full Page (B&W) $3,213.00. Half Page (B&W) $1,606.50. Full Page (Color) $3,863.00. Half Page (Color) $2,256.50. **Pub. Size:** Standard. **Wire Svcs.:** AP, JT. available on microfilm from University Microfilms International (UMI). ***Continues** Boston Advocate (Boston, Mass. : 1905); **Absorbed** Connecticut Hebrew Record.*

US
JEWISH CHRONICLE, THE. Vol. 1, No. 1 (Mar. 8, 1962)-. Newspaper. English. wk. $26.00 (PA residents); $28.00 (east of Miss.); $30.00 (west of Miss.); $50.00 (other). Jewish Chronicle / Pittsburgh, 5600 Baum Boulevard, Pittsburgh PA 15206. **Tel** (412) 687-1000, FAX (412) 687-5119. **LC** UNC. ***Formed by the union of** Jewish Criterion **and** American Jewish Outlook.*

UK/0021-633X
JEWISH CHRONICLE (LONDON, ENGLAND : 1845). **See** Religion and Theology-Judaism.

US
JEWISH EDUCATION NEWS. **See** Education.

US/0021-6453
JEWISH FRONTIER. **Added/Corp** League for Labor Palestine. Jewish Frontier Association. Vol. 1 (June 1933)-. Periodical. English. bm. $15.00 (one year), $25.00 (two years). Jewish Frontier, 275 7th Avenue, 17th Floor, New York NY 10001. **Tel** (212)645-8121. **ED** Nahum Guttman, David Twersky. **LC** DS149; .A324. **DD** 956.9. **Bk Rev. Ad Acc. Circ:** 4,500. available on microfilm and microfiche from University Microfilms International (UMI).
Desc: A Labor Zionist journal covering events in Israel, America and world Jewish communities. Contains analysis of world affairs, short stories, poetry and other writings related to Jewish and general culture.
Ind/Abst Guide Soc. Sci. Relig.; Index Jew. Period. (19??-199?); Middle East Abstr. Index.

●US
JEWISH HISTORICAL SOCIETIES' NETWORK : A PUBLICATION OF THE AMERICAN JEWISH HISTORICAL SOCIETY. **See** Religion and Theology-Judaism.

IS/0334-701X
JEWISH HISTORY. **See** Religion and Theology-Judaism.

US/0199-2929
JEWISH LIVING. V. 2, No. 2- Summer 1979-. Periodical. English. bm. $18.00. ADAR Communications Co, GPO Box 1859, New York NY 10009. **LC** DS101; .K65. **DD** 909/.04924082. ***Continues** Kosher Home's Jewish Living, 0194-6250.*

US/1070-5848
JEWISH NEWS OF GREATER PHOENIX. **See** Newspapers.

CN/0836-6063
JEWISH POST & NEWS, THE. [Jew. post news]. **VAT** Jewish Post and News. Vol. 1, No. 1 (Aug. 6, 1987)-. Periodical. English (summaries and/or abstracts in Hebrew and Yiddish). wk. 70.00Can$ Canada; 140.00Can$ other. Jewish Post / Canada, 117 Hutchings Street, Winnipeg Manitoba R2X 2V4 Canada. **Tel** (204)694-3332. **DD** 971.2/004924. ***Formed by the union of** Jewish Post., 0839-4687 **and** The Western Jewish News., 0839-4679.*

US/0021-6674
JEWISH PRESS (BROOKLYN), THE. (THE JEWISH PRESS.). [Jew. press]. (1949)-. Newspaper. English. wk. $30.00 (NY, NJ, CT, PA, & FL); $40.00 (all others US); $70.00 (all others except Israel). Jewish Press, Attn: J Hochberg, 338 Third Avenue, Brooklyn NY 11215. **Tel** (718)330-1100, FAX (718)797-2717. **ED** Rabbi S. Skass. **DD** 909. **Bk Rev. Ad Acc. Circ:** 175,000.
Desc: Items of interest to the Jewish community and more specifically the orthodox Jewish community. and children's section.

US/0021-6747
JEWISH STANDARD (JERSEY CITY, N.J.). (JEWISH STANDARD.). **VFOAT** Jewish Standard Center Record; Center Record. (1931)-. Newspaper. English. Fifty-two times a year. $25.00. Jewish Standard, 1086 Teaneck Road, Teaneck NJ 07666. **Tel** (201)837-8818.

US/0021-678X
JEWISH TRANSCRIPT, THE. **Added/Corp** Jewish Federation and Council of Greater Seattle. (1967)-. Newspaper. English. Twenty-two times a year. $22.50 One year; $39.50 two years. Jewish Transcript, 2031 3rd Avenue, Suite 200, Seattle WA 98121-2418. **Tel** (206)441-4553, FAX (206)441-2736. **ED** Craig Degginger. **Bk Rev. Ad Acc, Adv Mgr:** Karen Chachkes, **Tel** (206)441-4553. **Circ:** 4500. ***Continues** Transcript (Seattle, Wash.).*
Desc: A Jewish community newspaper for Washington State.

UK/0021-681X
JEWISH VEGETARIAN. [Jew. veg.]. (1966)-. Periodical. English. qt. £15.00. Jewish Vegetarian and Natural Health Society, Bet Teva 855 Finchley Road, London NW11 8LX United Kingdom. **Tel** 011 44 81 455 0692, FAX 011 44 81 455 0692. **DD** 613.

US/0047-2018
JEWISH VETERAN, THE. **Added/Corp** Jewish War Veterans of the United States of America. (1932)-. Periodical. English. Five times a year. $10.00. Jewish War Veterans of the US, 1811 R Street Northwest, Washington DC 20009. **Tel** (202)265-6280, FAX (202)234-5662. **ED** Al Schlossberg. **LC** DS101; .J567. **DD** 909/.04924/005. **Bk Rev. Ad Acc, Adv Mgr:** Howard Metzger. **Circ:** 55,000 (ctrl). available on microfilm.
Desc: Deals with veterans and the Jewish community.

US/0021-6860
JEWISH WEEKLY NEWS. [Jew. wkly. news]. **VFOAT** Jewish Weekly News of Western Massachusetts. (1945)-. Newspaper. English. wk (except one week in Aug.). $19.00 western Massachusetts; $35.00 other. Jewish Weekly News, PO Box 1569, Springfield MA 01101. **Tel** (413)739-4771. **DD** 296. **Bk Rev. Ad Acc. Circ:** 2,500.
Desc: Anglo-Jewish newspaper of western Massachusetts.

US/0199-4441
JEWISH WORLD (ALBANY), THE. (THE JEWISH WORLD.). **VFOAT** Schenectady Jewish World; Albany Jewish World. (1965)-. Newspaper. English. Fifty-two times a year. $21.00 New York; $25.00 other. The Jewish World, 1104 Central Avenue, Albany NY 12205. **Tel** (518)459-8455. **ED** Laurie J Clevenson. **Bk Rev. Ad Acc, Adv Mgr:** Lisa Shaw. **Circ:** 3,600 (ctrl). available on microfiche.
Desc: Covers local, national, and international events of interest and significance to Jewish people-events, peoples politics and affects.

US/0021-695X
JICARILLA CHIEFTAIN. **Added/Corp** Jicarilla Apache Tribe. (Jan. 1960)-. Newspaper. English (English). Twenty-six times a year. $12.00 Rio Arriba County; $18.00 North America; $24.00 other. Jicarilla Chieftain, PO Box 507, Dulce NM 87528. **Tel** (505)759-3242, FAX (505)759-3005. **ED** Mary F. Polanco and Lori M. Vicenti. **Bk Rev. Ad Acc. Circ:** 1,200.
Desc: Based on the needs of the Jicarilla Apache Tribe, Native Americans, and other minorities.

BL
JORNAL INDIGENA / UMA PUBLICACAO DA UNIAO DAS NACOES INDIGENAS, UNI. **Added/Corp** Uniao das Nacoes Indigenas (Brazil). No. 1 (July 1984)-. Periodical. Portuguese.
Ind/Abst Hum. Rights Intern. Rep.

AT/0819-0615
JOURNAL / AUSTRALIAN JEWISH HISTORICAL SOCIETY. **Added/Corp** Australian Jewish Historical Society. **VFOAT** Journal of the Australian Jewish Historical Society. Vol. 10, Pt. 1 (1986)-. Periodical. English. sa (May & Nov.). 25.00Aus$ (Australia), 35.00Aus$ (other) individuals. Australian Jewish Historical Society, 166 Castlereagh Street, Sydney NSW 2000 Australia. **Tel** 61 2 261 8407. **LC** DS135.A88; A8. **DD** 994/.004924/005. Index available (free). ***Continues** Australian Jewish Historical Society. Australian Jewish Historical Society.*
Ind/Abst APAIS, Aust. Public Aff. Inf. Ser. (1988-).

US
JOURNAL / GERMAN-TEXAN HERITAGE SOCIETY, THE. **See** Genealogy and Heraldry.

UK/0266-6952
JOURNAL / INSTITUTE OF MUSLIM MINORITY AFFAIRS. [J. - Inst. Muslim Minor. Aff.]. **Added/Corp** Jamiat Al-Malik Abd Al-Aziz. Mahad Shuun Al-Aqalliyat Al-Muslimah. Vol. 1, No. 1 (Summer 1979)-. English (Arabic). Twice a year (Jan., July). £23.90 (individual); £47.80 (institution). Institute of Muslim Minority Affairs, 46 Goodge Street/1st Floor, London W1P 1FJ United Kingdom. **Tel** 11 44 71 636 6740, FAX 11 44 71 255 1473, telex 296182. **ED** Syed and Saleha Abdein (editor's address: Journal Institute of Muslim Minority Affairs PO Box 8856 Jeddah 21492 - Saudi Arabia). **LC** BP52.5; .J68. **DD** 908/.82971. Index available. cum. index. **Bk Rev. Ad Acc. Circ:** 3,000. available on an online database from DIALOG; and BRS.
Desc: Devoted to the investigation of politics, economics, education, history, literature and sociology of Muslim and Minorities around the world.
Ind/Abst Hum. Rights Intern. Rep.; Index Book Rev. Relig.; Int. Bibliogr. Sociol.; Relig. Index One Period.; Soc. Plann. Policy Dev. Abstr.

●US/1063-4460
JOURNAL OF AFRICAN AMERICAN MALE STUDIES. [J. Afr. Am. male stud.]. **Added/Corp** National Council of African American Men. **VFOAT** JAAMS. Vol. 1, No. 1 (Winter 1993)-. Periodical. English. Twice a year. $20.00 (individuals); $40.00 (institutions). University of Kansas - Institute for Black Leaderhsip, 1028 Dole Road, Lawrence KS 66045. **Tel** (913)864-3990, FAX (913)864-5323. **DD** 305. **Ad Acc. Acid Free.**
Desc: To publish a scholarly journal on Black male studies that can enhance our knowledge of Black males and their families in American society. To research, develop and disseminate data and information on the status of Blacks in the region. To shape the direction of future leaders and foster a coalition of African American male organizations primarily concerned with the welfare of African American men. To promote better race relations by addressing important issues which affect Blacks.

US/0278-5927
JOURNAL OF AMERICAN ETHNIC HISTORY. [J. Am. ethn. hist.]. **VFOAT** American Ethnic History. Vol. 1, No. 1 (Fall 1981)-. Periodical. English. Four times a year. Fl125.00 (individual), Fl195.00 (institution). Transaction Publishers / Rutgers State University, New Brunswick NJ 08903. **Tel** (908)932-2280 Ext. 105, FAX (908)932-3138. **ED** Ronald H Bayor. **LC** E184.A1; J67. **DD** 305.8/00973. **[CCC]. Bk Rev. Ad Acc. Pr Rev. Circ:** 1300. available on labels; available on microfilm and microfiche from University Microfilms International (UMI). Documents available from The Genuine Article, UMI Article Clearinghouse.
Desc: Addresses various aspects of American immigration and ethnic history including background of emigration, ethnic and racial groups, Native-Americans, immigration policies, and the processes of acculturation. The official journal of the Immigration History Society.
Ind/Abst Acad. Search (July 1993-); Am. Hist. Life (1981-); Am. Bibliogr. Slavic East Europ. Stud.; Arts Humanit. Citation Index [Full Cov.]; Curr. Contents Arts Humanit.; Curr. Contents Soc. Behav. Sci.; Expand. Acad. Index (1989-); Hist. Source (July 1993-); Hum. Resour. Abstr.; Humanit. Index; Humanit. Source (Jul.

1993-); INFO-SOUTH Abstr.; Mag. Search; Newsp. Period. Abstr. (1990-); Res. Alert [Full Cov.]; Sage Fam. Stud. Abstr.; Soc. Sci. Cit. Index [Full Cov.]; West. Hist. Q.

US/0021-8731
JOURNAL OF AMERICAN INDIAN EDUCATION. See Education.

US/0095-7984
JOURNAL OF BLACK PSYCHOLOGY, THE. See Psychology.

US/0021-9347
JOURNAL OF BLACK STUDIES. [J. black stud.]. Vol. 1 (Sept. 1970)-. English. bm. $189.00. SAGE Periodical Press, 2455 Teller Road, Thousand Oaks CA 91320. **Tel** (805)499-0721, FAX (805)499-0871, telex 100799. **ED** Molefi Kete Asante (Temple University). **LC** E185.5; .J8. **DD** 909/.04/96. **[CCC]. Pr Rev. Acid Free.** available on microfilm and microfiche from University Microfilms International (UMI). Documents available from The Genuine Article, UMI Article Clearinghouse.
Desc: Sustains full analytical discussion of economic, political, sociological, historical, literary and philosophical issues related to persons of African descent.
Ind/Abst Abstr. Engl. Stud.; Acad. Ind. [Computer File] (1992-); Acad. Search (Jan. 1994-); Am. Hist. Life (1970-); Appl. Soc. Sci. Index Abstr.; Arts Humanit. Citation Index [Select. Cov.]; BHA : Biblio. Hist. Art; Book Rev. Index; Commun. Abstr.; Crim. Justice Abstr.; Curr. Contents Soc. Behav. Sci.; Curr. Index J. Educ.; Expand. Acad. Index (1992-); Geogr. Abstr. Human Geogr. (?-?); High. Educ. Abstr. (1985-); Hum. Resour. Abstr.; Humanit. Source (Jul. 1993-); INFO-SOUTH Abstr.; Int. Polit. Sci. Abstr.; Mag. Search; Newsp. Period. Abstr. (1990-); PAIS Int. Print (1991-); Res. Alert [Full Cov.]; Sage Public Adm. Abstr. (?-?); Sage Race Relat. Abstr.; Sage Urban Stud. Abstr (?-?); Soc. Plann. Policy Dev. Abstr.; Soc. Sci. Cit. Index [Full Cov.]; Soc. Sci. Index; Soc. Work Abstr. [Select. Cov.]; Sociol. Abstr.; U.S. Polit. Sci. Doc.; Urban Aff. Abstr.; Women Stud. Abstr.

SA/1015-2296
JOURNAL OF BLACK THEOLOGY IN SOUTH AFRICA. See Religion and Theology.

US/0146-2962
JOURNAL OF CHEROKEE STUDIES. [J. Cherok. stud.]. **Added/Corp** Museum of the Cherokee Indian. (Summer 1976)-. Academic Scholarly Publication. English. ir. Museum of the Cherokee Indian, PO Box 1599, Cherokee NC 28719. **Tel** (704)497-3481. **ED** Duane H. King. **LC** E99.C5; J68. **DD** 970/.004/97. Index available. **Circ:** 1,000.
Desc: A scholarly journal devoted to Cherokee history and culture.
Ind/Abst Am. Hist. Life (1976-); Anthropol. Lit.

US
JOURNAL OF EDUCATIONAL ISSUES OF LANGUAGE MINORITY STUDENTS. See Education.

US/0091-3219
JOURNAL OF ETHNIC STUDIES, THE. ***Ceased.*** [J. ethn. stud.]. **VFOAT** JES. Vol. 1 (Spring 1973). Ceased Vol. 19 (1992). Periodical. English. qt. Journal of Ethnic Studies, Western Washington University, American Cultural Studies, Bellingham WA 98225. **Tel** (206)647-4861. **ED** Jesse Hiraoka. **LC** E184.A1; J68. **DD** 301.45/1/0973. **Bk Rev. Ad Acc. Pr Rev. Circ:** 850 (ctrl). available on microfilm. Documents available from UMI Article Clearinghouse.
Desc: Interdisciplinary scholarship, opinion, and creative expression in the field of ethnic studies, international in scope and emphasis on theories of majority and minority relationships.
Ind/Abst Abstr. Anthropol.; Acad. Abstr. Full Text Elite (July 1990-Dec. 1991); Acad. Abstr. (July 1990-Dec. 1991); Acad. Search (July 1990-Dec. 1991); Am. Hist. Life (1973-19??); Am. Bibliogr. Slavic East Europ. Stud.; Annu. Bibliogr. Engl. Lang. Lit. (19??-19??); Anthropol. Lit. (-Vol. 13, 1991); Chicano Index; Curr. Index J. Educ.; Expand. Acad. Index (1989-); Geogr. Abstr. Human Geogr.; High. Educ. Abstr. (1986-19??); INFO-SOUTH Abstr.; Int. Dev. Abstr. (?-?); Int. Polit. Sci. Abstr.; Mag. Search; Middle East Abstr. Index; MLA Int. Bibl. Books Artic. Mod. Lang. Lit.; Multicult. Educ. Abstr.; Newsp. Period. Abstr. (1986-1992); Sage Race Relat. Abstr.; Soc. Plann. Policy Dev. Abstr.; Soc. Sci. Source (Jul. 1990-Dec. 1991); Soc. Sci. Index; Soc. Sci. Index Fulltext (Winter 1989-1992) [Full Txt.]; Soc. Work Abstr. (?-?); Sociol. Abstr. (?-?); Spec. Educ. Needs Abstr. (19??-1990); SportSearch; U.S. Polit. Sci. Doc.; West. Hist. Q.

US
JOURNAL OF HISPANIC LATINO THEOLOGY. See Religion and Theology.

AT/0725-6868
JOURNAL OF INTERCULTURAL STUDIES. See Emigration and Immigration.

NE/1044-8985
JOURNAL OF INTERDISCIPLINARY LITERARY STUDIES. See Literature.

US/0022-2089
JOURNAL OF JEWISH COMMUNAL SERVICE. [J. Jew. communal serv.]. **Added/Corp** National Conference of Jewish Communal Service. Vol. 32, No. 3 (Spring 1956)-. Periodical. English. Four times a year (Jan., Apr., July, Oct.). $30.00. Jewish Communal Service Association, 3084 State Highway 27, Suite 9, Kendall Park NJ 08824-1657. **Tel** (908)821-1871. **ED** Gail Naron Chalew. **NLM** W1 JO732N. Index available (Bound in each Summer issue.). **Bk Rev. Ad Acc. Circ:** 3,600 (ctrl). available on microfilm and microfiche from University Microfilms International (UMI). ***Continues*** *Jewish Social Service Quarterly.*
Desc: Covers professional trends and developments in all fields of Jewish communal service.
Ind/Abst Am. Bibliogr. Slavic East Europ. Stud.; Appl. Soc. Sci. Index Abstr.; Index Jew. Period. (19??-199?); Middle East Abstr. Index; PAIS Int. Print (1991-); Public Aff. Inf. Serv. Bull.; Ref. Sources; Soc. Work Abstr. (1987-) [Select. Cov.].

US/0742-6291
JOURNAL OF MINORITY AGING, THE. See Senior Citizens.

US/0743-7749
JOURNAL OF MODERN HELLENISM. [J. mod. Hellen.]. **Added/Corp** Hellenic College (Brookline, Mass.). Greek Studies Program. Queens College (New York, N.Y.). Center for Byzantine and Modern Greek Studies. (Apr. 1984)-. Periodical. English (Greek, Ancient and Greek, Modern). an. $10.00 US; $12.75 other. Holy Cross Greek Orthodox Press, 50 Goddard Avenue, Brookline MA 02146. **Tel** (617)232-4544. **ED** Rev. Dr. N. Michael Vaporis. **LC** DF701; .J67. **DD** 949.5. **Bk Rev**, (Qty: 10/year). ctrl circ. available on microfiche from Xerox.

US/1042-3265
JOURNAL OF NAVAJO EDUCATION. See Education.

US/0022-2984
JOURNAL OF NEGRO EDUCATION, THE. See Education.

UK/0022-4480
JOURNAL OF SEMITIC STUDIES. [J. Semit. stud.]. (Jan. 1956)-. Periodical. English. Twice a year. £59.00 UK and Europe; $110.00 other. Oxford University Press, Walton Street, Oxford OX2 6DP England. **Tel** 011 44 865 56767, FAX 011 44 865 267773, telex 837330 OXPRES G. **(Subscription address:** Oxford University Press / USA, Journals Marketing Department, Oxford University Press, 2001 Evans Road, Cary NC 27513.**) ED** C. E. Bosworth, S. P. Brock, M. E. J. Richardson. **LC** PJ3001; .J6. **[CCC].** Index available. **Bk Rev. Ad Acc. Circ:** 600. available on microfilm and microfiche. Documents available from The Genuine Article.
Desc: Emphasizes modern Near East research into language and literature interesting to orientalists and biblical scholars.
Ind/Abst Acad. Search (July 1993-); Am. Hist. Life (1956-1974); Arts Humanit. Citation Index [Full Cov.]; Curr. Contents Arts Humanit.; Humanit. Source (Jul. 1993-); Index Book Rev. Relig.; INFO-SOUTH Abstr.; Mag. Search; Middle East Abstr. Index; MLA Int. Bibl. Books Artic. Mod. Lang. Lit.; New Testam. Abstr.; Old Testam. Abstr.; Relig. Index One Period. (1956-); Relig. Theol. Abstr.; Res. Alert [Full Cov.]; Soc. Sci. Cit. Index [Select. Cov.].

US/1043-7916
JOURNAL OF SOVIET NATIONALITIES. ***Ceased.*** [J. Sov. natly.]. (1990)-(199?). Periodical. English. qt. Center for East-West Trade, Investment, and Communication, 2114 Campus Drive, Durham NC 27708. **Tel** (919)684-5551. **(Subscription address:** 2114 Campus Drive, Duke University, Durham, NC 27706**) ED** Jerry Hough. **LC** DK33; J68. **Bk Rev. Circ:** 2,000.
Desc: Looks at center periphery relations in the Soviet Union, and specific issues with regard to nationalities questions.
Ind/Abst Am. Hist. Life (1990-); Am. Bibliogr. Slavic East Europ. Stud.; PAIS Int. Print (1991-1992).

US/0272-1937
JOURNAL OF THE AFRO-AMERICAN HISTORICAL AND GENEALOGICAL SOCIETY. See Genealogy and Heraldry.

US/0021-6763
JTA WEEKLY NEWS DIGEST. Main/Corp Jewish Telegraphic Agency. **Added/Corp** Jewish Telegraphic Agency. Weekly News Digest. **VFOAT** Weekly News Digest. **VAT** Jewish Telegraphic Agency Weekly News Digest. (19??)-. Periodical. English. wk. $100.00. Jewish Telegraph Agency Inc, 330 Seventh Avenue, 11th Floor, New York NY 10001. **Tel** (212)643-1890, FAX (212)643-8498, telex 12-6978. **ED** Mark J. Joffe. **Bk Rev. Circ:** 5,000 (ctrl).
Desc: Summary of major stories and events from international Jewish news agency.

US/0276-2714
KAHANE. ***Title Change.*** [Kahane]. (April 1976)-(199?). Periodical. English. mo. Kahane, PO Box 425 Midwood Station, Brooklyn NY 11230. **LC** DS101; .K33. ***Continued by*** *Jewish Way Newsletter.*

CN/1187-3949
KAIKU (TORONTO). (KAIKU). [Kaiku]. **Added/Corp** Finnish Organization of Canada. **VFOAT** Echo. (Apr 15, 1991)-. Periodical. English (Finnish). mo. Free to members. Finnish Organization of Canada, PO Box 209, Station J, Toronto Ontario H4J 4Y1 Canada. **DD** 071/.1/08994541.

SP
KALATHOS : REVISTA DEL SEMINARIO DE ARQUEOLOGIA Y ETNOLOGIA TUROLENSE, COLEGIO UNIVERSITARIO DE TERUEL. See Archaeology.

US
KALENDAR. Added/Corp National Slovak Society of the United States of America. **VFOAT** Almanac; Narodny Kalendar; NSS Almanac. (1990)-. Slovak (English). National Slovak Society of the United States of America, 2325 East Carson Street, Pittsburgh PA 15203. **LC** WMLC 91/4548; AY76; .N232. ***Continues*** *Narodny Americko-Slovensky Kalendar.*

US
KALIFORNIISKII VESTNIK. (19??)-. Periodical. Russian. mo. $15.00. Californisky Vestnik, 4085 Leeward Avenue, Los Angeles CA 90005. **LC** F869.L89; R94. **DD** 979.4/940049171/005.

US/0022-8206
KAMPANA (NEW YORK, N.Y.). (KAMPANA.). [Kampana]. **VFOAT** Campana. (19??)-. Greek, Modern (English). sm (24 issues). $20.00 US; $25.00 other. Greek American Review, 600 West 188th Street, New York NY 10040. **Tel** (212)923-3580. **ED** Costas Athanasiades. Index available. **Circ:** 9,500.

US/1074-3502
KASHRUS MAGAZINE. See Food and Food Industry.

US
KHANG CHIEN. (19??)-. English. mo. $24.00. Khang Chien, PO Box 7826, San Jose CA 95150. **Tel** (408)363-1078, FAX (408)363-1178. **ED** Nguyen Linh. **Circ:** 10,000.
Desc: Presents Vietnamese community news and news from around the world.

US/0749-0763
KLANSMAN, THE. Added/Corp Ku Klux Klan (1915-). No. 1 (Jan. 1976)-. Periodical. English. mo. $12.00. Knightrider Publications, PO Box 700, Gulf NC 27256. **Tel** (203)929-7922. **ED** James W. Farrands. **Bk Rev. Ad Acc. Circ:** 29,000.
Desc: Documents the struggle of the invisible empire of the KKK against equal rights. Presses for an end to affirmative action and forced busing.

IS
KOL LUBLIN. VFOAT Lubliner Shtime. Periodical. Hebrew (Yiddish). an. Irgun Yotse Lublin Be-Yisrael, Rehov Dizengof 158, Tel-Aviv Israel. **LC** DS153.P62; L77.

US
KOREAM JOURNAL. VFOAT Kore Am Journal; KoreAm Journal News Magazine. (19??)-. Periodical. English. mo. $20.00. Korean Journal, 17813 South Main Street, Suite 112, Gardena CA 90248. **Tel** (213)769-4913, FAX (213)769-4903. **LC** F869.L89; K665. available on microfilm.

US/0743-2577
KORION PIPUL. [Korion pipul]. **VFOAT** Korean People. Periodical. Korean. mo. $18.00. Korea Publications Center, 2605 West Olympic Boulevard, Los Angeles CA 90006-2802. **LC** E184.K6; K66.

RM
KTAVET. Multiple languages. sm (24 issues). Ktavet, 9 Vineri St, Bucarest Romania.

US/1061-8457
KURDISH LIFE. See History(General)-History of the Middle East.

US/0746-4479
KYRIAKATIKA NEA. See Newspapers.

US
LAMATCHIL. (19??)-. Hebrew. bm (6 issues). $12.00. World Zionist Organization / New York, 110 East 59th Street, New York NY 10022. **Tel** (212)339-6000. **Circ:** 5,000.

CN/0707-8927
LAMBI, LE. [Lambi]. **VFOAT** Revue le Lambi. Mar./April 1979-. Periodical. French. $5.00. Revue le Lambi, 5174 Charleroi 2A1 Canada. **DD** 305.8/9697294/0714.

Ethnic Interests

US/1055-4661
LANDSMEN (WASHINGTON, D.C.). See Genealogy and Heraldry.

US
LATIN N.Y. Periodical. English. mo. $18.00. Latino Communications Inc, 316 5th Avenue/Suite 301, New York NY 10001. **Tel** (516)285-5770.

MX/0460-1955
LATINO AMERICA. Added/Corp Universidad Nacional Autonoma de Mexico. Centro de Estudios Latinoamericanos. (1968)-. Spanish. ir. Unam Facultad Ingenieria, Apartado Postal M 6987, 04510 Mexico DF Mexico. **LC** WMLC L 83/2474.
Ind/Abst HAPI Hisp. Am. Period. Index (19??-).

US
LATINO DATA BULLETIN. Added/Corp Latino Institute (Chicago, Ill.). Division of Research and Documentation. Vol. 1, No. 1 (Apr. 1991)-. Bulletin. English.

US/1066-1344
LATINO STUDIES JOURNAL. Title Change. [Lat. stud. j.]. **Added/Corp** DePaul University. Center for Latino Research. Vol. 1, Issue 1 (Jan. 1990)-(1993). Periodical. English. Three times a year. Center for Latino Research, 2323 North Seminary, Chicago IL 60614. **ED** Marisa Alicea. **LC** E184.S75; L38. **DD** 973/.0468. **CODEN** LSTJEZ. cum. index. **Continued by** Latino Studies Journal (Boston, Mass.).
Desc: Devoted to the contemporary and historic Latino life in American society; occasionally, individual issues will focus on themes such as language use and women's studies.
Ind/Abst Am. Hist. Life (1991-).

●US
LATINO STUDIES JOURNAL / NORTHEASTERN UNIVERSITY. Added/Corp Northeastern University (Boston, Mass.). Vol. 1, Issue 1 (Jan. 1994)-. Periodical. English. Three times a year. Center for Latino Research, 2323 North Seminary, Chicago IL 60614. **LC** E184.S75; .L382. **Continues** Latino Studies Journal, 1066-1344.
Ind/Abst Am. Hist. Life.

US/0890-863X
LATINOGRAMA. Ceased. Added/Corp Moraga & Associates. (1978)-(199?). Periodical. English. sm. Latinograma, 3752 Moore Street, Los Angeles CA 90066. **Tel** (310)397-6057. **ED** Peter Moraga. **Circ:** 1,000.

●US/1062-9505
LATVIAN DIMENSIONS. (LATVIAN DIMENSIONS / ALA.). [Latv. dimens.]. **Added/Corp** American Latvian Association in the United States. **VFOAT** ALA Latvian Dimensions. Vol. 1, No. 2 (Summer 1992)-. Periodical. English. Four times a year. $25.00 non-member; $20.00 member. American Latvian Association of America, PO Box 4578, Rockville MD 20849-4578. **Tel** (301)340-8174, FAX (301)340-8732. **ED** Martins Zvaners. **LC** DK504.8; .L38. **DD** 947/.43/005. **Ad Acc.** Circ: 2,000. **Continues** ALA Dimensions.
Desc: Reviews timely issues in Latvia and current affairs in the U.S. Latvian community.

US/0736-4903
LC FOLK ARCHIVE FINDING AID. See Sociology-Manners and Customs.

CN/0225-2287
LEGAL INFORMATION SERVICE - NATIVE LAW CENTRE. See Law.

US
LEGISLATIVE CONFERENCE REPORT. Main/Corp New York (State). Legislature. Assembly. Puerto Rican/Hispanic Task Force. **VFOAT** Annual New York State Assembly, Puerto Rican/Hispanic Task Force Conference. (1991)-. English.

US
LEGISLATIVE REPORT - COUNCIL ON BLACK MINNESOTANS. See Law.

US
LEGISLATIVE UPDATE / CONGRESSIONAL HISPANIC CAUCUS. Added/Corp Congressional Hispanic Caucus. Vol. 1, No. 1 (Sept. 1990)-. Periodical. English. mo. Congressional Hispanic Caucus, H2-557, Washington DC 20515.

US
LETRAS Y COLORES : A CULTURAL PUBLICATION BY EL CENTRO CULTURAL DE LA RAZA. Added/Corp Centro Cultural de la Raza (San Diego, Calif.). Vol. 1, No. 1 (Nov. 1990)-. Periodical. English. qt. $6.00 an issue. Centro Cultural de la Raza Publications, 2130-1 Pan American Plaza, #1, San Diego CA 92101. **Tel** (619)235-6135, FAX (619)595-0034. **ED** Sal Barajas.
Desc: A publication of Native American, Mexican, and Chicano culture featuring articles, short stories, and poetry.

US/0024-2950
LIETUVIU DIENOS. (LIETUVIU DIENOS. LITHUANIAN DAYS.). **VFOAT** Lithuanian Days. (1946)-. Periodical. English (Lithuanian). Ten times a year. $20.00. Lietuviu Dienos / Lithuanian Days, 4364 Sunset Boulevard, Los Angeles CA 90029-2195. **Tel** (310)664-2919. **LC** AP95.L5; L47. **Bk Rev. Ad Acc. Circ:** 5,000.
Desc: Pictorial magazine reflecting Lithuanian life in the free world.

US
LIFELINES. English. mo $36.00. Coalition to Free Soviet Jews, 8 West 40, Suite 1510, New York NY 10018. **Tel** (212) 354-1316.
Ind/Abst Hum. Rights Intern. Rep.

US/0199-2899
LONG ISLAND JEWISH WORLD. VFOAT Jewish World. Vol. 8., No. 9 (Apr. 20, 1979)-. Newspaper. English. ir. $26.00 US and Canada; $45.00 other. Empire Publishing Corporation, 115 Middle Neck Road, Great Neck NY 11021. **Tel** (516)829-4000. **Bk Rev. Ad Acc, Adv Mgr:** Harriet Lippman. **Continues** Jewish World.

US
LOUISIANA WEEKLY, THE. See Newspapers.

US
MALDEF. Added/Corp Mexican American Legal Defense and Educational Fund. (1967)-. Periodical. English (Spanish). Four times a year. $35.00 (two years). Mexican American Legal Defense and Educational Fund, 634 South Spring Street, 11th Floor, Los Angeles CA 90014. **Tel** (213)629-2512, FAX (213)629-1916. **ED** Abelardo de la Pena Jr. **Circ:** 15,000.

US/0737-8688
MALINI. Vol. 1, No. 1 (Oct. 1981)-. Periodical. English. Six times a year (Jan., Mar., May, July, Sept., Nov.). $6.00 Europe; $12.00 others. Malini Magazine, 2831 Rhodelia Avenue, Claremont CA 91711. **Tel** (213)826-1401. **ED** Chitra Chakraborty. **Bk Rev.** ctrl circ.
Desc: Promotes ethnic heritage of Pan-Asian cultures (India - Japan) in the United States through art and literature. Includes bibliography and/or suggested readings in every issue.

JA
MAN AND CULTURE IN OCEANIA. Added/Corp Japanese Society for Oceanic Studies. Vol. 1 (1985)-. English. an. $54.50. **(Subscription address:** Japan Publications Trading Company, Ltd., PO Box 5030, Tokyo International, Tokyo 100-31 Japan.**)**
Ind/Abst Int. Bibliogr. Sociol.

●US/1062-2543
MAN (CHICAGO, ILL.). (MAN.). [Man]. No. 1 (Spring 1992)-. Periodical. English. Four times a year (Seasonally). $19.99. Man / James Ray, PO Box 438801, Chicago IL 60643. **Tel** (312)239-2083. **ED** Lisa Wright, Jennifer Smith and Anthony Blackwell. **DD** 051. **Ad Acc. Pr Rev. Acid Free. Circ:** 2,000.
Desc: A magazine of African/African American peoples. It highlights their culture, history, and background. It features contemporary subjects such as style, fashion, art of these people. Advertising of African concerns is accepted.

CN/0834-6682
MANITOULIN EXPOSITOR. See Newspapers.

US/0892-1571
MARTYRDOM AND RESISTANCE. Added/Corp American Federation of Jewish Fighters, Camp Inmates, and Nazi Victims. Vol. 1 (Sept./Oct. 1974)-. Periodical. English. Five times a year. $10.00 (for postage). Martyrdom and Resistance Foundation, 48 West 37th, 9th Floor, New York NY 10018. **Tel** (212)564-1865. **ED** Dr. Harvey Rosenfeld. **DD** 940. **Bk Rev. Circ:** 26,000. available on microfiche; available with illustrations.
Desc: Information on the Jewish holocaust.

US/1046-5634
MAS (NEW YORK, N.Y.). Ceased. (MAS.). [Mas]. Vol. 1, No. 1 (Oct. 1989)-(1993). Periodical. Spanish. qt. Univision Publications, 330 Madison Avenue/26th Floor, New York NY 10017. **Tel** EDITORIAL: (212)455-5200, FAX (212)867-6710. **(Subscription address:** 605 Third Avenue, 12th Floor, New York, NY 10158-0180**) ED** Enrique Fernandez. **DD** 056. **Bk Rev. Ad Acc. Circ:** 500,000 (ctrl).
Desc: Designed for contemporary US Hispanics. Features topics as music, beauty, sports, fashion, cuisine, travel, political issue and arts.

GW
MATERIALIA TURCICA. See History(General)-History of Asia.

US
MEI CHIA HSUEH HSUN / MERICA NEWS. Added/Corp Merica Association. **VFOAT** Merica News. (19??-)-. Periodical. Chinese. sm. 351 - 11th Avenue, San Francisco CA 94118.

CN/0461-6871
MEIE ELU, TAHTRAAMAT. Began publication in 1950?. Estonian. an. Free to subscribers of Meie Elu, $2.00. Meie Elu, Estonian House, 985 Broadview Avenue, Toronto Ontario M4K 2R6 Canada. **DD** 971/.004/94545.

US
MEMORIES OF THE JEWISH MIDWEST. Added/Corp Nebraska Jewish Historical Society. **VFOAT** Journal of the Nebraska Jewish Historical Society. Vol. 1, No. 1 (Summer 1985)-. Periodical. English. **LC** F675.J5; M46.
Ind/Abst Am. Hist. Life (1987-).

US
MENOMINEE TRIBAL NEWS. (1976)-. Newspaper. English. sm. $20.00 institutions; $15.00 individuals. Menominee Indian Tribe, PO Box 910, Keshena WI 54135. **Tel** (715)799-5168, FAX (715)799-4525. **ED** Yvonne M. Kaquatosh-Aragon. **Ad Acc, Adv Mgr Tel** (715)799-5167. ctrl circ.
Desc: News of community and surrounding area and Native American news.

PO
MERIDIES. No. 1 (Dec. 1984)-. Periodical. French (Italian, Portuguese and Spanish). sa. **LC** HN371; .M47.

US/0026-0231
MESSAGE (NASHVILLE, TENN.). See Religion and Theology-Protestantism.

CN/0712-2713
METOIKOS. (O METOIKOS.). [Metoikos]. **VFOAT** Le Meteque. Vol. 1, No. 1 (June. 1980)-. Periodical. Greek, Modern. mo. Free to members of the Association Culturelle Helleno-Quebecoise, $1.00 each number nonmembers. O Metoikos, PO Box 382, Van Horne Station, Montreal Quebec H2V 1K0 Canada. **DD** 305.8/89/0714281.

US/0026-1580
METROPOLITAN STAR. Title Change. (19??)-(19??). Periodical. English. ir. Metropolitan Star, 823 UN Plaza/3rd Floor, New York NY 10017. **Continued by** Star (New York, N.Y.), 0745-8509.

US
MINNEAPOLIS SPOKESMAN. Vol. 1, No. 1 (Aug. 10, 1934)-. Newspaper. English. Fifty-two times a year. $29.00. Spokesman & Recorder Publishing Company, 3744 4th Avenue South, Minneapolis MN 55409. **Tel** (612)827-4021. **ED** Cecil E. Newman. **LC** Newspaper 8485. available on microfilm.

US/1053-2749
MINORITIES & WOMEN IN BUSINESS. Ceased. See Women's Interests.

US
MINORITY BUSINESS NEWS U.S.A. See Business.

US/0730-0034
MINORITY EDUCATION. Ceased. See Education.

US/0730-5141
MINORITY/ETHNIC MEDIA GUIDE, USA. See Communication.

US/1055-0690
MINORITY LITERARY EXPO. See Literary and Political Reviews.

●US/1061-2246
MINORITY LITERARY EXPO (BIRMINGHAM, ALA.). See Literary and Political Reviews.

US/0162-9034
MINORITY ORGANIZATIONS: A NATIONAL DIRECTORY. VFOAT Minority Organizations. (1978)-. Directory. English. te (every 3 years). $50.00. Garrett Park Press, PO Box 190 F, Garrett Park MD 20896. **Tel** (301)946-2553. **ED** Robert Calvert Jr. **LC** E184.A1; M544. **DD** 301.45/1/06173.
Desc: Lists over 7,700 organizations including minority membership organizations or programs developed by other groups to serve minority group members.

US
MINORITY PUPILS AND STAFF IN THE CONNECTICUT PUBLIC SCHOOLS. See Education.

CN/0825-012X
MINUTES OF PROCEEDINGS AND EVIDENCE OF THE SUB-COMMITTEE ON INDIAN WOMEN AND THE INDIAN ACT OF THE STANDING COMMITTEE ON INDIAN AFFAIRS AND NORTHERN DEVELOPMENT. See Law.

EC/0254-7678
MISCELANEA ANTROPOLOGICA ECUATORIANA. See Anthropology.

Ethnic Interests

US/0743-7641
MISSOURI ARCHAEOLOGICAL SOCIETY QUARTERLY. See Archaeology.

US/0746-1291
MISSOURI JEWISH POST & OPINION. Ceased. **VFOAT** Missouri Jewish Post and Opinion; Post and Opinion. Periodical. English. wk. Jewish Post and Opinion, 2120 North Meridian Street, Indianapolis IN 46202. **Tel** (317)927-7800, FAX (317)927-7807.

US
MONOGRAPH SERIES IN ETHNOMUSICOLOGY. See Music.

US/0002-905X
MONOGRAPHS OF THE AMERICAN JEWISH ARCHIVES. **Added/Corp** American Jewish Archives. No. 1 (1954)-. Monographic series. English. ir. Price varies per volume. American Jewish Archives, 3101 Clifton Avenue, Cincinnati OH 45220. **Tel** (513)221-1875 ext. 216, FAX (513)221-7812. **LC** UNC.

CN/0710-9695
MONTHLY NEWS - MULTICULTURAL COUNCIL OF WINDSOR AND ESSEX COUNTY. (MONTHLY NEWS.). [Mon. news - Multicult. Counc. Windsor Essex Cty.]. Periodical. English. mo. Free. Multicultural Council of Windsor and Essex, 1100 University Avenue West, Windsor Ontario N9A 5S7. **DD** 305.8/009713/32. ctrl circ.

US/0047-8121
MORNING STAR PEOPLE, THE. V. 1- 1965-. Periodical. English. qt. $1.00. St Labre Indian School, Ashland MT 59004.

●US/1058-9236
MULTICULTURAL REVIEW. (MULTICULTURAL REVIEW : DEDICATED TO A BETTER UNDERSTANDING OF ETHNIC, RACIAL, AND RELIGIOUS DIVERSITY.). [MultiCult. rev.]. Vol. 1, No. 1 (Jan. 1992)-. Periodical. English. qt. $59.00 US; $79.00 other. Greenwood Press Inc., PO Box 5007, Westport CT 06881-5007. **Tel** (203)226-3571, FAX (203)222-1502. **ED** Brenda Mitchell-Powell. **LC** Z711.8; .J68. **DD** 305. **Bk Rev. Ad Acc, Adv Mgr** Garance Inc, **Tel** (914)834-7070. **Pr Rev.** Absorbed Journal of Multicultural Librarianship, 0950-1649.
Desc: Provides a collection development direction and assistance to librarians and educators who are interested in locating materials that reflect the continually growing awareness of America's cultural, ethnic, and religious diversity.
Ind/Abst Mag. Artic. Summar. Elite (July 1994-).

AT/0818-8823
MULTICULTURALISM IN EDUCATION NEWSLETTER. See Education.

UK/0260-0226
MULTIRACIAL SCHOOL. Title Change. See Education.

US/1051-4147
MUNDO HISPANICO (ATLANTA, GA.). See Newspapers.

US/0739-8603
MUNDO HISPANO (AUSTIN, TEX.), EL. (EL MUNDO HISPANO.). Vol. 1, No. 1 (July 27, 1979)-. Periodical. English. Twenty-four times a year. $55.00. El Mundo Hispano National, 3206 McElroy Drive, Austin TX 78757. **Tel** (512)459-6394.

US
MUNDO LATINO, EL. **VFOAT** Latino. Vol. 4, No. 2 (May 5, 1991)-. Periodical. English. **Continues** National Latino News.

SZ
MUSEE NEUCHATELOIS. See History(General)-History of Europe.

GW
MUSIKETHNOLOGISCHE SAMMELBANDE. See Music.

CN/0708-5249
NACOI FORUM. [NACOI forum]. **Main/Corp** National Association of Canadians of Origins in India. V. 1- Jan. 1979-. Periodical. English. 10.00Can$. National Association of Canadians of Origins in Indis, 425 Gloucester Street, Ottawa K1R 5E9. **ED** B G Dillon. **DD** 971.00491411. **Bk Rev. Ad Acc.** Circ: 3,500. Supersedes Collage, 0708-9538.
Desc: Canadian issues pertaining to all aspects of integration and adaptation of people of Indian origin. Keys to the new system and cross cultural information especially groups and minority.

US/0744-737X
NAS GOLOS. (NASH HOLOS. OUR VOICE.). **Added/Corp** Asotsiiatsiia Ukraintsiv v Amerytsi. **VFOAT** Our Voice. (1972)-. Periodical. Ukrainian. sm. $119.95. **(Subscription address:** East View Publications Inc., 3020 Harbor Lane North, Suite 110, Minneapolis MN 55447.**)** **LC** E184.U5; N35. **Continues** Asotsiiatsiia Ukraintsiv v Amerytsi. Biuleten' Asotsiiasii Ukraintsiv v Amerytsi.

●RU
NASH DAGESTAN. See History(General)-History of Europe.

PL
NASHE SLOVO (WARSAW, POLAND). (NASHE SLOVO : ORHAN HOLOVNOHO PRAVLINNIA UKRAINSKOHO SUSPILNOKULTURNOHO TOVARYSTVA.). **Added/Corp** Ukrainske Suspilno-Kulturne Tovarystvo (Poland). Holovne Pravlinnia. **VFOAT** Nasze Slowo. (19??)-. Periodical. Ukrainian. wk. $52.00. **(Subscription address:** ARS Polona, PO Box 1001, 00068 Warsaw Poland.**)**

US/0896-0194
NATIONAL BLACK LAW JOURNAL. See Law.

AT/1037-6917
NATIONAL DIRECTORY OF ABORIGINAL AND TORRES STRAIT ISLANDER ORGANISATIONS. (19??)-. Directory. English. an. 140.00Aus$ Australia; 163.00Aus$ New Zealand, Papua New Guinea; 167.00Aus$ Indonesia, Malaysia, Singapore, 171.00Aus$ Japan, India; 177.00Aus$ US & Canada; 181.00Aus$ Europe. International Public Relations Pty Ltd, 33 Walsh Street, West Melbourne Victoria 3003 Australia. **Tel** 011 61 03 329 9333, FAX 011 61 03 329 7996.

US/0734-9920
NATIONAL HISPANIC JOURNAL. Suspended. [Natl. Hisp. j.]. **VFOAT** NHJ; N.H.J. Vol. 1, No. 1 (Summer 1981)-?. Periodical. English. qt. $9.00. National Hispanic Institute, PO Box 220, Maxwell TX 78656-0220. **Tel** (512)476-3595. **ED** Alex Avila. **Bk Rev. Ad Acc.** Circ: 1,500.
Desc: A diverse examination of issues affecting the multicultured youth, from education to analyses, to music and book reviews.

US
NATIONAL JEWISH LIFE, THE. (March 1987)-. Newspaper. English. Four times a year. Free on request. National Jewish Life, 350 5th Avenue, Suite 3304, New York NY 10118. **Tel** (212)431-6665.

US
NATIONAL MINORITY DIGEST. (19??)-. English. **LC** E184.A1; N295. **DD** 301.45/0973.

US/1057-1655
NATIONAL MINORITY POLITICS. [Natl. minor. polit.]. Vol. 1, No. 1 (Oct. 1988)-. Periodical. English. Twelve times a year. $29.00 (one year); $49.00 (two years). Richberg Communications Inc., 5757 Westheimer, Suite 3-296, Houston TX 77057. **Tel** (713)444-4265, FAX (713)583-9534. **ED** Gwen Daye Richardson. **LC** E184.A1; N296. **DD** 320. **Bk Rev,** (Qty: 6). **Ad Acc, Adv Mgr** Willie Richardson. **Circ:** 12,000 (ctrl). available on an online database from NEWSNET.
Desc: Opinions and features on trends, issues and elections involving minority groups; moderate to conservative in approach.

UK
NATIONALISM AND ETHNIC POLITICS. See Political Science.

US/0090-5992
NATIONALITIES PAPERS. [Natl. pap.]. Vol 1 (Fall 1972)-. Academic Scholarly Publication. English. sa (April and October). £48.00. Carfax Publishing Company, PO Box 25 Abingdon, Oxfordshire OX14 3UE England. **Tel** 011 44 235 555335, FAX (0279)31067, telex 817484. **(Subscription address:** US and Canada/ PO Box 2025, Dunnellon, FL 34430-2025; telephone:(904)489-6996**)** **ED** Henry R. Huttenbach. **LC** DR24; .N37. **DD** 301.45/1/05. Index available. **Bk Rev. Ad Acc.** Circ: 400. available on microfilm and microfiche from University Microfilms International (UMI).
Desc: Scholarly papers on minority nationalities in Eastern Europe and the Soviet Union.
Ind/Abst Am. Hist. Life (1972-); Am. Bibliogr. Slavic East Europ. Stud.; Hum. Rights Intern. Rep.; Int. Bibliogr. Sociol.; Int. Polit. Sci. Abstr.; MLA Int. Bibl. Books Artic. Mod. Lang. Lit.; PAIS Int. Print (1991-); Soc. Plann. Policy Dev. Abstr.; Sociol. Abstr.

US/0361-3399
NATIVE AERICAN TEXTS SERIES. V. 1-. Monographic series. English. Price varies per volume. University of Chicago Press / Book Department, 11030 South Langley Avenue, Chicago IL 60628. **Tel** (800)621-2736, (312)568-1550, FAX (312)753-0811, telex 23933. **ED** E P Hamp. available on microfilm and microfiche from University Microfilms International (UMI).

US
NATIVE AMERICAN, THE. Periodical. English. bm. US Department of Health and Human Services, 200 Independence Avenue Southwest, Washington DC 20201.

●US/1063-9632
NATIVE AMERICANS INFORMATION DIRECTORY. [Native Am. inf. dir.]. **Added/Corp** Gale Research Inc. **VFOAT** N D; ND; Native Directory. (1992)-. Directory. English. ir. $79.00. Gale Research Inc., 835 Penobscot Building, Detroit MI 48226. **Tel** (800)877-GALE, (313)961-2242, FAX (313)961-6083, telex TWX 810-221-7086. **LC** E76.2; .N38. **DD** 970.004/97/0025.

●US/1070-8014
NATIVE NORTH AMERICAN ALMANAC. **Added/Corp** Gale Research, Inc. (1993)-. English. ir. $75.00. Gale Research Inc., 835 Penobscot Building, Detroit MI 48226. **Tel** (800)877-GALE, (313)961-2242, FAX (313)961-6083, telex TWX 810-221-7086. **ED** Duane Champagne.
Desc: Provides coverage for all major aspects of the civilization and culture of the indigenous peoples of the US and Canada, including contemporary and historic information on all North American Indian groups and issues relevant to them.

US/0895-7606
NATIVE PEOPLES. See History(General)-History of North, South, and Central America.

CN/0703-9190
NATIVE SISTERHOOD. Began publication in 1969?. Periodical. English. $2.50. Native Sisterhood, Box 515, Kingston Ontario K7L 4WT Canada. **DD** 365/.9713/72.

CN/1187-3523
NATIVE SPORTS & CULTURE NEWS. [Native sports cult. news]. **VFOAT** Native Sports and Culture News; Native Sports News. Vol. 2, No. 4 (June/July 1991)-. Periodical. English. mo. Native Sports Publishing, Suite 205, 15517 Stony Plain Road, Edmonton Alberta T5P 3Z1 Canada. **DD** 790.1/9. **Continues** Native Sports News., 1185-2275.

CN/0381-4580
NATIVE STUDIES IN COLLEGES AND UNIVERSITIES. **Main/Corp** Ontario. Ministry of Colleges and Universities. 1975-. English. an. Free. Ministry of Colleges and Universities, Mowat Block/13th Floor, Queen's Park, Toronto Ontario M7A 1L2 Canada. **Tel** (416)965-6407. **LC** E76.6; .O58A. **DD** 301.2/07/11713.
Desc: A guide to courses in native studies offered in Ontario beyond the secondary school level.

CN/0831-585X
NATIVE STUDIES REVIEW. (1984)-. Academic Scholarly Publication. English. Twice a year. 20.00Can$ (individuals); 35.00Can$ (institutions). University of Saskatchewan / Native Studies Department, 104 McLean Hall, Saskatoon SASK S7N 0W0 Canada. **Tel** (306)966-6208, 966-6216, FAX (306)966-6242. **ED** Laurie Barron (editor's phone: (306)966-6212). Index available. **Bk Rev. Pr Rev.** Circ: 300.
Desc: A scholarly journal that explores the field of Native studies. Includes articles, research notes, commentaries, reviews, documents and a visual history section.

CN/0827-3944
NATIVE WOMEN'S NEWS. [Native women's news]. Suspended, Summer 1984- . Periodical. English. Free. Native Women's Association of the NWT, PO Box 2321, Yellowknife Northwest Territories X1A 2P7 Canada. **DD** 305.4/8897/07192.

US
NAVAJO NATION MESSENGER, THE. See Newspapers.

US/0466-6658
NAVAJO YEARBOOK. (THE NAVAJO YEARBOOK / COMPILED, WITH ARTICLES BY ROBERT W. YOUNG.). **Added/Corp** United States. Bureau of Indian Affairs. Navajo Agency. No. 6 (1957)-. English. an. US Bureau of Indian Affairs / Education Division, Navajo Area, Window Rock AZ 86515. **Tel** (602)871-4547. **DD** 970.1. **Continues** Navajo Yearbook of Planning in Action.

US/0161-2115
NCJW JOURNAL. [NCJW j.]. **Main/Corp** National Council of Jewish Women. **VAT** National Council of Jewish Women Journal. V. 1- Apr. 1978-. Periodical. English. qt. $2.00. National Council of Jewish Women, 53 W 23rd Street, New York NY 10010. **Tel** (212)645-4048. **ED** Michele Spirn. **Bk Rev. Ad Acc.** Circ: 100,000. **Continues** Council Woman, 0148-2106.
Desc: Publishes articles on the projects and programs of the National Council of Jewish Women, as well as articles on issues of social concern.

CN/0316-9782
NEDERLANDSE COURANT (WILLOWDALE). (DE NEDERLANDSE COURANT [MICROFORM].). [Ned. courant]. (19 Jan. 1966)-. Dutch (summaries and/or abstracts in English). bw. 22.10Can$ (1 year), 41.60Can$ (2 year) Canada; $35.00 (1 year), $65.00 (2 year) other. Dutch Canadian Biweekly, 3109 Harvester Rdn. A, Burlington ONT L7N 3G4 Canada. **Tel** (416)333-3615, FAX (416)333-5958.

Ethnic Interests

ED Theo Luykenaar. **DD** 071/.13541. **Ad Acc. Circ:** 5,000 (ctrl). **Continues** De Nederlandse Courant Voor Canada,, 0316-9790.
Desc: Dutch / Canadian news.

CN/0381-9477
NEGRO DIRECTORY. Vol. 1 (Mar. 1966)-.
Directory. English. sa. McLaren Micropublishing, PO Box 972 Station F, Toronto Ontario M4Y 2N9 Canada. **DD** 338/.0025/713541.
Desc: This is a partial list of businesses and services owned or opeated by Negroes.

US/0548-1457
NEGRO EDUCATIONAL REVIEW, THE.
See Education.

HU/0586-3716
NEPRAJZ ES NYELVTUDOMANY. See Anthropology.

HU/0077-6599
NEPRAJZI ERTESITO : NEPRAJZI MUZEUM EVKONYVE. Main/Corp Neprajzi Muzeum (Hungary). (1954)-. Periodical. Hungarian (English). an. Tankonyvkiado, Szalay u 10 14 Postfiok 20, H 1055 Budapest V Hungary. **Continues** Neprajzi Muzeum Ertesitoje.
Ind/Abst Anthropol. Index; BHA : Biblio. Hist. Art.

SP
NEVIPENS ROMANI : NOTICIAS GITANAS. Spanish. bm. 1500ptas. Nevipens Romani, Apartado de Correos 202, 08080 Barcelona Spain. **Tel** 011 34 3 3012833.

US
NEW AMERICAN, THE. See Newspapers.

US
NEW AMERICAN (NEW YORK, N.Y.). Vol. 30, No. 1 (Jan. 4th thru 10th, 1990)-. Periodical. English. wk. $33.00. Black American, Box 4233, New York NY 11247. **Tel** (718)399-2271, FAX (718)657-9115. **ED** Eleanor D. Branch. **LC** E185.5; .B6121. **Bk Rev. Ad Acc. Circ:** 54,355. available with charts; available with illustrations. **Continues** Black American, 0890-5983.

US
NEW BREED MICROFORM, THE.
Added/Corp Association of Metis and Non-Status Indians of Saskatchewan. (1970)-. Periodical. English. mo. $15.48. Association of Metis and Non-status Indians, 210-2505 11th Avenue, Regina Saskatchewan S4P 0K6 Canada. **Tel** (306)525-9501. **ED** Jean-Paul Claude. **Bk Rev. Ad Acc. Circ:** 4,000.
Desc: Exists to serve the communication needs of the Metis and non-status Indians of Saskatchewan, by providing information on relevant issues which affect them as individuals and communities.

CN/0707-5650
NEW CANADIAN SLOVENE DIARY, THE.
VFOAT Slovene Diary. V. 3, No. 31- Sept. 1978-. Periodical. English (Slovenian). mo. $5.00. the New Canadian Slovene Diary, PO Box 1371, Station B, Toronto Ontario M3H 5W3. **DD** 301.45/19/184071. **Continues** Dnevnik Slovene Canadian, 0702-8423.

UK/0047-9586
NEW COMMUNITY. [New community].
Added/Corp Great Britain. Community Relations Commission. Great Britain. Commission for Racial Equality. Vol. 1 (Oct. 1971)-. Periodical. English. Four times a year. £36.00 US; £48.00 other. Centre for Research on Ethnic Relations, University of Warwick, Coventry CV4 7AL England. **Tel** 44 203 523523 ext. 2364. **ED** Malcolm Cross. **LC** HN381; .N45. **DD** 309.1/42. **CODEN** NEWCEL. Index available. **Bk Rev. Ad Acc. Circ:** 2,000.
Desc: A journal of research and policy on ethnic relations.
Ind/Abst Appl. Soc. Sci. Index Abstr.; Br. Educ. Index; Br. Humanit. Index; Child. Lit. Abstr. (19??-); Geogr. Abstr. Human Geogr.; Health Serv. Abstr.; Index Islam. Lit.; Int. Bibliogr. Sociol.; Int. Labour Doc.; Lang. Teach.; Multicult. Educ. Abstr.; Soc. Plann. Policy Dev. Abstr.; Spec. Educ. Needs Abstr.

US/0747-4970
NEW ENGLAND JOURNAL OF BLACK STUDIES. [New. Engl. J. Black stud.]. **Added/Corp** National Council for Black Studies (U.S.). New England Regional Conference. No. 1 (1981)-. Periodical. English. an. $15.00 (institutions), $10.00 (individuals). Rhode Island Black Heritage Society, 46 Aborn Street, Providence RI 02903. **Tel** (401)751-3490. **ED** Melvin K. Hendrix. **LC** E185.5; .N457. **DD** 974/.00496073. **Bk Rev. Ad Acc. Circ:** 300.
Desc: Contains articles in African and Afro-American studies, research notes, and a section on archival and library holdings of interest to scholars in the field.

US
NEW ENGLAND MINORITY NEWS. (19??)-.
Newspaper. English. bw. $49.50. New England Minority News, PO Box 347, Hartford CT 06141. **Tel** (203)549-0809, (800)666-4696. **ED** James H. Monroe.

Ad Acc. Circ: 40,000.
Desc: Newspaper listing business and employment opportunities for minorities.

US/1043-5808
NEW GERMAN-AMERICAN STUDIES.
[New Ger.-Am. stud.]. **VFOAT** New German American Studies. (1990)-. Monographic series. English. ir. Price varies per volume. Peter Lang Publishing, 62 West 45th Street, 4th Floor, New York NY 10036. **Tel** (212)764-1471, (800)770-5264, telex 6973364 PLNY. **DD** 305.

US/0364-8184
NEW HORIZON (JERSEY CITY). (NEW HORIZON.). [New horiz.]. **VFOAT** New Horizon, Polish American Review. (1975)-. English. Ten times a year. $20.00. Bicentennial Publishing Company, 21 West 38th Street, New York NY 10018. **Tel** (212)354-0490. **ED** B. Wierzbianski. **LC** E184.P7; N48. **DD** 973/.04/9185. **Circ:** 5,000.

US
NEW JERSEY PUBLIC SCHOOL RACIAL/ETHNIC ENROLLMENTS AND DROPOUTS / STATE OF NEW JERSEY, DEPARTMENT OF EDUCATION. See Education.

US/0882-9462
NEW MOTON GUIDE TO AMERICAN COLLEGES WITH A BLACK HERITAGE, THE. See Education-Higher Education.

CN/0715-4445
NEW PERSPECTIVE (HAMILTON). (THE NEW PERSPECTIVE.). [New perspect.]. **Added/Corp** Hamilton Multicultural Centre. Hamilton and District Citizenship Council. Hamilton and District Multicultural Council. (1975)-. Periodical. English. mo. $10.00. New Perspective, 500 James Street North, Hamilton Ontario L8L 1J4 Canada. **Tel** (416)5280258. **DD** 305.8/009713/52. **Bk Rev. Ad Acc. Circ:** 600.

US
NEW VISIONS. English. bm. $7.50. Rodney Reynolds, 5007 Superior Avenue, Cleveland OH 44103. **Tel** (216)881-4112. **ED** Jane Littleton. **Circ:** 10,000.
Desc: Focuses on developments, activities and leaders in Cleveland's black community. Purpose is to provide a cohesive forum for the black community to discuss important and educational issues.

US
NEW VISIONS OF AZTLAN. Added/Corp Aztlan Cultural Arts Foundation. Vol. 1, Issue 1 (Spring 1990)-. Periodical. English (Spanish). sa. $10.00. Aztlan Cultural Arts Foundation, PO Box 5093, Riverside CA 92057.

US/0733-7809
NEW YORK FINE PRINT. (FINE PRINT.).
VFOAT Fine Print News. Began publication with Vol. 1, 1972. Periodical. English. wk. Fine Print News, PO Box 1208, Buffalo NY 14205.

US/0745-5356
NEW YORK JEWISH WEEK, THE. [N.Y. Jew. week]. **VFOAT** Jewish Week. Vol. 195, No. 10 (July 30, 1982)-. Newspaper. English. wk. $30.00 New York City, Nassau, Suffolk and Westchester; $35.00 other US and Canada; $52.00 other. Jewish Week, 1501 Broadway, Suite 505, New York NY 10036. **Tel** (212)921-7822, FAX (212)921-8420. **ED** Gary Rosenblatt (Editor-in-Chief) and Rob Goldblum (Managing Editor). **LC** DS101; .N388. **DD** 909/.04924/005. **Bk Rev**, (Qty: 26). **Photos. Ad Acc, Adv Mgr:** Richard Waloff. Full Page (B&W) $7,490.00. Half Page (B&W) $3,780.00. Full Page (Color) $8,290.00. Half Page (Color) $4,580.00.
Pub. Size: Tabloid. **Wire Svcs.:** JT. **Circ:** 109,000 (ctrl).
Continues New York Jewish Week and the American Examiner, 0737-352X.

US/1050-5490
NEW YORK LATINO. (1990)-. Periodical. English. bm. $12.00. Latinoamerica Spirit, 333 West 16th Street, Suite 1R, New York NY 10011.

US/0193-1814
NEWS CIRCLE, THE. [News circle]. **VFOAT** Halqat al-Akhbar; Dhi Niyuz Sirkil. (June 1972)-. Periodical. English (Arabic). Ten times a year (Jan./Feb. and Mar./Apr. issues combined). $25.00. The News Circle, PO Box 3684, Glendale CA 91201. **Tel** (818)545-0333, FAX (818)242-5039. **ED** Joseph Haiek. **Bk Rev**, (Qty: 10). **Ad Acc. Pr Rev. Circ:** 5,000. available on microfilm. **Absorbed** Mideast Business Exchange, 0193-189X.
Desc: Serving the Arab-American community, Arab world affairs, Arabic culture, social and Master calendar of Arab-American events.

US
NEWS FROM INDIAN COUNTRY : THE JOURNAL. Added/Corp Indian Country Communications (Hayward, Wis.). **VFOAT** News from Indian Country. Vol. 2, No. 8 (Aug. 1988)-. Newspaper. English. sm. $26.00 US; $48.00 Canada; $50.00 other.

Indian Country Communications, Route 2 Box 2900-A, Hayward WI 54843. **Tel** (715)634-5226, FAX (715)634-3243. **Continues** Journal (Hayward, Wis.).

US/0199-901X
NEWS INDIA (NEW YORK). Title Change.
(NEWS INDIA.). (19??)-(1993). Periodical. English. wk. Hanna Worldwide Publishing, 244 Fifth Avenue Suite 402, New York NY 10001. **Tel** (212)481-3115. **Continues** News & Cine India. **Continued by** News India-Times, 1071-0248.

●US/1071-0248
NEWS INDIA-TIMES. VFOAT News India Times. (July 2, 1993)-. Newspaper. English. Fifty-two times a year. $26.00 one year; $45.00 two years. Hanna Worldwide Publishing, 244 Fifth Avenue Suite 402, New York NY 10001. **Tel** (212)481-3115. **Continues** News India, 0199-901X.

US
NEWSBREAK / NATIONAL CONFERENCE ON SOVIET JEWRY.
Added/Corp National Conference on Soviet Jewry (U.S.). (Oct. 7, 1983)-. Periodical. English. wk. **Continues** Press Service (National Conference on Soviet Jewry (U.S.)).
Ind/Abst Hum. Rights Intern. Rep.

IS
NEWSLETTER. See Political Science.

US/0893-4290
NEWSLETTER - AFRICAN-AMERICAN FAMILY HISTORY ASSOCIATION. See Genealogy and Heraldry.

US/0882-8474
NEWSLETTER (AFRO-AMERICAN HISTORICAL AND GENEALOGICAL SOCIETY (WASHINGTON, D.C.) : 1983).
See History(General)-History of North, South, and Central America.

CN/0828-6965
NEWSLETTER - CROSS-CULTURAL COMMUNICATION CENTRE.
(NEWSLETTER.). [Newsl. - Cross-Cult. Commun. Cent.]. **Added/Corp** Cross Cultural Communication Centre (Toronto, Ont.). Vol. 6, No. 12 (Dec. 1977)-. Newsletter. English. Eleven times a year (July/August issues combined). 20.00Can$ (institutions), 15.00Can$ (individuals). Cross Cultural Communication Centre, 2909 Dundas Street West, Toronto Ontario M6P 1Z1 Canada. **Tel** (416)760-7855, FAX (416)767-4352. **ED** Terry Guerriero. **DD** 305.8/009713/541. **Circ:** 300 (ctrl).
Continues Cross Cultural Communication Centre (Toronto, Ont.). C.C.C.C. Newsletter., 0383-9346.

CN/0831-2885
NEWSLETTER / NATIVE ART STUDIES ASSOCIATION OF CANADA. [Newsl. - Native Art Stud. Assoc. Can.]. **Added/Corp** Native Art Studies Association of Canada. Vol. 1, No. 1 (Winter 1986)-. Newsletter. English. qt. 15.00Can$ Canada; 17.00Can$ other. Native Art Studies Association Canada, Carleton University, Department of Art/Blodgett, Ottawa Ontario K1S 5B6 Canada. **DD** 709/.01/1.
Desc: Information on the Indians of North America.
Ind/Abst Ethnoarts Index.

US/0889-6178
NEWSLETTER OF THE AFRO-AMERICAN RELIGIOUS HISTORY GROUP OF THE AMERICAN ACADEMY OF RELIGION. See History(General)-History of North, South, and Central America.

US/1056-5876
NEWSLETTER - SOUTH AND MESO-AMERICAN INDIAN INFORMATION CENTER (1990). Title Change. (NEWSLETTER / SOUTH AND MESO-AMERICAN INDIAN INFORMATION CENTER.). [Newsl. - South Meso-Am. Indian Inf. Cent.]. **Added/Corp** South and Meso-American Indian Information Center. **VFOAT** SAIIC Newsletter. Vol. 5, No. 3 & 4 (Dec. 1990)-(199?). Periodical. English. qt. South & Meso-American Indian Information Center, PO Box 28703, Oakland CA 94604. **Tel** (510)834-4263, FAX (510)834-4264. **LC** E59.G6; N48. **DD** 305. **Continues** SAIIC Newsletter, 1059-9673. **Continued by** Abya Yala News, 1071-3182.

CN/0712-1288
NEWSLETTER / VIETNAMESE ASSOCIATION, TORONTO. Added/Corp Vietnamese Association Toronto. (1979)-. Newsletter. English. mo. $10.00. Vietnamese Association of Toronto, 8 York Street, Toronto, Ontario M5J 1R2 Canada. **DD** 971/.0049592.

US
NHSF NEWS / NATIONAL HISPANIC SCHOLARSHIP FUND. **Added/Corp** National Hispanic Scholarship Fund. Vol. 1, No. 1 (Spring 1988)-. Periodical. English.

US/0164-6966
NINGAS. [Ningas]. V. 8, No. 3- Oct. 1978-. Periodical. English. mo. Ningas Magazine, 17E-16th Street/4th Floor, New York NY 10003. ***Continues** Ningas-Cogon, 0149-9289.*

US/0890-0485
NINNAU : THE NORTH AMERICAN WELSH NEWSLETTER. [Ninnau]. Vol. 1, No. 1 (Nov. 1, 1975)-. Newsletter. English (Welsh). mo (except Sept.). $15.00 US; 18.00Can$ Canada; £10.00 UK. Ninnau Publications, 11 Post Terrace, Basking Ridge NJ 07920. **Tel** (201)204-9254. **ED** Olga Williams. **DD** 973. **Bk Rev**, (Qty: 25). **Ad Acc. Circ:** 4,000.
Desc: News and feature articles of interest to the Welsh in North America.

PL/0546-1960
NIVA : ORHAN HALOUNAHA PRALENNIA BELARUSKAHA HRAMADSKA-KULTURNAHA TAVARYSTVA. **Added/Corp** Belaruskae Hramadska-Kulturnae Tavarystva. Haolunae Praulenne. (195?)-. Periodical. Byelorussian. wk. $39.00. **(Subscription address:** ARS Polona, PO Box 1001, 00068 Warsaw Poland.) **LC** WMLCF 83/62.

US/1056-683X
NOBO (HARLEM HEIGHTS, N.Y.). (NOBO : A JOURNAL OF AFRICAN AMERICAN DIALOGUE.). [NOBO]. **Added/Corp** Network of Black Organizers. **VAT** Network of Black Organizers. (Winter 1991)-. Periodical. English. qt. $12.00 North America; $20.00 other. NOBO, PO Box 1398, Jamaica Plain Station, Boston MA 02130. **DD** 305.

CN/0822-7942
NOMADIC PEOPLES. **Added/Corp** International Union of Anthropological and Ethnological Sciences. Commission on Nomadic Peoples. **VFOAT** Newsletter. No. 5 (Jan. 1980)-. Periodical. English (French). Twice a year. $52.00 (institutions), $42.00 (individuals). Nordiska Afrikaainstitutet, Sturegatan 9 1 TR EPOS, S 753 14 Uppsala Sweden. **Tel** 011 46 18 1833325. **ED** Philip Carl Salzman. **LC** GN387; .N594. **DD** 305.9/0693. **CODEN** NOPEES. **Bk Rev. Circ:** 500 (ctrl). ***Continues** Newsletter (Commission on Nomadic Peoples), 0822-7934.*
Desc: Contains material relevant to Third World studies. Development of anthropology, human ecology, cultural studies, livestock and range management agricultural economics.
Ind/Abst Abstr. Anthropol.; Anthropol. Lit.; Dairy Sci. Abstr.; Geogr. Abstr. Human Geogr.; Int. Dev. Abstr.; Int. Labour Doc.; Soc. Plann. Policy Dev. Abstr.

US
NOMMO : AFRICAN STUDENT NEWSMAGAZINE AT UCLA. Periodical. English. ASUCLA, Communications Board, 308 Westwood CA 90024. **LC** E185.5; .N66.

US/1051-0249
NORTHSTAR NEWS & ANALYSIS. ***Ceased.*** (NORTHSTAR NEWS & ANALYSIS : THE VOICE OF TODAY'S AFRICAN AMERICAN.). [NorthStar news anal.]. **VFOAT** NorthStar News and Analysis; North Star News & Analysis; North Star News and Analysis North Star NorthStar. Vol. 1, No. 1 (July 1989)-(1992). Periodical. English. mo. North Star Publishing Company / Chicago, 1169 South Plymouth Court, Suite 311, Chicago IL 60605. **Tel** (312)431-3310. **DD** 051.

US/0894-3109
NORTHWEST ETHNIC NEWS. (NORTHWEST ETHNIC NEWS / ETHNIC HERITAGE COUNCIL OF THE PACIFIC NORTHWEST.). [Northwest ethn. news]. **Added/Corp** Ethnic Heritage Council of the Pacific Northwest. **VFOAT** North West Ethnic News; Ethnic News. Vol. 1, No. 1 (Jan. 1984)-. Periodical. English. mo. $12.00 (individual); $30.00 (institution). Ethnic Heritage Council Pacific Northwest, 305 Harrison Street, Suite 326, Seattle WA 98109. **Tel** (206)443-1410. **ED** Sarah Sarai. **DD** 305. **Bk Rev**, (Qty: 8-14). **Ad Acc. Circ:** 15,000.

US/0146-1877
NORTHWEST INDIAN NEWS. Vol. 1, No. 1, (June 1971)-. Periodical. English. mo. $5.00. Seattle Indian Association, PO Box 4322, Pioneer Square Station, Seattle WA 98104. ***Continues** Indian Center News.*

UK
NOS. **VFOAT** Nos no Mundo; We, Around the World. Year 1, No. 1 (Feb. 1991)-. Periodical. English (Italian and Portuguese). mo.

MX
NOTICIAS INDIGENISTAS DE AMERICA. **Added/Corp** Inter-American Indian Institute. **VFOAT** Indian News from the Americas. (1979)-. Spanish (English and Spanish). qt. Inter-American Indian Institute, Insurgentes sur 1690, Col Florida, 01030 Mexico D. F.,, Mexico.

CN/0048-1017
NOVI DNI. (NOVI DNI. NOWI DNI.). [Novi dni]. **VFOAT** Nowi Dni. (1950)-. Periodical. Ukrainian. mo. 36.00Can$. Nowi Dni Publishing Ltd, PO Box 400 Station D, Toronto Ontario M6P 3J9 Canada. **Tel** (416)767-8440, FAX (416)234-1213. **ED** Mr. Maryan Horhota-Dalney (editor's address: #1112 260 Scarlett Road, Toronto Ontario M6N 4X6 Canada). **LC** AP58.U5; N6. Index available (bound in Dec. issue). cum. index. **Bk Rev**, (Qty: 24). **Ad Acc. Pr Rev. Circ:** 1,500 (ctrl).
Desc: Universal magazine: literature, arts, music, politics, particulars: social and political problems in Ukraine (USSR), life of Ukrainians anywhere. Articles on imperialism and communism.
Ind/Abst Am. Bibliogr. Slavic East Europ. Stud. (19??-19??); MLA Int. Bibl. Books Artic. Mod. Lang. Lit.

US/1045-2427
NUESTRAS RAICES (QUARTERLY). **See** Genealogy and Heraldry.

US/0147-3247
NUESTRO. [Nuestro]. Vol. 1 (April 1977)-. Periodical. English (summaries and/or abstracts in Spanish). Ten times a year. $22.00. Nuestro Publications, Inc, 461 Park Avenue South, PO Box 4078, Washington DC 20016. **ED** Daniel M. Lopez. **LC** E184.S75; N83. **DD** 973/.04/68. **Bk Rev. Ad Acc. Circ:** 210,000 (ctrl).
Desc: Serious analysis of socio-economic problems to personality profiles, sports and entertainment for Latinos in the US.
Ind/Abst Access (1978-1987); Gen. Period. Index (1985-1986); Mag. Search; Mag. Index (1980-?).

CN/0828-1513
OCCASIONAL PAPERS IN ETHNIC AND IMMIGRATION STUDIES. [Occas. pap. ethn. immig. stud.]. **Added/Corp** Multicultural History Society of Ontario. 3 (1978)-. Monographic series. English. ir. Price varies per volume. Multicultural History Society of Ontario, 43 Queens Park Crescent East, Toronto Ontario M5S 2C3 Canada. **Tel** (416)979-2973. **ED** Robert F. Harney. **LC** UNC. **Circ:** 500. ***Continues** Occasional Papers on Ethnic and Immigration Studies.*
Desc: Specific aspects of ethnic history and various ethnic communities in Ontario.

US/1068-5987
OFARI'S BI-MONTHLY. **See** Political Science.

CN/0821-5979
OJIBWAY CREE RESOURCE CENTRE CATALOGUE. [Ojibway Cree Resour. Cent. cat.]. **Main/Corp** Ojibway-Cree Resource Centre. 1982-. English. an. 35.00Can$. Ontario Library Service Voyageur, 334 Regent Street South, Sudbury Ontario P3C 4E2 Canada. **Tel** (705)675-6467. **LC** PAR. **DD** 016.971/00497.

US/0362-2770
OPTIONS (WAYNE, N.J.). (OPTIONS.). [Options]. (197?)-. Periodical. English. Twelve times a year (Published on the last Monday of each month). $21.00 US; $23.00 Canada; $24.00 other. Options Publishing Company, Box 311, Wayne NJ 07474-0311. **Tel** (201)694-2327. **ED** Betty J. Singer. Index available (Free with Nov. issue). **Bk Rev.**
Desc: Clearinghouse of American Jewish resources.

US/0733-477X
OREGON DIRECTORY OF AMERICAN INDIAN RESOURCES. [Or. dir. Am. Indian resour.]. **VFOAT** American Indian Resources. 1981-82-. Directory. English. be. $9.00. Commission on Indian Services, 454 State Capitol, Salem OR 97310. **Tel** (503)378-5481. **ED** Gladine G. Johnson. **LC** E78.O6; O72. **DD** 305.8/97/0795. **Circ:** 15,000 (ctrl).
Desc: Lists all American Indian tribes, organizations, interest groups, programs, etc. in the state of Oregon. Contains addresses, phone numbers and program or organization descriptions.

IS/0792-4615
OTHER ISRAEL : NEWSLETTER OF THE ISRAELI COUNCIL FOR ISRAELI-PALESTINIAN PEACE, THE. **Added/Corp** Israeli Council for Israeli-Palestinian Peace. No. 1 (July 1983)-. Newsletter. English. Six times a year. $50.00 (institution), $30.00 (individual), $15.00 (student/unemp.). The Other Israel, PO Box 2542, Holon 58125 Israel. **Tel** 011 972 3 5565804. **ED** Adam Keller and Beate Zilversmidt. **LC** DS119.7; .O85. **DD** 956/.04/05. **Bk Rev**, (Qty: 20). **Ad Acc. Circ:** 3,000.
Ind/Abst Hum. Rights Intern. Rep.

●CN/1196-1929
OTTAWA JEWISH BULLETIN (1993). (THE OTTAWA JEWISH BULLETIN.). (1993)-. English. Twenty times a year. 30.00Can$. Jewish Community Council of Ottawa, 151 Chapel Street, Ottawa Ontario K1N 7Y2 Canada. **Tel** (613)789-7306, FAX (613)789-4593. **ED** Myra Aronson. **Bk Rev. Ad Acc, Adv Mgr:** A. Baker. **Circ:** 2,400 / 3,700 (ctrl). ***Continues** Ottawa Jewish Bulletin & Review, 0319-1303.*
Desc: News and information of interest to the Jewish community in Ottawa.

CN/0319-1303
OTTAWA JEWISH BULLETIN & REVIEW. ***Title Change.*** [Ott. Jew. bull. rev.]. **Added/Corp** Jewish Community Council of Ottawa. Vol. 38, No. 2 (June 1974)-(1993). Bulletin. English. sm. Jewish Bulletin & Review, 151 Chapel Street, Ottawa Ontario K1N 7Y2 Canada. **Tel** (613)232-7306. **DD** 971.3/84/004924. ***Formed by the union of** Ottawa Jewish Bulletin, 0319-129X **and** Ottawa Jewish Digest and Review, 0319-1281. **Continued by** Ottawa Jewish Bulletin, 1196-1929.*

US/0739-9766
PAHA NEWSLETTER. (PAHA NEWSLETTER / POLISH AMERICAN HISTORICAL ASSOCIATION.). [PAHA newsl.]. **Added/Corp** Polish American Historical Association. **VFOAT** P.A.H.A. Newsletter. **VAT** Polish American Historical Association Newsletter. Vol. 33, No. 2 (June 1977)-. Periodical. English. Four times a year. $7.50 Comes with Polish American Historical Association membership. Polish American Historical Association, 1275 Harlem Road, Buffalo NY 14206. **Tel** (716)893-5771. ***Continues** PAHA Bulletin (Polish American Historical Association : 1969).*

CN/0711-4222
PAKIZAH INTIRNASHINAL. **See** Women's Interests.

US
PAMPHLET SERIES - UNIVERSITY OF CALIFORNIA, LOS ANGELES. CHICANO STUDIES CENTER. **Main/Corp** University of California, Los Angeles. Chicano Studies Center. No. 1-. Monographic series. English. Price varies per volume. Chicano Studies Center, UCLA, 405 Hilgard Avenue, Los Angeles CA 90024. **Tel** (310)825-2642. **ED** Oscar Marti. **Bk Rev. Circ:** 15,000.
Desc: Social studies on Chicanos and Mexicans in the United States and Mexico.

●US/1062-8428
PARDIS (WEST ORANGE, N.J.). (PARDIS: AN IRANIAN-AMERICAN PERSPECTIVE.). [Pardis]. Vol. 1, No. 1 (Spring 1992)-. Periodical. English. sa. $65.00 (institution). Pardis, Inc., PO Box 342, West Orange NJ 07052. **DD** 305.

CN/0824-359X
PATRIDES (TORONTO). (PATRIDES.). [Patrides]. **Added/Corp** Helleinic-Canadian Committee for the Truth About Macedonia. (1978)-. Periodical. Greek, Modern (summaries and/or abstracts in English). mo. Patrides, PO Box 266 Station O, Toronto Ontario M4A 2N3 Canada. **Tel** (416)921-4229, (416)921-8869, FAX (416)921-0723. **ED** Thomas Saras. **DD** 949.5/6/005. Index available. cum. index. **Bk Rev. Ad Acc. Circ:** 10,000 (ctrl). available on diskette.
Desc: For the Greek immigrant community in Canada. Included are news articles, government notices, interviews with government officials, editorials and reports on immigration status in Canada.

UK/0031-322X
PATTERNS OF PREJUDICE. [Patterns prejudice]. **Added/Corp** Institute of Jewish Affairs. Vol. 1 (Jan./Feb. 1967)-. Periodical. English. sa. £16.00 UK; $25.00 US. Institute of Jewish Affairs, 79 Wimpole Street, London W1M 7DD England. **Tel** 011 44 71 9358266, FAX 011 44 71 9353252, telex 21633. **ED** Tony Lerman. **LC** DS145; .P34. Index available. **Bk Rev. Circ:** 1,600. available on microfilm and microfiche from University Microfilms International (UMI).
Desc: Study of causes and manifestations of racial, religious and ethnic discrimination and prejudice, with particular reference to antisemitism.
Ind/Abst Am. Hist. Life (1970-); Hum. Rights Intern. Rep.; Index Book Rev. Relig.; Int. Bibliogr. Sociol.; Middle East Abstr. Index; Relig. Index One Period.; Sage Race Relat. Abstr.

US
PCNA MONTHLY / PALESTINE CONGRESS OF NORTH AMERICA. **Added/Corp** Palestine Congress of North America. Vol. 4, No. 4 (Apr. 1984)-. Periodical. English. mo. ***Continues** PCNA Newsletter.*
Ind/Abst Hum. Rights Intern. Rep.

PH/0116-5747
PEACEMAKER. [Peacemaker]. (1979)-. Periodical. English. qt. **DD** 320.9.
Ind/Abst Hum. Rights Intern. Rep.

US/0031-3793
PEDAGOGIC REPORTER, THE. ***Title Change.*** **See** Education.

CN/0715-5328
PEEL MULTICULTURAL SCENE. [Peel multicult. scene]. May 1979-. Periodical. English. bm. Free. Peel Multicultural Council, 1212 Melton Drive, Mississauga Ontario L4Y 4B1 Canada. **DD** 971.3/535. ***Continues** Peel Ethnic Scene, 0715-531X.*

US/8755-8416
PENNSYLVANIA ETHNIC STUDIES NEWSLETTER. **Added/Corp** Pennsylvania Ethnic Heritage Studies Center. Vol. 1, No. 1 (Sept. 1975)-. Newsletter. English. Three times a year (Feb., May, Nov.). $3.00. Pennsylvania Ethnic Heritage Studies, University of Pittsburg, 405 Bellefield Hall, Pittsburgh PA 15260. **Tel** (412)648-7420. **LC** F160.A1; P46. **DD** 974.8/005.
Ind/Abst Am. Bibliogr. Slavic East Europ. Stud.; Anthropol. Index.

FR/0245-9507
PEUPLE BRETON, LE. [Peuple breton]. (1965)-. Periodical. French. mo. 120.00F France; 150.00F other. Le Peuple Breton, BP 301 22304 Lannion Cedex 43, rue de Kerampont 22300, Lannion France. **ED** J. J. Monnier. **UDC** 329.17 (441.1/5). **Bk Rev. Ad Acc. Circ:** 5,000 to 10,000.
Desc: News about Brittany, Celtic countries, situation of minorities, culture, politics, economical development, folklore and ethnic interests.

CN/0822-1723
PEUPLES (MONTREAL). (PEUPLES : BULLETIN DE L'ASSOCIATION DES JOURNALISTES ETHNIQUES DU QUEBEC.). [Peuples]. **VFOAT** Bulletin de l'Association des Journalistes Ethniques du Quebec. Bulletin. French (English). bw. $5.00 members, $10.00 nonmembers. A.J.E.Q., Centre Multi-Ethnique St.Louis, 3553, Rue St.Urbain, Montreal Quebec H2X 2N6. **DD** 070.4/84/09714.

US/0032-0447
PLAINS ANTHROPOLOGIST. [Plains anthropol.]. **Added/Corp** Plains Anthropological Society. Vol. 1, No. 1 (May 1954)-. Periodical. English. qt (4 issues). comes with membership, $35.00 institution, $20.00 individual (membership). Plains Anthropological Society, 410 Wedgewood Drive, Lincoln NE 68510. **Tel** (402)488-3813. **ED** Patricia J O'Brien and Danny Walker. **LC** E78.G73; P52. **NLM** W1 PL101F. **CODEN** PLNAA3. Index available. cum. index. **Bk Rev. Pr Rev. Circ:** 1,200 (ctrl). available on microfilm and microfiche from University Microfilms International (UMI). Documents available from The Genuine Article, BIOSIS Document Express, UMI Article Clearinghouse. ***Supersedes*** *Plains Conference. News Letter.*
Desc: Publishes original papers on the anthropology of plains and adjacent areas of North America.
Ind/Abst Abstr. Anthropol. (19??-); Am. Hist. Life (1963-); Anthropol. Lit. (1963-); Arts Humanit. Citation Index [Select. Cov.]; Biol. Abstr.; Br. Archaeol. Bibliogr.; Curr. Contents Soc. Behav. Sci.; Ethnoarts Index (1963-); Expand. Acad. Index (1992-); Newsp. Period. Abstr. (1992-); Res. Alert [Full Cov.]; Soc. Sci. Cit. Index [Full Cov.].

●US/1057-932X
POBEREZE (PHILADELPHIA, PA.). (POBEREZHE). [Pobereze]. **VFOAT** Coast. (1992)-. Periodical. Russian. an. $15.00. Coast, 9921 Bustleton Avenue, Unit W-10, Philadelphia PA 19115. **DD** 891.

PL/0860-5882
POLISH-ANGLOSAXON STUDIES / UNIWERSYTET IM. ADAMA MICKIEWICZA W POZNANIU. Periodical. English. sa. Z2,500 Poland; $5.00 other. Adam Mickiewicz University Press, Nowowiejskiego 55, 61734 Poznan Poland. **Tel** 011 48 527-380, FAX 011 48 61-526425. **ED** Wojciech Liponski (editor's address: Adam Mickiewicz University Press, Poznan Poland). **Circ:** 1,000.

US
POLISH DIGEST & EASTERN EUROPEAN AFFAIRS. **VFOAT** Polish Digest and Eastern European Affairs; Polish Digest. Vol. 1, No. 1 (Sept. 1991)-. Periodical. English. mo. $20.00 (1 year), $38.00 (2 year). Artex Publishing Incorporated, 1924 North 7th Street, Sheboygan WI 53081. **Tel** (414)458-9987. **ED** L. Zieliuski. **LC** DK4449; .P66. **Ad Acc. Circ:** 5,000.

US
POLITICAL FOCUS / NATIONAL ASSOCIATION OF ARAB AMERICANS. **Added/Corp** National Association of Arab Americans. Vol. 1, No. 1 (Aug. 1978)-. Periodical. English. bw.
Ind/Abst Hum. Rights Intern. Rep.

BL
PORANTIM. **Added/Corp** Catholic Church. Conselho Indigenista Missionario. (19??)-. Periodical. Portuguese. mo. $20.00 (Latin America); $50.00 (other). CIMI - Conselho Indigenista Missionario, Caixa Postal 11 1159, Brasilia DF 70084, Brazil. **Tel** 011 55 61 2259457. **LC** F2519.3.G6; P67.
Ind/Abst Hum. Rights Intern. Rep.

US/8750-2143
PORTUGUESE AMERICAN, THE. **VFOAT** Jornal da Comunidade; Portuguese American Journal. Vol. 8, No. 375 (Mar. 21 1984)-. Newspaper. English (Portuguese). Fifty times a year (Except the first two weeks in July). $22.50 Rhode Island, Massachusetts, & Connecticut; $28.75 others. The Portuguese American, PO Box 3218, Providence RI 02906. **Tel** (401)274-4390. **LC** F89.P99; P86. **DD** 974.5/2004691. ***Continues*** *Portuguese American Journal.*

CN/0700-4249
POVUNGNITUK. **Added/Corp** Federation des Cooperatives du Nouveau-Quebec. Societe Cooperative de Povungnituk. (1963)-. Periodical. English (French; summaries and/or abstracts in Eskimo). ir. Federation des Cooperatives du Nouveau-Quebec, 880 Begin Street, Laurent Quebec H4M 2P6 Canada. **DD** 709.01/1.

US/0738-9183
PRENSA SAN DIEGO, LA. (1977)-. Periodical. English (Spanish). wk. $27.00. La Prensa San Diego, 1950 5th Avenue, San Diego CA 92101. **Tel** (619)231-2874, FAX (619)231-9180. **ED** Daniel Munoz. **Bk Rev**, (Qty: 6). **Ad Acc. Circ:** 25,000 (ctrl).
Desc: Provides general news of San Diego County's Hispanic community.

FR/0032-7638
PRESENCE AFRICAINE (PARIS, FRANCE : 1967). ***Suspended.*** (PRESENCE AFRICAINE.). [Presence afr.]. No. 61 (1st Quarter 1967)-Suspended. Periodical. French (English). qt. 280.00F France; $70.00 US. Revue Presence Africaine, 25 Bis rue des Ecoles, 75005 Paris France. **Tel** 011 33 1 43541374, telex AFRISAC 200891F. **ED** Mame Yande. **LC** DT348; .P75. **DD** 960. cum. index. **Bk Rev. Circ:** 2,000 (ctrl). ***Formed by the union of*** *Presence Africaine* ***and*** *Presence Africaine. English.*
Desc: A bilingual cultural revue containing articles mainly written by Africans on subjects of interest to Africa and the black diaspora.
Ind/Abst Am. Hist. Life (1986-); Bibliogr. Mission.; Hum. Rights Intern. Rep. (?-?); Int. Bibliogr. Sociol.; Int. Dev. Abstr. (?-?); MLA Int. Bibl. Books Artic. Mod. Lang. Lit.

CN/0829-1489
PROJECT NORTH JOURNAL. [Proj. North j.]. **Added/Corp** Project North. (1984)-. Periodical. English. mo. Project North, 80 Sackville Street, Toronto, Ontario, M5A 3E5 Canada. **DD** 323.1/197/071. ***Continues*** *Newsletter (Project North)., 0715-4003.*
Ind/Abst Hum. Rights Intern. Rep.

PL
PRZELAND POLONIJNY. **Added/Corp** Polska Akademia Nauk. Komitet Badania Problemow Polonii. Polska Akademia Nauk. Komitet Badania Polonii Zagranicznej. Polska Akademia Nauk. Komitet Badania Polonii. Vol. 1 (1975)-. Periodical. Polish. Four times a year. $28.00. **(Subscription address:** ARS Polona, PO Box 1001, 00068 Warsaw Poland.**)** **LC** DK4122; .P79. **CODEN** PRZPEI. ***Supersedes*** *Problemy Polonii Zagranicznej.*
Ind/Abst Am. Hist. Life (1987-).

PL/0079-7189
PRZESZOSC DEMOGRAFICZNA POLSKI. [Przesz. demogr. Pol.]. **Added/Corp** Polska Akademia Nauk. Sekcja Demografii Historycznej. (1967)-. Polish (summaries and/or abstracts in English and German). Polska Akademia Nauk, Rynek 9,, 50-106 Wroclaw, Poland. **Tel** 48-71-386-25, FAX 48-71-448-103, telex 0712771. **LC** HB3608.7; .P76.
Ind/Abst Popul. Index.

US/0090-7138
PUBLIC ASSISTANCE FOR MINNESOTA INDIANS. **Main/Corp** Minnesota. Dept. of Public Welfare. English. Department of Public Welfare / Minnesota, Centennial Office Building, St Paul MN 55155. **LC** E78.M7; A3. **DD** 362.9/776.

CN/0229-1916
QUAKER CONCERN. **See** Religion and Theology-Protestantism.

CN/0846-3093
R.E.P.P.: RESERVE EXECUTIVE PRACTICE POINTS / FIRST NATIONS RESOURCE COUNCIL. [R.E.P.P., Reserve exec. pract. points]. **Added/Corp** First Nations Resource Council. **VFOAT** Reserve Executive Practice Points. Vol. # 1, Issue # 1 (June 1991)-. Periodical. English. bm. Limited free distribution. First Nations Research Council, Number 502, 10036 Jasper Avenue, Edmonton Alberta T5J 2W2 Canada. **DD** 352.071/089/971.

UK/0306-3968
RACE & CLASS. [Race cl.]. **Added/Corp** Institute of Race Relations. **VAT** Race and Class. Vol. 16, No. 2 (Oct. 1974)-. Periodical. English. qt (Jan., Apr., July, Oct.). £16.00/£28.00 (individuals), £22.00/£48.00 (institutions) surface mail £26.00/£43.00 (individuals), £32.00/£63.00 (institutions) air mail. Institute of Race Relations, 2-6 Leeke Street, Kings Crossroad, London WC1X 9HS England. **Tel** 11 44 71 837 0041, FAX 071 278-0623. **ED** A Sivanandan and E Ahmad. **LC** HT1501; .R25. **DD** 301.45/1/04205. **NLM** W1 RA123. Index available. **Bk Rev. Ad Acc. Circ:** 5,000. Documents available from The Genuine Article. ***Continues*** *Race.*
Desc: Looks at third world issues; development, black affairs, migrant workers, liberation movements and race relations.
Ind/Abst Altern. Press Index; Am. Hist. Life (1988-); Anthropol. Index; Appl. Soc. Sci. Index Abstr.; Arts Humanit. Citation Index [Select. Cov.]; Br. Humanit. Index; Child. Lit. Abstr. (19??-); Curr. Contents Soc. Behav. Sci.; Geogr. Abstr. Human Geogr. (?-?); Hum. Rights Intern. Rep.; Index Islam. Lit.; Int. Bibliogr. Sociol.; Int. Dev. Abstr.; Int. Labour Doc.; Left Index; Middle East Abstr. Index; Multicult. Educ. Abstr.; Res. Alert [Full Cov.]; Sage Race Relat. Abstr.; Soc. Plann. Policy Dev. Abstr.; Soc. Sci. Cit. Index [Full Cov.]; Sociol. Abstr.

US
RACIAL AND ETHNIC REPORT : PUPIL ENROLLMENT. **See** Education.

US/0090-1059
RACIAL AND ETHNIC SURVEY. **Main/Corp** Oregon. Dept. of Education. English. an. Oregon Department of Education, 700 Pringle Parkway SE, Salem OR 97310. **Tel** (503)378-3573, FAX (503)378-7968. **LC** LC3732.O7; A3. **DD** 371.9/7.

US/0192-9879
RACIAL, ETHNIC, AND SEX ENROLLMENT DATA FROM INSTITUTIONS OF HIGHER EDUCATION. **See** Education-Higher Education.

AG
RAICES : JUDAISMO CONTEMPORANEO. **See** Religion and Theology-Judaism.

SP/0212-6753
RAICES (MADRID, SPAIN). (RAICES.). No. 1 (1986)-. Periodical. Spanish. qt (4 issues). 4800ptas Spain; 7200ptas Europe; 8000ptas The Americas and Israel; 9600ptas other. Sefarad Editores, Apartado de Correos 16110, 28080 Madrid Spain. **Tel** 011 34 1 637 5365, FAX 011 34 1 637 5365. **Bk Rev. Ad Acc. Pr Rev. Circ:** 6000.
Desc: A Jewish cultural magazine that offers the Spanish public, hispanephone or hispanist a platform for Jewish culture open to discussion and debate, a channel for thorough dissemination, yet within the reach of everyone, and an organ providing opinion, analysis, information and intercommunication.

US/0034-0219
RAZA, LA. Vol. 1 (1970)-. Periodical. Spanish. Fifty-two times a year. $19.00. La Raza Newspaper, 3909 North Ashland Avenue, Chicago IL 60613. **Tel** (312)525-9400. **ED** Fabio Marin. **LC** UNC. **Ad Acc. Circ:** 44,000. ***Continues*** *Raza.*
Desc: Covers international politics, local politics and the international economy.

US/8755-8815
RAZA LAW JOURNAL, LA. **See** Law.

HK/0034-0383
READER'S DIGEST BASIA ED. (READERS DIGEST HONG KONG. ENGLISH EDITION.). [Read. Dig.Basia Ed.]. (1963)- Vol.61 (Apr. 1993)- Vol. 4 No. 10. Periodical. English. Six times a year. $62.00. Readers Digest Association Far East, GPO Box 11852, Hong Kong Hong Kong. **Tel** 011 852 5 5681117, FAX 011 852 8853210, telex 74700. **ED** James Couch, 3Ah Kung Njam Village Road, Hong Kong. **UDC** 8-9. **Ad Acc.**

US/1049-1392
RECONSTRUCTION (CAMBRIDGE, MASS.). (RECONSTRUCTION.). [Reconstruction]. Vol. 1, No. 1 (Winter 1990)-. Periodical. English. qt. $40.00 (libraries), $25.00 (individuals). New Departures Inc., 1563 Massachusetts Avenue, Cambridge MA 02138. **Tel** (617)495-0907. **LC** E185.5; .R4. **DD** 973/.0496073/005.
Ind/Abst PAIS Int. Print.

US/1053-427X
RECURSIVE REASONING REPORTS. ***Title Change.*** **Added/Corp** American Association for the Advancement of Central & Eastern European White People. **VFOAT** Recursive Reasoning Mini Reports. Vol 1, No 1 (Jan. 1991)-(1992). Periodical. English. mo. Thomas F Kaus, PO Box 89-1432, Houston TX 77289-1432. **DD** 305. ***Merged with*** *Ap3sCEp2sWP : [Newsletter], 1053-4288* ***to form*** *NAp2sOP : [Newsletter], 1069-5710.*

US/0300-6344
RED CLOUD COUNTRY. **Added/Corp** Red Cloud Indian School. (19??)-. Periodical. English. Four times a year. $20.00. Red Cloud Indian School, Pine Ridge SD 57770. **Tel** (605)867-5491. **Circ:** 135,000 (ctrl).
Desc: News about our school for Sioux Indians.

US/1072-3625
RENAISSANCE (ARDMORE, PA.). (RENAISSANCE : THE NEW SPIRIT OF BLACK PHILADELPHIA.). (1989)-. English. Four times a year. $10.00 (one year), $18.00 (two year). RM Communications Group Inc., PO Box 842, Ardmore PA 19003. **Tel** (215)473-7060, FAX (215)473-7060. **ED** Suzanne Holloman. **Bk Rev**, (Qty: 4-20). **Ad Acc, Adv Mgr:** W. Nasir. **Circ:** 25,000.

Ethnic Interests

Desc: Lifestyle publication highlighting the achievements of African Americans in Pennsylvania, New Jersey, and Delaware.

US/0883-3389
RENATO ROSALDO LECTURE SERIES MONOGRAPH. (RENATO ROSALDO LECTURE SERIES MONOGRAPH.). [Renato Rosaldo lect. ser. monogr.]. **Added/Corp** University of Arizona. Mexican American Studies and Research Center. **VFOAT** Renato Rosaldo. A. Vol. 1 (1985)-. English (Spanish). an. $14.00 institutions, $12.00 individuals. Mexican American Studies & Research Center, The University of Arizona, Room 315, Tucson AZ 85721. **Tel** (602)621-7551. **ED** Thomas Gelsinon. **LC** E184.M5; R39. **DD** 973/.0046872/005. **Circ:** 500.
Desc: A compilation of lectures given each year as part of the Romato Ronaldo Lecture Series. It is an interdisciplinary in nature and its content is meant to stimulate research and writing concerning Mexican Americans.

US
REPORT OF THE MASSACHUSETTS COMMISSION ON INDIAN AFFAIRS. See Public Administration.

US/0548-3441
REPORT OF THE NEVADA INDIAN AFFAIRS COMMISSION. **Main/Corp** Nevada Indian Affairs Commission. (1965/66)-. Periodical. English. Nevada Indian Affairs Commission, 472 Galletti Way, Sparks NV 89431. **LC** E78.N4; N39. **DD** 970.1; 970.5.

US/0540-7109
REPORT - OFFICE OF THE STATE CO-ORDINATOR OF INDIAN AFFAIRS (MONTANA). **Main/Corp** Montana. Office of the State Co-Ordinator of Indian Affairs. English. an. Office of the State, Co-Ordinator of Indian Affairs, State Capital, Helena MT 59601.

UK/0305-6252
REPORTS / MINORITY RIGHTS GROUP. See Political Science-Civil Rights.

US/0195-7449
RESEARCH IN RACE AND ETHNIC RELATIONS. [Res. race ethn. relat.]. Vol. 1 (1979)-. English. ir. $73.25. JAI Press Inc., 55 Old Post Road, Suite 2, PO Box 1678, Greenwich CT 06836-1678. **Tel** (203)661-7602, FAX (203)661-0792. **ED** Rutledge Dennis. **LC** GN495.4; .R47. **DD** 305.8/005. [CCC].
Ind/Abst Psychol. Abstr. (1982-); PsycINFO (?-?); PsycLit; Soc. Plann. Policy Dev. Abstr.; Sociol. Abstr. [Full Cov.].

•US/1055-1158
RESEARCH IN RELIGION AND FAMILY--BLACK PERSPECTIVES. (1993)-. Monographic series. English. Price varies per volume. Peter Lang Publishing, 62 West 45th Street, 4th Floor, New York NY 10036. **Tel** (212)764-1471, (800)770-5264, telex 6973364 PLNY.

US/0749-2472
RESOUND. See Music.

US/1055-3703
RESPONSE (LOS ANGELES, CALIF.). Ceased. (RESPONSE : THE WIESENTHAL CENTER'S WORLD REPORT.). [Response]. **Added/Corp** Simon Wiesenthal Center. Vol. 1, No. 1 (Jan. 1990)-(19??). Periodical. English. **LC** D804.3; .R49. **DD** 909/.04924. **Continues** Response (Los Angeles, Calif.), 1055-3703.

US/1050-0022
RETURN (WASHINGTON, D.C.), THE. Suspended. (THE RETURN.). [Return]. (1988)-(19??). Periodical. English. Twelve times a year. $24.00. Jerusalem Press Service, 865 McArthur Boulevard, Suite 305, Washington DC 20007. **Tel** (202)338-2778. **LC** DS119.7; .R443.
Ind/Abst Hum. Rights Intern. Rep.

US/0034-6446
REVIEW OF BLACK POLITICAL ECONOMY, THE. See Economics.

XV
REVIJA ZA NARODNOSTNA VPRASANJA. **Added/Corp** Institut za Narodnostna Vprasanja. **VFOAT** Journal of Ethic Studies. (19??)-. Slovenian (English). an.
Ind/Abst Am. Hist. Life (1966-).

MX
REVISTA DE LA UNACH / UNIVERSIDAD AUTONOMA DE CHIAPAS. **VAT** Revista de la Universidad Autonoma de Chiapas. Vol. 1 (April 1985)-. Periodical. Spanish. qt. Departamento Editorial de la Unach, 2A sur Oriente 687, Tuxtla Gutierrez Chiapas Mexico. **LC** F1256; .R48. **DD** 972/.75/005. **Continues** Acuarimantima (Tuxtla Gutierrez, Mexico).

CN/0226-7284
REVUE AUTOCHTONE. See Law.

CN/0712-1350
REVUE ET BULLETIN DE L'ASSOCIATION CANADIENNE DES ENSEIGNANTS NOIRS. See Education.

US/0556-8609
RHODE ISLAND JEWISH HISTORICAL NOTES. [R.I. Jew. hist. notes]. **Added/Corp** Rhode Island Jewish Historical Association. (1954)-. English. an. $20.00 US; $22.36 Canada; $25.60 Australia; $24.33 other (postage included). Rhode Island Jewish Historical Association, 130 Sessions Street, Providence RI 02906. **Tel** (401)331-1360. **ED** Judith Weiss Cohen (editor's address: 97 Blaisdell Avenue, Pawtucket, RI 02860; telephone: (401)723-6315). **LC** F90.J5; R5. **DD** 325.2569309745. ctrl circ.
Desc: Historical facts about the Rhode Island Jewish community. Includes biographies on deceased community leaders.
Ind/Abst Am. Hist. Life (1973-); Writ. Am. Hist.

UK
RHODESIANS WORLDWIDE. See General Interest-General Interest-Africa.

CN/0824-5665
RMS NEWS. [RMS news]. **VAT** Regional Multilanguage Services News. Vol. 1, No. 1 (Feb. 1981)-. Periodical. English. mo (bi-monthly July and August). 6.00Can$ US. Languages and Literature Department, Metropolitan Toronto Reference Library, 789 Yonge Street, Toronto Ontario M4W 2G8 Canada. **Tel** (416)393-7007, telex 06-22232. **ED** Jaswinder Gundara and Ted J Uvanowski. **DD** 027.6/3. **Bk Rev. Circ:** 700 (ctrl).
Desc: A calendar of ethnic events in Metropolitan Toronto and news of library services to multicultural/multilanguage communities.

•US
ROBINSONS REDBOOK. A NATIVE AMERICAN GUIDE TO WASHINGTON D.C. See Public Administration.

XV/0557-2282
RODNA GRUDA SLOVENIJA. Periodical. Slovenian (Spanish and English). mo. $15.00 US; 20.00Can$ Canada; 23.00Aus$ Australia. Slovenska Matica, 61000 Ljubljana, Kongresni TRG 8, Slovenia. **Tel** (61)214200. **ED** Joze Preseren, Ivan Cimerman and Nada Sabec. **LC** AP58.S55; R6. **Bk Rev. Ad Acc. Circ:** 10,000 (ctrl). **Continues** Rodna Gruda.
Desc: Magazine for Slovene emigrants all over the world; informs them of developments in their native country.

US/0035-8053
ROMANIAN BULLETIN. V. 1- Jan. 1972-. Bulletin. English. mo. Romanian Library, 200 East 38th Street, New York NY 10016. **Tel** (212)687-0180. available on microfilm and microfiche from University Microfilms International (UMI). **Continues** Romanian Bulletin, 0035-8053.

US/0093-9951
ROSTER OF BLACK ELECTED OFFICIALS IN THE SOUTH. See Public Administration.

US/0036-0406
RUSSKII GOLOS (NEW YORK, N.Y.). (RUSSKII GOLOS / RUSSIAN VOICE / RUSSKY GOLOS.). **VFOAT** Russian Voice; Russky Golos. Vol. 1, No. 1 (Feb. 1, 1917)-. Newspaper. Russian (English). wk. $30.00. Russky Golos Publishing Corporation, 130 East 16th Street, New York NY 10003. **Tel** (212)475-7595. **ED** Pavel Vetrov. **Bk Rev. Ad Acc. Circ:** 3,000. available on microfilm from The Library of Congress Photoduplication Service. **Absorbed in part by** Novyi Mir.

US/0739-9103
S.E.M. NEWSLETTER (1981). See Music.

US/1056-2591
SAGARIN REVIEW, THE. See Literature.

US/0741-8639
SAGE (ATLANTA, GA.). Ceased. See Women's Interests.

US/0036-3847
SAMOSTIINA UKRAINA. **Added/Corp** Orhanizatsiia Derzhavnoho Vidrodzhennia Ukrainy. **VFOAT** Independent Ukraine. Vol. 1, No. 1 (1948)-. Periodical. Ukrainian. qt. $12.00. Organization Rebirth Ukraine, 2315 West Chicago Avenue, Chicago IL 60622. **Tel** (312)276-0066.
Ind/Abst MLA Int. Bibl. Books Artic. Mod. Lang. Lit.

CN/0380-2949
SANDESH (WINNIPEG). (SANDESH.). Began publication in Jan. 1976?. Monographic series. English (Lahnda). bw. Price varies per volume. Sandesh, 714 Campbell Street, Winnipeg Manitoba R3N 1C3 Canada. **DD** 071/.127/4.

CN/0714-9050
SASKATCHEWAN MULTICULTURAL MAGAZINE. [Sask. multicult. mag.]. **Added/Corp** Multicultural Council of Saskatchewan. Vol. 1, No. 1 (Spring/Summer 1981)-. Periodical. English. qt. 10.00Can$. Saskatchewan Multicultural Magazine, 369 Park Street, Regina Saskatchewan S4N 5B2 Canada. **Tel** (306)721-2767, FAX (306)721-3342. **ED** Maureen Murray. **DD** 305.8/0097124. **Ad Acc, Adv Mgr:** Elaine Lee. **Circ:** 3,000 (ctrl). **Absorbed** Bulletin (Multicultural Council of Saskatchewan), 0714-9034.
Desc: Multicultural issues.

US/1046-5790
SAZZ (NEW YORK, N.Y.). See Women's Interests.

CN/0836-2149
SCANDINAVIAN FORUM. [Scand. forum]. **Added/Corp** Scandinavian Canadian Business Association. Vol. 1, No. 1 (Winter 1985)-. Periodical. English. qt. $34.00 (institutions), $23.00 (individuals) Canada; $38.00 (institutions), $28.00 (individuals) other. E Terp Enterprises, 54 Lesgay Cresent, Willowdale Ontario M2J 2J1 Canada. **Tel** (416)495-8591. **DD** 971/.004395/05.

US/0098-857X
SCANDINAVIAN REVIEW. [Scand. rev.]. **Added/Corp** American-Scandinavian Foundation. Vol. 63, (Mar. 1975)-. Periodical. English. Three times a year. $15.00 US; $30.00 other. American Scandinavian Foundation, 725 Park Avenue, New York NY 10021. **Tel** (212)879-9779, FAX (212)249-3444, telex 661553. **LC** AP2; .A457. **DD** 051. available on microfilm and microfiche from University Microfilms International (UMI). Documents available from UMI Article Clearinghouse. **Continues** American-Scandinavian Review, 0003-0910.
Ind/Abst Acad. Abstr. Full Text Elite (July 1990-); Acad. Abstr. (July 1990-); Acad. Search (July 1990-); Am. Hist. Life (1975-1979); Annu. Bibliogr. Engl. Lang. Lit.; Humanit. Source (July 1990-); INFO-SOUTH Abstr.; Mag. Search; MLA Int. Bibl. Books Artic. Mod. Lang. Lit.; Newsp. Period. Abstr. (1988-); Soc. Sci. Source (July 1990-); Soc. Sci. Index.

US
SCANDINAVIAN REVIEW [MICROFORM]. **Added/Corp** American-Scandinavian Foundation. Vol. 63 (Mar. 1975)-. Periodical. English. qt. $15.00 US; $20.00 other. American Scandinavian Foundation, 725 Park Avenue, New York NY 10021. **Tel** (212)879-9779, FAX (212)249-3444, telex 661553. **ED** Patricia McFate and Adrienne Gyongy. Index available. **Bk Rev. Ad Acc. Circ:** 5,000. **Continues** American-Scandinavian Review, 0003-0910.
Desc: About politics, business and culture of contemporary Scandinavia.
Ind/Abst Soc. Sci. Index.

US/0883-3400
SCHOMBURG CENTER JOURNAL, THE. [Schomburg Cent. j.]. **Added/Corp** Schomburg Center for Research in Black Culture. Vol. 2, No. 1 (Winter 1983)-. Periodical. English. qt. Free to libraries and academic institutions, $35.00 other. Schomburg Center for Research in Black Culture, 515 Malcolm X Boulevard, New York NY 10037. **Tel** (212)491-2200. **ED** Glenderlyn Johnson. **DD** 973. **Bk Rev. Circ:** 5,000. **Continues** Journal -Schomburg Center for Research in Black Culture.
Desc: Information on the history and culture of blacks throughout the world.
Ind/Abst Index Free Period.

US/0145-8353
SCHOOL RACIAL-ETHNIC CENSUS. See Education.

GW
SCHRIFTENREIHE DER LANDSMANNSCHAFT DER BANATER SCHWABEN. **Added/Corp** Landsmannschaft der Banater Schwaben aus Rumanien in Deutschland. (1990)-. Periodical. German. **Continues** Veroffentlichung der Landsmannschaft der Banater Schwaben aus Rumanien in Deutschland e.V.

GW
SCHRIFTENREIHE DES KULTURINSTITUTS DER DONAUSCHWABEN IN WIEN. **Added/Corp** Kulturinstitut der Donauschwaben in Wien. 1981-. Monographic series. German. Price varies per volume. Wilhelm Braumueller, Servitengasse 5, A 1092 Vienna, Austria. **Tel** 011 43 1 3191482, 3191159.

CN/0707-073X
SCOTTISH BANNER, THE. [Scott. banner]. Vol.1 (July 1978). Periodical. English. mo $16.00 (one year), $28.00 (two year) Canada; $15.00 (one year), $26.00 (two year) US $30.00 other (one year) other. Scottish Banner, Box 34, Lewiston NY 14092. **Tel**

Ethnic Interests

800-729-8951, FAX 716 754-9020. **ED** Val Cairney. **DD** 971.3/004/9163. **Ad Acc. Circ:** 19,000 (ctrl). available on microfilm.
Desc: All matters related to Scots in Scotland and North America.

●US/1060-5606
SCRIBE (WASHINGTON, D.C.), THE. (THE SCRIBE: AN AFRICAN CENTERED MAGAZINE.). [Scribe]. Vol. 1, No. 1 (Dec.-Jan. 1992)-. Periodical. English. bm. $7.00. The Black Memorabilia Revue, PO Box 1586, Washington DC 20013. **DD** 305.

US/1047-4609
SEASONS (OAKLAND, CALIF.). See Public Health and Safety.

US/0363-5074
SEEDBED. See Religion and Theology.

US/0361-6622
SELECTED REPORTS IN ETHNOMUSICOLOGY. See Music.

US
SEPHARDI WORLD (JERUSALEM). (SEPHARDI WORLD : SW / WORLD SEPHARDI FEDERATION.). **VFOAT** S.W.; SW. June 1980-. Periodical. English. bm. World Zionist Organization, PO Box 92, Department of Education and Culture, Jerusalem Israel. **Tel** 011 972 2 513297. **LC** DS101; .S427. **DD** 305.8/0095694.

CN/0712-5704
SHAMA (TORONTO). (SHAMA.). [Shama]. **VFOAT** Monthly Shama Toronto. Vol. 1, No. 1 (April 1980)-. Periodical. Urdu (Hindi). Twelve times a year. 50.00Can$. Urdu Promotion Board, PO Box 1061 Station B, Mississauga Ontario L4Y 2E0 Canada. **Tel** (416)858-7525, FAX (416)858-7951. **ED** Alia Sultana. **DD** 971.3/54100491412.

US
SHOPTALK. See Beauty and Cosmetics.

IS
SHORASHIM. Added/Corp Mekhon Tabenkin le-Heker ve-Limud ha-Kibuts. **VFOAT** Roots. (1979)-. Periodical. Hebrew. Four times a year. $15.00 membership. Jewish Genealogical Society, 2370 1D Via Mariposa West, Laguna Hills CA 92653. **Tel** (714)855-4692. **LC** HX742.2.A3; S56.

US
SHUFAR : NASHRIYAH-I FIDIRASYUN-I YAHUDIYAN-I IRANI. VFOAT Shofar; Nashriyah-I Shufar. Periodical. Persian. Iranian Jewish Federation, 6505 Wilshire Boulevard/Suite 1101, Los Angeles CA 90048. **LC** E184.J5; S487.

PE/0254-2021
SHUPIHUI. Added/Corp Coordinacion Pastoral de la Selva (Peru) Centro Amazonico de Antropologia y Aplicacion Practica. Centro de Estudios Teologicos de la Amazonia (Iquitos, Peru). (19??)-. Periodical. Spanish. qt. S/20.00. Centro de Estudios Teologicos, de la Amazonia (CETA), Putumayo 355, Iquioos Peru. **Tel** 23.35.52. **LC** F3429; .S54. **DD** 985/.004/98005. Index available. cum. index. **Bk Rev. Ad Acc. Circ:** 700 (ctrl).
Desc: Anthropology, conservation and natural resources, general education and special aspects of education, ethnic issues, family, marriage, etc., linguistics, medicine, meetings and congresses, civil rights, international relations, and the Roman Catholic Church.
Ind/Abst Bibliogr. Mission.

US/1070-7786
SICANGU SUN TIMES. (SICANGU SUN TIMES / ROSEBUD RESERVATION, SICANGU LAKOTA NATION.). [Sicangu sun times]. **Added/Corp** Sicangu Lakota Nation. (199?)-. Periodical. English. wk. $25.00 Todd-Melette Co., South Dakota; $30.00 other US; $40.00 other the. Sicangu Sun Times, PO Box 750, Rosebud SD 57570. **Tel** (605)747-2058. **ED** P.R. Gregg. **DD** 970. cum. index. **Bk Rev. Ad Acc. Circ:** 2,000.

US/8755-6987
SICILIA PARRA. (SICILIA PARRA : NEWSLETTER OF ARBA SICULA, THE INTERNATIONAL SICILIAN ETHNIC AND CULTURAL ASSOCIATION.). [Sicil. parra]. Began in 1983?. Newsletter. English (Sicilian). Twice a year. $15.00. Arba Sicula Inc, PO Box 040328, Brooklyn NY 11204-0328. **Tel** (718)990-5114. **ED** Gaetano Cipolla. **DD** 305. cum. index. **Bk Rev. Ad Acc. Circ:** 1,500 (ctrl).
Desc: All aspects of ethnic Sicilian interests worldwide to the seventh generation. Contemporary articles on economics, linguistics, culture, history, etc.

PL/0080-9993
SLAVIA ANTIQUA. See Archaeology.

IT
SLOVENI IN ITALIA. Periodical. Italian. sm. Free. Via dei Montecchi 6, Trieste 34137 Italy. **ED** (040)7796600, FAX (040)772418, telex 460894 PD I. **ED** Vojmir Tavcar. **LC** DG457.S5; B64. **UDC** 945(=863). **Circ:** 3,000. Continues Bollettino d'Informazione Degli Sloveni in Italia.

XV
SLOVENIJA (SLOVENSKA IZSELJENSKA MATICA). (SLOVENIJA.). **Added/Corp** Slovenska Izseljenska Matica. (1987)-. Periodical. English. qt. $8.00 Slovenia; $15.00 other. Slovenska Matica, 61000 Ljubljana, Kongresni TRG 8, Slovenia. **Tel** (61)214200. **ED** Joze Preseren. **Bk Rev Ad Acc. Circ:** 8,000.
Desc: Serves as a means of communication for the Slovenian ethnic groups in the US, Canada, Australia, and the English-speaking European countries. Articles cover current social, political, and economic issues in Slovenia; the arts; Slovenian and Yugoslav history; literature; religion; and the situation of Slovenians and Yugoslav history; literature; and the situation of Slovenians living abroad.

US
SMITHSONIAN RUNNER. (19??)-. Newsletter. English. Six times a year. Comes with National Museum of the American Indian Charter membership. Smithsonian Institution / National Museum of the American Indian, PO Box 65303, Washington DC 20035. **Tel** (202)357-3164. **ED** Dan Agent.
Desc: Newsletter for Native Americans.

US/0741-5753
SOCIETY FOR GERMAN-AMERICAN STUDIES NEWSLETTER. [Soc. Ger.-Am. Stud. newsl.]. **Added/Corp** Society for German-American Studies (U.S.). **VFOAT** Society for German American Studies Newsletter; S.G.A.S. Newsletter; SGAS Newsletter. Vol. 4, No. 3 (1983)-. Newsletter. English. qt. comes with membership. Society for German-American Studies, 500 Belmont Road, Bettendorf IA 52722. **Tel** (319)359-7531. **ED** LaVern J. Rippley. **LC** E184.G3; N45. **DD** 973/.0431. **Bk Rev. Ad Acc. Circ:** 500. Continues Newsletter of the Society for German American Studies.
Desc: Reports on current activities of German ethnic groups. Book reviews of important publications, and reports on current SGAS activities.

US/1062-1462
SONS OF NORWAY VIKING, THE. Added/Corp Sons of Norway (U.S.). **VFOAT** Viking. Vol. 61, No. 8 (Aug. 1964)-. Periodical. English. Twelve times a year. $20.00. Viking Magazine, 1455 West Lake Street, Minneapolis MN 55408. **Tel** (612)827-3611, FAX (612)827-0658. **ED** Gaelyn Beal. **LC** HS1923.S6; A17. **DD** 369/.2481/097305. **Bk Rev. Ad Acc. Circ:** 65,000 (ctrl). Continues Viking (Minneapolis, Minn.).
Desc: Membership magazine for sons of Norway. Articles on Scandinavian travel, folklore, history, modern society, Norwegian-American culture.

NE
SOUTH ASIA NEWSLETTER. Newsletter. sa. Free. Documentatie Centrum Zuid Azie, Witte Singel 25, 2311 NL Leiden Netherlands. **Tel** 011 31 071 272498.

US/0094-372X
SOUTH DAKOTA INDIAN RECIPIENTS OF SOCIAL WELFARE. See Sociology-Social Services and Welfare.

US/0085-6525
SOUTHERN INDIAN STUDIES. See History(General)-History of North, South, and Central America.

US
SOUTHERN MEDIATOR. Southern Mediator Journal, PO Box 1257, Little Rock AR 72203. **Tel** (501)376-3000.

US/0587-0674
SOUTHERN UTE DRUM, THE. Added/Corp Southern Ute Tribe. Vol. 1, No. 1 (Aug. 23, 1969)-. Newspaper. English. bw (26 issues). $12.00. Southern Ute Drum, Tribal Affairs Building, PO Box 737, Ignacio CO 81137. **Tel** (303)563-4525. Index available. **Ad Acc.** ctrl circ.

US
SOUTHWESTERN SUN WAVE. See Newspapers.

US
SPEAKIN' OUT NEWS. (198?)-. Newspaper. English. wk (Published on Wednesdays). $20.00. Educator Information Services, 61 Livingston Avenue, North Brunswick NJ 08901. **Tel** (908)246-7046. **ED** William Smothers. **Bk Rev. Ad Acc, Adv Mgr Tel** (205)852-9449. **Circ:** 16,500. Continues Speakin' Out Weekly News.

CN/0315-0208
SPEAR (TORONTO). (SPEAR.). [Spear]. (Aug. 1971)-. English. Twelve times a year. Spear, PO Box 3243 Station D, Willowdale Ontario M2R 3G6 Canada. **Tel** (416)535-9727. **ED** Stanley Ansong. **Bk Rev. Ad Acc.**

US/0270-1766
SPECIAL SERIES / SOCIETY FOR ETHNOMUSICOLOGY. See Music.

US
SPICE. See Children and Youth Interests.

SA
SPOTLIGHT / SOUTH AFRICAN INSTITUTE OF RACE RELATIONS. See Sociology.

US/0279-1293
SRPSKA BORBA. (SRPSKA BORBA = SERBIAN STRUGGLE.). [Srp. borba]. **Added/Corp** Izdavac Srpsko Literarno Udruzelje (U.S.). **VFOAT** Serbian Struggle. (1946)-. Periodical. Serbian (English). mo (11 issues per year). $30.00. Serbian Literary Association Inc, PO Box 14 Little Neck Station, Flushing NY 11363. **Tel** (718)229-8973. **ED** Budimir Sreckovich. **Bk Rev. Ad Acc. Circ:** 2,500 (ctrl).
Desc: News, comments and opinions on political and economic events in Yugoslavia and Serbia in particular. News and events relative to ethnic Serbians and others originally from Yugoslavia.

US/0745-8509
STAR (NEW YORK, N.Y.), THE. (THE STAR / DISTRICT NO. ONE, B'NAI B'RITH.). Periodical. English. mo. District 1-B'Nai B'Rith, 823 United Nations Plaza, New York NY 10017. Continues Metropolitan Star, 0026-1580.

US/0148-6985
STATE OF BLACK AMERICA, THE. Main/Corp National Urban League. (1976)-. English. an (Jan.). $27.95. A G Publishing, 75 Varick Street, 6th Floor, New York NY 10013. **Tel** (212)274-9600. **ED** Janet Dewart. **LC** E185.5; .N317. **DD** 973/.04/96073.
Desc: A detailed record of significant trends and events in black America. Educators, public officials, and community leaders analyze recent developments in economics, education, housing, legislation, politics, and race relations as they affect and are affected by blacks.
Ind/Abst Am. Hist. Life (1987-); Stat. Ref. Index.

SA/1012-2338
STUDI D'ITALIANISTICA NELL'AFRICA AUSTRALE. Added/Corp Association of Professional Italianists. **VFOAT** Italian Studies in Southern Africa. No. 1 (1988)-. Italian (English).
Ind/Abst MLA Int. Bibl. Books Artic. Mod. Lang. Lit.

NE/0039-3347
STUDIA ROSENTHALIANA. [Stud. Rosenthaliana]. **Added/Corp** Bibliotheca Rosenthaliana. Vol. 1 (Jan. 1967)-. Periodical. Dutch (English, French and German; summaries and/or abstracts in French, German and English). sa. Fl90.00 Netherlands; Fl110.00 other. Van Gorcum & Company BV, PO Box 43, NL 9400 AA Assen Netherlands. **Tel** 011 31 5920 46846, FAX 011 31 5920 72064. **ED** A K Offenberg. **LC** DS135.N4; S8. **DD** 914.92. **Bk Rev. Ad Acc. Circ:** 400 (ctrl). Documents available from The Genuine Article.
Desc: The periodical is devoted to Jewish literature and history and aims to stimulate studies in this field.
Ind/Abst Am. Hist. Life (1973-); Arts Humanit. Citation Index (19??-19??) [Full Cov.]; BHA : Biblio. Hist. Art; Curr. Contents Arts Humanit.; Res. Alert [Full Cov.].

GW
STUDIEN ZUR KULTURKUNDE. Vol. 1 (1933)-. Monographic series. German. ir. Price varies per volume. Franz Steiner Verlag GmbH, Postfach 101061, D 70009 Stuttgart Germany. **Tel** 011 49 0711 2582372, FAX 011 49 0711 2582290, telex 723636 daz d. **ED** E. Haberland.
Desc: Ethnologic monographs, mostly dealing with Africa.

US/0740-8625
STUDIES IN CONTEMPORARY JEWRY. See Religion and Theology-Judaism.

●US/1058-5621
STUDIES IN SOUTHERN ITALIAN AND ITALIAN AMERICAN CULTURE. [Stud. South. Ital. Ital. Am. cult.]. **VFOAT** Studi Sulla Cultura dell'Italia Meridionale e Italo-Americana. Vol. 1 (1992)-. Monographic series. English (Italian). Price varies per volume. Peter Lang Publishing, 62 West 45th Street, 4th Floor, New York NY 10036. **Tel** (212)764-1471, (800)770-5264, telex 6973364 PLNY. **DD** 305.

US
SUCCESS GUIDE : THE GUIDE TO BLACK RESOURCES : CINCINNATI/DAYTON. (1991)-. English. Successource Inc, 1949 East 10th St. 100, Cleveland OH 44106. **Tel** (216)791-9330.

GW/0562-5297
SUDOSTDEUTSCHE VIERTELJAHRESBLATTER. Added/Corp Sudostdeutsches Kulturwerk, Munich. (1952)-. Periodical. German. qt (Jan., Apr., July, Oct.). DM44.00. Verlag Sudostdeutschen Kultur, Semmelweisstr 8, W 8033 Planegg Germany. **Tel** 011 49 89 85709397.

US/8750-6599
SURAJ (1984). (SURAJ.). [Suraj]. **VFOAT** The Rising Sun; Rising Sun. Began in 1984. Periodical. Panjabi (English). wk. $20.00 US; $26.00 other. Suraj, PO Box 855, El Sobrante CA 94803. **DD** 973. ***Continues in part*** *Sikh Times (El Sobrante, Calif.).*

US/0741-6571
SURVEY OF JEWISH AFFAIRS. ***Ceased.*** [Surv. Jew.]. (1982)-Ceased Dec. (1990). Academic Scholarly Publication. English. ir. Basil Blackwell Publishers Ltd, 108 Cowley Road, Oxford 0X4 1JF England. **Tel** 011 44 865 791100, FAX 011 44 865 791347, telex 837022 OXBOOK G. **(Subscription address:** Marston Book Services, Journal Subscription Department, PO Box 87, Oxford OX2 0DT England**) ED** William Frankel. **LC** DS101; .S86. **DD** 909/.04924.
Ind/Abst Int. Bibliogr. Sociol.

US/0892-6417
SWAIA UPDATE. [SWAIA update]. **VFOAT** S.W.A.I.A. Update; Newsletter of the Southwestern Association on Indian Affairs. **VAT** Southwestern Association on Indian Affairs Update. Vol. 1, No. 1 (April 1983)-. Periodical. English. qt (three to four no. a year). PO Box 1964, Santa Fe NM 87504. **DD** 708. ***Continues*** *Quarterly of the Southwestern Association on Indian Affairs, Inc.*

●US/1064-5977
SWEET B'S PAD. **See** Children and Youth Interests.

CN/0825-1886
SWEETGRASS. (May/June 1984)-. Periodical. English. bm. Sweetgrass Arts Publishing Inc, Toronto Ontario M5A IS5 Canada. ***Continues*** *Ontario Indian, 0707-3143.*

PL/0867-2814
SYBIRACY WARSZAWA. (SYBIRACY.). (1990)-. Periodical. Polish. wk. Price on Request. **(Subscription address:** ARS Polona, PO Box 1001, 00068 Warsaw Poland.**) UDC** 947.

US
SYMPHONY OF VOICES : AN ASIAN AMERICAN WOMEN'S JOURNAL, A. ***Title Change.*** **See** Women's Interests.

CN/0383-9192
TALKING DRUMS. (Dec. 17, 1975)-. Periodical. English. Talking Drums Magazine, Suite 301/Triller Avenue, Toronto Ontario M6K 3B7 Canada. **DD** 301.45/1/960713541.

US/0300-6247
TALKING LEAF (LOS ANGELES, CALIF. : 1972). (TALKING LEAF.). **Added/Corp** Los Angeles Indian Center. Vol. 1, No. 1 (Jan./Feb. 1972)-. Newspaper. English. Six times a year. $12.00, $20.00 (two years). Talking Leaf Newspaper, 1125 West 6th Street Suite 101, Los Angeles CA 90017. **ED** Mike Burgess. **Bk Rev. Ad Acc. Circ:** 7,000. ***Continues*** *Talking Leaf (Los Angeles, Calif. : 1935).*
Desc: A newspaper by, for, and about American Indians.

II
TAMIL INFORMATION. **Added/Corp** Tamil Information Centre. (198?)-. English. Tamil Information, E-114 16th Cross Street, Besant Nagar, Madras 600 090. **LC** DS489.25.T3; T36. **DD** 954.9/3/005. ***Continues*** *Tamil International.*

US
TECHQUA IKACHI. No. 1- Aug. 1975-. Periodical. English. Three times a year.

BL
TERRA INDIGENA : BOLETIM MENSAL DO G.E.I. KURUMIM. **Added/Corp** G.E.I. Kurumim (Araraquara, Brazil). (19??)-. Bulletin. Portuguese. mo. **LC** F2520; .T47.
Ind/Abst Hum. Rights Intern. Rep.

US/0040-4071
TEVYNE. [Tevyne]. Began in 1889?. Periodical. Lithuanian. mo. $4.00. Lithuanian Alliance of America, 307 West 30th Street, Ms Meilinunas, New York NY 10001. **Tel** (212)563-2210. **ED** Genevieve Meiliunas. **Circ:** 5,000.

US/0887-9982
TIKKUN. [Tikkun]. **Added/Corp** Institute for Labor and Mental Health (Oakland, Calif.). Vol. 1, No. 1 (1986)-. Periodical. English (English). bm (6 issues). $50.00 (institutions), $31.00 (individuals) US; $63.00 (institutions), $44.00 (individuals) Canada & Mexico; $66.00 (institutions), $47.00 (individuals) other. Tikkun Magazine, 5100 Leona Street, Oakland CA 94619. **Tel** (212)864-4110. **(Subscription address:** Tikkun Magazine, 508 West Mission, Suite 200, Escondido CA 92025.**) LC** DS101; .T54. **DD** 909/.04924. available on microfilm and microfiche from University Microfilms International (UMI). Documents available from UMI Article Clearinghouse.
Ind/Abst Acad. Abstr. Full Text Elite (Nov. 1990-); Acad. Abstr. (Nov. 1990-); Acad. Ind. [Computer File] (1989-); Acad. Search (Dec. 1990-); Altern. Press Index (199?-); Am. Bibliogr. Slavic East Europ. Stud.; Am. Humanit. Index; Book Rev. Index; Expand. Acad. Index (1989-); Gen. Period. Index (1989-); Index Book Rev. Relig.; Index Jew. Period. (199?-); INFO-SOUTH Abstr.; Mag. Index Plus (1989-); Mag. Search; Newsp. Period. Abstr. (1989-); Relig. Index One Period.; Mag. Index (1989-).

US/1045-8875
TQS NEWS. (TQS NEWS : A CONTEMPORARY NEWSLETTER OF ECLECTIC CHICANO THOUGHT.). [TQS news]. **VFOAT** T.Q.S. News. **VAT** Tonatiuh-Quinto Sol News. Vol. 6, No. 1 (Spring 1989)-. Newsletter. English (Spanish). qt. $14.00 (one year), $25.00 (two year), $36.00 (three year) US, Canada, and Mexico; $15.00 (one year), $27.00 (two year), $39.00 (three year) other. TQS Publications, PO Box 9275, Berkeley CA 94709. **Tel** (510)655-8036. **ED** Octavio I. Romano. **LC** E184.M5; G77. **DD** 306/.0896872073. ***Continues*** *Grito Del Sol Collection, 0742-1877.*
Desc: Newsletter of eclectic Chicano thought.

US/1047-7977
TRANSPACIFIC (VENICE, CALIF.). (TRANSPACIFIC.). Vol. 4, No. 5 (Sept./Oct. 1989)- Vol. 8 (July-Aug. 1993)-. Periodical. English. Ten times a year (Except August and December). $38.00 one year; $72.00 two year. Transpacific Media Incorporated, 23715 West Malibu Road, Suite 390, Malibu CA 90265. **Tel** (310)456-0790 x 112 Kagy, FAX (310)456-3724. **LC** E184.O6; A8. **DD** 973/.0495/005. **Bk Rev. Ad Acc. Circ:** 50,000. ***Continues*** *Asim, 0892-5747.*

US/0198-8891
TRIBAL AND BUREAU LAW ENFORCEMENT SERVICES AUTOMATED DATA REPORT: NAVAJO AREA. **See** Law-Law Enforcement and Criminology.

US/0198-8905
TRIBAL AND BUREAU LAW ENFORCEMENT SERVICES AUTOMATED DATA REPORT: TOTAL ALL AREAS. **See** Law-Law Enforcement and Criminology.

US
TRIBAL DIRECTORY. **Added/Corp** Arizona Commission of Indian Affairs. (1963)-. Directory. English. an. Arizona Commission of Indian Affairs, 1645 West Jefferson, Phoenix AZ 85007. **Tel** (602)255-3123. **LC** E78.A7; A33.

US/0041-3690
TRUTH (PHILADELPHIA), THE. (THE TRUTH.). **Added/Corp** Russian Brotherhood Organization of the U.S. (1902)-. Periodical. English. bm (6 issues). $5.00. Russian Brotherhood Organization USA, 1733 Spring Garden Street, Philadelphia PA 19130. **Tel** (215)563-2537. **ED** Stephen P. Kopestonsky. **Bk Rev. Circ:** 4,000.
Desc: A family-oriented fraternal paper.

US/0191-6106
TRY US. [Try us]. **VFOAT** National Minority Business Directory. (1972)-. English. an (Jan.). $45.00. Try Us Resources, Inc., 2105 Central Avenue Northeast, Minneapolis MN 55418. **Tel** (612)781-6819. **LC** HD2346.U5; N34. **DD** 338/.0025/73. **Ad Acc. Circ:** 8,000. ***Continues*** *National Black Business Directory.*
Desc: National directory of minority businesses, approximately 5,000 firms organized under 83 product/service categories.

US
TSA' ASZI'. ***Ceased.*** **VFOAT** Yucca. Vol. 1, No. 1 (1973)-(19??). Periodical. English (English). qt. Tsa Azsi Graphics Center, CPO Box 12, Pine Hill NM 87321. **Tel** (505)775-3242. **LC** E99.N3; T78. **DD** 970.004/97.

US/0896-2022
TURTLE QUARTERLY. [Turt. q.]. **Added/Corp** Native American Center for the Living Arts (Niagara Falls, N.Y.). Vol. 1, No. 1 (198?)-. Periodical. English. qt (Jan., Apr., July, Oct.). $15.00 US; $21.00 Canada; $50.00 other. Native American Center for the Living Arts, 25 Rainbow Blvd, Niagara Falls NY 14303. **Tel** (716)284-2427. **ED** Millicent Knapp. **LC** WMLC 93/1299. **DD** 974. **Bk Rev**, (Qty: 32). **Ad Acc. Circ:** 3,000.
Desc: The only educational publication suited for general readership about Native American life, history, art, dance, health, athletics, culture, conservation, cosmology and contemporary philosophy in North America.
Ind/Abst Ethnoarts Index.

US
TZU YU JEN. **VFOAT** Free Men. Began with Oct. 1971 issue. Periodical. Chinese. mo. $12.00. Free Men Magazine Inc, 39 Bowery, Box 747 Chinatown Mail Service, New York NY 10002. **LC** E184.C5; T96. **DD** 951.05/05.

US/0273-9348
UKRAINIAN WEEKLY, THE. **Added/Corp** Ukrainian National Association. Vol. 87, No. 1 (June 1, 1980)-. Newspaper. English. wk. $30.00. Ukrainian National Association Inc, 30 Montgomery Street, PO Box 76, Jersey City NJ 07303. **Tel** (201)451-2200. **ED** Roma Hadzewycz. **Bk Rev. Photos. Ad Acc, Adv Mgr:** Maria Szeparowycz, **Tel** (201)434-0237. Full Page (B&W) $600.00. Half Page (B&W) $310.00. **Pub. Size:** Tabloid. **Circ:** 10,500. available on microfilm. ***Separated from*** *Svoboda (Jersey City, N.J.).*
Desc: News and features about Ukrainian community worldwide and news about issues of concern to that community. Primarily focused on US and Canada.
Ind/Abst Hum. Rights Intern. Rep.

●US
UNBINDING THE FOOT : THE ASIAN/PACIFIC AMERICAN WOMEN'S JOURNAL. **VFOAT** Asian/Pacific American Women's Journal; APAWJ. Vol. 3 (Fall 1993)-. English. University of Michigan Press, PO Box 1104, Ann Arbor MI 48106. **Tel** (313)764-4392. ***Continues*** *Symphony of Voices.*

CN/0382-0610
UNDZER VEG (TORONTO). ***Ceased.*** (UNDZER VEG.). **VFOAT** View. Vol. 1 (196 -)-?. Periodical. English (Yiddish). Three times a year. Undzer Veg Toronto, 272 Codsell Avenue, Downsview Ontario M3H 3X2 Canada. **ED** J Kligman. **LC** DS150.L3; U5. **Bk Rev. Ad Acc. Circ:** 4,000. ***Supersedes*** *View: Undzer Veg, 0382-0165.*

CN/0829-4216
UNITY / ASSOCIATION OF IROQUOIS AND ALLIED INDIANS. [Unity - Assoc. Iroq. Allied Indians.]. **Added/Corp** Association of Iroquois and Allied Indians. Vol. 1, No. 1 (Feb. 1985)-. Periodical. English. qt. Association of Iroquois and Allied Indians, 920 Commissioners Road East, London Ontario N5Z 3J1 Canada. **DD** 971.3/00497. ***Continues*** *Strength in Unity., 0827-3685.*

US/1047-2592
UPSCALE (ATLANTA, GA.). (UPSCALE : THE SUCCESSFUL BLACK MAGAZINE.). [Upscale]. (198?)-. Periodical. English. bm. $12.95. Upscale Communications, PO Box 7477, Atlanta GA 30357. **Tel** (404)758-7467, 800-877-2253. **DD** 051.

US/0147-1740
URBAN LEAGUE REVIEW, THE. ***Ceased.*** [Urban Leag. rev.]. **Main/Corp** National Urban League. Research Dept. Vol. 1 (Spring 1975)-Vol. 16, No. 2 (Winter 1993). Periodical. English. sa. Transaction Publishers / Rutgers State University, New Brunswick NJ 08903. **Tel** (908)932-2280 Ext. 105, FAX (908)932-3138. **ED** Dionne J. Jones. **LC** E185.86; .N37A. **DD** 305.8/96073/05. **[CCC]. Bk Rev. Ad Acc. Pr Rev. Circ:** 500. available on labels; available on microfilm and microfiche from University Microfilms International (UMI). Documents available from The Genuine Article, UMI Article Clearinghouse.
Desc: Examines the social and economic conditions of blacks and other minorities in the United States. A central source of data and analysis of blacks in work, family, and educational contexts. A policy research journal of the National Urban League.
Ind/Abst Am. Hist. Life (1985-); Crim. Penol. Police Sci. Abstr.; Curr. Contents Soc. Behav. Sci.; Curr. Index J. Educ.; Expand. Acad. Index (1992-); Newsp. Period. Abstr. (1992-); PAIS Int. Print; Res. Alert [Full Cov.]; Soc. Plann. Policy Dev. Abstr.; Soc. Sci. Cit. Index [Full Cov.]; Soc. Work Abstr. [Select. Cov.].

US/1058-2428
US BLACK ENGINEER. [U S Black eng.]. **VAT** United States Black Engineer. (1984)-. Periodical. English. ir. $15.00 regular, $25.00 corporate. Career Communications Group, 729 East Pratt Street, Suite 504, Baltimore MD 21202. **Tel** (410)244-7101 ext. 30, FAX (410)752-1837. **LC** TA1; .U52. **DD** 620/.005. ***Continues*** *Umoja Sasa.*

US/0300-6808
UTE BULLETIN, THE. **Added/Corp** Ute Indian Tribe. (1960)-. Newspaper. English. Twenty-four times a year. $20.00. Ute Indian Tribe, PO Box 400, Fort Duchesne UT 84026. **Tel** (801)722-5141 ext. 161, (801)722-3736, FAX (801)722-3736. **ED** Larry Cesspooch.

US
VAN NGHE TIEN PHONG. (1???)-. Periodical. Vietnamese. sm. $150.00 US; $175.00 Canada & Mexico; $190.00 Europe; $220.00 other. Tien Phong Inc., 15 North Highland Street, Arlington VA 22201. **Tel** (703)522-7151.

GW
VAN NGHE TRE. ***Ceased.*** (19??)-No. 48 (Jan. 1992). Vietnamese. bm. Vidi Druckwerkstatt, Postfach 104122, 4600 Dortmund 1 Germany. ***Continues*** *Mang-Non.*

CN/0705-1867
VANI. Began publication in 1970. Telugu. an. $2.50 each number. Andhra Cultural Association, PO Box 3282, Postal Station D, Edmonton Alta T5L 4J7. **DD** 301.45/19/1411071233.

●US/1061-8333
VARIEGATED GOSPEL. **See** Religion and Theology.

US/0746-0627
VASA STAR, THE. (THE VASA STAR : VASASTJARNAN.). [Vasa Star]. **VFOAT** Vasastjarnan. Periodical. English. mo. $5.00 US; $10.00 other. Vasa Star, 50 Southeast Bush, Issaquah WA 98027. **ED** Alvalene P Karlsson. **Bk Rev. Ad Acc. Circ:** 19,000 (ctrl).
Desc: News, information, general and organizational.

US
VERDAD (CORPUS CHRISTI, TEX. : 1942). (LA VERDAD.). **VFOAT** Truth. (1942)-. Newspaper. English (Spanish). Fifty-two times a year. $6.00. La Verdad, 910 Francisca Street, Corpus Christi TX 78415. **ED** Santo de la Paz. **LC** Newspaper. **Bk Rev. Ad Acc. Circ:** 5,000 (ctrl).

US/1055-2278
VESTNIK (OWINGS MILLS, MD.). (VESTNIK.). [Vestnik]. (January 14, 1991)-. Periodical. Russian (English). sm. $48.00 US; $89.00 other. Vestnik Information Agency, 6100 Park Heights Avenue, Baltimore MD 21215-3625. **Tel** (410)358-0900, FAX (410)358-3867. **ED** Victor Blok. **LC** E184.R9; V47. **Bk Rev**, (Qty: 10). **Ad Acc, Adv Mgr:** Gennady Krochik. **Circ:** 5,000 (ctrl).
Desc: Diversified Russian language publication. Provides professional pieces on world politics and economics covering everything from US and the former Soviet Union to Western and Eastern Europe and the Middle East. Also features short stories, interviews, and much more.

US
VILLAGER, THE. (1973)-. Newspaper. English. Fifty-two times a year. $20.00. Villager Newspapers, 1223-A Rosewood Avenue, Austin TX 78702. **Tel** (512)476-0082, FAX (512)476-0179. **ED** T.L. Wyatt (editor's address: 1223 Rosewood Avenue, Austin, TX 78702) and Bobbie Hall (Managing Editor). **Photos. Ad Acc, Adv Mgr:** T. Wyatt. Full Page (B&W) $1,260.00. Half Page (B&W) $472.50. Full Page (Color) $1,860.00. Half Page (Color) $1,072.50. **Pub. Size:** Standard. **Wire Svcs.:** NP. **Circ:** 6,000 (ctrl). available in microform.
Desc: Newspaper with an Afro-American focus.

UK
VISION. See Women's Interests.

CN/0380-0369
VISTI - INSTYTUTU SV. VOLODYMYRA. **Main/Corp** Ukrainskyi Instytut SV. Volodymyra. **VFOAT** Newsletter - St. Vladimir Ukrainian Institute. Began publication in 1963. Periodical. Ukrainian (English). ir (4 or 5 issues a year). Free. St Vladimir Ukrainian Institute, 620 Spadina Avenue, Toronto Ontario M5S 2H4 Canada. **Tel** 923-3318. **DD** 971.3/541/00491791. **Bk Rev. Circ:** 4,000 (ctrl).
Desc: Newsletter reporting on activities within our community.

US/1056-6368
VITAL ISSUES (WASHINGTON, D.C.). (VITAL ISSUES : THE JOURNAL OF AFRICAN AMERICAN SPEECHES.). [Vital issues]. **VFOAT** Journal of African American Speeches. Vol. 1, No. 1 (Winter 1991)-. Periodical. English. Four times a year (Mar., June, Sept., Dec.). $35.00 (one year); $60.00 (two years). Bethune-Dubois Publications, 600 New Hampshire Avenue Northwest, Suite 1125, Washington DC 20037. **Tel** (202)625-7048, FAX (202)625-0499. **ED** Teta V. Banks (editor's address: 1809 Spring Garden Street, Philadelphia, PA 19130-3916 phone: (215)686-1873). **LC** E185.5; .V58. **DD** 973/.0496073/05. Index available. cum. index. **Circ:** 1,500.

US/0735-3154
VITO (SEATTLE, WASH.), LA. (LA VITO : ORGANO DE K.A.A. / KUNULARO DE ALKOHOLULOJ ANONIMAJ.). No. 0. (Autumn 1982)-. Periodical. Spanish. qt. $3.00. Kunularo De Alkoholuloj Anonimaj, 4743 Fifth Avenue NE, Seattle WA 98105.

AT/1035-4859
VIVA MT. LAWLEY. ***Ceased.*** (VIVA.). [Viva Mt. Lawley]. (1991)-Vol. 3, No. 3/4 (Dec. 1993). Periodical. English. Four times a year (Mar., June, Oct., Dec.). Campaign Against Racial Explotation, PO Box 159, Mt Lawley Wa, 6050 Australia. **Tel** 09 328 9396, 09 276 9144, telex 88765. **DD** 305.8005. ***Continues*** *CARE Newsletter - Campaign Against Racial Exploitation, 0726-6103.*

US/1054-4283
VOICES OF THE AFRICAN DIASPORA. (VOICES OF THE AFRICAN DIASPORA : THE CAAS RESEARCH REVIEW.). [Voices Afr. diaspora]. **Added/Corp** University of Michigan. Center for Afroamerican and African Studies. **VFOAT** Voices. Vol. 7, No. 1 (Fall 1990)-. Periodical. English. Three times a year. $18.00 (individuals), $24.00 (institutions). The Center for Afroamerican and African Studies, 200 West Engineering Building, University of Michigan, Ann Arbor MI 48109-1092. **Tel** (313)764-5513. **ED** Susanne Kocsis. **LC** E185.5; .V89. **DD** 973/.0496073/005. **Bk Rev. Ad Acc. Circ:** 1,800 (ctrl). ***Continues*** *Newsletter (University of Michigan. Center for Afroamerican and African Studies), 1054-4291.*
Desc: Academic journal focusing on Afroamerican, African, and Caribbean studies. Articles cover a wide range of disciplines from a cross-cultural perspective.

CN/0704-5352
VOIX SEFARAD. (LA VOIX SEPHARADE / COMMUNAUTE SEPHARADE DU QUEBEC.). **Added/Corp** Communaute Sepharade du Quebec. **VFOAT** Sepharade. Vol. 13, No. 1, (Feb. 1982)-. Periodical. French (English). Five times a year (Feb., Apr., June, Sept., Dec.). 25.00Can$ Quebec; 36.00Can$ other. Voix Sepharade, 4735 Chemin Cote Ste Catherine, Montreal Quebec H3W 1M1 Canada. **Tel** (514)733-8696, (514)733-4998, FAX (514)733-3158. **ED** M. Judah Castiel. **DD** 305.8/924/0714. **Bk Rev**, (Qty: 5). **Ad Acc, Adv Mgr:** Jean Claude Leon. **Circ:** 5,000 (ctrl). ***Continues*** *Voix Sefarad, 0704-5352.*
Desc: Community news, cultural and religious articles about Sephardic Jews.

US/0741-9414
WASHINGTON INFORMER, THE. VFOAT Informer. (19??)-. Newspaper. English. wk. $15.00 (1 year), $25.00 (2 year). Washington Informer Newspaper Company Limited, 3117 Martin Luther King Southeast, Washington DC 20032. **Tel** (202)561-4100, FAX (202)574-3785. **ED** Dr. Calvin Rolark and Denise Rolark Barnes. **Bk Rev**, (Qty: 10). **Ad Acc. Circ:** 17,000 (ctrl).
Desc: Newspaper focusing on the African-American in the Washington metropolitan area.

CN/0703-9387
WAWATAY NEWS. [Wawatay news]. **Added/Corp** Wa-Wa-Ta Native Communications Society. **VFOAT** Wawatay extra. (Nov. 1974)-. Periodical. English (Cree). Twenty-three times a year. 30.00Can$ institutions, 25.00 individuals, Canada; 40.00Can$ other. Wawatay Native Communications, Box 1180, Sioux Lookout Ontario P0V 2T0 Canada. **Tel** (807)737-2951, FAX 817-737-3224. **ED** Megan Williams, Anne Maxwell, Stu Cummings. **DD** 971.3/112. **Bk Rev. Ad Acc. Circ:** 5,500 (ctrl). available on microfilm and microfiche.
Desc: News pertaining to Indian people in 42 remote communities of northwestern Ontario.

●US/1065-5883
WAZO WEUSI. (WAZO WEUSI : A JOURNAL OF BLACK THOUGHT.). **Added/Corp** California State University, Fresno. Dept. of Political Science. (1992)-. Periodical. English. sa. Wazo Weusi, California State University, Fresno, Department of Political Science, Fresno CA 93740-0019.

US/0197-4327
WESTERN JOURNAL OF BLACK STUDIES, THE. [West. j. black stud.]. Vol. 1, No. 1 (March 1977)-. Periodical. English. qt. $20.00 individuals, $30.00 institutions. Washington State University Press, Cooper Publications, Room 40, Pullman WA 99164. **Tel** (509)335-3518. **ED** Fred Bohm. **LC** E185.5; .W54. **DD** 973/.0496. **Bk Rev. Ad Acc. Pr Rev. Circ:** 600 (ctrl). available on microfilm and microfiche from University Microfilms International (UMI). Documents available from UMI Article Clearinghouse.
Desc: Articles that focus on the social and intellectual experiences in America.
Ind/Abst Am. Humanit. Index; Curr. Index J. Educ.; Expand. Acad. Index (1992-); Multicult. Educ. Abstr.; Newsp. Period. Abstr. (1992-); Psychol. Abstr. (1986-); PsycINFO; PsycLit; Soc. Work Abstr. [Select. Cov.]; SportSearch.

US/0749-5471
WESTERN STATES JEWISH HISTORY. [West. states Jew. hist.]. **Added/Corp** Southern California Jewish Historical Society. Vol. 16, No. 1 (Oct. 1983)-. Periodical. English. Four times a year (Jan., Apr., July, Oct.). $20.00. Western States Jewish History Association, 3111 Kelton, C/O Professor W. Kramer, Los Angeles CA 90034. **Tel** (310)475-1415. **LC** F591; .W469. **DD** 978/.004924. Index available (Bound in 4th iss.). **Bk Rev.** ***Continues*** *Western States Jewish Historical Quarterly, 0043-4221.*
Desc: Jewish history of Western United States, including Alaska, Hawaii, Western Mexico, Western Canada, and Pacific Islands.
Ind/Abst Am. Hist. Life (1983-); Index Jew. Period.; West. Hist. Q.

US
WESTERN VIKING. (1889)-. Periodical. Multiple languages (English and Norwegian). Forty-seven times a year. $27.50 US; $30.00 Canada; $35.00 other. Western Viking, 2405 NW Market Street, PO Box 70408, Seattle WA 98107. **Tel** (206)784-4617, FAX (206)784-4856. **ED** Dr. Alf Lunder Knudsen. **Bk Rev**, (Qty: 10-15/year). **Ad Acc. Pr Rev. Circ:** 5,000.
Desc: A Norwegian and English language weekly with nationwide circulation.

US/0300-6565
WHISPERING WIND. [Whispering wind]. **Added/Corp** Louisiana Indian Hobbyist Association. **VFOAT** Whispering Wind Magazine. (1967)-. Periodical. English. Six times a year (Feb., Apr., June, Aug., Oct., Dec.). $16.00 one year; $28.00 two years. Written Heritage, 8009 Wales Street, New Orleans LA 70126. **Tel** (504)241-5866. **ED** Jack Heriard (phone: (504)246-3742). **LC** E75; .W46. **DD** 970.004/97. Index available. cum. index. **Bk Rev**, (Qty: 18). **Ad Acc. Circ:** 16,000.
Desc: American indian materials culture past and present. Illustrated crafts, traditions, and history.

●US/1052-7354
WHO'S WHO AMONG HISPANIC AMERICANS. [Who's who Hisp. Am.]. **Added/Corp** Gale Research Inc. **VFOAT** Hispanic Americans. 1st Ed. (1991-92)-. English. be. $89.95. Gale Research Inc., 835 Penobscot Building, Detroit MI 48226. **Tel** (800)877-GALE, (313)961-2242, FAX (313)961-6083, telex TWX 810-221-7086. **ED** Amy L Unterburger. **LC** E184.S75; W53; E184.S75; W36. **DD** 920/.009268. **NLM** E 184; S75.

US/0747-7538
WHO'S WHO IN INDIAN RELICS. See Biographies.

US
WIADOMO'SCI POLSKIE. No. 1- 1972-. Periodical. Polish (English). mo.

US
WOTANIN WOWAPI MICROFORM. (197?)-. Periodical. English. sm. $15.00. Wotanin Wowapi, Box 1027, Poplar MT 59255. **Tel** (406)768-5241. **ED** Bonnie C. Red Elk. **Bk Rev. Ad Acc. Circ:** 8,000. available in microform. ***Continues*** *Wotanin.*
Desc: Newspaper of tribal government news for Assiniboine and Sioux tribal members of the Fort Peck Indian Reservation, Montana.

UK/0075-8744
YEAR BOOK (LEO BAECK INSTITUTE). (YEAR BOOK - LEO BAECK INSTITUTE.). [Year b. - Leo Baeck Inst.]. Vol. 5 (1960)-. English (German). an. $40.00. Leo Baeck Institute, 129 East 73rd Street, New York NY 10021. **Tel** (212)744-6400. **ED** Arnold Paucker. **LC** DS135.G3; A262. **DD** 305.8/924/043. Index available. cum. index. **Circ:** 2,500. ***Continues*** *Year Book (Leo Baeck Institute of Jews from Germany).*
Ind/Abst Am. Hist. Life (1963-).

US/1050-8864
YIVO ANNUAL. See Religion and Theology-Judaism.

US/0084-4217
YIVO BLETER. See Literature.

US/0898-8358
YIVO NEWS. See Religion and Theology-Judaism.

US/1056-6198
YSB (WASHINGTON, D.C.). (YSB.). [YSB]. **VFOAT** Young Sisters and Brothers Magazine; Young Sisters & Brothers Magazine; YSB Magazine. Vol. 1, No. 1 (Sept. 1991)-. Periodical. English. Ten times a year. $14.95 (1 year), $22.00 (2 year), $34.00 (3 year). Paige Publications, 1700 North Moore, Suite 2200, Rosslyn VA 22209. **Tel** (703)875-0430. **(Subscription address:** CDS Agency Hard Copy, PO Box 4966, Des Moines, IA 50340**) LC** E185.5; .Y83. **DD** 305.

CN/0226-3068
ZAPAD. ***Title Change.*** [Zapad]. Vol. 1 April (1979)-(1992). Periodical. Czech (Slovak). bm. Zapad, PO Box 322, Waterloo Ontario N2J 4A4 Canada. **Tel** (519)742-6765. **ED** Milos Suchma, Josef Skvorecky, Ota Ulc, Stanislav Reinis, Vaclav Taborsky, Eva Liman, Jan Uhde. **LC** AP53; .Z36. **DD** 057/.86. Index available. cum. index. **Bk Rev. Ad Acc. Circ:** 5,000 (ctrl). ***Continued by*** *Zapad Today.*
Desc: Serves a large population of Czech and Slovaks all over the world. It's readership includes professionals, scholars, tradesmen, businessmen, students and newcomers.

●CN
ZAPAD TODAY. (1992)-. Periodical. Czech. Six times a year. $24.00 (one year), $40.00 (two years). Zapad, PO Box 322, Waterloo Ontario N2J 4A4 Canada. **Tel** (519)742-6765. **ED** S Reiuis (editor's address: Box 227 Heidelberg Ontario N2J 4A4 Canada; editor's phone: (519)699-4748). **Bk Rev. Ad Acc. Pr Rev. Circ:** 8,000 (ctrl). ***Continues*** *Zapad.*

AT
ZBORNIK AVSTRALSKIH SLOVENCEV. **Added/Corp** Slovenian-Australian Literary & Art Circle. **VFOAT** Anthology of Australian Slovenes. (19??)-. Slovenian (English). ir.

US
ZGODA. **Added/Corp** Polish National Alliance of the United States of North America. **VFOAT** Unity. (1881)-. Newspaper. English (Polish). Five times a year. $99.95. **(Subscription address:** East View Publications Inc., 3020 Harbor Lane North, Suite 110, Minneapolis MN 55447.**) LC** Newspaper. available on microfilm.

LV
ZINATNISKAS ATSKAITES SESIJAS MATERIALI PAR ARHEOLOGU UN ETNOGRAFU PETIJUMU REZULTATIEM. See Anthropology.

PL/0514-0188
ZIVOT WARSAWA. (1958)-. Periodical. Multiple languages. mo. Price on Request. **(Subscription address:** ARS Polona, PO Box 1001, 00068 Warsaw Poland.) **UDC** 008 (438). **CODEN** 885.4.

XR
ZPRAVODAJ KOORDINOVANE SITE VEDECKYCH INFORMACI PRO ETNOGRAFII A FOLKLORISTIKU. **Added/Corp** Ustav pro Etnografii a Folkloristiku (Ceskoslovenska Akademie Ved). Oborove Stredisko Vedeckych Informaci. (19??)-. Monographic series. Czech. Price varies per volume. **LC** DB2040; .Z68.

US/0277-9811
ZURNALS (LITTLETON, MASS.). (ZURNALS.). [Zurnals]. No. 1- (Aug. 1981)-. Periodical. Latvian. qt. $16.50. Zurnals, Gunara Indara Apgads, PO Box 2371, 550 Newtown Road, Littleton MA 01460. **LC** E184.L4; Z87.

ABSTRACTING, BIBLIOGRAPHIES AND STATISTICS

CN/0831-3180
ABSTRACTS OF NATIVE STUDIES. [Abstr. native stud.]. Vol. 1 (1984)-. English (French). Twice a year. 25.00Can$. Westarc Group Inc., Brandon University, 247 18th Street, Brandon Manitoba R7A 5A6 Canada. **Tel** (204)729-3440, FAX (204)729-9090. **ED** Robert C. Annis, (phone: (204)729-3444). **LC** E78.C2; A27. **DD** 305.897071. **Circ:** 250.
Desc: Analysis research to locate journal articles pertaining to the native people of North America.

AT
ANNUAL BIBLIOGRAPHY / AUSTRALIAN INSTITUTE OF ABORIGINAL AND TORRES STRAIT ISLANDER STUDIES. **Main/Corp** Australian Institute of Aboriginal and Torres Strait Islander Studies. (1989)-. Bibliography. English. an. 12.00Aus$. Australian Institute of Aboriginal and Torres Strait Island Studies, PO Box 553, Canberra ACT 2601 Australia. **Tel** 011 061 6 2461111, FAX 011 061 6 2497310. **LC** Z5116; .A78a. ***Continues*** *Australian Institute of Aboriginal Studies. Annual Bibliography.*

US/0360-2710
BIBLIOGRAPHIC GUIDE TO BLACK STUDIES. **Main/Corp** Schomburg Center for Research in Black Culture. 1975-. English. an. $95.00. GK Hall & Co, 100 Front Street, Riverside NJ 08075. **Tel** (800)257-5755 ext. 2223. **LC** Z1361.N39; S373A; E185. **DD** 016.973/04/96073.

US/0090-9513
FOCUS : BLACK AMERICAN BIBLIOGRAPHY SERIES. SUPPLEMENT. 1 (1971)-. Bibliography. English. Indiana University Libraries, Jennifer Paustenbaugh, Library C-2, Bloomington IN 47405. **Tel** (812)855-3403, FAX (812)855-2576. **LC** Z1361.N39; F584. **DD** 016.30145/19/6073.
Ind/Abst Bibliogr. Mission.

US/0737-7029
HISPANIC FOCUS. [Hisp. focus]. **Added/Corp** Library of Congress. Hispanic Division. No. 1 (1982)-. Monographic series. English. ir. Price varies per volume. Hispanic Division, Library of Congress, Washington DC 20540. **Tel** (202)707-5400. **LC** UNC. **Ad Acc.** ctrl circ.
Desc: Series of short bibliographies, reading lists, and reference aids on issues of contemporary relevance. The purpose is to acquaint the reader with materials in the Library of Congress' collections that bear on such issues, and to make them more accessible for research.

US
IHRC ETHNIC BIBLIOGRAPHY. **Main/Corp** University of Minnesota. Immigration History Research Center. No. 1 (1976)-. Monographic series. English. ir. Price varies per volume. Immigration History Research, University of Minnesota, 826 Berry Street, St Paul MN 55114. **Tel** (612)627-4208.

US/0899-6253
INDEX TO BLACK PERIODICALS. [Index Black period.]. **VFOAT** Index to Periodical Articles. (1984)-. Abstracting/Indexing Service. English. an (December). $101.72. GK Hall & Co, 100 Front Street, Riverside NJ 08075. **Tel** (800)257-5755 ext. 2223. **LC** AI3; .O4. **DD** 974. **Bk Rev.** ***Continues*** *Index to Periodical Articles by and About Blacks, 0161-8245.*
Desc: Provides librarians and patrons with a handy, single source to articles appearing each year in major black American journals, with interviews and book and drama reviews.

US/1066-9507
MINORITY & WOMEN DOCTORAL DIRECTORY. **See** Education-Higher Education.

US/0481-1356
QUARTERLY BIBLIOGRAPHY ON CULTURAL DIFFERENCES, A. No. 1- July 1964-. Bibliography. English. qt. California State Library / Training Division, State Personnel Board, 801 Capitol Mall, Sacramento CA 95814. **DD** 016.9173/06/09073.

FAMILY AND MARRIAGE

US/0001-5083
ACT (WHITING). **See** Religion and Theology.

BE/0776-4677
ACTUALQUARTO GERPINNES. [Actualquarto Gerpinnes]. (1973)-. Periodical. Dutch (French). Fifteen times a year. 100.00F Belguim; 150.00F others. Actualquarto, 20 Allee des Bouleaux, B6280 Gerpinnes Belguim. **Tel** 011 32 71 216153, FAX 011 32 71 217713. **ED** Jean Delahaut. **UDC** 082.

US/0899-5591
ADOLESCENT PREGNANCY PREVENTION CLEARINGHOUSE. ***Title Change.*** **See** Sociology-Social Services and Welfare.

US/0745-3167
ADOPTED CHILD. (1981)-. Periodical. English. Twelve times a year. $22.00 (one year); $40.00 (two years); $58.00 (three years). Adopted Child, PO Box 9362, Moscow ID 83843. **Tel** (208)882-1794. **ED** Lois Melina. Index available. cum. index. **Bk Rev**, (Qty: 1/yr). **Circ:** 3,000 (ctrl).
Desc: Sensitive and reassuring advice for adoptive families.

US/1046-3569
ADOPTION. **VFOAT** Adoption Magazine. Vol. 1, No. 1 (Nov./Dec. 1989)-. Periodical. English. bm. $30.00. Ulick Publication Company, PO Box 8551, Bartlett IL 60103. **Tel** (708)213-1300. **ED** Geoffrey Golson. **LC** HV875.55; .A363. **DD** 362.7/34/097305.
Desc: Special-interest magazine for prospective adoptive parents.

US
ADOPTION DIRECTORY, THE. 1989-. Directory. English. $55.00. Gale Research Inc., 835 Penobscot Building, Detroit MI 48226. **Tel** (800)877-GALE, (313)961-2242, FAX (313)961-6083, telex TWX 810-221-7086. **ED** Ellen Paul.
Desc: Provides a solid basis for making informed decisions. This helpful guide allows users to compare adoption resources state-by-state and country-by-country. Contains a glossary, annotated reading list, state-by-state listing of where to write for vital records, and information on the offices and requirements of the Immigration and Naturalization Service.

●US/1076-1020
ADOPTIVE FAMILIES. **See** Sociology-Social Services and Welfare.

US/1058-9155
ADOPTIVE FAMILIES TOGETHER : AFT. **Added/Corp** Adoptive Families Together. **VFOAT** AFT. Vol. 1, No. 1 (Dec./Jan. 1990/91)-. Periodical. English. mo. $20.00 (membership). Adoptive Families Together, PO Box 272963, Houston TX 77277-2963.

US/0044-7544
AMERICAN BABY. [Am. baby]. **Added/Corp** American Association of Maternal and Child Health. (1940)-. Periodical. English. mo. $23.94 US. Cahners Publishing Company, 249 West 17th Street, New York NY 10011. **Tel** (212)645-0067, FAX (212)242-6987. **(Subscription address:** Neodata / Colorado, PO Box 2606, Boulder Boulder CO 80322.) **ED** Judith Nolte. **LC** HQ750.A2; A2. **[CCC]. Bk Rev. Ad Acc. Circ:** 1,000,000 (ctrl). available on microfilm and microfiche from University Microfilms International (UMI). Documents available from UMI Article Clearinghouse, Magazine Collection.
Desc: A complete reference for expectant and new parents, focusing on all facets of childcare. It addresses the health and medical issues of pregnancy as well as infant and child care. American Baby also highlights new products, accessories and fashions.
Ind/Abst Acad. Abstr. Full Text Elite (Jan. 1992-); Acad. Abstr. (Jan. 1992-); AGRICOLA [Select. Cov.]; Consum. Health Nutr. Index; Gen. Period. Index (1985-); Health Index (1989-); Health Period. Database; Health Ref. Cent. (Jan. 1989-) [Full Cov.]; Health Source (Jan. 1992-); Mag. Artic. Summar. Elite (Jan. 1992-); Mag. Artic. Summar. CD-ROM (Jan. 1992-); Mag. Index Plus (1989-); Mag. Index. Sel. (1986-); Mag. Search; Newsp. Period. Abstr. (1988-); Mag. Index (1977-)(1959-).

US/0161-1178
AMERICAN FAMILY (WASHINGTON), THE. ***Title Change.*** (THE AMERICAN FAMILY.). [Am. fam.]. **Added/Corp** Wakefield Washington Associates Inc. Youth Policy Institute (Washington, D.C.). Vol. 1-15, No. 9 (Dec. 1977/Jan. 1978)-(Winter 1992). Periodical. English. Twelve times a year. Youth Policy Institute, 1221 Massachusetts Avenue Northwest, Suite B, Washington DC 20005. **Tel** (202)638-2144. ***Merged into*** *Youth Policy (Washington, D.C.), 8756-0909.*
Desc: A national newsletter dedicated to covering programs and policies that effect families. Topics covered are child care, divorce, parental-leave and welfare.
Ind/Abst AGRICOLA [Select. Cov.]; Curr. Lit. Fam. Plan. (19??-199?); Soc. Work Abstr. [Select. Cov.].

US/0192-6187
AMERICAN JOURNAL OF FAMILY THERAPY, THE. **See** Psychology.

US/1059-4469
ANNUAL CONFERENCE PROCEEDINGS - NATIONAL COUNCIL ON FAMILY RELATIONS. (ANNUAL CONFERENCE PROCEEDINGS.). [Annu. conf. proc. - Natl. Counc. Fam. Relat.]. **Main/Corp** National Council on Family Relations. Conference. **Added/Corp** National Council on Family Relations. **VFOAT** Families and Poverty. Vol. 1, No. 1 (Nov. 1991)-. English. Free to organizational members of the National Council on Family Relations. National Council of Family Relations, 3989 Central Avenue Northeast, Suite 550, Minneapolis MN 55421. **Tel** (612)781-9331, FAX (612)781-9348. **LC** IN PROCESS. **DD** 306.

AT
ANNUAL REPORT / BOARD OF MANAGEMENT, AUSTRALIAN INSTITUTE OF FAMILY STUDIES. **Main/Corp** Australian Institute of Family Studies. Board of Management. English. an. 6.00Aus$. Australian Institute of Family Studies, 300 Queen Street, Melbourne Victoria 3000 Australia. **Tel** 61 3 6086888, FAX 61 3 6000886. **LC** HQ706; .A9. **DD** 306.85/0994/05. **Circ:** 1,000.
Desc: Report focusing on the research and dissemination, finance, staffing and operation of this statutory authority.

UK/0307-6857
ANNUAL REPORT - INTERNATIONAL PLANNED PARENTHOOD FEDERATION. **Main/Corp** International Planned Parenthood Federation. (196?)-. Corporate Report. English (French, Spanish and Arabic). an. Free. International Planned Parenthood Federation, Regent's College, Inner Circle, Regent's Park, London NW1 4NS England. **Tel** 011 44 71 486 0741, FAX 011 44 71 487 7950, telex 919573 IPEPEE G. **ED** Jeremy Hamand. **LC** HQ750.A3; I5. **DD** 301.42/6/0621. **NLM** W1 IN827PB. **Circ:** 20,000 (ctrl). ***Continues*** *Report of the International Planned Parenthood Federation, 0309-2801.*
Desc: Seeks to inform the reader of what we are, what we do, and why we are deserving of continuing support internationally.

AT/0814-723X
AUSTRALIAN AND NEW ZEALAND JOURNAL OF FAMILY THERAPY, THE. [Aust. N. Z. j. family ther.]. Vol. 6 No. 1 (March 1985)-. Periodical. English. Four times a year (Mar., June, Sept., Dec.). 70.00Aus$ (individual), 90.00Aus$(institution). Australian and New Zealand Family Therapy, PO Box 633, Lane Cove NSW 2066 Australia. **Tel** 011 61 2 879 6144, FAX 011 61 2 879 6440. **NLM** W1; AU494. **CODEN** ANZTE7. Index available (Free). cum. index. ***Continues*** *Australian Journal of Family Therapy.*
Ind/Abst Linguist. Lang. Behav. Abstr.; Psychol. Abstr. (1983-); PsycINFO; PsycLit; Sage Fam. Stud. Abstr.; Soc. Plann. Policy Dev. Abstr.; Soc. Work Abstr. (Summer 1987-) [Select. Cov.]; Sociol. Abstr.

AT/0811-3661
AUSTRALIAN FAMILY MELBOURNE. (1980)-. Periodical. English. Four times a year (Mar., June, Sept., Dec.). 25.00Aus$. Australian Family Association, 582 Queensberry Street, N Melbourne VIC 3051 Australia. **Tel** 011 61 3 3265757, FAX 011 61 3 3282877. **ED** Bill Muehlenberg. Index available. cum. index. **Bk Rev**, (Qty: 2). **Circ:** 2,500 (ctrl).
Desc: An pro-family journal.

AT/1034-652X
AUSTRALIAN JOURNAL OF MARRIAGE & FAMILY. **Added/Corp** Family Life Movement of Australia. **VFOAT** Australian Journal of Marriage and Family. Vol. 11, No. 1 (Mar. 1990)-. Periodical. English. Three times a year (Mar., July, Nov.). 30.00Aus$ (individuals), 35.00Aus$ (institutions) Australia; 35.00Aus$ other. Australian Journal of Marriage & Family, PO Box 143, Concord New South Wales 2137 Australia. **Tel** 011 61 2 7362117, FAX 011 61 2 7362663. **LC** HQ1; .A97. Index available (bound in Mar. issue). **Bk Rev. Ad Acc. Circ:** 600. ***Continues*** *Australian Journal of Sex, Marriage & Family, 0159-1487.*

Desc: Writings on marital and family issues.
Ind/Abst APAIS, Aust. Public Aff. Inf. Ser. (1990-); Psychol. Abstr. (1983-); PsycINFO; PsycLit.

AT/1031-4830
AUSTRALIAN MOTHER AND BABY. [Aust. mother baby]. (1988)-. Periodical. English. Nine times a year. 22.00Aus$ (one year); 42.00Aus$ (two years); 59.00Aus$ (three years). Australian Mother & Baby, PO Box C117, Clarence Street, Sydney 2000 Australia. **Tel** 011 61 2 2812955, FAX 011 61 2 2812964. **DD** 649.12205. **Bk Rev**, (Qty: varies). **Ad Acc.**

AT
AUSTRALIA'S PARENTS : THE PRACTICAL PARENTING MAGAZINE. (19??)-. English. bm. 23.70Aus$ Australia; 77.70Aus$ Canada, US & Israel; 83.70Aus$ UK, Europe & Africa. Magazine House Pty Ltd, PO Box 1067, Crows Nest New South Wales 2065 Australia. **Tel** 011 61 2 4382399, FAX 011 61 2 4363014. ***Continues*** *Parents & Children Magazine.*

US/0894-3990
BABY CONNECTION, THE. See Education.

IT
BAMBINO INCOMPIUTO. Vol. 1 (May 1984)-. Periodical. Italian. Three times a year. Edizioni Unicopli SPA, Via Soperga 13, 20127 Milan Italy. **Tel** 011 39 2 66984682. **LC** HQ778.7.I8; B35.

UK/0952-4096
BILINGUAL FAMILY NEWSLETTER, THE. Vol. 1 No. 1 (Mar 1984)-. Newsletter. English. Four times a year. $16.00 US; £7.00 UK. Multilingual Matters Ltd., Frankfurt Lodge, Clevedon Hall, Clevedon Avon, BS21 7SJ England. **Tel** 011 44 275 876519, FAX 011 44 275 343096. **(Subscription address:** Kinokuniya Company Ltd., 38-1 Sakuragaoka 5, chome Setagaya-ku, Tokyo 156 Japan.**) ED** Goerge Saunders. **LC** P115; .B53. **CODEN** BFNEER. **Bk Rev. Ad Acc. Circ:** 1,200.
Desc: Gives information and encouragement to parents wishing to bring the children up bilingually.
Ind/Abst Linguist. Lang. Behav. Abstr.; Soc. Plann. Policy Dev. Abstr.; Sociol. Abstr.

AT/1032-9625
BIRTH ST. LEONARDS. (1989)-. English. an. $5.95. Magazine House Pty Ltd, PO Box 1067, Crows Nest New South Wales 2065 Australia. **Tel** 011 61 2 4382399, FAX 011 61 2 4363014. **ED** Carol Fallows. **Ad Acc, Adv Mgr:** Matthew Chivers, David Knight.
Desc: A guide to birth for parents-to-be.

IT
BOLLETTINO DEL CENTRO MILANESE DI TERAPIA DELLA FAMIGLIA. Italian. Three times a year. L30000 Italy; L40000 other. Centro Milan Terapia Famiglia, Via Leopardi 19, 20123 Milan Italy. **Tel** 011 39 2 4815350.

US/1059-1710
BOSTON PARENTS' PAPER, THE. [Boston parents' pap.]. (198?)-. Newspaper. English. Twelve times a year. $15.00 (one year), $22.00 (two year). Boston Parents Paper, PO Box 1777, Boston MA 02130. **Tel** (617)522-1515, FAX (617)522-1694. **ED** William Lindsay. **DD** 306. **Bk Rev**, (Qty: 12). **Ad Acc, Adv Mgr:** Clarke Williams. **Circ:** 80,000 (ctrl).
Desc: Articles, features, events and many more news for the parents.

CN/1183-0654
BOUNTY INFANT CARE GUIDE, THE. [Bounty infant care guide]. **VFOAT** Infant Care Guide. 1st Ed. (1991)-. English. Limited free distribution. Bounty Family Publications, Unite 2, 746 Ave Warden, Scarborough, Ontario M1L 4A2. **DD** 649.

US/1048-2881
BREAKAWAY (POMONA, CALIF.). (BREAKAWAY.). [Breakaway]. **VFOAT** Break Away; Breakaway Magazine. Vol. 1, No. 1 (Mar. 1990)-. Periodical. English. mo. $15.00. Focus on the Family, Colorado Springs CO 80995. **Tel** (800)232-6459. **DD** 051.

US
BRIDAL APPAREL NEWS. See Clothing Industry and Fashion.

US/0882-7451
BRIDAL GUIDE. (Summer 1985)-. Periodical. English. Six times a year (Jan., Mar., May, July, Sept., Nov.). $18.95 one year. Globe Communications Corporation, 441 Lexington Avenue, New York NY 10017. **Tel** (212)949-4040, FAX (212)286-0072. **ED** Erica Goldberg. **DD** 392. **Ad Acc. Circ:** 225,000.
Desc: The authority on wedding planning, fashions, honeymoons, travel and articles on purchasing your first home.

US/0730-1006
BRIDE GUIDE (LOS ANGELES, CALIF.), THE. (THE BRIDE GUIDE.). **VFOAT** Los Angeles Bride Guide. (1982)-. English. an. Bride Guide Enterprises, 8712 Wilshire Boulevard/Suite 100, Beverly Hills CA 90211. ***Continues*** *L.A. Bride Guide, 0278-2707.*

US/0730-0972
BRIDE GUIDE (SAN DIEGO, CALIF.), THE. (THE BRIDE GUIDE.). **VFOAT** San Diego Bride Guide. (1982)-. English. an. Bride Guide Enterprises, 8712 Wilshire Boulevard/Suite 100, Beverly Hills CA 90211.

UK/0006-9787
BRIDES AND SETTING UP HOME. [Brides setting home]. (1964)-. Periodical. English. bm. $42.00. Reed Business Publishing / West Sussex, England, Perrymount Road, Haywards Heath, West Sussex RH16 3DH England. **Tel** 011 44 81 6523500. **ED** Sandra Boler. **DD** 640. **Ad Acc, Adv Mgr:** Helen Fifield, **Tel** 011 44 71 499 9080. **Acid Free. Circ:** 65,727. ***Continues*** *Brides (British Edition).*

●US/1059-7476
BRIDE'S & YOUR NEW HOME. [Bride's your new home]. **VFOAT** Bride's and Your New Home; Bride's. Vol. 58, No. 6 (Dec. 1991/Jan. 1992)-. Periodical. English. bm (6 issues). $18.00. Conde Nast Publications / New York, 350 Madison Avenue, New York NY 10017. **Tel** (212)880-8800, (800)777-0700. **(Subscription address:** Neodata / Colorado, PO Box 2606, Boulder Boulder CO 80322.**) DD** 395. Documents available from UMI Article Clearinghouse. ***Continues*** *Bride's, 0161-1992.*
Ind/Abst Newsp. Period. Abstr. (1992-).

US/1048-2873
BRIO (POMONA, CALIF.). (BRIO.). [Brio]. Vol. 1, No. 1 (Mar. 1990)-. Periodical. English. mo. $15.00. Focus on the Family, Colorado Springs CO 80995. **Tel** (800)232-6459. **DD** 051.

CN/0840-464X
BRITISH COLUMBIA'S WEDDING BELLS. [B.C. wedd. bells]. **VFOAT** Wedding Bells. Vol. 4, No. 3 (Fall/Winter 1988)-. Periodical. English. Twice a year (Feb. and Aug.). 12.00Can$ Canada; 20.00Can$ other. Wedding Bells, 120 Front Street East, Suite 200, Toronto Ontario M5A 4L9 Canada. **Tel** (416)862-8479, FAX (416)862-2184. **ED** Crys Stewart. **DD** 392/.5/09711. **Ad Acc, Adv Mgr:** Alethea Wakefield. **Circ:** 100,000 (ctrl). ***Formed by the union of*** *Vancouver Island's Wedding Bells, 0831-7399* ***and*** *Vancouver's Wedding Bells, 0831-2192.*
Desc: Journal of wedding planning with two regional editions.

US/1045-5051
BROWN UNIVERSITY FAMILY THERAPY LETTER, THE. ***Title Change.*** [Brown Univ. fam. ther. lett.]. **Added/Corp** Brown University. **VFOAT** Family Therapy Letter. Vol. 1, No. 1 (June 1989)-(1992). Periodical. English. mo. Manisses Communications Group Inc., PO Box 3357, Providence RI 02906-0757. **Tel** (401)831-6020, (800)333-7771, FAX (401)861-6370. **ED** Linda Watts Jackim. **DD** 362. **NLM** W1; BR91I. **[CCC].** ***Continues*** *Family Therapy Today, 0887-9109.* ***Absorbed by*** *Psychotherapy Letter.*
Desc: Reports for professionals helping couples and families.

US/0742-9363
BUILDING A MARRIAGE. [Build. marriage]. Vol. 1, No. 1 (June 1984)-. Periodical. English. mo. $18.00. Coastal Air, 392 Jefferson Point, Rock Creek OH 44084. **DD** 362.

CN/0822-6768
BULLETIN DE LIAISON / FEDERATION DES ASSOCIATIONS DE FAMILLES MONOPARENTALES DU QUEBEC. [Bull. liaison - Fed. assoc. fam. monoparent. Que.]. **Added/Corp** Federation des Associations de Familles Monoparentales du Quebec. Vol. 9, No. 5 (Spring 1983)-. Bulletin. French. qt. 10.00Can$. Federation des Associations de Familles Monoparentales du Quebec, Piece 2320 890 Est rue Dorchester, Montreal Quebec H2L 2L4 Canada. **DD** 362.8/2. **Circ:** 700 (ctrl). ***Continues*** *Carrefour des Associations de Familles Monoparentales du Quebec. Bulletin de Liaison, 0704-7134.*

US
BUSINESSLINK. ***Ceased.*** **See** Business.

AT
BUYING FOR BABY. (19??)-. English. an. $5.95. Magazine House Pty Ltd, PO Box 1067, Crows Nest New South Wales 2065 Australia. **Tel** 011 61 2 4382399, FAX 011 61 2 4363014. **ED** Carol Fallows. **Ad Acc, Adv Mgr:** Matthew Chivers & David Knight. ***Continues*** *Parents Shopping Guide, 1030-1968.*

US/0742-4493
CALIFORNIA BRIDE. LOS ANGELES EDITION. ***Ceased.*** (CALIFORNIA BRIDE.). (1985)-?. Periodical. English. sa. California Bride Inc, 4444 Wilshire Boulevard/Suite 202, Los Angeles CA 90010.

●US/1069-4862
CATHOLIC PARENT (HUNTINGTON, IND.). See Religion and Theology-Catholicism.

US/8750-2259
CCC NEWS. (CCC NEWS : A COMMUNITY FAMILY NEWS WEEKLY FROM THE CONCERNED CITIZENS COMMITMENT.). Periodical. English. wk. $15.00 Evanston-Skokie Illinois; $22.00 other. CCC News, PO Box 955, Evanston IL 60204. ***Continues*** *CCC Newsette.*

US/1055-9221
CDF'S CHILD, YOUTH, AND FAMILY FUTURES CLEARINGHOUSE. ***Ceased.*** **See** Sociology-Social Services and Welfare.

RE
CHALLENGE. (19??)-. Periodical. English. $2.00. Challenge / Kenya, PO Box 7954, Nairobi Kenya. **LC** HQ799.K4; C47. **DD** 301.43/15/096762.

CN/1188-1879
CHARACTERISTICS OF DUAL-EARNER FAMILIES. (CHARACTERISTICS OF DUAL-EARNER FAMILIES / STATISTICS CANADA, HOUSEHOLD SURVEYS DIVISION.). [Charact. dual-earn. fam.]. **Added/Corp** Statistics Canada. Household Surveys Division. **VFOAT** Caracteristiques des Familles Comptant Deux Soutiens. (1989)-. English (French). an. 27.00Can$ Canada; $33.00 US; $38.00 other. Statistics Canada, Publications Sales & Services, Main Building Room 1710, Ottawa Ontario K1A 0T6 Canada. **Tel** (613)951-5078, (800)267-6677, FAX (613)951-1584, telex 053-3585. **DD** 331.4/3/0971021.
Desc: The purpose of this annual report is to highlight those families where both spouses work, to explore various characteristics of these families and to compare them with other kinds of husband-wife families.

CN/0708-5303
CHATELAINE'S NEW MOTHER. ***Title Change.*** [Chatelaine's new mother]. **VAT** New Mother. (1979)-(1992). English. qt. Maclean Hunter Canada / Montreal, 1001 bvd. de Maisonneuve W., Montreal, Quebec H3A 3E1 Canada. **Tel** 514-845-5141, FAX 514-845-4302, telex 055-60604. **DD** 649/.122/05. ***Continued by*** *New Mother, 1193-9397.*

US/0009-3882
CHILD AND FAMILY. [Child fam.]. **Added/Corp** National Commission on Human Life, Reproduction and Rhythm. **VFOAT** Child & Family. Vol. 1 (Jan. 1962)-. Periodical. English. qt. $12.00. Child & Family, Box 508, Oak Park IL 60303. **Tel** (312)383-8766. **ED** Herbert Ratner. **DD** 649. **NLM** W1 CH643. **CODEN** CHFMB. Index available (bound in Oct. issue). cum. index. **Bk Rev. Circ:** 1,500 (ctrl). ***Supersedes*** *Child-Family Digest.*
Desc: Scientific and philosophic articles illuminating the book of nature and the order of nature (sociobiologic oriented). Editorial comments are appended.
Ind/Abst Appl. Soc. Sci. Index Abstr.

US/1055-2448
CHILD CARE DIRECTORY & FAMILY RESOURCE GUIDE (DENVER METRO ED.), THE. (THE CHILD CARE DIRECTORY & FAMILY RESOURCE GUIDE.). [Child care dir. fam. resour. guide]. **VFOAT** Child Care Directory and Family Resource Guide; Family Resource Guide. (1991)-. Directory. English. $5.99 (single issue). **DD** 649.

CN/1187-4678
CHILD CARE (KITCHENER). (CHILD CARE.). [Child care]. **Added/Corp** Community Information Centre, Waterloo Region. **VFOAT** Child Care in Waterloo Region. (1991)-. English. Community Information Centre, Waterloo Region, 10 Water Street North, Kitchener Ontario N2H 5A5. **DD** 362.7. ***Continues*** *Child Care Handbook (Kitchener, Ont.), 1187-0559.*

US/0890-4715
CHILD CARE MANAGEMENT. ***Ceased.*** (1986)-(?). Periodical. English. mo. American Health Consultants, 3525 Piedmont Road, Suite 400, Atlanta GA 30305. **Tel** (800)688-2421, (404)262-7436.

CN/0708-997X
CHILD FOCUS. Vol. 1 (Jan./Feb. 1979)-. Periodical. English. ir. $6.95 Canada; $7.95 other. Child Focus Inc, PO Box 67 Station F, Toronto Ontario M4Y 2L4 Canada. **DD** 301.43/14/05. **Circ:** 25,000.

US/0894-7988
CHILD (NEW YORK, N.Y.). (CHILD.). [Child]. Vol. 1, No. 1 (Oct. 1986)-. Periodical. English. Ten times a year. $15.94. Family Circle Inc, 110 5th Avenue, New York NY 10011-5601. **Tel** (212)463-1000. **(Subscription address:** CDS Agency Hard Copy, PO Box 4966, Des Moines IA 50340.**) ED** Kate White and Laura Manske. **LC** WMLC L 90/0050. **DD** 649. **Bk Rev. Ad Acc. Circ:** 250,000.
Desc: Celebrates parenthood and is edited for parents with children birth to 12 years who are committed to raising healthy, joyful children. Every issue contains newsworthy, in-depth information of major concern to parents.

US/0738-4726
CHILD NURTURANCE. Vol. 1 (1982)-. Monographic series. English. ir. Price varies per volume. Plenum Press, 233 Spring Street, New York NY 10013-1578. **Tel** (212)620-8000, (800)221-9369, FAX

(212)463-0742, (212)807-1047, telex 23/421139. **ED** Marjorie J. Kostelnik and Hiram E. Fitzgerald. **LC** UNC. **DD** 649/.1/05. **NLM** W1; CH668D.

US
CHILD SUPPORT AND ALIMONY ... (ADVANCE REPORT). Began with 1978. Government Publication. English. US Department of Commerce, 14th Street & Constitution Avenue NW, Washington DC 20230. **Tel** (202)482-2000, FAX (202)482-3772.

US/0886-3792
CHILDREN FOR TODAY'S PARENT. ***Title Change.*** [Prev. child. today's parent]. (1986)-?. Periodical. English. sa. Children for Today's Parent, 33 East Minor Street, Emmaus PA 18049. **DD** 649. ***Continued by*** *Todale's Children, 0892-1296.*

CC
CHING NIEN I TAI. **VFOAT** Qingnian Yidai; Qingnian Yi Dai Shuangyuekan. Began in April 1979. Periodical. Chinese. bm. RMBY0.32. Hsin Hua Shu Tien / Shang-Hai Fa Hsing So, Shanghai, People's Republic of China. **LC** HQ799.C55; C5293. **DD** 305.2/35/0951.

US/0279-5310
CHRISTIAN FAMILY (BLOWNTVILLE, TEX.). **See** Religion and Theology.

US
CHRISTIAN HOME AND SCHOOL. **VFOAT** Christian Home & School. Vol. 51, No. 9 (May/June 1973)-. Periodical. English. mo. $11.95 (one year), $19.95 (two year) North America; $14.34 (one year), $23.94 (two year) other. Christian Home & School, PO Box 8709, Grand Rapids MI 49518. **Tel** (616)957-5070, FAX (616)957-1070. **ED** Gordon L Bordewyk. **Bk Rev. Ad Acc. Circ:** 50,000. ***Continues*** *Christian Home and School and Christian School Herald.*
Desc: To promote and explain the concept of Christian education while encouraging Christian parents in their daily walk as disciples of Jesus Christ and helping them to improve their parenting skills as a form of discipleship.

US/1065-7215
CHRISTIAN PARENTING TODAY. [Christ. parent. today]. (199?)-. Periodical. English. Six times a year (Jan., Mar., May, July, Sept., Nov.). $16.97 (one year), $24.97 (two years), $32.97 (three years). Good Family Magazines, PO Box 36630, Colorado Springs CO 80636. **Tel** (719)531-7776. **(Subscription address:** Kable Publishers Aide, 308 East Hitt Street, Subscription Department, Mt. Morris IL 61054-1473.**)** **DD** 649. ***Continues*** *Christian Parenting, 1040-8088.*
Ind/Abst Curr. Thoughts Trends.

US
CITIZEN. **See** Political Science.

US/1060-8222
CLEVELAND PARENT. [Clevel. parent]. (1991)-. Periodical. English. bm. $9.00. Media Associates, PO Box 770114, Lakewood OH 77107. **DD** 306.

SP
COLECCION JUVENIL MC. Spanish. mo. 3.300ptas Spain; 4.900ptas other. Ediciones Palabra SA, PO Castellana 210 2B, 28046 Madrid Spain. **Tel** 011 34 1 3507739, 011 34 1 3508311. **Bk Rev. Ad Acc. Circ:** 3,000 (ctrl).

UK/0591-017X
CONCERN LONDON. [Concern Lond.]. (1969)-. Periodical. English. qt. National Childrens Bureau Information Services, 8 Wakley Street, Islington, London EC1V 7QE England. **Tel** 011 44 71 2789441.

US/0892-2764
CONTEMPORARY FAMILY THERAPY. [Contemp. fam. ther.]. Vol. 8, No. 1 (Spring 1986)-. Periodical. English. Six times a year. £48.00 (individuals), £199.00 (institutions) UK & Europe; $255.00 US; $300.00 other. Human Sciences Press, PO Box 735, 233 Spring Street, New York NY 10013. **Tel** (212)620-8000, FAX (212)807-1047, telex 23421139. **(Subscription address:** Eurospan Ltd., Journals and Serials Division, 3 Henrietta Street, Covent Garden, London WC2E 8LU England.**)** **ED** William Nichols. **DD** 616. **NLM** W1; CO769MPEH. **CODEN** CFTHY. **[CCC].** available on microfilm and microfiche from University Microfilms International (UMI). Documents available from The Genuine Article, BIOSIS Document Express. ***Continues*** *International Journal of Family Therapy, 0148-8384.*
Desc: This comprehensive journal presents the latest developments in theory, research, and practice with an emphasis on examination of the family within the socioeconomic matrix of which it is an integral part. Demonstrating that the therapeutic relationship is most effective when family, individual, and society are seen as interacting systems, the journal examines essential factors which include family value systems, social class, and racial, religious, and ethnic backgrounds.
Ind/Abst Abstr. Res. Pastor. Care Couns. (19??-); Appl. Soc. Sci. Index Abstr.; Biol. Abstr. (1986-); Curr. Contents Soc. Behav. Sci.; Curr. Index J. Educ.; Multicult. Educ. Abstr.; Psychol. Abstr. (1979-); PsycINFO; PsycLit; Res. Alert [Full Cov.]; Sage Fam. Stud. Abstr.; Soc. Sci. Cit. Index [Full Cov.]; Soc. Work Abstr. [Select. Cov.]; Spec. Educ. Needs Abstr.

US/0147-1023
CONTRIBUTIONS IN FAMILY STUDIES. No. 1 (1977)-. Monographic series. English. ir. Price varies per volume. Greenwood Press Inc., PO Box 5007, Westport CT 06881-5007. **Tel** (203)226-3571, FAX (203)222-1502. **ED** Carol V. R. George. **LC** UNC.

CN/0384-5281
COUPLE ET FAMILLE. **Added/Corp** Mouvement Couple et Famille F.N.D. Foyers Notre-Dame Canadiens. Vol. 1, (Sept. 1968)-. Periodical. French. Four times a year (Feb., May, Aug., Nov.). $12.00. Revue Couple et Famille, 4101 Bordeaux, Montreal Quebec H2K 3Z4 Canada. **Tel** (514)526-5201. **Circ:** 3,000. ***Supersedes*** *Eternel Triangle.*

US/0092-3893
COUPLES (NEW YORK). (COUPLES.). Periodical. English. $1.00. NYM Corporation, 207 East 32nd Street, New York NY 10016. **LC** HQ1; .C68. **DD** 301.42/05.

CN/0225-2708
CRADLE CLUB MAGAZINE. [Cradle club mag.]. V. 1- Feb. 1980-. Periodical. English. qt. $1.50 per no. Girling Wade Marketing, Cradle Club Magazine, Suite 301/12 Sheppard Street, Toronto Ontario M5H 3A1 Canada. **DD** 649/.122/05.

US/0361-820X
CREEL FAMILY QUARTERLY. ***Ceased.*** Vol. 1 (Jan. 1976)-?. Periodical. English. qt. 1025 Middlecoff Drive, Akron OH 44313. **LC** CS71; .C912a. **DD** 929/.2/0973.

US/0092-6000
CURRENT LITERATURE IN FAMILY PLANNING. **See** Family and Marriage-Abstracting, Bibliographies and Statistics.

US/1040-2608
CURRENT PERSPECTIVES ON AGING AND THE LIFE CYCLE. [Curr. perspect. aging life cycle]. Vol. 1 (1985)-. Monographic series. English. an. $73.25. JAI Press Inc., 55 Old Post Road, Suite 2, PO Box 1678, Greenwich CT 06836-1678. **Tel** (203)661-7602, FAX (203)661-0792. **ED** Zena Smith Blau. **LC** HQ1060; .C87. **DD** 305.2/6. **NLM** W1; CU7995B. **CODEN** CALCEL. Documents available from BIOSIS Document Express.
Ind/Abst Biol. Abstr. (1985-); Linguist. Lang. Behav. Abstr.; Soc. Plann. Policy Dev. Abstr.; Sociol. Abstr.

US
DAD. (Jan. 1990)-. English. bm. $13.50. Creative Publishing Group Inc, 30 Moran Street, Newton NJ 07860. **Tel** (201)579-5900.
Desc: The magazine for today's involved father.

GW/0937-9614
DISKURS : STUDIEN ZU KINDHEIT, JUGEND, FAMILIE UND GESELLSCHAFT. **Added/Corp** Deutsches Jugendinstitut. (Summer 1990)-. Periodical. German. sa. DM54.00. Juventa Verlag GmbH, Ehretstrasse 3, D 69469 Weinheim Germany. **Tel** 011 49 6201 61035, FAX 011 49 6201 13135. **LC** HQ799.G5; D55.
Ind/Abst Linguist. Lang. Behav. Abstr.; Soc. Plann. Policy Dev. Abstr.; Sociol. Abstr.

AT
DIVORCES AUSTRALIA / AUSTRALIAN BUREAU OF STATISTICS. **See** Family and Marriage-Abstracting, Bibliographies and Statistics.

US
DOMESTIC VIOLENCE MONOGRAPH SERIES / NATIONAL CLEARINGHOUSE ON DOMESTIC VIOLENCE. No. 1 (May 1980)-. Periodical. English. mo. National Clearinghouse on Domestic Violence, PO Box 2309, Rockville MD 20852.

CN/0824-278X
DOUBLE FEATURE (LETHBRIDGE). (DOUBLE FEATURE : A PUBLICATION OF PARENTS OF MULTIPLE BIRTHS ASSOCIATIONS OF CANADA.). [Double feature]. Periodical. English. qt. 12.00Can$ Canada; $12.00 US. Parents of Multiple Births Associations of Canada, PO Box 2200, Lethbridge Alberta T1J 4K7 Canada. **Tel** (403)381-6868. **ED** Sheryl McInnes and Barbara Cooper. **DD** 155.4/44/05. Index available. **Bk Rev. Ad Acc. Circ:** 1,700.
Desc: Articles specific to parenting twins, triplets, and quads. Including resources and research.

KE/0419-7690
DRUM. EAST AFRICAN EDITION. (DRUM.). (19??)-. Periodical. English. Twelve times a year. Sh300.00 East Africa & Zambia; SH380.00 others in Africa; SH400.00 others. Drum Publications, PO Box 43372, Nairobi Kenya. **Tel** 011 254 2 714927. **ED** B. G. Bundeh. **LC** DT1; .D78. **DD** 960/.05. **Bk Rev. Ad Acc. Circ:** 60,000.
Desc: General interest family magazine.

UK/0300-4430
EARLY CHILD DEVELOPMENT AND CARE. (EARLY CHILD DEVELOPMENT AND CARE : ECDC.). [Early child dev. care]. **VFOAT** ECDC; E.C.D.C. (July 1971)-. Academic Scholarly Publication. English. Twelve times a year. $173.00 (academic institutions), $269.00 (corporate institutions). Gordon & Breach Science Publishers, PO Box 90, Reading RG1 8JL England. **Tel** 011 44 734 560080, FAX 011 44 734 568211. **(Subscription address:** International Publishers Distributor at one of the following addresses: 820 Town Center Drive, Langhorne, PA 19047; or PO Box 90, Reading Berkshire RG1 8JL UK; or Kent Ridge PO Box 1180, Singapore 9111, Republic of Singapore**)** **ED** Roy Evans. **LC** HQ767.8; .E23. **DD** 305.2/3/05. **NLM** W1 EA75. **CODEN** ECDCAD. **[CCC]. Bk Rev. Ad Acc.** available in microform. Documents available from BIOSIS Document Express.
Ind/Abst AGRICOLA; Appl. Soc. Sci. Index Abstr.; Biol. Abstr. (?-1984); Br. Educ. Index; Contents Pages Educ.; Curr. Index J. Educ.; Educ. Index; EMBASE; Multicult. Educ. Abstr.; Psychol. Abstr. (1973-); PsycINFO; PsycLit; Sociol. Educ. Abstr.

US/1065-2655
EASTSIDE PARENT. Vol. 1, No. 1 (April 1979)-. Periodical. English. Twelve times a year. $15.00. Seattles Child, 2107 Elliot Avenue, Suite 303, Seattle WA 98121. **Tel** (206)441-0191, FAX (206)441-4919. **ED** Ann Bergman. **Bk Rev. Ad Acc, Adv Mgr:** Alayne Sulkin. **Circ:** 20,000.
Desc: Parenting issues, books, video, software, nutrition, TV, and monthly calendar of events. Great for the parents with children aged 12 and under.

FR/0424-2238
ECOLE DES PARENTS, L'. [Ec. parents]. (1952)-. Periodical. French. mo (except Aug. and Oct.). 280.00F, 490.00F (combined with Groupe Familial) France; 360.00F, 590.00F (combined with Groupe Familial) other. Federation Nationale des Ecoles des Parents et des Educateurs, 5 Impasse Bon Secours, 75543 Paris Cedex 11 France. **Tel** 011 33 1 43480016, FAX 011 33 1 43488153. **UDC** 37. **Ad Acc.**

US
ELEGANT BRIDE. (Oct./Nov. 1990)-. Periodical. English. bm. $30.00 US; $34.00 Canada; $60.00 other. Pace Publications / North Carolina, 1301 Carolina Street, Greensboro NC 27401. **Tel** (919)378-6065, FAX (919)275-2864. **ED** Jackie Barret-Hirschhaut. **Ad Acc, Adv Mgr:** T.Reeves, **Tel** (919)378-6065. **Circ:** 200,000. ***Continues*** *Southern Bride, 0896-5838.*

GW
ELTERN. English. mo. $60.00. Gruner und Jahr Ag & Co, Abonnenten Service, D 20080 Hamburg Germany. **Tel** 011 49 40 37030.

CN/0823-6844
ETAIT DEUX FOIS, IL. (IL ETAIT DEUX FOIS ... : JOURNAL DES PARENTS DE JUMEAUX SAGAMIE.). [Il etait deux fois]. **Added/Corp** Association des Parents de Jumeaux Sagamie. **VFOAT** Journal des Parents de Jumeaux Sagamie. Vol. 1, No. 1 (Jan. 1981)-. Periodical. French. mo. Club Parents de Jumeaux, Segamie 120 rue Nicolet, Chicoutimi Nord Quebec G7J 1L8 Canada. **DD** 649/.144/06071414.

US/0046-9157
EXCEPTIONAL PARENT, THE. [Except. parent]. Vol. 1 (June/July 1971)-. Periodical. English. mo (12 issues). $24.00 US; $30.00 other. Exceptional Parent, 120 State Street, Hackensack NJ 07601. **Tel** (201)489-0871. **ED** Maxwell J. Schleifer and Stanley D. Klein. **DD** 649.1/5/105. **NLM** W1 EX198BP. **[CCC]. Bk Rev. Ad Acc. Circ:** 40,000 (ctrl). available on microfilm and microfiche from University Microfilms International (UMI); available on an online database (file 149/Full-Text) from DIALOG. Documents available from UMI Article Clearinghouse.
Desc: Practical information for parents and professionals concerned with the lives of children and young adults with disabilities.
Ind/Abst Acad. Abstr. Full Text Elite (Jan. 1992-); Acad. Abstr. (Jan. 1992-); Acad. Search (Jan. 1992-); Curr. Index J. Educ.; Educ. Index; Except. Child Educ. Resour.; Health Index (1989-); Health Period. Database [Full Txt.]; Health Ref. Cent. (Jan. 1989-) [Full Txt.] [Full Cov.]; Health Source (Jan. 1992-); INFO-SOUTH Abstr.; Mag. Search; Newsp. Period. Abstr. (1988-); Spec. Educ. Needs Abstr.; SportSearch.

US/1049-9717
FAMILIA DE HOY, LA. [Fam. hoy]. Vol. 1, No. 1 (March/April 1990)-. Periodical. Spanish (Spanish). bm. $11.95. Whittle Communications, 333 Main Avenue, Knoxville TN 37902. **Tel** (615)595-5000, FAX (615)595-5877. **DD** 051.

US/1077-3215
FAMILIA DE LA CIUDAD, LA. (199?)-. Periodical. English. Four times a year. $2.95. City Family Magazine, PO Box 748, Ansonia Station, New York NY 10023. **Tel** (212)362-3052.

US/0741-7403
FAMILIA LATINA. [Fam. lat.]. Dec. 1983-. Periodical. English (Spanish). mo. Familia Latina, PO Box 4958, Los Angeles CA 90051. **ED** Kirk Whisler. **Circ:** 400,000.

GW
FAMILIEN UND HAUSHALTE / HERAUSGEGEBEN VOM STATISTISCHEN LANDESAMT BADEN-WURTTEMBERG. Added/Corp Statistisches Landesamt Baden-Wurttemberg. (19??)-. German. Statistisches Landesamt Baden-Wuerttemberg, Postfach 10 60 33, 70049 Stuttgart Germany. **Tel** 011 49 771 6410, FAX 011 49 711 6412440. **LC** HA1320.B2; A32.

●US/1075-3184
FAMILIES IN CRISIS FUNDING REPORT. **See** Sociology-Social Services and Welfare.

MM
FAMILJA KANA. Maltese. Eleven times a year. +M2.50 (Malta); $40.00 (US). Cana Movement, Catholic Institute, Floriana Malta. **Tel** 238068, or 238942, FAX 250052. **ED** Rev Louis Camilleri, Paul A Attard. **Bk Rev**, (Qty: 11). **Ad Acc, Adv Mgr:** Crest Publicity, **Tel** 224876, 238467. **Circ:** 13,500 (ctrl).
Desc: The welfare of the Maltese family in its various aspects and situations. Articles on child rearing and education, youth, engaged and married couples, old people; psychological and physical development; counselling on personal, family, social, psychological, moral, medical and legal problems; news related to family affairs and interests.

FR
FAMILLE MAGAZINE. French. 130.00F France; 250.00F other. SPER (Societe de Publications et D'Editions Reunies), 21 rue du Faubourg St Antoine, 75550 Paris Cedex 11 France. **Tel** 011 33 1 40026262. **Ad Acc.** ctrl circ. ***Continues*** *Clair Foyer.*

CN/0318-0581
FAMILLE QUEBEC. Added/Corp Association des Parents Catholiques du Quebec. **VFOAT** Famille-Quebec. (1972)-. French. ir (10 issues per year). 8.00Can$. Association Parents Catholique Quebec, 3675 rue St Hubert, Montreal Quebec H2L 3Z9 Canada. **Tel** (514)526-0844. **DD** 301.42/3/09714. **Ad Acc. Pr Rev. Circ:** 18,000 (ctrl).
Desc: General information concerning the problems Catholic families are facing today.

US
FAMILY AFFAIRS. Added/Corp Institute for American Values. Vol. 1, No. 1 (Winter 1988)-. Periodical. English. qt. $40.00 (institutions), $25.00 (individuals), $50.00 (supporters), $100.00 (friends), $500.00 (donor), $1,000 (sponsors). Institute for American Values, 1841 Broadway Suite 211, New York NY 10023. **Tel** (212)246-3942, FAX (212)541-6665. **ED** Vesna Neskow. **Bk Rev**, (Qty: 1-4). **Ad Acc. Circ:** 12,000.
Desc: Review of research, public policy, and national debates on issues relating to family well-being. Newsletter presenting the activities of the Institute for American Values.

US/0272-992X
FAMILY (BOCA RATON). (FAMILY.). [Family]. V. 1, Article 1-. English. an. Social Issues Resources Series Inc, PO Box 2348, Boca Raton FL 33427. **Tel** (800)327-0513, (407)994-0079. **ED** Eleanor C Goldstein. **LC** HQ536; .F338. **DD** 306.8/5/05.
Desc: Interdisciplinary resource material consisting of reprinted articles from popular and professional journals, newspapers, magazines, and government documents.

US
FAMILY CHILD CARING. Newsletter. English. qt. Free. Redleaf Press, 450 North Syndicate Suite 5, St. Paul MN 55104. **Tel** (800)423-8309, (612)641-0305.
Desc: Information on family child care for associations and organizations who serve the field.

CN/0846-0353
FAMILY CONNECTION (REGINA). (FAMILY CONNECTION.). [Fam. connect.]. Vol. 1, No. 1 (Sept./Oct. 1990)-. Periodical. English. bm. $15.00. Family Connection, 2300 McAra Street, Regina, Saskatchewan S4N 2W3 Canada. **DD** 362.82/05.

CN/1195-9428
FAMILY CONNECTIONS. (19??)-. English. Four times a year. 15.00Can$ (individuals); 35.00Can$ (institutions). British Columbia Council for the Family, 2590 Granville Street, Suite 204, Vancouver British Columbia, V6H 3H1 Canada. **Tel** (604) 660-0675, FAX (604) 732-4813. **ED** Caroly Osher. Index available. cum. index. **Bk Rev**, (Qty: 10). **Ad Acc. Circ:** 3,000. ***Continues*** *Newsletter / British Columbia Council for the Family, 0706-9022.*
Desc: Concerned with family life education issues across the full spectrum of the family life cycle.

US/0747-024X
FAMILY GUIDE, THE. Vol. 1, No. 1 (Apr. 1984)-. Periodical. English. qt. $1.00. Woerner, PO Box 94368, Birmingham AL 35220-4368.

US/0892-2691
FAMILY IN AMERICA, THE. [Fam. Am.]. **Added/Corp** Rockford Institute. Vol. 1 No. 1 (Mar 1987)-. Academic Scholarly Publication. English. Twelve times a year. $24.00 (one year); $38.00 (two years); $54.00 (three years). The Rockford Institute, 934 North Main Street, Rockford IL 61103. **Tel** (815)964-5053, FAX (815)965-1826. **(Subscription address:** Kable Publishers Aide, 308 East Hitt Street, Subscription Department, Mt. Morris, IL 61054**) ED** Bryce J. Christensen. **DD** 173. cum. index. **Circ:** 3,000. ***Continues*** *Persuasion at Work, 0163-5387.*
Desc: Advocates family autonomy and reports on the latest scholarly research and statistical trends in family life.
Ind/Abst Curr. Thoughts Trends.

US/0732-0213
FAMILY-IN-TOUCH. VAT Family in Touch. Periodical. English. ir. Free to family members and allied families. Paul and Lora Marks, PO Box DD, Cabazon CA 92230.

CN/0703-7368
FAMILY INCOMES. CENSUS FAMILIES. **See** Family and Marriage-Abstracting, Bibliographies and Statistics.

US/1042-0878
FAMILY INFORMATION SERVICES. [Fam. inf. serv.]. (Jan. 1989)-. Periodical. English. mo. $159.00 (one focus issue), $179.00 (two focus issues), $199.00 (three focus issues). Family Information Services, 12565 Jefferson Street Northeast, Suite 102, Minneapolis MN 55434. **Tel** (800)852-8112, (612)755-6233, FAX (612)755-7355. **DD** 362.
Desc: Contains the latest demographics, changes and needs with our children youth and family TrendFacts. Keep up-to-date on current and future issues affecting children, youth and families.

●US/1066-4807
FAMILY JOURNAL (ALEXANDRIA, VA.), THE. (THE FAMILY JOURNAL : COUNSELING AND THERAPY FOR COUPLES AND FAMILIES.). [Fam. j.]. **Added/Corp** American Counseling Association. International Association of Marriage and Family Counselors. Vol. 1, No. 1 (Jan. 1993)-. Periodical. English. qt. $38.00. American Counseling Association, 5999 Stevenson Avenue, Alexandria VA 22304. **Tel** (703)823-9800, (800)347-6647, FAX (703)823-0252. **(Subscription address:** American Counseling Association, Subscription Office, PO Box 2513, Birmingham AL 35201-2513.**) LC** RC488.5; .F3252. **DD** 616.89/156/05.
Desc: Covers family and marital psychotherapy.

US/0272-2089
FAMILY JOURNAL (PUTNEY, VT.). (FAMILY JOURNAL.). [Fam. j.]. Vol. 1, No. 1 (Jan./Feb. 1981)-. English. bm. $9.00 US; $11.00 Canada. Family Journal, 58 Elliot Street, PO Box 815, Brattleboro VT 05301. **LC** HQ1; .F347. **DD** 306.8/5/05.

CN/0014-7303
FAMILY LIFE. Vol. 1 (Jan. 1968)-. Periodical. English (German). mo (11 issues per year). 9.00Can$ Canada; $9.00 US, Only Canadian subscribers need to add 7% G.S.T. Pathway Publishers, Route 4, Aylmer Ontario N5H 2R3 Canada. **Bk Rev**, (Qty: 11). **Circ:** 19,200. available on microfilm from Xerox; available on microfilm and microfiche from University Microfilms International (UMI).

UK
FAMILY LIFE. *Ceased.* (19??)-Vol. 14, No. 2 (July 1993). English. qt. Stanborough Press, Alma Park, Grantham Linc England. **ED** David Marshall. **Bk Rev. Ad Acc. Circ:** 25,000.
Desc: Features aimed at the whole family. Priority gives issues of current concern relating to the family.

US/0732-9962
FAMILY LIFE EDUCATOR. [Fam. life educ.]. **Added/Corp** National Family Life Education Network (U.S.). **VFOAT** F.L. Educator; FL Educator. Vol. 1, No. 1 (Fall 1982)-. Periodical. English. Four times a year (Feb., Apr., Sept., Nov.). $55.00 US; $60.00 Canada & Mexico; $70.00 others. ETR Associates Network Publications, PO Box 1830, Santa Cruz CA 95061. **Tel** (408)438-4060, FAX (408)438-4284. **ED** Kay Clark. **LC** HQ10; .F342. **DD** 306.8/5/0973. **Bk Rev. Circ:** 4,000.
Desc: Includes family life education articles, teaching ideas, book and film reviews, article abstracts and educator profiles.
Ind/Abst AGRICOLA [Full Cov.]; Curr. Lit. Fam. Plan.

US/1064-6167
FAMILY LIFE MATTERS. [Fam. life matters]. **Added/Corp** New Jersey Network for Family Life Education. Rutgers University. (19??)-. Periodical. English. Three times a year. $12.00 one year; $23.00 two years; $34.00 three years. Network for Family Life Education, Rutgers University, Building 4086, Livingston, New Brunswick NJ 08903. **Tel** (908)932-7929, FAX (609)683-9037. **DD** 613.

●US/1072-0332
FAMILY LIFE (NEW YORK, N.Y.). (FAMILY LIFE.). [Fam. life]. (Sept./Oct. 1993)-. Periodical. English. bm (6 issues). $12.97. Wenner Media Inc., 1290 Avenue of the Americas, 2nd Floor, New York NY 10104. **Tel** (212)484-1616, FAX (212)759-2966. **(Subscription address:** Neodata / Colorado, PO Box 2606, Boulder Boulder CO 80322.**) ED** Nancy Evans. **DD** 306. **Ad Acc.**
Desc: Designed for families with children aged three to twelve.
Ind/Abst Access (1993-).

US/0273-9054
FAMILY LIFE TODAY. *Ceased.* [Fam. life today]. Ceased (Oct. 1986). Periodical. English. ir. Moody Bible Institute, 820 North La Salle Boulevard, Chicago IL 60610. **Tel** (312)329-2164. **DD** 248. ***Absorbed*** *Creative Family Living, 0744-9690.*

CN/0319-5961
FAMILY LIFE (TORONTO). (FAMILY LIFE.). **VFOAT** J. F. & C. S. Family Life. Oct. 1973-. English. ir. Jewish Family and Child Service of Metropolitan Toronto, 150 Beverley Street, Toronto Ontario M5T 1Y6 Canada. **DD** 301.42/7/062713541. ***Supersedes*** *Family Matters, 0319-597X.*

AT/1030-2646
FAMILY MATTERS (MELBOURNE, VIC.). (FAMILY MATTERS : NEWSLETTER OF THE AUSTRALIAN INSTITUTE OF FAMILY STUDIES.). **Added/Corp** Australian Institute of Family Studies. **VFOAT** Newsletter of the Australian Institute of Family Studies; AIFS Newsletter; Family Matters, AIFS Newsletter. Issue No. 19 (Oct. 1987)-. Newsletter. English. Three times a year. 30.00Aus$ Australia; 45.00Aus$ other. Australian Institute of Family Studies, 300 Queen Street, Melbourne Victoria 3000 Australia. **Tel** 61 3 6086888, FAX 61 3 6000886. **ED** Meredith Michei. **LC** HQ706; .F36. **DD** 306.85/0994/05. **CODEN** FAMMEL. **Ad Acc, Adv Mgr:** Liz Sharmon. **Circ:** 4,000. ***Continues*** *Newsletter (Australian Institute of Family Studies).*
Ind/Abst Soc. Plann. Policy Dev. Abstr.

US/0014-7311
FAMILY PERSPECTIVE. Added/Corp Brigham Young University. Family and Demographic Research Institute. Brigham Young University. College of Family Living. Vol. 1 (Spring 1966)-. Periodical. English. Four times a year (Feb., May, Aug., Nov.). $30.00 (individuals); $60.00 (institutions). Family Perspective, 922 SWKT, Brigham Young University, Provo UT 84602. **Tel** (801)378-4452, FAX (801)378-5978. **ED** Stephen J. Bahr, Norene C. Peterson, and Pamela Toscano. **LC** HQ1; .F37. **DD** 301.42/1. **[CCC]. Pr Rev. Circ:** 700.
Desc: A multidisciplinary journal dedicated to the dissemination of information to those concerned about improving the quality of family life, emphasizing the practical application of religion, research, and theory.

US/0014-7354
FAMILY PLANNING PERSPECTIVES. See Birth Control.

US/0014-7370
FAMILY PROCESS. [Fam. proc.]. **Added/Corp** Mental Research Institute. Nathan W. Ackerman Family Institute. Palo Alto Medical Research Foundation. Mental Research Institute. Family Institute. Vol. 1 (March 1962)-. Periodical. English. qt. $68.00 (institutions), $39.00 (individuals) US; $72.00 (institutions), $42.00 (individuals) South America and Caribbean; $77.04 (institutions), $44.94 (individuals) Canada; $78.00 (institutions), $45.00 (individuals) other. Family Process Inc., 70 W Allendale Ave., Suite D, Allendale NJ 07401. **Tel** (201)236-8381. **(Subscription address:** Family Process Inc., Subscription Department, PO Box 6542, Syracuse NY 13217.**) ED** Carlos E Sluzki. **LC** RC488.5.A1; F3. **DD** 616.8/915. **NLM** W1 FA454E. **CODEN** FAPRA. **[CCC].** cum. index. **Bk Rev. Ad Acc. Pr Rev. Circ:** 10,000 (ctrl). available on microfilm and microfiche from University Microfilms International (UMI). Documents available from The Genuine Article.
Desc: A multidisciplinary journal of family study research and treatment.
Ind/Abst Abstr. Res. Pastor. Care Couns.; Appl. Soc. Sci. Index Abstr.; Commun. Abstr.; Curr. Contents Soc. Behav. Sci.; EMBASE; Health Plan. Adminis.; Index Med.; Middle East Abstr. Index; Psychol. Abstr. (1962-); PsycINFO; PsycLit; Res. Alert [Full Cov.]; Sage Fam. Stud. Abstr.; Soc. Plann. Policy Dev. Abstr.; Soc. Sci. Cit. Index [Full Cov.]; Soc. Work Abstr. [Select. Cov.]; Sociol. Abstr.; Stud. Women Abstr.

US/0197-6664
FAMILY RELATIONS. [Fam. relat.]. **Added/Corp** National Council on Family Relations. Vol. 29 (Jan. 1980)-. Periodical. English. qt. $85.00 US; add $7.00 postage other. National Council of Family Relations, 3989 Central Avenue Northeast, Suite 550, Minneapolis MN 55421. **Tel** (612)781-9331, FAX (612)781-9348. **ED** Timothy Brubaker. **LC** HQ1; .F36. **DD** 306.8/7/05. **NLM** W1 FA454H. **CODEN** FCOOBE. Index available. cum. index. **Bk Rev. Ad Acc. Pr Rev. Circ:** 4,200 (ctrl). available on microfilm and microfiche from University

Microfilms International (UMI). Documents available from The Genuine Article, UMI Article Clearinghouse. ***Continues*** *Family Coordinator, 0014-7214.*
Desc: A quarterly journal of information for educators and practicioners on marriage and family life issues and the application of theory to practice.
Ind/Abst Acad. Abstr. Full Text Elite (July 1990-); Acad. Abstr. (July 1990-); Acad. Ind. [Computer File] (1992-); Acad. Search (July 1990-); AGRICOLA [Full Cov.]; Book Rev. Index; Chicano Index; Crim. Penol. Police Sci. Abstr.; Curr. Contents Soc. Behav. Sci.; Curr. Index J. Educ.; Curr. Lit. Fam. Plan.; Expand. Acad. Index (1989-); High. Educ. Abstr. (1980-); Index Period. Lit. Aging; INFO-SOUTH Abstr.; Mag. Search; Med. Rev. Dig.; Middle East Abstr. Index; Multicult. Educ. Abstr.; Newsp. Period. Abstr. (1988-); Psychol. Abstr. (1980-); Res. Alert [Full Cov.]; Res. High. Educ. Abstr.; Sage Fam. Stud. Abstr.; Soc. Plann. Policy Dev. Abstr.; Soc. Sci. Source (Jul. 1990-); Soc. Sci. Cit. Index [Full Cov.]; Soc. Sci. Index; Soc. Sci. Index Fulltext (Oct. 1988-) [Full Txt.]; Soc. Work Abstr. [Select. Cov.]; Sociol. Abstr.; Sociol. Educ. Abstr.; Stud. Women Abstr.

US/1041-8660
FAMILY RESOURCE COALITION REPORT. [Fam. Resour. Coalit. rep.]. **Added/Corp** Family Resource Coalition (Chicago, Ill.). **VFOAT** FRC Report. (198u)-. Periodical. English. Three times a year (Jan., May., Sept.). comes with Family Resource Coalition membership. Family Resource Coalition, 200 South Michigan Avenue, Suite 1520, Chicago IL 60604. **Tel** (312)341-0900. **LC** HV699; .F319. **DD** 362.82/0973/05. ***Continues*** *Family Resource Coalition: [Newslatter], 1041-8652;* ***Absorbed*** *Prevention Report (Oakdale, Iowa), 1041-8679.*

US/0739-442X
FAMILY (ROCHESTER, N.Y.), THE. ***Ceased.*** (THE FAMILY.). [Family]. **Added/Corp** Center for Family Learning (New Rochelle, N.Y.) Georgetown U. Family Center. Vol. 1 (Fall 1973)-Vol. 13, No. 2 (Nov. 1986). Periodical. English. sa. Center for Family Learning, 16 Rye Ridge Plaza, Rye NY 10580.

●US/1070-0609
FAMILY SYSTEMS. (FAMILY SYSTEMS : A JOURNAL OF NATURAL SYTEMS THINKING IN PSYCHIATRY AND THE SCIENCES.). **Added/Corp** Georgetown Family Center. (1994)-. Periodical. English. sa. $20.00. Georgetown Family Center, 4400 MacArthur Boulevard, Suite 102, Washington DC 20007. **Tel** (202)965-0730.

US/0739-0882
FAMILY THERAPY NETWORKER, THE. [Fam. ther. newsl.]. **Added/Corp** Family Therapy Network. **VFOAT** Networker. Vol. 6, No. 1 (Jan./Feb. 1982)-. Periodical. English. bm. $20.00 (1 year), $38.00 (2 year) individuals US; $26.00 (1 year), $50.00 (2 year) institutions US; $26.00 (1 year), $50.00 (2 year) individuals other; $32.00 (1 year), $62.00 (2 year) institutions other. Family Therapy Networker, 7703 13th Street NW, Washington DC 20012. **Tel** (202)829-2452. **(Subscription address:** Family Therapy Networker, 8528 Bradford Road, Silver Springs MD 20901.**) LC** RC488.5; .F347. **DD** 616.89/156/05. **NLM** W1; FA454NC. ***Continues*** *Family Therapy Network Newsletter.*
Ind/Abst PsycINFO (?-?); Soc. Work Abstr. [Select. Cov.].

US/0277-6464
FAMILY THERAPY NEWS. See Psychology.

US/1056-9243
FAMILY TIMES (EAU CLAIRE, WIS.). (FAMILY TIMES : THE NEWSPAPER FOR CHIPPEWA VALLEY PARENTS.). (1990)-. Periodical. English. qt. $6.00. Family Times, PO Box 932, Eau Claire WI 54702.

CN/1187-5712
FAMILY TO FAMILY. [Fam. fam.]. **Added/Corp** Catholic Church. Archdiocese of Edmonton. Catholic Pastoral Centre. Vol. 1, No. 3 (Fall 1991)-. Periodical. English. bm. Free. Family Enrichment Centre, Catholic Pastoral Centre, Archdiocese of Edmonton, 8421-100 Avenue, Edmonton Alberta T6A 0L1. **DD** 362.82. ***Continues*** *Family Enrichment Notes., 1187-5704.*

US/1056-6333
FAMILYFUN (NEW YORK, N.Y.). (FAMILYFUN.). [Familyfun]. **VFOAT** Family Fun. (Summer 1991)-. Periodical. English. Ten times a year. $9.95. FamilyFun, c/o Beth Ifcher, 114 5th Avenue, 15th Floor, New York NY 10011. **Tel** (212) 633-3628. **(Subscription address:** CDS / SIFD Agency Control, 1901 Bell Avenue, Des Moines IA 50315.**) DD** 051. **Ad Acc. Circ:** 600,000.
Desc: Covers all the fun things you can do as a family: travelling, celebrations, arts & crafts, family computing, & weekends.

US/0887-1310
FLORIDA PARENT. Vol. 1, No. 1 (Spring 1986)-. Periodical. English. Six times a year. Florida Parent, PO Box 2321, Boca Raton FL 33427-2321. ***Continues*** *Guide to Child Care & Education (Palm Beach County Edition), 0883-878X.*

US/0894-3346
FOCUS ON THE FAMILY (ARCADIA, CALIF. 1982). (FOCUS ON THE FAMILY.). [Focus fam.]. **Added/Corp** Focus on the Family (Organization). (1982)-. Periodical. English. mo. Free on request. Focus on the Family, Colorado Springs CO 80995. **Tel** (800)232-6459. **ED** Dr. James Dobson. **DD** 248. ***Continues*** *Focus on the Family Newsletter.*
Desc: A Christian journal focusing on family issues and values.
Ind/Abst Christ. Period. Index (19??-); Curr. Thoughts Trends.

US/0895-1136
FOCUS ON THE FAMILY CLUBHOUSE. See Children and Youth Interests.

AU
FOHN. Added/Corp Gruppe Fohn (Austria). (19??)-. Periodical. German. ir. S30.00 (single issue). Gruppe Fohn, c/o Adolf Pichler Platz 6, 6020 Innsbruck, Austria. **LC** HQ799.G53; F63. **DD** 305.2/35/09431.

NO/0332-5415
FOKUS PA FAMILIEN. [Fokus fam.]. Vol. 1 (1973)-. Periodical. Norwegian (summaries and/or abstracts in English). qt. Kr415.00, $73.00. Scandinavian University Press, PO Box 2959 Toeyen, N 0608 Oslo 6 Norway. **Tel** 011 47 2 2575400, FAX 011 47 2 2575353, telex 71896 UROR N. **(Subscription address:** Scandinavian University Press, 200 Meacham Ave., Elmont NY 11003.**) ED** Sissel Gran and Bjoern Gunnar Saltnes. **DD** 158.24. **[CCC]. Bk Rev. Ad Acc. Circ:** 2,500.
Desc: The main family therapy journal in Scandinavia.

SP
FOLLETOS MUNDO CRISTIANO. (19??)-. Spanish. Twenty-one times a year. 3800ptas Spain and Portugal; 4800ptas other. Ediciones Palabra SA, PO Castellana 210 2B, 28046 Madrid Spain. **Tel** 011 34 1 3507739, 011 34 1 3508311. **UDC** 24. **Bk Rev. Ad Acc. Circ:** 4,000 (ctrl).

US/0277-612X
FOR PARENTS. ***Ceased.*** (1977)-Ceased (June 1991). Periodical. English. bm. Interpersonal Communication, S-7052 West Lane, Eden NY 14057. **Tel** (716)992-3316. **ED** Carolyn Shadle. **Bk Rev. Circ:** 4,000 (ctrl). ***Continues*** *Bows & Arrows.*
Desc: Goldmine of ideas, inspiration and resources to enhance parent-child communication and the development of strong values.

●US/1064-7996
FOR THE BRIDE BY DEMETRIOS (UNITED KINGDOM ED.). (FOR THE BRIDE BY DEMETRIOS.). (1993)-. Periodical. English. qt. $4.50 (single issue). For the Bride by Demetrios, 222 West 37th Street, New York NY 10018.

CN/0046-4767
FOSTER PARENT. ***Title Change.*** **VFOAT** Parent Nourricier. Vol. 3 (March 1968)-(19??). Periodical. English (French). qt. Children's Aid Society of Ottawa-Carleton, 1370 Bank Street, Ottawa Ontario K1H 7Y3 Canada. **DD** 362.7/33/05. ***Continues*** *Foster News, 0382-7402.* ***Continued by*** *Foster Parent Association Newsletter, 0382-7399.*

CN/0701-3418
FOSTERLETTER. (THE FOSTERLETTER.). 1964. English. mo. Free. Foster Letter, 1627 Fort Street, Department of Human Resources, Victoria British Columbia V8R 1H8 Canada. **Tel** (604)595-7559. **Bk Rev. Circ:** 600 (ctrl).
Desc: Newsletter for local foster parents and other local resources for children. Contains articles and notices of meetings and upcoming events.

US/0741-3505
FROM THE STATE CAPITALS. FAMILY RELATIONS. [From state cap., Fam. relat.]. **VFOAT** Family Relations. (Jan. 16, 1984)-. Periodical. English. wk. $211.50 (public, libraries, & institutions); $235.00 (others). Wakeman Walworth Inc., 300 North Washington Street #204, Alexandria VA 22314. **Tel** (703)549-8606. **ED** Emily Novick. **DD** 351. **[CCC].** ***Continues*** *From the State Capitals. Juvenile Delinquency and Family Relations, 0016-1764.*
Desc: Covers juvenile justice, marital rights, child support, adoption, abuse centers, counseling and shelter programs.

US/1055-2367
FULL-TIME DADS. [Full-time dads]. **VFOAT** Full Time Dads. Issue No. 1 (Apr./May 1991)-. Periodical. English. bm. $18.00. Chris Stafford, PO Box 12773, St. Paul MN 55112-0773. **DD** 306.

II/0252-1873
FUTURE (NEW DELHI, INDIA). (FUTURE.). **Added/Corp** UNICEF. Regional Office for South Central Asia. (4th Quarter 1981)-. Periodical. English. qt. $15.00. UNICEF / India, 73 Lodi Estate, New Delhi 110003 India. **Tel** 690401. **(Subscription address:** Prints India, 11 Darya Ganj, New Delhi, 110002 India, (Phone: 011 91 11 3268645)**) ED** Thomas P Matthai. **LC** HQ767.8; .F87. **DD** 305.2/3/091724. **NLM** W1 FU607. Index available. cum. index. **Bk Rev. Ad Acc. Circ:** 10,000 (ctrl).
Desc: Analysis of efforts for the neediest, mainly in South Asia; covers children, education, communication, nutrition, health care, sanitation, employment, income, community self-reliance, participation and freedom.

US/0891-1657
GETTING MARRIED. (19??)-. Periodical. English. Twice a year (July & Dec.). $4.50. Getting Married Inc., A Planning, PO Box 1424, Boston MA 02117. **Tel** (617)739-3369. **DD** 392. **Ad Acc. Circ:** 10,000 (ctrl).
Desc: A planning guide for brides and grooms to be.

NE/0921-9684
GEZIN LISSE. ***Ceased.*** (GEZIN). [GezinLisse]. (1989)-Vol. 5 (1993). Periodical. Dutch. qt. Swets & Zeitlinger BV, Heereweg 347B PO Box 825, 2160 SZ Lisse Holland. **Tel** 011 31 2521 35111, FAX 02521-15888, telex 41325. **ED** Prof J R M Gerris. **UDC** 314.6.

BE
GEZINSBELEID IN VLAANDEREN. (19??)-. Dutch. qt. 500.00F. Bond Van Grote Jonge Gezinnen, Troonstraat 125, B-1050 Brussels Belgium. **Tel** 02 5078871, FAX 02 5119065. **ED** Van Jonge Gezinnen, Bond Van Grote, Luk de Smet. Index available. cum. index. **Circ:** 6,000 (ctrl).

US/0733-4478
GOOD HOUSEKEEPING'S MOMS WHO WORK. VFOAT Moms Who Work. May/June 1982-. Periodical. English. $2.50 single issue. Single Copy Sales Department, 250 West 55th Street, New York NY 10019. **LC** HQ759; .G587. **DD** 640.

●US/1056-4551
GROOM'S GUIDE, THE. See Men's Interests.

FR/0180-9857
GROUPE FAMILIAL, LE. [Groupe fam.]. (1958)-. Periodical. French. qt. 270.00F, 490.00 (combined with L'Ecole des Parents) France; 290.00F, 590.00 (combined with L'Ecole des Parents) other. Federation Nationale des Ecoles des Parents et des Educateurs, 5 Impasse Bon Secours, 75543 Paris Cedex 11 France. **Tel** 011 33 1 43480016, FAX 011 33 1 43488153. **UDC** 37. ctrl circ.

CN/1183-0662
GUIDE BOUNTY DES SOINS AU NOURRISSON. [Guide Bounty soins nourrisson]. (1991)-. French. Limited free distribution. Bounty Family Publications, Unite 2, 746 Ave Warden, Scarborough, Ontario M1L 4A2. **DD** 649.

US
GUIDE TO PARENTERAL ADMIXTURES. (19??)-. English. Four times a year. $95.00 US & Canada; $125.00 others. Pace Marq Inc., 28 Geary Street, Suite 555, San Francisco CA 94108. **Tel** (415)989-4996. **(Subscription address:** King Guide, 11701 Borman Drive, Suite 100, St. Louis MO 63146.**)**

US/1049-2402
HAVING A BABY. [Having baby]. **VFOAT** Child Magazine's Guide to Having a Baby. Vol. 1, No. 1 (1990)-. Periodical. English. an. New York Times Company Magazine Group, Child Magazine Division, 110 5th Avenue, New York NY 10011. **DD** 618.

CN/1180-3126
HEALTH REPORTS. SUPPLEMENT. DIVORCES. See Family and Marriage-Abstracting, Bibliographies and Statistics.

US/1062-4236
HEALTHY KIDS. 4-10 YEARS. See Health and Personal Fitness.

●US/1063-0945
HEALTHY KIDS. BIRTH-3. See Health and Personal Fitness.

●US/1065-6405
HELPING CHILDREN LEARN. See Education.

US/0899-2673
HLI REPORT. [HLI rep.]. **VFOAT** HLI Reports. **VAT** Human Life International Report. Vol. 1, No. 4 (Sept. 1983)-. Periodical. English (French and Spanish). mo. $15.00 US; $20.00 Canada; $25.00 other. Human Life International, 7845-E Airpark Road, Gaithersburg MD 20879. **Tel** (301)670-7884, FAX (301)869-7363. **ED** William Marshner. **DD** 363. **Bk Rev. Circ:** 200,000 (ctrl). ***Continues*** *Loveline.*
Desc: International research, educational and service programs offering positive, pro-life/family alternatives described with emphasis on christian sexuality, NFP, and abortion.

US/0018-4071
HOME LIFE (NASHVILLE). See Religion and Theology-Protestantism.

US
HOUSEHOLD AND FAMILY CHARACTERISTICS. **Added/Corp** United States. Bureau of the Census. (April 1953)-. English. an. $14.00. Bernan Associates, 4611-F Assembly Drive, Lanham MD 20706-4391. **Tel** (301)459-7666, (800)274-4447 US, (800)233-0504 CANADA, FAX (301)459-0056, telex 7108260418.

SA
HUWELIKE EN EGSKEIDINGS / REPUBLIEK VAN SUID-AFRIKA, SENTRALE STATISTIEKDIENS / MARRIAGES AND DIVORCES / REPUBLIC OF SOUTH AFRICA, CENTRAL STATISTICAL SERVICE. **See** Population Studies.

US/1050-7949
IN BETWEEN YEARS, THE. [In between years]. **VFOAT** In-Between Years. Vol. 1, No. 1 (Apr. 1990)-. Periodical. English. qt. $19.95 (individual); $50.00 (school). Zeeter Inc, PO Box 575, Orono ME 04473. **Tel** (207)866-3187. **ED** Edward Brazee and Constance Carter. **DD** 155. **Circ:** 800.
Desc: Information for parents of 10-14 year olds.

●CN/1193-1833
INFO-PARENTS. [Info-parents]. **Added/Corp** Bourses Universitaires du Canada. Fondation Internationale des Bourses. (1992)-. Periodical. French. Limited free distribution. Bourses Universitaires du Canada, Suite 1500, 50 Ch Burmanthorpe Ouest, Mississauga Ontario L5B 4A5 Canada. **DD** 649. ***Continues*** *Rapport aux Parents., 1183-8868.*

CN/0711-2130
INSEPARABLES. (LES INSEPARABLES : JOURNAL OFFICIEL, CLUB DE PARENTS DE JUMEAUX LAVAL-LAURENTIDES INC.). [Inseparables]. Periodical. French. ir. Free to members. Club de Parents de Jumeaux Laval-Laurentides Inc, 153 Avenue 57 East, Saint-Eustache Quebec J7P 3L5 Canada. **DD** 649/.144/060714271.

US/0190-3187
INTERNATIONAL FAMILY PLANNING PERSPECTIVES. [Int. fam. plann. perspect.]. **Added/Corp** Alan Guttmacher Institute. Planned Parenthood Federation of America. Family Planning International Assistance Division. United States. Agency for International Development. (Mar. 1979)-. Periodical. English (summaries and/or abstracts in Spanish and French). Four times a year (Mar., June, Sept., Dec.). $36.00 (institutions), $26.00 (individuals) US; $46.00 other developed countries; Free to developing countries. Alan Guttmacher Institute, 120 Wall Street, New York NY 10005. **Tel** (212)248-1111, FAX (212)248-1951. **ED** Deirdre Wulf. **LC** HQ763; .I624. **DD** 363.9/6/05. **NLM** W1 IN748MAT. Index available (back issues, $10.00). **Bk Rev. Pr Rev. Circ:** 30,000. available on microfilm and microfiche from University Microfilms International (UMI). ***Continues*** *International Family Planning Perspectives and Digest, 0162-2749.*
Desc: Articles dealing with fertility, family planning, maternal and infant health, and population policy, with an emphasis on Africa, Latin America, the Caribbean and Asia.
Ind/Abst Biol. Dig.; Curr. Lit. Fam. Plan.; EMBASE; PAIS Int. Print; Popul. Index; Rural Dev. Abstr.; Soc. Plann. Policy Dev. Abstr.; Stud. Women Abstr.; Trop. Dis. Bull.

UK/0267-3843
INTERNATIONAL JOURNAL OF ADOLESCENCE AND YOUTH. Vol. 1, No. 1 (1987)-. Periodical. English. qt. £59.00 (add £20.00 airmail) UK; $109.00 (add $40.00 airmail) US. AB Academic Publishers, PO Box 42 Bicester, OXON OX6 7NW England. **Tel** 011 44 869 320949. **ED** Roy Evans. **NLM** W1; IN7652SE. cum. index. **Bk Rev. Ad Acc.**
Desc: Multidisciplinary international journal relative to problems and policies in all areas including psychology, health, education, social policy, etc.
Ind/Abst Appl. Soc. Sci. Index Abstr.; Br. Educ. Index; Multicult. Educ. Abstr.; Psychol. Abstr. (1987-); PsycINFO; PsycLit; Soc. Plann. Policy Dev. Abstr.; Sociol. Educ. Abstr.; Spec. Educ. Needs Abstr.

II/0020-7667
INTERNATIONAL JOURNAL OF SOCIOLOGY OF THE FAMILY. [Int. j. sociol. fam.]. (March 1971)-. Periodical. English. sa. $70.00. Lucknow Publishing House, 37 Cantonment Road, Lucknow, India. **(Subscription address:** Prints India, 11 Darya Ganj, New Delhi 110002 India.**) ED** Mansingh Dass. **LC** HQ1; .I53. **DD** 301.42/05. **NLM** W1 IN789H. available on microfilm and microfiche from University Microfilms International (UMI).
Ind/Abst AGRICOLA; Appl. Soc. Sci. Index Abstr.; Popul. Index; Soc. Plann. Policy Dev. Abstr.; Sociol. Abstr. [Full Cov.].

UK/0140-668X
INTERNATIONAL MONOGRAPH SERIES ON EARLY CHILD CARE. (INTERNATIONAL MONOGRAPH SERIES ON EARLY CHILD CARE / PREPARED BY THE INTERNATIONAL STUDY GROUP FOR EARLY CHILD CARE.). [Int. monogr. ser. early child care]. **Added/Corp** International Study Group for Early Child Care. **VFOAT** International Monographs on Early Child Care. (1972)-. Monographic series. English. ir. Price varies per volume. Gordon & Breach Science Publishers, PO Box 90, Reading RG1 8JL England. **Tel** 011 44 734 560080, FAX 011 44 734 568211. **(Subscription address:** International Publishers Distributor at one of the following addresses: 820 Town Center Drive, Langhorne, PA 19047; or PO Box 90, Reading Berkshire RG1 8JL UK; or Kent Ridge PO Box 1180, Singapore 9111, Republic of Singapore**) LC** UNC.

US/1047-5370
INTERRACE (SCHENECTADY, N.Y.). **See** Ethnic Interests.

US/0094-7814
INVENTORY OF MARRIAGE AND FAMILY LITERATURE. **Added/Corp** University of Minnesota. Dept. of Family Social Science. Vol. 3 (1974)-. English. an (March). $144.95 institutions and non-members; $89.95 NCFR members. National Council of Family Relations, 3989 Central Avenue Northeast, Suite 550, Minneapolis MN 55421. **Tel** (612)781-9331, FAX (612)781-9348. **ED** John Touliatis. **LC** Z7164.M2; I57; HQ728. **DD** 016.30142. **NLM** Z 7164.M2 I61. ***Continues*** *International Bibliography of Research in Marriage and the Family, 0095-4551.*
Desc: A comprehensive bibliographic listing of literature pertaining to the field of family social science.

UK/0019-0357
IPPF MEDICAL BULLETIN (ENGLISH EDITION). **See** Birth Control.

CN/0838-5505
ISLAND PARENT MAGAZINE. [Isl. parent mag.]. (July 1988)-. Periodical. English. Eleven times a year. 19.26Can$ Canada; 25.00Can$ other. Krayenhoff-Holland Enterprises Ltd, 941 Kings Road, Victoria British Columbia V8P 5L5 Canada. **Tel** (604)388-6905. **ED** Jim Holland. **DD** 649/.1/05. **Bk Rev. Ad Acc. Circ:** 26,000.
Desc: Information for parents on education, recreation, culture, products and services, plus articles on all aspects of parenting.

GW
JAHRBUCH - JUNGE UNION DEUTSCHLANDS. **Main/Corp** Junge Union Deutschlands. German. Junge Union Deutschlands, Annaberger Str 283, Bonn-Bad Godesberg Germany. **LC** HQ799.G5; J863A.

UA
JAMAAT SAYYIDAT MISR : KITAB SANAWI. **Main/Corp** Jamaat Sayyidat Misr. Arabic (English, French and German). an. Jamaat Sayyidat Misr, Al-Idarah 4 Shari Al-Awhadi Manshiyat Al-Bakri, Al-Qahirah Egypt. **LC** HQ1793; .A25A.

US/0160-7804
JOURNAL FOR GROWTH IN MARRIAGE, THE. **VFOAT** Growth in Marriage. Vol. 1, No. 1 (Oct. 1973)-. Periodical. English. sa. $6.00 individual, $8.00 institutions. Association for Professional for Growth in Marriage, Box 694, Paoli PA 19301. **Tel** (215)353-3555. **LC** HQ734; .J74. **DD** 306.8.

●US/1062-1024
JOURNAL OF CHILD AND FAMILY STUDIES. [J. child fam. stud.]. Vol. 1, No. 1 (Mar. 1992)-. Periodical. English. qt. $120.00 US; $140.00 other. Human Sciences Press, PO Box 735, 233 Spring Street, New York NY 10013. **Tel** (212)620-8000, FAX (212)807-1047, telex 23421139. **(Subscription address:** Eurospan Ltd., Journals and Serials Division, 3 Henrietta Street, Covent Garden, London WC2E 8LU England.**) ED** Nirbhay Singh. **LC** RJ499.A1; J595. **DD** 618.92/89. **NLM** W1; JO583KH. **CODEN** JCFSES. **[CCC].**
Desc: The international forum for topical issues pertaining to the mental well-being of children, adolescents, and their families. The journal translates the latest research developments into practical applications for clinicians and health care practicioners by addressing all facets of emotional disorders, including issues associated with identification, diagnosis, treatment, rehabilitation, and prevention.
Ind/Abst Sage Fam. Stud. Abstr.

CN/0047-2328
JOURNAL OF COMPARATIVE FAMILY STUDIES. [J. comp. fam. stud.]. Vol. 1, (Autumn 1970)-. Academic Scholarly Publication. English. Three times a year. $60.00 (institutions), $45.00 (individuals). University of Calgary Press, 2500 University Drive Northwest, Calgary Alberta T2N 1N4 Canada. **Tel** (403)220-7578. **ED** George Kurian. **LC** HQ1; .J44. **DD** 301.42/05. **NLM** W1 JO594H. **CODEN** JCFSAO. **[CCC]. Bk Rev. Ad Acc. Pr Rev. Circ:** 800. available on microfilm and microfiche from University Microfilms International (UMI). Documents available from The Genuine Article, UMI Article Clearinghouse.
Desc: Provides a unique cross cultural perspective on the study of the family. Its purpose is to promote the understanding of the interaction between different cultures and life styles.
Ind/Abst Acad. Abstr. Full Text Elite (Jan. 1992-); Acad. Abstr. (Jan. 1992-); Acad. Search (Jan. 1992-); AGRICOLA [Full Cov.]; Anthropol. Lit.; Appl. Soc. Sci. Index Abstr.; Curr. Contents Soc. Behav. Sci.; EMBASE; Expand. Acad. Index (1989-); Hum. Resour. Abstr. (?-?); INFO-SOUTH Abstr.; Int. Bibliogr. Sociol.; Int. Dev. Abstr. (?-?); Leis. Recreat. Tour. Abstr.; Mag. Search; Middle East Abstr. Index; Multicult. Educ. Abstr.; Newsp. Period. Abstr. (1991-); Popul. Index; Psychol. Abstr. (1971-); PsycINFO; PsycLit; Res. Alert [Full Cov.]; Rural Dev. Abstr.; Sage Fam. Stud. Abstr.; Sage Race Relat. Abstr.; Soc. Plann. Policy Dev. Abstr.; Soc. Sci. Source (Jan. 1992-); Soc. Sci. Cit. Index [Full Cov.]; Soc. Sci. Index Fulltext (Spring 1989-) [Full Txt.]; Sociol. Abstr. [Full Cov.]; Sociol. Educ. Abstr.; Spec. Educ. Needs Abstr.; Stud. Women Abstr.; World Agric. Econ.

US/0897-4446
JOURNAL OF COUPLES THERAPY. [J. couples ther.]. Vol. 1, No. 1 (1989)-. Periodical. English. qt. $95.00 US; $133.00 other. The Haworth Press Inc, 10 Alice Street, Binghamton NY 13904-1580. **Tel** (607)722-5857, (800)3-HAWORTH, FAX (607)722-1424. **ED** Jo Brothers (editor's address: 3500 St Charles Avenue, New Orleans, LA 70115). **LC** RC488.5; .J675. **DD** 616.89/156. **CODEN** JCTHEV. **Bk Rev. Ad Acc. Pr Rev. Acid Free. Circ:** 236. available on microfilm and microfiche from University Microfilms International (UMI). Documents available from Haworth Document Delivery Service.
Desc: Devoted entirely to the study of human bonding and intimacy for couples therapists and all marriage and family/clinical practitioners who deal with couples and intimacy/bonding issues as a focus in their practice.
Ind/Abst Soc. Plann. Policy Dev. Abstr.; Soc. Work Abstr. [Select. Cov.]; Stud. Women Abstr.

US/1050-2556
JOURNAL OF DIVORCE & REMARRIAGE. **VFOAT** Journal of Divorce and Remarriage. Vol. 14, No. 1 (1990)-. Periodical. English. qt. $225.00 US; $315.00 other. The Haworth Press Inc, 10 Alice Street, Binghamton NY 13904-1580. **Tel** (607)722-5857, (800)3-HAWORTH, FAX (607)722-1424. **ED** Craig A. Everett (editor's address: Arizona Institute of Family Therapy, Sonora Desert Professional Boulevard, Suite 150, 6060 North Fountain Plaza Drive, Tucson, AZ 95704). **LC** K10; .O8595. **DD** 346.7301/66/05; 347.30616605. **CODEN** JDREEJ. **Bk Rev. Ad Acc. Pr Rev. Acid Free. Circ:** 721. available on microfilm and microfiche from University Microfilms International (UMI). Documents available from The Genuine Article, UMI Article Clearinghouse, Haworth Document Delivery Service. ***Continues*** *Journal of Divorce, 0147-4022.*
Desc: Clinical studies and research in family therapy, family mediation, family studies and family law. This landmark journal will enrich the clinical skills of all marriage and family specialists and enhance the therapeutic and legal resources for couples and families needing specialized aid with divorce issues. This interdisciplinary resource covers all aspects of divorce, including predivorce marital and family treatment, marital separation and dissolution, children's responses to divorce and separation, single parenting, remarriage, and step families.
Ind/Abst Abstr. Res. Pastor. Care Couns. (19??-); Curr. Contents Soc. Behav. Sci.; Educ. Adm. Abstr.; Expand. Acad. Index (1992-); Newsp. Period. Abstr. (1989-); Psychol. Abstr. (1977-); PsycINFO; PsycLit; Res. Alert [Full Cov.]; Sage Fam. Stud. Abstr.; Soc. Plann. Policy Dev. Abstr.; Soc. Sci. Cit. Index [Full Cov.]; Soc. Work Abstr. [Select. Cov.].

US
JOURNAL OF FAMILY AND CULTURE, THE. **See** Sociology.

●US/1058-0476
JOURNAL OF FAMILY AND ECONOMIC ISSUES. [J. fam. econ. issues]. Vol. 13, No. 1 (Spring 1992)-. Periodical. English. qt. $195.00 US; $230.00 other. Human Sciences Press, PO Box 735, 233 Spring Street, New York NY 10013. **Tel** (212)620-8000, FAX (212)807-1047, telex 23421139. **(Subscription address:** Eurospan Ltd., Journals and Serials Division, 3 Henrietta Street, Covent Garden, London WC2E 8LU England.**) ED** Charles Hennon. **LC** HQ1; .A47. **DD** 301. **NLM** W1; JO6443G. **CODEN** JFEIEE. **[CCC]. *Continues*** *Lifestyles (New York, N.Y.), 0882-3391.*
Desc: Devoted exclusively to the interface of the family and its economic environment. The journal brings together work from a variety of disciplines that enhance understanding of family consumer behavior, household division of labor and productivity, the relationship between economic and non-economic decisions, interrelationships between work life and family life and other related topics.
Ind/Abst Curr. Contents Soc. Behav. Sci. (1992-); Educ. Index (1992-); Except. Child Educ. Resour. (1992-19??); Psychol. Abstr. (1992-); Sage Fam. Stud. Abstr. (1992-?).

US/0363-1990
JOURNAL OF FAMILY HISTORY. [J. fam. hist.]. **Added/Corp** National Council on Family Relations. **VFOAT** Family History. Vol. 1 (Autumn 1976)-. Academic Scholarly Publication. English. qt. $160.00 (institutions),

$60.00 (individuals), US; $180.00 (institutions), $80.00 (individuals) (surface mail), $200.00 (institutions), $100.00 (individuals) (air mail) other. JAI Press Inc., 55 Old Post Road, Suite 2, PO Box 1678, Greenwich CT 06836-1678. **Tel** (203)661-7602, FAX (203)661-0792. **ED** Tamara K. Hareven and Andrejs Plakans. **LC** HQ503; .J67. **DD** 301.42/05. **NLM** W1 JO6443R. **[CCC]. Pr Rev.** available on microfilm and microfiche from University Microfilms International (UMI). Documents available from The Genuine Article, UMI Article Clearinghouse. ***Supersedes*** *Family in Historical Perspective, 0360-3598.*
Desc: Publishes results of scholarly research concerning the family as an historical social form. Contributors have come from the disciplines of history, demography, anthropology, and sociology as well as from the liberal arts and the humanities.
Ind/Abst Acad. Search (Jan. 1993-); Am. Hist. Life (1976-); Am. Bibliogr. Slavic East Europ. Stud.; BHA : Biblio. Hist. Art; Curr. Contents Soc. Behav. Sci.; Expand. Acad. Index (1989-); Geogr. Abstr. Human Geogr.; Hist. Source (July 1993-); Humanit. Index; Humanit. Source (Jul. 1993-); INFO-SOUTH Abstr.; Int. Bibliogr. Sociol.; Mag. Search; Middle East Abstr. Index; Multicult. Educ. Abstr.; Newsp. Period. Abstr. (1991-); Popul. Index; Psychol. Abstr. (1976-); PsycINFO; PsycLit; Res. Alert [Full Cov.]; Sage Fam. Stud. Abstr.; Soc. Plann. Policy Dev. Abstr.; Soc. Sci. Source (Jul. 1993-); Soc. Sci. Cit. Index [Full Cov.]; Sociol. Abstr.; Sociol. Educ. Abstr.; Stud. Women Abstr.; West. Hist. Q.

US/0192-513X
JOURNAL OF FAMILY ISSUES. [J. fam. issues]. **Added/Corp** Sage Publications, Inc. National Council on Family Relations. Vol. 1 (March 1980)-. Periodical. English. bm. $198.00. SAGE Periodical Press, 2455 Teller Road, Thousand Oaks CA 91320. **Tel** (805)499-0721, FAX (805)499-0871, telex 100799. **ED** Patricia A. Voydanoff (University of Dayton). **LC** HQ1; .J463. **DD** 306.8/05. **NLM** W1 JO6443T. **[CCC]. Pr Rev. Acid Free.** available on microfilm and microfiche from University Microfilms International (UMI). Documents available from The Genuine Article, UMI Article Clearinghouse.
Desc: Devoted to contemporary social issues and social problems related to marriage and family life, and to theoretical and professional issues of current interest to those who work with and study families.
Ind/Abst Acad. Abstr. Full Text Elite (Jan. 1992-); Acad. Abstr. (Jan. 1992-); Acad. Search (Jan. 1992-); AGRICOLA [Full Cov.]; Am. Hist. Life (1985-1986); Crim. Justice Abstr.; Curr. Contents Soc. Behav. Sci.; Curr. Index J. Educ.; Curr. Lit. Fam. Plan.; Expand. Acad. Index (1989-); High. Educ. Abstr. (1985-); Hum. Resour. Abstr. (?-?); Humanit. Source (Jan. 1992-); Index Period. Artic. Relat. Law (19??-19??); INFO-SOUTH Abstr.; Mag. Search; Newsp. Period. Abstr. (1991-); Popul. Index; Psychoanal. Abstr.; Psychol. Abstr. (1990-); PsycINFO; PsycLit; PsycScan: Appl. Exp. Eng. Psych.; PsycScan: LD/MR; PsycScan: Neuropsych.; Res. Alert [Full Cov.]; Sage Fam. Stud. Abstr.; Soc. Plann. Policy Dev. Abstr.; Soc. Sci. Source (Jan. 1992-); Soc. Sci. Cit. Index [Full Cov.]; Soc. Sci. Index; Soc. Sci. Index Fulltext (Dec. 1988-) [Full Txt.]; Soc. Work Abstr. (Spring, Summer 1987) [Select. Cov.]; Sociol. Abstr.

US/0893-3200
JOURNAL OF FAMILY PSYCHOLOGY. **See** Psychology.

US/0897-5353
JOURNAL OF FAMILY PSYCHOTHERAPY. [J. fam. psychother.]. Vol. 1, No. 1 (1990)-. Periodical. English. qt. $105.00 US; $147.00 other. The Haworth Press Inc, 10 Alice Street, Binghamton NY 13904-1580. **Tel** (607)722-5857, (800)3-HAWORTH, FAX (607)722-1424. **ED** Terry Trepper (editor's address: Family Studies Center, Purdue University, Hammond IN 46323-2094). **DD** 616. **NLM** W1; JO6444T. **CODEN** JFAPEF. **Bk Rev. Ad Acc. Pr Rev. Acid Free. Circ:** 316. available on microfilm and microfiche from University Microfilms International (UMI). Documents available from BIOSIS Document Express, Haworth Document Delivery Service. ***Continues*** *Journal of Psychotherapy & the Family, 0742-9703.*
Desc: Provide an exchange for clinicians across the disciplines to share dynamic and creative solutions to difficult family problems. Will offer an expanded forum for detailed clinical case studies, descriptions of successful treatment programs, innovative strategies in clinical practice and other articles that will be of immediate practical use to therapists.
Ind/Abst Abstr. Res. Pastor. Care Couns.; Biol. Abstr.; Biol. Dig. (1991-); EMBASE; Index Med.; Psychol. Abstr. (1985-); PsycINFO; PsycLit; Ref. Z.; Sage Fam. Stud. Abstr.; Soc. Plann. Policy Dev. Abstr.; Soc. Work Abstr. [Select. Cov.]; Sociol. Abstr.; Stud. Women Abstr.

UK/0163-4445
JOURNAL OF FAMILY THERAPY. **See** Medical Science and Technology-Psychiatry.

US/0885-7482
JOURNAL OF FAMILY VIOLENCE. [J. fam. violence]. Vol. 1, No. 1 (March 1986)-. Periodical. English. Four times a year. $175.00 institutions, $42.00 individuals US; $205.00 institutions, $49.00 individuals other. Plenum Press, 233 Spring Street, New York NY 10013-1578. **Tel** (212)620-8000, (800)221-9369, FAX (212)463-0742, (212)807-1047, telex 23/421139. **ED** Vincent B. Van Hasselt and Michel Hersen. **LC** HQ809; .J68. **DD** 362.8/2. **NLM** W1; JO6445HG. **CODEN** JFVIEV. **[CCC].** available on microfilm and microfiche from University Microfilms International (UMI). Documents available from The Genuine Article, UMI Article Clearinghouse.
Desc: Publishes reports from a variety of fields addressing the problems of family violence and deviant family systems. Investigations utilize group comparisons or single case experimental designs, as well as clinically relevant and innovative case studies. All types of family violence and their precursors are examined.
Ind/Abst Chicano Index; Crim. Justice Abstr.; Crim. Penol. Police Sci. Abstr. (1990-); Curr. Contents Soc. Behav. Sci.; Expand. Acad. Index (1992-); Index Period. Artic. Relat. Law; Int. Bibliogr. Sociol.; Newsp. Period. Abstr. (1992-); Psychol. Abstr. (1986-); PsycINFO; PsycLit; Res. Alert [Full Cov.]; Soc. Plann. Policy Dev. Abstr.; Soc. Sci. Cit. Index [Full Cov.].

US/0895-2833
JOURNAL OF FEMINIST FAMILY THERAPY. [J. fem. fam. ther.]. Vol. 1, No. 1 (1989)-. Periodical. English. qt. $125.00 US; $175.00 other. The Haworth Press Inc, 10 Alice Street, Binghamton NY 13904-1580. **Tel** (607)722-5857, (800)3-HAWORTH, FAX (607)722-1424. **ED** Lois Braverman (editor's address: 3833 Woods Drive, Des Moines IA 50312). **LC** RC488.5; .J684. **DD** 616.89/156. **NLM** W1; JO648. **Bk Rev. Ad Acc. Pr Rev. Acid Free. Circ:** 605. available on microfilm and microfiche from University Microfilms International (UMI). Documents available from Haworth Document Delivery Service.
Desc: Provides a multidisciplinary forum to further explore the relationship between feminist theory and family therapy practice and theory. Articles include those of theoretical nature as well as those focusing on empirical research and clinical application. The contributors to the journal critique family therapy concepts and apply a feminist-oriented perspective to treatment issues of particular importance to therapy with women.
Ind/Abst Soc. Work Abstr.; Women Stud. Abstr.

US/0194-472X
JOURNAL OF MARITAL AND FAMILY THERAPY. **See** Psychology.

US/0022-2445
JOURNAL OF MARRIAGE AND THE FAMILY. [J. marriage fam.]. **Added/Corp** National Council on Family Relations. **VFOAT** Journal of Marriage & the Family. Vol. 26 (Feb. 1964)-. Periodical. English. qt. $95.00 US; add $7.00 postage other. National Council of Family Relations, 3989 Central Avenue Northeast, Suite 550, Minneapolis MN 55421. **Tel** (612)781-9331, FAX (612)781-9348. **ED** Alan Booth. **DD** 392. **NLM** W1; JO748N. **CODEN** JMFAA6. Index available. cum. index. **Bk Rev. Ad Acc. Pr Rev. Circ:** 6,800 (ctrl). available on microfilm and microfiche from University Microfilms International (UMI). Documents available from The Genuine Article, BIOSIS Document Express, UMI Article Clearinghouse. ***Continues*** *Marriage and Family Living (Menasha, Wis.), 0885-7059.*
Desc: Presents original theory, research interpretation, and critical discussion of materials related to marriage and the family.
Ind/Abst Abstr. Res. Pastor. Care Couns. (19??-); Acad. Abstr. Full Text Elite (Nov. 1990-); Acad. Abstr. (Nov. 1990-); Acad. Ind. [Computer File] (1987-); Acad. Search (Nov. 1990-); AGRICOLA [Select. Cov.]; Appl. Soc. Sci. Index Abstr.; Biol. Abstr. (-1984); Book Rev. Digest; Book Rev. Index; Chicano Index; Commun. Abstr.; Crim. Justice Abstr.; Curr. Contents Soc. Behav. Sci.; Curr. Index J. Educ.; Curr. Lit. Fam. Plan.; Expand. Acad. Index (1987-); High. Educ. Abstr. (1965-); Index Book Rev. Relig.; INFO-SOUTH Abstr.; Int. Bibliogr. Sociol.; Int. Dev. Abstr. (?-?); Mag. Search; Middle East Abstr. Index; Multicult. Educ. Abstr.; Newsp. Period. Abstr. (1986-); Popul. Index; Psychol. Abstr. (1964-); PsycINFO; PsycLit; Relig. Index One Period.; Res. Alert [Full Cov.]; Sage Fam. Stud. Abstr.; Soc. Plann. Policy Dev. Abstr.; Soc. Sci. Source (Jul. 1990-); Soc. Sci. Cit. Index [Full Cov.]; Soc. Sci. Index; Soc. Sci. Index Fulltext (Nov. 1988-) [Full Txt.]; Soc. Work Abstr. [Select. Cov.]; Sociol. Abstr.; Sociol. Educ. Abstr.; Stud. Women Abstr.; Trop. Dis. Bull.; Women Stud. Abstr.

US/0092-623X
JOURNAL OF SEX & MARITAL THERAPY. **See** Sexual Life.

US/1045-5205
JOYFUL CHILD JOURNAL. [Joyf. child j.]. Vol. 1 (Fall 1989)-. Periodical. English. qt. $20.00 (US); $25.00 (Canada); $28.00 (other). Joyful Child Journal, PO Box 5506, Scottsdale AZ 85261. **Tel** (602) 951-4111. **DD** 649.

CN/0823-776X
JUMELLO, LE. [Jumello]. Periodical. French. 7.00Can$. Club de Parents du Jumeaux de Montreal, 308 Brahms, Chateaugueay Quebec J6K 2W4 Canada. **Tel** (514)698-1183. **ED** C Pankratz. **DD** 649/.144/060714281. **Ad Acc. Circ:** 350 (ctrl).
Desc: Multiple birth articles for parents of twins, triplets, quads, on how to bring up children specific characteristics of multiples, tricks, statistics, education, and club activities.

CN/1183-6547
JUNIOR MODE. [Jr. mode]. Vol. 1, No 1 (Autumn 1991)-. Periodical. French. sa. 2.95Can$ per issue. Junior Mode, 428 Est Rue Rachel, Montreal Quebec H2J 2G7 Canada. **DD** 649/.05.

US
KALEIDOSCOPE / A SPECTRUM OF ARTICLES FOCUSING ON FAMILIES. English. Four times a year. $15.00 institutions; $5.00 individuals. University of Connecticut, J. Pappanikou Center, 1776 Ellington Road, South Windsor CT 06074. **Tel** (203)648-1205, FAX (203)644-2031. **ED** Lisa Glidden. **Bk Rev.** ctrl circ.

JA
KATEI SEIKATSU. **Added/Corp** Nihon Katei Seikatsu Mondai Kenkyu Kyokai. (19??)-. Periodical. Japanese. Shin Toranomon Jitsugyo Kaikan Minato-ku, Tokyo Japan. **LC** HQ1; .K38.

JA
KAZOKUSHI KENKYU / KAZOKUSHI KENKYU HENSHU IINKAI HEN. 1 (Spring 1980)-. Periodical. Japanese. sa. ¥2200 single issue. Otsuki Shoten, 11-9 Hongo 2 Bunkyo-ku, Tokyo 113 Japan. **LC** HQ503; .K29.

US/0740-5154
KEEPSAKE MAGAZINE FOR BRIDES. **VFOAT** Keepsake. Vol. 1, No. 1 (June 1984)-. Periodical. English. sa. $3.50. Keepsake Magazine for Brides, 3009 North 67th Place, Scottsdale AZ 85251.

GW
KEMENATE, DIE. (19??)-. German. Familienverband Berneburg e.v., Trettachstrasse 60, 8980 Oberstdorf Germany.

US
KIDS, KIDS, KIDZ MAGAZINE. English. mo. $12.00. J&J Publications, Box 24032, Omaha NE 68124-0032. **Tel** (402)391-0441. **ED** Melanie Morrissey. Index available. **Bk Rev. Ad Acc.** ctrl circ.
Desc: Upbeat and informative information for parents including a medical column, education column, and a spotlight on area events.

NE
KINDEREN. **See** Children and Youth Interests.

MY
LAPURAN TAHUNAN - PERSATUAN KELAB-KELAB BELIA MALAYSIA. **Main/Corp** Persatuan Kelab-Kelab Belia Malaysia. Malay. Wisma Belia, 40 Jalan Lornie, 08-04 Kuala Lumpur Malaysia. **LC** HQ799.M28; P47A.

US/8750-2011
LEAVEN (FRANKLIN PARK, ILL.). (LEAVEN.). [Leaven]. **Added/Corp** La Leche International. (19??)-. Periodical. English. bm. $15.00 (non-members); $10.00 (members). La Leche League International Inc, 9616 Minneapolis Avenue, PO Box 1209, Franklin Park IL 60131. **Tel** (708)455-7730, FAX (708)455-0125. **ED** Judy Targus. **DD** 649. Index available. **Bk Rev. Ad Acc. Circ:** 7,300 (ctrl).

US/0740-9613
LET'S PRAY TOGETHER. ***Ceased.*** **See** Religion and Theology-Catholicism.

CN/0849-1577
LIEN, LE. [Lien - Serv. orientat. foyers]. **Added/Corp** Service d'Orientation des Foyers. Vol. 19, No 2 (Dec. 1989)-. Periodical. French. Service d'Orientation des Foyers, 7559 Boulevard St-Laurent, Montreal Quebec H2B 1W9 Canada. **DD** 261.8/3581/060714. ***Continues*** *Lien National, 0828-5489.*

PH
LIFE FORUM. **See** Religion and Theology-Catholicism.

CN/0225-6975
LIFELINES (SHERWOOD PARK. 1979). **See** Birth Control.

US/0024-3450
LIGUORIAN. **See** Religion and Theology-Catholicism.

US/0456-3271
LIVING WITH CHILDREN. ***Title Change.*** **Added/Corp** Southern Baptist Convention. Sunday School Board. (197?)-(19??). Periodical. English. Four times a year. Southern Baptist Convention, 901 Commerce, Suite 750, Nashville TN 37203. **Tel** (615)244-2355, FAX (615)742-8919. **(Subscription address:** Sunday School Board, Customer Service, 127 9th Avenue North, Nashville TN 37234.) ***Merged with*** *Living with Preschoolers, 0162-4350* ***to form*** *ParentLife, 1074-326X.*
Ind/Abst South. Baptist Period. Index.

US/0162-4350
LIVING WITH PRESCHOOLERS. ***Title Change.*** **Added/Corp** Southern Baptist Convention. Sunday School Board. (19??)-(19??). Periodical. English.

Four times a year. Southern Baptist Convention, 901 Commerce, Suite 750, Nashville TN 37203. **Tel** (615)244-2355, FAX (615)742-8919. **(Subscription address:** Sunday School Board, Customer Service, 127 9th Avenue North, Nashville TN 37234.**)** ***Merged with*** *Living with Children, 0456-3271* ***to form*** *ParentLife, 1074-326X.*
Ind/Abst South. Baptist Period. Index.

US/0162-4261
LIVING WITH TEENAGERS. Added/Corp Southern Baptist Convention. Sunday School Board. Vol. 1 (Oct./Nov./Dec. 1978)-. Periodical. English. Four times a year. $15.50. Southern Baptist Convention, 901 Commerce, Suite 750, Nashville TN 37203. **Tel** (615)244-2355, FAX (615)742-8919. **(Subscription address:** Sunday School Board - Customer Service, 127 Ninth Avenue North, Nashville, TN 37234 USA; telephone: (800)458-2772**) ED** Jimmy Hester. **Bk Rev. Ad Acc. Circ:** 35,000 (ctrl).
Desc: A magazine for parents of youth (ages 12-17) designed to enrich their understanding and guidance of teenagers based on a Christian approach to living.
Ind/Abst South. Baptist Period. Index.

PL
MAGAZYN RODZINNY. MR. VFOAT MR. (19??)-. Polish. mo. Price on request. **(Subscription address:** ARS Polona, PO Box 1001, 00068 Warsaw Poland.**) LC** HQ1; .M254.

US/1059-5120
MANAGING TODAY'S FAMILY. *Ceased.* (1992)-Vol. 4 (1994). Periodical. English. mo. Whittle Communications, 333 Main Avenue, Knoxville TN 37902. **Tel** (615)595-5000, FAX (615)595-5877.

FR/0025-2980
MARIAGES. [Mariages]. (1960)-. Periodical. French. Four times a year. 180.00F (including VAT) France; 240.00F other. SEMP - Societe d'Editions Modernes Parisienne, 38 rue Jean Mermoz, 75008 Paris France. **Tel** 011 33 1 42669236, FAX 011 33 1 42666064, telex 650016. **UDC** 687.12.

US/0146-4213
MARITAL STATUS AND LIVING ARRANGEMENTS. [Marital status living arrange.]. Began with 1971. Government Publication. English. an. US Department of Commerce, 14th Street & Constitution Avenue NW, Washington DC 20230. **Tel** (202)482-2000, FAX (202)482-3772. **LC** HA195; .A53 subser; HB1127. **DD** 312/.0973 S; 312/.9. **NLM** W2; A B9cu. ***Continues*** *Marital Status and Family Status.*

US/0093-6146
MARRIAGE & DIVORCE. Mar./Apr. 1974-. Periodical. English. bm. $6.50. Abraxas Communications Corporation, 874 Malcolm Avenue, Los Angeles CA 90024. **LC** HQ1; .M27. **DD** 301.42/0973.

US/0272-7897
MARRIAGE & FAMILY. [Marriage fam.]. **VFOAT** Marriage and Family; Annual Editions: Marriage & Family. (1980/1981)-. English. an. $12.95. Dushkin Publishing Group Inc., Sluice Dock, Guilford CT 06437. **Tel** (203)453-4351, (800)243-6532, FAX (203)453-6000. **ED** Ollie Pocs. **LC** HQ536; .A57. **DD** 306.8/0973. ***Continues*** *Annual Editions. Readings in Marriage and Family, 0095-6155.*
Desc: Carefully selected articles provide an excellent overview of all aspects of family life. Articles encourage critical thinking and allow students to explore a variety of viewpoints.

US/0362-9341
MARRIAGE AND FAMILY NEWSLETTER. (1970)-. Periodical. English. qt. $20.00. Marriage and Family Newsletter, Ontario K9J 7A5 Canada. **Tel** (705)745-9637. **ED** John E. Harrington. **LC** HQ767; .M377. **DD** 301. **NLM** W1 MA68.

US/0149-4929
MARRIAGE & FAMILY REVIEW. [Marriage fam. rev.]. **VFOAT** Mariage and Family Review. **VAT** Marriage and Family Review. (Jan./Feb. 1978)-. Academic Scholarly Publication. English. qt. $200.00 US; $280.00 other. The Haworth Press Inc, 10 Alice Street, Binghamton NY 13904-1580. **Tel** (607)722-5857, (800)3-HAWORTH, FAX (607)722-1424. **ED** Marvin Sussman (editor's address: Unidel Professor of Human Behavior, Department of Individual and Family Studies, College of Human Resources, University of Delaware, Newark, DE 19716). **LC** HQ536; .M322. **DD** 306.8/0973. **NLM** W1 MA68C. **CODEN** MFARDJ. **Bk Rev. Ad Acc. Pr Rev. Acid Free. Circ:** 436. available on microfilm and microfiche from University Microfilms International (UMI). Documents available from The Genuine Article, UMI Article Clearinghouse, Haworth Document Delivery Service.
Desc: Each issue of this journal is a full-length, thematic, symposium-type issue dealing with a current topic in the marriage and family field in an in-depth manner. Presents new research and theory and also evaluates the importance of that research.
Ind/Abst Abstr. Soc. Gerontol.; Abstr. Res. Pastor. Care Couns. (19??-); Acad. Ind. [Computer File] (1992-); Acad. Search (July 1993-); AGRICOLA [Full Cov.]; Curr. Contents Soc. Behav. Sci.; EMBASE; Expand. Acad. Index (1989-); INFO-SOUTH Abstr.; Mag. Search; Middle East Abstr. Index; Multicult. Educ. Abstr.; Newsp. Period. Abstr. (1990-); Psychol. Abstr. (1978-); PsycINFO; PsycLit; Res. Alert [Select. Cov.]; Sage Fam. Stud. Abstr.; Soc. Plann. Policy Dev. Abstr.; Soc. Sci. Source (Jul. 1993-); Soc. Sci. Cit. Index [Select. Cov.]; Soc. Sci. Index; Soc. Sci. Index Fulltext (1988-) [Full Txt.]; Soc. Work Abstr. [Select. Cov.]; Sociol. Abstr.; Stud. Women Abstr.

US/1045-3407
MARRIAGE CONNECTION. *Title Change.* (MARRIAGE CONNECTION [COMPUTER FILE].). [Marriage connect.]. (Oct. 1989)-(19??). English. mo. Social Software Inc, 4586 Ashington Drive, Lithonia GA 30058-7010. **DD** 362. ***Continued by*** *Floppyland.*
Desc: 5 1/4" computer disks. System requirements: IBM PC and compatibles.

US/0897-5469
MARRIAGE PARTNERSHIP. See Religion and Theology.

●US/1063-1054
MARRIAGE (SAINT PAUL, MINN.). (MARRIAGE.). **Added/Corp** International Marriage Encounter. Vol. 21, No. 3 (May 1992)-. Periodical. English. ir (9 issues per year). $17.00 (one year), $32.00 (two year) US; $22.00 (one year), $42.00 (two year) other. Marriage Encounter, 955 Lake Drive, St. Paul MN 55120. **Tel** (612)454-6434, FAX (612)452-0466. **DD** 306. ***Continues*** *Marriage Encounter, 0734-0052.*

AT
MARRIAGES, AUSTRALIA. See Family and Marriage-Abstracting, Bibliographies and Statistics.

CN/1195-4140
MARRIAGES / STATISTICS CANADA, CANADIAN CENTRE FOR HEALTH INFORMATION. See Family and Marriage-Abstracting, Bibliographies and Statistics.

IO
MATRA : MAJALAH TREND PRIA. No. 1 (1986)-. Periodical. Indonesian. mo. Pusat Perdagangan, Senen Blok II Lantai III, Jakarta 10410 Indonesia. **LC** AP95.I5; M34.

UK
MATRIMONIAL DECISIONS OF GREAT BRITAIN AND IRELAND FOR .... See Religion and Theology.

US/0024-8908
MCCALL'S. See Women's Interests.

US/0270-0050
MCCALL'S BOOK FOR BRIDES. VFOAT Book for Brides. Vol. 1 (1979)-. English. $1.50 single issue. ABC Leisure Magazine Inc, 825 7th Avenue, New York NY 10019. **Tel** (212)265-8360. **LC** TT633; .M3. **DD** 646/.47.

BU
MLADEZH I OBSHTESTVO / NAUCHNOIZSLEDOVATELSKI INSTITUT ZA MLADEZHTA PRI TSK NA DKMS. **Added/Corp** Nauchnoizsledovatelski Institut za Mladezhta (Sofia, Bulgaria). Vol. 1 (1989)-. Periodical. Bulgarian. bm. Ul Chervena Iskra 17, Sofia 1619 Bulgaria. **LC** HQ799.B8; M477. ***Continues in part*** *Problemi za Mladezhta.*

AT/0729-5081
MODE FOR BRIDES. [Mode brides]. (1982)-. Periodical. English. qt. 30.00 Aus$ Australia; 36.80Aus$ New Zealand; 86.00Aus$ other. Australian Consolidated Press Ltd, GPO Box 5252, Sydney New South Wales 2001 Australia. **Tel** 011 61 2 2600000. **DD** 392.5. ***Continues*** *Australian Bride & Setting Up Home, 0729-5073.*

US/0026-7546
MODERN BRIDE. [Mod. bride]. Vol. 1 (Fall 1949)-. Periodical. English. bm. $17.97 US; $21.37 (includes GST) Canada; $36.97 other. Cahners Publishing Company, 249 West 17th Street, New York NY 10011. **Tel** (212)645-0067, FAX (212)242-6987. **(Subscription address:** Modern Bride, PO Box 2606, Boulder CO 80322-2606.**) ED** Cele Goldsmith Lalli. **LC** HQ1; .M63. **DD** 392.5. **[CCC]. Ad Acc.** available on microfilm and microfiche from University Microfilms International (UMI); available on an online database (file 647/Full-Text) from DIALOG.
Desc: The bridal magazine that will give readers fashion advice and options, and answer all their planning questions. Offering information and guidance for wedding preparations, the latest ideas in fashions, honeymoon travel as well as tips on married lifestyle.
Ind/Abst Mag. Index (1977-April 1984).

CN/0226-0891
MONDE NOUVEAU (THURSO). (MONDE NOUVEAU.). [Monde nouv.]. V. 1- Jan. 1980-. Periodical. French. mo. Free. Renouement Conjugal Canada, 208 rue Galipeau, Thurso Quebec J0X 3B0 Canada. **DD** 362.8/2/09714.

AT
MONOGRAPH / AUSTRALIAN INSTITUTE OF FAMILY STUDIES. VFOAT AIFS Monograph. No. 6; 1988-. Monographic series. English. Price varies per volume. Australian Institute of Family Studies, 300 Queen Street, Melbourne Victoria 3000 Australia. **Tel** 61 3 6086888, FAX 61 3 6000886. ***Continues*** *Institute of Family Studies Monograph, 0811-6091.*

US/0364-0396
MONTHLY VITAL STATISTICS REPORT. See Population Studies-Abstracting, Bibliographies and Statistics.

US/8756-9965
MOTC'S NOTEBOOK. VAT Mothers of Twins Clubs Notebook. Periodical. English. qt. $10.00. National Organization of Mothers of Twins Clubs, 5402 Amberwood Lane, Rockville MD 20853. **DD** 392.

AT
MOTHER & BABY. (19??)-. Periodical. English. Six times a year. 22.00Aus$ Australia; 29.00Aus$ other. Federal Publishing Co Pty Ltd, PO Box 199, 180 Bourke Road, Alexandria New South Wales, 2015 Australia. **Tel** 011 61 2 693 6666, FAX 011 61 2 693 9935. **(Subscription address:** Federal Publishing Co. Pty Ltd., PO Box 199, Alexandria NSW 2015 Australia.**)**

PK/0379-2617
MOTHER & CHILD (LAHORE). (MOTHER & CHILD.). **Added/Corp** Maternity & Child Welfare Association of Pakistan. **VAT** Mother and Child. (196?)-. Periodical. English. Four times a year. $20.00. Maternity & Child Welfare Association, MCH House, 30-F Gulberg-II, Lahore Pakistan. **Tel** 882146. **ED** A.K. Awan. **NLM** W1 MO941J. **Bk Rev. Ad Acc. Circ:** 2,500 (ctrl).
Desc: Concerned with both medical and social aspects of relationships between mothers and children.

US/0733-3013
MOTHERING. [Mothering]. **VFOAT** Mothering Magazine. (1976)-. Periodical. English. qt. $18.95 (one year), $32.00 (two year), $45.00 (three year). Mothering Publishing Inc, PO Box 1690, Santa Fe NM 87504. **Tel** (505)984-8116, FAX (505)986-8335. **(Subscription address:** Kable Publishers Aide, 308 East Hitt Street, Subscription Department, Mt. Morris IL 61054-1473.**) ED** Peggy O'Mara. **LC** WMLC L 83/9197. **DD** 306. Index available. cum. index. **Bk Rev. Ad Acc. Pr Rev. Circ:** 50,000. available on microfilm from University Microfilms International (UMI); available on an online database (file 149/Full-Text) from DIALOG.
Desc: Information on alternative parenting. Recognizes parents as the experts and provides information on which to base information choices.
Ind/Abst Acad. Abstr. Full Text Elite (Jan. 1992-); Acad. Abstr. (Jan. 1992-); Acad. Search (Jan. 1992-); Altern. Press Index; Child. Lit. Abstr. (19??-); Health Index (1989-); Health Period. Database [Full Txt.]; Health Ref. Cent. (Jan. 1989-) [Full Txt.] [Full Cov.]; Health Source (Jan. 1992-); INFO-SOUTH Abstr.; Mag. Search.

US/0272-6912
MOTHERS AND CHILDREN (WASHINGTON). (MOTHERS AND CHILDREN.). [Mothers child.]. Vol. 1 (Sept. 1980)-. Periodical. English. Three times a year. Free to developing countries; $10.00 other. American Public Health Association, 1015 15th Street Northwest, Washington DC 20005. **Tel** (202)789-5666. **DD** 618. **NLM** W1; MO9413.
Desc: Covers a range of nutrition and primary health care issues. Contains an annual supplement on education materials.

US/0744-8384
N.J. VASA HOME FAMILY. (N.J. VASA HOME FAMILY : THE OFFICIAL PUBLICATION OF DISTRICT NO. 6 V.O.A.). **VFOAT** NJ VASA Home Family. Periodical. English. mo. VOA New Jersey District No 6, 51 Scandia Road, Hackettstown NJ 07840.

IS
NAAMAT. See Women's Interests.

US
NANNY TIMES. Vol. 1, No. 1 (May 1989)-. English. mo. $9.95. Gillian Gordon and Publisher, Box 31, Rutherford NJ 07070. **Tel** (201)935-5575, FAX (201)935-7191. **ED** Gillian Gordon and Jack A Gordon. **Bk Rev. Ad Acc. Circ:** 30,000 (ctrl).
Desc: Provides articles pertinent to the childcare profession as well as nanny job listings. It's purpose is to portray the job of child care provides as a profession and a career and not merely as a temporary job.

US/0897-9847
NETWORK (CHARLOTTE, N.C.), THE. See Sociology-Social Services and Welfare.

US/0744-6861
NEW ENGLAND BRIDE. (19??)-. Periodical. English. Twelve times a year. $24.00. New England Publishing Group Inc, 215 Newbury Street, Peabody MA 01960. **Tel** (508)535-4186. **[CCC].**

Family and Marriage

US
NEW JERSEY BRIDE. Vol. 1, No. 1 (Spring/Summer 1988)-. Periodical. English. sm. $3.95 (each issue). MDR Publications, 55 Park Place, Box 920, Mirrorstown NJ 07960-0920. **Tel** (201)644-5522, FAX (201)538-2953. **ED** Jan Bresnick and Leah Roshe. **Ad Acc. Circ:** 40,000.
Desc: Offers in-depth wedding guide and planner for brides to-be in New Jersey area.

●CN/1193-9397
NEW MOTHER (1992). (NEW MOTHER.). [New mother]. No. 2 (1992)-. Periodical. English. qt. Free to new mothers. MacLean Hunter Publ. Limited / Toronto, 777 Bay Street, 8th Floor Agency Control, Toronto Ontario M5W 1A7 Canada. **Tel** (416)596-5000, (800)268-6811, FAX (416)596-5526. **DD** 649. ***Continues*** *Chatelaine's New other., 0708-5303.*

US/0278-0976
NEW PARENT ADVISER. [New parent advis.]. Periodical. English. an. 13-30 Corporation, 505 Market Street, Knoxville TN 37902. **Tel** (615)521-0600. **LC** HQ755.8; .N48. **DD** 649/.1/05.

CN/0706-9022
NEWSLETTER - BRITISH COLUMBIA COUNCIL FOR THE FAMILY. ***Title Change.*** [Newsl. - B.C. Counc. Fam.]. **Main/Corp** British Columbia Council for the Family. **VAT** Newsletter - BC Council for the Family. (Sept. 1977)-(19??). Newsletter. English. qt. British Columbia Council for the Family, 2590 Granville Street, Suite 204, Vancouver British Columbia, V6H 3H1 Canada. **Tel** (604) 660-0675, FAX (604) 732-4813. **ED** Rob Lees, John Lynn, Carol Matusicky and Phil Sunderland. **DD** 301.42/06/2711. Index available. **Bk Rev. Ad Acc. Circ:** 6,000 (ctrl). ***Continued by*** *Family Connections.*
Desc: Seeks to unite the efforts of all groups, agencies and citizens concerned about meeting the needs of families in British Columbia.

NE
NIEUWE REVU. Medianet BV, Postbus 6298, 2001 LN Haarlem Netherlands. **Tel** 011 31 23 173311.

US/1049-1821
NORTON NOTES. (NORTON NOTES : A NEWSLETTER FOR ALL NORTON RESEARCHERS.). [Norton notes]. Vol. 1, No. 1 (Sept. 1987)-. Newsletter. English. qt. Kinseeker Publications, Box 184, Grawn MI 49637. **ED** V. Wilson. **LC** CS71; .N886a. **DD** 929/.2/097305. Index available. **Bk Rev. Ad Acc. Circ:** 50.
Desc: Family information.

BE
NOUVELLES FEUILLES FAMILIALES. French. bm. 40.00F. Feuilles Familiales, Rue du Congres 27 Charme, 1000 Brussels Belgium. **Tel** (514)274-5468. ***Continues*** *Feuilles Familiales.*

UK/0029-6422
NURSERY WORLD. [Nurs. world]. (1925)-. Periodical. English. ir. £40.00 UK; £68.00 other. MRM Promotional Services Ltd., Premier House, Farndon Road, Market Hrbr. LEI LE16 9NR England. **Tel** 011 44 858 410510. **(Subscription address:** MRM Promotional Services Ltd., PO Box 500, Subscriptions Department, Leicester LE99 0AA England.**)** **DD** 649. ***Absorbed*** *Maternal and Child Care, 0025-5475.*

CN/0713-3898
NURTURING. ***Suspended.*** [Nurturing]. -Suspended (1985). Periodical. English. qt. $3.25 per no. Nurturing, 20 Papineau Drive, Don Mills Ontario M3C 2E7 Canada. **DD** 649/.1/05.

UK
OCCASIONAL PAPER (FAMILY POLICY STUDIES CENTRE (GREAT BRITAIN)). (OCCASIONAL PAPER / FAMILY POLICY STUDIES CENTRE.). **Added/Corp** Family Policy Studies Centre (Great Britain). No. 1 (1984)-. Monographic series. English. Price varies per volume. Family Policy Studies Centre, 231 Baker Street, London NW1 6XE England. ***Continues*** *Occasional Paper (Study Commission on the Family (Great Britain)).*

YU
OMLADINSKE : LIST SAVEZA SOCIJALISTICKE OMLADINE SRBIJE. Periodical. Serbo-Croatian (Cyrillic). wk. Republicka Konferencija Sso Srbije, 11070 Novi Belgrad, Ho Si Minova 27, Belgrad Yugoslavia. **LC** HQ793; .O45. ***Continues*** *Omladinske Novine.*

NE
OUDERS VAN NU. English. mo. Medianet BV, Postbus 6298, 2001 LN Haarlem Netherlands. **Tel** 011 31 23 173311.

CN/0030-6843
OUR FAMILY (BATTLEFORD). **See** Religion and Theology.

US/0899-9333
OURS (MINNEAPOLIS, MINN.). ***Title Change.*** **See** Sociology-Social Services and Welfare.

BL
PAIS & [I.E. E] FILHOS. Vol. 1, (Sept. 1968)-. Periodical. Portuguese. ir. Bloch Editoras SA, Rua do Russell 766 804, 22210 Rio de Janeiro Brazil. **Tel** 011 51 21 2652012, 011 51 21 2850033. **LC** HQ750.A2; P25.

US/1041-178X
PARENT & CHILD. ***Ceased.*** [Parent child]. **VFOAT** Parent and Child. Vol. 1, No. 1 (June 1988)-(March/April 1994). Periodical. English. Ten times a year (Monthly with Jan./Feb. and June/July issues combined). Parent Communications Inc, 7048 Wilson Lane, Bethesda MD 20817. **Tel** (301)229-2216, FAX (202)234-8231. **ED** Donna Hart. **DD** 649. **Bk Rev**, (Qty: 8). **Ad Acc, Adv Mgr:** Fran Gianaris. **Circ:** 55,000 (ctrl). ***Continues*** *Washington Parent.*
Desc: For Washington-area parents with children through the early teen years. Provides informative, balanced articles focusing on child development, education, and health while serving as a comprehensive source of information about community goods and services.

US/0887-0365
PARENT AND PRESCHOOLER : PP. **See** Education.

US/1058-5583
PARENT CARE (BETHANY, OKLA.). (PARENT CARE.). [Parent care]. **VFOAT** Parent Care Newsletter. (Oct. 1991)-. Periodical. English. mo. $19.95 US; $22.95 Canada. Betty Robertson, Box 216, Bethany OK 73008. **DD** 362.

CN/1195-1893
PARENT CARE / YOUR CHILD CARE NEWS-LINE. English. bm (6 issues). $12.00. CanDan Publishing Co., 4929 Cedar Crescent, PO Box 126, Canal Flats, BC, V0B 1B0 Canada. **Tel** (604)349-5677. **ED** Catherine M. Pruissen. **Bk Rev**, (Qty: 6-10). **Circ:** 1,000.
Desc: Dedicated to helping parents ensure their child receives quality daycare. Topics include safety, nutrition, child development through "fun" activities, and child abuse. Goal is to provide parents with the information they need to ensure their child is being properly cared for.

CN
PARENT-TO-PARENT. English. Ten times a year (Jan., Feb., Mar., Apr., May, June, Sept.,Oct., Nov., Dec.). 16.82Can$ (one year); 28.04Can$ (two year); 26091Can$ (three year). Positive Parenting Inc., PO Box 85324, Burlington ONT L7R 4K5 Canada. **Tel** (905)335-3549, FAX (905)336-0761. **ED** A. Greenway. **Bk Rev**, (Qty: 3). **Ad Acc, Adv Mgr:** D. Gonsalves, **Tel** (416)930-6877. **Circ:** 60,000 (ctrl).
Desc: For adults concerned about meeting children's emotional needs. Covers a variety of subjects from childbirth to young adults.

US/1060-0027
PARENT WORKSHOP, THE. [Parent workshop]. Vol. 1, Issue 1 (1991)-. Periodical. English. qt. $250.00 (minimum order 200 copies). National School Services, 610 South Wheeling Road, Wheeling IL 60090. **DD** 306.

US
PARENTAL GUIDANCE. (19??)-. Periodical. English. mo. $20.00. Focus on the Family, Colorado Springs CO 80995. **Tel** (800)232-6459.
Desc: A Christian magazine for parents.

CN/1183-6393
PARENTALK (RICHMOND HILL). (PARENTALK : A SERVICE TO PARENTS FROM SCHOLASTIC CANADA.). [ParenTalk]. **Added/Corp** Scholastic Canada Ltd. **VFOAT** Parent Talk. Vol. 1, No. 1 (Fall 1991)-. Periodical. English. sa. Free. Scholastic Canada Ltd, 123 Newkirk Road, Richmond Hill Ontario L4C 3G5 Canada. **Tel** (416)881-1446. **DD** 649/.58.

US/0896-1468
PARENTGUIDE NEWS. [Parentguide news]. **VFOAT** Parent Guide News; PG News. Vol. 3, No. 6 (May 1987)-. Periodical. English. mo. $16.90. Parents Guide Network Corporation, 475 Park Avenue South, Floor 75, New York NY 10016. **Tel** (212)213-8840. **ED** Leslie Elgort. **DD** 649. **Bk Rev. Ad Acc. Circ:** 205,000 (ctrl). ***Continues*** *Parentguide.*
Desc: Covers parenting concerns on a national and more specific New York/New Jersey metropolitan area.

US/0890-247X
PARENTING (SAN FRANCISCO, CALIF.). (PARENTING.). [Parenting]. **VFOAT** Parenting Magazine. (Feb. 1987)-. Periodical. English. Ten times a year. $12.00 (one year); $18.00 (two years). Parenting, 301 Howard Street, Suite 1700, San Francisco CA 94105. **Tel** (415)546-7575. **(Subscription address:** Neodata / Colorado, PO Box 2606, Boulder Boulder CO 80322.**)** **LC** WMLC 93/1611. **DD** 649. **Bk Rev.** Documents available from UMI Article Clearinghouse, Magazine Collection.
Desc: Covers health, childcare, relationships, finance, education, news, humor, movie and book reviews, etc. Includes ideas and information on raising kids today.
Ind/Abst Mag. Index Plus (1992-); Newsp. Period. Abstr. (1989-).

US/0737-5123
PARENTING STUDIES. ***Suspended.*** Vol. 1, No. 1 (Jan. 1984)-?. Periodical. English. qt. $40.00 multiple-reader institutions. Eterna Press, PO Box 157941, Chicago IL 60615. **Tel** (312)969-0318. **DD** 306. **NLM** W1; PA642T.
Ind/Abst Psychol. Abstr. (1984-); PsycINFO; PsycLit.

●US/1074-326X
PARENTLIFE (NASHVILLE, TENN.). (PARENTLIFE.). [ParentLife]. **Added/Corp** Southern Baptist Convention. Sunday School Board. **VFOAT** Parent Life. Vol. 1, No. 1 (July 1994)-. Periodical. English. mo. $19.95. Southern Baptist Convention, 901 Commerce, Suite 750, Nashville TN 37203. **Tel** (615)244-2355, FAX (615)742-8919. **(Subscription address:** Sunday School Board, Customer Service, 127 9th Avenue North, Nashville TN 37234.**)** **DD** 306. ***Formed by the union of*** *Living with Children, 0456-3271* ***and*** *Living with Preschoolers, 0162-4350.*
Ind/Abst South. Baptist Period. Index.

UK
PARENTS. English. Twelve times a year. £16.80 UK; £35.00 Europe & EIRE; £60.00 Southeast Asia & Mexico & Oceania; £52.00 others. EMAP Consumer Magazine Ltd., Sovereign Park, Market Harbor, Leics LE16 9EF England. **Tel** 011 44 858 468888.

US/1050-7108
PARENTS AND CHILDREN TOGETHER. ***Ceased.*** [Parents child. together]. (May 1990)-(Feb. 1993). Periodical. English. an. Family Literacy Center, 2805 East 10th Street, Suite 150, Bloomington IN 47408. **Tel** (812)855-5847, FAX (812)855-7901. **ED** Michael Shermis. **DD** 372. **Bk Rev. Ad Acc. Pr Rev. Circ:** 550. available on audiocassette.
Desc: An audio magazine developed to family literacy.

US/0897-8697
PARENTS & TEENAGERS. [Parents teenagers]. **VFOAT** Parents and Teenagers. (1988)- Vol. 6 (1993)-. Periodical. English. Six times a year (Jan., Mar., May, July, Sept., Nov.). $18.97. Parents of Teenagers, PO Box 850, 548 Sisters Parkway, Sisters OR 97759-0850. **Tel** FAX (503)549-0153. **(Subscription address:** Box 482, Mt Morris, IL 61054-0482**)** **ED** Gloria Chisholm. **DD** 649. **Ad Acc, Adv Mgr:** Debbie Mitchell, **Tel** (503)549-8261. **Circ:** 50,000.
Desc: Practical help for Christian parents of teenagers to help build closer family relationship and strengthen their teens faith.
Ind/Abst Christ. Period. Index (19??-); Curr. Thoughts Trends.

US
PARENTS' CHOICE. Vol. 2, No. 3 (1979)-. Periodical. English. qt (Mar., June, Nov., Dec.). $18.00 (1 year), $27.00 (2 year). Parents Choice, Box 185, Waban MA 02168. **Tel** (617)965-5913. **ED** Diana Hiuss Green. **Circ:** 90,000. ***Continues*** *It's The Parents' Choice.*

CN/0705-713X
PARENTS D'AUJOURD'HUI. No. 1- May 1978-. Periodical. French. mo. $15.00. Les Publications des Parents, 1429 rue Crescent, Montreal Quebec H3G 2B2 Canada. **DD** 301.43/1/05.

CN/1191-1727
PARENTS DE COEUR. (PARENTS AT HEART.). [Parents coeur]. **Added/Corp** Montreal General Hospital. Dept. of Community Health. Ville Marie Social Service Centre. Vol. 1, No. 1 (Winter 1991)-. Periodical. English (French). qt. Limited free distribution. Montreal General Hospital, Department of Community Health, Suite 300-A, 980 Guy Street, Montreal Quebec H3H 2K3 Canada. **DD** 362.7/33/05.

CN/0835-5754
PARENT'S DIGEST (CHILLIWACK). (THE PARENT'S DIGEST.). [Parent's dig.]. Vol. 3 (1987)-. Periodical. English. ir. $2.50 per no. $9.00 per year. $16.00 for 2 years. Sphoenix Productions, PO Box 369, Chilliwack British Columbia V2P 6J4, Canada. **DD** 649.1/05. ***Continues*** *Effective Parenting Magazine., 0826-6832.*

US/1059-9207
PARENTS' GUIDE TO CHILDREN'S ENTERTAINMENT. ***Ceased.*** **See** Communication-Broadcasting.

UK/0260-7514
PARENTS (LONDON). [Parents Lond.]. (1976)-. Periodical. English. mo. £16.80 UK. EMAP Consumer Magazine Ltd., Sovereign Park, Market Harbor, Leics LE16 9EF England. **Tel** 011 44 858 468888. **DD** 362.795.

US/1047-8574
PARENTS MAGAZINE (1985). (PARENTS MAGAZINE.). [Parents mag.]. **VFOAT** Parents. Vol. 60, No. 8, (Aug. 1985)-. Periodical. English. mo. $19.90. Gruner & Jahr AG & Co. / US, 685 Third Avenue, 23rd Floor, New York NY 10017. **Tel** (212)599-4040.

Family and Marriage

(Subscription address: CDS Agency Hard Copy, PO Box 4966, Des Moines IA 50340.) **ED** Ann Pleghette Murphy. **DD** 649. Index available. **Bk Rev**. **Ad Acc**. Circ: 1,725,000. available on microfilm and microfiche from University Microfilms International (UMI). Documents available from UMI Article Clearinghouse. **Continues** *Parents (Bergenfield, N.J.), 0195-0967*.
 Desc: Combines the authority of its 60+ years of experience with a fresh, modern outlook and bright, new graphics. Presents articles and columns on children, health, marriage, food, and family life.
 Ind/Abst Abr. Read. Guide Period. Lit.; Acad. Abstr. Full Text Elite (Jan. 1984-) [Full Txt.]; Acad. Abstr. (Jan. 1984-); Acad. Ind. [Computer File] (1984-); Acad. Search (Jan. 1984-); Book Rev. Index; Consum. Health Nutr. Index; Consum. Index Prod. Eval. Inf. Source; Cumul. Index Nurs. Allied Health Lit.; Curr. Lit. Fam. Plan.; Expand. Acad. Index (1984-); Gen. Period. Index (1985-); Health Index (1989-); Health Period. Database [Full Txt.]; Health Ref. Cent. (Jan. 1989-) [Full Txt.] [Full Cov.]; INFO-SOUTH Abstr.; Mag. Artic. Summar. Elite (Jan. 1984-) [Full Txt.]; Mag. Artic. Summar. Select (Jan. 1984-); Mag. Artic. Summar. CD-ROM (Jan. 1984-); Mag. ASAP Plus [Full Txt.]; Mag. ASAP Sel. [Full Txt.]; Mag. Index Plus (1989-); Mag. Index Sel. Microfiche (1990-) [Full Txt.]; Mag. Index Sel. (1986-); Mag. Search; Newsp. Period. Abstr. (1986-); Read. Guide Abstr. Select Ed.; Read. Guide Period. Lit.; Mag. Index (Aug. 1985); TOM Gen. Index (1985-) [Full Txt.]; Vocat. Search (Jan. 1984-) [Full Txt.].

US/1046-0446
PARENTS MAKE THE DIFFERENCE!.
[Parents make differ.]. **Added/Corp** Parent Institute. Vol. 1, No. 1 (Sept. 1989)-. Periodical. English. Nine times a year (published September through May). $77.00. Parent Institute, PO Box 7474, Fairfax Station VA 22039. **Tel** (703)569-9842, FAX (703)569-9842. **ED** Dr John Wherry. **DD** 649.

FR/0553-2159
PARENTS (PARIS), LES. (LES PARENTS.). [Parents]. No. 1 (Mar. 1969)-. Periodical. French. mo. 140.00F France; 250.00F other. EDI 7, 6 rue Ancelle, 92525 Neuilly Sur Seine, Cedex France. **Tel** 011 33 1 40886000. **(Subscription address:** EDI 7, 90 rue de Flandre Svc Abonmnts, 75947 Paris Cedex 19 France.) **LC** HQ768; .P24.
 Ind/Abst Point Repere (1983-).

US/0889-8863
PARENTS' PRESS. [Parents' press]. (June 1980)-. Periodical. English. mo. $16.28. Parents Press, 1454 Sixth Street, Berkeley CA 94710. **Tel** (510)524-1602. **ED** Lynne Verbeek. **DD** 649. **Bk Rev**, (Qty: 5-10). **Ad Acc**.
 Desc: For families with young children in San Francisco and the Bay Area. It provides information on Children's health, women's health, pregnancy, education, child development. It also has an extensive calendar of entertainment, classes, activities and resources for families.

AT/1030-1968
PARENTS SHOPPING GUIDE. *Title Change*. [Parents shopp. guide]. (1987)-(19??). English. an. Magazine House Pty Ltd, PO Box 1067, Crows Nest New South Wales 2065 Australia. **Tel** 011 61 2 4382399, FAX 011 61 2 4363014. **ED** Carol Fallows. **DD** 649.122029494. **Bk Rev**. **Ad Acc**. *Continued by Buying for Baby*.
 Desc: Covers everything you need to buy for 0-5 year olds.

CN/0841-7997
PARTENAIRE (SAINT-HUBERT). See Women's Interests.

FR/0031-2495
PARTICULIER, LE. No. 1 (Oct. 1949)-. French. mo. 213.52F. Le Particulier Ed, 21 Boulevard Montmartre, 75082 Paris Cedex 02 France. **Tel** 33 1 40207000, FAX 33 1 40207010, telex 220700. cum. index.

FR/0992-6054
PARTICULIER IMMOBILIER PARIS. 1986, LE. (LE PARTICULIER IMMOBILIER.). (1986)-. Periodical. French. Eleven times a year. 477.96F. Le Particulier Ed, 21 Boulevard Montmartre, 75082 Paris Cedex 02 France. **Tel** 33 1 40207000, FAX 33 1 40207010, telex 220700. **UDC** 339.4.

FR/0995-6840
PARTICULIER PRATIQUE PARIS, LE. (LE PARTICULIER PRATIQUE.). (1989)-. Periodical. French. Eleven times a year. 292.85F. Le Particulier Ed, 21 Boulevard Montmartre, 75082 Paris Cedex 02 France. **Tel** 33 1 40207000, FAX 33 1 40207010, telex 220700. **UDC** 64.01 (44). Index available. **Circ:** 80.000.
 Continues Comprendre, 0180-183X.
 Desc: Ideas, advice, lists on every aspect concerning family life.

US/0730-6725
PEDIATRICS FOR PARENTS. See Medical Science and Technology-Pediatrics.

IO/0126-3692
PELITA BPKS. See Sociology-Social Services and Welfare.

CN
PEOPLE AND PRACTICE. See Home Economics.

FI
PERHEET. VFOAT Familjer. Finnish (Swedish). an. Government Printing Centre, PO Box 516, SF-00101 Helsinki 10 Finland. **LC** HB3608.3.A3; T55 subser; HQ638. **DD** 306.8/5/094897. *Continues Finland. Tilastokeskus. Perhetilasto*.

UK/1350-4126
PERSONAL RELATIONSHIPS. (1994)-. Academic Scholarly Publication. English. qt. $120.00 US, Canada and Mexico; £74.00 other. Cambridge University Press, The Edinburgh Building, Shaftesbury Road, Cambridge CB2 2RU United Kingdom. **Tel** 011 44 223 312393, FAX 011 44 223 325959. **(Subscription address:** Cambridge University Press / North America, 110 Midland Avenue, Port Chester NY 10573.) **ED** Pat Noller.
 Desc: Devoted to the study of personal relationships. The aim is to promote scholarship in the field of personal relationships throughout a broad range of disciplines.

US/0190-3195
PERSPECTIVAS INTERNACIONALES EN PLANIFICACION FAMILIAR.
 Added/Corp Alan Guttmacher Institute. (1978)-. Periodical. Spanish (French). an. $10.00. Alan Guttmacher Institute, 120 Wall Street, New York NY 10005. **Tel** (212)248-1111, FAX (212)248-1951.
 Desc: Spanish- and French-language annual editions of International Family Planning Perspectives focusing on issues of particular concern to Latin America and francophone Africa.

CN/1185-9504
PINK & BLUE DIRECTORY, THE. See Women's Interests.

●UK
PLANNED PARENTHOOD CHALLENGES / INTERNATIONAL PLANNED PARENTHOOD FEDERATION. Added/Corp International Planned Parenthood Federation. **VFOAT** Challenges. (1993)-. Periodical. English. sa. Free. International Planned Parenthood Federation, Regent's College, Inner Circle, Regent's Park, London NW1 4NS England. **Tel** 011 44 71 486 0741, FAX 011 44 71 487 7950, telex 919573 IPEPEE G. **ED** Jeremy Hamand. **NLM** W1; PL104M. **Circ:** 6,000-10,000 (ctrl).
 Desc: Aims to debate and report on issues of topical interest to all those concerned with reproductive wellbeing, sexual health and family planning.

●US/1065-1969
POSITIVELY FOR KIDS. VFOAT Edgar Martinez; Patience Pays. (1992)-. Periodical. English. qt. $4.00 (single issue). Positively for Kids, 20912 33rd Avenue SE, Bothell WA 98201.

US/1047-384X
PRE-PARENT ADVISER. (PRE-PARENT ADVISER : A GUIDE TO GETTING READY FOR BIRTH.). [Pre-parent advis.]. **VFOAT** Pre Parent Adviser. (1981)-. Periodical. English. an. Whittle Communications, 333 Main Avenue, Knoxville TN 37902. **Tel** (615)595-5000, FAX (615)595-5877. **DD** 649.

NE
PRIVE. Dutch. wk. Dagblad Prive, Antwoordnummer 1313, 1000 PA Amsterdam Netherlands. **Tel** 011 31 20 6802802.

PL/0552-2234
PROBLEMY RODZINY. (1961)-. Periodical. Polish. bm. $60.00. **(Subscription address:** ARS Polona, PO Box 1001, 00068 Warsaw Poland.) **UDC** 37.018.1. **CODEN** 613.88.

US/0273-334X
PROCEEDINGS, ANNUAL CONVENTION - OHIO COUNCIL ON FAMILY RELATIONS. [Proc., annu. conv. - Ohio Counc. Fam. Relat.]. **Main/Corp** Ohio Council on Family Relations. (1980)-. Proceedings. English. an. **LC** HQ536; .O37a. **DD** 306.8/0973.

US/1054-2531
PROCEEDINGS OF THE ... ANNUAL CONFERENCE / ASSOCIATION FOR POPULATION/FAMILY PLANNING LIBRARIES AND INFORMATION CENTERS INTERNATIONAL. [Proc. annu. conf. - Assoc. Popul./Fam. Plann. Libr. Inf. Centers Int., Conf.]. **Main/Corp** Association for Population/Family Planning Libraries and Information Centers, International. Conference. 11th (1978)-. Proceedings. English. an. Association for Population/Family Planning Libraries and Information Centers, c/o Population Council Library, 1 Dag Hammarskjold Plaza, New York NY 10017. **Tel** (212)644-1620. **LC** HQ763; .A8A. **DD** 301. *Continues Proceedings of the Annual Conference - Association for Population/Family Planning Libraries and Information Centers, 0363-938X*.

CN/1183-045X
PROVIDER (VANCOUVER). *Ceased*. (PROVIDER.). [Provider]. **Added/Corp** British Columbia Council for the Family. Vol. 1, No. 1 (Nov. 1990)-(199?). Periodical. English. qt. British Council for the Family, 2590 Granville Street, Suite 204, Vancouver BC, V6H 3H1 Canada. **Tel** (604) 660-0675. **DD** 362.82/86.

IT
QUADERNI DEL CENTRO FAMIGLIA. (19??)-. Italian. ir. L10000.00. Vita e Pensiero, Pubblic University, Largo Gemelli 1, 20123 Milan Italy. **Tel** 011 39 2 72342310, 011 39 2 72342370.

CN/0705-3762
R A I F. RESEAU D'ACTION ET D'INFORMATION POUR LES FEMMES. See Women's Interests.

NE/0166-4298
RAAKPUNT (MAARSSEN). (RAAKPUNT.). [Raakpunt Maarssen]. (1976)-. Periodical. Dutch. ir (8 issues). Fl25.00. Vogg, Postbus 85274, 3508 AG Utrecht Netherlands. **Tel** 011 31 30 363744. **UDC** 376.4. *Continues in part Zorgenkind (Maarssen), 0926-1788 and Onze Taak, 0030-3216*.

US/1051-4295
RAISING ARIZONA KIDS. [Rais. Ariz. kids]. (1990)-. Periodical. English. Twelve times a year. $12.00. Raising Arizona Kids, PO Box 9500, Suite 215, Phoenix AZ 85068. **Tel** (602)494-0220. **DD** 649.

US/0895-3740
RAISING KIDS. *Ceased*. [Rais. kids]. Vol. 1, No. 1 (Dec. 1987)-?. Periodical. English. mo. Kattan-Wright Corporation, 56 Dudley Street, Cambridge MA 02140. **DD** 649.

CN/0847-3587
RAPPORT ANNUEL / CONSEIL DE LA FAMILLE. [Rapp. annu. - Cons. fam.]. **Main/Corp** Quebec (Province). Conseil de la Famille. (1988/1989)-. French. Editeur Officiel du Quebec, 1283 Boul Charest Ouest, Quebec Quebec G1N 2C9 Canada. **LC** HQ560.15.Q4; Q43a. **DD** 354.71484/82/05. *Continues in part Rapport Annuel - Conseil des Affaires Sociales et de la Famille, 0226-4323*.

US/0278-6168
REPORT / NATIONAL COUNCIL ON FAMILY RELATIONS. Added/Corp National Council on Family Relations. **VFOAT** Report from the National Council on Family Relations. (19??)-. Periodical. English. qt. Free to members; $110.00 organizational membership; $80.00 regular membership. National Council of Family Relations, 3989 Central Avenue Northeast, Suite 550, Minneapolis MN 55421. **Tel** (612)781-9331, FAX (612)781-9348. **ED** Kathy Collins Royce. **LC** HQ1; .N38a. **DD** 306.8/5/0973. **Ad Acc**. **Circ:** 4,000. *Continues Report from the National Council on Family Relations, 0278-6168*.
 Desc: Articles on family life issues; plus news on the council's activities and annual conference.

US/1051-3469
RESOURCES FOR CHILD CARE. [Resour. child care]. Vol. 1, No. 1 (Jan./Feb. 1991)-. Periodical. English. bm. $15.00. KRI Educational Resources, RR3, Box 8755, Union ME 04862. **DD** 649.

US
REVISTA PARA NOVIAS. English. ir. $14.95. White Lace Inc, 1751 Northeast 162 Street, North Miami FL 33162. **Tel** (305)944-9444, FAX (305)949-0544.

IT
RIVISTA CONSULTORIO FAMILIARE. (19??)-. Italian. tq. 4000000L Italy; 7000000 other. Associazione Culturale Cieffe, Via Ognissanti N 65, 35129 Padua Italy. **Tel** 011 39 49 8719943.

PL/0137-8287
RODZINA. (1960)-. Periodical. Polish. bm. $9.00. **(Subscription address:** ARS Polona, PO Box 1001, 00068 Warsaw Poland.) **UDC** 173.

BE/0773-4239
RONDOM GEZIN. [Rondom Gezin]. (1980)-. Periodical. Dutch. Four times a year. 400.00F Belgium; 500.00F other. Natle Raad Voor Gezinspastoraal, Moerstraat 40, 8000 Brugge Belgium. **Tel** 050334187. **ED** Paul Deleu. **UDC** 362.17. **Bk Rev**. **Circ:** 1,600 (ctrl). available on diskette.
 Desc: Pastoral concerns on family, marriage, lifestyles and on the relationship with the Catholic Church.

KO
SAE KAJONG. VFOAT Christian Home. Periodical. Korean (Korean). W4,000. Sae Kajong Sa, PO Box 420, Kwangwunmun 110, Seoul South Korea. **LC** HQ1; .S23.

US/0164-0283
SAGE FAMILY STUDIES ABSTRACTS. **See** Family and Marriage-Abstracting, Bibliographies and Statistics.

US/1064-4512
SEATTLE'S CHILD. Vol. 1, No. 1 (Apr. 1979)-. Newspaper. English. Twelve times a year. $15.00 (one year); $25.00 (two years). Northwest Parent Publishing, 2107 Elliott Avenue, Suite 303, Seattle WA 98121. **Tel** (206)441-0191, FAX (206)441-4919. **ED** Ann Bergman. **Bk Rev**, (Qty: varies). **Ad Acc, Adv Mgr:** Alayne Sulkin. **Circ:** 25,000.
Desc: The news magazine for parents with kids 12 and under. Parenting issues, book/video/software reviews, nutrition, tv, activities, and calendar of events for kids and parents.

SP
SER PADRES HOY. (19??)-. Periodical. Spanish. mo. 3900ptas Spain; 7400ptas Europe; 10200ptas other. G & J Espana SA, Marques de Villamagna 4, 28001 Madrid Spain. **Tel** 011 34 1 4316631, FAX 011 34 1 2767881, telex 43419 ORBSA E.

US
SESAME STREET PARENTS. (19??)-. English. ir. Children's Television Workshop, One Lincoln Plaza, Box TG, New York NY 10023. **Tel** (212)595-3456.
Ind/Abst Mid. Search (Nov. 1993-); Prim. Search (Nov. 1993-).

US
SESAME STREET PARENT'S GUIDE. (19??)-. English. ir. Included with Sesame Street Magazine. Children's Television Workshop, One Lincoln Plaza, Box TG, New York NY 10023. **Tel** (212)595-3456.
Ind/Abst Prim. Search (July 1993-Oct. 1993).

UK/0267-4653
SEXUAL AND MARITAL THERAPY. (SEXUAL AND MARITAL THERAPY : JOURNAL OF THE ASSOCIATION OF SEXUAL AND MARITAL THERAPISTS.). [Sex. marital ther.]. **Added/Corp** Association of Sexual and Marital Therapists. Vol. 1 No. 1 (1986)-. Periodical. English. Three times a year. £128.00. Carfax Publishing Company, PO Box 25 Abingdon, Oxfordshire OX14 3UE England. **Tel** 011 44 235 555335, FAX (0279)31067, telex 817484. **(Subscription address:** US and Canada/ PO Box 2025, Dunnellon, FL 34430-2025; telephone:(904)489-6996) **NLM** W1; SE996. **[CCC]. Bk Rev**. available on microfiche.
Ind/Abst Appl. Soc. Sci. Index Abstr.; Multicult. Educ. Abstr.; Psychol. Abstr. (1986-); PsycINFO (1990-); PsycLit; Sage Fam. Stud. Abstr. (?-?); Soc. Plann. Policy Dev. Abstr.; Stud. Women Abstr.

US
SIBLING INFORMATION NETWORK NEWSLETTER. Newsletter. English. Four times a year. $15.00 institutions; $8.50 individuals. Sibling Information Network, 1776 Ellington Road, South Windsor CT 06074. **Tel** (203)648-1205, FAX (203)644-2031. **ED** Lisa Glidden. **Bk Rev**. ctrl circ.

US/0739-8719
SINGLE DAD'S LIFESTYLE. V. 1- Feb. 1978-. Periodical. English. mo. $12.00. Phoenix Rising / Arizona, PO Box 4842, Scottsdale AZ 85261-4841.

US/1040-6557
SINGLE DAD'S MAGAZINE. (1989)-. Periodical. English. mo. $18.00. Castleton Publishing Inc, 6565 South Dayton/Suite 2000, Englewood CO 80111.

US/0037-5748
SINGLE PARENT, THE. [Single parent]. **Added/Corp** Parents without Partners, Inc. (1965)-. Periodical. English. bm (6 issues). $15.00. Parents Without Partners Inc, 401 North Michigan, Chicago IL 60611. **Tel** (312)644-6610. **DD** 649. **Bk Rev. Ad Acc, Adv Mgr Tel** (301)588-9354. **Circ:** 115,000 (ctrl). Documents available from UMI Article Clearinghouse. ***Continues*** *PWP Journal.*
Desc: Constructive, upbeat articles dealing with all aspects of single parenting. Covers legislation, books, finances and relationships. Includes stories for children.
Ind/Abst Acad. Abstr. Full Text Elite (Feb. 1984-); Acad. Abstr. (Feb. 1984-); Acad. Search (Feb. 1984-); INFO-SOUTH Abstr.; Mag. Artic. Summar. Elite (Feb. 1984-); Mag. Artic. Summar. Select (Feb. 1984-); Mag. Artic. Summar. CD-ROM (Feb. 1984-); Mag. Search; Newsp. Period. Abstr. (1989-); Vocat. Search (Feb. 1984-).

●US/1077-4092
SINGLE-PARENT FAMILY. VFOAT Single Parent Family. (1994)-. Periodical. English. mo. $12.00. Focus on the Family, Colorado Springs CO 80995. **Tel** (800)232-6459.
Desc: Christian guidance for single parents.

US/1042-3559
SPEAK OUT FOR CHILDREN. [Speak out child.]. **Added/Corp** National Council for Children's Rights (U.S.). Vol. 1, No. 1 (April 1986)-. Periodical. English. Four times a year. $35.00 Comes with National Council for Childrens Rights membership. National Council for Children's Rights Inc, 220 I Street Northeast, Suite 230, Washington DC 20002. **Tel** (202)547-6227, (202)546-6589. **LC** HQ834; .S67. **DD** 362.82/86.

US/1047-2878
SPECIAL REPORT ON FAMILY. *Title Change.* [Spec. rep. fam.]. **VFOAT** Family; Special Report, Family; Special Report. (Nov. 1988/Jan. 1989)-(199?). Periodical. English. qt. Whittle Communications, 333 Main Avenue, Knoxville TN 37902. **Tel** (615)595-5000, FAX (615)595-5877. **LC** PAR. **DD** 646. ***Merged with*** *Special Report, Fiction, 1047-2886; Special Report on Health, 1047-272X; Special Report on Living, 1047-0123; Special Report on Personalities, 1047-286X* ***and*** *Special Report on Sports, 1047-2851* ***to form*** *Special Report (Whittle Communications), 1059-5201.*

FR
STATISTIQUES ET RESULTATS COMPLEMENTAIRES. **See** Family and Marriage-Abstracting, Bibliographies and Statistics.

US/0195-5969
STEPFAMILIES. Added/Corp Stepfamily Association of America. Vol. 9, No. 3 (Fall 1989)-. Periodical. English. qt. $14.00 (individual) + $2.00 surface mail; $22.00 (institution). Stepfamily Association of America, 215 Centennial Mall South, Suite 212, Lincoln NE 68508. **Tel** (402)477-7837, FAX (402) 477-8317. **LC** HQ759.92; .S728. **DD** 306.874. ***Continues*** *Stepfamily Bulletin, 0195-5969.*

US
STEPFAMILIES & BEYOND. (19??)-. Newsletter. English. mo (July & August issues combined). $15.00. Listening Inc, 8716 Pine Avenue, Gary IN 46403. **Tel** (219)938-6962. **ED** Patricia Work Bennett. ***Continues*** *Stepparent News, 0271-3225.*

IT
STUDI INTERDISCIPLINARI SULLA FAMIGLIA. Italian. ir. Vita e Pensiero, Pubblic University, Largo Gemelli 1, 20123 Milan Italy. **Tel** 011 39 2 72342310, 011 39 2 72342370.

US/0191-4219
STUDYING ADULT LIFE AND WORK LESSONS. (19??)-. Periodical. English. Editor/Sunday School Board, 127 Ninth Avenue North, Nashville TN 37234.

AT/1034-6384
SYDNEY'S CHILD. [Syd. Child]. (1990)-. Periodical. English. Eleven times a year (Dec/Jan. issue combined). 25.00Aus$. Copeland Publishing, PO Box 171, Beecroft New South Wales, 2119 Australia. **Tel** 011 61 2 484-5334, FAX 011 61 2 484-5334. **ED** Lillian Hund. **DD** 649.105. **Bk Rev**, (Qty: 11). **Ad Acc, Adv Mgr:** Joanna, **Tel** 02 484-5334. **Circ:** 55,000 (ctrl).

US/0162-7171
SYNOPSIS OF FAMILY THERAPY PRACTICE. **See** Medical Science and Technology-Psychiatry.

GW/0933-3053
SYSTEM FAMILIE. Vol. 1, No. 1 (Jan. 1988)-. Periodical. German (summaries and/or abstracts in English; table of contents in English). Four times a year. DM158.00. Springer-Verlag GmbH & Company KG, Heidelberger Platz 3, D 14197 Berlin Germany. **Tel** 011 49 30 8207223, FAX 011 49 30 8214091, telex 183 319 SPBLN D. **(Subscription address:** Springer Verlag New York Inc. / for North America, 44 Hartz Way, Secaucus NJ 07096.) **ED** E J Brunner and L Reiter. **NLM** W1; SY688. **[CCC]**. available on microfilm and microfiche from University Microfilms International (UMI).
Ind/Abst Soc. Sci. Cit. Index [Full Cov.].

US/0277-4100
TEXAS FAMILY JOURNAL. Vol. 1 (1980)-. Periodical. English. Texas Institute for Families, 8002 Bellaire Blvd. #1122, Houston TX 77036. **LC** HQ536; .T44. **DD** 306.8/7.

SZ/0250-4952
THERAPIE FAMILIALE. **See** Psychology.

CN/0226-1758
TODAY'S BRIDE (DON MILLS). (TODAY'S BRIDE.). [Today bride]. Vol. 1 (Spring/Summer 1980)-. Periodical. English. sa. 9.90Can$. Today's Bride, 37 Hanna Avenue Unit 1, Toronto Ontario M6K 1X1 Canada. **Tel** (416)537-2604. **ED** Kathy Fremes. **DD** 392/.5/05. **Ad Acc. Acid Free. Circ:** 112,000 (ctrl).
Desc: Wedding and pre-marital planning.

US/1055-3169
TODAY'S FAMILY (ST. PAUL, MINN.). (TODAY'S FAMILY.). [Today's fam.]. Vol. 1, No. 1 (May/June 1991)-. Periodical. English. bm. $10.97 (one year), $19.97 (two year). Minnesota Ink, 27 Empire Drive, St Paul MN 55103. **Tel** (612)225-1306. **DD** 306.

CN/0823-9258
TODAY'S PARENT. [Today's parent]. Vol. 1, No. 1 (Dec. 1984)-. Periodical. English. Eight times a year. 14.95Can$ Canada; 20.95Can$ other. Professional Publishing Association, 955 Meyerside Drive, Mississauga Ontarion L5T 1P9 Canada. **Tel** (905)564-6232. **ED** Fran Fearnley and Holly Bennett. **DD** 649/.1/05. **[CCC]. Bk Rev. Ad Acc. Circ:** 150,000 (ctrl).
Desc: National Canadian parenting magazine targeted to parents with children 0-6 years with special emphasis on children 0-3 years. The service articles, profiles, columns and in-depth features are written in a positive manner and cover all aspects of the modern family.
Ind/Abst Can. Index (?-?); Can. Period. Index (19??-).

CN/0831-2184
TORONTO'S WEDDING BELLS. [Tor. wedd. bells]. **VFOAT** Wedding Bells. (Spring/Summer 1986)-. Periodical. English (French). Twice a year (Feb. and Aug.). 12.00Can$ Canada; 20.00Can$ other. Wedding Bells, 120 Front Street East, Suite 200, Toronto Ontario M5A 4L9 Canada. **Tel** (416)862-8479, FAX (416)862-2184. **ED** Crys Stewart. **DD** 392/.5/09713541. **Ad Acc, Adv Mgr:** Alethea Wakefield. **Circ:** 100,000 (ctrl). ***Continues*** *Wedding Bells (Toronto, Ont.), 0829-2973.*
Desc: Journal of wedding planning with two regional editions.

US/0193-1385
TOWARD INTERAGENCY COORDINATION: FEDERAL RESEARCH AND DEVELOPMENT ON ADOLESCENCE. Main/Corp George Washington University. Social Research Group. **Added/Corp** United States. Interagency Panel for Research and Development on Adolescence. George Washington University. Social Research Group. Federal Research and Development on Adolescence. **VFOAT** Federal Research and Development on Adolescence. 1st (1974)-. English. an. US Department of Health and Human Services, 200 Independence Avenue Southwest, Washington DC 20201. **LC** HQ796; .G4174a. **DD** 301.43/15/072073.

CN/0049-4429
TRANSITION (OTTAWA). (TRANSITION. VANIER INSTITUTE OF THE FAMILY.). [Transition]. **Added/Corp** Vanier Institute of the Family. Vol. 1, (Feb. 1970)-. Periodical. English (French). Four times a year (Mar., June, Sept., Dec.). 15.00Can$ Canada, 25.00Can$ other, (associate memberships); 60.00Can$ Canada, 70.00Can$ other, (organizational memberships); 25.00Can$ Canada , 35.00Can$ other (individuals memberships). Vanier Institute of the Family, 120 Holland, Suite 300, Ottawa Ontario, K1Y OX6 Canada. **Tel** (613)722-4007, FAX (613)729-5249. **ED** Ish Theilheimer. **Bk Rev**, (Qty: 4). **Circ:** 7,500 (ctrl).
Desc: Publication reporting on its work and on work of others concerned with family issues. Included are summaries from current journal reviews, guest opinions, reference materials, conference notices and calender events.

US/0890-3077
TWINS. (TWINS : THE MAGAZINE FOR PARENTS OF MULTIPLES.). [Twins]. **VFOAT** Twins Magazine. (198?)-. Periodical. English. bm. $24.00 (one year), $39.95 (two year), $53.95 (three year). Twins Magazine Inc., 6740 Antioch, Merriam KS 66204. **Tel** (800)821-5533, (913)722-1090, FAX (913)722-1767. **ED** Barbara C. Unell. **LC** WMLC 93/1062. **Ad Acc, Adv Mgr:** Brenda Schifman, **Tel** (913)722-1090. ctrl circ.
Desc: Designed to give guidance to help multiples, their parents, and professionals who care for them learn about twin facts and research. The magazine enables readers to share feelings, expectations, myths, joys and realities about being and living with multiples from their birth through adulthood.

NE
VIDEO UIT EN THUIS. **See** Classical Studies.

RW
VIE FAMILIALE. Periodical. French. 400. Bureau de l'Enseignement Familial au Ministere de l'Education Nationale, B P 622, Kigali Rwanda. **LC** HQ1; .V53. **DD** 301.42/0967/571. ***Continues*** *Vie Feminine et Enseignement Familial.*

US/0890-832X
VITAL CONNECTIONS. **See** Sociology-Manners and Customs.

US/8750-9563
WELCOME HOME. (WELCOME HOME. A PUBLICATION IN SUPPORT OF MOTHER'S WHO CHOOSE TO STAY HOME.). [Welcome home]. (1984)-. Periodical. English. Twelve times a year. $18.00. Mothers at Home Inc., 8310 Old Courthouse Road, Vienna VA 22182. **Tel** (703)827-5903, FAX (703)790-8587. **ED** Elizabeth Foss, Cheryl Hughes and Laura Jones, (phone: (703)827-5903). **Bk Rev**, (Qty: 3-4). **Pr Rev. Circ:** 18,000 (ctrl).
Desc: Is for the woman who has actively chosen to devote her exceptional skills and good mind to the nurturing of her family.

US
WESTERN NEW YORK FAMILY MAGAZINE. (19??)-. English. Twelve times a year. $18.00 (one year), $32.00 (2 year), $42.00 (3 year).

Western New York Family Magazine, 287 Parkside Avenue, PO Box 265, Buffalo NY 14215-0265. **Tel** (716)836-3486, FAX (716)836-3680. **ED** Michele Miller. **Bk Rev**, (Qty: 15 per year). **Ad Acc**, **Adv Mgr:** Doug Carpenter. **Circ:** 25,000 (ctrl).
Desc: Regional parenting publication for parents with children ages 0-12.

US/1040-0958
WORK & FAMILY LIFE. [Work fami. life]. **Added/Corp** Bank Street College. **VFOAT** Work and Family Life; WFL. (19??)-. Periodical. English. mo (except combined July/Aug.). $36.00. Work and Family Life, 6211 West Howard Street, Chicago IL 60714. **Tel** (708)647-6860. **DD** 646.

US
WORK & FAMILY SOURCEBOOK, THE. (1990)-. English. $89.00. Gale Research Inc., 835 Penobscot Building, Detroit MI 48226. **Tel** (800)877-GALE, (313)961-2242, FAX (313)961-6083, telex TWX 810-221-7086. **ED** Fairlee E Winfield. **DD** 658.3/12.
Desc: Important reference for human resource professionals, Employee Assistance Program counselors, benefits administrators, students, and anyone else interested in the study of American work and family relationships. Contributors to the 52 articles, studies, reports, and legislative proposals include the most knowledgeable, respected, and influential people in the field.

US/1060-930X
WORK-FAMILY ROUNDTABLE. (WORK-FAMILY ROUNDTABLE, ... / THE CONFERENCE BOARD.). [Work-fam. roundtable]. **Added/Corp** Conference Board. **VFOAT** Work Family Roundtable. Vol. 1, No. 1 (Dec. 1991)-. Periodical. English. qt. Free to associates of the Conference Board; $150.00 non-associates. Conference Board, 845 Third Avenue, New York NY 10022. **Tel** (212)759-0900 ext. 582, (800)872-6273, FAX (212)980-7014. **LC** HD4904.25; .W668. **DD** 331.25.

US/0278-193X
WORKING MOTHER (NEW YORK, N.Y. 1981). (WORKING MOTHER.). [Work. mother]. Vol. 4, No. 3 (May 1981)-. Periodical. English. mo. $7.97 (one year), $15.94 (two year). Lang Communications, 230 Park Avenue, New York NY 10169. **Tel** (212)551-9500, FAX (212)599-4597. **(Subscription address:** CDS Agency Hard Copy, PO Box 4966, Des Moines IA 50340.**) LC** HQ759; .M284. **DD** 306.8/7. **[CCC]. Ad Acc.** available on microfilm and microfiche from University Microfilms International (UMI). Documents available from UMI Article Clearinghouse. ***Continues*** *McCall's Working Mother, 0160-6131.*
Desc: The only magazine written for today's busy working mother. Provides expert advice and information on child development, your career, the latest health news, fashion and beauty, family finance, quick and easy recipes, and much more.
Ind/Abst Acad. Abstr. Full Text Elite (Jan. 1992-); Acad. Abstr. (Jan. 1992-); Acad. Search (Jan. 1992-); AGRICOLA; Gen. Period. Index (1992-); INFO-SOUTH Abstr.; Mag. Artic. Summar. Elite (Jan. 1992-); Mag. Artic. Summar. Select (Jan. 1992-); Mag. Artic. Summar. CD-ROM (Jan. 1992-); Mag. Index Plus (1992-); Mag. Search; Newsp. Period. Abstr. (1991-); Read. Guide Abstr. Select Ed.; Read. Guide Period. Lit.; Vocat. Search (Jan. 1992-); Work Relat. Abstr. (-19??).

US/0747-6140
WORKING PARENTS. ***Suspended.*** [Work. parents]. (1984)-?. Periodical. English. bm. $6.00. Mothers Manual Inc, Readers Services, Subscription Offices Box 279, Bronxville NY 10708. **LC** HQ755.8; .W68. **DD** 306.874/05.

US/0300-7006
WORLD EDUCATION REPORTS. **See** Education.

BG
YAUTUKA. **VFOAT** Dowry; Joutuk. June/December 1980-. Periodical. Bengali. sa. 10.00. Soukhin Prokasony, 120/40 North Sajahan Pur, Dacca Bangladesh. **LC** HQ1017; .Y38.

US/1055-6036
YOUR CHILD'S HEALTH AND DEVELOPMENT. (1991)-. Periodical. English. mo. $39.00. United States Medical Information Center, 1133 Fifteenth Street NW, Wahington DC 20005.

II
YUVA PRAGATI. Periodical. Hindi. Rs5.00. Bharatiya Yuvaka Kangresa, 1-C Ferozeshah Road, New Delhi India. **LC** HQ799.I5; Y86.

NP
YUVAKA. Periodical. Multiple languages (Nepali). 10.00. Yuvaka Sangathana, Jawalakhol Lalitpur, Kathamadaum Nepal. **LC** HQ799.N36; Y8.

US/1051-7804
ZOOMER & CO. ***Ceased.*** [Zoomer co.]. **VFOAT** Zoomer and Co.; Christian Parenting Today Presents Zoomer & Co. **VAT** Zoomer and Company. Vol. 1, No. 1 (Sept. 1990)-?. Periodical. English. qt. Good Family Magazines, PO Box 36630, Colorado Springs CO 80636. **Tel** (719)531-7776. **DD** 051.

US/0199-0071
ZPG REPORTER. **Added/Corp** Zero Population Growth, Inc. **VFOAT** Z.P.G. Reporter. **VAT** Zero Population Growth Reporter. Vol. 11, No.6 (Aug. 1979)-. Periodical. English. bm. $20.00, $10.00 (students, libraries, senior citizens). Zero Population Growth / Washington DC, 1400 Sixteenth Street Northwest, Suite 320, Washington DC 20036. **Tel** (202)332-2200, FAX (202)332-2302. **Acid Free. Circ:** 70,000. Documents available from Documents on Demand. ***Continues*** *Zero Population Growth National Reporter, 0049-8718.*
Desc: Includes news briefs, and articles on family planning. Serves as an advocate to stop over-population.
Ind/Abst Environ. Abstr.

ABSTRACTING, BIBLIOGRAPHIES AND STATISTICS

US/0098-390X
ANNUAL STATISTICAL SUMMARY OF THE STATE OF MARYLAND FAMILY PLANNING PROGRAM. **Main/Corp** Maryland. Dept. of Health and Mental Hygiene. Statistical Publication. English. an. Maryland Department of Health and Mental Hygiene, 201 West Preston Street, Baltimore MD 21201. **Tel** (410)225-6500. **LC** HQ766.5.U5; M33A. **DD** 362.8/2.

US/0092-6000
CURRENT LITERATURE IN FAMILY PLANNING. [Curr. lit. fam. plann.]. **Main/Corp** Katharine Dexter McCormick Library. **Added/Corp** Planned Parenthood Federation of America. Dept. of Education. (1972)-. Abstracting/Indexing Service. English. mo. $40.00. Planned Parenthood, 810 7th Avenue, K Medical Division, New York NY 10019. **Tel** (212)541-7800. **ED** Gloria A Roberts (telephone: (212)541-7800. **LC** Z7164.B5; K37a; HQ766. **DD** 016.3639/6. **NLM** Z 675.F4 C976. **Bk Rev. Circ:** 600. available on microfilm from University Microfilms International (UMI). ***Continues*** *Acquisitions List - Katharine Dexter McCormick Library.*
Desc: Classified annotated list of books and articles in the field of family planning received in the Library of Planned Parenthood Federation of America.
Ind/Abst Curr. Lit. Fam. Plan.; Popul. Index (?-?).

AT
DIVORCES AUSTRALIA / AUSTRALIAN BUREAU OF STATISTICS. **Added/Corp** Australian Bureau of Statistics. (1976)-. English. an. 12.20Aus$. Australian Bureau of Statistics, PO Box 10, Belconnen Australian Capital Territory, 2616 Australia. **Tel** 011 61 6 2527911, FAX 011 61 6 2516009. **LC** HQ960; .A23a. **DD** 306.8/9/0994. ***Continues*** *Divorces.*
Desc: Number of decrees granted for dissolution of marriage.

CN/0703-7368
FAMILY INCOMES. CENSUS FAMILIES. (FAMILY INCOMES (CENSUS FAMILIES) / DOMINION BUREAU OF STATISTICS, CONSUMER FINANCE RESEARCH STAFF.). [Fam. incomes, Census fam.]. **Main/Corp** Statistics Canada. Consumer Income and Expenditure Division. **Added/Corp** Canada. Dominion Bureau of Statistics. Consumer Finance Research Staff. Statistics Canada. Consumer Finance Research Staff. Statistics Canada. Consumer Income and Expenditure Division. Statistics Canada. Household Surveys Division. **VFOAT** Revenu de Familles (Familles de Recensement); Revenus de Familles (Familles de Recensement). (1967)-. Periodical. English (French). an. 37.00Can$ Canada; $33.00 North America; $38.00 other. Statistics Canada, Publications Sales & Services, Main Building Room 1710, Ottawa Ontario K1A 0T6 Canada. **Tel** (613)951-5078, (800)267-6677, FAX (613)951-1584, telex 053-3585. **LC** HC120.I5; C35c. **DD** 339.4/1/0971. **Circ:** 500.
Desc: Distributions of census families and persons not in families by size of income, region or province, age, sex and other characteristics. The family concept used is identical to the Canadian census. Statistics are derived from the Survey of Consumer Finances conducted annually since 1972.

CN/1180-3126
HEALTH REPORTS. SUPPLEMENT. DIVORCES. (HEALTH REPORTS. NO. 17, SUPPLEMENT. DIVORCES / STATISTICS CANADA, CANADIAN CENTRE FOR HEALTH INFORMATION.). [Health rep., Suppl., Divorces]. **Added/Corp** Canadian Centre for Health Information. **VFOAT** Divorces; Rapport sur la Sante. No 17, Divorces. (1988)-. English (French). an. 20.00Can$ Canada; $24.00 US; $28.00 other. Statistics Canada, Publications Sales & Services, Main Building Room 1710, Ottawa Ontario K1A 0T6 Canada. **Tel** (613)951-5078, (800)267-6677, FAX (613)951-1584, telex 053-3585. **LC** HQ838; .H4. **DD** 306.89/0971/021/. ***Continues in part*** *Marriages and Divorces, Vital Statistics, Volume II, 0825-298X.*
Desc: Presents data on divorces for Canada and the provinces.

AT
MARRIAGES, AUSTRALIA. **Added/Corp** Australian Bureau of Statistics. (19??)-. English. an. 12.50Aus$. Australian Bureau of Statistics, PO Box 10, Belconnen Australian Capital Territory, 2616 Australia. **Tel** 011 61 6 2527911, FAX 011 61 6 2516009. ***Continues*** *Australian Bureau of Statistics. Marriages.*
Desc: Registrations of marriages classified according to State or Territory of registration, age, previous marital status and country of birth of bridegrooms and brides, type of celebration, and month of celebration of marriage.

CN/1195-4140
MARRIAGES / STATISTICS CANADA, CANADIAN CENTRE FOR HEALTH INFORMATION. **Added/Corp** Canadian Centre for Health Information. **VFOAT** Mariages. (1991)-. English (French). 20.00Can$ Canada; $24.00 US; $28.00 other. Statistics Canada, Publications Sales & Services, Main Building Room 1710, Ottawa Ontario K1A 0T6 Canada. **Tel** (613)951-5078, (800)267-6677, FAX (613)951-1584, telex 053-3585. **LC** HB1149; .H43. **DD** 306.81/0971/021. ***Continues*** *Health Reports. Supplement. Marriages, 1180-3118.*

US/0164-0283
SAGE FAMILY STUDIES ABSTRACTS. [Sage fam. stud. abstr.]. **Added/Corp** Sage Publications, Inc. **VFOAT** Family Studies Abstracts. Vol. 1 (Feb. 1979)-. Abstracting/Indexing Service. English. qt (Feb., May, Aug., Nov.). $293.00. SAGE Periodical Press, 2455 Teller Road, Thousand Oaks CA 91320. **Tel** (805)499-0721, FAX (805)499-0871, telex 100799. **LC** HQ536; .S23. **DD** 301.42/0973. **NLM** Z 7164.F2 S129. **Bk Rev. Acid Free. Circ:** 750. available on microfilm and microfiche from University Microfilms International (UMI).
Desc: Abstracts major articles, reports, books and other materials on policy, theory and research relating to the family, interpersonal relations, human development, therapy and counseling.

FR
STATISTIQUES ET RESULTATS COMPLEMENTAIRES. **Main/Corp** Caisse Nationale des Allocations Familiales. (19??)-. French. **LC** HV700.F8; C33a. **DD** 362.8/2.

FIRE PREVENTION

US/1040-7316
9-1-1 MAGAZINE. **See** Communication.

US/0094-3932
ADVANCES IN FIRE RETARDANTS. Pt. 1, (1972)-. English. an. Technomic Publishing Company, Inc., 851 New Holland Avenue, Box 3535, Lancaster PA 17604. **Tel** (717)291-5609, (800)233-9936, FAX (717)295-4538. **LC** TP266.5; .A35. **DD** 628.9/22.

US
AERIAL APPLICATOR, FARM, FOREST AND FIRE. **See** Agriculture-Agricultural Equipment.

CN/0848-6794
ALBERTA FIRE NEWS (1990). (ALBERTA FIRE NEWS.). [Alta. fire news]. **Added/Corp** Alberta. Fire Prevention Branch. Vol. 11, No. 1 (May 1990)-. Periodical. English. sa. **DD** 354.71230078/2. ***Continues*** *Fire News., 0704-4259.*

BU/0204-8531
ALO, 160. (1991)-. Periodical. Bulgarian. mo. **LC** TH9111; .A45. ***Continues*** *Ogneborets.*

US/0739-3709
AMERICAN FIRE JOURNAL. [Am. fire j.]. Vol. 35, No. 9 (Sept. 1983)-. Periodical. English. mo. $19.95 (US); $35.50 (other). American Fire Journal, 9072 East Artesia Boulevard, Suite 7, Bellflower CA 90706-9990. **Tel** (310)866-1664, FAX (310)867-6434. **ED** John A. Ackerman. **LC** TH9111; .W47. **DD** 628.9/2/05. Index available in last issue of volume--attached. cum. index. **Ad Acc. Circ:** 5,800. ***Continues*** *Western Fire Journal, 0043-3705.*
Desc: Published for the progressive fire and rescue service. A forward-thinking, solution-oriented magazine. Focuses on current management and technical needs.
Ind/Abst Urban Aff. Abstr.

US/0278-1050
ANNUAL CONFERENCE ON FIRE RESEARCH. (ANNUAL CONFERENCE ON FIRE RESEARCH / CENTER FOR FIRE RESEARCH, NATIONAL ENGINEERING LABORATORY, NATIONAL BUREAU OF STANDARDS, U.S. DEPARTMENT OF COMMERCE.). [Annu. Conf. Fire Res.]. **Main/Conf** Conference on Fire Research. **Added/Corp** Center for Fire Research (U.S.). Began with (1977)-. Periodical. English. an. $9.00. National Technical Information

Service - NTIS, Room 2027S, 5285 Port Royal Road, Springfield VA 22161. **Tel** (703)487-4630, (703)487-4660, (703)487-4650, FAX (703)321-8547, telex 89-9405. **LC** TH9112; .C58a. **DD** 628.9/22/05.

US
ANNUAL FIRE REPORT (WASHINGTON). (ANNUAL FIRE REPORT.). **Main/Corp** United States. Bureau of Land Management. Government Publication. English. US Department of the Interior Bureau of Land Management, 1849 C Street NW, Room 5660, Washington DC 20240. **Tel** (202)208-3801, FAX (202)208-5902. **DD** 634.9.

US/0149-354X
ANNUAL MEETING, TECHNICAL COMMITTEE REPORTS. **Main/Corp** National Fire Protection Association. **Added/Corp** National Fire Protection Association. Technical Committee Reports. National Fire Protection Association. NFPA Technical Committee Reports. **VFOAT** NFPA Technical Committee Reports. (19??)-. English. be. Free on request. National Fire Protection Association, 1 Batterymarch Park, PO Box 9101, Quincy MA 02269-9101. **Tel** (617)770-3000, (800)344-3555. **LC** TH9111; .N322. **DD** 628.9/22.

US
ANNUAL REPORT OF THE COMMISSION ON FIRE PROTECTION, PERSONNEL STANDARDS, AND EDUCATION. **Main/Corp** Oklahoma State Fire Commission. Commission on Fire Protection, Personnel Standards, and Education. (June 30, 1982)-. English. **LC** TH9504; .O51a. **DD** 353.97660078/2. ***Continues*** *Oklahoma State Fire Commission. Commission on Fire Protection, Personnel Standards, and Education. Annual Report, 0732-9903.*

BE/0778-7383
ANPI MAGAZINE. [ANPI mag.]. **VFOAT** Association Nationale pour la Protection Contre l'Incendie et l'Intrusion Magazine. (1991)-. Periodical. French (Dutch). bm. Assn Nationale pour Protection, Parc Scientifique, 1348 Ottignies Belgium. **Tel** 11 32 10 475211, telex 010 47 52 70. **UDC** 614.84. Index available. **Ad Acc.** **Pr Rev.** ***Continues*** *Revue Belge du Feu, 0771-4033.*
Desc: Presents articles regarding fire, burglary prevention and protection. We also discuss the novelties, legal texts, standards and techniques concerning fire.

IT/0393-7089
ANTINCENDIO (1979). (ANTINCENDIO : SICUREZZA SUL LAVORO-PROTEZIONE CIVILE.). Vol. 5, No. 31 (Jan. 1979)-. Periodical. Italian. Twelve times a year. L185000.00 Italy; L200000.00 Europe; L220000.00 other. Edizioni Protezione Civile SPA, Via dell Acqua Traversa 187/189, 00135 Rome Italy. **Tel** 011 39 6 3313000, FAX 011 39 6 3313212, telex 626462 EPCINFI. Index available in last issue of volume--attached. **Bk Rev.** **Ad Acc**, **Adv Mgr:** Nunzio Rubino. **Circ:** 9,000. ***Continues*** *Antincendio e Protezione Civile.*
Desc: Deals with fire prevention and intervention techniques.

US
ARSON REPORTER. **Added/Corp** American Bar Association. Arson Project Committee. (19??)-. Periodical. English. mo. $16.00. American Bar Association, 750 North Lake Shore Drive, Chicago IL 60611. **Tel** (312)988-5522, (312)988-5241, FAX (312)988-5528, telex 270593. **LC** KF9377.A15; A77. **DD** 345.73/0264/005.

CN/0838-679X
ATLANTIC FIREFIGHTER. [Atl. firef.]. Vol. 1, Issue 1 (Sept. 1987)-. Periodical. English (French). mo. 10.00Can$. Cumberland Publishing Ltd, Box 280, Amherst Nova Scotia B4H 3Z2 Canada. **Tel** (902)667-5102. **DD** 363.3/78/09715. **Bk Rev.** **Ad Acc.** ctrl circ.
Desc: Coverage of all fire service related matters in Atlantic Canada.

US/0160-5291
AUDIT REPORT, STATE OF NEVADA DEPARTMENT OF COMMERCE, STATE FIRE MARSHAL DIVISION. **Main/Corp** Nevada. Legislative Auditor. English. an. Legislative Auditor, Legislative Building, Capitol Complex, Carson City NV 89710. **LC** TH9504.N31; N46A. **DD** 353.9/793/00782. **UDC** 614.84(047.33)(793).

US
AUTOMATIC SPRINKLER AND STANDPIPE SYSTEMS. (19??)-. English. ir. $55.65 nonmembers; $50.40 members. National Fire Protection Association, 1 Batterymarch Park, PO Box 9101, Quincy MA 02269-9101. **Tel** (617)770-3000, (800)344-3555.
Desc: Information on current sprinkler and standpipe technology.

US
AUTOMATIC SPRINKLER SYSTEMS HANDBOOK. (19??)-. English. an. $78.65 nonmembers; $71.15 members. National Fire Protection Association, 1 Batterymarch Park, PO Box 9101, Quincy MA 02269-9101. **Tel** (617)770-3000, (800)344-3555.

US
AUTOMOTIVE AND MARINE SERVICE STATION CODE. **See** Petroleum and Natural Gas.

US
BIENNIAL REPORT - NEVADA STATE FIRE MARSHAL DIVISION. **Main/Corp** Nevada. State Fire Marshal Division. English. be. State Fire Marshal Division, Kinkead Building, Capitol Complex/Room 302, 505 East King Street, Carson City NV 89710. **LC** TH9504.N31; N47A. **DD** 353.9/793/0078205. **UDC** 614.84(047.33)(793).

US/0897-0084
BOCA NATIONAL FIRE PREVENTION CODE, THE. [BOCA natl. fire prev. code]. **Main/Corp** Building Officials and Code Administrators International. **VFOAT** National Fire Prevention Code. **VAT** Building Officials and Code Administrators National Fire Prevention Code. 7th Edition (1987)-. English. ir (Every three years). $30.00 (members), $45.00 (non-members) soft cover; $34.00 (members), $49.00 (non-members) loose leaf. BOCA International, 4051 West Flossmoore Road, Country Club Hills IL 60478. **Tel** (708)799-2300, FAX (708)799-4981. **LC** KF3975; .B85. **DD** 344.73/0537; 347.304537. ***Continues*** *Building Officials and Code Administrators International. BOCA Basic/National Fire Prevention Code.*

GW/0006-906X
BRANDHILFE. [Brandhilfe]. (1954)-. Periodical. German. mo. DM45.50. Neckar Verlag GmbH, Klosterring 1, Postfach 1820, 78008 Villingen Germany. **Tel** 011 49 7721 89870, FAX 011 49 7721 8987 50. **UDC** 614.8. **[CCC].**

DK/0106-6072
BRANDVAERN. [Brandvrus]. **Added/Corp** Dansk Brandinspektorfreningen. Dansk Brandvrus-Komite. Vol. 1 (Jan. 1975)-. Periodical. Danish (English; summaries and/or abstracts in English). Twelve times a year. $15.25. Dansk Brandinspektoerforening / Danish Fire Protection Association, Datavej 48, DK 3460 Birkeroed Denmark. **Tel** 45 82 00 99, FAX 45 82 24 99. **ED** Ole B. Kristensen and H. C. Salomonsen. **LC** TH9549; .A27. Index available. **Ad Acc.** **Circ:** 5,600. ***Formed by the union of*** *Brandfare & i.e. OG Brandvaern* ***and*** *Dansk Brandvaern.*
Ind/Abst Saf. Health Work.

GW/0006-9116
BRANDWACHT. [Brandwacht]. Periodical. German. mo. DM16.20. Bayerisches Landesamt Katastro W-40, Germany. **Tel** (089)391053. **LC** TH9111; .B3. **UDC** 614.84. Index available. **Bk Rev.** **Ad Acc.** ctrl circ. ***Continues*** *Brandwacht.*
Ind/Abst Energy Res. Abstr. (March 1982-); Saf. Health Work.

UK/0265-962X
BRE NEWS OF FIRE RESEARCH. [BRE news fire res.]. **Added/Corp** Building Research Establishment. Fire Research Station. (May 1984)-. Periodical. English. qt. Free. Building Research Establishment, BRE Bookshop, Garston Watford WD27JR England. **Tel** 011 44 923 664444, FAX 011 44 923 664400. ctrl circ. ***Continues in part*** *BRE News, 0144-8358.*
Ind/Abst Avery Index Archit. Period. Suppl. Colum. Univ. (19??-199?); Fluid Abstr., Civil Eng.; Fluid Abstr. Proc. Eng.; FLUIDEX (-19??); J. Ferrocement.

AT
BUSH FIRE BULLETIN. **Added/Corp** Bush Fire Council of New South Wales. (19??)-. Periodical. English. qt. Bush Fire Council of New South Wales, Unit 3/175-179 James Ruse Drive, Rosehill New South Wales 2142 Australia. **Tel** (02)684-4411, FAX (02)638-7956, telex AA71438. **ED** Gilly Paxton. **LC** SD421.34.A8; B85. **DD** 363.3/79. **Bk Rev.** **Ad Acc**, **Adv Mgr:** John Jackson. Full Page (B&W) 880.00Aus$. Half Page (B&W) 460.00Aus$. Full Page (Color) 1150.00Aus$. Half Page (Color) 750.00Aus$. **Circ:** 30,000 (ctrl).
Desc: Reports on Bush Fire Council policies, staff, equipment, training and education program news from volunteer bushfire brigades. Articles on land management, fire prevention, mitigation, safety, etc.

CN/0846-3255
BYTOWN FIRE BRIGADE NEWSLETTER, THE. [Bytown Fire Brigade newsl.]. **Added/Corp** Bytown Fire Brigade. **VFOAT** B.F.B. Newsletter. **VAT** Newsletter - Bytown Fire Brigade. Vol. 1, No. 1 (June 1991)-. Newsletter. English. qt. Free to members (membership: $20.00). Bytown Fire Brigade, 2880 Sheffield Road, Ottawa Ontario K1B 1A4 Canada. **DD** 628.9.

CN/0706-1382
C A F C DIALOGUE. [C A F C dialogue]. **Main/Corp** Canadian Association of Fire Chiefs. **VFOAT** A C C P Dialogue. No. 1- Nov. 1975-. Periodical. English (French). bm. Free. Canadian Association of Fire Chiefs, 111-196 Bronson Avenue, Ottawa Ontario K1R 6H4 Canada. **DD** 628.9/2/0971. **UDC** 614.84(71). ctrl circ.

US
CALIFORNIA FIRE CONTROL NOTES (CALIFORNIA. DEPT. OF FORESTRY). (CALIFORNIA FIRE CONTROL NOTES / STATE OF CALIFORNIA, THE RESOURCES AGENCY, DEPARTMENT OF FORESTRY.). **VFOAT** Fire Control Notes. English. California Department of Forestry, 1416 9th Street, Sacramento CA 95814. **Tel** (916)445-9886. **LC** SD421; .C15b. **DD** 363.3/79. **UDC** 614.841(061)(794). ***Continues*** *Fire Control Notes (California. Division of Forestry : 1975), 0575-3031.*

US/1048-5074
CALIFORNIA FIRE SERVICE, THE. (CALIFORNIA FIRE SERVICE.). **Added/Corp** California State Firemen's Association. Vol. 1, No. 1 (Jan. 1990)-. Periodical. English. mo. $15.00. California State Firefighters Association, 3246 Ramos Circle, Sacramento CA 95827. ***Continues*** *California Fireman, 0739-0114.*

CN/0704-6391
CANADIAN FIREFIGHTER, THE. [Can. firef.]. **VAT** Firefighter (Toronto). Vol. 1 (March/April 1977)-. Periodical. English (French). bm. 11.22Can$ Canada; 36.00Can$ other. Canadian Firefighter, 480 Prince Edward Drive, Toronto ONT M8X 2M8 Canada. **Tel** (416)233-2516, FAX (416)233-2051. **ED** Lorne Campbell. **DD** 628.9/2/0971. **Ad Acc.** **Circ:** 12,000 (ctrl).
Desc: Educational training subjects in each issue. Latest equipment for firefighters and clothing for firefighting.

US
COURSE CATALOG / NATIONAL FIRE ACADEMY. ***Title Change.*** **Main/Corp** National Fire Academy. **Added/Corp** National Emergency Training Center (U.S.). (1983/1984)-(19??). Catalog. English. an. National Emergency Training Center, 16825 South Seton Avenue, Emmitsburg MD 21727. ***Continues*** *National Fire Academy. Catalog of Resident Courses.* ***Continued by*** *Catalog of On-Campus Courses.*

US
CSFM JOURNAL. **Added/Corp** California. Office of the State Fire Marshal. **VFOAT** SFM Journal. **VAT** California State Fire Marshal Journal; State Fire Marshal Journal. No. 6 (Jan./Feb. 1989)-. Periodical. English. bm. California State Fire Marshal, c/o Public Education Unit, 7171 Bowling Drive/Suite 600, Sacramento CA 95823. **Tel** (916)427-4178. ***Continues*** *SFM Journal.*

IT
ECO DEI VIGILI DEL FUOCO. EVF Eidzioni, Via Forze Armate 50, 20147 Milan Italy.

US
EMERGENCY MANAGEMENT OF HAZARDOUS MATERIALS INCIDENTS. **See** Industrial Health and Safety.

US/0362-2487
ENJINE! ENJINE!. **Added/Corp** Society for the Preservation and Appreciation of Antique Motor Fire Apparatus in America. (19??)-. Periodical. English. Four times a year. $20.00. SPAAMFAA, PO Box 2005, Syracuse NY 13220. **LC** TH9371; .E53. **DD** 628.9/252.

US
FALL MEETING, TECHNICAL COMMITTEE REPORTS. **Main/Corp** National Fire Protection Association. **VFOAT** NFPA Technical Committee Reports. (19??)-. English. be. Free on request. National Fire Protection Association, 1 Batterymarch Park, PO Box 9101, Quincy MA 02269-9101. **Tel** (617)770-3000, (800)344-3555. **LC** TH9503; .N19a. **DD** 628.9/2/0973. ***Continues*** *National Fire Protection Association. Technical Committee Reports.*

US
FIRE ALARM SIGNALING SYSTEMS. (19??)-. English. ir. $64.75 nonmembers; $58.25 members. National Fire Protection Association, 1 Batterymarch Park, PO Box 9101, Quincy MA 02269-9101. **Tel** (617)770-3000, (800)344-3555.
Desc: Addresses current technical applications and code requirements involving fire protection devices.

US/1059-7298
FIRE AND ARSON INVESTIGATOR, THE. [Fire arson invest.]. **Added/Corp** International Association of Arson Investigators. (19??)-. English. qt. International Association of Arson Investigators, 5428 Del Maria Way/Suite 201, Louisville KY 40291. **Tel** (502)491-7482. **LC** HV8079.A7; F57. **DD** 364.12. ***Continues*** *News Letter.*
Ind/Abst Crim. Justice Abstr.

US/0738-3940
FIRE & EMERGENCY WORLD. [Fire emerg. world]. **VFOAT** Fire and Emergency World. No. 1 (Thursday, Sept. 1, 1983)-. Periodical. English. Twelve times a year. $9.95. Fire & Emergency World Inc, 19 Joslin Street, Providence RI 02909. **Tel** (401)751-8509.

UK
FIRE & FLAMMABILITY BULLETIN. **VFOAT** Fire and Flammability Bulletin. (19??)-. Bulletin. English. Twelve times a year. $397.00 The Americas;

£266.00 other. Elsevier Advanced Technology, An Imprint of Elsevier Science Ltd., The Boulevard, Langford Lane, Kidlington, Oxford OX5 1GB United Kingdom. **Tel** 011 44 865 843000, 011 44 865 843699, FAX 011 44 865 843010. **(Subscription address:** Elsevier Science Ltd. Oxford Fulfillment Centre, PO Box 800, Kidlington, Oxford OX5 1DX United Kingdom.**)** **ED** Stephen J. Grayson, Carol Franks. available on microfilm from University Microfilms International (UMI). Documents available from Article Express International.
Desc: Provides a unique, comprehensive monitor of fire safety, prevention, detection, and control.
Ind/Abst Ei Page One; Eng. Index Annu.

UK/0308-0501
FIRE AND MATERIALS. **See** Building and Construction.

UK
FIRE AND RESCUE. English. qt. £30.00 Europe; £35.00 other. Kennedy Communications Limited, Unit 8, Old Yarn Mills West She, Dorset DT9 3RQ England. **Tel** 011 44 935 816030, FAX 011 44 935 817200.

UK
FIRE & SECURITY PROTECTION. ***Ceased.*** **See** Security Systems and Alarms.

US/0885-8837
FIRE APPARATUS JOURNAL. [Fire appar. j.]. Vol. 1, No. 1 (Summer 1984)-. Periodical. English. bm (Jan., Mar., May, July, Sept., Nov.). $21.00 (1 year), $40.00 (2 year) US; $24.00 (1 year), $46.00 (2 year) other. Fire Apparatus Journal, PO Box 141295, Staten Island NY 10314-1295. **Tel** (718)448-5009, FAX (718)981-2359. **ED** Elena Miranda. **LC** TH9371; .F53. **DD** 628.9/25. **Bk Rev**, (Qty: 6). **Ad Acc. Circ:** 7,000.
Desc: Devoted to firefighting apparatus of all types: contemporary, historical, military, new deliveries, rebuilt vehicles, fire boats, museums, upcoming shows, model fire trucks, books, and other items of interest. Each issue has regular columns and feature articles illustrated with color photos.

US/0015-2552
FIRE CHIEF. [Fire chief]. **VFOAT** Fire Chief Magazine. Vol. 1 (1956)-. Periodical. English. Twelve times a year. $52.00 (one year); $83.00 (two years). Argus Business, 6151 Powers Ferry Road, Atlanta GA 30339. **Tel** (404)995-2500, (800)233-3359. **(Subscription address:** Hallmark Data Systems, PO Box 1165, Skokie IL 60076.**)** **ED** William Randleman. **LC** TH9111; .F54. **[CCC]. Bk Rev. Ad Acc. Circ:** 32,000. available on microfilm and microfiche from University Microfilms International (UMI).
Desc: We carry articles of help to fire chiefs of city, county, and district fire departments- volunteer and paid.
Ind/Abst Urban Aff. Abstr.

US/0889-5740
FIRE CONTROL DIGEST. [Fire control dig.]. **VFOAT** Washington Fire News Services' Fire Control Digest; Washington Capital News Reports' Fire Control Digest. Vol. 1, No. 1 (Jan. 1975)-. Periodical. English. mo. $145.00 (one year), $225.00 (two year), $290.00 (three year). Washington Crime News Services, 3918 Prosperity Avenue, Suite 318, Fairfax VA 22031-3334. **Tel** (703)573-1600, (800)422-9267, FAX (703)573-1604. **DD** 628. **Bk Rev. Circ:** 1,000.
Desc: Independent monthly news service/information exchange for fire service professionals and those in related industries.

UK/0264-4827
FIRE DIRECTORY, THE. Directory. English. an. £68.90 UK; $114.00 other. Argus Press Group, Queensway House, 2 Queensway Redhill, Surrey RH1 1QS England. **Tel** 011 44 737 768611, 011 44 737 761685, FAX 011 44 737 760510, telex 948669 TOPJNL G.

US/0015-2587
FIRE ENGINEERING. [Fire eng.]. Vol. 79 (Jan. 10, 1926)-. Periodical. English. Twelve times a year. $24.95 US; $42.50 other. PennWell Publishing Company, 1421 South Sheridan, PO Box 1260, Tulsa OK 74101. **Tel** (918)835-3161, (800)331-4463, FAX (918)831-9497. **(Subscription address:** Fire Engineering, PO Box 1289, Tuylsa OK 74101.**)** **ED** Thomas F. Brennan. **LC** TH9111; .F52. **DD** 614.84105. **CODEN** FIENA2. **[CCC].** Index available. **Bk Rev. Ad Acc. Circ:** 39,018 (ctrl). available on microfilm and microfiche from University Microfilms International (UMI). Documents available from Article Express International, CASDDS. ***Supersedes in part*** *Fire and Water Engineering, 0367-2360;* ***Absorbed*** *Fire Engine; Fire Protection, 0096-2228.*
Desc: Objective is to inform chief officers of advances in management and fire prevention and suppression techniques to improve their professional capabilities.
Ind/Abst Appl. Sci. Technol. Index; Bioeng. Abstr.; Chem. Abstr.; Ei Page One; Eng. Index Annu.; Pollut. Abstr. Indexes; Saf. Health Work; Urban Aff. Abstr.

UK/0143-5337
FIRE ENGINEERS JOURNAL. [Fire eng. j.]. **Added/Corp** Institution of Fire Engineers (Great Britain). Vol. 33, No. 89 (Mar. 1973)-. Periodical. English. qt. £10.00 institutions; £20.00 individuals. Institution of Fire Engineers, 148 New Walk, Leicester LE1 7QB England. **Tel** 011 44 533 553654, FAX 011 44 533 471231. **ED** N. Anderson. **LC** TH9111; .I47. **DD** 628.9/2/05. **CODEN** FEGJA6. Index available. cum. index. **Bk Rev. Ad Acc. Circ:** 10,000 (ctrl). Documents available from Article Express International. ***Continues*** *Institution of Fire Engineers. Quarterly.*
Ind/Abst Bioeng. Abstr.; CIS Abstr.; Ei Page One; Energy Res. Abstr. (Dec. 1973-); Eng. Index Annu.; Int. Civil Eng. Abstr.; Saf. Health Work.

CN/0015-2595
FIRE FIGHTING IN CANADA. Vol. 1, (June 1957)-. Periodical. English. Ten times a year (Monthly except Jan. and July,). 20.00Can$ (one year), 29.00Can$ (two year), 36.00Can$ (three year), Canada; 50.00Can$ other. NCC Publishing, 222 Argyle Avenue, Delhi Ontario N4B 2Y2 Canada. **Tel** (519)582-2513, FAX (519)582-4040. **ED** Don Glendinning. **Ad Acc, Adv Mgr:** Dave Douglas, **Tel** (519)582-2513. **Circ:** 7,000 (ctrl).
Desc: Feature articles, technical papers and product news relating to fire prevention and protection in Canada.

US/0098-3276
FIRE INDEPENDENT, THE. V. 1- Jan./Feb. 1975-. English. bm. $15.00. Fire Independent Inc., Suite 909A, 1028 Conn. Avenue, Washington DC 20036. **LC** TH9111; .F566. **DD** 628.9/2/05. **UDC** 614.84.

UK/0015-2609
FIRE INTERNATIONAL. [Fire int.]. Vol. 1 (1963)-. Periodical. Multiple languages (English, French and German). qt. £58.95 UK; £67.70, $104.90 other. Argus Press Group, Queensway House, 2 Queensway Redhill, Surrey RH1 1QS England. **Tel** 011 44 737 768611, 011 44 737 761685, FAX 011 44 737 760510, telex 948669 TOPJNL G. **ED** Norman Anderson. **LC** TH9111; .F57. **NLM** W1 FI666. **CODEN** FINTAV. **Bk Rev. Ad Acc.** ctrl circ. Documents available from Article Express International.
Desc: Articles on the latest advances and developments in fire fighting and prevention.
Ind/Abst Bioeng. Abstr.; Ei Page One; Eng. Index Annu.; Health Saf. Sci. Abstr.; Pollut. Abstr. Indexes; Saf. Health Work.

CN/0821-820X
FIRE LOSSES IN BRITISH COLUMBIA IN ... . [Fire losses B.C.]. 1980-. English. an. Free. Province of British Columbia / Fire Commissioner, Ministry of Municipal Affairs, Office of the Fire Commissioner, 333 Quebec Street, Victoria British Columbia V8V 1X4 Canada. **Tel** (604)356-9000, FAX (604)356-9019. **ED** Paramjit Seran. **LC** TH9506.B8; B74B. **DD** 363.3/72/09711. **UDC** 368.1:614.84(711). **Circ:** 1,000 (ctrl). ***Continues*** *British Columbia. Office of the Fire Commissioner. Annual Report of the Fire Commissioner, 0227-1966.*
Desc: Fire statistics for province of British Columbia, Canada.

US/0194-214X
FIRE MANAGEMENT NOTES. ***Ceased.*** [Fire manage. notes]. **Added/Corp** United States. Forest Service. Vol. 37, No. 2, (Spring 1976)-(1992/1993 ed.). Government Publication. English. qt. Superintendent of Documents, US Government Printing Office, Washington DC 20402. **Tel** (202)275-3328, FAX (202)786-2377. **LC** SD421; .U58. **DD** 634.9/618/05. available on microfilm and microfiche from University Microfilms International (UMI). ***Continues*** *Fire Management, 0095-5450.*
Desc: Devoted to the techniques of forest fire control. Consists of articles written by foresters dealing with methods, plans and equipment found useful in preventing or fighting forest fires.
Ind/Abst AGRICOLA [Full Cov.]; For. Prod. Abstr.; For. Abstr.

US/0015-2625
FIRE NEWS (BOSTON). ***Title Change.*** (FIRE NEWS.). [Fire news]. **Added/Corp** National Fire Protection Association. (19??)-(19??). Periodical. English. mo. National Fire Protection Association, 1 Batterymarch Park, PO Box 9101, Quincy MA 02269-9101. **Tel** (617)770-3000, (800)344-3555. **DD** 363. available on microfilm and microfiche from University Microfilms International (UMI). ***Continues*** *Newsletter.* ***Continued by*** *Fire News (Quincy, Mass. : 1988), 0015-2625.*
Ind/Abst Fluid Abstr., Civil Eng.; Fluid Abstr. Proc. Eng.; FLUIDEX (-19??); Saf. Health Work.

US/0015-2625
FIRE NEWS (BOSTON). (FIRE NEWS / NATIONAL FIRE PROTECTION ASSOCIATION.). [Fire news]. **Added/Corp** National Fire Protection Association. Vol. 1, Issue 1 (Feb. 1988)-. Periodical. English. Six times a year. Comes with membership: $95.00. National Fire Protection Association, 1 Batterymarch Park, PO Box 9101, Quincy MA 02269-9101. **Tel** (617)770-3000, (800)344-3555. **LC** TH9111; .N165. **DD** 363. ***Continues*** *Fire News, 0015-2625.*
Ind/Abst Saf. Health Work; Vocat. Search (Jan. 1993-).

UK/0309-6866
FIRE PREVENTION (LONDON, 1971). (FIRE PREVENTION.). [Fire prev.]. **Added/Corp** Fire Protection Association. No. 90 (April 1971)-. Academic Scholarly Publication. English (French and German). Ten times a year. £131.00 (air mail), £82.00 (surface mail) UK; £89.00 (air mail) other, comes with Fire Protection Association membership. Fire Protection Association, 140 Aldersgate Street, London EC1A 4HX England. **Tel** 011 44 71 6063759, FAX 011 44 71 6001487. **ED** Lynn Jackson. **CODEN** FPRVD7. **[CCC].** Index available. cum. index. **Bk Rev. Ad Acc. Circ:** 7,500 (ctrl). available on microfilm and microfiche from University Microfilms International (UMI). Documents available from Article Express International, CASDDS. ***Continues*** *F.P.A. Journal.*
Desc: Complete coverage of fire subjects: news, views, special features, research papers, statistics, case studies, etc.
Ind/Abst Anbar Account. Finan. Abstr. [Full Txt.]; Anbar Mark. Distr. Abstr. [Full Txt.]; Anbar Top Manage. Abstr. [Full Txt.]; Archit. Period. Index; Bioeng. Abstr.; Chem. Abstr. (1971-1984); Chem. Hazards Ind.; Civ. Struct. Eng. Abstr.; Coal Abstr.; Ei Page One; Eng. Index Annu.; Fluid Abstr., Civil Eng.; Fluid Abstr. Proc. Eng.; FLUIDEX; Int. Build. Serv. Abstr.; Int. Civil Eng. Abstr.; Lab. Hazards Bull.; Manage. Bibliogr. Rev.; Oper. Prod. Manage. Abstr. [Full Txt.]; Person. Train. Abstr. [Full Txt.]; Saf. Health Work; Soft. Abstr. Eng.; Women Manage. Rev. [Full Txt.]; World Surf. Coat. Abstr.; World Text. Abstr.

US/0734-0702
FIRE PREVENTION NOTES. [Fire prev. notes]. No. 13- March 1977-. English. ir. California Department of Forestry, 1416 9th Street, Sacramento CA 95814. **Tel** (916)445-9886. **UDC** 614.841.3. ctrl circ. ***Continues*** *California Fire Prevention Notes.*
Ind/Abst For. Prod. Abstr.; For. Abstr.

US/1043-2485
FIRE PROTECTION CONTRACTOR, THE. [Fire prot. contract.]. **VFOAT** FPC. (Mar. 1978)-. Periodical. English. Twelve times a year. $65.00 (one year); $120.00 (two years); $165.00 (three years). Fire Protection Contractor, 12972 Earhart Avenue, Suite 302, Auburn CA 95602. **Tel** (916)823-0706, FAX (916)823-6937. **ED** Haden B. Brumbeloe and Brant Brumbeloe. **DD** 628. **Bk Rev. Ad Acc. Circ:** 1,800 (ctrl).
Desc: News and information on the automatic fire sprinkler industry.

US/0362-0786
FIRE PROTECTION GUIDE TO HAZARDOUS MATERIALS. **Added/Corp** National Fire Protection Association. **VFOAT** Fire Protection Guide to Hazardous Materials. 1st Ed. (1966)-. English. ir. $71.90 (members), $79.40 (nonmembers). National Fire Protection Association, 1 Batterymarch Park, PO Box 9101, Quincy MA 02269-9101. **Tel** (617)770-3000, (800)344-3555. **LC** TH9446.H38; F55; TH9115; .N28 subser. **DD** 614.8/31/0212.

US/0734-5984
FIRE PROTECTION HANDBOOK. [Fire prot. handb.]. **Added/Corp** National Fire Protection Association. 12th Ed. (1962)-. Monographic series. English. ir. Price varies per volume. National Fire Protection Association, 1 Batterymarch Park, PO Box 9101, Quincy MA 02269-9101. **Tel** (617)770-3000, (800)344-3555. **ED** John S. Petraglia. **LC** TH9150; .F47. **DD** 614.84. **Bk Rev. Pr Rev. Circ:** 7,000 (ctrl). ***Continues*** *NFPA Handbook of Fire Protection.*
Desc: International peer reviewed papers, book and software reviews, technical notes, current research activities, viewpoints, news and meetings concerning fire protection safety professionals.

US
FIRE PROTECTION SYSTEMS. (19??)-. English. ir. $51.50 nonmembers; $46.25 members. National Fire Protection Association, 1 Batterymarch Park, PO Box 9101, Quincy MA 02269-9101. **Tel** (617)770-3000, (800)344-3555.
Desc: Information on the inspection, testing, and maintenance of fire detection and suppression systems.

CN/1185-2607
FIRE PROTECTION VIDEO, FILM AND SLIDE CATALOGUE. [Fire prot. video film slide cat.]. **Added/Corp** Alberta. Alberta Labour. (1991)-. English. Alberta Department of Labour, 10808-99th Avenue/8th Floor, Edmonton Alberta T5K 0G5 Canada. **Tel** (403)427-8260. **DD** 016.36337/7. ***Continues*** *Fire Protection Film Catalogue, 0824-2674.*

●CN/1188-4053
FIRE RESEARCH NEWS. [Fire res. news]. **Added/Corp** Institute for Research in Construction (Canada). Iss No. 63 (Winter 1992)-. Periodical. English. qt. Institute for Research in Construction, National Research Council Canada, Ottawa Ontario K1A 0R6 Canada. **Tel** (613)993-9960, FAX (613)952-4040, telex 053-3145 NRC ADMIN OTT. **DD** 628.9. ***Continues*** *IRC Fire Research News., 0840-4968.*

UK/0261-1589
FIRE RESEARCH NEWS. [Fire res. news]. (1981)-. English. sa. FREE (governmental organizations except in UK). Home Office Fire Experimental Unit, Fire Research and Deveopment Group, c/o Fire Service College, Moreton-in-Marsh, Gloucestershire GL56 0RH UK. **Tel** 011-44-608-50004, FAX 011-44-608-51281. **ED** Martin Thomas. **DD** 628.92072041. **[CCC].**

US
FIRE RESISTANCE DIRECTORY.
Added/Corp Underwriters' Laboratories. (1977)-. English. an (Feb.). $26.00. Underwriters Laboratories Inc., 333 Pfingsten Road, Northbrook IL 60062. **Tel** (708)272-8800 Ext.3542, FAX (708)272-8129, telex 6502543343. ***Continues*** *Fire Resistance Index.*

US/1043-464X
FIRE RESISTANT MATERIALS AND PRODUCTS, PATENTS AND ABSTRACTS. ***Ceased.*** [Fire resist. mater. prod. pat. abstr.]. Vol. 1, No. 1 (July 1989)-(1992). Periodical. English. qt. Technomic Publishing Company, Inc., 851 New Holland Avenue, Box 3535, Lancaster PA 17604. **Tel** (717)291-5609, (800)233-9936, FAX (717)295-4538. **DD** 628. **[CCC].** available on microfilm and microfiche from University Microfilms International (UMI).
Desc: Review of new developments in fire retardance technology, materials, applications, and regulations. Each issue provides abstracts of international patents and items taken from the technical literature covering fire retardant chemicals, additives, compounded materials, structures, and products, also reports on flammability, combustibility, toxicity, degradation, heat and smoke generation and testing.

UK
FIRE SAFETY ENGINEERING. (19??)-. English. bm (6 issues). £25.00 UK; £30.00 other. Paramount Publishing Ltd, 17 21 Shenley Road, Borehamwood, Herts WD6 IRT England. **Tel** 011 44 81 207-5599, FAX 011 44 81 207-2598. ***Continues*** *Fire Surveyor.*

SZ/0379-7112
FIRE SAFETY JOURNAL. [Fire saf. j.]. Vol. 2 (Jan. 1980)-. Academic Scholarly Publication. English. Eight times a year. $544.00 The Americas; £365.00 other. Elsevier Applied Science, An Imprint of Elsevier Science Ltd., The Boulevard, Langford Lane, Kidlington, Oxford OX5 1GB United Kingdom. **Tel** 011 44 865 843000, 011 44 865 843699, FAX 011 44 865 843010. **(Subscription address:** Elsevier Science Ltd. Oxford Fulfillment Centre, PO Box 800, Kidlington, Oxford OX5 1DX United Kingdom.**) ED** D. J. Rasbash and D. D. Drysdale. **LC** TH9111; .F767. **DD** 628.9/22/05. **CODEN** FSJODZ. **[CCC]. Pr Rev.** available on microfilm and microfiche from University Microfilms International (UMI). Documents available from Article Express International, The Genuine Article, CASDDS. ***Continues*** *Fire Research (Lausanne), 0378-7761.*
Desc: Serves the rapidly developing field of fire safety engineering. This is a multidisciplinary subject whose aim is to make human activities and enterprise acceptably safe from fire.
Ind/Abst Appl. Sci. Technol. Index (1991-); Bioeng. Abstr.; Chem. Abstr.; Curr. Contents Clin. Med.; Ei Page One; EMBASE; Eng. Index Annu.; Health Saf. Sci. Abstr.; Res. Alert [Full Cov.]; SCISEARCH.

JA/0285-9521
FIRE SCIENCE AND TECHNOLOGY. [Fire sci. technol.]. V. 1, No. 1 (Nov. 5, 1981)-. Academic Scholarly Publication. English. sa. $50.00. Science University of Tokyo, Kagurazaka Shinuku-ku Ctr Fst, Tokyo 162 Japan. **Tel** 03 260 4271, FAX 81-3-235-2214. **ED** Kunio Kawagoe, Tadahiro Ishii, Yuji Hasemi, Toshisuke Hirano, Masahiro Morita, Philip H Thomas, John A Rockett, Takao Wakamatsu. **LC** TH9111; .F769. **DD** 628.9/2. **UDC** 614.84. **CODEN** FSCTDF. **Circ:** 300. available in microform. Documents available from CASDDS.
Ind/Abst Chem. Abstr.

US/0015-2668
FIRE SERVICE INFORMATION. **Added/Corp** Iowa State University. (19??)-. Periodical. English. Six times a year (Jan., Mar., May, July, Sept., Nov.). $10.00. Fire Service Education, Iowa State University, Ames IA 50011. **ED** Michelle Schlicht, (phone: (515)294-6817). **Ad Acc. Circ:** 2,000.
Desc: A service to fire related personnel in the state of Iowa in the interest of fire safety and the reduction of losses in human lives and property.

UK/0309-622X
FIRE SERVICE STATISTICS ... ACTUALS. English. an. Chartered Institute of Public Finance and Accountancy, 2 3 Robert Street, London WC2N 6BH England. **Tel** 011 44 1 895 8823. **LC** TH9537; .A27. **DD** 363.37/0941/021. ***Continues*** *Fire Service Actual Statistics.*

UK/0262-7981
FIRE SURVEYOR. ***Title Change.*** [Fire surv.]. **Added/Corp** Incorporated Association of Architects and Surveyors. Fire Surveyors Section. (19??)-(19??). Periodical. English. bm (6 issues). Paramount Publishing Ltd, 17 21 Shenley Road, Borehamwood, Herts WD6 IRT England. **Tel** 011 44 81 207-5599, FAX 011 44 81 207-2598. **ED** J.W. Northey. **LC** TH9111; .F775. **DD** 628.9/22/05. **Bk Rev. Ad Acc. Circ:** 5,500. ***Merged into*** *Fire Safety Engineering.*
Desc: Fire prevention and fire protection engineering journal. Authoritative and technical articles with current news coverage.
Ind/Abst Archit. Period. Index; Chem. Hazards Ind.; Fluid Abstr., Civil Eng.; Fluid Abstr. Proc. Eng.; FLUIDEX (-19??); Infomat Int. Bus.; Int. Build. Serv. Abstr.; Int. Civil Eng. Abstr.; Lab. Hazards Bull.; Soft. Abstr. Eng.

US/0015-2684
FIRE TECHNOLOGY. [Fire technol.]. **Added/Corp** National Fire Protection Association. Society of Fire Protection Engineers. Vol. 1, No. I (Feb. 1965)-. Periodical. English. qt. $44.50. National Fire Protection Association, 1 Batterymarch Park, PO Box 9101, Quincy MA 02269-9101. **Tel** (617)770-3000, (800)344-3555. **ED** John M Watts Jr and Marty Moore. **LC** TH9111; .F78. **CODEN** FITCAA. Index available. **Bk Rev. Pr Rev. Circ:** 5,400. available on microfilm and microfiche from University Microfilms International (UMI). Documents available from Article Express International, CASDDS.
Desc: Journal of records; informs the fire protection engineer on current fire protection technological developments.
Ind/Abst AGRICOLA; Appl. Sci. Technol. Index; Bioeng. Abstr.; Chem. Abstr.; Civ. Struct. Eng. Abstr.; Coal Abstr.; Comput. Inf. Syst. Abstr. J. [Full Cov.]; Ei Page One; EMBASE; Eng. Index Annu.; Fluid Abstr., Civil Eng.; Fluid Abstr. Proc. Eng.; FLUIDEX; Gas Abstr.; Health Plan. Adminis.; Hospit. Health Admin. Index; Int. Civil Eng. Abstr.; Manuf. Process Eng. Abstr.; Mater. Sci. Eng. Abstr.; Mech. Eng. Abstr.; Pollut. Abstr. Indexes; Saf. Health Work; Soft. Abstr. Eng.; Solid State Supercond. Abstr.; Urban Aff. Abstr.

US/0148-6675
FIRE TECHNOLOGY ABSTRACTS. (FIRE TECHNOLOGY ABSTRACTS / PREPARED BY APPLIED PHYSICS LABORATORY, THE JOHNS HOPKINS UNIVERSITY.). **Added/Corp** Johns Hopkins University. Applied Physics Laboratory. United States Fire Administration. Data Dissemination and Use Division. United States. Fire Reference Service. United States. National Fire Reference Service. Informatics General Corporation. Vol. 1, No. 1 (July/Oct. 1976)-. Periodical. English. bm (with annual cumulative index). Federal Emergency Management Agency, PO Box 70274, Washington DC 20024. **Tel** (202)646-3989. **LC** TH9111; .F79. **DD** 628.9/2/05.

UK/0142-2510
FIRE (TUNBRIDGE WELLS). (FIRE.). [Fire]. **VFOAT** UNISAF Fire. (1908)-. English. mo. £47.50 UK; £72.15, $111.80 other. Argus Press Group, Queensway House, 2 Queensway Redhill, Surrey RH1 1QS England. **Tel** 011 44 737 768611, 011 44 737 761685, FAX 011 44 737 760510, telex 948669 TOPJNL G. **ED** Val Hargreaves. **Bk Rev. Ad Acc. Circ:** 6,600. ***Absorbed*** *Industrial Hazards and Fire Prevention; Fire Pictorial.*
Desc: Cover of fire prevention and fire protection in all forms.
Ind/Abst Coal Abstr.; Infomat Int. Bus.; Int. Civil Eng. Abstr.; Saf. Health Work; Soft. Abstr. Eng.

USUS/1061-4818
FIREFIGHTER'S NEWS. [Firef. news]. **VFOAT** Fire Fighter's News. (1984)-. Periodical. English. Six times a year. $15.00 US; $30.00 Canada; $50.00 other; $25.00 combined subscription with Rescue-EMS Magazine. Lifesaving Communications, PO Box 100, Nassau DE 19969. **Tel** (302)645-5600, FAX (302)645-8747. **ED** Steve Stevenson. **DD** 363. **Ad Acc, Adv Mgr:** Al Frazier. **Circ:** 40,000 (ctrl).
Desc: Information and skills for fire, rescue, EMS and disaster management and leadership presented in capsulated "how-to" solution oriented style. Includes SOP's, safety, HazMat, tactical skills, wildfire and public education columns, new products, legislative and association news, calendar apparatus deliveries, and classified ads.

US/0145-4064
FIREHOUSE. Vol. 1 (Sept./Oct. 1976)-. Periodical. English. Twelve times a year. $24.00 US; $34.00 other. PTN Publishing Company, 445 Broad Hollow Road, Melville NY 11747. **Tel** (516)845-2700, FAX (516)845-7109. **ED** Janet Kimmerly. **LC** TH9111; .F82. **DD** 363.3/7/05. Index available. **Bk Rev. Ad Acc. Circ:** 110,000.
Desc: Devoted to the fire service, its primary audience is America's paid and volunteer firefighters.

US/0276-4881
FIREHOUSE MAGAZINE. BUYER'S GUIDE, THE. [Firehouse mag. buy. guid.]. **VFOAT** Firehouse Buyer's Guide. English. an. Firehouse Magazine Associates, 33 Irving Place/7th Floor, New York NY 10003-2316. **LC** TH9360; .F57. **DD** 628.9/25/029473. **UDC** 614.843/.847.

●US/1065-0210
FIRELINE. **VFOAT** Fire Line. (1993)-. Periodical. English. $50.00. International Association of Wildland Fire, PO Box 328, Fairfield WA 99012-0328. **Tel** (509)283-2397, FAX (509)283-2264.

AT/0812-0056
FIREMAN MELBOURNE, THE. (1947)-. Periodical. English. mo. 23.00Aus$ Australia; 33.00Aus$ other. H L King Publishing Pty Ltd., 1608 Rosebank Avenue, Clayton Victoria 3169 Australia. **Tel** 011 61 3 5584884, FAX 011 61 3 5584884. **ED** Alan E. King. **Bk Rev. Ad Acc. Circ:** 6,400.

AT/1035-2287
FIREPOINT ROSEVILLE. (1990)-. Periodical. English. qt. 50.00Aus$ (new subscription), 30.00Aus$ (renewal subscription). International Association Arson Investigators, PO Box 148, Nsw Chapter, Concord NSW 2137 Australia. **Tel** 61 2 7453359, FAX 61 2 7449726. **Ad Acc. Circ:** 200.
Desc: Articles on issues associated with arson and its detection & prevention.

US
FIREWATCH / NAFED. **Added/Corp** National Association of Fire Equipment Distributors (U.S.). (19??)-. Periodical. English. qt. $10.00. National Association Fire Equipment Distributors, 401 North Michigan Avenue, Chicago IL 60611. **Tel** (312)644-6610. **ED** Joe Ziemba. Index available. **Bk Rev. Ad Acc. Circ:** 4,000 (ctrl).
Desc: Items of interest to the fire equipment industry.

UK/0307-2118
FITECH. ***Title Change.*** [Fitech]. (1971)-(199?). Consumer Publication. English (French, German and Spanish). an. Argus Press Group, Queensway House, 2 Queensway Redhill, Surrey RH1 1QS England. **Tel** 011 44 737 768611, 011 44 737 761685, FAX 011 44 737 760510, telex 948669 TOPJNL G. **LC** TH9361; .F5. **DD** 338.4/7/628925025. **Ad Acc. Circ:** 12,000 (ctrl). ***Continued by*** *Fitech International.*
Desc: Buyer's guide to fire prevention, fire protection, fire-fighting and associated emergency equipment. Presenting products from over 20 countries.

UK
FITECH INTERNATIONAL. (199?)-. Consumer Publication. English (French, German, Russian and Spanish). an. $101.00. Argus Press Group, Queensway House, 2 Queensway Redhill, Surrey RH1 1QS England. **Tel** 011 44 737 768611, 011 44 737 761685, FAX 011 44 737 760510, telex 948669 TOPJNL G. **(Subscription address:** FMJ International Publications Ltd., Queensway House, 2 Queensway Redhill, Surrey RH1 1QS England.**) LC** TH9361; .F5. **DD** 338.44/7/628925025. **Ad Acc. Circ:** 12,000 (ctrl). ***Continues*** *Fitech, 0307-2118.*
Desc: Buyer's guide to fire prevention, fire protection, fire-fighting and associated emergency equipment. Presenting products from over 20 countries.

US/1058-0948
FLAME RETARDANCY NEWS. [Flame retard. news]. Vol. 1, No. 1 (Jan. 1991)-. Periodical. English. mo. $350.00. Business Communications Inc., 25 Van Zant Street, Suite 13, Norwalk CT 06855. **Tel** (203)853-4266. **DD** 668. available on an online database (files 16,636/Full-Text) from DIALOG.
Ind/Abst PROMT [Full Txt.]; PTS Newsl. Database [Full Txt.].

US/0361-6320
FLAME RETARDANCY OF POLYMERIC MATERIALS. See Textiles.

US
FLAMMABLE AND COMBUSTIBLE LIQUIDS CODE. See Industrial Health and Safety.

US
FLAMMABLE AND COMBUSTIBLE LIQUIDS CODE HANDBOOK. See Industrial Health and Safety.

US/0274-8797
FLORIDA FIREMAN. **Added/Corp** Florida State Firemen's Association. (19??)-. Periodical. English. Eleven times a year (June/July issues combined). $15.00. Florida Fireman, PO Box 968, Avon Park FL 33825. **Tel** (813)453-4817. **ED** H. M. Flowers. Index available. **Ad Acc. Circ:** 6,200 (ctrl).
Desc: News of interest to the members of the Florida State Fireman's Association.

US/0886-5841
FOREST FIRE NEWS. See Forestry.

US/0739-4349
GEORGIA FIREFIGHTER. **Added/Corp** Georgia State Firemen's Association. **VFOAT** Georgia Fire Fighter. (19??)-. Periodical. English. qt. Free to members. Callen Publishing, 720 Church Street, Decatur GA 30030. **Tel** (612)920-4848.

US
HAZARDOUS MATERIALS RESPONSE HANDBOOK. See Industrial Health and Safety.

US/1064-1831
HOT SHEET (FAIRFIELD, WASH.). ***Title Change.*** (HOTSHEET / THE INTERNATIONAL ASSOCIATION OF WILDLAND FIRE.). [Hotsheet]. **Added/Corp** International Association of Wildland Fire. **VFOAT** IAWF Hotsheet. (1992)-(1993). Periodical. English. mo. International Association of Wildland Fire, PO Box 328, Fairfield WA 99012-0328. **Tel** (509)283-2397, FAX (509)283-2264. **LC** SD420.5; .H68. **DD** 634.9/618/05. ***Continued by*** *tWildfire (Fairfield, Wash.), 1073-5658.*

US/0020-5974
IAEI NEWS. [IAEI news]. **VAT** International Association of Electrical Inspectors News. (19??)-. Periodical. English. bm. $36.00 (membership). International Association of Electrical Inspection, 901 Waterfall Suite 602, Richardson TX 75080. **Tel** (214)235-1455, FAX (214)235-3855. **ED** Jerri Smith and Phil Simmons. **DD** 621. Index available. **Ad Acc. Circ:** 30,000 (ctrl). available on microfilm.
Desc: Consists of material which explains articles of the National Electrical Code.
Ind/Abst Saf. Health Work.

US/0893-3936
IAFC ON SCENE. [IAFC scene]. **Added/Corp** International Association of Fire Chiefs. **VFOAT** On Scene. **VAT** International Association of Fire Chiefs on Scene. Vol. 1, No. 1 (April 15, 1987)-. Periodical. English. Twenty-three times a year. comes with membership. International Association of Fire Chiefs, 4025 Fair Ridge Drive, Fairfax VA 22033. **Tel** (703)273-0911. **DD** 363. ***Continues*** *Washington Scene, 0747-8992.*

●US/1061-5334
IFCI FIRE CODE JOURNAL. Added/Corp International Fire Code Institute. **VAT** International Fire Code Institute Fire Code Journal. (1992)-. Periodical. English. qt. $16.00. International Fire Code Institute, 5350 South Workman Mill Road, Whitter CA 90601.

UK/0964-9719
INDUSTRIAL FIRE JOURNAL. [Ind. fire j.]. **VFOAT** IFJ. (1990)-. Periodical. English. qt. £30.00 UK and Europe; $70.00 other (postage included). Kennedy Communications Limited, Unit 8, Old Yarn Mills West She, Dorset DT9 3RQ England. **Tel** 011 44 935 816030, FAX 011 44 935 817200. **ED** Aidan Turnbull. **DD** 628.922. **Ad Acc. Circ:** 6,500.
Desc: Reporting worldwide to the oil, gas, chemical, power and other high risk industries on passive and active fire protection.

US
INDUSTRIAL FIRE SAFETY. ***Ceased.*** (19??)-(1994). English. Six times a year. PennWell Publishing Company, 1421 South Sheridan, PO Box 1260, Tulsa OK 74101. **Tel** (918)835-3161, (800)331-4463, FAX (918)831-9497. **(Subscription address:** Industrial Fire Safety, PO Box 3046, Tulsa OK 74101.**)**
Desc: Trains and educates personnel of industrial facilities and commerical enterprises dedicated to fire protection/response and emergency preparedness. It is for brigade firefighters, plant fire chiefs, plant managers, corporate safety directors, fire protection engineers, industrial emergency medical personnel, rescue specialists and industrial training personnel.

US/0749-890X
INDUSTRIAL FIRE WORLD. [Ind. fire world]. Vol. 1, No. 1 (Jan./Feb. 1985)-. Periodical. English. Six times a year. $25.00 US; $30.00 Canada & Mexico; $45.00 others. Industrial Fire World, PO Box 9161, College Station TX 77840. **Tel** (409)693-7105. **ED** Leslie Hoffman. **DD** 628. **Bk Rev. Ad Acc. Circ:** 26,000.
Desc: Magazine published for the industrial fire protection professional, engineer, or manager. Considered the "Voice of Industrial Fire Protection".

CN/0708-2215
INSTALLATION DES SYSTEMES DE GICLEURS, L'. See Engineering.

US
INSTALLATION OF SPRINKLER SYSTEMS. (19??)-. English. ir (every three years). $27.50 nonmembers; $24.75 members. National Fire Protection Association, 1 Batterymarch Park, PO Box 9101, Quincy MA 02269-9101. **Tel** (617)770-3000, (800)344-3555.
Desc: Covers sprinkler design, installation, and acceptance testing.

US/1064-184X
INTERNATIONAL BIBLIOGRAPHIC BULLETIN OF WILDLAND FIRE. ***Title Change.*** [Int. bibliogr. bull. wildland fire]. **Added/Corp** International Association of Wildland Fire. **VFOAT** Bibliographic Bulletin of Wildland Fire; International Bulletin of Wildland Fire. (1992)-(1993). Bibliography. English. mo. International Association of Wildland Fire, PO Box 328, Fairfield WA 99012-0328. **Tel** (509)283-2397, FAX (509)283-2264. **LC** Z5991; .I625; SD421. **DD** 016.6349/618. ***Continues*** *International Bulletin of Wildland Fire, 1063-049X.* ***Continued by*** *Current Titles in Wildland Fire, 1073-6093.*

●US/1051-4201
INTERNATIONAL BIBLIOGRAPHY OF WILDLAND FIRE. Added/Corp Fire Research Institute. (1992)-. Bibliography. English. $125.00 members International Association of Wildland Fire; $225.00 non-members. Fire Research Institute, PO Box 328, Fairfield WA 99012. **Tel** (509)283-2397, FAX (509)283-2264.

US/1063-049X
INTERNATIONAL BULLETIN OF WILDLAND FIRE. ***Title Change.*** [Int. bull. wildland fire]. **Added/Corp** Fire Research Institute (Roslyn, Wash.) International Association of Wildland Fire. **VFOAT** Bulletin of Wildland Fire. (1992). Bulletin. English. mo. Fire Research Institute, PO Box 328, Fairfield WA 99012. **Tel** (509)283-2397, FAX (509)283-2264. **LC** Z5991; .I625; SD421. **DD** 016.6349/618. ***Continued by*** *International Bibliographic Bulletin of Wildland Fire, 1064-184x.*

UK/0961-3730
INTERNATIONAL FIRE AND SECURITY PRODUCT NEWS. [Int. fire secur. prod. news]. (1991)-. Periodical. English. qt (Jan., Apr., July, Oct.). Free upon request. Paramount Publishing Ltd, 17 21 Shenley Road, Borehamwood, Herts WD6 IRT England. **Tel** 011 44 81 207-5599, FAX 011 44 81 207-2598. **ED** C W Bridges. **DD** 658.473. **Ad Acc.** ctrl circ.
Desc: All aspects of fire prevention, detection and engineering of security projects and systems.

US/0020-6733
INTERNATIONAL FIRE FIGHTER. Added/Corp International Association of Fire Fighters. **VFOAT** Fire Fighter. (1918)-. Periodical. English. bm. International Association of Fire Fighters, 1750 New York Avenue NW, Washington DC 20006. **Tel** (202)872-8484. **LC** TH9111; .I55. **DD** 331.881161484. Index available. ctrl circ.
Ind/Abst Work Relat. Abstr. (-19??).

US/1049-8001
INTERNATIONAL JOURNAL OF WILDLAND FIRE, THE. [Int. j. wildland fire]. **Added/Corp** Fire Research Institute (Roslyn, Wash.) United States. Forest Service. San Francisco State University. Vol. 1, No. 1 (Mar. 1991)-. Periodical. English. qt. $60.00 members of IAWF Association; $150.00 non-member institutions; $95.00 non-member individual. International Association of Wildland Fire, PO Box 328, Fairfield WA 99012-0328. **Tel** (509)283-2397, FAX (509)283-2264. **ED** Mike Webber. **LC** SD420.5; .I57. **DD** 634.9/618. **Bk Rev. Ad Acc, Adv Mgr:** Lane Shaw, **Tel** (509)283-2397. **Pr Rev.** Documents available from Documents on Demand.
Ind/Abst Curr. Aware. Biol. Sci., CABS; Environ. Abstr.; Environ. Period. Bibliogr.

RU/0137-0243
ITOGI NAUKI I TEKHNIKI. SERIIA POZHARNAIA OKHRANA / GOSUDARSTVENNYI KOMITET SSSR PO NAUKE I TEKHNIKE, AKADEMIIA NAUK SSSR, VSESOIUZNYI INSTITUT NAUCHNOI I TEKHNICHESKOI INFORMATSII. Added/Corp Vsesoiuznyi Institut Nauchnoi I Tekhnicheskoi Informatsii (Soviet Union). **VFOAT** Seriia Pozharnaia Okhrana. (19??)-. Periodical. Russian. mo. 0.75rub. VINITI - Vsesoyuznyi Institut Nauchno-Tekhnicheskoi Informatsii, All-Union Scientific and Technical Information Institute, Baltiiskaia Ulitsa 14, 125219 Moscow Russia. **Tel** 238-46-00, FAX 9430060, telex 411160. **(Subscription address:** Victor Kamkin, 4956 Boiling Brook Parkway, Rockville MD 20852.**) LC** TH9111; .I87. **DD** 363.3/7/0947. ***Continues*** *Itogi Nauki I Tekhniki Pozharnaia Okhrana.*

US/1044-4300
JOURNAL OF APPLIED FIRE SCIENCE. [J. appl. fire sci.]. **VFOAT** Applied Fire Science. Vol. 1, No. 1 (1990)-. Periodical. English. Four times a year. $100.00. Baywood Publishing Company Inc., 26 Austin Avenue, PO Box 337, Amityville NY 11701. **Tel** (516)691-1270, (800)638-7819, FAX (516)691-1770. **ED** Paul R DeCicco.**DD** 628. **CODEN** JFSCEW. Index available. cum. index. **Bk Rev. Pr Rev.**
Desc: Directed to bridging the formidable and widening information gap between recent advances in fire chemistry, fire physics, and theoretical fire dynamics and the development and implementation of practical solutions to problems facing the fire protection community. Contains rigorously refereed, previously unpublished articles covering subjects of interest to those who design, evaluate, regulate, etc.
Ind/Abst Risk Abstr.

US/1042-3915
JOURNAL OF FIRE PROTECTION ENGINEERING. [J. fire prot. eng.]. **Added/Corp** Society of Fire Protection Engineers. Vol. 1, No. 1 (Jan/Feb/Mar. 1989)-. Periodical. English. Four times a year. $170.00 one year; $200.00 other. Society of Fire Protection Engineers, One Liberty Square, Boston MA 02109. **Tel** (617)482-0686, FAX (617)482-8184. **ED** J. R. Barnett (phone: (508)831-5593). **DD** 628. **CODEN** JFPEEN. Index available (No. 1 subsequent volume.). cum. index. **Bk Rev.** Documents available from Article Express International.
Ind/Abst Ei Page One; Eng. Index Annu.

US/0734-9041
JOURNAL OF FIRE SCIENCES. [J. fire sci.]. Vol. 1, No. 1 (Jan./Feb. 1983)-. Academic Scholarly Publication. English. bm (Jan., Mar., May, July, Spet., Nov.). $310.00 (one year), $610.00 (two year), $910.00 (three year). Technomic Publishing Company, Inc., 851 New Holland Avenue, Box 3535, Lancaster PA 17604. **Tel** (717)291-5609, (800)233-9936, FAX (717)295-4538. **ED** Gordon E. Hartzell. **LC** TH9446.3; .J68. **DD** 628.9/22/05. **CODEN** JFSCDV. **[CCC].** cum. index. **Pr Rev. Circ:** 700. available on microfilm and microfiche from University Microfilms International (UMI). Documents available from The Genuine Article, CASDDS. ***Formed by the union of*** *Journal of Fire & Flammability, 0022-1104; Journal of Combustion Toxicology, 0362-1669; Journal of Fire Retardant Chemistry, 0362-1693* ***and*** *Journal of Consumer Product Flammability, 0362-1677.*
Desc: Original research papers by leading fire scientists report on the advances in fire technology. The focus is on the fire behavior and fire safety of today's materials and products. Also includes dialogue and discussion among fire experts, scientists, and consultants.
Ind/Abst AGRICOLA [Select. Cov.]; Chem. Abstr. (1983-); Coal Abstr.; Crim. Justice Period. Index; Curr. Contents Eng. Tech. Appl. Sci.; EMBASE; Life Sci. Collect.; Res. Alert [Full Cov.]; Sci. Cit. Index; SCISEARCH; World Text. Abstr.

JA/0449-9042
KASAI : NIHON KASAI GAKKAISHI. [Kasai]. **VFOAT** Japanese Association of Fire Science and Engineering. (1951)-. Academic Scholarly Publication. Japanese. ir. $100.50. Nihon Kasai Gakkai, (Japanese Assoc. of Fire Science & Engineering), Gakkai Senta Biru, 4-16, Yayo 2 Chome, Bunkyoku, Tokyoto 113 Japan. **(Subscription address:** Japan Publications Trading Company, Ltd., PO Box 5030, Tokyo International, Tokyo 100-31 Japan.**) CODEN** KASIDP. Documents available from CASDDS.
Ind/Abst Chem. Abstr.

US
LAWS RELATING TO FIRES AND FIREMEN, STATE OF CALIFORNIA. See Law.

US/0192-1002
LIFE SAFETY CODE HANDBOOK. Main/Corp National Fire Protection Association. **VFOAT** NFPA Life Safety Code Handbook. 1st Ed. (1978)-. English. te. $64.90 (nonmembers), $71.65 (members). National Fire Protection Association, 1 Batterymarch Park, PO Box 9101, Quincy MA 02269-9101. **Tel** (617)770-3000, (800)344-3555. **LC** TH9445.P8; L54. **DD** 690/.22/0973.

US
LIQUEFIED PETROLEUM GASES HANDBOOK. See Petroleum and Natural Gas.

US/0737-3678
LOCAL 2 NEWS. (LOCAL 2 NEWS : OFFICIAL BULLETIN OF THE CHICAGO FIRE FIGHTERS UNION.). **Added/Corp** Chicago Fire Fighters Union. Local 2. **VFOAT** Local Two News. (19??)-. Periodical. English. Chicago Fire Fighters Union, 54 West Randolph, Chicago IL 60601. ***Continues*** *Chicago Fire Fighter, 0009-3548.*

US
MICHIGAN FIRE SERVICE NEWS. English. Twelve times a year. $15.00. Michigan Fire Chiefs Association, 1310 Nichols Road, Kalamazoo MI 49007. **Tel** (616)343-1811. **ED** Richard Marinucci (editor's address: 28711 Drake Road, Farmington Hills, MI 48331-2525, phone: (313)553-0740). **Ad Acc.** ctrl circ.

UK
MILITARY FIRE FIGHTER. English. Kennedy Communications Ltd, 3 Woodhurst Road, Action London W3 6SS England.

UK/0964-9700
MILITARY FIREFIGHTER. [Mil. firef.]. (198?)-. Periodical. English. qt (4 issues). £30.00 UK and Europe; $70.00 US. Kennedy Communications Limited, Unit 8, Old Yarn Mills West She, Dorset DT9 3RQ England. **Tel** 011 44 935 816030, FAX 011 44 935 817200.

US/0026-5470
MINNESOTA FIRE CHIEF. Added/Corp Minnesota State Fire Chiefs Association. (1964)-. Periodical. English. bm (6 issues). $10.00. Minnesota State Fire Chiefs, 10983 South Jackson Drive, Solon Springs WI 54873. **Tel** (800) 743-0911. **ED** Antona Richardson. Index available. **Bk Rev. Ad Acc, Adv Mgr:** James Heim. **Circ:** 2,800.
Desc: Publishes information relative to fire department operations.

US/0363-7131
NAFED DIRECTORY. [NAFED dir.]. **Main/Corp** National Association of Fire Equipment Distributors (U.S.). **VAT** National Association of Fire Equipment Distributors Directory. Directory. English. an. Free. National Association of Fire Equipment Distributors, 111 East Wacker Drive, Chicago IL 60601. **Tel** (312)644-6610. **ED** Colleen Wilmsen. **LC** HD9999.F53; U55. **DD** 381/.45/68. **UDC** 614.843. **Circ:** 2,000 (ctrl).
Desc: Directory of association members by state.

Fire Prevention

●US/1066-5609
NATIONAL DIRECTORY OF FIRE CHIEFS, RESCUE & EMERGENCY DEPARTMENTS. [Natl. dir. fire chiefs rescue emerg. dep.]. **VFOAT** National Directory of Fire Chiefs & Emergency Departments. (1992)-. Directory. English. an. $40.00. Span Publishing, Box 365, 1052 Main Street, Suite 207, Steven Point WI 54481-0365. **Tel** (715)345-2772, FAX (715)345-7288. **ED** Kathleen J. Nason. **LC** TH9503; .N188. **DD** 363.37/025/73. available on diskette.

US/0550-4406
NATIONAL ELECTRICAL CODE.
Added/Corp National Board of Fire Underwriters. National Fire Protection Association. **VFOAT** NEC. (19??)-. English. ir (published every three years). $37.50 nonmembers; $33.75 members. National Fire Protection Association, 1 Batterymarch Park, PO Box 9101, Quincy MA 02269-9101. **Tel** (617)770-3000, (800)344-3555.
Desc: The electrical code for the majority of states, counties and cities in the United States.

US/0193-7324
NATIONAL ELECTRICAL CODE HANDBOOK (1978), THE. (THE NATIONAL ELECTRICAL CODE HANDBOOK.]. [Natl. electr. code handb.]. **Main/Corp** National Fire Protection Association. (1978)-. English. an. $634.15 (members), $704.15 (nonmembers). National Fire Protection Association, 1 Batterymarch Park, PO Box 9101, Quincy MA 02269-9101. **Tel** (617)770-3000, (800)344-3555. **ED** W I Summers. **LC** TK260; .N47b. **DD** 621.319/24/0218.

US
NATIONAL FIRE ACADEMY ... RESIDENTIAL PROGRAM. **Main/Corp** National Fire Academy. English. National Fire Academy, 16825 South Seton Avenue, Emmitsburg MD 21727.

US
NATIONAL FIRE ALARM CODE. (19??)-. English. ir. $35.00 nonmembers; $31.50 members; With Handbook: $89.50 nonmembers; $80.50 members. National Fire Protection Association, 1 Batterymarch Park, PO Box 9101, Quincy MA 02269-9101. **Tel** (617)770-3000, (800)344-3555.
Desc: Covers all aspects of the installation, maintenance, and use of fire alarm systems.

CN/0700-124X
NATIONAL FIRE CODE OF CANADA.
[Natl. fire code Can.]. **Added/Corp** National Research Council of Canada. Associate Committee on the National Fire Code. National Research Council Canada. Associate Committee on the National Fire Code. 1st Ed. (1963)-. English. ir. $41.00. National Research Council of Canada, Receiver General for Canada, Ottawa Ontario K1A 0R6 Canada. **Tel** (613)993-0362, FAX (613)952-7656. **DD** 344.71/0537/02632.

US/0077-4545
NATIONAL FIRE CODES. [Natl. fire codes].
Main/Corp National Fire Protection Association. (1938)-. English. an. $661.15 (members), $734.15 (nonmembers). National Fire Protection Association, 1 Batterymarch Park, PO Box 9101, Quincy MA 02269-9101. **Tel** (617)770-3000, (800)344-3555. **LC** TH9111; .N375a. **DD** 614.8/41/0973.
Desc: Provides guidelines for code enforcement, inspection, design and maintenance of buildings in a single source reference.

US
NATIONAL FIRE CODES. SUPPLEMENT. **Main/Corp** National Fire Protection Association. (19??)-. Periodical. English. ir. Included with National Fire Code - $734.15 nonmembers, $661.15 members. National Fire Protection Association, 1 Batterymarch Park, PO Box 9101, Quincy MA 02269-9101. **Tel** (617)770-3000, (800)344-3555.

US
NATIONAL FORESTS FIRE REPORT. See Forestry.

●US
NEW JERSEY FIRE FOCUS : THE OFFICIAL NEWSLETTER OF THE NJ BUREAU OF FIRE SAFETY. **Added/Corp** New Jersey. Bureau of Fire Safety. New Jersey. Dept. of Community Affairs. **VFOAT** Fire Focus. (Jan./Feb./Mar. 1992)-. Newsletter. English. **Continues** Newsletter (New Jersey. Bureau of Fire Safety).

US/0094-8071
NEWS BULLETIN (DETROIT). (NEWS BULLETIN - FLAMMABILITY INSTITUTE.). [News bull.]. **Main/Corp** Flammability Institute. Bulletin. English. $55.00. Flammability Institute, 4001 West McNichols Road, Detroit MI 48221. **LC** TH1092; .F6. **DD** 628.9/22. **UDC** 614.841.41.

US
NFPA INSPECTION MANUAL. See Industrial Health and Safety.

US/1054-8793
NFPA JOURNAL. (NFPA JOURNAL : THE OFFICIAL MAGAZINE OF THE NATIONAL FIRE PROTECTION ASSOCIATION.). [NFPA j.]. **Added/Corp** National Fire Protection Association. **VAT** National Fire Protection Association Journal. Vol. 85, No. 1 Jan./Feb. (1991)-. Periodical. English. ir. Comes with membership/ $95.00. National Fire Protection Association, 1 Batterymarch Park, PO Box 9101, Quincy MA 02269-9101. **Tel** (617)770-3000, (800)344-3555. **DD** 628. **CODEN** NFJOEX. available on microfilm and microfiche from University Microfilms International (UMI). Formed by the union of Fire Journal (Boston, Mass.), 0015-2617 and Fire Command (Quincy, Mass.), 0746-9586.
Ind/Abst Acad. Search (Jan. 1994-); Appl. Sci. Technol. Index; Vocat. Search (Jan. 1993-).

●US
NFPA JOURNAL. BUYERS' GUIDE : FIRE PROTECTION AND FIRE SERVICE REFERENCE DIRECTORY. **Added/Corp** National Fire Protection Association. **VFOAT** NFPA Journal Buyers' Guide; Fire Protection and Fire Service Reference Directory; Buyers' Guide; NFPA Buyers' Guide. **VAT** National Fire Protection Association Journal. Buyers' Guide; National Fire Protection Association Buyers' Guide. (1992)-. Directory. English. an. $30.90. National Fire Protection Association, 1 Batterymarch Park, PO Box 9101, Quincy MA 02269-9101. **Tel** (617)770-3000, (800)344-3555. **Continues** NFPA Buyers' Guide.

CK/0120-5722
NOTICIERO TECNICO SOBRE INCENDIOS. [Not. tec. incendios]. (1982)-. Periodical. Spanish. qt. $35.00 (one year), $60.00 (two year). Organizacion Iberoamericano de Proteccion de Incendios, Apdo Postal 89120, Bogota Colombia. **DD** 350.782.

XR
POZARNI OCHRANA. Began in 1953. Periodical. Czech. mo. (**Subscription address:** Artia Pegas Press Ltd., Palac Metro Narodni Trida 25, 11210 Prague 1 Czech Republic.) **LC** TH9111; .P57. **Supersedes** Hasicske Rozhledy; **Absorbed** Pozarni Technika.
Ind/Abst Saf. Health Work.

RU
POZHARNOE DELO. **Added/Corp** Russia (1923- U.S.S.R.). Glavnoe Upravlenie Pozharnoi Okhrany. (Jan. 1955)-. Academic Scholarly Publication. Russian. mo. $99.95. (**Subscription address:** East View Publications Inc., 3020 Harbor Lane North, Suite 110, Minneapolis MN 55447.) **LC** TH9111; .P6. **CODEN** POZDAP. Documents available from CASDDS.
Ind/Abst Chem. Abstr. (?-1973).

NE
PREVENTIE. Samson Bedrijfsinformatie, Postbus 4, 2400 HA Alphen Rij Netherlands. **Tel** 011 31 1 72066633.

US
PROCEEDINGS - FIRE SERVICE EXTENSION SCHOOL, WEST VIRGINIA UNIVERSITY. **Main/Corp** Fire Service Extension School, West Virginia University. No. 1 (1931)-. Proceedings. English. **LC** TA7; .W4 no. -10.

US
PROCEEDINGS OF THE ANNUAL TALL TIMBER FIRE ECOLOGY CONFERENCE. See Forestry.

US/0193-306X
PROCEEDINGS OF THE INTERNATIONAL CONFERENCE ON FIRE SAFETY. [Proc. Int. Conf. Fire Saf.]. **Added/Corp** University of San Francisco. Fire Safety Center. 2nd (1977)-. Academic Scholarly Publication. English. an. $80.00. Product Safety Corporation, 1457 Firebird Way, Sunnyvale CA 94087. **Tel** (408)732-5325. **CODEN** PCFSDP. Documents available from Article Express International, CASDDS. **Continues** Conference Proceedings - International Conference on Fire Safety, 0193-3051.
Ind/Abst Bioeng. Abstr.; Chem. Abstr.; Ei Page One; Eng. Index Annu.

US/0092-9638
RC AND D RELEASE. Ceased. See Forestry.

US/0193-7359
REKINDLE. Title Change. Vol. 1 (1988)-(1988). Periodical. English. mo. International Society of Fire Service Instructors, 20 Main Street, Ashland MA 01721. **Tel** (508)881-5800, FAX (508)881-6829. **DD** 628. **UDC** 614.84. Ad Acc. **Continued by** Voice, 1040-1121.
Desc: Fire newsletter for exchange of information and ideas of value or concern to the instructor, educator and supervisor of fire and emergency personnel.

CN
REPERTOIRE DES SERVICES MUNICIPAUX DE PREVENTION DES INCENDIES DU QUEBEC. French. Editeur Officiel du Quebec, 1283 Boul Charest Ouest, Quebec Quebec G1N 2C9 Canada. **LC** TH9506.Q4; R45. **DD** 363.3/77/09714.

FJ
REPORT FOR THE YEAR ... / BOARD OF FIRE COMMISSIONERS. **Main/Corp** Fiji. Board of Fire Commissioners. English. an. **LC** J961; H835 subser; TH9599.F4. **DD** 300/.996/11; 354.96/1100782.

UK
REPORT OF THE FIREMASTER OF THE CITY OF GLASGOW. **Main/Corp** Glasgow. Fire Service. **VFOAT** Annual Report. English. an. Fire Service, 33 Ingram Street C 1, Glasgow Scotland. **LC** TH9543.G4; G45A. **DD** 363.3/7/0941435.

BE/0771-4033
REVUE BELGE DU FEU. Title Change. (1969)-(19??). Periodical. Multiple languages (French and Dutch). Five times a year. Assn Nationale pour Protection, Parc Scientifique, 1348 Ottignies Belgium. **Tel** 11 32 10 475211, telex 010 47 52 70. **UDC** 614.8. Index available. Bk Rev. Ad Acc. Circ: 12,000. **Continued by** ANPI Magazine.

JA
SAISHIN CHUKAI SHOBO HOREI.
Main/Corp Japan. **Added/Corp** Japan. Shobocho. Yoboka. Japan. Shobocho. Yobo Kyukyuka. Zenkoku Kajo Horei Shuppan. Japan. Laws, Statutes, etc. Shoboho. **VFOAT** Chukai Shobo Horei. (19??)-. Periodical. Japanese. ¥1750. Zenkoku Kajo Horei Shuppan Company Ltd., Dai 1 Zenkoku Biru 18 Saneicho, Shinjukuku Tokyoto 160 Japan. **LC** LAW.

FR/0036-469X
SAPEUR-POMPIER, LE. [Sapeur-pompier]. (1905)-. Periodical. French. Ten times a year. 88.15F France; 300.00F other. Fedn Natl des Sapeurs Francais, 75 rue de Dunkerque, 75010 Paris France. **Tel** 011 33 1 45261818. **UDC** 614.842.83.

US
SFPE HANDBOOK OF FIRE PROTECTION ENGINEERING. (19??)-. English. ir. $154.90 nonmembers; $139.90 members. National Fire Protection Association, 1 Batterymarch Park, PO Box 9101, Quincy MA 02269-9101. **Tel** (617)770-3000, (800)344-3555.
Desc: Combines theory, research results, and calculation methods.

JA/0426-2700
SHOBO KENKYUJO HOKOKU. [Shobo Kenkyujo hokoku]. **VFOAT** Report of the Fire Research Institute of Japan. Academic Scholarly Publication. Japanese (English). sa. Shobo Kenkyujo, 14-1 Nakahara 3-chome Mitakashi, Tokyo-to Japan. **CODEN** SHKHBF. Documents available from CASDDS.
Ind/Abst Chem. Abstr.

KO
SOBANG ANJON / FIRE SAFETY JOURNAL. **Added/Corp** Hanguk Sobang Anjon Hyophoe. **VFOAT** Fire Safety Journal. (19??)-. Periodical. Korean (Korean). bm. Hanguk Sobang Anjon Hyophoe, 1-582 Youido-dong Yongungpo-ku, Seoul Korea. **LC** TH9182; .S65.

US/0744-3730
SOUTH CAROLINA FIREMAN MAGAZINE, THE. **VFOAT** South Carolina Fireman. Vol. 1, No. 1 (Jan./Feb. 1982)-. Periodical. English. qt. Professional Publishing Company, 3020 Devine Street, Columbia SC 29205.

US/0896-2685
SPRINKLER AGE. [Sprink. age]. **Added/Corp** American Fire Sprinkler Association. (19??)-. Periodical. English. mo. Free to members, $75.00 nonmember US; $90.00 nonmember other. American Fire Sprinkler Association, 11325 Pegasus/Suite E-109, Dallas TX 75238. **DD** 338.

US
STANDARD FOR PORTABLE FIRE EXTINGUISHERS. (19??)-. English. ir. $21.50 nonmembers; $19.50 members. National Fire Protection Association, 1 Batterymarch Park, PO Box 9101, Quincy MA 02269-9101. **Tel** (617)770-3000, (800)344-3555.
Desc: Criteria on selection, distribution, inspection, maintenance, hydrostatic testing, etc., of fire extinguishers.

US
STANDARD FOR THE STORAGE AND HANDLING OF LIQUEFIED PETROLEUM GASES. See Petroleum and Natural Gas.

US/0362-6008
STATEWIDE SUMMARY OF FIRE PROTECTION DISTRICT FINANCE IN ILLINOIS. **Main/Corp** Illinois. Comptroller's Office. English. an. Illinois Comptroller's Office, 201 State House, Springfield IL 62706. **LC** TH9504.I31; I43A. **DD** 353.9/773/00782.

NE/0168-4639
STATISTIEK DER BRANDEN / CENTRAAL BUREAU VOOR DE STATISTIEK, HOOFDAFDELING STATISTIEKEN VAN RECHTSBESCHERMING EN VEILIGHEID. See Fire Prevention-Abstracting, Bibliographies and Statistics.

US
SUMMARY & ANALYSIS : CALIFORNIA FIRE INCIDENT REPORTING SYSTEM. **Main/Corp** California. Office of the State Fire Marshal. English. Office of State Fire Marshall, 7171 Bowling Drive/Suite 600, Sacramento CA 95823. **LC** TH9504.C21; C35B. **DD** 363.3/72/09794.

US/0278-9930
TEXAS FIREMEN. **Added/Corp** State Firemen's and Fire Marshalls' Association of Texas. Vol. 18, No. 10 (Oct. 1981)-. Periodical. English. Ten times a year. $15.00. State Firemens Fire Marshalls Association of Texas, PO Box 13326, Austin TX 78711. **Tel** (512)441-7388, FAX (512)441-9199. **ED** Sylvia Marshall-Polozeck (editor's telephone: (512)454-3743). **Ad Acc, Adv Mgr:** same as editor.

US/0738-9620
TEXTILE FLAMMABILITY DIGEST. Ceased. See Textiles.

US/0896-9736
UNIFORM FIRE CODE. [Unif. fire code]. **Main/Corp** International Conference of Building Officials. **Added/Corp** Western Fire Chiefs Association. (19??)-. English. ir (Published every three or four years). $36.70 (members) of ICBO; $47.80 (non-members). ICBO Evaluation Service Inc., 5360 South Workman Mill Road, Whittier CA 90601. **Tel** (213)699-0541, FAX (213)692-3853. **LC** KF3975.Z95; I58. **DD** 344.73/0537; 347.304537.
Desc: Sets out provisions necessary for fire prevention while achieving uniformity in terms and requirements with other codes.

US/0896-9744
UNIFORM FIRE CODE STANDARDS. [Unif. fire code stand.]. **Main/Corp** International Conference of Building Officials. **Added/Corp** Western Fire Chiefs Association. (19??)-. English. ir (Published every three years). $66.15 (three years) members of ICBO; $86.00 (three years) non-members. ICBO Evaluation Service Inc., 5360 South Workman Mill Road, Whittier CA 90601. **Tel** (213)699-0541, FAX (213)692-3853. **LC** KF3975.Z95; I59. **DD** 344.73/0537/02632; 347.30453702632.
Desc: A companion to the Uniform Fire Code. Contains National Fire Protection Association standards and Uniform Building Code standards referenced by the Uniform Fire Code.

US/0889-6038
US FIRE SPRINKLER REPORTER. [U. S. fire sprink. report.]. **VAT** United States Fire Sprinkler Reporter. (July 1986)-. Periodical. English. mo. $60.00. US Fire Sprinkler Reporter, 300 North Washington Street, Alexandria VA 22314. **Tel** (703)549-8606, FAX (703)549-1372. **DD** 338.

US/1056-7135
USER'S GUIDE TO ARTICLE 80, A. (A USER'S GUIDE TO ARTICLE 80 : A GUIDE TO SIMPLIFYING ARTICLE 80 OF THE UNIFORM FIRE CODE AND TO UNCOVERING THE MYSTERIES SURROUNDING THE STORAGE, USE, AND HANDLING OF HAZARDOUS MATERIALS.). [User's guide Artic. 80]. **VAT** User's Guide to Article Eighty. 1st Ed. (1991)-. Periodical. English. Western Fire Chiefs Association, Palm Brook Corporate Center, 3602 Inland Empire Boulevard, Suite B-205, Ontario CA 91764. **DD** 363.

US/1040-1121
VOICE, THE. Vol. 17, Issue 9 (Sept. 1988)-. Periodical. English. mo. $72.00. International Society of Fire Service Instructors, 20 Main Street, Ashland MA 01721. **Tel** (508)881-5800, FAX (508)881-6829. **DD** 628. **Ad Acc.** ctrl circ. **Continues** Rekindle, 0193-7359.
Desc: Fire newsletter for exchange of information and ideas of value or concern to the instructor, educator and supervisor of fire and emergency personnel.
Ind/Abst Bibliogr. Mission.

US
VOLUNTEERS IN FIRE PREVENTION. **Main/Corp** California. Dept. of Forestry. **VFOAT** Volunteers in Prevention. English. an. California Department of Forestry, 1416 9th Street, Sacramento CA 95814. **Tel** (916)445-9886. **LC** SD421.45.V64; C34A. **DD** 363.3/79.

US/1071-1767
WFS QUARTERLY. (WFS QUARTERLY / WOMEN IN FIRE SUPPRESSION.). [WFS q.]. **Added/Corp** Women in the Fire Service (Organization) Women in Fire Suppression (Organization). (1986)-. Periodical. English. Four times a year. $40.00 (institutions), $25.00 (individuals) US; $45.00 (institutions), $30.00 (individuals) other. Women in the Fire Service, PO Box 5446, Madison WI 53705. **Tel** (608)233-4768. **ED** Terese M. Floren. **DD** 628. Index available (bound in Jan. issue). cum. index. **Bk Rev. Ad Acc. Circ:** 280. **Continues** Firework (Dayton, Ohio).
Desc: Covers issues pertinent to the gender integration of the fire service.

US
WILDFIRE NEWS AND NOTES / SPONSORED BY NATIONAL FIRE PROTECTION ASSOCIATION ... [ET AL.]. **Added/Corp** National Fire Protection Association. **VFOAT** Wildfire News & Notes. Vol. 4, No. 3 (May/June 1990)-. Newsletter. English. qt. Free on request. National Fire Protection Association, 1 Batterymarch Park, PO Box 9101, Quincy MA 02269-9101. **Tel** (617)770-3000, (800)344-3555. **ED** Bill Baden. **Continues** Wildfire Strikes Home.

US/0360-8034
WILDFIRE STATISTICS. See Forestry-Abstracting, Bibliographies and Statistics.

US/1056-702X
WILDLAND/URBAN INTERFACE. [Wildland/urban interface]. **Added/Corp** Western Fire Chiefs Association. **VFOAT** Wildland Urban Interface; Development Strategies in the Wildland/Urban Interface. 1st Ed. (1991)-. English. WFCA Inc. Press, Palm Brook Corporate Center, 3602 Inland Empire Boulevard, Suite 205, Ontario CA 91764. **DD** 363.

US/0042-9775
WNYF. [WNYF]. **Added/Corp** New York (N.Y.). Fire Dept. **VFOAT** With New York Fire Fighters; W.N.Y.F. VAT With New York Firefighters. (19??)-. Periodical. English. Four times a year. $15.00 US / $18.00 other. WNYF, Fire Academy, Randalls Island NY 10035. **Tel** (212)860-9243. **ED** Gloria Sturzenacker (editor's phone: (212)860-9487). **LC** TH9111; .W2. **DD** 614.84. **Circ:** 15,000.
Desc: Training publication for uniformed members of the NYC fire department. Contains fire stories and technical articles.

ABSTRACTING, BIBLIOGRAPHIES AND STATISTICS

NE/0168-4639
STATISTIEK DER BRANDEN / CENTRAAL BUREAU VOOR DE STATISTIEK, HOOFDAFDELING STATISTIEKEN VAN RECHTSBESCHERMING EN VEILIGHEID. **VFOAT** Fire Statistics. Dutch. an. Fl11.00. Centraal Bureau voor de Statistiek, AFD ALG Zaken, Postbus 959, 2270 AZ Voorburg Netherlands. **Tel** 011 31 70 3373800, FAX 011 31 038 7429, telex 32692 CBS NL. **LC** TH9557; .A477.

FISH AND FISHERIES

US/0094-3630
ABSTRACTS OF FISHERY RESEARCH REPORTS. **Main/Corp** Missouri. Division of Fisheries. (19??)-. English. an. **LC** SK415; .M56a. **DD** 639.9/09778.

PL/0137-1592
ACTA ICHTHYOLOGICA ET PISCATORIA. [Acta ichthyolog. piscatoria]. **Added/Corp** Akademia Rolnicza w Szczecinie. Vol. 1 (1970)-. Academic Scholarly Publication. English (summaries and/or abstracts in Polish and Russian). sa. **(Subscription address:** ARS Polona, PO Box 1001, 00068 Warsaw Poland.) **CODEN** AIPSCJ. Documents available from BIOSIS Document Express, CASDDS. **Ind/Abst** Anim. Breed. Abstr.; Aquat. Sci. Fish. Abstr. (Computer File); Biol. Abstr. (1985-1988); Chem. Abstr.; Curr. Ref. Fish Res.; Fish Rev. (Jan. 1989-July 1992); Nutr. Abstr. Rev., Ser. B, Live Feeds and Feed.; Ocean. Abstr.; Life Sci. Collect.; Wildl. Rev. (Jan. 1989-July 1992).

PE
ACTUALIDAD PESQUERA. V. 1 No. 1 (May 1979)-. Periodical. Spanish (summaries and/or abstracts in English). mo. Jorge Luis Rojas Utrilla, Mariano de los Santos 198-404, San Isidro, Lima Peru. **LC** SH247; .A547. **DD** 639/.2/0985.

US
AFFIRMATIVE ACTION PLAN / ALASKA DEPARTMENT OF FISH AND GAME. **Main/Corp** Alaska. Dept. of Fish and Game. Calendar Year 1982-. English. an. Alaska Department of Fish and Game, PO Box 3-2000, Juneau AK 99802. **Tel** (907)465-4100, (907)465-4286. **LC** SH222.A4; .A55A. **DD** 353.9798001/3243.

GW/0001-1258
AFZ. ALLGEMEINE FISCHWIRTSCHAFTSZEITUNG. [AFZ. Allg. Fischwirtschaftsztg.]. **VFOAT** Allgemeine Fischwirtschaftszeitung. Vol. 9, No. 2 (Jan. 1957)-. Periodical. German. mo. DM37.40. Verlag Chmielorf GmbH, Fischwaid, Wilhelmstr 42, W-6200 Wiesbaden Germany. **Tel** 06121/39671. **CODEN** AAFIDK. **Bk Rev. Ad Acc. Circ:** 31,000. Documents available from CASDDS. **Continues** Allgemeine Fischwirtschaftszeitung.
Desc: Information on fishing gear, fishing waters, fishing rods, journeys and fishing clubs.
Ind/Abst Chem. Abstr.

AU/0157-8243
AGNOTE. English.
Ind/Abst Biocont. News Inf.; Soils Fert.

●CN/0849-2360
AGRI-FOOD AND FISHERIES PROJECT, THE. See Agriculture.

UK
AGRICULTURE, FISHERIES, FOOD. See Agriculture.

US/1051-9963
AIC SERIES. [AIC ser.]. **Added/Corp** Aquaculture Information Center (U.S.) National Agricultural Library (U.S.). **VAT** Aquaculture Information Center Series. (1990)-. English. National Agricultural Library, 10301 Baltimore Boulevard, Beltsville MD 20705. **DD** 639. **Ind/Abst** AGRICOLA [Full Cov.].

US/0360-7992
ALABAMA LANDINGS, ANNUAL SUMMARY. **Main/Corp** United States. National Marine Fisheries Service. English. an. National Marine Fisheries Services, Department of Commerce, Washington DC 20235. **LC** SH11; .A65A. **DD** 338.3/72/09761.

US
ALASKA CATCH AND PRODUCTION, COMMERCIAL FISHERIES STATISTICS. **Added/Corp** Alaska. Dept. of Fish and Game. Alaska. Division of Commercial Fisheries. (1965)-. English. ir. Price varies per volume. Alaska Department of Fish and Game / Juneau, PO Box 25526, Juneau AK 99802. **Tel** (907)465-4210, FAX (907)465-2604. **LC** SH222.A4; A32 subser. **DD** 338.3/72709798. **Continues** Alaska Commercial Fisheries Catch and Production Statistics.

US
ALASKA COMMERCIAL SALMON CATCHES / DIVISION OF COMMERCIAL FISHERIES, ALASKA DEPARTMENT OF FISH AND GAME. 1878-1981-. English. an. Alaska Department of Fish and Game, PO Box 3-2000, Juneau AK 99802. **Tel** (907)465-4100, (907)465-4286. **LC** SH348; .A47. **DD** 338.3/72755.

US/0164-8330
ALASKA FISHERMAN'S JOURNAL. (1978)-. Periodical. English. mo. 26.00Can$ (1year); 42.00Can$ (2 year); 57.00Can$ (3year); $21.00 (US); $70.00 (other). Waterfront Press Company, 1115 Northwest 46th Street, Seattle WA 98107. **Tel** (206)789-6506, FAX (206)789-9193, telex 272822 SFL UR. **ED** John Van Amerongen. **Bk Rev. Ad Acc. Circ:** 12,000 (ctrl).
Desc: Written for the men and women who make their livings fishing commercially in Alaska. Includes news from the fishing grounds, stories about fishermen and boats, etc.

US
ALASKA FISHERY RESEARCH BULLETIN. (19??)-. English. ir (4 to 6 bulletins per year). Free. Alaska Department of Fish and Game / Juneau, PO Box 25526, Juneau AK 99802. **Tel** (907)465-4210, FAX (907)465-2604. **ED** Robert Wilbur, (phone: (907)465-6105). **Pr Rev. Circ:** 500. **Continues** Fishery Research Bulletin.

US/0361-3984
ALASKA FISHING GUIDE. English. $3.95. Alaska Northwest Publishing Company, 130 Second

Fish and Fisheries

Avenue South, Edmonds WA 98020-3588. **Tel** (206)774-4111, (800)533-7381. **LC** SH467; .A63. **DD** 799.1/09798.

US/1060-2895
ALASKA MARINE RESOURCE QUARTERLY. See Earth Sciences-Oceanography.

CN/0318-4943
ALBERTA FISHING GUIDE. Began publication in 1972?. Periodical. English. an. George Mitchell, 10519 128A Avenue, Edmonton Alberta T5E 1T2 Canada. **DD** 799.1/1/097123.

CN/0833-0867
ALBERTA'S FISHING & HUNTING MAGAZINE. Ceased. [Alta. fish. hunt. mag.]. **VFOAT** Alberta Fishing & Hunting Magazine. **VAT** Alberta's Fishing and Hunting. Vol. 1, No. 1 (Oct. 1, 1985)-(Nov. 1992). Periodical. English. mo. Alberta's Fishing and Hunting, 12425 Jasper Avenue, Edmonton Alta T5N 3K9 Canada. **Tel** (403)482-1777, FAX (403)488-5427. **DD** 799/.097123.
Desc: This magazine publishes articles and columns on the how-to, where-to, when-to and what to use for fishing, hunting, and outdoors.

CN/0844-9031
ALIMENTATION QUEBEC, FISHERIES. [Aliment. Que. fish.]. Vol. 1, No. 4 (April 1982)-. Periodical. English. ir. Ministre des Finances, 200 Chemin Ste Foy, Quebec Quebec G1R 4X6 Canada. **DD** 639/.2/09714. **Continues** Alimentation Quebec, Pecheries. English, 0711-6128.

CN/1185-8591
ALLIANCE (WHITE ROCK). (ALLIANCE.). [Alliance]. **Added/Corp** Pacific Fishermen's Alliance. Vol. 1, No. 1 (Feb. 1991)-. Periodical. English. qt. Free to members. Pacific Fishermen's Alliance, 221-1450 Johnston Road, White Rock British Columbia Canada. **DD** 639.2.

US/1055-6737
AMERICAN ANGLER (INTERVALE, N.H.). (AMERICAN ANGLER : THE MAGAZINE OF FLY FISHING AND FLY TYING.). [Am. angler]. Vol. 14, Issue 1 (Jan./Feb. 1991)-. Periodical. English. Six times a year. $19.95 (one year); $37.90 (two years). American Angler Inc, PO Box 280, Intervale NH 03845. **Tel** (603)356-9425, FAX (603)356-9426. **(Subscription address:** America Angler, PO Box 434, Mt. Morris IL 61054.) **LC** SH451; .F567. **DD** 799.1/2. **Continues** American Angler & Fly Tyer.

US/1070-7352
AMERICAN CURRENTS. [Am. curr.]. **Added/Corp** North American Native Fishes Association. (19??)-. Periodical. English. Four times a year (Mar., June, Sept., Dec.). $11.00 US & Canada & Mexico; $14.00 other. North American Native Fishes Association, 123 West Mt. Airy Avenue, Philadelphia PA 19119. **Tel** (215)247-0384. **ED** Bruce Gebhardt. **DD** 639. Index available. cum. index. **Bk Rev**, (Qty: 8). **Ad Acc. Circ:** 350 (ctrl).
Desc: This magazine featuring articles on finding, collecting, keeping, observing, conserving, and breeding North American fishes. News about aquarists, laws, the environment, scientific literature and developments, and other sources of information.

US/0162-6728
AMERICAN FISHERIES DIRECTORY & REFERENCE BOOK, THE. [Am. fish. dir. ref. book]. **VFOAT** American Fisheries Directory and Reference Book; American Fisheries. 2nd Ed. (1981)-?. Directory. English. be. National Fisherman, PO Box 908, Rockland ME 04841-0908. **Tel** (207)594-6222. **LC** SH203; .A47. **DD** 338.3/72/02573. **Continues** American Fisheries Directory and Reference Book, 0162-6728.

US/0892-2284
AMERICAN FISHERIES SOCIETY SYMPOSIUM. (AMERICAN FISHERIES SOCIETY SYMPOSIUM : [PROCEEDINGS].). [Am. Fish. Soc. Symp.]. **VFOAT** Symposium; AFS Symposium. (1987)-. Monographic series. English. ir. Price varies per volume. American Fisheries Society, 5410 Grosvenor Lane, Suite 110, Bethesda MD 20814-2199. **Tel** (301)897-8616, (301)897-8621, FAX (301)897-8096. **LC** UNC. **DD** 639. **CODEN** AFSSEF. **[CCC]. Acid Free.**

US/0884-3562
AMERICAN FLY FISHER, THE. Added/Corp Museum of American Fly Fishing. Vol. 1 (Winter 1974)-. Periodical. English. qt. comes with membership. American Museum of Fly Fishing, PO Box 42, Manchester VT 05254. **Tel** (802)362-3300. **ED** Donald S. Johnson. **LC** SH456; .A53. **DD** 799.1/2/0973. Index available. **Bk Rev. Circ:** 1,500.
Desc: Published by the American Museum of Fly Fishing for its membership. Primary focus is on the history of fly fishing and its memorabilia.
Ind/Abst Am. Hist. Life (1985-).

US/1050-0839
AMERICAN SEAFOOD INSTITUTE REPORT. [Am. Seaf. Inst. rep.]. **Added/Corp** American Seafood Institute. **VFOAT** Report. (1990)-. Periodical. English. mo. Free to the U.S. seafood industry; $35.00 other. American Seafood Institute, 212 Main Street, Suite 3, Wakefield RI 02879. **Tel** (800)328-3474, (401)783-4200, FAX (401)789-9727. **DD** 338. **CODEN** ASIREJ.
Ind/Abst Foods Adlibra.

RM
ANALELE UNIVERSITATII DIN GALATI.FASCICULA VII, TEHNICA PISCICOLA. Added/Corp Universitatea din Galati. **VFOAT** Tehnica Piscicola; Tehnologia si Chimia Produselor Alimentare si Tehnica Piscicola, B.; Tehnica Piscicola, Constructii si Amenajari Piscicole, . (1983)-. Romanian (English and French). an. Price varies. Redactia Analelor, 6200 Galati, Str Domneasca Nr. 47 Romania. **Tel** 40 93 413602, FAX 40 93 412328. **ED** Mihai Jascanu. **LC** SH293.R8; B84. **Bk Rev. Ad Acc. Circ:** 250 (ctrl). **Continues** Buletinul Universitatii din Galati. Fascicula VII, Tehnica Piscicola.

US/0739-019X
ANGLERS' NEWS. Ceased. Periodical. English. wk. Anglers News, Brown Road, Middletown NY 10940. **Continues** N.J. Anglers News.

FR
ANNUAIRE DE LA MAREE ET DE LAQUACULTURE. Moreux SA, 190 Boulevard Haussmann, 75008 Paris France. **Tel** 011 33 1 44959992, telex NAVIMAR 290 131 F.

FR/0066-2623
ANNUAIRE DE L'ARMEMENT A LA PECHE. (1957)-. French. an. 370.00F. Moreux SA, 190 Boulevard Haussmann, 75008 Paris France. **Tel** 011 33 1 44959992, telex NAVIMAR 290 131 F. **ED** S. Marpaud. **LC** SH269; .A6. **Bk Rev. Ad Acc. Continues in part** Annuaire de la Maree et de l'Armement a la Peche.

US
ANNUAL LANDINGS SUMMARY. Added/Corp Florida. Marine Fisheries Information System. **VFOAT** Landings Summary. (1986)-. English. **Continues** Florida Landings, Annual Summary.

US
ANNUAL PROGRESS REPORT - DIVISION OF GAME AND FRESHWATER FISHERIES. Main/Corp South Carolina. Division of Game and Freshwater Fisheries. (19??)-. English. an. South Carolina Wildlife and Marine Resources Department, Charleston SC 29412. **LC** SK445; .S68a. **DD** 639/.09757.

US
ANNUAL REPORT / ALASKA SEA GRANT COLLEGE PROGRAM. Main/Corp Alaska Sea Grant College Program. (19??)-. English. an. Alaska Sea Grant College Program, University of Alaska, 138 Irving II, Fairbanks AK 99775. **LC** SH222.A4; A645a. **DD** 639.2/0720798.
Ind/Abst Aquat. Sci. Fish. Abstr. (Computer File).

US
ANNUAL REPORT - ARIZONA GAME & FISH DEPARTMENT. Main/Corp Arizona. Game and Fish Dept. English. an. Arizona Game & Fish Department, 2221 West Greenway Road, Phoenix AZ 85023. **Tel** (602)942-3000 ext.217. **LC** SH11.A75; A3. **DD** 353.9/791/008236. **Continues** Arizona. Game and Fish Commission. Report.

II
ANNUAL REPORT - CENTRAL INSTITUTE OF FISHERIES NAUTICAL & ENGINEERING TRAINING (INDIA). Main/Corp Central Institute of Fisheries Nautical & Engineering Training (India). English. an. Central Institute of Fisheries Nautical & Engineering Training, Dewan's Road, Cochin 682016 India. **Tel** 351490, telex 885 222 CENT IN. **ED** M Swaminath. **LC** SH299; .C39A. **Circ:** 500 (ctrl).
Desc: Deals with the activities and achievements of training programmes and fishing technology development conducted by the institute during the year under report. It also deals with the marine fisheries survey results of fishery training vessels of the institute.

AT
ANNUAL REPORT / DEPARTMENT OF FISHERIES. Main/Corp South Australia. Dept. of Fisheries. (19??)-. English. an. Department of Fisheries / South Australia, Adelaide SA Australia. **LC** SH318.S68; S66a. **DD** 354.94230082/362.

CN/0711-0782
ANNUAL REPORT / DEPARTMENT OF FISHERIES AND OCEANS. [Annu. rep. - Dep. Fish. Oceans]. **Main/Corp** Canada. Dept. of Fisheries and Oceans. **VFOAT** Rapport Annuel. 1979/80-. English (French). an. Bibliotheque, Institut Maurice-Lamontagne, Peches Et Oceans, C P 1000 850 Route de la Mer, Mont-Joli Quebec G5H 3Z4 Canada. **Tel** (613)995-2041. **LC** SH223; .C223A. **DD** 354.710082/362/06. **Continues in part** Canada. Fisheries and Environment Canada. Annual Report, 0706-2583.

US/0094-5021
ANNUAL REPORT - DIVISION OF FORESTRY, FISHERIES, AND WILDLIFE DEVELOPMENT, TENNESSEE VALLEY AUTHORITY. See Forestry.

CN/0068-7499
ANNUAL REPORT - FISHERIES RESEARCH BOARD OF CANADA. Main/Corp Canada. Fisheries Research Board. **VFOAT** Rapport Annuel. **VAT** Annual Report of the Fisheries Research Board of Canada; Rapport Annuel - Office des Recherches sur les Pecheries du Canada; Rapport Annuel de l'Office des Recherches sur les Pecheries du Canada (1940). 1937-. Periodical. English (French). an. Free. Fisheries Research Board of Canada, IC, Ottawa Ontario Canada. **LC** UNC. **CODEN** FBCAA6. **Continues** Annual Report of the Biological Board of Canada.

AT/0311-8959
ANNUAL REPORT - FISHING INDUSTRY RESEARCH COMMITTEE. (ANNUAL REPORT - FISHING INDUSTRY RESEARCH COMMITTEE (AUSTRALIA).). [Annu. rep. - Fish. Ind. Res. Comm.]. **Main/Corp** Australia. Fishing Industry Research Committee. English. 0.18Aus$. Government Printer / Australia, PO Box 84, Canberra, Australian Capital Territory, 2600 Australia. **LC** J905; .L3 subser; SH317. **DD** 328.94/01 S; 639/.2/072094.

NL
ANNUAL REPORT FOR THE YEAR ENDING ... / SKIPJACK SURVEY AND ASSESSMENT PROGRAMME. Main/Corp Skipjack Survey and Assessment Programme. Dec. 31, 1977-. English. an. South Pacific Commission, PO Box D5, Noumea Cedex New Caledonia. **Tel** (687)26 20 00, FAX (687)26 38 18. **LC** SH351.T8; S57A. **DD** 333.95/6.

US/0072-7296
ANNUAL REPORT - GREAT LAKES FISHERY COMMISSION. [Annu. rep. Great Lakes Fish. Comm.]. **Main/Corp** Great Lakes Fishery Commission. (1956)-. English. an. Free. Great Lakes Fishery Commission, 1451 Green Road, Ann Arbor MI 48105. **Tel** (313)662-3209, (800)378-2077. **ED** Barbara S. Staples. **LC** SH221; .G7. **DD** 639. **CODEN** GLFRAH. **Circ:** 500 (ctrl). Documents available from BIOSIS Document Express.
Ind/Abst Biol. Abstr.

US/0074-7238
ANNUAL REPORT - INTERNATIONAL PACIFIC HALIBUT COMMISSION. [Annu. rep. Int. Pac. Halibut Comm.]. **Main/Corp** International Pacific Halibut Commission (United States and Canada). (1969)-. English. an. International Pacific Halibut Commission, PO Box 95009, Seattle WA 98145-2009. **Tel** (206)634-1838, FAX (206)632-2983. **LC** WMLC L 83/1199. **CODEN** IPHCBX. Documents available from BIOSIS Document Express. **Continues in part** Report of the International Pacific Halibut Commission, 0096-1221.
Ind/Abst Biol. Abstr.

IE/0578-736X
ANNUAL REPORT - IRISH SEA FISHERIES BOARD. Main/Corp Ireland (Eire). Sea Fisheries Board. **VFOAT** Report and Accounts - Irish Sea Fisheries Board; Annual Report - Bord Iascaigh Mhara. 1st (1953)-. Multiple languages (English and Gaelic (Scots)). **DD** 639.

US
ANNUAL REPORT - NEW MEXICO DEPARTMENT OF GAME AND FISH. Main/Corp New Mexico. Department of Game and Fish. Periodical. English. **LC** SH11; .N65. **Continues** Report of the Game and Fish Warden of New Mexico.

AT/1034-7356
ANNUAL REPORT - NORTHERN TERRITORY. DEPARTMENT OF PRIMARY INDUSTRY AND FISHERIES. Main/Corp Northern Territory. Dept. of Primary Industry and Fisheries. (1988/89)-. English. an. 4.00Aus$. Department of Primary Industry & Fisheries, GPO Box 990, Darwin Northern Territory 5794 Australia. **Tel** 895511, telex 1410825. **LC** S387; .D46A. **DD** 354.94290082/33. **Circ:** 1,000 (ctrl). **Continues** Annual Report / Northern Territory. Dept. of Industries & Development, 1031-6221.
Ind/Abst Anim. Breed. Abstr.; Ornamental Hort. (1991-).

CN/0704-4798
ANNUAL REPORT / NORTHWEST ATLANTIC FISHERIES ORGANIZATION. [Annu. rep. - Northw. Atl. Fish. Organ.]. **Main/Corp**

Northwest Atlantic Fisheries Organization. (1979)-. English. an. 17.00Can$. Northwest Atlantic Fisheries Organization / NAFO, PO Box 638, Dartmouth Nova Scotia B2Y 3Y9 Canada. **Tel** (902)469-9105, telex 019-31475. **LC** SH1; .I532. **DD** 354.1/82362/091821. **Circ:** 500. ***Continues*** *International Commission for the Northwest Atlantic Fisheries. Annual Report, 0303-4151.*
Desc: Contains summarized reports of annual and special meetings of the scientific council, fisheries commission and general council of NAFO along with an administrative report.
Ind/Abst Fish Rev.; Wildl. Rev.

CN/0550-1717
ANNUAL REPORT OF DEPARTMENT OF FISHERIES (HALIFAX). (ANNUAL REPORT OF DEPARTMENT OF FISHERIES.). **Main/Corp** Nova Scotia. Dept. of Fisheries. **VAT** Annual Report - Department of Fisheries (Halifax). (1965)-. English. an. Free. Department of Fisheries, Box 2223, Halifax Nova Scotia B3J 3C4 Canada. **Tel** (902)424-4560.

US
ANNUAL REPORT OF THE ATLANTIC STATES MARINE FISHERIES COMMISSION. **Main/Corp** Atlantic States Marine Fisheries Commission. 3rd (1944)-. English. an. PO Box 2784, Tallahassee FL 32301. **LC** SH221; .A84. **DD** 639.2206174. ***Continues*** *Atlantic States Marine Fisheries Commission. Report to the Congress of the United States and to the Governors and the Legislatures of the Compacting States in Accordance with the Provisions of the Compact Creating such Commission.*
Ind/Abst Fish Rev. (199?-); Wildl. Rev. (199?-).

SA
ANNUAL REPORT OF THE DIRECTOR GENERAL, AGRICULTURE AND FISHERIES FOR THE PERIOD 1 APRIL ... TO 31 MARCH / REPUBLIC OF SOUTH AFRICA. **See** Agriculture.

AT
ANNUAL REPORT OF THE FISHERIES DEVELOPMENT AUTHORITY FOR THE YEAR ENDING 30 JUNE ... (TASMANIA). **Main/Corp** Tasmania. Fisheries Development Authority. English. an. Fisheries Development Authority, 23 Old Whard, Hobart Tasmania Australia. **LC** SH318.T3; T27A. **DD** 338.3/72/0994.

US/0074-1000
ANNUAL REPORT OF THE INTER-AMERICAN TROPICAL TUNA COMMISSION. [Annu. rep. Inter-Am. Trop. Tuna Comm.]. **Main/Corp** Inter-American Tropical Tuna Commission. **VFOAT** Informe Anual de la Comision Interamericana del Atun Tropical. 1950/51-. Multiple languages (English and Spanish). an. Inter-American Tuna Commission, Scripps Institute of Oceanography, La Jolla CA 92037. **Tel** (619)546-7025, telex 697115. **ED** William H Bayliff. **LC** SH351.T8. **DD** 639. Index available. cum. index. **Pr Rev. Circ:** 1,200. ***Continues*** *Inter-American Tropical Tuna Commission. Annual Report for the Years, 0074-1000.*
Desc: Contains progress reports on research on tunas in the Eastern Pacific, catch and effort statistics, accounts of commission meetings, financial statements, etc.

UK
ANNUAL REPORT / SEA FISH INDUSTRY AUTHORITY. **Main/Corp** Great Britain. Sea Fish Industry Authority. (1985)-. Corporate Report. English. an. Free. Sea Fish Industry Authority, 18 Logie Mill, Logie Green Road, Edinburgh EH7 4HG Scotland. **Tel** 011 44 31 558-3331 ext. 256, FAX 011 44 31 558-1442. Documents available from BLDSC. ***Continues*** *Annual Report and Accounts / Great Britain. Sea Fish Industry Authority.*

II
ANNUAL REPORT / STATE FISHERIES DEVELOPMENT CORPORATION LIMITED (CALCUTTA, INDIA). **Main/Corp** State Fisheries Development Corporation (Calcutta, India). English. an. Free. The State Fisheries Development Corporation Ltd, 43 Shakespeare Sarani, Calcutta 700017 India. **LC** HD4293; .S745A. **DD** 354.540092362/06.

CN/0837-1059
ANNUAL REPORT / THE ATLANTIC SALMON FEDERATION. [Annu. rep. - Atl. Salmon Fed.]. **Main/Corp** Atlantic Salmon Federation. (19??)-. English (French). an. Free upon request. Atlantic Salmon Federation, PO Box 429, St Andrews New Brunswick, E0G 2X0 Canada. **Tel** (506)529-4581, (506)529-1025, FAX (506)529-4438, telex 014-47458. **ED** Terry Davis. **LC** SH346; .A78a. **DD** 639/.2755. **Circ:** 7,500 (ctrl).
Desc: Deals with all aspects of the federation's continuing work in Atlantic salmon conservation and habitat restoration, as well as touching on its role in public education.
Ind/Abst Fish Rev. (Jan. 1989-July 1992); Wildl. Rev. (Jan. 1989-July 1992).

UG
ANNUAL REPORT / UGANDA FRESHWATER FISHERIES RESEARCH ORGANIZATION. **Main/Corp** Uganda Freshwater Fisheries Research Organization. (1977)-. English. an. Uganda Freshwater Fisheries Research Organization, PO Box 343, Jinja Uganda. **LC** SH315.E3; E37A. **DD** 354.676/1008236/06. **UDC** 639.21(047.1)(676.1). ***Continues*** *Director's Report / East African Freshwater Fisheries Research Organization.*

UK/0951-3752
ANNUAL REVIEW / FRESHWATER FISHERIES LABORATORY, PITLOCHRY. **Main/Corp** Freshwater Fisheries Laboratory (Pitlochry, Scotland). 1985-. English. an. Department of Agriculture and Fisheries for Scotland, PO Box 101 Victoria Road, Aberdeen AB9 8DB Scotland. **Tel** 0224 876544. ***Continues*** *Triennial Review of Research, 0140-5004.*

CN
ANNUAL REVIEW / NEWFOUNDLAND REGION. **Main/Corp** Canada. Dept. of Fisheries and Oceans. Newfoundland Region. (19??)-. English. an. Fisheries & Oceans Canada, Scientific Information & Publications Branch, 200 Kent Street/12th Floor, Ottawa Ontario K1A 0E6 Canada. **Tel** (613)993-0600, (800)267-6677, telex 053-3585. **LC** SH224.N7; C35a. **DD** 354.710082/362/097182. ***Continues*** *Canada. Dept. of Fisheries and Oceans. Newfoundland Region. Annual Report.*

US/0959-8030
ANNUAL REVIEW OF FISH DISEASES. Vol. 1 (1991)-. English. an. $224.00 The Americas; £150.00 other. Pergamon Press, An Imprint of Elsevier Science Ltd., The Boulevard, Langford Lane, Kidlington, Oxford OX5 1GB United Kingdom. **Tel** 011 44 865 843000, 011 44 865 843699, FAX 011 44 865 843010. **(Subscription address:** Elsevier Science Ltd. Oxford Fulfillment Centre, PO Box 800, Kidlington, Oxford OX5 1DX United Kingdom.**) ED** M. Faisal. **LC** SH171; .A56. **DD** 639.3. **CODEN** ARFDEN. **[CCC].** available on microfilm and microfiche from University Microfilms International (UMI).
Ind/Abst Curr. Aware. Biol. Sci., CABS; Environ. Period. Bibliogr.; Index Vet.

FR/0295-0448
AQUA REVUE. (1985)-. Periodical. French. bm. 250.00F France; 310.00F other. Societe Edition Aqua Presse, 55 Cours Georges Clemenceau, 33000 Bordeaux France. **Tel** 011 33 56 446208, FAX 011 33 56 442876. **UDC** 639.3.

HU/0138-9092
AQUACULTURA HUNGARICA. [Aquacult. Hung.]. **Added/Corp** Fisheries Research Institute (Szarvas, Hungary). Vol. 1 (1978)-. English (summaries and/or abstracts in Hungarian and Russian). **CODEN** AQHUD8.
Ind/Abst Aquat. Sci. Fish. Abstr. (Computer File).

UK/0144-8609
AQUACULTURAL ENGINEERING. [Aquac. eng.]. Vol. 1, No. 1 (Jan. 1982)-. Academic Scholarly Publication. English. Four times a year. $373.00 The Americas; £250.00 other. Elsevier Applied Science, An Imprint of Elsevier Science Ltd., The Boulevard, Langford Lane, Kidlington, Oxford OX5 1GB United Kingdom. **Tel** 011 44 865 843000, 011 44 865 843699, FAX 011 44 865 843010. **(Subscription address:** Elsevier Science Ltd. Oxford Fulfillment Centre, PO Box 800, Kidlington, Oxford OX5 1DX United Kingdom.**) ED** K. R. Murray and J. Colt. **LC** SH1; .A623. **DD** 639.3/05. **CODEN** AQEND6. **[CCC]. Bk Rev. Ad Acc. Pr Rev.** ctrl circ. available on microfilm and microfiche from University Microfilms International (UMI). Documents available from Article Express International, The Genuine Article, BIOSIS Document Express.
Desc: Emphasis is on the application of technology in aquaculture in the areas of engineering and design of aquacultural facilities; engineering-based commissioning and operation; materials selection and their uses and the quantification of biological data and constraints.
Ind/Abst AgBiotech News Inf.; Agric. Eng. Abstr. (19??-19??); Aquat. Sci. Fish. Abstr. (Computer File); Biodeter. Abstr.; Biol. Abstr. (1988-); Curr. Contents, Agric. Biol. Environ. Sci.; Curr. Ref. Fish Res.; Eng. Index Annu.; Fish Rev. (19??-199?); Fresh. Aqua. Contents Tables; Index Vet.; Mar. Sci. Contents Tables; Nutr. Abstr. Rev., Ser. B, Live Feeds and Feed.; Ocean. Abstr.; Res. Alert [Full Cov.]; Sci. Cit. Index; SCISEARCH; World Agric. Econ.

NE/0044-8486
AQUACULTURE. [Aquaculture]. (1972)-. Academic Scholarly Publication. English. Forty times a year (10 volumes). Fl3200.00. Elsevier Science Publishers BV, PO Box 211, 1000 AE Amsterdam Netherlands. **Tel** 011 31 20 5803642, FAX 011 31 20 5862696, telex 15682. **ED** G A E Gall and S J de Groot. **LC** SH1; .A626. **DD** 630/.9162. **CODEN** AQCLAL. **[CCC]. Pr Rev.** available on microfilm and microfiche from University Microfilms International (UMI). Documents available from The Genuine Article, BIOSIS Document Express, UMI Article Clearinghouse, CASDDS, Documents on Demand.
Desc: Journal for aquaculturists, fisheries scientists and marine biologists. Devoted to research on the exploration, improvement and management of all aquatic food resources, both floristic and faunistic, from freshwater, brackish and marine environments, related directly or indirectly to human consumption.
Ind/Abst AgBiotech News Inf.; AGRICOLA; Agric. Eng. Abstr. (1991-); Anim. Breed. Abstr.; AQUAREF; Aquat. Sci. Fish. Abstr. (Computer File); BioBusiness; Biodeter. Abstr. (1991-); Biol. Agric. Index; Biol. Abstr.; Biotechnol. Res. Abstr.; Chem. Abstr.; CSA Neuro. Abstr.; Curr. Aware. Biol. Sci., CABS; Curr. Contents, Agric. Biol. Environ. Sci.; Curr. Ref. Fish Res.; Ecol. Abstr.; Ecology Abstr.; EMBASE; Energy Inf. Abstr.; Energy Res. Abstr. (June 1977-); Environ. Abstr.; Fish Rev.; Food Sci. Technol. Abstr.; Fresh. Aqua. Contents Tables; Genet. Abstr.; Geogr. Abstr. Phys. Geogr.; Geogr. Abstr. Human Geogr.; Helminthol. Abstr. (19??-19??); Index Vet.; Int. Dev. Abstr.; Mag. Artic. Summar. Select; Mag. Artic. Summar. CD-ROM (July 1990-); Maize Abstr.; Mar. Sci. Contents Tables; Microbiol. Abstr. Sect. B (19??-19??); Microbiol. Abstr. Sect. C; Newsp. Period. Abstr. (1992-); Nutr. Abstr. Rev., Ser. B, Live Feeds and Feed.; Ocean. Abstr.; Life Sci. Collect.; Pollut. Abstr. Indexes; Potato Abstr.; Protozoolog. Abstr.; Res. Alert [Full Cov.]; Rev. Med. Vet. Entomol.; Rev. Med. Vet. Mycology; Rice Abstr.; Sci. Cit. Index; SCISEARCH; Soc. Sci. Cit. Index [Select. Cov.]; Soils Fert.; Soyabean Abstr.; Vet. Bull.; Vocat. Search (July 1990-); Wheat Barley Trit. Abstr.; World Agric. Econ.

UK/0266-996X
AQUACULTURE AND FISHERIES MANAGEMENT. ***Title Change.*** [Aquac. fish. manage.]. Vol. 16, No. 1 (Jan. 1985)-(1995). Academic Scholarly Publication. English. mo (12 issues). Blackwell Scientific Publications Ltd, Marston Book Services, PO Box 87, Oxford OX2 ODT UK. **Tel** 011 44 865 791155, FAX 011 44 865 791927, telex 837 515 MARDIS G. **LC** SH1; .F8185. **DD** 639/.8/05. **CODEN** AFMAEX. **[CCC].** Index available (bound in last issue). available on microfilm and microfiche from University Microfilms International (UMI). Documents available from BIOSIS Document Express, CASDDS. ***Continues*** *Fisheries Management, 0141-9862.* ***Continued in part by*** *Fisheries Management and Ecology, 0969-997X;* ***Continued by*** *Aquaculture Research.*
Ind/Abst Anim. Breed. Abstr.; Aquat. Sci. Fish. Abstr. (Computer File); Biol. Abstr. (1985-); Chem. Abstr. (1985-); Curr. Aware. Biol. Sci., CABS; Ecol. Abstr.; Environ. Period. Bibliogr. (?-?); Fish Rev.; Fresh. Aqua. Contents Tables; Geogr. Abstr. Human Geogr.; Index Vet.; Int. Dev. Abstr.; Nutr. Abstr. Rev., Ser. B, Live Feeds and Feed.; Ocean. Abstr.; Rev. Med. Vet. Entomol.; Rice Abstr.; Vet. Bull.; Wheat Barley Trit. Abstr.

US
AQUACULTURE & THE FISH FARMER. Vol. 1, No. 1 (May/June 1974)-. Periodical. English. bm. Damascus Publishing, PO Box 1837, Little Rock AR 72203. **UDC** 639.3.

UK/0953-2781
AQUACULTURE INFORMATION SERIES. [Aquacult. inf. ser.]. **Added/Corp** Great Britain. Dept. of Agriculture and Fisheries for Scotland. Marine Laboratory (Aberdeen, Scotland). No. 1 (1988)-. Monographic series. English.
Ind/Abst Index Vet.

●UK/0967-6120
AQUACULTURE INTERNATIONAL. (1993)-. English. qt. $225.00 US and Canada; £130.00 Europe; £145.00 other. Chapman & Hall, 2-6 Boundary Row, London SE1 8HN England. **Tel** 011 44 71 865 0066, FAX 011 44 71 522 9623, telex 290164 Chapmag. **(Subscription address:** Chapman & Hall, Cheriton House, North Way, Andover, Hampshire, SP10 5BE England.**)**
Ind/Abst Aquat. Sci. Fish. Abstr. (Computer File).

IE/0790-0929
AQUACULTURE IRELAND. [Aquac. Irel.]. **Added/Corp** Irish Aquaculture Association. **VFOAT** Ireland's Fish Farming Journal. (1983)-. Periodical. English. Six times a year. £15.00 Ireland; £20.00 other. Aquaculture Ireland, PO Box 12 Crofton Road, Dun Laughaire Co, Dublin Ireland. **Tel** 011 353 1 800078, FAX 011 353 1 800650, telex 93237. **ED** Deirde McKay. **LC** SH101.I73; A66. **DD** 639/.8/09417. Index available. **Bk Rev**, (Qty: 6). **Ad Acc. Circ:** 800 (ctrl). ***Absorbed in part by*** *Aquaculture Ireland Yearbook, 0790-3308.*

US/0199-1388
AQUACULTURE MAGAZINE. [Aquac. mag.]. **VFOAT** Aquaculture. Vol. 5, No. 6, (Sept./Oct. 1979)-. Periodical. English. Seven times a year (Jan., Mar., May, July, Sept., Nov. with Buyer's Guide in Dec.). $17.00 (one year), $32.00 (two year), $45.00 (three year) US; $21.00 (one year), $40.00 (two year) surface mail, $50.00 (one year) $90.00 (two year) airmail (other). Achill River Corporation, PO Box 2329, Asheville NC 28802. **Tel** (704)254-7334. **ED** Kay Homer. **LC** SH1; .C56. **DD** 639.3/05. **UDC** 639.3. **CODEN** AQMAE8. Index available.

Bk Rev. Ad Acc. Circ: 7,360 (ctrl). Documents available from Documents on Demand. ***Continues** Commercial Fish Farmer & Aquaculture News, 0099-0353.*
Desc: Leading the aquaculture (fish farming) expansion, features articles on actual operations and species. Columns on feed disease, nutrition, genetics and specific species.
Ind/Abst Acad. Abstr. Full Text Elite (July 1990-); Acad. Abstr. (July 1990-); Acad. Search (July 1990-); Agric. Eng. Abstr. (1991-); Anim. Breed. Abstr.; Aquat. Sci. Fish. Abstr. (Computer File); BioBusiness; Environ. Abstr.; Fish Rev.; Foods Adlibra; Gen. Sci. Source (Jul. 1990-); Helminthol. Abstr. (1991-); INFO-SOUTH Abstr.; Mag. Artic. Summar. Elite (July 1990-); Mag. Artic. Summar. Select (July 1990-); Mag. Artic. Summar. CD-ROM (July 1990-); Mag. Search; Ocean. Abstr.; Rev. Med. Vet. Mycology; Rural Dev. Abstr.; Wildl. Rev.; World Agric. Econ.

US/0898-9540
AQUACULTURE MAGAZINE. BUYER'S GUIDE ... AND INDUSTRY DIRECTORY. [Aquac. mag., Buy. guide ind. dir.]. **VFOAT** Buyer's Guide ... and Industry Directory. (1986)-. Directory. English. an. $17.00 (one year), $32.00 (two year), $45.00 (three year). Archill River Corporation, PO Box 2329, Asheville NC 28802. **Tel** (704)254-7334. **ED** K H Homer. **DD** 338. Index available. **Ad Acc. Circ:** 7,200 (ctrl). ***Continues** Aquaculture Magazine. Buyer's Guide.*
Desc: Alphabetical listings of products, service suppliers, manufacturers. Diagnostic, state extension, US soil conservation SVC. Institutions offering aquaculture courses.

●US
AQUACULTURE NEWS. (1992)-. English. Twelve times a year. $20.00 (one year); $35.00 (two years); $45.00 (three years). Aquaculture News, PO Box 416, Jonesville LA 71343. **Tel** (318)339-4660, FAX (318)339-4664. **ED** Stanley Nelson. **Ad Acc, Adv Mgr:** David Ryan. **Circ:** 6,000 (ctrl). ***Continues** Catfish and Aquaculture News.*
Desc: Covers the United States aquaculture industry. News and information to new products and services, and covers news in all aspects of fish farming and species.

●UK/1355-557X
AQUACULTURE RESEARCH. See Biology-Marine Biology.

IE/0332-2475
AQUACULTURE TECHNICAL BULLETIN. VFOAT Aquaculture. (1981)-. Bulletin. English. ir. Price varies per volume. National Board for Science and Technology, Shelbourne House Shelbourne Road, Dublin 4 Ireland. **Tel** (01)683311, telex 30327 NBSTE I.
Ind/Abst Aquat. Sci. Fish. Abstr. (Computer File).

UK/0003-7273
AQUARIST AND PONDKEEPER. VFOAT Aquarist and Pond Keeper; Aquarist. Vol. 2 No. 9 (1928)-. Periodical. English. mo. Buckley Press Ltd, 58 Fleet Street, London EC4Y 1JU England. **Tel** 011 44 71 5833030. **CODEN** AQPOAR. ***Continues** Amateur Aquarist & Reptilian Review.*
Ind/Abst Aquat. Sci. Fish. Abstr. (Computer File).

GW
AQUARIUM DIGEST INTERNATIONAL. ***Ceased.*** Vol. 1, No. 1 (1972)-(1991). Periodical. English. qt. Lewis Books, PO Box 41137, Cincinnati OH 45241. **UDC** 639.93.

FR/0990-7440
AQUATIC LIVING RESOURCES (MONTROUGE). (AQUATIC LIVING RESOURCES.). [Aquat. living resour.]. **VFOAT** Ressources Vivantes Aquatiques. Vol. 1, No. 1 (1988)-. Periodical. English (French and Spanish). Four times a year. 950.00F France; 1100.00F other. Gauthier-Villars, 15 rue Gossin, 92543 Montrouge Cedex France. **Tel** 33 1 40 92 65 00, FAX 33 1 40 92 65 97. **(Subscription address:** Centrale des Revues, 11 rue Gossin, 92543 Montrouge Cedex France.) **ED** R. Billard, B. Milcendeau. **CODEN** ALREEA. **[CCC]. Ad Acc. Circ:** 450. Documents available from BIOSIS Document Express. ***Continues** Revue des Travaux de l'Institut des Peches Maritimes, 0035-2276.*
Desc: Publishes original research papers, review articles and short communications dealing with the production and the exploitation of living resources of the oceans, coastal waters, rivers and lakes, including all fields of biology and environmental management and exploitation methods. Priority is given to the applied research without completely excluding basic aspects.
Ind/Abst Anim. Breed. Abstr.; Aquat. Sci. Fish. Abstr. (Computer File); Biol. Abstr.; Curr. Aware. Biol. Sci., CABS; Ecology Abstr.; Fish Rev.; Mar. Sci. Contents Tables; Ocean. Abstr.; Wildl. Rev.

US/1064-0460
AQUATIC SCIENCES & FISHERIES ABSTRACTS (CD-ROM ED.). See Fish and Fisheries-Abstracting, Bibliographies and Statistics.

US/0140-5373
AQUATIC SCIENCES AND FISHERIES ABSTRACTS. PART 1 : BIOLOGICAL SCIENCES AND LIVING RESOURCES. See Fish and Fisheries-Abstracting, Bibliographies and Statistics.

US/0140-5381
AQUATIC SCIENCES AND FISHERIES ABSTRACTS. PART 2 : OCEAN TECHNOLOGY, POLICY AND NON-LIVING RESOURCES. See Fish and Fisheries-Abstracting, Bibliographies and Statistics.

US/1045-6031
AQUATIC SCIENCES AND FISHERIES ABSTRACTS. PART 3 : AQUATIC POLLUTION AND ENVIRONMENTAL QUALITY. See Fish and Fisheries-Abstracting, Bibliographies and Statistics.

●CN/1188-553X
AQUATIC SURVIVAL. (AQUATIC SURVIVAL : BULLETIN OF THE AQUATIC CONSERVATION NETWORK.). [Aquat. surviv.]. **Added/Corp** Aquatic Conservation Network. Vol. 1, No. 1 (Mar. 1992)-. Bulletin. English. qt. $25.00 (membership). Aquatic Conservation Network, 540 Roosevelt Avenue, Ottawa, Ontario K2A 1Z8, Canada. **Tel** (613)729-4670, FAX (613)729-5613. **DD** 333.95/616/05.
Desc: Provides a forum for information exchange through articles and letters, outlines progress on Aquatic Conservation Network initiatives, and highlights the coming events of relevance to the aquatic conservation community.

GW/0003-9063
ARCHIV FUER FISCHEREIWISSENSCHAFT. ***Title Change.*** [Arch. Fischereiwiss.]. **Added/Corp** Bundesforschungsanstalt fuer Fischerei (Germany) Bundesanstalt fuer Fischerei (Germany). Vol. 1 (1948)-(1993). Academic Scholarly Publication. German (English and French). Three times a year. Gustav Fischer Verlag Stuttgart, Postfach 720143, Wollgrasweg 49, D 70577 Stuttgart Germany. **Tel** 011 49 711 458030, FAX 0711-4580334, telex 2627-7111488. **(Subscription address:** VCH Publishers Inc., 303 NW 12th Avenue, Deerfield Beach, FL 33442**) ED** Klaus Tiews and Dietrich Sahrhage. **LC** SH1; .H25. **DD** 639/.2. **CODEN** AVFSAO. Index available. cum. index. **Bk Rev. Ad Acc. Pr Rev. Circ:** 900. Documents available from The Genuine Article, BIOSIS Document Express, CASDDS. ***Continued by** Archiv fuer Fischerei und Meeresforschung.*
Desc: Scientific research papers concerned with fish and fisheries.
Ind/Abst Aquat. Sci. Fish. Abstr. (Computer File); Biol. Abstr.; Chem. Abstr.; Curr. Aware. Biol. Sci., CABS; Curr. Contents, Agric. Biol. Environ. Sci.; Curr. Ref. Fish Res.; Ecol. Abstr. (?-?); EMBASE; Energy Res. Abstr. (April 1974-); Fish Rev. (Jan. 1989-July 1992); Food Sci. Technol. Abstr.; Fresh. Aqua. Contents Tables; Helminthol. Abstr. (1991-); Index Vet.; Mar. Sci. Contents Tables; Nutr. Abstr. Rev., Ser. B, Live Feeds and Feed.; Ocean. Abstr.; Protozoolog. Abstr.; Res. Alert [Full Cov.]; Sci. Cit. Index; SCISEARCH; Wildl. Rev. (Jan. 1989-July 1992).

GW/0944-1921
ARCHIVE OF FISHERY AND MARINE RESEARCH. (19??)-. German. Three times a year. DM216.00 Germany; DM222.00 other. Gustav Fischer Verlag Stuttgart, Postfach 720143, Wollgrasweg 49, D 70577 Stuttgart Germany. **Tel** 011 49 711 458030, FAX 0711-4580334, telex 2627-7111488. **(Subscription address:** VCH Publishers Inc., 303 Northwest 12th Avenue, Journals Department, Deerfield FL 33442.) ***Continues** Archiv fuer Fischereiwissenschaft und Meeresforschung.*

US/0888-840X
ARIZONA HUNTER & ANGLER. See Recreation, Leisure-Sports.

BE/0775-454X
ARTEMIA NEWSLETTER. ***Title Change.*** [Artemia newsl.]. (1986)-(19??). Periodical. English. qt. Laboratory of Aquaculture, Artemia Reference Center, Rijksuniversiteit Gent, Rozier 44, B-9000 Gent Belgium. **Tel** 011 32 91 643754, FAX 011 32 91 644193. **(Subscription address:** Dr David Bengtson, University of Rhode Island, Dept of Zoology, Kingston RI 02881**) ED** P Sorgeloos and G Van Stappen. **UDC** 595.3. Index available. **Ad Acc. Circ:** 600. ***Continued by** Larviculture & Artemia Newsletter.*

US/0739-814X
ASFA AQUACULTURE ABSTRACTS. Added/Corp Cambridge Scientific Abstracts, Inc. United Nations. Dept. of International Economic and Social Affairs. Food and Agriculture Organization of the United Nations. Intergovernmental Oceanographic Commission. **VFOAT** A.S.F.A. Aquaculture Abstracts; Aquaculture Abstracts. **VAT** Aquatic Sciences and Fisheries Abstracts Aquaculture Abstracts. Vol. 1, No. 1 (Jan. 1984)-. English. bm (plus annual index). $350.00 US; $385.00 other. Cambridge Scientific Abstracts, 7200 Wisconsin Avenue, #601, Bethesda MD 20814-4823. **Tel** (301)961-6750, (800)843-7751, FAX (301)961-6720. **ED** Jonathan R. L. Sears. **LC** SH1; .A69. **DD** 639. Index available. cum. index. available on magnetic tape; available on an online database; available on CD-ROM; available via Internet (to the current year's abstracts and five-year backfiles) from Cambridge Scientific Abstracts.
Desc: The science, practice, management and economics of aquaculture, including biology and ecology of cultured species, aquaculture techniques, restocking, plant culture, and aquaria.

IT
ASFIS REFERENCE SERIES / AQUATIC SCIENCES AND FISHERIES INFORMATION SYSTEM. Added/Corp Aquatic Sciences and Fisheries Information System. No. 1 (1979)-. Monographic series. English. Food and Agriculture Organization (FAO) / Italy, GIPC166 via Terme di Caracalla, 00100 Rome Italy. **Tel** 011 39 6 522 52925, FAX 011 39 6 522 55784.
Ind/Abst Nematol. Abstr.

PH/0115-4974
ASIAN AQUACULTURE. [Asian aquaculture]. **Added/Corp** Southeast Asian Fisheries Development Center. Aquaculture Dept. **VFOAT** SEAFDEC Asian Aquaculture. Vol. 1, No. 1 (July 1978)-. Periodical. English. Twelve times a year. $27.00. Southeast Asian Fisheries Development Center - SEAFDEC, PO Box 256, Ililo City Philippines. **Tel** 011 63 2 7210428, FAX 011 63 2 7211342, telex 29078. **Bk Rev,** (Qty: 3). ctrl circ.
Ind/Abst Fish Rev. (Jan. 1989-July 1992); Life Sci. Collect.; Philip. Sci. Technol. Abstr.; Wildl. Rev. (Jan. 1989-July 1992).

PH/0116-6514
ASIAN FISHERIES SCIENCE. Added/Corp Asian Fisheries Society. Vol. 1, No. 1 (Dec. 1987)-. Periodical. English. Three times a year. $27.00 individuals; $60.00 institutions. Asian Fisheries Society, MC PO Box 1501, Makati Metro Manila Philippines. **Tel** 011 63 2 8180466.
Ind/Abst Aquat. Sci. Fish. Abstr. (Computer File); Food Sci. Technol. Abstr.

PH
ASIAN FISHING AND SHIPPING MAGAZINE. Vol. 1 (1974)-. Periodical. English. qt. 75.00 per copy. **LC** SH307.P5; A74. **DD** 338.3/72/095.
Ind/Abst Ocean. Abstr.

CN/0044-992X
ATLANTIC SALMON JOURNAL, THE. [Atl. salmon j.]. **Added/Corp** Atlantic Salmon Association. (May 1952)-. Periodical. English (French). Four times a year (Mar., June, Sept., Dec.). 40.00Can$ (individual), 25.00Can$ (libraries). Atlantic Salmon Federation, PO Box 429, St Andrews New Brunswick, E0G 2X0 Canada. **Tel** (506)529-4581, (506)529-1025, FAX (506)529-4438, telex 014-47458. **(Subscription address:** Atlantic Salmon Journal, PO Box 807, Calais ME 04619.**) ED** Terry Davis. **CODEN** ATSJAE. **Bk Rev. Ad Acc.** ctrl circ. Documents available from BIOSIS Document Express.
Desc: Magazine devoted to salmon conservation, habitat restoration, research projects and angling.
Ind/Abst AQUAREF; Biol. Abstr. (1986-); Fish Rev.; Ocean. Abstr.; Wildl. Rev.

CN/0826-5321
ATOSSEMENT VOTRE. (ATOSSEMENT VOTRE : REVUE TRIMESTRIELLE DE LA CONFRERIE DES PECHEURS A LA MOUCHE ATOS.). [Atossement votre]. Vol. 1, No. 1 Spring 1984-. Periodical. French. qt. $20.00 Canada; $25.00 other. Confrerie des Pecheure A la Mouche: Achigan Truite Omble et Saumon, C P 1120, Waterloo Quebec J0E 2N0 Canada. **ED** Claude Bernard. **DD** 799.1/2/05. **UDC** 799.12. **Bk Rev. Ad Acc. Circ:** 500 (ctrl). ***Continues** Atos, 0228-7366.*
Desc: Fly fishing promotion through education and conservation.

AT/0818-5522
AUSTASIA AQUACULTURE MAGAZINE. [Austasia aquac. mag.]. Vol. 1, No. 1 (Aug. 1986)-. Trade Publication. English. Six times a year. 38.00Aus$ Australia; 48.00Aus$ New Zealand; 72.00Aus$ others;. Turtle Press, 47 Sandy Bay Road, Sandy Bay Tasmania 7005 Australia. **Tel** 011 61 2 240581, FAX 011 61 2 232422. **(Subscription address:** PO Box 575, Sandy Bay Tasmania 7005 Australia**) ED** Dr. Tim Walker.
Desc: Trade magazine for aquaculture industry in Australasian, SE Asian and Indo-Pacific regions. Covers all spheres of aquaculture.
Ind/Abst Aquat. Sci. Fish. Abstr. (Computer File).

AT
AUSTASIA AQUACULTURE TRADE DIRECTORY. VFOAT Aust Asia Aquaculture Trade Directory; Trade Directory. (1988)-. English. an. 20.00Aus$ Australia. Turtle Press, 47 Sandy Bay Road, Sandy Bay Tasmania 7005 Australia. **Tel** 011 61 2

240581, FAX 011 61 2 232422. **(Subscription address:** Turtle Press, PO Box 279, Sandy Bay Tasmania 7005 Australia.)

AT
AUSTRALIA DEPARTMENT OF PRIMARY INDUSTRIES AND ENERGY BASIC FISH STATISTICS. English. mo. 45.00Aus$ Australia; 89.00Aus$ North America; 67.00Aus$ New Zealand; 81.00Aus$ India; 95.00Aus$ Europe;. Department of Primary Industry and Energy, Shop Front PO Box 858, Canberra Australian Capital Territory 2601 Australia. **Tel** 011 61 6 272550. **ED** Margaret Macreadie. Index available. cum. index. **Bk Rev. Ad Acc. Circ:** 2,000.
Desc: A broad base covering all aspects of the Australian and commercial fishing industry ranging from catching through to post harvest and marketing. It also focuses on environment issues and sustainable development.

AT/0159-6365
AUSTRALIAN AQUACULTURE. (1979)-. Periodical. English. sa. Free to members. Inland Fish Farmers Association of Australia, Rmb 626 Sturt Highway, Wagga Wagga NSW 2650 Australia. **Tel** 069 227360.
Ind/Abst Aquat. Sci. Fish. Abstr. (Computer File).

AT/0004-9115
AUSTRALIAN FISHERIES. [Aust. fish.]. **Added/Corp** Australia. Fisheries Branch. Australia. Fisheries Division. Vol. 28, No. 1 (Jan. 1969)-. Periodical. English. Twelve times a year. 50.00Aus$ Australia; 72.00Aus$ Papua New Guinea & New Zealand; 94.00Aus$ US & Canada; 86.00Aus$ India & Japan; 100.00Aus$ Europe; 79.00Aus$ others. Australian Fisheries Management Authority, Box 7051, Canberra Mail Centre, Canberra ACT 2601 Australia. **Tel** 011 61 6 2 25182, FAX 011 61 6 2725167. **LC** SH131; .A35. **DD** 338.3/72/0994. **[CCC].** Index available (Dec. issue). **Bk Rev**, (Qty: varies). **Ad Acc**, **Adv Mgr:** Angela, **Tel** 62 272 5182. **Circ:** 11,000 (ctrl). Documents available from Documents on Demand. ***Continues** Australian Fisheries Newsletter.*
Desc: Contains information about fishing industry including market prices, trade figures and book reviews.
Ind/Abst Aquat. Sci. Fish. Abstr. (Computer File); Curr. Ref. Fish Res.; Environ. Abstr.; Fish Rev. (Jan. 1989-July 1992); Food Sci. Technol. Abstr.; Life Sci. Collect.; Pollut. Abstr. Indexes; Wildl. Rev. (Jan. 1989-July 1992).

CN/0709-7778
B. C. FRESH WATER FISHING GUIDE. [B.C. fresh water fis. guide]. **VFOAT** Fresh Water Fishing Guide; Lee Straight's Updated, Enlarged B.C. Fresh Water Fishing Guide. **VAT** British Columbia Fresh Water Fishing Guide (1979) Lee Straight's Updated, Enlarged British Columbia Fresh Water Fishing Guide. V. 22-1979-. English. an. Maclean Hunter Canada / Montreal, 1001 bvd. de Maisonneuve W., Montreal, Quebec H3A 3E1 Canada. **Tel** 514-845-5141, FAX 514-845-4302, telex 055-60604. **DD** 917.11/044. **UDC** 639.21(711). ***Supersedes** B.C.'s Fresh Water Fishing Guide, 0315-4262.*

CN/0824-3190
B.C. REGIONAL FISHING GUIDE. CARIBOO, CHILCOTIN. [B.C. reg. fish. guide, Cariboo Chilcotin]. **VAT** British Columbia Regional Fishing Guide. Cariboo, Chilcotin. 1983-. English. an. $3.95 per vol. B C Regional Fishing Guide, 188 North 1st Avenue, Williams Lake British Columbia V2G 1Y8 Canada. **DD** 799.1/1/097112. **UDC** 799.1(711). ***Continues** Fishing Guide. Cariboo, Chilcotin, 0824-3204.*

US/0199-3291
BASS MASTER MAGAZINE. (BASSMASTER MAGAZINE.). **Added/Corp** Bass Anglers Sportsman Society of America. **VFOAT** Bass Master. (19??)-. Periodical. English. Ten times a year. $16.00 US; $20.00 other. Bassmaster Magazine, PO Box 17900, Montgomery AL 36117. **Tel** (205)272-9530, FAX (205)279-7148. **ED** Dave Precht. **LC** SH681; .B33. **DD** 799.1/7/58. Index available. **Ad Acc. Circ:** 550,000 (ctrl).
Desc: Articles on how to and where to on bass fishing.

US/0742-0609
BASS (NEW YORK, N.Y.). (BASS.). [Bass]. 1981 Ed.-. Periodical. English. an. $2.50 (per issue). The Hearst Corporation, 250 West 55th Street, New York NY 10019. **Tel** (212)649-4014. **ED** Mike Schwanz. **LC** SH681; .S68. **DD** 799.1/758. **UDC** 799.17. **Ad Acc. Circ:** 300,000. ***Continues** Sports Afield Bass, 0160-1822.*
Desc: How to articles about cabeling largemouth, smallmouth, striped and other bass species.

US/0884-4739
BASSIN'. [Bassin']. **VFOAT** Bassing. Vol. 13, Issue 6 (Aug./Sept. 1985)-. Periodical. English. Eight times a year. $18.60 (one year), $31.95 (two year). Natcom Inc, 5300 City Plex Tower, 2448 East 81st Street, Tulsa OK 74137-4207. **Tel** (918)491-6100, FAX (918)491-9410. **ED** Gordon Sprouse and Thayne Smith. **LC** WMLC L 83/6803. **DD** 796. **Ad Acc. Circ:** 225,000. ***Continues** Pro Bass, 0274-8908.*

II
BAY OF BENGAL NEWS. Added/Corp Bay of Bengal Programme. No. 1 (Jan. 1981)-. Periodical. English. qt. **LC** SH216.4; .B39. **DD** 338.3/727092764.
Ind/Abst Ocean. Abstr.

NE
BEDRIJFSRESULTATEN VAN DE KLEINE ZEEVISSERIJ. Main/Corp Hague. Landbouw-Economisch Instituut. Afdeling Visserij en Bosbouw. Dutch. an. Landbouw-Economisch Instituut, Conradkade 175, Hague Netherlands. **Tel** (070)614161. **ED** M N de Groot. **LC** SH275; .H35B. **UDC** 338.3:639.22(492). **Circ:** 300. ***Continues** Bedrijfsresultaten van de Kleine Zeevisserij.*
Desc: Outline of income and profitability of small scale sea fishery in the Netherlands.

US/0073-4519
BIENNIAL REPORT OF THE FISH AND GAME DEPARTMENT OF THE STATE OF IDAHO. Main/Corp Idaho. Fish and Game Dept. **VFOAT** Biennial Report. 18th- 1939/40-. Periodical. English. be. Idaho Department of Fish and Game, PO Box 25, Boise ID 83707. **Tel** (208)334-3748, FAX (208)334-2114. **LC** SH11; .I2. **DD** 639.061796. **UDC** 639(047.1)(796). ***Continues** Biennial Report of the Fish and Game Warden of the State of Idaho.*

US
BIENNIAL REPORT OF THE STATE GAME AND FISH COMMISSION TO THE REGULAR SESSION OF THE MISSISSIPPI LEGISLATURE. Main/Corp Mississippi. State Game and Fish Commission. **VFOAT** Biennial Report - State Game and Fish Commission; Biennial Report - Game and Fish Commission. 11th (1951/53)-. Periodical. English. be. Mississippi State Game and Fish Commission, Jackson MS 39205. **LC** SH11.M7; A3. **DD** 799.061762. ***Continues** Report of the State Game and Fish Commission to the Regular Session of the Mississippi Legislature.*

CN/0828-7899
BIG FISH COUNTRY FISHING GUIDE. [Big fish ctry. fish. guide]. 84-. English. an. $3.95 per vol. Big Fish Country Fishing Guide Columbia V8G 4B8 Canada. **DD** 799.1/09711/32. **UDC** 799.1(711).

US/1070-8340
BIG RIVER. [Big river]. (199?)-. Periodical. English. Twelve times a year. $20.00 (one year); $36.00 (two years). Big River, PO Box 741, Winona MN 55987. **Tel** (507)454-6758. **ED** Reggie McLeod. **DD** 333. **Bk Rev**, (Qty: 4). **Circ:** 500.
Desc: Covers anything that has to do with the Mississippi River from St. Cloud, Minnesota to Dubugue, Iowa.

PL/0209-0708
BIULETYN MORSKIEGO INSTYTUTU RYBACKIEGO. Added/Corp Morski Instytut Rybacki (Gdynia, Poland). **VFOAT** Bulletin of the Sea Fisheries Institute; Biulleten' Instituta Morskogo Rybolovstva. (19??)-. Periodical. Polish (summaries and/or abstracts in English; table of contents in Russian). bm. **LC** SH293.P7; B58.
Ind/Abst Aquat. Sci. Fish. Abstr. (Computer File).

BL/0046-9939
BOLETIM DO INSTITUTO DE PESCA. [Bol. Inst. Pesca]. **Main/Corp** Instituto de Pesca. Vol. 1 (Jan. 1971)-. Monographic series. Portuguese (English). Price varies per volume. Av Bartholomeu de Gusmao, 192 11.100, Santos Brazil. **Tel** (011)864 63 00. **(Subscription address:** Av Francisco Matarazzo 455, 05001 Sao Paulo SP Brasil) **LC** SH236; .I57A. **UDC** 639.2(81). **Bk Rev.**
Ind/Abst Anim. Breed. Abstr.; Nutr. Abstr. Rev., Ser. B, Live Feeds and Feed.; Nutr. Abstr. Rev., Ser. A, Hum. Exp.

BL/0103-1767
BOLETIM TECNICO - INSTITUTO DE PESCA. (BOLETIM TECNICO.). [Bol. tec. - Inst. Pesca]. (1988)-. Monographic series. Portuguese. ir. Price varies per volume. Instituto de Pesca, Sao Paulo Brazil. **UDC** 59.
Ind/Abst Nutr. Abstr. Rev., Ser. B, Live Feeds and Feed.

UY
BOLETIN COMERCIAL / INSTITUTO NACIONAL DE PESCA. See Economics-Industry and Production.

IT/0006-6575
BOLLETTINO DI PESCA, PISCICOLTURA E IDROBIOLOGIA. (BOLLETTINO DI PESCA, PISCICOLTURA E IDROBIOLOGIA / MINISTERO DELL'ECONOMIA NAZIONALE, ISPETTORATO GENERALE DELLA PESCA.). [Boll. pesca piscic. idrobiol.]. **Added/Corp** Italy. Ispettorato Generale della Pesca. Italy. Direzione Generale dell'Industria e delle Miniere. Laboratorio Centrale di Idrobiologia Applicata Alla Pesca (Rome, Italy) Italy. Commissariato Generale Per la Pesca. Ispettorato Servizi Scientifici. Italy. Ufficio Centrale per la Caccia e per la pesca. Italy. Ufficio Centrale per la Pesca e per la Caccia. Italy. Direzione Generale per la Produzione Agricola. Laboratorio Centrale di Idrobiologia (Rome, Italy). **VFOAT** Bollettino di Pesca, di Piscicoltura e di Iidrobiologia. (1925-. Periodical. Italian (English and French). sa. **LC** SH277; .A34.
Ind/Abst Aquat. Sci. Fish. Abstr. (Computer File); Life Sci. Collect.

UK
BOOKLET (GREAT BRITAIN. MINISTRY OF AGRICULTURE, FISHERIES AND FOOD). See Agriculture.

PH/0116-1377
BRACKISHWATER AQUACULTURE ABSTRACTS. [Brackishwater aquac. abstr.]. **Added/Corp** Brackishwater Aquaculture Information System. Vol. 2, No. 1 (July/Aug. 1985)-. Periodical. English. bm. Brackishwater Aquaculture Development Centre, Taman Pemandian Kartini, PO Box 1, Jepara Indonesia. **Tel** JEPARA 125. ***Continues** Brackishwater Aquaculture Bibliography, 0116-001X.*

US/8755-0075
BRIEFS / AMERICAN INSTITUTE OF FISHERY RESEARCH BIOLOGISTS. [Briefs - Am. Inst. Fish. Res. Biol.]. **Added/Corp** American Institute of Fishery Research Biologists. (19??)-. Periodical. English. bm. $25.00. American Institute of Fishery Research Biologists, 0-85 Morlot Avenue, c/o Dr. Rachlin, Fair Lawn NJ 07410. **Tel** (718)960-8239, FAX (718)960-8236. **ED** Oliver B Cope. **DD** 639. **Circ:** 1,200 (ctrl).
Desc: Professional activities of fishery biologists; meetings, publications, reviews, abstracts of theses and dissertations pertaining to fishery and biological oceanography.

CN/0827-2042
BRITISH COLUMBIA SPORT FISHING. [B.C. sport fish.]. **VFOAT** Sport Fishing. **VAT** Sport Fishing (New Westminster); British Columbia Sport Fishing Magazine. Vol. 3, No. 1 (March/April 1983)-. Periodical. English. ir. $10.50. First City Magazines, 628 Carnarvon Street, New Westminster BC V3M 1E5. **DD** 799.1/09711. **UDC** 799.1(711). ***Continues** British Columbia Sport Salmon Fishing News, 0827-2042.*

CN/0711-3862
BRITISH COLUMBIA SPORT SALMON FISHING NEWS. ***Title Change.*** [B.C. sport salmon fish. news]. **VFOAT** Salmon Fishing News; B.C. Sports Salmon Fishing News; Fishing News. **VAT** Fishing News (Vancouver); British Columbia Sports Salmon Fishing News. Vol. 1, No. 1 (July/Aug. 1980)-V. 2, No. 7 (Sept./Oct. 1982). Periodical. English. ir. Canada West Tourist Enterprises, 329 North Road, Coquitlam BC V3K 3V8. **DD** 799.1/755. **UDC** 799.1(711). ***Continued by** British Columbia Sport Fishing, 0827-2042.*

CZ/0007-389X
BULETIN VURH VODNANY. Added/Corp Vydava Vyzumny Ustav Rybarsky a Hydrobiologicky Vodnany. **VFOAT** Buletin. (19??)-. Periodical. Czech (summaries and/or abstracts in English; table of contents in English). qt.
Ind/Abst Index Vet.; Protozoolog. Abstr.

II/0008-9427
BULLETIN - CENTRAL INLAND FISHERIES RESEARCH INSTITUTE BARRACKPORE. (BULLETIN.). [Bull. - Cent. Inland Fish. Res. Inst. Barrackpore]. **Main/Corp** Central Inland Fisheries Research Institute (Barrackpore, India). **Added/Corp** Central Inland Fisheries Research Institute (Barrackpore, India). (196?)-. Monographic series. English. ir. Price varies per volume. Central Inland Fisheries Research Institute, 24 Parganas, Barrackpore West Bengal India. **Tel** 46-4265. **LC** SH299; .B28. **DD** 639/.3/0954; 639. **CODEN** CIFBA6. Documents available from BIOSIS Document Express.
Ind/Abst Aquat. Sci. Fish. Abstr. (Computer File); Biol. Abstr.; Protozoolog. Abstr.

CE/0588-4225
BULLETIN - COLOMBO, CEYLON. FISHERIES RESEARCH STATION. **Main/Corp** Colombo, Ceylon. Fisheries Research Station. V. 1- 1952-. Bulletin. English. Ceylon Fisheries Research Station, Columbo Ceylon. **UDC** 639.2(548.7).

CN/0821-6576
BULLETIN / EASTERN FISHERMEN'S FEDERATION. [Bull. - East. Fishermen's Fed.]. **Added/Corp** Eastern Fishermen's Federation. Vol. 1, No. 1 (Dec. 1980)-. Bulletin. English (French; summaries and/or abstracts in French). qt. Free. Eastern Fishermen's Federation, PO Box 384, Statio M, Halifax NS B3J 2P8 Canada. **DD** 639/.2/060715. ctrl circ.

CN/0046-3973
BULLETIN - FISHERIES COUNCIL OF CANADA. ***Ceased.*** **Main/Corp** Fisheries Council of Canada. (19??)-Number 3 (Sept. 1992). Periodical. English. ir. Fisheries Council of Canada, 77 Metcalfe Street, Room 505, Ottawa Ontario K1P 5L6 Canada. **Tel** (613)238-7751. **Circ:** 1,500.

Desc: Current developments affecting the industry, such as proposed legislative action, amendments to regulations, trade, treaties, tariff changes, and special statistics.

FR/0767-2861
BULLETIN FRANCAIS DE LA PECHE ET DE LA PISCICULTURE. [Bull. fr. peche piscic.]. **Added/Corp** Conseil Superieur de la Peche (France). No. 296 (1st Quarter 1985)-. Bulletin. French (summaries and/or abstracts in English). qt. 200.00F France; 260.00F other. Conseil Superieur de la Peche, BP No 5, 80440 Boves France. **Tel** 011 33 22 09-37-47. **ED** Erick Vigneux. **CODEN** BFPPE2. cum. index (1928-1984). **Bk Rev. Pr Rev. Circ:** 1,000 (ctrl). Documents available from The Genuine Article, BIOSIS Document Express. ***Continues*** *Bulletin Francais de Pisciculture, 0373-0514.*
Desc: Articles related to freshwater fish culture, pathology, management of aquatic resources, population dynamics, pollution impact study investigation methods (sampling statistics data processing).
Ind/Abst Aquat. Sci. Fish. Abstr. (Computer File); Biol. Abstr. (1985-); Curr. Aware. Biol. Sci., CABS; Curr. Contents, Agric. Biol. Environ. Sci.; Curr. Ref. Fish Res.; Fish Rev.; Fresh. Aqua. Contents Tables; Index Vet.; Res. Alert [Select. Cov.]; SCISEARCH.

CN/0074-7157
BULLETIN - INTERNATIONAL NORTH PACIFIC FISHERIES COMMISSION. [Bull. - Int. North Pac. Fish. Comm.]. **Added/Corp** International North Pacific Fisheries Commission. No. 1 (June 1955)-. Bulletin. English. ir. Price varies per volume. International North Pacific Fisheries Commission, 6640 Northwest Marine Drive, Vancouver British Columbia V6T 1X2 Canada. **Tel** (604)228-1128, FAX (604)228-1135. **LC** SH219.5; .I5A26. **DD** 639/.22/091644. **Circ:** 1,000 (ctrl).
Desc: Publications on fisheries and fauna of the North Pacific Ocean.
Ind/Abst Aquat. Sci. Fish. Abstr. (Computer File); Life Sci. Collect.

IT
BULLETIN OF FISHERY STATISTICS. **VFOAT** Bulletin Statistique des Peches; Boletin Estadistico de Pesca. (19??)-. Bulletin. English (French and Spanish). ir. $28.00 (latest edition). Food and Agriculture Organization (FAO) / Italy, GIPC166 via Terme di Caracalla, 00100 Rome Italy. **Tel** 011 39 6 522 52925, FAX 011 39 6 522 55784. **LC** SH1; .B85. **DD** 338.3/727/0021.

IO/0126-1924
BULLETIN OF THE BRACKISHWATER AQUACULTURE DEVELOPMENT CENTRE. Vol. 3, No. 1 & 2 (Jan. & July 1977)-. Bulletin. English (summaries and/or abstracts in Indonesian). ir. Brackishwater Aquaculture Development Centre, Taman Pemandian Kartini, PO Box 1, Jepara Indonesia. **Tel** JEPARA 125. **ED** Kisto Mintardjo, Made L Nurdjana, and Sudjiharno Saimun. **LC** SH380.6; .P87A. **UDC** 039.512. **Circ:** 500 (ctrl). ***Continues*** *Bulletin of the Shrimp Culture Research Centre.*
Ind/Abst Aquat. Sci. Fish. Abstr. (Computer File).

NE/0108-0288
BULLETIN OF THE EUROPEAN ASSOCIATION OF FISH PATHOLOGISTS. **Added/Corp** European Association of Fish Pathologists. (1981)-. Periodical. English. bm. Kr100.00 (institutions), Kr60.00 (individuals). EAFP Publications, National Veterinary Institute, c/o Dr. K. Thorud, PO Box 8156, 0033 Oslo Norway. **Ad Acc. Pr Rev. Circ:** 750.
Desc: Covers fish and shellfish diseases.
Ind/Abst Anim. Breed. Abstr.; Helminthol. Abstr. (1991-); Index Vet.; Nutr. Abstr. Rev., Ser. B, Live Feeds and Feed.; Protozoolog. Abstr.; Rev. Med. Vet. Entomol.; Rev. Med. Vet. Mycology; Vet. Bull.

JA
BULLETIN OF THE JAPANESE SOCIETY OF SCIENTIFIC FISHERIES. (19??)-. Periodical. Japanese. bm. $385.00. Nihon Suisan Gakkai, (Japanese Soc. of Scientific Fisheries), c/o Tokyo Suisan Daigaku, 5-7, Konan 4 Chome, Minatoku, Tokyoto 108, Japan. **(Subscription address:** Maruzen Company Ltd., PO Box 5050, Import & Export Department, Tokyo 100 31 Japan.)
Ind/Abst Sci. Cit. Index.

CN
BULLETIN - OFFICE DES RECHERCHES SUR LES PECHERIES DU CANADA. **See** Zoology.

US/0078-7582
BULLETIN / PACIFIC MARINE FISHERIES COMMISSION. **Main/Corp** Pacific Marine Fisheries Commission. No. 1- 1948-. Bulletin. English. Pacific Marine Fisheries Commission, 2000 SW 1st Avenue 420, Portland OR 97201-5302. **LC** SH11.A55; A1818.

US/1052-1984
CA SELECTS: OMEGA THREE FATTY ACIDS & FISH OIL. **See** Chemistry-Abstracting, Bibliographies and Statistics.

CN/0712-0613
CAHIER D'INFORMATION - MINISTERE DE L'AGRICULTURE DES PECHES ET DE L'ALIMENTATION. DIRECTION GENERALE DES PECHES MARITIMES. DIRECTION DE LA RECHERCHE SCIENTIFIQUE ET TECHNIQUE. (CAHIER D'INFORMATION.). [Cah. inf. - Minist. agric. pech. aliment., Dir. gen. peches marit., Dir. rech. sci. tech.]. (1980)-. Monographic series. French (summaries and/or abstracts in English and French). ir. Price varies per volume. Ministere of Agriculture, Pecheries et Alimentation, Bureau Exchanges, CP 340, Cte Gaspe Quebec G0C 1V0 Canada. **Tel** (418)385-2251. **CODEN** CIQTDG. Documents available from BIOSIS Document Express. ***Continues*** *Cahiers d'Information (Quebec (Province). Direction Generale des Peches Maritimes. Direction de la Recherque), 0707-9370.*
Ind/Abst Biol. Abstr.

CN/0832-7858
CAHIER SPECIAL D'INFORMATION - DIRECTION GENERAL DES PECHES MARITIMES. DIRECTION DE LA RECHERCHE SCIENTIFIQUE ET TECHNIQUE. (CAHIER SPECIAL D'INFORMATION.). [Cah. spec. inf. - Dir. gen. peches marit., Dir. rech. sci. tech.]. No. 5-. Monographic series. French (English). Price varies per volume. Gouvernement du Quebec, 600 St Amable 4E Etage, Quebec Quebec G1R 4Z1 Canada. **DD** 639/.2/09714. **UDC** 639.2(714). **CODEN** CIQTDG. Documents available from BIOSIS Document Express. ***Continues*** *Quebec (Province). Direction Generale des Peches Maritimes. Direction de la Recherche. Cahier Special d'Information, 0709-1699.*
Ind/Abst Biol. Abstr.

US/8750-8907
CALIFORNIA ANGLER. ***Ceased.*** [Calif. angler]. Vol. 1, No. 1 (March 1985)-(May 1994). Periodical. English. mo. California Angler, 1921 East Carnegie Suite N, Santa Ana CA 92705-5510. **Tel** (714)261-9779, FAX (714)261-9853. **ED** Jim Matthews. **LC** SH473; .C36. **DD** 799.1/09794. Index available. **Bk Rev. Ad Acc. Circ:** 27,841. ***Formed by the union of*** *Western Saltwater Fisherman, 0277-0644* ***and*** *Angler, 0745-3817.*
Desc: Guide to fresh and saltwater fishing on the west coast. Instructional as well as information on how, when and where to catch fish.

CN
CANADIAN ANGLER. (19??)-. Periodical. English. sa. 13.04Can$. Canadian Outdoor Publications, 140 Avenue F North, Saskatoon Sask S7L 1V8 Canada. **Tel** (306)665-6302, FAX (306)244-8859.

CN/0706-6503
CANADIAN BULLETIN OF FISHERIES AND AQUATIC SCIENCES. [Can. bull. fish. aquat. sci.]. **Added/Corp** Canada. Dept. of Fisheries and Oceans. (1979)-. Monographic series. English (French; summaries and/or abstracts in French). ir. Price varies per volume. National Research Council of Canada, Receiver General for Canada, Ottawa Ontario K1A 0R6 Canada. **Tel** (613)993-0362, FAX (613)952-7656. **DD** 574.971. **CODEN** CBFSDB. Documents available from BIOSIS Document Express, CASDDS. ***Continues*** *Fisheries Research Board of Canada. Bulletin - Fisheries Research Board of Canada, 0068-7537.*
Ind/Abst Aquat. Sci. Fish. Abstr. (Computer File); Biol. Abstr.; Chem. Abstr.; Food Sci. Technol. Abstr.; Ocean. Abstr.; Life Sci. Collect.; Protozoolog. Abstr.

CN/0706-6465
CANADIAN DATA REPORT OF FISHERIES AND AQUATIC SCIENCES. [Can. data rep. fish. aquatic sci.]. **Added/Corp** Canada. Dept. of Fisheries and Oceans. No. 161 (1979)-. Academic Scholarly Publication. English (summaries and/or abstracts in French). ir. Price varies per volume. Micromedia Limited, 20 Victoria Street, Toronto Ontario M5C 2N8 Canada. **Tel** (416)362-5211, (800)387-2689, FAX (416)362-6161, telex 06524668. Documents available from BIOSIS Document Express, CASDDS. ***Continues*** *Data Report (Canada. Dept. of Fisheries and Oceans), 0701-7634.*
Ind/Abst Biol. Abstr.; Chem. Abstr. (1979-1981); Ocean. Abstr.

CN/0711-6721
CANADIAN DATA REPORT OF HYDROGRAPHY AND OCEAN SCIENCES. (CANADIAN DATA REPORT OF HYDROGRAPHY AND OCEAN SCIENCES [MICROFORM].). [Can. data rep. hydrogr. ocean sci.]. **Added/Corp** Canada. Dept. of Fisheries and Oceans. **VFOAT** CDRHOS. (1982)-. Periodical. English (summaries and/or abstracts in French). **DD** 551.46.
Continues *Data Series (Bedford Institute of Oceanography)., 0067-4788.*
Ind/Abst Ocean. Abstr.

CN/0702-7966
CANADIAN FISH FANCIERS. V. 1- Winter 1973/1974-. Periodical. English. qt. $3.75. Canadian Fish Fanciers, 60 Polar Avenue, Islington Ontario M9B 3R4 Canada. **DD** 639/.34/05. **UDC** 639.34.

CN/0710-7641
CANADIAN FISHERIES AND OCEAN INDUSTRIES DIRECTORY, THE. [Can. fish. ocean ind. dir.]. No. 1-. Directory. English. be. $55.00 per no. Maritmie Ocean Resources Ltd., Po Box 2102, Station M, Halifax NS B3J 3B7 Canada. **DD** 338.3/727/002571. **UDC** 338.3:639.2(036)(71).

CN/0713-2158
CANADIAN FISHERIES ANNUAL STATISTICAL REVIEW. **See** Fish and Fisheries-Abstracting, Bibliographies and Statistics.

CN
CANADIAN FISHERIES. ANNUAL STATISTICAL REVIEW / ECONOMIC POLICY BRANCH, ECONOMIC DEVELOPMENT DIRECTORATE, FISHERIES AND OCEANS. **See** Fish and Fisheries-Abstracting, Bibliographies and Statistics.

CN/0713-1348
CANADIAN FISHERIES, LANDINGS. [Can. fish., Landings]. **VFOAT** Les Peches Canadiennes, Debarquements; Peches Canadiennes, Debarquements. **VAT** Peches Canadiennes. Debarquements. Jan. 1981-. Periodical. English (French). mo. Bibliotheque, Institut Maurice-Lamontagne, Peches Et Oceans, C P 1000 850 Route de la Mer, Mont-Joli Quebec G5H 3Z4 Canada. **Tel** (613)995-2041. **DD** 338.3/727/0971. **UDC** 338.3:639.2(71). ***Continues*** *Canadian Fisheries, Primary Sector Activities, 0225-7246.*

CN/0704-3694
CANADIAN INDUSTRY REPORT OF FISHERIES AND AQUATIC SCIENCES. [Can. ind. rep. fish. aquatic sci.]. **Added/Corp** Canada. Dept. of Fisheries and Oceans. **VFOAT** Rapport Canadien a l'Industrie sur les Sciences Halieutiques et Aquatiques. **VAT** Rapport a l'Industrie Canadien sur les Sciences Halieutiques et Aquatiques (Edition Anglaise et Francaise). No. 111 (1979)-. Academic Scholarly Publication. English (French; summaries and/or abstracts in French). ir. Price varies per volume. Canada Communication Group Publishers, Order Processing, Ottawa Ontario K1A 0S9 Canada. **Tel** (819)956-4800, (819)956-4802. **DD** 574.971. **CODEN** CRFSDL. Documents available from BIOSIS Document Express, CASDDS. ***Continues*** *Industry Report (Canada.) Dept. of Fisheries and Oceans, 0701-7642.*
Ind/Abst Biol. Abstr.; Chem. Abstr.; Fish Rev.; Ocean. Abstr.; Wildl. Rev.

CN/0706-652X
CANADIAN JOURNAL OF FISHERIES AND AQUATIC SCIENCES. [Can. j. fish. aquat. sci.]. **Added/Corp** Canada. Dept. of Fisheries and Oceans. **VFOAT** Journal Canadien des Sciences Halieutiques et Aquatiques. Vol. 37 (Jan. 1980)-. Academic Scholarly Publication. English (summaries and/or abstracts in French). mo. 365.00Can$ (institutions), 130.00Can$ (individuals) Canada; $395.00 (institutions), $145.00 (individuals) other. National Research Council of Canada, Receiver General for Canada, Ottawa Ontario K1A 0R6 Canada. **Tel** (613)993-0362, FAX (613)952-7656. **LC** QH1; .C143. **DD** 597/.05. **CODEN** CJFSDX. **[CCC]. Pr Rev.** available on microfilm and microfiche from University Microfilms International (UMI). Documents available from The Genuine Article, BIOSIS Document Express, CASDDS, Documents on Demand. ***Continues*** *Fisheries Research Board of Canada. Journal of the Fisheries Research Board of Canada, 0015-296X.*
Desc: Publishes original research articles and notes, critical reviews, perspectives (essays of opinion or hypothesis), comments, and book reviews.
Ind/Abst ASTIS Curr. Aware. Bull. (1980-); Abstr. Bull. Inst. Pap. Sci. Tech.; AgBiotech News Inf.; Anim. Behav. Abstr.; Anim. Breed. Abstr.; AQUAREF; Aquat. Sci. Fish. Abstr. (Computer File); ASTIS Bibliogr. (1980-); Biocont. News Inf. (1991-); Biol. Agric. Index; Biol. Abstr.; Chem. Abstr.; CSA Neuro. Abstr. (?-?); Curr. Aware. Biol. Sci., CABS; Curr. Contents, Agric. Biol. Environ. Sci.; Curr. Ref. Fish Res.; Ecol. Abstr.; Ecology Abstr.; EMBASE; Entomol. Abstr.; Environ. Abstr.; Fish Rev.; Food Sci. Technol. Abstr.; For. Prod. Abstr.; For. Abstr.; Fresh. Aqua. Contents Tables; Genet. Abstr.; Geogr. Abstr. Phys. Geogr.; Geogr. Abstr. Human Geogr.; Geol. Abstr.; GeoRef; Health Saf. Sci. Abstr.; Helminthol. Abstr. (1991-); Index Vet.; Key Word Index Wildl. Res.; Leadscan; Mar. Sci. Contents Tables; Microbiol. Abstr. Sect. C; Nutr. Abstr. Rev., Ser. B, Live Feeds and Feed.; Nutr. Abstr. Rev., Ser. A, Hum. Exp.; Ocean. Abstr.; Pollut. Abstr. Indexes; Protozoolog. Abstr.; Res. Alert [Full Cov.]; Rev. Med. Vet. Entomol.; Sci. Cit. Index; SCISEARCH; Soc. Sci. Cit. Index [Select. Cov.]; Soyabean Abstr.; Vet. Bull.; Weed Abstr.; Wildl. Rev.

CN/0706-6473
CANADIAN MANUSCRIPT REPORT OF FISHERIES AND AQUATIC SCIENCES. [Can. manuscr. rep. fish. aquat. sci.]. **Added/Corp** Canada. Dept. of Fisheries and Oceans. No. 1551 (1979)-. Periodical. English (French). Fisheries & Oceans Canada, Scientific Information & Publications Branch, 200 Kent Street/12th Floor, Ottawa Ontario K1A 0E6 Canada. **Tel** (613)993-0600, (800)267-6677, telex 053-3585. **DD** 574.971. **CODEN** CMRSDC. Documents available from BIOSIS Document Express. ***Continues*** *Manuscript Report (Canada. Dept. of Fisheries and Oceans)., 0701-7618.*
Ind/Abst Biol. Abstr.; Ocean. Abstr.

CN/0706-6481
CANADIAN SPECIAL PUBLICATION OF FISHERIES AND AQUATIC SCIENCES. [Can. spec. publ. fish. aquat. sci.]. **VFOAT** Publication Speciale Canadienne des Sciences Halieutiques et Aquatiques. **VAT** Publication Speciale Canadienne des Sciences Halieutiques et Aquatiques (Edition Anglaise et Francaise). (1979)-. Academic Scholarly Publication. English (summaries and/or abstracts in French). mo. Canada Communication Group Publishers, Order Processing, Ottawa Ontario K1A 0S9 Canada. **Tel** (819)956-4800, (819)956-4802. **DD** 333.91. **UDC** 597; 639.2(71). **CODEN** CSPSDA. Documents available from CASDDS. ***Continues in part*** *Canada. Dept. of Fisheries and Oceans. Miscellaneous Special Publication.*
Ind/Abst Chem. Abstr.; Fish Rev. (Jan. 1989-July 1992); Ocean. Abstr.; Wildl. Rev. (Jan. 1989-July 1992).

CN/0706-6457
CANADIAN TECHNICAL REPORT OF FISHERIES AND AQUATIC SCIENCES. [Can. tech. rep. fish. aquat. sci.]. **Added/Corp** Canada. Dept. of Fisheries and Oceans. No. 925 (1980)-. Academic Scholarly Publication. English (French; summaries and/or abstracts in French). ir. Free on request. Canada Communication Group Publishers, Order Processing, Ottawa Ontario K1A 0S9 Canada. **Tel** (819)956-4800, (819)956-4802. **LC** UNC. **DD** 574.971. **CODEN** CTRSDR. **[CCC]. Circ:** 350. Documents available from BIOSIS Document Express, CASDDS. ***Continues*** *Technical Report (Canada. Dept. of Fisheries and Oceans), 0701-7626.*
Desc: Medium for distribution of scientific and technical information which contributes to existing knowledge in the fields of fisheries and aquatic sciences.
Ind/Abst ASTIS Curr. Aware. Bull. (1980-); Agric. Eng. Abstr. (1991-); Aquat. Sci. Fish. Abstr. (Computer File); ASTIS Bibliogr. (1980-); BioBusiness; Biol. Abstr.; Chem. Abstr. (1980-1984); Ecol. Abstr. (?-?); Fish Rev.; Ocean. Abstr.; Wildl. Rev.

US
CATFISH AND AQUACULTURE NEWS. ***Title Change.*** Vol. 5, No. 1 (Late Summer 1990)-(1992). Periodical. English. mo. Catfish News, PO Box 199, Ridgeland MS 39158. **Tel** (601)853-1989. ***Continues*** *Catfish News.* ***Continued by*** *Aquaculture News.*

US
CATFISH PROCESSING / NATIONAL AGRICULTURAL STATISTICS SERVICE, UNITED STATES DEPT. OF AGRICULTURE. **Added/Corp** United States. National Agricultural Statistics Service. (199?)-. Periodical. English. mo. **LC** SH167.C35; C38. **DD** 338.3/713752. ***Continues*** *Catfish (Washington, D.C.), 0735-2077.*

US/0735-2077
CATFISH (WASHINGTON, D.C.). ***Title Change.*** (CATFISH / CROP REPORTING BOARD, ECONOMICS, STATISTICS, & COOPERATIVES SERVICE, U.S. DEPARTMENT OF AGRICULTURE.). **Added/Corp** United States. Crop Reporting Board. United States. Agricultural Statistics Board. Jan. (1980)-(199?). Government Publication. English. mo. US Department of Agriculture, 14th Street and Independence Avenue SW, Washington DC 20250. **Tel** (202)720-5457. **LC** SH167.C35; C38. **DD** 338.3/713752. available on microfiche (Vols. for (1986-) distributed to depository libraries). Documents available from Documents on Demand. ***Continues*** *Farm-Raised Catfish Processor's Report.* ***Continued by*** *Catfish Processing.*
Desc: Features short articles on current production and market trends.
Ind/Abst Am. Stat. Index.

US
CFEC REPORT. Monographic series. English. Price varies per volume. Alaska Commercial Fisheries Entry Commission, Pouch KB, Juneau AK 99811. **UDC** 338.3:639.2(798).

CL
CHILE PESQUERO. (197?)-. Periodical. Spanish. Five times a year. Revista Chile Pesquero LTDA, PO Box 2508, Santiago Chile. **Tel** 383882.
Ind/Abst Ocean. Abstr.

CH/0529-6471
CHUNG-KUO SHUI CHAN. **Added/Corp** Chung-Kuo Shui Chan Hsieh Hui. **VFOAT** China Fisheries Monthly. (1953)-. Periodical. Chinese. mo. **LC** SH298.5; .C48. **DD** 639.2/0951249.
Ind/Abst Aquat. Sci. Fish. Abstr. (Computer File).

MX/0185-0334
CIENCIA PESQUERA / DIRECCION GENERAL DEL INSTITUTO NACIONAL DE LA PESCA. **Added/Corp** Instituto Nacional de Pesca (Mexico). Vol. 1, No. 1 (July 1981)-. Periodical. Spanish. **LC** SH231; .C54. **CODEN** CIPEEZ. Documents available from BIOSIS Document Express.
Ind/Abst Aquat. Sci. Fish. Abstr. (Computer File); Biol. Abstr.

IT
CIFA OCCASIONAL PAPER. **Added/Corp** Food and Agriculture Organization of the United Nations. Committee for Inland Fisheries of Africa. **VFOAT** Document Occasionnel du CPCA. **VAT** Committee for Inland Fisheries of Africa Occasional Paper; Document Occasionnel du Comite des Peches Continentales Pour l'Afrique. No. 1 (1974)-. Monographic series. English (French). Price varies per volume. UNIPUB, 4611-F Assembly Drive, Lanham MD 20706-4391. **Tel** (800)274-4888, FAX (301)459-0056, telex 28787 GATT CH. **LC** UNC.

II/0378-2387
CMFRI BULLETIN. [CMFRI bull.]. **Added/Corp** Central Marine Fisheries Research Institute. **VFOAT** C.M.F.R.I. Bulletin. **VAT** Central Marine Fisheries Research Institute Bulletin. No. 27 (Mar. 1976)-. Bulletin. English. **LC** SH1; .C435. **DD** 636/.2/05. **CODEN** CMFBD3. Documents available from BIOSIS Document Express. ***Continues*** *Central Marine Fisheries Research Institute. Bulletin of the Central Marine Fisheries Research Institute, 0577-0844.*
Ind/Abst Aquat. Sci. Fish. Abstr. (Computer File); Biol. Abstr.

UK
COARSE ANGLING. (19??)-. Periodical. English. mo. £22.00 UK; £27.00 other. IPC Magazines Ltd., Perrymount Road, Haywards Heath, West Sussex RH16 3DH England. **Tel** 011 44 444 440421.

US/1062-3442
COASTLINES (STONY BROOK, N.Y.). (COASTLINES.). [Coastlines]. **Added/Corp** New York State Sea Grant Program. State University of New York at Stony Brook. Marine Sciences Research Center. New York State Sea Grant Institute. New York Sea Grant Advisory Service. New York Sea Grant Institute. New York Sea Grant Extension Program. Vol. 1, No. 1 (Dec. 1971)-. Periodical. English. qt. Free on request. New York Sea Grant Institute, 115 Nassau Hall, SUNY Stony Brook, Stony Brook NY 11794. **Tel** (516)632-6905. **ED** Julie Zeidner. **DD** 333.
Desc: Contains articles on New York Sea Grant projects and activities, short accounts of recent project results and programs, general articles, and the recipe of the month.

US
COLLECTED REPRINTS (SOUTHWEST FISHERIES CENTER). (COLLECTED REPRINTS / NATIONAL MARINE FISHERIES SERVICE, SOUTHWEST FISHERIES CENTER.). English. an. US Department of Commerce / National Marine Fisheries Service / CA, 300 Ferry Street, Suite 2005, Terminal Island CA 90731. **Tel** (310)514-6196, FAX (310)514-6194. **ED** Izadore Barrett. **UDC** 639.2(79); 597. **Circ:** 125 (ctrl).
Desc: A collection of scientific papers in fisheries and fishery biology published by scientists on the staff of the National Marine Fisheries Service Southwest Fisheries Center during a given calendar year.

SP
COLLECTIVE VOLUME OF SCIENTIFIC PAPERS. RECUEIL DE DOCUMENTS SCIENTIFIQUES. COLECCION DE DOCUMENTOS CIENTIFICOS. **Main/Corp** International Commission for the Conservation of Atlantic Tunas. **Added/Corp** International Commission for the Conservation of Atlantic Tunas. Recueil de Documents Scientifiques. International Commission for the Conservation of Atlantic Tunas. Coleccion de Documentos Cientificos. **VFOAT** Recueil de Documents Scientifiques; Colleccion de Documentos Cientificos. (19??)-. English (French and Spanish). International Commission for the Conservation of the Atlantic Tunas, Principe de Vergara 17, 28001 Madrid Spain. **Tel** 011 34 1 4310329.
Ind/Abst Ocean. Abstr.

US
COMMERCIAL FISH FARMER. 1- Sept./Oct. 1974-. Periodical. English. Catfish Farmers of America, 186 Rt 9W, New Windsor NY 12550. **UDC** 338.439.4:639.2(73).

US/0273-6713
COMMERCIAL FISHERIES NEWS. [Commer. fish. news]. **Added/Corp** Fisheries Communications. (1980)-. Periodical. English. mo. $18.00 (US); $28.00 (surface mail), $56.00 (airmail) Canada; $28.00 (surface mail); $97.00 (airmail) other. Compass Publications Inc, PO Box 37, Stonington ME 04681. **Tel** (207)367-2396, FAX (207)367-2490. **ED** Susan Jones. **DD** 338. **[CCC]. Ad Acc. Circ:** 8,500 (ctrl). ***Continues*** *Maine Commercial Fisheries, 0271-0501.*
Desc: Trade publication of the New England commercial fishing industry covering resource management, gear technology, trends, price reports by species, regulations, trade shows, boats and people.

UK/0143-652X
COMMERCIAL FISHING. ***Ceased.*** [Commer. fish.]. Vol. 1 No. 1 (1970)-(1992). Periodical. English. mo. Commercial Fishing Enterprises, 78 North Albert Street, Fleetwood Lancs FY7 6HS England. **Tel** 03917-2219, FAX 03917-6802, telex 677216. **ED** Peter Brady. **UDC** 338.439.4:639.2(410). **Bk Rev. Ad Acc. Circ:** 2,000 (ctrl). available on microfilm and microfiche.
Desc: Information for professional people in all spheres of the commercial fishing industry. Includes fish catching, processing and marketing information.
Ind/Abst Aquat. Sci. Fish. Abstr. (Computer File) (?-?); BMT Abstr. (?-?).

NZ/0110-1730
COMMERCIAL FISHING. ***Ceased.*** Vol. 14, No. 12 ( )-?. Periodical. English. mo. Trade Publications Ltd., 300 Great South Road Greenlane, Newmarket Auckland New Zealand. **Tel** 011 64 9 9293000. **ED** Norman Burns. **UDC** 338.439.4:639.2(931). **Ad Acc. Circ:** 2,000 (ctrl).
Desc: All aspects of commercial fishing in New Zealand. Coverage includes world fishing news, including Pacific area focus.
Ind/Abst Ocean. Abstr. (?-?).

US
COMMERCIAL OPERATORS. **Main/Corp** Alaska. Dept. of Fish and Game. 1967-. English. an. Alaska Department of Fish and Game, PO Box 3-2000, Juneau AK 99802. **Tel** (907)465-4100, (907)465-4286. **LC** SH222.A4; A32 subser. **DD** 338.4/7/66494025798. **UDC** 338.439.4:664.95(798). ***Continues*** *Alaska Commercial Fishery Operators.*

US/0590-8817
CORD SPORTFACTS FISHERMAN ANNUAL. **VFOAT** Fisherman Annual. English. an. $0.75. Cord Communications Corporation, 130 West 42nd Street, New York NY 10036. **Tel** (212)840-0660. **LC** SH1; .C84. **DD** 799.1/2/05. **UDC** 799.1.

US/0882-763X
CURRENT FEDERAL AID RESEARCH REPORT. FISH. [Curr. fed. aid. res. rep., Fish]. **VFOAT** Fish. Began in 1978. English. an. US Fish and Wildlife Service, Division of Federal Aid, 18th and C Streets NW, Washington DC 20240. **ED** Robert Sousa and Claude E Stephens. **LC** SH221; .C88. **DD** 639/.2/072073. **UDC** 639.2(73). ***Continues*** *Current Federal Aid Research. Fish, 0735-8849.*

US/0739-540X
CURRENT REFERENCES IN FISH RESEARCH. **See** Fish and Fisheries-Abstracting, Bibliographies and Statistics.

CN/0828-7902
CURRENT (RICHMOND). (CURRENT : PACIFIC TROLLERS' ASSOCIATION NEWSLETTER.). [Current]. Newsletter. English. ir. $20.00. Pacific Trollers Association, 5960 6 Road/Suite 625, Richmond British Columbia V6V 1Z1 Canada. **Tel** (604)273-4213. **DD** 338.3/72755. **UDC** 338.3:639.2(265). ***Continues*** *Pacific Trollers' Association. Newsletter, 0380-6359.*

FR/0399-0974
CYBIUM. [Cybium]. **Added/Corp** Laboratoire des Peches Coloniales (Museum National d'Histoire Naturelle). Association des Amis. Societe Francaise d'Ichtyologie. Laboratoire d'Ichtyologie Generale et Appliquee (Museum National d'Histoire Naturelle) Laboratoire des Peches Outre-Mer (France). (Oct. 1947)-. Periodical. French (English). qt. 450.00F. Societe Francaise d'Ichthyologie, 43 rue Cuvier, 75231 Paris Cedex 05 France. **Tel** 33 1 40793756, FAX 33 140793771. **ED** J C Hureau and T Y Sire. **LC** QL614; .C92. **DD** 597/.005. **CODEN** CYBIDK. **Bk Rev**, (Qty: 4). **Ad Acc. Circ:** 500 (ctrl). Documents available from BIOSIS Document Express.
Desc: Papers on fish and fisheries; topics include systematics, biology, growth, population dynamics and reproduction zoo geography.
Ind/Abst Aquat. Sci. Fish. Abstr. (Computer File); Biol. Abstr.; Curr. Ref. Fish Res.; GeoRef; Mar. Sci. Contents Tables; Ocean. Abstr.; Zool. Rec.

US/0145-613X
DAIWA FISHING ANNUAL. English. an. $1.75. Aqua Field Publications Inc, 66 West Gilbert Street, Shrewsbury NJ 07702. **Tel** (201)842-8300. **LC** SH401. **DD** 799.1/05. **UDC** 799.1.

DK/0106-553X
DANA (DANMARKS FISKERI- OG HAVUNDERSGELSER). **See** Biology-Marine Biology.

SP
DATA RECORD. RECUEIL DE DONNEES STATISTIQUES. COLECCION DE DATOS ESTADISTICOS. **Main/Corp** International Commission for the Conservation of Atlantic Tunas. **Added/Corp** International Commission for the Conservation of Atlantic Tunas. Recueil de Donnees Statistiques. International Commission for the Conservation of Atlantic Tunas. Coleccion de Datos Estadisticos. **VFOAT** Recueil de Donnees Statistiques; Coleccion de Datos Estadisticos. (June 1973)-. English (French and Spanish). an. $25.00. International Commission for the Conservation of the Atlantic Tunas, Principe de Vergara 17, 28001 Madrid Spain. **Tel** 011 34 1 4310329. **LC** SH351.T8; I53c. **DD** 338.3/72758.
Ind/Abst Ocean. Abstr.

US/0098-0765
DATA REPORT - U.S. DEPARTMENT OF COMMERCE, NATIONAL OCEANIC AND ATMOSPHERIC ADMINISTRATION NATIONAL MARINE FISHERIES SERVICE. (DATA REPORT - NATIONAL MARINE FISHERIES SERVICE.). **Main/Corp** United States. National Marine Fisheries Service. English. US Department of Commerce / National Marine Fisheries Service, 1335 East-West Highway, Silver Spring MD 20910. **Tel** (301)713-2239, FAX (301)713-2258. **LC** SH11; .A35D. **DD** 639/.2/0973. **UDC** 639.2(73).

IS/0011-7110
DAYIG U-MIDGEH BE-YISRAEL. **Added/Corp** Igud Ha-Dayagim (Israel) Irgun Megadle Dagim (Israel) Israel. Agaf Le-Dayig. **VFOAT** Fisheries and Fishbreeding in Israel. (July 1963)-. Periodical. Hebrew (summaries and/or abstracts in English). qt. **LC** SH307.I7; D35.
Ind/Abst Aquat. Sci. Fish. Abstr. (Computer File).

NE/0167-9309
DEVELOPMENTS IN AQUACULTURE AND FISHERIES SCIENCE. [Dev. aquac. fish. sci.]. V. 1-. Academic Scholarly Publication. English. ir. Price varies per volume. Elsevier Science Publishers BV, PO Box 211, 1000 AE Amsterdam Netherlands. **Tel** 011 31 20 5803642, FAX 011 31 20 5862696, telex 15682. **UDC** 639.2. **CODEN** DAFSDF. Documents available from CASDDS.
Ind/Abst Aquat. Sci. Fish. Abstr. (Computer File); Chem. Abstr. (1976-1983).

US/0098-4469
DIRECTORY OF AQUARIUM SPECIALISTS. 1974/75-. Directory. English. Waikiki Aquarium, 2777 Kalakaua Avenue, Honolulu HI 96815. **Tel** (808)923-9741. **LC** QH35; .D57. **DD** 574/.074. **UDC** 639.93.

PE
DOCUMENTA. Spanish. Ministerio de Pesqueria Oficina de Tramite Documentario, Lord Cochrane No 351, Lima Peru. **LC** SH247; .D63. **UDC** 338.3:639.2(460).

US/0899-0506
EAST COAST ANGLER. [East coast angler]. Periodical. English. wk. $15.00 North America. East Coast Angler Inc, 728 Beaver Dam Road, PO Box 3131, Pleasant NJ 08742. **Tel** (201)295-1080. **ED** Mickey Cooper. **DD** 799. **Bk Rev. Ad Acc.** ctrl circ.
Desc: Covers sportfishing both fresh and saltwater.

●DK/0906-6691
ECOLOGY OF FRESHWATER FISH. Vol. 1, Issue 1 (Sept. 1992)-. Periodical. English (summaries and/or abstracts in Spanish). qt. kr1000.00 US, Canada and Japan; kr990.00 other. Munksgaard International Publishers Ltd, PO Box 2148, DK-1016 Copenhagen K Denmark. **Tel** 011 45 33 12 70 30, FAX 011 45 33 12 93 87, telex 19431 MUNKS DK. **ED** E. Mortensen & J. Lobon-Cervia.
Desc: Features original articles on fish ecology and fishery sciences in lakes, rivers and estuaries.

US/0471-8208
EDUCATIONAL BULLETIN - FISH COMMISSION OF OREGON. **Main/Corp** Oregon. Fish Commission. No. 1- 1958-. Bulletin. English. Price varies per volume. Oregon Department of Fish & Wildlife, PO Box 59, 2501 Southwest 1st Street, Portland OR 97201. **Tel** (503)229-5400. **DD** 639. **UDC** 639.2(795).

JA/0388-2098
EHIME-KEN SUISAN SHIKENJO KENKYU HOKOKU. [Ehime-ken Suisan Shikenjo kenkyu hokoku]. **Main/Corp** Ehime-ken Suisan Shikenjo. **VFOAT** Bulletin of Ehime Prefectural Fisheries Experimental Station. No. 1- ; 1977-. Academic Scholarly Publication. Japanese (Japanese). Enimeken Suisan Shikenjo, Sakashizu 798, Uwajima Japan. **LC** SH302.E3; E36A. **UDC** 639.2(52). **CODEN** ESHODE. Documents available from CASDDS.
Ind/Abst Chem. Abstr. (1977-1978).

IT
EIFAC OCCASIONAL PAPER. **Main/Corp** European Inland Fisheries Advisory Commission. **VFOAT** EIFAC/OP. **VAT** European Inland Fisheries Advisory Commission Occasional Paper. No. 1 (1968)-. Monographic series. English (French). Price varies per volume. Food and Agriculture Organization (FAO) / Italy, GIPC166 via Terme di Caracalla, 00100 Rome Italy. **Tel** 011 39 6 522 52925, FAX 011 39 6 522 55784.
Ind/Abst Index Vet.; Vet. Bull.

IT/0532-940X
EIFAC TECHNICAL PAPER. [EIFAC tech. pap.]. **VFOAT** European Inland Fisheries Advisory Commission Technical Paper; EIFAC/T; E.I.F.A.C. Technical Paper. (1964)-. Academic Scholarly Publication. English. ir. Price varies per volume. Food and Agriculture Organization (FAO) / Italy, GIPC166 via Terme di Caracalla, 00100 Rome Italy. **Tel** 011 39 6 522 52925, FAX 011 39 6 522 55784. **CODEN** EIFPA2. Documents available from CASDDS.
Ind/Abst Chem. Abstr. (1964-1977); World Agric. Econ.

NE/0378-1909
ENVIRONMENTAL BIOLOGY OF FISHES. [Environ. biol. fishes]. Vol. 1 (Aug. 30, 1976)-. Academic Scholarly Publication. English. mo. $1,563.00. Kluwer Academic Publishers, Postbus 322, 3300 AH Dordrecht, The Netherlands. **Tel** 011 (31) 78 524400, FAX 011 31 78 183273, telex 20083. **ED** Eugene K Balon. **LC** QL614; .E58. **DD** 597/.05. **CODEN** EBFID3. **[CCC]. Bk Rev. Ad Acc. Pr Rev. Circ:** 500. available on microfilm and microfiche from University Microfilms International (UMI). Documents available from The Genuine Article, BIOSIS Document Express, CASDDS, Documents on Demand.
Desc: Publishes original research and theoretical monographs, papers and short notes on fishes as related to their natural or changed external and internal environments, advocating where possible wise use and maintenance of the global fish resources. Publishes empirical and theoretical papers that deal with the relationship between fish and their external and internal environment, whether natural or unnatural. In particular, the journal concentrates on papers which advance the scholarly understanding of life and which draw on a variety of disciplines in reaching this understanding.
Ind/Abst Anim. Behav. Abstr.; AQUAREF; Aquat. Sci. Fish. Abstr. (Computer File); Biol. Abstr.; Chem. Abstr.; CSA Neuro. Abstr. (?-?); Curr. Contents, Agric. Biol. Environ. Sci.; Curr. Ref. Fish Res.; Ecol. Abstr.; Ecology Abstr.; EMBASE; Environ. Abstr.; Environ. Period. Bibliogr.; Fish Rev.; Fresh. Aqua. Contents Tables; GeoRef; Mar. Sci. Contents Tables; Nutr. Abstr. Rev., Ser. B, Live Feeds and Feed.; Ocean. Abstr.; Life Sci. Collect.; Pollut. Abstr. Indexes; Protozoolog. Abstr.; Res. Alert [Full Cov.]; Sci. Cit. Index; SCISEARCH.

JA
ENYO SOKOBIKIAMI GYOGYO HOKUYO TENKANSEN GYOJOBETSU GYOKAKU TOKEI NEMPO. **Added/Corp** Suisancho Hokkaido-ku Suisan Kenkyujo. Japan. Suisancho. Hokkaido Gyogyo Chosei Jimusho. Zenkoku Sokobikiami Gyogyo Rengokai. (19??)-. Statistical Publication. Japanese. an. Zenkoku Sokobikiami Gyogyo Rengokai, (National Federation of Medium Trawlers), Chuo Biru 1-16 Toranomon 1 chome, Minatoku Tokyoto 105 Japan. **LC** SH344.6.T7; E58.

JA
ENYO : SUISAN KENKYUJO NYUSU. No. 1 (Aug. 1979)-. Periodical. Japanese. qt. Free. Far Seas Fisheries Research Laboratory, 7-1 5 Chome, Orido Shimizu 424 Japan. **Tel** 0543-34-0715. **LC** SH1; .E59 . **Circ:** 900 (ctrl).
Desc: To inform activity and results of research works in the far seas fisheries research laboratory in every three months.

SP
ESPANA AGRICOLA Y GANADERA. (ESPANA AGRICOLA GANADERA.). [Esp. agric. ganad.]. **VFOAT** Espana Agricola, Ganadera. No. 133 (Sept. 1985)-. Periodical. Spanish. mo (11 issues per year). 4000ptas Spain; 5000ptas Europe; 7000ptas other. Espana Agricola Ganadera, Gascuena 21, 28022 Madrid Spain. **Tel** 011 34 1 747-8000. ***Formed by the union of*** *Espana Agricola, 0210-8992* ***and*** *Espana Ganadera, 0210-5314.*

CN
ESTIMATES. PART III, FISHERIES AND OCEANS. **Main/Corp** Canada. **VFOAT** Budget des Depenses. Partie III, Peches et Oceans. (19??)-. English (French). $9.00 Canada; $10.80 other. Canada Communication Group Publishers, Order Processing, Ottawa Ontario K1A 0S9 Canada. **Tel** (819)956-4800, (819)956-4802. **LC** HD9464.C19; C34a. **DD** 354.710082/362.

UK/1040-8720
EUROFISH REPORT. English. bw. £530.00 UK; £557.00 Europe; £585.00 other. Agra Europe London Limited, 25 Frant Road, Tunbridge Wells, Kent TN2 5JT England. **Tel** 011 44 892 533813. **ED** Edgar Phillips. Index available. cum. index. **Circ:** 300.
Desc: Review of European and world fishing and fisheries, with comprehensive coverage of EEC legislation and the common fisheries policy.
Ind/Abst F&S Index Plus Text, Int. [Full Txt.] [Select. Cov.]; PROMT [Full Txt.].

UK/0142-937X
EUROPEAN SUPPLIES BULLETIN / FISHERY ECONOMICS RESEARCH UNIT, WHITE FISH AUTHORITY. **Added/Corp** Great Britain. Fishery Economics Research Unit. No. 1 (July 1979)-. Bulletin. English. Five times a year (Mar., Jun., Sept., Dec., plus annual issue). £85.00 United Kingdom; £105.00 U.S.; £95.00 other European countries. Sea Fish Industry Authority, 18 Logie Mill, Logie Green Road, Edinburgh EH7 4HG Scotland. **Tel** 011 44 31 558-3331 ext. 256, FAX 011 44 31 558-1442. **ED** F. I. MacLennan. **Circ:** 150.
Desc: Most recent data on landings and trade in sixteen European countries and North America.

CN/0848-6743
FACTSHEET - BRITISH COLUMBIA. AQUACULTURE AND COMMERCIAL FISHERIES BRANCH. ***Title Change.*** **See** Agriculture.

IT
FAO FISHERIES. Food and Agriculture Organization (FAO) / Italy, GIPC166 via Terme di Caracalla, 00100 Rome Italy. **Tel** 011 39 6 522 52925, FAX 011 39 6 522 55784.

US/0427-8038
FAO FISHERIES BIOLOGY REPORT. **Added/Corp** Food and Agriculture Organization of the United Nations. Fisheries Division. Biology Branch. No. 1 (19??)-. Periodical. Multiple languages (English and Spanish). Food and Agriculture Organization (FAO) / Italy, GIPC166 via Terme di Caracalla, 00100 Rome Italy. **Tel** 011 39 6 522 52925, FAX 011 39 6 522 55784. **DD** 591; 639.

IT/0429-9329
FAO FISHERIES CIRCULAR. (FAO FISHERIES CIRCULAR / FAO CIRCULAIRE SUR LES PECHES / FAO CIRCULAR DE PESCA.). [FAO fish. circ.]. **Added/Corp** Food and Agriculture Organization of the United Nations. **VFOAT** FAO Circulaire sur les Peches; FAO Circular de Pesca. **VAT** Food and Agriculture Organization of the United Nations Fisheries Circular. (19??)-. Monographic series. English (French and Spanish). ir. Price varies per volume. Food and Agriculture Organization (FAO) / Italy, GIPC166 via Terme di Caracalla, 00100 Rome Italy. **Tel** 011 39 6 522 52925, FAX 011 39 6 522 55784. **LC** SH1; .F8716. **DD** 639. Documents available from BIOSIS Document Express.
Ind/Abst AGRICOLA; Aquat. Sci. Fish. Abstr. (Computer File); Biol. Abstr.; Fish Rev. (Jan. 1989-July 1992); Ocean. Abstr.; Wildl. Rev. (Jan. 1989-July 1992).

IT/0429-9337
FAO FISHERIES REPORT. [FAO fish. rep.]. **Added/Corp** Food and Agriculture Organization of the United Nations. **VFOAT** FAO Fisheries Reports. **VAT** Food and Agriculture Organization Fisheries Reports. No. 1 (1962)-. Monographic series. English (French and Spanish). ir. Price varies per volume. Food and Agriculture Organization (FAO) / Italy, GIPC166 via Terme di Caracalla, 00100 Rome Italy. **Tel** 011 39 6 522 52925, FAX 011 39 6 522 55784. **LC** SH331; .F2. **CODEN** FOFRAR. Documents available from BIOSIS Document Express, CASDDS.
Ind/Abst Aquat. Sci. Fish. Abstr. (Computer File); Biodeter. Abstr. (1991-); Biol. Abstr. (1969-1977); Chem. Abstr. (1962-1979); Fish Rev. (Jan. 1989-July 1992); GeoRef; Index Vet.; Nutr. Abstr. Rev., Ser. B, Live Feeds and Feed.; Nutr. Abstr. Rev., Ser. A, Hum. Exp.; Ocean. Abstr.; Rural Dev. Abstr.; Wildl. Rev. (Jan. 1989-July 1992); World Agric. Econ.

IT
FAO FISHERIES SERIES. **Added/Corp** Food and Agriculture Organization of the United Nations. (19??)-. Periodical. English. ir. Price varies. Food and Agriculture Organization (FAO) / Italy, GIPC166 via Terme di Caracalla, 00100 Rome Italy. **Tel** 011 39 6 522 52925, FAX 011 39 6 522 55784. **(Subscription address:** UNIPUB, 4611 F Assembly Drive, Lanham MD 20706.**)**
Ind/Abst Aquat. Sci. Fish. Abstr. (Computer File); Nutr. Abstr. Rev., Ser. A, Hum. Exp.; Ocean. Abstr.

IT/0071-7037
FAO FISHERIES STUDIES. **Main/Corp** Food and Agriculture Organization of the United Nations. (July 1949)-. Monographic series. English. ir. Price varies per volume. Food and Agriculture Organization (FAO) / Italy, GIPC166 via Terme di Caracalla, 00100 Rome Italy. **Tel** 011 39 6 522 52925, FAX 011 39 6 522 55784. **DD** 639.

IT/0014-5602
FAO FISHERIES SYNOPSIS. **Added/Corp** Food and Agriculture Organization of the United Nations. **VFOAT** Fisheries Synopsis. **VAT** Food and Agriculture Organization of the United Nations Fisheries Synopsis. No. 24 (1964)-. Monographic series. English (French and Spanish). Food and Agriculture Organization (FAO) / Italy, GIPC166 via Terme di Caracalla, 00100 Rome Italy.

Tel 011 39 6 522 52925, FAX 011 39 6 522 55784. **LC** SH1; .F8725a. **DD** 597. Documents available from BIOSIS Document Express. ***Continues*** *FAO Fisheries Biology Synopsis.*
Ind/Abst Aquat. Sci. Fish. Abstr. (Computer File); Biol. Abstr.; Ocean. Abstr.

IT/0429-9345
FAO FISHERIES TECHNICAL PAPER. [FAO fish. tech. pap.]. **Added/Corp** Food and Agriculture Organization of the United Nations. Fishery Resources Division. Food and Agriculture Organization of the United Nations. Fisheries Division. Biology Branch. Food and Agriculture Organization of the United Nations. Fishery Resources and Exploitation Division. **VFOAT** Fisheries Technical Paper; Food and Agriculture Organization Fisheries Technical Paper. No. 45 (1964)-. Monographic series. English (French and Spanish). ir. Price varies per volume. Food and Agriculture Organization (FAO) / Italy, GIPC166 via Terme di Caracalla, 00100 Rome Italy. **Tel** 011 39 6 522 52925, FAX 011 39 6 522 55784. **LC** SH1; .F2. **DD** 574; 639. **CODEN** FFTPBT. Documents available from BIOSIS Document Express. ***Continues*** *FAO Fisheries Biology Technical Paper.*
Ind/Abst AGRICOLA; Anim. Breed. Abstr.; Aquat. Sci. Fish. Abstr. (Computer File); Biol. Abstr.; EMBASE; Fish Rev. (Jan. 1989-July 1992); Food Sci. Technol. Abstr.; For. Prod. Abstr.; For. Abstr.; GeoRef; Nutr. Abstr. Rev., Ser. B, Live Feeds and Feed.; Nutr. Abstr. Rev., Ser. A, Hum. Exp.; Rural Dev. Abstr.; Wildl. Rev. (Jan. 1989-July 1992); World Agric. Econ.

US/0014-8083
FARM POND HARVEST. [Farm pond harvest]. Vol. 1 (Spring 1967)-. Periodical. English. qt. $10.00. Professional Sportman Publishing Co., PO Box 197 RR 3, Momence IL 60954. **Tel** (815)472-2686.
Ind/Abst Aquat. Sci. Fish. Abstr. (Computer File).

US/0362-6652
FAWCETT'S FISHING JOURNAL. VFOAT Fishing Journal. No. 1- 1976-. English. an. $1.25. Fawcett Publications, 1 Fawcett Place, Greenwich CT 06830. **LC** SH401; .F37. **DD** 799.1/2/05. **UDC** 799.12.

US/0163-5468
FIELD & STREAM BASS FISHING ANNUAL. VAT Field and Stream Bass Fishing Annual. English. an. $1.50. Diamandis Communications Inc, 1499 Monrovia Avenue, New Port Beach CA 92663. **Tel** (714)720-5300. **LC** SH681; .F54. **DD** 799.1/7/58. **UDC** 799.17.

US/0362-6385
FIELD & STREAM FISHING ANNUAL. VAT Field and Stream Fishing Annual. English. an. $1.25. Diamandis Communications Inc, 1499 Monrovia Avenue, New Port Beach CA 92663. **Tel** (714)720-5300. **LC** SH401; .F45. **DD** 799.1/2/05. **UDC** 799.12.

FI/0301-908X
FINNISH FISHERIES RESEARCH. [Finnish fish. res.]. **Added/Corp** Riista- Ja Kalatalouden Tutkimuslaitos (Finland). Kalantutkimusosasto. (1972)-. English. an. Finnish Game and Fisheries Research Institute / Game Division, PO Box 202, FIN-00151 Helsinki Finland. **LC** SH1; .F47. **DD** 639/.2/05. **CODEN** FNFRAK. Documents available from BIOSIS Document Express.
Ind/Abst Aquat. Sci. Fish. Abstr. (Computer File); Biol. Abstr.; Fish Rev.; Wildl. Rev.

GW/0015-2854
FISCHERBLATT, DAS. [Fischerblatt]. (1953)-. Periodical. German. mo. **UDC** 639.2.
Ind/Abst Aquat. Sci. Fish. Abstr. (Computer File).

GW/0428-4984
FISCHEREI-FORSCHUNG. [Fisch.-Forsch.]. **Added/Corp** Institut fur Hochseefischerei und Fischverarbeitung. (1963)-. German. **LC** SH1; .F49. **CODEN** FISCA5. Documents available from BIOSIS Document Express, CASDDS.
Ind/Abst Aquat. Sci. Fish. Abstr. (Computer File); Biol. Abstr.; Chem. Abstr. (-1987); Ocean. Abstr.

GW/0722-706X
FISCHWAID (1982). (FISCHWAID.). [Fischwaid]. **VFOAT** AFZ-Fischwaid. Vol. 107 No. 2 (Feb. 1982)-. Periodical. German. mo. DM39.40. Verlag Chmielorf GmbH, Fischwaid, Wilhelmstr 42, W-6200 Wiesbaden Germany. **Tel** 06121/39671. Index available. **Bk Rev. Ad Acc. Circ:** 31,000. ***Continues*** *AFZ-Fischwaid, 0342-5320.*
Desc: Informations about fishing gear, fishing water, fishing rods, equipment, journey, informations about fishing-clubs.
Ind/Abst Energy Res. Abstr. (Feb. 1982-).

US/1043-299X
FISH AND FISH EGG DISTRIBUTION REPORT OF THE NATIONAL FISH HATCHERY SYSTEM. [Fish fish egg distrib. rep. Natl. Fish Hatch. Syst.]. **Added/Corp** U.S. Fish and Wildlife Service. (1986)-. English. an. United States Department of the Interior, Fish and Wildlife Service, Washington DC 20240. **LC** SH11; .A19. **DD** 639.3/0973. **CODEN** FEDSEM. Documents available from BIOSIS Document Express. ***Continues*** *Propagation and Distribution of Fish from National Fish Hatcheries for the Fiscal Year ..., 0197-4106.*
Ind/Abst Biol. Abstr. (1988-); Fish Rev. (19??-199?); Wildl. Rev.

●US/1069-9309
FISH & FISHERIES WORLDWIDE. (FISH & FISHERIES WORLDWIDE [COMPUTER FILE].). **Added/Corp** National Information Services Corporation. **VFOAT** Fish and Fisheries Worldwide. (1993)-. English. Twice a year. $711.00 US; $725.00 others. National Information Services Corp, 3100 St Paul Street, Wyman Towers, Suite 6, Baltimore MD 21218. **Tel** (410)243-0797, FAX (410)243-0982.

US/0899-3505
FISH AND WILDLIFE TECHNICAL REPORT. [Fish wildl. tech. rep.]. No. 1 (1985)-. Monographic series. English. ir. Price varies per volume. U S Fish and Wildlife Service / District of Columbia, Research and Development, Department of the Interior, Washington DC 20240. **UDC** 639(73). ***Formed by the union of*** *Special Scientific Report--Wildlife, 0096-123X* ***and*** *Technical Papers of the U.S. Fish and Wildlife Service, 0362-434X.*
Ind/Abst Ecol. Abstr.; Fish Rev. (19??-199?); Geogr. Abstr. Phys. Geogr.; Wildl. Rev. (19??-199?).

JA
FISH CATCH IN JAPANESE FISHERIES. Main/Corp Japan. Norinsho. Norin Keizaikyoku. Tokei Johobu. (19??)-. Periodical. English. Statistics and Information Department / Japan, Ministry of Agriculture and Forestry, 1-2-1 Kasumigaseki Chiyoda-ku, Tokyo Japan. **LC** SH301; .J24e. **DD** 338.3/72/7092052.

US/0430-6015
FISH CONSERVATION HIGHLIGHTS. 1956-. English. ir. Sport Fishing Institute, 1010 Massachusetts Avenue Northwest, Suite 320, Washington DC 20001. **Tel** (202)898-0770. **ED** Richard Stroud. **LC** SH34; .F5. **UDC** 664.95.

US/0015-2919
FISH CULTURIST, THE. Added/Corp Pennsylvania Fish Culturists' Association. (1921)-. Periodical. English. mo (except July and August). $8.00 US; $12.00 other. Pennsylvania Fish Culturist Association, 16 Wexford Road, Gibbsboro NJ 08026. **Tel** (609)783-8405. **ED** Robert W. Britton. cum. index. **Bk Rev. Ad Acc. Circ:** 750 (ctrl).
Desc: Covers ornamental fish cultivation and aquatic plants, plus propagation and maintenance.

US/0071-5492
FISH DISEASE LEAFLET. [Fish dis. leafl.]. English. $1.00 (one issue). Office of Biological Services, Fish & Wildlife Service, Department of the Interior, Washington DC 20240. **LC** SH171; .F54. **DD** 639.3. Documents available from BIOSIS Document Express.
Ind/Abst Biol. Abstr. (1986-).

CN/1180-5633
FISH FARM NEWS, THE. ***Title Change.*** [Fish farm news]. Vol. 1, No. 1 (Sept./Oct. 1988)-(19??). Periodical. English. mo. Fish Farm News, RR 4 Site 465 C-37, Courtenay British Columbia V9N 7J3 Canada. **Tel** (604)338-2455, FAX (604)338-2466. **ED** Ray Egan. **DD** 338.3/713/09711. Index available. **Bk Rev. Ad Acc, Adv Mgr:** Catherine Egan. **Circ:** 2,000 (ctrl). available on an online database. ***Continued by*** *Pacific Coast Aquaculture.*

UK
FISH FARMER. No. 1 (Nov. 1977)-. Periodical. English. bm. £30.00. Reed Business Publishing / West Sussex, England, Perrymount Road, Haywards Heath, West Sussex RH16 3DH England. **Tel** 011 44 81 6523500.
Ind/Abst Aquat. Sci. Fish. Abstr. (Computer File); Biocont. News Inf. (1991-); Fish Rev.; Index Vet.; Nutr. Abstr. Rev., Ser. B, Live Feeds and Feed.; Ocean. Abstr.; Rev. Med. Vet. Entomol.; Vet. Bull.; Wildl. Rev.

UK/0262-9615
FISH FARMER INTERNATIONAL FILE. Added/Corp Amber Publications. **VFOAT** International File. (19??)-. Periodical. English. bm (6 issues). £30.00 UK; £40.00 Europe; £45.00 other. Amber Publications, Perrymount Road Haywards Heath, West Sussex RH16 3DH England. **Tel** 011 44 444 440421. **(Subscription address:** Computer Action, Gerrard House, 2/6 Homesdale Road, Bromley BR2 9WL England.**)**

UK/0262-0820
FISH FARMING INTERNATIONAL. [Fish farming int.]. (1973)-. English. mo. £35.00 UK; £40.00 other. EMAP Heighway, Meed House, 21 John Street, London WC1N 2BP England. **Tel** 44 71 4045513, FAX 881 3483, telex 44 71 831 9362. **ED** Peter Hjul. **LC** SH1; .F806. **DD** 639/.3/05. **UDC** 639.3. **[CCC]. Bk Rev. Ad Acc. Circ:** 4,118. available on an online database (file 648/Full-Text) from DIALOG.
Desc: International coverage of all developments in aquaculture plus in-depth special features and country reports.
Ind/Abst AGRICOLA (19??-); Aquat. Sci. Fish. Abstr. (Computer File) (19??-); F&S Index Plus Text, Int. (19??-) [Select. Cov.]; Infomat Int. Bus. (19??-); Ocean. Abstr. (19??-); PROMT (19??-).

GW/0930-6552
FISH INTERNATIONAL. [Fish int.]. Vol. 1 & 2 (1986)-. Periodical. English. bm. DM80.00 Germany; DM108.00 (air mail), DM90.00 other. Fachpresse Verlag FPV, An der Alster 21, W-2000 Hamburg 1 Germany. **Tel** 011 49 40 2408523, FAX 011 49 40 2803788, telex 2165704. **ED** Herby Neubacher. **LC** WMLC 93/1434. **CODEN** FIINEQ. **Ad Acc, Adv Mgr:** Eckhard Preuss. ***Continues*** *AFZ International, 0177-2112.*
Desc: Includes reports on the people, powers and personalities behind the European fish industry.
Ind/Abst Aquat. Sci. Fish. Abstr. (Computer File); BioBusiness (1988-); Food Sci. Technol. Abstr.

US/0193-3558
FISH KILLS CAUSED BY POLLUTION IN ... (1975). (FISH KILLS CAUSED BY POLLUTION IN ... / U.S. ENVIRONMENTAL PROTECTION AGENCY, OFFICE OF WATER PLANNING AND STANDARDS, MONITORING AND DATA SUPPORT DIVISION, MONITORING BRANCH.). Began with 16th (1975). English. an. US Environmental Protection Agency / Office of Water Planning and Standards, Monitoring and Data Support, Division Monitoring Branch, 401 M Street SW, Washington DC 20460. **LC** TD223; .A26. **UDC** 639.331.5. ***Continues*** *Fish Kills Report, 0193-3450.*

PH
FISH MARKETING REVIEW. Added/Corp Philippine Fish Marketing Authority. Vol. 1, No. 1 (Sept. 1978)-. Periodical. English. qt.
Ind/Abst Aquat. Sci. Fish. Abstr. (Computer File).

US/0364-0140
FISH MEAL AND OIL. Periodical. English. qt. US Department of Commerce / National Marine Fisheries Service, 1335 East-West Highway, Silver Spring MD 20910. **Tel** (301)713-2239, FAX (301)713-2258. **LC** HD9469.F512; U64. **UDC** 664.95; 664.3. Documents available from Documents on Demand.
Ind/Abst Am. Stat. Index.

US
FISH PHYSIOLOGY. See Biology-Physiology.

NE/0920-1742
FISH PHYSIOLOGY AND BIOCHEMISTRY. [Fish physiol. biochem.]. Vol. 1, No. 1 (Jan. 1986)-. Academic Scholarly Publication. English. bm. $305.00 US; Fl550.00 Netherlands. Kugler Publications BV / Amsterdam, PO Box 11188, 1001 GD Amsterdam Netherlands. **Tel** 011 31 20 6278070. **ED** John F Leatherland, F W H Beamish and E D Stevens. **CODEN** FPBIEP. Index available. **Ad Acc. Pr Rev. Circ:** 300. available on microfilm and microfiche from University Microfilms International (UMI). Documents available from The Genuine Article, CASDDS.
Desc: An international journal publishing original research papers in all aspects of the physiology and biochemistry of fishes.
Ind/Abst AgBiotech News Inf.; Anim. Breed. Abstr.; Aquat. Sci. Fish. Abstr. (Computer File); Chem. Abstr. (1986-); CSA Neuro. Abstr.; Curr. Aware. Biol. Sci., CABS; Curr. Contents, Agric. Biol. Environ. Sci.; Curr. Ref. Fish Res.; Fish Rev. (Jan. 1989-July 1992); Index Vet.; Nutr. Abstr. Rev., Ser. B, Live Feeds and Feed.; Ocean. Abstr.; Res. Alert [Full Cov.]; Sci. Cit. Index; SCISEARCH; Soyabean Abstr.; Vet. Bull.; Wildl. Rev. (Jan. 1989-July 1992).

CN/0229-1924
FISH SUPPLIES INTERNATIONAL : PROCESSING & MARKETING NEWS. [Fish supplies int., Process. mark. news]. **VFOAT** Processing & Marketing News. **VAT** Processing & Marketing News (Ottawa). Vol. 1, No. 1 (Apr. 1981)-. Periodical. English. Twelve times a year. $30.95. Fish Supplies International Processing & Market, Box 4929 Station E, Ottawa Ontario K1S 5J1 Canada. **Tel** (613)235-7950. **ED** S. Gabrych. **DD** 380.1/4327. **Bk Rev. Ad Acc. Circ:** 10,000 (ctrl).
Desc: Fish processing and fish marketing information.

UK
FISH TRADER. (19??)-. Periodical. English. mo. £74.85 UK; £108.80, $168.80 other. Argus Press Group, Queensway House, 2 Queensway Redhill, Surrey RH1 1QS England. **Tel** 011 44 737 768611, 011 44 737 761685, FAX 011 44 737 760510, telex 948669 TOPJNL G. **LC** SH1; .F81. **DD** 338.3/727/0941. ***Continues*** *Fish Trades Gazette.*

UK/0953-8860
FISH TRADER YEARBOOK. [Fish trader yearb.]. (1988)-. English. an. £37.80 UK; $61.00 other. Argus Press Group, Queensway House, 2 Queensway Redhill, Surrey RH1 1QS England. **Tel** 011 44 737 768611, 011 44 737 761685, FAX 011 44 737 760510, telex 948669 TOPJNL G. ***Continues*** *Fish Trader Handbook, 0265-6450.*

US/0891-7523
FISHERIES AND WILDLIFE RESEARCH AND DEVELOPMENT. [Fish. wildl. res. dev.]. (1983)-. English. an. U S Fish and Wildlife Service / District of Columbia, Research and Development, Department of the Interior, Washington DC 20240. **LC** QL155; .U54A. **DD** 639. available on microfiche (Vols. for 1983- distributed to depository libraries). ***Continues*** *Fisheries and Wildlife Research, 0193-4163.*

AT
FISHERIES, AUSTRALIA. Added/Corp Australian Bureau of Statistics. (19??)-. English. an. Australian Bureau of Statistics, PO Box 10, Belconnen Australian Capital Territory, 2616 Australia. **Tel** 011 61 6 2527911, FAX 011 61 6 2516009. **LC** SH317; .A85a. **DD** 338.3/7270994. **Circ:** 1,000. ***Continues*** *Fisheries (Canberra, A.C.T.).*
Desc: Quantity and value of production of fish, crustaceans and molluscs by selected principal types; pearl culture and trochus shell fishing.
Ind/Abst Aquat. Sci. Fish. Abstr. (Computer File).

US/0363-2415
FISHERIES (BETHESDA). (FISHERIES.). [Fisheries]. **Added/Corp** American Fisheries Society. Vol. 1 (Jan./Feb. 1976)-. Periodical. English. mo. $425.00 US; $460.00 other (library). American Fisheries Society, 5410 Grosvenor Lane, Suite 110, Bethesda MD 20814-2199. **Tel** (301)897-8616, (301)897-8621, FAX (301)897-8096. **ED** Carl R. Sullivan. **LC** SH1; .F815. **DD** 338.3/72/0973. **[CCC]. Bk Rev. Ad Acc. Pr Rev. Acid Free. Circ:** 8,300 (ctrl). Documents available from The Genuine Article, BIOSIS Document Express, CASDDS, Documents on Demand. ***Supersedes*** *American Fisheries Society. Newsletter of the American Fisheries Society, 0044-7692.*
Desc: Provides for the exchange and dissemination of technical and scientific fisheries information.
Ind/Abst AGRICOLA; Aquat. Sci. Fish. Abstr. (Computer File); Biol. Agric. Index; Biol. Abstr.; Chem. Abstr.; Coal Abstr.; Curr. Ref. Fish Res.; Ecology Abstr.; EMBASE; Energy Res. Abstr. (May 1980-); Environ. Abstr.; Fish Rev.; Ocean. Abstr.; Life Sci. Collect.; Pollut. Abstr. Indexes; Res. Alert [Select. Cov.]; SCISEARCH; Soils Fert.

MW
FISHERIES BULLETIN. No. 1- 1971-. Bulletin. English. Fisheries Department of Malawi. **LC** SH315.M26; F58. **DD** 639/.2/096897.

US/0460-1815
FISHERIES BULLETIN (BATON ROUGE). (FISHERIES BULLETIN.). **Added/Corp** Louisiana Wild Life and Fisheries Commission. **VFOAT** Fish Division Bulletin. No. 1 (1960)-. Monographic series. English. Price varies per volume. Louisiana Wildlife & Fisheries Commission, PO Box 98000, Baton Rouge LA 70898-9000. **Tel** (504)765-2918. **DD** 639.

US
FISHERIES BULLETIN OF THE KENTUCKY DEPARTMENT OF FISH AND WILDLIFE RESOURCES. Bulletin. English. ir. Price varies per volume. Kentucky Department of Fish & Wildlife Resources, 1 Game Farm Road, Frankfort KY 40601. **Tel** (502)564-4336, FAX (502)564-6508. **LC** SH222.K4; A3. **DD** 639.3/09769. ***Continues*** *Kentucky Fisheries Bulletin, 0097-1057.*

SA/1015-6186
FISHERIES BULLETIN (PRETORIA). (FISHERIES BULLETIN.). [Fish. bull.]. No. 3 (1951)-. Bulletin. English. Price varies per volume. Pretoria Fisheries & Marine, Biological Survey Division, Pretoria South Africa. **LC** SH315.S7. ***Continues*** *Fishery Bulletin.*
Ind/Abst Curr. Contents, Agric. Biol. Environ. Sci.

CN/0225-9818
FISHERIES DATA REPORT. [Fish. data rep.]. 1-. Monographic series. English. Price varies per volume. Department of Northern Saskatchewan Resources Branch, PO Box 5000, La Ronge Saskatchewan S0J 1L0 Canada. **DD** 799.1/1/0971241.

CN
FISHERIES DEVELOPMENT ACT, ANNUAL REPORT. Main/Corp Canada. Dept. of Fisheries and Oceans. **VFOAT** Loi sur le Developpement de la Peche, Rapport Annuel. (198?)-. English (French). an. Bibliotheque, Institut Maurice-Lamontagne, Peches Et Oceans, C P 1000 850 Route de la Mer, Mont-Joli Quebec G5H 3Z4 Canada. **Tel** (613)995-2041. **LC** SH223; .C223c. **DD** 338.3/72/0971. **Circ:** 700. ***Continues*** *Canada. Dept. of Fisheries and Oceans. Report of Operations Under the Fisheries Development Act for the Fiscal Year Ended March 31 ....*

●UK/0969-997X
FISHERIES MANAGEMENT AND ECOLOGY. Added/Corp Institute of Fisheries Management. **VFOAT** FME. Vol. 1, No. 1 (Apr. 1994)-. Academic Scholarly Publication. English. Four times a year. $169.50 (institutions), $84.00 (individuals) US & Canada; £100.00 (institutions), £49.50 (individuals) Europe; £110.00 (institutions), £54.50 (individuals) other. Blackwell Scientific Publications Ltd, Marston Book Services, PO Box 87, Oxford OX2 ODT UK. **Tel** 011 44 865 791155, FAX 011 44 865 791927, telex 837 515 MARDIS G. **LC** SH1; .F575. ***Separated from*** *Aquaculture and Fisheries Management, 0266-996X.*

US/0740-4387
FISHERIES MANAGEMENT ANNUAL PROGRESS REPORT ON PROJECTS IN THE ... WORK SCHEDULE. Main/Corp Wyoming. Game and Fish Department. English. an. Wyoming Game & Fish Commission, 5400 Bishop Boulevard, Cheyenne WY 82006. **Tel** (307)777-4535, (800)548-9453. **LC** SH11.W83; G35A. **DD** 639/.2/09787. ***Continues*** *Wyoming. Game and Fish Commission. Fisheries Management Annual Progress Report on Projects in the Work Schedule, 0740-4387.*

CN/0707-8498
FISHERIES MANAGEMENT REPORT (ALBERTA. FISH AND WILDLIFE DIVISION). (FISHERIES MANAGEMENT REPORT.). **VFOAT** Management Report. **VAT** Management Report (Edmonton). (1967)-. Monographic series. English. Price varies per volume. Fish and Wildlife Division, Sun Building, 10363-108 Street Canada.

CN/0706-9596
FISHERIES MANUSCRIPT REPORT. Began with Oct. 1976 issue. Monographic series. English. Price varies per volume. Department of Northern Saskatchewan Resources Branch, PO Box 5000, La Ronge Saskatchewan S0J 1L0 Canada. **DD** 799.1/1/0971241.

CN/1183-3416
FISHERIES NEWS. [Fish. news]. **Added/Corp** Canada. Dept. of Fisheries and Oceans. Newfoundland Region. Vol. 1, No. 1 (Winter 1991)-. Periodical. English. qt. **DD** 338.3.

●US/1054-6006
FISHERIES OCEANOGRAPHY. See Earth Sciences-Oceanography.

JA
FISHERIES OF JAPAN. Main/Corp Dai Nihon Suisankai. (19??)-. English. **LC** SH301; .D34a. **DD** 338.3/7/0952. ***Continues*** *Dai Nihon Suisankai. Japan's Fishery Industry.*
Ind/Abst Aquat. Sci. Fish. Abstr. (Computer File).

US
FISHERIES OF THE UNITED STATES. Began in 1959. English. an. US Department of Commerce / National Marine Fisheries Service, 1335 East-West Highway, Silver Spring MD 20910. **Tel** (301)713-2239, FAX (301)713-2258. **LC** SH11; .A349. **DD** 338.3/72/7092073. ***Continues*** *Fisheries of the United States and Alaska, 0071-5565.*
Ind/Abst Predicasts Forecasts.

CN/0707-2783
FISHERIES POLLUTION REPORT (LETHBRIDGE). (FISHERIES POLLUTION REPORT.). **Added/Corp** Alberta. Fish and Wildlife Division. (1978)-. Monographic series. English. ir. Free on request. Environnement Canada Ottawa, Publication Section, Ottawa ONT K1A 0H3 Canada. **Tel** (819)997-1922. ***Continues*** *Pollution Report., 0707-2791.*

US/1047-2525
FISHERIES PRODUCT NEWS. [Fish. prod. news]. (1986)-. Periodical. English. bm. Free (North America); $25.00 (Canada), $35.00 (other) airmail. Compass Publications Inc, PO Box 37, Stonington ME 04681. **Tel** 207)367-2396, FAX (207)367-2490. **ED** Rick Martin. **DD** 639. **[CCC]. Bk Rev. Ad Acc. Circ:** 35,000 (ctrl).
Desc: Review of gear, equipment, services and new products for commercial fishing and seafood industries, aquaculture and boat building.

NE/0165-7836
FISHERIES RESEARCH. [Fish. res.]. Vol. 1, No. 1 (Nov. 1981)-. Academic Scholarly Publication. English. Sixteen times a year (4 vols.). Fl1432.00. Elsevier Science Publishers BV, PO Box 211, 1000 AE Amsterdam Netherlands. **Tel** 011 31 20 5803642, FAX 011 31 20 5862696, telex 15682. **ED** A D McIntyre. **LC** SH1 .F819. **DD** 639.2/05. **CODEN** FISRDJ. **[CCC]. Pr Rev.** available on microfilm and microfiche from University Microfilms International (UMI). Documents available from The Genuine Article, BIOSIS Document Express.
Desc: Provides an international forum for the publication of papers in the areas of fishing technology, fisheries science and fisheries management. Scope covers salt, brackish and freshwater systems, and fishing as an economic activity but not as a recreational one.
Ind/Abst Agric. Eng. Abstr. (1991-); Anim. Breed. Abstr.; Aquat. Sci. Fish. Abstr. (Computer File); Biodeter. Abstr. (1991-); Biol. Abstr.; Curr. Aware. Biol. Sci., CABS; Curr. Contents, Agric. Biol. Environ. Sci.; Curr. Ref. Fish Res.; Ecol. Abstr.; Environ. Period. Bibliogr.; Fish Rev.; Geogr. Abstr. Phys. Geogr.; Geogr. Abstr. Human Geogr.; Int. Dev. Abstr.; Mar. Sci. Contents Tables; Ocean. Abstr.; Res. Alert [Select. Cov.]; SCISEARCH; World Agric. Econ.

CN/0384-3149
FISHERIES RESEARCH BOARD OF CANADA REPORTS. [Fish. Res. Board Can. rep.]. **Main/Corp** Fisheries Research Board of Canada. **Added/Corp** Fisheries Research Board of Canada. **VFOAT** Les Series de Rapports de l'Office des Recherches sur les Pecheries du Canada. **VAT** Rapports de l'Office des Recherches sur les Pecheries du Canada; Rapport de l'ORP; Rapport de l'Office des Recherches sur les Pecheries du Canada; FRB Report; Fisheries Research Board Report. (1974)-. Monographic series. English (French). ir. Price varies per volume. Canada Communication Group Publishers, Order Processing, Ottawa Ontario K1A 0S9 Canada. **Tel** (819)956-4800, (819)956-4802.

UK/0264-5130
FISHERIES RESEARCH DATA REPORT. [Fish. res. data rep.]. **Added/Corp** Fisheries Laboratory, Lowestoft. (1983)-. Monographic series. English. Price varies per volume. Ministry of Agriculture Fisheries & Food, Directorate of Fisheries Research, Lowestoft Suffolk NR33 0HT England.

PH
FISHERIES RESEARCH JOURNAL OF THE PHILIPPINES. Added/Corp Fisheries Research Society of the Philippines. Vol. 1 (Jan./June 1976)-. Periodical. English.
Ind/Abst Philip. Sci. Technol. Abstr.

US/1042-6299
FISHERIES REVIEW (FORT COLLINS, COLO.). See Fish and Fisheries-Abstracting, Bibliographies and Statistics.

JA
FISHERIES SCIENCE. (19??)-. Periodical. Japanese. bm. $385.00. Nihon Suisan Gakkai, (Japanese Soc. of Scientific Fisheries), c/o Tokyo Suisan Daigaku, 5-7, Konan 4 Chome, Minatoku, Tokyoto 108, Japan. **(Subscription address:** Maruzen Company Ltd., PO Box 5050, Import & Export Department, Tokyo 100 31 Japan.**)**

UK/0955-2855
FISHERIES SPOTLIGHT. 1987/88-. English. an. Ministry of Agriculture Fisheries & Food, Directorate of Fisheries Research, Lowestoft Suffolk NR33 0HT England. **LC** SH257; .L68A. **DD** 338.3/72709411. ***Continues*** *Fishing Prospects, 0308-0935.*

JA
FISHERIES STATISTICS OF JAPAN. See Fish and Fisheries-Abstracting, Bibliographies and Statistics.

PH/0115-4443
FISHERIES TODAY. Began in Oct. 1978. Periodical. English. qt. Fishery Industry Development Council, Ministry of Natural Resources, 6th Floor/Philippines Heart Center for Asia, East Avenue, Quezon City Philippines. **LC** SH307.P5; F57. **DD** 338.3/727/09599.

CN/0015-2986
FISHERMAN, THE. Added/Corp Salmon Purse Seiners' Union of the Pacific. Pacific Coast Fishermen's Union. Vol. 1 (Feb. 28, 1937)-. Periodical. English. mo. 20.00Can$ Canada; 25.00Can$ other. Fisherman Publ Soc, 160-111 Victoria Drive, Vancouver British Columbia V5L 4C4 Canada. **Tel** (604)255-1366. **ED** Geoff Meggs. **Bk Rev. Ad Acc. Circ:** 9,100 (ctrl).
Desc: Deals mainly with commercial fishing, labor and environmental issues.

US/1059-5295
FISHERMAN (FLORIDA ED.), THE. (THE FISHERMAN.). [Fisherman]. **VFOAT** Florida Fisherman. Vol. 1, No. 1 (Jan. 3rd-Jan. 9th, 1991)-. Periodical. English. wk. FLF Publishing Corporation, 8110 Saturn Street, Suite 28, Jupiter FL 33477. **DD** 799.

US/8755-4216
FISHERMAN (GRAND HAVEN, MICH.), THE. (THE FISHERMAN.). [Fisherman]. **Added/Corp** Midwest Federated Fisheries Council (U.S.). (19??)-. Periodical. English. Ten times a year. $12.00 US; $15.00 others. Industrial Division of Great Lakes Fisheries Development Foundation, 1438 West Cortland, Chicago IL 60622. **Tel** (312)278-5814. **ED** Claude Ver Duin. **LC** SH219.6; .F57. **DD** 338.3/727092977. **Ad Acc. Circ:** 2,000 (ctrl). ***Continues*** *Great Lakes Journal.*

US/1040-0109
FISHERMAN (LONG ISLAND, METROPOLITAN NEW YORK ED.), THE. (THE FISHERMAN.). [Fisherman]. Vol. 18 (Jan. 1983)-. Periodical. English. wk. $23.00 (one year), $44.00 (two year). Fisherman Publishing Corporation, 14 Ramsey Road, Shirley NY 11967. **Tel** (516)345-5200. **DD** 799. ***Continues*** *Long Island Fisherman.*

US/1040-0125
FISHERMAN (NEW ENGLAND ED.), THE. (THE FISHERMAN.). [Fisherman]. (19??)-. Periodical. English. Fifty times a year (Except last 2 weeks of Dec.). $23.00 (one year); $44.00 (two years). New England Fisherman, 14 Ramsey Road, Shirley NY 11967. **Tel** (800)826-7531, (516)345-5200. **DD** 799. **Ad Acc, Adv Mgr Tel** (203)572-0564. ctrl circ. ***Continues*** *New England Fisherman.*

US
FISHERMAN'S HANDBOOK, THE. (19??)-. Periodical. English. Fisherman Press, PO Box 70, Oxford OH 45056. **LC** SH401; .F5. **DD** 799.1.

US/0015-2994
FISHERMEN'S NEWS, THE. [Fishermen's news]. (1945)-. Periodical. English. Twelve times a year. $16.00. Fishermens News, Fishermens Terminal, Room 110, Seattle WA 98119. **Tel** (206)282-7545. **ED** Richard H. Philips. **DD** 338. **Bk Rev. Ad Acc. Circ:** 14,000. ***Continued in part by*** *Pacific Fisheries Review, 0892-9076.*
Desc: Publishes news and information pertinent to commercial fishermen and the fishing industry along the US Pacific coast and Alaska.

US/0090-0656
FISHERY BULLETIN. (FISHERY BULLETIN / U.S. DEPT. OF COMMERCE, NATIONAL OCEANIC AND ATMOSPHERIC ADMINISTRATION, NATIONAL MARINE FISHERIES SERVICE.). [Fish. bull.]. **Added/Corp** United States. National Oceanic and Atmospheric Administration. United States. National Marine Fisheries Service. United States. National Marine Fisheries Service. Scientific Publications Office. Vol. 68, No. 2 (Feb. 1971)-. Government Publication. English. qt. $27.00 domestic; $33.75 other. Superintendent of Documents, US Government Printing Office, Washington DC 20402. **Tel** (202)275-3328, FAX (202)786-2377. **LC** SH11; .A25. **DD** 639/.2/05. **CODEN** FSYBAY. **Pr Rev.** available on microfilm and microfiche from University Microfilms International (UMI). Documents available from The Genuine Article, BIOSIS Document Express, CASDDS, Documents on Demand, Documents on Demand. ***Continues*** *Fishery Bulletin of the Fish and Wildlife Service, 0090-0656.*
Desc: Publishes original research papers, and occasionally, reviews of topical interest, in the broad discipline of fishery science. Research fields of particular interest are ecology, oceanography, limnology, mariculture, ocean pollution, physiology, behavior and taxonomy of marine organisms, particularly fishes, technology, gear development, and economics.
Ind/Abst AGRICOLA; Am. Stat. Index; Anim. Behav. Abstr.; AQUAREF; Aquat. Sci. Fish. Abstr. (Computer File); Biol. Agric. Index; Biol. Abstr.; Chem. Abstr.; Curr. Aware. Biol. Sci., CABS; Curr. Ref. Fish Res.; Ecol. Abstr.; Ecology Abstr.; Energy Res. Abstr. (April 1975-); Environ. Abstr.; Fish Rev. (19??-199?); Food Sci. Technol. Abstr.; Geogr. Abstr. Phys. Geogr.; Geogr. Abstr. Human Geogr.; Helminthol. Abstr.; INIS Atomindex [Micro.]; Mar. Sci. Contents Tables; Nutr. Abstr. Rev., Ser. B, Live Feeds and Feed.; Nutr. Abstr. Rev., Ser. A, Hum. Exp.; Ocean. Abstr.; Life Sci. Collect.; Protozoolog. Abstr.; Res. Alert [Full Cov.]; Sci. Cit. Index; SCISEARCH; Wildl. Rev. (19??-199?).

US
FISHERY MANAGEMENT REPORT. **Added/Corp** Alaska. Division of Sport Fish. Monographic series. English. Price varies per volume. Alaska Department of Fish and Game, PO Box 3-2000, Juneau AK 99802. **Tel** (907)465-4100, (907)465-4286.

US
FISHERY MARKET NEWS (SEATTLE, WASH.). (FISHERY MARKET NEWS.). Periodical. English. tw. $50.00. National Marine Fisheries Service / Seattle, 7600 Sandpoint Way NE, Seattle WA 98115. **Tel** (206)526-6150, FAX (206)526-6426. **ED** John Bishop. **Circ:** 500. Documents available from Documents on Demand.
Desc: Reports cover commercial fishing activities of Washington, Oregon, and Alaska. Three main topics are covered: foreign trade, landings and prices, and wholesale market.
Ind/Abst Am. Stat. Index.

US/0445-3034
FISHERY PUBLICATION (SPRINGFIELD). (FISHERY PUBLICATION.). **Added/Corp** Illinois. Division of Fisheries. (19??)-. Monographic series. English. ir. Price varies per volume. Illinois Division of Fisheries, Springfield IL 62704. **DD** 639.

US
FISHERY RESEARCH BULLETIN (JUNEAU, ALASKA). ***Title Change.*** (FISHERY RESEARCH BULLETIN.). **Added/Corp** Alaska. Division of Commercial Fisheries. No. 87-01 (1987)-(19??). Monographic series. English. ir. Alaska Department of Fish and Game / Juneau, PO Box 25526, Juneau AK 99802. **Tel** (907)465-4210, FAX (907)465-2604. **LC** SH11; .A74; F57. **DD** 639.2/05. **CODEN** FRBUE7. ***Continues*** *Informational Leaflet (Alaska. Dept. of Fish and Game), 0516-4303.* ***Continued by*** *Alaska Fishery Research Bulletin.*

US
FISHERY RESEARCH REPORT. **Main/Corp** Oregon. Wildlife Commission. Research Division. No.8-July 1974-. Periodical. English. ***Continues*** *Fishery Research Report.*

US/0095-7682
FISHERY STATISTICS OF THE UNITED STATES. **See** Fish and Fisheries-Abstracting, Bibliographies and Statistics.

II/0015-3001
FISHERY TECHNOLOGY. [Fish. technol.]. **Added/Corp** Society of Fisheries Technologists (India). (1964)-. Periodical. English. sa. $40.00. Society of Fisheries Technologists, Cochin, India. **(Subscription address:** Prints India, 11 Darya Ganj, New Delhi, 110002 India, (Phone: 011 91 11 3268645)) **LC** SH335; .F63. **CODEN** FITEAG. Documents available from BIOSIS Document Express, CASDDS.
Ind/Abst AGRICOLA; BioBusiness; Biol. Abstr.; Chem. Abstr.; Food Sci. Technol. Abstr.; SEA Abstr.

US
FISHES OF THE WESTERN NORTH ATLANTIC. English. Yale University Sears Foundation for Marine Research, Peabody M B Wheeler, PO Box 6666, New Haven CT 06511. **Tel** (203)432-6340. **LC** QH91.A1; Y3 no.1. pt.1. **DD** 597.0921.
Desc: Includes bibliographical references.

HK/1033-1247
FISHING BOAT WORLD. (1989)-. Periodical. English. mo. £35.00 UK; $65.00 other. Baird Publications Pty Ltd, PO Box 460, 573 Chapel Street, South Yarra Victoria, 3141 Australia. **Tel** 11 61 3 826-8741, FAX 011 61 3 827-0704, telex AA36720. **ED** Neil Baird and Tony Chester. **Bk Rev**, (Qty: 40). **Ad Acc. Circ:** 4,000 (ctrl).
Desc: News, fishing vessels, gear and equipment.

US/0899-9597
FISHING FACTS (NORTHERN ED.). (FISHING FACTS.). [Fish. facts (North. ed.)]. (19??)-. Periodical. English. mo. $14.97 US; $19.97 other. Fishing Facts Inc, PO Box 331, Milwaukee WI 53201. **Tel** (414)287-4333, FAX (414(273-0016. **ED** Carl Malz and Spence Petros. **DD** 799. **Ad Acc. Circ:** 125,000. ***Continues in part*** *Fishing Facts.*
Desc: Teaches methods and techniques of freshwater sport fishing.

US/0899-9589
FISHING FACTS (SOUTHERN ED.). (FISHING FACTS.). [Fish. facts (South. ed.)]. (19??)-. Periodical. English. Seven times a year. $14.97 US; $19.97 other. Fishing Facts Inc, PO Box 331, Milwaukee WI 53201. **Tel** (414)287-4333, FAX (414(273-0016. **ED** Carl Malz and Spence Petros. **DD** 799. **Ad Acc. Circ:** 125,000. ***Continues in part*** *Fishing Facts.*
Desc: Teaches methods and techniques of freshwater sport fishing.

US/0747-2250
FISHING GAZETTE (MARGATE, N.J.). (FISHING GAZETTE.). Vol. 1, No. 1 (Apr. 1984)-. Periodical. English. mo. $3.00 (Six Month Subscription). Fishing Gazette, 9317 Amherst Avenue, Margate NJ 08402.

US
FISHING GUIDEBOOK. **VFOAT** New Fishing Guidebook. (1974)-. English. an. Maco Publishing Company, 699 Madison Avenue, New York NY 10021. **Tel** (212)490-0172. **LC** SH401; .F5813. **DD** 799.1/05. ***Supersedes in part*** *New Fishing.*

US/1063-1577
FISHING HOLES. **See** Recreation, Leisure-Outdoor Life.

US/0164-0941
FISHING IN MARYLAND. [Fish. Md.]. (19??)-. Periodical. English. an. $6.95. Fishing in Maryland Inc, PO Box 201, Phoenix MD 21131. **Tel** (410)561-5452. **ED** W. Cary de Russy. **LC** SH505; .F52. **DD** 799.1/09752. **Ad Acc. Circ:** 29,000. available with illustrations. ***Supersedes in part*** *Fishing in Maryland & Virginia, 0363-8898* ***and*** *Fishing in the Mid Atlantic.*

US
FISHING IN NEW JERSEY. ***Ceased.*** (19??)-(19??). Periodical. English. ir. Fishing in Maryland Inc, PO Box 201, Phoenix MD 21131. **Tel** (410)561-5452. ***Supersedes in part*** *Fishing in the Mid Atlantic, 0363-552X.*

US/0192-9267
FISHING IN NEW YORK. 1979-. English. an. $4.50. Fishing in Maryland Inc, PO Box 201, Phoenix MD 21131. **Tel** (410)561-5452. **LC** SH529; .F57. **DD** 799.1/6/09747.

US/0363-552X
FISHING IN THE MID ATLANTIC. ***Ceased.*** (19??)-(19??). English. Fishing in Maryland Inc, PO Box 201, Phoenix MD 21131. **Tel** (410)561-5452. **LC** SH464.M53; F56. **DD** 799.1/2/0974. ***Superseded in part by*** *Fishing in Maryland, 0164-0941* ***and*** *Fishing in New Jersey.*

CN/0848-6913
FISHING INCOME TAX GUIDE. **See** Public Administration-Public Finance and Taxation.

US/0742-0587
FISHING (NEW YORK, N.Y.). (FISHING.). [Fishing]. **VFOAT** Sports Afield Special Fishing Annual; Sports Afield Fishing. 1981 Ed.-. Periodical. English. an. $8.95. Sports Afield, 250 West 55th Street, New York NY 10019. **Tel** (212)649-4014. **ED** Jay Cassell. **LC** SH401; .F566. **DD** 799.1/05. **Ad Acc. Circ:** 300,000. ***Continues*** *Sports Afield Fishing Annual, 0742-0579.*
Desc: Contains articles about fishing for fresh and saltwater gamefish.

UK/0015-3036
FISHING NEWS. [Fish. news]. (1913)-. Newspaper. English. wk. £30.00 UK; £40.00 Europe; £47.00 other. EMAP Heighway, Meed House, 21 John Street, London WC1N 2BP England. **Tel** 44 71 4045513, FAX 881 3483, telex 44 71 831 9362. **ED** Tim Oliver. **DD** 639.2. **Ad Acc, Adv Mgr:** Peter Darkins. **Circ:** 21,000. ***Absorbed*** *Seafood News, 0958-3246.*
Ind/Abst Ocean. Abstr. (19??-).

UK/0015-3044
FISHING NEWS INTERNATIONAL. [Fish. news int.]. (1961)-. Periodical. English. mo. £35.00 UK; £40.00 other. EMAP Heighway, Meed House, 21 John Street, London WC1N 2BP England. **Tel** 44 71 4045513, FAX 881 3483, telex 44 71 831 9362. **ED** Peter Hjul. **[CCC]. Bk Rev. Ad Acc. Circ:** 5,229. available on microfilm and microfiche from University Microfilms International (UMI).
Desc: Worldwide coverage of all trends and developments in the fisheries industries.
Ind/Abst Aquat. Sci. Fish. Abstr. (Computer File) (19??-); Curr. Technol. Index (19??-); F&S Index Plus Text, Int. (19??-) [Select. Cov.]; Food Sci. Technol. Abstr. (19??-); Foods Adlibra (19??-); Life Sci. Collect. (19??-); PROMT.

US/0742-0595
FISHING SECRETS. **VFOAT** Sports Afield Fishing Secrets. (1981)-. Periodical. English. an. $2.50 (per issue). The Hearst Corporation, 250 West 55th Street, New York NY 10019. **Tel** (212)649-4014. **ED** Lois Wilde. **LC** SH401; .S63. **DD** 799.1/05. **Ad Acc. Circ:** 250,000. ***Continues*** *Sports Afield Fishing Secrets, 0194-1143.*
Desc: Hundreds of angling tips and short how-to articles.

US/8750-1287
FISHING TACKLE RETAILER (1984). **See** Business.

US/0015-3060
FISHING TACKLE TRADE NEWS. (19??)-. Periodical. English. mo. $45.00; $70.00 (seamail); $135.00 (airmail). Fishing Tackle Trade News, PO Box 2669, Vancouver WA 98668-2669. **Tel** (206)693-4721, (800)325-6548, FAX (206)6936-3997. **ED** C. Boyd Pfeiffer and John Kirk. **Ad Acc. Circ:** 23,000 (ctrl).
Desc: Updating fishing tackle retailers on industry trends, product innovations and introductions, sales and management techniques, and product reviews.

●US/1065-5069
FISHING VESSELS OF THE UNITED STATES. (1993)-. English. $29.95. Nautilus Publishing, 2025 First Avenue, Number 1010, Seattle WA 98121.

US/0015-3079
FISHING WORLD. [Fish. world]. **Added/Corp** Fishing Club of America. Vol. 1, (1954)-. Periodical. English. Six times a year. $14.95 (on eyear), $24.90 (two year), $36.59 (three year). KC Publishing Inc., 700 West 47th Street, Suite 310, Kansas City MO 64112. **Tel** (816)531-5730, (800)444-0801. **(Subscription address:** CDS Agency Hard Copy, PO Box 4966, Des Moines IA 50340.) **ED** Keith Gardner. **LC** SH401; .F618. **DD** 799.1/05. Index available. **Bk Rev. Ad Acc. Circ:** 350,000.
Desc: Contains features on tackle and techniques that make for better anglers, regional fishing information and destinations.
Ind/Abst AQUAREF.

AT/0158-572X
FISHING WORLD SYDNEY. **See** Recreation, Leisure-Outdoor Life.

SW/0301-6668
FISKE (STOCKHOLM). (FISKE.). [Fiske]. Swedish. an. Box 39057, 100 54 39 Stockholm Sweden. **LC** SH637; .F57.

NO/0071-5638
FISKEN OG HAVET. [Fisken havet]. (1959)-. Periodical. Norwegian (Norwegian). ir. Havforskningsinstitutt Biblioteket, Postboks 1870 Nordnes, N-5024 Bergen Norway. **Tel** 011 47 5 238500.
Ind/Abst Aquat. Sci. Fish. Abstr. (Computer File); Energy

Res. Abstr. (May 1974-); Fish Rev. (Jan. 1989-July 1992); Ocean. Abstr.; Life Sci. Collect.; Wildl. Rev. (Jan. 1989-July 1992).

DK
FISKERI- OG FANGSTPRODUKTER KBT AF PRODUKTIONSANLG I GRNLAND / MINISTERIET FOR GRNLAND. **Added/Corp** Denmark. Ministeriet for Grnland. (19??)-. Danish. **LC** HD9465.D43; G734.

NO/0332-5083
FISKERIDIREKTORATETS SKRIFTER. SERIE ERNAERING. (FISKERIDEREKTORATETS SKRIFTER. SERIE ERNRING.). [Fiskeridir. skr., Ser. Ernaer.]. **Added/Corp** Norway. Fiskeridirektoratet. Vol. 1 No. 1 (1976)-. Periodical. English. Havforskningsinstitutt Biblioteket, Postboks 1870 Nordnes, N-5024 Bergen Norway. **Tel** 011 47 5 238500. **CODEN** FSSEDG. Documents available from CASDDS.
Ind/Abst Chem. Abstr. (1976-1984); Nutr. Abstr. Rev., Ser. B, Live Feeds and Feed.; Ocean. Abstr.

NO/0015-3117
FISKERIDIREKTORATETS SKRIFTER. SERIE HAVUNDERSKELSER. (FISKERIDIREKTORATETS SKRIFTER: SERIE HAVUNDERSKELSER / REPORT ON NORWEGIAN FISHERY AND MARINE INVESTIGATIONS / PUBLISHED BY THE DIRECTOR OF FISHERIES.). [Fiskeridir. skr., Ser. havunders.]. **Main/Corp** Norway. Fiskeridirektoratet. **Added/Corp** Norway. Fiskeridirektoratet. Havforskningsinstituttet (Norway). **VFOAT** Serie Havunderskelser; Report on Norwegian Fishery and Marine Investigations. Vol. 4 (1933)-. Periodical. English (Norwegian; summaries and/or abstracts in Norwegian and English). ir. Free. Havforskningsinstitutt Biblioteket, Postboks 1870 Nordnes, N-5024 Bergen Norway. **Tel** 011 47 5 238500. **CODEN** FDSHAJ. Documents available from BIOSIS Document Express. ***Continues*** *Report on Norwegian Fishery and Marine Investigations.*
Ind/Abst Aquat. Sci. Fish. Abstr. (Computer File); Biol. Abstr.; Fish Rev. (Jan. 1989-July 1992); Ocean. Abstr.; Life Sci. Collect.; Wildl. Rev. (Jan. 1989-July 1992).

US/0738-2359
FLAMING GORGE RESERVOIR FISHERIES INVESTIGATIONS. [Flaming Gorge Reserv. fish. invest.]. English. an. Department of Natural Resources / Utah, 1636 West North Temple, Suite 316, Salt Lake City UT 84116. **Tel** (801)538-7200, FAX (801)538-7315. **LC** SK453; .A25 subser. **DD** 333.95/611/0978785. ***Continues*** *Flaming Gorge Reservoir Postimpoundment Investigation, Annual Performance Report, 0272-250X.*

US/0164-5188
FLORIDA FISHING NEWS. (19??)-. Periodical. English. mo. $7.00. Aqualand Publishing, 1534 Northeast 147th Street, North Miami FL 33161. **Tel** (305)945-2373.

US/0015-4741
FLY FISHERMAN. (19??)-. Periodical. English. bm. $24.00. Cowles Magazines, PO Box 8200, Harrisburg PA 17105. **Tel** (717)657-9555, (800)435-9610. **LC** SH401; .F66. **DD** 799.1/2/05. **Bk Rev. Ad Acc. Circ:** 140,294. available on microfilm from University Microfilms International (UMI).
Desc: Edited for anglers who fish primarily with a fly rod. Articles include features on fly-fishing techniques, fly tying, tackle and where-to-go destinations.

US/1045-0149
FLY ROD & REEL. [Fly rod reel]. **VFOAT** Fly Rod and Reel. Vol. 11, No. 4 (July/Oct. 1989)-. Periodical. English. bm (Jan., Mar., Apr., May, July, Nov.). $19.95 US; $29.95 other. Fly Rod & Reel, PO Box 679, Camden ME 04843. **Tel** (207)594-9544, FAX (207)594-7215. **ED** Jim Bulter. **DD** 799. **Bk Rev**, (Qty: 6). **Ad Acc, Adv Mgr:** Bill Anderson, **Tel** (207)594-9544. **Circ:** 62,000. ***Continues*** *Rod & Reel, 0194-925X.*

US
FLY-TACKLE DEALER. English. bm. Free (fly-tackle dealers), $12.00 (other). Down East Enterprise Inc., PO Box 1357, Camden ME 04843. **Tel** (207)594-9544, FAX (207)594-5144. **ED** Jim Butler. **Ad Acc. Circ:** 11,000 (ctrl).
Desc: For makers and sellers of fly-fishing equipment.

US/0147-8834
FLYFISHER, THE. Periodical. English. qt. Federation of Fly Fishers, PO Box 1088, West Yellowstone MT 59758. **Tel** (406)646-9541. **LC** SH456; .F588. **DD** 799.1/2.

US/0744-7191
FLYFISHING. **VFOAT** Fly Fishing. (1978)-. Periodical. English. Five times a year (Jan., Mar., May, July, Nov.). $15.95 US, 20.95 others (one year); $29.95 US, $39.95 others (two years). $21.95 US, 31.95 others (one year); $39.95 US, $59.95 others (two years) combined with Salmon Trout Steelheader. Frank Amato Publications, PO Box 82112, Portland OR 97282. **Tel** (503)653-8108, (800)541-9498. **ED** Marty Sherman, PO Box 82112, Portland, OR 97282 (phone# (503)653-8108). **Bk Rev**, (Qty: varies). **Ad Acc, Adv Mgr:** Joyce Sherman, **Tel** (503)653-8108. **Circ:** 41,000. ***Continues*** *Flyfishing the West.*
Desc: Fly fishing, fly tying in U.S.A. Where to fish, how to fish. Flyfishing explored. Features articles on what to expect and how to catch.

FR/0986-5748
FRANCE-ECO-PECHE. **VFOAT** France Eco Peche. No 345 (Jan. 1990)-. Periodical. French. mo. **LC** SH1; .F732. ***Formed by the union of*** *France Peche, 0241-175X and Eco-Peche.*

●US/1060-5312
FRANKLIN PIERCE TIMES. (1992)-. Periodical. English. qt. $11.50. Pennsylvania Fish Culturist Association, 16 Wexford Road, Gibbsboro NJ 08026. **Tel** (609)783-8405.

US
FRED ... ANNUAL REPORT TO THE ALASKA STATE LEGISLATURE. **Main/Corp** Alaska. Division of Fisheries Rehabilitation, Enhancement, and Development. **VFOAT** Annual Report to the Alaska State Legislature. (198?)-. English. **LC** SH35.A62; A38b. **DD** 353.97980082/362. ***Continues*** *Alaska. Division of Fisheries Rehabilitation, Enhancement, and Development. Annual Report ... Division of Fisheries Rehabilitation, Enhancement, and Development (FRED).*
Desc: Deals with fish culture and the improvement of fish habitats.

IT
FRESHWATER AND AQUACULTURE CONTENTS TABLES. ACTUALITES DES EAUX DOUCES ET DE L'AQUACULTURE. **See** Fish and Fisheries-Abstracting, Bibliographies and Statistics.

US/0160-4317
FRESHWATER AND MARINE AQUARIUM. Vol. 1 (Jan. 1978)-. Periodical. English. mo. $22.00 (US); $27.50 (others). Freshwater and Marine Aquarium, 144 West Sierra Madre Boulevard, PO Box 487, Sierra Madre CA 91024. **Tel** (818)355-1476, (800) 523-1736, (800) 624-7354, FAX (818) 355-6415. **ED** Don Dewey. **LC** SF456; .F7. **DD** 639/.34/05. **Circ:** 30,000.
Desc: Every facet of the aquarium hobby is covered, money saving how-to articles, color photographs by renowned photographers, etc.
Ind/Abst Aquat. Sci. Fish. Abstr. (Computer File).

NZ/0111-3232
FRESHWATER CATCH. ***Ceased.*** [Freshwater catch]. (1979)-Vol. 49 (July 1992). Periodical. English. an. Freshwater Fisheries Centre, PO Box 8324, Christchurch, New Zealand. **Tel** 011 64 3 348 8939. **DD** _a639.21.
Ind/Abst Aquat. Sci. Fish. Abstr. (Computer File).

AT/1032-125X
FRESHWATER FISHING AUSTRALIA. English. qt (Jan., Apr., July, Oct.). 27.80Aus$ Australia; 39.80Aus$ other. Freshwater Fishing Australia, PO Box 436, Ringwood, Victoria, 3134 Australia. **Tel** 011 61 03 8702601, FAX 011 60 03 8791453. **ED** Bill and Helen Glassow. Index available (3.95Aus$). cum. index. **Bk Rev. Ad Acc, Adv Mgr:** Pamela Gibson. **Circ:** 25,000 (ctrl).

US/0364-0604
FROZEN FISHERY PRODUCTS. **Added/Corp** United States. National Marine Fisheries Service. **VFOAT** Frozen Fishery Products ... Preliminary. (1???)-. Periodical. English. Thirteen times a year (Publishes monthly with 1 annual issue). Free. US Department of Commerce / National Marine Fisheries Service, 1335 East-West Highway, Silver Spring MD 20910. **Tel** (301)713-2239, FAX (301)713-2258. **ED** Barbara O'Bannon. **Circ:** 1,500 (ctrl). Documents available from Documents on Demand.
Desc: Cold storage holdings by months and annual reports of fishery products.
Ind/Abst Am. Stat. Index.

IT
GAZZETTINO DELLA PESCA. (19??)-. Italian. Eleven times a year. L40000 Italy; L50000 Europe; L60000 other. Ente Fiera di Ancona, Lgo Fiera Pesca 11, 60125 Ancona Italy. **Tel** 011 39 71 58971.

US/0148-5245
GEORGIA LANDINGS, ANNUAL SUMMARY. **Main/Corp** United States. National Marine Fisheries Service. English. an. US Department of Commerce / National Marine Fisheries Service, 1335 East-West Highway, Silver Spring MD 20910. **Tel** (301)713-2239, FAX (301)713-2258.

IT
GLOBEFISH EUROPEAN FISH PRICE REPORT. **Added/Corp** GLOBEFISH (Project). **VFOAT** European Fish Price Report. (19??)-. Periodical. English (Spanish and French). Twelve times a year. $250.00 (members countries); $300.00 (developing countries); $350.00 (developed countries) Comes with Infofish Trade News. Infofish, PO Box 10899, 50728 Kuala Lumpur Malaysia. **Tel** 011 60 3 2914466, FAX 011 60 3 2916804, telex INFISH MA 31560.

IT/1014-9201
GLOBEFISH HIGHLIGHTS. [Globefish highlights]. **Added/Corp** GLOBEFISH (Project). **VFOAT** FAO Globefish Highlights; FAO/Globefish Highlights. (19??)-. Periodical. English (Spanish and French). Four times a year. $250.00 (members); $300.00 (developing countries); $350.00 (developed countries) Comes with Infofish Trade News. Infofish, PO Box 10899, 50728 Kuala Lumpur Malaysia. **Tel** 011 60 3 2914466, FAX 011 60 3 2916804, telex INFISH MA 31560.

PL
GOSPODARKA RYBNA. **Added/Corp** Panstwowe Wydawnictwo Rolnicze i Lesne. Vol. 28, No. 1 (Jan. 1976)-. Periodical. Polish. mo. $36.00. **(Subscription address:** ARS Polona, PO Box 1001, 00068 Warsaw Poland.**)**
Ind/Abst Food Sci. Technol. Abstr.; Nutr. Abstr. Rev., Ser. B, Live Feeds and Feed.; Nutr. Abstr. Rev., Ser. A, Hum. Exp.

CN/0847-0685
GREAT LAKES FISHERMAN. (THE GREAT LAKES FISHERMAN.). **VFOAT** Gr. Lakes Fisherman. (1973)-. Periodical. English. Twelve times a year. 20.00Can$. Nan Sea Publications, 542 George St, Port Stanley Ontario N5L 1H3 Canada. **Tel** (519)782-3412. **ED** Frank Prothero. **Bk Rev**, (Qty: 12). **Ad Acc. Circ:** 1,500 (ctrl).
Desc: Information and news about the commerical fishermen in the Great Lakes.

US/0194-5564
GREAT LAKES FISHERMAN (COLUMBUS, OHIO). ***Suspended.*** (GREAT LAKES FISHERMAN.). [Great Lakes fisherman]. Vol. 1 (Jan. 1979)-(19??). Periodical. English. Twelve times a year. Great Lakes Fisherman Publishing Company, PO Box 06355, Columbus OH 43206. **Tel** (614)882-5658. **ED** Ottie M. Snyder. **DD** 799. **Bk Rev. Ad Acc. Circ:** 40,000 (ctrl).
Desc: How, when and where for all fish of the region, with heavy emphasis on salmon and trout.

US/0749-0526
GREAT LAKES TROLLING ANNUAL. ***Ceased.*** English. an. Michigan Fisherman Inc, PO Box 977, East Lansing MI 48823. **Tel** (517)351-3074. **LC** SH457.7; .G74. **DD** 799.1/1.

JA/0388-788X
GYOBYO KENKYU. **Added/Corp** Nihon Gyobyo Gakkai. **VFOAT** Fish Pathology. (19??)-. Academic Scholarly Publication. Japanese (English). qt. $139.50. Business Center for Academic Societies Japan, Hon-Komagome 5-16-9, Bunkyo-ku, Tokyo 113 Japan. **Tel** 011 81 3 3817 5811. **(Subscription address:** Japan Publications Trading Company, Ltd., PO Box 5030, Tokyo International, Tokyo 100-31 Japan.**) ED** Y. Inui. **CODEN** GYKEDT. **Pr Rev.** Documents available from The Genuine Article, CASDDS.
Ind/Abst AgBiotech News Inf.; Aquat. Sci. Fish. Abstr. (Computer File); Chem. Abstr.; Curr. Ref. Fish Res.; Helminthol. Abstr. (1991-); Index Vet.; Protozoolog. Abstr.; Res. Alert [Full Cov.]; Sci. Cit. Index; SCISEARCH; Vet. Bull.

JA
GYOGYO HAKUSHO. **Main/Corp** Japan. Suisancho. **Added/Corp** Japan. Suisancho. Gyogyo no Doko ni Kansuru Nenji Hokoku. (19??)-. Japanese. ¥950. Norin Tokei Kyokai, (Association of Agriculture & Forestry Statistics), 11-14, Meguro 2 Chome, Meguroku, Tokyoto 153, Japan. **LC** SH301; .J28d.

JA
GYOGYO YOSHOKUGYO SEISAN TOKEI NEMPO. **Added/Corp** Japan. Norinsho. Norin Keizaikyoku. Tokei Chosabu. Japan. Norinsho. Norin Keizaikyoku. Tokei Johobu. (1963)-. Periodical. Japanese. Norin Tokei Kyokai, (Association of Agriculture & Forestry Statistics), 11-14, Meguro 2 Chome, Meguroku, Tokyoto 153, Japan. **LC** SH301; .K2. ***Continues*** *Gyogyo Yoshokugyo Gyokaku Tokei Hyo.*

JA
GYOMU NENPO. **Main/Corp** Chiba-Ken Suisan Shikenjo. **VFOAT** Chiba-Ken Suisan Shikenjo Gyomu Nenpo. Japanese. an. Chiba-Ken Suisan Shikenjo, 2492 Hiraiso, Chikura-Mach 8, Awa-gun 295, Chiba-Ken Japan. **LC** SH302.C48; C49A.

JA/0021-5090
GYORUIGAKU ZASSHI. (GYORUIGAKU ZASSHI / JAPANESE JOURNAL OF ICHTHYOLOGY.). [Gyoruigaku zasshi]. **Added/Corp** Nippon Gyogaku ShinkÅokai. **VFOAT** Japanese Journal of Ichthyology. Vol. 1 (1950)-. Periodical. Japanese (English; summaries and/or abstracts in English). qt. $95.00. Nihon Gyorui Gakkai, (Ichthyologu Society of Japan), Tokyo Suisan Daigaku, 5-7, Konan 4 Chome, Minatoku, Tokyoto 108 Japan. **(Subscription address:** Kyowa Book Company Inc., 1 38 Kanda Jinbocho Chiyoda-ku, Tokyo 101 Japan.**) DD** 597. **CODEN** GYOZA7. **Pr Rev.** Documents available from The Genuine Article, BIOSIS Document

Express, CASDDS.
Ind/Abst Aquat. Sci. Fish. Abstr. (Computer File); Biol. Abstr.; Chem. Abstr.; Curr. Contents, Agric. Biol. Environ. Sci.; Curr. Ref. Fish Res.; Ocean. Abstr.; Life Sci. Collect.; Res. Alert [Full Cov.]; Sci. Cit. Index; Zool. Rec.

CC/1004-2490
HAIYANG YUYE. **VFOAT** Marine Fisheries. (1979)-. Periodical. Chinese. bm. Zhongguo Shuichan Kexue Yuanjiuyuan, Donghai Shuichan Yanjiusuo, 300 Jungong lu, Shanghai 200090 People's Republic of China. **Tel** 86 21 5434690, FAX 86 21 5432926. **ED** Q. Yonggen. **Bk Rev. Ad Acc. Circ:** 5,500.
Ind/Abst Aquat. Sci. Fish. Abstr. (Computer File).

HU
HALASZAT. (1899)-. Periodical. English. Four times a year. Agroinform, Kitaibel Pal 4, 1024 Budapest Hungary. **Tel** 135-1927, FAX 135-0344, telex 224439. **ED** P. Karoly. **Ad Acc.**
Ind/Abst Agric. Eng. Abstr.; Index Vet.

CN/0846-3654
HALIBURTON FISHING GUIDE. [Haliburton fish. guide]. Vol. 1 (1991)-. English. $8.00 per year. Charasee Press, Box 28, RR2, Haliburton Ontario K0M 1S0 Canada. **DD** 799.1/1/0971361.

GR
HALIEIA. **VFOAT** Fishing. Periodical. Greek, Modern (summaries and/or abstracts in English). **LC** SH273; .H34.

KO/0374-8111
HAN-GUK SUSAN HAKHOIJI. (HAN'GUK SUSAN HAKHOE CHI.). [Han-guk Susan Hakhoiji]. **Main/Corp** Han'Guk Susan Hokhoe. **VFOAT** Bulletin of the Korean Fisheries Society. (19??)-. Academic Scholarly Publication. English (Korean). bm. W63 Korea; W23 other. National Fisheries, University of Busan, Busan Korea. **ED** Sung Yun Hong. **LC** SH1; .H28. **CODEN** HSHKAW. Index available. **Bk Rev. Circ:** 800. Documents available from BIOSIS Document Express, CASDDS.
Ind/Abst Aquat. Sci. Fish. Abstr. (Computer File); Biol. Abstr.; Chem. Abstr.; Fish Rev. (19??-199?); Wildl. Rev. (19??-199?).

US
HAWAII AQUACULTURE. (1992)-. Periodical. English.

US/0194-651X
HAWAII FISHING NEWS. (19??)-. Periodical. English. mo. $27.00 Hawaii; $30.00 US; $60.00 other. Hawaii Fishing News, PO Box 25413, Honolulu HI 96825. **Tel** (808)395-4499.

SP
HISTORICAL STATISTICAL BULLETIN. **See** Fish and Fisheries-Abstracting, Bibliographies and Statistics.

JA/0018-3458
HOKKAIDO DAIGAKU SUISANGAKUBU KENKYU IHO. [Hokkaido Daigaku Suisan Gakubu kenkyu iho]. **Main/Corp** Hokkaido Daigaku Suisangakubu, Hakodate. **VFOAT** Bulletin of the Faculty of Fisheries, Hokkaido University. (1950)-. Periodical. Multiple languages (Japanese and English). qt. Hokkaido University Faculty of Fisheries, 1 1 3 Chome Minato CHO, Hakodate Shi 040 Japan. **CODEN** HOSGAD. Documents available from BIOSIS Document Express, CASDDS.
Ind/Abst AGRICOLA; Biol. Abstr.; Chem. Abstr.; Ecol. Abstr.; Food Sci. Technol. Abstr.; Life Sci. Collect. (1985-).

JA
HOKKAIDO-KU SUISAN KENKYUJO KENKYU HOKOKU. **Added/Corp** Suisancho Hokkaido-Ku Suisan Kenkyujo (Japan). **VFOAT** Bulletin of the Hokkaido Regional Fisheries Research Laboratory; Bulletin of the Hokkaido National Fisheries Research Institute. Dai 52-Go (1988)-. Japanese (English). **LC** SH301; .H65. Documents available from BIOSIS Document Express. ***Continues*** *Suisancho Hokkaido-Ku Suisan Kenkyujo Kenkyu Hokoku, 0513-2541.*
Desc: Specifically looks at fisheries.
Ind/Abst Biol. Abstr.; Life Sci. Collect.

JA
HOKKAIDO OKIAI SOKOBIKIAMI GYOGYO-GYOJOBETSU GYOKAKU TOKEI NEMPO. **Added/Corp** Hokkaido Kisen Gyogyo Kyodo Kumiai Rengokai. Japan. Suisancho Hokkaido Gyogyo Chosei Jimusho. (19??)-. Periodical. Japanese. an. Mainichi Sapporo Kaikan, 1 Nishi 6-chome, Kita 4 jo Chuoku, Sapporishi Hokkaido 060 Japan. **LC** SH301; .H64.

JA
HOKKAIDORITSU HAKODATE SUISAN SHIKENJO JIGYO HOKOKUSHO. Japanese. an. free. Hokkaidoritsu Hakodate Suisan Shikenjo, 2-66 Yukawa-cho 1-chome, Hakodate-shi 042, Hokkaido Japan. **ED** Katsuo Saito. **LC** SH302.H6; H69. **Circ:** 350 (ctrl).

JA
HOKOKU. **Main/Corp** Hokkaido. Suisan Shikenjo, Yoichi. **VFOAT** Scientific Reports of Hokkaido Fisheries Experimental Station. No. 1 (March 1963)-. Monographic series. Japanese (summaries and/or abstracts in English; table of contents in English). Price varies per volume. Hokkaido University Faculty of Fisheries, 1 1 3 Chome Minato CHO, Hakodate Shi 040 Japan.
Ind/Abst Aquat. Sci. Fish. Abstr. (Computer File).

HK
HONG KONG CHENG FU YU NUNG CHU KAN WU. **See** Agriculture.

US
HOOKUP. (19??)-. Periodical. English. bm. Hookup, POB 1106, Poway CA 92064. Index available. cum. index. **Bk Rev. Ad Acc.** ctrl circ.
Desc: America's saltwater fishing journal.

UK/0262-3269
HOUSEHOLD FISH CONSUMPTION IN GREAT BRITAIN. [Househ. fish consum. G.B.]. (1981)-. English. qt. £75.00. Sea Fish Industry Authority, 18 Logie Mill, Logie Green Road, Edinburgh EH7 4HG Scotland. **Tel** 011 44 31 558-3331 ext. 256, FAX 011 44 31 558-1442. **DD** 339.486413920941.
Desc: Provides an analysis of the sales of fish by species for household consumption in Great Britain.

JA
HYOGO KENRITSU SUISAN SHIKENJO KENKYU HOKOKU. **Main/Corp** Hyogo Kenritsu Suisan Shikenjo. **VFOAT** Bulletin of the Hyogo Prefectural Fisheries Experimental Station. Japanese (Japanese). Hyogo Kenritsu Suisan Shikenjo, Japan. **LC** SH302.H9; H93A.

KO
HYONDAE HAEYANG. **VFOAT** The Fishing & Marine Industry Journal; Fishing and Marine Industry Journal; Fishing & Marine Industry Journal; Hyundai Haiyang. Periodical. Korean (Korean). mo. W2.700 single issue. Hyondae Haeyangsa, 151-8 Kwanhun-dong, Chongno-ku Seoul 110 Korea. **LC** SH302.5; .H96.

DK/0906-060X
ICES MARINE SCIENCE SYMPOSIA. **See** Earth Sciences-Oceanography.

GW/0936-9902
ICHTHYOLOGICAL EXPLORATION OF FRESHWATERS. Vol. 1, No. 1 (Jan. 1990)-. Periodical. English (French). Four times a year (Jan., Apr., July, Oct.). DM280.00 institution; DM140.00 individual. Verlag Dr Friedrich Pfeil, PO Box 65 00 86, W-8000 Munich 65 Germany. **Tel** (0043)89-8888196, FAX (0043)89-8341873. **ED** Dr. Maurice Kottelat. **CODEN** IEFRES. **Bk Rev. Pr Rev.**
Desc: This journal is devoted to the rapid information of high quality papers documenting biodiversity of freshwater fishes, taxonomic diversity, ecological diversity, ethological diversity, reproductive diversity and zoogeographic diversity.

PH/0115-4435
ICLARM CONFERENCE PROCEEDINGS. [ICLARM conf. proc.]. **VFOAT** International Center for Living Aquatic Resources Management Conference Proceedings. (1979)-. Periodical. English. International Center for Living Aquatic Resources Management, MCPO Box 2631, 0718 Makati, MM, Philippines. **Tel** 011 63 2 8180466, 011 63 2 8189283, FAX 011 63 2 8163183, telex 64794.
Ind/Abst Ocean. Abstr.

PH/0115-4494
ICLARM REPORT. **Main/Corp** International Center for Living Aquatic Resources Management. **VAT** International Center for Living Aquatic Resources Management Report. (19??)-. English. International Center for Living Aquatic Resources Management, MCPO Box 2631, 0718 Makati, MM, Philippines. **Tel** 011 63 2 8180466, 011 63 2 8189283, FAX 011 63 2 8163183, telex 64794. **LC** SH332; .I58a. **DD** 639.3/072.
Ind/Abst Ocean. Abstr.

PH/0115-4389
ICLARM STUDIES AND REVIEWS. **Added/Corp** International Center for Living Aquatic Resources Management. **VAT** International Center for Living Aquatic Resources Management Studies and Reviews. No. 1 (1979)-. Monographic series. English. International Center for Living Aquatic Resources Management, MCPO Box 2631, 0718 Makati, MM, Philippines. **Tel** 011 63 2 8180466, 011 63 2 8189283, FAX 011 63 2 8163183, telex 64794. **CODEN** ISRVES.
Ind/Abst Aquat. Sci. Fish. Abstr. (Computer File); Ocean. Abstr.

PH/0115-5547
ICLARM TECHNICAL REPORTS. **Added/Corp** International Center for Living Aquatic Resources Management. **VAT** International Center for Living Aquatic Resources Management Technical Reports. (1981)-. Monographic series. English. ir. Price varies per volume. International Center for Living Aquatic Resources Management, MCPO Box 2631, 0718 Makati, MM, Philippines. **Tel** 011 63 2 8180466, 011 63 2 8189283, FAX 011 63 2 8163183, telex 64794.
Ind/Abst Aquat. Sci. Fish. Abstr. (Computer File); Ocean. Abstr.; Philip. Sci. Technol. Abstr.

CN
ICNAF HANDBOOK. **Main/Corp** International Commission for the Northwest Atlantic Fisheries. (1965)-. Periodical. English. Northwest Atlantic Fisheries Organization / NAFO, PO Box 638, Dartmouth Nova Scotia B2Y 3Y9 Canada. **Tel** (902)469-9105, telex 019-31475. **DD** 639/.22/091634. ***Supersedes*** *International Commission for the Northwest Atlantic Fisheries. ICNAF Directory.*

US/0492-8539
IF REPORT SERIES. **Added/Corp** Texas. Parks and Wildlife Department. (19??)-. Monographic series. English. Price varies per volume. Texas Parks & Wildlife, 4200 Smith School Road, Austin TX 78744. **Tel** (512)707-0032. **DD** 639. ***Continues*** *IF Series,.*

US/0276-9905
IN-FISHERMAN, THE. (IN'FISHERMAN.). [In-fisherman]. **Added/Corp** Al Lindner's Outdoors, Inc. **VFOAT** In-Fisherman. Segment 1, Study Report 1-Segment 4, Study Report 2 ; Book #25 (June/July 1979)-. Periodical. English. Seven times a year. $16.00. In-Fisherman Inc., Two In-Fisherman Drive, Brainerd MN 56401. **Tel** (218)829-1648, FAX (218)829-3091. **ED** Doug Stange. **LC** SH401; .I48. **DD** 799.1/2/05. **Bk Rev**, (Qty: 15). **Ad Acc, Adv Mgr:** Jim Bessenfelder. **Circ:** 325,000.
Desc: Provides information on freshwater fishing.
Ind/Abst Access (1981-).

II/0537-1643
INDIAN FISHERIES BULLETIN. Vol. 1-1954-. Bulletin. English. ir. Government of India / Ministry of Agriculture and Irrigation, Department of Agriculture, New Delhi India.

II/0537-2003
INDIAN JOURNAL OF FISHERIES. [Indian j. fish.]. **Added/Corp** Indian Council of Agricultural Research. India. Ministry of Food and Agriculture. Vol. 1 (May 1954)-. Periodical. English. sa. $40.00. ICAR Unit-CMFRI, Post Bas No 1912, Cochin-18 Kerala 682018 India. **(Subscription address:** Prints India, 11 Darya Ganj, New Delhi, 110002 India, (Phone: 011 91 11 3268645)) **ED** E G Silas. **LC** SH1; .I45. **CODEN** IJFIAW. **Circ:** 500. Documents available from BIOSIS Document Express.
Desc: Covers fish, fisheries, marine biology, oceanography and aquaculture.
Ind/Abst Aquat. Sci. Fish. Abstr. (Computer File); Biol. Abstr.; Fish Rev. (19??-199?); Food Sci. Technol. Abstr.; Mar. Sci. Contents Tables; Life Sci. Collect.; Protozoolog. Abstr.; Wildl. Rev. (19??-199?).

US/0736-0460
INDO-PACIFIC FISHES. **See** Zoology.

SP
INDUSTRIAS PESQUERAS. (INDUSTRIAS PESQUERAS; REVISTA MARITIMA QUINCENAL.). **Added/Corp** Servicios Industriales Pesqueros. Vol. 1 (April 15, 1927)-. Periodical. Spanish. Twenty-six times a year. 6000ptas Spain; 8000ptas others. Servicios Industriales Pesquer Policarpo, Sanz 22 3, 36202 Vigo Spain. **Tel** 011 34 986 437004, 011 34 986 438597.

MY/0127-2012
INFOFISH INTERNATIONAL. **Added/Corp** INFOFISH (Project). No. 5/87 (Sept./Oct. 1987)-. Periodical. English. bm (Jan., March, May, July, Sep., Nov.). $15.00 (one year), $40.00 (three years) Infofish member countries; $25.00 (one year), $60.00 (three years) other developing countries; $50.00 (one year), $120.00 (three years) industrialized countries. Infofish, PO Box 10899, 50728 Kuala Lumpur Malaysia. **Tel** 011 60 3 2914466, FAX 011 60 3 2916804, telex INFISH MA 31560. **ED** Henri De Saram, Jeanette Low-Eu. Index available. **Bk Rev**, (Qty: 50-60 copies). **Ad Acc, Adv Mgr:** Paul H S Tan. **Pr Rev. Circ:** 5,500 (ctrl). ***Continues*** *INFOFISH Marketing Digest, 0127-2012.*
Desc: Bimonthly journal covering markets and marketing, aquaculture technological advances, product developments, and more.
Ind/Abst AgBiotech News Inf.; AGRICOLA; Agric. Eng. Abstr. (1991-); Anim. Breed. Abstr.; Food Sci. Technol. Abstr.; Index Vet.; Ocean. Abstr.; World Agric. Econ.

US
INFORMATION REPORTS (OREGON. DEPARTMENT OF FISH AND WILDLIFE. FISH DIVISION). (INFORMATION REPORTS / FISH DIVISION, OREGON DEPARTMENT OF FISH AND WILDLIFE.). Began in 1981. Monographic series. English. Price varies per volume. ***Continues*** *Information Report Series, Fisheries.*

US/0434-9474
INFORMATIONAL SERIES - GULF STATES MARINE FISHERIES COMMISSION. **Main/Corp** Gulf States Marine Fisheries Commission. No. 1 (1951)-. Monographic series. English. Price varies per volume. **DD** 639.

GW/0020-0344
INFORMATIONEN FUER DIE FISCHWIRTSCHAFT. [Inf. Fischwirtsch.]. **Added/Corp** Bundesforschungsanstalt fur Fischerei (Germany). **VFOAT** Infn Fischw. Vol. 6 (1959)-. Periodical. German. qt. DM40.00. Bundesforschungsanstalt fuer Fischerei, Palmaille 9, D 22767 Hamburg Germany. **Tel** 011 49 40 38905113. ***Continues*** *Wissenschaftliche Informationen fur die Fischereipraxis,.*
Ind/Abst Energy Res. Abstr. (Oct. 1979-); Ocean. Abstr.

SP
INTERNATIONAL COMMISSION FOR THE CONSERVATION OF THE ATLANTIC TUNAS STATISTICAL BULLETIN. Statistical Publication. Spanish. International Commission for the Conservation of the Atlantic Tunas, Principe de Vergara 17, 28001 Madrid Spain. **Tel** 011 34 1 4310329.
Ind/Abst Ocean. Abstr.

●CN
INTERNATIONAL DIRECTORY OF AQUARIST ORGANIZATIONS. (1994)-. Directory. English. an. $15.00 (members of ACN), $20.00 other. Aquatic Conservation Network, 540 Roosevelt Avenue, Ottawa, Ontario K2A 1Z8, Canada. **Tel** (613)729-4670, FAX (613)729-5613.
Desc: Facilitates worldwide communications in the aquarium hobby and between the hobby and professional aquarists.

CL
INVESTIGACIONES MARINAS. Main/Corp Valparaiso (City). Universidad Catolica. Centro de Investigaciones del Marinas. (19??)-. Spanish (English). anan. 33.00Chil$ US; 35.00Chil$ others. Ediciones Universitarias de Valparaiso, Casilla 1415, Valparaiso Chile. **Tel** 011 56 31 252900. **ED** Patricio M. Arana. **Circ:** 200 (ctrl).
Desc: Articles and information on oceanography, marine biology, fisheries, food science and technology all of the Pacific Southeast region and the Antarctic.
Ind/Abst Aquat. Sci. Fish. Abstr. (Computer File).

IS
ISRAEL FISHERIES IN FIGURES. Added/Corp Israel. Ha-Mahlakah Le-Dayig. (1???)-. Multiple languages (English and Hebrew).
Ind/Abst Ocean. Abstr.

IS/0792-156X
ISRAELI JOURNAL OF AQUACULTURE, BAMIDGEH. (THE ISRAELI JOURNAL OF AQUACULTURE.). [Isr. j. aquac. Bamidgeh]. **Added/Corp** Israel. Mahlakah le-Dayig. Irgun Megadle Dagim (Israel). **VFOAT** Bamidgeh. Vol. 40, No. 1 (Mar. 1988)-. Academic Scholarly Publication. English. qt (Mar., Jun., Sept., Dec.). $34.00 surface mail; $38.00 (one year), $39.00 (two years) airmail. Fish Breeders Association in Israel, Bamidgeh Editorial Office, NIR David 19150 Israel. **Tel** 011 972 65 585877, FAX 011 972 65 83900, telex 46832 ND. **ED** Dr. J. van Rijin (editor's address: The Hebrew University, Facul, Agriculture, P. O. Box 12, Rehovot 76-100, Israel). **LC** SH117.I75; B36. **DD** 639.3/05. **CODEN** IJABEO. Index available (Bound in 4th iss.). **Bk Rev. Ad Acc.** Documents available from The Genuine Article, BIOSIS Document Express, CASDDS. ***Continues*** *Bamidgeh, 0005-4577.*
Desc: Activities in the research and control of diseases and environmental factors influencing aquaculture.
Ind/Abst AgBiotech News Inf.; Anim. Breed. Abstr.; Aquat. Sci. Fish. Abstr. (Computer File); Biol. Abstr.; Chem. Abstr. (1988-); Curr. Aware. Biol. Sci., CABS; Curr. Contents, Agric. Biol. Environ. Sci.; Ecol. Abstr.; Fish Rev. (1988-); Fresh. Aqua. Contents Tables; Geogr. Abstr. Human Geogr.; Index Vet.; Nutr. Abstr. Rev., Ser. B, Live Feeds and Feed.; Ocean. Abstr.; Res. Alert [Full Cov.]; Sci. Cit. Index; SCISEARCH; Soyabean Abstr.; Wheat Barley Trit. Abstr.

GW/0075-2851
JAHRESBERICHT UBER DIE DEUTSCHE FISCHWIRTSCHAFT. VFOAT Annual Report on German Fisheries. (1958)-. German (summaries and/or abstracts in English). Kollen Druck & Verlag GmbH, Schontalweg 5, W5305 Alfter Oede Germany. ***Continues*** *Jahresbericht Uber die Deutsche Fischerei.*
Ind/Abst Ocean. Abstr.

JA
JAMARC. Added/Corp Kaiyo Suisan Shigen Kaihatsu Senta. (Sept. 1972)-. Japanese (Japanese). Kaiyo Suisan Shigen Kaihatsu Senta, c/o Godo Kaikan Building, 3-4 Kioicho, Chiyoda-ku Tokyo 102 Japan. **LC** SH327.5; .J34.
Ind/Abst Aquat. Sci. Fish. Abstr. (Computer File).

CH/0513-3483
JINGJI-BU GUOLI TAIWAN DAXUE HEBANYUVE SHENGWU SHIYAN-SUO YANJIU BAOGAO. ***Suspended.*** (REPORT OF THE INSTITUTE OF FISHERY BIOLOGY OF MINISTRY OF ECONOMIC AFFAIRS AND NATIONAL TAIWAN UNIVERSITY.). [Jingji- bu guoli Taiwan daxue hebanyuve shengwu shiyan-suo yanjiu baogao]. **Main/Corp** Yu Yeh Sheng Wu Shih Yen So, Tai-Pei. **VFOAT** Ching Chi Pu, Kuo Li Tai-Wan Ta Hsueh No Pan Yu Yeh Sheng Wu Shih Yen So Yen Chiu Pao Kao. Nov. (1956)-(19??). Multiple languages (English). Institute of Fishery Biology, National Taiwan University, 1 Roosevelt Road, Taipei, Taiwan. **LC** QL634.T28. **DD** 597/.008. **CODEN** RIFBAZ. Documents available from BIOSIS Document Express.
Ind/Abst Biol. Abstr.

●US/1049-6505
JOURNAL OF AGRICULTURAL & FOOD INFORMATION. **See** Agriculture.

US/1045-4438
JOURNAL OF APPLIED AQUACULTURE. [J. appl. aquac.]. Vol. 1, No. 1 (1991)-. Periodical. English. qt. $85.00 US; $119.00 other. The Haworth Press Inc, 10 Alice Street, Binghamton NY 13904-1580. **Tel** (607)722-5857, (800)3-HAWORTH, FAX (607)722-1424. **ED** Douglas Tave (editor's address: Department of Agriculture, University of Arkansas at Pine Bluff, Pine Bluff, AR 71601). **LC** SH1; .J67. **DD** 639/.8/05. **CODEN** JAAQEH. **Bk Rev. Ad Acc. Pr Rev. Acid Free.** available on microfilm and microfiche from University Microfilms International (UMI). Documents available from Haworth Document Delivery Service, Documents on Demand.
Desc: Devoted to innovative and significant research and ideas that will advance knowledge about the production, domestication, and husbandry of aquatic animals and plants. Covers the entire area of applied aquaculture including breeding, hatchery design and management, genetics, health management, nutrition, water quality management, physiology, production, harvest technology, marketing, processing, economics, technology transfer, development, and legal and regulatory aspects of aquaculture.
Ind/Abst Acad. Search (July 1993-); Curr. Aware. Biol. Sci., CABS; Ei Page One; Environ. Abstr.; Food Sci. Technol. Abstr.; Gen. Sci. Source (Jul. 1993-); INFO-SOUTH Abstr.

GW/0175-8659
JOURNAL OF APPLIED ICHTHYOLOGY. (ZEITSCHRIFT FUER ANGEWANDTE ICHTHYOLOGIE.). [J. appl. ichthyol.]. Vol. 1, 1 (May 1985)-. Academic Scholarly Publication. English (French and German). Four times a year. DM362.00 Europe; DM360.00 other. Blackwell Wissenschafts-Verlag, Kurfuerstendamm 57, D 10707 Berlin Germany. **Tel** 011 49 30 32790623, 011 49 30 32790624, FAX 011 49 30 327 90610. **ED** H. Rosenthal. **LC** QL614; .Z45. **DD** 597. **CODEN** ZAICEL. Index available. cum. index. **Bk Rev. Ad Acc. Pr Rev. Circ:** 2,500. Documents available from The Genuine Article, BIOSIS Document Express, CASDDS.
Desc: Publishes articles on ichthyology, aquaculture, and marine fisheries.
Ind/Abst Agric. Eng. Abstr.; Biol. Abstr. (1985-); Chem. Abstr. (1985-); Curr. Contents, Agric. Biol. Environ. Sci.; Curr. Ref. Fish Res.; Fish Rev. (19??-199?); Helminthol. Abstr. (1991-); Index Vet.; Nutr. Abstr. Rev., Ser. B, Live Feeds and Feed.; Ocean. Abstr.; Protozoolog. Abstr.; Res. Alert [Full Cov.]; Rev. Agric. Entomol.; Rev. Med. Vet. Entomol.; Sci. Cit. Index; SCISEARCH; Vet. Bull.; Weed Abstr.; Wildl. Rev. (19??-199?).

II/0970-0846
JOURNAL OF AQUACULTURE IN THE TROPICS. [J. aquac. trop.]. Vol. 1, No. 1 (May 1986)-. Periodical. English. Twice a year. Fl125.00 India; $110.00 US. AA Balkema, Box 1675, 3000 BR Rotterdam Netherlands. **Tel** 011 31 10 4145822, FAX 011 31 10 4135947, telex 41605. **(Subscription address:** Prints India, 11 Darya Ganj, New Delhi, 110002 India, (Phone: 011 91 11 3268645)) **ED** A N Bose. **[CCC]. Bk Rev. Circ:** 100. Documents available from BIOSIS Document Express.
Ind/Abst Anim. Breed. Abstr.; Aquat. Sci. Fish. Abstr. (Computer File); Biodeter. Abstr.; Biol. Abstr.; Curr. Aware. Biol. Sci., CABS; Fresh. Aqua. Contents Tables; Index Vet.; Nutr. Abstr. Rev., Ser. B, Live Feeds and Feed.; Rev. Med. Vet. Mycology; Rice Abstr.; World Agric. Econ.

US/0899-7659
JOURNAL OF AQUATIC ANIMAL HEALTH. [J. aquat. anim. health]. **Added/Corp** American Fisheries Society. Vol. 1, No. 1 (Mar. 1989)-. Academic Scholarly Publication. English. Four times a year. $425.00 US; $460.00 other (library). American Fisheries Society, 5410 Grosvenor Lane, Suite 110, Bethesda MD 20814-2199. **Tel** (301)897-8616, (301)897-8621, FAX (301)897-8096. **LC** WMLC 93/306. **DD** 639. **CODEN** JAAHEO. **[CCC]. Acid Free.** Documents available from BIOSIS Document Express, CASDDS, Documents on Demand.
Desc: Carries research papers on the causes, effects, treatments & prevention of diseases, particularly those of fish and shellfish. International is scope although the concentration is on North American science.
Ind/Abst AgBiotech News Inf.; Aquat. Sci. Fish. Abstr. (Computer File); Biodeter. Abstr. (1991-); Biol. Abstr.; Chem. Abstr.; Curr. Aware. Biol. Sci., CABS; Environ. Abstr.; Fish Rev.; Helminthol. Abstr. (1991-); Index Vet.; Nutr. Abstr. Rev., Ser. B, Live Feeds and Feed.; Ocean. Abstr.; Protozoolog. Abstr.; Rev. Med. Vet. Mycology; Soils Fert.; Vet. Bull.; Wildl. Rev.

●US/1049-8850
JOURNAL OF AQUATIC FOOD PRODUCTS TECHNOLOGY. [J. aquat. food prod. technol.]. **VFOAT** Aquatic Food Product Technology. Vol. 1, No. 1 (1992)-. Periodical. English. qt. $75.00 US; $105.00 other. The Haworth Press Inc, 10 Alice Street, Binghamton NY 13904-1580. **Tel** (607)722-5857, (800)3-HAWORTH, FAX (607)722-1424. **ED** George Pitgott (Editor's Address: Institute of Food Science and Technology, University of Washington, 3707 Brooklyn Avenue NE, Seattle, WA 98195). **LC** SH334.9; .J68. **DD** 664/.94/05. **CODEN** JAFPE5. **Bk Rev. Ad Acc. Pr Rev. Acid Free.** available on microfiche. Documents available from Haworth Document Delivery Service.
Desc: A primary source for the dissemination of international scientific information on aquatic food products. This journal will publish research papers, short communications, and review articles concerning the application of science and technology to all aspects of the research, development, production and distribution of food products originating from the marine and fresh water bodies of the world.
Ind/Abst AGRICOLA; Biol. Dig.; Environ. Period. Bibliogr.; Food Sci. Technol. Abstr.; Foods Adlibra (1992-).

UK/0022-1112
JOURNAL OF FISH BIOLOGY. [J. fish biol.]. Vol. 1 (Jan. 1969)-. Academic Scholarly Publication. English. mo. $790.00. Academic Press Ltd., A Division of Harcourt Brace & Company Ltd., 24-28 Oval Road, London NW1 7DX England. **Tel** 071 267 4466, FAX 071 482 2293, 071 485 4752, telex 25775 ACPRES G. **(Subscription address:** Harcourt Brace & Company, Ltd., Foots Cray, High Street, Sidcup Kent DA14 5HP England.) **ED** J. Thorpe. **LC** QL614. **DD** 598.2/05. **NLM** W1 JO65K. **CODEN** JFIBA9. **[CCC]. Bk Rev. Pr Rev.** Documents available from The Genuine Article, BIOSIS Document Express, CASDDS, Documents on Demand.
Desc: A leading international journal for scientists engaged in all aspects of fish and fisheries research, both freshwater and marine. The journal publishes high-quality papers relevant to the central theme of fish biology. Aims to bring together an overall picture of the research in progress and to provide international communication among researchers in many disciplines with a common interest in the biology of fish.
Ind/Abst AgBiotech News Inf.; Anim. Behav. Abstr.; Anim. Breed. Abstr.; AQUAREF; Aquat. Sci. Fish. Abstr. (Computer File); Biol. Abstr.; Chem. Abstr.; Chemorecept. Abstr.; Coal Abstr.; CSA Neuro. Abstr. (?-?); Curr. Aware. Biol. Sci., CABS; Curr. Contents, Agric. Biol. Environ. Sci.; Curr. Ref. Fish Res.; Ecol. Abstr.; Ecology Abstr.; EMBASE; Environ. Abstr.; Fish Rev. (Jan. 1989-July 1992); Fresh. Aqua. Contents Tables; Geogr. Abstr. Phys. Geogr.; Geogr. Abstr. Human Geogr.; Geol. Abstr.; Helminthol. Abstr. (19??-19??); Int. Dev. Abstr.; Mar. Sci. Contents Tables; Nutr. Abstr. Rev., Ser. B, Live Feeds and Feed.; Nutr. Abstr. Rev., Ser. A, Hum. Exp.; Ocean. Abstr.; Life Sci. Collect.; Pollut. Abstr. Indexes; Protozoolog. Abstr.; Res. Alert [Full Cov.]; Rev. Med. Vet. Entomol.; Sci. Cit. Index; SCISEARCH; Wildl. Rev. (Jan. 1989-July 1992).

UK/0140-7775
JOURNAL OF FISH DISEASES. [J. fish dis.]. Vol. 1 (Jan. 1978)-. Academic Scholarly Publication. English. bm (6 issues). $504.00 US & Canada; £295.00 Europe; £325.00 other. Blackwell Scientific Publications Ltd, Marston Book Services, PO Box 87, Oxford OX2 ODT UK. **Tel** 011 44 865 791155, FAX 011 44 865 791927, telex 837 515 MARDIS G. **ED** R. J. Roberts and R. Wootten. **CODEN** JFIDDI. **[CCC].** Index available (bound in last issue). **Bk Rev. Ad Acc. Pr Rev. Circ:** 600. available on microfilm and microfiche from University Microfilms International (UMI). Documents available from The Genuine Article, BIOSIS Document Express, CASDDS.
Desc: Covers all aspects of disease in wild and cultured fish and shellfish.
Ind/Abst AgBiotech News Inf.; AGRICOLA; AQUAREF; Aquat. Sci. Fish. Abstr. (Computer File); Biol. Abstr.; Chem. Abstr.; CSA Neuro. Abstr. (?-?); Curr. Aware. Biol. Sci., CABS; Curr. Contents, Agric. Biol. Environ. Sci.; Curr. Ref. Fish Res.; Ecol. Abstr.; EMBASE; Fish Rev.; Fresh. Aqua. Contents Tables; Geogr. Abstr. Phys. Geogr.; Helminthol. Abstr. (1991-); Index Vet.; Microbiol. Abstr. Sect. B; Microbiol. Abstr. Sect. C; Ocean. Abstr.; Life Sci. Collect.; PESTDOC; Protozoolog. Abstr.; Res. Alert [Full Cov.]; Rev. Med. Vet. Entomol.; Rev. Med. Vet. Mycology; Rev. Plant Pathol.; Sci. Cit. Index; SCISEARCH; Vet. Bull.; Virol. AIDS Abstr.

PH/0115-690X
JOURNAL OF FISHERIES & AQUACULTURE. ***Ceased.*** **Added/Corp** Mindanao State University. University Research Center. **VFOAT** Journal of Fisheries and Aquaculture. Vol. 1, No. 1 (1980)-(19??). Periodical. English. sa. University Research Center, Mindanao State University, PO Box 5594, 9200 Iligan City Philippines. **(Subscription address:** Mindanao State University, University

Research Center, PO Box 5594, 9200 Iligan City Philippines) **ED** Raymond Llorca. **LC** SH1; .J68. **DD** 639. **Pr Rev. Circ:** 500 (ctrl).

US/0032-9452
JOURNAL OF ICHTHYOLOGY. [J. ichthyol.]. **Added/Corp** American Fisheries Society. Scripta Technica, Inc. Vol. 10 (1970)-. Periodical. English (Russian). Nine times a year. $1,198.00 US; $1,288.00 Canada and Mexico; $1,321.75 other. Scripta Technica, A Subsidiary of John Wiley & Sons, Inc., 7961 Eastern Avenue, Silver Spring MD 20910. **Tel** (301)588-0484, FAX (301)588-5278. **(Subscription address:** John Wiley / Philadelphia, PO Box 7247, Philadelphia PA 19170.**) ED** Robert J. Behnke, Colorado State University. **LC** SH1; .V713. **DD** 597/.005. **CODEN** JITHAZ. **[CCC]. Ad Acc. Circ:** 425. available on microfilm and microfiche from University Microfilms International (UMI). Documents available from BIOSIS Document Express. ***Continues*** *Problems of Ichthyology, 0193-5119.*
Desc: Deals with fisheries management, fish culture, aquaculture, physiology, and biochemistry of both marine and freshwater fish, fish systematics and zoogeography. The emphasis is on promotion on reproducing commercially useful fish and their well-being for the purpose of ensuring the highest protein yields, rather than on sports fisheries.
Ind/Abst AgBiotech News Inf.; Aquat. Sci. Fish. Abstr. (Computer File); Biol. Abstr. (-1978); Ecol. Abstr. (?-?); EMBASE; Fish Rev.; Fresh. Aqua. Contents Tables; Geogr. Abstr. Phys. Geogr.; Geogr. Abstr. Human Geogr.; Index Vet.; Nutr. Abstr. Rev., Ser. B, Live Feeds and Feed.; Ocean. Abstr.; Rev. Agric. Entomol.; Rev. Med. Vet. Mycology; Vet. Bull.

CN/0250-6408
JOURNAL OF NORTHWEST ATLANTIC FISHERY SCIENCE. [J. Northwest Atl. fish. sci.]. **Added/Corp** Northwest Atlantic Fisheries Organization. Vol. 1 (1980)-. Periodical. English. ir. Northwest Atlantic Fisheries Organization / NAFO, PO Box 638, Dartmouth Nova Scotia B2Y 3Y9 Canada. **Tel** (902)469-9105, telex 019-31475. **ED** W. G. Doubleday, G. P. Ennis, M. G. Grosslein, R. G. Halliday, J. M. Colebrook, and V. M. Hodder. **LC** SH1; .I535. **DD** 639/.2/091631. **CODEN** JNFSD2. Index available. cum. index. **Circ:** 600. Documents available from BIOSIS Document Express. ***Continues*** *International Commission for the Northwest Atlantic Fisheries. Research Bulletin, 0074-2651.*
Desc: Primary publication of original research papers on fishery science in the Northwest Atlantic dealing with environmental, biological, ecological and fishery aspects of the living marine resources and ecosystems.
Ind/Abst Aquat. Sci. Fish. Abstr. (Computer File); Biol. Abstr.; Ecol. Abstr.; Fish Rev.; Geogr. Abstr. Human Geogr.; Mar. Sci. Contents Tables; Ocean. Abstr.; Life Sci. Collect.

US/0730-8000
JOURNAL OF SHELLFISH RESEARCH. [J. shellfish res.]. **Added/Corp** National Shellfisheries Association. Vol. 1, No. 1 (June 1981)-. Academic Scholarly Publication. English. sa (June and December). $125.00 US; $130.00 other. Sheridan Press, PO Box 465, Hanover PA 17331. **Tel** (800)352-2210, (717)632-3535, FAX (717)633-8900. **ED** Sandra Shumway. **LC** SH370.A1; N312. **DD** 639/.4/05. **CODEN** JSHRDA. **Bk Rev. Circ:** 1,000. available on CD-ROM. Documents available from BIOSIS Document Express, CASDDS. ***Continues*** *Proceedings of the National Shellfisheries Association, 0077-5711.*
Desc: Current research results from molluscan and crustacean shellfisheries studies. Topics include aquaculture, fisheries management, physiology, genetics, current membership list and past abstracts.
Ind/Abst Anim. Breed. Abstr.; Aquat. Sci. Fish. Abstr. (Computer File); Biol. Abstr.; Chem. Abstr.; Helminthol. Abstr. (1991-); Nutr. Abstr. Rev., Ser. B, Live Feeds and Feed.; Ocean. Abstr.; Life Sci. Collect.; Protozoolog. Abstr.; Sci. Cit. Index; Soyabean Abstr.

US/0002-967X
JOURNAL OF THE AMERICAN KILLIFISH ASSOCIATION, THE. **Added/Corp** American Killifish Association. Vol. 1, No. 1 (Spring 1964)-. Periodical. English. Six times a year (Feb., Apr., June, Aug., Oct., Dec.). $24.00 US, $30.00 Canada & Mexico, $40.00 others Comes with American Killifish Association membership. American Killifish Association, 903 Merrifield Place, Mishawaka IN 46544. **Tel** (219)255-6356. **ED** Albert J. Klee. **DD** 597. **Bk Rev. Circ:** 1,500 (ctrl). ***Absorbed*** *Killie Notes.*
Desc: News and information about freshwater fisheries, such as carps and minnows.

II/0971-1422
JOURNAL OF THE INDIAN FISHERIES ASSOCIATION. [J. Indian Fish. Assoc.]. (1971)-. Periodical. English. ir. **UDC** 639.2.
Ind/Abst Aquat. Sci. Fish. Abstr. (Computer File).

II/0379-3435
JOURNAL OF THE INLAND FISHERIES SOCIETY OF INDIA. [J. Inland Fish. Soc. India]. **Added/Corp** Inland Fisheries Society of India. (1969)-. Academic Scholarly Publication. English. Twice a year. Free. Central Inland Fish Research Institute, 24 Parganas, Barrackpore West Bengal India. **Tel** 46 4265. **LC** SH299; .I54. **DD** 639/.21/0954. **CODEN** JIFSBX. Documents available from BIOSIS Document Express, CASDDS.
Ind/Abst Aquat. Sci. Fish. Abstr. (Computer File); Biol. Abstr.; Chem. Abstr. (-1980); Fresh. Aqua. Contents Tables.

JA/0040-9014
JOURNAL OF THE TOKYO UNIVERSITY OF FISHERIES. [J. Tokyo Univ. Fish.]. **Main/Corp** Tokyo Suisan Daigaku. **Added/Corp** Tokyo Suisan Daigaku. Tokyo Suisan Daigaku Kenkyu Hokoku. **VFOAT** Tokyo Suisan Daigaku Kenkyu Hokoku. Vol. 36 No. 2 (1950)-. Periodical. English (French, German and Japanese). University of Tokyo / Plankton Society Japan, Ocean Research Institute, Minamidai Nakano Tokyo Japan. **LC** SH1; .T65. **CODEN** JTUFA9. Documents available from BIOSIS Document Express, CASDDS. ***Continues*** *Journal of the Tokyo College of Fisheries.*
Ind/Abst Aquat. Sci. Fish. Abstr. (Computer File); Biol. Abstr.; Chem. Abstr.; Fish Rev. (Jan. 1989-July 1992); Mar. Sci. Contents Tables; Ocean. Abstr.; Wildl. Rev. (Jan. 1989-July 1992).

US/0893-8849
JOURNAL OF THE WORLD AQUACULTURE SOCIETY. (JOURNAL OF THE WORLD AQUACULTURE SOCIETY.). [J. World Aquac. Soc.]. **Added/Corp** World Aquaculture Society. Vol. 17, No. 1-4 (1986)-. Academic Scholarly Publication. English. qt. $105.00 US; $115.00 Canada, Mexico and South America; $135.00 other. World Aquaculture Society, 143 J.M. Parker Coliseum, LSU, Baton Rouge LA 70803. **Tel** (504)388-3137, FAX (504)388-3493. **ED** Ronald L. Thune. **DD** 639. **CODEN** JWASE7. Index available. **Bk Rev. Circ:** 3,000 (ctrl). Documents available from BIOSIS Document Express, CASDDS. ***Continues*** *Journal of the World Mariculture Society, 0735-0147.*
Desc: Publishes papers concerning all aspects of the production of aquatic animals and plants for food. A partial list of species which are considered includes shrimp, lobster, oysters, clams, trout, catfish, tilapia and other finfish. Offers state-of-the-art information for researchers, students and entrepreneurs involved in the production of high quality seafood in culture.
Ind/Abst Anim. Breed. Abstr.; Aquat. Sci. Fish. Abstr. (Computer File); Biol. Abstr. (1987-); Chem. Abstr. (1986); Ecol. Abstr.; Fish Rev.; Geogr. Abstr. Phys. Geogr.; Geogr. Abstr. Human Geogr.; Helminthol. Abstr. (1991-); Index Vet.; Int. Dev. Abstr.; Nematol. Abstr.; Nutr. Abstr. Rev., Ser. B, Live Feeds and Feed.; Ocean. Abstr.; Protozoolog. Abstr.; Soyabean Abstr.; Vet. Bull.; Wildl. Rev.; World Agric. Econ.

IO/0216-8316
JURNAL PENELITIAN PASCA PANEN PERIKANAN. **Added/Corp** Balai Penelitian Perikanan Laut (Indonesia). **VFOAT** Journal of Post-harvest Fisheries Research; Jurnal Pen. Pasca Panen Perikanan. (1986)-. Periodical. Indonesian (English and Indonesian). Balai Penelitian Teknologi Perikanan, Jl K S Tubun, PO Box 30, Palmerah, Jakarta-Pusat Indonesia. **LC** SH307.I64; L36. ***Continues*** *Laporan Penelitian Teknologi Perikanan.*

IO/0216-7727
JURNAL PENELITIAN PERIKANAN LAUT. **Added/Corp** Balai Penelitian Perikanan Laut (Indonesia). **VFOAT** Journal of Marine Fisheries Research. Periodical. Multiple languages (English). Balai Penelitian Perikanan Laut, No.12 Sunda Kelapa, Jakarta. ***Continues*** *Laporan Penelitian Perikanan Laut.*

JA/0453-087X
KAGOSHIMA DAIGAKU SUISANGAKUBU KIYO. (KAGOSHIMA DAIGAKU SUISANGAKUBU KIYO. MEMOIRS OF THE FACULTY OF FISHERIES, KAGOSHIMA UNIVERSITY.). [Kagoshima Daigaku Suisangakubu kiyo]. **Added/Corp** Kagoshima Daigaku. Suisangakubu. Kagoshima Daigaku. Suisangakubu. Kagoshima Daigaku Suisangakubu Kiyo. Kagoshima Daigaku. Suisangakubu. Memoirs of the Faculty of Fisheries, Kagoshima University. **VFOAT** Memoirs of the Faculty of Fisheries, Kagoshima University. Vol. 2 (1952)-. Japanese. an. Kagoshima University / Fisheries, Faculty of Fisheries, Kagoshima Japan. **CODEN** KDSGA3. cum. index. Documents available from BIOSIS Document Express, CASDDS. ***Continues*** *Kagoshima Suisan Senmongakko. Kenkyu Hokoku.*
Ind/Abst Biol. Abstr.; Chem. Abstr.

JA
KANAGAWA-KEN SUISAN SHIKENJO KENKYU HOKOKU. **VFOAT** Bulletin of the Kanagawa Prefectural Fishery Experiment Station. No. 1- (1980)-. Japanese. Kanagawa-ken Suisan Shikenjo, Jogashima Misakicho Miura-shi, Kanagawa-ken 238-02 Japan. **LC** PAR.

JA
KANAGAWA-KEN TANSUIGYO ZOSHOKU SHIKENJO HOKOKU. **Main/Corp** Kanagawa-Ken Tansuigyo Zoshoku Shikenjo. Japanese. Kanagawa-Ken Tansuigyo Zoshoku Shikenjo Hokoku, 1902-3 Shimomizo 229, Sagamihara Japan. **LC** SH159; .K28A.

TH/0453-3453
KASETSART UNIVERSITY FISHERY RESEARCH BULLETIN. [Kasetsart Univ. fish. res. bull.]. **Main/Corp** Kasetsart University. Faculty of Fisheries. No. 1 (Dec. 1964)-. Bulletin. English. Price varies per volume. Kasetsart University Main Library, Bangkok 9 Thailand. **DD** 639. **CODEN** KUFRAM. **Circ:** 500. Documents available from BIOSIS Document Express.
Desc: Composed of one or two research publications.
Ind/Abst Biol. Abstr.; GeoRef.

JA
KENKYU HOKOKU. **Main/Corp** Enyo Suisan Kenkyujo. **VFOAT** Bulletin; F.S.F.R.L. Bulletin; Enyo Suisan Kenkyujo Kenkyu Hokoku. Vol. 1 (1969)-. Periodical. Japanese. Far Seas Fisheries Research Laboratory, 7-1 5 Chome, Orido Shimizu 424 Japan. **Tel** 0543-34-0715. **LC** SH1; .E58.

UK/0953-8348
KEY INDICATORS. [Key indic.]. (1988)-. English. qt. £35.00. Sea Fish Industry Authority, 18 Logie Mill, Logie Green Road, Edinburgh EH7 4HG Scotland. **Tel** 011 44 31 558-3331 ext. 256, FAX 011 44 31 558-1442. **DD** 338.37270941.
Desc: Contains information and statistical analyses of fish landings, the fishing fleet, imports and exports, and fish purchases in the United Kingdom.

JA
KUMAMOTO-KEN SUISAN SHIKENJO KENKYU HOKOKU. **Main/Corp** Kumamoto-ken Suisan Shikenjo. **VFOAT** Report of the Kumamoto Prefectural Fisheries Experimental Station. No. 1- ; 1979-. Japanese (Japanese). an. Kumamoto-Ken Suisan Shikenjo Kusuuramachi, Kumamoto-ken 863, Hondo Japan. **LC** SH109; .K84A.

JA
KYOTO FURITSU KAIYO SENTA KENKYU RONBUN. **VFOAT** Special Report. Vol. 1- (March 1982)-. Japanese (summaries and/or abstracts in English). Kyoto Furitsu Kaiyo Senta, (Kyoto Inst. of Oceanic & Fishery Science), Odashukuno, Miyazushi, Kyotofu 626 Japan. **LC** SH301; .K94.

JA/0285-6921
KYUSHU DAIGAKU NOGAKUBU FUZOKU SUISAN JIKKENJO HOKOKU. [Rep. Fish. Res. Lab., Kyushu Univ.]. **Main/Corp** Kyushu Daigaku. Nogakubu. Suisan Jikkenjo. **VFOAT** Report of Fishery Research Laboratory, Kyushu University. Academic Scholarly Publication. Japanese (English; summaries and/or abstracts in Japanese, English and Japanese). Kyushu Daigaku Nogakubu Fuzoku Suisan Jikkenjo, (Fishery Research Lab., Faculty of Agriculture, Kyushu University), Tsuyazakimachi, Munakatagun, Fukuokaken 811-33 Japan. **LC** SH301. **DD** 639/.3/0952. **CODEN** RFRUDW. Documents available from CASDDS.
Ind/Abst Chem. Abstr. (1971-1981).

US/0736-5586
LAKE POWELL FISHERIES INVESTIGATIONS. [Lake Powell fish. invest.]. English. an. **LC** SK453; .A25 subser; QL628.U8. **DD** 333.95/4 S; 333.95/611/0979251. ***Continues*** *Lake Powell Post-Impoundment Investigations, 0149-9564.*

GW/0072-3665
LAND- UND FORSTWIRTSCHAFT, FISCHEREI. REIHE 3 : VIEHWIRTSCHAFT. **Main/Corp** Germany (West). Statistisches Bundesamt. 1960-. German. ir. W Kohlhammer Verlag GMBH, Postfach 800430, D70549 Stuttgart Germany. **Tel** 011 49 711 78631. ***Supersedes*** *Germany (Federal Republic, 1949-) Statistische Berichte; Germany (Fedearl Republic, 1949-) Viehwirtschaft.*
Desc: Issued in pts: 1. Viehbestand; 2. Milch; 3. Schlachtungen und Fleischgewinnung; 4. Schlachttier- und Fleischbeschau; 5. Geflugel. (Some pts. continue the numbering of the Statistiche Berichts).

BE/0779-1119
LARVICULTURE & ARTEMIA NEWSLETTER. [Larvic. artemia newsl.]. **VFOAT** Larviculture and Artemia Newsletter. (1990)-. Periodical. English. qt. $35.00. Laboratory of Aquaculture, Artemia Reference Center, Rijksuniversiteit Gent, Rozier 44, B-9000 Gent Belgium. **Tel** 011 32 91 643754, FAX 011 32 91 644193. **(Subscription address:** Dr David Bengtson, University of Rhode Island, Dept of Zoology, Kingston RI 02881**) UDC** 595.3. ***Continues*** *Artemia Newsletter, 0775-454X.*

US/0080-2808
LAW OF THE SEA INSTITUTE: OCCASIONAL PAPERS. See Earth Sciences-Oceanography.

CN/0250-7811
LIST OF FISHING VESSELS - NORTHWEST ATLANTIC FISHERIES ORGANIZATION. (LIST OF FISHING VESSELS.). [List fish. vessels - Northwest Atl. Fish. Organ.]. (1980)-. English. te. Northwest Atlantic Fisheries Organization / NAFO, PO Box 638, Dartmouth Nova Scotia B2Y 3Y9 Canada. **Tel** (902)469-9105, telex 019-31475. **LC** SH344.8.B6; L57. **DD** 387.2/8/091634. ***Continues*** *List of Fishing Vessels, 0303-6138.*

US/0890-5207
LODE STAR, THE. (THE LODE STAR / ALASKA FISHERIES DEVELOPMENT FOUNDATION.). [Lode star]. **Added/Corp** Alaska Writers Group. Alaska Fisheries Development Foundation. **VFOAT** Lodestar Update; Lodestar. (198?)-. Periodical. English. qt. $30.00. Alaska Fisheries Development Foundation, 508 West 2nd Avenue, Suite 212, Anchorage AK 99501. **Tel** (907)276-7315. **DD** 338.
Ind/Abst Foods Adlibra.

US/0360-005X
MAINE FISH AND WILDLIFE. [Maine fish wildl.]. **Added/Corp** Maine. Dept. of Inland Fisheries and Game. Vol. 17 (Winter 1974/1975)-. Periodical. English. qt. $9.00 (one year), $15.00 (two year), $20.00 (three year). Maine Fish & Wildlife, 284 State Street, Station 41, Augusta ME 04333. **Tel** (207)287-5246, (800)288-8387. **(Subscription address:** CDS Agency Hard Copy, PO Box 4966, Des Moines, IA 50340; Phone: (515)247-7569**)** **ED** W. Thomas Shoener. **LC** SH11; .M204. **DD** 639/.97/605. **CODEN** MFWIDY. **Bk Rev**. **Circ:** 15,000. ***Continues*** *Maine Fish and Game.*
Desc: Describes the work of the Maine Fish and Wildlife Department, plus many articles on hunting, fishing, trapping, fly tying, and outdoor recreation.
Ind/Abst Fish Rev.; Wildl. Rev.

CU/0025-2735
MAR Y PESCA. ***Suspended.*** [Mar pesca]. No. 1-1956; New Ser. No. 1- Oct. 1965-?. Periodical. Spanish. mo. $20.00 US. Ediciones Cubanas, Obispo 527, Altos ESQ Bernaza, CP 10100 Havana Cuba. **Tel** 011 632980, 631942, FAX 011 631011, telex 512337, 6540. **LC** SH1; .M29. **DD** 639/.22/0916365. **Bk Rev**. **Ad Acc**. **Circ:** 30,000.
Desc: An illustrated magazine on topics related to fishing and sea navigation, scientific-technical developments and other activities in the sea.
Ind/Abst Aquat. Sci. Fish. Abstr. (Computer File).

US/0195-4555
MARINE FISH MANAGEMENT. (19??)-. English. mo. $87.50 (surface mail); $132.50 (airmail). Nautilus Press, 1045 National Press Building, Washington DC 20045. **Tel** (202)347-6643. **ED** John R. Botzum. **Bk Rev**.
Desc: Reports on fisheries in the US 200 mile zone, with special attention to the regional fishery councils and US fisheries policy.

US/1045-3555
MARINE FISH MONTHLY. [Mar. fish mon.]. (198?)-. Periodical. English. Twelve times a year. $20.00. Publishing Concepts, 3243 Highway 61 East, Luttrett TN 37779. **Tel** (615)992-3892, FAX (615)992-5259. **ED** Boyce E. Phipps. **DD** 639. cum. index. **Bk Rev**, (Qty: 3). **Ad Acc**, **Adv Mgr Tel** (615)992-3892. **Circ:** 32,000 (ctrl).

II
MARINE FISHERIES INFORMATION SERVICE. TECHNICAL AND EXTENSION SERIES. **Added/Corp** Central Marine Fisheries Research Institute. Indian Council of Agricultural Research. **VFOAT** Technical and Extension Series. No. 1 (Sept. 1978)-. Periodical. English. mo.
Ind/Abst Aquat. Sci. Fish. Abstr. (Computer File); Ocean. Abstr.; Life Sci. Collect.

US/0730-3394
MARINE FISHERIES MANAGEMENT REPORTER. ***Ceased.*** [Mar. fish. manage. rep.]. No. 1 (Aug. 1982)-(May 1994). Periodical. English. Six times a year. Jonathan Publishing Company, 3604 Pinnacle Road, Austin TX 78746. **Tel** (504)328-2480. **ED** Gary Knight. **Circ:** 150.
Desc: Five-volume, loose-leaf service covering all documents related to marine fisheries management - statutes, treaties, regulations and legal opinions.

SI
MARINE FISHERIES RESEARCH DEPARTMENT ANNUAL REPORT. **Main/Corp** Southeast Asian Fisheries Development Center. Marine Fisheries Research Dept. (1971)-. English. an. Free on request. Southeast Asian Fisheries Development / Thailand, 956 Rama IV Road Olympia Boulevard, Bangkok 10500 Thailand. **Tel** 011 66 2 2352071. **LC** SH295; .S63. **DD** 639/.2/072059. ***Continues*** *Southeast Asian Fisheries Development Center. Marine Fisheries Research Dept. Annual Report, (DLC) 87642191.*

US/0090-1830
MARINE FISHERIES REVIEW. [Mar. fish. rev.]. **Added/Corp** United States. National Marine Fisheries Service. Vol. 34, No. 7/8 (July/Aug. 1972)-. Government Publication. English. qt. $7.00 domestic; $8.75 other. Superintendent of Documents, US Government Printing Office, Washington DC 20402. **Tel** (202)275-3328, FAX (202)786-2377. **ED** Willis Hobart. **LC** SH11; .A4463. **DD** 338.3/72/7092. **CODEN** MFSRA4. Index available. cum. index. **Bk Rev**. **Pr Rev**. **Circ:** 2,400. available on microfilm and microfiche from University Microfilms International (UMI); available on an online database (file 648/Full-Text) from DIALOG. Documents available from BIOSIS Document Express, Documents on Demand. ***Continues*** *Commercial Fisheries Review, 0010-2989.*
Desc: Emphasizes developments that are relevant to the marine fisheries industries, such as: review articles on fishing areas and marine life; seafood preparation, preservation and marketing; in-depth specialized articles related to the industries, etc.
Ind/Abst Acad. Search (July 1993-); Am. Stat. Index; AQUAREF; Aquat. Sci. Fish. Abstr. (Computer File); Biol. Agric. Index; Biol. Abstr.; Bus. Index (1985-); Curr. Ref. Fish Res.; Ecol. Abstr.; Energy Res. Abstr. (Oct. 1975-); Fish Rev.; Food Sci. Technol. Abstr.; Foods Adlibra; Gen. BusinessFile (1985-); Gen. Period. Index (1985-); Geogr. Abstr. Human Geogr.; INFO-SOUTH Abstr.; Int. Dev. Abstr.; Mag. Search; Middle East Abstr. Index; Ocean. Abstr.; PAIS Int. Print (1991-?); Life Sci. Collect.; Pollut. Abstr. Indexes; Trade Ind. Index (1981-?); Wildl. Rev.; World Agric. Econ.

US/0161-522X
MARINE RECREATIONAL FISHERIES. No. 1- 1976-. English. an. $15.00. Sport Fishing Institute, 1010 Massachusetts Avenue Northwest, Suite 320, Washington DC 20001. **Tel** (202)898-0770. **LC** SH328; .M36. **DD** 333.95/6.
Ind/Abst Fish Rev.

US
MARINE RECREATIONAL FISHERY STATISTICS SURVEY. PACIFIC COAST. **See** Fish and Fisheries-Abstracting, Bibliographies and Statistics.

US/0738-1360
MARINE RESOURCE ECONOMICS. [Marin. resour. econ.]. Vol. 1, No. 1 (1984)-. Periodical. English. qt. $100.00 (1 year), $195.00 (2 year), $386.00 (3 year). American Seafood Institute, 212 Main Street, Suite 3, Wakefield RI 02879. **Tel** (800)328-3474, (401)783-4200, FAX (401)789-9727. **ED** Jon G Sutinen (editor's address: Department of Resource Economics, University of Rhode Island, Kingston RI 02881). **LC** SH328; .M38. **DD** 338.3/72/05. **CODEN** JMREDD. **[CCC]**. **Ad Acc**. available on microfilm from University Microfilms International (UMI).
Desc: Publishes studies of biological, social, political, legal and other issues clearly linked to economic factors. Papers present new theoretical and empirical developments, new techniques for practical application and analyses of institutions and policies related to the economics of marine resources.
Ind/Abst Contents Recent Econ. J.; Curr. Aware. Biol. Sci., CABS; Econ. Lit. Index; Environ. Period. Bibliogr.; Geogr. Abstr. Human Geogr.; J. Econ. Lit.; Mar. Sci. Contents Tables; Life Sci. Collect.; Pollut. Abstr. Indexes; Soyabean Abstr. (?-?).

US/0749-2006
MARLIN. [Marlin]. **Added/Corp** Marlin International Association. (198?)-. Periodical. English. bm (6 issues). $24.95 US: $45.00 other. World Publications, Inc., PO Box 2456, 809 South Orlando Ave., Winter Park FL 32790. **Tel** (407)628-4802, (800)394-6006. **ED** Wade Leftwich. **DD** 799. **Ad Acc**. **Circ:** 25,000.
Desc: Contains the latest news and articles on the world of off-shore fishing. Marlin, sailfish and other big game varieties of fish are covered in each publication.

US/0195-007X
MARYLAND ANGLER, THE. Vol. 1, Aug. (1978)-. Periodical. English. mo (12 issues). $12.00 one year, $22.00 two years. Maryland Angler, PO Box 2, Long Green MD 21092. **Tel** (301)592-5268.

US/0095-3334
MASSACHUSETTS LANDINGS, ANNUAL SUMMARY. English. an. US Department of Commerce / National Marine Fisheries Service, 1335 East-West Highway, Silver Spring MD 20910. **Tel** (301)713-2239, FAX (301)713-2258. **LC** SH11; .M75A. **DD** 338.3/72/70920744.

II/0253-9314
MATSYA. [Matsya]. **Added/Corp** Indian Society of Ichthyologists. No. 1 (1975)-. Academic Scholarly Publication. English. an. Price varies. Indian Society of Ichthyologists, 100 Santhome High Road, Madras 60028 India. **(Subscription address:** Prints India, 11 Darya Ganj, New Delhi, 110002 India, (Phone: 011 91 11 3268645)**)** **ED** K V Rama Rao. **CODEN** MTSYDO. **Bk Rev**. **Ad Acc**. Documents available from CASDDS.
Ind/Abst Chem. Abstr. (1975-1979).

JA/0018-3466
MEMOIRS OF THE FACULTY OF FISHERIES, HOKKAIDO UNIVERSITY. [Mem. Fac. Fish., Hokkaido Univ.]. **Main/Corp** Hokkaido Daigaku, Sapporo, Japan. Suisangakubu, Hakodate. Vol. 1 (Mar. 1953)-. Periodical. English. sa. Hokkaido University / Faculty of Fisheries, 3 1 1 C Minato-machi, Hakodate Hokkaido 041, Japan. **DD** 597. **CODEN** MFHOA8. Documents available from BIOSIS Document Express.
Ind/Abst Aquat. Sci. Fish. Abstr. (Computer File); Biol. Abstr.; Ecology Abstr.; Ocean. Abstr.; Life Sci. Collect.

US/0274-4783
MICHIGAN FISHERMAN, THE. ***Title Change.*** (197?)-(199?). Periodical. English. bm. Michigan Fisherman Inc, PO Box 977, East Lansing MI 48823. **Tel** (517)351-3074. ***Continued by*** *Michigan Hunting & Fishing, 1057-2856.*

JA/0915-0471
MIE DAIGAKU SEIBUTSU SHIGEN GAKUBU KIYO. **Added/Corp** Mie Daigaku. Seibutsu Shigen Gakubu. **VFOAT** Bulletin of the Faculty of Bioresources, Mie University. (1988)-. Japanese (English). Mie University / Agriculture, Faculty of Agriculture, Tsu Japan. Documents available from CASDDS. ***Formed by the union of*** *Mie Daigaku Nogakubu Gakujutsu Hokoku* ***and*** *Bulletin of the Faculty of Fisheries, Mie University.*
Ind/Abst Chem. Abstr.; Field Crop Abstr.; Food Sci. Technol. Abstr.; For. Prod. Abstr. (1991-); For. Abstr.; Hortic. Abstr.; Leis. Recreat. Tour. Abstr.; Postharvest News Inf.; Rice Abstr.

US
MISCELLANEOUS REPORT - BUREAU OF FISHERIES LABORATORY. **Main/Corp** Bureau of Fisheries Laboratory. Monographic series. English. Price varies per volume. Division of Fish Game and Shellfisheries, Bureau of Fisheries Laboratory, Trenton NJ 08625. ***Continues*** *Miscellaneous Report -Freshwater Fisheries Laboratory, 0275-2018.*

US/0098-0803
MISSISSIPPI LANDINGS, ANNUAL SUMMARY. English. an. US Department of Commerce / National Marine Fisheries Service, 1335 East-West Highway, Silver Spring MD 20910. **Tel** (301)713-2239, FAX (301)713-2258. **LC** SH11; .M73A. **DD** 338.3/72/70920762.

GW/0436-6425
MITTEILUNGEN AUS DEM INSTITUT FUER SEEFISCHEREI DER BUNDESFORSCHUNGSANSTALT FUER FISCHEREI. **Main/Corp** Institut fur Seefischerei. (1953)-. Monographic series. German. **DD** 597. ***Continues*** *Institut fur Seefischerei. Mitteilungen aus dem Institut fur Seefischerei der Bundesanstalt fur Fischerei.*
Ind/Abst Ocean. Abstr.

CN/0705-4149
MONDE AQUATIQUE. (LE MONDE AQUATIQUE.). **Added/Corp** Association Regionale des Aquariophiles de Quebec. (Nov. 1971)-. Periodical. French. Twelve times a year. $38.00 Canada; $30.26 US. Association Regionale Aquariophiles de Quebec Inc, CP 9574, C/O Luc Carrier, Ste Foy QUE G1V 4C2 Canada. **Tel** (418)653-3961. **DD** 639/.34/05.

US/0362-1715
MONOGRAPH - AMERICAN FISHERIES SOCIETY. [Monogr. - Am. Fish. Soc.]. **Main/Corp** American Fisheries Society. No. 1 (1976)-. Academic Scholarly Publication. English. ir. Price varies per volume. American Fisheries Society, 5410 Grosvenor Lane, Suite 110, Bethesda MD 20814-2199. **Tel** (301)897-8616, (301)897-8621, FAX (301)897-8096. **ED** Robert Kendall. **CODEN** MAFCDW. **[CCC]**. **Circ:** 2,000. Documents available from CASDDS.
Desc: Comprehensive field or laboratory research studies of fish biology and ecology that have a direct or ultimate bearing on fishery resource management.
Ind/Abst Chem. Abstr. (1976-1978).

CN
MONTHLY REVIEW OF CANADIAN FISHERIES STATISTICS. **See** Fish and Fisheries-Abstracting, Bibliographies and Statistics.

PH/0116-290X
NAGA, THE ICLARM QUARTERLY. **Added/Corp** International Center for Living Aquatic Resources Management. **VFOAT** NAGA, The I.C.L.A.R.M. Quarterly; ICLARM Quarterly. **VAT** NAGA, The International Center for Living Aquatic Resources Management Quarterly. Vol. 9, No. 1 (Jan. 1986)-. Periodical. English. Four times a year (Jan., Apr., July, Oct.). Free on request, surface mail; $20.00 airmail. International Center for Living Aquatic Resources Management, MCPO Box 2631, 0718 Makati, MM, Philippines. **Tel** 011 63 2 8180466, 011 63 2 8189283, FAX 011 63 2 8163183, telex 64794. **ED** J. L. Maclean. Index available (irregular). **Bk Rev**. **Ad Acc**. **Circ:** 4,000. ***Continues*** *ICLARM Newsletter;* ***Absorbed*** *Fishbyte, 0116-0079; Aquabyte, 0116-6972; Tropical Coastal Area Management, 0116-4082.*
Desc: General and technical articles, news, literature, and notices of meetings in courses in fisheries and aquaculture, especially in tropical and developing countries.

Ind/Abst Agrofor. Abstr. (1991-); Aquat. Sci. Fish. Abstr. (Computer File); For. Abstr.; Philip. Sci. Technol. Abstr.; Soils Fert.

KO
NAKSSI CHUNCHU. Periodical. Korean. mo. W36,000. Nakssi Chunchusa, 141 Songwol-dong Chongno-ku, Seoul 110 Korea. **LC** SH667.K8; N35.

JA
NANSEI KAIKU SUISAN KENKYUJO CHOSA HOKOKU. **Main/Corp** Nansei Kaiku Suisan Kenkyujo (Japan). No. 1 (1977)-. Periodical. Japanese. ir. Suisancho Nansei Kaiku Suisan Kenkyujo, (Nansei Regional Fisheries Research Lab, Fisheries Agency), 7782-9 Maruishi Onomachi, Saekigun Hiroshimaken 739-04 Japan. **LC** SH302.I54; N35a.

JA/0388-841X
NANSEI KAIKU SUISAN KENKYUJO KENKYU HOKOKU. [Nansei Kaiku Suisan Kenkyujo kenkyu hokoku]. **Main/Corp** Nansei Kaiku Suisan Kenkyujo (Japan). **VFOAT** Bulletin of the Nansei Regional Fisheries Research Laboratory. Began in 1968. Academic Scholarly Publication. Japanese (summaries and/or abstracts in English). an. Suisancho Nansei Kaiku Suisan Kenkyujo, (Nansei Regional Fisheries Research Lab., Fihseries Agency), 7782-9, Maruishi, Onomachi, Saekigun, Hiroshimaken 739-04, Japan. **CODEN** NRFBAK. Documents available from CASDDS.
Ind/Abst AGRICOLA; Chem. Abstr.

US/0027-9250
NATIONAL FISHERMAN. [Nal. fisherman]. Vol. 35, No. 5 (June 1954)-. Periodical. English. mo. $22.95 US; $32.95 other. Journal Publications, 120 Tillson Avenue, Suite 201, Rockland ME 04841. **Tel** (207)594-6222, FAX (207)594-8978. **(Subscription address:** National Fisherman, PO Box 908, Rockland ME 04841.**) ED** Jim Fullilove. **LC** SH1; .A8. **DD** 338.3727. Index available. **Bk Rev. Ad Acc. Circ:** 50,000. available on microfilm and microfiche from University Microfilms International (UMI); available on an online database (file 648/Full-Text) from DIALOG. ***Continues*** *Atlantic Fisherman, 0097-7101;* ***Absorbed*** *Maine Coast Fisherman; Pacific Fisherman, 0096-2864.*
Desc: Focus on commercial fishing. Articles and news stories are also of interest to boatbuilders and pleasure boaters.
Ind/Abst Aquat. Sci. Fish. Abstr. (Computer File); Bus. Index (1985-); Gen. BusinessFile (1985-); Gen. Period. Index (1985-); Health Source (Jul. 1993-); Mag. Search; Trade Ind. Index (1981-); Vocat. Search (Jan. 1993-).

US
NATIONAL FRESH WATER FISHING. (19??)-. English. an (Apr.). $7.00. Fresh Water Fishing Hall of Fame, PO Box 33, Hayward WI 54843. **Tel** (715)634-4440.
Desc: News and information about fresh water fishing.

US/0092-1734
NEW FISHING (NEW YORK). ***Title Change.*** (NEW FISHING.). English. an. Maco Publishing Company, 699 Madison Avenue, New York NY 10021. **Tel** (212)490-0172. **LC** SH401; .F582. **DD** 799.1/05. ***Supersedes*** *Fishing Guidebook.* ***Continued by*** *Fishing Guidebook.*

US/1054-4623
NEW JERSEY LAKE SURVEY FISHING MAPS GUIDE. [N. J. lake surv. fish. maps guide]. (1991)-. English. an. $8.95 ($1.55 postage). Comtech Lithographics Inc, POB 536, Building 20, 7300 Rt 130 North, Pennsauken NJ 08110. **Tel** (609)665-8350, FAX (609)665-8656. **(Subscription address:** New Jersey Sportsmen's Guides, PO Box 100, Somerdale, NJ 08083**) ED** Steve Perrone. **DD** 799. **Ad Acc, Adv Mgr:** Steve Perrone. **Pr Rev. Circ:** 6000. ***Continues*** *New Jersey Lake Survey Map Guide, 1043-6405.*
Desc: Edited for freshwater fishing for trout, bass, perch, catfish and other species. Contains 128 pages and approx. 112 full page maps of the surveyed lakes that illustrate contours, depths, bottom characteristics, shorelines and vegetation present at each location.

NZ
NEW ZEALAND CENSUS OF FISHING. ***Title Change.*** English. bm (five issues per year). Department of Statistics / New Zealand, PO Box 2922, Wellington New Zealand. **Tel** 011 64 4 4954600. **LC** SH318.5; .N48. **DD** 338.3/72/09931. ***Continued by*** *Economy Wide Census : Agricultural Services, Forestry and Fisheries.*
Desc: Contains statistics obtained from the first integrated economic census of fishing.

NZ/0113-2288
NEW ZEALAND FISHERIES DATA REPORT. [N.Z. fish. data rep.]. (1987)-. Monographic series. English. ir. Price varies per volume. **DD** 639.209931. ***Continues*** *Fisheries Research Division Occasional Publication. Data Series, 0111-5332.*
Ind/Abst Aquat. Sci. Fish. Abstr. (Computer File).

NZ/0113-227X
NEW ZEALAND FISHERIES OCCASIONAL PUBLICATION. [N.Z. fish. occas. publ.]. (1987)-. Monographic series. English. bm. Price varies per volume. **DD** 597.09931 639.209931. ***Continues*** *Occasional Publication - Fisheries Research Division, 0110-1765.*
Ind/Abst Aquat. Sci. Fish. Abstr. (Computer File).

NZ/0113-2261
NEW ZEALAND FISHERIES RESEARCH BULLETIN. [N. Z. fish. res. bull.]. **Added/Corp** MAFFish (Organization : New Zealand). No. 28 (1987)-. Bulletin. English. Price varies per volume. **CODEN** NZFBEC. Documents available from BIOSIS Document Express. ***Continues*** *Fisheries Research Bulletin (Wellington, N.Z.), 0110-1749.*
Ind/Abst Aquat. Sci. Fish. Abstr. (Computer File); Biol. Abstr.

NZ/0113-2180
NEW ZEALAND FISHERIES TECHNICAL REPORT. **Added/Corp** MAFFish (Organization : New Zealand). (1987)-. Monographic series. English. ir. Price varies per volume. New Zealand Marine Science Society, PO Box 297, Wellington New Zealand. **Tel** 011 64 4 861029. ***Continues in part*** *Fisheries Research Division Occasional Publication, 0110-1765.*
Ind/Abst Aquat. Sci. Fish. Abstr. (Computer File).

NZ/0113-9606
NEW ZEALAND FISHERMAN. **See** Recreation, Leisure-Sports.

CN/0576-0917
NEWFOUNDLAND FISHERIES. **Main/Corp** Canada. Fisheries and Marine Service. Newfoundland Region. English. Fisheries and Marine Service Newfoundland Region, 116 Lisgar Street, Ottawa Ontario K1A 0E6 Canada. **LC** SH224.N7; C36A. **DD** 354/.71/008236.

AT
NEWSDATA. (19??)-. English. mo. 60.00Aus$. National Fishing Industry Training Resource Centre, GPO Box 2851AA, Melbourne VIC 3001 Australia. **Tel** 011 61 3 6451088, FAX 011 61 3 6451740. **ED** Kathy Avingy. **Circ:** 150 (ctrl).
Desc: Offers broad coverage of major fishing industry topics within each State of Australia.

CN/0828-7236
NEWSLETTER (GOLDEN RODS & REELS, VICTORIA, B.C.). (NEWSLETTER / GOLDEN RODS & REELS, VICTORIA, B.C. SENIORS' FISHING CLUB.). [Newsl. - Golden Rod Reels Vic. B.C., Sr. Fish. Club]. Vol. 7, No. 9 (Sept. 1984)-. Newsletter. English. mo. Golden Rods & Reels, 4 Centennial Square, Victoria British Columbia V8W 1P7 Canada. **DD** 799.1/06/071134. ***Continues*** *News-Letter (Victoria Golden Rods and Reels), 0715-5107.*

US/1067-4454
NFI BLUE BOOK. (NFI BLUE BOOK / NATIONAL FISHERIES INSTITUTE.). [NFI blue book]. **Main/Corp** National Fisheries Institute. **VFOAT** Blue Book. (1984)-. English. ir. National Fisheries Institute, 1525 Wilson Boulevard, Suite 500, Arlington VA 22209. **Tel** (703)524-8880. **DD** 639. ***Continues*** *National Fisheries Institute. Blue Book, 0731-8847.*

JA/0021-4620
NIHON KAIKU SUISAN KENKYUJO KENKYU. (NIHON KAIKU SUISAN KENKYUJO KINKYU HOKOKU.). [Nihon Kaiku Suisan Kenkyujo kenkyu]. **Main/Corp** Nihon Kaiku Suisan Kenkyujo, Niigata. **VFOAT** Bulletin of the Japan Sea Regional Fisheries Research Laboratory. No. 1 (March 1951)-. Monographic series. Japanese. Price varies per volume. **LC** SH1; .N58. **DD** 639. **CODEN** TSKKA9. Documents available from BIOSIS Document Express.
Ind/Abst Biol. Abstr.; Life Sci. Collect. (1985-).

JA/0021-5392
NIHON SUISAN GAKKAI SHI. ***Title Change.*** [Nippon Suisan Gakkaishi]. **Main/Corp** Nihon Suisan Gakkai. **Added/Corp** Nihon Suisan Gakkai. Bulletin. **VFOAT** Bulletin of the Japanese Society of Scientific Fisheries. Vol. 1 (1932)-(19??). Academic Scholarly Publication. Japanese (English; summaries and/or abstracts in English; table of contents in English). mo. Nihon Suisan Gakkai, (Japanese Soc. of Scientific Fisheries), c/o Tokyo Suisan Daigaku, 5-7, Konan 4 Chome, Minatoku, Tokyoto 108, Japan. **(Subscription address:** Maruzen Company Ltd., PO Box 5050, Import & Export Department, Tokyo 100 31 Japan.**) ED** Tamotsu Iuai. **LC** SH1; .N5. **CODEN** NSUGAF. **[CCC]. Ad Acc. Pr Rev. Circ:** 4,400 (ctrl). Documents available from The Genuine Article, BIOSIS Document Express, CASDDS. ***Split into*** *Fisheries Science* ***and*** *Bulletin of the Japanese Society of Scientific Fisheries.*
Ind/Abst Aquat. Sci. Fish. Abstr. (Computer File); Biodeter. Abstr.; Biol. Abstr.; Chem. Abstr.; Curr. Contents, Agric. Biol. Environ. Sci.; Curr. Ref. Fish Res.; Fish Rev. (Jan. 1989-July 1992); Food Sci. Technol. Abstr.; Leadscan; Nutr. Abstr. Rev., Ser. B, Live Feeds and Feed.; Nutr. Abstr. Rev., Ser. A, Hum. Exp.; Life Sci. Collect.; Pollut. Abstr. Indexes; Res. Alert [Full Cov.]; Rev. Med. Vet. Entomol.; Sci. Cit. Index (19??-19??); SCISEARCH; Wildl. Rev. (Jan. 1989-July 1992).

JA/0303-0245
NIIGATA-KEN SUISAN SHIKENJO NEMPO. [Niigata-ken Suisan Shikenjo nenpo]. **Main/Corp** Niigata-ken Suisan Shikenjo. Japanese. an. Niigata-Ken Suisan Shikenjo, 2-ban 4-go Bandaijima, Niigata 950 Japan. **LC** SH301; .N6A.

US/1060-3654
NMFS FISHERIES MARKET NEWS REPORT. [NMFS fish. mark. news rep.]. **Added/Corp** United States. National Marine Fisheries Service. **VAT** National Marine Fisheries Service Fisheries Market News Report. Vol. 1, No. 17 (Thursday, Mar. 28, 1991)-. Periodical. English. tw. $239.00. Urner Barry Publications Inc., PO Box 389, Toms River NJ 08754. **Tel** (908)240-5330, (800)932-0617, FAX (908)341-0891. **LC** HD9454; .F585. **DD** 338. ***Continues*** *Fisheries Market News Report (Toms River, N.J.), 1055-2766.*

SW/1100-4096
NORDIC JOURNAL OF FRESHWATER RESEARCH. [Nord. j. freshw. res.]. **Added/Corp** Sotvattenslaboratoriet (Sweden). No. 64 (1988)-. English. an. Kr250.00. Institute of Freshwater Research, S-170-11 Drottningholm Sweden. **Tel** 11 46 8 7590040. **ED** Lennart Nyman. **LC** SH287; .D73. **DD** 591.92/948. **CODEN** NJFREG. Documents available from BIOSIS Document Express. ***Continues*** *Report (Sotvattenslaboratoriet (Sweden)), 0082-0032.*
Ind/Abst Biol. Abstr. (1991-); Fish Rev. (Jan. 1989-July 1992); Fresh. Aqua. Contents Tables (1991-); Wildl. Rev. (Jan. 1989-July 1992).

JA
NORIN GYOGYO JOHO. **Added/Corp** Japan. Kanto Noseikyoku. Tokei Johobu. (1962)-. Periodical. Japanese. mo. Norin Tokei Kyokai, (Association of Agriculture & Forestry Statistics), 11-14, Meguro 2 Chome, Meguroku, Tokyoto 153, Japan. **LC** HD2095.K37; N6.

US/1043-2450
NORTH AMERICAN FISHERMAN. (NORTH AMERICAN FISHERMAN : OFFICIAL PUBLICATION OF THE NORTH AMERICAN FISHING CLUB.). [North Am. fisherman]. **Added/Corp** North American Fishing Club. **VFOAT** Fisherman. Vol. 1, No. 1 (June/July 1988)-. Periodical. English. Six times a year. $18.00. North American Outdoor Group Inc, 12301 Whitewater Drive, Suite 260, Minnetonka MN 55343. **Tel** (612)936-0555, FAX (612)936-9755. **(Subscription address:** PO Box 3403, Minnetonka MN 55343**) LC** WMLC 93/1962. **DD** 799. **Ad Acc. Circ:** 140,000.
Desc: Covers fishing across North America.

US/0275-5947
NORTH AMERICAN JOURNAL OF FISHERIES MANAGEMENT. [North Am. j. fish. manage.]. **Added/Corp** American Fisheries Society. Vol. 1, No. 1 (1981)-. Academic Scholarly Publication. English. qt. $425.00 US; $460.00 other (library). American Fisheries Society, 5410 Grosvenor Lane, Suite 110, Bethesda MD 20814-2199. **Tel** (301)897-8616, (301)897-8621, FAX (301)897-8096. **ED** Mercer H. Patriarche. **LC** SH221; .N67. **DD** 639.3/05. **CODEN** NAJMDP. **[CCC].** Index available (free). **Acid Free. Circ:** 3,000 (ctrl). Documents available from BIOSIS Document Express, CASDDS, Documents on Demand.
Desc: Addresses the maintenance, enhancement, and allocation of fisheries resources. Its contents chronicle the development of practical monitoring and management programs for marine and freshwater fisheries.
Ind/Abst Anim. Breed. Abstr.; AQUAREF; Aquat. Sci. Fish. Abstr. (Computer File); Biol. Agric. Index; Biol. Abstr.; Chem. Abstr.; Curr. Aware. Biol. Sci., CABS; Ecology Abstr.; Environ. Abstr.; Fish Rev.; Index Vet.; Leis. Recreat. Tour. Abstr.; Mar. Sci. Contents Tables; Ocean. Abstr.; Life Sci. Collect.; Risk Abstr.; Vet. Bull.

CN/1183-2428
NORTHERN AQUACULTURE. [North. aquac.]. Vol. 7, No. 1 (Jan./Feb. 1991)-. Periodical. English. Seven times a year. 20.00Can$ US, 30.00Can$ others; 50.00Can$ (individuals), 85.00Can$ (institutions) Comes with Aquaculture Association of Canada membership. Harrison House Publishers, 4611 William Head Road, Victoria British Columbia V8X 3W9 Canada. **Tel** (604)478-9209, FAX (604)478-1184. **LC** SH33; .N67. **DD** 639/.8/097. ***Continues*** *Canadian Aquaculture, 0832-722X.*
Ind/Abst Can. Period. Index (Jan. 1991-)(Vol. 7, no. 1 (Jan./Feb. 1991)-); Food Sci. Technol. Abstr.

NN
NOTES ET DOCUMENTS D'OCEANOGRAPHIE. (1978)-. Monographic series. French (English). ir. Price varies per volume. Mission ORSTOM, BP 76, Port-Vila Vanuatu. **LC** SH319.V35; N67. **DD** 639.2/099595.

CN/0822-8736
ONTARIO FISHERMAN. [Ont. fisherman]. (1979)-. Periodical. English. bm. 13.00Can$ Canada; 16.00Can$ other. Ontario Fisherman, R R 2, Wiarton

Fish and Fisheries

Ontario, N0H 2T0 Canada. **Tel** (519)534-2889, FAX (519)534-2770. **ED** Darryl Choronzey. **DD** 799.1/1/09713. **Ad Acc, Adv Mgr:** same as editor.
Desc: Fishing techniques, methods of conservation, ideal fishing locations.

KO
OOP KISUL. VFOAT Bulletin of the Korean Fisheries Technological Society. Periodical. Korean (summaries and/or abstracts in English). sa. Hanguk Oop Kisul Hakhoe, c/o Pusan Susan Taehak, Taeyon-dong Nam-ku, Pusan 601-01 Korea. **LC** SH334.5; .O57.
Ind/Abst Energy Res. Abstr. (April 1982-).

US
OREGON AGRICULTURE & FISHERIES STATISTICS. See Agriculture.

US/0731-3306
OREGON SALMON AND STEELHEAD SPORT CATCH STATISTICS. See Fish and Fisheries-Abstracting, Bibliographies and Statistics.

KO
OSON. VFOAT The Journal of Korea Fishing Vessel Association; Journal of Korea Fishing Vessel Association. Periodical. Korean (Korean). qt. Hanguk Oson Hyophoe, 1-573 Youido-dong, Yongdungpo-ku, Seoul Korea. **LC** SH344.8.B6; O85.

AU/0029-9987
OSTERREICHS FISCHEREI. (1948)-. German (English). Eight times a year. $27.00 Austria; $33.00 other. Oesterreichischer Fischereiver, Scharfling 18, A 5310 Mondsee, Austria. **Tel** 11 43 6232 3847, or 3848, FAX 06232/384733. **ED** Albert Jagsch. Index available. **Bk Rev,** (Qty: 30-40). **Ad Acc. Circ:** 2,500.
Desc: Fisheries, fishery science, fish culture, angling, limnology, and news from fisheries organizations.
Ind/Abst Fish Rev. (19??-199?); Wildl. Rev. (19??-199?).

FR/0297-4932
OSTREICULTEUR FRANCAIS, L'. (L'OSTREICULTEUR FRANCAIS : JOURNAL D'INFORMATIONS PROFESSIONNELLES INTER BASSINS CONCHYLICOLES.). [Ostreiculteur fr.]. **VFOAT** O.F. (1986)-. Periodical. French. Ten times a year. 200.00F France; 290.00F other. L'Ostreiculteur Francais, Route de la Tremblade BP 22, 17920 Breuillet France. **Tel** 011 33 46 226161. **UDC** 639.41.

US
OUR LIVING OCEANS : THE ... ANNUAL REPORT ON THE STATUS OF U.S. LIVING MARINE RESOURCES. See Biology-Marine Biology.

TH
P F C REPORT, I. (19??)-. English. Indo-Pacific Fishery Commission, c/o Secretary FAO Regional Office for Asia and the Pacific, Maliwan Mansion / Phra Atit Road, Bangkok 10200 Thailand.

CN
PACIFIC COAST AQUACULTURE. (19??)-. Periodical. English. Twelve times a year. 25.00Can$ Canada; 35.00Can$ US; 40.00Can$ other. Fish Farm News, RR 4 Site 465 C-37, Courtenay British Columbia V9N 7J3 Canada. **Tel** (604)338-2455, FAX (604)338-2466. **Continues** Fish Farm News, 1180-5633.

US/0892-9076
PACIFIC FISHERIES REVIEW. [Pac. fish. rev.]. Vol. 14, (Mar. 1987)-. English. **DD** 338. **Continues in part** Fishermen's News, 0015-2994.

US/0195-6515
PACIFIC FISHING. [Pac. fish.]. (1980)-. Periodical. English. mo. $24.00 (1 year); $42.00 (2 year); $58.00 (3 year) US; $29.00 (1 year); $52.00 (2 year); $73.00 (3 year) Canada; $30.00 (1 year); $55.00 (2 year); $78.00 (3 year) (surface mail); $72.00 (1 year), $139.00 (2 year), $204.00 (3 year) (air mail) other. Salmon Bay Communications, 1515 Northwest 51st Street, Seattle WA 98107. **Tel** (206)789-5333, FAX (206)784-5545. **ED** Steve Shapiro. **LC** SH221.5.N65; P32. **DD** 639/.2/091645. Index available. cum. index. **Ad Acc. Circ:** 10,000. **Absorbed** Western Fisheries.
Desc: Commercial fishing magazine serving the Pacific Coast fishermen, processors and suppliers.
Ind/Abst Aquat. Sci. Fish. Abstr. (Computer File).

CN/1195-3365
PACIFIC GILLNETTER. VFOAT Pacific Gillnetters Association News Magazine. (1990)-. English. Four times a year (Mar., June, Sept., Dec.). 15.00Can$ (one year); 35.00Can$ (three years). Pacific Gillnetters Association, #7 17655 57th Avenue, Cloverdale BC V3S 1H1 Canada. **Tel** (604)576-8032, FAX (604)576-1054. **ED** Tom Sheaves. **Ad Acc. Circ:** 1,000 per issue (ctrl).
Desc: An industry organization of owner/operators of gillnet fishing vessels engaged in the commerical salmon and herring fisheries on the West Coast of Canada.

US
PACIFIC HALIBUT FISHERY REGULATIONS. (PACIFIC HALIBUT FISHERY REGULATIONS : EFFECTIVE ... / INTERNATIONAL FISHERIES COMMISSION.). **Added/Corp** International Fisheries Commission. International Pacific Halibut Commission. **VFOAT** International Pacific Halibut Commission Regulations; Regulations of the International Fisheries Commission Adopted Pursuant to the Pacific Halibut Fishery Convention ...; Regulations of the International Pacific Halibut Commission Adopted Pursuant to the Pacific Halibut Fishery Convention ...; Regulations Respecting the Convention between Canada and the United States of America for the Preservation of the Halibut Fishery of the Northern Pacific Ocean and Bering Sea. (19??)-. English. International Pacific Halibut Commission, PO Box 95009, Seattle WA 98145-2009. **Tel** (206)634-1838, FAX (206)632-2983. **LC** K3900.H35; A156. **DD** 343/.07692/091823; 342.37692091823.
Ind/Abst Ocean. Abstr.

FR/0031-3718
PECHE ET LES POISSONS PARIS, LA. (1935)-. Periodical. French. mo. 190.99F France; 255.00F other. Gerpresse, 8 10 rue Pierre Brossolette, 92300 Levallois Perr France. **Tel** 011 33 1 40874085. **UDC** 799.

US/0031-434X
PENNSYLVANIA ANGLER. Added/Corp Pennsylvania. Board of Fish Commissioners. Pennsylvania Fish Commission. (Oct.1931)-. Periodical. English. mo. $9.00 (1 year), $25.00 (3 year). Pennsylvania Fish Commission, PO Box 1673, Harrisburg PA 17105. **Tel** (717)657-4518. **ED** Art Michaels. **LC** SH1; .P45. **DD** 799.1. Index available. **Circ:** 52,000.

MY/0126-8856
PERANGKAAN TAHUNAN PERIKANAN. See Fish and Fisheries-Abstracting, Bibliographies and Statistics.

II
PERFORMANCE BUDGET - DEPARTMENT OF FISHERIES. Main/Corp Andhra Pradesh (India). Dept. of Fisheries. English. an. Director of Printing, Government of Andhra Pradesh, Government Central Press, Hyderabad India. **LC** SH300.A5; A52B. **DD** 354.54/840072/23682362.

II
PERFORMANCE BUDGET OF PORTS AND FISHERIES DEPARTMENT (FISHERIES). See Public Administration-Public Finance and Taxation.

IT
PESCARE. Editoriale Olimpia, Vale Milton 7, 50129 Florence Italy. **Tel** 011 39 55 473843.

IT
PESCE, IL. Pubblicita Italia Sas, Via Taglio 24, 41100 Modena Italy. **Tel** 011 39 59 216688.
Ind/Abst Aquat. Sci. Fish. Abstr. (Computer File).

PH/0048-377X
PHILIPPINE JOURNAL OF FISHERIES, THE. [Philipp. j. fish.]. **Added/Corp** Philippines. Bureau of Fisheries. Philippine Fisheries Commission. Philippines. Dept. of Agriculture and Natural Resources. Philippines. Bureau of Fisheries and Aquatic Resources. Vol. 1 (Jan./June 1951)-. Periodical. English. ir. Bureau of Fisheries and Aquatic Resources, 860 Quezon Avenu, Quezon City, Phillipines. **ED** Juanito B. Malig. **LC** SH1; .P492. **DD** 639.209914. **Circ:** 700.
Ind/Abst Life Sci. Collect.

CN/0825-7914
PISCES. [Pisces]. (Dec. 1980)-. Periodical. English (French). bm. Free. Fisheries & Oceans Canada, Scientific Information & Publications Branch, 200 Kent Street/12th Floor, Ottawa Ontario K1A 0E6 Canada. **Tel** (613)993-0600, (800)267-6677, telex 053-3585. **DD** 354.710082/362/05. **Formed by the union of** Fisheries and Oceans News, 0229-8511 **and** Nouvelles Peches et Oceans, 0229-8503.

FR/0335-2811
PISCICULTEUR DE FRANCE. [Piscic. Fr.]. (1974)-. Periodical. French. mo. **UDC** 63.
Ind/Abst Aquat. Sci. Fish. Abstr. (Computer File).

FR
PISCICULTURE FRANCAISE. French. Fedn Francaise d Aquaculture, 11 rue Milton, 75009 Paris France. **Tel** 011 33 1 42803031.
Ind/Abst Anim. Breed. Abstr.; Aquat. Sci. Fish. Abstr. (Computer File); Nutr. Abstr. Rev., Ser. B, Live Feeds and Feed.; World Agric. Econ.

FR/0295-317X
PISCICULTURE FRANCAISE D'EAU VIVE ET D'ETANG SAUMATRE ET MARINE, LA. See Biology.

US
PITTMAN-ROBERTSON BULLETIN (HARTFORD). (PITTMAN-ROBERTSON BULLETIN.). No. 1- 1944-. Bulletin. English. Price varies per volume. Connecticut State Board of Fisheries and Game, Hartford CT 06115. **LC** SH11; .C87.

XR
PRACE VURH VODNANY. Main/Corp Vyzkumny Ustav Rybarsky a Hydrobiologicky. **VFOAT** Papers of Fri Vodnany; Prace Vyzkumneho Ustav Rybarskeho a Hydrobiologickeho ve Vodnanech. V. 10-. Periodical. summaries and/or abstracts in Russian. **Continues** Vodnany, Czechoslovak Republic. Vyzkumny Ustav Rybarsky A Hydrobiologicky. Prace.
Ind/Abst AgBiotech News Inf.; AGRICOLA; Anim. Breed. Abstr.

US/1057-218X
PRACTICAL AQUACULTURE & LAKE MANAGEMENT. Ceased. [Pract. aquac. lake manage.]. **Added/Corp** Aquaculture Advisory Service. **VFOAT** Practical Aquaculture and Lake Management; PALM. Vol. 6, No. 4 (July/Aug. 1988)-Vol. 10 (April 1992). Periodical. English. bm. Aquaculture Advisory Service, PO Box 1294, Garner NC 27529. **Tel** (919)772-8548, FAX (919)662-0158. **DD** 639. Index available. **Bk Rev,** (Qty: 8). **Ad Acc, Adv Mgr:** Jean Roberts, **Tel** (919)772-8548. **Circ:** 3000 (ctrl). **Continues** Carolina Aquaculture News, 8755-9625.
Desc: Fish and shellfish farming and pond/lake management.
Ind/Abst AGRICOLA [Select. Cov.].

UK
PRACTICAL FISHKEEPING. (Dec. 1978)-. English. Twelve times a year. £25.00UK; £32.00 others. EMAP National Publications Ltd, Farndon Road, Market Harborough, Leicestershire, LE16 9NR England. **Tel** 011 44 733 555161. **Continues** Petfish Monthly.

SP
PROCEEDINGS AND REPORTS OF MEETINGS. Main/Corp International Commission for the Southeast Atlantic Fisheries. (19??)-. Proceedings. English.
Ind/Abst Ocean. Abstr.

US/1045-7127
PROCEEDINGS ... ANNUAL CONFERENCE OF THE TROPICAL AND SUBTROPICAL FISHERIES TECHNOLOGICAL SOCIETY OF THE AMERICAS. [Proc. - Trop. Subtrop. Fish. Technol. Soc. Am., Conf.]. **Main/Corp** Tropical and Subtropical Fisheries Technological Society of the Americas. Conference. 12th (1988)-. Proceedings. English. an. Marine Information Service, Sea Grant College Program, Texas A&M University, College Station TX 77843. **Tel** (409)845-7524. **LC** SH234; .T76A. **DD** 639.3/0913. **Continues** Proceedings of the ... Annual Tropical and Subtropical Fisheries Conference of the Americas, 0748-2965.

TH/0258-4190
PROCEEDINGS / INDO-PACIFIC FISHERY COMMISSION. [Proc. - Indo-Pac. Fish. Comm.]. **Main/Corp** Indo-Pacific Fishery Commission. 18th Session (March 8-17, 1978)-. Proceedings. English. FAO Regional Office for Asia & the Far East, Phra Atit Road, Bangkok 10200 Thailand. **LC** SH1; .I47. **DD** 333.956/09164. **Continues** Indo-Pacific Fisheries Council. Proceedings of Meeting, 0367-9675.

US/0276-7929
PROCEEDINGS OF THE ... ANNUAL CONFERENCE SOUTHEASTERN ASSOCIATION OF FISH AND WILDLIFE AGENCIES. See Recreation, Leisure-Sports.

US/0361-2953
PROCEEDINGS OF THE ANNUAL GULF AND CARIBBEAN FISHERIES INSTITUTE AND THE ANNUAL INTERNATIONAL GAME FISH RESEARCH CONFERENCE. [Proc. annu. Gulf Caribb. Fish. Inst. annu. Int. Game Fish Res. Conf.]. **Main/Corp** Gulf and Caribbean Fisheries Institute. **VFOAT** International Game Fish Research Conference. (1974)-. Academic Scholarly Publication. English. an. Gulf and Caribbean Fisheries Institute, 37 Wentworth Street, Adminsrtation Offices, Charleston SC 29401. **Tel** (803)577-5697, FAX (803)577-5697. **CODEN** UMPGAP. Documents available from BIOSIS Document Express, CASDDS. **Continues** Proceedings of the ... Annual Session.
Ind/Abst Biol. Abstr.; Chem. Abstr.; Mar. Sci. Contents Tables.

US
PROCEEDINGS OF THE DESERT FISHES COUNCIL. Main/Corp Desert Fishes Council (U.S.). Vol. 11 (1979)-. Proceedings. English. an. **Continues** Summary of the Proceedings of the ... Annual Symposium / Desert Fishes Council, 0734-2314.

US
PROCEEDINGS OF THE GULF AND CARIBBEAN FISHERIES INSTITUTE. Main/Corp Miami, University of, Coral Gables, Florida. Institute of Science. Proceedings. English (Spanish and

French). an (Summer). $30.00. Gulf and Caribbean Fisheries Institute, 37 Wentworth Street, Administration Offices, Charleston SC 29401. **Tel** (803)577-5697, FAX (803)577-5697. **ED** Melvin Goodwin. **Circ:** 500.
Ind/Abst Aquat. Sci. Fish. Abstr. (Computer File).

CN/0842-2990
PROCEEDINGS OF THE STANDING SENATE COMMITTEE ON FISHERIES. [Proc. Standing Senate Comm. Fish.]. **Main/Corp** Canada. Parliament. Senate. Standing Committee on Fisheries. **VFOAT** Deliberations du Comite Senatorial Permanent des Peches; Fisheries. Proceedings. English (French). ir. Canadian Government Publishing Center, Supply and Services Canada, Hull Quebec K1A 0S9 Canada. **Tel** (613)990-8116, telex 053-4296. **LC** HD9464.C19; C355A. **DD** 338.3/7270971. ***Continues in part*** *Proceedings of the Standing Senate Committee on Agriculture, Fisheries and Forestry, 0826-7820.*

US/0148-5296
PROCESSED FISHERY PRODUCTS, ANNUAL SUMMARY. **Added/Corp** United States. National Marine Fisheries Service. United States. National Marine Fisheries Service. Fisheries Statistics Division. (19??)-. English. an. Free on request. US Department of Commerce / National Marine Fisheries Service, 1335 East-West Highway, Silver Spring MD 20910. **Tel** (301)713-2239, FAX (301)713-2258. **LC** HD9451; .P76. **DD** 338.4/766494/0973021. ***Absorbed*** *Canned Fishery Products, Annual Summary, 0162-6140; U.S. Production of Fish Fillets and Steaks, Annual Summary, 0148-5318; Fish Sticks, Portions, and Breaded Shrimp* ***and*** *Industrial Fishery Products, Annual Summary, 0093-8726.*

IO
PRODUKSI PERIKANAN LAUT YANG DIJUAL DI PELELANGAN/TEMPAT PENDARATAN IKAN DI JAWA-MADURA. **Main/Corp** Indonesia Biro Pusat Statistik. **VFOAT** Marine Fishery Products Sold through Auctions/Landing Places in Java-Madura. Indonesian (English). an. Rp2,000 Indonesia; $2.00 US. Central Bureau of Statistics / Indonesia, c/o Dr. Sutomo, 8 Jalan, PO Box 3, Jakarta Indonesia. **Tel** 372808 374908 Ext.342. **LC** HD9466.I57; J33. **Ad Acc.** ctrl circ.

US/0033-0779
PROGRESSIVE FISH-CULTURIST, THE. [Prog. fish-cult.]. **Added/Corp** American Fisheries Society. U.S. Fish and Wildlife Service. **VFOAT** Progressive Fish Culturist. No. 1 (Dec. 1934)-. Academic Scholarly Publication. English. qt. $425.00 US; $460.00 other (library). American Fisheries Society, 5410 Grosvenor Lane, Suite 110, Bethesda MD 20814-2199. **Tel** (301)897-8616, (301)897-8621, FAX (301)897-8096. **ED** Mary J. Lewis. **LC** SH34; .P76. **DD** 639.3/00973. **CODEN** PFCUAY. **[CCC].** cum. index. **Ad Acc. Pr Rev. Acid Free. Circ:** 5,000. available on microfilm and microfiche from University Microfilms International (UMI). Documents available from The Genuine Article, BIOSIS Document Express, CASDDS, Documents on Demand. ***Absorbed*** *Fish Culture.*
Desc: Combines new research with practical experience to advance all aspects of intensive and extensive aquaculture -- freshwater and marine, vetebrates and invetebrates.
Ind/Abst AgBiotech News Inf.; Agric. Eng. Abstr. (1991-); Anim. Breed. Abstr.; AQUAREF; Aquat. Sci. Fish. Abstr. (Computer File); Biodeter. Abstr. (1991-); Biol. Abstr.; Chem. Abstr.; Curr. Aware. Biol. Sci., CABS; Curr. Contents, Agric. Biol. Environ. Sci.; Curr. Ref. Fish Res.; EMBASE; Energy Res. Abstr. (Sept. 1972-); Environ. Abstr.; Fish Rev.; Fresh. Aqua. Contents Tables; Helminthol. Abstr. (1991-); Nutr. Abstr. Rev., Ser. B, Live Feeds and Feed.; Ocean. Abstr.; Life Sci. Collect.; Res. Alert [Full Cov.]; Sci. Cit. Index; SCISEARCH; Weed Abstr.

IO/0426-7680
PURPOSE AND METHODS IN FISHERIES STATISTICS : DOCUMENT. **See** Fish and Fisheries-Abstracting, Bibliographies and Statistics.

US/1048-6259
QUARTERLY REPORT OF THE INTER-AMERICAN TROPICAL TUNA COMMISSION, THE. [Q. rep. Inter-Am. Trop. Tuna Comm.]. **Main/Corp** Inter-American Tropical Tuna Commission. **VFOAT** Informe Trimestral ... de la Comision Interamericana del Atun Tropical. (July/Sept. 1983)-. Periodical. English (Spanish). qt. Inter-American Tuna Commission, Scripps Institute of Oceanography, La Jolla CA 92037. **Tel** (619)546-7025, telex 697115. **LC** SH351.T8; I525. **DD** 639.
Ind/Abst Ocean. Abstr.

CN/1187-7693
QUEBEC MARINE FISHERIES, MONTHLY LANDING STATISTICS BY SPECIES. [Que. mar. fish. mon. land. stat. species]. **Added/Corp** Canada. Dept. of Fisheries and Oceans. Quebec Region. Statistics and Informatics Division. **VFOAT** Monthly Landing Statistics by Species. (Nov. 1991)-. Periodical. English. ir. **DD** 338.3. ***Continues*** *Landings Monthly Statistics by Species., 0829-9021.*

CN/0704-3708
RAPPORT CANADIEN A L'INDUSTRIE SUR LES SCIENCES HALIEUTIQUES ET AQUATIQUES. [Rapp. can. ind. sci. halieut. acquat.]. **VFOAT** Rapport A l'Industrie Canadien sur les Sciences Halieutiques et Aquatiques; Canadian Industry Report of Fisheries and Aquatic Sciences. Periodical. French (summaries and/or abstracts in English). Bibliotheque, Institut Maurice-Lamontagne, Peches Et Oceans, C P 1000 850 Route de la Mer, Mont-Joli Quebec G5H 3Z4 Canada. **Tel** (613)995-2041. **DD** 639/.2/0971.

FR
RAPPORT SUR LE COMMERCE EXTERIEUR DES PRODUITS DE LA PECHE EN ... . **Added/Corp** Comite Central des Peches Maritimes (France). (19??)-. French. an. 30.00F. Comite Central Peches Maritime, 51 rue Salvator Allende, 92027 Nanterre Cedex France. **Tel** 011 33 1 47750101. **LC** HD9462.1; .R36. **DD** 382/.4370944/021.
Desc: Information on the fish trade.

AT/0725-4598
REPORT - CSIRO MARINE LABORATORIES. (REPORT / COMMONWEALTH SCIENTIFIC AND INDUSTRIAL RESEARCH ORGANIZATION. MARINE LABORATORIES.). [Rep. - CSIRO Mar. Lab.]. **Main/Corp** CSIRO Marine Laboratories. **Added/Corp** CSIRO Marine Laboratories. **VFOAT** C.S.I.R.O. Marine Laboratories Report; CSIRO Marine Laboratories Report. (1981)-. Monographic series. English. Price varies per volume. CSIRO Publications, PO Box 89, 314 Albert Street, East Melborne Victoria 3002 Australia. **Tel** 011 61 3 4187333, 4187217, FAX 011 61 3 4190459, telex AA 30236. **CODEN** RCMLDR. Documents available from CASDDS. ***Continues*** *Commonwealth Scientific and Industrial Research (Australia). Division of Fisheries and Oceanography. Report.*
Ind/Abst Chem. Abstr. (1981-1983); Ocean. Abstr.; Life Sci. Collect.

SP/0377-368X
REPORT - INTERNATIONAL COMMISSION FOR THE CONSERVATION OF ATLANTIC TUNAS. ENGLISH VERSION. (REPORT - INTERNATIONAL COMMISSION FOR THE CONSERVATION OF ATLANTIC TUNAS.). **Main/Corp** International Commission for the Conservation of Atlantic Tunas. (19??)-. English (French and Spanish). be. International Commission for the Conservation of Atlantic Tunas, Principe de Vergara 17, 28001 Madrid Spain. **Tel** 431-03-29, FAX 576-19-68, telex 46339 ICCAT E. **LC** SH351.T8; I53a. **DD** 597/.58. **CODEN** RICTEA. cum. index. ctrl circ.
Ind/Abst Aquat. Sci. Fish. Abstr. (Computer File).

UK
REPORT OF THE DIRECTOR OF FISHERY RESEARCH. **Main/Corp** Fisheries Laboratory, Lowestoft, Eng. **VFOAT** Report of the Director of Marine Fishery Research. (19??)-. Periodical. English. ***Continues*** *Fisheries Laboratory, Lowestoft, Eng. Annual Report of the Director of Fishery Research.*
Ind/Abst Aquat. Sci. Fish. Abstr. (Computer File).

NZ
REPORT OF THE MINISTRY OF AGRICULTURE AND FISHERIES. ***Title Change.*** **See** Agriculture.

US/0093-9412
REPORT OF THE NATIONAL MARINE FISHERIES SERVICE. (REPORT OF THE NATIONAL MARINE FISHERIES SERVICE FOR THE CALENDAR YEAR ... / UNITED STATES DEPARTMENT OF COMMERCE, NATIONAL OCEANIC AND ATMOSPHERIC ADMINISTRATION, NATIONAL MARINE FISHERIES SERVICE.). **Main/Corp** United States. National Marine Fisheries Service. Began with 1970 and 1971. Government Publication. English. an. US Department of Commerce, 14th Street & Constitution Avenue NW, Washington DC 20230. **Tel** (202)482-2000, FAX (202)482-3772. **LC** SH11; .A35A. **DD** 639/.2/0973.

AT/0155-641X
REPORT OF THE NEW SOUTH WALES STATE FISHERIES FOR THE YEAR ENDED ... . **Main/Corp** New South Wales. State Fisheries. **VFOAT** Report on the Fisheries in New South Wales. English. an. $1.20. Government Printing Office / Australia, PO Box 4050, Sydney NSW 2001 Australia. **LC** SH318.N5; N46A. **DD** 338.3/72/099441. ***Continues*** *Report on Fisheries in New South Wales (1975/76).*

NZ/0110-9618
REPORT OF THE NEW ZEALAND FISHING INDUSTRY BOARD. [Rep. N.Z. Fish. Ind. Board]. (1979)-. English. an. Government Printing Office / New Zealand, 10 Mulgrave Street, Wellington New Zealand. **Tel** 011 64 4 4737211, FAX 011 64 4 734943, telex GOVPRINT NZ 31320. **DD** 354. ***Continues*** *Appendix to the Journals of the House of Representatives of New Zealand, 0110-3407.*
Ind/Abst Ocean. Abstr.

IT/0072-0755
REPORT OF THE ... SESSION / GENERAL FISHERIES COUNCIL FOR THE MEDITERRANEAN. **Main/Corp** General Fisheries Council for the Mediterranean (Food and Agriculture Organization of the United Nations). (196?)-. English (French). ir. Food and Agriculture Organization (FAO) / Italy, GIPC166 via Terme di Caracalla, 00100 Rome Italy. **Tel** 011 39 6 522 52925, FAX 011 39 6 522 55784. **(Subscription address:** UNIPUB, 4611 F Assembly Drive, Lanham MD 20706.**)** **LC** SH1; .G315. **DD** 338.3/727092/2. ***Continues*** *General Fisheries Council for the Mediterranean (Food and Agriculture Organization of the United Nations). Debats et Documents Techniques, 0072-0747.*
Ind/Abst Aquat. Sci. Fish. Abstr. (Computer File).

JA/0563-8372
REPORT OF THE TOKYO UNIVERSITY OF FISHERIES. (TOKYO SUISAN DAIGAKU RON SHU.). [Rep. Tokyo Univ. Fish.]. **Main/Corp** Tokyo Suisan Daigaku. **Added/Corp** Tokyo Suisan Daigaku. Report. **VFOAT** Report of the Tokyo University of Fisheries. No. 2 (1967)-. Periodical. Japanese (Japanese and English; summaries and/or abstracts in English). an. Tokyo University of Fisheries, Tokyo Suisan Daigaku, 4-5-7 Konan, Minato-Ku, Tokyo 108 Japan. **Tel** 03 471 1251. **ED** Kenzo Toyama. **LC** AS552.T7172; A28. ***Continues*** *Tokyo Suisan Daigaku Ron Shu.*
Ind/Abst Life Sci. Collect.

PO
REPORT - TECHNICAL MEETING ON FISHERIES. **Added/Corp** South Pacific Commission. English (French). an. Free (New Caledonia) and (Pacific Islands); $50.00 other. South Pacific Commission, PO Box D5, Noumea Cedex New Caledonia. **Tel** (687)26 20 00, FAX (687)26 38 18. **LC** SH319.A2; T42a. **DD** 639/.2/099. **Circ:** 500 (ctrl).

US/0575-3317
REPORTS - CALIFORNIA COOPERATIVE OCEANIC FISHERIES INVESTIGATIONS. [Rep. - Calif. Coop. Ocean. Fish. Invest.]. **Main/Corp** California Cooperative Oceanic Fisheries Investigations. Vol. 7 (1958-1959)-. English. ir. California Department of Fish and Game, 1416 9th Street, Sacramento CA 95814. **Tel** (916)653-7664. **DD** 639. **CODEN** COFRAS. **Pr Rev.** Documents available from The Genuine Article, BIOSIS Document Express, CASDDS. ***Continues*** *Progress Report - California Cooperative Oceanic Fisheries Investigations.*
Ind/Abst Aquat. Sci. Fish. Abstr. (Computer File); Biol. Abstr.; Chem. Abstr.; Curr. Aware. Biol. Sci., CABS; Curr. Contents, Agric. Biol. Environ. Sci.; Nutr. Abstr. Rev., Ser. B, Live Feeds and Feed.; Ocean. Abstr.; Life Sci. Collect.; Res. Alert [Select. Cov.]; SCISEARCH; World Agric. Econ.

US/0083-7555
RESEARCH IN FISHERIES. (RESEARCH IN FISHERIES : ANNUAL REPORT OF THE SCHOOL OF FISHERIES.). [Res. fish.]. **Main/Corp** University of Washington. School of Fisheries. (1981)-. English. an. University of Washington College of Fisheries, Seattle WA 98195. **LC** SH1; .W33. **DD** 639/.2/09797. **CODEN** UWRFAY. Documents available from BIOSIS Document Express. ***Continues*** *University of Washington. College of Fisheries. Research in Fisheries, 0083-7555.*
Ind/Abst Biol. Abstr. (?-1989).

US/0434-9490
RESEARCH PROSPECTUS - GULF STATES MARINE FISHERIES COMMISSION. **Main/Corp** Gulf States Marine Fisheries Commission. No. 1 (April 1961)-. Monographic series. English. Price varies per volume. Gulf States Marine Fisheries Commission, New Orleans LA 70122. **DD** 639.

CN
RESOURCE MANAGEMENT REPORT. **See** Environmental Issues-Conservation and Natural Resources.

FR/0078-6241
REVIEW OF FISHERIES IN OECD MEMBER COUNTRIES. **Main/Corp** Organisation for Economic Co-Operation and Development. **VFOAT** Review of Fisheries. (1967)-. English. an. $96.00. OECD Publications and Information Center, 2 rue Andre-Pascal, 75775 Paris Cedex 16 France. **Tel** 011 33 1 45248167, US:(202)785-6323, FAX 011 33 1 45248500 OR 45248176, telex 620 160 OCDE. **(Subscription address:** OECD Publications Center, 2001 L Street, Suite 700, Washington DC 20036.**)** **LC** SH334; .O74a. **DD** 338.3/72/709204.
Desc: Reports on major developments in fishery management, policy, production, and trade in OECD member countries.

UK/0960-3168
REVIEWS IN FISH BIOLOGY AND FISHERIES. (1991)-. English. qt. $235.00 US and Canada; £140.00 Europe; £155.00 other. Chapman & Hall, 2-6 Boundary Row, London SE1 8HN England. **Tel** 011 44 71 865 0066, FAX 011 44 71 522 9623, telex 290164 Chapmag. **(Subscription address:** Chapman & Hall, Cheriton House, North Way, Andover, Hampshire, SP10 5BE England.) **ED** Tony Pitcher.
Desc: Devoted to publishing important review articles on any aspect of fish and fisheries biology. Reviews are accepted in any field of fish biology where the emphasis is on the whole organism.
Ind/Abst Aquat. Sci. Fish. Abstr. (Computer File); Curr. Contents, Agric. Biol. Environ. Sci.; Sci. Cit. Index.

●US/1064-1262
REVIEWS IN FISHERIES SCIENCE. [Reviews fish. sci.]. **Added/Corp** American Fisheries Society. Vol. 1, Issue 1 (1993)-. Periodical. English. qt (4 issues). $225.00 institution. CRC Press Inc., 2000 Corporate Boulevard Northwest, Boca Raton FL 33431. **Tel** (407)994-0555, (800)272-7737, FAX (407)998-9784, telex 568689. **(Subscription address:** CRC Press Inc., PO Box 750, Pearl River, NY 10965) **ED** Robert R. Stickney. **DD** 639.
Desc: Provides an important forum for the publication of up-to-date reviews, historical articles, and experiential papers covering the broad range of subject areas in fisheries science.

CU/0138-8452
REVISTA CUBANA DE INVESTIGACIONES PESQUERAS / CENTRO DE INVESTIGACIONES PESQUERAS, MIRAMAR, LA HABANA, CUBA. ***Ceased.*** **Added/Corp** Centro de Investigaciones Pesqueras (Cuba). **VFOAT** Cuban Journal of Fisheries Research. Vol. 3, No. 1 (1978)-(19??). Periodical. Spanish (summaries and/or abstracts in English). qt. Centro de Investigaciones Pesqueras, M I P 1A y 26 Miramar Playa, Havana Cuba. **Tel** 0511345, 0511396. **Circ:** 780 (ctrl). ***Continues*** *Centro de Investigaciones Pesqueras (Cuba) Revista de Investigaciones.*
Desc: Publishes original research articles and notes on fisheries management, ocean science and aquatic environments relevant to Cuba.
Ind/Abst Aquat. Sci. Fish. Abstr. (Computer File); Fish Rev. (Jan. 1989-July 1992); Wildl. Rev. (Jan. 1989-July 1992).

AG/0325-6375
REVISTA DE INVESTIGACION Y DESARROLLO PESQUERO. **Added/Corp** Instituto Nacional de Investigacion y Desarrollo Pesquero (Argentina). Vol. 1, No. 1 (Nov. 1979)-. Periodical. Spanish (summaries and/or abstracts in English). Instituto Nacional de Investigacion y Desarrollo Pesquero, Casilla Correo 175, 7600 Mar Del Plata Argentina. **LC** QL614; .R48. **DD** 639.3/00982. **CODEN** RIDPE3. Documents available from BIOSIS Document Express. ***Continues*** *Boletin (Instituto de Biologia Marina (Mar del Plata, Argentina)), 0076-4299.*
Ind/Abst Biol. Abstr. (1986-).

PE/0250-2135
REVISTA LATINOAMERICANA DE ACUICULTURA. **Added/Corp** Latin American Economic System. Comite de Accion de Productos del Mar y de Agua Dulce. (19??)-. Spanish (summaries and/or abstracts in English). sa.
Ind/Abst Aquat. Sci. Fish. Abstr. (Computer File).

IC/0484-9019
RIT FISKIDEILDAR. [Rit Fiskid.]. Vol. 1, 1940-. Monographic series. English (Icelandic). ir. Price varies per volume. **LC** Sh293.12. **CODEN** RIFIAM. Documents available from BIOSIS Document Express.
Ind/Abst Biol. Abstr.; Life Sci. Collect.

PL/0080-3723
ROCZNIKI NAUK ROLNICZYCH. SERIA H. RYBACTWO. [Rocz. nauk roln., Ser. H]. **VFOAT** Annaly Selskokhoziaistvennykh Nauk; Polish Agricultural Annual. Series H. Fisheries. Vol. 90 (1967)-. Academic Scholarly Publication. Polish. qt. Panstwowe Wydawn Naukowe, Miodowa 10, PO Box 391, 00251 Warsaw Poland. **CODEN** RNRRB9. Documents available from BIOSIS Document Express, CASDDS. ***Continues in part*** *Roczniki Nauk Roniczych.*
Ind/Abst Biol. Abstr.; Chem. Abstr. (1967-1981); EMBASE; Fish Rev. (Jan. 1989-July 1992); Life Sci. Collect.; Wildl. Rev. (Jan. 1989-July 1992).

PL
ROZPRAWY - AKADEMIA ROLNICZA W SZCZECINIE. **See** Agriculture.

RU/0233-7754
RYBOLOV. **Added/Corp** Soviet Union. Ministerstvo Selskogo Khoziaistva. Soviet Union. Komitet po Fizicheskoi Kulture i Sportu. Soiuz Obshchestv Okhotnikov i Rybolovov RSFSR. (Jan./Feb. 1985)-. Russian. bm. $69.95. Agropromizdat, Sadovo-Spasskaia, 18, 107807 Moscow Russia. **(Subscription address:** East View Publications Inc., 3020 Harbor Lane North, Suite 110, Minneapolis MN 55447.)

KO
SAE OMIN. Periodical. Korean. mo. W300 single issue. Susanop Hyoptong Chohap Chunganghoe, 88 Kyongun-dong Chongno-ku, Seoul 110 Korea. **LC** SH302.5; .S23.

CN/0827-3472
SALAR. [Salar]. **Added/Corp** Atlantic Salmon Federation. (Aug. 1984)-. Periodical. English. Four times a year. Free to members. Atlantic Salmon Federation, PO Box 429, St Andrews New Brunswick, E0G 2X0 Canada. **Tel** (506)529-4581, (506)529-1025, FAX (506)529-4438, telex 014-47458. **ED** Martin Silverstone. **DD** 639/.2755. **Bk Rev. Ad Acc. Circ:** 5,000 (ctrl). ***Continues*** *Atlantic Salmon Newsletter, 0712-5933.*
Desc: Newsletter on the conservation and management. Includes news on councils and affiliates of The Atlantic Salmon Federation.

CN/0703-5810
SALMO SALAR. V. 1- Dec. 1976-. Periodical. French. bm. Free to members. Association des Pecheurs Sportifs de Saumons du Quebec, Bureau 225/1990 Ouest Boul Charest, Ste Foy Quebec G1N 4K8 Canada. **DD** 799.1/7/5509714.

UK/0036-3545
SALMON AND TROUT MAGAZINE, THE. ***Title Change.*** **Added/Corp** Salmon and Trout Association. Salmon and Trout Association. Journal. No. 1 (Dec. 1910)-(19??). Periodical. English. sa. Salmon & Trout Association, Fishmongers Hall, London Bridge, London EC4R 9EL England. **Tel** 011 44 71 283 5838, FAX 011 44 71 929 1389, telex 8956058. **ED** D.A. Orton. cum. index. **Bk Rev. Ad Acc. Circ:** 11,000 (ctrl). ***Continued by*** *Year Book.*
Desc: News of activities of the Salmon and Trout Association, articles on game fish, fishing and fisheries.
Ind/Abst Aquat. Sci. Fish. Abstr. (Computer File).

UK/0951-9882
SALMON FARMING. [Salmon farming]. **Added/Corp** Marine Laboratory (Aberdeen, Scotland). Library. Freshwater Fisheries Laboratory (Pitlochry, Scotland). Library. Great Britain. Dept. of Agriculture and Fisheries for Scotland. (1986)-. Periodical. English. mo. £30.00 EEC countries; £40.00 all except EEC countries. Auris Ltd., Librarian Marine Lab, PO Box 101 Victoria Road, Aberdeen AB9 8DB Scotland. **Tel** 011 44 424 876544 ext.5325, FAX 011 44 224 295511, telex 73587. **Bk Rev. Ad Acc. Circ:** 428.
Desc: Aims to provide coverage of the worldwide literature (scientific, technical, and non-technical) on the farming of Atlantic salmon and related species.

●US/1063-9624
SALMON MAGAZINE. (1992)-. Periodical. English. sa. $12.00. Andrew Tang, PO Box 440313, Somerville MA 02144.

UK/0962-6484
SALMON NET. [Salmon net]. English. an. **DD** 338.372755.
Ind/Abst Aquat. Sci. Fish. Abstr. (Computer File).

US/0029-3431
SALMON TROUT STEELHEADER. **See** Recreation, Leisure.

US/1071-1635
SALMONID (HARPERS FERRY, W.VA.). (SALMONID.). [Salmonid]. **Added/Corp** United States Trout Farmers Association. **VFOAT** Magazine of Cold Water Fishes. Vol. 1 (1977)-. Periodical. English. Four times a year. $60.00. US Trout Farmers Association, PO Box 220, Harpers Ferry WV 25425. **Tel** (304)876-6666, FAX (304)876-0946. **ED** Joseph P. McCraren and Kathryn M. Roderick. **DD** 639. **Ad Acc. Circ:** 1000.
Desc: Official quarterly publication of the U.S. Trout Farmers Association.

FR
SAUMONS. **Added/Corp** Association Nationale de Defense des Rivieres a Saumon. (19??)-. Periodical. French. Four times a year. 75.00F. Association Internationale de Defense du Saumon Atlantique, Institut Oceanigraphique, 195 rue Saint-Jacques, 75005 Paris France. **LC** QL638.S2; S26. **DD** 333.9/5.
Ind/Abst Aquat. Sci. Fish. Abstr. (Computer File).

RU/0367-7974
SBORNIK NAUCHNYKH TRUDOV / MINISTERVO RYBNOGO KHOZIAISTVA RSFSR, GOSUDARSTVENNYI NAUCHNO-ISSLEDOVATELSKII INSTITUT OZERNOGO I RECHNOGO RYBNOGO KHOZIAISTVA. [Sb. nauchn. tr. - Gos. nauchno-issled. inst. ozern. rechn. rybn. hoz.]. **Added/Corp** Gosudarstvennyi Nauchno-Issledovatelskii Institut Ozernogo i Rechnogo Rybnogo Khoziaistva (Russia). Vol. 139 (1979)-. Academic Scholarly Publication. Russian (summaries and/or abstracts in English; table of contents in English). ir. Price varies per volume. **LC** UNC. **CODEN** STKHDX. Documents available from CASDDS. ***Continues*** *Izvestiia Gosudarstvennogo Nauchno-Issledovatelskogo Instituta Ozernogo I Rechnogo Rybnogo Khoziaistva.*
Ind/Abst Chem. Abstr.; Potato Abstr.

AT/0314-4984
SCIENCE AND TECHNOLOGY INFORMATION BULLETIN. B10. FISH DISEASES. [Sci. technol. inf. bull., B10, Fish dis.]. **VFOAT** Fish Diseases. (1977)-. Periodical. English. mo. **DD** 597.02.
Ind/Abst Index Vet.

US/0271-5104
SCIENTIFIC ANGLERS FLY FISHING HANDBOOK. ***Ceased.*** [Sci. anglers fly fish. handb.]. **VFOAT** Fly Fishing Handbook. ( )-(1987). Periodical. English. an. Aqua Field Publications Inc, 66 West Gilbert Street, Shrewsbury NJ 07702. **Tel** (201)842-8300. **LC** SH456; .S36. **DD** 799.1/2/05.

CN/0250-6416
SCIENTIFIC COUNCIL REPORTS. (SCIENTIFIC COUNCIL REPORTS / NORTHWEST ATLANTIC FISHERIES ORGANIZATION.). [Sci. Counc. rep.]. **Main/Corp** Northwest Atlantic Fisheries Organization. Scientific Council. (1979/1980)-. English. an. 20.00Can$. Northwest Atlantic Fisheries Organization / NAFO, PO Box 638, Dartmouth Nova Scotia B2Y 3Y9 Canada. **Tel** (902)469-9105, telex 019-31475. **ED** V. M. Hodder. **LC** SH213.5; .I57a. **DD** 639/.2/091634. **Circ:** 500 (ctrl). ***Continues*** *International Commission for the Northwest Atlantic Fisheries. Redbook., 0074-2643.*
Desc: Reports of NAFO Scientific Council Meetings involving assessment and recommendations for management of selected finfish and invertebrates stocks in the Northwest Atlantic.
Ind/Abst Ocean. Abstr.

CN/0250-6432
SCIENTIFIC COUNCIL STUDIES. (SCIENTIFIC COUNCIL STUDIES / NORTHWEST ATLANTIC FISHERIES ORGANIZATION.). [Sci. Counc. stud.]. **Added/Corp** Northwest Atlantic Fisheries Organization. Scientific Council. No. 1 (1981)-. Monographic series. English. ir. Price varies per volume. Northwest Atlantic Fisheries Organization / NAFO, PO Box 638, Dartmouth Nova Scotia B2Y 3Y9 Canada. **Tel** (902)469-9105, telex 019-31475. **ED** V.M. Hodder. **LC** SH213.5; .S34. **DD** 639/.2/091631. Index available. cum. index. **Circ:** 600. Documents available from BIOSIS Document Express. ***Formed by the union of*** *Special Publication (International Commission for the Northwest Atlantic Fisheries), 0074-2678* ***and*** *International Commission for the Northwest Atlantic Fisheries. Selected Papers, 0380-4933.*
Desc: Selected scientific papers of topical interest from meetings of the NAFO Scientific Council, considered worthy of secondary publication but not of sufficiently high quality for primary publication.
Ind/Abst Biol. Abstr.; Fish Rev. (19??-199?); Mar. Sci. Contents Tables; Life Sci. Collect.; Wildl. Rev. (19??-199?).

US/0304-016X
SCIENTIFIC REPORT / INTERNATIONAL PACIFIC HALIBUT COMMISSION. [Sci. rep. Int. Pac. Halibut Comm.]. **Added/Corp** International Pacific Halibut Commission. No. 53 (1971)-. Monographic series. English. ir. Price varies per volume. International Pacific Halibut Commission, PO Box 95009, Seattle WA 98145-2009. **Tel** (206)634-1838, FAX (206)632-2983. **LC** SH351.H2; I54. **CODEN** IPHRBA. Documents available from BIOSIS Document Express. ***Continues*** *Report of the International Pacific Halibut Commission, 0096-1221.*
Ind/Abst Biol. Abstr.; Life Sci. Collect.

JA/0441-0769
SCIENTIFIC REPORTS OF THE HOKKAIDO SALMON HATCHERY. **Main/Corp** Hokkaido Sake Masu Fukajo. **Added/Corp** Hokkaido Sake Masu Fukajo. Hokkido Sake Masu Fukajo Kenkyu Hokoku. **VFOAT** Hokkaido Sake Masu Fukajo Kenkyu Hokoku. (19??)-. Japanese (English and Japanese; summaries and/or abstracts in English). an. Suisancho Hokkaido Sake Masu Fukajo, (Hokkaido Salmon Hatchery, Fisheries Agency), 2 Chome, Nakanoshima 2 Jo, Toyohiraku, Sapporoshi, Hokkaido 062 Japan. **LC** SH109; .H64a. **CODEN** HSHSAM.
Ind/Abst Aquat. Sci. Fish. Abstr. (Computer File); Fish Rev. (Jan. 1989-July 1992); Ocean. Abstr.; Life Sci. Collect. (1985-); Wildl. Rev. (Jan. 1989-July 1992).

UK
SCOTTISH FISH FARMER. English. Alister Barnett, PO Box 1, Oban Argyll PA 34 5PY Scotland.

UK/0309-9105
SCOTTISH FISHERIES INFORMATION PAMPHLET. **Added/Corp** Great Britain. Dept. of Agriculture and Fisheries for Scotland. No. 1 (1977)-. Monographic series. English. Price varies per volume. Department of Agriculture and Fisheries for Scotland, PO Box 101 Victoria Road, Aberdeen AB9 8DB Scotland. **Tel** 0224 876544.
Ind/Abst Fish Rev. (Jan. 1989-July 1992); Index Vet.; Wildl. Rev. (Jan. 1989-July 1992).

Fish and Fisheries

UK
SCOTTISH FISHERIES RESEARCH REPORT. **Added/Corp** Great Britain. Dept. of Agriculture and Fisheries for Scotland. (1975)-. Monographic series. English. bm. free on request. Department of Agriculture and Fisheries for Scotland, PO Box 101 Victoria Road, Aberdeen AB9 8DB Scotland. **Tel** 0224 876544.

IE
SEA AND INLAND FISHERIES REPORT FOR ... / AN ROINN IASCAIGH AGUS FORAOISEACHTA (DEPT. OF FISHERIES AND FORESTRY). **Main/Corp** Ireland. Dept. of Fisheries and Forestry. **VFOAT** Report of the Minister for Fisheries and Forestry on the Sea and Inland Fisheries for the Year ... . (19??)-. English. an. 1.20p per copy. Government Publications, 4 5 Harcourt Road, Dublin 2 Ireland. **Tel** 011 353 1 6613111 Ext.4005. **LC** SH261; .I7a. **DD** 338.3/72709417. **Circ:** 1,000. *Continues Ireland. Dept. of Fisheries. Sea and Inland Fisheries Report.*

US/0271-7069
SEA GRANT REPORT (COLLEGE). (SEA GRANT REPORT.). [Sea grant rep.]. **Main/Corp** University of Alaska (College). **Added/Corp** Alaska Sea Grant Program. **VFOAT** Alaska Sea Grant Report. (19??)-. Monographic series. English. Alaska Sea Grant College Program, University of Alaska, 138 Irving II, Fairbanks AK 99775.
Ind/Abst ASTIS Curr. Aware. Bull. (1978-); ASTIS Bibliogr. (1978-); GeoRef; Ocean. Abstr.

TH
SEAFDEC NEWSLETTER / SOUTHEAST ASIAN FISHERIES DEVELOPMENT CENTER. **Added/Corp** Southeast Asian Fisheries Development Center. **VFOAT** S.E.A.F.D.E.C. Newsletter; Newsletter. **VAT** Southeast Asian Fisheries Development Center Newsletter. (19??)-. Periodical. English. Four times a year (Mar., June, Sept., Dec.). 20B Thailand; $10.00 (airmail), $6.00 (surface mail) North America. SEAFDEC Newsletter, Rama 4 Road, 956 Olympia Building, Bangkok 10500 Thailand. **Tel** 66 2 235-2071, 66 2 233-1470, telex 82156 COMSERV TH. **ED** Amanda Owden Challali. **Bk Rev. Circ:** 2,500.
Desc: A newsletter containing information about three departments of SEAFDEC in Thailand, Singapore and the Philippines; fisheries articles of interest to Southeast Asia.

US/0272-4294
SEAFOOD AMERICA. [Seaf. Am.]. Vol. 1, No. 1 (Oct. 1980)-. Periodical. English. bm. Free to qualified personnel in the seafood industry; $25.00 others, US; $40.00 others, Canada and Mexico. Seafood America Inc, PO Box 181, Kensington MD 20895. **LC** SH334.9; .S42. **DD** 664/.94/05.

II/0037-010X
SEAFOOD EXPORT JOURNAL. [Seaf. export j.]. **Added/Corp** Sea Food Exporters Association of India. (19??)-. Periodical. English. mo. $15.00. Seafood Exporters Association of India, Cochin, India. **(Subscription address:** Prints India, 11 Darya Ganj, New Delhi, 110002 India, (Phone: 011 91 11 3268645)**)** **LC** SH299; .S4.
Ind/Abst Aquat. Sci. Fish. Abstr. (Computer File); Food Sci. Technol. Abstr.; Ocean. Abstr.

UK/0268-1293
SEAFOOD INTERNATIONAL. [Seaf. int.]. (1986)-. Periodical. English (Japanese). mo. £35.00 UK; £40.00 other. EMAP Heighway, Meed House, 21 John Street, London WC1N 2BP England. **Tel** 44 71 4045513, FAX 881 3483, telex 44 71 831 9362. **ED** Mike Urch. **CODEN** SEINE5. Index available. cum. index. **Bk Rev**. **Ad Acc. Circ:** 10,000. available on an online database (file 648/Full-Text) from DIALOG.
Desc: Covers seafood processing.
Ind/Abst BioBusiness (19??-); F&S Index Plus Text, Int. (19??-) [Select. Cov.]; Food Sci. Technol. Abstr. (19??-); Foods Adlibra (19??-); PROMT (19??-); World Agric. Econ. (19??-).

US/0744-4664
SEAFOOD LEADER. [Seaf. lead.]. (1981)-. Periodical. English (French, Spanish and Japanese). Six times a year (Jan., Mar., May, July, Sept. and Nov.). $24.00 (US); $50.00 (other); 31.00Can$ (1 year); 51.00Can$ (2 year); 71.00Can$ (3 year). Waterfront Press Company, 1115 Northwest 46th Street, Seattle WA 98107. **Tel** (206)789-6506, FAX (206)789-9193, telex 272822 SFL UR. **ED** Peter Redmayne. **LC** SH334.9; .S44. **DD** 338.3/727/05. **CODEN** SELEDG. **Bk Rev**. **Ad Acc. Circ:** 16,000 (ctrl). *Continues Ocean Leader, 0279-8549.*
Desc: Written for those who make their living buying, selling, processing, handling, cooking and serving seafood. Includes reports on new seafood products, species and price information, etc.
Ind/Abst BioBusiness (1990-); F&S Index Plus Text, Int. [Select. Cov.]; Foods Adlibra; PROMT.

US/1048-1303
SEAFOOD YELLOW PAGES. (SEAFOOD YELLOW PAGES : A BUSINESS TO BUSINESS DIRECTORY.). [Seaf. yellow pages]. **Added/Corp** American Seafood Insitute. Rhode Island Seafood Council. (1990)-. Directory. English. $59.95 (single issue). Rhode Island Seafood Council, American Seafood Institute, 406-A Main Street, Wakefield RI 02879. **DD** 639.

US
SEMI-MONTHLY MEANS OF SEA SURFACE TEMPERATURE, WEST COAST. (Jan. 1-15, 1981)-. English. sm. National Meteorological Center. *Continues Fishing Information. Supplement.*

JA
SETO NAIKAI RENGO KAIKU GYOGYO CHOSEI IINKAI GIJIROKU. **Main/Corp** Japan. Seto Naikai Rengo Kaiku Gyogyo Chosei Iinkai. (19??)-. Periodical. Japanese. Seto Naikai Gyogyo Chosei Jimukyoku, Shin Minatocho, Ikuta-ku 650 Kobe Japan. **LC** SH302.I54; J37a.

JA
SETO NAIKAI SAIBAI GYOGYO HORYU GIJUTSU KAIHATSU CHOSA. Japanese. Hyogo Kenritsu Suisan Shikenjo, Japan. **LC** SH109; .S47.

US/0085-6592
SFI BULLETIN. See Recreation, Leisure-Sports.

US/0276-2137
SHELL MANAGEMENT ANNUAL REPORT. [Shell manage. annu. rep.]. **Main/Corp** Texas. Coastal Fisheries Branch. (19??)-. English. an. Texas Parks & Wildlife, 4200 Smith School Road, Austin TX 78744. **Tel** (512)707-0032. **LC** TD195.D72; T49a. **DD** 333.91/817/09764.

US/0191-2054
SHELLFISH MARKET REVIEW. [Shellfish mark. rev.]. Began with Nov. 1978. English. US Department of Commerce / National Marine Fisheries Service, 1335 East-West Highway, Silver Spring MD 20910. **Tel** (301)713-2239, FAX (301)713-2258. **LC** HD9471.U5; U54A. **DD** 381/.435/3840973. *Continues Shellfish Market Review and Outlook, 0098-8014.*

US/0559-9296
SHRIMP LANDINGS, ANNUAL SUMMARY. English. an. US Department of Commerce / National Marine Fisheries Service, 1335 East-West Highway, Silver Spring MD 20910. **Tel** (301)713-2239, FAX (301)713-2258. **LC** SH380; .S55. **DD** 639.5.

●US/1076-7568
SHRIMP NEWS INTERNATIONAL. [Shrimp news int.]. Vol. 19, No. 3 (Mar./Apr. 1994)-. Periodical. English. Six times a year. Aquaculture Digest, 9434 Kearney Mesa Road, San Diego CA 92126. **LC** SH380.6; .W673. **DD** 639. *Continues World Shrimp Farming (Bimonthly Report), 1047-5672.*

SI/0129-6485
SINGAPORE JOURNAL OF PRIMARY INDUSTRIES. See Agriculture.

US/1042-8569
SMALLMOUTH (EDGEFIELD, S.C.). (SMALLMOUTH.). **VFOAT** Small Mouth; Smallmouth Magazine. (1988)-. Periodical. English. Six times a year. $15.00. Smallmouth Inc, PO Box 670, Edgefield SC 29824. **Tel** (803)637-5722. **DD** 799.

SA/0080-5076
SOUTH AFRICAN FISHING INDUSTRY HANDBOOK AND BUYER'S GUIDE, THE. (1951)-. English. be (Publishes once every 2 years in Apr.). R93.50. Marine Information Services Pty. Ltd., PO Box 487, Stellenbosch 7600 South Africa. **Tel** 011 27 2231 900280. **LC** SH315.S7; S6. **DD** 338.372; 639.

SA/0038-2671
SOUTH AFRICAN SHIPPING NEWS AND FISHING INDUSTRY REVIEW, THE. See Transportation-Ships and Shipping.

NL
SOUTH PACIFIC COMMISSION FISHERIES NEWSLETTER, THE. **Main/Corp** South Pacific Commission. No. 11 (1974)-. Newsletter. English. South Pacific Commission, PO Box D5, Noumea Cedex New Caledonia. **Tel** (687)26 20 00, FAX (687)26 38 18. **LC** SH319.A2; S66a. **DD** 639/.22/0996. *Continues South Pacific Islands Fisheries Development Agency. Newsletter - South Pacific Islands Fisheries Deveopment Agency.*
Ind/Abst Aquat. Sci. Fish. Abstr. (Computer File).

SA/1018-9688
SOUTHERN AFRICAN JOURNAL OF AQUATIC SCIENCES. **Added/Corp** Southern African Society of Aquatic Scientists. Vol. 15, No. 1 (June 1989)-. Academic Scholarly Publication. English. sa. South African Society of Aquatic Scientists, University Cape Town, Zoology Department, 7700 Rondebosch South Africa. **Tel** 011 27 21 6503638. **CODEN** SAASEK. Documents available from CASDDS. *Continues Journal of the Limnological Society of Southern Africa.*
Ind/Abst Chem. Abstr.

GW
SPANIEN, LAND- UND FORSTWIRTSCHAFT, FISCHEREI / BUNDESSTELLE FUER AUSSENHANDELSINFORMATION. See Agriculture.

US/0445-3042
SPECIAL FISHERIES REPORT - STATE OF ILLINOIS. [Spec. fish. rep.]. No. 1 (1964)-. Monographic series. English. Price varies per volume. Illinois Division of Fisheries, Springfield IL 62704. **LC** SH11; .I297. **DD** 639. **CODEN** IDDSAA. Documents available from BIOSIS Document Express.
Ind/Abst Biol. Abstr.

US/0097-0638
SPECIAL PUBLICATION - AMERICAN FISHERIES SOCIETY. [Spec. publ., Am. Fish. Soc.]. **Added/Corp** American Fisheries Society. (1948)-. Monographic series. English. ir. Price varies per volume. American Fisheries Society, 5410 Grosvenor Lane, Suite 110, Bethesda MD 20814-2199. **Tel** (301)897-8616, (301)897-8621, FAX (301)897-8096. **(Subscription address:** American Fisheries Society, PO Box 1056, Evans City PA 16033.**)** **LC** UNC. **CODEN** AFPUA2. **[CCC]**.

US/0193-1245
SPECIAL PUBLICATION - DIVISION OF FISH AND WILDLIFE, SECTION OF FISHERIES. (SPECIAL PUBLICATION - DIVISION OF FISH AND WILDLIFE, SECTION OF FISHERIES (MINNESOTA).). **Main/Corp** Minnesota. Section of Fisheries. Monographic series. English. ir. Price varies per volume. Department of Natural Resources / Minnesota, 350 Centennial Building, St Paul MN 55155. **LC** SH11.M68; D58A. **DD** 639.9/7709776. Index available. cum. index. **Circ:** 300 (ctrl).

BE/0774-0689
SPECIAL PUBLICATION / EUROPEAN AQUACULTURE SOCIETY. **Added/Corp** European Aquaculture Society. **VFOAT** EAS Special Publication; EAS Special Publication Series. No. 9 (1986)-. Monographic series. English (French). ir. Price varies per volume. European Aquaculture Society, Coupure Rechts 168, B 9000 Gent Belgium. **Tel** 011 32 9 2237722, FAX 011 32 9 2237604. *Continues Special Publication (European Mariculture Society).*
Ind/Abst Anim. Breed. Abstr.

GR
SPECIAL PUBLICATION - INSTITUTE OF OCEANOGRAPHIC AND FISHERIES RESEARCH. See Earth Sciences-Oceanography.

US
SPECIAL PUBLICATION SERIES (ATLANTIC SALMON FEDERATION). (SPECIAL PUBLICATION SERIES.). **VFOAT** ASF Special Publication Series. No. 11 (1983)-. Monographic series. English. ir. Price varies per volume. Atlantic Salmon Federation, PO Box 429, St Andrews New Brunswick, E0G 2X0 Canada. **Tel** (506)529-4581, (506)529-1025, FAX (506)529-4438, telex 014-47458. *Continues IASF Special Publication Series.*
Desc: Subjects include salmon genetics, economics, management, aquaculture, fisheries and acid rain.

JA/0493-4008
SPECIAL PUBLICATIONS - TOKAI REGIONAL FISHERIES RESEARCH LABORATORY. **Main/Corp** Tokai-ku Suisan Kenkyujo. No. 1 (1952)-. Monographic series. English. **DD** 639.
Ind/Abst Aquat. Sci. Fish. Abstr. (Computer File).

US/0099-5541
SPECIAL REPORT - MONTANA FISH AND GAME DEPARTMENT. **Main/Corp** Montana. Fish and Game Department. No. 1 (1966)-. Monographic series. English. Price varies per volume.

SA
SPECIAL REPORT / REPUBLIC OF SOUTH AFRICA, DEPARTMENT OF ENVIRONMENT AFFAIRS, SEA FISHERIES RESEARCH INSTITUTE. **Added/Corp** Sea Fisheries Research Institute (South Africa). **VFOAT** Spesiale Verslag; Spec. Rep. Sea Fish. Res. Inst. S. Afr.; Spes. Versl. NavorsInst. Seeviss. S.-Afr. (1984)-. Monographic series. English. Price varies per volume. Sea Fisheries Research Institute, Private Bag X2, Rogge Bay, 8012, Cape Town, South Africa.
Ind/Abst Aquat. Sci. Fish. Abstr. (Computer File).

Fish and Fisheries

US/0734-3914
SPECIAL SCIENTIFIC REPORT - NORTH CAROLINA. DIVISION OF MARINE FISHERIES. (SPECIAL SCIENTIFIC REPORT / DIVISION OF MARINE FISHERIES, NORTH CAROLINA DEPARTMENT OF NATURAL AND ECONOMIC RESOURCES.). [Spec. sci. rep. - N.C., Div. Mar. Fish.]. Monographic series. English. ir. Price varies per volume. Department of Natural Resources and Community Development / Morehead City North Carolina, Division of Marine Fisheries, PO Box 769, Morehead City NC 28557. **Tel** (919)726-7021. **ED** Michael W Street. **Circ:** 100. *Continues* Special Scientific Report (North Carolina. Division of Commercial and Sports Fisheries).
Desc: Life histories, habitat, and management of marine and estuarine fisheries, including estuarine, marine, and anadromous finfishes, crustaceans, and bivalve shellfish.

US/0172-6161
SPRINGER SERIES ON ENVIRONMENTAL MANAGEMENT. *See* Environmental Issues-Conservation and Natural Resources.

CN/0527-6942
STATISTICAL BASEBOOK SERIES - ECONOMICS SERVICE, DEPARTMENT OF FISHERIES OF CANADA. *See* Fish and Fisheries-Abstracting, Bibliographies and Statistics.

CN/0250-6394
STATISTICAL BULLETIN / NORTHWEST ATLANTIC FISHERIES ORGANIZATION. *See* Fish and Fisheries-Abstracting, Bibliographies and Statistics.

CN/0535-1588
STATISTICAL YEARBOOK / INTERNATIONAL NORTH PACIFIC FISHERIES COMMISSION. *See* Fish and Fisheries-Abstracting, Bibliographies and Statistics.

II
STATISTICS OF MARINE PRODUCTS EXPORTS. *See* Fish and Fisheries-Abstracting, Bibliographies and Statistics.

CN/0319-9436
STEELHEAD HARVEST ANALYSIS. [Steelhead harvest anal.]. English. an. Ministry of the Environment, Parliament Building, Water Investigation, Victoria British Columbia V8V 1X5 Canada. **Tel** (604)387-1111. **LC** SH687.7; .S75. **DD** 333.95/613. **Circ:** 125 (ctrl).
Desc: Annual analysis of provincial steelhead catch in the recreational fishery of British Columbia.

US/0279-0610
STRIPED BASS MAGAZINE. (STRIPED BASS MAGAZINE / AMERICAN STRIPED BASS SOCIETY.). Periodical. English. bm. American Striped Bass Society, PO Box 50, Striped Bass Building, Edgefield SC 29824.

US/0199-5634
STRIPER. VFOAT Striper Magazine. Periodical. English. bm. $15.00. Sunbelt Fulfillment Services, PO Box 41094, Nashville TN 37204. **Tel** (202)337-7000. **ED** Will Landers. **Ad Acc. Circ:** 31,000.
Desc: Content dedicated to sportfishing, resource management, fishing education and better understanding of our outdoors.

IT/0433-3519
STUDIES AND REVIEWS - GENERAL FISHERIES COUNCIL FOR THE MEDITERRANEAN. Main/Corp General Fisheries Council for the Mediterranean. **VFOAT** Etudes et Revues - Conseil General des Peches pour la Mediterranee. No. 1- 1957-. Monographic series. Multiple languages (French). Price varies per volume. UNIPUB, 4611-F Assembly Drive, Lanham MD 20706-4391. **Tel** (800)274-4888, FAX (301)459-0056, telex 28787 GATT CH. **LC** SH1. **DD** 639. **Circ:** 1,200.
Desc: Scientific and technical papers dealing with subjects related to the programme of work or GFCM or with topics of interest for fisheries management and development in the mediterranean.

KO
SUHYOP TONGGYE WOLBO. VFOAT Monthly Statistics. V. 16- No. 1 (Jan. 1984)-. English (Korean). mo. Susanop Hyoptong Chohap Chunganghoe, 88 Kyongun-dong Chongno-ku, Seoul 110 Korea. **LC** SH302.5; .S94A. *Continues* Suhyop Chosa Wolbo.

JA/0370-9361
SUISAN DAIGAKKO KENKYU HOKOKU. [Suisan Daigakko kenkyu hokoku]. **VFOAT** Journal of the Shimonoseki University of Fisheries. Vol. 12 (Feb. 1963)-. Academic Scholarly Publication. Japanese. Three times a year. Suisancho Suisan Daigakko, (Shimonoseki University of Fisheries, Fisheries Agency), 1944, Nagata Honcho, Yoshimi, Shimonosekishi, Yamaguchiken 759-65, Japan. **CODEN** SDKHAK. Documents available from BIOSIS Document Express, CASDDS. *Continues* Kenkyu Hokoku.
Ind/Abst Biol. Abstr.; Chem. Abstr.; SEA Abstr.

JA/0286-6536
SUISAN FUKAJO KENKYU HOKOKU. [Suisan Fukajo kenkyu hokoku]. **Added/Corp** Hokkaidoritsu Suisan Fukajo. **VFOAT** Scientific Reports of the Hokkaido Fish Hatchery. (Dec. 1957)-. Japanese (summaries and/or abstracts in English). Hokkaidoritsu Suisan Fukajo, (Hokkaido Fish Hatchery), 3, Kitakashiwagicho, Eniwashi, Hokkaido 061-14, Japan. **CODEN** HSFHDG. Documents available from CASDDS. *Continues* Fukajo Shiken Hokoku.
Ind/Abst Aquat. Sci. Fish. Abstr. (Computer File); Chem. Abstr.; Index Vet.; Protozoolog. Abstr.

JA/0916-1562
SUISAN KAIYO KENKYU. Added/Corp Suisan Kaiyo Gakkai. **VFOAT** Bulletin of the Japanese Society of Fisheries Oceanography. (1989)-. Periodical. Japanese. Four times a year. ¥114.00. Japanese Society of Fisheries and Oceanography, c/o Tokyo University of Fisheries, 5-7 Konan 4 Minato-ku, Tokyo 108 Japan. **Tel** 11 81 3 34711251 Ext. 274. **ED** Naofumi Inoue. **LC** SH1; .S86. **Bk Rev. Ad Acc. Circ:** 1,000 (ctrl). *Continues* Suisan Kaiyo Kenkyukai Ho, 0388-9149.
Desc: Studies on the influence of oceanographical conditions on fishing from physical, chemical and biological approaches. Reviews of symposium on the correlation between marine and environmental conditions and fisheries.

JA/0388-9718
SUISAN KOGAKU KENKYUJO HOKOKU. [Suisan Kogaku Kenkyujo hokoku]. **VFOAT** Bulletin of National Research Institute of Fisheries Engineering. Vol. 1 (March 1980)-. Periodical. English (Japanese). Suisan Kogaku Kenkyujo, Ebidai 314-04, Ibaraki-ken Japan. **LC** SH334.5; .S9.

FI
SUOMEN KALASTUSLEHTI. Added/Corp Suomen Kalastusyhdistys. (1892)-. Periodical. Finnish. Eight times a year. Fmk170.00. Kalatalouden Keskusliitto, Federation of Finnish Fisheries Associations, Koydenpunojankatu 7 B 23, 00180 Helsinki 10 Finland. **Tel** 358 0 640 126, FAX 358 0 608 309. **ED** Markku Myllyla. **LC** SH1; .S9. Index available. **Bk Rev. Circ:** 4,392 (ctrl). available with charts; available with illustrations.
Desc: Provides information on fisheries.

FI/0085-6940
SUOMEN KALATALOUS. [Suom. Kalatal.]. **VFOAT** Finlands Fiskerier. (1912)-. Periodical. Finnish (summaries and/or abstracts in English). ir. Finnish Game and Fisheries Research Institute / Game Division, PO Box 202, FIN-00151 Helsinki Finland. **LC** SH293.F5; F5.

IO
SURVEI PERIKANAN LAUT. Indonesian. ir. Rp1500 Indonesia; $1.00 US. Central Bureau of Statistics / Indonesia, c/o Dr. Sutomo, 8 Jalan, PO Box 3, Jakarta Indonesia. **Tel** 372808 374908 Ext.342. **LC** HD9466.I55; S87. ctrl circ.

US
SURVEY OF BLACK BASS TOURNAMENT FISHING IN TEXAS, A. Added/Corp Texas. Parks and Wildlife Dept. Inland Fisheries Branch. English. an. P Durocher, Texas Parks and Wildlife Department, Austin TX 78744. **LC** SH681; .D87. **DD** 799.1/758.

KO
SUSANMUL KYETONG PANMAEGO TONGGYE YONBO. *See* Fish and Fisheries-Abstracting, Bibliographies and Statistics.

US/1048-9215
TACKLE TEST. Title Change. [Tack. test]. Vol. 1, No. 1 (April 1990)-(1993). Periodical. English. mo. Belvoir Publications Inc., 75 Holly Hill Lane, Greenwich CT 06836. **Tel** (203)661-6111, FAX (203)661-4802. **ED** W. Todd Woodard. **DD** 799. *Continued by* Tackle Tester, 1068-5812.
Desc: Provides insightful, researched evaluations and ratings of freshwater fishing equipment including boats, electronics, lines, rods, reels, lures and accesories.

AT
TASMANIAN FISHERIES RESEARCH. Added/Corp Tasmania. Sea Fisheries Division. (196?)-. Periodical. English. **LC** SH318.T3; T3.
Ind/Abst Aquat. Sci. Fish. Abstr. (Computer File).

UK/0072-6729
TECHNICAL BULLETIN - MINISTRY OF AGRICULTURE, FISHERIES AND FOOD. *See* Agriculture.

US
TECHNICAL FISHERY REPORT. Added/Corp Alaska. Division of Commercial Fisheries. **VFOAT** Technical Fisheries Report; Technical Fisheries Report Series. No. 1 (1987)-. Monographic series. English. ir. Price varies per volume. Alaska Department of Fish and Game, PO Box 3-2000, Juneau AK 99802. **Tel** (907)465-4100, (907)465-4286. **LC** SH11; .A7252a. **DD** 639.2/09798. **CODEN** TFRAET. *Continues* ADF&G Technical Data Report, 0095-4632.

US/0579-3920
TECHNICAL REPORT - INTERNATIONAL PACIFIC HALIBUT COMMISSION. (TECHNICAL REPORT.). [Tech. rep. - Int. Pac. Halibut Comm.]. **Main/Corp** International Pacific Halibut Commission (Canada and United States). **Added/Corp** International Pacific Halibut Commission. No. 1 (1969)-. Monographic series. English. ir. Price varies per volume. International Pacific Halibut Commission, PO Box 95009, Seattle WA 98145-2009. **Tel** (206)634-1838, FAX (206)632-2983. **DD** 639/.27/58. **CODEN** IHCTB3. Documents available from BIOSIS Document Express.
Ind/Abst Biol. Abstr.; Fish Rev.; Ocean. Abstr.; Wildl. Rev.

UK/0308-5589
TECHNICAL REPORT SERIES - FISHERIES LABORATORY. (FISHERIES RESEARCH TECHNICAL REPORT.). [Tech. rep. ser. - Fish. lab.]. Academic Scholarly Publication. English. Price varies per volume. Ministry of Agriculture Fisheries & Food, Directorate of Fisheries Research, Lowestoft Suffolk NR33 0HT England. **CODEN** FRTRDJ. Documents available from BIOSIS Document Express, CASDDS.
Ind/Abst Biol. Abstr. (-1988); Chem. Abstr. (-1982); Geogr. Abstr. Human Geogr.

NZ/0111-932X
TECHNICAL REPORT SOUTHERN SOUTH ISLAND REGION, AGRICULTURAL RESEARCH DIVISION, MINISTRY OF AGRICULTURE & FISHERIES. *See* Agriculture.

US/0083-7474
TECHNICAL REPORT - WASHINGTON DEPARTMENT OF FISHERIES. (TECHNICAL REPORT / STATE OF WASHINGTON DEPARTMENT OF FISHERIES.). No. 1 (1970)-. Monographic series. English. Price varies per volume. Washington State Department of Fisheries, Olympia WA 98504. **LC** UNC. **CODEN** WDFTA7. Documents available from BIOSIS Document Express.
Desc: Includes abstracts of some reports.
Ind/Abst Biol. Abstr.; Fish Rev. (Jan. 1989-July 1992); Wildl. Rev. (Jan. 1989-July 1992).

US
TECHNICAL SERIES - FISHERIES SECTION (DES MOINES). (TECHNICAL SERIES - FISHERIES SECTION.). **Main/Corp** Iowa. Fisheries Section. **VFOAT** Iowa Fisheries Research. No. 71 (1971)-. Monographic series. English. Price varies per volume. Iowa Conservation Commission, Fisheries Section, State Office Building, 300 4th Street, Des Moines IA 50319. **LC** SH11; .I813. **DD** 639.

US/0434-9504
TECHNICAL SUMMARY - GULF STATES MARINE FISHERIES COMMISSION. Main/Corp Gulf States Marine Fisheries Commission. No. 1 (Oct. 1958)-. Monographic series. English. Price varies per volume. Gulf States Marine Fisheries Commission, New Orleans LA 70122. **DD** 639.

CN/0225-199X
TECHNIQUES DE PECHE. [Tech. peche]. No. 1- ; 1978-. Periodical. French. qt. $2.00 Each Number. La Maison Faits de Peche, CP 400, St-Pie Quebec J0H 1W0 Canada. **Tel** (514)772-5160. **ED** R Denys Benoit. **DD** 799.1/1/05. **Ad Acc. Circ:** 30,000.
Desc: The magazine is the only French Annual in the province of Quebec that specializes in teaching fishing methods that really work, how to use and be efficient with the new equipment, rods and reels, lures, electronic equipment, boats and outboards.

MX
TECNICA PESQUERA. Ceased. (1968)-(199?). Periodical. Spanish. mo. Ediciones Mundo Marino SA, PO Box 21-500 Coyoacan, Mexico DF 04000 Mexico. **Tel** 549 5103 OR 544 3988. **ED** Rosa Maria Oliver. **Bk Rev. Ad Acc. Circ:** 4,000.
Desc: All about commercial fisheries and investigations in the oceans. Technology, economy, methodology and information on commercial fishing.
Ind/Abst Aquat. Sci. Fish. Abstr. (Computer File).

US/0734-7278
TEXAS COMMERCIAL HARVEST STATISTICS. *See* Fish and Fisheries-Abstracting, Bibliographies and Statistics.

US/8750-7951
TEXAS FISHERMAN. Title Change. [Tex. fisherman]. (19??)-(19??). Periodical. English. mo. Sports Magazines of America, 7633 East 63rd Place/Suite 420, Tulsa OK 74133. **DD** 799. *Merged into* Texas Fish & Game.

GR/0250-3298
THALASSOGRAFIKA. (THALASSOGRAPHIKA / INSTITOUTON OKEANOGRAPHIKON KAI ALIEUTIKON EREUNON.). [Thalassografika]. **Added/Corp** Institouton Okeanographikon kai Alieutikon Ereunon (Greece). **VFOAT** Thalassographica. (Oct. 1976)-. Periodical. English (French and Greek, Modern). ir. **LC** QH90.A1; H44a. **CODEN** THALDO. ***Continues*** *Hellenike Okeanologia kai Limnologia.*
Ind/Abst Aquat. Sci. Fish. Abstr. (Computer File).

FI/0355-0648
TIEDONANTOJA - RIISTA- JA KALATALOUDEN TUTKIMUSLAITOS KALANTUKIMUSOSASTO. **Main/Corp** Riista-Ja Kalatalouden Tutkimuslaitos. Kalantukimusosasto. Vol. 1 (1971)-. Finnish. Riista- Ja Kalatalouden Tutkimuslaitos, Kalantutkimusosasto PL 202, 00151 Helsinki 15 Finland. ***Continues in part*** *Finland. Kalataloudellinen Tutkimustoimisto. Monistettuja Julkaisuja., 0430-5183.; Kalataloudellisen Tutkimustoimiston Tiedonantoja.*

JA
TOKAI-KU SUISAN KENKYUJO GYOSEKI MOKUROKU. **Main/Corp** Tokai-ku Suisan Kenkyujo, Tokyo. No. 1- 1972-. Japanese. Tokai-ku Suisan Kenkyujo, Kachideki 5-chome Chuo-ku, Tokyo 104 Japan. **LC** Z5972; .T57A.

JA/0495-7490
TOKAI-KU SUISAN KENKYUJO GYOSEKISHU. **Main/Corp** Tokai-Ku Suisan Kenkyujo. **VFOAT** Collected Reprints from the Tokai Regional Fisheries Research Laboratory. Japanese (English). Tokai-ku Suisan Kenkyujo, Kachideki 5-chome Chuo-ku, Tokyo 104 Japan. **LC** SH302.P33; T63A.

TRANSACTIONS - NORTHEAST FISH & WILDLIFE CONFERENCE. **Main/Corp** Northeast Fish and Wildlife Conference. (19??)-. English.
Ind/Abst Key Word Index Wildl. Res.

US/0002-8487
TRANSACTIONS OF THE AMERICAN FISHERIES SOCIETY (1900). (TRANSACTIONS OF THE AMERICAN FISHERIES SOCIETY.). [Trans. Am. Fish. Soc.]. **Main/Corp** American Fisheries Society. Vol. 29 (1900)-. Academic Scholarly Publication. English. bm. $425.00 US; $460.00 other (library). American Fisheries Society, 5410 Grosvenor Lane, Suite 110, Bethesda MD 20814-2199. **Tel** (301)897-8616, (301)897-8621, FAX (301)897-8096. **LC** SH1; .A51. **CODEN** TAFSAI. **[CCC].** Index available in last issue of volume--attached. cum. index. **Ad Acc. Pr Rev. Acid Free.** available on microfilm from University Microfilms International (UMI). Documents available from The Genuine Article, BIOSIS Document Express, CASDDS, Documents on Demand. ***Continues*** *Proceedings of the American Fisheries Society.*
Desc: Provides for the exchange and dissemination of technical and scientific fisheries information.
Ind/Abst Abstr. Bull. Inst. Pap. Sci. Tech.; AGRICOLA; Agric. Eng. Abstr.; Anim. Breed. Abstr.; AQUAREF; Aquat. Sci. Fish. Abstr. (Computer File); Biol. Agric. Index; Biol. Abstr.; Chem. Abstr.; CSA Neuro. Abstr. (?-?); Curr. Aware. Biol. Sci., CABS; Curr. Contents, Agric. Biol. Environ. Sci.; Curr. Ref. Fish Res.; Ecology Abstr.; EMBASE; Energy Res. Abstr.; Environ. Abstr.; Fish Rev.; Fresh. Aqua. Contents Tables; Helminthol. Abstr.; Index Vet.; Mar. Sci. Contents Tables; Nutr. Abstr. Rev., Ser. B, Live Feeds and Feed.; Ocean. Abstr.; Life Sci. Collect.; Pollut. Abstr. Indexes; Protozoolog. Abstr.; Res. Alert [Full Cov.]; Sci. Cit. Index; SCISEARCH; Vet. Bull.; Wildl. Rev.

US/0041-3259
TROPICAL FISH HOBBYIST. [Trop. fish hobbyist]. (1953)-. Periodical. English. Twelve times a year. $30.00 (one year), $55.00 (two year), $75.00 (three year). T F H Publications, Inc, 1 TFH Plaza, 3rd and Union Avenues, Neptune City NJ 07753. **Tel** (908)988-8400, FAX (908)988-5466, telex 132468. **ED** Ray Hunziker. **LC** SF456; .T75. **DD** 639.3/4/05. Index available (bound in issue). cum. index. **Bk Rev. Ad Acc, Adv Mgr:** Amy Manning. **Circ:** 50,000.
Desc: Tropical fish magazine featuring timely articles about rare and popular fish.
Ind/Abst Aquat. Sci. Fish. Abstr. (Computer File); Fish Rev.; Mag. Search; Vocat. Search (Jan. 1993-).

UK/0041-3372
TROUT AND SALMON. [Trout salmon]. (1955)-. Periodical. English. Twelve times a year. £18.00 UK, £23.50 others (surface mail); £30.50 Europe, £33.50 Middle East & North Africa, £40.50 others, £43.50 Pacific Island, Australasia & Far East (airmail). EMAP National Publications Ltd, Farndon Road, Market Harborough, Leicestershire, LE16 9NR England. **Tel** 011 44 733 555161. **ED** Sandy Leventon. **[CCC]. Bk Rev. Ad Acc. Circ:** 55,000.
Desc: Features, news on all aspects of game fishing.
Ind/Abst AGRICOLA.

UK
TROUT FISHERMAN. **See** Recreation, Leisure-Outdoor Life.

UK/0954-7037
TROUT NEWS. [Trout news]. (1987)-. Periodical. English. qt. **DD** 338.3727550941.
Ind/Abst Index Vet.

RU/0372-2864
TRUDY - VSESOJUZNYJ NAUCNO-ISSLEDOVATELSKIJ INSTITUT MORSKOGO RYBNOGO HOZJAISTVA I OKEANOGRAFII. (TRUDY VSESOIUZNOGO NAUCHNO-ISSLEDOVATELSKOGO INSTITUTA MORSKOGO RYBNOGO KHOZIAISTVA I OKEANOGRAFII / NARODNYI KOMISSARIAT PISHCHEVOI PROMYSHLENNOSTI SSSR.). [Tr. - Vses. naucno-issled. inst. morsk. rybn. hoz. okeanogr.]. **Added/Corp** Vsesoiuznyi Nauchno-Issledovatelskii Institut Morskogo Rybnogo Khoziaistva i Okeanografii (Soviet Union) Soviet Union. Narodnyi Komissariat Rybnoi Promyshlennosti. Soviet Union. Narodnyi Komissariat Pishchevoi Promyshlennosti. Tikhookeanskii Nauchno-Issledovatelski Institut Rybnogo Khoziastva i Okeanografii (Soviet Union). **VFOAT** Transactions of the Institute of Marine Fisheries and Oceanography; Trudy VNIRO; Proceedings - All-Union Research Institute of Marine Fisheries and Oceanography. Vol. 1 (1935)-. Academic Scholarly Publication. Russian (summaries and/or abstracts in English and German; table of contents in English and German). Price varies per volume. **LC** SH1; .M65. **CODEN** TVKOA8. Documents available from CASDDS. ***Separated from*** *Trudy Gosudarstvennogo Okeanograficheskogo Instituta.*
Ind/Abst Chem. Abstr. (?-1978); GeoRef.

FR/0396-518X
TRUITE OMBRE SAUMON. **VFOAT** T.O.S. Truite Ombre Saumon. (1963)-. Periodical. French. bm. **UDC** 63.
Ind/Abst Aquat. Sci. Fish. Abstr. (Computer File).

SP
TUNA CATCH AND EFFORT, AND SIZE DATA FOR ... LONGLINE FISHERY, COLLECTED AT TRANSSHIPMENT PORTS IN THE ATLANTIC. **VFOAT** Donnes Thonieres de Prise et Effort et de Taille, ... , Pecherie Palangriere, Recueillies dans les Ports Atlantiques de Transbordement. English (English). Calle del Principe de Vergara 17-7O, Madrid 1 Spain. **LC** SH351.T8; T78. **DD** 338.3/72758.

US/1064-6418
TWINE LINE : OHIO SEA GRANT PROGRAM NEWSLETTER. [Twine line]. **Added/Corp** Ohio Sea Grant Program. Ohio Sea Grant College Program. **VFOAT** Ohio Sea Grant Twine Line. (19??)- Vol. 15 (Feb. 1993)-. Newsletter. English. Six times a year (Feb., Apr., June, Aug., Oct., Dec.). $4.50. Ohio State University / Sea Grant, 1314 Kinnear, Columbus OH 43212. **Tel** (614)292-8949, FAX (614)292-4364. **ED** Maran Brainard. **DD** 574. **Circ:** 4,000 (ctrl).

SA/0041-476X
TYDSKRIF VIR LETTERKUNDE. [Tydskr. letterkd.]. **Added/Corp** Afrikaanse Skrywerskring. Vol. 1 (March 1951)-. Periodical. Afrikaans. qt. R17.55 South Africa; R20.00 other. Foundation for Education Science & Technology, PO Box 1758, Pretoria 0001 South Africa. **Tel** 011 27 12 3226404, FAX 011 27 12 3207803. **ED** N. H. Gopal Dutt. **Bk Rev. Ad Acc. Circ:** 700.
Desc: Covers fish taxonomy, ecology, biogeography, fish behavior, toxicology, reviews, applied fisheries, and all aspects of fish research.
Ind/Abst MLA Int. Bibl. Books Artic. Mod. Lang. Lit.

US/0148-5318
U.S. PRODUCTION OF FISH FILLETS AND STEAKS, ANNUAL SUMMARY. ***Title Change.*** **Added/Corp** United States. National Marine Fisheries Service. **VAT** United States Production of Fish Fillets and Steaks, Annual Summary. (19??)-(19??). English. an. US Department of Commerce / National Marine Fisheries Service, 1335 East-West Highway, Silver Spring MD 20910. **Tel** (301)713-2239, FAX (301)713-2258. ***Absorbed by*** *Processed Fishery Products, Annual Summary, 0148-5296.*

UK/0963-9446
UK TRADE BULLETIN IMPORTS & EXPORTS OF FISH & FISH PRODUCTS. [UK trade bull. imports exports fish fish prod.]. **VFOAT** Monthly Trade Bulletin of United Kingdom Imports and Exports of Fish and Fish Products; United Kingdom Trade Bulletin Imports and Exports of Fish and Fish Products. (198?)-. Bulletin. English. mo. £35.00 UK; £45.00 Europe; £55.00 other. Sea Fish Industry Authority, 18 Logie Mill, Logie Green Road, Edinburgh EH7 4HG Scotland. **Tel** 011 44 31 558-3331 ext. 256, FAX 011 44 31 558-1442. ***Continues*** *Trade bulletin.*
Desc: Provides information on the value and quantity of imports and exports of fish intended for human consumption based on HM Customs and Excise data.

US/0747-9832
UNITED FLY TYERS' ROUNDTABLE. **Added/Corp** United Fly Tyers. **VFOAT** Roundtable. (19??)-. Periodical. English. qt. $15.00 US; $18.00 Canada; $20.00 (surface mail), $25.00 (airmail) other. United Fly Tyers Inc, PO Box 220, Maynard MA 01754. **LC** SH451; .R64. **DD** 688.7/912. **Bk Rev. Ad Acc. Circ:** 2,000 (ctrl). ***Continues*** *Roundtable (Boston, Mass.), 0161-9861.*
Desc: Non-profit organization dedicated to the education, promotion, and preservation of the art and science of fly tying.

US/0747-6493
UP-LAND FISHING. **VFOAT** Upland Fishing Annual; Upland Fishing. English. an. $3.25. Upland Publishing Company, Swamp Road, PO Box 527, West Stockbridge MA 01266-0527. **LC** SH464.N48; U6. **DD** 799.1/10974.

US/0278-9345
USDC APPROVED LIST OF FISH ESTABLISHMENTS AND PRODUCTS. English. Twice a year. Free. DOC/NOAA/NMFS/NSIL, 3209 Frederic Street, Pascagoula MS 39567. **Tel** (601)762-1892, FAX (601)769-1436. **ED** George J Haines. **LC** SH335.5.Q35; A66. **Circ:** 3,000. available on microfiche (Vols. for (1981-) distributed to libraries).
Desc: Listing sanitary fish plants and products produced under federal inspection bearing federal marks for use by institutional and retail purchasing agents in purchasing inspected fishery products.

US/0092-5810
VERMONT'S FISHERIES ANNUAL. **Main/Corp** Vermont. Fish and Game Dept. 1st- 1973-. English. an. Vermont Fish and Wildlife Department, 103 South Main, Building 10-S, Waterbury VT 05671. **Tel** (802)244-7331. **LC** SH11; .V52A. **DD** 639/.2/09743.

GW/0343-2203
VEROFFENTLICHUNGEN DES INSTITUTS FUER KUSTEN- UND BINNENFISCHEREI HAMBURG. [Veroff. Inst. Kusten- Binnenfisch. Hambg.]. (1950)-. Monographic series. German. ir. Price varies per volume. **UDC** 551.463/.464(083.53).
Ind/Abst Aquat. Sci. Fish. Abstr. (Computer File).

●US/1064-4768
VIRGINIA ACQUACULTURE MARKET NEWS REPORT. (VIRGINIA ACQUACULTURE MARKET NEWS REPORT / VIRGINIA DEPARTMENT OF AGRICULTURE AND CONSUMER SERVICES.). [Va. acquac. mark. news rep.]. **Added/Corp** Virginia. Dept. of Agriculture and Consumer Services. Virginia. Market Information Program. (July 10, 1992)-. Periodical. English. bw. Free. Virginia Department of Agriculture & Consumer Services, 1100 Bank Street, Washington Building, Suite 210, Richmond VA 23219. **Tel** (804)786-2373, FAX (804)371-7679. **DD** 338.

RU/0042-8752
VOPROSY IKHTIOLOGII. [Vopr. ihtiol.]. **Added/Corp** Akademiia Nauk SSSR. Akademiia Nauk SSSR. Ikhtiologicheskaia Komissiia. (1953)-. Academic Scholarly Publication. Russian. bm. $173.00. Izdatelstvo Nauka / Akademiia Nauk, Publishing House of the Russian Academy of Sciences, Leninskii Porspekt 14, 117901 Moscow Russia. **Tel** 011 95 954-21-53, FAX 011 95 938-21-44, telex 411964. **(Subscription address:** East View Publications Inc., 3020 Harbor Lane North, Suite 110, Minneapolis MN 55447.) **LC** QL614; .V6. **CODEN** VOIKAR. **[CCC].** Index available. **Bk Rev.** Documents available from BIOSIS Document Express, CASDDS.
Ind/Abst Aquat. Sci. Fish. Abstr. (Computer File); Biol. Abstr.; Chem. Abstr.

US/1068-2112
WALLEYE IN-SIDER. [Walleye in-sider]. (199?)-. Periodical. English. bm. $9.97. In-Fisherman Inc., Two In-Fisherman Drive, Brainerd MN 56401. **Tel** (218)829-1648, FAX (218)829-3091. **ED** Doug Stange. **DD** 799. **Ad Acc, Adv Mgr:** Jim Besenfelder. **Circ:** 50,000. ***Continues*** *In-Fisherman Walleye In-Sider.*
Desc: Provides information on walleye fishing. Includes features on tackle, tournaments and topics that blend fishery science with practical fishing experience.

US/1051-0583
WATER FARMING JOURNAL. (WATER FARMING JOURNAL : NORTH AMERICA'S AQUACULTURE NEWSPAPER.). [Water farming j.]. July (1986)-. Periodical. English. ir. $24.00 (one year), $45.00 (two-year). Carroll Trosclair & Association Inc., 3400 Neyrey Drive, Metairie LA 70002. **Tel** (504)454-8934, FAX (504)488-4135. **ED** Carroll Paul Trosclair. **DD** 639. **Ad Acc, Adv Mgr:** B. Rombach, **Tel** (504)454-8934. **Circ:** 6,000 (ctrl).
Desc: Topics covered include; aquaculture, production, marketing, legislation, technology and equipment.

PL/0867-3195
WEDKARZ POLSKI. (1990)-. Periodical. Polish. mo. Price on Request. **(Subscription address:** ARS Polona, PO Box 1001, 00068 Warsaw Poland.) **UDC** 438.

CN/0836-8600
WESTCOAST FISHERMAN (VANCOUVER). (THE WESTCOAST FISHERMAN.). [Westcoast fisherman]. (July 1986)-. Periodical. English. Twelve times a year. 30.00Can$ Canada; 40.00Can$ other. Westcoast Publishing Ltd., 1496 West 72nd Avenue, Vancouver British Columbia V6P 3C8 Canada. **Tel** (800)972-1060, (604)266-7433, FAX (604)263-8620. **ED** Peter Robson. **DD** 338.3/727/09711. **Bk Rev**. **Ad Acc**, **Adv Mgr:** Joyce Haughian.

AT/1035-493X
WESTERN ANGLER. (1988)-. Periodical. English. bm (Feb., Apr., June, Aug., Oct., Dec.). 52.00Aus$ Australia; 72.00 other. Western Angler, PO Box 362, Mountain Hawthorn NA 6016 Australia. **Tel** 011 61 9 244 3411, FAX 011 61 9 244 1709. **ED** Ian Stagles. **Bk Rev**, (Qty: 3). **Ad Acc**, **Adv Mgr Tel** 09 227 7266. **Circ:** 7,000 (ctrl). ***Continues*** *Western Angler and Diver, 0818-4070.*
Desc: Focus on fishing in WA only. Encompasses all facts including product reviews, junior angler tips, current news and events, various fishing locations within the state.

AT/1033-4149
WESTERN FISHERIES MAGAZINE. (WESTERN FISHERIES MAGAZINE : WF.). [West. fish. mag.]. **Added/Corp** Western Australia. Fisheries Dept. **VFOAT** WF; Western Fisheries. (Jan./Feb. 1989)-. Periodical. English. Six times a year. Free. Department of Fisheries / Western Australia, 108 Adelaide Terrace, Perth Western Australia 6000 Australia. **Tel** (09)325-5988, FAX (09)325-3134, telex 93832. **ED** Clifford Young. **CODEN** WFMAE3. Index available. **Bk Rev**. **Circ:** 9,000. ***Continues*** *FINS, 0046-2993.*
Ind/Abst BioBusiness (1990-); Fish Rev. (Jan. 1989-July 1992); Wildl. Rev. (Jan. 1989-July 1992).

US/0270-160X
WHO'S WHO IN THE FISH INDUSTRY. (1981)-. English. ir. $95.00. Urner Barry Publications Inc., PO Box 389, Toms River NJ 08754. **Tel** (908)240-5330, (800)932-0617, FAX (908)341-0891. **ED** Paul B. Brown. **LC** HD9453; .W47. **DD** 380.1/43/929473. Index available (free). **Bk Rev**. **Ad Acc**. **Circ:** 5,000 (ctrl).
Desc: Revised and expanded to 6,000 company listings with sixty product categories detailing regions or country of origin.

US/1040-7804
WHO'S WHO IN THE FISH INDUSTRY, CANADA. [Who's who fish ind. Can.]. (1989)-. English. an. $95.00. Urner Barry Publications Inc., PO Box 389, Toms River NJ 08754. **Tel** (908)240-5330, (800)932-0617, FAX (908)341-0891. **ED** Paul B. Brown, Jr. **LC** HD9464.C2; W46. **DD** 338. **Ad Acc**. **Circ:** 3,500.
Desc: Contains 6,000 company listings with sixty product categories detailing regions or country of origin.

●US/1064-931X
WHO'S WHO IN THE FISH INDUSTRY, CENTRAL & SOUTH AMERICA. **VFOAT** Central & South America; Who's Who in the Fish Industry. Central & South America; Central and South America. (1992)-. English. $35.00. Urner Barry Publications Inc., PO Box 389, Toms River NJ 08754. **Tel** (908)240-5330, (800)932-0617, FAX (908)341-0891.

US/1046-6479
WILDLIFE & FISH WORLDWIDE. VOLUME 1. ***Title Change.*** **See** Environmental Issues-Conservation and Natural Resources.

●US/1070-499X
WILDLIFE REVIEW & FISHERIES REVIEW. **See** Environmental Issues-Conservation and Natural Resources.

US/1041-5602
WORLD AQUACULTURE. [World aquac.]. **Added/Corp** World Aquaculture Society. **VFOAT** World Aquaculture Magazine. Vol. 19 (3) (Sept. 1988)-. Periodical. English. Four times a year (Mar., June, Sept., Dec.). $30.00 (one year); $50.00 (individuals), $85.00 (institutions) Comes with Aquaculture Association of Canada membership & World Aquaculture Society membership. World Aquaculture Society, 143 J.M. Parker Coliseum, LSU, Baton Rouge LA 70803. **Tel** (504)388-3137, FAX (504)388-3493. **ED** David E. Aiken. **LC** SH1; .W59. **DD** 639/.8. **CODEN** WOAQEK. **Ad Acc**. **Pr Rev**. **Circ:** 4,300 (ctrl). ***Continues*** *World Aquaculture Society Newsletter.*
Desc: Devoted to the advancement of aquaculture science and technology worldwide. Through a network of members, affiliates, associates and chapters, the society represents over 4,000 individuals from more than 100 countries. Attains its objectives by sponsoring scientific meetings, workshops and symposia, and by publishing aquaculture information.
Ind/Abst Anim. Breed. Abstr.; BioBusiness; Food Sci. Technol. Abstr.; World Agric. Econ.

UK/0043-8480
WORLD FISHING. [World fish.]. Vol.1 (Apr. 1952)-. Periodical. English. mo. £35.00 UK; £50.00 Europe; £90.00 US and Canada; £60.00 other. World Fishing, Royston House, Caroline Park, Edinburgh Scotland. **Tel** 011 44 631 63058, FAX 011 44 631 65470. **ED** Martin Gill. **LC** SH1; .W6. **DD** 338.3/72/05. **Bk Rev**. **Ad Acc**. **Circ:** 5,874 (ctrl). available on microfilm and microfiche from University Microfilms International (UMI). ***Absorbed*** *Fish Industry.*
Desc: An international journal serving, catching, processing, and manufacturing industries.
Ind/Abst Aquat. Sci. Fish. Abstr. (Computer File); BMT Abstr.; Curr. Technol. Index; Ocean. Abstr.; Pollut. Abstr. Indexes.

US/0194-3340
WORLD RECORD GAME FISHES. [World rec. game fishes]. **Added/Corp** International Game Fish Association. (1979)-. English. an. $11.75 US; $12.75 other. International Game Fish Association, 1301 East Atlantic Boulevard, Pompano Beach FL 33060. **Tel** (305)467-0161, FAX (305)467-0331. **ED** Ray Crawford. **LC** SH455; .W67. **DD** 799.1/05. **Ad Acc**. **Circ:** 25,000. ***Continues*** *World Record Marine Fishes, 0535-059X.*
Desc: Contains updated listing of world records for freshwater, saltwater and fly rod fishing; scientific articles, species descriptions, references, etc.

US/1047-5672
WORLD SHRIMP FARMING (BIMONTHLY REPORT). ***Title Change.*** (WORLD SHRIMP FARMING : A BIMONTHLY REPORT ON SHRIMP AND PRAWN FARMING.). Vol. 14, No. 5 (May 1989)-Vol. 19, No. 1 (Jan./Feb. 1994). Periodical. English. bm. Aquaculture Digest, 9434 Kearney Mesa Road, San Diego CA 92126. **LC** SH380.6; .W673. **DD** 639. ***Continues in part*** *Aquaculture Digest, 0193-3140.* ***Continued by*** *Shrimp News International, 1076-7568.*
Ind/Abst Aquat. Sci. Fish. Abstr. (Computer File).

US/1051-4155
X MAGAZINE. **See** General Interest.

US
YAKIMA & KLICKITAT FISHERIES / YAKIMA/KLICKITAT PRODUCTION PROJECT. **Added/Corp** Yakima/Klickitat Production Project. Yakima Indian Nation. Washington (State). Dept. of Fisheries. Washington (State). Dept. of Wildlife. **VFOAT** Yakima and Klickitat Fisheries. No. 1 (Jan. 1990)-. English. **LC** SH222.W3; Y34.

JA
YAMAGUCHI-KEN GAIKAI SAIBAI GYOGYO SENTA HOKOKU. **Main/Corp** Yamaguchi-Ken Gaikai Saibai Gyogyo Senta. Vol. 1 (1976)-. Japanese. Yamaguchi-Ken Gaikai Saibai Gyogyo Senta, Aza Kurose Kayoi, Nagato 759-43 Japan. **LC** SH109; .Y35A.

JA/0386-3816
YAMAGUCHI-KEN GAIKAI SUISAN SHIKENJO KENKYU HOKOKU. **Added/Corp** Yamaguchi-ken Gaikai Suisan Shikenjo. (19??)-. English (Japanese). Yamaguchi-Ken Gaikai Suisan, Shikenjo Senzaki, Nagato Japan. **LC** SH138; .Y38.

JA
YAMAGUCHI-KEN NAIKAI SUISAN SHIKENJO HOKOKU. Japanese. ir. Yamaguchi-Ken Naikai Suisan Shikenjo, Akiho Futajima, Yamaguchi Japan. **LC** SH109; .Y36.

JA
YAMAGUCHI-KEN NAIKAI SUISAN SHIKENJO NEMPO. Japanese. an. Yamaguchiken Naikai Suisan Shikenjo, (Yamaguchi Prefectural Naikai Fisheries Experiment Station), 437-77, Aio Futajima, Yamaguchishi, Yamaguchiken 754, Japan. **LC** SH109; .Y365.

CH
YANG SHUI CHAN YEN CHIU, HAI. **Added/Corp** Kuo Chia Shui Chan Tsung Chu Huang-Hai Shui Chan yen Chiu so. **VFOAT** Marine Fisheries Research. (1980)-. Chinese (summaries and/or abstracts in English; table of contents in English). Documents available from BIOSIS Document Express.
Ind/Abst Aquat. Sci. Fish. Abstr. (Computer File); Biol. Abstr.

IT/0084-375X
YEARBOOK OF FISHERY STATISTICS. **See** Fish and Fisheries-Abstracting, Bibliographies and Statistics.

UK/0969-1405
YEARBOOK - SALMON AND TROUT ASSOCIATION. (YEARBOOK.). [Yearb. - Salmon and Trout Assoc.]. **VFOAT** Salmon and Trout Association Yearbook. (19??)-. Periodical. English. an. £10.00 Europe; £15.00 other. Salmon & Trout Association, Fishmongers Hall, London Bridge, London EC4R 9EL England. **Tel** 011 44 71 283 5838, FAX 011 44 71 929 1389, telex 8956058. **DD** 799.1755. ***Continues*** *Salmon and Trout Magazine, 0036-3545.*

JA/0389-5858
YOSHOKU KENKYUJO KENKYU HOKOKU. [Yoshoku Kenkyujo kenkyu hokoku]. **VFOAT** Bulletin of National Research Institute of Aquaculture. Academic Scholarly Publication. English (Japanese). an. ¥3780000. National Research Institute of Aquaculture, Nansei Mie 516-01 Japan. **Tel** 05996-6-1830, FAX 05996-6-1962. **LC** SH109. **DD** 639.3. **CODEN** YKHKDU. **Circ:** 1,000 (ctrl). Documents available from BIOSIS Document Express, CASDDS. ***Continues*** *Tansuiku Suisan Kenkyujo Kenkyu Hokoku.*
Ind/Abst Agrindex; Biol. Abstr.; Chem. Abstr.

CN/1186-2394
YOUTH FISHERIES EDUCATION PROGRAM : [NEWSLETTER]. [Youth Fish. Educ. Program]. **Main/Corp** Ontario. Youth Fisheries Education Program. **Added/Corp** Ontario. Ministry of Natural Resources. (1991)-. English. Ministry of Natural Resources / Ontario, Whitney Block, Parliament Buildings, Toronto Ontario M7A 1W3 Canada. **DD** 333.95.

CH
YU YEH NIEN CHIEN / CHUNG-HUA YEH TSA CHIH SHE PIEN. Chinese. an. NT$600.00. Chung-Hua Yu Yeh Tsa Chih She, 125 Lo-Ssu-Fu Rd, 3 Section, Taipei Taiwan. **LC** SH298.5; Y8. **DD** 338.3/72/0951249.

ABSTRACTING, BIBLIOGRAPHIES AND STATISTICS

US/1064-0460
AQUATIC SCIENCES & FISHERIES ABSTRACTS (CD-ROM ED.). (AQUATIC SCIENCES & FISHERIES ABSTRACTS [COMPUTER FILE] : ASFA / CAMBRIDGE SCIENTIFIC ABSTRACTS.). [Aquat. sci. fish. abstr.]. **Added/Corp** Cambridge Scientific Abstracts, Inc. **VFOAT** ASFA; Aquatic Sciences and Fisheries Abstracts. (19??)-. Abstracting/Indexing Service. English. ir (Parts 1 & 2 published monthly, Part 3 published bimonthly). $1585.00 US; $1745.00 other. Cambridge Scientific Abstracts, 7200 Wisconsin Avenue, #601, Bethesda MD 20814-4823. **Tel** (301)961-6750, (800)843-7751, FAX (301)961-6720. **LC** Z5970. **DD** 639. available on an online database; available in print; available via Internet (to the current year's abstracts and five-year backfiles) from Cambridge Scientific Abstracts.
Desc: Brings together worldwide information from numerous fields. Provides detailed information on biology, ecology, living aquatic resources, oceanography, limnology, geoscience, ocean technology, non-living resources, pollution, and related sociopolitical issues. Covers proceedings, books, dissertations and grey literature. Covers technical reports by over 2,000 national and international organizations and governments including: Sea Grant, US Navy, US EPA, Fish and Wildlife Service, Minerals Management Service, US Geological Survey, US Army Corps of Engineers, Department of Fisheries and Oceans, US Department of Energy, UK Department of Energy, FAO, UNDP, ICES, IMO, UNESCO, WMO, WHO, IAEA, UN, UNEP, IOC, INFOFISH, IUCN, IEEE, MAFF, NASA, USDA, EEC, NMFS, and NWS.

US/0140-5373
AQUATIC SCIENCES AND FISHERIES ABSTRACTS. PART 1 : BIOLOGICAL SCIENCES AND LIVING RESOURCES. [Aquat. sci. fish. abstr., 1 Biol. sci. living resour.]. **Added/Corp** United Nations. Dept. of Economic and Social Affairs. Food and Agriculture Organization of the United Nations. Intergovernmental Oceanographic Commission. Information Retrieval Limited. Cambridge Communications Corporation. **VFOAT** Biological Sciences and Living Resources; ASFA 1. **VAT** Aquatic Sciences and Fisheries Abstracts 1. Vol. 8 (Jan. 1978)-. Abstracting/Indexing Service. English. mo (includes annual index). $985.00 US; $995.00 other. Cambridge Scientific Abstracts, 7200 Wisconsin Avenue, #601, Bethesda MD 20814-4823. **Tel** (301)961-6750, (800)843-7751, FAX (301)961-6720. **ED** Jonathan Sears. Index Available, published separately, free-automatically sent. cum. index. available on CD-ROM (ASFA) from Cambridge Scientific Abstracts; available on magnetic tape; available on an online database; available via Internet (to the current year's abstracts and five-year backfiles) from Cambridge Scientific Abstracts. ***Supersedes in part*** *Aquatic Sciences & Fisheries Abstracts, 0044-8516.* ***Continued in part by*** *Aquatic Sciences and Fisheries Abstracts. Part 3, Aquatic Pollution and Environmental Quality, 1045-6031.*
Desc: Covers aquatic organisms and their marine, freshwater and brackish environments, including general biology, microbiology, aquatic ecology, pollution, environmental, conservation, fisheries, marketing and use of aquatic products.
Ind/Abst Fish Rev.; Wildl. Rev.

US/0140-5381
AQUATIC SCIENCES AND FISHERIES ABSTRACTS. PART 2 : OCEAN TECHNOLOGY, POLICY AND NON-LIVING RESOURCES. [Aquat. sci. fish. abstr., 2 Ocean technol. policy nonliving resour.]. **Added/Corp** United Nations. Dept. of Economic and Social Affairs. Food and Agriculture Organization of the United Nations. Intergovernmental Oceanographic Commission. Information Retrieval Limited. Cambridge Scientific Abstracts, Inc. **VFOAT** Ocean Technology, Policy and Non-Living Resources; ASFA 2. Vol. 8 (Jan. 1978)-. Abstracting/Indexing Service. English. mo (includes annual index). $735.00 US; $835.00 other. Cambridge Scientific Abstracts, 7200 Wisconsin Avenue, #601, Bethesda MD 20814-4823. **Tel** (301)961-6750, (800)843-7751, FAX (301)961-6720. **ED** Jonathan Sears. **DD** 551. **NLM** Z 6004.P6 A658. Index available. cum. index. available on CD-ROM (ASFA CD-ROM) from Cambridge Scientific Abstracts; available on magnetic tape; available on an online database; available via Internet (to the current year's abstracts and five-year backfiles) from Cambridge Scientific Abstracts. ***Continues in part*** *Aquatic Sciences & Fisheries Abstracts, 0044-8516;* ***Absorbed*** *Marine and Coastal Technology Abstracts.* ***Continued in part by*** *Aquatic Sciences and Fisheries Abstracts. Part 3, Aquatic Pollution and Environmental Quality, 1045-6031.*
Desc: Focuses on international and national policy and legislation, descriptive and dynamical oceanography and limnology, geochemistry, geology and geophysics, meteorology and climatology, technology and engineering, non-living resources and commerce, and pollution.

US/1045-6031
AQUATIC SCIENCES AND FISHERIES ABSTRACTS. PART 3 : AQUATIC POLLUTION AND ENVIRONMENTAL QUALITY. [Aquat. sci. fish. abstr., Pt. 3 Aquat. pollut. environ. qual.]. **Added/Corp** United Nations. Office for Ocean Affairs and the Law of the Sea. **VFOAT** Aquatic Pollution and Environmental Quality; ASFA 3. Vol. 20, No. 1 (Feb. 1990)-. Abstracting/Indexing Service. English. bm (plus annual index). $275.00 US; $295.00 other. Cambridge Scientific Abstracts, 7200 Wisconsin Avenue, #601, Bethesda MD 20814-4823. **Tel** (301)961-6750, (800)843-7751, FAX (301)961-6720. **ED** Jonathan Sears. **DD** 551. **NLM** Z 5322.M3; A6567a. available on magnetic tape; available on an online database; available on CD-ROM; available via Internet (to the current year's abstracts and five-year backfiles) from Cambridge Scientific Abstracts. ***Continues in part*** *Aquatic Sciences and Fisheries Abstracts. Part 1, Biological Sciences & Living Resources, 0140-5373* ***and*** *Aquatic Sciences and Fisheries Abstracts. Part 2, Ocean Technology, Policy and Non-Living Resources, 0140-5381.*
Desc: Adopting a wide range of perspectives, the journal examines a spectrum of current aquatic and environmental issues including: acid rain, eutrophication, radioactive waste disposal, and much more. Contains information that will prove essential to specialists who deal in any capacity with aquatic environments and marine pollution problems, including biologists, oceanographers, limnologists, government officials, etc.

CN/0713-2158
CANADIAN FISHERIES ANNUAL STATISTICAL REVIEW. (ANNUAL STATISTICAL REVIEW, CANADIAN FISHERIES / ECONOMIC POLICY BRANCH, ECONOMIC DEVELOPMENT DIRECTORATE.). [Can. fish. annu. stat. rev.]. **VFOAT** Revue Statistique Annuelle, Les Peches Canadiennes. **VAT** Peches Canadiennes. Revue Statistique Annuelle. Vol. 12 (1979)-. Statistical Publication. English (French). an. Fisheries & Oceans Canada, Scientific Information & Publications Branch, 200 Kent Street/12th Floor, Ottawa Ontario K1A 0E6 Canada. **Tel** (613)993-0600, (800)267-6677, telex 053-3585. **LC** SH223; .A52. **DD** 338.3/72/7092071. **UDC** 338.3:639.2(71). ***Continues*** *Annual Statistical Review of Canadian Fisheries, 0382-2249.*

CN
CANADIAN FISHERIES. ANNUAL STATISTICAL REVIEW / ECONOMIC POLICY BRANCH, ECONOMIC DEVELOPMENT DIRECTORATE, FISHERIES AND OCEANS. **VFOAT** Les Peches Canadiennes. Revue Statistique Annuelle; Peches Canadiennes. Revue Statistique Annualle. Vol. 12 (1979)-. Statistical Publication. English (French). Bibliotheque, Institut Maurice-Lamontagne, Peches Et Oceans, C P 1000 850 Route de la Mer, Mont-Joli Quebec G5H 3Z4 Canada. **Tel** (613)995-2041. **UDC** 338.3:639.2(71). **Circ:** 1,000 (ctrl). ***Continues*** *Annual Statistical Review of Canadian Fisheries.*
Desc: Statistical information on the commercial activities of Canadian fisheries, giving breakdown of quantity and value of catch statistics, exports, imports, and employment.

US/0739-540X
CURRENT REFERENCES IN FISH RESEARCH. [Curr. ref. fish res.]. Vol. 1 (1976)-. Abstracting/Indexing Service. English. an (Jan.). $18.00. Current References in Fish Research, Route No 1 Box 84, Chippewa Falls WI 54729. **Tel** (715)723-0098. **ED** Victor Cvancara. **LC** Z7996.F5; C87; QL614. **DD** 016.597/005. cum. index. **Pr Rev. Circ:** 2,000.
Desc: Listing of current references in fisheries research. Includes author, keyword, and scientific name index.

UK/0309-4294
FISHERIES ECONOMICS NEWSLETTER. [Fish. econ. newsl.]. **Added/Corp** Great Britain. White Fish Authority. No. 1, (Apr. 1976)-. Newsletter. English. Twice a year (May, Nov.). £30.00. Sea Fish Industry Authority, 18 Logie Mill, Logie Green Road, Edinburgh EH7 4HG Scotland. **Tel** 011 44 31 558-3331 ext. 256, FAX 011 44 31 558-1442. **ED** G. W. R. Buck. Index available. cum. index. **Bk Rev. Circ:** 300.
Desc: Abstracts on fisheries economics with articles by leading fisheries economists.
Ind/Abst Life Sci. Collect.

US/1042-6299
FISHERIES REVIEW (FORT COLLINS, COLO.). (FISHERIES REVIEW.). **Added/Corp** U.S. Fish and Wildlife Service. Vol. 31, No. 1 (1986)-. Abstracting/Indexing Service. English. qt. $31.00. US Fish and Wildlife Service, 1201 Oak Ridge Drive, Suite 200, Fort Collins CO 80525-5589. **Tel** (303)223-9709. **(Subscription address:** Superintendent of Documents, US Government Printing Office, Washington DC 20402.) **LC** SH1; .S82. **DD** 639/.2. **Circ:** 2,000. available on CD-ROM from National Information Service Corporation (NISC). ***Continues*** *Sport Fishery Abstracts, 0038-786X;* ***Absorbed*** *Fish Health News, 0736-1726.*
Desc: Contains citations to current fisheries/aquatic resource literature. Citations are taken selectively from over 950 journals and periodicals. In addition, reference to more than 500 books and symposia proceedings concerning fisheries and aquatic resources is included annually. All citations are comprehensively cross-referenced in appended indices.

JA
FISHERIES STATISTICS OF JAPAN. **Added/Corp** Japan. Norinsho. Norin Keizaikyoku. Tokei Chosabu. Japan. Norinsho. Norin Keizaikyoku. Tokei Johobu. Japan. Norin Suisansho. Keizaikyoku. Tokei Johobu. (1963)-. Statistical Publication. English. an. Price varies per volume. Government Publishing Service Center, 2-1 Kasumigaseki, 1-Chome Chiyoda-ku, Tokyo 100 Japan. **Tel** 011 81 3 3504-3885, FAX 011 81 3 3504-3889. **LC** SH301; .J26a. **DD** 338.3/72/7092052. ctrl circ.
Ind/Abst Ocean. Abstr.

US/0095-7682
FISHERY STATISTICS OF THE UNITED STATES. **VFOAT** Fishery Statistics of the U.S. Began in 1939. English. an. US Department of Commerce / National Marine Fisheries Service, 1335 East-West Highway, Silver Spring MD 20910. **Tel** (301)713-2239, FAX (301)713-2258. **LC** SH11; .A443. **DD** 338.3/72/7092073. ***Continues*** *Fishery Industries of the United States.*

NO
FISKERISTATISTIKK. **VFOAT** Fishery Statistics. Began in 1962. Norwegian (English). an. 13.00. **LC** HA1501; subser; SH279. **DD** 314.81 338.3/727/09481. ***Continues*** *Norges Fiskerier.*
Ind/Abst Ocean. Abstr.

IT
FRESHWATER AND AQUACULTURE CONTENTS TABLES. ACTUALITES DES EAUX DOUCES ET DE L'AQUACULTURE. **Added/Corp** Food and Agriculture Organization of the United Nations. Fishery Information, Data and Statistics Service. **VFOAT** Actualites des Eaux Douces et de l'Aquaculture. Vol. 1 (Jan. 1978)-. Abstracting/Indexing Service. English (French, Russian and Spanish). mo. Free on request. Food and Agriculture Organization (FAO) / Italy, GIPC166 via Terme di Caracalla, 00100 Rome Italy. **Tel** 011 39 6 522 52925, FAX 011 39 6 522 55784. **Circ:** 2,400.

SP
HISTORICAL STATISTICAL BULLETIN. **VFOAT** Bulletin Statistique Historique. Vol. 1 (1950-1959)-. Statistical Publication. English (French and Spanish). an. International Commission for the Conservation of the Atlantic Tunas, Principle de Vergara 17, 28001 Madrid Spain. **Tel** 011 34 1 4310329. **LC** SH351.T8; H57. **DD** 338.3/7278.
Ind/Abst Ocean. Abstr.

PH/0115-5997
ICLARM BIBLIOGRAPHIES. **Added/Corp** International Center for Living Aquatic Resources Management. **VAT** International Center for Living Aquatic Resources Management Bibliographies. No. 2 (1981)-. Monographic series. English. ir. Price varies per volume. International Center for Living Aquatic Resources Management, MCPO Box 2631, 0718 Makati, MM, Philippines. **Tel** 011 63 2 8180466, 011 63 2 8189283, FAX 011 63 2 8163183, telex 64794. **CODEN** ICLCEX. Documents available from BIOSIS Document Express. ***Continues*** *Bibliographies (International Center for Living Aquatic Resources Management).*
Ind/Abst Biol. Abstr. (1987-); Ocean. Abstr.

US
MARINE RECREATIONAL FISHERY STATISTICS SURVEY. PACIFIC COAST. **VFOAT** Pacific Coast. 1979-1980-. English. an. US Department of Commerce / National Marine Fisheries Service, 1335 East-West Highway, Silver Spring MD 20910. **Tel** (301)713-2239, FAX (301)713-2258. **LC** SH464.P3; M37. **DD** 333.95/6.

CN
MONTHLY REVIEW OF CANADIAN FISHERIES STATISTICS. **Main/Corp** Statistics Canada. Manufacturing and Primary Industries Division. **VFOAT** La Statistique Mensuelle des Peches du Canada. Vol. 26 (Jan. 1972)-. Periodical. English (French). mo. Statistics Canada, Publications Sales & Services, Main Building Room 1710, Ottawa Ontario K1A 0T6 Canada. **Tel** (613)951-5078, (800)267-6677, FAX (613)951-1584, telex 053-3585. ***Continues*** *Canada. Bureau of Statistics. Manufacturing and Primary Industries Division. Monthly Review of Canadian Fisheries Statistics.*

US/0731-3306
OREGON SALMON AND STEELHEAD SPORT CATCH STATISTICS. **VFOAT** Steelhead Sport Catch Statistics; Salmon and STeelhead Sport Catch Statistics. 1970-79-. English. an. Oregon Department of Fish & Wildlife, PO Box 59, 2501 Southwest 1st Street, Portland OR 97201. **Tel** (503)229-5400. **LC** SH686; .O73. **DD** 333.95/6.

MY/0126-8856
PERANGKAAN TAHUNAN PERIKANAN. [Perangkaan tahunan perikanan]. **Main/Corp** Malaysia. Bahagian Perikanan. **VFOAT** Annual Fisheries Statistics. Malay (English and Malay). Secretary General, Minis Agriculture, Swettenham Road, Kuala Lumpur Malaysia. **Tel** 2982011. **LC** SH307.M3; M34A.

IO/0426-7680
PURPOSE AND METHODS IN FISHERIES STATISTICS : DOCUMENT. **Added/Corp** Food and Agriculture Organization of the United Nations. **VFOAT** Buts et Methodes en Matiere de Statistiques des Peshes. No. 1 (1952)-. Monographic series. Multiple languages (English and French). Price varies per volume. UNIPUB, 4611-F Assembly Drive, Lanham MD 20706-4391. **Tel** (800)274-4888, FAX (301)459-0056, telex 28787 GATT CH. **DD** 338.3.

UK/0080-8202
SCOTTISH SEA FISHERIES STATISTICAL TABLES. **Added/Corp** Scotland. Home Dept. Great Britain. Dept. of Agriculture and Fisheries for Scotland. (1948)-. Statistical Publication. English. an. £11.50. Scottish Office Library, Room 1-44 New St. Andrews House, Edinburgh EH1 3TG Scotland. **Tel** 011 44 31 2444771, FAX 011 44 31 2444785. **DD** 338.3. ***Continues*** *Sea Fisheries: Statistical Tables.*
Ind/Abst Ocean. Abstr.

CN/0527-6942
STATISTICAL BASEBOOK SERIES - ECONOMICS SERVICE, DEPARTMENT OF FISHERIES OF CANADA. **Main/Corp** Canada. Department of Fisheries. Economics Service. No. 3 (1958)-. Statistical Publication. English. Price varies per volume. Department of Fisheries of Canada, Economics Service, Ottawa Ontario Canada. **DD** 639. ***Continues*** *Basebook on Fishery Statistics.*

CN/0250-6394
STATISTICAL BULLETIN / NORTHWEST ATLANTIC FISHERIES ORGANIZATION. [Stat. bull. - Northwest Atl. Fish. Organ.]. **Added/Corp** Northwest Atlantic Fisheries Organization. **VFOAT** N.A.F.O. Statistical Bulletin; NAFO Statistical Bulletin. Vol. 29 (1979)-. Statistical Publication. English. an. 35.00Can$. Northwest Atlantic Fisheries Organization / NAFO, PO Box 638, Dartmouth Nova Scotia B2Y 3Y9 Canada. **Tel** (902)469-9105, telex 019-31475. **ED** V. M. Hodder. **LC** SH1; .I54. **DD** 338.3/727092/11. **Circ:** 600. ***Continues*** *International Commission for the Northwest Atlantic Fisheries. Statistical Bulletin (International Commission for the Northwest Atlantic Fisheries)., 0074-266X.*
Desc: Publication of detailed catch and effort statistics by type and size of fishing vessel, fishing gear, statistical area and country for all fishing activity in the Northwest Atlantic.
Ind/Abst Ocean. Abstr.

CN/0535-1588
STATISTICAL YEARBOOK / INTERNATIONAL NORTH PACIFIC FISHERIES COMMISSION. [Stat. yearb. - Int. North Pac. Fish. Comm.]. **Added/Corp** International North Pacific Fisheries Commission. (1952)-. Statistical Publication. English (Japanese). an. International North Pacific Fisheries Commission, 6640 Northwest Marine Drive, Vancouver British Columbia V6T 1X2 Canada. **Tel** (604)228-1128, FAX (604)228-1135. **DD** 639/.22/091644.

II
STATISTICS OF MARINE PRODUCTS EXPORTS. English. an. Marine Products Exports Development Authority Etc, M G Road, Cochin India. **LC** HD9466.I5; S73. **DD** 382/.437/092054.

TU
SU URUNLERI ISTATISTIKLERI. **VFOAT** Fishery Statistics. (1986)-. English (Turkish). an. **LC** HA1911; .A3 subser; HD9466.T9. **DD** 315.61. ***Continues*** *Su Urunleri Anket Sonuclar.*

KO
SUSANMUL KYETONG PANMAEGO TONGGYE YONBO. **VFOAT** Statistics on Cooperative Sale of Fishery Products. 1981-. English (Korean). an. Susanop Hyoptong Chohap Chunganghoe, 88 Kyongun-dong Chongno-ku, Seoul 110 Korea. **LC** HD9466.K58; S95. ***Continues*** *Susanmul Kyetong Panmaego Tonggye.*

US/0734-7278
TEXAS COMMERCIAL HARVEST STATISTICS. [Tex. commer. harvest stat.]. **Added/Corp** Texas. Coastal Fisheries Branch. (19??)-. English. an. Texas Parks & Wildlife, 4200 Smith School Road, Austin TX 78744. **Tel** (512)707-0032. **LC** SH222.T4; T53. **DD** 333.3/72/09764.

IT/0084-375X
YEARBOOK OF FISHERY STATISTICS. **VFOAT** Annuaire Statistique des Peches; Anuario Estadistico de Pesca. Vol. 1 (1947)-. Monographic series. Multiple languages (English, French and Spanish). ir. Price varies per volume. Food and Agriculture Organization (FAO) / Italy, GIPC166 via Terme di Caracalla, 00100 Rome Italy. **Tel** 011 39 6 522 52925, FAX 011 39 6 522 55784. **(Subscription address:** UNIPUB, 4611 F Assembly Drive, Lanham MD 20706.**)** **LC** SH1. **DD** 338.3727.
Ind/Abst Aquat. Sci. Fish. Abstr. (Computer File); Ocean. Abstr.

FOLKLORE

QA
AL-MATHURAT AL-SHABIYAH. **VFOAT** Folk Heritage; Mathurat Al Shabiyyah. (1986)-. Periodical. Arabic (Arabic). qt. PO Box 7996, Doha Qatar. **LC** DS215; .M34.
Ind/Abst Middle East J.

US/0748-5905
AMERICAN FOLK MUSIC AND FOLKLORE RECORDINGS. **See** Music.

US/0092-5519
AMERICAN FOLKLIFE. Periodical. English. mo. $4.00. American Folklore Society, PO Box 295, Oley PA 19547. **LC** E161; .A38. **DD** 917.3/03/05.

•US
AMERICAN FOLKLORE SOCIETY NEWS. (1993)-. English. Twice a year. $10.00 Comes with American Forklore Society AFS Archiving Section Membership. American Folklore Society Archiv, 4350 North Fairfax Drive, Suite 640, Arlington VA 22203. **Tel** (202)232-8800.

US/0745-5178
AMERICAN FOLKLORE SOCIETY NEWSLETTER, THE. ***Title Change.*** [Am. Folk. Soc. newsl.]. **Added/Corp** American Folklore Society. Vol. 11, No. 5 (Oct. 1982)-(1993). Newsletter. English. bm. American Anthropological Association, 4350 North Fairfax Dr, Suite 640, Arlington VA 22203. **Tel** (703)528-1902 ext. 3031, FAX (703)528-3546. **ED** Timothy Lloyd. **LC** GR105; .A66. **DD** 398/.0973. **Bk Rev. Circ:** 2,216 (ctrl). ***Continues*** *American Folklore Newsletter, 0199-3526.* ***Continued by*** *American Folklore Society News.*
Desc: Society news and developments in the field of American folklore.

UK/0951-2500
AMMONITE GILLINGHAM, DORSET. (1987)-. Periodical. English. ir. £3.50 UK; £7.50 North America; £5.00 others. Ammonite Publications, 12 Priory Mead, Bruton, Somerset, BA10 0DZ England. **Tel** 0749-813349. **ED** John Howard Greaves. **Bk Rev**, (Qty: 12). **Ad Acc. Pr Rev. Circ:** 250.

US/0363-2318
APPALACHIAN HERITAGE. **See** Literature.

CN/0085-5243
ARCHIVES DE FOLKLORE, LES. [Arch. folk.]. Vol. 1 (1946)-. Monographic series. French. ir. Price varies per volume. Presses de l'Universite Laval, CP 2447 Avenue de la Medicine, Saint Foy Quebec G1K 7P4 Canada. **Tel** (418)656-5106, (418)656-2590.
Ind/Abst MLA Int. Bibl. Books Artic. Mod. Lang. Lit.

US
ARCHIVES OF APPALACHIA NEWSLETTER / EAST TENNESSEE STATE UNIVERSITY. **Main/Corp** Archives of Appalachia. **Added/Corp** East Tennessee State University. Vol. 1, No. 1 (Mar. 1, 1979)-. Newsletter. English. qt. Free on request. Archives of Appalachia, East Tennessee State University, PO Box 22450A, Johnson City TN 37614. **Tel** (615)929-4337. **LC** Z1251.A7; A76a.

IT/0392-1050
ARCHIVIO PER L'ALTO ADIGE. **See** Ethnic Interests.

VE/0254-1572
ARTESANIA Y FOLKLORE DE VENEZUELA. **See** The Arts-Art.

SW/0066-8176
ARV. [Arv]. **Added/Corp** Kungl. Gustav Adolfs Akademien (Uppsala, Sweden). **VFOAT** Journal of Scandinavian Forklore. Vol. 1 (1945)-. Swedish (English). ir. 218.00F. Scandinavian University Press, PO Box 2959 Toeyen, N 0608 Oslo 6 Norway. **Tel** 011 47 2 2575400, FAX 011 47 2 2575353, telex 71896 UROR N. **(Subscription address:** Scandinavian University Press, 200 Meacham Ave., Elmont NY 11003.**)** **LC** GR1; .G823. ***Supersedes*** *Folkminnen Och Folktankar.*
Ind/Abst Am. Hist. Life (1964-1970, 1979-)(1964-); MLA Int. Bibl. Books Artic. Mod. Lang. Lit.

JA/0385-2342
ASIAN FOLKLORE STUDIES. [Asian folk. stud.]. **Added/Corp** Asian Folklore Institute. Society for Asian Folklore. Vol. 22 (1963)-. Periodical. English (French and German). sa. $102.00. **(Subscription address:** Japan Publications Trading Company, Ltd., PO Box 5030, Tokyo International, Tokyo 100-31 Japan.**)** **LC** GR330; .F6. **DD** 398.2/095. available on microfilm and microfiche from University Microfilms International (UMI). Documents available from The Genuine Article, UMI Article Clearinghouse. ***Continues*** *Folklore Studies.*
Ind/Abst Acad. Search (July 1993-); Anthropol. Index; Arts Humanit. Citation Index [Full Cov.]; Curr. Contents Arts Humanit.; Expand. Acad. Index (1989-); Humanit. Index; Humanit. Source (Jul. 1993-); Index Book Rev. Relig.; INFO-SOUTH Abstr.; Mag. Search; MLA Int. Bibl. Books Artic. Mod. Lang. Lit.; Newsp. Period. Abstr. (1991-); Relig. Index One Period.; Res. Alert [Full Cov.]; Soc. Sci. Source (Jul. 1993-); Soc. Sci. Cit. Index [Select. Cov.].

AT/0819-0852
AUSTRALIAN FOLKLORE. **Added/Corp** Curtin University of Technology. Centre for Australian Studies. No. 1 (March 1987)-. English. an. 25.00Aus$ (institutions), 20.00Aus$ (individuals) Australia; 30.00Aus$ (institutions), 25.00Aus$ (individuals) other. Department of English Communication Studies, University of New England, Armidale NSW 2351 Australia. **Tel** 011 61 67 732601, FAX 011 61 67 732623. **ED** J.S. Ryan. **LC** GR365; .A873. **DD** 398/.0994/05. Index available. **Bk Rev. Ad Acc. Pr Rev. Circ:** 140. ***Absorbed*** *Australian Folklore. Bulletin.*
Ind/Abst MLA Int. Bibl. Books Artic. Mod. Lang. Lit.

IE/0332-270X
BEALOIDEAS. (BEALOIDEAS : THE JOURNAL OF THE FOLKLORE OF IRELAND SOCIETY.). [Bealoideas]. **Added/Corp** Folklore of Ireland Society. Vol. 1, No. 1 (May 1927)-. Periodical. Irish (English). ir. 24.00p. Folklore of Ireland Society, University College, Irish Folklore Department, Belfield Dublin 4 Ireland. **Tel** 011 353 1 693244 ext. 8216. **ED** Padraig O'Healai, Bo Almqvist. **LC** GR1; .B4. Index available. **Bk Rev. Circ:** 1,000 (ctrl).
Desc: Covers all aspects of Irish folklore and tradition.
Ind/Abst MLA Int. Bibl. Books Artic. Mod. Lang. Lit.

GW/0408-8220
BEITRAEGE ZUR DEUTSCHEN VOLKS- UND ALTERTUMSKUNDE. [Beitr. dtsch. Volks-Altertumskd.]. **Added/Corp** Museum fur Hamburgische Geschichte. (1954-). German. **LC** DD60; .B43.
Ind/Abst BHA : Biblio. Hist. Art; MLA Int. Bibl. Books Artic. Mod. Lang. Lit.; Numis. Lit.

SZ
BEITRAEGE ZUR VOLKSKUNDE. **VFOAT** Contributions a l'Ethnologie de la Suisse et de l'Europe; Contributi all-Ethnologia della Svizzera e dell'Europa. Vol. 1 (1981)-. German (French and Italian). ir. Schweizerische Gesellschaft fuer Volkskunde, Augustinergasse 19, CH 4051 Basel Switzerland. **Tel** 011 41 61 2619900, . **Circ:** 1,000.
Desc: Series on Swiss folklore, linguistics, sociology, manners and customs.

AU/0006-4459
BLATTER FUER HEIMATKUNDE ... . **See** History(General).

BL
BOLETIM - COMISSAO GOIANA DE FOLCLORE. **Main/Corp** Comissao Goiana de Folclore. Vol. 1, No. 1 (Dec. 1977)-. Bulletin. Portuguese. Comissao Goiana de Folclore, rua 82 No 455 Sector Sul 74.000, Goiania Brazil.

MX
BOLETIN DEL DEPARTAMENTO DE INVESTIGACION DE LAS TRADICIONES POPULARES. **Main/Corp** Mexico. Departamento de Investigacion de las Tradiciones Populares. 1-. Periodical. Spanish. Direccion General de Arte Popular, Apartado Postal 1856, Mexico City Mexico. **LC** GR115; .M47A. **DD** 390/.0972.

FR/1151-2709
BULLETIN DE LA SOCIETE DE MYTHOLOGIE FRANCAISE. **Added/Corp** Societe de Mythologie Francaise. No 156 (1989)-. Bulletin. French. qt. Societe de Mythologie Francaise, 175 rue de Pontoise, 6000 Beauvais France. **LC** GR160; .S58. ***Continues*** *Mythologie Francaise, 0769-0525.*

US
BULLETIN DE LA SOCIETE HISTORIQUE ET FOLKLORIQUE FRANCAISE. Began with 1958/59 issue. Bulletin. French. an. $6.00. French Folklore Society, 56-52 203rd Street, Bayside NY 11364. **Tel** (718)225-4453. **ED** Ida Courtinas. **LC** GR160; .F713. **DD** 398.2/0944. **Bk Rev. Circ:** 200. ***Continues*** *Bulletin de la Societe Folklorique et Historique Francaise de New York.*
Desc: Covers French folklore and history published in French and subscribed to by college and university libraries here and abroad.

CN/0705-1115
BULLETIN OF THE FOLKLORE STUDIES ASSOCIATION OF CANADA. **Main/Corp** Folklore Studies Association of Canada. **VFOAT** Bulletin de l'Association Canadienne pour les Etudes du Folklore; Bulletin FSAF; Bulletin ACEF; Bulletin de l'Association Canadienne d'Ethnologie et de Folklore. Vol. 13 (May 1989)-. Bulletin. English (French). sa. 50.00Can$ US; 51.50Can$ Canada; 53.00Can$ other (institutions); 35.00Can$ US; 36.50Can$ Canada; 38.00Can$ other (individuals). Folklore Studies Association of Canada, 37 Fairbank Street, Dartmouth NS B3A 1B9 Canada. **Tel** (902)464-8990. **LC** GR113; .F634A. **DD** 398/.06/271. ***Continues*** *Folklore, 0705-1158.*

BL
CADERNOS DE FOLCLORE. **Added/Corp** Brazil. Campanha de Defesa do Folclore Brasileiro. (1968)-. Periodical. Portuguese. **LC** GR1; .C25.
Ind/Abst MLA Int. Bibl. Books Artic. Mod. Lang. Lit.

FR/0396-891X
CAHIERS DE LITTERATURE ORALE. [Cah. litt. orale]. (1976)-. Periodical. French (English). Twice a year. 160.00F (surface mail); 203.00F (airmail). Publications Langues O'Inalco, 2 rue de Lille, 75343 Paris Cedex 07 France. **Tel** 011 33 1 49264274. **LC** GR1; .C254. **DD** 398.2/09. **CODEN** CLOREM. **Bk Rev.**
Desc: Covers the study of genres of spoken literature, as well as all topics relating to the spoken word.
Ind/Abst Linguist. Lang. Behav. Abstr.; Soc. Plann. Policy Dev. Abstr.; Sociol. Abstr.

CN/0843-9559
CAHIERS FRANCO-CANADIENS DE LOUEST. **See** Linguistics.

US/0889-1648
CALIFORNIA, FOLKS & LORE. [Calif. folks lore]. **VFOAT** California, Folks and Lore. (198?)-. Periodical. English. bm. $6.00. California Folks and Lore, PO Box 1437, San Capistrano CA 92693. **DD** 979.

CN/0225-2899
CANADIAN FOLKLORE (FOLKLORE STUDIES ASSOCIATION OF CANADA). (CANADIAN FOLKLORE.). [Can. folk.]. **VFOAT** Folklore Canadien. Vol. 1, No. 1/2 (1979)-. Periodical. English (French). sa. $10.00 (individual members),. Folklore Studies Association of Canada, 37 Fairbank Street, Dartmouth NS B3A 1B9 Canada. **Tel** (902)464-8990. **LC** GR113; .C368. **DD** 398/.0971.

CN/0576-5277
CANADIAN-GERMAN FOLKLORE. Began with: Vol. No. 1, published in 1961. Periodical. English. ir. Pennsylvania Folklore Society, 100 Pollack Drive, Orwigsberg PA 17961. **Tel** (717)544-6705. **LC** F1059.7.G3; C3. **DD** 398.

CN/0710-197X
CELAT-INFORMATION. [CELAT-information]. Periodical. French. Centre d'Etudes sur la Langue, Faculte des Lettres, Universite Laval, Ste Foy Quebec G1K 7P4 Canada. **Tel** (418)656-3834. **DD** 378.714/47. ***Continues*** *Folklore-Information, 0710-1961.*

US/0739-5558
CHILDREN'S FOLKLORE REVIEW, THE. [Child. folk. rev.]. **Added/Corp** American Folklore Society. East Carolina University. Vol. 11, No. 1 (fall 1988)-. Periodical. English. sa. C W Sullivan Children's Folklore Newsletter, Department of English, East Carolina University, Greenville NC 27834-4353. **Tel** (919)757-6411. **ED** Chip Sullivan. **LC** GR43.C4; C55. ***Continues*** *Children's Folklore Newsletter, 0739-5558.*

CH
CHU FENG / CHUNG-KUO MIN CHIEN WEN I YEN CHIU HUI HU-NAN FEN HUI. See Literature.

US/0736-6132
COME-ALL-YE (HATBORO, PA.). (COME-ALL-YE.). **VFOAT** Come All Ye. Vol. 1, (Summer 1977)-. Periodical. English. qt (Mar., June, Sept., Dec.). $6.00 US; $7.00 Canada & Pan American nations; $8.00 other. Legacy Books, PO Box 494, Hatboro PA 19040. **Tel** (215)675-6762, FAX (215)674-2826. **ED** Richard K. Burns and Lillian Krelove. Index available. cum. index. **Bk Rev. Ad Acc. Circ:** 2,000 (ctrl).
Desc: A book review journal of monographs in the broad fields of folklore/folklife to provide reference, selection and advisory guides for libraries and scholars.
Ind/Abst Book Rev. Index.

UK/0963-8334
CONTEMPORARY LEGEND : THE JOURNAL OF THE INTERNATIONAL SOCIETY FOR CONTEMPORARY LEGEND RESEARCH. Added/Corp International Society for Contemporary Legend Research. Vol. 1 (1991)-. English. an. £20.00 EEC countries; £22.00 other. Hisarlik Press, 4 Catisfield Road, Enfield Lock, Middlesex EN3 6BD England. **Tel** 011 44 992 700898. **LC** GR1; .C65.

AT/0818-7339
CORNSTALK GAZETTE. See The Arts-Performing Arts.

UK/0269-8773
COSMOS. (COSMOS : THE YEARBOOK OF THE TRADITIONAL COSMOLOGY SOCIETY.). [Cosmos]. Vol. 1 (1985)-. English. an. **LC** BL300; .C65. **DD** 291.2/4/05.
Ind/Abst Anthropol. Lit. (-Vol. 11, 1989).

CN/0701-0184
CULTURE & TRADITION. [Cult. tradit.]. **Added/Corp** Universite Laval. Association des Etudiants en Arts et Traditions Populaires. Memorial University of Newfoundland. Folklore Students Association. **VAT** Culture and Tradition. Vol. 1 (1976)-. Periodical. English (French). an. 6.00Can$ Canada; 9.00Can$ other. Culture and Tradition, Memorial University, PO Box 115, St John's Newfoundland A1C 5S7 Canada. **Tel** (709)737-8402. **(Subscription address:** CELAT, Faculte des Lettres, Universite Lavai, Quebec G1K 7P4 Canada) **ED** J. Moreira and M. Roberge. **LC** GR113; .C84. **DD** 398/.042/0971. **Bk Rev. Pr Rev. Circ:** 250 (ctrl).
Desc: Journal edited by the folklore students of MUN and Laval. It includes articles relevant to all areas of folklore in Canada.
Ind/Abst MLA Int. Bibl. Books Artic. Mod. Lang. Lit.

●UK
CURRENT FOLKLORE. Added/Corp London Hisarlik Press on Behalf of the Folklore Society Library. **VFOAT** Folklore in Use. (1992)-. English. Twice a year (June & Dec.). £10.00 (individuals); £20.00 (institutions). Hisarlik Press, 4 Catisfield Road, Enfield Lock, Middlesex EN3 6BD England. **Tel** 011 44 992 700898. ***Continues*** *Current Contents in Folklore, 0955-7725.*

US
DANCE AND MOVEMENT ANALYSIS NEWSLETTER. Newsletter. English. Twice a year. $10.00 Comes with American Folklore Society AFS Dance and Movement Analysis Section Membership. American Folklore Society Archiv, 4350 North Fairfax Drive, Suite 640, Arlington VA 22203. **Tel** (202)232-8800.

DK/0106-4525
DANSKE STUDIER. See Literary and Political Reviews.

US/1049-0892
DEAD OF NIGHT. See Romance and Adventure.

GR/1012-229X
DELTION TES HISTORIKES KAI ETHNOLOGIKES HETAIREIAS TES HELLADOS. [Delt. Ist. Ethnol. Etair. Ell.]. **Added/Corp** Historike kai Ethnologike Hetaireia tes Hellados. **VFOAT** Bulletin de la Societe Historique et Ethnologique de la Grece. (1883)-. Periodical. Greek, Modern (English and French). an. Dodone Bookstore, 3 Asklepeou Street, 10679 Athens Greece. **LC** DF701; .H6.
Ind/Abst Am. Hist. Life (1956-1964).

GW
DGV INFORMATIONEN. Main/Corp Deutsche Gesellschaft fuer Volkskunde. No. 79 (July 1970)-. Newsletter. German. Four times a year. Comes with membership. Deutsche Gesellschaft fuer Volkskunde e.V., Friedlaender Weg 2, D 37085 Goettingen Germany. **Tel** 044 49 551 399489, 395352. **LC** GN2; .D423. ***Continues*** *Mitteilungen der Deutschen Gesellschaft fuer Volkskunde e.V.*

NE
DRIEMAANDELIJKSE BLADEN. See Linguistics.

GW
ENZYKLOPAEDIE DES MAERCHENS. (19??)-. German. ir. Vol. 7 $112.00. Walter de Gruyter Inc., PO Box 303421, D 10728 Berlin Germany. **Tel** 011 49 30 260050, FAX 011 49 30 26005251. Index available. cum. index.
Desc: Encyclopedia about the fairy tale. Compares narrative material from the most diverse ethnic groups transmitted orally and through the medium of literature and points out its social, historical, psychological, and religious background.

GR
EPETERIS TOU KENTROU EREUNES TES HELLENIKES LAOGRAPHIAS. Added/Corp Kentron Ereunes tes Hellenikes Laographias (Akademia Athenon). **VFOAT** Annuaire du Centre de Recherches du Folklore Hellenique. (1965)-. Greek, Modern (French). **LC** GR170; .A33. ***Continues*** *Epeteris tou Laographikou Archeiou.*
Ind/Abst MLA Int. Bibl. Books Artic. Mod. Lang. Lit.

BE/0774-3297
ETHNOLOGIA FLANDRICA. Added/Corp Leuvense Vereniging voor Volkskunde. 1 (1985)-. Academic Scholarly Publication. Dutch (summaries and/or abstracts in English, French and German). an. 500F. Leuvense Vereniging voor Volkskunde, Blijde-Inkomststraat 21, B-3000 Leuven Belgium. **Tel** 011 16 284856, FAX 011 32 16 285068. **LC** GR186.F57; E87. **DD** 398/.09493/1. available on diskette.
Desc: Contains the proceedings of the conference held every year.

SW/0348-9698
ETHNOLOGIA SCANDINAVICA. [Ethnol. Scand.]. **Added/Corp** Kungl. Gustav Adolfs Akademien (Uppsala, Sweden) Statens Humanistiska Forstningsrad (Sweden). (1971)-. English (German). an (June). Kr225.00. Ethnologia Scandinavica, Box 65, S 237 00 Bjarred Sweden. **Tel** 11 46 46 291314. **(Subscription address:** BTJ Trycle AB, Traktorvagen 13 S-222 60 Lund Sweden, 011 46 46 304400, Attention: Birgitta Lung) **ED** Nils Arvid Bringeus and Margareta Tellenbach. **LC** GN1; .F62. Index available. **Bk Rev**, (Qty: 30). **Circ:** 800. ***Supersedes*** *Folk-Liv.*
Desc: Examines trends in various fields of research within the discipline, as social and material culture in the Nordic countries.
Ind/Abst Anthropol. Index; Anthropol. Lit.; MLA Int. Bibl. Books Artic. Mod. Lang. Lit.

FR/0046-2616
ETHNOLOGIE FRANCAISE. See Ethnic Interests.

●BO
ETNOFOLK : REVISTA DEL COMITE DEPARTAMENTAL DE ETNOGRAFIA Y FOLKLORE. Added/Corp Oruro (Bolivia : Dept.). Comite Departamental de Etnografia y Folklore. Vol.1, No.1 (1992)-. Periodical. Spanish. tq. Comite Departamental de Etnografia y Folklore, Oruro, Bolivia. **ED** Alberto Guerra Guiterrez.

GW/0014-6242
FABULA. (FABULA : ZEITSCHRIFT FUER ERZAHLFORSCHUNG : JOURNAL OF FOLKTALE STUDIES : REVUE D'ETUDES SUR LE CONTE POPULAIRE.). [Fabula]. **VFOAT** Zeitschrift fuer Erzahlforschung; Journal of Folktale Studies; Revue d'Etudes sur le Conte Populaire. Vol. 1 (1957)-. Periodical. German (English and French). Twice a year. $132.65. Walter de Gruyter Inc., PO Box 303421, D 10728 Berlin Germany. **Tel** 011 49 30 260050, FAX 011 49 30 26005251. **ED** K. Ranke. **LC** GR1; .F25. **[CCC]. Bk Rev. Ad Acc. Circ:** 600. Documents available from The Genuine Article.
Desc: Publishes papers and reports in different languages concerning the study of folklore.
Ind/Abst Arts Humanit. Citation Index [Full Cov.]; Child. Lit. Abstr. (19??-); MLA Int. Bibl. Books Artic. Mod. Lang. Lit.; Res. Alert [Full Cov.].

AF
FARHANG-I MARDUM. VFOAT Farhang-E-Mardom; Folklore. Persian. bm. $15.00. Kummitah-I Dawlati-I Kaltur, Manzil-I 4 Mudiriyat-I Majallah-I Farhang-I Mardum, Kabul Afghanistan. **LC** GR302.5; .F37.

US/1056-6805
FESTIVAL OF AMERICAN FOLKLIFE / SMITHSONIAN INSTITUTION AND NATIONAL PARK SERVICE. Main/Corp Festival of American Folklife. Began with 1968. English. an. $2.00. Festival of American Folklife, Smithsonian Institute, Washington DC 20560. **Tel** (202)3816525. **LC** GR105; .F47. **DD** 398/.0973.

FI/0014-5815
FF COMMUNICATIONS. Main/Corp Folklore Fellows. **Added/Corp** Suomalainen Tiedeakatemia, Helsingfors. Vol. 1 No. 1 (1910)-. Monographic series. English. ir. Price varies per volume. Suomalainen Tiedeakatemia / Academia Scientiarum Fennica, Mariankatu 5, SF-00170 Helsinki Finland. **(Subscription address:** Academic Bookstore Akateeminen, Postilokero 23, FIN 00371 Helsinki Finland.) **LC** GR1; .F55. Documents available from The Genuine Article.
Ind/Abst Arts Humanit. Citation Index (19??-19??) [Full Cov.]; Curr. Contents Arts Humanit.; MLA Int. Bibl. Books Artic. Mod. Lang. Lit.; Res. Alert [Full Cov.].

GW/0302-752X
FOLCLORICA (GOIANIA). (FOLCLORICA.). [Folclorica]. Yearly V. 1- August/Oct. 1972-. Periodical. Portuguese. qt. Editora Oriente Etc, Praca Civica No 13, Goiania Brazil. **LC** GR133.B6; F64.

US/1043-5026
FOLK ART MESSENGER. See The Arts-Art.

UK/0430-8778
FOLK LIFE. [Folk life]. **Added/Corp** Society for Folk Life Studies. Vol. 1 (1963)-. English. an. £12.50 Comes with Society for Folk Life Studies membership. Society Folk Life Studies, Welsh Folk Museum, St Fagans Cardiff CF5 6XB Wales England. **Tel** 011 44 222 569441 ext. 220, FAX 011 44 222 578413. **ED** Roy Brigden (editor's address: Museum of English Rural Life, Whiteknights, Reading, Belkshire United Kingdom, phone: 011 44 734 318663). **LC** GR140; .F6. Index available. cum. index. **Bk Rev. Ad Acc. Circ:** 500 (ctrl). Documents available from The Genuine Article. ***Supersedes*** *Gwerin.*
Desc: Ethnological studies such as agriculture, crafts and industries, linguistics, vernacular architecture, costume, traditional sports, customs and folklore.
Ind/Abst Annu. Bibliogr. Engl. Lang. Lit.; Anthropol. Index; Art Archaeol. Tech. Abstr.; Arts Humanit. Citation Index [Full Cov.]; BHA : Biblio. Hist. Art; Br. Archaeol. Bibliogr.; Curr. Contents Arts Humanit.; MLA Int. Bibl. Books Artic. Mod. Lang. Lit.; Res. Alert [Full Cov.].

UK/0531-9684
FOLK MUSIC JOURNAL. See Music.

DK/0105-1024
FOLK OG KULTUR. [Folk kult.]. **Added/Corp** Foreningen Danmarks Folkeminder. (1972)-. Danish (summaries and/or abstracts in English and German). **LC** DL131; .F64.
Ind/Abst MLA Int. Bibl. Books Artic. Mod. Lang. Lit.

UK/0951-1326
FOLK ROOTS. See Music.

US/0149-6840
FOLKLIFE CENTER NEWS. [Folklife Cent. news]. **Added/Corp** American Folklife Center. (Jan. 1978)-. Periodical. English. Four times a year (within the season of the year). free on request. American Folklife Center, Library of Congress, Washington DC 20540. **Tel** (202)707-6590, FAX (202)707-2076. **ED** James Hardin. **LC** GR105; .A63a. **DD** 973/.06/073. **Circ:** 13,000 (ctrl).
Desc: Describes the Folklife Center's activities--field projects, conferences, research initiatives, etc. Pursuant to its mandate to preserve and present American folklife.

HU
FOLKLOR ARCHIVUM. 1-. Periodical. Hungarian (summaries and/or abstracts in English, Slovak, Romanian and German). ir. MTA Neprajzi Kutato Csoport, 1250 Budapest, Pf 29, Budapest Hungary. **Tel** 36-1-56-99-39. **ED** Mihaly Hoppal. **LC** GR154.5; .F64. **Bk Rev. Ad Acc. Circ:** 500 (ctrl).
Desc: Ethnic Hungarian folk narrative on folk beliefs, mythological legends, ethno-medicine, funeral customs, decorative folk art and carved gravestones.

RU
FOLKLOR (MOSCOW, R.S.F.S.R.). (FOLKLOR / AKADEMIIA NAUK SSSR, INSTITUT MIROVOI LITERATURY IMENI A.M. GORKOGO.). **Added/Corp** Institut Mrovoi Lteratury Ieni A.M. Gorkogo. (1981)-. Russian. ir. 2.90rub. Izdatelstvo Nauka / Akademiia Nauk, Publishing House of the Russian Academy of Sciences, Leninskii Porspekt 14, 117901 Moscow Russia. **Tel** 011 95 954-21-53, FAX 011 95 938-21-44, telex 411964. **LC** GR1; .F322. **DD** 398/.05. ***Continues*** *Tipologiia i Vzaimosviazi Folklora Narodov SSSR.*

RU
FOLKLOR NARODOV RSFSR. Added/Corp Bashkirskii Gosudarstvennyi Universitet Imeni 40-Letiia Oktiabriia. **VAT** Folklor Narodov Rossiiskoi Sovetskoi Federativnoi Sotsialisticheskoi Respubliki. Vol. 1 (1974)-. Russian. **LC** GR203.R88; F64.

BG
FOLKLORE. V. 1- No. 1; Jan. 1976-. Periodical. English. TK.5 single issue. Ishurdi Road, Kushita Bangladesh. **LC** GR304.5; .F64. **DD** 390/.09549/2.

PE/0071-6774
FOLKLORE AMERICANO. Added/Corp Pan American Institute of Geography and History. Commission on History. Comite Interamericano de Folklore. No. 1 (1953)-. Spanish (English and French). sa. $19.00 US, Canada & Central America; $21.50 South America & Europe; $24.00 other. Instituto Panamericano de Geographico Historia, APDO 18879 Secretaria General, 11870 Mexico DF Mexico. **Tel** 011 52 5 2775888, 011 52 5 2775791, FAX 011 52 5 2716172. **ED** Celso A. Lara Figueroa. **LC** GR1; .F327. Index available. **Pr Rev. Circ:** 500. Documents available from The Genuine Article.

Desc: Publishes essays, works and research material related to the cultural habits and customs of ethnic groups in Latin America.
Ind/Abst Anthropol. Index; Arts Humanit. Citation Index (19??-19??) [Full Cov.]; Curr. Contents Arts Humanit.; Ethnoarts Index; HAPI Hisp. Am. Period. Index; Res. Alert [Full Cov.].

US/0272-5711
FOLKLORE AND FOLKLIFE IN VIRGINIA. Added/Corp Virginia Folklore Society. Journal of the Virginia Folklore Society. **VFOAT** Journal of the Virginia Folklore Society. Vol. 1 (1979)-. Periodical. English. ir. The Virginia Folklore Society, 115 Wilson Hall, University of Virginia, Charlottesville VA 22903. **Tel** (804)924-7813. **ED** Charles L. Perdue Jr. **LC** GR110.V8; F64. **DD** 390/.009755. **Circ:** 200.
Desc: Articles on the traditional culture of Virginia.

US/0162-6280
FOLKLORE AND MYTHOLOGY STUDIES (LOS ANGELES, CALIF. : 1977). (FOLKLORE AND MYTHOLOGY STUDIES.). **Added/Corp** University of California, Los Angeles. Folklore Graduate Students' Association. Vol. 1 (Spring 1977)-. English. an. $8.50 (add $1.00 postage & handling) US; $8.50 (add $2.50 postage & handling) other. Folklore Graduate Students Association, University of California, Los Angeles CA 90024. **Tel** (310)825-4242. **(Subscription address:** Folklore and Mythology Studies, UCLA, 1037 GSM-Library Wing, Los Angeles CA 90024-1459) **LC** GR1; .F329. **DD** 390/.05. **Bk Rev. Pr Rev.**
Desc: Folklore and mythology articles on multiple genres and areas.
Ind/Abst Am. Hist. Life (1985-1988).

US/0731-1524
FOLKLORE AND MYTHOLOGY STUDIES (LOS ANGELES, CALIF. : 1980). (FOLKLORE AND MYTHOLOGY STUDIES.). [Folk. myth. stud.]. **Added/Corp** University of California, Berkeley Publications: Folklore Studies. No. 31 (1980)-. Monographic series. English. ir. Price varies per volume. University of California Press, 2120 Berkeley Way, Berkeley CA 94720. **Tel** (510)642-4191, (510)642-3907, FAX (510)642-9917. **Circ:** 800 (ctrl). ***Continues*** *University of California Publications. Folklore Studies.*
Ind/Abst MLA Int. Bibl. Books Artic. Mod. Lang. Lit.

BE/0015-590X
FOLKLORE BRABANCON. [Folk. brabancon]. **Added/Corp** Brabant (Belgium). Service de Recherches Historiques et Folkloriques. **VFOAT** Brabantsche Folklore. No. 1 (Aug. 1921)-. Bulletin. French (Dutch). qt. 350F. Folklore Brabancon, rue du Marche aux Herbes 61, 1000 Bruxelles Belgium. **Tel** 02 504 0430, FAX 02 504 0495. **ED** Gilbert Menne. Index available. **Bk Rev. Pr Rev. Circ:** 1,000 (ctrl). Documents available from FAXON Xpress.
Desc: History, folklore and popular traditions of the province of Brabant.
Ind/Abst BHA : Biblio. Hist. Art.

II/0015-5896
FOLKLORE (CALCUTTA). (FOLK-LORE.). [Folklore]. **VFOAT** Folklore. Vol. 1 (Jan. 1960)-. Periodical. English (Hindi). mo. $24.00. **(Subscription address:** Prints India, 11 Darya Ganj, New Delhi, 110002 India, (Phone: 011 91 11 3268645)) **ED** Kanad Dasgupta. **LC** GR305; .F63. Index available. cum. index. **Bk Rev. Ad Acc. Circ:** 5,472. available on microfilm and microfiche from University Microfilms International (UMI). ***Continues in part*** *Indian Folk Lore.*
Desc: Devoted to the cause of the Indian Folklore Society.
Ind/Abst MLA Int. Bibl. Books Artic. Mod. Lang. Lit.; RILM Abstr.

FR
FOLKLORE DE CHAMPAGNE. Began with No. 27, published in 1971. Periodical. French. qt. 80.00F. Jean Daunay, Rumilly-les-Vandes, 10260 Saint-Parre-les-Vaudes France. **LC** GR162.C43; F65. **DD** 398.2/0944/3. ***Continues*** *Revue du Folklore de l'Aube.*

FR/0015-5918
FOLKLORE DE FRANCE. (19??)-. Periodical. French. Four times a year. 158.00F. Conference National Groups Folkloriques Francais, 8 Avenue du General Leclerc, 30000 Nimes France. **Tel** 33 66 848777. **ED** Lachaud (editor's address: 160 Traverse du Russan 30000 Nimes France). **DD** 398. **Bk Rev**, (Qty: 4). **Ad Acc, Adv Mgr:** Feybesse JC. **Pr Rev. Circ:** 4,500 (ctrl). ***Continues*** *Folklore.*

US/0015-5926
FOLKLORE FORUM. [Folk. forum]. Vol. 1 (March 1968)-. Periodical. English. sa. $8.00 (individuals), $10.00 (institutions). Folklore Forum Society, 504 North Fess Street, Bloomington IN 47405. **Tel** (812)855-0426. **ED** CG Kelley, R Veatch, T Vaughan. **LC** GR1; .F564. **DD** 398/.05. Index available. **Bk Rev**, (Qty: 15-20). **Pr Rev. Circ:** 400 (ctrl).
Desc: Articles and book reviews on current topics in folklore and folkloristics.

Ind/Abst Am. Hist. Life (1976-); Am. Bibliogr. Slavic East Europ. Stud. (19??-19??); Annu. Bibliogr. Engl. Lang. Lit.; MLA Int. Bibl. Books Artic. Mod. Lang. Lit.

US/1041-8644
FOLKLORE HISTORIAN (MIDDLETOWN, DAUPHIN COUNTY, PA.), THE. (THE FOLKLORE HISTORIAN.). [Folk. hist.]. **Added/Corp** Pennsylvania State University. Folklore and American Studies. Vol. 1 No. 1 (1984)-. English. an. $5.00. Indiana State University, Department of English, Terre Haute IN 47809. **Tel** (812)237-3163, FAX (812)237-3156. **LC** GR1; .F34. **DD** 398/.05.
Ind/Abst Am. Hist. Life (1990-); MLA Int. Bibl. Books Artic. Mod. Lang. Lit.

UK/0015-587X
FOLKLORE (LONDON). (FOLKLORE.). [Folklore]. **Added/Corp** Folklore Society (Great Britain). **VAT** Folk Lore. Vol.1 (Mar. 1890)-. Periodical. English. an (June). £32.00. Folklore Society, University College, Gower Street, London WC1E 6BT England. **Tel** 011 44 71 3875894. **ED** Dr. Gillian Bennett. **LC** GR1; .F5. **DD** 398/.05. Index available. cum. index. **Bk Rev**, (Qty: 12 - 15). **Ad Acc. Circ:** 1,500. available on microfilm and microfiche from University Microfilms International (UMI). Documents available from The Genuine Article, UMI Article Clearinghouse. ***Formed by the union of*** *Archaeological Review* ***and*** *Folklore Journal.*
Ind/Abst Acad. Search (July 1993-); Annu. Bibliogr. Engl. Lang. Lit.; Anthropol. Index; Arts Humanit. Citation Index [Full Cov.]; BHA : Biblio. Hist. Art; Br. Humanit. Index; Child. Lit. Abstr. (19??-); Curr. Contents Arts Humanit.; Humanit. Index; Humanit. Source (Jul. 1993-); Index Book Rev. Humanit.; INFO-SOUTH Abstr.; Mag. Search; MLA Int. Bibl. Books Artic. Mod. Lang. Lit.; Newsp. Period. Abstr. (1989-); Res. Alert [Full Cov.]; RILM Abstr.

CN/0824-3085
FOLKLORE (MOOSE JAW). (FOLKLORE / SASKATCHEWAN HISTORY & FOLKLORE SOCIETY.). [Folklore]. **Added/Corp** Saskatchewan History & Folklore Society. Vol. 1, No. 1, Summer (1979)-. Periodical. English. Four times a year. 15.00Can$ Canada; 19.00Can$ US; 25.00Can$ other. Saskatchewan History & Folklore Society, 1870 Lorne Street, Regina Saskatchewan S4P 2L7 Canada. **Tel** (306)780-9204, FAX (306)781-6021. **ED** Richard J. Wood. **DD** 971.24/005. **[CCC].** Index available (published separately). cum. index. **Bk Rev. Ad Acc. Circ:** 1,800.
Desc: Covers the history and folklore of the province of Saskatchewan from the point of view of personalized sources.

US
FOLKLORE OF AMERICAN HOLIDAYS, THE. (1991)-. English. ir (every five years). $85.00. Gale Research Inc., 835 Penobscot Building, Detroit MI 48226. **Tel** (800)877-GALE, (313)961-2242, FAX (313)961-6083, telex TWX 810-221-7086. **ED** Hennig Cohen and Tristram Potter Coffin. Index available.
Desc: Reference source that vividly illustrates the rich body of history and lore behind 133 holidays celebrated in the United States. Chronologically arranged, entries include well known religious and secular celebrations. A description of the holiday's origins, historical background, and general characteristics are provided, followed by a wide variety of folklore.

CN/0705-1158
FOLKLORE (OTTAWA). ***Title Change.*** (FOLKLORE.). Vol. 1, No. 2 (March 1977)-?. Periodical. English (French). qt. Folklore Studies Association of Canada, 37 Fairbank Street, Dartmouth NS B3A 1B9 Canada. **Tel** (902)464-8990. **LC** GR113; .F63. **DD** 398/.06/271. ***Continues*** *Bulletin of the Folklore Studies Association of Canada, 0705-1115.* ***Continued by*** *Bulletin of the Folklore Studies Association of Canada, 0705-1115.*

US/0730-3181
FOLKLORE PAPERS OF THE UNIVERSITY FOLKLORE ASSOCIATION. [Folk. pap. Univ. Folk. Assoc.]. No. 9-. Academic Scholarly Publication. English. ir. Center for Intercultural Studies in Folklore and Ethnomusicology, University of Texas at Austin, Austin TX 78712. **Tel** (512)471-1288. **LC** GR1; .T38A. **DD** 398/.05. Index available. **Circ:** 1,000 (ctrl). ***Continues*** *Folklore Annual of the University Folklore Association, 0071-6782.*
Desc: Scholarly publications on folklore by students at the University of Texas graduate program in folklore and other scholarly disciplines.

US
FOLKLORE SOCIETY OF GREATER WASHINGTON NEWSLETTER. Main/Corp Folklore Society of Greater Washington. (19??)-. Newsletter. English. Twelve times a year. $16.00. Folklore Society of Greater Washington, 307 Broadleaf Drive, Vienna VA 22180. **Tel** (703)281-2228. **ED** Cecily Pilzer (phone: ()301)565-8818). **LC** GR105; .F65. **DD** 398/.0973.

SZ/0015-5969
FOLKLORE SUISSE. Added/Corp Schweizerische Gesellschaft fuer Volkskunde. Vol. 33 (1943)-. Periodical. German (Italian). Four times a year (Mar., July, Sep., Dec.). 45.00F. Schweizerische Gesellschaft fuer Volkskunde, Augustinergasse 19, CH 4051 Basel Switzerland. **Tel** 011 41 61 2619900, . Index available. **Bk Rev. Ad Acc. Circ:** 600.
Desc: Journal of the Swiss Society for Folklore.
Ind/Abst MLA Int. Bibl. Books Artic. Mod. Lang. Lit.

GW
FOLKLORE VERZEICHNIS FUER EUROPA. VFOAT Folklore Directory for Europe. (19??)-. English (German). Floricica News, Dorrei Schafer Danziger Str 17, W-6113 Babenhausen Germany. **LC** GV1643; .F64. **DD** 793.3/194.

US/0160-9831
FOLKLORE WOMEN'S COMMUNICATION. No. 14 (Winter 1978)-. Periodical. English. ir. $7.00 (individuals), $7.50 (institutions), $5.00 (students). Folklore Women's Communication, Folklore Institute, 506 North Fess, Indiana University, Bloomington IN 47405. **Tel** (812)331-0832. **ED** Patricia E. Sawin and Jan Laude. **LC** GR470; .F64. **DD** 398/.02/4042. **Bk Rev. Circ:** 125. ***Continues*** *Folklore Feminists' Communication, 0093-8475.*
Desc: Newsletter of the women's section of the American Folklore Society. Includes short articles, book reviews and notices regarding women's folklore and folk art and feminist approaches to folklore.

TU
FOLKOR VE ETNOGRAFYA ARASTRMALAR. (1984)-. summaries and/or abstracts in English; table of contents in English and Turkish. an. **LC** GR280; .F63.

US/0145-3009
FORGET ME NOT (ANCHORAGE). (FORGET-ME-NOT.). **Added/Corp** Folk Magazine Workshop. Vol. 1 (1976)-. English. an. $3.50. Folk Magazine Workshop, 2533 Providence Avenue, Anchorage AK 99504. **LC** GR110.A4; F65. **DD** 398.2/09798.

US/0892-2500
FRIENDS OF FLORIDA FOLK. Added/Corp Friends of Florida Folk. **VFOAT** Friends of Florida Folk Newsletter. (19??)-. Periodical. English. Twelve times a year (Sometimes July/Aug. issues are combined). $10.00. Friends of Florida Folk, 1625 Vereda Verde, Sarasota FL 34232-2164. **Tel** (813)377-9256. **ED** Jean Hewitt. **Ad Acc. Circ:** 400 (ctrl).
Desc: Contains information about folk personalities. Includes a calendar of folk events. Networking regarding the folk world in Florida.

US/1070-8898
FROM THE BROTHERS GRIMM. [From Brothers Grimm]. **Added/Corp** Davenport Films. **VFOAT** From the Brothers Grimm Newsletter. Vol. 1, No. 1 (1988)-. Periodical. English. sa. $6.00 (one year), $10.00 (two year). Davenport Films, Route 1 Box 527, Delaplane VA 22025. **Tel** (703)592-3701, FAX (703)592-3717. **ED** Tom Davenport. **LC** LB1583.8; .F76. **DD** 372.6/4. **Bk Rev**, (Qty: 2). **Circ:** 500.

US/0532-7334
FROM THE SOURDOUGH CROCK. English. $1.00. California Folklore Society, State College, Department of Anthropology, Northridge CA 91324. **LC** GR1; .C258. **DD** 398/.05.

JA
GAKUSHUIN MINZOKU. No. 1 (1980)-. Japanese. Gakushuin Daigaku Minzoku Kenkyukai, 5-1 Mejiro-1 Toshima-ku, Tokyo-to 171 Japan. **LC** GR339; .G34.

FI/0782-0011
GLIMTAR UR ALANDS FOLKKULTUR. [Glimtar Alands folkkult.]. (1984)-. Periodical. Swedish.

US/0099-0159
GOLDENSEAL. [Goldenseal]. **Added/Corp** West Virginia. Dept. of Commerce. West Virginia Arts and Humanities Council. Vol. 1 (April/June 1975)-. Periodical. English. qt (Mar., June, Sep., Dec.). $15.00. Goldenseal, The Cultural Center, 1900 Kanawha Blvd East, Charlestown WV 25305. **Tel** (304) 558-0220, FAX (304)558-2779. **ED** Ken Sullivan. **LC** F241; .G64. **DD** 975.5/04. Index available. cum. index. **Bk Rev. Circ:** 32,000 (ctrl).
Desc: Documents the traditional culture of West Virginia, including the folk, arts, crafts, folklife and oral history, relying mainly on interviews with older citizens.

CN/0318-0042
GOLOS INSTYTUTU. **See** Ethnic Interests.

●US/1047-7225
GOOD COUNTRY PEOPLE. (1992)-. English. ir. $12.00. North Carolina Wesleyan College Press, 3400 North Wesleyan Boulevard, Rocky Mount NC 27804. **Tel** (919)985-5193, FAX (919)977-3701. **ED** Arthur Mann Kaye (Department of English, NC Wesleyan College, Rocky Mount, NC 27804).

Desc: The subtitle is "an irregular journal of the cultures of eastern North Carolina." Interested in essays of all types which focus on the region.

UK
GYPSY. See Anthropology.

US/0095-6910
HOMEGROWN (ROHNERT PARK). (HOMEGROWN.). V. 1- Fall 1973-. English. Division of American Ethnic Studies, California State College Sonoma, Rohnert Park CA 94928. **LC** GR105; .H65. **DD** 390/.08.

CC
HSIN-CHIANG MIN CHIEN WEN HSUEH. See Literature.

US/0885-7970
I AIN'T LYING. **Added/Corp** Mississippi: Cultural Crossroads. Vol. 1, No. 1 (Spring 1981)-. Monographic series. English. ir. Price varies per volume. Mississippi Cultural Crossroads, Box 89, Alcorn State University, Lorman MS 39096. **Tel** (601)437-8905. **LC** WMLC 93/207.

CU/0047-1542
ISLAS. [Islas]. No. 1 (1958)-. Periodical. Spanish. ir. $13.00. Empresa Ediciones Cubanas, Oreilly No 407, Haban Vieja Ciudad de la Habana Cuba. **Tel** 6-6074. **LC** AP63. **Circ:** 10,000 (ctrl).
Desc: Essays, poetry, fiction, research and documentation about folklore, drawings and song lyrics.
Ind/Abst Am. Hist. Life (1970-1973, 1978-); ARTbibliogr. Mod.; HAPI Hisp. Am. Period. Index; Soc. Plann. Policy Dev. Abstr.; Sociol. Abstr.

BE/0778-5607
JAARBOEK / KONINKLIJKE BELGISCHE COMMISSIE VOOR VOLKSKUNDE, VLAAMSE AFDELING. ***Title Change.*** **Added/Corp** Commission Royale Belge de Folklore. Section Flamande. (1959)-(19??). Dutch. an. **LC** GR187.F54; J3. ***Continues*** *Jaarboek (Commission Nationale Belge de Folklore. Vlaamse Afdeling), 0778-5593.* ***Continued by*** *Jaarboek met Volkskundige Bibliografie.*
Ind/Abst MLA Int. Bibl. Books Artic. Mod. Lang. Lit.

BE
JAARBOEK MET VOLKSKUNDIGE BIBLIOGRAFIE / KONINKLIJKE BELGISCHE COMMISSIE VOOR VOLKSKUNDE, VLAAMSE AFDELING. **Added/Corp** Commission Royale Belge de Folklore. Section Flamande. Belgium. Ministerie van de Vlaamse Gemeenschap. (19??)-. Dutch. an. ***Continues*** *Jaarboek (Commission Royale Belge de Folklore. Section Flamande), 0778-5607.*

GW/0075-2738
JAHRBUCH FUER OSTDEUTSCHE VOLKSKUNDE. [Jahrb. ostdtsch. Volkskd.]. Vol. 7 (1962/63)-. German (summaries and/or abstracts in English). an. N G Elwert Verlag, Postfach 1128, Reitgasse 7+9, W-3550 Marburg Germany. **Tel** 06421 25023, FAX 06421 15487. **ED** Von Ulrich Tolksdorf. **LC** DD61.8; .J3. **DD** 305.8/31/005. Index available. ctrl circ. ***Continues*** *Jahrbuch fur Volkskunde der Heimatvertriebenen.*
Ind/Abst BHA : Biblio. Hist. Art; MLA Int. Bibl. Books Artic. Mod. Lang. Lit.

GW/0171-9904
JAHRBUCH FUER VOLKSKUNDE. **Added/Corp** Gorres-Gesellschaft. (1978)-. Periodical. German. an. Echter Wuerzburg, Postfach 5560, Julius Promenade 64, D 97070 Wuerzburg Germany. **Tel** 011/49/931/3091153, FAX 011/49/931/16735.
Ind/Abst BHA : Biblio. Hist. Art.

CN/0228-3689
JARNIGOINE. (LA JARNIGOINE : TRADITIONS ET ARTS POPULAIRES AU QUEBEC.). [Jarnigoine]. Vol. 1, No. 1 (Jan. 1981)-. Periodical. French. bm. $8.51. La Jarnigoine, Federation des Loisirs-Danse du Quebec, 4545 Pierre de Coubertin, Case Postale 1000 Station M, Montreal Quebec H1V 3R2. **Tel** (514)252-3029. **DD** 398/.09714.
Desc: Folklore from all points of view, mainly traditional dance, music and folk song.

US/0890-9113
JEWISH FOLKLORE AND ETHNOLOGY REVIEW. [Jew. folk. ethnol. rev.]. **Added/Corp** American Folklore Society. Jewish Folklore and Ethnology Section. Max Weinreich Center for Advanced Jewish Studies. Tisch School of the Arts. Dept. of Performance Studies. **VFOAT** Jewish Folklore and Ethnology. Vol. 9, No. 1 (1987)-. Periodical. English. sa (Mar., Oct.). $20.00 US; $23.00 other. Jewish Folklore Ethnology Section, 3822 South Troostoc, Tulsa OK 74105. **Tel** (918)745-9251. **ED** Guy Haskell. **DD** 305. **Bk Rev**. **Ad Acc**, **Adv Mgr:** A. Fromm. **Circ:** 500. ***Continues*** *Jewish Folklore and Ethnology Newsletter, 0737-559X.*
Desc: Resources, directories, and articles relating to the study and teaching of all facets of Jewish folklore and ethnology of Jewish communities.

US/1053-3664
JOURNAL / CALIFORNIA TRADITIONAL MUSIC SOCIETY. [J. - Calif. Tradit. Music Soc.]. **Added/Corp** California Traditional Music Society. **VFOAT** CTMS Journal. Vol. 1, No. 1 (Sept. 1984-Jan. 1985)-. Periodical. English. Twice a year (Aug. and Dec.). Free. California Traditional Music Society, 4401 Trancas Place, Tarzana CA 91356. **Tel** (818)342-7664, FAX (818)609-0106. **ED** Elaine and Clark Weissman. **LC** IN PROCESS. **DD** 781. **Bk Rev**, (Qty: 6-12). **Ad Acc**. **Circ:** 18,000. ***Continues*** *House Concerts.*
Desc: Information on all aspects of folk music.

US/0021-8715
JOURNAL OF AMERICAN FOLKLORE. (THE JOURNAL OF AMERICAN FOLK-LORE.). [J. Am. folk.]. **Added/Corp** American Folklore Society. **VFOAT** Journal of American Folklore. Vol. 1, No. 1 (April/June 1888)-. Periodical. English. qt. $60.00. American Anthropological Association, 4350 North Fairfax Dr, Suite 640, Arlington VA 22203. **Tel** (703)528-1902 ext. 3031, FAX (703)528-3546. **ED** Bruce Jackson and Lyle Green. **LC** GR1; .J8. Index available. **Bk Rev**. **Ad Acc**. **Circ:** 3,000 (ctrl). available on microfilm and microfiche from University Microfilms International (UMI). Documents available from The Genuine Article, UMI Article Clearinghouse.
Desc: Articles covering all aspects of world folklore, reviews of books, records, and films of current interest to folklorists.
Ind/Abst Abstr. Anthropol.; Acad. Abstr. Full Text Elite (July 1990-); Acad. Abstr. (July 1990-); Acad. Ind. [Computer File] (1987-); Acad. Search (July 1990-); Am. Hist. Life (1965-); Am. Bibliogr. Slavic East Europ. Stud.; Annu. Bibliogr. Engl. Lang. Lit.; Anthropol. Index; Anthropol. Lit.; Arts Humanit. Citation Index [Full Cov.]; Book Rev. Index; Chicano Index; Child. Lit. Abstr. (19??-); Curr. Contents Arts Humanit.; Expand. Acad. Index (1987-); Hist. Source (July 1990-); Humanit. Index; Humanit. Source (Jul. 1990-); Index Book Rev. Humanit.; INFO-SOUTH Abstr.; Mag. Search; MLA Int. Bibl. Books Artic. Mod. Lang. Lit.; Music Index; Newsp. Period. Abstr. (1989-); Recent. Publ. Artic.; Ref. Sources; Res. Alert [Full Cov.]; Romant. Move.; West. Hist. Q.; Women Stud. Abstr.

●US/1064-752X
JOURNAL OF COMMUNICATION AND TRANSFORMATIONAL MYTH. (JOURNAL OF COMMUNICATION AND TRANSFORMATIONAL MYTH : EXPLORATIONS ON THE CULTURAL, HISTORICAL AND PERSONAL IMPLICATIONS OF MYTH.). **Added/Corp** Human Communication Cooperative. (1993)-. Periodical. English. sa. $6.00. Human Communication Cooperative, Department of Speech Communication, 2801 South University Avenue, Little Rock AR 72204.

US/0737-7037
JOURNAL OF FOLKLORE RESEARCH. [J. folk. res.]. **Added/Corp** Indiana University, Bloomington. Folklore Institute. Vol. 20, No. 1 (May 1983)-. Academic Scholarly Publication. English. tq (Jan., May, Sept.). $25.00 (institutions), $18.00 (individuals), $15.00 (students). Indiana University Folklore Institute, 504 North Fess Street, Bloomington IN 47405. **Tel** (812)855-0043. **ED** Mary Ellen Brown. **LC** GR1; .I5. **DD** 398/.05. **[CCC]**. Index available. cum. index. **Bk Rev**. **Ad Acc**. **Pr Rev. Circ:** 700. available on microfilm and microfiche from University Microfilms International (UMI). Documents available from The Genuine Article. ***Continues*** *Journal of the Folklore Institute, 0015-5934.*
Desc: Devoted to the scholarly study of folklore. Provides an international forum for current theory and research, emphasizing articles that investigate issues and assess scholarship.
Ind/Abst Abstr. Anthropol.; Am. Hist. Life (1964-); Annu. Bibliogr. Engl. Lang. Lit.; Anthropol. Index; Arts Humanit. Citation Index (19??-19??) [Full Cov.]; Curr. Contents Arts Humanit.; Humanit. Index; Middle East Abstr. Index; MLA Int. Bibl. Books Artic. Mod. Lang. Lit.; Music Index; Res. Alert [Full Cov.]; Soc. Sci. Cit. Index [Select. Cov.]; Soc. Sci. Index.

US/0360-1927
JOURNAL OF LATIN AMERICAN LORE. [J. Lat. Am. lore]. **Added/Corp** University of California, Los Angeles. Latin American Center. Vol. 1 (Summer 1975)-. Periodical. English (Spanish). Twice a year. $30.00 (individuals), $40.00 (institutions). Regents of the University of California at Los Angeles, 405 Hilgard Avenue, Los Angeles CA 90024-1447. **Tel** (310)825-6634. **ED** Johannes Wilbert. **LC** GR114; .J67. **DD** 390/.098. **CODEN** JLALEB. **Ad Acc**. **Circ:** 400. Documents available from The Genuine Article.
Desc: Latin American lore is found in the records of ancient civilizations, among surviving tribal societies, indigenous groups, peasant communities and in both the elite and popular sectors of modern urban society.
Ind/Abst Abstr. Anthropol.; Acad. Abstr. (July 1993-); Acad. Search (July 1993-); Am. Hist. Life (1975-); Anthropol. Index; Anthropol. Lit.; Arts Humanit. Citation Index (19??-19??) [Full Cov.]; Curr. Contents Arts Humanit.; Ethnoarts Index; HAPI Hisp. Am. Period. Index; Mag. Artic. Summar. Elite; Mag. Artic. Summar. CD-ROM (July 1993-); MLA Int. Bibl. Books Artic. Mod. Lang. Lit.; Res. Alert [Full Cov.].

US/0017-6087
JOURNAL OF THE GYPSY LORE SOCIETY. [J. Gypsy Lore Soc.]. **Added/Corp** Gypsy Lore Society. Vol. 1 (July 1888)-. Periodical. English. sa (Feb. and Aug.). $35.00 US and Canada; $40.00 other. Gypsy Lore Society, 5607 Greenleaf Road, Cheverly MD 20785. **Tel** (301)341-1261, FAX (301)341-1261. **ED** Sheila Salo. **LC** DX101; .G6. **DD** 398/.08991497. **CODEN** GYLJAC. **[CCC]**. Index available (bound in 2nd issue). cum. index (published each August). **Bk Rev**, (Qty: 5). **Ad Acc**. **Circ:** 250.
Desc: Features articles on the cultures of groups traditionally known as Gypsies as well as travelers and peripatetic groups. These groups include those referring to themselves as Ludar, Rom, Roma, Romnichels, Sinti, and Travellers.
Ind/Abst Am. Hist. Life (1991-); Br. Humanit. Index; MLA Int. Bibl. Books Artic. Mod. Lang. Lit.; Soc. Plann. Policy Dev. Abstr.

MW
KALULU. V. 1 (June 1976)-. Periodical. English. K0.50 single issue. University of Malawi English Department, Box 280, Zomba Malawi Central Africa. **LC** GR358.5; .K34. **DD** 398.2/096897.

US/0164-2537
KARIKAZO. ***Ceased.*** ( )-(1989). Periodical. English. qt. Karikazo/Hungarian Folklore, Box 262, Bogota NJ 07603. **Tel** (201)836-4869. **Ad Acc**.

US/0149-8444
KEYSTONE FOLKLORE. ***Suspended.*** (KEYSTONE FOLKLORE : A PUBLICATION OF THE PENNSYLVANIA FOLKLORE SOCIETY.). [Keyst. folk.]. (1973)-Suspended with Vol. 4, No. 2. Periodical. English. qt. $10.00. Pennsylvania Folklore Society, 100 Pollack Drive, Orwigsberg PA 17961. **Tel** (717)544-6705. **ED** Thomas E Graves. **LC** GR1; .K45. **DD** 398/.05. **Bk Rev**. **Ad Acc**. **Circ:** 300. available on microfilm and microfiche from University Microfilms International (UMI). ***Continues*** *Keystone Folklore Quarterly, 0023-0987.*
Desc: General interest articles and reviews on the folklore of Pennsylvania.
Ind/Abst Am. Hist. Life (1976-1989); Annu. Bibliogr. Engl. Lang. Lit.; MLA Int. Bibl. Books Artic. Mod. Lang. Lit.

FI/0047-3677
KOTISEUTU. ***Title Change.*** (KOTISEUTU : KOTISEUTULIITON AIKAKAUSLEHTI.). [Kotiseutu]. **Added/Corp** Kotiseutuliitto (Finland) Suomen Kotiseutuliitto. (1929)-(1993). Periodical. Finnish. qt. **LC** GR200; .K6. ***Merged with*** *Elias (Helsinki, Finland), 0785-5249* ***and*** *Kieliposti, 0783-2958,* ***to form*** *Hiidenkivi (Helsinki, Finland), 1236-794X.*
Ind/Abst Am. Hist. Life (1964-).

IT/0394-2791
LACIO DROM : RIVISTA BIMESTRALE DI STUDI ZINGARI. **Added/Corp** Centro Studi Zingari (Rome, Italy). **VFOAT** Buon Cammino. (1965)-. Periodical. Italian (Romany). Six times a year (Feb., Apr., June, Aug., Oct., Dec.). L22.000 Italy; L28.000 other. Lacio Drom, Centro Studi Zingar, Via dei Barbieri 22, 00186 Rome Italy. **Tel** 011 39 6 6541397. **ED** Lacio Drom. **LC** DX101; .L33. Index available (6th iss.). cum. index (Nov/Dec. iss.). **Bk Rev**, (Qty: 30). **Ad Acc**. **Circ:** 2,100.
Desc: Information on anthropology, education, linguistics, literature, poetry and history.

GR/1010-7266
LAOGRAPHIA. [Laografia]. **Added/Corp** Hellenike Laographike Hetaireia. (1909)-. Greek, Modern (French and English). ir (every 3 years). $7.00 (per copy). Hellenike Laographike Etaireia, Odos Didotou 12, Athens 144 Greece. **Tel** 3633110. **ED** Demetrios Loukatos. **LC** GR1; .L3. Index available. cum. index. **Bk Rev**. **Ad Acc**. **Circ:** 1,000 (ctrl).
Desc: The organ of the Greek Society of Laography. Rich source material, as well as research studies on folklore, ethnography, social life and popular culture in Greece.
Ind/Abst Am. Hist. Life; MLA Int. Bibl. Books Artic. Mod. Lang. Lit.

CY
LAOGRAPHIKE KYPROS. Vol. 1, No. 1 (Jan./April 1971)-. Periodical. Greek, Modern. PO Box 1034, Leukosia Ceylon. **LC** GR295.C9; L34.

IT
LARES (FIRENZE). See Anthropology.

FR/0024-0761
LEMOUZI. **VFOAT** Lemouzi, Revue Franco-Limousine. (1893)-. Periodical. French. Four times a year. 240.00F France; 300.00F other. Soc. Historique du bas Limousin, 13 Place Municipale, 19000 Tulle France. **Tel** 16 55 26 22 62. **ED** Robert Joudoux. **LC** UNC. Index available (Published 2 to 3 times a year). **Bk Rev**, (Qty: 3-4). **Ad Acc**. **Circ:** 3,000 (ctrl).
Desc: Archeological, ethnology and language in history. Limousines, traditions, biographies, bibliographies and literature.

PL/0024-4708
LITERATURA LUDOWA. [Lit. lud.]. **Added/Corp** Polskie Towarzystwo Ludoznawcze. (1957)-. Periodical. Polish (summaries and/or abstracts in English). bm. $54.00. **(Subscription address:** ARS Polona, PO Box 1001, 00068 Warsaw Poland.**) LC** GR195; .L5. **DD** 398.2/09438.
Ind/Abst Anthropol. Index; MLA Int. Bibl. Books Artic. Mod. Lang. Lit.

UK
LONDON LORE. Vol. 1, Pt. 1 (Mar. 1978)-. Periodical. English. ir. £2.80 (4 parts). Monica & Roy Vickery, 12 Eastwood Street, London SW16 6PX United Kingdom. **LC** GR142.L66; L66. **DD** 398/.09421.

UK/0307-7144
LORE AND LANGUAGE. [Lore lang.]. **Added/Corp** Sheffield Survey of Language and Folklore. Sheffield Survey of Language and Folklore. Archives of Cultural Tradition. University of Sheffield. Dept. of English Language. University of Sheffield. Dept. of Extramural Studies. University of Sheffield. Language Centre. Centre for English Cultural Tradition and Language. No. 1 (July 1969)-. Periodical. English. sa (Jan. & July). $88.00 (institutions), $29.50 (individuals) US and Canada. Sheffield Academic Press Ltd, 343 Fulwood Road, Sheffield S10 3BP England. **Tel** 011 44 742 670044, 011 44 742 668431, FAX 011 44 742 660291. **ED** J. D. A. Widdowson. **LC** GR140; .L67. **DD** 390/.0942. Index available (free). cum. index. **Bk Rev. Ad Acc. Circ:** 150 (ctrl).
Desc: Modern approaches to the study of folklore. Covers linguistics, anthropology, sociology, psychology, history (especially oral history) and literary studies.
Ind/Abst Annu. Bibliogr. Engl. Lang. Lit.; MLA Int. Bibl. Books Artic. Mod. Lang. Lit.; Soc. Plann. Policy Dev. Abstr.; Sociol. Abstr.

US/0090-9769
LOUISIANA FOLKLORE MISCELLANY. **Added/Corp** Louisiana Folklore Society. (19??)-. Periodical. English. an. $10.00. Louisiana Folklore Miscellany, Loyola University, Department of English, New Orleans LA 70118. **Tel** (504)865-2476. **ED** Frank de Caro. **LC** GR110.L5; L68. **DD** 390/.09763. Index available. **Circ:** 150.
Desc: Covers folklore in Louisiana.

PL/0076-1435
LUD. (LUD : ORGAN POLSKIEGO TOWARZYSTWA LUDOZNAWCZEGO.). [Lud]. **Added/Corp** Polskie Towarzystwo Ludoznawcze. (1985)-. Periodical. Polish (summaries and/or abstracts in English and Russian). **LC** GR1; .L8.
Ind/Abst Anthropol. Index; Anthropol. Lit.; MLA Int. Bibl. Books Artic. Mod. Lang. Lit.

XN/0542-2108
MAKEDONSKI FOLKLOR. [Maked. folk.]. **Added/Corp** Institut za Folklor (Skopje, Macedonia). **VFOAT** Folklore Macedonien. Vol. 1, No. 1 (1968)-. Macedonian (summaries and/or abstracts in French and Russian). sa. **LC** GR1; .M25.
Ind/Abst Anthropol. Index; MLA Int. Bibl. Books Artic. Mod. Lang. Lit.

US/0363-3659
MALEDICTA. See Linguistics.

NO/0024-855X
MALL OG MINNE. See Linguistics.

RU
MATERIALY I ISSLEDOVANIIA PO FOLKLORU BASHKIRII I URALA. **Added/Corp** Bashkirskii Gosudarstvennyi Universitet. Vol. 1 (1974)-. Russian. 1.60rub. **LC** GR203.B37; M37.

NE
MEDEDELINGEN VAN HET P.J. MEERTENS-INSTITUUT. No. 31 (Dec. 1979)-. Periodical. Dutch. an. Free. PJ Meertens-Instituut, Keizersgracht 569-571, Postbus 19888, 1017 DR Amsterdam Netherlands. **Tel** 020-234698. **ED** P J Meertens and J Berns. **LC** PF701.; M46. **Circ:** 2,000 (ctrl). ***Continues*** *Mededelingen van het Instituut voor Dialectologie, Volkskunde en Naamkunde.*

US/1048-857X
MEDIEVAL FOLKLORE. [Mediev. folk.]. Vol. 1 (Spring 1991)-. Periodical. English (French). sa. $19.95 (paperbound), $29.95 (casebound). Edwin Mellen Press, PO Box 450, Lewiston NY 14092. **Tel** (716)754-2788. **LC** GR1; .M36. **DD** 398.2/09/0205.

IS
MEHKERE HA-MERKAZ LE-HEKER HA-FOLKLOR. Main/Corp Universitah Ha-Ivrit Bi-Yerushalayim. Merkaz Le-Heker Ha-Folklor. **VFOAT** Folklore Research Center Studies. Vol. 1 (1970)-. Monographic series. English (French and Hebrew). an. Price varies per volume. Magnes Press, Hebrew University of Jerusalem, PO Box 7695, Jerusalem 91076 Israel. **Tel** 011 972 2 660341, 011 972 2 635291, FAX 011 972 2 633370, telex 25391. **LC** GR98.A1; J46.

IS/0333-7030
MEHKERE YERUSHALAYIM BE-FOLKLOR YEHUDI / HA-UNIVERSITAH HA-IVRIT BI-YERUSHALAYIM, HA-FAKULTAH LE-MADAE HA-RUAH, HA-MAKHON LE-MADAE HA-YAHADUT. Added/Corp Universitah Ha-Ivrit Bi-Yerushalayim. Makhon Le-Madae Ha-Yahadut. **VFOAT** Jerusalem Studies in Jewish Folklore. (1981)-. Periodical. Hebrew (summaries and/or abstracts in English). sa. Magnes Press, Hebrew University of Jerusalem, PO Box 7695, Jerusalem 91076 Israel. **Tel** 011 972 2 660341, 011 972 2 635291, FAX 011 972 2 633370, telex 25391. **LC** GR97.8; .M44. **DD** 398/.089924.
Desc: Contains Hebrew and Yiddish folk literature.

US/0193-1598
MEMBERSHIP DIRECTORY - GYPSY LORE SOCIETY, NORTH AMERICAN CHAPTER. Main/Corp Gypsy Lore Society. North American Chapter. (19??)-. Directory. English. an. $2.00 (available to Chapter Members only). Gypsy Lore Society, 5607 Greenleaf Road, Cheverly MD 20785. **Tel** (301)341-1261, FAX (301)341-1261. **ED** Sheila Salo. **LC** DX101; .G765. **DD** 909/.04/91497. **Ad Acc. Circ:** 250 (ctrl).
Desc: Aid to communication among scholars and others interested in Gypsy Studies. Lists members, their areas of interest, their contributions to the field.

US/0275-6013
MID-AMERICA FOLKLORE. [MidAm. folk.]. **Added/Corp** Ozark States Folklore Society. Southwest Missouri State University. English Dept. Arkansas College. Regional Culture Center. Kansas Folklore Society. Mid-America Folklore Society. **VAT** Mid America Folklore. Vol. 7 (Spring 1979)-. Periodical. English. sa. $10.00. Mid-America Folklore Society, Arkansas College, Batesville AR 72501. **Tel** (501)793-9813. **(Subscription address:** Secretary/Treasurer, c/o Ozark Folk Center, Mountain View AR 72560**) ED** George Lankford. **LC** GR108; .M53. **DD** 398/.0973. **Bk Rev. Ad Acc. Circ:** 200 (ctrl). ***Continues*** *Mid-South Folklore, 0099-2356.*
Desc: Analytical articles and collections of folklore, with emphasis on central parts of the United States.
Ind/Abst Annu. Bibliogr. Engl. Lang. Lit.; MLA Int. Bibl. Books Artic. Mod. Lang. Lit.; West. Hist. Q.

US/1074-0244
MIDDLE EAST & SOUTH ASIA FOLKLORE BULLETIN, THE. Added/Corp Ohio State University. Division of Comparative Studies in the Humanities. **VFOAT** Middle East and South Asia Folklore Bulletin; Folklore Bulletin. Vol. 8, No. 1 (Winter 1991)-. Bulletin. English. Three times a year (Autumn, Winter, and Spring). $10.00 (institutions); $6.00 (individuals). Ohio State University Division of Comparative Studies in the Humanities, 308 Dulles Hall, 230 West 17th Avenue, Columbus OH 43210. **Tel** (614)292-9255, (614)292-0389. **ED** Anupama G. Mande and Sabra J. Webber. **LC** GR270; .M5. **Bk Rev**, (Qty: 15). available on diskette. ***Continues*** *Middle East & South Asia Folklore Newsletter.*

US/0894-4059
MIDWESTERN FOLKLORE. [Midwest. folkl.]. Vol. 13, No. 1 (Spring 1987)-. Periodical. English. sa. $7.00 North America; $10.00 other. Indiana State University, Department of English, Terre Haute IN 47809. **Tel** (812)237-3163, FAX (812)237-3156. **ED** Ronald L Baker. **LC** GR1; .M5. **DD** 398/.05. **Pr Rev. Circ:** 200 (ctrl). ***Continues*** *Midwestern Journal of Language and Folklore, 0363-9967.*
Ind/Abst Am. Hist. Life (1989-); Annu. Bibliogr. Engl. Lang. Lit.; MLA Int. Bibl. Books Artic. Mod. Lang. Lit.

PH
MINDANAO ART AND CULTURE. VFOAT Mindanao Art & Culture. No. 1-. Monographic series. English. Price varies per volume. University Research Center, Mindanao State University, PO Box 5594, 9200 Iligan City Philippines. **ED** Raymond Llorca. **Circ:** 500 (ctrl).

JA
MINWA NO TECHO. Added/Corp Minwa No Kenkyukai. (Spring 1978)-. Periodical. Japanese. qt. ¥3520 Japan; $23.00 US. Nihon Minwa No Kai, 6-8-28 Higashi-Oizumi, Nerima-ku, Tokyo 178 Japan. **Tel** 03(925)7018. **ED** Kazuo Yoshizawa, Miyoko Matsutani, Shozo Mizutani, Isao Shibuya, Yoichi Yoneya, Atsushi Higuchi, Ichiro Wakabayashi, and Shinzaburo Mochizuki. **LC** GR339; .M56. **Bk Rev. Ad Acc. Circ:** 5,000.

JA
MINZOKUGAKU RONSO. VFOAT Japanese Folklore Review; Minzoku-Gaku Ronso. Aug. 1979 Ed.-. Periodical. Japanese (Japanese). Sagami Minzokugakkai, 3996 Totsukamachi Totsuka-ku, Yokohama 244 Japan. **LC** GR339; .M57.

US/0026-6248
MISSISSIPPI FOLKLORE REGISTER. [Miss. folk. regist.]. **Added/Corp** Mississippi Folk-Lore Society. Vol. 1 (Spring 1967)-. Periodical. English. an (Dec.). $7.00. Mississippi Folklore Society, University of Mississippi, Center for the Study of Southern Culture, University MS 38677. **Tel** (601)232-5574. **ED** Thomas S. Rankin. **LC** GR1; .M56. **DD** 398/.09762. **Bk Rev. Ad Acc. Circ:** 400.
Desc: Original research on Mississippi and Southern folklore, but will consider articles on all aspects of folklore.
Ind/Abst Annu. Bibliogr. Engl. Lang. Lit.; Lit. Crit. Regist.; MLA Int. Bibl. Books Artic. Mod. Lang. Lit.

US/0731-2946
MISSOURI FOLKLORE SOCIETY JOURNAL. [Mo. Folk. Soc. j.]. **Added/Corp** Missouri Folklore Society. **VFOAT** Journal. Vol. 1 (1979)-. Periodical. English. an. $12.00. Missouri Folklore Society Journal, Box 1757, Columbia MO 65201. **Tel** (314)882-6066. **ED** Donald M Lance. **LC** GR110.M77; M57. **DD** 398/.09778. Index available. **Bk Rev. Pr Rev. Circ:** 500 (ctrl).
Desc: Articles on traditions and customs in Missouri with primary focus on non-academic and non-commercial topics.
Ind/Abst MLA Int. Bibl. Books Artic. Mod. Lang. Lit.

US
MLA INTERNATIONAL BIBLIOGRAPHY OF BOOKS AND ARTICLES ON THE MODERN LANGUAGES AND LITERATURES. VOLUME 5, FOLKLORE. **Added/Corp** Modern Language Association of America. (1981)-. Bibliography. English. an (Dec.). $100.00. Modern Language Association of America, 10 Astor Place, New York NY 10003-6981. **Tel** (212)614-6382, FAX (212)477-9863. ***Continues*** *Modern Language Association of America. MLA International Bibliography of books and articles on the Modern Languages and Literatures, 0024-8215.*

FR
MONDE ALPIN ET RHODANIEN, LE. See Sociology-Manners and Customs.

US/0278-2286
MOTIF (COLUMBUS, OHIO). ***Suspended.*** (MOTIF.). [Motif]. No. 1 (Oct. 1981)-?. Periodical. English. sa. $3.00. Ohio State University / Department of English, 164 West 17th Avenue, Columbus OH 43210. **Tel** (614)292-6555, (614)488-8634. **ED** Daniel R Barnes. cum. index. **Bk Rev. Pr Rev. Circ:** 256.
Desc: Publishes notes, queries, and reviews, bibliographies and checklists, some longer articles. Directed to folklorists and literary scholars interested in the relationship between folklore and literature.
Ind/Abst MLA Int. Bibl. Books Artic. Mod. Lang. Lit.

AT
MYTHOS : A NEWSLETTER ABOUT STORY TELLING. Newsletter. English. an.
Ind/Abst Aust. Educ. Index.

UN/0130-6936
NARODNA TVORCHIST TA ETNOGRAFIIA. See The Arts-Crafts and Decorative Arts.

CI
NARODNA UMJETNOST. Added/Corp Zagreb. Institut za Narodnu Umjetnost. (1962)-. Serbo-Croatian (Roman) (summaries and/or abstracts in English, French and German). an. **LC** GR259; .N34. **DD** 398/.09497.
Ind/Abst Anthropol. Index; MLA Int. Bibl. Books Artic. Mod. Lang. Lit.

YU/0027-8017
NARODNO STVARALASTVO. FOLKLOR. [Nar. stvar., Folk.]. **VFOAT** Folklor. V. 1- (No. 1-20); Jan. 1962-. Periodical. Serbo-Croatian (Roman) (summaries and/or abstracts in French and Russian). qt. **LC** GR259; .N3.
Ind/Abst MLA Int. Bibl. Books Artic. Mod. Lang. Lit.

SP
NARRIA. Added/Corp Universidad Autonoma de Madrid. No. 1 (Jan. 1976)-. Periodical. Spanish. sa. $10.00. Museo Artes Tradiciones Poplrs, Universidad Autonoma Cantoblanco, 28049 Madrid Spain. **Tel** 011 34 1 3974270. **LC** GR229; .N37.

US
NATIONAL DIRECTORY OF STORYTELLING. Directory. English. an. NAPPS National Association for the Preservation & Perpetuation of Storytelling, PO Box 309, Jonesborough TN 37659. **Tel** (615)753-2171. **LC** GR105; .N37. **DD** 398.2/025/73. ***Continues*** *National Directory of Storytellers.*

II
NATYAM : NATYA PARISHAD, SAGARA KA PRAKASANA. Vol. 1, No. 1-. Periodical. Hindi (Hindi). qt. 20.00. Drama Council Sanskrit Department, Sagar University, Sagar India. **LC** PK2971; .N38.

US/0887-8048
NEW JERSEY FOLKLIFE. [N.J. folklife]. **Added/Corp** Douglass College. American Studies Dept. New Jersey Folklore Society. New Jersey Folk Festival. **VFOAT** New Jersey Folk Life. Vol. 11 (1986)-. English. an

(published in May). $10.00 (individual and institutional membership), $8.50 (student membership). New Jersey Folklore Society Popular Studies, 3718 Locust Walk, F Thomsen, Philadelphia PA 19104. **Tel** (215)898-7885. **LC** F134; .N55. **DD** 974.9/005. ***Continues** New Jersey Folklore, 0886-201X.*
Ind/Abst Am. Hist. Life (1986-); MLA Int. Bibl. Books Artic. Mod. Lang. Lit.

US/0160-2330
NEW MEXICO FOLKLORE RECORD, THE. **Added/Corp** New Mexico Folklore Society. Vol. 1 (1947)-. English. ir. New Mexico Folklore Society, 616 Vassar Drive NE, Albuquerque NM 87106. **Tel** (505)255-7102. **LC** GR1; .N47. **DD** 398.

US/0361-204X
NEW YORK FOLKLORE. [N. Y. folk.]. **Added/Corp** New York Folklore Society. Vol.1 (Summer 1975)-. Academic Scholarly Publication. English. sa. $50.00 (US), $55.00 (other) institution; $35.00 (US), $40.00 (other) individual. New York Folklore Society, PO Box 130, Newfield NY 14867. **Tel** (607)273-9137, FAX (607)273-8225. **ED** Ray Allen & Egle Zygas. **LC** GR1; .N472. **DD** 398/.042/09747. **Bk Rev. Ad Acc. Circ:** 1,000 (ctrl). available on microfilm and microfiche from University Microfilms International (UMI). Documents available from The Genuine Article. ***Supersedes** New York Folklore Quarterly, 0028-7229.*
Desc: Essays and scholarly papers specifically related to folkloristic studies, primarily in New York State.
Ind/Abst Abstr. Anthropol.; Am. Hist. Life (1975-); Annu. Bibliogr. Engl. Lang. Lit.; Arts Humanit. Citation Index (19??-19??) [Full Cov.]; Curr. Contents Arts Humanit.; Music Index; Res. Alert [Full Cov.].

US/0015-5950
NEWSLETTER. **See** Music.

US
NEWSLETTER - KANSAS FOLKLORE SOCIETY. **Main/Corp** Kansas Folklore Society. Newsletter. English. Kansas Folklore Society, Kansas State Historical Society, 120 SW 10th Street, Topeka KS 66612. **LC** GR105; .K27. **DD** 398/.06/2781.

US/1070-4604
NEWSLETTER OF THE GYPSY LORE SOCIETY. [Newsl. Gypsy Lore Soc.]. **Added/Corp** Gypsy Lore Society. **VFOAT** GLS Newsletter; Newsletter. (19??)-. Newsletter. English. qt. Gypsy Lore Society, 5607 Greenleaf Road, Cheverly MD 20785. **Tel** (301)341-1261, FAX (301)341-1261. **LC** DX101; .N48. **DD** 970.004/91497/05. ***Continues** Newsletter of the Gypsy Lore Society, North American Chapter, 0731-4841.*

US/0731-4841
NEWSLETTER OF THE GYPSY LORE SOCIETY, NORTH AMERICAN CHAPTER. ***Title Change.*** [Newsl. Gypsy Lore Soc. North Am. Chapter]. **Added/Corp** Gypsy Lore Society. North American Chapter. Vol. 1, No. 1 (Spring 1978)-(19??). Newsletter. English. qt. Gypsy Lore Society, 5607 Greenleaf Road, Cheverly MD 20785. **Tel** (301)341-1261, FAX (301)341-1261. **ED** Matt T Salo and Sheila Salo. **LC** DX101; .N48. **DD** 970.004/91497/05. **[CCC]. Bk Rev. Ad Acc. Circ:** 300 (ctrl). ***Continued by** Newsletter of the Gypsy Lore Society, 1070-4604.*
Desc: Interdisciplinary publication in gypsy studies. News of conferences, research, bibliography, reviews, articles, anthropology, linguistics, folklore, history, sociology, literature, and arts.

US/0888-6121
NEWSLETTER OF THE NORTH CAROLINA FOLKLORE SOCIETY. [Newsl. N.C. Folk. Soc.]. **Added/Corp** North Carolina Folklore Society. (19??)-. Newsletter. English. qt. North Carolina Folklore Society, Department of English, Appalachian State University, Boone NC 28608. **Tel** (704)262-2323. **ED** Thomas McGowan. **DD** 390. **Bk Rev. Circ:** 500.
Desc: Studies of North Carolina folklore and folklife, use of folklore in literature and news of folklife activities. Includes short articles, media notes, queries, state directory and calendar, and a teachers' column.

FI
NIF NEWSLETTER. **Main/Corp** Nordic Institute of Folklore. Vol. 1, (1972)-. Newsletter. English. Three times a year. Free. Nordic Institute of Folklore, PO Box 107, SF-20501 Turku Finland. **Tel** 011 358 21 326206. **LC** GR205; .N67a.

DK
NORD NYTT. **Added/Corp** Nordisk Etnologisk-Folkloristisk Arbetsgrupp. (1963-1978); New Series No. 1 (Nov. 1978)-. Periodical. Danish. Nefa-Norden, Museumstjenesten Lysgard, DK-8800 Viborg Lyngby Denmark. **LC** GR205; .N65.
Ind/Abst Am. Hist. Life (1987-); For. Prod. Abstr.; Int. Bibliogr. Sociol.; Soc. Plann. Policy Dev. Abstr.

US/0090-5844
NORTH CAROLINA FOLKLORE JOURNAL. [N.C. folk. j.]. **Added/Corp** North Carolina Folklore Society. North Carolina State University. Dept. of English. North Carolina State University. School of Liberal Arts. Appalachian State University. Vol. 21 (April 1973)-. Periodical. English. Twice a year (May & Nov.). $10.00 Comes with North Carolina Folklore Society membership & Newsletter. North Carolina Folklore Society, Department of English, Appalachian State University, Boone NC 28608. **Tel** (704)262-2323. **ED** Dr. Thomas McGowan. **LC** GR110.N8; N6. **DD** 390/.09756. **Bk Rev. Circ:** 500. ***Continues** North Carolina Folklore, 0029-246X.*
Desc: Studies of North Carolina folklore and folklife, use of folklore in literature.
Ind/Abst Am. Hist. Life (1969-1973, 1986-); Annu. Bibliogr. Engl. Lang. Lit.; MLA Int. Bibl. Books Artic. Mod. Lang. Lit.; Music Index.

US/0078-1681
NORTHEAST FOLKLORE. [Northeast folk.]. **Added/Corp** Northeast Folklore Society. University of Maine. Dept. of English. Northeast Archives of Folklore and Oral History. Maine Folklife Center. Vol. 1 (Spring 1958)-. English. an. $10.00 US and Canada; $15.00 other. Maine Folklife Center, University of Maine, 5773 South Stevens Hall, Orono ME 04469. **Tel** (207)581-1891. **ED** Edward D. Ives. **LC** GR1; .N65. **DD** 398/.0974. **Circ:** 600.
Desc: Regional material including songs, legends, tales, and traditions of New England and the Atlantic Provinces of Canada.
Ind/Abst Am. Hist. Life (1963-); MLA Int. Bibl. Books Artic. Mod. Lang. Lit.

US/0029-3369
NORTHWEST FOLKLORE. [Northwest folk.]. **Added/Corp** College of Idaho (Caldwell, Idaho). Regional Studies Center. University of Oregon. Vol. 1, No. 1 (Summer 1965)-. Periodical. English. sa (2 issues). $15.00 (individuals), $30.00 (institutions). Northwest Folklore, Center for Humanities, DV-11 University of Washington, Seattle WA 98195. **Tel** (206)543-6884. **ED** Louie W. Attebery. **DD** 398. **Bk Rev. Pr Rev. Circ:** 150. ***Continues** Oregon Folklore Bulletin, 0474-4489.*
Desc: Voice for the region's efforts to collect, interpret and disseminate its oral-aural lore and studies of its traditional material culture.
Ind/Abst MLA Int. Bibl. Books Artic. Mod. Lang. Lit.

US
NOTES ON AMERICA'S FOLK ART ENVIRONMENTS. **See** The Arts-Art.

CK/0120-8195
NUEVA REVISTA COLOMBIANA DE FOLCLOR. 1986-. Spanish. Three times a year. 1,000Col$ Colombia. Patronato Colombiano de Artes y Ciencias, Carrera 15 No 33-76, Bogota DE Colombia. **Tel** 2 85 43 09. **ED** Alvaro Chaves Mendoza. **LC** GR1; .R295. **DD** 398/.09861. **Circ:** 1,500. ***Continues** Revista Colombiana de Folclor.*
Desc: Dedicated to divulge the Colombian folclor, a tool for researchers on this subject.

US/0194-3464
NUGGETS (YREKA). (NUGGETS.). **Added/Corp** Siskiyou County Historical Society. (19??)-. Periodical. English. ir. $15.00 (individuals), $25.00 (institutions) Comes with Siskiyou County Historical Society membership. Siskiyou County Historical Society, 910 South Main Street, Yreka CA 96097. **Tel** (916)842-3836.

HU/0547-0196
NYIREGYHAZI JOSA ANDRAS MUZEUM EVKONYVE, A. **Added/Corp** Josa Andras Muzeum. (1958)-. Hungarian. an. **LC** DB975.S9; N99.
Ind/Abst BHA : Biblio. Hist. Art.

AU/0029-9669
OESTERREICHISCHE ZEITSCHRIFT FUER VOLKSKUNDE. [Osterr. Z. Volkskd.]. **Added/Corp** Verein fuer Volkskunde in Wien. Vol. 1 (1947)-. Periodical. German. qt. S240.00. Verein fuer Volkskunde, Laudongasse 15-19, A-1080 Vienna Austria. **Tel** (0222)438905, FAX (0222)4085342. **ED** Klaus Beitl and Franz Grieshofer. **LC** GR1; .O37. **DD** 398/.05. Index available. **Bk Rev. Ad Acc. Circ:** 1,300. Documents available from The Genuine Article. ***Continues** Wiener Zeitschrift fuer Volkskunde, 0257-4764.*
Desc: Essays, information, chronicles and reviews concerning Austrian and European folklore.
Ind/Abst Arts Humanit. Citation Index [Full Cov.]; BHA : Biblio. Hist. Art; MLA Int. Bibl. Books Artic. Mod. Lang. Lit.; Numis. Lit.; Res. Alert [Full Cov.]; Romant. Move.; Soc. Sci. Cit. Index [Select. Cov.].

US/0733-4737
OHIO FOLKLORE. (OHIO FOLKLIFE : JOURNAL OF THE OHIO FOLKLORE SOCIETY.). New Ser. V. 6 (79-81)-. Periodical. English. $10.00. Ohio Folklore Society, 2366 Glenmawr Avenue, #2, Columbus OH 43202. **LC** GR110.O48; O5. **DD** 398/.09771. available on microfilm and microfiche from University Microfilms International (UMI). ***Continues** Journal of the Ohio Folklore Society, 0473-9817.*

JA
OKINAWA MINWA NO KAI KAIHO. **Main/Corp** Okinawa Minwa no Kai. (June 1976)-. Japanese. Endo Kenkyushitsu, Okinasw Kokusai Daigaku 267-2, Ginowan Japan. **LC** GR339; .O38a.

CN/0384-5052
ONTARIO FOLKDANCER. **See** Dance.

US/0883-5365
ORAL TRADITION. [Oral tradit.]. **VFOAT** OT. Vol. 1, No. 1 (Jan. 1986)-. Periodical. English. Three times a year (three numbers per volume). $20.00 (individuals), $35.00 (institutions). Slavica Publishers Inc., PO Box 14388, Columbus OH 43214-0388. **Tel** (614)268-4002. **ED** John Miles Foley. **LC** GR72; .O68. **DD** 398/.05. **Bk Rev. Pr Rev. Circ:** 500.
Desc: Contains studies in oral literature and related fields, research and scholarship on the creation, transmission, and interpretation of all forms of oral expression.
Ind/Abst MLA Int. Bibl. Books Artic. Mod. Lang. Lit.; RILM Abstr.

ER/0552-7155
PAAR SAMMUKEST EESTI KIRJANDUSE UURIMISE TEED. **See** Literature.

AT/0362-1596
PARABOLA (MT. KISCO). (PARABOLA.). [Parabola]. **Added/Corp** Tamarack Press. Society for the Study of Myth and Tradition. Vol. 1, Iss. 1 (Winter 1976)-. Periodical. English. Four times a year (Feb., May, Aug., Nov.). $20.00 one year; $35.00 two years; $49.00 three years. Society for Study Myth & Tradition, 656 Broadway, Subs Department, New York NY 10012. **Tel** (212)505-6200. **ED** D. Tacon and R. James. **LC** BL1; .P25. **DD** 291.1/3/05. Index available. cum. index. **Ad Acc. Circ:** 36,000. available on microfilm and microfiche from University Microfilms International (UMI). Documents available from The Genuine Article, UMI Article Clearinghouse.
Desc: Explores the universal themes found in myth, legend, ritual and religion of the world's traditions, relating them to our modern search for meaning.
Ind/Abst Abstr. Engl. Stud.; Acad. Search (July 1993-); Am. Humanit. Index; Arts Humanit. Citation Index [Full Cov.]; Book Rev. Index; Child. Lit. Abstr. (19??-); Except. Hum. Exp.; Expand. Acad. Index (1989-); Humanit. Index; Humanit. Source (Jul. 1993-); Index Book Rev. Relig.; INFO-SOUTH Abstr.; Mag. Search; Middle East Abstr. Index; MLA Int. Bibl. Books Artic. Mod. Lang. Lit.; Newsp. Period. Abstr. (1991-); Relig. Index One Period. (1976-); Relig. Theol. Abstr.; Res. Alert [Full Cov.]; Romant. Move.; Soc. Sci. Cit. Index [Select. Cov.].

US/0031-4498
PENNSYLVANIA FOLKLIFE. **See** History(General)-History of North, South, and Central America.

US/0743-782X
PROVERBIUM (COLUMBUS, OHIO). (PROVERBIUM.). [Proverbium]. **Added/Corp** Ohio State University. University of Vermont. Universitah ha-Ivrit bi-Yerushalayim. Vol. 1 (1984)-. Periodical. English (French and German). an (Sept.). $25.00 (individuals); $30.00 (institutions). Proverbium, University of Vermont, Department of English, Burlington VT 05405. **Tel** (802)656-3063. **ED** Wolfgang Mieder. **LC** PN6401; .P77. **DD** 398/.9/05. **Bk Rev**, (Qty: 5-10). **Ad Acc. *Continues** Proverbium Paratum, 0209-9950.*
Ind/Abst Lit. Crit. Regist.; MLA Int. Bibl. Books Artic. Mod. Lang. Lit.

US/0890-0655
PUBLIC PROGRAMS NEWSLETTER. [Public programs newsl.]. **Added/Corp** American Folklore Society. Public Programs Section. State Historical Society of Iowa. (1983)-. Newsletter. English. Twice a year (Apr., Oct.). $10.00. American Folklore Society Archiv, 4350 North Fairfax Drive, Suite 640, Arlington VA 22203. **Tel** (202)232-8800. **ED** Steve Ohrn. **LC** GR105; .P86. **DD** 398/.05. **Circ:** 150 (ctrl).

US/8756-7245
PUBLICATIONS / GYPSY LORE SOCIETY, NORTH AMERICAN CHAPTER. [Publ. - Gypsy Lore Soc., North Am. Chapter]. No. 1-. Monographic series. English. ir. Price varies per volume. Gypsy Lore Society, 5607 Greenleaf Road, Cheverly MD 20785. **Tel** (301)341-1261, FAX (301)341-1261. **ED** Matt T Salo. **DD** 390. **Circ:** 250.
Desc: Selected papers from meetings and conferences sponsored by the Gypsy Lore Society, North American Chapter.

US/0741-7896
PUBLICATIONS OF THE AMERICAN FOLKLIFE CENTER. [Publ. Am. Folklife Cent.]. No. 1-. Monographic series. English. ir. Price varies per volume. American Folklife Center, Library of Congress, Washington DC 20540. **Tel** (202)707-6590, FAX (202)707-2076. **DD** 398/.0973.

US
PUBLICATIONS OF THE AMERICAN FOLKLORE SOCIETY. **Added/Corp** American Folklore Society. Vol. 1 (1980)-. Monographic series. English. The University of Pennsylvania Press, 418 Service Drive, 1300 Blockley Hall, Philadelphia PA 19104. **Tel** (215)898-6264. **LC** UNC.
Ind/Abst MLA Int. Bibl. Books Artic. Mod. Lang. Lit.

US/0082-3023
PUBLICATIONS OF THE TEXAS FOLK-LORE SOCIETY. [Publ. Tex. Folk. Soc.]. **Added/Corp** Texas Folklore Society. No. 1 (1916)-. English. Texas Folklore Society, University Station, Austin TX 78712. **LC** GR1; .T4. **DD** 398/.05.
Ind/Abst Annu. Bibliogr. Engl. Lang. Lit.; MLA Int. Bibl. Books Artic. Mod. Lang. Lit.

SP/0034-7981
REVISTA DE DIALECTOLOGIA Y TRADICIONES AND POULARES. **Added/Corp** Spain. Consejo Superior de Investigaciones Cientificas. Centro de Estudios de Etnologia Peninsular. Spain. Consejo Superior de Investigaciones Cientificas. Instituto Antonio de Nebrija. Seccion de Tradiciones Populares. Vol. 1 (1944)-. Periodical. Spanish. qt. 4000ptas Spain; 5000ptas other. Consejo Superior Investigacion Cientificas (CSIC), Vitruvio 8, 28006 Madrid Spain. **Tel** 011 34 1 5612833, FAX 011 34 1 4113077, telex 42182. **LC** GR1; .R293.

SP/0034-7981
REVISTA DE DIALECTOLOGIA Y TRADICIONES POPULARES. (REVISTA DE DIALECTOLOGIA Y TRADICIONES POPULARES / CONSEJO SUPERIOR DE INVESTIGACIONES CIENTIFICAS, INSTITUTO ANTONIO DE NEBRIJA, SECCION DE TRADICIONES POPULARES.). [Rev. dialectol. tradic. pop.]. **Added/Corp** Centro de Estudios de Etnologia Peninsular (Spain) Instituto Antonio de Nebrija. Seccion de Tradiciones Populares. (1945)-. Spanish. qt. 4000ptas Spain; 500ptas other. Consejo Superior Investigacion Cientificas (CSIC), Vitruvio 8, 28006 Madrid Spain. **Tel** 011 34 1 5612833, FAX 011 34 1 4113077, telex 42182. **LC** GR1; .R293. **DD** 398/.0946. Documents available from The Genuine Article. ***Continues** Revista de Tradiciones Populares.*
Ind/Abst Am. Hist. Life (1967-1973); Arts Humanit. Citation Index [Full Cov.]; BHA : Biblio. Hist. Art; Curr. Contents Arts Humanit.; Int. Bibliogr. Sociol.; MLA Int. Bibl. Books Artic. Mod. Lang. Lit.; Res. Alert [Full Cov.]; Soc. Sci. Cit. Index [Select. Cov.].

RM/0034-8198
REVISTA DE ETNOGRAFIE SI FOLCLOR. **See** Anthropology.

VE
REVISTA INIDEF. **See** Music.

VE/0035-0575
REVISTA VENEZOLANA DE FOLKLORE. [Rev. venez. folk.]. **Added/Corp** Servicio de Investigaciones Folkloricas Nacionales (Venezuela) Instituto Nacional de Folklore (Venezuela) Instituto Nacional de Culture y Bellas Artes. Vol. 1, No. 1-2, (Jun./Jul./Dic. 1947)- Segunda Epoca, Ano 1 (Mayo 1968)-. Periodical. Spanish.
Ind/Abst Anthropol. Index; HAPI Hisp. Am. Period. Index (19??-); RILM Abstr.

GW/0080-2697
RHEINISCHES JAHRBUCH FUER VOLKSKUNDE. [Rhein. Jahrb. Volkskd.]. (1950)-. German. ir. Ferdinand Dummler Verlag, Postfach 1480, D 53004 Bonn Germany. **Tel** 011 49 228 223031. **ED** K. Meisen. **LC** GR1; .R47.
Ind/Abst MLA Int. Bibl. Books Artic. Mod. Lang. Lit.

IT/0391-9099
RICERCA FOLKLORICA, LA. 1 (June 1980)-. Periodical. Italian (summaries and/or abstracts in English). sa. L70000 Italy; L85000 other. Grafo Edizioni, Via A Bassi 10, 25123 Brescia Italy. **Tel** 39 30 393221, FAX 39 30 307397. **ED** Glavco Sanga (editor's phone: 39 2 70001773). **LC** GR1; .R49. **DD** 390/.005.
Ind/Abst Anthropol. Lit. (-Vol. 9, 1987).

RU/0136-7447
RUSSKIJ FOLKLOR. (RUSSKII FOLKLOR.). [Rus. folk.]. **Added/Corp** Institut Russkoi Literatury (Pushkinskii Dom). (1956)-. Academic Scholarly Publication. Russian. ir. Izdatelstvo Nauka / Akademiia Nauk, Publishing House of the Russian Academy of Sciences, Leninskii Porspekt 14, 117901 Moscow Russia. **Tel** 011 95 954-21-53, FAX 011 95 938-21-44, telex 411964. **LC** GR190; .R86.
Desc: Information on Russian folklore.
Ind/Abst MLA Int. Bibl. Books Artic. Mod. Lang. Lit.

PK
SANG-I MIL. **VFOAT** Intarneshnal Fok Lor Jarnal. V. 1- August/Sept. 1973-. Periodical. Urdu (Urdu). 20.00. **ED** Farigh Bukhari. **LC** GR303; .S24.

SZ/0080-732X
SCHRIFTEN DER SCHWEIZERISCHEN GESELLSCHAFT FUER VOLKSKUNDE. **Main/Corp** Schweizerische Gesellschaft fuer Volkskunde. **Added/Corp** Schweizerische Gesellschaft fuer Volkskunde. **VFOAT** Publications de la Societe Suisse des Traditions Populaires. (1902)-. Monographic series. German (French and Italian). ir. Price varies per volume. Schweizerische Gesellschaft fuer Volkskunde, Augustinergasse 19, CH 4051 Basel Switzerland. **Tel** 011 41 61 2619900, . **LC** GR240; .S3. **Circ:** 1,000-2,000.
Desc: Monograph series on Swiss folklore - stories, songs, games, legends, fairy tales, and costumes.

GW
SCHRIFTEN ZUR ANTIKEN MYTHOLOGIE. **Added/Corp** Heidelberger Akademie der Wissenschaften. Kommission fur Antike Mythologie. Vol. 1, (1972)-. Monographic series. German. ir. Price varies per volume. Verlag Phillip Von Zabern, Postfach 190930, D 80609 Munich Germany. **Tel** 011 49 89 12151661.
Desc: Covers mythology.

GW
SCHRIFTENREIHE - DEUTSCHE GESELLSCHAFT FUR VOLKSKUNDE. KOMMISSION FUR OSTDEUTSCHE VOLKSKUNDE. **Main/Corp** Deutsche Gesellschaft fur Volkskunde. Kommission fur Ostdeutsche Volkskunde. Periodical. German. ir. N G Elwert Verlag, Postfach 1128, Reitgasse 7+9, W-3550 Marburg Germany. **Tel** 06421 25023, FAX 06421 15487.

SZ/0048-9522
SCHWEIZER VOLKSKUNDE. **Added/Corp** Schweizerische Gesellschaft fuer Volkskunde. Schweizerische Gesellschaft fuer Volkskunde. Annual Reports. **VFOAT** Folk-Lore Suisse; Folklore Suisse. Vol. 1 (1911)-. Periodical. German. Four times a year (Mar., July, Sep., Dec.). 45.00F. Schweizerische Gesellschaft fuer Volkskunde, Augustinergasse 19, CH 4051 Basel Switzerland. **Tel** 011 41 61 2619900, . **ED** Rolf Thalmann. **LC** GR1; .S37. **DD** 398.05. Index available (bound in Dec. issue). **Bk Rev**, (Qty: 10-15). **Circ:** 1,800. ***Continued in part by** Folk-Lore Suisse.*
Desc: Journal of the Swiss Society of Folklore.
Ind/Abst BHA : Biblio. Hist. Art; MLA Int. Bibl. Books Artic. Mod. Lang. Lit.

SZ/0036-794X
SCHWEIZERISCHES ARCHIV FUER VOLKSKUNDE. [Schweiz. Arch. Volkskd.]. **VFOAT** Archives Suisses des Traditions Populaires. Vol. 1 (1897)-. Periodical. German (French). Twice a year (June and December). 65.00F. Schweizerische Gesellschaft fuer Volkskunde, Augustinergasse 19, CH 4051 Basel Switzerland. **Tel** 011 41 61 2619900, . **ED** Prof. Dr. Gyr. **LC** GR1; .S4. Index available (bound in 2nd issue, published in December). **Bk Rev**, (Qty: 40-50). **Circ:** 800. Documents available from The Genuine Article.
Desc: Journal with scientific articles in the authors languages and with illustrations also included.
Ind/Abst Anthropol. Index; Arts Humanit. Citation Index [Full Cov.]; BHA : Biblio. Hist. Art; Curr. Contents Arts Humanit.; MLA Int. Bibl. Books Artic. Mod. Lang. Lit.; Res. Alert [Full Cov.]; Soc. Sci. Cit. Index [Select. Cov.].

US
SFS FLYER. **Main/Corp** Seattle Folklore Society. **VFOAT** Flyer. **VAT** Seattle Folklore Society Flyer. (19??)-. Periodical. English. mo.

CC
SHAN CHA. **See** Literature.

IE/0332-2653
SINSEAR. Periodical. English (Gaelic (Scots)). **LC** GR153.5; .S55. **DD** 398/.09415.
Ind/Abst Annu. Bibliogr. Engl. Lang. Lit.

US/0196-0725
SISKIYOU PIONEER IN FOLKLORE, FACT AND FICTION, THE. [Siskiyou pioneer folk. fact fict.]. **Added/Corp** Siskiyou County Historical Society. **VFOAT** Siskiyou Pioneer in Folklore, Fact and Fiction and Yearbook; Siskiyou Pioneer in Folklore, Fact and Fiction and Guidebook to Siskiyou's Gold fields; Siskiyou Pioneer in Fact and Folklore and Yearbook; Siskiyou Pioneer; Siskiyou Pioneer and Yearbook. Vol. 3 (1947)-. English. ir. $15.00 (individuals), $25.00 (institutions) Comes with Siskiyou County Historical Society membership. Siskiyou County Historical Society, 910 South Main Street, Yreka CA 96097. **Tel** (916)842-3836. **DD** 979. Index available. cum. index. **Bk Rev**. **Ad Acc**. **Circ:** 1,500 (ctrl). ***Absorbed** Siskiyou County Historical Society. Yearbook, 1056-7771.*
Ind/Abst Am. Hist. Life.

US/0038-1462
SONS OF NORWAY VIKING, THE. **See** Ethnic Interests.

US/0899-594X
SOUTHERN FOLKLORE. [South. folk.]. **Added/Corp** Western Kentucky University. Vol. 46, No. 1 (1989)-. Periodical. English. Three times a year. $25.00 US; $28.00 other. University Press of Kentucky, 663 South Limestone Street, Lexington KY 40508. **Tel** (606)257-8439, FAX (606)257-2984. **ED** Erika Brady (editor's address: Folklore Program, Western Kentucky University, Bowling Green, KY 42101; phone: (502)745-5902). **LC** GR1; .S648. **DD** 398/.05. Index available in last issue of volume--attached. **Bk Rev**, (Qty: 15-20 per year). **Ad Acc**, **Adv Mgr:** K. Shaw. **Pr Rev.** **Circ:** 500. available on microfilm and microfiche from University Microfilms International (UMI). Documents available from FAXON Xpress. ***Formed by the union of** Kentucky Folklore Record, 0023-0227 **and** Southern Folklore Quarterly, 0038-4127.*
Desc: Scholarly journal containing articles on various aspects of folklore. Also reviews of books on folklore.
Ind/Abst Am. Hist. Life (1959-); Am. Humanit. Index (199?-); MLA Int. Bibl. Books Artic. Mod. Lang. Lit.; Music Index.

US
SOUTHERN FOLKLORE REPORTS. No. 1-. Monographic series. English. Price varies per volume. Center for Southern Folklore, 1216 Peabody Avenue, PO Box 4081, Memphis TN 38104.

UK/0038-7533
SPIN. Began in 1961. Periodical. English. qt. **LC** ML5; .S724. **DD** 784.4/005.

US/0888-3319
SPRINGHOUSE, THE. [Springhouse]. Vol. 1, No. 1 (Fall 1983)-. Periodical. English. bm. $15.00 US; $20.00 other. Springhouse - Journal of the Illinois Ozarks, PO Box 61, Herod IL 62947. **Tel** (618)252-3341. **ED** Gary DeNeal & Judy DeNeal. **DD** 977. **Bk Rev**. **Ad Acc**. **Circ:** 2,000.
Desc: Regional publication with emphasis on history, folklore, nostalgia, and humor.

US/1048-1354
STORYTELLING MAGAZINE. [Storytell. mag.]. **Added/Corp** National Association for the Preservation and Perpetuation of Storytelling (U.S.). **VFOAT** Storytelling. Vol. 1, No. 1 (Summer 1989)-. Periodical. English. Six times a year. $40.00. NAPPS National Association for the Preservation & Perpetuation of Storytelling, PO Box 309, Jonesborough TN 37659. **Tel** (615)753-2171. **DD** 808. **Ad Acc**. **Circ:** 12,000. ***Continues** National Storytelling Journal, 0743-1104.*
Desc: Features news of NAPPS and the broader storytelling community.
Ind/Abst Child. Lit. Abstr. (19??-).

●FI/1235-1946
STUDIA FENNICA. FOLKLORISTICA. **VFOAT** Folkloristica. (1992)-. Monographic series. English. ir. Price varies per volume. Finnish Literature Society, Hallituskatu 1, PB 259, 00171 Helsinki Finland. **Tel** 011 358 0 131231. **LC** GR1; .S78. ***Continues in part** Studia Fennica, 0085-6835.*

NO
STUDIA NORVEGICA ETHNOLOGICA ET FOLKLORISTICA. ***Ceased.*** (19??)-(19??). Multiple languages (English and Norwegian). ir. Universitetsforlaget, Kolstadgt. 1, Box 2959-Toeyen, Oslo 6 Norway. **LC** GR1; .S85. **DD** 301.2. ***Continues** Studia Norvegica.*

SW/0347-1837
SVENSKA LANDSMAL OCH SVENSKT FOLKLIV. **See** Linguistics.

US/0738-7911
TALKIN' UNION (TAKOMA PARK MD.). ***Ceased.*** **See** Economics-Labor.

US/0040-3253
TENNESSEE FOLKLORE SOCIETY BULLETIN. [Tenn. Folk. Soc. bull.]. **Added/Corp** Tennessee Folklore Society. Middle Tennessee State University. Vol. 3, No. 1 (Feb. 1937)-. Bulletin. English. qt (Mar., June, Sept., Dec.). $12.00 institution, $10.00 individual. Tennessee Folklore Society, c/o G. Anderson, Middle Tennessee State University, Murfreesboro TN 37132. **Tel** (615)898-2576. **ED** Charles K. Wolfe. **DD** 398. Index available (published separately, $5.00). **Bk Rev**, (Qty: 6-10). **Circ:** 350 (ctrl). available on microfilm from Tennessee Microfilms. ***Continues** Bulletin of the Tennessee Folklore Society.*
Desc: Devoted to the preservation and documentation of traditional culture. Articles are written by specialists and are designed to appeal to the scholar and general reader alike. Information about folk festivals and related events is also included.
Ind/Abst Am. Hist. Life (1969-); Annu. Bibliogr. Engl. Lang. Lit.; MLA Int. Bibl. Books Artic. Mod. Lang. Lit.; Music Index.

CN/0381-6109
THEM DAYS. **See** History(General)-History of North, South, and Central America.

AU/1013-8919
TIROLER HEIMAT. **See** History(General)-History of Europe.

GT
TRADICION POPULAR, LA. Spanish. Universidad de San Carlos de Guatemala / Folkloricos, Centro de Estudios Folkloricos, Ciudad Universitaria, San Carlos Guatemala, 12 Guatemala. **Tel** 011 502 2 319171. **LC** GR118.G8; T68.
Ind/Abst HAPI Hisp. Am. Period. Index.

GT/0564-0571
TRADICIONES DE GUATEMALA. [Tradic. Guatem.]. **Added/Corp** Universidad de San Carlos de Guatemala. Centro de Estudios Folkloricos. 1 (1968)-. Periodical. Spanish. sa. Universidad de San Carlos de Guatemala / Folkloricos, Centro de Estudios Folkloricos, Ciudad Universitaria, San Carlos Guatemala, 12 Guatemala. **Tel** 011 502 2 319171. **LC** GR118.G8; T7.
Ind/Abst Am. Hist. Life (1968-); Anthropol. Lit.

NO/0332-5997
TRADISJON. [Tradisjon]. No. 1 (1971)-. Norwegian. an. Kr240.00 Scandinavia; Kr285.00 other. Vett & Viten, PO Box 4, N-1321 Stabekk Norway. **Tel** 011 47 67 12 50 90, FAX 011 47 67 12 50 94. **ED** Reimund Kvideland. **LC** GR220; .T73. **Bk Rev. Ad Acc. Circ:** 600.
Desc: Folkloristic science with perspectives of the present times.
Ind/Abst MLA Int. Bibl. Books Artic. Mod. Lang. Lit.

SA
TYDSKRIF VIR VOLKSKUNDE EN VOLKSTAAL. **Added/Corp** Genootskap vir Afrikaanse Volkskunde. Vol. 1 (Aug. 1944)-. Periodical. Afrikaans. Twice a year. R25.00 South Africa; R30.00 other. Genootskap Vir Africaanse Volkskunde, PO Box 3038, Coetzenburg 7602 South Africa. **Tel** 011 7823784. **ED** Dr. Willie Loots. **LC** GR1; .G373. (y). cum. index. **Bk Rev. Ad Acc. Pr Rev. Circ:** 250 (ctrl).
Desc: Devoted to folklore, folklife, and cultural history in South America.

NL/0082-7347
ULSTER FOLKLIFE. [Ulster folklife]. **Added/Corp** Committee on Ulster Folklife and Traditions. Ulster Folklife Society. Ulster Folk and Transport Museum. Ulster Folk Museum. (1955)-. English. an. 7.00CFPF. Ulster Folk & Transport Museum, Cultra Manor, Holywood Co Down, Northern Ireland. **ED** J. Bell. **LC** GR148.N6; U43. **DD** 398/.09416. Index available. cum. index. **Bk Rev. Circ:** 500. Documents available from The Genuine Article.
Ind/Abst Annu. Bibliogr. Engl. Lang. Lit.; Anthropol. Index; Arts Humanit. Citation Index (19??-19??) [Full Cov.]; Br. Archaeol. Bibliogr. -?; Curr. Contents Arts Humanit.; MLA Int. Bibl. Books Artic. Mod. Lang. Lit.; Res. Alert [Full Cov.].

NR/0189-2320
UWA NDI IGBO. See Literature.

GW/0067-5989
VEROFFENTLICHUNGEN. ABTEILUNG SUDSEE. **Main/Corp** Berlin. Museum fur Volkerkunde (West Berlin). 1- 1961-. Periodical. German. Duncker und Humblot Verlag, Postfach 410329, D-12113 Berlin Germany. **Tel** 011 49 30 79000612, 011 49 30 79000613.

US/0042-6253
VILTIS. Vol. 1 (May 1942)-. Periodical. English. Six times a year. $20.00. Viltis Magazine, 1337 Marion Street, Denver CO 80218. **Tel** (303)839-1589. **ED** V.F. Beliajus. **LC** GR1; .V74. **Bk Rev**, (Qty: 6). **Ad Acc. Circ:** 2,100. available on microfilm and microfiche from University Microfilms International (UMI).
Desc: Folklore, folkdance, ethnic news and activities, histories, recipes, reviews of books, records, dance and concerts, travel, etc.

BE/0775-3128
VOLKSKUNDE (1940). (VOLKSKUNDE.). [Volkskunde]. **Added/Corp** Koninklijke Nederlandse Akademie van Wetenschappen. Volkskunde-Commissie. Vereniging voor Volkskunde. Commission Royale Belge de Folklore. (1940)-. Periodical. Dutch. qt. 500F Belgium; 600F other. Instituut voor Volkskunde, Centrum voor Studie en Documentatie vzw., Gildekamersstraat 7-9, 2000 Antwerpen Belgium. **Tel** 011 32 3 2329409. Index available. **Bk Rev**, (Qty: approx. 20-25 per year). ctrl circ. Documents available from The Genuine Article. ***Continues** Nederlandsch Tijdschrift voor Volkskunde.*
Ind/Abst Arts Humanit. Citation Index [Full Cov.]; BHA : Biblio. Hist. Art; Curr. Contents Arts Humanit.; MLA Int. Bibl. Books Artic. Mod. Lang. Lit.; Res. Alert [Full Cov.]; Soc. Sci. Cit. Index [Select. Cov.].

NE
VOLKSKUNDIG BULLETIN. **Added/Corp** Koninklijke Nederlandse Akademie van Wetenschappen. Volkskunde-Commissie. (Oct. 1975)-. Bulletin. Dutch. an. 3500F. Department of Folklore of the P J Meertens-Instituut, Keizersgracht 569-571, 1017 DR Amsterdam The Netherlands. **Tel** 020-23 46 98. **(Subscription address:** P J Meertens-Instituut, Postbus 1988, 1000 GW Amsterdam The Netherlands**)** **ED** K Roelandts and D P Blok and others. **LC** GR1; .V63. cum. index. **Bk Rev. Circ:** 500 (ctrl).
Desc: Cultural history, the spiritual and material culture of the Netherlands since the Middle ages.
Ind/Abst BHA : Biblio. Hist. Art; Int. Bibliogr. Sociol.

SJ
WAZA / MARKAZ DIRASAT AL-FULKLUR. 1 (March 1980)-. Periodical. Arabic (English). qt. Markaz Dirasat Al-Fullur Wa-Al-Tawthiq Al-Thaqafi, Jumhuriyat Al-Sudan Al-Dimuqratiyah S B 437, Al-Khartum Sudan. **LC** DT154.9; .W39.

GW/0511-4225
WEGWEISER ZUR VOLKERKUNDE. No. 1- 1951-. Monographic series. German. ir. Price varies per volume. Klaus Renner Fachbuchhdlg Verlag, Am Sonnenhang 8, D 82069 Hohenschftlrn Germany.

US/0196-2175
WEST VIRGINIA FOLKLORE JOURNAL. Periodical. English. sa. West Virginia Folklore Society, Box 446, Fairmont WV 26554. **LC** GR110.W4; W473. **DD** 398/.05.

US/0043-373X
WESTERN FOLKLORE. [West. folk.]. **Added/Corp** California Folklore Society. Vol. 6, No. 1 (Jan. 1947)-. Periodical. English. qt (Jan., April, July, Oct.). $30.00 (1 year), $90.00 (3 year) institutions; $25.00 (1 year), $70.00 (3 year) individuals. California State Polytechnic University, 3801 West Temple Avenue, Pomona CA 91768. **Tel** (714)869-3888. **ED** Jay Mechling. **LC** GR1; .C26. **DD** 398/.05. cum. index. **Bk Rev. Ad Acc. Circ:** 1,100. available on microfilm and microfiche from University Microfilms International (UMI). Documents available from The Genuine Article, UMI Article Clearinghouse. ***Continues** California Folklore Quarterly.*
Desc: A journal devoted to the description and analysis of regional, national and international folklore and customs.
Ind/Abst Abstr. Anthropol.; Acad. Search (July 1993-); Am. Hist. Life (1963-); Annu. Bibliogr. Engl. Lang. Lit.; Arts Humanit. Citation Index [Full Cov.]; Curr. Contents Arts Humanit.; Expand. Acad. Index (1989-); Humanit. Index; Humanit. Source (Jul. 1993-); INFO-SOUTH Abstr.; Mag. Search; MLA Int. Bibl. Books Artic. Mod. Lang. Lit.; Music Index; Newsp. Period. Abstr. (1990-); Res. Alert [Full Cov.]; Soc. Sci. Cit. Index [Select. Cov.]; West. Hist. Q.

UK
WILTSHIRE FOLKLIFE. Periodical. English. Three times a year. £5.00. Wiltshire Folklife Society, General Fanshawe, Farley Farm, Farley Salisburg, Wiltshire England. **LC** GR142.W54; W57. **DD** 390/.009423/1.

IS/0334-4053
YEDDA IAM. (YEDA-AM : BAMAH LE-FOLKLOR YEHUDI.). [Yed. iam]. **Added/Corp** Israel Folklore Society. Vol. 1 No. 1 (Jan./Feb. 1948)-. Hebrew (summaries and/or abstracts in English). be. **LC** GR98.A1; Y2.
Ind/Abst MLA Int. Bibl. Books Artic. Mod. Lang. Lit.

GW/0044-3700
ZEITSCHRIFT FUER VOLKSKUNDE. (ZEITSCHRIFT FUER VOLKSKUNDE / IM AUFTRAGE DES VERBANDES DEUTSCHER VEREINE FUER VOLKSKUNDE.). [Z. Volkskd.]. **Added/Corp** Verband Deutscher Vereine fuer Volkskunde. Verband der Vereine fuer Volkskunde. Deutsche Gesellschaft fuer Volkskunde. Vol. 1 (1929)-. Periodical. German (summaries and/or abstracts in English). Twice a year (May & Oct). DM86.00. Verlag Otto Schwartz & Company, Annastrasse 7, D 37075 Goettingen Germany. **Tel** 011 49 551 31051, 011 49 551 31052, FAX 011 49 551 372812. **LC** GR1; .Z4. **[CCC]**. available on microfilm from Indiana University Libraries Preservation Department. Documents available from The Genuine Article. ***Formed by the union of** Zeitschrift des Vereins fuer Volksunde.*
Ind/Abst Arts Humanit. Citation Index [Full Cov.]; Curr. Contents Arts Humanit.; MLA Int. Bibl. Books Artic. Mod. Lang. Lit.; Music Index; Res. Alert [Full Cov.]; RILM Abstr.; Soc. Sci. Cit. Index [Select. Cov.].

XR
ZPRAVODAJ KOORDINOVANE SITE VEDECKYCH INFORMACI PRO ETNOGRAFII A FOLKLORISTIKU. See Ethnic Interests.

ABSTRACTING, BIBLIOGRAPHIES AND STATISTICS

US/0272-8494
FOLKLORE BIBLIOGRAPHY. [Folk. bibliogr.]. 1973-. Bibliography. English. an. Institute for the Study of Human Issues, 3401 Science Center, Philadelphia PA 19104. **LC** Z5981; .S532; GR66. **DD** 016.398.

GW
INTERNATIONAL FOLKLORE BIBLIOGRAPHY. Bibliography. English. Dr. Rudolf Habelt GmbH, Postfach 150104, D 53040 Bonn Germany. **Tel** 011 49 228 232015.

GW
INTERNATIONALE VOLKSKUNDLICHE BIBLIOGRAPHIE. **Added/Corp** International Commission on Folk Arts and Folklore. International Society for Ethnology and Folklore. **VFOAT** International Folklore Bibliography. (1949)-. English (French and German). ir. DM195.00. Dr. Rudolf Habelt GmbH, Postfach 150104, D 53040 Bonn Germany. **Tel** 011 49 228 232015. **LC** Z5982; .I523. **DD** 016.398. ***Continues** Bibliographie Internationale des Arts et Traditions Populaires.*

US/0736-4911
LC FOLK ARCHIVE REFERENCE AID. [LC Folk Arch. ref. aid]. **VFOAT** L.C. Folk Archive Reference Aid. **VAT** Library of Congress Folk Archive Reference Aid. LCFARA No. 1 (June 1983)-. Monographic series. English. ir. Price varies per volume. Archive of Folk Culture, Library of Congress, Washington DC 20540. **Tel** (202)707-5510. **ED** Joseph C Hickerson. **LC** Z5982; .L36; GR105. **DD** 973. **Circ:** 2,000 (ctrl).
Desc: Periodic publications of bibliographies and related lists covering a variety of subjects in the fields of folklife, folk music and ethnomusicology.

AU
OSTERREICHISCHE VOLKSKUNDLICHE BIBLIOGRAPHIE. Began with 1965/67 vol. Periodical. German. ir. Verband der Wissenschaftlichen Gesellschaften Osterreichs, Lindengasse 37, A-1070 Vienna Austria. **Tel** 011 43 1 932166, 011 43 1 934756, telex 847/134981. **ED** Klaus Beitl. **LC** Z5984.A9; O85; GR155. **DD** 016.9436. **Circ:** 500.
Desc: Lists publications by: Austrian authors, about Austria, and by foreign authors as far as Austrian folklore is concerned.

FOOD AND FOOD INDUSTRY

NE
AANVULLINGEN OP WARENWET. Koninklijke Vernmande, Antwoordnummer 234, 8200 VB Lelystad Netherlands.

FR/0994-2653
ABRICOT PARIS. (ABRICOT.). Periodical. French. Eleven times a year. 292.00F France, French speaking Africa, Dom Tom; 316.00F other. Fleurus Presse International, 21 rue Faubourg St Antoine, 75550 Paris Cedex 11 France. **Tel** 011 33 1 40026300. **(Subscription address:** Fleurus Presse Service Abonn, BP 72, 77932 Perthes Cedex France**)** **UDC** 087.5.

UK/0430-7941
ABSTRACTS - FLOUR MILLING AND BAKING RESEARCH ASSOCIATION. [Abstr. - Flour Mill. Bak. Res. Assoc.]. **Main/Corp** Flour Milling and Baking Research Association. (19??)-. English. bm. £170.00. Flour Milling and Baking Research Association, Chorleywood Herts, WD3 5SH England. **Tel** 011 44 9278 4111, FAX 011 44 9278 4539, telex 8952883. Index available. **Circ:** 1,400.
Ind/Abst Int. Packag. Abstr.

US/0565-1921
ACREAGE-MARKETING GUIDES, WINTER VEGETABLES AND POTATOES. **Main/Corp** United States. Consumer and Marketing Service. Government Publication. English. an. US Department of Agriculture, 14th Street and Independence Avenue SW, Washington DC 20250. **Tel** (202)720-5457. **LC** HD9220.U5; U55A. **DD** 380.1/41/50973. ***Continues** Acreage-Marketing Guides, Winter Vegetables, Winter Potatoes.*

HU/0139-3006
ACTA ALIMENTARIA (BUDAPEST). (ACTA ALIMENTARIA.). [Acta aliment.]. **Added/Corp** Magyar Tudormanyos Akademia. Elelmezestudomanyi Bizottsag. Vol. 5 (1976)-. Academic Scholarly Publication. English. qt. $144.00. Akademiai Kiado, Publishing House of the Hungarian Academy of Sciences, Prielle Kornelia u. 19-35, H-1117 Budapest Hungary. **Tel** 011 36 1 1811991, FAX 011 36 1 1811991, telex 22-6228 AKNYO H. **ED** Janos Hollo and Ivan Varsanyi (editorial address: Acta Alimentaria, Editorial Office, Central Food Research Institute, PO Box 102, H-1525 Budapest Hungary). **NLM** W1 AC743K. **CODEN** ACALDI. **[CCC]. Bk Rev. Ad Acc. Pr Rev. Circ:** 300. Documents available from The Genuine Article, BIOSIS Document Express, CASDDS, Documents on Demand. ***Continues** Acta Alimentaria Academiae Scientiarum Hungaricae, 0302-7368.*
Desc: Publishes original papers on food science and technology. The main subjects covered are: physics, physical chemistry, chemistry, analysis, biology, microbiology, enzymology, engineering, instrumentation, automation and economics of foods and food production.
Ind/Abst Anal. Abstr.; Biodeter. Abstr.; Biol. Abstr. (1985-); Chem. Abstr.; Curr. Biotechnol.; Curr. Contents, Agric. Biol. Environ. Sci.; Dairy Sci. Abstr.; Energy Inf. Abstr.; Environ. Abstr.; Food Sci. Technol. Abstr.;

Helminthol. Abstr.; Hortic. Abstr.; Index Vet.; Nutr. Abstr. Rev., Ser. B, Live Feeds and Feed.; Nutr. Abstr. Rev., Ser. A, Hum. Exp.; Life Sci. Collect.; PESTDOC; Pig News Inf.; Postharvest News Inf.; Protozoolog. Abstr.; Res. Alert [Select. Cov.]; SCISEARCH; Sug. Indus. Abstr.; Vitis Vitic. Enol. Abstr.

US/0198-0181
ACTIVITIES REPORT OF THE R & D ASSOCIATES. [Act. rep. R & D Assoc.]. **Main/Corp** Research and Development Associates for Military Food and Packaging Systems. **VFOAT** Activities Report of the R and D Associates. **VAT** Activities Report of the Research and Development Associates; Activities Report of the R&D Associates. Vol. 30, No. 2 (1978)-. Academic Scholarly Publication. English. Twice a year (May & Oct.). $60.00 US; $100.00 other. Research & Development Association, 16607 Blanco Road, Suite 305, San Antonio TX 78232-1940. **Tel** (512)493-8024, FAX (512)493-8036. **ED** Anna May Schenck. **DD** 355. **NLM** W1 AC98D. **CODEN** ARYTDT. **Circ:** 700. Documents available from Article Express International, CASDDS. ***Continues*** *Research and Development Associates for Military and Food Packaging Systems. Activities Report, 0742-1974.*
Desc: Technical proceedings of meetings held by R&D Associates twice a year.
Ind/Abst AGRICOLA [Full Cov.]; Bioeng. Abstr.; Chem. Abstr.; Ei Page One; Eng. Index Annu.; Foods Adlibra.

SP
ACTUALIDAD PANADERA DE CATALUNA. Trade Publication. Castilian (Catalan). free. Gremio de Panaderos de Barcelona, Pau Claris 134, 08009 Barcelona Spain. **Tel** 215 55 00, FAX 216 05 39. **Circ:** 3,500.
Desc: Trade journal with technical information about bakeries and union matters.

US/0362-1634
ADVANCES IN CEREAL SCIENCE AND TECHNOLOGY. ***Ceased.*** [Adv. cereal sci. technol.]. **Added/Corp** American Association of Cereal Chemists. Vol. 1 (1976)-Completed Series (19??). English. ir. American Association of Cereal Chemists, 3340 Pilot Knob Road, St. Paul MN 55121. **Tel** (612)454-7250, FAX (612)454-0766, telex 6502439657. **ED** Y. Pomeranz. **LC** TP434; .A37. **DD** 664/.7/05. **NLM** W1; AD531V. **CODEN** ACSTDU. Documents available from Article Express International, CASDDS.
Desc: Intended to supply intermediary information between the AACC journals and the AACC monograph series. Collections of cereal research information.
Ind/Abst AGRICOLA [Full Cov.]; BioBusiness; Chem. Abstr.; Eng. Index Annu.; Food Sci. Technol. Abstr.; Maize Abstr.; Rev. Med. Vet. Mycology; Rev. Plant Pathol.

UK
AFRICAN FARMING AND FOOD PROCESSING. See Agriculture.

UK/0950-4958
AGRAFILE. LIVESTOCK & MEAT. See Agriculture.

NE
AGRARISCHE BUITENLANDSE HANDEL VAN POLEN, DE. **Main/Corp** Netherlands (Kingdom, 1815-). Ministerie Van Landbouw en Visserij. Directie Algemene Zaken. Afdeling Statistiek en Documentatie. Dutch. Ministerie van Landbouw en Visserij, Directie Algemene Zaken Afdeling Statistiek en Documentatie, Koningin Julianaplein 3, S-Gravenhage Netherlands. **LC** HD9015.P7; N47A. **DD** 382/.41/509438.

CN/1182-9133
AGRI-FOOD BUSINESS IN P.E.I. See Agriculture.

US/0364-7994
AGRICULTURE & FOOD. ***Title Change.*** See Agriculture.

UK
AGRICULTURE, FISHERIES, FOOD. See Agriculture.

KZ/0235-2958
AGROPROMYSHLENNYI KOMPLEKS KAZAKHSTANA. **Added/Corp** Qazaqstan KP Ortalyq Komiteti. (1987)-. Periodical. Russian. mo. Izdatelstvo TSK Kompartii Kazakhstana, Ulitsa M. Gorkogo 50, Alma-Ata 480044 Kazakhstan. **LC** S13; .S432. ***Continues*** *Selskoe Khoziaistvo Kazakhstana (Alma-Ata, Kazakh S.S.R. : 1953).*

US/0892-4236
AIRLINE, SHIP & CATERING ONBOARD SERVICES MAGAZINE. **Added/Corp** Inflight Food Service Association. MHC&DF Association. Independent Fundamental Churches of America. **VFOAT** Airline, Ship and Catering Onboard Services Magazine; Onboard Services Magazine; Onboard Services. Vol. 19, No. 2 (Feb. 1987)-. Periodical. English. mo. $25.00 US; $65.00 other. International Publishing Company of America, 665 La Villa Drive, Miami Springs FL 33166. **Tel** (305)887-1701, FAX (305)885-1923, telex 6811546. **DD** 338. ***Continues*** *Airline & Travel Food Service, 0161-1755.*

JA/0385-3152
AKITA-KEN KAJU SHIKENJUO KENKYUU HUOKOKU. See Gardening and Horticulture.

SZ/0002-5402
ALIMENTA. [Alimenta]. **Added/Corp** Institute for Scientific Information. (1962)-. Academic Scholarly Publication. German (English and French). Six times a year. 95.00F. Cicero-Verlag AG, Stauffacherstr 5, Postfach 8021, CH 8021 Zurich Switzerland. **Tel** 011 41 1 72429700, FAX 011 41 1 2419458. **ED** Cicero-Verlag. **CODEN** ALMTBR. **Bk Rev. Ad Acc. Pr Rev. Circ:** 5,800. Documents available from The Genuine Article, CASDDS.
Desc: Publication concerning fabrication, packaging and transport of food, hygiene, chemistry and technology.
Ind/Abst Chem. Abstr.; Curr. Biotechnol.; Curr. Contents, Agric. Biol. Environ. Sci.; Dairy Sci. Abstr.; Food Sci. Technol. Abstr.; Index Vet.; Int. Packag. Abstr.; Life Sci. Collect.; Res. Alert [Select. Cov.]; SCISEARCH; Vet. Bull.

BL/0100-9397
ALIMENTACAO (SAO PAULO). (ALIMENTACAO / ASSOCIACAO BRASILEIRA DAS INDUSTRIAS DA ALIMENTACAO.). [Alimentacao]. Academic Scholarly Publication. Portuguese. bm. Abia, Av Nove de Julho 3452, CEP 01406, Sao Paulo SP Brazil. **LC** TX341; .A83A. **DD** 664/.005. **CODEN** ALIMDM. Documents available from BIOSIS Document Express, CASDDS. ***Continues*** *Revista (Associacao Brasileira das Industrias da Alimentacao. Setor de Alimentos Calorico-Proteicos), 0100-0993.*
Ind/Abst Biol. Abstr.; Chem. Abstr.; Nutr. Abstr. Rev., Ser. B, Live Feeds and Feed.; Nutr. Abstr. Rev., Ser. A, Hum. Exp.

SP/0214-803X
ALIMENTALEX (MADRID). (ALIMENTALEX : INTERNATIONAL FOOD LAW REVIEW.). [Alimentalex]. **Added/Corp** European Food Law Association. Asociacion Iberoamericana Para el Derecho Alimentario. **VFOAT** International Food Law Review. No. 1 (June 1989)-. Periodical. English (French and Spanish). Twice a year. 10300ptas Spain; 14300ptas Europe; 15300ptas others. Eypasa, Sandoval 12 1 5, 28010 Madrid Spain. **Tel** 011 34 1 4469659, FAX 011 34 1 5933744. **ED** C. Barros. **CODEN** ALMTEU. **Bk Rev. Ad Acc. Circ:** 1,000 (ctrl).
Ind/Abst BioBusiness; Foods Adlibra; PAIS Int. Print (1991-).

IT/0394-8404
ALIMENTARISTA, L'. [Alimentarista]. (1966)-. Periodical. Italian. bm (6 issues). L40000.00 Italy; L80000.00 other. Agepe Agenzia Gestione Per SRL, Via Trentacoste 9, 20134 Milan Italy. **Tel** 011 39 2 2640009. **UDC** 658.87.

CN/0834-2431
ALIMENTATION (MONTREAL). (L'ALIMENTATION.). [Alimentation]. Vol. 25 (Sept. 1986)-. Periodical. French. ir. 30.00Can$ Canada; 52.00Can$ other. Editions du Marchand, 1298 Saint Zotique, Montreal Quebec H2S 1N7 Canada. **Tel** (514)271-6922, FAX (514)271-1308. **DD** 381/.456413/009714. ***Continues*** *L'Alimentation au Quebec, 0002-5410.*

CN/0823-9355
ALIMENTOLOGUE. (L'ALIMENTOLOGUE : BULLETIN DE L'ASSOCIATION DES DETAILLANTS EN ALIMENTATION DU QUEBEC.). [Alimentologue]. **Added/Corp** Association des Detaillants en Alimentation du Quebec. Vol. 1, No. 1 (Sept. 1981)-. Bulletin. French. bm. Free. Association des d'Etaillants en Alimentation du Quebec, Bureau 813/1100 Est rue Cremazie, Montreal Quebec H2P 2X2 Canada. **DD** 381/.45664/0060714. ctrl circ.
Desc: Information on the food industry and grocery trade.

BL/0103-4235
ALIMENTOS E NUTRICAO / UNIVERSIDADE ESTADUAL PAULISTA. See Nutrition and Dietetics.

US/0744-625X
ALIMENTOS PROCESADOS. Vol. 1, No. 1 (Mar. 1982)-. Periodical. Spanish. mo. $59.00 US; $139.00 (surface mail), $199.00 (airmail) other. Cahners Publishing Company, 249 West 17th Street, New York NY 10011. **Tel** (212)645-0067, FAX (212)242-6987. **(Subscription address:** Cahners Publishing Company / Colorado, Paid Subscription Service Center, PO Box 7610, Highlands Ranch CO 80126-7610.**)** **ED** Mario Schacher. **Ad Acc. Circ:** 21,000 (ctrl). available on microfilm from University Microfilms International (UMI).
Desc: Brings the world of food processing to over 20,000 food and beverage processors in Mexico, Central and South America. Features information on new technologies, products and ideas, and includes processor profiles, trade show coverage and critical issue analysis. Includes Buyer's Guide and Top 75 Latin American Processors issues.

IT/0304-8918
ALINORM. (ALINORM / CODEX ALIMENTARIUS COMMISSION OF THE FOOD AND AGRICULTURE ORGANIZATION OF THE UNITED NATIONS AND THE WORLD HEALTH ORGANIZATION.). [Alinorm]. English. ir. UNIPUB, 4611-F Assembly Drive, Lanham MD 20706-4391. **Tel** (800)274-4888, FAX (301)459-0056, telex 28787 GATT CH. **LC** TX537; .A42. **DD** 363.1/926/05. **NLM** W1 AL395.
Desc: Consists of reports of the various Codex committees.

II
ALL INDIA PREVENTION OF FOOD ADULTERATION CASES. See Law.

GW
ALLGEMEINE FLEISCHER ZEITUNG. **Added/Corp** Deutscher Fleischer-Verband. (1???)-. Periodical. German. Fifty-two times a year. DM528.85 Germany; DM401.31 others. Deutscher Fachverlag GmbH, Verlagsgruppe, D 60264 Frankfurt Germany. **Tel** 011 49 69 75951001, telex 411 862.

US/0891-3331
AMERICAN DELI-BAKERY NEWS. [Am. deli-bak. news]. **VFOAT** American Deli Bakery News. Vol. 1, No. 1 (Jan. 15, 1987)-. Periodical. English. ir (18 issues). $145.00. American Deli Bakery News, PO Box 194130, San Francisco CA 94119. **Tel** (415)777-0604. **ED** Richard Kanes. **DD** 338. **CODEN** ADNEE2. ctrl circ.
Ind/Abst BioBusiness.

US/1065-3775
AMERICAN FOOD AND AG EXPORTER. [Am. food ag export.]. **VFOAT** Exporter. Vol. 2, Issue 6 (Oct. 1990)-. Periodical. English. ir (4 issues). Free on request; Includes American Food & Ag Exporter Directory. AG Coallier Publishing, 1060 Fulton Mall, Suite 1202, Fresno CA 93721. **Tel** (714)237-1167. **ED** Richard Van Brackle. **LC** HF1416.5; .A447. **DD** 382. **Ad Acc. Circ:** 12,500 (ctrl). ***Continues*** *American Agricultural Exporter.*
Desc: Promotion of American food products in 70 countries around the world.

US
AMERICA'S FUTURE FOOD TRENDS. English. bm (Plus two two special reports). $195.00. Technomic Inc, 300 South Riverside Plaze, 1940S, Chicago IL 60606. **Tel** (312)876-0004, FAX (312) 876-1158. **ED** John Hofer. **Bk Rev.** ***Continues*** *Ron Paul's Future Food Trends.*

US
AMS FOOD PURCHASES. WEEKLY SUMMARY / UNITED STATES DEPARTMENT OF AGRICULTURE, AGRICULTURAL MARKETING SERVICE. **Added/Corp** United States. Agricultural Marketing Service. **VFOAT** A.A.M.S. Food Purchases. Weekly Summary. **VAT** Agricultural Marketing Service Food Purchases. Weekly Summary. Vol. 11, No. 3 (Oct. 1981)-. Periodical. English. Fifty-two times a year. $96.00. United States Department of Agriculture / California, 1320 East Olympic Boulevard, Suite 212, Los Angeles CA 90021. **Tel** (213)894-3077. **Circ:** 60. available on microfiche (Vols. for 1986 distributed to depository libraries). Documents available from Documents on Demand. ***Continues*** *FSQS Food Purchases. Weekly Report.*
Ind/Abst Am. Stat. Index.

US/1052-1666
ANDRE GAYOT'S TASTES, WITH THE BEST OF GAULT MILLAU. [Andre Gayot's Tastes Best Gault Millau]. **Added/Corp** Gault Millau (Firm). **VFOAT** Tastes. (Apr./May 1990)-. Periodical. English. bm (Feb., Apr., June, Aug., Oct., Dec.). $40.00. Gault Millau, PO Box 361144, Los Angeles CA 90036. **Tel** (213)965-3481, FAX (213)936-2883. **DD** 642.

IT/0304-0569
ANNALI DELL'ISTITUTO SPERIMENTALE PER LA FRUTTICOLTURA. See Agriculture.

IT/0304-0577
ANNALI DELL'ISTITUTO SPERIMENTALE PER LA VALLORIZZAZIONE TECNOLOGICA DEI PRODOTTI AGRICOLI. **Main/Corp** Istituto Sperimentale per la Valorizzazione Tecnologica dei Prodotti Agricoli. Vol. 1 (1970)-. Multiple languages (English and Italian). Istituto Sperimentale per la Valorizzazione Technologica dei Prodotti Agricoli, Via XXVIII, Aprile 26 31015 Conegliano, Treviso Italy. **CODEN** AISMDH. Documents available from BIOSIS Document Express, CASDDS.
Ind/Abst Biol. Abstr. (1986-); Chem. Abstr.; Crop Physiol. Abstr.; Dairy Sci. Abstr.; Postharvest News Inf.

FR
ANNUAIRE NATIONAL DE LA CONSERVE. **VFOAT** A.N.C.; ANC. French. an. Les Editions Comindus, 1 rue Descombes, Paris 75017 France. **Tel** (1)43807916. **LC** HD9323.3; .A56. **DD** 338.4/7664028/0944.
Desc: All about the industry of conserve in France.

US/0276-4458
ANNUAL DIRECTORY / TEXAS RETAIL GROCERS ASSOCIATION. **Main/Corp** Texas Retail Grocers Association. **Added/Corp** Texas Retail Grocers Association. TRGA ... Annual Directory. **VFOAT** TRGA ... Annual Directory. 1st (1981)-. Directory. English. an. Associated Business Publishing Inc, 41 East 42nd Street/Suite 921, New York NY 10017. **Tel** (212)490-3999. **LC** HD9321.3; .T47a. **DD** 381/.45664/0025764.
Desc: Information on the grocery, produce and food trade industry.

SZ/0251-3986
ANNUAL ECE/FAO PRICE REVIEW. [Annu. ECE/FAO price rev.]. **VFOAT** Annual Economic Commission for Europe / Food and Agriculture Organization of the United Nations Price Review. (1961)-. Periodical. English. an. **UDC** 338.5.
Ind/Abst Potato Abstr.; Soyabean Abstr.

US/0192-379X
ANNUAL FINANCIAL REVIEW - FOOD MARKETING INSTITUTE. **Main/Corp** Food Marketing Institute. English. an. $15.00. Food Marketing Institute Research Division / Chicago, 303 East Ohio Street, Chicago IL 60611. **Tel** (202)452-8444. **LC** HF5469; .F67A. **DD** 338.4/3.
Desc: A financial picture of the supermarket companies, including data on profits, return on investment, capital structure, debt and equity. Also included is an annual balance sheet and income statement.

US
ANNUAL FINANCIAL REVIEW - SUPER MARKET INSTITUTE. **Main/Corp** Super Market Institute. (1975)-. English. an. Super Market Institute, 303 East Ohio Street, Chicago IL 60611. **LC** HF5469; .S88a. **DD** 381.

JM
ANNUAL REPORT AND ACCOUNTS FOR THE YEAR ENDED DECEMBER 31ST, ... / THE COCONUT INDUSTRY BOARD, JAMAICA, WEST INDIES. **Main/Corp** Jamaica. Coconut Industry Board. Began in 1961. English. an. **LC** HD9259.C6; J3. **DD** 354.72920082/333. ***Continues*** *Jamaica. Coconut Industry Board. Annual Report and Statements of Accounts.*

US
ANNUAL REPORT / BUREAU OF FRUIT, VEGETABLE, AND PEANUT MARKETING SERVICES. **Main/Corp** Virginia. Bureau of Fruit, Vegetable, and Peanut Marketing Services. (June 30, 1981)-. English. an. Bureau of Fruit Vegetable and Peanut Marketing Services, Main Office, Washington Building/Room 701, 1100 Bank Street, Richmond VA 23219. **LC** HD9240.9.U7; V88A. **DD** 353.97550082/615/06. ***Formed by the union of*** *Virginia. Fruit and Vegetable Section. Annual Report; Virginia. Processed Foods Section. Annual Report* ***and*** *Virginia. Apple and Peach Section. Annual Report.*

US
ANNUAL REPORT CMA/ACRI. **Main/Corp** Chocolate Manufacturers Association of the United States of America. **Added/Corp** America Cocoa Research Institute. (197?)-. Periodical. English. ***Continues*** *American Cocoa Research Institute. Annual Report of the Director of Research to the Board of Directors.*
Desc: Information on the chocolate and cocoa research and industry.

AT
ANNUAL REPORT / DRIED FRUITS RESEARCH COUNCIL. **Main/Corp** Dried Fruits Research Council (Australia). (19??)-. English. an. Dried Fruits Research Council, Canberra ACT Australia. **LC** HD9258.A8; D74a. **DD** 388.4/766484/06094.

US/0361-8706
ANNUAL REPORT - FIRST NATIONAL STORES INC. [Annu. rep. - First Natl. Stores Inc.]. **Main/Corp** First National Stores, Inc. (19??)-. English. an. Free. Treasurer's Office Finast, 5 Middlesex Avenue, Somerville MA 02143. **LC** HD9321.9.F5; A3. **DD** 381/.45/641300973. ***Continues*** *First National Stores, Inc. President's Report to the Stockholders.*
Desc: Information on grocery trade.

TZ
ANNUAL REPORT - KILOMBERO SUGAR COMPANY. **Main/Corp** Kilombero Sugar Company. (19??)-. English. Kilombero Sugar Company, PO Box 4355, Dar es Salaam Tanzania. **LC** HD9117.T34; K544. **DD** 338.7/66/412209678.

CN/0837-6875
ANNUAL REPORT OF THE SASKATCHEWAN PORK PRODUCERS MARKETING BOARD. (ANNUAL REPORT OF THE SASKATCHEWAN PORK PRODUCERS MARKETING BOARD FOR THE YEAR.). [Annu. rep. Sask. Pork Prod. Mark. Board]. **Main/Corp** Saskatchewan Pork Producers Marketing Board. (1984)-. English. an. Saskatchewan Pork Producers Marketing Board, 502-45th Street West, Saskatoon Saskatchewan S7L 6H2 Canada. **Tel** (306)653-3014, FAX (306)244-2918, telex 074-2764. **ED** Jack McClung. **DD** 354.71240082/65/0005. ***Continues*** *Annual Report - Saskatchewan Hog Marketing Commission, 0228-6114.*

AT
ANNUAL REPORT / WESTERN AUSTRALIAN EGG MARKETING BOARD. **Main/Corp** Western Australian Egg Marketing Board. (19??)-. English. an. Western Australian Egg Marketing Board, 43-45 McGregor Road, Palmyra Western Australia 6156 Australia.

US
ANNUAL REVIEW OF RETAIL GROCERY STORE TRENDS. **Added/Corp** A.C. Nielsen Company. Nielsen Marketing Research (Firm). **VFOAT** Nielsen Review. (1990)-. English. A. C. Nielsen Company, Media Research Division, Neilsen Plaza, Northbrook IL 60062. **Tel** (312)498-6300. ***Continues*** *Nielsen Annual Review of Retail Grocery Store Trends.*
Desc: Information on the grocery trade.

IT
ANNUARIO DELL'ALIMENTAZIONE E DELLE ATTIVITA RICETTIVE. Yearly V. 1-1977/78-. Italian. Seat, Via Aurelio Saffi 18, Turin 10138 Italy. **Tel** 011-33301-212248 I, FAX 4472953, telex 212248 I. **LC** HD9015.I6; A65.

CN/0711-0944
APERITIF. (L'APERITIF / ASSOCIATION CANADIENNE DES CADRES DES SERVICES ALIMENTAIRES). **Added/Corp** Canadian Food Service Executives Association. (Sept. 1981)-. Periodical. English (French). mo. L'Aperitif, Compagnie des Editions du Saint-Laurent, Suite 400/625 President Kennedy, Montreal Quebec H3A 1K9 Canada. **DD** 647/.95/06071.

AT/1031-0533
APPARENT CONSUMPTION OF FOODSTUFFS AND NUTRIENTS, AUSTRALIA. **See** Food and Food Industry-Abstracting, Bibliographies and Statistics.

CN/0226-823X
APPARENT PER CAPITA FOOD CONSUMPTION IN CANADA. PART 1. (APPARENT PER CAPITA FOOD CONSUMPTION IN CANADA, PART I / STATISTICS CANADA, AGRICULTURE STATISTICS DIVISION, CROPS SECTION.). [Apparent per capita food consum. Can., 1]. **Added/Corp** Statistics Canada. Crops Section. Statistics Canada. Horticultural Crops Unit. **VFOAT** Consommation Apparente des Aliments par Personne au Canada, Partie I. (1979)-. English (French). an. 30.00Can$ Canada; $36.00 US; $42.00 other. Statistics Canada, Publications Sales & Services, Main Building Room 1710, Ottawa Ontario K1A 0T6 Canada. **Tel** (613)951-5078, (800)267-6677, FAX (613)951-1584, telex 053-3585. **LC** HD9014.C2; A66. **DD** 339.4/8664/00971. ***Formed by the union of*** *Apparent Per Capita Food Consumption in Canada., 0708-2657* ***and*** *Estimates of Production and Disappearance of Meats., 0575-8440.*

CN/0226-8248
APPARENT PER CAPITA FOOD CONSUMPTION IN CANADA. PART 2. (APPARENT PER CAPITA FOOD CONSUMPTION IN CANADA, PART II / STATISTICS CANADA, AGRICULTURE STATISTICS DIVISION, CROPS SECTION.). [Apparent per capita food consum. Can., 2]. **Added/Corp** Statistics Canada. Crops Section. Statistics Canada. Horticultural Crops Unit. **VFOAT** Consommation Apparente des Aliments Par Personne au Canada, Partie II. (1979)-. English (French). an. 30.00Can$ Canada; $36.00 US; $42.00 other. Statistics Canada, Publications Sales & Services, Main Building Room 1710, Ottawa Ontario K1A 0T6 Canada. **Tel** (613)951-5078, (800)267-6677, FAX (613)951-1584, telex 053-3585. **LC** HD9014.C2; C27c. **DD** 339.4/8664/00971. ***Continues in part*** *Apparent Per Capita Food Consumption in Canada., 0708-2657.*
Desc: Contains supply, disposition and per capita disappearance data for the following food groups: oils and fats, fruits, vegetables, potatoes and fish.

AT/1033-9280
AQIS BULLETIN. [AQIS bull.]. **Added/Corp** Australian Quarantine and Inspection Service. **VFOAT** Bulletin. **VAT** Australian Quarantine and Inspection Service Bulletin. Vol. 1, No. 1 (Sept. 1989)-. Periodical. English. mo (11 issues). Free on request. AQUIS, GPO Box 858, Canberra 2601 Australia. **Tel** 011 61 06 272-4730.
Ind/Abst Potato Abstr.

SP/1130-8109
ARAL MADRID. (ARAL.). [Aral Madr.]. (1967)-. Periodical. Spanish. wk. 28100ptas Spain; 45400ptas other. Tecnipublicaciones SA, C Fernando VI No 27, 28004 Madrid Spain. **Tel** 011 34 1 3197889, FAX 341 4101069, telex 43905 YEBE E. **UDC** 641.
Ind/Abst Infomat Int. Bus.; PROMT.

GW/0233-0652
ARBEITEN ZUR MECHANISIERUNG DER PFLANZEN- UND TIERPRODUKTION. [Arb. Mech. Pflanzen-Tierprod.]. (1984)-. Monographic series. German. ir. **UDC** 63.
Ind/Abst Agric. Eng. Abstr.; Field Crop Abstr.; Hortic. Abstr.; Nutr. Abstr. Rev., Ser. B, Live Feeds and Feed.; Postharvest News Inf.; Potato Abstr.

GW/0003-925X
ARCHIV FUER LEBENSMITTELHYGIENE. (ARCHIV FUER LEBENSMITTELHYGIENE, FLEISCH-, FISCH- UND MILCHHYGIENE.). [Arch. lebensmittelhyg.]. **VFOAT** Archives of Meat, Fish and Dairy Science. (19??)-. Academic Scholarly Publication. German (summaries and/or abstracts in English). qt. DM162.20 Germany; DM167.00 other. Verlag M & H Schaper GmbH & Co, Postfach 16 42, D 31046 Alfeld Leine Germany. **Tel** 011 49 5181 80090. **NLM** W1 AR238. **CODEN** ALMHAO. **[CCC]**. Documents available from CASDDS. ***Continues*** *Lebensmitteltierarzt.*
Ind/Abst Biodeter. Abstr. (19??-19??); Chem. Abstr.; Coal Abstr.; EMBASE; Energy Res. Abstr.; Food Sci. Technol. Abstr.; Helminthol. Abstr. (19??-19??); Index Vet.; Nutr. Abstr. Rev., Ser. B, Live Feeds and Feed.; Life Sci. Collect.; Pig News Inf.; Rev. Med. Vet. Mycology.

GW
ARGENTINIEN, LANDWIRTSCHAFTLICHE ANBAUPRODUKTE / BUNDESSTELLE FUR AUSSENHANDELSINFORMATION. German. DM5.00. Bundesstelle fuer Aussenhandelsinformation, Agrippastr 87 93, D 50676 Cologne Germany. **Tel** 011 49 221 2057316, FAX 011 49 221 2057212. **LC** HD9014.A7; A73. **DD** 338.1/75/0982.

US/0004-1505
ARIZONA GROCER. **Added/Corp** Retail Grocers Association of Arizona. (1943)-. Periodical. English. mo. $50.00. Arizona Grocers Publishing Company, 120 East Pierce, Phoenix AZ 85004. **Tel** (602)252-9761. **ED** Shelley S Davidson. **Ad Acc. Circ:** 2,600 (ctrl).
Desc: Articles and features concerning the retail food industry in Arizona with information on national products, issues and concerns of the Arizona food industry.

US/0004-1815
ARKANSAS GROCER. (19??)-. Periodical. English. bm (6 issues). $3.00. Arkansas Grocer Publishing Company, Box 7806, Pine Bluff AR 71601. **Tel** (501)534-8803. **ED** George T. Anderson. **Ad Acc. Circ:** 3,100.

SW
ARSBERATTELSE - SIK-SVENSKA LIVSMEDELSINSTITUTET. **Main/Corp** Sik-Svenska Livsmedelsinstitutet. **VFOAT** Annual Report - Sik-Swedish Food Institute. English (Swedish). SIK/FACK, 400 23 Goteborg Sweden. **LC** TX341; .G63 subser.

US/0895-6200
ART OF EATING, THE. [Art eat.]. (Fall 1986)-. Periodical. English. Four times a year (Jan., Apr., July, Oct.). $25.00. Art of Eating, Box 242, Peacham VT 05862. **ED** Edward Behr. **DD** 641. **Bk Rev**, (Qty: 12). **Circ:** 2,200.
Desc: In-depth essays on gastronomic subjects.

IT
ARTE BIANCA : LA PANIFICAZIONE ITALIANA, L'. **Added/Corp** Federazione Italiana Panificatori, Panificatori-Pasticceri e Affini. **VFOAT** Panificazione Italiana. (1946)-. Periodical. Italian. Forty-Five times a year. L40000 Italy; L80000 others. Federazione It Panificatori, Via Alessandria 159 D, 00198 Rome Italy. **Tel** 011 39 6 8549559.

MY/0127-7324
ASEAN FOOD JOURNAL. [ASEAN food j.]. **Added/Corp** ASEAN Food Handling Bureau. **VFOAT** A.S.E.A.N. Food Journal. **VAT** Association of South East Asian Nations Food Journal. Vol. 1, No. 1 (March 1985)-. Academic Scholarly Publication. English. Four times a year (Jan., Apr., July, Oct.). $10.00 (individuals in Brunei, Indonesia, Malaysia, Philippines, Singapore and Thailand; $25.00 institutions and individuals other, Surface mail; $50.00 US & Europe & Africa; $40.00 other Airmail. Asean Food Handling Bureau, Level 3, G14 and G15, Damansara Town Centre, 50490 Lumpur Malaysia.

Tel 2544199, FAX 2552787, telex MA 31555 AFHBKL. **ED** Peter Soosai. **LC** TX341; .A74. **CODEN** AFJOEQ. **Bk Rev**, (Qty: 12). **Ad Acc. Circ:** 1,500 (ctrl). Documents available from BIOSIS Document Express, CASDDS.
Ind/Abst AGRICOLA [Select. Cov.]; Agric. Eng. Abstr. (1991-); Biodeter. Abstr. (19??-19??); Biol. Abstr. (1988-); Chem. Abstr. (1985-); Crop Physiol. Abstr.; Dairy Sci. Abstr.; Field Crop Abstr.; Food Sci. Technol. Abstr.; Foods Adlibra; Hortic. Abstr.; Postharvest News Inf.; Rev. Med. Vet. Mycology; Rev. Plant Pathol.; Rice Abstr.; Seed Abstr.; Soyabean Abstr.

CU/0366-242X
ATAC, ASOCIACION DE TECNICOS AZUCAREROS DE CUBA. (ATAC.). **Main/Corp** Asociacion de Tecnicos Azucareros de Cuba. **VAT** Asociacion de Tecnicos Azucareros de Cuba. Spanish. bm. $15.00 US. Ediciones Cubanas, Obispo 527, Altos ESQ Bernaza, CP 10100 Havana Cuba. **Tel** 011 632980, 631942, FAX 011 631011, telex 512337, 6540. **LC** TP375; .A76. **Circ:** 10,000 (ctrl).
Desc: Purely technical articles by Cuban specialists with experience in this important sector of the economy. Information, interviews and feature articles about raising and industrially processing sugarcane, both nationally and internationally.
Ind/Abst Biodeter. Abstr.; Food Sci. Technol. Abstr.; Hortic. Abstr.; Nutr. Abstr. Rev., Ser. B, Live Feeds and Feed.; Plant Genet. Resour. Abstr.; Rev. Plant Pathol.; Sug. Indus. Abstr.

AT/0004-8283
AUSTRALIAN CITRUS NEWS. [Aust. citrus news]. Vol. 41 (1965)-. Periodical. English. Twelve times a year. 20.00Aus$ Australia $30.00 other. Australian Citrus Growers Federation, 118 King Will Street, Room 107 10th Floor, Adelaide South Australia 5000 Australia. **Tel** 11 61 8 2124245, FAX 11 61 8 2313413. **ED** Hugh Cope. Index Bound in First Issue. **Bk Rev**, (Qty: 1-2). **Ad Acc, Adv Mgr:** Martin, **Tel** 11 61 8 2319056. **Circ:** 3,000 (ctrl). ***Continues*** *Citrus News.*
Desc: Statistics, reports and information concerning the Australian citrus industry; research papers and information concerning the world citrus situation.
Ind/Abst AGRICOLA; Hortic. Abstr.; Postharvest News Inf.; Rev. Plant Pathol.

AT/0815-208X
AUSTRALIAN DRIED FRUITS NEWS. [Aust. dried fruits news]. **Added/Corp** Australian Dried Fruits Association. **VFOAT** Dried Fruits News. (19??)-. Periodical. English. bm. Australian Dried Fruits Association, 9 Queens Road, Melbourne VIC 3004 Australia. **Tel** (03)2678322, telex AA39479. ***Supersedes*** *Australian Dried Fruits Journal.*

AT/1034-9006
AUSTRALIAN GOURMET TRAVELLER 1989. (AUSTRALIAN GOURMET TRAVELLER.). [Aust. gourmet travel. 1989]. (1989)-. Periodical. English. mo. 57.00Aus$ Australia & New Zealand; 117.00Aus$ other. Australian Consolidated Press Ltd, GPO Box 5252, Sydney New South Wales 2001 Australia. **Tel** 011 61 2 2600000. **DD** 641.51405. ***Continues*** *Gourmet Traveller, 1032-8009.*

AT/0156-2681
AUSTRALIAN MEAT INDUSTRY BULLETIN. [Aust. meat ind. bull.]. (1978)-. Bulletin. English. Six times a year (Feb., Apr., June, Aug., Oct., Dec.). 30.00Aus$. Meat & Allied Trades Federation of Australia, PO Box 1208, Crows Nest New South Wales, 2065 Australia. **Tel** 011 61 2 9067767, FAX 011 61 2 9068022, telex AA22480. **ED** Joy Allen. **DD** 338.47664900994. **Ad Acc.** ctrl circ.

AT/1033-6656
AUSTRALIAN SUGAR CRAFT. [Aust. sugar craft]. **Added/Corp** Australian National Cake Decorators' Association. National Committee. (1989)-. Periodical. English. Four times a year (Mar., June, Sept., Dec.). 18.00Aus$ Australia; 24.00Aus$ other. Australis National Cake Decorators Association, PO Box 321, Plympton SA 2038 Australia. **Tel** 011 61 8 2933367. **ED** Elizabeth Brookes. **DD** 641.8653. **Bk Rev**, (Qty: 3-4). **Ad Acc, Adv Mgr:** Maxine Halliday, **Tel** (08)2933367. **Circ:** 2,000.
Desc: Cake decorating for special occasions. Subscribers are encouraged to provide articles, photographs, tips, recipes, news and bulletins.

AT/0067-2173
AUSTRALIAN SUGAR YEAR BOOK, THE. **Added/Corp** Australian Cane Grower's Association. Australian Sugar Producers Association. Vol. 1 (1940/41)-. English. an. 35.00Aus$ Australia; 55.00Aus$ other. Rural Press Pty Ltd / Queensland, PO Box 586, Cleveland Queensland 4163 Australia. **Tel** 011 61 7 2865688. **ED** Jenny Hallson. **LC** TP375.3; A8. **DD** 664.1. **Ad Acc. Circ:** 1,500.
Desc: A directory of Australian sugar organizations and mills and a review of the year's events.

●US/1061-1797
AUTOMATIC MERCHANDISER. [Autom. merch.]. Vol. 34, No. 1 (Jan. 1992)-. Trade Publication. English. mo. $35.00 US; $55.00 Canada and Mexico; $120.00 other. Johnson Hill Press Inc., 1233 Janesville Avenue, PO Box 803, Fort Atkinson WI 53538-0803. **Tel** (414)563-1749, FAX (414)563-1704. **ED** Elliott Maras. **LC** TJ1560; .A46. **DD** 338. **Ad Acc.** Full Page (B&W) $2370.00. Full Page (Color) $3510.00 (4-color). **Circ:** 13,642. available on an online database (files 16,570/Full-Text) from DIALOG. ***Continues*** *American Automatic Merchandiser, 0002-7545.*
Desc: Serves the merchandise vending, contract food service and coffee service industries. This magazine delivers business management and marketing information in addition to vending equipment information and industry news.
Ind/Abst Mark. Advert. Ref. Serv. [Full Txt.]; PROMT [Full Txt.].

GW/0005-383X
BACKER UND KONDITOR. [Backer Konditor]. Academic Scholarly Publication. German (Russian and English). mo. 21.00M. Fachbuchverlag, Leninstrasse 16, DDR-701 Leipzig German Democratic Republic. **Tel** 49500. **CODEN** BAKOD6. Index available. **Bk Rev. Ad Acc.** ctrl circ. Documents available from CASDDS.
Desc: Special journal for bakery, confectionery, biscuit manufacture and ice cream production. Deals with new technologic, technical and economic developments in industry and retail trade; informs of conferences and fairs.
Ind/Abst Chem. Abstr. (-1982); Food Sci. Technol. Abstr.; Life Sci. Collect.

US/0191-6114
BAKER'S DIGEST. [Baker's dig.]. **VFOAT** BD, Baker's Digest. Vol. 14, No. 7 (Jan. 1940)-. Periodical. English. bm. $11.00. Sosland Publishing Company / Missouri, 4800 Main Street, Suite 100, Kansas City MO 64112. **Tel** (816)756-1000, FAX (816)756-0494, telex 820182. **ED** Laurie Gorton. **LC** TX341; .B3. **DD** 664/.725/05. **UDC** 664.61. **CODEN** BADIAI. **Bk Rev. Ad Acc. Circ:** 6,700. Documents available from CASDDS. ***Continues*** *Baker's Technical Digest, 0096-4433.*
Desc: Summarization of the current state of the art in baked foods and ingredient technology.
Ind/Abst Chem. Abstr.; Dairy Sci. Abstr.; Life Sci. Collect.

CN/0005-4097
BAKERS JOURNAL. [Bak. j.]. (1938)-. Periodical. English. Ten times a year. 24.00Can$ Canada; 28.00Can$ US; 45.00Can$ others. NCC Publishing, 222 Argyle Avenue, Delhi Ontario N4B 2Y2 Canada. **Tel** (519)582-2513, FAX (519)582-4040. Index available. **Bk Rev. Ad Acc, Adv Mgr:** Anna Spencer, **Tel** (416)271-1366. **Circ:** 6,400 (ctrl). available in microform. ***Absorbed*** *Focus on the Baking Industry, 0702-0945.*
Desc: National magazine for the Canadian bakery industry. Reports on new products, techniques, news, and developments.
Ind/Abst Foods Adlibra.

UK/0005-4100
BAKERS' REVIEW (WATFORD). (BAKERS' REVIEW.). [Bakers' rev.]. **Added/Corp** National Association of Master Bakers, Confectioners and Caterers. Vol. 73, No. 27 (1956)-. Periodical. English. mo. £71.00 UK; £57.00 other. Turret Group, 177 Hagden Lane, Watford Herts WD1 8LN United Kingdom. **Tel** 011 44 923 228577, FAX 011 44 923 221346. **ED** Debra Clay. **CODEN** BAKREG. **Bk Rev. Ad Acc. Circ:** 5,000.
Ind/Abst BioBusiness; Food Sci. Technol. Abstr.; Foods Adlibra.

US/1049-3174
BAKERY NEWSLETTER. (BAKERY NEWSLETTER : PRODUCTION AND MARKETING.). [Bak. newsl.]. (19??)-. Periodical. English. wk (50 issues). $245.00 US; $295.00 other. Cahners Publishing Company, 249 West 17th Street, New York NY 10011. **Tel** (212)645-0067, FAX (212)242-6987. **(Subscription address:** Cahners Publishing Company / Colorado, Paid Subscription Service Center, PO Box 7610, Highlands Ranch CO 80126-7610.) **DD** 338. **CODEN** BANEDP. **[CCC].** available on an online database (file 648/Full-Text) from DIALOG.
Desc: Brings four pages of information to help your bakery compete more effectively. Helps readers stay on top of market strategies, mergers and acquisitions, competitive moves, government regulations and more.
Ind/Abst BioBusiness (1990-); Foods Adlibra.

US/0005-4127
BAKERY PRODUCTION AND MARKETING. [Bak. prod. mark.]. **VFOAT** Bakery Production and Marketing, Buyers Guide; Retail Bakery Annual Report; Bakery Production; Bakery. (Sept. 1966)-. Periodical. English. mo. $90.00 US; $158.00 (surface mail), $295.00 (airmail) other. Cahners Publishing Company, 249 West 17th Street, New York NY 10011. **Tel** (212)645-0067, FAX (212)242-6987. **(Subscription address:** Cahners Publishing Company / Colorado, Paid Subscription Service Center, PO Box 7610, Highlands Ranch CO 80126-7610.) **ED** Ray Lahvic. **LC** TX761; .B32. **DD** 338.4/7/6647520973. **CODEN** BPMKA4. **[CCC]. Ad Acc. Circ:** 40,000 (ctrl). available on microfilm and microfiche from University Microfilms International (UMI). ***Absorbed*** *Bakers Weekly.*
Desc: Unbiased resource of industry news and information with an editorial blend of professional journalism and "hands-on" baker experience.
Ind/Abst BioBusiness; Bus. ASAP (1990-) [Full Txt.]; Bus. Index (1991-); F&S Index Plus Text, Int. [Select. Cov.]; Foods Adlibra; Gen. BusinessFile (1981-); PROMT; Trade Ind. ASAP [Full Txt.]; Trade Ind. Index [Full Txt.].

IE/0790-2239
BAKERY WORLD. (1975)-. English. bm. 11.00p Ireland; 17.00p other. Jemma Publications Ltd, PO Box 1973, Rathmines Dublin 6 Ireland. **Tel** 011 353 1 975500, FAX 011 353 1 977190.
Ind/Abst Foods Adlibra.

US/1040-9254
BAKING & SNACK SYSTEMS. [Baking snack sys.]. **VFOAT** Baking and Snack Systems. (Jan. 1988)-. Periodical. English. Eleven times a year. Free to qualified readers; $30.00 (US), $60.00 (other) non-qualified readers. Sosland Publishing Company / Missouri, 4800 Main Street, Suite 100, Kansas City MO 64112. **Tel** (816)756-1000, FAX (816)756-0494, telex 820182. **ED** Laurie Gorton. **LC** WMLC 93/101. **DD** 338. **CODEN** BSSYEX. **Ad Acc. Circ:** 9,400 (ctrl). ***Absorbed*** *Baking Equipment.*
Ind/Abst Foods Adlibra.

US/1056-6007
BAKING BUYER. [Bak. buy.]. (19??)-. Periodical. English. mo. free. Sosland Publishing Company / Missouri, 4800 Main Street, Suite 100, Kansas City MO 64112. **Tel** (816)756-1000, FAX (816)756-0494, telex 820182. **DD** 381. Full Page (B&W) $3,835.00. Half Page (B&W) $2,265.00.
Desc: A resource of new ideas, products and services for bakers. Includes dates and locations of seminars, and lists of manufacturers and suppliers to the baking industry.

NE/0026-5934
BAKKERSWERELD. [Bakkerswereld]. (1937)-. Periodical. Dutch. wk. Fl280.63. Misset Uitgeverij BV, Postbus 9000, 6800 DA Arnhem Netherlands. **Tel** 011 31 85 209911. **UDC** 664.6. ***Absorbed*** *Banketbakkerij, 0005-5484.*

US/0896-4653
BALTIMORE MENU DIRECTORY. [Baltim. menu dir.]. (1990)-. English. ir. $7.95. Menu Directory Publishers, PO Box 1000, Exton PA 19341. **DD** 642.

FR/0154-5752
BAROMETRE PORC. **See** Agriculture-Livestock and Poultry.

UK/0957-588X
BBC GOOD FOOD. [BBC good food]. **VFOAT** Good Food (London); British Broadcasting Corporation Good Food. (1989)-. Periodical. English. mo. £17.40 UK; £36.40 other Europe; £49.35 other. Redwood Publishing, Fulham House Goldsworth Road, Woking Surrey GU21 1LZ England. **Tel** 011 44 483747008. **DD** 641.

BE/0005-8467
BELGISCHE FRUITREVUE. [Belg. fruitrev.]. (1948)-. Periodical. Dutch. Eleven times a year (monthly with July/Aug. issues combined). $66.67. Belgische Fruitrevue, Krommehamlaan 27, 9031 Drongen Belgium. **Tel** 32 9 2272401, FAX 32 9 2279896. Index available. **Ad Acc. Pr Rev.**

●CN/1189-4172
BERRY & VEGETABLE INFORMER. **See** Agriculture.

US/0897-0386
BEST RECIPES. [Best recipes]. (19??)-. Periodical. English. bm. $15.00. Capper's, 1503 Southwest 42nd Street, Topeka KS 66609. **Tel** (913)274-4366. **ED** Barbara Miller. **DD** 641. cum. index. **Bk Rev. Ad Acc. Circ:** 214,000.
Desc: Features over 100 recipes in every issue. Recipes focus on creating meals with ingredients commonly found in the average kitchen.

II/0970-6240
BHARATIYA SUGAR. **See** Agriculture-Crop Production and Soil.

US/0884-6081
BIENNIAL REPORT ON THE SPECIAL SUPPLEMENTAL FOOD PROGRAM FOR WOMEN, INFANTS, AND CHILDREN, AND ON THE COMMODITY SUPPLEMENTAL FOOD PROGRAM. (BIENNIAL REPORT ON THE SPECIAL SUPPLEMENTAL FOOD PROGRAM FOR WOMEN, INFANTS, AND CHILDREN, AND ON THE COMMODITY SUPPLEMENTAL FOOD PROGRAM / NATIONAL ADVISORY COUNCIL ON MATERNAL, INFANT, AND FETAL NUTRITION.). [Bienn. rep. spec. suppl. food program women infants child. commod. suppl. food program]. **Main/Corp** United States. National Advisory Council on Maternal, Infant, and Fetal Nutrition. **Added/Corp** United States. Food and Nutrition Service.

Food and Food Industry

(198?)-. English. be. **LC** HV696.F6; U625b. **DD** 363.8/83/0973. *Continues* United States. National Advisory Council on Maternal, Infant, and Fetal Nutrition. National Advisory Council on Maternal, Infant, and Fetal Nutrition ... Biennial Report.

●CN/1188-8555
BIERE MAG. [Biere mag.] **Added/Corp** Ordre de Saint-Arnould. Vol. 1, No 1 (1992)-. Periodical. French. qt. Free for members. Ordre de Saint-Arnould, CP 1411, Succursale B, Hull Quebec J8X 3Y1 Canada. **DD** 641.2.

UK
BINSTED'S DIRECTORY OF FOOD TRADE MARKS AND BRAND NAMES.
(1959)-. Directory. English. te. £50.00. Food Trade Press Ltd, Station House, Hortons Way, Westerham Kent TN16 1BZ England. **Tel** 011 44 689 50551, 011 44 689 53070, FAX 011 44 689 561285. **ED** Adrian Binsted. Index available. cum. index. **Ad Acc. Acid Free. Circ:** 2,000. available on diskette; available on CD-ROM. Documents available from BLDSC.
Desc: Provides descriptions of trade marks and brand names used in the United Kingdom. Plus company names and addresses.

US/0149-0958
BIORESEARCH TODAY. FOOD ADDITIVES & RESIDUES. Ceased. VFOAT Food Additives & Residues. **VAT** Bioresearch Today. Food Additives and Residues. Ceased (Dec. 1991). English. mo. BioSciences Information Service, Biological Abstracts / BIOSIS, 2100 Arch Street, Philadelphia PA 19103-1399. **Tel** (800)523-4806 US, (215)587-4800 Pennsylvania and worldwide, FAX (215)587-2016, telex 831739.
Desc: Current awareness journal including abstracts and content summaries of studies involving food additives and residues.

PL/0137-1576
BIULETYN INSTYTUTU ZIEMNIAKA. [Biul. inst. ziemn.]. **Main/Corp** Instytut Ziemniaka Bonin. (1968)-. Polish (summaries and/or abstracts in English and Russian). Insytut Ziemniaka (Institute for Potato Research), Bonin 75-016 Koszalin, Poland. **LC** SB211.P8; I56b. **CODEN** BIZIDH. Documents available from CASDDS.
Ind/Abst Agric. Eng. Abstr.; Biodeter. Abstr.; Chem. Abstr. (?-1980); Field Crop Abstr.; Nutr. Abstr. Rev., Ser. B, Live Feeds and Feed.; Pig News Inf.; Plant Breed. Abstr.; Postharvest News Inf.; Potato Abstr.; Rev. Agric. Entomol.; Rev. Plant Pathol.

US
BLUE BOOK : MEMBERSHIP DIRECTORY & BUYER'S GUIDE.
Main/Corp Food Processing Machinery and Supplies Association. **VFOAT** Membership Directory & Buyer's Guide; Membership Directory and Buyer's Guide. (1988)-. Directory. English (summaries and/or abstracts in French, German and Spanish). an. Free to food processors; $50.00 (US), $53.00 (Canada), $66.00 (other) other. Food Processing Machinery and Supplies, 200 Daingerfield Road, Alexandria VA 22314. **Tel** (703)684-1080, FAX (703)548-6563. Index available. **Ad Acc. Circ:** 20,000. *Continues* Food Processing Machinery and Supplies Association. Membership Directory.
Desc: Directory for members of the Food Processing Machinery & Supplies Association. Provides access to food and beverage packaging and processing machinery, supplies, and services.

CN/0316-9537
BLUE BOOK OF FOOD STORE OPERATORS AND WHOLESALERS.
Added/Corp Grocer Management. (1968)-. Periodical. English (French). an (Published in Summer). 27.00Can$. Sanford Evans Communications Ltd., Box 6900, 1700 Church Avenue, Winnipeg Manitoba R3C 3B1 Canada. **Tel** (204)632-2768, FAX (204)694-2347. **ED** G B Henry. **DD** 658.8/09/664002571. Index available.
Desc: Information on the food industry and grocery trade.

BL
BOLETIM DA SOCIEDADE BRASILEIRA DE CIENCIA E TECNOLOGIA DE ALIMENTOS / SOCIEDADE BRASILEIRA DE CIENCIA E TECNOLOGIA DE ALIMENTOS, SBCTA. Vol. 15, No. 1 (Jan./March 1981)-. Bulletin. Portuguese. qt. Sociedade Brasileira de Ciencia e tecnologia de Alimentos, Caixa Postal 271, 13.100 Campinas, Sao Paulo Brazil. **LC** TX341; .B64. **DD** 664/.005. *Continues* Bol. SBCTA.

FR/0006-713X
BONNE CUISINE. French. Twenty-six times a year. $58.00. Editions Presse Professionelle, 8 10 rue Pierre Brossolette, 92300 Levallois Perret France. **Tel** 011 33 140874146.

FR
BONNE TABLE ET TOURISME : ORGANE OFFICIEL DE LA CHAINE DES ROTISSEURS, DE L'ACADEMIE DE GASTRONOMIE BRILLAT-SAVARIN, DE L'ORDRE MONDIAL DES GOURMETS DEGUSTATEURS. Added/Corp Chaine des Rotisseurs. Academie de Gastronomie Brillat-Savarin. Ordre Mondial des Gourmets Degustateurs. (19??)-. Periodical. French. bm. Bonne Table et Tourisme Revue, 7 rue d'Aumale, F 75009 Paris France. **Tel** 4281 30 12.

US
BOSTON, FRESH FRUIT AND VEGETABLE WHOLESALE MARKET PRICES. Main/Corp Federal-State Market News Service. **Added/Corp** United States. Agricultural Marketing Service. Fruit and Vegetable Division. Market News Branch. Massachusetts. Dept. of Food and Agriculture. **VFOAT** Fresh Fruit and Vegetable Wholesale Market Prices, Boston. (1976)-. Periodical. English.

FR
BOUCHERIE FRANCAISE, LA. (19??)-. Periodical. French. ir. Sepeta, 98 Boulevard Pereire, 75850 Paris Cedex France. **Tel** 380/24-02. **Bk Rev. Ad Acc.**
Desc: Only professional journal for everything concerning the butcher and meat cutter in France.

FR/0224-5027
BOULANGER PATISSIER 1979, LE. Title Change. (1979)-(1989). Periodical. French. Eleven times a year. Presse Corporative Francaise, 43 rue de la Roquette, 75011 Paris France. **UDC** 641(44). *Continues* Le Boulanger Patissier et le Boulanger-Patissier Confiseur Glacier Reunis, 0224-5035. *Continued by* La Patisserie Francaise Illustree (Paris), 0243-7600; *Absorbed by* Patisserie Boulangerie (Neuilly-sur-Seine), 0998-4933.

GW/0520-7568
BRAUER-UND MAELZER-LEHRLING. (April 1963)-. Academic Scholarly Publication. German. ir. DM186.40 Germany; DM233.00 other. Westkreuz Druckerei und Verlag, Toepchiner Weg 198-200, D-12309 Berlin Germany. **Tel** 011 49 30 7452047, FAX 011 49 30 7453066. **CODEN** BMLEDV. Documents available from CASDDS.
Ind/Abst Chem. Abstr. (1963-1982).

GW/0724-696X
BRAUWELT (1978). (BRAUWELT.). [Brauwelt]. Vol. 118, No. 14 (April 6, 1978)-. Academic Scholarly Publication. German. wk. DM226.00. Verlag Hans Carl GmbH & Company KG, Andernacher Strasse 33A, D 90411 Nuernberg Germany. **Tel** 011 49 911 952850. **CODEN** BRUWAQ. [CCC]. Index available. cum. index. **Bk Rev. Ad Acc. Circ:** 6,375 (ctrl). Documents available from CASDDS. *Formed by the union of* Brauwelt. Ausgabe A *and* Brauwelt. Ausgabe B.
Desc: Covers science, technology, sales, marketing, management, organisation, training, further education. Qualified survey of all economical and technical developments of the trade.
Ind/Abst BioBusiness; Chem. Abstr.; EMBASE; Food Sci. Technol. Abstr.; Int. Packag. Abstr.; Microbiol. Abstr. Sect. A; Saf. Health Work.

●US/1061-2718
BREAD MACHINE NEWSLETTER, THE. [Bread mach. newsl.]. Vol. 1, No. 1 (Mar./Apr. 1992)-. Newsletter. English. bm. $11.95. Donna Rathmell German, 976 Houston Northcutt Blvd., Suite 3, Mt. Pleasant SC 29464. **DD** 641.

AT/0818-8653
BRIEFS/ BREAD RESEARCH INSTITUTE OF AUSTRALIA. [Briefs - Bread Res. Inst. Aust.]. (1985)-. Periodical. English. bm. comes with membership. Bread Research Institute of Australia, PO Box 7, North Ryde NSW 2112 Australia. **Tel** 011 61 2 8889600. **DD** 664.75230994.
Ind/Abst Foods Adlibra.

UK/0007-0300
BRITISH BAKER. [Br. bak.]. Vol. 171, No. 16 (1975)-. Periodical. English. Fifty times a year. £32.75 UK; £62.00 Europe; £83.00 others. EMAP Readerlink, Audit House, 260 Field End Road, Ruislip Middlesex HA4 9LT England. **Tel** 011 44 081 868 4499, FAX 011 44 081 429 3117. **CODEN** BRBAE5. [CCC]. available on microfilm from University Microfilms International (UMI).
Ind/Abst BioBusiness; Trade Index.

UK/0007-070X
BRITISH FOOD JOURNAL (1966). (BRITISH FOOD JOURNAL.). [Br. food j.]. (1966)-. Periodical. English. Eleven times a year. $2389.00. MCB University Press, 60 62 Toller Lane, Bradford West Yorkshire BD8 9BX England. **Tel** 011 44 274 499821, FAX 011 44 274 547143, telex 51317 MCBUNI G. **(Subscription address:** MCB University Press / US and Canada Subscriptions, PO Box 10812, Birmingham AL 35201-0812.**) ED** Brian Beharrell. **LC** TX501; .B7. **DD** 363.1/926. **NLM** W1 BR432. **CODEN** BFOJA9. **Bk Rev.** *Continues* British Food Journal and Hygienic Review; *Absorbed* Food Marketing (Bradford, West Yorkshire, England), 0267-4394.
Desc: Aims to foster a greater understanding of the methods and motives among all those involved in the food sector.
Ind/Abst AGRICOLA [Select. Cov.]; BioBusiness (1989-1990); Biodeter. Abstr. (19??-19??); Dairy Sci. Abstr.; Food Sci. Technol. Abstr.; Int. Packag. Abstr.; Manage. Market. Abstr.; Nutr. Abstr. Rev., Ser. B, Live Feeds and Feed.; Nutr. Abstr. Rev., Ser. A, Hum. Exp.; Rice Abstr.; Trop. Dis. Bull.; World Agric. Econ.

GW/0172-8180
BROT & BACKWAREN. VFOAT Brot und Backwaren. (1980)-. Periodical. German. Twelve times a year. DM96.00 Germany; DM108.00 other. Rhenania Fachverlag GmbH, Postfach 601220, Possmoorweg 5, W-2000 Hamburg 60 Germany. **Tel** 011 49 40 27170, FAX 011 49 40 27172056, telex 2173465 or 213214. **UDC** 664.6. Index available. cum. index. **Bk Rev**, (Qty: 30). **Ad Acc. Circ:** 7,200 (ctrl). *Formed by the union of* Brotindustrie, 0007-246X *and* Backtechnik, 0344-4686.
Ind/Abst Food Sci. Technol. Abstr.

FR/0243-5314
BULLETIN ANALYTIQUE - CIE. Title Change. VFOAT Bulletin Analytique - Centre Institut Ecole. (1980)-(1992). Periodical. French. Nine times a year. CTCPA, 44 rue d'Alesia, 75682 Paris Cedex 14 France. **Tel** 011 33 1 43218321, FAX 011 33 1 43212352. **ED** C. Divin. **UDC** 577. **Bk Rev. Circ:** 1,000. *Continued by* CT Infos, 1165-4651.
Desc: Technical literature on the canning and preserving industry.

II/0536-8502
BULLETIN ON FOOD STATISTICS.
(BULLETIN ON FOOD STATISTICS / ISSUED BY THE ECONOMIC AND STATISTICAL ADVISER, MINISTRY OF AGRICULTURE.). **Added/Corp** India. Directorate of Economics and Statistics. **VFOAT** Khadya Sankhyiki Buletina. (1951)-. Statistical Publication. English (Hindi). an. Price varies. Directorate of Economics and Statistics / Agriculture, Ministry of Agriculture, A-Block 2E/3, Curzoor Old Barracks, Kasturba Ganothi Marg 110001 New Delhi. **Tel** 381523. **(Subscription address:** Prints India, 11 Darya Ganj, New Delhi, 110002 India, (Phone: 011 91 11 3268645)**) LC** HD9016.I4; A33.

BE
BULLETIN STATISTIQUE INTERNATIONAL : CHOCOLAT SUCRE BISCUITERIE. (19??)-. Bulletin. English (French). an. $37.00. IOCCC, c/o Mlle. MacNeall, Avenue de Cortenberg 172, 1040 Brussels Belgium. **Tel** 011 32 2 7351072.

UK
BULLETIN - THE INSTITUTE OF MEAT.
Main/Corp Institute of Meat. **Added/Corp** Institute of Meat. No. 85 (Aug. 1974)-. Trade Publication. English. qt. £11.00 England; £16.00 other. Institute of Meat, 57 60 St John Street, London EC1M 6DT England. **Tel** 011 44 1 253 2971. **ED** D W Leith. **Ad Acc.** ctrl circ.
Desc: Technical and educational journal available to institute members and the meat industry.
Ind/Abst Anim. Breed. Abstr.; Food Sci. Technol. Abstr.

UK/0268-1781
BUTCHER & PROCESSOR. [Butch. process.]. **VFOAT** Butcher and Processor. (1984)-. Trade Publication. English. Eight times a year. £25.00 UK; £35.00 other. Smithfield Publishing Ltd., High Street Castle Campus, Cambs CB1 6SN England. **Tel** 0799 504 879, FAX 0799 584 883. **ED** Tony Pike. **DD** 338.4766490041. **Bk Rev. Ad Acc, Adv Mgr:** Peter Fleming. **Tel** 0799 584 879. **Circ:** 10,000 (ctrl). available in print. Documents available from BLDSC.

US/0890-1813
CA SELECTS: ARTIFICIAL SWEETENERS. *See* Chemistry-Abstracting, Bibliographies and Statistics.

US/0895-5913
CA SELECTS: FOOD & FEED ANALYSIS. *See* Chemistry-Abstracting, Bibliographies and Statistics.

US/1051-3914
CA SELECTS. FOOD, DRUGS, & COSMETICS. *See* Chemistry-Abstracting, Bibliographies and Statistics.

US/0162-7813
CA SELECTS: FOOD TOXICITY. *See* Chemistry-Abstracting, Bibliographies and Statistics.

Food and Food Industry

BL/0102-7344
CABRA & BODES. See Agriculture-Crop Production and Soil.

JM/0376-7655
CAJANUS. See Nutrition and Dietetics.

US/0749-1824
CAKE DECORATING. [Cake decor.]. **VFOAT** Wilton Yearbook of Cake Decorating. English. an. Wilton Enterprises Inc, 2240 West 75th Street, Woodridge IL 60517. **LC** TX771; .C292. **DD** 641.8/653.

US/1047-9481
CALIFORNIA FOOD. [Calif. food]. (1990)-. Periodical. English. mo. California Food, PO Box 7495, Van Nuys CA 91409. **Tel** (818)703-6177. **DD** 338.

US/0270-384X
CALIFORNIA FRESH FRUIT AND VEGETABLE SHIPMENTS BY RAIL, TRUCK, AND AIR. **Main/Corp** Federal-State Market News Service. 1978-. English. an. $2.00. Federal-State Market News Service, 1220 N Street/Suite 216, Sacramento CA 95814. **Tel** (202)872-4600, (800)227-5558, **FAX** (202)872-4615. **LC** HE199.5.F3; F43A. **DD** 380.1/41/09794. *Continues* Shipments of California Fruits and Vegetables by Rail, Truck, and Air, 0361-4697.

US/1061-9658
CALIFORNIA FRUIT GROWER ANNUAL. [Calif. fruit grow. annu.]. **Added/Corp** Blue Anchor, Inc. (1991)-. English. California Fruit Grower, 730 Howe Avenue, Sacramento CA 95825. **DD** 338. **CODEN** CFGAEP. *Continues* California Fruit Grower, 1049-3166.
Ind/Abst BioBusiness.

US
CALIFORNIA GROCER. (19??)-. English. mo (10 issues per year). $25.00. Southern California Grocers Association, 906 G Street, Suite 700, Sacremento CA 95814. **Tel** (916)448-3545. *Continues* Grocer Journal of California, 0745-4104.
Desc: Information on the food industry and grocery trade.

US/0744-4834
CALIFORNIA POTATO & ONION REPORT. Periodical. English. sw. Federal-State Market News Service, 1220 N Street/Suite 216, Sacramento CA 95814. **Tel** (202)872-4600, (800)227-5558, **FAX** (202)872-4615.

US/0194-8504
CALIFORNIA STRAWBERRY REPORT. **Added/Corp** California. Bureau of Market News. United States. Agricultural Marketing Service. Fruit and Vegetable Division. (19??)-. English. ir (Feb-Oct). $99.00 US & Canada; $198.00 other. US Department of Agriculture / Federal-State Market News, 630 Sansome Street, Room 727, San Francisco CA 94111. **Tel** (415)705-1300. **ED** F. Teensma. **Circ:** 100 (ctrl).
Desc: Shipping point information on strawberries and raspberries.

● US
CAMERON'S FOODSERVICE MARKETING REPORTER. **VFOAT** Cameron's Food Service Marketing Reporter; Foodservice Marketing; Food Service Marketing Reporter; Food Service Marketing Reporter. Vol. 11, No. 1 (Jan. 1, 1992)-. Periodical. English. Twenty-four times a year. $197.00 US; $227.00 other. Camerons Publications, 5325 Sheridan Drive, PO Box 1160, Williamsville NY 14231-1160. **Tel** (716)833-4369, **FAX** (716)834-4159. **ED** Nina Cameron. ctrl circ.
Continues Cameron's Foodservice Promotions Reporter, 0735-5548.

UK/0260-7352
CANADEAN WORLD NEW PRODUCTS. [Canadean world new prod.]. **VFOAT** World New Products. No. 1(23 Oct., 1980)-. Periodical. English. mo. Sosland Publishing Company / Missouri, 4800 Main Street, Suite 100, Kansas City MO 64112. **Tel** (816)756-1000, **FAX** (816)756-0494, telex 820182. **ED** Celia Radice. ctrl circ. *Continues in part* Eurofood.
Desc: Details of new products in the food and drink industry worldwide.

CN/0008-3704
CANADIAN GROCER. [Can. grocer]. Vol. 18, No. 12 (Mar. 18, 1904)-. Trade Publication. English. mo. 42.00Can$ Canada; 95.00Can$ other. MacLean Hunter Ltd. Business Publishers / Canada, Box 9100, Station A, Toronto ONT M5W 1A5 Canada. **Tel** (416)946-8420, (800)567-0444. **Subscription address:** Indas, 35 Riviera Drive, Building 17, Markham Ontario L3R 8N4 Canada.} **ED** George H. Condon. **CODEN** CAGRE7. **Circ:** 18,200. available on microfilm and microfiche from University Microfilms International (UMI). *Continues* Canadian Grocer & General Storekeeper, 1180-6400.
Desc: Canada's national trade magazine for supermarket operators and the food distribution industry; includes directory and statistical issues.
Ind/Abst BioBusiness; Infomat Int. Bus.

US
CANDY BUYERS' DIRECTORY; A CLASSIFIED DIRECTORY OF CANDY MANUFACTURERS SELLING NATIONALLY OR SECTIONALLY, THE. (19??)-. Directory. English. an. $45.00. MC - Manufacturing Confectioner Publishing Company Inc, 175 Rock Road, Glen Rock NJ 07452. **Tel** (201)652-2655. **LC** TX784; .C3. **Ad Acc.**
Desc: Covers confectionery information.

US/0745-1032
CANDY INDUSTRY (1982). (CANDY INDUSTRY.). [Candy ind.]. (1982)-. Periodical. English. mo. $32.00 US and possessions; $42.00 Canada; $48.00 other. Advanstar Communications Inc., 131 West First Street, Duluth MN 55802. **Tel** (218)723-9477, (800)346-0085. **ED** Patricia Magee. **LC** HD9999.C72; C2. **DD** 338.4/7664153/05. **CODEN** CANIDE. **[CCC].** **Circ:** 3,706. available on an online database (file 16/Full-Text) from DIALOG. *Continues* Candy & Snack Industry, 0744-9453.
Desc: The leading publication in the confectionery industry.
Ind/Abst BioBusiness; Bus. Index (1985-); F&S Index Plus Text, Int. [Full Txt.] [Select. Cov.]; Food Sci. Technol. Abstr.; Foods Adlibra; Gen. BusinessFile (1985-); Gen. Period. Index (1985-); Mag. Search; PROMT [Full Txt.]; Trade Ind. Index (1982-); Vocat. Search (July 1993-).

US/0739-8921
CANDY INDUSTRY BUYING GUIDE. [Candy ind. buy. guide]. Vol. 36 (1983)-. Consumer Publication. English. an. $25.00. Advanstar Communications Inc., 131 West First Street, Duluth MN 55802. **Tel** (218)723-9477, (800)346-0085. **ED** Patricia Magee. **LC** HD9330.C65; C3. **DD** 664/.153/029473. **Circ:** 3,976. *Continues* Candy & Snack Industry Buying Guide, 0734-3183.
Desc: Information on the confectionery and candy industry.

US
CANDY INDUSTRY CATALOG & FORMULA BOOK. (1947)-. Catalog. English. an. Magazine for Industry, 747 3rd Avenue, New York NY 10017. **Tel** (212)838-7778. **LC** TX761; .C4. **DD** 664.1.

US/0886-3741
CANDY MARKETER (1985). **Ceased.** (CANDY MARKETER.). [Candy mark.]. Vol. 1, No. 1 (Jan./Feb. 1985)-(Mar./April 1994). Periodical. English. bm. Advanstar Communications Inc., 131 West First Street, Duluth MN 55802. **Tel** (218)723-9477, (800)346-0085. **LC** HD9330.C65; C36. **DD** 381; 381/.45664153/05. **CODEN** CMARER. **[CCC].** **Circ:** 10,417. available on an online database (files 16,570/Full-Text) from DIALOG. *Continues* Candy Marketer Quarterly, 0733-9070.
Ind/Abst BioBusiness; F&S Index Plus Text, Int. [Full Txt.] [Select. Cov.]; Foods Adlibra; Mark. Advert. Ref. Serv. [Full Txt.]; PROMT [Full Txt.].

US/0162-5136
CANDY WHOLESALER. **Added/Corp** National Candy Wholesalers Association. (19??)-. Periodical. English. Ten times a year (Jan./Feb. and July/Aug. issues combined). $36.00 US; $46.00 other. National Candy Wholesalers Association, 1128 16th Street Northwest, Washington DC 20036. **Tel** (202)463-2124, **FAX** (202)467-0559. **ED** Joyce Grimley. **LC** HD9999.C72; N3. **DD** 658.8/6. **Ad Acc**, **Adv Mgr:** Mary Ann Paniccia, **Tel** (800)482-2962 or (202)463-2124. **Circ:** 11,597 (ctrl). *Continues* National Candy Wholesaler.
Desc: Distribution management and sales marketing publication for candy, tobacco, and snack wholesalers throughout the U.S.

CN/0702-6528
CANNED AND FROZEN FRUITS AND VEGETABLES. [Cann. frozen fruits veg.]. **Added/Corp** Statistics Canada. Manufacturing and Primary Industries Division. Statistics Canada. Industry Division. **VFOAT** Fruits et Legumes en Boites et Congeles. Vol. 44, No. 1 (Jan. 1, 1977)-. Periodical (French). mo. 60.00Can$ Canada; $72.00 US; $84.00 other. Statistics Canada, Publications Sales & Services, Main Building Room 1710, Ottawa Ontario K1A 0T6 Canada. **Tel** (613)951-5070, (800)267-6677, **FAX** (613)951-1584, telex 053-3585. **DD** 338.4/76648/00971. *Continues* Pack, Shipments and Stocks of Selected Canned Fruits and Vegetables, 0702-6536.
Desc: Pack in terms of total cases, and stocks by container size of selected canned fruits and vegetables by major geographic area.

II
CARDAMOM STATISTICS (INDIA). See Food and Food Industry-Abstracting, Bibliographies and Statistics.

IT
CARNE. Editoriale CIM, via Aureliana 25, 00187 Rome Italy.

US/0744-2483
CAROLINA FOOD DEALER, THE. **Added/Corp** North Carolina Food Dealers Association. (19??)-. Periodical. English. mo. $2.50. North Carolina Food Dealers Association Inc, PO Box 6066, Charlotte NC 28207.

CN/1186-6217
CARREFOUR BIO-ALIMENTAIRE. (CARREFOUR BIO-ALIMENTAIRE : PERIODIQUE DU SOUS-MINISTERIAT DES AFFAIRES ECONOMIQUES.). [Carrefour bio-aliment.]. **Main/Corp** Quebec (Province). Ministere de l'Agriculture, des Pecheries et de l'Alimentation. Sous-Ministeriat des Affaires Economiques. (April 1991)-. Periodical. French. bm. **DD** 338.1.

US
CATEGORY REPORT. English. mo. $1030.00 US & Canada; $1055.00 Europe & Pan America; $1070.00 other. Marketing Intelligence Service Ltd, 6473D Route 64, Naples NY 14512. **Tel** (716)374-6326, (800)836-5710, **FAX** (714)374-5217, telex 469979. **ED** Tom Vierhile.
Desc: Reports on new packaged goods by major industries. It combines North American and international coverage with in-depth reports of potentially influential new products and selected print advertising.

UK/0008-7777
CATERER & HOTELKEEPER. [Cater. hotelk.]. **VFOAT** Caterer and Hotelkeeper. (19??)-. Periodical. English. wk (published on Thurs.). $169.00 US and Canada. Reed Business Publishing / West Sussex, England, Perrymount Road, Haywards Heath, West Sussex RH16 3DH England. **Tel** 011 44 81 6523500. **DD** 647.9.
Ind/Abst Infomat Int. Bus.

UK
CATERING. (19??)-. Periodical. English. bm. £139.55. Croner Publ Ltd, Croner House, London Road, Kingston upon Thames, Surrey KT2 6SR England. **Tel** 011 44 81 5473333, **FAX** 081 547-2637. Index available (Free).

UK
CATERING. English. mo. £60.00 UK and Northern Ireland; $150.00 other. Morgan Grampian, 40 Beresford Street Woolwich, London SE18 6BQ England. **Tel** 011 44 81 855 7777, **FAX** 011 44 81 855 5548, telex 896238.

UK/0267-3851
CATERING & HEALTH. **VFOAT** Catering and Health. Vol. 1, No. 1 (1988)-. Periodical. English. Four times a year. £89.00. AB Academic Publishers, PO Box 42 Bicester, OXON OX6 7NW England. **Tel** 011 44 869 320949. **ED** R. H. G. Charles. **NLM** W1; CA959U. **Bk Rev.** **Ad Acc.** **Pr Rev.**
Desc: This journal includes the health and educational aspects of hygiene and microbiological problems in institutional foodservice.
Ind/Abst Food Sci. Technol. Abstr.; Health Plan. Adminis.; Hospit. Health Admin. Index (Vol. 1, No. 1, 1988-).

UK
CATERING BUYERS GUIDE. See Business-Purchasing.

US/1057-042X
CATERING IMPACT. [Cater. impact]. (May/June 1991)-. Periodical. English. bm. Free (to caterers). Catering Impact, PO Box 14899, Chicago IL 60614. **DD** 642.

US/0008-7815
CATERING INDUSTRY EMPLOYEE. See Economics-Labor.

NE
CATERING MAGAZINE. (1986)-. English. mo (10 issues). Fl135.00. Koggeschip Vakbladen BV, Postbus 1198, 1000 BD Amsterdam Netherlands. **Tel** 011 31 20 6916666.

NZ/0113-2326
CATERING MANAGEMENT (AUCKLAND, N.Z.). **Title Change.** (CATERING MANAGEMENT.). **VFOAT** Catering and Accommodation Management. (19??)-Vol. 28, No. 11 (Nov. 1992). Periodical. English. Six times a year. Trade Publications Ltd., 300 Great South Road Greenlane, Newmarket Auckland New Zealand. **Tel** 011 64 9 9293000. *Merged with* Hospitality *to form* Hospitality & Catering.

UK
CATERING RECORDS AND PROCEDURES. (19??)-. Periodical. English. £86.00. Croner Publ Ltd, Croner House, London Road, Kingston upon Thames, Surrey KT2 6SR England. **Tel** 011 44 81 5473333, **FAX** 081 547-2637.

SP
CATERING : REVISTA DE ALIMENTACION RESTAURACION Y EQUIPAMIENTO PARA GRANDES COLECTIVIDADES. **Ceased.** (19??)-(19??). Spanish. bm. Elsevier Prensa SA, Avenida Paral Lel 180, 08015 Barcelona Spain. **Tel** 011 34 3 3255350, **FAX** 011 34 3 4252880.

US
CATERING SERVICE IDEA NEWSLETTER. Newsletter. English. be. $8.50 US; $11.50 other. Continnuus / Houston, PO Box 570213, Houston TX 77257. **Tel** (713)867-3438. **ED** A.C. Doyle. **Circ:** 2,400.
Desc: Ideas for catering services.

UK/0269-7696
CATERING UPDATE. [Cater. update]. (1986)-. Periodical. English. ir (10 issues). $65.00 US and Canada. Reed Business Publishing / West Sussex, England, Perrymount Road, Haywards Heath, West Sussex RH16 3DH England. **Tel** 011 44 81 6523500.

GW/0341-2601
CCB : REVIEW FOR CHOCOLATE, CONFECTIONERY AND BAKERY. [CCB, rev. choc., confect. bak.]. (1976)-. Academic Scholarly Publication. English. qt. Verlag Eduard F Beckmann KG, Postfach 1120, Haus Heideck, D-31251 Lehrte Germany. **Tel** 011 49 5132 85910, FAX 011 49 5132 53100. **CODEN** CCBKD8. Documents available from CASDDS.
Desc: Information on chocolate processing, bakers, bakeries and confectionery.
Ind/Abst Chem. Abstr. (1976-1983); Dairy Sci. Abstr.

US/0744-2351
CENTRAL CALIFORNIA VEGETABLE REPORT. (CENTRAL CALIFORNIA VEGETABLE REPORT : FRUIT AND VEGETABLE MARKET NEWS.). **VFOAT** Fruit and Vegetable Market News. Periodical. English. da. Federal-State Market News Service, 1220 N Street/Suite 216, Sacramento CA 95814. **Tel** (202)872-4600, (800)227-5558, FAX (202)872-4615.

CU/0253-5777
CENTRO AZUCAR. ***Suspended.*** [Cent. azucar]. Vol. 1, No. 1/2 (Jan./Aug. 1974)-?. Academic Scholarly Publication. Spanish (summaries and/or abstracts in English; table of contents in English). qt. 29.94Cub$ North and South America; 35.93Cub$ other. Ediciones Cubanas, Obispo 527, Altos ESQ Bernaza, CP 10100 Havana Cuba. **Tel** 011 632980, 631942, FAX 011 631011, telex 512337, 6540. **LC** SB215; .C45. **CODEN** CEAZDS. Documents available from CASDDS. ***Continues*** *Centro. Serie Azucar, 0253-5769.*
Ind/Abst Chem. Abstr.; Field Crop Abstr.; Food Sci. Technol. Abstr.; Hortic. Abstr.; Plant Breed. Abstr.; Soils Fert.; Sug. Indus. Abstr.

US/0146-6283
CEREAL FOODS WORLD. [Cereal foods world]. **Added/Corp** American Association of Cereal Chemists. Vol. 20 (Jan. 1975)-. Periodical. English. mo. $90.00 US; $125.00 other. American Association of Cereal Chemists, 3340 Pilot Knob Road, St. Paul MN 55121. **Tel** (612)454-7250, FAX (612)454-0766, telex 6502439657. **ED** Jody Grider. **DD** 664. **CODEN** CFWODA. **[CCC]. Bk Rev. Ad Acc. Pr Rev. Circ:** 4,000 (ctrl). available on microfilm and microfiche from University Microfilms International (UMI). Documents available from The Genuine Article, CASDDS, Documents on Demand. ***Continues*** *Cereal Science Today, 0009-0360.*
Desc: Contains information on applied research, features, columns by experts in various fields, and news for food processors.
Ind/Abst AGRICOLA [Full Cov.]; Agric. Eng. Abstr. (1991-); Anal. Abstr.; BioBusiness; Biodeter. Abstr.; Chem. Abstr.; Curr. Aware. Biol. Sci., CABS; Curr. Biotechnol.; Curr. Contents, Agric. Biol. Environ. Sci.; Dairy Sci. Abstr.; Environ. Abstr. (Dec. 16, 1991-); Field Crop Abstr.; Food Sci. Technol. Abstr.; Foods Adlibra; Grasslands For. Abstr.; Int. Aerosp. Abstr.; Int. Packag. Abstr.; Maize Abstr.; Nutr. Abstr. Rev., Ser. A, Hum. Exp.; Life Sci. Collect.; Plant Breed. Abstr.; Postharvest News Inf.; Protozoolog. Abstr.; Res. Alert [Full Cov.]; Rev. Med. Vet. Mycology; Rice Abstr.; Sci. Cit. Index; SCISEARCH; Seed Abstr.; Soils Fert.; Sug. Indus. Abstr.; Wheat Barley Trit. Abstr.

UK
CEREALS & BAKERY. English. ir. Derwent Publications Ltd., Derwent House 14, Great Queen Street, London WC2B 5DF England. **Tel** 011 44 71 3442800.

CH
CHAO CHI SHIH CHANG SHIH PIN PAI HUO TSAI KOU NIEN CHIEN / CHEN FENG-JEN PIEN. **VFOAT** Modern Super Market Operation and Almanac; Modern Super Market Operation & Almanac. 1981-1982-. Chinese. an. $1,900.00. Chao Chi Chu Pan She, PO Box 8-198, Taipei Shin Taiwan. **LC** HF5469.23.T28; C47. **DD** 658.8/78/0951249.

FR/0222-0377
CHARCUTERIE ET GASTRONOMIE PARIS. (1979)-. Periodical. French. mo. 420.00F France; 468.00F other. Soc Editions Publ Alimentation, 15 rue Jacques Bingen, F 75017 Paris France. **Tel** 011 33 1 47660122. **UDC** 66. **Ad Acc. Circ:** 26,000.

●US
CHEF. **VFOAT** Chef Institutional. (Sept./Oct. 1992)-. Periodical. English. bm (6 issues). $20.00. Talcott Communications Corporation, 20 North Wacker Drive, Suite 3230, Chicago IL 60606. **Tel** (312)664-4040. **CODEN** CHEFEA. ***Continues*** *Chef Institutional.*

SZ
CHEFS. 1939-. Periodical. French. ir. Association D'Organization Scientific, Switzerland.

GW/0366-7154
CHEMIE, MIKROBIOLOGIE, TECHNOLOGIE DER LEBENSMITTEL. (CHEMIE, MIKROBIOLOGIE, TECHNOLOGIE DER LEBENSMITTEL / FOOD CHEMISTRY, MICROBIOLOGY, TECHNOLOGY.). [Chem., Mikrobiol., Technol. Lebensm.]. **VFOAT** Food Chemistry, Microbiology, Technology; Chimie, Microbiologie, Technologie Alimentaire. Vol. 1 (Oct. 1971)-. Academic Scholarly Publication. German (English and French; table of contents in French). Three times a year (Jan., May, Oct.). DM210.00. Lehrst Chemisch Tech Anaylse, Technishe Universite Muenchen, W 8050 Freising F R Germany. **Tel** 011 49 89 8161 713823. **ED** F. Drawert. **NLM** W1; CH291R. **CODEN** CMTLBX. **Bk Rev. Ad Acc.** Documents available from CASDDS.
Desc: Contains food chemistry, microbiology technology, biotechnology analysis, residues enzymes, proteins, fats, carbohydrates, vitamins, minerals, flavors, natural compounds, equipment storage, and processing.
Ind/Abst BioBusiness; Chem. Abstr.; Chemorecept. Abstr.; Dairy Sci. Abstr.; EMBASE; Energy Res. Abstr. (Aug. 1976-); Food Sci. Technol. Abstr.; Life Sci. Collect.; Rice Abstr.; Vitis Vitic. Enol. Abstr.

US/1069-7985
CHILE PEPPER. [Chile pepper]. Vol. 4, No. 3 (May/June 1990)-. Periodical. English. Six times a year. $18.95 (one year), $33.95 (two year). Chile Pepper Magazine, PO Box 80780, Albuquerque NM 87198. **Tel** (505)266-8322, (800)959-5468, FAX (505)266-2127. **(Subscription address:** Stark Services, 12444 Victory Boulevard #300, North Hollywood CA 91606.**) ED** Dave DeWitt. **DD** 641. ***Continues*** *Whole Chile Pepper, 0898-0020.*
Desc: A consumer food magazine devoted to spicy foods.

US/0193-323X
CHILTON'S FOOD ENGINEERING. [Chilton's food eng.]. **VFOAT** Food Engineering. Vol. 49, No. 1 (Jan. 1977)-. Periodical. English. mo. $55.00. Chilton Company, 201 King of Prussia Road, Radnor PA 19089. **Tel** (610)964-4122, (800)695-1214, FAX (610)964-4978, telex 6851035 CHILTON UW. **LC** TX341; .F87. **DD** 664. **CODEN** CFENDJ. **[CCC]. Ad Acc. Circ:** 60,130 (ctrl). available on microfilm and microfiche from University Microfilms International (UMI). ***Continues*** *Food Engineering, 0015-637X.*
Desc: The latest developments in manufacturing and processing techniques, packaging, ingredients, research and development, machinery, for the food and beverage industry's management and engineering personnel.
Ind/Abst Appl. Sci. Technol. Index; BioBusiness (1988-); Dairy Sci. Abstr.; F&S Index Plus Text, Int. [Select. Cov.]; Food Sci. Technol. Abstr.; Foods Adlibra; Infobank (1977-); Mark. Advert. Ref. Serv.; Life Sci. Collect.; PROMT; Soyabean Abstr.; Stat. Ref. Index; Sug. Indus. Abstr.; Trade Ind. ASAP [Full Txt.]; Trade Ind. Index [Full Txt.].

US/0148-4478
CHILTON'S FOOD ENGINEERING INTERNATIONAL. [Chilton's food eng. int.]. **VFOAT** Food Engineering International. (1976)-. Periodical. English (French, German and Spanish). Six times a year. $55.00. Chilton Company, 201 King of Prussia Road, Radnor PA 19089. **Tel** (610)964-4122, (800)695-1214, FAX (610)964-4978, telex 6851035 CHILTON UW. **ED** James N Wagner and Marla S Feder. **DD** 664. **CODEN** FEINDV. **[CCC]. Ad Acc. Circ:** 14,000 (ctrl). available on microfilm and microfiche from University Microfilms International (UMI). Documents available from Article Express International. ***Continues*** *Food Engineering International, 0885-0461.*
Desc: Covers new products, equipment, ingredients, packaging and monthly segments: trade show calendar, supermarket (focuses on marketing of new products), industry focus section, world report and great food labs.
Ind/Abst Appl. Sci. Technol. Index; BioBusiness (1988-); Dairy Sci. Abstr.; Ei Page One; Eng. Index Annu.; Food Sci. Technol. Abstr.; Int. Packag. Abstr.; Trade Ind. ASAP [Full Txt.]; Trade Ind. Index [Full Txt.].

US/0192-6098
CHILTON'S FOOD ENGINEERING MASTER. **Added/Corp** Chilton Company. **VFOAT** Food Engineering Master. (19??)-. English. Thirteen times a year. $130.00. Chilton Company, 201 King of Prussia Road, Radnor PA 19089. **Tel** (610)964-4122, (800)695-1214, FAX (610)964-4978, telex 6851035 CHILTON UW. **LC** TP373; .C3. **DD** 381/.45/681766402573.

UK
CHOCOLATE NEWS. ***Ceased.*** 1 (Feb. 1981)-?. Periodical. English. bm. Zel Publishing Inc, Box 1745, FDR Station, New York NY 10150. **Tel** (212)206-0735. **ED** Milton Zelman. **Bk Rev. Ad Acc. Circ:** 16,000.
Desc: News, recipes and information pertaining to chocolate and chocolate events.

FR/0009-4943
CHOCOLATERIE, CONFISERIE DE FRANCE. Began publication in 1946. Periodical. French. ir. Inter Presse Service, 12 rue Paul Lelong, 75095 Paris Cedex 02 France.

US/0887-591X
CHOCOLATIER. [Chocolatier]. Vol. 1, No. 1 (1984)-. Periodical. English. Six times a year. $19.95 US; $23.45 other. Haymarket Group Ltd, 45 West 34th Street, New York NY 10001. **Tel** (212)239-0855. **(Subscription address:** Kable Publishers Aide, 308 East Hitt Street, Subscription Department, Mt. Morris IL 61054-1473.**) LC** TX767.C5; C54. **DD** 641.6/374/05. **Bk Rev. Ad Acc. Circ:** 350,000.
Ind/Abst Foods Adlibra.

CC
CHUNG-KUO SHIH PIN KUNG YEH NIEN CHIEN. **VFOAT** China Food Industry Almanac. (1984)-. Chinese. an. $23.00. China National Publishing Import & Export Corporation, 16 Gongti E Rd., Chaoyang Dist., Beijing 100704, People's Republic of China. **Tel** 011 8601 50630169, 5066688, FAX 011 8601 5063101, 5063010, telex 22313. **LC** HD9016.C6; C57. **DD** 338.4/76664/00951.

CU
CIENCIA Y TECNICA EN LA AGRICULTURA. ARROZ. **Added/Corp** Centro de Informacion y Documentacion Agropecuario (Cuba) Estacion Central de Investigaciones de Arroz "Nina Bonita.". **VFOAT** Arroz. (197?)-. Spanish (summaries and/or abstracts in English; table of contents in English). Ediciones Cubanas, Obispo 527, Altos ESQ Bernaza, CP 10100 Havana Cuba. **Tel** 011 632980, 631942, FAX 011 631011, telex 512337, 6540.
Ind/Abst Field Crop Abstr.; Rev. Agric. Entomol.; Rice Abstr.

CU
CIENCIA Y TECNICA EN LA AGRICULTURA. CITRICOS Y OTROS FRUTALES. **See** Agriculture-Crop Production and Soil.

US/0362-014X
CITRUS FRUIT INDUSTRY STATISTICAL BULLETIN. **See** Food and Food Industry-Abstracting, Bibliographies and Statistics.

US
CITRUS INDUSTRY (BARTOW, FLA. : 1982), THE. (THE CITRUS INDUSTRY.). Vol. 63, No. 3 (March 1982)-. Periodical. English. mo. $16.00 US; $42.00 other. Citrus Industry Magazine, POB 89, 495 East Summerlin, Bartow FL 33830. **Tel** (813)533-4114. **ED** Mariann Holland. **CODEN** CIINAN. **Ad Acc, Adv Mgr:** Jane Kutler. Documents available from Article Express International. ***Continues*** *Citrus Industry Magazine, 0278-2197.*
Ind/Abst Bioeng. Abstr.; Ei Page One; Eng. Index Annu.; Food Sci. Technol. Abstr.

SZ/1012-9707
CLIPPER (BASEL), THE. (THE CLIPPER.). [Clipper]. **Added/Corp** AgroPress Ltd. (1988)-. Periodical. English (French, German, Portuguese and Spanish). Four times a year (Jan., Apr., July, Oct.). 100.00F Europe; 150.00F other. Agropress Ltd, Aeschengraben 16, CH-4051 Basel Switzerland. **Tel** 011 41 61 2721170, FAX 011 41 61 2721126, telex 845/962185.

US
CODE OF FEDERAL REGULATIONS. 21, FOOD AND DRUGS. **See** Law.

BL/0100-350X
COLETANEA DO INSTITUTO DE TECNOLOGIA DE ALIMENTOS. (COLETANEA.). [Colet. Inst. Tecnol. Aliment.]. **Main/Corp** Instituto de Tecnologia de Alimentos (S‰ao Paulo, Brazil). (19??)-. Monographic series. Portuguese (summaries and/or abstracts in English). sa. $70.00. Instituto Tecnologia Alimentos, Caixa Postal 139, 13073 001 Campinas SP Brazil. **Tel** 011 55 192 415222, FAX 011 55 192 415034, telex 0191009. **LC** TP368; .I55a. **DD** 664. **CODEN** CITAC7. Index available. **Circ:** 600. Documents available from CASDDS.
Ind/Abst Biodeter. Abstr.; Chem. Abstr.; Nutr. Abstr. Rev., Ser. A, Hum. Exp.; Postharvest News Inf.; Rev. Med. Vet. Entomol.; Rev. Med. Vet. Mycology; Rev. Plant Pathol.

US/0896-3177
COLORADO CONNOISSEUR, THE. ***Ceased.*** [Colo. connoiss.]. ( )-(1992). Periodical. English. mo. The Colorado Connoisseur, PO Box 134, Buffalo Creek CO 80425. **DD** 978.

SP
COMER Y BEBER. Spanish. mo. $83.15. El Hogar y La Moda Sa, Diputacion 211, 08011 Barcelona Spain. **Tel** 011 34 3 2541004.

MX
COMERCIALIZACION EXTERNA DEL CAFE MEXICANO EN EL CICLO ... / INSTITUTO MEXICANO DEL CAFE, LA. Spanish. an. **LC** HD9199.M6; C65. **DD** 382/.41373/0972.

US/0275-7184
COMMERCIAL FOOD PATENTS, U.S. [Commer. food. pat. U.S.]. (1970)-. English. an. AVI Publishing Company, 115 Fifth Avenue VNR, New York NY 10003-1004. **Tel** (203)226-0738. **LC** TP370.5; .N67. **DD** 664/.00272.

FR
COMPTE RENDU DES ESSAIS. **See** Agriculture.

BE
COMPTES-RENDUS DE LA ASSEMBLEE GENERALE DE LA COMMISSION INTERNATIONALE TECHNIQUE DE SUCRERIE. **Main/Corp** Commission Internationale Technique de Sucrerie. 7th (1953)-. French (English and German). CITS, Aandorenstraat 1, B-3300 Tienen Belgium. **Tel** 011 32 16 801211.

BL/0101-5508
COMUNICADO TECNICO - CENTRO DE TECNOLOGIA AGRICOLA E ALIMENTAR. **See** Agriculture.

US/1047-8345
CONFECTIONER (1989), THE. (THE CONFECTIONER.). [Confectioner]. Vol. 74, No. 7-8 (Nov./Dec. 1989)-. Periodical. English. bm. $35.00. American Publishing Corp, 17400 Dallas Parkway, Suite 125, Dallas TX 75287. **Tel** (800)826-8586, (214)250-3630. **ED** Pamela Roy. **DD** 338. **Ad Acc. Circ:** 12,200 (ctrl). ***Continues*** *Confectioner Magazine, 0898-5790.*
Desc: Original confectionery marketing and merchandising magazine. Original features and product information presented in an easy-to-read format.
Ind/Abst BioBusiness (1989-); Foods Adlibra (1989-).

UK/0010-5473
CONFECTIONERY PRODUCTION. [Confect. prod.]. (19??)-. Academic Scholarly Publication. English. mo (12 issues). £50.00 UK; £60.00 other. Specialized Publications Ltd, 5 Grove Road Surbiton, Surrey KT6 4BT England. **Tel** 011 44 81 390 0222. **ED** Dennis A. Buckley. **CODEN** CNFPAF. Index available. **Bk Rev. Ad Acc. Circ:** 5,400. Documents available from CASDDS. ***Absorbed*** *Chocolate Production.*
Desc: Machinery, ingredients, packaging and marketing, etc. in the chocolate and sugar confectionery industry.
Ind/Abst BioBusiness; Chem. Abstr. (1935-1983); Dairy Sci. Abstr.; Food Sci. Technol. Abstr.; Foods Adlibra; Int. Packag. Abstr.; Life Sci. Collect.; Sug. Indus. Abstr.

GW/0016-2213
CONFRUCTA. [Confructa]. Vol. 15 (1970)-. Academic Scholarly Publication. English. bm. Verlag Fluessiges Obst GmbH, Diezer Str 7, Postfach 1, 5429 Schoenborn Germany. **CODEN** CONFAW. Documents available from CASDDS. ***Continues*** *Fruchtsaft-Industrie ver. Confructa.*
Ind/Abst Chem. Abstr. (1961-1981/1982); Energy Res. Abstr. (March 1972-).

UK
CONSUMER BRIEF. (1977)-. Newsletter. English. ir (10 issues per year). Hernderson Crosthwaite Institutional Brokers, 32 St Mary at Hill, London EC3P 3AJ England. **Tel** 011 44 71 623 9992, FAX 011 44 71 528 0884. **ED** David P. Lang & Michael R. Landymore. Index available.

CN/0317-2058
CONSUMER FOOD BULLETIN. V. 1- Nov. 1973-. Bulletin. English. Consumer Food Bulletin, 6000 East Metropolitain/Suite 122, Montreal Quebec H1S 1B2 Canada. **DD** 641.3/1/0971.

US/1055-8071
COOKBOOK COLLECTOR, THE. Vol. 1, No. 1 (Jan., Feb., Mar 1991)-. Periodical. English. qt. The Cookbook Collector, 2721 Church Street, Zachary LA 70791. **DD** 641.

●US/1061-0537
COOKBOOK (STEUBEN, ME.). (COOKBOOK: THE FOOD BOOK REVIEW FOR COOKS WHO LIKE TO READ.). [Cookbook]. (1992)-. Periodical. English. bm (6 issues). $18.00. Cookbook, PO Box 88, Steuben ME 04680. **Tel** (207)546-7209. **DD** 641.

US/1061-4729
COOKING CONTEST NEWSLETTER, THE. [Cook. contest newsl.]. (1991)-. Newsletter. English. mo. $19.95. Joyce G Campagna, PO Box 339, Summerville SC 29484. **DD** 641.

US/1040-1903
COOKING EDGE, THE. ***Title Change.*** [Cook. edge]. **Added/Corp** Cuisinart Cooking Club. Periodical. English. mo. Cuisinart Cooking Club, 150 Milford Road, East Windsor NJ 08520. **Tel** (203)323-0854. **DD** 641. ***Continues*** *Cuisinart Cook, 0890-0833.* ***Continued by*** *Connoisseur's Choice, 1051-3582.*

US/0091-861X
COOKING FOR PROFIT. [Cook. profit]. (1932)-. Periodical. English. mo. $24.00 US; $38.00 Canada and Mexico; $52.00 other. Cooking for Profit, PO Box 267, Fond du Lac WI 54936-0267. **Tel** (414)923-3700, FAX (414)923-6805. **ED** Colleen Phalen. **DD** 338. **Ad Acc. Circ:** 23,000. available on microfilm and microfiche from University Microfilms International (UMI).
Desc: A professional-level foodservice publication targeted to owners, operators and staff of restaurants, schools, health care facilities and other volume operations. Emphasis is on recipes, food preparation, kitchen techniques, foodservice equipment, management and other back-of-the-house topics. Features an in-depth profile of a successful foodservice operation every month.
Ind/Abst AGRICOLA [Select. Cov.].

US
COOKING SCHOOL ALTERNATIVE NEWSLETTER. (1992)-. Newsletter. English. Four times a year. $7.00 North America; $14.00 other. Prosperity & Profits Unlimited, PO Box 416, Denver CO 80201-0416. **ED** A. Doyle. **Circ:** 4500.
Desc: Instructions on cooking various foods.

US
COOPERATIVE GROCER. English. bm. $22.00 (one year). Cooperative Grocer, PO Box 597, Athens OH 45701. **Tel** (614) 592-1912.

II
COOPERATIVE SUGAR / NATIONAL FEDERATION OF COOPERATIVE SUGAR FACTORIES LTD. **Added/Corp** National Federation of Co-operative Sugar Factories Ltd. (19??)-. Periodical. English. mo. **LC** HD9116.I39; C65. **DD** 334/.6836/0954.
Ind/Abst Field Crop Abstr.; Hortic. Abstr.; Plant Breed. Abstr.; Potato Abstr.; Rev. Agric. Entomol.; Rev. Plant Pathol.; Soils Fert.; Sug. Indus. Abstr.; Weed Abstr.; World Agric. Econ.

US
COST OF FOOD AT HOME ESTIMATED FOR FOOD PLANS AT THREE COST LEVELS. WESTERN REGION. English. an. US Department of Agriculture / Science and Education Administration / Maryland, Beltsville MD 20705.

US
COST OF FOOD AT HOME FOR FOOD PLANS AT FOUR COST LEVELS. U.S. AVERAGE. English. qt. US Department of Agriculture / Science and Education Administration / Maryland, Beltsville MD 20705.

US/0737-0466
COYOTE (TUCSON, ARIZ.). (COYOTE.). [Coyote]. **Added/Corp** Food Conspiracy. Food Conspiracy Community Access Project. Vol. 1, No. 1 [Jan. 1982]-. Periodical. English. mo. $10.00. Food Conspiracy Cooperative, 1145 East 6th Street, Tucson AZ 85719. ***Continues*** *Food Conspiracy Newsletter.*
Ind/Abst Hum. Rights Intern. Rep.

US/1040-8398
CRITICAL REVIEWS IN FOOD SCIENCE AND NUTRITION. [Crit. rev. food sci. nutr.]. **VFOAT** CRC Critical Reviews in Food Science and Nutrition. **VAT** Chemical Rubber Company Critical Reviews in Food Science and Nutrition. Vol. 12, Issue 3 (June 1980)-. Academic Scholarly Publication. English. Six times a year. $420.00 institution. CRC Press Inc., 2000 Corporate Boulevard Northwest, Boca Raton FL 33431. **Tel** (407)994-0555, (800)272-7737, FAX (407)998-9784, telex 568689. **(Subscription address:** CRC Press Inc., PO Box 750, Pearl River NY 10965.**) ED** Fergus M. Clydesdale. **LC** TP368; .C46. **DD** 664/.005. **NLM** W1; C555F. **CODEN** CRFND6. **[CCC].** Documents available from The Genuine Article, BIOSIS Document Express, CASDDS, Documents on Demand. ***Continues*** *CRC Critical Reviews in Food Science and Nutrition, 0099-0248.*
Desc: Provides critical viewpoints of selected topics of food technology, food science, and nutrition.
Ind/Abst AgBiotech News Inf.; AGRICOLA [Full Cov.]; Agric. Eng. Abstr.; BioBusiness; Biodeter. Abstr. (19??-19??); Biol. Abstr.; Chem. Abstr.; Curr. Aware. Biol. Sci., CABS; Curr. Contents, Agric. Biol. Environ. Sci.; Dairy Sci. Abstr.; EMBASE; Energy Inf. Abstr.; Energy Res. Abstr.; Environ. Abstr.; Food Sci. Technol. Abstr.; Foods Adlibra; Health Plan. Adminis.; Hortic. Abstr.; Index Med. (1980-); Index Sci. Rev. [Full Cov.]; INIS Atomindex [Micro.]; Maize Abstr.; Nutr. Abstr. Rev., Ser. A, Hum. Exp.; Life Sci. Collect.; Plant Breed. Abstr.; Postharvest News Inf.; Res. Alert [Full Cov.]; Sci. Cit. Index; Soc. Sci. Cit. Index [Select. Cov.]; Sug. Indus. Abstr.; Vitis Vitic. Enol. Abstr.; Wheat Barley Trit. Abstr.

US/1041-3081
CROWLEY REVIEW. Vol. 1, No. 1 (May 7, 1987)-. Newspaper. English. Fifty-two times a year (every Thursdays). $13.50 Johnson & Tarrant counties in Texas; $16.00 Texas; $19.50 other. Burleson Publishing Company, 319 North Burleson Boulevard, Burleson TX 76028. **Tel** (817)295-0486. **(Subscription address:** Burleson & Star, PO Drawer 909, Burleson, TX 76097) **ED** Nancy Huckaby, (editor's address: PO Box 300, Crowley, TX 76036). **Ad Acc, Adv Mgr:** Cathy Smith, **Tel** (817)295-0486. **Circ:** 3,500.

US/0277-1268
CSM'S ... EQUIPMENT BUYERS' GUIDE FOR THE FOOD INDUSTRY. **VFOAT** Equipment Buyers' Guide for the Food Industry; Convenience Store Merchandiser's ... Equipment Buyers' Guide; EBG Industry. **VAT** Convenience Store Merchandiser's ... Equipment Buyers' Guide for the Food Industry. 1979-. Consumer Publication. English. an. Associated Business Publishing Inc, 41 East 42nd Street/Suite 921, New York NY 10017. **Tel** (212)490-3999. **LC** HF5469.25; .C8. **DD** 680.

FR/1165-4651
CT INFOS PARIS. (CT INFOS.). **VFOAT** Centre Technique Infos (Paris). (1993)-. Periodical. French. bm (6 issues). 710.00F. CTCPA, 44 rue d'Alesia, 75682 Paris Cedex 14 France. **Tel** 011 33 1 43213821, FAX 011 33 1 43212352. **ED** C. Divin. **UDC** 577(44). **Bk Rev. Circ:** 1,000. ***Continues*** *Bulletin Analytique - CTCPA, 1167-9603.*

CU/0590-2916
CUBA AZUCAR. [Cuba azucar]. Vol. 1 (Jan./Feb. 1966)-. Academic Scholarly Publication. Multiple languages (English and Spanish). qt. 23.89Can$ North and South America; 28.83Can$ other. Ediciones Cubanas, Obispo 527, Altos ESQ Bernaza, CP 10100 Havana Cuba. **Tel** 011 632980, 631942, FAX 011 631011, telex 512337, 6540. **CODEN** CUAZAZ. Documents available from CASDDS.
Ind/Abst Chem. Abstr.; Food Sci. Technol. Abstr.; Sug. Indus. Abstr.

FR/0045-9208
CUISINE COLLECTIVE. (April 1960)-. French. Ten times a year. 100.00F (1 year), 150.00F (2 year) France; 200.00F (1 year), 300.00F (2 year) other. Cuisine Collective, 22 24 rue du President Wilson, F-92300 Levllois Perret France. **Tel** 011 33 1 47393481, FAX 011 33 1 47393479.

FR
CUISINE DE AAZ. Periodical. French. Editions du Hennin, BP 26, F 77932 Perthes Cedex France. **Tel** 011 33 1 64380328.

FR
CUISINEWS. Cuisinews, 11 rue Dulong, F 75017 Paris France.

US
CUKORIPAR. **Added/Corp** Mezogazdasagi- es Elelmiszeripari Tudomanyos Egyesulet. Cukoripari Szakosztaly. (1948)-. Periodical. Hungarian (summaries and/or abstracts in German and Russian). qt. $14.00. Delta Szaklapkiado, 1093 Budapest IX Kozraktar U 4 Hungary. **Tel** 632 000, telex 22-4677. **(Subscription address:** Kultura, PO Box 149, H-1389, Budapest 62 Hungary 8) **ED** Albert Vigh. **LC** Microfilm 04103TP; TP375. **Bk Rev. Circ:** 1,400. Documents available from CASDDS.
Desc: Advanced methods of growing and recent development of sugar production to the technical staff of the factories.
Ind/Abst Chem. Abstr.; Nutr. Abstr. Rev., Ser. B, Live Feeds and Feed.; Plant Genet. Resour. Abstr.; Sug. Indus. Abstr.

US/1057-3453
CULINARY TRENDS. [Culin. trends]. (1990)-. Periodical. English. qt. $21.60 US; $27.60 Canada and Mexico; $31.60 other. Culinary Trends, 6285 East Spring Street #107, Long Beach CA 90808. **Tel** (213)496-2558. **LC** TX901; .C85. **DD** 647.95/05.
Ind/Abst Foods Adlibra.

US/0270-0352
CUMULATIVE INDEX - FOOD MARKETING INSTITUTE, INFORMATION SERVICE. ***Title Change.*** [Cumul. index - Food Mark. Inst., Inf. Serv.]. **Main/Corp** Food Marketing Institute. Information Service. English. an. Karen Bonz, Index Service Coordinator, The Information Service, Food Marketing Institute, 303 East Ohio Street, Chicago IL 60611. **Tel** (202)452-8444. **ED** Barbara L McBride. **LC** HD9001; .F63A. **DD** 381/.456413/00973. **Circ:** 300. ***Continued by*** *Reference Point. Cumulative Index.*
Desc: A compilation of abstracts of all major articles on food distribution which appear in trade, business, and government publications; classified by subject.

US/0882-7915
CURRENTS (CHAPEL HILL, N.C.). **See** Nutrition and Dietetics.

US
DAILY MARKET REPORT - NEW YORK COFFEE AND SUGAR EXCHANGE. **Main/Corp** New York Coffee and Sugar Exchange. July 1, 1976-. Periodical. English. da. New York Coffee &

Sugar Exchange, 4 World Trade Center/8th Floor, New York NY 10048. **Tel** (212)938-2800. ***Formed by the union of*** *Daily Market Report, Coffee* ***and*** *Daily Market Report, Sugar.*

US/1043-3546
DAIRY, FOOD AND ENVIRONMENTAL SANITATION. (DAIRY, FOOD, AND ENVIRONMENTAL SANITATION : A PUBLICATION OF THE INTERNATIONAL ASSOCIATION OF MILK, FOOD AND ENVIRONMENTAL SANITARIANS.). [Dairy food environ. sanit.]. **Added/Corp** International Association of Milk, Food, and Environmental Sanitarians. Vol. 9, No. 1 (Jan. 1989)-. Periodical. English. mo. $120.00, $205.00 (combined with Journal of Food Protection) US; $142.50, $250.00 (combined with Journal of Food Protection) other. IAMFES, 6200 Aurora Avenue, Suite 200W, Des Moines IA 50322. **Tel** (515)276-3344, (800)369-6337, FAX (515)276-8655. **LC** SF257; .D34. **DD** 363. **NLM** W1; DA239F. **CODEN** DFESEC. available on microfilm and microfiche from University Microfilms International (UMI). ***Continues*** *Dairy and Food Sanitation, 0273-2866.*
Ind/Abst AgBiotech News Inf.; AGRICOLA [Full Cov.]; Agric. Eng. Abstr. (1991-); BioBusiness (1989-); Biodeter. Abstr. (1991-); Dairy Sci. Abstr.; Food Sci. Technol. Abstr.; Index Vet.; Poult. Abstr.; Rev. Med. Vet. Mycology.

US
DAIRY INDUSTRY NEWSLETTER. ***Title Change.*** **See** Agriculture-Dairy Industry.

US/0011-7862
DELI NEWS. **Added/Corp** Delicatessen Council of Southern California. (19??)-. Periodical. English. Twelve times a year. $25.00. Delicatessen Council of Southern California, 12631 Imperial Highway, Suite 215 A, Santa Fe Springs CA 90670-4753. **Tel** (310)929-6788, FAX (213)929-1978. **ED** Robert A. Boyajian. **Ad Acc. Circ:** 6,000 (ctrl).
Desc: Dedicated to food industry news, company profiles, personal profiles, opinion, commentary, new products, broker news and more.

US
DELICIOUS MAGAZINE. English. mo. $20.00. New Hope Communications, PO Box 600, Boulder CO 80306. **Tel** (303)939-8440, FAX (303)939-9559. **ED** Sue Frederick. **Ad Acc, Adv Mgr:** Rick Prill. **Circ:** 250,000.
Desc: A monthly magazine that urges health conscious people to take responsibility for their health and well-being. Provides medical and scientific research that motivates readers to make healthy choices for themselves and their families.

JA/0021-5406
DENPUN KAGAKU. **Added/Corp** Nihon Denpun Gakkai. **VFOAT** Journal of the Japanese Society of Starch Science. Vol. 19, No. 1 (1972)-. Academic Scholarly Publication. Japanese (English). qt. $110.00. Nihon Denpun Gakkai, c/o National Food Research Institute, Kannondai 2-1-2 Tsukuba-shi 305 Japan. **Tel** 810298-38-8053. **(Subscription address:** Kyowa Book Company Inc., 1-38 Kanda Jinbo-Cho, Chiyoda-Ku Tokyo 101, Japan) **ED** Susumu Hizukuri. **LC** QP702.S75; D45. **CODEN** DPNKAV. **Bk Rev. Ad Acc. Circ:** 1,200 (ctrl). Documents available from CASDDS. ***Continues*** *Denpun Kogyo Gakkai Shi.*
Desc: Publishes original papers on starch (and related carbohydrates), chemistry and enzymology.
Ind/Abst Chem. Abstr.; Food Sci. Technol. Abstr.; Maize Abstr.; Plant Breed. Abstr.; Sug. Indus. Abstr.

US/1072-639X
DESSERTS!. ***Title Change.*** (1991)-(1993). English. qt. House of White Birches, 306 East Parr Road, Berne IN 46711. **Tel** (219)589-8741, FAX (219)589-8093. **ED** Judi K. Merkel. **Circ:** 21,529. ***Continued by*** *Recipe Digest.*
Desc: Contains easy-to-fix dessert recipes for all occasions.

GW/0046-0117
DEUTSCHE BACKERZEITUNG. [Dtsch. Backerztg.]. **VFOAT** DBZ. Deutsche Backerzeitung. (1970)-. Periodical. German. wk. DM270.10 Germany; DM378.10 other. Deutscher Baecker Verlag GmbH, Bergstr 79/81, Postfach 102050, D-44720 Bochum Germany. **Tel** 011 49 234 51841, 51842. **UDC** 664.6.
Ind/Abst Food Sci. Technol. Abstr.

GW/0720-1206
DEUTSCHE LEBENSMITTEL-EINZELHANDEL IM SPIEGEL DER STATISTIK, DER. [Dtsch. Lebensm.-Einzelhand. Spieg. Stat.]. (1974)-. German. an. Hauptyerband des Deutschen Lebensmittel-Einzelhandels E V, Heilsbachstr 15, W-5300 Bonn 1 Germany. **Tel** (02 28) 64 30 36. **UDC** (663/664:339.37):31. Index available.

GW/0012-0413
DEUTSCHE LEBENSMITTEL-RUNDSCHAU. [Dtsch. Lebensm.-Rundsch.]. **Added/Corp** Bund Deutscher Lebensmittel-Fabrikanten u.- Handler fuer Lebensmittelkunde und Lebensmittelrecht. Wirtschaftsgruppe Lebensmittelindustrie. Vol. 1 (1903)-. Academic Scholarly Publication. German (English). mo. DM218.40. Wissenschaftliche Verlagsgesellschaft mbH, Postfach 101061, D 70009 Stuttgart Germany. **Tel** 011 49 711 258200, FAX 011 49 711 2582290, telex 723636 DAZ D. **ED** K. G. Bergner. **LC** HD9013.1; .D4. **DD** 381/.41/505. **CODEN** DLRUAJ. **[CCC].** Index available. **Bk Rev. Ad Acc. Pr Rev. Circ:** 1,700 (ctrl). Documents available from The Genuine Article, BIOSIS Document Express, CASDDS.
Desc: Publishes articles on food chemistry, food technology, and food law.
Ind/Abst AGRICOLA; Anal. Abstr.; Anim. Breed. Abstr.; Biodeter. Abstr. (19??-19??); Biol. Abstr.; Chem. Abstr.; Curr. Aware. Biol. Sci., CABS; Curr. Contents, Agric. Biol. Environ. Sci.; Dairy Sci. Abstr.; EMBASE; Energy Res. Abstr.; Food Sci. Technol. Abstr.; Hortic. Abstr.; Index Vet.; Int. Packag. Abstr.; Leadscan; Maize Abstr.; Nucl. Sci. Abstr.; Nutr. Abstr. Rev., Ser. A, Hum. Exp.; Life Sci. Collect.; Pig News Inf.; Postharvest News Inf.; Poult. Abstr.; Res. Alert [Full Cov.]; Rev. Med. Vet. Mycology; Sci. Cit. Index; SCISEARCH; Soc. Sci. Cit. Index [Select. Cov.]; Soyabean Abstr.; Sug. Indus. Abstr.; Vet. Bull.; Vitis Vitic. Enol. Abstr.; Wheat Barley Trit. Abstr.

UK/0262-1606
DEVELOPMENTS IN FOOD COLOURS... . [Dev. food colours]. (1980)-. Academic Scholarly Publication. English. Elsevier Science Publishing Company Inc, Madison Square Station, PO Box 882, New York NY 10159-0882. **Tel** (212)633-3950, FAX (212)633-3990. **CODEN** DFOCDD. Documents available from CASDDS.
Ind/Abst Chem. Abstr.

UK/0263-3752
DEVELOPMENTS IN FOOD PACKAGING. **See** Packaging.

UK/0263-4376
DEVELOPMENTS IN FOOD PRESERVATION. [Dev. food preserv.]. (1981)-. English. ir. £71.00 (latest edition). Chapman & Hall, 2-6 Boundary Row, London SE1 8HN England. **Tel** 011 44 71 865 0066, FAX 011 44 71 522 9623, telex 290164 Chapmag. **LC** TP368; .D47. **DD** 664/.028/05. **CODEN** DEFPDY. Documents available from CASDDS.
Ind/Abst AGRICOLA [Select. Cov.]; Chem. Abstr. (1981-1983).

UK/0263-3728
DEVELOPMENTS IN FOOD PRESERVATIVES. [Dev. food preserv.]. 1-. Academic Scholarly Publication. English. ir. $48.75. Elsevier Science Publishers Ltd, Crown House, Linton Road, Barking Essex IG11 8JU England. **Tel** 011 44 81 5947272, FAX 081-594-5942, telex 896950. **ED** R H Tilbury. **NLM** W1; DE997VXDD. **CODEN** DFOPDI. Documents available from CASDDS.
Ind/Abst Chem. Abstr. (1980).

UK/0263-4708
DEVELOPMENTS IN FOOD PROTEINS. [Dev. food proteins]. (1982)-. Academic Scholarly Publication. English. ir. $101.00. Routledge Chapman & Hall Inc, 29 West 35th Street, New York NY 10001. **Tel** (212)244-3336, (212)244-6412. **ED** B.J.F. Hudson. **LC** TX553.P7; D48. **DD** 641.1/2/05. **NLM** W1; DE997VXH. **CODEN** DVFPDH. Documents available from BIOSIS Document Express, CASDDS.
Ind/Abst AGRICOLA [Full Cov.]; Biol. Abstr.; Chem. Abstr.

NE/0167-4501
DEVELOPMENTS IN FOOD SCIENCE. [Dev. food sci.]. (1978)-. Academic Scholarly Publication. English. ir. Price varies per volume. Elsevier Science Publishers BV, PO Box 211, 1000 AE Amsterdam Netherlands. **Tel** 011 31 20 5803642, FAX 011 31 20 5862696, telex 15682. **NLM** W1 DE997VY. **CODEN** DFSCDX. **[CCC].** Documents available from BIOSIS Document Express, CASDDS.
Ind/Abst AGRICOLA [Full Cov.]; Biol. Abstr. (1985-); Chem. Abstr.; Crop Physiol. Abstr.; Curr. Biotechnol.; Dairy Sci. Abstr.; Food Sci. Technol. Abstr.; Hortic. Abstr.; Ornamental Hort. (1991-); Postharvest News Inf.

UK/0144-8811
DEVELOPMENTS IN MEAT SCIENCE. [Dev. meat sci.]. (1980)-. Academic Scholarly Publication. English. ir. Price varies per volume. Routledge Chapman & Hall Inc, 29 West 35th Street, New York NY 10001. **Tel** (212)244-3336, (212)244-6412. **LC** TS1960; .D48. **DD** 664/.9/005. **CODEN** DMSCDE. Documents available from CASDDS.
Ind/Abst Chem. Abstr.

UK/0950-6438
DEVELOPMENTS IN SWEETENERS. [Dev sweeteners]. (1979)-. Monographic series. English. ir. Price varies per volume. Elsevier Science Publishers BV, PO Box 211, 1000 AE Amsterdam Netherlands. **Tel** 011 31 20 5803642, FAX 011 31 20 5862696, telex 15682. **LC** TP421; .D49. **DD** 664.5.

US/0885-159X
DICKINSON'S FDA. ***Title Change.*** **See** Public Administration.

US/1063-2433
DICKINSON'S FDA INSPECTION. ***Title Change.*** **See** Public Administration.

●US/1073-4414
DICKINSON'S FDA REVIEW. **See** Public Administration.

US/0737-7703
DIGEST - UNIVERSITY OF PENNSYLVANIA. DEPT. OF FOLKLORE AND FOLKLIFE, THE. (THE DIGEST.). [Digest - Univ. Pa., Dept. Folk. Folklife]. **Added/Corp** University of Pennsylvania. Dept. of Folklore and Folklife. Vol. 1, No. 1 (Nov. 1977)-. Periodical. English. Three times a year. $9.00 US; $12.00 other. Subscription Manager of The Digest, Department of Folklore/Folklife, 415 Logan Hall, CN University of Pennsylvania, Philadelphia PA 19104. **Tel** (215)898-7352. **ED** Kathy Neustadt. **LC** GT2850; .D53. **DD** 394.1/05. Index available. **Bk Rev. Circ:** 200.
Desc: A clearinghouse for people interested in the study of food and culture, from diverse points of view, anthropological, historical, gastronomic, etc.

VE
DIRECTORIO INDUSTRIAL AZUCARERO. 1972-. Spanish. Bs50.00. Edificio Luz Electrica de Venezuela, Piso 7 Ave Urdaneta, Esquina de Urapal, Venezuela. **LC** HD9114.V4; D5.

US/0271-7662
DIRECTORY OF FOOD SERVICE DISTRIBUTORS (BUSINESS GUIDES, INC.). (DIRECTORY OF FOOD SERVICE DISTRIBUTORS). [Dir. food serv. distrib.]. **VFOAT** Food Service Distributors; Directory of Foodservice Distributors. (1980)-. Directory. English. an. $89.00. Lebhar Friedman Inc., 3922 Coconut Palm Drive, Tampa FL 33619. **Tel** (800)927-9292, (813)664-6707. **(Subscription address:** 3922 Coconut Palm Drive, Tampa, FL 33619) **ED** Jim Smethurst. **LC** HD9321.3; .D53. **DD** 380.1/456838/02573. Index available. ctrl circ. ***Continues*** *Food Service Distributors, 0091-9152.*
Desc: Provides complete company profiles on 4,000 distributors who supply food, equipment, supplies to restaurants and institutional accounts.

US
DIRECTORY OF MAJOR U.S. CORPORATIONS INVOLVED IN AGRIBUSINESS. **See** Agriculture.

US/0896-2162
DIRECTORY OF SINGLE-UNIT SUPERMARKET OPERATORS. [Dir. single-unit supermark. oper.]. **Added/Corp** Business Guides, Inc. **VFOAT** Chain Store Guide; Single-Unit Supermarket Operators. **VAT** Directory of Single Unit Supermarket Operators; Single Unit Supermarket Operators. (1989)-. Directory. English. an. $224.00 Continental US; $234.00 Alaska, Hawaii, Puerto Rico, Mexico & Canada; $249.00 other. Lebhar Friedman Inc., 3922 Coconut Palm Drive, Tampa FL 33619. **Tel** (800)927-9292, (813)664-6707. **LC** HF5469.23.U6; D57. **DD** 381/.45664/002573.
Desc: Information on supermarkets and the grocery trade.

US/0196-1845
DIRECTORY OF SUPERMARKET, GROCERY, AND CONVENIENCE STORE CHAINS. **VFOAT** Directory of Supermarket, Grocery and Convenience Store Chains; Chain Store Guide; Guide to the Supermarket and Grocery Chains; Supermarket and Grocery Chains; Supermarket. (1981)-. Directory. English. an. $290.00 continental US; $300.00 Alaska, Hawaii; $315.00 other. Lebhar Friedman Inc., 3922 Coconut Palm Drive, Tampa FL 33619. **Tel** (800)927-9292, (813)664-6707. **ED** Jim Smithurst. **LC** HD9321.3; .C43. **DD** 381/.45664/002573. Index available. ctrl circ. ***Continues*** *Directory of Supermarket, Grocery, and Convenience Store Chains, 0196-1845.*
Desc: Provides company profiles on 3,700 or more store chains operating 75,000 units.

US/0419-3717
DIRECTORY OF THE CANNING, FREEZING, PRESERVING INDUSTRIES, THE. 1st Ed., (1967)-. Directory. English. an (June). $135.00 (two years). Edward E. Judge & Sons Inc., PO Box 866, Westminster MD 21158. **Tel** (301)876-2052, (800)729-5517, FAX (301)848-2034. **ED** Daniel P. Judge. **LC** TX600; .D55. **DD** 338.4/7/664.
Desc: Lists over 2,600 United States and Canadian plants operated by over 2,200 companies processing canned, frozen, dehydrated foods. Provides full information, including personnel and factory locations and products, by alphabetical, geographical, product and brand listings. Includes 17 page index of over 3,500 products.

UK/0951-7812
DIY SUPERSTORE. [Diy superst.]. **VFOAT** Do it Yourself Superstore. (1981)-. Periodical. English. mo. £40.00 UK; £60.00. Faversham House Group Ltd,

Faversham House, 111 Saint James Road, Croydon Surrey CR9 2TH England. **Tel** 011 44 81 684 4082. **DD** 338.47684080941.

GW/0938-9369
DMZ, LEBENSMITTELINDUSTRIE UND MILCHWIRTSCHAFT. VFOAT DMZ; Magazine for Food and Dairy Industry; Journal d'Industrie Alimentaire et de Laiterie. **VAT** Deutsche Molkerei-Zeitung Lebensmittelindustrie und Milchwirtschaft. (Jan. 1990)-. Periodical. German. wk. ***Continues*** *Deutsche Molkerei-Zeitung (Munich, Germany : 1951).*

BL/0101-5494
DOCUMENTOS / EMPRESA BRASILEIRA DE PESQUISA AGROPECUARIA, VINCULADA AO MINISTERIO DA AGRICULTURA, CENTRO NACIONAL DE PESQUISA DE SOJA. See Agriculture-Crop Production and Soil.

XV
DRUZBENA PREHRANA. Main/Corp Zavod Sr Slovenije Za Statistiko. 1976-. Slovenian. an. Zavod Sr Slovenije za Statistiko, Vozarski Pot 12, Ljubljana Slovenia. **LC** TX946.5.A1; S552A.

GW/0722-6950
DYNAMIK IM HANDEL 1982. (1982)-. Periodical. German. mo (12 issues). DM250.70. Deutsches Handelsinstitut GmbH, Spichernstrasse 55, W 5000 Cologne 1 Germany. **Tel** 011 49 221 579930. **UDC** 658.628. **CODEN** 381.

UK/0965-0717
EC FOOD LAW. See Law.

HU/0013-0842
EDESIPAR. [Edesipar]. **Added/Corp** Magyar Elelmiszeripari Tudomanyos Egyesulet. Edesipari Szakosztalya. Vol. 27, No. 2 (1976)-. Periodical. Hungarian (summaries and/or abstracts in German, Russian and Hungarian). qt. $18.00. Lapkiado Vallalat, Lenin Korut 9-11, 1073 Budapest 7, Hungary. **Tel** 222-408. **(Subscription address:** Kultura, PO Box 149, H 1389 Budapest 62 Hungary.**) ED** S. Szanto. **CODEN** EDESA5. **Ad Acc. Circ:** 725.
Desc: Contains confectionery information.
Ind/Abst AGRICOLA; Food Sci. Technol. Abstr.

UK
EDIBLE NUT STATISTICS. English. an. £30.00. Gill & Duffus Group PLC, 201 Borough High Street, St Dunstan, London SE1 1HW England.

UK
EEC FOOD LEGISLATION MANUAL. English. (updated twice a year). £180.00. British Food Manufacturing Industries Research Association, Randalls Road, Leatherhead Surrey KT22 7RY England. **Tel** 011 44 372 376761, FAX 011 44 372 386228, telex 929846.

US/0148-9828
EGG MARKETING GUIDE. [Egg mark guide]. **Main/Corp** United States. Consumer and Marketing Service. Government Publication. English. sa. US Department of Agriculture, 14th Street and Independence Avenue SW, Washington DC 20250. **Tel** (202)720-5457. **LC** HD9284.U4; U55A. **DD** 338.1/7/7540973.

UA/0378-2700
EGYPTIAN JOURNAL OF DAIRY SCIENCE. [Egyptian j. dairy science]. **Added/Corp** Egyptian Society of Dairy Science. Vol. 1, (June 1973)-. Academic Scholarly Publication. English (summaries and/or abstracts in Arabic). Twice a year (June and December). $45.00. Egyptian Society of Dairy Science, National Research Center/Dokki, Cairo Egypt. **Tel** 011 20 2 701211 415, FAX 700931, telex 94022 NAREC ON. **ED** M. H. Abad El-Salam. **CODEN** EJDSDB. **Bk Rev. Ad Acc. Pr Rev. Circ:** 400. Documents available from CASDDS.
Desc: Research papers in the areas of processing milk products and milk production.
Ind/Abst AGRICOLA; Anim. Breed. Abstr.; Biodeter. Abstr. (19??-19??); Chem. Abstr.; Dairy Sci. Abstr.; Food Sci. Technol. Abstr.; Nutr. Abstr. Rev., Ser. B, Live Feeds and Feed.; Nutr. Abstr. Rev., Ser. A, Hum. Exp.; Poult. Abstr.; Rev. Agric. Entomol.; Rev. Med. Vet. Entomol.; Rice Abstr.; Soyabean Abstr.

UA/0301-8571
EGYPTIAN JOURNAL OF FOOD SCIENCE. Added/Corp Jamiyat Ulum wa-TiknulujiyÂa al-Aghdhiyah. **VFOAT** Majallah Al-Misriyah Li-Ulum Al-Aghdhiyah. Vol. 1 (1973)-. Periodical. English (summaries and/or abstracts in Arabic). ir. $75.00 (latest volume). National Information & Documentation Center, A1-Tahrir St Dokki AGWAF, Cairo Egypt. **Tel** 011 20 2 701696, telex 93069. **LC** TX341; .E38. **DD** 641.1/05. **NLM** W1 EG913KT. **CODEN** EJFSAI. Documents available from CASDDS.
Ind/Abst Biodeter. Abstr. (1991-); Chem. Abstr.; Dairy Sci. Abstr.; Food Sci. Technol. Abstr.; Hortic. Abstr.; Postharvest News Inf.; Rev. Agric. Entomol.; Rev. Med. Vet. Entomol.; Rev. Med. Vet. Mycology; Wheat Barley Trit. Abstr.

HU/0422-9576
ELELMISZERVIZSGALATI KOZLEMENYEK. [Elelmiszervizsg. kozl.]. (1955)-. Periodical. Hungarian (summaries and/or abstracts in English, French, German and Russian). bm. Lapkiado Vallalat, Lenin Korut 9-11, 1073 Budapest 7, Hungary. **Tel** 222-408. **NLM** W1 EL453T. **CODEN** EMKZAH. Documents available from CASDDS.
Ind/Abst AGRICOLA; Chem. Abstr.; Food Sci. Technol. Abstr.

FI/0785-0522
ELINTARVIKETEOLLISUUS. VFOAT Livsmedelsindustri. Finnish (Swedish). an. Tilastokeskus, PL 504, Annankatu 44, 00101 Helsinki Finland. **Tel** 358-0-17341, FAX 358-0-17342474, telex 1002111 TILASTO SF. **LC** HD9015.F5; E46.

US/1050-2688
EMERGING FOOD R & D REPORT. [Emerg. food R D rep.]. **Added/Corp** Food Technology Intelligence (Firm). **VFOAT** Emerging Food R and D Report. **VAT** Emerging Food Research & Development Report; Emerging Food Research and Development Report. Vol. 1, No. 1 (Apr. 1990)-. Periodical. English. mo. $365.00 (one year), $630.00 (two year). Food Technology Intelligence, PO Box 322, 215 Goodwin Avenue, Midland Park NJ 07432. **Tel** (201)445-4227, FAX (201)447-5904. **ED** Joseph Constance. **DD** 664. **CODEN** EFRREH. Index available.
Desc: Covers food research and development with the intent of promoting technology transfer.
Ind/Abst Foods Adlibra.

US
EMPIRE STATE FOOD SERVICE NEWS. VFOAT Food Service News. (19??)-. Periodical. English. mo. $24.00. Empire State Food Service News, PO Box 89, Skaneateles NY 13152. **Tel** (315)497-1750. ***Continues*** *Food Industry News.*

BL/0100-7947
ENGARRAFADOR MODERNO. [Engarrafador Mod.]. Academic Scholarly Publication. Portuguese. Engarrafador Moderno, rua Marcos Fernandes 977, Cep 04149 Sao Paulo Brasil. **CODEN** ENMOD4. Documents available from CASDDS.
Ind/Abst Chem. Abstr. (1979-1982).

CN/0826-4546
ENTREFILET (POINTE CLAIRE). (L'ENTREFILET.). [Entrefilet]. **Added/Corp** Centre d'Information sur le Boeuf. Vol. 1, No. 1 (Winter 1983)-. Periodical. French (English). Four times a year (Seasonally). 7.50Can$. L'Entrefilet, 110, rue del la Barre, #214, Longueuil, Quebec J4K 1A3 Canada. **DD** 641.3/6. Index available. cum. index. **Pr Rev. Circ:** 9,000 (ctrl).
Desc: Publication which studies topics relating to meat and meat consumption.

CN/0013-9521
EPICIER (MONTREAL). ***Ceased.*** (L'EPICIER.). (1946)-(19??). Periodical. French. ir. Maclean Hunter Canada / Montreal, 1001 bvd. de Maisonneuve W., Montreal, Quebec H3A 3E1 Canada. **Tel** 514-845-5141, FAX 514-845-4302, telex 055-60604. **ED** Benoit Dutrisae. **Ad Acc. Circ:** 12,000 (ctrl).
Desc: Serves the food distribution and food retailing industry in the province of Quebec.
Ind/Abst Infomat Int. Bus.

GW/0174-0008
ERNAHRUNGS-UMSCHAU 1977. [Ernahr.-Umsch.1977]. (1977)-. Periodical. German. mo. DM150.00 Germany; DM159.00 other. Umschau Verlag, Postfach 110262, D-60037 Frankfurt Germany. **Tel** 011 49 69 2600692, FAX 011 49 69 2600223, telex 411964. **UDC** 613.2. ***Formed by the union of*** *Ernahrungs-Umschau. Ausgabe B, 0340-2371* ***and*** *Ernahrungs-Umschau. Ausgabe M, 0340-2320.*
Ind/Abst Index Vet.

GW
ERNAHRUNGSWIRTSCHAFT. ***Title Change.*** **Added/Corp** Bundesvereinigung der Deutschen Ernahrungsindustrie. (????)-(19??). Periodical. German. mo. Rhenania-Fachverlag GmbH, Postfach 60 1220, W-2000 Hamburg 11 Germany. **Tel** 40/2717-3600. **ED** Herr Hermann. **Bk Rev. Ad Acc. Circ:** 6,335. ***Continued by*** *EW Ernaehrungswirtschaft, 0179-8812.*
Desc: Forum for experience and exchange of ideas and options from experts of all aspects of the production of food and drink.
Ind/Abst Food Sci. Technol. Abstr.

GW/0721-9776
ESSEN & TRINKEN. VFOAT Essen und Trinken. (1971)-. Periodical. German. mo. $70.00. Gruner und Jahr Ag & Co, Abonnenten Service, D 20080 Hamburg Germany. **Tel** 011 49 40 37030. **(Subscription address:** US: German Language Publications, Inc., 153 South Deanstreet, Englewood, NJ 07631**) UDC** 641/642.

FR
EURO VIANDE. French. Euro Viande, 34 rue Laroche, 33000 Bordeaux France.

IT/0394-2910
EUROCARNI. [Eurocarni]. (1986)-. Periodical. Multiple languages. mo. L72000 Italy; L120000 other. Pubblicita Italia Sas, Via Taglio 24, 41100 Modena Italy. **Tel** 011 39 59 216688. **UDC** 637.5.

UK/0955-5404
EUROFOOD. English. mo. £195.00 UK; £505.00 Europe; £215.00 other. Agra Europe London Limited, 25 Frant Road, Tunbridge Wells, Kent TN2 5JT England. **Tel** 011 44 892 533813. **ED** Janet Nunn. Index available. cum. index. available on an online database (file 16/Full-Text) from DIALOG.
Desc: The monthly newsletter for the European food and drink industry. Company news, Brussels report, political scene, special features and new EC legislation.
Ind/Abst F&S Index Plus Text, Int. [Full Txt.] [Select. Cov.]; PROMT [Full Txt.].

UK/0960-7943
EUROFOOD MONITOR. English. sa. £480.00 UK and Europe; £540.00 other. Agra Europe London Limited, 25 Frant Road, Tunbridge Wells, Kent TN2 5JT England. **Tel** 011 44 892 533813.
Desc: An information service for the food industry. Gives complete consolidated text of European Community directives and amendments on foodstuffs as published in the Official Journal.

UK
EUROPEAN BAKER. (19??)-. Trade Publication. English. qt. £20.00 UK and Europe; £30.00 other. EMAP Readerlink, Audit House, 260 Field End Road, Ruislip Middlesex HA4 9LT England. **Tel** 011 44 081 868 4499, FAX 011 44 081 429 3117. **(Subscription address:** EMAP Business Publishing, Ferrari House Audit House, Field End, Ruislip Middlesex HA4 9UY England.**)**

UK/0955-4416
EUROPEAN FOOD AND DRINK REVIEW. [Eur. food drink rev.]. (1989)-. Periodical. English. qt. $135.00. Euromoney Publications PLC, Nestor House, Playhouse Yard, London EC4Z 5EX England. **Tel** 011 44 71 779 8888, FAX 011 44 71 779 8617, telex 290700 EUROMON G. **DD** 664.0094.
Desc: Review of this vital manufacturing industry developed to provide European food manufacturers with the latest in developments in food ingredients, process technology, analysis and control, packaging and transportation and storage.
Ind/Abst Dairy Sci. Abstr.; Index Vet.; Nutr. Abstr. Rev., Ser. A, Hum. Exp.

US
EUROPEAN GOURMET: THE GRAND DINING TOUR OF EUROPE, THE. (1992)-. English. an. $22.95. European Gourmet, 331 West 57th Street, No. 379, New York NY 10019-3101. **Tel** (800)523-5503. **ED** D. Easton. **Ad Acc. Circ:** 100,000. available with illustrations.
Desc: An in-depth guide to Europe's restaurants. Selections are conducted by a panel of five American food reviewers and experts.

UK/0142-937X
EUROPEAN SUPPLIES BULLETIN / FISHERY ECONOMICS RESEARCH UNIT, WHITE FISH AUTHORITY. See Fish and Fisheries.

GW/0179-8812
EW. ERNAHRUNGSWIRTSCHAFT. [EW, Ernahr.wirtsch.]. **VFOAT** Ernahrungswirtschaft (Grafelfing. 1983). (1983)-. Periodical. German. ir. DM120.00 (Germany); DM140.00 (other). E Albrecht Verlags-KG, Freihamer Strasse 2 PF 1120, W-8032 Graefelfing Germany. **Tel** 49 89 858530. **UDC** 664. ***Continues*** *Ernahrungswirtschaft, 0014-0244;* ***Absorbed*** *EuroMagazin (Grafelfing), 0936-9775.*

CN/1180-3568
EXPOSURE (SASKATOON). (EXPOSURE.). [ExPOSure]. **Added/Corp** POS Pilot Plant Corp. **VFOAT** Ex-POS-Ure; Proteins, Oils and Starch. Vol. 1, No. 1 (May 1990)-. Periodical. English. qt. POS Pilot Plant Corporation, 118 Veterinary Road, Saskatoon, Saskatchewan S7N 2R4 Canada. **DD** 664/.00971.

UK/0958-0549
EXTRUSION COMMUNIQUE. [Extrus. commun.]. (1989)-. Periodical. English. Four times a year (Mar., June, Sept., Dec.). £25.00. Asbury Publications Ltd., Stoke Road, Bishops Cleeve, Gloucestershire 52 4RW England. **Tel** 011 44 242 676645, FAX 011 44 242 674032. **ED** R. Gilbert. **DD** 664. **Bk Rev**, (Qty: 4). **Ad Acc, Adv Mgr:** Ms. Taylor, **Tel** 011 44 242 676645. **Circ:** 9,500 (ctrl).
Desc: Focus on the hardware and the mechanics of extrusion cooking and processing of bio-polymers.
Ind/Abst Foods Adlibra.

US/1040-7537
F & B MARKETPLACE. See Business-Marketing.

US/0732-233X
FACTS ABOUT STORE DEVELOPMENT. [Facts store dev.]. **Added/Corp** Food Marketing Institute. Research Division. (19??)-. English. an (Published in August). $15.00 FMI members, $30.00 nonmembers. Food Marketing Institute, 1750 K Street Northwest, Washington DC 20006. **Tel** (202)452-8444. **(Subscription address:** Food Marketing Institute, 800 Connecticut Avenue Northwest, Washington DC 20006.) **LC** HF5469; .S88b. **DD** 381/.456413/00973. ***Continues*** *Food Marketing Institute. Facts about New Super Markets Opened, 0081-9522.*
Desc: Examines areas such as new store size, costs of building and opening new stores, store remodelings, rental and leasing data.
Ind/Abst Stat. Ref. Index.

US/1046-2880
FANCY FOOD. [Fancy food]. (19??)-. Periodical. English. mo. Talcott Communications Corporation, 20 North Wacker Drive, Suite 3230, Chicago IL 60606. **Tel** (312)664-4040. **DD** 664. **CODEN** FAFOEQ. ***Continues*** *Fancy Food & Candy.*
Ind/Abst Foods Adlibra.

US
FANCY FOOD. BUYERS GUIDE. **VFOAT** Buyers Guide. Consumer Publication. English. an. $10.00. 1414 Merchandise Mart, Chicago IL 60654. **LC** HD9320.1; .F34. **DD** 664.

IT
FAO-DOC CURRENT BIBLIOGRAPHY (MICROFORM). **Main/Corp** Food and Agriculture Organization of the United Nations. **VAT** Food and Agriculture Organization Documentation Current Bibliography. Began with issue for 1976/77. Bibliography. English. Food and Agriculture Organization (FAO) / Italy, GIPC166 via Terme di Caracalla, 00100 Rome Italy. **Tel** 011 39 6 522 52925, FAX 011 39 6 522 55784.

IT
FAO RESEARCH AND TECHNOLOGY PAPER. **VAT** Food and Agriculture Organization of the United Nations Research and Technology Paper. 1-1986-. Monographic series. English. ir. Price varies per volume. Food and Agriculture Organization (FAO) / Italy, GIPC166 via Terme di Caracalla, 00100 Rome Italy. **Tel** 011 39 6 522 52925, FAX 011 39 6 522 55784.

US/1059-2393
FBN (SPARTA, N.J.). (FBN [COMPUTER FILE].). **Added/Corp** Parker and Associates, Food Industry Consultants. **VAT** Food Byte News. (1991)-. Periodical. English. mo. $195.00. Parker and Associates Food Industry Consultants, 66 Woodport Road, Sparta NJ 07871. **DD** 338.
Desc: Online via Foodbytes Online System. Available in PC compatible or Amiga format.

●US/1069-5109
FDA NEWS. (FDA NEWS : DRUGS, COSMETICS, DEVICES, AND BIOLOGICS.). [FDA news]. **Added/Corp** Association of Food and Drug Officials. **VFOAT** Food and Drug Administration News. Vol. 1, No. 1 (July 1993)-. Periodical. English. mo. $190.00 (one year), $370.00 (two year), $50.00 (three year). Technomic Publishing Company, Inc., 851 New Holland Avenue, Box 3535, Lancaster PA 17604. **Tel** (717)291-5609, (800)233-9936, FAX (717)295-4538. **DD** 363. **[CCC].**

US/0363-2288
FEDERAL-STATE MARKET NEWS REPORTS. Government Publication. English. US Department of Agriculture / Agricultural Marketing Service / Washington, DC, Market News Branch, Fruit and Vegetable Division, Washington DC 20250. **Tel** (202)720-2745, (202)720-3343, FAX (202)720-7502. **LC** HD9003; .F43. **DD** 016.3801/41/072073.

IT
FILIERA CARNE. Italian. Six times a year. L42000.00 Italy; L55000.00 other. Essepiesse Srl, Via G Galilei 14, 20124 Milan Italy. **Tel** 011 39 2 29003781.

FR
FILIERE GOURMANDE. French. mo (10 issues). 416.26F France; 510.00F other. SEPP, 13 rue Ganneron, 75018 Paris France. **Tel** 011 33 1 42932243, FAX 011 33 1 42875024. ***Formed by the union of*** *Strategies Gourmande, 0299-7584* ***and*** *Filiere Farine.*

FR/1143-7375
FILIERES VIANDE ET PECHE LEVALLOIS-PERRET. ***Title Change.*** (FILIERE VIANDE ET PECHE.). (1990)-(1992). Periodical. French. Eleven times a year. CEP Communications Groupe LSA, 6 rue Marius Aufan, 92300 Levallois Perret France. **Tel** 011 33 1 47 582000, FAX 011 33 1 47 586070. **UDC** 636. ***Continues*** *Filiere Viande., 0182-0427.* ***Absorbed by*** *Produits Frais.*

●US
FIRST PLACE [COMPUTER FILE]. (Jan. 1992)-. Periodical. English. Twelve times a year. $895.00. Automated Catalogue Services, Inc., 487 Devon Park Drive, Suite 215, Wayne PA 19087. **Tel** (215)687-7500.
Desc: System requirements: IBM AT or XT, or compatible; MS-DOS or PC-DOS 3.1 or higher; Microsoft Windows; CD-ROM drive.

UK
FISH AND CHIPS AND FAST FOODS. English. qt. £21.20 UK; £23.98, $37.15 other. Argus Press Group, Queensway House, 2 Queensway Redhill, Surrey RH1 1QS England. **Tel** 011 44 737 768611, 011 44 737 761685, FAX 011 44 737 760510, telex 948669 TOPJNL G.

UK/0882-5734
FLAVOUR AND FRAGRANCE JOURNAL. [Flavour fragr. j.]. Vol. 1, No. 1 (Nov. 1985)-. Academic Scholarly Publication. English. Six times a year. $395.00. John Wiley & Sons Ltd., Baffins Lane, Chichester West Sussex PO19 1UD England. **Tel** 0243 779777, FAX 0243 776128 BTG:JWP001, telex 86290 WIBOOKG. **(Subscription address:** John Wiley / Philadelphia, PO Box 7247, Philadelphia PA 19170.) **ED** Roger Stevens. **LC** WMLC 93/1371. **DD** 152. **CODEN** FFJOED. **[CCC]. Bk Rev. Ad Acc. Circ:** 2,000. available on microfilm and microfiche from University Microfilms International (UMI). Documents available from BIOSIS Document Express, CASDDS.
Desc: Devoted to the rapid publication of scientific and technical papers on natural and synthetically derived flavours, fragrances and colouring agents used in foodstuffs. Its comprehensive coverage is reflected in the wide range of product types discussed, such as frangrances and their compositions, and the flavour, colours and odours of foodstuffs.
Ind/Abst AgBiotech News Inf.; Anal. Abstr.; Biodeter. Abstr.; Biol. Abstr. (1988-); Chem. Abstr. (1985-); Chemorecept. Abstr.; Crop Physiol. Abstr.; Curr. Aware. Biol. Sci., CABS; EMBASE; Field Crop Abstr.; Food Sci. Technol. Abstr.; Foods Adlibra; For. Prod. Abstr. (19??-19??); For. Abstr.; Hortic. Abstr.; Ornamental Hort. (1991-); Plant Breed. Abstr.; Plant Genet. Resour. Abstr.; Plant Grow. Reg. Abstr.; Rev. Med. Vet. Mycology; Seed Abstr.

GW/0015-3575
FLEISCH. [Fleisch]. (19??)-. Academic Scholarly Publication. German. mo. DM79.00 Germany; DM101.50 other. Verlag Karlheinz Holz, Rheingaustr 85, Postfach 3329, D-65023 Wiesbaden Germany. **Tel** 011 49 611 9450751, FAX 011 49 611 261124. **ED** Karlheinz Holz. **CODEN** FLCHAT. cum. index. **Ad Acc.** Documents available from CASDDS.
Ind/Abst AGRICOLA; Chem. Abstr. (1988-); Food Sci. Technol. Abstr.; Life Sci. Collect.; Pig News Inf.; World Agric. Econ.

GW/0015-3613
FLEISCHEREI. (DIE FLEISCHEREI.). [Fleischerei]. (1950)-. Periodical. German (English, French, Italian and Spanish). Twelve times a year. DM205.60 Germany; DM245.20 other. Hans Holzmann Verlag KG, Postfach 1342, D 86816 BD Woerishofen Germany. **Tel** 011 49 8247 35401. **ED** Fhia Mautes. **CODEN** FLEIEC. Index available. cum. index. **Bk Rev. Ad Acc. Pr Rev. Circ:** 8,200 (ctrl).
Desc: International magazine for meat processors in trade and industry.
Ind/Abst AGRICOLA; BioBusiness; Food Sci. Technol. Abstr.

US/0191-9857
FLORIDA FOOD DEALER. Periodical. English. mo. $12.00. Retail Grocers Association, 3500 East Silver Springs Boulevard/Suite 3, Ocala FL 32670.

US/0191-586X
FLORIDA GROCER. Vol. 1 (1956)-. Periodical. Multiple languages (English and Spanish). mo. $21.00. Florida Grocer Publishing Inc, PO Box 430760, South Miami FL 33243-0760. **Tel** (315)441-1138, FAX (305)661-6720. **ED** Dennis M Kane. **Bk Rev. Ad Acc. Circ:** 16,000.
Desc: A food trade newspaper serving the Florida food industry.

US
FLORIDA VEGETABLES. CABBAGE REPORT. **Added/Corp** Florida Crop and Livestock Reporting Service. **VFOAT** Cabbage Report. (19??)-. Periodical. English.

GW/0015-4539
FLUSSIGES OBST. [Fluss. obst]. **VFOAT** Liquifruit; Liquid Fruit. Vol. 1, No. 2 (Mar./Apr. 1930)-. Academic Scholarly Publication. German (English). mo. DM115.50. Verlag Flussiges Obst GmbH, Postfach 11, D 56370 Schoenborn Germany. **Tel** 011 49 6486 801618, telex 484802. **ED** Philipp Possmann. **CODEN** FLOBA3. Index available. cum. index. **Bk Rev. Ad Acc. Circ:** 2,000 (ctrl). Documents available from CASDDS.
Desc: Technical and marketing Information for fruit processing and fruit juice industry, developments, and news commentaries, etc.
Ind/Abst Chem. Abstr.; EMBASE; Energy Res. Abstr. (Oct. 1972-); Food Sci. Technol. Abstr.; Int. Packag. Abstr.; Life Sci. Collect.; Vitis Vitic. Enol. Abstr.

US/0275-8059
FMI ISSUES BULLETIN. **See** Business-Marketing.

US/0888-1332
FNP NEWSLETTER. FOOD INDUSTRY REPORT. [FNP newsl., Food ind. rep.]. **VFOAT** Food Industry Report. Vol. 1, No. 1 (Jan. 1984)-. Newsletter. English. mo (12 issues per volume). $60.00 US, Canada & Mexico; $80.00 other. Food & Nutrition Press Inc, 2 Corporate Drive, PO Box 374, Trumbull CT 06611. **Tel** (203)261-8587, FAX (203)261-9724. **ED** Samuel A. Matz. **DD** 338.

US/0160-8053
FNP NEWSLETTER : FOOD, NUTRITION AND HEALTH. **See** Nutrition and Dietetics.

US/0194-2980
FNP NEWSLETTER, FOOD PACKAGING AND LABELING. **See** Packaging.

US/0194-2972
FNP NEWSLETTER : PRICE TRENDS OF FOOD INGREDIENTS. ***Ceased.*** **VFOAT** Price Trends of Food Ingredients Newsletter. **VAT** Food and Nutrition Press Newsletter. Price Trends of Food Ingredients. Vol. 1, No. 1 (Jan. 1977)-(19??). Periodical. English. mo. Food & Nutrition Press Inc, 2 Corporate Drive, PO Box 374, Trumbull CT 06611. **Tel** (203)261-8587, FAX (203)261-9724.
Desc: Covers food prices and additives.

CN/0229-1770
FOCUS ON FOOD SERVICE. [Focus food serv.]. Vol. 1, No. 1 (Feb. 1981)-. Periodical. English. mo. $12.00 Canada $18.00 other countries. Kerry Hill Publications, 2425 Truscott Drive, Mississauga Ontario L5J 2B4 Canada. **DD** 338.4/7664/00971.

US
FOOD ADDITIVES ANALYTICAL MANUAL. **Main/Corp** United States. Food and Drug Administration. **VFOAT** FAAM. (1983)-. English. ir. US Food and Drug Administration / FDA, 5600 Fishers Lane, Room 14-71, Rockville MD 20857. **Tel** (301)443-2410, FAX (301)443-0755.

UK/0265-203X
FOOD ADDITIVES AND CONTAMINANTS. (FOOD ADDITIVES AND CONTAMINANTS : ANALYSIS, SURVEILLANCE, EVALUATION, CONTROL.). [Food addit. contam.]. Vol. 1, No. 1 (Jan.-Mar. 1984)-. Academic Scholarly Publication. English. bm. £272.00 UK; $449.00 other. Taylor & Francis Ltd., Rankine Road, Basingstoke Hampshire, RG24 8PR United Kingdom. **Tel** 011 44 256 840366, FAX 011 44 256 479438, telex 858540. **(Subscription address:** Taylor & Francis Inc., 1900 Frost Road, Suite 101, Bristol PA 19007-1598.) **ED** R. Walker, M. E. Knowles and S. A. Miller. **LC** TX553.A3; F567. **DD** 664/.06/05. **NLM** W1; FO402. **CODEN** FACOEB. **[CCC]. Pr Rev.** available on microfilm and microfiche from University Microfilms International (UMI). Documents available from The Genuine Article, BIOSIS Document Express, CASDDS, Documents on Demand.
Desc: Contains original research and review articles relating to the detection, determination, occurrence, persistence, safety evaluation and control of naturally occurring and man-made additives and contaminants in the food chain. Contributions cover the chemistry, biochemistry and bioavailability of these substances; factors affecting levels of potentially toxic compounds that may arise during production, processing, packaging and storage, and in the development of novel foods and processes; surveillance data and exposure estimates.
Ind/Abst Abstr. Bull. Inst. Pap. Sci. Tech.; AgBiotech News Inf.; AGRICOLA [Full Cov.]; Agrofor. Abstr. (1991-); Anal. Abstr.; BioBusiness; Biodeter. Abstr. (19??-19??); Biol. Abstr. (1984-); Chem. Abstr. (1984-); Curr. Aware. Biol. Sci., CABS; Curr. Contents, Agric. Biol. Environ. Sci.; Dairy Sci. Abstr.; EMBASE; Environ. Abstr.; Environ. Period. Bibliogr.; Food Sci. Technol. Abstr.; Foods Adlibra; For. Abstr.; Health Plan. Adminis.; Helminthol. Abstr. (1991-); Hortic. Abstr.; Index Med. (Vol. 1, No. 1, 1984-); Index Vet.; Int. Packag. Abstr.; Maize Abstr.; Nutr. Abstr. Rev., Ser. B, Live Feeds and Feed.; Nutr. Abstr. Rev., Ser. A, Hum. Exp.; Nutr. Res. Newsl.; Pig News Inf.; Postharvest News Inf.; Potato Abstr.; Poult. Abstr.; Res. Alert [Select. Cov.]; Rev. Med. Vet. Entomol.; Rev. Med. Vet. Mycology; Rev. Plant Pathol.; SCISEARCH; Soyabean Abstr.; Vet. Bull.; Weed Abstr.; Wheat Barley Trit. Abstr.

UK
FOOD ADDITIVES INFORMATION FILE. Vol. 1, No. 1 (April 1976)-. Periodical. English. bw.

UK
FOOD AID CONVENTION. **See** Sociology-Social Services and Welfare.

IT
FOOD AID MONITOR / WORLD FOOD PROGRAMME, THE. **Added/Corp** World Food Programme. No. 1 (Autumn 1989)-. English. qt. World Food Programme, Via Cristoforo Colombo, 426, 00145 Rome, Italy. **Tel** 011 39 6 626675, FAX 52282840, telex 626675 WFP I. **LC** HV696.F6; F618. **DD** 363.8/83/021.

Continues *Food Aid Deliveries.*
Ind/Abst Nutr. Abstr. Rev., Ser. A, Hum. Exp.; World Agric. Econ.

IT/0015-6221
FOOD AND AGRICULTURAL LEGISLATION. **Added/Corp** Food and Agriculture Organization of the United Nations. Vol. 1, No. 1 (1952)-. Periodical. English (French and Spanish). sa. $12.00. UNIPUB, 4611-F Assembly Drive, Lanham MD 20706-4391. **Tel** (800)274-4888, FAX (301)459-0056, telex 28787 GATT CH. cum. index. ***Continues*** *Annuaire International de Legislation Agricole.*
Desc: Presents in some depth, significant and illustrative information on laws and regulations currently in force and governing food and agriculture in FAO member states. The bulletin's objective is to provide comprehensive, up-to-date coverage of pertinent legislation and legislative activities within those nations.
Ind/Abst For. Abstr.

ET
FOOD AND AGRICULTURE IN AFRICA / UNITED NATIONS ECONOMIC COMMISSION FOR AFRICA, FOOD AND AGRICULTURE ORGANIZATION OF THE UNITED NATIONS. **See** International Assistance and Development.

US/0731-3799
FOOD & BEVERAGE MARKETING. [Food beverage mark.]. **VFOAT** Food and Beverage Marketing. Vol. 1, No. 1 (Jan. 1982)-. Periodical. English. mo. $190.00. Charleson Publishing Company, 505 8th Avenue, New York NY 10018. **Tel** (212) 695-0704. **LC** HD9000.1; .F54. **DD** 664/.0068/8. **CODEN** FBEMDL. available on an online database (file 648/Full-Text) from DIALOG.
Ind/Abst BioBusiness; F&S Index Plus Text, Int. [Select. Cov.]; Mark. Advert. Ref. Serv.; PROMT; Trade Ind. ASAP [Full Txt.]; Trade Ind. Index [Full Txt.].

UK/0960-3085
FOOD AND BIOPRODUCTS PROCESSING : TRANSACTIONS OF THE INSTITUTION OF CHEMICAL ENGINEERS, PART C. **Added/Corp** Institution of Chemical Engineers (Great Britain). **VFOAT** Transactions of the Institution of Chemical Engineers. Part C; Trans IChem Part C. Vol. 69, No. C1 (Mar. 1991)-. Periodical. English. qt. £149.00 UK; $249.00 other. Taylor & Francis Ltd., Rankine Road, Basingstoke Hampshire, RG24 8PR United Kingdom. **Tel** 011 44 256 840366, FAX 011 44 256 479438, telex 858540. **(Subscription address:** Taylor & Francis Inc., 1900 Frost Road, Suite 101, Bristol PA 19007-1598.) **ED** G. F. Hewitt. **CODEN** FBPREO. **Pr Rev.** available on microfilm and microfiche from University Microfilms International (UMI). Documents available from Article Express International, The Genuine Article.
Desc: Focuses on the processing aspects of food, drink including raw materials operations, hygiene, environmental concerns and packaging, and therefore excludes food chemistry. On the biochemical engineering side it includes such activities as bioreactor design and performance, microbial and enzymic reactions, fermentation, upstream and downstream processing, instrumentation and control, economic analysis, while excluding protein and genetic engineering.
Ind/Abst AGRICOLA; Curr. Technol. Index; Ei Page One; Eng. Index Annu.; Food Sci. Technol. Abstr.; Res. Alert [Full Cov.].

UK
FOOD & COOKERY REVIEW. **VFOAT** Food and Cookery Review. Began in Jan. 1935. Periodical. English. mo. Publishing Dimension Ltd, 11 St Marks Road, Windsor Berkshire SL4 3BD England. **Tel** 0753 830909. ***Continues*** *Bulletin / Universal Cookery & Food Association.*

US
FOOD & DRINK DAILY. **VFOAT** Food and Drink Daily. Vol. 1, No. 2 (Mar. 11, 1991)-. Periodical. English. da. $925.00. King Publishing Group, 627 National Press Building, Washington DC 20045. **Tel** (202)638-4260, FAX (202)662-9744. available on an online database (file 16,636/Full-Text) from DIALOG. ***Formed by the union of*** *Food & Drink Daily* ***and*** *World Food & Drink Report.*
Ind/Abst PROMT [Full Txt.]; PTS Newsl. Database [Full Txt.].

US/1053-9034
FOOD AND DRUG LAW REPORTS. ***Title Change.*** **See** Law.

US/0362-6466
FOOD & DRUG LETTER, THE. **VAT** Food and Drug Letter. (1976)-. Periodical. English. bw (published every other Friday). $945.00 US, Canada and Mexico; $1,000.00 other. Washington Business Information Inc., 1117 North 19th Street, Suite 200, Arlington VA 22209. **Tel** (703)247-3433, (800)426-0416, FAX (703)247-3421. **ED** Mike Dolan. **NLM** W1 FO4046. **[CCC].** available on an online database (file 158/Full-Text) from DIALOG.
Desc: Studies and interprets key issues in federal control of foods, drugs and cosmetics. Focuses on major regulatory questions of interest to executives.

●US/1071-8869
FOOD AND DRUG REPORT. **See** Law.

UK/0266-9366
FOOD & DRUGS INDUSTRY BULLETIN. (1983)-. Bulletin. English. ir. £132.00. Legal Studies and Services Publishing Ltd., 9 13 St. Andrew Street, London EC4A 3AE England. **Tel** 011 44 71 936 2016. **(Subscription address:** IBC House, Vickers Drive, Weybridge, Surrey KT13 OXS England; Telephone: 011 44 932 254020)
Desc: The latest legal developments, plus expert commentary, affecting the food and drinks industry in the UK and the European community.
Ind/Abst Foods Adlibra.

US/0739-6791
FOOD & FIBER LETTER, THE. (THE FOOD & FIBER LETTER : A PUBLICATION OF WEBSTER COMMUNICATIONS CORPORATION.). [Food fiber lett.]. **Added/Corp** Webster Communications Corporation. **VFOAT** Food and Fiber Letter. (198?)-. Periodical. English. wk (48 issues). $445.00 North America; $495.00 other. Sparks Companies Inc., 6708 Whittier Avenue, McLean VA 22101. **Tel** (703)734-8787, FAX (703)893-1065. **ED** Phil Wallace. **Bk Rev**, (Qty: 20).
Desc: Food and agricultural policy and legislative issues for executives.

SZ/0740-9710
FOOD & FOODWAYS. **See** Sociology.

US/0885-0704
FOOD AND JUSTICE. **See** Agriculture-Crop Production and Soil.

GH
FOOD AND NUTRITION IN AFRICA. **Added/Corp** Food and Agriculture Organization of the United Nations. Joint FAO/WHO/OAU Regional Food and Nutrition Commission for Africa. (Dec. 1964)-. English. ir. Secretariat of the Joint FAO/WHO/OAU Food and Nutrition Commission for Africa, PO Box 1628, Accra Ghana. **LC** TX360.A26; F66. **DD** 362.5.

UK
FOOD AND NUTRITION UPDATE. (19??)-. English. Twelve times a year. £395.00. Leatherhead Food Research Association, Randalls Road, Leatherhead Surrey KT22 7RY United Kingdom. **Tel** 011 44 372 376761, FAX 011 44 372 386228, telex 929846.

US/0046-4384
FOOD AND NUTRITION (WASHINGTON. 1971). **See** Nutrition and Dietetics.

US/0891-0154
FOOD & SERVICE / TEXAS RESTAURANT ASSOCIATION. **VFOAT** Food and Service. Vol. 47, No. 3 (Oct. 1986)-. Periodical. English. mo. Texas Restaurant Association, PO Box 1429, Austin TX 78767. **Tel** (512)444-6543. **ED** Bland Crowder. **Bk Rev.** **Ad Acc.** **Circ:** 5,000 (ctrl). ***Continues*** *Texas Food & Service News, 0746-5211.*
Desc: Gives business solutions to problems in restaurant/food service industry.

US/1042-9123
FOOD ARTS. [Food arts]. Vol. 1, No. 1 (1988)-. Periodical. English. Ten times a year. $30.00 US; $36.00 Canada; $50.00 other. M. Shanken Communications, Inc., 387 Park Avenue South, New York NY 10016. **Tel** (212)684-4224, FAX (212)684-5424, telex 422687 MSHANK UI. **(Subscription address:** Food Arts, PO Box 7809, Riverton NJ 08077.) **LC** TX945; .F58. **DD** 647.94/05. **CODEN** FOARE6.
Ind/Abst Foods Adlibra.

AT/1032-5298
FOOD AUSTRALIA : OFFICIAL JOURNAL OF CAFTA AND AIFST. [Food Aust.]. **Added/Corp** Council of Australian Food Technology Associations. Australian Institute of Food Science and Technology. Vol. 40, No. 9 (Sept. 1988)-. Academic Scholarly Publication. English. mo. 58.00Aus$ Australia; 90.00Aus$ (surface mail), 114.00Aus$ (air mail) other. Council of Australian Food Technology Associations, PO Box 1493, North Sydney NSW 2059 Australia. **Tel** 011 61 2 9637672, FAX 011 61 2 9544327. **ED** Jack Kefford. **LC** TP368; .F68. **DD** 664/.00994. **CODEN** FOAUEF. Index available. **Bk Rev.** **Ad Acc.** **Circ:** 3,325 (ctrl). Documents available from The Genuine Article, CASDDS. ***Continues*** *Food Technology in Australia, 0015-6647.*
Desc: Designed to promote the scientific and technical aspects of the food manufacturing industries in Australia, research papers, scientific reviews and general-interest papers, news items, and reports of meetings.
Ind/Abst AGRICOLA [Full Cov.]; BioBusiness (1988-); Biodeter. Abstr. (1991-); Chem. Abstr. (-1989); Chemorecept. Abstr.; Curr. Contents, Agric. Biol. Environ. Sci.; Dairy Sci. Abstr.; Food Sci. Technol. Abstr.; Foods Adlibra; Health Saf. Sci. Abstr.; Nutr. Abstr. Rev., Ser. A, Hum. Exp.; Res. Alert [Select. Cov.]; Rev. Med. Vet. Entomol.; SCISEARCH; Soc. Sci. Cit. Index [Select. Cov.].

US/0890-5436
FOOD BIOTECHNOLOGY. **See** Medical Science and Technology-Biotechnology.

UK/0952-357X
FOOD BIOTECHNOLOGY (LONDON). **See** Medical Science and Technology-Biotechnology.

US/0884-7185
FOOD BROKER QUARTERLY. (FOOD BROKER QUARTERLY : FBQ.). [Food brok. q.]. **Added/Corp** National Food Brokers Association (U.S.). **VFOAT** FBQ. (Winter 1985)-. Periodical. English. Four times a year (Mar., June, Sept., Dec.). $40.00 (nonmembers), $15.00 (members). National Food Brokers Association, 1010 Massachusetts Avenue NW, Washington DC 20001. **Tel** (202)789-2844, FAX (202)842-0839. **ED** Alan Goldstein. **DD** 381. **Ad Acc.** **Circ:** 4,000 (ctrl).
Desc: Reports on the dynamics of progress and change in the food broker profession, with special emphasis on food industry topics and issues presenting near and long-term challenges and opportunities for food brokers.

US/1057-6959
FOOD BUSINESS ANNUAL. [Food bus. annu.]. **Added/Corp** Food Research & Innovation Enterprises. Vol. 1, (1991)-. English. an (Mar.). $500.00 (one year), $880.00 (two years), $1275.00 (three years). F. R. I. Enterprises, PO Box 67, New Berlin WI 53151. **Tel** (414)782-3330, FAX (414)782-8228. **ED** Dr. T Shukla. **LC** HD9000.1; .F58933. **DD** 338.4/7664/00973021. ctrl circ.
Desc: Covers the market, technology, intelligence work, analysis and market research for the food industry.

US/1049-5568
FOOD BUSINESS (CHICAGO, ILL.). (FOOD BUSINESS.). [Food bus.]. (19??)-. Periodical. English. Twenty-three times a year. $80.00 US; $120.00 (surface mail), $225.00 (airmail) other; $5.00 (single issue). Putnam Publishing Company, 301 East Erie Street, Chicago IL 60611. **Tel** (312)644-2020, FAX (312)644-1131. **LC** HD9000.1; .F5893. **DD** 338.4/7664/005. **CODEN** FBUSEI. **[CCC].** available on microfilm and microfiche from University Microfilms International (UMI).
Ind/Abst Foods Adlibra.

US/8756-8772
FOOD BUSINESS MERGERS & ACQUISITIONS. [Food bus. mergers acquis.]. **VFOAT** Food Business Mergers and Acquisitions. Began in 1949?. Periodical. English. an. $330.00. The Food Institute, 28-12 Broadway, Fair Lawn NJ 07410. **Tel** (201)791-5570. **ED** Frank Panyko. **LC** HD9001; .F62. **DD** 338.8/36413/00973. **Circ:** 600.
Desc: Annual study by the Food Institute on merger and acquisition activity involving companies concerned with the distribution of food products.

US/1062-8665
FOOD CHANNEL, THE. [Food channel]. (1988)-. Periodical. English. sm. $195.00. Noble Communications, PO Box 9011, Springfield MO 65890. **Tel** (417)882-5050, ext. 431, FAX (312)644-0493. **DD** 641. available on an online database (file 636/Full-Text) from DIALOG.
Ind/Abst Foods Adlibra.

US
FOOD CHEMICAL NEWS GUIDE. English. wk (52 issues). $897.00. Food Chemical News Inc, 1101 Pennsylvania Avenue Southeast, Washington DC 20003. **Tel** (202)544-1980, FAX (202)546-3890.

UK/0308-8146
FOOD CHEMISTRY. **See** Chemistry-Chemical Technology.

US
FOOD CONSUMPTION, PRICES, AND EXPENDITURES / UNITED STATES DEPARTMENT OF AGRICULTURE, ECONOMIC RESEARCH SERVICE. **Added/Corp** United States. Dept. of Agriculture. Economic Research Service. (19??)-. Government Publication. English. ir. Superintendent of Documents, US Government Printing Office, Washington DC 20402. **Tel** (202)275-3328, FAX (202)786-2377. **LC** HD1751; .A5 subser.; HD9001. **DD** 338.1/0973 S; 339.4.
Ind/Abst Predicasts Forecasts.

UK
FOOD CONTROL. Vol. 1, No. 1 (Jan. 1990)-. Periodical. English. Six times a year. $358.00 The Americas; £240.00 other. Butterworth Heinemann Publishers, Linacre House, Jordan Hill, Oxford OX2 8DP England. **Tel** 011 44 865 310366. **(Subscription address:** Elsevier Science Ltd. Oxford Fulfillment Centre, PO Box 800, Kidlington, Oxford OX5 1DX United Kingdom.) **NLM** W1; FO4457. **CODEN** FOOCEV. **Bk Rev.** **Ad Acc.** **Circ:** 1,000 (ctrl). available on microfilm and microfiche from University Microfilms International (UMI).

Desc: International journal for all managers, scientists and technologists in the food industry.
Ind/Abst Foods Adlibra; Index Vet.

US/1048-8197
FOOD DISTRIBUTION MAGAZINE : FDM. [Food distrib. mag.]. **VFOAT** FDM. Vol. 31, No. 1 (Jan. 1990)-. Periodical. English. mo. $49.00 (one year), $75.00 (two year). Food Distribution Magazine, PO Box 10378, Clearwater FL 34617. **Tel** (813)443-2723, (800)541-6336. **ED** Tim Parolini (editor's address: 406 Water Street, Warren, RI 02885; Phone: (401)245-4500). **DD** 338. **Bk Rev. Ad Acc, Adv Mgr:** Ray Rehn. **Circ:** 34,000 (ctrl). ***Formed by the union of*** *Food Distributors Magazine, 0744-2769* ***and*** *Grocery Communications, 0017-4416.*
Desc: Editorial features on retail operations, ideas, and techniques regarding sales, store displays, DSD, merchandising, promotions, legislative views of manufacturers and supermarket executives about food industry.

US/0730-1413
FOOD ENGINEERING'S ... DIRECTORY OF U.S. FOOD & BEVERAGE PLANTS. [Food eng. dir. U.S. food beverage plants]. **VFOAT** Food Engineering's ... Directory of US Food & Beverage Plants; Directory of U.S. Food & Beverage Plants; Directory of US Food and Beverage Plants. **VAT** Food Engineering's Directory of United States Food and Beverage Plants. (19??)-. English. be (published in even years). $295.00. Chilton Company, 201 King of Prussia Road, Radnor PA 19089. **Tel** (610)964-4122, (800)695-1214, FAX (610)964-4978, telex 6851035 CHILTON UW. **LC** HD9003; .F58. **DD** 338.4/7664/002573. **Circ:** 1,500.
Desc: Complete listing of U.S. food and beverage plants with 20 or more employees showing: address, primary end product(s), phone number, and number of employees.

UK/0956-6783
FOOD EUROPE ENGLISH ED. (FOOD EUROPE). [Food Eur. Engl. ed.]. (1985)-. Periodical. English. Six times a year. £100.00. IML Group, Blair House, 184-186 High Street, Tonbridge Kent, TN9 1BQ England. **Tel** 011 44 732 359990, FAX 011 44 732 770049. **ED** Caroline Scoular. **Ad Acc, Adv Mgr:** Frank Blackwell.

UK/0967-5302
FOOD FILE. [Food File]. (1990)-. Trade Publication. English. sm (combined issues in Summer and Christmas). £415.00. ERC Publications, Lanwades House, Moulton Road, Kennett, Newmarket, Suffolk CB8 7PW England. **Tel** 011 44 638 552113, FAX 011 44 638 552109. **ED** Fiona Dyer. **DD** 338.476640094. Index available. cum. index. Documents available from BLDSC.
Desc: Topical, factual and statistical publication for the world's food industry.
Ind/Abst Infomat Int. Bus.

●US
FOOD FIRST NEWS & VIEWS. Added/Corp Institute for Food and Development Policy (Oakland, Calif.). **VFOAT** Food First News and Views. Vol. 14, No. 47 (Summer 1992)-. Periodical. English. qt. Food First News, 145 9th Street, San Francisco CA 94103-2626. **LC** TX341; .F662. ***Continues*** *Food First News.*

US/0199-5286
FOOD FREEZING AND PROCESSING EQUIPMENT. VFOAT Food Freezing; Food Freezing/Processing Equipment. (197?)-. Periodical. English. bm (6 issues). $45.00. Davies Publishing Company, 241 Frontage/Suite 32, Hinsdale IL 60521. **Tel** (708)325-2930.

US/1067-1951
FOOD HISTORY NEWS. [Food hist. news]. (1989)-. Periodical. English. qt (Mar., June, Sept., Dec.). $12.00 (individual); $15.00 (institutions). Food History News, HCR 61 Box 354A, Isleboro ME 04848. **Tel** (207)734-8140. **ED** Sandra Oliver. **DD** 641. Index available. **Bk Rev**, (Qty: 12). **Circ:** 500 (ctrl).

UK/0268-005X
FOOD HYDROCOLLOIDS. See Chemistry-Organic Chemistry.

GW
FOOD + I.E. UND NONFOOD. VFOAT Food + I.E. Und Non-Food. Periodical. German. E Albrecht Verlags-KG, Freihamer Strasse 2 PF 1120, W-8032 Graefelfing Germany. **Tel** 49 89 858530. **LC** HD9324.1; .F66. ***Supersedes*** *Lebensmittel-Grosshandel; Susswaren-Zeitung.*

CN/0317-3364
FOOD IN CANADA BUYERS' DIRECTORY & SERVICES INDEX. Added/Corp Food in Canada. (1973)-. Periodical. English. an. 38.00Can$ Canada; 49.00Can$ other. MacLean Hunter Ltd. Business Publishers / Canada, Box 9100, Station A, Toronto ONT M5W 1A5 Canada. **Tel** (416)946-8420, (800)567-0444. **DD** 338.4/7/664002571. ***Continues*** *Food in Canada. Buyers' Guide, 0317-3372.*

SA/0015-6450
FOOD INDUSTRIES OF SOUTH AFRICA. ***Title Change.*** (FOOD INDUSTRIES OF SOUTH AFRICA FOR THE MANUFACTURE, EXPORTER, WHOLESALER, AND RETAILER.). [Food ind. S. Afr.]. Periodical. English. mo. Thomson Publications Pty, PO Box 56182, Pinegowrie 2123 South Africa. **Tel** 011 27 11 7892144. **ED** Paddy Attwell. **Bk Rev. Ad Acc. Circ:** 3,000 (ctrl). ***Continued by*** *Food Industries (Randburg, South Africa), 0015-6450.*
Desc: Founded in 1948, this magazine is the only monthly journal for all the food and beverage industries in South Africa.
Ind/Abst AGRICOLA; BioBusiness.

SA/0015-6450
FOOD INDUSTRIES OF SOUTH AFRICA. (FOOD INDUSTRIES.). [Food ind. S. Afr.]. **VFOAT** Food Industries of SA. (19??)-. Periodical. English. mo. R60.00. Thomson Publications Pty, PO Box 56182, Pinegowrie 2123 South Africa. **Tel** 011 27 11 7892144. **CODEN** FISAAX. ***Continues*** *Food Industries of South Africa for the Manufacture, Exporter, Wholesaler, and Retailer, 0015-6450.*
Ind/Abst AGRICOLA; BioBusiness.

CN/0835-0000
FOOD INDUSTRIES (OTTAWA). (FOOD INDUSTRIES / STATISTICS CANADA, INDUSTRY DIVISION, CENSUS OF MANUFACTURES SECTION.). [Food ind.]. **Added/Corp** Statistics Canada. Census of Manufactures Section. Statistics Canada. Industry Division. **VFOAT** Industries des Aliments. (1985)-. English (French). an. 38.00Can$ Canada; $46.00 US; $54.00 other. Statistics Canada, Publications Sales & Services, Main Building Room 1710, Ottawa Ontario K1A 0T6 Canada. **Tel** (613)951-5078, (800)267-6677, FAX (613)951-1584, telex 053-3585. **LC** HD9014.C2; F658. **DD** 338.4/7664/00971021; 338.4/7664/00971/021. ***Formed by the union of*** *Biscuit Industry (1984), 0832-8455; Bread and Other Bakery Products Industry (1984), 0832-8463; Dairy Products Industries (Ottawa Ont. : 1983), 0318-2711; Confectionery Manufacturers, 0575-8246; Feed Industry (Statistics Canada : Final), 0700-0073; Fish Products Industry (Final), 0527-5172; Fruit and Vegetable Processing Industries (Statistics Canada), 0384-4420; Cane and Beet Sugar Industry, 0833-5710; Vegetable Oil Mills (Final), 0527-6403; Miscellaneous Food Processors (Final), 0384-3696; Meat and Poultry Products Industry, 0700-0324* ***and*** *Flour and Breakfast Cereal Products Industries, 0319-888X.*

UK/0965-4682
FOOD INDUSTRY BULLETIN. [Food ind. bull.]. (1989)-. Periodical. English. mo. £345.00. Leatherhead Food Research Association, Randalls Road, Leatherhead Surrey KT22 7RY United Kingdom. **Tel** 011 44 372 376761, FAX 011 44 372 386228, telex 929846. **DD** 338.4766400941.

US/0145-3610
FOOD INDUSTRY DIRECTORY, THE. VFOAT Washington Food Industry Directory. Directory. English. $3.00 single issue. Washington State Food Dealers Association, 480 19th Street East, Tacoma WA 98421. **Tel** (206)272-2966. **LC** HD9007.W2; F66. **DD** 338.4/7/64130025797.

US/0046-4414
FOOD INDUSTRY FUTURES. [Food ind. futures]. (1972)-. Periodical. English. sm. $150.00 US and Canada; $180.00 other. Food Industry Futures, PO Box 430, Fayetteville NY 13066. **Tel** (315)682-7455. **ED** Merritt L. Kastens. **DD** 338.
Desc: A strategy service for decision makers planning five/ten years out. Keyword terms: agribusiness, agriculture, eating, food industry (processing, distribution, retailing, service).

NZ/0113-8901
FOOD INDUSTRY NEWS AUCKLAND. (FOOD INDUSTRY NEWS.). [Food ind. news Auckl.]. (1987)-. Periodical. English. Eleven times a year. 35.75NZ$. Minty's Media, 22 Heather Street, Private Bag 93218, Parnell Auckland New Zealand. **Tel** 011 64 9 3794233, FAX 011 64 9 3093575. **ED** Allison Oosterman. **DD** 338.4766409931. **Ad Acc, Adv Mgr:** Heather Braae. ***Continues*** *Food Industry (Auckland), 0111-6843.*

US/0890-720X
FOOD INDUSTRY NEWSLETTER (FAIRFAX, VA.), THE. (THE FOOD INDUSTRY NEWSLETTER.). (1972)-. Newsletter. English. Twenty-two times a year. $245.00. Newsletters Inc., PO Box 2730, Bethesda MD 20827. **Tel** (301)469-8507, FAX (301)469-7271. **ED** Max Busetti. **DD** 338. ctrl circ.
Desc: Issued for food manufacturers.

US/1040-9076
FOOD INDUSTRY REPORT. [Food ind. rep.]. Vol. 1, No. 1 (Sept. 19, 1988)-. Periodical. English. ir. $297.00 US, Canada & Mexico; $325.00 others. Food Industry Report, PO Box 651, South Elgin IL 60177. **Tel** (312)742-7676. **DD** 338.
Ind/Abst Foods Adlibra.

US
FOOD INDUSTRY TOPICS. English. sa. Free on request. Michigan State University / 51 Kellogg Center, East Lansing MI 48824. **Tel** (517)355-8295.
Ind/Abst Foods Adlibra.

●US/0968-574X
FOOD INGREDIENTS AND ANALYSIS INTERNATIONAL. VFOAT Food Ingredients & Analysis International. (1993)-. English. Six times a year. £58.00 UK; £70.00 other. Turret Group, 177 Hagden Lane, Watford Herts WD1 8LN United Kingdom. **Tel** 011 44 923 228577, FAX 011 44 923 221346. ***Continues*** *Food Ingredients & Processing International, 0968-574X.*

UK/0968-574X
FOOD INGREDIENTS & PROCESSING INTERNATIONAL. ***Title Change.*** [Food ingred. process. int.]. **VFOAT** Food Ingredients and Processing International. (Aug. 1991)-(Mar. 1993). Periodical. English. mo. Turret Group, 177 Hagden Lane, Watford Herts WD1 8LN United Kingdom. **Tel** 011 44 923 228577, FAX 011 44 923 221346. **CODEN** FIPIEC. ***Continues*** *Food FIPP, 0143-8441.* ***Continued by*** *Food Ingredients and Analysis International.*
Ind/Abst AGRICOLA; Foods Adlibra.

UK
FOOD INGREDIENTS & PROCESSING INTERNATIONAL. ***Title Change.*** (19??)-(19??). English. mo. Turret Group, 177 Hagden Lane, Watford Herts WD1 8LN United Kingdom. **Tel** 011 44 923 228577, FAX 011 44 923 221346. ***Continued by*** *Food Ingredients & Analysis International.*

UK
FOOD INNOVATION INTERNATIONAL. (19??)-. English. mo. £254.00 UK; $445.00 US. World Business Publications Ltd., 960 High Road, Britannia 4th Floor, London N12 9RY England. **Tel** 11 44 81 446 5141, FAX 11 44 81 446 3659, telex 9419208.

US/1065-1497
FOOD INSIGHT. (FOOD INSIGHT / INTERNATIONAL FOOD INFORMATION COUNCIL.). [Food insight]. **Added/Corp** International Food Information Council. IFIC Food Education Foundation. (19??)-. Periodical. English. bm. Free on request to health professionals, journalist educators and other professionals. International Food Information Council, 1100 Connecticut Avenue Northwest #430, Washington DC 20036. **Tel** (202)296-6540. **DD** 613.
Ind/Abst Foods Adlibra.

US/0745-4503
FOOD INSTITUTE REPORT, THE. (THE FOOD INSTITUTE REPORT / FI, THE AMERICAN INSTITUTE OF FOOD DISTRIBUTION INC.). [Food Inst. rep.]. **Added/Corp** American Institute of Food Distribution. (19??)-. Periodical. English. Fifty-one times per year (Except Christmas week). $155.00 US (schools); $535.00 others Comes with American Institue of Food Distribution membership. American Institute of Food Distribution, 2812 Broadway, Fair Lawn NJ 07410. **Tel** (201)791-5570, FAX (201)791-5222. **ED** Roy Harrison and Jack Rengstorff. Index available. cum. index. **Bk Rev. Circ:** 5,600. ***Continues*** *Food Institute's Weekly Digest, 0002-8959; Food Institute's Washington Food Report, 0162-5233; Food Institute's Report on Food Markets, 0002-8940.*
Desc: Posting for all segments of the nation's largest industry, raw product to consumer purchase. Features pertinent and timely information on food distribution developments and trends.
Ind/Abst Infomat Int. Bus.; Trade Ind. Index.

US/1067-9871
FOOD INVESTMENT REPORT. ***Ceased.*** [Food invest. rep.]. Vol. 1, No. 1 (Jan. 1993)-(199?). Periodical. English. Fifteen times a year. Food & Nutrition Press Inc, 2 Corporate Drive, PO Box 374, Trumbull CT 06611. **Tel** (203)261-8587, FAX (203)261-9724. **ED** Gerald C. Melson. **DD** 332.
Desc: Provides a market analysis of the food and related industries.

IE/0790-0430
FOOD IRELAND. [Food Irel.]. (1978)-. Periodical. English. mo. 25.00p. Tara Publishing Co Ltd, 1 Poolbeg Street, Poolbeg House, Dublin 2 Ireland. **Tel** 011 353 1 719244. **DD** 664. ***Continues*** *Irish Packaging, 0790-1380.*
Ind/Abst Food Sci. Technol. Abstr.

AU/1011-2588
FOOD IRRADIATION NEWSLETTER. (FOOD IRRADIATION NEWSLETTER / JOINT FAO/IAEA DIVISION OF ATOMIC ENERGY IN FOOD AND AGRICULTURE, INTERNATIONAL ATOMIC ENERGY AGENCY.). [Food irradiat. newsl.]. **Added/Corp** Joint FAO/IAEA Division of Atomic Energy in Food and Agriculture. Joint FAO/IAEA Division of Isotope and Radiation Applications of Atomic Energy for Food and Agricultural Development. Joint FAO/IAEA Division of Nuclear Techniques in Food and Agriculture. Issue No. 1 (Mar. 1977)-. Periodical. English. sa. Free on request. International Atomic Energy Agency / IAEA, Wagramerstrasse 5, PO Box 100, A-1400 Vienna Austria. **Tel** 011 43 1 2360 ext. 2530, FAX 011 43 1 234564.

(Subscription address: UNIPUB, 4611 F Assembly Drive, Lanham MD 20706.**)**
Desc: Covers the radiation preservation of food.

●US/1065-142X
FOOD IRRADIATION UPDATE. (1993)-. Periodical. English. bm. $95.00 US; $124.00 Canada; $122.00 other. Technomic Publishing Company, Inc., 851 New Holland Avenue, Box 3535, Lancaster PA 17604. **Tel** (717)291-5609, (800)233-9936, FAX (717)295-4538.

US
FOOD IRRADIATION [COMPUTER FILE]. Periodical. English. National Agricultural Library, 10301 Baltimore Boulevard, Beltsville MD 20705.

●US/1064-6329
FOOD LABELING NEWS. [Food labeling news]. **VFOAT** FLN. Vol. 1, No. 1 (Oct. 8, 1992)-. Periodical. English. wk. $755.00. Food Chemical News Inc, 1101 Pennsylvania Avenue Southeast, Washington DC 20003. **Tel** (202)544-1980, FAX (202)546-3890. **DD** 344. **[CCC].**

SW/1100-3227
FOOD LABORATORY NEWS. ***Suspended.*** [Food lab. news]. **Added/Corp** Sweden. Statens Livsmedemsverk. No. 15 (1989)-(19??). Periodical. English. Four times a year. Food Laboratory News, Stephen Blattmann Strasse 11, D 7743 Furtwangen Germany. **Tel** 011 49 7723 4459. ***Continues*** *Food Laboratory Newsletter, 0282-1338.*
Ind/Abst Biodeter. Abstr. (1991-); Dairy Sci. Abstr.; Food Sci. Technol. Abstr.; Hortic. Abstr.; Maize Abstr.; Nutr. Abstr. Rev., Ser. A, Hum. Exp.; Postharvest News Inf.; Rev. Med. Vet. Mycology; Sug. Indus. Abstr.; World Agric. Econ.

UK/0965-4690
FOOD LAUNCH AWARENESS BULLETIN. [Food Launch aware. bull.]. (1991)-. Bulletin. English. Twelve times a year. £395.00. Leatherhead Food Research Association, Randalls Road, Leatherhead Surrey KT22 7RY United Kingdom. **Tel** 011 44 372 376761, FAX 011 44 372 386228, telex 929846. **DD** 016.641.

UK
FOOD LAW MONTHLY. **See** Law.

UK/0953-5047
FOOD MAGAZINE LONDON. 1988. (THE FOOD MAGAZINE). [Food mag.Lond., 1988]. (1988)-. Periodical. English. qt. £17.50 (individuals), £35.00 (institutions) UK; £25.00 (individuals), £40.00 (institutions) other. The Food Magazine, Third Floor, 5/11 Worship Street, Third Floor, London EC2A 2BH England. **Tel** 011 44 71 628-7774, FAX 011 44 71 628-0817. **ED** Tim Lobstein and Sue Dibb. **DD** 641.3005. Index available. cum. index. **Bk Rev. Pr Rev. Circ:** 4,000 (ctrl). ***Continues*** *London Food News.*
Desc: News, opinions and features about food and the food business.
Ind/Abst Food Sci. Technol. Abstr.

US/0091-018X
FOOD MANAGEMENT. [Food manage.]. Vol. 7 (Aug./Sept. 1972)-. Periodical. English. Twelve times a year. $50.00 US; $75.00 Canada; $95.00 Mexico; $125.00 other. Penton Publishing, 1100 Superior Avenue, Cleveland OH 44114-2543. **Tel** (216)696-7000, FAX (216)696-0836. **(Subscription address:** Penton Publishing, PO Box 96732, Chicago IL 60693.**) ED** Donna Boss. **DD** 647. **CODEN** FOMADE. **[CCC]. Ad Acc. Circ:** 56,870 (ctrl). available on microfilm and microfiche from University Microfilms International (UMI). ***Formed by the union of*** *Hospital & Nursing Home Food Management* ***and*** *School & College Food Management.*
Desc: Serves the field of food service in schools and colleges, hospitals and nursing homes, contract feeders and inplant operators.
Ind/Abst AGRICOLA [Select. Cov.]; BioBusiness; Foods Adlibra; Health Plan. Adminis.; Hospit. Health Admin. Index.

NE/0168-325X
FOOD MANAGEMENT AMERSFOORT. (FOOD MANAGEMENT). [Food manage.Amersfoort]. (1983)-. Periodical. Dutch. Eighteen times a year. Fl98.00 Netherlands; Fl140.00 other. Industriele Pers, Postbus 1297, 3800 BG Amersfoort, Netherlands. **Tel** 011 31 33 637977, FAX 011 31 33 638300. **ED** F D Noordhoek and J van Haastrecht. **UDC** 664. Index available. **Bk Rev. Ad Acc. Pr Rev. Circ:** 4,500.
Desc: Reports on the developments in the food and beverage industry in Holland and Belgium. Technological developments are reported in a readable way for general management.

AT
FOOD MANAGEMENT NEWS. (19??)-. English. mo. 38.00Aus$ Australia; 105.00Aus$ other. Yaffa Publishing Group Pty Ltd., GPO Box 606, Sydney NSW 2001 Australia. **Tel** 011 61 2 2812333, FAX 011 61 2 2812750. ***Continues*** *Food Manufacturing News.*

UK/0015-6477
FOOD MANUFACTURE. [Food manuf.]. Vol. 1 (May 1927)-. Periodical. English. mo. £70.00 UK and Northern Ireland; $170.00 other. Morgan Grampian, 40 Beresford Street Woolwich, London SE18 6BQ England. **Tel** 011 44 81 855 7777, FAX 011 44 81 855 5548, telex 896238. **LC** TX341; .F9. **CODEN** FOMAAB. **[CCC].** available on microfilm and microfiche from University Microfilms International (UMI); available on an online database (files 16,648/Full-Text) from DIALOG.
Ind/Abst AGRICOLA; BioBusiness (1989-); Curr. Technol. Index; Dairy Sci. Abstr.; EMBASE; F&S Index Plus Text, Int. [Select. Cov.]; Food Sci. Technol. Abstr.; Foods Adlibra; Infomat Int. Bus.; Int. Packag. Abstr.; Life Sci. Collect.; Pollut. Abstr. Indexes; PROMT [Full Txt.]; Trade Ind. ASAP [Full Txt.]; Trade Ind. Index [Full Txt.].

UK
FOOD MANUFACTURE INGREDIENT & MACHINERY SURVEY. **VFOAT** Ingredient & Machinery Survey; Ingredient Survey. 1977/78-. English. an. £21.00. Morgan Grampian, 40 Beresford Street Woolwich, London SE18 6BQ England. **Tel** 011 44 81 855 7777, FAX 011 44 81 855 5548, telex 896238. **ED** Hugh Darrington. Index available. **Ad Acc.** ***Continues*** *Food Manufacture Ingredient Survey, 0532-0925.*

UK/0267-1506
FOOD MANUFACTURE INTERNATIONAL. [Food manuf. int.]. (1984)-. Periodical. English (English; table of contents in French, German and Italian). bm. £50.00 UK and Northern Ireland; $130.00 other. Morgan Grampian, 40 Beresford Street Woolwich, London SE18 6BQ England. **Tel** 011 44 81 855 7777, FAX 011 44 81 855 5548, telex 896238. **CODEN** FMINEK. available on an online database (file 16/Full-Text) from DIALOG.
Ind/Abst BioBusiness (1989-); Dairy Sci. Abstr.; Food Sci. Technol. Abstr.; Foods Adlibra; PROMT [Full Txt.]; Soyabean Abstr.; Sug. Indus. Abstr.

AT/0816-3634
FOOD MANUFACTURING NEWS. ***Title Change.*** (1974)-(19??). Periodical. English. Seven times a year. Yaffa Publishing Group Pty Ltd., GPO Box 606, Sydney NSW 2001 Australia. **Tel** 011 61 2 2812333, FAX 011 61 2 2812750. ***Continued by*** *Food Management News.*

UK/0268-0408
FOOD MARKET ABSTRACTS. [Food mark. abstr.]. (1984)-. English. mo. £340.00. Leatherhead Food Research Association, Randalls Road, Leatherhead Surrey KT22 7RY United Kingdom. **Tel** 011 44 372 376761, FAX 011 44 372 386228, telex 929846. **DD** 016.33847641.

CN/0709-5864
FOOD MARKET COMMENTARY. [Food mark. comment.]. **Added/Corp** Canada. Food Markets Analysis Division. Vol. 1 (1979)-. Government Publication. English. Free on request. Agriculture Canada, Communications Branch, Ottawa Ontario K1A 0C7 Canada. **LC** HD9014.C2; F66. **DD** 381/.456413/00971.
Ind/Abst World Agric. Econ.

GW/0932-2744
FOOD MARKETING & TECHNOLOGY. (INTERNATIONAL FOOD MARKETING AND TECHNOLOGY.). [Food mark. technol.]. **VFOAT** International Food Marketing and Technology; Food Marketing & Technology. (1986)-. Periodical. English. Six times a year. $66.00. Harnisch Verlagsgesellschaft, Blumenstrasse 15, D 90402 Nuernberg Germany. **Tel** 011 49 911 203658, FAX 011 49 911 204579. **ED** Juliane Neutsch. **CODEN** IFMTE8. **Bk Rev. Ad Acc. Circ:** 26,000.
Desc: The international magazine for executives and specialists in the food industry. Reports on new marketing strategies and trends, equipment and processing methods, innovative technologies, raw materials and additives, packaging systems and other topics of selling and purchasing marketing. Addresses factory managers, food technologies, and the product developers in the food industry.
Ind/Abst Foods Adlibra; Infomat Int. Bus.

US/0896-4203
FOOD MARKETING BRIEFS. [Food mark. briefs]. Vol. 1, No. 1 (May 1987)-. Periodical. English. Twelve times a year. $97.00. Newsletters Inc., PO Box 2730, Bethesda MD 20827. **Tel** (301)469-8507, FAX (301)469-7271. **ED** Ray Marsili. **DD** 658. **CODEN** FMABEC. ctrl circ. available on an online database (file 636/Full-Text) from DIALOG.
Desc: National digest of food marketing information.
Ind/Abst PTS Newsl. Database [Full Txt.].

US/0190-3349
FOOD MARKETING INDUSTRY SPEAKS, THE. **Added/Corp** Food Marketing Institute. (1977)-. English. an. $22.00 members, $44.00 nonmembers. Food Marketing Institute, 1750 K Street Northwest, Washington DC 20006. **Tel** (202)452-8444. **(Subscription address:** Food Marketing Institute, 800 Connecticut Avenue Northwest, Washington DC 20006**) LC** HD9321.1; .F58. **DD** 381. ***Supersedes*** *Super Market Industry Speaks, 0081-9530.*
Desc: Reviews sales, profit, and other operating ratios, operating and merchandising practices, and other subjects of current interest. Data is for store-level operations and distribution center operations.

US/0190-504X
FOOD MARKETING INDUSTRY SPEAKS : DETAILED TABULATIONS, THE. English. an. $7.50 members, $15.00 nonmembers. Food Marketing Institute, 1750 K Street Northwest, Washington DC 20006. **Tel** (202)452-8444. **LC** HD9004; .F74. **DD** 381/.45/66400973.

US
FOOD MARKETING POLICY CENTER RESEARCH REPORT. **Added/Corp** University of Connecticut. Food Marketing Policy Center. **VFOAT** Research Report. No. 1 (1989)-. Monographic series. English.
Ind/Abst World Agric. Econ.

US
FOOD MARKETS IN REVIEW. **Added/Corp** American Institute of Food Distribution. (19??)-. English. ir. $646.00 US; $683.99 other. American Institute of Food Distribution, 2812 Broadway, Fair Lawn NJ 07410. **Tel** (201)791-5570, FAX (201)791-5222. **LC** HD9001; .F64. **DD** 381/.45664/00973. Index available. **Bk Rev.**
Desc: Information on the food industry and the grocery trade.

US/0279-3105
FOOD MERCHANDISING FOR NON-FOOD RETAILERS. (FOOD MERCHANDISING FOR NON-FOOD RETAILERS : FM.). **VFOAT** FM; F.M. **VAT** Food Merchandising for Non Food Retailers. Vol. 1, No. 1 (Aug. 1981)-. Periodical. English. qt. Free upon request. Lebhar Friedman Inc., 3922 Coconut Palm Drive, Tampa FL 33619. **Tel** (800)927-9292, (813)664-6707. **LC** HD9001; .F65. **DD** 664/.0068/8.
Desc: Information on the food industry and the grocery trade.

US/0015-6493
FOOD MERCHANTS ADVOCATE. **Added/Corp** New York State Food Merchants Association. (1935)-. Periodical. English. mo (Nov./Dec. combined). $10.00. Food Merchants Advocate, 50 Broadway 26th Floor, New York NY 10004. **Tel** (212)558-6500. **ED** Christopher Pellnat. **CODEN** FMADEI. **Ad Acc. Circ:** 27,000 (ctrl).
Desc: Covers retail food industry, legislation, new store openings, personnel, etc.

UK/0740-0020
FOOD MICROBIOLOGY. **See** Biology-Microbiology.

US/1057-7785
FOOD NEWS FOR CONSUMERS / UNITED STATES DEPT. OF AGRICULTURE, FOOD SAFETY AND QUALITY SERVICE. ***Ceased.*** (Jan. 1980)-Vol. 10, No. 4. Government Publication. English. Three times a year. Superintendent of Documents, US Government Printing Office, Washington DC 20402. **Tel** (202)275-3328, FAX (202)786-2377. **CODEN** FNCNEV.
Desc: Contains news items pertaining to food safety, food and nutrition agricultural research, economic research, human nutrition, and agricultural marketing. Also includes current news on the activities of the United States Department of Agriculture's Food Safety and Inspection Service, Food and Nutrition Service, Agricultural Research Service, Economic Research Service, Human Nutrition Information Service, and Agricultural Marketing Service.

IT
FOOD OUTLOOK (ROME, ITALY). (FOOD OUTLOOK.). **Added/Corp** Food and Agriculture Organization of the United Nations. **VFOAT** Global Information and Early Warning System on Food and Agriculture. (19??)-. Periodical. English. Eleven times a year. Food and Agriculture Organization (FAO) / Italy, GIPC166 via Terme di Caracalla, 00100 Rome Italy. **Tel** 011 39 6 522 52925, FAX 011 39 6 522 55784. **LC** HD9000.1.F593. **DD** 338.1/9.

IT
FOOD OUTLOOK. STATISTICAL SUPPLEMENT. **See** Food and Food Industry-Abstracting, Bibliographies and Statistics.

UK/0957-5189
FOOD PACKER INTERNATIONAL. **See** Packaging.

US/1062-0192
FOOD PAPER (LOS ANGELES, CALIF.), THE. (THE FOOD PAPER.). [Food pap.]. (1991)-. Periodical. English. qt. $16.00 US; $18.00 Canada & Mexico; $22.00 Europe & Japan. Gault Millau, PO Box 361144, Los Angeles CA 90036. **Tel** (213)965-3481, FAX (213)936-2883. **ED** Andre Gayot. **DD** 647.
Desc: Guide to food and restaraunts in Southern California.

US/0279-9839
FOOD PEOPLE AND THEIR COMPANIES. **VFOAT** Food People. (198?)-. Trade Publication. English. Twelve times a year. $28.00 (one

year); $46.00 (two years); $54.00 (three years). Olson Publications Inc., PO Box 1208, Woodstock GA 30188. **Tel** (404)928-8994. **ED** Johnnie S. Nelson (phone: (404)974-1077 or (800)647-3724). **CODEN** FPTCET. **Ad Acc, Adv Mgr:** Laura Mikszan, **Tel** (404)974-1077 or (800)647-3724. **Circ:** 37,856 (ctrl).
Desc: A national trade journal serving the retail food industry from a feature perspective. Features the people, companies, issues and trends important to the industry.

NE/0925-8051
FOOD PERSONALITY. [Food pers.]. **VFOAT** Vakblad Food Personality. (1985)-. Periodical. Dutch. mo (12 issues). Fl175.00. Mediaset Uitgeverij BV, Postbus 499, 6500 AL Nijmegen, Netherlands. **Tel** 011 31 080 580722, FAX 011 31 080 581540. **ED** W. Spaan. **UDC** 641. **Ad Acc. Circ:** 9,400.

US/0887-3895
FOOD PLANT EQUIPMENT. (FOOD PLANT EQUIPMENT : FPE.). [Food plant equip.]. **VFOAT** FPE. Periodical. English. bm. $16.00 US; $35.00 other. Machalek Publishing Company, 15 South Ninth Street, Minneapolis MN 55402. **Tel** (612)370-0413. **ED** Dale Thompson. **DD** 664. **Ad Acc. Circ:** 48,000 (ctrl). ***Continues** Food Plant Industry, 8750-7099.*
Desc: Food plant equipment (formerly Food Plant Industry) is a product news publication containing news of equipment and supplies for the food, drug and cosmetics processing industries.

●US/1072-298X
FOOD PLANT STRATEGIES. [Food plant strat.]. Vol. 1, No. 1 (Oct. 1993)-. Periodical. English. mo. $295.00 (one year), $560.00 (two year) US, Canada & Mexico; $345.00 (one year), $640.00 (two year) other. Packaging Strategies, 122 South Church Street, West Chester PA 19382. **Tel** (215)436-4220, FAX (215)436-6277, telex 757674. **ED** Mike Pehanich. **DD** 658. **Circ:** Not disclosed.
Desc: Covers innovations and trends in the design and construction of new food factories, expansions, and renovations. Also focuses on plant location strategies and new manufacturing technologies.

UK/0306-9192
FOOD POLICY. [Food policy]. Vol. 1, No. 1 (Nov. 1975)-. Periodical. English. bm. $395.00 The Americas; £265.00 other. Butterworth Heinemann Publishers, Linacre House, Jordan Hill, Oxford OX2 8DP England. **Tel** 011 44 865 310366. **(Subscription address:** Elsevier Science Ltd. Oxford Fulfillment Centre, PO Box 800, Kidlington, Oxford OX5 1DX United Kingdom.**) ED** Jennifer Nicholson. **LC** HD9000.1; .F5643. **DD** 338.1/9. **[CCC].** Index available. **Bk Rev. Ad Acc. Pr Rev.** available on microfilm and microfiche from University Microfilms International (UMI). Documents available from The Genuine Article, Documents on Demand.
Desc: An international journal which publishes refereed articles on the politics, economics and planning aspects of food, agriculture and nutrition. It provides the reader with a single source of information on the many factors which influence the formulation and implementation of food policy.
Ind/Abst AgBiotech News Inf.; AGRICOLA [Select. Cov.]; BioBusiness; Biol. Agric. Index; Contents Recent Econ. J.; Curr. Contents, Agric. Biol. Environ. Sci.; Curr. Lit. Sci. Sci.; Dairy Sci. Abstr.; Environ. Abstr.; Environ. Period. Bibliogr.; Food Sci. Technol. Abstr.; For. Abstr.; Geogr. Abstr. Human Geogr.; Int. Dev. Abstr.; Int. Labour Doc.; J. Plan. Lit.; Leis. Recreat. Tour. Abstr.; Maize Abstr.; Nutr. Abstr. Rev., Ser. B, Live Feeds and Feed.; Nutr. Abstr. Rev., Ser. A, Hum. Exp.; PAIS Int. Print (1991-); Life Sci. Collect.; Plant Breed. Abstr.; Res. Alert [Full Cov.]; Rice Abstr.; Rural Dev. Abstr.; Sci. Cit. Index; SCISEARCH; Seed Abstr.; Soc. Sci. Cit. Index [Full Cov.]; Sug. Indus. Abstr.; Wheat Barley Trit. Abstr.; World Agric. Econ.

BE/0778-7065
FOOD POLICY INTERNATIONAL. See Agriculture.

US
FOOD PRICE SPREADS IN CALIFORNIA. Main/Corp California. Bureau of Market News. English. ir. California Department of Food and Agriculture, 1220 N Street, Sacramento CA 95814. **Tel** (916)654-0433, FAX (916)324-1681. **LC** HD9007.C2; C223A. **DD** 338.4/36413/009794.

US/0015-6523
FOOD PROCESSING. [Food process.]. (Sept. 1968)-. Periodical. English. Twelve times a year. $68.00 US; $115.00 (surface mail), $225.00 (airmail) other; $10.00 (single issue). Putnam Publishing Company, 301 East Erie Street, Chicago IL 60611. **Tel** (312)644-2020, FAX (312)644-1131. **LC** TP373; .F55. **DD** 664/.005. **CODEN** FOPRA9. **[CCC].** available on microfilm and microfiche from University Microfilms International (UMI). Documents available from BIOSIS Document Express, CASDDS. ***Continues** Management's Food Processing-Marketing.*
Desc: Reaches more than 16,000 food processing plants worldwide, with special sections.
Ind/Abst AGRICOLA; BioBusiness (1985-); Biol. Abstr.; Chem. Abstr. (1950-1983); Dairy Sci. Abstr.; Food Sci. Technol. Abstr.; Foods Adlibra; Gen. Period. Index (1985-); Gen. Sci. Source (Jan. 1993-); Mag. Search; Soyabean Abstr.; Sug. Indus. Abstr.; Vocat. Search (Jan. 1993-).

UK/0264-9462
FOOD PROCESSING (BROMLEY, LONDON, ENGLAND). (FOOD PROCESSING.). [Food process.]. (Jan. 1983)-. Academic Scholarly Publication. English. mo. £55.00 UK; £75.00 Europe; £100.00 other. IML Group, Blair House, 184-186 High Street, Tonbridge Kent, TN9 1BQ England. **Tel** 011 44 732 359990, FAX 011 44 732 770049. **ED** Caroline Scoular. **LC** TP368; .F66. **DD** 664/.005. **CODEN** FOPRED. **Bk Rev. Ad Acc, Adv Mgr:** Frank Blackwell. **Circ:** 8,000 (ctrl). ***Continues** Food Processing Industry, 0015-6531.*
Desc: Directed to managers, engineers, directors, and technologists engaged in food and drink processing. Contains feature articles on food processing ingredients, techniques, packaging, marketing, food processing machinery and systems.
Ind/Abst BioBusiness; Bus. Index (1985-); Dairy Sci. Abstr.; EMBASE; F&S Index Plus Text, Int. [Select. Cov.]; Food Sci. Technol. Abstr.; Gen. BusinessFile (1985-); Infomat Int. Bus.; Int. Packag. Abstr.; PROMT; Sug. Indus. Abstr.; Trade Ind. ASAP [Full Txt.]; Trade Ind. Index [Full Txt.].

UK
FOOD PROCESSING EQUIPMENT AND TESTING. English. Derwent Publications Ltd., Derwent House 14, Great Queen Street, London WC2B 5DF England. **Tel** 011 44 71 3442800.

AT
FOOD PROCESSOR. English. bm. $50.00 Australia; $105.00 other. Reed Business Publishing Pty Ltd. / Australia, 1 5 Railway Street, Level 12 North Tower, Chatswood W 2067 NSW Australia. **Tel** 011 61 2 3725222, FAX 011 61 2 4197533. **ED** Jennifer Larson. **Bk Rev. Ad Acc, Adv Mgr:** Ros Richards. **Circ:** 3727 (ctrl).
Desc: FOOD PROCESSOR is written for the food manufacturing industry to keep them up to date with plant, equipment, ingredients and services enabling readers to get their products safely and economically through the factory and to the distribution system.

US/1065-772X
FOOD PRODUCT DESIGN. [Food prod. des.]. (1991)-. Periodical. English. Twelve times a year. $80.00 (one year), $110.00 (two years). Weeks Publishing Company, 3400 Dundee Road, Suite 100, Northbrook IL 60062. **Tel** (708)559-0385. **LC** WMLC 93/1526. **DD** 664. **CODEN** FPDEEN.
Ind/Abst Foods Adlibra.

US/0191-6181
FOOD PRODUCTION MANAGEMENT. [Food prod./manage.]. **VFOAT** Food Production/Management. (July 1971)-. Periodical. English. mo. $25.00 (one year), $45.00 (two year) US; $40.00 (one year), $75.00 (two year) other. CTI Publications Inc., 2619 Maryland Avenue, Baltimore MD 21218. **Tel** (410)467-3338, FAX (410)467-7434. **ED** Arthur I. Judge. **LC** TX599; .T7. **DD** 664/.028/068. **CODEN** FPMNAN. **Bk Rev. Ad Acc, Adv Mgr:** R.Gerstmyer. **Circ:** 5,200 (ctrl). available on microfilm from University Microfilms International (UMI). ***Continues** Canning Trade.*
Desc: Information on firms which can, freeze, glass pack and preserve foods; manufacturers' representatives, distributors, dealers and suppliers to the food processing and preserving industry; trade associations, government agencies, libraries and others allied to the field.
Ind/Abst BioBusiness; Food Sci. Technol. Abstr.; Int. Packag. Abstr. (1986-); Life Sci. Collect.

US/1056-5078
FOOD PRODUCTS & EQUIPMENT. [Food prod. equip.]. **VFOAT** Food Products and Equipment. (198?)-. Periodical. English. mo (11 issues). $23.00 US, Canada & Mexico; $35.00 (surface mail), $70.00 (airmail) other. Cahners Publishing Company, 249 West 17th Street, New York NY 10011. **Tel** (212)645-0067, FAX (212)242-6987. **(Subscription address:** Gordon Publications, Inc., Paid Circulation Department, 301 Gibraltar Drive, Box 650, Morris Plains NJ 07950-0650.**) DD** 664. **[CCC].**
Desc: Reaches corporate administrators, plant/process managers, engineering managers and others responsible for buying, handling and packaging for processing plants engaged in meat, dairy, beverage, baked foods, preserved fruits/vegetables and other food product production.

US/1046-2414
FOOD PROFESSIONAL'S GUIDE, THE. (THE FOOD PROFESSIONAL'S GUIDE : A NATIONAL DIRECTORY OF PEOPLE, PRODUCTS AND SERVICES.). (1990)-. Directory. English. an. $35.00. American Showcase, 915 Broadway, 14th Floor, New York NY 10010. **Tel** (212)673-6600, FAX (212)673-9795, telex 880356 AMSHOW P. **LC** TX650; .F66. **DD** 641/.02573.

US/0884-0806
FOOD PROTECTION REPORT. [Food prot. rep.]. **Added/Corp** Charles Felix Associates. (1985)-. Periodical. English. mo (July/Aug. issue combined). $135.00 (one year), $240.00 (two year), $340.00 (three year). Charles Felix Associates, PO Box 1581, Leesburg VA 22075. **Tel** (703)777-7448, FAX (703)777-4453. **ED** Charles W. Felix. **DD** 641. **CODEN** FPREEP. Index available (Bound in December issue). cum. index.
Ind/Abst BioBusiness (1990-); Foods Adlibra.

US/0091-7605
FOOD PURITY PERSPECTIVES. [Food purity perspect.]. Periodical. English. mo. EMS Inc, 5321 Valley Trail, Racine WI 53402. **Tel** (414)552-8874. **LC** TP373.6; .F66. **DD** 614.3/1/05.

UK/0950-3293
FOOD QUALITY AND PREFERENCE. [Food qual. prefer.]. Vol. 1, No. 1 (1988)-. Academic Scholarly Publication. English. Four times a year. $298.00 The Americas; £200.00 other. Elsevier Applied Science, An Imprint of Elsevier Science Ltd., The Boulevard, Langford Lane, Kidlington, Oxford OX5 1GB United Kingdom. **Tel** 011 44 865 843000, 011 44 865 843699, FAX 011 44 865 843010. **(Subscription address:** Elsevier Science Ltd. Oxford Fulfillment Centre, PO Box 800, Kidlington, Oxford OX5 1DX United Kingdom.**) CODEN** FQPRER. **[CCC].** available on microfilm and microfiche from University Microfilms International (UMI).
Ind/Abst AGRICOLA [Full Cov.]; BioBusiness (1990-); Hortic. Abstr.; Postharvest News Inf.

UK
FOOD R.A. ABSTRACTS FROM CURRENT SCIENTIFIC AND TECHNICAL LITERATURE. Added/Corp British Food Manufacturing Industries Research Association. Food Research Association. Vol. 26, No. 1 (Jan. 1973)-. Periodical. English. mo. £340.00. British Food Manufacturing Industries Research Association, Randalls Road, Leatherhead Surrey KT22 7RY England. **Tel** 011 44 372 376761, FAX 011 44 372 386228, telex 929846.

●CN/0963-9969
FOOD RESEARCH INTERNATIONAL. [Food res. int.]. **Added/Corp** Canadian Institute of Food Science and Technology. Vol. 25, No. 1 (1992)-. Academic Scholarly Publication. English. Six times a year. $462.00 The Americas; £310.00 other. Elsevier Applied Science, An Imprint of Elsevier Science Ltd., The Boulevard, Langford Lane, Kidlington, Oxford OX5 1GB United Kingdom. **Tel** 011 44 865 843000, 011 44 865 843699, FAX 011 44 865 843010. **(Subscription address:** Elsevier Science Ltd. Oxford Fulfillment Centre, PO Box 800, Kidlington, Oxford OX5 1DX United Kingdom.**) LC** TP368; .C3. **NLM** W1; FO482C. **CODEN** FORIEU. **[CCC].** Documents available from The Genuine Article. ***Continues** Canadian Institute of Food Science and Technology. Canadian Institute of Food Science and Technology Journal, 0315-5463.*
Ind/Abst AGRICOLA; Curr. Aware. Biol. Sci., CABS; Curr. Contents, Agric. Biol. Environ. Sci.; Food Sci. Technol. Abstr.; Foods Adlibra; Res. Alert [Full Cov.]; Sci. Cit. Index; Soc. Sci. Cit. Index [Select. Cov.].

SA/0257-8867
FOOD REVIEW. (FOOD REVIEW : OFFICIAL JOURNAL OF THE SOUTH AFRICAN ASSOCIATION FOR FOOD SCIENCE & TECHNOLOGY.). [Food rev.]. **Added/Corp** South African Association for Food Science & Technology. (19??)-. Academic Scholarly Publication. English. Six times a year (Feb., Apr., June, Aug., Oct., Dec.). R70,00 South Africa & Namibia & Homelands; R130,00 others. National Publishing Pty Ltd, 155 2nd Avenue Kenilworth 7700, PO Box 2271, Clareinch 7740 South Africa. **Tel** (021)61-1140, FAX (021)611389, telex 9555542+. **ED** Gill Loubser. **CODEN** FORVDY. **Ad Acc, Adv Mgr:** G Wells. **Circ:** 3,300 (ctrl). available on an online database (file 15/Full-Text) from DIALOG. Documents available from CASDDS. ***Continues** South African Food Review, 0379-6000.*
Desc: Circulates to executives in the food and beverage industry in South Africa. Covers development in technology, processing methods, packaging and distribution.
Ind/Abst BioBusiness; Bus. Index (1991-); Bus. Period. Index; Chem. Abstr. (1983-); Expand. Acad. Index (1992-); F&S Index Plus Text, Int. [Select. Cov.]; Food Sci. Technol. Abstr.; Foods Adlibra; Gen. BusinessFile (1991-); Gen. Period. Index (1991-); Predicasts Forecasts; Trade Ind. ASAP [Full Txt.]; Trade Ind. Index [Full Txt.]; Wilson Bus. Abstr.

US/8755-9129
FOOD REVIEWS INTERNATIONAL. [Food rev. int.]. Vol. 1, No. 1 (1985)-. Academic Scholarly Publication. English. Four times a year. $495.00 US; $509.00 other. Marcel Dekker Inc., 270 Madison Avenue, New York NY 10016. **Tel** (212)696-9000, (800)228-1160, FAX (212)685-4540, telex 421419. **(Subscription address:** Marcel Dekker Inc, PO Box 5017, Monticello NY 12701.**) ED** Roy Teranishi and Irwin Hornstein. **LC** TX341; .F929. **DD** 641.3/005. **NLM** W1; FO482H. **CODEN** FRINEL. **[CCC].** available on microfiche. Documents available from BIOSIS Document Express, CASDDS.
Desc: Provides multidisciplinary, state-of-the-art reviews concerned with food production, food processing, food acceptability, and nutritional values. This journal examines the relationship between food and nutrition and

health, as well as the differing food problems affecting both affluent and developing nations. The insights provided by these articles offer guidance to the various scientists seeking technical solutions to critical global food problems and shortages.
Ind/Abst AGRICOLA [Full Cov.]; Biodeter. Abstr. (1991-); Biol. Abstr. (1985-); Chem. Abstr. (1985-); Curr. Contents, Agric. Biol. Environ. Sci.; Food Sci. Technol. Abstr.; Foods Adlibra; Nutr. Abstr. Rev., Ser. A, Hum. Exp.; Postharvest News Inf.; Ref. Upd. Deluxe Ed.; Rev. Med. Vet. Mycology; Rice Abstr.; Sci. Cit. Index; Soyabean Abstr.

●UK/0964-4164
FOOD SAFETY & SECURITY. [Food saf. secur.]. **VFOAT** Food Safety and Security. (1992)-. English. mo. $363.00 The Americas; £243.00 other. Elsevier Advanced Technology, An Imprint of Elsevier Science Ltd., The Boulevard, Langford Lane, Kidlington, Oxford OX5 1GB United Kingdom. **Tel** 011 44 865 843000, 011 44 865 843699, FAX 011 44 865 843010. **(Subscription address:** Elsevier Science Ltd. Oxford Fulfillment Centre, PO Box 800, Kidlington, Oxford OX5 1DX United Kingdom.) **DD** 363.192. **[CCC].**

UK/0968-1647
FOOD SAFETY CONCERNS BULLETIN, THE. [Food saf. concerns bull.]. (1991)-. English. mo. £160.00. Leatherhead Food Research Association, Randalls Road, Leatherhead Surrey KT22 7RY United Kingdom. **Tel** 011 44 372 376761, FAX 011 44 372 386228, telex 929846. **DD** 363.192.

US/1050-1843
FOOD SAFETY NOTEBOOK. [Food saf. noteb.]. **Added/Corp** Lyda Associates. **VFOAT** FSN. Vol. 1 (Sept./Oct. 1990)-. Periodical. English. Ten times a year. $55.00 US, Canada & Mexico; $65.00 other. Lyda Associates, Inc., PO Box 700, Palisades NY 10964. **Tel** (914)359-8282, FAX (914)359-1229. **ED** Lillian Langseth. **DD** 363. **NLM** W1; FO483. **Circ:** 1,000.

●UK
FOOD SAFETY SERIES. (1992)-. Monographic series. English. ir. Price varies per volume. Chapman & Hall, 2-6 Boundary Row, London SE1 8HN England. **Tel** 011 44 71 865 0066, FAX 011 44 71 522 9623, telex 290164 Chapmag. **ED** M.H. Lessof. **NLM** W1; FO485.

US/0532-0984
FOOD SCIENCE AND TECHNOLOGY: A SERIES OF MONOGRAPHS. (1965)-. Monographic series. English. ir. Price varies per volume. Academic Press, Inc., 6277 Sea Harbor Drive, Orlando FL 32887. **Tel** (800)543-9534, (407)345-4100, FAX (407)363-9661. **ED** Fergus M. Clydesdale and Kathryn L. Wiemer.

UK/0015-6574
FOOD SCIENCE AND TECHNOLOGY ABSTRACTS. **See** Food and Food Industry-Abstracting, Bibliographies and Statistics.

US/0891-8961
FOOD SCIENCE AND TECHNOLOGY (NEW YORK, N.Y. 1984). (FOOD SCIENCE AND TECHNOLOGY.). [Food sci. technol.]. (1984)-. Academic Scholarly Publication. English. ir. Price varies per volume. Marcel Dekker Inc., 270 Madison Avenue, New York NY 10016. **Tel** (212)696-9000, (800)228-1160, FAX (212)685-4540, telex 421419. **(Subscription address:** Marcel Dekker Inc, PO Box 5017, Monticello NY 12701.) **DD** 664. **NLM** W1; FO509P. **CODEN** FSTEEM. Documents available from The Genuine Article, BIOSIS Document Express, CASDDS. ***Continues*** *Food Science, 0071-7223.*
Desc: Presents topics relevant in food science and technology, including food additives, flavor research, preservation of foods, and more.
Ind/Abst Biol. Abstr. (1988-); Chem. Abstr. (1984); Res. Alert [Full Cov.]; Sci. Cit. Index; SCISEARCH.

JA
FOOD SCIENCE AND TECHNOLOGY SERIES. **Added/Corp** Kyoto Daigaku. Nogakubu. **VFOAT** Food sci. and tech. ser. No. 1 (Nov. 1971)-. English.
Ind/Abst Nutr. Abstr. Rev., Ser. A, Hum. Exp.

UK/0950-9623
FOOD SCIENCE & TECHNOLOGY TODAY. [Food sci. technol. today]. **Added/Corp** Institute of Food Science and Technology (U.K.). **VFOAT** Food Science and Technology Today. Vol. 1, No. 1 (Mar. 1987)-. Periodical. English. qt (Mar., June, Sept., Dec.). £56.00 UK & EC; £62.00 other. Institute of Food Science and Technology, 210 Shepherds Bush Road, 5 Cambridge Court, London W6 7NL United Kingdom. **Tel** 011 44 71 603 6316, FAX 011 44 71 6029936. **ED** Heather Payne (081-874-5059). **NLM** W1; FO509R. **[CCC]. Bk Rev**, (Qty: 4). **Ad Acc, Adv Mgr:** Mr. B. Broome, **Tel** 0732-866360. **Pr Rev. Circ:** 3,400. ***Formed by the union of*** *Institute of Food Science and Technology (U.K.). Proceedings - Institute of Food Science and Technology (U.K.), 0144-1493* ***and*** *Focus (Institute of Food Science and Technology (U.K.)).*
Desc: The journal covers research and activity in the food service industry.
Ind/Abst AgBiotech News Inf.; Curr. Technol. Index; Dairy Sci. Abstr.; Food Sci. Technol. Abstr.; Int. Packag. Abstr.; Soyabean Abstr.

US/0885-6877
FOOD-SERVICE EAST. [Food-serv. east]. **VFOAT** Food Service East; Lodging East. Vol. 60, No. 3 (Sept. 1985)-. Periodical. English. Seven times a year. $20.00. The Newbury Street Group Inc., 76 Summer Street, Boston MA 02110. **Tel** (617)695-9080. **ED** Susan Holaday. **DD** 647. **Ad Acc, Adv Mgr:** Richard E. Dolby, **Tel** (800)852-5212. **Circ:** 24,000 (ctrl). ***Continues*** *Lodging and Food-Service East.*
Desc: Trade publication for northeast food service, lodging operators, trends, analysis, products.

US
FOOD SERVICE RECIPE NEWSLETTER; MAKE IT TASTY SPICE BLENDS. English. Twice a year. $30.00 North America; $40.00 other. Prosperity & Profits Unlimited, PO Box 416, Denver CO 80201-0416. **ED** A. Doyle.
Desc: Spice and herb blend recipes.

US/0532-0992
FOOD SERVICE RESEARCH ABSTRACTS. [Food serv. res. abstr.]. **Added/Corp** Society for the Advancement of Food Service Research (U.S.). Began in (1966)-. English. an. Society for the Advancement of Food Service Research, Box One, Hope KY 40334. **LC** TX943; .F68. **DD** 647/.95/05.

●BG
FOOD SITUATION REPORT FOR THE MONTH OF ... [MICROFORM]. **See** Sociology-Social Services and Welfare.

US/1046-705X
FOOD STRUCTURE. [Food struct.]. **Added/Corp** Scanning Microscopy International. (1990)-. Academic Scholarly Publication. English. qt (Mar., June, Sept., Dec.). $100.00. Scanning Microscopy International, PO Box 66507, AMF O'Hare, Chicago IL 60666-0507. **Tel** (708)529-6677, FAX (708)980-6698. **LC** TX543; .F67. **DD** 664/.07. **CODEN** FSTUE2. **[CCC].** Documents available from The Genuine Article, BIOSIS Document Express, CASDDS. ***Continues*** *Food Microstructure, 0730-5419.*
Ind/Abst Agric. Eng. Abstr. (1991-); Biodeter. Abstr. (1991-); Biol. Abstr.; Chem. Abstr.; Curr. Contents, Agric. Biol. Environ. Sci.; Dairy Sci. Abstr.; EMBASE; Field Crop Abstr.; Food Sci. Technol. Abstr.; Foods Adlibra; Hortic. Abstr.; Life Sci. Collect.; Plant Breed. Abstr.; Res. Alert [Full Cov.]; Sci. Cit. Index; SCISEARCH; Seed Abstr.; Sorghum Mill. Abstr.

UK/0141-8521
FOOD SURVEILLANCE PAPER. (FOOD SURVEILLANCE PAPER / MINISTRY OF AGRICULTURE, FISHERIES AND FOOD.). [Food surveill. pap.]. **Added/Corp** Great Britain. Ministry of Agriculture, Fisheries and Food. No. 1 (1978)-. Monographic series. English. ir. Her Majesty's Stationery Office, 51 Nine Elms Lane, London SW8 5DR England. **Tel** 011 44 71 873 8459, 011 44 71 873 8499, FAX 011 44 71 873 8499, 011 44 71 873 8456, telex 297138. **CODEN** FSPAEO. Documents available from BIOSIS Document Express, CASDDS.
Ind/Abst Biol. Abstr.; Chem. Abstr.; Nutr. Abstr. Rev., Ser. A, Hum. Exp.

US
FOOD TALK. English. mo (11 issues). $110.00. Charles Felix Associates, PO Box 1581, Leesburg VA 22075. **Tel** (703)777-7448, FAX (703)777-4453. **ED** Charles W. Felix.

US/0015-6639
FOOD TECHNOLOGY (CHICAGO). (FOOD TECHNOLOGY.). [Food technol.]. **Added/Corp** Institute of Food Technologists. Vol. 1 (Jan. 1947)-. Periodical. English. mo. $82.00 US, Canada & Mexico; $92.00 other. Institute of Food Technologists, 221 North LaSalle Street, Chicago IL 60601. **Tel** (312)782-8424, FAX (312)782-8348. **ED** John B. Klis. **LC** TP370; .F63. **DD** 664.05. **NLM** W1 FO511. **CODEN** FOTEAOFOTEAD. **[CCC]. Bk Rev. Ad Acc. Pr Rev. Circ:** 25,000. available on microfilm and microfiche from University Microfilms International (UMI). Documents available from The Genuine Article, BIOSIS Document Express, UMI Article Clearinghouse, CASDDS, Documents on Demand. ***Formed by the union of*** *Proceedings - Institute of Food Technologists, 0097-2118; Institute of Food Technologists. Newsletter* ***and*** *Institute of Food Technologists. Transactions.*
Desc: Covers all aspects of food, ranging from harvesting to consumption. Topics include biology, chemistry, nutrition, engineering, production, microbiology, packaging, quality assurance, regulations, research and development, and consumerism.
Ind/Abst Acad. Ind. [Computer File] (1987-); Acad. Search (Jan. 1993-); AgBiotech News Inf.; AGRICOLA [Full Cov.]; Appl. Sci. Technol. Index; BioBusiness (1984-); Biodeter. Abstr. (19??-19??); Biol. Agric. Index; Biol. Abstr.; Chem. Abstr.; Chemorecept. Abstr.; Curr. Aware. Biol. Sci., CABS; Curr. Biotechnol.; Curr. Contents, Agric. Biol. Environ. Sci.; Dairy Sci. Abstr.; EMBASE; Energy Inf. Abstr.; Environ. Abstr.; Expand. Acad. Index (1987-); F&S Index Plus Text, Int. [Select. Cov.]; Food Sci. Technol. Abstr.; Foods Adlibra; Gen. Sci. Index; Gen. Sci. Source (Jan. 1993-); Helminthol. Abstr.; Hortic. Abstr.; Index Vet.; INFO-SOUTH Abstr.; INIS Atomindex [Micro.]; Int. Packag. Abstr.; Mag. Search; Newsp. Period. Abstr. (1989-); Nucl. Sci. Abstr.; Nutr. Abstr. Rev., Ser. B, Live Feeds and Feed.; Nutr. Abstr. Rev., Ser. A, Hum. Exp.; Nutr. Res. Newsl.; Life Sci. Collect.; Pig News Inf.; Predicasts; PROMT; Res. Alert [Full Cov.]; Sci. Cit. Index; SCISEARCH; Sel. Water Resour. Abstr.; Soc. Sci. Cit. Index [Select. Cov.]; Stat. Theory Method Abstr. (1959-1963); Sug. Indus. Abstr.; Vet. Bull.; Vocat. Search (Jan. 1993-); World Agric. Econ.

NZ/0015-6655
FOOD TECHNOLOGY IN NEW ZEALAND. [Food technol. N.Z.]. **VFOAT** Food Technology. (1965)-. Periodical. English. mo. 60.00NZ$ New Zealand; 75.00NZ$ other. Trade Publications Ltd., 300 Great South Road Greenlane, Newmarket Auckland New Zealand. **Tel** 011 64 9 9293000. **ED** Pam Parsons. **CODEN** FTNZAO. **[CCC]. Ad Acc. Circ:** 2,600 (ctrl). Documents available from CASDDS.
Desc: New, technical articles and research papers on all aspects of food and beverage processing, packaging and marketing, including new equipment and technology; also a yearbook directory.
Ind/Abst AGRICOLA; BioBusiness (1989-1991); Chem. Abstr.; Dairy Sci. Abstr.; Food Sci. Technol. Abstr.

CN/0829-643X
FOOD (TORONTO). (FOOD.). [Food]. **VFOAT** Food in Canada. Vol. 44, i.e. 45, No. 4 (Apr. 1985)-. Periodical. English. Ten times a year. 53.00Can$ Canada; 105.00Can$ other. MacLean Hunter Ltd. Business Publishers / Canada, Box 9100, Station A, Toronto ONT M5W 1A5 Canada. **Tel** (416)946-8420, (800)567-0444. **(Subscription address:** Indas, 35 Riviera Drive, Building 17, Markham Ontario L3R 8N4 Canada.) **DD** 338.1/9/71. **CODEN** FOODEY. available on microfilm and microfiche from University Microfilms International (UMI). ***Continues*** *Food in Canada, 0015-6442.*
Ind/Abst BioBusiness; Foods Adlibra.

US/0015-6663
FOOD TRADE NEWS. (19??)-. Periodical. English. mo. $36.00. Food Trade News, 2 Elm Street, Suite 104, Conshohocken PA 19428. **Tel** (215)834-3760. **(Subscription address:** 5537 Twin Knolls Road, #438, Columbia, MD 21045; phone (410)730-5013) **ED** Bob Ingram. Index available. **Ad Acc. Circ:** 23,000 (ctrl).
Desc: Publishes the news of the food industry in the Pennsylvania, New Jersey, Delaware and Maryland markets.

UK/0015-6671
FOOD TRADE REVIEW. [Food trade rev.]. **VFOAT** FTR. (1939)-. Trade Publication. English. Twelve times a year. £38.00 UK, £49.00 other (surface mail); £49.00 Europe, £69.00 other (airmail). Food Trade Press Ltd, Station House, Hortons Way, Westerham Kent TN16 1BZ England. **Tel** 011 44 689 50551, 011 44 689 53070, FAX 011 44 689 561285. **ED** Howard Binsted. **CODEN** FTRVAW. **[CCC].** Index available. **Bk Rev**, (Qty: 120). **Ad Acc, Adv Mgr:** Adrain Rinsted. **Circ:** 5,152. available on an online database, CD-ROM, magnetic tape, and microfilm from INFO ACCESS; available on an online database (file 648/Full-Text) from DIALOG. ***Continues*** *Food Industries Review.*
Desc: Britain's oldest trade journal on the food industry.
Ind/Abst AGRICOLA; BioBusiness; Curr. Technol. Index; Dairy Sci. Abstr.; F&S Index Plus Text, Int. [Select. Cov.]; Food Sci. Technol. Abstr.; Foods Adlibra; Int. Packag. Abstr.

US
FOOD TRENDS NEWSLETTER. Newsletter. English. Twenty-four times a year. $195.00. Food Trends Newsletter, 937 Elm Court, Palatine IL 60067. **Tel** (708)358-8487, FAX (708)358-8772. **ED** Robert P. Messenger. **Ad Acc. Circ:** 4,000.
Desc: News and information on the manufacturing of the food & beverage industry.

HK
FOOD WORLD. Chinese. mo. $70.00 US; $77.00 Canada. **(Subscription address:** Evergreen Publishing & Stationery, 136 South Atlantic Boulevard, Monterey Park, CA 91754)

US/0191-619X
FOOD WORLD (COLUMBIA). (FOOD WORLD.). (19??)-. Periodical. English. mo. $36.00. Food World, 5537 Twin Knolls Road/Suite 438, Columbia MD 21045-3240. **Tel** (410)730-5013, FAX (410)740-4680. **ED** Shari Simmons. **Ad Acc, Adv Mgr:** Nina Weiland. **Circ:** 23,000 (ctrl).
Desc: Food trade newspaper covering the state of Maryland, Southern PA, Virginia, Delaware, and District of Columbia.

UK/0260-1974
FOOD WORLD NEWS. [Food world news]. (1982)-. Periodical. English. bm. $60.00. Food World News, 130 Wigmore Street, London W1H 0AT England. **Tel** 01 486 6757.

II
FOODCORP. **Added/Corp** Food Corporation of India. Vol. 4, No. 1 (Feb. 1973)-. Periodical. English. mo. ***Continues*** *Foodcorp Quarterly.*

US/8756-1514
FOODLETTER. [Foodletter]. **VFOAT** Food Letter. (July 1984)-. Periodical. English. mo (except combined May/June and Nov./Dec.). $95.00 (1 year), $180.00 (2 year). Foodletter, PO Box 204, Mahwah NJ 07430. **Tel** (201)529-3835. **ED** Doreen Higgins. **DD** 641.
Desc: Ideas and insights on food and beverages.

UK/0951-130X
FOODNEWS. [Foodnews]. (19??)-. Periodical. English. wk. £240.00 UK; DM795.00 Europe and Middle East; $520.00 other. Food News, 22A Sidcup High Street, Sidcup Kent DA14 6EH England. **Tel** 011 44 81 3007864, FAX 011 44 81 3038121, telex 8954109. **ED** Godfrey Brown. **DD** 637. ***Continues*** *Roy Ellard's Foodnews.*
Desc: Weekly commodity newspaper reporting on prices, supply and demand trends, on canned/frozen foods, fruit juice concentrates, dairy products and dried fruit and nuts. Foodnews readers also receive supplements/features which provide in-depth product reviews, statistical and market briefings. Concise, easy-to-digest: That's what Foodnews offers you.

NE/0015-6701
FOODPRESS. [Foodpress]. (19??)-. Periodical. Dutch. wk (50 issues per year). Fl300.00. Uitgeverij Nocerizon BV, Postbus 276, 3770 Ag Barnaveld, Netherlands. **Tel** 011 31 4320 92556. **UDC** 641.

US/1056-327X
FOODREVIEW (WASHINGTON, D.C.). (FOODREVIEW.). [FoodReview]. **Added/Corp** United States. Dept. of Agriculture. Economic Research Service. United States. Dept. of Agriculture. Commodity Economics Division. **VFOAT** Food Review. Vol. 14, Issue 1 (January-March 1991)-. Government Publication. English. Three times a year. $8.50 domestic; $10.65 other. Superintendent of Documents, US Government Printing Office, Washington DC 20402. **Tel** (202)275-3328, FAX (202)786-2377. **LC** HD9001; .N275. **DD** 338.1/973/05. **NLM** W1; FO482D. **CODEN** FORVEZ. available on microfilm and microfiche from University Microfilms International (UMI). Documents available from UMI Article Clearinghouse. ***Continues*** *National Food Review, 0164-3428.*
Desc: Offer developments in food prices, product safety, nutrition programs, consumption patterns and marketing.
Ind/Abst Bus. ASAP (199?-) [Full Txt.]; Bus. Source (Jan. 1993-); Foods Adlibra; Gen. Sci. Source (Jan. 1993-) [Full Txt.]; Health Source (Jan. 1993-) [Full Txt.]; Mag. Search; Newsp. Period. Abstr. (1992-); PAIS Int. Print; Vocat. Search (Jan. 1993-) [Full Txt.].

US/0146-9304
FOODS ADLIBRA (1975). **See** Food and Food Industry-Abstracting, Bibliographies and Statistics.

●US/1063-4169
FOODS INTELLIGENCE ON COMPACT DISC. **See** Food and Food Industry-Abstracting, Bibliographies and Statistics.

US/0897-7208
FOODSERVICE DIRECTOR. [FoodServ. dir.]. **VFOAT** Food Service Director. Vol. 1, No. 1 (May 15, 1988)-. Periodical. English. mo. $50.00 US. Bill Communications Inc., 355 Park Avenue South, New York NY 10010-1789. **Tel** (800)821-6897, (212)592-6262, FAX (212)592-6209. **ED** Walter Schruntek. **LC** TX901; .F62. **DD** 647.95/0973/05.
Desc: Targeted to professionals at schools, colleges, hospitals, nursing homes, airlines, contract feeders, penal institutions, military installations and other noncommercial corporations and organizations.

US/0883-1912
FOODSERVICE DIRECTORY. [Foodservice dir.]. **VFOAT** Food Service Directory; C-Store Business ... Foodservice Directory; C-Store Business ... Food Service Directory. 1985-. Directory. English. $25.00 single copy. C-Store Business Foodservice Directory, 1351 Washington Boulevard, Stamford CT 06902. **LC** TX912; .F638.

US/0199-9400
FOODSERVICE DISTRIBUTION NEWS. Began with Vol. 5, No. 5, May 1980. Periodical. English. ir. $20.00. 270 St Paul Street, Denver CO 80206. **LC** TX901; .F63. **DD** 642/.5/05. ***Continues*** *Foodservice Distribution Sales, 0192-8708.*

US/0896-4505
FOODSERVICE DISTRIBUTOR, THE. [Foodserv. distrib.]. **VFOAT** Food Service Distributor. Vol. 1, No. 1 (March 1987)-. Periodical. English. Twelve times a year. $50.00 US; $80.00 Canada; $85.00 Mexico; $95.00 other. Penton Publishing, 1100 Superior Avenue, Cleveland OH 44114-2543. **Tel** (216)696-7000, FAX (216)696-0836. **(Subscription address:** Penton Publishing, PO Box 96732, Chicago IL 60693.**)** **LC** HD9001; .F652. **DD** 664/.0068/8. **CODEN** FODIES. **[CCC].** Index available. **Ad Acc.** ctrl circ. available on microfilm from University Microfilms International (UMI).
Ind/Abst BioBusiness; Foods Adlibra.

US/0888-8515
FOODSERVICE EQUIPMENT & SUPPLIES SPECIALIST. [Foodserv. equip. supplies spec.]. **VFOAT** Foodservice Equipment and Supplies Specialist. (1986)-. Periodical. English. mo (13 issues). $75.00 US; $112.00 Canada; $105.00 Mexico; $135.00 (surface mail) other. Cahners Publishing Company, 249 West 17th Street, New York NY 10011. **Tel** (212)645-0067, FAX (212)242-6987. **(Subscription address:** Cahners Publishing Company / Colorado, Paid Subscription Service Center, PO Box 7610, Highlands Ranch CO 80126-7610.**)** **LC** TX943; .F6. **DD** 641. **CODEN** FESSET. **[CCC].** available on microfilm and microfiche from University Microfilms International (UMI). ***Continues*** *Foodservice Equipment Specialist, 0148-4958.*
Desc: The standard journal of the foodservice equipment industry is intended for buyers, specifiers and distributors of foodservice equipment for commercial and institutional use. Features include new products, kitchen design and decor, distribution, sales and marketing. Includes the annual Suppliers Source Guide.

US/0363-1303
FOODSERVICE EQUIPMENT DEALER. BUYERS GUIDE AND PRODUCT DIRECTORY. (1975)-. Directory. English. an. $10.00. Circulation Office / Denver, 270 St. Paul Street, Denver CO 80206. **LC** TX912; .F64. **DD** 338.4/7/642502573. ***Continues*** *Foodservice Equipment Product Directory.*

US
FOODSERVICE EQUIPMENT SPECIALIST. BUYERS GUIDE AND PRODUCT DIRECTORY. 1978-. Directory. English. an. $55.00. Foodservice Equipment & Supplies Specialist, 1350 East Touhy Avenue, Des Plaines IL 60018. **Tel** (312)635-8800. **(Subscription address:** 270 St Paul Street, Denver CO 80206**)** **ED** Gregory B Richards. **Ad Acc. Circ:** 20,203 (ctrl). ***Continues*** *Foodservice Equipment Dealer. Buyers Guide and Product Directory.*
Desc: The standard journal of the foodservice equipment industry intended for buyers, specifiers and distributors of foodservice equipment for commercial and institutional use.

US/1040-4546
FOODSERVICE OPERATORS GUIDE. [Foodserv. oper. guide]. (1989)-. English. an. $207.00. Foodservice Database Company Inc, 5724 West Diversey Avenue, Chicago IL 60639. **Tel** (312)745-9400. **ED** Raymond Mitchell. **DD** 647. Index available. **Ad Acc.**
Desc: Reference of major restaurants in US.

US/0199-7696
FOODSERVICE PRODUCT NEWS. [Foodserv. prod. news]. Vol. 13, No. 5 (Mar. 1980)-. Periodical. English. Eight times a year. $40.00. Young/Conway Publications Inc., 1101 Richmond Avenue, Suite 201, Point Pleasant BC NJ 08742. **Tel** (908)295-5959. **DD** 642. ***Continues*** *Food & Equipment Product News, 0015-6280.*

●US/1062-7324
FOODSERVICE YEARBOOK INTERNATIONAL. **VFOAT** Expo; Foodservice Yearbook International Expo; Foodservice Yearbook International Directory. (1992)-. Periodical. English. Three times a year. $39.95. Keller Publishing Corporation, 150 Great Neck Road, Great Neck NY 11021. **Tel** (516)829-9210, FAX (516)829-5414, telex 221574 KELLE.

CN/0834-3365
FOODSTORE MAGAZINE. [Foodstore mag.]. **VFOAT** Food Store Magazine. Vol. 1, No. 1 (June/July 1986)-. Periodical. English. bm. $19.95. LDL Magazines Inc, 468 Queen Street East/Suite 203, Toronto Ontario M5A 1T7 Canada. **DD** 381/.45664/00971.
Desc: Information on the food industry and grocery trade.

GW/0936-0646
FOODTEC. ***Ceased.*** [FoodTec]. (1988)-(Jan. 1993). Periodical. German. qt (4 issues). Deutscher Fachverlag GmbH, Verlagsgruppe, D 60264 Frankfurt Germany. **Tel** 011 49 69 75951001, telex 411 862. **UDC** 663/664.

AT
FOODWEEK. English. ir. 365.00Aus$. Ian Huntley Publishers Pty Limited, PO Box 99, Cremorne NSW, 2090 Australia. **Tel** 11 61 2 9535788.

US
FOODWEEK NEWSLETTER. Newsletter. English. wk. $295.00US; $375.00 (airmail) other. Putnam Publishing Company, 301 East Erie Street, Chicago IL 60611. **Tel** (312)644-2020, FAX (312)644-1131.

CN/0015-9158
FOURNEE, LA. (1947)-. Periodical. French. bm. 25.00Can$ Canada; 30.00Can$ US; 40.00Can$ other. Communications Vero Inc, 1600 Henri Bourassa Boulevard, Montreal Quebec H3M 3E2 Canada. **Tel** (514)332-8376, FAX (541)332-2666. **ED** Dominique LaMarche. cum. index. **Ad Acc. Circ:** 4,500 (ctrl).
Desc: Articles about exhibition, for people in the pastry and bakery business. There are also articles about new products, or people who have received honors in their field.

FR
FRED : FOOD REGULATIONS EUROPEAN DIRECTORY. Directory. English. qt. 2800.00F. APRIA, 14 16 rue Claude Bernard, 75005 Paris France. **Tel** 011 33 1 47073900.

UK/0306-5782
FREEZE. [Freeze]. Vol. 1 (Jan./Mar. 1972)-. Periodical. English. qt. Hereford Press Ltd, 25 Elystan Place, London SW3 3JY England. **LC** TX610; .F73. **DD** 641.4/53/05.

US/1062-2705
FRESH TRENDS. (FRESH TRENDS / CONDUCTED FOR THE PACKER MAGAZINE BY VANCE RESEARCH SERVICES.). [Fresh trends]. **Added/Corp** Vance Research Services. (1987)-. Periodical. English. an. $20.00 (comes also with Packer Magazine). Vance Publishing Corporation, 400 Knightsbridge Parkway, Lincolnshire IL 60069. **Tel** (800)255-5113, (708)634-2600. **LC** HD9001; .F67. **DD** 381/.415/0973021.

UK/0265-6485
FROZEN & CHILLED FOODS. [Frozen chill. foods]. **VFOAT** Frozen and Chilled Foods. Vol. 37, No. 1/2 (Jan./Feb. 1984)-. Periodical. English. mo. £58.65 UK; £70.50, $109.30 other. Argus Press Group, Queensway House, 2 Queensway Redhill, Surrey RH1 1QS England. **Tel** 011 44 737 768611, 011 44 737 761685, FAX 011 44 737 760510, telex 948669 TOPJNL G. **CODEN** FCFOE6. ***Continues*** *Frozen Foods.*
Desc: Specialist journal for frozen and chilled food retailers; manufacturers; wholesalers and caterers
Ind/Abst BioBusiness (1989-); Curr. Technol. Index; F&S Index Plus Text, Int. [Full Txt.] [Select. Cov.]; Food Sci. Technol. Abstr.; Infomat Int. Bus.; Int. Packag. Abstr.; PROMT [Full Txt.]; Trade Ind. ASAP [Full Txt.]; Trade Ind. Index [Full Txt.].

UK
FROZEN & CHILLED FOODS YEAR BOOK. **VFOAT** Frozen and Chilled Foods Yearbook; Frozen & Chilled Foods. (1985)-. English. an. £76.20 UK; $126.00 other. Argus Press Group, Queensway House, 2 Queensway Redhill, Surrey RH1 1QS England. **Tel** 011 44 737 768611, 011 44 737 761685, FAX 011 44 737 760510, telex 948669 TOPJNL G. **LC** TP493.5; .F75. ***Continues*** *Frozen Foods Year Book.*

US/0016-2191
FROZEN FOOD AGE. [Frozen food age]. Vol. 1 (Aug. 1952)-. Periodical. English. mo. $75.00 US; $86.00 Canada; $96.00 other. Frozen Food Age Publishing Corporation, Four Stamford Forum, Stamford CT 06901. **Tel** (203)325-3500. **LC** HD9001; .F68. **DD** 338.4/7/6640285. **CODEN** FFOADT. available on an online database (file 648/Full-Text) from DIALOG.
Ind/Abst BioBusiness; Infomat Int. Bus.; Int. Packag. Abstr.; Trade Ind. ASAP [Full Txt.]; Trade Ind. Index [Full Txt.].

US/0889-5902
FROZEN FOOD DIGEST. [Frozen food dig.]. Vol. 1, No. 1 (Oct. 1985)-. Periodical. English. Four times a year (Feb., Apr., July, Oct.). $30.00. Saul Beck, 271 Madison Avenue, New York NY 10016. **Tel** (212)557-8600, FAX (212)986-9868. **ED** Audrey Beck. **LC** TP493.5.A1; Q5. **DD** 664/.02853/025. **CODEN** FFDIEX. cum. index. **Ad Acc. Circ:** 16,000 (ctrl). ***Continues*** *Quick Frozen Foods (New York, N.Y. : 1952), 0033-6408.*
Desc: Complete coverage of retail and food service marketplace, packers, processing plants, brokers, distributors, food service operations, warehousing, refrigerated transportation, freezing equipment, machinery and supplies.
Ind/Abst AGRICOLA; BioBusiness (1990-); Bus. Index (1988-); Bus. Period. Index (1985-); F&S Index Plus Text, Int. [Select. Cov.]; Foods Adlibra; Gen. BusinessFile (1988-); Gen. Period. Index (1988-); Infobank (1985-); Mag. Search; PROMT; Stat. Ref. Index; Trade Ind. ASAP [Full Txt.]; Trade Ind. Index [Full Txt.].

US/0279-1498
FROZEN FOOD EXECUTIVE, THE. (THE FROZEN FOOD EXECUTIVE. NATIONAL FROZEN FOOD ASSOCIATION.). **Added/Corp** National Frozen Food Association (U.S.). (19??)-. Periodical. English. Twelve times a year. $30.00 members; $60.00 non-members. National Frozen Food Association, PO Box 6069, Harrisburg PA 17112. **Tel** (717)534-1601. **ED** Cindi Rockwell, (phone: (717)651-8601). **Ad Acc, Adv Mgr:** JoAnne Meyers. **Circ:** 4,000 (ctrl).
Desc: Monthly magazine printed for members of the National Frozen Food Association. Content of magazine includes frozen food statistics, industry trends, new products, government and regional news and views.

UK
FROZEN FOOD MANAGEMENT. bm. £18.00 UK; £40.00 US; £35.00 other. Winlove Publications Ltd, 4

High Street, Croydon CR0 1YA England. **Tel** 081-688 2696. **ED** Kirsti Corbert. ctrl circ.
Desc: Covers all items in the frozen food sector.

US/0469-7405
FROZEN FOOD PACK STATISTICS. See Food and Food Industry-Abstracting, Bibliographies and Statistics.

US/0192-0367
FROZEN FOOD REPORT. [Frozen food rep.]. **Added/Corp** American Frozen Food Institute. **VFOAT** AFFI Frozen Food Report. (19??)-. Periodical. English. bm. Comes with American Frozen Food Institute membership. American Frozen Food Institute, 1764 Old Meadow Road, Suite 350, McLean VA 22102. **Tel** (703)821-0770, FAX (703)821-1350. **ED** Traci D. Vasilik. **DD** 338. **Bk Rev. Ad Acc. Circ:** 3,500 (ctrl).
Desc: Provides complete coverage of the American Frozen Food Institute and developments/issues affecting the frozen food industry.

DK/0106-004X
FRUGTAVLEREN. [Frugtavleren]. **Added/Corp** Dansk Erhvervsfrugtavl. (1972)-. Periodical. Danish. mo. ***Supersedes*** *Erhvervsfrugtavleren.*
Ind/Abst Crop Physiol. Abstr.; Hortic. Abstr.; Plant Breed. Abstr.; Postharvest News Inf.; Soils Fert.

US
FRUIT AND VEGETABLE NATIONAL SHIPPING POINT TRENDS. See Business-Commerce.

CN/0380-5042
FRUIT AND VEGETABLE PRESERVATION. ***Title Change.*** (FRUIT AND VEGETABLE PRESERVATION / MANUFACTURING AND PRIMARY INDUSTRIES DIVISION / CONSERVATION DE FRUITS ET DE LEGUMES / DIVISION DES INDUSTRIES MANUFACTURIERES ET PRIMAIRES.). [Fruit veg. preserv.]. **Added/Corp** Statistics Canada. Manufacturing and Primary Industries Division. Statistics Canada. Industry Division. **VFOAT** Conservation de Fruits et de Legumes. Vol. 1, No. 1 (Jan. 1972)-(1990). Periodical. English (French). an. Statistics Canada, Publications Sales & Services, Main Building Room 1710, Ottawa Ontario K1A 0T6 Canada. **Tel** (613)951-5078, (800)267-6677, FAX (613)951-1584, telex 053-3585. **DD** 338.4/76648/00971. ***Continued by*** *Pack of Processed Asparagus, 1180-5900; Pack of Apples and Apple Products, 1180-5986.*
Desc: Seasonal pack of selected individual canned and frozen fruits and vegetables, by major region, by container size at the Canada level.

FR/0754-0698
FRUITS & LEGUMES. VFOAT Fruits et Legumes. (1983)-. Periodical. French. mo. (July and Aug. combined). 240.00F (1 year), 395.00F (2 year) France; 305.00F (1 year), 520.00F (2 year) Switzerland and Austria; 365.00F (1 year), 605.00F (2 year) other. Agropole - Alphagro, BP 200, 47931 Agen Ct, Cedex 9 France. **Tel** 011 33 53 772130, FAX 011 33 53 772131. **ED** Guy DuBon. **UDC** 634. **Bk Rev**, (Qty: 1). **Ad Acc. Circ:** 7,500 (ctrl).

US/1072-0758
FSIS FOOD SAFETY REVIEW. [FSIS food saf. rev.]. **Added/Corp** United States. Food Safety and Inspection Service. **VFOAT** Food Safety Review. **VAT** Food Safety and Inspection Service Food Safety Review. Vol. 1, No. 1 (Summer 1991)-. Periodical. English. Four times a year. Free. Food Safety Inspection Service, Information Office 116 2 A, USDA, Washington DC 20250. **Tel** (202)720-9113. **LC** TX501; .F78. **DD** 363.19/26/097305.
Ind/Abst AGRICOLA.

US/0271-7328
GF NEWS. [GF news]. **Main/Corp** General Foods Corporation. **VAT** General Foods News. Periodical. English. bm. General Foods, 250 North Street, White Plains NY 10625.

US/1040-3140
GOOD FOOD + FITNESS=A WINNING LIFESTYLE. [Good food + fit. = win. lifestyle]. **VFOAT** Good Food Plus Fitness Equals a Winning Lifestyle. No. 1 (Summer 1988)-. Periodical. English. qt. $12.00. Sunamita MK Lim, 433 13th Avenue East/Suite 106, Seattle WA 98102. **DD** 641.

US/0885-0690
GOOD FOOD MAGAZINE. ***Ceased.*** [Good food mag.]. Vol. 3, No. 1 (Feb. 1986)-(1988). Periodical. English. mo. Triangle Communications, 850 Third Avenue, New York NY 10022. **Tel** (212)759-8100. **DD** 641. **Ad Acc. Circ:** 650,000. ***Continues*** *Good Food.*
Desc: A unique service magazine, with food being its special interest and total environment.

GW/0017-2243
GORDIAN (1948). (GORDIAN.). [Gordian (1948)]. (1895)-. Academic Scholarly Publication. German. Ten times a year (monthly with Jan./Feb. and Jul./Aug. issues combined). DM107.00 Germany; DM115.00 other. A Gordian GmbH & Company, Postfach 605128, D 22246 Hamburg Germany. **Tel** 49 40 275481, FAX 49 40 2799012. **ED** Peter Pries (editor's phone: 49 40 2793809). **CODEN** GORDAM. Index available. **Bk Rev. Ad Acc. Circ:** 3400. Documents available from CASDDS.
Desc: Topics include raw material, quality control, products development, packaging and storage, microbiology, sanitation, modern production plants, etc.
Ind/Abst AGRICOLA; Chem. Abstr.; Dairy Sci. Abstr.; EMBASE; Energy Res. Abstr. (March 1982-); Food Sci. Technol. Abstr.; Hortic. Abstr.; Int. Packag. Abstr.; Nutr. Abstr. Rev., Ser. A, Hum. Exp.; Soyabean Abstr.

US/1052-4630
GOURMET NEWS (YARMOUTH, ME.). (GOURMET NEWS.). [Gourmet news]. Vol. 55, No. 4 (1990)-. Periodical. English. mo. Free (to specialty food trade professionals). United Publications Inc., PO Box 995, 38 Lafayette Street, Yarmouth ME 04096. **Tel** (207)846-0600, FAX (207)846-0657. **LC** TX901; .G69. **DD** 338.4/76415/05. **CODEN** GONEE9. ***Continues*** *Gourmet Today (Birmingham, Mich. : 1986).*
Ind/Abst Foods Adlibra (1990-).

US/0199-0357
GOURMET RETAILER, THE. [Gourmet retail.]. Vol. 1 (Sept. 1979)-. Periodical. English. mo. Free inside US; $24.00 postage other. Specialty Media, Inc., 3301 Ponce de Leon Boulevard, Suite 300, Coral Gables FL 33134. **Tel** (800)397-1137, (305)446-3388, FAX (305)446-2868. **LC** HD9321.1; .G68. **DD** 381/.45664/00973.

US/0279-8247
GOURMET'S NOTEBOOK, A. ***Ceased.*** Vol. 1, No. 1 (Dec. 1972)-(July 1992). Periodical. English. Ten times a year. Gourmet's Notebook, PO Box 12171, Seattle WA 98112. **Tel** (206)322-5882. **ED** D. M. Huey and P. L. Siggs. Index available. ctrl circ.

CN/0824-6181
GPMC NEWSLETTER. [GPMC newsl.]. **Added/Corp** Grocery Products Manufacturers of Canada. (Nov. 1982)-. Newsletter. English. bm. Free to Canada. Grocery Products Manufacturers of Canada, 1185 Eglinton Avenue East, Don Mills Ontario M3C 3C6 Canada. **Tel** (416)429-4444. **ED** S K Watanabe. **DD** 338.4/7664/00971. **Circ:** 1,500. ***Continues*** *Newsletter (Grocery Products Manufacturers of Canada), 0824-619X.*
Desc: Contains items of interest to grocery product manufacturers in Canada regarding association activities, including government, and trade liaison, and upcoming meeting dates.

US/0160-8894
GR. GROCERS REPORT. VFOAT Grocers Report. Periodical. English. mo. Super Markets Productions Ltd, PO Box 6124, San Rafael CA 94903. **Tel** (415)479-0211. **ED** Lori Abrams. Index available. **Ad Acc. Pr Rev. Circ:** 15,000 (ctrl).
Desc: A how-to magazine devoted to supermarket retailing.

UK
GRAIN AND OILSEEDS. See Agriculture.

US
GRAPE RESEARCH NEWS. Added/Corp New York State Agricultural Experiment Station. New York Wine & Grape Foundation. Vol. 1, No. 1 (Jan. 1990)-. English.

SP/0017-3495
GRASAS Y ACEITES (SEVILLA). See Biology-Biochemistry.

US/8756-2553
GREAT FOODS MAGAZINE. [Great foods mag.]. **VFOAT** Great Foods. V. 1, No. 1 (May/June 1984)-. Periodical. English. bm. Great Foods Magazine Inc, 333 Sylvan Avenue, Englewood Cliffs NJ 07632. **DD** 641.

US/0272-796X
GREAT RECIPES OF THE WORLD. [Gt. recipes world]. Vol. 1, No. 1 (March 1981)-. Periodical. English. mo (except Aug./Sept.). $9.87. Digest Publishing Inc, 333 Sylvan Avenue, Englewood Cliffs NJ 07632.

US/0886-3504
GREAT TASTE. [Great taste]. **VFOAT** Great Taste Newsletter. Vol. 1, No. 1 (Mar. 1986)-. Periodical. English. mo. $18.00. Great Taste Newsletter, PO Box 10985, Des Moines IA 50340. **DD** 641.

US
GRIFFIN REPORT, THE. ***Title Change.*** **VFOAT** The Griffin Report of New England. V. 10, No. 1 (Jan. 1975)-. Periodical. English. mo. Griffin Publishing Company, PO Box 983, Dennis MA 02638. **Tel** (617)385-8335. **ED** John H Griffin Jr. **Ad Acc.** ctrl circ. ***Continued by*** *Griffin Report of Food Marketing, 0192-4400.*
Desc: Food trade newspaper.

US/0192-4400
GRIFFIN REPORT OF FOOD MARKETING, THE. VFOAT Griffin Report. Vol. 12, No. 9 (Sept. 1977)-. Periodical. English. mo. $42.00. Griffin Publishing Co Inc, 1099 Hingham Street, Rockland MA 02370. **Tel** (617)878-5300 or, (508)385-5700, FAX (508)385-8134. **ED** Heather Reesse. **Ad Acc, Adv Mgr:** Kevin Griffin. **Circ:** 14,780 (ctrl). ***Continues*** *Griffin Report.*
Desc: Reports the news and happenings of the New England and upstate New York grocery and food retailing industries. Issues include annual top selling item studies, annual market studies, and food broker studies. 50% of the space is devoted to editorial features including personnel changes, new stores, new products, local trends and up-coming events.

UK
GRIST INTERNATIONAL. English. bm (Jan., Mar., May, July, Sept., Dec.). 90.00 Aus$. The Grist Interantional, 2 Balfour Road, Highbury, London, N5 2HB England. **Tel** 011 44 71 3598323, FAX 011 44 71 3543962.
Desc: Concerned with the beverage industry of Europe.

●UK/0967-5892
GROCER FOOD & DRINK DIRECTORY, THE. [Groc. food & drink dir.]. **VFOAT** Grocer Food and Drink Directory. (1992)-. Directory. English. an. £85.00. William Reed Ltd, Broadfield Park, Crawley, West Sussex RH11 9RJ England. **Tel** 011 44 293 613400, FAX 0293-613156. **Ad Acc.**

UK
GROCER. MONTHLY SUPPLEMENT, THE. Vol. 1, No. 1 (May 1950)-. Periodical. English. £40.00 UK; £80.00 Europe; £140.00 other. William Reed Ltd, Broadfield Park, Crawley, West Sussex RH11 9RJ England. **Tel** 011 44 293 613400, FAX 0293-613156. available on an online database (files 771,772,799/Full-Text) from DIALOG.
Desc: Information grocers and the grocery trade.
Ind/Abst F&S Index Plus Text, Int. [Select. Cov.]; Foods Adlibra; Infomat Int. Bus.

US/0745-4104
GROCERS JOURNAL OF CALIFORNIA. ***Title Change.*** **Added/Corp** Southern California Grocers Association. Vol. 64, No. 1 (Jan. 1979)-(19??). Periodical. English. mo (11 issues per year - Nov/Dec issue combined). Southern California Grocers Association, 906 G Street, Suite 700, Sacremento CA 95814. **Tel** (916)448-3545. **ED** Jackie Binkow. **Ad Acc. Circ:** 8,500. ***Continues*** *South California Grocers Journal.* ***Continued by*** *California Grocer.*
Desc: Covers the California food industry, providing information on government, new products and personnel changes. Features include guest editorials, current trends, convention coverage.

NZ/0113-1850
GROCERS' REVIEW. [Groc. rev.]. (1974)-. Periodical. English. Eleven times a year (monthly except Jan.). 45.00NZ$ New Zealand; 150.00NZ$ other. Grocer's Review, PO Box 4378, 479 Parnell Road, Auckland, New Zealand. **Tel** 64 9 798747, FAX 64 9 377817. **ED** Peter Mitchell (editor's phone: 64 9 6310373). **DD** 641.3009931. **Bk Rev**, (Qty: 10). **Ad Acc. Circ:** 5,600 (ctrl). ***Continues*** *New Zealand Grocers' Review, 0468-009X.*
Ind/Abst Infomat Int. Bus.

US/0361-4034
GROCERY DISTRIBUTION. [Groc. distrib.]. (Sept./Oct. 1975)-. Trade Publication. English. bm (Jan., Mar., May, July, Sept., Nov.). $30.00 (one year), $40.00 (two year), $50.00 (three year) US; $75.00 (one year), $100.00 (two year) other. Grocery Distribution, 455 South Frontage Road #116, Burr Ridge IL 60521. **Tel** (708)986-8767. **ED** R.W. Mulville. **LC** HD9320.1; .G73. **DD** 381/.41. **Ad Acc. Circ:** 15,000 (ctrl).
Desc: Trade magazine for food industry concentrating on physical handling of products from food manufacturer to retail store.

US/0749-551X
GROCERY DISTRIBUTION ANALYSIS AND GUIDE (1983). (GROCERY DISTRIBUTION ANALYSIS AND GUIDE / COMPILED AND PUBLISHED BY METRO MARKET STUDIES.). [Groc. distrib. anal. guide]. **Added/Corp** Metro Market Studies (Firm). **VFOAT** Grocery Distribution Guide. (1983)-. English. an (Published in April). $250.00. Metro Market Studies Inc, Box 602, Weston MA 02193. **Tel** (617)891-8527. **DD** 381. **[CCC].** Index available (Bound in each issue). ***Continues*** *Grocery Distribution Guide.*
Desc: Analysis of grocery distribution in 220 metropolitan areas. Provides names of retailers and wholesalers, number of stores, market share and location of buying office.

●US
GROCERY EQUIPMENT PRODUCT NEWS. (Oct. 1994)-. English. bm. $80.00 (one year), $125.00 (two year) US; $150.00 (one year), $245.00 (two year). Trend Publishing Inc, 625 North Michigan Avenue, Suite 2500, Chicago IL 60611-3109. **Tel** (312)654-2300, FAX (312)654-2323.

US
GROCERY INDUSTRY ANNUAL REPORT, THE. (1921)-. English. an. $15.00. Progressive Grocer, 263 Tresser Boulevard, Stamford CT 06901. **Tel** (203)977-7640. Index available. **Ad Acc.**

Circ: 90,000 (ctrl).
Desc: Statistical report of the grocery industry for previous year, with sales, number of stores, consumer information, wholesaler data, and store operations.

US/0888-0360
GROCERY MARKETING. [Groc. mark.]. Vol. 52, No. 5 (Feb. 1986)-. Trade Publication. English. mo (11 issues per year - not published in July). $80.00 (one year), $125.00 (two year) US and Possessions; $150.00 (one year), $245.00 (two year) other. Trend Publishing Inc, 625 North Michigan Avenue, Suite 2500, Chicago IL 60611-3109. **Tel** (312)654-2300, FAX (312)654-2323. **ED** Ollie Bieniemy and Bryan Salvage. **LC** HD9321.1; .G76. **DD** 381. **CODEN** GRMAED. **Ad Acc. Circ:** 65,213 (ctrl). available on microfilm from University Microfilms International (UMI); available on an online database (file 648/Full-Text) from DIALOG. ***Continues** Grocers' Spotlight, 0017-4394.*
Desc: Marketing magazine of product movement and financial management for the grocery industry; edited for chain headquarters, independent grocers, wholesalers, brokers and manufacturers. Editorial focus is on new product marketing, sales promotion and merchandising, general merchandising, trade practices and issues, news trends, and analysis.
Ind/Abst BioBusiness (1990-); Foods Adlibra; Mark. Advert. Ref. Serv.; Trade Ind. ASAP [Full Txt.]; Trade Ind. Index [Full Txt.].

II
GROUNDNUT NEWS. **Added/Corp** National Research Centre for Groundnut (India). Vol. 1, No. 1 (Jan. 1989)-. Periodical. English. sa.
Ind/Abst Field Crop Abstr.; Plant Breed. Abstr.; Weed Abstr.

MX
GUIA DE LA INDUSTRIA ALIMENTARIA. (19??)-. Spanish. an. Litoimpresores, Espana 396 Col Granjas, Estrella/Mexico 09880 DF Mexico. **Tel** 670-3485. **ED** Cesar Macazaga. **LC** HD9014.M6; G85. **Bk Rev. Ad Acc. Circ:** 5,000 (ctrl).
Desc: Yearly food and drink industries suppliers directory.

US/1040-2616
GUIDE TO COOKING SCHOOLS, THE. [Guide cook. sch.]. 1st Ed. (1989)-. English. an. $19.95. Shaw Associates, 625 Biltmore Way, Suite 1406, Coral Gables FL 33134. **Tel** (305)446-8888, FAX (305)446-1837. **LC** TX667; .G85. **DD** 641.5/025/73.

US
GUIDE TO U.S. FOOD LABELING LAW. English. mo. $537.00. Thompson Publishing Group, 7711 Anderson Road, Tampa FL 33634. **Tel** (800)677-3789, (813)282-8607.
Ind/Abst Foods Adlibra.

IO
GULA INDONESIA. **See** Agriculture-Crop Production and Soil.

GW/0342-376X
GV-PRAXIS. **VFOAT** Gemeinschaftsverpflegungs-Praxis. (1973)-. Periodical. German. mo. DM168.13 Germany; DM186.15 other. Deutscher Fachverlag GmbH, Verlagsgruppe, D 60264 Frankfurt Germany. **Tel** 011 49 69 75951001, telex 411 862. **UDC** 664.8.037.5.

GW/0935-1574
GV SWISS. [GV Swiss]. **VFOAT** Grossverpflegung Swiss. (1988)-. Periodical. German. mo. 66.00F. Deutscher Fachverlag GmbH, Verlagsgruppe, D 60264 Frankfurt Germany. **Tel** 011 49 69 75951001, telex 411 862. **UDC** 641.5.022.

KO/0253-3154
HANGUG NYENNYAN SIGRYAN HAGHOI JI. **See** Nutrition and Dietetics.

KO/0367-6293
HAN'GUK SIKPUM KWAHAKHOE CHI. **Main/Corp** Han'Guk Sikpum Kwahakhoe. **VFOAT** Korean Journal of Food Science & Technology. Academic Scholarly Publication. English (Korean). Hanguk Sikpum Kwahakhoe, 125-1 4-ka Chungmu-ro, Chung-ku, Seoul South Korea. **LC** TP368. **NLM** W1; HA524H. **CODEN** HSKCAN. Documents available from CASDDS.
Ind/Abst AGRICOLA; Chem. Abstr.; Food Sci. Technol. Abstr.; Potato Abstr.; Rice Abstr.; Soyabean Abstr.

KO
HANGUK SIKPUM SANOP PYOLLAM. **VFOAT** Food Industry in Korea. Korean (Korean). Nongochon Kaebal Kongsa, 13-8 Noryangjin-dong, Kwanak-ku, Seoul Korea. **LC** HD9106.K6; H367.

US
HAWAII FOOD PROCESSOR / COOPERATIVE EXTENSION SERVICE, UNIVERSITY OF HAWAII, U.S. DEPARTMENT OF AGRICULTURE, COOPERATING. Periodical. English.
Ind/Abst AGRICOLA [Full Cov.].

US/0149-9602
HEALTH FOODS BUSINESS. [Health foods bus.]. (19??)-. Periodical. English. Twelve times a year. $33.00 US; $37.00 Canada; $50.00 other. PTN Publishing Company, 445 Broad Hollow Road, Melville NY 11747. **Tel** (516)845-2700, FAX (516)845-7109. **LC** HD9001; .H44. **DD** 338.4/7/6413. **CODEN** HFBUED. **Bk Rev. Ad Acc. Circ:** 11,500 (ctrl).
Desc: Geared primarily for the health foods shop retailer/buyer and mass market foods buyer.
Ind/Abst AGRICOLA; BioBusiness; Foods Adlibra.

US/0194-5343
HEALTH FOODS COMMUNICATOR, THE. (19??)-. Periodical. English. bm (6 issues). $12.00. Communicator Publications, 5050 France Avenue South, Suite 220, Edina MN 55410. **Tel** (612)929-3329.

US/0163-304X
HEALTH FOODS RETAILING MERCHANDISING HANDBOOK. 1978-. Periodical. English. an. $10.00. Syndicate Magazines, Inc., 6 East 43rd Street, New York NY 10017. **LC** HD9003; .H42. **DD** 381/.45641302/029473.

CN/0823-7352
HEALTHY HORIZONS. [Healthy horiz.]. Periodical. English. 5.00Can$. Healthy Horizons Association, 609 Temperance Street, Saskatoon Saskatchewan S7N 0M4 Canada. **Tel** 244-8820. **ED** Marge Jenkin. **DD** 613/.05. **Bk Rev.**
Desc: Information on skills, nutrition, and chemistry in the food chain, along with the hazards of chemical additives.

US/1050-9941
HERB AND SPICE SAMPLER. [Herb spice sampl.]. (1990)-. Periodical. English. bm. $30.00. Miralta Press, PO Box 309, Kent WA 98035-0309. **DD** 641.

US/1040-581X
HERB COMPANION, THE. [Herb companion]. (Oct./Nov. 1988)-. Periodical. English. Six times a year (Feb., Apr., June, Aug., Oct., Dec.). $21.00 (one year); $38.00 (two years). Interweave Press, 201 East 4th Street, Loveland CO 80537. **Tel** (303)669-7672. **LC** WMLC 93/1287. **DD** 635.
Desc: Dedicated to exploring and celebrating the history, culture, and applications of herbs. Covers on how to grow them, cook with them, use them for scent, and crafts.
Ind/Abst Garden Lit. (1992-); Index Inf. (June 1990-).

NO/0800-5419
HERBA. [Herba]. (1965)-. Periodical. Norwegian. qt. **DD** 641.302.
Ind/Abst Plant Grow. Reg. Abstr.; Seed Abstr.

NO
HL-INFORMASJON. **Main/Corp** Hermetikkindustriens Laboratorium (Stravanger Norway). **VAT** HL Informasjon. Norwegian. Postboks 68-4001, Stavanger Norway. **LC** TP370.8; .H473A. ***Absorbed** Hermetikkindustriens Laboratorium (Stavanger, Norway). Arsberetning.*

SP
HOJA DE INFORMACION (INTERNATIONAL OLIVE OIL COUNCIL). (HOJA DE INFORMACION.). **VFOAT** Feuille d'Information. (1964)-. Spanish. sm. 5,000ptas Spain; $50.00 Spain; $65.00 Europe and North Africa; $105.00 America and Near East; $132.00 other. Consejo Oleicola Internacional, Madrid Spain. **Tel** 34-1-431 61 27, telex 577 47 3548197 IOOC E. **LC** HD9490.5.O463; E874.

US
HONOLULU ARRIVALS, FRESH FRUITS AND VEGETABLES. (1983)-. English. an. Hawaii Department of Agriculture / Market News Service Branch, PO Box 22159, Honolulu HI 96822. **LC** HE199.5.F3; H38A. **DD** 380.1/414/09969021. ***Continues** Honolulu Unloads Fresh Fruits and Vegetables, 0149-5178.*

US/0360-9626
HONOLULU PRICES, WHOLESALE FRESH FRUITS AND VEGETABLES. **Main/Corp** Hawaii. Federal-State Market News Service. English. an. Department of Agriculture / Hawaii, PO Box 22159, Honolulu HI 96823. **Tel** (808)973-9599, FAX (808)973-9613. **LC** HD9220.U53; H63A. **DD** 338.1/34/099693.

NE
HORECA. (19??)-. Dutch. wk (52 issues). Fl181.00. Misset Uitgeverij BV, Postbus 9000, 6800 DA Arnhem Netherlands. **Tel** 011 31 85 209911.

US/0046-7979
HOSPITAL FOOD SERVICE. **See** Medical Science and Technology-Hospital Administration and Medical Centers.

●NZ
HOSPITALITY. **See** Hotels/Motels.

UK
HOSPITALITY. **Added/Corp** Hotel, Catering & Institutional Management Association. No. 1 (Jan. 1980)-. Periodical. English. Ten times a year. £23.00 United Kingdom; £32.00 other. Hotel Catering and Institutional Management Association, 191 Trinity Road, London SW17 7HN England. **Tel** 11 44 81 6724251, FAX 11 44 81 6821707. ***Supersedes** HCIMA Journal.*

NZ
HOSPITALITY & CATERING. ***Title Change.*** **VFOAT** Hospitality and Catering. (1992)-(1993). Periodical. English. Trade Publications Ltd., 300 Great South Road Greenlane, Newmarket Auckland New Zealand. **Tel** 011 64 9 9293000. ***Formed by the union of** Hospitality **and** Catering Management, 0113-2326. **Split into** Hospitality (Auckland, N.Z. : 1993) **and** Food & Beverage (Auckland, N.Z.).*

AT
HOSPITALITY FOODSERVICE. **VFOAT** Hospitality. (19??)-. Periodical. English. Eleven times a year. 65.00Aus$ Australia; 84.00Aus$ Pacific Region; 95.00Aus$ other. Peter Isaacson Publications, 46-50 Porter Street, Prahran Victoria, 3181 Australia. **Tel** 011 61 3 2457777, FAX 011 61 3 2457605. **LC** TX943; .H67.

SA
HOTELIER & CATERER : OFFICIAL MAGAZINE OF FEDHASA. **See** Hotels/Motels.

YU/0018-6872
HRANA I ISHRANA. (HRANA I ISHRANA. FOOD AND NUTRITION.). **Added/Corp** Drustvo za Unapreenje Ishrane Naroda Jugoslavije. **VFOAT** Food and Nutrition. Vol. 1 (1960)-. Periodical. Serbo-Croatian (Roman) (summaries and/or abstracts in English and French). mo. **LC** TX341; .H7. **DD** 641.1/05. **NLM** W1; HR8144. **CODEN** HRISAK. Documents available from BIOSIS Document Express, CASDDS.
Ind/Abst AGRICOLA; Biodeter. Abstr.; Biol. Abstr.; Chem. Abstr.; Dairy Sci. Abstr.; Hortic. Abstr.; Nutr. Abstr. Rev., Ser. A, Hum. Exp.; Soyabean Abstr.; Sug. Indus. Abstr.

BU/0205-177X
HRANITELNOPROMISHLENA NAUKA. (KHRANITELNO-PROMISHLENA NAUKA.). [Hranitelnoprom. nauka]. **Added/Corp** Selskostopanska Akademiia (Bulgaria). **VFOAT** Khranitelno Promishlena Nauka; Food Industry Science; Khranitelnopromishlena Nauka. (1985)-. Academic Scholarly Publication. Bulgarian (summaries and/or abstracts in English and Russian; table of contents in English and Russian). bm. Bulgarska Akademiia na Naukite, 7 Noemvri 1, Sofia Bulgaria. **LC** TP368; .K52. **CODEN** KHNAEQ. Documents available from CASDDS.
Ind/Abst Chem. Abstr. (1985-); Sug. Indus. Abstr.

HU/0018-8085
HUTOIPAR. [Hutoipar]. **Added/Corp** Mezogazdasagi es Elelmizesipari Tudomanyos Egyesulet, Hutoipari Szakosztaly. (1954)-. Trade Publication. Hungarian (summaries and/or abstracts in English and Russian). qt. $24.00. Lapkiado Vallalat, Lenin Korut 9-11, 1073 Budapest 7, Hungary. **Tel** 222-408. **(Subscription address:** Kultura, PO Box 149, H 1389 Budapest 62 Hungary.) **ED** L. B. Laczko. **Ad Acc. Circ:** 850. available with illustrations.
Ind/Abst AGRICOLA; Food Sci. Technol. Abstr.

AU
ICC STANDARDS METHODS. (19??)-. English (French and German). be. DM148.00. International Association for Cereal Science Technology, Weiner Strasse 22A, PO Box 77, A 2320 Schwechat Austria. **Tel** 011 43 1 7077202.

UK
ICE CREAM AND FROZEN CONFECTIONERY. **Added/Corp** Ice Cream Alliance Ltd. **VFOAT** Ice Cream & Frozen Confectionery. (19??)-. Periodical. English. Eleven times a year (Dec/Jan. issued combined). £100.00. Ice Cream Alliance Ltd, 90-94 Grays Inn Road, London WCIX 8AH England. **Tel** 011 44 1 405 0712. **ED** Lisa Gnef. **CODEN** ICFZAY. **Ad Acc. Circ:** 1,500.
Ind/Abst BioBusiness (1988-); Biodeter. Abstr. (1991-); Dairy Sci. Abstr.; Food Sci. Technol. Abstr.

US/0897-3261
ICE CREAM REPORTER. [Ice cream report.]. Vol. 1, No. 1 (Dec. 1, 1987)-. Periodical. English. mo. $395.00. Find/SVP, 625 Avenue of Americas, New York NY 10011. **Tel** (212)645-4500. **DD** 338.

US/0731-518X
ID HANDBOOK OF FOODSERVICE DISTRIBUTION. [ID handb. foodserv. distrib.]. **VFOAT** Handbook of Foodservice Distribution; I.D. Handbook of Foodservice Distribution; ID Handbook of Food Service Distribution; I.D. Handbook of Food Service Distribution. **VAT** Institutional Distribution Handbook of Foodservice Distribution. (1982)-. English. an. $337.00 (postage included). Bill Communications Inc., 355 Park Avenue South, New York NY 10010-1789. **Tel** (800)821-6897, (212)592-6262, FAX (212)592-6209. **ED** Edith F. Walker. **LC** HD9003; .I3. **DD** 381/.456413/002573. **Circ:** 800. available on diskette (or computer tape). ***Continues** ID Directory of Foodservice Distributors, 0275-3561.*
Desc: A directory of foodservice (institutional) distributors

in the United States, alphabetically arranged by state, city and company name, cross-referenced by MSA and product lines.

US/8755-0334
IFMA ENCYCLOPEDIA OF THE FOODSERVICE INDUSTRY, THE. [IFMA encycl. foodserv. ind.]. **Added/Corp** International Foodservice Manufacturers Association. **VFOAT** IFMA Encyclopedia of the Food Service Industry; Encyclopedia of the Foodservice Industry; Encyclopedia of the Food Service Industry. **VAT** International Foodservice Manufacturers Association Encyclopedia of the Foodservice Industry. (1972)-. English. te. $400.00. International Food Service Manufacturers Association, 875 North Michigan Avenue, Suite 3460, Chicago IL 60610. **Tel** (312)467-0810. **LC** TX901; .I37. **DD** 647.95/0973/021.
Desc: The most comprehensive source of current information for marketers to the foodservice market.

UK
IFR NEWS. Newsletter. English. qt. Free. Institute of Food Research / Norwich, England, Norwich Laboratory, Research Park Colney, Norwich NR4 7UA England. **Tel** (0603)255000, FAX (0603)507723. **Circ:** 2,500 (ctrl). ***Continues*** *Norwich Newsletter.*
Desc: Review of work and activities of the Institute of Food Research (IFR).

US
IFT SHORT COURSE MANUALS. (19??)-. Monographic series. English. ir. price varies per volume. Institute of Food Technologists, 221 North LaSalle Street, Chicago IL 60601. **Tel** (312)782-8424, FAX (312)782-8348.

US/0018-9766
IGA GROCERGRAM. [IGA grocergram]. **Added/Corp** IGA Inc. Independent Grocers' Alliance Distributing Co. Independent Grocers' Alliance of America. **VFOAT** Grocergram. **VAT** Independent Grocers' Alliance Grocergram. (1950)-. Periodical. English. mo (12 issues). $40.00. IGA Grocergram, 8725 West Higgins Road, Chicago IL 60631. **Tel** (312)693-4520. **DD** 658. ***Continues*** *Independent Grocergram.*
Ind/Abst AGRICOLA.

UK
IMAC, INTERNATIONAL MARINE AND AIR CATERING. **VFOAT** International Marine and Air Catering. V. 139, No. 874- Jan. 1980-. Periodical. English. mo. £10.00 UK; £14.00 Europe; £12.00 other. JoCast Ltd, 63 Shelton Street, London WC2 England. **LC** VK224; .C5. **DD** 387.5/42. ***Continues*** *Marine and Air Catering, 0025-3138.*

FR
IMAGES ECONOMIQUES DES ENTREPRISES. INDUSTRIES AGRICOLES ET ALIMENTAIRES AU ... . **See** Agriculture-Abstracting, Bibliographies and Statistics.

US/0898-9877
IMS LIST, SANITATION COMPLIANCE AND ENFORCEMENT RATINGS OF INTERSTATE MILK SHIPPERS. **See** Agriculture-Dairy Industry.

US/0733-4796
IN-STORE BAKERY PRODUCTION AND MARKETING. ***Ceased.*** [In-store bak. prod. mark.]. **VFOAT** In-Store Bakery. Ceased (1989). English. an. Gorman Publishing Company, 5725 East River Road, Chicago IL 60631. **LC** TX761; .I5. **DD** 664/.752/068.

DR/1013-980X
INAZUCAR. [Inazucar]. Periodical. Spanish. bm. $3.00. Instituto Azucarero Dominicano Centro de los Heroes, Santo Domingo Dominican Republic. **LC** HD9114.D6; I55.

II/0019-4484
INDIAN CASHEW JOURNAL. **Added/Corp** Cashew Export Promotion Council. Vol. 1 (Oct. 1956)-. Periodical. English. qt (Mar., June, Sept., Dec.). Rs150.00 India; Rs300.00, $30.00 other. Cashew Export Promotion Council, Chittoor Road, Cochin 682016 India. **Tel** 011 91 11 361459, FAX 011 91 11 8856677, telex 0885-6677. **(Subscription address:** Prints India, 11 Darya Ganj, New Delhi 110002 India.**)** **ED** Dr. K.G. Nayar. **LC** HD9210.A1; I5. **Ad Acc. Circ:** 1,700.
Ind/Abst Agrofor. Abstr. (1991-); Food Sci. Technol. Abstr.; Hortic. Abstr.; Plant Grow. Reg. Abstr.

II/0253-5025
INDIAN FOOD INDUSTRY. [Indian food ind.]. **Added/Corp** Association of Food Scientists & Technologists (India). Vol. 1, No. 1 & 2 (Jan./June 1982)-. Academic Scholarly Publication. English. bm. $66.00. Association of Food Scientists & Technologists, India Mysore-550 013 India. **Tel** 21747, telex 0846-241. **(Subscription address:** Prints India, 11 Darya Ganj, New Delhi, 110002 India, (Phone: 011 91 11 3268645)**)** **ED** Darly Thomas, J Hemalatha Rao, Malathi Prabhakara, N Nagaraja and V H Potty. **LC** HD9016.I4; I55. **DD** 338.4/7664/00954. **CODEN** IFIND3. **Ad Acc. Circ:** 2,000 (ctrl). Documents available from CASDDS.
Ind/Abst Chem. Abstr.; Food Sci. Technol. Abstr.; Int. Packag. Abstr.

II/0019-4808
INDIAN FOOD PACKER. [Indian food pack.]. **Added/Corp** All India Food Preservers' Association. (1946)-. Periodical. English. bm. $75.00. All India Food Preservers' Association, Bangalore, India. **(Subscription address:** Prints India, 11 Darya Ganj, New Delhi 110002 India.**)** **ED** V B Oberol. **LC** TP368; .I45. **DD** 664/.09. **NLM** W1 IN204N. **CODEN** IFPAAU. **Bk Rev. Ad Acc. Circ:** 1,000 (ctrl). Documents available from CASDDS.
Desc: Covers food processing, particularly fruits and vegetables. Includes research, review and subjects of interest to the industry.
Ind/Abst AGRICOLA; Chem. Abstr.; Dairy Sci. Abstr.; Food Sci. Technol. Abstr.

II/0019-6401
INDIAN SPICES. **See** Business-Commerce.

II/0019-6428
INDIAN SUGAR. [Indian sugar]. **Added/Corp** Indian Sugar Mills Association. (1938)-. Academic Scholarly Publication. English. mo. $30.00. Indian Sugar, Sugar House, 39 Nehru Place, New Delhi 110024 India. **Tel** 6416601. **(Subscription address:** Prints India, 11 Darya Ganj, New Delhi, 110002 India, (Phone: 011 91 11 3268645)**)** **ED** J S Mehta. **CODEN** ISUGAS. **Bk Rev. Ad Acc. Circ:** 1,000. Documents available from CASDDS.
Desc: The main feature includes articles on sugarcane, sugar technology, commercial and economic aspects of the sugar industry and also statistical analysis of the industry's present position and progress.
Ind/Abst AGRICOLA; Chem. Abstr. (1938-1980); Field Crop Abstr.; Food Sci. Technol. Abstr.; Grasslands For. Abstr.; Hortic. Abstr.; Plant Breed. Abstr.; Rev. Agric. Entomol.; Rev. Plant Pathol.; Soils Fert.; Sug. Indus. Abstr.; Weed Abstr.; World Agric. Econ.

II/0537-2631
INDIAN SUGAR YEAR BOOK. **Added/Corp** Indian Sugar Mills Association. (19??)-. English. an. $30.00. Indian Sugar Mills Association, Calcutta, India. **(Subscription address:** Prints India, 11 Darya Ganj, New Delhi, 110002 India, (Phone: 011 91 11 3268645)**)** **LC** TP379.I5; I5.

CU
INDUSTRIA ALIMENTICIA. ***Suspended.*** **Added/Corp** Cuba. Ministerio de la Industria Alimenticia. No. 1 (1968)-(1989). Periodical. Spanish. qt. $10.00. Ediciones Cubanas, Obispo 527, Altos ESQ Bernaza, CP 10100 Havana Cuba. **Tel** 011 632980, 631942, FAX 011 631011, telex 512337, 6540. **LC** HD9014.C9; I542. **Circ:** 25,000.
Desc: Devoted to offer full information on the alimentary development in the whole country.

IT/0019-7483
INDUSTRIA CONSERVE. [Ind. conserve]. **Added/Corp** Stazione Sperimentale per l'Industria Delle Conserve Alimentari. (1953)-. Academic Scholarly Publication. Italian. Four times a year. L80000 Italy; L100000 others. Stazione Sperimentale IND Conserve Alimentari, Viale Faustino Tanara 31A, 43100 Parma Italy. **Tel** 011 39 521 795222. **ED** A. Porrella. **CODEN** ICOPAF. Index available. **Bk Rev. Ad Acc. Circ:** 5,000. Documents available from BIOSIS Document Express, CASDDS. ***Continues*** *Industria Italiana Delle Conserve, 0367-9284.*
Desc: Covers food technology, food analysis, food processing waste water treatment.
Ind/Abst AGRICOLA; Biodeter. Abstr. (1991-); Biol. Abstr.; Chem. Abstr.; Dairy Sci. Abstr.; Food Sci. Technol. Abstr.; Int. Packag. Abstr.; Life Sci. Collect.; Rev. Med. Vet. Mycology.

IT
INDUSTRIA DELLE CARNI. Italian. sm. L61000 Italy; L88000 other. Ass i Ca Service Srl, Via Carlo G Merio 1, 20122 Milan Italy. **Tel** 011 39 2 791428.

IT/0019-7734
INDUSTRIA SACCARIFERA ITALIANA. (L'INDUSTRIA SACCARIFERA ITALIANA.). [Ind. sac. ital.]. **Added/Corp** Associazione Nazionale fra i Tecnici dello Zucchero e dell'Alcole. (1???)-. Academic Scholarly Publication. Italian (summaries and/or abstracts in English). Six times a year. L60000. Industria Saccarifera Italiana, Via Tito Speri 5, 44100 Ferrara Italy. **Tel** 11 39 532 206009. **CODEN** INSIAN. Index available in last issue of volume--attached. **Bk Rev. Ad Acc. Circ:** 900. Documents available from CASDDS.
Desc: Covers sugar industry, sugar beet agriculture, beet sugar production, sugar processing, and sugar technology.
Ind/Abst AGRICOLA; Biodeter. Abstr.; Chem. Abstr.; Field Crop Abstr.; Food Sci. Technol. Abstr.; Grasslands For. Abstr.; Plant Breed. Abstr.; Postharvest News Inf.; Rev. Plant Pathol.; Soils Fert.; Sug. Indus. Abstr.

IT/0019-901X
INDUSTRIE ALIMENTARI (PINEROLO). (INDUSTRIE ALIMENTARI.). [Ind. aliment.]. (1962)-. Academic Scholarly Publication. Italian (summaries and/or abstracts in English). mo. L70000 (Italy); L120000 (other). Chiriotti Editori, PO Box 66, 10064 Pinerolo Italy. **Tel** 121 794493, FAX 121/794480, telex 211 820 CHIED I. **CODEN** INALBB. **[CCC]**. Index available. **Bk Rev. Ad Acc. Pr Rev. Circ:** 6,500. Documents available from The Genuine Article, CASDDS. ***Continues*** *Technica e Chimica Perle Industrie Alimentari.*
Desc: Italian magazine for technological scientific economical and legislative information in the different fields of food industry.
Ind/Abst AGRICOLA; Agric. Eng. Abstr. (1991-); BioBusiness (1988-); Biodeter. Abstr. (1991-); Chem. Abstr.; Curr. Biotechnol.; Curr. Contents, Agric. Biol. Environ. Sci.; Dairy Sci. Abstr.; Food Sci. Technol. Abstr.; Foods Adlibra; Helminthol. Abstr. (1991-); Index Vet.; Leadscan; Leis. Recreat. Tour. Abstr.; Nutr. Abstr. Rev., Ser. B, Live Feeds and Feed.; Nutr. Abstr. Rev., Ser. A, Hum. Exp.; Life Sci. Collect.; Pig News Inf.; Postharvest News Inf.; Poult. Abstr.; Protozoolog. Abstr.; Res. Alert [Select. Cov.]; Rev. Med. Vet. Entomol.; Rural Dev. Abstr.; SCISEARCH; Soc. Sci. Cit. Index [Select. Cov.]; Soyabean Abstr.; Sug. Indus. Abstr.; Vet. Bull.; Weed Abstr.; Wheat Barley Trit. Abstr.; World Agric. Econ.

GW/0367-939X
INDUSTRIELLE OBST- UND GEMUESEVERWERTUNG, DIE. [Ind. Obst-Gemueseverwert.]. **Main/Corp** Bundesverband der Obst- und Gemueseverwertungsindustrie. (1948)-. Academic Scholarly Publication. German. Twelve times a year. DM206.00 Germany; DM219.00 others. Verlag Gunter Hempel, Postfach 100706, Poststrasse 44, D 38440 Wolfsburg 1 Germany. **Tel** 011 49 5361 12042. **CODEN** INOGAV. **Bk Rev. Ad Acc.** Documents available from BIOSIS Document Express, CASDDS.
Desc: Industrial processing of fruit and vegetables.
Ind/Abst AGRICOLA; Biol. Abstr.; Chem. Abstr.; Energy Res. Abstr.; Food Sci. Technol. Abstr.; Int. Packag. Abstr.; Rice Abstr.; Vitis Vitic. Enol. Abstr.

FR/0245-985X
INDUSTRIES AGRO-ALIMENTAIRES. (INDUSTRIES AGRO-ALIMENTAIRES / CNRS, CDIUPA.). [Ind. agro-aliment.]. **Added/Corp** Centre de Documentation Internationale des Industries Utilisatrices de Produits Agricoles. Centre National de la Recherche Scientifique (France). Centre de Documentation Scientifique et Technique. **VFOAT** Industries Agroalimentaires; Bibliographie Internationale. (1983)-. Periodical. French. Twelve times a year. 5876.59F France; 6000.00F others. Apria Documentation, CDIUPA, 1 Ave des Olympiades, 91300 Massy France Recherche Scientifique, 26 rue Boyer, 75971 Paris Cedex 20 France. **Tel** 011 33 1 69209738. Index Available, published separately, free-automatically sent. **Ad Acc.** ***Continues*** *Bulletin Signaletique. 380: Produits Alimentaires.*

CN/1184-9762
INFOOD (EDMONTON). (INFOOD / ALBERTA RESTAURANT AND FOODSERVICES ASSOCIATION.). [Infood]. **Added/Corp** Alberta Restaurant & Foodservices Association. **VFOAT** Newsletter for the Alberta Food and Beverage Industry. Vol. 8, Issue 5 (Mar. 1991)-. Periodical. English. bm. Free to members. Alberta Restaurant & Foodservice Association, 210 9930 106th Street, Edmonton Alberta T5K 1C7 Canada. **DD** 647.95. ***Continues*** *Provincial News (Alberta Restaurant & Foodservices Association)., 0844-5842.*

UK
INFORMATION SHEETS. Bulletin. English. mo. £300.00. British Food Manufacturing Industries Research Association, Randalls Road, Leatherhead Surrey KT22 7RY England. **Tel** 011 44 372 376761, FAX 011 44 372 386228, telex 929846. ctrl circ.

BU/0453-8315
INFORMATSIONEN BIULETIN. KHRANITELNA PROMISHLENOST. **Added/Corp** Bulgaria. Ministerstvo na Zemedelieto i Khranitelnata Promishlenost. **VFOAT** Khranitelna Promishlenost. (19??)-. Bulgarian. Four times a year. **LC** HD9000.1; .I425. **CODEN** KPRSAG. Documents available from CASDDS.
Ind/Abst AGRICOLA; Chem. Abstr.; Soyabean Abstr.; Sug. Indus. Abstr.

FR/0758-5373
INFOS PARIS. **See** Agriculture.

IT/0394-588X
INGEGNERIA ALIMENTARE. LE CONSERVE ANIMALI. [Ing. aliment., Conser. anim.]. (1985)-. Periodical. Italian (summaries and/or abstracts in English). bm. L50000 Italy; L90000 Europe; L160000 other. GM Editoriale Sas, Via Lanzone 22, 20123 Milan Italy. **Tel** 011 39 2 8055531, 8055534. **ED** Eloisa Stella. Index available. **Bk Rev**, (Qty: 20/yr). **Ad Acc, Adv Mgr:** Wanda Moroni. **Pr Rev. Circ:** 13,000.
Desc: International publication about technology and processing of meat products from raw material to the finished merchandised.
Ind/Abst Index Vet.; Pig News Inf.; Vet. Bull.

US/0020-3572
INSTITUTIONAL DISTRIBUTION. [Inst. distrib.]. **VFOAT** ID. Vol. 1 (Jan. 1965)-. Periodical. English. ir (15 issues). $80.00 US; $100.00 Canada; $110.00 other. Bill Communications Inc., 355 Park Avenue South, New York NY 10010-1789. **Tel** (800)821-6897, (212)592-6262, FAX (212)592-6209. **(Subscription address:** Bill Communications, PDS

Distribution Center, PO Box 231, Hopkinton MA 01748.) **ED** Robert Ciuin. **LC** HD9001; .I52. **DD** 658.86. **Bk Rev. Ad Acc. Circ:** 32,000 (ctrl). available on microfilm and microfiche from University Microfilms International (UMI); available on an online database (file 648/Full-Text) from DIALOG.
Desc: Serves the field of foodservice distributors, foodservice brokers and foodservice equipment distributors who sell to the away-from-home eating market.
Ind/Abst Bus. ASAP (1990-) [Full Txt.]; Bus. Index (1985-); Foods Adlibra; Gen. BusinessFile (1985-); Gen. Period. Index (1985-); Mag. Search; Trade Ind. ASAP [Full Txt.]; Trade Ind. Index (1981-) [Full Txt.]; Vocat. Search (July 1993-).

US/0095-0777
INSTRUMENTATION IN THE FOOD AND BEVERAGE INDUSTRY. (INSTRUMENTATION IN THE FOOD AND BEVERAGE INDUSTRY; PROCEEDINGS.). [Instrum. food beverage ind.]. **Main/Conf** International ISA Food Instrumentation Division Symposium. **Added/Corp** Instrument Society of America. Food Industry Division. Vol. 1, (1972)-. Proceedings. English. ir. Instrument Society of America, 67 Alexander Drive, Research Triangle NC 27709. **Tel** (919)549-8411, FAX (919)549-8288, telex 802 540. **LC** TP373; .I55a. **DD** 664/.02/05. **CODEN** IFDBB8. Documents available from CASDDS.
Ind/Abst Chem. Abstr.

US
INTERNATIONAL ASSOCIATION OF MILK FOOD AND ENVIRONMENTAL SANITARIANS 3A SANITARY STANDARDS. (19??)-. Periodical. English. $78.25 (nonmembers), $54.25 (members). IAMFES, 6200 Aurora Avenue, Suite 200W, Des Moines IA 50322. **Tel** (515)276-3344, (800)369-6337, FAX (515)276-8655.

UK
INTERNATIONAL EGG MARKET REVIEW; SITUATION AND OUTLOOK REPORT. **Main/Corp** International Egg Commission. No. 13 (Dec. 1974)-. Periodical. English. sa.

NE/0924-5863
INTERNATIONAL FOOD INGREDIENT. (1989)-. English. bm. £100.00 EEC countries; £120.00 Europe. Expoconsult Publishers, Industrieweg 54, PO Box 325, 3600 AH Maarssen Netherlands. **Tel** 31 3465 73777, FAX 31 3465 73811. **ED** Emile B. Blomme. Index available. **Bk Rev. Ad Acc. Circ:** 9,000 (ctrl).
Desc: Covers food ingredients and additives including new research and new applications.
Ind/Abst Foods Adlibra.

UK
INTERNATIONAL FOOD INGREDIENTS DIRECTORY. **VFOAT** Food Ingredients Directory. (19??)-. Directory. English. an. £50.00 UK; £55.00 other. Turret Group, 177 Hagden Lane, Watford Herts WD1 8LN United Kingdom. **Tel** 011 44 923 228577, FAX 011 44 923 221346.

●UK/0960-9784
INTERNATIONAL FOOD SAFETY NEWS. [Int. food saf. news]. (Jan. 1992)-. Periodical. English. mo (10 issues per year). $309.24. Churchill Livingstone, 1-3 Baxter's Place, Leith Walk, Edinburgh EH1 3AF Scotland. **Tel** 011 44 31 556 2424, FAX 011 44 31 558 1278, telex 727511. **(Subscription address:** Maruzen Company Ltd., PO Box 5050, Import & Export Department, Tokyo 100 31 Japan.) **ED** Gordon Paterson. **DD** 363.192.
Desc: Provides up-to-date and international news analyses of information on food pathogens and all aspects of food safety. It will also promote ideas on the prevention of food-borne disease.

SZ/0250-944X
INTERNATIONAL FRUIT WORLD. [Int. fruit world]. (1942)-. Periodical. English (French, German and Spanish). Three times a year (May, Sept., Dec.). 135.00F Europe; 270.00F other. Agropress Ltd, Aeschengraben 16, CH-4051 Basel Switzerland. **Tel** 011 41 61 2721170, FAX 011 41 61 2721126, telex 845/962185. **ED** G. H. Breuer. **Bk Rev. Ad Acc. Circ:** 5,500. ***Continues*** *Fruchte und Gemuse.*
Desc: World trade in fruit and vegetables: fresh and dried, and juices.
Ind/Abst AGRICOLA; Food Sci. Technol. Abstr.

NE/0168-1605
INTERNATIONAL JOURNAL OF FOOD MICROBIOLOGY. [Int. j. food microbiol.]. **Added/Corp** International Union of Microbiological Societies. International Union of Microbiological Societies. Committee on Food Microbiology and Hygiene. Vol. 1, No. 1 (Feb. 1984)-. Academic Scholarly Publication. English. Twelve times a year (4 vols.). Fl1804.00. Elsevier Science Publishers BV, PO Box 211, 1000 AE Amsterdam Netherlands. **Tel** 011 31 20 5803642, FAX 011 31 20 5862696, telex 15682. **ED** M Jacobsen. **NLM** W1; IN766JM. **CODEN** IJFMDD. **[CCC]. Pr Rev.** available on microfilm and microfiche from University Microfilms International (UMI). Documents available from The Genuine Article, BIOSIS Document Express, CASDDS.
Desc: Publishes full-length original research papers, short communications, review articles and book reviews covering all aspects of microbiological safety, quality and acceptability of foods.
Ind/Abst AGRICOLA [Full Cov.]; Biodeter. Abstr. (19??-19??); Biol. Abstr. (1985-); Chem. Abstr. (1984-); Curr. Aware. Biol. Sci., CABS; Curr. Contents, Agric. Biol. Environ. Sci.; Dairy Sci. Abstr.; EMBASE; Food Sci. Technol. Abstr.; Foods Adlibra; Health Plan. Adminis.; Index Vet.; Maize Abstr.; Life Sci. Collect.; Pig News Inf.; Postharvest News Inf.; Poult. Abstr.; Res. Alert [Full Cov.]; Rev. Med. Vet. Mycology; Rice Abstr.; Sci. Cit. Index; SCISEARCH; Soc. Sci. Cit. Index [Select. Cov.]; Soyabean Abstr.; Vet. Bull.; Wheat Barley Trit. Abstr.

UK/0950-5423
INTERNATIONAL JOURNAL OF FOOD SCIENCE AND TECHNOLOGY. [Int. j. food sci. technol.]. **Added/Corp** Institute of Food Science and Technology (U.K.). **VFOAT** International Journal of Food Science and Technology. Vol. 22, No. 1 (Feb. 1987)-. Academic Scholarly Publication. English. bm (6 issues). $332.00 US & Canada; £195.00 Europe; £214.00 other. Blackwell Scientific Publications Ltd, Marston Book Services, PO Box 87, Oxford OX2 ODT UK. **Tel** 011 44 865 791155, FAX 011 44 865 791927, telex 837 515 MARDIS G. **ED** D. L. Land. **LC** TX341; .J583. **DD** 664/.005. **CODEN** IJFTEZ. **[CCC]. Bk Rev. Ad Acc. Pr Rev. Circ:** 2,750. available on microfilm and microfiche from University Microfilms International (UMI). Documents available from The Genuine Article, BIOSIS Document Express, CASDDS. ***Continues*** *Journal of Food Technology, 0022-1163.*
Desc: Covers food processing, technology, storage, and cultural food processing.
Ind/Abst AGRICOLA [Select. Cov.]; Agric. Eng. Abstr. (1991-); BioBusiness; Biodeter. Abstr. (19??-19??); Biol. Abstr. (1987-); Chem. Abstr. (1987-); Crop Physiol. Abstr.; Curr. Aware. Biol. Sci., CABS; Curr. Contents, Agric. Biol. Environ. Sci.; Curr. Technol. Index; Dairy Sci. Abstr.; Food Sci. Technol. Abstr.; Foods Adlibra; Hortic. Abstr.; Int. Packag. Abstr.; Microbiol. Abstr. Sect. A; Nutr. Abstr. Rev., Ser. B, Live Feeds and Feed.; Nutr. Abstr. Rev., Ser. A, Hum. Exp.; Nutr. Res. Newsl.; Pig News Inf.; Postharvest News Inf.; Potato Abstr.; Res. Alert [Full Cov.]; Rice Abstr.; Sci. Cit. Index; SCISEARCH; Sorghum Mill. Abstr.; Soyabean Abstr.; Wheat Barley Trit. Abstr.

UK
INTERNATIONAL NEW PRODUCT REPORT. English. mo. $175.00 North America; $250.00 other. International New Product Newsletter, PO Box 1146, Marblehead MA 01945. **Tel** (508)741-0224, FAX (508)741-0224. **ED** Pamela Michaelsen. Index available. cum. index. **Circ:** 500.
Desc: A fortnightly review of all new products launched in the food, drink, and toiletries industries in Europe, Africa and Asia.

US
INTERNATIONAL PRODUCT ALERT. English. Twenty-four times a year. $650.00 US & Canada; $705.00 Pan America & Europe; $735.00 other. Marketing Intelligence Service Ltd, 6473D Route 64, Naples NY 14512. **Tel** (716)374-6326, (800)836-5710, FAX (714)374-5217, telex 469979. **ED** Sherie Meeker-Barton. available on an online database (files 16,570,636/Full-Text) from DIALOG.
Desc: International news and reports on the packaged goods.
Ind/Abst Mark. Advert. Ref. Serv. [Full Txt.]; PROMT [Full Txt.]; PTS Newsl. Database [Full Txt.].

UK/0020-8841
INTERNATIONAL SUGAR JOURNAL. [Int. sugar j.]. Vol. 1 (Jan. 1899)-. Academic Scholarly Publication. English (summaries and/or abstracts in French, German and Spanish). Twelve times a year. $165.00. International Media Ltd., PO Box 26, Port Talbot, W Glamorgan SA13 1NX England. **Tel** 011 44 639 887498, FAX 011 44 639 899830. **ED** Desmond Leighton. **LC** TP375; .I6. **CODEN** ISUJA3. **Bk Rev. Ad Acc. Circ:** 3,500. available on microfilm and microfiche from University Microfilms International (UMI). Documents available from Article Express International, The Genuine Article, CASDDS. ***Continues*** *Sugar Cane, 0371-4012.* ***Continued in part by*** *Sugar Cane (High Wycombe, England), 0265-7406.*
Desc: Articles and abstracts on the processing of beet and cane sugar, refining, by-products, laboratory analysis, techniques, etc.
Ind/Abst AGRICOLA [Select. Cov.]; Anal. Abstr.; BioBusiness; Chem. Abstr.; Curr. Biotechnol.; Curr. Contents, Agric. Biol. Environ. Sci.; Curr. Technol. Index; Ei Page One; EMBASE; Eng. Index Annu.; Field Crop Abstr.; Food Sci. Technol. Abstr.; Grasslands For. Abstr.; Hortic. Abstr.; Leis. Recreat. Tour. Abstr.; Life Sci. Collect.; Postharvest News Inf.; Protozoolog. Abstr.; Res. Alert [Select. Cov.]; Rural Dev. Abstr.; SCISEARCH; Soc. Sci. Cit. Index [Select. Cov.]; Soils Fert.; Sug. Indus. Abstr.; Weed Abstr.; World Agric. Econ.

US
IOWA FOOD DEALER, THE. V. 1- 1932-. Periodical. English. mo. Iowa Food Dealer, 607-616 Empire Building, Des Moines IA 50309.

●IE/0791-6833
IRISH JOURNAL OF AGRICULTURAL AND FOOD RESEARCH. See Agriculture.

IT/1120-1770
ITALIAN JOURNAL OF FOOD SCIENCE. [Ital. j. food sci.]. **VFOAT** IJFS; Rivista Italiana di Scienza Degli Alimenti. Vol. 1 No. 1 (1989)-. English. qt. L150000. Chiriotti Editori, PO Box 66, 10064 Pinerolo Italy. **Tel** 121 794493, FAX 121/794480, telex 211 820 CHIED I. **ED** Paolo Fantozzi. **CODEN** ITFSEY. **[CCC].** Index available. cum. index. **Pr Rev. Circ:** 1,500. Documents available from BIOSIS Document Express.
Desc: Basic and applied papers in food chemistry, analysis, microbiology, food technology and related areas.
Ind/Abst AGRICOLA [Full Cov.]; Biodeter. Abstr. (1991-); Biol. Abstr.; Dairy Sci. Abstr.; Food Sci. Technol. Abstr.; Foods Adlibra (1990-); Nutr. Abstr. Rev., Ser. A, Hum. Exp.; Postharvest News Inf.; Trop. Dis. Bull.; Vitis Vitic. Enol. Abstr.

SP/1130-6017
ITEA. PRODUCCION VEGETAL. See Agriculture-Crop Production and Soil.

RU/0579-3009
IZVESTIA VYSSIH UCEBNYH ZAVEDENIJ. PISEVAA TEHNOLOGIA. (IZVESTIIA VYSSHIKH UCHEBNYKH ZAVEDENII. PISCHEVAIA TEKHNOLOGIIA.). [Izv. vyss. ucebn. zaved., Pis. tehnol.]. **Added/Corp** Krasnodarskii Institut Pishchevoi Promyshlennosti. Krasnodarskii Politekhnicheskii Institut. **VFOAT** Pishchevaia Tekhnologiia. (1957)-. Academic Scholarly Publication. Russian (table of contents in English). bm. **(Subscription address:** Victor Kamkin, 4956 Boiling Brook Parkway, Rockville MD 20852.) **NLM** W1 IZ653. **CODEN** IVUPA8. Documents available from BIOSIS Document Express, Ask*IEEE, CASDDS.
Ind/Abst Biol. Abstr.; Ceram. Abstr. (19??-); Chem. Abstr.; Curr. Biotechnol.; INSPEC (1970-); Life Sci. Collect.; Sug. Indus. Abstr.

US/0021-387X
JACOBSEN'S FATS AND OILS BULLETIN. [Jacobsen's fats oils bull.]. **VFOAT** Fats and Oils Bulletin. (19??)-. Bulletin. English. da. $288.00 US; $448.00 other. Jacobsen Publishing Company, 300 West Adams Street / Room 835, Chicago IL 60606. **Tel** (312)726-6600, FAX (312)726-6654.

AU
JAHRESBERICHT DER VIEH- UND FLEISCHKOMMISSION BEIM BUNDESMINISTERIUM FUER LAND- UND FORSTWIRTSCHAFT. **Main/Corp** Vieh- und Fleischkommission. (1976/77)-. German. ir. **LC** LAW. **DD** 343/.436/076.

UK/0264-3812
JAPANSCAN. FOOD SCIENCE AND THE FOOD INDUSTRY. (JAPANSCAN FOOD INDUSTRY BULLETIN.). [Japanscan. Food sci. food ind.]. **VFOAT** Food Science & the Food Industry; Japanscan. Food Science and the Food Industry. (1983)-. English. Twelve times a year. £325.00. Japanscan, Anville, Upper Quinton, Stratford on Avon CV37 8SX United Kingdom. **Tel** 011 44 789720395, FAX 011 44 926332990, telex 311195. **ED** Carole Burke. Index available (Bound in each issue.). **Circ:** 200.
Desc: Provides Japanese food industry market information. Covers new products launched, company information, market intelligence (market size, brand leaders share, imports, exports, trends, forecasts), patent application, and changes in legislation.
Ind/Abst Foods Adlibra.

US/1075-6302
JOURNAL - AMERICAN SOCIETY OF SUGAR CANE TECHNOLOGISTS. FLORIDA DIVISIONS. See Agriculture-Crop Production and Soil.

FR
JOURNAL DU PATISSIER: CONFISEUR GLACIER. CHOCOLATIER TRAITEUR, LE. French. mo (11 issues). 293.83F France; 450.00F Europe; 570.00F other. Le Journal du Patissier, 4 rue Hanovre, 75002 Paris France. **Tel** 011 33 1 47424137.

●US/1053-8739
JOURNAL OF COLLEGE & UNIVERSITY FOODSERVICE. [J. coll. univ. foodserv.]. **VFOAT** Journal of College and University Foodservice. Vol. 1, No. 1 (1992)-. Periodical. English. qt. $60.00 US; $84.00 other. The Haworth Press Inc, 10 Alice Street, Binghamton NY 13904-1580. **Tel** (607)722-5857, (800)3-HAWORTH, FAX (607)722-1424. **ED** Mahmood A. Khan (Editor's Address: Virginia Polytechnic Institute and State University, Department of Hotel, Restaurant and Institutional Mgmt., Blacksburg, VA 24061). **LC** TX946; .J68. **DD** 647.95/05. **CODEN** JCUFEU. **Bk Rev. Ad Acc. Pr Rev. Acid Free.** available on microfiche. Documents available from Haworth Document Delivery Service.

Desc: A ground breaking publication covering the broad spectrum of topics in institutional food service.
Ind/Abst Food Sci. Technol. Abstr.

●US/1052-9241
JOURNAL OF CULINARY PRACTICE. ***Suspended.*** (1992)-(199?). Periodical. English. qt. $36.00 US; $50.40 other. The Haworth Press Inc, 10 Alice Street, Binghamton NY 13904-1580. **Tel** (607)722-5857, (800)3-HAWORTH, FAX (607)722-1424. **ED** F. H. Waskey (editor's address: Conrad N Hilton College of Hotel and Restaurant Mgmt., University of Houston, Houston, TX 77204). **Bk Rev**. **Ad Acc**. **Pr Rev**. **Acid Free.** available on microfiche. Documents available from Haworth Document Delivery Service.
Desc: Devoted entirely to research based articles on food preparation and cooking.
Ind/Abst Food Sci. Technol. Abstr.

NR/0794-7194
JOURNAL OF FOOD & AGRICULTURE. **VFOAT** Journal of Food and Agriculture. Vol. 1, No. 1 (Apr. 1987)-. Periodical. English. tq. **CODEN** JFAGEM. Documents available from BIOSIS Document Express.
Ind/Abst Agric. Eng. Abstr.; Biocont. News Inf.; Biol. Abstr.; Potato Abstr.

US/0145-8884
JOURNAL OF FOOD BIOCHEMISTRY. [J. food biochem.]. **VFOAT** FNP Journal of Food Biochemistry. **VAT** Food and Nutrition Press Journal of Food Biochemistry. Vol. 1 (Jan. 1977)-. Academic Scholarly Publication. English. Six times a year (6 issues per volume). $150.00 US, Canada & Mexico; $170.00 other. Food & Nutrition Press Inc, 2 Corporate Drive, PO Box 374, Trumbull CT 06611. **Tel** (203)261-8587, FAX (203)261-9724. **ED** Herb Hultin, N. F. Hoard and J. R. Whitaker. **LC** TX545; .J68. **DD** 664/.001/574192. **NLM** W1 JO65Q. **CODEN** JFBIDW. **Bk Rev**. **Ad Acc**. **Pr Rev.** Documents available from The Genuine Article, BIOSIS Document Express, CASDDS.
Desc: Now established as the leading journal for all disciplines that bear on the problems of food biochemistry.
Ind/Abst AGRICOLA [Full Cov.]; BioBusiness; Biol. Abstr. (1985-); Chem. Abstr.; Curr. Aware. Biol. Sci., CABS; Curr. Contents, Agric. Biol. Environ. Sci.; Dairy Sci. Abstr.; Food Sci. Technol. Abstr.; Foods Adlibra; Life Sci. Collect.; Res. Alert [Full Cov.]; Sci. Cit. Index; SCISEARCH; Soyabean Abstr.

US/0047-245X
JOURNAL OF FOOD DISTRIBUTION RESEARCH. [J. food distrib. res.]. **Added/Corp** Food Distribution Research Society. (1970)-. Periodical. English. sa (Feb., Sept.). $50.00 Libraries and Professional Individuals; $35.00 Professors or Government Employees; $135.00 Companies; $250.00 life membership. Food Distribution Research Society, 937 Cypress Lane, Greentown PA 18426. **Tel** (302)831-1320, (717)857-1445, FAX (302)831-3651. **ED** John Strovinsky. **LC** HD9001; .J68. **DD** 381/.45/66400973. **Bk Rev**, (Qty: 300). **Pr Rev. Circ:** 300. available on microfilm.
Desc: Research on food distribution.
Ind/Abst AGRICOLA [Full Cov.]; Foods Adlibra; Postharvest News Inf.; Potato Abstr.; World Agric. Econ.

UK/0260-8774
JOURNAL OF FOOD ENGINEERING. [J. food eng.]. Vol. 1, No. 1 (1982)-. Academic Scholarly Publication. English. Twelve times a year. $887.00 The Americas; £595.00 other. Elsevier Applied Science, An Imprint of Elsevier Science Ltd., The Boulevard, Langford Lane, Kidlington, Oxford OX5 1GB United Kingdom. **Tel** 011 44 865 843000, 011 44 865 843699, FAX 011 44 865 843010. **(Subscription address:** Elsevier Science Ltd. Oxford Fulfillment Centre, PO Box 800, Kidlington, Oxford OX5 1DX United Kingdom.**)** **ED** Ronald Jowitt and J. T. Clayton. **CODEN** JFOEDH. **[CCC]**. **Bk Rev**. **Ad Acc**. available on microfilm and microfiche from University Microfilms International (UMI). Documents available from Article Express International, The Genuine Article, BIOSIS Document Express, CASDDS.
Desc: Publishes papers on any subject at the interface between food and engineering, particularly those of relevance to industry and industrial scale operations.
Ind/Abst AGRICOLA [Full Cov.]; Agric. Eng. Abstr. (1991-); BioBusiness; Biol. Abstr. (1985-); Chem. Abstr.; Civ. Struct. Eng. Abstr.; Curr. Aware. Biol. Sci., CABS; Curr. Contents, Agric. Biol. Environ. Sci.; Dairy Sci. Abstr.; Ei Page One; Eng. Index Annu.; Environ. Eng. Abstr.; Food Sci. Technol. Abstr.; Foods Adlibra; Mech. Eng. Abstr.; Life Sci. Collect.; Postharvest News Inf.; Proc. Chem. Eng.; Res. Alert [Full Cov.]; Rice Abstr.; Sci. Cit. Index; Soc. Sci. Cit. Index [Select. Cov.]; Theoret. Chem. Eng.

●US/1065-7258
JOURNAL OF FOOD LIPIDS. [J. food lipids]. Vol. 1, No. 1 (1993)-. Periodical. English. qt (4 issues per volume). $95.00 US, Canada & Mexico; $115.00 other. Food & Nutrition Press Inc, 2 Corporate Drive, PO Box 374, Trumbull CT 06611. **Tel** (203)261-8587, FAX (203)261-9724. **LC** TX553.L5; J68. **DD** 613.2/8. **CODEN** JFFLES.
Desc: Information on lipids in human nutrition.

US/0145-8876
JOURNAL OF FOOD PROCESS ENGINEERING. [J. food process eng.]. **VFOAT** FNP Journal of Food Process Engineering. **VAT** Food and Nutrition Press Journal of Food Process Engineering. Vol. 1 (Jan. 1977)-. Periodical. English. qt (4 issues per volume). $142.00 US, Canada & Mexico; $162.00 other. Food & Nutrition Press Inc, 2 Corporate Drive, PO Box 374, Trumbull CT 06611. **Tel** (203)261-8587, FAX (203)261-9724. **ED** D. R. Heldman. **LC** TP368; .J66. **DD** 664/.005. **CODEN** JFPEDM. **Bk Rev**. **Ad Acc**. Documents available from Article Express International, BIOSIS Document Express, CASDDS.
Desc: Specializes in the engineering aspects of equipment and process design for the food industry, including packaging and sanitation.
Ind/Abst AGRICOLA [Full Cov.]; BioBusiness; Bioeng. Abstr.; Biol. Abstr. (1985-); Chem. Abstr. (-1987); Dairy Sci. Abstr.; Ei Page One; Eng. Index Annu.; Food Sci. Technol. Abstr.; Foods Adlibra; Int. Aerosp. Abstr.; Int. Packag. Abstr.; Life Sci. Collect.; Potato Abstr.; Rice Abstr.

US/0145-8892
JOURNAL OF FOOD PROCESSING AND PRESERVATION. [J. food process. preserv.]. **VFOAT** FNP Journal of Food Processing and Preservation. Vol. 1 (Jan. 1977)-. Academic Scholarly Publication. English. Six times a year (6 issues per volume). $150.00 US, Canada & Mexico; $170.00 other. Food & Nutrition Press Inc, 2 Corporate Drive, PO Box 374, Trumbull CT 06611. **Tel** (203)261-8587, FAX (203)261-9724. **ED** Daryl B. Lund. **LC** TP368; .J67. **DD** 664/.005. **NLM** W1 JO65R. **CODEN** JFPPDL. **Bk Rev**. **Ad Acc**. **Pr Rev.** Documents available from The Genuine Article, BIOSIS Document Express, CASDDS.
Desc: Covers the broad areas of chemistry, microbiology and engineering of food systems with respect to processing and preservation.
Ind/Abst AGRICOLA [Full Cov.]; BioBusiness; Biodeter. Abstr. (1991-); Biol. Abstr.; Chem. Abstr.; Curr. Aware. Biol. Sci., CABS; Curr. Contents, Agric. Biol. Environ. Sci.; Dairy Sci. Abstr.; Energy Res. Abstr. (April 1978-); Food Sci. Technol. Abstr.; Foods Adlibra; INIS Atomindex [Micro.]; Int. Packag. Abstr.; Maize Abstr.; Nutr. Abstr. Rev., Ser. A, Hum. Exp.; Life Sci. Collect.; Postharvest News Inf.; Potato Abstr.; Res. Alert [Select. Cov.]; Rev. Plant Pathol.; SCISEARCH; Soyabean Abstr.

●US/1045-4446
JOURNAL OF FOOD PRODUCTS MARKETING. [J. food prod. mark.]. **VFOAT** Journal of Food Products Marketing. Vol. 1, No. 1 (1991)-. Periodical. English. qt. $90.00 US; $126.00 other. The Haworth Press Inc, 10 Alice Street, Binghamton NY 13904-1580. **Tel** (607)722-5857, (800)3-HAWORTH, FAX (607)722-1424. **ED** John Stanton (editor's address: St Josephs University, 5600 City Avenue, Philadelphia, PA 19131). **LC** HD9000.1; .J677. **DD** 664/.0068/8. **CODEN** JFPMED. **Bk Rev**. **Ad Acc**. **Pr Rev**. **Acid Free.** available on microfilm and microfiche from University Microfilms International (UMI). Documents available from Haworth Document Delivery Service.
Desc: Devoted entirely to the full range of food products marketing, from food promotion and advertising to new food product development and consumer behavior research. The goal of this journal is to provide timely, practical articles that will keep food marketers on the cutting edge of their profession.
Ind/Abst Contents Pages Manage.; Food Sci. Technol. Abstr.; Foods Adlibra (1991-); Sage Fam. Stud. Abstr.; Soc. Plann. Policy Dev. Abstr.; Sociol. Abstr.; Vet. Bull.

US/0362-028X
JOURNAL OF FOOD PROTECTION. [J. food prot.]. **Added/Corp** International Association of Milk, Food, and Environmental Sanitarians. Vol. 40 (Jan. 1977)-. Academic Scholarly Publication. English. mo. $155.00, $205.00 (combined with Dairy, Food, and Environmental Sanitation) US; $177.50, $250.00 (combined with Dairy, Food, and Environmental Sanitation) other. IAMFES, 6200 Aurora Avenue, Suite 200W, Des Moines IA 50322. **Tel** (515)276-3344, (800)369-6337, FAX (515)276-8655. **ED** LLoyd Bullerman. **LC** SF221; .I532. **DD** 664. **NLM** W1 JO65T. **CODEN** JFPRDR. Index available. **Ad Acc**. **Pr Rev. Circ:** 3,500 (ctrl). available on microfilm from Xerox; available on microfilm and microfiche from University Microfilms International (UMI). Documents available from The Genuine Article, BIOSIS Document Express, CASDDS, Documents on Demand. ***Continues** Journal of Milk and Food Technology, 0022-2747.*
Desc: Publishes research and review papers dealing with causes and control of all forms of foodborne illness. Covers contamination and its control in raw foods and in foods during processing, distribution and preparing and serving to consumers, and the causes of and methods for control of food spoilage. Also covers food quality and methods to measure the various attributes of food quality, the food service industry, and wastes from the food industry and means to use or treat the wastes.
Ind/Abst AgBiotech News Inf.; AGRICOLA [Full Cov.]; BioBusiness; Biodeter. Abstr. (19??-19??); Biol. Agric. Index; Biol. Abstr.; Chem. Abstr.; Curr. Biotechnol.; Curr. Contents, Agric. Biol. Environ. Sci.; Dairy Sci. Abstr.; EMBASE; Energy Inf. Abstr.; Environ. Abstr.; Food Sci. Technol. Abstr.; Foods Adlibra; Helminthol. Abstr.; Hortic. Abstr.; Index Vet.; Int. Packag. Abstr.; Nutr. Abstr. Rev., Ser. B, Live Feeds and Feed.; Nutr. Abstr. Rev., Ser. A, Hum. Exp.; Life Sci. Collect.; PESTDOC; Pig News Inf.; Postharvest News Inf.; Potato Abstr.; Protozoolog. Abstr.; Res. Alert [Full Cov.]; Rev. Med. Vet. Mycology; Rev. Plant Pathol.; Rice Abstr.; Sci. Cit. Index; SCISEARCH; Soils Fert.; Soyabean Abstr.; Vet. Bull.; Weed Abstr.; Wheat Barley Trit. Abstr.

US/0146-9428
JOURNAL OF FOOD QUALITY. [J. food qual.]. **VFOAT** FNP Journal of Food Quality. **VAT** Food & Nutrition Press Journal of Food Quality. Vol. 1 (April 1977)-. Academic Scholarly Publication. English. Six times a year (6 issues per volume). $150.00 US, Canada & Mexico; $170.00 other. Food & Nutrition Press Inc, 2 Corporate Drive, PO Box 374, Trumbull CT 06611. **Tel** (203)261-8587, FAX (203)261-9724. **ED** M. P. de Figueiredo. **LC** TP372.5; .J68. **DD** 664/.07. **NLM** W1 JO65W. **CODEN** JFQUD7. **Bk Rev**. **Ad Acc**. **Pr Rev.** Documents available from The Genuine Article, BIOSIS Document Express, CASDDS.
Desc: Publishes all aspects of food quality assurance and regulations including environmental factors.
Ind/Abst AGRICOLA [Full Cov.]; BioBusiness; Biodeter. Abstr. (1991-); Biol. Abstr. (1985-); Chem. Abstr.; Curr. Contents, Agric. Biol. Environ. Sci.; Dairy Sci. Abstr.; EMBASE; Food Sci. Technol. Abstr.; Foods Adlibra; Int. Packag. Abstr.; Pig News Inf.; Postharvest News Inf.; Res. Alert [Select. Cov.]; Rev. Med. Vet. Mycology; Rev. Plant Pathol.; Rice Abstr.; SCISEARCH; Soc. Sci. Cit. Index [Select. Cov.].

US/0149-6085
JOURNAL OF FOOD SAFETY. [J. food. saf.]. **VFOAT** FNP Journal of Food Safety. **VAT** Food & Nutrition Press Journal of Food Safety. Vol. 1 (Aug. 1977)-. Academic Scholarly Publication. English. qt (4 issues per volume). $115.00 US, Canada & Mexico; $135.00 other. Food & Nutrition Press Inc, 2 Corporate Drive, PO Box 374, Trumbull CT 06611. **Tel** (203)261-8587, FAX (203)261-9724. **ED** M. Solberg and J. Rosen. **LC** TX501; .J68. **DD** 614.3/1/05. **NLM** W1 JO65Y. **CODEN** JFSADP. **Bk Rev**. **Ad Acc**. **Pr Rev.** Documents available from The Genuine Article, BIOSIS Document Express, CASDDS.
Desc: Emphasizes chemical and microbiological coverage of food safety. Chemical includes toxicology, metabolism, and environmental conversion of materials entering the food supply.
Ind/Abst AGRICOLA [Full Cov.]; BioBusiness; Biodeter. Abstr. (19??-19??); Biol. Abstr. (1985-); Chem. Abstr.; Curr. Aware. Biol. Sci., CABS; Curr. Contents, Agric. Biol. Environ. Sci.; Dairy Sci. Abstr.; Food Sci. Technol. Abstr.; Foods Adlibra; For. Prod. Abstr.; Health Saf. Sci. Abstr.; Life Sci. Collect.; Plant Breed. Abstr.; Res. Alert [Full Cov.]; Rev. Med. Vet. Mycology; Sci. Cit. Index; SCISEARCH; Soc. Sci. Cit. Index [Select. Cov.]; Soyabean Abstr.

US/0022-1147
JOURNAL OF FOOD SCIENCE. (JOURNAL OF FOOD SCIENCE : AN OFFICIAL PUBLICATION OF THE INSTITUTE OF FOOD TECHNOLOGISTS.). [J. food sci.]. **Added/Corp** Institute of Food Technologists. Vol. 26, No. 1 (Jan./Feb. 1961)-. Academic Scholarly Publication. English. bm. $100.00 US, Canada and Mexico; $125.00 other. Institute of Food Technologists, 221 North LaSalle Street, Chicago IL 60601. **Tel** (312)782-8424, FAX (312)782-8348. **ED** Aaron E. Wasserman. **LC** TX1; .F65. **NLM** W1 JO651. **CODEN** JFDSAZ. **[CCC]**. Index available in last issue of volume--attached. **Pr Rev. Circ:** 12,000. available on microfilm and microfiche from University Microfilms International (UMI). Documents available from The Genuine Article, BIOSIS Document Express, UMI Article Clearinghouse, CASDDS, Documents on Demand. ***Continues** Food Research, 0095-974X.*
Desc: Research articles which report original work and have a relationship to foods.
Ind/Abst Acad. Search (Jan. 1993-); AgBiotech News Inf.; AGRICOLA [Full Cov.]; Agric. Eng. Abstr. (1991-); Anal. Abstr.; Anim. Breed. Abstr.; AQUAREF; BioBusiness; Biodeter. Abstr. (19??-19??); Biol. Agric. Index; Biol. Abstr.; Biol. Dig.; Can. Environ.; Chem. Abstr.; Chemorecept. Abstr.; Crop Physiol. Abstr.; Curr. Aware. Biol. Sci., CABS; Curr. Biotechnol.; Curr. Contents, Agric. Biol. Environ. Sci.; Dairy Sci. Abstr.; EMBASE; Energy Inf. Abstr.; Energy Res. Abstr.; Environ. Abstr.; Expand. Acad. Index (1992-); Field Crop Abstr.; Food Sci. Technol. Abstr.; Foods Adlibra; Gen. Sci. Index; Gen. Sci. Source (Jan. 1993-); Helminthol. Abstr. (1991-); Index Vet.; INFO-SOUTH Abstr.; INIS Atomindex [Micro.]; Int. Packag. Abstr.; Leadscan; Mag. Search; Maize Abstr.; Microbiol. Abstr. Sect. B (19??-19??); Microbiol. Abstr. Sect. A; Microbiol. Abstr. Sect. C; NAPRALERT; Newsp. Period. Abstr. (1991-); Nucl. Sci. Abstr.; Nutr. Abstr. Rev., Ser. B, Live Feeds and Feed.; Nutr. Abstr. Rev., Ser. A, Hum. Exp.; Nutr. Res. Newsl.; Life Sci. Collect.; PESTDOC; Pig News Inf.; Plant Breed. Abstr.; Plant Grow. Reg. Abstr.; Postharvest News Inf.; Potato Abstr.; Protozoolog. Abstr.; Res. Alert [Full Cov.]; Rev. Plant Pathol.; Rice Abstr.; Sci. Cit. Index; SCISEARCH; Seed Abstr.; Sel. Water Resour. Abstr.; Soc. Sci. Cit. Index [Select. Cov.]; Soils Fert.; Soyabean Abstr.; Sug. Indus. Abstr.; Vet. Bull.; Trop. Dis. Bull.; Vocat. Search (Jan. 1993-); Wheat Barley Trit. Abstr.

II/0022-1155
JOURNAL OF FOOD SCIENCE AND TECHNOLOGY. **See** Nutrition and Dietetics.

US/0196-4283
JOURNAL OF FOODSERVICE SYSTEMS. [J. food serv. syst.]. **Added/Corp** Society for Foodservice Systems. **VFOAT** Journal of Food Service Systems. Vol. 1, No. 1 (Summer 1980)-. Periodical. English. qt (4 issues per volume). $85.00 US, Canada & Mexico; $105.00 other. Food & Nutrition Press Inc, 2 Corporate Drive, PO Box 374, Trumbull CT 06611. **Tel** (203)261-8587, FAX (203)261-9724. **ED** O. P. Snyder, Jr. **Bk Rev. Ad Acc.**
Desc: Designed to keep all professionals in food service informed of new developments and trends.
Ind/Abst AGRICOLA [Full Cov.]; Food Sci. Technol. Abstr.; Foods Adlibra.

CC/1001-7364
JOURNAL OF FRUIT SCIENCE. **See** Agriculture.

US/0747-7368
JOURNAL OF GASTRONOMY, THE. [J. gastron.]. **Added/Corp** American Institute of Wine & Food. Vol. 1 (Summer 1984)-. Periodical. English. an (Spring). $8.00 (one year); $60.00 (associate), $85.00 (associate couple), $125.00 (contributing & professional), $250.00 (supporting) Comes with American Institue of Wine and Food Dedicated Consumers membership. American Institute of Wine and Food, 1550 Bryant, Suite 700, San Francisco CA 94103. **Tel** (415)255-3000, FAX (415)255-2874. **ED** Nancy Harmon Jenkins. **DD** 641. cum. index. **Bk Rev. Circ:** 9,000 (ctrl).

US/0897-4438
JOURNAL OF INTERNATIONAL FOOD & AGRIBUSINESS MARKETING. [J. int. food agribus. mark.]. **VFOAT** Journal of International Food and Agribusiness Marketing; Food & Agribusiness Marketing; Food and Agribusiness Marketing. Vol. 1, No. 1 (1989)-. Periodical. English. qt. $135.00 US; $189.00 other. The Haworth Press Inc, 10 Alice Street, Binghamton NY 13904-1580. **Tel** (607)722-5857, (800)3-HAWORTH, FAX (607)722-1424. **ED** Erdener Kaynak (editor's address: International Business Press, PO Box 231, Middletown, PA 17057). **LC** HD9000.1; .J68. **DD** 382. **CODEN** JIFMEI. **Bk Rev. Ad Acc. Pr Rev. Acid Free. Circ:** 149. available on microfilm and microfiche from University Microfilms International (UMI). Documents available from Haworth Document Delivery Service.
Desc: Created to study food and agribusiness marketing systems in a variety of socioeconomic and political systems around the world. Places a special emphasis on exporting and importing food products between developed and developing countries. Methods for improving food and agribusiness marketing practice in developing countries and the transfer of food marketing technology from advanced countries are discussed.
Ind/Abst AGRICOLA [Full Cov.]; BioBusiness; Cot. Trop. Fibr. Abstr. Bibliogr.; Dairy Sci. Abstr.; Food Sci. Technol. Abstr.; Foods Adlibra; Maize Abstr.; Postharvest News Inf.; Sug. Indus. Abstr.; World Agric. Econ.

US/1073-3124
JOURNAL OF ITALIAN FOOD & WINE. **VFOAT** Journal of Italian Food and Wine. (199?)-. Periodical. English. Six times a year. $17.00 US; $21.00 Canada; $23.00 Pan America; $25.00 Europe; $27.00 other. Journal of Italian Food & Wine, 609 West 114 Street, Suite 77, New York NY 10025. **Tel** (212)316-3026. **ED** Robert DiZallo. **Bk Rev**, (Qty: 12-18). **Ad Acc, Adv Mgr:** Andrew Pappas. **Circ:** 40,000.

US/1046-0756
JOURNAL OF MUSCLE FOODS. [J. muscle foods]. **VFOAT** FNP Journal of Muscle Foods. (1989)-. Periodical. English. qt (4 issues per volume). $117.00 US, Canada & Mexico; $137.00 other. Food & Nutrition Press Inc, 2 Corporate Drive, PO Box 374, Trumbull CT 06611. **Tel** (203)261-8587, FAX (203)261-9724. **DD** 664. **CODEN** JMFOEI.
Ind/Abst Food Sci. Technol. Abstr.; Foods Adlibra.

●US/1060-3999
JOURNAL OF RAPID METHODS AND AUTOMATION IN MICROBIOLOGY. [J. rapid methods autom. micribiol.]. Vol. 1, No. 1 (Mar. 1992)-. Academic Scholarly Publication. English. qt (4 issues per volume). $105.00 US, Canada & Mexico; $125.00 other. Food & Nutrition Press Inc, 2 Corporate Drive, PO Box 374, Trumbull CT 06611. **Tel** (203)261-8587, FAX (203)261-9724. **LC** QR69.A88; J68. **DD** 576/.028. **NLM** W1; JO865D. **CODEN** JRMMEE. Documents available from CASDDS.
Ind/Abst Chem. Abstr.

●US/1052-214X
JOURNAL OF RESTAURANT & FOODSERVICE MARKETING. **See** Restaurants.

US/0887-8250
JOURNAL OF SENSORY STUDIES. [J. sens. stud.]. **VFOAT** FNP Journal of Sensory Studies. **VAT** Food & Nutrition Press Journal of Sensory Studies. Vol. 1, No. 1 (1986)-. Academic Scholarly Publication. English. qt (4 issues per volume). $125.00 US, Canada & Mexico; $145.00 other. Food & Nutrition Press Inc, 2 Corporate Drive, PO Box 374, Trumbull CT 06611. **Tel** (203)261-8587, FAX (203)261-9724. **LC** TX546; .J68. **DD** 664/.07/05. **CODEN** JSSDEO. Documents available from CASDDS.
Ind/Abst BioBusiness (1989-); Chem. Abstr. (1986-); Chemorecept. Abstr.; Dairy Sci. Abstr.; Food Sci. Technol. Abstr.; Foods Adlibra.

UK/0022-474X
JOURNAL OF STORED PRODUCTS RESEARCH. [J. stored prod. res.]. Vol. 1 (Sept. 1965)-. Periodical. English. qt. $485.00 The Americas; £325.00 other. Pergamon Press, An Imprint of Elsevier Science Ltd., The Boulevard, Langford Lane, Kidlington, Oxford OX5 1GB United Kingdom. **Tel** 011 44 865 843000, 011 44 865 843699, FAX 011 44 865 843010. **(Subscription address:** Elsevier Science Ltd. Oxford Fulfillment Centre, PO Box 800, Kidlington, Oxford OX5 1DX United Kingdom.**) ED** C. E. Dyte. **LC** TX599; .J6. **NLM** W1 JO904R. **CODEN** JSTPAR. **[CCC]. Pr Rev.** available on microfilm and microfiche from University Microfilms International (UMI). Documents available from The Genuine Article, BIOSIS Document Express, CASDDS, Documents on Demand.
Ind/Abst AGRICOLA [Full Cov.]; Agric. Eng. Abstr. (1991-); Agrofor. Abstr. (1991-); BioBusiness; Biocont. News Inf. (19??-19??-); Biodeter. Abstr. (19??-19??); Biol. Abstr.; Chem. Abstr.; Curr. Contents, Agric. Biol. Environ. Sci.; EMBASE; Energy Inf. Abstr.; Entomol. Abstr.; Environ. Abstr.; Food Sci. Technol. Abstr.; Hortic. Abstr.; Nutr. Abstr. Rev., Ser. B, Live Feeds and Feed.; Life Sci. Collect.; PESTDOC; Plant Genet. Resour. Abstr.; Plant Grow. Reg. Abstr.; Postharvest News Inf.; Protozoolog. Abstr.; Res. Alert [Full Cov.]; Rev. Agric. Entomol.; Rev. Med. Vet. Mycology; Rev. Plant Pathol.; Rice Abstr.; Sci. Cit. Index; SCISEARCH; Sorghum Mill. Abstr.; Soyabean Abstr.

US/0022-4901
JOURNAL OF TEXTURE STUDIES. [J. texture stud.]. Vol. 1 (Nov. 1969)-. Periodical. English. Six times a year (6 issues per volume). $183.00 US, Canada & Mexico; $203.00 other. Food & Nutrition Press Inc, 2 Corporate Drive, PO Box 374, Trumbull CT 06611. **Tel** (203)261-8587, FAX (203)261-9724. **ED** M. L. Bourne and P. Sherman. **LC** TX341; .J597. **DD** 664/.02. **NLM** W1 JO906C. **CODEN** JTXSBU. **Bk Rev. Ad Acc. Pr Rev.** Documents available from The Genuine Article, BIOSIS Document Express, CASDDS.
Desc: Publication on texture of foods and pharmaceuticals.
Ind/Abst AGRICOLA [Select. Cov.]; Agric. Eng. Abstr. (1991-); BioBusiness; Biol. Abstr.; Chem. Abstr.; Curr. Contents, Agric. Biol. Environ. Sci.; Dairy Sci. Abstr.; Field Crop Abstr.; Food Sci. Technol. Abstr.; For. Prod. Abstr. (1991-); Life Sci. Collect.; Postharvest News Inf.; Potato Abstr.; Res. Alert [Full Cov.]; Rice Abstr.; Sci. Cit. Index; SCISEARCH; Sug. Indus. Abstr.

US/0898-4131
JOURNAL OF THE ASSOCIATION OF FOOD AND DRUG OFFICIALS. **See** Public Health and Safety.

II/0302-9808
JOURNAL OF THE FOOD MARKETING CENTRE. [J. Food Mark. Cent.]. **Main/Corp** Xavier Institute. Food Marketing Centre. V. 1- Mar. 1973-. Periodical. English. qt. 25.00. Xavier Institute, Food Marketing Center, PO Box 47-831001, Jamshedpur India. **LC** TX341; .X36A. **DD** 338.1/9/54.

KO
JOURNAL OF THE KOREAN SOCIETY OF FOOD AND NUTRITION. **See** Nutrition and Dietetics.

UK/0022-5142
JOURNAL OF THE SCIENCE OF FOOD AND AGRICULTURE. [J. sci. food agric.]. **Added/Corp** Society of Chemical Industry (Great Britain). Vol. 1 (Jan. 1950)-. Academic Scholarly Publication. English. mo. $775.00. John Wiley & Sons Ltd., Baffins Lane, Chichester West Sussex PO19 1UD England. **Tel** 0243 779777, FAX 0243 776128 BTG:JWP001, telex 86290 WIBOOKG. **(Subscription address:** John Wiley / Philadelphia, PO Box 7247, Philadelphia PA 19170.**) ED** E. R. Dinnis, I. G. Burns, W. F. J. Cuthbertson, R. J. Dowdell, H. F.ore, M. P. Tombs, C. H. S. Hitchcock, A. J. MacLeod and P. J. van Soest. **LC** TX341; .J6. **NLM** W1 JO954. **CODEN** JSFAAE. **[CCC]. Pr Rev.** available on microfilm from University Microfilms International (UMI). Documents available from The Genuine Article, BIOSIS Document Express, CASDDS, ADONIS.
Desc: Provides an ideal forum for presentation of papers relevant to food science, food technology, agriculture, and the important area of interaction between food and agriculture research.
Ind/Abst ADONIS; AgBiotech News Inf.; AGRICOLA [Full Cov.]; Agrofor. Abstr. (1991-); Anal. Abstr.; Anim. Breed. Abstr.; AQUAREF; BioBusiness; Biodeter. Abstr. (19??-19??); Biol. Agric. Index; Biol. Abstr.; Chem. Abstr.; Chemorecept. Abstr.; Cot. Trop. Fibr. Abstr. Bibliogr.; Crop Physiol. Abstr.; Curr. Aware. Biol. Sci., CABS; Curr. Biotechnol.; Curr. Contents, Agric. Biol. Environ. Sci.; Curr. Technol. Index; Dairy Sci. Abstr.; EMBASE; Field Crop Abstr.; Fish Rev.; Food Sci. Technol. Abstr.; Foods Adlibra; For. Prod. Abstr.; For. Abstr.; Grasslands For. Abstr.; Hortic. Abstr.; Index Med.; Irr. Drain. Abstr.; Key Word Index Wildl. Res.; Leadscan; Maize Abstr.; NAPRALERT; Nutr. Abstr. Rev., Ser. B, Live Feeds and Feed.; Nutr. Abstr. Rev., Ser. A, Hum. Exp.; Life Sci. Collect.; PESTDOC; Pig News Inf.; Plant Breed. Abstr.; Plant Genet. Resour. Abstr.; Plant Grow. Reg. Abstr.; Postharvest News Inf.; Potato Abstr.; Poult. Abstr.; Proc. Chem. Eng.; Ref. Upd. Deluxe Ed.; Res. Alert [Full Cov.]; Rev. Agric. Entomol.; Rev. Med. Vet. Mycology; Rev. Plant Pathol.; Rice Abstr.; Sci. Cit. Index; SCISEARCH; Seed Abstr.; Soils Fert.; Sorghum Mill. Abstr.; Soyabean Abstr.; Stat. Theory Method Abstr. (1970, 1974-1975); Sug. Indus. Abstr.; Theoret. Chem. Eng.; Vitis Vitic. Enol. Abstr.; Wildl. Rev.

FR/0767-9874
JOURNEES DE LA RECHERCHE PORCINE EN FRANCE. **See** Veterinary Sciences.

GW/0022-7838
KAKAO + ZUCKER. (KAKAO + I.E. UND ZUCKER.). [Kakao + Zucker]. (1956)-. Periodical. German. mo. DM144.00. Zeitschriftenverlag RBDV, Postfach 14 02 20, 80452 Muenchen Germany. **Tel** 011 49 211 5050. **ED** M Lotsch and Anton Corda. **[CCC].** Index available. **Ad Acc. Circ:** 1,500.
Desc: Chocolate and candy manufacturing and packaging, ice cream in West Germany, advertising and export. Special section on people and news in the industry.
Ind/Abst AGRICOLA; Food Sci. Technol. Abstr.

US/0022-8753
KANSAS RESTAURANT. **See** Restaurants.

JA
KANZUME JIHO. **Added/Corp** Nihon Kanzume Kyokai. **VFOAT** Canners Journal. (1952)-. Periodical. Japanese. mo. $110.00. Canners Association of Japan, c/o Maru Building/2-2 Marunouchi, Chiyoda-ku Tokyo Japan. **Tel** 213-4781, telex 211-1430. **ED** K Numajiri. Index available. **Ad Acc. Circ:** 3,000 (ctrl). ***Continues*** *Kanbinzume Jiho.*
Desc: Contains information on food marketing and new technology (to produce prepared foods). Also includes domestic and trade statistics (especially canned and bottled foods).
Ind/Abst Food Sci. Technol. Abstr.

US/1074-3502
KASHRUS MAGAZINE. [Kashrus mag.]. **Added/Corp** Yeshiva Birkas Reuven (New York, N.Y.). Vol. 10, No. 4 (Apr. 1990)-. Periodical. English. Five times a year. $20.00 US; $25.00 Canada; $34.00 other. Kashrus Magazine, PO Box 204, Brooklyn NY 11204. **Tel** (718)336-8544. **ED** Rabbi Yosef Wikler. **LC** BM710; .K2644. **DD** 296.7/3/05. Index available. cum. index. **Bk Rev**, (Qty: 3). **Ad Acc. Circ:** 10,000. ***Continues*** *Kashrus, 0886-2753.*
Desc: Kosher food information: new products, mislabeled products, and technology.

UN/0554-2081
KHARCHOVA PROMYSLOVIST. **Added/Corp** Ukraine. Ministerstvo Vyshchoi i Serendoi Spetsialnoi Osvity. **VFOAT** Pishchevaia Promyshlennost. (19??)-. Academic Scholarly Publication. Ukrainian. mo. $89.95. Tekhnika, Pushkinskaia 28, Kiev Ukraine. **Tel** 282243. **LC** TX368; .K473. **CODEN** PPMVAL. Documents available from CASDDS.
Ind/Abst Chem. Abstr. (1965-1988).

RU/0235-2508
KHLEBOPRODUKTY : EZHEMESIACHNYI TEORETICHESKII I NAUCHNO-PRAKTICHESKII ZHURNAL MINISTERSTVA KHLEBOPRODUKTOV SSSR I GOSUDARSTVENNOGO AGROPROMYSHLENNOGO KOMITETA SSSR. **Added/Corp** Soviet Union. Ministerstvo Khleboproduktov. Gosudarstvennyi Agropromyshlennyi Komitet SSSR. (1988)-. Periodical. Russian. mo. Agropromizdat, Sadovo-Spasskaia, 18, 107807 Moscow Russia. **CODEN** KHLEES. Documents available from CASDDS. ***Continues*** *Zakupki Selskokhoziaistvennykh Produktov, 0130-1357.*
Ind/Abst Chem. Abstr.; Seed Abstr.

JA/0368-5365
KOGYO GIJUTSUIN BISEIBUTSU KOGYO GIJUTSU KENKYUSHO KENKYU HOKOKU. **See** Chemistry-Chemical Technology.

GW/0023-3234
KONDITOREI UND CAFE. (1948)-. Periodical. German. wk. DM426.00. Hugo Matthaes Druckerei Verlag, Postfach 103144, W-7000 Stuttgart 10 Germany. **Tel** 011 49 711 21331. **UDC** 664.68. **CODEN** 664.143/.148.
Ind/Abst Food Sci. Technol. Abstr.

HU
KONZERV- ES PAPRIKAIPAR. See Home Economics.

GW/0344-4376
KUCHE. (1???)-. Periodical. German. Twelve times a year. DM95.00 Germany; DM154.00 other. Rhenania Fachverlag GmbH, Postfach 601220, Possmoorweg 5, W-2000 Hamburg 60 Germany. **Tel** 011 49 40 27170, FAX 011 49 40 27172056, telex 2173465 or 213214. **ED** Sabine Romeis (phone: 011 49 40 27173625. **UDC** 641. **Bk Rev**, (Qty: 20). **Ad Acc. Circ:** 7,200 (ctrl).

JA/0289-3827
KYOTO JOSHI DAIGAKU SHOKUMOTSU GAKKAI SHI. [Shokumotsu Gakkaishi]. **Added/Corp** Kyoto Joshi Daigaku. Shokumotsu Gakkai. **VFOAT** Shokumotsu Gakkai Shi; Journal of Food Science, Kyoto Women's University. (1957)-. Periodical. Japanese. Kyoto Joshi Daigaku, (Kyushu Women's University), c/o Kyoto joshi daigaku kaseigakubu, Kitahiyoshimachi, Imagumano, Higashiyamaku, Kyotoshi, Kyotofu 605 Japan. **LC** TX341; .K93. **NLM** W1 KY9927. **CODEN** KJDSB7.

FR
LAMY DEHOVE. (19??)-. French. ir. 1100.00F. Editions Lamy SA, 187-189 Quai de Valmy, 75490 Paris Cedex 10 France. **Tel** 011 33 1 44721200, 011 33 1 44721212, FAX 011 33 1 44721395. Index available.
Desc: Covers regulation in the food regulation.

CN/0710-569X
LANCE K. LERAY'S BAKERY WORLD OF CANADA. [Lance K. LeRay's bak. world Can.]. **VFOAT** Bakery world of Canada. Vol. 1, No. 1 (Jan./Feb. 1977)-. Periodical. English. bm. 12.00p Ireland; 18.00p other. Jemma Publications Ltd, PO Box 1973, Rathmines Dublin 6 Ireland. **Tel** 011 353 1 975500, FAX 011 353 1 977190. **ED** Frank Dillon. **DD** 338.4/7664752/0971. **Ad Acc, Adv Mgr:** Frank Grennan. **Circ:** 1,800 (ctrl).

US/0732-0620
LATEST SCOOP, THE. [Latest scoop]. **Added/Corp** International Association of Ice Cream Manufacturers. (1978)-. English. an. $10.00. International Association of Ice Cream Manufacturers, 888 16th Street Northwest, Washington DC 20006. **Tel** (202)296-4250. **LC** HD9281.A1; L37. **DD** 338.1/774. ***Continues*** *Production Index, 0534-7025.*

GW
LEBENSMITTEL PRAXIS. (19??)-. Periodical. German. Twenty-four times a year. DM105.60. Lebensmittel Praxis Verlag, Hermannstr 40, W 5450 Neuwied 1 F R Germany. **Tel** 011 49 263187790.
Ind/Abst Infomat Int. Bus.; PROMT.

SZ
LEBENSMITTEL TECHNOLOGIE. (1973)-. Periodical. German (English and French). Ten times a year. 106.00F Switzerland; 112.80F Europe; 120.00F other. Frieden Verlag AG, Guestrasse 50, CH-8700 Kuesnacht Switzerland. **Tel** 011 41 1 9105054, FAX 011 41 1 9110189. **ED** Eva Friedman. Index available in last issue of volume--attached. **Bk Rev. Ad Acc, Adv Mgr:** W. Frieden. **Circ:** 6,000.
Desc: Covers food technology, new food processings, food packaging and storage, food chemistry and food biology.
Ind/Abst Dairy Sci. Abstr.

AU/0254-9298
LEBENSMITTEL- UND BIOTECHNOLOGIE. (LEBENSMITTEL- & BIOTECHNOLOGIE / OFFIZIELLES ORGAN DES VEREINS OSTERREICHISCHER LEBENSMITTEL- UND BIOTECHNOLOGEN.). [Lebensm. Biotechnol.]. **Added/Corp** Verein Osterreichischer Lebensmittel- und Biotechnologen. **VFOAT** Lebensmittel- und Biotechnologie. (1984)-. Periodical. English (English). ir. Fachverlag Wien, Krottenbachstrasse 31 10 S Fischer, A-1190 Vienna Austria. **Tel** (0222)367973, FAX (022)3691949. **ED** S. K. Fischer. **NLM** W1; LE317H. **CODEN** LEBIEE. **Bk Rev. Ad Acc. Circ:** 2,000 (ctrl). Documents available from BIOSIS Document Express, CASDDS.
Ind/Abst Biol. Abstr. (1988-); Chem. Abstr.; Curr. Biotechnol.; Food Sci. Technol. Abstr.

UK/0023-6438
LEBENSMITTEL-WISSENSCHAFT + I.E. UND TECHNOLOGIE. [Lebensm.-Wiss. Technol.]. **VFOAT** Food Science + Technology; Science + Technologie Alimentaire; Lebensmittel-Wissenschaft und -Technologie; Food Science and Technology; Science et Technologie Alimentaire. Vol. 1 (1968)-. Academic Scholarly Publication. English (German and French). bm (6 issues). $295.00. Academic Press Ltd., A Division of Harcourt Brace & Company Ltd., 24-28 Oval Road, London NW1 7DX England. **Tel** 071 267 4466, FAX 071 482 2293, 071 485 4752, telex 25775 ACPRES G. **(Subscription address:** Harcourt Brace & Company, Ltd., Foots Cray, High Street, Sidcup Kent DA14 5HP England.) **ED** A. Temperli and K. Lorenz. **LC** TP368. **DD** 664/.005. **CODEN** LBWTAP. **[CCC]**. Index available. **Bk Rev. Ad Acc. Circ:** 1,500. Documents available from BIOSIS Document Express, CASDDS.
Desc: International journal pertaining to all aspects of food science. Papers are published in the fields of chemistry, microbiology, biotechnology and food processing. Welcomes contributions in the form of review articles, research papers, and research notes. Research areas include biochemistry, food processing, microbiology, and nutrition.
Ind/Abst AGRICOLA [Select. Cov.]; BioBusiness; Biodeter. Abstr. (19??-19??); Biol. Abstr.; Chem. Abstr.; Chemorecept. Abstr.; Crop Physiol. Abstr.; Curr. Biotechnol.; Dairy Sci. Abstr.; Field Crop Abstr.; Food Sci. Technol. Abstr.; Foods Adlibra; For. Abstr.; Hortic. Abstr.; Maize Abstr.; Microbiol. Abstr. Sect. A; Nutr. Abstr. Rev., Ser. B, Live Feeds and Feed.; Nutr. Abstr. Rev., Ser. A, Hum. Exp.; Life Sci. Collect.; Plant Breed. Abstr.; Postharvest News Inf.; Potato Abstr.; Poult. Abstr.; Seed Abstr.; Sorghum Mill. Abstr.; Soyabean Abstr.

GW/0024-0001
LEBENSMITTEL-ZEITUNG. (June 1948)-. Periodical. German. Fifty-two times a year. DM253.80 Germany; DM368.00 other. Deutscher Fachverlag GmbH, Verlagsgruppe, D 60264 Frankfurt Germany. **Tel** 011 49 69 75951001, telex 411 862. **LC** HD9324.1; .L4.
Ind/Abst Infomat Int. Bus.; PROMT.

GW/0937-1478
LEBENSMITTELCHEMIE : ZEITSCHRIFT DER LEBENSMITTELCHEMISCHEN GESELLSCHAFT, FACHGRUPPE IN DER GESELLSCHAFT DEUTSCHER CHEMIKER. **Added/Corp** Lebensmittelchemische Gesellschaft. Vol. 44, No. 1 (Jan. 1990)-. Academic Scholarly Publication. German. Six times a year. $250.00. VCH Gesellschaft GmbH, Postfach 101161, D 69451 Weinheim Germany. **Tel** 011 49 6201 606459, FAX 011 49 6201 606184. **(Subscription address:** VCH Publishers Inc., 303 Northwest 12th Avenue, Journals Department, Deerfield FL 33442.) **LC** TP372.5; .G47a. **DD** 664/.07/05. **NLM** W1; LE317L. **CODEN** LEBEE2. **[CCC]**. Documents available from CASDDS. ***Continues*** *Lebensmittelchemie und Gerichtliche Chemie, 0341-5309.*
Ind/Abst Chem. Abstr.; Food Sci. Technol. Abstr.

GW/0047-4290
LEBENSMITTELTECHNIK. **VFOAT** Food Technology. (19??)-. Periodical. German. Twelve times a year. DM124.00 Germany; DM155.00 other. Rhenania Fachverlag GmbH, Postfach 601220, Possmoorweg 5, W-2000 Hamburg 60 Germany. **Tel** 011 49 40 27170, FAX 011 49 40 27172056, telex 2173465 or 213214. **UDC** 663/664. **Bk Rev**, (Qty: 25). **Ad Acc. Circ:** 7,300 (ctrl).
Ind/Abst AgBiotech News Inf.; Biodeter. Abstr. (1991-); Dairy Sci. Abstr.; Food Sci. Technol. Abstr.; Sug. Indus. Abstr.

US/1070-9940
LI GUIDE TO DINING & WINING NEWSLETTER. ***Ceased.*** [LI guide dining wining newsl.]. (1992)-(Oct. 1993). Newsletter. English. Twelve times a year. Vine Venture International Inc., PO Box 4234, Great neck NY 11023. **Tel** (516)487-1981, FAX (516)487-1981. **ED** Robert Schoolsky. **DD** 641. cum. index. **Bk Rev**, (Qty: 12).
Desc: News of food and wine with reviews of six Long Island restaurants each month.

US/0748-3082
LIST OF PROPRIETARY SUBSTANCES AND NONFOOD COMPOUNDS AUTHORIZED FOR USE UNDER USDA INSPECTION AND GRADING PROGRAMS. (LIST OF PROPRIETARY SUBSTANCES AND NONFOOD COMPOUNDS AUTHORIZED FOR USE UNDER USDA INSPECTION AND GRADING PROGRAMS / UNITED STATES DEPARTMENT OF AGRICULTURE, FOOD SAFETY AND INSPECTION SERVICE.). [List propr. subst. nonfood compd. auth. use USDA inspec. grad. programs]. **Added/Corp** United States. Food Safety and Inspection Service. **VAT** List of Proprietary Substances and Nonfood Compounds Authorized for Use Under United States Department of Agriculture Inspection and Grading Programs. (Jan. 1, 1982)-. Government Publication. English. an (one change over one year period). $21.00 domestic; $26.25 other. Superintendent of Documents, US Government Printing Office, Washington DC 20402. **Tel** (202)275-3328, FAX (202)786-2377. **LC** S21; .A46 subser; TP12. **DD** 630 S; 664/.01/05. available on microfiche (Vols. for (1983-) distributed to depository libraries). ***Continues*** *List of Chemical Compounds Authorized for Use Under USDA Inspection and Grading Programs.*
Desc: Part 1 is a new listing which includes substances used in the preparation of meat, poultry, and rabbit products; part 2 is a list of nonfood compounds used in the plant environment.

GW/0343-6632
LITERATURDIENST / HERAUSGEBER ; BUND FUER LEBENSMITTELRECHT UND LEBENSMITTELKUNDE. **Added/Corp** Bund fuer Lebensmittelrecht und Lebensmittelkunde. (19??)-. Periodical. German. ir. CH Beck Verlagsbuchhandlung, D 80791 Munich Germany. **Tel** 011 49 89 381891.

US
LIVESTOCK REVIEW / WISCONSIN. Trade Publication. English. mo. $10.00. Wisconsin Agricultural Statistics Service, 801 West Badger Road, PO Box 9160, Madison WI 53713. **Tel** (608)264-5317.
Desc: Summary of livestock information including hogs, cattle, sheep, honey production, cold storage holdings and prices.

SW/0024-5399
LIVSMEDELSTEKNIK. [Livsmedelsteknik]. (1953)-. Periodical. Swedish. Nine times a year. kr260.00. Livsmedelsteknik, Katarinavagen 20 5 Tr, S 116 45 Stockholm, Sweden. **Tel** 011 46 8 7145045, FAX 011 46 8 6408045. **UDC** 663/664.
Ind/Abst Nutr. Abstr. Rev., Ser. A, Hum. Exp.; Potato Abstr.; Rice Abstr.

US/0740-3860
LOOKOUT. FOODS. **Added/Corp** Marketing Intelligence Service Ltd. **VFOAT** Foods. (19??)-. English. Twenty-four times a year. $655.00 US and Canada; $705.00 Europe and Pan America; $735.00 other. Marketing Intelligence Service Ltd, 6473D Route 64, Naples NY 14512. **Tel** (716)374-6326, (800)836-5710, FAX (714)374-5217, telex 469979. **ED** Tom Vierhile. **[CCC]**. Index available.
Desc: Reports on new foods and beverages that are potentially influential. Coverage includes full page package illustrations, package copy, and in depth background and opinion commentary.
Ind/Abst F&S Index Plus Text, Int. [Select. Cov.]; Mark. Advert. Ref. Serv.; PROMT.

US/0740-3852
LOOKOUT. NON-FOODS. **Added/Corp** Marketing Intelligence Service Ltd. **VFOAT** Non-Foods. (19??)-. English. Fifty-one times per year. $655.00 US and Canada; $705.00 Europe and Pan America; $735.00 other. Marketing Intelligence Service Ltd, 6473D Route 64, Naples NY 14512. **Tel** (716)374-6326, (800)836-5710, FAX (714)374-5217, telex 469979. **ED** Tom Vierhile. **[CCC]**. Index available.
Desc: Reports on new health and beauty aids, household products, miscellaneous products, and pet products that are potentially influential because of their innovation or the importance of the manufacturer.
Ind/Abst F&S Index Plus Text, Int. [Select. Cov.]; Mark. Advert. Ref. Serv.; PROMT.

US
LOUISIANA GROCER, THE. Periodical. English. mo. Louisiana Grocer, PO Box 53431, New Orleans LA 70153.

RM/1010-1349
LUCRARI STIINTIFICE - INSTITUTUL DE CERCETARI SI PROIECTARI PENTRU VALORIFICAREA SI INDUSTRIALIZAREA LEGUMELOR SI FRUCTELOR. See Agriculture.

CN/0228-8966
MANITOBA FOOD PRODUCTS DIRECTORY. [Man. food prod. dir.]. **Added/Corp** Manitoba. Dept. of Agriculture. Marketing Branch. (1981)-. Directory. English. an. Free to US. Manitoba Agriculture Marketing Branch, Norquay Building, 916-401 York Avenue, Winnipeg Manitoba Canada. **Tel** (204)945-4529, FAX TELEX 07-587881(204)945-8692. **LC** HD9014.C4; M276. **DD** 381/.456413/00257127. **Circ:** 2,500 (ctrl). ***Continues*** *Listing of Manitoba Food Products for ..., 0228-8974.*

US/8750-9881
MAPLE SYRUP JOURNAL, THE. [Maple syrup j.]. (198?)-. Periodical. English. Four times a year. Maple Syrup Journal Inc, PO Box 680, Fairfax VT 05454. **DD** 664.

US
MARKETING CALIFORNIA AND ARIZONA MELONS, INCLUDES CANTALOUPS-HONEYDEWS-WATERMELONS. **VFOAT** California and Arizona Melons. Began in 1979. English. an. Federal-State Market News Service, 1220 N Street/Suite 216, Sacramento CA 95814. **Tel** (202)872-4600, (800)227-5558, FAX (202)872-4615. ***Continues*** *Marketing California Melons.*

US
MARKETING CALIFORNIA APRICOTS. **Main/Corp** Federal-State Market News Service. 1976-. Periodical. English. an. $4.00. Federal-State Market News Service, 1220 N Street/Suite 216, Sacramento CA 95814. **Tel** (202)872-4600, (800)227-5558, FAX (202)872-4615.

US/0098-7360
MARKETING CALIFORNIA ARTICHOKES. **Main/Corp** Federal-State Market News Service. (19??)-. English. Federal-State Market

Food and Food Industry

News Service, 1220 N Street/Suite 216, Sacramento CA 95814. **Tel** (202)872-4600, (800)227-5558, FAX (202)872-4615. **LC** HD9235.A72; C23a. **DD** 381/.41/53209794.

US
MARKETING CALIFORNIA ASPARAGUS. **Main/Corp** Federal-State Market News Service. English. an. $4.00. Federal-State Market News Service, 1220 N Street/Suite 216, Sacramento CA 95814. **Tel** (202)872-4600, (800)227-5558, FAX (202)872-4615. **LC** HD9235.A82; C23A. **DD** 381/.41531/09794. *Continues Marketing Asparagus from California.*

US/0148-4966
MARKETING CALIFORNIA BROCCOLI. **Main/Corp** Federal-State Market News Service. English. $4.00. Federal-State Market News Service, 1220 N Street/Suite 216, Sacramento CA 95814. **Tel** (202)872-4600, (800)227-5558, FAX (202)872-4615. **LC** HD9235.B762; C24. **DD** 380.1/41/535.
 Desc: Includes a review of season shipping point, wholesale market prices, shipments, unload distribution and product information.

US/0146-0676
MARKETING CALIFORNIA CARROTS. **Main/Corp** Federal-State Market News Service. English. $4.00. Federal-State Market News Service, 1220 N Street/Suite 216, Sacramento CA 95814. **Tel** (202)872-4600, (800)227-5558, FAX (202)872-4615. **LC** HD9235.C342; U553. **DD** 381/.41/51309794.

US/0148-4974
MARKETING CALIFORNIA CELERY. **Main/Corp** Federal-State Market News Service. English. $4.00. Federal-State Market News Service, 1220 N Street/Suite 216, Sacramento CA 95814. **Tel** (202)872-4600, (800)227-5558, FAX (202)872-4615. **LC** HD9235.C442; U54. **DD** 381/.41/55309794.
 Desc: Includes a review of season shipping point, wholesale market prices, shipments, unload distribution and product information.

US
MARKETING CALIFORNIA CHERRIES. **Main/Corp** Federal-State Market News Service. Periodical. English. an. Federal-State Market News Service, 1220 N Street/Suite 216, Sacramento CA 95814. **Tel** (202)872-4600, (800)227-5558, FAX (202)872-4615. *Continues Marketing California Cherries for Fresh Market.*

US/0094-2510
MARKETING CALIFORNIA DRIED FRUITS. (MARKETING CALIFORNIA DRIED FRUITS : PRUNES, RAISINS, DRIED APRICOTS & PEACHES.). English. ir. $2.00. Federal-State Market News Service, 1220 N Street/Suite 216, Sacramento CA 95814. **Tel** (202)872-4600, (800)227-5558, FAX (202)872-4615. **LC** HD9247.C2; M37. **DD** 381/.45/6648.
 Desc: Includes a review of season shipping point, wholesale market prices, shipments, unload distribution and product information.

US
MARKETING CALIFORNIA ONIONS. **Main/Corp** Federal-State Market News Service. (19??)-. English. an. Federal-State Market News Service, 1220 N Street/Suite 216, Sacramento CA 95814. **Tel** (202)872-4600, (800)227-5558, FAX (202)872-4615. **LC** HD9235.O62; U33a. **DD** 381/.41/5250973.
 Desc: Information on onions, includes garlic statistics.

US/0277-1489
MARKETING CALIFORNIA PEARS. [Mark. Calif. pears]. English. an. $4.00. Federal-State Market News Service, 1220 N Street/Suite 216, Sacramento CA 95814. **Tel** (202)872-4600, (800)227-5558, FAX (202)872-4615. **LC** HD9259.P333; U53A. **DD** 381/.41413/09794. *Continues Marketing California Pears for Fresh Market, 0098-8928.*

US
MARKETING CALIFORNIA PLUMS. **Main/Corp** Federal-State Market News Service. English. an. $6.00. Federal-State Market News Service, 1220 N Street/Suite 216, Sacramento CA 95814. **Tel** (202)872-4600, (800)227-5558, FAX (202)872-4615.
 Desc: Includes a review of season shipping point, wholesale market prices, shipments, unload distribution and product information.

US
MARKETING CALIFORNIA POTATOES. **Main/Corp** Federal-State Market News Service. **Added/Corp** United States. Agricultural Marketing Service. Fruit and Vegetable Division. Market News Branch. California. Dept. of Food and Agriculture. Division of Marketing Services. Bureau of Market News. (1976)-. Periodical. English. an.

US
MARKETING CALIFORNIA POTATOES, FEATURING THE KERN DISTRICT. VFOAT California Potatoes. English. an. Federal-State Market News Service, 1220 N Street/Suite 216, Sacramento CA 95814. **Tel** (202)872-4600, (800)227-5558, FAX (202)872-4615.

US/0363-7964
MARKETING CALIFORNIA POTATOES FROM THE KERN DISTRICT AND STOCKTON DELTA DISTRICT. **Main/Corp** Federal-State Market News Service. English. ir. Federal-State Market News Service, 1220 N Street/Suite 216, Sacramento CA 95814. **Tel** (202)872-4600, (800)227-5558, FAX (202)872-4615. **LC** HD9235.P82; U435. **DD** 381/.41/349109794.

US
MARKETING CALIFORNIA TOMATOES. **Main/Corp** Federal-State Market News Service. **Added/Corp** United States. Agricultural Marketing Service. Fruit and Vegetable Division. Market News Branch. California. Dept. of Food and Agriculture. Division of Marketing Services. (1974)-. Periodical. English. an. $4.00. Federal-State Market News Service, 1220 N Street/Suite 216, Sacramento CA 95814. **Tel** (202)872-4600, (800)227-5558, FAX (202)872-4615.

US
MARKETING EASTERN NORTH CAROLINA VEGETABLES ... CROP / FEDERAL STATE MARKET NEWS SERVICE. English. an.

US/0160-0370
MARKETING FLORIDA AVOCADOS, LIMES, MANGOS. **Main/Corp** Federal-State Market News Service. (19??)-. English. PO Box 3275, Homestead FL 33030. **LC** HD9259.A953; U54. **DD** 380.1/41/4.

US/0732-9768
MARKETING FLORIDA TROPICAL FRUITS & VEGETABLES. [Mark. Fla. trop. fruits veg.]. **VFOAT** Marketing Florida Tropical Fruits and Vegetables. English. Federal-State Market New Service, PO Box 1148, Winter Park FL 32790. **LC** HD9247.F6; M37. **DD** 380.1/41/09759.

US/0193-242X
MARKETING FLORIDA VEGETABLES : SUMMARY. English. an. Federal-State Market News Service, 1220 N Street/Suite 216, Sacramento CA 95814. **Tel** (202)872-4600, (800)227-5558, FAX (202)872-4615. **LC** HD9220.U53; F66. **DD** 381/.41/509759.

US/0732-7625
MARKETING LETTUCE FROM SALINAS-WATSONVILLE, OTHER CENTRAL CALIFORNIA DISTRICTS AND COLORADO. English. ir. $4.00. Federal-State Market News Service, 1220 N Street/Suite 216, Sacramento CA 95814. **Tel** (202)872-4600, (800)227-5558, FAX (202)872-4615. **LC** 381/.41552/09794. *Continues Marketing Lettuce from Salinas-Watsonville-King City and Other Central California Districts, 0145-6396.*
 Desc: Includes a review of season shipping point, wholesale market prices, shipments, unload distribution and product information.

US
MARKETING MICHIGAN APPLES, PEACHES, AND PRUNES. English. an. *Formed by the union of Marketing Michigan Apples and Marketing Michigan Peaches and Prunes.*

US
MARKETING MICHIGAN ONIONS AND POTATOES. 1977-. Periodical. English. an. *Formed by the union of Marketing Michigan Onions and Marketing Michigan Potatoes.*

US
MARKETING MICHIGAN VEGETABLES. **Main/Corp** Federal-State Market News Service. **Added/Corp** United States. Agricultural Marketing Service. Fruit and Vegetable Division. Market News Branch. Michigan. Dept. of Agriculture. Marketing Division. (1976)-. Periodical. English. an (Published in June). $10.00. Michigan Department of Agriculture, PO Box 30017, Lansing MI 48909. **Tel** (517)373-1050, FAX (517)335-0628.
 Desc: Emphasis on vegetables.

US
MARKETING SELECTED CALIFORNIA VEGETABLES. English. an. Federal-State Market News Service, 1220 N Street/Suite 216, Sacramento CA 95814. **Tel** (202)872-4600, (800)227-5558, FAX (202)872-4615. **LC** HD9225.U53; C238. **DD** 380.1/415/09794.

UK/0142-7571
MASTER BAKERS' HANDBOOK AND BUYERS GUIDE. [Master bak. handb. buy. guide]. (1976)-. Periodical. English. an. £29.00 UK; £31.00 other. Turret Group, 177 Hagden Lane, Watford Herts WD1 8LN United Kingdom. **Tel** 011 44 923 228577, FAX 011 44 923 221346. *Continues Annual Report of National Association of Master Bakers, Confectioners of Caterers.*

US
MASTERING FOOD ALLERGIES. Newsletter. English. Ten times a year. $20.00. Mast Enterprises Inc., 2615 North 4th Street, Suite 616, Coeur D'Alene ID 83184. **Tel** (208)772-8213. Index available (Dec./Jan. every two years). **Ad Acc.**
 Desc: List any problems that concerns those with food allergies. Introduction to new foods as they become available, simple methods of preparation, the psychological aspects of coping with "being different" and coping with family problems that seem to rise.

●AT
MEAT & LIVESTOCK REVIEW / PRODUCED BY THE AUSTRALIAN MEAT AND LIVESTOCK CORPORATION, MARKETING INTELLIGENCE UNIT. **Added/Corp** Australian Meat and Live-stock Corporation. Market Intelligence Unit. **VFOAT** Meat and Livestock Review. (Jan. 1992)-. Periodical. English. mo. Free, Australia; 50.00Aus$ other. Australian Meat & Livestock Corporation, GPO Box 4129, Sydney 2001 Australia. **Tel** 011 61 2 260-3111, FAX 011 61 02 2676620, telex AA22887. *Continues In Brief (Sydney, N.S.W.).*
 Desc: Covers domestic and overseas markets for cattle, sheep, and goats.

US/0892-6077
MEAT & POULTRY. [Meat poult.]. **VFOAT** Meat and Poultry Magazine; Meat and Poultry; Meat & Poultry Magazine. Vol. 32, No. 12 (Dec. 1986)-. Periodical. English. Twelve times a year. $40.00 US; $45.00 Canada & Mexico; $75.00 other. Oman Publishing Inc, 90 Throckmorton Avenue, PO Box 72, Mill Valley CA 94941. **Tel** (415)388-7575, FAX (415)388-4961. **ED** Steve Bjerklie. **LC** HD9411; .W4. **DD** 338.4/76649/00973. **CODEN** MEAPE7. **Ad Acc. Circ:** 20,000 (ctrl). *Continues Meat Industry, 0099-2011.*
 Desc: Contains information for managers in the animal protein industry, including processing, slaughtering, labor, marketing, and government regulation.
 Ind/Abst BioBusiness (1990-); Foods Adlibra; Trade Ind. Index.

US/1049-5908
MEAT BUSINESS MAGAZINE. [Meat bus. mag.]. Vol. 51, No. 2 (Feb. 1990)-. Periodical. English. Twelve times a year. $19.95 (one year); $33.00 (two years); $47.88 (three years). EROMDA Publishing Company, 109 West Washington, Milstadt IL 62260. **Tel** (314)621-0176, FAX (618)476-1616. **LC** HD9410.1; .M4. **DD** 664. *Continues Meat Business, 1049-6688.*

UK/0308-7050
MEAT HYGIENIST, THE. (1972)-. English. Four times a year. £10.00. Association of Meat Inspectors Ltd, 44 Parkfield Road, P Comrie, Taunton TA1 4SF England. **Tel** 011 44 823 333201.

AT
MEAT INDUSTRY DIGEST. (19??)-. English. mo (with Jan./Feb. and Nov./Dec. issues combined). 22.50Aus$. Master Butchers Limited, 432 Churchill Road, Kilburn SA 5084 Australia. **Tel** 011 61 8 2625433, FAX 011 61 8 3496043. **ED** T.K. Ford. **Ad Acc, Adv Mgr:** D. Curtis. **Circ:** 1,000 (ctrl).
 Desc: Contains articles relevant to the benefit of the meat and poultry industry.

CN/0826-4554
MEAT PROBE. [Meat probe]. **Added/Corp** Beef Information Centre. Vol. 1, No. 1 (Winter 1983)-. Periodical. English (French). Four times a year (Seasonally). 7.50Can$. Beef Information Centre, 1081 Roosevelt Cresent, North Vancouver British Columbia, V7P 1M9 Canada. **Tel** (604)985-0113, FAX (604)985-8284. **ED** Pat Scarlett. **DD** 641.3/6. Index available (bound in fourth issue). **Pr Rev. Circ:** 9,000 (ctrl).
 Desc: A newsletter for health professionals and educators which covers topics relating to meat and the meat industry.

US/0025-6390
MEAT PROCESSING. (MEAT PROCESSING : MP.). [Meat process.]. **VFOAT** MP; MPSM. Vol. 4, No. 5 (May 1965)-. Periodical. English. mo. $54.00. Watt Publishing Company, 122 South Wesley Avenue, Mount Morris IL 61054. **Tel** (815)734-4171, FAX (815)734-7021, telex TWX 910-642-2891. **ED** Mark Lefens. **LC** TS1950; .M2. **DD** 664/.9/005. **[CCC]. Circ:** 15,822. *Continues Meat Processing, Sausage Manufacturing.*
 Desc: Provides information for companies that process, slaughter, and market red meat, poultry, and/or fish.
 Ind/Abst AGRICOLA; BioBusiness (1990-); F&S Index Plus Text, Int. [Select. Cov.]; Foods Adlibra; PROMT.

US
MEAT REPORT FROM THE UNIVERSITY OF ILLINOIS AT URBANA-CHAMPAIGN. **Added/Corp** University of Illinois at Urbana-Champaign. **VFOAT** Meat Report. (19??)-. Periodical. English. Six

times a year. $3.00. Agricultural Newsletter Service, University of Illinois, 116 Mumford Hall, Urbana IL 61801. **Tel** (217)333-2666.

AT/0815-676X
MEAT RESEARCH NEWSLETTER. See Agriculture-Livestock and Poultry.

UK/0309-1740
MEAT SCIENCE. See Agriculture-Livestock and Poultry.

US/0889-3608
MEAT SHEET, THE. [Meat sheet]. (19??)-. Periodical. English. da. $375.00 (one year), $725.00 (two year), $1030.00 (three year) US; $400.00 (one year), $875.00 (two year), $1255.00 (three year) Pan American nations; $425.00 (one year), $875.00 (two year), $1255.00 (three year) other. Meat Sheet Inc., Box 124, Westmont IL 60559. **Tel** (708)963-2252, FAX (708)963-2980. **DD** 338. cum. index.

US/0887-9214
MEAT SOURCE. ***Ceased.*** [Meat source]. Vol. 1, No. 1 (June 1986)-(1988). Periodical. English. mo. Meat Information Services Inc, PO Box 22316, Lexington KY 40522. **Tel** (606)269-3534. **ED** Leonard Berkowitz, Jill E Provan. **DD** 338. **Circ:** 200.
Desc: Covers current news, trends, and basics about meats, fish, and poultry for food industry professionals in business and education.

UK
MEAT TRADES JOURNAL. No. 4101 (Jan. 5, 1967)-. Periodical. English. wk. £43.00 UK; £55.00 Europe; £76.00 other. **(Subscription address:** BKT Subscription Services, Lansdowne Mews 196 High Street, Tonbridge Kent TN9 1EF United Kingdom.)
Ind/Abst Infomat Int. Bus.

US/0884-1101
MEMBERSHIP/COMMITTEE DIRECTORY - NATIONAL ASSOCIATION OF MEAT PURVEYORS (U.S.). (MEMBERSHIP/COMMITTEE DIRECTORY / NAMP.). **Main/Corp** National Association of Meat Purveyors (U.S.). **VFOAT** Membership, Committee Directory. (19??)-. Directory. English. an. National Association of Meat Purveyors, 1920 Association Dr. #400, Reston VA 22102. **LC** HD9411; .N37a. **DD** 380.1/456649/002573.

US/0361-0888
MEMBERSHIP DIRECTORY AND BUYERS' GUIDE - AMERICAN FROZEN FOOD INSTITUTE. **Main/Corp** American Frozen Food Institute. (19??)-. Consumer Publication. English. an. $100.00. American Frozen Food Institute, 1764 Old Meadow Road, Suite 350, McLean VA 22102. **Tel** (703)821-0770, FAX (703)821-1350. **ED** Traci Carnel. **LC** TP493.5.A1; A5. **DD** 338.4/7/664028502573. **Ad Acc. Circ:** 2,800. ***Continues*** *American Frozen Food Institute. Directory.*
Desc: The easy-to-use, comprehensive format features complete information on frozen food products, containerization, brand names, distribution, plant locations and key personnel.

US/0275-6595
MICRO WAVE NEWS. [Micro wave news]. **VFOAT** Microwave News. Vol. 1, No. 1, (Jan. 1981)-. Periodical. English. bm. $285.00 (1 year), $550.00 (2 year), $800.00 (3 year) US; $315.00 (1 year), $600.00 (2 year), $875.00 (3 year) other. Slesin, PO Box 1799 Grand Central Station, New York NY 10163. **Tel** (212)517-2800. **CODEN** MIWNE3.

US
MICROWAVES AND FOOD. Newsletter. English. mo (12 issues per volume). $60.00 US, Canada and Mexico; $80.00 other. Food & Nutrition Press Inc, 2 Corporate Drive, PO Box 374, Trumbull CT 06611. **Tel** (203)261-8587, FAX (203)261-9724.
Ind/Abst Foods Adlibra.

US/0888-5311
MID-ATLANTIC FOODSERVICE NEWS. [Mid-Atl. foodserv. news]. **VFOAT** Mid-Atlantic Food Service News; Food Service News; Foodservice News. Periodical. English. mo. $24.00. Best-Met Publishing Company, 5537 Twin Knolls/Suite 438, Columbia MD 21045. **Tel** (410)730-5013, FAX (410)730-4680. **ED** Dick Bestany. **Ad Acc. Circ:** 23,000 (ctrl).
Desc: News of the food service industry in the mid-Atlantic

LE
MIDDLE EAST AND WORLD FOOD DIRECTORY. Directory. English. te. $90.00 Lebanon; $110.00 other. Chatila Publishing House, PO Box 13-5121, Beirut Lebanon. **Tel** 352413/19, telex 23008 MIYAH LE. **ED** Saad Chehab and Khaled Choukair. Index available. **Ad Acc. Circ:** 5,000 (ctrl).
Desc: Listings of firms serving the food, catering and beverage industry.

UK/0265-6469
MIDDLE EAST FOOD TRADE & CATERING EQUIPMENT. [Middle East food trade cater. equip.]. (1984)-. Periodical. Multiple languages. qt. $36.00 (1 year), $68.00 (2 year), $96.00 (3 year). J Latka Verlag GmbH, Borsigallee 6, D-53125 Bonn, FR Germany. **Tel** 011 49 228 919320, FAX 011 49 228 9193217. **ED** Patrick Murray. **DD** 380.145641300956. **Ad Acc. Circ:** 18,000.
Desc: Journal for food, beverages, and technology.

US
MIDWEST FOODSERVICE NEWS. English. mo. $18.00. Target Publishing Company, 2470 East Main Street, Columbus OH 43209. **Tel** (614)235-1022.
Ind/Abst Foods Adlibra.

US/0886-8832
MILITARY CLUB & HOSPITALITY. [Mil. club hospit.]. **VFOAT** Military Club and Hospitality. Vol. 20, No 1 (Feb. 1986)-. Periodical. English. bm (Feb., Mar., Apr., June, Aug., Sept., Oct., Dec.). $35.00 (one year), $60.00 (two year). Executive Business Media, PO Box 1500, Westbury NY 11590. **Tel** (516)334-3030. **ED** Robert Moran. **DD** 338. **Ad Acc.** ctrl circ. ***Continues*** *Club & Food Service, 0192-7981.*

US/0091-4843
MILLING AND BAKING NEWS. See Agriculture-Feed Grain and Milling.

US
MINNESOTA GROCER. Vol. 1, No. 1 (Jan./Feb. 1986)-. English. bm. $30.00. Minnesota Grocers Association, 533 Saint Clair Avenue, St Paul MN 55102-2859. **Tel** (612)228-0973. **ED** Randy Schubring. **Ad Acc. Circ:** 3,400 (ctrl). ***Continues*** *Minnesota Food Guide, 0026-5489.*
Desc: Represents every segment of food and grocery industry. Keeps grocers in touch with what is happening in their industry.

CN
MINUTES OF PROCEEDINGS AND EVIDENCE OF THE SPECIAL COMMITTEE ON TRENDS IN FOOD PRICES. **Main/Corp** Canada. Parliament. House of Commons. Special Committee on Trends in Food Prices. **VFOAT** Proces-Verbaux et Temoignages du Comite Special sur les Tendances des Prix de l'Alimentation. Jan. 30, 1973-. Proceedings. English (French). Information Canada, 171 Slater Street, Ottawa Ontario K1A 0S9 Canada. **Tel** (819)997-1095.

US/0897-6201
MODERN BAKING. [Mod. bak.]. (19??)-. Periodical. English. Twelve times a year. $60.00. Donohue Meehan Publishing Company, 2700 River Road, Suite 306, Des Plaines IL 60018. **Tel** (708)299-4430. **DD** 641. **CODEN** MOBAE3.
Ind/Abst BioBusiness (1990-).

US/0026-7805
MODERN GROCER. [Mod. groc.]. (19??)-. Periodical. English. Twenty-three times a year. $32.00 one year, $55.00 two years. Grocers Publishing Company, 15 Emerald Street, Hackensack NJ 07601. **Tel** (201)488-1800. **ED** Robert Reis. **Ad Acc, Adv Mgr:** K. Gallagher. **Circ:** 22,000 (ctrl).
Desc: A food trade publication providing news, legislative information, sales, marketing and merchandising topics to retailers, wholesalers, distributors and brokers in metro New York.

US/0065-7107
MONOGRAPH SERIES - AMERICAN ASSOCIATION OF CEREAL CHEMISTS. [Monogr. ser. - Am. Assoc. Cereal Chem.]. **Main/Corp** American Association of Cereal Chemists. Monographic series. English. ir. Price varies per volume. American Association of Cereal Chemists, 3340 Pilot Knob Road, St. Paul MN 55121. **Tel** (612)454-7250, FAX (612)454-0766, telex 6502439657. **CODEN** ACHMBK. Documents available from BIOSIS Document Express, CASDDS.
Desc: Reference book series which includes references on production, utilization, structure, quality, chemical components, milling, breadmaking, and durum and soft wheat end products of major world cereals.
Ind/Abst Biol. Abstr.; Chem. Abstr. (1946-1976).

US/0047-7931
MONTANA FOOD DISTRIBUTOR. Periodical. English. mo. $3.95. Montana Food Distributors Association, 2700 Airport Way, Box 5775, Helena MT 59604-5775. **Tel** (406)449-6394. **ED** W E Stevens. **Ad Acc. Circ:** 1,100 (ctrl).

US
MONTHLY IMPORT DETENTION LIST / DEPT. OF HEALTH AND HUMAN SERVICES, FOOD AND DRUG ADMINISTRATION. **Added/Corp** United States. Food and Drug Administration. **VFOAT** Import Detention Monthly Report. Report No. 81-07 (July 1 to July 31, 1981)-. Periodical. English. mo. US Department of Health and Human Services, 200 Independence Avenue Southwest, Washington DC 20201. **(Subscription address:** National Technical Information Service, 5285 Port Royal Road, Springfield, VA 22161**)** available on microfiche (Vols. for (1981-) distributed to depository libraries). ***Continues*** *Commercial Import Detentions, 0363-6852.*

JA
MONTHLY NEW FOOD PRODUCTS IN JAPAN. **VFOAT** New Food Products in Japan. (197?)-. Periodical. English. mo. $825.00. Pacific Research Consulting, 18 2 Shikahama 4 Chome, Adachi Ku Tokyo 123 Japan. **Tel** 011 81 3 3899 9953.
Ind/Abst Foods Adlibra; Mark. Advert. Ref. Serv. [Full Txt.]; PROMT [Full Txt.]; PTS Newsl. Database [Full Txt.].

US/0566-3628
MONTHLY PRICE REVIEW. **Main/Corp** Urner Barry Publications. (1???)-. English. ir. $113.00 US; $115.00 Canada and Mexico; $121.00 other. Urner Barry Publications Inc., PO Box 389, Toms River NJ 08754. **Tel** (908)240-5330, (800)932-0617, FAX (908)341-0891.
Desc: Lists prices for the month and compares the monthly average to the previous year. Includes eggs, turkeys, chickens, fowl, butter, margarine, cheese, and concentrated milk products.

FR
MOSELLE FRUIT. (19??)-. French. Four times a year. 46.00F France; 56.00F other. Moselle Fruit, Ctr Departemental Exp Fruitier, 57530 Laquenexy France. **Ad Acc. Pr Rev. Acid Free. Circ:** 850.
Desc: News and information on fruits and fruits trees.

JA/0286-102X
NAGANO-KEN SHOKUHIN KOGYO SHIKENJO KENKYU HOKOKU. [Nagano-ken Shokuhin Kogyo Shikenjo kenkyu hokoku]. **VFOAT** Research Report of the Nagano State Laboratory of Food Technology. Began in 1973. Academic Scholarly Publication. Japanese. an. Nagano-ken Shokuhin Kogyo Shikenjo, 205-1 Nishi Banjo Kurita, Nagano-shi 380 Japan. **CODEN** NKHKDB. Documents available from CASDDS.
Ind/Abst Chem. Abstr.; Rice Abstr.; Soyabean Abstr.

US/0747-7716
NATIONAL CULINARY REVIEW, THE. (THE NATIONAL CULINARY REVIEW : OFFICIAL MAGAZINE OF THE AMERICAN CULINARY FEDERATION.). [Natl. culin. rev.]. **Added/Corp** American Culinary Federation. (1977)-. Periodical. English. mo. $35.00 US; $53.00 other. American Culinary Federation, 10 San Bartola Drive, St Augustine FL 32086. **Tel** (904)824-4468, FAX (904)825-4758. **ED** Brent T Frei. **DD** 641. **Bk Rev**, (Qty: 6-12). **Ad Acc. Circ:** 20,000 (ctrl). ***Continues*** *Culinary Review.*
Desc: The official publication of America's largest professional association of chefs, cooks and pastry chefs. Editorial content focuses on food, trends, techniques, and industry news.

US/0895-9722
NATIONAL DIPPER, THE. [Natl. dipper]. (198?)-. Periodical. English. Nine times a year. Free on request. US Exposition Corporation, 1850 Oak Street, Northfield IL 60093. **Tel** (708)446-8434. **DD** 338.
Desc: Magazine for the ice cream retailer.

CN/0823-2717
NATIONAL DIRECTORY / CANADIAN INSTITUTE OF FOOD SCIENCE AND TECHNOLOGY. [Natl. dir. - Can. Inst. Food Sci. Technol.]. **Main/Corp** Canadian Institute of Food Science and Technology. **VFOAT** Registre National. Directory. English (French). an. $50.00 membership. Canadian Institute of Food Science and Technology, 309-1335 Carling Avenue, Ottawa Ontario K1Z 8N8 Canada. **Tel** (613)724-5572. **ED** Carol Mueller. **DD** 664/.006/071. **Ad Acc. Circ:** 2,500 (ctrl).

US/1066-2162
NATIONAL DIRECTORY OF ORGANIC WHOLESALERS. ***Title Change.*** [Natl. dir. org. wholes.]. **Added/Corp** California Agrarian Action Project. **VFOAT** National Organic Directory and Yearbook. (1991)-(199?). English. California Action Network, PO Box 464, Davis CA 95617. **Tel** (916)756-8518. **DD** 338. ***Continues*** *Organic Wholesalers Directory & Yearbook.* ***Continued by*** *National Organic Directory, 1073-0540.*

US
NATIONAL HONEY MARKET NEWS. See Agriculture.

AT/1030-8784
NATIONAL MARKET PLACE NEWS. (19??)-. English. Eleven times a year. 25.00Aus$. National Market Place News, 16 Napier Street, St Arnaud Victoria 3478, Australia. **Tel** 011 61 054 951055, FAX 011 61 054 951937. **ED** Rob Suggett. **Ad Acc, Adv Mgr:** Brian Garrett. **Circ:** 11,300 (ctrl).

●US/1073-0540
NATIONAL ORGANIC DIRECTORY, THE. [Natl. org. dir.]. **Added/Corp** Community Alliance with Family Farmers. (1994)-. Directory. English. an.

Food and Food Industry

$34.95. California Action Network, PO Box 464, Davis CA 95617. **Tel** (916)756-8518. **DD** 630. **Continues** National Directory of Organic Wholesalers, 1066-2162.

US/1073-6948
NATIONAL PACKING NEWS. (1990)-. Periodical. English. mo. $25.00. National Packing News, PO Box 1349, Murphys CA 95247. **Tel** (209)728-1455, FAX (209)728-3277. **ED** Jack Soward. **Bk Rev. Ad Acc.** Circ: 2,000. **Formed by the union of** Eastern Packing News **and** Western Packing News.
 Desc: News for and about the US food processing industry. Covers the people, plants and products.

US/0027-996X
NATIONAL PROVISIONER, THE. [Natl. provis.]. **Added/Corp** American Meat Institute. Vol. 1, (1889)-. Periodical. English. Twenty-six times a year. $50.00 US, $75.00 Canada, $100.00 other (surface mail); $210.00 (one year) airmail. Stagnito Publishing Company, 1935 Sherner Road, Suite 100, Northbrook IL 60062. **Tel** (708)205-5660, FAX (708)205-5680. **ED** John N. Frank. **DD** 664. **CODEN** NAPRAX. Index available. **Ad Acc.** available on microfilm and microfiche from University Microfilms International (UMI). Documents available from CASDDS.
 Ind/Abst BioBusiness; Chem. Abstr.

US
NATURAL FIBERS UTILIZATION RESEARCH ANNUAL PROGRESS REPORT FOR THE PERIOD OF ... TO THE NATURAL FIBERS & FOOD PROTEIN COMMISSION OF TEXAS. **VFOAT** Annual Progress Report for the Period of ... to the Natural Fibers & Food Protein Commission of Texas; Annual Report to the Natural Fibers & Food Protein Commission for the Period ... . English. an. College of Nutrition Textiles & Human Development, Department of Fashion and Textiles, Texas Woman's University, Denton TX 76204. **LC** TS1449; .N35. **DD** 677/.02832/05.

US/0164-338X
NATURAL FOODS MERCHANDISER. Vol. 1, (Feb. 1979)-. Trade Publication. English. Twelve times a year. $45.00. New Hope Communications, PO Box 600, Boulder CO 80306. **Tel** (303)939-8440, FAX (303)939-9559. **ED** Frank Lampe. **CODEN** NFMEEI. Index available (Bound in the 12th issue, for $12.00). **Bk Rev. Ad Acc, Adv Mgr:** Cassandra, **Tel** (303)939-8440. Circ: 12,500 (ctrl).
 Desc: Natural products retail trade magazine covering industry topics, new products, trends and marketing strategies.
 Ind/Abst BioBusiness (1990-).

US/0145-4218
NAWGA DIRECTORY OF MEMBERS. [NAWGA dir. memb.]. **Main/Corp** National-American Wholesale Grocers' Association. **VAT** National-American Wholesale Grocers' Association Directory of Members. (19??)-. Directory. English. National-American Wholesale Grocers' Association, 51 Madison Avenue, New York NY 10010. **LC** HD9321.3; .N24a. **DD** 381.
 Desc: Information on the food industry and grocery trade.

US/0028-1948
NEBRASKA RETAILER. **Added/Corp** Federation of Nebraska Retailers. (190?)-. Periodical. English. Six times a year. Omaha Food Retailers Association Inc., 4563 Cuming Street, Omaha NE 68132. **Tel** (402)558-2252.

US
NEGM : THE VOICE OF THE NEW ENGLAND FOOD INDUSTRY : THE NEW NEW ENGLAND GROCERY AND MARKET MAGAZINE. **Added/Corp** Massachusetts Retail Grocers and Provision Dealers Association. Vermont Retail Grocers Association. Rhode Island Grocers & Marketmens Association. **VFOAT** The New New England Grocery and Market Magazine; The New NEGM Magazine; N.E.G.M. **VAT** New England Grocery Magazine. Vol. 20, No. 4 (Feb. 1952)-. Periodical. English. mo. **Continues** New England Grocery and Market Magazine.
 Desc: Information on the food industry and grocery trade.

JA/0547-0277
NEW FOOD INDUSTRY. (NYU FUDO INDASUTORI. NEW FOOD INDUSTRY.). [New food ind.]. **Added/Corp** Shokuhin Shizai Kenkyukai. **VFOAT** New Food Industry; Shukuhin Kako Oyobi Shizai No Shinchishiki. (1959)-. Academic Scholarly Publication. Japanese. mo. $354.00. **(Subscription address:** Kyowa Book Company Inc., 1-38 Kanda Jinbo-Cho, Chiyoda-Ku Tokyo 101, Japan**) NLM** W1 NY9983. **CODEN** NYFIAM. Documents available from CASDDS.
 Ind/Abst Chem. Abstr.; Food Sci. Technol. Abstr.

US/8756-498X
NEW ORLEANS MENU, THE. **VFOAT** Menu. Vol. 2, No. 1 (Nov. 1981)- . Periodical. English. Eight times a year. $14.00 (1 year), $23.00 (2 year). Menu Subscriber Service, P.O. Box 51831, New Orleans LA 70151. **Tel** (504)821-3100.

UK
NEW TECHNOLOGIES BULLETIN / CAMPDEN FOOD & DRINK RESEARCH ASSOCIATION. **Added/Corp** Campden Food and Drink Research Association. No. 1 (Apr. 1990)-. Bulletin. English.

NZ
NEW ZEALAND MEAT PRODUCER : OFFICIAL JOURNAL OF THE NEW ZEALAND MEAT PRODUCERS, THE. **Added/Corp** New Zealand. Meat-Producers Board. (19??)-. Periodical. English. Four times a year (Mar., June, Oct., Dec.). Free. New Zealand Meat Producers, PO Box 121, Wellington New Zealand. **Tel** 011 64 4 4739150, FAX 011 64 4 723172, telex NZ3525. **ED** Anita Busby. Index available. cum. index. Circ: 13,500 (ctrl).
 Desc: Deals with in-depth New Zealand meat industry issues and all aspects which impact on them.

SZ
NEWS BULLETIN - INTERNATIONAL UNION OF FOOD & ALLIED WORKERS' ASSOCIATIONS. See Economics-Labor.

AU/0254-5837
NEWSLETTER - INTERNATIONAL ASSOCIATION FOR CEREAL CHEMISTRY. (I C C NEWSLETTER.). **VFOAT** Newsletter - Association Internationale de Chimie Cerealiere; Newsletter - Internationale Gesellschaft fur Getreidechemie; Newsletter - Mezdunarodnoe Obscestvo po Himii Zerna. (1983)-. Newsletter. English. Four times a year (Mar., June, Sept., Dec.). $8.00. International Association for Cereal Science and Technology, PO Box 77, Wiener Str 22, A-2320 Schwechat Austria. **Tel** 011 43 222 777202, FAX 011 43 222 7077204, telex 133316. **ED** Dr. H. Glattes. **UDC** 54:633.1. Circ: 200.

CN/0228-202X
NEWSLETTER - ONTARIO MINISTRY OF AGRICULTURE AND FOOD. Title Change. See Agriculture.

US
NEWSLETTER / THE AMERICAN INSTITUTE OF WINE & FOOD. **Added/Corp** American Institute of Wine & Food. **VFOAT** AIWF Newsletter. Vol. 1, No. 1 (Nov. 1982)-. Periodical. English. ir. $8.00 (one year); $60.00 (associate), $85.00 (associate couple), $125.00 (contributing & professional), $250.00 (supporting) Comes with American Institue of Wine and Food Dedicated Consumers membership. American Institute of Wine and Food, 1550 Bryant, Suite 700, San Francisco CA 94103. **Tel** (415)255-3000, FAX (415)255-2874.

JA/0029-0394
NIHON SHOKUHIN KOGYO GAKKAI SHI. [Nippon Shokuhin Kogyo Gakkai-Shi]. **Added/Corp** Norin Suisansho Shokuhin Sogo Kenkyujo (Japan) Nihon Shokuhin Kogyo Gakkai. **VFOAT** Journal of Food Science and Technology; Journal of Japanese Society of Food Science and Technology. Vol. 9, (Feb. 1962)-. Academic Scholarly Publication. Japanese (English). Twelve times a year. ¥21630.00 Japan; ¥19800.00 other. Japanes Society Food Science & Technology, 2-1-2 Kannondai, Tsuluba City Ibaraki 305 Japan. **Tel** FAX 0298-38-7153. **(Subscription address:** Japan Publications Trading Company, PO Box 5030, Tokyo International, Tokyo 100-31 Japan.**) ED** H. Aoki. **CODEN** NSKGAX. Index available (Bound in Dec. iss). **Bk Rev**, (Qty: 30). **Ad Acc. Pr Rev.** Circ: 4,000 (ctrl). Documents available from The Genuine Article, BIOSIS Document Express, CASDDS. **Continues** Nosan Kako Gijutsu Kenkyukaishi, 0369-5174.
 Desc: Features different articles on Japanese foods and food industries.
 Ind/Abst Biol. Abstr. (1985-); Chem. Abstr.; Food Sci. Technol. Abstr.; Maize Abstr.; Nutr. Abstr. Rev., Ser. A, Hum. Exp.; PESTDOC; Postharvest News Inf.; Res. Alert [Select. Cov.]; SCISEARCH; Seed Abstr.; Sug. Indus. Abstr.

JA/0914-7675
NIHON SHOKUHIN TEION HOZO GAKKAISHI. [Nihon Shokuhin Teion Hozo Gakkaishi]. **VFOAT** Journal of the Japanese Society for Cold Preservation of Food. (1987)-. Periodical. Multiple languages. qt. Nihon Shokuhin Teion Hozo Gakkai, (Japanese Soc. for Cold Preservation of Food), c/o Tokyo Nogyo Daigaku Nosan, Setogakugaku Kenkyushitsu, 1-1, Sakuragaoka 1 Chome, Setagayaku, Tokyoto 156, Japan. **DD** 664.028. **Continues** Shokuhin to Teion, 0285-1385.
 Ind/Abst Potato Abstr.

US/0029-103X
NON-FOODS MERCHANDISING. **VFOAT** Non-Foods Merchandising. Buyer's Guide and Directory.; Buyer's Guide and Directory. (19??)-. Periodical. English. Twelve times a year. $85.00 US; $150.00 other. Network Publishing Company, 298 5th Avenue 7th Floor, New York NY 10001. **Tel** (212)563-5301. available on an online database (file 648/Full-Text) from DIALOG.
 Desc: News related to supermarkets and wholesale non-food merchandising.

KO/1013-9443
NONGSA SIHOM YON'GU NONMUNJIP. SUDO P'YON. See Agriculture.

DK/0903-9759
NORTH EUROPEAN FOOD AND DAIRY JOURNAL. Title Change. [North Eur. food dairy j.]. Vol. 53, 5 (Aug. 1987)-?. Periodical. Danish (English and German). mo. North European Food and Dairy Journal, PO Box 9083, S-250 09 Helsingborg Sweden. **Tel** 042 11 63 70, FAX 042 11 34 22. **CODEN** NEFJEP. Circ: 8,000. **Continues** North European Dairy Journal, 0109-3207. **Continued by** SDI - Scandinavian Dairy Information.
 Desc: One of the largest dairy periodicals in the world read by managers of dairy and ice cream factories and importers of dairy products across the world.
 Ind/Abst AgBiotech News Inf.; BioBusiness; Dairy Sci. Abstr.; Food Sci. Technol. Abstr.; Int. Packag. Abstr.

US/0892-8363
NORTHWEST PALATE, THE. [Northwest palate]. **VFOAT** NW Palate. Vol. 1, Issue 1 (March/April 1987)-. Periodical. English. bm (Jan., Mar., May, July, Sept., Nov.). $21.00 (one year), $39.00 (two year). Northwest Palate, PO Box 10860, Portland OR 97210. **Tel** (503)228-4897, FAX (503)294-4324. **(Subscription address:** PO Box 9481, Seattle, WA 98109) **ED** Cameron Nagel (phone: (503)224-6039). **DD** 641. Index available. cum. index. **Bk Rev**, (Qty: 12). **Ad Acc.** Circ: 15,000. **Continues** Oregon Wine Review, 0736-8496.
 Desc: Wine reviews and new releases from Oregon, Washington, and Idaho. Also contains news of regional cuisine, articles/recipes, travel, and more.

US
NSF FOOD SERVICE EQUIPMENT STANDARDS. Main/Corp National Sanitation Foundation (U.S.). **VFOAT** Food Service Equipment Standards. Periodical. English.

US
NTIS ALERT. AGRICULTURE & FOOD. See Agriculture.

●US/1065-7967
NY FOOD LETTER, THE. [NY food lett.]. **VFOAT** New York Food Letter. **VAT** New York food letter. (1992)-. Newsletter. English. mo. $20.00 US; $25.00 Canada and Mexico; $30.00 other. New York Food Letter, PO Box 238, Bowling Green Station, New York NY 10274. **Tel** FAX (212)873-9068. **ED** Patricia MacKenzie and William Gillen. **DD** 363. **Bk Rev.** ctrl circ.
 Desc: Gives tips on where to buy food and wine, and announces new restaurant openings.

IT
OCCASIONAL PAPERS / WORLD FOOD PROGRAMME. **Added/Corp** World Food Programme. No. 1 (1985)-. Monographic series. English. **LC** UNC.
 Ind/Abst Nutr. Abstr. Rev., Ser. A, Hum. Exp.; Rice Abstr.; World Agric. Econ.

●US
OCCUPATIONAL COMPENSATION SURVEY--PAY ONLY. BELL COUNTY, TX--FAST FOOD RESTAURANTS / U.S. DEPARTMENT OF LABOR, BUREAU OF LABOR STATISTICS. See Economics-Labor.

US
OCCUPATIONAL COMPENSATION SURVEY--PAY ONLY. ESCAMBIA COUNTY, FL--FAST FOOD RESTAURANTS / U.S. DEPARTMENT OF LABOR, BUREAU OF LABOR STATISTICS. See Economics-Labor.

●US
OCCUPATIONAL COMPENSATION SURVEY--PAY ONLY. LAKE COUNTY, IL--FAST FOOD RESTAURANTS / U.S. DEPARTMENT OF LABOR, BUREAU OF LABOR STATISTICS. See Economics-Labor.

●US
OCCUPATIONAL COMPENSATION SURVEY--PAY ONLY. WASHINGTON, DC--FAST FOOD RESTAURANTS / U.S. DEPARTMENT OF LABOR, BUREAU OF LABOR STATISTICS. See Economics-Labor.

US
OFFICIAL REPORT / GENERAL ASSEMBLY. Main/Conf General Assembly of the International Office of Cocoa and Chocolate and the International Sugar Confectionery Manufacturers' Association. (19??)-. English. MC - Manufacturing Confectioner Publishing Company Inc, 175 Rock Road, Glen Rock NJ 07452. **Tel** (201)652-2655. **LC** HD9200.A1;

G45a. **DD** 338.1/7374.
Desc: Information on the cocoa trade and the chocolate industry.

SP/0255-9994
OLIVAE (MADRID, SPAIN : ENGLISH EDITION). (OLIVAE.). **Added/Corp** International Olive Oil Council. No. 1 (April 1984)-. Periodical. English (Spanish, French and Italian). Five times a year. $45.00. Consejo Oleicola, C Principe de Vergara 154, 28002 Madrid Spain. **Tel** 011 34 1 5630071, FAX 34-1-4316127, telex 48197 IOOC-E. **LC** WMLC 93/434.
Desc: Information regarding olives.
Ind/Abst AGRICOLA; Biocont. News Inf.; Hortic. Abstr.; Irr. Drain. Abstr.; Plant Breed. Abstr.; Plant Grow. Reg. Abstr.; Rev. Agric. Entomol.; Rev. Plant Pathol.; Soyabean Abstr.; World Agric. Econ.

CN/1180-2251
ORCHARD (KELOWNA). **See** Agriculture.

AU/1015-0811
OSTERREICHISCHE ZEITSCHRIFT FUER STATISTIK UND INFORMATIK. [Osterr. Z. Stat. Inform.]. (1970)-. Periodical. German. mo. S65.00. Verlag Orac GmbH and Company, Graben 17, A-1014 Vienna Austria. **Tel** 011 43 222 534520, FAX 011 43 222 55162178, telex 136365. **Circ:** 173,000.

UK
OVERSEAS FOOD LEGISLATION MANUAL. English. (updated 3 times a year). £300.00. Leatherhead Food Research Association, Randalls Road, Leatherhead Surrey KT22 7RY United Kingdom. **Tel** 011 44 372 376761, FAX 011 44 372 386228, telex 929846. ctrl circ.

BL/0205-1710
OVOSHTARSTVO, GRADINARSTVO I KONSERVNA PROMISHLENOST. **See** Agriculture-Crop Production and Soil.

CN/1182-5790
PACIFIC FOOD & DRINK NEWS. ***Ceased.*** [Pac. food drink news]. **VFOAT** Food & Drink News; Pacific Food and Drink News. Vol. 1, No. 1 (May 1990)-(March 1994). Periodical. English. mo. Pacific Community News Ltd., PO Box 2455, Sidney, British Columbia V8L 3Y3 Canada. **DD** 647.95711/05.

US/0030-8668
PACIFIC FRUIT NEWS. [Pac. fruit news]. (19??)-. Periodical. English. wk. $40.00 North America; $42.00 other. Pacific Fruit News, PO Box 460, Copperopolis CA 95228. **Tel** (209)785-3377. **ED** Frank Crawford. **DD** 338. **Ad Acc. Circ:** 1,200. ***Continues*** *California Fruit News.*
Desc: Reports on West Coast processed fruit and vegetables, including frozen and dried fruit and tree nuts. Covers domestic and international markets, and political actions affecting these products and markets.

CN/1180-5986
PACK OF APPLES AND APPLE PRODUCTS. **Added/Corp** Statistics Canada. Industry Division. **VFOAT** Conserves de Pommes et des Produits de la Pomme. (1989)-. English (French). an. 14.00Can$ Canada; $17.00 US; $20.00 other. Statistics Canada, Publications Sales & Services, Main Building Room 1710, Ottawa Ontario K1A 0T6 Canada. **Tel** (613)951-5078, (800)267-6677, FAX (613)951-1584, telex 053-3585. **LC** WMLC 91/2448. ***Continues in part*** *Fruit and Vegetable Preservation.*
Desc: Provides information on annual seasonal packs of apples, including crabapples.

CN/1180-5943
PACK OF CANNED TOMATOES AND TOMATO PRODUCTS. [Pack cann. tomatoes tomato prod.]. **Added/Corp** Statistics Canada. Industry Division. **VFOAT** Conserves de Tomates et de Produits de Tomates, en Boites. (1990)-. English (French). an. 14.00Can$ Canada; $17.00 US; $20.00 other. Statistics Canada, Publications Sales & Services, Main Building Room 1710, Ottawa Ontario K1A 0T6 Canada. **Tel** (613)951-5078, (800)267-6677, FAX (613)951-1584, telex 053-3585. **DD** 338.4/7664805642/0971021. ***Continues in part*** *Fruit and Vegetable Preservation., 0380-5042.*
Desc: Provides data on annual seasonal packs of canned tomatoes and tomato products.

CN/1180-5900
PACK OF PROCESSED ASPARAGUS. [Pack process. asparagus]. **Added/Corp** Statistics Canada. Industry Division. **VFOAT** Conserves d'Asperges Conditionnees. (1990)-. English (French). an. 14.00Can$ Canada; $17.00 US; $20.00 other. Statistics Canada, Publications Sales & Services, Main Building Room 1710, Ottawa Ontario K1A 0T6 Canada. **Tel** (613)951-5078, (800)267-6677, FAX (613)951-1584, telex 053-3585. **LC** WMLC 91/3428. **DD** 338.4/766480531/0971021. ***Continues in part*** *Fruit and Vegetable Preservation, 0380-5042.*
Desc: Data is provided on annual seasonal packs of asparagus.

CN/1180-5951
PACK OF PROCESSED BEANS, GREEN AND WAX. [Pack process. beans green wax]. **Added/Corp** Statistics Canada. Industry Division. **VFOAT** Conserves de Haricots Verts et Jaunes Conditionnes. (1990)-. English (French). an. 14.00Can$ Canada; $17.00 US; $20.00 other. Statistics Canada, Publications Sales & Services, Main Building Room 1710, Ottawa Ontario K1A 0T6 Canada. **Tel** (613)951-5078, (800)267-6677, FAX (613)951-1584, telex 053-3585. **LC** WMLC 91/2449. **DD** 338.4/766480565. ***Continues in part*** *Fruit and Vegetable Preservation., 0380-5042.*
Desc: Provides data on annual seasonal packs of green and wax beans.

CN/1180-596X
PACK OF PROCESSED CARROTS. [Pack process. carrots]. **Added/Corp** Statistics Canada. Industry Division. **VFOAT** Conserves de Carottes Conditionnees. (1990)-. English (French). an. 14.00Can$ Canada; $17.00 US; $20.00 other. Statistics Canada, Publications Sales & Services, Main Building Room 1710, Ottawa Ontario K1A 0T6 Canada. **Tel** (613)951-5078, (800)267-6677, FAX (613)951-1584, telex 053-3585. **LC** WMLC 91/2447. **DD** 338.4/766480513/0971021. ***Continues in part*** *Fruit and Vegetable Preservation., 0380-5042.*
Desc: Provides data on annual seasonal packs of carrots.

CN/1180-5935
PACK OF PROCESSED CORN. [Pack process. corn]. **Added/Corp** Statistics Canada. Industry Division. **VFOAT** Conserves de Mais Conditionnees. (1990)-. English (French). an. 14.00Can$ Canada; $17.00 US; $20.00 other. Statistics Canada, Publications Sales & Services, Main Building Room 1710, Ottawa Ontario K1A 0T6 Canada. **Tel** (613)951-5078, (800)267-6677, FAX (613)951-1584, telex 053-3585. **LC** WMLC 91/2450. **DD** 338.4/766480567/0971021. ***Continues in part*** *Fruit and Vegetable Preservation., 0380-5042.*
Desc: Provides data on annual seasonal packs of corn.

CN/1180-5927
PACK OF PROCESSED PEAS. [Pack process. peas]. **Added/Corp** Statistics Canada. Industry Division. **VFOAT** Conserves de Pois Conditionnees. (1990)-. English (French). an. 14.00Can$ Canada; $17.00 US; $20.00 other. Statistics Canada, Publications Sales & Services, Main Building Room 1710, Ottawa Ontario K1A 0T6 Canada. **Tel** (613)951-5078, (800)267-6677, FAX (613)951-1584, telex 053-3585. **LC** WMLC 91/2446. **DD** 338.4/7664805656/0971021. ***Continues in part*** *Fruit and Vegetable Preservation., 0380-5042.*
Desc: Provides data on annual seasonal packs of peas. Data on canned and frozen peas are listed in separate tables showing current and previous years' weight and number of cases by major regions and container sizes.

CN/1180-5919
PACK OF SELECTED PROCESSED FRUITS (EXCL. APPLES). [Pack sel. process. fruits exclud. apples]. **Added/Corp** Statistics Canada. Industry Division. **VFOAT** Certaines Conserves de Fruits Conditionnes (Sauf les Pommes). (1991)-. English (French). an. 14.00Can$ Canada; $17.00 US; $20.00 other. Statistics Canada, Publications Sales & Services, Main Building Room 1710, Ottawa Ontario K1A 0T6 Canada. **Tel** (613)951-5078, (800)267-6677, FAX (613)951-1584, telex 053-3585. **DD** 338.4/76648/00971021. ***Continues in part*** *Fruit and Vegetable Preservation., 0380-5042.*

CN/1180-5919
PACK OF SELECTED PROCESSED FRUITS (EXCL. APPLES). [Pack sel. process. fruits exclud. apples]. **Added/Corp** Statistique Canada. Division de l'Industrie. **VFOAT** Certaines Conserves de Fruits Conditionnes (Sauf les Pommes). (1991)-. French (English). an. 14.00Can$ Canada; $17.00 US; $20.00 other. Statistics Canada, Publications Sales & Services, Main Building Room 1710, Ottawa Ontario K1A 0T6 Canada. **Tel** (613)951-5078, (800)267-6677, FAX (613)951-1584, telex 053-3585. **DD** 338.4/76648/00971021. ***Continues in part*** *Fruit and Vegetable Preservation., 0380-5042.*
Desc: Provides information on annual seasonal packs of selected individual canned or frozen fruits. Tables present weight of current and previous years' packs by major regions and container sizes.

CN/1180-5978
PACK OF SELECTED PROCESSED VEGETABLES. [Pack sel. process. veg.]. **Added/Corp** Statistics Canada. Industry Division. **VFOAT** Certaines Conserves de Legumes Conditionnes. (1990)-. English (French). an. 14.00Can$ Canada; $17.00 US; $20.00 other. Statistics Canada, Publications Sales & Services, Main Building Room 1710, Ottawa Ontario K1A 0T6 Canada. **Tel** (613)951-5078, (800)267-6677, FAX (613)951-1584, telex 053-3585. **DD** 338.4/7664805/0971021. ***Continues in part*** *Fruit and Vegetable Preservation, 0380-5042.*
Desc: Provides data on annual seasonal packs of selected individual vegetables.

US/0030-9168
PACKER, THE. [Packer]. Vol. 1 (1893)-. Periodical. English. Fifty-two times a year (published weekly on Saturday). $49.00 US; $80.00 other (surface mail); Includes Packer's Produce Availability and Merchandising Guide and Fresh Trends). Vance Publishing Corporation, 400 Knightsbridge Parkway, Lincolnshire IL 60069. **Tel** (800)255-5113, (708)634-2600. **ED** Bill O'Neill. **DD** 338. **[CCC]. Ad Acc. Circ:** 15,000 (ctrl). available on microfilm and microfiche from University Microfilms International (UMI).
Desc: Newspaper of the fruit and vegetable industry.
Ind/Abst BioBusiness (1990-).

PK/1010-3562
PAKISTAN SEAFOOD DIGEST. Vol. 1, No. 1 (April 1987)-. English. qt. $60.00. Press Associates Pvt Ltd, Press Center, Shahrah-e-kamal Ataturk, Karachi Pakistan. **Tel** 219262, 219905, 213408, FAX 217754, telex 23868-PPIX. **ED** Owais Aslam Ali. **LC** HD9466.P3; P35. **DD** 338.4/766494/09549105. **Bk Rev. Ad Acc. Circ:** 5,000.
Desc: The only magazine on the seafood industry in Pakistan.

●US/1061-7701
PALATE AND SPIRIT. (PALATE AND SPIRIT : A QUARTERLY GUIDE TO CULINARY LEARNING ADVENTURES.). [Palate spirit]. (1992)-. Periodical. English. qt. $49.00. Palate and Spirit, 2443 Fillmore Street #347, San Francisco CA 94115. **Tel** (415)563-2830. **LC** TX661; .P35. **DD** 641/.05.

US/0893-0244
PALATE PLEASERS. [Palate pleas.]. **VFOAT** Palate Pleasers of Japan. Vol. 4 (1987)-. Periodical. English. Twice a year. $17.90 US; $19.90 Canada; $31.90 Europe; $33.90 Australia and Japan; $23.90 Brazil and Panama. Apcon International Inc., 420 Boyd Street / Suite 502, Los Angeles CA 90013. **Tel** (213)680-9101, telex 194955. **ED** Jack Cooper, Hiro'omi Tanaka, and Susan Hirano. **LC** TX724.5.J3; P34. **DD** 641.5952/05. **Bk Rev. Circ:** 50,000. ***Continues*** *Palate Pleasers of Japan, 8756-6656.*
Desc: Features Japanese cuisine and culture.

MX
PAN. (1???)-. Periodical. Spanish. Twelve times a year. $60.00. Bravo Grupo Edit SA, c/o Jose M. Bustillos, #49 Col Algarin, 06880 Mexico DF Mexico. **Tel** 011 52 5 5306062, FAX 011 52 5 5388679. **ED** Lazaro Bravo Bernabe. **Bk Rev. Ad Acc, Adv Mgr:** Dulce Ma.Perarta. **Pr Rev. Circ:** 10,000 (ctrl).
Desc: Wheat processing industries: milling, bakery, pastries and wheat derivatives.

SP
PANADERIA NOTICIAS. (19??)-. Trade Publication. Spanish. mo. 9850ptas Spain; $135.00 North America; $220.00 other. Montagud Editores SA, Ausias Marc 25 1, 08010 Barcelona Spain. **Tel** 93-3182082, FAX 93-3025083. **ED** Frederico Montegud Bosoms. Index available. cum. index. **Bk Rev. Ad Acc. Circ:** 7,000.
Desc: Newspaper on baking industry.

SP
PANORAMA CONTITERO. Spanish. Twelve times a year. $100.00. Panorama Contitero, Almirante 9, 28004 Madrid Spain. **Tel** 011 34 1 5215194, FAX 011 34 1 5212177. **Ad Acc, Adv Mgr:** Marisa Hernandez, **Tel** 011 34 1 5219228. **Pr Rev. Circ:** 5,000.
Desc: News about cakes, ice cream, chocolates, recipes, dessert fashion, company information and interviews.

SP/0212-6524
PANORAMA PANADERO. [Panorama panad.]. **VFOAT** PP. Panorama Panadero. (1982)-. Periodical. Spanish. Thirteen times a year (Publish with 2 issues in July). $100.00 one year. Panorama Panadero, Almirante 9 1 Derecha, 28004 Madrid Spain. **Tel** 011 34 1 4138289, FAX 011 34 1 5212177. **ED** A. M. Ediciones, (phone: (91) 5215285). **UDC** 664.6. **Ad Acc, Adv Mgr:** Marisa Hernandez, **Tel** 91-5215194. **Circ:** 8,000. ***Continues*** *P.H. Panorama Harinero, 0210-5535.*
Desc: Making and the makers of bread.

●US/1064-8224
PARTY TIMES. [Party times]. **VFOAT** PT. (1993)-. Periodical. English. mo. $15.97. New Way Publications, PO Box 1125, Scarsdale NY 10583-1125. **DD** 642.

US/8750-9393
PASTA JOURNAL. (PASTA JOURNAL / NATIONAL PASTA ASSOCIATION.). [Pasta j.]. **Added/Corp** National Pasta Association (U.S.). Vol. 1, No. 1 (Jan. 1985)-. Periodical. English. bm. $28.00. National Pasta Association, 2101 Wilson Boulevard, Suite 920, Arlington VA 22201. **Tel** (703)841-0818, FAX (703)528-6507. **ED** Donna Chowning Reid. **CODEN** PASJEG. **Ad Acc.** Full Page (B&W) $660.00. Half Page (B&W) $480.00. **Circ:** 900.
Ind/Abst BioBusiness (1990-); Foods Adlibra.

IT/0392-4718
PASTICCERIA INTERNAZIONALE. (19??)-. Italian. bm. L55000 (Italy); L80000 (other). Chiriotti Editori, PO Box 66, 10064 Pinerolo Italy. **Tel** 121 794493, FAX 121/794480, telex 211 820 CHIED I. **[CCC]. Bk**

Food and Food Industry

Rev. **Ad Acc. Circ:** 16,000.
Desc: Technical-professional magazine for master bakers and confectioners that deal with modern technology, new products, machines, and recipes from all over the world.

AT/0818-6561
PASTRYCOOKS AND BAKERS NEWS MONTHLY. (1979)-. Periodical. English. Twelve times a year. 50.00Aus$ Australia; 80.00Aus$ others. Pastrycooks & Bakers Pty. Ltd., PO Box 270, Crows News NSW 2065 Australia. **Tel** 011 61 2 9565155, FAX 011 61 2 9544045. **ED** Norman Baxter (editor's address: 68 Blues Point Road, McMahons Point, NSW 2060 Australia). **Bk Rev**, (Qty: 3-4). **Ad Acc, Adv Mgr:** R. J. Corner. **Circ:** 3,131.

FR/0998-4933
PATISSERIE BOULANGERIE NEUILLY-SUR-SEINE. (PATISSERIE BOULANGERIE.). **VFOAT** Patisserie Boulangerie vie Pratique. (1989)-. Periodical. French. mo (10 issues). 142.02 France; 250.00F other. Editions MBD, 4 rue Santerre, 75012 Paris France. **Tel** 011 33 1 43450333. **UDC** 641(44). *Absorbed Boulanger Patissier Confiseur Glacier*, 0224-5027.

US/0734-6530
PC/SFA ... SNACK FOOD MANAGEMENT REPORT. [PC/SFA snack food manage. rep.]. **VFOAT** P.C./S.F.A. ... Snack Food Management Report. **VAT** Potato Chip/Snack Food Association Snack Food Management Report. 1981-. English. an. Potato Chip/Snack Food Association, Crystal Sq. III/ Suite 903, 1735 Jeff Davis Highway, Arlington VA 22202. **LC** TX803.P8; P37. **DD** 338.4/76646.

US/0740-2562
PEANUT INDUSTRY GUIDE. See Agriculture.

US/0031-3661
PEANUT JOURNAL AND NUT WORLD. *Ceased*. Vol. 10, No. 4 (Feb. 1931)-?. English. mo. Peanut Journal Publishing Company, PO Box 347, Suffolk VA 23434. *Continues Peanut Journal.*

US
PERISHABLES HANDLING. Added/Corp California. University. Extension Service. California. University. Agricultural Extension Service. **VFOAT** Fruit and Vegetables; Perishables Handling. No. 1 (Sept. 1962)-. Periodical. English. ir. University of California Agriculture Engineering Extension, L. Johnston, Davis CA 95616. **Tel** (916)752-0506.

UK/0142-4857
PETITS PROPOS CULINAIRES. See Nutrition and Dietetics.

PH
PHILIPPINE FOOD BALANCE SERIES. No. 6-. English. an. National Economic and Development Authority, PO Box 419, Greenhills Metro Manila Philippines. **Tel** 011 63 2 6313281. *Continues NEDA Food Balance Series.*

PH/0115-6500
PHILIPPINE JOURNAL OF COCONUT STUDIES, THE. See Agriculture-Crop Production and Soil.

PH
PHILIPPINE JOURNAL OF FOOD SCIENCE AND TECHNOLOGY. VFOAT Journal of Food Science and Technology. Vol. 1 (1977)-. Academic Scholarly Publication. English. sa. Documents available from CASDDS.
Ind/Abst Chem. Abstr.; Index Philip. Period.; Philip. Sci. Technol. Abstr.

US/1059-8073
PILLSBURY FAST AND HEALTHY MAGAZINE. *Title Change.* See Nutrition and Dietetics.

UN/0136-9172
PISCEVAJA PROMYSLENNOST (KIEV. 1977). (PISHCHEVAIA PROMYSHLENNOST.). [Pisc. prom-st.]. **Added/Corp** Ukraine. Ministerstvo Kharchovoi Promyshlovosti. Ukraine. Ministerstvo M'iasnoi i Molochnoi Promyslovosti. Ukrains'ke Naukovo Tekhnichne Tovarystvo Kharchovoi Promyslovosti. (1977)-. Periodical. Russian. qt. **CODEN** PIPRDC. Documents available from BIOSIS Document Express. *Continues Kharchova Promyslovist.*
Ind/Abst Biol. Abstr.; Soyabean Abstr.

RU/0235-2486
PISHCHEVAIA PROMYSHLENNOST. Added/Corp Gosudarstvennyi Agropromyschlennyi Komitet SSSR. (1988)-. Periodical. Russian. mo. $119.95. Agropromizdat, Sadovo-Spasskaia, 18, 107807 Moscow Russia. **(Subscription address:** East View Publications Inc., 3020 Harbor Lane North, Suite 110, Minneapolis MN 55447.**) CODEN** PSPREF. Documents available from CASDDS. *Continues Pishchevaia i Pererabatyvaiushchaia Promyshlennost*, 0233-7738.
Ind/Abst Chem. Abstr.; Sug. Indus. Abstr.

US
PIZZA AND PASTA. English. bm. $18.00. Talcott Communications Corporation, 20 North Wacker Drive, Suite 3230, Chicago IL 60606. **Tel** (312)664-4040.
Ind/Abst Foods Adlibra; Infomat Int. Bus.

US/0743-3115
PIZZA TODAY. Added/Corp National Association of Pizza Operators (U.S.). (1983)-. Periodical. English. mo. $24.00 (one year), $35.95 (two year), $42.46 (three year) US; $39.00 (one year), $62.00 (two year), $61.20 (three year) other. Pro-Tech Publishing, PO Box 1347, New Albany IN 47151. **Tel** (812)949-0909, , FAX (812)941-9711. **ED** Gerry Durnell. **LC** TX770.P58; P59. **Bk Rev. Ad Acc, Adv Mgr:** Kaye Durnell. **Circ:** 50,000.
Ind/Abst Foods Adlibra.

II/0032-0978
PLANTERS' CHRONICLE, THE. [Plant. chron.]. (Sept. 1906)-. Periodical. English. Twelve times a year. **(Subscription address:** Prints India, 11 Darya Ganj, New Delhi, 11002 India, telephone: 011 91 11 3268645**)**
Ind/Abst AGRICOLA; Plant Grow. Reg. Abstr.

●PL/1230-0322
POLISH JOURNAL OF FOOD AND NUTRITION SCIENCES / POLISH ACADEMY OF SCIENCES. Added/Corp Polska Akademia Nauk. Division of Food Science. Polska Akademia Nauk. Komitet Technologii i Chemii Zywnosci. Polish Food Technologists' Society. Polish Society of Nutritional Sciences. Vol. 42, No. 1 (Mar. 1992)-. Periodical. English (summaries and/or abstracts in Polish; table of contents in Polish). qt. $40.00. **LC** TP368; .A3. **CODEN** PJFSE7. *Continues Acta alimentaria Polonica.*

MY/0127-0249
PORIM BULLETIN. [PORIM bull.]. **Added/Corp** Institut Penyelidikan Minyak Kelapa Sawit Malaysia. **VAT** Palm Oil Research Institute of Malaysia Bulletin. No. 1 (Nov. 1980)-. Bulletin. English. sa. PORIM, PO Box 10620, Kuala Lumpur Malaysia. **Tel** 011 3 335155, telex MA31604.
Ind/Abst Agric. Eng. Abstr.; Biodeter. Abstr.; Crop Physiol. Abstr.; Hortic. Abstr.; Rev. Agric. Entomol.

US/1070-9320
POSITIVELY PASTA!. (POSITIVELY PASTA! : THE NEWSLETTER ON PASTA.). [Posit. pasta!]. **Added/Corp** National Pasta Association (U.S.). (19??)-. Newsletter. English. Three times a year. $4.00. National Pasta Association, 2101 Wilson Boulevard, Suite 920, Arlington VA 22201. **Tel** (703)841-0818, FAX (703)528-6507. **DD** 641. *Continues Pastahhh.*

●UK/0968-7661
POTATO BUSINESS WORLD. VFOAT PBW. Vol. 1, Issue No. 1 (Jan. 1993)-. Periodical. English. qt. $180.00. Crier Publications Limited, Arctic House, Rye Lane, Sevenoak Kent TN14 5HB England. **Tel** 011 44 71 732-451515, FAX 011 44 71 732 451383. **ED** Alwyn Brice. **Ad Acc, Adv Mgr:** David Brenchley. **Circ:** 4,000.
Desc: For executives involved in producing products from potatoes.

PE
POTATOES IN FOOD SYSTEMS RESEARCH SERIES. Added/Corp International Potato Center. No. 1 (1984)-. Monographic series. English (summaries and/or abstracts in Spanish). **LC** SB211.P8; P7984. **DD** 635/.21.
Ind/Abst World Agric. Econ.

XR
POTRAVINARSKE VEDY. Added/Corp Ceskoslovenska Akademie Zemedelska. Ustav Vedeckotechnickych Informaci pro Zemedelstvi. **VFOAT** Sbornik UVTIZ. Potravinarske Vedy. (1990)-. Periodical. Czech (English and Slovak; summaries and/or abstracts in English, German and Russian; table of contents in English, German and Russian). qt. *Continues Sbornik UVTIZ. Potravinarske Vedy.*
Ind/Abst Postharvest News Inf.

US/0898-4565
POULTRY PROCESSING. [Poult. process.]. (19??)-. Periodical. English. bm. $20.00 US and possessions; $25.00 other. Advanstar Communications Inc., 131 West First Street, Duluth MN 55802. **Tel** (218)723-9477, (800)346-0085. **DD** 664. **CODEN** POPREL.
Ind/Abst BioBusiness (1989-).

UK
PRACTICAL FOOD HYGIENE. (19??)-. Periodical. English. tq. £138.35. Croner Publ Ltd, Croner House, London Road, Kingston upon Thames, Surrey KT2 6SR England. **Tel** 011 44 81 5473333, FAX 081 547-2637.

YU/0352-9193
PREHRAMBENO-TEHNOLOSKA I BIOTEHNOLOSKA REVIJA. [Prehrambeno-tehnol. biotehnol. rev.]. **VFOAT** Food Technology and Biotechnology Review. Vol. 24, No. 1 (1986)-. Academic Scholarly Publication. Serbo-Croatian (Roman). qt. **CODEN** PTBREK. Documents available from CASDDS. *Continues Prehrambeno-Tehnoloska Revija*, 0556-4158.
Ind/Abst AGRICOLA; Chem. Abstr. (1986-); Curr. Biotechnol.

US/0747-2536
PREPARED FOODS. [Prep. foods]. Vol. 153, No. 3, March (1984)-. Periodical. English. mo (13 issues). $85.00 US; $123.00 (GST included) Canada; $115.00 Mexico; $150.00 other. Cahners Publishing Company, 249 West 17th Street, New York NY 10011. **Tel** (212)645-0067, FAX (212)242-6987. **(Subscription address:** Cahners Publishing Company / Colorado, Paid Subscription Service Center, PO Box 7610, Highlands Ranch CO 80126-7610.**) LC** TP368; .P78. **DD** 664/.6. **CODEN** PRFOEH. **[CCC].** available on microfilm and microfiche from University Microfilms International (UMI); available on an online database (file 648/Full-Text) from DIALOG. Documents available from BIOSIS Document Express. *Continues Processed Prepared Foods*, 0192-7132.
Desc: Edited for processors of prepared foods, fruits, vegetables, meats, prepared and convenience bakery foods, dairy specialties, beverages and snack foods. Covers the food business and trends, plant operations and product development.
Ind/Abst BioBusiness (1985-); Biol. Abstr. (1985-); Bus. ASAP (1990-) [Full Txt.]; Bus. Index (1985-); Dairy Sci. Abstr.; F&S Index Plus Text, Int. [Select. Cov.]; Food Sci. Technol. Abstr.; Foods Adlibra; Gen. BusinessFile (1985-); Gen. Period. Index (1985-); Int. Packag. Abstr.; Mag. Search; Life Sci. Collect.; PROMT; Soyabean Abstr.; Sug. Indus. Abstr.; Trade Ind. ASAP [Full Txt.]; Trade Ind. Index [Full Txt.].

●US/1064-7503
PREVENTION'S QUICK AND HEALTHY LOW-FAT COOKING. (1993)-. English. $20.95. Rodale Press Inc., 400 South 10th Street, Emmaus PA 18098. **Tel** (215)967-5171, (800)666-2503.

US
PRICES RECEIVED. MINNESOTA-WISCONSIN MANUFACTURING GRADE MILK /UNITED STATES DEPARTMENT OF AGRICULTURE, STATISTICAL REPORTING SERVICE, CROP REPORTING BOARD. See Agriculture.

US/0090-5631
PROCEEDINGS. ANNUAL MEAT SCIENCE INSTITUTE. (PROCEEDINGS.). [Proc., Annu. Meat Sci. Inst.]. **Main/Corp** Meat Science Institute. Academic Scholarly Publication. English. an. **LC** TS1970; .M42. **DD** 664/.9/005. **CODEN** PAMIDG. Documents available from CASDDS.
Ind/Abst Chem. Abstr.

US/0742-5546
PROCEEDINGS - DISTILLERS FEED CONFERENCE (1980). (PROCEEDINGS.). [Proc. - Distill. Feed Conf.]. **Added/Corp** Distillers Feed Research Council (Cincinnati, Ohio). Vol. 35 (Mar. 27, 1980)-. Academic Scholarly Publication. English. an (March). $20.00. Distillers Feed Research Council, 1885 Dixie Hwy, Suite 270, Fort Wright KY 41011. **Tel** (606)344-8008. **CODEN** PDFCDI. Documents available from CASDDS. *Continues Distillers Feed Research Council (Cincinnati, Ohio). Proceedings*, 0192-2661.
Ind/Abst AGRICOLA; Chem. Abstr. (-1988).

UK/0144-1493
PROCEEDINGS - INSTITUTE OF FOOD SCIENCE AND TECHNOLOGY (U.K.). *Title Change.* [Proc. - Inst. Food Sci. Technol. (U.K.)]. **Main/Corp** Institute of Food Science and Technology. **Added/Corp** Institute of Food Science and Technology (U.K.) IFST Proceedings. **VFOAT** IFST Proceedings. Vol. 1 (1968)-(19??). Proceedings. English. qt. Taylor & Clifton Ltd, 130 High Street Uppermill Oldham, Lancashire England. **NLM** W1; PR583ZT. **[CCC].** *Supersedes in part Journal of Food Technology*, 0022-1163. *Merged with Focus (Institute of Food Science and Technology (U.K.) to form Food Science & Technology Today*, 0950-9623.
Desc: Contains papers presented at meetings, symposia and congresses of the various branches of the institute.
Ind/Abst AGRICOLA.

US/0092-2633
PROCEEDINGS - NATIONAL PEACH COUNCIL. (PROCEEDINGS, ANNUAL CONVENTION - NATIONAL PEACH COUNCIL.). [Proc. - Nat. Peach Counc.]. **Main/Corp** National Peach Council. (19??)-. Proceedings. English. an. $15.00. National Peach Council, PO Drawer 1085, Martinsburg WV 25401. **Tel** (304)267-6024. **ED** Lillie Hoover-Largent. **Circ:** 300 (ctrl). *Supersedes in part National Peach Council Annual*, 0092-3036.
Desc: Speaker presentations regarding production and marketing of fresh peaches.
Ind/Abst AGRICOLA.

SA/0373-045X
PROCEEDINGS OF THE ANNUAL CONGRESS OF THE SOUTH AFRICAN SUGAR TECHNOLOGISTS' ASSOCIATION. (PROCEEDINGS OF THE ... ANNUAL CONGRESS.). [Proc. annu. congr. S. Afr. Sugar Technol. Assoc.]. **Main/Corp** South African Sugar Technologists' Association. Congress. **VFOAT** Proceedings of the ... Annual Congress of the South African Sugar Technologists' Association. (1933)-. Academic Scholarly Publication. English. an (Sept.). R15.00 South Africa; R17.00 others. South African Sugar Technologist's, SASA Experiment Station, Mt Edgecombe 4300 Republic of South Africa. **Tel** 031-593205, telex 6-23020. **CODEN** PSATAA. cum. index. **Ad Acc. Circ:** 1,100 (ctrl). Documents available from BIOSIS Document Express, CASDDS. ***Continues*** *South African Sugar Technologists' Association. Proceedings of the ... Annual General Meeting and Congress.*
Desc: Proceedings of Annual Congress of South African Sugar Technologists Association (agricultural and factory papers). Includes laboratory manual for South African sugar factories.
Ind/Abst Agric. Eng. Abstr.; Biocont. News Inf.; Biol. Abstr.; Chem. Abstr.; Field Crop Abstr.; Hortic. Abstr.; Soils Fert.

US/0066-0582
PROCEEDINGS OF THE ... ANNUAL MEETING / AMERICAN SOCIETY OF BAKERY ENGINEERS. [Proc. annu. meet. Am. Soc. Bak. Eng.]. **Main/Corp** American Society of Bakery Engineers. (1925)-. Proceedings. English. American Society of Baking Engineers, 2 Riverside Plaza, Room 1921, Chicago IL 60606. **Tel** (312)332-2246. **LC** TX761; .A7. **DD** 664.
Ind/Abst AGRICOLA [Full Cov.]; Foods Adlibra.

US/0081-1483
PROCEEDINGS OF THE CONFERENCE - SOCIETY FOR THE ADVANCEMENT OF FOOD SERVICE RESEARCH. **Main/Corp** Society for the Advancement of Food Service Research. 1st- 1959-. Proceedings. English. an. Society for the Advancement, 2710 North Salisburg Street, West Lafayette IN 47906. **Tel** (312)763-7350.

US
PROCEEDINGS OF THE PRODUCTION CONFERENCE. **Main/Corp** Pennsylvania Manufacturing Confectioners' Association. **Added/Corp** Lehigh University, Bethlehem, Pa. Institute of Research. (1947)-. Proceedings. English. an. **LC** TX761; .P4. **DD** 664.15062748.
Desc: Contains confectionery and food industry information.

FR
PROCESS MAGAZINE : LE MENSUEL DES TECHNIQUES LAITIERES ET ALIMENTAIRES. French (English). mo. 476.00F France; 576.00F other (one year), 878.75F France; 1078.75F other (two year). Editions du Boisbaudry, BP 6359, 35036 Rennes Cedex France. **Tel** 011 33 99 322121. **Ad Acc. Circ:** 4,350. ***Continues*** *Technique Laitiere & Marketing.*
Desc: Journal for the food and dairy industry. Techniques for milk and food processing.
Ind/Abst Food Sci. Technol. Abstr.

US/1053-1556
PROCESS (WASHINGTON, D.C.). ***Ceased.*** (PROCESS : THE NEWSMAGAZINE OF THE NATIONAL FOOD PROCESSORS ASSOCIATION.). [Process]. **Added/Corp** National Food Processors Association (U.S.). Vol. 1, No. 1 (Dec. 1990)-(19??). Periodical. English. qt. National Food Processors Association, 1401 New York Avenue Northwest, Suite 400, Washington DC 20005. **Tel** (202)639-5900. **LC** HD9001; .P68. **DD** 338.4/7664/0097305. **CODEN** PRWAEQ.
Ind/Abst Foods Adlibra.

UK
PROCESSED & PACKAGED FOOD DIGEST. English. Mintel International Group Ltd., 18-19 Long Lane, London EC1A 9HE England. **Tel** 011 44 71 606 4533.

US/0886-5663
PRODUCE BUSINESS. [Prod. bus.]. (1985)-. Periodical. English. Eight times a year. $29.70 (one year); $53.70 (two years); $76.70 (three years). Produce Business, PO Box 810425, Boca Raton FL 33481. **Tel** (407)241-4333, FAX (407)241-4486. **DD** 338. **CODEN** PRBSE9. Index available. **Bk Rev. Ad Acc, Adv Mgr:** Whit Acre, **Tel** (407)241-4333.
Desc: The marketing, merchandising and management publication serving the fresh fruit, vegetable and floral industries.

US/0032-969X
PRODUCE NEWS. (1901)-. Periodical. English. wk. $49.00 US; $89.00 Canada; $119.00 other. ZIM-MER Trade Publications Inc, 2185 Lemoine Avenue, Fort Lee NJ 07024. **Tel** (201)592-9100, FAX (201)592-0809. **ED** Gordon Hochberg. **LC** HD9001; .P7. **DD** 338.05. **Ad Acc. Circ:** 10,000 (ctrl). ***Continues*** *Produce Barometer.*
Desc: Covers fresh fruit and vegetable industry.

US/0740-3801
PRODUCT ALERT. **Added/Corp** Marketing Intelligence Service Ltd. (19??)-. English. Fifty-one times per year. $690.00 US; $700.00 Canada; $780.00 Europe and Pan America; $830.00 other. Marketing Intelligence Service Ltd, 6473D Route 64, Naples NY 14512. **Tel** (716)374-6326, (800)836-5710, FAX (714)374-5217, telex 469979. **ED** Diane Beach and Pat Peck. **[CCC].** Index available. available on an online database (files 16,570,636/Full-Text) from DIALOG.
Desc: Reports on new packaged goods in North America.
Ind/Abst Mark. Advert. Ref. Serv. [Full Txt.]; PROMT [Full Txt.]; PTS Newsl. Database [Full Txt.].

US
PRODUCT PROMOTION. **See** Economics-Industry and Production.

CN/0227-1761
PRODUCTION OF SELECTED BISCUITS. [Prod. sel. biscuits]. **Added/Corp** Statistics Canada. Manufacturing and Primary Industries Division. Statistics Canada. Industry Division. **VFOAT** Production de Certains Biscuits. Vol. 2, No. 1 (Mar. 1980)-. English (French). sa. 16.00Can$ Canada; $20.00 US; $23.00 other. Statistics Canada, Publications Sales & Services, Main Building Room 1710, Ottawa Ontario K1A 0T6 Canada. **Tel** (613)951-5078, (800)267-6677, FAX (613)951-1584, telex 053-3585. **LC** HD9058.B573; C26. **DD** 338.4/7664752/0971. ***Continues*** *Production of Biscuits and Cones, 0708-7551.*
Desc: Production of selected biscuits is provided in this semi-annual publication. It includes survey coverage and a list of reporting firms and their plant locations.

FR/1167-539X
PRODUITS FRAIS LEVALLOIS-PERRET. (PRODUITS FRAIS.). (1992)-. Periodical. French. Eleven times a year. 171.40F France; 275.00F other. CEP Communications Groupe LSA, 6 rue Marius Aufan, 92300 Levallois Perret France. **Tel** 011 33 1 47 582000, FAX 011 33 1 47 586070. **UDC** 339.372(44). ***Absorbed*** *Filieres Viande et Peche, 1143-7375.*

NE/0168-5813
PRODUKTIESTATISTIEKEN : BROOD-, BESCHUIT-, BANKET-, KOEKEN BISCUITFABRIEKEN (W.O. BROOD- EN BANKETBAKKERIJEN). **Main/Corp** Netherlands (Kingdom, 1815-) Centraal Bureau voor de Statistiek. Dutch. 4.00. Centraal Bureau voor de Statistiek, AFD ALG Zaken, Postbus 959, 2270 AZ Voorburg Netherlands. **Tel** 011 31 70 3373800, FAX 011 31 038 7429, telex 32692 CBS NL. **LC** HD9057.N4; N48A.

II
PROFODCIL BULLETIN. **Added/Corp** Processed Foods Export Promotion Council. (19??)-. Bulletin. English. qt. Processed Foods Export Promotion Council, New Dehli India.
Ind/Abst Food Sci. Technol. Abstr.

MX
PROGRAMA SIEMBRA-EXPORTACION DE CHILE BELL / DGEA. **VFOAT** Programa Siembra Exportacion de Chile Bell. Spanish. Direccion General de Economia Agricola-Sarh, Carolina No 132-120, Piso 18 DF Mexico. **LC** HD9235.P462; .M66. **DD** 338.1/75643/0972.

MX
PROGRAMA SIEMBRA-EXPORTACION DE FRESA / DGEA. **VFOAT** Programa Siembra Exportacion de Fresa. Spanish. Secretaria de Agricultura y Recursos Hidraulicos, Direccion General de Economia, Agricola Carolina No 132 - 120, Piso Delegacion Benito, Juarez Codigo Postal 03720 Mexico DF. **LC** HD9259.S83; M66. **DD** 382/.41475/0972.

MX
PROGRAMA SIEMBRA-EXPORTACION DE PEPINO / DGEA. **VFOAT** Programa Siembra Exportacion de Pepino. Spanish. Secretaria de Agricultura y Recursos Hidraulicos, Direccion General de Economia, Agricola Carolina No 132 - 120, Piso Delegacion Benito, Juarez Codigo Postal 03720 Mexico DF. **LC** HD9235.C832; M66. **DD** 338.1/7563/0972.

MX
PROGRAMA SIEMBRA-EXPORTACION DE PIMIENTA GORDA / DGEA. **VFOAT** Programa Siembra Exportacion de Pimienta Gorda; Programa Siembra-Exportacion de Pimienta. Spanish. Secretaria de Agricultura y Recursos Hidraulicos, Direccion General de Economia, Agricola Carolina No 132 - 120, Piso Delegacion Benito, Juarez Codigo Postal 03720 Mexico DF. **LC** HD9211.A443; M66. **DD** 382/.4566453.

MX
PROGRAMA SIEMBRA-EXPORTACION DE SANDIA / DGEA. **VFOAT** Programa Siembra Exportacion de Sandia. Spanish. Direccion General de Economia Agricola-Sarh, Carolina No 132-120, Piso 18 DF Mexico. **LC** HD9259.W353; M496. **DD** 338.1/75615/0972.

MX
PROGRAMA SIEMBRA-EXPORTACION DE TOMATE / DGEA. **Added/Corp** Mexico. Direccion General de Economia Agricola. **VFOAT** Programa Siembra Exportacion de Tomate. (19??)-. Spanish. Direccion General de Economia Agricola-Sarh, Carolina No 132-120, Piso 18 DF Mexico. **LC** HD9235.T62; M596. **DD** 382/.415642/0972.

US/0033-0787
PROGRESSIVE GROCER, THE. [Prog. groc.]. (1922)-. Periodical. English. mo. $75.00 US; $86.00 Canada; $96.00 other. Progressive Grocer, 263 Tresser Boulevard, Stamford CT 06901. **Tel** (203)977-7640. **ED** Richard K. Hofler. **LC** TX343; .P7. **DD** 381/.456413/00973. **Ad Acc. Circ:** 72,166. available on microfilm and microfiche from University Microfilms International (UMI); available on an online database (files 15,648/Full-Text) from DIALOG. Documents available from UMI Article Clearinghouse.
Ind/Abst ABI/INFORM Glob. Ed.; ABI Inform Ondisc (Jan. 1991-); AGRICOLA; Bus. ASAP (1990-) [Full Txt.]; Bus. Index (1985-); Bus. Period. Index; F&S Index Plus Text, Int. [Select. Cov.]; Foods Adlibra; Gen. BusinessFile (1985-); Gen. Period. Index (1985-); Infobank (1979-); Mag. Search; Mark. Advert. Ref. Serv.; PROMT; Stat. Ref. Index; Trade Ind. ASAP [Full Txt.]; Trade Ind. Index [Full Txt.]; UMI ABI/Inform--Bus. Period. Ondisc (Jan. 1991-) [Full Txt.]; Vocat. Search (Jan. 1993-); Wilson Bus. Abstr.

US/8755-0571
PROGRESSIVE GROCER EXECUTIVE REPORT. ***Ceased.*** [Prog. groc. exec. rep.]. **VFOAT** Executive report. (Nov. 1984)-?. Periodical. English. bm (5 issues a year). Progressive Grocer Executive Report, 4 Stamford Forum, Stamford CT 06901. **Tel** (416)596-5284, FAX (416)596-5526. **DD** 658. ***Absorbed*** *Management Challenges, 8756-6818; Mid-Year Executive Report, 8756-6826.*

US
PROGRESSIVE GROCER'S ... MARKET SCOPE. **VFOAT** Market Scope. (198?)-. English. an. $299.00. Progressive Grocer, 263 Tresser Boulevard, Stamford CT 06901. **Tel** (203)977-7640. **LC** HD9321.2; .M37. ***Continues*** *Market Scope, 0146-9223.*

US/0079-6921
PROGRESSIVE GROCER'S MARKETING GUIDEBOOK. **See** Business-Marketing.

PL
PRZEGLAD PIEKARSKI I CUKIERNICZY. Vol. 24, No. 1 (Jan. 1976)-. Periodical. Polish (German; table of contents in Russian and German). mo. $75.00. **(Subscription address:** ARS Polona, PO Box 1001, 00068 Warsaw Poland.**)**
Ind/Abst Food Sci. Technol. Abstr.

PL
PRZEMYS ROLNY I SPOZYWCZY. (19??)-. Periodical. Polish. **LC** TP370; .P7.

PL/0033-250X
PRZEMYS SPOZYWCZY. (1955)-. Academic Scholarly Publication. Polish (summaries and/or abstracts in English, French, German and Russian). mo. $117.00. **(Subscription address:** ARS Polona, PO Box 1001, 00068 Warsaw Poland.**)** **CODEN** PRSPAD. Documents available from CASDDS. ***Continues*** *Przemys Rolny i Spozywczy.*
Ind/Abst AGRICOLA; Biodeter. Abstr.; Chem. Abstr.; Food Sci. Technol. Abstr.; Hortic. Abstr.; Nutr. Abstr. Rev., Ser. B, Live Feeds and Feed.; Postharvest News Inf.; Potato Abstr.; Rev. Med. Vet. Mycology; Seed Abstr.; Soyabean Abstr.

US/0099-9032
PUBLICATION OF TECHNICAL PAPERS AND PROCEEDINGS OF THE ANNUAL MEETING OF SUGAR INDUSTRY TECHNOLOGISTS, INC. [Publ. tech. pap. proc. annu. meet. Sugar Ind. Technol. inc.]. **Main/Corp** Sugar Industry Technologists, Inc. 24th (1965)-. Academic Scholarly Publication. English. an. $37.50 Canada; $38.00 US; $40.00 other. Sugar Industry Technologists, PO Box 632 Ste. Therese, Blainville Quebec J7E 4K3 Canada. **Tel** (514)621-3524. **LC** TP375; .S833a. **DD** 664/.12/05. **CODEN** PTPPAC. Documents available from CASDDS. ***Continues*** *Sugar Industry Technicians. Publication of Technical Papers and Proceedings of the Annual Meeting.*
Ind/Abst AGRICOLA; Chem. Abstr.

Food and Food Industry

US/1058-0352
PUBLICATIONS IN FOOD MICROBIOLOGY. See Biology-Microbiology.

NE
PUBLIKATIE - INSTITUUT VOOR BEWARING EN VERWERKING VAN LANDBOUWPRODUKTEN. Main/Corp Instituut voor Bewaring en Verwerking van Landbouwprodukten. No. 273B (Oct. 1974)-. Monographic series. Dutch. Price varies per volume. *Continues* Publikatie, Series A. / Instituut Voor Bewaring en Verwerking Onderzoek Landbouw. Van Landbouwprodukten.
Ind/Abst Postharvest News Inf.; Potato Abstr.

DK/0903-9783
PUBLIKATION - SUNDHEDSMINISTERIET. LEVNEDSMIDDELSTYRELSEN. (PUBLIKATION.). [Publ. - Sundh.minist., Levnedsm.styr.]. **VFOAT** Publikation - Levnedsmiddelstyrelsen, Sundhedsministeriet; Publikation - Levnedsmiddelstyrelsen. (1988)-. Monographic series. Multiple languages. ir. Price varies per volume. Sundhedsministeriet, Levnedsmiddelstyrelsen, Moerkhoej Bygade 19, DK 2860 Soeborg Denmark. **DD** 351.489 007 782. *Continues* Publikation - Miljoministeriet Levnedsmiddelstyrelsen, 0901-4322.
Ind/Abst Pig News Inf.

US
PUBLISHED SEARCH BIBLIOGRAPHIES FROM THE NTIS BIBLIOGRAPHIC DATA BASE. AGRICULTURE AND FOOD / U.S. DEPARTMENT OF COMMERCE, NATIONAL TECHNICAL INFORMATION SERVICE. See Agriculture-Abstracting, Bibliographies and Statistics.

US/1057-7351
PURCHASING PERFORMANCE BENCHMARKS FOR THE U.S. FOOD MANUFACTURING INDUSTRY. See Business-Purchasing.

US/0464-8005
QUALITY PUBLICATION. No. 16- Dec. 1959-. Monographic series. English. Price varies per volume. Malting Barley Improvement Association, 2040 West Wisconsin Avenue, Milwaukee WI 53233. *Continues* Publication - Malt Research Institute, 0096-8943.

UK/0308-4469
QUARTERLY BULLETIN OF COCOA STATISTICS / BULLETIN TRIMESTRIEL DE STATISTIQUES DU CACAO. See Food and Food Industry-Abstracting, Bibliographies and Statistics.

US
QUARTERLY NEWSLETTER / FOOD DISTRIBUTION RESEARCH SOCIETY, INC. Title Change. Main/Corp Food Distribution Research Society. **Added/Corp** Food Distribution Research Society. **VFOAT** Food Distribution Research Society Quarterly Newsletter. (Jan. 1975)-(199?). Newsletter. English. qt. Food Distribution Research Society, 937 Cypress Lane, Greentown PA 18426. **Tel** (302)831-1320, (717)857-1445, FAX (302)831-3651. *Continued by* Newsletter (Food Distribution Research Society).

US/0890-5517
QUICK FROZEN FOODS ANNUAL PROCESSORS' DIRECTORY AND BUYERS' GUIDE. (ANNUAL PROCESSORS' DIRECTORY AND BUYERS' GUIDE.). [Quick frozen foods annu. process. dir. buy. guide]. **VFOAT** Quick Frozen Foods Processors Directory; Directory of Frozen Food Processors. 37th Annual Ed. (1985 Ed.)-. Consumer Publication. English. an. $98.00 US and Canada; $135.00 other. Saul Beck, 271 Madison Avenue, New York NY 10016. **Tel** (212)557-8600, FAX (212)986-9868. **ED** Audrey Beck. **LC** TP493.5.A1; A56. **DD** 664/.0285/02573. cum. index. **Ad Acc.** *Continues* Directory of Frozen Food Processors.
Desc: This directory provides everything you need to know about the frozen food industry.

US/0033-6416
QUICK FROZEN FOODS INTERNATIONAL. [Quick frozen foods int.]. **VFOAT** Quick Frozen Foods. Vol. 1 (June 1959)-. Periodical. English (French, German and Japanese). qt. $20.00 (one year), $35.00 (two year). E W Williams Publications Company, 80 Eighth Avenue, New York NY 10011. **Tel** (212)989-1101, FAX (212)242-5991, telex 427380 QFFI. **ED** John M Saulnier. **LC** TP493.5.A1; Q52. **DD** 641. **CODEN** QFFIAO. **Ad Acc.** **Circ:** 11,000 (ctrl). available on an online database (file 648/Full-Text) from DIALOG.
Ind/Abst BioBusiness (1989-); Bus. ASAP (1990-) [Full Txt.]; Bus. Index (1985-); Food Sci. Technol. Abstr.; Gen. BusinessFile (1985-); Gen. Period. Index (1985-); Infomat Int. Bus.; Int. Packag. Abstr.; Mag. Search; Trade Ind. ASAP [Full Txt.]; Trade Ind. Index (1981-) [Full Txt.]; Vocat. Search (Jan. 1993-).

FR/0035-4244
R.I.A. (PARIS, 1977). (RIA, REVUE ECONOMIQUE ET TECHNIQUE DE L'INDUSTRIE ALIMENTAIRE EUROPEENNE.). [R.I.A.]. **VFOAT** Revue Economique et Technique de l'Industrie Alimentaire Europeenne. (19??)-. Periodical. French. Nineteen times a year. 534.00F France; 670.00F EEC countries; 795.00F other. Nouvelles Edns Publs Agricoles, 8 Cite Paradis, F 75010 Paris France. **Tel** 011 33 1 40227900. **LC** TP368; .R49. **DD** 338.4/7/66400944. **Bk Rev. Ad Acc. Circ:** 4,000. *Continues* Revue Technique et Economique de l'Industrie Alimentaire, 0220-813X.
Desc: Economics, technology and marketing for the food industry.
Ind/Abst AGRICOLA; Food Sci. Technol. Abstr.

JA/0385-0218
RAKUNO KAGAKU, SHOKUHIN NO KENKYU. See Agriculture-Dairy Industry.

FR
RAPPORT STATISTIQUE - COMITE NATIONAL DE LA POMME DE TERRE. Main/Corp Comite National de la Pomme de Terre. 1974/75-. French. 50.00. Documentation Francaise, 29 Quai Voltaire, 75344 Paris Cedex 7 France. **Tel** 011 33 1 40157000, FAX 011 33 1 40157230, telex 204 826 DOCFRAN. **LC** HD9235.P82; F73. **DD** 338.1/7/5210944.

IT/0392-7113
RASSEGNA DI DIRITTO E TECNICA DELLA ALIMENTAZIONE. [Rass. diritto tec. alim.]. (1966)-. Periodical. Italian. bm (6 issues). L120000 Italy; L160000 other. Franco Angeli Riviste SRL, Viale Monza 106, 20127 Milan Italy. **Tel** 011 39 2 2827651, 011 39 2 289562. **UDC** 613.2.

●US
RECIPE DIGEST. (1993)-. English. bm (6 issues). $12.97. House of White Birches, 306 East Parr Road, Berne IN 46711. **Tel** (219)589-8741, FAX (219)589-8093. **(Subscription address:** Palm Coast Data, PO Box 420235, Agency Department, Palm Coast FL 32142.**)** *Continues* Desserts, 1072-639X.
Desc: Over 500 reader-tested recipes per year.

US/0889-2113
REFERENCE POINT. (REFERENCE POINT; FOOD INDUSTRY ABSTRACTS.). [Ref. point]. **Added/Corp** Food Marketing Institute. Information Service. **VFOAT** Food Industry Abstracts. (Jan. 1980)-. Periodical. English. mo. $55.00 members; $77.00 non-members (includes postage). Food Marketing Institute, 1750 K Street Northwest, Washington DC 20006. **Tel** (202)452-8444. **DD** 381. Index available. cum. index (included in subscription). *Continues* Food Marketing Institute. Information Service. Monthly Index Listings.
Desc: Articles of particular interest to food retailers, wholesalers, and manufacturers. Also abstracts of general business periodicals relating to food marketing. Easy-to-follow indexing system and key retail terms.

US/0889-2113
REFERENCE POINT. CUMULATIVE INDEX : FOOD INDUSTRY ABSTRACTS. **Added/Corp** Food Marketing Institute. Information Service. **VFOAT** Cumulative Index. (1980)-. English. Food Marketing Institute, 1750 K Street Northwest, Washington DC 20006. **Tel** (202)452-8444. *Continues* Cumulative Index (Food Marketing Institute. Information Service).

US
REFERENCE SOURCE. (19??)-. English. an (Nov.). $30.00 US and Canada; $40.00 other. Sosland Publishing Company / Missouri, 4800 Main Street, Suite 100, Kansas City MO 64112. **Tel** (816)756-1000, FAX (816)756-0494, telex 82051. Full Page (B&W) $3,835.00. Half Page (B&W) $2,265.
Desc: A statistical reference manual and specification guide for the baked foods specialist. Includes statistics, formulations and troubleshooting information .

US/1061-6152
REFRIGERATED & FROZEN FOODS. [Refrig. frozen foods]. **VFOAT** Refrigerated and Frozen Foods. (19??)-. Periodical. English. Twelve times a year. $55.00. Stagnito Publishing Company, 1935 Sherner Road, Suite 100, Northbrook IL 60062. **Tel** (708)205-5660, FAX (708)205-5680. **DD** 664.
Ind/Abst Foods Adlibra.

US/0090-8932
RENDER. [Render]. **Added/Corp** National Renderers Association. Pacific Coast Renderers Association. (19??)-. Periodical. English. bm. free. Editor's West, PO Box 7595, c/o Frank Burnham, Riverside CA 92504. **Tel** (312)827-8151. **ED** Frank A. Burnham (editor's phone: (909)795-4240). **LC** IN PROCESS. **DD** 664. **Ad Acc. Circ:** 7,000 (ctrl).

GY
REPORT AND ACCOUNTS - GUYANA SUGAR CORPORATION. Main/Corp Guyana Sugar Corporation. (1976)-. Corporate Report. English. an. Free. Guyana Sugar Corporation, 22 Church Street, Georgetown Guyana. **Tel** 592 2 66841, FAX 592 2 57274, telex GY 2265. **LC** HD9114.G84; G84. **DD** 338.7/63/36109881. **Circ:** 1,000.
Desc: An assessment of the industry's performance. An opening statement, usually a synopsis of the entire report, is followed by sectionalised commentary of key operation areas. Audited financial statements close each issue.

AT
REPORT OF RESEARCH / COMMONWEALTH SCIENTIFIC AND INDUSTRIAL RESEARCH ORGANIZATION, AUSTRALIA, DIVISION OF FOOD RESEARCH. Main/Corp Commonwealth Scientific and Industrial Research Organization (Australia). Division of Food Research. (1970/1971)-. English. an. CSIRO Publications, PO Box 89, 314 Albert Street, East Melbourne Victoria 3002 Australia. **Tel** 011 61 3 4187333, 4187217, FAX 011 61 3 4190459, telex AA 30236. *Formed by the union of* Commonwealth Scientific and Industrial Research Organization (Australia) Division of Food Preservation Annual Report *and* Commonwealth Scientific and Industrial Research Organization. Division of Dairy Research. Report.

AT
REPORT OF RESEARCH - DIVISION OF FOOD RESEARCH. Main/Corp Commonwealth Scientific and Industrial Research Organization (Austria). Division of Food Research. (19??)-. English. be. 5.00Aus$. CSIRO Publications, PO Box 89, 314 Albert Street, East Melborne Victoria 3002 Australia. **Tel** 011 61 3 4187333, 4187217, FAX 011 61 3 4190459, telex AA 30236. **ED** Colin Chandler. **LC** TX341; .A92a. **DD** 664. **Bk Rev. Ad Acc. Circ:** 2,000 (ctrl).

JA/0915-5457
REPORT OF STUDY GROUP ON INTERNATIONAL ISSUES, FAPRC. See Agriculture.

SA
REPORT OF THE AUDITOR-GENERAL ON THE ACCOUNTS OF THE MEAT BOARD FOR THE FINANCIAL YEAR ... . **VFOAT** Verslag van die Ouditeur-Generaal oor die Rekenings van die Vleisraad vir die Boekjaar. Afrikaans (English). an. Bosman Street, Private Bag X85, Pretoria 0001 South Africa. **LC** HD9427.S6; R47.

IT
REPORT OF THE CODEX COMMITTEE ON COCOA PRODUCTS AND CHOCOLATE. Main/Corp Joint FAO/WHO Codex Alimentarius Commission. Codex Committee on Cocoa Products and Chocolate. (19??)-. English. Codex Committee on Cocoa Products and Chocolate, Via Delle Terme di Caracalla, Rome 00100 Italy. **LC** TP640; .J56a. **DD** 664.

IT
REPORT OF THE CONFERENCE OF FAO. Main/Corp Food and Agriculture Organization of the United Nations. Conference. 16th (1971)-. Monographic series. English. ir. Price varies per volume. Food and Agriculture Organization (FAO) / Italy, GIPC166 via Terme di Caracalla, 00100 Rome Italy. **Tel** 011 39 6 522 52925, FAX 011 39 6 522 55784. *Continues* Food and Agriculture Organization of the United Nations. Conference. Report of the ... Session of the Conference.

IT
REPORT OF THE COUNCIL OF FAO (ENGLISH EDITION). See Agriculture.

IT
REPORT OF THE SESSION OF THE CODEX COMMITTEE ON FOODS FOR SPECIAL DIETARY USES. Main/Corp Joint FAO/WHO Codex Alimentarius Commission. Codex Committee on Foods for Special Dietary Uses. English. Codex Committee on Foods for Special Dietary Uses, Via Delle Terme di Caracalla, Rome 00100 Italy. **LC** TX537; .J62A. **DD** 614.3/1/05.

IT
REPORT OF THE SESSION OF THE JOINT ECE/CODEX ALIMENTARIUS GROUP OF EXPERTS ON STANDARDIZATION OF QUICK FROZEN FOODS. See Law.

US/0886-7372
RESEARCH REPORT / INTERNATIONAL FOOD POLICY RESEARCH INSTITUTE. [Res. rep. - Int. Food Policy Res. Inst.]. **Added/Corp** International Food Policy Research Institute. No. 1

(1976)-. Monographic series. English. ir. Price varies per volume. **LC** UNC. **DD** 363.
Ind/Abst AGRICOLA; Geogr. Abstr. Human Geogr.; Int. Dev. Abstr.; Maize Abstr.; Potato Abstr.; Rural Dev. Abstr.; World Agric. Econ.

US/0146-2210
RETAIL BAKING TODAY. V. 1- Apr. 1974-. Periodical. English. mo. $5.00 US; $20.00 other. Sosland Publishing Company / Missouri, 4800 Main Street, Suite 100, Kansas City MO 64112. **Tel** (816)756-1000, FAX (816)756-0494, telex 820182. **LC** HD9057.U58; R48. **DD** 338.4/7/6647520973.

CN
RETAIL FOOD PRICE INDEXES. **See** Business-Retail.

NR
RETAIL MARKET PRICES OF SOME FOOD ITEMS IN PLATEAU STATE, SELECTED FROM SOME LOCAL GOVERNMENT IN THE STATE. **Main/Corp** Nigeria. Ministry of Finance and Economic Planning. Economic Planning Division. English. Ministry of Finance & Economic Planning, Economic Planning Division, Lagos Nigeria. **LC** HD9017.N53; P545. **DD** 338.4/3641/30096695.

AG/0326-0550
REVISTA ARGENTINA DE PRODUCCION ANIMAL. **See** Veterinary Sciences.

CU/1010-2752
REVISTA DE PROTECCION VEGETAL. **See** Agriculture-Crop Production and Soil.

BL/0100-3674
REVISTA DO INSTITUTO DE LATICINIOS CANDIDO TOSTES. [Rev. Inst. Laticinios Candido Tostes]. **Added/Corp** Instituto de Laticinios Candido Tostes (Brazil). **VFOAT** Revista do ILCT. (19??)-. Periodical. Portuguese. bm. **CODEN** RILCAY. Documents available from CASDDS.
Ind/Abst Biodeter. Abstr.; Chem. Abstr. (-1988); Dairy Sci. Abstr.; Food Sci. Technol. Abstr.

●SP/1131-799X
REVISTA ESPANOLA DE CIENCIA Y TECNOLOGIA DE ALIMENTOS / EDITADA POR EL CONSEJO SUPERIOR DE INVESTIGACIONES CIENTIFICAS. **Added/Corp** Consejo Superior de Investigaciones Cientificas (Spain) Instituto de Agroquimica y Tecnologia de Alimentos (Valencia, Spain). **VFOAT** Ciencia y Tecnologia de Alimentos. (1992)-. Periodical. Spanish (English). Six times a year. 9,500.00ptas Spain; $125.00 other. Instituto de Agroquimica, Jaime ROIG 11, 46010 Valencia Spain. **Tel** 34 6 3690800. **CODEN** RCTAEU. Index available in last issue of volume--attached. cum. index. **Bk Rev. Ad Acc. Circ:** 1,000 (ctrl). Documents available from The Genuine Article, CASDDS. ***Continues*** *Revista de Agroquimica y Tecnologia de Alimentos.*
Desc: Publishes manuscripts in the area of food science and technology. Reviews scientific and technical articles; includes book reviews.
Ind/Abst Chem. Abstr.; Curr. Contents, Agric. Biol. Environ. Sci.; Res. Alert [Select. Cov.]; SCISEARCH; Soc. Sci. Cit. Index [Select. Cov.].

FR
RIBC BISCUITERIE CHOCOLATERIE. French. ir. 225.00F France; 295.00F other. Sepaic, 42 rue du Louvre, BP 551, 75001 Paris France. **Tel** 011 33 1 42335740.

IT/1120-6039
RISTORAZIONE COLLETTIVA. [Ristor. collettiva]. (1976)-. Periodical. Italian. mo (Jan/Feb & July/Aug issues combined). L90000 Italy; L155000 other. Unisco SRL, Via a Pestalozza 31, 20131 Milan Italy. **Tel** 011 39 2 236-1556, FAX 011 39 2 26680526. **ED** Stefania Porro. **UDC** 641.5. Index available. **Bk Rev. Ad Acc. Circ:** 24,500.
Desc: Supply of goods and services, designing, and management for the institutionalized food industry.

IT/0391-4887
RIVISTA DELLA SOCIETA ITALIANA DI SCIENZA DELL'ALIMENTAZIONE, LA. [Riv. Soc. Ital. Sci. Aliment.]. **Main/Corp** Societa Italiana De Scienza Dell'Alimentazione. Vol. 1 (Feb. 1972)-. Academic Scholarly Publication. Italian (summaries and/or abstracts in English). Four times a year. L150000.00 Italy; L250000.00 other. Societa Editrice Alimenti Alimentazione Nutrizione, Via Tiberio Imperatore 65, 00145 Rome Italy. **Tel** 11 39 6 5137436. **LC** TX341; .S57a. **CODEN** RSISAZ. Index available in last issue of volume--attached. **Bk Rev. Ad Acc. Pr Rev. Circ:** 2,500. Documents available from BIOSIS Document Express, CASDDS.
Desc: Includes chemical and microbiological new analytical methods of foodstuffs, nutritional evaluation of nutrients and special diets, and jurisprudence book recensions.
Ind/Abst Anim. Breed. Abstr.; Biodeter. Abstr. (1991-); Biol. Abstr. (1987-); Chem. Abstr.; Dairy Sci. Abstr.; Food Sci. Technol. Abstr.; Nutr. Abstr. Rev., Ser. B, Live Feeds and Feed.; Nutr. Abstr. Rev., Ser. A, Hum. Exp.; Potato Abstr.; Poult. Abstr.; Rev. Agric. Entomol.; Rev. Med. Vet. Mycology; Sug. Indus. Abstr.

US/1044-8330
ROCKY MOUNTAIN FOOD DEALER BULLETIN : NEWSLETTER FOR MEMBERS OF THE ROCKY MOUNTAIN FOOD DEALERS ASSOCIATION, THE. **VFOAT** Rocky Mountain Food Dealer. Newsletter. English. bm. Rocky Mountain Food Dealers Association, 1015 Kipling, Lakewood CO 80215. ***Continues*** *Rocky Mountain Food Dealer, 0035-7588.*

GW/0341-0668
RUNDSCHAU FUER FLEISCHUNTERSUCHUNG UND LEBENSMITTELUBERWACHUNG. **Added/Corp** Bundesverband Deutscher Fleischbeschauer, Trichinenschauer, Lebensmittel- und Geflugelfleischkontrolleure. Issue No. 4 (Apr. 1976)-. Trade Publication. German. mo. DM72.00. Verlag M & H Schaper GmbH & Co, Postfach 16 42, D 31046 Alfeld Leine Germany. **Tel** 011 49 5181 80090. **ED** Eberhard Ruppert. **NLM** W1 RU684L. **Bk Rev. Ad Acc. Circ:** 2,600. ***Continues*** *Rundschau fur Fleischbeschauer, Trichinenschauer und Geflugelfleischkontrolleure, 0340-1219.*
Desc: Trade journal for butchering and meat inspection. Control of traffic for food, tobacco, cosmetics and utensils.
Ind/Abst Helminthol. Abstr.; Index Vet.; Pig News Inf.; Vet. Bull.

RU/0235-2583
SAKHARNAIA SVEKLA--PROIZVODSTVO I PERERABOTKA. ***Ceased.*** **VFOAT** Sakharnaia Svekla, Proizvodstvo i Pererabotka; Sakharnaia Svekla. Vol. 1 (1988)-(19??). Periodical. Russian. bm. **(Subscription address:** Victor Kamkin, 4956 Boiling Brook Parkway, Rockville MD 20852.**)** ***Continues*** *Sakharnaia Svekla, 0036-3359* ***and*** *Sakharnaia Promyshelnnost, 0036-3340.*
Ind/Abst Agric. Eng. Abstr.; Field Crop Abstr.; Food Sci. Technol. Abstr.; Postharvest News Inf.; Rev. Plant Pathol. (?-?); Seed Abstr.; Sug. Indus. Abstr.

US
SALES PRO. English. mo. $640.00 US & Canada; $670.00 Europe & Pan America; $695.00 other. Marketing Intelligence Service Ltd, 6473D Route 64, Naples NY 14512. **Tel** (716)374-6326, (800)836-5710, FAX (714)374-5217, telex 469979. **ED** Tom Vierhile. available on an online database from DATA-STAR; and DIALOG.
Desc: Monitors and analyzes current consumer sales promotional material for packaged goods.
Ind/Abst Mark. Advert. Ref. Serv.

CN/0848-5313
SASKATCHEWAN FOOD PROCESSORS DIRECTORY. [Sask. food process. dir.]. **Added/Corp** Saskatchewan. Saskatchewan Agriculture and Food. Canada. Agriculture Canada. (1990)-. Directory. English. **LC** WMLC 90/0644. **DD** 338.4/7664/0025714.

XR/0554-9701
SBORNIK VYSOKE SKOLY CHEMICKO-TECHNOLOGICKE V PRAZE ... POTRAVINY. [Sb. Vys. sk. chem.-technol. Praze, Potraviny]. **Added/Corp** Vysoka Skola Chemicko-Technologicka v Praze. **VFOAT** Scientific Papers of the Institute of Chemical Technology, Prague ... Food; Potraviny; Food. (1966)-. Monographic series. Czech (English, German, Russian and Slovak; summaries and/or abstracts in English and Russian). Statni Pedagogicke Nakladatelstvi, Ostrovni 30, 113 01 Prague 1 Czech Republic. **Tel** (2)203787, FAX (2)293883. **CODEN** SVSCAZ. Documents available from CASDDS. ***Continues*** *Sbornik Vysoke Skoly Chemicko-Technologicke v Praze. Potravinarska Technologie.*
Ind/Abst Chem. Abstr.

US/0741-4838
SCHOOL FOOD SERVICE DIRECTOR. [Sch. food serv. dir.]. **Added/Corp** Federal News Services. Vol. 1, No. 1 (Jan. 11, 1984)-. Periodical. English. Twenty-two times a year. $107.00. Federal News Services Inc., PO Box 13460, Silver Spring MD 20911. **Tel** (301)608-9322, FAX (301)608-9057. **[CCC].**

US/0160-6271
SCHOOL FOOD SERVICE JOURNAL. ***Title Change.*** [School foodserv. j.]. **Added/Corp** American School Food Service Association. **VFOAT** School Foodservice Journal. Vol. 25, No. 8, Sept. (1971)-(1994). Periodical. English. Eleven times a year (With June/July issues combined). American School Food Service Association, 1600 Duke Street, 7th Floor, Alexandria VA 22314-3421. **Tel** (800)728-0728, (703)739-3900, FAX (703)739-3915. **ED** Adrienne Gall Tufts. **LC** LB3475.A1; S3. **DD** 371.7/16/05. **CODEN** SFSJAC. Index available. cum. index. **Bk Rev. Ad Acc, Adv Mgr:** Tina Farah, **Tel** (703)739-3900. **Circ:** 65,000. ***Continues*** *School Lunch Journal.* ***Continued by*** *School Foodservice & Nutrition, 1075-3885.*
Desc: These are primarily members of ASFSA, who are principally elementary and high school food service professionals, who are involved in child nutrition research and education.
Ind/Abst AGRICOLA [Select. Cov.]; BioBusiness (1990-).

●US/1075-3885
SCHOOL FOODSERVICE & NUTRITION. [School foodserv. nutr.]. **Added/Corp** American School Food Service Association. **VFOAT** School Foodservice and Nutrition. Vol. 48, No. 6 (June/July 1994)-. Periodical. English. mo (11 issues). $125.00. American School Food Service Association, 1600 Duke Street, 7th Floor, Alexandria VA 22314-3421. **Tel** (800)728-0728, (703)739-3900, FAX (703)739-3915. **ED** Adrienne Gall Tufts. **LC** LB3475.A1; S3. **DD** 371.7/16/05. Index available. cum. index. **Bk Rev. Ad Acc, Adv Mgr:** Tina Farah, **Tel** (703)739-3900. **Circ:** 65,000. ***Continues*** *School Food Service Journal, 0160-6271.*
Desc: These are primarily members of ASFSA, who are principally elementary and high school food service professionals, who are involved in child nutrition research and education.

US/0149-6808
SCHOOL FOODSERVICE RESEARCH REVIEW. [Sch. foodserv. res. rev.]. **Added/Corp** American School Food Service Association. Vol. 1 (Summer 1977)-. Periodical. English. Twice a year (Mar. & Nov.). $24.00 (nonmembers), $20.00 (members). American School Food Service Association, 1600 Duke Street, 7th Floor, Alexandria VA 22314-3421. **Tel** (800)728-0728, (703)739-3900, FAX (703)739-3915. **ED** Deborah Cantor Ph.D. **LC** TX945; .S344. **DD** 642/.58/05. **NLM** W1; SC237. cum. index. **Bk Rev. Circ:** 500.
Desc: This highlights current research on the subject of nutrition, school food service, and education.
Ind/Abst AGRICOLA [Full Cov.]; Foods Adlibra.

GW/0724-8784
SCHRIFTENREIHE LEBENSMITTELCHEMIE, LEBENSMITTELQUALITAT. **Added/Corp** Gesellschaft Deutscher Chemiker. Arbeitsgruppe Zusatzstofftechnologie und -Analytik. **VFOAT** Lebensmittelchemie, Lebensmittelqualitat; Technologie der Lebensmittel-Zusatzstoffe. (1983)-. Monographic series. German (English). Behrs Verlag, Averhoffstr 10, D 22085 Hamburg Germany. **Tel** 49 40 22700818. **NLM** W1; SC343H. **CODEN** LELBD8. Documents available from CASDDS.
Ind/Abst Chem. Abstr.

JA
SCIENCE OF COOKERY. CHORI KAGAKU. Japanese. Four times a year. $80.00. Nihon Chori Kagakkai, (Japanese Soc. for Science of Cookery), Ochanomizu Joshi Daigaku, Kaseigakubu Chorigaku Kenkyushitsu, 1-1, Otsuka 2 Chome, Bunkyoku, Tokyoto 112, Japan. **(Subscription address:** Maruzen Company Ltd., PO Box 5050, Import & Export Department, Tokyo 100 31 Japan.**)**

US/0738-9310
SCIENCE OF FOOD AND AGRICULTURE. [Sci. food agric.]. **Added/Corp** Council for Agricultural Science and Technology. Vol. 1, No. 1 (Sept. 1988)-. Periodical. English. sa. $10.00 (two year). Council for Agricultural Science and Technology, 4420 West Lincoln Way, Ames IA 50010. **Tel** (515)292-2125, FAX (515)292-4512. **ED** Robert J Ver Straeten. **LC** S1; .S342. **DD** 630. Index available. cum. index. **Circ:** 30,000. available on an online database from NSTA Science Line. ***Continues*** *Science of Food and Agriculture, 0738-9310.*
Desc: Articles, exercises, research news, resources that are published for use by high school science teachers and students.
Ind/Abst Dairy Sci. Abstr.; Foods Adlibra.

FR/0240-8813
SCIENCES DES ALIMENTS. [Sci. aliments]. Vol. 1, No. 1 (1981)-. Academic Scholarly Publication. English (French; summaries and/or abstracts in English). qt. $197.00. Lavoisier Abonnements, 14 rue de Provigny, F 94236 Cachan Cedex France. **Tel** 011 33 1 47406700. **(Subscription address:** VCH Publishers Inc., 303 Northwest 12th Avenue, Journals Department, Deerfield FL 33442.**)** **ED** J.L. Multon. **LC** TX341; .S33. **NLM** W1 SC789C. **CODEN** SCALDC. **[CCC].** Index available. cum. index. **Bk Rev. Pr Rev. Circ:** 1,000 (ctrl). Documents available from The Genuine Article, CASDDS. ***Continues*** *Annales de Technologie Agricole, 0003-4223.*
Desc: Journal of a high standard devoted to food science and technology: fruit, vegetable, cereals, milk, meat, and drinks. Including food engineering, nutrition, animal feeding and hygiene.
Ind/Abst Agric. Eng. Abstr. (1991-); BioBusiness; Biodeter. Abstr. (1991-); Chem. Abstr.; Crop Physiol. Abstr.; Curr. Contents, Agric. Biol. Environ. Sci.; Dairy Sci. Abstr.; Field Crop Abstr.; Food Sci. Technol. Abstr.; Grasslands For. Abstr.; Hortic. Abstr.; Index Vet.; Maize Abstr.; Nutr. Abstr. Rev., Ser. B, Live Feeds and Feed.;

Nutr. Abstr. Rev., Ser. A, Hum. Exp.; Life Sci. Collect.; Pig News Inf.; Postharvest News Inf.; Potato Abstr.; Poult. Abstr.; Res. Alert [Select. Cov.]; Rev. Agric. Entomol.; Rev. Plant Pathol.; Rice Abstr.; Seed Abstr.; Sorghum Mill. Abstr.; Soyabean Abstr.; Sug. Indus. Abstr.; Vet. Bull.; Vitis Vitic. Enol. Abstr.; Wheat Barley Trit. Abstr.

UK/0144-2074
SCIENTIFIC AND TECHNICAL SURVEYS - BRITISH FOOD MANUFACTURING INDUSTRIES RESEARCH ASSOCIATION. (SCIENTIFIC AND TECHNICAL SURVEYS.). [Sci. tech. surv. - Br. Food Manuf. Ind. Res. Assoc.]. **Main/Corp** British Food Manufacturing Industries Research Association. (Mar. 1947)-. Academic Scholarly Publication. English. ir. Price varies per volume. British Food Manufacturing Industries Research Association, Randalls Road, Leatherhead Surrey KT22 7RY England. **Tel** 011 44 372 376761, FAX 011 44 372 386228, telex 929846. **LC** TP370; .B817. **CODEN** SBFMAU. ctrl circ. Documents available from CASDDS.
Ind/Abst Chem. Abstr.; Food Sci. Technol. Abstr.

US/0272-4294
SEAFOOD AMERICA. See Fish and Fisheries.

AT/1320-9663
SEAFOOD AUSTRALIA. (19??)-. English. bm (6 issues). 36.00Aus$ Australia; 48.00Aus$ other. Firecrest Publications, Suite 3, 382 Pacific Highway, Crows Nest NSW 2065 Australia. **Tel** 011 61 2 437 5691, FAX 011 61 2 437 5827. **ED** Norman Grant, Nick Ruello. **Bk Rev. Ad Acc. Circ:** 6,000 (ctrl).

US/0889-3217
SEAFOOD BUSINESS (CAMDEN, ME.). (SEAFOOD BUSINESS.). [Seaf. bus.]. Vol. 5, No. 3 (May/June 1986)-. Periodical. English. bm (plus additional issue in Aug.). $30.00 (one year), $50.00 (two year), $65.00 (three year) US, Canada and Mexico; $70.00 (one year), $130.00 (two year), $180.00 (three year) other. Journal Publications, 120 Tillson Avenue, Suite 201, Rockland ME 04841. **Tel** (207)594-6222, FAX (207)594-8978. **LC** HD9451; .S4. **DD** 338.4/766494/0973. **CODEN** SEFBEM. **Bk Rev. Ad Acc. Circ:** 15,500 (ctrl).
Continues *Seafood Business Report, 0733-0464;*
Absorbed *Seafood Buyer's Catalog, 0897-3687.*
Desc: Price, supply, marketing information for North America seafood.
Ind/Abst BioBusiness; Foods Adlibra; Stat. Ref. Index.

UK/0958-3246
SEAFOOD NEWS FOR UK AND IRELAND. ***Title Change.*** **VFOAT** Seafood News. (19??)-(19??). Periodical. English. mo. EMAP Heighway, Meed House, 21 John Street, London WC1N 2BP England. **Tel** 44 71 4045513, FAX 881 3483, telex 44 71 831 9362. **LC** WMLC L 83/9347. **CODEN** SEWSEM.
Merged into *Fishing News.*
Ind/Abst Foods Adlibra (?-?).

US/0270-417X
SEAFOOD PRICE - CURRENT. (19??)-. English. sw (Tues. & Thurs.). $252.00 US; $264.00 Canada; $269.00 Mexico; $323.00 others. Urner Barry Publications Inc., PO Box 389, Toms River NJ 08754. **Tel** (908)240-5330, (800)932-0617, FAX (908)341-0891. **ED** Paul B. Brown. **Ad Acc. Circ:** 500.
Desc: Extensive report on all types of fin and shellfish, both fresh and frozen. Covers all regions of the country.

US/1057-2708
SEAFOOD TREND NEWSLETTER. [Seaf. trend newsl.]. (1990)-. Newsletter. English. Twenty-four times a year. $220.00. Seafood Trend, 8227 Ashworth Avenue North, Seattle WA 98103. **Tel** (206)523-2280, FAX (206)526-8719. **ED** Ken Talley (editor's phone; (206)523-8830). **DD** 338. **CODEN** STRNEJ. cum. index.
Continues *Seafood Trend, 0892-5666.*
Desc: Provides information on the seafood markets.
Ind/Abst BioBusiness (1990-).

NE
SERIES IN FOOD MATERIAL SCIENCE. Vol. 1 (1975)-. Academic Scholarly Publication. English. ir. Price varies per volume. Reidel Publishing, 101 Philip Drive, Norwell MA 02061-1677. **Tel** (617)871-6600, telex 200190. **CODEN** SFMSDC. Each issue contains an index to its own contents (no volume index)--loose. Documents available from CASDDS.
Ind/Abst Chem. Abstr. (1975).

II
SHARKARA : QUARTERLY BULLETIN OF THE NATIONAL SUGAR INSTITUTE, KANPUR. **Added/Corp** National Sugar Institute, Kanpur, India. Vol. 1, No. 1 (1958)-. Bulletin. English. Four times a year. National Sugar Institute, Kanpur, India. **(Subscription address:** Prints India, 11 Darya Ganj, New Delhi 110002 India.**)**
Ind/Abst Sug. Indus. Abstr.

US/0194-1968
SHELBY REPORT OF THE SOUTHEAST, THE. (1968)-. Periodical. English. mo. $25.00 (one year), $45.00 (two year), $65.00 (three year). Shelby Publishing Company, 517 Green Street, Gainesville GA 30501. **Tel** (404)534-8380, FAX (404)535-0110. **ED** Gary Shelby (Publisher and Editor). **Ad Acc, Adv Mgr:** D. Heller. **Circ:** 22,000 (ctrl).
Desc: News of retail, wholesale food industry covering all new products in supermarkets and all other news pertaining to supermarket industry in the Sunbelt.

US/0192-916X
SHELBY REPORT OF THE SOUTHWEST. (1978)-. English. Twelve times a year. $25.00 one year; $45.00 two years; $65.00 three years. Shelby Publishing Company, 517 Green Street, Gainesville GA 30501. **Tel** (404)534-8380, FAX (404)535-0110. **ED** Lorne Griffith. **Ad Acc, Adv Mgr:** D. Heller, **Tel** (404)534-8380. **Circ:** 19,000 (ctrl).
Desc: News of retail and wholesale food industry. Covering all new products in supermarkets and all other news pertaining to supermarket industry in the Southwest.

CC/0253-8997
SHIPIN KEXUE. (SHIH PIN KO HSUEH.). [Shipin kexue]. **Main/Corp** Shin Pin Ko Hsueh (Peking, China). **VFOAT** Food Science. Academic Scholarly Publication. Chinese (Chinese). RMBY6.00. Pei-Ching Shih Shih Pin Yen Chiu So, Fa Hsing Tsu 3, Tung Tan Tung Tsung Pu Hu Tung Hugn Tung Hsiang, Beijing, People's Republic of China. **LC** TP368; .S49. **DD** 641.3/005. **CODEN** SPKHD5. Documents available from CASDDS.
Ind/Abst Chem. Abstr.; Curr. Biotechnol.; NAPRALERT; Soyabean Abstr.

CC/0253-990X
SHIPIN YU FAXIAO GONGYE. (SHIH PIN YU FA HSIAO KUNG YEH.). [Shipin yu faxiao gongye]. **Added/Corp** Ching Kung Yeh pu Shih Pin fa Hsiao Kung Yeh ko Hsueh Yen Chiu so (China) Chuan Kuo Shih Pin yu fa Hsiao Kung Yeh ko Chi Ching Pao Chan (China). (19??)-. Academic Scholarly Publication. Chinook jargon. bm. RMBYO.50. **LC** TP368; .S494. **CODEN** SPYYDO. Documents available from CASDDS.
Ind/Abst Chem. Abstr.

JA/0287-1734
SHOKU NO KAGAKU. [Shoku no kagaku]. (1971)-. Academic Scholarly Publication. Japanese. mo. $192.00. Marunouchi Shuppan, Maru Biru 5-kai, Marunouchi 2-4-1 Chiyoda-ku, Tokyo-to 100 Japan. **(Subscription address:** Kyowa Book Company Inc., 1-38 Kanda Jinbo-Cho, Chiyoda-Ku Tokyo 101, Japan**)** **CODEN** SNKAD4. Documents available from CASDDS.
Ind/Abst Chem. Abstr.

JA/0559-8974
SHOKUHIN EISEI KENKYU. See Public Health and Safety.

JA/0583-1121
SHOKUHIN KAIHATSU. [Shokuhin kaihatsu]. **Added/Corp** Shokuhin Kenkyusha. (1966)-. Academic Scholarly Publication. Japanese. mo. $458.00. **(Subscription address:** Kyowa Book Company Inc., 1-38 Kanda Jinbo-Cho, Chiyoda-Ku Tokyo 101, Japan**)** **CODEN** SKAIAM. Documents available from CASDDS.
Ind/Abst Chem. Abstr.; Food Sci. Technol. Abstr.; Soyabean Abstr.

JA
SHOKUHIN KAIHATSU. UP-TO-DATE FOOD PROCESSING. (Feb 1977-). Periodical. Japanese. mo. Kenko Sangyo Shinbunsha, (Health Food News), 2-19, Kanda Tsukasacho, Chiyodaku, Tokyoto 101, Japan.
Ind/Abst Rice Abstr.

JA
SHOKUHIN KIKAI SOCHI. [Shokuhin kikai sochi]. **VFOAT** Machinery and Equipment for Food Industry; Machinery & Equipment for Food Industry. (1964)-. Academic Scholarly Publication. Japanese. Twelve times a year. $206.00. Bijinesu Sentasha, 2-6, Kanda Tsukasacho, Chiyodaku, Tokyoto 101, Japan. **(Subscription address:** Kyowa Book Company Inc., 1 38 Kanda Jinbocho Chiyoda-ku, Tokyo 101 Japan.**)** **CODEN** SKISAO. Documents available from CASDDS.
Ind/Abst Chem. Abstr.

JA/0559-8990
SHOKUHIN KOGYO. THE FOOD INDUSTRY. **VFOAT** The Food Industry. Vol. 19, No. 1 (1976)-. Academic Scholarly Publication. Japanese (English). sm. $528.00. Korin, (Kohrin Publishing Co., Ltd.), 27-4, Iriya 1 Chome, Taitoku, Tokyoto 110, Japan. **(Subscription address:** Kyowa Book Company Inc., 1 38 Kanda Jinbocho Chiyoda-ku, Tokyo 101 Japan.**)** Documents available from CASDDS.
Ind/Abst Chem. Abstr.; Food Sci. Technol. Abstr.

JA/0388-3388
SHOKUHIN SANGYO SENTA GIJUTSU KENKYU HOKOKU. [Shokuhin Sangyo Senta gijutsu kenkyu hokoku]. **Added/Corp** Shokuhin Sangyo Senta (Japan). **VFOAT** Technical Report of Japan Food Industry Center. (1977)-. Academic Scholarly Publication. Japanese (summaries and/or abstracts in English). Japan Food Industry Center, 3-22 Toranomon-2, Minato-ku, Tokyo 105 Japan. **CODEN** SSGHD6. Documents available from CASDDS.
Ind/Abst Chem. Abstr.

JA/0387-1975
SHOKUHIN SHOSHA. (SHOKUHIN SHOSHA. FOOD IRRADIATION, JAPAN.). [Shokuhin shosha]. **Added/Corp** Nihon Shokuhin Shosha Kenkyu Kyogikai. **VFOAT** Food Irradiation, Japan. (1966)-. Academic Scholarly Publication. Japanese (English). sm. Nihon Shokuhin Shosha Kenkyu Kyogikai, (Japanese Research Assoc. for Food Irradiation), Norin Suisansho Shokuhin Sogo, Kenkyujo, 1-2, Kannondai 2 Chome, Tsukubashi, Ibarakinken 305, Japan. **LC** TP371.8; .S5. **CODEN** SNNSB3. Documents available from BIOSIS Document Express, CASDDS.
Ind/Abst Biol. Abstr. (1984-); Chem. Abstr.; Energy Res. Abstr. (Aug. 1973-).

JA/0910-8637
SHOKUHIN TO BISEIBUTSU. [Shokuhin to biseibutsu]. **Added/Corp** Shokuhin Eisei Biseibutsu Kenkyukai. **VFOAT** Japanese Journal of Food Microbiology. (1984)-. Japanese. Shokuhin Eisei Biseibutsu Kenkyukai, (Japanese Assoc. for Food Microbiologist), Tokyo Toritsu Eisei kenkyujo, Biseibutsubu Saikin Dai 1, Kenkyuka, 24-1, Hyakunincho, 3 Chome, Shinjukuku, Tokyoto 160 Japan. **NLM** W1; SH514Y. **CODEN** SHBIEA. Documents available from CASDDS.
Ind/Abst Biodeter. Abstr.; Chem. Abstr. (1986-); Nutr. Abstr. Rev., Ser. A, Hum. Exp.

JA
SHOKUHIN TO KAGAKU. [Shokuhin to kagaku]. **VFOAT** Food Science. (1959)-. Academic Scholarly Publication. Japanese. mo. $306.00. Shokuhin To Kagakusha, 8-5, Nishitenma 5 Chome, Kitaku, Osakashi, Osakafu 530 Japan. **(Subscription address:** Kyowa Book Company Inc., 1 38 Kanda Jinbocho Chiyoda ku, Tokyo 101 Japan**)** **CODEN** SHTKAY. Documents available from CASDDS.
Ind/Abst Chem. Abstr.

JA
SHOKURYO KEIZAI HAKUSHO. **Added/Corp** Nosei Kenkyu Senta (Japan). (1974)-. Periodical. Japanese. ¥2,000. Tokyo Kampo Company Ltd, c/o Norin Chuo Kinko 13-2, Yurakucho 1 Chiyoda-ku, Tokyo 100 Japan. **Tel** (03)287-1891. **ED** Masayoshi Namiki. **LC** HD9016.J4; S54. **Bk Rev. Circ:** 1,500.
Desc: Publishes articles of interest on nutrition and manners.

JA/0387-9836
SHOKURYO SEISAKU KENKYU. **VFOAT** Food Policy Study. (Jan. 1975)-. Periodical. Japanese. qt. ¥5000 (private), ¥10000 (organizations). Nosei Kenkyu Senta, c/o Norin Chuo Kinko, Yurakucho Building Tokyo-to 100 Japan. **Tel** (03)287-1891. **ED** Toshimune Hayashi. **LC** HD9016.J4; S55. **Bk Rev. Circ:** 1,000 (ctrl).
Desc: Publishes articles on the competition within the food industry.
Ind/Abst Plant Breed. Abstr.; Postharvest News Inf.; Rice Abstr.; Soyabean Abstr.; World Agric. Econ.

SW/0436-2071
SIK-RAPPORT. See Nutrition and Dietetics.

KO
SIKPUM KONGOP. **VFOAT** Food Industry. Periodical. Korean (Korean). bm. **LC** HD9016.K6; S54.

KO
SIKPUM KWAHAK. **VFOAT** Food Science. Began with Nov. 1968 issue. Periodical. Korean (Korean). W5,000. **LC** TP368; .S56. **NLM** W1; SI423.

US/1056-8611
SIMPLY SEAFOOD. Feb. (1991)-. Periodical. English. Four times a year. $8.95 (US); $11.00 (Mexico); $30.00 (other);. Waterfront Press Company, 1115 Northwest 46th Street, Seattle WA 98107. **Tel** (206)789-6506, FAX (206)789-9193, telex 272822 SFL UR. **DD** 641.

NE
SLAGER. Dutch. wk. Audet Tijdschtiften BV, Postbus 16, 6500 AA Nijmegen Netherlands. **Tel** 31 80 239561, FAX 31 80 228316. **ED** A Hackmann, P Verhamme, and W Busser. **Bk Rev. Ad Acc. Circ:** 7,310 (ctrl).
Desc: Information on the latest market developments in the meat trade and the average sales prices but it does not fail to elaborate on business practice and to describe trade techniques in detail.

US/0736-122X
SN DISTRIBUTION STUDY OF GROCERY STORE SALES. [SN distrib. study groc. store sales]. **Added/Corp** Fairchild Publications. **VFOAT** Distribution Study of Grocery Store Sales. **VAT**

Supermarket News Distribution Study of Grocery Store Sales. (197?)-. English. an. $72.95. Fairchild Publications Inc, 7 West 34th Street, 4th Floor, New York NY 10001. **Tel** (212)630-4230. **ED** Joseph Miranda. **LC** HD9321.1; .S64. **DD** 381/148/0973021. **Circ:** 1,500 (ctrl). ***Continues*** *Distribution Study of Grocery Store Sales in ... Cities.*
Desc: Itemizes the number of supermarkets in over 300 leading American and Canadian cities.

US/0037-7406
SNACK FOOD. [Snack food]. (1968)-. Periodical. English. mo. $50.00 US; $110.00 other. Stagnito Publishing Company, 1935 Sherner Road, Suite 100, Northbrook IL 60062. **Tel** (708)205-5660, FAX (708)205-5680. **ED** Jerry L. Hess. **LC** TX761. **DD** 664/.6. **CODEN** SNFOAI. **Circ:** 9,249. available on microfilm from University Microfilms International (UMI); available on an online database (files 16,570/Full-Text) from DIALOG. ***Continues*** *Biscuit and Cracker Baker, 0273-4826.*
Desc: The business magazine for the snack food industry.
Ind/Abst AGRICOLA; BioBusiness; F&S Index Plus Text, Int. [Full Txt.] [Select. Cov.]; Foods Adlibra; Int. Packag. Abstr.; Mark. Advert. Ref. Serv. [Full Txt.]; PROMT [Full Txt.]; Trade Ind. Index.

US/0148-8872
SNACK FOOD BLUE BOOK. ***Ceased.*** (19??)-(1992). English. an. Advanstar Communications Inc., 131 West First Street, Duluth MN 55802. **Tel** (218)723-9477, (800)346-0085. **LC** TP451.S57; S64. **DD** 664/.6.

NE
SNACK KOERIER. Dutch. bw. Misset Uitgeverij BV, Postbus 9000, 6800 DA Arnhem Netherlands. **Tel** 011 31 85 209911.

US/0896-1670
SNACK WORLD. (SNACK WORLD : OFFICIAL MAGAZINE OF THE INTERNATIONAL SNACK FOOD ASSOCIATION.). [Snack world]. **Added/Corp** Snack Food Association. (Sept. 1987)-. Periodical. English. mo. $60.00 (non-members), $30.00 (members) US; $90.00 (non-members), $60.00 (members) other. Potato Chip / Snack Food Association, 1711 King Street / Suite 1, Alexandria VA 22314. **Tel** (703)836-4500, FAX (703)836-4500. **ED** Jane Wuerthner. **LC** TX803.P8; P6. **DD** 664. **CODEN** SNWOE5. **Ad Acc. Circ:** 5,400 (ctrl). ***Continues*** *Chipper Snacker, 0192-933X.*
Desc: Trends in the snack industry; new products and technology and events in the snack industry are covered.
Ind/Abst BioBusiness (1988-); Food Sci. Technol. Abstr.; Maize Abstr.; Mark. Advert. Ref. Serv.; Postharvest News Inf.; Potato Abstr.; Trade Ind. Index.

UK
SNACKS MAGAZINE, THE. (19??)-. Periodical. English. Four times a year. £35.00 (one year), £60.00 (two years). Creative Business Communications, Lion House 4 Russell Street, Leek Staffordshire ST13 5JF England. **Tel** 011 44 0 538399155, FAX 011 44 0 538382165. **ED** Christine Horton. **Bk Rev. Ad Acc, Adv Mgr:** Dawn Dubsky, **Tel** 44 33 46090756. **Circ:** 2,000. ***Continues*** *International Chips Snacks Management, 0952-293X.*

CU/0049-0849
SOBRE LOS DERIVADOS DE LA CANA DE AZUCAR. ***Title Change.*** **See** Agriculture.

CU
SOBRE LOS DERIVADOS DE LA CANA DE AZUCAR (HAVANA, CUBA : 1983). (SOBRE LOS DERIVADOS DE LA CANA DE AZUCAR / ICIDCA.). **Added/Corp** ICIDCA. **VFOAT** Revista I.C.I.D.C.A.; Revista ICIDCA. (198?)-. Academic Scholarly Publication. Spanish (summaries and/or abstracts in English). Three times a year. $12.00. Ediciones Cubanas, Obispo 527, Altos ESQ Bernaza, CP 10100 Havana Cuba. **Tel** 011 632980, 631942, FAX 011 631011, telex 512337, 6540. **ED** Jesus Hernandez Ramirez. **LC** TP375; .S67. **DD** 664/.118/05. **Bk Rev. Ad Acc. Circ:** 1,400 (ctrl). Documents available from CASDDS. ***Continues*** *Revista Sobre los Derivados de la Cana de Azucar.*
Desc: Specialized scientific technical publication on sugar cane by products, organic synthesis, pulp and paper, economics, and others.
Ind/Abst Abstr. Bull. Inst. Pap. Sci. Tech.; Chem. Abstr.; Food Sci. Technol. Abstr.; Sug. Indus. Abstr.

US
SOURCE (SHAWNEE MISSION, KAN.). ***Title Change.*** (SOURCE / BAKERS DIGEST.). **VFOAT** Bakers Digest Source. (1985)-(19??). English. an. Sosland Publishing Company / Missouri, 4800 Main Street, Suite 100, Kansas City MO 64112. **Tel** (816)756-1000, FAX (816)756-0494, telex 820182. ***Continued by*** *Reference Source.*

US
SOURCEBOOK ON FOOD AND NUTRITION. ***Ceased.*** **See** Nutrition and Dietetics.

SA
SOUTH AFRICAN SUGAR YEAR BOOK, THE. **See** Agriculture.

US/0145-5796
SOUTH CAROLINA FOOD AND AGRICULTURAL PRODUCTS : EXPORT DIRECTORY. [S. C. food agric. prod. export dir.]. Directory. English. Wade Hampton State Office Building, PO Box 11280, Columbia SC 29211. **LC** HD9007.S6; S68. **DD** 382/.41/025757.

US/0199-2805
SOUTHEAST FOOD SERVICE NEWS. (1977)-. Periodical. English. mo. $30.00. Southeast Publishing Company, PO Box 47719, Atlanta GA 30362. **Tel** (404)452-1807. **ED** R Dal Rasmussen. **Ad Acc. Circ:** 18,300.
Desc: Concentrates on news dealing with segments of the food service industry in the nine state, Southeastern region.

US
SOUTHWEST INTERNATIONAL WINE & FOOD REVIEW. **VFOAT** Wine & Food Review; Southwest International Wine and Food Review. Holiday issue (1988)-. English. bm. $15.00 North America; $25.00 other. Richard Jones, Rt 2 Box 20-A, Sapello NM 87745. **Tel** (505)425-5077. **ED** Richard Jones and Shirley Jones. Index available. **Bk Rev. Circ:** 300.
Desc: Contains reviews of food and wines of Southwest Texas, New Mexico, Colorado, Utah, Oklahoma, and Arizona.

CH/0258-3097
SOYBEAN RUST NEWSLETTER. **See** Biology-Botany.

US/8755-1683
SOYFOODS INDUSTRY AND MARKET, DIRECTORY AND DATABOOK, THE. **VFOAT** Directory and Databook. 1983-. Directory. English. sa. $135.00. Soyfoods Center, PO Box 234, Lafayette CA 94549. **Tel** (510)283-2991. **ED** William Shurtleff. **LC** HD9235.S6; S64. **DD** 338.4/7664805655/05. Index available. **Circ:** 300. ***Continues*** *Soyfoods Industry Directory & Databook.*
Desc: Analysis of the soyfoods industry and market, plus a directory of all manufacturers of tofu soymilk, tempeh soy sauce, miso and soy protein products.

●US/1066-1417
SPECIAL EVENTS NEWS. (SPECIAL EVENTS NEWS : OFFICIAL PUBLICATION OF THE AMERICAN VENDORS ASSOCIATION.). [Spec. events news]. **Added/Corp** American Vendors Association. **VFOAT** Fair Times Special Events News. (1992)-. Periodical. English. mo. $40.00. 21st Century Marketing, 930 Fox Pavilion, Jenkintown PA 19046. **Tel** (215)887-5700, FAX (215)887-7536. **DD** 338. ***Continues*** *Fair Times, 0889-0714.*

GH/0378-2239
SPECIAL PAPER - JOINT FAO/WHO/OAU REGIONAL FOOD AND NUTRITION COMMISSION FOR AFRICA. **VAT** Special Paper - Joint Food and Agriculture Organization-World Health Organization-Organization for African Unity Regional Food and Nutrition Commission for Africa. No. 1- 1967-. Monographic series. English. Price varies per volume. Secretariat of the Joint FAO/WHO/OAU Food and Nutrition Commission for Africa, PO Box 1628, Accra Ghana. **NLM** W1 SP295DJ.

US/0194-1429
SPECIALTY FOOD MERCHANDISING. [Spec. food merch.]. (19??)-. Periodical. English. Twelve times a year. Tarter Communications Inc., 29 Park Avenue, Manhasset NY 11030. **Tel** (516)365-9088. **DD** 641. **CODEN** SFMEE5.
Ind/Abst BioBusiness.

II
SPICE NEWSLETTER. **Added/Corp** Spices Export Promotion Council. (19??)-. Newsletter. English. ir. Rs12.00 India; Rs20.00 others; Rs65.00Europe; Rs75.00 US & Canada. Spices Board, PO Box 1909, Ernakulam, Cochin 682018 India. **Tel** 011 91 484 353837, 011 91 484 366403, FAX 011 91 484 370429, telex 885-6480, 885-6534. **ED** M. Balaraman Nair. **LC** HD9210.I5; S69. **DD** 382/.41/3830954. **Bk Rev. Ad Acc. Circ:** 1,050.
Desc: Markets news and trends of prices for spices.

US
STANDARDS AND LABELING POLICY BOOK / UNITED STATES DEPARTMENT OF AGRICULTURE, FOOD SAFETY AND INSPECTION SERVICE, REGULATORY PROGRAMS, STANDARDS AND LABELING DIVISION. **Main/Corp** United States. Food Safety and Inspection Service. Standards and Labeling Division. **Added/Corp** United States. Meat and Poultry Inspection Service. Meat and Poultry Inspection Regulations. United States. Meat and Poultry Inspection Program. Meat and Poultry Inspection Manual. **VFOAT** Policy Book. (19??)-. Government Publication. English. ir. $98.00 US; $122.50 other. Superintendent of Documents, US Government Printing Office, Washington DC 20402. **Tel** (202)275-3328, FAX (202)786-2377.

US
STATE ADMINISTRATIVE EXPENSE PLAN FOR FISCAL YEAR. English. an. free. Kansas State Department of Education, Kansas State Education Building, 120 East 10th Street, Topeka KS 66612. **Tel** (913)296-4961, FAX (913)296-7933. **Circ:** 100 (ctrl). ***Continues*** *School Food Service : State Plan for Fiscal Year ... .*
Desc: It is a compliance plan for outlining activities to be completed with State Administrative Expense Funds.

KO
STATE OF FOOD AND AGRICULTURE. **See** Agriculture.

US/0277-3724
STATISTICAL SUMMARY, FEDERAL MEAT AND POULTRY INSPECTION FOR FISCAL YEAR. **See** Food and Food Industry-Abstracting, Bibliographies and Statistics.

US/0430-7585
STATISTICAL SUMMARY - FLORIDA CANNERS ASSOCIATION. ***Ceased.*** **See** Food and Food Industry-Abstracting, Bibliographies and Statistics.

US/0270-7691
STATISTICAL SUMMARY - FLORIDA CITRUS PROCESSORS ASSOCIATION. **Main/Corp** Florida Citrus Processors Association. (19??)-. Statistical Publication. English. an. $15.00. Florida Citrus Processors Association, PO Box 780, Winter Haven FL 33882. **Tel** (813)293-4171. **LC** HD9259.C54; U5873a. **DD** 338.4/766480435/09759.

CN/0703-7333
STOCKS OF FROZEN MEAT PRODUCTS. ***Ceased.*** [Stocks frozen meat prod.]. **Added/Corp** Canada. Dominion Bureau of Statistics. Livestock and Animal Products Section. Statistics Canada. Livestock and Animal Products Section. **VFOAT** Stocks de Viandes Congelees. Vol. 53, No. 9 (Sept. 1, 1970)-(Feb. 1993). Periodical. English (French). mo. Statistics Canada, Publications Sales & Services, Main Building Room 1710, Ottawa Ontario K1A 0T6 Canada. **Tel** (613)951-5078, (800)267-6677, FAX (613)951-1584, telex 053-3585. **DD** 338.1/760883/0971. ***Continues*** *Stocks of Meat Products, 0703-7341.*
Desc: Stocks by kinds in cold storage on first day of each month, for Canada and by province.

CN/0705-4289
STOCKS OF FRUIT AND VEGETABLES. ***Ceased.*** [Stocks fruit veg.]. **VFOAT** Stocks of Fruit and Vegetables as at ...; Stocks de Fruits et de Legumes. Jan. 1, 1944-?. Periodical. English. mo. Statistics Canada, Publications Sales & Services, Main Building Room 1710, Ottawa Ontario K1A 0T6 Canada. **Tel** (613)951-5078, (800)267-6677, FAX (613)951-1584, telex 053-3585. **LC** HD9254.C18; C35A. **DD** 338.1/74/0971. ***Continues*** *Stocks of Canadian Fruit and Vegetables, 0827-1135.*
Desc: Stocks in cold and common storage on first day of each month.

FR/0987-7541
STRATEGIES GOURMANDES PARIS. ***Title Change.*** (STRATEGIES GOURMANDES.). (1988)-(1993). Periodical. French. mo. SEPP, 13 rue Ganneron, 75018 Paris France. **Tel** 011 33 1 42932243, FAX 011 33 1 42875024. **UDC** 664.14. ***Merged with*** *Filiere Farine, 1140-5104* ***to form*** *Filiere Gourmande, 1243-9681.*

SJ/1016-5711
SUDAN JOURNAL OF ANIMAL PRODUCTION, THE. **See** Veterinary Sciences.

SJ/0254-0789
SUDAN JOURNAL OF FOOD SCIENCE AND TECHNOLOGY. [Sudan j. food sci. technol.]. Began in 1971. Academic Scholarly Publication. Arabic (English). an. Government Printing Press / Sudan, Editorial Board, PO Box 213, Khartoum Sudan. **LC** TP368. **DD** 664/.005. **CODEN** SJFTD8. Documents available from BIOSIS Document Express, CASDDS. ***Continues*** *Journal of Food Science and Technology in the Sudan.*
Ind/Abst Biol. Abstr.; Chem. Abstr. (1971-1979).

US/0039-4726
SUGAR BULLETIN, THE. [Sugar bull.]. **Added/Corp** American Sugar Cane League. (Nov. 1922)-. Bulletin. English. Twelve times a year. $15.00 US; $50.00 other. American Sugar Cane League of USA, 206 E Bayon Road, PO Box 938, Thibodaux LA 70302. **Tel** (504)448-3707, FAX (504)448-3722. **ED** Charles J. Melancon. **LC** HD9100.1; .S83. **DD** 380.1/41/3610973. **Ad Acc. Circ:** 1,700 (ctrl).
Desc: Contains news and research for the Louisiana sugar industry.
Ind/Abst AGRICOLA; Life Sci. Collect.

US/0585-881X
SUGAR CLUB ANNUAL, THE. Main/Corp Sugar Club. No. 1- 1960/61-. English. an. Wine & Spirits Wholesalers of America, 1023 15th Street Northwest, 4th Floor, Washington DC 20005. **Tel** (202)371-9792. **LC** HD9100.1; .S85. **DD** 338.1/7/36.

US/0199-8498
SUGAR PRODUCER, THE. [Sugar prod.]. (19??)-. Periodical. English. bm. $8.00 US; $20.00 Canada; $30.00 other. Harris Publishing Inc, 520 Park Avenue, Idaho Falls ID 83402. **Tel** (208)524-7000, FAX (208)522-5241. **Ad Acc**. ctrl circ.

NE
SUGAR SERIES. Vol. 1 (1981)-. Academic Scholarly Publication. English. ir. Price varies per volume. Elsevier Science Publishers BV, PO Box 211, 1000 AE Amsterdam Netherlands. **Tel** 011 31 20 5803642, FAX 011 31 20 5862696, telex 15682. **CODEN** SUGSEK. Documents available from CASDDS.
Ind/Abst Chem. Abstr.

CN/0380-8378
SUGAR SITUATION, THE. [Sugar situat.]. **Added/Corp** Canada. Bureau Federal de la Statistique. Division de l'Agriculture. Canada. Bureau Federal de la Statistique. Section des Cultures. Canada. Bureau Federal de la Statistique. Division des Industries Manufacturieres et Primaires. Statistique Canada. Division des Industries Manufacturieres et Primaires. Statistique Canada. Division de l'Industrie. **VFOAT** Situation du Sucre. Vol. 51, (Jan. 1972)-. Periodical. French (English). mo. 60.00Can$ Canada; $72.00 US; $84.00 other. Statistics Canada, Publications Sales & Services, Main Building Room 1710, Ottawa Ontario K1A 0T6 Canada. **Tel** (613)951-5078, (800)267-6677, FAX (613)951-1584, telex 053-3585. **DD** 338.4/766412/0971. ***Continues** The Sugar Situation in Canada, 0380-8386.*
Desc: Covers acquisitions, stocks, production and shipments of raw cane sugar and refined cane and beet sugar. Detailed shipments of sugar by type and package size.

CN/0229-737X
SUGAR WORLD. (SUGAR WORLD : A NEWSLETTER ON ISSUES OF CONCERN TO SUGAR WORKER.). [Sugar world]. No. 1 (Oct. 1, 1977)-. Newsletter. English (Spanish). bm. $10.00. ICCSASW, PO Box 66 Station B, Toronto Ontario M5T 2T2 Canada. **Tel** (416)597-8454. **DD** 338.1/7361/05. Index available. cum. index. **Bk Rev**. ctrl circ.
Desc: A newsletter on issues of concern to sugar workers.
Ind/Abst Hum. Rights Intern. Rep.

US/0039-4742
SUGAR Y AZUCAR. See Agriculture.

US/0081-9212
SUGAR Y AZUCAR. YEARBOOK. Vol. 36 (1968)-. English (Spanish). an. $55.00. Ruspam Communications, 452 Hudson Terrace, Englewood Cliffs NJ 07632. **Tel** (201)871-9200, FAX (201)871-9639. **LC** TP375.3; .S85. **Ad Acc, Adv Mgr:** A. Berg. **Circ:** 1,500. ***Continues** Sugar. Azucar. Yearbook.*

US/1069-3475
SUNBELT FOODSERVICE. [Sunbelt foodserv.]. **VFOAT** Sunbelt Food Service. (1984)-. Periodical. English. Twelve times a year. $25.00 (one year); $45.00 (two years), $65.00 (three years). Shelby Publishing Company, 517 Green Street, Gainesville GA 30501. **Tel** (404)534-8380, FAX (404)535-0110. **ED** Chuck Gilmer. **DD** 338. **Ad Acc, Adv Mgr:** D. Heller. **Circ:** 18.500 (ctrl).
Desc: News and features pertaining to the foodservice industry throughout Southeast and Southwest US.

US/0196-5700
SUPERMARKET BUSINESS. [Supermark. bus.]. Vol. 34, No. 10 (Oct. 1979)-. Periodical. English. mo. $70.00 US; $88.00 Canada; $125.00 other. Howfrey Communication, 1086 Teaneck Road, Teaneck NJ 07666. **Tel** (210)833-1900. **LC** HD9321.1; .F6. **DD** 658.8/78/0973. **CODEN** SUPBDD. **[CCC]**. available on microfilm and microfiche from University Microfilms International (UMI); available on an online database (file 648/Full-Text) from DIALOG. Documents available from UMI Article Clearinghouse. ***Continues** Supermarketing, 0039-5811.*
Desc: Information on supermarkets and grocery trade.
Ind/Abst ABI/INFORM Glob. Ed.; ABI Inform Ondisc (March 1988-); Bus. ASAP (1990-) [Full Txt.]; Bus. Index (1985-); Bus. Source (Jan. 1993-); F&S Index Plus Text, Int. [Select. Cov.]; Foods Adlibra; Gen. BusinessFile (1985-); Gen. Period. Index (1985-); Mag. Search; Mark. Advert. Ref. Serv.; PROMT; Stat. Ref. Index; Trade Ind. ASAP [Full Txt.]; Trade Ind. Index (1981-) [Full Txt.]; Vocat. Search (Jan. 1993-).

US/0039-5803
SUPERMARKET NEWS. [Supermark. news]. Vol. 1 (April 21, 1952)-. Periodical. English. wk. $175.00. Fairchild Publications Inc, 7 West 34th Street, 4th Floor, New York NY 10001. **Tel** (212)630-4230. **LC** HD9321.1; .S863. **DD** 658.8/78. **[CCC]**. available on microfilm and microfiche from University Microfilms International (UMI); available on an online database (files 16,648/Full-Text) from DIALOG.
Ind/Abst Bus. ASAP (1990-) [Full Txt.]; Bus. Index (1985-); Bus. Source (Jan. 1993-); F&S Index Plus Text, Int. [Full Txt.] [Select. Cov.]; Foods Adlibra; Gen. BusinessFile (1985-); Gen. Period. Index (1985-); Mag. Search; PROMT [Full Txt.]; Trade Ind. ASAP [Full Txt.]; Trade Ind. Index [Full Txt.]; Vocat. Search (Sept. 1993-).

AT
SUPERMARKET NEWS. English. Twenty-five times a year. 90.00Aus$ Australia; 120.00Aus$ other. Reed Business Publishing Pty Ltd. / Australia, 1 5 Railway Street, Level 12 North Tower, Chatswood W 2067 NSW Australia. **Tel** 011 61 2 3725222, FAX 011 61 2 4197533.

US/0039-5803
SUPERMARKET NEWS. [Supermark. news]. Vol. 1 (Apr. 21, 1952)-. English. $190.00. Fairchild Publications Inc, 7 West 34th Street, 4th Floor, New York NY 10001. **Tel** (212)630-4230. **LC** Microfilm (o) 83/343. **[CCC]**.

US/1065-3260
SUPERMARKET SCOOP. [Supermark. scoop]. (Jan./Feb. 1988)-. Periodical. English. Six times a year. $77.00 (one year); $150.00 (two years). Supermarket Savvy, PO Box 666, Herndon VA 22070-0666. **Tel** (703)742-3364, FAX (703)742-3316. **ED** Leni Reed. **DD** 641. **Ad Acc. Circ:** 2,000. ***Continues** Supermarket Savvy Newsletter.*
Desc: News & analysis of brand-name foods of interest to the health care professional.

US/0163-9528
SUPERMARKET SHOPPER. Periodical. English. mo. American Coupon Club, 2 Broadlawn Avenue, Great Neck NY 11023-1537. **Tel** (516)328-6222.

US/1053-3648
SUPERMARKET STRATEGIC ALERT. [Supermark. strateg. alert]. (1990)-. Periodical. English. Twelve times a year. $795.00 one year; $1,500.00 two year. Pollack Associates, 140 East 81 Street, Suite 5E, New York NY 10028. **Tel** (212)734-0753, FAX (212)988-9394. **ED** Mary S. Pollack. **DD** 338. **[CCC]**. Index available (In all issues.). cum. index. **Circ:** 250.
Desc: Summarizes news and information about the supermarket industry.

NZ/0112-949X
SUPERMARKETING AUCKLAND. [Supermarketing Auckl.]. (1985)-. Periodical. English. Eleven times a year. 44.00NZ$ New Zealand; 76.00NZ$ Australia & The Pacific; 113.00NZ$ others. Minty's Media, 22 Heather Street, Private Bag 93218, Parnell Auckland New Zealand. **Tel** 011 64 9 3794233, FAX 011 64 9 3093575. **ED** Maxine Wrennall. **DD** 658.8709931.
Desc: Articles and information of supermarket buying.

BL
SUPERVAREJO. (19??)-. Periodical. Portuguese. mo. 40.00. M & Z Representatives, 112 Ferry Street, Newark NJ 07105. **LC** HF5469; .S9.
Desc: Information on supermarkets, grocery and retail trade.

CN
SURVEY OF CHAINS AND GROUPS. (1965)-. Trade Publication. English. mo. 32.00Can$. Canadian Grocer, MacLean Hunter Building, 777 Bay Street, Toronto Ontario M5W 1A7 Canada. **Tel** (416)596-5284, FAX (416)596-5526, telex 06-219547. **ED** George H Condon. **DD** 381/.45/664. **Bk Rev. Ad Acc. Circ:** 17,200.
Desc: Canada's national trade magazine for supermarket operators and the food distribution industry. Includes directory and statistical issues.

GW/0039-4653
SUSSWAREN. [Susswaren]. **VFOAT** Susswaren (1957). (1957)-. German. mo. DM154.00 Germany; DM176.00 other. Rhenania Fachverlag GmbH, Postfach 601220, Possmoorweg 5, W-2000 Hamburg 60 Germany. **Tel** 011 49 40 27170, FAX 011 49 40 27172056, telex 2173465 or 213214. **UDC** 664.1 :338.45. **CODEN** SUSWAK.
Ind/Abst Food Sci. Technol. Abstr.

●US
SWEETENER MARKET DATA / UNITED STATES DEPARTMENT OF AGRICULTURE, AGRICULTURAL STABILIZATION AND CONSERVATION SERVICE. Added/Corp United States. Agricultural Stabilization and Conservation Service. Vol. 1, Issue 1 (June 12, 1992)-. Government Publication. English. mo. US Department of Agriculture / Agricultural Stabilization and Conservation, 14th and Independence Avenue SW, Washington DC 20250.

SZ/0251-1681
SWISS FOOD. [Swiss food]. (1979)-. Academic Scholarly Publication. German (French, English and Italian). Twelve times a year. 100.00F Switzerland; 120.00F Europe; 200.00F other. Verlag Dr Felix Wuest AG, Seestrasse 5/Postfach, CH-8700 Kuesnacht Switzerland. **Tel** 011 41 1 9110055, FAX (01)9106080, telex 825705. **CODEN** SWFODG. Index available. ctrl circ. Documents available from CASDDS.
Ind/Abst Chem. Abstr. (1979-1984); Int. Packag. Abstr.

US
TASTE FULL. English. qt (Mar., June, Sep., Dec.). $15.00 US; $25.00 Canada; $30.00 other. Great Menus Inc., PO Box 1712, Wilminton NC 28402. **Tel** (910)763-1601, FAX (910)763-0321. **ED** Elizabeth K. Norfleet. **Bk Rev**, (Qty: 25-30). **Ad Acc. Circ:** 15,000.
Desc: Focuses on food, travel and entertaining in North Carolina.

●US/1072-5121
TAUNTON'S FINE COOKING. [Taunton's fine cook.]. **VFOAT** Fine cooking. No. 1 (Feb./Mar. 1994)-. Periodical. English. bm (Feb., Apr., June, Aug., Oct., Dec.). $26.00 (one year), $42.00 (two year), $58.00 (three year). Taunton Press, 63 South Main Street, PO Box 5506, Newtown CT 06470-5506. **Tel** (203)426-8171, (800)283-7252, FAX (203)426-3434, telex 5106004860. **DD** 641.

IT/0394-7181
TAVOLA, A. [A tavola]. (1987)-. Periodical. Italian. mo. $125.00. RCS Rizzoli Periodici, Via A Rizzoli 2, 20132 Milan Italy. **Tel** 011 39 2 27200720. **UDC** 641.

UK/0265-9441
TCS&D BUYERS' GUIDE. [TCS&D buy. guide]. **VFOAT** Temperature Controlled Storage & Distribution ... Buyers' Guide. (1984)-. English. an. £53.40 UK; $91.00 other. Argus Press Group, Queensway House, 2 Queensway Redhill, Surrey RH1 1QS England. **Tel** 011 44 737 768611, 011 44 737 761685, FAX 011 44 737 760510, telex 948669 TOPJNL G. **DD** 621.5602541.

US
TECHNICAL BULLETIN / AIB RESEARCH DEPARTMENT. Added/Corp American Institute of Baking. **VFOAT** AIB Research Department Technical Bulletin. Vol. 1, No. 1 (Jan. 1979)-. Bulletin. English. mo. $30.00. American Institute of Baking, 1213 Bakers Way, Manhattan KS 66502. **Tel** (913)537-4750, FAX (913)537-1493.
Ind/Abst Foods Adlibra.

CH/0379-7627
TECHNICAL BULLETIN - ASPAC, FOOD & FERTILIZER TECHNOLOGY CENTER. (TECHNICAL BULLETIN - FOOD & FERTILIZER TECHNOLOGY CENTER.). [Tech. bull. - ASPAC Food Fertil. Tech. Cent.]. **Main/Corp** Asian and Pacific Council. Food & Fertilizer Technology Center. (1970)-. Periodical. English. ir. Food and Fertilizer Technology Center for the Asian and Pacific Region, Agriculture Building, 114 Wen Chow Street, PO Box 22-149, Taipei, Taiwan. **CODEN** APFBAX. Documents available from CASDDS.
Ind/Abst AGRICOLA; Chem. Abstr. (1970-1982); Crop Physiol. Abstr.; Field Crop Abstr.; For. Abstr.; Hortic. Abstr.; Plant Grow. Reg. Abstr.; Soils Fert.; Weed Abstr.

UK
TECHNICAL MEMORANDUM. Added/Corp Campden Food and Drink Research Association. (198?)-. Monographic series. English. ***Continues** Technical Memorandum (Campden Food Preservation Research Association).*
Ind/Abst Potato Abstr.; Sug. Indus. Abstr.

PL/0324-9212
TECHNOLOGIA ALIMENTORUM. Added/Corp Akademia Rolniczo-Techniczna w Olsztynie. (1985)-. Periodical. Polish (summaries and/or abstracts in English and Russian). Akademia Rolniczo-Techniczna, Biblioteka Glowna, Kortowo bl.41 10-957 Olsztyn, Poland. Documents available from CASDDS. ***Continues** Akademia Rolniczo-Techniczna w Olsztynie. Zeszyty Naukowe: Technologia Zywnosci.*
Ind/Abst Chem. Abstr.

YU/0494-9846
TEHNOLOGIJA MESA. See Manufacturing.

UK/0143-750X
TEMPERATURE CONTROLLED STORAGE AND DISTRIBUTION. [Temp. control. storage distrib.]. (1977)-. Periodical. Multiple languages. Eight times a year. £51.35 UK; £66.10, $102.50 other. Argus Press Group, Queensway House, 2 Queensway Redhill, Surrey RH1 1QS England. **Tel** 011 44 737 768611, 011 44 737 761685, FAX 011 44 737 760510, telex 948669 TOPJNL G. **DD** 658.785.

US/0040-4322
TEXAS FOOD MERCHANT. (19??)-. Periodical. English. Eleven times a year (May/June issues combined). $24.00 one year. Texas Food Industry Association, 7333 Highway 290 East, Austin TX 78723. **Tel** (512)926-9285 or (800)856-TFIA, FAX (512)926-0917. **ED** Val McLean. **Ad Acc. Circ:** 3,500 (ctrl).
Desc: Information on grocery industry, equipment and services for grocers.

US/0092-2005
TEXAS FRUIT AND PECAN STATISTICS. See Food and Food Industry-Abstracting, Bibliographies and Statistics.

Food and Food Industry

US/1061-284X
THOMAS FOOD INDUSTRY REGISTER.
[Thomas food ind. regist.]. (1991)-. English. an (Published in May). $255.80. Thomas Publishing Company / Food Industry, 5 Penn Plaza, New York NY 10001. **Tel** (212)290-8700. **LC** HD9321.3; .T5. **DD** 380.1/456413/0029473. *Continues* Thomas Grocery Register, 0082-4151.
 Desc: Information on the food industry and grocery trade.

US/0894-184X
THOMAS GROCERY REGISTER. FOOD MARKETERS' HANDBOOK. [Thomas groc. regist., Food mark. handb.]. **VFOAT** Food Marketers' Handbook; Thomas Grocery Register's Food Marketers' Handbook. (198?)-. English. an. $8.50. Todd Publications, 18 North Greenbush Road, West Nyack NY 10994. **Tel** (914)358-6213, FAX (914)358-6213. **DD** 381. *Continues* Thomas Grocery Register. Food Marketers' Handbook, Key Industry Statistics and Trade Calendar, 0739-3423.
 Desc: Information on the food industry and grocery trade.

NE
TIP. (19??)-. English. ir (13 issues). Fl55.25 (latest issue). Medianet BV, Postbus 6298, 2001 LN Haarlem Netherlands. **Tel** 011 31 23 173311.

GW/0723-5054
TK REPORT. [Tk-rep.]. **VFOAT** Ff Report; Ff-Report. **VAT** Tiefkuhl Report; Frozen Food Report. (19??)-. Periodical. German.
 Ind/Abst F&S Index Plus Text, Int. [Select. Cov.].

US/1060-8966
TOTAL FOOD SERVICE : TFS. [Total food serv.]. **VFOAT** TFS. Vol. 1, No. 1 (June 1991)-. Periodical. English. mo. IDA Publishing, Inc., 282 Railroad Avenue, Greenwich CT 06830. **DD** 338.

US/0890-5134
TRA FOODSERVICE DIGEST. [TRA foodserv. dig.]. **VFOAT** Foodservice Digest; TRA Food Service Digest; Food Service Digest. (19??)-. Periodical. English. mo. $165.00 (delivered to same address); $70.00 (delivered to separate address). Technomic Inc, 300 South Riverside Plaza, 1940S, Chicago IL 60606. **Tel** (312)876-0004, FAX (312) 876-1158. **ED** Mary Doherty. **DD** 338.

US/0278-6346
TRENDS--CONSUMER ATTITUDES AND THE SUPERMARKET ... UPDATE.
VAT Trends, Consumer Attitudes and the Supermarket Update. 1981-. English. an. Food Marketing Institute, 1750 K Street Northwest, Washington DC 20006. **Tel** (202)452-8444. **LC** HC110.C6; T67. **DD** 381/.0973. *Continues* Supermarket Trends.
 Ind/Abst Stat. Ref. Index.

UK/0924-2244
TRENDS IN FOOD SCIENCE & TECHNOLOGY. [Trends food sci. technol.]. **VFOAT** Trends in Food Science and Technology; Food Science & Technology; Food Science and Technology. Vol. 1, No. 1 (July 1990)-. Periodical. English. mo. $514.00 The Americas; £345.00 other. Elsevier Science Journals, An Imprint of Elsevier Science Ltd., The Boulevard, Langford Lane, Kidlington, Oxford OX5 1GB United Kingdom. **Tel** 011 44 865 843000, 011 44 865 843699, FAX 011 44 865 843010. **(Subscription address:** Elsevier Science Ltd. Oxford Fulfillment Centre, PO Box 800, Kidlington, Oxford OX5 1DX United Kingdom.**) LC** TP368; .T74. **DD** 664. **CODEN** TFTEEH. **[CCC].** available on microfilm and microfiche from University Microfilms International (UMI). Documents available from Article Express International, CASDDS.
 Desc: International news and review journal providing scientists and all those concerned with the science and technology of food manufacture, distribution, storage and marketing. Links basic scientific research and its application in the food industry.
 Ind/Abst AGRICOLA [Full Cov.]; Biodeter. Abstr. (1991-); Chem. Abstr.; Curr. Aware. Biol. Sci., CABS; Dairy Sci. Abstr.; Ei Page One; Eng. Index Annu. [Select. Cov.]; Food Sci. Technol. Abstr.; Foods Adlibra (1990-); Nutr. Abstr. Rev., Ser. A, Hum. Exp.; Sci. Cit. Index; Soc. Sci. Cit. Index [Select. Cov.].

US/0041-249X
TRI-STATE FOOD NEWS. (19??)-. Periodical. English. Twelve times a year. $10.00 (one year); $18.00 (two years); $25.00 (three years). Gateway Press Inc., 610 Beatty Road, Monroeville PA 15146. **Tel** (412)856-7400. **ED** Jim Damp. **Ad Acc. Circ:** 26,000.
 Desc: Trade publication serving the food industry geared toward retail wholesalers/brokers and manufacturers in Pennsylvania Ohio, West Virginia, Maryland and Buffalo.

US
U. S. FOOD PRODUCTS DIRECTORY, THE BLUE BOOK OF FOOD PACKERS AND DISTRIBUTORS. Added/Corp Western Canner and Packer. Directory. English. Gorman Publishing Company, 5725 East River Road, Chicago IL 60631. **LC** HD9003; .U5. **DD** 664.058. *Continues* California Food Products Directory.

US/0749-5005
U.S. REGULATORY REPORTER. See Sociology-Social Services and Welfare.

FR
UNILET INFORMATIONS / UNION NATIONALE INTERPROFESSIONNELLE DES LEGUMES TRANFORMES. See Agriculture.

UK/0954-5875
UNITED KINGDOM MEAT MARKET REVIEW. See Agriculture-Livestock and Poultry.

US
UPDATE - FOOD AND DRUG LAW INSTITUTE. See Law.

US/0278-9345
USDC APPROVED LIST OF FISH ESTABLISHMENTS AND PRODUCTS. See Fish and Fisheries.

SW/0042-2657
VAR FODA. See Nutrition and Dietetics.

DK/0107-0967
VARESTATISTIK FOR INDUSTRI. SERIE A, ANIMALSKE OG VEGETABILSKE PRODUKTER, SAMT ANDRE NRINGS OG NYDELSESMIDLER. Added/Corp Danmarks Statistik. **VFOAT** Animalske og Vegetabilske Produkter, Samt Andre Nrings og Nydelsesmidler. (1980)-. Danish. qt. kr100.00. Danmarks Statistik, Sejrgade 11, DK-2100 Copenhagen Denmark. **Tel** 011 45 3 9173917, FAX 011 45 31 18 48 01, telex 1 62 36. **LC** HD9735.D4; V37. *Continues* Kvartalsstatistik for Industrien. Varestatistik, 0107-7031.

DK/0107-0975
VARESTATISTIK FOR INDUSTRI. SERIE B, MINERALSKE OG KEMISKE PRODUKTER, TROG PAPIR SAMT VARER DERAF. Added/Corp Danmarks Statistik. **VFOAT** Mineralske og Kemiske Produkter, Trog Papir Samt Varer Deraf. (1980)-. Danish. qt. kr100.00. Danmarks Statistik, Sejrgade 11, DK-2100 Copenhagen Denmark. **Tel** 011 45 3 9173917, FAX 011 45 31 18 48 01, telex 1 62 36. **LC** HD9735.D4; V372. *Continues* Kvartalsstatistik for Industrien. Varestatistik, 0107-7031.

DK/0107-0983
VARESTATISTIK FOR INDUSTRI. SERIE C, TEKSTILVARER, FODTJ, SPORTSARTIKLER M.V. Added/Corp Danmarks Statistik. **VFOAT** Tekstilvarer, Fodtj, Sportsartikler M.V. (1980)-. Danish. qt. kr100.00. Danmarks Statistik, Sejrgade 11, DK-2100 Copenhagen Denmark. **Tel** 011 45 3 9173917, FAX 011 45 31 18 48 01, telex 1 62 36. **LC** HD9735.D4; V373. *Continues* Kvartalsstatistik for Industrien. Varestatistik, 0107-7031.

DK/0107-0991
VARESTATISTIK FOR INDUSTRI. SERIE D, METALLER, METALVARER, MASKINER, APPARATER OG INSTRUMENTER, SAMT TRANSPORTMIDLER. Added/Corp Danmarks Statistik. **VFOAT** Metaller, Metalvarer, Maskiner, Apparater og Instrumenter, Samt Transportmidler. (1980)-. Danish. qt. kr100.00. Danmarks Statistik, Sejrgade 11, DK-2100 Copenhagen Denmark. **Tel** 011 45 3 9173917, FAX 011 45 31 18 48 01, telex 1 62 36. **LC** HD9735.D4; V374. *Continues* Kvartalsstatistik for Industrien. Varestatistik, 0107-7031.

US/0749-6664
VEALER, THE. Added/Corp American Veal Association. (198?)-. Periodical. English. mo. $20.00 US; $30.00 Canada; $40.00 other. Graphicom Inc, PO Box 8246, Madeira Beach FL 33738. **Tel** (606)986-1495. **ED** Lea Schultz. **DD** 338. **Bk Rev**. **Ad Acc. Circ:** 2,000 (ctrl).
 Desc: Directed to the growers and producers of milk-fed veal meat.

XO
VEDECKE PRACE VYSKUMNEHO USTAVU RASTLINNEJ VYROBY V PIESTANOCH. OBILNINY - STRAKOVINY / SCIENTIFIC PAPERS OF THE RESEARCH INSTITUTE FOR PLANT PRODUCTION AT PIESTANY. CEREALS - LEGUMES. See Agriculture-Crop Production and Soil.

●US/1065-6340
VEGETARIAN GOURMET. [Veg. gourmet]. No. 1 (Spring 1992)-. Periodical. English. Five times a year. $15.95 (one year); $29.95 (two year). Chariot Publishing, 2 Public Avenue, Montrose PA 18801. **Tel** (717)278-1984, FAX (717) 278-2223. **(Subscription address:** Vegel, PO Box 7641, Riverton NJ 08077.**) ED** Christiane Meunier and Jessica Dubey. **LC** TX837; .V4264. **DD** 641.5/636/05. **Bk Rev**. **Circ:** 80,000.
 Desc: Includes quick recipes and cooking tips for easy vegetarian cooking.

US/0164-8497
VEGETARIAN TIMES. See Nutrition and Dietetics.

●US/1065-2728
VEGGIE LIFE. [Veggie life]. (1993)-. Periodical. English. bm. $17.00. EGW Publishing Company, 1041 Shary Circle, Concord CA 94518. **Tel** (510)671-9852, (800)777-1164, FAX (510)671-0692. **LC** WMLC 93/4704. **DD** 641.

UK/0954-6235
VENDING INTERNATIONAL. VFOAT International Vending Times. Vol. 5, No. 7 (July 1972)-. Periodical. English. mo. £50.00 UK; £75.00 Europe; £95.00 other. Datateam Publishing Limited, Datateam House Tovil Hill, Maidstone KT ME15 6QS England. **Tel** 011 44 622 687031, FAX 011 44 622 757646. *Continues* International Vending Times & Food Service News.
 Ind/Abst F&S Index Plus Text, Int. (19??-) [Select. Cov.]; Infomat Int. Bus. (19??-); PROMT (19??-).

NE
VERSLAG LEVENSMIDDELEN EN KEURING VAN WAREN. Main/Corp Netherlands. Ministerie van Volksgezondheid en Milieuhygiene. Dutch. Ministerie van Volksgezondheid en Milieuhygiene, Dokter Reijersstraat 12, Leidschendam Netherlands. **LC** TX501; .N48A.

NE
VERSLAG / PROEFSTATION VOOR DE AKKERBOUW ON DE GROENTETEELT IN DE VOLLEGROND. Added/Corp Proefstation voor de Akkerbouw en de Groenteteelt in de Vollegrond. (19??)-. Monographic series. Dutch (summaries and/or abstracts in English).
 Ind/Abst Agric. Eng. Abstr.

SA
VERSLAG VAN DIE OUDITEUR-GENERAAL OOR DIE REKENINGS VAN DIE RAAD VIR INMAAKVRUGTE VIR DIE BOEKJAAR ... . VFOAT Report of the Auditor-General on the Accounts of the Canning Fruit Board for the Financial Year ... . Afrikaans (English). an. R0.90. Staatsdrukker, Bosmanstraat, Privaatsak X85, Pretoria 0001 South Africa. **LC** HD9257.S7; S65B. *Continues* Report of the Controller and Auditor-General on the Accounts of the Canning Fruit Board and the Balance Sheet.

FR/0241-0389
VIANDES ET PRODUITS CARNES AUBIERE. (VIANDES ET PRODUITS CARNES.). [Viandes prod. carnes Aubiere]. **Added/Corp** Association pour le Developpement de l'Institut de la Viande (Aubiere, Puy-de-Dome). **VFOAT** Viandes et Produits Carnes (Clermont-Ferrand); VPC (Aubiere). (1980)-. Periodical. French. Six times a year. 509.30F France; 548.48F others. Association pour le Developpment d le Institut de la Viande / Adiv VPC, 2 rue Chappe, 63039 Clermont Ferr 02 France. **Tel** 011 33 73 907297, FAX 011 33 73 921777, telex 990227. **UDC** 637.5.
 Ind/Abst Anim. Breed. Abstr.; Food Sci. Technol. Abstr.

US/0049-6456
VINTAGE (NEW YORK, N.Y. 1971). *Ceased*. (VINTAGE.). [Vintage]. Ceased (1987). Periodical. English. mo. Vintage Magazines Inc, 2700 Westchester Avenue, c/o Ira Green, Purchase NY 10577-2560. **Tel** (212)570-6111. **ED** Philip Seldon. **LC** TP544; .V55. **DD** 641.2/05. **Bk Rev**. **Ad Acc. Circ:** 100,000.
 Desc: Lavish full color "coffee table" magazine on gourmet food, fine wine, and the accouterments of gracious living. Includes coverage on china, glass, silver, etc. and gourmet related travel.
 Ind/Abst Consum. Index Prod. Eval. Inf. Source; Gen. Period. Index (1985-1986); Mag. Index (1977-?).

●US/1064-4083
VIRGINIA FRUIT AND VEGETABLE MARKET INFORMATION. (VIRGINIA FRUIT AND VEGETABLE MARKET INFORMATION / VIRGINIA DEPARTMENT OF AGRICULTURE AND CONSUMER SERVICES.). [Va. fruit veg. bull.]. **Added/Corp** Virginia. Dept. of Agriculture and Consumer Services. Virginia. Market Information Program. Issue 92.1 (May 15, 1992)-. Periodical. English. mo. Free. Virginia Department of Agriculture & Consumer Services, 1100 Bank Street, Washington Building, Suite 210, Richmond VA 23219. **Tel** (804)786-2373, FAX (804)371-7679. **DD** 338.

Food and Food Industry

NE
VLEES EN VLEESWAREN. Misset Uitgeverij BV, Postbus 9000, 6800 DA Arnhem Netherlands. **Tel** 011 31 85 209911.

NE/0042-7934
VOEDINGSMIDDELEN TECHNOLOGIE. (VOEDINGSMIDDELENTECHNOLOGIE.). [Voedingsm. technol.]. **VFOAT** Voedings Middelen Technologie; Voedingsmiddelen Technologie; VMT. (1970)-. Periodical. Dutch. Twenty-six times a year (Wed.). F220.00. Keesing Uitgeversmaatschappij, Hogehilweg 13, Postbus 1118, 1000 BC Amsterdam Netherlands. **Tel** 011 31 020 5641183, 5641184. *Formed by the union of Conserva and Voeding en Techniek.*
Ind/Abst Dairy Sci. Abstr.; Food Sci. Technol. Abstr.; Infomat Int. Bus.; Int. Packag. Abstr.; Potato Abstr.; Soyabean Abstr.

MY/0126-5903
WARTA PASARAN LADA / PEPPER MARKET BULLETIN. (WARTA PASARAN LADA.). [Warta Pasaran Lada.]. **Added/Corp** Jemaah Pemasaran Lada Hitam. **VFOAT** Pepper Market Bulletin. (19??)-. Periodical. English (English). qt. $12.00. Jemaah Pemasaran Lada Hitam, Tanah Putih (Berdekatan KPA), Peti Surat 1653/93916 Kuching, Sarawak Malaysia. **Tel** 082-331811, telex MA 70987 PMBKG. **LC** HD9210.M25; W37. **Circ:** 350 (ctrl).
Desc: Review of pepper market situation, export performance, price tables and graphs for Sarawak pepper exports.

US/0043-0560
WASHINGTON FOOD DEALER MAGAZINE, THE. **Added/Corp** Washington State Food Dealers Association. **VFOAT** Washington Food Dealer; Food Dealer. (19??)-. Trade Publication. English. Four times a year (Wed.). $20.00 US; $25.00 Canada. Washington State Food Dealers Association, 480 19th Street East, Tacoma WA 98421. **Tel** (206)272-2966. **ED** Bob Sheffels. **Ad Acc. Circ:** 1,600 (ctrl).
Desc: Trade publication for the grocery industry in Washington and Alaska.

US
WASHINGTON RICELETTER. Ceased. Vol. 2, No. 1 (Feb. 6, 1976)-(1993). Periodical. English. bw. Washington Riceletter, PO Box 14260 Benjamin Franklin Station, Washington DC 20044. **Tel** (202)547-5633. **ED** David Morrison. **Bk Rev.**
Desc: Information on rice production and marketing.

US/0043-1923
WEEKLY STATISTICAL SUGAR TRADE JOURNAL. See Food and Food Industry-Abstracting, Bibliographies and Statistics.

GW/0375-8818
WEIN-WISSENSCHAFT, DIE. [Wein-Wiss.]. Academic Scholarly Publication. German (English and French). bm. $30.44. Fachverlag Dr Fraund GmbH, Postfach 1329, D 61364 Friedrichsdorf Germany. **Tel** 011 49 6172 71060. Documents available from CASDDS.
Ind/Abst AGRICOLA; Chem. Abstr.; Food Sci. Technol. Abstr.; Vitis Vitic. Enol. Abstr.

CN
WESTERN COMMERCE & INDUSTRY MAGAZINE. English. Six times a year (Jan., Mar., May, July, Sept., Nov.). 39.00Can$ Canada; 58.50Can$ other. Mercury Publications Ltd., 945 King Edward Street, Winnipeg Manitoba R3H 0P8 Canada. **Tel** (204)775-0387, FAX (204)775-7830. **ED** Kelly Gray. **Ad Acc. Circ:** 10,400.

US/0164-6001
WESTERN FRUIT GROWER. See Agriculture.

CN/0705-906X
WESTERN GROCER MAGAZINE (1977). (WESTERN GROCER MAGAZINE.). **VFOAT** Western Grocer and Food Store Manager. **VAT** Western Grocer and Food Store Manager (1977). Vol. 62, No. 5 (Aug./Sept. 1977)-. Periodical. English. Six times a year (Feb., Apr., June, Aug., Oct., Dec.). 39.00Can$ Canada; 58.50Can$ other. Mercury Publications Ltd. / Manitoba, 945 King Edward Street, Winnipeg Manitoba R3H 0P8 Canada. **Tel** (204)775-0387, FAX (204)775-7830. **ED** Kelly Gray. **DD** 658.8/09/641305. **Ad Acc. Circ:** 10,400 (ctrl). *Continues Western Grocer and Food Store Manager, 0043-3780.*
Desc: This journal serves The Grocery, Allied Non-Food and Institutional Industries throughout Western Canada, (NW Ontario, Manitoba, Saskatchewan, Alberta and BC).

UK/0300-0923
WHO FOOD ADDITIVES SERIES. [WHO food addit. ser.]. **Added/Corp** World Health Organization. **VAT** World Health Organization Food Additives Series. No.1 (1972)-. Monographic series. English. sa. Price varies per volume. World Health Organization, Distribution and Sales, 20 Avenue Appia, CH-1211 Geneva 27 Switzerland. **Tel** 011 41 22 7912111, FAX 011 41 22 7880401. **LC** TX553.A3; W67a; S401; .F63 subser. **DD** 664/.06/08. **NLM** W1 W14H.
Desc: Serves as a record of the extensive toxicological data assessed by the Joint FAO/WHO Expert Committee on Food additives when establishing acceptable daily intakes for international food additives and tolerable intakes for contaminants.
Ind/Abst EMBASE; Food Sci. Technol. Abstr.; Helminthol. Abstr. (1991-); Index Vet.; Nutr. Abstr. Rev., Ser. A, Hum. Exp.; Protozoolog. Abstr.; Vet. Bull.; Trop. Dis. Bull.

US/0193-1504
WHOLE FOODS. [Whole foods]. (1976)-. Periodical. English. Thirteen times a year (Publish monthly source directory, annually in May.). $30.00 US; $40.00 Canada & Mexico; $150.00 other. WFC Corporation, 3000 Hadley Road, South Plainfield NJ 07080. **Tel** (201)769-1160, FAX (201)769-1171. **ED** Daniel McSweeney. **LC** HD9001; .W48. **DD** 641.3/02/068. **CODEN** WHFOEO. **Ad Acc. Circ:** 11,000 (ctrl).
Desc: An trade in which covers the natural foods industry. With the news, statistics, articles on trends and plus new product coverage.
Ind/Abst BioBusiness (1990-).

CN/0227-3837
WINE & DINE. [Wine dine]. V. 1- Summer 1980-. Periodical. English. qt. Wine & Dine, PO Box 15, Nuns Island Province of Quebec H3E 1J8 Canada. **Tel** (514)933-5027. **DD** 641.3/005.

US/1053-4776
WINE ON LINE. See Food and Food Industry-Beverage Industry.

IO
WORKING PAPER. See Agriculture-Crop Production and Soil.

PH
WORKING PAPER (INTERNATIONAL FOOD POLICY RESEARCH INSTITUTE). See Engineering-Hydraulic Engineering.

US
WORKING PAPERS ON FOOD SUBSIDIES / INTERNATIONAL FOOD POLICY RESEARCH INSTITUTE. (1985)-. English. IFPRI, 1776 Massachusetts Avenue NW, Washington DC 20036. **Tel** (202)862-5600, FAX (202)467-4439, telex 440054.
Ind/Abst World Agric. Econ.

US/1060-9741
WORLD AGRICULTURE (WASHINGTON, D.C. 1991). See Agriculture.

UK
WORLD COMMODITY FORECASTS. FOOD, FEEDSTUFFS AND BEVERAGES. See Economics.

●US/1073-2357
WORLD FOOD CHEMICAL NEWS. (1994)-. English. wk. $1,450.00. Food Chemical News Inc, 1101 Pennsylvania Avenue Southeast, Washington DC 20003. **Tel** (202)544-1980, FAX (202)546-3890.

IT/0084-179X
WORLD FOOD PROBLEMS. **Added/Corp** Food and Agriculture Organization of the United Nations. No. 1 (1956)-. Monographic series. English. Price varies per volume. UNIPUB, 4611-F Assembly Drive, Lanham MD 20706-4391. **Tel** (800)274-4888, FAX (301)459-0056, telex 28787 GATT CH. **DD** 338.1.

UK/0963-4894
WORLD FOOD REGULATION REVIEW. [World food regul. rev.]. **Added/Corp** BNA International Inc. Vol. 1, No. 1 (June 1991)-. Periodical. English. mo. £336.00 UK; $595.00 other. BNA International Inc., Herron, HSE Dean 10 Farrar Street, 6th Floor, London SW1H 0DL England. **Tel** (44) 71 222 8831, FAX (44) 71 222 0294, telex 262570 BNA LONG. **NLM** W1; WO868L. **[CCC].**

IT
WORLD FOOD SURVEY. See Agriculture.

US
WORLD SUGAR SITUATION AND OUTLOOK / UNITED STATES DEPARTMENT OF AGRICULTURE, FOREIGN AGRICULTURAL SERVICE. See Business-Commerce.

US/0195-2552
YANKEE FOOD SERVICE. Vol. 1 (Sept. 1979)-. Periodical. English. mo. Free (food service operators), $40.00 other. Griffin Publishing Co Inc, 1099 Hingham Street, Rockland MA 02370. **Tel** (617)878-5300 or, (508)385-5700, FAX (508)385-8134. **ED** Heather Reese. **Ad Acc, Adv Mgr:** Kevin Griffin. **Circ:** 25,250 (ctrl).
Desc: Reports the news and happenings of the food service and hospitality industry in New England and upstate New York. 50% of the space is devoted to editorial news, personnel changes, business expansions, and end user profiles including current events on restaurants, colleges, health care, hospitality, captive food service and the distributors.

US/0748-0423
YEAR IN REVIEW (RICHMOND, VA.), THE. (THE YEAR IN REVIEW / VIRGINIA DEPARTMENT OF AGRICULTURE AND CONSUMER SERVICES.). **Main/Corp** Virginia. Dept. of Agriculture and Consumer Services. 1980-81-. English. an. Virginia Department of Agriculture & Consumer Services, 1100 Bank Street, Washington Building, Suite 210, Richmond VA 23219. **Tel** (804)786-2373, FAX (804)371-7679. **LC** HD1775.V5; V465A. **DD** 353.97550082/33043. *Continues in part Bulletin - The Virginia Department of Agriculture and Consumer Services, 0198-8298.*

US/0068-5720
YEARBOOK - CALIFORNIA MACADAMIA SOCIETY. See Gardening and Horticulture.

GW/0044-3026
ZEITSCHRIFT FUER LEBENSMITTEL-UNTERSUCHUNG UND -FORSCHUNG. [Z. Lebensm.-Unters. forsch.]. Vol. 86 (July/Aug. 1943)-. Periodical. English (German). Twelve times a year. DM1896.00. Springer-Verlag GmbH & Company KG, Heidelberger Platz 3, D 14197 Berlin Germany. **Tel** 011 49 30 8207223, FAX 011 49 30 8214091, telex 183 319 SPBLN D. **(Subscription address:** Springer Verlag New York Inc. / for North America, 44 Hartz Way, Secaucus NJ 07096.**) ED** F Kiermeier. **NLM** W1 ZE445. **CODEN** ZLUFAR. **[CCC].** Pr Rev. available on microfilm from University Microfilms International (UMI). Documents available from The Genuine Article, BIOSIS Document Express, CASDDS, Documents on Demand. *Formed by the union of Zeitschrift fur Untersuchung der Lebensmittel, 0373-0174 and Vorratspflege und Lebensmittelforschung, 0372-6509.*
Desc: A source of critical and up-to-date information on scientific research into all aspects of food and related products.
Ind/Abst AGRICOLA; Anal. Abstr.; Biodeter. Abstr. (1991-); Biol. Abstr.; Chem. Abstr.; Crop Physiol. Abstr.; Curr. Contents, Agric. Biol. Environ. Sci.; Dairy Sci. Abstr.; EMBASE; Energy Inf. Abstr.; Energy Res. Abstr.; Environ. Abstr.; Field Crop Abstr.; Food Sci. Technol. Abstr.; Hortic. Abstr.; Index Med.; Index Vet.; Mass Spect. Bull.; NAPRALERT; Nutr. Abstr. Rev., Ser. B, Live Feeds and Feed.; Nutr. Abstr. Rev., Ser. A, Hum. Exp.; Life Sci. Collect.; PESTDOC; Pig News Inf.; Postharvest News Inf.; Poult. Abstr.; Protozoolog. Abstr.; Res. Alert [Full Cov.]; Rev. Agric. Entomol.; Rev. Med. Vet. Mycology; Rev. Plant Pathol.; Sci. Cit. Index; SCISEARCH; Seed Abstr.; Soc. Sci. Cit. Index [Select. Cov.]; Soyabean Abstr.; Sug. Indus. Abstr.; Vet. Bull.; Vitis Vitic. Enol. Abstr.; Wheat Barley Trit. Abstr.

GW/0722-5733
ZFL : INTERN. ZEITSCHRIFT FUER LEBENSMITTEL-TECHNOLOGIE UND -VERFAHRENSTECHNIK. [ZFL, Int. Z. Lebensm.-Technol. -Verfahr.tech.]. **Added/Corp** Verband der Legensmitteltechnologen. Bundesverband des Deutschen Feinkostindustrie. **VFOAT** International Journal of Food Technology and Food Process Engineering. (1982)-. Academic Scholarly Publication. German. Ten times a year. DM258.00 Germany; DM275.40 other. Dr. Alfred Huethig Verlag GmbH, Postfach 102869, D 69018 Heidelberg Germany. **Tel** 011 49 6221 489281. **(Subscription address:** Huethig Publishing Inc., 29 Macintosh Drive, Oxford CT 06478.**) CODEN** ZIZVEF. **[CCC].** Documents available from CASDDS.
Ind/Abst Chem. Abstr. (1986-).

CH/1000-8047
ZHONGGUO GUOSHU. See Agriculture-Crop Production and Soil.

CH/1001-7216
ZHONGGUO SHUIDAO KEXUE. **VFOAT** Chinese Journal of Rice Science. (1986)-. Periodical. Chinese. qt. **DD** 633.18.
Ind/Abst Crop Physiol. Abstr.; Plant Breed. Abstr.; Rev. Plant Pathol.; Seed Abstr.

CC/1000-9973
ZHONGGUO TIAOWEIPIN. (1984)-. Academic Scholarly Publication. Chinese. mo. Harbin Shipin Weisheng Gongye Yanjiusuo, 66 Shitoudao Jie, Daoli-qu, Harbin Heilongjiang, 150010 People's Republic of China. **Tel** 416701. **ED** Z. Yi. **DD** 664.5. Documents available from CASDDS.
Desc: Magazine of Chinese spices.
Ind/Abst Chem. Abstr.

PL/0302-7716
ZIEMNIAK. See Agriculture-Crop Production and Soil.

GW/0342-3476
ZLR, ZEITSCHRIFT FUER DAS GESAMTE LEBENSMITTELRECHT. See Law.

GW
ZMP BILANZ. **Main/Corp** Zentrale Markt- und Preisberichtstelle fur Erzeugnisse der Land-, Forst- und

Ernahrungswirtschaft. **VAT** Zentrale Markt- und Preisberichtstelle Bilanz. 1976-. German. an. Zentrale Market und Preisberichtstelle fur Erzeugnisse der Land, Forst und Ernahrungswirtschaft GmbH (ZMP), Godesberger Allee 142-148, 5300 Bonn 2 Germany. **Tel** 888-0, telex 88576759. **LC** HD9013.4; .A6. ***Continues*** *Agrarmarkte Br Deutschland, Ewg und Weltmarkt.*

GW/0373-0204
ZUCKER- UND SUSSWAREN WIRTSCHAFT. [Zucker-Susswaren-Wirtsch.]. **VFOAT** Revue Internationale de Sucre et de Confiserie; International Review for Sugar and Confectionery; ZSW. (1948)-. Periodical. German. mo. DM144.00 Germany; DM174.00 other. Verlag Eduard F Beckmann KG, Postfach 1120, Haus Heideck, D-31251 Lehrte Germany. **Tel** 011 49 5132 85910, FAX 011 49 5132 53100. **LC** HD9999.C73; G398. **CODEN** ZUSUAN. Index available. **Bk Rev. Ad Acc.**
Desc: Machines for manufacturing sweets, sugar industries, and recipes for making sweets.
Ind/Abst BioBusiness (1989-1990); Food Sci. Technol. Abstr.

ABSTRACTING, BIBLIOGRAPHIES AND STATISTICS

US/0887-4999
ALMANAC OF THE CANNING, FREEZING, PRESERVING INDUSTRIES, THE. [Alm. cann. freez. preserv. ind.]. **VFOAT** Almanac. (1958)-. English. Twice a year. $65.00 US; $75.00 Canada and Mexico; $89.00 other. Edward E. Judge & Sons Inc., PO Box 866, Westminster MD 21158. **Tel** (301)876-2052, (800)729-5517, FAX (301)848-2034. **ED** Daniel P. Judge. **LC** TX599; .C4. **DD** 338.4/7/6640280973. Each issue contains an index to its own contents (no volume index)--loose. **Ad Acc.** ***Continues*** *Canning Trade Almanac.*
Desc: Contains U.S. food law, labeling and packaging regulations, food standards, USDA quality grades, pack statistics, canned and frozen, crop statistics, US census of food manufacturers, and international trade data.

UK/0305-2370
ANNUAL BULLETIN OF STATISTICS. **Main/Corp** International Tea Committee. (May 1946)-. English. an. £185.00. International Tea Committee Ltd, 5 High Timber Street, Sir John Lyon House, London EC4V 3NH United Kingdom. **Tel** 011 44 71 4284672, FAX 011 44 71 2483011, telex 887911 TELTEA G "ITC". **LC** HD9198.A1; I56. Index available. **Ad Acc. Circ:** 500. ***Supersedes in part*** *International Tea Committee. Monthly Bulletin of Statistics.*
Desc: Statistics relating to all aspects of tea trade e.g. production, consumption, exports, imports, acreage, supply, absorption.

NR
ANNUAL BULLETIN OF STATISTICS ON COCOA, COFFEE & TEA. **VFOAT** Nigerian Cocoa Board Statistical Bulletin. 1979-. Bulletin. English. an. Nigerian Cocoa Board Statistics Section, P M B 5032, Ibadan Nigeria. **LC** HD9017.N53; W467A. **DD** 338.1/7374/09669. ***Continues*** *Statistical Information on Western State of Nigeria Controlled Produce.*

AT/1031-0533
APPARENT CONSUMPTION OF FOODSTUFFS AND NUTRIENTS, AUSTRALIA. [Apparent consum. foodst. nutr. Aust.]. **Added/Corp** Australian Bureau of Statistics. (1971)-. English. an. 37.70Aus$. Australian Bureau of Statistics, PO Box 10, Belconnen Australian Capital Territory, 2616 Australia. **Tel** 011 61 6 2527911, FAX 011 61 6 2516009. **DD** 339.4864130994.
Desc: General overview of the supply and use of approximately 130 basic foodstuffs, level of nutrient intake and estimated supply of selected types of nutrients available for consumption.

US/0164-4831
BEER STATISTICS NEWS. [Beer stat. news]. Vol. 3, No. 6 (July 1977)-. Periodical. English. Twelve times a year. $280.00. Beer Marketers Insights, 51 Virginia Avenue, West Nyack NY 10994. **Tel** (914)358-7751, FAX (914)358-7860. **ED** James Sullivan. **DD** 338. ***Continues*** *Beer Statistics Monthly, 0164-4467.*
Desc: Computerized data service, with reports highlighting data, showing trends for major brewers in 39 states in US. States grouped by region, and regional analyses are also made.

II
CARDAMOM STATISTICS (INDIA). **Main/Corp** India. Cardamon Board. English. Government of India Cardamon Board, Chittoor Road, Cochin 682018 India. **LC** HD9210.I5; I45A. **DD** 338.1/7/383.

US/0362-014X
CITRUS FRUIT INDUSTRY STATISTICAL BULLETIN. [Citrus fruit ind. stat. bull.]. **Main/Corp** Sunkist Growers, Inc. Information Systems Dept. Statistical Publication. English. Sunkist Growers Inc, 14130 Riverside Drive, Sherman Oak CA 91423. **LC** HD9259.C54; U589A. **DD** 338.1/7/430973.

FR
FOOD CONSUMPTION STATISTICS. **Added/Corp** Organisation for Economic Co-Operation and Development. **VFOAT** Basic Statistics OECD/OCDE Statistiques de Base; Statistiques de la Consommation des Denrees Alimentaires. (1966)-. English (French). ir. 425.00F. OECD Publications and Information Center, 2 rue Andre-Pascal, 75775 Paris Cedex 16 France. **Tel** 011 33 1 45248167, US:(202)785-6323, FAX 011 33 1 45248500 OR 45248176, telex 620 160 OCDE. **(Subscription address:** OECD Publications Center, 2001 L Street, Suite 700, Washington DC 20036.**) LC** HD9000.1; .F5894. **DD** 339.4/86413/00212. available on microfiche.

IT
FOOD OUTLOOK. STATISTICAL SUPPLEMENT. **Added/Corp** Food and Agriculture Organization of the United Nations. **VFOAT** Food Outlook Statistical Supplement. (1981)-. Statistical Publication. English. an. Food and Agriculture Organization (FAO) / Italy, GIPC166 via Terme di Caracalla, 00100 Rome Italy. **Tel** 011 39 6 522 52925, FAX 011 39 6 522 55784. **LC** HD9000.1; .F594. **DD** 338.1/9.

UK/0015-6574
FOOD SCIENCE AND TECHNOLOGY ABSTRACTS. **Added/Corp** International Food Information Service. Vol. 1 (Jan. 1969)-. Abstracting/Indexing Service. English. mo. $1,520.00 US and Canada; £825.00 other. International Food Information Service, c/o H Brookes, Lane End House, Shinfield, Reading Berkshire RG9 2BB England. **Tel** 011/44/734/883895, telex 847204. **ED** H Brookes. **LC** TP368; .F678. **DD** 664/.008. **NLM** Z 5776.F7 F686. **Ad Acc. Circ:** 1,250. available on CD-ROM (Pollution/Toxicology CD-ROM) from Cambridge Scientific Abstracts.
Desc: Over 1100 primary journals scanned, making this journal the prime world source for information used by specialists in government, food industry and academic research establishments.

II/0253-4924
FOOD TECHNOLOGY ABSTRACTS. [Food technol. abstr.]. (1966)-. Periodical. English. mo. $20.00. **(Subscription address:** Prints India, 11 Darya Ganj, New Delhi 110002 India.**) UDC** 612.392.

US/0146-9304
FOODS ADLIBRA (1975). (FOODS ADLIBRA.). **VFOAT** Alibra. Vol. 1 (Feb. 15, 1974)-. Abstracting/Indexing Service. English. sm. $200.00 US; $275.00 other. Foods Adlibra Publications, 9000 Plymouth Avenue North, Minneapolis MN 55427. **Tel** (612)540-2720, FAX (612)540-3166, telex 882122. **ED** Judith O'Connell. available on an online database (Dialog). Documents available.
Desc: Coverage content includes food trade business and technical literature citations with descriptive highlights.

●US/1063-4169
FOODS INTELLIGENCE ON COMPACT DISC. (FOODS INTELLIGENCE ON COMPACT DISC [COMPUTER FILE].). [Foods intell. compact disc]. **Added/Corp** BioSciences Information Service of Biological Abstracts. SilverPlatter Information, Inc. (1992)-. English. qt. $1560.00 US & Canada; $1720.00 other. Silverplatter Information Inc., 100 River Ridge Drive, Norwood MA 02062. **Tel** (800)343-0064, (617)769-2599, FAX (617)235-1715. **DD** 338.
Desc: Offers a vital combination of references to scientific research and related business literature. Covers biological and medical journals, conferences and workshops, research reports, business publications, and more.

US/0469-7405
FROZEN FOOD PACK STATISTICS. (FROZEN FOOD PACK STATISTICS / AMERICAN FROZEN FOOD INSTITUTE.). [Frozen food pack stat.]. **Main/Corp** American Frozen Food Institute. (1969)-. English. an (May). $10.00 (members); $100.00 (non-members). American Frozen Food Institute, 1764 Old Meadow Road, Suite 350, McLean VA 22102. **Tel** (703)821-0770, FAX (703)821-1350. **Circ:** 1,000 (ctrl).
Desc: United States production of frozen fruit, vegetables and potatoes, broken out by commodity, region, and container size.
Ind/Abst Predicasts Forecasts.

UK/0309-0477
INTERNATIONAL TEA COMMITTEE MONTHLY STATISTICAL SUMMARY. **Added/Corp** International Tea Committee. **VFOAT** I.T.C. Monthly Statistical Summary. (19??)-. Statistical Publication. English. mo. £140.00. International Tea Committee Ltd, 5 High Timber Street, Sir John Lyon House, London EC4V 3NH United Kingdom. **Tel** 011 44 71 4284672, FAX 011 44 71 2483011, telex 887911 TELTEA G "ITC".

US/0730-3254
MONTHLY COFFEE STATISTICS. [Mon. coffee stat.]. V. 1- (No. 1-); Jan. 1979-. Periodical. English. mo. $85.00. R Mondschein, 114 Libersty Street, New York NY 10016.

US
NEW YORK CITY WHOLESALE FRUIT AND VEGETABLE REPORT. **Added/Corp** United States. Agricultural Marketing Service. Fruit and Vegetable Division. Vol. 68, No. 147 (Aug. 3, 1982)-. Periodical. English. da. $120.00 US; 240.00 other. US Department of Agriculture / Agricultural Marketing Service / New York, Fruit and Vegetable Market News Branch, 4A New York City Terminal Market, New York NY 10474. **Tel** (212)542-2225. ***Continues*** *New York City Fruit and Vegetable Report.*
Desc: Covers the ever changing fruit and vegetable market situation in New York City.

UK/0308-4469
QUARTERLY BULLETIN OF COCOA STATISTICS / BULLETIN TRIMESTRIEL DE STATISTIQUES DU CACAO. **Added/Corp** International Cocoa Organization. **VFOAT** Bulletin Trimestriel de Statistiques du Cacao. (Dec. 1974)-. Bulletin. English (French, Russian and Spanish). Four times a year. £40.00 UK & Europe; £50.00 other. International Cocoa Organization, 22 Berners Street, London W1P 3DB United Kingdom. **Tel** 011 44 71 6373211, FAX 011 41 71 6310114, telex 28173. **LC** HD9200.A1; Q37. **DD** 382/.41374/0212.
Desc: Statistics on world cocoa economy, prediction, consumption, exports, imports, prices.

US/0363-0072
STATISTICAL SUMMARY - COMMONWEALTH OF VIRGINIA, STATE MILK COMMISSION. **Main/Corp** Virginia. Milk Commission. Statistical Publication. English. **LC** HD9282.U5; V964A. **DD** 338.1/7/7109755.

US/0277-3724
STATISTICAL SUMMARY, FEDERAL MEAT AND POULTRY INSPECTION FOR FISCAL YEAR. (STATISTICAL SUMMARY, FEDERAL MEAT AND POULTRY INSPECTION FOR FISCAL YEAR ... / UNITED STATES DEPARTMENT OF AGRICULTURE, FOOD SAFETY AND QUALITY SERVICE, MEAT AND POULTRY INSPECTION PROGRAM.). 1980-. Statistical Publication. English. an. US Department of Agriculture, 14th Street and Independence Avenue SW, Washington DC 20250. **Tel** (202)720-5457. **LC** HD9410.9.U5; C64A. **DD** 353.0082/336043. ***Continues*** *Federal Meat and Poultry Inspection Statistical Summary for ... .*

US/0430-7585
STATISTICAL SUMMARY - FLORIDA CANNERS ASSOCIATION. ***Ceased.*** **Main/Corp** Florida Canners Association. (19??)-?. Statistical Publication. English. an. PO Box 780, Winter Haven FL 33880. **LC** HD9259.C54; U587a. **DD** 338.4/7/6648.

II
TEA STATISTICS (CALCUTTA, INDIA : 1982). (TEA STATISTICS.). English. an. J Thomas & Company, Private Limited Nilhat House 11 R N Mukherjee Road, Calcutta 700001 India. **LC** HD9198.I4; T395. **DD** 338.1/7372/0954.

US/0092-2005
TEXAS FRUIT AND PECAN STATISTICS. **Main/Corp** Texas Crop and Livestock Reporting Service. English. PO Box 70, Austin TX 78767. **LC** HD9247.T4; T48A. **DD** 338.1/7/409764.

GW/0175-8292
VITIS, VITICULTURE AND ENOLOGY ABSTRACTS. [Vitis vitic. enol. abstr.]. **Added/Corp** Bundesforschungsanstalt fuer Rebenzuchtung Geilweilerhof. International Food Information Service. **VFOAT** Viticulture and Enology Abstracts. Vol. 23, No. 1 (March 1984)-. Abstracting/Indexing Service. English (French, German, Italian and Spanish). qt. DM64.00 (per volume), DM16.00 (per issue). Vitis / Bundesanstalt fuer Zuechtungsforschung, Forschung Wein/ Geilweilerhof, W 6741 Siebeldingen Germany. **Tel** 011 49 6345 410. Index available. **Bk Rev. Circ:** 700 (ctrl). available on an online database from IFIS. ***Separated from*** *Vitis, 0042-7500.*
Desc: Abstracts of scientific papers on viticulture, enology and grapevine breeding.

US/0043-1923
WEEKLY STATISTICAL SUGAR TRADE JOURNAL. **VFOAT** Willet & Gray's Weekly Statistical Sugar Trade Journal. **VAT** Willet and Gray's Weekly Statistical Sugar Trade Journal. (1842)-. Statistical Publication. English. wk. $65.00. Willett & Gray Inc, PO Box N, Brightwaters NY 11718. **LC** HD9100.1; .W3. **DD** 380.1/41/360973. available on microfilm.

AT
WINE PRODUCTION, AUSTRALIA AND STATES / AUSTRALIAN BUREAU OF STATISTICS. **Added/Corp** Australian Bureau of Statistics. (19??)-. English. an. 10.70Aus$. Australian Bureau of Statistics, PO Box 10, Belconnen Australian Capital Territory, 2616 Australia. **Tel** 011 61 6 2527911, FAX 011 61 6 2516009. **ED** G.D. Carey. **LC** HD9388.A8; W56. **DD** 338.4/76632/00994. **Bk Rev**. **Ad Acc**. **Circ:** 1,500 (ctrl).
Desc: Contains information on commercial production of wine, stocks of wine and grade spirit and materials used in winemaking.

BEVERAGE INDUSTRY

US/1067-3105
ALCOHOL ISSUES INSIGHTS. [Alcohol issues insights]. **VFOAT** Insights. (198?)-. Periodical. English. Twelve times a year. $215.00. Beer Marketers Insights, 51 Virginia Avenue, West Nyack NY 10994. **Tel** (914)358-7751, FAX (914)358-7860. **ED** Eric Sheppard. **DD** 363.
Desc: Covers brewer-wholesaler relations, industry association activities, beer and health, media portrayal, advertising and other trends of interest to beer brewers, suppliers, wholesalers and associated executives with focus on exclusive stories and analysis.

NE
ALCOHOLFABRIEKEN EN DISTILLEERDERIJEN, BIERBROUWERIJEN EN MOUTERIJEN, FRISDRANKENINDUSTRIE PRODUKTIESTATISTIEKEN. **Main/Corp** Netherlands. Centraal Bureau voor de Statistiek. Hoofdafdeling Statistieken van Industrie en Bouwnijverheid. **VFOAT** Distilling Factories, Breweries and Malt-Houses, Non-Alcoholic Carbonated Drinks Industry Production Statistics. Dutch (summaries and/or abstracts in English). an. Fl8.00. Centraal Bureau voor de Statistiek, AFD ALG Zaken, Postbus 959, 2270 AZ Voorburg Netherlands. **Tel** 011 31 70 3373800, FAX 011 31 038 7429, telex 32692 CBS NL. **LC** HD9390.N4; N47A.

US/0889-3519
ALCOHOLIC BEVERAGE EXECUTIVES' NEWSLETTER INTERNATIONAL. [Alcohol. beverage exec. newsl. int.]. **VFOAT** Alcoholic Beverage Newsletter International; Alcoholic Beverage Executives' Newsletter. (19??)-. Periodical. English. Fifty-two times a year. $225.00. Alcoholic Beverage Executives, PO Box 3188, Omaha NE 68103. **Tel** (402)397-5514, FAX (402)397-3843. **ED** Patricia Kennedy. **DD** 338. **Bk Rev**. **Ad Acc**. ***Continues*** *Alcoholic Beverage Executives' Newsletter.*
Desc: Covers issues and articles beer, wine, and other beverages.

FR/1142-1983
ALCOOLOGIE (PARIS). (ALCOOLOGIE.). [Alcool. Paris]. (1989)-. Periodical. French. qt (4 issues). 225.27F France; 350.00F other. Societe Francaise Alcoologie, 19 rue de la Tour, 75116 Paris France. **Tel** 011 33 1 45243336. **UDC** 615.9. ***Continues*** *Bulletin de la Societe Francaise d'Alcoologie, 0245-6664.*

US/0898-9001
ALL ABOUT BEER. [All beer]. Periodical. English. qt. $13.00. Bosak Publ Inc, PO Box 566402, Oceanside CA 92056. **DD** 641.

GW/0175-8314
ALLES UBER WEIN. **VFOAT** Wein (Mainz). (1983)-. Periodical. German. bm. DM108.00. Woschek Verlags Gmbh, Wilhelm Theo Roemheld STR 34, D 55130 Mainz Germany. **Tel** 011 49 6131 81035, FAX 011 49 6131 839898. **UDC** 634.8. Index available. cum. index. **Bk Rev**, (Qty: 60). **Ad Acc**, **Adv Mgr:** Beata Kratz. ctrl circ.
Desc: Covers wine, sparkling wines and spirits, tourism, and gastronomy; covers producers and markets, analyzes the trends and gives manifold information.

FR
AMATEUR DE BORDEAUX, L'. (19??)-. French. qt. 430.00F France; 480.00F other. l'Amateur de Bordeaux, 22 rue des Reculettes, 75013 Paris France. **Tel** 011 33 1 43314499, FAX 011 33 1 43314115.

CN/0316-6317
AMATEUR ENOLOGIST, THE. ***Title Change.*** V. 1- Summer 1971-. Periodical. English. qt. Amateur Enologist, PO Box 2701 V6B 3X2 Canada. **DD** 641.8/72/05. ***Continued by*** *Pump & Press, 0318-9260.*

UK/0002-6883
AMATEUR WINE MAKER. [Amat. winemaker]. (1957)-. Periodical. English. mo. £13.70 UK; £17.00, £36.00 (airmail) other. ASP, 1 Golden Square, London W1R 3AB England. **Tel** 01-437 0626. **ED** Terry Bentley. **Bk Rev**. **Ad Acc**. **Circ:** 15,000. ***Continues*** *Winemaker & Brewer.*
Desc: Magazine for those interested in home winemaking and brewing of beer. News, recipes, technical features, product reviews and test results of wine and beer kits are included.

US/1055-470X
AMERICAN BREWER (HAYWARD, CALIF.). (AMERICAN BREWER.). [Am. brew.]. **VFOAT** American Brewer Magazine. Vol. 3, No. 34 (Fall 1987)-. Periodical. English. qt. $18.00 (one year), $30.00 (two year) US; $21.00 (one year), $35.00 (two year) other. American Brewer, PO Box 510, Hayward CA 94541. **Tel** (415)538-9500 (a.m.), FAX (415)538-0948. **ED** Bill Owens. **LC** HD9397.U5; A47. **DD** 338.4/76633/097305. **Bk Rev**, (Qty: (8-10)). **Ad Acc**, **Adv Mgr:** Bill Owens. **Pr Rev. Circ:** 6000. ***Formed by the union of*** *Amateur Brewer, 0887-7416* ***and*** *Home Fermenter's Digest, 0742-4590.*
Desc: Focus on micro and pub brewing.

US/0748-8343
AMERICAN BREWERIANA JOURNAL. (AMERICAN BREWERIANA JOURNAL : OFFICIAL PUBLICATION OF THE AMERICAN BREWERIANA ASSOCIATION, INC.). **Added/Corp** American Breweriana Association. (198?)-. Periodical. English. Six times a year. 25.00Can$ Canada; 30.00Can$ (surface mail); $40.00 (airmail) others. American Breweriana Association, PO Box 11157, Pueblo CO 81001. **Tel** (719)544-9267. **ED** Bob Pirie (editor's address: P. O. Box 456, Chanhassen, MN 55317). ***Continues*** *ABA Journal (Colorado Springs, Colo.).*
Desc: An literary and educational magazine organized to advance the public knowledge of brewing and breweriana.

US/0002-9254
AMERICAN JOURNAL OF ENOLOGY AND VITICULTURE. [Am. j. enol. vitic.]. **Added/Corp** American Society of Enologists. Vol. 10, (1959)-. Academic Scholarly Publication. English. qt (Feb., May, Aug., Nov.). $120.00 US; $130.00 other. American Society for Enology & Viticulture, PO Box 1855, Davis CA 95617. **Tel** (916)753-3142, , FAX (916)753-3318, telex 9103337496. **ED** Joanne M. Rantz. **CODEN** AJEVAC. Index available. cum. index. **Bk Rev**. **Ad Acc**. **Pr Rev. Circ:** 3,400 (ctrl). available on microfilm from University Microfilms International (UMI). Documents available from The Genuine Article, BIOSIS Document Express, CASDDS. ***Continues*** *American Journal of Enology.*
Desc: Technical research related to enology and viticulture.
Ind/Abst AGRICOLA [Full Cov.]; Agric. Eng. Abstr. (1991-); BioBusiness; Biol. Abstr.; Chem. Abstr.; Chemorecept. Abstr.; Crop Physiol. Abstr.; Curr. Aware. Biol. Sci., CABS; Curr. Biotechnol.; Curr. Contents, Agric. Biol. Environ. Sci.; EMBASE; Food Sci. Technol. Abstr.; Hortic. Abstr.; Microbiol. Abstr. Sect. A; Microbiol. Abstr. Sect. C; Nematol. Abstr.; Nutr. Abstr. Rev., Ser. A, Hum. Exp.; Life Sci. Collect.; PESTDOC; Plant Breed. Abstr.; Plant Genet. Resour. Abstr.; Plant Grow. Reg. Abstr.; Postharvest News Inf.; Res. Alert [Full Cov.]; Rev. Plant Pathol.; Sci. Cit. Index; SCISEARCH; Seed Abstr.; Soils Fert.

US/0149-676X
AMERICAN WINE SOCIETY MANUAL, THE. **Added/Corp** American Wine Society. (19??)-. Monographic series. English. ir. Price varies per volume. American Wine Society, 3006 Latta Road, Rochester NY 14612. **Tel** (716)225-7613. **LC** UNC.

US
ANNUAL BEER REPORT / ALABAMA ALCOHOLIC BEVERAGE CONTROL BOARD. **Main/Corp** Alabama. Alcoholic Beverage Control Board. (19??)-. English. Twelve times a year. $5.00 (per issue). Alabama ABC Board, Box 1151, Montgomery AL 36192. **Tel** (205)271-3840. **LC** HD9397.U53; A22a. **DD** 381/.4566342/09761.

UK/0305-2370
ANNUAL BULLETIN OF STATISTICS. **See** Food and Food Industry-Abstracting, Bibliographies and Statistics.

NR
ANNUAL BULLETIN OF STATISTICS ON COCOA, COFFEE & TEA. **See** Food and Food Industry-Abstracting, Bibliographies and Statistics.

US/0360-3075
ANNUAL PERFORMANCE STUDY - WINE AND SPIRITS WHOLESALERS OF AMERICA. **Main/Corp** Wine and Spirits Wholesalers of America. English. an. Harbor City, 1617 West 261st Street, Harbor City CA 90710. **LC** HD9354; .W5. **DD** 381/.45/663200973. ***Continues*** *Annual Operations Survey.*

AT
ANNUAL REPORT FOR THE YEAR ENDED 30TH JUNE ... / AUSTRALIAN WINE AND BRANDY CORPORATION. **Main/Corp** Australian Wine and Brandy Corporation. (1981/82)-. English. an. **LC** TP559.A8; A85A. **DD** 338.4/7663/200994. ***Continues*** *Annual Report of the Australian Wine Board ... .*

US/0742-0390
ANNUAL REPORT / NATIONAL SOFT DRINK ASSOCIATION. **Main/Corp** National Soft Drink Association. **VFOAT** N.S.D.A Annual Report; NSDA Annual Report. English. an. National Soft Drink Association, 1101 16th Street NW, Washington DC 20036. **Tel** (202)833-2450. **LC** HD9349.S63; N37A. **DD** 338.4/766362/0973.

TZ
ANNUAL REVIEW OF COFFEE. English. an. United Republic of Tanzania / Ministry of Agriculture & Livestock Development, PO Box 2066, Dar Es Salaam Tanzania. **LC** HD9199.T3; A55. **DD** 338.1/7373/09678021. ***Continues*** *Annual Review of the Tanzania Coffee Industry.*

US
ANNUAL STATEMENT / STATE OF NEW HAMPSHIRE, LIQUOR COMMISSION. **Main/Corp** New Hampshire. Liquor Commission. (198?)-. English. **LC** HV5297.N4; A35. ***Continues*** *New Hampshire. Liquor Commission. Annual Statement of Operations.*

US/0164-6281
ARIZONA BEVERAGE ANALYST. Vol. 42, No. 11 (Nov. 1978)-. Periodical. English. Twelve times a year. $15.00 (one year), $25.00 (two years). Bell Publications, 2403 Champa Street, Denver CO 80205. **Tel** (303)296-1600. **ED** Mariette Bell. **Ad Acc**. **Circ:** 5,000 (ctrl). ***Continues*** *Arizona Beverage Journal.*
Desc: Liquor, wine and beer trade publication including wholesaler price listings. Updated monthly with local editorial and national coverage.

US/0746-1151
ARIZONA BEVERAGE GUIDE. (19??)-. English. mo. $15.00 (one year), $25.00 (two year). Arizona Beverage Guide, 2701 North 16th Street/#220, Phoenix AZ 85006. **Tel** (602)279-0978. **ED** Kristin Halsted. **Ad Acc**. **Circ:** 4,225.

US/1054-657X
ATLANTIC CONTROL STATES/NORTH CAROLINA BEVERAGE JOURNAL. **VFOAT** Atlantic Control States North Carolina Beverage Journal; Beverage Journal; Atlantic Control States Beverage Journal. (19??)-. Periodical. English. mo. $10.00. Arnold Lazarus, 3 Twelfth Street, Wheeling WV 26003. **Tel** (304)232-7620, FAX (304)233-1236. ***Continues in part*** *Atlantic Control States Beverage journal, 0044-9881.*

US/1054-6561
ATLANTIC CONTROL STATES/VIRGINIA BEVERAGE JOURNAL. **VFOAT** Atlantic Control States Virginia Beverage Journal; Beverage Journal; Atlantic Control States Beverage Journal. (19??)-. Periodical. English. mo. $10.00. Arnold Lazarus, 3 Twelfth Street, Wheeling WV 26003. **Tel** (304)232-7620, FAX (304)233-1236. ***Continues in part*** *Atlantic Control States Beverage Journal, 0044-9881.*

US
ATLANTIC CONTROL STATES/WEST VIRGINIA BEVERAGE JOURNAL. (19??)-. Trade Publication. English. Twelve times a year. $12.00. Arnold Lazarus, 3 Twelfth Street, Wheeling WV 26003. **Tel** (304)232-7620, FAX (304)233-1236. **Ad Acc**, **Adv Mgr:** Arnold Lazarus. **Circ:** 7,600.
Desc: Information and news on liquor industry, and also includes list of products and prices.

AT/1033-7954
AUSTRALIAN AND NEW ZEALAND WINE INDUSTRY DIRECTORY. [Aust. N.Z. wine ind. dir.]. (1987)-. Directory. English. an. 60.00Aus$ Australia & New Zealand; 70.00Aus$ other. Winetitles, PO Box 1140, Cowandilla SA, 5033 Australia. **Tel** 011 61 8 2346055, FAX 011 61 8 2346050. **ED** Michael Deves. **DD** 663.20994. **Ad Acc**, **Adv Mgr:** Paul Clancy. **Circ:** 2,500. ***Continues*** *Australian Wine Industry Directory, 0811-1324.*
Desc: Complete listing of all wineries in Australia & New Zealand. Listing of suppliers to wine industry, consultants, personnel, brands, and maps of wine making areas.

AT
AUSTRALIAN AND NEW ZEALAND WINE INDUSTRY JOURNAL. [Aust. N. Z. wine ind. j.]. (1986)-. English. Four times a year. 60.00Aus$ Australia & New Zealand; 90.00Aus$ other. Winetitles, PO Box 1140, Cowandilla SA, 5033 Australia. **Tel** 011 61 8 2346055, FAX 011 61 8 2346050. **ED** Michael Deves. Index available. **Bk Rev**. **Ad Acc**. **Pr Rev. Circ:** 2,500. ***Continues*** *Australian Wine Industry Journal, 0817-427X.*
Desc: Technical articles on winemaking and grapegrowing.
Ind/Abst Agric. Eng. Abstr. (1991-); Crop Physiol. Abstr.; Food Sci. Technol. Abstr.; Hortic. Abstr.; Irr. Drain. Abstr.; Rev. Plant Pathol.

Food and Food Industry —Beverage Industry

AT/0727-3606
AUSTRALIAN GRAPEGROWER AND WINEMAKER. (THE AUSTRALIAN GRAPEGROWER & WINEMAKER : JOURNAL OF THE AUSTRALIAN WINE INDUSTRY.). [Aust. grapegrow. winemak.]. **Added/Corp** Federal Grapegrowers' Council of Australia. **VFOAT** The Australian Grapegrower and Winemaker. (1963)-. Periodical. English. mo. 45.00Aus$ Australia and New Zealand; 48.00Aus$ other. Ryan Publications, 95 Currie Street, Adelaide South Australia 5000 Australia. **Tel** 011 61 8 2316082, FAX 011 61 8 2127504. **ED** John Ryan and Justin Brady. **CODEN** AGWIEC. Index available (annual index in Jan. issue). **Bk Rev. Ad Acc. Circ:** 4,300 (ctrl).
Desc: News related items and specialist articles on viticulture and oenology.
Ind/Abst BioBusiness (1989-); Food Sci. Technol. Abstr.; Vitis Vitic. Enol. Abstr.

AT/1033-6044
AUSTRALIAN LIQUOR TRADER. **Ceased.** (1989)-(1992). English. bm. Winestate Magazine, 254 Franklin Street, Adelaide SA 5000 Australia. **Tel** 011 61 8 2314133, FAX 011 61 8 2312113.

CN/0006-0348
BAR: BEVERAGE ALCOHOL REPORTER. (1949)-. Trade Publication. English. mo (except combined Jan.-Feb. and July-Aug.). 20.00Can$ Canada; $35.00 US; $40.00 other. Clarke Publishing Company Ltd., 26 Bannatyne Drive, Willowdale Ontario M2L 2Y9 Canada. **ED** Patricia Clarke. **Bk Rev. Ad Acc. Circ:** 16,000 (ctrl).
Desc: Trade magazine for the beverage alcohol industry.

CN/0824-1899
BARRIQUE (1984). (LA BARRIQUE.). [Barrique]. Vol. 14, No 4 (1984)-. Periodical. French. Seven times a year. 23.00Can$ Canada; 36.00Can$ other. Kylix Media Inc, 5165 Sherbrooke Street West, Montreal Quebec H4A 1T6 Canada. **Tel** (514)481-5892, FAX (514)481-9699. **ED** Nicole Barrette Ryan. **DD** 663/.1/09714. **Ad Acc. Circ:** 11,000 (ctrl). **Continues** Barrique & Marmite, 0228-5452.
Desc: Covers wine, spirits, and liqueurs.

US/0199-8404
BARTENDER. **VFOAT** Bartender Magazine. (19??)-. Periodical. English. Four times a year (Spring, Summer, Fall and Winter). $25.00. Foley Publ, PO Box 158, Liberty Corner NJ 07938. **Tel** (908)766-6006, FAX (908)766-6607. **ED** Jaclyn W. Foley. **Bk Rev.** (Qty: 15). **Ad Acc, Adv Mgr:** Jamie, **Tel** (908)766-6006. ctrl circ.
Desc: Serves all full-service drinking establishments. Serves single locations including individual restaurants, hotel, motels, bars, taverns, lounges and all other full-service on-premise licensee's.

US/0005-7533
BEBIDAS. [Bebidas]. (1942)-. Academic Scholarly Publication. Spanish. bm (6 issues). $18.00 (one year), $36.00 (two years). International Beverage Publishers, 8575 West 110th Street, Suite 218, Overland Park KS 66210. **Tel** (913) 341-0020, FAX (913) 341-3025. **ED** Floyd E. Sagaser. **CODEN** BBDSDO. **Ad Acc. Pr Rev. Circ:** 8,800 (ctrl). Documents available from CASDDS.
Desc: Covers items of interest to soft drink bottlers, brewers, vintners, and distillers.
Ind/Abst Chem. Abstr.

US
BEER INDUSTRY UPDATE. (19??)-. English. an. $450.00. Beer Marketers Insights, 51 Virginia Avenue, West Nyack NY 10994. **Tel** (914)358-7751, FAX (914)358-7860. **LC** HD9397.U5; B42. **DD** 338.4/766342/0973021.

US/0300-7480
BEER MARKETER'S INSIGHTS. [Beer mark. insights]. **VFOAT** Insights. (1970)-. Trade Publication. English. Twenty-three times a year. $335.00. Beer Marketers Insights, 51 Virginia Avenue, West Nyack NY 10994. **Tel** (914)358-7751, FAX (914)358-7860. **ED** Benjamin Steinman. **DD** 338.
Desc: Covers sale, marketing, legal, social issues concerning beer industry.

US/0738-8799
BEER PAPER, THE. [Beer pap.]. Vol. 1, No 1 (Apr. 24, 1978)-. Periodical. English. Twenty-four times a year (Monday). $85.00. The Beer Paper, 404 East 41st Street, Loveland CO 80538-2314. **Tel** (303)663-4244. **ED** Stan Vlantes. **Circ:** 860 (ctrl).
Desc: US and the international news, comments and features about brewing and marketing trends.

US/0164-4831
BEER STATISTICS NEWS. See Food and Food Industry-Abstracting, Bibliographies and Statistics.

US/0005-7770
BEER WHOLESALER. [Beer wholes.]. (19??)-. Periodical. English. Six times a year (Feb., Apr., June, Aug., Oct., Dec.). $50.00. Beverage Management Associates, 11460 West 44th Avenue, Suite 4, Wheat Ridge CO 80033. **Tel** (303)425-4668. **ED** Kenneth Breslauer. **DD** 338. **Bk Rev. Ad Acc. Circ:** 3,800 (ctrl).

US/0191-5312
BEVARAGE ANALYST. OREGON. [Beverage anal., Or.]. Periodical. English. mo. Bell Publications, 2403 Champa Street, Denver CO 80205. **Tel** (303)296-1600. **ED** Mariette Bell. **DD** 338. **Circ:** 1,898.

US/0191-5347
BEVARAGE ANALYST. WASHINGTON. [Beverage anal., Wash.]. Periodical. English. mo. Bell Publications, 2403 Champa Street, Denver CO 80205. **Tel** (303)296-1600. **ED** Mariette Bell. **DD** 338. **Circ:** 2,255.

●US/1060-9180
BEVERAGE AISLE. [Beverage aisle]. Vol. 1, No. 1 (Jan. 1992)-. Periodical. English. Twelve times a year. $48.00 US; $65.00 others. Keller Publishing Corporation, 150 Great Neck Road, Great Neck NY 11021. **Tel** (516)829-9210, FAX (516)829-5414, telex 221574 KELLE. **LC** WMLC 93/276. **DD** 338.

US/0736-220X
BEVERAGE ALCOHOL MARKET REPORT. **VFOAT** B/A Market Report; BA Market Report. (1982)-. Periodical. English. Twenty-six times a year. $175.00 US; $195.00 other. Perry Luntz, 160 East 48th Street, New York NY 10017. **Tel** (212)371-5237. **ED** Perry Luntz. Index available. **Bk Rev. Ad Acc. Circ:** 3,000.
Desc: Executive newsletter for beer, wine, and spirits producers, importers, marketers, and their distributors and retailers worldwide.

US/0191-5304
BEVERAGE ANALYST. MONTANA. [Beverage anal., Mont.]. Periodical. English. mo. Bell Publications, 2403 Champa Street, Denver CO 80205. **Tel** (303)296-1600. **DD** 338.

CN/0835-0019
BEVERAGE AND TOBACCO PRODUCTS INDUSTRIES. (BEVERAGE AND TOBACCO PRODUCTS INDUSTRIES / STATISTICS CANADA, INDUSTRY DIVISION, CENSUS OF MANUFACTURES SECTION.). [Beverage tob. prod. ind.]. **Added/Corp** Statistics Canada. Census of Manufactures Section. Statistics Canada. Industry Division. Statistics Canada. Annual Survey of Manufactures Section. **VFOAT** Industries des Boissons et du Tabac. (1985)-. English (French). an. 38.00Can$ Canada; $46.00 US; $54.00 other. Statistics Canada, Publications Sales & Services, Main Building Room 1710, Ottawa Ontario K1A 0T6 Canada. **Tel** (613)951-5078, (800)267-6677, FAX (613)951-1584, telex 053-3585. **LC** HD9348.C3; B48. **DD** 338.4/7663/0971/021. **Formed by the union of** Soft Drink Industry, 0833-7497; Tobacco Products Industries, 0300-0249 **and** Alcoholic Beverage Industries, 0319-8871.

US/0148-6187
BEVERAGE INDUSTRY. [Beverage ind.]. Vol. 52, No. 6 (March 1972)-. Periodical. English. mo. $55.00 US; $110.00 other. Stagnito Publishing Company, 1935 Sherner Road, Suite 100, Northbrook IL 60062. **Tel** (708)205-5660, FAX (708)205-5680. **ED** Gary Hemphill. **LC** HD9348.U5. **DD** 338.4/7/6636. **CODEN** BEVIAY. **Circ:** 24,915. available on microfilm and microfiche from University Microfilms International (UMI); available on an online database (files 16,570/Full-Text) from DIALOG. **Continues** Soft Drink Industry.
Desc: For those who manufacture, market and distribute soft-drinks, water, beer, wine, juice and other similar beverages.
Ind/Abst BioBusiness; Bus. Index (1985-); F&S Index Plus Text, Int. [Full Txt.] [Select. Cov.]; Foods Adlibra; Gen. BusinessFile (1985-); Gen. Period. Index (1985-); Infobank (Jan. 1979-); Infomat Int. Bus.; Int. Packag. Abstr.; Mag. Search; Mark. Advert. Ref. Serv. [Full Txt.]; PROMT [Full Txt.]; Stat. Ref. Index; Trade Ind. Index (1981-); Vocat. Search (July 1993-).

US/8755-0717
BEVERAGE INDUSTRY ANNUAL MANUAL. [Beverage ind. ann. man.]. (1973)-. English. an (Sept.). $55.00. Stagnito Publishing Company, 1935 Sherner Road, Suite 100, Northbrook IL 60062. **Tel** (708)205-5660, FAX (708)205-5680. **ED** Gary Hemphill. **LC** HD9348.U5; B63. **DD** 338.4/7663/0973. **Circ:** 8,774. **Continues** Soft Drink Industry Annual Manual.
Ind/Abst Predicasts Forecasts; Stat. Ref. Index.

US
BEVERAGE INDUSTRY NEWS. English. Industry Publications Inc / San Francisco, 703 Market Street, San Francisco CA 94103. **Tel** (415)986-2360.

US/0271-9894
BEVERAGE INDUSTRY NEWS MERCHANDISER. (BEVERAGE INDUSTRY NEWS MERCHANDISER; BIN.). [Beverage ind. news merch.]. **VFOAT** BIN; Merchandiser; BIN Merchandiser. Began Dec. 1970?. Periodical. English. mo. $22.00. BIN Publications Inc, 703 Market Street, San Francisco CA 94103. **DD** 338. **Continues** BIN. Beverage Industry News Merchandiser of Northern California.

US/0279-7070
BEVERAGE MARKET, THE. Periodical. English. mo. Beverage Publishing Corporation, 662 Main Street, New Rochelle NY 10805.

US
BEVERAGE MARKETING DIRECTORY. **Added/Corp** Beverage Marketing Corporation. 13th Ed. (1991)-. Directory. English. an. $695.00 (softcover), $715.00 (hardcover). Beverage Marketing Corporation, 2670 Commercial Avenue, Mingo Junction OH 43938. **Tel** (614)598-4133, FAX (614)598-3977. **Continues** National Beverage Marketing Directory, 0197-3061.

US/0006-0372
BEVERAGE MEDIA. (1977)-. Periodical. English. Twelve times a year. $69.90 metro edition; $34.85 upstate edition. Beverage Media Ltd., 161 Avenue of the Americas, New York NY 10013. **Tel** (212)620-0100.

US/0744-4958
BEVERAGE RETAILER WEEKLY. **Ceased.** [Beverage retail. wkly.]. **VFOAT** Beverage Retailer. ( )-(May 1989). Periodical. English. wk (44 no. a year). Beverage Retailers Weekly, 1661 Route 23 Box 283, Wayne NJ 07470. **DD** 381.

US/0098-2318
BEVERAGE WORLD. [Beverage world]. **VFOAT** Beverage World. Periscope Edition. Vol. 93, No 1214 (Jan. 1975)-. Periodical. English. mo. $39.95 US & Canada; $49.95 other. Keller Publishing Corporation, 150 Great Neck Road, Great Neck NY 11021. **Tel** (516)829-9210, FAX (516)829-5414, telex 221574 KELLE. **ED** Larry Jabbonsky. **LC** TP659.A1; N3. **DD** 338.4/7/6630973. **CODEN** BEWODQ. **[CCC].** Index available. **Bk Rev. Ad Acc. Circ:** 34,000 (ctrl). available on microfilm and microfiche from University Microfilms International (UMI); available on an online database (files 15,648/Full-Text) from DIALOG. Documents available from UMI Article Clearinghouse. **Continues** Soft Drinks, 0038-0571. **Continued in part by** Beverage World (Periscope Ed.), 1064-8909.
Desc: News and information for and about the beverage producing and distributing industries.
Ind/Abst ABI/INFORM Glob. Ed.; ABI Inform Ondisc (January 1991); BioBusiness; Bus. ASAP (1990-) [Full Txt.]; Bus. Index (1985-); Bus. Period. Index; Bus. Source (Jan. 1993-); F&S Index Plus Text, Int. [Select. Cov.]; Foods Adlibra; Gen. BusinessFile (1985-); Gen. Period. Index (1985-); Infomat Int. Bus.; Int. Packag. Abstr.; Mag. Search; Mark. Advert. Ref. Serv.; PAIS Int. Print (1991-?); PROMT; Trade Ind. ASAP [Full Txt.]; Trade Ind. Index (1981-) [Full Txt.]; Vocat. Search (July 1993-); Wilson Bus. Abstr.

US
BEVERAGE WORLD ... DATABANK. (1985/1986)-. English. an. $49.78. Keller Publishing Corporation, 150 Great Neck Road, Great Neck NY 11021. **Tel** (516)829-9210, FAX (516)829-5414, telex 221574 KELLE. **Continues** Beverage World's Daily Desk Reference and Living Directory, 0882-0333.
Ind/Abst Mark. Advert. Ref. Serv.; Trade Ind. Index [Full Txt.].

US
BEVERAGE WORLD INTERNATIONAL. Vol. 1, No. 1 (Apr. 1983)-. Periodical. English (Spanish). Six times a year. $30.00 US; $45.00 other. Keller Publishing Corporation, 150 Great Neck Road, Great Neck NY 11021. **Tel** (516)829-9210, FAX (516)829-5414, telex 221574 KELLE. **ED** Larry Jabbonsky and Jeanne Lukasick. **LC** TP500; .B46. **DD** 663/.05. Index available. cum. index. **Bk Rev. Ad Acc. Circ:** 10,400 (ctrl).
Desc: Content consists of articles and regular departments dedicated to explaining new technological developments which impact upon the international beverage marketplace. Marketing trends and events pertinent to the industry are featured.

US/0409-2945
BEVERAGES. **Ceased.** [Beverages]. Vol. 1 (Dec. 1963)-(19??). Periodical. English. bm. International Beverages Publishers Inc, PO Box 7406, Overland Park KS 66207. **Tel** (913)341-0020, FAX (913)341-3025. **(Subscription address:** 10741 El Monte, Overland Park, KS 66211**) ED** Floyd E Sageser. **DD** 641. **CODEN** BEVEEQ. **Ad Acc. Circ:** 9,000.
Ind/Abst BioBusiness (1989-).

GW/0937-1958
BIER & GETRANKE. [Bier Getranke]. **VFOAT** Bier und Getranke; B & G. Bier & Getranke. (1990)-. Periodical. German. bw (26 issues per year). DM120.00 Germany; DM170.00 other. Verlag Hans Carl GmbH & Co KG, Andernacher Str 33A, D-90411 Nuernberg Germany. **Tel** 011 49 911 952850. **UDC** 33. **Circ:** 9,000.
Desc: Information on the beverage industry.

FR/0366-2284
BIOS (PARIS). (BIOS.). [Bios]. Vol.1 (Jan. 1970)-. Academic Scholarly Publication. French (English). mo. 490.00F France; 650.00F other. Institut Francais Boissons Brasseur, Malterie Bios BP 268, F-54512 Vandoeuvre Cedex France. **Tel** 83 44 25 32, FAX 83 44 12 90, telex 960568F. **ED** Muriel Deymie. **CODEN** BOSSBI. cum. index. **Bk Rev. Ad Acc. Circ:** 3,500.

Documents available from CASDDS. ***Formed by the union of*** *Brasserie* ***and*** *Biotechnique.*
Desc: Covers beer, malt and beverage packaging, processing, marketing and new equipment.
Ind/Abst Chem. Abstr.; Curr. Biotechnol.; Dairy Sci. Abstr.; Food Sci. Technol. Abstr.; PESTDOC.

FR/0760-1999
BOISSONS DE FRANCE, JEAN PRIMUS. (1984)-. Periodical. French. mo. Boissons de France, 49 Rue de la Glaciere, 75013 Paris France. **UDC** 331.88:663.
Ind/Abst Infomat Int. Bus.

CR
BOLETIN DE PROMECAFE. Periodical. Spanish. qt.
Ind/Abst Hortic. Abstr.; Rev. Plant Pathol.

US/1046-543X
BOTTLED WATER REPORTER. [Bottled water report.]. (19??)-. Periodical. English. bm. $40.00 (US & Canada); $75.00 (others). Intl Bottled Water Assn, 113 N Henry Street, Alexandria VA 22314. **Tel** (703)683-5213, FAX (703)683-4074, telex 5106017836, IBWA VA UQ. **ED** Valerie H. Peterson, (703)683-5213. **DD** 338. **Ad Acc.**

GW
BRANNTWEINWIRTSCHAFT, DIE. **Added/Corp** Versuchs- und Lehranstalt fuer Spiritusfabrikation. (19??)-. Periodical. German. Twenty-four times a year. DM240.00 Germany; DM293.00 other. Spiritusfabrikation, Seestrasse 13, D 13353 Berlin Germany. **Tel** 011 49 30 45091, FAX 011 49 30 4536067, telex 841 184403. Index available. **Bk Rev. Ad Acc. Circ:** 3,000.
Desc: Technology and research of alcohol manufacture. Political, economical and legal themes for the management of alcohol, vinegar, and yeast industries.
Ind/Abst Biodeter. Abstr. (1991-); Dairy Sci. Abstr.; Food Sci. Technol. Abstr.; Sug. Indus. Abstr.

GW/0179-2466
BRAUEREI FORUM. [Brau.-Forum]. (1985)-. Periodical. German. Thirty-six times a year. DM185.00 Germany; DM225.00 other. Westkreuz Druckerei und Verlag, Toepchiner Weg 198-200, D-12309 Berlin Germany. **Tel** 011 49 30 7452047, FAX 011 49 30 7453066. **UDC** 663.4. ***Formed by the union of*** *Der Brauer- und Malzer-Lehrling, 0520-7568; Forum der Brauerei, 0723-6891* ***and*** *Tageszeitung fur Brauerei, 0039-8942.*

GW/0172-0589
BRAUEREI-JOURNAL. [Brau.-J.]. (1972)-. Periodical. German. Twenty-one times a year. Dreistern Verlag GmbH, Andreas Hoffer Strasse 1, D 81547 Munich Germany. **Tel** 011 49 89 6970088. **UDC** 663.4 : 338. ***Continues*** *DBB. Der Brauereibesitzer und Braumeister, 0172-0600.*

SZ
BRAUEREI- UND GETRANKE-RUNDSCHAU. **Added/Corp** Versuchsstation Schweizerischer Brauereien. **VFOAT** Brauerei-Rundschau; Revue de la Brasserie et des Boisons. Vol. 102, No. 1/2 (Jan./Feb. 1991)-. Periodical. German. mo. 188.00F. Versuchsstation Schweizerischer Brauereien, Ute Luttgen, Bahnhofplatz 9 Postfach, CH 8023 Zurich Switzerland. Documents available from CASDDS. ***Continues*** *Brauerei-Rundschau mit Allgemeiner Getranke-Rundschau.*
Ind/Abst Chem. Abstr.

GW
BRAUEREIEN UND MALZEREIEN IN EUROPA. **VFOAT** Brasseries et Malteries en Europe; Breweries and Malteries in Europe. (1962/1963)-. German (French and English). an. DM360.00. Verlag Hoppenstedt & Company, Postfach 100139, D 64201 Darmstadt Germany. **Tel** 011 49 6151 380436. **LC** TP572; .B7. **DD** 338.4/7/66330254. ***Continues*** *Brauerein und Malzereien.*

GW/0341-7115
BRAUINDUSTRIE. **VFOAT** Der Brauer und Malzer. (1976)-. Academic Scholarly Publication. German (English). mo. DM88.00 Germany; DM112.00 other. Verlag W Sachon, Postfach 325, Schloss Mindelheim, D-8948 Mindelheim Germany. **Tel** 49 8261 9990, FAX 49 8261 999132. **ED** Verlag Sachon. **CODEN** BRINDA. Index available. cum. index. **Ad Acc. Circ:** 7,000 (ctrl). Documents available from CASDDS. ***Continues*** *Brauer und Malzer, 0045-2718.*
Desc: Marketing, technic, technology, packaging, logistics in the brewing industry.
Ind/Abst Chem. Abstr.

GW/0934-9340
BRAUWELT INTERNATIONAL. [Brauwelt int.]. (1983)-. English. qt. DM112.00. Verlag Hans Carl GmbH & Company KG, Andernacher Strasse 33A, D 90411 Nuernberg Germany. **Tel** 011 49 911 952850. **LC** HD9397.A1; B72. **DD** 338.4/76633/05. **CODEN** BRINEB. **Bk Rev. Ad Acc. Circ:** 6,210.
Desc: Publishes original articles of authors of science, research and practical work as well as of the specialized beverage and allied industries: technics, technology, raw materials, and market.
Ind/Abst BioBusiness; Food Sci. Technol. Abstr.

NE
BREW INFO MONTHLY INDUSTRY REVIEW. (19??)-. English. mo. Fl400.00. European Brewery Convention, PO Box 510, 2380 BB Zoeterwoude Netherlands. **Tel** 011 31 71 456047, FAX 011 31 71 410013, telex 39390.
Desc: Contains the most recent published references on brewing and related topics.

UK/0006-9736
BREWER (LONDON). (THE BREWER.). [Brewer]. **Added/Corp** Incorporated Brewer's Guild. Vol. 57 No. 675 (Jan. 1971)-. Academic Scholarly Publication. English. Twelve times a year. £53.00 UK; £63.00 other. Brewers Guild Publications, 8 Ely Place Holborn, London EC1N 6SD England. **Tel** 011 44 71 4054565, FAX 011 44 71 8314995. **ED** Judy Simpson. **CODEN** BREWDH. Index available. cum. index. **Bk Rev. Ad Acc. Circ:** 2,500 (ctrl). Documents available from CASDDS. ***Continues*** *Brewer's Guild Journal, 0366-2764.*
Desc: This journal is about the decisions on the choice of plant and material for breweries.
Ind/Abst BioBusiness (-1983)(1989-); Chem. Abstr. (-1983); Food Sci. Technol. Abstr.; Int. Packag. Abstr.; Plant Breed. Abstr. (1989-).

US
BREWERS' ALMANAC. **Added/Corp** United States Brewers' Association. United States Brewers Foundation. Beer Institute. **VFOAT** Brewing Industry in the United States; Centennial Issue. (1940)-. English. an (Oct.). $140.00. The Beer Institute, 1225 I Street, Suite 825, Washington DC 20005. **Tel** (202)737-2337. **LC** HD9397.U5; B7. **DD** 338.476633.

US/0006-9701
BREWERS BULLETIN, THE. (1907)-. Bulletin. English. sw (104 issues). $45.00. Brewers Bulletin, PO Box 677, Thiensville WI 53092. **Tel** (414)242-6105. **ED** Marge Jones. **Bk Rev. Ad Acc. Circ:** 1,000.
Desc: An international trade publication for brewing industry. It features articles on brewing personalities, facilities and equipment.

US/0006-971X
BREWER'S DIGEST, THE. [Brew. dig.]. Vol. 13, No. 1 (Dec. 1937)-. Academic Scholarly Publication. English. mo (12 issues per year). $25.00 US; $40.00 other. Siebel Publishing Company, 4049 West Peterson Avenue, Chicago IL 60646. **Tel** (312)463-3400. **LC** TP500; .B82. **DD** 663. **CODEN** BRDGAT. Documents available from CASDDS. ***Continues*** *Brewer's Technical Review, 0096-6606.*
Ind/Abst AGRICOLA; Chem. Abstr.; Curr. Biotechnol.; Food Sci. Technol. Abstr.; Int. Aerosp. Abstr.; Int. Packag. Abstr.; Life Sci. Collect.

US
BREWER'S DIGEST. BUYERS' GUIDE & DIRECTORY, THE. **VFOAT** Brewer's Digest. Buyers' Guide and Brewery Directory; Brewer's Digest. Buyers' Guide and Directory. (1962)-. Consumer Publication. English. an. Siebel Publishing Company, 4049 West Peterson Avenue, Chicago IL 60646. **Tel** (312)463-3400. **LC** TP572; .B78. ***Continues*** *Brewer's Digest. Annual Buyers' Guide & Directory.*

UK/0006-9728
BREWERS' GUARDIAN. [Brew. guard.]. (19??)-. Periodical. English. Twelve times a year. £38.00 UK, £58.00 surface mail; £72.00 airmail. Hampton Publishing Limited, 10 Belgrade Roadhampton, Middlesex TW12 2 AZ England. **Tel** 011 44 81 941 7750. **ED** Hazel Thompson. **LC** TP500; .B785. **DD** 663/.3/05. **Bk Rev. Ad Acc. Circ:** 3,000 (ctrl). available on microfilm from University Microfilms International (UMI). ***Continues*** *Brewer & Wine Merchant & Brewers' Guardian;* ***Absorbed*** *International Brewer & Distiller.*
Desc: In-depth coverage of every aspect of the United Kingdom brewing industry.
Ind/Abst Food Sci. Technol. Abstr.; Int. Packag. Abstr.

GW
BREWING AND BEVERAGE INDUSTRY INTERNATIONAL. **VFOAT** Industrie Internationale de la Biere et des Boissons; BBII. (1989)-. Academic Scholarly Publication. English (French). sa. DM12.00 per issue (plus postage). Verlag W Sachon, Postfach 325, Schloss Mindelheim, D-8948 Mindelheim Germany. **Tel** 49 8261 9990, FAX 49 8261 999132. **CODEN** BBIIEK. Documents available from CASDDS.
Ind/Abst Chem. Abstr.

UK/0308-1265
BREWING & DISTILLING INTERNATIONAL. [Brew. distill. int.]. Vol. 4 (Jan. 1974)-. Periodical. English (French and German). mo. £40.00 UK; £70.00 other. Brewery Traders Publications Ltd, Burton Road, Branston Burton Upon Trent, Staffs DE14 3DP England. **Tel** 44 283 66784, FAX 44 283 510674, telex 334419. **ED** Bruce Stevens (editor's address: 52 Glenhouse Road, Eltham London SE9 1JQ England; editor's phone: 44 81 8594300). **DD** 663. **CODEN** BDINDE. **Ad Acc, Adv Mgr:** Kath Adkin, **Tel** 44 283 66784. **Circ:** 4,000 (ctrl). ***Continues*** *International Brewing & Distilling.*
Desc: News and technical features on production and marketing of beer, spirits and soft drinks.
Ind/Abst Food Sci. Technol. Abstr.; Infomat Int. Bus.; Int. Packag. Abstr.

US/0273-5768
BREWING INDUSTRY NEWS, THE. [Brew. ind. news]. (1979)-. Periodical. English. sm. $65.00. Brewing Industry News, PO Box 27037, Riverdale IL 60627. **Tel** (312)841-1639. **ED** James J. Shannon. **Bk Rev. Ad Acc. Circ:** 800.
Desc: General news pertaining to brewers, wholesalers and allied industry members, strong on political and legislative issues as they pertain to industry.

DK/0007-2737
BRYGMESTEREN. (BRYGMESTEREN. SCANDINAVIAN BREWERS' REVIEW.). [Brygmesteren]. **Added/Corp** Dansk Brygmester Forening. Norsk Bryggerlaug. Sveriges Bryggmastare Forening. **VFOAT** Scandinavian Brewers' Review. Vol. 34, No. 1 (Jan. 1977)-. Academic Scholarly Publication. Danish (English; summaries and/or abstracts in English). bm. kr210.00. Dansk Brygmesterforening, Strandvejen 50, DK 2900 Hellerup Denmark. **ED** S Kledal. **CODEN** BRYGAW. **Bk Rev. Ad Acc. Circ:** 1,000 (ctrl). Documents available from CASDDS.
Desc: Covers the processing of beer and soft drinks, raw materials, equipment, quality control, research, logistics, personnel and statistics.
Ind/Abst Chem. Abstr. (-1988); Food Sci. Technol. Abstr.

JA/0521-7237
BULLETIN OF BREWING SCIENCE. ***Ceased.*** Vol. 1 (1955)-Ceased Vol.28. Academic Scholarly Publication. English (German and Japanese). The Brewing Science Research Institute, Mita 141 Meguro-Ku, Tokyo Japan. **CODEN** BBRSAN. Documents available from CASDDS.
Ind/Abst Chem. Abstr.; Food Sci. Technol. Abstr.; Plant Breed. Abstr.; Vitis Vitic. Enol. Abstr.

US/1056-280X
BUYERS GUIDE - NATIONAL SOFT DRINK ASSOCIATION. (BUYERS GUIDE.). [Buy. guide - Natl. Soft Drink Assoc.]. **Added/Corp** National Soft Drink Association. (1991)-. English. National Soft Drink Association, 1101 16th Street NW, Washington DC 20036. **Tel** (202)833-2450. **LC** HD9349.S633; U625. **DD** 681/.7664.

IV
CAFE D'AFRIQUE / ORGANISATION INTERAFRICAINE DU CAFE. **Added/Corp** Interafrican Coffee Organisation. **VFOAT** African Coffee. (198?)-. Periodical. English (French). qt. $30.00 Africa; $40.00 Europe; $50.00 other. Interafrican Coffee Organisation, PO Box V210, Abidjan Ivory Coast. **Tel** 011 225 216131, 011 225 216185. **LC** HD9199.A35; C33. **DD** 338.1/7373/096.
Desc: Information on the coffee trade.

BL
CAFE: RESULTADOS OBTIDOS. **Main/Corp** Instituto Brasileiro do Cafe. (19??)-. Portuguese. Ministerio da Industria e do Comercio / Instituto Brasileiro do Cafe, Assessoria de Relacoes Publicas, 129 - 90 Andar, Rio de Janeiro Brazil. **LC** HD9199.B69; I52b.

●GT
CAFETAL: REVISTA BIMESTRAL DE ANACAFE. **Added/Corp** Asociacion Nacional del Cafe (Guatemala). (1992)-. Periodical. Spanish. bm. Asociacion Nacional del Cafe, Edificio Etisa, Plazuela Espana,, Zona 9, Guatemala City, Guatemala. **Tel** 011 502 2 367487. **ED** Byron Dardon. **Ad Acc. Circ:** 5,000. available with charts; available with illustrations. ***Continues*** *Revista Cafetalera.*

US/0194-0406
CALIFORNIA GOLD BOOK. **VFOAT** Bin California Gold Book. 1969-. English. an. Leroy W Page, San Francisco Office, Central Tower Building, San Francisco CA 94103. **LC** HD9350.1; B4. **DD** 338.4/7/663109794. ***Continues*** *Beverage Industry News. California Yearbook.*

US/0273-8961
CALIFORNIA GRAPEVINE. (19??)-. Periodical. English. bm (6 issues). $30.00 US; $34.00 Canada and Mexico; $40.00 other. California Grapevine, PO Box 22152, San Diego CA 92122. **Tel** (619)457-4818.

US/0731-9436
CALIFORNIA WINE MERCHANT'S GAZETTE & COLLECTOR'S INDEX. [Calif. wine merch. gaz. collect. index]. **VFOAT** California Wine Merchant's Gazette; California Wine Merchant's Gazette and Collector's Index. Vol. 1, No. 1 (Jan. 1982)-. Periodical. English. mo. $48.00. Evento-Gamina Publications, PO Box 77291, San Francisco CA 94107. **Tel** (510)285-7333. **ED** Ed Everett and John Gay.

US
CALIFORNIA WINE PURCHASING GUIDE. English. $12.95. The California Wine Experience Inc, PO Box 530, La Canada CA 91011. **LC** TP557; .C34. **DD** 641.2/22/09794.

US
CALIFORNIA WINE REPORT / UNITED STATES DEPARTMENT OF AGRICULTURE, AGRICULTURAL MARKETING SERVICE, FRUIT AND VEGETABLE MARKET NEWS SERVICE. ***Ceased.*** (19??)-(Dec. 1992). English. wk. California Wine Report, 630 Sansome Street, Room 727, San Francisco CA 94111. **Tel** (415)516-5587.

US/0883-4423
CALIFORNIA WINE WINNERS. (19??)-. English. an. $7.00 North America; $10.00 other. Varietal Fair, 4022 Harrison Grade Road, Sebastopol CA 95472. **Tel** (707)874-3105. **ED** Compiled by: Trudy Ahlstrom and J.T. Devine. **LC** TP557; .C35. **DD** 641.2/22/09794. **Circ:** 4,000.
Desc: Annual compilation of awards given in California state wine competitions each year.

UK/0260-7352
CANADEAN WORLD NEW PRODUCTS. **See** Food and Food Industry.

SP/0210-5543
CARNICA 2000. [Carnica 2000]. **VFOAT** Carnica Dos Mil. (1973)-. Periodical. Spanish. mo (10 issues). 11500.00ptas Spain; 21500.00ptas other. Pub. Tecnicas Alimentarias S A, Triana 52 Bajo IZQ, 28016 Madrid Spain. **Tel** 011 34 1 3505319 OR 3595798. **UDC** 664.9.

BE/0778-2640
CEREVISIA AND BIOTECHNOLOGY. [Cerevisia biotechnol.]. **Added/Corp** Associations d'Anciens Etudiants des Ecoles de Brasserie Belges. Vol. 16 No. 1 (1991)-. Periodical. French (Dutch and English). Four times a year. F2100 Belgium; F2500 others. S C Cepia, Groene Dreef 11, 9830 Sint Marten Latem Belgium. **Tel** 011 32 91 825695. **NLM** W1; CE585H. **CODEN** CERBE8. Documents available from CASDDS. ***Formed by the union of*** *Cerevisia, 0770-1713* ***and*** *Belgian Journal of Food Chemistry and Biotechnology, 0773-6177.*
Ind/Abst BioBusiness (1991-); Chem. Abstr.

SP/0300-4481
CERVEZA Y MALTA. **Added/Corp** Asociacion Espanola de Tecnicos de Cerveza y Malta. (1964)-. Periodical. Spanish. qt. $74.00 Spain; $100.00 other. Cerveza y Malta, Bustamente 21 Bajo, 28045 Madrid Spain. **Tel** 34 1 5277255. **CODEN** CEMADD. Documents available from CASDDS.
Ind/Abst Chem. Abstr.

FR
CHAMPAGNE VITICOLE, LA. (19??)-. French. mo. La Champagne Viticole, BP 325, 51334 Eperway Cedex France. **Tel** 2651 0444, FAX 26 54 97 27, telex 842753. **Ad Acc, Adv Mgr:** Blaques Jawes. Full Page (B&W) 3000.00F. Half Page (B&W) 1500.00F.

KO
CHILLO. Periodical. Korean. qt. Chusik Hoesa Chillo, 170-8 Singil-dong Yongdungpo-ku, Seoul 150 Korea. **LC** HD9366.K64; C473.

US/8756-2286
CHRONICLE / SOCIETY OF WINE EDUCATORS. [Soc. wine educ. chron.]. **Added/Corp** Society of Wine Educators (U.S.). **VFOAT** Wine Educators Chronicle. (19??)-. Periodical. English. qt. Comes with the Society of Wine Educators membership. Society of Wine Educators, 132 Shaker Road, Suite 14, East Longmeadow MA 01028. **Tel** (413)567-8272. **LC** TP544; .C48. **DD** 641.

KO
CHURYU KONGOP. Periodical. Korean. sa. Taehan Churyu Kongop Hyophoe, 1-499 Youido-dong Yongdungpo-ku, Seoul Korea. **LC** HD9366.K6; C47.

IT/0390-1572
CIVILITA DEL BERE. [Civ. bere]. (1974)-. Periodical. Italian. mo (11 issues). L72000.00 Italy; L110000.00 Europe; L130000.00 North & South America, Asia and Africa; L135000.00 Australia & New Zealand. Editoriale Lariana Spa, Via G Gallina 8, 20129 Milan Italy. **Tel** 011 39 2 76110206, FAX 011 39 2 713847. **UDC** 663.

IT/0393-4926
CODICE ENOLOGICO. [Codice enol.]. (1984)-. Periodical. Italian. qt. L436800. Branka Publisher SRL, C So Caribaldi 50, 12042 BRA / CN Italy. **Tel** 011 39 172 422971. **UDC** 663.2:34.

UK/0262-5938
COFFEE & COCOA INTERNATIONAL. [Coffee cocoa int.]. **VFOAT** Coffee And Cocoa International. (19??)-. Periodical. English (summaries and/or abstracts in French, German, Portuguese and Spanish). bm. £77.00 UK; £93.00, $170.00 other. Argus Press Group, Queensway House, 2 Queensway Redhill, Surrey RH1 1QS England. **Tel** 011 44 737 768611, 011 44 737 761685, FAX 011 44 737 760510, telex 948669 TOPJNL G. **ED** Michael Segal. **LC** HD9199.A1; C64. **DD** 382/.41373/05. **CODEN** COCIEO. **Bk Rev. Ad Acc. Circ:** 5,000 (ctrl). ***Continues*** *Coffee International, 0309-331X.*
Desc: The number one international business journal dealing with the coffee and cocoa trades world wide. Gives in-depth coverage to the news and views affecting both major commodities.
Ind/Abst BioBusiness (1988-); Food Sci. Technol. Abstr.

UK/0309-331X
COFFEE INTERNATIONAL. ***Title Change.*** [Coffee int.]. (19??)-(19??). Periodical. English (summaries and/or abstracts in French, German, Portuguese and Spanish). an. Argus Press Group, Queensway House, 2 Queensway Redhill, Surrey RH1 1QS England. **Tel** 011 44 737 768611, 011 44 737 761685, FAX 011 44 737 760510, telex 948669 TOPJNL G. **LC** HD9199.A1; C64. **DD** 382/.41/37305. ***Continued by*** *Coffee & Cocoa International, 0262-5938.*

UK
COFFEE INTERNATIONAL DIRECTORY : CID. **VFOAT** CID. (19??)-. Directory. English. an. £97 UK; £107.00, $189.00 other. Argus Press Group, Queensway House, 2 Queensway Redhill, Surrey RH1 1QS England. **Tel** 011 44 737 768611, 011 44 737 761685, FAX 011 44 737 760510, telex 948669 TOPJNL G.

SZ
COLLOQUE SCIENTIFIQUE INTERNATIONAL SUR LE CAFE : [PROCEEDINGS]. **See** Agriculture.

US/0010-1516
COLORADO BEVERAGE ANALYST. **VFOAT** Beverage Analyst. Periodical. English. mo. Bell Publications, 2403 Champa Street, Denver CO 80205. **Tel** (303)296-1600. **ED** Mariette Bell. **Circ:** 3,200.

GW/0177-7440
CONFRUCTA. ***Ceased.*** Vol. 21, No. 1/2 (Feb./April 1976)-(1992). Periodical. Multiple languages (English and German). bm. Verlag Fluessiges Obst GmbH, Diezer Str 7, Postfach 1, 5429 Schoenborn Germany. **ED** Philipp Possmann. ***Absorbed*** *Fruchtsaft-Industrie.*
Ind/Abst AGRICOLA; Vitis Vitic. Enol. Abstr.

US/0744-1843
CONNECTICUT BEVERAGE JOURNAL. (1944)-. Periodical. English. Twelve times a year. $17.00. Beverage Publications Inc, PO Box 5157, 2508 Whitney Avenue, Hamden CT 06518. **Tel** (203)288-3375, FAX (203)288-2693. **ED** Gerald P. Slone. **Ad Acc. Circ:** 6,850. ***Continues*** *Connecticut Beverage Journal and Blue Book, 0191-8818.*
Desc: Classified ads, news in the liquor industry and tax reports. All types of advertising.

US/0161-6668
CONNOISSEURS' GUIDE TO CALIFORNIA WINE. [Connoiss. guide Calif. wine]. (1974)-. Periodical. English. mo. $42.00 US & Canada & Mexico; $67.00 other. Connisseurs Guide to California Wines, PO Box V, Alameda CA 94501. **Tel** (415)865-3150. **ED** Charles E. Olken and Earl G. Singer. **DD** 663. Index available. **Circ:** 12,000.
Desc: Newsletter featuring tasting notes and reviews of California premium wines.

CN/0705-4319
CONTROL AND SALE OF ALCOHOLIC BEVERAGES IN CANADA, THE. ***Suspended.*** [Control sale alcohol. beverages Can.]. **Main/Corp** Statistics Canada. Provincial Government Section. **VFOAT** Controle et la Vente des Boissons Alcooliques au Canada. (1943)-. Periodical. English (French). an. For further information on current data still available, please contact Tom Capland (613)951-0885 or Patti Phillips (613)951-0767. Statistics Canada, Publications Sales & Services, Main Building Room 1710, Ottawa Ontario K1A 0T6 Canada. **Tel** (613)951-5078, (800)267-6677, FAX (613)951-1584, telex 053-3585. **LC** HD9364.C3; A3. **DD** 338.4/76631/0971. ***Continues*** *Control and Sale of Alcoholic Beverages in Canada.*
Desc: Presents historical tables of government revenue from the control, sales and taxation of alcoholic beverages. Contains data on the sale of beverages by volume and by value, by type, by province and per capita, on warehousing transactions, imports, exports and retail sales by nongovernment outlets, as well as balance sheet information of provincial liquor boards and commissions.

FR/0337-8810
CUISINE ET VINS DE FRANCE (1975). (CUISINE ET VINS DE FRANCE.). [Cuis. vins Fr.]. **VFOAT** CVF. **VAT** Cuisine & Vins de France. (1947)-. Periodical. French. Twelve times a year. 290.00F France; 390.80F others. Societe Marie-Claire, 11 Bis rue Boissy d'Anglas, F-75008 Paris France. **Tel** 011 33 1 42668888.

BL
CUSTOS DE PRODUCAO E PERSPECTIVAS DA AGROINDUSTRIA DO ACUCAR E DO ALCOOL. **Main/Corp** Cooperativa Central dos Produtores de Acucar e Alcool do Estado de Sao Paulo. Divisoa Economica. (19??)-. Portuguese. **LC** HD9114.B7; S34.

UK/0954-4240
DECANTER (LONDON. 1985). (DECANTER.). [Decanter]. (198?)-. Periodical. English. mo. $80.00 (US); $90.00 (Canada & Mexico); £33.00 (UK); £45.00 (Europe); £59.00 (other). Decanter Magazine Ltd, Priority House, 8 Battersea Park, London SW8 4BG England. **Tel** 44 71 627 8181, FAX 71-738 8688. **(Subscription address:** North America/ 2323 Randolph Ave, Avenel, NJ 07001, Tel. (800)688-6247; Uk/ 1st Floor, Stephenson House, Brunel Centre, Bletchley, Milton Keynes MKZ ZEW England**)** Index available (bound in Dec. issue). **Bk Rev. Ad Acc, Adv Mgr:** John Cullimore. **Circ:** 35,000. ***Continues*** *Decanter Magazine, 0141-6014.*

GW
DEUTSCHE WEINBAU, DER. (1921)-. Periodical. German. Three times a year. DM120.20. Fachverlag Dr Fraund GmbH, Postfach 1329, D 61364 Friedrichsdorf Germany. **Tel** 011 49 6172 71060. **UDC** 634.8(430.1). **Ad Acc. Circ:** 11,273 (ctrl).
Desc: Wine-economy, wine marketing policy, wine rights, every subject of wine growing, cellar economy, and wine marketing.
Ind/Abst Leis. Recreat. Tour. Abstr.; Rural Dev. Abstr.; World Agric. Econ.

GW/0012-0979
DEUTSCHE WEINBAU. ***Title Change.*** (DER DEUTSCHE WEINBAU : ORGAN DES DEUTSCHEN WEINBAUVERBANDES.). [Dtsch. Weinb.]. **Added/Corp** Deutscher Weinbauverband. (1952)-(1992). Academic Scholarly Publication. German. tm. Deutscher Weinwirtschaftsverlag Meininger GmbH & Company KG, Maximillianstr 7-17, Postfach 312, W-6730 Neustadt an Der Weinstrasse Germany. ***Continues*** *Weinbau, 0342-5924.* ***Continued by*** *Deutsche Weinmagazin, 0943-089X.*
Ind/Abst EMBASE.

UK
DI, DRINKS INTERNATIONAL. **VFOAT** Drinks International. (19??)-. Periodical. English. Ten times a year. $135.00. Reed Business Publishing / West Sussex, England, Perrymount Road, Haywards Heath, West Sussex RH16 3DH England. **Tel** 011 44 81 6523500. **LC** HD9390.A1; D18. **DD** 382/.45/6631.
Ind/Abst Infomat Int. Bus.

US/0278-050X
DIRECTORY OF MEMBERS - NATIONAL SOFT DRINK ASSOCIATION. (DIRECTORY OF MEMBERS.). **Main/Corp** National Soft Drink Association. (1980)-. Directory. English. an. $15.00. National Soft Drink Association, 1101 16th Street NW, Washington DC 20036. **Tel** (202)833-2450. **LC** HD9348.U5; N37b. **DD** 338.4/766362/06073. ***Continues*** *National Soft Drink Association. Directory of Members and Services, 0190-0587.*

US/0162-5993
DISCUS NEWS LETTER. (DISCUS NEWSLETTER.). **Main/Corp** Distilled Spirits Council of the U.S. **Added/Corp** Distilled Spirits Council of the U.S. Newsletter. **VFOAT** News Letter - Distilled Spirits Council of the U.S.; Newsletter - Distilled Spirits Council of the United States. **VAT** Distilled Spirits Council of the United States News Letter. (1974)-. Periodical. English. mo (summer months combined). Distilled Spirits Council of the United States, 1250 Eye Street Northwest, Suite 900, Washington DC 20005. **Tel** (202)628-3544. ***Supersedes*** *Licensed Beverage Industries Newsletter.*

UK/0966-4661
DRINKS FILE. [Drinks file]. (1991)-. Trade Publication. English. sm (24 issues). £395.00. ERC Publications, Lanwades House, Moulton Road, Kennett, Newmarket, Suffolk CB8 7PW England. **Tel** 011 44 638 552113, FAX 011 44 638 552109. **ED** Fiona Dyer. **DD** 338.76412. Index available. cum. index. Documents available from BLDSC.

US/0735-6145
ECONOMIC RESEARCH REPORT (SAN FRANCISCO, CALIF.). (ECONOMIC RESEARCH REPORT / WINE INSTITUTE.). **Added/Corp** California. Wine Advisory Board. Wine Institute (San Francisco, Calif.). No. 1 (1967)-. English. ir. **LC** HD9377.C2; W5. **DD** 338.4/7/6632009794.

CN/0705-6761
EMBOUTEILLEUR QUEBECOIS, L'. **Added/Corp** Association des Embouteilleurs de Boissons Gazeuses du Quebec. Vol. 1, (Jan. 1978)-. Periodical. French. qt. Free. L'Association des Embouteilleurs de Boissons Gazeuses du Quebec, 1080 Cote de Beaver Hall/Bureau 904, Montreal Quebec H2Z 1S8 Canada. **DD** 663.62/05. ctrl circ.

Food and Food Industry — Beverage Industry

CN/0705-8578
EMBOUTEILLEUR QUEBECOIS (EDITION ANGLAISE). (L'EMBOUTEILLEUR QUEBECOIS.). V. 1, No. 3- July 1978-. Periodical. English. qt. Quebec Soft-Drink Bottlers Association, 904 - 1080 Cote du Beaver Hall, Montreal Quebec H2Z 1S8 Canada. **DD** 338.4/7/6636209714. *Continues Quebec Bottler, 0707-4972.*

IT
ENOTRIA. **Added/Corp** Unione Italiana Vini. No. 1 (May 8, 1972)-. Periodical. Italian. an. comes with Il Corriere Vinicolo. Unione Italiana Vinicolo, Via S Vittore Al Teatro 8, 20123 Milan Italy. **Tel** 011 39 2 801595.

GW/0342-2232
ERFRISCHUNGSGETRANK, DAS. **VFOAT** Mineralwasser-Zeitung (1968). (1968)-. Periodical. German. bw. DM273.60. Hugo Matthaes Druckerei Verlag, Postfach 103144, W-7000 Stuttgart 10 Germany. **Tel** 011 49 711 21331. **ED** A. M. Mattlaes. **UDC** 663.64. Index available. **Bk Rev**. **Ad Acc**. **Circ**: 3,300 (ctrl).

GW
ERNAHRUNGSWIRTSCHAFT. *Title Change.* See Food and Food Industry.

GW/0179-8812
EW. ERNAHRUNGSWIRTSCHAFT. See Food and Food Industry.

US/1040-7537
F & B MARKETPLACE. See Business-Marketing.

US/1055-8993
F. PAUL PACULT'S SPIRIT JOURNAL. [F Paul Pacult's spirit j.]. **VFOAT** Spirit Journal. Vol. 1, Issue 1 (Feb. 1991)-. Periodical. English. bm. $49.00. F Paul Pacult's Spirit Journal, PO Box 218, Lake Ariel PA 18436. **DD** 641.

UK/0957-7041
FERMENT (LONDON). (FERMENT.). [Ferment]. **Added/Corp** Institute of Brewing (Great Britain). (Feb. 1988)-. Periodical. English. bm £105.00. Institute of Brewing, 33 Clarges Street, London W1Y 8EE England. **Tel** 11 44 71 499 8144, **FAX** 11 44 71 499 1156. **ED** J S Pierce, Northwoods, Inner Ting Tong, Budleigh Sacterton, Devon EX9 7AP. **LC** TP500; .F47. **DD** 663/.13/05. **CODEN** FEREEG. **Ad Acc, Adv Mgr:** F. Bolton. **Circ:** 500 (ctrl). Documents available from BIOSIS Document Express. *Continues Newsletter.*
Desc: A learned journal of the brewing, fermentation, and distilling industry.
Ind/Abst BioBusiness (1990-); Biol. Abstr.; Curr. Biotechnol.; Food Sci. Technol. Abstr.

CN/0709-4531
FINANCIAL STATEMENTS / BRITISH COLUMBIA LIQUOR DISTRIBUTION BRANCH. **Main/Corp** British Columbia. Liquor Distribution Branch. Fiscal Year ended Mar. 31, 1978-. English. an. **LC** HV5309.B7; B74A. **DD** 354.7110076/1.

US/0891-0774
FINIGAN WINE LETTER, THE. [Finigan wine lett.]. Vol. 1, No. 1 (August 1986)-. Periodical. English. bm. $45.00 (one year), $75.00 (two year), $105.00 (three year). Winecom Inc, 2040 Polk Street/Suite 344, San Francisco CA 94109. **Tel** (415)474-3064. **DD** 641.
Desc: Nationally distributed critical review of domestic and imported wine.

GW/0015-4539
FLUSSIGES OBST. See Food and Food Industry.

US/0731-3799
FOOD & BEVERAGE MARKETING. See Food and Food Industry.

FI/0780-6655
FOUNDATION FOR BIOTECHNICAL AND INDUSTRIAL FERMENTATION RESEARCH. [Found. Biotech. Ind. Ferment. Res.]. **Added/Corp** Foundation for Biotechnical and Industrial Fermentation Research. **VFOAT** Stiftelsen for Bioteknisk och Jasningsindustriell Forskning. Vol. 1 (1983)-. Monographic series. English (Norwegian). **CODEN** FBIREN. Documents available from BIOSIS Document Express, CASDDS.
Ind/Abst Biol. Abstr.; Chem. Abstr.

US/0364-9474
FRIENDS OF WINE, THE. [Friends wine]. V. 12, No. 4- July/Aug. 1975-. Periodical. English. bm. $18.00. Les Amis du Vin, International Wine Association, 2302 Perkin Place, Silver Spring MD 20910. **Tel** (301)588-0980. **ED** Ron Fonte. **LC** TP544; .A4823. **DD** 641.2/2/05. available on microfilm from University Microfilms International (UMI). *Continues Amis du Vin, 0364-9482.*
Desc: Magazine of Les Amis du Vin Society for the appreciation of fine wine through a program of continuing education by renowned wine experts.
Ind/Abst Consum. Index Prod. Eval. Inf. Source.

CN/0832-2589
FUT / BREWERS ASSOCIATION OF CANADA / L'ASSOCIATION DES BRASSEURS DU CANADA, EN. [En f„ut]. **Added/Corp** Association des Brasseries du Canada. Vol. 1, No 2 (Oct. 1986)-. Periodical. French. qt. Free. Brewers Association of Canada, International Survey, Suite 1200, 155 Queen Street, Ottawa ONT K1P 6L1 Canada. **Tel** (613)232-9601, **FAX** (613)232-2283, telex 053-4370. **DD** 338.4/76633/0971. *Continues On Tap. Francais., 0832-2570.*

GW
GERMAN WINE REVIEW : THE GERMAN WINE & BEVERAGE MAGAZINE. *Ceased.* (19??)-(1993). German (English). sa. Verlag & Druckerei Meininger GmbH, Postfach 100762, D 67407 Neustadt Wein Germany. **Tel** 011 49 6321 890830.

GW
GETRANKETECHNIK. (Nov. 1984)-. Periodical. German. bm. DM68.50. Verlag Hans Carl GmbH & Co Kg, Andernacher Str 33A, PF 990153, W-8500 Nuernberg 10 Germany. **Tel** 011 49 911 952850. **CODEN** GTMAER. **Circ:** 7,500.

US/0742-7700
GRAPPA. *Suspended.* [GRAPPA]. (19??)-Suspended. Periodical. English. qt. $20.00. Grappa, Dept A, PO Box 221127, Carmel CA 93922. **Tel** (408)649-8727. **LC** TP557; .G73. **DD** 663/.2/009794.

CN/0823-6682
GUIDE DU VIN, LE. [Guide vin]. French. an. $8.95 per vol. Guide du Vin, 7 rue St-Jacques, Montreal Quebec H2Y 1K9 Canada. **DD** 641.2/22/05.

●CN/1191-1522
GUIDE EXPRESS DES VINS. (LE GUIDE EXPRESS DES VINS.). [Guide express vins]. (1992)-. French. 17.95Can$. XYZ Editeur, Bureau 201, 815 Est, Rue Ontario Montreal, Quebec H2L 1P1. **DD** 641.2.

FR
GUIDE HACHETTE DES VINS DE FRANCE. **VFOAT** Guide Hachette ... des Vins. French. **LC** TP553; .G85. **DD** 641.2/22/0944.

US/0191-7838
GUIDE TO VINTAGE WINE PRICES. 1979/80-. English. Warner Books Inc, 666 Fifth Avenue, New York NY 10103. **LC** HD9371; .A18. **DD** 663/.2/00294.

UK
HARPERS DIRECTORY. Directory. English. an. £8.50. Harper Trade Journals Ltd., Harling House, 47-51 G Suffolk Street, London SE1 0BS England. **Tel** 011 44 71 261 1604. **LC** TP500.5; .H37. **DD** 380.1/456631/025. *Continues Harpers Directory and Manual.*

UK/0017-7903
HARPERS WINE AND SPIRIT GAZETTE. **VFOAT** Wine and Spirit Gazette. No. 4726 (Aug. 15, 1975)-. Periodical. English. wk. £65.00 UK; £70.00 other. Harper Trade Journals Ltd., Harling House, 47-51 G Suffolk Street, London SE1 0BS England. **Tel** 011 44 71 261 1604. *Continues Wine and Spirit Gazette (Harper's Weekly).*
Ind/Abst Infomat Int. Bus.

US/0017-8543
HAWAII BEVERAGE GUIDE. [Hawaii beverage guide]. (19??)-. Periodical. English. mo. $29.00. Hawaii Beverage Guide, PO Box 853, Honolulu HI 96808. **Tel** (808)591-0049, **FAX** (808)591-0038. **ED** Campbell Mansfield. Index available (Free). **Ad Acc. Circ:** 2,000 (ctrl).
Desc: A combination price book and news magazine serving the buyers of beverages in Hawaii.

US/0270-4668
HOME WINE AND BEER MAKERS INFORMATION. **Added/Corp** American Wine Society. (1979)-. English. an. $1.50 US; $2.50 other. American Wine Society, 3006 Latta Road, Rochester NY 14612. **Tel** (716)225-7613. **ED** Angel Nardone. **Circ:** 3,000. *Continues Home Winemakers Information.*
Desc: List of books and articles on wine making.

US/0739-5434
HOME WINEMAKER, THE. [Home winemak.]. Vol. 1, No. 1 (Spring-Summer 1983)-. Periodical. English. qt. $8.00. The Home Winemaker, PO Box 4260 Old Village Station, Great Neck NY 11027.

US/0191-5290
IDAHO BEVERAGE ANALYST. [Beverage anal., Ida.]. Periodical. English. mo. Bell Publications, 2403 Champa Street, Denver CO 80205. **Tel** (303)296-1600. **ED** Mariette Bell. **DD** 338. **Circ:** 1,385.

SP
ILE : INDUSTRIAS LACTEAS ESPANOLAS. Spanish. ir. 11000ptas. Industrias Lacteas Espanolas (ILE), C/ Triana 52 Bajo Izda, 28016 Madrid Spain. **Tel** 011 34 1 2505319, 011 34 1 2595798.

US/0019-1892
ILLINOIS BEVERAGE JOURNAL. (19??)-. Periodical. English. mo $30.00. Illinois Beverage Journal, 540 Frontage Road, Suite 344, North Field IL 60093. **Tel** (312)441-7776. **Ad Acc.**

IT/0392-792X
IMBOTTIGLIAMENTO. [Imbottigliamento]. (1982)-. Periodical. Italian. bm (6 issues). L35000 Italy; L55000 Europe; L90000 other. Tecniche Nuove SPA, Via Ciro Menotti 14, 20129 Milan Italy. **Tel** 011 39 2 75701, **FAX** 011 39 2 7610351, telex 334647 TECHS I. **UDC** 683.5. *Continues in part Tecnologie Alimentari, 0392-3835.*
Ind/Abst Food Sci. Technol. Abstr.

US/0882-6277
IMPACT BEVERAGE TRENDS IN AMERICA REVIEW AND FORECAST, THE. [Impact beverage trends Am. rev. forecast]. **VFOAT** Beverage Trends in America; Impact. (1985)-. English. an. $695.00. M. Shanken Communications, Inc., 387 Park Avenue South, New York NY 10016. **Tel** (212)684-5424, **FAX** (212)684-5424, telex 422687 MSHANK UI. **(Subscription address:** PO Box 1960, Marion, OH 43305) **ED** Marvin R. Shanken. **LC** HD9348.U5; I48. **DD** 338.4/7663/0973.
Desc: A factual and statistical report on the US beverage market. Products covered include wine, liquor, beer, soft drinks, coffee, tea, milk, juice, and water.

US/0268-8212
IMPACT INTERNATIONAL (NEW YORK, N.Y.). (IMPACT INTERNATIONAL.). [Impact int.]. Vol. 1, No. 1 (Jan. 15, 1986)-. Periodical. English. Twenty-four times a year (published the 1st and 15th of each month). $345.00. M. Shanken Communications, Inc., 387 Park Avenue South, New York NY 10016. **Tel** (212)684-4224, **FAX** (212)684-5424, telex 422687 MSHANK UI. **(Subscription address:** Impact International, PO Box 3083, Southeastern PA 19398.) **DD** 338.
Desc: Global news and research for the international drinks industry.

US/0363-9444
IMPACT (NEW YORK. 1970). (IMPACT.). [Impact]. **VFOAT** Impact Newsletter. Vol. 1 (Sept. 15, 1970)-. Periodical. English. sm. $300.00 (one year) $550.00 (two year) US; $315.00 (one year) $575.00 (two year) Canada; $330.00 (one year), $600.00 (two year) other. M. Shanken Communications, Inc., 387 Park Avenue South, New York NY 10016. **Tel** (212)684-4224, **FAX** (212)684-5424, telex 422687 MSHANK UI. **(Subscription address:** Impact, PO Box 3083, Southeastern PA 19398.) Index available (published in Dec.).

●US
IMPACT WORLD DIRECTORY : LEADING SPIRITS, WINE & BEER COMPANIES : WHO'S WHO OF INDUSTRY EXECUTIVES. (1992 Ed.)-. Directory. English. an. $310.00. M. Shanken Communications, Inc., 387 Park Avenue South, New York NY 10016. **Tel** (212)684-4224, **FAX** (212)684-5424, telex 422687 MSHANK UI. **LC** HD9350.3; .I47. **DD** 338.7/6631/02573. *Continues Impact International Directory, 1048-2253 and Impact Yearbook.*

US/0749-7946
IMPACT YEARBOOK. *Title Change.* [Impact yearb.]. **VFOAT** Impact Year Book. (1985)-(199?). English. an. M. Shanken Communications, Inc., 387 Park Avenue South, New York NY 10016. **Tel** (212)684-4224, **FAX** (212)684-5424, telex 422687 MSHANK UI. **(Subscription address:** PO Box 1960, Marion, OH 43305) **ED** Marvin R Shanken. **LC** HD9353; .I56. **DD** 338.7/6631/02573. **Ad Acc. Circ:** 14,000. *Merged into Impact World Directory.*
Desc: A directory of people and companies in the wine and spirits industry.

US/0730-8728
IMPORTED WINE MARKET IN AMERICA, THE. [Import. wine mark. Amer.]. (1990)-. English. an. M. Shanken Communications, Inc., 387 Park Avenue South, New York NY 10016. **Tel** (212)684-4224, **FAX** (212)684-5424, telex 422687 MSHANK UI. **(Subscription address:** PO Box 1960, Marion, OH 43305)

US
INDIANA BEER BOOK. English. $695.00. Beverage Marketing Corporation, 2670 Commercial Avenue, Mingo Junction OH 43938. **Tel** (614)598-4133, **FAX** (614)598-3977.

US/0274-547X
INDIANA BEVERAGE JOURNAL. (1945)-. Periodical. English. mo. $20.00 (one year), $35.00 (two year). Indiana Beverage Journal, 2511 East 46th Street, Indianapolis IN 46205. **Tel** (317)545-5262. **ED** Richard V. Baxter. **Ad Acc. Circ:** 7,750 (ctrl).
Desc: Provides price and product information for retailers of alcoholic beverages in Indiana. New products, promotions and current issues are discussed.

IT/0390-0541
INDUSTRIE DELLE BEVANDE. [Ind. bevande]. (1972)-. Academic Scholarly Publication. Italian (summaries and/or abstracts in English). bm. L50000 (Italy); L75000 (other). Chiriotti Editori, PO Box 66, 10064 Pinerolo Italy. **Tel** 121 794493, FAX 121/794480, telex 211 820 CHIED I. **CODEN** INBEEW. **[CCC].** Index available. **Bk Rev. Ad Acc. Circ:** 4,600. Documents available from CASDDS.
Desc: Deals with technological, scientific and practical articles concerning the production and bottling of mineral waters, soft drinks, aperitifs, carbonated drinks, beer, wines, spirits, liqueurs, fruit juices, etc.
Ind/Abst AGRICOLA; BioBusiness; Biodeter. Abstr.; Chem. Abstr. (1986-); Curr. Biotechnol.; Food Sci. Technol. Abstr.; Int. Packag. Abstr.; Vitis Vitic. Enol. Abstr.

HK/0954-7541
INTERNATIONAL JOURNAL OF WINE MARKETING. **Added/Corp** South Australian Institute of Technology. **VFOAT** IJWM. (19??)-. English. qt. $750.00. MCB University Press, 60 62 Toller Lane, Bradford West Yorkshire BD8 9BX England. **Tel** 011 44 274 499821, FAX 011 44 274 547143, telex 51317 MCBUNI G. **(Subscription address:** MCB University Press / US and Canada Subscriptions, PO Box 10812, Birmingham AL 35201-0812.**)** **ED** Michael Howley. **LC** HD9370.1; .I57. **DD** 380.1/456632/005. **Bk Rev. Ad Acc.** Documents available from UMI Article Clearinghouse.
Desc: Provides an invaluable interface between wine marketing practitioners and academics, bringing current academic research and development to marketing managers and strategists.
Ind/Abst ABI/INFORM Glob. Ed.; World Agric. Econ.

UK/0309-0477
INTERNATIONAL TEA COMMITTEE MONTHLY STATISTICAL SUMMARY. See Food and Food Industry-Abstracting, Bibliographies and Statistics.

NE
INTERNATIONAL TEA JOURNAL. **VFOAT** Tea; Tea, International Journal. Periodical. English. I.T.P.A., PO Box 30007, NL-3011 AE Rotterdam The Netherlands.

US/1061-9305
INTERNATIONAL WINE MARKET: IMPACT DATABANK REPORT, THE. [Int. wine mark.]. (1992)-. English. $7500.00. M. Shanken Communications, Inc., 387 Park Avenue South, New York NY 10016. **Tel** (212)684-4224, FAX (212)684-5424, telex 422687 MSHANK UI. **LC** HD9370.1; .I58. **DD** 382/.456632/005.

IT
ITALIAN WINES & SPIRITS. **VFOAT** Italian Wines and Spirits. (197?)-. Periodical. English. qt. $20.00. **(Subscription address:** International Subscription Inc., 30 Montgomery Street, 7th Floor, Jersey City, NJ 07302; Phone: (800)544-6748 or (201)451-9420**)**

GW/0072-422X
JAHRBUCH / GESELLSCHAFT FUER DIE GESCHICHTE UND BIBLIOGRAPHIE DES BRAUWESENS E.V. **Main/Corp** Gesellschaft fur die Geschichte und Bibliographie des Brauwesens (Berlin, Germany). (1928)-. German. an. DM73.50. Gesellschaft Fur Die Geschichte Und Bibliographie Des Brauwesens, E.V. D-1000 Berlin 65 Germany. **Tel** 030 4509264, FAX 030 4536069. **ED** Hans Gunter Schultze-Berndt. **LC** HD9397.G2; G48a. **DD** 338.4/76633/0943. Index available. cum. index. **Bk Rev. Circ:** 600.
Desc: History of brewing and malting including packaging and matters of interest to brewing historians. History of methods as well as of brewing regions, towns, families, and companies.

US/0738-8853
JESSE MEYER'S BEVERAGE DIGEST. **VFOAT** Beverage Digest. (198?)-. Periodical. English. sm. $175.00. Jesse Meyer's Beverage Digest, PO Box 238, Old Greenwich CT 06870. **Tel** (203)358-8198, FAX (203)327-9761.

US
JOBSON'S BEER HANDBOOK. **VFOAT** Beer Handbook. (19??)-. Periodical. English. an. $265.00. Jobson Publishing Corporation, 100 Avenue of the Americas, New York NY 10013. **Tel** (212)274-7084, 274-7000, FAX (212)431-0500.

US/1046-1973
JOBSON'S BEVERAGE DYNAMICS. [Jobson's beverage dyn.]. **VFOAT** Beverage Dynamics. Vol. 100, No. 3 (Apr. 1989)-. Periodical. English. Nine times a year. $35.00 US; $50 Canada; $80 Asia; $70 other. Jobson Publishing Corporation, 100 Avenue of the Americas, New York NY 10013. **Tel** (212)274-7084, 274-7000, FAX (212)431-0500. **(Subscription address:** Jobson's Beverage Dynamics, PO Box 7648, Riverton NJ 08077.**)** **LC** HD9350.1; .L55. **DD** 338. ***Continues*** *Liquor Store (New York, N.Y.), 1058-5273.*
Desc: Targets off-premise sellers of beverage alcohol.

US/1051-564X
JOBSON'S CHEERS. (JOBSON'S CHEERS : THE PREMIUM ON-PREMISE BEVERAGE ALCOHOL BUSINESS MAGAZINE.). [Jobson's cheers]. **VFOAT** Cheers. Vol. 1, No. 1 (Sept./Oct. 1990)-. Periodical. English. bm. $24.00 US; $35.00 Canada; $80.00 Asia; $70.00 other. Jobson Publishing Corporation, 100 Avenue of the Americas, New York NY 10013. **Tel** (212)274-7084, 274-7000, FAX (212)431-0500. **(Subscription address:** Jobson's Cheers, PO Box 7633, Riverton NJ 08077.**)** **LC** TX950.7; .J63. **DD** 647.95/05. ctrl circ.
Desc: Targets high-volume, premium on-premise accounts in the beverage alcohol industry. Includes articles on spirits, wine, beer, non-alcoholic beverages and food.
Ind/Abst Foods Adlibra.

US/1047-918X
JOBSON'S HANDBOOK ADVANCE. [Jobson's handb. adv.]. **VFOAT** Jobson's Hand Book Advance; Handbook Advance; Hand Book Advance. (1988)-. Periodical. English. an. $225.00. Jobson Publishing Corporation, 100 Avenue of the Americas, New York NY 10013. **Tel** (212)274-7084, 274-7000, FAX (212)431-0500. **LC** HD9351; .J63. **DD** 380. ***Continues*** *Jobson's Liquor Handbook Advance.*

●US
JOBSON'S LICENSED BEVERAGE MARKETING & MERCHANDISING FACT BOOK. **VFOAT** Jobson's Licensed Beverage Marketing and Merchandising Fact book; Jobson's Licensed Beverage Fact Book. (1993)-. Periodical. English. an. $245.00. Jobson Publishing Corporation, 100 Avenue of the Americas, New York NY 10013. **Tel** (212)274-7084, 274-7000, FAX (212)431-0500.

US/1046-8250
JOBSON'S LIQUOR HANDBOOK. [Jobson's liquor handb.]. **VFOAT** Liquor Handbook. (1985)-. Periodical. English. an. $265.00. Jobson Publishing Corporation, 100 Avenue of the Americas, New York NY 10013. **Tel** (212)274-7084, 274-7000, FAX (212)431-0500. **LC** HD9352; .L5. **DD** 380.1/456631/0973021. ***Continues*** *Liquor Handbook, 0459-4843.*
Ind/Abst F&S Index Plus Text, Int. [Select. Cov.]; Predicasts Forecasts; Stat. Ref. Index.

US
JOBSON'S WINE & SPIRITS INDUSTRY MARKETING. **Added/Corp** Wine and Spirits Wholesalers of America. **VFOAT** Jobson's Wine and Spirits Industry Marketing; Wine & Spirits Industry Marketing; Wine and Spirits Industry Marketing. (1989)-. Periodical. English. an. $150.00. Jobson Publishing Corporation, 100 Avenue of the Americas, New York NY 10013. **Tel** (212)274-7084, 274-7000, FAX (212)431-0500. **LC** HD9351; .L56. **DD** 381/.456631/02573. ***Continues*** *Jobson's Liquor Industry Marketing, 1041-651X.*
Desc: Information on the alcoholic beverage industry, wine and liquor.

US
JOBSON'S WINE HANDBOOK. (19??)-. Periodical. English. an. $265.00. Jobson Publishing Corporation, 100 Avenue of the Americas, New York NY 10013. **Tel** (212)274-7084, 274-7000, FAX (212)431-0500.

US
JOBSON'S WINE MARKETING HANDBOOK. ***Title Change.*** **VFOAT** Wine Marketing Handbook. (1985)-(19??). English. an. Jobson Publishing Corporation, 100 Avenue of the Americas, New York NY 10013. **Tel** (212)274-7084, 274-7000, FAX (212)431-0500. **LC** HD9372; .W5. **DD** 338.4/76632/005. ***Continues*** *Wine Marketing Handbook, 0364-5738.* ***Continued by*** *Jobson's Wine Handbook.*

US/0364-698X
JOURNAL - AMERICAN WINE SOCIETY. [J. - Am. Wine Soc.]. **Main/Corp** American Wine Society. (19??)-. English. Four times a year (Mar., June, Sept., Dec.). $32.00; Comes also with American Wine Society membership. American Wine Society, 3006 Latta Road, Rochester NY 14612. **Tel** (716)225-7613. **ED** Jane Moulton. **LC** TP544.A46; A3. Index available. cum. index. **Bk Rev. Ad Acc. Pr Rev. Circ:** 3,800.
Desc: An consumer organization devoted to educating people on all aspects of wine. For the wine lovers who want to learn more about wine.
Ind/Abst AGRICOLA [Select. Cov.].

FR/1151-0985
JOURNAL INTERNATIONAL DES SCIENCES DE LA VIGNE ET DU VIN. See Agriculture-Crop Production and Soil.

FR/1151-0285
JOURNAL INTERNATIONAL DES SCIENCES DE LA VIGNE ET DU VIN. Vol. 24 No. 1 (1990)-. Periodical. French (summaries and/or abstracts in English). Four times a year. 362.39F France; 470.00F other. Vigne et Vin Publications Internationales, Bordeaux Technopolis, Site Montesquieu, 33651 Martillac cedex France. **Tel** 011 33 56 648230, FAX 011 33 56 648205, telex 550 415F. **CODEN** JISVE8. Documents available from CASDDS. ***Continues*** *Connaissance de la Vigne et du Vin, 0010-577X.*
Ind/Abst Chem. Abstr.

UK/0046-9750
JOURNAL OF THE INSTITUTE OF BREWING. [J. Inst. Brew.]. Vol. 9 (1904)-. Academic Scholarly Publication. English. bm. £190.00. Institute of Brewing, 33 Clarges Street, London W1Y 8EE England. **Tel** 11 44 71 499 8144, FAX 11 44 71 499 1156. **ED** J S Pierce. **CODEN** JINBAL. Index available. **Ad Acc, Adv Mgr:** F. Bolton, **Tel** (071)499-8144. **Circ:** 4300 (ctrl). Documents available from The Genuine Article, CASDDS. ***Continues*** *Journal of the Federated Institutes of Brewing.*
Desc: This is a learned journal of the brewing, fermentation, and distilling industry.
Ind/Abst AGRICOLA [Select. Cov.]; Anal. Abstr.; BioBusiness; Biodeter. Abstr.; Chem. Abstr.; Curr. Contents, Agric. Biol. Environ. Sci.; Curr. Technol. Index; Dairy Sci. Abstr.; Field Crop Abstr.; Food Sci. Technol. Abstr.; Grasslands For. Abstr.; Hortic. Abstr.; Microbiol. Abstr. Sect. A; Microbiol. Abstr. Sect. C; Nutr. Abstr. Rev., Ser. B, Live Feeds and Feed.; Nutr. Abstr. Rev., Ser. A, Hum. Exp.; Life Sci. Collect.; PESTDOC; Plant Breed. Abstr.; Res. Alert [Full Cov.]; Saf. Health Work; Sci. Cit. Index; SCISEARCH; Vitis Vitic. Enol. Abstr.; Wheat Barley Trit. Abstr.

UK/0957-1264
JOURNAL OF WINE RESEARCH / THE INSTITUTE OF MASTERS OF WINE. **Added/Corp** Institute of Masters of Wine. Vol. 1, No. 1 (1990)-. Periodical. English. tq. £162.00. Carfax Publishing Company, PO Box 25 Abingdon, Oxfordshire OX14 3UE England. **Tel** 011 44 235 555335, FAX (0279)31067, telex 817484. **(Subscription address:** US and Canada/ PO Box 2025, Dunnellon, FL 34430-2025; telephone:(904)489-6996**)** **ED** Jasper Morris & Tim Unwin. **[CCC].** available on microfiche.
Desc: Reports the results of research in all aspects of the wine trade.
Ind/Abst Curr. Aware. Biol. Sci., CABS; Geogr. Abstr. Human Geogr.; Hortic. Abstr.; Int. Dev. Abstr.; Soils Fert.

FR
JOURNEE VINICOLE, LA. Periodical. French. Le Mas d'Astre/CD 132, 34000 Montpellier France.

JA/0911-4785
KAGOSHIMA-KEN CHAGYO SHIKENJO KENKYU HOKOKU. See Agriculture.

US/0882-2573
KANE'S BEVERAGE WEEK. [Kane's beverage week]. (1985)-. Periodical. English. Forty-seven times a year (weekly except biweekly in July and August and not between Christmas and New Year's). $380.00 (one year), $750.00 (two year). Whitaker Newsletter, PO Box 340, 313 South Avenue, Suite 202, Fanwood NJ 07023-0340. **Tel** (201)889-6336, FAX (201)889-6339. **(Subscription address:** Whitaker Newsletters, PO Box 192, Fanwood, NJ 07023-0192**)** **ED** Joel Whitaker. **DD** 338. **[CCC]. Bk Rev.** ***Continues*** *Kane Report, 0732-9679.*
Desc: Regular coverage of federal and state bev/al regulations, excise taxes, BATF policies and rulings, warning labels, and activities of anti-alcohol activists.

XR/0023-5830
KVASNY PRUMYSL. [Kvasny prum.]. **Added/Corp** Czechoslovak Republic. Ministerstvo Potravinarskeho Prumyslu. Vol. 1 (1955)-. Academic Scholarly Publication. Czech (summaries and/or abstracts in English, German and Multiple languages; table of contents in English and German). Twelve times a year. $111.60. **(Subscription address:** Artia Pegas Press Ltd., Palac Metro Narodni Trida 25, 11210 Prague 1 Czech Republic.**)** **LC** TP500; .K9. **CODEN** KVPRAB. Documents available from CASDDS.
Ind/Abst AGRICOLA; Chem. Abstr.; Curr. Biotechnol.; Food Sci. Technol. Abstr.; Microbiol. Abstr. Sect. A; Microbiol. Abstr. Sect. C; Life Sci. Collect.; Vitis Vitic. Enol. Abstr.

●GW
LAND- UND FORSTWIRTSCHAFT, FISCHEREI. REIHE 3.2.3, WEINBESTAENDE / STATISTISCHES BUNDESAMT. **Added/Corp** Germany. Statistisches Bundesamt. **VFOAT** Weinbestaende; Fachserie 3. (1992)-. Statistical Publication. German. W Kohlhammer Verlag GMBH, Postfach 800430, D70549 Stuttgart Germany. **Tel** 011 49 711 78631. **LC** HD9383.1; .L36. **DD** 338.4/76632/00943021. ***Continues*** *Land- und Forstwirtschaft, Fischerei. Reihe 3.2.3, Weinbestaende und Lagerbehaelter.*

GW
LAND- UND FORSTWIRTSCHAFT, FISCHEREI. REIHE 3.2.2, WEINERZEUGUNG. **Added/Corp** Germany (West). Statistisches Bundesamt. **VFOAT** Weinerzeugung; Fachserie 3. (1985)-. German. W

Kohlhammer Verlag GMBH, Postfach 800430, D70549 Stuttgart Germany. **Tel** 011 49 711 78631. **LC** HD9383.1; .L358. ***Continues in part*** *Land- und Forstwirtschaft, Fischerei. Reihe 3.2.2, Weinerzeugung und Bestand, Weinbestande und Lagerbehalter.*

CN
LEGISLATION DIGEST. English. ir. 93.46Can$. Brewers Association of Canada, International Survey, Suite 1200, 155 Queen Street, Ottawa ONT K1P 6L1 Canada. **Tel** (613)232-9601, FAX (613)232-2283, telex 053-4370.

US/1040-3736
LEISURE BEVERAGE INSIDER NEWSLETTER. [Leis. beverage insid. newsl.]. **VFOAT** Leisure Beverage Newsletter; Leisure Beverage Insider. (198?)-. Newsletter. English. bw. $285.00 (one year), $550.00 (two year). Whitaker Newsletter, PO Box 340, 313 South Avenue, Suite 202, Fanwood NJ 07023-0340. **Tel** (201)889-6336, FAX (201)889-6339. **(Subscription address:** Whitaker Newsletters, PO Box 192, Fanwood, NJ 07023-0192) **ED** Anne Bittner. **DD** 338. **[CCC]. Bk Rev.** ***Continues*** *Leisure Beverage Insider, 0148-6713.*
Desc: News pertaining to the beverage industry with particular emphasis on soft drinks, mixers and bottled water.

US/0024-2764
LICENSED BEVERAGE JOURNAL. (1965)-. Periodical. English. Twenty-four times a year. $10.00. Licensed Beverage Journal, 2917 Bruckner Boulevard, Brons NY 10461. **ED** Kamell Abdenour. **Bk Rev. Ad Acc. Circ:** 5,200 (ctrl).
Desc: Metro New York liquor industry news.

AT
LIQUOR RETAILING HANDBOOK. (19??)-. English. an. 90.00Aus$ Australia; 95.00Aus$ New Zealand, Papua New Guinea; 100.00Aus$ Malaysia, Indonesia, Fiji, Japan, India, Hong Kong; 110.00Aus$ US, Canada, Lebanon; 120.00Aus$ Europe, Africa, former USSR. Thomson Publications / Australia, 47 Chippen Street, Chippendale New South Wales, 2008 Australia. **Tel** 011 61 2 6992411, FAX 011 61 2 698 3920, telex 122226. **(Subscription address:** Thomson Publications Australia, PO Box 815, Strawberry Hills, New South Wales, 2012 Australia.**)**

SA
LIQUOR STORE MONTHLY. (19??)-. English. mo. R111.00 South Africa, Namibia and TVCB countries; R135.00 other. Ramsay Son & Parker Pty Ltd., PO Box 180, Howard Place, Pinelands 7450 South Africa. **Tel** 011 27 21 531 1391, FAX 011 27 21 531 3333, telex 526933. **ED** Mike Froud. Index available. **Bk Rev. Ad Acc. Circ:** 5,500 (ctrl).
Desc: Covers items of interest to liquor producers and retailers.

BE/0777-8805
LOUVAIN BREWING LETTERS. (1988)-. Periodical. English (French). qt. $400.00 Belgium; $500.00 other. Laboratoire de Brasserie, Place Croix du Sud 3, B-1348 Louvain La Neuv Belgium. **Tel** 011 32 10 47 36 92, FAX 32 10 47 27 78, telex UCLB 59 532. **ED** J. P. Dufor. **CODEN** 378.4. Index available. cum. index. **Bk Rev. Ad Acc. Pr Rev.**
Desc: Scientific papers, conferences and technical news on malting and brewing research and technology.
Ind/Abst Food Sci. Technol. Abstr.

FI/0356-3014
MALLAS JA OLUT. [Mallas olut]. (1977)-. Academic Scholarly Publication. Finnish. bm. Fmk90.00 Finland; Fmk130.00 (Europe); Fmk160.00 (other). Mallasjuomalehti Oy, Tekniikantie 17, SF-02150 Espoo Finland. **Tel** 358-0-4565100. **ED** Matti Linko. **LC** TP577; .M33. **CODEN** MAOLD2. Index available. **Bk Rev. Ad Acc. Circ:** 400. Documents available from CASDDS. ***Continues*** *Mallasjuomat.*
Desc: Malting, brewing technology and science.
Ind/Abst AGRICOLA; Chem. Abstr. (1977-1983).

●US/1062-1032
MARK SPIVAK'S FLORIDA WINE BULLETIN. [Mark Spivak's Fla. wine bull.]. **VFOAT** Florida Wine Bulletin. Issue No. 1 (May 1992-). Bulletin. English. mo. $24.00. Sunshine Wine Concepts, 6265 West Sample Road, Suite 204, Coral Springs FL 33067. **DD** 641.

US/0277-9277
MARKET WATCH (NEW YORK, N.Y.). (MARKET WATCH.). [Mark. watch]. **Added/Corp** M. Shanken Communications. Vol. 1, No. 1 (Sept. 1981)-. Periodical. English. Eight times a year. $60.00 (one year), $100.00 (two year) US; $70.00 (one year), $120.00 (two year) Canada; $85.00 (one year), $150.00 (two year) other. M. Shanken Communications, Inc., 387 Park Avenue South, New York NY 10016. **Tel** (212)684-4224, FAX (212)684-5424, telex 422687 MSHANK UI. **(Subscription address:** PO Box 7807 Riverton, NJ 08077) **ED** Michael Moaba. **LC** HD9350.1; .M37. **DD** 338.4/76631/05. **Bk Rev. Ad Acc.**
Desc: Market intelligence on the wine, spirits and beer industry business. Covers latest drink trends, profiles of successful retail and restaurant operations.

US/1052-5785
MARTHA'S VINEYARD. See Agriculture.

●US/1058-935X
MARYLAND BEVERAGE JOURNAL. [Md. beverage j.]. **VFOAT** Maryland-Washington Beverage Journal; Maryland-Washington, D.C. Beverage Journal. (199?)-. Periodical. English. mo. $30.00. Beverage Journal, 7451 Race Road, Box 1002, Hanover MD 21076. **Tel** (301)235-1717, FAX (301)243-8505. **DD** 641. ***Continues*** *Maryland-Washington Beverage Journal (Maryland Ed.), 1051-9777.*

US
MEDIAMARK RESEARCH BEER, WINE & LIQUOR REPORT. **Added/Corp** Mediamark Research Inc. **VFOAT** Beer, Wine & Liquor Report; Beer, Wine and Liquor Report. (198?)-. Periodical. English. sa. Mediamark Research Inc, 341 Madison Avenue, New York NY 10017. **LC** HF5415.3; .M43 pt. P-3. ***Continues*** *Beer, Wine, Soft Drinks.*

US
MERCADO DE CAFE NOS ESTADOS UNIDOS E NO CANADA, O. **Main/Corp** Instituto Brasileiro do Cafe Escritorio de New York. **VFOAT** The Coffee Market in the United States and Canada. No. 2 (1978)-. English (Portuguese). Brazil Coffee Institute, 477 Madison Avenue/#703, New York NY 10022-5802. **LC** HD9199.U47; I57C. ***Formed by the union of*** *Mercado de Cafe. Instituto Brasilerio do Cafe. Escritorio de New York* ***and*** *Coffee Market, 0196-0253.*

US/0026-2021
MICHIGAN BEVERAGE NEWS. Periodical. English. sm. $28.50. Michigan Beverage News, 27716 Franklin Road, Southfield MI 48034-2352. **Tel** (313)357-6397. **ED** David A Brown. **Bk Rev. Ad Acc. Circ:** 6,000.
Desc: Reports news to holders of liquor licenses in Michigan.

US/0026-2978
MID-CONTINENT BOTTLER. (19??)-. Periodical. English. bm. $9.00 (one year), $16.00 (two year), $22.00 (three year). Mid-Continent Bottler, 8575 West 110th Street, Suite 218, Overland Park KS 66210. **Tel** (913)469-8611. **ED** Floyd E. Sageser. **Bk Rev. Ad Acc. Circ:** 3,000 (ctrl).
Desc: Merchandising and marketing magazine for soft drink bottlers. Covers a 21-state area from Ohio to Colorado.

AU/0007-5922
MITTEILUNGEN KLOSTERNEUBURG : REBE UND WEIN, OBSTBAU UND FRUCHTEVERWERTUNG. [Mitt. Klosterneuburg Rebe Wein Obstb. Fruchtevewert.]. **Added/Corp** Hohere Bundeslehr- und Versuchsanstalt fur Wein- und Obstbau. Vol. 27, No. 1 (Jan. 1977)-. Academic Scholarly Publication. German (summaries and/or abstracts in English and French). Six times a year. S1055.00. Hohere Bundeslehr Versuchsanstalt Wein Obstbau, Weinerstr 74, A3400 Klosterneuburg Austria. **Tel** 011 43 2243 2159. **CODEN** MIKLD4. Index available. **Bk Rev. Ad Acc.** Documents available from BIOSIS Document Express, CASDDS. ***Continues*** *Mitteilungen : Rebe und Wein, Obstbau und Fruchteverwertung.*
Ind/Abst AgBiotech News Inf.; Biol. Abstr.; Chem. Abstr.; Crop Physiol. Abstr.; Food Sci. Technol. Abstr.; Hortic. Abstr.; Plant Breed. Abstr.; Plant Genet. Resour. Abstr.; Plant Grow. Reg. Abstr.; Postharvest News Inf.; Rev. Agric. Entomol.; Rev. Plant Pathol.; Seed Abstr.; Soils Fert.; Vitis Vitic. Enol. Abstr.

US/0026-7538
MODERN BREWERY AGE. [Mod. brew. age]. Vol. 23, No. 3-Vol. 78, No. 1, (Mar . 1940)-(Jan./Feb. 1970)-. Periodical. English. wk. $170.00. Business Journals Inc, PO Box 5550, Norwalk CT 06856. **Tel** (203)853-6015, FAX (203)852-8175, telex 353706. **ED** Peter Reid and Glenn Schute. **Bk Rev. Ad Acc. Circ:** 6,000. available on an online database (file 648/Full-Text) from DIALOG. ***Formed by the union of*** *Brewery Age, 0096-445X* ***and*** *Modern Brewer, 0096-4972.*
Desc: Complete coverage of the brewing and beverage fields worldwide.
Ind/Abst BioBusiness (1990-); Predicasts; Trade Ind. ASAP [Full Txt.]; Trade Ind. Index [Full Txt.].

US
MODERN BREWERY AGE BLUE BOOK. **VFOAT** MBA Blue Book. (19??)-. English. an. $165.00. Business Journals Inc, PO Box 5550, Norwalk CT 06856. **Tel** (203)853-6015, FAX (203)852-8175, telex 353706. **ED** Terri Finnegan. **Bk Rev. Ad Acc. Circ:** 6,000.
Desc: Complete coverage of the brewing industry. From news to ingredients and everything in between.

GW/0723-1520
MONATSSCHRIFT FUER BRAUWISSENSCHAFT. [Monatsschr. Brauwiss.]. **Added/Corp** Technische Universitat Munchen. Fakultat fur Brauwesen, Lebensmitteltechnologie und Milchwissenschaft. Versuchs- und Lehranstalt fur Brauerei in Berlin. Wissenschaftliche Station fur Brauerei in Munchen. Vol. 36, No. 1 (1983)-. Academic Scholarly Publication. German (French; table of contents in French and English). mo. DM196.00. Verlag Hans Carl GmbH & Company KG, Andernacher Strasse 33A, D 90411 Nuernberg Germany. **Tel** 011 49 911 952850. **CODEN** MOBRDJ. **[CCC].** Documents available from The Genuine Article, CASDDS. ***Formed by the union of*** *Brauwissenschaft, 0006-9337* ***and*** *Monatsschrift fur Brauerei.*
Ind/Abst AGRICOLA; Anal. Abstr.; Biodeter. Abstr. (19??-19??); Chem. Abstr. (1983-); Crop Physiol. Abstr.; Curr. Contents, Agric. Biol. Environ. Sci.; EMBASE (1983-); Energy Res. Abstr. (1983-); Field Crop Abstr.; Food Sci. Technol. Abstr.; Int. Packag. Abstr.; Life Sci. Collect. (1983-); Postharvest News Inf.; Res. Alert [Select. Cov.]; Rev. Med. Vet. Mycology; SCISEARCH; Seed Abstr.; Wheat Barley Trit. Abstr.

GW/0255-7045
MONOGRAPH / EUROPEAN BREWERY CONVENTION. [Monogr. - Eur. Brew. Conv.]. **Added/Corp** European Brewery Convention. (1975)-. Academic Scholarly Publication. English. ir. Price varies per volume. Verlag Hans Carl GmbH & Company KG, Andernacher Strasse 33A, D 90411 Nuernberg Germany. **Tel** 011 49 911 952850. **CODEN** MEBCD6. Documents available from CASDDS.
Ind/Abst Chem. Abstr.

US/0730-3254
MONTHLY COFFEE STATISTICS. See Food and Food Industry-Abstracting, Bibliographies and Statistics.

CN/0527-575X
MONTHLY PRODUCTION OF SOFT DRINKS. [Mon. prod. soft drinks]. **Added/Corp** Canada. Bureau Federal de la Statistique. Division de l'Industrie. Canada. Bureau Federal de la Statistique. Division des Industries Manufacturieres et Primaires. Statistique Canada. Division des Industries Manufacturieres et Primaires. Statistique Canada. Division de l'Industrie. **VFOAT** Production Mensuelle de Boissons Gazeuses. Vol. 11, No. 1 (Jan. 1964)-. French (English). mo. 30.00Can$ Canada; $36.00 US; $42.00 other. Statistics Canada, Publications Sales & Services, Main Building Room 1710, Ottawa Ontario K1A 0T6 Canada. **Tel** (613)951-5078, (800)267-6677, FAX (613)951-1584, telex 053-3585. **DD** 338.4/766362/0971. ***Continues*** *Monthly Production of Carbonated Beverages, 0380-593X.*
Desc: Production data for month and cumulative period together with comparisons with earlier periods.

AT/0816-0430
NATIONAL LIQUOR NEWS. [Natl. liquor news]. (1984)-. Periodical. English. mo. 73.00Aus$ Australia; 95.00Aus$ New Zealand, Papua New Guinea; 100.00Aus$ Malaysia, Indonesia, Fiji; 101.00Aus$ Japan, India, Hong Kong; 110.00Aus$ US, Canada, Lebanon; 118.00Aus$ Europe, Africa, former USSR. Thomson Publications / Australia, 47 Chippen Street, Chippendale New South Wales, 2008 Australia. **Tel** 011 61 2 6992411, FAX 011 61 2 698 3920, telex 122226. **(Subscription address:** Thomson Publications Australia, PO Box 815, Strawberry Hills, New South Wales, 2012 Australia.**) DD** 380.14566310994. ***Continues*** *National Thomson's Liquor Guide, 0812-3705.*

US/0028-1808
NEBRASKA BEVERAGE ANALYST. **VFOAT** Beverage Analyst. Periodical. English. mo. Bell Publications, 2403 Champa Street, Denver CO 80205. **Tel** (303)296-1600. **ED** Mariette Bell. **Circ:** 4,219.

US/1053-6345
NEVADA BEVERAGE ANALYST. [Nev. beverage anal.]. (19??)-. Periodical. English. mo. $12.00. Bell Publications, 2403 Champa Street, Denver CO 80205. **Tel** (303)296-1600. **DD** 338. ***Continues*** *Nevada Beverage Index, 0191-4723.*

US/0191-4723
NEVADA BEVERAGE INDEX. ***Title Change.*** [Nev. beverage index]. Periodical. English. mo. Nevada Publishing Company, PO Box 99, Reno NV 89504. **DD** 338. ***Continued by*** *Nevada Beverage Analyst, 1053-6345.*

US/0741-0506
NEW BREWER, THE. (THE NEW BREWER / INSTITUTE FOR BREWING AND FERMENTATION STUDIES.). [New brew.]. **Added/Corp** Institute for Brewing and Fermentation Studies (Boulder, Colo.). Vol. 1 (Nov. 1983)-. Periodical. English. Six times a year (Jan., Mar., May, July, Sept., Nov.). $55.00 US; $65.00 other. Association of Brewers, 734 West Pearl Street, Boulder CO 80302. **Tel** (303)447-0816. **(Subscription address:** Institute of Brewing Studies, PO Box 1679, Boulder CO 80306.**) ED** Virginia Thomas. Index available. cum. index. **Bk Rev. Ad Acc. Circ:** 850.

US/0192-6462
NEW HAMPSHIRE BEVERAGE JOURNAL. **VFOAT** Beverage Journal. (19??)-. English. mo. $6.00 (one year), $10.00 (two year), $14.00 (three year). New England Beverage Publ, 227 East Main Street, PO Box 608, Avon MA 02322. **Tel** (617)786-9600.

US/0028-5552
NEW JERSEY BEVERAGE JOURNAL. (19??)-. Periodical. English. mo. $25.00. New Jersey Beverage Journal, 2414 Morris Avenue, Union NJ 07083. **Tel** (908)964-5060. **ED** Harry Slone. **Bk Rev. Ad Acc. Circ:** 10,000 (ctrl).
Desc: Editorial information, brand information, and some price information directed towards beverage alcohol licensees in the state of New Jersey.

US/0194-813X
NEW MEXICO BEVERAGE ANALYST. VFOAT Beverage Analyst. (19??)-. Periodical. English. mo. Beverage Analyst Group, 2403 Champa Street, Denver CO 80205. **ED** Mariette Bell. **Circ:** 1,217.

AT/0816-0694
NEWSLETTER - INSTITUTE OF BREWING, AUSTRALIA AND NEW ZEALAND SECTION. [Newsl. - Inst. Brew. Aust. N. Z. Sect.]. (1983)-. Periodical. English. be. 76.00Aus$ (Australia); 86.00Aus$ (other). Institute of Brewing / Asia Pacific Section, PO Box 229, Brooklyn Park SA 5032, Australia. **Tel** 011 61 8 3560996, FAX 011 61 8 2351061. **DD** 663.30994.

US
NORTHWEST GRAPE GROWER AND WINEMAKER. VFOAT N.W. Grape Grower/Winemaker. Vol. 1, No. 5 (Dec. 1982)-. Periodical. English. mo. Dawson House Publishing, PO Box 477, Othello WA 99344. ***Continues** Northwest Grape Grower.*

US
NSDA SALES SURVEY OF THE SOFT DRINK INDUSTRY. Main/Corp National Soft Drink Association. (19??)-. English. an (July). free (first copy), $1.50 (each additional copy). National Soft Drink Association, 1101 16th Street NW, Washington DC 20036. **Tel** (202)833-2450.

UK/0043-5775
OFF LICENCE NEWS. [Off licence news]. (1969)-. Newspaper. English. wk. £55.00 UK; £95.00 Europe; £150.00 other. William Reed Ltd, Broadfield Park, Crawley, West Sussex RH11 9RJ England. **Tel** 011 44 293 613400, FAX 0293-613156. ***Continues** Wine & Spirit Trade Review.*
Ind/Abst Infomat Int. Bus.

US
OHIO BEER BOOK. (19??)-. Periodical. English. Six times a year. $695.00. Beverage Marketing Corporation, 2670 Commercial Avenue, Mingo Junction OH 43938. **Tel** (614)598-4133, FAX (614)598-3977.

US/0740-1361
OHIO BEVERAGE JOURNAL. (19??)-. Periodical. English. Twelve times a year. $12.00 (one year), $18.00 (two year). Ohio Beverage Journal, 3 12th Street, Wheeling WV 26003. **Tel** (304)232-7620, FAX (304)233-1236. **ED** Arnold Lazarus. **Ad Acc. Circ:** 6,800. ***Continues** Buckeye Beverage Journal, 0007-2826.*
Desc: Covers local and national industry news, product and industry promotions of beer, wine and liquor, new merchandising and staff editorials. Each issue contain Ohio's distilled spirits wholesale price list by case and bottle, and retailer service features.

CN/0832-2562
ON TAP (ENGLISH ED.). (ON TAP / BREWERS ASSOCIATION OF CANADA / L'ASSOCIATION DES BRASSEURS DU CANADA.). [On tap]. **Added/Corp** Brewers Association of Canada. Vol. 1, No. 1 (July 1986)-. Periodical. English. qt. Free. Brewers Association of Canada, International Survey, Suite 1200, 155 Queen Street, Ottawa ONT K1P 6L1 Canada. **Tel** (613)232-9601, FAX (613)232-2283, telex 053-4370. **DD** 338.4/76633/0971.

CN/0380-6057
ONTARIO GRAPE GROWER, THE. **See** Gardening and Horticulture.

BL/0102-9738
PESQUISA EM ANDAMENTO - CENTRO NACIONAL DE PESQUISA DE UVA E VINHO. (PESQUISA EM ANDAMENTO.). [Pesqui. Andam. - Cent. Nac. Pesqui. Uva Vinho]. **VFOAT** Pesquisa em Andamento / CNPUV. (1986)-. Monographic series. Portuguese. ir. **UDC** 63. ***Continues** Pesquisa em Andamento - Unidade de Execucao de Pesquisa de Ambito Estadual de Bento Goncalves, 0101-9694.*
Ind/Abst Grasslands For. Abstr.; Plant Grow. Reg. Abstr.; Rev. Plant Pathol.

BE/0031-6253
PETIT JOURNAL DU BRASSEUR. (LE PETIT JOURNAL DU BRASSEUR / HET KLEINE BROUWERSBLAD.). [Petit j. brass.]. **VFOAT** Kleine Brouwersblad; Kleine Brouwers Blad. (1893)-. Periodical. Dutch (French). Ten times a year. 2014.00F Belgium; 3150.00F other. Confederation des Brasseurs Belgique, Msn Brasseurs Grand Place 10, B-1000 Brussels Belgium. **Tel** 011 32 2 5114987. **Ad Acc.**
Desc: News and articles about the world of beers.
Ind/Abst Food Sci. Technol. Abstr.

NE/1380-6084
PINT NIEUWS. VFOAT Promotie Informatie Traditioneel Bier Nieuws. (1980)-. Periodical. English. bm (6 issues). FI33.02. Pint, PO Box 3757, 1001 AN Amsterdam, Netherlands. **Tel** 011 31 20 0180711376.

US/1057-2694
PRACTICAL WINERY/VINEYARD. [Pract. winery vineyard]. **VFOAT** Practical Winery & Vineyard; Practical Winery and Vineyard; PWV. Vol. 8, No. 2 (July/Aug. 1987)-. Periodical. English. bm. $30.00 (US), $38.00 (other) one year; $56.00 (US), $72.00 (other) two year. Practical Winery/Vineyard, 15 Grande Pasco, San Rafael CA 94903. **Tel** (415)479-5819. **ED** Don Neel. **DD** 663. **CODEN** PWVIEC. Index available. **Bk Rev. Ad Acc. Pr Rev. Circ:** 2,500 (ctrl). ***Continues** Practical Winery, 0739-8077.*
Desc: No-nonsense in-depth information on grapegrowing, winemaking, marketing and finance.
Ind/Abst BioBusiness.

NE/0071-2531
PROCEEDINGS OF THE CONGRESS - EUROPEAN BREWERY CONVENTION. Main/Conf European Brewery Convention. **VFOAT** Progress in Brewing Science. (19??)-. Academic Scholarly Publication. English (French and German). ir. Price varies per volume. European Brewery Convention, PO Box 510, 2380 BB Zoeterwoude Netherlands. **Tel** 011 31 71 456047, FAX 011 31 71 410013, telex 39390. **(Subscription address:** Oxford University Press / USA, Journals Marketing Department, Oxford University Press, 2001 Evans Road, Cary NC 27513.**)** **LC** TP570.A1; E8. **DD** 663.30634; 663.4063*. Index available. **Circ:** 1,500. Documents available from CASDDS.
Desc: Provides an opportunity for reviewing the latest scientific research and technological developments and applications in the fields of malting and brewing.
Ind/Abst Chem. Abstr.

AT/0367-6897
PROCEEDINGS OF THE CONVENTION - INSTITUTE OF BREWING AUSTRALIAN AND NEW ZEALAND SECTION. [Proc. Conv. - Inst. Brew., Aust. N. Z. Sect.]. (1968)-. Academic Scholarly Publication. English. be. **CODEN** IBAZA2. Documents available from CASDDS. ***Continues** Proceedings of the Convention - Institute of Brewing. Australian Section, 0534-1671.*
Ind/Abst Chem. Abstr.

CN/0709-2768
PRODUCTION AND STOCKS OF TEA, COFFEE, AND COCOA. [Prod. stocks tea coffee cocoa]. **Added/Corp** Statistics Canada. Manufacturing and Primary Industries Division. Statistics Canada. Industry Division. **VFOAT** Production et Stocks de The, Cafe et Cacao. Vol. 1, No. 1 (Quarter ended Mar. 1979)-. English (French). qt. 32.00Can$ Canada; $39.00 US; $45.00 other. Statistics Canada, Publications Sales & Services, Main Building Room 1710, Ottawa Ontario K1A 0T6 Canada. **Tel** (613)951-5078, (800)267-6677, FAX (613)951-1584, telex 053-3585. **LC** HD9195.C2; P76. **DD** 338.47/6639/0971. ***Formed by the union of** Miscellaneous Food Preparations., 0575-9013.*
Desc: Shows production and stock of tea and coffee and stocks and grindings of cocoa beans. It includes sources and methods and lists of reporting firms and their plant locations.

NE
PRODUKTIESTATISTIEKEN. BIERBROUWERIJEN EN MOUTERIJEN. Main/Corp Netherlands. Centraal Bureau voor de Statistiek. **Added/Corp** Netherlands. Centraal Bureau voor de Statistiek. Production Statistics; Brewies and Malt-Houses. **VFOAT** Production Statistics Breweries and Malt-Houses. (1971)-. Dutch (summaries and/or abstracts in English). ir (unnumbered series). Price varies. SDU Uitgeverij, Postbus 20014, Christoffel Plan, 2500 EA Den Haag Netherlands. **Tel** 011 31 70 3789911. **LC** HD9397.N4; N47a.

US/0148-0863
PUBLIC REVENUES FROM ALCOHOL BEVERAGES. [Public revenues alcohol beverages]. 1973-. English. Distilled Spirits Council of the United States, 1250 Eye Street Northwest, Suite 900, Washington DC 20005. **Tel** (202)628-3544. **LC** HD9350.8.U5; A12. **DD** 336.2/786631/0973. ***Continues** Public Revenues from Alcoholic Beverages, 0148-0863.*

CN/0318-9260
PUMP & PRESS. V. 1- Summer 1975-. Periodical. English. qt. $6.00. Pump and Press, Suite 304, 1847 West Broadway, Vancouver BC V6J 1Y6. **DD** 641.8/72/05. ***Supersedes** Amateur Enologist, 0316-6317.*

MW
QUARTERLY NEWSLETTER - TEA RESEARCH FOUNDATION OF CENTRAL AFRICA. **See** Agriculture-Crop Production and Soil.

US/0740-1248
QUARTERLY REVIEW OF WINES. [Q. rev. wines]. **VFOAT** QRW. (19??)-. Periodical. English. Four times a year. $14.95. Quarterly Review of Wines, 24 Garfield Avenue, Winchester MA 01890. **Tel** (617)729-7132, FAX (617)721-0572. **ED** Richard Elia and Randy Sheahan. **DD** 641. cum. index. **Bk Rev**, (Qty: 4). **Ad Acc, Adv Mgr:** Jack Lynch, **Tel** same as editor. **Circ:** 65,000.
Desc: Dedicated to fine wines, selected fine spirits and fine foods.

IT
RASSEGNA ALIMENTARE. (19??)-. Italian. Five times a year. L100000. Editrice Zeus Sas, Corso Buenos Aires 47, 20124 Milan Italy. **Tel** 011 39 2 29406358.

GW/0034-1118
REBE UND WEIN WEINSBERG. VFOAT Rebe Wein (Weinsberg). (194?)-. Periodical. German. Twelve times a year. DM33.60 Germany; DM53.60 other. Jahrbuch Verlag, Postfach 1180, D 74183 Weinsberg Germany. **Tel** 011 49 7134 8061, FAX 011 49 7134 2652. **UDC** 634.8. Index available. **Circ:** 6,600.
Desc: Covers the wine industry.

CN/0715-6618
REPERTOIRE DES VINS ET DES SPIRITUEUX, QUEBEC. (REPERTOIRE DES VINS ET SPIRITUEUX / SOCIETE DES ALCOOLS DU QUEBEC.). V. 1, No. 1, (Dec. 1982)-. Periodical. French. ir. Free. Publicite BM, 85 Ouest, De Castelnau, Montreal Quebec H2R 2W3 Canada. **DD** 663/.1/0294714.

US
REPORT OF ACTIVITIES - NEW MEXICO. DEPT. OF ALCOHOLIC BEVERAGE CONTROL. Main/Corp New Mexico. Dept. of Alcoholic Beverage Control. Office of Director. **VFOAT** Biennial Report of the Director. English. New Mexico Department of Alcoholic Beverage Control, State Capital, Santa Fe NM 87503. **LC** HV5297.N6; N48A. **DD** 353.9/789/0076105.

BL
RESUMOS - CONGRESSO BRASILEIRO DE PESQUISAS CAFEEIRAS. **See** Agriculture-Crop Production and Soil.

US/0416-0525
RETAIL OUTLETS FOR THE SALE OF DISTILLED SPIRITS. **See** Business-Retail.

FR/0035-273X
REVUE DU VIN DE FRANCE (ENGLISH EDITION). (REVUE DU VIN DE FRANCE.). (19??)-. English. Nine times a year. 284.00F France; 580.00F others. Leader International Press, 10 rue Guymener, 92136 Issy L Moulineaux France. **Tel** 011 33 1 41093000, 41093198.

FR/0395-899X
REVUE FRANCAISE D'OENOLOGIE. [Rev. fr. oenol.]. (1966)-. Periodical. French. qt. 385.00F France; 450.00F other. Revue Francaise d'Oenologie, Maison Agriculteurs/Mas Saport, 34970 Lattes France. **Tel** 011 33 67 586906, FAX 011 33 67 586891. **UDC** 663.2. Index available. **Ad Acc. Circ:** 14,000. Documents available from CASDDS.
Ind/Abst Chem. Abstr.

FR
REVUE VINICOLE INTERNATIONALE. THE INTERNATIONAL WINE REVIEW. (1???)-. Periodical. French. mo. 675.81F France; 780.00F other. Leader International Press, 10 rue Guymener, 92136 Issy L Moulineaux France. **Tel** 011 33 1 41093000, 41093198. **(Subscription address:** Leader International Press, 18 20 Rue Guynemer, 92441 Issy L Moulineaux France**)**
Ind/Abst Infomat Int. Bus.

US/0197-1565
ROSTER/INDUSTRY DIRECTORY. Main/Corp Wine and Spirits Wholesalers of America. **VAT** Roster, Industry Directory. 24th Ed. (1973)-. Directory. English. an. $25.00 (members of Wine and Spirits Wholesalers of America); $100.00 (nonmembers). Wine & Spirits Wholesalers of America, 1023 15th Street Northwest, 4th Floor, Washington DC 20005. **Tel** (202)371-9792. ***Continues** Blue Book, Industry Directory, 0364-751X.*

US/0741-6288
SALES OF DISTILLED SPIRITS. (SALES OF DISTILLED SPIRITS : RETAIL SALES IN CONTROL STATES, SUPPLIER SHIPMENTS IN LICENSE STATES BY CLASS AND TYPE / DISTILLED SPIRITS COUNCIL OF THE U.S.). 1978-. English. an. Distilled Spirits Council of the United States, 1250 Eye Street Northwest, Suite 900, Washington DC 20005. **Tel** (202)628-3544. **LC** HD9390.U6; S24. **DD** 381/.456635/00973. ***Continues** Apparent Consumption of Distilled Spirits by Class and Type.*

SP/0037-184X
SEMANA VITIVINICOLA, LE. [Sem. vitivinic.]. (1945)-. Academic Scholarly Publication. Spanish. wk. La Semana Vitivinicola, Apartado 642, 46080 Valencia Spain. **CODEN** SEVIAH. Documents available from

CASDDS.
Ind/Abst Chem. Abstr. (1945-1983); Food Sci. Technol. Abstr.; Vitis Vitic. Enol. Abstr.

JA/0371-3768
SODA TO ENSO. [Soda to enso]. Began in 1950. Academic Scholarly Publication. Japanese. mo. ¥42.00. Nihon Soda Kogyokai, (Japan Soda Industry Assoc.), 6-1, Kajicho 2 Chome, Chiyodaku, Tokyoto 101, Japan. **(Subscription address:** Maruzen Company Ltd., PO Box 5050, Import & Export Department, Tokyo 100 31 Japan.) **ED** Reizo Murai. **CODEN** STOEB8. **Ad Acc. Circ:** 2,800 (ctrl). Documents available from CASDDS.
Desc: An organ of Japan Soda Industry Association. Technical monograph of the Soda Industry.
Ind/Abst Chem. Abstr.

UK/0953-4776
SOFT DRINKS MANAGEMENT INTERNATIONAL. [Soft drinks manag. int.]. **Added/Corp** British Soft Drink Association. (Jan. 1988)-. Periodical. English. mo. £50.00. British Soft Drinks Association Ltd., 20 / 22 Stukeley Street, London WC2B 5LR England. **Tel** 011 44 71 4300356, FAX 011 44 71 8316014. **ED** Stewart Farr. **CODEN** SDMIE3. **Ad Acc, Adv Mgr:** Keith Bailey. ctrl circ. ***Continues*** *Soft Drinks (Twickenham, London, England).*
Ind/Abst BioBusiness; Food Sci. Technol. Abstr.; Infomat Int. Bus.; Int. Packag. Abstr.; Sug. Indus. Abstr.

HU/0560-8538
SORIPAR. [Soripar]. **Added/Corp** Soripari Vallalatok Trosztje. Magyar Elelmezesipari Tudomanyos Egyesulet. Soripari Szakosztaly. (1954)-. Academic Scholarly Publication. Hungarian (summaries and/or abstracts in German). Four times a year. $18.00. Akademiai Kiado, Publishing House of the Hungarian Academy of Sciences, Prielle Kornelia u. 19-35, H-1117 Budapest Hungary. **Tel** 011 36 1 1811991, FAX 011 36 1 1811991, telex 22-6228 AKNYO H. **(Subscription address:** Kultura, Hungarian Foreign Trading Company, PO Box 149, H-1389 Budapest Hungary) **CODEN** SORIBY. Documents available from CASDDS.
Ind/Abst AGRICOLA; Chem. Abstr. (1954-1982); Food Sci. Technol. Abstr.

SA/0253-939X
SOUTH AFRICAN JOURNAL FOR ENOLOGY AND VITICULTURE. (SOUTH AFRICAN JOURNAL FOR ENOLOGY AND VITICULTURE / SAWWV, SASEV.). [S. Afr. j. enol. vitic.]. **Added/Corp** South African Society for Enology and Viticulture. (1980)-. Academic Scholarly Publication. English. sa. $15.00 US; R30.00 other. South African Society of Enology and Viticulture, PO Box 2092 / Dennesig, Stellenbosch 7600 South Africa. **Tel** 011 27 2211 631001. **ED** P.G. Goussard. **CODEN** SAJVD5. Index available. cum. index. **Ad Acc.** ctrl circ. Documents available from BIOSIS Document Express, CASDDS.
Ind/Abst Biocont. News Inf.; Biol. Abstr. (1988-); Chem. Abstr.; Crop Physiol. Abstr.; Food Sci. Technol. Abstr.; Irr. Drain. Abstr.; Rev. Agric. Entomol.; Rev. Plant Pathol.; Soils Fert.

US/0193-0613
SOUTHERN BEVERAGE JOURNAL. [South. beverage j.]. (19??)-. Periodical. English. Twelve times a year. $200.00. Southern Beverage Journal, PO Box 561107, Miami FL 33256. **Tel** (305)233-7230, FAX (305)252-2580. **ED** Jacqueline N. Preston. **DD** 338. **Bk Rev. Ad Acc. Circ:** 30,000 (ctrl).
Desc: An independent publication devoted to liquor, wine and beer licensees in package stores, bars, clubs, restaurants and hotels.

US/0192-1835
SOUTHERN CALIFORNIA BEVERAGE BULLETIN. **VFOAT** Beverage Bulletin. (19??)-. Bulletin. English. mo. $24.00. Beverage Bulletin, 8383 Wilshire Boulevard, Suite 345, Beverly Hills CA 90211. **Tel** (213)653-4445. **ED** Michael Lynn. **Bk Rev. Ad Acc. Circ:** 16,000 (ctrl).
Desc: Business newspaper mailed to every retail merchant in Southern California, with distilled spirits, beer and wine coverage.

US/0747-3206
SPIRITS, WINE & BEER MARKETING IN MINNESOTA, NORTH AND SOUTH DAKOTA. **VFOAT** Spirits, Wine and Beer Marketing in Minnesota, North and South Dakota. (198?)-. Periodical. English. ir. Beverage Journal Inc. / Minnesota, 4504 Excelsior Boulevard, Minneapolis MN 55416. **Tel** (612)920-7711. ***Continues*** *Northwest Beverage Journal.*

US/0747-3214
SPIRITS, WINE & BEVERAGE MARKETING IN IOWA. **VFOAT** Spirits, Wine and Beer Marketing in Iowa. Periodical. English. mo. $5.00. Beverage Journal Inc. / Minnesota, 4504 Excelsior Boulevard, Minneapolis MN 55416. **Tel** (612)920-7711. ***Continues*** *Iowa Beverage Journal, 0191-4650.*

CE/1010-4208
SRI LANKA JOURNAL OF TEA SCIENCE. **Added/Corp** Tea Research Institute of Sri Lanka. (1985)-. Periodical. English. Twice a year. $20.00 other. Tea Research Institute of Sri Lanka, Publications Officer, Talawakele Republic Sri Lanka. **Tel** 11 94 8244. **ED** P. Sivapalan and A. Kathiravetpillai. Index available. ***Continues*** *Tea Quarterly, 0040-036X.*
Desc: Information of interest to the tea industry.
Ind/Abst Crop Physiol. Abstr.; For. Abstr.; Hortic. Abstr.; Nematol. Abstr.; Plant Breed. Abstr.; Plant Grow. Reg. Abstr.; Postharvest News Inf.; Rev. Agric. Entomol.; Soils Fert.; Weed Abstr.

US/0363-0072
STATISTICAL SUMMARY - COMMONWEALTH OF VIRGINIA, STATE MILK COMMISSION. **See** Food and Food Industry-Abstracting, Bibliographies and Statistics.

US/0081-931X
SUMMARY OF STATE LAWS AND REGULATIONS RELATING TO DISTILLED SPIRITS. **See** Law.

UN/0230-2241
SZOLOTERMEZTESES BORASZAT. (VINOGRADARSTVO I VINODELIE.). [Szolotermezt. borasz.]. **Added/Corp** Ukraine. Ministerstvo Silskoho Hospodarstva. **VFOAT** Szolotermezteses Boraszat. No. 7 (1969)-. Russian. 1.06rub (single issue). Ul B Podvalnaia 10, Kiev Ukraine. **LC** SB396.5; .V54. ***Continues*** *Vinogradarstvo.*
Ind/Abst AGRICOLA.

US/0040-0343
TEA & COFFEE TRADE JOURNAL, THE. [Tea coffee trade j.]. **VFOAT** Tea and Coffee Trade Journal. **VAT** Tea and Coffee Trade Journal. (1903)-. Periodical. English. Twelve times a year. $30.00 US & Canada & Mexico; $46.00 others. Lockwood Trade Journal Co. Inc., 130 West 42nd Street, 22nd Floor, New York NY 10036. **Tel** (212)391-2060. **ED** Jane Phillips McCabe. **DD** 382. **CODEN** TCTJA7. **Ad Acc. Circ:** 8,500. available on an online database (file 648/Full-Text) from DIALOG. ***Continues*** *Tea, Coffee and Sugar.*
Desc: Reaches executives and managers of International Tea and Coffee Inc. Editorializes on green trade, roasting coffee and packaging of tea.
Ind/Abst BioBusiness; F&S Index Plus Text, Int. [Select. Cov.]; Food Sci. Technol. Abstr.; Predicasts Forecasts; Trade Ind. ASAP [Full Txt.]; Trade Ind. Index [Full Txt.].

CE/1012-3962
TEA BULLETIN. [Tea bull.]. (1981)-. Periodical. English.
Ind/Abst Biodeter. Abstr.; Rev. Plant Pathol.; Weed Abstr.

II
TEA DIRECTORY. 1966-. Directory. English. Rs16.00. Tea Board, 14 Biplabi Trailokya Maharaj Sarani, Calcutta-700 001 India. **LC** HD9195.A1; T32. **DD** 380.1/41/37202554. ***Continues*** *All-India Tea Directory.*

II
TEA STATISTICS (CALCUTTA, INDIA : 1982). **See** Food and Food Industry-Abstracting, Bibliographies and Statistics.

AT/0313-0568
THOMSON'S LIQUOR GUIDE. [Thomson's liquor guide]. (1976)-. Periodical. English. mo. 128.00Aus$ Australia; 151.00Aus$ New Zealand, Papua New Guinea; 156.00Aus$ Malaysia, Indonesia, Fiji; 158.00Aus$ Japan, India, Hong Kong; 170.00Aus$ US, Canada, Lebanon; 181.00Can$ Europe, Africa, former USSR. Thomson Publications / Australia, 47 Chippen Street, Chippendale New South Wales, 2008 Australia. **Tel** 011 61 2 6992411, FAX 011 61 2 698 3920, telex 122226. **(Subscription address:** Thomson Publications Australia, PO Box 815, Strawberry Hills, New South Wales, 2012 Australia.) **DD** 641.20994.

CN/0824-1465
TRAVERS LES VIGNES, A. **VFOAT** On the Grapevine. Periodical. English. bm. Society for American Wines, PO Box 4901 Station E, Ottawa Ontario K1S 5J1 Canada. **Tel** (613)233-9039. **ED** Marcia Almey. **DD** 641.2/22/05. **Bk Rev. Circ:** 1,200 (ctrl). ***Continues*** *Newsletter (Society for American Wines).*
Desc: Newsletter for private club members on American wine. The purpose is educational.

US/1059-6887
U.S. BEER MARKET. [U. S. beer mark.]. **VFOAT** US Beer Market; Impact Databank Review and Forecast. **VAT** United States Beer Market. (1989)-. English. an. $806.46 New York City, $745.00 other. M. Shanken Communications, Inc., 387 Park Avenue South, New York NY 10016. **Tel** (212)684-4224, FAX (212)684-5424, telex 422687 MSHANK UI. **LC** HD9397.U5; I46. **DD** 380.1/4566342/0973. ***Continues*** *Impact American Beer Market Review and Forecast, 0198-9952.*

US
U.S. DISTILLED SPIRITS MARKET. **VFOAT** US Distilled Spirits Market; Impact Databank Review and Forecast; Impact. (1989)-. English. an. $806.46 New York City; $745.00 other. M. Shanken Communications, Inc., 387 Park Avenue South, New York NY 10016. **Tel** (212)684-4224, FAX (212)684-5424, telex 422687 MSHANK UI. **LC** HD9390.U6; I47. **DD** 380.1/456635/0097305. ***Continues*** *Impact American Distilled Spirits Market Review and Forecast, 0163-9536.*

US/0163-9544
U.S. WINE MARKET. **VFOAT** Impact Databank Review and Forecast; US Wine Market; Impact. **VAT** United States Wine Market. (1989)-. English. an. $806.46 New York City, $745.00 other. M. Shanken Communications, Inc., 387 Park Avenue South, New York NY 10016. **Tel** (212)684-4224, FAX (212)684-5424, telex 422687 MSHANK UI. **LC** HD9374; .I56. **DD** 381/.456632/0097305. ***Continues*** *Impact American Wine Market Review and Forecast, 0163-9544.*

●US
ULTIMATE GUIDE TO BUYING WINE / THE WINE SPECTATOR. **VFOAT** Wine Spectator's Ultimate Guide to Buying Wine. 1993 Ed. (1993)-. English. $14.95. **LC** TP544; .W558. **DD** 641.2/2/05. ***Continues*** *Wine Spectator's Ultimate Guide to Buying Wine, 1058-5729.*

US/1047-6865
UNDERGROUND WINE JOURNAL, THE. [Undergr. wine j.]. **VFOAT** Wine Journal. Vol. 10, No. 1 (Aug. 1988)-. Periodical. English. Twelve times a year. $48.00 US; $60.00 Canada; $78.00 others. Wine Journal Enterprises, PO Box 3567, South Pasadena CA 91031. **Tel** (818)441-6617, FAX (818)441-6765. **ED** John Tilson, Ted Swinnerton, and Joseph L. Sullivan. **LC** TP544; .U53. **DD** 641. **Ad Acc.** ***Continues*** *Wine Journal, 0892-3833.*
Desc: A defintive guide to the finest wines of the world.

FR/1145-5799
VIGNE PARIS, LA. (LA VIGNE.). (1990)-. Periodical. French. Ten times a year. 347.70F France; 405.00F other. Nouvelles Edns Publs Agricoles, 8 Cite Paradis, F 75010 Paris France. **Tel** 011 33 1 40227900. **UDC** 634.8. ***Continues*** *La France Agricole. Edition France Viticole, 0981-3918.*

FR
VIGNERON CHAMPENOIS, LE. **Added/Corp** Association Viticole Champenoise. (1???)-. Periodical. French. Eleven times a year (July/Aug., issues combined). 195.89F Marne Aisne & Aube, 254.65F others Depts of France; 370.00F others. Le Vigneron Champenois, 5 rue Henri Martin, 51204 Epernay Cedex France. **Tel** 011 33 26 544561, FAX 26.55.19.79, telex AVE 830516F. **Circ:** 5,400.
Desc: Dedicated to the viniculture, in particularly the producing of champagne.
Ind/Abst AGRICOLA.

IT/0390-0479
VIGNEVINI. [Vignevini]. Vol. 1 (Nov./Dec. 1974)-. Academic Scholarly Publication. Italian. mo. L88000. Edagricole, PO Box 2157, 40100 Bologna Italy. **Tel** 011 39 51 492211 Ext. 22, FAX 011 39 51 493660, telex 510336 EDAGRI. **LC** SB387; .V634. **CODEN** VIGNDL. Index available in last issue of volume--attached. Documents available from CASDDS.
Ind/Abst AGRICOLA; Agric. Eng. Abstr. (1991-); Chem. Abstr.; Crop Physiol. Abstr.; Food Sci. Technol. Abstr.; Hortic. Abstr.; Nematol. Abstr.; Life Sci. Collect.; Plant Breed. Abstr.; Soils Fert.; Vitis Vitic. Enol. Abstr.; Weed Abstr.; World Agric. Econ.

IT
VIN VALDATAIN, PIEMONTEIS, LIGURE. Yearly V. 1- ; Oct./Dec. 1974-. Periodical. Italian (Italian). 6000. Eda, Via Avogadro 22, Turin Italy. **LC** TP559.I8; V54.

US/0276-4687
VINEYARD ALMANAC & WINE GAZETTEER, THE. **VFOAT** Vineyard Almanac and Wine Gazetteer. English. an. $2.25. Vineyard Almanac and Wine Gazetteer, 960 North San Antonia Road, Suite 125, Los Altos CA 94022. **LC** TP557; .V55. **DD** 641.2/22/05.

US/1047-4951
VINEYARD & WINERY MANAGEMENT. [Vineyard winery manage.]. Vol. 12, No. 2 (May/June 1986)-. Periodical. English. Six times a year. $25.00 (one year), $46.00 (two year), $69.00 (three year) US; $37.00 (one year), $70.00 (two year), $132.00 (three year) other. Vineyard and Winery Management, PO Box 231, Watkins Glen NY 14891. **Tel** (607)535-7133, (607)535-5670, FAX (607)535-2998. **ED** J William Moffett. **LC** TP544; .V53. **DD** 634.8/09. **CODEN** VWMAE9. cum. index. **Ad Acc, Adv Mgr:** Hope Merletti, **Tel** (800)535-5670. **Circ:** 3,500 (ctrl). ***Continues*** *Eastern Grape Grower & Winery News, 0194-5254.*
Desc: Bottom line resource for vineyard and winery owners and operators outlining basic how-tos of the grape industry.
Ind/Abst BioBusiness (1989-).

US
VINEYARD VIEW. Periodical. English. Greyton H Taylor Wine Museum, Greyton Taylor Memorial Drive, Hammondsport NY 14840.

IT/0042-630X
VINI D'ITALIA. ***Ceased.*** [Vini Ital.]. **VFOAT** Wines of Italy. Vol. 14, No. 76 (Jan./Feb. 1972)-(1992). Periodical.

Italian (English, French and Spanish). bm. Edizioni AEB Spa, Via Vittorio Arici 92, San Polo 25010 Brescia Italy. **Tel** +39 30 2301761, FAX +39 30 2302679, telex 301271 AEB I. **ED** Pietro Giacomini. **CODEN** VIITAC. **Circ:** 8,000 (ctrl). Documents available from CASDDS.
Desc: International oenological review.
Ind/Abst AGRICOLA; Chem. Abstr.; Food Sci. Technol. Abstr.; Vitis Vitic. Enol. Abstr.

US/0095-3563
VINIFERA WINE GROWERS JOURNAL, THE. ***Ceased.*** **See** Agriculture-Crop Production and Soil.

IT
VINO, IL. Elemond Arte SRL, Via Trentacoste 7, 20134 Milan Italy. **Tel** 011 39 2 215631.

XR/0042-6326
VINOHRAD. [Vinohrad]. **Added/Corp** Slovak Socialist Republic (Czechoslovakia). Ministerstvo Poinohospodarstva a Vyzivy. (1963)-. Academic Scholarly Publication. Czech. mo. **CODEN** VINOAM. Documents available from CASDDS. ***Continues*** *Vinarstvi.*
Ind/Abst Chem. Abstr.; Life Sci. Collect.

FR
VINS D'ALSACE. French. mo. 138.00F France; 165.00F other. Assn Viticulteurs d'Alsace, BP 396, 68007 Colmar Cedex France. **Tel** 011 33 89 242400.
Desc: All about vineyards, wines and their promotion.

US/0737-6626
VINTAGE BUYERS GUIDE. (VINTAGE.). [Vintage buy. guide]. Vol. 13, No. 2 (July 1984)-. Periodical. Serbo-Croatian (Cyrillic). an. $20.00. Philip Seldon, 301 East 79th Street/Suite 27E, New York NY 10021. **DD** 641.

SZ/0177-2570
VINUM. (1989)-. Periodical. German (French). Ten times a year (French edition only 4 issues per year). 45.00F Switzerland; 52.00F other. Vinum Verlags AG, Klosbachstrasse 85, CH 8030 Zurich Switzerland. **Tel** 011 41 1 2622618, FAX 011 41 1 2519953. **LC** TP544; .V57. **DD** 641.2/2/05. cum. index. **Bk Rev**, (Qty: 1-2). **Ad Acc.** ctrl circ.

GW/0175-8292
VITIS, VITICULTURE AND ENOLOGY ABSTRACTS. **See** Food and Food Industry-Abstracting, Bibliographies and Statistics.

US/0890-8060
WASHINGTON BEVERAGE INSIGHT. (WASHINGTON BEVERAGE INSIGHT / GEORGE WELLS.). [Wash. beverage insight]. **Added/Corp** George Wells & Associates. (19??)-. English. wk. $350.00. George Wells and Associates, 2942 South Columbus Street, Suite A-2, Arlington VA 22206. **Tel** (703)671-8140. **ED** George Wells. **DD** 338. Index available. cum. index. available on an online database (files 16,636/Full-Text) from DIALOG.
Ind/Abst PROMT [Full Txt.]; PTS Newsl. Database [Full Txt.].

●US/1058-9341
WASHINGTON BEVERAGE JOURNAL. [Wash. beverage j.]. **VFOAT** Maryland-Washington Beverage Journal; Maryland Washington, D.C. Beverage Journal. (199?)-. Periodical. English. mo. $30.00. Beverage Journal, 7451 Race Road, Box 1002, Hanover MD 21076. **Tel** (301)235-1717, FAX (301)243-8505. **DD** 641. ***Continues*** *Maryland-Washington Beverage Journal (Washington, D.C. Ed.), 1051-9785.*

GW/0341-6364
WEINWIRTSCHAFT, DIE. [Weinwirtschaft]. (19??)-. Academic Scholarly Publication. German (English). an. Fachverlag Dr Fraund GmbH, Postfach 1329, D 61364 Friedrichsdorf Germany. **Tel** 011 49 6172 71060. **LC** HD9383.1; .W44. **DD** 338.4/76632/00943. **CODEN** WEMADT. Documents available from CASDDS.
Ind/Abst Chem. Abstr.

GW/0723-1350
WEINWIRTSCHAFT. MARKT, DIE. **VFOAT** Markt; WW. Markt. (Jan. 1983)-. Periodical. German. bw. DM234.00 Germany; DM282.00 other. Verlag & Druckerei Meininger GmbH, Postfach 100762, D 67407 Neustadt Wein Germany. **Tel** 011 49 6321 890830. **LC** HD9383.1; .W443. **DD** 338.4/76632/00943. **[CCC].** ***Continues in part*** *Weinwirtschaft.*
Ind/Abst Food Sci. Technol. Abstr.; Vitis Vitic. Enol. Abstr.

GW/0723-1369
WEINWIRTSCHAFT. TECHNIK, DIE. ***Title Change.*** [Weinwirtsch., Tech.]. **VFOAT** Technik. (1983)-(Jan. 1993). Academic Scholarly Publication. German. wk. DM8.50 single issue. Deutscher Weinwirtschaftsverlag Meininger GmbH & Company KG, Maximillianstr 7-17, Postfach 312, W-6730 Neustadt an Der Weinstrasse Germany. **LC** TP559.G3; W445. **DD** 663/.22/05. **CODEN** WETED8. **[CCC].** Documents available from CASDDS. ***Continues in part*** *Weinwirtschaft.* ***Merged into*** *Der Deutsche Weinbau.*
Ind/Abst Chem. Abstr.; Food Sci. Technol. Abstr.; Sug. Indus. Abstr.; Vitis Vitic. Enol. Abstr.

CN/0714-2056
WHAT'S BREWING. (WHAT'S BREWING : CAMPAIGN FOR REAL ALE CANADA NEWSLETTER.). [What's brew.]. Vol. 1, No. 1 (Apr. 1981)-. Newsletter. English. qt. 18.00Can$. Campaign for Real Ale Canada, PO Box 2036 Station D, Ottawa Ontario K1P 5W3 Canada. **Tel** (613)236-6256. **ED** David Bowyer. **DD** 641.2/3/0971. **Bk Rev. Ad Acc. Circ:** 2,000 (ctrl).
Desc: Provides information on Canadian and US small breweries and home brewing advice for amateurs and advanced brewers.

UK/0043-5791
WINE. **VFOAT** Wine Magazine. (19??)-. Periodical. English. mo (12 issues). £27.50 UK; £35.00 Eire & Europe; £50.00 America; Middle East, Africa & India; £53.00 Australia, New Zealand & Japan. Haymarket Publishing Ltd., 12 14 Ansdell Street, London W8 5TR England. **Tel** 011 44 483 733800, FAX 011 44 483 776573. **(Subscription address:** Haymarket Publishing Ltd, PO Box 219, Subscriptions Department, Woking Surrey GU21 1ZW, United Kingdom.**)** ***Continues*** *Wine Quarterly Review.*

US/0887-8463
WINE ADVOCATE, THE. [Wine advocate]. **VFOAT** Robert M. Parker's The Wine Advocate. (19??)-. Periodical. English. bm. $35.00 (one year), $60.00 (two years), $85.00 (three years). Wine Advocate, Robert Parker Jr, PO Box 311, Monkton MD 21111. **Tel** (301)329-6477, telex 198169 WINE ADVOCATE. **Bk Rev.**

CN/0227-3837
WINE & DINE. **See** Food and Food Industry.

US
WINE & LIQUOR SALES. **Main/Corp** Florida. State Beverage Dept. Periodical. English. mo.

UK
WINE & SPIRIT INTERNATIONAL. **VFOAT** Wine and Spirit International; Wine and Spirit; Wine & Spirit. (1986)-. Periodical. English. mo (12 issue). £80.00 UK; £85.00 Eire & Europe; £100.00 America, Middle East, Africa & India; £105.00 Australia, New Zealand & Japan. Haymarket Publishing Ltd., 12 14 Ansdell Street, London W8 5TR England. **Tel** 011 44 483 733800, FAX 011 44 483 776573. **(Subscription address:** Haymarket Publishing Ltd, PO Box 219, Subscriptions Department, Woking Surrey GU21 1ZW, United Kingdom.**)** ***Continues*** *Wine & Spirit, 0264-4897.*

US/0890-0299
WINE & SPIRITS (BERKELEY, CALIF.). (WINE & SPIRITS.). [Wine spirits]. **VFOAT** Wine and Spirits. (198?)-. Periodical. English. Eight times a year. $22.00. Winestate Publications Inc, PO Box 1548, Princeton NJ 08542. **Tel** (415)255-7736, (609)921-1060, FAX (415)255-9659, (609)921-2566. **ED** Joshua Greene, (editor's address: 82 Linden Lane, Princeton, NJ 08542, phone: (609)921-2196). **LC** WMLC 93/2517. **DD** 641. **Ad Acc, Adv Mgr:** Michael Kinney, **Tel** (415)255-9659. **Circ:** 60,000 (ctrl). ***Continues*** *Wine & Spirits Buying Guide, 0748-6065; International Wine Review.*
Desc: Consumer magazine promoting the greater appreciation and enjoyment of wine and fine spirits. Features include articles on food and travel as well as results of the American Wine Competition, and restaurant and retail surveys.

US/1057-8544
WINE BUSINESS INSIDER. [Wine bus. insider]. Vol. 1, No. 8 (June 10, 1991)-. Periodical. English. Fifty times a year. $159.00 US; $219.00 other. Wine Business Publications, 867 West Napa Street, Sonoma CA 95476. **Tel** (707)939-0822, FAX (707)939-0833. **ED** Rich Cartiere. **DD** 641. **Circ:** 1,000. available on an online database (file 16,636/Full-Text) from DIALOG. ***Continues*** *Napa/Sonoma Wine Business, 1056-1447.*
Desc: A weekly information service for the wine industry.
Ind/Abst PROMT [Full Txt.]; PTS Newsl. Database [Full Txt.].

US/1048-0455
WINE COUNTRY INTERNATIONAL. [Wine ctry. int.]. **VFOAT** Wine Country. Periodical. English. bm. Wine Country, 985 Lincoln Avenue, Benicia CA 94510. **Tel** (707)746-0741. **LC** F868.N2; W56. **DD** 979.4/18. ***Continues*** *Wine Country, 0278-047X.*

US/0892-662X
WINE EAST. [Wine east]. (198?)-. Periodical. English. Six times a year. $18.00 US; $26.00 other. Wine East, 620 North Pine Street, Lancaster PA 17603. **Tel** (717)393-0943. **ED** Hudson Cattell and Linda Jones McKee. **LC** TP544; .W54. **DD** 663/.2/00974. **Bk Rev. Ad Acc.**

US/1046-6851
WINE EDUCATOR, THE. (THE WINE EDUCATOR : THE JOURNAL OF THE SOCIETY OF WINE EDUCATORS.). [Wine educ.]. **Added/Corp** Society of Wine Educators (U.S.). Vol. 1, No. 1 (1990)-. Periodical. English. sa. $150.00 (institution). The Society of Wine Educators, 132 Shaker Road, Suite 14, East Longmeadow MA 01028. **LC** WMLC L 83/9177. **DD** 641.

US/0889-4256
WINE INVESTOR. EXECUTIVE EDITION, THE. [Wine investor, Exec. ed.]. **VFOAT** Wine Investor/Executive Edition. (19??)-. Periodical. English. Thirty-six times a year. $300.00. Paul Gillete, 3284 Barham Boulevard, Suite 201, Los Angeles CA 90068. **Tel** (213)876-7590. **ED** Paul Gillette. **DD** 338. **Bk Rev. Ad Acc.**

US
WINE NEWS, THE. English. bm (begins with Feb.). $18.00 US; $38.00 Canada; $48.00 other. Wine News, 353 Alcazar Ave/Ste 101-B, Coral Gables FL 33134. **Tel** (305)444-7250. **ED** Kathy Sinnes and Elizabeth Smith, (305)444-7309. **Bk Rev**, (Qty: 12/yr). **Ad Acc, Adv Mgr:** Elizabeth Kuehner, **Tel** (303)444-6110. **Circ:** 40,000.
Desc: Informative, educational, entertaining, authoritative, incisive wine and food consumer-oriened editorial.

US/1065-4895
WINE NEWS (CORAL GABLES, FLA.), THE. (THE WINE NEWS.). [Wine news]. (198?)-. Periodical. English. bm. $18.00 US; $38.00 Canada. Wine News, 353 Alcazar Ave/Ste 101-B, Coral Gables FL 33134. **Tel** (305)444-7250. **ED** Elizabeth K. Smith. **LC** TP544; .W5527. **DD** 641.2/2/05. cum. index. **Bk Rev. Ad Acc. Circ:** 40,000. ***Continues*** *Eastside Wine News.*

US/0094-5153
WINE NOW. Periodical. English. bm. Wine Journal, 575 West End Avenue, New York NY 10024. **LC** TP544; .W553. **DD** 641.2/2/05.

US/1053-4776
WINE ON LINE. (WINE ON LINE [COMPUTER FILE] : INTERNATIONAL FOOD & WINE MAGAZINE.). [Wine line]. Issue 1, Vol. 1 (Nov. 1, 1990)-. Periodical. English. mo. $35.00. Enterprises Publishing, 400 East 59th Street, Suite 9F, New York NY 10022. **Tel** (212)755-4363, FAX (212)755-4365. **DD** 641. available on CD-ROM.

AT
WINE PRODUCTION, AUSTRALIA AND STATES / AUSTRALIAN BUREAU OF STATISTICS. **See** Food and Food Industry-Abstracting, Bibliographies and Statistics.

US/0193-497X
WINE SPECTATOR, THE. [Wine spect.]. (197?)-. Periodical. English. Twenty times a year (published twice monthly except 1 issue in Jan. and Aug.). $40.00 (one year), $75.00 (two year), $105.00 (three year) US; $53.50 (one year), $96.30 (two year), Canada; $110.00 (one year) $200 (three year) other. M. Shanken Communications, Inc., 387 Park Avenue South, New York NY 10016. **Tel** (212)684-4224, FAX (212)684-5424, telex 422687 MSHANK UI. **(Subscription address:** Wine Spectator, PO Box 50463, Boulder CO 80323.**) ED** Marvin R. Shanken. **DD** 641. **CODEN** WISPEV. **Bk Rev. Ad Acc. Circ:** 55,000. Documents available from UMI Article Clearinghouse.
Desc: A newspaper for wine enthusiasts with international coverage.
Ind/Abst Foods Adlibra; Gen. Period. Index (1989-); Mag. Index Plus (1989-); Mag. Index. Sel. (1989-); Mark. Advert. Ref. Serv.; Newsp. Period. Abstr. (1988-); PROMT; Mag. Index (1989-).

US/1058-5729
WINE SPECTATOR ULTIMATE GUIDE TO BUYING WINE, THE. ***Title Change.*** [Wine spect. ultim. guide buy. wine]. **VFOAT** Ultimate Guide to Buying Wine. Vol. 1 (1992)-(1992). English. Wine Spectator Press, 601 Van Ness Avenue, Suite 2014, San Francisco CA 94102. **LC** TP544; .W558. **DD** 641.2/2/05. ***Continued by*** *Ultimate Guide to Buying Wine.*

US/0749-033X
WINE SPECTATOR'S GUIDE TO SELECTED WINES, THE. **VFOAT** Guide to Selected Wines. English. an. $7.95. Wine Spectator Press, 601 Van Ness Avenue, Suite 2014, San Francisco CA 94102. **LC** TP546.5; .W56. **DD** 641.2/22.

US/0897-8492
WINE SPECTATOR'S WINE COUNTRY GUIDE TO CALIFORNIA, THE. [Wine spect. wine ctry. guide Calif.]. **VFOAT** Wine Spectator's Guide to California Wine Country; Wine Country Guide to California; Wine Spectator. (1988/89)-. English. an. $4.95. M. Shanken Communications, Inc., 387 Park Avenue South, New York NY 10016. **Tel** (212)684-4224, FAX (212)684-5424, telex 422687 MSHANK UI. **(Subscription address:** PO Box 1960, Marion, OH 43305**) LC** TP557; .W687. **DD** 663/.2/0025794. ***Continues*** *Wine Maps, 0882-7206.*

CN/0228-6157
WINE TIDINGS. [Wine tidings]. **VFOAT** Tidings. **VAT** Tidings (Montreal. 1980). No. 49 (July/Aug. 1980)-. Periodical. English. Eight times a year (monthly except

Jan. & Feb. with May/June & July/Aug. issues combined). 24.50Can$ (one year), 42.00Can$ (two years) Canada; 35.00Can$ US; 39.00Can$ other. Kylix Media Inc, 5165 Sherbrooke Street West, Montreal Quebec H4A 1T6 Canada. **Tel** (514)481-5892, FAX (514)481-9699. **ED** Tony Aspler. **DD** 663/.2/00971. **Bk Rev. Ad Acc. Circ:** 17,000. ***Continues*** *Tidings, 0381-730X.*
Desc: Canadian magazine for discerning wine lovers. Features articles on wine appreciation, winemaking and travel to the wine-producing countries. Reviews wine price trends, vintage reports, restaurant cellars in Canada and abroad and wine lovers' recipes. Comparative tasting notes by panel gives insight into making selections.

US/0196-1381
WINE TRADE (SAN FRANCISCO), THE. (THE WINE TRADE.). V. 1- Nov. 1979-. Periodical. English. mo. $48.00. The Wine Trade, PO Box 77291, San Francisco CA 94107. **Tel** (415)285-7333. **ED** Ed Everett.

US/0199-7483
WINE WORLD. [Wine world]. (Oct./Nov. 1971)-. Periodical. English. qt. $16.00. Wine World Publishing Company, 6433 Topanga Cyn Boulevard, Suite 412, Canoga Park CA 91303. **Tel** (818)346-9326. **ED** Dee Sindt. **LC** TP544; .W56. **DD** 641.2/2/05. **Bk Rev. Ad Acc. Circ:** 50,000 (ctrl).
Desc: Entertains and informs the novice as well as the expert. Features wineries and vineyards of the world. Contains buyer's guide.
Ind/Abst Consum. Index Prod. Eval. Inf. Source; Gen. Period. Index (1985-1987); Mag. Index (1977-?).

US/0043-583X
WINES AND VINES. [Wines vines]. **VFOAT** Wines & Vines. (1935)-. Periodical. English. mo. $32.50 (1 year), $59.00 (2 year), $86.00 (3 year) US; $39.00 (1 year), $72.00 (2 year), $106.00 (3 year) Canada and Mexico; $50.00 (1 year), $94.00 (2 year), $139.00 (3 year) other. Wines & Vines, 1800 Lincoln Avenue, San Rafael CA 94901. **Tel** (415)453-9700, FAX (415)453-2517. **ED** Philip Hiaring Jr. and Larry Walker. **DD** 663. **Bk Rev. Ad Acc. Circ:** 4,300. available on an online database (file 648/Full-Text) from DIALOG. ***Continues*** *California Grape Grower;* ***Absorbed*** *Wine Review, 0096-8471.*
Desc: Technical trade publication for the wine industry, with statistics and an emphasis on grape growing and grape product processing of various levels such as wine and juice processing and marketing.
Ind/Abst AGRICOLA; Predicasts; Trade Ind. ASAP [Full Txt.]; Trade Ind. Index [Full Txt.]; Vitis Vitic. Enol. Abstr.

US/0043-583X
WINES & VINES. BUYER'S GUIDE ISSUE. **VFOAT** Buyer's Guide Issue; Wines & Vines. Directory Issue; Directory of the Wine Industry in North America. (19??)-. English. an. $45.00 US; $55.00 Canada and Mexico; $65.00 other. The Hiaring Company, 1800 Lincoln Avenue, San Rafael CA 94901. **Tel** (415)453-9700, FAX (415)453-2517. **ED** Dorthy Kubota-Cordery. **Bk Rev. Ad Acc. Circ:** 4,500. ***Continues*** *Directory of the Wine Industry in North America, 0749-9272.*
Desc: A technical trade publication for the wine industry.

AT/0156-6490
WINESTATE. [Winestate]. (1978)-. Periodical. English. Six times a year (Jan., Mar., May, July, Sept., Nov.). 28.00Aus$ Australia, 40.00Aus$ others (surface mail); 45.00Aus$ New Zealand, 55.00Aus$ others (airmail). Winestate Magazine, 254 Franklin Street, Adelaide SA 5000 Australia. **Tel** 011 61 8 2314133, FAX 011 61 8 2312113. **ED** Larry Ellenwood. **DD** 641.220994. **Bk Rev**, (Qty: 6). **Ad Acc, Adv Mgr:** P. Simic. **Circ:** 20,000.

AU/0043-5953
WINZER : FACHBLATT DES OSTERREICHISCHE WEINHAUS, DER. **Added/Corp** Bundesverband der Weinbautreibenden Osterreichs. (1954)-. Periodical. German. mo. S630.00 Austria; S780.00 other. Osterreichischer Agrarverlag, Inkustr 1 7 Bueropark Donau, A 3400 Klosterneuberg Austria. **Tel** 011 43 2243 33300.

US/1071-1090
WORLD BEER REVIEW. [World beer rev.]. (1987)-. Periodical. English. bm. $18.50 (1 year), $33.00 (2 year). World Beer Review, PO Box 71, Clemson SC 29633. **Tel** (803)654-3360, FAX (803)654-5067. **ED** Steve Johnson. **DD** 641. **Circ:** 950.

US/0043-8340
WORLD COFFEE & TEA. [World coffee tea]. **VFOAT** World Coffee and Tea. Vol. 1 (May 1960)-. Periodical. English. mo. $24.00 (one year), $40.00 (two year), $60.00 (three year) US; $30.00 (one year), $55.00 (two year), $75.00 (three year) surface mail, $90.00 (one year), $175.00 (two year), $255.00 (three year) airmail other. World Coffee & Tea, PO Box 507, West Haven CT 06516. **Tel** (203)934-5288, (203)934-4631, telex 963453. **ED** Richard F. Hanley. **LC** HD9195.A1; W6. **Ad Acc. Circ:** 6,500 (ctrl).
Desc: Edited for those responsible for growing, exporting, importing, processing and marketing coffee and/or tea.
Ind/Abst Life Sci. Collect.

IT/1121-158X
WORLD OF BEER, THE. [World of beer]. (1988)-. Periodical. English (Italian). Twice a year (Mar. & Oct.). $21.00 US & Europe; $36.00 Middle East; $51.00 Africa, Asia & South America; $56.00 Australia. Tuttopress Editrice SRL, via Cagliero 21, 20125 Milan Italy. **Tel** 011 39 2 6682834, FAX 011 39 2 6072185. **UDC** 663.4. **Bk Rev. Ad Acc, Adv Mgr:** Edwin Janus, **Tel** 02 6682834. **Circ:** 15,000.

US/0145-9848
WORLD WINE ALMANAC & WINE ATLAS. (WORLD WINE ALMANAC & WINE ATLAS COMPLETE WINE BUYING GUIDE & CATALOGUE OF WINE LABELS.). **VAT** World Wine Almanac and Wine Atlas Complete Wine Buying Guide and Catalogue of Wine Labels. 1976-. Consumer Publication. English. International Wine Society, 304 East 45th Street, New York NY 10017. **LC** TP544; .T74. **DD** 641.2/2/0275.

SA/0043-9657
WYNBOER. (DIE WYNBOER.). [Wynboer]. **Added/Corp** Ko-operatieve Wynbouwers Vereniging. (1931)-. Periodical. Afrikaans (English). Twelve times a year. R59.50 South Africa; R85.00 others. Ko-operatieve Wynbouwers Vereniging - KWV, PO Box 528, Suider Paarl 7624 South Africa. **Tel** 011 27 2233 631001, FAX 011 27 2211 631562. **(Subscription address:** National News Distributors, PO Box 53085, Troyville 2139 South Africa.) **ED** Henry Hopkins.
Desc: This magazine is for the wine lovers.
Ind/Abst AGRICOLA.

JA/0916-6858
YASAI CHAGYO SHIKENJO KENKYU HOKOKU. B, CHAGYO. **Added/Corp** Norin Suisansho Yasai Chagyo Shikenjo (Japan). **VFOAT** Chagyo; Tea; Bulletin of the National Research Institute of Vegetables, Ornamental Plants and Tea. Series B, Tea. (Mar. 1991)-. Periodical. Japanese (summaries and/or abstracts in English; table of contents in English). Norin Suisansho Yasai Chagyo Shikenjo, (National Research Institute of Vegetables, Ornamental Plants & Tea, Ministry of Agriculture, Forestry & Fisheries), 360, Kusawa, Anocho, Agegun, Mieken 514-23, Japan. ***Continues*** *Yasai Chagyo Shikenjo Kenkyu Hokoku. B, Kanaya, 0914-6652.*
Ind/Abst Rev. Plant Pathol.

CC/0254-5071
ZHONGGUO NIANGZAO. (CHUNG-KUO NIANG TSAO.). [Zhongguo niangzao]. **Added/Corp** Chung-Kuo Wei Sheng wu Hsueh Hui. Niang Tsao Hsueh Hui. Shang Yeh Pu Shih Pin Niang Tsao Yen Chiu So (China). **VFOAT** Zhongguo Niangzao; China Brewing. (1982)-. Academic Scholarly Publication. Chinese. **LC** TP500; .C49. **DD** 663/.13/05. **CODEN** ZHNIDA. Documents available from CASDDS.
Ind/Abst Chem. Abstr.

US/0196-5921
ZYMURGY. **Added/Corp** American Homebrewers Association. (197?)-. Periodical. English. qt (plus one special issue). $21.00 US; $26.00 other. American Homebrewers Association, Box 287, Boulder CO 80306. **Tel** (303)447-0816. **ED** Charlie Papazian. Index available. cum. index. **Bk Rev. Ad Acc. Circ:** 8,000. Documents available from UMI Article Clearinghouse.
Desc: Contains articles and columns to help the homebrewer, from beginner to advanced, brew better beer. Also, examines specialty beers, domestic and abroad, and the brewing scene around the country.
Ind/Abst Newsp. Period. Abstr. (1988-).

FORESTRY

US/0271-1532
ACCOMPLISHMENTS OF FISCAL YEAR - NORTHEASTERN AREA, STATE AND PRIVATE FORESTRY. [Accomp. fiscal year, Northeast. Area, State Priv. For.]. **Main/Corp** United States. State and Private Forestry. Northeastern Area. English. an. US Department of Agriculture/ Pennsylvania, Agricultural Research Service, Northeastern Forest Experiment Station, 370 Reed Road, Broomall PA 19008. **LC** SD11; .S8A. **DD** 333.75/0974.

PL/0065-0927
ACTA AGRARIA ET SILVESTRIA. SERIES SILVESTRIS. [Acta agrar. silv., ser. silv.]. **Added/Corp** Polska Akademia Nauk. Komisja Nauk Rolniczych i Lesnych. (1966)-. Academic Scholarly Publication. Polish (summaries and/or abstracts in English and Russian). an. **(Subscription address:** ARS Polona, PO Box 1001, 00068 Warsaw Poland.) ***Continues*** *Acta Agraria et Silvestria. Seria Lesna.*
Ind/Abst EMBASE; For. Prod. Abstr. (1991-); For. Abstr.; Rev. Agric. Entomol.; Rev. Plant Pathol.

XO/0231-5785
ACTA FACULTATIS FORESTALIS, ZVOLEN. (ACTA FACULTATIS FORESTALIS ZVOLEN, CZECHOSLOVAKIA.). [Acta Fac. for. Zvolen]. **Added/Corp** Vysoka Skola Lesnicka a Drevarska vo Zvolene. Lesnicka Fakulta. **VFOAT** Acta Facultatis Forestalis. (1979)-. Periodical. Slovak (English, French and German). bm. **CODEN** AFFCE4. Documents available from CASDDS. ***Continues*** *Vysoka Skola Lesnicka a Drevarska vo Zvolene. Lesnicka Fakulta. Zbornik Vedeckych Prac Lesnickej Fakulty Vysokej Skoly Lesnickej a Drevarskej vo Zvolene, 0139-5572.*
Ind/Abst Chem. Abstr. (1985-); Plant Grow. Reg. Abstr.

FI/0001-5636
ACTA FORESTALIA FENNICA. [Acta for. Fenn.]. **Added/Corp** Suomen Metsatieteelinen Seura. Metsantutkimuslaitos. Vol. 1 (1913)-. Monographic series. Finnish (English, German, French and Swedish). ir. Price varies per volume. Academic Bookstore Akateeminen, Postilokero 23, FIN-00371 Helsinki Finland. **Tel** 011 358 0 12141. **LC** SD1; .A3. **CODEN** AFRFAZ. cum. index. Documents available from BIOSIS Document Express. ***Absorbed*** *Communicationes Instituti Forestalis Fenniae, 0358-9609.*
Ind/Abst Abstr. Bull. Inst. Pap. Sci. Tech.; Agrindex; Agrofor. Abstr. (1991-); Biol. Abstr.; Ecol. Abstr.; Fish Rev. (Jan. 1989-July 1992); For. Prod. Abstr.; For. Abstr.; Geogr. Abstr. Phys. Geogr.; Geogr. Abstr. Human Geogr.; Nematol. Abstr.; Life Sci. Collect.; Plant Breed. Abstr.; Rev. Med. Vet. Mycology; Rev. Plant Pathol.; Soils Fert.; Wildl. Rev. (Jan. 1989-July 1992).

XR/0524-7438
ACTA UNIVERSITATIS AGRICULTURAE FACULTAS SILVICULTURAE. [Acta univ. agric. fac. silvic.]. **Main/Corp** Brunn. Vysoka Skola Zemedelska. Fakulta Lesnicka. **VFOAT** Acta Universitatis Agriculturae (Brno). Series C. (Facultas Silviculturae). (1967)-. Periodical. Czech (English, French, German and Russian). qt. **CODEN** AUAFAL. Documents available from BIOSIS Document Express, CASDDS. ***Continues*** *Brunn. Vysoka Skola Zemedelska. Fakulta Lesnicka. Sbornik. Rada C. Spisy.*
Ind/Abst Biol. Abstr. (1967-1987); Chem. Abstr.; For. Abstr.; Life Sci. Collect.; Rev. Agric. Entomol.; Seed Abstr.

II
ADVANCES IN FORESTRY RESEARCH IN INDIA. Vol. 1 (1988)-. Periodical. English. Price varies. **(Subscription address:** Prints India, 11 Darya Ganj, New Delhi, 110002 India, (Phone: 011 91 11 3268645))

II/0971-0507
ADVANCES IN HORTICULTURE AND FORESTRY. **See** Gardening and Horticulture.

CN/0225-6533
ADVENTURING IN CONSERVATION. **See** Environmental Issues-Conservation and Natural Resources.

US
AFA'S RESOURCE HOTLINE : THE COMMUNICATION NETWORK OF THE AMERICAN FORESTRY ASSOCIATION. **VFOAT** A.F.A.'s Resource Hotline. **VAT** American Forestry Association's Resource Hotline. Began in 1986. Periodical. English. bw. 1319 Eighteenth Street NW, Washington DC 20036.

GW
AFZ : ALLGEMEINE FORST ZEITSCHRIFT FUER WALDWIRTSCHAFT UND UMWELTVORSORGE. **VFOAT** Allgemeine Forst Zeitschrift fur Waldwirtschaft und Umweltvorsorge. Vol. 44, No. 1-2 (Jan. 14, 1989)-. Periodical. German. wk. BLV Verlagsgesellschaft MBH, Lothstrasse 29, D80797 Munich Germany. **Tel** 011 49 89 12705214. ***Continues*** *Allgemeine Forstzeitschrift, 0002-5860.*
Ind/Abst Key Word Index Wildl. Res.

NE/0168-1923
AGRICULTURAL AND FOREST METEOROLOGY. **See** Earth Sciences-Meteorology.

CN/0705-3983
AGRICULTURE AND FORESTRY BULLETIN. ***Suspended.*** **See** Agriculture.

JA
AGRICULTURE, FORESTRY, AND FISHERIES FINANCE CORPORATION : REPORT. **See** Agriculture.

AU
AGRO BONUS. (19??)-. German. Eight times a year. S650.00 Austria; S750.00 other. Osterreichischer Agrarverlag, Inkustr 1 7 Bueropark Donau, A 3400 Klosterneuberg Austria. **Tel** 011 43 2243 33300. ***Absorbed*** *Der Land und Forstwirtschaftliche Betrieb; Praktische Landtechnik.*

UK/0952-1453
AGROFORESTRY ABSTRACTS. **See** Forestry-Abstracting, Bibliographies and Statistics.

KE/0255-8173
AGROFORESTRY TODAY. **See** Agriculture.

PO
AITIM : BOLETIN DE INFORMACION TECNICA / ASOCIACION DE INVESTIGACION TECHNICA DE LAS INDUSTRIAS DE LA MADERNA Y CORCHO. **Added/Corp** Sindicato Nacional de la Madera y Corcho (Spain) Asociacio'n de Investigacio'n Te'cnica de las Industrias de la Madera y Corcho (Spain). **VFOAT** Boletin de Informacion Tecnica. **VAT** Asociacio'n de Investigacio'n T'ecnica de las Industrais y Corcho. (1962)-. Periodical. English (French). Four times a year. 5500ptas Spain; 8800ptas other. Impreso en Casalo AG, Sanz Raso 5, 28038 Madrid Spain. **Tel** 242 58 64. **ED** Ricardo Velez Munoz. Index available. cum. index. **Bk Rev.** **Ad Acc.** **Pr Rev.** ctrl circ.
Desc: Technical articles, news, markets, architecture and design related to forestry and the wood industry.

US/0275-6625
ALABAMA FORESTS. [Ala. for.]. Vol. 21 (Jan. 1978)-. Periodical. English. Six times a year. $30.00 others; Free to schools and public libraries in Alabama. Alabama Forestry Association, 555 Alabama Street, Montgomery AL 36104. **Tel** (205)265-8733, FAX (205)262-1258. **ED** Rei Boyce. **DD** 634. **Ad Acc.** **Circ:** 3,500 (ctrl). available on diskette. ***Continues*** *Alabama Forest Products, 0002-4228.*
Desc: Forestry-related articles and information.

US/0737-3961
ALASKA REGION REPORT. (ALASKA REGION REPORT / UNITED STATES DEPARTMENT OF AGRICULTURE, FOREST SERVICE.). [Alsk. Reg. rep.]. Monographic series. English. Price varies per volume. US Department of Agriculture, 14th Street and Independence Avenue SW, Washington DC 20250. **Tel** (202)720-5457. **LC** SD144.A4; A73. **DD** 634.9/09798.

CN/0840-6146
ALBERTA OIL & FORESTRY REVIEW QUARTERLY. ***Title Change.*** **See** Petroleum and Natural Gas.

GW/0002-5852
ALLGEMEINE FORST UND JAGDZEITUNG. [Allg. Forst- Jagdztg.]. (1825)-. Periodical. German (summaries and/or abstracts in English and French). mo. DM274.60 Germany; DM280.00 others. J. D. Sauerlaender Verlag, Finkenhofstrasse 21, D 60322 Frankfurt Germany. **Tel** 011 49 69 555217. **ED** H. Steinlin and H. Kramer. **CODEN** AFJZAL. Index available. **Bk Rev.** **Ad Acc.** **Pr Rev.** Documents available from The Genuine Article, BIOSIS Document Express, CASDDS. ***Supersedes*** *Annalen der Forst- und Jagdwissenschaft.*
Desc: Forestry, ecology, forest botany, soil science, biology, tree timber, wood, wild life management and landscape planning.
Ind/Abst Biol. Abstr.; Chem. Abstr.; Coal Abstr.; Crop Physiol. Abstr.; Curr. Contents, Agric. Biol. Environ. Sci.; Ecol. Abstr. (?-?); Ecology Abstr.; EMBASE; Fish Rev. (Jan. 1989-July 1992); For. Prod. Abstr. (19??-19??); For. Abstr.; Geogr. Abstr. Phys. Geogr. (?-?); GeoRef; Key Word Index Wildl. Res.; Life Sci. Collect.; Plant Breed. Abstr.; Res. Alert [Select. Cov.]; Rev. Med. Vet. Mycology; Rev. Plant Pathol.; SCISEARCH; Soils Fert.; Wildl. Rev. (Jan. 1989-July 1992).

US/0569-3845
AMERICAN CHRISTMAS TREE JOURNAL. **See** Agriculture.

US/0002-8541
AMERICAN FORESTS. [Am. for.]. **Added/Corp** American Forestry Association. Vol. 37, No. 1 (Jan. 1931)-. Periodical. English. Six times a year. $24.00 (one year), $40.00 (two year), $72.00 (three year). American Forestry Association, PO Box 2000, Washington DC 20013. **Tel** (202)667-3300. **ED** Bill Rooney. **LC** SD1; .A55. **DD** 634.905. **CODEN** AMFOAH. Index available. **Bk Rev.** **Ad Acc.** **Circ:** 30,000. available on microfilm and microfiche from University Microfilms International (UMI); available on an online database (files 647,648/Full-Text) from DIALOG. Documents available from BIOSIS Document Express, UMI Article Clearinghouse, CASDDS, Documents on Demand, Magazine Collection. ***Continues*** *American Forests and Forest Life.*
Desc: Dedicated to people who care about trees and forests. Explores recreation, conservation, wildlife, urban forests, wilderness, genetics, air pollution effects, tropical deforestation, changing recreational attitudes, unfolding legislation, and the future of national forests. Learn about Urban forestry, greenways, and the development of new natural areas.
Ind/Abst Abstr. Bull. Inst. Pap. Sci. Tech.; Acad. Abstr. Full Text Elite (May 1991-); Acad. Abstr. (May 1991-); Acad. Ind. [Computer File] (1992-); Acad. Search (May 1991-); AGRICOLA [Select. Cov.]; Biol. Agric. Index; Biol. Abstr.; Biol. Dig.; Book Rev. Index; Bus. ASAP (1990-) [Full Txt.]; Bus. Index (1985-); Chem. Abstr.; Coal Abstr.; Energy Res. Abstr. (Sept. 1978-); Environ. Abstr.; Environ. Period. Bibliogr.; Expand. Acad. Index (1984-); For. Prod. Abstr.; For. Abstr.; Gen. BusinessFile (1985-); Gen. Period. Index (1985-); Gen. Sci. Index; GeoRef; Index Sci. Rev.; INFO-SOUTH Abstr.; Key Word Index Wildl. Res.; Mag. Artic. Summar. Elite (May 1991-); Mag. Artic. Summar. Select (July 1990-); Mag. Artic. Summar. CD-ROM (May 1991-); Mag. ASAP Plus [Full Txt.]; Mag. Index Plus (1989-); Mag. Search; Newsp. Period. Abstr. (1991-); Ocean. Abstr.; Pollut. Abstr. Indexes; Read. Guide Period. Lit.; Mag. Index (1977-); Trade Ind. ASAP [Full Txt.]; Trade Ind. Index (1981-) [Full Txt.].

US
AMERICA'S GREAT OUTDOORS : NEWSLETTER FOR THE NATIONAL RECREATION STRATEGY. **Added/Corp** United States. Forest Service. **VFOAT** National Forests, America's Great Outdoors. No. 1 (Jan. 1991)-. Newsletter. English. Three times a year. **LC** GV191.67.F6; A44.

US
AMES FORESTER. **Added/Corp** Iowa State University. Forestry Club. Iowa State College. Forestry Club. (19??)-. Periodical. English. an. $4.00 students, $8.00 alumni. Iowa State University Forestry Club, Ames IA 50012. **Tel** (515)294-1167. **(Subscription address:** Department of Forestry, 251 Bessey Hall, Iowa State University, Ames IA 50011**)** **ED** Scott Davis. **LC** SD1; .A56. **DD** 634.9/05. **Ad Acc.** **Circ:** 400.
Desc: Publication about activities and articles dealing with students and staff in forestry at Iowa State University.

MR/0483-8009
ANNALES DE LA RECHERCHE FORESTIERE AU MAROC : RAPPORT ANNUEL. [Ann. rech. for. Maroc]. **VFOAT** Hawliyat Al-Bahth Al-Ghabawi Fi Al-Maghrib. 1951-. Academic Scholarly Publication. French. an. **LC** WMLC L 83/2433. **CODEN** AFRMAM. Documents available from CASDDS.
Ind/Abst Biocont. News Inf.; Chem. Abstr. (1984-); For. Prod. Abstr.

FR/0398-494X
ANNALES DE RECHERCHES SYLVICOLES. [Ann. rech. sylvic.]. **VFOAT** AFOCEL; A.F.O.C.E.L. (1976)-. Multiple languages (English, French and German). an. 225.00F European Union; 250.00F others. Afocel Service Des Publishing, Domaine De L Etancon, F 77370 Nangis France. **Tel** 011 33 1 60670030. ***Continues*** *AFOCEL, 0398-4931.*
Ind/Abst Abstr. Bull. Inst. Pap. Sci. Tech.; For. Prod. Abstr.; For. Abstr.; Soils Fert.

FR/0003-4312
ANNALES DES SCIENCES FORESTIERES. (ANNALES DES SCIENCES FORESTIERES / L'ECOLE NATIONALE DES EAUX & LE CENTRE NATIONAL DE RECHERCHES FORESTIERES.). [Ann. sci. for.]. **Added/Corp** Ecole Nationale des Eaux et Forets (France) Centre National de Recherches Forestieres (France) Ecole Nationale du Genie Rural, des Eaux et des Forets (France) Institut National de la Recherche Agronomique (France). Vol. 21 (1964)-. Academic Scholarly Publication. French (English and German). bm (6 issues). 1275.00F France; 1550.00F other. Editions Scientifique Elsevier, 141 rue de Javel, 75747 Paris Cedex 15 France. **Tel** 011 33 1 47 07 11 22, FAX 011 33 1 43 36 80 93. **(Subscription address:** Editions Scientifiques Elsevier / for North America, PO Box 7247-7576, Philadelphia PA 19170-7576.**)** **ED** G. Aussenac. **LC** SD1; .N23. **CODEN** ANSFAS. **[CCC].** Index available. **Bk Rev.** **Pr Rev.** **Circ:** 900. available on microfilm and microfiche from University Microfilms International (UMI). Documents available from The Genuine Article, BIOSIS Document Express, CASDDS. ***Continues*** *Ecole Nationale des Eaux et Forets (France). Annales de l'Ecole Nationale des Eaux et Forets et de la Station de Recherches et Experiences, 0365-1827.*
Desc: Covers forestry: pedology, forest tree breeding, physiology, forest protection, wood technology.
Ind/Abst Abstr. Bull. Inst. Pap. Sci. Tech.; Art Archaeol. Tech. Abstr.; Biol. Abstr.; Chem. Abstr. (1964-1985); Curr. Contents, Agric. Biol. Environ. Sci.; Ecol. Abstr.; EMBASE; Entomol. Abstr.; Environ. Period. Bibliogr.; For. Prod. Abstr. (19??-19??); For. Abstr.; Geogr. Abstr. Phys. Geogr.; Life Sci. Collect.; Plant Breed. Abstr.; Res. Alert [Full Cov.]; Sci. Cit. Index; SCISEARCH; Soils Fert.

IT/0390-0010
ANNALI DELL'ISTITUTO SPERIMENTALE PER LA SELVICOLTURA. [Ann. ist. sper. selvic.]. **Main/Corp** Istituto Sperimentale per la Selvicoltura. (1970)-. Italian (summaries and/or abstracts in English and French). Arezzo Oistituto Sperimentale per la Selvicoltura, Via Eritrea, 9, 52100 Italy. **LC** SD201; .I76a.
Ind/Abst Abstr. Bull. Inst. Pap. Sci. Tech.; For. Prod. Abstr. (1991-); For. Abstr.; Soils Fert.

PL/0208-5704
ANNALS OF WARSAW AGRICULTURAL UNIVERSITY - SGGW-AR. FORESTRY AND WOOD TECHNOLOGY. [Ann. War. Agric. Univ. - SSGW-AR, for. wood technol.]. **VFOAT** Forestry and Wood Technology. No. 29 (1982)-. Academic Scholarly Publication. English (French, German and Russian). ir. Z1120.00 single issue. Warsaw Agricultural University Press, Ul Nowoursynowska 166, 02-766 Warsaw Poland. **CODEN** AWATDC. **Ad Acc.** ctrl circ. Documents available from CASDDS. ***Formed by the union of*** *Zeszyty Naukowe Szkoy Gownej Gospodarstwa Wiejskiego--Akademii Rolniczej w Warszawie. Lesnictwo, 0511-1684* ***and*** *Technologia Drewna.*
Ind/Abst Chem. Abstr.; For. Prod. Abstr. (1991-); For. Abstr.; Rev. Agric. Entomol.; Rev. Plant Pathol.

US
ANNUAL FINANCIAL REPORT - SOUTH DAKOTA DEPARTMENT OF WILDLIFE, PARKS AND FORESTRY. **See** Recreation, Leisure-Outdoor Life.

US/0091-438X
ANNUAL GRAZING STATISTICAL REPORT. ***Title Change.*** **See** Forestry-Abstracting, Bibliographies and Statistics.

PR
ANNUAL LETTER. **Main/Corp** Institute of Tropical Forestry (Rio Piedras, San Juan, P.R.). (19??)-. Multiple languages (English and Spanish). an. free. Institute of Tropical Forestry, Call Box 25000, Rio Piedras Puerto Rico 00928-2500. **Tel** (809)753-4335. **ED** Dr. Ariel E. Lugo. **Circ:** 3000. ***Continues*** *Institute of Tropical Forestry (Rio Piedras, San Juan, P.R.). Letter Presenting some of the Highlights of Activities and Progress at Institute of Tropical Forestry.*
Desc: Details recent research efforts by Institute of Tropical Forestry scientists and collaborators. Research problems include plantation management, secondary forests, watersheds, tropical forest ecology, and global change.

CN/0832-6916
ANNUAL REPORT / ALBERTA FORESTRY, LANDS AND WILDLIFE. [Annu. rep. - Alta. For. Lands Wildl.]. **Main/Corp** Alberta. Alberta Forestry, Lands and Wildlife. (1986)-. English. an. Department of Energy and Natural Resources / Alberta, Petroleum Plaza/South Tower, 9915-108 Street, Edmonton Alberta T5K 2C9 Canada. **LC** HC117.A6; A51625a. **DD** 354.71230082/3. ***Continues in part*** *Alberta. Alberta Energy and Natural Resources. Annual Report -Alberta Energy and Natural Resources., 0700-2645.*

UK
ANNUAL REPORT AND ACCOUNTS OF THE FORESTRY COMMISSION. (ANNUAL REPORT AND ACCOUNTS OF THE FORESTRY COMMISSION TOGETHER WITH THE COMPTROLLER AND AUDITOR GENERAL'S REPORT ON THE ACCOUNTS.). **Main/Corp** Great Britain. Forestry Commission. 48th (1967)-. Periodical. English. an. price varies per volume. Her Majesty's Stationery Office, 51 Nine Elms Lane, London SW8 5DR England. **Tel** 011 44 71 873 8459, 011 44 71 873 8499, FAX 011 44 71 873 8499, 011 44 71 873 8456, telex 297138. **(Subscription address:** Her Majesty's Stationery Office, PO Box 276, Publications Centre, London SW8 5DT England.**)** ***Continues*** *Annual Report of the Forestry Commissioners.*

US/8756-8292
ANNUAL REPORT / ARKANSAS FORESTRY COMMISSION. **Main/Corp** Arkansas Forestry Commission. SFY 1982-1983-. English. an. Arkansas Forestry Commission, Box 4523, Asher Station, Little Rock AR 72214. **LC** SD12; .A8. **DD** 353.97670082/338/06. ctrl circ. ***Continues*** *Annual Report of the Arkansas Forestry Commission for the Fiscal Year ..., 8756-8284.*
Desc: Describes the activities of the Forestry commission during a fiscal year.

US/0882-8326
ANNUAL REPORT - CALIFORNIA. DEPT. OF FORESTRY. (ANNUAL REPORT / THE CALIFORNIA DEPARTMENT OF FORESTRY.). [Annu. rep. - Calif., Dep. For.]. **Main/Corp** California. Dept. of Forestry. 1981-. English. an. California Department of Forestry, 1416 9th Street, Sacramento CA 95814. **Tel** (916)445-9886. **LC** SD12.C3; D46A. **DD** 353.97940082/338/06. ***Continues*** *California Department of Forestry ... Review.*

US/0094-5021
ANNUAL REPORT - DIVISION OF FORESTRY, FISHERIES, AND WILDLIFE DEVELOPMENT, TENNESSEE VALLEY AUTHORITY. **Main/Corp** Tennessee Valley Authority. Division of Forestry, Fisheries, and Wildlife Development. English. an. Springer-Verlag GmbH & Company KG, Heidelberger Platz 3, D 14197 Berlin Germany. **Tel** 011 49 30 8207223, FAX 011 49 30 8214091, telex 183 319 SPBLN D. **(Subscription address:** Springer Verlag New York Inc. / for North America, 44 Hartz Way, Secaucus NJ 07096.**)** **LC** SD11; .T4 subser. **DD** 353.008/233. ***Continues*** *Tennessee Valley Authority. Division of Forestry Development. Annual Report.*

CN/0826-1725
ANNUAL REPORT - FOREST RESEARCH COUNCIL OF BRITISH COLUMBIA. (ANNUAL REPORT FOR THE YEAR ENDING MARCH 31 ... / FOREST RESEARCH COUNCIL OF BRITISH COLUMBIA.). [Annu. rep. - For. Res. Counc. B.C.]. **Main/Corp** Forest Research Council of British Columbia. 1st (1982)-. English. an. **LC** SD356.54.C22; F673A. **DD** 354.7110082/338.

AT/1031-7740
ANNUAL REPORT / FORESTRY COMMISSION OF TASMANIA. **Main/Corp** Tasmania. Forestry Commission. (1988/1989)-. English. ***Continues*** *Tasmania. Forestry Commission. Report.*

KE
ANNUAL REPORT / INTERNATIONAL CENTRE FOR RESEARCH IN AGROFORESTRY. **Main/Corp** International Centre for Research in Agroforestry. (199?)-. English. International Centre for Research in Agroforestry, POB 30677, Nairobi Kenya. **LC** S494.5.A45; I5. ***Continues*** *International Council for Research in Agroforestry. Annual Report of the International Council for Research in Agroforestry.*

US/0362-6482
ANNUAL REPORT OF OPERATIONS AND FOREST PEST CONDITIONS. **Main/Corp** Pennsylvania. Division of Forest Pest Management. English. an. Pennsylvania Department of Environmental Resources, PO Box 2063, Harrisburg PA 17105. **Tel** (717)787-2814, FAX (717)783-2802. **LC** SB763.P4; P46A. **DD** 634.9/6/609748.

NR/0331-3751
ANNUAL REPORT OF THE FORESTRY RESEARCH INSTITUTE OF NIGERIA FOR THE PERIOD ... . **Main/Corp** Forestry Research Institute of Nigeria. **VFOAT** Annual Report. (Apr. 1 1976-Mar. 31 1977)-. English. **LC** SD356.54.N62; F673a. **DD** 634.9/0720669/2. ***Continues*** *Nigeria. Federal Dept. of Forest Researh. Annual Report of the Federal Dept. of Forest Research.*

KE
ANNUAL REPORT OF THE INTERNATIONAL COUNCIL FOR RESEARCH IN AGROFORESTRY. ***Title Change.*** **Main/Corp** International Council for Research in Agroforestry. **VFOAT** Annual Report. (19??)-(199?). English. ***Continues*** *Report / International Council for Research in Agroforestry.* ***Continued by*** *International Centre for Research in Agroforestry. Annual Report.*

US/0734-6565
ANNUAL REPORT - PENNSYLVANIA. BUREAU OF FORESTRY. (ANNUAL REPORT / BUREAU OF FORESTRY.). [Annu. rep. - Pa., Bur. For.]. **Main/Corp** Pennsylvania. Bureau of Forestry. (1979)-. English. an. Bureau of Forestry, PO Box 1467, Harrisburg PA 17120. **Tel** 9717)787-2703. **LC** SD12.P42; B8a. **DD** 353.97480082/338/06.
Desc: Summary of activities and accomplishments of The Pennsylvania Bureau of Forestry for each calendar year.

AT
ANNUAL REPORT / QUEENSLAND FOREST SERVICE. **Main/Corp** Queensland Forest Service. (1989/1990)-. English. **LC** WMLC 91/5541. ***Continues*** *Queensland. Dept. of Forestry. Annual Report.*

SA
ANNUAL RESEARCH REPORT / INSTITUTE FOR COMMERCIAL FORESTRY RESEARCH. **Added/Corp** University of Natal. Institute for Commercial Forestry Research. **VFOAT** ICFR Annual Research Report. **VAT** Institute for Commercial Forestry Research Annual Research Report. (1990)-. English. an. **LC** SD356.54.S62; U55a. ***Continues*** *University of Natal. Institute for Commercial Forestry Research. Annual Report.*
Ind/Abst Agrofor. Abstr.; For. Abstr.; Seed Abstr.; Soils Fert.; Weed Abstr.

SW/0280-4158
ARBETSRAPPORT / SVERIGES LANTBRUKSUNIVERSITET, INSTITUTIONEN FOR SKOGSEKONOMI. [Arbetsrapp. - Sver. lantbruksuniv. Inst. skogsekon.]. **Added/Corp** Sveriges Lantbruksuniversitet. Institutionen for Skogsekonomi. (1981)-. Monographic series. Swedish (English).
Ind/Abst Agrofor. Abstr. (1991-); For. Prod. Abstr. (1991-); For. Abstr.; Irr. Drain. Abstr.; Maize Abstr.

US/0279-0106
ARBOR AGE. [Arbor age]. Vol. 1, No. 1 (May/June 1981)-. Periodical. English. mo. $33.00 US; $55.00 other. Adams Publishing, 68860 Perez Road, PO Box 2150, Cathedral City CA 92235. **Tel** (619)770-4370, (800)776-1036. **(Subscription address:** Adams Publishing, PO Box 2150, Cathedral City CA 92235.) **ED** Anne Goldstein. **Ad Acc. Circ:** 15,000 (ctrl).
Desc: Tree care for the professional, commercial, residential, municipal, and utility arborist.
Ind/Abst AGRICOLA [Select. Cov.]; Environ. Period. Bibliogr. (?-?).

FR/0767-337X
ARBORESCENCES (PARIS). (ARBORESCENCES.). [Arborescences]. **Added/Corp** France. Office National des Forets. (1985)-. Periodical. French. bm. 180.00F. Dept Commun Ofc Natl Forets, 2 Avenue de St Mande, 75570 Paris Cedex 12 France. **Tel** 33 1 40195800. **ED** Jean-Claude Gachet. **Bk Rev**, (Qty: 6). ctrl circ. ***Continues*** *Bulletin d'Information (France. Office National des Forets), 0767-3388.*

UK/0307-1375
ARBORICULTURAL JOURNAL, THE. [Arboric. j.]. **Added/Corp** Arboricultural Association. Vol. 2, No. 7 (Sept. 1974)-. Periodical. English. qt. $213.75 (airmail), $161.23 (surface mail). AB Academic Publishers, PO Box 42 Bicester, OXON OX6 7NW England. **Tel** 011 44 869 320949. **ED** T.H.R. Hall. **LC** SB435; .A72. **CODEN** ARJOD7. **[CCC]**. Index available. **Bk Rev**. **Ad Acc**. Documents available from BIOSIS Document Express. ***Continues*** *Arboricultural Association Journal.*
Desc: Research and review articles in all areas of urban and amenity forestry, etc. Reading and reference in a growing field.
Ind/Abst Biol. Abstr.; Ecol. Abstr.; Environ. Period. Bibliogr.; For. Prod. Abstr.; For. Abstr.; Geogr. Abstr. Human Geogr.; Hortic. Abstr.; Ornamental Hort. (1991-); Rev. Med. Vet. Mycology; Rev. Plant Pathol.; Soils Fert.

UK
ARBORICULTURE RESEARCH NOTE. **Added/Corp** Great Britain. Forestry Commission. (19??)-. Monographic series. English.
Ind/Abst For. Abstr.; Hortic. Abstr.; Soils Fert.

CN/1188-2891
ARNEWS ANNUAL REPORT. **Main/Corp** Canada. Forestry Canada. Science and Sustainable Development Directorate. **VFOAT** Rapport Annuel ... sur le Dispositif National d'Alerte Rapide pour les Pluies Acides (DNARPA). (1991)-. English. **DD** 634.9/619/0971.

SI/0217-4421
ASIAN TIMBER (SINGAPORE). (ASIAN TIMBER : THE MAGAZINE OF THE ASIAN TIMBER INDUSTRY : LOGGING, PROCESSING & TRADING.). [Asian Timber Singapore]. (1982)-. Periodical. English. bm. $140.00. Toucan Publications PTE Ltd, 322-C King George's Avenue, Singapore 0820. **Tel** 011 65 2997121, FAX 011 65 2997545.

CN/0832-5502
ATLANTIC FORESTRY JOURNAL. ***Ceased.*** [Atl. for. j.]. Vol. 1, No. 1 (Aug. 1987)-(19??). Periodical. English. mo. Nova Scotia Business Publishing Ltd., 2099 Gottingen Street, Halifax NS B3K 3B2 Canada. **Tel** (902)420-0437, FAX (902)423-8212. **ED** Ken Partidge. **DD** 634.9/09715. **Ad Acc.** ctrl circ.
Desc: Forestry related subjects from throughout Atlantic Canada.

CN/0316-3733
AUBELLE, L'. **Added/Corp** Corporation Professionnelle des Ingenieurs Forestiers du Quebec. Vol. 28, No. 4 (Sept. 1973)-. Periodical. French. Six times a year. Ordre des Ingenieurs Forestiers du Quebec, 2022 rue Lavoisier Bureau 165, Ste Foy Quebec G1N 4L5 Canada. **DD** 634.9/06/2714. ***Continues*** *Chronique., 0316-3741.*

GW/0519-4555
AUS DEM WALDE. [Aus Walde]. No. 1, (1957)-. Periodical. German.
Ind/Abst For. Prod. Abstr.

AT
AUSTRALIAN FOREST GROWER. (197?)-. Periodical. English. Four times a year. 28.00Aus$ Australia; 36.00Aus other. Australian Forest Growers, PO Box E18, Queen Victoria Terrace, Australian Capital Territory 2600 Australia. **Tel** 011 61 6 2853833, FAX 011 61 6 2853855. **ED** Josef Vondra (editor's address: PO Box 5, South Yarra VIC 3141 Australia). **Ad Acc.** Full Page (B&W) $675.00. Half Page (B&W) $400.00. Full Page (Color) $975.00. **Circ:** 3,000. ***Absorbed*** *Tree Farmer.*
Desc: Hands on and most up-to-date supplement to all aspects of commerical forest in Australia.
Ind/Abst For. Prod. Abstr.; For. Abstr.; Soils Fert.

AT/0812-2792
AUSTRALIAN FOREST INDUSTRIES JOURNAL (1982). (AUSTRALIAN FOREST INDUSTRIES JOURNAL & LOGGER.). [Aust. for. ind. j.]. **VFOAT** Australian Forest Industries Journal and Logger; Australian Forest Industries Journal & Australian Logger; Australian Forest Industries Journal; AFIJ. Vol. 48, No. 5 (June 1982)-. Periodical. English. mo. **CODEN** AFILEC. ***Continues*** *Australian Forest Industries Journal & Australian Logger, 0812-2784.*
Ind/Abst BioBusiness (1991-); For. Prod. Abstr. (1991-).

AT/0004-914X
AUSTRALIAN FOREST RESEARCH. ***Ceased.*** [Aust. for. res.]. Vol. 1 (1964)-Vol. 17 (?). Periodical. English. sa. CSIRO Publications, PO Box 89, 314 Albert Street, East Melborne Victoria 3002 Australia. **Tel** 011 61 3 4187333, 4187217, FAX 011 61 3 4190459, telex AA 30236. **ED** John Ienaghan. **CODEN** AUFRAE. **[CCC]**. **Ad Acc. Circ:** 202. available on microfilm from University Microfilms International (UMI). Documents available from BIOSIS Document Express, Documents on Demand.
Desc: Original reports on forestry, forest products and forest science including descriptions and assessments of field and laboratory techniques.
Ind/Abst Abstr. Bull. Inst. Pap. Sci. Tech.; AGRICOLA [Full Cov.]; Biol. Abstr. (1986-1987); Environ. Abstr.; For. Prod. Abstr. (19??-19??); For. Abstr.; Life Sci. Collect.; Pollut. Abstr. Indexes; Protozoolog. Abstr.; Rev. Med. Vet. Mycology; Rev. Plant Pathol.; Soils Fert.

AT/0004-9158
AUSTRALIAN FORESTRY. [Aust. for.]. **Added/Corp** Institute of Foresters of Australia. Vol. 1 (June 1936)-. Periodical. English. Four times a year. 100.00Aus$ Australia; 120.00Aus$ others. Institute Foresters of Australia, PO Box E/73, Queen Victoria Terrace, Canberra Australian Capital Territory 2600 Australia. **Tel** 011 61 62813992, FAX 011 61 062901014. **ED** D. Doley. **LC** SD1; .A93. **DD** 634.9/0994. **CODEN** AUFOA5. Index available. **Bk Rev. Circ:** 2,000 (ctrl). Documents available from CASDDS. ***Continues*** *Research Activity.*
Desc: Concerned with forestry, in Australia and in general.
Ind/Abst Abstr. Bull. Inst. Pap. Sci. Tech.; AGRICOLA [Full Cov.]; Agrofor. Abstr. (1991-); Biocont. News Inf. (1991-); Chem. Abstr.; For. Prod. Abstr. (19??-19??); For. Abstr.; GeoRef; Leis. Recreat. Tour. Abstr.; Plant Breed. Abstr.; Protozoolog. Abstr.; Rev. Agric. Entomol.; Rev. Med. Vet. Mycology; Rev. Plant Pathol.; Rural Dev. Abstr.; Soils Fert.; Weed Abstr.; Wildl. Rev.; World Agric. Econ.

CN
AUTOUR DE NOS BOISES. **Added/Corp** Nouveau-Brunswick. Ministere des Ressources Naturelles et de l'energie. **VFOAT** Around Your Woodlot. Vol. 1, No. 1 (Spring 1991)-. Periodical. French (English). Three times a year. **DD** 634.9. ***Continues*** *Around Your Woodlot.*

NP/1016-0582
BANKO JANAKARI : A JOURNAL OF FORESTRY INFORMATION FOR NEPAL. **Added/Corp** Forest Research and Information Centre (Nepal). **VFOAT** Banako Janakari; Journal of Forestry Information for Nepal. Vol. 1, No. 1 (Spring 1987)-. Periodical. English. qt. **LC** SD235.N4; B36. **DD** 634.9/095496.
Ind/Abst Grasslands For. Abstr.; Plant Grow. Reg. Abstr.; Soils Fert.

BG/0254-4539
BANO BIGGYAN PATRIKA. **Added/Corp** Forest Research Institute (Bangladesh). **VFOAT** Journal of Forest Science; Bana Bijnana Patrika. Vol. 4, No. 2-3 (Jan./April 1972)-. Academic Scholarly Publication. English (summaries and/or abstracts in Bengali and English). sa. Free on request. Forest Research Institute of Bangladesh, PO Box 273, Chittagong Bangladesh. **LC** SD97.P3; F6. **CODEN** BBPADU. Documents available from CASDDS. ***Continues*** *Forestdale News.*
Ind/Abst Biocont. News Inf. (1991-); Chem. Abstr.; For. Prod. Abstr. (1991-); For. Abstr.; Rev. Plant Pathol.; Seed Abstr.; Weed Abstr.

CN/0705-3274
BC-X - PACIFIC FOREST RESEARCH CENTRE. (INFORMATION REPORT - PACIFIC FOREST RESEARCH CENTRE.). [BC-X - Pac. For. Res. Cent.]. **VAT** Report BC-X - Pacific Forest Research Center; Information Report BC-X - Pacific Forest Research Centre. Academic Scholarly Publication. English (summaries and/or abstracts in French). Price varies per volume. Pacific Forest Research Centre, 506 West Burnside Road, Victoria British Columbia V8Z 1M5 Canada. **DD** 634.9'09711. **CODEN** RBCPDG. Documents available from CASDDS. ***Continues*** *Canada. Forest Research Laboratory, Victoria, B.C. Information Report, 0576-1921.*
Ind/Abst AGRICOLA; Chem. Abstr. (-1983).

CN/0834-5414
BEALE'S INDUSTRY LETTER, VANCOUVER. [Beale's ind. lett.]. **VFOAT** Beale's Letter. No. 339 (Oct. 14, 1986)-. Periodical. English. bw. $197.00. Beale's Industry Letter Vancouver, PO Box 48651, Vancouver British Columbia V7X 1A3 Canada. **DD** 338.1/749/09711. ***Continues*** *Beale's Letter, 0318-6482.*

GW/0323-4673
BEITRAEGE FUER DIE FORSTWIRTSCHAFT. [Beitr. Forstwirtsch.]. Periodical. German. qt. DM88.00. Forschungsanst

Forestry

Holzwirtschaft, Alfred Moeller Str, D 16225 Eberswalde Germany. **Tel** 011 49 3334 65343. **CODEN** BFORD2. Documents available from BIOSIS Document Express, CASDDS. *Absorbed Archiv fur Forstwesen.*
Ind/Abst Agric. Eng. Abstr. (1991-); Agrofor. Abstr.; Biol. Abstr. (1986-); Chem. Abstr.; EMBASE; For. Prod. Abstr. (1991-); For. Abstr.; Irr. Drain. Abstr.; Plant Breed. Abstr.; Plant Grow. Reg. Abstr.; Rev. Agric. Entomol.; Rev. Plant Pathol.; Seed Abstr.; Soils Fert.

AU
BERICHT - KAMMER FUR LAND- UND FORSTWIRTSCHAFT IN SALZBURG. See Agriculture.

GW
BERICHTE DES FORSCHUNGSZENTRUMS WALDOKOSYSTEM/WALDSTERBEN REIHE B. Vol. 1 (1986)-. Monographic series. German. ir. Price varies per volume. *Continues in part Berichte des Forschungszentrums.*

GW/0930-7044
BERICHTE DES FORSCHUNGSZENTRUMS WALDOKOSYSTEME/WALDSTERBEN REIHE A. Monographic series. German. ir. Price varies per volume. *Continues in part Berichte des Foschungszentrums Waldokosystems/Waldsterben.*

VE
BIBLIOGRAPHICAL BULLETIN - LATIN AMERICAN FORESTRY INSTITUTE. See Forestry-Abstracting, Bibliographies and Statistics.

AT/0313-9093
BIENNIAL REPORT / CSIRO DIVISION OF FOREST RESEARCH. Main/Corp Commonwealth Scientific and Industrial Research Organization (Australia). Division of Forest Research. (1981-). English. be. CSIRO Publications, PO Box 89, 314 Albert Street, East Melborne Victoria 3002 Australia. **Tel** 011 61 3 4187333, 4187217, FAX 011 61 3 4190459, telex AA 30236. *Continues Commonwealth Scientific and Industrial Research Organization (Australia). Division of Forest Research. Annual Report, 0313-9093.*

US
BIG BOOK / RANDOM LENGTHS. VFOAT Random Lengths ... Big Book; Random Lengths Directory. (19??)-. English. an. $160.00. Random Lengths Publications Inc, PO Box 867, Eugene OR 97440. **Tel** (503)686-9925, FAX (800)874-7979, (503)686-9629. **LC** TS803; .R35. *Continues Random Lengths Buyers' & Sellers' Guide, 0891-7833.*

IO/0216-5023
BIOTROPIA. Vol. 1, No. 1 (July/Dec. 1987)-. Periodical. English. ir $14.00 (latest edition). SE Asian Regional Center, PO Box 17, Bogor 16001 Indonesia. **Tel** 011 62 251 323848. **LC** SD235.S67; B56. **DD** 634.9/0959. **CODEN** BITREF. *Formed by the union of Biotrop Bulletin in Tropical Biology; Seameo-Biotrop Newsletter and Biotrop Technical Bulletin, 0215-1081.*
Ind/Abst Agrofor. Abstr. (19??-19??); Postharvest News Inf.; Rev. Agric. Entomol.; Rev. Med. Vet. Entomol.; Weed Abstr.

US/0194-8148
BLACK HILLS NATIONAL FOREST PRODUCTS NEWS. Vol. 1 (May 1976)-. Periodical. English. Twelve times a year. $5.00. The Black Hills National Forest Products News, Box 337, Hill City SD 57745. **Tel** (605)574-4218. *Supersedes in part Hill City Prevailer.*

FR/0006-579X
BOIS ET FORETS DES TROPIQUES. [Bois for. trop.]. **Added/Corp** Comite National des Bois Tropicaux. Societe pour le Developpement de l'Utilisation des Bois Tropicaux de l'Union Francaise. (1947)-. Periodical. French. Four times a year. CIRAD Foret / Centre de Cooperation International en Recherche Agronomique pour le Developpement, 45 Bis Avenue de la Belle Gabrielle, 94736 Nogent-sur-Marne France. **Tel** 011 33 43944300. **LC** SD1; .B6.
Ind/Abst Abstr. Bull. Inst. Pap. Sci. Tech.; Agrofor. Abstr.; Biodeter. Abstr.; Field Crop Abstr.; Fish Rev.; For. Prod. Abstr. (1991-); For. Abstr.; Grasslands For. Abstr.; Hortic. Abstr.; Leis. Recreat. Tour. Abstr.; Nutr. Abstr. Rev., Ser. B, Live Feeds and Feed.; Nutr. Abstr. Rev., Ser. A, Hum. Exp.; Life Sci. Collect.; Rev. Plant Pathol.; Soils Fert.; Wildl. Rev.

FR
BOIS NATIONAL (EDITION VERTE), LE. (LE BOIS NATIONAL.). (19??)-. Periodical. French. Forty-three times a year. 470.00F France; 660.00F other. Bois National, 3 rue Claude Odde, BP 523, 42007 St. Etienne Cedex France. **Tel** 011 33 77743399, FAX 011 33 77931126, telex 300818. **ED** Francois Goutin. **Bk Rev. Ad Acc, Adv Mgr:** J. Andre. **Circ:** 23,000 (ctrl). *Absorbed Bois Hebdo.*

BL/0101-1057
BOLETIM DE PESQUISA FLORESTAL. No. 1 (Dec. 1980)-. Bulletin. Portuguese (summaries and/or abstracts in English).
Ind/Abst Agrofor. Abstr. (19??-19??); For. Prod. Abstr. (1991-); For. Abstr.; Seed Abstr.; Soils Fert.; Weed Abstr.

MX/0188-4360
BOLETIN MENSUAL DE INFORMACION BASICA DEL SECTOR AGROPECUARIO Y FORESTAL / SECRETARIA DE AGRICULTURA Y RECURSOS HIDRAULICOS, SUBSECRETARIA DE PLANEACION, DIRECCION GENERAL DE ESTADISTICA. See Agriculture.

MX/0185-2310
BOLETIN TECNICO. No. 60 (Dec. 1979)-. Monographic series. Spanish (summaries and/or abstracts in English). Price varies per volume. Instituto Nacional de Investigaciones Agricolas, Apartado Postal 6 882, Mexico 6 DF Mexico. **LC** SD147; .B64. *Continues Boletin Tecnico (Mexico. Direccion General de Investigaciony Capacitacion Forestales).*
Ind/Abst Biocont. News Inf.

CL/0304-5560
BOLETIN TECNICO / UNIVERSIDAD DE CHILE, FACULTAD DE CIENCIAS AGRARIAS, VETERINARIAS Y FORESTALES, ESCUELA DE CIENCIAS FORESTALES. Added/Corp Universidad de Chile. Escuela de Ciencias Forestales. No. 63 (1981)-. Monographic series. Spanish. *Continues Universidad de Chile. Facultad de Ciencias Forestales. Boletin Tecnico.*
Ind/Abst Hortic. Abstr.

NE/0923-7488
BOS NIEUWSLETTER. [BOS nieuwsl.]. **Added/Corp** Stichting voor Nederlandse Bosbouw Ontwikkelings Samenwerking Foundation for Dutch Forestry Development Cooperation. **VFOAT** Bosbouw Ontwikkelings Samenwerking Nieuwsletter. (1982)-. Periodical. Dutch. qt. Stichting voor Nederlandse Bosbouw Ontwikkelings Samenwerking; Foundation for Dutch Forestry Development Cooperation, PO Box 23, 6700 AA, Wageningen, Netherlands. **UDC** 630.
Ind/Abst Agrofor. Abstr. (1991-); For. Prod. Abstr. (1991-); For. Abstr.

SA
BOSBOUNUUS. VFOAT Forestry News : Official Newsletter of the Department of Forestry; Forestry News. Periodical. Afrikaans (English). qt. Directorate of Forestry, Private Bag X447, Pretoria Republic of South Africa. **Tel** (12)310-3911, FAX 310-3584, telex 320142. **ED** Jackie de Klerk. **LC** SD242.S6; B64. **DD** 634.9/0968. **Circ:** 5,600.

CL/0304-8799
BOSQUE. Added/Corp Universidad Austral de Chile. Facultad de Ingenieria Forestal. Vol.1, No.1 (1975)-. Periodical. Spanish. sa.
Ind/Abst Biocont. News Inf. (1991-); Biodeter. Abstr. (1991-); For. Prod. Abstr. (1991-); For. Abstr.; Plant Grow. Reg. Abstr.; Rev. Agric. Entomol.; Rev. Plant Pathol.; Weed Abstr.

FR
BRANCHES EXPLOITATION FORESTIERE, CARBONISATION EN FORET ET SCIERIE : RESULTATS STATISTIQUES. French. Lter, Avenue de Lowendal, Paris 75700 France. **LC** SD59; .A27. **DD** 338.1/7/490944. *Continues Production de la Branche Exploitation Forestiere et Production des Branches Scierie et Carbonisation en Foret.*

BL/0045-270X
BRASIL FLORESTAL. Suspended. [Bras. florest.]. (Jan/March 1970)-Suspended. Portuguese. qt. $12.00. IBDF-Biblioteca, Sector de Areas Isoladas L4 Norte, 70800 Brasilia DF Brazil. **Tel** 223-5966, telex 061-1711. **LC** SD159; .B73. Index available. **Bk Rev. Desc:** A publication of the Brazilian Institute for Forestry Development (IBDF). Contains scientific and technical articles written by national and international scientists on conservation, preservation, management and utilization of renewable natural resources. Editorial norms must be followed by all authors submitting articles for publication.
Ind/Abst Agrofor. Abstr.; For. Prod. Abstr.; For. Abstr.; Hortic. Abstr.; Ornamental Hort. (1991-); Soils Fert.

BL
BRASIL MADEIRA. Periodical. Portuguese. 900. Caixa Postal 1425, 80.000 Curitiba Brazil. **LC** SD159; .B74.

CN/0706-1056
BRITEQ PRESSE. See Energy.

IO/0215-028X
BULETIN PENELITIAN HUTAN. (BULETIN PENELITIAN HUTAN / DEPARTEMEN KEHUTANAN, BADAN PENELITIAN DAN PENGEMBANGAN KEHUTANAN, PUSAT PENELITIAN DAN PENGEMBANGAN HUTAN.). [Bul. penelitian hutan]. **Added/Corp** Pusat Penelitian dan Pengembangan Hutan (Indonesia). **VFOAT** Forest Research Bulletin. (1984-)-. Periodical. Indonesian (summaries and/or abstracts in English); table of contents in English). ir. **CODEN** BPHUED. Documents available from BIOSIS Document Express. *Continues Laporan (Pusat Penelitian dan Pengembangan Hutan).*
Ind/Abst Agric. Eng. Abstr. (1991-); Agrofor. Abstr. (1991-); Biocont. News Inf. (1991-); Biodeter. Abstr. (1991-); Biol. Abstr. (1985-); Field Crop Abstr.; Fish Rev. (Jan. 1989-July 1992); For. Prod. Abstr. (1991-); For. Abstr.; Plant Breed. Abstr.; Plant Grow. Reg. Abstr.; Rev. Plant Pathol.; Seed Abstr.; Soils Fert.; Weed Abstr.; Wildl. Rev. (Jan. 1989-July 1992).

IO/0215-0190
BULETIN PENELITIAN KEHUTANAN. [Bul. penelitian kehutanan]. **VFOAT** Forestry Research Bulletin. (1985)-. Periodical. English. Balai Penelitian Kehutanan, Jalen Viyata Yudha Pematang Siantar, Sumatera Utara Indonesia. **DD** 634.9.
Ind/Abst Crop Physiol. Abstr.; For. Abstr.; Grasslands For. Abstr.; Hortic. Abstr.; Plant Grow. Reg. Abstr.; Seed Abstr.; Weed Abstr.

RM/1010-3589
BULETINUL INFORMATIV AL ACADEMIEI DE STIINTE AGRICOLE SI SILVICE. [Bul. inf. Acad. Stiinte Agric. Silv.]. **Added/Corp** Academia de Stiinte Agricole si Silvice. (19??)-. Academic Scholarly Publication. Romanian (summaries and/or abstracts in English; table of contents in English). Documents available from CASDDS.
Ind/Abst Biodeter. Abstr.; Chem. Abstr.; Maize Abstr.; Wheat Barley Trit. Abstr.

RM
BULETINUL UNIVERSITATII DIN BRASOV. SERIA B : ECONOMIE FORESTIERA. Main/Corp Universitatea din Brasov. **VFOAT** Economie Forestiera. Vol. 19 (1977)-. Periodical. Romanian (summaries and/or abstracts in English, French, German and Russian); table of contents in English, French, German and Russian). an. $35.00. **(Subscription address:** Ilexim Press Department, PO Box 1, 136-1-137, Bucharest, Romania.) *Continues Noutati in Economie Forestiera.*
Ind/Abst For. Prod. Abstr.; For. Abstr.

CN/0822-773X
BULLETIN / FONDS DE RECHERCHES ET DE DEVELOPPEMENT FORESTIER. [Bull. - Fonds rech. dev. for.]. Bulletin. French. Fonds de Recherches et de Developpement Forestier, 3083 Chemin des Quatre-Bourgeois, Ste Foy Quebec G1W 2K6 Canada. **DD** 634.9/05. *Continues Universite Laval. Fonds de Recherches Forestieres. Bulletin.*

UK
BULLETIN - FOREST PRODUCTS RESEARCH. DEPARTMENT OF THE ENVIRONMENT. Main/Corp Forest Products Research Laboratory, Princes Risborough. No. 53- 1970-. Bulletin. English. Price varies per volume. *Continues Gt. Brit. Dept. of Scientific and Industrial Research. Forest Products Research Dept. Bulletin.*

AT/0085-7742
BULLETIN - FORESTS COMMISSION, VICTORIA. Main/Corp Victoria. Forests Commission. Bulletin. English. ir. Price varies per volume. Forest and Land Service, 601 Bourke Street, Melbourne 3000 Victoria Australia.

AT/0085-8129
BULLETIN - FORESTS DEPARTMENT. Main/Corp Western Australia. Forests Dept. 1- 1919-. Bulletin. English. ir. Price varies per volume. Forests Department, 54 Barrack Street, Perth Western Australia 6000 Australia.
Ind/Abst For. Prod. Abstr.; For. Abstr.; Soils Fert.

US/0898-0497
BULLETIN (MISSISSIPPI AGRICULTURAL AND FORESTRY EXPERIMENT STATION). See Agriculture.

●US
BULLETIN OF TALL TIMBERS RESEARCH, INC. Added/Corp Tall Timbers Research, Inc. Bulletin 26 (1992)-. Bulletin. English. Price varies per volume. Tall Timbers Research Station, Route 1 Box 678, Tallahassee FL 32312. **Tel** (904)893-4153. *Continues Bulletin (Tall Timber Research Station).*

JA
BULLETIN OF THE KYUSHU UNIVERSITY FORESTS. Main/Corp Kyushu Daigaku. Fukuoka, Japan. Bulletin. English. Kyushu Daigaku Nogakubu Fuzoku Enshurin, (Research Institution of University Forests, Faculty of Agriculture, Kyushu University), 10-1, Hakozaki 6 Chome, Higashiku,

Fukuokashi, Fukuokaken 812 Japan.
Ind/Abst For. Prod. Abstr. (1991-); Leis. Recreat. Tour. Abstr.; Nematol. Abstr.; World Agric. Econ.

JA
BULLETIN OF THE TOKYO UNIVERSITY FORESTS. **Main/Corp** Tokyo Daigaku. Nogakubu. Experimental Forest. (19??)-. Bulletin. English. Tokyo Daigaku Nogakubu Fuzoku Enshurin, (Tokyo University Forests), 1-1, Yayoi 1 Chome, Bunkyoku, Tokyoto 113, Japan.
Ind/Abst Biodeter. Abstr.; Crop Physiol. Abstr.; Irr. Drain. Abstr.; Nematol. Abstr.; Plant Breed. Abstr.; Rev. Agric. Entomol.; Rev. Plant Pathol.

FR/0395-7497
BULLETIN TECHNIQUE - OFFICE NATIONAL DES FORETS. [Bull. tech. - off. natl. for.]. (1971)-. Periodical. French (English). qt. 120.00F. Bulletin Technique Office National Forets, Boulevard de Constance, 77305 Fontainebleau France. **Tel** 011 33 1 64274807. **UDC** 634.0. Index available. **Circ:** 7,500.
Desc: Forestry techniques for internal use in French Foresty Administration.

FR
BULLETIN TRIMESTRIEL / SOCIETE FORESTIERE DE FRANCHE-COMTE ET DES PROVINCES DE L'EST. **Added/Corp** Societe Forestiere de Franche-Comte et des Provinces de l'Est. **VFOAT** Bulletin de la Societe Forestiere de Franche-Comte et des Provinces de l'Est. (1923)-. Periodical. French. qt. Societe Forestiere de Franche-Comte, 2 Place Rene Payot, 25000 Besancon France. **Tel** 011 33 81 803086. **Continues** Bulletin Trimestriel (Societe Forestiere de Franche-Comte & Belfort).

US/0748-1268
BULLETIN / WEST VIRGINIA UNIVERSITY AGRICULTURAL AND FORESTRY EXPERIMENT STATION. **See** Agriculture.

US/0361-4425
BULLETIN - YALE UNIVERSITY, SCHOOL OF FORESTRY AND ENVIRONMENTAL STUDIES. [Bull. Yale Univ. Sch. For. Environ. Stud.]. Bulletin. English. Price varies per volume. Yale University / Forestry, School of Forestry and Environmental Studies, 205 Prospect Street, New Haven CT 06511. **Tel** (203)432-5100. **CODEN** BYSSDM. Documents available from CASDDS. **Continues** Bulletin - Yale University, School of Forestry, 0097-2592.
Ind/Abst Chem. Abstr.

FR
CAHIERS SCIENTIFIQUES. **Added/Corp** Centre Technique Forestier Tropical. No. 1 (1972)-. Periodical. French.
Ind/Abst For. Prod. Abstr. (1991-).

US/0889-0102
CALIFORNIA FORESTRY NOTE. [Calif. for. note]. **Added/Corp** California. Dept. of Forestry. (1978)-. Monographic series. English. ir (two to four issues per year). Price varies per volume. California Resources Agency, Department of Forestry, 1416 Ninth Street, Sacramento CA 95814. **Tel** (916)445-5571. **(Subscription address:** PO Box 944246, Sacramento, CA 94244-2460) **ED** Clifford E Fago. **LC** SD144.C2; S7. **DD** 634.9/09794. Index available. cum. index. **Circ:** 750 (ctrl). **Continues** State Forest Notes, 0068-5577.
Desc: Reporting results of forestry studies in California. Generally in non-technical language suitable for layman.
Ind/Abst Field Crop Abstr.; For. Abstr.

US/1057-1736
CAMCORE BULLETIN ON TROPICAL FORESTRY. **Added/Corp** Central America and Mexico Resources Cooperative. **VFOAT** C.A.M.C.O.R.E. Bulletin on Tropical Forestry. **VAT** Central America and Mexico Resources Cooperative Bulletin on Tropical Forestry. No. 1 (June 1984)-. Bulletin. English. CAMCORE Cooperative, PO Box 8007, N C State School-Forestry, Raleigh NC 27695.
Ind/Abst AGRICOLA [Full Cov.]; For. Prod. Abstr. (1991-); For. Abstr.; Seed Abstr.

CN
CANADA'S FOREST INVENTORY / BY G.M. BONNOR. **Added/Corp** Canadian Forestry Service. Forestry Statistics and Systems Branch. (19??)-. English (French). ir (every five years). $26.95. Petawawa National Forestry Institute, PO Box 2000, Chalk River Ontario K0J 1J0 Canada. **Tel** (613)589-2880. **LC** SD145; .C25. **DD** 333.75/0971.

CN/0575-805X
CANADIAN FORESTRY STATISTICS. **See** Forestry-Abstracting, Bibliographies and Statistics.

CN/0045-5067
CANADIAN JOURNAL OF FOREST RESEARCH. [Can. j. for. res.]. **Added/Corp** National Research Council of Canada. **VFOAT** Journal Canadien de la Recherche Forestiere. Vol. 1 (March 1971)-. Academic Scholarly Publication. English (French; summaries and/or abstracts in French). mo. 366.00Can$ (institutions), 119.00Can$ (individuals) Canada; $366.00 (institutions), $123.00 (individuals) other. National Research Council of Canada, Receiver General for Canada, Ottawa Ontario K1A 0R6 Canada. **Tel** (613)993-0362, FAX (613)952-7656. **ED** B. P. Dancik. **LC** SD255; .C35. **DD** 634.9/0971. **CODEN** CJFRAR. **[CCC].** Index available. **Ad Acc. Pr Rev. Circ:** 1,000. available on microfilm and microfiche from University Microfilms International (UMI). Documents available from The Genuine Article, BIOSIS Document Express, CASDDS, Documents on Demand.
Desc: Research papers, notes, discussions, reviews, and rapid communications cover all aspects of forestry, including silviculture, forest ecology, tree physiology, forest entomology and pathology, fire science, and land management.
Ind/Abst ASTIS Curr. Aware. Bull. (1978-); Abstr. Bull. Inst. Pap. Sci. Tech.; AgBiotech News Inf.; AGRICOLA [Full Cov.]; Agrofor. Abstr.; AQUAREF; ASTIS Bibliogr. (1978-); BioBusiness; Biocont. News Inf. (1991-); Biodeter. Abstr.; Biol. Abstr.; Chem. Abstr.; Coal Abstr.; Crop Physiol. Abstr.; Curr. Contents, Agric. Biol. Environ. Sci.; Ecol. Abstr.; Ecology Abstr.; EMBASE; Environ. Abstr.; Environ. Period. Bibliogr.; Field Crop Abstr.; For. Prod. Abstr. (19??-19??); For. Abstr.; Geogr. Abstr. Phys. Geogr.; Geogr. Abstr. Human Geogr.; Geol. Abstr.; Grasslands For. Abstr.; Hortic. Abstr.; Index Vet.; INIS Atomindex [Micro.]; Int. Dev. Abstr.; Irr. Drain. Abstr.; Key Word Index Wildl. Res.; Environ.; Microbiol. Abstr. Sect. A; Microbiol. Abstr. Sect. C; Nematol. Abstr.; Life Sci. Collect.; Plant Breed. Abstr.; Plant Grow. Reg. Abstr.; Protozoolog. Abstr.; Res. Alert [Full Cov.]; Rev. Agric. Entomol.; Rev. Med. Vet. Mycology; Rev. Plant Pathol.; Sci. Cit. Index; SCISEARCH; Seed Abstr.; Soc. Sci. Cit. Index [Select. Cov.]; Soils Fert.; Vet. Bull.; Weed Abstr.; Wheat Barley Trit. Abstr.; Wildl. Rev.

CN/1196-1376
CANADIAN RESOUCRES REVIEW. (199?)-. Periodical. English. qt. Consolidated Communications, 807 Manning Road Northeast, Suite 200, Calgary Alberta T2E 7M8 Canada. **Tel** (403)569-9520, FAX (403)569-9590. **Continues** Forestry, Gas and Oil Review.

PH/0115-0960
CANOPY INTERNATIONAL. **Added/Corp** Forest Research Institute (College, Philippines). **VFOAT** Canopy. Vol. 5, No. 6 (June 1979)-. Periodical. English. Six times a year. Free on request. Forest Research Institute / Philippines, College of Laguna, Laguna 3720 Philippines. **Tel** 011 63 3481. **Continues** Canopy.
Ind/Abst Abstr. Bull. Inst. Pap. Sci. Tech.; Agrofor. Abstr. (1991-); Biocont. News Inf. (1991-); For. Prod. Abstr. (1991-); For. Abstr.; Philip. Sci. Technol. Abstr.; Rev. Agric. Entomol.

US/0742-7921
CATALOG - FORESTRY SUPPLIERS, INC. [Cat. - For. Suppl., Inc.]. **Main/Corp** Forestry Suppliers, Inc. (19??)-. Catalog. English. an. Free. Forestry Suppliers Inc, PO Box 3897, 205 West Eankin Street, Jackson MS 39204. **Tel** (800)647-5368.

AU/0008-9583
CENTRALBLATT FUER DAS GESAMTE FORSTWESEN. **Title Change.** [Centralbl. gesamte Forstwes.]. Vol. 1 (1875)-. Academic Scholarly Publication. German. qt. F Fluck-Wirth-International Booksellers for Botany and Natural History, CH-9053 Teufen Switzerland. Documents available from CASDDS. **Continued by** Zeitschrift fur das Gesamte Forstwesen.
Ind/Abst Biocont. News Inf. (1991-); Chem. Abstr. (1958-1983); For. Prod. Abstr. (19??-19??); For. Abstr.; Key Word Index Wildl. Res.; Rev. Agric. Entomol.

US/0748-1721
CFRU PROGRESS REPORT. [CFRU prog. rep.]. **VFOAT** C.F.R.U. Progress Report. **VAT** Cooperative Forest Research Unit Progress Report. Monographic series. English. ir. Price varies per volume. CRFU, University of Maine at Orono, Life Sciences & Agriculture Experiment Station, Orono ME 04469.
Ind/Abst For. Prod. Abstr.; For. Abstr.

US/0748-1748
CFRU RESEARCH NOTE. (COOPERATIVE FORESTRY RESEARCH UNIT RESEARCH NOTE.). [CFRU res. note]. **VFOAT** C.F.R.U. Research Note. Monographic series. English. ir. Price varies per volume. CFRU, University of Maine at Orono, Life Sciences & Agriculture Experiment Stations, Orono ME 04469. **DD** 634.

CC
CHE-CHIANG LIN HSUEH YUAN HSUEH PAO. **Added/Corp** Che-Chiang lin Hsueh Yuan. **VFOAT** Journal of Zhejiang Forestry College; Zhejiang Linxueyuan Xuebao. (1984)-. Periodical. Chinese (summaries and/or abstracts in English). sa. **LC** SD222.C479; C48. **DD** 634.9/0951/242.
Ind/Abst For. Prod. Abstr. (1991-); For. Abstr.; Hortic. Abstr.; Soils Fert.

CL/0716-1190
CHILE FORESTAL. **Added/Corp** Corporacion Nacional Forestal. Vol. 1, No. 1 (Aug. 1975)-. Periodical. Spanish. mo. $80.00 Chile; $88.00 US and Canada; $96.00 other. Corporacion Nacional Forestal, Avda Bulnes 259 of 706, Santiago Chile. **Tel** 011 56 2 6966724, telex 240001 CONAF CL. Index available. **Ad Acc. Circ:** 6,700.
Desc: Specialized magazine which deals with the situation, behavior and development of Chilean forestry sector.
Ind/Abst Agrofor. Abstr. (1991-); Field Crop Abstr.; For. Prod. Abstr. (1991-); For. Abstr.

CL
CHILEAN FORESTRY NEWS. (1978)-. Periodical. English. mo (11 issues). $96.00 North America; $88.00 Latin America; $104.00 other. Corporacion Nacional Forestal, Avda Bulnes 259 of 706, Santiago Chile. **Tel** 011 56 2 6966724, telex 240001 CONAF CL. **ED** Maria Eugenia Diaz. **Ad Acc. Circ:** 1,300.
Desc: Analysis and review of the Chilean forestry sector and its relations with external markets.
Ind/Abst Field Crop Abstr.; For. Abstr.

US/0199-0217
CHRISTMAS TREES. Vol. 1 (April 1973)-. Periodical. English. Four times a year (Jan., Apr., July, Oct.). $10.00 US; $16.20 Canada & Mexico; $17.80 others. Tree Publishers Inc, Box 107, Lecompton KS 66050. **Tel** (913)887-6324, FAX (913)887-6734. **ED** Charles W. Wright. **Ad Acc, Adv Mgr:** Alice Wright. **Circ:** 8,000 (ctrl).
Desc: This magazine is about plantation management for Christmas Trees. Its articles cover various aspects of the grower's operations from planting, insect and weed control, to shearing, shaping and marketing.

CC/0529-6315
CHUNG-KUO LIN YEH / ZHONGGUO LINYE / FORESTRY OF CHINA. **VFOAT** Forestry of China; Zhongguo Linye. (June 1950)-. Periodical. Chinese. Twelve times a year. $18.97. Linye Bu - Ministry of Forestry, Hepingli, Beijing 100013, People's Republic of China. **Tel** 4217381. **(Subscription address:** China International Book Trading Corporation, PO Box 399, Library Service Department, Beijing 100044 People's Republic of China.) **ED** Zhao Shengtie. **LC** SD221; .C5125. **DD** 634.9/0951.

CH/0716-5994
CIENCIA E INVESTIGACION FORESTAL. **Added/Corp** Instituto Forestal (Santiago, Chile). Vol. 1, No. 1 (Apr. 1987)-. Periodical. Spanish. sa. Ciencia e Investigacion Forest, Huerfanos 554, Casilla 3085, Santiago Chile. **Tel** 011 56 2 6333864. **LC** SD161; .C54. **DD** 634.9/0983.
Ind/Abst Abstr. Bull. Inst. Pap. Sci. Tech.

MX/0185-2418
CIENCIA FORESTAL. **Suspended.** (CIENCIA FORESTAL : REVISTA DEL INSTITUTO NACIONAL DE INVESTIGACION ES FORESTALES.). [Cienc. for.]. **Added/Corp** Instituto Nacional de Investigaciones Forestales (Mexico). (May/June 1976)-(19??). Academic Scholarly Publication. Spanish (summaries and/or abstracts in English). bm. $3,000 Mexico; $15.00 US. Revista Ciencia Forestal, Progreso 5, Coyoacan DF Mexico. **Tel** 658 43 33. **ED** Carlos E Gonzalez Vicente, Avelino B Villa Salas. **LC** SD147; .C53. **DD** 634.9/05. Index available. cum. index. **Ad Acc. Circ:** 2,000 (ctrl). Documents available from BIOSIS Document Express, CASDDS.
Desc: Topics include forestry science, genetic recourse, forest ecology, forestry products, multiple uses, forestry entomology, inventions relating to forestry, cold, tropical and temperate zones. Dry zones/regions and urban forestry.
Ind/Abst Abstr. Bull. Inst. Pap. Sci. Tech.; Agrofor. Abstr. (1991-); Biocont. News Inf.; Biol. Abstr.; Chem. Abstr.; For. Prod. Abstr. (1991-); For. Abstr.; Weed Abstr.

US
CINTRAFOR NEWS. (19??)-. Newsletter. English. Four times a year. Free on request. College of Forest Resources, University of Washington AR-10, Seattle WA 98195. **Tel** (206)543-8684, FAX (206)685-0790, telex 47-40096 VW;UI. **ED** John Dirks. **Circ:** 1,200.
Desc: Contains summaries of research relating to the forest products trade.

BL/0101-1847
CIRCULAR TECNICA. **Added/Corp** Empresa Brasileira de Pesquisa Agropecuaria. Unidade Regional de Pesquisa Florestal Centro-Sul. (19??)-. Monographic series. Portuguese.
Ind/Abst Agrofor. Abstr.; For. Abstr.

UK
COMMONWEALTH FORESTRY HANDBOOK, THE. **Added/Corp** Commonwealth Forestry Association. (19??)-. English. Free to Members. Commonwealth Forestry Association, South Parks Road, Oxford OX1 3RB England. **Tel** 011 44 865 275072, telex 3147 ATTN FOROX. Index available. **Bk Rev. Ad Acc. Continues** Empire Forestry Handbook.

Forestry

XR/0507-5548
COMMUNICATIONES INSTITUTI FORESTALIS CECHOSLOVENIAE. **Added/Corp** Vyzkumny Ustav Lesniho Hospodarstvi a Myslivosti (Ceskoslovenska Akademie Zemedelskych Ved). **VFOAT** Communications. (1959)-. English (summaries and/or abstracts in Czech, German and Russian). be. **LC** WMLC L 83/2352. **CODEN** CIFCA9. Documents available from BIOSIS Document Express. **Ind/Abst** Agric. Eng. Abstr. (1991-); Biol. Abstr. (?-1983); For. Prod. Abstr. (19??-19??); Irr. Drain. Abstr.; Soils Fert.

CN/0839-8585
COMPREHENSIVE PUBLICATION LIST - MINISTRY OF FORESTS AND LANDS (VICTORIA). (COMPREHENSIVE PUBLICATION LIST.). [Compr. publ. list - Minist. For. Lands]. **Main/Corp** British Columbia. Ministry of Forests and Lands. **VFOAT** Ministry of Forests and Lands Comprehensive Publication List. (Oct. 30, 1987)-. English. Ministry of Forests, 1450 Government Street Information Center, Victoria British Columbia V8W 3E7 Canada. **DD** 016.33375/09711. **Continues** Publications List., 0710-9776.

US/0749-2111
CONFERENCE PROCEEDINGS - WESTERN FORESTRY COUNCIL (U.S.) CONFERENCE. (CONFERENCE PROCEEDINGS / WESTERN FORESTRY NURSERY COUNCIL.). [Conf. proc. - West. For. Nurs. Counc. (U.S.), Conf.]. **Main/Corp** Western Forestry Nursery Council (U.S.). Conference. **Added/Corp** Southern Oregon Regional Services Institute. **VFOAT** Proceedings of the ... Western Nurserymen's Conference. (198?)-. Periodical. English. qt. Western Forestry and Conservation, 4033 Southwest Canyon Road, Portland OR 97221. **Tel** (503)226-4562. **DD** 634.

US
CONSULTANT, THE. **Added/Corp** Association of Consulting Foresters. (19??)-. Periodical. English. qt. $20.00. Association of Consulting Foresters Inc, 5400 Grosvenor Lane/Suite 300, Bethesda MD 20814. **Tel** (301)530-6795. **ED** Arthur F. Ennis. **Bk Rev**. **Ad Acc**. **Circ**: 750.
Desc: The journal of the Association of Consulting Foresters, Inc. Owners/managers of forest land will find information of value on management, harvest, protection, taxation, estate planning, etc.

US/0010-7085
CONSULTANT - ASSOCIATION OF CONSULTING FORESTERS OF AMERICA, THE. (THE CONSULTANT.). [Consult. - Assoc. Consult. For. Am.]. **Main/Corp** Association of Consulting Foresters of America. Vol. 1 (Feb. 1956)-. Periodical. English. Four times a year (Jan., Apr., July, Oct.). $20.00. Association of Consulting Forresters Inc., 5400 Grosvenor Lane, Suite 300, Bethesda MD 20814-2198. **Tel** (301)530-6795, FAX (301)530-5128. **ED** Michael Webb (editor's address: 309 Church Street, Columbia, MS 39429; phone: (601)736-4956). **DD** 634. **Bk Rev**, (Qty: 4). **Ad Acc**.

US/0071-6146
COOPERATIVE FOREST GENETICS RESEARCH PROGRAM. (COOPERATIVE FOREST GENETICS RESEARCH PROGRAM; PROGRESS REPORT.). **Main/Corp** University of Florida. School of Forest Resources and Conservation. No. 14 (1972)-. English. University of Florida / Forest Research, School of Forest Resources and Conservation, 118 Newins Ziegler Hall, Institute of Food and Agricultural Science, Gainesville FL 32611. **LC** SD399.5; .F64a. **DD** 582/.1601/505. **Continues** Cooperative Forest Genetics Research Program, 0071-6146.

US/0097-4536
CROSSTIES. **Added/Corp** Railway Tie Association. Vol. 49 No. 12 (Dec. 1968)-. Periodical. English. bm. $35.00 US, $50.00 other. Covey Communications, PO Box 2267, Gulf Shores AL 36547. **Tel** (205)968-5300, FAX (205) 968-4532. **ED** D B Mabry. **Bk Rev**. **Ad Acc**. **Circ**: 1,800 (ctrl). **Continues** Cross Tie Bulletin, 0011-197X.
Desc: Articles involving the manufacture, procurement and treatment of wood railroad ties including conservation of forest, forest products and reforestation.

US
CROW'S. **VFOAT** Forest Industry Journal; Crow's Forest Industry Journal. Vol. 5, No. 6 (July 1990)-. Periodical. English. CC Crow Publishers Inc., PO Box 25749, Portland OR 97255. **Tel** (503)646-8075. **LC** HD9750.1; .C76. **Continues** Crow's Digest.

US/0897-313X
CRUISER (1985), THE. (THE CRUISER : NEWSLETTER OF THE FOREST HISTORY SOCIETY.). [Cruiser]. **Added/Corp** Forest History Society. Vol. 8, No. 2 (Summer 1985)-. Periodical. English. qt (4 issues). Comes with Forest History Society membership. Forest History Society, 701 Vickers Avenue, Durham NC 27701. **Tel** (919)682-9319. **ED** Harold K. Steen. **DD** 634. **Circ**: 2,500. **Continues** Forest History Cruiser (1981).
Desc: News of Forest History Society and its members.

US/0748-1616
CURRENT PUBLICATIONS FROM THE FOREST, WILDLIFE AND RANGE EXPERIMENT STATION. [Curr. publ. For. Wildl. Range Exp. Stn.]. English. sa. Free. Forest Wildlife and Range Experiment Station, University of Idaho, Moscow ID 83843. **Tel** (208)885-6674. **ED** George Savage. **DD** 630. **Circ**: 3,000.
Desc: List of publications available.

DK
DANSK SKOVBRUGS TIDSSKRIFT : DST. **Added/Corp** Dansk Skovforening. **VFOAT** DST. (1989)-. Periodical. Danish. qt. kr190.00. Danish Forestry Society, Amalievej 20 1875, DK 1875 Fredeiksberg C Denmark. **Tel** 011 45 31 244266, FAX 011 45 31 240242. **LC** SD1; .D3. **CODEN** DSTEEY. **Continues** Dansk Skovforenings Tidsskrift, 0011-6475.
Ind/Abst For. Abstr.

SZ
DECISION ADOPTED BY THE INTERNATIONAL TROPICAL TIMBER COUNCIL. **Main/Corp** International Tropical Timber Council. (19??)-. English.

IT
DENDRONATURA / ASSOCIAZIONE FORRESTALE DEL TRENTINO. **Added/Corp** Associazione Forrestale del Trentino. (19??)-. Periodical. Italian (summaries and/or abstracts in English). sa.
Ind/Abst For. Abstr.; Rev. Agric. Entomol.; Rev. Plant Pathol.

US/0193-8223
DEPARTMENT OF FORESTRY TECHNICAL PAPER. [Dep. For. tech. pap.]. **Main/Corp** Clemson University. Dept. of Forestry. No. 1-. Monographic series. English. Price varies per volume. Clemson University / Forestry, College of Forest and Recreation Resources, Department of Forestry, Clemson SC 29631. **CODEN** CUFTA8. Documents available from BIOSIS Document Express.
Ind/Abst AGRICOLA [Full Cov.]; Biol. Abstr.; GeoRef.

DK/0367-2174
DET FORSTLIGE FORSOEGSVAESEN I DANMARK : BERETNINGER UTGIVNE VED DEN FORSTLIGE FORSOEGSKOMMISSION. **Ceased**. **VFOAT** Beretninger Utgivne ved den Forstlige Forsgskommission; Danish Forest Experiment Station : Reports. Began in 1905-Ceased 1992. Periodical. Danish (English). ir. Statens Forstlige Forsoegsvaesen, Skovbrynet 16, 2800 Lyngby Denmark. **Tel** 45 93 12 00, FAX 45 93 48 49. **ED** E Holmsgaard. **LC** SD191; .F67. Index available. cum. index. **Circ**: 800 (ctrl).
Desc: Forestry research.
Ind/Abst For. Abstr.

GW/0011-992X
DEUTSCHE BAUMSCHULE. **See** Gardening and Horticulture.

●**US/1075-1653**
DIFFERENT DRUMMER MAGAZINE. [Differ. drummer mag.]. **Added/Corp** Cascade Holistic Economic Consultants. **VFOAT** Different Drummer. Vol. 1, No. 1 (Winter 1994). Periodical. English. Four times a year. $27.50 (one year), $49.95 (two year). Cascade Holistic Economic Consultants / CHEC, 14417 Southeast Laurie, Oak Grove OR 97267. **Tel** (503)652-7049. **LC** IN PROCESS; SD143; .D53. **DD** 333. **Separated from** Forest Watch, 1057-2724.

CN/0705-1875
DIRECTORY AND NEWSLETTER - FORESTRY ALUMNI ASSOCIATION, UNIVERSITY OF TORONTO. **See** College and School Publications-Alumni.

MY
DIRECTORY OF FOREST INDUSTRIES IN MALAYSIA. **See** Forestry-Lumber and Wood.

US/1053-8453
DIRECTORY OF FORESTRY AND NATURAL RESOURCES COMPUTER SOFTWARE. **See** Computers.

US/0748-1276
DIVIDENDS FROM WOOD RESEARCH. (DIVIDENDS FROM WOOD RESEARCH / UNITED STATES DEPARTMENT OF AGRICULTURE, FOREST SERVICE, FOREST PRODUCTS LABORATORY.). [Divid. wood res.]. (June 30/Dec. 31, 1967)-. Periodical. English. sa. Free on request. Forest Products Laboratory, One Gifford Pinchot Drive, Madison WI 53705-2398. **Tel** (608)231-9200, FAX (608)231-9592. **DD** 634. **Circ**: 8,000. available on microfiche. **Continues** Forest Products Laboratory (U.S.). List of Publications.
Desc: Listing of recent publications resulting from wood utilization at the forest products laboratory.
Ind/Abst Abstr. Bull. Inst. Pap. Sci. Tech.

US
DIVISION OF FORESTRY IN THE CALIFORNIA CONSERVATION CAMP PROGRAM, THE. **Main/Corp** California. Division of Forestry. **VFOAT** California Conservation Camp Program. 196?-. Periodical. English. an. California Department of Forestry, 1416 9th Street, Sacramento CA 95814. **Tel** (916)445-9886. **LC** WMLC L 83/8013. **DD** 634.9. **Continues** Conservation Camp Program, 0526-9970.

AT
DIVISIONAL REPORT - CSIRO DIVISION OF FOREST RESEARCH. **Main/Corp** Australia. Commonwealth Scientific and Industrial Research Organization. Division of Forest Research. No. 1 (1977)-. Monographic series. English. ir. Price varies per volume. CSIRO Publications, PO Box 89, 314 Albert Street, East Melborne Victoria 3002 Australia. **Tel** 011 61 3 4187333, 4187217, FAX 011 61 3 4190459, telex AA 30236.
Ind/Abst For. Prod. Abstr.; For. Abstr.

TU/1011-0917
DOGA BILIM DERGISI. SERI D2, TARIM V ORMANCILIK. **Title Change**. **See** Agriculture.

TU/1010-7649
DOGA. TURK TARIM VE ORMANCLK DERGISI. **See** Agriculture.

SW
DOMANKONCERNEN. **Main/Corp** Sweden. Domanverket. Swedish. an. Pelle Bergs Backe 3, Falun Sweden. **LC** HA1521; .D3. **Continues** Domanverket.

IO/0126-1118
DUTA RIMBA / PERUM PERHUTANI. (June 1974)-. Indonesian (English). mo.
Ind/Abst Agrofor. Abstr. (19??-19??); Biodeter. Abstr. (1991-); For. Prod. Abstr. (19??-19??); For. Abstr.; Seed Abstr.; Soils Fert.

KE/0012-8325
EAST AFRICAN AGRICULTURAL AND FORESTRY JOURNAL. **See** Agriculture.

IT/0012-9836
ECONOMIA MONTANA ROMA. **See** Environmental Issues-Ecology.

US
ECONOMIC ANALYSIS SERIES FOR SCREENING PROPOSED TIMBER MANAGEMENT PROJECTS / U.S. DEPARTMENT OF THE INTERIOR, BUREAU OF LAND MANAGEMENT, AN. **Added/Corp** United States. Bureau of Land Management. Denver Service Center. Report No. 1 (1979)-. Monographic series. English. ir. Price varies per volume.

JA/0424-6845
EHIME DAIGAKU NOGAKUBU ENSHURIN HOKOKU. **VFOAT** Bulletin of the Ehime University Forest. (1963)-. Periodical. Multiple languages. an. University Forest, College of Agriculture, Ehime University,, Matsuyama, Japan. **DD** 634.9.
Ind/Abst For. Prod. Abstr. (1991-); For. Abstr.

US/0363-8685
EISENHOWER CONSORTIUM BULLETIN. [Eisenhower Consortium bull.]. **Main/Corp** Eisenhower Consortium for Western Environmental Forestry Research. No. 1-. Academic Scholarly Publication. English. Price varies per volume. Rocky Mountain Forest and Range Experiment Station, 240 West Prospect Road, Fort Collins CO 80526. **CODEN** ECOBDY. Documents available from BIOSIS Document Express, CASDDS.
Ind/Abst AGRICOLA; Biol. Abstr.; Chem. Abstr.

RU/0134-4978
EKOLOGIIA I ZASHCHITA LESA : MEZHVUZOVSKII SBORNIK NAUCHNYKH TRUDOV / LENINGRADSKAIA LESOTEKHNICHESKAIA AKADEMIIA IMENI S.M. KIROVA. **See** Environmental Issues-Ecology.

RU
EKONOMICHESKIE PROBLEMY LESNOI, DEREVOOBRABATYVAIUSHCHEI PROMYSHLENNOSTI I LESNOGO KHOZIAISTVA. **Added/Corp** Leningradskaia Lesotekhnicheskaia Akademiia Imeni S. M. Kirova. (19??)-. Periodical. Russian. **LC** SD207; .E338.

UK
ENTOPATH NEWS, THE. No. 7 (Oct. 1955)-. Newsletter. English. Twice a year. Free. Northern Research Station, Roswn Midlothian EH25 9SY England.

Tel 031 445 2176, FAX 031 445 5124. **ED** Stuart Heritage. Index available. cum. index. **Bk Rev**, (Qty: varies). **Acid Free. Circ:** 1,000 (ctrl). Documents available from BLDSC. ***Continues*** *Entopath News Letter.*
Desc: Provides current information on all aspects of forest and amenity tree health. Helpful information to local authorities, foresters, and scientists with an interest to forest reviews and recent events in forest pathology.
Ind/Abst Nematol. Abstr.

HU/0209-9306
ERDESZETI ES FAIPARI TUDOMANYOS KOZLEMENYEK. [Erdesz. faip. tud. kozl.]. **Added/Corp** Erdeszeti es Faipari Egyetem. **VFOAT** Scientific Publications of Forestry and Timber Industry; Erdeszeti es Faipari Egyetem Tudomanyos Kozlemenyei. (1980)-. Periodical. Hungarian (summaries and/or abstracts in English, German and Russian). sa. **LC** SD217.H8; E69. ***Continues*** *Erdeszeti es Faipari Egyetem Tudomanyos Kozlemenyei, 0584-1291.*
Ind/Abst AGRICOLA; Biodeter. Abstr.; Fish Rev. (Jan. 1989-July 1992); For. Prod. Abstr.; For. Abstr.; Wildl. Rev. (Jan. 1989-July 1992).

HU/1215-0389
ERDESZETI LAPOK : AZ ORSZAGOS ERDESZETI EGYESULET LAPJA. (1992)-. Periodical. Hungarian. mo. $36.00 Austria, Croatia, Czech Republic, Slovakia, Romania, Yugoslavia, Slovenia & Ukraine; $45.00 other. **(Subscription address:** Kultura, PO Box 149, H 1389 Budapest 62 Hungary.**)** ***Continues*** *Erdo, 0014-0031.*
Ind/Abst Abstr. Bull. Inst. Pap. Sci. Tech.; For. Prod. Abstr.; Vitis Vitic. Enol. Abstr.

HU/0014-0031
ERDO, AZ. ***Title Change.*** [Erdo]. **Main/Corp** Orszagos Erdeszeti Egyesulet. **Added/Corp** Orszagos Erdeszeti Egyesuelet (Hungary). (1952)-(199?). Periodical. Hungarian (table of contents in English, French and Russian). mo. **(Subscription address:** Kultura, PO Box 149, H 1389 Budapest 62 Hungary.**)** ***Continues*** *Erdeszeti Lapok (Budapest, Hungary : 1862).* ***Continued by*** *Erdeszeti Lapok (Budapest, Hungary : 1992), 1215-0398.*
Ind/Abst Abstr. Bull. Inst. Pap. Sci. Tech. (?-?); For. Prod. Abstr. (?-?); Vitis Vitic. Enol. Abstr. (?-?).

US
ESTIMATED 25% PAYMENTS TO BE MADE TO COUNTIES IN FISCAL YEAR ... FROM GOVERNMENT OWNED LANDS ADMINISTERED BY THE FOREST SERVICE / U.S. DEPT. OF AGRICULTURE, FOREST SERVICE. English. an.

CN/1183-3548
ETAT DES FORETS AU CANADA, RAPPORT AU PARLEMENT, L'. [Etat for. Can. rapp. Parlem.]. **Main/Corp** Canada. Forets Canada. **VFOAT** Le Plan Vert du Canada. (1991)-. Periodical. French. **DD** 634.9/0971/05.

GW/0300-1237
EUROPEAN JOURNAL OF FOREST PATHOLOGY. (EUROPEAN JOURNAL OF FOREST PATHOLOGY. JOURNAL EUROPEEN DE PATHOLOGIE FORESTIERE. EUROPAISCHE ZEITSCHRIFT FUER FORSTPATHOLOGIE.). [Eur. j. forest pathol.]. **VFOAT** Journal Europeen de Pathologie Forestiere; Europaische Zeitschrift fuer Forstpathologie. Volume 1 (Sept. 1971)-. Academic Scholarly Publication. Multiple languages (English, French and German). Seven times a year. DM721.00 Europe; DM719.00 other. Blackwell Wissenschafts-Verlag, Kurfuerstendamm 57, D 10707 Berlin Germany. **Tel** 011 49 30 32790623, 011 49 30 32790624, FAX 011 49 30 327 90610. **ED** O. Holdenrieder. **CODEN** EJFPA9. **[CCC].** Index available. cum. index. **Bk Rev. Ad Acc. Pr Rev. Circ:** 2,500. Documents available from The Genuine Article, BIOSIS Document Express, CASDDS, Documents on Demand.
Desc: Covers forest pathological problems worldwide. Includes compilation of titles of relevant articles from other current publications.
Ind/Abst AgBiotech News Inf.; AGRICOLA; Agrofor. Abstr. (1991-); Biol. Abstr.; Chem. Abstr.; Curr. Aware. Biol. Sci., CABS; Curr. Contents, Agric. Biol. Environ. Sci.; EMBASE; Energy Inf. Abstr.; Environ. Abstr.; Environ. Period. Bibliogr.; For. Prod. Abstr. (19??-19??); For. Abstr.; Irr. Drain. Abstr.; Key Word Index Wildl. Res.; Microbiol. Abstr. Sect. A; Microbiol. Abstr. Sect. C; Nematol. Abstr.; Life Sci. Collect.; PESTDOC; Plant Breed. Abstr.; Protozoolog. Abstr.; Res. Alert [Full Cov.]; Rev. Agric. Entomol.; Rev. Med. Vet. Mycology; Rev. Plant Pathol.; Sci. Cit. Index; SCISEARCH; Seed Abstr.; Soils Fert.; Weed Abstr.

II/0254-6426
EVERGREEN (PEECHI, INDIA). (EVERGREEN / KERALA FOREST RESEARCH INSTITUTE.). **Added/Corp** Kerala Forest Research Institute. No. 5 (Mar. 1979)-. Periodical. English. Twice a year. Free. Kerala Forest Research Institute, Peechi 680653 Trichur District, Kerala India. **Tel** 22375. ***Continues*** *Kerala Forest Research Institute. Newsletter.*

US
EXPERIENCE THE WILLAMETTE NATIONAL FOREST. Added/Corp Willamette National Forest (Or.). **VFOAT** Experience the Willamette. Vol. 1, Issue 1 (Winter 1991)-. Periodical. English. qt. Willamette National Forest, PO Box 10607, 211 East 7th Avenue, Eugene OR 97440-2607. **LC** SD428.W55; E97.

HU/0014-6897
FAIPAR. [Faipar]. **Added/Corp** Faipari Tudomanyos Egyesaulet (Hungary). (1951)-. Academic Scholarly Publication. English (Hungarian; table of contents in German and Russian). Twelve times a year. $15.00. Akademiai Kiado, Publishing House of the Hungarian Academy of Sciences, Prielle Kornelia u. 19-35, H-1117 Budapest Hungary. **Tel** 011 36 1 1811991, FAX 011 36 1 1811991, telex 22-6228 AKNYO H. **(Subscription address:** Kultura, PO Box 149, H 1389 Budapest 62 Hungary.**)**
Ind/Abst AGRICOLA; Biodeter. Abstr.; For. Prod. Abstr.; World Agric. Econ.

IT/0071-7029
FAO FORESTRY DEVELOPMENT PAPER. No. 1 (1956)-. Monographic series. English. Price varies per volume. UNIPUB, 4611-F Assembly Drive, Lanham MD 20706-4391. **Tel** (800)274-4888, FAX (301)459-0056, telex 28787 GATT CH. **LC** SD121; .F6.

IT/0258-6150
FAO FORESTRY PAPER. [FAO for. pap.]. **Added/Corp** Food and Agriculture Organization of the United Nations. **VFOAT** Etude FAO, Forets; Etudio FAO, Montes. **VAT** Food and Agriculture Organization Forestry Paper. (1977)-. Monographic series. English (French and Spanish). ir. Price varies per volume. Food and Agriculture Organization (FAO) / Italy, GIPC166 via Terme di Caracalla, 00100 Rome Italy. **Tel** 011 39 6 522 52925, FAX 011 39 6 522 55784. **(Subscription address:** UNIPUB, 4611 F Assembly Drive, Lanham MD 20706.**)**
Ind/Abst Agrofor. Abstr.; For. Prod. Abstr. (1991-).

IT
FAO FORESTRY SERIES. Monographic series. English (French and Spanish). Price varies per volume. UNIPUB, 4611-F Assembly Drive, Lanham MD 20706-4391. **Tel** (800)274-4888, FAX (301)459-0056, telex 28787 GATT CH. ***Formed by the union of*** *FAO Forestry and Forest Products Studies, 0532-0283* ***and*** *FAO Forestry Development Paper, 0071-7029.*

US/1061-5539
FARM FORESTRY NEWS. (FARM FORESTRY NEWS / FORESTRY/FUELWOOD RESEARCH AND DEVELOPMENT PROJECT.). [Farm for. news]. **Added/Corp** Forestry/Fuelwood Research and Development Project. United States. Agency for International Development. Bureau for Science and Technology. Winrock International Institute for Agricultural Development. No. 1 (Summer 1986)-. Periodical. English. qt. **DD** 338.
Ind/Abst Agrofor. Abstr.; For. Abstr.

PO
FICHA DE CARACTERISTICAS. VFOAT Information on Characteristics. No. 1- Dec. 1963-. Monographic series. Portuguese (English). Price varies per volume.
Ind/Abst Int. Civil Eng. Abstr.; Soft. Abstr. Eng.

US/0272-9407
FINANCIAL REPORT AND PROGRESS REPORT ON SPRUCE BUDWORM PROGRAMS. Main/Corp Maine. Bureau of Forestry. **VFOAT** Spruce Budworm Programs. (1978)-. English. an. Maine Department of Conservation, State House, Station 22, Augusta ME 04333. **Tel** (207)289-3821. **LC** SB945.S7; M32a. **DD** 634.9/7526781/09741.

US/0470-0384
FINGERTIP FACTS & FIGURES. [Fingertip facts fig.]. **Added/Corp** National Forest Products Association. National Lumber Manufacturers Association. **VFOAT** Fingertip Facts and Figures. (June 1958)-. English. mo. National Forest Products Association, 1250 Connecticut Avenue NW, Washington DC 20036. **Tel** (202)463-2721, FAX (202)463-2785, telex 140950 NFPA DC.

GW
FINNLAND, LAND-, FORST- UND HOLZWIRTSCHAFT / BUNDESSTELLE FUER AUSSENHANDELSINFORMATION. **See** Agriculture.

US/0194-214X
FIRE MANAGEMENT NOTES. ***Ceased.*** **See** Fire Prevention.

CN/0229-1886
FIVE YEAR FOREST AND RANGE RESOURCE PROGRAM. (FIVE YEAR FOREST AND RANGE RESOURCE PROGRAM / MINISTRY OF FORESTS.). [Five year for. range resour. program]. **Main/Corp** British Columbia. Ministry of Forests. **VFOAT** Five-Year Forest and Range Resource Program. March 1980-. English. an. Ministry of Forests and Lands, Government of British Columbia, Parliament Buildings, Victoria British Columbia V8V 1X4 Canada. **Tel** (604)387-3484. **LC** SD568.B7; B74A. **DD** 333.75/09711.

BL/0015-3826
FLORESTA. [Floresta]. **VFOAT** Revista Floresta. Vol. 1 (1969)-. Periodical. English. Universidade Federal Parana, Biblitoeca Central Caixa Pst 441, 80001 Curitiba Parana Brazil. **Tel** 011 55 41 2527022, 2527244.
Ind/Abst AGRICOLA; Biodeter. Abstr.

FI/0015-5543
FOLIA FORESTALIA. [Folia for.]. Vol. 1 (1963)-. English (Finnish). ir. Free on request. Finnish Forest Research Institute Library, PL 18, 01301 Vantaa Finland. **Tel** 358/0/831941. **ED** Seppo Oja and Tommi Salomen.
Desc: Concerns all aspects of forestry and forestry science.
Ind/Abst Abstr. Bull. Inst. Pap. Sci. Tech.; AGRICOLA; Agric. Eng. Abstr. (1991-); Ecology Abstr.; Energy Res. Abstr. (March 1972-); Fish Rev.; For. Prod. Abstr. (1991-); For. Abstr.; Life Sci. Collect.; Rev. Agric. Entomol.; Seed Abstr.; Soils Fert.; Wildl. Rev.

PL/0071-6677
FOLIA FORESTALIA POLONICA. SERIA A. LESNICTWO. [Fol. for. Pol. Ser. A.]. (1958)-. Polish (Russian, German and English). Panstwowe Wydawn Naukowe, Miodowa 10, PO Box 391, 00251 Warsaw Poland. **LC** SD217.P7; F6.
Ind/Abst AGRICOLA; Fish Rev. (Jan. 1989-July 1992); For. Abstr.; Life Sci. Collect.; Wildl. Rev. (Jan. 1989-July 1992).

US
FOR. Main/Corp Kentucky. University. Dept. of Forestry. **Added/Corp** Kentucky. University. Cooperative Extension Service. (Feb. 1974)-. Periodical. English.
Ind/Abst AGRICOLA.

US/1046-7009
FOREST & CONSERVATION HISTORY. [For. conserv. hist.]. **Added/Corp** Forest History Society. **VFOAT** Forest and Conservation History. Vol. 34, No. 1 (Jan. 1990)-. Periodical. English. qt (Jan., Apr., July, Oct.). $45.00 (comes with membership to Forest History Society). Forest History Society, 701 Vickers Avenue, Durham NC 27701. **Tel** (919)682-9319. **ED** Kevin C. Foy. **LC** SD140; .F6. **DD** 333.75/0973. **Bk Rev**, (Qty: 60 /yr). **Ad Acc. Circ:** 1,800. available on microfilm and microfiche from University Microfilms International (UMI). ***Continues*** *Journal of Forest History, 0094-5080.*
Desc: Deals with the history of the forests and history of conservation.
Ind/Abst AGRICOLA [Select. Cov.]; Am. Hist. Life (1963-); Environ. Period. Bibliogr.; For. Prod. Abstr. (1991-); For. Abstr.; Soils Fert.

NE/0378-1127
FOREST ECOLOGY AND MANAGEMENT. [For. ecol. manage.]. Vol. 1 (Dec. 1976)-. Academic Scholarly Publication. English. Twenty-seven times a year (9 volumes). Fl2835.00. Elsevier Science Publishers BV, PO Box 211, 1000 AE Amsterdam Netherlands. **Tel** 011 31 20 5803642, FAX 011 31 20 5862696, telex 15682. **ED** L Roche. **LC** SD1; .F57. **DD** 634.9/05. **CODEN** FECMDW. **[CCC]. Pr Rev.** available on microfilm and microfiche from University Microfilms International (UMI). Documents available from The Genuine Article, BIOSIS Document Express, CASDDS, Documents on Demand.
Desc: Provides easy access to papers concerned with forest science and conservation, and in particular, the application of ecological knowledge to the management of man-made and natural forests. The scope of the journal includes all forest ecosystems of the world.
Ind/Abst Abstr. Bull. Inst. Pap. Sci. Tech.; AgBiotech News Inf.; AGRICOLA; Agrofor. Abstr. (19??-19??); Biocont. News Inf. (1991-); Biol. Agric. Index; Biol. Abstr.; Chem. Abstr.; Crop Physiol. Abstr.; Curr. Contents, Agric. Biol. Environ. Sci.; Ecol. Abstr.; Ecology Abstr.; EMBASE; Energy Inf. Abstr.; Entomol. Abstr.; Environ. Abstr.; Environ. Period. Bibliogr.; For. Prod. Abstr. (19??-19??); For. Abstr.; Geogr. Abstr. Phys. Geogr.; Geogr. Abstr. Human Geogr.; Geol. Abstr.; GeoRef; Grasslands For. Abstr.; Int. Dev. Abstr.; Irr. Drain. Abstr.; Key Word Index Wildl. Res.; Life Sci. Collect.; Plant Breed. Abstr.; Plant Genet. Resour. Abstr.; Plant Grow. Reg. Abstr.; Res. Alert [Full Cov.]; Rev. Agric. Entomol.; Rev. Med. Vet. Mycology; Rev. Plant Pathol.; Sci. Cit. Index; SCISEARCH; Seed Abstr.; Soc. Sci. Cit. Index [Select. Cov.]; Soils Fert.; Weed Abstr.; Wildl. Rev.

US/0015-7406
FOREST FARMER. [For. farmer]. Vol. 1, No. 8 (1942)-. Trade Publication. English. Six times a year. $40.00 US; $45.50 other (includes postage). Forest Farmer, PO Box 95385, Atlanta GA 30347-0385. **Tel** (404)325-2954, FAX (404)325-2955. **ED** Jack Warren. **Bk Rev. Ad Acc, Adv Mgr:** Janet Webb. **Circ:** 5,500 (ctrl).
Desc: Forestry trade magazine. Covers timber, wildlife watershed, aesthetics, and recreation management for private forest land.
Ind/Abst Abstr. Bull. Inst. Pap. Sci. Tech.; Fish Rev.; Leis. Recreat. Tour. Abstr.; Wildl. Rev.; World Agric. Econ.

US/0886-5841
FOREST FIRE NEWS. (FOREST FIRE NEWS / NORTH AMERICAN FORESTRY COMMISSION.). [For. fire news]. **Added/Corp** United States. Dept. of Agriculture. North American Forestry Commission. Fire Management Study Group. (1973)-. Periodical. English. sa. Free. Canadian Forestry Service / Hull, 351 St Joseph Boulevard, 19th Floor, Hull Quebec K1A 1G5 Canada. **Tel** (819)997-1107. **DD** 634; 634.
Ind/Abst AGRICOLA.

IT/0259-2894
FOREST GENETIC RESOURCES INFORMATION. [For. genet. resour. inf.]. Began in 1973. Periodical. English. Food and Agriculture Organization (FAO) / Italy, GIPC166 via Terme di Caracalla, 00100 Rome Italy. **Tel** 011 39 6 522 52925, FAX 011 39 6 522 55784.
Ind/Abst Abstr. Bull. Inst. Pap. Sci. Tech.; Agrofor. Abstr. (1991-); For. Prod. Abstr.; For. Abstr.; Hortic. Abstr.; Plant Breed. Abstr.; Seed Abstr.; Weed Abstr.

●XO/1335-048X
FOREST GENETICS. (Spring 1994)-. English. Four times a year. $115.00. Arbora Publishers SPOL SRO, PO Box 22, SK - 960 06, Zvolen 6 Slovakia. **ED** Ladislav Paule.
Desc: Information on recent advances in forest genetics and forest breeding.

US
FOREST-GRAM SOUTH. **Added/Corp** United States. Forest Service. Southern Region. United States. Forest Service. Southeastern Area. Division of State and Private Forestry. No. 1 (Sept. 1971)-. English. ir. Free. US Department of Agriculture / Georgia, Southern Region, Forest Service, 1720 Peachtree St NW, Atlanta GA 30367. **Tel** (404)347-4177, FAX (404)347-3608. **ED** David M. Webb. **Circ:** 6,000.
Desc: Newsletter on research and technology having a practical application of forestry in the South.
Ind/Abst AGRICOLA.

AT
FOREST INDUSTRIES DIRECTORY, BUYERS' AND SELLERS' GUIDE. ***Ceased.*** (19??)-(19??). Consumer Publication. English. be. Australian Forest Industries Journal, 203 Castlereagh Street, Sydney New South Wales 2000 Australia. **Tel** (02)264-6273, FAX (02)261-1473, telex AA72621. **Ad Acc. Circ:** 1,500.
Desc: Directory devoted to forest industries in Australia; 7,600 companies listed in more than 61 categories. Includes a buyers and sellers section devoted to 908 equipment manufacturers and suppliers and their agents.

CN
FOREST INDUSTRY LECTURE SERIES. **Added/Corp** University of Alberta. Dept. of Forest Science. No. 1 (1977)-. Monographic series. English. sa. Free on request. University of Alberta / Forest Science, Department of Forest Science, Edmonton Alberta T6G 2P5 Canada. **Tel** (403)432-4413, telex 037-2979. **ED** Peter J. Murphy. cum. index. **Circ:** 500.
Desc: Covers topics on forest resource management. Text of lectures by visiting speakers.

CN/0226-3793
FOREST INSECT AND DISEASE CONDITIONS : CARIBOO FOREST REGION. [For. insect dis. cond., Cariboo for. reg.]. 1973-. English. an. Pacific Forest Research Centre, 506 West Burnside Road, Victoria British Columbia V8Z 1M5 Canada. **DD** 634.9/6/097112. ***Continues in part*** *Canada. Forest Insect and Disease Survey. Annual District Report.*

CN/0226-9759
FOREST INSECT AND DISEASE CONDITIONS IN CANADA. [For. insect dis. cond. Can.]. **Added/Corp** Forest Insect and Disease Survey (Canada). (1980)-. English. an. Environment Canada / Emergencies Science Division, Ottawa Ontario K1A 0H3 Canada. **Tel** (819)998-9622. **LC** SB764.C36; F67. **DD** 634.9/6/0971. ***Continues*** *Forest Insect and Disease Survey (Canada). Annual Report of the Forest Insect and Disease Survey., 0068-7588.*
Ind/Abst Rev. Plant Pathol.

US/0195-8410
FOREST INSECT AND DISEASE CONDITIONS IN THE NORTHERN REGION. [For. insect dis. cond. north. reg.]. **Main/Corp** United States. Forest Service. Northern Region. English. an. Montana Department of Agriculture, PO Box 7669, Missoula MT 59807. **LC** SB763.N68; U54A. **DD** 634.9/6/09795. ***Continues*** *Forest Insect and Disease Conditions in the Northern Region, 0195-8410.*

US/0198-8018
FOREST INSECT AND DISEASE CONDITIONS IN THE PACIFIC NORTHWEST. [For. insect dis. cond. Pac. Northwest]. **Main/Corp** Oregon. Dept. of Forestry. 31st-1978-. English. an. US Department of Agriculture / Portland, Forest Service, Pacific Northwest Region, 319 SW Pine Street, Portland OR 97204. **Tel** (503)326-3625, FAX (503)326-2272. **LC** SB761; .U77. **DD** 634.9/6709795. ***Continues*** *Forest Pest Conditions in the Pacific Northwest, 0090-1784.*

US/0160-5143
FOREST INSECT AND DISEASE CONDITIONS IN THE UNITED STATES. [For. insect dis. cond. U. S.]. 1971-. Government Publication. English. an. US Department of Agriculture / Forest Service, 201 14th Street SW, Washington DC 20250. **Tel** (202)205-1661, FAX (202)205-1181. **LC** SB762; .U55A. **DD** 634.9/6. Each issue contains an index to its own contents (no volume index)--loose. ***Continues*** *Forest Insect Conditions in the United States, 0071-7487.*
Ind/Abst AGRICOLA; Rev. Med. Vet. Mycology; Rev. Plant Pathol.

US/0272-8737
FOREST INSECT AND DISEASE CONDITIONS. INTERMOUNTAIN REGION. [For. insect dis. cond., Intermt. reg.]. English. an. Free. Forest Pest Management, State and Private Forestry, 342 25th Street, Odgen UT 84401. **Tel** (801)625-5252. **LC** SB763.R62; U54A. **DD** 634.9/6/0978. **Circ:** 125. available on microfiche (Vols. for (1984-) distributed to depository libraries).
Desc: Important forest insect and disease problems occurring in the Intermountain Region. Information from aerial surveys, ground examinations and biological evaluations determine population status and trends.

CN/0226-3777
FOREST INSECT AND DISEASE CONDITIONS : KAMLOOPS FOREST REGION. [For. insect dis. cond., Kamloops for. reg.]. 1973-. English. an. Pacific Forest Research Centre, 506 West Burnside Road, Victoria British Columbia V8Z 1M5 Canada. **DD** 634.9/6/0971141. ***Continues in part*** *Canada. Forest Insect and Disease Survey. Annual District Report.*

CN/0226-3785
FOREST INSECT AND DISEASE CONDITIONS: NELSON FOREST REGION. [For. insect dis. cond., Nelson for. reg.]. (1973)-. English. an. Pacific Forest Research Centre, 506 West Burnside Road, Victoria British Columbia V8Z 1M5 Canada. **DD** 634.9/6/0971144. ***Continues in part*** *Canada. Forest Insect and Disease Survey. Annual District Report, 0226-417X.*

CN/0226-3769
FOREST INSECT AND DISEASE CONDITIONS : PRINCE GEORGE FOREST REGION. [For. insect dis. cond., Prince George for. reg.]. 1973-. English. an. Pacific Forest Research Centre, 506 West Burnside Road, Victoria British Columbia V8Z 1M5 Canada. **DD** 634.9/6/0971132. ***Continues in part*** *Canada. Forest Insect and Disease Survey. Annual District Report.*

CN/0226-3750
FOREST INSECT AND DISEASE CONDITIONS : PRINCE RUPERT FOREST REGION. [For. insect dis. cond., Prince Rupert for. reg.]. 1973-. English. an. Pacific Forest Research Centre, 506 West Burnside Road, Victoria British Columbia V8Z 1M5 Canada. **DD** 634.9/6/0971132. ***Continues in part*** *Canada. Forest Insect and Disease Survey. Annual District Report.*

CN/0226-3742
FOREST INSECT AND DISEASE CONDITIONS: VANCOUVER FOREST REGION. [For insect dis. cond., Vanc. for. reg.]. (1973)-. English. an. Pacific Forest Research Centre, 506 West Burnside Road, Victoria British Columbia V8Z 1M5 Canada. **DD** 634.9/6/0971133. ***Continues in part*** *Canada. Forest Insect and Disease Survey. Annual District Report, 0226-417X.*

CN/0226-4188
FOREST INSECT AND DISEASE CONDITIONS : YUKON TERRITORY. [For. insect dis. cond., Yukon Territ.]. 1974-. English. an. Pacific Forest Research Centre, 506 West Burnside Road, Victoria British Columbia V8Z 1M5 Canada. **DD** 634.9/6/097191.

US/0015-7449
FOREST LOG (SALEM). (FOREST LOG.). **Added/Corp** Oregon. Dept. of Forestry. Oregon. State Board of Forestry. Vol. 1 (May 1930)-. Periodical. English. Six times a year. Free on request. Oregon State Department of Forestry, 2600 State Street, Salem OR 97310. **Tel** (503)945-7422, FAX (503)945-7212. **ED** Brian Ballou. **Circ:** 5,000 (ctrl).
Desc: Forestry information of interest to Oregon forest landowners and other Oregon residents.

US
FOREST MANAGEMENT UPDATE. English. Twice a year. Free. Forest Resources Management, 180 Canfield Street, Morgantown WV 26505. **Tel** (304)285-1525, FAX (304)285-1505. **ED** Brenda Wilkins, (phone: (304)285-1533). **Circ:** 3,000 (ctrl).

US/0015-7457
FOREST NOTES. [For. notes]. **Added/Corp** Society for the Protection of New Hampshire Forests. (1937)-. Periodical. English. Five times a year. Free to members of the Society for the Protection of New Hampshire Forests. Society for the Protection of New Hampshire Forests, 54 Portsmouth Street, Concord NH 03301. **Tel** (603)224-9945. **ED** Richard Ober. **DD** 634. Index available. **Bk Rev. Ad Acc. Circ:** 10,000 (ctrl). ***Absorbed*** *Society for the Protection of New Hampshire Forests. Action* ***and*** *Action (Concord, N.H.).*
Desc: News and special features on forestry and conservation in New Hampshire with a concentration on land protection.
Ind/Abst AGRICOLA.

●CN/1195-0560
FOREST PEOPLE (WILLOWDALE). (FOREST PEOPLE / ONTARIO FORESTRY ASSOCIATION.). [For. people]. **Added/Corp** Ontario Forestry Association. **VFOAT** News from the OFA, Forest People. No. 1 (1993)-. Periodical. English. bm. Free to members (membership $25.00 per year). Ontario Forestry Association, 150 Consumers Road, Suite 209, Willowdale ONT M2J 1P9 Canada. **Tel** (416)493-4565, FAX (416)493-4608. **DD** 634.9. ***Continues*** *Newsletter (Ontario Forestry Association)., 0834-2008.*

US/0160-6492
FOREST PEST CONDITIONS IN THE NORTHEAST. **Main/Corp** United States. Forest Service. Northeastern Area. State and Private Forestry. Government Publication. English. an. US Department of Agriculture / Forest Service, 201 14th Street SW, Washington DC 20250. **Tel** (202)205-1661, FAX (202)205-1181.

AT
FOREST PESTS AND DISEASES / FORESTRY COMMISSION, TASMANIA. **Added/Corp** Tasmania. Forestry Commission. No. 1 (1976)-. Periodical. English.
Ind/Abst Rev. Plant Pathol.

CN/0832-1655
FOREST PLANNING-CANADA. ***Title Change.*** [For. plan. Can.]. **Added/Corp** Forest Planning-Canada (Organization). Vol. 1, No. 1 (Feb./March (1985)-(19??). Periodical. English. bm. Forest Planning Canada, PO Box 5885 Station B, Victoria BC V8R 6S8 Canada. **Tel** (604)598-2363. **ED** Bob Nixon. **DD** 333.75/0971. **[CCC]. Bk Rev. Ad Acc. Circ:** 1,100 (ctrl). ***Continued by*** *International Journal of Eco-Forestry.*

UK/0951-581X
FOREST PRODUCTS. (1989)-. English. Drewry Shipping Consultants Ltd, 11 Heron Quay, London E14 4JF England. **Tel** 011 44 71 5380191, FAX 01-987-9396, telex 21167 HPDLDG.

IT
FOREST PRODUCTS. **Added/Corp** Food and Agriculture Organization of the United Nations. **VFOAT** Produits Forestiers; Productos Forestales; FAO Yearbook Forest Products. (1987)-. Monographic series. English (French and Spanish). ir (Every 3 years). Price varies per volume. Food and Agriculture Organization (FAO) / Italy, GIPC166 via Terme di Caracalla, 00100 Rome Italy. **Tel** 011 39 6 522 52925, FAX 011 39 6 522 55784. **LC** HD9750.4; .Y4. **DD** 338.1/7498/021. ***Continues*** *Yearbook of Forest Products, 0084-3768.*

UK/0140-4784
FOREST PRODUCTS ABSTRACTS. **See** Forestry-Abstracting, Bibliographies and Statistics.

US
FOREST PRODUCTS DIRECTORY FOR THE STATE OF WASHINGTON. Directory. English. Evergreen Partnership, World Trade Center, 3600 Pt of Tacoma Road East, Tacoma WA 98424. **LC** TS803; .F63. **DD** 333.75/09797 S; 338. 4/7674/009797.

US/0015-7473
FOREST PRODUCTS JOURNAL. [For. prod. j.]. **Added/Corp** Forest Products Research Society. Forest Products Society. Vol. 5 (Feb. 1955)-. Academic Scholarly Publication. English. mo (except Jul./Aug. and Nov./Dec.). $135.00 US; $145.00 Canada and Mexico; $175.00 other. Forest Products Society, 2801 Marshall Court, Madison WI 53705-2295. **Tel** (608)231-1361, FAX (608)231-2152. **DD** 338. **CODEN** FPJOAB. **[CCC].** Index available. **Circ:** 4,500. available on microfilm and microfiche; available in reprints. Documents available from Article Express International, The Genuine Article, BIOSIS Document Express, CASDDS, Documents on Demand. ***Continues*** *Forest Products Research Society. Journal of the Forest Products Research Society, 0096-5693.*
Desc: A vital reference work for anyone interested in the wood products industry. Contains special feature articles of interest to the industry and a section for practical abstracts of new patents of interest to the forest products industry.

Ind/Abst Abstr. Bull. Inst. Pap. Sci. Tech.; AGRICOLA [Full Cov.]; Art Archaeol. Tech. Abstr.; Biodeter. Abstr. (19??-19??); Biol. Abstr.; Chem. Abstr.; Curr. Aware. Biol. Sci., CABS; Curr. Contents, Agric. Biol. Environ. Sci.; Ei Page One; Energy Inf. Abstr.; Eng. Index Annu.; Environ. Abstr.; For. Prod. Abstr. (1991-); For. Abstr.; INIS Atomindex [Micro.]; Res. Alert [Full Cov.]; Sci. Cit. Index; SCISEARCH; Soc. Sci. Cit. Index [Select. Cov.].

US
FOREST PRODUCTS NEWS. **Main/Corp** Louisiana State University and Agricultural and Mechanical College. Cooperative Extension Service. No. 1- Apr. 1974-. Periodical. English. sa. Louisiana State University / Extension Service, Louisiana Cooperative Extension Service, Baton Rouge LA 70803. **Tel** 01 592-899. ***Continues*** *Forest Products Newsletter.*

TH
FOREST RESEARCH BULLETIN. **Main/Corp** Kasetsart University. Faculty of Forestry. Bulletin. Thai (summaries and/or abstracts in English).
Ind/Abst For. Prod. Abstr.; For. Abstr.

US/0748-1586
FOREST RESEARCH IN THE SOUTHEAST. (FOREST RESEARCH IN THE SOUTHEAST : RECENT PUBLICATIONS OF THE SOUTHEASTERN FOREST EXPERIMENT STATION.). [For. res. Southeast]. **Main/Corp** Southeastern Forest Experiment Station (Asheville, N.C.). 1976-. Periodical. English. sa. Free. Southeastern Forest, PO Box 2680, Asheville NC 28802-2680. **Tel** (704)259-0327. **ED** R C Biesterfeldt. **DD** 634. **Circ:** 5,000 (ctrl). ***Continues*** *Research Information Digest, 0160-1717.*
Desc: New research findings are listed and includes journal articles, proceedings, resource statistics and specialized technical compendia.
Ind/Abst AGRICOLA; For. Prod. Abstr. (1991-).

CN/0319-9118
FOREST RESEARCH INFORMATION PAPER. [For. res. inf. pap.]. **Main/Corp** Ontario. Division of Forests. (19??)-. Periodical. English. Ministry of Natural Resources, Ontario Tree Improvement and Forest Biomass Institute, Maple Ontario L0J 1E0 Canada. **ED** D. Bates and G. Gillmeister. cum. index. **Circ:** 1,000 (ctrl).
Desc: Review of selected research activities for a calendar year period.
Ind/Abst AGRICOLA.

US
FOREST RESEARCH NOTE. **Main/Corp** United States. Pacific Southwest Forest and Range Experiment Station, Berkeley, California. English. Department of Forest Service, Pacific Southwest Forest and Range Experiment Station, PO Box 245, Berkeley CA 94701. **LC** SD11; .A455. **DD** 634.9072.
Ind/Abst For. Abstr.

CN/0381-2650
FOREST RESEARCH NOTE. [For. res. note]. **Added/Corp** Ontario. Forest Research Branch. Ontario Forest Research Centre. Ontario Tree Improvement and Forest Biomass Institute. No. 1 (1975)-. English. Ministry of Natural Resources, Ontario Tree Improvement and Forest Biomass Institute, Maple Ontario L0J 1E0 Canada.
Ind/Abst Crop Physiol. Abstr.

BP
FOREST RESEARCH NOTE / SOLOMON ISLANDS, FORESTRY DIVISION. **Added/Corp** Solomon Islands. Forestry Division. (1979)-. Monographic series. English. ***Continues in part*** *Technical Note (British Solomon Islands. Forestry Dept.).*
Ind/Abst Agrofor. Abstr.; For. Abstr.; Plant Breed. Abstr.; Seed Abstr.

CN
FOREST RESEARCH REPORT. **Main/Corp** Ontario. Ministry of Natural Resources. No. 91 (Dec. 1972)-. Monographic series. English. ir. Price varies per volume. Ministry of Natural Resources, Ontario Tree Improvement and Forest Biomass Institute, Maple Ontario L0J 1E0 Canada. ***Continues*** *Ontario. Dept. of Lands and Forests. Research Report.*
Ind/Abst For. Abstr.; Soils Fert.

MY
FOREST RESEARCH REPORT. Periodical. English.
Ind/Abst Biocont. News Inf.; Nematol. Abstr.

US
FOREST RESEARCH SERIES / DEPARTMENT OF FORESTRY. **Added/Corp** Clemson University. Dept. of Forestry. No. 20 (Dec. 1970)-. Monographic series. English. Clemson University / Forestry, College of Forest and Recreation Resources, Department of Forestry, Clemson SC 29631. ***Continues*** *South Carolina Agricultural Experiment Station. Dept. of Forestry. Forest Research Series.*
Ind/Abst AGRICOLA; For. Abstr.

CN/0704-2809
FOREST RESEARCH (TORONTO). (FOREST RESEARCH / ONTARIO TREE IMPROVEMENT AND FOREST BIOMASS INSTITUTE.). [For. res.]. **Main/Corp** Ontario Tree Improvement and Forest Biomass Institute. **Added/Corp** Ontario. Ministry of Natural Resources. (1982)-. English. an. Ministry of Natural Resources, Ontario Tree Improvement and Forest Biomass Institute, Maple Ontario L0J 1E0 Canada. **ED** G. Gillmeister. **LC** SD356.54.C22; O576a. **DD** 634.9/0720713. **Pr Rev. Circ:** 1,000. ***Continues*** *Ontario Forest Research Centre. Forest Research, 0704-2809.*
Desc: Review of selected research activities for a calendar year period.
Ind/Abst Int. Dev. Abstr.

US/0071-755X
FOREST RESOURCE REPORT - UNITED STATES. FOREST SERVICE. **Main/Corp** United States. Forest Service. No. 1 (1950)-. Monographic series. English. Price varies per volume. US Department of Agriculture / Forest Service, 201 14th Street SW, Washington DC 20250. **Tel** (202)205-1661, FAX (202)205-1181. **LC** SD11; .A4546. **CODEN** XAFSAS. Documents available from CASDDS.
Ind/Abst Chem. Abstr.; For. Prod. Abstr.; For. Abstr.

CN/0046-4589
FOREST SCENE, THE. [For. scene]. V. 1- Apr. 1970-. Periodical. English. Ontario Forest Information, 15 Toronto Street/Suite 200, Toronto Ontario M5C 2E3 Canada. ***Supersedes*** *Logger, 0047-4975.*

US/0015-749X
FOREST SCIENCE. [For. sci.]. **Added/Corp** Society of American Foresters. Vol. 1 (March 1955)-. Periodical. English. qt (Feb., May, Aug., Nov.). $100.00 (institutions), $50.00 (non-member individuals) US and Canada; $130.00 (institution), $75.00 (non-member individuals) other. Society of American Foresters, 5400 Grosvenor Lane, Bethesda MD 20814-2198. **Tel** (301)897-8720, FAX (301)897-3690, telex 9102501089 SAFFOREST UQ. **ED** Gregory Buhyoff. **LC** SD1; .F655. **DD** 634.905. **CODEN** FOSCAD. Index available (bound in issue). **Bk Rev. Ad Acc. Pr Rev. Circ:** 1,800. available on microfilm and microfiche from University Microfilms International (UMI). Documents available from The Genuine Article, BIOSIS Document Express, CASDDS, Documents on Demand.
Desc: Previously unpublished basic research on subjects fundamental to forestry: soils, physiology, genetics, biometrics, economics, wood, anatomy and chemistry, insects, diseases, land management, wildlife, recreation and ecology.
Ind/Abst Abstr. Bull. Inst. Paper Chem.; Abstr. Bull. Inst. Pap. Sci. Tech.; AgBiotech News Inf.; AGRICOLA [Full Cov.]; Biol. Agric. Index; Biol. Abstr.; Chem. Abstr.; Coal Abstr.; Crop Physiol. Abstr.; Curr. Aware. Biol. Sci., CABS; Curr. Contents, Agric. Biol. Environ. Sci.; Ecol. Abstr.; Ecology Abstr.; EMBASE; Energy Inf. Abstr.; Energy Res. Abstr.; Environ. Abstr.; Environ. Period. Bibliogr. (?-?); For. Prod. Abstr. (19??-19??); For. Abstr.; Geogr. Abstr. Phys. Geogr.; Geogr. Abstr. Human Geogr.; Geol. Abstr.; Grasslands For. Abstr.; Hortic. Abstr.; INIS Atomindex [Micro.]; Int. Dev. Abstr. (?-?); Irr. Drain. Abstr.; Nucl. Sci. Abstr.; Life Sci. Collect.; Plant Breed. Abstr.; Plant Genet. Resour. Abstr.; Plant Grow. Reg. Abstr.; Res. Alert [Full Cov.]; Rev. Agric. Entomol.; Rev. Med. Vet. Mycology; Rev. Plant Pathol.; Sci. Cit. Index; SCISEARCH; Sel. Water Resour. Abstr.; Soc. Sci. Cit. Index [Select. Cov.]; Soils Fert.; Stat. Theory Method Abstr. (1963); Weed Abstr.; Wildl. Rev.

US/0071-7568
FOREST SCIENCE. MONOGRAPH. ***Ceased.*** **VFOAT** Monograph. Vol. 1 (1959)-Ceased Vol. 28. Monographic series. English. qt (March, June, Sept. and Dec.). Society of American Foresters, 5400 Grosvenor Lane, Bethesda MD 20814-2198. **Tel** (301)897-8720, FAX (301)897-3690, telex 9102501089 SAFFOREST UQ. **ED** Harold E. Burkhart. **DD** 634.9. Index available. **Bk Rev. Ad Acc. Circ:** 1,700.
Desc: Basic research subjects fundamental to forestry: soils, physiology, genetics, biometrics, economics, wood anatomy and chemistry, insects, diseases, land management, wildlife, recreation and ecology.
Ind/Abst Abstr. Bull. Inst. Pap. Sci. Tech.; For. Prod. Abstr. (1991-); For. Abstr.; Soils Fert.

US/0160-9904
FOREST SERVICE ORGANIZATIONAL DIRECTORY. (FOREST SERVICE ORGANIZATIONAL DIRECTORY / UNITED STATES DEPARTMENT OF AGRICULTURE, FOREST SERVICE.). **Main/Corp** United States. Forest Service. **VFOAT** Organizational Directory. Directory. English. an. US Department of Agriculture / Forest Service, 201 14th Street SW, Washington DC 20250. **Tel** (202)205-1661, FAX (202)205-1181. **LC** SD11; .F67D. **DD** 353.0082/338/025. ***Continues*** *Directory, Forest Service.*

US/0090-239X
FOREST SERVICE RESEARCH ACCOMPLISHMENTS. (RESEARCH ACCOMPLISHMENTS.). **VFOAT** Forest for our Needs; Improving Productivity on Forests and Rangelands; Research for Tomorrow's Forests; Research Accomplishments Report. Government Publication. English. an. US Department of Agriculture / Forest Service, 201 14th Street SW, Washington DC 20250. **Tel** (202)205-1661, FAX (202)205-1181. **LC** SD252; .A17. **DD** 634.9/05. available on microfiche (Vols. for (1983-) distributed to depository libraries). ***Continues*** *Forest Service Research Accomplishments.*

PR/0565-6338
FOREST SERVICE RESEARCH PAPER ITF. **Main/Corp** Institute of Tropical Forestry (Rio Piedras, P.R.). No. 1- 1964-. Monographic series. English. ir. Price varies per volume. Institute of Tropical Forestry, Call Box 25000, Rio Piedras Puerto Rico 00928-2500. **Tel** (809)753-4335.

US
FOREST SERVICE RESOURCE BULLETIN SE. ***Title Change.*** Bulletin. English. **LC** SD11; .A45756. **DD** 333.7/5/0975. ***Continues*** *USDA Forest Service Resource Bulletin SE, 0363-6208.* ***Continued by*** *Resource Bulletin SE, 0885-8381.*

US/0146-4159
FOREST STATISTICS FOR IOWA. **See** Forestry-Abstracting, Bibliographies and Statistics.

CN/0706-7747
FOREST TIMES. **Added/Corp** Nova Scotia. Dept. of Lands and Forests. Vol. 1 (Jan. 1979)-. Periodical. English. Six times a year. Free. Department of Land & Forest, Box 68, Truro Nova Scotia B2N 5B8 Canada. **Tel** (902)424-5444. **ED** Jim Guild. **Bk Rev.**
Desc: Provides information, features on forest improvement practices, innovations and programs to private landowners and others interested in the forests of Nova Scotia, Canada.

US/1057-2724
FOREST WATCH. ***Title Change.*** [For. watch]. **Added/Corp** Cascade Holistic Economic Consultants. Vol. 6, No. 8 (March 1986)-(1993). Periodical. English. mo (11 issues). Cascade Holistic Economic Consultants / CHEC, 14417 Southeast Laurie, Oak Grove OR 97267. **Tel** (503)652-7049. **LC** SD143; .F63. **DD** 333.75/0973. **CODEN** FOWAEV. ***Continues*** *Forest Planning, 0738-0585.* ***Split into*** *Different Drummer Magazine, 1075-1653* ***and*** *Wild Forest Review.*
Ind/Abst BioBusiness.

CN/0711-5660
FORESTERIE ATOUT. [For. atout]. French. an. Foresterie Atout, CP 1935, Quebec 2 Quebec C1K 7M1 Canada. **DD** 634.9/06/0714.

CN/0844-6334
FORESTERIE SANS DETOUR, LA. [For. detour]. No. 1 (Dec. 1986)-. Periodical. French. Ministere des Forets, Service du transfert de technologie, 2700 rue Einstein, Sainte-Foy Quebec, Canada G1P 3WP. **DD** 634.9/09714.

IT
FORESTRY. **Main/Corp** Food and Agriculture Organization of the United Nations. Documentation Center. **VFOAT** Forets; Montes. (1966)-. English (French and Spanish). ir. $338.00. Food and Agriculture Organization (FAO) / Italy, GIPC166 via Terme di Caracalla, 00100 Rome Italy. **Tel** 011 39 6 522 52925, FAX 011 39 6 522 55784.
Ind/Abst Ecol. Abstr.; Ecology Abstr.; Environ. Period. Bibliogr.; Fish Rev.; Geogr. Abstr. Phys. Geogr.; Geogr. Abstr. Human Geogr.; Wildl. Rev.

UK/0015-7538
FORESTRY ABSTRACTS. **See** Forestry-Abstracting, Bibliographies and Statistics.

AT
FORESTRY, ANNUAL REPORT. **Main/Corp** Queensland Department of Forestry. **VFOAT** Forestry. Began with v. for 1978-79. English. an. Queensland Department of Forestry, Box 944, Government Printing Office, Brisbane 4001 Queensland Australia. **LC** SD111.Q8; A25. **DD** 353.9430082/338/06. ***Continues*** *Annual Report of the Department of Forestry.*

US/0093-0083
FORESTRY BULLETIN (CLEMSON, S.C.). (FORESTRY BULLETIN / DEPARTMENT OF FORESTRY, CLEMSON UNIVERSITY.). [For. bull,]. **Added/Corp** Clemson University. Dept. of Forestry. No. 1 (Nov. 1967)-. Bulletin. English. Clemson University / Forestry, College of Forest and Recreation Resources, Department of Forestry, Clemson SC 29631. **LC** UNC.
Ind/Abst AGRICOLA [Full Cov.]; For. Abstr.

CN/0015-7546
FORESTRY CHRONICLE, THE. [For. chron.]. **Added/Corp** Canadian Society of Forest Engineers. Canadian Institute of Forestry. Vol. 1 (July 1925)-. Multiple languages (English and French). bm. $87.00 (institutions), $79.00 (individuals) Canada; $105.00 (institutions), $92.00 (individuals) other. Canadian Institute of Forestry, 151 Slater Street, Suite 1005, Ottawa, Ontario Canada K1P 5H3. **Tel** (613)234-2242, FAX (613)234-6181, telex 053-3329. **LC** SD1; .F666. **CODEN** FRCRAX. **[CCC]. Bk Rev. Ad Acc. Pr Rev. Circ:** 2,700. Documents available from The Genuine Article, BIOSIS Document Express, CASDDS,

Documents on Demand. ***Absorbed*** *Annual Report of the Canadian Institute of Forestry, 0068-8991.*
Desc: Information on improving the management and use of the forest land resources and encourage a wider understanding of forestry within Canada and internationally.
Ind/Abst Abstr. Bull. Inst. Pap. Sci. Tech.; AGRICOLA [Full Cov.]; Agrofor. Abstr. (1991-); AQUAREF; Arts Humanit. Citation Index [Select. Cov.]; Biol. Abstr.; Chem. Abstr.; Coal Abstr.; Curr. Aware. Biol. Sci., CABS; Curr. Contents, Agric. Biol. Environ. Sci.; Ecol. Abstr.; Ecology Abstr.; Environ. Abstr.; Environ. Period. Bibliogr.; Fish Rev. (Jan. 1989-July 1992); For. Prod. Abstr. (19??-19??); For. Abstr.; Geogr. Abstr. Phys. Geogr.; Geogr. Abstr. Human Geogr.; Int. Dev. Abstr.; Key Word Index Wildl. Res.; Environ.; Leis. Recreat. Tour. Abstr.; Life Sci. Collect.; Plant Breed. Abstr.; Res. Alert [Select. Cov.]; Rev. Agric. Entomol.; Rev. Plant Pathol.; Rural Dev. Abstr.; SCISEARCH; Seed Abstr.; Soc. Sci. Cit. Index [Select. Cov.]; Soils Fert.; Weed Abstr.; Wildl. Rev. (Jan. 1989-July 1992); World Agric. Econ.

UK
FORESTRY COMMISSION BULLETIN. **Added/Corp** Great Britain. Forestry Commission. No. 39 (1969)-. Monographic series. English. ir. Price varies per volume. Her Majesty's Stationery Office, 51 Nine Elms Lane, London SW8 5DR England. **Tel** 011 44 71 873 8459, 011 44 71 873 8499, FAX 011 44 71 873 8499, 011 44 71 873 8456, telex 297138. **(Subscription address:** Her Majesty's Stationery Office, PO Box 276, Publications Centre, London SW8 5DT England.**)** **LC** SD45; .A4. ***Continues*** *Bulletin (Great Britain. Forestry Commission).*
Ind/Abst Agrofor. Abstr.; Ecol. Abstr.; For. Prod. Abstr. (19??-19??); For. Abstr.; Geogr. Abstr. Phys. Geogr.; Geogr. Abstr. Human Geogr.; Rev. Agric. Entomol.; Soils Fert.; Weed Abstr.

UK
FORESTRY COMMISSION FIELD BOOK. **Main/Corp** Great Britain. Forestry Commission. (1987)-. Monographic series. English. Her Majesty's Stationery Office, 51 Nine Elms Lane, London SW8 5DR England. **Tel** 011 44 71 873 8459, 011 44 71 873 8499, FAX 011 44 71 873 8499, 011 44 71 873 8456, telex 297138. **CODEN** FCFBEZ. Documents available from BIOSIS Document Express. ***Continues*** *Great Britain. Forestry Commission. Forestry Commission Leaflet.*
Ind/Abst Biol. Abstr. (1990-); For. Prod. Abstr. (1991-); For. Abstr.

US
FORESTRY-GEOLOGICAL REVIEW. **Added/Corp** Georgia. State Board of Forestry. Georgia. Dept. of Forestry and Geological Development. Vol. 1 (Jan. 1931)-. Periodical. English. mo. United States Department of Agriculture / Forest Service, Capital Square, Atlanta GA 30334. **LC** SD1; .F67. **DD** 634.909758.

BP
FORESTRY INFORMATION PAMPHLET / SOLOMON ISLANDS, FORESTRY DIVISION. (1979)-. Monographic series. English. Price varies per volume. Forestry Division, Munda Solomon Islands. ***Continues in part*** *Technical Note (British Solomon Islands. Forestry Dept.).*
Ind/Abst Agrofor. Abstr.

AT
FORESTRY LOG. **Main/Corp** Australian National University, Canberra. Forestry Students' Society. Periodical. English. an. Anutech Pty Limited, GPO Box 4, Canberra Act, 2601 Australia. **Tel** 011 61 6 2492479, FAX 011 61 6 2575088.

UK/0015-752X
FORESTRY (LONDON). (FORESTRY : THE JOURNAL OF THE SOCIETY OF FORESTERS OF GREAT BRITAIN.). [Forestry]. **Added/Corp** Society of Foresters of Great Britain. Institute of Foresters (Great Britain) Institute of Chartered Foresters (Great Britain). (1927)-. Periodical. English. qt (4 issues). £11500 UK and Europe; $185.00 other. Oxford University Press, Walton Street, Oxford OX2 6DP England. **Tel** 011 44 865 56767, FAX 011 44 865 267773, telex 837330 OXPRES G. **(Subscription address:** Oxford University Press / USA, Journals Marketing Department, Oxford University Press, 2001 Evans Road, Cary NC 27513.**)** **ED** J. Evans. **LC** SD1; .S67. **DD** 634.905. **CODEN** FRSTAH. **[CCC].** cum. index. **Bk Rev. Ad Acc. Pr Rev. Circ:** 1,600. available on microfilm and microfiche from University Microfilms International (UMI). Documents available from The Genuine Article, BIOSIS Document Express. ***Continues*** *Forestry (Society of Foresters of Great Britain).*
Desc: Covers the entire range of forest science, including physiology, maintenance, management, techniques, the ecology and productivity of growth, etc. Includes regional accounts and book reviews.
Ind/Abst AGRICOLA (19??-) [Full Cov.]; Agrofor. Abstr. (19??-); Biol. Abstr. (19??-); Curr. Aware. Biol. Sci., CABS (19??-); Curr. Contents, Agric. Biol. Environ. Sci. (19??-); Field Crop Abstr. (19??-); For. Prod. Abstr. (1991-); For. Abstr. (19??-); Hortic. Abstr. (19??-); Life Sci. Collect. (19??-); Plant Breed. Abstr. (19??-); Plant Grow. Reg. Abstr. (19??-); Res. Alert (19??-) [Full Cov.]; Rev. Med. Vet. Mycology (19??-); Rev. Plant Pathol. (19??-); Risk Abstr. (19??-); Sci. Cit. Index (19??-); SCISEARCH (19??-); Soils Fert. (19??-).

US/0164-4661
FORESTRY NEWSLETTER (AVONDALE ESTATES). (FORESTRY NEWSLETTER.). **Added/Corp** Society of American Foresters. Southeastern Section. (19??)-. Newsletter. English. qt.
Ind/Abst Soils Fert.

CN/0825-1770
FORESTRY NEWSLETTER (SAULT STE. MARIE). (FORESTRY NEWSLETTER / GREAT LAKES FOREST RESEARCH CENTRE.). [For. newsl.]. **Added/Corp** Great Lakes Forest Research Centre. Canadian Forestry Service. (Spring 1984)-. Periodical. English (French). Four times a year. Free. Forestry Canada Ontario Region, Box 490, Sltste Marie Ontario P6A 5M7 Canada. **Tel** (705)949-9461. **DD** 354.710082/338042/09713132. ***Continues*** *Forestry Research Newsletter, 0705-520X.*
Ind/Abst Abstr. Bull. Inst. Pap. Sci. Tech.; Agrofor. Abstr.; For. Abstr.

●CN/1196-278X
FORESTRY, OIL & GAS REVIEW. ***Title Change.*** [For. oil gas rev.]. **VFOAT** Forestry Oil and Gas Review. Vol. 5, No. 1 (Winter 1993)-(1993). Periodical. English. qt. Consolidated Communications, 807 Manning Road Northeast, Suite 200, Calgary Alberta T2E 7M8 Canada. **Tel** (403)569-9520, FAX (403)569-9590. **DD** 338.1/749. ***Continues*** *Alberta Oil & Forestry Review Quarterly., 0840-6146.* ***Continued by*** *Canadian Resources Review, 1196-1376.*

CN/1185-9598
FORESTRY ON THE HILL. ***Ceased.*** [For. Hill]. **Added/Corp** Canadian Forestry Association. (1991)-(1994). Periodical. English. bm. Canadian Forestry Association, 185 Somerset Street West, Suite 203, Ottawa Ontario K2P 0J2 Canada. **Tel** (613)232-1815, FAX (613)232-4210. **ED** Edwinna von Baeyer. **DD** 634.9/0971. **Bk Rev. Ad Acc. Circ:** 150 (ctrl). ***Continues*** *What They Say About Forestry on the Hill., 0828-6299.*

CN/0824-3824
FORESTRY REPORT (OTTAWA). (THE FORESTRY REPORT.). [For. rep.]. No. 1 (Spring 1982)-. Periodical. English. Free. Forestry Report, c/o New Democratic Party, House of Commons, Ottawa Ontario K1A 0A6 Canada. **DD** 333.75/0971.

US/1057-2139
FORESTRY REPORT R8-FR. [For. rep. R8-FR]. (1983)-. Monographic series. English. ir. Price varies per volume. Department of Agriculture / Foreign Agricultural Service, 14th Street and Independence Avenue SW, Washington DC 20250-1000. **Tel** (202)720-3935, FAX (202)720-7729. ***Continues*** *Forestry Report SA-FR, 0889-9843.*
Ind/Abst AGRICOLA [Full Cov.]; Rev. Plant Pathol.

US/0094-4181
FORESTRY RESEARCH NOTE (CAMAS). ***Ceased.*** (FORESTRY RESEARCH NOTE.). **Main/Corp** Crown Zellerbach Corporation. Central Research. No. 1 (1972)-(1992). Monographic series. English. an (Published in January). University of Wisconsin Forestry Department, 1630 Linden Drive, Madison WI 53706.

US/0091-1313
FORESTRY RESEARCH REPORT. [For. res. rep.]. **Main/Corp** University of Illinois at Urbana-Champaign. Agricultural Experiment Station. **Added/Corp** University of Illinois at Urbana-Champaign. Dept. of Forestry. (1970)-. Periodical. English. Illinois Agricultural Experiment Station, 211 Mumford Hall, 1301 West Gregory Drive, Urbana IL 61801. **Tel** (217)333-2548. **CODEN** IFRRAN. Documents available from BIOSIS Document Express, CASDDS.
Ind/Abst AGRICOLA [Full Cov.]; Biol. Abstr.; Chem. Abstr.; For. Prod. Abstr. (1991-); For. Abstr.; Soils Fert.

US/0195-5861
FORESTRY RESEARCH WEST. [For. res. west]. (Jan. 1979)-. Periodical. English. Four times a year. Rocky Mountain Station Publications, 3825 East Mulberry, Fort Collins CO 80524. **Tel** (303)498-1719. **LC** SD254.W4; F67. **DD** 634.9/0978. available on microfiche (Vols. for (1986-) distributed to depository libraries). Documents available from Documents on Demand. ***Continues*** *Forestry Research: What's New in the West, 0093-0148.*
Ind/Abst AGRICOLA [Full Cov.]; Coal Abstr.; Energy Res. Abstr. (Oct. 1982-); Environ. Abstr.

NE/0924-5480
FORESTRY SCIENCES. [For. sci.]. Monographic series. English. Price varies per volume. Martinus Nijhoff Publishers, Subsidiary of Kluwer Academic Publishers, Koraalrood 50, 2713 SC Zoetermeer Netherlands. **Tel** 011 31 79 684400.
Ind/Abst AGRICOLA [Full Cov.].

CN/0381-1786
FORESTRY TECHNICAL REPORT. [For. tech. rep.]. **Added/Corp** Canadian Forestry Service. **VFOAT** Forestry Technical Publication. (1974)-. Periodical. English. **CODEN** FTRSDQ. Documents available from CASDDS.
Ind/Abst Chem. Abstr. (1974-1981); For. Abstr.; Seed Abstr.

US/0015-7589
FORESTS AND PEOPLE. [For. people]. **Added/Corp** Louisiana Forestry Association. Vol. 1 (1951)-. Periodical. English. qt (March, June, Sept., Dec.). $11.00 US; $25.00 other. Louisiana Forestry Association, PO Drawer 5067, Alexandria LA 71302. **Tel** (318)443-2558. **ED** Janet Tompkins. **DD** 333. **CODEN** FOPEA4. Index available. **Ad Acc. Circ:** 7,000 (ctrl). Documents available from CASDDS.
Desc: Contains stories about forestry and people who work in Louisiana's forests in any and every capacity.
Ind/Abst Chem. Abstr.

SZ
FORET, LA. Periodical. English. mo. Societe Forestiere Suisse, I4 Rosenweg Fores Central Suis, 4500 Solothurn Switzerland.

CN/0380-321X
FORET CONSERVATION. [For. conserv.]. **Added/Corp** Association Forestiere Quebecoise. **VFOAT** Foret-Conservation. (1952)-. Periodical. French. Ten times a year. 24.00Can$ Canada; 29.08Can$ other. Foret-Conservation, 175 rue Saint Jean 4E Etage, Quebec G1R 1N4 Canada. **Tel** (418)529-2542. **ED** Marie Bissonnette. **CODEN** FRCVAB. **Bk Rev. Ad Acc. Circ:** 8,000 (ctrl). Documents available from BIOSIS Document Express. ***Continues*** *Foret et Conservation.*
Desc: Forest, environment, natural sciences, science and technology, private forests, sylviculture, pulp and paper, logging and sawmilling and urban forestry are covered.
Ind/Abst AQUAREF; Biol. Abstr.; Environ.; Life Sci. Collect.; Point Repere (1983-); Rev. Agric. Entomol.

CN/1180-4270
FORET DE CHEZ-NOUS (1990). (FORET DE CHEZ-NOUS.). [For. chez-nous]. **Added/Corp** Union des Producteurs Agricoles. Vol. 1, No 1 (1990)-. Periodical. French. qt. Free for members. Union des Producteurs Agricoles, 555 Boul Roland Therrien, Longueuil Quebec J4H 3Y9 Canada. **Tel** (514)679-0535. **DD** 634.9/09714/05.

FR/0245-484X
FORET MEDITERRANEENNE. [For. mediterr.]. **Added/Corp** Association Foret Mediterraneenne. Vol. 1 (Oct. 1979)-. Periodical. French. qt. 230.00F. Assn Foret Mediteraneenne, 14 Rue Louis Astouin, F 13002 Marseille France. **Tel** 33 91 560691.
Ind/Abst Agrofor. Abstr.; For. Abstr.; Geogr. Abstr. Human Geogr.; Life Sci. Collect.; Rev. Agric. Entomol.; Rev. Plant Pathol.; Wheat Barley Trit. Abstr.

FR/0153-0216
FORET PRIVEE (1977), LA. (LA FORET PRIVEE.). [For. priv. (1977)]. No. 114, (Mar./Apr. 1977)-. Periodical. French. Six times a year (Jan., Mar., May, July, Sept., Nov.). 285.00F France; 350.00F other. La Foret Privee, 61 Ave de la Grande Armee, 75782 Paris Cedex 16 France. **Tel** 011 33 1 45004661. **ED** Madame Lucile Decoufle. Index available (Mar. iss.). **Bk Rev.** (Qty: 5-6). **Ad Acc, Adv Mgr:** C. Chavet. **Pr Rev. Circ:** 4,000. ***Continues*** *Foret Privee Francaise et Revue Forestiere Europeenne.*
Desc: Covers all aspects of forestry, including production, the nursery and wood industries, commerce of wood, environment, biology and pathology of trees.
Ind/Abst AGRICOLA; For. Prod. Abstr.; For. Abstr.

BE
FORET WALLONE. (19??)-. Bulletin. French. Three times a year. 450F Belgium; 990.00F other. Asbl Foret Wallone, 33 rue de la Terre Franche, B-5310 Longchamps Belgium. **Tel** 32 81 51 20 93. **ED** Vincent Felten. Index available. **Bk Rev. Ad Acc. Pr Rev.**
Desc: Touches on all aspects of economics, society, ecology and forestry.

FR
FORETS DE FRANCE ET ACTION FORESTIERE. **Added/Corp** Federation Nationale des Syndicats de Proprietaires Forestiers Sylviculteurs. (19??)-. Periodical. French. Ten times a year. 259.55F France; 300.00F other. Federation Nationale Syndicates Proprietare Forestiers Sylviculteurs, 6 rue de la Tremoille, 75008 Paris France. **Tel** 011 33 1 47203632.

PH
FORPRIDECOM TECHNICAL NOTE. No. 103 (1971)-. Periodical. English. Forest Products Research Development Institute, College Laguna 3720 Philippines. ***Continues*** *Technical Note (Forest Products Research and Development Commission).*
Ind/Abst Abstr. Bull. Inst. Pap. Sci. Tech.; Philip. Sci. Technol. Abstr.

GW/0931-2277
FORSCHUNGSREPORT, ERNAHRUNG, LANDWIRTSCHAFT, FORSTEN. **See** Agriculture.

GW/0939-7701
FORSCHUNGSVORHABEN / ZENTRALSTELLE FUER AGRARDOKUMENTATION UND -INFORMATION. **See** Agriculture.

GW/0932-9315
FORST UND HOLZ (HANNOVER, GERMANY : 1988). (FORST UND HOLZ.). Vol. 43, No. 1 (Jan. 1988)-. Periodical. German. sm. DM158.60. Verlag M & H Schaper GmbH & Co, Postfach 16 42, D 31046 Alfeld Leine Germany. **Tel** 011 49 5181 80090. **LC** SD1; .F75. **DD** 634.9. **CODEN** FOHOEW. ***Continues*** *Forst und Holzwirt, 0015-7961.*
Ind/Abst Fish Rev. (Jan. 1989-July 1992); For. Prod. Abstr. (19??-19??); For. Abstr.; Rev. Agric. Entomol.; Rev. Plant Pathol.; Seed Abstr.; Soils Fert.; Weed Abstr.; Wildl. Rev. (Jan. 1989-July 1992).

GW/0300-4112
FORSTARCHIV. [Forstarchiv]. 1.- Yearly volume; July 1925-. Periodical. German. bm. DM189.40 Germany; DM192.10 other. Verlag M & H Schaper GmbH & Co, Postfach 16 42, D 31046 Alfeld Leine Germany. **Tel** 011 49 5181 80090. **LC** SD1; .F753. **[CCC].** ***Absorbed*** *Mitteilungen aus Forstwirtschaft und Forstwissenschaft.*
Ind/Abst AGRICOLA; Agric. Eng. Abstr. (1991-); Agrofor. Abstr.; EMBASE; For. Prod. Abstr. (19??-19??); For. Abstr.; Irr. Drain. Abstr.; Key Word Index Wildl. Res.; Leis. Recreat. Tour. Abstr.; Plant Breed. Abstr.; Rev. Plant Pathol.; Rural Dev. Abstr.; Soils Fert.; World Agric. Econ.

GW/0174-1810
FORSTLICHE FORSCHUNGSBERICHTE MUNCHEN. No.46 (1980)-. Monographic series. German. ***Continues*** *Forstliche Forschungsanstalt, Munchen. Forschungsberichte.*
Ind/Abst Agrofor. Abstr.; For. Abstr.; Irr. Drain. Abstr.; Plant Genet. Resour. Abstr.; Rev. Plant Pathol.; Soils Fert.

GW/0015-7988
FORSTLICHE UMSCHAU. ***Ceased.*** Vol. 1 (1958)-Ceased Dec. 1991. Periodical. German. qt. Blackwell Wissenschafts-Verlag, Kurfuerstendamm 57, D 10707 Berlin Germany. **Tel** 011 49 30 32790623, 011 49 30 32790624, FAX 011 49 30 327 90610. **ED** H Loeffler and E Niesslein. **[CCC].** Index available. cum. index. **Bk Rev. Ad Acc. Circ:** 2,500.
Desc: Abstracts major literature on forestry.

GW/0427-0029
FORSTTECHNISCHE INFORMATIONEN. [Forsttech. Inf.]. **Added/Corp** Kuratorium fuer Waldarbeit und Forsttechnik. (19??)-. Periodical. German. mo. DM70.00. Fritz and Philipp Nauth Erben, Bonifaziusplatz 3, D 55118 Mainz Germany. **Tel** 011 49 6131 674443.
Ind/Abst AGRICOLA; For. Prod. Abstr.; For. Abstr.

SZ
FORSTWISSENSCHAFTLICHE BEITRAEGE / ETH ZURICH, FACHBEREICH FORSTOKONOMIE UND FORSTPOLITIK. **Added/Corp** Eidgenossische Technische Hochschule Zurich. Fachbereich Forstokonomie und Forstpolitik. (1984)-. Monographic series. German.
Ind/Abst AGRICOLA; For. Prod. Abstr. (1991-); For. Abstr.

GW/0015-8003
FORSTWISSENSCHAFTLICHES CENTRALBLATT. [Forstwiss. Centralbl.]. Vol. 1 (1879)-. Academic Scholarly Publication. German. bm (6 issues). DM417.00 Europe; DM416.00 other. Blackwell Wissenschafts-Verlag, Kurfuerstendamm 57, D 10707 Berlin Germany. **Tel** 011 49 30 32790623, 011 49 30 32790624, FAX 011 49 30 327 90610. **ED** V. Ammer and W. Bosshard. **[CCC].** Index available. cum. index. **Bk Rev. Ad Acc. Pr Rev. Circ:** 2,500. Documents available from The Genuine Article, Documents on Demand. ***Supersedes*** *Monatschrift fuer das Forst-und Jadgwesen;* ***Absorbed*** *Forstliche Wochenschrift Silva.*
Desc: Scientific journal on forestry.
Ind/Abst Biocont. News Inf.; Crop Physiol. Abstr.; Curr. Contents, Agric. Biol. Environ. Sci.; EMBASE; Energy Inf. Abstr.; Environ. Abstr.; For. Prod. Abstr. (19??-19??); For. Abstr.; GeoRef; Key Word Index Wildl. Res.; Leis. Recreat. Tour. Abstr.; Life Sci. Collect.; Plant Breed. Abstr.; Protozoolog. Abstr.; Res. Alert [Select. Cov.]; Rev. Plant Pathol.; Rural Dev. Abstr.; SCISEARCH; Seed Abstr.; Soils Fert.; Wheat Barley Trit. Abstr.; World Agric. Econ.

NP
FRD OCCASIONAL PAPER. **Added/Corp** Nepal. Forestry Research Division. **VAT** Forestry Research Division Occasional Paper. (199?)-. Monographic series. English (Hindi). ir. Price varies per volume. ***Continues*** *FRIC Occasional Paper.*
Ind/Abst For. Abstr.; Rev. Plant Pathol.

CN/0835-0752
FRDA REPORT. [FRDA rep.]. **Added/Corp** British Columbia. Ministry of Forests and Lands. Forest Resource Development Agreement (Canada) Canadian Forestry Service. **VFOAT** Forest Resource Development Agreement Report; F.R.D.A. Report. Vol. 1 (1986)-. Monographic series. English. **LC** IN PROCESS. **CODEN** FREPE7.
Ind/Abst AGRICOLA [Full Cov.]; Nematol. Abstr.

NZ/0111-8129
FRI BULLETIN / FOREST RESEARCH INSTITUTE, NEW ZEALAND FOREST SERVICE. **Added/Corp** Forest Research Institute (N.Z.). **VFOAT** F.R.I. Bulletin. **VAT** Forest Research Institute Bulletin. No. 1 (1982)-. Bulletin. English. ir. Forest Research Institute, Private Bag 3020, Rotorua, New Zealand. **Tel** 011 64 73 475899, FAX 011 64 73 479380, telex 21080. **[CCC].**
Ind/Abst AGRICOLA [Full Cov.]; Biocont. News Inf. (1991-); Ecol. Abstr.; Field Crop Abstr.; For. Prod. Abstr. (1991-); For. Abstr.; Geogr. Abstr. Phys. Geogr.; Geogr. Abstr. Human Geogr.; Rev. Agric. Entomol.; Rev. Plant Pathol.; Seed Abstr.; Soils Fert.; Weed Abstr.; Wheat Barley Trit. Abstr.

NP
FRIC OCCASIONAL PAPER. ***Title Change.*** **Added/Corp** Forest Research and Information Centre (NepaL). **VFOAT** Occassional Paper. **VAT** Forest Research and Information Centre Occasional Paper. (198?)-(199?). Monographic series. English. ir. Price varies per volume. ***Continued by*** *FRD Occasional Paper.*
Ind/Abst For. Abstr. (19??-19??); Rev. Plant Pathol. (19??-19??).

MY/0127-9793
FRIM TECHNICAL INFORMATION. [FRIM tech. inf.]. **VFOAT** Forest Research Institute Malaysia Technical Information. (1988)-. Monographic series. Malay. ir. **DD** 634.909595.
Ind/Abst For. Abstr.

US
FWS. **Main/Corp** Virginia Polytechnic Institute and State University. School of Forestry and Wildlife Resources. (197?)-. Monographic series. English. Price varies per volume. Virginia Polytechnic Institute and State University / Forestry & Wildlife, School of Forestry and Wildlife Resources, Blacksburg VA 24061. Documents available from Documents on Demand. ***Continues*** *Virginia Polytechnic Institute and State University. Division of Forestry and Wildlife Resources. FWS.*
Ind/Abst AGRICOLA [Full Cov.]; Environ. Abstr.

US/0748-1209
GENERAL TECHNICAL REPORT INT. [Gen. tech. rep. INT]. **Added/Corp** Intermountain Forest and Range Experiment Station (Ogden, Utah). **VFOAT** General Technical Report I.N.T. **VAT** General Technical Report Intermountain. No. 111 (Apr. 1981)-. Monographic series. English. ir. Price varies per volume. Intermountain Research Station, 507 25th Street, Ogden UT 84401. ctrl circ. ***Continues*** *USDA Forest Service General Technical Report INT, 0363-6186.*
Ind/Abst AGRICOLA [Full Cov.]; Agric. Eng. Abstr.; For. Prod. Abstr. (1991-); Life Sci. Collect.; Rev. Plant Pathol.

US
GENERAL TECHNICAL REPORT NC. **Added/Corp** North Central Forest Experiment Station (Saint Paul, Minn.). **VAT** General Technical Report North Central. (1981)-. Monographic series. English. ir. Price varies per volume. North Central Forest Experiment Station, Forest Service, US Department of Agriculture, 1992 Folwell Avenue, St Paul MN 55108. **Tel** (612)642-5233. **ED** Robert D Wray. **LC** UNC. ctrl circ. available on microfiche. ***Continues*** *USDA Forest Service General Technical Report NC, 0363-616X.*
Desc: Series publication reporting technical information, proceedings, computer programs, bibliographies, etc.
Ind/Abst For. Prod. Abstr. (1991-); For. Abstr.; Life Sci. Collect.; Rev. Plant Pathol.

US/0748-1314
GENERAL TECHNICAL REPORT NE. (GENERAL TECHNICAL REPORT NE / NORTHEASTERN FOREST EXPERIMENT STATION.). [Gen. tech. rep. NE]. **Added/Corp** Northeastern Forest Experiment Station (Radnor, Pa.). **VAT** General Technical Report Northeastern. (1980)-. Monographic series. English. ir. Price varies per volume. Northeastern Forest Experiment Station / Broomall, PA, US Department of Agriculture / Forest Service, Broomall PA 19008. **LC** UNC. **DD** 333. ***Continues*** *Forest Service General Technical Report NE, 0886-7429.*
Ind/Abst AGRICOLA [Full Cov.]; Biocont. News Inf. (1991-); For. Prod. Abstr. (19??-19??); For. Abstr.; Rev. Agric. Entomol.; Rev. Plant Pathol.

US/0887-4840
GENERAL TECHNICAL REPORT PNW. [Gen. tech. rep. PNW]. **Added/Corp** Pacific Northwest Forest and Range Experiment Station (Portland, Or.). **VFOAT** USDA Forest Service General Technical Report. **VAT** General Technical Report Pacific Northwest. (1978)-. Monographic series. English. Price varies per volume. Pacific Northwest Forest and Range Experiment Station, 809 Northeast Sixth Avenue, Portland OR 97232. **Tel** (503)231-2081. **LC** UNC. **DD** 634. ***Continues*** *Pacific Northwest Forest and Range Experiment Station (Portland, Or.). USDA Forest Service General Technical Report PNW, 0363-6224.*
Ind/Abst ASTIS Curr. Aware. Bull. (1978-); AGRICOLA [Full Cov.]; Agrofor. Abstr.; ASTIS Bibliogr. (1978-); For. Prod. Abstr. (1991-); For. Abstr.; Life Sci. Collect.

US/0196-2094
GENERAL TECHNICAL REPORT PSW. [Gen. tech. rep. PSW]. **Added/Corp** Pacific Southwest Forest and Range Experiment Station (Berkeley, Calif.). **VAT** General Technical Report Pacific Southwest. (1978)-. Monographic series. English. Price varies per volume. Pacific Southwest Forest and Range Experiment Station, PO Box 245, Berkeley CA 94701. **LC** SD11; .P3a. **DD** 634.9/09794. Documents available from CASDDS. ***Continues*** *USDA Forest Service General Technical Report PSW, 0092-9662.*
Ind/Abst AGRICOLA; Chem. Abstr.; For. Abstr.; GeoRef; Life Sci. Collect.; Weed Abstr.

US/0277-5786
GENERAL TECHNICAL REPORT RM. [Gen. tech. rep. RM]. **Added/Corp** Rocky Mountain Forest and Range Experiment Station (Fort Collins, Colo.). **VAT** General Technical Report Rocky Mountain. (1972)-. Monographic series. English. ir. Price varies per volume. Rocky Mountain Forest and Range Experiment Station, 240 West Prospect Road, Fort Collins CO 80526. **LC** UNC. **DD** 634. ***Continues*** *USDA Forest Service General Technical Report RM, 0094-4823.*
Ind/Abst AGRICOLA [Full Cov.]; Biocont. News Inf.; For. Prod. Abstr. (1991-); For. Abstr.; GeoRef; Hortic. Abstr.; Leis. Recreat. Tour. Abstr.; Nematol. Abstr.; Ornamental Hort. (1991-); Life Sci. Collect.; Rev. Agric. Entomol.; Rev. Plant Pathol.; Rural Dev. Abstr.; Seed Abstr.; Soyabean Abstr.

US/0887-4859
GENERAL TECHNICAL REPORT SE (1981). (GENERAL TECHNICAL REPORT SE / UNITED STATES DEPARTMENT OF AGRICULTURE, SOUTHEASTERN FOREST EXPERIMENT STATION, FOREST SERVICE.). [Gen. tech. rep. SE]. **Added/Corp** Southeastern Forest Experiment Station (Asheville, N.C.). **VAT** General Technical Report Southeastern. (1981)-. Monographic series. English. **DD** 634. available on microfilm. ***Continues*** *Forest Service General Technical Report SE, 0748-1292.*
Ind/Abst For. Abstr.; Leis. Recreat. Tour. Abstr.; Life Sci. Collect.

US/0887-4875
GENERAL TECHNICAL REPORT SO. (GENERAL TECHNICAL REPORT SO / U.S. DEPARTMENT OF AGRICULTURE, FOREST SERVICE.). [Gen. tech. rep. SO]. **Added/Corp** Southern Forest Experiment Station (New Orleans, La.) United States. Forest Service. **VAT** General Technical Report Southern. (1977)-. Monographic series. English. Price varies per volume. Southern Forest Experiment Station, T-10210 US Postal Services Building, US Department of Agriculture, 701 Loyola Avenue, New Orleans LA 70113. **Tel** (504)589-6800, FAX (504)589-3961. **LC** UNC. **DD** 634. ***Continues*** *Forest Service General Technical Report SO, 0093-4887.*
Ind/Abst AGRICOLA [Full Cov.]; Ecol. Abstr.; For. Prod. Abstr. (1991-); For. Abstr.; Life Sci. Collect.; Seed Abstr.

US/0197-6109
GENERAL TECHNICAL REPORT WO. (GENERAL TECHNICAL REPORT WO - FOREST SERVICE.). [Gen. tech. rep. WO]. **Main/Corp** United States. Forest Service. **VFOAT** GTR-WO. **VAT** General Technical Report Washington Office. (197?)-. Academic Scholarly Publication. English. ir. Price varies per volume. Superintendent of Documents, US Government Printing Office, Washington DC 20402. **Tel** (202)275-3328, FAX (202)786-2377. **DD** 634. **CODEN** GTRWDF. Documents available from BIOSIS Document Express, CASDDS. ***Continues*** *USDA Forest Service General Technical Report WO.*
Ind/Abst Abstr. Bull. Inst. Pap. Sci. Tech.; AGRICOLA [Full Cov.]; Biol. Abstr. (-1982); Chem. Abstr. (1977-1983); Geogr. Abstr. Phys. Geogr.; Geogr. Abstr. Human Geogr.

US/0435-5377
GEORGIA FOREST RESEARCH PAPER. [Ga. for. res. pap.]. **Added/Corp** Georgia Forestry Commission. Research Division. **VFOAT** Georgia Forest Research Report. Vol. 1 (1979)-. Monographic series. English. **DD** 634. **CODEN** GFRPAT. Documents available from BIOSIS Document Express. ***Continues*** *Georgia Forest Research Paper, 0435-5377.*
Ind/Abst AGRICOLA [Full Cov.]; Biol. Abstr.; Soils Fert.

US
GEORGIA FORESTRY / [GEORGIA FORESTRY COMMISSION]. **Added/Corp** Georgia. Forestry Commission. (194?)-. Periodical. English. Four times a year. Free on request. Georgia Forestry Commission, Box 819, Macon GA 31298. **Tel** (912)744-3364. **ED** Howard Bennett. ctrl circ.

IO/0852-0070
GFG REPORT. [GFG rep.]. **VFOAT** German Forestry Group Report. (1985)-. Periodical. Multiple languages. qt. **DD** 634.905.
Ind/Abst Agrofor. Abstr.; For. Prod. Abstr. (1991-); For. Abstr.

US/0091-7680
GIFFORD PINCHOT NATIONAL FOREST. **Main/Corp** United States. Forest Service. (19??)-. English. an. Supervisor's Office, 500 West 12th Street, PO Box 449, Vancouver WA 98660. **LC** SD428.G45; U5a. **DD** 333.7/5/0979784.

US/1054-0563
GIS APPLICATION NOTE. [GIS appl. note]. **Added/Corp** United States. Forest Service. Southern Region. **VAT** Geographic Information System Application Note. No. 1 (Aug. 1990)-. English. **LC** SD144.A15; G57. **DD** 634.9/0975.
Ind/Abst AGRICOLA [Full Cov.].

YU
GLASNIK PRIRODNJACKOG MUZEJA U BEOGRADU. SERIJA C. SUMARSTVO I LOV. **Main/Corp** Belgrad. Prirodnjacki Muzej. **VFOAT** Bulletin du Museum d'Histoire Naturelle de Belgrade. Forets et Chasse. Vol. 7-. Periodical. Serbo-Croatian (Cyrillic) (summaries and/or abstracts in German and Russian). Prirodnjacki Muzej U Beogradu, Njegoseva 51 PB 401, Belgrad Yugoslavia. **LC** SD1; .B4215A. ***Continues*** *Glasnik Muzeja Sumarstva i Lova.*

CI/0352-3861
GLASNIK ZA SUMSKE POKUSE. [Glas. sumske pokuse]. **VFOAT** Annales pro Experimentis Foresticis. (1926)-. Academic Scholarly Publication. Multiple languages. an. DEM100. Sumarski Fakultet Sveucilista u Zagrebu, University of Zagreb, Svetosimunska 25, 41000 Zabreb Croatia. **Tel** 385 041 218 288, FAX 385 041 218 616. **UDC** 630. **Circ:** 1,000 (ctrl).
Ind/Abst For. Prod. Abstr. (1991-); For. Abstr.

YU/0017-2723
GOZDARSKI VESTNIK. [Gozd. vestn.]. **VFOAT** Slowenische Forstzeitschrift; Slovenian Journal of Forestry. (1938)-. Periodical. Multiple languages. mo. **UDC** 630.
Ind/Abst For. Abstr.

NE/0167-2932
GRASDUINEN. **See** Biology-Botany.

US/0090-8088
GREEN AMERICA. (GREENAMERICA.). [Green Am.]. **Added/Corp** American Forest Institute. Vol. 1 (Summer 1972)-. Periodical. English. qt. Greenamerica, Department S, American Forest Institute, 1619 Massachusetts Avenue NW, Washington DC 20036. **DD** 634.9.

CN/0380-8572
GREEN LEAVES. BRITISH COLUMBIA EDITION. (THE GREEN LEAVES.). **VFOAT** Green Leaves, Directory of Suppliers. **VAT** Green Leaves. Western Canada Edition. (Fall 1973)-. Periodical. English. an. Greencrest Industrial Publications, 201-5600 Cedarbridge Way, Richmond BC V6X 2A7. **DD** 338.4/7/634982028.

CN/0705-1697
GREEN LEAVES. WESTERN CANADA ED, THE. (Spring 1977)-. Periodical. English. sa. Free. Greencrest Industrial Publications, 201-5600 Cedarbridge Way, Richmond BC V6X 2A7. **DD** 338.4/7/634982028. ctrl circ. ***Continues*** *Green Leaves. British Columbia Ed., 0380-8572.*

KO
HANGUK IMHAKHOE CHI. **Main/Corp** Hanguk Imhakhoe. **Added/Corp** Hanguk Imhakhoe. Journal. **VFOAT** Journal of the Korean Forestry Society. (19??)-. Periodical. Korean (summaries and/or abstracts in English). Seoul National University College of Agriculture, Suweon Korea. **LC** SD1; .H25a. ***Continues*** *Imop kwa Imhak, 0445-4650.*
Ind/Abst Agrofor. Abstr.; Crop Physiol. Abstr.; For. Prod. Abstr. (1991-); For. Abstr.; Hortic. Abstr.; Leis. Recreat. Tour. Abstr.; Ornamental Hort. (1991-); Rev. Plant Pathol.; Seed Abstr.

CN/0708-2169
HIBALLER FOREST MAGAZINE. **VFOAT** Forest Magazine; Hiballer. **VAT** Hiballer (1976). Vol. 27, No. 8 (Aug. 1976)-. Periodical. English. Six times a year. 25.00Can$ Canada; 55.00Can$ others. HB Publishers Ltd., 206 525 Seymour Street, Vancouver BC V6B 3H7 Canada. **Tel** (604)984-2002. **ED** Paul Young. **DD** 338.1/7/498209711. **Bk Rev. Ad Acc. Circ:** 10,000 (ctrl). ***Continues*** *Hiballer, 0318-7632.*

US
HIGHLIGHTS: WALLOWA-WHITMAN NATIONAL FOREST. **Main/Corp** United States. Forest Service. (19??)-. Government Publication. English. US Department of Agriculture / Forest Service, 201 14th Street SW, Washington DC 20250. **Tel** (202)205-1661, FAX (202)205-1181.

JA/0367-6129
HOKKAIDO DAIGAKU NOGAKUBU ENSHURIN KENKYU HOKOKU. (RESEARCH BULLETINS OF THE COLLEGE EXPERIMENT FORESTS.). [Hokkaido Daigaku Nogakubu Enshurin Kenkyu Hokoku]. **Main/Corp** Hokkaido Daigaku. Nogakubu. (1920)-. English. Hokkaido Daigaku Nogakubu Enshurin, (College Experiment Forests, Faculty of Agriculture, Hokkaido University), Nishi 9 Chome, Kita 9 Jo, Kitaku, Sapporoshi, Hokkaido 060 Japan. **CODEN** HOKDAW. Documents available from BIOSIS Document Express, CASDDS. ***Continues*** *Hokkaido Daigaku. College of Experimental Forests. Research Bulletins.*
Ind/Abst Abstr. Bull. Inst. Pap. Sci. Tech.; Biol. Abstr.; Chem. Abstr.; For. Abstr.

JA
HOKKAIDO EIRINKYOKU JIGYO TOKEISHO : CHOKKATSU. **Main/Corp** Japan. Hokkaido Eirinkyoku. Japanese. Hokkaido Eirinkyoku, Kita 2-jo Nishi 1-chome, Chuo-ku, Sapporo Japan. **LC** SD90.H64; J36A.

AU
HOLZ KURIER. **VFOAT** Holz-Kurier. (1946)-. Periodical. German. wk. S1935.00 (Austria); S2360.00 (other). Osterreichischer Agrarverlag, Inkustr 1 7 Bueropark Donau, A 3400 Klosterneuberg Austria. **Tel** 011 43 2243 33300. **LC** HD9750.1; .H64.
Ind/Abst Abstr. Bull. Inst. Pap. Sci. Tech.

GW/0018-3792
HOLZ-ZENTRALBLATT. [Holz-zentralbl.]. (1874)-. Periodical. German. tw. DM324.00 Germany; DM448.20 other. DRW Verlag Weinbrenner GmbH and Company, Fasanenweg 18, W 7022 Leinfelden 1 Germany. **Tel** 011 49 711 75911, FAX 011 49 711 7591266, telex 7 255609. **ED** Lieselotte Drabarczyk. **[CCC].** Index available. **Bk Rev. Ad Acc. Circ:** 18,000 (ctrl).
Desc: Covers forestry, logging, sawmilling, log and timbermarket, timber import and export, woodworking, furniture production, particleboard and fibreboard production, woodworking and sawmilling machinery.
Ind/Abst Biodeter. Abstr.; Coal Abstr.; For. Prod. Abstr.; For. Abstr.

GW/0437-7168
HOLZZUCHT, DIE. [Holzzucht]. (1947)-. Periodical. German. Twice a year. Schriftleitung-Die Holzzucht, Prof Oelkers Str 6, 3510 Hann Munden 1 Germany. **Tel** 05541/7004-46. **DD** 634.9. Index available. cum. index. **Bk Rev. Circ:** 1,200.
Desc: Research on fast growing tree species, cultivation, utilization, and diseases.
Ind/Abst AGRICOLA; For. Prod. Abstr. (1991-); For. Abstr.; Plant Breed. Abstr.

KE
ICRAF WORKING PAPER. **VFOAT** Working Paper; I.C.R.A.F. Working Paper. **VAT** International Council for Research in Agroforestry Working Paper. (1985)-. Monographic series. English. Price varies per volume. ***Continues*** *Working Paper (International Council for Research in Agroforestry).*
Ind/Abst Agrofor. Abstr. (19??-19??); For. Abstr.

KO
IMOP YONGUQON YONGU POGO. **Added/Corp** Imop Yonguwon (Korea). **VFOAT** Research Reports of the Forestry Research Institute. (1987)-. Periodical. Korean (summaries and/or abstracts in English). an. Sallimchong Imop Sihomjang, San 1, Chongyangni-dong, Tongdaemun-ku, Seoul South Korea. **LC** SD235.K6; I48a. **CODEN** IYYPEJ. ***Continues*** *Imop Sihomjang Yongu Pogo.*
Ind/Abst For. Prod. Abstr. (1991-); For. Abstr.; Irr. Drain. Abstr.; Rev. Agric. Entomol.; Rev. Plant Pathol.; Seed Abstr.; Soils Fert.; Weed Abstr.

US/0198-8042
IMPAC REPORTS. **See** Business-General Management.

II/0019-4816
INDIAN FORESTER, THE. [Indian for.]. Vol. 1 (1975)-. Periodical. English. mo. $100.00. Indian Forester, PO New Forest Pin Code 248006, Dehra Dun 248006 India. **Tel** 27021, telex 595-258. **(Subscription address:** Prints India, 11 Darya Ganj, New Delhi, 110002 India, (Phone: 011 91 11 3268645)) **ED** A P Dwivedi. **LC** SD1; .I3. **DD** 634.9/0954. **CODEN** IFORA8. Index available. **Bk Rev. Ad Acc. Circ:** 2,500. Documents available from BIOSIS Document Express, CASDDS.
Desc: Journal of forestry and forestry research.
Ind/Abst Abstr. Bull. Inst. Pap. Sci. Tech.; AgBiotech News Inf.; AGRICOLA; Agrofor. Abstr. (1991-); Biocont. News Inf.; Biodeter. Abstr.; Biol. Abstr.; Chem. Abstr.; Crop Physiol. Abstr.; Energy Res. Abstr. (Feb. 1980-); Field Crop Abstr.; For. Prod. Abstr. (19??-19??); For. Abstr.; Grasslands For. Abstr.; Hortic. Abstr.; Ornamental Hort. (19??-19??); Life Sci. Collect.; Plant Breed. Abstr.; Plant Genet. Resour. Abstr.; Plant Grow. Reg. Abstr.; Rev. Agric. Entomol.; Rev. Med. Vet. Mycology; Rev. Plant Pathol.; Rural Dev. Abstr.; Seed Abstr.; Soils Fert.; Soyabean Abstr.; Weed Abstr.; Wildl. Rev.

II/0250-524X
INDIAN JOURNAL OF FORESTRY. [Indian j. for.]. Vol. 1 (Mar. 1978)-. Academic Scholarly Publication. English. qt. $45.00. Bishen Singh Mahendra Pal Sing, 23A Connaught Place, PO Box 137, Dehra Dun 248 001 India. **Tel** 011 91 935 24048. **(Subscription address:** Prints India, 11 Darya Ganj, New Delhi, 110002 India, (Phone: 011 91 11 3268645)) **ED** M B Raizada. **CODEN** IJFODJ. cum. index. **Bk Rev.** ctrl circ. Documents available from CASDDS.
Desc: Journal on forestry, agriculture, natural history, botany and zoology, etc.
Ind/Abst AgBiotech News Inf.; AGRICOLA; Agrofor. Abstr. (1991-); Biocont. News Inf. (1991-); Biodeter. Abstr.; Chem. Abstr.; Crop Physiol. Abstr.; For. Prod. Abstr. (19??-19??); For. Abstr.; Grasslands For. Abstr.; Hortic. Abstr.; Irr. Drain. Abstr.; NAPRALERT; Nematol. Abstr.; Ornamental Hort. (19??-19??); Plant Breed. Abstr.; Plant Grow. Reg. Abstr.; Potato Abstr.; Rev. Med. Vet. Mycology; Rev. Plant Pathol.; Seed Abstr.; Soils Fert.; Weed Abstr.

RM
INDUSTRIA LEMNULUI (BUCHAREST, ROMANIA : 1986). (INDUSTRIA LEMNULUI.). **Added/Corp** Romania. Ministerul Industrializarii Lemnului si Materialelor de Constructii. Vol. 37, No. 1 (1986)-. Periodical. Romanian (English; summaries and/or abstracts in French and Russian). qt. $120.00. Forest Infodoc SA, Bd. Magheru Nr. 31, Sector 1, 70162 Bucharest Romania. **Tel** 659 6865. **(Subscription address:** Rompresfilatelia, PO Box 12 201, Bucharest Romania.) **LC** TS840; .I32. **Bk Rev. Ad Acc. Circ:** 4,300. ***Continues*** *Revista Padurilor-Industria Lemnului, Celuloza si Hirtie. Industria Lemnului, 0250-5487.*
Ind/Abst Abstr. Bull. Inst. Pap. Sci. Tech.

CR
INFORMACION AL DIA: ALERTA DASONOMOS. ***Ceased.*** **Added/Corp** Programa Cooperativo para el Desarrollo del Tropico Americano. No. 1 (1974)-(19??). Periodical. Spanish. Biblioteca Commemorativa Orton, IICA / CATIE, Turrialba Costa Rica.
Desc: Includes tables of contents reprinted from forestry periodicals.

US
INFORMATION BULLETIN - MISSISSIPPI. AGRICULTURAL AND FORESTRY EXPERIMENT STATION, MISSISSIPPI STATE. **See** Agriculture.

CN
INFORMATION REPORT. **Added/Corp** Northern Forestery Centre.(Canada). Northwest Region. **VFOAT** Information Report NOR. **VAT** Information Report NOR-X (1990). (1990)-. Periodical. English. ***Continues*** *Information Report (Northern Forestry Centre).*
Ind/Abst Rev. Plant Pathol.

CN
INFORMATION REPORT BC-X/ FORESTRY CANADA, PACIFIC AND YUKON REGION, PACIFIC FORESTRY CENTRE. English.
Ind/Abst Rev. Plant Pathol.

CN/0705-324X
INFORMATION REPORT DPC-X. [Inf. rep. DPC-X]. **VFOAT** Rapport d'Information DPX (Ed. Anglaise et Francaise); Information Report - Program Development Branch. Canadian Forestry Service; DPC-X (English Edition); Information Report - Directorate of Program Coordination. Canadian Forestry Service; Information Report - Program Coordination and Evaluation Branch. Canadian Forestry Service. (197?)-. Monographic series. English. ir. price varies per volume. **DD** 634.90971.
Ind/Abst For. Abstr.; Rev. Agric. Entomol.; Rev. Plant Pathol.; Seed Abstr.

CN
INFORMATION REPORT / FORESTRY CANADA. **Added/Corp** Canada. Forestry Canada. Newfoundland and Labrador Region. (1989)-. Monographic series. English. available on microfiche. ***Continues*** *Information Report (Newfoundland Forestry Centre), 0831-8255.*
Desc: Reports on the forests of and the forestry in Canada.

CN/0832-7122
INFORMATION REPORT - GREAT LAKES FORESTRY CENTRE. (INFORMATION REPORT / GREAT LAKES FORESTRY CENTRE, ONTARIO REGION, FORESTRY CANADA.). [Inf. rep. - Gt. Lakes For. Cent.]. **Added/Corp** Great Lakes Forestry Centre. (1985)-. Monographic series. English. Free. **CODEN** IRFCE6. available on microfilm. Documents available from BIOSIS Document Express. ***Continues*** *Information Report (Great Lakes Forest Research Centre), 0822-210X.*
Ind/Abst Biol. Abstr. (1989-); For. Prod. Abstr. (19??-19??).

CN/0835-1570
INFORMATION REPORT - LAURENTIAN FORESTRY CENTRE. (INFORMATION REPORT LAU-X.). [Inf. rep. - Laurent. For. Cent.]. **Added/Corp** Laurentian Forestry Centre. (1985)-. English (summaries and/or abstracts in French).
Ind/Abst Biocont. News Inf.; For. Abstr.; Rev. Agric. Entomol.; Seed Abstr.

CN/0831-8255
INFORMATION REPORT - NEWFOUNDLAND FORESTRY CENTRE. ***Title Change.*** (INFORMATION REPORT / CANADIAN FORESTRY SERVICE, NEWFOUNDLAND FORESTRY CENTRE.). [Inf. rep. - Nfld. For. Cent.]. **Added/Corp** Newfoundland Forestry Centre. (1985)-(198?). Monographic series. English (summaries and/or abstracts in French). ***Continues*** *Information Report (Newfoundland Forest Research Centre), 0704-7657.* ***Continued by*** *Information Report (Canada. Forestry Canada. Newfoundland and Labrador Region).*
Ind/Abst Plant Grow. Reg. Abstr.; Rev. Agric. Entomol.

CN/0831-8247
INFORMATION REPORT - NORTHERN FORESTRY CENTRE. (INFORMATION REPORT.). [Inf. rep. - North. For. Cent.]. **Added/Corp** Northern Forestry Centre (Canada). **VFOAT** Information Report Northern Forestry Centre. **VAT** Information Report NOR-X (1985). Vol. 273, (1985)-. Academic Scholarly Publication. English (summaries and/or abstracts in French). ir. Price varies per volume. Northern Forestry Centre, Canadian Forestry Service, 5320 122nd Street, Edmonton Alberta T6H 3S5 Canada. **Tel** (403)435-7210. **ED** J. K. Samoil. **Circ:** 1,000. Documents available from CASDDS. ***Continues*** *Information Report (Northern Forest Research Centre (Canada)), 0704-7673.*
Desc: Scientific and technical reports of forestry research studies.
Ind/Abst Chem. Abstr.; For. Prod. Abstr.; For. Abstr.

CN/0706-1854
INFORMATION REPORT / PETAWAWA NATIONAL FORESTRY INSTITUTE. [Inf. rep. - Petawawa Natl. For. Inst.]. **Added/Corp** Petawawa National Forestry Institute. (1980)-. Periodical. English. ir. Petawawa National Forestry Institute, PO Box 2000, Chalk River Ontario K0J 1J0 Canada. **Tel** (613)589-2880. **LC** UNC. **DD** 634.9/0971. **CODEN** IRPID5. Documents available from BIOSIS Document Express. ***Continues*** *Petawawa Forest Experiment Station. Information Report., 0705-3223.*
Ind/Abst Biol. Abstr.; For. Abstr.

BL/0100-9508
INFORME DA PESQUISA. [Inf. Pesqui.]. (1977)-. Monographic series. Portuguese. tw. Fundacao Instituto Agronomico do Parana, Caixa Postal 1331, Londrina 86.100 Brazil. **UDC** 63:167.
Ind/Abst For. Abstr.

CL/0581-6378
INFORME TECNICO (INSTITUTO FORESTAL (SANTIAGO, CHILE)). (INFORME TECNICO / INSTITUTO FORESTAL.). **Added/Corp** Instituto Forestal (Santiago, Chile) Instituto Forestal (Santiago, Chile). Division Estudios Economicos. Instituto Forestal (Santiago, Chile). Division Industrias. Instituto Forestal (Santiago, Chile). Gerencia Tecnica. Instituto Forestal (Santiago, Chile). Division Regional. Corporacion de Fomento de la Produccion (Chile). Gerencia de Desarrollo. (1962)-. Monographic series. Spanish. Price varies per volume. **LC** SD29; .S352a.
Ind/Abst AGRICOLA.

FR/1156-1653
INRA MENSUEL LES DOSSIERS. (1989)-. Periodical. French. ir. Free. INRA Direction Info Communicat, 47 rue de l Universite, 75341 Paris Cedex 07 France. **Tel** 011 33 1 42759000. **UDC** 631(44).

US
INTERCOM. **Main/Corp** Intermountain Research Station (Ogden, Utah). Periodical. English. Intermountain Research Station, 507 25th Street, Ogden UT 84401. ***Continues*** *Intercom, 0146-3551.*

US
INTERMOUNTAIN REGION ANNUAL QUALITY PLAN. **Main/Corp** United States. Forest Service. Intermountain Region. **VFOAT** Annual Quality Plan. (1991)-. English.

CN
INTERNATIONAL JOURNAL OF ECO FORESTRY. (19??)-. Periodical. English. qt. $60.00 (institutions), $30.00 (individuals). Woodland Planning Publications, PO Box 5885 Station B, Victoria BC V8R 6S8 Canada. **Tel** (604)598-2363. ***Continues*** *Forest Planning Canada, 0832-1655.*

UK/0143-5698
INTERNATIONAL TREE CROPS JOURNAL, THE. [Int. tree crops j.]. Vol. 1 (1980)-. Periodical. English (summaries and/or abstracts in French and Spanish). qt. £69.00 (add £25.00 airmail) UK; $129.00 (add $50.00 airmail) US. AB Academic Publishers, PO Box 42 Bicester, OXON OX6 7NW England. **Tel** 011 44 869 320949. **ED** A. Grainger; L. D. Hills. **CODEN** ITRJDW. **[CCC]**. Index available. **Bk Rev. Ad Acc.** Documents available from BIOSIS Document Express.
Desc: Research and review papers in fields of nonwood tree crops, agroforestry, afforestation, environmental management, multiple land use and community development.
Ind/Abst AgBiotech News Inf.; AGRICOLA [Full Cov.]; Agrofor. Abstr. (1991-); BioBusiness; Biol. Abstr.; Crop Physiol. Abstr.; Ecol. Abstr.; Environ. Period. Bibliogr.; Field Crop Abstr.; Food Sci. Technol. Abstr.; For. Prod. Abstr. (19??-19??); For. Abstr.; Grasslands For. Abstr.; Hortic. Abstr.; Int. Dev. Abstr.; Maize Abstr.; Plant Breed. Abstr.; Plant Grow. Reg. Abstr.; Rural Dev. Abstr.; Seed Abstr.; Soils Fert.; Weed Abstr.; World Agric. Econ.

CN
INVENTAIRE DES INSECTES ET DES MALADIES DES ARBRES, AU QUEBEC.
Main/Corp Canada. Centre de Recherches Forestieres des Laurentides. Published since 1973. Periodical. French. an. Free. Service Canadian des Forets, Centre de Forestieres des Laurentides, CP 3800, Sainte-Foy Quebec G1V 4C7 Canada. **Tel** (418)648-5788.

US/0898-9737
INVENTORY AND CRUISING NEWSLETTER / JOHN BELL & ASSOCIATES. [Inventory cruis. newsl.]. No. 1 (Jan. 1988)-. Newsletter. English. qt. $15.00 (individuals), $50.00 (institutions). John Bell and Associates, PO Box 1538, Corvallis OR 97330. **Tel** (503)758-4939. **ED** John Bell. **DD** 634.

BL/0100-4557
IPEF, INSTITUTO DE PESQUISAS E ESTUDOS FLORESTAIS. (IPEF.). [IPEF, Inst. Pesqu. Estud. Flor.]. **Main/Corp** Escola Superior de Agricultura "Luiz de Queiroz." Instituto de Pesquisas e Estudos Florestaia. **VAT** Instituto de Pesquisas e Estudos Florestais. No. 1 (1970)-. Periodical. Portuguese (summaries and/or abstracts in English). Twice a year (June, Dec.). $40.00. Institute Pesquis Estud Florestais, Caixa Postal 530, Biblioteca 13400, Piracicaba SP Brazil. **Tel** 011 55 194 334124, telex (019)1141. **(Subscription address:** Instituto de Pesquisan e Estudos, Florestais, Caisca Postal 530, 13400 Piracicaba SP Brasil**) ED** Walter De Paula Lima and Marialice Metzker Poggiani. **LC** SD1; .I4a. **CODEN** PSIFDB. **Bk Rev. Ad Acc. Circ:** 1,500 (ctrl). Documents available from CASDDS.
Desc: Presents research papers on silvicultural, technological, environmental, social economic and energy aspects of forestry.
Ind/Abst Abstr. Bull. Inst. Pap. Sci. Tech.; AGRICOLA; Agrofor. Abstr. (1991-); Biocont. News Inf. (1991-); Biodeter. Abstr. (1991-); Chem. Abstr.; Field Crop Abstr.; For. Prod. Abstr. (19??-19??); For. Abstr.; Maize Abstr.; Rev. Agric. Entomol.; Rev. Plant Pathol.; Rice Abstr.; Seed Abstr.; Soils Fert.

IE/0021-1192
IRISH FORESTRY. [Ir. for.]. **Added/Corp** Society of Irish Foresters. No. 1 (1943)-. Periodical. English. Twice a year. $12.00. Society of Irish Foresters, c/o Royal Dublin Society, Thomas Prior House/Ballsbridge, Dublin 4 Ireland. **Tel** 011 353 1 867751. **ED** A. Pfeifer. Index available. cum. index. **Bk Rev. Ad Acc. Circ:** 800 (ctrl).
Desc: Forest biomass, economics, genetics, history, management, nutrition, protection and silviculture.
Ind/Abst AGRICOLA; Biodeter. Abstr. (1991-); Ecol. Abstr.; Fish Rev. (Jan. 1989-July 1992); For. Prod. Abstr. (19??-19??); For. Abstr.; Geogr. Abstr. Human Geogr. (?-?); Life Sci. Collect. (?-1986); Soils Fert.; Wildl. Rev. (Jan. 1989-July 1992).

TU/0535-8418
ISTANBUL UNIVERSITESI ORMAN FAKULTESI DERGISI. SERI A. [Istanbul Univ., Orman Fak. Derg., Seri A]. **Main/Corp** Istanbul Universitesi. Orman Fakultesi. **VFOAT** Revue de la Faculte des Sciences, Foresteeres de l'Universite d'Istanbul. Vol. 1 (1951)-. Periodical. Turkish. sa.
Ind/Abst AGRICOLA; EMBASE; For. Prod. Abstr. (1991-); For. Abstr.; Irr. Drain. Abstr.; Rev. Agric. Entomol.; Rev. Plant Pathol.; Soils Fert.

US/0276-2056
ISTF NEWS. (ISTF NEWS / INTERNATIONAL SOCIETY OF TROPICAL FORESTERS.). [ISTF news]. **Added/Corp** International Society of Tropical Foresters. **VFOAT** I.S.T.F. News. **VAT** International Society of Tropical Foresters News. (March 1979)-. Periodical. English (Spanish). Four times a year (Mar., June, Sept., Dec.). $20.00 (regular), $100.00 (sustaining), $1,000.00 (donor) US, Canada, Europe, Japan, Australia, & New Zealand (members); $10.00 (regular), $50.00 (sustaining), $600.00 (donor) others (non-members). International Society of Tropical Foresters, 5400 Grosvenor Lane, Bethesda MD 20814. **Tel** (301)897-8720, FAX (301)897-3690. **ED** Frank Wadsworth. **Bk Rev. Ad Acc. Circ:** 1,700 (ctrl).
Desc: Activities, meetings, and publications of interest to tropical foresters. Also results of specific forest management practices in tropical countries.

US/0743-5991
ISTF NOTICIAS. **Added/Corp** International Society of Tropical Foresters. **VFOAT** I.S.T.F. Noticias. (19??)-. Newsletter. Spanish (English). qt. $25.00. International Society of Tropical Foresters, 5400 Grosvenor Lane, Bethesda MD 20814. **Tel** (301)897-8720, FAX (301)897-3690. **ED** Frank Wadsworth, Warren Doolittle (Managing Editor). **Bk Rev**, (Qty: 8). **Ad Acc**, **Adv Mgr:** Rodney Young. **Pub. Size:** Standard. ctrl circ.
Desc: Deals with problems in tropical forestry and discussions of possible solutions. Lists recent publications and reviews the ones.

US/8755-5506
ISTF NOUVELLES. [ISTF nouv.]. **VFOAT** I.S.T.F. Nouvelles. **VAT** International Society of Tropical Foresters Nouvelles. Periodical. French. qt. $10.00 members, $20.00 libraries. International Society of Tropical Foresters, 5400 Grosvenor Lane, Bethesda MD 20814. **Tel** (301)897-8720, FAX (301)897-3690. **DD** 634.

AU/1016-3263
IUFRO WORLD SERIES. [IUFRO world ser.]. **Added/Corp** International Union of Forestry Research Organizations. **VAT** International Union of Forestry Research Organizations World Series. Vol. 1 (1990)-. Monographic series. Multiple languages (English, French, German, Italian, Russian and Spanish). International Union Forestry Res Organ, Zuercherstrasse 111, CH8903 Birmensdorf Switzerland. **Tel** 011 41 1 7392111.
Ind/Abst For. Prod. Abstr. (1991-).

RU/0536-1036
IZVESTIIA VYSSHIKH UCHEBNYKH ZAVEDENII. LESNOI ZHURNAL. [Izv. vyss. uchebn. zaved. Lesn. z.]. **Added/Corp** Soviet Union. Ministerstvo Vysshego Obrazovaniia. Soviet Union. Ministerstvo Vysshego i Srednego Spetsialnogo Obrazovaniia. Arkhangelskii Lesotekhnicheskii Institut Im. V.V. Kuibysheva. Soviet Union. Gosudarstvennyi Komitet Po Narodnomu Obrazovaniiu. **VFOAT** Lesnoi Zhurnal. (1958)-. Periodical. Russian. ir (156 issues). **(Subscription address:** East View Publications Inc., 3020 Harbor Lane North, Suite 110, Minneapolis MN 55447.**) LC** SD1; .R92. **CODEN** IVZLAL. Documents available from BIOSIS Document Express, CASDDS. ***Absorbed*** *Nauchnye Doklady Vysshei Shkoly. Lesoinzhenernoe Delo.*
Ind/Abst Abstr. Bull. Inst. Paper Chem.; Abstr. Bull. Inst. Pap. Sci. Tech.; AGRICOLA; Biol. Abstr.; Chem. Abstr.; For. Prod. Abstr. (19??-19??); For. Abstr.; Maize Abstr.; Plant Grow. Reg. Abstr.; Rev. Plant Pathol.; Seed Abstr.; Soils Fert.

CC
JE TAI LIN YEH K'O CHI. **Added/Corp** Chung-Kuo Lin Yeh K'o Hsueh Yen Chiu Yuan. Je Tai Lin Yeh Yen Chiu So. **VFOAT** Tropical Forestry : Science and Technology. (19??)-. Periodical. Chinese (summaries and/or abstracts in English). qt.
Ind/Abst Agrofor. Abstr.; For. Abstr.; Rev. Plant Pathol.; Seed Abstr.

DK/0906-7043
JORD OG VIDEN. **See** Agriculture.

BL
JORNAL DOS REFLORESTADORES. (19??)-. Periodical. Portuguese. Editora Florestal Ltda, Rua Joao Annes 153 Alta Da Lapa, 05060 Sao Paulo SP Brazil. **LC** SD159; .J67.

CN/0843-5243
JOURNAL OF FOREST ENGINEERING. [J. for. eng.]. **Added/Corp** University of New Brunswick. Dept. of Forest Engineering. Vol. 1, No. 1 (July 1989)-. Periodical. English. Twice a year (Jan. & July). $93.46. University of New Brunswick, PO Box 4400, Fredericton New Brunswick, E3B 5A3 Canada. **Tel** (506)453-4506, FAX (506)453-3538, telex 014-46202. **LC** SD388; .J68. **DD** 634.9.
Desc: Devoted to dissemination of scientific knowledge in all areas related to forest operations such as tree harvesting/processing; machine management; transportation; road design; wood processing; wood engineering; operations planning.
Ind/Abst For. Prod. Abstr. (1991-).

US/0022-1201
JOURNAL OF FORESTRY. [J. for.]. **Added/Corp** Society of American Foresters. Vol. 15 (Jan. 1917)-. Academic Scholarly Publication. English. mo. $100.00 (institutions), $130.00 (non-member individuals) US and Canada; $130.00 (institution), $85.00 (non-member individuals) other. Society of American Foresters, 5400 Grosvenor Lane, Bethesda MD 20814-2198. **Tel** (301)897-8720, FAX (301)897-3690, telex 9102501089 SAFFOREST UQ. **ED** Wendy B. Osborne. **LC** SD1; .S63. **CODEN** JFUSAI. cum. index. **Bk Rev. Ad Acc. Circ:** 23,000 (ctrl). available on microfilm and microfiche from University Microfilms International (UMI). Documents available from Article Express International, The Genuine Article, BIOSIS

Document Express, CASDDS, Documents on Demand. ***Formed by the union of** Forestry Quarterly **and** Proceedings of the Society of American Foresters.* ***Superseded in part by** Society of American Foresters. Proceedings of the Meeting 1947.*
Desc: Editorial coverage, analysis, and commentary of forest technology, management, measurement, protection, resource policy, and forest uses, plus book reviews, meetings, and national and association activities.
Ind/Abst Abstr. Bull. Inst. Pap. Sci. Tech.; AGRICOLA [Select. Cov.]; Agrofor. Abstr.; Art Archaeol. Tech. Abstr.; BioBusiness; Biocont. News Inf.; Biol. Agric. Index; Biol. Abstr.; Biol. Dig.; Chem. Abstr.; Curr. Contents, Agric. Biol. Environ. Sci.; Curr. Geogr. Publ. (199?-); Ecol. Abstr.; Ei Page One; EMBASE; Energy Res. Abstr. (Sept. 1971-); Eng. Index Annu.; Environ. Abstr.; Environ. Period. Bibliogr.; Fish Rev. (Jan. 1989-19??); For. Prod. Abstr.; For. Abstr.; Geogr. Abstr. Phys. Geogr.; Geogr. Abstr. Human Geogr.; Highw. Res. Abstr.; INIS Atomindex [Micro.]; Int. Aerosp. Abstr.; Int. Dev. Abstr.; J. Plan. Lit.; Key Word Index Wildl. Res.; Life Sci. Collect.; Res. Alert [Full Cov.]; Rev. Agric. Entomol.; Sci. Cit. Index; SCISEARCH; Soc. Sci. Cit. Index [Select. Cov.]; Stat. Theory Method Abstr. (1959-1963); Wildl. Rev. (Jan. 1989-19??).

CC
JOURNAL OF NORTHEAST FORESTRY UNIVERSITY. Chinese. bm. **(Subscription address:** China Intl Book Trading Corp, PO Box 399, Beijing China, Tel. 86 1 8414284**)**
Ind/Abst Agric. Eng. Abstr.; Anim. Breed. Abstr.; Biodeter. Abstr.; Crop Physiol. Abstr.; For. Abstr.; Grasslands For. Abstr.; Hortic. Abstr.; Rev. Agric. Entomol.; Rev. Plant Pathol.; Seed Abstr.; Soils Fert.

●US/1054-9811
JOURNAL OF SUSTAINABLE FORESTRY. (1993)-. Periodical. English. qt (4 issues). $60.00 US; $84.00 other. The Haworth Press Inc, 10 Alice Street, Binghamton NY 13904-1580. **Tel** (607)722-5857, (800)3-HAWORTH, FAX (607)722-1424. **ED** Graeme P. Berlyn, Yale University School of Forestry and Environmental Studies. **Acid Free.** available on microfiche. Documents available from Haworth Document Delivery Service, Documents on Demand.
Desc: The broad scope encompasses topics from biotechnology, physiology, silviculture, wood science, economics and forest management. Research dealing with above and/or below ground perspectives will also be published.
Ind/Abst Abstr. Bull. Inst. Pap. Sci. Tech.; Abstr. Anthropol.; AGRICOLA; Biostatistica; Ecol. Abstr.; Environ. Abstr.; Environ. Period. Bibliogr.; Fish Rev.; GeoRef; Hum. Resour. Abstr.; Ref. Z.; Sage Public Adm. Abstr.; Sage Urban Stud. Abstr.

TZ/0856-0269
JOURNAL OF THE TANZANIA ASSOCIATION OF FORESTERS. **Added/Corp** Tanzania Association of Foresters. Vol. 5, No. 1 (1984)-. Periodical. English. ***Continues** TAF Newsletter.*
Ind/Abst Agric. Eng. Abstr. (1991-); Agrofor. Abstr. (1991-); For. Prod. Abstr. (1991-); For. Abstr.; Rev. Agric. Entomol.; Soils Fert.

II
JOURNAL OF TREE SCIENCES. **Added/Corp** Indian Society of Tree Scientists. Vol. 1, No. 1 & 2 (1982)-. Periodical. English. sa. $50.00. HP Agricultural University Department of Forestry, SNS Nagar-173 230 Solan India. **Tel** 26 86 45. **(Subscription address:** Prints India, 11 Darya Ganj, New Delhi, 110002 India, (Phone: 011 91 11 3268645)**) ED** P K Khosla. **LC** SB170; .J68. **DD** 634.9/05. **Bk Rev. Circ:** 600.
Desc: International journal on research and development in tree sciences and environmental conservation.
Ind/Abst Agrofor. Abstr. (1991-); Crop Physiol. Abstr.; For. Prod. Abstr. (1991-); Plant Grow. Reg. Abstr.

MY/0128-1283
JOURNAL OF TROPICAL FOREST SCIENCE. [J. trop. for. sci.]. **Added/Corp** Institut Penyelidikan Perhutanan Malaysia. **VFOAT** Tropical Forest Science. Vol. 1, No. 1 (Sept. 1988)-. Periodical. English. qt. $90.00 (institutions), $45.00 (individuals). Forest Research Institute of Malaysia, Kepong, PO Box 201, 52109 Kuala Lumpur Malaysia. **Tel** 011 60 3 6342633, FAX 011 60 3 6367753, telex FIRM-MA-27007. **ED** K. C. Khoo. **CODEN** JTFSEB. Index available. cum. index. **Bk Rev. Circ:** 300-400. Documents available from BIOSIS Document Express.
Ind/Abst Abstr. Bull. Inst. Pap. Sci. Tech.; Agric. Eng. Abstr. (1991-); Agrofor. Abstr. (1991-); Biodeter. Abstr. (1991-); Biol. Abstr. (1969-); Crop Physiol. Abstr.; Field Crop Abstr.; For. Prod. Abstr. (1991-); For. Abstr.; Grasslands For. Abstr.; Plant Breed. Abstr.; Rev. Agric. Entomol.; Rev. Plant Pathol.; Seed Abstr.; Soils Fert.; Weed Abstr.

II/0970-1494
JOURNAL OF TROPICAL FORESTRY. [J. trop. for.]. **Added/Corp** Society of Tropical Forestry Scientists (Jabalpur, India). Vol. 1, No. 1 (March 1985)-. Academic Scholarly Publication. English. qt. $100.00. Society of Tropical Forestry Scientists, Jabalpur, India. **(Subscription address:** Prints India, 11 Darya Ganj, New Delhi, 110002 India, (Phone: 011 91 11 3268645)**) LC** SD247; .J68. **DD** 634.9/0913. **CODEN** JTFOEX. Documents available from CASDDS.
Ind/Abst AgBiotech News Inf.; AGRICOLA; Biocont. News Inf. (19??-19??); Chem. Abstr. (1986-); Crop Physiol. Abstr.; Field Crop Abstr.; For. Prod. Abstr. (1991-); For. Abstr.; Grasslands For. Abstr.; Hortic. Abstr.; Irr. Drain. Abstr.; Key Word Index Wildl. Res.; Plant Grow. Reg. Abstr.; Rev. Agric. Entomol.; Rev. Plant Pathol.; Rural Dev. Abstr.; Seed Abstr.; Soils Fert.; Weed Abstr.; Wheat Barley Trit. Abstr.

UK/0261-4286
JOURNAL OF WORLD FOREST RESOURCE MANAGEMENT. (THE JOURNAL OF WORLD FOREST RESOURCE MANAGEMENT.). [J. world for. resour. manage.]. **VFOAT** World Forest Resource Management. Vol. 1, No. 1 (1984)-. Periodical. English (summaries and/or abstracts in French). Twice a year. £59.00. AB Academic Publishers, PO Box 42 Bicester, OXON OX6 7NW England. **Tel** 011 44 869 320949. **ED** Alan Grainger. **LC** SD1; .J68. **DD** 333.75/05. **[CCC].** Index available. **Bk Rev. Ad Acc.** Documents available from Documents on Demand.
Desc: Focuses on forest policy, economics, modelling, forecasting, ecology, resource assessment and all aspects of forests and global resource.
Ind/Abst AGRICOLA [Full Cov.]; Agrofor. Abstr.; Curr. Aware. Biol. Sci., CABS; Ecol. Abstr. (?-?); Environ. Abstr.; Environ. Period. Bibliogr.; For. Prod. Abstr.; Geogr. Abstr. Phys. Geogr. (?-?); Geogr. Abstr. Human Geogr.; Int. Dev. Abstr.

IO/0216-9525
JURNAL PENELITIAN DAN PENGEMBANGAN KEHUTANAN. [J. Penelitian Pengembangan Kehutanan]. **VFOAT** Journal of Forestry Research and Development. (1985)-. Periodical. Multiple languages. sa. **DD** 634.9.
Ind/Abst Agric. Eng. Abstr.; Agrofor. Abstr.; Biocont. News Inf.; For. Abstr.; Rev. Agric. Entomol.; Soils Fert.

JA/0372-7785
KAIHO. See Agriculture.

JA/0288-6510
KANTO RINBOKU IKUSHUJO NENPO. [Kanto Rinboku Ikushujo nenpo]. **VFOAT** Annual report - Kanto Forest Tree Breeding Institute. (1960)-. Periodical. Multiple languages. an. Rinyacho Kanto Rinboku Ikushujo, (Kanto Forest Tree Breeding Inst., Forestry Agency), 978, Kasaharacho, Mitoshi, Ibarakiken 310 Japan. **DD** 634.9.
Ind/Abst For. Abstr.

JA
KENKYU HOKOKU. RESEARCH BULLETINS OF THE COLLEGE EXPERIMENT FORESTS, HOKKAIDO UNIVERSITY. **Main/Corp** Hokkaido Daigaku, Sapporo, Japan. Nogakubu. Enshurin. **Added/Corp** Hokkaido Daigaku, Sapporo, Japan. Nogakubu. Enshurin. Research Bulletin of the College Experiment Forests, Hokkaido University. **VFOAT** Research Bulletins of the College Experiment Forests, Hokkaido University. Vol. 1 (1915)-. Periodical. Japanese (English). Hokkaido University College Experiment Forests, North 9 West 7, Kita-ku, Sapporo 060 Japan.
Ind/Abst Agric. Eng. Abstr.; For. Prod. Abstr. (1991-); Soils Fert.

JA/0386-9032
KENKYU KIYO / TOKUGAWA RINSEISHI KENKYUJO. **Added/Corp** Tokugawa Rinseishi Kenkyujo. **VFOAT** Tokugawa Rinseishi Kenkyujo Kenkyo Kiyo; Bulletin of the Tokugawa Institute for the History of Forestry. (19??)-. Periodical. Japanese. Tokugawa Reimeikai 8, Mejiro 3-chome Toshima-ku, Tokyo-to 171 Japan. **LC** SD225; .K46.

US
KENTUCKY'S GROWING GOLD. **Added/Corp** Kentucky. Division of Forestry (1936-). (19??)-. Periodical. English. Four times a year (Jan., Apr., July, Oct.). Free. Kentucky Division of Forestry, 618 Teton Trail, Frankfort KY 40601. **Tel** (502)564-4496. **ED** C. J. Lohr. **Ad Acc. Circ:** 800.

II/0970-8103
KFRI RESEARCH REPORT. **VFOAT** K.F.R.I. Research Report. **VAT** Kerala Forest Research Institute Research Report. Monographic series. English. Price varies per volume. Kerala Forest Research Institute, Peechi 680653 Trichur District, Kerala India. **Tel** 22375.
Ind/Abst Agrofor. Abstr.; For. Prod. Abstr.; For. Abstr.; Grasslands For. Abstr.; Plant Grow. Reg. Abstr.

PP
KLINKII : THE JOURNAL OF THE FORESTRY SOCIETY OF THE PAPUA NEW GUINEA UNIVERSITY OF TECHNOLOGY. Vol. 1, No. 1 (Oct. 1977)-. English. an.
Ind/Abst Biodeter. Abstr. (1991-); For. Prod. Abstr. (1991-); For. Abstr.; Rev. Plant Pathol.

JA
KOKUYU RINYA JIGYO TOKEISHO. **Main/Corp** Japan. Rinyacho. Japanese. Rinyacho. (Forestry Agency), 2-1, Kasumigaseki 1 Chome, Chiyodaku, Tokyoto 100, Japan. **LC** SD647; .J36A.

SW/0023-5350
KUNGL. SKOGS- OCH LANTBRUKSAKADEMIENS TIDSKRIFT. **See** Agriculture.

JA/0368-511X
KYOTO DAIGAKU NOGAKUBU ENSHURIN HOKOKU. [Kyoto Daigaku Nogakubu enshurin hokoku]. **Added/Corp** Kyoto Daigaku. Fuzoku Enshurin. **VFOAT** Bulletin of the Kyoto University Forests. (1930)-. Academic Scholarly Publication. Japanese (summaries and/or abstracts in English). Kyoto Daigaku Nogakubu Fuzoku Enshurin, (Kyoto University Forests), Oiwakecho, Kitashirakawa, Sakyoku, Kyotoshi, Kyotofu 606, Japan. ***Continues** Kyoto Teikoku Daigaku Nogakubu Enshurin Hokoku.*
Ind/Abst AGRICOLA; Agric. Eng. Abstr.; EMBASE; For. Prod. Abstr. (1991-); Hortic. Abstr.; Ornamental Hort. (1991-); Rev. Agric. Entomol.; Soils Fert.

JA
KYOTO FURITSU DAIGAKU NOGAKUBU ENSHURIN HOKOKU. **Added/Corp** Kyoto Furitsu Daigaku. Fuzoku Enshurin. **VFOAT** Bulletin of the Kyoto Prefectural University Forests. (19??)-. Japanese (summaries and/or abstracts in English; table of contents in English). Kyoto Furitsu Daigaku Nogakubu Fuzoku Enshurin, (Kyoto Prefectural University Forests), 1, Shimogamo Hangicho, Sakyoku, Kyotoshi, Kyotofu 606, Japan.
Ind/Abst Nematol. Abstr.

CN/1183-2894
LAKEHEAD FOREST : A NEWSLETTER FROM THE SCHOOL OF FORESTRY, LAKEHEAD UNIVERSITY, THE. [Lakehead for.]. **Added/Corp** Lakehead University. School of Forestry. Winter (1991)-. Newsletter. English. Three times a year. Limited free distribution. Lakehead University / School of Forestry, Thunder Bay Ontario P7B 5E1 Canada. **DD** 634.9/071/1713133.

US/0196-7878
LAND AREAS OF THE NATIONAL FOREST SYSTEM. (LAND AREAS OF THE NATIONAL FOREST SYSTEM AS OF ... / UNITED STATES DEPARTMENT OF AGRICULTURE, FOREST SERVICE.). [Land areas Natl. for. syst.]. **VFOAT** National Forest Areas Report. Began with 1977. Government Publication. English. an. US Department of Agriculture / Forest Service, 201 14th Street SW, Washington DC 20250. **Tel** (202)205-1661, FAX (202)205-1181. **LC** SD426; .L36. **DD** 333.75/11/0973. available on microfiche (Vols. for (1982-) distributed to depository libraries). ***Continues** National Forest System Areas.*

CN/0229-1622
LAND MANAGEMENT HANDBOOKS / PROVINCE OF BRITISH COLUMBIA, MINISTRY OF FORESTS. Monographic series. English. ir. Price varies per volume. Ministry of Forests and Lands, Government of British Columbia, Parliament Buildings, Victoria British Columbia V8V 1X4 Canada. **Tel** (604)387-3484. **ED** Tim Mock.

CN/0702-9861
LAND MANAGEMENT REPORT. [Land manage. rep.]. Monographic series. English. Price varies per volume. Ministry of Forests and Lands, Government of British Columbia, Parliament Buildings, Victoria British Columbia V8V 1X4 Canada. **Tel** (604)387-3484.
Ind/Abst For. Prod. Abstr.; For. Abstr.

AU
LAND- UND FORSTWIRTSCHAFLICHE BETRIEB, DER. ***Title Change.*** **Added/Corp** Verband Landwirtschaftlicher Gutsbetriebe in Osterreich. (19??)-(19??). Periodical. German. mo. Osterreichischer Agrarverlag, Inkustr 1 7 Bueropark Donau, A 3400 Klosterneuberg Austria. **Tel** 011 43 2243 33300. **ED** Arnold Kolterer. **Bk Rev. Ad Acc. Circ:** 3,500. ***Absorbed by** Agro Bonus.*

IO
LAPORAN TAHUNAN. **Main/Corp** Indonesia. Perhutani, Djawa Tengah. Direksi. **Added/Corp** Indonesia. Direktorat Djenderal Kehutanan. (19??)-. Periodical. Indonesian.

IO
LAPORAN TAHUNAN - DINAS KEHUTANAN PROPINSI SUMATERA UTARA. **Main/Corp** Sumatera Utara, Indonesia. Dinas Kehutanan. Indonesian. Dinas Kehutanan Propinsi Sumatera Utara, Jln Sei Galang No 26, Medan Indonesia. **LC** SD97.I6; S84A.
Desc: Vols. for 1973/74-include an evaluation of the 1st-five year plan, 1969/74.

VE/0798-1945
LATINAMERICAN FORESTRY BIBLIOGRAPHY / INSTITUTO FORESTAL LATINOAMERICANO. **Added/Corp** Instituto Forestal Latinoamericano. No. 1 (1982)-. Bibliography. English. Three times a year. $60.00. Instituto Forestal Latino-Americano, Apartado 36, Merida Venezuela. **Tel** 011 58 74 440535, FAX 011 58 74 448906, telex 74104. cum. index. **Bk Rev. Circ:** 300.
Desc: Provides summaries and review of Latin American forestry literature.

RU/0368-7619
LESNAIA PROMYSHLENNOST (MOSKVA). (LESNAIA PROMYSHLENNOST.). [Lesn. prom.]. **Added/Corp** Soviet Union. Ministerstvo Lesnoi Promyshlennosti. (1941)-. Periodical. Russian. Six times a year. $79.95. **(Subscription address:** East View Publications Inc., 3020 Harbor Lane North, Suite 110, Minneapolis MN 55447.**)** **LC** SD1; .L387. **CODEN** LESNA8. available on microfilm from University Microfilms International (UMI). Documents available from CASDDS.
Ind/Abst Abstr. Bull. Inst. Pap. Sci. Tech.; AGRICOLA; Agric. Eng. Abstr.; Chem. Abstr. (-1972); Energy Res. Abstr. (Oct. 1980-); For. Prod. Abstr. (1991-); For. Abstr.

XR/0322-9254
LESNICKA PRACE. [Lesn. pr.]. (1922)-. Periodical. Czech. Twelve times a year. **(Subscription address:** Artia Pegas Press Ltd., Palac Metro Narodni Trida 25, 11210 Prague 1 Czech Republic.**)**
Ind/Abst AGRICOLA; For. Prod. Abstr. (1991-); Saf. Health Work.

XO/0323-1046
LESNICKY CASOPIS. [Lesn. cas.]. **Added/Corp** Slovenska Akademia vied. (1955)-. Periodical. Czech. bm. Slovenska Akademia Vied / Slovak Academy of Sciences, PO Box 57, 81005 Bratislava Slovakia. **Tel** 011 42 7 3782715, 011 42 7 3782925, FAX 011 42 7 496849, telex 93261. **(Subscription address:** Translibris GMbH, PO Box 301373, D 50783 Cologne Germany; telephone: 011 49 221 542085**)**
Ind/Abst Irr. Drain. Abstr.; Rev. Agric. Entomol.

XR/0024-1105
LESNICTVI. [Lesnictvi]. **Main/Corp** Czechoslovak Republic. Ministerstvo Zemdelstvi, Lesniho a Vodniho Hospodarstvi. Ustav Vedecko-Technickych Informaci. **Added/Corp** Ceskoslovenska Akademie Zemedelskych Ved. Vol. 1 (1955)-. Academic Scholarly Publication. Czech (English; summaries and/or abstracts in English and Russian; table of contents in Russian and English). Twelve times a year. $117.70. **(Subscription address:** Artia Pegas Press Ltd., Palac Metro Narodni Trida 25, 11210 Prague 1 Czech Republic.**)** **LC** SD83.C9; A33. **CODEN** LSNCAE. **Bk Rev. Circ:** 1,000 (ctrl). Documents available from BIOSIS Document Express, CASDDS. ***Supersedes in part** Ceskoslovenska Akademie Zemedelska. Sbornik.*
Desc: Papers from all spheres of forestry science, game management and environment conservation. Topical problems are treated in subject issues. Secondary information included at the end of issues.
Ind/Abst Abstr. Bull. Inst. Pap. Sci. Tech.; AGRICOLA; Biocont. News Inf. (19??-19??); Biol. Abstr.; Chem. Abstr.; Crop Physiol. Abstr.; EMBASE; For. Prod. Abstr. (1991-); For. Abstr.; Irr. Drain. Abstr.; Life Sci. Collect.; Plant Grow. Reg. Abstr.; Rev. Agric. Entomol.; Rev. Plant Pathol.; Saf. Health Work.

RU/0024-1113
LESNOE KHOZAJSTVO (MOSKVA). (LESNOE KHOZIAISTVO.). [Lesn. hoz.]. **Added/Corp** Soviet Union. Ministerstvo Lesnogo Khoziaistvo. Gosudarstvennyi Komitet SSSR Po Lesnomu Khoziaistvu. Nauchno-tekhnicheskoe Obshchestvo Lesnoi Promyshlennosti i Lesnogo Khoziaistva. Tsentralnoe Pravlenie. (1948)-. Academic Scholarly Publication. Russian. Six times a year. $89.95. **(Subscription address:** East View Publications Inc., 3020 Harbor Lane North, Suite 110, Minneapolis MN 55447.**)** **CODEN** LKHOAW. Index available. **Bk Rev. Circ:** 31,932. Documents available from CASDDS.
Ind/Abst Abstr. Bull. Inst. Paper Chem.; Abstr. Bull. Inst. Pap. Sci. Tech.; Agric. Eng. Abstr.; Agrofor. Abstr. (19??-19??); Biocont. News Inf. (19??-19??); Chem. Abstr. (-1972); Field Crop Abstr.; For. Prod. Abstr. (19??-19??); For. Abstr.; Hortic. Abstr.; Ornamental Hort. (19??-19??); Plant Grow. Reg. Abstr.; Rev. Plant Pathol.; Seed Abstr.; Soils Fert.

RU/0134-5710
LESOSECHNYE, LESOSKLADSKIE RABOTY I SUKHOPUTNYI TRANSPORT LESA : MEZHVUZOVSKII SBORNIK NAUCHNYKH TRUDOV / LENINGRADSKAIA LESOTEKHNICHESKAIA AKADEMIIA IMENI S.M. KIROVA. [Lesosecnye, lesoskladskie rab. suhoputnyj trans. lesa]. **Added/Corp** Leningradskaia Lesotekhnicheskaia Akademiia Imeni S.M. Kirova. (1972-). Academic Scholarly Publication. Russian. **CODEN** LLRLDF. Documents available from CASDDS.
Ind/Abst Abstr. Bull. Inst. Pap. Sci. Tech.; Chem. Abstr. (1972-1981).

RU/0024-1148
LESOVEDENIE. [Lesovedenie]. **Added/Corp** Akademiia Nauk SSSR. (1967)-. Academic Scholarly Publication. Russian (summaries and/or abstracts in English). Six times a year. $128.00. Izdatelstvo Kniga, 50 Gorky Ulitsa, 125047 Moscow Russia. **(Subscription address:** East View Publications Inc., 3020 Harbor Lane North, Suite 110, Minneapolis MN 55447.**)** **LC** SD1; .L424. **CODEN** LESOAB. Documents available from BIOSIS Document Express, CASDDS.
Ind/Abst Abstr. Bull. Inst. Paper Chem.; Abstr. Bull. Inst. Pap. Sci. Tech.; AGRICOLA; Agrofor. Abstr.; Biol. Abstr.; Chem. Abstr.; Crop Physiol. Abstr.; EMBASE; For. Prod. Abstr.; For. Abstr.; Plant Grow. Reg. Abstr.

UN/0459-1216
LESOVODSTVO I AGROLESOMELIORATSIIA. [Lesovod. agrolesomelior.]. **Added/Corp** Ukraine. Ministerstvo Lisovoho Hospodarstva. Vol. 1 (1965)-. Periodical. Russian. **CODEN** LSVAAE.
Ind/Abst AGRICOLA; Agric. Eng. Abstr.; Agrofor. Abstr. (19??-19??); Field Crop Abstr.; For. Abstr.; Maize Abstr.; Rev. Plant Pathol.; Seed Abstr.; Soils Fert.

RU/0130-9099
LESOVODSTVO, LESNYE KULTURY I POCHVOVEDENIE. [Lesovod. lesn. kul't. pocvoved.]. **Added/Corp** Russian S.F.S.R. Ministerstvo Vysshego i Srednego Spetsialnogo Obrazovaniia. Vol. 1 (1973)-. Russian. 0.70rub (single issue). St Petersburg State University / Izdatelstvo Leningradskogo Universiteta, Universitetskaia Nab 7/9, 199034 St Petersburg Russia. **Tel** 011 95 218-97-88, FAX 011 95 218-51-52, telex 121481. **LC** SD207; .L47.
Ind/Abst Abstr. Bull. Inst. Pap. Sci. Tech.

CC
LIN YEH K'O CHI TNG HSUN. **Added/Corp** Chung-kuo lin yeh ko Hsueh yen Chiu Yuan. K'o chi Ching pao yen Chiu so. **VFOAT** Forestry Technical Newsletter; Linye Keji Tongxun; Forest Science and Technology. (19??)-. Periodical. Chinese. mo. RMBY0.15. Science Press, 16 Donghuangchenggen North Street, Beijing 100707, People's Republic of China. **Tel** 011 86 1 4019821, 011 86 1 4010642, FAX 011 86 1 4012180, 011 86 1 4019810, telex 210147. **LC** SD1; .L56. **DD** 634.9/05.

CH
LIN YEH SHIH YEN SO YEN CHIU PAO KAO. **VFOAT** Bulletin of Taiwan Forestry Research Institute. Periodical. Chinese (summaries and/or abstracts in English). qt. **LC** SD86.5; .L56. **DD** 634.9/0951/249. ***Continues** Shih Yen Pao Kao.*
Ind/Abst Agrofor. Abstr.

CH/1010-5204
LIN YEH SHIH YEN SO YEN CHIU PAO KAO CHI KAN. **Added/Corp** Tai-wan Sheng lin yeh Shih yen so. **VFOAT** Bulletin of the Taiwan Forestry Research Institute. (1986)-. Periodical. Chinese (summaries and/or abstracts in English; table of contents in English). qt. ***Continues** Yen Shiu pao kao chi kan (Tai-wan Sheng lin yeh Shih yen so), 0253-9586.*
Ind/Abst Agrofor. Abstr.; Biodeter. Abstr.; For. Prod. Abstr. (1991-); For. Abstr.; Plant Grow. Reg. Abstr.; Seed Abstr.; Soils Fert.

CC/0253-2417
LINCHAN HUAXUE YU GONGYE. (LIN CHAN HUA HSUEH YU KUNG YEH.). [Linchan huaxue yu gongye]. **Added/Corp** Chung-kuo lin yeh ko Hsueh yen Chiu Yuan. Lin Chan hua Hsueh Kung yeh yen chiu so. **VFOAT** Chemistry and Industry of Forestry Products. (1981)-. Periodical. Chinese (English). qt. Chinese Academy of Forestry, Long Pan Road, Nanjing, People's Republic of China. **LC** WMLC L 83/7290. **CODEN** LHYGD7. Documents available from CASDDS.
Ind/Abst Abstr. Bull. Inst. Pap. Sci. Tech.; AGRICOLA; Agrofor. Abstr.; Chem. Abstr.; For. Prod. Abstr. (1991-); For. Abstr.

CH/1001-9499
LINYE KE-JI. **VFOAT** Forest Science & Technology. (1973)-. Periodical. Chinese. bm. **DD** 634.9.
Ind/Abst Rev. Plant Pathol.

CC/1001-7488
LINYE KEXUE (1979). (LIN YUEH K'O HSUEH.). [Linye kexue]. **Added/Corp** Chung-Kuo Lin Hsueh Hui. **VFOAT** Scientia Silvae Sinicae. Vol. 15, No. 1 (1979)-. Academic Scholarly Publication. Chinese (summaries and/or abstracts in English; table of contents in English). qt. $35.58. **(Subscription address:** China International Book Trading Corporation, PO Box 399, Library Service Department, Beijing 100044 People's Republic of China.**)** **CODEN** LYKSAL. Documents available from CASDDS. ***Continues** Chung-Kuo Lin Yeh K'o Hsueh, 0250-3271.*
Desc: Contains information forestry science.
Ind/Abst AGRICOLA; Agric. Eng. Abstr.; Agrofor. Abstr.; Biocont. News Inf.; Biodeter. Abstr.; Chem. Abstr.; Crop Physiol. Abstr.; For. Prod. Abstr. (1991-); For. Abstr.; Hortic. Abstr.; Irr. Drain. Abstr.; Plant Grow. Reg. Abstr.; Protozoolog. Abstr.; Rev. Agric. Entomol.; Rev. Plant Pathol.; Seed Abstr.; Soils Fert.

CC/1001-1498
LINYE KEXUE YANGJIU. (LIN YEH KO HSUEH YEN CHIU.). [Linye kexue yangjiu]. **Added/Corp** Chung-kuo lin yeh ko Hsueh yen Chiu Yuan. **VFOAT** Forest Research. (1988)-. Periodical. Chinese (summaries and/or abstracts in English). bm. **CODEN** LKYAEB. Documents available from BIOSIS Document Express.
Ind/Abst Biol. Abstr. (1990-); Ecol. Abstr.; For. Prod. Abstr. (1991-); Geogr. Abstr. Human Geogr.

CN/0709-4590
LRIS NEWSLETTER. (LRIS NEWSLETTER / ALBERTA LAND-RELATED INFORMATION SYSTEMS.). [LRIS newsl.]. **Main/Corp** Alberta. Land-Related Information Services Branch. **Added/Corp** Alberta. Alberta Forestry, Lands and Wildlife. Vol. 10, No. 4 (July/Aug. 1989)-. Newsletter. English. Six times a year. Free on request. Land-Related Information Systems Branch, Land Information Services Division, 910/108th Street NW, Edmonton Alberta T5K 2J5 Canada. **Tel** (403)422-1413, FAX 427-0360. **DD** 025.06/3337. ***Continues** Alberta. Land-Related Information Services Group. LRIS Newsletter., 0709-4590.*

US/0076-1109
LSU WOOD UTILIZATION NOTES. [LSU wood util. notes]. **Added/Corp** Louisiana State University (Baton Rouge, La.). School of Forestry. Louisiana State University (Baton Rouge, La.). School of Forestry and Wildlife Management. Louisiana Agricultural Experiment Station. **VAT** Louisiana State University Wood Utilization Notes. No. 1 (Oct. 1960)-. Periodical. English. Louisiana State University / School of Forestry, Wildlife, and Fish, 227 Forestry, Wildlife, and Fish Building, Baton Rouge LA 70803. **Tel** (504)388-4131. **LC** WMLC 90/0221. **DD** 674. Index available. cum. index.
Desc: Technical and scientific reports in relation to wood properties and use.
Ind/Abst Abstr. Bull. Inst. Pap. Sci. Tech.; AGRICOLA [Full Cov.]; For. Prod. Abstr.

FI/0357-5527
MAA- JA METSATALOUS. See Agriculture.

US/0091-4460
MAFES RESEARCH HIGHLIGHTS. See Agriculture.

MY/0302-2935
MALAYSIAN FORESTER, THE. [Malays. for.]. Vol. 36 No. 1 (Jan. 1973)-. English. Four times a year. Maylaysian Forester for Department Headquarters, Jalan Sultan Salahuddin, 50660 Kuala Lumpur Malaysia. **LC** SD1; .M33. **DD** 634.9/09595. ***Continues** Malayan Forester.*
Ind/Abst Abstr. Bull. Inst. Pap. Sci. Tech.; Agrofor. Abstr. (19??-19??); Biodeter. Abstr. (1991-); Crop Physiol. Abstr.; EMBASE; For. Prod. Abstr. (19??-19??); For. Abstr.; Life Sci. Collect.; Plant Grow. Reg. Abstr.; Rev. Agric. Entomol.; Wildl. Rev.

CL/0581-6386
MANUAL - INSTITUTO FORESTAL, CHILE. **Main/Corp** Santiago de Chile. Instituto Forestal. (1963)-. Monographic series. Spanish.
Ind/Abst For. Prod. Abstr. (1991-).

CN/1185-9075
MANUEL D'EXPLOITATION FORESTIERE DES TERRES DE LA COURONNE. [Man. exploit. for. terres Couronne]. **Added/Corp** Nouveau-Brunswick. Ministere des Ressources naturelles et de l'energie. (April 1991)-. French. te. **DD** 346.715/104675/05.

IT/0390-6736
MB : MONTI E BOSCHI. **VFOAT** Monti d Boschi. Vol. 33, No. 1/2 (Jan./Apr. 1982)-. Periodical. Italian (summaries and/or abstracts in English). bm. L62000. Edagricole, PO Box 2157, 40100 Bologna Italy. **Tel** 011 39 51 492211 Ext. 22, FAX 011 39 51 493660, telex 510336 EDAGRI. **LC** SD201; .M58. **DD** 634.9/0945. ***Continues** Montanaro d'Italia, Monti e Boschi, 0390-6736.*
Ind/Abst Agrofor. Abstr. (1991-); For. Prod. Abstr. (1991-); For. Abstr.; Plant Genet. Resour. Abstr.; Rev. Agric. Entomol.; Rev. Plant Pathol.; Seed Abstr.

SW/0532-2499
MEDDELANDE / FORSKNINGSSTIFTELSEN SKOGSARBETEN. **Added/Corp** Forskningsstiftelsen Skogsarbeten. No. 1 (1964)-. Monographic series. Swedish (English; table of contents in English and Swedish). ir. Price varies per volume. Forskningstiftelsen Skogsforsk Glunten, S 751 83 Uppsala Sweden. **Tel** 011 46 18 188500.
Desc: Information on timber, logging, and forestry.

NO/0803-2866
MEDDELELSER FRA SKOGFORSK / NORSK INSTITUTT FOR SKOGFORSKNING, INSTITUTT FOR SKOGFAG, NLH. **Added/Corp** Norsk Institutt for Skogforskning. Norges Landbrukshgskole. Institutt for Skogfag. **VFOAT** Communications of Skogforsk;

Forestry

Skogsfork. (1991)-. Monographic series. English (Norwegian). **Continues** Meddelelser fra Norsk Institutt for Skogforskning, 0332-5709.

US
MEMBER NEWSLETTER - FOREST PRODUCTS RESEARCH SOCIETY.
Main/Corp Forest Products Research Society. **VFOAT** FPRS Newsletter. - . Periodical. English. qt. $52.00 (non-members) $20.00 (members) US; $56.00 (non-members) $22.00 (members) Canada and Mexico; $64.00 (non-members), $24.00 (members) other;. Forest Products Society, 2801 Marshall Court, Madison WI 53705-2295. **Tel** (608)231-1361, FAX (608)231-2152.

US
MEMBERSHIP DIRECTORY - FOREST HISTORY SOCIETY.
Main/Corp Forest History Society. (Summer 1975)-. Directory. English.

FI
METSAHALLITUKSEN VUOSIKERTOMUS.
Title Change. Main/Corp Finland. Metsahallitus. **VFOAT** Forststyrelsens Arsberattelse; Annual Report of the National Board of Forestry; Vuosikertomus. (1987)-. Finnish (summaries and/or abstracts in English and Swedish). an. Metsahallitus, H 94, H Fin-01301 Vantaa Finland. **Tel** 358 0 857841, FAX 358 0 85784200. **ED** Sirbba Nurmi. **LC** SD83.F5; M38a. Index available. **Circ:** 5,000 (ctrl). **Continues** Metsahallituksen Toimintakertomus.

ER/0135-2466
METSANDUSLIKUD UURIMUSED.
Added/Corp Zoologia ja Botaanika Instituut (Eesti NSV Teaduste Akadeemia) Metsanduse Teadusliku Uurimise Laboratoorium. Eesti Metsamajanduse ja Looduskaitse Teadusliku Uurimise Instituut. **VFOAT** Lesovodcheskie Issledovaniia; Lesovodstvennye Issledovaniia. (1957)-. Monographic series. Estonian (Russian; summaries and/or abstracts in English and German). **LC** SD217.E8; M4. **CODEN** MUURAH.
Ind/Abst For. Abstr.

FI/0358-4283
METSANTUTKIMUSLAITOKSEN TIEDONONTOJA. Added/Corp
Metsantutkimuslaitos. (19??)-. Periodical. Finnish.
Ind/Abst For. Prod. Abstr. (1991-); For. Abstr.; Rev. Plant Pathol.

FI/0356-7257
METSATEHON TIEDOTUS. [Metsatehon tied.].
VFOAT Metsateho Report. (1945)-. Monographic series. Multiple languages. ir. Price varies per volume. Suomen Metsateollisuuden Keskusliitto ry Metsatyontutkimusosasto (METSATHEHO), PL 194 (Fabianinkatu 9B), 00131 Helsinki 13, Finland. **UDC** 630.
Ind/Abst Agric. Eng. Abstr. (1991-); For. Prod. Abstr. (1991-); For. Abstr.

US
MICHIGAN FORESTS.
English. Four times a year. $25.00. Michigan Forest Association, 1558 Barrington, Ann Arbor MI 48103. **Tel** (313)665-8279. **ED** Don Ingle (editor's address: PO Box 78, Baldwin MI 49304).

JA/0493-4326
MISCELLANEOUS INFORMATION, THE TOKYO UNIVERSITY FORESTS. Main/Corp
Tokyo Daigaku. Nogakubu. Experimental Forest. Periodical. English. Tokyo Daigaku Nogakubu Fuzoku Enshurin, (Tokyo University Forests), 1-1, Yayoi 1 Chome, Bunkyoku, Tokyoto 113, Japan.
Ind/Abst For. Abstr.; Irr. Drain. Abstr.

CN/0832-7130
MISCELLANEOUS REPORT - GREAT LAKES FORESTRY CENTRE.
(MISCELLANEOUS REPORT.). [Misc. rep. - Gt. Lakes For. Cent.]. (1985)-. Monographic series. English. ir. Great Lakes Forest Research Centre, Canadian Forestry Service, PO Box 490, 1189 Queen Street East/Sault Ste, Marie Ontario P6A 5M7 Canada. **DD** 634.909713. **Continues** Miscellaneous Report - Great Lakes Forest Research Centre, 0826-0222.

US
MISCELLANEOUS REPORT - U. S. LAKE STATES FOREST EXPERIMENT STATION, ST. PAUL. Main/Corp
United States. Lake States Forest Experiment Station. English. Minnesota Department of Agriculture, 90 Plato Boulevard West, St Paul MN 55107. **Tel** (612)297-3219, FAX (612)297-5522. **LC** SD11; .A455455. **DD** 634.9072.

US/0739-893X
MISSOURI FOREST PEST REPORT. [Mo. forest pest rep.].
Began with Vol. for 1978. English. an. Missouri Department of Conservation, 2901 North Ten Mile Drive, Jefferson City MO 65101. **LC** SB763.M8; M57A. **DD** 632/.7/09778. **Continues** Forest Pest Activity in Missouri, 0161-4495.

GW/0067-5849
MITTEILUNGEN AUS DER BIOLOGISCHEN BUNDESANSTALT FUER LAND- UND FORSTWIRTSCHAFT, BERLIN- DAHLEM.
[Mitt. Biol. Bundesanst. Land-Forstwirtsch.]. No. 80 (1954)-. Monographic series. German (English). ir. Price varies per volume. Paul Parey (Berlin), Seelbuschring 9-17, 1000 Berlin 42 Germany. **Tel** 030-70784-00. **LC** S231; .A4. **CODEN** MBBLA9. Documents available from BIOSIS Document Express. **Continues** Mitteilungen aus der Biologischen Zentralanstalt fur Land-und Fortswirtschaft, Berlin-Dahlem.
Ind/Abst Biocont. News Inf.; Biodeter. Abstr.; Biol. Abstr.; Food Sci. Technol. Abstr.; For. Abstr.; Nematol. Abstr.; PESTDOC; Plant Breed. Abstr.; Postharvest News Inf.; Rev. Med. Vet. Entomol.; Rev. Plant Pathol.; Soils Fert.; Soyabean Abstr.; Weed Abstr.; Wheat Barley Trit. Abstr.

GW/0368-8798
MITTEILUNGEN DER BUNDESFORSCHUNGSANSTALT FUER FORST- UND HOLZWIRTSCHAFT REINBEK BEI HAMBURG.
(MITTEILUNGEN DER BUNDESFORSCHUNGSANSTALT FUER FORST- UND HOLZWIRTSCHAFT.). [Mitt. Bundesforschungsanst. Forst- Holzwirtsch. Reinbek Hambg.]. **Main/Corp** Bundesforschungsanstalt fur Forst- und Holzwirtschaft (Germany). Vol. 1-. Monographic series. German. Price varies per volume. **LC** SD1; .R33. **Continues** Mitteilungen der Bundesanstalt fur Forst- und Holzwirtschaft.
Ind/Abst Abstr. Bull. Inst. Pap. Sci. Tech.; AGRICOLA; For. Prod. Abstr.; For. Abstr.; Life Sci. Collect.; Rev. Plant Pathol.; Soils Fert.

SZ/1016-3158
MITTEILUNGEN DER EIDGENOSSISCHEN FORSCHUNGSANSTALT FUER WALD, SCHNEE UND LANDSCHAFT. Added/Corp
Eidgenossische Forschungsanstalt fur Wald, Schnee und Landschaft. **VFOAT** Mitteilungen; Mitt. Eidgenoss. Forsch.anst. Wald Schnee Landsch.; Mitteilungen WSL. Bd. 56, Heft 1 (1991)-. Monographic series. French (German and Italian; summaries and/or abstracts in English). **CODEN** MEFLEK. **Continues** Mitteilungen (Schweizerische Anstalt fur das Forstliche Versuchswesen), 0251-4133.
Desc: Speaks of forests and forestry, the protection of landscape, and the impact of snow.

AU/0374-9037
MITTEILUNGEN DER FORSTLICHEN BUNDES-VERSUCHSANSTALT WIEN.
[Mittl. Forstl. Bundes- Versuchsanst. Wien.]. **Added/Corp** Forstliche Bundes-Versuchsanstalt Wien. **VFOAT** Mitteilungen der Forstlichen Bundesverschsanstalt Wien. (1967)-. Academic Scholarly Publication. German (English and French; summaries and/or abstracts in Russian). Price varies per volume. **CODEN** MFBWA2. Documents available from CASDDS. **Continues** Mitteilungen der Forstlichen Bundes-Versuchsanstalt Mariabrunn, 0374-9029.
Ind/Abst Chem. Abstr.

GW/0178-3165
MITTEILUNGEN DER FORSTLICHEN VERSUCHS- UND FORSCHUNGSANSTALT BADEN-WRTTEMBERG.
(MITTEILUNGEN DER FORSTLICHEN VERSUCHS UND FORSCHUNGSANSTALT.). [Mitt. Forstl. Vers.-Forsch.anst. Baden-Wrtt.]. **Added/Corp** Forstlichen Versuchs- und Forschungsanstalt Baden-Wurrttemberg. (1973)-. Monographic series. German. ir. Price varies per volume. Forstliche Versuchs und Forschungsanstalt, Postfach 708, W-7800 Freiburg F R Germany. **Tel** 011 49 761 40180.
Ind/Abst For. Prod. Abstr. (1991-); For. Abstr.

GW/0171-2446
MITTEILUNGEN DER VERSUCHSANSTALT FUER PILZANBAU DER LANDWIRTSCHAFTSKAMMER RHEINLAND, KREFELD-GROSSHUTTENHOF.
[Mitt. Versuchsanst. Pilzanbau Landwirtschaftskam. Rheinl. Krefeld-Grosshuttenhof]. **Added/Corp** Landwirtschaftskammer Rheinland. Versuchsanstalt fur Pilzanbau. Gemeinschaft der Freunde und Forderer der Versuchsanstalt fur Pilzanbau der Landwirtschaftskammer Rheinland. (1977)-. German (summaries and/or abstracts in English).
Ind/Abst For. Prod. Abstr. (1991-); Rev. Plant Pathol.; Soils Fert.

GW/0506-7049
MITTEILUNGEN DES VEREINS FUER FORSTLICHE STANDORTSKUNDE UND FORSTPFLANZENZUCHTUNG.
[Mitt. Ver. Forstl. Standortsk. Forstpflanzenzucht.]. (1957)-. Periodical. German. an. Verlag Eugen Ulmer, Postfach 700561, D 70574 Stuttgart Germany. **Tel** 011 49 711 4507108, FAX 011 49 711 4507120, telex 7-23634.
Ind/Abst For. Prod. Abstr. (1991-); For. Abstr.; Plant Breed. Abstr.

IT
MONTANARO D'ITALIA (TORINO, ITALY).
(IL MONTANARO D'ITALIA.). Periodical. Italian. mo. Edagricole, PO Box 2157, 40100 Bologna Italy. **Tel** 011 39 51 492211 Ext. 22, FAX 011 39 51 493660, telex 510336 EDAGRI. **Continues** Montanaro d'Italia, Monti e Boschi, 0390-6736.

US
MONTHLY ALERT / INFOSOUTH.
Added/Corp INFOSouth (Organization). Vol. 8, No. 10 (Aug. 1988)-. Periodical. English. mo. $50.00. USDA INFOSouth, University of Georgia, Science Library, Room 496, Athens GA 30602. **Tel** (404)546-2477, FAX (404)546-2465. **Circ:** 400. **Continues** Southern Forestry Information Network (U.S.). Monthly Alert.
Desc: A current awareness bibliography focusing on forestry and related topics in the Southeastern United States.

JA
MORI.
VFOAT Kikan Mori. Periodical. Japanese (Japanese). ¥350. Rinya Kosaikai, 7-12 Koraku 1, Bunkyo-ku 112, Tokyo Japan. **LC** SD225; .M58.

AT/0818-8238
MULGA RESEARCH CENTRE JOURNAL.
See Aeronautics, Astronautics-Abstracting, Bibliographies and Statistics.

II
MYFOREST.
Periodical. English. **LC** SD88.M7; A25. **DD** 634.9/0954/87.
Ind/Abst AgBiotech News Inf.; Agrofor. Abstr.; Biocont. News Inf.; Biodeter. Abstr.; Crop Physiol. Abstr.; Ecol. Abstr.; For. Prod. Abstr.; Geogr. Abstr. Phys. Geogr.; Geogr. Abstr. Human Geogr.; Int. Dev. Abstr.; Nematol. Abstr.; Ornamental Hort.; Plant Grow. Reg. Abstr.

CN/0705-4831
N. S. TRAPPER'S NEWSLETTER. No. 13
(Oct. 1977)-. Newsletter. English. an. Free. Department of Land & Forest, Box 68, Truro Nova Scotia B2N 5B8 Canada. **Tel** (902)424-5444. **Continues** Trapper's Newsletter, 0705-484X.

CC/1000-2006
NANJING LINYE DAXUE XUEBAO.
(NAN-CHING LIN YEH TA HSUEH HSUEH PAO.). [Nanjing linye daxue xuebao]. **Added/Corp** Nan-ching lin yeh ta Hsueh. **VFOAT** Journal of Nanjing Forestry University. (1986)-. Periodical. Chinese (summaries and/or abstracts in English). qt. **CODEN** NLDXE4. Documents available from CASDDS. **Continues** Nan-Ching lin Hsueh Yuan Hsueh pao.
Ind/Abst Agric. Eng. Abstr.; Agrofor. Abstr.; Biocont. News Inf.; Biodeter. Abstr.; Chem. Abstr. (1986-); For. Prod. Abstr. (1991-); For. Abstr.; Rev. Agric. Entomol.; Rev. Plant Pathol.; Seed Abstr.

US
NATIONAL FORESTS FIRE REPORT.
1969-. Government Publication. English. an. US Department of Agriculture / Forest Service, 201 14th Street SW, Washington DC 20250. **Tel** (202)205-1661, FAX (202)205-1181. **ED** John W Chambers. **Circ:** 4,000. available on microfiche (Vols. for (1981-) distributed to depository libraries). **Continues** Annual Fire Report for the National Forests.
Desc: Report of wildfire statistics on national forest lands.

US/0279-9812
NATIONAL WOODLANDS. [Natl. woodl.].
Added/Corp National Woodland Owners Association. Vol. 1, No. 10 (July 1979)-. Periodical. English. Six times a year (Feb., Mar., May, June, Aug., Sept., Nov., Dec.). $15.00 (one year), $17.00 (two year), US; $28.00 (one year), $32.00 (two year), Canada. National Woodlands Owners Association, 374 Maple Avenue, Suite 210, Vienna VA 22180. **Tel** (703)255-2700. **ED** Eric Johnson (phone: (315)369-3078). **LC** WMLC 93/1913. **Bk Rev**. **Ad Acc**. **Circ:** 5,000. **Continues** National Woodlands Magazine.
Desc: Emphasizes the stewardship of the woodland resources. Provides useful information on management, ecology, tax issues, wood energy and legislative matters.
Ind/Abst Abstr. Bull. Inst. Pap. Sci. Tech.

RU/0540-9691
NAUCHNYE TRUDY / MOSKOVSKII LESOTEKHNICHESKII INSTITUT.
[Naucn. tr. - Moskovskij lesoteh. inst.]. **Added/Corp** Moskovskii Lesotekhnicheskii Institut. (1950)-. Academic Scholarly Publication. Russian. Price varies per volume. **LC** SD388; .M572. **CODEN** NTMLAV. Documents available from CASDDS.
Ind/Abst Chem. Abstr.; For. Prod. Abstr. (1991-); For. Abstr.; Math. Rev.

BU/0861-007X
NAUKA ZA GORATA.
(NAUKA ZA GORATA / FOREST SCIENCE / BULGARSKA AKADEMIIA NA

NAUKITE.). [Nauka gorata]. **Added/Corp** Bulgarska Akademiia na Naukite. **VFOAT** Forest Science. (1988)-. Academic Scholarly Publication. Bulgarian (summaries and/or abstracts in English and Russian; table of contents in English and Russian). qt. 1.22lv (single issue). Bulgarska Akademiia na Naukite, 7 Noemvri 1, Sofia Bulgaria. **CODEN** NAGOEH. ***Continues*** *Gorskostopanska Nauka, 0017-2286.*
Ind/Abst Agric. Eng. Abstr.; Biocont. News Inf.; Biodeter. Abstr.; Crop Physiol. Abstr.; For. Prod. Abstr. (1991-); For. Abstr.; Plant Breed. Abstr.; Rev. Agric. Entomol.; Rev. Plant Pathol.; Seed Abstr.; Soils Fert.

NE/0369-3651
NEDERLANDS BOSBOUW TIJDSCHRIFT. [Ned. bosbouw tijdschr.]. **Added/Corp** Koninklijke Nederlandsche Bosbouw Vereniging. **VFOAT** Bosbouw, Nederlands Bosbouw Tijdschrift. Vol. 1 (1928)-. Periodical. Dutch (summaries and/or abstracts in English). Eleven times a year. Nederlands Bosbouw, BP 23, Wageningen The Netherlands. **Tel** 05370-95111. **ED** H.M. Heybroek. Index available. **Bk Rev. Ad Acc.** ctrl circ.
Ind/Abst AGRICOLA; Biocont. News Inf.; EMBASE; For. Prod. Abstr.; Plant Breed. Abstr.

CC
NEI MENG-KU LIN YEH. **VFOAT** Neimenggu Linye. Periodical. Chinese. mo. RMBY0.50. Post Office, Hu-Ho-Hao-T E Shih, People's Republic of China. **LC** SD222.I55; N44. **DD** 634.9/0951/77.

JA/0910-5115
NETTAI RINGYO 1984. [Nettai ringyo 1984]. **VFOAT** Tropical Forestry (Tokyo. 1984). (1984)-. Periodical. Multiple languages. tq. Kaigai Ringyo Konsarutantsu Kyokai, (Japan Overseas Forestry Consultants Assocd.), 7, Rokubancho, Chiyodaku, Tokyoto 102 Japan. **DD** 634.9. ***Continues*** *Nettai Ringyo, 0386-2674.*

JA
NETTAI RINGYO KANKEI BUNKEN BUNRUI MOKUROKU. No. 1- ; 1976-. Japanese (English). Rinyacho Ringyo Shikenjo, (Forestry & Forest Products Research Inst., Forestry Agency), 1, Matsunosato, Kukizakimachi, Inashikigun, Ibarakiken 305, Japan. **LC** Z5991; .N34; SD247.

●UK/0968-2627
NETWORK PAPER / ODI, RURAL DEVELOPMENT FORESTRY NETWORK. [Netw. pap. - Soc. For. Netw.]. **Added/Corp** Rural Development Forestry Network (Overseas Development Institute). (1992)-. Monographic series. English (summaries and/or abstracts in French and Spanish). ir. Price varies per volume. **LC** SD387.S55; N4. ***Continues*** *Network Paper (Social Forestry Network (Overseas Development Institute)), 0951-1857.*
Ind/Abst Agrofor. Abstr. (?-?); For. Abstr. (?-?).

NE/0169-4286
NEW FORESTS. [New for.]. Vol. 1, No. 1 (1986)-. Periodical. English. bm. $536.00. Kluwer Academic Publishers, Postbus 322, 3300 AH Dordrecht, The Netherlands. **Tel** 011 (31) 78 524400, FAX 011 31 78 183273, telex 20083. **ED** Mary L. Duryea. **LC** SD409; .N49. **DD** 634.9/56/05. **CODEN** NEFOE6. **[CCC]. Pr Rev. Acid Free.** available on microfilm and microfiche from University Microfilms International (UMI). Documents available from BIOSIS Document Express.
Desc: Publishes papers dealing with fundamental and applied aspects of afforestation and reforestation for an audience comprising forest scientists, foresters, nursery managers, conservationists, and stuudents in temperate and tropical countries. Emphasis is placed on papers presenting the results of original research or the development of a theory or technique, although occasional reviews on important topics are also carried. The papers published focus on such subjects as the physiology, genetics, ecology, economics, protection, and management of the six stages of afforestation and reforestation; propagation methods (sexual and asexual); nursery cultural practices; handling, planting and stock quality; matching stock types, species and seed source to sites; site preparation; early stand growth and development.
Ind/Abst Abstr. Bull. Inst. Pap. Sci. Tech.; AGRICOLA [Full Cov.]; Agrofor. Abstr. (1991-); Bibliogr. Agric.; Biol. Abstr. (1991-); Curr. Aware. Biol. Sci., CABS; Ecol. Abstr.; For. Prod. Abstr. (1991-); For. Abstr.; Geogr. Abstr. Phys. Geogr.; Geogr. Abstr. Human Geogr.; Int. Dev. Abstr.; Irr. Drain. Abstr.; Plant Breed. Abstr.; Seed Abstr.; Soils Fert.; Weed Abstr.

US/0094-2782
NEW MEXICO FOREST PRODUCTS DIRECTORY. ***Title Change.*** [N. M. for. prod. dir.]. Directory. English. New Mexico Department of State Forestry & Resources Conservation Division, PO Box 1948, Santa Fe NM 87504-1948. **Tel** (505)827-5830, FAX (505)827-3903. **LC** HD9757.N65; N49A. **DD** 338.1/7/498025789. ***Continued by*** *Wood Industries of New Mexico.*

NZ/0113-3128
NEW ZEALAND FOREST INDUSTRIES. **See** Forestry-Lumber and Wood.

NZ/0112-9597
NEW ZEALAND FORESTRY. (NEW ZEALAND FORESTRY : JOURNAL OF THE N.Z. INSTITUTE OF FORESTERS INC.). [N. Z. for]. **Added/Corp** N.Z. Institute of Foresters. **VFOAT** NZ Forestry; N.Z. Forestry. Vol. 31, No. 1 (May 1986)-. Academic Scholarly Publication. English. qt (Apr., July, Oct., Dec.). 38.00NZ$ (individuals), 60.00NZ$ (institutions) New Zealand; 53.00NZ$ (individuals), 75.00NZ$ (institutions) other. New Zealand Institute of Forestry, PO Box 19-840, Christchurch 8002 New Zealand. **Tel** 011-64-3-842432. **ED** D J Mead. **LC** SD1; .N543. **DD** 338.1/749/09931. **CODEN** NZFOEH. **[CCC].** Index available. **Bk Rev. Ad Acc. Circ:** 1,350 (ctrl). Documents available from BIOSIS Document Express, CASDDS. ***Continues*** *New Zealand Journal of Forestry, 0028-8284.*
Desc: Publishes articles on forestry philosophy, policy, science, technology and practice as well as information and comment on current events and changes in New Zealand forestry.
Ind/Abst Abstr. Bull. Inst. Pap. Sci. Tech.; AGRICOLA; Biol. Abstr. (1986-); Chem. Abstr.; Fish Rev. (Jan. 1989-July 1992); For. Prod. Abstr. (19??-19??); For. Abstr.; Life Sci. Collect.; Plant Breed. Abstr.; Seed Abstr.; Wildl. Rev. (Jan. 1989-July 1992).

NZ/0048-0134
NEW ZEALAND JOURNAL OF FORESTRY SCIENCE. [N. Z. j. for. sci.]. **Added/Corp** Forest Research Institute (N.Z.) New Zealand Forest Service. Vol. 1 (May 1971)-. Periodical. English. Three times a year (June, Oct., Dec.). 100.00NZ$ (institutions), 50.00NZ$ (individuals). Forest Research Institute, Private Bag 3020, Rotorua, New Zealand. **Tel** 011 64 73 475899, FAX 011 64 73 479380, telex 21080. **ED** J.A. Griffith. **LC** SD111.N7; A27. **DD** 634.9/09931. **CODEN** NZFSAP. **[CCC].** Index available. **Bk Rev. Pr Rev. Circ:** 550. Documents available from BIOSIS Document Express, CASDDS, Documents on Demand.
Desc: Concerned with production forestry, protection forestry, watershed rehabilitation, pathology, entomology, wood quality and processing, timber engineering, and composite wood products.
Ind/Abst Abstr. Bull. Inst. Pap. Sci. Tech.; AGRICOLA; Agrofor. Abstr. (1991-); Biocont. News Inf. (1991-); Biol. Abstr.; Chem. Abstr.; Ecol. Abstr.; Energy Inf. Abstr.; Environ. Abstr.; For. Prod. Abstr. (1991-); For. Abstr.; Geogr. Abstr. Phys. Geogr. (?-?); Geogr. Abstr. Human Geogr.; Grasslands For. Abstr.; Int. Dev. Abstr.; Key Word Index Wildl. Res.; Life Sci. Collect.; Plant Breed. Abstr.; Rev. Agric. Entomol.; Rev. Plant Pathol.; Seed Abstr.; Soils Fert.; Vitis Vitic. Enol. Abstr.; Weed Abstr.; Wildl. Rev.

NZ/0111-2694
NEW ZEALAND TREE GROWER. [N.Z. tree grow.]. **VFOAT** Tree Grower; N.Z. Tree Grower. (1980)-. Periodical. English. Four times a year (Feb., May, Aug., Nov.). 45.00NZ$. NZ Farm Forestry Association, PO Box 715, Wellington 1 New Zealand. **Tel** 011 64 4 737269. **DD** 634.9. ***Continues*** *Farm Forestry, 0428-0113.*
Ind/Abst Agrofor. Abstr.; Biocont. News Inf.; For. Abstr.; Plant Breed. Abstr.

CN/0834-2008
NEWSLETTER / ONTARIO FORESTRY ASSOCIATION. ***Title Change.*** [Newsl. - Ont. For. Assoc.]. **Added/Corp** Ontario Forestry Association. (197?)-(19??). Newsletter. English. Four times a year. Ontario Forestry Association, 150 Consumers Road, Suite 209, Willowdale ONT M2J 1P9 Canada. **Tel** (416)493-4565, FAX (416)493-4608. **ED** Jim Coats. **DD** 634.9/09713. **Bk Rev**, (Qty: varies). **Ad Acc, Adv Mgr:** J.D.C., **Tel** (416)493-4565. **Circ:** 700 (ctrl). ***Continued by*** *Forest People.*
Desc: A non-profit, non-political educational organization dedicated to the care and wise use of forests and related resources.

US
NFT HIGHLIGHTS. **Added/Corp** Nitrogen Fixing Tree Association. **VAT** Nitrogen Fixing Tree Highlights. (1982)-. Periodical. English.
Ind/Abst Agrofor. Abstr.; Field Crop Abstr.; For. Prod. Abstr. (1991-); For. Abstr.; Grasslands For. Abstr.; Rev. Agric. Entomol.; Soils Fert.; Weed Abstr.

NR/0331-0353
NIGERIA FORESTRY INFORMATION BULLETIN. Bulletin. English. Price varies per volume. Nigeria Federal Department of Forestry, Ibadan Nigeria. **LC** SD103.N6; A318. **DD** 634.9/09669.

NR/0374-9584
NIGERIAN JOURNAL OF FORESTRY. (1971)-. Periodical. English. sa (published Jan. and July). $25.00. Forestry Association of Nigeria, Box 4185, Ibadan Nigeria. **ED** J. A. Okojie. **Ad Acc. Circ:** 500.
Desc: Survey evaluation of problems and trends in forest management or forest industries. Research reports on new findings, techniques, and equipment.

JA/0021-485X
NIHON RINGAKKAI SHI. (NIHON RINGAKKAI SHI. JOURNAL OF THE JAPANESE FORESTRY SOCIETY.). [Nihon Ringakkai shi]. **Main/Corp** Nihon Ringakkat. **Added/Corp** Japanese Forestry Society. Journal. **VFOAT** Journal of the Japanese Forestry Society. No. 1-38 (1919-1926); Vol. 9 (1927)-. Periodical. Japanese (English; summaries and/or abstracts in English, French and German). mo. $178.00. Nihon Ringakkai, (Japanese Forestry Society), Nihon Ringyo Gijutsu Kyokai, Kaikan, 7, Rokubancho, Chiyodaku, Tokyoto 102, Japan. **(Subscription address:** Kyowa Book Company Inc., 1 38 Kanda Jinbocho Chiyoda-ku, Tokyo 101 Japan.**) LC** SD1; .N56. **CODEN** NIRKAA.
Ind/Abst AGRICOLA; Agric. Eng. Abstr.; Agrofor. Abstr.; Biocont. News Inf.; Crop Physiol. Abstr.; Fish Rev. (19??-199?); For. Prod. Abstr. (1991-); For. Abstr.; Nematol. Abstr.; Life Sci. Collect.; Plant Breed. Abstr.; Plant Genet. Resour. Abstr.; Plant Grow. Reg. Abstr.; Rev. Agric. Entomol.; Rev. Plant Pathol.; Seed Abstr.; Soils Fert.; Sug. Indus. Abstr.; Weed Abstr.; Wildl. Rev. (19??-199?); World Agric. Econ.

JA/0549-4818
NIIGATA DAIGAKU NOGAKUBU ENSHURIN HOKOKU. [Niigata Daigaku Nogakubu Enshurin hokoku]. **Added/Corp** Niigata Daigaku. Nogakubu. Fuzoku Enshurin. **VFOAT** Bulletin of the Niigata University Forests. (1962)-. Japanese. an. Niigata Daigaku Nogakubu Fuzoku Enshurin, (Niigata University Forests), 8050, Igarashi Ninocho, Niigatashi, Niigataken 950-21, Japan. **CODEN** NDNHAE. Documents available from CASDDS.
Ind/Abst Chem. Abstr.; For. Prod. Abstr. (1991-); Soils Fert.

CH/1002-204X
NINGXIA NONG-LIN KE-JI. **See** Agriculture.

TH
NITROGEN FIXING TREE RESEARCH REPORTS : A PUBLICATION OF THE NITROGEN FIXING TREE ASSOCIATION (NFTA). **Added/Corp** Nitrogen Fixing Tree Association. Sathaban Wichai Witthayasat ThÂeknoloyi Hng Prathet Thai. **VFOAT** NFTRR. Vol. 1 (Mar. 1983)-. Periodical. English. an. comes with membership. Nitrogen Fixing Tree Association, Route 3 Box 376, Morrilton AR 72110. **Tel** (501)727-5435. **ED** Dale Withington and James Brewbaker. **Bk Rev. Circ:** 1,300.
Desc: Contains reports on research and development activities using nitrogen fixing trees for fuelwood, fodder, fertilizer and other products and services.
Ind/Abst AGRICOLA [Full Cov.]; Irr. Drain. Abstr.; Maize Abstr.; Rev. Agric. Entomol.; Seed Abstr.; Soils Fert.; Wheat Barley Trit. Abstr.

CN/1188-4444
NOEUD (CHARLESBOURG). (LE NOEUD : LA REVUE INFORMATIQUE DU MINISTERE DES FORETS.). [Noeud]. **Added/Corp** Quebec (Province). Ministere des Forets. Vol. 1, No 1 (Nov. 1991)-. Periodical. French. qt. **DD** 004.

CH/0550-3744
NONG-LIN XUE BAO. **See** Agriculture.

KO
NONGNIM NONJIP. **See** Agriculture.

NO
NORDEN; NORD-NORGES LANDBRUKSTIDSSKRIFT. **See** Agriculture.

JA
NORIN-SUISANGYO SEISAN SHISU. **Main/Corp** Japan. Norin Suisansho. Keizaikyoku. Tokei Johobu. Periodical. Japanese. an. Norin Tokei Kyokai, (Association of Agriculture & Forestry Statistics), 11-14, Meguro 2 Chome, Meguroku, Tokyoto 153, Japan. **LC** HD2091; .N65J. ***Continues*** *Norin-Suisangyo Seisan Shisu.*

NO/0029-2087
NORSK SKOGBRUK. [Nor. skogbr.]. **VFOAT** Norwegian Forestry. Began in 1955. Periodical. Norwegian. mo. Kr320.00 Norway; Kr420.00 other. Norsk Skogselskap, Wegelandsvn 23B, 0167 Oslo 1 Norway. **Tel** (02)466940, FAX (02)604189. **ED** Johs Bjorndal. **LC** SD203; .N67. Index available. cum. index. **Bk Rev. Ad Acc. Circ:** 5,900 (ctrl). ***Continues*** *Skogbrukeren, 0801-1743;* ***Absorbed*** *Skogen, 0333-4937.*
Desc: Articles, reports, interviews, research, results and abstracts, official policies, etc. for foresters on a professional level.

US/0742-6348
NORTHERN JOURNAL OF APPLIED FORESTRY. [Northern j. appl. for.]. **Added/Corp** Society of American Foresters. **VFOAT** Northern Forestry. Vol. 1, No. 1 (April 1984)-. Periodical. English. qt (March, June, Sept. and Dec.). $85.00 (institutions), $40.00 (non-member individuals) US and Canada; $120.00 (institutions), $60.00 (non-member individuals) other. Society of American Foresters, 5400 Grosvenor Lane, Bethesda MD 20814-2198. **Tel** (301)897-8720, FAX (301)897-3690, telex 9102501089 SAFFOREST UQ. **ED** Harry V. Wiant. **LC** SD144.A127; N67. **DD** 634.9/0974. **CODEN** NJAFEN. **Bk Rev. Ad Acc. Circ:** 1,000. available on microfilm from University Microfilms International (UMI). Documents available from BIOSIS Document Express, Documents on Demand.

Desc: New ideas and research for practical application by practicing foresters, landowners and resource managers in the Northern US and Canada.
Ind/Abst Abstr. Bull. Inst. Pap. Sci. Tech.; AGRICOLA [Full Cov.]; Agrofor. Abstr.; Biocont. News Inf.; Biol. Abstr.; Ecol. Abstr.; Environ. Abstr.; Fish Rev.; For. Prod. Abstr.; For. Abstr.; Geogr. Abstr. Phys. Geogr.; Geogr. Abstr. Human Geogr.; Plant Breed. Abstr.; Plant Grow. Reg. Abstr.; Rev. Agric. Entomol.; Rev. Plant Pathol.; Seed Abstr.; Soils Fert.; Weed Abstr.; Wildl. Rev.

CN/0712-0680
NOTE - SERVICE DE LA RECHERCHE FORESTIERE. (NOTE.). [Note - Serv. rech. for.]. **VAT** Note - Gouvernement du Quebec, Ministere de l'Energie et des Ressources, Service de la Recherche Forestiere. Periodical. French. Publication du Quebec, CP1005, Quebec Quebec G1K 7B5 Canada. **Tel** (418)643-5150, (800)463-2100. **DD** 634.9/07/20714. ***Continues*** *Note (Quebec (Province) Direction Generale des Forets. Service de la Recherche), 0712-0672.*

CN
NOTE TECHNIQUE - LE FONDS DE RECHERCHES FORESTIERES DE L'UNIVERSITE LAVAL. **Main/Corp** Laval University. Forest Research Foundation. No. 2 (Jan. 1976)-. Monographic series. French. ir. Price varies per volume. Universite Laval / Foresterie, Faculte Foresterie Geodesie, Quebec Canada.

CN/0832-8293
NOVA SCOTIA CHRISTMAS TREE JOURNAL. [N.S. Christmas tree j.]. **Added/Corp** Christmas Tree Council of Nova Scotia. (July 1986)-. Periodical. English. qt. $20.00 per year. Christmas Tree Council Nova Scotia, P.O.Box 696, Truro NS B2N 5E5 Canada. **Tel** (902)766-4869. **ED** Caryl Worden. **DD** 338.1/7597752/09716. **Bk Rev. Ad Acc. Circ:** 1,000.
Desc: For and about Christmas tree growers in Nova Scotia and Canada's Atlantic provinces.

KO/0073-9294
NYENGU BOGO - RIMMOG NYUGJON NYENGUSO. (YONGU POGO / IMMOK YUKCHONG YONGUSO.). [Nyengu bogo - Rimmog Nyugjon Nyenguso]. **Added/Corp** Immok Yukchong Yonguso (Korea). **VFOAT** Research Report of the Institute of Forest Genetics; Immok Yukchong Yonguso Yonguso Yongu Pogo. (1959)-. Academic Scholarly Publication. English (Korean; summaries and/or abstracts in English). an. Free. Forest Genetics Research Institute, PO Box 24, Suwon, Kyonggi-do 441-350, South Korea. **Tel** 0331-290-1114, FAX 0331-292-4458. **ED** B. Lee. **LC** SD399.5; .Y64. **CODEN** IYYYA8. **Pr Rev. Circ:** 1,000. Documents available from CASDDS.
Desc: Contains information on tree breeding.
Ind/Abst Chem. Abstr.; For. Abstr.; Hortic. Abstr.; Seed Abstr.

SW/0347-5883
NYTT - FORSKNINGSSTIFTELSEN SKOGSARBETEN. (NYTT.). [Nytt - Forsk.stift. Skogsarb.]. **Main/Corp** Forskinigsstiftelsen Skogsarbeten (Stockholm, Sweden). (19??)-. Periodical. Swedish (English). Five times a year. Free on request. Forskningstiftelsen Skogsforsk Glunten, S 751 83 Uppsala Sweden. **Tel** 011 46 18 188500. **ED** Gunilla Sundquist. **Circ:** 4,700.
Desc: Provides general information on the activities of the forest operations institute "Skogsarbeten".
Ind/Abst AGRICOLA.

UK/0269-5790
O.F.I. OCCASIONAL PAPERS. [O.F.I. occas. pap.]. **VFOAT** OFI Occasional Papers. Monographic series. English. ir. Price varies per volume. Oxford Forestry Institute, South Parks Road, Oxford OX1 3RB England. **Tel** 0865 275082, telex 83147. **CODEN** OPOIEJ. Documents available from BIOSIS Document Express. ***Continues*** *C.F.I. Occasional Papers.*
Ind/Abst AGRICOLA; Agrofor. Abstr.; Biol. Abstr. (1987-); For. Prod. Abstr.

UK
OCCASIONAL PAPER (GREAT BRITAIN. FORESTRY COMMISSION). (OCCASIONAL PAPER.). **Added/Corp** Great Britain. Forestry Commission. (19??)-. Monographic series. English. Price varies per volume.
Ind/Abst Agrofor. Abstr.; Dairy Sci. Abstr.; For. Prod. Abstr.; For. Abstr.; Geogr. Abstr. Phys. Geogr.; Maize Abstr.; Rev. Plant Pathol.; Weed Abstr.

US
OHIO WOODLANDS. **Added/Corp** Ohio Forestry Association. **VFOAT** Conservation in Action. Vol. 14, No. 3 (Fall 1976)-. Periodical. English. qt (Feb., May, Aug., Nov.). $8.00 US; $15.00 Canada; $30.00 other. Ohio Forestry Association, 1335 Dublin Road, Suite 203 D, Columbus OH 43215. **Tel** (614)486-6767, FAX (614)486-6769. **ED** Ronald C. Cornell. **Ad Acc, Adv Mgr:** AgComm Advertising Agency, **Tel** (614)889-6604. **Circ:** 3,000 (ctrl). ***Continues*** *Woodlands, 0361-8730.*
Desc: Covers forest resources management, harvesting and utilization to communities in Ohio and surrounding states.

CN/0030-3631
OPERATIONS FORESTIERES ET DE SCIERIE. [Oper. for. scierie]. Vol. 1 (Feb. 1966)-. Periodical. French. Seven times a year. 34.00Can$ US; 23.00Can$ Canada; 60.00Can$ other. Forest Communications, 1 Pacifique Street, St. Ann Bell Quebec H9X 1C5 Canada. **Tel** (514)457-2211.
Ind/Abst Environ.; Point Repere (1979-1980).

US/0164-5536
OREGON CONIFER. **Added/Corp** Sierra Club. Oregon Chapter. Vol. 1 (Aug. 1978)-. Periodical. English. Four times a year (Feb., May, Aug., Nov.). $3.00. Oregon Chapter Sierra Club, 2941 N W Luray, Portland OR 97210. **Tel** (503)687-3964. ***Supersedes*** *Northwest Conifer.*

AU
OSTERREICHISCHE FORSTZEITUNG (1987). (OSTERREICHISCHE FORSTZEITUNG.). **VFOAT** Forstzeitung. (Jan. 1987)-. Periodical. German (English). mo. 1030.00Aus$ Australia; 1210Aus$ other. Osterreichischer Agrarverlag, Inkustr 1 7 Bueropark Donau, A 3400 Klosterneuberg Austria. **Tel** 011 43 2243 33300. **(Subscription address:** Osterreichischer Agrarverlag, Bankgasse 1-3, A-1014 Vienna Austria**) ED** Franz-Werner Hillgarter. Index available. cum. index. **Bk Rev. Ad Acc. Circ:** 2,500. ***Continues*** *Allgemeine Forstzeitung, 0002-5879.*
Desc: Covers forest technologies, forest protection, harvesting, and forestry in general.
Ind/Abst For. Prod. Abstr.

CN/1182-7696
OUTAOUAIS FORESTIER. (L'OUTAOUAIS FORESTIER : REVUE DE L'ASSOCIATION FORESTIERE DE L'OUTAOUAIS.). [Outaouais for.]. **Added/Corp** Association Forestiere de l'Outaouais. (May 1990)-. Periodical. French. qt. Free for members. Association Forestiere de l'Outaouais, CP 158, Maniwaki, Quebec J9E 3B4 Canada. **DD** 634.9/09714/2205.

UK
OXFORD FORESTRY MEMOIRS. ***Ceased.*** (19??)-(19??). English. ir. Oxford University Press, Walton Street, Oxford OX2 6DP England. **Tel** 011 44 865 56767, FAX 011 44 865 267773, telex 837330 OXPRES G.

PK/0030-9818
PAKISTAN JOURNAL OF FORESTRY, THE. [Pak. j. for.]. **Added/Corp** Pakistan Forest Institute, Peshawar. Vol. 1 (Jan. 1951)-. Periodical. English (Urdu). qt (Feb., May, Aug., Nov.). $18.00. Pakistan Forest Institute, PO Peshawar, NWFP Pakistan. **ED** K M Siddiqui. **LC** SD1; .P23. **DD** 634.9/09549/1. **CODEN** PAJFAN. Index available. cum. index. **Bk Rev. Ad Acc. Circ:** 400 (ctrl). Documents available from BIOSIS Document Express, CASDDS.
Desc: Articles on sylviculture management, range management, forest production, zoology wildlife managers, watershed managements, etc.
Ind/Abst AGRICOLA; Agrofor. Abstr.; Biodeter. Abstr.; Biol. Abstr.; Chem. Abstr. (1951-1982); Field Crop Abstr.; Fish Rev.; For. Prod. Abstr. (19??-19??); For. Abstr.; Grasslands For. Abstr.; Hortic. Abstr.; Maize Abstr.; Nutr. Abstr. Rev., Ser. B, Live Feeds and Feed.; Ornamental Hort. (1991-); Life Sci. Collect.; Plant Grow. Reg. Abstr.; Potato Abstr.; Rev. Agric. Entomol.; Rev. Plant Pathol.; Rural Dev. Abstr.; Soils Fert.; Weed Abstr.; Wildl. Rev.; World Agric. Econ.

●US
PAPER AND FOREST PRODUCTS / SALOMON BROTHERS. **Added/Corp** Salomon Brothers. **VFOAT** United States Equity Research. (1992)-. English. Salomon Brothers Center Finance, 7 World Trade Center, 36th Floor, New York NY 10004. **Tel** (212)747-7000. ***Continues*** *Forest Products and Paper Monthly, 0895-3511.*
Ind/Abst Abstr. Bull. Inst. Pap. Sci. Tech.

US
PAPERS IN FOREST POLICY. **Added/Corp** Oregon State University. Forest Research Laboratory. (1990)-. Monographic series. English. Price varies per volume. Forest Research Laboratory, Oregon State University, Corvallis OR 97331. **Tel** (503)754-4271.

US/1180-9175
PAPERTREE LETTER. **See** Paper and Pulp Industry.

CC/1000-1522
PEI-CHING LIN YEH TA HSUEH HSUEH PAO. **Added/Corp** Pei-Ching Lin Yeh ta Hsueh. **VFOAT** Journal of Beijing Forestry University. (1985)-. Academic Scholarly Publication. Chinese (summaries and/or abstracts in English). qt. Pei-Ching Lin Yeh Ta Hsueh Pao, PO Box 2820, Pei-Ching, People's Republic of China. **LC** SD221; .P45. **CODEN** BLDXE8. Documents available from CASDDS. ***Continues*** *Pei-Ching Lin Hsueh Yuan Hsueh Pao.*
Ind/Abst Biocont. News Inf.; Chem. Abstr.; Crop Physiol. Abstr.; Field Crop Abstr.; For. Prod. Abstr. (1991-); Hortic. Abstr.; Ornamental Hort. (1991-); Rev. Agric. Entomol.; Rev. Med. Vet. Mycology; Rev. Plant Pathol.; Soils Fert.

US/0031-4501
PENNSYLVANIA FORESTS. [Pa. for.]. **Added/Corp** Pennsylvania Forestry Association. Vol. 36, No. 346 (1951)-. Periodical. English. Four times a year. $10.00 one year; $20.00 other. Pennsylvania Forestry Association, 56 East Main Street, Mechanicsburg PA 17055. **Tel** (717)766-5371. **ED** Sue Haskins. **Bk Rev**, (Qty: 4). **Ad Acc. Circ:** 2,500 (ctrl). ***Continues*** *Forest Leaves, 0097-1294.*
Desc: Contains information encouraging widespread public support for all forest values, including timber, water, wildlife, recreation, aesthetics and minerals.
Ind/Abst AGRICOLA.

CN/0317-1388
PEOPLE'S FOREST, THE. **Added/Corp** People's Wood Producers Board. (Summer 1974)-. English. Free. Peoples Wood Producers Board, 37 13th Street East, Prince Albert Sask. S6V 1C7. **DD** 634.9/82/097124.

CN/0715-0830
PEST LEAFLET (VICTORIA). **See** Pest Control.

PH
PHILIPPINE FORESTRY STATISTICS. **See** Forestry-Abstracting, Bibliographies and Statistics.

US
PINES & NEEDLES. **Added/Corp** Florida Forestry Association. Vol.1 (1965)-. Periodical. English. mo (Except September). $20.00. Florida Forestry Association, PO Box 1696, Tallahassee FL 32302. **Tel** (904)222-5646.

VE
PITTIERIA. **Added/Corp** Universidad de los Andes (Merida, Venezuela). Facultad de Ciencias Forestales. No. 1 (Feb. 1967)-. Periodical. English (Spanish). **LC** QK273; .P59.
Ind/Abst For. Prod. Abstr. (1991-); For. Abstr.

PL
POLSKI, LAS. **Added/Corp** Poland. Ministerstwo Lesnictwa. Poland. Centralny Zarzad Lasow Panstwowych. Stowarzyszenie Inzynierow i Technikow Lesnictwa i Drzewnictwa. (1921)-. Periodical. Polish. sm. Price on Request. **(Subscription address:** ARS Polona, PO Box 1001, 00068 Warsaw Poland.**) LC** SD1; .L28.
Ind/Abst Biocont. News Inf. (1991-); For. Prod. Abstr. (1991-); For. Abstr.; Rev. Agric. Entomol.; Rev. Plant Pathol.; Seed Abstr.

CI
POPIS SUMSKOG FONDA ... GODINE / SOCIJALISTICKA REPUBLIKA SRBIJA, REPUBLICKI ZAVOD ZA STATISTIKU. 1979-. Serbo-Croatian (Roman). 100.00. Republicki Zavod za Statistiku, Central Bureau of Statistics of the Republic of Croatia, Ilica 3, Zagreb Croatia. **Tel** 011 385 41 45 44 22, FAX 011 385 41 42 94 13, 011 385 41 42 37 11, telex 21130 DZSTAT RH. **LC** SD217.Y8; P66. **Circ:** 400.

PL
PRACE INSTYTUTU BADAWCZEGO LESNICTWA. (1958)-. Periodical. Polish. Panstwowe Wydawn Naukowe, Miodowa 10, PO Box 391, 00251 Warsaw Poland. **LC** SD1; .P745. ***Continues*** *Roczniki Nauk Lesnych.*
Ind/Abst Agrofor. Abstr. (1991-); Crop Physiol. Abstr.; For. Prod. Abstr. (1991-); For. Abstr.

XR/0139-5807
PRACE VYZKUMNEHO USTAVU LESNIHO HOSPODARSTVI A MYSLIVOSTI. [Pr. Vyzk. ustavu les. hospod. mysliv.]. **VFOAT** Trudy Nauchno-Issledovatelskogo Instituta Lesnogo i Okhotnichego Khoziaistva; Reports of the Forestry and Game Management Research Institute; Arbeiten der Forschungsanstalt fur Fortswirtschaft und Jagdwesen; Prace Vulhm. (1966)-. Periodical. Czech. **LC** SD1; .P747. **CODEN** PVLHAG. Documents available from BIOSIS Document Express. ***Continues*** *Prace Vyzkumnych Ustavu Lesnickych CSSR.*
Ind/Abst Biol. Abstr. (-1985); Fish Rev. (Jan. 1989-July 1992); Wildl. Rev. (Jan. 1989-July 1992).

US/1044-2200
PRACTICAL FORESTRY. [Pract. for.]. Vol. 1, No. 1 (Sept. 1989)-. Periodical. English. Six times a year. Practical Forestry Inc., PO Box 482, Lexington TN 38351. **DD** 338.
Desc: Aimed at the national population. An educational magazine that strives to help people learn how to do a better job of managing their timberland.

XR
PREHLED LESNICKE A MYSLIVECKE LITERATURY. **Added/Corp** Ceskoslovenska Akademie Zemedeskych Ved. ODIS Lesniho Hospodarstvi a Myslivosti. Vyzkumny Ustav Lesniho Hospodarstvi a Myslivosti (Ceskoslovenska Akademie Zemedelskych Ved). (1957)-. Periodical. Czech. mo. **(Subscription address:** Artia Pegas Press Ltd., Palac

Forestry

Metro Narodni Trida 25, 11210 Prague 1 Czech Republic.) **LC** SD1; .P78. **Continues in part** Prehled Zahranicni Zemedelske a Lesnicke Literatury.

US/0160-2284
PRIMARY FOREST INDUSTRY OF WEST VIRGINIA, THE. English. 1800 Washington Street East, Charleston WV 25305. **LC** TS803; .P74. **DD** 338.4/7/6742025754.

US/0489-555X
PROCEEDINGS ANNUAL MEETING / SOCIETY OF AMERICAN FORESTERS, NORTHERN CALIFORNIA SECTION. [Proc. annu. meet. - Soc. Am. For., North. Calif. Sect.]. **Main/Corp** Society of American Foresters. Northern California Section. (19??)-. Proceedings. English. an. Society of American Foresters, 5400 Grosvenor Lane, Bethesda MD 20814-2198. **Tel** (301)897-8720, FAX (301)897-3690, telex 9102501089 SAFFOREST UQ. **Continues** Proceedings / Society of American Foresters. Northern California Section, 0732-8702.

US/0549-8929
PROCEEDINGS - NORTHEASTERN FOREST TREE IMPROVEMENT CONFERENCE. **Main/Conf** Northeastern Forest Tree Improvement Conference. **VFOAT** Proceedings of the Northeastern Forest Tree Improvement Conference. (1953)-. English. an. $14.00 (two year). Northeastern Forest Experiment Station / Durham, NH, PO Box 640, Durham NH 03824. **Tel** (603)868-5692. **LC** SD118; .N86. **DD** 634.9.
Ind/Abst AGRICOLA.

NR
PROCEEDINGS OF THE ANNUAL CONFERENCE OF THE FORESTRY ASSOCIATION OF NIGERIA. Main/Corp Forestry Association of Nigeria. No. 1 (1970)-. Proceedings. English. sm. $19.33. Forestry Association of Nigeria, Box 4185, Ibadan Nigeria. **ED** Miss O O Okoro and I Verinumbe. **Ad Acc.**
Desc: Survey evaluation of problems and trends in forest management or forest industries. Research reports on new findings, techniques, and equipment.

US/0160-2950
PROCEEDINGS OF THE ANNUAL NORTHEASTERN FOREST INSECT WORK CONFERENCE. See Environmental Issues-Pollution and Waste Management.

US
PROCEEDINGS OF THE ANNUAL TALL TIMBER FIRE ECOLOGY CONFERENCE. Main/Corp Tall Timber Fire Ecology. Conference. No. 1- 1962-. Proceedings. English.

US/0899-370X
PROCEEDINGS OF THE SOCIETY OF AMERICAN FORESTERS NATIONAL CONVENTION (1985). (PROCEEDINGS OF THE ... SOCIETY OF AMERICAN FORESTERS NATIONAL CONVENTION.). [Proc. Soc. Am. For. Natl. Conv.]. **Main/Corp** Society of American Foresters. Convention. (1985)-. Proceedings. English. Society of American Foresters, 5400 Grosvenor Lane, Bethesda MD 20814-2198. **Tel** (301)897-8720, FAX (301)897-3690, telex 9102501089 SAFFOREST UQ. **DD** 634. **Continues** Society of American Foresters. Convention. Proceedings of the ... Convention of the Society of American Foresters, 0884-285X.
Ind/Abst AGRICOLA [Full Cov.].

BL
PRODUCAO DA EXTRACAO VEGETAL E DA SILVICULTURA. Added/Corp Fundacao Instituto Brasileiro de Geografia E Estatistica. Departamento de Agropecuaria. Vol. 1 (1986)-. Polish. an. Instituto Brasileiro de Geografia e Estatistica, Rua General Canabarro 666 AN2, 20271 Rio de Janeiro RJ Brazil. **Tel** 011 55 21 2847690, 011 55 21 2342043. **Formed by the union of** Producao Extrativa Vegetal **and** Silvicultura (Fundacao Instituto Brasileiro de Geografia E Estatistica).

AT
PROGRAM OF RESEARCH. Main/Corp Commonwealth Scientific and Industrial Research Organization. Division of Forest Products. Periodical. English. an. 9.22Aus$. CSIRO Publications, PO Box 89, 314 Albert Street, East Melborne Victoria 3002 Australia. **Tel** 011 61 3 4187333, 4187217, FAX 011 61 3 4190459, telex AA 30236.

CN/1185-9806
PROGRAMS AT WORK / BRITISH COLUMBIA FORESTRY ASSOCIATION. [Programs work - B.C. For. Assoc.]. **Added/Corp** British Columbia Forestry Association. (Jan./Mar. 1991)-. Periodical. English. sa. British Columbia Forestry Association, 9800-A-140th Street, Surrey British Columbia V3T 4M5 Canada. **DD** 634.9/06/0711. **Continues** Update (British Columbia Forestry Association)., 1187-3566.

CN/0705-4130
PROGRES FORESTIER, LE. Periodical. French (English). qt. 0.50Can$ per no. Association Forestiere des Cantons de l'Est, 178 Nord rue Wellington, Sherbrooke Quebec J1H 5C5 Canada. **DD** 634.9/06/27146.

US/1061-7825
PROTECTION REPORT R8. [Prot. rep. R8]. **Added/Corp** United States. Forest Service. Southern Region. **VFOAT** Southern Pine Beetle Fact Sheet. **VAT** Protection Report Region Eight. (May 1987)-. Monographic series. English. US Department of Agriculture / Georgia, Southern Region, Forest Service, 1720 Peachtree St NW, Atlanta GA 30367. **Tel** (404)347-4177, FAX (404)347-3608. **DD** 634. **Continues** Forestry Bulletin R8-FB/P.
Ind/Abst For. Abstr.

CN/0828-6256
PROVINCIAL REPORT - CANADIAN FORESTRY ASSOCIATION OF BRITISH COLUMBIA. **Title Change.** (PROVINCIAL REPORT / CANADIAN FORESTRY ASSOCIATION OF BRITISH COLUMBIA.). [Prov. rep. - Can. For. Assoc. B.C.]. **Added/Corp** Canadian Forestry Association of British Columbia. Vol. 1, No. 1 (May 1984)-Vol. 2, No. 1 (June 1985). Periodical. English. sa. Canadian Forestry Association of British Columbia, Suite 410, 1200 West Pender Street, Vancouver BC V6E 2S9. **DD** 634.9/06/0711. **Continued by** Update (British Columbia Forestry Association), 1187-3566.

CN/0300-5844
PUBLICATION - CANADIAN FORESTRY SERVICE. (PUBLICATION.). [Publ. - Can. For. Serv.]. **Added/Corp** Canadian Forestry Service. **VFOAT** Canadian Forestry Service Publication; Publication ... du Service Canadian des Forets. **VAT** Canadian Forestry Service Publication. (19??)-. Monographic series. English. $3.00 (no. 1313) varies. Canadian Forestry Service / Hull, 351 St Joseph Boulevard, 19th Floor, Hull Quebec K1A 1G5 Canada. **Tel** (819)997-1107. **LC** SD13; .A215. **DD** 634.9/08. **Continues** Canada. Forestry Branch. Forestry Branch Publication.
Ind/Abst Abstr. Bull. Inst. Pap. Sci. Tech.

IT
QUADERNI DI RICERCA (SOCIETA AGRICOLA E FORESTALE). (QUADERNI DI RICERCA.). No. 1 (1984)-. Periodical. Italian (English; summaries and/or abstracts in Italian). qt. **LC** SD1; .S636.

● AT/1038-4243
QUARTERLY FOREST PRODUCTS STATISTICS. Added/Corp Australian Bureau of Agricultural and Resource Economics. **VFOAT** Forest Products Statistics. (1992)-. Periodical. English. qt. 48.00Aus$ Australia; 56.50Aus$ Asia and Pacific; 60.00Aus$ other. ABARE / Australian Bureau of Agriculture and Resource Economics, GPO Box 1563, Canberra ACT 2601 Australia. **Tel** 011 61 6 2722000, FAX 011 61 6 272 2001. **Formed by the union of** Forest Products Trade **and** Timber Supply Review, 0040-778X Australian Forest Resources, 0157-8189.

UK/0033-5568
QUARTERLY JOURNAL OF FORESTRY. [Q. j. for.]. **Added/Corp** Royal Forestry Society of England, Wales and Northern Ireland. Royal English Arboricultural Society. Royal English Forestry Society. Vol. 1 (1907)-. Periodical. English. qt. $128.00 all except UK. Hall-McCartney Ltd, PO Box 21, Unit 7, Campus 5, Hertfordshire SG6 2JF England. **Tel** 11 44 462 675848, FAX 11 44 462 679356. **ED** T W Wright. **CODEN** QJFOA2. Index available. **Bk Rev. Ad Acc.** **Circ:** 5,000. Documents available from BIOSIS Document Express. **Supersedes** Royal English Arboricultural Society. Transactions.
Desc: The official journal of the Royal Forestry Society of England, Wales and Northern Ireland.
Ind/Abst AGRICOLA; Agrofor. Abstr. (1991-); Biol. Abstr.; Curr. Aware. Biol. Sci., CABS; Ecology Abstr.; For. Prod. Abstr.; For. Abstr.; Life Sci. Collect.; Soils Fert.; Wildl. Rev.

CH/0255-6014
QUARTERLY JOURNAL OF THE EXPERIMENTAL FOREST OF NATIONAL TAIWAN UNIVERSITY. (19??)-. Chinese.
Ind/Abst Agrofor. Abstr.; For. Prod. Abstr. (1991-); For. Abstr.; Seed Abstr.; Soils Fert.

CN/0710-0566
QUARTERLY NEWSLETTER / CANADIAN FORESTRY ASSOCIATION OF BRITISH COLUMBIA. [Q. newsl. - Can. For. Assoc. B.C.]. **Added/Corp** Canadian Forestry Association of British Columbia. Vol. 1, No. 1 (June 1976)-. Newsletter. English. ir. Free. Canadian Forestry Association of British Columbia, Suite 410, 1200 West Pender Street, Vancouver BC V6E 2S9. **DD** 634.9/06/0711. ctrl circ.

US
R8-RG / USDA, FOREST SERVICE, SOUTHERN REGION. (1990)-. Periodical. English.
Ind/Abst For. Prod. Abstr. (1991-).

BN/0581-748X
RADOVI SUMARSKOG FAKULTETA I INSTITUTA ZA SUMARSTVO U SARAJEVU. [Rad. Sumar. fak. inst. sumar. Sarajevu]. Vol. 12 (1967)-. Monographic series. Serbo-Croatian (Roman). ir. Price varies per volume. **LC** SD1; .S26. **Continues** Radovi Sumarskog Fakulteta i Instituta za Sumarstvo i Drvnu Industriju u Sarajevu.
Ind/Abst AGRICOLA.

US/1055-0895
RANDOM LENGTHS YARDSTICK. (RANDOM LENGTHS YARDSTICK : THE MONTHLY MEASURE OF FOREST PRODUCTS STATISTICS.). **VFOAT** Random Lengths Yard Stick; Yardstick. (Jan. 1991)-. Periodical. English. mo. $195.00 US; $200.00 Canada; $235.00 other. Random Lengths Publications Inc, PO Box 867, Eugene OR 97440. **Tel** (503)686-9925, FAX (800)874-7979, (503)686-9629. **ED** Joseph Heitz. **DD** 333. [CCC].
Desc: A monthly, 24-page report of statistics, prices, and other economic indicators related to the North American Forest Products Industry. Product prices, production data, export data, housing market data, and financial market data are included.

AT/1036-9872
RANGELAND JOURNAL, THE. [Rangeland j.]. **Added/Corp** Australian Rangeland Society. Vol. 13 (1991)-. Periodical. English. sa. 50.00Aus$, 75.00Aus$ (combined with Rangeland Newsletter), Australia and New Zealand; 55.00Aus$, 85.00Aus$ (combined with Rangeland Newsletter) other. Australian Rangeland Society, PO Box 718, Victoria Park WA 6100 Australia. **Tel** 011 61 9 2227084, FAX 011 61 9 3221598. **Continues** Australian Rangeland Journal, 0313-4555.
Ind/Abst AGRICOLA.

CM
RAPPORT ANNUEL - CENTRE TECHNIQUE FORESTIER TROPICAL DU CAMEROUN. Main/Corp Centre Technique Forestier Tropical du Cameroun. French. Centre Technique Forestier Tropical du Cameroun, BP 832, Douala Cameroon. **LC** SD105.C3; C47. **DD** 634.9/0967/11.

FR/0984-5453
RAPPORT ANNUEL / OFFICE NATIONAL DES FORETS. [Rapp. annu. - Off. nat. for]. **Main/Corp** France. Office National des Forets. (198?)-. French. an. Office National des Forets, 2 Avenue de Saint-Mande, 75570 Paris Cedex 12 France. **LC** SD59; .A25. **DD** 354.440082/338. **Continues** France. Office National des Forets. Rapport au Parlement.

CN/0824-2089
RAPPORT - FORINTEK CANADA CORP., LABORATOIRE DE L'EST. (RAPPORT.). [Rapp. - Forintek Can. Corp. Lab. Est]. Monographic series. French (English). Price varies per volume. Forintek Canada Corporation, 800 Montreal Road, Ottawa Ontario K1G 3Z5 Canada. **Tel** (613)744-0963. **DD** 634.9/8/05. **Continues** Rapport (Laboratoire des Produits Forestiers de l'Est (Canada)), 0704-7746.

CN/0824-3832
RAPPORT SUR L'INDUSTRIE FORESTIERE. [Rapp. ind. for.]. No. 1 (Spring 1982)-. Periodical. French. Free. Rapport sur l'Industrie Forestiere, c/o Nouveau Parti Democratique, Chambre des Communes, Ottawa Ontario K1A 0A6 Canada. **DD** 333.75/0971.

SW/0348-4599
RAPPORT - SVERIGES LANTBRUKSUNIVERSITET, INSTITUTION FOR VIRKESLARA. [Rapp. - Sver. lantbruksuniv., inst. virkesl.]. **Main/Corp** Sveriges Lantbruksuniversitet. Institutionen for Virkeslara. **VFOAT** Report - Swedish University of Agricultural Sciences, Department of Forest Products. No. 104 (1978)-. Monographic series. Swedish. Price varies per volume. **Continues** Rapporter. Research Notes.
Ind/Abst AGRICOLA; For. Abstr.

SW/0348-422X
RAPPORT / SVERIGES LANTBRUKSUNIVERSITET, INSTITUTIONEN FOR EKOLOGI OCH MILJOVARD. [Rapp. - Sver. lantbruksv., Inst. ekol. miljovard]. **Added/Corp** Sveriges Lantbruksuniversitet. Institutionen for Ekologi och Miljovard. **VFOAT** Report. (1978)-. Monographic series. English (Swedish). **CODEN**

Forestry

RSLME2. Documents available from BIOSIS Document Express.
Ind/Abst Biol. Abstr.; For. Abstr.

SW/0348-7954
RAPPORT - SVERIGES LANTBRUKSUNIVERSITET. INSTITUTIONEN FOR SKOGLIG GENETIK OCH VAXTFYSIOLOGI. REPORT - SWEDISH UNIVERSITY OF AGRICULTURAL SCIENCES, DEPARTMENT OF FOREST GENETICS AND PLANT PHYSIOLOGY. Main/Corp Sveriges Lantbruksuniversitet. Institutionen for Skoglig Genetik och Vaxtfysiologi. **VFOAT** Report - Swedish University of Agricultural Sciences, Department of Forest Genetics and Plant Physiology. No. 1 (1979)-. Monographic series. English.
Ind/Abst For. Abstr.; Plant Breed. Abstr.

SW/0348-7636
RAPPORT (SVERIGES LANTBRUKSUNIVERSITET. INSTITUTIONEN FOR SKOGSPRODUKTION). (RAPPORT / SVERIGES LANTBRUKSUNIVERSITET. INSTITUTIONEN FOR SKOGSPRODUKTION.--). **Added/Corp** Sveriges Lantbruksuniversitet. Institutionen for Skogsproduktion. (1979)-. Monographic series. Swedish (summaries and/or abstracts in English). Price varies per volume. *Formed by the union of Skogshogskolan (Stockholm, Sweden). Institutionen for Skogsproduktion. Rapporter och Uppsatser. and Skogshogskolan (Stockholm, Sweden). Institutionen for Skogsforyngring. Rapporter och Uppsatser.*

SW/0348-565X
RAPPORTER OCH UPPSATSER - SVERIGES LANTBRUKSUNIVERSITET INSTITUTIONEN FOR SKOGSGENETIK. [Rapp. upps. - Sver. lantbruksuniv. inst. skogsgenet.]. **Added/Corp** Skogshogskolan (Stockholm, Sweden). Institutionen for Skogsgenetik. Sveriges Lantbruksuniversitet. Institutionen for Skogsgenetik. **VFOAT** Research Notes. (19??)-. Monographic series. Swedish. Price varies per volume. Swedish University of Agricultural Sciences / Ekonomi & Statistik, Sveriges Lantruksuniversitet, Institutionen for Ekonomi och Statistik, S-75007 Uppsala Sweden. **Tel** 011 46 18 671000, telex 003939. **LC** UNC.
Desc: Information on forest genetics and tree breeding.
Ind/Abst AGRICOLA; For. Abstr.; Plant Breed. Abstr.

US/0092-9638
RC AND D RELEASE. Ceased. [R.C. D. release]. **Main/Corp** Utah. Forestry and Fire Control Section. No. 1 (1972)-(19??). Periodical. English. Forestry and Fire Control, 1596 West North Temple, Salt Lake City UT 84116. **LC** SD12; .U87a. **DD** 634.9/09792.

CN/0824-8826
REALISATIONS RECENTES A PETAWAWA. Ceased. [Realis. recent. Petawawa]. **Main/Corp** Petawawa National Forestry Institute. Vol. 1, No. 1 (July 1983)-(19??). Periodical. French. an. Petawawa National Forestry Institute, PO Box 2000, Chalk River Ontario K0J 1J0 Canada. **Tel** (613)589-2880. **DD** 634.9/07/2071. **Circ:** 1,600. *Continues Station d'Experiences Forestiere de Petawawa. Recherches Accomplies a Petawawa.*

US
RECENT PUBLICATIONS OF THE PACIFIC NORTHWEST RESEARCH STATION. Added/Corp Pacific Northwest Research Station (Portland, Or.). 3rd Quarter (1985)-. Periodical. English. qt. US Department of Agriculture / Portland, Forest Service, Pacific Northwest Region, 319 SW Pine Street, Portland OR 97204. **Tel** (503)326-3625, FAX (503)326-2272. *Continues Recent Publications of the Pacific Northwest Forest and Range Experiment Station.*

US
RECENT PUBLICATIONS (SOUTHERN FOREST EXPERIMENT STATION (NEW ORLEANS, LA.)). (RECENT PUBLICATIONS / UNITED STATES DEPARTMENT OF AGRICULTURE, FOREST SERVICE, SOUTHERN FOREST EXPERIMENT STATION.). English. qt. Southern Forest Experiment Station, T-10210 US Postal Services Building, US Department of Agriculture, 701 Loyola Avenue, New Orleans LA 70113. **Tel** (504)589-6800, FAX (504)589-3961. **Circ:** 7,000. *Continues Research Accomplished (Southern Forest Experiment Station).*

US
RECENT REPORTS (INTERMOUNTAIN RESEARCH STATION (OGDEN, UTAH)). (RESEARCH REPORTS / INTERMOUNTAIN RESEARCH STATION.). **Added/Corp** Intermountain Research Station (Ogden, Utah). No. 65 (April 1985)-. Periodical. English. qt. Intermountain Research Station, 507 25th Street, Ogden UT 84401. *Continues Recent Reports (Intermountain Forest and Range Experiment Station (Ogden, Utah), 0364-8494.*

RU
REFERATIVNYI ZHURNAL. LESOVODSTVO I AGROLESOMELIORATSIIA / MINISTERSTVO SELSKOGO KHOZIAISTVA SSSR. VFOAT Lesovodstvo I Agrolesomelioratsia. Abstracting/Indexing Service. Russian. mo. VINITI - Vsesoyuznyi Institut Nauchno-Tekhnicheskoi Informatsii, All-Union Scientific and Technical Information Institute, Baltiiskaia Ulitsa 14, 125219 Moscow Russia. **Tel** 238-46-00, FAX 9430060, telex 411160.
Ind/Abst Plant Breed. Abstr.

CN/0836-5709
REPERTOIRE DES MEMBRES - ORDRE DES INGENIEURS FORESTIERS DU QUEBEC. (REPERTOIRE DES MEMBRES.). [Repert. memb. - Ordre ing. for. Que.]. **Main/Corp** Ordre des Ingenieurs Forestiers du Quebec. (1987)-. French. Missions des Franciscains, 2080 Ouest Boulevard Rene-Levesque, Montreal Quebec H3H 1R6 Canada. **Tel** (514)932-6094, FAX (514)259-7407. **DD** 634.9/025/714. *Continues Ordre des Ingenieurs Forestiers du Quebec. Membres - Ordre des Ingenieurs Forestiers du Quebec., 0703-6876.*

CN/0704-772X
REPORT - FOREST PEST MANAGEMENT INSTITUTE. [Rep. - For. Pest Manag. Inst.]. **Added/Corp** Forest Pest Management Institute (Canada). (1977)-. Monographic series. English (French). **CODEN** RFFID4. Documents available from BIOSIS Document Express. *Formed by the union of Canada. Insect Pathology Research Institute. Information Report., 0704-7665 and Canada. Chemical Control Research Institute. Report., 0704-7711.*
Ind/Abst Biol. Abstr.; For. Abstr.; Rev. Agric. Entomol.

US
REPORT - FOREST SERVICE. SOUTHEASTERN AREA. DIVISION OF FOREST PEST MANAGEMENT. (REPORT - DIVISION OF FOREST PEST MANAGEMENT.). **Main/Corp** United States. Forest Service. Southeastern Area. Division of Forest Pest Management. (19??)-. Monographic series. English. Price varies per volume. *Continues Report - Division of Forest Pest Control.*

KE
REPORT / INTERNATIONAL COUNCIL FOR RESEARCH IN AGROFORESTRY. Title Change. Main/Corp International Council for Research in Agroforestry. (1979)-?. English. *Continued by Annual Report of the International Council for Research in Agroforestry. International Council for Research in Agroforestry.*

US/0731-8316
REPORT - NORTHEASTERN FOREST EXPERIMENT STATION (BROOMALL, PA.) (1977/78). (REPORT / NORTHEASTERN FOREST EXPERIMENT STATION.). [Rep. - Northeast. For. Exp. Stn. (Broomall, Pa.)]. **Main/Corp** Northeastern Forest Experiment Station (Radnor, Pa.) (1978)-. English. Northeastern Forest Experiment Station / Durham, NH, PO Box 640, Durham NH 03824. **Tel** (603)868-5692. **LC** SD356.52.P42; N676a. **DD** 634.9/0974. *Continues Northeastern Forest Experiment Station (Radnor, Pa.) At the Northeastern Forest Experiment Station, 0731-8421.*

US/0270-4080
REPORT OF ACTIVITIES - NEW MEXICO FORESTRY DIVISION. Main/Corp New Mexico. Forestry Division. 66th- 1977/78-. English. Department of Natural Resources / New Mexico, Forestry Division, PO Box 2167, Santa Fe NM 87503. **LC** SD12; .N63A. **DD** 353.97890082/338/06. *Continues Activities - New Mexico Department of State Forestry, 0149-6247.*

AT/0311-0893
REPORT OF RESEARCH ACTIVITIES - DIVISION OF TECHNICAL SERVICES, QUEENSLAND DEPARTMENT OF FORESTRY. Title Change. Main/Corp Queensland. Dept. of Forestry. Division of Technical Services. **Added/Corp** Queensland. Dept. of Forestry. Division of Technical Services. Research Report. **VFOAT** Research Report. No. 1 (1977)-?. English. be. Director Division of Technical Services, Department of Forestry, PO Box 631, Indooroopilly Queensland 4068 Australia. **Tel** (07)377 6400, FAX (07)371 2217. **ED** Paul Nielsen. **LC** SD111.Q8; D43b. **DD** 634.9/07/0943. **Circ:** 1,000 (ctrl). *Continued by Research Report (Queensland. Dept. of Forestry. Division of Technical Services (Research and Utlization)).*
Desc: Report of research activities.

US/0272-1007
REPORT OF THE FOREST SERVICE (WASHINGTON). (REPORT OF THE FOREST SERVICE.). [Rep. For. Serv.]. **Main/Corp** United States. Forest Service. Began with 1977/78. Government Publication. English. an. US Department of Agriculture / Forest Service, 201 14th Street SW, Washington DC 20250. **Tel** (202)205-1661, FAX (202)205-1181. **LC** SD11; .F67C. **DD** 333.75/0973. available on microfiche (Vols. for (1982-) distributed to depository libraries). *Continues United States. Forest Service. Report of the Chief, 0083-1069.*
Desc: Combined reports of: Report to Congress and Report for the Secretary of Agriculture.

CN
REPORT OF THE PFRA SHELTERBELT CENTRE / AGRICULTURE CANADA, PRAIRIE FARM REHABILITATION ADMINSTRATION. Added/Corp PFRA Shelterbelt Centre (Canada). **VFOAT** Report. (1987)-. English. *Continues PFRA Tree Nursery (Canada).; Report of the PFRA Tree Nursery.*

UK/0436-4120
REPORT ON FOREST RESEARCH. (REPORT ON FOREST RESEARCH / FORESTRY COMMISSION.). [Rep. for. res.]. **Main/Corp** Great Britain. Forestry Commission. **Added/Corp** Great Britain. Forestry Commission. (1949)-. English. an. £16.00. Her Majesty's Stationery Office, 51 Nine Elms Lane, London SW8 5DR England. **Tel** 011 44 71 873 8459, 011 44 71 873 8499, FAX 011 44 71 873 8499, 011 44 71 873 8456, telex 297138. **(Subscription address:** Her Majesty's Stationery Office, PO Box 276, Publications Centre, London SW8 5DT England.) **ED** D. A. Berdekin. **LC** SD45; .A453. **CODEN** GIFFAS. Index available. **Circ:** 1,500. Documents available from BIOSIS Document Express.
Ind/Abst Biol. Abstr.

US
REPORT - USDA FOREST SERVICE, NORTHERN REGION, STATE AND PRIVATE FORESTRY. Main/Corp United States. Forest Service. Northern Region. Division of State and Private Forestry. **VFOAT** Insect Disease Report. (19??)-. Monographic series. English.
Ind/Abst For. Abstr.; Rev. Plant Pathol.

CN/0846-6610
REPORTS AND PUBLICATIONS - PACIFIC FORESTRY CENTRE. [Rep. publ. - Pac. For. Cent.]. **Main/Corp** Pacific Forestry Centre. **VFOAT** Rapports et Publications. (1984)-. English (French). an. Pacific Forest Research Centre, 506 West Burnside Road, Victoria British Columbia V8Z 1M5 Canada. **DD** 016.6349. *Continues Reports and Publications - Pacific Forest Research Centre, 0707-557X.*

●US
RESEARCH CONTRIBUTION. Added/Corp Oregon State University. Forest Research Laboratory. (1993)-. Monographic series. English. Forest Research Laboratory, Oregon State University, Corvallis OR 97331. **Tel** (503)754-4271. **LC** SD133.A13; R48. *Formed by the union of Research Bulletin (Oregon State University. Forest Research Laboratory); Oregon State University. Forest Research Laboratory. Research Note - School of Forestry, Forest Research Laboratory, Oregon State University; Oregon State University. Forest Research Laboratory. Research Paper - Forest Research Laboratory, Oregon State University and Special Publication (Oregon State University. Forest Research Laboratory).*
Ind/Abst Bibliogr. Agric.

UK/0267-2375
RESEARCH INFORMATION NOTE - FORESTRY COMMISSION RESEARCH & DEVELOPMENT DIVISION. (RESEARCH INFORMATION NOTE.). [Res. inf. note - For. Comm. Res. Dev. Div.]. **Added/Corp** Great Britain. Forestry Commission. Research and Development Division. Great Britain. Forestry Commission. Research Division. (1975)-. Monographic series. English.
Ind/Abst Agrofor. Abstr.; For. Prod. Abstr. (1991-); For. Abstr.; Plant Genet. Resour. Abstr.; Rev. Agric. Entomol.; Seed Abstr.; Soils Fert.

US/0163-3643
RESEARCH NOTE FPL. [Res. note FPL]. **Added/Corp** Forest Products Laboratory (U.S.). **VAT** Research note Forest Products Laboratory. (19??)-. Monographic series. English. **LC** SD433; .U35. *Continues U.S.D.A. Forest Service Research Note FPL, 0093-1683.*
Ind/Abst AGRICOLA [Full Cov.]; For. Prod. Abstr. (1991-); Rev. Agric. Entomol.

US/0099-3468
RESEARCH NOTE INT. (RESEARCH NOTE INT / INTERMOUNTAIN FOREST AND RANGE EXPERIMENT STATION, FOREST SERVICE, UNITED STATES DEPARTMENT OF AGRICULTURE.). [Res.

note INT]. **VAT** Research Note Intermountain. 299 (Oct. 1981)-. Monographic series. English. ir. Price varies per volume. Intermountain Research Station, 507 25th Street, Ogden UT 84401. **LC** SD11; .A4544755. **DD** 634.9/05. ctrl circ. ***Continues*** *USDA Forest Service Research Note INT, 0099-3468.*
Ind/Abst AGRICOLA [Full Cov.]; Ecol. Abstr.; For. Prod. Abstr. (1991-); For. Abstr.; Life Sci. Collect.

US/0361-2449
RESEARCH NOTE NC. [Res. note NC]. **Added/Corp** North Central Forest Experiment Station (Saint Paul, Minn.). **VFOAT** Research Note RN-NC; Research Note RN NC. **VAT** Research Note North Central. (1966)-. Monographic series. English. Price varies per volume. 1992 Folwell Avenue, St Paul MN 55108. **Tel** (612)649-5276. **LC** SD11; .N66. **DD** 634.9/0977. **CODEN** XAFNBE. **Circ:** 2,000 (ctrl). available on microfiche. Documents available from BIOSIS Document Express. ***Formed by the union of*** *U.S. Forest Service Research Note CS, 0270-6113* ***and*** *U.S. Forest Service Research Note LS.*
Desc: Brief or preliminary results of research.
Ind/Abst AGRICOLA [Full Cov.]; Biol. Abstr.; EMBASE; Life Sci. Collect.

US/0737-7150
RESEARCH NOTE PNW. (RESEARCH NOTE PNW / UNITED STATES DEPARTMENT OF AGRICULTURE, FOREST SERVICE, PACIFIC NORTHWEST FOREST AND RANGE EXPERIMENT STATION.). [Res. note PNW]. **VFOAT** Research Note P.N.W. **VAT** Research Note Pacific Northwest. 356-. English. ir. US Department of Agriculture / Portland, Forest Service, Pacific Northwest Region, 319 SW Pine Street, Portland OR 97204. **Tel** (503)326-3625, FAX (503)326-2272. **LC** SD11; .A45613. **DD** 634.9/09795. ***Continues*** *PNW Research Note, 0889-9738.*
Ind/Abst AGRICOLA [Full Cov.]; For. Prod. Abstr.; Geogr. Abstr. Phys. Geogr.; Life Sci. Collect.

CN/0226-9368
RESEARCH NOTE - PROVINCE OF BRITISH COLUMBIA, MINISTRY OF FORESTS. [Res. note - Prov. B.C., Minist. For.]. **Added/Corp** British Columbia. Ministry of Forests. **VAT** Research Note - Research Branch, Ministry of Forests, Province of British Columbia. No. 78 (1977)-. Monographic series. English. ir. Price varies per volume. Ministry of Forests and Lands, Government of British Columbia, Parliament Buildings, Victoria British Columbia V8V 1X4 Canada. **Tel** (604)387-3484. **ED** A R Scott. **LC** UNC. Index available. ***Continues*** *British Columbia. Forest Research Division. Research Notes.*
Ind/Abst AGRICOLA [Full Cov.].

US/0196-3376
RESEARCH NOTE PSW. [Res. note PSW]. **Added/Corp** Pacific Southwest Forest and Range Experiment Station (Berkeley, Calif.). **VAT** Research Note Pacific Southwest. (1978)-. Monographic series. English. Price varies per volume. Pacific Southwest Forest and Range Experiment Station, PO Box 245, Berkeley CA 94701. **LC** SD11; .P3c. **DD** 634.9/09794. ***Continues*** *USDA Forest Service Research Note PSW, 0363-6356.*
Ind/Abst AGRICOLA [Full Cov.]; GeoRef; Life Sci. Collect.; Rev. Agric. Entomol.

US/0277-5794
RESEARCH NOTE RM. (RESEARCH NOTE RM / USDA FOREST SERVICE, ROCKY MOUNTAIN FOREST AND RANGE EXPERIMENT STATION.). [Res. note RM]. **Added/Corp** Rocky Mountain Forest and Range Experiment Station (Fort Collins, Colo.). **VAT** Research Note Rocky Mountain. No. 353 (1978)-. Academic Scholarly Publication. English. ir. Price varies per volume. Rocky Mountain Forest and Range Experiment Station, 240 West Prospect Road, Fort Collins CO 80526. **LC** SD144.A14; R47. **DD** 634.9/0978. available on microfiche. ***Continues*** *Rocky Mountain Forest and Range Experiment Station (Fort Collins, Colo.). USDA Forest Service Research Note RM, 0161-410X.*
Ind/Abst AGRICOLA [Full Cov.]; EMBASE; Life Sci. Collect.; Rev. Agric. Entomol.; Soils Fert.

US/0748-1217
RESEARCH NOTE SE. [Res. note SE]. **VFOAT** Research Note Southeastern. 320-. Academic Scholarly Publication. English. ir. Price varies per volume. USDA Forest Service, Southeastern Forest Experiment Station, PO Box 2570, Asheville NC 28802. **DD** 634. ***Continues*** *Forest Service Research Note SE, 0192-2866.*
Ind/Abst AGRICOLA [Full Cov.]; EMBASE; Life Sci. Collect.

US/0197-8373
RESEARCH NOTE SO. [Res. note SO]. **Main/Corp** United States. Southern Forest Experiment Station, New Orleans. English (Spanish). Southern Forest Experiment Station, T-10210 US Postal Services Building, US Department of Agriculture, 701 Loyola Avenue, New Orleans LA 70113. **Tel** (504)589-6800, FAX (504)589-3961. **LC** SD11.; S67A. **DD** 634.9/0976. ***Continues*** *U.S. Forest Service Research Note SO.*
Ind/Abst AGRICOLA [Full Cov.]; EMBASE; Life Sci. Collect.

MY
RESEARCH PAMPHLET - FOREST RESEARCH INSTITUTE. **Main/Corp** Institiut Penyelidekan Perhutanan. (19??)-. English (Malay). qt. Institut Penyelidikan Perhutanan Malaysia, Kepong, 52109 Kuala Lumpur, Malaysia. **Tel** 03-6342633, FAX 603-6367753. **ED** Khoo Kean Choon. Index available. **Bk Rev**, (Qty: 1-4/yr). **Circ:** 300.

AT/1035-9796
RESEARCH PAPER. **Added/Corp** Queensland Forest Service. **VFOAT** Forest Research Institute Research Paper. No. 16 (19??)-. Monographic series. English. ir. Price varies per volume. Manager Forest Research Branch, PO Box 631, Indooroopilly Queensland, 4068 Australia. **Tel** (07)377 6400, FAX (07)371 2217. **ED** Paul Nielsen. **Circ:** 350 (ctrl). Documents available from BIOSIS Document Express. ***Continues*** *Research Paper (Queensland. Dept. of Forestry), 0155-9672.*
Desc: Reports on substantial research work carried out by officers of the Queensland Forest Service.
Ind/Abst Biol. Abstr.

NR/0331-6793
RESEARCH PAPER. FOREST SERIES. [Res. pap., For. ser.]. **VFOAT** Forest Series. No. 34-. Monographic series. English. Price varies per volume. **CODEN** RFRSDQ. Documents available from BIOSIS Document Express. ***Continues*** *Research Paper (Forest Series).*
Ind/Abst Biol. Abstr. (-1982).

US/0163-3376
RESEARCH PAPER FPL. (RESEARCH PAPER FPL / FOREST PRODUCTS LABORATORY, FOREST SERVICE, U.S. DEPARTMENT OF AGRICULTURE.). [Res. pap. FPL]. **VAT** Research Paper Forest Products Laboratory. Began in 1978. Academic Scholarly Publication. English. Price varies per volume. Forest Products Laboratory, One Gifford Pinchot Drive, Madison WI 53705-2398. **Tel** (608)231-9200, FAX (608)231-9592. **LC** TS801; .U493. **DD** 634.9/8. **CODEN** XAFLA7. available on microfiche. Documents available from Article Express International, CASDDS. ***Continues*** *U.S.D.A. Forest Service Research Paper FPL, 0362-7268.*
Desc: Research reports resulting from wood utilization research at the forest products laboratory.
Ind/Abst AGRICOLA [Full Cov.]; Bioeng. Abstr.; Chem. Abstr.; Ecol. Abstr.; Ei Page One; Eng. Index Annu.

US/0886-7380
RESEARCH PAPER INT. [Res. pap. INT]. **Added/Corp** Forestry Sciences Laboratory (Missoula, Mont.). **VAT** Research Paper Intermountain. (Apr. 1981)-. Monographic series. English. ir. Price varies per volume. **LC** SD11; .A455453. **DD** 634.9/0978. ***Continues*** *USDA Forest Service Research Paper INT, 0363-6232.*
Ind/Abst AGRICOLA [Full Cov.]; Leis. Recreat. Tour. Abstr.; Life Sci. Collect.; Rev. Agric. Entomol.; Soils Fert.

US/0888-9686
RESEARCH PAPER NC. [Res. pap. NC]. **VFOAT** Research Paper N.C. 202-. Monographic series. English. ir. Price varies per volume. **LC** SD11; .A45476. **DD** 634.9/0978. ***Continues*** *U.S.D.A. Forest Service Research Paper NC, 0886-3873.*
Ind/Abst AGRICOLA [Full Cov.]; Life Sci. Collect.

US
RESEARCH PAPER PNW-RP / UNITED STATES, DEPARTMENT OF AGRICULTURE, FOREST SERVICE, PACIFIC NORTHWEST RESEARCH STATION. **Added/Corp** Pacific Northwest Research Station (Portland, Or.). **VFOAT** Research Paper PNW RP. (1986)-. Monographic series. English. Price varies per volume. ***Continues*** *Research Paper PNW, 0882-5165.*
Ind/Abst Geogr. Abstr. Phys. Geogr.

US/0196-1993
RESEARCH PAPER PSW. [Res. pap. PSW]. **Added/Corp** Pacific Southwest Forest and Range Experiment Station (Berkeley, Calif.). **VAT** Research Paper Pacific Southwest. (19??)-. Monographic series. English. Price varies per volume. Pacific Southwest Forest and Range Experiment Station, PO Box 245, Berkeley CA 94701. **LC** SD11; .A45628. **DD** 634.9/09794. available on microfiche. ***Continues*** *USDA Forest Service Research Paper PSW, 0363-5988.*
Ind/Abst AGRICOLA [Full Cov.]; For. Abstr.; Life Sci. Collect.; Rev. Agric. Entomol.

US/0502-5001
RESEARCH PAPER RM. [Res. pap. RM]. **Added/Corp** Rocky Mountain Forest and Range Experiment Station (Fort Collins, Colo.). **VAT** Research Paper Rocky Mountain. (1978)-. Monographic series. English. Price varies per volume. Rocky Mountain Forest and Range Experiment Station, 240 West Prospect Road, Fort Collins CO 80526. **LC** SD11; .A4568. **DD** 634.9/0978. ***Continues*** *USDA Forest Service Research Paper RM, 0363-6259.*
Ind/Abst AGRICOLA [Full Cov.]; For. Prod. Abstr.; Life Sci. Collect.; Seed Abstr.

US/0888-9678
RESEARCH PAPER SE. [Res. pap. SE]. **Added/Corp** Southeastern Forest Experiment Station (Asheville, N.C.). **VAT** Research Paper Southeast. (1981)-. Monographic series. English. ir. Price varies per volume. Southeastern Forest Experiment Station, Box 2680, Asheville NC 28802. **LC** SD11; .A4576. **DD** 634. ***Continues*** *Forest Service Research Paper SE, 0272-6041.*
Ind/Abst Agrofor. Abstr.; For. Prod. Abstr.; Life Sci. Collect.

US/0748-1225
RESEARCH PAPER SO. [Res. pap. SO]. **VAT** Research Paper Southern. (1977)-. Monographic series. English. ir. Price varies per volume. Southern Forest Experiment Station, T-10210 US Postal Services Building, US Department of Agriculture, 701 Loyola Avenue, New Orleans LA 70113. **Tel** (504)589-6800, FAX (504)589-3961. **LC** SD11; .A45792. **DD** 634.9/0975. **Circ:** 5,000 (ctrl). available on microfilm. ***Continues*** *Forest Service Research Paper SO (1972).*
Ind/Abst AGRICOLA [Full Cov.]; Life Sci. Collect.

AT/0311-0893
RESEARCH REPORT / DIVISION OF TECHNICAL SERVICES (RESEARCH AND UTILIZATION), QUEENSLAND DEPARTMENT OF FORESTRY. **Added/Corp** Queensland. Dept. of Forestry. Division of Technical Services (Research and Utlization). (19??)-. English. be. Queensland Department of Forestry, Box 944, Government Printing Office, Brisbane 4001 Queensland Australia. **LC** SD111.Q8; D43b. **DD** 634.9/072/0943. ***Continues*** *Queensland. Dept. of Forestry. Division of Technical Services. Report of Research Activities - Division of Technical Services, Queensland Department of Forestry.*

AT
RESEARCH REPORT - FORESTRY COMMISSION OF N.S.W. **Main/Corp** New South Wales. Forestry Commission. 1973/74- 1974-. Periodical. English. an. Forestry Commission of New South Wales, 95-99 York Street, Sydney New South Wales, 2000 Australia. **Tel** 02 234- 1513. ***Continues*** *Annual Research Report - Forestry Commission of N.S.W.*

US/0147-2186
RESEARCH REPORT - MISSISSIPPI AGRICULTURAL & FORESTRY EXPERIMENT STATION. **See** Agriculture.

AT/0814-9992
RESEARCH REVIEW / DIVISION OF CHEMICAL AND WOOD TECHNOLOGY. **See** Chemistry.

US/0748-1241
RESOURCE BULLETIN INT. [Resour. bull. INT]. **VFOAT** Resource Bulletin I.N.T. **VAT** Resource Bulletin Intermountain. 25 (Oct. 1981)-. Bulletin. English. ir. Price varies per volume. Intermountain Research Station, 507 25th Street, Ogden UT 84401. ctrl circ. ***Continues*** *USDA Forest Service Resource Bulletin INT, 0098-6313.*
Ind/Abst AGRICOLA; For. Prod. Abstr.; Life Sci. Collect.

US/0748-1357
RESOURCE BULLETIN NE. [Resour. bull. NE]. **Added/Corp** Northeastern Forest Experiment Station (Radnor, Pa.). **VFOAT** Resource Bulletin N.E. **VAT** Resource Bulletin Northeastern. No. 67 (1981)-. Monographic series. English. ir. Price varies per volume. Northeastern Forest Experiment Station / Broomall, PA, US Department of Agriculture / Forest Service, Broomall PA 19008. **DD** 634. ***Continues*** *U.S.D.A. Forest Service Resource Bulletin NE, 0363-633X.*
Ind/Abst AGRICOLA; For. Prod. Abstr.

US/0748-1284
RESOURCE BULLETIN PNW. [Resour. bull. PNW]. **VAT** Resource Bulletin Pacific Northwest. Bulletin. English. ir. Price varies per volume. Pacific Northwest Forest and Range Experiment Station, 809 Northeast Sixth Avenue, Portland OR 97232. **Tel** (503)231-2081. **LC** SD11; .A45616. **DD** 333.75/09795. Documents available from BIOSIS Document Express. ***Continues*** *USDA Forest Service Resource Bulletin PNW, 0363-6240.*
Ind/Abst AGRICOLA; Biol. Abstr.; Ecol. Abstr.; Life Sci. Collect.

US/0888-9708
RESOURCE BULLETIN RM. [Resour. bull. RM]. **Main/Corp** Rocky Mountain Forest and Range Experiment Station (Fort Collins, Colo.). **VAT** Resource Bulletin Rocky Mountain. 1-. Bulletin. English. ir. Price varies per volume. Rocky Mountain Forest and Range Experiment Station, 240 West Prospect Road, Fort Collins CO 80526. **DD** 634.
Ind/Abst AGRICOLA [Full Cov.]; For. Prod. Abstr.; Life Sci. Collect.

US/0885-8381
RESOURCE BULLETIN SE. [Resour. bull. SE]. **VAT** Resource Bulletin Southeastern. (1981)-. Bulletin. English. ir. Price varies per volume. Southeastern Forest, PO Box 2680, Asheville NC 28802-2680. **Tel** (704)259-0327. **DD** 634. available in microform. ***Continues*** *Forest Service Resource Bulletin SE.*
Ind/Abst For. Abstr.; Geogr. Abstr. Human Geogr.; Life Sci. Collect.

US/0887-4832
RESOURCE BULLETIN SO. (RESOURCE BULLETIN SO / FOREST SERVICE, U.S. DEPARTMENT OF AGRICULTURE.). [Resour. bull. SO]. **Added/Corp** United States. Forest Service. Southern Forest Experiment Station (New Orleans, La.). **VAT** Resource Bulletin Southern. (1978)-. Bulletin. English. Price varies per volume. Southern Forest Experiment Station, T-10210 US Postal Services Building, US Department of Agriculture, 701 Loyola Avenue, New Orleans LA 70113. **Tel** (504)589-6800, FAX (504)589-3961. **DD** 634. ***Continues*** *Forest Service Resource Bulletin SO, 0363-6321.*
Ind/Abst For. Abstr.; Life Sci. Collect.

SW/0280-1892
RESULTS (FORSKNINGSSTIFTELSEN SKOGSARBETEN). (RESULTS / FORSKNINGSSTIFTELSEN SKOGSARBETEN.). **Added/Corp** Forskningsstiftelsen Skogsarbeten (Stockholm, Sweden). (19??)-. Periodical. English. Forskningstiftelsen Skogsforsk Glunten, S 751 83 Uppsala Sweden. **Tel** 011 46 18 188500. **LC** SD538.3.S8; R475.
Desc: Information on logging, forestry, and forest machinery.
Ind/Abst For. Prod. Abstr. (1991-); For. Abstr.

CN/0824-2135
REVIEW REPORT - FORINTEK CANADA CORP., EASTERN LABORATORY. (REVIEW REPORT.). [Rev. rep. - Forintek Can. Corp. East. Lab.]. 1981-. Monographic series. English (French). Price varies per volume. Forintek Canada Corporation, 800 Montreal Road, Ottawa Ontario K1G 3Z5 Canada. **Tel** (613)744-0963. **DD** 634.9/8/05. ***Continues*** *Review Report (Eastern Forest Products Laboratory (Canada)), 0711-1339.*

BL/0100-6762
REVISTA ARVORE. (REVISTA ARVORE / SOCIEDADE DE INVESTIGACOES FLORESTAIS.). [Rev. ,arvore]. **Added/Corp** Sociedade de Investigacoes Florestais (Brazil) Universidade Federal de Vicosa. (1976)-. Periodical. Portuguese (summaries and/or abstracts in English; table of contents in English). sa. **CODEN** RARVDY. Documents available from CASDDS.
Ind/Abst Chem. Abstr.; Irr. Drain. Abstr.; Plant Grow. Reg. Abstr.

CU
REVISTA BARACOA. **Added/Corp** Centro de Informacion y Documentacion Agropecuario (Cuba). Vol. 21, No. 1 (1991)-. Periodical. Spanish (English). Three times a year. Ediciones Cubanas, Obispo 527, Altos ESQ Bernaza, CP 10100 Havana Cuba. **Tel** 011 632980, 631942, FAX 011 631011, telex 512337, 6540. **LC** WMLC 93/4331. ***Formed by the union of*** *Revista Forestal Baracoa, 0138-6441* ***and*** *Ciencia y Tecnica en la Agricultura. Cafe y Cacao, 1013-9834.*

BL/0103-2674
REVISTA DO INSTITUTO FLORESTAL. Vol. 1, No. 1 (July 1989)-. Portuguese (summaries and/or abstracts in English). sa. Instituto Florestal, Caixa Postal 1.322, Sao Paulo 01051 Brazil. **Tel** (011)203 01 22, telex (011)22877 SAGR BR. **LC** SD160.S26; R48. ***Formed by the union of*** *Silvicultura Em Sao Paulo, 0583-3132* ***and*** *Boletim Tecnico (Sao Paulo (Brazil : State). Instituto Florestal), 0100-3151.*
Ind/Abst For. Abstr.

CU/0138-6441
REVISTA FORESTAL BARACOA. [Rev. for. baracoa]. (19??)-. Periodical. Spanish. sa.
Ind/Abst Agrindex; Agrofor. Abstr.; Biocont. News Inf.; Biodeter. Abstr.; Field Crop Abstr.; For. Prod. Abstr. (1991-); For. Abstr.; Grasslands For. Abstr.; Maize Abstr.; Rev. Agric. Entomol.; Rev. Plant Pathol.

PE
REVISTA FORESTAL DEL PERU. Periodical. Spanish.
Ind/Abst Agric. Eng. Abstr. (1991-); Agrofor. Abstr. (1991-); For. Prod. Abstr. (1991-); For. Abstr.; Hortic. Abstr.; Maize Abstr.; Soils Fert.; Weed Abstr.

VE/0556-6606
REVISTA FORESTAL VENEZOLANA. [Rev. for. venez.]. **Added/Corp** Universidad de los Andes (Merida, Venezuela). Facultad de Ciencias Forestales. No. 1 (1958)-. Periodical. Spanish. ***Supersedes*** *Universidad de los Andes (Merida, Venezuela). Facultad de Ciencias Forestales. Boletin.*
Ind/Abst AGRICOLA; Biocont. News Inf.; Crop Physiol. Abstr.; Field Crop Abstr.; For. Prod. Abstr. (1991-); For. Abstr.

RM
REVISTA PADURILOR (BUCHAREST, ROMANIA : 1986). (REVISTA PADURILOR.). **Added/Corp** Romania. Ministerul Silviculturii. Romania. Ministerul Industrializarii Lemnului si Materialelor de Constructii. Vol. 101, (1986)-. Periodical. Romanian (summaries and/or abstracts in English). qt. DM225.00. **(Subscription address:** Kubon & Sagner, ABT Zeitschriftenimport, D 80328 Munich Germany.**)** ***Continues*** *Revista Padurilor-Industria Lemnului, Celuloza Si Hirtie. Silvicultura Si Exploatarea Padurilor, 0250-5495.*
Ind/Abst Grasslands For. Abstr.; Irr. Drain. Abstr.; Rev. Agric. Entomol.

FR/0035-2829
REVUE FORESTIERE FRANCAISE. [Rev. for. fr.]. **Added/Corp** Ecole Nationale du Genie Rural, des Eaux et des Forets (France) Ecole Nationale des Eaux et Forets (France) France. Ministere de l'Agriculture et du Developpement Rural. Vol. 1 (April 1949)-. Academic Scholarly Publication. French. bm (plus 1 special issue per year). 225.00F France; 243.00F other. Ecole Nationale du Genie Rural des Eaux et des Forets, 14 rue Girardet, F-54042 Nancy Cedex France. **Tel** 83 39 08 00, telex 83 30 22 54. **[CCC]**. Index available (published separately). cum. index. **Bk Rev.** ctrl circ. Documents available. ***Supersedes*** *Revue des Eaux et Forets.*
Desc: Ideas in the area of forestry. Specific topics include biology, economy of forests, and forests in other countries.
Ind/Abst Abstr. Bull. Inst. Paper Chem.; Abstr. Bull. Inst. Pap. Sci. Tech.; AGRICOLA; EMBASE; Key Word Index Wildl. Res.; Wildl. Rev.

SP/1130-958X
RFE. REVISTA FORESTAL ESPANOLA. [RFE, Rev. for. esp.]. **VFOAT** Revista Forestal Espanola. (1991)-. Periodical. Spanish. qt. 5000.00ptas. GAESA, Calle Gran Via 31-7-2, 28013 Madrid Spain. **Tel** 011 34 1 5227320. **UDC** 630. **Ad Acc, Adv Mgr:** Angel Garcia-Rodrigo, **Tel** 532-3875.
Desc: Magazine for specialists in forestry, environmental studies, and ecology.

IO/0035-5372
RIMBA INDONESIA. V. 1- 1952-. Periodical. Multiple languages (Dutch, English and Indonesian; summaries and/or abstracts in Dutch and English). qt. **LC** SD1; .R53.

JA/0287-5136
RINBOKU IKUSHUJO KENKYU HOKOKU. **Added/Corp** Kant o Rinboku Ikushujo (Japan). **VFOAT** Kenkyu Hokoku; Bulletin of the Forest Tree Breeding Institute. No. 1 (March 1983)-. Japanese (summaries and/or abstracts in English).
Ind/Abst AGRICOLA; For. Prod. Abstr. (1991-); Seed Abstr.

JA/0388-8614
RINGYO KEIZAI. **Added/Corp** Ringyo Keizai Kenkyujo (Tokyo, Japan). **VFOAT** Forest Economy. (1948)-. Periodical. Japanese. mo. $137.50. **(Subscription address:** Japan Publications Trading Company, Ltd., PO Box 5030, Tokyo International, Tokyo 100-31 Japan.**)** **LC** SD393; .R55.

JA
RINGYO SEISAN TOKEI NEMPO. **Main/Corp** Japan. Norinsho. Norin Keizaikyoku. Tokei Johobu. (1971)-. Periodical. Japanese. Norin Tokei Kyokai, (Association of Agriculture & Forestry Statistics), 11-14, Meguro 2 Chome, Meguroku, Tokyoto 153, Japan. **LC** SD225; .J28a. ***Continues*** *Ringyo Seisan Tokei Nempo.*

JA
RINGYO SHIKENJO JIHO. **Added/Corp** Fukuoka-ken Ringyo Shikenjo. **VFOAT** Bulletin of Fukuoka-ken Forest Experiment Station; Fukuoka-ken Ringyo Shikenjo Jiho. (19??)-. Periodical. Japanese (summaries and/or abstracts in English; table of contents in English). an.
Ind/Abst AGRICOLA; Biocont. News Inf.; For. Abstr.

JA/0082-4720
RINGYO SHIKENJO KENKYU HOKOKU. [Ringyo Shikenjo kenkyu hokoku]. **Added/Corp** Ringyo Shikenjo. **VFOAT** Bulletin of the Government Forest Experiment Station; Bulletin of the Forestry and Forest Products Research Institute. No. 42 (July 1949)-. Academic Scholarly Publication. Japanese. Forestry & Forest Products Research Institute, PO Box 16, Tsukuba Norin Kenkyu Danchi-nai, Ibaraki 305 Japan. **CODEN** RSHKA6. Documents available from CASDDS. ***Continues*** *Ringyo Shiken Hokoku.*
Ind/Abst Abstr. Bull. Inst. Pap. Sci. Tech.; Chem. Abstr.

JA
RINSAN SHIKENJO KENKYU HOKOKU. [Rinsan Shikenjo kenkyu hokoku]. **VFOAT** Report of the Hokkaido Forest Products Research Institute. (1975)-. Academic Scholarly Publication. Japanese (English). ir. Hokkaido Forest Products Research Institute, 1-10 Nishikagura Asahikawa, Hokkaido 070-01 Japan. **Tel** 0166-75-4233, telex 0166-75-36-21. **ED** Hisashi Shida and Tetsuo Takeno. **CODEN** HRSKAC. Index available. **Circ:** 600 (ctrl). Documents available from CASDDS.
Desc: Publishes results of testing by the Hokkaido Forest Products Research Institute.
Ind/Abst Abstr. Bull. Inst. Pap. Sci. Tech.; Chem. Abstr.

JA/0913-140X
RINSAN SHIKENJOHO. [Rinsan Shikenjoho]. **Added/Corp** Hokkaidoritsu Rinsan Shikenjo. **VFOAT** Journal of the Hokkaido Forest Products Research Institute. (1987)-. Periodical. Japanese (summaries and/or abstracts in English). mo. Hokkaido Forest Products Research Institute, 1-10 Nishikagura Asahikawa, Hokkaido 070-01 Japan. **Tel** 0166-75-4233, telex 0166-75-36-21. **CODEN** RSHOEM. Documents available from CASDDS. ***Continues*** *Hokkaidoritsu Rinsan Shikenjo. Rinsan Shikenjo Geppo, 0370-7296.*
Ind/Abst Chem. Abstr.

US
ROSTER OF CURRENT LICENSES - GEORGIA. STATE BOARD OF REGISTRATION FOR FORESTERS. **Main/Corp** Georgia. State Board of Registration for Foresters. English. State Examining Boards, 166 Pryor Street SW, Atlanta GA 30303. **LC** SD12; .G47. **DD** 634.9/025/758.

US/0196-7533
ROSTER OF REGISTERED FORESTERS OF MISSISSIPPI. [Roster regist. for. Miss.]. English. an. Mississippi Board of Registration for Foresters, Suite 201/620 North State Street, Jackson MS 39202. **Tel** (601)354-4936. **LC** SD144.M7; R67. **DD** 634.9/025/762.

US
ROSTER OF REGISTERED FORESTERS : STATE OF ALABAMA. **Main/Corp** Alabama. State Board of Registration for Foresters. English. be. Alabama State Board of Registration for Foresters, Montgomery AL. **Tel** (205)240-9368. **ED** Pamela B Sears. Index available.
Desc: Listing of Registered Foresters all over the US licensed by the Alabama State Board of Registration for Foresters.

●US/1068-669X
RUSSIAN FOREST SCIENCES. [Russ. for. sci.]. No. 1 (1992)-. Periodical. English (translations available in Russian). Six times a year. $590.00. Allerton Press, Inc., 150 Fifth Avenue, New York NY 10011. **Tel** (212)924-3950, FAX (212)463-9684, telex 427441 ALPRES. **LC** SD1; .L425. **DD** 634.9. **[CCC]**. ***Continues*** *Lesovedenie. English. Soviet Forest Sciences, 0891-0324.*

KO
SALLIM. Periodical. Korean. mo. Sallim Chohap Chunganghoe, 192-2 Ssangnim-dong Chung-ku, Seoul 100 Korea. **LC** SD235.K6; S23.

JA/0911-615X
SAN'IN CHIIKI KENKYU. [San'in chiiki kenkyu]. **VFOAT** Studies of the San'in Region. (1985)-. Periodical. Multiple languages. an. **DD** 060. ***Continues*** *San'in Bunka Kenkyu Kiyo, 0558-4825.*
Ind/Abst For. Abstr.

JA/0911-6168
SAN'IN CHIIKI KENKYU. SHIRO-HEN. [San'in Chiiki Kenkyu. Shiryo-hen]. **VFOAT** Studies of the San'in Region. Research Data and Source Material. (1985)-. Periodical. Multiple languages. an. Centre for Studies of the San'in Region, Shimane University, 1060 Nishikawatsu-cho Matsue,, Shimane 606, Japan. **DD** 060.
Ind/Abst For. Prod. Abstr. (1991-).

FI/0355-032X
SCANDINAVIAN FOREST ECONOMICS. **Added/Corp** Nordic Forest Economic Seminar. (19??)-. Periodical. English. ir. Scandinavian Forest Economics, PL 37, SF00381, Helsinki 38 Finland. **ED** Ashley Selby. **Bk Rev. Circ:** 200 (ctrl).
Desc: Occasional news and proceedings bulletin of the Scandinavian Society of Forest Economics.
Ind/Abst For. Prod. Abstr.

SW/0282-7581
SCANDINAVIAN JOURNAL OF FOREST RESEARCH. [Scand. j. for. res.]. (1986)-. Periodical. English. qt. Kr945.00, $153.00. Scandinavian University Press, PO Box 2959 Toeyen, N 0608 Oslo 6 Norway. **Tel** 011 47 2 2575400, FAX 011 47 2 2575353, telex 71896 UROR N. **(Subscription address:** Scandinavian University Press, 200 Meacham Ave., Elmont NY 11003.**)** **ED** Sven-Uno Skarp. **LC** SD217.S34; S26. **DD** 634.9/0948. **CODEN** SJFRE3. **Pr Rev.** Documents available from BIOSIS Document Express.
Desc: Aim is to cover the whole field of forest research from basic to more applied subjects. This means articles within basic forestry sciences, silviculture, forest operations, forest planning management and economics, forest utilization and marketing.
Ind/Abst Abstr. Bull. Inst. Pap. Sci. Tech.; AGRICOLA; Biol. Abstr. (1986-); Crop Physiol. Abstr.; Curr. Aware. Biol. Sci., CABS; Environ. Period. Bibliogr.; Fish Rev. (Jan. 1989-July 1992); For. Prod. Abstr. (1991-); For. Abstr.; Plant Breed. Abstr.; Plant Grow. Reg. Abstr.; Rev.

Agric. Entomol.; Rev. Plant Pathol.; Sci. Cit. Index; Seed Abstr.; Soc. Sci. Cit. Index [Select. Cov.]; Soils Fert.; Weed Abstr.; Wildl. Rev. (Jan. 1989-July 1992).

GW/0344-5666
SCHRIFTEN AUS DER FORSTLICHEN FAKULTAT DER UNIVERSITAT GOTTINGEN UND DER NIEDERSACHSISCHEN FORSTLICHEN VERSUCHSANSTALT. **Added/Corp** Universitat Gottingen. Forstliche Fakultat. Niedersachsische Forstliche Versuchsanstalt (Germany). (1978)-. Monographic series. German. **LC** SD195; .G6. ***Continues*** *Schriftenreihe der Forstlichen Fakultat der Universitat Gottingen und Mitteilungen der Niedersachsischen Forstlichen Versuchsanstalt.*
Ind/Abst For. Abstr.

GW
SCHWEDEN FORST- UND HOLZWIRTSCHAFT / BUNDESSTELLE FUR AUSSENHANDELSINFORMATION. German. 5.00. Bundesstelle fuer Aussenhandelsinformation, Agrippastr 87 93, D 50676 Cologne Germany. **Tel** 011 49 221 2057316, FAX 011 49 221 2057212. **LC** HD9765.S8; S38. **DD** 338.1/749/09485.

SZ/0036-7818
SCHWEIZERISCHE ZEITSCHRIFT FUER DAS FORSTWESEN. **VFOAT** Journal Forestier Suisse. (19??)-. Periodical. Multiple languages (German and French). Twelve times a year. 115.00F. Schweizerischer Forstverein, Eth-Zentrum Schmekzbergstr 25, CH-8092 Zurich Switzerland. **Tel** 011 41 1 2565205, FAX 011 262 45 43. Index available (Feb issue). **Bk Rev. Ad Acc. Circ:** 1,800 (ctrl).
Desc: Information on forestry, science, experiences, research environment (mostly in Switzerland).
Ind/Abst Fish Rev. (Jan. 1989-July 1992); For. Prod. Abstr. (19??-19??); Irr. Drain. Abstr.; Key Word Index Wildl. Res.; Soils Fert.; Wildl. Rev. (Jan. 1989-July 1992).

KE
SCIENCE AND PRACTICE OF AGROFORESTRY. **See** Agriculture.

UK/0036-9217
SCOTTISH FORESTRY. [Scott. for.]. **Added/Corp** Royal Scottish Forestry Society. Vol. 1 (July 1947)-. Periodical. English. Four times a year (Jan., Apr., July, Oct.). £40.00. Royal Scottish Forestry Society, Camsie House Charlestown, DUN Fife KY11 3EE Scotland. **Tel** 011 44 383 873014, FAX 011 44 383 872863. **ED** Ms. J. Johnston, (phone: 0383 873 014). **LC** SD1; .S457. **DD** 634.905. **CODEN** SFORAG. Index Bound in First Issue. cum. index. **Ad Acc. Circ:** 1,800. Documents available from BIOSIS Document Express. ***Supersedes*** *Scottish Forestry Journal.*
Desc: Technical papers, news and reviews on a wide variety of subjects connected with forestry in Scotland.
Ind/Abst AGRICOLA; Biol. Abstr.; Curr. Aware. Biol. Sci., CABS; For. Prod. Abstr.; For. Abstr.; Life Sci. Collect.; Soils Fert.; Wildl. Rev.

CN/0834-938X
SELECTED FORESTRY STATISTICS, CANADA. (SELECTED FORESTRY STATISTICS, CANADA / ECONOMICS BRANCH, CANADIAN FORESTRY SERVICE, GOVERNMENT OF CANADA.). [Sel. for. stat. Can.]. **Added/Corp** Canadian Forestry Service. Economics Branch. (198?)-. English. Free. **LC** HD9764.C2; S44. **DD** 338.1/7498/0971021.
Ind/Abst For. Prod. Abstr. (19??-19??).

CC/0253-3669
SENGONG KEJI TONGXUN. (SEN KUNG KO CHI TUNG HSUN.). [Sengong keji tongxun]. **VFOAT** Forest Industry Technical Newsletter. Began in 1980. Academic Scholarly Publication. Chinese. mo. **CODEN** SKTHDF. Documents available from CASDDS.
Ind/Abst Chem. Abstr.

CK/0121-0254
SERIE DE DOCUMENTACION / CORPORACION NACIONAL DE INVESTIGACION Y FOMENTO FORESTAL. **Added/Corp** Corporacion Nacional de Investigacion y Fomento Forestal (Colombia). **VFOAT** Serie Documentacion. No. 1 (1976)-. Monographic series. Spanish. **LC** SD163; .S47. **DD** 634.9/09861.
Ind/Abst For. Abstr.

CC
SHAN-HSI LIN YEH KO CHI. **Added/Corp** Shan-Hsi Sheng Lin Yeh Ko Hsueh Yen Chiu So (Shensi Province, China) Shan-Hsi Sheng Lin Hsueh Hui (Shensi Province, China). **VFOAT** Shaanxi Forest Science and Technology. (19??)-. Periodical. Chinese (summaries and/or abstracts in English). qt.
Ind/Abst For. Prod. Abstr. (1991-); Plant Grow. Reg. Abstr.

CC
SHIH CHIEH LIN YEH CHIU. **VFOAT** World Forestry Research. English (French). bm (6 issues). $90.00. World Forestry Research Board, Editorial Department, Wan Shou Shan, 100091 Beijing, People's Republic of China. **(Subscription address:** China International Book Trading Corporation, PO Box 399, Library Service Department, Beijing 100044 People's Republic of China.**)**

CH/1001-4241
SHIJIE LINYE YANJIU. **VFOAT** World Forestry Research. (1988)-. Periodical. Chinese (French). Six times a year. $90.00. World Forestry Research Board, Editorial Department, Wan Shou Shan, 100091 Beijing, People's Republic of China. **(Subscription address:** China International Book Trading Corporation, PO Box 399, Library Service Department, Beijing 100044 People's Republic of China.**)** **ED** Li Weichang. **DD** 634.9. Index available.

JA
SHIMANE DAIGAKU NOGAKUBU ENSHURIN HOKOKU. **Main/Corp** Shimane Daigaku, Matsue, Japan. Nogakubu. **VFOAT** Bulletin of the Shimane University Forests. No. 1 (1972)-. Japanese. Shimane Daigaku Nogakubu Enshurin Hokoku, 1060 Nishi Kawatsucho, 690 Matsue Japan. **LC** SD226.S55; S54A.

JA
SHINRIN BOEKI. **VFOAT** Forest Protection. Periodical. Japanese (Japanese). Zenkoku Shinrin Byochujugai Bogo Kyokai, c/o Kobu Building Chiyoda-ku, Tokyo Japan. **LC** SD414.J3; S54.

JA/0385-9088
SHINRIN REKURIESHON KENKYU. (SHINRIN REKURYESHON KENKYU. FOREST RECREATION RESEARCH.). [Shinrin rekurieshon kenkyu]. **Added/Corp** Tokyo Noko Daigaku. Ringakuka. **VFOAT** Forest Recreation Research. No. 1 (1977)-. Japanese (summaries and/or abstracts in English). Tokyo Noko Daigaku Nogakubu Ringakuka, 8-1 Harumicho 3-chome, Fuchu 183 Japan. **LC** SD647; .S538. **CODEN** FRERDC. Documents available from BIOSIS Document Express.
Ind/Abst Biol. Abstr. (?-1984).

JA/0916-4405
SHINRIN SOGO KENKYUJO KENKYU HOKOKU. **VFOAT** Bulletin of the Forestry and Forest Products Research Institute (1989). (1989)-. Academic Scholarly Publication. Multiple languages. ir. **DD** 634.9. Documents available from CASDDS. ***Continues*** *Ringyo Shikenjo Kenkyu Hokoku, 0082-4720.*
Ind/Abst Chem. Abstr.

BE
SILVA BELGICA. Vol. 96, No. 1 (Jan./Feb. 1989)-. Periodical. French (Dutch and Flemish). bm. 1050.00F Belgium; 1700.00F other. Societe Royale Forestiere de Belgique, Galerie du Centre, Bloc 2-5, B-1000 Brussels Belgium. **Tel** 011 32 2 2230766, FAX 011 32 2 2230145. ***Continues*** *Bulletin de la Societe Royale Forestiere de Belgique.*

FI
SILVA FENNICA (HELSINKI, FINLAND : 1926). (SILVA FENNICA.). **Added/Corp** Suomen Metsatieteellinen Seura. Vol. 1, No 1 (1967)-. Periodical. English (Finnish and Swedish). Four times a year. Fmk600.00. Academic Bookstore Akateeminen, Postilokero 23, FIN-00371 Helsinki Finland. **Tel** 011 358 0 12141. **LC** SD217.F5; S55. **DD** 333.75/094897. ***Continues*** *Silva Fennica (Helsinki, Finland : 1926), 0037-5330.*
Ind/Abst Biocont. News Inf.; Ecol. Abstr.; Ecology Abstr.; Fish Rev. (Jan. 1989-July 1992); For. Prod. Abstr. (19??-19??); For. Abstr.; Geogr. Abstr. Phys. Geogr.; Geogr. Abstr. Human Geogr.; Int. Dev. Abstr.; Rev. Plant Pathol.; Soils Fert.; Wildl. Rev. (Jan. 1989-July 1992).

GW/0037-5349
SILVAE GENETICA. **See** Biology-Botany.

CN
SILVICULTURAL OPERATIONS NEWSLETTER. Newsletter. English. sa (June & Dec.). (Free upon request). Forest Engineering Research Institute of Canada, 143 Place Frontenac, Pointe-Claire Quebec H9R 4Z7 Canada.
Ind/Abst Abstr. Bull. Inst. Pap. Sci. Tech.

SW/1101-9506
SKOG & FORSKNING. [Skog forsk.]. **Main/Corp** Sveriges Skogsvardsforbund. **Added/Corp** Sveriges Skogsvardsforbund. **VFOAT** Skog Och Forskning. (1991)-. Periodical. Swedish (summaries and/or abstracts in English). Four times a year. Kr400.00 Europe; Kr440.00 others. Sveriges Skogsvardsforbund, Box 500, S 18215 Danderyd Sweden. **Tel** 011 46 8 7530390, FAX 011 46 8 7558602. **ED** Bengt Ek. **LC** SD1; .S83. **Bk Rev. Ad Acc. Circ:** 1,500 (ctrl). ***Continues*** *Sveriges Skogsvardsforbunds Tidskrift, 0371-2907.*
Ind/Abst AGRICOLA; For. Abstr.; Life Sci. Collect.

SW/0283-1007
SMALL SCALE FORESTRY. **Added/Corp** Sveriges Lantbruksuniversitet. Dept. of Operational Efficiency. Sveriges Lantbruksuniversitet. Research Group for Small Scale Forestry. (198?)-. Periodical. English. sa. $16.00 (individuals), $45.00 (institutions). Swedish University, Agricultural Sciences, Department of Forest Ext., c/o V. Karhu, S770 73 Garpenburg Sweden. **Tel** 011 46 225 22100, FAX 011 46 225 22193, telex 74551.

SW
SOEDRA SKOG. Swedish. Six times a year. free to members, Kr120.00 other. Soedra Skogsaegarna AB, S-351 89, Vaxjo 1 Sweden. **Tel** 0470-89466, FAX 0470-21738. **Ad Acc.**
Desc: Forestry, advertisements and other information regarding forestry machines.

KO
SOUL TAEHAKKYO NONGKWA TAEHAK YONSUMNIM YONGU POGO. **VFOAT** Yonsumnim Yongu Pogo; Research Bulletin of the Seoul National University Forests. Vol. 18-. Periodical. Korean (summaries and/or abstracts in English). an. W6000 S. Korea; $6.00 US. Office of the University Forest College of Agriculture, Seoul National University, 103 Seodoon-dong, Suwon 170 Korea. **Tel** (0331)44-2121. **ED** D Lee, T Kim, H Kim, H Chung, K Woo and B Woo. **LC** SD235.K6; S63A . Index available. cum. index. **Circ:** 500 (ctrl). ***Continues*** *Bulletin of the Seoul National University Forests.*
Desc: Publication accepts research data primarily concerned with the Seoul National University Forests.

SA/0038-2167
SOUTH AFRICAN FORESTRY JOURNAL. **Added/Corp** South African Forestry Association. South African Forestry Association. Journal. South African Forestry Association. Tydskrif. South African Institute of Forestry. **VFOAT** Suid-Afrikaa Bosboutydskrif. No. 1 (Oct. 1938)-. Periodical. Multiple languages (English and Afrikaans). qt. $18.36 South Africa; $50.00 other. South African Forestry Association, PO Box 1022, Pretoria 0001 South Africa. **Tel** 012-627851. **ED** J V Jordaan. Index available. cum. index. **Bk Rev. Ad Acc. Circ:** 1,183 (ctrl).
Desc: Scientific and general papers on all aspects of forestry, including conservation, economics, management, culture production and research.
Ind/Abst Ecol. Abstr. (?-?); Ecology Abstr.; For. Prod. Abstr. (1991-); For. Abstr.; Geogr. Abstr. Human Geogr. (?-?); Irr. Drain. Abstr.; Seed Abstr.; Weed Abstr.; Wildl. Rev.

US/0148-4419
SOUTHERN JOURNAL OF APPLIED FORESTRY. [South. j. appl. for.]. **Added/Corp** Society of American Foresters. Vol. 1, No. 1 (Feb. 1977)-. Academic Scholarly Publication. English. qt (Feb., May, Aug., and Nov.). $85.00 (institutions), $40.00 (non-member individuals) US and Canada; $120.00 (institutions), $60.00 (non-member individuals) other. Society of American Foresters, 5400 Grosvenor Lane, Bethesda MD 20814-2198. **Tel** (301)897-8720, FAX (301)897-3690, telex 9102501089 SAFFOREST UQ. **ED** J. S. McKnight. **LC** SD144.A15; S66. **DD** 634.9/0975. **CODEN** SJAFD9. Index available. **Bk Rev. Ad Acc. Circ:** 1,600 (ctrl). available on microfilm and microfiche from University Microfilms International (UMI). Documents available from BIOSIS Document Express, CASDDS, Documents on Demand.
Desc: New ideas and research for practical application by landowners and resource managers in the South.
Ind/Abst Abstr. Bull. Inst. Pap. Sci. Tech.; AGRICOLA [Full Cov.]; Biol. Abstr.; Chem. Abstr.; Ecol. Abstr.; Environ. Abstr.; For. Prod. Abstr. (1991-); For. Abstr.; Geogr. Abstr. Phys. Geogr. (?-?); Geogr. Abstr. Human Geogr.; Rev. Agric. Entomol.; Weed Abstr.; Wildl. Rev.

GW
SPANIEN, LAND- UND FORSTWIRTSCHAFT, FISCHEREI / BUNDESSTELLE FUER AUSSENHANDELSINFORMATION. **See** Agriculture.

US/1059-2512
SPECIAL PUBLICATION / FOREST RESEARCH LAB, SCHOOL OF FORESTRY, OREGON STATE UNIVERSITY. ***Title Change.*** [Spec. publ. - Or. State Univ., For. Res. Lab.]. **Added/Corp** Oregon State University. Forest Research Laboratory. (1981)-(1992). Monographic series. English. Forest Research Laboratory, Oregon State University, Corvallis OR 97331. **Tel** (503)754-4271. **LC** UNC. **DD** 634. ***Merged with*** *Research Bulletin (Oregon State University. Forest Research Laboratory); Oregon State University. Forest Research Laboratory. Research Note - School of Forestry, Forest Research Laboratory, Oregon State University* ***and*** *Oregon State University. Forest Research Laboratory. Research Paper - Forest Research Laboratory, Oregon State University* ***to form*** *Research Contribution.*
Ind/Abst AGRICOLA (?-?) [Full Cov.]; For. Prod. Abstr. (1991-?).

CN/0381-7733
SPECIAL REPORT (FOREST ENGINEERING RESEARCH INSTITUTE OF CANADA). (SPECIAL REPORT / FERIC, FOREST ENGINEERING RESEARCH INSTITUTE OF

CANADA.). [Spec. rep. - For. Eng. Res. Inst. Can.]. No. 1 (Jan. 1976)-. Monographic series. English. ir. Price varies per volume. Forest Engineering Research Institute of Canada, 143 Place Frontenac, Pointe-Claire Quebec H9R 4Z7 Canada. **DD** 634.9/0971.
Ind/Abst Agric. Eng. Abstr. (1991-); For. Prod. Abstr. (19??-19??); For. Abstr.; Weed Abstr.

CE/0258-624X
SRI LANKA FORESTER, THE. [Sri Lanka for.]. New Series, V. 10, No. 3/4 (Jan./Dec. 1972)-. Periodical. English. sa. $2.50. Sri Lanka Forester, Forest Department, Colombo 2 Sri Lanka Ceylon. **LC** SD235.S72; C48. **DD** 634.9/05. **CODEN** SLFOD7. Documents available from BIOSIS Document Express. ***Continues** Ceylon Forester, 0045-6195.*
Ind/Abst Agrofor. Abstr. (1991-); Biol. Abstr.; For. Abstr.; Life Sci. Collect.; Rev. Agric. Entomol.; Seed Abstr.

US
STAFF PAPER SERIES / DEPARTMENT OF FOREST RESOURCES. Added/Corp University of Minnesota. Dept. of Forest Resources. No. 1 (1978)-. Monographic series. English.
Ind/Abst For. Abstr.

US
STATION PAPER - U. S. FOREST SERVICE. LAKE STATES FOREST EXPERIMENT STATION, ST. PAUL. **Main/Corp** United States. Forest Service. Lake States Forest Experiment Station. English. Minnesota Department of Agriculture, 90 Plato Boulevard West, St Paul MN 55107. **Tel** (612)297-3219, FAX (612)297-5522. **LC** SD11.A455; 47. **DD** 634.92577.

US
STATISTICAL ROUNDUP. See Forestry-Abstracting, Bibliographies and Statistics.

IT
STATISTICHE FORESTALI. Added/Corp Istituto Centrale di Statistica (Italy). Vol. 37 (1986)-. Italian. an. Istituto Nazionale Statistica, GBP SEZ4 Via Cesare Balbo 16, 00184 Rome Italy. **Tel** 011 39 6 46735118. **LC** SD67; .A3. ***Continues** Annuario di Statistica Forestale, 0269-6960.*

IO
STATISTIK EKSPOR HASIL HUTAN BUKAN KAYU. See Forestry-Abstracting, Bibliographies and Statistics.

FR
STATISTIQUES FORESTIERES EN ... / REPUBLIQUE FRANCAISE, MINISTERE DE L'AGRICULTURE, SERVICE CENTRAL DES ENQUETES ET ETUDES STATISTIQUES. French. SCEES - Service Central des Enquetes et Etudes Statistiques, 4 Avenue de Saint-Mande, 75570 Paris Cedex 12 France. **Tel** 011 33 1 49558576. **LC** SD193; .S73. **DD** 333.75/0944/021.

SW/0039-3150
STUDIA FORESTALIA SUECICA. [Stud. for. Suec.]. **Added/Corp** Skogshogskolan (Stockholm, Sweden) Svenska Skogsvardsforeningen. Sveriges Skogsvardsforbund. Sveriges Lantbruksuniversitet. Skogsvetenskapliga Fakulteten. (1963)-. Monographic series. English (French, German, Russian and Swedish). ir. Price varies per volume. Scandinavian University Press, PO Box 2959 Toeyen, N 0608 Oslo 6 Norway. **Tel** 011 47 2 2575400, FAX 011 47 2 2575353, telex 71896 UROR N. **(Subscription address:** Scandinavian University Press, 200 Meacham Ave., Elmont NY 11003.**)** **LC** SD211; .S86. **CODEN** SFSUAB. Documents available from BIOSIS Document Express. ***Formed by the union of** Kungl. Skogshogskolans Skrifter **and** Meddelanden Fran Statens Skogsforskningsinstitut.*
Ind/Abst Abstr. Bull. Inst. Pap. Sci. Tech.; AGRICOLA; Biol. Abstr.; EMBASE; Fish Rev. (Jan. 1989-July 1992); For. Prod. Abstr.; For. Abstr.; Life Sci. Collect.; Wildl. Rev. (Jan. 1989-July 1992).

US/0272-3298
STUDIES IN CULTURAL RESOURCE MANAGEMENT. [Stud. cult. resour. manage.]. No. 1-. Monographic series. English. Price varies per volume. US Department of Agriculture / Portland, Forest Service, Pacific Northwest Region, 319 SW Pine Street, Portland OR 97204. **Tel** (503)326-3625, FAX (503)326-2272.

SJ/0562-5122
SUDAN SILVA. [Sudan silva]. **Added/Corp** Sudan Forestry Society. Majlis al-Qawmi lil-Buhuth (Sudan). (1949)-. Periodical. English. Sudan Forestry Society, PO Box 658, Khartoum Sudan. **LC** SD242.S73; S84.
Ind/Abst For. Prod. Abstr.; Irr. Drain. Abstr.; Life Sci. Collect.

SA/0038-2167
SUID-AFRIKAANSE BOSBOUTYDSKRIF. (SOUTH AFRICAN FORESTRY JOURNAL.). [S.-Afr. bosb.tydskr.]. **Added/Corp** South African Forestry Association. South African Institute of Forestry. **VFOAT** Suid-Afrikaanse Bosboutydskrif. No. 41 (April/June 1962)-. Periodical. English (Afrikaans). qt. $80.00 South Africa; $130.00 (air mail) other. South African Institute of Forestry, PO Box 1022, Pretoria 0001 South Africa. **Tel** 011 27 12 3103591. **ED** H.A. Van der Syde. **LC** SD1; .S69. **DD** 634.9/05. cum. index. **Bk Rev. Pr Rev. Circ:** 1,200. ***Continues** Journal of the South African Forestry Association.*
Desc: Scientific and general papers, book reviews, editorials, on forestry from nursery to timber, including conservation, vegetation, hydrology pulp and paper, harvesting and sawmilling.
Ind/Abst AGRICOLA [Full Cov.]; Agrofor. Abstr.; Curr. Aware. Biol. Sci., CABS; For. Prod. Abstr. (1991-); For. Abstr.; Hortic. Abstr.; Life Sci. Collect.; Plant Grow. Reg. Abstr.; Rev. Plant Pathol.

CN/0701-8347
SUMMARY OF TECHNICAL REPORT - FOREST ENGINEERING RESEARCH INSTITUTE OF CANADA. (SUMMARY OF TECHNICAL REPORT / FERIC, FOREST ENGINEERING RESEARCH INSTITUTE OF CANADA.). [Summ. tech. rep. - For. Eng. Res. Inst. Can.]. **VFOAT** Sommaire du Rapport Technique. **VAT** Sommaire de Rapport Technique - Institut Canadien de Recherches en Genie Forestier; Sommaire du du Rapport Technique - Institut Canadien de Recherches. Monographic series. English (French). Price varies per volume. FERIC, 143 Place Frontenac, Pointe-Claire Quebec H9R 4Z7 Canada. **DD** 634.9/0971.

FI/0039-5471
SUO. See Agriculture.

IT
SUPERFICIE FORESTALE NELLE COMUNITA MONTANE AL 31 DICEMBRE, LA. Italian. Istituto Nazionale Statistica, GBP SEZ4 Via Cesare Balbo 16, 00184 Rome Italy. **Tel** 011 39 6 46735118. **LC** SD201; .S86. **DD** 333.75/0945/021.

PH/0115-0022
SYLVATROP. *Title Change.* (SYLVATROP, THE PHILIPPINE FOREST RESEARCH JOURNAL.). [Sylvatrop]. **Added/Corp** Forest Research Institute (Philippines). Vol. 1, No. 2, Apr.-June (1976)-(19??). Academic Scholarly Publication. English. qt. Forest Product Research and Development Institute, College, Laguna 3720 Philippines. **Tel** 2586, 2377. **ED** Eliseo M Baltazar. **CODEN** SYLVDD. Index available. **Bk Rev. Circ:** 1,000. Documents available from CASDDS. ***Continues** Philippine Forest Research Journal. **Continued by** Sylvatrop (College, Philippines : 1991).*
Desc: Covers tropical forest, social forestry, agroforestry, dipterocarps, pines, forestation, range management, watershed wildlife, outdoor recreation, lesser used species, silviculture and forest seed research.
Ind/Abst AGRICOLA; Agrofor. Abstr. (1991-); Chem. Abstr. (-1985); Field Crop Abstr.; For. Prod. Abstr.; For. Abstr.; Grasslands For. Abstr.; Hortic. Abstr.; Life Sci. Collect.; Plant Grow. Reg. Abstr.; Rev. Plant Pathol.; Sug. Indus. Abstr.

PL/0039-7660
SYLWAN : CZASOPISMO MIESIECZNE DLA LESNIKOW I WASCICIELI ZIEMSKICH / ORGAN GALIC. TOWARZYSTWA LESNEGO. Added/Corp Polskie Towarzystwo Lesne. Galicyjskiego Towarzystwa Lesnego. Polska Akademia Nauk. Wydzia Nauk Rolniczych i Lesnych. (1820)-. Periodical. Polish (summaries and/or abstracts in Multiple languages; table of contents in Multiple languages). mo. Price on Request. **(Subscription address:** ARS Polona, PO Box 1001, 00068 Warsaw Poland.**)**
Ind/Abst Agric. Eng. Abstr. (1991-); Biocont. News Inf. (1991-); Biodeter. Abstr. (1991-); Crop Physiol. Abstr.; For. Prod. Abstr. (1991-); For. Abstr.; Nematol. Abstr.; Plant Grow. Reg. Abstr.; Rev. Agric. Entomol.; Rev. Plant Pathol.; Seed Abstr.; Soils Fert.; Weed Abstr.

CN/0712-3094
TALLYBOARD. [Tallyboard]. Periodical. English. bm. Free. Forest Products Accident Prevention Association, PO Box 270, North Bay Ontario P1B 8H2 Canada. **DD** 363.1/1963498/060713.

TU
TARM, ORMAN, VE KOYISLERI BAKANLG DERGISI. *Title Change.* See Agriculture.

TU
TARM VE KOYISLERI BAKANLG DERGISI. See Agriculture.

AT/1033-8306
TASFORESTS. [Tasforests]. (1989)-. Periodical. English. tq. **DD** 634.909946.
Ind/Abst Plant Genet. Resour. Abstr.

US/0277-5506
TECHNICAL BULLETIN - MISSISSIPPI AGRICULTURAL AND FORESTRY EXPERIMENT STATION. See Agriculture.

CN/0381-7741
TECHNICAL NOTE - FOREST ENGINEERING RESEARCH INSTITUTE OF CANADA. Added/Corp Forest Engineering Research Institute of Canada. **VFOAT** Fiche Technique. **VAT** Fiche Technique - Institut Canadien de Recherches en Genie Forestie. No. 1 (May 1976)-. Monographic series. English (French). ir. Price varies per volume. Forest Engineering Research Institute of Canada, 143 Place Frontenac, Pointe-Claire Quebec H9R 4Z7 Canada. **DD** 634.9'82. ***Continued in part by** Fiche Technique (Forest Engineering Institute of Canada).*
Ind/Abst AGRICOLA [Full Cov.]; For. Prod. Abstr.

AT/0548-6807
TECHNICAL PAPER - FORESTRY COMMISSION OF NEW SOUTH WALES. (TECHNICAL PAPER.). [Tech. pap. - For. Comm. N. S. W.]. **Main/Corp** New South Wales. Forestry Commission. (1963)-. Periodical. English. Forestry Commission of New South Wales, 95-99 York Street, Sydney New South Wales, 2000 Australia. **Tel** 02 234- 1513.
Ind/Abst AGRICOLA; For. Prod. Abstr. (1991-).

AT
TECHNICAL PUBLICATION. Main/Corp New South Wales. Forestry Commission. (19??)-. English. ir. Forestry Commission of New South Wales, 95-99 York Street, Sydney New South Wales, 2000 Australia. **Tel** 02 234- 1513. **LC** SD111.N5; F66a. **DD** 634.9/09944.

US/0749-5536
TECHNICAL PUBLICATION R8-TP / UNITED STATES DEPARTMENT OF AGRICULTURE, FOREST SERVICE, SOUTHERN REGION. [Tech. publ. R8-TP]. **VFOAT** Technical Publication R.8-T.P. **VAT** Technical Publication Region Eight Technical Publication. 1-. Monographic series. English. ir. Price varies per volume. Department of Agriculture / Foreign Agricultural Service, 14th Street and Independence Avenue SW, Washington DC 20250-1000. **Tel** (202)720-3935, FAX (202)720-7729. **DD** 634. ***Continues** Technical Publication SA-TP.*
Ind/Abst AGRICOLA [Full Cov.].

CN/0318-7063
TECHNICAL REPORT (FOREST ENGINEERING RESEARCH INSTITUTE OF CANADA). (TECHNICAL REPORT - FOREST ENGINEERING RESEARCH INSTITUTE OF CANADA.). [Tech. rep. - For. Eng. Res. Inst. Can.]. **Added/Corp** Forest Engineering Research Institute of Canada. No. 1 (Dec. 1975)-. Monographic series. English (French; summaries and/or abstracts in French). Price varies per volume. Forest Engineering Research Institute of Canada, 143 Place Frontenac, Pointe-Claire Quebec H9R 4Z7 Canada. **DD** 634.9/82. ***Supersedes** Logging Research Reports, 0316-4853.*
Ind/Abst AGRICOLA [Full Cov.]; Agric. Eng. Abstr. (1991-); For. Prod. Abstr. (1991-); For. Abstr.

CN/0709-4523
TECHNICAL REPORT - FORINTEK CANADA CORP., EASTERN LABORATORY. (TECHNICAL REPORT.). [Tech. rep. - Forintek Can. Corp. East. Lab.]. Academic Scholarly Publication. English (summaries and/or abstracts in French). Price varies per volume. Forintek Canada Corporation, 800 Montreal Road, Ottawa Ontario K1G 3Z5 Canada. **Tel** (613)744-0963. **DD** 634.9/8/05. **CODEN** TFELDU. Documents available from CASDDS. ***Continues** Technical Report (Eastern Forest Products Laboratory (Canada)), 0824-2070.*
Ind/Abst Chem. Abstr.

US/0090-0664
TECHNICAL REPORT - SCHOOL OF FOREST RESOURCES. NORTH CAROLINA STATE UNIVERSITY. [Tech. rep. Sch. For. Resour., North Carolina State Univ.]. **Main/Corp** North Carolina State University at Raleigh. School of Forest Resources. (19??)-. Monographic series. English. ***Continues** Technical Report - School of Forestry, North Carolina State University.*
Ind/Abst For. Abstr.

CN/0823-2784
TERRE DE CHEZ NOUS. DOSSIER D'INFORMATION TECHNIQUE ET PROFESSIONNELLE, LA. See Agriculture.

US/0739-1463
TEXAS FORESTRY (LUFKIN, TEX.). (TEXAS FORESTRY.). **Added/Corp** Texas Forestry Association. Vol. 1 (1960)-. Periodical. English. mo. $15.00. Texas Forestry Association, PO Box 1488, Lufkin TX 75901. **Tel** (409)632-8733. ***Continues** Texas Forests and Texans.*

US/1047-7667
TEXAS TREES. [Tex. trees]. **Added/Corp** Texas Forest Service. Vol. 68, No. 3 (1989)-. Periodical. English. qt. Texas Forest Service Systems Building, Texas A & M University, College Station TX 77843. **Tel** (409)845-2641. **LC** SD1; .T45. **DD** 634.9/09764. ***Continues** TF News, 0363-2431.*

UK/0040-7763
TIMBER GROWER. (1961)-. Periodical. English. Four times a year (Feb., May, Aug., Nov.). £15.00 UK; £21.00 others. BC Publications / UK, 16C Market Place /

Diss, Norfolk 1P22 3AB England. **Tel** 011 44 379 644200, FAX 011 44 379 650480. **ED** David Steers. **Bk Rev**, (Qty: varies). **Ad Acc. Circ:** 3,000 (ctrl).
Desc: For the decision-makers in the forest industry and priced equipment.

AT
TIMBER NOTE. (TIMBER NOTE / QUEENSLAND DEPARTMENT OF FORESTRY.). [Timber note]. **Added/Corp** Queensland. Dept. of Forestry. Queensland. Dept. of Forestry. Division of Technical Services. (1982)-. Monographic series. English. ir. Price varies per volume. Queensland Department of Forestry, Box 944, Government Printing Office, Brisbane 4001 Queensland Australia.

CN/0833-0689
TIMBERLINES. [Timberlines]. **Added/Corp** Northern Forestry Centre (Canada). **VFOAT** Timber Lines. No. 1 (Winter 1986)-. Periodical. English. qt. Free on request. Canadian Forestry Service / Alberta, Research Center, 5320 122nd Street, Edmonton Alberta, T6H 335 Canada. **Tel** (403)435-7210, FAX (403)435-7359.

JA/0371-6007
TOKYO DAIGAKU NOGAKUBU ENSHURIN HOKOKU. [Tokyo Daigaku Nogakubu Enshurin Hokoku]. **VFOAT** Bulletin of the Tokyo University Forests. (1920)-. Multiple languages. ir. Tokyo University / Forests, Yayoi 1-1-1 Bunkyoku, Tokyo, Japan. **CODEN** TDNEA3.
Ind/Abst For. Prod. Abstr. (1991-); For. Abstr.; Soils Fert.

US/0563-9093
TOPS. [Tops]. **Added/Corp** Georgia Forestry Association. **VFOAT** Tops Magazine. (19??)-. Periodical. English. an. $30.00 Comes with Georgia Forestry Association Inc. membership. Georgia Forestry Association Inc, 500 Pinnacle Court, Suite 505, Norcross GA 30071. **Tel** (404)416-7621. **ED** Leon Brown. **DD** 634. **Circ:** 5,696.

US
TRAILHEAD. English. Six times a year. $10.00 (individuals); $20.00 (institutions). Trailhead, PO Box 1629, Sun Valley ID 83353. **Tel** (208)622-3046 or 522-4088. **ED** Bernice E. Paige. **Ad Acc. Circ:** 200.
Desc: News and summaries on the trail in Idaho and the US.

CN/0829-318X
TREE PHYSIOLOGY. [Tree physiol.]. Vol. 1, No. 1 (June 1986)-. Periodical. English. mo. 520.00Can$ Canada, $382.00 other. Heron Publishing, 202-3994 Shelbourne Street, Victoria BC V8R 6S4 Canada. **Tel** (604)721-9921, FAX (604)721-9924. **ED** Dr. Rozanne Poulson (address: Department of Biochemistry, University of Victoria, (604)721-8887). **DD** 582.16/01/05. **CODEN** TRPHEM. **[CCC].** Index available (Bound in 12th iss.). cum. index (Electroninc form only). **Bk Rev**, (Qty: 4). **Ad Acc. Pr Rev. Circ:** 650 (ctrl). Documents available from the publisher, CASDDS, Documents on Demand.
Desc: These articles are responsed to forest, crop, and ornamental tree species to acid rain, air pollutants, ultraviolet radiation, and global warming. The genetic transformation and micropropagtion of tree; tree growth, reproduction, nutrition, photosynthesis, and wnvironmental environmental and the relation between tree structure and function.
Ind/Abst AGRICOLA [Full Cov.]; Agrofor. Abstr. (1991-); Biol. Abstr. (1986-); Chem. Abstr.; Crop Physiol. Abstr.; Curr. Aware. Biol. Sci., CABS; Curr. Contents, Agric. Biol. Environ. Sci.; Ecol. Abstr.; Ecology Abstr.; Environ. Abstr.; For. Prod. Abstr. (1991-); For. Abstr.; Hortic. Abstr.; Irr. Drain. Abstr.; Plant Breed. Abstr.; Plant Genet. Resour. Abstr.; Plant Grow. Reg. Abstr.; Res. Alert [Select. Cov.]; Rev. Plant Pathol.; Seed Abstr.; Soils Fert.

US/0732-0329
TREE PLANTER, THE. (THE TREE PLANTER / AGRI-SILVICULTURE INSTITUTE.). [Tree plant.]. Periodical. English. sa. Free to members. Youth Resources Inc, PO Box DD, Cabazon CA 92230-0770. ***Continues*** *Communicator.*

US/0096-8714
TREE PLANTERS' NOTES. [Tree plant. notes]. **Added/Corp** United States. Forest Service. **VFOAT** Planters' Notes. Vol. 1, No. 1 (Nov. 1950)-?. Government Publication. English. qt. $8.00 domestic; $10.00 other. Superintendent of Documents, US Government Printing Office, Washington DC 20402. **Tel** (202)275-3328, FAX (202)786-2377. **LC** SD391; .T69. **DD** 634.9/56/0973. Documents available from BIOSIS Document Express. ***Continued in part by*** *Forest and Windbarrier Planting and Seeding in the United States, 0094-8799.*
Desc: Contains information on a wide range of topics pertaining to planting of trees, reforestation, and related areas of forestry.
Ind/Abst Abstr. Bull. Inst. Pap. Sci. Tech.; AGRICOLA [Full Cov.]; Agric. Eng. Abstr.; Agrofor. Abstr.; Biol. Abstr.; For. Abstr.; Irr. Drain. Abstr.; Plant Genet. Resour. Abstr.; Plant Grow. Reg. Abstr.; Rev. Agric. Entomol.; Rev. Plant Pathol.; Seed Abstr.; Soils Fert.; Weed Abstr.

US
TREE PLANTING IN THE UNITED STATES / UNITED STATES DEPARTMENT OF AGRICULTURE, FOREST SERVICE, STATE AND PRIVATE FORESTRY, COOPERATIVE FORESTRY. **Added/Corp** United States. State and Private Forestry. Cooperative Forestry. (1990)-. English. **LC** SD143; .U15. ***Continues*** *U.S. Forest Planting Report, 0740-4751.*

US/0041-2198
TREE-RING BULLETIN. [Tree-ring bull.]. **Added/Corp** Tree-Ring Society. University of Arizona. Laboratory of Tree-Ring Research. Vol. 1 July (1934)-. English. an. $15.00. Tree Ring Society - Tree Ring Laboratory, University of Arizona, Tucson AZ 85721. **Tel** (602)621-6469, FAX (602)621-8229. **ED** Jeffrey S. Dean (editor's address: 105 West Stadium , Tree Ring Laboratory, University of Arizona, Tucson, AZ 85721 phone: (602)621-2320). **LC** QK477; .T75. **CODEN** TRBUAL. Index available. cum. index. **Circ:** 350 (ctrl). Documents available from BIOSIS Document Express.
Desc: To promote and encourage research in dendrochronology (tree-ring dating) all over the world; to sponsor and promote application of dendrochronology to related fields.
Ind/Abst AGRICOLA [Full Cov.]; Anthropol. Lit.; Biol. Abstr. (1969-1988); Br. Archaeol. Bibliogr.; GeoRef.

GW/0931-1890
TREES (BERLIN, WEST). (TREES : STRUCTURE AND FUNCTION.). [Trees]. Vol. 1 No. 1 (1986)-. Academic Scholarly Publication. English. Six times a year. DM598.00. Springer-Verlag GmbH & Company KG, Heidelberger Platz 3, D 14197 Berlin Germany. **Tel** 011 49 30 8207223, FAX 011 49 30 8214091, telex 183 319 SPBLN D. **(Subscription address:** Springer Verlag New York Inc. / for North America, 44 Hartz Way, Secaucus NJ 07096.) **ED** H Ziegler. **CODEN** TRESEY. **[CCC].** available on microfilm and microfiche from University Microfilms International (UMI). Documents available from The Genuine Article, BIOSIS Document Express, CASDDS.
Desc: Features original articles on the physiology, biochemistry, functional anatomy, structure and ecology of trees.
Ind/Abst Abstr. Bull. Inst. Pap. Sci. Tech.; AGRICOLA; Agrofor. Abstr. (1991-); Bibliogr. Agric. (1990-); Biol. Abstr. (1989-); Chem. Abstr. (?-1988); Crop Physiol. Abstr.; Curr. Aware. Biol. Sci., CABS; Curr. Contents, Agric. Biol. Environ. Sci.; For. Prod. Abstr. (1991-); For. Abstr.; Hortic. Abstr.; Ornamental Hort. (1991-); Res. Alert [Select. Cov.]; Rev. Agric. Entomol.; Rev. Plant Pathol.; Seed Abstr.; Soils Fert.; Weed Abstr.

SA/0041-2236
TREES IN SOUTH AFRICA. [Trees S. Afr.]. V. 1- April/June 1949-. Periodical. English. qt. **LC** SB435; .T7. **DD** 635.977. ***Supersedes*** *Arboricultural News.*
Ind/Abst Life Sci. Collect.

UK/0141-9668
TROPICAL FORESTRY PAPERS. [Trop. for. pap.]. **Added/Corp** University of Oxford. Commonwealth Forestry Institute. No. 7 (1975)-. Monographic series. English. ir. Price varies per volume. Commonwealth Forestry Association, South Parks Road, Oxford OX1 3RB England. **Tel** 011 44 865 275072, telex 3147 ATTN FOROX. **LC** SD434; .F33. **DD** 634.9/0913. **Circ:** 1,000. Documents available from BIOSIS Document Express. ***Continues*** *Fast Growing Timber Trees of the Lowland Tropics, 0430-1099.*
Desc: Occasional series of research reports on tropical forestry.
Ind/Abst Biol. Abstr.; For. Abstr.; Life Sci. Collect.

FI/0786-8170
TROPICAL FORESTRY REPORTS. [Trop. for. rep.]. (1989)-. Monographic series. Multiple languages. ir. **UDC** 630.
Ind/Abst For. Abstr.

RU
TRUDY LESOSTEPNOI NAUCHNO-ISSLEDOVATELSKOI STANTSII LENINGRADSKOGO UNIVERSITETA "LES NA VORSKLE.". **Main/Corp** Leningrad. Universitet. Lesostepnaia Nauchno-Issledovatelskaia Stantsiia. (1939)-. Russian. 1.44rub (single issue). St Petersburg State University / Izdatelstvo Leningradskogo Universiteta, Universitetskaia Nab 7/9, 199034 St Petersburg Russia. **Tel** 011 95 218-97-88, FAX 011 95 218-51-52, telex 121481. **LC** AS262; .L422 subser.

CC/1000-5382
TUNG-PEI LIN YEH TA HSUEH HSUEH PAO. **Added/Corp** Tung-Pei Lin Yeh Ta Hsueh (China). **VFOAT** Journal of NEFU; Journal of N.E. Forestry Univ.; Journal of North-East Forestry University. (1985)-. Periodical. Chinese (summaries and/or abstracts in English; table of contents in English). bm. $33.06. **(Subscription address:** China International Book Trading Corporation, PO Box 399, Library Service Department, Beijing 100044 People's Republic of China.) **LC** SD85; .T86. ***Continues*** *Tung-Pei Lin Hsueh Yuan Hsueh Pao, 0253-2271.*
Ind/Abst Agrofor. Abstr.; Biocont. News Inf.; Biodeter. Abstr.; For. Prod. Abstr.; Nematol. Abstr.; Plant Grow. Reg. Abstr.

FI/0355-0710
TYOTEHOSEURAN JULKAISUJA. **See** Agriculture.

US/0502-3548
U. S. FOREST SERVICE RESEARCH NOTE NOR. **Main/Corp** Northern Forest Experiment Station. 1- Feb. 1963-. Monographic series. English. Price varies per volume. US National Forest Experiment Station, Juneau AK 99811. **LC** A99.9.F7672; U. ***Continues*** *Technical Note - Northern Forest Experiment Station.*
Ind/Abst For. Prod. Abstr.

IT/0041-6436
UNASYLVA. (UNASYLVA / FOOD AND AGRICULTURAL ORGANIZATION OF THE UNITED NATIONS.). [Unasylva]. **Added/Corp** Food and Agriculture Organization of the United Nations. Food and Agriculture Organization of the United Nations. Division of Forestry and Forest Products. Vol. 1, No. 1 (July/Aug. 1947)-Vol. 25, 2-3-4; Special Issue No. 104 (1972); Vol. 26, No. 105 (Summer 1974)-. Periodical. English. Four times a year. $24.00. Food and Agriculture Organization (FAO) / Italy, GIPC166 via Terme di Caracalla, 00100 Rome Italy. **Tel** 011 39 6 522 52925, FAX 011 39 6 522 55784. **LC** SD1; .U5. **DD** 634.905. cum. index.
Desc: Features illustrated articles, international data and book reviews pertaining to policymaking, economics, education, research, forest and watershed management, logging and transport, national parks, saw milling, the pulp and paper industries and related subjects. Special emphasis is placed on events and developments in the tropics and in developing countries.
Ind/Abst Abstr. Bull. Inst. Pap. Sci. Tech.; AGRICOLA; Agrofor. Abstr. (19??-19??); Biol. Dig.; Ecol. Abstr.; For. Prod. Abstr.; For. Abstr.; Geogr. Abstr. Human Geogr.; Int. Bibliogr. Sociol.; Int. Dev. Abstr.; Life Sci. Collect.; World Agric. Econ.

CN/0707-1957
UNB FORESTRY FOCUS. (UNB FORESTRY FOCUS : A QUARTERLY PUBLICATION OF THE FACULTY OF FORESTRY, UNIVERSITY OF NEW BRUNSWICK.). [UNB for. focus]. **Added/Corp** University of New Brunswick. Faculty of Forestry. **VAT** University of New Brunswick Forestry Focus; Forestry Focus. (Summer 1976)-. Periodical. English. qt. Free on request. University of New Brunswick / Faculty of Forestry, Bag No. 44555, Fredericton New Brunswick E3B 6C2, Canada. **Tel** (506)453-4501, FAX (506)453-3538. **ED** Ardith Armstrong. **DD** 634.9/09715. **Circ:** 900 (ctrl).
Desc: Newsletter of the University of New Brunswick Faculty of Forestry.

GW
UNSER WALD : ZEITSCRIFT DER SCHUTZGEMEINSCHAFT DEUTSCHER WALD. **Added/Corp** Schutzgemeinschaft Deutscher Wald. (1950)-. Periodical. German. bm. DM25.00. Verlagsgesellschaft Unser Wald GmbH, Meckenheimer Allee 79, 53115 Bonn 1 Germany. **Tel** 0228-658462, FAX 0228 656980. **Bk Rev**, (Qty: 30). **Ad Acc, Adv Mgr:** Ulrike Migende. **Pr Rev. Acid Free. Circ:** 10,000 (ctrl). ***Continues*** *Grune Blatt.*
Desc: German association for the protection of forests, woodlands and landscape.

SW/0349-8913
UPPSATSER - SVERIGESLANTBRUKSUNIVERSITET, INSTITUTIONEN FOR VIRKESLARA. [Uppsats. - Sver. lantbr.univ. Inst. virkesl.]. **VFOAT** Research Notes - Swedish University of Agricultural Sciences, Department of Forest Products. (1977)-. Monographic series. Multiple languages. ir. Institutionen for Virkeslara, Sveriges Lantbruksuniversiter, Box 7008 S-750 07, Uppsala, Sweden. ***Continues*** *Uppsatser - Institutionen for Virkeslara, Skogshogskolan, 0082-0059.*
Ind/Abst For. Prod. Abstr. (1991-).

US/1052-2484
URBAN FORESTS. [Urban for.]. **Added/Corp** American Forestry Association. Vol. 10, No. 3 (June/July 1990)-. Periodical. English. bm (6 issues). Free in the US; $18.00 other. American Forestry Association, PO Box 2000, Washington DC 20013. **Tel** (202)667-3300. **LC** SB436; .N34. **DD** 333. Documents available from Documents on Demand. ***Continues*** *Urban Forest Forum.*
Ind/Abst Abstr. Bull. Inst. Pap. Sci. Tech. (19??-); Environ. Abstr. (19??-); Garden Lit. (1992-).

JA/0286-8733
UTSUNOMIYA DAIGAKU NOGAKUBU ENSHURIN HOKOKU. **VFOAT** Bulletin of the Utsunomiya University Forests. (1961)-. Japanese. an. Utsunomiya University, 350 Mine-Machi, Utsunomiyashi, Japan. **UDC** 634.9.
Ind/Abst For. Prod. Abstr. (1991-); For. Abstr.; Soils Fert.

II/0970-3071
VAN VIGYAN. [Van Vigyan]. (1967)-. Periodical. English. qt. $40.00. **(Subscription address:** Prints India, 11 Darya Ganj, New Delhi, 110002 India, (Phone: 011 91 11 3268645)) ***Continues** Journal of the Society of Indian Foresters, 0560-6306.*
Ind/Abst Agrofor. Abstr.; Seed Abstr.; Soils Fert.

VE
VENEZUELA FORESTAL : PUBLICACION CUATRIMESTRAL DE LA COMPANIA NACIONAL DE REFORESTACION, CONARE. **Added/Corp** Compania Nacional de Reforestacion (Venezuela). (197?)-. Periodical. Spanish (summaries and/or abstracts in English). tq.
Ind/Abst Agrofor. Abstr.; For. Abstr.; Maize Abstr.

SA
VERSLAE VAN DIE GEKOSE KOMITEE VOOR DIE BOSWETSONTWERP. **See** Law.

SA
VERSLAG - BOSBOURAAD. **Main/Corp** South Africa. Forestry Council. **VFOAT** Report - Forestry Council. 1973/75-. Multiple languages (Afrikaans and English). 2.10. Forestry Council, The Government Printer, Private Bag X85, Pretoria South Africa. **LC** SD103.S8; F66A.

US/0740-011X
VIRGINIA FORESTS (1974). (VIRGINIA FORESTS.). [Va. for.]. **Added/Corp** Virginia Forests, Inc. Virginia Forestry Association. Vol. 29, No. 3 (Fall 1974)-. Periodical. English. Four times a year (Jan., Apr., July, Oct.). $30.00 Comes with Virginia Forestry Association Membership. Virginia Forestry Association, 1205 East Main Street, Richmond VA 23219-3627. **Tel** (804)644-8462, FAX (804)788-0734. **ED** Charles F. Finley Jr. Index available ($5.00). cum. index. **Bk Rev. Ad Acc. Circ:** 4,200. ***Continues** Virginia Forests Magazine.*
Desc: Documents issues affecting trees and tree farmers, and through a variety of articles, interest and encourage landowners to reforest their land after harvest.

CN/0848-3809
VISION, TERRE ET FORET. [Vis. terre for.]. Vol. 1, No 1 (Sept. 1988)-. Periodical. French. Twelve times a year. 12.96Can$. Group Bellavance, 73, St-Germain Est., Rimouski Quebec G5L 7C4 Canada. **Tel** (418)723-4800. **DD** 634.9/09714/77.

GW/0043-0048
WALDARBEIT, DIE. [Waldarbeit]. Periodical. German. mo. Wirtschafts und Forstverlag, Euting KG, Tannenstrasse, W-5451 Strassenhaus Germany.
Ind/Abst Saf. Health Work.

GW/0511-0939
WALDHYGIENE. [Waldhygiene]. **Added/Corp** Julius-Maximilians-Universitat. Institut fur Angewandte Zoologie. Vol. 1 1954-. Periodical. German. **CODEN** WLDHAH. Documents available from BIOSIS Document Express.
Ind/Abst AGRICOLA; Biol. Abstr.; For. Abstr.; Life Sci. Collect.; Rev. Agric. Entomol.; Rev. Med. Vet. Entomol.

US/1041-5769
WALNUT COUNCIL BULLETIN. [Walnut Counc. bull.]. **Added/Corp** Walnut Council. Purdue University. Dept. of Forestry and Natural Resources. Forestry Sciences Laboratory (Carbondale, Ill.). Vol. 7, No. 1 (April 1980)-. Bulletin. English. qt. $20.00. Walnut Council, 5603 West Raymond Street, Suite O, Indianapolis IN 46241. **Tel** (317)244-3311. **DD** 634. **Ad Acc.** ctrl circ. ***Continues** Member Newsletter (Walnut Council), 1041-5777.*
Desc: Articles on research findings and other general subjects including woodland and plantation management, use of herbicides and pesticides, fertilization, pruning, thinning, harvesting, and marketing.

US/0197-1387
WEST VIRGINIA FORESTRY NOTES. [West Va. for. notes]. **Added/Corp** West Virginia University. College of Agriculture and Forestry. No. 1 (19??)-. Academic Scholarly Publication. English. sa. Free. West Virginia University / 105 Communications Building, Morgantown WV 26505. **Tel** (304)293-6366. **ED** John Luchok and Harry V. Wiant Jr. **CODEN** WVFNDG. **Circ:** 2,500 (ctrl). Documents available from BIOSIS Document Express, CASDDS.
Desc: Reports results of forestry research at West Virginia University which is of special interest in the Appalachian hardwood region.
Ind/Abst AGRICOLA (19??-) [Full Cov.]; Biol. Abstr. (19??-); Chem. Abstr. (19??-); For. Prod. Abstr. (19??-); Plant Grow. Reg. Abstr. (19??-); Wildl. Rev. (1987).

US/0885-6095
WESTERN JOURNAL OF APPLIED FORESTRY. [West. j. appl. for.]. **Added/Corp** Society of American Foresters. **VFOAT** WJAF; Western Forestry. Vol. 1, No. 1 (Jan. 1986)-. Periodical. English. qt (Jan., April, July and Oct.). $85.00 (institutions), $40.00 (non-member individuals) US and Canada; $120.00 (institutions), $60.00 (individuals) other. Society of American Foresters, 5400 Grosvenor Lane, Bethesda MD 20814-2198. **Tel** (301)897-8720, FAX (301)897-3690, telex 9102501089 SAFFOREST UQ. **ED** Ronald M. Lanner. **LC** SD144.A18; W43. **DD** 634.9/0978. **CODEN** WJAFEK. **Bk Rev. Ad Acc. Circ:** 950. available on microfilm from University Microfilms International (UMI). Documents available from BIOSIS Document Express, Documents on Demand.
Desc: New ideas and research for practical application by practicing foresters, landowners and resource managers in the Western US and Canada.
Ind/Abst Abstr. Bull. Inst. Pap. Sci. Tech.; AGRICOLA [Full Cov.]; Agric. Eng. Abstr. (1991-); Agrofor. Abstr. (1991-); Biol. Abstr.; Ecol. Abstr.; Environ. Abstr.; Fish Rev.; For. Prod. Abstr. (1991-); For. Abstr.; Geogr. Abstr. Phys. Geogr. (?-?); Geogr. Abstr. Human Geogr.; Plant Breed. Abstr.; Rev. Agric. Entomol.; Rev. Plant Pathol.; Seed Abstr.; Soils Fert.; Weed Abstr.; Wildl. Rev.

US/0191-2984
WEYERHAEUSER SCIENCE SYMPOSIUM. [Weyerhaeuser Sci. Symp.]. **Added/Corp** Weyerhaeuser Company. (Apr. 30-May 3, 1979)-. English. **LC** SD118; .W45a. **DD** 634.9/05. **CODEN** WSSYDP. Documents available from CASDDS.
Ind/Abst AGRICOLA [Full Cov.]; Bioeng. Abstr.; Chem. Abstr.

NZ/0110-1048
WHAT'S NEW IN FOREST RESEARCH. [What's new for. res.]. **Added/Corp** Forest Research Institute (N.Z.). No. 1 (May 1973)-. Periodical. English. (Free upon request). Forest Research Institute, Private Bag 3020, Rotorua, New Zealand. **Tel** 011 64 73 475899, FAX 011 64 73 479380, telex 21080. **[CCC].**
Ind/Abst For. Abstr.; Seed Abstr.

CN/0825-477X
WHISTLE PUNK. [Whistle punk]. **VFOAT** B.C. Forest History Magazine. **VAT** British Columbia Forest History Magazine. (1984)-. Periodical. English. Four times a year (Feb., May, Aug., Nov.). 12.00Can$ Canada; $12.00 US. Whistle Punk, 2035 Stanley Avenue, Victoria British Columbia V8R 3X7 Canada. **Tel** (604)592-8799. **ED** Gordon D. Currie. **DD** 338.1/749/09711. **Bk Rev. Ad Acc. Circ:** 2,000 (ctrl).
Desc: Descriptive and entertaining periodical chronicling the history of the forest industry in British Columbia from the 1850's on. Well illustrated with vintage photographs and maps.

US/1074-3650
WILD FOREST REVIEW. [Wild forest rev.]. **Added/Corp** Save the West. **VFOAT** WFR. Vol. 1, No. 1 (Nov. 1993)-. Periodical. English. mo (11 issues). $25.00 (one year), $45.00 (two year). Save the Forest, 3758 Southeast Milwaukie, Portland OR 97202. **Tel** (503)234-0093. **DD** 634. ***Separated from** Forest Watch.*

US/0360-8034
WILDFIRE STATISTICS. **See** Forestry-Abstracting, Bibliographies and Statistics.

US
WILLAMETTE, THE. **Main/Corp** Willamette National Forest. English. an. Willamette National Forest, PO Box 10607, 211 East 7th Avenue, Eugene OR 97440-2607. **LC** SD428.W54; A3. **DD** 333.7/5.

US/0485-764X
WILLIAM L. HUTCHESON MEMORIAL FOREST BULLETIN. **Main/Corp** Rutgers University, New Brunswick, New Jersey. Bulletin. English. ir. Rutgers University / Nelson Lab, PO Box 1059, Nelson Biological Lab, Piscataway NJ 08854. **Tel** (201)932-2363.

US/0887-8927
WISCONSIN ARBORIST, THE. (THE WISCONSIN ARBORIST : THE NEWSLETTER OF THE WISCONSIN ARBORIST ASSOCIATION, INC.). **Added/Corp** Wisconsin Arborist Association. (198?)-. Newsletter. English. bm. Free (members), $15.00 (non-members). Wisconsin Arborist Association, 5730 Forsythia Place, Madison WI 53705. **Tel** (608)267-0843. **ED** Melinda Myers. **DD** 580. **Bk Rev. Ad Acc, Adv Mgr:** David Eastman, **Tel** 471-8420. **Circ:** 600. ***Continues** Wisconsin Arborist Association Newsletter.*

US
WOMEN IN NATURAL RESOURCES. **See** Women's Interests.

CN/0713-7826
WORK PROGRAM / FERIC. [Work program - FERIC]. **Main/Corp** Forest Engineering Research Institute of Canada. 1978-. Periodical. English. Free to members. Forest Engineering Research Institute of Canada, 143 Place Frontenac, Pointe-Claire Quebec H9R 4Z7 Canada. **DD** 634.9/07/2. ctrl circ.

US/0148-5741
YALE FOREST SCHOOL NEWS. V. 1- Jan. 1, 1913-. Periodical. English. qt. $10.00 membership. Yale University / Forestry, School of Forestry and Environmental Studies, 205 Prospect Street, New Haven CT 06511. **Tel** (203)432-5100. **ED** David M Smith. **LC** SD254; .Y25. **Circ:** 2,200.

TU
YILLIK BULTENI - KAVAK VE HIZLI GELISEN YABANCI TUR ORMAN AGACLARI ARASTIRMA ENSTITUSU. **Main/Corp** Kavak ve Hizli Gelisen Yabanci Tur Orman Agaclari Arastirma Enstitusu. No. 9- 1974-. Periodical. Turkish. ***Continues** Yillik Bulteni.*
Ind/Abst AGRICOLA; For. Abstr.

KO
YONGU POGO / SALLIMCHONG, SUWON YUKCHONG CHIJANG. **Added/Corp** Suwon Yukchong Chijang (Korea). (19??)-. Korean (English). ***Continues** Yongu Pogo (Imop Sihomjang (Korea). Suwon Yukchong Chijang), 0536-5651.*
Ind/Abst Plant Grow. Reg. Abstr.

AU
ZAHLEN AUS OESTERREICHS LAND- UND FORSTWIRTSCHAFT. (19??)-. German. Osterreichischer Agrarverlag, Inkustr 1 7 Bueropark Donau, A 3400 Klosterneuberg Austria. **Tel** 011 43 2243 33300. **LC** HD1395; .Z34. **DD** 338.1/09436.

XV
ZBORNIK GOZDARSTVA IN LESARSTVA. **Main/Corp** Ljubljana. Univerza. Institut za Gozdno in Lesno Gospodarstvo. **VFOAT** Research Reports : Forestry and Wood Technology. 11- 1973-. Periodical. Slovenian (summaries and/or abstracts in English and German). ***Continues** Institut za Gozdno in Lesno Gospodarstvo Slovenije. Zbornik; Proceedings / Institut za Gozdno in Lesno Gospodarstvo Slovenije.*

XO
ZBORNIK VEDECKYCH PRAC DREVARSKEJ FAKULTY VYSOKEJ SKOLY LESNICKEJ A DREVARSKEJ VO ZVOLENE. **Added/Corp** Vysoka Skola Lesnicka a Drevarska vo Zvolene. Drevarska Fakulta. (19??)-. Slovak (summaries and/or abstracts in English, German and Russian). **CODEN** ZVPZEY. Documents available from CASDDS.
Ind/Abst Chem. Abstr. (?-1991); For. Prod. Abstr. (1991-); For. Abstr.

CC/1001-3776
ZHEJIANG LINYE KE JI. (CHE-CHIANG LIN YEH KO CHI.). **Added/Corp** Che-Chiang Sheng Lin Yeh Ko Hsueh Yen Chiu So. Che-Chiang Sheng Lin Hsueh Hui. Che-Chiang Sheng Lin Yeh Ko Chi Cing Pao Chung Hsin. **VFOAT** Journal of Zhejiang Forestry Science and Technology. (19??)-. Periodical. Chinese (summaries and/or abstracts in English; table of contents in English). bm. Zhejiang Linye Kexue Yanjiusuo, Liuxua, Hangzhou, Zhejiang 310023 People's Republic of China. **Tel** 529277. **ED** Fan Fusheng.
Ind/Abst Biocont. News Inf.; Crop Physiol. Abstr.; For. Prod. Abstr. (1991-); For. Abstr.; Hortic. Abstr.; Rev. Agric. Entomol.; Rev. Plant Pathol.; Seed Abstr.; Soils Fert.

CH/0578-1345
ZHONGHUA LINXUE JIKAN. (CHUNG HUA LIN HSUEH CHI KAN.). [Zhonghua linxue jikan]. **VFOAT** Quarterly Journal of Chinese Forestry. Vol. 1, No. 1, (Dec. 1967)-. Periodical. Chinese (English). qt. Chinese Forestry Association, 2 Sec. 1 Hongchu South Road, Taipei, Taiwan. **CODEN** CLHKEY. ***Continues** Tai-Wan Lin Yeh Chi Kan.*
Ind/Abst Agrofor. Abstr.; For. Prod. Abstr. (1991-); For. Abstr.; Hortic. Abstr.; Nematol. Abstr.; Ornamental Hort. (1991-); Rev. Plant Pathol.; Soils Fert.

ABSTRACTING, BIBLIOGRAPHIES AND STATISTICS

UK/0952-1453
AGROFORESTRY ABSTRACTS. [Agrofor. abstr.]. **Added/Corp** C.A.B. International. International Council for Research in Agroforestry. Vol. 1, No. 1 (June 1988)-. Abstracting/Indexing Service. English. qt. $160.00 US. CAB International Centre, Wallingford, Oxon OX10 8DE United Kingdom. **Tel** 44 491 832111, FAX 44 491 833508, telex 847964 (COMAGG G). **ED** R. E. H. Haynes. available on magnetic tape and CD-ROM; available on an online database from Tsukuba Daigaku; CAN/OLE; STN International; JICST; DATA-STAR; DIMDI; ESA-IRS; BRS; and DIALOG.
Desc: Covers journal articles, reports, conferences and books. Includes agroforestry in general, agroforestry systems, agroforestry components and processes - trees, animals and crops; production, service, conservation, human ecology, social and economic aspects; development issues; research and methodology.
Ind/Abst Agrofor. Abstr. (1991-); For. Abstr.; Nematol. Abstr.

US/0091-438X
ANNUAL GRAZING STATISTICAL REPORT. ***Title Change.*** (ANNUAL GRAZING STATISTICAL REPORT. USE SUMMARY / UNITED STATES DEPARTMENT OF AGRICULTURE, FOREST

SERVICE, RANGE MANAGEMENT STAFF.). **Added/Corp** United States. Forest Service. Range Management Staff. (19??)-(19??). Statistical Publication. English. an. US Department of Agriculture / Forest Service, 201 14th Street SW, Washington DC 20250. **Tel** (202)205-1661, FAX (202)205-1181. **LC** SD427.G8; U54a. ***Continued by*** *Annual Grazing Statistical Use Summary.*

VE
BIBLIOGRAPHICAL BULLETIN - LATIN AMERICAN FORESTRY INSTITUTE. **Main/Corp** Instituto Forestal Latino-Americano de Investigacion y Capacitacion. **VFOAT** Information on Forestry in Latin America. (1976)-. Bulletin. English.

CN/0575-805X
CANADIAN FORESTRY STATISTICS. [Can. for. stat.]. **Main/Corp** Canada. Statistics Canada. Forestry Section. **Added/Corp** Canada. Dominion Bureau of Statistics. Industry and Merchandising Division. Canada. Dominion Bureau of Statistics. Industry Division. Canada. Dominion Bureau of Statistics. Manufacturing and Primary Industries Division. Statistics Canada. Forestry Section. Statistics Canada. Machinery, Wood and Metal Products Section. Statistics Canada. Census of Manufactures Section. Statistics Canada. Annual Survey of Manufactures Section. **VFOAT** Statistiques Forestieres du Canada. (1959)-. English (French). an. 29.00Can$ Canada; $35.00 US; $41.00 other. Statistics Canada, Publications Sales & Services, Main Building Room 1710, Ottawa Ontario K1A 0T6 Canada. **Tel** (613)951-5078, (800)267-6677, FAX (613)951-1584, telex 053-3585. **LC** SD13; .A382. **DD** 634.9/0971.
Desc: Forest land by type, by tenure; forest inventories of timber by species; forest fire statistics; estimates of primary forest production; principal statistics of the logging, wood, pulp, paper and allied industries; shipments and exports of principal commodities; imports of roundwood; capital and expenditures of the forest industries.

UK/0140-4784
FOREST PRODUCTS ABSTRACTS. [For. prod. abstr.]. **Added/Corp** Commonwealth Agricultural Bureaux. University of Oxford. Commonwealth Forestry Bureau. Vol. 1 (Jan. 1978)-. Abstracting/Indexing Service. English. bm. $332.00 US. CAB International Centre, Wallingford, Oxon OX10 8DE United Kingdom. **Tel** 44 491 832111, FAX 44 491 833508, telex 847964 (COMAGG G). **ED** J. R. Metcalfe. **Ad Acc.** available on magnetic tape and CD-ROM; available on an online database from Tsukuba Daigaku; CAN/OLE; STN International; JICST; DATA-STAR; DIMDI; ESA-IRS; BRS; and DIALOG.
Desc: Covers all aspects of forest products from harvesting to marketing.
Ind/Abst Abstr. Bull. Inst. Pap. Sci. Tech.; Pap. Board Abstr.

US/0146-4159
FOREST STATISTICS FOR IOWA. **Main/Corp** North Central Forest Experiment Station (St. Paul, Minn.). English. ir. Free. St Paul North Forest Experiment Station, Folwell Avenue, St Paul MN 55108. **Tel** (612)642-5233. **(Subscription address:** Forest Products Laboratory, 1 Gifford Pinchot Drive, Madison, WI 53705-2398) **ED** Robert D Wray. **LC** SD11; .A45533 subser; SD144.I8. **DD** 333.7/5/0977 S; 333.7/5/09777. **Circ:** 4,000 (ctrl). available on microfiche. Documents available from BIOSIS Document Express.
Desc: One of a series (Resource Bulletins) reporting on periodic statewide inventories of forest resources.
Ind/Abst AGRICOLA; Biol. Abstr.

UK/0015-7538
FORESTRY ABSTRACTS. [For. abstr.]. **Added/Corp** C.A.B. International. Commonwealth Agricultural Bureaux. University of Oxford. Commonwealth Forestry Bureau. Vol. 1 (1940)-. Abstracting/Indexing Service. English. mo. $664.00. CAB International Centre, Wallingford, Oxon OX10 8DE United Kingdom. **Tel** 44 491 832111, FAX 44 491 833508, telex 847964 (COMAGG G). **ED** C. A. D. Elbourn MSc. **LC** SD1; .F66. **DD** 634.905. **Ad Acc.** **Circ:** 1,000. available on magnetic tape and CD-ROM; available on an online database from Tsukuba Daigaku; CAN/OLE; STN International; JICST; DATA-STAR; DIMDI; ESA-IRS; BRS; and DIALOG.
Desc: Covers the world-wide literature on aspects of forestry, including land use and nature conservation topics.
Ind/Abst Abstr. Bull. Inst. Pap. Sci. Tech.; Field Crop Abstr.; Fish Rev.; For. Prod. Abstr. (1991-); Grasslands For. Abstr.; Leis. Recreat. Tour. Abstr.; Rural Dev. Abstr.; Weed Abstr.; Wildl. Rev.; World Agric. Econ.

JA
GOHAN TOKEI. **VFOAT** Statistics of Plywood. Japanese (Japanese). Nihon Gohan Kogyo Kumiai Rengokai, c/o Meisan Building, 18-17 Nishi Shinbashi 1-chome, Minato-ku, Tokyo-to Japan. **LC** HD9769.P63; J34.

JA
HAKODATE EIRINKYOKU TOSHO MOKUROKU. **Main/Corp** Japan. Hakodate Eirinkyoku. Keirika. Toshoshitsu. 1974-. Multiple languages (Japanese, English and German). Hakodate Eirinkyoku, 4-9 Komabacho, Hakodate 042 Japan. **LC** Z5991; .J36A; SD373.

CN/0834-440X
LOGGING INDUSTRY. (LOGGING INDUSTRY / STATISTICS CANADA, INDUSTRY DIVISION, CENSUS OF MANUFACTURES SECTION.). [Logging ind.]. **Added/Corp** Statistics Canada. Census of Manufactures Section. Statistics Canada. Annual Survey of Manufactures Section. **VFOAT** Exploitation Forestiere. (1983)-. English (French). an. 33.00Can$ Canada; $40.00 US; $47.00 other. Statistics Canada, Publications Sales & Services, Main Building Room 1710, Ottawa Ontario K1A 0T6 Canada. **Tel** (613)951-5078, (800)267-6677, FAX (613)951-1584, telex 053-3585. **ED** Jacques Lepage. **LC** HD9764.C2; A594. **DD** 338.1/74982/0971. **Circ:** 495. ***Continues*** *Statistics Canada. Manufacturing and Primary Industries Division. Logging, 0701-645X.*
Desc: Principal statistics of the logging industry, including number of establishments, number of employees, salaries and wages, costs of fuel and electricity, costs of materials, value of shipments and value added. Commodity detail by province on inputs and outputs; includes estimates of total forest production by products and province.

PH
PHILIPPINE FORESTRY STATISTICS. English. an. Bureau of Forest Development, Diliman, Quezon City Philippines. **Tel** 96-21-41. **LC** SD229; .P46. **DD** 333.75/09599. **Circ:** 700 (ctrl).
Desc: Forestry activities, forest resources, forest land uses, products utilization, trade and revenues derived from the utilization of forest resources.

US
STATISTICAL ROUNDUP. **Added/Corp** National Forest Products Association. (198?)-. Statistical Publication. English. Twelve times a year. $57.00 (members); $157.00 (non-members). American Forest & Paper Association, 1111 19th Street Northwest, Suite 800, Washington DC 20036. **Tel** (202)463-2721, FAX (202)463-2787, telex 140950 AF+PA DC. ***Continues*** *NFPA Economics Monthly.*

US/0195-931X
STATISTICAL YEARBOOK OF THE WESTERN LUMBER INDUSTRY. (STATISTICAL YEARBOOK OF THE WESTERN LUMBER INDUSTRY / WESTERN WOOD PRODUCTS ASSOCIATION.). **Added/Corp** Western Wood Products Association. Western Wood Products Association. Economic Services Dept. (197?)-. Statistical Publication. English. an. $20.00. Western Wood Products Association, Yeon Building, 522 Southwest Fifth Avenue, Portland OR 97204-2122. **Tel** (503)224-3930, FAX (503)224-3934. **LC** HD9757.A17; S73. **DD** 338.4/7674/0978. ***Continues*** *Western Wood Products Association. Statistical Yearbook, 0511-8301.*
Desc: Contains tables of statistics covering production in coast and inland regions by state, county and species; summaries of industry production, new orders, etc. for each region by month; import and export data; forest products statistics for each western state; other data relevant to the lumber industry.

IO
STATISTIK EKSPOR HASIL HUTAN BUKAN KAYU. **Main/Corp** Indonesia. Direktorat Bina Sarana Usaha Kehutanan. Indonesian. mo. Rp2,000 Indonesia; $1.00 US. Central Bureau of Statistics / Indonesia, c/o Dr. Sutomo, 8 Jalan, PO Box 3, Jakarta Indonesia. **Tel** 372808 374908 Ext.342. **LC** HD9766.I7; I48A. ctrl circ. ***Continues*** *Statistik Ekspor Hasil Hutan Non Kayu.*

UK/0269-980X
TROPICAL TIMBERS. [Trop. timbers]. (1986)-. Periodical. English. Twelve times a year. £86.00 UK; £96.00 others. Tropical Timbers, 2 Bug Hill, Woldingham Surrey CR3 7LB England. **Tel** 011 44 883 653326, FAX 011 44 883 652505. **ED** Geoffrey Pleydell. **DD** 338.47674. **Bk Rev.**
Desc: Marketing news and statistics related to tropical countries, forest, and international trade.

US/0360-8034
WILDFIRE STATISTICS. [Wildfire stat.]. Began with 1968. Government Publication. English. an. US Department of Agriculture / Forest Service, 201 14th Street SW, Washington DC 20250. **Tel** (202)205-1661, FAX (202)205-1181. **LC** SD421; .W545. **DD** 634.9/6/180973. available on microfiche (Vols. for (1979-) distributed to depository libraries). ***Continues*** *Forest Fire Statistics.*
Ind/Abst AGRICOLA.

LUMBER AND WOOD

FR/1155-4495
AGRESTE. SERIES, COMMERCE EXTERIEUR BOIS ET DERIVES. (1991)-. Periodical. French. Four times a year. 125.00F France; 145.00F other. Ministere de l'Agriculture et de la Peche, Direction des Affaires Financieres et Economiques, Service Central des Enquetes et Etudes Statistiques, 4 Avenue de Saint-Mande, 75570 Paris Cedex 12 France. **Tel** 011 33 1 43444633, 16 61288305. **UDC** 31(44). **CODEN** 630(44). ***Continues*** *Commerce Exterieur Bois & Derives (Paris), 0243-8283.*
Desc: Exports and imports by product.

US
APA STRUCTURAL PANEL STATISTICS. Weekly Report No. 85-27 (July 6, 1985)-. Periodical. English. wk. American Plywood Association, 7011 South 19th Street 2, PO Box 11700, Tacoma WA 98411. **Tel** (206)565-6600, FAX (206)565-7265. ***Continues*** *Plywood Statsitics.*

UK
ASIAN TIMBER. (198?)-. Periodical. English. mo. $140.00 Singapore and Malaysia; $170.00 other. Toucan Publications PTE Ltd, 322-C King George's Avenue, Singapore 0820. **Tel** 011 65 2997121, FAX 011 65 2997545. **ED** Martin C Pearce. **CODEN** ASITEP. **Circ:** 4,222.
Desc: Covers logging, forestry, timber processing, panels, veneer and value-added processing, within Southeast Asia, looking at news, current affairs, markets and statistics.
Ind/Abst BioBusiness (1990-).

CN/0383-0047
AU FIL DU BOIS. ***Ceased.*** Vol. 2 (Sept. 1975)-(1992). Periodical. French. bm. Assn Manufacturiers Bois Sciag 200, Quebec Quebec G2E 2G6 Canada. **Tel** (418)872-5610. **ED** Guy Gauvin. **DD** 338.4/7/674009714. Index available. cum. index. **Bk Rev.** **Ad Acc.** **Pr Rev.** **Circ:** 5,000 (ctrl). ***Continues*** *Bulletin Mensuel d'Information de l'Association des Manufacturiers de Bois de Sciage du Quebec.*
Desc: Official magazine of the Quebec Lumber Manufacturers Association containing forestry reports.

US/0511-8255
BAROMETER (PORTLAND). (BAROMETER.). **Main/Corp** Western Wood Products Association. No.1 (Mar. 20, 1965). Periodical. English. wk. $48.00. Western Wood Products Association, Yeon Building, 522 Southwest Fifth Avenue, Portland OR 97204-2122. **Tel** (503)224-3930, FAX (503)224-3934.
Desc: Summary of softwood lumber production, new and unfilled orders, shipments and inventory for industry.

UK/0306-4123
BOARD MANUFACTURE AND PROCESSING. [Board manuf. process.]. (1973)-. Periodical. English. bm. £25.00 UK; £30.00 other; $70.00 US. Chandler Publications Ltd, 10 South Street, Totnes Devon TQ9 5DZ England. **Tel** 0803 864668, FAX 0803 805049, telex 42928. **ED** J.R. Heming. **LC** TS875; .B57. **DD** 338.4/7/67483. **Bk Rev.** **Ad Acc.** **Circ:** 2,000. ***Continues*** *Board Practice.*
Desc: A news sheet for manufacturers and converters of wood-based sheet materials, plastic finishes and appropriate machinery.

CN
BRITISH COLUMBIA LUMBERMAN. V. 1-1917-. Periodical. English. mo. Journal of Commerce Ltd, Box 82230, North Burnaby British Columbia V5C 6E7 Canada. **Tel** (604)433-8164.
Ind/Abst For. Prod. Abstr.; For. Abstr.

US/0742-5694
BUILDING PRODUCTS DIGEST. [Build. prod. dig.]. (March 1982)-. Periodical. English. mo. $25.00 (one year), $41.00 (two years), $55.00 (three years) US; $62.00 (one year) Canada; $64.00 (one year) other. The Merchant Magazine Inc, 4500 Campus Drive/Suite 480, Newport Beach CA 92660. **Tel** (714)852-1990. **ED** Juanita Lovret. **Bk Rev.** **Ad Acc.** **Circ:** 12,750 (ctrl).
Desc: Independently-owned publication for the retail, wholesale and distribution levels of the lumber and home center markets in 13 southern states.

US/0145-5915
BUYERS' GUIDE & DEALER DIRECTORY: NORTHEASTERN AREA. **See** Business-Commerce.

SW
BYGG OCH TRAVARUHANDELN. No. 1-Jan. 1976-. Periodical. Swedish. mo. Travarhandeln, Grevgatan 3, Box 14109, S-104 40 Stockholm Sweden. ***Continues*** *Tra & Byggvaruhandlaren.*

CN/0318-4277
CANADIAN FOREST INDUSTRIES. [Can. for. ind.]. Vol. 84, No.3 (March 1964)-. Periodical. English. Eight times a year. 41.95Can$ Canada; 48.00Can$ US; 65.00Can$ other. Forest Communications, 1 Pacifique Street, St. Ann Bell Quebec H9X 1C5 Canada. **Tel** (514)457-2211. **[CCC].** available on microfilm and microfiche from University Microfilms International (UMI). ***Formed by the union of*** *Canada Lumberman, 0318-4285 and Timber of Canada, 0318-4269.*
Ind/Abst For. Prod. Abstr.; For. Abstr.; Life Sci. Collect.

UK/0010-3381
COMMONWEALTH FORESTRY REVIEW, THE. [Commonw. for. rev.]. **Added/Corp** Commonwealth Forestry Association. (Dec. 1962)-. Periodical. English. qt. £40.00. Commonwealth Forestry Association, South Parks Road, Oxford OX1 3RB England. **Tel** 011 44 865 275072, telex 3147 ATTN FOROX. **ED** Maurice T. Rogers. **LC** SD1; .E573. Index available. **Bk Rev. Ad Acc. Circ:** 1,600. available on microfilm; available in microform. ***Continues** Empire Forestry Review.*
Desc: Features reports of international forestry meetings, international coverage of forestry-related developments; plus academic and practical papers on all aspects of forestry; research notes.
Ind/Abst AgBiotech News Inf.; AGRICOLA; Agrofor. Abstr. (1991-); Ecol. Abstr.; Fish Rev.; For. Prod. Abstr. (19??-19??); For. Abstr.; Geogr. Abstr. Phys. Geogr.; Geogr. Abstr. Human Geogr.; Int. Dev. Abstr.; Life Sci. Collect.; Plant Breed. Abstr.; Plant Grow. Reg. Abstr.; Rev. Agric. Entomol.; Rev. Plant Pathol.; Soils Fert.; Wildl. Rev.

US/0742-2784
COMPILER, THE. See Computers.

CN/0708-6229
CONSTRUCTION TYPE PLYWOOD. [Constr. type plywood]. **Added/Corp** Statistics Canada. Manufacturing and Primary Industries Division. Statistics Canada. Industry Division. **VFOAT** Contre-Plaques de Construction. Vol. 27, No. 1 (Jan. 1979)-. Periodical. English (French). mo. 60.00Can$ Canada; $72.00 US; $84.00 other. Statistics Canada, Publications Sales & Services, Main Building Room 1710, Ottawa Ontario K1A 0T6 Canada. **Tel** (613)951-5078, (800)267-6677, FAX (613)951-1584, telex 053-3585. **LC** HD9769.P63; C33a. **DD** 338.4/7674834/0971021. ***Continues** Peeler Logs, Veneers and Plywoods, 0410-5702.*
Desc: Production, domestic and export shipments and month-end stocks of construction-type plywood; monthly and cumulative.

US
CROW'S BUYER'S & SELLER'S GUIDE TO THE FOREST PRODUCTS INDUSTRIES. 1983-. English. an. $120.00. CC Crow Publishers Inc., PO Box 25749, Portland OR 97255. **Tel** (503)646-8075. **ED** Sam Sherrill. **Ad Acc. Circ:** 1,200. ***Continues in part** Crow's Buyer's and Seller's Guide of the Forest Products Industries.*

US
CROW'S PLYWOOD GUIDE. (1975)-. Periodical. English. an. $69.50. CC Crow Publishers Inc., PO Box 25749, Portland OR 97255. **Tel** (503)646-8075.

US
CROW'S WEEKLY MARKET REPORT OF LUMBER & PANEL PRODUCTS. **VFOAT** Crow's; Weekly Market Report of Lumber & Panel Products; Crow's Weekly Letter; Crow's Market Report (Dec. 23, 1993-). (Sept. 21, 1990)-. Periodical. English. wk. CC Crows Publishing Company, PO Box 25749, Portland OR 97255. **Tel** (503)646-8075. **LC** HD9754; .C76. ***Continues** Crow's Weekly Letter.*

FR
CTBA INFO. 370.00F. CTBA, 10 Avenue de Sainte Mande, F-75012 Paris, France. **Tel** 011 33 1 40194905.
Desc: Technical review on wood and furniture industry.

•US
DESTINATION OF SHIPMENTS OF WESTERN U.S. SOFTWOOD LUMBER BY STATE, EXCEPT REDWOOD LUMBER. **Added/Corp** Western Wood Products Association. (Jan.-Mar. 1992)-. English. qt. Western Wood Products Association, Yeon Building, 522 Southwest Fifth Avenue, Portland OR 97204-2122. **Tel** (503)224-3930, FAX (503)224-3934. **LC** HD9757.A5; W393. ***Continues** Destination of Shipments of Western Wood Species by State, 0195-9336.*

MY
DIRECTORY OF FOREST INDUSTRIES IN MALAYSIA. (1974)-. Directory. English. qt. The Malaysian Forester, Forestry Department Headquarters, Jalan Mahameru, 50660 Kuala Lumpur Malaysia. **Tel** 03-2988244. **ED** Nik Muhamad Majid, Yong Chai Ting, Ong Meng Seng and Abdul Rashid Bin Mat Amin. **LC** TS803; .D49. **DD** 338.1/7/4982025595. Index available. **Bk Rev. Ad Acc. Circ:** 1,000.

CN
DIRECTORY OF MANUFACTURERS OF LUMBER, PLYWOOD, AND BUILDING MATERIALS ... MADE IN B.C. Directory. English. Ministry of Economic Development, 315 Robson Square British Columbia B6Z 2C5 Canada. **LC** HD9764.C4; B76. **DD** 338.7/674/0025711.

US/0070-6477
DIRECTORY OF THE FOREST PRODUCTS INDUSTRY. ***Title Change.*** 44th (1963)-(1993). Periodical. English. an. Miller Freeman Inc., 600 Harrison Street, San Francisco CA 94107. **Tel** (415)905-2337, FAX (415)905-2240, telex 278273. **ED** Pamela G Malpas. **LC** TS803; .D5. **[CCC]. Ad Acc.** ***Merged into** Directory of the Wood Products Industry, 1064-749X.*

US/1063-9985
DIRECTORY OF THE FOREST PRODUCTS INDUSTRY. ***Title Change.*** (DIRECTORY OF THE FOREST PRODUCTS INDUSTRY : DFPI.). [Dir. for. prod. ind.]. **VFOAT** DFPI. (1963)-(1993). Directory. English. Miller Freeman Inc., 600 Harrison Street, San Francisco CA 94107. **Tel** (415)905-2337, FAX (415)905-2240, telex 278273. **LC** TS803; .D5. **DD** 674/.0029/473. ***Continues** Directory of the Wood Products Industry; **Absorbed** Secondary Wood Products Manufacturers Directory, 1047-370X. **Continued by** Directory of the Wood Products Industry (San Francisco, Calif. : 1992), 1064-749X.*

•US/1064-749X
DIRECTORY OF THE WOOD PRODUCTS INDUSTRY (1992). (DIRECTORY OF THE WOOD PRODUCTS INDUSTRY.). [Dir. wood prod. ind.]. **Added/Corp** Miller Freeman Inc. **VFOAT** Wood Products Industry; DWPI. (1993)-. Directory. English. an. $243.00 US; $246.50 Canada; $262.00 other. Miller Freeman Inc., 600 Harrison Street, San Francisco CA 94107. **Tel** (415)905-2337, FAX (415)905-2240, telex 278273. **LC** TS803; .D5. **DD** 674/.0029/473. ***Absorbed** Directory of the Forest Products Industry, 1063-9985.*

US/0046-0435
DIXIE LOGGER AND LUMBERMAN MAGAZINE. ***Title Change.*** Periodical. English. mo. Dixie Publishing, Box 487, Wadley GA 30477. **Tel** (912)252-5237. **ED** Jane K Smith. **Ad Acc. Circ:** 25,000 (ctrl). ***Continued by** Logger and Lumberman Magazine, 0192-7124.*

US/0417-741X
DIXIE LUMBERMAN. V. 1, No. 1- April, 1952-. Periodical. English. Dixie Lumberman, Box 483, Jackson MS 39505.

XO/0012-6136
DREVARSKY VYSKUM. [Drev. vysk.]. **Added/Corp** Drevarsky Vyskumny Ustav. Vol. 1 (Oct. 1956)-. Academic Scholarly Publication. Slovak (Czech, Russian, English and German; summaries and/or abstracts in Russian, English and German). Twice a year. $56.00. Forest Products Research Institute, Lamacska Cesta 1, Bratislava 84411 Slovakia. **Tel** 011 42 7 373 301, telex 09333. **ED** Marian Babiak. **DD** 634.9. **CODEN** DRVYAP. **Pr Rev. Circ:** 700. Documents available from CASDDS.
Desc: Fundamental wood research from biological, chemical and physical standpoint, also including mechanical and chemical processing of wood.
Ind/Abst Abstr. Bull. Inst. Pap. Sci. Tech.; AGRICOLA; Biodeter. Abstr.; Chem. Abstr.; For. Prod. Abstr.; Life Sci. Collect.

CI/0012-6772
DRVNA INDUSTRIJA. [Drvna ind.]. Vol. 1 (Dec. 1950)-. Academic Scholarly Publication. Serbo-Croatian (Roman). ir. $66.00. Technicki Centar Za Drvo, Zagreb Ul 8 Maja 82, 41001 Zagreb Croatia. **Tel** 041/448-611, telex 22367 IDZG YU. **ED** Stanislav Badjun and Dinko Tusun. **LC** TS800; .D7. **DD** 338. **CODEN** DRINAT. Index available. cum. index. **Bk Rev. Ad Acc. Circ:** 2,000 (ctrl). Documents available from CASDDS.
Desc: Sawmilling, hydrothermal wood treatment, veneer and board manufacture, wood chemistry, wood preserving, forest product manufacture organization, furniture and joinery manufacture and woodworking machinery.
Ind/Abst Abstr. Bull. Inst. Pap. Sci. Tech.; AGRICOLA; Chem. Abstr.; For. Prod. Abstr. (1991-); For. Abstr.

BE
ECHO DES BOIS, L'. (19??)-. Periodical. French. Forty-eight times a year. 5960F. L'Echo des Bois SA, rue de l'Abattoir 29, B 1000 Bruxelles Belgium. **Tel** 011 32 2 5135047, FAX 011 32 2 5118641. **ED** C. Castelo. Index available. cum. index. **Bk Rev. Ad Acc. Circ:** 3,500.
Desc: Timber and wood products, markets and technology.

HU/0014-0066
ERDOGAZDASAG ES FAIPAR. [Erdogazdasag faip.]. V. 11, No. 7-. Periodical. Hungarian. mo. $2.00. Lapkiado Vallalat, Lenin Korut 9-11, 1073 Budapest 7, Hungary. **Tel** 222-408. **ED** Pal Kiraly. Index available. **Bk Rev. Ad Acc. Circ:** 4,500.
Ind/Abst AGRICOLA.

US/0730-5176
EXPORT REPORT - WESTERN WOOD PRODUCTS ASSOCIATION. [Export rep.]. (19??)-. Periodical. English. mo. $28.00. Western Wood Products Association, Yeon Building, 522 Southwest Fifth Avenue, Portland OR 97204-2122. **Tel** (503)224-3930, FAX (503)224-3934.
Desc: Covers species produced in the inland area showing volume and average price per M board feet by product and grade within product for current month, previous month and year-to-date.

US
FLORIDA'S WOOD-USING INDUSTRY. **Added/Corp** Florida. Division of Forestry. (19??)-. English. be. Florida Department of Agriculture & Consumer Services, State Capitol, 10th Floor, Tallahassee FL 32399. **Tel** (904)488-6971, FAX (904)488-8087. **LC** HD9757.F6; F58. **DD** 338.4/7/6740025759.

US
FLORIDA'S WOOD USING INDUSTRY, A DIRECTORY. Directory. English. Florida Department of Agriculture & Consumer Services, State Capitol, 10th Floor, Tallahassee FL 32399. **Tel** (904)488-6971, FAX (904)488-8087. **LC** HD9757.F6. **DD** 338.4/7/6740025759.

AT/0015-7392
FOREST AND TIMBER. ***Suspended.*** [For. timber]. **Added/Corp** New South Wales. Forestry Commission. (1963)-(19??)-. Periodical. English. an. Free Australia; 6.00Aus$ (per issue) other. Government Information Service / Australia, PO Box 258, Regents Park, New South Wales 2143 Australia. **Tel** 011 61 2 7521108. **ED** Ted Sheil. **CODEN** FOTIB3. **Circ:** 20,000. Documents available from BIOSIS Document Express.
Desc: Articles of general interest on forests, recreation, silviculture, and timber use.
Ind/Abst Biol. Abstr.; For. Prod. Abstr.; For. Abstr.

US/0015-7430
FOREST INDUSTRIES (SAN FRANCISCO, CALIF.). ***Title Change.*** (FOREST INDUSTRIES.). [Forest ind.]. **Added/Corp** Miller Freeman Publications, Inc. Vol. 89 No. 7 (July 1962)-Vol. 119 No. 5 (Sept./Oct. 1992). Periodical. English. bm. Miller Freeman Inc., 600 Harrison Street, San Francisco CA 94107. **Tel** (415)905-2337, FAX (415)905-2240, telex 278273. **LC** TS800; .W412. **DD** 634. **CODEN** FOINBV. **[CCC]. Circ:** 24,993. available on magnetic tape, an online database, and CD-ROM; available on microfilm and microfiche from University Microfilms International (UMI); available on an online database (files 15,648/Full-Text) from DIALOG. Documents available from UMI Article Clearinghouse. ***Formed by the union of** Timberman, 0097-3092 **and** Lumberman and Wood Industries, 0360-1560. **Continued by** Wood Technology, 1067-1064.*
Desc: Edited for North American operations and management personnel in forestry and logging (growth and harvesting of raw materials) and for those engaged in manufacture of lumber, plywood and wood-based panels. Content includes logging and forestry know-how and news, mill operations and industry-at-large coverage.
Ind/Abst ABI/INFORM Glob. Ed.; ABI Inform Ondisc (Dec. 1971-April 1975); Abstr. Bull. Inst. Pap. Sci. Tech.; Biol. Agric. Index; Bus. ASAP (1990-) [Full Txt.]; Bus. Index (1985-); Bus. Period. Index; Bus. Source (Jul. 1993-); EMBASE (Dec. 1971-Apr. 1975); Expand. Acad. Index (1992-); F&S Index Plus Text, Int. [Select. Cov.]; For. Prod. Abstr.; For. Abstr.; Gen. BusinessFile (1985-); Gen. Period. Index (1985-); Mag. Search; Newsp. Period. Abstr. (1992-); PROMT; Soils Fert.; Trade Ind. ASAP [Full Txt.]; Trade Ind. Index (1981-) [Full Txt.]; UMI ABI/Inform--Bus. Period. Ondisc [Full Txt.]; Wilson Bus. Abstr.

RM
FORESTA: ROMANIAN WOOD AND FURNITURE REVIEW. **Added/Corp** Camera de Comert a Republicii Socialiste Romania. Vol. 1, No. 2 (1969)-. Periodical. English. qt. DM232.00. **(Subscription address:** Kubon & Sagner, ABT Zeitschriftenimport, D 80328 Munich Germany.**)**

UK
FORESTRY AND BRITISH TIMBER. Vol. 5, No. 3 (June/July 1976)-. Periodical. English. Twelve times a year. £49.00 UK; £57.00 other. Benn Publications Ltd., Sovereign Way, Tonbridge TNQ 1RW England. **Tel** 011 44 732 364422, FAX 011 44 732 361534, telex 0732 95132 BENTON G. **ED** Tony Reardon. **Bk Rev. Ad Acc. Circ:** 3,000. ***Continues** Forestry and Home Grown Timber.*
Desc: Business magazine covering the forestry industry from silviculture to lumber processing.
Ind/Abst Agric. Eng. Abstr.; Agrofor. Abstr.; For. Prod. Abstr. (19??-19??); For. Abstr.; Soils Fert.; Weed Abstr.

US/0190-1257
FORSIM REVIEW. V. 9, No. 2- Apr. 1978-. Periodical. English. DRI McGraw Hill, 24 Hartwell Avenue, Lexington MA 02173. **Tel** (617)863-5100. **LC** HD9751; .F67. **DD** 338.1/7/498097. ***Continues** Forsim Review of the North American Forest Products Market, 0149-0001.*

PH/0115-0456
FPRDI JOURNAL : A PUBLICATION OF THE FOREST PRODUCTS RESEARCH AND DEVELOPMENT INSTITUT, NATIONAL SCIENCE AND TECHNOLOGY AUTHORITY. Vol. 12, No. 1 & 2 (Jan.-June 1983)-. Academic Scholarly Publication.

English. sa. Forest Products Research Development Institut, Laguna 3720 Philippines. **LC** TS800; .F59. **DD** 338.4/7674/009599. **CODEN** FPJOEF. Documents available from CASDDS. ***Continues*** *Forpride Digest.*
Ind/Abst Abstr. Bull. Inst. Pap. Sci. Tech.; Agrofor. Abstr. (1991-); Biocont. News Inf. (1991-); Chem. Abstr. (1983-); For. Prod. Abstr. (1991-); For. Abstr.; Hortic. Abstr.; Philip. Sci. Technol. Abstr.; Seed Abstr.

US/0196-321X
GENERAL TECHNICAL REPORT FPL. [Gen. tech. rep. FPL]. **VAT** General Technical Report Forest Products Laboratory. (19??)-. Academic Scholarly Publication. English. Price varies per volume. US Department of Agriculture / Wisconsin, PO Box 8911, Madison WI 53708. **Tel** (608)264-5254, FAX (608)264-5011. **LC** TS800; .U532A. **DD** 674/.005. **CODEN** XFPLAO. Documents available from Article Express International, CASDDS. ***Continues*** *USDA Forest Service General Technical Report FPL, 0094-4815.*
Ind/Abst AGRICOLA; Bioeng. Abstr.; Chem. Abstr.; Ei Page One; Eng. Index Annu.; For. Prod. Abstr. (1991-).

RU/0016-9706
GIDROLIZNAIA I LESOKHIMICHESKAILA PROMYSHLENNOST. **Added/Corp** U.S.S.R. Ministerstvo Tselliulozno-Bumazhnoi Promyshlennosti. U.S.S.R. Glavnoe Upravlenie Mikrobiologicheskoi Promyshlennosti. Nauchno-Tekhnicheskoe Obshchestvo Bumazhnoi i Derevoobrabatvaiushchei Promyshlennosti. (1955)-. Academic Scholarly Publication. Russian. Four times a year. $67.00. Ministerstvo Tselliulozno-Bumazhnoi Promyshlennosti, Moscow Russia. **(Subscription address:** Victor Kamkin, 4956 Boiling Brook Parkway, Rockville MD 20852.**)** **CODEN** GLKPA2. Index available. **Bk Rev.** Documents available from CASDDS. ***Continues*** *Gidroliznaia Promyshlennost SSSR.*
Ind/Abst Abstr. Bull. Inst. Paper Chem.; Abstr. Bull. Inst. Pap. Sci. Tech.; AGRICOLA; Chem. Abstr.; Coal Abstr.; Curr. Biotechnol.; Sel. Water Resour. Abstr.

JA
GOHAN TOKEI. **See** Forestry-Abstracting, Bibliographies and Statistics.

US/0882-4568
GREEN BOOK (MEMPHIS, TENN.). **See** Economics-Industry and Production.

US/0884-7894
GREEN BOOK'S HARDWOOD LUMBER MARKETING DIRECTORY. [Green Book's hardwood lumber mark. dir.]. **VFOAT** Hardwood Lumber Marketing Directory. (19??)-. Directory. English. an. Leases for $1,100.00 per year to North American firms. International Wood Trade Publications, PO Box 34908, Memphis TN 38184. **Tel** (901)372-8280 or (800)844-1280. **LC** HD9753; .G733. **DD** 381/.45674142/02573.
Desc: New sales opportunities for your slow moving species and lower grades of hardwoods and imported wood.

US/0745-6603
GULF COAST LUMBERMAN AND BUILDING MATERIAL DISTRIBUTOR (HOUSTON, TEX. : 1982). (THE GULF COAST LUMBERMAN AND BUILDING MATERIAL DISTRIBUTOR.). [Gulf Coast lumberman build. mater. distrib.]. **VFOAT** Gulf Coast Lumberman. (Aug. 1982)-. Periodical. English. qt. Gulf Cost Lumberman, 6633 Hillcroft, Suite 252C, Houston TX 77081. ***Continues*** *Gulf Coast Lumberman, 0192-4389.*

US/0897-022X
HARDWOOD FLOORS. (HARDWOOD FLOORS : THE MAGAZINE OF THE NATIONAL WOOD FLOORING ASSOCIATION.). [Hardwood floors]. **Added/Corp** National Wood Flooring Association. (Feb./March 1988)-. Periodical. English. bm. $36.00 (nonqualified readers). Directors Commercial Corp, PO Box 16428/ NACDA, Cleveland OH 44116. **Tel** (216)892-4000, FAX (216)892-4007. **ED** Rick Berg. **DD** 338. **Ad Acc. Circ:** 20,000 (ctrl).
Desc: Created for floor covering retailers, builders and interior designers. Editorial covers design applications, association news and major issues facing the industry.

US/0888-9104
HARDWOOD MARKET REPORT (MEMPHIS, TENN.). (HARDWOOD MARKET REPORT.). [Hardwood mark. rep.]. (19??)-. Periodical. English. wk. $189.44 (includes 8.25% sales tax) Tennessee; $175.00 other. Hardwood Market Report, PO Box 241325, Memphis TN 38124. **Tel** (901)767-9126, FAX (901)767-7534. **DD** 338.

US
HARDWOOD PURCHASING HANDBOOK. (1971)-. English. an. $150.00 US; $175.00 other. International Wood Trade Publications, PO Box 34908, Memphis TN 38184. **Tel** (901)372-8280 or (800)844-1280. **LC** TS803; .H37.
Desc: In one easy step, you'll have the digest size directory and you will have all the major suppliers in the USA.

US/1063-9322
HARDWOOD REVIEW EXPORT. [Hardwood rev. export]. (1989)-. Periodical. English. mo. $40.00 US; $50.00 Canada; $75.00 other (postage included). Hardwood Publishing Co., PO Box 471307, Charlotte NC 28247-1307. **Tel** (704)543-4408. **LC** HD9769.H393; U64. **DD** 338.
Desc: Monthly newsletter covering prices and market activity for exported North American hardwood lumber.

LV/0201-7474
HIMIJA DREVESINY. (KHIMIIA DREVESINY.). [Him. drev.]. **Added/Corp** Latvijas PSR Zinatnu Akademija. (Sept./Oct. 1974)-. Periodical. Russian (summaries and/or abstracts in English; table of contents in English). Six times a year. $99.95. **(Subscription address:** East View Publications Inc., 3020 Harbor Lane North, Suite 110, Minneapolis MN 55447.**)** **LC** TS920; .K48. **CODEN** KHDRDQ. **[CCC].** Documents available from CASDDS. ***Continues*** *Khimiia Drevesiny (Riga, Latvia : 1968).*
Ind/Abst Abstr. Bull. Inst. Pap. Sci. Tech.; AGRICOLA; Biodeter. Abstr.; Chem. Abstr.; For. Prod. Abstr. (1991-); For. Abstr.; Maize Abstr.

GW/0018-3768
HOLZ ALS ROH- UND WERKSTOFF. [Holz Roh- Werkst.]. **Added/Corp** Deutsche Gesellschaft fuer Holzforschung. Centre International de Sylviculture. Internationaler Ausschuss fuer Holzverwertung. (Oct./Nov. 1937)-. Academic Scholarly Publication. German. Six times a year. DM574.00. Springer-Verlag GmbH & Company KG, Heidelberger Platz 3, D 14197 Berlin Germany. **Tel** 011 49 30 8207223, FAX 011 49 30 8214091, telex 183 319 SPBLN D. **(Subscription address:** Springer Verlag New York Inc. / for North America, 44 Hartz Way, Secaucus NJ 07096.**)** **ED** H Schulz. **LC** TA419.A1; H58. **DD** 620.1/2/05. **CODEN** HOZWAS. **[CCC]. Bk Rev. Pr Rev.** available on microfilm from University Microfilms International (UMI). Documents available from The Genuine Article, CASDDS.
Desc: Reports on biological, chemical, physical and technological properties of wood. Includes original research on processes and handling as well as management and computer ramifications.
Ind/Abst Abstr. Bull. Inst. Pap. Sci. Tech.; Abstr. AIT Rep. Publ. Energy; AgBiotech News Inf.; AGRICOLA; Art Archaeol. Tech. Abstr.; Biodeter. Abstr. (19??-19??); Chem. Abstr.; Curr. Contents Eng. Tech. Appl. Sci.; EMBASE; Energy Res. Abstr.; For. Prod. Abstr. (19??-19??); For. Abstr.; Nucl. Sci. Abstr.; Res. Alert [Full Cov.]; Rev. Med. Vet. Mycology; Rev. Plant Pathol.; SCISEARCH.

GW
HOLZ-KUNSTSTOFF. Periodical. German. bm. DM166.00. Holzverlag GmbH & Co KG, VdK Strasse 25, D 86438 Kissing Germany. **Tel** 011 44 8233 5029, telex 533 295. **LC** TS840; .H717. Index available. **Bk Rev. Ad Acc.**

GW/0018-3830
HOLZFORSCHUNG. [Holzforschung]. (1947)-. Academic Scholarly Publication. German (English and French). bm. $748.00. Walter de Gruyter Inc., PO Box 303421, D 10728 Berlin Germany. **Tel** 011 49 30 260050, FAX 011 49 30 26005251. **ED** G. Stegmann. **CODEN** HOLZAZ. **[CCC]. Bk Rev. Ad Acc. Pr Rev. Circ:** 600. Documents available from The Genuine Article, BIOSIS Document Express, CASDDS.
Desc: Publishes reports on basic and applied research investigations relative to the biology, chemistry, physics, and technology of wood and wood components including biomass utilization.
Ind/Abst Abstr. Bull. Inst. Pap. Sci. Tech.; AgBiotech News Inf.; AGRICOLA; Agrofor. Abstr.; Biodeter. Abstr. (19??-19??); Biol. Abstr.; Chem. Abstr.; Chem. Titles; Curr. Contents, Agric. Biol. Environ. Sci.; EMBASE; Energy Res. Abstr.; For. Prod. Abstr. (1991-); For. Abstr.; Hortic. Abstr.; Life Sci. Collect.; Res. Alert [Full Cov.]; Rev. Agric. Entomol.; Rev. Plant Pathol.; Sci. Cit. Index; SCISEARCH.

AU/0018-3849
HOLZFORSCHUNG UND HOLZVERWERTUNG. [Holzforsch. holzverwert.]. **Added/Corp** Osterreichische Gesellschaft fuer Holzforschung. (1957)-. Academic Scholarly Publication. German (English). bm. S1,650 Austria; S1,705 other. Osterreichischer Agrarverlag, Inkustr 1 7 Bueropark Donau, A 3400 Klosterneuberg Austria. **Tel** 011 43 2243 33300. **ED** Alfred Teischinger. **CODEN** HOZVAP. Index available. cum. index. **Bk Rev. Ad Acc. Circ:** 5,000 (ctrl). Documents available from CASDDS. ***Continues*** *Mitteilungen der Osterreichische Gesellschaft fuer Holzforschung.*
Desc: Covers the field of mechanical and chemical wood technology including pulp and paper.
Ind/Abst Abstr. Bull. Inst. Pap. Sci. Tech.; AGRICOLA; Art Archaeol. Tech. Abstr.; Chem. Abstr.; EMBASE; For. Prod. Abstr. (19??-19??); For. Abstr.; Int. Civil Eng. Abstr.; Pap. Board Abstr.; Soft. Abstr. Eng.

NE/0254-3915
IAWA BULLETIN. ***Title Change.*** [IAWA bull.]. **Main/Corp** International Association of Wood Anatomists. **VFOAT** I.A.W.A. Bulletin. (1970-1992). Periodical. English. Four times a year. International Association of Wood Anatomists, Rijksherbarium/Schelpenkade 6, PO Box 9514, NL 2300 Ra Leiden Netherlands. **Tel** 011 31 71-130541, 011 30-532643. **LC** QK647; .I58. **CODEN** IAWABV. **[CCC]. Pr Rev.** Documents available from The Genuine Article, BIOSIS Document Express. ***Continues*** *Bulletin (International Association of Wood Anatomists).* ***Continued by*** *IAWA Journal.*
Ind/Abst Abstr. Bull. Inst. Pap. Sci. Tech.; Art Archaeol. Tech. Abstr.; Biodeter. Abstr. (1991-); Biol. Abstr.; Curr. Aware. Biol. Sci., CABS; Curr. Contents, Agric. Biol. Environ. Sci.; Field Crop Abstr.; For. Prod. Abstr. (19??-19??); For. Abstr.; Life Sci. Collect.; Plant Breed. Abstr.; Res. Alert [Select. Cov.]; Rev. Plant Pathol.; SCISEARCH; Vitis Vitic. Enol. Abstr.

NE
IAWA BULLETIN. NEW SERIES. Vol. 1, No. 1-2 (1980)-. Bulletin. English. qt. Fl90.00 Netherlands; $45.00 US; $6.00 (cum. index). International Association of Wood Anatomists, Rijksherbarium/Schelpenkade 6, PO Box 9514, NL 2300 Ra Leiden Netherlands. **Tel** 011 31 71-130541, 011 30-532643. **ED** P Baas. Index available. cum. index. **Bk Rev. Circ:** 750. ***Continues*** *I.A.W.A. Bulletin.*
Desc: Studies of microscopic wood structure related to problems in botany (morphogenesis, anatomy, physiology, taxonomy), forestry (growth, pollution, breeding), and wood technology.
Ind/Abst Abstr. Bull. Inst. Pap. Sci. Tech.; For. Prod. Abstr.; For. Abstr.

●NE/0928-1541
IAWA JOURNAL / INTERNATIONAL ASSOCIATION OF WOOD ANATOMISTS. **Added/Corp** International Association of Wood Anatomists. Vol. 14, No. 1 (1993)-. Periodical. English. Four times a year. Fl100.00. International Association of Wood Anatomists, Rijksherbarium/Schelpenkade 6, PO Box 9514, NL 2300 Ra Leiden Netherlands. **Tel** 011 31 71-130541, 011 30-532643. **LC** QK647; .I58. **CODEN** IAJOEB. ***Continues*** *International Association of Wood Anatomists. IAWA Bulletin, 0254-3915.*

US/0194-1186
IMPORT/EXPORT WOOD PURCHASING NEWS. [Import/export wood purch. news]. **VAT** Import Export Wood Purchasing News. (19??)-. Periodical. English. Six times a year (Feb., Apr., June, Aug., Oct., Dec.). $40.00 US; $70.00 Canada; $115.00 other. International Wood Trade Publications, PO Box 34908, Memphis TN 38184. **Tel** (901)372-8280 or (800)844-1280. **DD** 382. ***Continues*** *Imported Wood Purchasing News.*
Desc: This tabloid has an lot of information on "what happening" in the imports and exports international forest products industry.

US
IMPORTED WOOD PURCHASING GUIDE. **Added/Corp** International Wood Trade Publications. (19??)-. English. an. $150.00 US; $175.00 other. International Wood Trade Publications, PO Box 34908, Memphis TN 38184. **Tel** (901)372-8280 or (800)844-1280. **LC** TA419.A1; I47. **DD** 382/.45674/002573.
Desc: This directory tells you where to find anything you need in the US or Canada, on imported forest products. This gives you a wide variety of imported suppliers of lumber, mouldings, veneers, wall paneling, furniture components, flooring, plywood, logs, hardboard, doorskins, and millworks etc.

SZ
INDUSTRIEL SUR BOIS. French. mo. 48.00F. FRM, Case Postale 660, 1001 Lausanne Switzerland. **Tel** 011 41 21 274422, FAX 011 41 21 265662. **Ad Acc. Circ:** 2,800.

US
INLAND LUMBER PRICE INDEX. **VFOAT** Lumber Price Index. Sept. 1982-. English. mo. $28.00. Western Wood Products Association, Yeon Building, 522 Southwest Fifth Avenue, Portland OR 97204-2122. **Tel** (503)224-3930, FAX (503)224-3934. Index available. ***Continues*** *Lumber Price Index.*
Desc: Reflects the trend of weighted index prices for inland species.

US/0300-7405
INTERMOUNTAIN LOGGING NEWS. ***Ceased.*** (1965)-Vol. 23 No. 5 (1987). Periodical. English. mo. The Statesman Examiner Inc, 220 South Main Street, Colvill WA 99114. **Tel** (509)684-4567. **ED** Chris Lowbrough. **Ad Acc. Circ:** 3,200.

US/0890-5142
INTERNATIONAL TRADE REPORT. (INTERNATIONAL TRADE REPORT / NFPA.). [Int. trade rep.]. **Added/Corp** National Forest Products Association. International Trade Dept. National Forest Products Association. International Trade Division. **VFOAT** International Trade Council. (19??)-. Periodical. English.

Twelve times a year. Free (members); $97.00 (non-members). American Forest & Paper Association, 1111 19th Street Northwest, Suite 800, Washington DC 20036. **Tel** (202)463-2721, FAX (202)463-2787, telex 140950 AF+PA DC. **ED** Lori Kisch. **DD** 333. ctrl circ.

AU/0020-9422
INTERNATIONALER HOLZMARKT. [Int. Holzmarkt]. No. 1/2 (Jan. 9, 1943)-. Periodical. German. Twenty-six times a year. S1200.00. Internationaler Holzmarkt, Anton Frank Gasse 17, 1180 Vienna Austria. **Tel** 011 43 222 4706756, FAX 011 43 222 4706723. **ED** H. Rauscher. **LC** HD9750.1; .I65. **DD** 338.47674. Index available. **Ad Acc. Circ:** 8,000.
Desc: An wood journal of European standard which has given authentic complete and up-to-date information all on the forestry and timber industry from logging to wood and paper processing.
Ind/Abst AGRICOLA.

SW
IRG AND ITS MEMBERS AND SPONSORS. **Main/Corp** International Research Group on Wood Preservation. **VAT** International Research Group and its Members and Sponsors. English (German, Spanish and French). Kr1,800. IRG Secretariat, Drottning Kristinas Vag 47C, S-114 28 Stockholm Sweden. **Tel** 46-8-101 453, FAX 46-8-20-00 63, telex 143 75 STURES. **LC** TA422; .I55A. **DD** 674. **Circ:** 500. ***Continues** List of Members and Sponsors.*

AU/0256-5145
IUFRO NEWS. [IUFRO news]. **Main/Corp** International Union of Forestry Research Organizations. **VAT** International Union of Forestry Research Organizations News. No. 1, (Sept. 1972)-. Periodical. English (Spanish). Four times a year. International Union Forestry Res Organ, Zuercherstrasse 111, CH8903 Birmensdorf Switzerland. **Tel** 011 41 1 7392111. **Bk Rev. Circ:** 7,000 (ctrl). available on diskette.
Ind/Abst Abstr. Bull. Inst. Pap. Sci. Tech.

GW/0075-2878
JAHRESBERICHTE UBER HOLZSCHUTA. ***Ceased.*** **VFOAT** Annual Report on Wood Protection. Ceased 1975. German (English). ir. Springer-Verlag GmbH & Company KG, Heidelberger Platz 3, D 14197 Berlin Germany. **Tel** 011 49 30 8207223, FAX 011 49 30 8214091, telex 183 319 SPBLN D. **(Subscription address:** Springer Verlag New York Inc. / for North America, 44 Hartz Way, Secaucus NJ 07096.**)** ***Continues** Jahresberichte uber Holzschutz Gegen Holzpilze, Tierische Schadlinge und Feuer.*

JA
JAPAN LUMBER JOURNAL. Vol. 14, No. 1 (Jan. 1973)-. Periodical. Japanese. sm. $280.00. Japan Lumber Journal Inc, 1-36-1 Higashi-Ikebukuro #2 YH, Toshima-Ku Tokyo 170 Japan. **Tel** 011-81-3-5950-2251, FAX 011-81-3-5950-2252.

JA
JAPAN LUMBER REPORTS. (19??)-. Periodical. English. sm (24 issues). $245.00. Japan Forest Products Journal, 23 4 Fuyuki Koto Ku, Tokyo 135 Japan. **Tel** 011 81 3 38203511.

II/0379-5497
JOURNAL OF THE INDIAN ACADEMY OF WOOD SCIENCE. (JOURNAL.). [J. Indian Acad. Wood Sci.]. **Main/Corp** Indian Academy of Wood Science. Vol. 1 (Jan./June 1970)-. Periodical. English. sa. $25.00. **(Subscription address:** Prints India, 11 Darya Ganj, New Delhi, 110002 India, (Phone: 011 91 11 3268645)**) LC** TS800; .I5. **DD** 647/.05. **CODEN** JIAWAJ.

UK/0020-3203
JOURNAL OF THE INSTITUTE OF WOOD SCIENCE. [J. Inst. Wood Sci.]. **Main/Corp** Institute of Wood Science. No. 1, (Mar. 1958)-. Periodical. English. Twice a year. £42.00. Institute of Wood Science, Stocking Lane, Hughenden Valley, High Wycombe, Bucks HP14 4NU United Kingdom. **Tel** 011 44 494 565374. **ED** Richard Murphy. **LC** TA419.A1; I55. **CODEN** JIWSAF. **Bk Rev. Ad Acc. Circ:** 1,700. Documents available from CASDDS.
Desc: Covers wood science and technology.
Ind/Abst Abstr. Bull. Inst. Pap. Sci. Tech.; AGRICOLA; Art Archaeol. Tech. Abstr.; Biodeter. Abstr. (1991-); Chem. Abstr.; Ei Page One; For. Prod. Abstr. (19??-19??); For. Abstr.

US/0277-3813
JOURNAL OF WOOD CHEMISTRY AND TECHNOLOGY. **See** Chemistry-Physical and Theoretical Chemistry.

II/0377-936X
JOURNAL - TIMBER DEVELOPMENT ASSOCIATION OF INDIA. [J. Timber Dev. Assoc. India]. **Main/Corp** Timber Development Association of India. **Added/Corp** Timber Dryer's and Preserver's Association of India. Journal. (19??)-. Periodical. English. Four times a year (Jan., Apr., July, Oct.). $20.00 (one year), $35.00 (two years), $50.00 (three years). Timber Development Association of India, New Forest, Dehradun India. **Tel** 011 91 135 27021 ext 367, FAX 011 91 135 23258, telex 595-258.

(Subscription address: Prints India, 11 Darya Ganj, New Delhi 110002 India.**) ED** Satish Kumar. **CODEN** TDIJAR. Index available. cum. index. **Bk Rev. Ad Acc. Pr Rev. Circ:** 400 (ctrl). Documents available from CASDDS.
Desc: Wood science, wood processing utilisation, physical mechanical properties, drying chemical treatment, durability, wood based panels and engineered wood products.
Ind/Abst AGRICOLA; Agrofor. Abstr.; Biodeter. Abstr. (1991-); Chem. Abstr.; For. Prod. Abstr. (1991-); Hortic. Abstr.; Pollut. Abstr. Indexes; Rev. Agric. Entomol.

RU/0134-5710
LESOSECHNYE, LESOSKLADSKIE RABOTY I SUKHOPUTNYI TRANSPORT LESA : MEZHVUZOVSKII SBORNIK NAUCHNYKH TRUDOV / LENINGRADSKAIA LESOTEKHNICHESKAIA AKADEMIIA IMENI S.M. KIROVA. **See** Forestry.

CC
LIN CHAN KUNG YEH. **VFOAT** Linchan Gongye. Periodical. Chinese. bm. RMBY0.35. Pei-Ching Pao Kan Fa Hsing Chu, Beijing, People's Republic of China. **Tel** 483531. **LC** TS800; .L36. **DD** 674/.05.

US/0192-7124
LOGGER AND LUMBERMAN MAGAZINE, THE. **VFOAT** Logger and Lumberman. Periodical. English. mo. Dixie Publications and Arts Company, 210 North Main Street, Wadley GA 30477. **DD** 674. ***Continues** Dixie Logger and Lumberman Magazine, 0046-0435.*

●CN/1193-5855
LOGGER (VANCOUVER). (LOGGER.). [Logger]. **VFOAT** Westcoast Logger. (Feb. and Apr./May 1992)-. Periodical. English. Six times a year. 10.00Can$ Canada; 20.00Can$ other. Westcoast Publishing Ltd., 1496 West 72nd Avenue, Vancouver British Columbia V6P 3C8 Canada. **Tel** (800)972-1060, (604)266-7433, FAX (604)263-8620. **ED** Robert Allington. **DD** 634.9. **Bk Rev. Ad Acc.** ***Continues** Westcoast Logger, 1189-3575.*

US/0047-4983
LOGGERS WORLD. Vol. 1, No. 1 (Oct. 1964)-. Periodical. English. mo. $10.00 (one year) $18.00 (two year) US; $35.00 (one year) $63.00 (two year) other. Loggers World, 4206 Jackson Highway, Chehalis WA 98532. **Tel** (206)262-3376. **ED** Michael Crouse. **LC** SD538.2.W4; L65. **Bk Rev. Ad Acc, Adv Mgr:** Kevin Core. **Circ:** 15,500.
Desc: Covers the logging and lumbering areas of the west coast of the United States. Also contains articles about logging operations and related subjects.

CN/0714-363X
LOGGING & SAWMILLING JOURNAL. [Logging sawmilling j.]. **VFOAT** Logging and Sawmilling Journal. Vol. 13, No. 1 (Jan. 1982)-. Periodical. English. Nine times a year. $30.18. Maclean Hunter Canada / Montreal, 1001 bvd. de Maisonneuve W., Montreal, Quebec H3A 3E1 Canada. **Tel** 514-845-5141, FAX 514-845-4302, telex 055-60604. **DD** 634.9/82/0971. available on microfilm from University Microfilms International (UMI). ***Continues** Journal of Logging & Sawmilling, 0710-3433.*
Ind/Abst AQUAREF.

CN/0834-440X
LOGGING INDUSTRY. **See** Forestry-Abstracting, Bibliographies and Statistics.

CN/0318-2541
LOGGING RESEARCH PROGRESS REPORT. No. 40- March 1972-. Periodical. English. Pulp and Paper Research Institute of Canada, 570 St John's Boulevard, Pointe-Claire Quebec H9R 3J9 Canada. **Tel** (514)630-4100, telex 05-821541. **DD** 634.9/82. ***Continues** Woodlands Progress Report.*

US/8756-8314
LOUISIANA FOREST PRODUCTS. (LOUISIANA FOREST PRODUCTS : QUARTERLY MARKET REPORT.). [La. for. prod.]. **Added/Corp** Louisiana. Dept. of Agriculture. (1972)-. Periodical. English. qt. Free. Louisiana Department of Marketing/Marketing News, PO Box 44184 Capitol Station, Baton Rouge LA 70804. **Tel** (504)925-4638, (504)925-4639. **ED** Dave Foster and Diana Landry. **LC** HD9757.L8; L68. **DD** 338.1/3498/09763. **Circ:** 939. ***Continues** Louisiana Timber Products.*
Desc: Lists price information on timber sold in Louisiana during the quarter. Products included are: sawtimber, pulpwood, and poles.

US/0024-7294
LUMBER CO-OPERATOR, THE. **Added/Corp** Northeastern Retail Lumbermens Association, inc., Rochester, N.Y. (1917)-. Periodical. English. mo. $15.00 (members), $20.00 (nonmembers) US; $20.00 (members), $25.00 (nonmembers) other. Northeastern Retail Lumberman, 339 East Avenue, Rochester NY 14604. **Tel** (716)325-1626, FAX (716)325-6179. **Ad Acc, Adv Mgr:** Christine S. Mattke.

Circ: 3,800.
Desc: News on industry affairs, legislation, trade promotion, new products, current events in the industry, human interest stories, and convention. Special issues on subjects related to the industry.

US/0276-5551
LUMBER PRODUCTION AND MILL STOCKS. (CURRENT INDUSTRIAL REPORTS. MA-24T, LUMBER PRODUCTION AND MILL STOCKS / U.S. DEPARTMENT OF COMMERCE, BUREAU OF THE CENSUS.). [Lumber prod. mill stocks]. Government Publication. English. an. $1.25. US Department of Commerce, 14th Street & Constitution Avenue NW, Washington DC 20230. **Tel** (202)482-2000, FAX (202)482-3772. **LC** HD9751; .L85. **DD** 338.4/7674/0973.
Desc: Presents timely data on the production, inventories, and orders of approximately 5,000 products, which represents 40 percent of all US manufacturing.

MX
MADERA Y SU USO, LA. **Added/Corp** Laboratorio de Ciencia y Tecnologia de la Madera (Mexico). Universidad Autonoma Metropolitana. Unidad Azcapotzalco. Departamento de Materiales. No. 15 (1988)-. Periodical. Spanish. ***Formed by the union of** Madera y Su Uso en la Construccion **and** Nota Tecnica (Laboratorio de Ciencia y Tecnologia de la Madera (Mexico)).*
Ind/Abst For. Prod. Abstr. (1991-).

CN/0316-6414
MADISON'S CANADIAN LUMBER DIRECTORY. **Added/Corp** Madison's Canadian Lumber Reporter. (1952)-. Directory. English. an. 100.00Can$ US and Canada; 135.00Can$ other. Madison's Canadian Lumber Directory, PO Box 2486, Vancouver British Columbia, V6B 3W7 Canada. **Tel** (604)681-6838, FAX (604)681-6585, telex 04-54643. **ED** Laurence Cater (editor's address: 430-845 Cambre Street, Vancouver BC V6B 2P4 Canada). **DD** 338.4/7/67402571. **Ad Acc, Adv Mgr:** same as editor. **Circ:** 1,300.
Desc: A single authoritative guide to Canada's lumber industry. Includes wholesalers, lumber and plywood manufacturers, wood preservers, remanufacturers, statistics, price graphs, personnel and lumber transporters.

CN/0715-5468
MADISON'S CANADIAN LUMBER REPORTER. [Madison's Can. lumber report]. (19??)-. Periodical. English (French; summaries and/or abstracts in French). Fifty times a year. $165.00. Madison's Canadian Lumber Directory, PO Box 2486, Vancouver British Columbia, V6B 3W7 Canada. **Tel** (604)681-6838, FAX (604)681-6585, telex 04-54643. **DD** 381/.41498/029471.

US
MANAGEMENT REPORT. **Main/Corp** American Plywood Association. (19??)-. Periodical. English. Twelve times a year. Free (members), $25.00 (non-members). American Plywood Association, 7011 South 19th Street 2, PO Box 11700, Tacoma WA 98411. **Tel** (206)565-6600, FAX (206)565-7265. **ED** Jack Merry. **Circ:** Y (ctrl).
Desc: News and information on structural panels and engineered wood trade newsletter.

SW/0346-7090
MEDDELANDEN / SVENSKA TRAASKYDDSINSTITUTET / REPORTS / THE SWEDISH WOOD PRESERVATION INSTITUTE. [Medd. - Sven. traaskyddsinst.]. **Added/Corp** Svenska Traaskyddinstitutet. **VFOAT** Reports. (1974)-. Monographic series. Swedish (summaries and/or abstracts in English). ir. Price varies per volume. Swedish Wood Preservation Institute, Box 5607, S 114 865 Stockholm Sweden. **ED** Joran Jermer. **LC** UNC. **Circ:** 750.
Desc: Technical and research reports on wood preservation.
Ind/Abst AGRICOLA; Biodeter. Abstr.

US/0739-9723
MERCHANT MAGAZINE, THE. (July 1975)-. Periodical. English. mo. $11.00 (one year), $17.00 (two year), $22.00 (three year) US; $41.00 (one year) other. The Merchant Magazine Inc, 4500 Campus Drive/Suite 480, Newport Beach CA 92660. **Tel** (714)852-1990. **ED** David Cutler. **Bk Rev. Ad Acc. Circ:** 5,011 (ctrl). ***Continues** Western Lumber and Building Materials Merchant.*
Desc: Serving the lumber and home center markets in the 13 Western states since 1922.

US
MESQUITE MESSENGER. (19??)-. English. Four times a year. $12.50 US; $16.50 other. Mesquite Messenger, Reagan Wells Route Box 122, Uvalde TX 78801. **Tel** (512)232-6167. **ED** J. Lee. **Bk Rev,** (Qty: 12 or more). **Ad Acc. Circ:** 300.
Desc: Industrial and technical data on all aspects of mesquite and related products.

KO
MOKCHAE KONGHAK. **VFOAT** Wood Science & Technology. Periodical. English (Korean). Hanguk Mokchae Konghakhoe, San 1 Chongnyangni-dong, Tongdaemun-ku, Seoul South Korea. **LC** TA419.A1; M63. ctrl circ. ***Continues*** *Mokchae Kongop.*

JA/0021-4795
MOKUZAI GAKKAISHI. [Mokuzai gakkaishi]. **Main/Corp** Nihon Mokuzai Gakkai. **Added/Corp** Nihon Mokuzai Gakkai. **VFOAT** Journal of the Japan Wood Research Society. (1955)-. Academic Scholarly Publication. Japanese. mo. $252.00. Nihon Mokuzai Gakkai, (Japan Wood Research Society), 21-4-407, Hongo 6 Chome, Bunkyoku, Tokyoto 113, Japan. **(Subscription address:** Kyowa Book Company Inc., 1 38 Kanda Jinbocho Chiyoda-ku, Tokyo 101 Japan.**)** **CODEN** MKZGA7. **[CCC]. Pr Rev.** Documents available from The Genuine Article, CASDDS.
Ind/Abst Abstr. Bull. Inst. Pap. Sci. Tech.; AgBiotech News Inf.; AGRICOLA; Art Archaeol. Tech. Abstr.; Biodeter. Abstr. (19??-19??); Chem. Abstr.; Crop Physiol. Abstr.; Curr. Contents Eng. Tech. Appl. Sci.; For. Prod. Abstr. (19??-19??); For. Abstr.; Ornamental Hort.; Plant Breed. Abstr.; Plant Grow. Reg. Abstr.; Res. Alert [Full Cov.]; Rev. Agric. Entomol.; Sci. Cit. Index; SCISEARCH; Soc. Sci. Cit. Index [Select. Cov.].

JA
MOKUZAI RYUTSU KOZO HOKOKUSHO. **Main/Corp** Japan. Norinsho. Norin Keizaikyoku. Tokei Johobu. (19??)-. Periodical. Japanese. Norin Tokei Kyokai, (Association of Agriculture & Forestry Statistics), 11-14, Meguro 2 Chome, Meguroku, Tokyoto 153, Japan. **LC** HD9766.J3; J36a.

AU
MONATSHEFT DER OSTERREICHISCHEN HOLZAUSFUHR-STATISTIK. **Added/Corp** Bundesholzwirtschaftsrat (Austria). Statistische Abteilung. (19??)-. German. ir. **LC** HD9765.A9; M66.

US/0195-9409
MONTHLY F.O.B. PRICE SUMMARY PAST SALES. INLAND MILLS. **Main/Corp** Western Wood Products Association. **VFOAT** Coast Mills. (19??)-. English. mo. $45.00. Western Wood Products Association, Yeon Building, 522 Southwest Fifth Avenue, Portland OR 97204-2122. **Tel** (503)224-3930, FAX (503)224-3934. ***Supersedes*** *Weekly FOB Price Summary, Past Sales, Inland Mills.*
Desc: Covers species produced in the inland area showing volume and average price per M board feet by grade for current month, pervious month, and year-to-date.

CH/1001-8654
MUCAI GONGYE. **VFOAT** Wood Industry. (1987)-. Periodical. Chinese. qt. **DD** 674.
Ind/Abst For. Abstr.

US/0164-4580
NAVAL STORES REVIEW (1979). (NAVAL STORES REVIEW.). [Naval stores rev.]. (Jan./Feb. 1979)-. Academic Scholarly Publication. English. bm (6 issues). $58.00. Kriedt Enterprises LTD, 129 South Cortez Street, New Orleans LA 70119. **Tel** (504)482-3914, FAX (504)482-4205. **ED** Don E. Neighbors (editor's phone: (904)272-0108). **LC** TP977; .S3. **DD** 668/.372/05. **CODEN** NSTRED. Index available. cum. index. **Bk Rev. Ad Acc. Circ:** 500 (ctrl). Documents available from CASDDS. ***Continues*** *Naval Stores Review & Terpene Chemicals, 0028-1468.*
Desc: Directed to producers and processors of pine gum and wood naval stores; producers and processors of pulp chemicals such and black liquor soap skimmings, tall oil, and turpentine; and producers and processors of pine derivative chemicals for the adhesives, coating, printing ink, paper chemicals, flavor and fragrance, solvent, and household products industries.
Ind/Abst Abstr. Bull. Inst. Pap. Sci. Tech.; AGRICOLA [Select. Cov.]; Chem. Abstr. (1986-); Stat. Ref. Index.

NZ/0113-3128
NEW ZEALAND FOREST INDUSTRIES. [N. Z. for. ind.]. **Added/Corp** Forest Industry Engineering Association (N.Z.) Timber Machinists Educational Association (N.Z.). **VFOAT** Forest Industries. Vol. 17, No. 10 (Oct. 1986)-. Periodical. English. mo (12 issues per year). 55.00NZ$ New Zealand; 85.00NZ$ Australia and South Pacific; 125.00NZ$ other. Profile Publishing Ltd, PO Box 5544, Wellesley Street, Auckland New Zealand. **Tel** 011 64 9 3585455, FAX 011 64 9 3585462. **CODEN** NZFIEX. ***Continues*** *Forest Industries (Auckland, N.Z.);* ***Absorbed*** *Logging and Wood Processing.*
Ind/Abst BioBusiness (1990-); For. Prod. Abstr. (1991-).

NZ
NEW ZEALAND JOURNAL OF TIMBER CONSTRUCTION, THE. ***Title Change.*** **VFOAT** NZ Journal of Timber Construction. (Dec. 1984) - Vol. 3, No. 2 (June 1987). Periodical. English. qt. New Zealand Timber Industry Marketing, PO Box 308, Wellington New Zealand. ***Continued by*** *New Zealand Timber Today.*

NZ
NEW ZEALAND TIMBER TODAY. ***Title Change.*** ***Added/Corp*** New Zealand Timber Industry Marketing Ltd. New Zealand Timber Industry Federation. **VFOAT** Timber Today. (19??)-(199?). Periodical. English. qt. New Zealand Timber Industry Marketing, PO Box 308, Wellington New Zealand. ***Continued by*** *New Zealand and Timber Design Journal, 1171-8323.*

CN/0711-0480
NEWSBOARD (MONTREAL, QUEBEC). (NEWSBOARD.). [Newsboard]. Vol. 1, No. 1 (May 1981)-. Periodical. English. ir. $150.00. Lamb, Guay Inc., Suite 200, 1155 Sherbrooke Street West, Montreal Quebec H3A 2N3. **DD** 338.4/7674/00971.

US/0029-3156
NORTHERN LOGGER AND TIMBER PROCESSOR, THE. [North. logger timber process.]. **Added/Corp** Northeastern Loggers' Association. Vol. 14, No. 12 (June 1966)-. Periodical. English. mo. $10.00 (one year), $16.00 (two year), $22.00 (three year) US; $15.00 (one year), $26.00 (two year), $37.00 (three year). Northern Logger & Timber Process, PO Box 69, Old Forge NY 13420. **Tel** (315)369-3078, FAX (315)369-3736. **ED** Eric A Johnson. **LC** TS800; .N79. **DD** 634.9/82/0974. Index available. cum. index. **Bk Rev. Ad Acc, Adv Mgr:** Pamela Leach, **Tel** (315)369-3078. **Circ:** 13,500. ***Continues*** *Northern Logger, 0147-815X.*
Desc: Material devoted to covering the professions of logging and sawmilling, as well as forest management.
Ind/Abst Abstr. Bull. Inst. Pap. Sci. Tech.; AGRICOLA.

RU
NOVOE V TEKHNIKE I TEKHNOLOGII PROIZVODSTVA FANERY, DREVESNOSTRUZHECHYNKH PLIT I DREVESNOSLOISTYKH PLASTIKOV. **Added/Corp** Tsentralnyi Nauchno-Issledovatelskii Institut Fanery. (19??)-. Periodical. Russian. 1.50rub. Izdatelstvo Lesnaia Promyshlennost, Ulitsa Kirova 40 A, Moscow Russia. **LC** TS870; .N65.

US/0732-0981
ORIGIN TO DESTINATION. SHIPMENTS OF WESTERN LUMBER BY STATE AND MODE OF TRANSPORTATION. [Orig. destin., Shipm. west. lumber state mode transp.]. **Added/Corp** Western Wood Products Association. **VFOAT** Origin to Destination. (1981)-. Periodical. English. sa. $20.00. Western Wood Products Association, Yeon Building, 522 Southwest Fifth Avenue, Portland OR 97204-2122. **Tel** (503)224-3930, FAX (503)224-3934.
Desc: Year-to-date analysis of lumber shipments originating in the Western woods region from state of origin to state of destination by mode of transportation. Summary is in board feet; state of origin data is in thousand board feet.

US/1065-3651
PALLET ENTERPRISE. [Pallet enterp.]. Vol. 1, No. 6 (Dec. 1981)-. Trade Publication. English. mo (10 issues). Free (trade), $35.00 (non-trade) US; $45.00 Canada; $75.00 other. Pallet Enterprise Magazine, 1893-D1 Billingsgate Circle, Richmond VA 23233-4239. **Tel** (804)740-1567, FAX (804)740-2826. **(Subscription address:** CWPCA ACMPC / Canadian Subscriptions, PO Box 640, c/o Gordon Hughes, Pickering Ontario L1V 3T3 Canada.**)** **ED** Edward C. Brindley, Jr., PhD. **DD** 338. **Ad Acc, Adv Mgr:** E. Scott Brindley.
Desc: Trade magazine for the wooden pallet and container industry.

US/1048-826X
PANEL WORLD. (PANEL WORLD : VENEER, PLYWOOD, COMPOSITES.). [Panel world]. Vol. 31, No. 1 (Jan. 1990)-. Periodical. English. Six times a year. $18.00 US; $25.00 Canada; $35.00 (surface mail), $55.00 (airmail) other. Hatton Brown Publishers Inc, PO Box 2268, Montgomery AL 36197. **Tel** (205)834-1170, FAX (205)834-4525, telex 782350. **LC** HD9769.P6; P55. **DD** 338.4/7674834/05. ***Continues*** *Plywood & Panel World, 0744-6853.*

CN/1180-5099
PARTICLEBOARD, WAFERBOARD, AND FIBREBOARD. [Particleboard waferboard fibreboard]. **Added/Corp** Statistics Canada. Industry Division. **VFOAT** Panneaux Agglomeres, Panneaux Gaufres et Panneaux de Fibres; Panneaux Agglomeres, Gaufres et de Fibres. Vol. 26, No. 1 (Jan. 1990)-. English (French). mo. 60.00Can$ Canada; $72.00 US; $84.00 other. Statistics Canada, Publications Sales & Services, Main Building Room 1710, Ottawa Ontario K1A 0T6 Canada. **Tel** (613)951-5078, (800)267-6677, FAX (613)951-1584, telex 053-3585. **LC** HD9769.P33; C37. **DD** 338.4/7674836/0971021. ***Continues*** *Particleboard, Waferboard and Hardboard, 0714-1629.*
Desc: Shows the production, domestic and export shipments of particleboard, waferboard and fibreboard in monthly and cumulative totals.

PH/0024-7316
PHILIPPINE LUMBERMAN, THE. (1955)-. Periodical. English. mo. $75.00. Jacobo & Sons, PO Box 1899, Manila Philippines. **Tel** 63 2 711 1020. **Ad Acc.**
Ind/Abst Agrofor. Abstr. (1991-); For. Prod. Abstr.; For. Abstr.; Grasslands For. Abstr.

US/0735-066X
PNW COAST LUMBER PRICE INDEX. **VFOAT** P.N.W. Coast Lumber Price Index. **VAT** Pacific Northwest Coast Lumber Price Index. (Oct. 1992)-. English. mo. $28.00. Western Wood Products Association, Yeon Building, 522 Southwest Fifth Avenue, Portland OR 97204-2122. **Tel** (503)224-3930, FAX (503)224-3934.
Desc: Reflects the trend of weighted index prices for coast species.

US/0884-8823
POPULAR WOODWORKING. [Pop. woodwork.]. Vol. 5, No. 3 (Oct./Nov. 1985)-. Periodical. English. bm (6 issues). $19.97 US; $26.97 other. F&W Publications, 1507 Dana Avenue, Cincinnati OH 45207. **Tel** (513)531-2222, FAX (513)531-1843. **(Subscription address:** Neodata / Colorado, PO Box 2606, Boulder Boulder CO 80322.**)** **ED** David Camp. **DD** 684. **Bk Rev. Ad Acc. Circ:** 70,000. ***Continues*** *Popular Woodworker, 0743-6203.*
Ind/Abst Index Inf.

PL/0032-6240
PRACE INSTYTUT TECHNOLOGII DREWNA. [Pr. inst. technol. Drew.]. **Main/Corp** Instytut Technologii Drewna (Poznan, Poland). (1954)-. Academic Scholarly Publication. Polish (summaries and/or abstracts in English and Russian). qt. **(Subscription address:** ARS Polona, PO Box 1001, 00068 Warsaw Poland.**)** **LC** TA401; .P6. **DD** 620.1/2/05. **CODEN** PITDAL. Documents available from CASDDS. ***Continues in part*** *Roczniki Nauk Lesnych.*
Ind/Abst Abstr. Bull. Inst. Pap. Sci. Tech.; AGRICOLA; Chem. Abstr.

CN/0700-5075
PREVENIR (QUEBEC). (PREVENIR.). **Added/Corp** Association de Securite des Industriels Forestiers du Quebec. Vol. 1 (Jan/Feb 1975)-. Periodical. French (English; summaries and/or abstracts in English). qt. Free. Association De Securite Des Industriles Forestiers Du Quebec, Bureau 60, 580 Est, Av. Grande-Allee, Quebec, Quebec G1R 2K2. **DD** 338.4/7/67409714.

US/0066-1198
PROCEEDINGS, ... ANNUAL MEETING OF THE AMERICAN WOOD-PRESERVERS' ASSOCIATION. [Proc., annu. meet. Am. Wood-Preservers' Assoc.]. **Main/Corp** American Wood-Preservers' Association. (1949)-. Academic Scholarly Publication. English. an. **CODEN** PAWPAG. Documents available from CASDDS. ***Continues*** *American Wood-Preservers' Association. Proceedings of the ... Annual Meeting of the American Wood Preservers' Association, 0066-1198.*
Ind/Abst Chem. Abstr.

US/0066-1198
PROCEEDINGS, ANNUAL MEETING OF THE AMERICAN WOOD-PRESERVERS' ASSOCIATION. (PROCEEDINGS - AMERICAN WOOD PRESERVERS' ASSOCIATION.). [Proc. annu. meet. Am. Wood Preservers' Assoc.]. **Main/Corp** American Wood Preservers' Association. Proceedings. English. an. $50.00 (paper back), $55.00 (cloth back). American Wood Preservers Association, PO Box 849, Stevensville MD 21666. **Tel** (410)643-4163. **CODEN** PAWPAG. cum. index. **Ad Acc. Circ:** 2,000 (ctrl).
Desc: Proceedings of annual meeting.

US/0193-8495
PROCEEDINGS - HARDWOOD SYMPOSIUM OF THE HARDWOOD RESEARCH COUNCIL. [Proc. - Hardwood Symp. Hardwood Res. Counc.]. **Main/Conf** Hardwood Symposium. **Added/Corp** Hardwood Research Council. **VFOAT** Hardwood Symposium Proceedings. (1973)-. Proceedings. English. an. $10.00 (nonmembers), $5.00 (members). Hardwood Research Council, PO Box 34518, Memphis TN 38184. **Tel** (901)377-1824, FAX (901)382-6419. **ED** John A. Pitcher. **LC** HD9769.H393; U64a. **DD** 338.4/7674142/0973. **Circ:** 3,000.
Ind/Abst AGRICOLA [Full Cov.].

US/0198-0130
PROCEEDINGS - LIGHTWOOD RESEARCH CONFERENCE. [Proc. - Annu. Lightwood Res. Conf.]. **Main/Conf** Lightwood Research Conference. Academic Scholarly Publication. English. an. Southeastern Forest, PO Box 2680, Asheville NC 28802-2680. **Tel** (704)259-0327. **CODEN** PALCDR. Documents available from CASDDS. ***Continues*** *Proceedings - Lightwood Research Coordinating Council, 0161-5327.*
Ind/Abst AGRICOLA; Chem. Abstr.

US/0078-1797
PROCEEDINGS OF THE ANNUAL NORTHWEST WOOD PRODUCTS CLINIC. ***Title Change.*** [Proc. annu. Northwest Wood Prod. Clin.]. **Main/Conf** Northwest Wood Products Clinic.

Added/Corp Washington State University. Engineering Extension Service. Forest Products Research Society. Inland Empire Section. **VFOAT** Proceedings - Northwest Wood Products Clinic. (19??)-(19??). Proceedings. English. an. Washington State University / Engineering, College of Engineering, Pullman WA 99163. **LC** TS801; .F63. **DD** 634.98072. **CODEN** NWPCA6. Documents available from CASDDS. ***Continued by*** *Annual Northwest Wood Products Clinic Proceedings.*
Ind/Abst AGRICOLA; Chem. Abstr.

US
PROCEEDINGS OF THE ... WASHINGTON STATE UNIVERSITY INTERNATIONAL PARTICLEBOARD/COMPOSITE MATERIALS SYMPOSIUM. **Added/Corp** Washington State University. Wood Technology Section. Washington State University. College of Engineering. Conferences and Institutes. Washington State University. Wood Materials and Engineering Laboratory. **VFOAT** Proceedings ... International Particleboard/Composite Materials Symposium; Proceedings-W.S.U. Particleboard. (1985)-. Academic Scholarly Publication. English. an. Documents available from CASDDS. ***Continues*** *Washington State University International Particleboard/Composite Materials Series Symposium. Proceedings of the ... Washington State University International Particleboard/Composite Materials Series.*
Ind/Abst Chem. Abstr.

US/0364-1252
PRODUCTION, PRICES, EMPLOYMENT, AND TRADE IN NORTHWEST FOREST INDUSTRIES. **See** Economics-Industry and Production.

CN/0380-464X
PRODUCTION, SHIPMENTS, AND STOCKS ON HAND OF SAWMILLS EAST OF THE ROCKIES. (PRODUCTION, SHIPMENTS AND STOCKS ON HAND OF SAWMILLS EAST OF THE ROCKIES, EXCLUDING NEWFOUNDLAND AND PRINCE EDWARD ISLAND / STATISTICS CANADA, MANUFACTURING AND PRIMARY INDUSTRIES DIVISION.). [Prod. shipm. stocks hand sawmills east Rock.]. **Main/Corp** Statistics Canada. Manufacturing and Primary Industries Division. **Added/Corp** Statistics Canada. Manufacturing and Primary Industries Division. Statistics Canada. Industry Division. **VFOAT** Production, Livraison et Stocks en Mains des Scieries a l'Est des Rocheuses (Sauf Terre-Neuve et l'Ile-du-Prince-Edouard); Production, Expeditions et Stocks en Mains des Scieries a l'Est des Rocheuses (Sauf Terre-Neuve et l'Ile-du-Prince-Edouard); Production, Livraisons et Stocks en Mains des Scieries a l'Est des Rocheuses (Sauf Terre-Neuve et l'Ile-du-Prince-Edouard); Production, Livraison et Stocks en Mains des Scieries a l'Est des Rocheuses (Sauf Terre-Neuve et l'Ile-du-Prince-Edouard). Vol. 32 No. 1 (Jan. 1977)-. English (French). mo. 110.00Can$ Canada; $132.00 US; $154.00 other. Statistics Canada, Publications Sales & Services, Main Building Room 1710, Ottawa Ontario K1A 0T6 Canada. **Tel** (613)951-5078, (800)267-6677, FAX (613)951-1584, telex 053-3585. **LC** HD9764.C2; A585. **DD** 338.4/76742/09713021. ***Continues*** *Production, Shipments, and Stocks on Hand of Sawmills East of the Rockies, Excluding Newfoundland, Prince Edward Island, and Manitoba, 0380-464X.*
Desc: Production, shipments and stocks of sawed lumber by kind of wood, of sawmills east of Rockies; provincial totals.

FR
PRODUITS D'EXPLOITATION FORESTIERE ET DE SCIERIE, ET PRINCIPAUX PRODUITS DERIVES. **Main/Corp** France. Service Central des Enquetes et Etudes Statistiques. Periodical. French. Ministere de l'Agriculture, 78 rue de Varenne, 75007 Paris France. **Tel** 011 33 1 49554955 ext. 2718. **LC** HD9762.1; .F7A. **DD** 382/.45/67400944.

CN/0575-9536
PULPWOOD AND WOOD RESIDUE STATISTICS. [Pulpwood wood residue stat.]. **Main/Corp** Statistics Canada. Manufacturing and Primary Industries Division. **Added/Corp** Canada. Dominion Bureau of Statistics. Industry and Merchandising Division. Canada. Dominion Bureau of Statistics. Industry Division. Canada. Dominion Bureau of Statistics. Manufacturing and Primary Industries Division. Statistics Canada. Manufacturing and Primary Industries Division. Statistics Canada. Industry Division. **VFOAT** Statistiques de Bois a Pate et Dechets de Bois. Vol. 6, No. 1 (Jan. 1963)-. English (French). mo. 70.00Can$ Canada; $84.00 US; $98.00 other. Statistics Canada, Publications Sales & Services, Main Building Room 1710, Ottawa Ontario K1A 0T6 Canada. **Tel** (613)951-5078, (800)267-6677, FAX (613)951-1584, telex 053-3585. **LC** HD9769.W53; C35a. **DD** 338.4/7/676120971. ***Continues*** *Canada. Dominion Bureau of Statistics. Pulpwood Production, Consumption and Inventories., 0833-2371.*
Desc: Cumulative data on production, consumption and inventories of pulpwood and wood residue for Canada and the provinces.

US/0891-7833
RANDOM LENGTHS BUYERS' & SELLERS' GUIDE. [Randon Lengths buy. sellers' guide]. **VFOAT** Random Lengths Buyers' and Sellers' Guide; Buyers' and Sellers' Guide. Vol. 1 (1987)-. Consumer Publication. English. an. $130.00 North America; $160.00 other. Random Lengths Publications, PO Box 867, Eugene OR 97440-0867. **Tel** (503)686-9925, FAX (503)686-9629. **ED** David R Bartel. **DD** 338. **[CCC]**. **Ad Acc. Circ:** 1,900.
Desc: Directory of the North American products industry. Producers, wholesalers, remanufacturers, and other related firms are listed.

US/0483-9420
RANDOM LENGTHS (EUGENE, OR.). (RANDOM LENGTHS.). [Random lengths]. (1952)-. Periodical. English. wk. $193.50 US; $202.50 Canada; $230.00 other. Random Lengths Publications Inc, PO Box 867, Eugene OR 97440. **Tel** (503)686-9925, FAX (800)874-7979, (503)686-9629. **ED** Burrle Elmore. **DD** 381. **[CCC]**. **Circ:** 11,000. available via electronic mail.
Desc: Random Lengths is a weekly report on the trading and marketing of North American softwood lumber and panel products. Includes prices reported for more than 1,000 items. Feature articles on conditions in the industry and in the housing industry. Charts and graphs included. Industry News Section Weekly and Advertising Supplement Monthly.

US/1052-942X
RANDOM LENGTHS EXPORT. [Random lengths export]. **VFOAT** Export. Vol. 1, (1985)-. Periodical. English. bw. $90.00 North America; $120.00 other. Random Lengths Publications, PO Box 867, Eugene OR 97440-0867. **Tel** (503)686-9925, FAX (503)686-9629. **ED** David R Bartel. **DD** 382. **Circ:** 1,400. ***Continues*** *Random Lengths Export Market Report.*
Desc: Newsletter covering the overseas markets for North American forest products. Price guide included. Market news and analysis.

US/1045-2796
RANDOM LENGTHS YEARBOOK (1985). (RANDOM LENGTHS YEARBOOK.). [Random lengths yearb.]. **Added/Corp** Random Lengths Publications. Vol. 21 (1985)-. English. an. $34.95. Random Lengths Publications Inc, PO Box 867, Eugene OR 97440. **Tel** (503)686-9925, FAX (800)874-7979, (503)686-9629. **ED** Terri L Richards. **DD** 338. **[CCC]**. **Circ:** 1,800. ***Continues*** *Yearbook, Random Lengths.*
Desc: Statistical reference. Forest products market prices and related data covering previous eleven years.

US
REDWOOD NEWS. **Main/Corp** California Redwood Association. Periodical. English. sa. Free. California Redwood Association, 405 Enfrente Drive/Suite 200, Novato CA 94949-7206. **Tel** (415)382-0662, FAX (415)382-8531. **Bk Rev. Circ:** 25,000 (ctrl).
Desc: Architectural designing using redwood.

AT/1032-0407
REPORT - WOOD UTILISATION RESEARCH CENTRE, DEPARTMENT OF CONSERVATION AND LAND MANAGEMENT. (REPORT.). [Rep. - Wood Util. Res. Cent. Dep. Conserv. Land Manage.]. (1988)-. Monographic series. English. ir. **DD** 338.1749809941.
Ind/Abst Biodeter. Abstr.

UK
RESEARCH STUDY TD/RS. **Main/Corp** Timber Research and Development Association. No. 1-1975-. Monographic series. English. Price varies per volume.

FR/0373-5133
REVUE DU BOIS ET DE SES APPLICATIONS. [Rev. bois appl.]. (1946)-. Academic Scholarly Publication. French. Nine times a year (monthly with Jan./Feb., Jun./Jul. & Aug./Sep. issues combined.). 360.00F France; 480.00F other. SOPROGE SA, 7 Ter Cour des Petites Ecuries, 75010 Paris France. **Tel** 011 33 1 42471205, FAX 011 33 1 47703394. **ED** Nell Boix. **Bk Rev. Ad Acc. Circ:** 4,000.
Ind/Abst EMBASE; Saf. Health Work.

FR/0984-2810
REVUE DU BOIS STRASBOURG. (REVUE DU BOIS.). Periodical. French. qt. 380.00F France; 500.00F other. SOPROGE SA, 7 Ter Cour des Petites Ecuries, 75010 Paris France. **Tel** 011 33 1 42471205, FAX 011 33 1 47703394. **UDC** 671 (443.831). ***Continues*** *Revue Mensuelle des Industries du Bois (Strasbourg), 0398-0340.*

CN/0829-8653
RIGID INSULATING BOARD, WOOD FIBRE AND MINERAL PRODUCTS. [Rigid insul. board wood fibre miner. prod.]. **Added/Corp** Canada. Dominion Bureau of Statistics. Industry Division. Canada. Dominion Bureau of Statistics. Manufacturing and Primary Industries Division. Statistics Canada. Manufacturing and Primary Industries Division. Statistics Canada. Industry Division. **VFOAT** Panneaux Isolants Rigides, Produits a Base de Fibres Ligneuses et de Mineraux. Vol. 19, No. 2 (Feb. 1965)-. Periodical. English (French). mo. 60.00Can$ Canada; $72.00 US; $84.00 other. Statistics Canada, Publications Sales & Services, Main Building Room 1710, Ottawa Ontario K1A 0T6 Canada. **Tel** (613)951-5078, (800)267-6677, FAX (613)951-1584, telex 053-3585. **DD** 338.4/767483/0971. ***Continues*** *Rigid Insulating Board., 0318-7934.*
Desc: Provides production, domestic and export shipments of building board, asphalted sheathing board, and roof insulating board.

SW
SAAGVERKEN. No. 8 (Sept. 1974)-. Trade Publication. Swedish (Finnish). ir. Kr275.00 Sweden; Kr290.00 other. Arbor Publishing AB, Box 26212, S 100 41 Stockholm Sweden. **Tel** 011 46 8 6799011, FAX 011 46 8 6643005. **ED** Lennart Johansson. **Bk Rev. Ad Acc. Circ:** 3,880 (ctrl). ***Continues*** *Saagverken/Traevaruindustrien.*
Desc: A technical and commercial journal for sawmill and woodworking industries, timber trade and forestry.

US/0190-7379
SAWMILL TECHNIQUES FOR SOUTHEAST ASIA. (SAWMILL TECHNIQUES FOR SOUTHEAST ASIA : PROCEEDINGS OF THE SOUTHEAST ASIA SAWMILL SEMINAR.). **Main/Corp** Southeast Asia Sawmill Seminar. **Added/Corp** Southeast Asia Sawmill Seminar. Proceedings of the Southeast Asia Sawmill Seminar. Vol. 1 (1975)-. Proceedings. English. be. $30.00. Miller Freeman Inc., 600 Harrison Street, San Francisco CA 94107. **Tel** (415)905-2337, FAX (415)905-2240, telex 278273. **LC** TS840; .S66a. **DD** 674/.0959.

US
SF NEWSLETTER. **Added/Corp** Southern Forest Products Association (U.S.). **VFOAT** S.F. Newsletter. (1976)-. Periodical. English. wk. $25.00. Southern Forest Products Association, PO Box 641700, Kenner LA 70064-1700. **Tel** (504)443-4464, FAX (504)443-6612, telex 756854. **ED** David Kellogg. **Circ:** 1,500. available on microfilm.
Desc: Report of Association activities plus news and analysis of developments at regional and national levels affecting the Southern lumber industry.

US/0744-2106
SOUTHERN LOGGIN' TIMES. (198?)-. Periodical. English. mo. $12.00 (qualified), $30.00 (non-qualified) US; $40.00 Canada; $50.00 (surface mail), $70.00 (airmail) other. Hatton Brown Publishers Inc, PO Box 2268, Montgomery AL 36197. **Tel** (205)834-1170, FAX (205)834-4525, telex 782350. **ED** David Knight. **[CCC]**. **Ad Acc. Circ:** 13,227 (ctrl). ***Continues*** *Loggin' Times, 0191-5568.*
Desc: Monitors the South's forest products industry; editorial thrust slanted toward the region's logging trade through feature stories and news articles about logging, timber dealers, sawmills and logging equipment.

US/0038-4313
SOUTHERN LUMBERMAN. (THE SOUTHERN LUMBERMAN.). [South. lumberman]. Vol. 1 (1881)-. Periodical. English. mo. $21.00 US; $38.00 Canada; $150.00 other. Greysmith Publishing Company Inc., PO Box 681629, Franklin TN 37064. **Tel** (615)791-1953, FAX (615)790-6188. **ED** Nanci P. Gregg. **LC** TS800; .S7. **DD** 338. **Ad Acc, Adv Mgr:** Lori Fisher, **Tel** (615)790-0790. **Circ:** 11,500 (ctrl). ***Absorbed*** *Lumber Journal.*
Desc: Serves those engaged in wood processing industries.
Ind/Abst AGRICOLA.

CN/0824-2119
SPECIAL PUBLICATION - FORINTEK CANADA CORP. EASTERN LABORATORY. (SPECIAL PUBLICATION / FORINTEK CANADA CORPORATION.). [Spec. publ. - Forintek Can. Corp.]. **Added/Corp** Forintek Canada Corp. Western Laboratory. Forintek Canada Corp. Forintek Canada Corp. Eastern Laboratory. (1980)-. Academic Scholarly Publication. English (summaries and/or abstracts in French). Price varies per volume. Forintek Canada Corporation / Vancouver, Western Laboratory, 6620 NW Marine Drive, Vancouver British Columbia V6T 1X2 Canada. **DD** 634.9/8/05. **CODEN** SPCCDI. **Circ:** 300-3,000. Documents available from CASDDS. ***Formed by the union of*** *Special Publication (Western Forest Products Laboratory (Canada)), 0226-1170* ***and*** *Special Publication (Eastern Forest Products Laboratory (Canada)), 0824-2240.*
Ind/Abst Chem. Abstr. (1980-1982).

US/0195-931X
STATISTICAL YEARBOOK OF THE WESTERN LUMBER INDUSTRY. **See** Forestry-Abstracting, Bibliographies and Statistics.

SI
STATISTICS OF TIMBER EXPORTS FROM SINGAPORE IN ... . English. an. **LC** HD9766.S55; S7. **DD** 382/.41498/095957021.

SW/0348-2650
STFI-MEDDELANDE. SERIE A. ***Ceased.*** (19??)-(1992). Monographic series. English. ir.
Ind/Abst Abstr. Bull. Inst. Pap. Sci. Tech.

US/0889-339X
STUMPAGE PRICE REPORT (EUGENE, OR.). (STUMPAGE PRICE REPORT.). **Added/Corp** Timber Data Company (Eugene, Or.). (198?)-. Periodical. English. mo. $280.00. Timber Data Company, PO Box 10065, Eugene OR 97440. **Tel** (503)485-6239, FAX (503)485-8310. **DD** 338. **Circ:** 125.
Desc: Includes price of stumpage by species, by geographical area and by agency.

SW/0039-6796
SVENSK TRAVARU- OCH PAPPERSMASSETIDNING. **VFOAT** The Swedish Timber and Woodpulp Journal. Periodical. Multiple languages (Swedish and English). mo (with annual special issue). Kr215.00 Sweden; $35.00 US. Absvensk Traevarutidning, Observatoriegatan 17, S-113 29 Stockholm Sweden. **Tel** 468230515, telex 468318328. **ED** Jan Westlin and Gustav Printz. **Ad Acc. Circ:** 2,600 (ctrl).
Desc: Technical and commercial journal for the exporting wood processing industries of Scandinavia; covers timber, paper, wood pulp, cardboard and chipboard.

CN/0381-7741
TECHNICAL NOTE - FOREST ENGINEERING RESEARCH INSTITUTE OF CANADA. (FICHE TECHNIQUE - INSTITUT CANADIEN DE RECHERCHES EN GENIE FORESTIER.). [Tech. note - For. Eng. Res. Inst. Can.]. **Added/Corp** Institut Canadien de Recherches en Genie Forestier. **VFOAT** Technical Note. No. 1 (May 1976)-. Monographic series. French (English). ir. Price varies per volume. Forest Engineering Research Institute of Canada, 143 Place Frontenac, Pointe-Claire Quebec H9R 4Z7 Canada. **DD** 634.9'82. ***Continued in part by*** *Technical Note (Institut Canadien de Recherches en Genie Forestier).*

PL
TECHNOLOGIA DREWNA. ***Title Change.*** **Added/Corp** Akademia Rolnicza w Warszawie. (19??)-(19??). Polish (summaries and/or abstracts in English and Russian). Dzia Wydawnictw Akademii Rolniczej, Ksiegarnia Domu Ksiazki Ul Rakowiecka 41, Warszawa Poland. **LC** TS800; .T4. ***Merged with*** *Zeszyty Naukowe Szkoy Gownej Gospodarstwa Wiejskiego--Akademii Rolniczej w Warszawie. Lesnictwo* ***to form*** *Annals of Warsaw Agricultural University - SGGW-AR. Forestry and Wood Technology, 0208-5704.*
Ind/Abst AGRICOLA.

SZ/0255-4356
TIMBER BULLETIN. [Timber bull.]. **Added/Corp** United Nations. Economic Commission for Europe. Food and Agriculture Organization of the United Nations. **VFOAT** Bulletin du Bois. Vol. 38, No. 1 (Jan. 1985)-. Government Publication. English (French). Seven times a year. $95.00. United Nations Publications, 2 United Nations Plaza, Room DC2 0853, Department 007C, New York NY 10017. **Tel** (212)963-8303, (800)253-9646. **(Subscription address:** United Nations Publications, Subscription Office, PO Box 361, Birmingham AL 35201-0361.**)** **LC** HD9765.A2; T5. **DD** 338.1/7498/094. ***Absorbed*** *Annual Forest Products Market Review; ECE Timber Committee Yearbook; Forest Products Market Trends in ... and Prospects for ...; Monthly Prices for Forest Products;* ***Continues*** *Timber Bulletin for Europe, 0040-7747.*
Desc: Contains information on forest products, including monthly prices, production statistics, a market review and trade flow data.
Ind/Abst Abstr. Bull. Inst. Pap. Sci. Tech.; For. Prod. Abstr. (1991-).

UK
TIMBER ECONOMY. **Main/Corp** Great Britain. Directorate of Constructional Design. (194?)-. English. ir. Her Majesty's Stationery Office, 51 Nine Elms Lane, London SW8 5DR England. **Tel** 011 44 71 873 8459, 011 44 71 873 8499, FAX 011 44 71 873 8499, 011 44 71 873 8456, telex 297138.

UK
TIMBER FOR ARCHITECTS. (19??)-. Periodical. English. Four times a year. £20.00. Benn Publications Ltd., Sovereign Way, Tonbridge TNQ 1RW England. **Tel** 011 44 732 364422, FAX 011 44 732 361534, telex 0732 95132 BENTON G.

US/0160-6433
TIMBER HARVESTING. [Timber harvest.]. Vol. 25, No. 11 (Nov. 1977)-. Periodical. English. mo. $30.00 US; $40.00 Canada; $55.00 (surface mail), $75.00 (airmail) other. Hatton Brown Publishers Inc, PO Box 2268, Montgomery AL 36197. **Tel** (205)834-1170, FAX (205)834-4525, telex 782350. **ED** David Knight. **LC** TS1171; .P87. **DD** 634.9/82/0973. **CODEN** TIHAEY. **[CCC]. Ad Acc. Circ:** 23,750 (ctrl). ***Continues*** *Pulpwood Production & Timber Harvesting, 0097-7357.*
Desc: Publication edited for those engaged in harvesting, managing and handling timber in the US. Issues report on all aspects of logging and timber operations, industry news and trends.
Ind/Abst Abstr. Bull. Inst. Pap. Sci. Tech.

US/0194-5955
TIMBER MART-SOUTH. **VFOAT** Timber Mart South. **VAT** Timber Mart South. (19??)-. Periodical. English. mo. Timber Mart-South, PO Box 1278, Highlands NC 28741. **Tel** (704)526-3653. **ED** F.W. Norris. **Circ:** 500.
Desc: Market price survey and report of raw forest products.

US/0882-732X
TIMBER MART-SOUTH ... YEARBOOK. [Timber mart-south yearb.]. **VFOAT** Timber Mart South ... Yearbook. 1983-. English. an. $125.00. DRI McGraw Hill, 24 Hartwell Avenue, Lexington MA 02173. **Tel** (617)863-5100. **LC** HD9757.A13; T56. **DD** 338.1/3498/0975.

US/0885-906X
TIMBER PROCESSING. [Timber process.]. Vol. 10, No. 8 (Aug. 1985)-. Periodical. English. Ten times a year. $30.00 US; $40.00 Canada; $55.00 (surface mail), $75.00 (airmail) other. Hatton Brown Publishers Inc, PO Box 2268, Montgomery AL 36197. **Tel** (205)834-1170, FAX (205)834-4525, telex 782350. **ED** D K Knight. **DD** 674. **CODEN** TIPREN. **[CCC]. Ad Acc. Circ:** 14,000 (ctrl). ***Continues*** *Timber Processing Industry, 0194-0864.*
Ind/Abst BioBusiness (1990-).

US/0886-1242
TIMBER PRODUCER, THE. [Timber prod.]. **Added/Corp** Timber Producers Association of Wisconsin and Michigan. Vol. 13, No. 6 (June 1957)-. Periodical. English. Twelve times a year. $15.00 (one year); $27.00 (two years). Timber Producer Association, PO Box 39, Tomahawk WI 54487. **Tel** (715)453-5159. **DD** 338. ***Continues*** *Timber Producers Bulletin.*
Ind/Abst Abstr. Bull. Inst. Pap. Sci. Tech.

US/0748-9129
TIMBER REVIEW. [Timber rev.]. **VFOAT** Data Resources Timber Review. Periodical. English. DRI McGraw Hill, 24 Hartwell Avenue, Lexington MA 02173. **Tel** (617)863-5100. **LC** HD9751; .T53. **DD** 338.1/7498/0973.

●US/1065-7010
TIMBER TIMES. (1992)-. Periodical. English. qt. $14.00. Timber Times, PO Box 219, Hillsboro OR 97123.

MY
TIMBER TRADE REVIEW. **See** Economics-Industry and Production.

UK
TIMBER TRADES JOURNAL & WOOD PROCESSING. ***Title Change.*** **VFOAT** Timber Trades Journal and Wood Processing; TTJ; Timber Trades Journal. Vol. 314, No. 5433 (Nov. 1980)-Vol. 361 No. 6005 (May 1992). Periodical. English. wk. Benn Business Information Service Ltd, Riverbank House, Angel Lane, Tonbridge Kent TN9 1SE England. **Tel** 011 44 732 362666, FAX 011 44 732 770483, telex 95454 BBIS. **LC** HD9750.1; .T6. available on microfilm and microfiche from University Microfilms International (UMI). ***Formed by the union of*** *Timber Trades Journal, 0040-7798* ***and*** *Woodworking Industry, 0043-7786.* ***Continued by*** *TTJ.*

US/0740-9877
TIMBER UPDATE, TIMBER MARKETS THROUGH 1990. [Timber update, timber mark.]. **VFOAT** Timber Update. Vol. 1, No. 1 (June 1983)-. Periodical. English. DRI McGraw Hill, 24 Hartwell Avenue, Lexington MA 02173. **Tel** (617)863-5100. **LC** HD9751; .T55. **DD** 338.4/7674/00973.

US/0192-0642
TIMBER/WEST. **VFOAT** Timber West. (Dec. 1975)-. Periodical. English. Ten times a year. $20.00. Timber/West, PO Box 610, Edmonds WA 98020. **Tel** (206)778-3388. **ED** John L. Nederlee. **LC** SD538.2.P33; T56. **DD** 634. **Bk Rev. Ad Acc. Circ:** 8,500 (ctrl).
Desc: Field articles on logging, forest roadbuilding, log trucking, cutting and allied timber harvesting activities in Western US; industry news, and legislation.

US/0744-8511
TIMBERTALK. (TIMBERTALK / OLA, OHIO LUMBERMEN'S ASSOCIATION.). [Timbertalk]. **VFOAT** Timber Talk. Periodical. English. mo (except combined July and Aug.). $25.00 US. Timbertalk, 41 Croswell Road, Columbus OH 43214. **Tel** (614)267-7816. **Ad Acc. Circ:** 550 (ctrl).

AT/1035-4298
TIMBERTRADER NEWS (1990). (1990)-. Periodical. English. mo. 68.00Aus$ Australia; 95.00Aus$ other. Timbertrader News, 4 Brinsley Road, Camberwell Victoria 3124 Australia. **Tel** 011 61 3 8821972, FAX 011 61 3 8825713. **ED** Helen Hatty (editor's telephone: 054 282 104). **Ad Acc, Adv Mgr:** Mr. King, **Tel** 011 61 3 8821972. **Circ:** 1,700.
Desc: Contains information on timber marketing.

UK
TRADA : REPORT OF THE DIRECTOR OF THE TIMBER RESEARCH AND DEVELOPMENT ASSOCIATION. **Main/Corp** Timber Research and Development Association. 1971-. Periodical. English. an. ***Continues*** *Timber Research and Development Association. Annual Report.*

●UK
TTJ. **VFOAT** Timber Trades Journal. Vol. 361, No. 6006 (6 June 1992)-. Periodical. English. wk. £98.00 UK; £125.00 other. Benn Publications Ltd., Sovereign Way, Tonbridge TNQ 1RW England. **Tel** 011 44 732 364422, FAX 011 44 732 361534, telex 0732 95132 BENTON G. **LC** HD9750.1; .T6. ***Continues*** *Timber Trades Journal & Wood Processing.*
Desc: Covers the lumber trade and forest products industry.

UK/0141-5735
TTJ TELEPHONE ADDRESS BOOK. (TIMBER TELEPHONE ADDRESS BOOK.). [TTJ teleph. addr. book]. **Added/Corp** Benn Business Information Services Ltd. **VFOAT** TTJ; Timber Telephone Address Book. **VAT** Timber Trades Journal timber telephone address book. (1992)-. English. £52.00. Benn Business Information Service Ltd, Riverbank House, Angel Lane, Tonbridge Kent TN9 1SE England. **Tel** 011 44 732 362666, FAX 011 44 732 770483, telex 95454 BBIS. **ED** Doreen Barnwell. **Circ:** 3,200. ***Continues*** *Timber Trades Directory.*
Desc: Comprehensive ready-reference book of the UK's timber industry.

US/0274-970X
UNION REGISTER, THE. **Added/Corp** Western Council of Lumber Production and Industrial Workers. (19??)-. Periodical. English. mo (Publish 4th Friday of each month). $9.00. Union Register, 721 Southwest Oak Street, Portland OR 97205. **Tel** (503)228-0780, FAX (503)228-0245. **ED** Merle A. Reinikka. **Circ:** 26,000 (ctrl).

US/1063-9314
WEEKLY HARDWOOD REVIEW. [Wkly. hardwood rev.]. (1985)-. Periodical. English. wk. $155.00 US; $175.00 Canada; $260.00 other (postage included). Hardwood Publishing Co., PO Box 471307, Charlotte NC 28247-1307. **Tel** (704)543-4408. **LC** HD9769.H393; U68. **DD** 338.

CN/1189-3575
WESTCOAST LOGGER. ***Title Change.*** (THE WESTCOAST LOGGER.). [Westcoast logger]. Vol. 1, No. 1 (1990)-(1992). Periodical. English. mo. Westcoast Publishing Ltd., 1496 West 72nd Avenue, Vancouver British Columbia V6P 3C8 Canada. **Tel** (800)972-1060, (604)266-7433, FAX (604)263-8620. **DD** 634.9/8/071105. ***Continued by*** *Logger (Vancouver, B.C.), 1193-5855.*

CN/0049-7371
WESTERN CANADIAN LUMBER WORKER, THE. Began publication in 1939. Periodical. English. mo. International Woodworkers of America #1, 2859 Commercial Drive, Vancouver 12 British Columbia Canada.

US/0049-7398
WESTERN FLOORS. **See** Interior Design.

US/0511-7704
WESTERN LUMBER FACTS. (19??)-. English. mo. $36.00. Western Wood Products Association, Yeon Building, 522 Southwest Fifth Avenue, Portland OR 97204-2122. **Tel** (503)224-3930, FAX (503)224-3934. **LC** HD9757.A4; W47.
Desc: Charts and tables covering industry statistics of production, new and unfilled orders, shipments, and inventories.

US
WISCONSIN WOOD MARKETING BULLETIN. **Added/Corp** Wisconsin. Dept. of Natural Resources. (Oct. 1973)-. Bulletin. English. bm. Free. Forest Products Specialist, 3911 Fish Hatchery Road, Route 4, Madison WI 53711. **Tel** (608)275-3276, FAX (715)453-5998. **ED** Terry Mace. **Ad Acc. Circ:** 4,400. ***Continues*** *Wisconsin's Forest Products Marketing Bulletin.*
Desc: Industry newsletter with classified ads.

AT
WOOD ANALYSIS CENTRE NEWSLETTER. (19??)-. Newsletter. English. Four times a year (Mar., June, Sept., Dec.). 25.00Aus$. Wood Analysis Centre, Rural House, Southgate 87 Canning Highway, Victoria Park Western Australia, 6001 Australia. **Tel** 011 61 9 4703567.

UK
WOOD AND EQUIPMENT NEWS. (19??)-. Periodical. English. Ten times a year. £33.00 UK; £42.00 (surface), £63.00 (air mail) other. Turret Group, 177 Hagden Lane, Watford Herts WD1 8LN United Kingdom. **Tel** 011 44 923 228577, FAX 011 44 923 221346. **DD** 694.

UK/0263-1180
WOOD & EQUIPMENT NEWS + WOODWORKING MATERIALS. [Wood equip. news woodwork. mater.]. **VFOAT** Wood and Equipment News and Woodworking Materials. (1977)-. Periodical. English. Ten times a year. £33.00 UK; £42.00 (surface), £63.00 (air mail) other. Turret Group, 177

Hagden Lane, Watford Herts WD1 8LN United Kingdom. **Tel** 011 44 923 228577, FAX 011 44 923 221346. **DD** 694. ***Continues** Wood & Equipment News, 0043-7646.*

US/0735-6161
WOOD AND FIBER SCIENCE. (WOOD AND FIBER SCIENCE : JOURNAL OF THE SOCIETY OF WOOD SCIENCE AND TECHNOLOGY.). [Wood fiber sci.]. **Added/Corp** Society of Wood Science and Technology (U.S.) Forest Products Research Society. Vol. 15, No. 1 (Jan. 1983)-. Academic Scholarly Publication. English. qt. $110.00. Society of Wood Science and Technology, One Gifford Pinchot Drive, Madison WI 53705. **Tel** (608)231-9200, FAX (608)231-9592. **ED** Thomas Elder. **LC** TA419.A1; W58. **DD** 674/.05. **CODEN** WFSCD4. Index available. cum. index. **Bk Rev. Pr Rev. Circ:** 800 (ctrl). Documents available from The Genuine Article, CASDDS. ***Formed by the union of** Wood and Fiber, 0043-7654 **and** Wood Science, 0043-7700.*
Desc: Publishes manuscripts in the wood and fiber sciences that make original contributions in these disciplines and which are judged of value and interest by the scientific community through peer review.
Ind/Abst Abstr. Bull. Inst. Pap. Sci. Tech.; AGRICOLA [Select. Cov.]; Biocont. News Inf. (1991-); Biodeter. Abstr. (1991-); Chem. Abstr. (1983-); Curr. Contents, Agric. Biol. Environ. Sci.; Curr. Contents Eng. Tech. Appl. Sci.; For. Prod. Abstr. (1983-19??); For. Abstr.; Life Sci. Collect.; Plant Breed. Abstr.; Res. Alert [Full Cov.]; Rev. Agric. Entomol.; Sci. Cit. Index; SCISEARCH; Soc. Sci. Cit. Index [Select. Cov.].

US/0043-7662
WOOD & WOOD PRODUCTS. (WOOD AND WOOD PRODUCTS; THE NATIONAL AUTHORITY ON WOOD & APPLIED PRODUCTS MANAGEMENT AND OPERATIONS.). [Wood wood prod.]. (March 1952)-. Academic Scholarly Publication. English. Thirteen times a year (includes annual reference). $45.00 North America; $125.00 other. Vance Publishing Corporation, 400 Knightsbridge Parkway, Lincolnshire IL 60069. **Tel** (800)255-5113, (708)634-2600. **DD** 674. **[CCC].** available on microfilm and microfiche from University Microfilms International (UMI). ***Continues** Wood, Combined with Wood Products.*
Ind/Abst Appl. Sci. Technol. Index; Bus. ASAP (1990-) [Full Txt.]; Bus. Index (1985-); Coal Abstr.; EMBASE; Gen. BusinessFile (1985-); Gen. Period. Index (1985-); Mag. Search; Trade Ind. ASAP [Full Txt.]; Trade Ind. Index [Full Txt.]; Vocat. Search (Jan. 1993-).

US
WOOD & WOOD PRODUCTS. RED BOOK. VFOAT Wood and Wood Products. Red Book; Wood and Wood Products. Red Book Buying Guide; Wood & Wood Products. Red Book Buying Guide; Wood & Wood Products/RB; Red Book. (198?)-. English. an (published in March). $40.00. Vance Publishing Corporation, 400 Knightsbridge Parkway, Lincolnshire IL 60069. **Tel** (800)255-5113, (708)634-2600. **LC** IN PROCESS. ***Continues** Wood & Wood Products. Reference Buying Guide.*

UK/0040-7798
WOOD BASED PANELS INTERNATIONAL. (19??)-. Periodical. English. Six times a year. £52.00 UK; £63.00 other. Benn Publications Ltd., Sovereign Way, Tonbridge TNQ 1RW England. **Tel** 011 44 732 364422, FAX 011 44 732 361534, telex 0732 95132 BENTON G. available on an online database (file 16/Full-Text) from DIALOG.
Ind/Abst PROMT [Full Txt.].

CN/0835-0078
WOOD INDUSTRIES. (WOOD INDUSTRIES / STATISTICS CANADA, INDUSTRY DIVISION, CENSUS OF MANUFACTURES DIVISION.). [Wood ind.]. **Added/Corp** Statistics Canada. Census of Manufactures Section. Statistics Canada. Industry Division. Statistics Canada. Annual Survey of Manufactures Section. **VFOAT** Industries du Bois. (1985)-. English (French). an. 53.00Can$ Canada; $64.00 US; $75.00 other. Statistics Canada, Publications Sales & Services, Main Building Room 1710, Ottawa Ontario K1A 0T6 Canada. **Tel** (613)951-5078, (800)267-6677, FAX (613)951-1584, telex 053-3585. **LC** HD9764.C2; W66. **DD** 338.4/76748/0971021. ***Formed by the union of** Sawmill, Planing Mill and Shingle Mill Products Industries, 0828-9867; Sash, Door and Other Millwork Industries, 0828-9875; Veneer and Plywood Industries, 0828-9883 **and** Miscellaneous Wood Industries (Final), 0575-9056.*

US
WOOD INDUSTRIES OF NEW MEXICO. English. ir. free. New Mexico Department of State Forestry & Resources Conservation Division, PO Box 1948, Santa Fe NM 87504-1948. **Tel** (505)827-5830, FAX (505)827-3903. ***Continues** New Mexico Forest Products Directory.*
Desc: List of primary and secondary wood products and manufacturers.

US/0743-5231
WOOD MACHINING NEWS. [Wood mach. news]. **Added/Corp** Wood Machining Institute (Berkeley, Calif.). **VFOAT** WM News. Vol. 1, No. 1 (Jan./Feb. 1984)-. Periodical. English. Six times a year. $72.00 North America; $78.00 other. Wood Machining Institute, PO Box 476, Berkeley CA 94701. **Tel** (510)943-5240, FAX (510)945-0947. **ED** Dr. Ryszard Szymani. cum. index. **Bk Rev**, (Qty: 6). ctrl circ.
Desc: An international newsletter, designed to keep users and manufacturers of cutting tools and equipment informed of the latest world-wide developments in wood machining. It includes technical information on technology of sawing, planing and sanding, production of veneer and chips, and associated equipment.

US
WOOD PRODUCTS, INTERNATIONAL TRADE AND FOREIGN MARKETS. ***Title Change.*** **Added/Corp** United States. Foreign Agricultural Service. (198u)-(1992). Government Publication. English. qt. Department of Agriculture / Foreign Agricultural Service, 14th Street and Independence Avenue SW, Washington DC 20250-1000. **Tel** (202)720-3935, FAX (202)720-7729. **LC** HD9750.1; .F58. **DD** 338.4/7674/00973. available on microfiche (Vols. for (Feb. 1987-) distributed to depository libraries). ***Continues** Foreign Agriculture Circular. Wood Products, International Trade and Foreign Markets. **Continued by** Wood Products Trade and Foreign Markets.*

US
WOOD PRODUCTS TRADE AND FOREIGN MARKETS / UNITED STATES DEPARTMENT OF AGRICULTURE, FOREIGN AGRICULTURAL SERVICE. **Added/Corp** United States. Foreign Agricultural Service. (Mar. 1993)-. Government Publication. English. qt. Department of Agriculture / Foreign Agricultural Service, 14th Street and Independence Avenue SW, Washington DC 20250-1000. **Tel** (202)720-3935, FAX (202)720-7729. **LC** HD9750.1; .F58. **DD** 338.4/7674/00973. ***Continues** Wood Products, International Trade and Foreign Markets.*

UK/0960-3220
WOOD PROTECTION. (19??)-. English. sa (Jan. and Sept.). £35.00. British Wood Preservation Damp Proofing Association, Building 6, 4 Ronford Road, Stratford E15 4EA England. **Tel** 011 44 81 5192588. **ED** Luke Whale. **Bk Rev. Circ:** 500 (ctrl).
Desc: Published for the international community of researchers and technologists involved in wood protection. It will contain original research articles, major and minor reviews and short communications on all aspects of the protection of wood and wood products.

JA/0372-719X
WOOD RESEARCH. **Added/Corp** Kyoto Daigaku. Mokuzai Kenkyujo. No. 50 (Oct. 1970)-. Academic Scholarly Publication. English. Kyoto University, C O Yukawa Hall, Kyoto 606 Japan. **Tel** 075 722 3540. **LC** TA419.A1; W66. **CODEN** WDRSAU. Documents available from BIOSIS Document Express, CASDDS. ***Continues** Mokuzai Kenkyu.*
Ind/Abst Biodeter. Abstr.; Biol. Abstr.; Chem. Abstr.; For. Prod. Abstr.; For. Abstr.; Life Sci. Collect.; Rev. Agric. Entomol.; Rice Abstr.; Sug. Indus. Abstr.

US/0043-7719
WOOD SCIENCE AND TECHNOLOGY. [Wood sci. technol.]. **Added/Corp** International Academy of Wood Science. Vol. 1 (1967)-. English. Six times a year. DM744.00. Springer-Verlag GmbH & Company KG, Heidelberger Platz 3, D 14197 Berlin Germany. **Tel** 011 49 30 8207223, FAX 011 49 30 8214091, telex 183 319 SPBLN D. **(Subscription address:** Springer Verlag New York Inc. / for North America, 44 Hartz Way, Secaucus NJ 07096.**) ED** H Schulz, W Liese, T E Timell, and K A Sorg. **LC** TA419; .W83. **CODEN** WOSTBE. **[CCC]. Pr Rev.** available on microfilm from University Microfilms International (UMI). Documents available from The Genuine Article, CASDDS.
Desc: Publishes original research contributions and reviews within the entire field of wood science and technology.
Ind/Abst Abstr. Bull. Inst. Pap. Sci. Tech.; AgBiotech News Inf.; AGRICOLA [Full Cov.]; Biocont. News Inf.; Biodeter. Abstr. (1991-); Chem. Abstr.; Coal Abstr.; Curr. Contents, Agric. Biol. Environ. Sci.; Curr. Contents Eng. Tech. Appl. Sci.; For. Prod. Abstr. (19??-19??); Life Sci. Collect.; Plant Grow. Reg. Abstr.; Res. Alert [Full Cov.]; Sci. Cit. Index; SCISEARCH.

●US/1067-1064
WOOD TECHNOLOGY. [Wood technol.]. **Added/Corp** Miller Freeman Publications, Inc. **VFOAT** WT. Vol. 119, No. 6 (Nov./Dec. 1992)-. Academic Scholarly Publication. English. bm. $85.00 US; $95.00 Canada; $105.00 (surface mail), $170.00 (airmail) other. Miller Freeman Inc., 600 Harrison Street, San Francisco CA 94107. **Tel** (415)905-2337, FAX (415)905-2240, telex 278273. **(Subscription address:** Hallmark Data Systems, PO Box 1165, Skokie IL 60076.**) LC** TS800; .W412. **DD** 634. ***Continues** Forest Industries (Portland, Or.), 0015-7430; **Absorbed** World Wood, 0043-9258.*
Ind/Abst Abstr. Bull. Inst. Pap. Sci. Tech. (19??-); Biol. Agric. Index (19??-); Bus. Period. Index (19??-); EMBASE (19??-); Trade Ind. Index (?-?).

CN/0227-1001
WOOD TECHNOLOGY NOTES. [Wood technol. notes]. Vol. 1 (Feb. 1981)-. Periodical. English. qt. Wood Technology Notes, Forintek Canada Corporation, Eastern Laboratory, 800 Montreal Road, Ottawa Ontario K1G 3Z5 Canada. **DD** 674/.8/0971. ***Continues in part** Wood Research Notes, 0706-9405.*
Ind/Abst Pap. Board Abstr.

US/0161-7893
WOODBOOK, THE. **Added/Corp** Wood Products Publications (Firm). **VFOAT** Wood Book. (1978)-. English. an. $15.00. Avery Phares Inc., 2815 2nd Avenue, Suite 240, Seattle WA 98121-1261. **Tel** (206)621-1030. **LC** TA419; .W84. **DD** 674/.005.

US
WOODCHUCK, THE. Vol. 4, No. 1 (1976)-. Periodical. English. mo.

US/0894-5403
WOODSHOP NEWS. NORTHEAST. Vol. 1, No. 1 (Dec. 1986)-. Periodical. English. Twelve times a year. $14.97 one year; $21.97 two years; $28.97 three years. Soundings Publications, 35 Pratt Street, Essex CT 06426. **Tel** (203)767-8227, FAX (203) 767-1048. **ED** Ian Bowen. **Ad Acc. Circ:** 81,000.
Desc: News for and about people who work with wood.

CN/0838-4185
WOODWORKING (MARKHAM). (WOODWORKING.). [Woodworking]. Vol. 1 No. 1 (Nov. 1987)-. Periodical. English. Six times a year (Jan., March, May, June, Aug., Sept., Nov.). Free on request to woodworking companies in Canada; 35.00Can$ Canada; 55.00Can$ other. Action Communications Inc, 135 Spy Ct, Markham Ontario L3R 5H6 Canada. **Tel** (416)477-3222. **ED** Maurice Holtham. **DD** 684/.08/0971. **Bk Rev. Ad Acc. Circ:** 11,020 (ctrl).
Desc: New product tabloid including features for the wood and wood products manufacturing industries in Canada.

US/0043-9258
WORLD WOOD. ***Title Change.*** [World wood]. (1960)-(19??). Periodical. English. bm. Miller Freeman Inc., 600 Harrison Street, San Francisco CA 94107. **Tel** (415)905-2337, FAX (415)905-2240, telex 278273. **ED** David Pease. **LC** TS800; .W6. **[CCC]. Circ:** 8,118. available on microfilm and microfiche from University Microfilms International (UMI); available on an online database (file 648/Full-Text) from DIALOG. ***Merged into** Wood Technology, 1067-1064.*
Desc: Journal for loggers, foresters and manufacturers of lumber, plywood and wood-based panels outside North America. Mill and forestry methods emphasized with focus on machinery and techniques. Editorial includes mill and logging operations, industry news, new machinery and suppliers, forest management and resources.
Ind/Abst Abstr. Bull. Inst. Pap. Sci. Tech.; AGRICOLA; Agrofor. Abstr. (1991-); F&S Index Plus Text, Int. [Select. Cov.]; For. Prod. Abstr. (1991-); For. Abstr.; Int. Civil Eng. Abstr.; Life Sci. Collect.; PROMT; Trade Ind. ASAP [Full Txt.]; Trade Ind. Index [Full Txt.].

FUNERAL SERVICE

US/0002-7804
AMERICAN CEMETERY, THE. (19??)-. Periodical. English. Twelve times a year. $18.00 US; $20.00 other. American Cemetery, 1501 Broadway, New York NY 10036. **Tel** (212)398-9266.

US/0002-8576
AMERICAN FUNERAL DIRECTOR. [Am. funer. dir.]. (19??)-. Periodical. English. Twelve times a year. $23.00 US; $29.00 others. Kates Boyleston Publishing Company, 1501 Broadway, New York NY 10036. **Tel** (212)398-9266.

CN/0319-3225
CANADIAN FUNERAL DIRECTOR. Vol. 1 (May 1973)-. Periodical. English. mo (11 issues). 60.00Can$ Canada; 70.00Can$ other. Halket Publishing, 174 Harwood Avenue South/Suite 206, Ajax Ontario L1S 2H7 Canada. **Tel** (905)427-6121. **ED** Ray Halket. **Bk Rev. Ad Acc. Circ:** 1,635 (ctrl). ***Supersedes** Canadian Funeral Service, 0008-364X.*

CN/0382-5876
CANADIAN FUNERAL NEWS. **VFOAT** C F N. Vol. 1 (Nov. 1975)-. Periodical. English. Eleven times a year. 75.00Can$. Consolidated Communications, 807 Manning Road Northeast, Suite 200, Calgary Alberta T2E 7M8 Canada. **Tel** (403)569-9520, FAX (403)569-9590. **ED** Randi Berting. **DD** 338.4/7/614640971. Index available. **Bk Rev. Ad Acc. Circ:** 1,400.
Desc: A trade publication going out to funeral directors across Canada. New issues, products and events which affect funeral profession.

CN/0846-0019
CANADIAN OBITUARY RECORD. (THE CANADIAN OBITUARY RECORD / ROBERT M. STAMP.). [Can. obit. rec.]. (1988)-. Periodical. English. an (June). 39.99Can$ Canada. Dundurn Press, 2181 Queen Street East, Suite 301, Toronto Ontario M4E 1E5 Canada. **Tel** (416)698-0454. **LC** CT283; .S73. **DD** 920.071/09/04505; B.

US/0008-7327
CASKET & SUNNYSIDE. (CASKET & SUNNYSIDE : C & S.). [Casket sunnyside]. **VFOAT** Casket and Sunnyside; C & S; C&S; C and S. Periodical. English. mo. $16.00. Casket & Sunnyside, 274 Madison Avenue, New York 10016. **Tel** (212)685-8310. **DD** 338. available on microfilm from University Microfilms International (UMI).

US/0162-4237
CEMETERY BUSINESS & LEGAL GUIDE. **VAT** Cemetery Business and Legal Guide. (19??)-. Periodical. English. Ten times a year. $110.00. CB Legal Publishing Corporation, 555 Skokie Boulevard, Suite 500, Northbrook IL 60062. **Tel** (708)480-1020, FAX (708)509-1027. **ED** Cheryl A. Lapin. **LC** KF3781.A15; C45. cum. index. **Circ:** 500.
Desc: A newsletter discussing business and legal problems and solutions pertinent to your operation. Question/Answer format, in-depth analysis, layman language. Up-to-date coverage of antitrust, tax matters, OSHA, consumer trade practices, government regulations, EPA information and more. One subject covered in each issue with suggestions for implication.

US
CEMETERY - FUNERAL SERVICE LEGAL COMPASS. English. mo. $69.00. American Cemetery Association, 5201 Leesburg Pike, Suite 1111, Falls Church VA 22041. **Tel** (703)379-5838, (800)645-7700, FAX (703)998-0162. **ED** Robert M. Fells. Index available. cum. index. **Circ:** 600. ***Continues*** *Cemetery Legal Compass.*

US/0270-5281
CEMETERY MANAGEMENT. [Cemet. manage.]. **Added/Corp** National Association of Cemeteries. American Cemetery Association. Vol. 40 (Jan. 1980)-. Periodical. English. mo. $35.00 members, $45.00 others. American Cemetery Association, 5201 Leesburg Pike, Suite 1111, Falls Church VA 22041. **Tel** (703)379-5838, (800)645-7700, FAX (703)998-0162. **LC** RA626; .N314. **DD** 614/.6. ***Continues*** *Correspondent (Arlington), 0364-1066.*

US/0199-3186
DIRECTOR (MADISON, WIS.), THE. (THE DIRECTOR.). [Director]. Periodical. English. mo. $16.00. National Funeral Directors Association, 11121 West Oklahoma Avenue, Milwaukee WI 53227-4033. **Tel** (414)541-2500. **ED** Sue Simon. **DD** 338. **Bk Rev. Ad Acc. Circ:** 16,000.
Desc: Journal of the National Funeral Directors Association.

US/0272-2674
DIRECTORY OF MEMBERS, LOT EXCHANGE, MAUSOLEUM CRYPT EXCHANGE, DOLLAR CREDIT PLANS. [Dir. memb. lot exch. mausol. crypt exch. dollar credit plans]. **Main/Corp** National Association of Cemeteries. Directory. English. National Association of Cemeteries, 1911 North Fort Myer Drive, Suite 409, Arlington VA 22209. **LC** RA626; .N322. **DD** 363.7/5/02573. ***Continues*** *Membership Directory - National Association of Cemeteries, 0360-2095.*

US/0095-1862
DIRECTORY OF UNITED STATES CEMETERIES. V. 1- 1974-. Directory. English. Cemetery Research, Inc., Po Box 6616, San Jose CA 95150. **LC** RA626.3; .D57. **DD** 363.

US/0273-9747
FLORIDA FUNERAL DIRECTOR, THE. Vol. 1 (1932)-. Trade Publication. English. bm. $12.00. Florida Funeral Directors Services Inc, PO Box 6009, Tallahassee FL 32314. **Tel** (904)224-1969, FAX (904)224-7965. **ED** Jan Scheff and Karen Thurston. **Ad Acc. Circ:** 1,000 (ctrl).
Desc: A journal dealing with the concerns and interests of the Florida funeral service industry.

CN/0575-8629
FUNERAL DIRECTORS. (FUNERAL DIRECTORS / PREPARED IN THE WHOLESALE TRADE AND SERVICES SECTION, INDUSTRY AND MERCHANDISING DIVISION.). [Funer. dir.]. **Added/Corp** Canada. Dominion Bureau of Statistics. Wholesale Trade and Services Section. Canada. Dominion Bureau of Statistics. Current Surveys Section. Canada. Dominion Bureau of Statistics. Merchandising and Services Division. Statistics Canada. Merchandising and Services Division. Statistics Canada. Services Division. **VFOAT** Directeurs de Funerailles. (1956)-. English (French). ir. 20.00Can$ Canada; $21.00 other. Statistics Canada, Publications Sales & Services, Main Building Room 1710, Ottawa Ontario K1A 0T6 Canada. **Tel** (613)951-5078, (800)267-6677, FAX (613)951-1584, telex 053-3585. **LC** HD9999.U53; C33a. **DD** 338.4/7/61464.
Desc: Contains information on types of services, average funeral costs, inventory, purchases and expenditures.

US/1051-3779
FUNERAL SERVICE INSIDER NEWSLETTER. [Funer. serv. insid. newsl.]. (19??)-. Newsletter. English. Fifty times a year (3 combined issues). $255.00. United Communications Group, 11300 Rockville Pike, Suite 1100, Rockville MD 20852. **Tel** (301)816-8950 ext. 223, FAX (301)816-8945. **DD** 338. ***Continues*** *Funeral Service Insider, 0148-6705.*

UK
FUNERAL SERVICE JOURNAL ENGLAND. English. Twelve times a year. £13.00 UK; £20.00 other. John Horbury & Associates, 43 Stockens Green Knebworth, Herts SG3 6DQ England. **Tel** 011 44 438 814441, FAX 011 44 438 814002.

US/0882-2883
INSCRIPTIONS (STEVENS POINT, WIS.). **See** Genealogy and Heraldry.

US/0739-0289
MORTICIANS OF THE SOUTHWEST. (19??)-. Periodical. English. mo. $18.00 (1 year), $34.00 (2 year) US; $22.00 (1 year), $42.00 (2 year) other. Farring Incorporated, 2514 National Drive, Garland TX 75041. **Tel** (214)480-1060.

US/0027-1268
MORTUARY MANAGEMENT. (1914)-. Periodical. English. mo (11 issues). $27.00. Mortuary Management, 315 Silver Lake Boulevard, Los Angeles CA 90026. **Tel** (213)665-0101. **ED** Ronald A. Hast. **LC** RA622; .A295. **DD** 658/.91/614605. **Bk Rev. Ad Acc. Circ:** 5,000. available on microfilm and microfiche from University Microfilms International (UMI).
Desc: Designed for funeral directors and allied professionals, including manufacturers and jobbers of mortuary supplies, equipment and merchandise.

US
NATIONAL FUNERAL DIRECTOR AND EMBALMER. **Added/Corp** National Funeral Directors and Morticians Association, Inc. (1948)-. Periodical. English. bm. $24.00. National Funeral Director / Morticians Association, 734 West 79th Street, Chicago IL 60620. **Tel** (312)487-3600.

US/1054-8238
NATIONAL YELLOW BOOK OF FUNERAL DIRECTORS, THE. [Natl. yellow book fun. dir.]. **VFOAT** Yellow Book. (1988)-. English. an. $65.00 standard size; $35.00 pocket size. Nomis Publications Inc, PO Box 5122, Youngstown OH 44501. **Tel** (216)788-9608 or (800)321-7479. **LC** HD9999.U53; U555. **DD** 363.7/5/02573. ***Continues in part*** *Yellow Book of Funeral Directors & Suppliers, 1054-822X.*

CN/0711-3838
NEWSLETTER - FEDERATION OF ONTARIO MEMORIAL SOCIETIES. (NEWSLETTER.). [Newsl. - Fed. Ont. Meml. Soc.]. Vol. 1 (1981)-. Newsletter. English. Hamilton Memorial Society, PO Box 164, Hamilton Ontario L8N 3A2 Canada. **DD** 393/.09713. ***Absorbed*** *Hamilton Memorial Society Newsletter, 0711-3846.*

CN/0701-1377
NEWSLETTER - MEMORIAL SOCIETY ASSOCIATION OF CANADA. **Main/Corp** Memorial Society Association of Canada. V. 1 (Summer 1975)-. Newsletter. English. Memorial Society Association of Canada, Box 96 Station A, Weston Ontario M9N 3M6 Canada. **DD** 614/.64/06271.

US/0198-9162
RED BOOK (WORTHINGTON). (RED BOOK.). **Added/Corp** American Monument Association. (1979)-. English. an. American Monument Association, 933 High Street / Suite 220, Worthington OH 43085-4046. **Tel** (614)885-2713. **LC** HD9999.S463; U56. **DD** 338.4/769068.

●US/1073-273X
REDBOOK (CHAGRIN FALLS, OHIO), THE. (THE REDBOOK : THE NATIONAL DIRECTORY OF MORTICIANS.). (1992)-. Directory. English. an. $85.00. National Directory of Morticians, PO Box 73, Chagrin Falls OH 44022. **Tel** (216)247-3561. ***Continues*** *National Directory of Morticians.*

US/0038-4135
SOUTHERN FUNERAL DIRECTOR. [South. funer. dir.]. (1919)-. Periodical. English. mo. $30.00 US; $45.00 other. John W Yopp Publications Inc., PO Box 1147, Beaufort SC 29901. **Tel** (803)521-0239, FAX (803)521-1398. **ED** John W Yopp. **DD** 338. **Bk Rev. Ad Acc. Circ:** 5,659 (ctrl).
Desc: Dedicated to funeral directors in the South and Southwest, with news among funeral homes and updates concerning state and national associations.

US/1062-5909
TEXAS FUNERAL SERVICES DIRECTORY. [Tex. funer. serv. dir.]. **VFOAT** Funeral Services Directory. (1991)-. Directory. English. Texas State Directory Press, PO Box 12186 Capitol Station, Austin TX 78711. **Tel** (512)477-5698, (800)388-8075, FAX (512)473-2447. **DD** 393.

GARDENING AND HORTICULTURE

US/0098-5228
AAN ANNUAL CONVENTION REPORT. **Main/Corp** American Association of Nurserymen. **VAT** American Association of Nurserymen Annual Convention Report. English. an. American Association of Nurserymen, 230 Southern Building, 15th & H Street NW, Washington DC 20005. **LC** SB1; .A35. **DD** 635.9/06/273. ***Continues*** *American Association of Nurserymen. Annual Meeting.*

US/0565-1905
ACREAGE MARKETING GUIDES. SPRING VEGETABLES AND MELONS. (SPRING VEGETABLES AND MELONS.). Government Publication. English. an. Department of Agriculture / Foreign Agricultural Service, 14th Street and Independence Avenue SW, Washington DC 20250-1000. **Tel** (202)720-3935, FAX (202)720-7729. **LC** SB320.6; .A25. **DD** 338.1/8. ***Continues*** *Spring Vegetables, Spring Melons.*

XO/0567-7432
ACTA FYTOTECHNICA. [Acta fytotech.]. **Added/Corp** Vysoka Skola Polnohospodarska v Nitre. Agronomicka Fakulta. (1966)-. Academic Scholarly Publication. Czech (summaries and/or abstracts in Russian and English). ir. **CODEN** ACFYAB. Documents available from CASDDS. ***Supersedes in part*** *Vysoka Skola Polnohospodarska v Nitre. Agronomicka Faculta. Sbornik Vysokej Skoly Polnohospodarskej v Nitre.*
Ind/Abst Chem. Abstr.; Crop Physiol. Abstr.; Field Crop Abstr.; Grasslands For. Abstr.; Hortic. Abstr.; Maize Abstr.; Plant Breed. Abstr.; Rev. Med. Vet. Mycology; Rev. Plant Pathol.

NE/0567-7572
ACTA HORTICULTURAE. [Acta hortic.]. **Added/Corp** International Society for Horticultural Science. No. 1 (Oct. 1963)-. Monographic series. English (French and Multiple languages). ir. Price varies per volume. International Society for Horticultural Science / ISHS, Englaan 1, 6703 ET Wageningen The Netherlands. **Tel** 011 31 8370 21747, FAX 011 31 8370 21586, telex 45760. **LC** SB13; .A182. **CODEN** AHORA2. **Circ:** 300 (ctrl). Documents available from BIOSIS Document Express, CASDDS.
Ind/Abst AgBiotech News Inf.; AGRICOLA [Full Cov.]; Agric. Eng. Abstr. (1991-); Agrofor. Abstr. (19??-19??); Biocont. News Inf. (1991-); Biodeter. Abstr. (19??-19??); Biol. Abstr.; Chem. Abstr.; Crop Physiol. Abstr.; Field Crop Abstr.; Food Sci. Technol. Abstr.; For. Prod. Abstr. (19??-19??); For. Abstr.; Grasslands For. Abstr.; Hortic. Abstr.; Irr. Drain. Abstr.; Leis. Recreat. Tour. Abstr.; Maize Abstr.; Nematol. Abstr.; Nutr. Abstr. Rev., Ser. A, Hum. Exp.; Ornamental Hort. (19??-19??); Plant Breed. Abstr.; Plant Genet. Resour. Abstr.; Plant Grow. Reg. Abstr.; Postharvest News Inf.; Potato Abstr.; Protozoolog. Abstr.; Rev. Agric. Entomol.; Rev. Med. Vet. Mycology; Rev. Plant Pathol.; Rural Dev. Abstr.; Seed Abstr.; Soils Fert.; Soyabean Abstr.; Vitis Vitic. Enol. Abstr.; Weed Abstr.; Wheat Barley Trit. Abstr.; World Agric. Econ.

US/0092-8348
ACTIVITY REPORT OF THE VIRGINIA STATE APPLE COMMISSION. (ACTIVITY REPORT.). **Main/Corp** Virginia State Apple Commission. (19??)-. English. State Apple Commission, PO Box 718, Staunton VA 22401. **LC** SB363.2.U6; V52. **DD** 353.9/755/008233.

IT/0394-6169
ADVANCES IN HORTICULTURAL SCIENCE. [Adv. hortic. sci.]. **Added/Corp** Universita di Firenze. Dipartimento di Ortoflorofrutticoltura. (1987)-. Periodical. English. Four times a year. L50000 Italy; L60000 other. Universita de Firenze / Dipartimento di Ortoflorofrutticoltura, Via Donizetti 6, 50144 Firenze Italy. **Tel** 011 39 55 333462, 333463. ***Continues*** *Rivista della Ortoflorofrutticoltura Italiana, 0035-5968.*
Ind/Abst AGRICOLA [Full Cov.]; Crop Physiol. Abstr.; Curr. Aware. Biol. Sci., CABS; Food Sci. Technol. Abstr.; Hortic. Abstr.; Irr. Drain. Abstr.; Nematol. Abstr.; Ornamental Hort. (19??-19??); Plant Breed. Abstr.; Plant Genet. Resour. Abstr.; Plant Grow. Reg. Abstr.; Postharvest News Inf.; Rev. Plant Pathol.; Vitis Vitic. Enol. Abstr.

II/0971-0507
ADVANCES IN HORTICULTURE AND FORESTRY. [Adv. Hortic. For.]. **VFOAT** Advances in Horticulture and Forestry Research. Vol. 1 (1990)-. Periodical. English. an. Rs360.00. Scientific Publishers, PO Box 91, Ratanada Road, Jodhpur 342011 India. **ED** S.P. Singh. **UDC** 63.
Desc: Main aim is to communicate current advancements which are made in the fields of horticulture and forestry. Carries recent findings from the field as well as from the laboratories, and information on the present

state of knowledge on various topics on pomology, olericulture, floriculture, fruit and vegetable preservation and landscaping gardening.

US/0002-0265
AFRICAN VIOLET MAGAZINE. [African violet mag.]. **Added/Corp** African Violet Society of America. Vol. 1 (1947/48)-. Periodical. English. bm. $15.00 US; $17.00 other. African Violet Society of America, PO Box 3609, Beaumont TX 77704-3609. **Tel** (409)839-4725, FAX (409)839-4329. **ED** Jane Birge (editor's address: PO Box 1238 Nederland TX 77627; editor's phone: (409)724-0999). **DD** 635. Index available (bound in Jan. issue). cum. index. **Ad Acc, Adv Mgr:** D Richardson, **Tel** (410)686-4667. **Circ:** 12,000 (ctrl).
Desc: Contains articles written by the nation's leading growers, hybridizers, recognized experts in their fields and by amateur growers. Each issue contains beautiful color pictures of new varieties, older specimens and scenes from shows around the country.
Ind/Abst AGRICOLA.

US/8756-7733
AGACCESS. ***Title Change.*** **See** Agriculture.

SW/0002-1172
AGRI HORTIQUE GENETICA. (AGRI HORTIQUE GENETICA : MEDDELANDEN FRAN WEIBULLSHOLMS VAXTFORADLINGSANSTALT, LANDSKRONA.). [Agri. hort. genet.]. **Added/Corp** Weibullsholms Vaxtforadlingsanstalt, Landskrona. Vol. 1 (1943)-. Periodical. English (German and Swedish). ir. Plant Breeding Institute, Weibullsholn, Landskrona Sweden. **CODEN** AHWVAK. cum. index. Documents available from BIOSIS Document Express.
Ind/Abst Biol. Abstr.; Field Crop Abstr.; Plant Breed. Abstr.; Wheat Barley Trit. Abstr.

US
AGRICULTURAL BOOKS AND INFORMATION. **See** Agriculture.

SA
AGROPLANTAE. **See** Agriculture.

JA/0385-3152
AKITA-KEN KAJU SHIKENJUO KENKYUU HUOKOKU. (BULLETIN OF THE AKITA FRUIT-TREE EXPERIMENT STATION.). [Akita-ken Kaju Shikenjuo kenkyuu huokoku]. **Main/Corp** Akita, Japan, Akita Fruit-Tree Experiment Station. (1969)-. Bulletin. Japanese. Akita Fruit-Tree Experiment Station, Daigo, Hiraka Akita, Japan.
Ind/Abst Crop Physiol. Abstr.; Hortic. Abstr.; Plant Breed. Abstr.

CN
ALBERTA GREENHOUSE NOTES. Periodical. English. mo. Free. Alberta Tree Nursery and Horticulture Centre, RR #6, Edmonton Alberta T5B 4K3 Canada. **Tel** (403)973-3351. **ED** Mirza Mohyuddin. Index available. **Circ:** 700 (ctrl).
Desc: An extension publication reporting on crop condition; current problems, future events, new chemicals and growers viewpoints.

US/0098-793X
ALLIED LANDSCAPE INDUSTRY MEMBER DIRECTORY. **Added/Corp** American Association of Nurserymen. American Association of Nurserymen. Member Directory. (19??)-. Directory. English. American Association of Nurserymen, 230 Southern Building, 15th & H Street NW, Washington DC 20005. **LC** SB44; .A5. **DD** 338.1/7/5902573.

US/0886-4365
ALMOND FACTS. **Main/Corp** California Almond Growers Exchange, Sacramento, Calif. Vol. 1 (1937)-. Periodical. English. Six times a year. $25.00 US; $45.00 other. Blue Diamond Growers, PO Box 1768, Sacramento CA 95812. **Tel** (916)442-0771. **ED** Dan Campbell. **DD** 634. **Ad Acc. Circ:** 9,000 (ctrl).
Desc: Published for the 5,800 grower/members of the California Almond Growers Exchange, with information on cultural practices, and on the cooperative which markets under the Blue Diamond label.
Ind/Abst Bibliogr. Agric.

UK
AMATEUR GARDENING. (19??)-. Periodical. English. wk (52 issues). $95.00 US and Canada. IPC Magazines Ltd., Perrymount Road, Haywards Heath, West Sussex RH16 3DH England. **Tel** 011 44 444 440421. ***Absorbed*** *Popular Gardening.*

US/0065-762X
AMERICAN CAMELLIA YEARBOOK, THE. [Am. camellia yearb.]. **Added/Corp** American Camellia Society. 1st (1946)-. English. an (Dec.). $20.00 Comes with American Camellia Society membership only. American Camellia Society, One Massee Lane, Fort Valley GA 31030. **Tel** (912)967-2358, (912)967-2722, FAX (912)967-2083. **ED** Ann Blair Brown. **LC** SB413.C18; A5. **DD** 635.933166. Index available. **Bk Rev. Circ:** 4,000 (ctrl).
Desc: Articles promoting interest in the genus Camellia, including its culture. New varieties and events of interest to camellia growers.
Ind/Abst AGRICOLA [Select. Cov.]; Hortic. Abstr.

US/0002-8568
AMERICAN FRUIT GROWER (WILLOUGHBY, OHIO : 1931). (AMERICAN FRUIT GROWER.). [Am. fruit grow.]. Vol. 51 (Jan. 1931)-. Periodical. English. mo. $11.96 (one year), $20.96 (two year). Meister Publishing Company, 37733 Euclid Avenue, Willoughby OH 44094-5992. **Tel** (216)942-2000, (800)572-7740, FAX (216)942-0662. **CODEN** AMFGAR. **[CCC].** available on microfilm and microfiche from University Microfilms International (UMI). Documents available from Documents on Demand. ***Continues*** *American Fruit Grower Magazine.*
Ind/Abst Biocont. News Inf. (1991-); Biol. Agric. Index; Energy Inf. Abstr.; Environ. Abstr.; Hortic. Abstr.; Postharvest News Inf.; Rev. Agric. Entomol.; Rev. Plant Pathol.; Weed Abstr.

US/0194-3456
AMERICAN FUCHSIA SOCIETY BULLETIN. **Main/Corp** American Fuchsia Society. **Added/Corp** American Fuchsia Society. Bulletin. (1929)-. Periodical. English. Six times a year. $15.00. American Fuchsia Society, 9th Avenue and Lincoln Way, Hall Flower, San Francisco CA 94122. **Tel** (415)697-6278. **ED** Charles T. Hassett. **Ad Acc. Circ:** 1,400 (ctrl).
Desc: Covers fuchsia culture, registration, taxonomy and exhibitions; organizational news.

US/0096-4417
AMERICAN HORTICULTURIST (ALEXANDRIA). (AMERICAN HORTICULTURIST.). [Am. hortic.]. **Added/Corp** American Horticultural Society. Vol. 51 (March 1972)-. Periodical. English. Twelve times a year. $35.00 US; $50.00 others. American Horticultural Society, 7931 East Boulevard Drive, Alexandria VA 22308-1300. **Tel** (800)777-7931, (703)768-5700, FAX (703)765-6032. **ED** Kathleen Fisher. **LC** SB1; .N3. **DD** 635.9/0973. Index available (back issues, $3.00). **Bk Rev. Ad Acc. Circ:** 25,000. available on microfilm and microfiche from University Microfilms International (UMI). ***Continues*** *American Horticultural Magazine, 0002-8800.*
Desc: These publications provide a treasury of gardening information for both the amateur and professional.
Ind/Abst Acad. Search (Jan. 1993-); Biol. Agric. Index; Biol. Dig.; Garden Lit. (1992-); Gen. Sci. Index; Gen. Sci. Source (Jan. 1993-); Hortic. Abstr.; INFO-SOUTH Abstr.; Mag. Search; Life Sci. Collect.; Plant Breed. Abstr.; Rev. Med. Vet. Mycology; Rev. Plant Pathol.; Vocat. Search (Jan. 1993-).

US
AMERICAN HORTICULTURIST NEWS. **Added/Corp** American Horticultural Society. Vol. 59, No. 6 (Nov. 1980)-. Periodical. English. bm (published in alternate months with American Horticulturist). $35.00 one year, $60.00 two year (new subscription); $45.00 one year, $80.00 two year (renewal). American Horticultural Society, 7931 East Boulevard Drive, Alexandria VA 22308-1300. **Tel** (800)777-7931, (703)768-5700, FAX (703)765-6032. **(Subscription address:** American Horticultural Society, 7931 East Boulevard Drive, Alexandria, Virginia 22308-1300) **ED** Barbara W Ellis. **Bk Rev. Ad Acc. Circ:** 40,000. ***Continues*** *News Views, 0002-8819.*
Desc: Practical, how-to approach to gardening in this country. Articles on plants, gardeners, projects and research as well as public and private gardens.

US/0003-0198
AMERICAN NURSERYMAN. [Am. nurserym.]. (Aug. 1, 1940)-. Periodical. English. Twelve times a year. $45.00 (one year); $80.00 (two years). American Nurseryman Publishing Company, 77 West Washington Street, Suite 2100, Chicago IL 60602. **Tel** (800)621-5727, (312)782-5505, FAX (312)782-3232. **ED** Cynthia Champney Urbano. **LC** SB354; .A2. **DD** 634.05. Index available. **Bk Rev. Ad Acc. Circ:** 16,500. available on microfilm and microfiche from University Microfilms International (UMI). ***Continues*** *American Nurseryman and the National Nurseryman.*
Desc: Professional magazine for growers of landscape plants, garden center operators and landscapers. Articles on everything from research to basic how-to's to profiles to business management.
Ind/Abst AGRICOLA [Select. Cov.]; Agric. Eng. Abstr. (1991-); Agrofor. Abstr. (1991-); Biocont. News Inf. (19??-19??); Biol. Agric. Index; Crop Physiol. Abstr.; For. Prod. Abstr.; For. Abstr.; Garden Lit. (1992-); Hortic. Abstr.; Irr. Drain. Abstr.; Mag. Search; Nematol. Abstr.; Ornamental Hort. (19??-19??); Plant Breed. Abstr.; Plant Grow. Reg. Abstr.; Rev. Agric. Entomol.; Rev. Plant Pathol.; Soils Fert.; Vocat. Search (July 1993-); Weed Abstr.

US/0003-0252
AMERICAN ORCHID SOCIETY BULLETIN. [Am. Orchid Soc. bull.]. **Main/Corp** American Orchid Society. **Added/Corp** American Orchid Society. Bulletin. Vol. 1 (June 1932)-. Bulletin. English. mo. $30.00 (one year), $57.00 (two year) US; $36.00 (one year), $69.00 (two year) other. American Orchid Society Inc, 6000 South Olive Avenue, West Palm Beach FL 33405. **Tel** (407)585-8666, FAX (407)585-0654. **ED** James Watson. **LC** SB409.A1; A62. **DD** 635.9341506273. Index available in last issue of volume--attached (free of charge). cum. index. **Bk Rev**, (Qty: 6-12). **Ad Acc. Circ:** 27,000 (ctrl).
Desc: Have a wealth of orchid information at your fingertips with our monthly AOS bulletin which includes more than 110 pages of fullcolor orchid photographs, articles on culture, breeding, natural habitats, history and conservation as well as a special advertising section. New subscriptions include our complimentary handbook on orchid culture and more.
Ind/Abst AGRICOLA [Select. Cov.]; Hortic. Abstr.; Ornamental Hort. (19??-19??); Plant Breed. Abstr.; Plant Genet. Resour. Abstr.

US
AMERICAN PEONY SOCIETY BULLETIN, THE. **Main/Corp** American Peony Society. **Added/Corp** American Peony Society. Bulletin. (Aug. 1924)-. Bulletin. English. qt. $7.50 one year, $20.00 three years. American Peony Society, 250 Interlachen Road, Hopkins MN 55343. **Tel** (612)938-4706. **ED** Greta M. Kessenich. **LC** SB413.P4; A6. **DD** 635.933111. **Ad Acc. Circ:** 1,000. ***Continues*** *Bulletin of Peony News.*
Desc: Emphasis on peonies.

US/0066-0000
AMERICAN ROSE ANNUAL / AMERICAN ROSE SOCIETY, THE. ***Title Change.*** **Added/Corp** American Rose Society. (1916)-(199?). English. an. American Rose Society, PO Box 30000, Shreveport LA 71130. **Tel** (318)938-5402. **LC** SB411; .A42. **DD** 635.9/33372. cum. index. ***Continues*** *American Rose Society. Annual Proceedings and Bulletin.* ***Absorbed by*** *American Rose Magazine (American Rose Society : 1991).*
Ind/Abst AGRICOLA [Select. Cov.].

US
AMERICAN ROSE MAGAZINE, THE. **Added/Corp** American Rose Society. **VFOAT** Rose Annual. Vol. 31, No. 5 (May 1991)-. Periodical. English. mo. $25.00. American Rose Society, PO Box 30000, Shreveport LA 71130. **Tel** (318)938-5402. ***Absorbed*** *American Rose Annual;* ***Continues*** *American Rose (American Rose Society : 1988), 0003-0899.*

US/1042-3427
AMERICAN ROSE REGISTRY. [Am. rose regist.]. (1988)-. English. be. $10.00. American Rose Society, PO Box 30000, Shreveport LA 71130. **Tel** (318)938-5402. **ED** Thomas Cairns. **LC** SB411.6; .A56. **DD** 635.9/33372. **Circ:** 2,000.

FR/0044-8095
AMI DES JARDINS ET DE LA MAISON, L'. (1960)-. Periodical. French. Ten times a year. 184.13F France; 250.00F other. L'Amie des Jardins de la Maison, BP 58, 77932 Perthes Cedex France. **Tel** 011 33 64 380221. **UDC** 35.

FR/0003-1844
AMIS DES ROSES, LES. [Amis roses]. **Added/Corp** Societe Francaise des Roses. (1897)-. Periodical. French. Three times a year (Apr., July, Nov.). $14.00 one year, US; 200.00F other. Societe Francaise des Roses, Parc de la Tete d'Or, 69459 Lyon Cedex 3 France. **ED** Zinsch Amand (phone: 78 25 17 69). **Circ:** 3,000.
Desc: Information of interest to botanist, gardners, and all lovers of flowers. It offers useful tips in flower growing.
Ind/Abst AGRICOLA.

GW
AMTLICHE PFLANZENSCHUTZBESTIMMUNGEN. Vol. 1 (1949)-. Periodical. German. Six times a year. Price varies. Saphir Druck Verlag, Guttsstrasse 15, D 38851 Ribbesbuettel Germany. **Tel** 011 49 5374 6578.
Ind/Abst Rev. Med. Vet. Mycology; Rev. Plant Pathol.

FR/0373-8701
ANNALES DE LA SOCIETE D'HORTICULTURE ET D'HISTOIRE NATURELLE DE L'HERAULT. (ANNALES.). [Ann. Soc. hortic. hist. nat. Herault]. **Main/Corp** Societe d'Horticulture et d'Histoire Naturelle de l'Herault. V. 1 (1861)-. Periodical. French. an.
Ind/Abst GeoRef.

IT/0304-0550
ANNALI DELL'ISTITUTO SPERIMENTALE PER LA FLORICOLTURA. **Main/Corp** Istituto Sperimentale per la Floricoltura. Vol. 1 (1970)-. Monographic series. Italian (summaries and/or abstracts in English; table of contents in English). Price varies per volume.
Ind/Abst Biocont. News Inf.; Plant Grow. Reg. Abstr.

IT/0304-0585
ANNALI DELL'ISTITUTO SPERIMENTALE PER LA PATOLOGIA VEGETALE. **Added/Corp** Istituto Sperimentale per la Patologia Vegetale. (1970)-. Italian (summaries and/or abstracts in English). an. Istituto Sperimentale per la Patologia Vegetale, via Bertero 22, 00156 Roma. **LC** SB732.54.I8; A56. **DD** 632/.05.
Ind/Abst Biodeter. Abstr.; Hortic. Abstr.; Seed Abstr.

II/0970-9924
ANNALS OF PLANT PHYSIOLOGY AKOLA. [Ann. Plant Physiol.Akola]. (1987)-. Periodical. English. sa. Dr. S. B. Lall, Editor-in-Chief, RDG College Hostel-1, Amt Road, Akola 444001, Maharashtra, India. **UDC** 581.1.
Ind/Abst Agrofor. Abstr. (1991-); Crop Physiol. Abstr.; Field Crop Abstr.; For. Prod. Abstr. (1991-); Hortic. Abstr.; Plant Breed. Abstr.; Plant Grow. Reg. Abstr.; Rice Abstr.; Seed Abstr.; Soils Fert.; Sorghum Mill. Abstr.; Soyabean Abstr.

PL/0208-5747
ANNALS OF WARSAW AGRICULTURAL UNIVERSITY, SGGW-AR. HORTICULTURE. [Ann. Warsaw Agric. Univ. SGGW-AR, Hortic.]. **VFOAT** Horticulture. (1984)-. English. ir. Z1100.00 (single issue). Warsaw Agricultural University Press, Ul Nowoursynowska 166, 02-766 Warsaw Poland. **CODEN** AWAHEB. Documents available from BIOSIS Document Express. ***Continues*** *Zeszyty Naukowe Szkoy Gownej Gospodarstwa Wiejskiego--Akademii Rolniczej w Warszawie. Ogrodnictwo, 0083-7288.*
Ind/Abst Biol. Abstr. (-1986); Hortic. Abstr.; Ornamental Hort. (1991-); Rev. Plant Pathol.; Seed Abstr.

UK/0305-2443
ANNOTATED BIBLIOGRAPHY (WEED RESEARCH ORGANIZATION). (ANNOTATED BIBLIOGRAPHY.). Bibliography. English.

CN/0319-1915
ANNUAL - CANADIAN GLADIOLUS SOCIETY. **Main/Corp** Canadian Gladiolus Society. (1938)-. English. an. comes with membership. Canadian Gladiolus Society, 3073 Grand Road, Regina Saskatchewan S4S 5G9 Canada. **Tel** (604)796-2548. **ED** Grant Wilson. **DD** 584/.24. **Bk Rev. Ad Acc. Circ:** 300. ***Continues*** *Quarterly of the Canadian Gladiolus Society.*
Desc: Symposium of gladiolus varieties articles about growing, showing and propagation of gladiolus shows, reports and results, also information on dahlias.

US
ANNUAL REPORT. **Main/Corp** Vegetable Growers Association of America, Inc. (19??)-. English.

US/0885-7849
ANNUAL REPORT ... ANNUAL MEETING / OREGON HORTICULTURAL SOCIETY. [Annu. rep. annu. meet. - Or. Hortic. Soc., Meet.]. **Main/Corp** Oregon Horticultural Society. Meeting. **VFOAT** Proceedings of the Oregon Horticultural Society. Began with 54th ... 77th (Nov. 28-30, 1962). English. an. $15.00. Oregon Horticultural Society, PO Box 1246, McMinnville OR 97128. **Tel** (503)472-7910. **ED** W Wayne Roberts. **DD** 635. **Ad Acc. Circ:** 700 (ctrl). ***Continues*** *Oregon State Horticultural Society. Annual Report.*
Desc: Report of the annual meeting covering information and education on production, marketing and management.

US
ANNUAL REPORT / DESERT BOTANICAL GARDEN. **See** Biology-Botany.

US
ANNUAL REPORT / DIVISION OF PLANT INDUSTRY. **Main/Corp** Colorado. Division of Plant Industry. (19??)-. English. an. **LC** SB21.C67; D58a. **DD** 353.97880082/333/06.

UK/0963-3235
ANNUAL REPORT / HORTICULTURE RESEARCH INTERNATIONAL. **Main/Corp** Horticulture Research International (Great Britain). (1991)-. English. an. ***Formed by the union of*** *nstitute of Horticultural Research (Great Britain). Annual Report, 0953-2455* ***and*** *Stockbridge House Experimental Horticulture Station. Annual Review Annual review for ... (Efford Experimeal Horticulture Station), 0263-0281 Kirton Experimental Horticulture Station. Annual Report.*

US/0096-7688
ANNUAL REPORT OF THE SECRETARY OF THE STATE HORTICULTURAL SOCIETY OF MICHIGAN. [Annu. rep. secr. State Hortic. Soc. Mich.]. **Main/Corp** Michigan State Horticultural Society. **VFOAT** Michigan State Horticultural Society. (18??)-. English. an (Published in February). $20.00. Michigan State Horticulture Society, 338 Plant and Soil Science Building, Michigan State University, East Lansing MI 48824. **Tel** (517)355-5194, FAX (517)353-0890. **ED** Jerome Hull. **LC** SB21; .M55. **DD** 635. Index available. **Circ:** 2,200 (ctrl). ***Continues*** *State Pomological Society of Michigan. Annual Report of the Secretary of the State Pomological Society of Michigan.*
Desc: Information relating to production, handling and marketing of fruit crops.
Ind/Abst AGRICOLA [Select. Cov.].

US/0092-3745
ANNUAL ROSTER - TEXAS STATE BOARD OF LANDSCAPE ARCHITECTS. (ANNUAL ROSTER.). **Main/Corp** Texas. State Board of Landscape Architects. English. an. State Board of Landscape Architects, 1011 Sam Houston Building, Austin TX 78701. **LC** SB469.34.T4; T48A. **DD** 712/.025/764. **UDC** 712(066)(764).

CN/0319-3098
ANNUELLES ET LEGUMES. RESULTATS DES CULTURES D'ESSAI. (ANNUELLES ET L'EGUMES.). **Main/Corp** Jardin Botanique de Montreal. 1969-. Periodical. French. an. Free to exchangists and professionals. Jardin Botanique de Montreal, 4101 Sherbrooke Street East, Montreal Quebec H1X 2B2 Canada. **Tel** (514)872-1430. **DD** 635.9/31. **UDC** 635.1/.8-15(714). **Circ:** 500 (ctrl). ***Supersedes*** *Jardin Botanique de Montreal. Annualles, 0319-3101.*
Desc: Contains results of vegetables and annual trials.

GW
ANREGUNGEN FUR PRODUKTION UND ABSATZ. **Added/Corp** Landwirtschaftskammer Rheinland. Abteilung Erzeugung. Gruppe Gartenbau. No. 1 (Sept. 1972)-. Periodical. German. Rheinischer Landwirtschafts, Verlag GmbH, Rochusstrasse 18, W-5300 Bonn Germany. **Tel** 0228 520060.

SZ/0003-5424
ANTHOS; GARTEN- UND LANDSCHAFTSGESTALTUNG. **Added/Corp** Bund Schweizerischer Garten- und Landschaftsarchitekten. International Federation of Landscape Architects. Vereinigung Schweizerischer Gartenbauamter. Vol. 1 (Mar. 1962)-. Periodical. German (French and English). Four times a year (Feb., May, Aug., Nov.). 68.00F Europe; 70.00F others. Graf & Neuhaus AG, Hermetschloostr 77, CH 8010 Zurich Switzerland. **Tel** 011 41 1 4320276. **ED** H. Mathys. **Bk Rev. Ad Acc.**
Desc: Landscape architecture and landscape planning.
Ind/Abst Archit. Period. Index (1977-); Avery Index Archit. Period. Suppl. Colum. Univ. (1989-); Garden Lit. (1992-); Life Sci. Collect.

SP
ANUARIO HORTOFRUTICOLA ESPANOL. (1975)-. Periodical. Spanish. an. 6.000ptas. Sucro SA, Herran Cortes 5, 46004 Valencia Spain. **Tel** 352 53 01, FAX (96)352 57 52. **ED** Fidel Pascual Tecles. **Circ:** 2,000.
Desc: International annual on horticulture and fruit growing.

US/0094-3789
APHIS 81. **VFOAT** A.P.H.I.S. 81. **VAT** Animal and Plant Health Inspection Service Eighty One. Periodical. English. University of Georgia School of Accounting, Athens GA 30602. **Tel** (404)542-1616. **UDC** 632.
Ind/Abst AGRICOLA [Full Cov.].

CN
AQUATIC PLANT MANAGEMENT PROGRAM PROPOSALS FOR ... . **Main/Corp** British Columbia. Aquatic Plant Management Program. English. Aquatic Plant Management Program of the Ministry of Environment, Parliament Buildings, Victoria British Columbia V8V 1X4 Canada. **LC** SB614.3.C2; B74A. **DD** 354.7110077/2.

LE/0255-982X
ARAB JOURNAL OF PLANT PROTECTION. Periodical. English (Arabic).
Ind/Abst Biocont. News Inf. (19??-19??); Biodeter. Abstr.; For. Prod. Abstr. (1991-); For. Abstr.; Hortic. Abstr.; Nematol. Abstr.; Ornamental Hort. (1991-); Plant Breed. Abstr.; Postharvest News Inf.; Potato Abstr.; Rev. Agric. Entomol.; Rev. Plant Pathol.; Rice Abstr.; Seed Abstr.; Weed Abstr.; Wheat Barley Trit. Abstr.

US/0518-2662
ARBORETUM LEAVES. **See** Biology-Botany.

US
ARBORICULTURAL ABSTRACTS. **Added/Corp** International Society of Arboriculture. (197?)-. Periodical. English. an (Includes 6 sections (must specify name or number)). $1.00 per copy (latest edition). International Society of Arboriculture, PO Box GG, Savoy IL 61874. **Tel** (217)355-9411.

US
ARBORICULTURE. - . Periodical. English. ir. International Society of Arborculture, Chicago IL.

US/0004-2633
ARNOLDIA (JAMAICA PLAIN). (ARNOLDIA.). [Arnoldia]. **Added/Corp** Arnold Arboretum. Vol. 1 (Mar. 14, 1941)-. Periodical. English. Four times a year (seasonally). $20.00. Arnold Arboretum Harvard University, The Arborway, Jamaica Plain MA 02130. **Tel** (617)524-1718, FAX (617)524-1418. **ED** Karen Madsen (editor's address: Arnold Arboretum, 125 Arborway, Jamaica Plain, MA 02130, phone: (617)524-1718 Ext. 114). **LC** QK479; .A7. **DD** 582.1605. **CODEN** ARNOAO. Index available (bound in 4th issue). **Circ:** 4,000 (ctrl). Documents available from BIOSIS Document Express. ***Supersedes*** *Bulletin of Popular Information, 0196-6057.*
Desc: A magazine for amateur and professional horticulturists. News and information on articles dealing with botany, horticulture and plant and exploration.
Ind/Abst AGRICOLA [Full Cov.]; Biol. Abstr.; Crop Physiol. Abstr.; Garden Lit. (1992-); Hortic. Abstr.; Key Word Index Wildl. Res.; Ornamental Hort.; Plant Genet. Resour. Abstr.; Plant Grow. Reg. Abstr.

US/0197-4033
AROIDEANA. [Aroideana]. **Added/Corp** International Aroid Society. Vol. 1 (May 1978)-. Periodical. English. qt. $15.00 individuals; $20.00 institutions. International Aroid Society, PO Box 43-1853, South Miami FL 33143. **Tel** (305)271-3767. **ED** John Banta. cum. index. **Bk Rev. Ad Acc. Circ:** 450 (ctrl).
Desc: Clearing house for information on culture, propagation and taxonomy of aroids and promotes interest in aroids.

US/0747-8976
ARS ROSACEAE. (ARS ROSACEAE / FEDERATION OF INTERNATIONAL ROSE EXHIBITORS.). Periodical. English. qt. $15.00. Cowley Victor Francis, 2204 Hyde Street, San Francisco CA 94109. **DD** 635. **UDC** 633.811.

IT
ARTE DEI GIARDINI. **VFOAT** Artedeigiardini. (1991)-. Periodical. Italian. sa. L50000 Italy; L100000 other. Karta Sas, Via Slataper 10, 50134 Florence, Italy. **Tel** 011 39 55 496502.
Ind/Abst BHA : Biblio. Hist. Art.

UK/0309-1120
ASHINGTONIA. **See** Biology-Botany.

US/0192-5067
ASLA MEMBERS' HANDBOOK. **Main/Corp** American Society of Landscape Architects. **VFOAT** Members' Handbook. **VAT** American Society of Landscape Architects Members' Handbook. (1978)-. English. an. $25.00. American Society of Landscape Architects, 4401 Connecticut Avenue Northwest, 5th Floor, Washington DC 20008. **Tel** (202)686-2752. **LC** SB469; .A632a. **DD** 712/.06/073. ***Continues*** *American Society of Landscape Architects. ASLA Membership Roster.*

NZ
ASPARAGUS RESEARCH NEWSLETTER. **Added/Corp** Massey University. Dept. of Horticulture & Plant Health. Vol. 1, No. 1 (June 1983)-. Periodical. English. sa. Massey University / Department of Plant Science, c/o M. Nichols, Palmerston North New Zealand. **Tel** 011 64 63 69099.
Ind/Abst Agric. Eng. Abstr. (1991-); Hortic. Abstr.; Ornamental Hort.; Plant Breed. Abstr.; Plant Genet. Resour. Abstr.; Plant Grow. Reg. Abstr.; Rev. Agric. Entomol.; Rev. Plant Pathol.; Seed Abstr.; Weed Abstr.

IT
ASPETTI STRUTTURALI DELLE PRINCIPALI COLTIVAZIONI LEGNOSE AGRARIE. Italian. Istituto Nazionale Statistica, GBP SEZ4 Via Cesare Balbo 16, 00184 Rome Italy. **Tel** 011 39 6 46735118. **LC** SB354.6.I8; A84. **DD** 338.1/74/0945021.

AT/1033-3673
AUSTRALIAN GARDEN HISTORY. [Aust. gard. hist.]. **Added/Corp** Australian Garden History Society. (1989)-. Periodical. English. Five times a year. 23.00Aus$ (Australia); 36.00Aus$ (other). Australian Garden Journal, PO Box 588, Bowral New South Wales, 2576 Australia. **Tel** 11 61 48 614999, FAX 11 61 48 614576. **ED** Tim North. **DD** 635.0994. **Bk Rev. Ad Acc. Circ:** 6,000.

AT/0812-9495
AUSTRALIAN GARDEN JOURNAL, THE. [Aust. gard. j.]. **Added/Corp** Australian Garden History Society. (1983)-. Periodical. English. bm. **DD** 635.05. ***Formed by the union of*** *Garden Cuttings, 0729-8692* ***and*** *Journal of the Australian Garden History Society, 0727-3517.* ***Continued in part by*** *Australian Garden History., 1033-3673.*
Ind/Abst Garden Lit. (19??-19??).

AT/0726-2256
AUSTRALIAN HORTICULTURE. Vol. 79, No. 6, June (1981)-. Periodical. English. mo. 54.00Aus$ (Australia); 69.00Aus$ (New Zealand, Papua, New Guinea, Fiji, Indonesia, Malaysia, India, Japan & China); 77.00Aus$ (other). Rural Press / Victoria, PO Box 160, Port Melbourne Victoria 3207 Australia. **Tel** 11 61 3 2870900, telex 35668. **UDC** 634(94). ***Continues*** *Seed and Nursery Trader.*
Ind/Abst Hortic. Abstr.; Ornamental Hort. (1991-); Rev. Agric. Entomol.

AT
AUSTRALIAN HOUSE AND GARDEN. **See** Interior Design.

UK
AUSTRALIAN INDUSTRIAL RELATIONS COMMISSION AWARDS : GARDENING, NURSERIES AND GREENKEEPING. English. ir. Collect Pub Money, Aus Indu Reg, GPO Box 19945, Melbourne Victoria 3001 Australia. **Tel** 011 61 3 6538369.

AT/0045-0782
AUSTRALIAN ORCHID REVIEW. [Aust. orchid rev.]. Vol. 1 (1936)-. Periodical. English. qt. 29.50Aus$ (one year), 55.00Aus$ (two years) Australia; 34.00Aus$ (one year), 64.00Aus$ (two years) New Zealand. Graphic World, 14 McGill Street, Lewisham New South Wales 2049 Australia. **Tel** 61 2 560 6166, FAX (02)560-6677. **ED** David Wallace. Index available. **Bk Rev. Ad Acc. Circ:** 10,000 (ctrl).
Desc: A colour magazine specialising in all aspects of orchid culturing. Also carries news and information from all major orchid societies in Australia.

AT
AUSTRALIAN PLANT INTRODUCTION REVIEW. Added/Corp Commonwealth Scientific and Industrial Research Organization (Australia). Division of Plant Industry. (1975)-. Periodical. English. sa. free. CSIRO / Division of Plant Industry, GPO Box 1600, Canberra ACT 2601 Australia. **Tel** 062 465 483. ***Continues** Plant Introduction Review.*
Ind/Abst Field Crop Abstr.; Grasslands For. Abstr.; Maize Abstr.; Plant Breed. Abstr.; Plant Genet. Resour. Abstr.; Rice Abstr.; Soyabean Abstr.

AT/0005-0008
AUSTRALIAN PLANTS. [Aust. plants]. Vol. 1, No. 1, (Dec. 1959)-. Periodical. English. qt. 18.00Aus$ Australia; 30.00Aus$ other. Society for Growing Australian Plants, PO Box 410, Padstow NSW 2211 Australia. **Tel** 11 61 2 6308201. **(Subscription address: PO Box 410, Padstow New South Wales 2211 Australia) ED** W H Payne. **UDC** 582(94); 633/635(94). **CODEN** ANPLAV. Index available. cum. index. **Ad Acc. Circ:** 9,500 (ctrl). available on microfilm and microfiche from University Microfilms International (UMI). Documents available from BIOSIS Document Express.
Desc: The horticultural application of the Australian flora. Descriptions of species in the flora with keys sketches and color plates.
Ind/Abst Biol. Abstr.; Hortic. Abstr.; Ornamental Hort. (1991-); Plant Genet. Resour. Abstr.; Seed Abstr.; Soils Fert.

US/0005-1926
AVANT GARDENER, THE. Vol. 1 (1968)-. Periodical. English. mo. $18.00 (one year), $45.00 (three year) US; $20.00 (one year), $50.00 (three year) other. Horticultural Data Processors, PO Box 489, New York NY 10028. **ED** Thomas Powell. Index available. **Bk Rev**, (Qty: 25). available on microfilm from University Microfilms International (UMI).
Desc: Covers news of new plants, products and techniques, plus articles on all aspects of indoor and outdoor gardening.
Ind/Abst Garden Lit. (1992-).

US/0404-6927
BALLS AND BURLAPS. Added/Corp Washington State Nurserymen's Association. **VFOAT** Balls & Burlaps. Vol. 1 (1951)-. Trade Publication. English. mo. $9.00. Washington State Nurserymens Association, PO Box 670, Sumner WA 98390. **Tel** (206)863-1802. **ED** Jill Palmer. **Bk Rev. Ad Acc. Circ:** 1,600 (ctrl).
Desc: Produced by the Washington State Nursery and Landscape Association as a service to its membership and the ornamental horticulture industry in the Pacific Northwest. Provides technical, business and educational information of interest to nurserymen and landscapers.

BG/0379-4288
BANGLADESH HORTICULTURE. [Bangladesh hortic.]. **Added/Corp** Bangladesh Society for Horticultural Science. (19??)-. Periodical. English. sa. **CODEN** BAHODP. Documents available from BIOSIS Document Express, CASDDS.
Ind/Abst Biodeter. Abstr. (1991-); Biol. Abstr.; Chem. Abstr. (1973-1980); Field Crop Abstr.; Food Sci. Technol. Abstr.; Hortic. Abstr.; Maize Abstr.; Plant Breed. Abstr.; Plant Grow. Reg. Abstr.; Postharvest News Inf.; Potato Abstr.; Rev. Agric. Entomol.; Rev. Plant Pathol.; Seed Abstr.; Soils Fert.

BG/1018-0818
BANGLADESH JOURNAL OF CROP SCIENCE. [Bangladesh j. crop sci.]. (1990)-. Periodical. English. sa.
Ind/Abst Field Crop Abstr.; Rice Abstr.

BL
BATATINHA : RESUMOS INFORMATIVOS. Main/Corp Empresa Brasileira de Perquisa Agropecuaria. Unidade de Execucao de Perquisa de Ambito Estadual de Brasilia. Portuguese. Unidade de Execucao de Pesquisa de Ambito Estadual de Brasilia, Caixa Postal 1316, 70.000 Brasilia Brazil. **LC** Z5074.P75; E48A; SB211.P8.

PK
BEGINNER'S GARDENING. Vol. 1, No. 1 (May/Aug. 1984)-. Periodical. English. qt.

US/0096-8684
BEGONIAN, THE. Added/Corp American Begonia Society. (1938)-. Periodical. English. Six times a year. $17.00 US; $23.00 Canada & Mexico; $27.00 others. American Begonia Society, c/o John Ingles Jr., 157 Monument Road, Rio Dell CA 95562. **Tel** (909)371-8042. **ED** Tamsin Boardman. **Ad Acc. Circ:** 2,000 (ctrl). ***Continues** Bulletin - American Begonia Society.*
Desc: Promotes interest in begonias and other shade loving plants. Goal is to standardize homeculture, to gather and publish information on begonias.
Ind/Abst Crop Physiol. Abstr.; Hortic. Abstr.; Ornamental Hort. (19??-19??); Plant Breed. Abstr.

BE/0005-8483
BELGISCHE TUINBOUW. INTERNATIONALE EDITIE, DE. Added/Corp Chamber Syndicale des Horticulteurs Belges. **VFOAT** L'Horticulture Belge. Edition Internationale; Belgian Horticulture. International Edition; Die Belgische Zierpflanzencultur. Internationale Auflage. Vol. 58, No. 1 (1919)-. Periodical. Dutch (French). Eleven times a year. Free (members), 2830.19F (nonmembers). Syndicale Kamer Belgische Tuin, Kasteellaan 66, 9000 Gent Belgium. **Tel** 091/25-74-60, FAX 091/257336. Index available. **Bk Rev. Ad Acc. Circ:** 1,350.

MY/0127-6581
BERITA ISOPB. [Ber. ISOPB]. **VFOAT** Berita International Society for Oil Palm Breeders; Newsletter ISOPB. (1984)-. Periodical. English. qt. **DD** 633.851.
Ind/Abst Plant Breed. Abstr.

NE
BESCHRIJVENDE RASSENLIJST VOOR GROENTEGEWASSEN. VOLLEGRONDSGROENTEN. Added/Corp Commissie voor de Samenstelling van de Rassenlijst voor Groentgewassen (Netherlands). **VFOAT** Vollegrondsgroenten. (198?)-. Dutch. an. Fl51.50 (includes postage). De Boer Mailingservice, Postbus 507, 1200 AM Hiversum Netherlands. **Tel** 011 31 30 258611. ***Continues** Rassenlijst voor Groentegewassen. Vollegrondsgroenten.*
Desc: Information on plant-breeding, horticulture, and field grown crops.

SW/0345-1410
BETODLAREN. (BETODLAREN : ORGAN FOR SVERIGES BETODLARES CENTRALFORENING.). [Betodlaren]. **Added/Corp** Sveriges Betodlares Centralforening. (1964)-. Periodical. Swedish. qt. ***Continues** Sveriges Betodlares Centralforenings Tidskrift.*
Ind/Abst Field Crop Abstr.; Seed Abstr.

●US
BETTER HOMOS AND GARDENS. See Homosexuality.

AG
BIBLIOGRAFIA FORRAJERA. Added/Corp Estacion Experimental Agropecuaria Oliveros. (1967)-. Spanish. **LC** Z5074.F7; B5.

UK/0144-8765
BIOLOGICAL AGRICULTURE & HORTICULTURE. See Agriculture.

JA/0289-0011
BIOTRONICS. [Biotronics]. **Added/Corp** Kyushu Daigaku. Biotron Institute. Vol. 1 (1971)-. English (Japanese). Kyushu Daigaku Seibutsu Kankyo Chosetsu Kenkyu Senta, (Biotron Inst., Kyushu University), 10-1, Hakozaki 6 Chome, Higashiku,, Fukuokashi, Fukuokaken 812 Japan.
Ind/Abst Agric. Eng. Abstr.; Crop Physiol. Abstr.; Field Crop Abstr.; Hortic. Abstr.; Irr. Drain. Abstr.; Ornamental Hort. (1991-); Weed Abstr.

PL/0509-6839
BIULETYN WARZYWNICZY. BULLETIN OF VEGETABLE CROPS RESEARCH WORK. BIULLETEN PO OVOSHCHEVODSTVU. Added/Corp Instytut Warzywictwa. Warsaw. Instytut Uprawy, Nawozenia i Gleboznawstwa. Zakad Warzywnictwa. **VFOAT** Bulletin of Vegetable Crops Research Work; Biulleten po Ovoshchevodstvu. (19??)-. Bulletin. Polish (summaries and/or abstracts in English and Russian). **CODEN** BIWAA9. Documents available from CASDDS.
Ind/Abst Agric. Eng. Abstr. (1991-); Chem. Abstr. (1953-1979); Field Crop Abstr.; Hortic. Abstr.; Plant Breed. Abstr.; Plant Grow. Reg. Abstr.; Rev. Plant Pathol.; Seed Abstr.; Weed Abstr.

NE
BLOEMBOLLENCULTUUR. Vol. 81, No. 1 (1970)-. Periodical. Dutch. sa. Fl139.50. Uitgeversmaatschappij C Misset Doetinchem, Netherlands. **Tel** 08340-49911, FAX (08340)44479, telex 45481. **Circ:** 4,810.
Ind/Abst Irr. Drain. Abstr.; Ornamental Hort.; Plant Breed. Abstr.; Plant Grow. Reg. Abstr.; Soils Fert.

NE
BLOEMEN EN PLANTEN. Dutch. Uitgeverij Vipmedia, POB 7185, 4800 GD Breda Netherlands.

US
BLUE BOOK. OFFICIAL LAWN MOWER TRADE-IN GUIDE. Added/Corp Intertec Publishing Corporation. Technical Publications Division. **VFOAT** Official Lawn Mower Trade-In Guide; Lawn Mower Trade-In Guide. (19??)-. English. an. $13.95. Intertec Publishing Corporation, 9800 Metcalf, Overland Park KS 66212. **Tel** (913)341-1300. **LC** HD9486.6.L373; U63. **DD** 681/.7631. **Bk Rev.**
Desc: A comprehensive valuation guide which offers complete appraisals and comparative specifications for both riding and walk-behind lawn mowers.

NE
BOER EN TUINDER. Added/Corp Roomsch-Katholieke Nederlandsche Boeren- en Tuindersbond. Vol. 1 (Jan. 4, 1947)-. Periodical. Dutch. Fifty times a year. Fl112.26 Netherlands & Belgium; Fl278.30 others. Boer en Tuinder, Postbus 29708, Scheveningseweg 46, NL 2500 Den Haag Netherlands. **Tel** 011 31 70 6514191, FAX 011 31 70 3524853.

BL/0102-292X
BOLETIM DE PESQUISA. See Agriculture-Crop Production and Soil.

US
BONSAI BULLETIN. Added/Corp Bonsai Society of Greater New York. Vol. 1, No. 1 (May 1963)-. Bulletin. English. qt. comes with membership. Bonsai Society of Greater New York Inc, PO Box 154, Malverne NY 11565.

US/0744-3277
BONSAI CLUBS INTERNATIONAL. *Title Change.* [Bonsai Clubs Int.]. **Added/Corp** Bonsai Clubs International. Vol. 20, No. 1 (Jan./Feb. 1981)-(19??). Periodical. English. bm. Bonsai Clubs International, 2636 West Mission Road 277, Tallahassee FL 32304-2556. **Tel** (904)575-1442. **ED** J Smith. **DD** 635. Index available. **Bk Rev. Ad Acc. Circ:** 3,600 (ctrl). ***Continues** Bonsai International, 0273-6934.* ***Continued by** Bonsai Magazine, 1068-6193.*

AT
BONSAI JOURNAL OF AUSTRALIA. Added/Corp Western Suburbs Bonsai Group, Sydney. Vol. 8, No. 1 (Feb. 1976)-. Periodical. English. bm.

US
BONSAI : JOURNAL OF THE AMERICAN BONSAI SOCIETY. Added/Corp American Bonsai Society. **VFOAT** Bonsai Journal. Vol. 19, No. 2 (Summer 1985)-. Periodical. English. Four times a year. $20.00 Comes with American Bonsai Society membership. American Bonsai Society, PO Box 358, Keene NH 03431. **Tel** (603)352-9034. **ED** Arch Hawkins (editor's address: 421 Malabar, Austin, TX 78734, phone: (512)261-4780). **LC** SB433.5; .B64. **DD** 635.9/772/05. **Bk Rev. Ad Acc. Circ:** 1,600. ***Continues** Bonsai Journal, 0149-9726.*

US/1068-6193
BONSAI MAGAZINE. (BONSAI MAGAZINE : THE OFFICIAL PUBLICATION OF BONSAI CLUBS INTERNATIONAL.). [Bonsai mag.]. **Added/Corp** Bonsai Clubs International. (19??)-. Periodical. English. bm. $25.00. Bonsai Clubs International, 2636 West Mission Road 277, Tallahassee FL 32304-2556. **Tel** (904)575-1442. **DD** 635. Index available. **Bk Rev. Ad Acc. *Continues** Bonsai Club International, 0744-3277.*

US/0362-4447
BONSAI (PHOENIX). (BONSAI.). V. 1- Jan. 1976-. English. qt. Bonsai Press-Jama Press, PO Box 580, Prescott AZ 86302. **UDC** 635.9.
Ind/Abst Hortic. Abstr.; Ornamental Hort. (1991-).

US/1044-2529
BONSAI TODAY. [Bonsai today]. (May/June, 1989)-. Periodical. English. Six times a year (Jan., Mar., May, July, Sept., Nov.). $42.00 US; $48.00 Canada & Mexico; $52.50 other. Stone Lantern, PO Box 816, Sudbury MA 01776. **Tel** (508)443-7110, FAX (508)443-9115. **ED** W. John Palmer. **LC** SB433.5; .B683. **DD** 635.9/772. Index available. cum. index. **Ad Acc, Adv Mgr:** Pat Palmer, **Tel** (508)443-7110. **Circ:** 9,000 (ctrl).
Desc: Devoted to the art technique of growing miniature trees and forests.

NE
BOOMWEKERIJ. Misset Uitgeverij BV, Postbus 9000, 6800 DA Arnhem Netherlands. **Tel** 011 31 85 209911.

US
BOSLEY PLANT NEWS. Main/Corp Bosley Nurseries. English. an. ***Continues** Bosley Rose News.*

US/0897-0785
BROOKGREEN GARDENS NEWSLETTER. [Brookgreen Gard. newsl.]. **Added/Corp** Brookgreen Gardens. **VFOAT** Newsletter. (19??)-. Newsletter. English. qt. **DD** 580.
Ind/Abst Garden Lit.

US/0884-8815
BROOKGREEN JOURNAL. See The Arts-Art.

US
BROOKLYN BOTANIC GARDEN 21ST CENTURY GARDENING SERIES. (19??)-. English. Four times a year (Mar., June, Sept., Dec.). $25.00 (subscribing), $50.00 (sustaining), $125.00 (supporting), $300.00 (contributing) Comes with Brooklyn

Botanic Garden Subscribing membership. Brooklyn Botanic Garden, 1000 Washington Avenue, Brooklyn NY 11225. **Tel** (718)622-4433, FAX (718)857-2430. ***Continues*** *Plants and Gardens.*

US/0736-9050
BU$INESS OF HERBS, THE. (THE BUSINESS OF HERBS.). [Bu$. herbs]. **VFOAT** Business of Herbs. Vol. 1, No. 1 (March/April 1983)-. Periodical. English. Six times a year (Jan., Mar., May, July, Sept., Nov.). $20.00 (one year); $36.00 (two years); $52.00 (three years). Northwind Farm Publications, Route 2 Box 246, Shevlin MN 56676-9535. **Tel** (218)657-2478, FAX (218)657-2447. **ED** Paula and David Oliver. **DD** 338. **CODEN** BUSHEU. Index available. cum. index (all years, (individually)). **Bk Rev. Ad Acc. Circ:** 2,000 subscribers, 10,000 readership (ctrl).
Desc: The latest research news, market trends, and the most accurate information about herbs.
Ind/Abst BioBusiness (1991-); Garden Lit. (1992-).

US
BULLETIN. (19??)-. Periodical. English. mo. $12.50. Cleveland Botanical Garden, 11030 East Boulevard, Cleveland OH 44106. **Tel** (216)721-1600. **ED** Marilyn Sommer. **Bk Rev**, (Qty: 6). **Ad Acc. Circ:** 4,250 (ctrl). ***Continues*** *Garden Center Bulletin, 0892-564X.*

AT
BULLETIN. Main/Corp Queensland. Division of Plant Industry. (1924)-. Periodical. English. CSIRO / Division of Plant Industry, GPO Box 1600, Canberra ACT 2601 Australia. **Tel** 062 465 483. **LC** SB187.Q4; A3.
Ind/Abst Plant Breed. Abstr.

US
BULLETIN - AMERICAN ORCHID SOCIETY. Main/Corp American Orchid Society. V. 1-June 1932-. Bulletin. English. mo. $28.00 US; $34.00 other. American Orchid Society Inc, 6000 South Olive Avenue, West Palm Beach FL 33405. **Tel** (407)585-8666, FAX (407)585-0654. **UDC** 582.594.2(73). **Bk Rev. Ad Acc. Circ:** 23,000.
Desc: Articles on the culture, hybridization, photography, history and botany of orchids.

US/0897-0599
BULLETIN OF AMERICAN GARDEN HISTORY, A. [Bull. Am. gard. hist.]. Vol. 1, No. 1 (Fall 1985)-. Periodical. English. Four times a year. Bulletin of American Garden History, PO Box 397A Planetarium Station, New York NY 10024. **DD** 635.

US/0002-8150
BULLETIN OF THE AMERICAN DAHLIA SOCIETY, INC. (BULLETIN OF THE AMERICAN DAHLIA SOCIETY.). [Bull. Am. Dahlia Soc. Inc.]. **Main/Corp** American Dahlia Society. Vol. 1 (1915)-. Bulletin. English. qt (March, June, Sept., Dec.). $14.00. American Dahlia Society, 771 Cambridge Road, Hueytown AL 35023. **Tel** (205)491-6296. **ED** Donald L Brown, editor/ Terry Smith, co-editor, address:771 Cambridge Road, Hueytown, Alabama 35023; phone:(205)491-6296. **Bk Rev. Ad Acc, Adv Mgr:** Charles S. Conerty, Jr., **Tel** (201)694-4864. **Circ:** 1,800 (ctrl).
Desc: The growing, showing and listing of dahlias grown throughout the world. All phases of dahlia culture from seed to roots and uses of fertilizers and chemicals to forward the dahlia. The journal of the American Dahlia Society. Its purpose is to promote the culture and to stimulate interest in the dahlia, a native American flower.

US/0747-4172
BULLETIN OF THE AMERICAN IRIS SOCIETY. [Bull. Am. Iris Soc.]. **Main/Corp** American Iris Society. No. 1- 1920-. Bulletin. English. qt. Free to members. The American Iris Society, 7414 East 60th Street, Tulsa OK 74145. **Tel** (918)627-0706. **ED** Ronald Mullin. **LC** SB413.I8; A6. **DD** 635. **UDC** 582.594.2(73). **Ad Acc. Circ:** 6,000 (ctrl).

US/0065-9584
BULLETIN OF THE AMERICAN PENSTEMON SOCIETY. Main/Corp American Penstemon Society. (19??)-. English. Twice a year (Winter & Summer). $10.00 Comes with American Penstemon Society membership. American Penstemon Society, 1569 South Holland Court, Lakewood CO 80232. **Tel** (303)986-8096. **ED** Jack Ferreri, (editor's address: 3118 Timber Lane, Verona, WI 53593, phone: (608)845-8674). **LC** SB413.P37; A47a. **DD** 635.9/33/81. **Ad Acc. Circ:** 500.

US/0003-0864
BULLETIN OF THE AMERICAN ROCK GARDEN SOCIETY. [Bull. Am. Rock Gard. Soc.]. **Added/Corp** American Rock Garden Society. Vol. 1 (Jan./Feb. 1943)-. Periodical. English. Four times a year (Jan., Apr., July, Oct.). $25.00 (one year); $50.00 (two years). American Rock Garden Society, c/o Jacques Mommens, Box 67, Millwood NY 10546. **ED** Gwen Kelaidis, (editor's address: 1410 Eudora Street, Denver, CO 80822, phone: (303)322-1410). **DD** 635. Index available. cum. index. **Bk Rev**, (Qty: 10). **Ad Acc, Adv Mgr:** Al Deurbrouck. **Circ:** 4,500 (ctrl).
Desc: Articles on rock garden plants, their culture, habitat and geographic distribution, as well as construction, design, and maintenance of rock gardens.
Ind/Abst Garden Lit. (1992-).

FR
BULLETIN OF THE INTERNATIONAL GROUP FOR THE STUDY OF MIMOSOIDEAE. Added/Corp Groupe International pour l'Etude des Mimosoideae. No. 12 (1984)-. Bulletin. English (French). an. 120.00F. Laboratorie de Botanique, 39 Allees J Guesde, 31400 Toulouse Cedex France. **Tel** 011 33 61 530235, FAX 011 33 61 259033. **ED** J. Vassal. **Bk Rev. Pr Rev.** ***Continues*** *Bulletin (Groupe International pour l'Etude des Mimosoideae).*
Desc: Contains recent literature, reviews, and original papers dealing with the leguminosae mimosoideae - interdisciplinary research reported.

IO/0126-1436
BULLETIN PENELITIAN HORTIKULTURA. [Bull. penelitian hortik.]. **Added/Corp** Lembaga Penelitian Hortikultura. Vol. 1 (1973)-. Bulletin. Indonesian (summaries and/or abstracts in English). qt. **CODEN** BPHODS. Documents available from CASDDS.
Ind/Abst Biocont. News Inf.; Chem. Abstr. (1973-1980); EMBASE; Field Crop Abstr.; Nematol. Abstr.; Ornamental Hort. (1991-); Potato Abstr.; Rev. Plant Pathol.; Seed Abstr.

CN/0711-6446
BULLETIN - SOCIETE DES AMIS DU JARDIN VAN DEN HENDE INC. (BULLETIN.). [Bull. - Soc. amis Jardin Van den Hende inc.]. V. 1, No. 1, (Dec. 1981)-. Bulletin. French. qt. 10.00Can$ Canada; 8.00Can$ US. Societe des Amis du Jardin Van den Hende Inc, Chambre 2601, Department de Phytologie FSAA, Pavillon des Services Universite Laval, 2450 Boulevard Hochelaga, Ste Foy Quebec G1K 7P4 Canada. **Tel** (418)656-3410. **ED** Genette Deschenes. **DD** 635/.09714. **UDC** 58.006(714). cum. index. **Bk Rev. Ad Acc. Circ:** 850 (ctrl).
Desc: Original articles describing garden plants, often in a review manner, with special reference to the Van Den Hende Garden.

US
BULLETIN - VIRGINIA. TRUCK EXPERIMENT STATION, NORFOLK. Main/Corp Virginia. Truck Experiment Station, Norfolk. Bulletin. English. qt. **LC** SB21; .V82. **DD** 635.

US
BUNTINGS' ... BERRIES. Main/Corp Buntings' Nurseries. English. an. **UDC** 634.7. ***Continues*** *Buntings' Book of Top-Quality Berries.*

US/0749-4653
BURPEE GARDENS. Main/Corp W. Atlee Burpee Company. (1983)-. English. an. Free. W Atlee Burpee Company, 300 Park Avenue, Warminster PA 18974. **Tel** (215)674-4900. **Ad Acc.** ctrl circ. ***Continues*** *Burpee Seeds.*

US
BURPEE SPRING FLOWERING BULBS : ... PRE-SEASON SALE CATALOG. Main/Corp W. Atlee Burpee Company. **VFOAT** Spring Flowering Bulbs. Catalog. English. an. **UDC** 635.073.

US
BURPEE'S IMPORTED DUTCH BULBS : ... WHOLESALE PRICES FOR THE TRADE. Main/Corp W. Atlee Burpee Company. **VFOAT** Imported Dutch Bulbs. English. an. W Atlee Burpee Company, 300 Park Avenue, Warminster PA 18974. **Tel** (215)674-4900. **UDC** 635.073.

AT
CACTUS AND SUCCULENT JOURNAL. Added/Corp Cactus and Succulent Society of New South Wales. Vol. 10, No. 1 (1975)-. Periodical. English. qt. $5.90. Cactus Succulent Society of New South Wales, PO Box 36, Woollhara New South Wales 2025 Australia. Index Available in last issue of volume--loose--unpaged.

US/0007-9367
CACTUS AND SUCCULENT JOURNAL (SANTA BARBARA). (CACTUS AND SUCCULENT JOURNAL.). [Cactus succul. j.]. Vol. 3, No. 1 (July 1931)-. Periodical. English. bm. $40.00 institute. Cactus and Succulent Journal, c/o Mindy Fusaro, PO Box 35034, Des Moines IA 50315-0301. **Tel** (515)245-8294. **LC** SB438; .J68. **DD** 635.9/3347. **UDC** 635.9; 582.852. Index available (published separately). cum. index. **Ad Acc, Adv Mgr:** Mindy Fusaro, **Tel** (515)285-7760. **Acid Free. Circ:** 5,000. available on microfilm and microfiche from University Microfilms International (UMI). ***Continues*** *Journal of the Cactus and Succulent Society of America, 0190-468X.*
Desc: Devoted to cacti and other succulents for the dissemination of information and the recording of hitherto unpublished data in order that the culture and study of these particular plants may attain the popularity which is justly theirs. This journal is useful to horticulturists, teachers, botanists, researchers, hobbyists, and librarians to keep abreast of current research and discoveries in the field.
Ind/Abst AGRICOLA [Full Cov.]; Hortic. Abstr.; Ornamental Hort. (1991-); Plant Breed. Abstr.; Plant Genet. Resour. Abstr.; Rev. Agric. Entomol.; Seed Abstr.

AT/0526-7196
CACTUS AND SUCCULENT JOURNAL WOOLLAHRA. (CACTUS AND SUCCULENT JOURNAL.). (1957)-. Periodical. English. Four times a year (Mar., June, Sept., Dec.). 15.00Aus$. Cactus & Succulent Society New South Wales, PO Box 36, Woollhara NSW 2025 Australia. **Tel** 011 61 2 3631107. **ED** R. Johnstone (phone: (02)525-2554). Index available. **Bk Rev**, (Qty: 5-6). **Ad Acc.** ctrl circ.

CN/0828-7449
CAHIER DES JOURNEES HORTICOLES ORNEMENTALES. [Cah. journ. hortic. ornem.]. (1977)-. French. an. **DD** 635.9.
Ind/Abst Irr. Drain. Abstr.; Plant Grow. Reg. Abstr.; Weed Abstr.

US/0008-1116
CALIFORNIA GARDEN. Added/Corp San Diego Floral Association. Vol. 1 (1909)-. Periodical. English. Six times a year (Jan., Mar., May, July, Sept., Nov.). $7.00 (one year), $13.00 (two years). San Diego Floral Association, Casa del Prado-Balboa Park, San Diego CA 92101-1619. **Tel** (619)232-5762. **ED** Jacqueline Coleman. Index available (bound in Nov./Dec. issue). **Bk Rev**, (Qty: 45). **Ad Acc, Adv Mgr:** Maianne Truby, **Tel** (619)232-5762. **Circ:** 2,100.
Desc: Concerned with horticulture and floriculture applicable to a Mediterranean-type climate, with a calendar of planting and plant care, coverage of floral events and garden club information.
Ind/Abst Calif. Period. Index (19??-).

US/0888-1502
CALIFORNIA LANDSCAPE MAGAZINE. ***Title Change.*** [Calif. landsc. mag.]. **Added/Corp** California Landscape Contractors Association. **VFOAT** CLM. Vol. 11 No. 1 (Feb. 1986)-(19??). Periodical. English. Six times a year. Communications Group Inc., 206 South Galena, Suite 090, Freeport IL 61032. **Tel** (815)232-5176. **DD** 712. ***Continues*** *California Landscape Management, 0197-7660.* ***Continued by*** *California Landscaping.*

●US
CALIFORNIA LANDSCAPING. Added/Corp California Landscape Contractors Association. Vol. 17, No. 1 (Jan./Feb. 1992)-. Periodical. English. Eleven times a year (June/July issues combined). Free on request. Adams Publishing, 68860 Perez Road, PO Box 2150, Cathedral City CA 92235. **Tel** (619)770-4370, (800)776-1036. **(Subscription address:** Adams Publishing, PO Box 2150, Cathedral City CA 92235.) **LC** SB472.535.C2; C3. ***Continues*** *California Landscape Magazine.*

US/0527-1622
CALIFORNIA TURFGRASS CULTURE. [Calif. turfgrass cult.]. **Added/Corp** Federated Turfgrass Council. University of California, Riverside. Dept. of Plant Science. University of California (System). Cooperative Extension. Vol. 10, No. 1 (Jan. 1960)-. Periodical. English. Four times a year. Free. University of California Cooperative Extension, 174 224 West Winston Avenue, Hayward CA 94544. **Tel** (510)670-5200. ***Continues*** *Southern California Turfgrass Culture, 0278-0429.*
Ind/Abst AGRICOLA [Full Cov.]; Agric. Eng. Abstr. (1991-); Field Crop Abstr.; Grasslands For. Abstr.; Hortic. Abstr.; Ornamental Hort. (19??-19??); Plant Breed. Abstr.; Rev. Plant Pathol.; Soils Fert.

US
CALIFORNIA WEED SCIENCE SOCIETY PROCEEDINGS. (1993)-. Proceedings. English. an. $15.00 US; $17.50 Pan-American nations; $19.00 other. California Weed Conference, PO Box 609, Fremont CA 94537. **Tel** (510)790-1252, FAX (510)790-2419. ***Continues*** *Procedings - California Weed Conference, 0097-1731.*

US/0008-204X
CAMELLIA JOURNAL, THE. [Camellia j.]. **Added/Corp** American Camellia Society. Vol. 16, No. 3 (Sept. 1961)-. Periodical. English. Four times a year (Feb., May, Aug., Nov.). $20.00 US; $21.50 other $20.00 Comes with American Camellia Society membership. American Camellia Society, One Massee Lane, Fort Valley GA 31030. **Tel** (912)967-2358, (912)967-2722, FAX (912)967-2083. **ED** Ann Blair Brown. **Bk Rev. Ad Acc. Circ:** 4,000 (ctrl). ***Continues*** *Camellias.*
Desc: Articles promoting interest in the genus camellia, including its culture, new varieties, and events of interest to camellia growers.
Ind/Abst AgBiotech News Inf.; AGRICOLA; Hortic. Abstr.; Ornamental Hort. (1991-); Plant Breed. Abstr.; Plant Genet. Resour. Abstr.; Plant Grow. Reg. Abstr.; Rev. Plant Pathol.

US
CAMELLIA NOMENCLATURE. 6th Rev. Ed., (1958)-. Periodical. English. ir. Free to members.

Gardening and Horticulture

Southern California Camellia Society, 7475 Brydon Road, La Verne CA 91750. **Tel** (818)447-7598. **Continues** Camellia, Its Culture and Nomenclature.

CN/0703-5667
CANADA GREEN. Began with May 1976 issue. Periodical. English. bm. 0.75Can$ per number. Canada Green, 39 Enterprise Road, Rexdale Ontario M9W 1C4 Canada. **DD** 635/.0971. **UDC** 635(71).

CN/0045-4885
CANADIAN FRUITGROWER. [Can. fruitgrow.]. Vol. 12 (1956)-. Periodical. English. Nine times a year (Jan., Feb., Mar., Apr., May, June, July, Sept., Nov.). 14.00Can$ (one year), 22.00Can$ (two year), 28.00Can$ (three year) Canada; 38.00Can$ other. NCC Publishing, 222 Argyle Avenue, Delhi Ontario N4B 2Y2 Canada. **Tel** (519)582-2513, FAX (519)582-4040. **ED** Ben Steidman. **CODEN** CAFRAW. **Ad Acc, Adv Mgr:** Jim Countryman. **Circ:** 4,000 (ctrl). **Continues** Canadian Fruitgrower and Gardener.

CN/0828-7619
CANADIAN GARDEN NEWS. [Can. gard. news]. No. 1 (1983)-. Periodical. English. ir (10 issues). Canadian Garden News, 36 Head Street, Dundas Ontario L9H 3H3 Canada. **DD** 635/.0971.

CN/0847-3463
CANADIAN GARDENING. [Can. gard.]. Vol. 1, No. 1 (Feb./Mar. 1990)-. Periodical. English. Seven times a year. 24.56Can$. Camar Publications Ltd., 130 Spy Court, Markham Ontario L3R 5H6 Canada. **Tel** (416)475-8440, FAX (416)475-9246. **DD** 635/.0971.
Ind/Abst Garden Lit.

CN/0828-8259
CANADIAN HORTICULTURAL HISTORY. **Suspended.** [Can. hortic. hist.]. **Added/Corp** Centre for Canadian Historical Horticultural Studies. Royal Botanical Gardens (Hamilton, Ont.). **VFOAT** Histoire de l'Horticulture au Canada. Vol. 1, No. 1 (1985)-(1993). Periodical. English (French). qt. 18.00Can$ per volume. Royal Botanical Gardens/CCHHS, PO Box 399, Hamilton Ontario L8N 3H8 Canada. **Tel** (416)527-1158, FAX (416)577-0375. **DD** 635/.0971.
Ind/Abst Am. Hist. Life (1985-); Garden Lit. (1992-).

US
CANADIAN HORTICULTURAL THERAPY ASSOCIATION NEWSLETTER. Newsletter. English. Four times a year (Feb., May, Aug., Nov.). $18.00 (individuals); $40.00 (institutions). Royal Botanical Gardens/CCHHS, PO Box 399, Hamilton Ontario L8N 3H8 Canada. **Tel** (416)527-1158, FAX (416)577-0375.

CN/0848-9629
CANADIAN JOURNAL OF HERBALISM. (THE CANADIAN JOURNAL OF HERBALISM : THE QUARTERLY OF THE ONTARIO HERBALISTS' ASSOCIATION.). [Can. j. herbal.]. **Added/Corp** Ontario Herbalists' Association. **VFOAT** Herbalism. Vol. 10, No. 1 (Jan. 1989)-. Periodical. English. qt. 25.00Can$. Ontario Herbalists Association, 11 Winthrop Place, Stoney Creek Ontario L8G 3M3 Canada. **Tel** (416)664-6715. **ED** Keith Stelling. **DD** 615/.321. **NLM** W1; CA588M. **Bk Rev**, (Qty: 12). **Ad Acc. Pr Rev. Circ:** 2,000. **Continues** Newsletter (Ontario Herbalists' Association).

CN/0008-4220
CANADIAN JOURNAL OF PLANT SCIENCE. **See** Biology-Botany.

CN/0824-1554
CANADIAN ORCHID JOURNAL, THE. [Can. orchid j.]. **Added/Corp** Canadian Orchid Journal Society. **VFOAT** Bulletin Canadien des Orchidees. (Spring 1981)-. Periodical. English. qt. Canadian Orchid Society, PO Box 9472, Station B, St. Johns New Foundland A1A 2Y4 Canada. **ED** Edward A. Speers. **DD** 635.9/3415/0971. Index available. **Bk Rev. Ad Acc. Circ:** 1,500. **Continues** Orchid Journal.
Desc: Publishes articles on the growing and culturing of orchid species. Also describes experiences of orchid growers in the field and in the home/greenhouses.

CN/0826-743X
CANADIAN ROSE ANNUAL (1983). (THE CANADIAN ROSE ANNUAL.). [Can. rose annu.]. **Added/Corp** Canadian Rose Society. (1983)-. English. an. Membership 18.00Can$. Canadian Rose Society, 10 Fairfax Crescent, Scarborough Ontario M1L 1Z8 Canada. **Tel** (416)751-4850. **ED** Ethel Freeman. **DD** 635.9/33372. **Circ:** 800 (ctrl). **Continues** Canadian Rose Guide, 0821-5618.

US/1049-460X
CAPE COD HOME & GARDEN. [Cape Cod home gard.]. **VFOAT** Cape Cod Home and Garden. Vol. 1, No. 1 (March/April 1990)-. Periodical. English. Four times a year (Feb., Mar., Apr., Nov.). $15.00 US; $23.00 other. Cape Cod Compass, 60 Munson Meeting, Chatham MA 02633. **Tel** (508)945-3542. **LC** NK2002; .C37. **DD** 747.2144/9/05. **Continues** Cape Cod Compass Magazine, 1045-7771.

IT
CAPSICUM NEWSLETTER. (1982)-. Newsletter. English. an. Institute of Plant Breeding and Seed Production, Via P Giuria, 15-10126 Turin Italy.
Ind/Abst Hortic. Abstr.; Nematol. Abstr.; Plant Genet. Resour. Abstr.; Rev. Agric. Entomol.; Rev. Plant Pathol.; Seed Abstr.

US/0197-7679
CARNIVOROUS PLANTS DIGEST. [Carniv. plants dig.]. V. 1- Jan. 1978-. Periodical. English. bm. $10.00. Carnivorous Plants Digest, PO Box 331, Hamilton NY 13346.

US/1063-7451
CAROLINA GARDENER. [Carol. gard.]. (19??)-. Periodical. English. bm. $14.95 (1 year), $26.50 (2 year), $38.00 (3 year). Carolina Gardener, PO Box 4504, Greensboro NC 27404. **Tel** (919)294-8199, (800)245-0142, FAX (919)294-8290. **ED** L.A. Jackson. **DD** 635. Index available. cum. index. **Bk Rev**, (Qty: 12-15). **Ad Acc. Circ:** 25,000.

IT
CASA E GIARDINO. Italian. Ten times a year. L63000.00 Italy; L119000.00 other. Casa & Giardino Editrice Srl, Via F T Marinetti 3, 20127 Milan Italy. **Tel** 011 39 2 26140371.

KO
CHAYONMI SAENGHWAL. Periodical. Korean. bm. W15,000. Punjae Susoksa, 12-13 Pongik-dong Chongno-ku, Seoul 110 Korea. **LC** SB403.C44. **Continues** Punjae Susok.

UK
CHELSEA YEAR : THE YEARBOOK OF THE ROYAL HORTICULTURAL SOCIETY, THE. 1988/89-. English. an.

JA/0069-3227
CHIBA DAIGAKU ENGEI GAKUBU GAKUJUTSU KOKOKU. [Chiba Daigaku Engeigakubu gakujutsu hokoku]. **VFOAT** Technical Bulletin of Faculty of Horticulture, Chiba University. (1953)-. Academic Scholarly Publication. Japanese (summaries and/or abstracts in English). an. Chiba Daigaku Engeigakubu, (Faculty of Horiculture, Chiba University), 648, Matsudo, Matsudoshi, Chibaken 271 Japan. **LC** SB317.5. **CODEN** CDEGAF. Documents available from CASDDS.
Ind/Abst Chem. Abstr.; Field Crop Abstr.; Irr. Drain. Abstr.; Plant Grow. Reg. Abstr.; Poult. Abstr.; Rev. Plant Pathol.; Rice Abstr.

JA
CHIBA-KEN DANCHI ENGEI SHIKENJO KENKYU HOKOKU. **Main/Corp** Chiba-Ken Danchi Engei Shikenjo. No. 1- 1969-. Japanese. Chiba-ken Danchi Engei Shikenjo, 1762 Yamatoto, Tateyama Japan. **LC** SB99.J28; C45A.

US
CHICAGO FRUIT & VEGETABLE REPORTER. **Added/Corp** Chicago Fruit & Vegatable Reporter (Firm). **VFOAT** Chicago Fruit and Vegetable Reporter. (19??)-. Periodical. English. da. Chicago Produce Publishing Company, 1656 West 35th Street, Chicago IL 60609.

UK
CHILEANS, THE. **See** Biology-Botany.

NE/0578-039X
CHRONICA HORTICULTURAE. [Chron. hortic.]. **Added/Corp** International Society for Horticultural Science. Vol. 1 (March 1961)-. Bulletin. English (French). Four times a year. Fl100.80. International Society for Horticultural Science / ISHS, Englaan 1, 6703 ET Wageningen The Netherlands. **Tel** 011 31 8370 21747, FAX 011 31 8370 21586, telex 45760. **ED** G. Slettenhaar. **DD** 635. **Ad Acc. Circ:** 3,500 (ctrl).
Desc: Bulletin of the International Society for Horticultural Science (ISHS). Includes short articles, news of symposia held, calendar of events, news of the sections, commissions and working groups within the society.
Ind/Abst Agric. Eng. Abstr.; Hortic. Abstr.

US/0090-5771
CHRYSANTHEMUM. [Chrysanthemum]. **Added/Corp** National Chrysanthemum Society. (Dec. 1972)-. Periodical. English. qt (Mar., Jun., Sept., Dec.). $12.50 US; $16.50 (surface mail) other. National Chrysanthemum Society Inc, 10107 Homar Pond Drive, Fairfax Station VA 22039-1650. **Tel** (703)978-7981. **ED** Robert M. Knox. **LC** SB413.C55; B84. **DD** 635. Index available. **Ad Acc. Circ:** 1,800 (ctrl). **Continues** Chrysanthemum Bulletin.
Desc: Promotes a wider interest in the cultivation of the chrysanthemum, teaches the procedures for the propagation and cultivation of the chrysanthemum, and increases the bond of fellowship between the growers of the chrysanthemum.

CH
CHUNG-HUA MIN KUO ... LAN I NIEN CHIEN / LAN HUA SHIH CHIEH TSA CHIH SHE CHU PIEN. **VFOAT** Lan I Nien Chien; Annual of Orchids Republic of China. (1983)-. Chinese. an. $600.00. Lan Hua Shih Chien Tsa Chih She, 138 Lo-ssu-fu Road, 3 Section Fourth Floor, Taipei Shih Taiwan. **LC** SB409.A1; C47. **DD** 635/.9415/0951249.

CC
CHUNG-KUO KUO SHU / ZHONG GUO GUOSHU. **Added/Corp** Chung-Kuo Nung Yeh Ko Hsueh Yuen. Kuo Shu Yen Chiu So. **VFOAT** Zhong Guo Guoshu. (19??)-. Periodical. Chinese. **LC** SB354; .C48. **DD** 634/.05.

XXU
CLASSIFICATION AND HANDBOOK OF DAHLIAS. **Added/Corp** American Dahlia Society. (1986)-. English. **Continues** American Dahlia Society. Classification of Dahlias.
Desc: Specifically focuses on dahlias.

US/0195-0045
COLORADO GREEN. **Added/Corp** Associated Landscape Contractors of Colorado. (19??)-. Periodical. English. Four times a year. $12.00. ALCC, 3895 Upham Street, Wheat Ridge CO 80033. **Tel** (303)425-4862. **ED** Sally D. Benson. **DD** 338. **Bk Rev. Ad Acc. Circ:** 7,500 (ctrl). available on microfilm from University Microfilms International (UMI).
Desc: Landscape industry trade publication.

IT/0390-0444
COLTURE PROTETTE. [Colt. prot.]. Vol. 4, No. 6-7 (June/July 1975)-. Periodical. Italian. mo. L90000. Edagricole, PO Box 2157, 40100 Bologna Italy. **Tel** 011 39 51 492211 Ext. 22, FAX 011 39 51 493660, telex 510336 EDAGRI.
Ind/Abst AGRICOLA; Agric. Eng. Abstr. (1991-); Biocont. News Inf.; Crop Physiol. Abstr.; For. Abstr.; Hortic. Abstr.; Irr. Abstr. Abstr.; Maize Abstr.; Nematol. Abstr.; Ornamental Hort. (19??-19??); Plant Breed. Abstr.; Plant Grow. Reg. Abstr.; Potato Abstr.; Soils Fert.

US/0538-9143
COMBINED PROCEEDINGS / INTERNATIONAL PLANT PROPAGATORS' SOCIETY. [Comb. proc. - Int. Plant Propag. Soc.]. **Main/Corp** International Plant Propagators' Society. Began publication with Vol. 13 (1963). Proceedings. English. an. $75.00. International Plant Propagators Society Inc, University of Washington, Urban Horticulture GF-15, Seattle WA 98195. **Tel** (206)543-8602. **ED** J A Wott. Index available. cum. index. **Circ:** 3,500 (ctrl). **Continues** Plant Propagators's Society. Combined Proceedings.
Desc: Papers summarized from six regional meetings, three in the United States, Great Britain and Ireland, Australia, New Zealand. Latest information on how and why to propagate plants. Only world's authority in latest techniques.
Ind/Abst AGRICOLA; Biodeter. Abstr.; Crop Physiol. Abstr.; For. Prod. Abstr.; For. Abstr.; Hortic. Abstr.; Ornamental Hort. (19??-19??); Plant Breed. Abstr.; Plant Grow. Reg. Abstr.; Seed Abstr.; Soils Fert.

US/0538-9143
COMBINED PROCEEDINGS - INTERNATIONAL PLANT PROPAGATORS' SOCIETY. **Main/Corp** International Plant Propagators' Society. **Added/Corp** Plant Propagators' Society. (1951)-. English. an. IPPS Center for Urban Horticulture, University of Washington, GF 15, Seattle WA 98195. **Tel** (206)543-8602. cum. index.
Ind/Abst Irr. Drain. Abstr.; Weed Abstr.

AT/0069-7435
COMMONWEALTH SCIENTIFIC & INDUSTRIAL RESEARCH ORGANISATION. DIVISION OF HORTICULTURE. REPORT. English. be. Division of Horticulture, Box 350/GPO, Adelaide South Australia 5001 Australia. **ED** B L Loveys and A M Brennan. **Circ:** 1000 (ctrl).

BL/0100-8854
COMUNICADO TECNICO (CENTRO NACIONAL DE PESQUISA DE MANDIOCA E FRUTICULTURA (BRAZIL)). (COMUNICADO TECNICO / EMBRAPA, CNP MANDIOCA E FRUTICULTURA.). **Added/Corp** Centro Nacional de Pesquisa de Mandioca e Fruticultura (Brazil). (19??)-. Portuguese. Embrapa, Caixa Postal 040-315, 70700 Brasilia DF Brazil. **Tel** 011 55 61 2724241, 011 55 61 3484236.
Ind/Abst Anim. Breed. Abstr.; Nutr. Abstr. Rev.; Ser. B, Live Feeds and Feed.

US
CONNECTICUT GREENHOUSE NEWSLETTER. **Added/Corp** Connecticut. University. Cooperative Extension Service. No. 20 (Jan. 1968)-. Newsletter. English. bm. $4.00. University of

Connecticut Department of Plant Science, U-67, Storrs CT 06268. **Tel** (203)486-3435. **ED** Jay Sanford Koths. **Circ:** 900 (ctrl). **Continues** Florists News Letter.
Desc: A cooperative extension service publication concerning the production of plants in greenhouses.
Ind/Abst Hortic. Abstr.; Ornamental Hort.; Plant Grow. Reg. Abstr.

FR/0010-9711
COTON ET FIBRES TROPICALES.
Ceased. [Coton fibres trop.]. **Added/Corp** Institut de Recherches du Coton et des Textiles Exotiques. Institut de Recherches du Coton et des Textiles Exotiques. Bibliographie Signaletique. Vol. 1 (June 1946)-Vol. 48 (1993). Academic Scholarly Publication. French (summaries and/or abstracts in English and Spanish). qt. IRCT - Service Edition, CIRAD, BP 5035, 34032 Montpellier Cedex France. **Tel** 011 67 61 58 00, telex 480 762 F. **LC** SB245; .C62. **CODEN** CTFTAZ. Index available. cum. index. **Bk Rev. Ad Acc. Circ:** 500. Documents available from CASDDS. **Absorbed** Coton et Fibres Tropicales. Bulletin Bibliographique, 0010-972X.
Desc: Research results on cotton and tropical fibers in the fields of genetics, agronomy plant protection and technology.
Ind/Abst AGRICOLA; Agric. Eng. Abstr. (1991-); Agrindex; Biocont. News Inf. (1991-); Chem. Abstr.; Cot. Trop. Fibr. Abstr. Bibliogr.; Field Crop Abstr.; Grasslands For. Abstr.; Leis. Recreat. Tour. Abstr.; Life Sci. Collect.; PESTDOC; Plant Breed. Abstr.; Postharvest News Inf.; Rev. Agric. Entomol.; Rev. Med. Vet. Mycology; Rev. Plant Pathol.; Rural Dev. Abstr.; Seed Abstr.; Soils Fert.; Sorghum Mill. Abstr.; Text. Technol. Dig.; Weed Abstr.; World Agric. Econ.; World Text. Abstr.

UK/0954-7843
COUNTRY TIMES AND LANDSCAPE. See Architecture.

US/0735-2689
CRITICAL REVIEWS IN PLANT SCIENCES. See Biology-Botany.

UK/0263-9459
CRUCIFERAE NEWSLETTER. See Agriculture.

US
CULTIVATOR (STATE ARBORETUM OF UTAH). (THE CULTIVATOR.). Added/Corp State Arboretum of Utah. (19??)-. Periodical. English. qt. free. State Arboretum of Utah, University of Utah, Salt Lake City UT 84112. Tel (801)581-5322.

II/0253-7125
CURRENT RESEARCH ON MEDICINAL & AROMATIC PLANTS. [Curr. res. med. aromat. plants.] **Added/Corp** Central Institute of Medicinal and Aromatic Plants, Lucknow. **VFOAT** CROMAP; C.R.O.M.A.P. (19??)-. Academic Scholarly Publication. English. qt. $65.00. Central Institute of Medicinal & Aromatic Plants, Lucknow, India. (Subscription address: Prints India, 11 Darya Ganj, New Delhi 110002 India.) LC Discard. NLM ZQV 766 C997. CODEN CRMPDD. Documents available from BIOSIS Document Express, CASDDS.
Ind/Abst Biol. Abstr. (1986-); Chem. Abstr.

US
CUTT : CORNELL UNIVERSITY TURFGRASS TIMES. Added/Corp Cornell Cooperative Extension. Cornell University. Turfgrass Science Program. VFOAT Cornell University Turfgrass Times. Vol. 1, No. 1 (Spring 1990)-. Periodical. English. qt. $8.00. Cornell Cooperative Extension for Turfgrass Science, Cornell University, 20 Plant Science Building, Ithaca NY 14853. Tel (607)255-1629.

RU/0041-4905
CVETOVODSTVO. (TSVETOVODSTVO.).
[Cvetovodstvo]. **Added/Corp** Soviet Union. Ministerstvo Selskogo Khoziaistva. Soviet Union. Ministerstvo Plodoovoshchnogo Khoziaistva. Nauchno-Tekhnicheskoe Obshchestvo Selskogo Khoziaistva. TSentralnoe Pravlenie. Gosudarstvennyi Agropromyshlennyi Komitet SSSR. (1958)-. Academic Scholarly Publication. Russian. Six times a year. $79.95. Ministerstvo Selskogo Khoziastva, Moscow Russia. (Subscription address: East View Publications Inc., 3020 Harbor Lane North, Suite 110, Minneapolis MN 55447.) CODEN TSVTAN. Index available. Bk Rev. Documents available from CASDDS.
Ind/Abst Chem. Abstr. (?-1973).

US/0011-5290
DAFFODIL JOURNAL, THE. Added/Corp
American Daffodil Society. Vol. 1 (Sept. 1964)-. Periodical. English. Four times a year (Mar., June, Sept., Dec.). $5.00 (junior -18 years of age); $20.00 (individuals & institutions); $25.00 (family & sustaining); $50.00 (contributing), includes membership. American Daffodil Society Inc., 1686 Grey Fox Trails, Milford OH 45150. **Tel** (513)248-9137. **ED** Lee Kitchens, (editor's address: 351 Buttonwood Avenue, Cinnaminson, NJ, 08077, phone: (609)829-6557). **DD** 635. Index available (bound in Sept. issue). **Bk Rev. Ad Acc, Adv Mgr:** L. Kitchens, **Tel** (609)829-6557. **Circ:** 1,400 (ctrl).
Desc: Articles principally are on the breeding, growing and exhibiting of daffodils.

UK
DAFFODILS. Added/Corp Royal Horticultural Society (Great Britain). (1972)-. English. qt $4.25. American Daffodil Society Inc., 1686 Grey Fox Trails, Milford OH 45150. Tel (513)248-9137. LC SB413.D12; D312. DD 635.9/34/25. Supersedes Daffodil and Tulip Year Book.
Ind/Abst Rev. Med. Vet. Mycology; Rev. Plant Pathol.

US/0744-0219
DAYLILY JOURNAL, THE. Added/Corp
American Hemerocallis Society. Vol. 35, No. 3 (Fall 1981)-. Periodical. English. qt (4 issues). Comes with American Hemerocallis membership. The American Hemerocallis Society, 1454 Rebel Drive, Jackson MS 39211. **Tel** (601)366-4362. **ED** Frances L. Gatlin. **LC** SB413.D3; H4. **DD** 635.9/3432. **Ad Acc. Circ:** 5,000. **Continues** Hemerocallis Journal, 0018-0297.
Desc: Journal of the American Hemerocallis Society featuring information, articles and photos pertaining to daylilies.

SA/0302-7074
DECIDUOUS FRUIT GROWER, THE.
[Decid. fruit grow.]. **Added/Corp** Deciduous Fruit Board (South Africa). **VFOAT** Die Sagtevrugteboer. Vol. 26, Pt. 3 (March 1976)-. Academic Scholarly Publication. English (Afrikaans). mo. R46.80 South Africa; R100.80 (surface mail), R282.00 (air mail) other. Deciduous Fruit Board, Parc du Cap Mispel Road, PO Box 1801, Bellville 7530 South Africa. **Tel** 011 27 21 946-1040, FAX 011 27 21 946 1967. **ED** H. Wenhold. **Bk Rev. Ad Acc. Circ:** 5,000. **Formed by the union of** Delicious Fruit Grower and Sagtevrugteboer.
Desc: Scientific and technical reports on deciduous fruit growing and research. Also covers dried and canning, marketing, packaging and general information on cape fruit industry.
Ind/Abst AgBiotech News Inf.; AGRICOLA; Agrofor. Abstr. (19??-19??); Biocont. News Inf.; Biodeter. Abstr. (1991-); Crop Physiol. Abstr.; EMBASE; Hortic. Abstr.; Irr. Drain. Abstr.; Nematol. Abstr.; Plant Breed. Abstr.; Plant Grow. Reg. Abstr.; Postharvest News Inf.; Rev. Plant Pathol.; Soils Fert.

NE/0374-7247
DENDROFLORA. [Dendroflora]. Added/Corp
Vereniging voor Boskoopse Culturen. Nederlandse Dendrologische Vereniging. No. 1 (1964)-. Monographic series. Dutch. an. Price varies per volume. Dendroflora, PO Box 133, 2770 AC Boskoop Netherlands. **LC** WMLC L 83/9879. Index Available Published separately--free--upon request.
Ind/Abst For. Abstr.; Ornamental Hort.; Life Sci. Collect.; Plant Genet. Resour. Abstr.

GW/0011-992X
DEUTSCHE BAUMSCHULE. [Dtsch.
Baumsch.]. Vol. 1, No. 1 (Jan. 1, 1949)-. Periodical. German. Twelve times a year. DM213.00 Germany; DM220.00 other. Georgi GMBH, Postfach 407, D-52005 Aachen, Germany. **Tel** 011 49 241 4779118. **[CCC].**
Ind/Abst AGRICOLA; For. Abstr.; Hortic. Abstr.; Leis. Recreat. Tour. Abstr.; Ornamental Hort. (1991-); Plant Grow. Reg. Abstr.; Rev. Agric. Entomol.; Rural Dev. Abstr.; Soils Fert.; Weed Abstr.; World Agric. Econ.

GW/0940-2454
DEUTSCHE GARTNERPOST. (1991)-.
Periodical. German. wk. **Continues** Gartnerpost.

GW
DEUTSCHER GARTENBAU. Vol. 29 (1975)-.
Periodical. German. wk. DM286.00 Germany; DM338.70 other. Verlag Eugen Ulmer, Postfach 700561, D 70574 Stuttgart Germany. **Tel** 011 49 711 4507108, FAX 011 49 711 4507120, telex 7-23634. **ED** Roland Ulmer. **Bk Rev. Ad Acc. Circ:** 7,000 (ctrl). **Continues** Der Erwerbsgartner.
Desc: Magazine for horticulture and plant culture in Germany.
Ind/Abst Agric. Eng. Abstr. (1991-); Biocont. News Inf. (1991-); Crop Physiol. Abstr.; Grasslands For. Abstr.; Hortic. Abstr.; Leis. Recreat. Tour. Abstr.; Ornamental Hort. (19??-19??); Plant Breed. Abstr.; Plant Grow. Reg. Abstr.; Postharvest News Inf.; Rev. Agric. Entomol.; Rev. Plant Pathol.; Rural Dev. Abstr.; Seed Abstr.; Soils Fert.; Weed Abstr.; World Agric. Econ.

NE
DEVELOPMENTS IN LANDSCAPE MANAGEMENT AND URBAN PLANNING. Vol. 1 (1975)-. Monographic series. English. ir. Price varies per volume. Elsevier Science Publishing Company Inc, Madison Square Station, PO Box 882, New York NY 10159-0882. Tel (212)633-3950, FAX (212)633-3990. DD 711.
Ind/Abst GeoRef.

US/1054-9161
DIRECTORY OF MASTER GARDENING PROGRAMS IN THE UNITED STATES AND CANADA. VFOAT Master Gardening Programs in the United States and Canada. (1991)-. Directory. English. $10.00 (members), $15.00 (non-members). Master Gardeners International Corporation, 2904 Cameron Mills Road, Alexandria VA 22302.

US/8756-0178
DIRECTORY OF NEW JERSEY CERTIFIED NURSERIES AND PLANT DEALERS. [Dir. N.J. certif. nurs. plant deal.]. (1984)-. Directory. English. an. New Jersey Department of Agriculture, John Fitch Plaza, CN-330, Trenton NJ 08625. Tel (609)292-3976, FAX (609)292-3978. LC SB118.487.N5; D57. DD 381/.415/025749. UDC 635.037(036)(749). Continues New Jersey Certified Nurserymen and Dealers.
Desc: Includes statistics of the New Jersey nursery industry.

US/0099-1589
DIRECTORY OF NURSERYMEN AND OTHERS LICENSED TO SELL NURSERY STOCK IN CALIFORNIA, AND SUMMARY OF LAWS AND REGULATIONS. VFOAT Directory of Nurserymen-Laws and Regulations. Directory. English. Federal-State Market News Service, 1220 N Street/Suite 216, Sacramento CA 95814. Tel (202)872-4600, (800)227-5558, FAX (202)872-4615. (Subscription address: PO Box 57136 West End Station, Washington DC 20037) LC SB44; .C3. DD 338.1/7/59025794. UDC 635.037(036)(794). Continues Directory of Nurserymen and Others Licensed to Sell Nursery Stock in California.

NZ
DISCUSSION PAPER. Added/Corp Lincoln College (University of Canterbury). Dept. of Horticulture, Landscape, and Parks. No. 1 (1981)-. English. Royal New Zealand Institute of Horticulture, PO Box 12, Lincoln College, Canterbury New Zealand. Tel 011 03 252811 ext 788. ED R.L. Sheppard. Circ: 300.
Desc: Economic and marketing papers on agricultural subjects including policy, management, transport, business, resources and education.

US
DWARF CONIFER NOTES. Vol. 1, No. 1 (Jan. 1980)-. Periodical. English. qt. Free. Theophrastus, PO Box 458, Little Compton RI 02837. UDC 633.877.

PL/0137-7930
DZIALKOWIEC. [Dzialkowiec]. Added/Corp
Centralna Rada Zwiazkow Zawodowych w Polsce. Polski Zwiazek Dziakowcow. Krajowa Rada. (1949)-. Periodical. Polish. mo. $27.00. (Subscription address: ARS Polona, PO Box 1001, 00068 Warsaw Poland.)

US/0749-3312
ECONOMIC POISONS ... REPORT (BISMARCK, N.D.). (ECONOMIC POISONS ... REPORT / NORTH DAKOTA STATE LABORATORIES DEPARTMENT.). Added/Corp North Dakota. State Laboratories Dept. (19??)-. English. an. North Dakota State Laboratories Department, Lock Box 937, Bismarck ND 58502. LC SB960; .E28. DD 632/.95.

UA/0301-8164
EGYPTIAN JOURNAL OF HORTICULTURE. [Egypt. j. hort.]. Added/Corp
Jamiyat Filahat al-Basatin al-Misriyah. **VFOAT** Majallah al-Misriyah lil-Basatin. Vol. 1 (1974)-. Periodical. English (Arabic). ir. $50.00. National Information & Documentation Center, A1-Tahrir St Dokki AGWAF, Cairo Egypt. **Tel** 011 20 2 701696, telex 93069. **CODEN** EJHCAE. Documents available from CASDDS.
Ind/Abst AGRICOLA; Agric. Eng. Abstr.; Chem. Abstr.; Crop Physiol. Abstr.; Field Crop Abstr.; Food Sci. Technol. Abstr.; Grasslands For. Abstr.; Hortic. Abstr.; Plant Breed. Abstr.; Postharvest News Inf.; Rev. Med. Vet. Mycology; Rev. Plant Pathol.; Rice Abstr.; Seed Abstr.; Soils Fert.; Weed Abstr.

SA/1012-9987
ENCEPHALARTOS. [Encephalartos]. (1985)-.
Periodical. Multiple languages. qt. R40.00 South Africa; R65.00 other. Cycad Society of South Africa, PO Box 189, Port Elizabeth 6000 South Africa. **ED** Isabella Claasen. Index available. cum. index. **Circ:** 1,000 (ctrl).

JA/0013-7626
ENGEI GAKKAI ZASSHI. [Engei Gakkai zasshi].
Main/Corp Engei Gakkai (Japan). **VFOAT** Journal of the Horticultural Association of Japan; Journal of the Japanese Society for Horticultural Science. Vol. 1 (July 1925)-. Academic Scholarly Publication. Multiple languages (Japanese and English). qt. $178.00. Engei Gakkai, (Japanese Society for Horticultural Science), Kyoto Daigaku Nogakubu Nogaku, Kyoshitsu, Kitashirakawa, Oiwakecho, Sakyoku,, Kyotoshi, Kyotofu 606 Japan. (**Subscription address:** Kyowa Book Company Inc, 1 38 Kanda Jinbocho Chiyoda-ku, Tokyo 101 Japan.) **CODEN** EGKZA9. **[CCC]. Pr Rev.** Documents available from The Genuine Article, BIOSIS Document Express, CASDDS.
Ind/Abst AGRICOLA; Biol. Abstr.; Chem. Abstr.; Crop Physiol. Abstr.; EMBASE; Hortic. Abstr.; Ornamental Hort. (1991-); Life Sci. Collect.; Plant Breed. Abstr.; Plant Grow.

Reg. Abstr.; Postharvest News Inf.; Potato Abstr.; Res. Alert [Full Cov.]; Rev. Plant Pathol.; Sci. Cit. Index; SCISEARCH; Seed Abstr.; Soils Fert.; Soyabean Abstr.

JA
ENGEI SHINCHISHIKI. HANA NO GO.
Added/Corp Takii Shubyo Kabushiki Kaisha. **VFOAT** Hana no go. (199?)-. Periodical. English. mo. Takii Shubyo K.K. Shuppanbu, (Takii & Co., Ltd.), 180, Inokuma Higashi Iru, Umekoki, Shimogyoku, Kyotoshi, Kyotofu 600-91 Japan. ***Continues*** *Engei Shinchishiki. Hana to Midori no Johoshi.*

CN/0846-5339
ESPACES VERTS. [Espaces verts]. Vol. 1, No. 6 (July/Aug. 1989)-. Periodical. French. Seven times a year. 28.56Can$ regular; 23.36Can$ student. Editions Versicolores Inc., 1320 Boulevard Saint-Joseph, A Marchand Quebec, G2K 1G2 Quebec, Canada. **Tel** (418)628-8690, (800)463-1576, FAX (418)628-0524. **DD** 712/.09714. ***Continues*** *Bulletin d'Information sur l'Entretien et l'Amenagement des Espaces Verts., 0840-7428.*

UK
ESSEX SUCCULENT REVIEW. Periodical. English. qt. £2.50. Essex Succulent Review, c/o E A and D L Harris, 49 Chestnut Glen, Hornchurch Essex RM12 4HL England. **Tel** 011 44 708 447778. **ED** E. A. Harris and D. L. Harris. **Bk Rev. Ad Acc. Circ:** 200.
Desc: Covers various aspects of the hobby of collecting and growing cacti and other succulents.

US/0737-8823
EUPHORBIA JOURNAL, THE. VFOAT Euphorbia. Vol. 1, (1983)-. English. an (Sept.). $48.50. Strawberry Press, 227 Strawberry Drive, Mill Valley CA 94941. **Tel** (415)388-5017. **ED** Herman Schwartz, Ron Lafon and Daryl Koutnik. **LC** SB413.E95; E9. **DD** 635.9/3395. Index available. cum. index. **Bk Rev. Pr Rev. Circ:** 3,000.
Desc: Covers all of the worlds euphorbias, articles by world authorities, and magnificent color plates of all the plants discussed.

UK
EUROFRUIT. Vol. 4, No. 8 (Aug.1976)-. Periodical. Multiple languages (French, Italian, Spanish, English and German). mo (Jan./Dec. is combined). £72.00 UK; £79.00 Europe; £89.00 others. Market Intelligence Ltd, 440/441 Market Towers, New Covent Garden, London SW8 5NQ England. **Tel** 011 44 71 498 6711, FAX 011 44 71 498 6472, telex 8950975. **ED** Chris White. Index available (Bound in Dec. issue). cum. index. **Bk Rev. Ad Acc, Adv Mgr:** Erica Nicholson. **Circ:** 7,000 (ctrl).
Desc: The international marketing magazine for producers, exporters, importers and buyers of fruit and vegetables as well as associated service industries.

US/0014-6943
FAIRCHILD TROPICAL GARDEN BULLETIN. ***Title Change.*** [Fairchild Trop. Gard. bull.]. **Main/Corp** Fairchild Tropical Garden, Coconut Grove, Fla. **Added/Corp** Fairchild Tropical Garden. Bulletin. Vol.1 (1945)-(1992). Bulletin. English. qt. Fairchild Tropical Garden, 10901 Old Cutler Road, Miami FL 33156. **Tel** (305)667-1651. **ED** Karen Nagle. **LC** QK73.U62; F34. **Bk Rev. Circ:** 5,000 (ctrl). ***Absorbed*** *Annual Report - Fairchild Tropical Garden.* ***Continued by*** *Garden News (Miami, Fla.).*
Desc: Gardening, horticultural, and botanical information about issues related to the unique area of south Florida.
Ind/Abst AGRICOLA [Full Cov.]; Garden Lit. (1992-).

IT
FAO PLANT PRODUCTION AND PROTECTION PAPERS. Added/Corp Food and Agriculture Organization of the United Nations. **VFOAT** Plant Production and Protection Papers; FAO Plant Production and Protection Paper; Etude FAO, Production Vegetale et Protection des Plantes. **VAT** Food and Agriculture Organization of the United Nations Plant Production and Protection Papers. (1976)-. Monographic series. English. ir. Price varies per volume. Food and Agriculture Organization (FAO) / Italy, GIPC166 via Terme di Caracalla, 00100 Rome Italy. **Tel** 011 39 6 522 52925, FAX 011 39 6 522 55784. **LC** UNC.
Ind/Abst AGRICOLA; Life Sci. Collect.

IT/0259-2525
FAO PLANT PRODUCTION AND PROTECTION SERIES. See Agriculture-Crop Production and Soil.

IT/0014-5637
FAO PLANT PROTECTION BULLETIN. [FAO plant prot. bull.]. **Added/Corp** Food and Agricultural Organization of the United Nations. World Reporting Service on Plant Diseases and Pest. **VFOAT** Plant Protection Bulletin. **VAT** Food and Agricultural Organization Plant Protection Bulletin. Vol. 1, No. 1 (Oct. 1952)-. Academic Scholarly Publication. English. Four times a year. $26.00. Food and Agriculture Organization (FAO) / Italy, GIPC166 via Terme di Caracalla, 00100 Rome Italy. **Tel** 011 39 6 522 52925, FAX 011 39 6 522 55784. **CODEN** FAOPA2. cum. index. available on microfilm from University Microfilms International (UMI). Documents available from BIOSIS Document Express. ***Continues*** *Plant Protection Bulletin.*
Desc: Medium for dissemination of information received by the World Reporting Service on Plant Diseases and Pests; of value to professionals in plant protection and quarantine; publishes reports on the incidence, outbreak and control of plant pests of economic significance, plant quarantine announcements and related topics.
Ind/Abst Biodeter. Abstr.; Biol. Agric. Index; Biol. Abstr.; Ecol. Abstr.; EMBASE; Entomol. Abstr.; Field Crop Abstr.; For. Prod. Abstr.; For. Abstr.; Grasslands For. Abstr.; Hortic. Abstr.; Int. Dev. Abstr.; Microbiol. Abstr. Sect. B (19??-19??); Microbiol. Abstr. Sect. A; Microbiol. Abstr. Sect. C; Nematol. Abstr.; Life Sci. Collect.; PESTDOC; Plant Breed. Abstr.; Plant Genet. Resour. Abstr.; Potato Abstr.; Rev. Agric. Entomol.; Rev. Plant Pathol.; Rice Abstr.; Seed Abstr.; Sorghum Mill. Abstr.; Soyabean Abstr.; Weed Abstr.; Wheat Barley Trit. Abstr.

GW/0932-6154
FARMING SYSTEMS AND RESOURCE EECONOMICS IN THE TROPICS. [Farming syst. resour. econ. trop.]. (1988)-. Monographic series. English. ir.
Ind/Abst Irr. Drain. Abstr.; Soils Fert.

US
FENNELL'S ORCHID NEWS. Main/Corp Fennell Orchid Company. English. **UDC** 582.594.2.

CH/0253-9616
FFTC BOOK SERIES. [FFTC book ser.]. **Added/Corp** Asian and Pacific Council. Food & Fertilizer Technology Center. **VFOAT** F.F.T.C. Book Series. **VAT** Food and Fertilizer Technology Center Book Series. No. 1 (1978)-. Monographic series. English. ASPAC Food & Fertilizer Technology Center, Agriculture Building, 14 Wen Chow Street, Taipei Taiwan. **CODEN** FBSEDX. Documents available from CASDDS.
Ind/Abst Biodeter. Abstr.; Chem. Abstr.; Maize Abstr.; Postharvest News Inf.; Rev. Agric. Entomol.

US/0896-6281
FINE GARDENING. [Fine gard.]. No. 1 (May/June 1988)-. Periodical. English. bm (Jan., Mar., May, July, Sept. and Nov.). $28.00 (one year), $48.00 (two year), $64.00 (three year). Taunton Press, 63 South Main Street, PO Box 5506, Newtown CT 06470-5506. **Tel** (203)426-8171, (800)283-7252, FAX (203)426-3434, telex 5106004860. **ED** Rita Buchanan, Nancy Beaubaire and Mark Kane. **LC** WMLC 93/1412. **DD** 635. Index available. **Bk Rev. Ad Acc. Circ:** 125,000.
Desc: Targeted to the serious gardener, the publication includes three practical science applications, such as plant pathology and irrigation. Focuses on two individual plants, as well as landscaping. Concentrates on ornamental and landscape gardening, with some food gardening.
Ind/Abst Garden Lit. (1992-); Index Inf. (1988-).

CN/1180-159X
FLEURS, PLANTES ET JARDINS. [Fleurs plantes jard.]. (1990)-. Periodical. French. Eight times a year. 25.05Can$ Canada; 41.49Can$ other. Editions Versicolores Inc., 1320 Boulevard Saint-Joseph, A Marchand Quebec, G2K 1G2 Quebec, Canada. **Tel** (418)628-8690, (800)463-1576, FAX (418)628-0524. **DD** 712/.09714/05.

US/1051-9076
FLORACULTURE INTERNATIONAL. [FloraCult. int.]. **VFOAT** Flora Culture International. (1991)-. Periodical. English (summaries and/or abstracts in French, German and Spanish). Six times a year (Jan., Mar., May, July, Oct., Nov.). $51.00 US & Canada; $65.00 other. International Horticulture Publications, PO Box 9, Batavia IL 60510. **Tel** (708)208-9080, FAX (708)208-9350. **ED** Debbie Hamrick. **DD** 635. **Ad Acc. Circ:** 10,500 (ctrl).
Desc: Devoted to the production of cut flowers, flowering and foliage potted plants and garden flowers. These articles brings you the latest news, new technology, research, and reports on successful growers worldwide.

US/0272-6793
FLORICULTURE CROPS. [Floric. crops]. **Added/Corp** United States. Crop Reporting Board. United States. Agricultural Statistics Board. (1978)-. Government Publication. English. an. $12.00 (one year) $22.00 (two year), $32.00 (three year). US Department of Agriculture / National Agricultural Statistics Service (NASS), Room 5829 South Building, Washington DC 20250. **Tel** (202)720-4020, FAX (314)875-5231. **(Subscription address:** ERS NASS, 341 Victory Drive, Herndon VA 22070.) **LC** SB405; .U54. **DD** 338.1/759/0973. ***Continues*** *Flowers and Foliage Plants.*

US/1043-9137
FLORICULTURE DIRECTIONS. ***Ceased.*** [Floric. dir.]. **Added/Corp** Herb Mitchell Associates. (1976)-Vol. 15 (May 1990). Periodical. English. mo. Herb Mitchell Associates, 234 East 17th Street/Suite 206, Costa Mesa CA 92627. **Tel** (714)631-5551, FAX (714)631-4010. **ED** Herb Mitchell. **DD** 658. **Circ:** 30,000.
Desc: A black and white, eight page newsletter containing editorial of interest to those engaged in the floriculture industry.

US
FLORIDA CITRUS TREE INVENTORY. Main/Corp Florida Crop and Livestock Reporting Service. **Added/Corp** Florida. Division of Plant Industry. (19??)-. English. USDA NASS Florida Agricultural Statistics Service, 1222 Woodward Street, Orlando FL 32803. **Tel** (407)648-6013. **LC** SB369.2.F6; F65a. **DD** 338.1/7/4309759.

US
FLORIDA FOLIAGE. (1978)-. English. mo. $30.00 US; $50.00 other. Florida Foliage Association, PO Box 2507, Apopka FL 32704. **Tel** (407)886-1036, FAX (407)886-9585. **ED** Richelle Calvert. **Ad Acc. Circ:** 3,500 (ctrl).
Desc: Includes foliage updates, articles, thoroughly covered events, product advertising.

US/0426-5750
FLORIDA GARDENER, THE. Vol. 1, Sept. (1951)-. Periodical. English. bm. $5.00. Florida Federation of Garden Clubs, 2815 Northwest 29th Street, Gainsville FL 32605. **Tel** (904)378-9186. **(Subscription address:** FFGC Headquarters, PO Box 1604, Winter Park, FL 32790-1604**)** **ED** Elizabeth Harrer. **Bk Rev. Ad Acc. Circ:** 30,000 (ctrl).
Desc: Federation activities and educational opportunities are covered with feature articles on horticulture, floral design, landscape design, conservation and other environmental subjects.

US
FLORIDA NURSERYMAN. Vol. 1 (1956)-. Trade Publication. English. mo. $24.00 North America; $50.00 other. Florida Nurserymen Grower Association, 5401 Kirkman Road/Suite 650, Orlando FL 32819. **Tel** (407)345-8137, FAX (407)351-2610. **ED** Janice M Herbster. **UDC** 635.037(759). **Ad Acc. Circ:** 6,000 (ctrl).
Desc: A trade journal for southeast nursery industry. Reports latest industry business trends, research and "how-to" stories.

US/0430-778X
FLORIDA ORCHIDIST, THE. Added/Corp South Florida Orchid Society. Florida-Caribbean Orchid Association. Vol. 1, No. 1 (Nov. 1958)-. Periodical. English. Three times a year (Mar., Jul., Nov.). $17.50. South Florida Orchid Society, 6940 Southwest 111 Place, Miami FL 33173. **Tel** (305)274-3741, FAX (305)274-3741. **ED** Sally Taylor, (editor's address: 4305 Stirling Road, Ft. Lauderdale, FL 33314, (305)581-1409). **LC** SB409.A1; F5. Index available. **Ad Acc, Adv Mgr:** S. Taylor. **Circ:** 1,300.
Desc: A magazine with regular features by noted authors on orchid culture and awards judging.

IT
FLORTECNICA. Added/Corp Giovani Florovivaisti Associati. Vol. 1, No. 1 (April 1977)-. Periodical. Italian. Ten times a year. L80000 Italy; L110000 other. Ace International, Via Mocomero 26, 29010 Vernasca PC Italy. **Tel** 011 39 523 9910719, FAX 011 39 523 9910719. **ED** Arturo Croci. Index available. cum. index. **Bk Rev,** (Qty: 15-20). **Ad Acc.**
Desc: Information in horticulture.

US/0891-9534
FLOWER AND GARDEN (KANSAS CITY, MO. : 1982). (FLOWER AND GARDEN.). [Flower garden]. **VFOAT** Flower and Garden Magazine. Vol. 26, No. 1 (Jan. 1982)-. Periodical. English. bm (6 issues). $14.95 (one year), $24.90 (two year), $36.59 (three year). KC Publishing Inc., 700 West 47th Street, Suite 310, Kansas City MO 64112. **Tel** (816)531-5730, (800)444-0801. **(Subscription address:** CDS Agency Hard Copy, PO Box 4966, Des Moines IA 50340.**)** **ED** Kay M. Olson. **DD** 635. Index available. **Bk Rev. Ad Acc. Circ:** 550,000. available on an online database from DIALOG. Documents available from UMI Article Clearinghouse. ***Formed by the union of*** *Flower and Garden. Western Ed.; Flower and Garden. Northern Ed., 0162-3222; Flower and Garden. Southern Ed.* ***and*** *Flower and Gardening. Mid-American Ed., 0162-3249.*
Ind/Abst Acad. Abstr. Full Text Elite (Jan. 1989-); Acad. Abstr. (Jan. 1989-); Acad. Search (Jan. 1989-); Biol. Dig.; Garden Lit. (1992-); Gen. Period. Index (1985-); Index Inf.; INFO-SOUTH Abstr.; Mag. Artic. Summar. Elite (Jan. 1989-); Mag. Artic. Summar. Select (Jan. 1989-); Mag. Artic. Summar. CD-ROM (Jan. 1989-); Mag. Index Plus (1989-); Mag. Search; Newsp. Period. Abstr. (1988-); Read. Guide Abstr. Select Ed.; Read. Guide Period. Lit.; Mag. Index (1977-); Vocat. Search (Jan. 1989-).

US/0886-5833
FLOWER AND NURSERY REPORT FOR COMMERCIAL GROWERS. [Flower nurs. rep. commer. grow.]. **Added/Corp** University of California (System). Cooperative Extension. University of California Agricultural Extension Service. (May 1970)-. Periodical. English. bm. **DD** 635.
Ind/Abst AGRICOLA [Full Cov.]; Ornamental Hort. (1991-).

US/0015-4490
FLOWER NEWS : THE FLORAL INDUSTRY'S NATIONAL WEEKLY. (19??)-. Periodical. English. Fifty-two times a year. Flower News, 549 West Randolph Street, Chicago IL 60606. **Tel** (312)236-8648. **ED** Lauren C. Oates. **Bk Rev. Ad Acc. Circ:** 15,000 (ctrl).
Desc: For various segments of the floriculture and

ornamental horticulture industry, florist and nursery growers, wholesale florists and florist supply jobbers, florist retailers and allied tradesmen.

US/1061-9011
FLOWERING PLANT INDEX. (FLOWERING PLANT INDEX : FPI.). [Flower. plant index]. **Added/Corp** Andersen Horticultural Library. **VFOAT** FPI. Vol. 1, No. 1 (1991)-. Periodical. English. sa. $120.00. Andersen Horticultural Library, Minnesota Landscape Arboretum, 3675 Aboretum Drive, Box 39, Chanhassen MN 55317. **Tel** (612)442-2440. **ED** Richard T. Isaacson. **LC** Z5353; .F46. **DD** 582.

SA/0015-4504
FLOWERING PLANTS OF AFRICA, THE. **Added/Corp** Botanical Research Institute (South Africa) South Africa. Dept. of Agricultural Technical Services. (1945)-. Monographic series. English. an. Price varies per volume. National Botanical Institute, Private Bag X101, Pretoria 0001 South Africa. **Tel** 11 27 12 861164, **FAX** 11 27 12 861194. **LC** QK396; .F6. **DD** 582.0968. ***Continues*** *Flowering Plants of South Africa.*

IT
FOLIA. (1991)-. Italian. Il Verde Editoriale, Via Bolchini 12, 21100 Varese Italy. **Tel** 011 39 332 457288. ***Continues*** *Folia di Acer.*

PL/0867-1761
FOLIA HORTICULTURAE. [Folia Hortic.]. (1989)-. Multiple languages. tq. **UDC** 635.
Ind/Abst Crop Physiol. Abstr.; Field Crop Abstr.; Hortic. Abstr.; Nutr. Abstr. Rev., Ser. A, Hum. Exp.; Ornamental Hort. (1991-); Postharvest News Inf.; Seed Abstr.

US/1047-000X
FOSTER'S BOTANICAL & HERB REVIEWS. [Foster's bot. herb rev.]. **VFOAT** Botanical & Herb Reviews; Botanical and Herb Reviews; Foster's Botanical and Herb Reviews; B&H Reviews. (198?)-. Periodical. English. Four times a year (Mar., June, Sept., Dec.). $10.00 one year; $19.00 two years. Botanical Herb Review, PO Box 106, Eureka Springs AR 72632. **Tel** (501)253-7309, FAX (501)253-7442. **DD** 635. **Bk Rev**. **Circ:** 150. ***Continues*** *Herb Business Bulletin.*
Desc: News and information on the natural resources and the human health and plants of medicinal and nutritional value it has on them.
Ind/Abst Garden Lit. (1992-).

US/1055-4564
FRATERNA (CENTRAL POINT, OR.). (FRATERNA : OFFICIAL BULLETIN FOR INTERNATIONAL HOYA ASSOCIATION.). [Fraterna]. **Added/Corp** International Hoya Association. 3rd Quarter (1991)-. Bulletin. English. qt. $12.00 (membership). International Hoya Association, PO Box 5130, Central Point OR 97502. **DD** 635. ***Continues*** *Newsletter (International Hoya Society).*

BE/0016-2248
FRUIT BELGE, LE. [Fruit Belge]. **Added/Corp** Ligues Pomologiques Wallonnes. (1933)-. Academic Scholarly Publication. French. Six times a year. 1132.07F Belgium; 1400F other. Fruit Belge, 69 rue du Village, B 4460 Velroux Belgium. **Tel** 011 33 41 792336. **ED** A. Sansdrap. **CODEN** FRUBA7. Index available. **Bk Rev**. **Ad Acc. Circ:** 1,500 (ctrl). Documents available from CASDDS.
Desc: Contains all subjects related to fruit culture.
Ind/Abst Agric. Eng. Abstr. (1991-); Chem. Abstr. (1933-1976); Food Sci. Technol. Abstr.; Hortic. Abstr.; Plant Breed. Abstr.; Postharvest News Inf.; Rev. Agric. Entomol.; Weed Abstr.

US/1049-4545
FRUIT GARDENER, THE. [Fruit gard.]. **Added/Corp** California Rare Fruit Growers. Vol. 18, No. 3 (Third Quarter 1986)-. Periodical. English. Six times a year (Feb., Apr., June, Aug., Oct., Dec.). $16.00 US; $25.00 Canada & Mexico; $30.00 others Comes with California Rare Fruit Growers Membership. California Rare Fruit Growers Inc., PO Box W, El Cajon CA 92022. **Tel** (619)441-7395. **ED** Clytia Chambers, (phone: (818)762-0730). **DD** 634. cum. index. **Bk Rev**, (Qty: 6). **Ad Acc. Circ:** 3,000. ***Continues*** *California Rare Fruit Growers Newsletter, 0742-8049.*

US/0091-3642
FRUIT VARIETIES JOURNAL. [Fruit var. j.]. Vol. 27 (Jan. 1973)-. Periodical. English. qt. $20.00 US; $32.00 (airmail) other. American Pomological Society, c/o Dr R M Crassweller, 103 Tyson Building, University Park PA 16802. **Tel** (814)863-6163, FAX (814)863-6139. **ED** David C Ferree. **LC** SB354; .A54. **DD** 634/.04/705. **UDC** 634.1. **CODEN** FVRJAA. cum. index. **Bk Rev**. **Ad Acc. Pr Rev. Circ:** 1,000 (ctrl). available on microfilm and microfiche from University Microfilms International (UMI). Documents available from The Genuine Article, BIOSIS Document Express. ***Continues*** *Fruit Varieties and Horticultural Digest, 0016-2272.*
Desc: Promotes fruit variety and rootstock improvement through breeding and testing. Publishes latest information on fruit variety introductions and performance of existing varieties.
Ind/Abst AgBiotech News Inf.; AGRICOLA [Full Cov.]; Biol. Abstr.; Curr. Aware. Biol. Sci., CABS; Curr. Contents, Agric. Biol. Environ. Sci.; Food Sci. Technol. Abstr.; Hortic. Abstr.; Irr. Drain. Abstr.; Nematol. Abstr.; Life Sci. Collect.; Plant Breed. Abstr.; Plant Grow. Reg. Abstr.; Postharvest News Inf.; Res. Alert [Select. Cov.]; Rev. Agric. Entomol.; Rev. Plant Pathol.; SCISEARCH; Seed Abstr.; Soils Fert.; Vitis Vitic. Enol. Abstr.

FR/0016-2299
FRUITS. **Added/Corp** Institut des Fruits et Agrumes Coloniaux. Institut Francais de Recherches Fruitieres Outre-mer. Institut de Recherches sur ls Fruits et Agrumes. Vol. 6, (1951)-. Academic Scholarly Publication. French (Spanish and English; summaries and/or abstracts in English, German and Spanish). Six times a year (1 special iss. included). 370.00F France; 470.00F other. IRFA Inst Rech Fruits Agrumes, BP 5035, 34032 Montpellier France. **Tel** 011 33 1 45531692, telex 610992. **ED** Chantal Cabot. **CODEN** FRUIAS. Index available. cum. index. **Bk Rev. Ad Acc. Circ:** 1,000. Documents available from CASDDS. ***Continues*** *Fruits d'Outre Mer, 0367-2816.*
Desc: Information on culture, plant protection, maturation, harvest, conservation and industrial transformation of tropical and subtropical fruits.
Ind/Abst AGRICOLA; Agrofor. Abstr.; Chem. Abstr.; Field Crop Abstr.; Food Sci. Technol. Abstr.; For. Abstr.; Nematol. Abstr.; Life Sci. Collect.; PESTDOC; Plant Genet. Resour. Abstr.; Postharvest News Inf.; Rev. Agric. Entomol.; Rev. Plant Pathol.; Seed Abstr.; Soils Fert.

UK
GARDEN ANSWERS. (1982)-. Periodical. English. Twelve times a year. £16.50UK; £18.50 others. EMAP National Publications Ltd, Farndon Road, Market Harborough, Leicestershire, LE16 9NR England. **Tel** 011 44 733 555161. ***Absorbed*** *Greenhouse and Garden.*

US
GARDEN BOOK / WHITE FLOWER FARM, THE. **Main/Corp** White Flower Farm. English. Three times a year. $5.00. White Flower Farm, Litchfield CT 06759. **Tel** (203)496-9624. **ED** Amos Pettingill. **Circ:** 1,000,000.

US/0892-564X
GARDEN CENTER BULLETIN, THE. ***Title Change.*** (THE GARDEN CENTER BULLETIN. GARDEN CENTER OF GREATER CLEVELAND.). [Gard. Cent. bull.]. **Added/Corp** Garden Center of Greater Cleveland. **VFOAT** Bulletin. (1967)-(19??). Periodical. English. mo. Cleveland Botanical Garden, 11030 East Boulevard, Cleveland OH 44106. **Tel** (216)721-1600. **ED** Marilyn Sommer. **DD** 635. Index available. **Ad Acc. Circ:** 4,000 (ctrl). ***Continues*** *Your Garden Center Bulletin.* ***Continued by*** *Bulletin.*

CN/0318-7705
GARDEN CLIPPINGS. ***Ceased.*** **Added/Corp** Saskatoon Horticultural Society. (1???)-(1???). Periodical. English. ir. Saskatoon Horticultural Society, PO Box 211, Prairie Garden Guil, Saskatoon Saskatchewan S7K 3K4 Canada. **Tel** 343-8679. **ED** Monty Zary. Index available. cum. index. **Bk Rev. Ad Acc. Circ:** 2,300 (ctrl).
Desc: Covers all areas concerning gardening, plant culture and house plants. Keeps articles so they cover the immediate time period-which is three months for each issue.

US/0896-8373
GARDEN CLUB OF AMERICA NEWSLETTER, THE. [Gard. Club Am. newsl.]. **Added/Corp** Garden Club of America. **VFOAT** Newsletter; GCA Bulletin. Vol. 76, No. 1 (1987)-. Newsletter. English. bm. Garden Club of America, 598 Madison Avenue, New York NY 10022. **LC** SB403; .G3. **DD** 635.9/06/073. ***Continues*** *Bulletin of the Garden Club of America.*
Ind/Abst Garden Lit. (1992-).

US/0733-4923
GARDEN DESIGN. [Gard. des.]. **VFOAT** Garden Design Magazine; GD. Vol. 1, No. 1 (Spring 1982)-. Periodical. English. bm (6 issues). $24.00 (one year), $42.00 (two year). Circulation Specialists Inc., 49 Richmondville Avenue, Westport CT 06880. **Tel** (203)454-0344. **ED** Karen Fishler. **LC** SB469; .G27. **DD** 712/.6/05. **UDC** 712. **Bk Rev. Ad Acc. Circ:** 50,000.
Desc: Beautiful four-color magazine on outdoor residential design.
Ind/Abst Avery Index Archit. Period. Suppl. Colum. Univ. (1990-); Garden Lit. (1992-).

UK/0307-1243
GARDEN HISTORY. [Gard. hist.]. **Added/Corp** Garden History Society (Great Britain). (1972)-. Periodical. English. Twice a year. £15.00 UK; £18.00 other. Garden History Society, c/o Anne Richards, 5 The Knoll, Hereford HR1 1RU England. **Tel** 44 432 354479. **ED** Mrs. J Crawley and Mrs. E Whittle. **LC** SB451; .G34. **DD** 635.9/09. Index available (bound in each issue). cum. index. **Bk Rev. Circ:** 1,800 (ctrl). ***Continues*** *Occasional Paper (Garden History Society); Garden History Society Newsletter.*
Desc: Garden history in all aspects; garden and landscape design and its relation to architecture, etc. plant introduction, estate planning and maintenance.
Ind/Abst Archit. Period. Index (1974-); Avery Index Archit. Period. Suppl. Colum. Univ. (1990-); BHA : Biblio. Hist. Art; Br. Archaeol. Bibliogr.; Garden Lit. (1992-).

US/0733-0340
GARDEN IDEAS & OUTDOOR LIVING. **VFOAT** Garden Ideas and Outdoor Living. (19??)-. Periodical. English. an. Available on newsstand only. Meredith Corporation, Locust at 17th, Des Moines IA 50309. **Tel** (515)284-3000. **LC** SB450.9; .G36. **DD** 643/.55/05.

UK/0308-5457
GARDEN (LONDON 1975). (THE GARDEN.). [Garden]. **Added/Corp** Royal Horticultural Society (Great Britain). Vol. 100, Pt. 6 (June 1975)-. Periodical. English. mo. £34.00 (airmail); £19.00 UK; £27.00 other. New Perspectives Publishing Ltd, Vincent Square, London SW1 England. **LC** SB4; .R8. **DD** 635.9/0941. available on microfilm and microfiche from University Microfilms International (UMI). ***Continues*** *Royal Horticultural Society (Great Britain). Journal of the Royal Horticultural Society, 0035-8924.*
Ind/Abst AGRICOLA; Biol. Agric. Index; Biol. Dig.; EMBASE; Hortic. Abstr.; Ornamental Hort. (19??-19??); Life Sci. Collect.; Plant Breed. Abstr.; Plant Genet. Resour. Abstr.; Rev. Med. Vet. Mycology; Rev. Plant Pathol.; Seed Abstr.

●US
GARDEN NEWS / FAIRCHILD TROPICAL GARDEN. **Added/Corp** Fairchild Tropical Garden. Vol. 48, No. 1 (Spring 1993)-. Periodical. English. Four times a year. $40.00 (individuals); $60.00 (institutions) Comes with Fairchild Tropical Garden membership. Fairchild Tropical Garden, 10901 Old Cutler Road, Miami FL 33156. **Tel** (305)667-1651. **LC** QK73.U62; F34. **UDC** 1. ***Continues*** *Fairchild Tropical Garden Bulletin, 0014-6943.*
Desc: Information concerning tropical plants and botanical gardens.

US/0016-4607
GARDEN PATH, THE. **Added/Corp** Ohio Association of Garden Clubs. (19??)-. Periodical. English. Four times a year. $3.00. Mrs Fred Schuster/President, 4135 Strobridge Road, Vandalia OH 45377. **Tel** (513)898-6389.

US/0897-280X
GARDEN TALK. [Gard. talk]. **Added/Corp** Chicago Horticultural Society. Chicago Botanic Garden. (1986)-. Periodical. English. mo. Chicago Botanic Garden, PO Box 400, Glencoe IL 60022. **Tel** (312)835-5440. ***Continues*** *Garden Talk (Chicago, Ill. : 1974), 0897-280X.*

●US/1062-6093
GARDEN TOURIST, THE. (THE GARDEN TOURIST: A GUIDE TO GARDEN TOURS, GARDEN DAYS, SHOWS AND SPECIAL EVENTS.). [Gard. tour.]. (Jan.-Dec. 1992)-. English. an. $14.50. The Garden Tourist Press, 290 West End Avenue, New York NY 10023. **Tel** (212)874-6211. **LC** SB317.74; .G37. **DD** 712/.07473.

US
GARDEN WRITERS NEWSLETTER. Newsletter. English. bm. part of $75.00 membership. Garden Writers Association of America, 1218 Overlook Road, Eustis FL 32726. **Tel** (704)252-9143. **Bk Rev**. **Circ:** 1,250.
Desc: Articles to improve member skills. Includes information about future association meetings, book reviews, and a calendar of events.

US/0016-464X
GARDENER. [Gardener]. **Added/Corp** Men's Garden Clubs of America. (1958)-. Periodical. English. Six times a year (Jan., Mar., May, July, Sept., Nov.,). $15.00. The Gardeners of America, Inc., 5560 Merele Hay Road, Box 241, Johnston IA 50131. **Tel** (515)278-0295. ***Continues*** *MECA.*

CN/0821-5855
GARDENERS DIGEST. (GARDENERS DIGEST : THE OFFICIAL PUBLICATION OF THE GARDENERS GUILD.). [Gard. dig.]. Vol. 1, No. 1 (Fall 1982)-. Periodical. English. bm. Free to members. Gardeners Guild, PO Box 200, Georgetown Ontario L7G 4Y5 Canada. **DD** 635/.05. **UDC** 635.

US/1041-2875
GARDENER'S EYE, THE. [Gard. eye]. (Jan. 1989)-. Periodical. English. mo. $24.00 US; $28.00 other. Hurricane Publishing Company, PO Box 22382, Denver CO 80222. **DD** 635.

IT/0393-585X
GARDENIA. [Gardenia]. (1984)-. Periodical. Italian. mo. L62000 Italy; L100000 other. Giorgio Mondadori Intl, Via A Ponti 10, 20143 Milan Italy. **Tel** 011 39 2 891661. **UDC** 63. Index available. **Circ:** 95,000 (ctrl).

AT
GARDENING AUSTRALIA. (19??)-. Periodical. English. mo. 34.00Aus$ Australia; 69.00Aus$ New Zealand & Papua New Guinea; 93.00Aus$ US & Canada; 100.00Aus$ Europe & Africa; 75.00Aus$ Singapore, Indonesia, Malaysia; 84.00Aus$ other. Federal Publishing Co Pty Ltd, PO Box 199, 180 Bourke Road, Alexandria New South Wales, 2015 Australia. **Tel** 011 61 2 693

6666, FAX 011 61 2 693 9935. **(Subscription address:** Federal Publishing Co. Pty Ltd., PO Box 199, Alexandria NSW 2015 Australia.**)**

•CN/1188-2972
GARDENING IN ALBERTA. [Gard. Alta.]. Vol. 1, No. 1 (Mar./Apr. 1992)-. Periodical. English. Eight times a year. 18.00Can$ Canada; 32.00Can$ other. Bobbsey Publishing, PO Box 39043, Edmonton AB T5B 4TB Canada. **Tel** (403)491-0010, FAX (403)491-0010. **ED** Caroyln Dack (phone: (403)349-6745). **DD** 635. **Bk Rev**, (Qty: 3). **Ad Acc**, **Adv Mgr:** C. Dack. **Circ:** 4,000, 17,000.

AT
GARDENING NEWS. (19??)-. English. qt. Free to members. Box Hill Horticultural Society Inc., Box 287, Box Hill 3128 Australia. **ED** Flora Miller. **Ad Acc**. Full Page (B&W) 80.00Aus$. Half Page (B&W) 50.00Aus$. **Circ:** 250 (ctrl).
Desc: Editorial reports from president, secretary and treasurer. Reports on activities of morning group meetings, and reports on the floral art group. Contains a children's page, articles of information and general interest.

US/0164-7482
GARDENING NEWSLETTER. (197?)-. Newsletter. English. mo. $15.95. Bob Flagg Gardening Newsletter, PO Box 2306, Houston TX 77001. **Tel** (713) 522-7671. ***Continues** Compton's Gardening Newsletter.*

UK
GARDENING WHICH. (19??)-. Periodical. English. Ten times a year. £47.00. Consumers Association, Castlemead, Gascoyne Way, Hertford SG14 1LH England. **Tel** 011 44 992 587773.

UK/0953-8550
GARDENS OF ENGLAND AND WALES 1988. [Gard. Engl. Wales 1988]. **VFOAT** Gardens of England and Wales Open to the Public (1988). (1988)-. Periodical. English. an. £3.75 UK; £4.75 other Europe. National Gardens Scheme, Hatchland Park, East Clandon / Guildford, Surrey GU4 7RT England. **DD** 914.2. ***Continues** Gardens of England and Wales Open to the Public (1970), 0141-2361.*

CN/0836-4974
GARDENS WEST. [Gard. west]. Vol. 1, No. 1 (April 1987)-. Periodical. English. Nine times a year. 20.00Can$ (one year), 36.00Can$ (two year). Cornwall Publishing, P.O.Box 2680, Vancouver BC V6B 3W8 Canada. **Tel** (604)879-4991, FAX (604)879-5110. **DD** 635/.09711. Index available. **Ad Acc**, **Adv Mgr:** T.Wilson, **Tel** (604)879-4991. **Circ:** 50,000.
Ind/Abst Garden Lit. (1992-).

GW
GARTEN ORGANISCH. ***Title Change.*** No. 1 (Feb./Mar. 1990)-(1993). Periodical. German. bm. ***Continues** Garten + Landbau Organisch. **Continued by** Natuerlich Gaertnern.*

GW/0016-4720
GARTEN UND LANDSCHAFT. [Gart. Landsch.]. **Added/Corp** Deutsche Gesellschaft fur Gartenkunst und Landschaftspflege. **VFOAT** Journal for Landscape Architecture and Landscape Planning. (19??)-. Academic Scholarly Publication. German (English). mo. DM114.00. Verlag Georg DW Callwey GmbH, Postfach 800409, D 81604 Munich Germany. **Tel** 011 49 89 43600533. **[CCC].**
Ind/Abst AGRICOLA; Avery Index Archit. Period. Suppl. Colum. Univ. (1989-); EMBASE; Leis. Recreat. Tour. Abstr.

GW/0016-4739
GARTENAMT, DAS. [Gartenamt]. (1952)-. Periodical. German. mo. DM147.00 Germany; DM180.00 other. Patzer Verlag, Postfach 330460, D 14174 Berlin Germany. **Tel** 011 49 30 8959030. **UDC** 712.
Ind/Abst Agric. Eng. Abstr.; Hortic. Abstr.; Irr. Drain. Abstr.; Leis. Recreat. Tour. Abstr.; Ornamental Hort. (1991-); Rev. Plant Pathol.; Soils Fert.; World Agric. Econ.

GW
GARTENBAU. FORSCHUNG, TECHNIK, MANAGEMENT FUER PRODUKTION-SBETRIEBE. **Added/Corp** Akademie der Landwirtschaftswissenschaften zu Berlin. Vol. 38 No. 1, (1991)-. Periodical. German. mo. Deutsche Akademie der Landwirtschaftswissenschaften, Berlin Germany. ***Continues** Gartenbau.*

•GW/0942-0118
GARTENBAU MAGAZIN. [Gart.bau-Mag.]. **Added/Corp** Kuratorium fuer Technik und Bauwesen in der Landwirtschaft. **VFOAT** Gartenbau-Magazin. (Jan./Feb. 1992)-. Periodical. German (summaries and/or abstracts in English). mo. DM69.00 Germany; DM89.40 other. Bernhard Thalacker Verlag, Hamburger Str 277, Postfach 3361, D 38023 Braunschweig Germany. **Tel** 011 49 531 380040, FAX 011 49 531 3800425. ***Continues** Gartenbau.*
Desc: Journal aimed at those with an interest in gardening.

AU
GARTENBAU- UND FELDGEMUSE-ANBAUERHEBUNG / BEARBEITET IM OSTERREICHISCHEN STATISTISCHEN ZENTRALAMT. **See** Gardening and Horticulture-Abstracting, Bibliographies and Statistics.

GW
GARTENBAU UND WEINWIRTSCHAFT. III. WEINWIRTSCHAFT. **Main/Corp** Germany (Federal Republic) Statistisches Bundesamt. No.15 (May 1967)-. Periodical. German. ir. ***Continues** Germany (Federal Republic Statistisches Bundesamt. Gartenbau und Weinbau. III. Wein.*

GW
GARTENBAULICHE VERSUCHSBERICHTE. **Main/Corp** Landwirtschaftskammer Rheinland. Abteilung Erzeugung. Gruppe Gartenbau. (1972)-. Periodical. German. an (Sept.). Rheinischer Landwirtschafts Verlag GmbH, Rochusstrasse 18, D-53123 Bonn Germany. **Tel** 011 49 228 520060. ***Continues** Landwirtschaftskammer Rheinland. Abteilung Gemuse-, Obst- und Gartenbau. Gartenbauliche Versuchsberichte.*

GW
GARTENBAUTECHNISCHE INFORMATIONEN. Vol. 1 (1974)-. Monographic series. German. an. Price varies per volume.
Ind/Abst Agric. Eng. Abstr. (1991-); Hortic. Abstr.; Ornamental Hort. (1991-).

GW/0016-478X
GARTENBAUWISSENSCHAFT. [Gartenbauwissenschaft]. Vol. 1 (April 1928)-. Periodical. Multiple languages (English and German; summaries and/or abstracts in English, German, Russian and French). bm. DM549.00. Verlag Eugen Ulmer, Postfach 700561, D 70574 Stuttgart Germany. **Tel** 011 49 711 4507108, FAX 011 49 711 4507120, telex 7-23634. **ED** Rulund Ulmer. **LC** SB10; .G264. **CODEN** GTBWAY. **[CCC]. Pr Rev.** Documents available from The Genuine Article, CASDDS. ***Absorbed** Archiv fuer Gartenbau, 0003-908X.*
Ind/Abst Agric. Eng. Abstr. (1991-); Chem. Abstr.; Crop Physiol. Abstr.; Curr. Aware. Biol. Sci., CABS; Curr. Contents, Agric. Biol. Environ. Sci.; Energy Res. Abstr. (Feb. 1972-); Field Crop Abstr.; Food Sci. Technol. Abstr.; For. Prod. Abstr.; For. Abstr.; Hortic. Abstr.; Irr. Drain. Abstr.; Leis. Recreat. Tour. Abstr.; Ornamental Hort. (1991-); Life Sci. Collect.; Plant Breed. Abstr.; Plant Genet. Resour. Abstr.; Postharvest News Inf.; Res. Alert [Full Cov.]; Rev. Med. Vet. Mycology; Rev. Plant Pathol.; Rural Dev. Abstr.; Sci. Cit. Index; SCISEARCH; Seed Abstr.; Soils Fert.; Vitis Vitic. Enol. Abstr.; World Agric. Econ.

GW/0935-0519
GARTENKUNST, DIE. (1989)-. Periodical. German. sa. DM90.00. Wernersche Verlagsgesellschaft GmbH, Liebfrauenring 17, D-67547 Worms Germany. **Tel** 011 49 6241 43574. **(Subscription address:** Brockhaus Commission, Kreidlerstrasse 9, D 70803 Kornwestheim Germany.**)**
Ind/Abst BHA : Biblio. Hist. Art.

GW/0341-2105
GARTENPRAXIS. [Gartenpraxis]. No. 1 (Jan. 1975)-. Consumer Publication. German. mo. DM130.80. Verlag Eugen Ulmer, Postfach 700561, D 70574 Stuttgart Germany. **Tel** 011 49 711 4507108, FAX 011 49 711 4507120, telex 7-23634. **ED** Roland Ulmer. **[CCC].** Index available. **Bk Rev**, (Qty: 3). **Ad Acc**, **Adv Mgr:** Mr. Kretschmer, **Tel** 49 711 4507-126. **Acid Free. Circ:** 14,296 each month (ctrl). Documents available.
Ind/Abst AGRICOLA.

DK/0106-8393
GARTNER-TIDENDE : ORGAN FOR ALMINDELIG DANSK GARTNERFORENING. **Added/Corp** Almindelig Dansk Gartnerforening. (1885)-. Periodical. Danish. wk.
Ind/Abst For. Abstr.; Hortic. Abstr.; Nematol. Abstr.; Ornamental Hort. (1991-); Plant Breed. Abstr.; Plant Grow. Reg. Abstr.; Postharvest News Inf.; Rev. Agric. Entomol.; Soils Fert.

•GW/0945-9111
GARTNERBORSE. (Jan. 1994)-. Periodical. German. wk. DM279.00. Georgi GMBH, Postfach 407, D-52005 Aachen, Germany. **Tel** 011 49 241 4779118. **CODEN** GAGADX. ***Continues** Gartnerborse und Gartenwelt, 0342-4731.*
Desc: Contains information on gardening and horticulture.

GW/0936-3734
GARTNERBORSE, GARTENWELT. ***Title Change.*** **VFOAT** Gb + Gw. Gartnerborse, Gartenwelt. (1989)-(19??). Periodical. German. wk. Blackwell Wissenschafts-Verlag, Kurfuerstendamm 57, D 10707 Berlin Germany. **Tel** 011 49 30 32790623, 011 49 30 32790624, FAX 011 49 30 327 90610. ***Continued by** Gartnerborse.*
Ind/Abst Agric. Eng. Abstr.

SZ
GARTNERMEISTER. (1976)-. Periodical. German. wk. Verband Schweizerischer Gaertnermeister, 8029 Zurich Switzerland. ***Continues** Schweizerische Gartnerzeitung.*
Ind/Abst Biocont. News Inf.; For. Abstr.; Hortic. Abstr.; Nematol. Abstr.; Ornamental Hort. (1991-).

GW/0342-4731
GB+GW; GARTNERBORSE UND GARTENWELT. ***Title Change.*** [Gb+Gw; Gartnerborse und Gartenwelt]. **VFOAT** Gartnerborse und Gartenwelt. Vol. 77, No. 26 (July 2, 1977)-(199?). Periodical. German. wk. Georgi GMBH, Postfach 407, D-52005 Aachen, Germany. **Tel** 011 49 241 4779118. Index available. cum. index. **Bk Rev. Ad Acc.** ***Formed by the union of** Gartenwelt, 0016-4798 **and** Deutsche Gartnerborse. **Continued by** Gartnerborse.*
Ind/Abst AGRICOLA; Agric. Eng. Abstr. (1991-); For. Prod. Abstr. (1991-); For. Abstr.; Irr. Drain. Abstr.; Ornamental Hort. (1991-); Plant Grow. Reg. Abstr.; Postharvest News Inf.; Rev. Agric. Entomol.; Rev. Plant Pathol.; Seed Abstr.; Soils Fert.; World Agric. Econ.

GW/0721-4499
GC. GRUNER MARKT, GARTENCENTER +. **VFOAT** Gartencenter, Gruner Markt, Gartencenter +; GC. Gruner Markt, Gartencenter und Freizeit. (1981)-. Periodical. German. mo. DM142.00. Klette Druck Verlag Euroflora, Freunder Landstrasse 25, D 52078 Aachen Brand Germany. **Tel** 011 49 241 521021. **UDC** 634.

PL/0016-6715
GENETICA POLONICA. [Genet. pol.]. **Added/Corp** Zakad Genetyki Roslin PAN. Polska Akademia Nauk. Wydzia V. **VFOAT** Polish Journal of Theoretical and Applied Genetics; Polish Journal of Genetics and Plant Breeding. Vol. 1 (Dec. 1960)-. Periodical. English (summaries and/or abstracts in Polish and Russian). qt. Price on Request. **(Subscription address:** ARS Polona, PO Box 1001, 00068 Warsaw Poland.**) LC** SB123; .G42. **NLM** W1 GE287K. **CODEN** GPOLA4. **[CCC].** Documents available from BIOSIS Document Express, CASDDS.
Ind/Abst AgBiotech News Inf.; Anim. Breed. Abstr.; Biol. Abstr.; Chem. Abstr.; Field Crop Abstr.; Grasslands For. Abstr.; Index Vet.; Maize Abstr.; Life Sci. Collect.; Pig News Inf.; Plant Breed. Abstr.; Plant Genet. Resour. Abstr.; Plant Grow. Reg. Abstr.; Potato Abstr.; Poult. Abstr.; Protozoolog. Abstr.; Rev. Agric. Entomol.; Rev. Plant Pathol.; Seed Abstr.; Soils Fert.; Vet. Bull.; Wheat Barley Trit. Abstr.

BU/0016-6766
GENETIKA I SELEKTSIYA. (GENETIKA I SELEKTSIIA / GENETICS AND PLANT BREEDING.). [Genet. sel.]. **Added/Corp** Akademiia na Selskostopanskite Nauki. **VFOAT** Genetics and Plant Breeding. Vol. 1 (1968)-. Academic Scholarly Publication. Bulgarian (summaries and/or abstracts in English, German and Russian). bm (6 issues). DM143.00. Academie Bulgare des Sciences, Bibliotheque, 1 rue 7 Noemvri, 1040 Sofia Bulgaria. **Tel** 70-40-54. **(Subscription address:** Kubon & Sagner, ABT Zeitschriftenimport, D 80328 Munich Germany.**) ED** Manol Stoilov. **NLM** W3 ME959W. **CODEN** GESKAC. **Bk Rev. Ad Acc. Circ:** 930 (ctrl). Documents available from BIOSIS Document Express, CASDDS.
Desc: Journal of the Bulgarian Academy of Sciences.
Ind/Abst AgBiotech News Inf.; AGRICOLA; Anim. Breed. Abstr.; BioBusiness; Biol. Abstr.; Chem. Abstr.; Field Crop Abstr.; Genet. Abstr.; Grasslands For. Abstr.; Hortic. Abstr.; Index Vet.; Maize Abstr.; Nematol. Abstr.; Ornamental Hort. (1991-); Life Sci. Collect.; Pig News Inf.; Plant Breed. Abstr.; Plant Genet. Resour. Abstr.; Plant Grow. Reg. Abstr.; Potato Abstr.; Poult. Abstr.; Rev. Agric. Entomol.; Rev. Plant Pathol.; Soyabean Abstr.; Wheat Barley Trit. Abstr.

US
GEORGIA LICENSED NURSERIES. **Added/Corp** Georgia. Dept. of Agriculture. Georgia. Nursery and Plant Protection Program. **VFOAT** Licensed Nurseries. (19??)-. English. Georgia Department of Agriculture, Agriculture Building, Capitol Square, Atlanta GA 30334. **Tel** (404)656-3600, FAX (404)656-9380. **LC** SB118.487.G4; G46. **DD** 381/.415969/025758.

US/0016-8599
GERANIUMS AROUND THE WORLD. **Added/Corp** International Geranium Society. Vol. 1 (Aug./Sept. 1953)-. Periodical. English. Four times a year (Mar., June, Sept., Dec.). $12.50. International Geranium Society, PO Box 92734, Pasadena CA 91109. **Tel** (619)727-0309. Index available. **Bk Rev**, (Qty: 1). **Ad Acc. Circ:** 1,000 (ctrl).
Desc: Contains articles by both professionals and hobbyists on all aspects of geranium culture. Advertisers are often welcome sources for collectors. Members are encouraged, but by no means expected, to contribute articles, photographs and art work to the magazine.

US
GESNERIAD JOURNAL. **Added/Corp** Gesneriad Society International. Vol. 1, No. 1 (May/June 1989)-. Periodical. English. bm. $16.50 US; $21.50 other.

Gesneriad Society International, 11510 124th Terrace, Largo FL 34648. **Tel** (813)585-4247. ***Separated from*** *Gesneriad Saintpaulia News, 0016-3627.*

IT/0394-0853
GIARDINI. [Giardini]. (1986)-. Periodical. Italian. mo. $87.00. Zanfi Editori SRL, Via Emilia Ovest 954, CP 433, 41100 Modena Italy. **Tel** 011 39 59 891700, FAX 011 39 59 225719, telex 52 22 72. **UDC** 635.

IT
GIARDINO FIORITO, IL. Added/Corp Societa Italiana "Amici dei Fiori". (?)-. Periodical. Italian. Ten times a year. L73000 (Italy); L98000 (other). Edagricole, PO Box 2157, 40100 Bologna Italy. **Tel** 011 39 51 492211 Ext. 22, FAX 011 39 51 493660, telex 510336 EDAGRI. Index available in last issue of volume--attached.

US/0431-9168
GLADIO GRAMS. *Ceased.* [Gladio grams]. **Added/Corp** North American Gladiolus Council. Commercial Growers Division. (1970)-(1993). Periodical. English. qt. Florida Flower Association, PO Box 1569, Ft Myers FL 33902. **DD** 635.

UK/0072-4580
GLADIOLUS ANNUAL : BEING THE YEARBOOK OF THE BRITISH GLADIOLUS SOCIETY, THE. Added/Corp British Gladiolus Society. (1927)-. English. an. Comes with British Gladiolus Society membership; £8.50 UK, £12.00 other (membership). British Gladiolus Society, 24 Terrace Mayfield, Ashbourne, Derbyshire DE6 2JL England. **Tel** 011 44 335 345443. **LC** SB413.G5; G64.

US/1049-0000
GOLF & SPORTSTURF. *Title Change.* (GOLF & SPORTSTURF : THE OFFICIAL PUBLICATION OF THE SPORTS TURF MANAGERS ASSOCIATION.). [Golf sportsTURF]. **Added/Corp** Sports Turf Managers Association. **VFOAT** Golf & Sports Turf; Golf and SportsTurf; Golf and Sports Turf; SportsTurf Magazine. Vol. 6, No. 1 (Jan. 1990)-(Jan. 1992). Periodical. English. mo. Golf & SportsTurf, PO Box 8420, Van Nuys CA 91409. **DD** 716. ***Continues*** *SportsTurf, 0890-0167.* ***Continued by*** *SportsTURF (Van Nuys, Calif.), 1061-687X.*

AT
GOOD FRUIT & VEGETABLES. English. mo. 39.00Aus$ (Australia); 58.00Aus$ (China, Papua, New Guinea, Fiji, Indonesia, Malaysia, India, China, & Japan); 66.50Aus$ (other). Rural Press / Victoria, PO Box 160, Port Melbourne Victoria 3207 Australia. **Tel** 11 61 3 2870900, telex 35668. **ED** Tony Biggs. Index available. **Bk Rev. Ad Acc. Circ:** 9,000.
Desc: Catered to fruit and vegetable growers. Provides technical and market information to growers.

US/0046-6174
GOODFRUIT GROWER, THE. [Goodfruit grow.]. **VAT** Good Fruit Grower. (1946)-. Periodical. English. Seventeen times a year. $30.00 (one year), $75.00 (three year). Washington State Fruit Commission, PO Box 9219, 1005 Tieton Drive, Yakima WA 98902. **Tel** (509)575-2315. **ED** Phillip D. Shelton. **DD** 634. Index available. **Ad Acc. Circ:** 12,600.
Desc: Covers Pacific Northwest tree fruit industry: production, handling, storage, packaging, marketing, promotion, research and economics of apples, pears, cherries, plums, nectarines and grapes.
Ind/Abst Hortic. Abstr.; Postharvest News Inf.

US/0147-3891
GREEN BOOK BUYERS' GUIDE FOR GARDEN MERCHANDISE. (HOME AND GARDEN SUPPLY MERCHANDISER. GREEN BOOK.). **VFOAT** Annual Green Book Buyers' Guide. English. an. $10.00. Garden Supply Retailer, PO Box 2400, Minnetonka MN 55343. **Tel** (612)931-0211, telex 910-576-2905. **ED** Kay M Olson. **LC** HD9999.G36; H65. **DD** 380.1/45/681763105. **Bk Rev. Ad Acc. Circ:** 41,000 (ctrl). ***Continues in part*** *Home and Garden Supply Merchandiser, 0018-3954.*
Desc: Directory of products, brands, manufacturers, representatives, distributors, organizations and power equipment specifications. Published as the Garden Supply Retailer's November issue.

US/0895-772X
GREEN MARKETS DEALER REPORT. [Green mark. deal. rep.]. **VFOAT** GM Dealer Report; Dealer Report. (1987)-. Periodical. English. Fifty-two times a year. $267.00 North America; $495.00 other. Pike & Fischer Inc., 4600 East-West Highway, Suite 200, Bethesda MD 20814-1438. **Tel** (301)654-6262, FAX (301)654-6297. **DD** 338.

US/1064-0118
GREEN PRINTS. [Green prints]. (1990)-. Periodical. English. qt. $14.00 US; $17.00 Canada and Mexico; $23.00 Europe. Green Prints, PO Box 1355, Fairview NC 28730. **Tel** (704)628-1902. **ED** Pat Stone. **DD** 635. **Circ:** 1,000.

US/0190-9789
GREEN SCENE, THE. Added/Corp Pennsylvania Horticultural Society, Philadelphia. (1972)-. Periodical. English. Six times a year (Jan., Mar., May, July, Sept., Nov.). $9.75 one year; $19.50 two years. Pennsylvania Horticultural Society, 325 Walnut Street, Philadelphia PA 19106-2777. **Tel** (215)625-8250, FAX (215)625-9342. **ED** Jean Byrne. Index available (Vol. 20, (July iss., $15.00)). cum. index. **Ad Acc, Adv Mgr:** Joe Robinson, **Tel** (215)625-8280. **Circ:** 13,500 (ctrl).
Desc: Feature articles about horticulture in the Delaware Valley. Written by local professional and amateur horticulturists, botanists and landscape architects.
Ind/Abst Garden Lit. (1992-).

US/0749-2138
GREEN THUMB NEWS. (GREEN THUMB NEWS / DENVER BOTANIC GARDENS.). **Added/Corp** Denver Botanic Gardens. Denver Botanic Gardens. Educational Dept. No. 83-4 (April 1983)-. Periodical. English. mo. $25.00 (comes with membership). Denver Botanic Gardens, 909 York Street, Denver CO 80206. **Tel** (303)575-3751. **ED** Patricia A. Pachuta. **Bk Rev. Circ:** 7,000 (ctrl). ***Continues*** *Green Thumb Newsletter.*
Desc: Special gardens events and horticultural information.
Ind/Abst Garden Lit. (1992-).

US/0160-3965
GREEN THUMB (OAKLAND). (GREEN THUMB.). Periodical. English. mo. $3.50 US; $5.00 other. Green Thumb, PO Box 2941, Oakland CA 94618.

CN/0712-4996
GREENHOUSE CANADA. [Greenh. Can.]. Vol. 1, No. 1 (Dec. 1980)-. Periodical. English. mo. 25.00Can$ (one year), 40.00Can$ (two year) Canada; 36.00Can$ (one year), 65.00Can$ (two year) US; 48.00Can$ other. NCC Publishing, 222 Argyle Avenue, Delhi Ontario N4B 2Y2 Canada. **Tel** (519)582-2513, FAX (519)582-4040. **ED** James Brown. **DD** 635/.0483. **Ad Acc, Adv Mgr:** Mark Crandon, **Tel** (519)582-2513. **Circ:** 4,500 (ctrl).
Desc: Editorial comment of interest to growers and affiliated persons in Canada's national commercial greenhouse industry.

US/0745-7324
GREENHOUSE GROWER. [Greenh. grow.]. Vol. 1, No. 1 (Jan. 1983)-. Periodical. English. Fourteen times a year. $18.75 (one year), $33.75 (two year). Meister Publishing Company, 37733 Euclid Avenue, Willoughby OH 44094-5992. **Tel** (216)942-2000, (800)572-7740, FAX (216)942-0662. **DD** 338. **[CCC].**
Desc: Targeted to commercial growers.
Ind/Abst Vocat. Search (Jan. 1993-).

CN/0527-5369
GREENHOUSE INDUSTRY. [Greenh. ind.]. **Main/Corp** Canada. Statistics Canada. Horticultural Crops Unit. **Added/Corp** Canada. Dominion Bureau of Statistics. Crops Section. Statistics Canada. Crops Section. Statistics Canada. Horticultural Crops Unit. Statistics Canada. Horticultural Crops Unit. L'Industrie des Cultures de Serre. **VFOAT** Industrie des Cultures de Serre. (1955)-. English (French). an. 30.00Can$ Canada; $36.00 US; $42.00 other. Statistics Canada, Publications Sales & Services, Main Building Room 1710, Ottawa Ontario K1A 0T6 Canada. **Tel** (613)951-5078, (800)267-6677, FAX (613)951-1584, telex 053-3585. **LC** SB415.6.C2; C35a. **DD** 338.1/750483/0971. ***Continues*** *Greenhouse Industry, 0527-5369.*
Desc: Identifies a number of establishments, area under glass, value of sales, flower production by type of crops and financial statistics for Canada and the provinces.

US
GREENHOUSE IPM UPDATE. Added/Corp Cornell Cooperative Extension. **VAT** Greenhouse Integrated Pest Management Update. (1992)-. Periodical. English. Twenty-six times a year. $30.00. Cooperative Extension of Suffolk County, 246 Griffing Avenue, Riverhead NY 11901. **Tel** (516)727-7850, FAX (516)727-7130. **ED** Ralph N. Freeman. **Circ:** 70.
Desc: Information for greenhouse growers.

US/0744-8988
GREENHOUSE MANAGER. [Greenh. manager]. **VFOAT** News for the Greenhouse Manager. 1982-. Periodical. English. mo. $24.00 (one year), $44.00 (two years), $59.00 (three years). Branch-Smith Publishing, PO Box 1868, Fort Worth TX 76101. **Tel** (817)332-8236, FAX (817)877-1862. **ED** Mike Branch. **Bk Rev. Ad Acc. Circ:** 15,000 (ctrl).
Desc: Commercial greenhouse growers read Greenhouse Manager to learn ways to grow and market better bedding plants, foliage plants, flowering pot plants, cut flowers and vegetables.

US/1053-7104
GREENHOUSE PRODUCT NEWS. [Greenh. prod. news]. Vol. 1, No. 1 (Sept. 1990)-. Periodical. English. mo. $24.00 (one year), $40.00 (two year), $60.00 (three year) US; $45.00 (onw year), $60.00 (two year), $75.00 (three year) other. Scranton Gillette Communications Inc., 380 East Northwest Highway, Des Plaines IL 60016-2282. **Tel** (708)298-6622, FAX (708)390-0408. **DD** 635. cum. index. **Ad Acc. Circ:** 20,000.
Desc: Contains information on basic care of greenhouses, also lists up coming shows.

CN/0712-1822
GREENSCAPE. (GREENSCAPE : CANADIAN LANDSCAPE AND OUTDOOR LIVING.). [Greenscape]. **VFOAT** Greenscape Magazine. Vol. 1, No. 1 (Apr. 1981)-. Periodical. English. ir. Free. Greenscape Pala Graphics Ltd, Suite 19/6219 Dorman Road, Mississauga Ontario L4V 1H2 Canada. **DD** 712/.0971. ctrl circ.

DK/0903-0719
GRN VIDEN. HAVEBRUG / STATENS PLANTEAVLSFORSG. Added/Corp Statens Planteavlsforsg (Denmark). **VFOAT** Havebrug. (19??)-. Monographic series. Danish. ir. Price varies per volume.
Ind/Abst Biocont. News Inf.; Ornamental Hort. (1991-); Plant Breed. Abstr.; Plant Grow. Reg. Abstr.; Seed Abstr.

NE
GROEI EN BLOEI. See Biology-Botany.

NE/0166-3534
GROEN. [Groen]. **Added/Corp** Stichting Vakblad voor de Boomkwekerij (Netherlands). (1970)-. Academic Scholarly Publication. Dutch. mo. Fl74.53. S I Publikaties B V, Postbus 3184, 3760 DD Soest Netherlands. **Tel** 011 31 02155 24385.
Ind/Abst EMBASE; For. Prod. Abstr.; For. Abstr.; Hortic. Abstr.; Leis. Recreat. Tour. Abstr.; Rural Dev. Abstr.; Soils Fert.; World Agric. Econ.

NE/0017-4491
GROENTEN EN FRUIT : G & F. Added/Corp Netherlands. Centraal Bureau van de Tuinbouwveilingen. **VFOAT** G & F. (1945)-. Periodical. Dutch. ir. Fl537.00 (includes Glasgroenten, Fruit, Vollegrondsgroenten and Paddestoelen sections). Misset Uitgeverij BV, Postbus 9000, 6800 DA Arnhem Netherlands. **Tel** 011 31 85 209911. **Bk Rev. Ad Acc. Circ:** 17,000. ***Absorbed*** *Tuinderij.*
Desc: Professional journal on growing vegetables and fruit.
Ind/Abst Agric. Eng. Abstr. (1991-); Biodeter. Abstr.; Crop Physiol. Abstr.; Hortic. Abstr.; Irr. Drain. Abstr.; Leis. Recreat. Tour. Abstr.; Maize Abstr.; Ornamental Hort. (19??-19??); Plant Breed. Abstr.; Plant Grow. Reg. Abstr.; Postharvest News Inf.; Rev. Agric. Entomol.; Rev. Plant Pathol.; Rural Dev. Abstr.; Seed Abstr.; Soils Fert.; World Agric. Econ.

NE/0925-9708
GROENTEN + FRUIT. ALGEMEEN. [Groenten + fruit, Alg.]. **VFOAT** Groenten en Fruit. Algemeen. (1991)-. Periodical. Dutch. ir. Misset Uitgeverij BV, Postbus 4, 7000 BA Doetinchem, Netherlands. **Tel** 011 31 8340 49911. **UDC** 634 + 635. ***Continues in part*** *Groenten & Fruit (Den Haag. 1988), 0924-3585; Tuinderij, 0041-3984* ***and*** *Vollegrond (Doetinchem), 0922-3576.*

NE/0925-9694
GROENTEN + FRUIT. FRUIT. [Groenten + fruit, Fruit]. **VFOAT** Groenten en Fruit. Fruit. (1991)-. Periodical. Dutch. ir. Fl311.00. Misset Uitgeverij BV, Postbus 4, 7000 BA Doetinchem, Netherlands. **Tel** 011 31 8340 49911. **UDC** 634. ***Continues in part*** *Groenten & Fruit (Den Haag. 1988), 0924-3585; Tuinderij, 0041-3984* ***and*** *Vollegrond (Doetinchem), 0922-3576.*

NE/0925-9686
GROENTEN + FRUIT. GLASGROENTEN. [Groenten + Fruit, Glasgroenten]. **VFOAT** Groenten en Fruit. Glasgroenten. (1991)-. Periodical. Dutch. ir. Fl372.00. Misset Uitgeverij BV, Postbus 4, 7000 BA Doetinchem, Netherlands. **Tel** 011 31 8340 49911. **UDC** 635 :631.544. ***Continues in part*** *Groenten & Fruit (Den Haag. 1988), 0924-3585; Tuinderij, 0041-3984* ***and*** *Vollegrond (Doetinchem), 0922-3576.*
Ind/Abst Agric. Eng. Abstr.

NE/0925-9716
GROENTEN + FRUIT. PADDESTOELEN. [Groenten fruit, Paddest.]. **VFOAT** Groenten en Fruit. Paddestoelen. (1991)-. Periodical. Dutch. ir. Fl276.00. Misset Uitgeverij BV, Postbus 4, 7000 BA Doetinchem, Netherlands. **Tel** 011 31 8340 49911. **UDC** 635.8. ***Continues in part*** *Groenten & Fruit (Den Haag. 1988), 0924-3585; Tuinderij, 0041-3984* ***and*** *Vollegrond (Doetinchem), 0922-3576.*

NE/0925-9678
GROENTEN + FRUIT. VOLLEGRONDSGROENTEN. [Groenten + fruit, Vollegrondsgroenten]. **VFOAT** Groenten en Fruit. Vollegrondsgroenten. (1991)-. Periodical. Dutch. ir. Misset Uitgeverij BV, Postbus 4, 7000 BA Doetinchem, Netherlands. **Tel** 011 31 8340 49911. **UDC** 635. ***Continues in part*** *Groenten & Fruit (Den Haag. 1988), 0924-3585; Tuinderij, 0041-3984* ***and*** *Vollegrond (Doetinchem), 0922-3576.*

US/0017-4688
GROUNDS MAINTENANCE. [Grounds maint.]. Vol. 1 (Jan. 1966)-. Periodical. English. mo. $30.59 US; $36.47 other. Intertec Publishing Corporation, 9800 Metcalf, Overland Park KS 66212. **Tel** (913)341-1300. **(Subscription address:** Intertec Publishing Corporation, PO Box 2901, Overland Park KS 66282.**) ED** Kathy Copley. **LC** SB469; .G7. **DD** 635.9,05. **[CCC]. Bk Rev. Ad Acc. Circ:** 45,000 (ctrl). available on microfilm and microfiche from University Microfilms International (UMI).
Desc: Provides technical and managerial guidance for professional grounds care managers and golf course superintendents; covers grounds care, irrigation

techniques, turf management, equipment, chemical selection and management principles.
Ind/Abst AGRICOLA [Select. Cov.].

US/0742-5511
GROUNDS MANAGEMENT FORUM. [Grounds manage. forum]. V. 3, No. 7 (July 1979)-. Periodical. English. mo. Free membership. Prof Grounds Management Society, 12 Galloway Avenue/Suite 1E, Cockeysville MD 21030. **Tel** (410)667-1833. ***Continues*** *Manager's Memo.*

UK/0017-4696
GROUNDSMAN. [Groundsman]. (1952)-. Periodical. English. Twelve times a year. £39.50 UK; £44.00 other; £69.00 US. The Institute of Groundsmanship, 19-23 Church Street, The Agora, Wolverton, Milton Keynes, Buckinghamshire MK12 5LG England. **Tel** 011 44 908312511, FAX 011 44 908 311140. **(Subscription address:** Anthony Harvey Associates, 111 High Holborn, London WC1V 6JS England.**) ED** Richard Frost. **Bk Rev. Ad Acc, Adv Mgr:** Anthony Harvey, **Tel** (077)837-9363. **Circ:** 5000 (ctrl).
Desc: The official international journal of the Institute of Groundsmanship.

UK
GROW ELECTRIC HANDBOOK. V. 1 May 1972-. Periodical. English.

UK/0017-4785
GROWER. Vol. 1, (19??)-. Periodical. English. wk. £47.50 UK; £55.00 Eire; £62.00 other. Grower Publications Ltd, 50 Doughty Street, London WC1N 2LS England. **Tel** 071 405-0364, FAX 01 831 2230, telex 8954111. **ED** Peter Rogers. Index available. **Bk Rev. Ad Acc. Circ:** 14,000.
Desc: Commercial horticulture's top selling paper with the latest news, market prices, experimental reports, cultural information and recent developments occurring in the industry.
Ind/Abst Hortic. Abstr.; Plant Breed. Abstr.

US/0737-9935
GROWER ADVISOR. (GROWER ADVISOR / CALIFORNIA AVOCADO ADVISORY BOARD.). [Grow. advis.]. Periodical. English. mo. California Avocado Advisory Board, 4533-B Macarthur Blvd., Newport CA 92660.

US/0276-9433
GROWER TALKS. [Grow. talks]. Vol. 1 (May 1937)-. Periodical. English. mo. $22.00 US; $28.00 Canada and Mexico; $75.00 other. Growth Talks, 335 North River Street, Batavia IL 60510. **Tel** (708)208-9080. **ED** Debbie Hamrick. **Ad Acc. Circ:** 16,000.
Desc: Edited for the commercial greenhouse grower of bedding plants, pot plants, foliage and cut flowers.
Ind/Abst Garden Lit. (1992-).

CN/0017-4777
GROWER (TORONTO). (THE GROWER.). **Added/Corp** Ontario Fruit and Vegetable Growers' Association. (Mar. 1952)-. Periodical. English. Twelve times a year. 25.00Can$ Canada; 35.00Can$ other. Ontario Fruit and Vegetable Growers Association, 355 Elmira Road Unit 103, Guelph Ontario N1K 1S5 Canada. **Tel** (519)763-6160, FAX (519)763-6604. **ED** Blair Adams (phone: (519)763-8728). **Ad Acc, Adv Mgr:** James Shaw, **Tel** (416)463-0007. **Circ:** 11,500 (ctrl). ***Supersedes*** *Canadian Grower.*
Ind/Abst Crop Physiol. Abstr.

US/1043-2906
GROWING EDGE (CORVALLIS, OR.), THE. (THE GROWING EDGE.). [Grow. edge]. (1989)-. Periodical. English. Four times a year. $24.95 US and Canada; $45.00 other. New Moon Publishing Inc., PO Box 90, Corvallis OR 97339. **Tel** (503)757-8477, FAX (503)757-0028. **ED** Don Parker, PO Box 1027, Corvallis, OR 97339; Telephone: (503)757-2511. **LC** SB450.9; .G76. **DD** 635. Index available. **Bk Rev. Ad Acc. Circ:** 40,000.
Desc: High tech indoor and outdoor gardening including hydroponics, controlled environment, HID lighting, organic methods, water conservation, environmental gardening.
Ind/Abst Garden Lit. (1992-).

AT
GROWING NATIVE PLANTS. ***Ceased.*** **Added/Corp** Canberra Botanic Gardens. Vol. 1 (1971)-Vol. 12 (19??). Periodical. English. an. Australian Government Publishing Service, GPO Box 84, Canberra ACT 2601 Australia. **Tel** 011 61 6 2954411, FAX 011 61 6 2954455. **LC** SB439; .G76. **DD** 635.9,676,0994.

US
GROWING POINTS, CENTRAL COAST COUNTRIES. **Main/Corp** California. University, Berkeley. Cooperative Extension Service. (June 1975)-. Periodical. English. Twelve times a year. Free (Cooperative Extension Programs); $8.00 others. University of California Cooperative Extension, 174 224 West Winston Avenue, Hayward CA 94544. **Tel** (510)670-5200. **(Subscription address:** UC Regents, UCCE 1682 Novato Boulevard, Novato CA 94947.**)** cum. index.
Ind/Abst AGRICOLA [Full Cov.].

CN/1187-2268
GUIDE DE L'ACHETEUR ANNUEL - EXPOSITION COMMERCIALE DE L'HORTICULTURE ORNEMENTALE. (GUIDE DE L'ACHETEUR ANNUEL.). [Guide achet. annu. - Expo. commer. hortic. ornem.]. **Added/Corp** Exposition Commerciale de l'Horticulture Ornementale. (1991)-. French. $25.00. Editions Versicolores Inc., 1320 Boulevard Saint-Joseph, A Marchand Quebec, G2K 1G2 Quebec, Canada. **Tel** (418)628-8690, (800)463-1576, FAX (418)628-0524. **DD** 635. ***Continues*** *Guide de l'Acheteur ... des Produits et Equipements Horticoles., 1187-2292.*

US/0271-3373
GUIDE TO SPECIFICATIONS FOR INTERIOR LANDSCAPING, A. [Guide specif. inter. landsc.]. **Main/Corp** Associated Landscape Contractors of America. English. Associated Landscape Contractors, 405 North Washington Street, Falls Church VA 22046. **Tel** (703)241-4004. **LC** SB419; .A77A. **DD** 635.9/65/0212.

HU
GYUMOLCSTERMESZTES. **Added/Corp** Gyumolcstermesztes, Feldolgozas es Tarolas Korszerusitese Kutatasi Celprogram. Kerteszeti Kutato Intezet. **VFOAT** Fruit Growing. Vol. 1 (1974)-. Periodical. Hungarian (summaries and/or abstracts in English, German, French and Russian).

KO
HANGUK CHONGWON HAKHOE CHI. **VFOAT** Journal of the Korean Traditional Garden Research Association. V. 1- No. 1- (Oct. 1982)-. Periodical. Korean (summaries and/or abstracts in English). Hanguk Chongwon Hakhoe, 108-5 Chongun-dong Chongno-ku, Seoul 1 Korea. **LC** SB451.36.K6; H36.

KO/0253-6498
HANGUK WONYE HAKHOE CHI. [Hangug nwennyei haghoi ji]. **Main/Corp** Hanguk Wonye Hakhoe. **VFOAT** Journal of the Korean Society for Horticultural Science. Academic Scholarly Publication. English (Korean). Korean Society for Horticultural Sciene, c/o Department of Horticulture, College of Agriculture, Seoul National University, Suweon Korea. **LC** SB317.5; .H36A. **CODEN** HWHCD5. Documents available from BIOSIS Document Express, CASDDS.
Ind/Abst AGRICOLA; Biol. Abstr. (1989-); Chem. Abstr.; Crop Physiol. Abstr.; Food Sci. Technol. Abstr.; Hortic. Abstr.; Ornamental Hort. (1991-); Plant Grow. Reg. Abstr.; Rev. Plant Pathol.; Seed Abstr.; Soils Fert.

UK/0266-0539
HARDWARE & GARDEN REVIEW. [Hardw. gard. rev.]. **VFOAT** Hardware and Garden Review; HGR + DIY. Hardware & Garden Review. (1983)-. Periodical. English. mo. £28.00 UK; £34.00 other. Faversham House Group Ltd, Faversham House, 111 Saint James Road, Croydon Surrey CR9 2TH England. **Tel** 011 44 81 684 4082. ***Continues*** *Hardware Review, 0017-7733.*

II
HARYANA JOURNAL OF HORTICULTURAL SCIENCES. **Added/Corp** Horticultural Society of Haryana. Vol. 1 (Jan./Dec. 1972)-. Periodical. English (summaries and/or abstracts in Sanskrit). qt. $75.00. Horticulture Society of Haryana, Hissar, India. **(Subscription address:** Prints India, 11 Darya Ganj, New Delhi, 110002 India, (Phone: 011 91 11 3268645)**)**
Ind/Abst Agrofor. Abstr. (1991-); Biodeter. Abstr. (19??-19??); Crop Physiol. Abstr.; Field Crop Abstr.; Food Sci. Technol. Abstr.; Hortic. Abstr.; Ornamental Hort. (19??-19??); Plant Breed. Abstr.; Plant Grow. Reg. Abstr.; Postharvest News Inf.; Potato Abstr.; Protozoolog. Abstr.; Rev. Agric. Entomol.; Rev. Plant Pathol.; Seed Abstr.; Soils Fert.; Weed Abstr.

PL
HASLO OGRODNICZE. **Added/Corp** Towarzystwo Ogrodnicze w Krakowie. Panstwowe Wydawnictwo Rolnicze i Lesne. Vol. 33, No. 1 (1976)-. Periodical. Polish. mo. $51.00. **(Subscription address:** ARS Polona, PO Box 1001, 00068 Warsaw Poland.**)**

YU/1018-1806
HELIA (NOVI SAD). (HELIA : SCIENTIFIC BULLETIN OF THE F.A.O. RESEARCH NETWORK ON SUNFLOWER.). [Helia]. **Added/Corp** F.A.O. Research Network on Sunflower. Poljoprivredni Fakultet u Novom Sadu. Institut za Ratarstvo i Povrtarstvo. (19??)-. Bulletin. English (Spanish; summaries and/or abstracts in French and Spanish).
Ind/Abst Field Crop Abstr.; Plant Breed. Abstr.; Plant Genet. Resour. Abstr.; Rev. Plant Pathol.; Seed Abstr.

US/0163-9900
HERB QUARTERLY, THE. [Herb q.]. No. 1, (Apr. 1979)-. Periodical. English. Four times a year (Mar., June, Sept., Dec.). $24.00 one year; $45.00 two years. Herb Quarterly, PO Box 689, San Anselmo CA 94960. **Tel** (415)455-9540. **(Subscription address:** P.O. Box 548, Boiling Springs, PA 17007-0548**) ED** Linda Sparrowe. **LC** SB351.H5; H357. **DD** 635/.7/05. Index available. **Bk Rev**, (Qty: 20). **Ad Acc, Adv Mgr:** J. Keough, **Tel** (415)455-9540. **Circ:** 25,000.
Desc: Articles concerning herbs as they relate to gardens, garden design cooking, crafts, remedies, cosmetics, folk wisdom and lore, business and history.
Ind/Abst Garden Lit. (1992-).

US/1048-3160
HERB, SPICE, AND MEDICINAL PLANT DIGEST, THE. (THE HERB, SPICE, AND MEDICINAL PLANT DIGEST / PREPARED BY THE DEPARTMENT OF PLANT AND SOIL SCIENCES.). [Herb spice med. plant dig.]. **Added/Corp** University of Massachusetts at Amherst. Dept. of Plant and Soil Sciences. University of Massachusetts at Amherst. Cooperative Extension Service. Vol. 1, No. 1 (Winter 1983)-. Periodical. English. Four times a year (Mar., June, Sept., Dec.). $10.00. University of Massachusetts / Department of Plant Soil Science, C/O Le Craker, Amherst MA 01003. **Tel** (413)545-2347, FAX (413)545-1242. **ED** Lyle E. Craker. **DD** 633. **Bk Rev**, (Qty: 4-5). **Circ:** 1,000.
Desc: Growing marketing and information on herbs.
Ind/Abst AGRICOLA [Full Cov.]; Garden Lit. (1992-).

NO/0800-5419
HERBA. **See** Food and Food Industry.

US/1055-8578
HERBAL ROSE REPORT, THE. [Herb. rose rep.]. (1990)-. Periodical. English. qt. $20.00 US; $28.00 Canada. Jeanne Rose, the Grand-Dame of Herbs, Anne Labe - Editor, 194 Cypress Place, Sausalito CA 94965-1509. **DD** 615.

US/0740-5979
HERBARIST, THE. [Herbarist]. **Added/Corp** Herb Society of America. Vol. 1 (1935)-. Periodical. English. an. $7.50. Herb Society of America Inc., 9019 Kirtland Chardon Road, Mentor OH 44060. **Tel** (216)256-0514, FAX (216)256-0541. **ED** Mrs. Dorothy Fish. Index available. cum. index. **Ad Acc, Adv Mgr:** Linda Wells. **Circ:** 3,000.
Ind/Abst AGRICOLA [Select. Cov.]; Garden Lit. (1992-).

US/8756-9418
HERBERTIA (1984). (HERBERTIA.). [Herbertia]. **Added/Corp** American Plant Life Society. Vol. 40 (1984)-. English. an. $30.00 (one year), $55.00 (two year), $80.00 (three year). International Bulb Society, PO Box 4928, Culver City CA 90230. **Tel** (310)827-3229. **ED** R. Mitchel Beauchamp. **LC** QK1; .P67. **DD** 584/.25/05. Index available. cum. index. **Bk Rev. Pr Rev. Circ:** 850. ***Continues*** *Plant Life, 0275-0783.*
Desc: Covers the taxonomy and culture of bulbous plants.
Ind/Abst AGRICOLA [Full Cov.].

II
HIMALAYAN PLANT JOURNAL. Vol. 1, No. 1 (June 1982)-. Periodical. English. sa. $35.00 institutions, $25.00 individuals. Himalayan Plant Journal, Primulaceae Books, Abhijit Villa, BPO Ecchey, Kalimpong 734301 India. **Tel** KALIMPONG 673. **(Subscription address:** Prints India, 11 Darya Ganj, New Delhi 110002 India.**) ED** Udai C Pradhan, Tej K Pradhan. Index available. **Bk Rev. Ad Acc. Circ:** 300 (ctrl).
Desc: A scientific journal devoted to the dissemination of knowledge on Himalayan Flora. Non-profit, supported by subscriptions and profits generated by primulaceae books.

●US/1067-5973
HISTORICAL GARDENER, THE. [Hist. gard.]. (Spring 1992)-. Periodical. English. qt. **DD** 635.
Ind/Abst Garden Lit. (1992-).

US
HO. **Main/Corp** Purdue University. Cooperative Extension Service. **Added/Corp** Purdue University. Horticultural Dept. No. 1 (1975)-. Monographic series. English. Price varies per volume.
Ind/Abst AGRICOLA [Select. Cov.].

US/1040-6212
HOBBY GREENHOUSE. [Hobby greenh.]. **Added/Corp** Hobby Greenhouse Association (Bedford, Mass.). Vol. 8, No. 1 (Winter 1986)-. Periodical. English. qt (Feb., May, Aug., Nov.). $12.00 (comes with membership). Hobby Greenhouse Association, 8 Glen Terrace, Bedford MA 01730. **Tel** (617)275-0377, FAX (617)275-5693. **ED** Janice L. Hale. **DD** 635. Index available. **Bk Rev**, (Qty: 20). **Ad Acc. Circ:** 2,100 (ctrl). ***Continues*** *Planter.*

US
HOME AND CONDO. English. mo (with combined April/May, June/July/Aug., Sept./Oct., and Nov./Dec.). $10.95 US; $30.90 other. Gulfshore Publishing Company, 2900 Horseshoe Drive South, Suite 400, Naples FL 33942. **Tel** (813)643-3933. **ED** Janis Lyn Johnson. **Ad Acc. Circ:** 25,000 (ctrl).

US/1048-8537
HOME LANDSCAPE PLANS. [Home landsc. plans]. **VFOAT** Landscape Plans. (1990)-. English. an. $4.95. Practical Homeowner Publishing Company, 825 7th Avenue/4th Floor, New York NY 10019. **DD** 712.

BL/0103-3700
HORTI SUL. [Horti sul]. (1989)-. Periodical. Portuguese. ir.
Ind/Abst Plant Breed. Abstr.; Weed Abstr.

BL
HORTICULTURA BRASILEIRA. Added/Corp Sociedade de Olericultura do Brasil. Vol. 1, No. 1 (Maio 1983)-. Periodical. Portuguese (English). sa. ***Continues*** *Revista de Olericultura.*
Ind/Abst Field Crop Abstr.; Hortic. Abstr.; Irr. Drain. Abstr.; Plant Breed. Abstr.; Rev. Agric. Entomol.; Rev. Plant Pathol.; Seed Abstr.; Soils Fert.; Sug. Indus. Abstr.

UK/0018-5280
HORTICULTURAL ABSTRACTS. See Gardening and Horticulture-Abstracting, Bibliographies and Statistics.

NE
HORTICULTURAL ECONOMIC NEWSLETTER. (19??)-. Newsletter. English. sa. $15.00. International Society for Horticultural Science, Postbus 29703, 2502 LS Den Haag Netherlands. **Tel** 011 31 70 3614161.

UK
HORTICULTURAL ENTERPRISES.
Main/Corp Great Britain Agricultural Development and Advisory Service. **Added/Corp** Great Britain. Agricultural Development and Advisory Service. (1973)-. Monographic series. English. Price varies per volume.

US/0886-5779
HORTICULTURAL NEWS (NEW BRUNSWICK, N.J.). (HORTICULTURAL NEWS.). **VFOAT** State Horticultural Society News. Vol. 23, No. 1 (Jan. 1942)-. Periodical. English. qt (4 issues). $20.00 (membership dues for 1 year to the NJSHS, includes subscription to "Horticultural News"), $10.00 (library) US; $15.00 (library), $25.00 other. New Jersey State Horticultural Society, PO Box 116, Clayton NJ 08312-0116. **Tel** (609)863-0110, FAX (609)881-4191. **DD** 635. Index available. cum. index. **Bk Rev. Ad Acc. Circ:** 300 (ctrl). ***Continues*** *New Jersey State Horticultural Society News.*
Desc: Contains news pertaining to horticulture in New Jersey.
Ind/Abst AGRICOLA.

US/0894-8429
HORTICULTURAL PRODUCTS REVIEW. ***Title Change.*** [Hortic. prod. rev.]. **Added/Corp** United States. Foreign Agricultural Service. United States. World Agricultural Outlook Board. (Jan. 1987)-(1993). Government Publication. English. mo. Department of Agriculture / Foreign Agricultural Service, 14th Street and Independence Avenue SW, Washington DC 20250-1000. **Tel** (202)720-3935, FAX (202)720-7729. **LC** HD9000.1; .F66. **DD** 338.1/75/05. **CODEN** HPREED. **Circ:** 916. available on microfiche. Documents available from Documents on Demand. ***Continues*** *Foreign Agriculture Circular. Horticultural Products.* ***Continued by*** *World Horticultural Trade & U.S. Export Opportunities.*
Desc: Features information on general developments in the world fruit and vegetable industry. Covers fresh and dried fruit and nuts, processed fruits, nursery products, wine, beer and hops. Includes production, consumption, trade data and analysis.
Ind/Abst AGRICOLA [Full Cov.]; Am. Stat. Index (1987-); BioBusiness.

US/0163-7851
HORTICULTURAL REVIEWS. [Hortic. rev.]. **Added/Corp** American Society for Horticultural Science. Vol. 1 (1979)-. Academic Scholarly Publication. English. ir. John Wiley & Sons, Inc., 605 Third Avenue, New York NY 10158-0012. **Tel** (212)850-6000, (212)850-6645, FAX (212)850-6088, telex 12-7063. **(Subscription address:** John Wiley & Sons / England, Baffins Lane, Chichester, West Sussex PO19 1UD England.**) ED** Jules Jamick. **LC** SB317.5; .H67. **DD** 635/.05. **CODEN** HORED5. Documents available from CASDDS.
Desc: A continuing resource series reporting current advances in horticulture.
Ind/Abst AGRICOLA [Full Cov.]; Chem. Abstr.; Crop Physiol. Abstr.; Food Sci. Technol. Abstr.; For. Abstr.; Hortic. Abstr.; Ornamental Hort. (1991-); Plant Grow. Reg. Abstr.; Postharvest News Inf.; Rev. Agric. Entomol.; Rev. Med. Vet. Mycology; Rev. Plant Pathol.; Seed Abstr.; Soils Fert.

US/0018-5329
HORTICULTURE. [Horticulture]. **Added/Corp** Massachusetts Horticultural Society. Vol. 1, No. 1 (Dec. 3, 1904)-Vol. 37, No. 14 (July 25, 1923) ; New Series, Vol. 1, No. 1 (Aug. 1, 1923)-. Periodical. English. Ten times a year. $24.00 (one year), $42.00 (two year), $56.00 (three year). Horticulture, 98 Washington Street, Boston MA 02114. **Tel** (617)742-5600. **(Subscription address:** Neodata / Colorado, PO Box 2606, Boulder Boulder CO 80322.**) LC** SB1; .H86. Index available. **Bk Rev. Ad Acc. Circ:** 125,000 (ctrl). available on microfilm and microfiche from University Microfilms International (UMI). Documents available from UMI Article Clearinghouse, Magazine Collection.
Desc: Authoritative articles by and about expert gardeners, as well as practical advice, photography, and useful information for both the novice and expert gardener.
Ind/Abst Acad. Abstr. Full Text Elite (Jan. 1984-) [Full Txt.]; Acad. Abstr. (Jan. 1984-); Acad. Ind. [Computer File] (1992-); Acad. Search (Jan. 1984-); Access (1980-); Biogr. Index; Biol. Agric. Index; Biol. Dig.; Book Rev. Index; Consum. Index Prod. Eval. Inf. Source; Expand. Acad. Index (1984-1988); Garden Lit. (1992-); Gen. Period. Index (1988-); Gen. Sci. Index; Index Inf.; INFO-SOUTH Abstr.; Mag. Artic. Summar. Elite (Jan. 1984-) [Full Txt.]; Mag. Artic. Summar. Select (Jan. 1984-) [Full Txt.]; Mag. Artic. Summar. CD-ROM (Jan. 1984-); Mag. Index Plus (1989-); Mag. Search; Newsp. Period. Abstr. (1986-); Read. Guide Period. Lit.; Mag. Index (1977-); Vocat. Search (Jan. 1984-) [Full Txt.].

II
HORTICULTURE ADVANCE. English. an. Government Horticulture Research Institute, Saharanpur U P India.

US
HORTICULTURE AND HOME PEST NEWSLETTER. Added/Corp Iowa State University. Cooperative Extension Service. (Apr. 8, 1987)-. Newsletter. English. ir. $15.00. Iowa State University Printing and Publications Building, Ames IA 50011. **Tel** (515) 294-1101.

US/0046-6964
HORTICULTURE DIGEST. [Hortic. dig.]. No. 1-Oct. 1970-. Periodical. English. qt. Free. University of Hawaii / Maile Way, 3190 Maile Way, c/o Fred Rauch, Honolulu HI 96822. **ED** Fred D Rauch. **DD** 631. ctrl circ.
Ind/Abst AGRICOLA [Full Cov.].

FR/0395-8531
HORTICULTURE FRANCAISE. (L'HORTICULTURE FRANCAISE.). [Hortic. fr.]. (1970)-. Periodical. French. mo. Editions du Lien, BP 30, F-34471 Perols Cedex 1 France. **Tel** 33 67 500618, , FAX 33 67 501902, telex 480755.
Ind/Abst AGRICOLA; Agric. Eng. Abstr.; Ornamental Hort.; Rev. Plant Pathol.; Weed Abstr.

NZ/1170-1803
HORTICULTURE IN NEW ZEALAND : JOURNAL OF THE ROYAL NEW ZEALAND INSTITUTE OF HORTICULTURE. Added/Corp Royal New Zealand Institute of Horticulture. **VFOAT** Journal of the Royal New Zealand Institute of Horticulture. Vol. 1, No. 1 (Summer 1990)-. Periodical. English. sa. Royal New Zealand Institute of Horticulture, PO Box 12, Lincoln College, Canterbury New Zealand. **Tel** 011 03 252811 ext 788. **ED** R Davison. **Bk Rev. Ad Acc. Circ:** 900 (ctrl). ***Continues*** *Royal New Zealand Institute of Horticulture. Annual Journal, 0110-5760.*
Desc: Articles on all aspects of horticulture and related sciences with emphasis on research and education. Separate garden history section.
Ind/Abst AgBiotech News Inf.; Garden Lit. (1992-); Plant Breed. Abstr.; Potato Abstr.; Weed Abstr.

NZ
HORTICULTURE NEWS. English. mo. 60.00NZ$ New Zealand; 75.00NZ$ other. Trade Publications Ltd., 300 Great South Road Greenlane, Newmarket Auckland New Zealand. **Tel** 011 64 9 9293000.
Desc: Information for those in the business of keeping New Zealand growing; its columns have pointed the way as this sector has progressed from a commercial backwater to a major export earner.

CN/0823-8472
HORTICULTURE REVIEW. [Hortic. rev.]. (1983)-. Periodical. English. Twenty-four times a year. 30.00Can$. Landscape Ontario, 1293 Matheson Boulevard, Mississauga Ontario L4W 1R1 Canada. **Tel** (416)629-1184, FAX (416)629-4438. **ED** Rita Weerdenburg. **DD** 635/.09713. **Bk Rev. Ad Acc. Circ:** 3,000. ***Continues*** *Ontario Landscape & Nursery Trades Newsletter.*
Desc: All articles of interest to the wholesale horticultural trades, i.e. industry activities, current events, relevant plants and products, research updates, company profiles, etc.

UK/0269-9478
HORTICULTURE WEEK. (HORTICULTURE WEEK : GARDENER'S CHRONICLE & HORTICULTURAL TRADE JOURNAL.). [Hortic. week]. **VFOAT** Gardener's Chronicle & Horticultural Trade Journal Gardener's Chronicle and Horticultural Trade Journal. Vol. 199, No. 2 (Jan. 10, 1986)-. Periodical. English. wk (52 issues). £55.00 UK; £60.00 Eire & Europe; £85.00 America, Middle East, Africa & India; £95.00 Australia, New Zealand & Japan. Haymarket Publishing Ltd., 12 14 Ansdell Street, London W8 5TR England. **Tel** 011 44 483 733800, FAX 011 44 483 776573. **(Subscription address:** Haymarket Publishing Ltd, PO Box 219, Subscriptions Department, Woking Surrey GU21 1ZW, United Kingdom.**) LC** SB4; .G3. **DD** 635/.0941. ***Continues*** *GC & HTJ, 0309-1147.*
Desc: Information on ornamental horticulture.
Ind/Abst Agric. Eng. Abstr. (1991-); Ornamental Hort.

●UK/0964-8992
HORTICULTURIST/ INSTITUTE OF HORTICULTURE, THE. Added/Corp Institute of Horticulture (Great Britain). Vol. 1 No. 1 (Jan. 1992)-. Periodical. English. qt. £37.00 UK & Ireland; £42.00 other. Institute of Horticulture, 80 Vincent Square, London SW1P 2PE United Kingdom. **Tel** 011 44 71 9765951. **ED** Barbara Segall. Index available. cum. index. **Bk Rev**, (Qty: 20). **Ad Acc.** ***Formed by the union of*** *Professional Horticulture* ***and*** *IOH News.*
Desc: This journal contains articles and information on product developments, research results, and EC regulations.
Ind/Abst AGRICOLA; Garden Lit. (1992-).

US/0742-8219
HORTIDEAS. [HortIdeas]. Vol. 1, No. 1 (Jan. 1984)-. Periodical. English. Twelve times a year. $15.00 US; $17.50 Canada and Mexico; $20.00 (surface mail), $30.00 (airmail) other. HortIdeas, 460 Black Lick Road, Gravel Switch KY 40328. **Tel** (606)332-7606. **ED** Gregory Williams. Index available (June and Dec.). **Bk Rev**, (Qty: 30/per yr.). **Circ:** 1,500.
Desc: Reports on the latest research methods, tools, plants, and books for adventurous vegetable, fruit and flower growers, gathered from hundreds of popular and technical sources.
Ind/Abst Garden Lit. (1992-).

US/0018-5345
HORTSCIENCE. (HORTSCIENCE : A PUBLICATION OF THE AMERICAN SOCIETY FOR HORTICULTURAL SCIENCE.). [HortScience]. **Added/Corp** American Society for Horticultural Science. **VFOAT** Hort Science. Vol. 1 (Winter 1966)-. Academic Scholarly Publication. English. mo. $165.00 US, Canada, and Mexico; $200.00 other. American Society for Horticultural Science, 113 South West Street, Suite 400, Alexandria VA 22314-2824. **Tel** (703)836-4606, FAX (703)836-2024. **ED** W. Lipton. **LC** SB317.5; .H675. **DD** 635/.05. **CODEN** HJHSAR. Index available (free). cum. index. **Bk Rev. Ad Acc. Pr Rev. Acid Free. Circ:** 6,200. available on microfilm. Documents available from The Genuine Article, BIOSIS Document Express, CASDDS.
Desc: An international publication of horticultural science for rapid reporting of results of preliminary or on-going research, progress reports, research notes, and brief announcements of new concepts, methods, applications and findings. Containing more than 500 papers per year, it emphasizes innovative developments in horticultural science and the horticultural industry, as well as changes and trends in horticultural education and extension.
Ind/Abst Abstr. Bull. Inst. Pap. Sci. Tech.; AgBiotech News Inf.; AGRICOLA [Full Cov.]; Agric. Eng. Abstr. (1991-); Agrofor. Abstr. (1991-); BioBusiness; Biocont. News Inf. (1991-); Biodeter. Abstr. (19??-19??); Biol. Agric. Index; Biol. Abstr.; Biol. Dig.; Chem. Abstr.; Crop Physiol. Abstr.; Curr. Aware. Biol. Sci., CABS; Curr. Biotechnol.; Curr. Contents, Agric. Biol. Environ. Sci.; EMBASE; Field Crop Abstr.; Food Sci. Technol. Abstr.; For. Abstr.; Genet. Abstr.; Grasslands For. Abstr.; Hortic. Abstr.; INIS Atomindex [Micro.]; Int. Aerosp. Abstr.; Irr. Drain. Abstr.; Leadscan; Maize Abstr.; Microbiol. Abstr. Sect. A; Microbiol. Abstr. Sect. C; Nematol. Abstr.; Nutr. Abstr. Rev., Ser. A, Hum. Exp.; Ornamental Hort. (19??-19??); Life Sci. Collect.; PESTDOC; Philip. Sci. Technol. Abstr.; Plant Breed. Abstr.; Plant Genet. Resour. Abstr.; Plant Grow. Reg. Abstr.; Postharvest News Inf.; Potato Abstr.; Res. Alert [Full Cov.]; Rev. Agric. Entomol.; Rev. Plant Pathol.; Rice Abstr.; Sci. Cit. Index; SCISEARCH; Seed Abstr.; Soc. Sci. Cit. Index [Select. Cov.]; Soils Fert.; Sorghum Mill. Abstr.; Soyabean Abstr.; Vitis Vitic. Enol. Abstr.; Weed Abstr.; World Agric. Econ.

US/1063-0198
HORTTECHNOLOGY (ALEXANDRIA, VA.). (HORTTECHNOLOGY.). [HortTechnology]. **Added/Corp** American Society for Horticultural Science. **VFOAT** Hort Technology. Vol. 1, No. 1 (Oct./Dec. 1991)-. Periodical. English. qt. $60.00 US, Canada and Mexico; $70.00 other. American Society for Horticultural Science, 113 South West Street, Suite 400, Alexandria VA 22314-2824. **Tel** (703)836-4606, FAX (703)836-2024. **DD** 635. **Ad Acc. Acid Free.**
Desc: An international publication of applied horticultural science and technology. Regular features include technology and product reports, production and marketing reports, research updates, comprehensive crop reports, technology transfer and teaching methods, and resources available.
Ind/Abst AGRICOLA; Curr. Aware. Biol. Sci., CABS; Food Sci. Technol. Abstr.

UK/0950-1657
HORTUS (FARNHAM). (HORTUS.). [Hortus]. No. 1 (Spring 1987)-. Periodical. English. qt (Mar., July, Sept., Dec.). £25.00 UK; £30.00 Europe; £35.00 other. Hortus / A Gardening Journal, The Neuadd Rhayader, Powys LD6 5HH Wales. **Tel** 44 597 810227. **ED** David Wheeler. Index available (bound in first issue). **Bk Rev**, (Qty: 1-20). **Ad Acc, Adv Mgr:** same as editor. **Circ:** 3,000.
Desc: Essays on decorative elements of gardening: history, design and ornament, places, people and books.
Ind/Abst Garden Lit. (1992-).

US
HORTUS NORTHWEST. Issue 1 (1989/1990)-. English. Hortus Northwest, PO Box 955, Canby OR 97013. **LC** SB1; .H67.
Ind/Abst Garden Lit. (1992-).

GW
HORTUS TUBIGENSIS INDEX SEMINUM. **Main/Corp** Botanischer Garten der Universitat Tubingen. Periodical. German. ***Continues*** *Tubingen. Universitat. Botanischer Garten. Semenverzeichnis.*

UK/0043-5759
HOUSE & GARDEN (BRITISH EDITION, 1948). **See** Interior Design.

US/0271-2881
HOUSE & GARDEN PLANS GUIDE (1979). (HOUSE & GARDEN PLANS GUIDE.). **VFOAT** House and Garden Plan Guide; Plans. (1980)-. English. an. Conde Nast Publications / New York, 350 Madison Avenue, New York NY 10017. **Tel** (212)880-8800, (800)777-0700. **LC** NA7127; .H823. ***Continues*** *House & Garden Plans, 0161-2336.*

●US/1061-4079
HOUSEPLANT MAGAZINE. English. qt (Feb., May, Aug., Nov.). $19.95 (one year), $34.00 (two year), $3.00 (single copy) US; $24.95 (one year), $45.00 (two year), $5.00 (single copy) Canada and Mexico. Houseplant Inc., Route 1 Box 271 2 Airport, Elkins WV 26241. **Tel** (304)636-1212, FAX (304)636-9723. **(Subscription address:** Houseplant Magazine, PO Box 1638, Elkins WV, 26421**) ED** Larry Hodgeson and Bonnie Branciaroli. **Bk Rev**, (Qty: 12). **Ad Acc**, **Adv Mgr:** Mark Branciaroli, **Tel** (304)636-1212. **Circ:** 200,000 (ctrl).
Desc: Dedicated to the indoor gardener and house plant enthusiast. Issues include full-color extravaganzas of plants, places, growing tips, greenhouses, hydroponics and travel.
Ind/Abst Garden Lit. (1992-).

US/0095-4705
HOW TO (INDIANAPOLIS). **See** Building and Construction.

US
IDAHO FRUIT TREE CENSUS / U.S. DEPARTMENT OF AGRICULTURE, ECONOMICS AND STATISTICS SERVICE AND IDAHO DEPARTMENT OF AGRICULTURE. English. be. Idaho Crop and Livestock Reporting Service, PO Box 1699, Boise ID 83701. **Tel** (208)554-1507. **ED** R C Max. **LC** SB354.6.U5; I3. **DD** 634/.09796. **Bk Rev**. **Ad Acc**. **Circ:** 150 (ctrl).

US
ILLINOIS NURSERY NOTES FOR THE PLANT INDUSTRIES. **Added/Corp** University of Illinois at Urbana-Champaign. Cooperative Extension Service. **VFOAT** Illinois Nursery Notes. (19??)-. Periodical. English. Six times a year. $6.00. Agricultural Newsletter Service, University of Illinois, 116 Mumford Hall, Urbana IL 61801. **Tel** (217)333-2666.

US
ILLUSTRATED GARDEN BOOK / KRIDER'S. **Main/Corp** Krider Nurseries. **VFOAT** Glories of the Garden. (19??)-. English.

GW/0170-8414
IMMERGRUNE BLATTER. [Immergrune Bl.]. (No. 15- 1976-). Periodical. German.
Ind/Abst AGRICOLA; Hortic. Abstr.

US/1042-7562
IN-SITE (VERNON HILLS, ILL.). ***Suspended.*** (IN-SITE.). [In-site]. **VFOAT** In Site. Vol. 1, No. 1 (Nov./Dec. 1987)-(19??). Periodical. English. bm. $149.00. James Martin Associates, 24380 North Highway 45, Vernon Hills IL 60061. **Tel** (708)634-8888. **DD** 712.

UK
IN TOUCH WITH FLOWERS. English. wk. £78.00. Orbis Publishing Ltd, Marlborough Road Aldbourne, Wiltshire SN8 2DO England.

NO
INDEX SEMINUM. **Main/Corp** Oslo. Universitet. Botanisk Have. Periodical. English (summaries and/or abstracts in German, French and Russian). ***Continues*** *Delectus Seminum Fructum, Sporarum ... Quem pro Mutua Commutatione Hortus Botanicus Universitatis Osloensis Offert.*

PO
INDEX SEMINUM. JARDIM-MUSEU AGRICOLA TROPICAL. Portuguese. be. free. Instituto de Investigacao Cientifica Tropical, Centro de Documentacao e Informacao, rua Jau 47, 1 300 Lisbon Portugal. **Tel** 645321. **Circ:** 500 (ctrl).

II/0019-4875
INDIAN HORTICULTURE. [Indian hortic.]. **Added/Corp** Indian Council of Agricultural Research. Vol. 1 (Oct. 1956)-. Periodical. English. qt. $20.00. Indian Council of Agricultural Research, Mgr Krishi Anusandham Bhavan, New Delhi 110 012 India. **Tel** 011 91 11 5713657, telex 031-62249 ICAR IN. **(Subscription address:** Prints India, 11 Darya Ganj, New Delhi, 110002 India, (Phone: 011 91 11 3268645)**) ED** Neelam Chhabra. **CODEN** INHOAK. **Bk Rev**. **Ad Acc**. **Circ:** 10,000. Documents available from BIOSIS Document Express.
Desc: Information on fruit cultivation, vegetable growing, floriculture, landscaping and home gardening. Illustrated.
Ind/Abst AGRICOLA; Agric. Eng. Abstr. (1991-); Agrindex; Biocont. News Inf. (1991-); Biol. Abstr.; Field Crop Abstr.; Food Sci. Technol. Abstr.; Grasslands For. Abstr.; Hortic. Abstr.; Nutr. Abstr. Rev., Ser. B, Live Feeds and Feed.; Nutr. Abstr. Rev., Ser. A, Hum. Exp.; Ornamental Hort. (1991-); Life Sci. Collect.; Plant Breed. Abstr.; Plant Genet. Resour. Abstr.; Postharvest News Inf.; Potato Abstr.; Protozoolog. Abstr.; Rev. Agric. Entomol.; Rev. Plant Pathol.; Seed Abstr.

II/0970-6429
INDIAN JOURNAL OF HILL FARMING. [Indian J. Hill Farming]. (1987)-. Periodical. English. sa.
Ind/Abst Index Vet.; Irr. Drain. Abstr.

II/0019-5251
INDIAN JOURNAL OF HORTICULTURE, THE. [Indian j. hortic.]. **Added/Corp** Horticultural Society of India. Vol. 1 (June 1943)-. Periodical. English. qt. $60.00. Horticultural Society of India, 255 Upper Palace Orchards, Bangladore 6 India. **(Subscription address:** Prints India, 11 Darya Ganj, New Delhi, 110002 India, (Phone: 011 91 11 3268645)**) LC** SB13; .H65. **CODEN** IJHOAQ. Documents available from BIOSIS Document Express, CASDDS.
Ind/Abst AgBiotech News Inf.; AGRICOLA; Agric. Eng. Abstr. (1991-); Agrofor. Abstr. (1991-); Biodeter. Abstr.; Biol. Abstr.; Chem. Abstr.; Crop Physiol. Abstr.; Field Crop Abstr.; Food Sci. Technol. Abstr.; For. Abstr.; Hortic. Abstr.; Irr. Drain. Abstr.; Nematol. Abstr.; Ornamental Hort. (19??-19??); Philip. Sci. Technol. Abstr.; Plant Breed. Abstr.; Plant Grow. Reg. Abstr.; Postharvest News Inf.; Potato Abstr.; Rev. Agric. Entomol.; Rev. Plant Pathol.; Seed Abstr.; Soils Fert.; Sug. Indus. Abstr.; Vitis Vitic. Enol. Abstr.; Weed Abstr.; World Agric. Econ.

US/8750-4081
INDOOR GARDEN, THE. [Indoor gard.]. **Added/Corp** Indoor Gardening Society of America. Vol. 21 No. 4 (July-Aug. 1984)-. Periodical. English. bm. $15.00 US and Canada; $17.00 other. Indoor Light Gardening Society of America, 128 West 58th Street, New York NY 10019. **Tel** (216)835-2947. **LC** SB126; .L53. **DD** 635.9/65. **Ad Acc**. ctrl circ. ***Continues*** *Light Garden, 0194-0317.*
Ind/Abst Garden Lit. (1992-).

AU
INDUSTRIELLER PFLANZENBAU. **Main/Conf** Symposium fur Industriellen Pflanzenbau. **Added/Corp** Gesellschaft zur Forderung des Industriellen Pflanzenbaues. Vol. 1 (1964)-. Multiple languages (English and German).

US
INDUSTRY REFERENCE GUIDE. **VFOAT** Nursery Business. Industry Reference Guide. (1976)-. Periodical. English. ir. Brantwood Publications Inc, 3023 Eastland Boulevard/Suite 103, Clearwater FL 34621. **Tel** (813)796-3877, FAX (813)791-4126.

CK
INFORME ... DEL PROGRAMA NACIONAL DE FISIOLOGIA VEGETAL. **Main/Corp** Instituto Colombiano Agropecuario. Programa Nacional de Fisiologia Vegetal. 1975-. Periodical. Spanish.

EC
INFORME TECNICO DE BANANO. **Main/Corp** Instituto Nacional de Investigaciones Agropecuarias. **VFOAT** Convenio Para el Programa de Investigacion en Banano. Spanish. Instituto Nacional de Investigaciones Agropecuarias, Casilla 2600, Quito Ecuador. **LC** SB379.B2; I57A.

FR
INFOS / CENTRE TECHNIQUE INTERPROFESSIONNEL DES FRUITS ET LEGUMES. **Added/Corp** Centre Technique Interprofessionnel des Fruits et Legumes (France). No. 1 (Apr. 1984)-. Periodical. French. Ten times a year. 293.83F France; 450.00F other. Centre Technique Interprofessionel des Fruits et Legumes, 22 rue Bergere, F-75009 Paris France. **Tel** 011 33 1 47701693. ***Continues*** *CTIFL-Documents.*
Ind/Abst Biodeter. Abstr.; Irr. Drain. Abstr.; Plant Grow. Reg. Abstr.; Postharvest News Inf.; Rev. Agric. Entomol.; Rev. Plant Pathol.; Soils Fert.; World Agric. Econ.

NR
INTERAFRICAIN PHYTOSANITARY BULLETIN. **VFOAT** Bulletin d'Informations Phytosanitaires Interafricain; Bulletin Interafricain d'Informations Phytosanitaires. Bulletin. Multiple languages (English and French). Interafricain Phytosanitary Council, BP 4170 Nglongkak, Yaounde Africa. **LC** SB599; .I67. **DD** 632.

●US/1063-1607
INTERIOR LANDSCAPE. [Inter. landsc.]. Vol. 9, No. 5 (May 1992)-. Periodical. English. Four times a year. $16.00. American Nurseryman Publishing Company, 77 West Washington Street, Suite 2100, Chicago IL 60602. **Tel** (800)621-5727, (312)782-5505, FAX (312)782-3232. **DD** 635. ***Continues*** *Interior Landscape Industry, 0742-1648.*

US/0742-1648
INTERIOR LANDSCAPE INDUSTRY. ***Title Change.*** [Int. landsc. ind.]. Vol. 1, No. 1 (Jan. 1984)-(199?). Periodical. English. mo. Interior Landscape Industry, 111 North Canal Street/Suite 545, Chicago IL 60606-7203. **Tel** (312)782-5505. **ED** Brent Marchant. **DD** 635. Index available. **Bk Rev**. **Ad Acc**. **Circ:** 7,000. available on microfilm from University Microfilms International (UMI). ***Continued by*** *Interior Landscape, 1063-1607.*
Desc: Devoted to professionals in the design, installation, and maintenance of interior landscapes for commercial and residential settings.

US/0744-8635
INTERIORSCAPE. [Interiorscape]. Vol. 1, No. 1 (Jan./Feb. 1982)-. Periodical. English. bm. $12.00 (one year), $30.00 (three year) US; $35.00 (one year), $60.00 (three year) other. Brantwood Publications Inc, 3023 Eastland Boulevard/Suite 103, Clearwater FL 34621. **Tel** (813)796-3877, FAX (813)791-4126. **ED** Jeff Morey. **Bk Rev**. **Ad Acc**.
Desc: America's leading magazine for professionals who design, install and maintain interior plantings.

US/0198-9561
INTERNATIONAL BONSAI. [Int. bonsai]. **Added/Corp** International Bonsai Arboretum. Vol. 1 (Spring 1979)-. Periodical. English. Four times a year. $24.00 US; $32.00 other. International Bonsai Arboretum, 1070 Martin Road, West Henrietta NY 14586. **Tel** (716)334-2595. **ED** William N. Valvavanis. Index available. **Bk Rev**. **Ad Acc**. **Circ:** 5,000.
Desc: Bonsai design techniques and appreciation are graphically and photographically presented to help all levels of Bonsai hobbyists.

US/0159-656X
INTERNATIONAL CAMELLIA JOURNAL. (INTERNATIONAL CAMELLIA JOURNAL : AN OFFICIAL PUBLICATION OF THE INTERNATIONAL CAMELLIA SOCIETY.). [Int. camellia j.]. **Added/Corp** International Camellia Society. **VFOAT** Kokusai Tsubaki Kaishi. (Dec. 1962)-. English. an. Free to members of the International Camellia Society; L20000 (membership) Italy; $13.00 (membership) US. International Camellia Society, 1486 Yosemite Circle, Clayton CA 94517. **Tel** (415)672-6941.

UK/0534-7750
INTERNATIONAL CAMELLIA SOCIETY JOURNAL, THE. **Added/Corp** International Camellia Society. No. 6 (Nov. 1974)-. Periodical. English.
Ind/Abst Crop Physiol. Abstr.; Hortic. Abstr.; Ornamental Hort. (1991-); Plant Breed. Abstr.; Plant Grow. Reg. Abstr.

AT
INTERNATIONAL SUNFLOWER YEARBOOK. **Added/Corp** International Sunflower Association. (1985)-. English. an. International Sunflower Association / France, 174 Avenue Victor Hugo, 75116 Paris France. **Tel** 011 44 34 7246.

UN/0579-4005
INTRODUKTSIIA I AKKLIMATIZATSIIA RASTENII (KIEV, UKRAINE). (INTRODUKTSIIA I AKKLIMATIZATSIIA RASTENII / AKADEMIIA NAUK UKRAINSKOI SSR, DONETSKII BOTANICHESKII SAD.). **Added/Corp** Donetskyi Botanichnyi Sad. (1984)-. Periodical. Russian. Izdatelstvo Naukova Dumka / Ukrainian Academy of Sciences, Vladimirskaia Ulitsa 54, 252601 Kiev Ukraine. **Tel** 225-63-66, telex 131376. ***Continues*** *Introduktsiia ta Aklimatyzatsiia Roslyn na Ukraini.*
Ind/Abst Plant Breed. Abstr.

UK/0075-0700
IRIS YEAR BOOK / BRITISH IRIS SOCIETY, THE. **Added/Corp** Iris Society (London, England) British Iris Society. (1930)-. English. an. £9.20 Comes with British Iris Society membership. British Iris Society, c/o Neville Watkins, 31 Larkfield Road, Farnham Surrey GU9 7DB England. **Ad Acc**. **Circ:** 700 (ctrl). ***Continues*** *Bulletin (London, England).*

CN/0827-2824
ISLAND GROWER, THE. [Isl. grow.]. Vol. 1, No. 1 (Apr. 1984)-. Periodical. English. Ten times a year. 18.00Can$ Canada; 35.00Can$ other. Greenhart Publications, 7007 Richview Drive, Rural Route 4, Sooke BC VOS 1NO Canada. **Tel** (604)642-4129. **ED** Phyllis Kusch. **DD** 635/.09711/34. Index available. cum. index. **Bk Rev**, (Qty: 5-10). **Ad Acc**. **Circ:** 8,400 (ctrl).
Desc: A gardening magazine for Vancouver Island with a wide range of gardening and related topics. Information relevant to all gardeners.

US
IWSS. **Main/Corp** International Weed Science Society. **Added/Corp** Oregon State University. International Weed Science Society. **VFOAT** IWSS Newsletter. Vol. 1, No. 1 (June 1976)-. Newsletter. English. sa (June, Dec.). $10.00. International Weed Science Society, OSU, Cordley Hall 2040, Corvallis OR 97331-2915. **Tel** (503)737-3541, FAX (503)737-3080. **ED** Susan Larson. **Bk Rev. Circ:** 450.
Desc: Newsletter of the International Weed Science Society. Dedicated to encourage, promote, and assist development of weed science and weed control technology.

NE/0074-0446
JAARSVERSLAG - INSTITUUT VOOR PLANTENZEIKTENKUNDIG ONDERZOEK. **Main/Corp** Instituut Voor Plantenziektenkundig Onderzoek (Wegeningen, Netherlands). 1950-. Dutch (English). an. Instituut voor Plantenziektekundig Onderzoek, Bibnnehaven 12, 6700 Wageningen Netherlands. **LC** SB599; .W26. **DD** 632/.3/05. Each issue contains an index to its own contents (no volume index)--loose.

FR/0021-5481
JARDINS DE FRANCE PARIS. (1947)-. Periodical. French. Ten times a year. 220.00F France; 300.00F other. Societe Nationale Horticulture France, 84 rue de Grenelle, 75007 Paris France. **Tel** 33 1 45488100, FAX 33 1 45669657. **ED** Jean Paul Collnert. **UDC** 635(44). cum. index. **Bk Rev**, (Qty: 10). **Circ:** 13,000 (ctrl).

●DK/0906-7043
JORD OG VIDEN. **See** Agriculture.

US/0745-7839
JOURNAL / AMERICAN RHODODENDRON SOCIETY. [Journal - Am. Rhododendr. Soc.]. **Added/Corp** American Rhododendron Society. Vol. 36, No. 1 (Winter 1982)-. Periodical. English. Four times a year (Jan., Apr., July, Oct.). $25.00 (individuals & regular); $60.00 (commerical & corporate) Comes with American Rhododendron Society Membership. American Rhododendron Society, PO Box 1380, Gloucester VA 23061. **Tel** (804)693-4433. **ED** Sonja Nelson (editor's address: 201A South State Street, Bellingham, WA 98225, phone: (206)738-1894). **LC** SB413.R47; A5. **DD** 635.9/3362. Index available. cum. index. **Bk Rev. Ad Acc. Circ:** 6,000. ***Continues*** *Quarterly Bulletin (American Rhododendron Society), 0003-0821.*
Desc: For people who explore and love the world of rhododendrons and azaleas. For home gardeners, nurserymen and horticulturists, from the eager beginner to the acknowledged specialist.
Ind/Abst Biocont. News Inf. (1991-); Crop Physiol. Abstr.; For. Abstr.; Hortic. Abstr.; Ornamental Hort. (1991-); Plant Breed. Abstr.; Plant Genet. Resour. Abstr.; Plant Grow. Reg. Abstr.; Rev. Plant Pathol.

US/0431-0233
JOURNAL (GARDEN CLUB OF VIRGINIA). (JOURNAL / THE GARDEN CLUB OF VIRGINIA.). **Added/Corp** Garden Club of Virginia. **VFOAT** Garden Club of Virginia Journal. Vol. 1, No. 1 (Sept. 1955)-. Periodical. English. Six times a year. $8.00. Mrs. W. D. Bayles, 1939 Blue Ridge Road, Charlottesville VA 22903. ***Continues*** *Garden Gossip.*

US/0278-5226
JOURNAL OF ARBORICULTURE. [J. arboric.]. **Added/Corp** International Society of Arboriculture. Vol. 1 (Jan. 1975)-. Periodical. English. mo. $70.00 (surface mail); $100.00 (airmail). International Society of Arboriculture, PO Box GG, Savoy IL 61874. **Tel** (217)355-9411. **ED** Dan Neely. **DD** 635. Index available. cum. index. **Bk Rev. Ad Acc. Circ:** 4,500. ***Formed by the union of*** *Arborist's News, 0003-7958* ***and*** *International Shade Tree Conference. Proceedings of Annual Meeting.*
Desc: Devoted to the dissemination of knowledge in the science and art of growing and maintaining shade and ornamental trees.
Ind/Abst AGRICOLA [Select. Cov.]; Agric. Eng. Abstr. (1991-); Agrofor. Abstr.; Biol. Agric. Index; For. Prod. Abstr.; For. Abstr.; Garden Lit. (1992-); Geogr. Abstr. Human Geogr.; Hortic. Abstr.; Irr. Drain. Abstr.; Ornamental Hort. (19??-19??); Plant Breed. Abstr.; Plant Grow. Reg. Abstr.; Rev. Agric. Entomol.; Rev. Plant Pathol.; Soils Fert.; Weed Abstr.

US/0738-632X
JOURNAL OF COMMUNITY GARDENING. (JOURNAL OF COMMUNITY GARDENING / ACGA, AMERICAN COMMUNITY GARDENING ASSOCIATION.). [J. community gard.]. Periodical. English. qt. $30.00. American Community Gardening Association, PO Box 8645, Ann Arbor MI 48107-8645.

US/0738-2898
JOURNAL OF ENVIRONMENTAL HORTICULTURE. [J. environ. hortic.]. **Added/Corp** Horticultural Research Institute. Vol. 1, No. 1 March (1983)-. Academic Scholarly Publication. English. qt (Mar., June, Sept., Dec.). $60.00 US; $80.00 other. Horticultural Research Institution, 1250 Eye Street Northwest, Suite 500, Washington DC 20005. **Tel** (202)789-2900, FAX (202)789-1893. **ED** Thomas Fretz. **LC** SB118.48; .J68. **DD** 635/.05. **CODEN** JEHOD5. Index available. cum. index. **Pr Rev. Circ:** 700. Documents available from BIOSIS Document Express, CASDDS.
Desc: Publishes peer-reviewed scientific reports with a section providing a non-technical summary of the research results.
Ind/Abst AGRICOLA [Full Cov.]; Agric. Eng. Abstr. (1991-); Biodeter. Abstr. (1991-); Biol. Abstr. (1988-); Chem. Abstr. (1983-); Crop Physiol. Abstr.; For. Abstr.; Hortic. Abstr.; Irr. Drain. Abstr.; Ornamental Hort. (1991-); Plant Breed. Abstr.; Plant Genet. Resour. Abstr.; Plant Grow. Reg. Abstr.; Rev. Agric. Entomol.; Rev. Plant Pathol.; Rice Abstr.; Seed Abstr.; Soils Fert.; Weed Abstr.; World Agric. Econ.

UK/0144-5170
JOURNAL OF GARDEN HISTORY. [J. gard. hist.]. Vol. 1, No. 1 (Jan.-Mar. 1981)-. Periodical. English. qt. £124.00 UK; $205.00 other. Taylor & Francis Ltd., Rankine Road, Basingstoke Hampshire, RG24 8PR United Kingdom. **Tel** 011 44 256 840366, FAX 011 44 256 479438, telex 858540. **(Subscription address:** Taylor & Francis Inc., 1900 Frost Road, Suite 101, Bristol PA 19007-1598.**) ED** John Dixon Hunt (editorial address: 3 Pembroke Studios, Pembroke Gardens, London W8 6HX, UK). **LC** SB451; .J76. **DD** 712/.09. **[CCC].** available on microfilm from University Microfilms International (UMI). Documents available from The Genuine Article.
Desc: Addresses itself to readers with a serious interest in gardening. Emphasis is on documentation of individual gardens in all parts of the world, with articles on other topics such as iconography, aesthetics, botany and horticulture, technology, social and economic history, conservation and restoration of historic gardens, geography and history of ideas.
Ind/Abst Am. Hist. Life (1981-); Archit. Period. Index (1981-); Art Archaeol. Tech. Abstr.; Art Index; ARTbibliogr. Mod.; Arts Humanit. Citation Index [Full Cov.]; Avery Index Archit. Period. Suppl. Colum. Univ. (1989-); BHA : Biblio. Hist. Art; Br. Archaeol. Bibliogr.; Br. Humanit. Index; Curr. Contents Arts Humanit.; Garden Lit. (1992-); Recent. Publ. Artic.; Res. Alert [Full Cov.]; RILA, Int. Rep. Lit. Art.

●US/1049-6475
JOURNAL OF HERBS, SPICES & MEDICINAL PLANTS. [J. herbs spices med. plants]. **VFOAT** Journal of Herbs, Spices, and Medicinal Plants. Vol. 1, No. 1/2 (1992)-. Periodical. English. qt (Published during the academic year). $75.00 US; $105.00 other. The Haworth Press Inc, 10 Alice Street, Binghamton NY 13904-1580. **Tel** (607)722-5857, (800)3-HAWORTH, FAX (607)722-1424. **ED** Lyle Craker (editor's address: Department of Plant and Soil Sciences, University of Massachusetts, Amherst, MA 01003). **LC** SB351.H5; J68. **DD** 635/.7. **NLM** W1; JO67I. **CODEN** JHEPEF. **Bk Rev. Ad Acc. Pr Rev. Acid Free.** available on microfiche. Documents available from Haworth Document Delivery Service. ***Absorbed*** *Herbs, Spices & Medicinal Plants.*
Desc: Features original articles and short reviews associated with the production and development of herbs, spices, and medicinal plants. Includes information related to such areas as physiology, breeding, productivity, commercial applications and marketing.
Ind/Abst Food Sci. Technol. Abstr.; Foods Adlibra (1992-); Int. Pharm. Abstr.

●US/1054-4682
JOURNAL OF HOME & CONSUMER HORTICULTURE. **VFOAT** Journal of Home and Consumer Horticulture. (1994)-. Periodical. English. Twice a year. $60.00 US; $84.00 other. The Haworth Press Inc, 10 Alice Street, Binghamton NY 13904-1580. **Tel** (607)722-5857, (800)3-HAWORTH, FAX (607)722-1424. **ED** Raymond P. Poincelot, Fairfield University, Fairfield, Connecticut. **Acid Free.** available on microfiche. Documents available from Haworth Document Delivery Service.
Desc: Focus is on both academics and business professionals concerned with home and consumer horticulture. Publishes a broad spectrum of information for all levels of horticulturists.
Ind/Abst Abstr. Anthropol.; AGRICOLA; Biol. Dig.; Environ. Period. Bibliogr.; Food Sci. Technol. Abstr.; Foods Adlibra; Garden Lit.; Ref. Z.

UK/0022-1589
JOURNAL OF HORTICULTURAL SCIENCE, THE. [J. hortic. sci.]. Vol. 24 (1948)-. Academic Scholarly Publication. English. bm. £90.00. Headley Brothers Ltd., The Invicta Press, Queens Road, Ashford Kent TN24 8HH England. **Tel** 011 44 233 623131. **ED** A.R. Rees. **CODEN** JHSCA8. Index available. **Pr Rev. Circ:** 1,000 (ctrl). Documents available from The Genuine Article, BIOSIS Document Express, CASDDS. ***Continues*** *Journal of Pomology and Horticultural Science.*
Desc: Results of original research on temperate, tropical fruit, other perennial crops, vegetables and flowers in Britain and overseas.
Ind/Abst AgBiotech News Inf.; AGRICOLA [Full Cov.]; Agric. Eng. Abstr. (19??-19??); Agrofor. Abstr.; Biocont. News Inf. (1991-); Biodeter. Abstr. (19??-19??); Biol. Agric. Index; Biol. Abstr.; Chem. Abstr.; Crop Physiol. Abstr.; Curr. Aware. Biol. Sci., CABS; Curr. Contents, Agric. Biol. Environ. Sci.; EMBASE; Field Crop Abstr.; Food Sci. Technol. Abstr.; For. Abstr.; Grasslands For. Abstr.; Hortic. Abstr.; Irr. Drain. Abstr.; Leadscan; Maize Abstr.; Nematol. Abstr.; Ornamental Hort. (19??-19??); Life Sci. Collect.; PESTDOC; Plant Breed. Abstr.; Plant Genet. Resour. Abstr.; Plant Grow. Reg. Abstr.; Postharvest News Inf.; Potato Abstr.; Protozoolog. Abstr.; Res. Alert [Full Cov.]; Rev. Med. Vet. Mycology; Rev. Plant Pathol.; Sci. Cit. Index; Seed Abstr.; Soils Fert.; Stat. Theory Method Abstr. (1972, 1974-1975); Vitis Vitic. Enol. Abstr.; Wheat Barley Trit. Abstr.

UK
JOURNAL OF KEW GUILD. English. an (May). £15.00. Kew Guild, Royal Botanic Gardens, Kew Richmond Surrey TW9 3AB England. **Tel** 011 44 81 332 5116, FAX 011 44 81 332 5197. **ED** Richard Ward (editor's telephone: 011 44 81 948 2970). **Ad Acc, Adv Mgr:** Mr. Gaggini, **Tel** 0604 811839. **Circ:** 500.
Desc: Kew Guild annual reporting on activities of Kewites, awards made and activities at the Royal Botanic Gardens.

US/0003-1062
JOURNAL OF THE AMERICAN SOCIETY FOR HORTICULTURAL SCIENCE. [J. Am. Soc. Hortic. Sci.]. **Main/Corp** American Society for Horticultural Science. Vol. 94 (Jan. 1969)-. Academic Scholarly Publication. English. bm. $165.00 US, Canada and Mexico; $200.00 other. American Society for Horticultural Science, 113 South West Street, Suite 400, Alexandria VA 22314-2824. **Tel** (703)836-4606, FAX (703)836-2024. **ED** Lincoln C. Pierce. **LC** SB1; .A6A. **DD** 635/.05. **CODEN** JOSHB5. Index available (free). cum. index. **Pr Rev. Circ:** 5,300. available on microfilm. Documents available from The Genuine Article, BIOSIS Document Express, CASDDS. ***Continues*** *American Society for Horticultural Science. Proceedings.*
Desc: An international journal of horticultural science and the primary publication for more than 200 detailed papers per year presenting the results of original and completed basic or fundamental research in all phases of horticultural science.
Ind/Abst AgBiotech News Inf.; AGRICOLA [Full Cov.]; Agric. Eng. Abstr. (1991-); BioBusiness; Biocont. News Inf.; Biodeter. Abstr. (19??-19??); Biol. Agric. Index; Biol. Abstr.; Chem. Abstr.; Crop Physiol. Abstr.; Curr. Aware. Biol. Sci., CABS; Curr. Contents, Agric. Biol. Environ. Sci.; EMBASE; Field Crop Abstr.; Food Sci. Technol. Abstr.; For. Prod. Abstr.; For. Abstr.; Grasslands For. Abstr.; Hortic. Abstr.; INIS Atomindex [Micro.]; Irr. Drain. Abstr.; Maize Abstr.; Nematol. Abstr.; Ornamental Hort. (19??-19??); Life Sci. Collect.; PESTDOC; Plant Breed. Abstr.; Plant Genet. Resour. Abstr.; Plant Grow. Reg. Abstr.; Postharvest News Inf.; Potato Abstr.; Protozoolog. Abstr.; Res. Alert [Full Cov.]; Rev. Agric. Entomol.; Rev. Med. Vet. Mycology; Rev. Plant Pathol.; Sci. Cit. Index; SCISEARCH; Seed Abstr.; Soils Fert.; Soyabean Abstr.; Vitis Vitic. Enol. Abstr.; Weed Abstr.

US
JOURNAL OF THE ARNOLD ARBORETUM. SUPPLEMENTARY SERIES / HARVARD UNIVERSITY. **Added/Corp** Harvard University. **VFOAT** Supplementary Series. Vol. 1 (1991)-. Monographic series. English. ir. Price varies per volume. Harvard University Department of Botany, 22 Divinity Avenue, Cambridge MA 02138. **Tel** (617)495-2368.

●US
JOURNAL OF THE INTERNATIONAL OAK SOCIETY. **Added/Corp** International Oak Society. **VFOAT** International Oak Society Journal; IOS Journal. Issue No. 1 (Mar. 1992)-. Periodical. English. International Oak Society, 1093 Ackermanville Road, Pen Argyl PA 18072.
Desc: Information on oak trees.

US/1053-2617
JOURNAL OF THE NEW ENGLAND GARDEN HISTORY SOCIETY. [J. N. Engl. Gard. Hist. Soc.]. **Added/Corp** New England Garden History Society. Vol. 1 (Fall 1991)-. Periodical. English. Twice a year. $25.00 Comes with New England Garden History Society membership. New England Garden History Society, 300 Massachusetts Avenue, Boston MA 02115. **Tel** (617)536-9280. **LC** SB466.U65; N482. **DD** 712/.0974/05.
Ind/Abst Garden Lit. (1992-).

US/0485-2044
JOURNAL OF THE RIO GRANDE VALLEY HORTICULTURAL SOCIETY. [J. Rio Grande Val. Hortic. Soc.]. **Main/Corp** Rio Grande Valley Horticultural Society. Vol. 10 (1956)-. Periodical. English. an (Feb.). $16.00. Journal of the Rio Grande, PO Box 107, Weslaco TX 78595. **ED** Gene Lester. **CODEN** JRGVA7. **Ad Acc. Pr Rev.** ctrl circ. Documents available from BIOSIS Document Express, CASDDS. ***Continues*** *Rio Grande Valley Horticultural Institute. Proceedings.*
Desc: Scientific articles concerning production, horticulture, citrus, vegetables and fruits, and ornamentals.
Ind/Abst AgBiotech News Inf.; AGRICOLA [Full Cov.];

Gardening and Horticulture

Biocont. News Inf.; Biodeter. Abstr. (1991-); Biol. Abstr.; Chem. Abstr.; Crop Physiol. Abstr.; Food Sci. Technol. Abstr.; For. Abstr.; Hortic. Abstr.; Nematol. Abstr.; Ornamental Hort.; Plant Breed.; Plant Grow. Reg. Abstr.; Seed Abstr.

UK
JOURNAL OF THE SCOTTISH ROCK GARDEN CLUB, THE. Main/Corp Scottish Rock Garden Club. (1937)-. Periodical. English. sa. £9.00 UK; $20.00 US. Scottish Rock Garden Club, c/o K M Gibb, 21 Merchiston Park, Edinburgh EH10 4PW Scotland. **Tel** 031 229 8138. **ED** D. Bainbridge. **Circ**: 4,000.
Desc: Articles on the cultivation of plants of interest to Alpine gardeners and travelogues to areas of the world where the plants grow wild.

US
JOURNAL OF THERAPEUTIC HORTICULTURE. Added/Corp National Council for Therapy and Rehabilitation through Horticulture. American Horticultural Therapy Association. Vol. 1 (1986)-. Periodical. English. an. $15.00. **NLM** W1; JO966E.
Ind/Abst Garden Lit. (1992-).

II
JOURNAL OF TREE SCIENCES. See Forestry.

●US/1070-437X
JOURNAL OF TURFGRASS MANAGEMENT. (March 1994)-. Periodical. English. qt. $60.00 US; $84.00 other. The Haworth Press Inc, 10 Alice Street, Binghamton NY 13904-1580. **Tel** (607)722-5857, (800)3-HAWORTH, FAX (607)722-1424. **ED** William A. Torello. **Bk Rev. Ad Acc. Pr Rev. Acid Free.** available on microfiche. Documents available from Haworth Document Delivery Service.
Desc: Will gather and disseminate current advances in basic as well as applied turfgrass research for the benefit of the turfgrass scientist as well as the practicing turfgrass manager.

US/1040-8134
JOY OF HERBS, THE. Ceased. [Joy herbs]. Vol. 1, No. 1 (1988)-( ). Periodical. English. qt. Brook Publishing Company, PO Box 7617, Birmingham AL 35253-0617. **Tel** (205)933-1804. **DD** 635. Index available. **Bk Rev. Ad Acc.**

JA
KAJU BYOGAICHU BOJO HANDOBUKKU. Japanese. an. Shiga-ken Kaju Kumiai Rengoki, c/o Shiga-Kencho Nosan-Fukyuka, 1-1 Kyomachi, 4-chome, Otsu 520 Japan. **Tel** 0775-24-1121, FAX 0775-23-1581. **LC** SB950.3.J3; K3.

JA
KAJU SHIKENJO NYUSU. Main/Corp Norinsho Kaju Shikenjo (Japan). No. 10- May 1978-. Japanese. Norinsho Kaju Shikenjo, 2-1 Fujimoto Yatabecho, Tsukuba-gun, Ibaraki-ken, Yatabecho Japan. **LC** SB29.J3; K34A.

GW/0022-7846
KAKTEEN UND ANDERE SUKKULENTEN. See Biology-Botany.

KO
KAMGYUL. Periodical. Korean. Cheju Kamgyul Hyoptong Chohap, 586-10 Sogi 3-Ni, Sogiup Korea. **LC** SB369.5.K7; K35.

JA/0387-1002
KANSAI BYOCHUGAI KENKYUKAI HO. [Kansai ByochÂugai Kenkyukaiho]. **Added/Corp** Kansai Byochugai Kenkyukai. **VFOAT** Proceedings of the Kansai Plant Protection Society. (1958)-. Japanese (summaries and/or abstracts in English). Kansai Plant Protection Society, c/o Vegetable and Ornamental Crops Research Station, Ishinden-Ogoso, Tsu-City Japan. **CODEN** KBKNA4.
Ind/Abst Biocont. News Inf.; Hortic. Abstr.; Rev. Agric. Entomol.; Seed Abstr.

US
KANSAS CITY HOMES & GARDENS. English. bm. $21.00 (one year), $28.00 (two year), $34.00 (three year). Showcase Publishing Inc, 5301 West 75th, Prairie Village KS 66208. **Tel** (913) 648-5757, FAX (913) 648-5783.

RU
KARTOPLIARSTVO. Added/Corp Ukraine. Ministerstvo sil'Shskoho Hospodarstva. (19??)-. Periodical. Russian.
Ind/Abst Agric. Eng. Abstr.; Biocont. News Inf.; Postharvest News Inf.

RU
KATALOG SADOVOE ZAVEDENIE "SINOP" E I.V. VELIKAGO KNIAZIA ALEKSANDRA MIKHAILOVICHA.
Main/Corp Sadovoe Zavedenie Sinop. (19??)-. Russian. an.

US/1062-0745
KERR'S COST DATA FOR LANDSCAPE CONSTRUCTION. Added/Corp Kerr Associates. **VFOAT** Cost Data for Landscape Construction. 10th Ed. (1990)-. English. Kerr Associates Inc, 1207 Iowa Avenue, Ames IA 50010. **Tel** (515)292-5377. *Continues* Cost Data for Landscape Construction, 0271-2067.

HU/0023-0677
KERTESZET ES SZOLESZET. (1952)-. Periodical. Hungarian. wk. $60.00. (**Subscription address:** Kultura, PO Box 149, H 1389 Budapest 62 Hungary)
Ind/Abst Plant Breed. Abstr.; Rev. Med. Vet. Entomol.

HU/0238-6852
KERTESZETI ES ELELMISZERIPARI EGYETEM KOEZLEMENYEI / PUBLICATIONES UNIVERSITATIS HORTICULTURAE INDUSTRIAEQUE ALIMENTARIAE, A. Added/Corp Kerteszeti es Elelmiszeripari Egyetem. **VFOAT** Publicationes Universitatis Horticulturae Industriaeque Alimentariae. (1987)-. Monographic series. Hungarian (summaries and/or abstracts in English and Russian). ir. **LC** SB13; .B923. *Continues* Kerteszeti Egyetem Koezlemenyei, 0368-5217.
Ind/Abst Vitis Vitic. Enol. Abstr.; World Agric. Econ.

II
KFRI INFORMATION BULLETIN. Added/Corp Kerala Forest Research Institute. Division of Botany. **VFOAT** K.F.R.I. Information Bulletin; Information Bulletin. **VAT** Kerala Forest Research Institute Information Bulletin. (19??)-. Bulletin. English. Price varies per volume.
Ind/Abst Biodeter. Abstr.; For. Prod. Abstr.

US/0883-7333
KITCHEN GARDEN (NEWARK, DEL.), THE. (THE KITCHEN GARDEN.). [Kitchen garden]. Vol. 1, No. 1 (July/Aug. 1985)-. Periodical. English. bm. $12.00. F. Weldon Burge, PO Box 1067, Newark DE 19715. **DD** 635.

US/0748-7320
KOI USA. [Koi USA]. **Added/Corp** Associated Koi Clubs of America. **VFOAT** KOI U.S.A. **VAT** KOI United States of America. (19??)-. Periodical. English. Six times a year (Jan., Mar., May, July, Sept., Nov.). $20.00. Associated KOI Clubs of America, PO Box 1, Midway City CA 92655. **Tel** (714)548-3690. **ED** Mark Whalen (editor's address: 3687 Conquista Avenue, Longbeach, CA 90808). **DD** 639. Index available. cum. index ($3.00 each). **Ad Acc, Adv Mgr**: T. Graham, **Tel** (619)673-0955. **Circ**: 5,000.
Desc: Interesting and technical information on ponds, filters, fish and landscaping. Lot of pages are in full color. Captures the beauty of fish coloration and pond decoration.

JA
KOKUFU BONSAI TEN. Added/Corp Nihon Bonsai Kyokai. (19??)-. Periodical. Japanese (English). an. ¥5800. Nippon Bonsai Association, 8-1 Ikenohata 2-chome Taitoku, Tokyo Japan. **Tel** 03-821-3059, FAX 03-828-9150. **LC** SB433.5; .K647. **Circ**: 25,000.

KO
KORYO INSAM HAKHOE CHI. Main/Corp Koryo Insam Hakhoe. (19??)-. **VFOAT** Korean Journal of Ginseng Science. (1976)-. Periodical. English (summaries and/or abstracts in Korean). **LC** SB295.G5; K77a. Documents available from CASDDS.
Ind/Abst Chem. Abstr.; NAPRALERT; Rev. Plant Pathol.

PL/0324-8011
KWIATY. [Kwiaty]. **Added/Corp** Panstwowe Wydawnictwo Rolnicze I Lesne. No. 1 (1976)-. Periodical. Polish. qt. $19.00. (**Subscription address:** ARS Polona, PO Box 1001, 00068 Warsaw Poland.)
Ind/Abst AGRICOLA.

US/0733-0642
LA FILE. (LAFILE.). [LA file]. **Added/Corp** American Society of Landscape Architects. **VFOAT** L.A. File; LA File. **VAT** Landscape Architecture File. (1982)-. English. an. Landscape Architecture, 1733 Connecticut Avenue NW, Washington DC 20009-1108.

US/1053-2625
LABYRINTH (BOSTON, MASS.). (LABYRINTH : NEWSLETTER OF THE NEW ENGLAND GARDEN HISTORY SOCIETY OF THE MASSACHUSETTS HORTICULTURAL SOCIETY.). [Labyrinth]. **Added/Corp** New England Garden History Society. Vol. 1, No. 1 (Fall/Winter 1990)-. Newsletter. English. sa. comes with membership. New England Garden History Society, 300 Massachusetts Avenue, Boston MA 02115. **Tel** (617)536-9280. **DD** 635.
Ind/Abst Garden Lit. (1992-).

US/0146-910X
LAIFS. Main/Corp Los Angeles International Fern Society. **Added/Corp** Los Angeles International Fern Society. Bulletin. **VAT** Los Angeles International Fern Society. (19??)-. Periodical. English. bm (6 issues). Free to members of the Los Angeles International Fern Society. Los Angeles International Fern Society, PO Box 90943, Pasadena CA 91109. **Tel** (818)798-1046. **ED** Phyllis Bates. **LC** SB429; .L6714. **DD** 587/.31/05. Index available. **Ad Acc. Circ**: 500 (ctrl).
Desc: Articles and lessons on ferns and fern culture.

II/0023-7388
LAL-BAUGH; JOURNAL OF THE MYSORE HORTICULTURAL SOCIETY, THE. Added/Corp Mysore Horticultural Society. **VFOAT** Journal of the Mysore Horticultural Society. (1956)-. Periodical. English (Kannada). qt. Horticultural Society of India, 255 Upper Palace Orchards, Bangalore 6 India. **LC** SB429; .M914.
Ind/Abst Plant Grow. Reg. Abstr.; Rev. Agric. Entomol.; Rev. Plant Pathol.

GW
LAND- UND FORSTWIRTSCHAFT, FISCHEREI. REIHE 3.1.6, ANBAU VON ZIERPFLANZEN / HERAUSGEBER : STATISTISCHES BUNDESAMT. VFOAT Anbau von Zierpflanzen; Fachserie 3. 1981-. German. te. DM2.60. W Kohlhammer Verlag GMBH, Postfach 800430, D70549 Stuttgart Germany. **Tel** 011 49 711 78631. **LC** SB404.6.G4; G47B. **DD** 338.1/759/0943. *Continues* Land- und Forstwirtschaft. Reihe 3.6, Anbau von Zierpflanzen.

CN/0843-459X
LANDMARK (CALGARY). (LANDMARK.). [Landmark]. Vol. 1, No. 1 (Mar. 1989)-. Periodical. English. Six times a year. 30.00Can$ Canada; $45.00 other. Consolidated Communications, 807 Manning Road Northeast, Suite 200, Calgary Alberta T2E 7M8 Canada. **Tel** (403)569-9520, FAX (403)569-9590. **ED** Kathleen Peirera. **DD** 712/.0971. **Bk Rev. Ad Acc, Adv Mgr**: W. Whalen, **Tel** (613)930-9020. ctrl circ.
Desc: Covers gardening and horticulture.

NZ/0110-1439
LANDSCAPE, THE. Ceased. [Landscape]. No. 1 (Sept. 1976)-(1992). Periodical. English. Four times a year. New Zealand Institute of Landscape Architects, Box 10-022, The Terrace, Wellington 1 New Zealand. **Tel** 011 64 4 4722313. **Bk Rev. Ad Acc.** ctrl circ. *Supersedes* Nzila Newsletter.
Ind/Abst Avery Index Archit. Period. Suppl. Colum. Univ. (1989-).

UK
LANDSCAPE AND GARDEN CONTRACTOR. English. bm £24.00 UK; £28.00 Europe; £30.00 other. Peter Neale & Assn, 28 London Road, Maltravers House, Cheltenham Glo GL526DX England. **Tel** 011 44 242 221456.

US/0745-3795
LANDSCAPE & IRRIGATION. [Landsc. irrig.]. **VFOAT** Landscape and Irrigation. Vol. 6, No. 3 (Jan. 1983)-. Periodical. English. mo. $33.00 US; $55.00 other. Adams Publishing, 68860 Perez Road, PO Box 2150, Cathedral City CA 92235. **Tel** (619)770-4370, (800)776-1036. (**Subscription address:** Adams Publishing, PO Box 2150, Cathedral City CA 92235.) **ED** Anne Goldstein. **LC** SB472.53; .L34. **Ad Acc. Circ**: 30,500 (ctrl). *Continues* Landscape West & Irrigation News, 0199-6959; *Absorbed* Western Landscaping, 8750-412X.
Desc: Residential and commercial landscape and irrigation construction and maintenance.

●US/1071-3697
LANDSCAPE & NURSERY DIGEST. **VFOAT** Landscape and Nursery Digest. (1993)-. Periodical. English. Twelve times a year. $29.95 US; $48.95 others. Betrock Information Systems, 1601 North Palm Avenue, Suite 303, Pembroke Pines FL 33026. **Tel** (800)627-3819, (305)434-4440. *Continues* Southern Nursey Digest.

US/1060-9962
LANDSCAPE ARCHITECT & SPECIFIER NEWS. [Landsc. archit. specif. news]. **VFOAT** LASN; Landscape Architect and Specifier News. (19??)-. English. Twelve times a year. $29.95 one year; $34.95 two year. Landscape Arch & Specifier New, PO Box 30087, Santa Ana CA 92705. **ED** George Schmok. **DD** 712. **Bk Rev. Ad Acc, Adv Mgr**: Bob Erber, **Tel** (714)979-5276. ctrl circ.
Desc: The aim of this publication is to inform and promote the landscape architectural profession. LASN firmly believes that the principal consultant in every development should be the landscape architect.

CN/0228-6963
LANDSCAPE ARCHITECTURAL REVIEW. Ceased. [Lands. archit. rev.]. Vol. 1, No. 1 (May/June 1980)-Vol. 14. Periodical. English (summaries and/or abstracts in French). Five times a year. Landscape Architectural Review, 24 Kensington Avenue, Willowdale Ontario M2M 1R6 Canada. **Tel** (416)223-3956, FAX (416)366-9238. **ED** Nick van Vliet. **DD** 712/.09713. Index available. **Bk Rev. Ad Acc. Pr Rev. Circ**: 1,500 (ctrl). *Continues* OALA Review, 0383-9052.
Desc: Forum for articles, papers and reports related to landscape architecture, environmental sciences and

allied professions.
Ind/Abst Avery Index Archit. Period. Suppl. Colum. Univ. (Mar., Dec. 1989, Mar. 1990-); Can. Index (?-?); Garden Lit. (1992-).

US/0023-8031
LANDSCAPE ARCHITECTURE. [Landsc. archit.]. **Added/Corp** American Society of Landscape Architects. **VFOAT** Landscape Architecture Magazine. Vol. 1, No. 1 (Oct. 1910)-. Periodical. English. Twelve times a year. $48.00 (institutions), $44.00 (individuals) US; $76.00 (institutions), $74.00 (individuals) other. American Society Landscape Architects, 4401 Connecticut Avenue Northwest, 5th Floor, Washington DC 20008. **Tel** (202)686-2752. **ED** James Trulove. **LC** SB469; .L3. **DD** 712. Documents available from The Genuine Article.
Desc: Directed to the professional landscape architect, the main focus is on common problems of developers, builders, and ambitious laypersons give it a much wider dimension.
Ind/Abst Archit. Period. Index (1958,1978-); Art Index; Arts Humanit. Citation Index [Full Cov.]; Avery Index Archit. Period. Suppl. Colum. Univ. (1990-); Constr. Index (199?-); Curr. Contents Arts Humanit.; Ecol. Abstr. (?-?); Environ. Period. Bibliogr.; Garden Lit. (1992-); Geogr. Abstr. Human Geogr.; J. Plan. Lit.; Middle East Abstr. Index; Res. Alert [Full Cov.]; Soc. Sci. Cit. Index [Select. Cov.].

US/0278-8373
LANDSCAPE ARCHITECTURE. HOME LANDSCAPE. [Landsc. archit., Home landsc.]. **VFOAT** Home Landscape. Periodical. English. an. $42.00 US and Canada; $44.00 other. American Society of Landscape Architects / Kentucky, 1190 East Broadway, Louisville KY 40204. **LC** SB473; .L347. **DD** 712/.6/05.

US/0023-754X
LANDSCAPE ARCHITECTURE NEWS DIGEST. (LANDSCAPE ARCHITECTURAL NEWS DIGEST : LAND). [Landsc. archit. news dig.]. **Added/Corp** American Society of Landscape Architects. **VFOAT** LAND; Landscape Architecture News Digest. Vol. 1 (1960)-. Periodical. English. mo (except Dec. and Jan.). $19.00. American Society Landscape Architects, 4401 Connecticut Avenue Northwest, 5th Floor, Washington DC 20008. **Tel** (202)686-2752. **LC** SB469; .L27. available on microfilm and microfiche from University Microfilms International (UMI). ***Continues*** *Bulletin - American Society of Landscape Architects.*

AT/0310-9011
LANDSCAPE AUSTRALIA. [Landsc. Aust.]. **Added/Corp** Australian Institute of Landscape Architects. (1971)-. Periodical. English. qt. 36.00Aus$ Australia; 42.00Aus$ New Zealand; 45.00Aus$ other. Landscape Publications, 17 Carlyle Crescent, Mont Albert Victoria 3127 Australia. **Tel** 011 61 3 8905764, FAX 011 61 3 8996789. **ED** Ralph Neale. Index available. cum. index. **Bk Rev**. **Ad Acc. Circ:** 3,400.
Desc: Journal in landscape design. Covers technical articles, private gardens, Australian flora, landscape-related events in Australia, landscape construction and management.
Ind/Abst Archit. Period. Index (1979-); Avery Index Archit. Period. Suppl. Colum. Univ. (19??-199?); Garden Lit. (1992-).

US/0194-7257
LANDSCAPE CONTRACTOR, THE. [Landsc. contract.]. **Added/Corp** Illinois Landscape Contractors Association. (19??)-. Periodical. English. Twelve times a year. $65.00. Landscape Contractors Association, 2200 South Main Street, Suite 304, Lombard IL 60148-5334. **Tel** (708)932-8443. **ED** Deborah Slott. **DD** 712. **CODEN** LACOE9. Index available (bound in Dec. issue). **Ad Acc, Adv Mgr:** Esther Baricza, **Tel** (708)932-8443. **Circ:** 2,200 (ctrl). ***Absorbed*** *Midwest Landscaping.*
Desc: Carries news and features relating to landscape contracting, maintenance and designs.

UK/0020-2908
LANDSCAPE DESIGN. [Landsc. des.]. No. 93 (Feb. 1971)-. Periodical. English. ir (24 issues). £45.00 US. Landscape Design, c/o C. Hodder, 13A West Street, Reigate Surrey RH2 9BL England. **Tel** 011 44 73 7223294. **ED** Ken Fieldhouse. **LC** SB469; .L33. **DD** 712/.05. Index available (free). **Bk Rev. Ad Acc. Circ:** 5,000. ***Continues*** *Institute of Landscape Architects. Journal.*
Desc: Landscape architecture, design, ecology, landscape management, town and country planning, and land development.
Ind/Abst Archit. Period. Index (1971, 1977-); ARTbibliogr. Mod.; Avery Index Archit. Period. Suppl. Colum. Univ. (1989/1990-); EMBASE; Garden Lit. (1992-); J. Plan. Lit.

US/1070-3853
LANDSCAPE DESIGN (VAN NUYS, CALIF.). (LANDSCAPE DESIGN.). [Landsc. des.]. (199?)-. Periodical. English. mo (10 issues). $25.00 US; $55.00 other. Adams Publishing, 68860 Perez Road, PO Box 2150, Cathedral City CA 92235. **Tel** (619)770-4370, (800)776-1036. **(Subscription address:** Adams Publishing, PO Box 2150, Cathedral City CA 92235.**) DD** 712.

UK/0143-3768
LANDSCAPE HISTORY. (LANDSCAPE HISTORY : JOURNAL OF THE SOCIETY FOR LANDSCAPE STUDIES.). [Landsc. hist.]. **Added/Corp** Society for Landscape Studies (Great Britain). Vol. 1 (1979)-. Periodical. English. an. £15.00 (individuals), £10.00 (students & pensioners), £20.00 (institutions) UK; £20.00 (individuals), £15.00 (students & pensioners), £25.00 (institutions) other. Society for Landscape Studies, 22 Raleigh Crescent, c/o Graham Brown, Amesbury SP4 7QE England. **Tel** (011-44-980)623-723. **ED** Dr. D. Hooke. **LC** GF101; .L35. **DD** 333.73/09. Index available. **Bk Rev**, (Qty: 40). **Circ:** 450.
Desc: This journal is a testing ground for the study of landscape and a vehicle for bridging the disciplinary boundaries.
Ind/Abst Am. Hist. Life (1983-); Archit. Period. Index (1979-); Avery Index Archit. Period. Suppl. Colum. Univ. (1989); BHA : Biblio. Hist. Art; Br. Archaeol. Bibliogr.; Geogr. Abstr. Phys. Geogr. (?-?); Geogr. Abstr. Human Geogr. (?-?).

US/0277-2426
LANDSCAPE JOURNAL. [Landsc. j.]. **Added/Corp** University of Wisconsin--Madison. Dept. of Landscape Architecture. Council of Educators in Landscape Architecture. Vol. 1, No. 1 (Spring 1982)-. Academic Scholarly Publication. English. sa. $58.00 (one year), $114.00 (two year), $169.00 (three year), institution; $25.00 (one year), $50.00 (two year), $75.00 (three year), individuals. University of Wisconsin Press, Journal Division, 114 North Murray Street, Madison WI 53715. **Tel** (608)262-4952, FAX (608)262-8909. **LC** SB469; .L35. **DD** 333.73/05. **[CCC]. Ad Acc.** available on microfilm and microfiche from University Microfilms International (UMI).
Desc: Academic research, scholarly investigation, and technical information of interest to practitioners, academicians, and students of landscape architecture.'A significant contribution to the field', states Library Journal.
Ind/Abst AGRICOLA [Select. Cov.]; Archit. Period. Index (1984-); Avery Index Archit. Period. Suppl. Colum. Univ. (1990-); BHA : Biblio. Hist. Art; Curr. Aware. Biol. Sci., CABS; Environ. Period. Bibliogr.; Fish Rev. (Jan. 1989-July 1992); Garden Lit. (1992-); J. Plan. Lit.; Wildl. Rev. (Jan. 1989-July 1992).

US/0894-1254
LANDSCAPE MANAGEMENT. [Landsc. manage.]. Vol. 26, No. 4 (Apr. 1987)-. Academic Scholarly Publication. English. mo. $39.00 US and possessions; $66.00 Canada; $130.00 other. Advanstar Communications Inc., 131 West First Street, Duluth MN 55802. **Tel** (218)723-9477, (800)346-0085. **LC** SB610; .W37. **DD** 635.9/642. **[CCC].** ***Continues*** *Weeds, Trees & Turf, 0043-1753.*
Ind/Abst Acad. Search (July 1993-); AGRICOLA; EMBASE (Apr. 1987-); INFO-SOUTH Abstr.; Mag. Search; Vocat. Search (July 1993-).

UK/0142-6397
LANDSCAPE RESEARCH. [Landsc. res.]. **Added/Corp** Landscape Research Group (Great Britain). Vol. 2, No. 1 (Winter 1976)-. Periodical. English. Three times a year (Apr., Aug., and Dec.). £58.00 (institutions), £27.00 (individuals) UK & EEC countries; £65.00 (institutions), £33.00 (individuals) other. Landscape Research Group Ltd., Faculty of Arts and Design, University of Plymouth, Exeter Devon EX2 6AS England. **Tel** 011 44 525 60428, FAX 011 44 525 61527, telex 265871Monrefgeum300. **ED** Peter J. Howard. **CODEN** LAREDJ. Index available (to 1990). cum. index. **Bk Rev**, (Qty: 30). **Ad Acc. Pr Rev. Circ:** 500. Documents available from BIOSIS Document Express. ***Continues*** *Landscape Research News.*
Desc: Deals with recent research in landscape from all disciplines.
Ind/Abst Archit. Period. Index; BHA : Biblio. Hist. Art; Biol. Abstr.; Ecol. Abstr. (?-?); Environ. Period. Bibliogr.; Garden Lit. (1992-); Geogr. Abstr. Phys. Geogr. (?-?); Geogr. Abstr. Human Geogr.; Int. Dev. Abstr.; Leis. Recreat. Tour. Abstr.; Ornamental Hort.; Life Sci. Collect.; Rural Dev. Abstr.

UK
LANDSCAPE RESEARCH. EXTRA. No. 1 (Winter 1988)-. English. **LC** QH75.A1; L3.

UK/0266-0954
LANDSCAPE SCOTLAND QUARTERLY. **VFOAT** LSQ. (1984)-. English. qt.
Ind/Abst Archit. Period. Index (June 1984-).

UK/0195-489X
LANDSCAPE SYSTEMS. Monographic series. English. Price varies per volume. John Wiley & Sons Ltd., Baffins Lane, Chichester West Sussex PO19 1UD England. **Tel** 0243 779777, FAX 0243 776128 BTG:JWP001, telex 86290 WIBOOKG. **(Subscription address:** North, South and Central America/ John Wiley & Sons, Inc., Subscription Department, 605 Third Avenue, New York, NY 10158-0012, USA; telephone: (212)850-6645; FAX: (212)850-6021**)**

CN/0225-6398
LANDSCAPE TRADES. [Landsc. trades]. **Added/Corp** Landscape Ontario. Vol. 1 (Oct. 1979)-. Periodical. English. Ten times a year. 30.00Can$. Landscape Ontario, 1293 Matheson Boulevard, Mississauga Ontario L4W 1R1 Canada. **Tel** (416)629-1184, FAX (416)629-4438. **ED** Rosemary Dexter. **DD** 338.1/75/0971. **Bk Rev. Ad Acc. Circ:** 5,000 (ctrl).
Desc: National publication of interest to landscapers and other horticultural trades. Includes research, reports, industry information, international techniques, new products and articles of general interest.

AT
LANDSCAPER. (19??)-. English. Eleven times a year. 55.00Aus$. Landscape Contractors Association NSW, PO Box 1226, Bankstown NSW 2200 Australia. **Tel** 011 61 2 7905151, FAX 011 61 2 7962726. **Ad Acc.** ctrl circ.

US/0737-1632
LANDSCAPING HOMES & GARDENS GARDEN PLANS. **VFOAT** Landscaping Homes and Gardens Garden Plans; Garden Plans. Issue #1-. Periodical. English. Arden Communications Inc., PO Box 99, Amawalk NY 10501. **LC** SB473; .L3695. **DD** 712/.6/05.

US/0271-9126
LANDSCAPING, LAWNS AND GARDENS. [Landsc. lawns gard.]. Periodical. English. an. $2.25. Landscaping Lawns and Garden, 19 Arden Drive, Amawalk NY 10501. **LC** SB473; .L37. **DD** 634.9/05.

GW/0323-3162
LANDSCHAFTSARCHITEKTUR. Vol. 1, (1972)-. Periodical. German. bm. DM58.80 Germany; DM64.80 other. Bernhard Thalacker Verlag, Hamburger Str 277, Postfach 3361, D 38023 Braunschweig Germany. **Tel** 011 49 531 380040, FAX 011 49 531 3800425. **LC** SB469; .L36. **DD** 712/.05. **Bk Rev. Ad Acc.** ***Supersedes*** *Deutsche Gartenarchitektur.*
Desc: The only special journal for green planning, landscape architecture and horticulture in the socialist countries. It is indispensable to all, dealing with questions of landscape gardening, landscape architecture, projecting, construction and tending of parks.

DK/0023-8066
LANDSKAB. (LANDSKAB : TIDSSKRIFT FOR PLANLNING AF HAVE OG LANDSKAB : REVIEW FOR GARDEN AND LANDSCAPE PLANNING.). [Landskab]. Vol. 62 No. 1 (Feb. 1981)-. Periodical. Danish (summaries and/or abstracts in English). Eight times a year. kr390.00 Scandinavia; kr440.00 others. Arkitektens Forlag / The Danish Architectural Press, Nyhavn 43, DK-1051 Copenhagen K Denmark. **Tel** 011 45 33 136200, FAX 011 45 33 912770. available on microfilm from University Microfilms International (UMI). ***Continues*** *Landskap.*
Desc: Journal on garden and landscape planning.
Ind/Abst Archit. Period. Index (1981-); Avery Index Archit. Period. Suppl. Colum. Univ. (1989-); BHA : Biblio. Hist. Art.

US
LAWN AND GARDEN MARKETING. ***Ceased.*** (19??)-(19??). English. Intertec Publishing Corporation, 9800 Metcalf, Overland Park KS 66212. **Tel** (913)341-1300.
Ind/Abst F&S Index Plus Text, Int. [Select. Cov.].

CN/0705-212X
LAWN & GARDEN TRADE. Vol. 6, No. 2 (Spring 1977)-. Periodical. English. Four times a year (Feb., May, Aug., Nov.). 15.00Can$. CRV Publications, 2585 Skymark Ave, Suite 306, Mississauga Ontario L4W 4L5 Canada. **Tel** (416)624-8218, FAX (416)624-6764. **ED** Peter Tasler. **DD** 338.4/7/6817631. **Bk Rev. Ad Acc. Circ:** 15,000 (ctrl). ***Continues*** *Recreational Vehicles Trade, 0317-5308.*
Desc: Published to further the development and growth of Canada's lawn and garden and outdoor power equipment industries.

US/1046-154X
LAWN & LANDSCAPE MAINTENANCE. [Lawn landsc. maint.]. **VFOAT** Lawn & Landscape Maintenance. Vol. 10, No. 7 (July 1989)-. Periodical. English. Twelve times a year. $30.00 US; $35.00 Canada; $98.00 others. GIE Publishing Company, 4012 Bridge Avenue, Cleveland OH 44113. **Tel** (216)961-4130, (800)456-0707, FAX (216)961-0364. **ED** Cindy Code. **Ad Acc, Adv Mgr:** M Mertz. **Circ:** 43,000 (ctrl). ***Continues*** *ALA Lawn and Landscape Maintenance (OCoLC)19294454.*

US/0148-7906
LAWN, GARDEN AND HOME SHOWTIME. ***Ceased.*** **VFOAT** Showtime. Vol. 1 (1978)-(19??). English. an. Intertec Publishing Corporation, 9800 Metcalf, Overland Park KS 66212. **Tel** (913)341-1300.

CN/1193-767X
LIAISON - AMIS DU JARDIN BOTANIQUE DE MONTREAL. (LIAISON / LES AMIS DU JARDIN BOTANIQUE DE MONTREAL.). [Liaison - Amis Jard. bot. Montr.]. **Added/Corp** Amis du Jardin Botanique de Montreal. No. 58 (Autumn 1991)-. Periodical. French. tq. Les Amis du Jardin Botanique, 4101 Est Rue Sherbrooke 125, Montreal Quebec H1X

2B2 Canada. **Tel** (514)872-1493. **DD** 581. ***Continues*** *Societe d'Animation du Jardin et de l'Institut Botanique. Liaison - S A J I B., 0704-948X.*

FR/0293-6852
LIEN HORTICOLE. [Lien hortic.]. (1964)-. Periodical. French. Forty-eight times a year. 347.70F France; 680.00F other. Editions du Lien, BP 30, F-34471 Perols Cedex 1 France. **Tel** 33 67 500618, , FAX 33 67 501902, telex 480755. Index available. **Bk Rev. Ad Acc.** ctrl circ.

UK/0075-949X
LILIES AND OTHER LILIACEAE. 1973-. English. an. £95.00. Royal Horticultural Society, 80 Vincent Square, London SW1P 2PE England. **Tel** 011 44 71 834 4333. **LC** SB413.L7; L47. **DD** 635.9/34/32405. ***Continues*** *Lily Yearbook.*

US/0741-9910
LILY YEARBOOK OF THE NORTH AMERICAN LILY SOCIETY, INC, THE. [Lily yearb. North Am. Lily Soc. Inc.]. **Added/Corp** North American Lily Society. (19??)-. Periodical. English. an. $12.50 (individuals), $18.75 (sustaining) Comes with North American Lily Society membership. North American Lily Society, PO Box 272, Owatonna MN 55060. **Tel** (507)451-2170. **ED** Robert Gilman. Index available. cum. index. **Ad Acc. Circ:** 1,500. ***Continues*** *Lily Yearbook.*
Desc: Information on the propagation and culture of true (bulb) lilies and the research being done with them around the world.
Ind/Abst AGRICOLA [Select. Cov.].

IT/0394-3704
LINEA VERDE. [Linea verde]. (1975)-. Periodical. Italian. Twelve times a year. L100000 Italy; L160000 others. Aquarius Editrice, via A Gramsci 803, 50019 Sesto Fiorentino Italy. **Tel** 011 39 55 4250271, FAX 011 39 55 452504. **UDC** 712.4.

US
LINING OUT STOCK FOR ... / APPALACHIAN NURSERIES. Main/Corp Appalachian Nurseries. (Spring 1981)-. English. an. ***Continues*** *Lining Out Stock.*

US/0092-6825
LIST OF INTERCEPTED PLANT PESTS. (LIST OF INTERCEPTED PLANT PESTS / UNITED STATES DEPARTMENT OF AGRICULTURE, PLANT QUARANTINE AND CONTROL ADMINISTRATION.). [List intercept. plant pests]. **Added/Corp** United States. Plant Quarantine and Control Administration. United States. Bureau of Plant Quarantine. United States. Bureau of Entomology and Plant Quarantine. United States. Agricultural Research Service. United States. Plant Quarantine Branch. United States. Plant Quarantine Division. United States. Animal and Plant Health Inspection Service. Plant Protection and Quarantine Programs. (Jan. 1, 1930/June 30, 1931)-. English. an. US Department of Agriculture / Animal & Plant Health Inspection Service, 741 Federal Building 1, 6505 Belcres Road, Hyattsville MD 20782. **Tel** (301)436-7817. **LC** SB981; .A334 subser. **DD** 632/.93/0973. **Circ:** 2,000 (ctrl). ***Continues*** *List of Pests Intercepted on Imported Plants and Plant Year ... .*

US/0738-7687
LIVING OFF THE LAND. [Living land]. Vol. 1, No. 1 (Apr. 1, 1975)-. Periodical. English. Five times a year (Jan., March, May, Sept., Nov.). $14.00 US; $16.00 other. Geraventure Corp., PO Box 2131, Melbourne FL 32902. **Tel** (407)723-5554. **ED** Marian Van Atta. **Circ:** 600.

US
LONG ISLAND GARDENING. Added/Corp Cooperative Extension Association of Nassau County. Cooperative Extension Association of Suffolk County. (Jan. 1986)-. Periodical. English. bm. $10.00. Cooperative Extension of Suffolk County, 246 Griffing Avenue, Riverhead NY 11901. **Tel** (516)727-7850, FAX (516)727-7130. **Circ:** 1,500. ***Formed by the union of*** *Suffolk Living* ***and*** *Nassau Living.*

USUS/1057-3224
LONGWOOD GRADUATE PROGRAM SEMINARS, THE. [Longwood Grad. Program semin.]. **Added/Corp** Longwood Graduate Program in Public Horticulture Administration. Vol. 17 (1985)-. English. University of Delaware / Longwood, Longwood Graduate Program in Public Horticulture Administration, Newark DE 19717-1303. **DD** 580. ***Continues*** *Longwood Program Longwood Program Seminars, 0886-6384.*
Ind/Abst AGRICOLA [Select. Cov.].

BU/0458-4244
LOZARSTVO I VINARSTVO. [Lozar. vinar.]. **Added/Corp** Bulgaria, Ministerstvo na Zemedelieto i Khranitelnata Promishlenost. Vol. 1 (Feb. 1952)-. Academic Scholarly Publication. Bulgarian. mo. DM144.00. **(Subscription address:** Kubon & Sagner, ABT Zeitschriftenimport, D 80328 Munich Germany.**)** **CODEN** LOVIAA. Documents available from CASDDS.
Ind/Abst AGRICOLA; Chem. Abstr.; Food Sci. Technol. Abstr.; Hortic. Abstr.; Plant Breed. Abstr.; Plant Grow. Reg. Abstr.; Rev. Agric. Entomol.; Vitis Vitic. Enol. Abstr.; World Agric. Econ.

IO
LUAS & INTENSITAS SERANGAN HAMA & PENYAKIT DI INDONESIA. **Main/Corp** Indonesia. Biro Pusat Statistik. **VAT** Luas dan Intensitas Serangan Hama dan Penyakit di Indonesia. 1976-. Indonesian. an. Rp2500 Indonesia; $2.60 US. Central Bureau of Statistics / Indonesia, c/o Dr. Sutomo, 8 Jalan, PO Box 3, Jakarta Indonesia. **Tel** 372808 374908 Ext.342. **LC** SB605.I53; I53A. **Ad Acc.** ctrl circ.

US/1054-9153
MAGNOLIA (WINSTON-SALEM, N.C.). (MAGNOLIA : BULLETIN OF THE SOUTHERN GARDEN HISTORY SOCIETY.). [Magnolia]. **Added/Corp** Southern Garden History Society. (198?)-. Bulletin. English. qt. Free to members; $30.00 (institutions), $20.00 (individuals) membership fee. Southern Garden History Society, Old Salem, Inc., Drawer F, Salem Station, Winston-Salem NC 27108. **Tel** (919)721-7300. **ED** Peggy C. Newcomb (Editor's Address: Monticello, PO Box 316, Charlottesville, VA 22902; Phone: (804)979-5283). **DD** 635. **Bk Rev**, (Qty: 4). **Circ:** 600.
Desc: Strives to stimulate interest in Southern garden and landscape history, in historical horticulture, and in the preservation and restoration of historic gardens and landscapes in the South.
Ind/Abst Garden Lit. (1992-).

FR/0025-0945
MAISON & JARDIN. **See** Interior Design.

AG
MALEZAS / ASOCIACION ARGENTINA PARA EL CONTROL DE MALEZAS. **See** Biology-Botany.

GW
MEIN SCHONER GARTEN. Vol. 3, No. 3 (Mar. 1974)-. Periodical. German. mo. $60.00. Burda GmbH, Postfach 1230, D-7602 Offenburg Germany. **Tel** 011 49 781-8401. **(Subscription address:** US: German Language Publications, Inc., 153 South Deanstreet, Englewood, NJ 07631**)**

●CN/1191-3363
MEMBERSHIP DIRECTORY, PLANT SOURCE LIST. [Membsh. dir. plant source list]. **Main/Corp** Landscape Alberta Nursery Trades Association. **VFOAT** Plant Source List; LANTA. (1992/1993)-. Directory. English. Landscape Alberta Nursery Trades Association, 10215-176 St., Edmonton Alberta T5S 1M1 Canada. **DD** 338.1/759/02947123. ***Formed by the union of*** *Landscape Alberta Nursery Trades Association. Membership Roster., 0832-0160* ***and*** *Plant Source List (Edmonton, Alta. : 1989)., 0843-0861.*

US
MENTZELIA. Added/Corp Northern Nevada Native Plant Society. No. 1, (1975)-. Periodical. English. ir. $7.50 (one year), $20.00 (three years) Comes with Northern Nevada Native Plant Society membership. Northern Nevada Native Plant Society, Box 8965, Reno NV 89507. **Tel** (702)358-7759. **Circ:** 500.

NE/0169-2267
MESTSTOFFEN. [Meststoffen]. **Added/Corp** Nederlands Meststoffen Instituut. (1985)-. Periodical. Dutch. an. F35.00. Ned Meststoffen Institute, Agro Business Park 20, 6708 PW Wageningen, Netherlands. **Tel** 011 31 8370 79620. ***Continues*** *Stikstof, 0585-3060.*
Ind/Abst Agric. Eng. Abstr.; Dairy Sci. Abstr.; Grasslands For. Abstr.

US/0026-5500
MINNESOTA HORTICULTURIST, THE. [Minn. hortic.]. **Added/Corp** Minnesota State Horticultural Society. Vol. 22, No. 1 (Feb. 1894)-. Periodical. English. mo (except July, Sept., Nov.). $25.00 (comes with membership). Minnesota State Horticultural Society, 1755 Prior Avenue North, Falcon Heights MN 55113. **Tel** (612)624-7752, (800)676-6747. **ED** Lynn M. Steiner. Index available. cum. index. **Bk Rev. Ad Acc. Circ:** 14,000.
Desc: Non-technical magazine for gardening and horticultural activities in the northern climates.
Ind/Abst AGRICOLA; Garden Lit. (1992-); Ornamental Hort.

SZ/1016-3158
MITTEILUNGEN DER EIDGENOSSISCHEN FORSCHUNGSANSTALT FUER WALD, SCHNEE UND LANDSCHAFT. **See** Forestry.

GW/0178-2916
MITTEILUNGEN DES OBSTBAUVERSUCHSRINGES DES ALTEN LANDES. (MITTEILUNGEN DES OBSTBAUVERSUCHSRINGES DES ALTEN LANDES E.V. UND DER ARBEITSGEMEINSCHAFT BAUMSCHULEN IM OBSTBAUVERSUCHSRING.). [Mitt. Obstbauvers.ringes Alten Landes]. **Main/Corp** Obstbauversuchsring des Alten Landes, Jork. (1947)-. Periodical. German. mo. DM100.00 Germany; DM115.00 other. Obstbauversuchsring d Alten Landes EV, Postfach 1220, W 2155 Jork Germany. **Tel** 011 49 4162 60160. cum. index.
Ind/Abst AGRICOLA; Agric. Eng. Abstr.; Soils Fert.

UK
MONOGRAPH / BRITISH SOCIETY FOR PLANT GROWTH REGULATION. **Added/Corp** British Society for Plant Growth Regulation. **VFOAT** BSPGR Monograph. **VAT** British Society for Plant Growth Regulation Monograph. No. 19 (1990)-. Monographic series. English. **CODEN** MBSREE. ***Continues*** *Monograph (British Plant Growth Regulator Group), 0952-6463.*
Ind/Abst Hortic. Abstr.; Irr. Drain. Abstr.; Rev. Plant Pathol.; Seed Abstr.; Soils Fert.; Soyabean Abstr.

IE/0332-4273
MOOREA : THE JOURNAL OF THE IRISH GARDEN PLANT SOCIETY. **Added/Corp** Irish Garden Plant Society. Vol. 1 (Mar. 1982)-. Periodical. English. an. £7.50 (comes with Irish Garden Plant Society membership). Irish Garden Plant Society, c/o National Botanic Gardens Glasnevin, Dublin 9 Republic of Ireland. **Tel** 011 353 1 37163617, FAX 011 353 1 337329. **ED** Board. **Bk Rev. Circ:** 600 (ctrl).
Desc: History of gardens and gardening in Ireland; nomenclature and cultivation of exotic plants in Ireland.

AT/1037-1842
MOOREANA : JOURNAL OF THE PALMETUM. **See** Biology-Botany.

FR/0998-495X
MOTOCULTURE MAGAZINE NEUILLY-SUR-SEINE. (MOTOCULTURE MAGAZINE.). (1989)-. Periodical. French. mo. $103.00. Masson SA, Avenue Beauregard 12, CH-1701 Fribourg Switzerland. **Tel** 011 41 37 249585, FAX 011 41 37 247559, telex 942658 SEMI CH. **UDC** 631.3.

US/1057-5049
MOUNTAIN, PLAIN AND GARDEN. **See** Biology-Botany.

UK/0144-0551
MUSHROOM JOURNAL. (THE MUSHROOM JOURNAL.). [Mushroom j.]. **Added/Corp** Mushroom Growers' Association. (1973)-. Academic Scholarly Publication. English. Twelve times a year. $217.46 (non-trade), $453.05 (trade). Mushroom Growers Association, 2 St Pauls Street Stanford, Lincolnshire PE39 2BE England. **Tel** 011 44 780 66888, FAX 0780-66558. **ED** K. I. James. **CODEN** MUSJDK. Index available. **Ad Acc. Circ:** 1,000 (ctrl). Documents available from CASDDS. ***Supersedes*** *Mushroom Growers' Association. MGA Bulletin.*
Desc: Comprehensive news and information on all aspects of the industry and is highly valued among our members. Also contains advertisers of the latest equipment.
Ind/Abst AgBiotech News Inf.; AGRICOLA [Full Cov.]; Agric. Eng. Abstr. (1991-); Biodeter. Abstr.; Chem. Abstr. (1973-1983); Food Sci. Technol. Abstr.; Hortic. Abstr.; Microbiol. Abstr. Sect. A; Microbiol. Abstr. Sect. C; Nematol. Abstr.; Life Sci. Collect.; Plant Breed. Abstr.; Postharvest News Inf.; World Agric. Econ.

UK/0029-6430
N&GC : JOURNAL OF THE HORTICULTURAL TRADES ASSOCIATION. **Added/Corp** Horticultural Trades Association (Great Britain). **VFOAT** N. &. G. C.; N and GC; N&GC Nurseryman & Garden Centre; Nurseryman & Garden Centre. **VAT** Nurseryman and Garden Centre. Vol. 174, No. 17 (June 12, 1986)-. Periodical. English. Twenty-four times a year. £44.00 UK; £59.00 others. Bouverie Publishing Company Ltd, 141 147 Temple Chambers, London EC4Y ODT England. **Tel** 011 44 825 765075, 011 44 71 5836463. ***Continues*** *Nurseryman & Garden Centre.*

UK
N&GC NURSERYMAN & GARDEN CENTRE. - . English.

US
NATIONAL APPLE NEWS / INTERNATIONAL APPLE INSTITUTE. V. 1- July 1970-. Periodical. English. bm. International Apple Institute, 6707 Old Dominion Drive/Suite 210, PO Box 1137, McLean VA 22101. ***Continues*** *National Apple News.*

US/0027-9331
NATIONAL GARDENER, THE. [Natl. gard.]. **Added/Corp** National Council of State Garden Clubs. Vol. 19, Nos. 6-8 (July/Aug. 1948)--. Periodical. English. bm (6 issues). $6.50. National Council of State Garden Clubs, 4401 Magnolia Avenue, St Louis MO 63110-3492. **Tel** (314)776-7574, FAX (314)776-5108. **(Subscription address:** National Gardener, Circulation Department, NCSGC, 4401 Magnolia Avenue, St. Louis MO 63110-3492.**)** **ED** Susan Davidson (editor's address and telephone: 102 South Elm Avenue, St. Louis, MO 63119, (314)968-1664). **LC** SB1; .N2947. **DD** 635.905. **Ad Acc. Circ:** 31,000. ***Continues*** *Bulletin of the National Council of State Garden Clubs, Inc.*

Desc: Ideas in the area of gardening, environment and natural resources.
Ind/Abst Garden Lit. (1992-).

US/1052-4096
NATIONAL GARDENING. [Natl. gard.]. **Added/Corp** National Gardening Association (U.S.). **VFOAT** National Gardening Magazine. (1986)-. Periodical. English. Six times a year. $18.00 US; $24.00 other. National Gardening Association, 180 Flynn Avenue, Burlington VT 05401. **Tel** (802)863-1308. **DD** 635. Index available. **Ad Acc, Adv Mgr:** Bob Bennett. **Circ:** 219,000. ***Continues*** *National Gardening Association, 0887-8447.*
Desc: Provides solid gardening information and excellent color photography with a gardener-to-gardener style, sence of humor and commitment to the founding principles that have become the trademark of its parent organization, The National Gardening Association.
Ind/Abst Garden Lit. (1992-).

US
NATIONAL GARDENING MAGAZINE'S ... GARDEN HANDBOOK. Added/Corp National Gardening Association (U.S.). **VFOAT** Garden Handbook. (1991)-. English. National Gardening Association, 180 Flynn Avenue, Burlington VT 05401. **Tel** (802)863-1308.

US/0270-0816
NATIONAL GARDENING SURVEY. [Natl. gard. surv.]. **Main/Corp** Gallup Organization. **Added/Corp** Gardens for All, Inc. (19??)-. English. an. $50.00 nonprofit organizations; $250.00 other. National Gardening Association, 180 Flynn Avenue, Burlington VT 05401. **Tel** (802)863-1308. **ED** Bruce W. Butterfield. **LC** SB320.6; .G35a. **DD** 635/.0973. **Circ:** 200.
Desc: Consumer market research study of lawn and garden participation, spending and interests of US households.

US/0883-8313
NATIONAL GREENHOUSE GARDENER. [Natl. greenh. gard.]. (Oct. 1985)-. Periodical. English. qt. $10.00 U.S.; $12.00 Canada. Andmar Press, PO Box 217, Mills WY 82644. **Tel** (307)472-3107. **ED** Francis X. Jozwik. **DD** 635. **Bk Rev. Ad Acc. Circ:** 18,000 (ctrl).
Desc: Presents cultural, marketing and environmental subjects concerning greenhouse crops. Edited for professional and serious amateur horticulturists.

US
NATIONAL RETAIL FLORAL INDEX SPECIAL CONSUMER STUDY. English. Floral Index Inc, Twenty North Wacker Drive, Chicago IL 60606. **LC** SB443.3; .N37. **DD** 381/.4159/0973.

GW
NATURSCHUTZ UND LANDSCHAFTSPLANUNG. Vol. 23 Issue 1 (Jan./Feb. 1991)-. Periodical. German. bm. DM98.20 Germany; DM105.80 other. Verlag Eugen Ulmer, Postfach 700561, D 70574 Stuttgart Germany. **Tel** 011 49 711 4507108, FAX 011 49 711 4507120, telex 7-23634. ***Continues*** *Landschaft + Stadt, 0023-8058.*
Ind/Abst Leis. Recreat. Tour. Abstr.; World Agric. Econ.

RU/0202-5361
NAUCHNO-TEKHNICHESKII BIULLETEN VSESOIUZNOGO ORDENA LENINA I ORDENA DRUZHBY NARODOV NAUCHNO-ISSELDOVATELSKOGO INSTITUTA RASTENIEVODSTVA IMENI N.I. VAVILOVA / VSESOIUZNAIA ORDENA LENTINA I ORDENA TRUDOGO KRASNOGO ZNAMENI AKADEMIIA SELSKOKHOZIAISTVENNYKH NAUK IMENI V.I. LENINA. Added/Corp Vsesoiuznyi Nauchno-Issledovatelskii Institut Rastenievodstva Imenii N.I. Vavilova. Vsesoiuznaia Akademiia Selskokhoziaistvennykh Nauk Imeni V.I. Lenina. No. 127 (1983)-. Periodical. Russian. ***Continues*** *Biulleten' Vsesoiuznogo Ordena Lenina I Ordena Druzhby Narodov Nauchno-Issledovatel'skogo Instituta Rastenievodstva Imeni N.I. Vavilova.*
Ind/Abst Cot. Trop. Fibr. Abstr. Bibliogr.; Field Crop Abstr.; For. Abstr.; Grasslands For. Abstr.; Maize Abstr.; Ornamental Hort. (1991-); Plant Breed. Abstr.; Plant Genet. Resour. Abstr.; Plant Grow. Reg. Abstr.; Potato Abstr.; Rev. Plant Pathol.; Rice Abstr.; Seed Abstr.; Soyabean Abstr.

●US/1061-3994
NEIL SPERRY'S GARDENS. [Neil Sperry's gard.]. **VFOAT** Gardens. Vol. 6, No.1 (Jan. 1992)-. Periodical. English. Ten times a year. $21.50 one year; $40.00 two years; $56.00 three years. Gardens South, PO Box 864, McKinney TX 75069. **Tel** (214)562-5050. **ED** Mike Goldman. **DD** 635. **Bk Rev. Ad Acc. Circ:** 25,000. ***Continues*** *Gardens and More, 1052-3243.*

JA
NEMPO - NORINSHO KANTO RINBOKU IKUSHUJO. Main/Corp Norinsho Kanto Rinboku Ikushujo. **Added/Corp** Norinsho Kanto Rinboku Ikushujo. Annual Report. **VFOAT** Annual Report. No. 1 (1960)-. Japanese (summaries and/or abstracts in English). 978 Kasahara, Mito Japan. **LC** SB399.5; .N67a.

US
NEW ENGLAND FARM BULLETIN & GARDEN GAZETTE. (19??)-. Bulletin. English. mo. $17.00 (one year), $31.00 (two year), $45.00 (three year). Jacob's Meadow Inc, PO Box 67, Taunton MA 02780. **Tel** (508)824-1186. **ED** Pam Comstock. **Bk Rev. Ad Acc. Circ:** 10,000.
Desc: Bulletin on gardening and horticulture.

US/0896-8160
NEW ENGLAND GARDENER. *Ceased.* [N. Engl. gard.]. **Added/Corp** New England Farm and Home, Assn. New England Horticultural Services. (19??)-(1992). Periodical. English. mo. New England Gardener, 180 Flynn Avenue, Burlington VT 05401. **Tel** (802)863-1308. **ED** Warren Schultz. **DD** 635. **Bk Rev**, (Qty: 10).
Desc: Gardening techniques for New England gardeners.
Ind/Abst Garden Lit. (1992-?).

US/0197-5633
NEW GARDENS NEWSLETTER. Vol. 1 (1980)-. Newsletter. English. mo. $9.96. Garden Center Publishing Ltd, Box 222, Greece NY 14515. **Tel** (716)458-7952, (716)235-2350.

AT/0028-249X
NEW IDEA MELBOURNE. See Home Economics.

JA/0914-3238
NEW ORCHIDS. [New orchids]. **VFOAT** Nyu Okiddo; Shumi no Yoran, New Orchids; Bonsai Sekai. Zokan. (1983)-. Periodical. Japanese. Five times a year. $130.00. Shinkikaku Co., 4-17-17 Jingumae Shibuya-ku, Tokyo Japan. **Tel** 011 81 3 354748621. **DD** 635.934.

●UK/1352-4186
NEW PLANTSMAN, THE. Added/Corp Royal Horticultural Society (Great Britain). Vol. 1, Pt. 1 (March 1994)-. Periodical. English. qt. £25.00 British Isles; £29.00 other. Royal Horticultural Society, 80 Vincent Square, London SW1P 2PE England. **Tel** 011 44 71 834 4333. **LC** QK1; .N48. ***Continues*** *Plantsman, 0143-0106.*
Desc: Includes articles on plants that are less commonly grown, their cultivation and garden value; fruit and vegetables are included, although the main emphasis is on decorative plants for both outdoors and in.

NZ
NEW ZEALAND COMMERCIAL GROWER : OFFICIAL JOURNAL OF THE NEW ZEALAND VEGETABLE AND PRODUCE GROWERS' FEDERATION. Added/Corp New Zealand Vegetable and Produce Growers' Federation. (19??)-. Periodical. English. Ten times a year (Jan./Feb. & Nov./Dec. issues combined). 30.00NZ$ New Zealand; 60.00NZ$ others. Vegetable Producers Publishers Limited, PO Box 10232, Wellington, New Zealand. **Tel** 011 64 4 723795. **ED** David Poterson. **Ad Acc. Circ:** 5,800.
Desc: The magazine is in research and education institutes, business houses, produce merchants, exporters, processing factories, government department and service organizations.
Ind/Abst Hortic. Abstr.; Plant Breed. Abstr.

NZ/0028-8136
NEW ZEALAND GARDENER. [N.Z. gard.]. **VFOAT** N.Z. Gardener; Gardener. (1944)-. Periodical. English. Eleven times a year. 52.50NZ$ New Zealand; 78.00NZ$ (surface mail) other. New Zealand Gardener, PO Box 6341, Wellesley Street, Auckland, New Zealand. **Tel** 011 64 9 377889, FAX 011 64 9 777765. **DD** _a635. **[CCC].**
Ind/Abst Garden Lit. (1992-).

NZ/0114-0671
NEW ZEALAND JOURNAL OF CROP AND HORTICULTURAL SCIENCE. [N.Z. j. crop hortic. sci.]. **Added/Corp** New Zealand. Dept. of Scientific and Industrial Research. Vol. 17, No. 1 (1989)-. Academic Scholarly Publication. English. qt (Mar., June, Sep., Dec.). £130.00 (institution), £35.00 (individual). SIR Publishing, PO Box 399, Wellington, New Zealand. **Tel** 011 64 4 472 7421, FAX 011 64 4 473 1841. **CODEN** NZJSEF. **[CCC]. Ad Acc. Pr Rev.** Documents available from The Genuine Article, BIOSIS Document Express, CASDDS. ***Continues*** *New Zealand Journal of Experimental Agriculture, 0301-5521.*
Desc: Covers all aspects of horticulture and field crops.
Ind/Abst AgBiotech News Inf.; Agric. Eng. Abstr. (1991-); BioBusiness; Biocont. News Inf. (1991-); Biodeter. Abstr. (1991-); Biol. Abstr. (1989-); Chem. Abstr.; Crop Physiol. Abstr.; Curr. Aware. Biol. Sci., CABS; Curr. Contents, Agric. Biol. Environ. Sci.; Ecol. Abstr.; Field Crop Abstr.; Geogr. Abstr. Phys. Geogr.; Hortic. Abstr.; Irr. Drain. Abstr.; Plant Breed. Abstr.; Plant Genet. Resour. Abstr.; Plant Grow. Reg. Abstr.; Postharvest News Inf.; Potato Abstr.; Res. Alert [Full Cov.]; Rev. Agric. Entomol.; Rev. Plant Pathol.; Sci. Cit. Index; SCISEARCH; Seed Abstr.; Soils Fert.; Soyabean Abstr.; Weed Abstr.; Wheat Barley Trit. Abstr.

US/0401-913X
NEWS CAST - AMERICAN IRIS SOCIETY. REGION 4. [News cast - Am. Iris Soc., Reg. 4]. **Main/Corp** American Iris Society. Region 4. **VFOAT** Newscast. Periodical. English. Three times a year. **DD** 635. ***Continues*** *American Iris Society. Region 4. Newsletter.*
Ind/Abst AGRICOLA.

US/0569-2423
NEWSLETTER / AMERICAN ASSOCIATION OF BOTANICAL GARDENS AND ARBORETA. See Biology-Botany.

US/1046-2627
NEWSLETTER - CATALOG OF LANDSCAPE RECORDS IN THE UNITED STATES (PROJECT). (NEWSLETTER / THE CATALOG OF LANDSCAPE RECORDS IN THE UNITED STATES.). [Newsl. - Cat. Landsc. Rec. U. S. (Proj.)]. **Added/Corp** American Garden and Landscape History Program at Wave Hill. Catalog of Landscape Records in the United States (Project) Wave Hill, Inc. **VFOAT** Catalog of Landscape Records in the United States Newsletter. Vol. 1, No. 1 (Summer 1987)-. Catalog. English. qt. $25.00. Wave Hill, 675 West 252nd Street, Bronk NY 10471. **DD** 712.
Ind/Abst Garden Lit. (1992-).

UK/0269-4123
NEWSLETTER - GARDEN HISTORY SOCIETY (1981). (NEWSLETTER / THE GARDEN HISTORY SOCIETY.). [Newsl. - Gard. Hist. Soc.]. **Main/Corp** Garden History Society (Great Britain). (Winter 1981)-. Newsletter. English. tq. Garden History Society, c/o Anne Richards, 5 The Knoll, Hereford HR1 1RU England. **Tel** 44 432 354479. **LC** SB451; .G37.

US/0739-1609
NEWSLETTER - NATIONAL COUNCIL FOR THERAPY AND REHABILITATION THROUGH HORTICULTURE (U.S.). (NEWSLETTER.). [Newsl. - Natl. Counc. Ther. Rehabil. Hortic. (U.S.)]. **Main/Corp** National Council for Therapy and Rehabilitation Through Horticulture. Vol. 1 (Jan. 1974)-. Newsletter. English. mo (eleven times per year). comes with membership. American Horticultural Therapy Association, 362 A Christopher Avenue, Gaithersburg MD 20879. **Tel** (301)948-3010. **ED** Steven H. Davis. Index available. **Bk Rev. Ad Acc. Circ:** 1,000 (ctrl).
Desc: For therapists and rehabilitation using horticulture.

US/0897-3091
NEWSLETTER (NEW ENGLAND WILDFLOWER SOCIETY : 1985). (NEWSLETTER / NEW ENGLAND WILD FLOWER SOCIETY.). [Newsl. - N. Engl. Wild Flower Soc.]. **Added/Corp** New England Wildflower Society. (Spring 1985)-. Newsletter. English. qt. New England Wild Flower Society, Garden in the Woods, Hemenway Road, Framingham MA 01701. **DD** 635. ***Continues in part*** *Wild Flower Notes and News.*
Ind/Abst Garden Lit. (1992-).

US/1065-2108
NEWSLETTER OF THE GARDEN CONSERVANCY, THE. [Newsl. Gard. Conserv.]. **Main/Corp** Garden Conservancy. **Added/Corp** Tides Foundation. (Spring/summer 1990)-. Newsletter. English. sa. $50.00. The Garden Conservancy, Box 219, Main Street, Cold Spring NY 10516. **Tel** 914 265-2029. **DD** 635.
Ind/Abst Garden Lit. (1992-).

JA/0077-4847
NOGYO GIJUTSU KENKYUJO HOKOKU. C : BYORI KONCHU. [Nogyo Gijutsu Kenkyusho Hokoku C]. **Main/Corp** Norinsho Nogyo Gijutsu Kenkyujo (Japan). **VFOAT** Bulletin of the National Institute of Agricultural Sciences. Plant Pathology and Entomology. No. 1- ; 1952-. Academic Scholarly Publication. Multiple languages (Japanese and English). an. Norinsho Nogyo Gijutsu Kenkyujo, Nishigata 2, Kita-Ku (114), Tokyo Japan. **LC** SB599. **CODEN** NGKCA5. Documents available from BIOSIS Document Express, CASDDS.
Ind/Abst AGRICOLA; Biol. Abstr.; Chem. Abstr. (1952-1984); EMBASE.

JA/0369-5247
NOGYO OYOBI ENGEI. See Agriculture.

JA
NOKO TO ENGEI. See Agriculture.

KO/1013-9370
NONGSA SIHOM YON'GU NONMUNJIP. T'OYANG PIRYO P'YON. VFOAT Research Reports of the Rural Development Administration. Soil & Fertilizer; Research Reports of R.D.A., S & F. (1988)-.

Periodical. Multiple languages. ir.
Ind/Abst Agric. Eng. Abstr.; Hortic. Abstr.; Rice Abstr.; Seed Abstr.; Soyabean Abstr.

KO/1010-562X
NONGSA SIHOM YON'GU NONMUNJIP. WONYE P'YON. **VFOAT** Research Reports of the Rural Development Administration. Horticulture; Research Reports of R.D.A., H. (1985)-. Periodical. Multiple languages. sa. ***Continues*** *Nongsa Sihom Yon'gu Pogo. Wonye p'Yon, 1013-7092.*
Ind/Abst Hortic. Abstr.; Plant Breed. Abstr.; Plant Grow. Reg. Abstr.; Postharvest News Inf.; Potato Abstr.; Rev. Plant Pathol.; Seed Abstr.

KO
NONGSA SIHOM YONGU POGO. WONYE. **VFOAT** Research Reports of the Office of Rural Development. Vol. 24 (Dec. 1982)-. Periodical. Korean (summaries and/or abstracts in English). sa. Office of Rural Development, Ministry of Agriculture and Fisheries, Suweon Korea. ***Continues*** *Nongsa Sihom Yongu Pogo. Wonye, Jamup.*

NO
NORDEN; NORD-NORGES LANDBRUKSTIDSSKRIFT. **See** Agriculture.

NO/0029-1986
NORSK HAGETIDEND. **Added/Corp** Norske Hageselskap. Havedyrkningens Venner (Norwey). **VFOAT** Norsk Havetidende. Vol. 1 (1885)-. Periodical. Norwegian. mo. Kr225.00. Det Norske Hageselskap, Postboks 9008, Vaterland Oslo 1 Norway. **Tel** 2670595, FAX 2673626. **ED** Dagfinn Tveito and Knut Lono. **[CCC].** Index available. **Bk Rev. Ad Acc. Circ:** 58,751 (ctrl).
Desc: Gardening, outdoor life in gardens, development areas, garden planning, furniture, vegetables, fruits, herbs, tools and sundries.

US
NORTH CAROLINA FLOWER GROWERS' BULLETIN. **VFOAT** Flower Growers' Bulletin. Bulletin. English. ir.
Ind/Abst Hortic. Abstr.; Ornamental Hort. (1991-); Plant Grow. Reg. Abstr.; Rev. Plant Pathol.

JA/0389-1763
NOSAGYO KENKYU. [Nosagyo Kenkyu]. **VFOAT** Japanese Journal of Farm Work Research; Farm Work Research; Journal of Farm Work Society of Japan. (1966)-. Periodical. Multiple languages. tq. Nihon Nosagyo Gakkai, (Japanese Soc. of Farm Work Research), Norin Suisansho Nogyo Kenkyu Senta, 1-1, Kannondai 3 Chome, Tsukubashi, Ibarakiken 305, Japan. **DD** 631.
Ind/Abst Agric. Eng. Abstr.

US/1050-6217
NURSERY BUSINESS GROWER. [Nurs. bus. grow.]. **VFOAT** Nursery Business, Grower Edition; Nursery Business-Grower Edition. Vol. 1, No. 1 (Feb. 1990)-. Periodical. English. bm. $15.00 (one year), $35.00 (three year) US; $35.00 (one year), $60.00 (three year) other. Brantwood Publications Inc, 3023 Eastland Boulevard/Suite 103, Clearwater FL 34621. **Tel** (813)796-3877, FAX (813)791-4126. **LC** SB118.73; .N88. **DD** 338. ***Continues in part*** *Nursery Business (Clearwater, Fla.), 0029-6406.*

US
NURSERY MANAGER. Vol. 1, No. 1 (Jan. 1985)-. Periodical. English. mo. $24.00 (one year), $44.00 (two years), $59.00 (three years). Branch-Smith Publishing, PO Box 1868, Fort Worth TX 76101. **Tel** (817)332-8236, FAX (817)877-1862. **ED** Mike Branch. **Bk Rev. Ad Acc. Circ:** 12,000 (ctrl). ***Continues*** *SF & N, 0746-973X.*
Desc: A national magazine concentrating exclusively on garden centers, including landscaping, interiorscaping and other departments often found in retail nurseries. Also including growing foliage under shade and in greenhouses, growing and selling bedding and pot plants.

US/0192-3625
NURSERYMEN'S DIGEST. ***Title Change.*** (1966)-?. Periodical. English. mo. Betrock Publications Inc, 10400 Griffin Road/Suite 301, Copper City FL 33328. **Tel** (305)434-4440. **ED** Bette Betrock. **Bk Rev. Ad Acc. Circ:** 8,651. ***Continued by*** *Nursery Digest.*
Desc: A nursery industry publication, concerns landscape, foliage and plants.

US/0738-596X
NUT KERNEL, THE. **Added/Corp** Pennsylvania Nut Growers Association. Vol. 1 (1948)-. Periodical. English. Three times a year. $5.00 Comes with Pennsylvania Nut Growers Association membership. Pennsylvania Nut Growers Association, Tucker Hill, 654 Beinhower Road, Etters PA 17319. **Tel** (717)326-3669. **Bk Rev. Ad Acc. Circ:** 300 (ctrl).
Desc: Pennsylvania growing nut species trees, grafting techniques, practices, resources, diseases, insects, and nut using recipes.

US
NUTSHELL, THE. **Added/Corp** Northern Nut Growers Association. Vol. 1 (1967)-. Periodical. English. Four times a year. $15.00. Northern Nut Growers Association, 9870 South Palmer Road, New Carlisle OH 45344. **Tel** (513)878-2610.

CN/0847-3080
OALA NEWS. (OALA NEWS / ONTARIO ASSOCIATION OF LANDSCAPE ARCHITECTS.). [OALA news]. **Added/Corp** Ontario Association of Landscape Architects. **VFOAT** Ontario Association of Landscape Architects News. (Feb. 1990)-. Periodical. English. bm. Free to members. Ontario Association of Landscape Architects, Suite 120, 170 the Donway West, Don Mills, Ontario M3C 2G3 Canada. **DD** 712/.06/0713. ***Continues*** *OALA News Flash., 0848-8517.*

GW/0029-7798
OBST UND GARTEN. (19??)-. Periodical. German. mo. DM45.40 Germany; DM59.10 other. Verlag Eugen Ulmer, Postfach 700561, D 70574 Stuttgart Germany. **Tel** 011 49 711 4507108, FAX 011 49 711 4507120, telex 7-23634. **ED** Roland Ulmer. **[CCC].** Index available (bound in last issue). **Bk Rev. Ad Acc. Circ:** 20,000 (ctrl). ***Continues*** *Obstbau.*
Desc: Magazine for fruit growing in Baden-Wuerttemberg, Germany.
Ind/Abst Hortic. Abstr.; Plant Breed. Abstr.; Postharvest News Inf.

UK/0957-0985
OCCASIONAL PAPER / WYE COLLEGE, UNIVERSITY OF LONDON, DEPARTMENT OF AGRICULTURE, HORTICULTURE AND THE ENVIRONMENT. **See** Agriculture.

NR/0795-4123
OCCASIONAL PAPERS - NATIONAL HORTICULTURAL RESEARCH INSTITUTE. [Occas. pap. - Natl. Hortic. Res. Inst.]. (1988)-. Monographic series. English. ir. **DD** 634.4'89'09669.
Ind/Abst Agric. Eng. Abstr.; Agrofor. Abstr.; For. Abstr.; Hortic. Abstr.; Postharvest News Inf.; Rev. Plant Pathol.

US
OFFERINGS FOR ... . **Main/Corp** Fennell Orchid Company. '81-. English. an. ***Continues*** *Fennell. Fennell Orchid Company. Fennell.*

PL/0239-9326
OGRODNICTWO. **Added/Corp** Wyzsza Szkoa Rolnicza w Krakowie. Akademia Rolnicza w Krakowie. Akademia Rolnicza im. H. Koataja w Krakowie. (19??)-. Polish (summaries and/or abstracts in English and Russian; table of contents in English).
Ind/Abst Agric. Eng. Abstr.; Postharvest News Inf.

US
OHIO FLORISTS ASSOCIATION FLOWER GROWERS HOTLINE. **See** Gardening and Horticulture-Florist Trade.

US/0099-8745
OKIKA O HAWAII, NA. [Okika Hawaii]. **Added/Corp** Honolulu Orchid Society. Pacific Orchid Society. **VFOAT** Hawaii Orchid Journal. Vol. 1 (March 1972)-. Periodical. English. qt. $15.00. Pacific Orchid Society of Hawaii, 3335 Huelani Drive, Honolulu HI 96822. **Tel** (808)455-7541. **ED** Yoneo Sagawa. **LC** SB409.5.U6; N3. **DD** 635.9/3415/09969. **CODEN** OKHAAN. **Bk Rev. Ad Acc. Circ:** 1,000 (ctrl). Documents available from BIOSIS Document Express. ***Formed by the union of*** *Bulletin of the Pacific Orchid Society of Hawaii, 0030-8838* ***and*** *Pua Okika O Hawaii Nei, 0027-7304.*
Desc: Describes the new developments in orchid hybrids and culture. Helpful for both beginners and veteran orchid hobbyists.
Ind/Abst AGRICOLA; Biol. Abstr.

US/0274-6956
OLD DOMINION GARDENER. **Added/Corp** Virginia Federation of Garden Clubs. Vol. 1 (Fall 1959)-. Periodical. English. qt. $2.00. Old Dominion Gardner, 8710 Mapleton Road, Richmond VA 23229. **Tel** (804)741-1187. **ED** Mrs. Herbert E. Bickel and Stephen Mann. **Bk Rev. Ad Acc. Circ:** 11,000 (ctrl).

US/0892-578X
ONION WORLD. [Onion world]. (Jan. 1985)- Vol. 9 & 10 (Jan. 1993-94)-. Periodical. English. Eight times a year. $15.00 US; $27.00 Canada & Mexico; $45.00 other. Onion World, PO Box 1467, Yakima WA 98907. **Tel** (509)248-2452, (800)900-2452, FAX (509)248-4056. **ED** D. Brent Clement. **DD** 635. **Ad Acc, Adv Mgr:** Mike Stoken. **Circ:** 6,109 (ctrl).
Desc: Includes information on onion production and marketing. Grower and shipper feature stories, onion research, from herbicide an a pesticide studies to promising new varieties, market reports, feedback from major onion meetings and conventions, spot reports on overseas production and marketing, and other key issues and trends of interest to U. S. and Canadian onion growers.

CN/0380-6057
ONTARIO GRAPE GROWER, THE. **Added/Corp** Ontario Grape Growers' Marketing Board. Vol. 1 (Sept. 1968)-. Periodical. English. qt. Free. Ontario Grape Growers' Marketing Board, PO Box 100 Vineland Station, St Catharines Ontario L0R 2E0 Canada. **Tel** (416)688-0990, FAX (416)688-3211. **ED** Brian Leyden. **Circ:** 8,500 (ctrl).
Desc: Current data on Ontario's vineyards and on Ontario wines.

CN/0838-1674
OPTION SERRE. [Option serre]. (Mar. 1988)-. Periodical. French. Ten times a year. 28.56Can$ regular; 23.36Can$ student. Editions Versicolores Inc., 1320 Boulevard Saint-Joseph, A Marchand Quebec, G2K 1G2 Quebec, Canada. **Tel** (418)628-8690, (800)463-1576, FAX (418)628-0524. **DD** 635/.0483.

AT/0474-3342
ORCHADIAN, THE. **Added/Corp** Australasian Native Orchid Society. Vol. 1, No. 12 (Aug. 1963)-. Periodical. English. qt (Mar., June, Sept., Dec.). 26.00Aus$ Australia; 30.00Aus$ New Zealand, New Guinea, Fiji; 32.00Aus$ India, Japan, Asia; 35.00Aus$ other. Australasian Native Orchid Society, GPO Box 978, Sydney NSW 2001 Australia. **Tel** 011 61 2 274097. **ED** M. Penberthy. Index available. **Bk Rev. Circ:** 900 (ctrl).
Desc: To publish information on a technical basis on Australasian native orchids and hybrids. Also, growing information and all other subjects associated within these guidelines.

US/0097-9546
ORCHID ADVOCATE, THE. [Orchid advocate]. **Added/Corp** Cymbidium Society of America. Vol. 1, (Jan/Feb. 1975)-. Periodical. English. bm. $20.00. Cymbidium Society of America, PO Box 2244, Orange CA 92669. **Tel** ((805)684-8811. **ED** Don Burkey. **LC** SB409.A1; O78. **DD** 635.9/34/1505. **Bk Rev. Ad Acc. Circ:** 2,000 (ctrl). ***Supersedes*** *Cymbidium Society News.*
Desc: International coverage of cymbidiums, paphiopedilums and other selected genera for beginners and advanced growers.

US/0199-9559
ORCHID DIGEST, THE. [Orchid dig.]. Vol.1 (1937)-. Periodical. English (Japanese). qt. $20.00 US; $22.00 other. Orchid Digest, PO Box 916, Carmichael CA 95609. **Tel** (916)485-8317. **ED** J.A. Fowlie. Index available. cum. index. **Bk Rev. Ad Acc. Circ:** 4,500.
Desc: News of orchid events.
Ind/Abst AGRICOLA [Select. Cov.]; Rev. Plant Pathol.

NE
ORCHID MONOGRAPHS. **Added/Corp** Rijksherbarium (Netherlands). Vol. 1 (1986)-. Monographic series. English. ir. Price varies per volume. Rijksherbarium, PO Box 9514, 2300 RA Leiden Netherlands. **Tel** 011 31 71 273500. **CODEN** ORMOE7.

GW/0473-1425
ORCHIDEE, DIE. **Added/Corp** Deutsche Orchideen-Gesellschaft. Vol. 1, (Oct./Dec. 1949)-. Periodical. German. Six times a year (Jan., Mar., May, July, Sept., Nov.). DM110.00. Deutsche Orchideen Gesellschaf, Schoenbrunner STR 8/E Wermuth, W 8071 Denkendorf Germany. **Tel** 011 49 8466 8228, , FAX 011 49 8466 8332. **ED** Gerd Roellke (phone: 0049 52 441384). **LC** SB409.A1; O787. Index Available Published separately--free--upon request (First issue of the next year). cum. index. **Bk Rev**, (Qty: 10-20). **Ad Acc, Adv Mgr:** E. Wermuth, **Tel** (08466)8228. **Circ:** 7,000 (ctrl).
Desc: Journal of the members of the German Orchid Society.
Ind/Abst Rev. Plant Pathol.; Soils Fert.

US/0897-3792
ORGANIC GARDENING (1988). (ORGANIC GARDENING.). [Org. gard.]. (April 1988)-. Periodical. English. Nine times a year. $25.00 US; $41.00 other. Rodale Press Inc., 400 South 10th Street, Emmaus PA 18098. **Tel** (215)967-5171, (800)666-2503. **(Subscription address:** CDS Agency Hard Copy, PO Box 4966, Des Moines, IA 50340**)** **LC** S605.5; .O7. **DD** 635.0484. available on microfilm and microfiche from University Microfilms International (UMI). Documents available from UMI Article Clearinghouse, Magazine Collection. ***Continues*** *Rodale's Organic Gardening, 0884-3252.*
Ind/Abst Acad. Abstr. Full Text Elite (Jan. 1984-) [Full Txt.]; Acad. Abstr. (Jan. 1984-); Acad. Search (Jan. 1984-); Biol. Agric. Index; Biol. Dig.; Environ. Period. Bibliogr. (?-?); Garden Lit. (1992-); Gen. Period. Index (1985-); Health Source (Jan. 1984-) [Full Txt.]; INFO-SOUTH Abstr.; Mag. Artic. Summar. Elite (Jan. 1984-) [Full Txt.]; Mag. Artic. Summar. Select (Jan. 1984-) [Full Txt.]; Mag. Artic. Summar. CD-ROM (Jan. 1984-); Mag. Index Plus (1989-); Mag. Index. Sel. (1987-); Mag. Search; Newsp. Period. Abstr. (1988-); Read. Guide Abstr. Select Ed.; Mag. Index; Vocat. Search (Jan. 1984-) [Full Txt.].

UK/0305-4934
ORNAMENTAL HORTICULTURE. **See** Gardening and Horticulture-Abstracting, Bibliographies and Statistics.

US/0030-4778
ORNAMENTALS NORTHWEST (1981). ***Suspended.*** (ORNAMENTALS NORTHWEST.). [Ornam. northwest]. **Added/Corp** British Columbia. Ministry of Agriculture. Oregon State University. Extension Service.

University of Idaho. Cooperative Extension Service. Washington State University. Cooperative Extension Service. USDA Horticultural Crops Research Laboratory. Urban Horticulture Center at the University of Washington. **VFOAT** Ornamentals Northwest Newsletter; ONW Newsletter. Vol. 5, No. 2 (Mar./Apr. 1981)-(Dec. 1990). Periodical. English. bm. Oregon State University / Horticulture, James Green, Department of Horticulture, Corvallis OR 97331. **Tel** (503)754-3464. **DD** 635. ***Continues*** *Ornamentals Northwest Newsletter.*
Ind/Abst AGRICOLA; Garden Lit. (1992-).

CK/0120-1433
ORQUIDEOLOGIA. [Orquideologia]. **Added/Corp** Sociedad Colombiana de Orquideologia. No. 4-5, (July/Nov. 1967)-. Periodical. Spanish (English). ir. $40.00. Sociedad Colombiana de Orquide, Apartado Aereo 4725, Medellin Colombia. **Tel** 011 57 4 2448384, 011 57 4 2773702. ***Continues*** *Sociedad Colombiana de Orquideologia. Revista de la Sociedad Colombiana de Orquideologia.*
Ind/Abst AGRICOLA.

BL/0205-1710
OVOSHTARSTVO, GRADINARSTVO I KONSERVNA PROMISHLENOST. **See** Agriculture-Crop Production and Soil.

PL
OWOCE, WARZYWA, KWIATY. **Added/Corp** Centralna Spolozielnia Oggrodnicza. No. 1 (July 1/15, 1961)-. Periodical. Polish. sm (24 issues). $54.00. **(Subscription address:** ARS Polona, PO Box 1001, 00068 Warsaw Poland.**)**

FR
P.H.M. - REVUE HORTICOLE. **VFOAT** Pepinieristes, Horticulteurs, Maraichers - Revue Horticole. (19??)-. Periodical. French. Twelve times a year. 337.90F France; 450.00F other. PHM Revue Horticole, 11 rue des Messageries, 75010 Paris France. **Tel** 011 33 1 40229897. Index available. cum. index. **Bk Rev. Ad Acc. Circ:** 12,500 (ctrl). ***Continues*** *Pepinieristes, Horticulteurs, Maraichers. Revue Horticole.*
Desc: Technical information and articles for nurserymen, horticulturists and market-gardeners.
Ind/Abst Ornamental Hort.

US/0192-7159
PACIFIC COAST NURSERYMAN & GARDEN SUPPLY DEALER. **VFOAT** Pacific Coast Nurseryman; Pacific Coast Nurseryman and Garden Supply Dealer. Vol. 15, No. 2 (Feb. 1956)-. Periodical. English. mo (12 issues). $20.00 US & Canada; $30.00 other. Pacific Coast Nurseryman, 306 West Foothill Boulevard, PO Box 1477, Glendora CA 91740. **Tel** (818)914-3916. **ED** Harold R. Young. **Bk Rev. Ad Acc. Circ:** 10,500 (ctrl). ***Continues*** *Pacific Coast Nurseryman.*
Desc: Business publication for managers and owners of production nurseries and retail nurseries, and those in landscaping professions. A chronicle of the nursery industry in the western states.

US/0163-7843
PACIFIC HORTICULTURE. [Pac. hortic.]. **Added/Corp** Pacific Horticultural Foundation (U.S.). (Jan. 1976)-. Periodical. English. qt. $15.00 (also comes with Southern California Horticulture Institute Membership). Pacific Horticultural Foundation, PO Box 485, Berkeley CA 94701. **Tel** (510)526-2853. **LC** SB453.2.P33; P3. **DD** 635/.0979. ***Continues*** *California Horticultural Journal.*
Ind/Abst AGRICOLA; Calif. Period. Index (19??-); Garden Lit. (1992-).

US
PACIFIC NORTHWEST PLANT DISEASE CONTROL HANDBOOK. ***Suspended.*** **Added/Corp** University of Idaho. Cooperative Extension Service. Oregon State University. Extension Service. Washington State University. Cooperative Extension. Washington State University. Cooperative Extension Service. **VFOAT** PNW Plant Disease Control. (March 1978)-Suspended. English. an. Agricultural Communications, Publications Orders, Oregon State University, Administrative Services/Room 422, Corvallis OR 97331-2119. **Tel** (503)737-2513, FAX (503)737-2400. **ED** Paul Koepsell. **Bk Rev. Ad Acc. Circ:** 1,000 (ctrl). ***Continues*** *Oregon Plant Disease Control Handbook.*
Desc: Reference to recommend control measures for more important Pacific Northwest plant diseases.

US/0899-3041
PACIFIC NORTHWEST WEED CONTROL HANDBOOK. ***Suspended.*** [Pac. Northwest weed control handb.]. **Added/Corp** Oregon State University. Extension Service. Washington State University. Cooperative Extension Service. University of Idaho. Cooperative Extension Service. **VFOAT** Weed Control Handbook; Pacific North West Weed Control Handbook; PNW Weed Control Handbook. (Jan. 1985)-Suspended. English. Agricultural Communications, Publications Orders, Oregon State University, Administrative Services/Room 422, Corvallis OR 97331-2119. **Tel** (503)737-2513, FAX (503)737-2400. **DD** 632. ***Formed by the union of*** *Idaho Weed Control Handbook; Oregon Weed Control Handbook* ***and*** *Washington State University Weed Control Handbook.*
Ind/Abst AGRICOLA [Full Cov.].

US/0276-4164
PALMETTO (ORLANDO, FLA.), THE. (THE PALMETTO / FLORIDA NATIVE PLANT SOCIETY.). [Palmetto]. **Added/Corp** Florida Native Plant Society. Florida Conservation Foundation. Vol. 1, No. 1 (Feb. 1981)-. Periodical. English. Four times a year (Mar., June, Sept., Dec.). $20.00 (individual), $25.00 (family), $50.00 (organizations) Comes with Florida Native Plant Society membership. Florida Native Plant Society, PO Box 680008, Orlando FL 32868. **Tel** (407)299-1472. **ED** Peggy S. Lantz. **LC** QK154; .P3. **Bk Rev. Ad Acc. Circ:** 1,500 (ctrl).

US/0566-330X
PAPERS FROM THE ANNUAL CONFERENCE. **Added/Corp** Pittsburgh. University. Institute of Local Government. Pittsburgh. University. Knowledge Availability Systems Center. American Society of Planning Officials. (1964)-. English. an. Urban Regional Information Systems Association, 900 Second Street Northeast, Suite 304, Washington DC 20002. **Tel** (202)289-1685, FAX (202)842-1850. **DD** 711.

SA
PARKS AND GROUNDS. 1977-. English. bm. R23.00 South Africa; $10.00 US. Avonwold Publishing Company Pty Limited, PO Box 52068, Saxonwold 2132, South Africa. **Tel** 11 27 11 7881610. **ED** Christine Michelson. **Bk Rev. Ad Acc. Circ:** 3,945 (ctrl).
Desc: Covers turf management, horticulture landscape design and construction.

FR/0395-2916
PAYSAGE ACTUALITES. (197?)-. Periodical. French. mo. 397.00F France. Sepem SRL, Via G Livraghi 9, 20126 Milan, Italy. **Tel** 011 39 2 27001110, FAX 011 39 2 27000652. ***Absorbed*** *Espaces Verts.*

US/0031-3610
PEACH TIMES. Periodical. English. mo. $10.00 US; 12.00 other. National Peach Council, PO Drawer 1085, Martinsburg WV 25401. **Tel** (304)267-6024. **ED** Lillie Hoover-Largent. **Bk Rev. Ad Acc. Circ:** 1,800 (ctrl).
Desc: Published by the National Peach Council. Information relative to the fresh peach industry.

US
PENN STATE HORTICULTURAL REVIEWS. Vol. 1, No. 1 (Mar. 1953)-. Periodical. English. qt. Free. 103 Tyson Building, University Park PA 16802. **Tel** (814)863-2198. **ED** L D Tukey. **Bk Rev. Circ:** 2,500.
Desc: Short topics relating to horticulture of interest to growers, researchers, extension specialists as information, reviews, and announcements.

•US/1060-5398
PENNSYLVANIA LAWN, AND GARDEN MAGAZINE. (1992)-. Periodical. English. mo. Pennsylvania Publishing Company, PO Box 170, Coalport PA 16627.

US/0090-0737
PENNSYLVANIA ORCHARD AND VINEYARD SURVEY. **Main/Corp** Pennsylvania Crop Reporting Service. English. Pennsylvania Crop Reporting Service, 2301 North Cameron Street, Harrisburg PA 17120. **LC** SB354.6.U5; P43. **DD** 338.1/7/409748. ***Continues*** *Fruit Tree and Grapevine Survey.*

US
PERENNIAL PLANTS. English. qt. Perennial Plant Association, 3383 Schirtzinger Road, Hilliard OH 43026. **Tel** 614 771-8431.
Ind/Abst Garden Lit. (1992-).

GW/0170-0405
PFLANZENSCHUTZ-NACHRICHTEN BAYER (ENGLISH ED.). (PFLANZENSCHUTZ-NACHRICHTEN BAYER.). [Pflanzenschutz-Nachr. Bayer]. **Added/Corp** Farbenfabriken Bayer Aktiengesellschaft. **VFOAT** Pflanzenschutz Nachrichten Bayer. (1962)-. Periodical. English (summaries and/or abstracts in French, German and Spanish). tq. Bayer AG, Bayerwerk, W 5090 Leverkusen Germany. **CODEN** PNBED6. ***Continues*** *Hofchen-Briefe (English ed.), 0437-6404.*
Ind/Abst Potato Abstr.

GW
PFLANZENSCHUTZMITTEL-VERZEICHNIS. TEIL 2: GEMUSEBAU, OBSTBAU, ZIERPFLANZENBAU. **See** Pest Control.

GW
PFLANZENSOZIOLOGIE; EINE REIHE VEGETATIONSKUNDLICHER GEBIETSMONOGRAPHIEN. (19??)-. Monographic series. German. ir. Price varies per volume. Gustav Fischer Verlag Jena, Postfach 100537, D 07705 Jena Germany. **Tel** 011 49 3641 27332, FAX 011 49 3641 626500. **ED** Erich Oberdorfer. **Bk Rev.**

US/1043-0083
PJG (MIAMI, FLA.). (PJG.). [PJG]. **VAT** Parrot Jungle Gardens. Vol. 1, No. 1 -. Periodical. English. qt. $9.00. Parrot Jungle and Garden, 11000 SW 57th Avenue, Miami FL 33156. **Tel** (305)666-7834, FAX (305)661-2230. **DD** 636. **Bk Rev. Ad Acc. Circ:** 20,000.
Desc: A magazine for garden and bird fanciers.

CN
PLANT & GARDEN. English. qt (Feb., May, Aug., Nov.). 13.95Can$ (one year), 25.90Can$ (two year), 36.35Can$ (three year). Gardenvale Publishing, 1 rue Pacifique, Ste Anne de Bellevue, Quebec H9X 1C5 Canada. **Tel** (514)457-2744, FAX (514)457-6255. **ED** Kathryn Spracklin (613)230-9021. Index available (published in November issue). cum. index. **Bk Rev. Ad Acc, Adv Mgr:** Barbara Paul. **Circ:** 40,000.
Desc: Aims to impart both the pleasures and skills of indoor and outdoor gardening. Provides information about plants, gardening techniques, tools and the science of gardening.

US/0886-683X
PLANT BIBLIOGRAPHY. [Plant bibliogr.]. **Added/Corp** Council on Botanical and Horticultural Libraries (U.S.). **VFOAT** CBHL Plant Bibliography. No. 1 (Jan. 1978)-. Monographic series. English. ir. Price varies per volume. Council Botanical Horticulture Libraries, New York Botanical Garden, Bronx NY 10458. **Tel** (212)220-8728, FAX (212)220-6504. **ED** Meryl Miasek Barney. **LC** UNC. **DD** 631. cum. index. **Circ:** 400.
Ind/Abst AGRICOLA.

US/0730-2207
PLANT BREEDING REVIEWS. [Plant breed. rev.]. **Added/Corp** American Society for Horticultural Science. (1983)-. Academic Scholarly Publication. English. ir. $110.00. John Wiley & Sons, Inc., 605 Third Avenue, New York NY 10158-0012. **Tel** (212)850-6000, (212)850-6645, FAX (212)850-6088, telex 12-7063. **(Subscription address:** John Wiley & Sons / England, Baffins Lane, Chichester, West Sussex PO19 1UD England.**)** **LC** SB123; .P55. **DD** 631.5/3/05. **CODEN** PBREE3. Documents available from CASDDS.
Ind/Abst AgBiotech News Inf.; Chem. Abstr. (1983-); Maize Abstr.; Nematol. Abstr.; Life Sci. Collect.; Plant Breed. Abstr.; Rev. Agric. Entomol.; Seed Abstr.; Soyabean Abstr.; Wheat Barley Trit. Abstr.

US
PLANT CONSERVATION. English. qt. $25.00. Center for Plant Conservation, PO Box 299, St. Louis MO 63166-0299. **Tel** 314 664-1200.
Ind/Abst Garden Lit. (1992-).

US
PLANT DOCTOR. CD-ROM. English. $57.95 (Minnesota residents); $54.95 other. Quanta Press, Inc., 1313 Fifth Street Southeast, Suite 208C, Minneapolis MN 55414. **Tel** (612)379-3956, FAX (612)623-4570. available in print.
Desc: Electronic, multi-media database on trees, turf, flowers, shrubs, and other plantings that flourish in an urban environment. Hundreds of plant disorders and cures are available. Available in DOS format.

US
PLANT HEALTH GUIDE. (19??)-. Directory. English. an. $27.75 US; $33.00 Canada; $36.75 other. Meister Publishing Company, 37733 Euclid Avenue, Willoughby OH 44094-5992. **Tel** (216)942-2000, (800)572-7740, FAX (216)942-0662.
Desc: Listings of registered disease control products. Crop specific descriptions, with individual use recommendations, restrictions, and new registrations.

US/0361-9974
PLANT INVENTORY. (PLANT INVENTORY / UNITED STATES DEPARTMENT OF AGRICULTURE.). **Added/Corp** United States. Bureau of Plant Industry. Division of Plant Exploration and Introduction. United States. Agricultural Research Service. Horticultural Crops Research Branch. United States. Dept. of Agriculture. United States. Agricultural Research Service. Crops Research Division. New Crops Research Branch. Agricultural Research Center-West (U.S.). Northeastern Region. United States. Science and Education Administration. Federal Research. No. 133 (Oct. 1/Dec. 31, 1937)-. English. ir. Free on request. National Technical Information Service - NTIS, Room 2027S, 5285 Port Royal Road, Springfield VA 22161. **Tel** (703)487-4630, (703)487-4660, (703)487-4650, FAX (703)321-8547, telex 89-9405. **LC** SB109; .U5. **DD** 630.5/2/0973. available on microfiche (Vols. for (Jan./Dec. 1978)- distributed to depository libraries). ***Continues*** *Inventory (United States. Dept. of Agriculture), 0888-6369.*

US/0097-8787
PLANT PROTECTION AND QUARANTINE PROGRAMS. (PLANT PROTECTION AND QUARANTINE PROGRAMS, FY ... PROGRESS REPORT.). English. US Department of Agriculture / Animal & Plant Health Inspection Service, 741 Federal Building 1, 6505 Belcres Road, Hyattsville MD 20782. **Tel** (301)436-7817. **LC** SB950.2.A1; U53A. **DD** 632/.9/0973.

UK/0952-3863
PLANT VARIETIES & SEEDS. [Plant var. seeds]. **Added/Corp** National Institute of Agricultural Botany (Great Britain). **VFOAT** Plant Varieties and Seeds. Vol. 1, No. 1 (July 1988)-. Periodical. English. Three times a year. £44.00 UK; £45.00 Europe; £49.00 other. National Institute of Agricultural Botany, Huntingdon Road, Cambridge CB3 OL3 England. **Tel** 11 44 223 276381, FAX 11 44 223 277602. **CODEN** PVSEEC. **[CCC].** Index available in last issue of volume--attached. **Bk Rev. Pr Rev. Circ:** 1,100 (ctrl). available on microfilm and microfiche from University Microfilms International (UMI). Documents available from BIOSIS Document Express. ***Continues** National Institute of Agricultural Botany (Great Britain). Journal of the National Institute of Agricultural Botany, 0077-4790.*
Desc: Research papers on all aspects of variety and seed improvement. Emphasis is on practical applications rather than theoretical research and interest extends across agricultural and vegetable species.
Ind/Abst AgBiotech News Inf.; AGRICOLA [Full Cov.]; Biol. Abstr. (1989-); Crop Physiol. Abstr.; Curr. Aware. Biol. Sci., CABS; Field Crop Abstr.; Food Sci. Technol. Abstr.; Grasslands For. Abstr.; Hortic. Abstr.; Maize Abstr.; Nutr. Abstr. Rev., Ser. B, Live Feeds and Feed.; Plant Breed. Abstr.; Plant Genet. Resour. Abstr.; Plant Grow. Reg. Abstr.; Potato Abstr.; Rice Abstr.; Seed Abstr.; Sorghum Mill. Abstr.; Wheat Barley Trit. Abstr.

AT/1030-9748
PLANT VARIETIES JOURNAL. Added/Corp Australia. Bureau of Rural Science. Registrar of Plant Variety Rights. Vol. 1, No. 1 (March 1988)-. Periodical. English. Four times a year (Mar., Jun., Sep., Dec.). 30.00Aus$. Plant Variety Rights Office, GPO Box 858, Canberra ACT 2601 Australia. **Tel** 011 61 6 2724228, FAX 011 61 6 2723650. cum. index. **Ad Acc.**
Ind/Abst Field Crop Abstr.; Grasslands For. Abstr.; Hortic. Abstr.; Nematol. Abstr.; Ornamental Hort. (19??-19??); Plant Breed. Abstr.; Plant Genet. Resour. Abstr.; Seed Abstr.; Soyabean Abstr.

US/0740-6002
PLANT VARIETY PROTECTION OFFICE OFFICIAL JOURNAL. [Plant Var.. Prot. Off. off. j.]. **Added/Corp** United States. Plant Variety Protection Office. Vol. 7 No. 2 (Apr/June 1979)-. Periodical. English. qt (Jan., April, July, Oct.). Free. Plant Variety Protection Office, National Agricultural Library Building/Room 500, Room 500, Beltsville MD 20705. **Tel** (301)504-5518. **ED** Kenneth H Evans. **LC** SB123.5; .P57. **DD** 631.5/7. Index available. cum. index. **Circ:** 1,500. ***Continues** Official Journal of the Plant Variety Protection Office, 0091-5327.*
Desc: The purpose is to inform the public and the seed industry of applications for plant variety protection of seed-reproduced plants and certificates of protection issued.
Ind/Abst Field Crop Abstr.; Grasslands For. Abstr.; Maize Abstr.; Plant Breed. Abstr.; Rice Abstr.; Soyabean Abstr.

CN/0823-6984
PLANTE-A-TOUT. Vol. 1, No. 1 (May 1983)-. Periodical. French. mo. $1.00 per number. Entreprises Teledition, 850 Est, Rue Sherbrooke, Montreal Quebec H2L 1K9. **DD** 635.9/65/05.

NE
PLANTENBEURS, DE. Randstad Publication BV, P B 151, 1430 AD Aalsmeer Netherlands.

FR/0476-9813
PLANTES DE MONTAGNE / BULLETIN DE LA SOCIETE DES AMATEURS DE JARDINS ALPINS. V. 1, No. 1-. Bulletin. French. qt. Soc des Amateurs de Jardins, 43 rue Buffon, 75005 Paris France.

US/1071-3670
PLANTFINDER (PEMBROKE PINES, FLA.). (PLANTFINDER.). [PlantFinder]. **VFOAT** Plant Finder. (Mar. 1987)-. Periodical. English. Twelve times a year. $59.95. Betrock Information Systems, 1601 North Palm Avenue, Suite 303, Pembroke Pines FL 33026. **Tel** (800)627-3819, (305)434-4440. **DD** 338. ***Continues** PlantFinder with InteriorScan Section.*

MY/0127-306X
PLANTI NEWS. [Planti news]. **VFOAT** Plant Quarantine Centre and Training Institute News. (1982)-. Periodical. English. qt. Asean - Planti, Post Bag 209, UPM Post Serdang, Selangor, Malaysia. **DD** 632.93.
Ind/Abst Helminthol. Abstr. (1991-); Nematol. Abstr.; Potato Abstr.; Rev. Plant Pathol.; Rice Abstr.

MY
PLANTING MANUAL. ***Title Change.*** No. 1 (1928)-. Monographic series. English. **LC** SB290; .K8. **DD** 633.8/952. ***Continued by** R.R.I.M. Planting Manual.*

US/0146-3659
PLANTS ALIVE. Vol. 1 (Oct. 1972)-. Periodical. English. mo. $9.60 US; $11.60 other. Plants Alive, 529 South Crest, Wheaton IL 60187.

US/0362-5850
PLANTS & GARDENS. ***Title Change.*** [Plants gard.]. **Added/Corp** Brooklyn Botanic Garden. **VFOAT** Plants and Gardens. Vol. 1, No. 1 (Spring 1945)-(19??). Periodical. English. qt. Brooklyn Botanic Garden, 1000 Washington Avenue, Brooklyn NY 11225. **Tel** (718)622-4433, FAX (718)857-2430. **ED** Barbara B Pesch. **LC** SB1; .P56. **DD** 635.905. **CODEN** PLGAA. cum. index. **Bk Rev. Circ:** 25,000 (ctrl). Documents available from BIOSIS Document Express, CASDDS. ***Continues** Brooklyn Botanic Garden Record, 0096-5251.* ***Continued by** Brooklyn Botanic Garden 21st Century Gardening Series.*
Ind/Abst AGRICOLA; Biogr. Index; Biol. Agric. Index; Biol. Abstr.; Chem. Abstr.; Garden Lit. (1992-); Life Sci. Collect.

US
PLANTS & GARDENS NEWS / BROOKLYN BOTANIC GARDEN.
Added/Corp Brooklyn Botanic Garden. **VFOAT** Plants and Gardens Views. **VAT** Plants and Gardens News. Vol. 1 No. 1 (1986)-. Periodical. English. Four times a year (Mar., June, Aug., Nov.). $25.00 (subscribing), $50.00 (sustaining), $125.00 (supporting), $300.00 (contributing) Comes with Brooklyn Botanic Garden Subscribing membership. Brooklyn Botanic Garden, 1000 Washington Avenue, Brooklyn NY 11225. **Tel** (718)622-4433, FAX (718)857-2430. **ED** Betsy Kissam. **Bk Rev. Circ:** 25,000 (ctrl). ***Continues** Newsletter (Brooklyn Botanic Garden).*
Desc: A digest of timely planting tips, great new gardening products, sources for seeds, plants and tools, research reports from university laboratories, and the "trade secrets" of BBG's own skilled gardeners.
Ind/Abst Garden Lit. (1992-).

UK/0143-0106
PLANTSMAN, THE. ***Title Change.*** [Plantsman]. **Added/Corp** Royal Horticultural Society (Great Britain). Vol. 1, (June 1979)-(1994). Periodical. English. qt. Royal Horticultural Society, 80 Vincent Square, London SW1P 2PE England. **Tel** 011 44 71 834 4333. **ED** Elspeth Napier. **LC** QK1; .P55. Index available. **Ad Acc. Circ:** 2,500. ***Continued by** New Plantsman.*
Desc: Includes articles on plants that are less commonly grown, their cultivation and garden value; fruit and vegetables are included, although the main emphasis is on decorative plants for both outdoors and in.
Ind/Abst Agrofor. Abstr. (1991-?); Crop Physiol. Abstr. (?-?); Field Crop Abstr. (?-?); For. Abstr. (?-?); Garden Lit. (1992-?); Hortic. Abstr. (?-?); Ornamental Hort. (19??-19??); Plant Breed. Abstr. (?-?); Plant Genet. Resour. Abstr. (?-?).

US/0748-6510
POMONA : NORTH AMERICAN FRUIT EXPLORERS' QUARTERLY. [Pomona]. **Added/Corp** North American Fruit Explorers. Vol. 14, No. 2 (Spring 1981)-. Periodical. English. qt. $8.00 (1 year), $15.00 (2 year) US; $12.00 (1 year), $23.00 (2 year) other; comes with North American Fruit Explorers membership. North American Fruit Explorers, Route 1 Box 94, Chapin IL 62628. **Tel** (217)245-7589. **(Subscription address:** Rt 1, Box 94, Chapin, IL 62628) **ED** John English. **DD** 634. Index available. cum. index. **Bk Rev. Ad Acc. Circ:** 3,000. ***Continues** North American Pomona.*
Desc: Fruit growing for the hobbyist. Test and report on all kinds of fruit in all parts of North America and the world.

US/0147-4723
POPULAR GARDENING INDOORS. Periodical. English. bm. $7.50. CBS Publications, 1515 Broadway, New York NY 10036. **Tel** (212)503-5064. **LC** SB419; .P64. **DD** 635.9/65/05.

US
POTATOES / NATIONAL AGRICULTURAL STATISTICS SERVICE, UNITED STATES DEPARTMENT OF AGRICULTURE, AGRICULTURAL STATISTICS BOARD.
Added/Corp United States. Agricultural Statistics Board. (198?)-. English. an. ***Continues** Potatoes and Sweet Potatoes (Annual), 0499-0587.*

PL/0324-8437
PRACE INSTYTUTU SADOWNICTWA I KWIACIARSTWA W SKIERNIEWICACH. SERIA B, ROSLINY OZDOBNE. Added/Corp Instytut Sadownictwa i Kwiaciarstwa (Skierniewice, Poland). **VFOAT** Rosliny Ozdobne; Ornamental Plants; Experimental Work of the Institute of Pomology and Floriculture Skierniewice--Poland. Series B, Ornamental Plants. (19??)-. Polish (English; summaries and/or abstracts in Russian). ***Continues** Prace Instytutu Sadownictwa i Kwiaciarstwa w Skierniewicach, 0583-5759.*
Ind/Abst Crop Physiol. Abstr.; Hortic. Abstr.; Ornamental Hort. (1991-); Plant Breed. Abstr.; Rev. Agric. Entomol.; Rev. Plant Pathol.; Seed Abstr.; Soils Fert.

UK/0032-6399
PRACTICAL GARDENING. [Pract. gard.]. **VFOAT** Practical Gardening Monthly. (1960)-. Periodical. English. Twelve times a year. £14.50 UK; £28.00 others. EMAP National Publications Ltd, Farndon Road, Market Harborough, Leicestershire, LE16 9NR England. **Tel** 011 44 733 555161. **DD** 635. **[CCC].** ***Absorbed** Gardening World (Brentwood), 0144-3828.*

AT/1037-5457
PRACTICAL HYDROPONICS. [Pract. hydroponics]. (1991)-. Periodical. English. Six times a year. 35.70Aus$ Australia; 51.90Aus$ New Zealand & Papua New Guinea. Federal Publishing Co Pty Ltd, PO Box 199, 180 Bourke Road, Alexandria New South Wales, 2015 Australia. **Tel** 011 61 2 693 6666, FAX 011 61 2 693 9935. **(Subscription address:** Federal Publishing Co. Pty Ltd., PO Box 199, Alexandria NSW 2015 Australia.) **DD** 631.5850994.

CN/0315-6850
PRAIRIE GARDEN. (THE PRAIRIE GARDEN.). **Added/Corp** Winnipeg Horticultural Society. (1944)-. Periodical. English. an. 5.50Can$. Winnipeg Horticultural Society; The Prairie Garden, PO Box 517, Winnipeg Man R3C 2J3 Canada. **ED** Frances Wershler. **DD** 635/.09712. **Circ:** 8000.
Desc: Covers all aspects of horticulture.
Ind/Abst Garden Lit. (1992-).

CN/0820-6848
PRAIRIE LANDSCAPE MAGAZINE. [Prairie landsca. mag.]. Vol. 4, No. 1 (Jan. 1981)-. Periodical. English. bm. Free to Members. Prairie Landscape Magazine, Suite 695/10123-99th Street, Edmonton Alberta T5J 1H3 Canada. **DD** 338.1/759/09712. ***Continues** Landscape Alberta, 0712-5003.*

US
PRICE LIST / BARWAL DAHLA FARM.
Main/Corp Barwal Dahlia Farm. (19??)-. English.

US
PRICE LIST / ENVIRONMENTAL SEED PRODUCERS, INC. Main/Corp Environmental Seed Producers, Inc. (19??)-. English.

US/0162-6671
PRIMROSES. [Primroses]. **Added/Corp** American Primrose Society. **VFOAT** American Primrose Society Quarterly. Vol. 35, No. 2 (Spring 1977)-. Periodical. English. Four times a year (Jan., Apr., July, Oct.). $15.00 one year, $40.00 three years (membership). American Primrose Society, 9705 Southwest Spring Crest Drive, Portland OR 97225. **Tel** (503)640-4582. **ED** Richard Critz. **LC** SB413.P7; A5. **DD** 635.9/33672. Index available. cum. index. **Bk Rev. Ad Acc. Circ:** 800. ***Continues** Quarterly of the American Primrose Society, 0003-0619.*
Desc: A plant society journal devoted to the history, culture and collection of primulas.

US/0890-829X
PRINCE WILLIAM NEWSLETTER. **See** Building and Construction.

US/1041-5610
PRO (FORT ATKINSON, WIS.). (PRO.). Vol. 1, No. 1 (Nov./Dec. 1988)-. Trade Publication. English. Seven times a year. $24.00 US; $55.00 Canada and Mexico; $120.00 other. Johnson Hill Press Inc., 1233 Janesville Avenue, PO Box 803, Fort Atkinson WI 53538-0803. **Tel** (414)563-1749, FAX (414)563-1704. **ED** Karla Raye Cuculi. **DD** 338. **Ad Acc.** Full Page (B&W) $4545.00. Full Page (Color) $5990.00 (4-color). **Circ:** 44,044.
Desc: Magazine for lawn maintenance and landscape contractors and building/grounds maintenance professionals.

US/0149-6905
PROCEEDINGS, ANNUAL MEETING - WASHINGTON STATE HORTICULTURAL ASSOCIATION.
Main/Corp Washington State Horticultural Association. **Added/Corp** Washington State Horticultural Association. Annual Proceedings - Washington State Horticultural Association. Washington State Horticultural Association. Report of the Annual Convention of the Washington State Horticultural Association. Washington State Horticultural Association. Report of the Annual Meeting of the Washington State Horticultural Association. **VFOAT** Annual Proceedings - Washington State Horticultural Association. (1905)-. Proceedings. English. an. $35.00. Washington State Horticultural Association, PO Box 136, Wenatchee WA 98801. **Tel** (509)548-4728, FAX (509)548-6840. Index available (bound in 1990 issue). cum. index. **Ad Acc. Circ:** 4,600.
Desc: Contains speeches on all aspects of the fruit growing, post harvest, marketing.
Ind/Abst AGRICOLA [Select. Cov.]; Food Sci. Technol. Abstr.

US/0097-1731
PROCEEDINGS - CALIFORNIA WEED CONFERENCE. ***Title Change.*** [Proc. - Calif. Weed Conf.]. **Main/Conf** California Weed Conference. (1949)-(1993). Proceedings. English. an. California Weed Conference, PO Box 609, Fremont CA 94537. **Tel** (510)790-1252, FAX (510)790-2419. **LC** SB612.C2; C34a. **DD** 632/.58/05. **CODEN** PCWCAP. Index available. **Circ:** 1,000. Documents available from CASDDS. ***Continued by** California Weed Science*

Society Proceedings.
Desc: Papers and abstracts of papers presented at annual conference.
Ind/Abst AGRICOLA [Select. Cov.]; Chem. Abstr. (1949-1984); PESTDOC.

US
PROCEEDINGS / NORTH CENTRAL WEED SCIENCE SOCIETY. **Main/Corp** North Central Weed Science Society (U.S.). **VFOAT** NCWSS Proceedings. Vol. 44 (1989)-. Proceedings. English. an. $20.00. North Central Weed Science Society, 1508 West University, Champaign IL 61821. **Tel** (217)356-3182. **LC** SB610; .N57. ***Continues*** *Proceedings of Annual Meeting.*
Ind/Abst PESTDOC.

US/0749-4327
PROCEEDINGS OF THE ANNUAL MEETING / ARKANSAS STATE HORTICULTURAL SOCIETY. (PROCEEDINGS OF THE ANNUAL MEETING.). [Proc. annu. meet. - Ark. State Hortic. Soc.]. **Main/Corp** Arkansas State Horticultural Society. 1st (1893)-. Proceedings. English. an. $12.50. Arkansas State Horticultural Society, Plant Science Building/Room 306, University of Arkansas, Fayetteville AR 72701. **Tel** (501)575-2603. **ED** Roy C Rom. **DD** 635. **Ad Acc. Circ:** 400.
Desc: Research reports and general papers on peach, apple, grape, small fruits, vegetables and ornamental crops; production and marketing.

US/0886-7283
PROCEEDINGS OF THE ANNUAL MEETING OF THE FLORIDA STATE HORTICULTURAL SOCIETY. [Proc. annu. meet. Fla. State Hort. Soc.]. **Main/Conf** Florida State Horticultural Society. Meeting. **Main/Corp** Florida State Horticultural Society. Meeting. **VFOAT** Proceedings of the Florida State Horticultural Society. (1977)-. Proceedings. English. an (June). $28.00. Florida State Horticultural Society, PO Box 1146, Lake Alfred FL 33850. **Tel** (813)299-1702, FAX (813)956-5318. **ED** Norman Childers (editor's address: University of Florida, IFAS Horticultural Sciences Department, 2115 Fifield Hall, Gainesville, FL 32611-0511; (904)392-4711. **LC** SB1; .F55. **DD** 635. Index available. cum. index. **Circ:** 1,600. available on an online database from Federal Document Retrieval. Documents available from BIOSIS Document Express. ***Continues*** *Annual Meeting of the Florida State Horticultural Society, 0097-1219.*
Desc: Growing, handling, and processing of horticulture crops in Florida.
Ind/Abst AGRICOLA [Full Cov.]; Agric. Eng. Abstr. (1991-); Biodeter. Abstr.; Biol. Abstr.; Crop Physiol. Abstr.; Food Sci. Technol. Abstr.; For. Abstr.; Hortic. Abstr.; Irr. Drain. Abstr.; Nematol. Abstr.; Ornamental Hort.; PESTDOC; Plant Breed. Abstr.; Plant Grow. Reg. Abstr.; Postharvest News Inf.; Rev. Plant Pathol.; Seed Abstr.; Soils Fert.; Sug. Indus. Abstr.; World Agric. Econ.

US/0160-1156
PROCEEDINGS OF THE ANNUAL MEETING, WESTERN WASHINGTON HORTICULTURAL ASSOCIATION. **Main/Corp** Western Washington Horticultural Association. (19??)-. Proceedings. English. an (may). $22.00. Western Washington Horticultural Association, 625 Commerce Street, Old City 3200, Tacoma PA 98402. **Tel** (206)627-5897.

CN/0315-6877
PROCEEDINGS OF THE CANADIAN SOCIETY FOR HORTICULTURAL SCIENCE. (PROCEEDINGS OF THE CANADIAN SOCIETY FOR HORTICULTURAL SCIENCE, ANNUAL MEETING.). **Main/Corp** Canadian Society for Horticultural Science. Meeting. Vol. 3 (1964)-. English. an. 25.00Can$. Canadian Society for Horticultural Science, BC Min. Ag. Fish Food, Vernon BC VIT 4K7 Canada. **Tel** (604)549-5580. **ED** D. Buszard. **DD** 635/.06/271. **Circ:** 350 (ctrl). ***Continues*** *Proceedings of the Annual Meeting, Canadian Society for Horticultural Science., 0576-6095.*
Desc: Abstracts of papers presented at the annual meeting, minutes and reports of business meetings of the Canadian Society for Horticultural Science.

US
PROCEEDINGS OF THE FLORIDA TURF-GRASS MANAGEMENT CONFERENCE. **Main/Conf** Florida Turf-Grass Management Conference. 1st- 1953-. Proceedings. English. an. Florida Turf-Grass Association, 302 South Graham Avenue, Orlando FL 32803. **LC** SB433. cum. index.

CR
PROCEEDINGS OF THE INTERAMERICAN SOCIETY FOR TROPICAL HORTICULTURE. **Main/Corp** Interamerican Society for Tropical Horticulture. (198?)-. English (Spanish). an. $20.00. Interamerican Society for Tropical Horticulture, 18905 Southwest 280 Street, Homestead FL 33031. **Tel** (305)247-3597, FAX (305)247-3597. **ED** Dr. Richard Campbell (editor's address: Fairchild Tropical Garden, Homestead, FL 33156 USA; phone: (305)666-4019). **Pr Rev. Circ:** 400. ***Continues*** *American Society for Horticulture Science. Tropical Region. Proceedings of the Tropical Region, Annual Meeting, 0254-2528.*
Ind/Abst For. Abstr.; Hortic. Abstr.; Irr. Drain. Abstr.; Plant Breed. Abstr.; Plant Grow. Reg. Abstr.; Postharvest News Inf.; Rev. Agric. Entomol.; Seed Abstr.; Soils Fert.; Weed Abstr.

US/0149-7685
PROCEEDINGS OF THE PLANT GROWTH REGULATOR WORKING GROUP. ***Title Change.*** [Proc. Plant Growth Regul. Work. Group]. **Main/Conf** Plant Growth Regulator Working Group. **VFOAT** Proceedings, Annual Meeting: Plant Growth Regulator Working Group. (1977)-. Proceedings. English. an. Sugar Mill Road, 11939 Sugarmill Road, Longmont CO 80501. **LC** SB128; .P55A. **DD** 631.8. ***Continues*** *Program and Abstracts, Meeting of the Plant Growth Regulator Working Group, 0271-4590.* ***Continued by*** *Proceedings of the Plant Growth Regulator Society of America.*
Ind/Abst AGRICOLA; Crop Physiol. Abstr. (-19??).

US/0091-4487
PROCEEDINGS OF THE WESTERN SOCIETY OF WEED SCIENCE. **See** Agriculture-Crop Production and Soil.

US/0362-4463
PROCEEDINGS, SOUTHERN WEED SCIENCE SOCIETY. [Proc. S. Weed Sci. Soc.]. **Main/Corp** Southern Weed Science Society (U.S.). Vol. 22 (1969)-. Proceedings. English. an. $16.50. Southern Weed Science Society, 309 West Clark Street, Champaign IL 61820. **Tel** (217)356-3182, FAX (217)398-4119. **LC** SB610.2; .S68A. **DD** 632/.58/05. **CODEN** SWSPBE. Documents available from BIOSIS Document Express, CASDDS. ***Continues*** *Proceedings: Annual Meeting of the Southern Weed Conference.*
Ind/Abst AGRICOLA [Select. Cov.]; Biol. Abstr.; Chem. Abstr. (1969-1983); PESTDOC.

US/0510-9221
PROCEEDINGS - WORLD ORCHID CONFERENCE. **Main/Corp** World Orchid Conference. (19??)-. English. ir (every 3 years). World Orchid Conference, PO Box 59 5150, Miami FL 33159. **Tel** (305)635-6144. **LC** SB409; .W8. **DD** 635.93415; 635.

RM
PRODUCTIA VEGETALA : HORTICULTURA. ***Ceased.*** (1974)-(19??). Periodical. Romanian. mo. **(Subscription address:** Orion Press SRL, SPL Independentei 202-A, Bucharest 6 Romania.)
Desc: Studies in the field of horticulture.
Ind/Abst Hortic. Abstr.; Plant Breed. Abstr.; Potato Abstr.; Rev. Plant Pathol.

UK
PROFESSIONAL LANDSCAPER. (1986)-. English. bm (6 issues). £12.00 UK; £20.00 other. Albatross Publications, PO Box 193, Dorking Surrey RH5 5YF England. **Tel** 0306 712712. **ED** Carol Andrews. **Bk Rev. Ad Acc. Circ:** 4,000 (ctrl).
Desc: Covers all aspects of landscaping and groundsmanship.

II/0970-3020
PROGRESSIVE HORTICULTURE. [Progress. Hortic.]. (1969)-. Periodical. English. qt. $50.00. Directorate of Fruit Utilization, Hill Horticulture Development Board, 18-B Outram, Lucknow Uttar Pradesh India. **(Subscription address:** Prints India, 11 Darya Ganj, New Delhi, 110002 India, (Phone: 011 91 11 3268645)) **ED** J N Seth. **CODEN** PGHCBD. cum. index. Documents available from BIOSIS Document Express.
Ind/Abst AGRICOLA; Agric. Eng. Abstr. (1991-); Agrofor. Abstr. (1991-); Biocont. News Inf. (1991-); Biodeter. Abstr.; Biol. Abstr.; Crop Physiol. Abstr.; Field Crop Abstr.; Hortic. Abstr.; Irr. Drain. Abstr.; Nematol. Abstr.; Ornamental Hort. (19??-19??); Plant Breed. Abstr.; Plant Grow. Reg. Abstr.; Postharvest News Inf.; Potato Abstr.; Rev. Agric. Entomol.; Rev. Plant Pathol.; Seed Abstr.

US/0885-3894
PUBLIC GARDEN, THE. (THE PUBLIC GARDEN : THE JOURNAL OF THE AMERICAN ASSOCIATION OF BOTANICAL GARDENS AND ARBORETA.). [Public gard.]. **Added/Corp** American Association of Botanical Gardens and Arboreta. Vol. 1, No. 1 (Jan. 1986)-. Periodical. English. Four times a year. $24.00 (one year); $50.00 Combined with AABGA Newsletter. American Association of Botanical Gardens, 786 Church Road, Wayne PA 19087. **Tel** (215)688-1120, FAX (215)293-0149. **ED** Sharon A. Lee. **DD** 581. Index available. **Bk Rev. Ad Acc. Circ:** 1,800. ***Continues*** *Bulletin - American Association of Botanical Gardens and Arboreta, 0190-5155.*
Ind/Abst AGRICOLA [Select. Cov.]; Garden Lit. (1992-); Plant Genet. Resour. Abstr.

II/0033-4324
PUNJAB HORTICULTURAL JOURNAL, THE. [Punjab hortic. j.]. **Added/Corp** Punjab State Co-operative Fruit Development Federation. Vol. 1, (1961)-. Periodical. English. Four times a year. $26.00. Indian Books and Periodicals, 2429 Tilak Street, Pahar Ganj, New Delhi 110005 India.
Ind/Abst AGRICOLA; Crop Physiol. Abstr.; Food Sci. Technol. Abstr.; For. Abstr.; Hortic. Abstr.; Nematol. Abstr.; Ornamental Hort. (19??-19??); Plant Breed. Abstr.; Plant Grow. Reg. Abstr.; Postharvest News Inf.; Potato Abstr.; Rev. Agric. Entomol.; Seed Abstr.; Weed Abstr.

UK/0002-6476
QUARTERLY BULLETIN OF THE ALPINE GARDEN SOCIETY. [bull. Alp. Gard. Soc.]. **Added/Corp** Alpine Garden Society (Great Britain). Scottish Rock Garden Club. **VFOAT** A.G.S. Bulletin; Alpine Garden Society Bulletin. (1933)-. Periodical. English. Four times a year. £13.00 UK; £16.00 other. Alpine Garden Society / Worcestershire, AGS Centre, Avon Bank, Pershore, Worcestershire, WR10 3JP England. **Tel** 011 44 386 554790, FAX 011 44 386 554801. **ED** Dr. C. Grey-Wilson (phone: 0284-89205). Index available (Dec. issue). cum. index. **Bk Rev. Ad Acc. Circ:** 11,000 (ctrl). ***Continues*** *Bulletin of the Alpine Garden Society;* ***Absorbed*** *Alpine Gardening.*
Desc: An amateur publication of high professional standards and international reputation, it caters for all interested in rock and alpine plants both in cultivation and in the wild.
Ind/Abst Garden Lit. (1992-).

US
QUARTERLY BULLETIN OF THE NORTH AMERICAN LILY SOCIETY, INC. **Added/Corp** North American Lily Society. Vol. 17, No. 3 (Dec. 1963)-. Periodical. English. Four times a year (Mar., June, Sept., Dec.). $12.50 (individuals), $18.75 (sustaining) Comes with North American Lily Society membership. North American Lily Society, PO Box 272, Owatonna MN 55060. **Tel** (507)451-2170. **ED** Robert Gilman. **Ad Acc. Circ:** 1,500. ***Continues*** *North American Lily Society. Quarterly Bulletin.*
Ind/Abst Hortic. Abstr.; Ornamental Hort. (1991-); Plant Breed. Abstr.

US/1042-3524
QUARTERLY - PLANT GROWTH REGULATOR SOCIETY OF AMERICA. (QUARTERLY / PGRSA.). [Q. - Plant Growth Regul. Soc. Am.]. **Added/Corp** Plant Growth Regulator Society of America. **VFOAT** PGRSA Quarterly. Vol. 16, No. 4 (Oct./Dec. 1988)-. Academic Scholarly Publication. English. qt. $20.00. Plant Growth Regulator Society of America, PO Box 12014, Research Triangle NC 27709. **Tel** (919)549-2408. **DD** 581. **CODEN** PGQUED. Documents available from CASDDS. ***Continues*** *Bulletin, Plant Growth Regulator, 0163-6367.*
Desc: Theoretical and practical papers on all plant growth regulator subjects. PGR industry announcements of general interest.
Ind/Abst AGRICOLA [Full Cov.]; Chem. Abstr.; Cot. Trop. Fibr. Abstr. Bibliogr.; Crop Physiol. Abstr.; Curr. Aware. Biol. Sci., CABS; Field Crop Abstr.; Hortic. Abstr.; Ornamental Hort. (1991-); Plant Grow. Reg. Abstr.

FR/0242-4959
QUATRE SAISONS DU JARDINAGE, LES. (1980)-. Periodical. French. bm. 153.77F, 210.00F other. Editions Terre Vivante, 6 rue Saulnier, 75009 Paris France. **Tel** 011 33 1 42463788, FAX 45 23 38 17. **ED** Terre Vivante. **UDC** 634. Index available. cum. index. **Bk Rev. Ad Acc. Circ:** 22,000.
Desc: Organic gardening, ecology, and health.

CN/0820-5515
QUATRE-TEMPS. **See** Biology-Botany.

AT/0033-6122
QUEENSLAND FRUIT AND VEGETABLE NEWS. **Added/Corp** Queensland. Committee of Direction of Fruit Marketing. Vol. 1 (Nov. 3, 1950)-. Trade Publication. English. Twenty-three times a year. 40.00Aus$ (Australia); 60.00Aus$ (Asia & Pacific); 70.00Aus$ (other). Committee of Direction Fruit Marketing, PO Box 19, Brisbane Queensland 4106 Australia. **Tel** 11 61 7 2132463, telex AA 42111. **ED** Helen O'Brien. Index available. **Bk Rev. Ad Acc. Circ:** 11,500 (ctrl).
Desc: Trade journal for Queensland's fruit and vegetable growers.

FR
RAPPORT - SECTION D'EXPERIMENTATION DE BOBO-DIOULASSO, INSTITUT DE RECHERCHES DU COTON ET DES TEXTILES EXOTIQUES. **Main/Corp** Institut de Recherches du Cotton et des Textiles Exotiques. Section d'Experimentation de Bobo-Dioulasso. French. Paris Institut de Recherches du Cotton et des Textiles, 34 rue des Renaudes, Paris 75016 France. **LC** SB251.U65; I57A. **DD** 633/.51/096625.

SW/0348-4157
RAPPORT / SVERIGES LANTBRUKSUNIVERSITE. INSTITUTIONEN FOR TRADGARDSVETENSKAP. [Rapp. - Sver. lantbruksuniv., Inst. tradgardsvetensk.]. **VFOAT** Report / Swedish University of Agricultural Sciences. Department

of Horticultural Sciences. 1-. Monographic series. Swedish (summaries and/or abstracts in English). Five times a year. Price varies per volume. Sveriges Lantbruksuniversitet / Alnarp, Konsulentaudelningen/Tradgard, S-230 53 Alnarp Sweden. **Tel** 040/415000. **CODEN** RSLTDM. Index available. cum. index. Documents available from BIOSIS Document Express.
Ind/Abst Biol. Abstr.; Hortic. Abstr.; Ornamental Hort.; Plant Breed. Abstr.; Plant Grow. Reg. Abstr.

AT/0726-1470
RARE FRUIT COUNCIL OF AUSTRALIA INC. NEWSLETTER. [Newsl. - Rare Fruit Counc. Aust.]. (1980)-. Newsletter. English. Six times a year (Jan., Mar. May, July, Sept., Nov.). 35.00Aus$ Australia; 40.00Aus$ other. Rare Fruit Council of Australia Inc., PO Box 707, Cairns QLD 4870 Australia. **Tel** 011 61 7 552824. **ED** Thea Verstegen. **DD** 634.0994. **Ad Acc.** ctrl circ.

GW/0341-9789
RASEN. [Rasen]. **VFOAT** Rasen, Grunflachen, Begrunungen; Turf/Gazon. (970)-. Academic Scholarly Publication. German (English and French). qt. DM61.00. Hortus Verlag GmbH, Rheinallee 4B, D 53173 Bonn Germany. **Tel** 011 49 288 353030, 011 49 288 353033. **CODEN** RASNDF. Documents available from CASDDS.
Ind/Abst Chem. Abstr. (1970-1985).

BU/0568-465X
RASTENIEVDNI NAUKI. ***Suspended.*** [Rastenievdni nauki]. **VFOAT** Plant Growing; Plant Science. (1964)-(1991). Periodical. Russian (summaries and/or abstracts in English). mo. **(Subscription address:** Hemus Foreign Trade Organization, 6 Tzar Osvoboditel Boulevard, 1000 Sofia Bulgaria.**) CODEN** RSTNA7. Documents available from BIOSIS Document Express, CASDDS. ***Supersedes*** *Akademiia na Selskostopanskite Nauki. Izvestiia.*
Ind/Abst Biocont. News Inf.; Biodeter. Abstr.; Biol. Abstr.; Chem. Abstr.; Cot. Trop. Fibr. Abstr. Bibliogr.; Crop Physiol. Abstr.; Field Crop Abstr.; Food Sci. Technol. Abstr.; For. Abstr.; Hortic. Abstr.; Maize Abstr.; Ornamental Hort. (1991-); Plant Breed. Abstr.; Postharvest News Inf.; Potato Abstr.; Rev. Agric. Entomol.; Rev. Plant Pathol.; Rice Abstr.; Seed Abstr.; Soils Fert.; Weed Abstr.; Wheat Barley Trit. Abstr.

BL
RELATORIO ANUAL DE PESQUISA. HORTICULTURA / EMPRESA DE PESQUISA AGROPECUARIA DO CEARA. **Main/Corp** Empresa de Pesquisa Agropecuaria do Ceara. (19??)-. Portuguese. an.
Ind/Abst Field Crop Abstr.

NE
RENTABILITEIT EN FINANCIERING VAN DE BOOMKWEKERIJ IN NEDERLAND OVER. Dutch. an. Landbouw-Economisch Instituut, Conradkade 175, Hague Netherlands. **Tel** (070)614161. **LC** SB118.75.N4; R45.

CN/0849-8334
REPERTOIRE DES PRODUITS ET SERVICES HORTICOLES DE LAVAL. ***Title Change.*** [Repert. prod. serv. hortic. Laval]. **Added/Corp** Corporation de Developpement Economique de Laval. Union des Producteurs Agricoles--Laval. Societe d'Agriculture de Laval. (1990)-(199?). French. CODEL, Bureau 100, 1555 Boulevard Chomedey, Laval Quebec H7V 3Z1 Canada. **DD** 338.1/75/0294714271. ***Continued by*** *Repertoire des Entreprises Horticoles de Laval, 1202-1199.*

AT/0069-7435
REPORT / DIVISION OF HORTICULTURAL RESEARCH. **Main/Corp** Commonwealth Scientific and Industrial Research Organization (Australia). Division of Horticultural Research. (1967)-. English. be. CSIRO Publications, PO Box 89, 314 Albert Street, East Melborne Victoria 3002 Australia. **Tel** 011 61 3 4187333, 4187217, FAX 011 61 3 4190459, telex AA 30236. **LC** SB317.65.A8; C65a. **DD** 635/.0994. ***Continues*** *Commonwealth Scientific and Industrial Research Organization (Australia). Horticultural Research Section. Report.*
Ind/Abst Vitis Vitic. Enol. Abstr.

CK
REPORT OF THE TREE NUT AUTHORITY. **Main/Corp** Tree Nut Authority. 1st-1975/76-. English. **LC** HD9259.N7; M37. **DD** 354/.689/7008233. ***Supersedes*** *Tung Board. Final Report of the Tung Board; Tung Board. Final Report of the Tung Board.*

CN/0083-8810
REPORTS OF PROCEEDINGS OF ANNUAL MEETING - WESTERN CANADIAN SOCIETY FOR HORTICULTURE. (REPORTS OF PROCEEDINGS - WESTERN CANADIAN SOCIETY FOR HORTICULTURE.). **Main/Corp** Western Canadian Society for Horticulture. Meeting. 12th (1956)-. English (French). an. 40.00Can$. University of Alberta / Botanic Garden, Devonian, c/o Roger Vick, Edmonton Alberta T6G 2E1 Canada. **ED** S. H. Nelson. Index available. **Circ:** 300 (ctrl). ***Continues*** *Western Canadian Society for Horticulture. Report of Proceedings of the Western Canadian Society for Horticulture., 0315-5110.*
Desc: Report of proceedings of the annual meeting including scientific presentations and committee reports pertaining to horticulture in Prairie Canada.

NR/0795-414X
RESEARCH BULLETIN - NATIONAL HORTICULTURAL RESEARCH INSTITUTE. [Res. bull. - Natl. Hortic. Res. Inst.]. (1988)-. Monographic series. English. bm. **DD** 635.05.
Ind/Abst Hortic. Abstr.; Nematol. Abstr.; Rev. Plant Pathol.; Soils Fert.

US/0733-9283
RESULTS FROM THE COOPERATIVE COORDINATED OAT BREEDING NURSERIES, AND THE UNIFORM WINTER-HARDINESS NURSERIES. **See** Economics-Cooperatives.

•UK
REVIEW OF AROMATIC AND MEDICINAL PLANTS. (199?)-. English. bm. $230.00. CAB International Centre, Wallingford, Oxon OX10 8DE United Kingdom. **Tel** 44 491 832111, FAX 44 491 833508, telex 847964 (COMAGG G).

US/1042-4148
REVIEWS OF WEED SCIENCE. (REVIEWS OF WEED SCIENCE / WSSA, WEED SCIENCE SOCIETY OF AMERICA.). [Rev. weed sci.]. **Added/Corp** Weed Science Society of America. Vol. 1 (1985)-. Monographic series. English. ir. Price varies per volume. Weed Science Society of America, 1508 West University Avenue, Champaign IL 61821. **Tel** (217)352-4212, FAX (217)398-4114. **LC** SB610; .R48. **DD** 632/.58/05. **CODEN** RWSCEZ. Documents available from BIOSIS Document Express, CASDDS.
Ind/Abst Biol. Abstr.; Chem. Abstr.; Maize Abstr.; Plant Grow. Reg. Abstr.; Seed Abstr.; Soyabean Abstr.; Weed Abstr.

SZ/0370-5323
REVUE HORTICOLE SUISSE. [Rev. hortic. suisse]. Vol. 1 (Sept. 1927)-. Periodical. French. mo. 55.00F Switzerland; 70.00F other. Centre Horticole de Lullier, CH Moncousin, CH 1254 Jussy, Switzerland. **Tel** 11 41 22 7591814. **LC** SB7; .R52.
Ind/Abst AGRICOLA; For. Abstr.; Hortic. Abstr.; Ornamental Hort. (1991-); Plant Breed. Abstr.; Plant Genet. Resour. Abstr.; Rev. Agric. Entomol.

SZ/0375-1430
REVUE SUISSE DE VITICULTURE, ARBORICULTURE, HORTICULTURE. [Rev. suisse vitic., arboric., hortic.]. (1972)-. Academic Scholarly Publication. French (summaries and/or abstracts in English, German and Italian). bm. 42.00F; 52.00F (combined subscription with Revue Suisse de Agriculture). Revue Suisse d'Agriculture, M Magnenat, Case Postale 190, CH-1260 Nyon Switzerland. **Tel** 011 41 22 615454, FAX 011 41 22 621325. **ED** Michel Magnenat. **CODEN** RVAHAH. Index available. cum. index. **Bk Rev. Ad Acc. Circ:** 6,500 (ctrl). Documents available from CASDDS. ***Continues*** *Revue Suisse de Viticulture et Arboriculture.*
Desc: All about viticulture, arboriculture and horticulture.
Ind/Abst Biocont. News Inf.; Chem. Abstr.; Crop Physiol. Abstr.; EMBASE; Food Sci. Technol. Abstr.; Hortic. Abstr.; Nematol. Abstr.; Ornamental Hort. (19??-19??); PESTDOC; Plant Breed. Abstr.; Plant Genet. Resour. Abstr.; Plant Grow. Reg. Abstr.; Postharvest News Inf.; Rev. Agric. Entomol.; Rev. Plant Pathol.; Soils Fert.; Weed Abstr.; World Agric. Econ.

AT/0485-0637
RHODODENDRON, THE. V. 1- May 1962-. Periodical. English. qt. 20.00Aus$ Australia. Australian Rhododendron Society, PO Box 21, Olinda Victoria 3788 Australia. **Tel** 751 1980. **ED** L Marshall. **Bk Rev. Ad Acc. Circ:** 500 (ctrl). ***Supersedes*** *Journal of the Australian Rhododendron Society.*

GW/0482-9905
RHODODENDRON UND IMMERGRUNE LAUBGEHOLZE JAHRBUCH. **Added/Corp** Deutsche Rhododendron Gesellschaft. Deutsche Rhododendron Gesellschaft. Jahrbuch der Rhododenron Gesellschaft. (1937)-. German. cum. index.
Ind/Abst Hortic. Abstr.; Ornamental Hort. (1991-); Plant Breed. Abstr.; Plant Genet. Resour. Abstr.

IT
RIVISTA DI FRUTTICOLTURA E DI ORTOFLORICOLTURA. Vol. 45, No. 1 (Jan. 1983)-. Periodical. Italian. Eleven times a year. L63000 (one year), L114000 (two year) Italy; L80000 Spain; L90000 other. Edagricole, PO Box 2157, 40100 Bologna Italy. **Tel** 011 39 51 492211 Ext. 22, FAX 011 39 51 493660, telex 510336 EDAGRI. Index available in last issue of volume--attached. ***Continues*** *Frutticoltura, 0016-2310.*
Ind/Abst Crop Physiol. Abstr.; Hortic. Abstr.; Plant Genet. Resour. Abstr.; Postharvest News Inf.

US/1054-9552
ROCKY MOUNTAIN GARDENER. [Rocky Mt. gard.]. Vol. 1, No. 1 (Winter 1990)-. Periodical. English. Four times a year (published seasonally). $12.00 US; $14.00 Canada. Westwind Publications, 403 North Pine, PO Box 1230, Gunnison CO 81230. **Tel** (303)641-5091. **ED** Susan Martineau and Judy Allen. **DD** 635. **Bk Rev**, (Qty: 20/year). **Ad Acc.**
Ind/Abst Garden Lit. (1992-).

US
ROSTER OF REGISTERED LANDSCAPE ARCHITECTS, COMMONWEALTH OF KENTUCKY. **Main/Corp** Kentucky. State Board of Examiners and Registration of Landscape Architects. English. an. Capitol Annex, Suite 168, Frankfort KY 40601. **LC** SB469.34.K4; K46A. **DD** 712/.025/769.

RU/0131-3568
SADOVODSTVO. ***Title Change.*** **Added/Corp** Russia (1923-U.S.S.R.). Ministerstvo Selskogo Khoziaistva. (1960)-(19??). Periodical. Russian. bm. Ministerstvo Selskogo Khoziastva, Moscow Russia. **(Subscription address:** Victor Kamkin, 4956 Boiling Brook Parkway, Rockville MD 20852.**)** ***Formed by the union of*** *Priusadebnyi Sad* ***and*** *Sad I Ogorod.* ***Continued by*** *Sadovodstvo i Vinogradarstvo, 0235-2591.*
Ind/Abst Agrofor. Abstr.; Plant Breed. Abstr.

RU/0235-2591
SADOVODSTVO I VINOGRADARSTVO. **Added/Corp** Soviet Union. Gosudarstvennyi Agropromyshlennyi Komitet. (1988)-. Academic Scholarly Publication. Russian. Six times a year. $69.95. Agropromizdat, Sadovo-Spasskaia, 18, 107807 Moscow Russia. **(Subscription address:** East View Publications Inc., 3020 Harbor Lane North, Suite 110, Minneapolis MN 55447.**) LC** SB319.3.S65; S25. **DD** 635/.0947. **CODEN** SAVIER. Documents available from CASDDS. ***Formed by the union of*** *Sadovodstvo, 0131-3568* ***and*** *Vinodelie i Vinogradarstvo SSSR, 0042-6318.*
Ind/Abst Agric. Eng. Abstr. (1991-); Agrofor. Abstr. (1991-); Biocont. News Inf. (1991-); Chem. Abstr.; Food Sci. Technol. Abstr.; Hortic. Abstr.; Irr. Drain. Abstr.; Plant Breed. Abstr.; Postharvest News Inf.; Rev. Agric. Entomol.; Rev. Plant Pathol.; Seed Abstr.; Soils Fert.; Weed Abstr.; Wheat Barley Trit. Abstr.; World Agric. Econ.

KO
SAE NONGSA. Began with Jan. 1956 issue. Periodical. Korean. mo. W400 single issue. Chungang Chongmyo Chusik Hoesa. **LC** SB317.5; .S33.

US
SAINTPAULIA INTERNATIONAL NEWS. Vol. 1, No. 1 (June 1989)-. English. Six times a year (Feb., Apr., June, Aug., Oct., Dec.). $12.00 US; $15.00 other. Saintpaulia International News, 780 Suzanne, Las Cruces NM 88005. **ED** Roberta M. Hale (editor's address: 1650 Cherry Hill Road South, State College, PA 16803, phone: (814)237-7410). **Bk Rev. Ad Acc. Circ:** 1,350. ***Continues*** *Gesneriad Saintpaulia News, 0016-3627.*
Desc: Informative publication on growing and caring for African violets and other gesneriads.

JA/0385-3675
SAITAMA-KEN ENGEI SHIKENJO KENKYU HOKOKU. [Saitama-ken Engei Shikenjo kenkyu hokoku]. **Added/Corp** Saitama-ken Engei Shikenjo. **VFOAT** Bulletin of the Saitama Horticultural Experiment Station. (1970)-. Japanese (summaries and/or abstracts in English). Saitamaken Engei Shikenjo, (Saitama Horticultural Experiment Station), 91, Rokumanbu, Kukishi, Saitamaken 346 Japan. **CODEN** BSHSDR. Documents available from CASDDS.
Ind/Abst Chem. Abstr. (1970-1983); Crop Physiol. Abstr.; Hortic. Abstr.; Ornamental Hort. (1991-); Plant Breed. Abstr.; Plant Genet. Resour. Abstr.; Soils Fert.

US
SAN DIEGO HOME / GARDEN. ***Title Change.*** **See** Home Economics.

•US/1073-6891
SAN DIEGO HOME/GARDEN LIFESTYLES. **See** Home Economics.

US/0273-6004
SAN FRANCISCO WHOLESALE ORNAMENTAL CROPS REPORT. (SAN FRANCISCO WHOLESCALE ORNAMENTAL CROPS REPORT / FEDERAL-STATE MARKET NEWS SERVICE.). **Added/Corp** Federal-State Market News Service. California. Bureau of Market News. United States. Agricultural Marketing Service. Fruit and Vegetable Division. **VFOAT** Ornamental Crops Market News. (19??)-. English. Fifty-two times a year. $96.00 North America; $192.00 others. US Department of Agriculture / Federal-State Market News, 630 Sansome Street, Room 727, San Francisco CA 94111. **Tel** (415)705-1300. **ED** F. Teensma. **Circ:** 100 (ctrl).
Desc: Information on cut flowers on San Francisco's market.

●US/1062-8908
SANSEVIERIA JOURNAL, THE. [The Sansevieria j.]. (1992)-. Periodical. English. qt (Mar., June, Sept., Dec.). $10.00 (US); $12.00 (other). Trans Terra, 9821 White Oak Avenue, Northride CA 91325. **Tel** (818) 349-9798. **ED** Juan Chahinian 18618 Erwin St., Reseda CA 91335 (818) 344-4096. Index available. **Ad Acc. Circ:** 250.

UN/0201-7997
SBORNIK NAUCHNYKH TRUDOV / VSESOIUZNAIA ORDENA LENINA I ORDENA TRUDOVOGO KRASNOGO ZNAMENI AKADEMIIA SELSKOKHOZIAISTVENNYKH NAUK IMENI V.I. LENINA, GOUDARSTVENNYI ORDENA TRUDOVOGO KRASNOGO ZNAMENI NIKITSKII BOTANICHESKII SAD. See Biology-Botany.

RU/0375-2232
SBORNIK NAUCHNYKH TRUDOV (VSESOIUZNYI NAUCHNO-ISSLEDOVATELSKII INSTITUT SADOVODSTVA IM. I.V. MICHURINA). (SBORNIK NAUCHNYKH TRUDOV / MINISTERSTVO SELSKOGO KHOZIAISTVA SSSR, VSESOIUZNYI NAUCHNO-ISSLEDOVATELSKII INSTITUT SADOVODSTVA IM. I.V. MICHURINA.). **Added/Corp** Vsesoiuznyi Nauchno-Issledovatelskii Institut Sadovodstva Im. I.V. Michurina. Vol. 26 (1978)-. Monographic series. Russian. Price varies per volume. ***Continues** Sbornik Nauchnyky Rabot (Vsesoiuxnyi Nauchno-Issledovatelskii Institut Sadovodstva Im. I.V. Michurina).*

XR/0231-567X
SBORNIK UVTI. ZAHRADNICTVI. [Sb. UVTIZ. Zahrad.]. **Main/Corp** Ustav Vedeckotechnickych Informac Pro Zemedelstvi. **VFOAT** Zahradnictvi. V. 3, No. 1/2-. Periodical. Czech (summaries and/or abstracts in English, German and Russian). qt. **(Subscription address:** Artia Pegas Press Ltd., Palac Metro Narodni Trida 25, 11210 Prague 1 Czech Republic.**)** ***Continues** Sbornik Uvti. Zahradnictvi.*
Ind/Abst AGRICOLA; Agrofor. Abstr.; Crop Physiol. Abstr.; Hortic. Abstr.; Irr. Drain. Abstr.; Ornamental Hort. (19??-19??); Plant Breed. Abstr.; Plant Grow. Reg. Abstr.; Postharvest News Inf.; Rev. Plant Pathol.; Seed Abstr.

SZ/0371-4942
SCHWEIZERISCHE ZEITSCHRIFT FUER OBST- UND WEINBAU. [Schweiz. Z. Obst-Weinb.]. (1892)-. Academic Scholarly Publication. German. Twenty-six times a year. 59.00F. Verlag Stutz & Company AG, Postfach, CH-8820 Waedenwil Switzerland. **Tel** 011 41 1 7800837. **CODEN** SZOWAZ. Documents available from CASDDS.
Ind/Abst AgBiotech News Inf.; AGRICOLA; Agric. Eng. Abstr.; Agrofor. Abstr.; Biocont. News Inf. (1991-); Chem. Abstr. (1892-1984); EMBASE; Food Sci. Technol. Abstr.; Hortic. Abstr.; PESTDOC; Plant Grow. Reg. Abstr.; Rev. Agric. Entomol.; Rev. Plant Pathol.; Weed Abstr.; World Agric. Econ.

NE/0304-4238
SCIENTIA HORTICULTURAE. [Sci. hortic.]. **Added/Corp** International Society for Horticultural Science. (1973)-. Academic Scholarly Publication. English. Twenty times a year (5 vols.). Fl1845.00. Elsevier Science Publishers BV, PO Box 211, 1000 AE Amsterdam Netherlands. **Tel** 011 31 20 5803642, FAX 011 31 20 5862696, telex 15682. **ED** J van Bragt and S J Wellensiek. **LC** SB4; .S33. **DD** 635/.05. **CODEN** SHRTAH. **[CCC]. Pr Rev.** available on microfilm and microfiche from University Microfilms International (UMI). Documents available from The Genuine Article, BIOSIS Document Express, CASDDS, Documents on Demand.
Desc: Deals with horticulture under moderate subtropical and tropical conditions, as well as with open and protected crop growing of vegetables, fruits, mushrooms, bulbs and ornamentals.
Ind/Abst AgBiotech News Inf.; Agric. Eng. Abstr. (1991-); Agrofor. Abstr. (1991-); BioBusiness; Biodeter. Abstr. (1991-); Biol. Abstr.; Chem. Abstr.; Crop Physiol. Abstr.; Curr. Contents, Agric. Biol. Environ. Sci.; Ecol. Abstr.; EMBASE; Energy Inf. Abstr.; Environ. Abstr.; Field Crop Abstr.; Food Sci. Technol. Abstr.; For. Abstr.; Hortic. Abstr.; Irr. Drain. Abstr.; Leadscan; Nutr. Abstr. Rev., Ser. A, Hum. Exp.; Ornamental Hort. (19??-19??); Life Sci. Collect.; PESTDOC; Plant Breed. Abstr.; Plant Genet. Resour. Abstr.; Plant Grow. Reg. Abstr.; Postharvest News Inf.; Potato Abstr.; Res. Alert [Full Cov.]; Rev. Agric. Entomol.; Rev. Plant Pathol.; Sci. Cit. Index; SCISEARCH; Seed Abstr.; Soils Fert.; Vitis Vitic. Enol. Abstr.; Weed Abstr.

US/0091-567X
SEASON SUMMARY - OREGON BARTLETT PEAR COMMISSION. (SEASON SUMMARY.). **Main/Corp** Oregon Bartlett Pear Commission. English. an. Oregon Bartlett Pear Commission, 601 Woodlark Building, Portland OR 97205. **LC** HD9259.P333; O75A. **DD** 338.1/7/413.

CN/0317-350X
SEASONAL FRUIT & VEGETABLE REPORT (ANNUAL SUMMARY). (FRUIT AND VEGETABLE PRODUCTION IN ONTARIO, ANNUAL SUMMARY.). **Main/Corp** Ontario. Ministry of Agriculture and Food. Economics Branch. **Added/Corp** Ontario. Ministry of Agriculture and Food. Economics Branch. Seasonal Fruit & Vegetable Report. 0474-1560. **VAT** Fruit and Vegetable Production in Ontario (Annual Summary). (19??)-. Periodical. English. an. Parliament Building, Queen's Park, Toronto Ontario M7A 1B6 Canada. **LC** SB29.C2; O63. **DD** 338.1/7/409713. ***Continues** Ontario. Dept. of Agriculture and Food. Farm Economics, Cooperatives and Statistics Branch. Fruit and Vegetable Production in Ontario, Annual Summary., 0317-350X.*

US
SEATTLE HOME AND GARDEN. ***Title Change.*** Vol. 1, No. 1 (Fall 1989)-(Feb. 1992). Periodical. English. Seven times a year. Pacific Northwest Media Inc., 701 Dexter Avenue North, Suite 101, Seattle WA 98109. **Tel** (206)284-1750, FAX (206)284-2550. **ED** Jo Brown. **LC** NA7238.S4; S43. **Bk Rev. Ad Acc. Circ:** 31,000 (ctrl). ***Continued by** Greater Seattle.*
Desc: Seattle area home, garden, and lifestyle publication.

US/0149-1296
SEED ANALYSIS REPORT. Main/Corp Pennsylvania. Bureau of Plant Industry. English. an. Pennsylvania Department of Agriculture, 2301 North Cameron Street, Harrisburg PA 17110. **Tel** (717)772-2853, FAX (717)787-2387. **LC** SB114.U7; P45A. **DD** 631.5/21.

US
SEED SAVERS EXCHANGE. (19??)-. English. Three times a year (Jan., Aug., Nov.). $25.00 US; $30.00 Canada and Mexico; $40.00 other. Seed Savers Exchange, Kent Whealy, Route 3 Box 239, Decorah IA 52101. **Tel** (319)382-5990.

US
SEEDHEAD NEWS, THE. Added/Corp Native Seeds/Search. **VFOAT** Seed Head News. No. 1 (1983)-. Periodical. English. qt. $18.00. Native Seeds Search Association, 2509 North Campbell, #325, Tucson AZ 85719. **Tel** (602) 327-9123.

IT
SEMENTI SILE : CATALOGO. Main/Corp Sementi Sile (Firm). Periodical. Italian. sa.

US
SHADE TREE : MONTHLY BULLETIN OF THE NEW JERSEY FEDERATION OF SHADE TREE COMMISSIONS, THE. Began in 1928. Bulletin. English. mo. ***Continues** Bulletin of the New Jersey Federation Shade Tree Commissions; **Absorbed** Proceedings, Annual Meeting of the New Jersey Federation of Shade Tree Commissions. New Jersey Federation of Shade Tree Commissions.*
Ind/Abst For. Abstr.; Hortic. Abstr.; Ornamental Hort. (1991-); Weed Abstr.

JA/0387-0707
SHOKUBUTSU BOEKIJO CHOSA KENKYU HOKOKU. [Shokubutsu Boekijo chosa kenkyu hokoku]. **Main/Corp** Norinsho Yokohama Shokubutsu Boikijo. (1961)-. Academic Scholarly Publication. Japanese (summaries and/or abstracts in English). ir. Norinsho Yokohama Shokubutsu Boekijo 57, Kitanakadori-5, Naka-ku 231, Yokohama Japan. **LC** SB989.J3; N67A. **CODEN** SBCKA9. Documents available from BIOSIS Document Express, CASDDS.
Ind/Abst Biodeter. Abstr.; Biol. Abstr.; Chem. Abstr.; For. Prod. Abstr. (1991-); Rev. Med. Vet. Entomol.

MY
SIARAN PEKEBUN. Periodical. Malay. $2.00 single issue. Institut Penyelidikan Getah Malaysia, 260 Jl Ampang, Peti Surat 150, Kuala Lumpur 01-02 Malaysia. **LC** SB290.5.M4; R82A. ***Continues** Siaran Pekebun Pusat Penyelidikan Getah Malaysia.*

US
SIGNA. Added/Corp American Iris Society. Species Iris Study Group. No. 1 (April 1968)-. Periodical. English.

US/1049-3352
SITUATION AND OUTLOOK REPORT. VEGETABLES AND SPECIALTIES. [Situat. outlook rep., Veg. spec.]. **VFOAT** Vegetables and Specialties; Situation and Outlook Yearbook. Vegetable and Specialities; Vegetables and Specialities, Situation and Outlook. TVS-244 (Feb. 1988)-. Government Publication. English. Three times a year. $8.00; $3.00 (single issues) US; $10.00; $3.75 (single issues) other. US Department of Agriculture, 14th Street and Independence Avenue SW, Washington DC 20250. **Tel** (202)720-5457. **LC** HD9220.U5; S58. **DD** 338.1/75/0973021. **CODEN** VSSRES. available on microfiche (Vols. for 1988 distributed to depository libraries). ***Continues** Situation and Outlook Report. Vegetable (Washington, D.C. : 1987).*
Desc: Reports, consisting chiefly of tables and statistics, containing information on supply, demand and price research.
Ind/Abst BioBusiness (1990-); Trade Ind. ASAP [Full Txt.]; Trade Ind. Index [Full Txt.]; World Agric. Econ.

US
SONORAN QUARTERLY, THE. Added/Corp Desert Botanical Garden (Ariz.). Vol. 45, No. 1 (Spring 1991)-. Periodical. English. qt (4 issues). $25.00. Desert Botanical Garden, 1201 North Galvin Parkway, Phoenix AZ 85008. **Tel** (602)941-1225. ***Continues** Saguaroland Bulletin, 0275-6919; **Absorbed** Agave.*

SA
SOUTH AFRICAN NURSERYMAN : THE OFFICIAL JOURNAL OF SANA / DIE SUID-AFRIKAANSE KWEKER : DIE AMPTELIKE TYDSKRIF VAN DIE SAKU, THE. Added/Corp South African Nurserymen's Association. **VFOAT** Die Suid-Afrikaanse Kweker : Die Amptelike Tydskrif van die Saku; Suid-Afrikaanse Kweker; SA Nurseryman. (198?)-. Periodical. English (Afrikaans). qt. $34.00. South African Nursery Association, PO Box 514, 1685 Halfway House South Africa. **Tel** 011 27 11 3151920, FAX 011 27 11 3151636. ***Continues** Sa Kweker Vio Mooi Suid-Afrika.*

SA
SOUTH AFRICAN ORCHID JOURNAL. SUID-AFRIKAANSE ORGIDEEJOERNAAL. Added/Corp South African Orchid Council. **VFOAT** Suid-Afrikaanse Orgideejoernaal. (19??)-. Periodical. English. qt. R42.00 South Africa; $26.00 other. South African Orchid Council, PO Box 81, Constantia, 7848, South Africa. **Tel** 011 27 11 7888306. **ED** H. Rogers. **Bk Rev. Ad Acc, Adv Mgr:** L. Davies. **Circ:** 1,500 (ctrl).

II/0038-3473
SOUTH INDIAN HORTICULTURE. [South Indian hortic.]. **Added/Corp** South Indian Horticultural Association. Vol. 1 (May 1953)-. Periodical. English. bm. $25.00. South Indian Horticulture Association, Coimbatore, India. **(Subscription address:** Prints India, 11 Darya Ganj, New Delhi, 110002 India, (Phone: 011 91 11 3268645)**)**
Ind/Abst Agrofor. Abstr. (19??-19??); Crop Physiol. Abstr.; Field Crop Abstr.; Food Sci. Technol. Abstr.; For. Abstr.; Hortic. Abstr.; Irr. Drain. Abstr.; Maize Abstr.; Nematol. Abstr.; Nutr. Abstr. Rev., Ser. A, Hum. Exp.; Ornamental Hort. (1991-); Plant Breed. Abstr.; Plant Genet. Resour. Abstr.; Plant Grow. Reg. Abstr.; Postharvest News Inf.; Rev. Agric. Entomol.; Rev. Plant Pathol.; Seed Abstr.; Soils Fert.; World Agric. Econ.

US/0149-516X
SOUTHERN ACCENTS. See Interior Design.

US
SOUTHERN LAWNMOWERS DEALERS NEWSLETTER. Newsletter. English. mo. $8.00 (one year), $14.00 (two year), $18.00 (three year). Southern Lawnmower, PO Box 6426, Maryville TN 37802. **Tel** (615)983-1477, FAX (615)984-9902. **ED** Roger R. Stewart. **Ad Acc. Circ:** 3,000 (ctrl).

US/1048-2318
SOUTHERN LIVING ... GARDEN ANNUAL. [South. living gard. annu.]. **VFOAT** Garden Annual. (1990)-. English. an. $14.95 (single issue). Oxmoor House, PO Box 2463, Birmingham AL 35201. **Tel** (205)877-6000. **LC** SB453.2.S66; S66. **DD** 635/.05.

US
SOUTHERN NURSERY DIGEST. ***Title Change.*** **VFOAT** Nursery Digest. (19??)-(19??). Periodical. English. mo. Betrock Information Systems, 1601 North Palm Avenue, Suite 303, Pembroke Pines FL 33026. **Tel** (800)627-3819, (305)434-4440. ***Continues** Nursery Digest. **Continued by** Landscape & Nursey Digest, 1071-3697.*

US
SOUTHERN NURSERYMEN'S ASSOCIATION RESEARCH CONFERENCE, ANNUAL REPORT. Main/Corp Southern Nurserymen's Association. **VFOAT** Proceedings of SNA Research Conference, Annual Report. 16th- 1971-. Periodical. English. an. ***Continues** Annual Report on Ornamental Research in Each Southern State.*
Ind/Abst AGRICOLA.

US/0190-8723
SPECIAL PUBLICATION - CALIFORNIA NATIVE PLANT SOCIETY. No. 1-. Monographic series. English. Price varies per volume. California Native Plant Society, 909 12th Street/Suite 116, Sacramento CA 95814. **Tel** (916)447-2677.

UK
SPON'S LANDSCAPE AND EXTERNAL WORKS PRICE BOOK. English. an (includes three updates). £39.50. International Thompson Publishing Services Ltd, North Way, Cheriton House, Andover Hampshire SP10 5BE England. **Tel** 011 44 264 342840.

●US/1061-687X
SPORTSTURF (1992). (SPORTSTURF : THE OFFICIAL MAGAZINE OF THE SPORTS TURF MANAGERS ASSOCIATION.). [SportsTURF]. **Added/Corp** Sports Turf Managers Association. **VFOAT** Sports TURF; SportsTURF Magazine. Vol. 8, No. 2 (Feb. 1992)-. Periodical. English. mo (11 issues). $33.00 US; $55.00 other. Adams Publishing, 68860 Perez Road, PO Box 2150, Cathedral City CA 92235. **Tel** (619)770-4370, (800)776-1036. **(Subscription address:** Adams Publishing, PO Box 2150, Cathedral City CA 92235.**) DD** 716. ***Continues*** *Golf & SportsTURF, 1049-0000.*

US
SPRING CATALOGUE / BERKSHIRE GARDEN SUPPLY. Main/Corp Berkshire Garden Supply. (1965)-. English. an. ***Continues*** *Berkshire Garden Supply. Spring Catalog.*

US
SPRING ... PRICE LIST - ECCLES NURSERIES. Main/Corp Eccles Nurseries. **VFOAT** Northern Grown Evergreen Seedlings, Transplants, Christmas Trees. 1981-. English. an. ***Continues*** *Eccles Northern Grown Evergreen Seedlings, Transplants, Christmas Trees.*

US/0190-4205
ST. LOUIS HOME/GARDEN. See Interior Design.

SW/0280-4549
STAD OCH LAND. (STAD & LAND.). [Stad land]. **Added/Corp** Stiftelsen Anpassning till liv och Arbete. MOVIUM. Sveriges Lantbruksuniversitet. Institutionen for Landskapsplanering. **VFOAT** Stad och Land. (1982)-. Monographic series. Swedish (English). **CODEN** STLAEI. Documents available from BIOSIS Document Express. ***Formed by the union of*** *Rapport - ALA, 0348-2375* ***and*** *ALA Arbetsgruppen Lantbruk och Samhalle, 0348-2383 Konsulentavdelningens Rapporter. Landskap, 0347-9676.*
Ind/Abst Biol. Abstr. (-1986); For. Abstr.; Leis. Recreat. Tour. Abstr.

AT
SUCCESSFUL HORTICULTURE. English. Six times a year. 24.00Aus$ Australia; 36.00Aus$ New Zealand; 55.00Aus$ others. Sterling Media, PO Box 392, Baulkham Hills, 2153 Australia. **Tel** 11 61 2 6862033, FAX 11 61 2 6861939.
Desc: Keeping abreast of what's going on in the industry.

NE/0039-4467
SUCCULENTA. [Succulenta]. **Added/Corp** Nederlands - Belgische Vereniging van Liefhebbers van Cactussen en Andere Vetplanten. Nederlandsche Vereeniging van vetplantenverzamelaars. Vol. 1 (1919)-. Periodical. Dutch. bm. Fl40.00 Netherlands and Belgium; Fl65.00 other. Succulenta, Clarionlaan 12, 2082 HZ Santpoort Netherlands. Index Available, published separately, free-automatically sent. **Ad Acc.** ctrl circ.
Desc: Contains information on cactus and succulent plants.
Ind/Abst AGRICOLA.

BL/0100-5405
SUMMA PHYTOPATHOLOGICA. [Summa phytopathol.]. **Added/Corp** Sociedade Brasileira de Fitopatologia. Grupo Paulista de Fitopatologia. (1975)-. Academic Scholarly Publication. Portuguese (English and Spanish). Four times a year. Free to institutions; $10.00 individuals. Grupo Paulista Fitopatologia, Caixa Postal 69, 13820 Jaguariuna SP Brazil. **Tel** 011 52 192 671721. **CODEN** SUPHDV. Documents available from BIOSIS Document Express, CASDDS.
Ind/Abst Biol. Abstr.; Chem. Abstr.; For. Abstr.; Hortic. Abstr.; Ornamental Hort. (1991-); Potato Abstr.; Rev. Plant Pathol.; Rice Abstr.; Soyabean Abstr.; Weed Abstr.; Wheat Barley Trit. Abstr.

US/0899-8809
SUN-DIAMOND GROWER. [Sun-Diam. grow.]. **VFOAT** Sun Diamond Grower. Vol. 1, No. 1 (Oct./Nov. 1980)-. Periodical. English. qt. $12.00 US; $45.00 other. Sun-Diamond Growers of California, 1050 South Diamond Street, Stockton CA 95205. **ED** Sandra J McBride. **DD** 634. **Ad Acc. Circ:** 10,000 (ctrl). ***Continues*** *Diamond/Sunsweet News, 0899-8876.*
Desc: Key resource for California's agribusiness community, providing current information about production techniques and industry affairs for the walnut, hazelnut, raisin grapes, prune and fig industries.

US/1052-2247
SUNDEW GARDENS REPORTS. *Ceased.* (SUNDEW GARDENS REPORTS : NATURAL VEGETABLE GARDENING AND LANDSCAPING FOR FLORIDA.). [Sundew Gard. rep.]. **Added/Corp** Sundew Gardens. (Aug. 1990)-(Dec. 1993). Periodical. English. Six times a year. Sundew Gardens, PO Box 214, Oviedo FL 32765. **Tel** (407)366-5303. **ED** Tom Carey, (407)365-6024. **DD** 635. Index Bound in First Issue. cum. index. **Bk Rev. Circ:** 500 (ctrl).
Desc: Organic vegetable gardening and landscaping methods applicable to Florida.

NE
SUNFLOWER NEWSLETTER, THE. ***Ceased.*** Ceased 1987. Newsletter. English. qt. International Sunflower Association / Netherlands, PO Box 7, 6900 AA Zevenaar Netherlands.

US/0273-7671
SUNFLOWER WORLD. [Sunflower world]. (19??)-. Periodical. English. Twelve times a year. $8.50. Sunflower World Publications, PO Box 3189, Davenport IA 52808.

US/1058-4803
SUPERMARKET FLORAL. [Supermark. floral]. (19??)-. Periodical. English. mo. $25.00 US; $40.00 other. Vance Publishing Corporation, 400 Knightsbridge Parkway, Lincolnshire IL 60069. **Tel** (800)255-5113, (708)634-2600. **DD** 380.

CN/0318-5184
SURVEY OF CANADIAN NURSERY TRADES INDUSTRY. (SURVEY OF CANADIAN NURSERY TRADES INDUSTRY / DOMINION BUREAU OF STATISTICS, AGRICULTURE DIVISION, CROPS SECTION.). [Surv. Can. nurs. trades ind.]. **Main/Corp** Canada. Statistics Canada. Horticultural Crops Unit. **Added/Corp** Canada. Dominion Bureau of Statistics. Crops Section. Statistics Canada. Crops Section. Statistics Canada. Horticultural Crops Unit. **VFOAT** Enquete sur l'Industrie des Pepinieres Canadiennes. (1969)-. Periodical. English (French). an. 26.00Can$ Canada; $32.00 US; $37.00 other. Statistics Canada, Publications Sales & Services, Main Building Room 1710, Ottawa Ontario K1A 0T6 Canada. **Tel** (613)951-5078, (800)267-6677, FAX (613)951-1584, telex 053-3585. **LC** SB29.C2; S72a. **DD** 338.1/7/590971. ***Continues*** *Shipments of Fruit and Ornamental Nursery Stock.*
Desc: Sales and purchases of fruit and ornamental nursery stock, with financial statistics for Canada and the provinces.
Ind/Abst J. Econ. Lit.

UN/0230-2241
SZOLOTERMEZTESES BORASZAT. See Food and Food Industry-Beverage Industry.

GW/0177-5014
TASPO MAGAZIN. [TASPO-Mag.]. No. 1, (1976)-. Trade Publication. German. mo. DM164.40 Germany; DM201.60 other. Bernhard Thalacker Verlag, Hamburger Str 277, Postfach 3361, D 38023 Braunschweig Germany. **Tel** 011 49 531 380040, FAX 011 49 531 3800425. Index available. cum. index. **Bk Rev. Ad Acc. Circ:** 22,000.
Desc: This is a publication for gardening and horticulture with a full colored supplement for the weekly trade-journal THSPO.
Ind/Abst AGRICOLA.

NR/0795-4131
TECHNICAL BULLETIN - NATIONAL HORTICULTURAL RESEARCH INSTITUTE. [Tech. bull. - Natl. Hortic. Res. Inst.]. (1988)-. Monographic series. English. **DD** 635.05.
Ind/Abst Hortic. Abstr.; Rev. Agric. Entomol.; Rev. Plant Pathol.; Weed Abstr.

UK/0959-2164
TECHNICAL REPORT - LONG ASHTON RESEARCH STATION, WEED RESEARCH DEPARTMENT. (TECHNICAL REPORT / INSTITUTE OF ARABLE CROPS RESEARCH, LONG ASHTON RESEARCH STATION, WEED RESEARCH DEPARTMENT.). [Tech. rep. - Long Ashton Res. Stn., Weed Res. Dep.]. **Added/Corp** Long Ashton Research Station. Weed Research Dept. (1987)-. Monographic series. English. Long Ashton Research Station, Bristol BS18 9AF England. **Tel** 011 44 272 392181. ***Continues*** *Technical Report (Long Ashton Research Station. Weed Research Division).*
Ind/Abst Soyabean Abstr.

AT/0312-9764
TELOPEA. (TELOPEA / NEW SOUTH WALES DEPARTMENT OF AGRICULTURE, NATIONAL HERBARIUM OF NEW SOUTH WALES [AND] ROYAL BOTANICAL GARDENS, SYDNEY.). [Telopea]. **Added/Corp** National Herbarium of New South Wales. Royal Botanical Gardens, Sydney. Vol. 1, No. 1 (1975)-. Periodical. English. sa. 40.00Aus$ (institution), 20.00Aus$ (individual) Australia; 43.00Aus$ other. Royal Botanic Gardens and National Herbarium, Sydney Australia. **Tel** 2318011, FAX 2514403. **CODEN** TELODX. Documents available from BIOSIS Document Express. ***Supersedes*** *Contributions From the New South Wales National Herbarium.*
Ind/Abst AGRICOLA [Full Cov.]; Biol. Abstr.; Ecol. Abstr.; For. Abstr.; Grasslands For. Abstr.; Plant Breed. Abstr.; Plant Genet. Resour. Abstr.

US/0095-1927
TEXAS CERTIFIED SEED DIRECTORY. 1971-. Directory. English. an. Texas Department of Agriculture, 18th & Congress Street, PO Box 12847, Austin TX 78711. **Tel** (512)463-7435, FAX (512)463-7643. **LC** SB113.4; .T5. **DD** 338.1/7. ***Continues*** *Texas Seed Directory.*

US/0744-0987
TEXAS GARDENER (WACO, TX.). (TEXAS GARDENER.). Vol. 1, No. 1 (Nov./Dec. 1981)-. Periodical. English. Six times a year. $16.95. Suntex Communications, PO Box 9005, Waco TX 76714. **Tel** (817)772-1270. **ED** Chris S. Corby. **Bk Rev. Ad Acc. Circ:** 36,000.
Desc: Deals with all aspects of home gardening under tough Texas conditions. Topics include vegetable, fruit and ornamental production.
Ind/Abst Garden Lit. (1992-).

US
TEXAS HORTICULTURIST, THE. Added/Corp Texas Pecan Growers Association. Texas State Horticultural Society. (1989)-. Periodical. English. Twelve times a year. $12.00. Texas State Horticultural Society, PO Drawer CC, College Station TX 77841. **Tel** (409)846-3285. **ED** Cindy Loggins Wise. **Ad Acc.** ***Continues*** *Horticulturist.*

CN/0835-3271
TLC -- FOR PLANTS. *Title Change.* [TLC plants]. Vol. 1, No. 1 (Summer 1988)-(Spring 1994). Periodical. English. qt (4 issues). Gardenvale Publishing, 1 rue Pacifique, Ste Anne de Bellevue, Quebec H9X 1C5 Canada. **Tel** (514)457-2744, FAX (514)457-6255. **ED** Kathryn Spracklin. **DD** 635.9/0971. Index available (bound in Nov. issue). cum. index. **Bk Rev. Ad Acc, Adv Mgr:** Josee Brault, **Tel** same as publisher. **Circ:** 30,000. ***Continued by*** *Plant & Garden.*
Desc: Aims to impart both the pleasure and the skills of gardening both indoors and out. It provides accurate and authoritive information about plants, gardening techniques, tools and the science of gardening. With a wide variety of articles and columns, it attracts both amateur and serious gardeners, as well as professionals in the gardening business who use it as a teaching and informational resource.

US
TODAY'S HERBS. See Medical Science and Technology-Homeopathy.

JA
TOKYO NO IKEBANA. Added/Corp Tokyo-to Kado Kyokai. (19??)-. Periodical. Japanese. an. Tokyo-To Kado Kyokai, Shinkosha Building, 2-1-8 Koraku Bunkyo-ku, Tokyo Japan. **LC** SB450; .T64.

US
TOMPKINS COUNTY HOME & GARDEN. See Home Economics.

US
TRANSACTIONS OF THE ILLINOIS STATE HORTICULTURAL SOCIETY FOR THE YEAR. (1991)-. Proceedings. English. an. $12.00. Illinois State Horticultural Society, 611 County Road 2000 E, Sidney IL 61877. **Tel** (217)688-2590. ***Continues*** *Proceedings ... Illinois Specialty Growers Association Convention and Transactions of the Illinois State Horticultural Society for the Year.*

CN/0380-1470
TRELLIS. Began publication in 1974. Periodical. English. mo. 10.00Can$. Civic Garden Centre, 777 Lawrence Avenue East, Don Mills Ontario M3C 1P2 Canada. **Tel** 445-1552. **ED** Gordon D Wick. **DD** 635/.09713. **Bk Rev. Ad Acc. Circ:** 3,600 (ctrl). available on microfilm and microfiche from University Microfilms International (UMI).
Desc: Calendar of garden related events in metropolitan Toronto area, timely gardening hints column, in-depth gardening focus articles, new product and book reviews, news of Civic Garden Centre members programs.

JA/0289-3568
TSUKUBA JIKKEN SHOKUBUTSUEN KENKYU HOKOKU. VFOAT Annals of the Tsukuba Botanical Garden. No. 1-. Periodical. English (Japanese). Kokuritsu Kagaku Hakubutsukan Tsukuba Jikken Shokubutsuen, Amakubo 4-1-1 Sakura-mura Niihari-gun, Ibaraki-ken 305 Japan. **LC** QK1; .T84. **DD** 581/.05.

NE
TUIN EN LANDSCHAP. Dutch. sm. Uitgeversmaatschappij C Misset Doetinchem, Netherlands. **Tel** 08340-49911, FAX (08340)44479, telex 45481. **ED** J S Horsting. **Bk Rev. Ad Acc.**
Desc: Information on the layout and maintenance of gardens, parks and other greenspaces, material used, machinery and tools.

BE/0776-4472
TUINBOUW VISIE. [Tuinbouw vis.]. (1989)-. Periodical. Dutch. wk. 1200F Belgium; 3950F other. Fr Editions Rurales, Ave Leon Grosjean 92, B-1140 Brussels Belgium. **UDC** 635. **Bk Rev. Ad Acc.**
Desc: Magazine for professional growers.

NE/0440-0771
TUINBOUWCIJFERS. See Gardening and Horticulture-Abstracting, Bibliographies and Statistics.

Gardening and Horticulture

BE
TUINBOUWMAGAZINE. Dutch. ir. 750.00F. Rekad, Geelsesteenweg 47, 2410 Herentals Belgium. **Tel** 011 32 13 219600.

US/0163-0059
TULIP TIDINGS. V. 1- Mar. 1948-. Periodical. English. sa. National Tulip Society, 401 22nd Avenue SE, St. Petersburg FL 33705.

CN/1186-0170
TURF & RECREATION. [Turf recreat.]. **VAT** Turf and recreation. (1988)-. Periodical. English. Eight times a year. Free upon request. MRK Publishing Ltd, 1 9613 192nd Street, Surrey BC V3T 4W2 Canada. **Tel** (604)888-8843, FAX (604)944-9096. **ED** R A Kendall. **DD** 635.9/642/05. **Bk Rev. Ad Acc. Circ:** 13,600 (ctrl).
Desc: Covers golf course and landscape management.

US/1059-6348
TURF CENTRAL. [Turf cent.]. (1990)-. Periodical. English. Twelve times a year. $12.00. NEF Publishing Company, 50 Bay Street, Box 391, St Johnsbury VT 05819. **Tel** (802)748-8908, FAX (802)748-1866. **DD** 635. *Continues in part Turf, 1045-6503.*

UK/0262-0669
TURF MANAGEMENT. [Turf manage.]. (1982)-. Periodical. English. mo (12 issues). £20.00 UK; £40.00 Eire & Europe; £50.00 America, Middle East, Africa & Indial; £60.00 Australia, New Zealand & Japan; £40.00 other. Haymarket Publishing Ltd., 12 14 Ansdell Street, London W8 5TR England. **Tel** 011 44 483 733800, FAX 011 44 483 776573. **(Subscription address:** Haymarket Publishing Ltd, PO Box 219, Subscriptions Department, Woking Surrey GU21 1ZW, United Kingdom.**) DD** 635.96420288.

US/0899-417X
TURF NEWS. (TURF NEWS : A PUBLICATION OF THE AMERICAN SOD PRODUCERS ASSOCIATION.). [Turf news]. **VFOAT** ASPA Turf News. **VAT** American Sod Producers Association Turf News. Periodical. English. bm. $6.00 (included in membership). American Sod Producers Association, 1855-A Hicks Road, Rolling Meadows IL 60008. **DD** 635.

US
TURF NORTH. (19??)-. English. Twelve times a year. $12.00. NEF Publishing Company, 50 Bay Street, Box 391, St Johnsbury VT 05819. **Tel** (802)748-8908, FAX (802)748-1866. *Continues in part Turf.*

US/1071-4995
TURF WEST. [Turf west]. (19??)-. Periodical. English. Twelve times a year. $12.00. NEF Publishing Company, 50 Bay Street, Box 391, St Johnsbury VT 05819. **Tel** (802)748-8908, FAX (802)748-1866. **DD** 635. *Continues in part Turf, 1045-6503.*

NE
VAKBLAD VOOR DE BLOEMISTERIJ. Vol. 4, No. 29 (1949)-. Periodical. Dutch. Fifty-two times a year. F400.00 (latest volume) Comes with Bloemistry plus Tuin en Landschap. Misset Uitgeverij BV, Postbus 9000, 6800 DA Arnhem Netherlands. **Tel** 011 31 85 209911. **ED** J. S. Horsting. **Bk Rev. Ad Acc.**
Desc: Information on all aspects of growing pot plants and cut flowers. New equipment and techniques, financial management, trade and organisation news, also featured.
Ind/Abst AgBiotech News Inf.; Agric. Eng. Abstr. (1991-); Crop Physiol. Abstr.; Hortic. Abstr.; Ornamental Hort. (1991-); Plant Breed. Abstr.; Postharvest News Inf.; Rev. Agric. Entomol.; Soils Fert.

SW
VAXTODLING. Added/Corp Lantbrukshogskolan. Institutionen for Vaxtodling. Uppsala. Lantbrukshogskolan och Statens Lantbruksforsok. Institutionen for Vaxtodlingslara. **VFOAT** Plant Husbandry. No 1 (1944)-. Multiple languages (English and Swedish). Documents available from BIOSIS Document Express.
Ind/Abst Biol. Abstr.; Potato Abstr.; Seed Abstr.

CN/1181-9782
VEGETABLE GARDEN RESEARCH. [Veg. gard. res.]. **Added/Corp** Garden Research Exchange. (1990)-. English. $12.00 Canada. Garden Research Exchange, 536 MacDonnell Street, Kingston, Ontario K7K 4W7 Canada. **DD** 635.

US
VEGTATIONSMONOGRAPHIEN DER EINZELNEN GROSSRAUME. Vol. 1 (1965)-. German. ir. VCH Publishers Inc, 220 East 23rd Street, New York NY 10010. **Tel** (212)683-8333, , FAX (212)481-0897. **(Subscription address:** VCH Publishers Inc., 303 Northwest 12th Avenue, Journals Department, Deerfield FL 33442.**)**

NE
VERSLAG / PROEFSTATION VOOR DE AKKERBOUW ON DE GROENTETEELT IN DE VOLLEGROND. See Food and Food Industry.

NE/0466-9959
VERZAMELDE OVERDRUKKEN - PLANTENZIEKTENKUNDIGE DIENST.
Main/Corp Netherlands. Plantenziektenkundige. **VFOAT** Collected Reprints - Plant Protection Service of the Netherlands. 1954-. Periodical. Multiple languages (English and Dutch). Tav Mevr Urannie Postbus 9102, 6700 Wageningen Netherlands.

IT/0042-6237
VILLE GIARDINI. [Ville, Giard.]. **VFOAT** VilleGiardini; Ville-Giardini. (19??)-. Periodical. Italian. Eleven times a year. $175.00 US. **(Subscription address:** Agenzia Italiana Esportazione, Via Manzoni 12, 20089 Rozzano Milan, Italy.**)** *Continues Ville e Giardini, 0042-6237.*
Desc: Covers landscape gardening and domestic architecture.
Ind/Abst Archit. Period. Index (19??-); Avery Index Archit. Period. Suppl. Colum. Univ. (Nov. 1989, Jan. 1990-).

US/0097-1782
VIRGINIA FRUIT. Added/Corp Virginia State Horticultural Society. Virginia State Horticultural Society. Report. (19??)-. Periodical. English. bm. $15.00. Virginia State Horticultural Society, PO Box 718, Staunton VA 76401. **Tel** (703)885-9046. **LC** SB354; .V58. **DD** 634./1/09755. **Ad Acc. Circ:** 500.

US/1057-3003
VIRGINIA GARDENER, THE. *Title Change.* (THE VIRGINIA GARDENER / DEPARTMENT OF HORTICULTURE.). [Va. gard.]. **Added/Corp** Virginia Polytechnic Institute and State University. Extension Division. Virginia Cooperative Extension Service. Virginia Polytechnic Institute and State University. Dept. of Horticulture. Virginia Cooperative Extension. (Jan. 1982)-Vol. 11, No. 4 (Apr. 1992). Periodical. English. mo. Treasurer of Virginia Tech, Department of Horticulture, Blacksburg VA 24061. **Tel** (703)231-6254. **DD** 635.
Continued by Virginia Gardener Newsletter.
Ind/Abst AGRICOLA (?-1990) [Full Cov.].

●US
VIRGINIA GARDENER NEWSLETTER / DEPARTMENT OF HORTICULTURE, COOPERATIVE EXTENSION DIVISION, VIRGINIA TECH. Main/Corp Virginia Cooperative Extension Service. **Added/Corp** Virginia Polytechnic Institute and State University. Virginia Cooperative Extension Service. Vol. 11, No. 5 (May 1992)-. Periodical. English. Twelve times a year. $5.00. Treasurer of Virginia Tech, Department of Horticulture, Blacksburg VA 24061. **Tel** (703)231-6254. **ED** Diane Relf. **Bk Rev,** (Qty: varies). **Circ:** 9,500. *Continues Virginia Gardener., 1057-3003.*
Desc: Containing horticulture information for the general public.
Ind/Abst Bibliogr. Agric.

US
VOICE, THE. Main/Corp Michigan Nursery and Landscape Association. English. bm. $15.00 members; $18.00 other. Michigan Nursery & Landscape Association, 819 North Washington Avenue, Suite 2, Lansing MI 48906. **Tel** (517)487-1282, FAX (517)487-0969. **ED** Kathy Polega & Laurie Donaldson. **Ad Acc.**

US/0505-8708
VOICE M.A.N, THE. *Title Change.* (THE VOICE OF MAN : OFFICIAL PUBLICATION OF MICHIGAN ASSOCIATION OF NURSERYMEN.). [Voice M.A.N.]. **Added/Corp** Michigan Association of Nurserymen. **VFOAT** Voice of M.A.N. **VAT** Voice of Michigan Association of Nurserymen. Vol. 1, No. 1 (Jan. 1957)-(19??). Periodical. English. bm. Michigan Nursery & Landscape Association, 819 North Washington Avenue, Suite 2, Lansing MI 48906. **Tel** (517)487-1282, FAX (517)487-0969. **ED** Kathy Polega. cum. index. **Bk Rev,** (Qty: 24-30). **Ad Acc, Adv Mgr:** (same as editor): **Circ:** 1,800 (ctrl). *Continued by Voice.*
Desc: Publishes the most up-to-date research findings, new products and feature articles for growers, contractors, designers and wholesalers.

US
VOICE. OFFICIAL PUBLICATION OF MICHIGAN ASSOCIATION OF NURSERYMEN. (19??)-. English. Six times a year (Jan., Mar, May, July, Sept., Nov.). $18.00 (one year); $32.00 (two years). Michigan Nursery & Landscape Association, 819 North Washington Avenue, Suite 2, Lansing MI 48906. **Tel** (517)487-1282, FAX (517)487-0969. **ED** Kristin S. Ebert. **Ad Acc, Adv Mgr:** K. Ebert. **Circ:** 1,200 (ctrl).
Desc: Up-to-date industry news, covering each segment of the nursery and landscape industry.

US/1046-8749
WASHINGTON PARK ARBORETUM BULLETIN. [Wash. Park Arbor. bull.]. **Added/Corp** University of Washington. Arboretum Foundation (Seattle, Wash.). **VFOAT** UW Arboretum Bulletin. Vol. 49, No. 2 (Summer 1986)-. Periodical. English. qt. $35.00 (institution); $20.00 (individual). Arboretum Foundation, University of Washington, XD-10, Seattle WA 98195. **ED** Jan Silver. **LC** SB1; .A7. **DD** 580. Index available. **Bk Rev. Ad Acc. Circ:** 3,000 (ctrl). *Continues University of Washington Arboretum Bulletin, 0737-643X.*
Ind/Abst AGRICOLA (19??-); Garden Lit. (1992-).

US/0741-9856
WEED CONTROL MANUAL. [Weed control man.]. (1976)-. Periodical. English. an. $40.50 US; $42.75 Canada; $48.00 other. Meister Publishing Company, 37733 Euclid Avenue, Willoughby OH 44094-5992. **Tel** (216)942-2000, (800)572-7740, FAX (216)942-0662. **[CCC].** *Continues Weed Control Manual and Herbicide Guide.*
Desc: Identification photos of weeds in the US. Includes use reminders for each crop.

IO/0215-1367
WEEDWATCHER. [Weedwatcher]. (1986)-. Periodical. English. qt. **DD** 632.58.
Ind/Abst Field Crop Abstr.; Seed Abstr.

US
WHOLESALE PRICE AND ORDER SHEET / APPLEWOOD SEED CO. Main/Corp Applewood Seed Co. (19??)-. English.

US
WHOLESALE PRICE LIST / BULK'S NURSERIES. Main/Corp Bulk's Nurseries. Periodical. English. *Absorbed Bulk's Nurseries (Freehold, N.J.). Wholesale Price List.*

US/0730-7225
WHO'S WHO IN LANDSCAPE CONTRACTING (1979). (WHO'S WHO IN LANDSCAPE CONTRACTING : MEMBERSHIP DIRECTORY ASSOCIATED LANDSCAPE CONTRACTORS OF AMERICA.). [Who's who landsc. contract.]. **Main/Corp** Associated Landscape Contractors of America. (1979)-. Directory. English. an. $25.00 (non-members), $3.00 (members). Associated Landscape Contractors, 405 North Washington Street, Falls Church VA 22046. **Tel** (703)241-4004. **LC** SB472.55; .A84a. **DD** 338.7/61712/02573. Index available. **Ad Acc. Circ:** 4,000. *Continues ALCA Membership Directory.*
Desc: Membership listing of landscape contracting firms located throughout the country.

US/0890-3786
WILD BLUEBERRY GROWER. (198?)-. Periodical. English. mo. Wild Blueberry Grower, PO Box 354, Machias ME 04654-0354. **DD** 634.

US
WILD FLOWER NOTES / NEW ENGLAND WILD FLOWER SOCIETY. Vol 1 No 1 (1985)-. Periodical. English. sa. *Continues in part Wild Flower Notes and News.*
Ind/Abst Garden Lit. (1992-).

US/0898-8803
WILDFLOWER (AUSTIN, TEX. 1984). See Biology-Botany.

US/0896-4858
WILDFLOWER (AUSTIN, TEX. 1988). *Suspended.* See Biology-Botany.

US
WILDFLOWERS. V. 1-. Monographic series. English. Price varies per volume. Touchstone Press, PO Box 81, Beaverton OR 97005.

US/0887-8927
WISCONSIN ARBORIST, THE. See Forestry.

US
WISH LETTER / GRIGSBY CACTUS GARDENS. Main/Corp Grigsby Cactus Gardens. (19??)-. Periodical. English.

UK
WISLEY HANDBOOK. Main/Corp Royal Horticultural Society (Great Britain). (19??)-. Periodical. English.

US/0161-2344
WOMAN'S DAY VEGETABLE GARDENING, CANNING & FREEZING. VFOAT Vegetable Gardening, Canning & Freezing. **VAT** Woman's Day Vegetable Gardening, Canning and Freezing. No. 1-. English. Fawcett Publications, 1 Fawcett Place, Greenwich CT 06830. **LC** SB320; .W6. **DD** 635/.05.

●US
WORLD HORTICULTURAL TRADE & U.S. EXPORT OPPORTUNITIES / UNITED STATES DEPARTMENT OF AGRICULTURE, FOREIGN AGRICULTURAL SERVICE. Added/Corp United States. Foreign Agricultural Service. United States. World Agricultural Outlook Board. **VFOAT** World Horticultural Trade and U.S. Export Opportunities. (Jan. 1994)-. Trade Publication. English. mo. $30.00. Department of Agriculture / Foreign Agricultural Service,

14th Street and Independence Avenue SW, Washington DC 20250-1000. **Tel** (202)720-3935, FAX (202)720-7729. **LC** HD9000.1; .F66. **DD** 338.1/75/05. **Circ:** 916. Documents available from Documents on Demand. ***Continues** Horticultural Products Review, 0894-8429.*
Desc: Features information on general developments in the world fruit and vegetable industry. Covers fresh and dried fruit and nuts, processed fruits, nursery products, wine, beer and hops. Includes production, consumption, trade data and analysis.
Ind/Abst AGRICOLA.

US/0148-9089
WORLD OF HOUSE PLANTS, THE. English. an. $1.25. Maco Publishing Company, 699 Madison Avenue, New York NY 10021. **Tel** (212)490-0172. **LC** SB419; .W84. **DD** 635.9/65/05.

US
WSSA ABSTRACTS : MEETING OF THE WEED SCIENCE SOCIETY OF AMERICA. **See** Agriculture-Abstracting, Bibliographies and Statistics.

US
YANKEE NURSERY QUARTERLY. **Main/Corp** University of Connecticut. Dept. of Plant Science. **Added/Corp** University of Connecticut. Cooperative Extension System. University of Massachusetts at Amherst. Cooperative Extension System. University of Rhode Island. Cooperative Extension Service. **VFOAT** Yankee Nursery. Vol. 1, No. 1 (Spring 1991)-. Periodical. English. qt. $12.00. University of Connecticut Department of Plant Science, U-67, Storrs CT 06268. **Tel** (203)486-3435. ***Formed by the union of** Connecticut Nursery Newsletter **and** Nursery Notes (Amherst, Mass.).*
Ind/Abst AGRICOLA.

US/0896-6834
YARD & GARDEN. [Yard gard.]. **VFOAT** Yard and Garden. (198?)-. Trade Publication. English. Nine times a year. $21.00 US; $28.00 Canada and Mexico; $120.00 other. Johnson Hill Press Inc., 1233 Janesville Avenue, PO Box 803, Fort Atkinson WI 53538-0803. **Tel** (414)563-1749, FAX (414)563-1704. **ED** Dan Kirkpatrick. **DD** 658. **Ad Acc.** Full Page (B&W) $3575.00. Full Page (Color) $4970.00 (4-color). **Circ:** 33,959. ***Continues** Yard and Garden Product News, 0163-4127.*
Desc: Serves retailers selling outdoor power equipment and lawn and garden products. Provides business management information to dealers and retailers who sell and service yard and garden equipment and products.

JA/0916-684X
YASAI CHAGYO SHIKENJO KENKYU HOKOKU. A, YASAI, KAKI. **Added/Corp** Norin Suisansho Yasai Chagyo Shikenjo (Japan). **VFOAT** Yasai, Kaki; Vegetables and Ornamental Plants; Bulletin of the National Research Institute of Vegetables, Ornamental Plants and Tea. Series A, Vegetables and Ornamental Plants. Vol. 4 (Mar 1991)-. Periodical. Japanese (summaries and/or abstracts in English; table of contents in English). Norin Suisansho Yasai Chagyo Shikenjo, (National Research Institute of Vegetables, Ornamental Plants & Tea, Ministry of Agriculture, Forestry & Fisheries), 360, Kusawa, Anocho, Agegun, Mieken 514-23, Japan. ***Continues** Yasai Chagyo Shikenjo Kenkyu Hokoku. A, 0914-6644.*
Ind/Abst Plant Grow. Reg. Abstr.

UK
YEAR BOOK - NATIONAL AURICULA & PRIMULA SOCIETY (SOUTHERN SECTION). **Main/Corp** National Auricula and Primula Society. Southern Section. English. an. $4.60. National Auricula & Primula Society, 146 Queens Road, Cheadle Cheshire SK8 5HY England. **Tel** 061-485-6371.

US/0068-5720
YEARBOOK - CALIFORNIA MACADAMIA SOCIETY. [Yearb. - Calif. Macadamia Soc.]. **Main/Corp** California Macadamia Society. (19??)-. Periodical. English. an. $17.50 US; $24.00 other. California Macademia Society, PO Box 1298, Fallbrook CA 92088. **Tel** (619)743-0358. **ED** Jim Teeter. Index available. **Ad Acc. Circ:** 500 (ctrl).
Ind/Abst AGRICOLA [Select. Cov.].

US/0096-5960
YEARBOOK OF THE CALIFORNIA AVOCADO SOCIETY. (YEARBOOK OF THE CALIFORNIA AVOCADO SOCIETY FOR THE YEAR ...). [Yearb. Calif. Avocado Soc.]. **Main/Corp** California Avocado Society. (1941)-. English. an (July). $50.00. California Avocado Society, PO Box 4816, Saticoy CA 93003. **Tel** (805)644-1184. **ED** J. S. Shepherd. **LC** SB379.A9; C3. **DD** 634. **Bk Rev. Ad Acc. Circ:** 2,000. ***Continues** California Avocado Association. Yearbook of the California Avocado Association for the Year ... .*
Desc: Compendiums of information on every aspect of avocado industry: culture, marketing, pests and diseases, economics, basic research reports and applied research "how-to" articles, popular and technical.
Ind/Abst AGRICOLA; Biocont. News Inf.; Crop Physiol. Abstr.; Hortic. Abstr.; Plant Breed. Abstr.; Postharvest News Inf.; Rev. Agric. Entomol.; Rev. Plant Pathol.; Seed Abstr.; Soils Fert.

AT/0044-1031
YOUR GARDEN CLAYTON. [Your gard. Clayton]. (1947)-. Periodical. English. mo. 39.60Aus$ Australia; 48.60Aus$ other. Pacific Publications Pty Ltd, 32 Walsh Street, Melbourne VIC 3000 Australia. **Tel** 011 61 3 3207000. **DD** 635.05.

CC/0372-784X
YUAN I HSUEH PAO. [Yuan i hsueh pao]. **VFOAT** Yuanyi Xuebao; Acta Horticulturae Sinica. (1962)-. Periodical. Chinese. qt. $6.12. Science Press, 16 Donghuangchenggen North Street, Beijing 100707, People's Republic of China. **Tel** 011 86 1 4019821, 011 86 1 4010642, FAX 011 86 1 4012180, 011 86 1 4019810, telex 210147. **CODEN** AHTSAU. Documents available from BIOSIS Document Express.
Ind/Abst AGRICOLA; Biol. Abstr.; Crop Physiol. Abstr.; Hortic. Abstr.; Plant Grow. Reg. Abstr.; Seed Abstr.

GW/0342-6556
ZB. ZIERPFLANZENBAU. [ZB, Zierplanzenbau]. **VFOAT** Zierpflanzenbau; ZB.Zierpflanzenbau mit Internationaler Gartenbautechnik; ZB. Zierpflanzenbau, Gartenbautechnik. (196?)-. Periodical. German. Twenty-six times a year. DM172.70. Klette Druck Verlag Euroflora, Freunder Landstrasse 25, D 52078 Aachen Brand Germany. **Tel** 011 49 241 521021. **UDC** 635.9-1. **CODEN** 635.9-1.
Ind/Abst Agric. Eng. Abstr.; Hortic. Abstr.; Ornamental Hort.; Plant Grow. Reg. Abstr.; Rev. Agric. Entomol.; Rev. Plant Pathol.; World Agric. Econ.

JA
ZOEN ZASSHI. **Added/Corp** Nihon Zoen Gakkai. **VFOAT** Journal of the Japanese Institute of Landscape Architects. (Feb. 1934)-. Periodical. Japanese (English). Five times a year. $166.00. **(Subscription address:** Kyowa Book Company Inc., 1-38 Kanda Jinbo-Cho, Chiyoda-Ku Tokyo 101, Japan**)**

HU
ZOLDFELULETGAZDALKODAS. **Added/Corp** Fovarosi Kerteszeti Vallalat. Kerteszeti Egyetem. Taj- es Kertepiteszeti Tanszek. No. 3 (1972)-. Periodical. Hungarian. qt.

HU/0133-3682
ZOLDSEGTERMESZTESI KUTATO INTEZET BULLETINJE. [Zoldsegtermesztesi Kut. Intez. bull.]. **Added/Corp** Zoldsegtermesztesi Kutato Intezet. **VFOAT** Bulletin of the Vegetable Crops Research Institute. Vol. 6 (1971)-. Monographic series. Hungarian. **CODEN** ZKIBDJ. Documents available from CASDDS. ***Continues** Duna-Tisza Kosi Mezogazdasagi Kiserlei Intezet Bulletinje.*
Ind/Abst Chem. Abstr.; Crop Physiol. Abstr.; Food Sci. Technol. Abstr.; For. Prod. Abstr. (1991-); Hortic. Abstr.; Seed Abstr.

HU
ZOLDSEGTERMESZTESI KUTATO INTEZET BULLETINJE. **Main/Corp** Zoldsegtermesztesi Kutato Intezet. **Added/Corp** Duna-Tisza Kosi Mezogazdasagi Kiserleti Intezet. **VFOAT** Bulletin of the Vegetable Crops Research Institute; Bulletin of the Agricultural Experiment Institute of Duna-Tisza koz; Biulleten Selskokhoziaistvennogo Issledovatelskogo Instituta Oblasti Duna-Tisake. Vol. 1 (1967)-. Monographic series. Hungarian (summaries and/or abstracts in English and Russian).
Ind/Abst AGRICOLA; For. Prod. Abstr. (1991-); Plant Breed. Abstr.

ABSTRACTING, BIBLIOGRAPHIES AND STATISTICS

GW/0006-1387
BIBLIOGRAPHIE DER PFLANZENSCHUTZLITERATUR. [Bibliogr. Pflanzenschutz-lit.]. **Added/Corp** Biologische Reichsanstalt fuer Land- und Forstwirtschaft (Germany) Biologische Zentralanstalt fuer Land- und Forstwirtschaft in Berlin-Dahlem. Biologische Bundesanstalt fuer Land- und Forstwirtschaft. **VFOAT** Bibliography of Plant Protection; Bibliographie der Pflanzenschutz-Literatur. Vol. 1, No. 1-4 (1919)-. Periodical. German (English and French). Four times a year. DM410.00 Europe; DM437.00 other. Blackwell Wissenschafts-Verlag, Kurfuerstendamm 57, D 10707 Berlin Germany. **Tel** 011 49 30 32790623, 011 49 30 32790624, FAX 011 49 30 327 90610. **ED** W. Laux. **[CCC]**. Index available in last issue of volume--attached. cum. index. **Bk Rev. Ad Acc. Circ:** 500. ***Continues** Jahresbericht Uber das Gebiet der Pflantxenkrankheiten.*
Ind/Abst For. Prod. Abstr.; For. Abstr.; Nematol. Abstr.; Rev. Agric. Entomol.; Rev. Plant Pathol.; Weed Abstr.

●US/1061-3722
GARDEN LITERATURE. (GARDEN LITERATURE : AN INDEX TO PERIODICAL ARTICLES AND BOOK REVIEWS.). [Gard. lit.]. Vol. 1, No. 1 (Jan./Mar. 1992)-. Abstracting/Indexing Service. English. qt (4 issues). $75.00 (institutions), $50.00 (individuals). Garden Literature Press, 398 Columbus Avenue, Suite 181, Boston MA 02116. **Tel** (617)424-1784, FAX (617)424-1712. **ED** Sally Williams. **DD** 635.
Desc: Indexes over 130 periodicals including magazines, newsletters, newspapers and annuals of interest to gardeners, garden designers, growers and retailers, horticulturists, landscape architects, historians, preservationists, and all those who work in and enjoy the plant world. Covers international and national interests. Represents titles from all US regions. Brings together in one bibliographical source garden and landscape subjects now scattered over several different indexes. Includes titles not previously indexed.

AU
GARTENBAU- UND FELDGEMUSE-ANBAUERHEBUNG / BEARBEITET IM OSTERREICHISCHEN STATISTISCHEN ZENTRALAMT. **Added/Corp** Osterreichisches Statistisches Zentralamt. **VFOAT** Gartenbau- und Feldgemuseanbauerhebung. (1982)-. Statistical Publication. German. ir (issued every ten years). S270.00. Osterreichische Statistische Zentralamt, Hintere Zollamtstrasse 2B, A-1033 Vienna Austria. **Tel** 0222 711 28 7654, FAX 0222 715 68 28. **LC** HA1173; .A27 subser.; SB319.3.A9. Index available. **Bk Rev. Circ:** 350 (ctrl).
Desc: Covers all establishments of horticulture and all production lines which have at least 1,000 square meters of area, also covers cultivation of field crops.

UK/0018-5280
HORTICULTURAL ABSTRACTS. [Hortic. abstr.]. **Added/Corp** C.A.B. International. Commonwealth Bureau of Horticulture and Plantation Crops. Imperial Bureau of Fruit Production. Imperial Bureau of Horticulture and Plantation Crops. Vol. 1 (March 1931)-. Abstracting/Indexing Service. English. mo. $949.00 US. CAB International Centre, Wallingford, Oxon OX10 8DE United Kingdom. **Tel** 44 491 832111, FAX 44 491 833508, telex 847964 (COMAGG G). **ED** J. R. Metcalfe. **LC** SB1; .H65. **DD** 634.05. Index available. cum. index. **Ad Acc.** available on magnetic tape and CD-ROM; available on an online database from Tsukuba Daigaku; CAN/OLE; STN International; JICST; DATA-STAR; DIMDI; ESA-IRS; BRS; and DIALOG.
Desc: Covers the literature on all fruits, nuts, vegetables, plantation and ornamental plants.
Ind/Abst Agric. Eng. Abstr.; Field Crop Abstr.; For. Prod. Abstr.; For. Abstr.; Grasslands For. Abstr.; Leis. Recreat. Tour. Abstr.; Plant Breed. Abstr.; Protozoolog. Abstr.; Rev. Med. Vet. Mycology; Rev. Plant Pathol.; Rural Dev. Abstr.; Soils Fert.; Vitis Vitic. Enol. Abstr.; Weed Abstr.; World Agric. Econ.

UK/0305-4934
ORNAMENTAL HORTICULTURE. Vol. 1 (1975)-. Abstracting/Indexing Service. English. bm. $253.00. CAB International Centre, Wallingford, Oxon OX10 8DE United Kingdom. **Tel** 44 491 832111, FAX 44 491 833508, telex 847964 (COMAGG G). **Circ:** 300. available on magnetic tape and CD-ROM; available on an online database from Tsukuba Daigaku; CAN/OLE; STN International; JICST; DATA-STAR; DIMDI; ESA-IRS; BRS; and DIALOG.
Desc: Meets the information needs of horticultural scientists dealing with ornamentals, horticulturalists concerned with public parks, gardens and other amenities, nurserymen, students and serious amateur gardeners.

NE/0440-0771
TUINBOUWCIJFERS. **Main/Corp** Hague. Landbouw-Economisch Instituut. 1968-. Dutch. an. $10.00. Landbouw Economisch Instituut, Postbus 29703, 2502 LS Den Haag Netherlands. **Tel** 011 31 70 3308330, FAX 011 31 70 615624. **ED** W van Veen. **LC** SB319.N4; H34A. Index available. **Circ:** 1,200.
Desc: Statistical data on horticultural holdings, areas, means of production and produce of Dutch horticulture.

FLORIST TRADE

NE
BLOEM & BLAD. **VFOAT** Bloem en Blad. (1979)-. Periodical. Dutch. mo. Misset Uitgeverij BV, Postbus 9000, 6800 DA Arnhem Netherlands. **Tel** 011 31 85 209911. **ED** J S Horsting. **Bk Rev. Ad Acc.**
Desc: Information on all aspects of the retail in pot plants, purchase and sale of cut flowers. Entrepreneurial news.

GW
BLUMEN EINZELHANDEL. German. mo. DM116.40. Verlag Eugen Ulmer, Postfach 700561, D 70574 Stuttgart Germany. **Tel** 011 49 711 4507108, FAX 011 49 711 4507120, telex 7-23634. **ED** Roland Ulmer. **Bk Rev. Ad Acc. Circ:** 4,200 (ctrl).
Desc: Magazine for florists and flower sale in Germany.

US
BULLETIN OF THE ILLINOIS STATE FLORISTS' ASSOCIATION. Bulletin. English. bm.
Ind/Abst Hortic. Abstr.

US/0030-090X
BULLETIN - OHIO FLORISTS' ASSOCIATION. **Main/Corp** Ohio Florists' Association. (1949)-. Bulletin. English. Twelve times a year. $50.00 (members without greenhouses); $50.00 (members with greenhouse space 25,000 sq. ft.); $80.00 (members with greenhouse space 25,000-100,000 sq. ft.); $110.00 (members with greenhouse over 100,000 sq. ft.). Ohio Florists Association, 2130 Satella Court, Suite 200, Columbus OH 43215. **Tel** (614)487-1117, FAX (614)487-1216. **Pr Rev.** ***Continues*** *Ohio Florists' Association. Monthly Bulletin - Ohio Florists' Association.*
Ind/Abst Hortic. Abstr.; Ornamental Hort. (1991-); Plant Grow. Reg. Abstr.; Rev. Agric. Entomol.; Rev. Plant Pathol.; Soils Fert.

US/0031-448X
BULLETIN - PENNSYLVANIA FLOWER GROWERS. [Bull. - Pa. Flower Grow.]. **Main/Corp** Pennsylvania Flower Growers. **Added/Corp** Pennsylvania Flower Growers. **VFOAT** Florist Bulletin. (Dec. 1950)-. Periodical. English. Eight times a year. $30.00. Pennsylvania Flower Growers, 16 Hertzel Strive, Warren PA 19365. **Tel** (814)726-3779, FAX (814)726-3779. **ED** Gary Olson. **DD** 635. **Ad Acc. Circ:** 300.
Desc: Information on culture, pest control, marketing, greenhouses and flowering crops.
Ind/Abst Garden Lit. (1992-); Hortic. Abstr.; Ornamental Hort. (19??-19??); Plant Grow. Reg. Abstr.; Soils Fert.

US/0744-2653
CALIFORNIA ORNAMENTAL CROPS REPORT. [Calif. ornam. crops rep.]. **Added/Corp** California. Bureau of Market News. United States. Agricultural Marketing Service. Fruit and Vegetable Division. (19??)-. Periodical. English. sw (104 per year). $132.00 North America; $264.00 other. US Department of Agriculture / Federal-State Market News, 630 Sansome Street, Room 727, San Francisco CA 94111. **Tel** (415)705-1300. **ED** F. Teensma. **Circ:** 200 (ctrl).
Desc: Shipping point information on cut flowers for California and other areas.

CN/0008-3585
CANADIAN FLORIST, GREENHOUSE AND NURSERY. Vol. 56 (Jan. 1961)-. Periodical. English. Twelve times a year. $12.00 Canada; $18.00 other. Horticulture Publications Ltd, 1090 Aerowood Drive, Unit 1, Mississauga Ontario L4W 1Y5 Canada. **Tel** (416)625-2730, FAX (416)625-1355. **ED** Peter B. Heywood. **Ad Acc. Circ:** 2,600. ***Continues*** *Canadian Florist, 0315-5641.*
Desc: The only independent Canadian publication that covers all segments of the ornamental horticulture industry.

NE/0923-0203
DETAILHANDEL IN BLOEMEN, PLANTEN EN TUINBENODIGDHEDEN, DIEREN EN DIERBENODIGDHEDEN / CENTRAAL BUREAU VOOR DE STATISTIEK, HOOFDAFDELING STATISTIEKEN VAN BIENNENLANDSE HANDEL EN DIENSTVERLENING. **VFOAT** Retail Trade in Flowers, Plants, and Gardening Requirements, Pets and Requisites for the Care Thereof. Dutch (summaries and/or abstracts in English). an. Fl8.00. Centraal Bureau voor de Statistiek, AFD ALG Zaken, Postbus 959, 2270 AZ Voorburg Netherlands. **Tel** 011 31 70 3373800, FAX 011 31 038 7429, telex 32692 CBS NL. **LC** SB443.4.N4; D47.

CN/0827-150X
FLEUR DESIGN. [Fleur des.]. Vol. 1, No. 1 (Nov. 1985)-. Periodical. French. Seven times a year. 23.36Can$ regular; 19.04Can$ student. Editions Versicolores Inc., 1320 Boulevard Saint-Joseph, A Marchand Quebec, G2K 1G2 Quebec, Canada. **Tel** (418)628-8690, (800)463-1576, FAX (418)628-0524. **DD** 338.1/759/09714.

CN/0380-3163
FLEURISTE DU QUEBEC. Published since 1971. Periodical. French. bm. $10.00. Fleuriste du Quebec, C P 103, Grand'Mere Quebec Canada.

●US/1062-855X
FLORA-LINE, THE. **VFOAT** Flora Line. (1992-. Periodical. English. qt. $16.95 US; $20.00 other. Berry Hill Press, 7336 Berry Hill, Palos Verdes CA 90274-4404. **ED** Dody Lyness. **Bk Rev**, (Qty: (unlimited)). **Ad Acc, Adv Mgr:** Dody Lyness, **Tel** (310)377-7040. **Circ:** 1,200 (ctrl). ***Continues*** *Potpourri Party-Line, 0882-3790.*
Desc: A semi-trade publication targeted to the home-based manufacturer of dried floral home decor, the manufacturer of fragrance items and the grower of flowers for drying and use by those professional artisans.

UK/0306-882X
FLORA (LONDON). (FLORA INTERNATIONAL MAGAZINE.). [Flora]. **VFOAT** Flora for Gardeners and Flower Arrangers. No. 6 (1976)-. Periodical. English. bm. £12.95 Great Britain and Northern Ireland; £14.95 other. Flora International Magazine, 77 Bulbridge Road, Wilton Salisbury England. **ED** Russell Bennett (editor's address: 46 Merlin Grove Eden Park, Beckenham Kent BR3 3HU England; editor's phone: 44 81 658180). **Bk Rev. Ad Acc. Pr Rev. Circ:** 20,000.
Desc: Filled with fascinating floral features for flower arrangers and florists-abstract to traditional styles.
Ind/Abst AGRICOLA; Life Sci. Collect.

US
FLORAL MARKETING DIRECTORY & BUYER'S GUIDE. See Business-Marketing.

IT
FLORICULTURE. Agrital Editrice, Casella Postale 573, 22100 Como 4 Italy.

US/0744-3714
FLORIDA CUT FLOWER AND FERN REPORT. (FLORIDA CUT FLOWER AND FERN REPORT / FEDERAL/STATE MARKET NEWS SERVICE.). Vol. 1, No. 1 (Tues., Feb. 22, 1982)-. English. sw. Federal-State Market News Service, 1220 N Street/Suite 216, Sacramento CA 95814. **Tel** (202)872-4600, (800)227-5558, FAX (202)872-4615.

GW/0015-4393
FLORIST (GUNZBURG, GERMANY). (FLORIST : FACHORGAN DER DEUTSCHEN FLORISTEN; ANZEIGENBLATT DER BLUMENGESCHAFTE UND IHRER LIEFERFIRMEN.). **Added/Corp** Fachverband Deutscher Floristen. (1948)-. Periodical. German. sm. DM124.80. Donau Verlag, Postfach 1154, D-89301 Gunzburg Germany. **Tel** 0881 34527, FAX 08221 34527. **Bk Rev. Ad Acc, Adv Mgr:** D. Winkler. Full Page (B&W) DM4140.00. Half Page (B&W) DM3028.00. **Acid Free. Circ:** 3,800. available on diskette.

US/0015-4385
FLORIST (SOUTHFIELD, MICH.). (FLORIST.). [Florist]. **Added/Corp** Florists' Transworld Delivery Association. Vol.1 (June 1967)-. Periodical. English. mo. $28.00 (one year), $48.00 (two year). Florists Transworld Delivery, PO Box 2227, Publishing Department, Southfield MI 48037. **Tel** (313)355-9300, FAX (313)355-6350. **ED** William P. Golden. **Ad Acc, Adv Mgr:** Denise Mazzetti, **Tel** (810)355-6264. **Circ:** 30,000. ***Continues*** *Florists' Transworld Delivery Association. FTD News.*
Ind/Abst AGRICOLA [Select. Cov.].

UK/0015-4415
FLORIST TRADE MAGAZINE. (1949)-. Trade Publication. English. mo. £33.00, £25.00 (students) UK; £60.00 other. Lonsdale Publications Ltd, 120 Lower Ham Road, Surrey Kingston-Upon-Thames England. **Tel** 081 546 1535, FAX 081 547 3682. **ED** Caroline Marshall-Foster. **Bk Rev. Ad Acc. Circ:** 3,800 (ctrl).
Desc: Covers professional use of flowers, plants and allied products within a retailing environment.

US/0015-4423
FLORISTS' REVIEW. [Flor. rev.]. Vol. 30, No. 761 (June 27, 1912)-. Periodical. English. Thirteen times a year (June issue includes sourcebook material). $36.00 (one year), $65.00 (two year) US; $46.00 (one year), $75.00 (two year) other. Florists' Review Enterprises, PO Box 4368, Topeka KS 66604. **Tel** (913)266-0888, FAX (913)266-0333. **(Subscription address:** P O Box 5716; Topeka,KS 66605-0716) **ED** Judith Lennox. **DD** 338. **Ad Acc. Circ:** 22,000. available on microfilm and microfiche from University Microfilms International (UMI). ***Continues*** *Weekly Florists' Review.* ***Continued in part by*** *Growers' Review Marketletter, 0886-1048.*
Desc: Practical design techniques, with specific how-to information. Latest product information. Shop management methods, useful tips on displays, promotions, industry trends. The only independent magazine in floral industry.
Ind/Abst AGRICOLA [Select. Cov.].

UK/0046-421X
FLOWER ARRANGER. English. qt (4 issues). £7.50 UK; £9.00 (surface mail), £12.00 (airmail) other. Nafas Flower Arranger, Taylor Bloxham Ltd, Nugent Street, Leicester LE3 5HH England.

CN/0836-3749
FLOWER SHOP. ***Ceased.*** [Flower shop]. Vol. 1, No. 1 (Nov. 1986)-(19??). Periodical. English. mo. NCC Publishing, 222 Argyle Avenue, Delhi Ontario N4B 2Y2 Canada. **Tel** (519)582-2513, FAX (519)582-4040. **DD** 381/.456359/0971.

UK
FLOWER TRADES JOURNAL. (19??)-. Periodical. English. mo. £41.00 UK; £53.00 Europe; £74.00 others. Yewtree Publishing Company Limited, 17 Wickham Road, Beckenham, Kent, BR3 2JS England. **Tel** 011 44 81 658-8688, 011 44 81 658-8689, FAX 011 44 81 658-2250.

US/0199-4751
FLOWERS&. **VFOAT** Flowers &; Flowers And. Vol. 1 (Jan. 1980)-. Periodical. English. mo. $32.95 (one year), $59.95 (two years) US; $46.75 (one year), $88.50 (two year) Canada; $42.95 (one year), $79.95 (two year) other. Teleflora Inc, 12233 Olympic Blvd, Suite 118, Los Angeles CA 90064. **Tel** (310)826-5253, FAX (310)447-0228. **(Subscription address:** Stark Services, PO Box 16029 N. Hollywood, CA 91615 (818)760-8983) **ED** Bruce Wright. Index available (December issue; $3.25). cum. index. **Bk Rev. Ad Acc, Adv Mgr:** Peter Nicolaysen, **Tel** (310)826-5253. **Pr Rev. Circ:** 30,000. ***Continues*** *Teleflorist.*

US/0745-4201
FTD FAMILY. [FTD fam.]. **Added/Corp** Florists' Transworld Delivery Association. **VAT** Florists' Transworld Delivery Association Family. (19??)-. Periodical. English. mo. FTD Headquarters, 29200 Northwestern Highway, PO Box 2227, Southfield MI 48037.

KO
HWAHWE HYOPHOE PO. **Added/Corp** Hanguk Hwahwe Hyophoe. (19??)-. Periodical. Korean. ir. Hanguk Hwahwe Hyophoe, San 120-11-ho Socho-dong Kangnam-ku, Seoul 135 Korea. **LC** SB403; .H86.

UK
INTERNATIONAL FLORICULTURE QUARTERLY REPORT. Vol. 1, No. 1 (March 1989)-. Periodical. English. qt (4 issues). £120.00. Pathfast Publishing, 31 2nd Avenue, Frinton on Sea, Essex CO13 9ER England. **Tel** 011 44 255 678755, FAX 011 44 255 850258. **ED** Jeremy Pertwee. Index available. **Circ:** 300 (ctrl).

JA
KADO: ART OF FLOWER ARRANGEMENT. Japanese. mo. $100.00. **(Subscription address:** Japan Publications Trading Company, Ltd., PO Box 5030, Tokyo International, Tokyo 100-31 Japan.)

US/0737-1004
LIST OF NURSERYMEN, FLORISTS & DEALERS AND PLANT INSPECTION AND QUARANTINE OFFICIALS. [List nurserym., flor., deal. plant insp. quar. off.]. **VFOAT** List of Nurserymen, Florists and Dealers and Plant Inspection and Quarantine Officials; Texas Floral and Nursery Directory. 1982-. English. an. Texas Department of Agriculture, 18th & Congress Street, PO Box 12847, Austin TX 78711. **Tel** (512)463-7435, FAX (512)463-7643. **LC** SB44; .L57. **DD** 338.1/759/025764. ***Continues*** *List of Nurserymen, Florists & Dealers and the Texas Nursery and Floral Inspection Law.*

UK/0891-589X
MARKETLETTER (MARKET ED.). (MARKETLETTER.). [MarketLetter]. **VFOAT** Market Letter; Grower's Review MarketLetter. Vol. 1, No. 33 (Aug. 18, 1986)-. Periodical. English. Fifty times a year. $490.00. Marketletter Publications Ltd, 54-55 Wilton Road, London SW1V 1DE England. **Tel** 011 44 71 8287272, FAX 011 44 71 8280415. **DD** 635. available on an online database (files 16,636/Full-Text) from DIALOG. ***Continues in part*** *Growers' Review Marketletter, 0886-1048.*
Ind/Abst F&S Index Plus Text, Int. [Select. Cov.]; Trade Ind. Index.

US/0026-217X
MICHIGAN FLORIST, THE. **Added/Corp** Michigan State Florist Associaion. Michigan Floral Association. (19??)-. Periodical. English. bm. $50.00. Michigan State Florists Association, PO Box 24065, Lansing MI 48909. **Tel** (517)349-2900. **ED** Sue Ann Steuver. **Ad Acc, Adv Mgr:** Barbara Doyle. **Circ:** 1,800 (ctrl).
Desc: Features keyed to retailers, wholesalers and growers in the floral industry in the areas of sales, production, marketing, personnel, general business and association activities.

US
MINNESOTA COMMERCIAL FLOWER GROWERS ASSOCIATION BULLETIN. **Added/Corp** Minnesota Extension Service. Minnesota Commercial Flower Growers Association. Vol. 40, No. 6 (Nov. 1991)-. Bulletin. English. bm. ***Continues*** *Minnesota Flower Grower Association Bulletin, 1064-4415.*

US
NURSERY RETAILER. Vol. 36, No. 3 (May 1991)-. Periodical. English. bm. $15.00 (one year), $35.00 (three year) US; $35.00 (one year), $60.00 (three year) other. Brantwood Publications Inc, 3023 Eastland Boulevard/Suite 103, Clearwater FL 34621. **Tel** (813)796-3877, FAX (813)791-4126. **LC** SB118.73; .N87. ***Continues*** *Nursery Business Retailer.*

US
OHIO FLORISTS ASSOCIATION FLOWER GROWERS HOTLINE. (19??)-. Trade Publication. English. Ten times a year. $15.00. Ohio Florists Association, 2130 Satella Court, Suite 200, Columbus OH 43215. **Tel** (614)487-1117, FAX (614)487-1216. **ED** Harry Tayama. **Circ:** 1,000 (ctrl).
Desc: Newsletter featuring timely information on insect out-breaks, disease epidemics, and changing cultural procedures faced by commercial flower growers.

CN/0833-2274
OPERATING RESULTS. RETAIL FLORISTS. (OPERATING RESULTS, RETAIL FLORISTS / STATISTICS CANADA, MERCHANDISING AND SERVICES DIVISION, ANALYSIS AND DEVELOPMENT SECTION.). [Oper. results, Retail flor.]. **Added/Corp** Statistics Canada. Merchandising and Services Division. Analysis and Development Section. Statistics Canada. Retail Trade Section. **VFOAT** Resultats de l'Exploitation, Magasins de Vente au Detail de Fleuristes; Resultats de l'Exploitation, Fleuristes Detaillants. (1979)-. English (French). an. 15.00Can$ Canada; $16.00 other. Statistics Canada, Publications Sales & Services, Main Building Room 1710, Ottawa Ontario K1A 0T6 Canada. **Tel** (613)951-5078, (800)267-6677, FAX (613)951-1584, telex 053-3585. **LC** SB443.4.C2; O65. **DD** 381/.456359/0971.
Desc: Presents data on retail florists: operating results, gross profit, detailed expense items and net profit as a percentage of net sales for incorporated and unincorporated firms. Includes data analysis, methodology and bibliography.

UK/0030-4476
ORCHID REVIEW. (THE ORCHID REVIEW.). [Orchid rev.]. (1893)-. Periodical. English. Twelve times a year. £22.17. Royal Horticultural Society, 80 Vincent Square, London SW1P 2PE England. **Tel** 011 44 71 834 4333. **ED** C. Bailes. Index available. **Bk Rev.** **Ad Acc.** **Circ:** 2,000.
Desc: Magazine for orchid growers, professional and amateur, founded in 1893. Worldwide subscription with articles ranging from basic cultural notes to the latest techniques. Also show and exhibition reports.
Ind/Abst Ornamental Hort.; Plant Breed. Abstr.

US/0889-9924
PROFESSIONAL FLORAL DESIGNER, THE. (THE PROFESSIONAL FLORAL DESIGNER / AFS.). [Prof. floral des.]. **Added/Corp** American Floral Services. (1981)-. Periodical. English. Six times a year. $60.00. American Floral Services Inc., PO Box 12309, Oklahoma City OK 73157. **Tel** (800)456-7890, (405)947-3373. **LC** SB449; .P76. **DD** 745.92.
Ind/Abst Mag. Search; Vocat. Search (Jan. 1993-).

CN/0824-0442
SUBSCRIBERS DIRECTORY - TELEFLORA CANADA. (SUBSCRIBERS DIRECTORY / ANNUAIRE DES ABONNES / TELEFLORA CANADA.). **Main/Corp** Teleflora Canada. **VFOAT** Annuaire des Abonnes. (Dec. 1983/Jan. 1984)-. Periodical. English (French). bm. Free to subscribers of Teleflora Canada. Teleflora Canada, 350 Bay Street, Toronto Ontario M5H 3N9 Canada. **DD** 338.1/759/02571. ***Continues** United Flowers-by-Wire Canada. Membership and Delivery Directory, 0820-9537.*

BE
VERBONDSNIEUWS VOOR DE BELGISCHE SIERTEELT. (1969)-. Trade Publication. Dutch (English, French and German). sm. 2.000F Belgium; 3.000F other other. Belgische Boerenbond, Minderbroederstraat 8, B3000 Leuven Belgium. **Tel** 011 32 16 242111. **ED** E Bolckaert, M Van Niewerburgh and W De Geest. Index available. **Bk Rev.** **Ad Acc.** **Pr Rev.** **Circ:** 2,500 (ctrl).
Desc: The most important trade journal for the horticultural branch in Belgium.
Ind/Abst AgBiotech News Inf.; Biodeter. Abstr.; Crop Physiol. Abstr.; For. Abstr.; Hortic. Abstr.; Ornamental Hort. (19??-19??); Plant Breed. Abstr.; Plant Grow. Reg. Abstr.

GENEALOGY AND HERALDRY

US/1044-7350
3-D DATA. (3-D DATA : NEWSLETTER OF THE DYCKMAN/DIKEMAN/DYKEMAN FAMILY ASSOCIATION.). [3-D data]. **Added/Corp** Dyckman/Dikeman/Dykeman Family Association. **VFOAT** Three-D Data; 3 D Data; Newsletter of the Dyckman/Dikeman/Dykeman Family Association. **VAT** Dyckman/Dikeman/Dykeman Data. Vol. 1, No. 1 (Winter 1985)-. Periodical. English. qt. $10.00. Marjorie Chamberlain, PO Box 25, East Poland ME 04230. **DD** 929.

CN/0381-145X
21ST GENERATION, THE. V. 1- 1975-. English (French). an. P B Merey, 113 Hiltz Avenue, Toronto Ontario M4L 2N7 Canada. **DD** 929/.2/05. **UDC** 929.5.

UK/0263-5712
1851 CENSUS INDEX SERIES. Vol. 1, No. 1- 1982-. English. East Surrey Family History Society, 18 Roseville Road, London SW10 8RB England. **LC** CS436.L7; A242. **DD** 929/.342.

US/0883-1173
ABOUT ALFORDS. [About Alfords]. **Added/Corp** Alford, Mary. Alford, Gilbert K. (198?)-. Periodical. English. qt. $12.00. About Alfords, 1403 Kingsford Drive, Florissant MO 63031. **Tel** (314)831-8648. **DD** 929.

US/0199-9591
ACADIAN GENEALOGY EXCHANGE. **VFOAT** Acadian Newsletter. Vol. 1, No. 1 (1972)-. Periodical. English. Four times a year (Jan., Apr., July, Oct.). $15.00. Acadian Genealogy Exchange, 863 Wayman Branch Road, Convington KY 41015. **Tel** (606)356-9825, FAX (606)356-9825. **ED** Janet B. Jehn. **LC** F380.A2; A27. **DD** 929/.1/089410763. Index available (Bound in 4th iss, in (Oct).). **Bk Rev**, (Qty: 15). **Ad Acc.** **Circ:** 750 (ctrl).
Desc: Genealogical and historical material geared towards the Acadian and French-Canadian Acadian interests. Ancestor charts and free queries related to the above are welcome.
Ind/Abst Genealogical Period. Annu. Index.

US
ACORNS TO OAKS. English. Four times a year. $10.00 US, $15.00 Other. Oakland Co Genealogical Society, PO Box 1094, Birmingham MI 48012. **ED** Pamela Epple.

US/1053-0614
ACROSS THE BORDER (BLOOMINGTON, MINN.). (ACROSS THE BORDER : FOR ALL FAMILY HISTORY RESEARCHERS INTERESTED IN THE NORTHERN VERMONT COUNTIES OF ESSEX, LAMOILLE, CHITTENDEN, CALEDONIA, GRAND ISLE, FRANKLIN, WASHINGTON AND ORLEANS, AND THE EASTERN TOWNSHIPS OF QUEBEC.). [Across bord.]. (1988)-. Periodical. English. qt. $16.00. Claudette Maerz, PO Box 37010, Bloomington MN 55431. **Tel** (613)257-5355, (612)881-4864. **ED** Diana Hibbert Bailey (editor's address: RR 2 McOreger Ridge, Carleton Place K7C 3P2 Canada). **LC** F48; .A64. **DD** 929/.1/0720743.

US/1063-9926
ADAIR COUNTY REVIEW. **Added/Corp** Adair County Genealogical Society (Adair County, Ky.). (1987)-. Periodical. English. Four times a year. $10.00. Adair County Genealogical Society, PO Box 613, Columbia KY 42728. **Tel** (502)384-5906. **LC** F457.A3; A32. **DD** 929/.3769675. **Bk Rev.** **Circ:** 250.

US/0739-0076
ADAMS ADDENDA. Vol. 1, (Spring 1971)-. Periodical. English. Twice a year (Mar., Oct.). $14.00. Adams Addenda, 9514 Minerva Avenue, C/O D. A. Griffith, St Louis MO 63114. **ED** Dorothy A. Griffith (phone: (314)428-7048). **DD** 929.2/0973. Index available (Oct. iss.). **Bk Rev**, (Qty: 4). **Ad Acc.** **Circ:** 300.
Desc: Records, family histories, Bibles, and all other materials are pre-1900, for an serious research of the Adamses family histories.

AT
ADDRESS BOOK FOR FAMILY HISTORY SEARCHERS AND HISTORIANS / WHOLLY COMPILED BY JAMES MCCLELLAND RESEARCH. **Added/Corp** James McClelland Research. (1982)-. English. an. Keith Ainsworth Pty Ltd, 7 Clifton Avenue, Glenbrook New South Wales Australia. **LC** CS5; .A33. **DD** 929/.1/025.

AU/0001-8260
ADLER (WIEN). (ADLER.). [Adler]. **Added/Corp** Heraldisch-Genealogische Gesellschaft "Adler". Vol. 1 (May 1947)-. German. qt. S490.00 Austria; DM70.00 Germany. Heraldisch Genealogische Gesellschaft Adler, 1 Haarhof 4A, Vienna A-1014 Austria. **ED** Horst Dolezal. **LC** CS1; .A4. **DD** 929/.1/05. Index available. **Bk Rev**, (Qty: 40). **Ad Acc.** **Pr Rev.** **Circ:** 800.
Ind/Abst Am. Hist. Life (1964-1978).

US/1060-6645
ADVANCE NOTICE (PRINCETON, N.J.). ***Suspended.*** **See** Library and Information Sciences.

US/0884-6669
AGE. (AGE / ALABAMA GENEALOGICAL EXCHANGE.). **Added/Corp** Alabama Genealogical Exchange. **VFOAT** Alabama Genealogical Exchange Quarterly; Quarterly. Vol. 1, No. 1 (Summer 1984)-. Periodical. English. qt. $20.00. Wood Publishing Company, 814 35th Avenue, Tuscaloosa AL 35401. **LC** F325; .A25. **DD** 929/.3761.

US/0091-1607
AKIKI, THE. [Akiki]. **VFOAT** A-Ki-Ki. Periodical. English. qt. $10.00. Kankakee Valley Genealogical Society, c/o Kankakee Public Library, 304 South Indiana Avenue, Kankakee IL 60901. **Tel** (815)939-4564. **ED** Marsha Stang. **LC** F532.K2; T47. **DD** 929/.377363. **UDC** 929.5(773). **Bk Rev.** **Circ:** 150 (ctrl).
Desc: Summaries of meetings and articles on Kankakee area history and families, family genealogy charts.

US
ALABAMA FAMILY HISTORY AND GENEALOGY NEWS (1984). (ALABAMA FAMILY HISTORY AND GENEALOGY NEWS.). **Added/Corp** North Central Alabama Genealogical Society. Vol. 5, No. 1 (1984)-. Periodical. English. qt (Jan., Apr., July, Oct.). $15.00. North Central Alabama Genealogical Society, PO Box 13, Cullman AL 35056. **Tel** (205)352-4170. **ED** Carolina Nigg, PO Box 32, Hanceville, AL 35007-0032. Each issue contains an index to its own contents (no volume index)--loose. **Bk Rev.** **Circ:** 200. ***Continues** Alabama Family History, 0738-5730.*
Ind/Abst Genealogical Period. Annu. Index.

US/0516-396X
ALABAMA GENEALOGICAL REGISTER / BY BETTY WOOD THOMAS, THE. (June 1959)-. English. qt. $25.00. Alabama Genealogical Register, PO Box 84, Columbus MS 39701. **LC** CS42; .A48. **DD** 929/.3761. ***Continues** Alabama Genealogical Registrar.*

US
ALAMANCE GENEALOGIST. English. Three times a year (Jan., May, Sept.). $10.00. Alamance County Genealogical Society, PO Box 3052, Burlington NC 27215-3052. **Tel** (919)226-0449. **ED** W. Ray Kinnin Jr. **Bk Rev.** **Circ:** 150.
Desc: Deals with data of genealogical interest of Alamance and Orange counties in North Carolina.

CN/0228-9288
ALBERTA FAMILY HISTORIES SOCIETY QUARTERLY. [Alta. Fam. Hist. Soc. q.]. **Added/Corp** Alberta Family Histories Society. Vol. 1, No. 1 (Sept. 1980)-. Periodical. English. qt. $23.44 institutions; $18.75 individuals. Alberta Family Histories Society, P.O.Box 30270 Station B, Calgary Alberta T2M 4P1 Canada. **Tel** (403)255-8660. **DD** 929/.2/097123. **Bk Rev.** **Ad Acc.** **Circ:** 180 (ctrl).

US/0742-5910
ALL-IRELAND HERITAGE, THE. ***Suspended.*** [All-Ireland her.]. **VFOAT** All Ireland Heritage. Vol. 1, No. 1 (Feb. 1984)-Suspended. Periodical. English. Three times a year. $18.00. D R H Associates, 2255 Cedar Lane, Vienna VA 22180. **LC** CS480; .A45. **DD** 929/.1/0720415. **UDC** 929.5(415).

US/0883-5926
ALLEE'S ALL AROUND. Vol. 1, No. 1 (July 1984)-. Periodical. English. qt. $10.00. Allees All Around, PO Box 347, Friendswood TX 77546. **LC** CS71; .A4442. **DD** 929/.2/0973. **UDC** 929.5(73).

US/1041-9381
ALLEN COUNTY-FORT WAYNE HISTORICAL SOCIETY BULLETIN. **See** History(General)-History of North, South, and Central America.

US
ALLEN COUNTY LINES. Vol. 3, No. 2 (Dec. 1978)-. Periodical. English. qt. Allen County Genealogical Society of Indiana, PO Box 12003, Ft Wayne IN 46862. **LC** CS42; .L55. **DD** 929/.1/072077274. **UDC** 929.5(772). ***Continues** Lines, 0149-7669.*
Ind/Abst Genealogical Period. Annu. Index.

●US/1059-7719
ALLTON-ALTON-AULTON ASSOCIATION FAMILY NEWSLETTER. **VFOAT** Allton Alton Aulton Association Family Newsletter. (1992)-. Newsletter. English. qt. $15.00. AAAAFN, 15510 Laurel Ridge Road, Dumfries VA 22026.

CN/1183-1529
ALOGNON (SILLERY). (ALOGNON : JOURNAL DE L'ASSOCIATION DES FAMILLES LOIGNON.). [Alognon]. **Added/Corp** Association des Familles Loignon. Vol. 1, No 1 (Dec. 1990)-. Periodical. French. sa. Free for members. Association des Familles Loignon, CP 6700, Sillery, Quebec G1T 2W2 Canada. **DD** 929/.2/0971.

US/1076-3902
AMERICAN-CANADIAN GENEALOGIST. (AMERICAN-CANADIAN GENEALOGIST : OFFICIAL JOURNAL OF THE AMERICAN-CANADIAN GENEALOGICAL SOCIETY.). [Am.-Can. geneal.]. **Added/Corp** American-Canadian Genealogical Society. **VAT** American Canadian Genealogist. Vol. 17, No. 3 (Summer 1991)-. Periodical. English. Four times a year (Jan., Apr., July, Oct.). $25.00 Comes with American Canadian Genealogical Society membership. American-Canadian Genealogical Society Inc, PO Box 668, Manchester NH 03105. **Tel** (603)622-1554. **ED** Anne-Marie Perrzult, (editor's address: RFD 6, Goffstown, NH, 03045, phone: (603)622-1591). **LC** E184.F85; G46. **DD** 929/.1/089114073. Index available. cum. index. **Bk Rev**, (Qty: 5 to 10). **Ad Acc.** **Circ:** 2,000. ***Continues** Genealogist (Manchester, N.H.), 0196-4259.*
Desc: Many articles on genealogy, history, and family along the ancestors lines.

US/0736-9794
AMERICAN ELM, THE. (THE AMERICAN ELM : WMGS QUARTERLY.). [Am. elm]. **Added/Corp** Western Massachusetts Genealogical Society. Vol. 1, No. 1 (April 1972)-. Periodical. English. qt (4 issues). $6.00. Western Massachusetts Genealogical Society, PO Box 80206,

Springfield MA 01108. **ED** Christopher Broderick. **LC** F63; .A46. **DD** 929/.1/060744. Index available (Bound in May issue). **Circ:** 225 (ctrl).
Desc: Matters pertaining to area history and members genealogical findings.

US/0002-8592
AMERICAN GENEALOGIST (DES MOINES). (THE AMERICAN GENEALOGIST.). [Am. geneal.]. Vol. 14, No. 1 (July 1937)-. Periodical. English. Four times a year (Jan., Apr., July, Oct.). $20.00 (one year), $39.00 (two year), $58.00 (three year). American Genealogist, PO Box 398, Demorest GA 30535. **Tel** (706)865-6440. **ED** D. L. Greene and Ric Anderson. **LC** F104.N6; A6. **DD** 929/.1/072073. Index available (Annual index in October issue.). cum. index. **Bk Rev. Pr Rev. Circ:** 1,600. available on microfilm and microfiche from University Microfilms International (UMI). ***Continues*** *American Genealogist and New Haven Genealogical Magazine, 0197-6915.*
Desc: Dedicated to the elevation of genealogical scholarship, through carefully documented analyses of genealogical problems and through short compiled genealogies.
Ind/Abst Genealogical Period. Annu. Index.

US/1049-6696
AMERICAN GENEALOGY MAGAZINE. [Am. geneal. mag.]. **Added/Corp** Datatrace Systems (Firm). (1989)-. Periodical. English. Six times a year. $22.50. Datatrace Systems, PO Box 1587, Stephenville TX 76401. **Tel** (817)965-6979. **DD** 929. ***Continues*** *American Genealogy.*
Ind/Abst Genealogical Period. Annu. Index.

US/1045-9960
AMERICAN SCHLESWIG-HOLSTEIN HERITAGE SOCIETY NEWSLETTER. [Am./Schleswig-Holstein Herit. Soc. newsl.]. **Added/Corp** American Schleswig-Holstein Heritage Society. **VFOAT** American Schleswig, Holstein Heritage Society Newsletter; ASHHS Newsletter. Vol. 1, No. 1 (Jan./Feb. 1989)-. Newsletter. English. Six times a year (Feb., Apr., June, Aug., Oct., Dec.). $15.00. American Schleswig Holstein, PO Box 313, Davenport IA 52805. **ED** Merl Arp (phone: (301)681-3464). **DD** 929. **Circ:** 600 (ctrl).
Desc: This newsletter has articles and news on the family history, cultural changing, and calendar of events.

US/0743-2801
AMONG THE COLES. (AMONG THE COLES / COLES COUNTY ILLINOIS GENEALOGICAL SOCIETY.). **Added/Corp** Coles County Genealogical Society. (19??)-. Periodical. English. Ten times a year. $7.00 (individuals), $8.00 (family) Comes with Among the Coles membership. Coles County / Illinois Genealogical Society, PO Box 225, Charleston IL 61920. **Tel** (217)345-7359. **ED** Cathy Hartley. **LC** F547.C6; A45. **DD** 929/.1/072077372. Index available. **Circ:** 250 (ctrl).
Desc: Genealogical material of interest to Coles county and related articles.

AT/0044-8222
ANCESTOR. **Added/Corp** Genealogical Society of Victoria. (196?)-. Periodical. English. qt (Mar., June, Sept., Dec.). 30.00Aus$ Australia, (add 10.00Aus$ for postage) other. Genealogical Society of Victoria Inc, Curtin House/5th Floor, 252 Swanston Street, Melbourne 3000 Australia. **Tel** 011 61 3 663 7033. **ED** J. Ray (phone: 03 6637034). Index available. **Bk Rev. Ad Acc, Adv Mgr:** Julie Taylor, **Tel** 03 6637034. **Circ:** 6,500 (ctrl).
Desc: A family history/genealogical magazine for people interested in tracking their family history. It provides information for beginners and experienced researchers together with up-to-date fees, addresses and record releases for both Australia and overseas.

US/0742-7212
ANCESTOR CHARTS. Vol. 1, Ser. 1-. English. $8.00. Nebraska State Genealogical Society, 3507 South 116th Avenue, Omaha NE 68144. **Tel** (402)291-1411. **ED** Allen W Dripps. **LC** F665; .A5. **DD** 929/.3782. **UDC** 929.5(782).

US/0736-9115
ANCESTOR HUNT. (ANCESTOR HUNT : QUARTERLY PUBLICATIONS OF THE ASHTABULA GENEALOGICAL SOCIETY OF OHIO.). **Added/Corp** Ashtabula County Genealogical Society. (19??)-. Periodical. English. Four times a year (Feb., May, Aug., Nov.). $10.00 Comes with Ashtabula County Genealogical Society membership. Ashtabula County Genealogical Society Inc OGS, Henderson Memorial Library, 54 East Jefferson Street, Jefferson OH 44047. **Tel** (216)992-6343. **ED** Marion Holmes (editor's address: 958 Mineral Springs Road, Ashtabula, OH 44004, phone: (216)998-0238). **LC** F497.A73; A53. **DD** 929/.1/072077134. Index available. **Bk Rev**, (Qty: 4). **Circ:** 325 (ctrl).
Desc: News and information in Ashtabula County, Ohio.
Ind/Abst Genealogical Period. Annu. Index.

CN/0704-6618
ANCESTOR INDEX. **Main/Corp** Alberta Genealogical Society. V. 1- 1977-. English. an. Alberta Genealogical Society, PO Box 12015, Fort McMurray BR, Alberta T9H 4W1 Canada. **Tel** (403)791-2913, telex KS4337. **ED** Joachim Nuthack. **DD** 929/.37123. **UDC** 929.53(712). Index available. **Circ:** 800. ***Absorbed*** *Alberta Genealogical Society. Surnames Register, 0704-6618.*

US
... ANCESTOR SURNAME DIRECTORY, THE. **Added/Corp** Forsyth County Genealogical Society. **VFOAT** Ancestor Surname Index. Directory. English. Forsyth County Genealogical Society, PO Box 5715, Winston Salem NC 27113. **Tel** (919)724-0714. **LC** F262.F7; A53. **DD** 929/.375667. ***Continues*** *Index of Surnames (Winston-Salem, N.C.), 8755-4275.*

●US/1064-0738
ANCESTOR UPDATE. (ANCESTOR UPDATE / THE GENEALOGICAL SOCIETY OF HENRY & CLAYTON COUNTIES, INC.). [Ancestor update]. **Added/Corp** Genealogical Society of Henry & Clayton Counties (Georgia). Vol. 1, No. 1 (Spring 1992)-. Periodical. English. qt. Free to members, $15.00 (non-members). Genealogical Society of Henry and Clayton Counties Georgia, PO Box 1296, McDonough GA 30253. **Tel** (404)954-1456. **ED** Gladys Rutan Daw (Editor's Address: 50 Tanglewood Court, McDonough , GA 30253). **LC** F292.H73; A52. **DD** 929. Index available. ctrl circ. ***Continues*** *Ancestors Unlimited Edition (College Park, Ga. : 1982), 0889-3039.*
Desc: Genealogical and historical information about Henry and surrounding counties.

US/0272-0426
ANCESTORING. **Added/Corp** Augusta Genealogical Society. (1980)-. Periodical. English. sa. Free to members of the Augusta Geneaological Society. Augusta Genealogical Society, PO Box 3743, Augusta GA 30914. **Tel** (404)722-4073. **ED** Carrie M. Adamson. **LC** CS1; .A48. **DD** 929/.1/05. **Pr Rev. Circ:** 1,000.
Desc: Abstracts of 18th and 19th Century Georgia/South Carolina cemetery, family, Bible, marriage, birth, baptism, funeral, naturalization, amnesty, voter, census, land, etc., records; historical background articles.
Ind/Abst Genealogical Period. Annu. Index.

US/0888-5273
ANCESTORS UNLIMITED (MCCOOK, NEB.). (ANCESTORS UNLIMITED.). **Added/Corp** Southwest Nebraska Genealogical Society. (197?)-. Periodical. English. Six times a year. $6.00 Comes with Southwest Nebraska Genealogical Society membership. Southwest Northest Genealogical Society, PO Box 156, McCook NE 69001. **Tel** (308)345-1763. **DD** 929.
Ind/Abst Genealogical Period. Annu. Index.

US/0734-4988
ANCESTORS WEST. [Ancestors west]. **Added/Corp** Santa Barbara County Genealogical Society. Vol. 4, No. 1 (Mar. 1978)-. Periodical. English. Four times a year (Mar., June, Sept., Dec.). $10.00 one year; $15.00 other. Santa Barbara County Genealogical Society, PO Box 1303, Goleta CA 93116-1303. **Tel** (805)967-8954. **ED** Lilian Fish. **LC** F868.S23; A52. **DD** 929/.1/072079491. **Bk Rev**, (Qty: 4). **Circ:** 450 (ctrl).
Desc: General articles on genealogy; records of Santa Barbara County; members ancestry charts; queries.
Ind/Abst Genealogical Period. Annu. Index.

US/0894-8895
ANCESTRAL PURSUIT. ***Ceased.*** (1987)-?. Periodical. English. qt. Ancestral Pursuit, 10 Quiet Hills Circle, Pomona CA 91766. **LC** CS42; .A66. **DD** 929/.373. **UDC** 929.5(794).

US
ANCESTREE / LOGAN COUNTY GENEALOGICAL SOCIETY. **Added/Corp** Logan County Genealogical Society (W. Va.). Vol. 7, No. 1 (Spring 1984)-. Periodical. English. qt. $6.00 (individual membership), $10.00 (family membership). Logan County Genealogical Society, PO Box 1959, Logan WV 25601. **LC** F247.L8; L63. **DD** 929/.1/072075444. ***Continues*** *Logan County Ancestree.*

US
ANCESTRY. **Added/Corp** Palm Beach County Genealogical Society. Vol. 1 (Jan. 1966)-. Periodical. English. qt (Jan., April, July, Oct.). $15.00. Palm Beach County Genealogical Society, PO Box 1746, West Palm Beach FL 33402. **Tel** (407)832-3279. **ED** Ellen Gardner Brown & Jane M. Allen. **LC** CS1; .P3. **DD** 929.3/05. Index available (Bound in Oct. issue). **Bk Rev**, (Qty: 8). **Ad Acc, Adv Mgr:** Jane Allen. **Circ:** 400.
Desc: Covers Florida genealogy, original manuscripts, library acquisitions and general genealogy. Exchanges are made with about 100 periodicals.
Ind/Abst Genealogical Period. Annu. Index.

US/0749-5927
ANCESTRY NEWSLETTER. ***Title Change.*** [Ancestry newsl.]. (198?)-(19??). Periodical. English. Six times a year. Ancestry, Inc., PO Box 476, Salt Lake City UT 84110. **Tel** (800)531-1790. **ED** Robb Barr. **LC** CS1; .A49. **DD** 929/.1/072073. cum. index. **Bk Rev. Circ:** 7,000 (ctrl). ***Continued by*** *Ancestry (Salt Lake City, Utah), 1075-475X.*
Desc: Publishes genealogical "how-to" pieces, ranging in scope from record source types to regional focus (U.S. and foreign). Occasionally publishes genealogical general interest on societies, etc.

●US/1075-475X
ANCESTRY (SALT LAKE CITY, UTAH). (ANCESTRY.). [Ancestry]. Vol. 12, No. 1 (Jan./Feb. 1994)-. Periodical. English. Six times a year (Jan., Mar., May, July, Sept., Nov.). $18.00 US; $23.00 Canada & Mexico; $28.00 others. Ancestry, Inc., PO Box 476, Salt Lake City UT 84110. **Tel** (800)531-1790. **ED** Anne Lemmon. **LC** CS1; .A493. **DD** 929/.1/072073. Index available ($4.00). cum. index. **Ad Acc. Pr Rev. Circ:** 8,600. ***Continues*** *Ancestry Newsletter, 0749-5927.*

US/1054-2310
ANCESTRY TRAILS. [Ancestry trails]. (Oct. 1982)-. Periodical. English. mo. $8.00. Ohio Genealogical Society / Warren Ohio Chapter, PO Box 309, Warren OH 44482. **DD** 929. ***Continues*** *News Bulletin (Ohio Genealogical Society. Trumbull County Chapter).*

CN/0316-0513
ANCETRE (QUEBEC). (L'ANCETRE.). [Ancetre]. **Added/Corp** Societe de Genealogie de Quebec. Vol. 1 (Sept. 1974)-. Periodical. French. Ten times a year. $25.00 Canada; $30.00 other. Societe de Genealogie de Quebec, CP 9066, Sainte-Foy Quebec G1V 4A8 Canada. **Tel** (418)651-9127. **DD** 929/.1/09714. (June). cum. index. **Bk Rev. Ad Acc. Circ:** 1,250 (ctrl).
Desc: Bulletin of the Society of Genealogy in Quebec.

US
ANCHORAGE GENEALOGICAL SOCIETY QUARTERLY. English. qt. $15.00. Anchorage Genealogical Society, PO Box 212265NE, Anchorage AK 99521. **Tel** (907)344-9581.
Ind/Abst Genealogical Period. Annu. Index.

US/1072-8953
ANCIENT CITY GENEALOGIST, THE. **Added/Corp** St. Augustine Geneological Society. (19??)-. Periodical. English. Four times a year (Mar., June, Sept., Dec.). $15.00. St. Augustine Genealogical Society, C/O St. Johns County Public Library, 1960 North Ponce deLeon Boulevard, St. Augustine FL 32084. **ED** Gil Wilson (editor's address: 6 Sanchez Avenue, St. Augustine, FL 32084-3228, telephone: (904)823-1270). Index available. **Circ:** 150 (ctrl).

US/8756-7571
ANDERSON FAMILY COURIER. [Anderson fam. cour.]. Vol. 1, (April 1985)-. Periodical. English. qt. $15.00. Courier Publications, PO Box 1320, Winnfield LA 71483. **Tel** (318)628-2019. **ED** Annette Carpenter Womack. **DD** 929. **UDC** 929.5(714).
Desc: Contains facts, queries, figures and charts on the history of Anderson families of the United States.

US/0003-5246
ANSEARCHIN' NEWS. **Added/Corp** Tennessee Genealogical Society. Memphis Genealogical Society. Vol. 1 (Jan. 1954)-. Periodical. English. Four times a year (Mar., June, Sept., Dec.). $22.00. Tennessee Genealogical Society Board, PO Box 111249, Memphis TN 38111. **Tel** (901)327-3273. **ED** Betsy West. Index available. **Bk Rev. Pr Rev. Circ:** 2,100 (ctrl).
Desc: Printing unpublished material dating primarily before 1850. Bible records, wills, deeds, petitions, census records, and review books. All printing pertains to genealogy.

US/1041-8466
APPALACHIAN FAMILIES. [Appalach. fam.]. Vol. 1, No. 1 (1988)-. Periodical. English. qt. $15.00. Mountain Press, PO Box 4810, Sevierville TN 37864. **Tel** (615)428-0746. **ED** James L Douthat. **LC** F217.A65; A655. **DD** 929/.2/097305. Index available. **Bk Rev. Ad Acc. Circ:** 500 (ctrl).
Desc: A publication in the genealogical/heraldic field - traces families across the appalachian area of the mid-Atlantic states in their migration and movement from time period to time period.

US/0888-6814
APPALACHIAN ROOTS. [Appalach. roots]. (1983)-. Periodical. English. mo. $16.00 US; $18.00 Canada; $19.00 other. Appalachian Roots, PO Box 4004, Parkersburg WV 26104-4004. **Tel** (304)422-6001. **ED** Mary Jo Brown. **DD** 929. **Bk Rev**, (Qty: 50). **Circ:** 450 (ctrl).
Desc: A newsletter for genealogists researching the Appalachian Mountain area of the U.S.
Ind/Abst Genealogical Period. Annu. Index.

US/0736-0800
APPLELAND BULLETIN, THE. **Added/Corp** Genealogical Society of North Central Washington. (19??)-. Bulletin. English. Four times a year (Mar., June, Sept., Dec.). $7.50. Genealogical Society of North Central Washington, PO Box 613, Wenatchee WA 98807-0613. **Tel** (509)664-5989 Ext. 20004. **ED** Frances Caldwell Miller. **LC** F890; .A66. **DD** 929/.3797. Index available. **Bk Rev. Circ:** 400.
Ind/Abst Genealogical Period. Annu. Index.

US/0736-7082
ARCHIBALD CLAN NEWSLETTER. Vol. 1, No. 1 (Jan. 1981)-. Periodical. English. qt (4 issues). $10.00. Clan Archibald Family Association, 273 Crestwood Drive, Hobart IN 46342. **Tel** (219)931-2616. **LC** CS71; .A67392. **DD** 929/.2/0973.

GW/0003-9403
ARCHIV FUR SIPPENFORSCHUNG UND ALLE VERWANDTEN GEBIETE. Began in 1928?. Periodical. German. qt. DM36.00 (add DM6.00 for postage). CA Starke Verlag, PO Box 1310, 6250 Limburg Frankfurt 51-53 Germany. **Tel** 06431-42033. **ED** C A Starke-Verlag. **LC** CS610; .A57. **UDC** 929.52. **[CCC]**. Index available. **Bk Rev. Ad Acc.** ctrl circ. ***Continues*** *Kultur und Leben.*
Desc: Popular science journal including essays and dissertations.

SZ
ARCHIVES HERALDIQUE SUISSES. (19??)-. Periodical. Multiple languages. sa. $80.00. Societe Suisse d'Heraldique, Sichtenstrasse 35, CH 4410 Liestal Switzerland. **Tel** 011 41 61 9211644. ***Absorbed*** *Archivum Heraldicum, 0004-0673.*

US/0736-4024
AREA FOOTPRINTS. Added/Corp Genealogical Society of Butler County. (19??)-. Periodical. English. Twice a year (June, Nov.). $12.00. Genealogical Society of Butler County, PO Box 426, Poplar Bluff MO 63901. **Tel** (314)785-2174. **LC** F472.B96; A73. **DD** 929/.1/072077893.

US/0571-0472
ARKANSAS FAMILY HISTORIAN, THE. [Ark. fam. hist.]. **Added/Corp** Arkansas Genealogical Society. Vol. 1 (Mar. 1962)-. Periodical. English. Four times a year (Mar., June, Sept., Dec.). $15.00. Arkansas Genealogical Society, PO Box 908, Hot Springs AR 71902. **Tel** (501)262-4513, FAX (501)262-4513. **ED** Margaret Harrison Hubbard (editor's address: 1411 Shady Grove Road, Hot Springs, AR 71901). **LC** F410; .A7. Index available. **Bk Rev. Circ:** 1,200 (ctrl). available on microfiche.
Desc: Census, cemetery, marriage, Bible, county records and pensions.
Ind/Abst Genealogical Period. Annu. Index.

PO
ARMAS E TROFEUS. Began in 1932; Second Series began in 1959. Periodical. Portuguese. Three times a year. **LC** CR680; .A8. **UDC** 929.6.

US/8756-6842
ARMCHAIR RESEARCHERS. QUERIES & BOOK REVIEWS, THE. VFOAT Armchair Researcher. Book Reviews and Queries. Vol. 1, No. 1-. Periodical. English. 810 McDonough Road, Hampton GA 30228. **LC** F208; .A76. **DD** 929/.1/072075. **UDC** 929.5(75).

US/0898-1329
ARMSTRONG CHRONICLES. [Armstrong chron.]. **Added/Corp** Armstrong Clan Society. Vol. 6, No. 4 (Winter 1987)-. Periodical. English. qt. free to members; $18.00 other. Armstrong Clan Society Inc, 1910 Wensley Drive, Charlotte NC 28210. **Tel** (704)553-9977. **ED** Charles H. Armstrong Jr. and Gene F. Armstrong. **LC** CS71; .A7394. **DD** 929/.2/0973. Index available. **Bk Rev. Ad Acc. Circ:** 200 (ctrl). ***Continues*** *Journal of the Strong Arm, 0738-1735.*
Desc: Published to collect and preserve historical, literary and genealogical records and documents relating to the Armstrong Clan and descendents throughout the world.

US/0749-517X
AROUND THE BEND (RICHMOND, TEX.). (AROUND THE BEND.). **Added/Corp** Fort Bend County Genealogical Society. (19??)-. English. qt. $12.50. Fort Bend County Genealogical Society, PO Box 274, Richmond TX 77469. **Tel** (713)341-6861. **ED** Elizabeth (Betsy) Barr, Margaret Elizabeth Isbell, and Mary Bennett. **LC** F392.F7; A76. **DD** 929/.1/0720764135. cum. index. **Bk Rev. Circ:** 100.
Desc: Contains book reviews, courthouse, cemetery and Bible records. Family histories, queries, calendar of upcoming events, census records, pedigree charts, and notes from librarian's desk of local library.

US/0096-1469
ASHLEYS OF AMERICA QUARTERLY. Main/Corp Ashleys of America, Inc. Periodical. English. qt. Ashleys of America Inc, 165 Elm Street, South Dartmouth MA 02748. **LC** CS71; .A8A. **DD** 929/.2/0973. **UDC** 929.5(73).

US/0004-4377
ASHTREE ECHO. Added/Corp Fresno Genealogical Society. **VAT** Ash Tree Echo. Vol. 1 (Jan. 1965)-. Periodical. English. sa (2 issues). $12.00. Fresno Genealogical Society, PO Box 1429, Fresno CA 93716. **ED** Loretta Brimhall. Index Available, published separately, free-automatically sent (Free). **Bk Rev. Circ:** 300 (ctrl).
Desc: Nucleus of magazine is devoted to genealogical and historical information pertaining to San Joaquin Valley but not limited to the area. The scope is nationwide.

CN/0833-1685
ASSOCIATION DES FAMILLES KIROUAC : BULLETIN, L'. [Assoc. fam. Kirouac]. No. 1 (Dec. 1983)-. Bulletin. French. ir. Free to members. Association des Familles Kirouac, 116 Place Jouvence, Ste Foy Quebec G2G 1K6 Canada. **DD** 929/.2. **UDC** 929.52(714).

CN/0836-3102
AU "PAYS" DE MATANE. See History(General)-History of North, South, and Central America.

US
AUGUSTAN. Augustan Society, Society Headquarters and Library, PO Box P, Torrance CA 90507-0210. **Tel** (310)320-7766.

US/0272-5525
AUGUSTAN SOCIETY OMNIBUS, THE. VFOAT Omnibus. 1986-. English. Augustan Society, Society Headquarters and Library, PO Box P, Torrance CA 90507-0210. **Tel** (310)320-7766. **LC** CS1; .A95. **DD** 929/.1/05. **UDC** 929.5. ***Formed by the union of*** *Augustan; Colonial Genealogist; English Genealogist; Genealogical Library Journal; Germanic Genealogist; Heraldry* ***and*** *Irish-American Genealogist.*
Ind/Abst Genealogical Period. Annu. Index.

US
AUSTIN GENEALOGICAL SOCIETY : [QUARTERLY]. Added/Corp Austin Geneological Society. **VFOAT** AGS Quarterly. (19??)-. Periodical. English. Four times a year (Mar., June, Sept., Dec.). $15.00. Austin Genealogical Society, PO Box 1507, Austin TX 78767. **ED** Bill Koehler, (editor's address: 4500 Hyridge Drive, Austin, TX 78759-8054, phone: (512)345-4409). Index available. cum. index (Price varies). **Bk Rev**, (Qty: 10). **Circ:** 500. available on microfilm from the publisher.
Desc: Genealogical information on family sheets, articles and other reviews.
Ind/Abst Genealogical Period. Annu. Index.

●US/1071-3425
AUTOGRAPH COLLECTOR. [Autogr. collect.]. **VFOAT** AC. Vol. 1, No. 1 (Mar. 1992)-. Periodical. English. Twelve times a year. $38.00 US; $72.00 Canada & Mexico; $93.60 others. Autograph Collector, 541 North Main Street, Suite 104-283, Corona CA 91720. **Tel** (909)734-9636, FAX (909)371-7139. **ED** Kevin Sherman, (editor's address: 510-A South Corona Mall, Corona, CA 91719). **DD** 929. **Bk Rev**, (Qty: 12). **Ad Acc. Circ:** 20,000 (ctrl). ***Continues*** *Autograph Collector's Magazine, 1069-8264.*

US
AVI AVOT. ***Ceased.*** (19??)-((19??). English. qt. Avi Avot, PO Box 2034, Cypress CA 90630. **Tel** (714)827-8243.

US/0882-6501
AVOTAYNU. [Avotaynu]. Vol. 1, No. 1 (Jan. 1985)-. Periodical. English. Four times a year (seasonally). $29.00 (one year); $56.00 (two years); $82.00 (three years). Avotaynu, PO Box 1134, Teaneck NJ 07666. **Tel** (201)837-8300, FAX (201)837-6272. **ED** Gary Mikotoff, (editor's address: 1485 Teaneck Road, Teaneck, NJ 07666). **LC** DS101; .A87. **DD** 929/.1/089924. cum. index. **Bk Rev**, (Qty: 12). **Ad Acc. Circ:** 2,000 (ctrl).
Desc: News and information of interest to research of Jewish genealogy.
Ind/Abst Genealogical Period. Annu. Index (?-?).

CN/1192-1137
B & D HEIR LINES. (B & D HEIR LINES : NEWSLETTER, ALBERTA GENEALOGICAL SOCIETY, BROOKS & DISTRICT BRANCH.). [B D heir lines]. **Added/Corp** Alberta Genealogical Society. Brooks & District Branch. **VFOAT** Brooks and District Heir Lines. Vol. 1 No. 1 (Spring 1988)-. Newsletter. English. Twice a year (Spring and Fall). 7.50Can$. Alberta Genealogy Society, Brooks & District BR, Box 1538, Brooks Alberta T0J 0J0 Canada. **Tel** (403)362-3216. **ED** Carol Anderson, (phone: (403)362-4608). **DD** 929/.1/072071234. cum. index. **Bk Rev**, (Qty: 3 or more). **Ad Acc. Circ:** 55.
Desc: News and information on research aids, local history, and others news.

US/0094-6915
BACKTRACKER, THE. [Backtracker]. **Added/Corp** Northwest Arkansas Genealogical Society. (1971)-. Periodical. English. qt. $10.00. Northwest Arkansas Genealogical Society, P.O.Box 796, Rogers AR 72757. **ED** George Crabtree. **LC** F410; .B3. **DD** 929/.3767. **Bk Rev. Circ:** 550.
Desc: Cemetery, family Bible, census, probate and other country records. Also pedigree charts. Queries and research hints.

US/8756-7237
BALL BEGINNINGS. [Ball begin.]. (1984)-. Periodical. English. Three times a year. Claudette Maerz, PO Box 37010, Bloomington MN 55431. **Tel** (613)257-5355, (612)881-4864. **ED** Claudette Maerz. **LC** CS71; .B1993. **DD** 929/.2/0973. **Circ:** 200.
Desc: Explores the family tree of the name Ball.

US/1046-4247
BALLEW FAMILY JOURNAL, THE. [Ballew fam. j.]. Vol. 1, No. 1-. Periodical. English. $10.00. 2711 Leslie Drive NE, Atlanta GA 30345. **LC** CS71; .B2193. **DD** 929/.2/0973. **UDC** 929.52(73).

US/0735-8695
BARNER FAMILY NEWSLETTER, THE. No. 1 (May 1974)-. Newsletter. English. an. Barner Family, Sandy Gipe, 2338 Boas Street, Harrisburg PA 17103. **LC** CS71; .B96333. **DD** 929/.2/0973. **UDC** 929.52(73).

●US/1062-6859
BARNES BULLETIN 2.0. [Barnes bull. 2.0]. **VFOAT** Barnes Bulletin Two Point Zero. (1992)-. Bulletin. English. $6.00 (single issue). KARD Files, 19305 SE 243rd Place, Kent WA 98042-4820. **Tel** (206)432-1659. **DD** 929. ***Continues*** *Barnes Bulletin, 1056-6961.*

US/0882-8202
BARRON FAMILY NEWSLETTER, THE. [Barron fam. newsl.]. Newsletter. English. bm. $16.50. Family Heritage Publications, 1465 South West Temple Street, Salt Lake City UT 84115-5241. **ED** William P Barron Jr. **DD** 929. **UDC** 929.52. **Ad Acc. Circ:** 50 (ctrl).
Desc: Genealogy and history of the Barron family with spelling variants in America and European roots. Maps, photos and general interest articles, and family and pedigree charts are included.

US/0882-0791
BARTON BULLETIN OF THE BARTON HISTORICAL SOCIETY, INC, THE. [Barton bull. Barton Hist. Soc. Inc.]. 1979-1980-. Bulletin. English. an. Barton Historical Society Inc, c/o Thelma B Gilreath, PO Box 157, Whitley City KY 42653. **ED** Thelma B Gilreath. **LC** CS71; .B3353. **DD** 929/.2/0973. **UDC** 929.5(73). **Circ:** 350. ***Continues*** *Barton Bulletin, 0882-0805.*

US/1042-671X
BARTON COUNTY GENEALOGICAL SOCIETY QUARTERLY. ***Title Change.*** [Barton Cty. Geneal. Soc. q.]. **Added/Corp** Barton County Genealogical Society. **VFOAT** Barton County Quarterly; BCGSQ. Vol. 5, No. 1 (Winter 1985)-(199?). Periodical. English. qt. Barton County Genealogical Society, PO Box 425, Great Bend KS 67530. **Tel** (316)793-7182. **LC** F687.B2; N49. **DD** 929/.378152/05. ***Continues*** *Newsletter (Barton County Genealogical Society).* ***Continued by*** *Quarterly (Barton County Genealogical Society).*
Ind/Abst Genealogical Period. Annu. Index.

US/0897-7429
BATCHELDER REVIEW. [Batchelder rev.]. (1988)-. Periodical. English. ir. $6.00. Pioneer Publications, PO Box 397, Black Eagle MT 59414-0397. **Tel** (406)453-4266. **ED** Shirley Penna Oaks. **DD** 929. Index available. **Bk Rev.**

US/0741-7632
BATEMAN DATUM. (BATEMAN DATUM : ANNUAL NEWSLETTER OF THE BATEMAN FAMILY ASSOC.). Newsletter. English. an. Bateman Family Association, Lebo Rt, Box 211, West Plains MO 65773. **LC** CS71; .B36743. **DD** 929/.2/0973. **UDC** 929.52(73).

US
BATON ROUGE, LE. (19??)-. English. Four times a year. $20.00. Baton Rouge Genealogical & Historical Society, PO Box 80565, SE Station, Baton Rouge LA 70898-0565. **Tel** (504)766-4900. **ED** Karen Strawn, (phone: (504)766-7789). Index available (bound in 4th issue). **Bk Rev**, (Qty: 16). **Circ:** 325.
Desc: Promote interest in genealogical and historical research.

UK
BEDFORDSHIRE FAMILY HISTORY SOCIETY JOURNAL. Added/Corp Bedfordshire Family History Society. **VFOAT** Journal. (19??)-. Periodical. English. Four times a year (Mar., June, Sept., Dec.). £6.00 UK; £7.00 other Comes with Bedsfordshire Family History Society membership. Bedfordshire Family Historical Society, c/o Kathy Gerrard, 34 Jubilee Street, Luton Bedford LU2 OEA England. **Tel** 011 44 0582 429602. **ED** A. J. Weston. **LC** CS435.B3; B42. **DD** 929/.1/07204256. **Bk Rev. Ad Acc. Circ:** 700 (ctrl).

GW/0005-8114
BEITRAEGE ZUR NAMENFORSCHUNG. [Beitr. Namenforsch.]. Vol. 1-16, (1949/50-1965); New Series Vol. 1 (1966)-. Periodical. German (English). Four times a year (Feb., Apr., Aug., Oct.). DM174.50 Germany; DM182.00 others. Universitatsverlag Carl Winter, POB 106140, D 69051 Heidelberg Germany. **Tel** 011 49 6221 770260. **ED** Rudolf Schuetzeichel. **LC** P769; .B45. **Bk Rev. Ad Acc. Circ:** 550 (ctrl).
Desc: News and information on the names, genealogy and heraldry.
Ind/Abst Annu. Bibliogr. Engl. Lang. Lit.; MLA Int. Bibl. Books Artic. Mod. Lang. Lit.

US/1046-0462
BELGIAN LACES. [Belg. laces]. **Added/Corp** Belgian Researchers (Organization) Belgian American Heritage (Organization). No. 7 (Aug. 1978)-. Periodical. English. Four times a year (Feb., May, Aug., Nov.). $12.00 US & Canada; $14.00 others. Belgian Researchers, Fruitdale Lane 62073, La Grande OR 97850. **Tel** (503)963-6697. **ED** Leeh J. Inghels. **LC**

Genealogy and Heraldry

E184.B2; N48. **DD** 929/.1/0893932073. Index available. cum. index. **Circ:** 350. ***Continues*** *Newsletter (Belgian Researchers (Organization)).*

US/0749-6168
BELL FAMILY NEWSLETTER, THE. **Main/Corp** Marrs, Janet Kay. Issue No. 1 (Jan. 1984)-. Newsletter. English. mo. Jan Marrs, 912 East 6th Street, Newburg OR 97132. **LC** CS71; .B45196. **DD** 929/.2/0973. **UDC** 929.53(73).

US/0884-6510
BENNETT EXCHANGE, THE. [Bennett exch.]. English. qt. $7.50. Miller Families Exchanges, PO Box 31, Napa CA 94559. **LC** PAR. **DD** 929. **UDC** 929.52(73). ***Continues*** *Bennett Exchange Newsletter.*

US/0275-1720
BENSON MAGAZINE OF RESEARCH. Vol. 1, No. 1 (May 1980)-. English. sa. $7.00. Christine Knox Wood, 2410 47th Street, Lubbock TX 79412. **LC** CS71; .B46993. **DD** 929/.2/0973. **UDC** 929.52(73).

US/0734-0214
BENSON TRACE, THE. V. 1, No. 1 (April/June 1980)-. Periodical. English. qt. cost on request only. Nettie Lee Benson, 2834 Shoal Crest, Austin TX 78705. **Tel** (512)472-2735. **ED** Nettie Lee Benson. **LC** CS71; .B46992. **DD** 929/.2/0973. **UDC** 929.52(73). Index available. **Bk Rev. Circ:** 300 (ctrl).
Desc: Devoted to tracing Benson families in the United States from 1607 to present from censuses historical sources, and personal communications from descendants.

US/0887-0713
BERKSHIRE GENEALOGIST, THE. [Berks. geneal.]. **Added/Corp** Berkshire Family History Association. Vol. 1 No. 1 (1982)-. Periodical. English. Four times a year (Feb., May, Aug., Nov.). $8.00 US; $12.00 Canada; $13.00 other. Berkshire Family History Association Inc, PO Box 1437, Pittsfield MA 01202. **Tel** (413)445-5521. **ED** Donald L. Lutes. **DD** 929. Index available. cum. index. **Bk Rev**, (Qty: 12). **Pr Rev. Circ:** 700 (ctrl).
Desc: Deals exclusively with resources and records of Berkshire County, Massachusetts area.
Ind/Abst Genealogical Period. Annu. Index.

US/0749-9108
BETHEL COURIER (BETHEL, ME 1976), THE. **See** History(General)-History of North, South, and Central America.

US/1073-838X
BEYOND GERMANNA. (19??)-. English. Six times a year. $10.00 (individuals), $5.00 (libraries). Beyond Germanna, PO Box 120, J. Blankenbaker, Chadds Ford PA 19317. **Tel** (215)388-1305. **ED** John Blankenbaker. Index available in last issue of volume--attached. **Bk Rev**, (Qty: 6). **Circ:** 250.
Ind/Abst Genealogical Period. Annu. Index.

US
BIENNIAL MEMBERSHIP BOOK / GENEALOGICAL FORUM OF PORTLAND, OREGON. **Main/Corp** Genealogical Forum of Oregon. **VFOAT** Membership Directory. P.Supplement. (1986)-. English. be. $18.00 (libraries & societies membership), $25.00 (individual membership), $35.00 (family membership), $51.00 (contributing membership), $99.00 (patron membership), 375.00 (single life membership), $500.00 (joint life membership). Genealogical Forum of Oregon, 1410 SW Morrison Street, Suite 812, Portland OR 97205. **Tel** (503)227-2398. **LC** F884.P853; A25a. **DD** 929/.1/02579549. ***Continues*** *Biennial Membership Book / The Genealogical Forum of Portland, Oregon, 0742-1397.*

US/0736-7074
BIG BEND REGISTER. **Added/Corp** Grant County Genealogical Society (Wash.). Vol. 1, No. 1 (Mar. 1980)-. English. qt. Free to members; $10.00 membership. Grant County Genealogical Society, 45 Alder Street Northwest, Public Library, Ephrata WA 98823. **Tel** (509)754-3971. **ED** Beverly Dell. **LC** F897.G75; B53. **DD** 929/.1/072079732. **Bk Rev. Ad Acc. Circ:** 100 (ctrl).
Desc: Contains obituaries, marriages, births, articles on local history, cemetery records, Grant county 1910 census, family records and queries.

US
BIIOGRAPHY AND GENEOLOGY MASTER INDEX. English. an. $299.00. Taft Group, 835 Penobscott Building, Customer Service, Detroit MI 48226. **Tel** (800)877-8238, FAX (313)961-6083.

US/0899-1707
BILLINGSLEY YESTERDAY & TODAY. (BILLINGSLEY YESTERDAY & TODAY / BY THE K.A.R.D. FILES.). [Billingsley yesterday today]. **Added/Corp** K.A.R.D. Files (Firm). **VFOAT** Billingsley Yesterday and Today. Vol. 1 (Oct. 1984)-. English. ir. $6.00 (per volume). Abshire Abstracts, 19305 Southeast 243rd Place, Kent WA 98042. **Tel** (206)432-1659. **ED** Judy K. Dye. **LC** CS71; .B6273a. **DD** 929/.2/0973. Index available. **Bk Rev.** ctrl circ.
Desc: Raw data regarding the Billingsley surname. Queries, lineages and data are published free of charge.

US/1066-4831
BILYEU BLOOD LINES. ***Title Change.*** [Bilyeu blood lines]. **VFOAT** Bilyeu Blood Lines Newsletter. Vol. 1, Issue 1 (Jan. 1993)-(1993). Periodical. English. qt. Bilyeu Blood Lines, 5628 60th Drive NE, Marysville WA 98270. **DD** 929. ***Continued by*** *Bilyeu/Workman Blood Lines, 1069-2738.*

US/0730-1316
BIOGRAPHY AND GENEALOGY MASTER INDEX. **See** Biographies.

US
BIOGRAPHY AND GENEALOGY MASTER INDEX. SUPPLEMENT. **See** Biographies.

US/0270-5583
BITS OF BARK FROM THE FAMILY TREE. **Added/Corp** Batesville Genealogical Society. Vol. 1 (1976)-. English. qt. $10.00. Batesville Genealogical Society, PO Box 3883, Batesville AR 72503-3883. **Tel** (501)793-7725. **ED** Mary Cooper Miller. **LC** F410; .B57. **DD** 929/.1/09767. **Circ:** 250.
Desc: Publishes genealogical information from independence and surrounding counties.

US/0523-7203
BLACK HILLS NUGGETS. **Added/Corp** Rapid City Society for Genealogical Research. (May 1968)-. Periodical. English. qt. $12.00. Rapid City Society of Genealogical Research, PO Box 1495, Rapid City SD 57701. **Tel** (605)343-1708. **ED** Genevieve Howard. Index available. **Bk Rev. Circ:** 300.
Desc: General genealogical helps; history of the area; cemetery readings, county and state records, stories of families, family group sheets, excerpts of helpful articles in other genealogy publications.
Ind/Abst Genealogical Period. Annu. Index.

GW/0006-4424
BLAETTER FUER FRAENKISCHE FAMILIENKUNDE. **Added/Corp** Gesellschaft fuer Familienforschung in Franken. (1926)-. Periodical. German. sa (2 issues). Price varies per volume. Gesellschaft fuer Familienforschung in Franken, Archivstrasse 17, W 8500 Nuernberg FR Germany. **LC** WMLC L 83/1816.

CN/0712-127X
BLAIN FAMILY NEWSLETTER, THE. [Blain fam. newsl.]. Vol. 1, No. 1 (Jan. 1981)-. Newsletter. English. sa. Free. The Blain Family Newsletter, c/o D H Blain, 6 Athlone Road, Cambridge Ontario N1R 1H8 Canada. **DD** 929/.2. **UDC** 929.52. ctrl circ.

US
BLA(Y)LOCK GENEALOGY NEWS, THE. **VFOAT** Blaylock Genealogy News; Blalock Genealogy News. Vol. 8, No. 6 (Nov./Dec. 1987)-. Periodical. English. bm. $18.00. Bla(y)lock Newsletter, Route 1 Box 1280, Ripley OK 74062. **Tel** (918)372-4405. **LC** CS71; .B647144. **DD** 929/.2/0973. ***Continues*** *Genealogy News of the Blalock-Blaylock Clans, 0882-5068.*

US/1056-6252
BLOUNT JOURNAL, THE. (THE BLOUNT JOURNAL: A PUBLICATION OF BLOUNT COUNTY GENEALOGICAL & HISTORICAL SOCIETY.). [Blount j.]. **Added/Corp** Blount County Genealogical & Historical Society (Blount County, Tenn.). Vol. 1, No. 1 & 2 (Nov. 1985)-. Periodical. English. sa. $10.00. Blount County Genealogical & Historical Society, PO Box 4986, Maryville TN 37802. **Tel** (615)982-5661. **ED** Dr. Elmer E. Mize Ph.d, 615 South Washington Street, Maryville, TN 37801-5045 (phone: (615)982-0302). **DD** 976. **Bk Rev. Pr Rev. Circ:** 350 (ctrl).
Desc: Information of an historical and/or genealogical nature concerning the history and people of Blount County, Tennessee.

US/0742-1389
BLUE BOOK (BALTIMORE, MD.). (BLUE BOOK.). **VFOAT** Baltimore Society Visiting List; Society Visiting List. English. an. $44.00. Blub Book, Inc., 229 North Charles Street, Baltimore MD 21201. **LC** F189.B13; B57. **DD** 929/.37526. **UDC** 929.5(752).

US/0278-8071
BLUE GRASS ROOTS. **Added/Corp** Kentucky Genealogical Society. **VFOAT** Bluegrass Roots. (1974)-. Periodical. English. qt. $10.00. Kentucky Genealogical Society, PO Box 153, Frankfort KY 40602. **Tel** (502)875-4452. **LC** F450; .B6. **DD** 929/.3769. **Bk Rev. Circ:** 1,500 (ctrl).
Desc: Contains articles and listings of Kentucky's counties: wills, marriages, land records, bibles, military, pensioners, book reviews, and members of genealogical queries, etc.

US/0743-183X
BLUE MOUNTAIN HERITAGE. **Added/Corp** Walla Walla Valley Genealogical Society. (1974)-. Periodical. English. qt (published seasonally). $8.00. Walla Walla Valley Genealogical Society, PO Box 115, Walla Walla WA 99362-0003. **Tel** (509)529-2534. **ED** Gayle Van Winkle Cavalli. **LC** F899.W2; B49. **DD** 929/.379748. **Bk Rev. Ad Acc. Circ:** 100 (ctrl).
Desc: Southeast Washington and Northeast Oregon records with genealogical interest and articles of general genealogical information.

US/0883-7775
BOATMAN NEWSLETTER. [Boatman newsl.]. No. 1 (Dec. 26, 1981)-. English. an. $5.00. Boatman Newsletter, c/o L. Swindell, 7009 65th Place, Tulsa OK 74133. **Tel** (405)234-3496. **DD** 929.

AG
BOLETIN DEL CENTRO DE ESTUDIOS GENEALOGICOS DE CORDOBA. **Added/Corp** Centro de Estudios Genealogicos de Cordoba. **VFOAT** Boletin. (19??)-. Periodical. Spanish. an. $3.00. Pasaje Chicoana 330, Cordoba Argentina. **Tel** 051-31236. **ED** Alejandro Moyano Aliaga. **LC** CS288.C67; B64. **DD** 929/.1/072082. **Bk Rev. Ad Acc. Circ:** 500.

US/0743-0957
BONNET-T-E'S & KIN, THE. **VFOAT** Bonnet-T-E'S and Kin. Vol. 1, 1 & 2 (June 1973)-. Periodical. English. ir. H Bonnett, 314 East Glenwood Road, Lake Forest IL 60045. **Tel** (312)234-4804. **ED** H T Bonnett. **LC** CS71; .B714723. **DD** 929/.2/0973. **UDC** 929.52. Index available. **Circ:** 450.
Desc: The publication is a vehicle for disseminating genealogical information about Bonnet-t-e and allied families. The information is obtained from published sources, public records and family members.

US
BOONE COUNTY HISTORIAN. Vol. 1 (Dec. 1978)-. Periodical. English. Four times a year (Mar., June, Sept., Dec.). $10.00 (individuals), $25.00 (institutions); $20.00 (individuals), $35.00 (institutions) Comes with Boone County Historical & Railroad Society membership. Boone County Historical and Railroad Society, Box 1094, Harrison AR 72601. **ED** Sammie Rose & Virginia Phillips, (phone: (501)741-3312). Documents available from the publisher.
Desc: Contains genealogical data and general Boone County area history; and also Oak Leaves, reporting historical information about the Missouri and Arkansas Railroad.
Ind/Abst Ozark Period. Index (19??-199?).

US/0145-5060
BOONE SCOUT OF THE BOONE FAMILY ASSOCIATION OF WASHINGTON, THE. (THE BOONE SCOUT.). [Boone scout Boone Fam. Assoc. Wash.]. Began with Oct. 1956 issue. Periodical. English. qt. Boone Family Association of Washington, 2068 Interlaken East, Seattle WA 98112. **LC** CS71; .B725A. **DD** 929/.2/0973. **UDC** 929.52(73).

CN/0826-8428
BOTTIN QUEBECOIS DES CHERCHEURS EN GENEALOGIE. [Bottin que. cherch. geneal.]. **Added/Corp** Federation des Societes d'Histoire du Quebec. Conseil de Genealogie. Federation des Societes d'Histoire du Quebec. (1984)-. Periodical. French. te. Limited free distribution. Secretariat de la Federation des Societes d'Histoire du Quebec, 4544 Ave Pierre-de-Coubertin, Montreal Quebec H1V 3R2. **DD** 929/.1/025714.

NE
BRABANTSE LEEUW, DE. (19??)-. Periodical. Dutch. Four times a year. F37.50 Netherlands; F40.50 others. Noordbrabants Genootschap, Postbus 1104, 5200 BD der Bosch Netherlands. **Tel** 011 31 73 139484. **ED** L. Adriaensseu. **LC** WMLC L 82/303. Index available. cum. index. **Bk Rev. Ad Acc. Circ:** 500. available on diskette.

US/0892-9238
BRADFORD COMPACT NEWSLETTER. (BRADFORD COMPACT NEWSLETTER / THE GOVERNOR WILLIAM BRADFORD COMPACT.). [Bradford Compact newsl.]. **Added/Corp** Governor William Bradford Compact. **VFOAT** Descendants of Governor William Bradford of Plymouth Colony, The Governor William Bradford Compact. Spring (1987)-. Newsletter. English. an. $8.00. Bradford Compact Newsletter, Attn: Mrs. Mary Ellen E. Pogue, Governor William Bradford Compact, 5204 Kinwood Avenue, Chevy Chase MD 20815-6604. **Tel** (301)654-7233. **ED** John M. Pogue, M.D. **DD** 929. **Bk Rev**, (Qty: varies). **Acid Free. Circ:** 570. ***Continues*** *Newsletter (Governor William Bradford Compact), 0892-9246.*
Desc: A newsletter of the Governor William Bradford Compact, a genealogical society in existence since 1946, with information on the society's meetings, current events, new books, projects, genealogical and other information on descendants of Governor William Bradford of Plymouth Colony. Has essays, obituaries, art work, photographs, news notes, and a president's letter.

CN/0383-7505
BRANCH NOTES / WATERLOO-WELLINGTON BRANCH, ONTARIO GENEALOGICAL SOCIETY. **Main/Corp** Ontario Genealogical Society

Waterloo-Wellington Branch. Began with June 1973 issue. Periodical. English. qt. $7.00 U.S. Waterloo-Wellington Branch of Ontario Genealogical Society, PO Box 603, Kitchener Ontario N2G 4A2 Canada. **Tel** (519)578-8945. **ED** Frances Hoffman. **LC** CS88.W37; O57A. **DD** 929/.1/06271342. **UDC** 929.5(713). **Bk Rev. Circ:** 500 (ctrl).
Desc: Genealogy of Waterloo and Wellington counties in Ontario.

US
BRANCHES AND ACORNS. Vol. 1, No. 1 (Sept. 1985)-. Periodical. English. qt. Southwest Texas Genealogical Society, El Progresso, 129 Nopal Street, Uvalde TX 78801. **LC** F385; .B76. **DD** 929/.1/0720764. **UDC** 929.5(764).

US/0742-9851
BRANCHES & TWIGS : NEWSLETTER OF GENEALOGICAL SOCIETY OF VERMONT. **Added/Corp** Genealogical Society of Vermont. **VFOAT** Branches and Twigs. (Winter 1972)-. Newsletter. English. qt. $20.00 US; $25.00 Canada; $30.00 other. Genealogical Society of Vermont, PO Box 422, Pittsford VT 05763. **Tel** (802)483-2957. **ED** Carol Church. **LC** F48; .B73. **DD** 929/.1/0720743. **Bk Rev**, (Qty: 24). **Circ:** 1,250.
Desc: Members submit queries, articles, cemetary lists, Bible records and other material especially focusing on Vermont genealogical records.
Ind/Abst Genealogical Period. Annu. Index.

US/8755-9749
BRANCHING OUT FROM ST. CLAIR COUNTY, ILLINOIS. **Added/Corp** Marissa Historical and Genealogical Society. **VFOAT** Branching Out from Saint Clair County, Illinois. Vol. 1, No. 2 (Winter 1974)-. Periodical. English. Four times a year (Feb., May, Aug., Nov.). $15.00. The Marissa Historical and Genealogical Society, PO Box 47, Marissa IL 62257. **Tel** (618)295-2562. **LC** F547.S2; B73. **DD** 929/.377389. available on microfiche; available on microfilm. ***Continues*** *Branching Out from St. Clair County, 8755-9757.*

CN/0848-841X
BRANTCHES - ONTARIO GENEALOGICAL SOCIETY. BRANT COUNTY BRANCH. (BRANTCHES.). [Brantches - Ont. Geneal. Soc., Brant Cty. Branch]. **Added/Corp** Ontario Genealogical Society. Brant County Branch. **VFOAT** Branches. Vol. 9, No. 4 (Sept. 1989)-. Periodical. English. bm. Free to members. Brant County Branch OGS, PO Box 2181, Brantford Ontario N3T 5Y6 Canada. **Tel** 753-4140. **DD** 929.1/072071347. ***Continues*** *Newsletter (Ontario Genealogical Society. Brant County Branch), 0824-4804.*

US/0896-7415
BREMER COUNTY BROWSINGS. (BREMER COUNTY BROWSINGS : NEWSLETTER OF THE BREMER COUNTY GENEALOGICAL SOCIETY.). **Added/Corp** Bremer County Genealogical Society. (198?)-. Periodical. English. Four times a year (Feb., May, Aug., Nov.). $6.00 Comes with Bremer County Genealogical Society membership. Bremer County Genealogical Society, 1378 Badger Avenue, Plainfield IA 50666. **Tel** (319)276-3234. **ED** Nancy Robinson. **DD** 929. **Circ:** 60-80 (ctrl).
Desc: Topics and articles of interest to genealogists. Includes various family group sheets, generation charts, news and events of the society.

US/8756-0445
BRENGLE BRANCHES. [Brengle branches]. (198?)-. Periodical. English. qt. $12.00. Charles Brengle, 6619 Pheasant Road #16, Baltimore MD 21220. **Tel** 335-3948. **ED** Charles Brengle. **DD** 929. **Circ:** 50.
Desc: To bring together our Brengle family.

US/0897-7879
BRICKER BRANCHES. [Bricker branches]. (1985)-. Periodical. English. qt. $7.35. Pioneer Publications, PO Box 397, Black Eagle MT 59414-0397. **Tel** (406)453-4266. **ED** Shirley Penna-Oakes. **LC** CS71; .B848763. **DD** 929/.2/0973. Index available. **Bk Rev. Ad Acc.**

US/0743-8958
BRIDGE BUILDER (SCHENECTADY, N.Y.), THE. (THE BRIDGE BUILDER.). Vol. 1, No. 1 (Feb. 1968)-. English. sa. $7.50. National Pontius Association, 126 Maplewood Estates, Scott Depot WV 25660-9744. **Tel** (518)374-1965. **ED** James W Pontius. **LC** CS71; .P79943. **DD** 929/.2/0973. Index available. cum. index. **Circ:** 310.
Desc: Devoted to research, education, and preservation of family history and genealogy.

CN/0840-7738
BRIDGING THE GAP (LANCASTER). ***Ceased.*** (BRIDGING THE GAP.). [Bridg. gap]. **Added/Corp** Glengarry Genealogical Society. Vol. 1, No. 5 (Sept./Oct. 1988)-Vol. 7 No. 4 (1994). Periodical. English. Six times a year. Alex W. Fraser Highland Heritage, Rural Route 1, Lancaster ONT K0C 1NO Canada. **Tel** (613)347-2363 or 3180. **ED** Alex W. Fraser and Rhoda Ross. **DD** 929/.1/072071377. **Bk Rev**, (Qty: varies). **Ad Acc**, **Adv Mgr:** Alex W. Fraser. **Pr Rev. Circ:** 115. ***Continues*** *Bi-Monthly News Notes (Glengarry Genealogical Society), 0842-9782.*

CN/0315-3835
BRITISH COLUMBIA GENEALOGIST, THE. **Added/Corp** British Columbia Genealogical Society. **VFOAT** B.C.G.S. Genealogist; BCGS Genealogist. Vol. 1 (Fall 1971)-. Periodical. English. Four times a year (Mar., June, Sept., Dec.). 30.00Can$. British Columbia Society, PO Box 88054, Richmond British Columbia V6X 3T6 Canada. **Tel** (604)270-6025. **ED** Grace Darney. **LC** CS88.B74; B77. **DD** 929.1/09711/05. **Bk Rev. Ad Acc. Circ:** 1,500 (ctrl).
Desc: Articles on British Columbia history and genealogy, aids to genealogical research, book reviews, and genealogical queries.
Ind/Abst Genealogical Period. Annu. Index.

US/0736-7066
BROOKS FAMILY QUERY EXCHANGE, THE. Vol. 1, Issue No. 1 (May 1980)-. Periodical. English. qt. $7.50. Madeline S Mills Editor, 3348 East 83rd Place, Tulsa OK 74136. **LC** CS71; .B869813. **DD** 929/.2/0973. **UDC** 929.52(73).

US
BROWER FAMILY CIRCLE, THE. V. 1- Apr. 1976-. Periodical. English. qt. Jay Brower, 350 Regents Boulevard, Tacoma WA 98466. **LC** CS71; .B878A. **DD** 929/.2/0973. **UDC** 929.52(53).

US/1068-9931
BROWN FAMILY NEWS AND GENEALOGICAL SOCIETY, THE. ***Ceased.*** [Brown fam. news geneal. soc.]. **VFOAT** Brown Family News & Genealogical Society; Brown Family; Brown Family News. Vol. 20, Issue no. 1 (Mar. 1, 1991)-(1993). Periodical. English. tq. Hal Gordon Brown, 19 Terrace Street, Keene NH 03431. **LC** CS71; .B88b. **DD** 929/.2/0973. ***Continues*** *Brown Family, 0147-0019.*

UK
BROWNE RECORDS. No. 1- Jan. 1978-. Periodical. English. qt. £2.50. 51 Amersham Hill, High Wycombe England. **LC** CS71; .B88A. **DD** 929/.2/0973. **UDC** 929.52(73).

CN/0849-0848
BRUCE & GREY BRANCH OF O.G.S. (BRUCE & GREY BRANCH OF O.G.S. (NEWSLETTER)). [Bruce Grey Branch O.G.S.]. **Added/Corp** Ontario Genealogical Society. Bruce and Grey Branch. **VFOAT** Bruce & Grey Branch of the Ontario Genealogical Society. Vol. 15, (Mar. 1985)-. Periodical. English. qt (Feb., May, Aug., Nov.). 12.00Can$ (with membership). Ontario Genealogical Society / Bruce & Grey Branch, Box 66, Owen Sound Ontario N4K 5P1 Canada. **ED** Wendy Bachiu. **DD** 929/.1/06071318. **Circ:** 700 (ctrl). ***Continues*** *Branches of Bruce and Grey., 0703-9506.*
Desc: Branch news and tips on doing genealogical research.

CN/1184-7387
BRUCE BULLETIN. [Bruce bull.]. **Added/Corp** Bruce County Genealogical Society. Vol. 2, Issue 1 (Feb. 1991)-. Bulletin. English. qt. Free to members. Bruce County Genealogical Society, General Delivery, Port Elgin Ontario N0H 2C0 Canada. **DD** 929/.1/06071321. ***Continues*** *Bruce County Genealogical Society Newsletter., 1185-0353.*

US/0146-1990
BRYANT BACKTRAILS. V. 1- Jan./Mar. 1977-. Periodical. English. qt. $12.95. Kenma Publishing Company, PO Box 2786, Evansville IN 47714. **LC** CS71; .B916A. **DD** 929/.2/0973. **UDC** 929.52(73).

US/0736-2463
BUFFALO CHIPS. ***Ceased.*** (BUFFALO CHIPS / FT. KEARNY GENEALOGICAL SOCIETY.). [Buffalo chips]. Vol. 1, No. 1 (Spring 1978)-Ceased ?. Periodical. English. qt. Ft Kearney Genealogical Society, Box 22, Kearney NE 68848. **Tel** (308)237-7010. **ED** Luaine Smith. **LC** F687.B85; B83. **DD** 929/.378245. **UDC** 929.5(782). **Circ:** 100 (ctrl).

US/1077-095X
BULLETIN (CALIFORNIA CENTRAL COAST GENEALOGICAL SOCIETY : 1993). (BULLETIN / SAN LUIS OBISPO COUNTY GENEALOGICAL SOCIETY, INC.). [Bulletin]. **Added/Corp** California Central Coast Genealogical Society. (19??)-. Periodical. English. Four times a year. $10.00. San Luis Ohispo County Genealogical Society, PO Box 4, Atascadero CA 93423-0004. **LC** F860; .C34a. **DD** 929/.1/072079478. ***Continues*** *San Luis Obispo County Genealogical Society, Inc., 1047-5893.*

US/1075-3605
BULLETIN / CAPE COD GENEALOGICAL SOCIETY. (19??)-. Bulletin. English. Four times a year. $10.00 membership. Cape Cod Genealogical Society, Brooks Library, Main Street, Harwich MA 02646. **Tel** (617)432-8593. **DD** 929. ***Continues*** *Bulletin of the Cape Code Genealogical Society, 0737-3279.*

US
BULLETIN / GENEALOGICAL FORUM OF OREGON, INC. Vol. 36, Quarterly No. 1 (Sept. 1986)-. Bulletin. English. qt. $10.00. Membership Chairman, 1410 Morrison Street/Room 812, Portland OR 97205. **Tel** (503)227-2398. **ED** Ruth C Bishop. **LC** CS42; .G456A. **DD** 929/.1/0720795. **UDC** 929.5(795). Index available. **Bk Rev. Ad Acc. Circ:** 950. ***Continues*** *Bulletin - Genealogical Forum of Portland, Oregon, Inc., 0433-3179.*
Desc: Covers vital records, Bible records, local history, book reviews and other materials of interest to local and family historians.
Ind/Abst Genealogical Period. Annu. Index.

US/0092-7953
BULLETIN - GENEALOGICAL SOCIETY OF OLD TYRON COUNTY. (BULLETIN.). **Main/Corp** Genealogical Society of Old Tryon County. Bulletin. English. qt. Genealogical Society of Old Tryon County, PO Box 745, Spindale NC 28160. **LC** F253; .G45A. **DD** 929/.3756. **UDC** 92935(756).

US/1047-6121
BULLETIN / GERMAN GENEALOGICAL SOCIETY OF AMERICA. ***Suspended.*** [Bull. - Ger. Geneal. Soc. Am.]. **Added/Corp** German Genealogical Society of America. **VFOAT** GGSA Bulletin. **VAT** German Genealogical Society of America Bulletin. Vol. 1, No. 1 (Oct. 1986)-Vol. 5, No. 5 (1993). Bulletin. English. mo. $15.00. German Genealogical Society of America, PO Box 291818, Los Angeles CA 90029. **Tel** (909)626-1362. **LC** E184.G3; B85. **DD** 929/.1/08931.
Desc: Award winning newsletter of German Genealogical Society of America. Packed with information for Americans of German descent.
Ind/Abst Genealogical Period. Annu. Index.

US/0363-8847
BULLETIN - HUDSON FAMILY ASSOCIATION, SOUTH. (HUDSON FAMILY ASSOCIATION, SOUTH, BULLETIN.). [Bull. - Hudson Fam. Assoc. South]. **Main/Corp** Hudson Family Association (South). Bulletin. English. Birdie P Hudson, 1211 S Mobeetie Street/Suite B2N, Wheeler TX 79095. **LC** CS71; .H885A. **DD** 929/.2/0973. **UDC** 929.52(73). ***Absorbed*** *Hudsoniana Bulletin., 1044-1743.*

CN/0842-5159
BULLETIN: KAWARTHA BRANCH, ONTARIO GENEALOGICAL SOCIETY, THE. [Bull. - Kawartha Branch, Ont. Geneal. Soc.]. **Added/Corp** Ontario Genealogical Society. Kawartha Branch. Vol. 9, No. 1 (Jan. 1984)-. Periodical. English. qt. 8.00Can$. Ontario Genealogical Society / Kawartha Branch, Kawartha Branch, P.O.Box 162, Peterborough ONT K9J6Y8 Canada. **Tel** (705)745-8334. **DD** 929/.1/0607136. ***Continues*** *Kawartha Branch Bulletin., 0842-5140.*

CN/1183-4455
BULLETIN LA PARENTELE : BULLETIN DE L'ASSOCIATION DES FAMILLES MARCHAND. [Bull. parent.]. **Added/Corp** Association des Familles Marchand. **VFOAT** Parentele. Vol. 1, No 1 (Winter 1991)-. Bulletin. French. qt. Free for Members. Association des Familles Marchand, CP 117, Montreal Quebec H1X 3B6 Canada. **DD** 929/.2/0971.

US/1070-8677
BULLETIN - NORTHERN ARIZONA GENEALOGICAL SOCIETY. (THE BULLETIN.). [Bull. - North. Ariz. Geneal. Soc.]. **Added/Corp** Northern Arizona Genealogical Society. (198?)-. Bulletin. English. qt (4 issues). Free to members. Northern Arizona Genealogical Society, PO Box 695, Prescott AZ 86302. **Tel** (602)445-4783. **DD** 929.
Ind/Abst Genealogical Period. Annu. Index.

US/0887-5413
BULLETIN OF THE GLOUCESTER COUNTY HISTORICAL SOCIETY. **See** History(General)-History of North, South, and Central America.

US/0091-8857
BULLETIN OF THE WATAUGA ASSOCIATION OF GENEALOGISTS. [Bull. Watauga Assoc. Geneal.]. (1972)-. English. sa. Watauga Association of Genealogists, PO Box 117, Johnson City TN 37601. **DD** _a929/.373.
Ind/Abst Genealogical Period. Annu. Index.

US
BULLETIN OF THE WEST-CENTRAL KENTUCKY FAMILY RESEARCH ASSOCIATION. Bulletin. English. $15.00. West Central Kentucky Family Research Association, PO Box 1932, Owensboro KY 42302. **Tel** (502)684-4150.
Ind/Abst Genealogical Period. Annu. Index.

US/0748-2507
BULLETIN OF THE WHATCOM GENEALOGICAL SOCIETY. **Added/Corp** Whatcom Genealogical Society. (Nov. 1970)-. Bulletin. English. qt. comes with membership. Whatcom

Genealogical Society, PO Box 1493, Bellingham MA 98227. **Tel** (206)734-4673. **LC** F897.W57; B85. **DD** 929/.1/072079773. ***Continues** Whatcom Genealogical Society. Whatcom Genealogical Society : [Bulletin].*
Ind/Abst Genealogical Period. Annu. Index.

US/0742-8472
BULLETIN / OVERHOLSER FAMILY ASSOCIATION. [Bull. - Overholser Fam. Assoc.]. **Added/Corp** Overholser Family Association. **VFOAT** Overholser Family Association Bulletin. Vol. 1, No. 1 (Feb. 1979)-. Bulletin. English. sa. Free. Overholser Family Association, 413 Appletree Road, Camp Hill PA 17011. **Tel** (215)828-2464. **ED** John Oswald. **LC** CS71; .O12293. **DD** 929/.2/0973. **Circ:** 450 (ctrl).
Desc: News of members, genealogical queries, news of reunions, and contributions by members.

US/1056-568X
BULLETIN / POLISH GENEALOGICAL SOCIETY, CALIFORNIA. [Bull. - Pol. Geneal. Soc. Calif.]. **Added/Corp** Polish Genealogical Society, California. **VFOAT** Polish Genealogical Society California Newsletter; Polish Genealogical Society California Bulletin. (19??)-. Bulletin. English. Four times a year (Jan., Apr., July, Oct.). $20.00 Comes with Polish Genealogical Society membership/California Chapter. Polish Genealogical Society - California, PO Box 713, Midway City CA 92655. **ED** Jacque Penstone (editor's address: PO Box 651, Midway City, CA 92655, phone: (714)890-1618). **DD** 929. **Bk Rev. Ad Acc. Pr Rev. Circ:** 300 (ctrl).
Desc: Devoted to Polish researchers whether researching in the US or any others countries.

CN/0048-9182
BULLETIN - SASKATCHEWAN GENEALOGICAL SOCIETY. Main/Corp Saskatchewan Genealogical Society. Vol. 1 (Apr. 1970)-. Bulletin. English (French). qt. 30.00Can$; $30.00 other. The Saskatchewan Genealogical Society, 1870 Lorne Street, Box 1984, Regina Saskatchewan SP4 2L7 Canada. **Tel** (306)780-9207, FAX (306)781-6021. **ED** Marie Suedahl. **Bk Rev. Circ:** 1,100 (ctrl).
Desc: Articles on research and methodology, book reviews, updates on library additions and queries.

US/0559-2526
BULLETIN - SEATTLE GENEALOGICAL SOCIETY. Main/Corp Seattle Genealogical Society. (19??)-. Bulletin. English. qt. $20.00. Seattle Genealogical Society, PO Box 1708, Seattle WA 98111. **Tel** (206)522-8658. **ED** Sally Gene Mahoney. **LC** CS42; .S412. **DD** 929/.2/0973. Index available (included in each issue). **Bk Rev**, (Qty: 100+). **Ad Acc. Circ:** 1800.
Desc: 60 page genealogical publication of a non-profit educational society, containing how-to, original research, publication of old records from various sources and other articles in the field.
Ind/Abst Genealogical Period. Annu. Index.

US
BULLETIN - WATAUGA ASSOCIATION OF GENEALOGISTS. Main/Corp Watauga Association of Genealogists. V. 1- Winter/Spring 1972-. Bulletin. English. sa. East Tennessee State University / Sherrod Library, Room 301, Johnson City TN 37601. **LC** CS42; .W37A. **DD** 929/.373. **UDC** 929.5(73).
Desc: Winter/spring issue includes directory of members.

US/0883-9069
BULLETIN / WESTERN RESERVE HISTORICAL SOCIETY. GENEALOGICAL COMMITTEE. [Bull. - West. Reserve Hist. Soc., Geneal. Comm.]. **Added/Corp** Western Reserve Historical Society. Genealogical Committee. **VFOAT** Genealogical Committee Bulletin. (198?)-. Bulletin. English. Four times a year (Jan., Apr., July, Oct.). $4.00. Western Reserve Historic Society, 10825 East Boulevard, Cleveland OH 44106. **Tel** (216)721-5722, FAX (216)721-0645. **ED** Gina Hamister. **DD** 929. **Bk Rev**, (Qty: 4).
Desc: Family search is a collection of easy to use files on compact discs developed to help individuals search for information about their ancestors which was developed and is the property of The Church of Jesus Christ of Latter-Day Saints.

US/0513-6776
BULLETIN - YAKIMA VALLEY GENEALOGICAL SOCIETY. (BULLETIN.). **Main/Corp** Yakima Valley Genealogical Society. Vol. 1 (1969)-. Bulletin. English. qt. $12.00. Yakima Valley Genealogical Society, Box 445, Yakima WA 98907. **Tel** (509)248-1328. **ED** Ellen Brzoska (editor's address: 402 West Nob Hill Blvd., Yakima WA 98902-4536; editor's phone:(509)453-2626). **LC** DS42; .Y34. **DD** 929.2. Index available (bound in Dec. issue). **Bk Rev**, (Qty: as received). **Ad Acc. Pr Rev. Circ:** 550.
Desc: Concerns Yakima, and surrounding counties. Contains miscellaneous records and genealogical queries. New acquisitions and society publications for sale.
Ind/Abst Genealogical Period. Annu. Index.

US/0892-5895
BULLETIN - YELL COUNTY HISTORICAL & GENEALOGICAL ASSOCIATION (ARK.). (BULLETIN / YELL COUNTY HISTORICAL & GENEALOGICAL ASSOCIATION.). [Bull. - Yell Cty. Hist. Geneal. Assoc. (Ark.)]. **Added/Corp** Yell County Historical & Genealogical Association (Ark.). **VFOAT** Yell County Historical & Genealogical Association Bulletin. (19??)-. Bulletin. English. Three times a year. $15.00. Yell County Historical Genealogical Association, PO Box 622, Dardanelle AR 72834. **DD** 929. ***Continues** Yell County Historical & Genealogical Society Bulletin.*

US
BUNKER BANNER / BUNKER FAMILY ASSOCIATION OF AMERICA. Vol. 1, No. 1-. English. qt. $10.00 US; $12.00 other. Editor B Banner, 9 Sommerset Road, Turnersville NY 08012. **Tel** (609)589-6140. **ED** Carole Bunker. **LC** CS71; .B93793. **DD** 929/.2/0973. **UDC** 929.52(73). Index available. **Bk Rev. Circ:** 500 (ctrl).
Desc: Includes genealogical information as well as articles and events of general interest by or about Bunkers and information about family reunions.

US/1071-7013
BURBANK BANNER. [Burbank banner]. Issue 34/35 (June 1991)-. Periodical. English. Four times a year. $4.00. John R. Burbank, 31 Congress Street, St Albans VT 05478. **Tel** (802)524-3529. **LC** CS71; .B94483. **DD** 929/.2/0973. ***Continues** Burbank Family News, 0736-4040.*

US/0736-4040
BURBANK FAMILY NEWS. ***Title Change.*** [Burbank fam. news]. Issue 2 (June 1980)-(199?). Periodical. English. qt. John R. Burbank, 31 Congress Street, St Albans VT 05478. **Tel** (802)524-3529. **ED** John R. Burbank. **LC** CS71; .B94483. **DD** 929/.2/0973. **Circ:** 175. ***Continues** Burbank, 0736-4032. **Continued by** Burbank Banner, 1071-7013.*
Desc: A genealogical newsletter of the Burbank/Burbanck families in America with an emphasis on updating the 1928 genealogy by George Burbank Sedgley.

US/0882-5653
BURIED TREASURES. (BURIED TREASURES : A QUARTERLY PUBLICATION OF THE CENTRAL FLORIDA GENEALOGICAL AND HISTORICAL SOCIETY.). **Added/Corp** Central Florida Genealogical & Historical Society. Vol. 10 No. 4 (Oct. 1978)-. Periodical. English. Four times a year (Jan., Apr., July, Oct.). $20.00 (one year); $25.00 (family) Comes with Central Florida Genealogical & Historical Society membership. Central Florida Genealogical and Historical Society Inc., PO Box 177, Orlando FL 32802. **Tel** (407)351-9282. **ED** Dorothy McAdams Westenhofer. **LC** F310; .N48. **DD** 929/.1/0720759. Index available. **Bk Rev. Circ:** 225 (ctrl). available on microfilm. ***Continues** Newsletter (Central Florida Genealogical & Historical Society), 0882-1194.*
Desc: Includes family histories, Bible records, wills, cemetery records, tombstone inscriptions and queries; includes a geographical and surname index, articles from the Central Florida area and items from other state sources.

UK
BURKE'S IRISH FAMILY RECORDS. 5th-Ed.; 1976-. English. ir. Burkes Peerage Ltd, 56 Walton Street, London SW3 1RB England. **UDC** 929.52(415). ***Continues** Burke's Genealogical and Heraldic History of the Landed Gentry of Ireland, 0068-4260.*

US/0730-1405
BURLESON FAMILY BULLETIN. [Burleson fam. bull.]. Vol. 1, No. 1 (Aug. 1981)-. Bulletin. English. qt. Burleson Family Association, PO Box 155, Karnes City TX 78118. **Tel** (512)780-2533. **LC** CS71; .B96063. **DD** 929/.2/0973. **UDC** 929.52(73).

US/0730-4978
BURNETT FAMILY NEWSLETTER. Vol. 1, No. 1 (Apr./June 1981)-. Newsletter. English. qt. $15.00 US; $20.00 (surface mail), $25.00 (airmail) other. Burnett Family Genealogical Association, 3891 Commander Drive, Chamblee GA 30341-0016. **Tel** (404)455-6445. **ED** Thomas Robley Burnett. **LC** CS71; .B96393. **DD** 929/.2/0973. **UDC** 929.52(73). Index available. cum. index. **Bk Rev. Circ:** 100 (ctrl). available on microfiche.
Desc: Contains census and other vital statistics' indexes; ancestor charts, family group worksheets; biographicals, news articles on Burnetts' and other spellings.

US/1071-0523
BUSH-MEETING DUTCH, THE. **See** Religion and Theology.

US/1070-8243
BUSHWHACKER MUSINGS : VERNON COUNTY HISTORICAL SOCIETY NEWSLETTER. **See** History(General)-History of North, South, and Central America.

US
C.C.G.S. NEWSLETTER. Main/Corp Clark County Genealogical Society. **VFOAT** CCGS Newsletter. (19??)-. Periodical. English. Ten times a year. $12.00 Clark County Genealogical Society membership. Clark County Genealogical Society / Washington, PO Box 2728, Vancouver WA 98668. **Tel** (206)256-0977. **LC** Discard.

FR/0339-9354
CAHIERS D'HERALDIQUE. [Cah. her.]. (1975)-. Periodical. French. Leopard d'Or, 8 Rue de Couedic, F-75014 Paris France. **Tel** 011 33 1 43275798. **UDC** 9.

CN/0225-9303
CAHIERS GEN-HISTO. [Cah. gen-histo]. No. 1- Oct. 1979-. Periodical. French. $4.00 per number. Groupe d'Etudes Gen-Histo Inc, 9249 24 E Avenue, Montreal Quebec H1Z 4A2 Canada. **DD** 929/.2/09714. **UDC** 929.5(714).

FR/0756-9750
CAHIERS SAVOYARDS DE GENEALOGIE. [Cah. savoyards geneal.]. No. 1 (1982)-. French. an. **LC** CS597.S4; C33. **DD** 929/.1/07204448.

CN/0049-1098
CAHIERS--SOCIETE HISTORIQUE ACADIENNE, LES. **See** History(General)-History of North, South, and Central America.

US/0747-4849
CALDWELL COUNTY GENEALOGICAL SOCIETY, INC. (CALDWELL COUNTY GENEALOGICAL SOCIETY : NEWSLETTER.). Newsletter. English. qt. $10.00. Caldwell County Genealogical Society Inc, PO Box 2476, Lenoir NC 28645. **Tel** 754-5806. **ED** John O Hawkins. **LC** F262.C15; N48. **DD** 929/.1/0720756845. **UDC** 929.5(756). **Bk Rev. Circ:** 225 (ctrl). ***Continues** Newsletter (Caldwell County Genealogical Society), 0742-9533.*
Desc: Publishes county records and genealogical information. Queries accepted.
Ind/Abst Genealogical Period. Annu. Index.

US/0895-8939
CALVERT CO. MARYLAND GENEALOGY NEWSLETTER. VFOAT Calvert County Maryland Genealogy Newsletter; Calvert Co. Md. Genealogy Newsletter. Vol. 2, No. 4 (July 1987)-. Newsletter. English. mo. $12.00 (US); $15.00 (other). Calvert County Maryland Genealogy Newsletter, PO Box 9, Sunderland MD 20689. **Tel** (301)535-0829. **ED** Mildred E O'Brien. **LC** F187.C15; C35. **DD** 929/.1/072075244. **Bk Rev. Ad Acc. *Continues** Calvert County Genealogy Newsletter, 0895-8939.*

US/1041-1240
CANADIAN ANCESTRAL TIES. Periodical. English. ir. $6.00 (single issue). Images Past Publications, PO Box 852, Pullman WA 99163-0852.

US/0732-0590
CANADIAN COUNTY CONNECTIONS. ***Ceased.*** Vol. 1, No. 1-Ceased Vol. 10, No. 4 (Nov. 1987). Periodical. English. qt. Canadian County Genealog Soc, PO Box 866, El Reno OK 73036. **LC** F702.C18; C36. **DD** 929/.1/072076639. **UDC** 929.5(71).

CN/0824-6637
CANADIAN ROSE ROOTS. [Can. Rose roots]. Vol. 1, No. 1 (Winter 1983)-. Periodical. English. qt. $12.00. Canadian Rose Roots, c/o S R Mooney, PO Box 3, Plenty Saskatchewan S0L 2R0 Canada. **DD** 929/.2. **UDC** 929.5(71).

US/0094-6907
CANTWELL TAPESTRY, A. Added/Corp Cantwell-Conteville Family Association. Vol. 1 (Jan. 1974)-. Periodical. English. qt. $8.00. Cantwell-Conteville Family Association, Rural Route 1, Reese Road, Clayton NY 13624. **ED** Gene Cantwell. **LC** CS71; .C237a. **DD** 929/.2/0973.

US/0885-4718
CAPITAL (RHINEBECK, N.Y.), THE. (THE CAPITAL.). Vol. 1, No. 1 (1st Quarter 1986)-. Periodical. English. qt. $14.00 US; $16.00 other. Kinship, 60 Cedar Heights Road, Rhinebeck NY 12572. **Tel** (914)876-4592. **ED** Arthur C.M. Kelly. **LC** F127.A3; C37. **DD** 929/.374741. Index available. cum. index. **Bk Rev. Ad Acc. Circ:** 200.

US/0882-5181
CAQUELIN CHRONICLE, THE. [Caquelin chron.]. Began with: No. 1, issued in Nov. 1982. Periodical. English. Three times a year. $5.00. Velma G Clark, 3933 Zoozer Drive, Jackson MS 39212. **DD** 929. **UDC** 929.5(73).

US/0008-6029
CAR-DEL SCRIBE. ***Ceased.*** [Car-del scr.]. (1963)-Ceased Vol. 26, No. 4. Periodical. English. bm. Car-Del Publications, Box 73, Ludlow MA 01056-0073. **Tel** (413)543-5804. **ED** Elizabeth Bentley. **LC** CS1; .C34. **DD** 929.1/05. **UDC** 929.5(73). Index available. **Bk Rev. Ad Acc. Circ:** 1,700. ***Absorbed** Missing Links.*
Desc: How-to articles, reader queries, book and serial reviews.

Genealogy and Heraldry

US/0363-440X
CAROLINAS GENEALOGICAL SOCIETY BULLETIN, THE. Main/Corp Carolomas Genealogical Society. Bulletin. English. qt. $10.00. Carolinas Genealogical Society, 2005 Irby Road, Monroe NC 28110. **Tel** (704)283-2933. **ED** Frances Small. **LC** F253; .C35B. **DD** 929/.2/0973. **UDC** 929.5(756). **Bk Rev. Circ:** 250 (ctrl).

US/0363-1826
CAROLINAS GENEALOGICAL SOCIETY YEARBOOK. Main/Corp Carolinas Genealogical Society. **Added/Corp** Carolinas Genealogical Society. Yearbook. (19??)-. English. an. 306 South Thompson Street, Monroe NC 28110. **LC** F253; .C35a. **DD** 929/.1/09756.

US/0740-6673
CARPENTER AND RELATED FAMILY HISTORICAL JOURNAL, THE. Vol. 1, No. 1 (Jan./Mar. 1981)-. Periodical. English. qt. $10.00. Carpenter and Related Family Historical Journal, PO Box 1356, Bowling Green KY 42101-1004. **Tel** (502)842-7803. **ED** James A. Carpenter. **LC** CS71; .C2977. **DD** 929/.2/0973. **Circ:** 280. ***Continues*** *Carpenter and Related Family Paper, 0740-9400.*

US/8755-7207
CARPENTER FAMILY COURIER. [Carpenter fam. cour.]. Vol. 1, No. 1 (April 1985)-. Periodical. English. Twice a year (Apr., & Oct.). $15.00. Courier Publications, PO Box 1320, Winnfield LA 71483. **Tel** (318)628-2019. **DD** 929.

US/0892-2152
CARROLL CABLES. [Carroll cables]. Vol. 1, No. 1 (April 1987)-. Periodical. English. qt. $10.00. Kinseeker Publications, Box 184, Grawn MI 49637. **ED** V Wilson. **DD** 929. **Bk Rev. Ad Acc. Circ:** 50.
Desc: Contains genealogical information on Carroll families.

US/0734-5682
CARROLL COUNTY GENEALOGICAL QUARTERLY. Added/Corp Carroll County Genealogical Society (Ga.). Vol. 1, No. 1 (Spring 1980)-. Periodical. English. Four times a year. $15.00. Carroll County Genealogical Society, PO Box 576, Carrollton GA 30117. **Tel** (404)832-6138. **ED** Shirley Gardner. **LC** F292.C19; C37. **DD** 929/.1/072075839. Index available. **Bk Rev. Circ:** 225 (ctrl).

US/0747-4873
CARROLL COUSINS. (CARROLL COUSINS / CARROLL COUNTY GENEALOGICAL SOCIETY.). [Carroll cousins]. **Added/Corp** Carroll County Genealogical Society (Ohio). Vol. 5, No. 1 (Jan. 1982)-. Periodical. English. mo. Carroll County Genealogical Society / Ohio, 59 Third Street NE, Carrollton OH 44615. **LC** F497.C2; N48. **DD** 929/.1/072077167. ***Continues*** *Newsletter (Carroll County Genealogical Society Ohio), 0747-4865.*

US/0882-1631
CARROLLTONIAN. [Carrolltonian]. Periodical. English. qt. Carroll County Genealogical Society / Maryland, 50 East Main Street, Westminister MD 21157. **Tel** (301)848-4250. **LC** F187.C25; C38. **DD** 929/.1/072075277. **UDC** 929.5(752). **Circ:** 250.
Ind/Abst Genealogical Period. Annu. Index.

US/0749-4890
CARTMEL, CARTMELL, CARTMILL FAMILY QUARTERLY, THE. VFOAT CCC Family Quarterly; C.C.C. Family Quarterly. No. 1 (Fall 1979)-. Periodical. English. qt. $18.95. William Patrick Cartmel, Box 7074, Bend OR 97708. **LC** CS71; .C32514. **DD** 929/.2/0973.

US/0092-7694
CASON QUARTERLY, THE. Spring 1973-. Periodical. English. qt. $6.00. William R Cason, The Cason Family Association, PO Box 88393, Atlanta GA 30338. **LC** CS71; .C33933. **DD** 929/.2/0973. **UDC** 929.5(73).

●US/1074-5742
CASS COUNTY CONNECTIONS. Added/Corp Cass County Genealogical Society. Vol. 18, No. 4 (Dec. 1992)-. Periodical. English. Four times a year (Mar., June, Sept., Dec.). $10.00. Cass County Genealogical Society, PO Box 880, Atlanta TX 75551. **Tel** (903) 796-6750. **ED** Mary Echols, (editor's address: Rt. 1 Box 80, Bivins, TX 75555, phone: (903)796-0553). **LC** F392.C29; C38. **DD** 929/.1/0720764195. Index available (Bound in 4th issue (Dec.)). **Bk Rev. *Continues*** *Cass County Genealogical Society Quarterly.*

US
CASS COUNTY GENEALOGICAL SOCIETY QUARTERLY. ***Title Change.*** **Added/Corp** Cass County Genealogical Society. **VFOAT** Quarterly. (198?)-(1992). English. Four times a year (Mar., June, Sept., Dec.). Cass County Genealogical Society, PO Box 880, Atlanta TX 75551. **Tel** (903) 796-6750. **ED** Mellodene Banks. **LC** F392.C29; C38. **DD** 929/.1/0720764195. Index available. **Bk Rev.** ctrl circ. ***Continues*** *The Cass County Genealogical Society, 0737-190X.* ***Continued by*** *Cass County Connections, 1074-5742.*

UK
CATHOLIC ANCESTOR. English. Three times a year. £8.00 UK; £12.00 other. Catholic Family History Society, 2 Winscombe Crescent, c/o Ms. Murray, Ealing London W5 1AZ England. **Tel** 011 081 9978115. **ED** A.G. Butler (editor's address: 6 Wyndcroft Close, Enfield, Middlesex EN27BJ; phone: 011 081 3636484). **Bk Rev.** ctrl circ. ***Continues*** *ECA Journal.*
Desc: Articles on history of Catholic families in great Britain.

US/0738-1905
CEDAR TREE, THE. ***Ceased.*** **Added/Corp** Northeast Iowa Genealogical Society. (1971)-(1992). Periodical. English. an. Northeast Iowa Genealogical Society, c/o Grout Museum of History and Science, 503 South Street, Waterloo IA 50701. **Tel** (319)235-0489. **ED** Mrs Robert W Ross. **LC** CS42; .C35. **DD** 929/.1/072073. **Bk Rev. Ad Acc. Circ:** 130.
Desc: Each issue features a Black Hawk County, Iowa township and includes history, 1860 census, cemetery records, etc. of township featured.

US/0743-4979
CELLE NEWSLETTER. No. 5 (Jan. 1970)-. Newsletter. English. qt. $1.75. Carolyn Cell Choppin, 17524 Eagle Bend Boulevard, Jacksonville FL 32226-1110. **Tel** (904)751-2515. **ED** Carolyn Cell Choppin. **LC** CS71; .S45964. **DD** 929/.2/0973. **UDC** 929.5(73). Index available. cum. index. **Bk Rev. Ad Acc. Circ:** 120 (ctrl). available on diskette (5.25). ***Continues*** *Cell Newsletter, 0743-4960.*
Desc: Issues of queries, records, history, and genealogy of the American Cell(e), Gsell(e), Seal(e), Sell(s), Sill(s), Zell(e) families primarily of Pennsylvania German origin.

●US/1071-8729
CEMETERIES OF THE U.S. (CEMETERIES OF THE U.S. : A GUIDE TO CONTACT INFORMATION FOR U.S. CEMETERIES AND THEIR RECORDS.). **Added/Corp** Gale Research, Inc. (1993)-. English. te. $149.95. Gale Research Inc., 835 Penobscot Building, Detroit MI 48226. **Tel** (800)877-GALE, (313)961-2242, FAX (313)961-6083, telex TWX 810-221-7086. **ED** Deborah Burek.
Desc: Contains basic contact information, descriptions and citations for sources of further information for approximately 8,000 operating and up to 7,000 closed cemeteries.

US
CENTRAL ALABAMA GENEALOGICAL SOCIETY : NEWSLETTER. Added/Corp Central Alabama Genealogical Society. Vol. 1, No. 1 (Sept. 24, 1975)-. Newsletter. English. qt (Jan., Apr., July, Oct.). $12.50. Central Alabama Genealogical Society, PO Box 125, Selma AL 36702. **Tel** (205)874-9290. **ED** June Carter. **LC** F325; .C4. **DD** 929/.1/0720761. Index available. **Bk Rev. Circ:** 350 (ctrl).

US/0577-0807
CENTRAL ILLINOIS GENEALOGICAL QUARTERLY. [Cent. Ill. geneal. q.]. **Main/Corp** Decatur Genealogical Society. Vol. 1 (Oct. 1965)-. Periodical. English. qt (Mar., June, Sept., Dec.). $15.00 single; $20.00 family. Decatur Genealogical Society, PO Box 1548, Decatur IL 62525. **Tel** (217)429-0135. **ED** Martha Pulliam (phone: (217)876-8761. **DD** 929. **Bk Rev**, (Qty: 20-25). **Circ:** 800 (ctrl).
Desc: Articles on Macon County, Illinois families, subjects, and Bible records. Includes other articles on other Illinois counties and other states.
Ind/Abst Genealogical Period. Annu. Index.

US/0095-1439
CENTRAL KENTUCKY RESEARCHER. [Cent. Ky. res.]. **Added/Corp** Taylor County Historical Society. Vol. 1 (Jan. 1971)-. Periodical. English. qt (Feb., May, Aug., Nov.). $7.50. Taylor County Historical Society, PO Box 14, Campbellsville KY 42719. **Tel** (502)465-8748. **ED** Aileen McKinley and Gwynette Sullivan. **LC** F457.T25; C45. **DD** 929/.3769/673. Index available. cum. index. **Circ:** 300.
Desc: Twenty-one pages of historical research.
Ind/Abst Am. Hist. Life.

US/0883-9603
CENTRAL MONTANA WAGON TRAILS. (CENTRAL MONTANA WAGON TRAILS / LEWISTOWN GENEALOGY SOCIETY.). **Added/Corp** Lewistown Genealogy Society. Vol. 1, No. 1 (Aug. 1979)-. Periodical. English. Four times a year (Feb., May, Aug., & Nov.). $6.00. Lewistown Genealogy Society, 701 West Main, Lewistown MT 59457. **Tel** (406) 538-5212. **ED** Mary Ann Quiring. **LC** F730; .C46. **DD** 929/.1/0720786. Index available in last issue of volume--attached. **Bk Rev. Ad Acc. Circ:** 125 (ctrl).

US/1043-4895
CENTRAL VIRGINIA HERITAGE. [Cent. Va. herit.]. **VFOAT** CVGA Heritage. Vol. 2, No. 3 (Fall 1984)-. Periodical. English. Four times a year (Jan., Apr., July, Oct.). $12.50 (individuals), $15.00 (family). Central Virginia Genealogical Association, PO Box 5583, Charlottesville VA 22905-5583. **Tel** (804)295-1861. **LC** F225; .C42. **DD** 929/.1/0720755; 929. Index available. cum. index. **Bk Rev**, (Qty: 50). **Circ:** 200. ***Continues*** *Central Virginia Genealogical Association, 1046-6533.*
Desc: Articles on Central Virginia Genealogy.
Ind/Abst Genealogical Period. Annu. Index.

US/0749-5684
CERTIFIED COPY, THE. (THE CERTIFIED COPY / GREATER CLEVELAND GENEALOGICAL SOCIETY.). **Added/Corp** Greater Cleveland Genealogical Society. Vol. 1, No. 2 (Aug. 1972)-. Periodical. English. Four times a year. $9.00. Greater Cleveland Genealogical Society, Box 40254, Cleveland OH 44140. **Tel** (216)871-3286. **LC** F499.C653; A24. **DD** 929/.1/072077132. Index available. cum. index. **Circ:** 250 (ctrl). available on microfilm. ***Continues*** *Greater Cleveland Genealogical Society, 0749-5676.*
Desc: Abstracts of vital records; cemetery and church.
Ind/Abst Genealogical Period. Annu. Index.

US/1058-5133
CGS NEWS - CALIFORNIA GENEALOGICAL SOCIETY. (CGS NEWS : A PUBLICATION OF THE CALIFORNIA GENEALOGICAL SOCIETY.). [CGS news - Calif. Geneal. Soc.]. **Added/Corp** California Genealogical Society. (19??)-. Periodical. English. Six times a year. $30.00 Comes with California Genealogical Society membership. California Genealogical Society, 300 Brannan Street, Suite 409, San Francisco CA 94107. **Tel** (415)777-9936. **(Subscription address:** California Genealogical Society, PO Box 77105, San Francisco CA 94107.) **LC** F865; .N58. **DD** 929/.1/0720794. ***Continues*** *Newsletter (California Genealogical Society), 8756-694X.*

US/1056-2095
CGS NEWSLETTER. [CGS newsl.]. **Added/Corp** Colorado Genealogical Society. **VAT** Colorado Genealogical Society newsletter. Vol. 15, No. 3 (Mar. 1991)-. Newsletter. English. mo. Colorado Genealogical Society, PO Box 9218, Denver CO 80209. **Tel** (303)571-1535. **DD** 929. ***Continues*** *Newsletter, 1040-340X.*

US/0882-987X
CHAMBERLAIN ASSOCIATION NEWS. [Chamberlain Assoc. news]. Series 2, V. 1, No. 1 (Jan. 1981)-. Periodical. English. Three times a year. Chamberlain Association, 1303 Weatherstone Drive, c/o F Forbes, Paoli PA 19301. **ED** Helen H Woodro. **LC** CS71; .C44293. **DD** 929/.2/0973. **UDC** 929.52(73). Index available. cum. index. **Circ:** 300 (ctrl).

US/0736-2390
CHAMBERS HELPING CHAMBERS. [Chambers help. Chambers]. (19??)-. Periodical. English. Twice a year. $12.00. Claudette Maerz, PO Box 37010, Bloomington MN 55431. **Tel** (613)257-5355, (612)881-4864. **ED** Claudette Maerz. **LC** CS71; .C44393. **DD** 929/.2/0973. **Circ:** 200.
Desc: A publication for people interested in the name Chambers.

US/0277-2086
CHAMPAIGN COUNTY GENEALOGICAL SOCIETY QUARTERLY. [Champaign Cty. Geneal. Soc. q.]. **Main/Corp** Champaign County Genealogical Society. **Added/Corp** Champaign County Genealogical Society. Quarterly. Vol. 1, No. 1 (Fall 1979)-. Periodical. English. qt. comes with membership. Champaign County Genealogical Society, 201 South Race Street, Urbana IL 61801. **Tel** (217)367-4025. **ED** Fonda D. Baselt. **LC** F547.C4; C47a. **DD** 929/.1/072077366. Index available. cum. index. **Bk Rev. Circ:** 320 (ctrl).
Desc: Includes courthouse records, cemetery listings, ancestry, book reviews, census, Bible records, free queries, county history, lineage charts, newspaper gleanings, naturalizations, maps, announcements, etc.
Ind/Abst Genealogical Period. Annu. Index.

US/0883-1181
CHAPMAN CHATTER. [Chapman chatter]. Began in 1983?. Periodical. English. qt. $12.00. Chapman Chatter, 1403 Kingsford Drive, Florissant MO 63031. **DD** 929. **UDC** 929.5(73).

US/1046-5901
CHARBONNEAU CONNECTION. [Charbonneau connect.]. (1984)-. Periodical. English. qt (4 issues). $5.00. Charbonneau Connection, 9040 Farley Road, Pinckney MI 48169. **ED** Milton E. Charboneau (editor's telephone: (313)878-3680). **DD** 929.

US/0737-2655
CHART AND QUILL. Added/Corp Northeastern Nevada Genealogical Society. Vol. 1, Book 1 (May 1979)-. Periodical. English. sa (Spring and Fall). $25.00 institution. Northeastern Nevada Genealogical Society, PO Box 1903, Elko NV 89801. **Tel** (702)738-4071. **ED** Judy Swett. **LC** F840; .C43. **DD** 929/.1/0720793. Index available. **Bk Rev. Ad Acc. Circ:** 100 (ctrl).
Desc: Genealogical information from northeastern Nevada and society member research material.

US
CHEROKEE FAMILY HISTORY. English. sa. $6.50. Cherokee Family Researcher, 516 North 38th Street, Mesa AZ 85205. **Tel** (602)832-1467. **ED** Donna

Williams. Index available. **Ad Acc. Circ:** 100 (ctrl).
Desc: Queries and information to help with research on Indian ancestry.

US
CHEROKEE FAMILY RESEARCHER. (19??)-. English. Twice a year (Spring & Fall). $7.95. Cherokee Family Researcher, 516 North 38th Street, Mesa AZ 85205. **Tel** (602)832-1467. **ED** Donna Williams. Index available. cum. index. **Bk Rev. Ad Acc. Circ:** 300.
Ind/Abst Genealogical Period. Annu. Index.

US/1073-8363
CHEROKEE TRACER, THE. (1991)-. English. Four times a year (Jan., Apr., July, Oct.). $20.00. Cherokee Tracer, 5802 East 22nd Place, Tulsa OK 74114. **Tel** (918)835-1031. **ED** Marybelle W. Chase. Index available (Back issues in 1991 & 1992, 4 issues sets, ($20.00)).
Desc: News and information for the Cherokee Indian genealogical research.

US/0882-1208
CHESAPEAKE COUSINS. (CHESAPEAKE COUSINS / UPPER SHORE GENEALOGICAL SOCIETY OF MARYLAND.). **Added/Corp** Upper Shore Genealogical Society of Maryland. Vol. 1, No. 1 (Aug. 1974)-. Periodical. English. sa (June and December). comes with membership. Upper Shore Genealogical Society of Maryland, PO Box 275, Easton MD 21601. **Tel** (301)364-5336. **LC** F187.E2; C43. **DD** 929/.1/07207521. Index available. cum. index.

US/0363-4493
CHESTNUT TREE, THE. Periodical. English. mo. Piere Chastain Family Association, 1100 East Teresa, Sapulpa OK 74066. **LC** CS71; .C488A. **DD** 929/.2/0973. **UDC** 929.5(73).

US/0009-3556
CHICAGO GENEALOGIST. [Chic. geneal.]. **Added/Corp** Chicago Genealogy Club. (1969)-. Periodical. English. Four times a year (Jan., Apr., July, Oct.). $16.00. Chicago Genealogical Society, PO Box 1160, Chicago IL 60690. **Tel** (312)725-1306. **ED** Ms. Kathy O'Leary. **LC** CS1; .C45. **DD** 929.1/09773/11. cum. index. **Bk Rev**, (Qty: 11). **Circ:** 800 (ctrl). ***Continues*** *Chicago Genealogy Club Newsletter.*
Ind/Abst Genealogical Period. Annu. Index.

US
CHILDREN OF THE AMERICAN REVOLUTION MAGAZINE. Added/Corp National Society, Children of the American Revolution. **VFOAT** CAR Magazine. Vol. 23, No. 2 (March 1933)-. Periodical. English. Four times a year (Mar., June, Sept., Dec.). $6.00. Children of the American Revolution, 1776 D Street Northwest, Washington DC 20006. **Tel** (202)638-3153. **ED** Tami Ambrose. **LC** E202.9; .A13. **DD** 369/.13. **Circ:** 5,000 (ctrl). ***Continues*** *Children of the American Revolution.*

CN/1192-8190
CHINOOK (CALGARY. 1993). (CHINOOK : THE JOURNAL OF THE ALBERTA FAMILY HISTORIES SOCIETY.). [Chinook]. **Added/Corp** Alberta Family Histories Society. (1993)-. Periodical. English. qt. $30.00 institutions; $25.00 individuals. Alberta Family Histories Soc., PO 30270 Station B, Calgary Alberta T2M 4P1. **Tel** (403)255-8660. **DD** 929/.2/097123. ***Continues*** *Alberta Family Histories Society Quarterly., 0228-9288.*

US
CHISHOLM TRAIL, THE. Vol. 1, No. 1 (Jan. 1982)-. Periodical. English. qt. $12.00 US. Williamson County Genealogical Society, PO Box 585, Round Rock TX 78664. **ED** Linda Emry. **UDC** 929.5(73). Index available. **Bk Rev. Ad Acc. Circ:** 230.

US/0897-408X
CHRISTIAN COUNTY GENEALOGICAL SOCIETY. (CHRISTIAN COUNTY GENEALOGICAL SOCIETY : [QUARTERLY].). [Christ. Cty. Geneal. Soc.]. **Added/Corp** Christian County Genealogical Society (Christian County, Ill.). **VFOAT** Christian County Genealogical Quarterly; CCGS. (198?)-. Periodical. English. qt. Free to members. Christian County Genealogical Society, PO Box 174, Taylorville IL 62568. **Tel** (217)824-9435. **DD** 929.
Ind/Abst Genealogical Period. Annu. Index.

US/0196-8947
CHRISTIAN CROSE FAMILY NEWSLETTER. V. 1, Issue No. 1 (July 1976)-. Newsletter. English. Henry A Hamann, 5907 Walton Avenue, Camp Springs MD 20748. **LC** CS71; .C95193. **DD** 929/.2/0973. **UDC** 929.52(73).

US/0893-2921
CHRONICLES (PHILADELPHIA, PA.). (CHRONICLES / JEWISH GENEALOGICAL SOCIETY OF PHILADELPHIA.). [Chronicles]. **Added/Corp** Jewish Genealogical Society of Philadelphia. (198?)-. Periodical. English. Four times a year. $20.00 (individuals within 100 miles of Philadelphia), $12.00 (outside Philadelphia) US; $15.00 other. Jewish Genealogical Society of Philadelphia, 332 Harrison Avenue, Elkins Park PA 19027-2662. **Tel** (215)635-3263. **ED** Tammy Pegg. **DD** 929. **Bk Rev. Ad Acc.** ctrl circ. ***Continues*** *Newsletter (Jewish Genealogical Society of Philadelphia).*

CN/0711-0359
CHRONIQUES DE LA DROUINERIE, LES. [Chron. Drouinerie]. V. 1 No. 1 (Jan./June 1981)-. Periodical. French. sa. $3.00 members, $3.75 nonmembers. Societe Historique de Drouin d'Amerique, CP 7362, Vanier Ontario K1L 8E3 Canada. **DD** 929/.2. **UDC** 929.5(71).

US/0741-8264
CIRCUIT RIDER (SPRINGFIELD, ILL.), THE. (THE CIRCUIT RIDER.). **Added/Corp** Sangamon County Genealogical Society of Illinois. (19??)-. Periodical. English. Four times a year (Jan., Apr., July, Oct.). $12.00 Comes with Sangamon County Genealogical Society membership. Sangamon County Genealogical Society, PO Box 1829, Springfield IL 62705. **Tel** (217)529-0542. **ED** Manford R. White (phone: (217)546-9238). **LC** F547.S3; C57. **DD** 929/.377356. Index available. **Bk Rev. Pr Rev. Circ:** 450 (ctrl).
Desc: Genealogy and historical events primarily in areas in and near Sangamon County in Illinois.
Ind/Abst Genealogical Period. Annu. Index.

US/1047-4358
CLACKAMAS LEGACY. Added/Corp Clackamas County Family History Society (Clackamas County, Or.). Vol. 1, No. 1 (July, Aug., Sept. 1988). Periodical. English. qt. $12.00 (includes membership). Clackamas County Family Historical Society, Post Office Box 995, Oregon City OR 97045. **Tel** (503)786-0166. **DD** 929.

US
CLALLAM COUNTY GENEALOGICAL SOCIETY BULLETIN. Bulletin. English. Four times a year. $12.00 Comes with Clallam County Genealogical Society membership. Clallam County Genealogical Soceity, 223 East 4th Street, Port Angeles WA 98362. **Tel** (206)452-3821.

US/0731-3845
CLAN CHATTER. (CLAN CHATTER / MACDUFFEE CLAN OF AMERICA.). Periodical. English. qt. PO Box 5006, Albany NY 12205. **LC** CS71; .M138395. **DD** 929/.2/0973. **UDC** 929.52(73).

US/8755-3635
CLAN DIGGER. Periodical. English. mo. $10.00. Pacific County Genealogical Society, PO Box 843, Ocean Park WA 98640. **ED** Kathleen Johnson. **LC** F897.P2; C47. **DD** 929/.379792. **UDC** 929.5(797). **Bk Rev. Circ:** 100 (ctrl). ***Continues*** *South Pacific County Genealogical Society.*
Desc: Book reviews, genealogy conferences and work shops, queries, genealogy information.
Ind/Abst Genealogical Period. Annu. Index (?-?).

CN/0226-2436
CLANDIGGER (EDMONTON). (THE CLANDIGGER / THE ALBERTA GENEALOGICAL SOCIETY, EDMONTON BRANCH.). [Clandigger]. **Added/Corp** Alberta Genealogical Society. Edmonton Branch. (1980)-. Periodical. English. qt. 10.00Can$. Alberta Genealogical Society / Edmonton Branch, PO Box 12015, Edmonton Alberta T5J 3L2 Canada. **Tel** (403)424-4429. **ED** R. Muriel Jones. **DD** 929/.1/06071233. **Bk Rev. Circ:** 400 (ctrl).
Desc: Articles mainly of interest to those in Edmonton and the surrounding 50-mile radius.

US/0883-2692
CLARK CLARION, THE. [Clark clar.]. (1977)-. Periodical. English. qt. $8.00. Merle Ganier, 2108 Grace Street, Fort Worth TX 76111. **Tel** (817)838-5727. **LC** CS71; .C5993. **DD** 929/.2/0973. **Bk Rev. Circ:** 100 (ctrl).
Desc: Provides data and communication for researchers of Clark, Clerk and Clarke families.

US
CLARK COUNTY KIN. Added/Corp Ohio Genealogical Society. Clark County Chapter. (Jan. 1983)-. English. qt. $7.00. Clark County Genealogical Society / Ohio, PO Box 1412, Springfield OH 45501. **LC** F497.C5; C53. **DD** 929/.1/072077149.
Ind/Abst Genealogical Period. Annu. Index.

US/0883-7716
CLEARY NEWS. (19??)-. Periodical. English. Four times a year. $12.00. The Cleary News, c/o Stephen A. Lamb, 2983 Bayside Court, Wantagh NY 11793. **Tel** (516)826-7273. **ED** Stephen A. Lamb. **DD** 929. **Bk Rev. Ad Acc. Circ:** 150 (ctrl).
Desc: Family name association, specializing in the surname Cleary.

US/0883-0940
CLOUD FAMILY JOURNAL. (CLOUD FAMILY JOURNAL : CFJ.). [Cloud fam. j.]. **Added/Corp** Cloud Family Association. **VFOAT** CFJ. Vol. 7, No. 1 (1984-1985)-. Periodical. English. Four times a year (Jan., Apr., July, Oct.). $20.00 Comes with Cloud Family Association Membership. Cloud Family Association, 400 Mountain Drive, Santa Barbara CA 93103. **Tel** (713)781-6803. **ED** Jan Cloud. **LC** CS71; .C64263. **DD** 929/.2/0973. **Circ:** 200. ***Continues*** *Cloud Family Newsletter, 0736-1947.*
Desc: Publish primary source material and family data on persons with the surname Cloud-all branches, all locales.

UK/0010-003X
COAT OF ARMS, THE. [Coat arms]. **Added/Corp** Heraldry Society (Great Britain). Vol. 1, No. 1 (1950)-. Periodical. English. qt. £14.50. Heraldry Society, 44-45 Museum Street, London WC1A 1LY England. **Tel** 011 44 71 430 2172. **ED** J.P. Brooke-Little, Rachel Cullen. Index available. **Bk Rev. Ad Acc. Circ:** 1,200.
Ind/Abst BHA : Biblio. Hist. Art; MLA Int. Bibl. Books Artic. Mod. Lang. Lit.

US
COATNEY/COURTNEY EXCHANGE. English. qt. $9.00. Carol Peterson, Box 536, Freeman SD 57029. **Tel** (605)925-7186. **ED** Carol Peterson. **Bk Rev. Ad Acc.**
Desc: Family trees, history and census records pertaining to Coatney/Courtney genealogy.

US/0891-5296
COCKRELL CONNECTION, THE. [Cockrell connect.]. Vol. 1, Issue 1 (Jan. 1986)-. Periodical. English. Four times a year. $12.00. The Cockrell Connection, 505 Church Street, Brenham TX 77833. **Tel** (409)830-9116. **DD** 929. Index available. cum. index. **Bk Rev. Ad Acc. Circ:** 85.

US
COFFEY COUNTY FOOTPRINTS. (19??)-. English. Four times a year. $16.00. Coffey County Genealogical Society, c/o Della Meyer, 712 Sanders, Burlington KS 66839. **Tel** (316) 364-8795.

US/0749-758X
COFFEY COUSINS' CLEARINGHOUSE. VFOAT CCC; C.C.C. No. 1 (Jan. 1981)-. Periodical. English. qt. $8.00. Coffee Cousins' Clearinghouse, 1416 Green Berry Road, Jefferson City MO 65101. **Tel** (314)635-9057. **ED** L.N. Coffey. **LC** CS71; .C67393. **DD** 929/.2/0973. Index available. cum. index. **Bk Rev. Circ:** 150.
Desc: Information about the Coffee/Coffey families of North America.

US/0887-1264
COLE CHRONICLE. [Cole chron.]. (1986)-. Periodical. English. qt. $15.00. Clovis Byars Herring, Route 1 Box 123A, Buffalo TX 75831. **Tel** (214)322-5462. **DD** 929. Index available. cum. index. **Bk Rev. Circ:** 1,250.
Desc: Covers the surname Cole.

US/1060-0949
COLLIN CHRONICLES. [Collin chron.]. **Added/Corp** Collin County Genealogical Society. Vol. 1, No. 1 (Jan.-Feb. 1981)-. English. qt (4 issues). $15.00. Collin County Genealogical Society, Box 865052, Plano TX 75086. **Tel** (214)596-3567. **ED** Aurora Chancy. **LC** F392.C56; C64. **DD** 929/.1/0720764556. Index available. cum. index. **Bk Rev. Ad Acc. Circ:** 225.
Desc: Devoted to publication of the genealogical records of Collin County Texas.

US/0010-1613
COLORADO GENEALOGIST, THE. [Colo. geneal.]. **Added/Corp** Colorado Genealogical Society. Vol.1 (1939)-. Periodical. English. qt. $20.00. Colorado Genealogical Society, PO Box 9218, Denver CO 80209. **Tel** (303)571-1535. **ED** Birdie Monk Holslaw (editor's address: 7472 Mountain Sherman Street, Longmont CO 80503; editor's phone: (303)530-4054). **DD** 929. Index available (bound in fourth issue). cum. index. **Bk Rev. Ad Acc, Adv Mgr:** Barbara Henritze, **Tel** (303)499-3750. **Pr Rev. Circ:** 650 (ctrl). available on microfiche.
Desc: Information articles on methods of family research, genealogical records location and family history material.
Ind/Abst Genealogical Period. Annu. Index (?-?).

US/0896-9590
COLTON CLARION. [Colton clar.]. Vol. 1, No. 1 (Feb. 1988)-. Periodical. English. sa. $10.00. Surname Publications, PO Box 96, Broderick CA 95605. **Tel** (916)373-1262. **ED** Verna Ellis. **LC** CS71; .C72a. **DD** 929/.2/0973. **Bk Rev. Ad Acc. Circ:** 100.
Desc: Contains Colton family records, census biographies, diaries, etc.

US/8755-2914
COLUMBIA (RHINEBECK, N.Y.), THE. (THE COLUMBIA.). Vol. 1, No. 1 (1st Quarter 1985)-. Periodical. English. qt. $14.00 US; $16.00 Canada. Kinship, 60 Cedar Heights Road, Rhinebeck NY 12572. **Tel** (914)876-4592. **ED** Arthur C.M. Kelly. **LC** F127.C8; C694. **DD** 929/.1/072074739. Index available. cum. index. **Bk Rev. Ad Acc. Circ:** 200.
Desc: Contains subscriber's queries and vital records never before published.
Ind/Abst Am. Humanit. Index (?-199?).

US/0743-7919
COMPUTERIZED SURNAME MAGAZINE. [Comput. surname mag.]. Began in July 1981. Periodical. English. ir. $16.00. Genealogical Center Library, Box 88534, Atlanta GA 30356-8534. **LC** CS42; .C58. **DD** 929/.373. **UDC** 929.52.

UK/0263-3248
COMPUTERS IN GENEALOGY. See Computers-Microcomputers, Personal Computers.

US/0197-2103
CONNECTICUT ANCESTRY. Added/Corp Stamford Geneaological Society. Vol. 14, No. 2 (Nov. 1971)-. Periodical. English. qt. $20.00 US; $24.00 Canada; $26.00 other. Connecticut Ancestry Society Inc, PO Box 249, Stamford CT 06904. **Tel** (203)328-5173. **ED** Patricia F. Larrabee. **LC** CS42; .S75. **DD** 929/.1/05. Index available. cum. index. **Bk Rev**. **Circ:** 400 (ctrl). ***Continues*** *Stamford Genealogical Society. Bulletin of the Stamford Genealogical Society.*
Ind/Abst Genealogical Period. Annu. Index.

US/0045-8120
CONNECTICUT NUTMEGGER, THE. Added/Corp Connecticut Society of Genealogists. (June 1970)-. English. qt. $12.00. Connecticut Society of Genealogists Inc, Box 435, Glastonbury CT 06033. **Tel** (203)569-0002. **ED** Jacquelyn L. Ricker. **LC** F93; .C64. **Bk Rev**. **Ad Acc**. **Circ:** 4,300 (ctrl). ***Continues*** *Nutmegger, 0190-9495.*
Desc: Genealogies, bible records, vital records, surname listings, book reviews, articles, stories, church records.
Ind/Abst Genealogical Period. Annu. Index.

CN/0707-7130
CONNECTIONS (POINTE CLAIRE). (CONNECTIONS.). **Added/Corp** Societe de l'Histoire des Familles du Quebec. Vol. 1 (Sept. 1978)-. Periodical. English. Four times a year. $20.00 Comes with Quebec Family History Society membership. Quebec Family History Society, PO Box 1026 Postal Station, Pointe-Claire Quebec H9S 4H9 Canada. **Tel** (514)695-1502. **ED** C. Truesdell. **LC** CS88.Q4; C64. **DD** 929/.1/09714; 929/.3714. **Bk Rev**. **Ad Acc**. **Circ:** 800.
Desc: Concentrates on genealogy and family history about the English speaking people of Quebec.

US/0591-2083
COOS GENEALOGICAL BULLETIN. ***Ceased.*** **Main/Corp** Coos Genealogical Forum. **VFOAT** Bulletin. Vol. 1 (July 1964)-(June 1992). Bulletin. English. sa. Coos Genealogical Forum, PO Box 1067, North Bend OR 97459. **ED** Lona P Downing. **Ad Acc**. **Circ:** 150.
Desc: Genealogical information.

US/0098-4841
COPPER STATE BULLETIN. Added/Corp Arizona State Genealogical Society. Vol. 7, No. 1 (Fall 1971)-. Periodical. English. qt. $12.00. Arizona State Genealogical Society, PO Box 42075, Tucson AZ 85733. **Tel** (602)624-5206. **ED** Floyd Negley. **LC** F810; .C64. **DD** 929/.3791. **Bk Rev**. **Ad Acc**. **Circ:** 450 (ctrl). ***Continues*** *Bulletin (Southern Arizona Genealogical Society), 0584-4339.*
Desc: Covers Arizona and Southwest history.
Ind/Abst Genealogical Period. Annu. Index.

US/0739-0904
CORNERSTONE CLUES. Added/Corp Cornerstone Genealogical Society. Vol. 1 (1975)-. Periodical. English. qt (Feb., May, Aug., Nov.). $12.00. Cornerstone Genealogical Society, PO Box 547, Wayneburg PA 15370. **Tel** (412)627-5896. **ED** Norma T. Bell. **Circ:** 700 (ctrl).
Desc: Contains Greene County genealogical information - births, deaths, marriages - and local historical articles.

US/0731-8375
CORNSILK. (CORNSILK : QUARTERLY OF THE GENEALOGICAL SOCIETY OF DEKALB COUNTY, ILLINOIS.). **Added/Corp** Genealogical Society of DeKalb County, Illinois. **VFOAT** Cornsilk Quarterly; Cornsilk Quarterly, Dekalb Co., IL. Vol. 1, No. 1 (Spring 1982)-. Periodical. English. qt. $10.00. Dekalb County Historical and Genealogical Society, PO Box 295, Sycamore IL 60178. **ED** Gay Edens Carrigan. **LC** F547.D3; C63. **DD** 929/.377328/05. **Bk Rev**. **Circ:** 250.
Desc: Genealogy and history of DeKalb County Illinois. Research news and aids, and queries.
Ind/Abst Genealogical Period. Annu. Index.

US/0748-3309
CORYELL KIN. Added/Corp Coryell County Genealogical Society. Vol. 1, No. 1 (Jan. 1982)-. English. qt. $7.50 individual, $10.00 family. Coryell County Genealogical Society, 811 Main Street, Gatesville TX 76528. **Tel** (817)865-5367. **LC** CS71; .C83393. **DD** 929/.2/0973.

US/0883-7600
CORYELL NEWSLETTER. [Coryell newsl.]. Vol. 1 (Fall Ed. 1970)-. Newsletter. English. ir. Voluntary donations excepted, $0.25 back issues. Coryell Newsletter, PO Box 662, Santa Barbara CA 93102-0662. **Tel** (805)965-3749. **ED** N Burr Coryell. **DD** 929. **UDC** 929.52(73). **Bk Rev**. **Circ:** 200 (ctrl).
Desc: To record genealogy and secure family data of the Coryell-Coryell family. A one name study; four family lines.

US/1046-641X
COUNCIL OF GENEALOGY COLUMNISTS NEWSLETTER. [Counc. Geneal. Columnists newsl.]. **Added/Corp** Council of Genealogy Columnists. **VFOAT** CGC Newsletter. (1987)-. Periodical. English. qt. $15.00 US; $18.00 other. Council of Genealogy Columnists, 3607 Arlington, Lawton OK 73505. **Tel** (405)355-7432, FAX (405)355-7053. **ED** Aulena S. Gibson. **DD** 929. **Bk Rev**, (Qty: 350). **Pr Rev**. **Circ:** 80-90 (ctrl).

US/0888-2851
COUNTY LINE. English. qt (Mar., June, Sept., Dec.). $10.00. Genealogical Society of Bay County, PO Box 662, Panama City FL 32402. **Tel** (904)785-3457. **ED** Cliff Loper. **Bk Rev**, (Qty: 4). **Circ:** 100.
Desc: Bay county genealogical and historical articles, books, and upcoming events.

US/0888-2851
COUNTY LINE (PANAMA CITY, FLA.), THE. (THE COUNTY LINE.). [Cty. line]. **Added/Corp** Genealogical Society of Bay County (Fla.). (198?)-. Periodical. English. qt (Mar., June, Sept., Oct.). $10.00. Genealogical Society of Bay County, PO Box 662, Panama City FL 32402. **Tel** (904)785-3457. **ED** Cliff Loper. **DD** 929. **Bk Rev**, (Qty: 4). **Ad Acc**. **Circ:** 110.
Desc: Bay county, Florida genealogical and historical articles, book reviews, upcoming events, etc.
Ind/Abst Genealogical Period. Annu. Index.

US/1070-4922
COUNTY LINES (PRINCETON, IND.). (COUNTY LINES / GIBSON COUNTY HISTORICAL SOCIETY.). [Cty. lines]. **Added/Corp** Gibson County Historical Society. (199?)-. Periodical. English. mo. Gibson County Historical Society, PO Box 516, Princeton IN 47670. **Tel** (812)385-3874. **LC** F532.G4; G53. **DD** 929/.1/072077235. ***Continues*** *Gibson County Lines, 1053-4946.*

US/1058-2703
COUNTY SEAT SCRAPS. [Cty. seat scraps]. **Added/Corp** County Seat Genealogical Society--Primary Sources. Vol. 1, No. 1 (Jan. 1988)-. Periodical. English. qt. $12.00. County Seat Scraps, 310 Urban Street, Danville IN 46122. **Tel** (317)745-2628. **(Subscription address:** County Seat Scraps, c/o Betty Hadley, Sec./Treas., 172 S Road 225 East, Danville IN 46122.**) ED** Patricia J. Cox. **LC** F532.H5; C68. **DD** 929/.377253/05. Index available. **Circ:** 100.
Desc: Includes wills, deeds, miscellaneous records, and other genealogically related data.

US
COURIER OF HISTORICAL EVENTS. See History(General).

US/0882-8806
COURTNEY CHRONICLE. [Courtney chron.]. Vol. 1, No. 1 (Oct. 1983)-. Periodical. English. Four times a year (Jan., Apr., July, Oct.). $15.00. Courtney Chronicles S. Courtney, Rt. 1 Box 778, Pawnee IL 62558. **Tel** (217)625-7751. **LC** CS71; .C863514. **DD** 929/.2/0973.

US/0740-3046
COUSINS ET COUSINES. (COUSINS ET COUSINES : A NEWSLETTER FOR MEMBERS OF THE NORTHWEST TERRITORY FRENCH AND CANADIAN HERITAGE INSTITUTE, A SECTION OF THE MINNESOTA GENEALOGICAL SOCIETY.). **Added/Corp** Northwest Territory French and Canadian Heritage Institute. (Aug. 1978)-. Newsletter. English. qt. comes with membership. Northwest Territory Canadian and French Heritage Center, PO Box 26372, Brooklyn Center MN 55429. **Tel** (612)560-9086. **ED** Judith Bougie. **LC** F358.2.F85; C68. **DD** 929/.3/097705. **Bk Rev**. **Ad Acc**. **Circ:** 600 (ctrl). ***Continues*** *Digging for Roots.*

US/0736-2404
COWETA COUNTY GENEALOGICAL SOCIETY MAGAZINE. ***Title Change.*** [Coweta Cty. Geneal. Soc. maga.]. **Main/Corp** Coweta County Genealogical Society. Vol. 1, No. 1 (Spring 1982)-(19??). Periodical. English. qt. Coweta County Genealogical Society, PO Box 1014, Newman GA 30264. **Tel** (404)251-2877. **ED** Frances Christopher. **LC** F292.C8; C67a. **DD** 929/.3758423/05. **Circ:** 225. ***Continues*** *Norma's Coweta Chatter.* ***Continued by*** *Coweta Courier.*
Desc: Contains records of Coweta County, Georgia of interest to genealogists and historians. It also includes family information from throughout every region.
Ind/Abst Genealogical Period. Annu. Index.

US
COWETA COURIER. (19??)-. English. Four times a year. Free to members of the Coweta County Genealogical Society. Coweta County Genealogical Society, PO Box 1014, Newman GA 30264. **Tel** (404)251-2877. ***Continues*** *Coweta County Genealogical Society Magazine.*

US/1061-1088
CRABB NEWSLETTER, THE. [Crabb newsl.]. Vol. 1, No. 1 (Mar. 1991)-. Newsletter. English. qt. Richard Prall, 14104 Piedras Road NE, Albuquerque NM 87123. **DD** 929.

US
CRACKER CRUMBS. Added/Corp Manasota Genealogical Society. (1984)-. Periodical. English. qt. $8.00. Manasota Genealogical Society, 1405 4th Avenue West, Bradenton FL 34205. **Tel** (813)792-3006. **LC** F317.M2; N48. **DD** 929/.1/072075961. ***Continues*** *Newsletter (Manasota Genealogical Society : 1983).*
Ind/Abst Genealogical Period. Annu. Index.

US
CRAIG-LINKS. Vol. 1, No. 1 (Feb.-March 1980)-. Periodical. English. qt. $14.50. Martha Nell Craig, PO Box 645, Twain Harte CA 95383. **Tel** (209)586-4939. **ED** Martha Nell Craig. **LC** CS71; .C88548. **DD** 929/.2/0973. **UDC** 929.52(73). Index available. **Bk Rev**. **Circ:** 1,200.
Desc: Offers a forum for the sharing and publishing of information relating to any Craig, or related family. Research is conducted by individuals and shared with subscribers via our publication.

US/1059-0374
CRAWFORD COUNTY IOWA GENEALOGICAL SOCIETY. (CRAWFORD COUNTY IOWA GENEALOGICAL SOCIETY : [NEWSLETTER].). [Crawford Cty. Iowa Geneal. Soc.]. **Added/Corp** Crawford County Iowa Genealogical Society. **VFOAT** CCIGS Newsletter. (Nov. 1986)-. Periodical. English. qt (Feb., May, Aug., Nov.). $5.00. Crawford County Genealogical Society / Charter Oak, PO Box 29, c/o Nancy L Rosburg, Charter Oak IA 51439. **Tel** (712)263-3678. **ED** Nancy Rosburg (phone: (712)678-3454). **DD** 929. **Circ:** 55 (ctrl).
Desc: All included items refer to genealogy, both general and Crawford County, IA.

US/0883-1009
CROSS COUNTY GENEALOGICAL PUBLICATION. Vol. 1, No. 1 (Sept. 1982)-. Periodical. English. ir. Cross County Genealogical Society, PO Box 1274, Wynne AR 72396. **LC** F417.C95; C75. **UDC** 929.5(791).

US/0735-6196
CROSSROAD TRAILS. [Crossroad trails]. **Added/Corp** Effingham County Genealogical Society. **VAT** Cross Road Trails. Vol. 1, No. 1 (Summer 1980)-. Periodical. English. Ten times a year. $10.00. Effingham County Genealogical Society, PO Box 1166, Effingham IL 62401. **Tel** (217)342-2464. **ED** Eleanor Poe Bounds. **LC** F547.E4; C76. **DD** 929/.1/0720773796. Index available. **Bk Rev**. **Circ:** 250 (ctrl).
Desc: To promote and preserve genealogical data. Includes births, marriages, family charts, queries, deaths, obituaries, indexes, book reviews, cemetery readings, and other information.
Ind/Abst Genealogical Period. Annu. Index.

CN/0824-7730
DADSWELL FAMILY BULLETIN. [Dadswell fam. bull.]. No. 1 (Spring 1982)-. Bulletin. English. Twice a year. 5.00Can$. Dadswell Family Bulletin, c/o Barbara Balch Nethercott, 1310 Brydges Street, London Ontario N5W 2C4 Canada. **Tel** (519)451-7594. **ED** Barbara Balch Nethercott. **DD** 929/.2/05. Index available. **Circ:** 125 (ctrl).
Desc: Follow-up to "A Dadswell Family History and Genealogy C1560-1980", published 1980. Additions, corrections and updates in genealogy. Includes information not in the book received since publication.

US/1044-6524
DAKOTA COUNTY GENEALOGIST, THE. (THE DAKOTA COUNTY GENEALOGIST : NEWSLETTER OF THE DAKOTA COUNTY GENEALOGICAL SOCIETY.). [Dak. Cty. geneal.]. **Added/Corp** Dakota County Genealogical Society (Minn.). (Mar. 1987)-. Newsletter. English. qt. $10.00. Dakota County Genealogical Society, PO Box 74, South St Paul MN 55075. **Tel** (612)455-3626. **ED** Vicki Albu. **DD** 929. **Bk Rev**, (Qty: (2)). **Circ:** 300 (ctrl).
Desc: Newsletter for genealogists and historians with interest in families of Dakota County, Minnesota.
Ind/Abst Genealogical Period. Annu. Index.

US/0045-9518
DAKOTA TERRITORY. Vol. 1 (Fall 1969)-. Periodical. English. ir. $3.50. Dakota Territory, PO Box 372, Rapid City SD 57701. **LC** F650; .D34. **DD** 929.1/09783/05.

US/0890-8125
DALLAS QUARTERLY, THE. [Dallas q.]. **Added/Corp** Dallas Genealogical Society. Dallas Public Library. Vol. 30, No. 1 (Mar. 1984)-. Periodical. English. qt. Free to members. Dallas Genealogical Society, PO Box 25556, Dallas TX 75225. **LC** CS42; .D3. **DD** 929/.1/0973. Index available (Free). ***Continues*** *Dallas Genealogical Society. Quarterly - Dallas Genealogical Society, 0163-1381.*
Ind/Abst Genealogical Period. Annu. Index.

US
DARKE COUNTY KINDLING. English. ir. $9.00. Darke County Genealogical Society, PO Box 908, Greenville OH 45331. **Tel** (513)548-5250.

US/0011-7013
DAUGHTERS OF THE AMERICAN REVOLUTION MAGAZINE. See History(General)-History of North, South, and Central America.

US/0736-2633
DAVENPORT NEWSLETTER, THE. Vol. 1, No. 1 (Jan. 1979)-. Newsletter. English. qt. $9.00. Gene Davenport, 3510 McMillan, Tyler TX 75701. **LC** CS71; .D2464. **DD** 929/.2/0973. **UDC** 929.52(73). **Circ:** 165.

US/0893-5408
DAWSON COUNTY GENEALOGICAL NEWSLETTER. [Dawson Cty. geneal. newsl.]. **Added/Corp** Lexington Genealogy Society (Lexington, Neb.). Vol. 1, No. 1 (Sept. 1986)-. Periodical. English. Three times a year. $5.00. Lexington Genealogy Society, PO Box 778, Lexington NE 68850. **Tel** (308)324-2151. **DD** 929.

US/0743-216X
DAY RESEARCHER. **VFOAT** Day Family Researcher. (1983)-. Periodical. English. Four times a year. $15.00. Addie Paramore Howell, 319 Houston Lake Boulevard, Centerville GA 31028. **Tel** (912)953-3114. **ED** Addie P. Howell. **LC** CS71; .D27293. **DD** 929/.2/0973. Index available. **Circ:** 70 (ctrl).

UK
DEBRETT'S PEERAGE AND BARONETAGE. (1976)-. English. ir (published every 5 years). Debrett's Peerage Ltd., 73-77 Britannia Road, London SW6 2JY England. **Tel** 011 44 71 736 6524. **(Subscription address:** Macmillan Distribution Ltd. / UK, Brunel Road, Basingstoke, Hampshire RG21 2XS England.**)** **LC** CS420; .D32. **DD** 929.7/2. ***Continues*** *Debrett's Peerage, Baronetage, Knightage, and Companionage.*
Desc: Information on gentry, heraldry, knights and knighthood.

US/0418-4904
DEEP SOUTH GENEALOGICAL QUARTERLY. **Added/Corp** Mobile Genealogical Society. Vol. 1 No. 1; (Aug. 1963)-. Periodical. English. qt. comes with membership. Mobile Genealogical Society Inc, PO Box 6224, Mobile AL 36660. **Tel** (205)479-3512. **ED** Marie A. Nichols. **LC** CS42; .D4. **DD** 929. **Bk Rev. Circ:** 320.
Desc: Specializes in biographical and genealogical source material for Mobile, Alabama and the surrounding areas.
Ind/Abst Genealogical Period. Annu. Index.

●US/1062-6468
DELAWARE COUNTY GENEALOGIST. [Del. Cty. geneal.]. **Added/Corp** Delaware County Historical Alliance (Delaware County, Ind.). Vol. 1, No.1 Mar. (1992)-. Periodical. English. qt. $20.00. Delaware County Historical Alliance, PO Box 1266, Muncie IN 47308. **DD** 929.

US/0731-3896
DELAWARE GENEALOGICAL SOCIETY JOURNAL. **Added/Corp** Delaware Genealogical Society. Vol. 1, No. 1 (Oct. 1980)-. English. sa (Apr. & Oct.). Comes with Delaware Genealogical Society membership. Delaware Genealogical Society, 505 Market Street Mall, Wilmington DE 19801. **Tel** (302)478-3859. **ED** Caroline Sparks and Mary Richards. **LC** F163; .D35. **DD** 929/.3751. Index available (bound in all issues). **Pr Rev. Circ:** 250 (ctrl).
Desc: Publication of previously unpublished material useful for research on Delaware families.
Ind/Abst Genealogical Period. Annu. Index.

US/1065-4887
DELAWARE GENEALOGIST, THE. (THE DELAWARE GENEALOGIST : PUBLICATION OF THE DELAWARE COUNTY GENEALOGY SOCIETY, CHAPTER OF THE OHIO GENEALOGICAL SOCIETY.). [Del. geneal.]. **Added/Corp** Delaware County Genealogy Society. Vol. 1, No. 1 (Mar. 1985)-. Periodical. English. qt (Jan., April, July, Oct.). $8.00. Delaware County Genealogy Society, PO Box 1126, Delaware OH 43015. **Tel** (614)369-3831. **LC** F497.D3; D45. **DD** 929/.1/0720771535.
Ind/Abst Genealogical Period. Annu. Index.

UK/0142-7938
DELICHON URBICA. **Added/Corp** Family History Society of Martin. **VFOAT** House Martin. Vol. 1, Serial No. 1 (Jan. 1980)-. Periodical. English. qt (4 issues). £2.00 UK; £3.00 other. Family History Society of Martin, 21 Lyndhurst Road, Exmouth Devon 3X8 3DS England. **LC** CS439; .M3394. **DD** 929/.2/0941.

US/0736-3931
DES MOINES COUNTY GENEALOGICAL SOCIETY. (DES MOINES COUNTY GENEALOGICAL SOCIETY : QUARTERLY.). Periodical. English. qt. $5.00. Des Moines County Genealogical Society, Box 493, Burlington IA 52601. **ED** Vivian Setterberg. **LC** F627.D4; D48. **DD** 929/.1/072077796. **UDC** 929.5(777). **Circ:** 175 (ctrl). ***Continues*** *Des Moines County Genealogical Society Quarterly, 0736-394X.*
Desc: Genealogical information and research done in Des Moines County as well as queries form members of the society.

US/0420-0063
DESCENDER, THE. **Added/Corp** Montgomery County Genealogy Society (Montgomery County, Kan.) Montgomery County Genealogical Society (Montgomery County, Kan.). Vol. 1, No. 1 (Feb. 1968)-. Periodical. English. Twice a year. $7.00. Montgomery City Genealogical Society, Box 444, Coffeyville KS 67337. **Tel** (316)251-0716. **ED** Carol Durall. **LC** CS42; .D47. **DD** 929/.373. **Bk Rev. Ad Acc. Circ:** 100 (ctrl).
Desc: Includes local records to aid family genealogists and to preserve the records.

AT/0084-9731
DESCENT (SYDNEY). (DESCENT.). [Descent]. **Added/Corp** Society of Australian Genealogists. (1961)-. Periodical. English. Four times a year. 48.00Aus$. Society of Australian Genealogists, Richmond Villa, 120 Kent Street, Sydney New South Wales 2000 Australia. **Tel** 011 61 02 2473953. **ED** Mr. E.C. Best and Miss H.E. Garnsey. **LC** CS2000; .S6513. **DD** 929/.394. Index available. cum. index. **Bk Rev**, (Qty: 25,000). **Ad Acc. Circ:** 6,500 (ctrl). ***Continues*** *Australian Genealogist.*
Desc: Genealogical articles on sources in Australia and overseas - "how to" articles, news of new finding aids, members inquiries.
Ind/Abst APAIS, Aust. Public Aff. Inf. Ser. (1973-); Genealogical Period. Annu. Index (?-?).

US/0749-5633
DESPENCER, LE. (LA DESPENCER : NEWSLETTER OF THE SPENCER FAMILY ASSOCIATION.). **Added/Corp** Spencer Family Association. Vol. 1, No. 2 (Sept. 1978)-. Newsletter. English. qt. $13.00. Spencer Family Association, 915 White Gate Drive, Mt. Prospect IL 60056. **ED** Frances Spencer Powell. **LC** CS71; .S74493. **DD** 929/.2/0973. Index available. **Circ:** 700. ***Continues*** *Bulletin (Spencer Family Association), 0749-5625.*
Desc: For all persons interested in the Spencer surname.

US/0011-9687
DETROIT SOCIETY FOR GENEALOGICAL RESEARCH MAGAZINE. **Added/Corp** Detroit Society for Genealogical Research. (19??)-. Periodical. English. qt. comes with membership. Detroit Society for Genealogical Research Inc., 5201 Woodward Avenue, Detroit MI 48202. **Tel** (313)833-1480. available on microfilm and microfiche from University Microfilms International (UMI).
Ind/Abst Genealogical Period. Annu. Index.

GW/0012-1193
DEUTSCHES ADELSBLATT. **Added/Corp** Vereinigung der Deutschen Adelsverbande. (1962)-. Periodical. German. ir. DM69.00 (latest edition). Verlag Deutsches Adelsblatt, Westerbrakk 10, D 37619 Kirchbrak Germany. **Tel** 011 49 5533 2790.

US/0890-4456
DEWITT COUNTY GENEALOGICAL QUARTERLY. **Added/Corp** DeWitt County Genealogical Society. (Winter 1975)-. Periodical. English. Four times a year. $15.00. Dewitt County Genealogical Society, PO Box 632, Clinton IL 61727. **Tel** (217)935-3493. **ED** Betty Adcock. **DD** 929. Index available in last issue of volume--attached. **Bk Rev. Circ:** 200.
Desc: Genealogical and historical articles relating to DeWitt County, Illinois.
Ind/Abst Genealogical Period. Annu. Index.

US
DICK DOCUMENTS. (Aug. 1984)-. Periodical. English. Three times a year. The Legacy, PO Box 2040, Pinetop AZ 85935. **ED** Kay O'Dell.

US
DICKINSON DIGGINGS : THE QUARTERLY PUBLICATION OF THE DICKINSON COUNTY GENEALOGICAL SOCIETY. **Added/Corp** Dickinson County Genealogical Society (Mich.). Vol. 1, No. 1 (Jan. 1982)-. Periodical. English. Four times a year (Feb., May, Aug., Nov.). $8.00 (comes with Dickinson County Genealogical Society membership). Dickinson County Genealogical Society, 401 Iron Mountain Street, Iron Mountain MI 49801. **Tel** (906)563-5242.

US
DICKSON HERALD DEATH NOTICES. (1984/85)-. English. an. Donald G Luke, 825 Footpath Terrace, Nashville TN 37221.

US/0740-9079
DIGGER'S DIGEST (YUBA CITY, CALIF. : 1980), THE. ***Ceased.*** (THE DIGGER'S DIGEST.). [Digger's dig. (Yuba City, Calif. : 1980)]. Vol. 7, No. 2 (Spring 1980)-(Ceased Dec. 1991). Periodical. English. qt. Sutter-Yuba Genealogical Society, PO Box 1274, Yuba City CA 95992-1274. **LC** F868.S9; S94. **DD** 929/.379434. **UDC** 929.5(794). ***Continues*** *Sutter-Yuba Digger's Digest (Yuba City, Calif.), 0740-9060.*

UK
DIRECTORY OF MEMBERS' RESEARCH. SUPPLEMENT / OXFORDSHIRE FAMILY HISTORY SOCIETY. **Main/Corp** Oxfordshire Family History Society. (1981-1982)-. Directory. English. an. Oxfordshire Family History Society, 47 Bull Street, Aston Oxford OX18 2DT England. **Tel** 011 44 0865 820493. **LC** CS435.O9; O93 1981 Suppl. **DD** 929/.1/0604257.

US/1055-6710
DIRECTORY OF PROFESSIONAL GENEALOGISTS. [Dir. prof. geneal.]. **Added/Corp** Association of Professional Genealogists (U.S.). (19??)-. English. ir. $15.00 (two years). Association of Professional Genealogists, 3421 M Street Northwest, Suite 236, Washington DC 20007. **Tel** (703)920-2385, (504)766-3018. **ED** Eileen Polakoff. **DD** 929. **Bk Rev**, (Qty: 50-75). **Ad Acc, Adv Mgr:** Suzanne McVetty, **Tel** (516)997-8393. **Circ:** 770. ***Continues*** *Directory of Professional Genealogists and Related Services, 0272-3387.*

US/0272-3387
DIRECTORY OF PROFESSIONAL GENEALOGISTS AND RELATED SERVICES. ***Title Change.*** [Dir. prof. geneal. relat. serv.]. **Added/Corp** Association of Professional Genealogists (U.S.) Utah Genealogical Association. Professional Genealogists Chapter. (1979)-(19??). Directory. English. Association of Professional Genealogists, 3421 M Street Northwest, Suite 236, Washington DC 20007. **Tel** (703)920-2385, (504)766-3018. **ED** Eileen Polakoff. **LC** CS5; .D57. **DD** 929/.1/02573. **Bk Rev**, (Qty: 50-75). **Ad Acc. Circ:** 600. ***Continued by*** *Directory of Professional Genealogists, 1055-6710.*
Desc: Lists professional genealogists by specialty or service, with addresses, phone numbers and sometimes fees charged.

CN/0823-7891
DIRECTORY OF SURNAMES - ONTARIO GENEALOGICAL SOCIETY. (DIRECTORY OF SURNAMES.). [Dir. surnames - Ont. Geneal. Soc.]. **Main/Corp** Ontario Genealogical Society. (May 1982)-. Directory. English. an. 16.50Can$ Canada; 18.00Can$ other. Ontario Genealogical Society / Toronto, 40 Orchard View Boulevard, Suite 251, Toronto Ontario M4R 1B9 Canada. **Tel** (416)489-0734, FAX (416)489-9803. **DD** 929/.3713.

●US
DISTANT CROSSROADS. (1994)-. English. Four times a year (Jan., Apr., July, Oct.). $10.00. Hawkins County Genealogical and Historical Society, PO Box 429, Rogersville TN 37857. **ED** Sheila Johnston (editor's phone: (615)272-9387). Index available (published separately). **Bk Rev. Circ:** 450.

US/0736-2854
DODD DIGGINGS. Vol. 3, No. 12 (Oct. 1982)-. Periodical. English. Four times a year. $7.00. Avlyn Dodd Conley, 7543 B and A Boulevard, Glen Burnie MN 21061. **Tel** (410)766-2262. **ED** Avlyn Dodd Conley. **LC** CS71; .D63894. **DD** 929/.2/0973. Index available. **Bk Rev. Circ:** 125. ***Continues*** *Dodd Newsletter, 0736-0924.*
Desc: Genealogical information on surname Dodd(s) for anywhere, anytime, plus free queries to subscribers only.

US/0736-2412
DOHNER FAMILY NEWSLETTER. [Dohner fam. newsl.]. No. 1 (Feb. 1980)-. Newsletter. English. qt. $5.00. Dohner and Dudley, 40701 Rancho Vista Bl #68, Palmdale CA 93551. **Tel** (805)943-3416. **ED** Dudley Dohner. **LC** CS71; .D74793. **DD** 929/.2/0973. **UDC** 929.52(73). **Bk Rev. Ad Acc. Circ:** 100 (ctrl).
Desc: Family history, tracing roots.

US/8755-2353
DORCHESTER COUNTY GENEALOGICAL MAGAZINE, THE. [Dorchester Cty. geneal. mag.]. **VFOAT** Dorchester County Maryland Genealogy Magazine; Dorchester County, Maryland Genealogical Magazine. Vol. 1, No. 6 (Mar. 1982)-. Periodical. English. bm. $12.00. Dorchester County Genealogical Magazine, Route 4 Box 67, Madison MD 21648. **Tel** (410)228-5442. **ED** Debra Smith Moxey. **LC** F187.D6; D67. **DD** 929/.1/072075227. **UDC** 929.5(752). Index available. **Bk Rev. Ad Acc. Circ:** 250. ***Continues*** *Dorchester Genealogical Magazine, 8755-2337.*
Desc: Genealogical material from Dorchester County, Maryland.

US/0886-2796
DOROT. (DOROT : THE JOURNAL OF THE JEWISH GENEALOGICAL SOCIETY.). [Dorot]. (1985)-. Periodical. English. qt. $12.00 US, (add $6.00 for postage) other. Jewish Genealogical Society (NY), PO Box 6398, New York NY 10128. **Tel** (212)722-8456. **ED** Alex Friedlander. **LC** CS31; .D67. **DD** 929/.1/089924. **UDC** 929.5(73=924). **Bk Rev. Circ:** 900.
Desc: The journal of The Jewish Genealogical Society, Inc., with both New York-area and out-of-town membership.

US/0742-0846
DORSEY DREAMS. (DORSEY DREAMS : THE DORSEY FAMILY NEWSLETTER.). Vol. 1 No. 1 (Oct./Dec. 1982)-. Newsletter. English. Four times a year. $12.00. Lois Colette Dorsey Bennington, 15252 Seneca Road 6, Victorville CA 92392. **LC** CS71; .D7173. **DD** 929/.2/0973.

UK/0141-237X
DOUBLE TRESSURE : JOURNAL OF THE HERALDRY SOCIETY OF SCOTLAND, THE. **VFOAT** Journal of the Heraldry Society of Scotland. English. sa. **LC** CR510; .D68. **DD** 929.6/09411. **UDC** 929.6(411).

US/0897-3350
DOUGHTY TREE, THE. [Doughty tree]. Vol. 1, No. 1 (Mar. 1977)-. Periodical. English. Three times a year. $10.00. Doughty Family Association, PO Box 203, Mays Landing NJ 08330. **Tel** (609)625-5459. **ED** Clarence E Doughty. **LC** CS71; .D7243. **DD** 929/.2/0973. **UDC** 929.52(100). Index available. cum. index. **Bk Rev. Circ:** 250 (ctrl).
Desc: Records and articles of Doughty family worldwide. Various spellings, Dowty, Dowdy, Doty, Doten, Doughtie, Dowtie, Doutty, etc.

US/0895-7444
DOUGLAS COUNTY PIONEER. (DOUGLAS COUNTY PIONEER / GENEALOGICAL SOCIETY OF DOUGLAS COUNTY.). **Added/Corp** Genealogical Society of Douglas County (Douglas County, Or.). **VFOAT** DCP. Vol. 1, No. 1 (Mar. 1987)-. Periodical. English. qt (March, June, Sep., Dec.). $10.00. Genealogical Society of Douglas County, PO Box 579, Roseburg OR 97470. **Tel** (503)673-6940 or, (503)440-6178. **ED** Kay Livermore. **DD** 979.

US/0741-6954
DOUGLAS TRAILS AND TRACES. (DOUGLAS TRAILS AND TRACES : A PUBLICATION OF THE DOUGLAS COUNTY, ILLINOIS GENEALOGICAL SOCIETY.). **Added/Corp** Douglas County Illinois Genealogical Society. Vol. 4, No. 2 (June 1981)-. Periodical. English. Four times a year (Mar., June, Sept., Dec.). $7.50. Douglas County Illinois Genealogical Society, Box 113, Tuscola IL 61953. **Tel** (217)268-3551. **ED** M. Tracy Carpenter (phone: (217)253-4635). **LC** F547.D7; D68. **DD** 929/.1/072077368. **Circ:** 150. ***Continues** Douglas County, Illinois Genealogical Society Quarterly, 0741-6962.*
Desc: News from newspapers on microfilm, wills, county court records or minutes, queries, and surnames that members are researching.

US/0891-0960
DOWNEAST ANCESTRY. [Downeast ancestry]. V. 1- (June 1977)-. Periodical. English. bm. $20.00. Downeast Ancestry, PO Box 191, Biddeford Pool ME 04006. **Tel** (207)284-7132. **ED** Mary Dormer. **LC** F18; .D69. **DD** 929. **UDC** 929.5(741). Index available. **Bk Rev. Ad Acc.**
Desc: Covers Maine family history and genealogy.
Ind/Abst Genealogical Period. Annu. Index (?-?).

US/0090-483X
DUDLEY GENEALOGICAL REVIEW, THE. V. 1- July 1972-. Periodical. English. qt. $10.00. C.W. Dudley, PO Box 6474, Richmond VA. **LC** CS71; .D849. **DD** 929/.2/0973. **UDC** 929.52(73).

US/0735-6242
DUTCHESS, THE. [Dutchess]. **Added/Corp** Dutchess County Genealogical Society. Vol. 1, No. 2 (Sept. 1973)-. Periodical. English. Four times a year (Mar., June, Sept., Dec.). $15.00. Dutchess County Genealogical Society, Box 708, Poughkeepsie NY 12602. **Tel** (914)454-1614. **ED** Arthur Kelly. **LC** F127.D8; D65. **DD** 929/.1/072074733. Index available. **Bk Rev. Ad Acc. Circ:** 250 (ctrl). ***Continues** Duchess, 0735-6234.*
Desc: All previously unpublished records, will abstracts and genealogical source material from Dutchess County, New York.

US/0732-1007
EAGLET, THE. (THE EAGLET / POLISH GENEALOGICAL SOCIETY OF MICHIGAN.). **Added/Corp** Polish Genealogical Society of Michigan. Vol. 1, No. 1 (May 198?)-. Periodical. English. Three times a year (Jan., May, Sept.). $15.00 family membership. Polish Genealogical Society of Michigan, Detroit Public Library, 5201 Woodward Avenue, Detroit MI 48202. **Tel** (313)833-1480. **ED** Pamela L. Lazar. **LC** WMLC 93/1315. **Bk Rev. Circ:** 450.
Ind/Abst Genealogical Period. Annu. Index.

US/0424-107X
EAST KENTUCKIAN, THE. (June 1965)-. Periodical. English. qt (Mar., June, Sept., Dec.). $14.00. The East Kentuckian, Box 24202, Lexington KY 40524. **Tel** (606)277-4569. **ED** Clayton R. Cox. **LC** F450; .E17. **DD** 976.9/005. **Bk Rev. Circ:** 780 (ctrl).
Desc: Intended for those doing family research or library source files in eastern Kentucky.
Ind/Abst Genealogical Period. Annu. Index.

US/0885-4025
EAST TENNESSEE ROOTS. [East Tenn. roots]. Vol. 1, No. 1 (March 1984)-. Periodical. English. Four times a year. $20.00. East Tennessee Roots, 1345 Oakridge Turnpike 318, Oak Ridge TN 37830. **Tel** (615)691-8760. **ED** Paula Gammell. **LC** WMLC 93/1360. **DD** 929. Index available. **Bk Rev. Ad Acc. Circ:** 600.
Desc: News and information on local and family history. Includes regular columns-queries, transcripts, research, art and letters.
Ind/Abst Genealogical Period. Annu. Index.

US/0272-4405
EAST TEXAS FAMILY RECORDS. **Added/Corp** East Texas Genealogical Society. Vol. 1 (1977)-. Periodical. English. qt (4 issues). Comes with East Texas Genealogical Society membership; $12.00 regular membership, $25.00 sustaining membership. East Texas Genealogical Society, PO Box 6967, Tyler TX 75711. **Tel** (214)561-3830. **ED** Martha Ann Glover. **LC** F385; .E22. **DD** 929/.3764. Index available. cum. index. **Bk Rev. Circ:** 450.
Desc: Contains vital statistics, biographical sketches of early East Texas families, court, cemetery and bible records, queries and other genealogical resource material.

US
EATON COUNTY QUEST. English. qt. $15.00 US; $21.00 other. Eaton County Genealogical Society, 100 West Lawrence, Charolotte MI 48813. **ED** Joyce Liepins (phone: (517)645-2988). Index available. **Pr Rev. Circ:** 150 (ctrl).

CN/0228-5908
ECHO DES BASQUES. (L'ECHO DES BASQUES / SOCIETE HISTORIQUE ET GENEALOGIQUE DE TROIS-PISTOLES.). [Echo Basques]. **Added/Corp** Societe Historique et Genealogique de Trois-Pistoles. Vol. 1, No. 1 (Dec. 1980)-. French. an. 7.00Can$; Comes also with membership. Societe Historique & Genealogique de Trois-Pistoles, CP 1586, Trois-Pistoles Quebec GOL 4KO Canada. **Tel** (418)851-3144. **DD** 971.4/76.

CN/0828-8151
ECHOS GENEALOGIQUES. (ECHOS GENEALOGIQUES / SOCIETE DE GENEALOGIE DES LAURENTIDES : SOCIETE GENEALOGIQUE DE LA RIVIERE DU NORD.). [Echos geneal.]. **Added/Corp** Societe de Genealogie des Laurentides. Vol. 1, No. 1 (Autumn 1984)-. Periodical. French. Four times a year. 18.00Can$ (individuals); 30.00Can$ (institutions). Societe de Genealogie des Laurentides, CP 131, St-Jerome Quebec J7Z 5T7 Canada. **DD** 929/.1/07207144.

US/0743-8591
EDWARDS JOURNAL, THE. Vol. 1 No. 1 (Jan./Mar. 1983)-. Periodical. English. Four times a year. $12.00. Conley Publications, PO Box 2617, Laurel MD 20708. **Tel** (301)776-6853. **ED** Elaine Nelson. **LC** CS71; .E2593. **DD** 929/.2/0973.

●US/1061-690X
EILRICH FAMILY SNAPSHOTS. [Eilrich fam. snapshots]. Vol. 1, No.1 Mar. (1992)-. Periodical. English. ir. Free. William Eilrich, 1021 Maple Way, Santa Clara CA 95051-4214. **DD** 929.

US/0740-1477
ELLIS COUSINS NEWSLETTER, THE. Vol. 1, No. 1 (Mar. 1979)-. Periodical. English. qt. $12.00. Ellis Cousins Newsletter, 1201 Maple Street, Friona TX 79035. **Tel** (806)247-3053. **ED** Bill and Carol Ellis. **LC** CS71; .E46914. **DD** 929/.2/0973. Index available. **Bk Rev. Circ:** 700.
Desc: Covers queries, old photos, family records, source materials and research articles.

US/0361-7157
ENGLISH GENEALOGICAL HELPER. 1975-. English. $5.00. Union of International Associations, Rue Washington 40, 1050 Brussels Belgium. **Tel** 011 32 2 6404109, FAX 011 32 2 646 05 25, telex 65080 INAC B. **LC** CS410; .E52. **DD** 929/.1/0941. **UDC** 929.5.

CN/0226-6245
ENTRAIDE GENEALOGIQUE. (L'ENTRAIDE GENEALOGIQUE.). **Added/Corp** Societe Genealogique des Cantons de l'Est. Vol. 1 (1979)-. Periodical. French. Four times a year (Jan., Apr., July, Oct.). 20.00Can$. Societe de Genealogie des Cantons de l'Est Inc, CP 635 Sherbrooke Quebec J1H 5K5 Canada. **Tel** (819)562-7741. **DD** 929/.1/0607146. **Circ:** 800.

CN/0711-1789
ENTRE NOUS, LES MARTIN. [Entre nous, Martin]. **Added/Corp** Societe Genealogique des Martin. Vol. 1 No. 1 (Jan. 1982)-. Periodical. French. sa. $10.00. Entre Nous les Martin, La Societe Genealogique des Martin, App 608, 30 Chemin Lakeshore, Pointe-Claire Quebec H9S 4H2 Canada. **DD** 929/.2.

US
ESCAMBIA COUNTY HISTORICAL QUARTERLY. **See** History(General).

UK/0140-7503
ESSEX FAMILY HISTORIAN, THE. **Added/Corp** Essex Society for Family History. (19??)-. Periodical. English. Four times a year (Feb., May, Aug., Nov.). £10.00 Comes with Essex Society for Family History membership. Essex Society for Family History, 1 Robin Close Great Bentley, Colchester Essex CO7 SQH England. **LC** CS435.E7; E84. **DD** 929/.1/07204267. **Bk Rev. Ad Acc. Circ:** 1,700 (ctrl). available on microfiche.

US/0279-067X
ESSEX GENEALOGIST, THE. **Added/Corp** Essex Society of Genealogists. **VFOAT** T.E.G.; TEG. Vol. 1, No. 1 (Feb. 1981)-. Periodical. English. qt (Feb., May, Aug., Nov.). $13.00 US; $18.50 other. Essex Society of Genealogists, PO Box 313, Lynnfield MA 01940-0313. **Tel** (508)657-7232. **ED** Marcia Wiswall Lindberg. **LC** F72.E7; E54. **DD** 929/.1/07207445. Index available. **Circ:** 750 (ctrl).
Desc: Family history, local history, news, queries, tips relating to Essex County, Massachusetts.
Ind/Abst Genealogical Period. Annu. Index.

US/0737-481X
ESTES TRAILS. Vol. 1, No. 1 (July 1980)-. Periodical. English. qt. $10.00. Historic Trails Library, Route 1 Box 373, Mrs. Mary Estes Beckham, Philadelphia MS 39350-9762. **Tel** (601)656-3506. **ED** Mary Estes Beckham. **LC** CS71; .E7893. **DD** 929/.2/0973. **Bk Rev. Ad Acc. Circ:** 250 (ctrl).
Desc: For and about Estes, various spelling, everywhere. Queries, lineage charts, marriage, death, deeds, etc. Census records, genealogies, book reviews. All areas of the US and the world.

CN/0824-4936
ESTUAIRE GENEALOGIQUE, L'. **Added/Corp** Societe Genealogique de l'Est du Quebec. Vol. 1, No. 1 (Jan. 1982)-. Periodical. French. Four times a year (Jan., Apr., July, Oct.). 20.00Can$ Canada; 22.00Can$ other. Societe Genealogique de l'Est du Quebec, CP 253, Rimouski Quebec G5L 7C1 Canada. **Tel** (418)724-2862. **ED** Pierre Rioux. **DD** 929/.1/072071477. Index available. **Circ:** 400.
Ind/Abst Genealogical Period. Annu. Index.

US/0747-5810
ESWAU HUPPEDAY. **Added/Corp** Broad River Genealogical Society. Vol. 1, No. 1 (Feb. 1981)-. Periodical. English. Four times a year (Feb., May, Aug., Nov.). $12.50. Broad River Genealogical Society, PO Box 2261, Shelby NC 28150. **Tel** (704)482-3016. **ED** JoAnn F. Surratt, (phone: (704)487-6168). **LC** F277.B73; E84. Index Available Received separately--bound from publisher. **Bk Rev. Circ:** 500.
Desc: This publications contains historical and genealogical material about the Broad River.

●US/1016-6359
EVERTON'S GENEALOGICAL HELPER. **VFOAT** Genealogical Helper. (Jan./Feb. 1992)-. Periodical. English. bm (6 issues). $21.00 US; $24.15 other. Everton Publishing Inc, PO Box 368, Logan UT 84321. **Tel** (801)752-6022, (800)443-6325. **LC** CS1; .G38. **DD** 929.105. ***Continues** Genealogical Helper, 0016-6359.*

US/0738-5234
EWGS BULLETIN. **Added/Corp** Eastern Washington Genealogical Society. **VFOAT** E.W.G.S. Bulletin; Bulletin; Bulletin of the Eastern Washington Genealogical Society. **VAT** Eastern Washington Genealogical Society Bulletin. Vol. 19, No. 1 (Mar. 1982)-. Bulletin. English. Four times a year. $20.00. Eastern Washington Genealogical Society, PO Box 1826, Spokane WA 99210. **Tel** (509)535-2847. **ED** Doris Woodward, 2121 South Lincoln, Spokane, WA 99203-1252; Telephone: (509)456-7553. **LC** F890; .B85. **DD** 929/.1/0720797. Each issue contains an index to its own contents (no volume index)--loose. **Bk Rev. Ad Acc.** ***Continues** Bulletin (Eastern Washington Genealogical Society), 0738-5188.*
Desc: Extraction of local records of interest to genealogy; articles on genealogy.
Ind/Abst Genealogical Period. Annu. Index.

US/0892-2144
EWING EXCHANGE. [Ewing exch.]. Vol. 1, No. 1 (March 1987)-. Periodical. English. qt. $10.00. Kinseeker Publications, Box 184, Grawn MI 49637. **ED** V. Wilson. **DD** 929. Index available. **Bk Rev. Ad Acc. Circ:** 50.
Desc: Contains genealogical information on Ewing families.

US/0736-2269
FACTS AND FINDINGS. [Facts find.]. **Added/Corp** Frankfort Area Genealogy Society. Vol. 1, No. 1 (Fall 1975)-. Periodical. English. qt (4 issues). $12.00. Frankfort Area Genealogical Society, PO Box 427, West Frankfort IL 62896. **Tel** (618)937-4458, (618)932-6159. **ED** Helen Lino. **LC** F549.W52; F32. **DD** 929/.1/072077394. Index available (bound in all issues). **Circ:** 250.
Desc: This magazine offers concise, readable analysis of our latest research in vocational education.

US
FAIRFIELD HERITAGE QUARTERLY. English. Four times a year (Jan., Apr., July, Oct.). $10.00 (individual), $15.00 (family), $25.00 (sustaining), $50.00 (patron) members; Comes with Fairfield Heritage Association membership. Fairfield Heritage Association, 105 East Wheeling Street, Lancaster OH 43130. **Tel** (614)654-9923.

US
FAIRFIELD TRACE. English. Free to members. Ohio Genealogical Society - Fairfield County Chapter, PO Box 203, Lancaster OH 43130.
Ind/Abst Genealogical Period. Annu. Index.

US/0093-6634
FAIT-FEIGHT-FATE. English. $1.50. AIMS Education Foundation, PO Box 8120, Fresno CA 93747. **Tel** (209)255-4094. **LC** CS71; .F1742. **DD** 929/.2/0973. **UDC** 929.52(73).

SA/0014-7117
FAMILIA. **Added/Corp** Genealogical Society of South Africa. Vol. 1 (1964/65)-. Periodical. Multiple languages (Afrikaans, Dutch and English). Four times a year. R40.00. Genealogical Society of South Africa, PO Box 1344, Kelvin 2054 South Africa. **ED** Cornelis Pama. **LC** CS1590; .F3. Index available (Free). **Bk Rev. Ad Acc. Circ:** 1,500.
Desc: Articles on the Socio-cultural review, genealogy and family history of South Africa.
Ind/Abst Annu. Bibliogr. Engl. Lang. Lit.

CN/0030-2945
FAMILIES. [Families]. **Added/Corp** Ontario Genealogical Society. Vol. 10 (Winter 1971)-. Periodical. English. qt. Ontario Genealogical Society / Toronto, 40 Orchard View Boulevard, Suite 251, Toronto Ontario M4R 1B9 Canada. **Tel** (416)489-0734, FAX (416)489-9803. ***Continues*** *Ontario Genealogical Society. Bulletin., 0474-2036.*
Ind/Abst Can. Period. Index; Genealogical Period. Annu. Index.

US/0890-0353
FAMILIES OF WYOMING CO., WV. [Fam. Wyo. Co. WV]. **VFOAT** Families of Wyoming County, WV. **VAT** Families of Wyoming County, West Virginia. Vol. 1, Issue 1 (1986)-. Periodical. English. Four times a year (Feb., May, Aug., Nov.). $10.00. Ancestor Seminars Library, PO Box 1035, North Highlands CA 95660-1035. **Tel** (916)991-4165. **ED** Sally Seaman Williams. **DD** 929. Each issue contains an index to its own contents (no volume index)--loose. **Bk Rev. Circ:** 200.
Desc: Included in each issue are ancestor charts, family groups, Bible records, cemetery records, queries, photographs, vital records and family histories. Each issue is indexed by both surname and given name.
Ind/Abst Genealogical Period. Annu. Index.

US/0890-0361
FAMILIES OF YANCEY COUNTY, NC. **VFOAT** Families of Yancey Co., NC.; FOYC. **VAT** Families of Yancey County, North Carolina. (198?)-. Periodical. English. Four times a year (Mar., June, Sept., Dec.). $10.00. Ancestor Seminars Library, PO Box 1035, North Highlands CA 95660-1035. **Tel** (916)991-4165. **ED** Sally Seaman Williams. **DD** 929. Each issue contains an index to its own contents (no volume index)--loose. cum. index. **Bk Rev. Circ:** 255.
Desc: Each issue contains records such as birth, marriage, death, Bible, Civil War, cemetery, land, census, topographic maps, photographs and family histories.
Ind/Abst Genealogical Period. Annu. Index.

US/0749-4505
FAMILY ASSOCIATION NEWSLETTER, DRODDY, DRODY, DRAWDY & VARIANTS, THE. Began with Jan. 1981. Newsletter. English. sa. $10.00. Trend Publications Inc, 4528 Wyndale Avenue SW, Roanoke VA 24018. **ED** Margaret Drody Thompson. **LC** CS71; .D78414. **DD** 929/.2/0973. **UDC** 929.52(73). **Bk Rev. Ad Acc. Circ:** 100.
Desc: Intended for descendants of Irish immigrant Daniel Droddy, who immigrated to America in pre-colonial times. Feature articles based on historical research. Area of concern encompasses contemporary and historical United States, Canada, England and Ireland, as well as Germany. Includes interviews, news of research, calendar of events, reports of meetings, book reviews, columns on military services, obituaries, births, marriages.

US/0735-682X
FAMILY BACKTRACKING. [Family backtrack.]. **Added/Corp** Olympic Genealogical Society. Puget Sound Genealogical Society. Vol. 1, No. 1 (Feb. 1976)-. Periodical. English. Four times a year. $12.00. Puget Sound Genealogical Society, 4430 Pine Avenue Northeast, Bremerton WA 98310. **Tel** (206)377-3955. **LC** F897.P9; F35. **DD** 929/.1/07207977.

GW/1040-4821
FAMILY FINDER (HEIDELBERG, GERMANY). (FAMILY FINDER.). [Fam. finder]. (1988)-. Periodical. English. mo. Genealogical Association of English-Speaking Researchers in Europe, c/o USAREUR Library and Resource Center, APO 09063, Heidelberg Germany. **DD** 929.

US/0533-0939
FAMILY FINDINGS. English. Four times a year. $12.00. Mid-West Tennessee Genealogical Society, PO Box 3343, Jackson TN 38303. **ED** Darlene Wiggins. Index available. **Bk Rev.**

US/0277-6936
FAMILY FOOTPRINTS. **VFOAT** Kiser Family Footprints; Kiser, A Supplement and Newsletter. 1981-. English. an. Ralph T Kiser, PO Box 54, Ashland AL 36251. **LC** CS71; .K1344. **DD** 929/.2/0973. **UDC** 929.5(73).

US/0894-0487
FAMILY FOOTSTEPS QUARTERLY. **Added/Corp** Comal County Genealogical Society. **VFOAT** Family Footsteps. (198?)-. Periodical. English. Three times a year (Mar., June, Oct.). $15.00 one year. Comal County Genealogy Society, PO Box 310583, New Braunfels TX 78131. **Tel** (512)625-8766. **ED** Tom Call. **LC** F392.C7; F35. **DD** 929/.1/0720764887. Index available (Bound in 3rd issue, publish in October.). cum. index. **Circ:** 150 (ctrl).
Desc: New Braunfels, Comal County, Texas and other material of interest to Germans Texans and Genealogists.

US/0895-061X
FAMILY GROUP SHEETS OF THE WORLD INTERNATIONAL. 1989-. Periodical. English. an. Multi-Family Publications, PO Box 28215, Sacramento CA 95828. **LC** CS25; .F36. **DD** 929/.3.

US/1057-946X
FAMILY HISTORIAN QUARTERLY, THE. ***Ceased.*** [Fam. hist. q.]. **Added/Corp** Madison County Genealogical Society (Madison County, Tex.). **VFOAT** Family Historian. (1985)-Vol. 12, No. 2 (Feb. 1993). Periodical. English. qt. Madison County Genealogical Society / Texas, PO Box 24, Madisonville TX 77864. **Tel** (409)348-2639. **DD** 929. ***Continues*** *Past & Present (Madisonville, Tex.).*

UK/0014-7265
FAMILY HISTORY. [Fam. hist.]. **Added/Corp** Institute of Heraldic and Genealogical Studies. Vol. 1, No. 1 (Oct. 1962)-. Periodical. English. qt. £12.00 (1 year), £30.00 (3 year). Institute of Heraldic Genealogical Studies, Northgate Canterbury, Kent CT1 1BA England. **Tel** 011 44 227 68664, FAX 011 44 227 65617. **ED** Cecil R. Humphery-Smith. **LC** CR1; .F3. **Bk Rev. Ad Acc. Circ:** 1,000. available on microfilm and microfiche from University Microfilms International (UMI).
Desc: Covers heraldry, genealogy, and family history.
Ind/Abst Am. Hist. Life; Br. Humanit. Index.

US/0742-1419
FAMILY HISTORY CAPERS. **Added/Corp** Genealogical Society of Washtenaw Co. Michigan. (19??)-. English. Four times a year. $14.00 Comes with Genealogical Society of Washtenaw County Michigan membership. The Genealogical Society of Washtenwaw County, PO Box 7155, Ann Arbor MI 48107. **Tel** (313)668-6422. **ED** Nancy H. Krohn (editors' address: 905 Robin Road, Ann Arbor, MI 48103; telephone: (313)668-6422). **LC** F572.W3; F35. **DD** 929/.1/072077435. Index available. **Bk Rev.** ctrl circ.
Desc: Aids and assists members in genealogical studies, to encourage collection and preservation of family and public records and to promote the exchange of genealogical information.
Ind/Abst Genealogical Period. Annu. Index.

AT/0815-3922
FAMILY HISTORY FOR BEGINNERS. [Fam. hist. begin.]. (1985)-. English. ir. 9.50Aus$. Heraldy and Genealogy Society of Canberra, GPO 585, Canberra, ACT 2601 Australia. **Tel** 011 61 62 411942. **DD** 929.1072094. **Bk Rev.** ctrl circ. ***Continues*** *Information Leaflet - Heraldry & Genealogy Society of Canberra, 0726-030X.*

UK/0309-8559
FAMILY HISTORY NEWS AND DIGEST. Vol. 1 (Summer 1977)-. Periodical. English (table of contents in French and German). Four times a year. £3.80 UK; £4.40 other. Federation of Family History Societies, 15 Dover Close Fareham, Hampshire PO14 3S4 England. **Tel** 44 329662512. **LC** CS1; .F36. **DD** 929/.1/05.

US/1057-9451
FAMILY PEDIGREES. (FAMILY PEDIGREES / NORTHWEST ARKANSAS GENEALOGICAL SOCIETY.). [Fam. pedigrees]. **Added/Corp** Northwest Arkansas Genealogical Society. Vol. No. 1 (Feb. 1991)-. English. Northwest Arkansas Genealogical Society, P.O.Box 796, Rogers AR 72757. **DD** 929.

US/0736-1858
FAMILY RECORDS TODAY. [Fam. rec. today]. **Added/Corp** American Family Records Association. **VFOAT** AFRA Family Records Today; A.F.R.A. Family Records Today. Vol. 1, No. 1 (April 1980)-. English. Four times a year (Jan., Apr., June, Oct.). $22.00 (one year); $44.00 (two years); $66.00 (three years). American Family Records Association, 311 East 12th Street, PO Box 15505, Kansas City MO 64106. **Tel** (816)453-1294. **ED** Nita Neblock, (editor's address: 4429 South Union, Independence, MO 64055-4663, phone: (816)373-6570). **LC** CS42; .F34. **DD** 929/.1/072073. Index available (Oct., in 4th issue). **Bk Rev**, (Qty: 150-200). **Ad Acc.**
Desc: This journal is devoted to the study of genealogy and family history.
Ind/Abst Genealogical Period. Annu. Index.

UK
FAMILY ROOTS : JOURNAL OF THE FAMILY ROOTS FAMILY HISTORY SOCIETY. EASTBOURNE AND DISTRICT. (1986)-. English. qt. £6.00 (individual), £8.00 (family membership), £7.00 (air mail). Family Roots Family History Society, 22 Abbey Road, Eastbourne SX BN20 8TE England. **Tel** (0323)731206. **ED** N. Weir. cum. index. **Bk Rev. Ad Acc. Circ:** 350 (ctrl).
Desc: Information, articles, members research and points of interest.

US
FAMILY SNOOP. English. Twelve times a year. $10.00. Merced County Genealogical Society, PO Box 3061, Merced CA 95344. **Tel** (209)723-9019. **ED** Chastain, Padilla and Jimenez.

US/0736-9883
FAMILY TIES (HOLLAND GENEALOGICAL SOCIETY). (FAMILY TIES.). [Fam. ties]. Vol. 1 (Winter 1974)-. Periodical. English. Three times a year. $10.00 US; $12.50 other. Holland Genealogical Society, 300 River Avenue, Holland MI 49423. **Tel** (616)394-1400. **ED** William Robertson. **LC** F574.H6; F35. **DD** 929/.37741. **UDC** 929.5(741). **Ad Acc. Circ:** 125 (ctrl).

US/1047-0956
FAMILY TREE (DAYTON, OHIO). (FAMILY TREE : A PUBLICATION OF THE MONTGOMERY COUNTY CHAPTER. OGS.). [Fam. tree]. **Added/Corp** Ohio Genealogical Society. Montgomery County Chapter. **VFOAT** MCC-OGS Family Tree. **VAT** Montgomery County Chapter-Ohio Genealogical Society Family Tree. (Nov. 1979)-. Periodical. English. Twelve times a year. $10.00. Ohio Genealogical Society Montgomery County, PO Box 1584, Dayton OH 45401. **ED** Jesse Walsh (editor's address: 2630 Normont Court, Dayton, OH 45414-5033). **DD** 929. ***Continues*** *Ohio Genealogical Society. Montgomery County Chapter. Montgomery County Chapter, Ohio Genealogical Society : [Newsletter].*

US/1064-1106
FAMILY TREE (HOWARD COUNTY, MD), THE. (THE FAMILY TREE.). [Fam. tree]. **Added/Corp** Howard County Genealogical Society. Issue No. 3 (Mar. 30, 1977)-. Periodical. English. Ten times a year (Except July & Aug.). $10.00 Comes with Howard County Genealogical Society membership. Howard County Genealogical Society, PO Box 274, Columbia MD 21045. **Tel** (301)730-8070. **DD** 929. ***Continues*** *H.C.G.S. Newsletter.*
Ind/Abst Genealogical Period. Annu. Index.

UK/0267-1131
FAMILY TREE MAGAZINE. **VFOAT** Family Tree. (Nov./Dec. 1984)-. Periodical. English. Twelve times a year. $35.00 (surface mail), $46.00 (airmail), US; 45.00Can$ (surface mail), 58.00Can$ (airmail), Canada; £21.75 (surface mail), £30.72 (airmail), other. J M Armstrong Publishing, 15/16 Highlode, Stocking Fen Road, Huntingdon PE17 1RB England. **Tel** 011 44 487 814050. **ED** Avril Cross. **Bk Rev. Ad Acc, Adv Mgr:** J. Boon. ctrl circ. available on microfiche from the publisher.

US/1059-0803
FAMILY TREE QUARTERLY : A PUBLICATION OF THE COBB COUNTY, GEORGIA, GENEALOGICAL SOCIETY, INC. [Fam. tree q.]. **Added/Corp** Cobb County Genealogical Society (Cobb County, Ga.). **VFOAT** Cobb County Genealogical Society Quarterly. Vol. 1, Issue 1 (Mar. 1991)-. Periodical. English. qt. Cobb County Genealogical Society, PO Box 1413, Marietta GA 30061-1413. **LC** F292.C6; F36. **DD** 929/.1/0720758245.
Ind/Abst Genealogical Period. Annu. Index.

US/0747-9441
FAMILY TREE TALK. (FAMILY TREE TALK / THE MUSKEGON COUNTY GENEALOGICAL SOCIETY.). Periodical. English. qt. $7.50. Muskegon County Genealogical Society, c/o Hackley Public Library, 316 West Webster Avenue, Muskegon MI 49440. **ED** Tressa LaFayette. **LC** F572.M9; F35. **DD** 929/.1/072077457. **UDC** 929.5(774). Index available. **Bk Rev. Ad Acc. Circ:** 150 (ctrl).
Desc: Local genealogy and little known biographical material. Emphasizes is on material not readily available to anyone including local researchers.

US/0749-1530
FAMILY VINES. (FAMILY VINES / MANITOWOC COUNTY GENEALOGICAL SOCIETY.). **Added/Corp** Manitowoc County Genealogical Society. (198?)-. English. qt. $5.00 (includes membership). Manitowoc County Genealogical Society, PO Box 1745, Manitowoc WI 54221. **Tel** (414)684-1402. **ED** Bob Bjerke (Editor's address: University of Wisconsin Center, 705 Viebahn Street, Manitowoc Wisconsin 54220; Editor's telephone: (414)683-4718). **LC** F587.M2; F22. **DD** 929/.377567. **Circ:** 200.
Desc: Publishes news of the Manitowoc County Genealogical Society, items of interest to members, records of genealogical and historical importance from or concerning Manitowoc County, Wisconsin.

US/1063-4711
FAMILYSEARCH. INTERNATIONAL GENEALOGICAL INDEX. BRITISH ISLES. (FAMILYSEARCH. INTERNATIONAL GENEALOGICAL INDEX. BRITISH ISLES [COMPUTER

FILE].). [FamilySearch, Int. geneal. index, Br. Isles]. **Added/Corp** Church of Jesus Christ of Latter-Day Saints. **VFOAT** Family Search. British Isles; International Genealogical Index. British Isles. (19??)-. English. The Church of Jesus Christ of Latter-Day Saints, Genealogical Department, 50 East North Temple Street, Salt Lake City UT 84150. **LC** CS1. **DD** 929.
Desc: System requirements: PC, DOS, two disk drives, or one disk drive and a hard drive; monochrome or color monitor; printer; CD-ROM drive; FamilySearch retrieval/search software.

US/1063-4738
FAMILYSEARCH. INTERNATIONAL GENEALOGICAL INDEX. DENMARK. (FAMILYSEARCH. INTERNATIONAL GENEALOGICAL INDEX. DENMARK [COMPUTER FILE].). [FamilySearch, Int. geneal. index, Den.]. **Added/Corp** Church of Jesus Christ of Latter-Day Saints. **VFOAT** Family Search. Denmark; International Genealogical Index. Denmark. (198?)-. English. The Church of Jesus Christ of Latter-Day Saints, Genealogical Department, 50 East North Temple Street, Salt Lake City UT 84150. **LC** CS1. **DD** 929. available on microfiche.
Desc: World-wide index of more than one hundred forty-seven million names of deceased persons. Most names come from forms submitted by members of the Church of Jesus Christ of Latter-Day Saints. System requirements: PC, DOS, two disk drives (one hard disk and one floppy drive), monitor (color or monochrome), printer, CD-ROM drive, FamilySearch retrieval/search software.

US/1063-4703
FAMILYSEARCH. INTERNATIONAL GENEALOGICAL INDEX. U.S. AND CANADA. (FAMILYSEARCH. INTERNATIONAL GENEALOGICAL INDEX. U.S. AND CANADA [COMPUTER FILE].). [FamilySearch, Int. geneal. index, U. S. Can.]. **Added/Corp** Church of Jesus Christ of Latter-Day Saints. **VFOAT** Family Search. U.S. and Canada; International Genealogical Index. U.S. and Canada. (19??)-. English. The Church of Jesus Christ of Latter-Day Saints, Genealogical Department, 50 East North Temple Street, Salt Lake City UT 84150. **LC** CS1. **DD** 929.
Desc: Worldwide index of more than one hundred forty-seven million names of deceased persons. Most names come from forms submitted by members of the Church of Jesus Christ of Latter-Day Saints. System requirements: PC; DOS; two disk drives (one disk drive and one hard disk); monitor (color or monochrome); printer; CD-ROM drive; FamilySearch retrieval/search software.

US/1063-472X
FAMILYSEARCH. INTERNATIONAL GENEALOGICAL INDEX. WALES. (FAMILYSEARCH. INTERNATIONAL GENEALOGICAL INDEX. WALES [COMPUTER FILE].). [FamilySearch, Int. geneal. index, Wales]. **Added/Corp** Church of Jesus Christ of Latter-Day Saints. **VFOAT** Family Search. Wales; International Genealogical Index. Wales. (19??)-. English. The Church of Jesus Christ of Latter-Day Saints, Genealogical Department, 50 East North Temple Street, Salt Lake City UT 84150. **LC** CS1. **DD** 929.
Desc: World-wide index of more than one hundred forty-seven million names of deceased persons. Most names come from forms sumbitted by members of the Church of Jesus Christ of Latter-Day Saints.

US/0897-778X
FARR FOOTNOTES. [Farr footnotes]. Vol. 1 (May 1985)-. Periodical. English. Four times a year. $7.35. Pioneer Publications, PO Box 397, Black Eagle MT 59414-0397. **Tel** (406)453-4266. **ED** Shirley Penna Oakes. **LC** CS71; .F239a. **DD** 929/.2/0973. Index available. **Bk Rev**. **Ad Acc**.

US/0732-6661
FAYETTE ANCESTORS SURNAME INDEX. [Fayette ancestors surname index]. **VFOAT** Fayette Ancestors. 3rd Ed.-. English. an. $10.00. Dean Publications, 3690 Peacock Court, Apt. 2, Santa Clara CA 95051. **LC** F157.F2; F38. **DD** 929/.1/072074884. **UDC** 929.52(748). ***Continues*** *Fayette Ancestors Magazine.*

US/0739-8093
FAYETTE CONNECTION, THE. Main/Corp Fayette County Genealogical Society (Ohio). Vol. 2, No. 1 (Aug. 1982)-. Periodical. English. qt (August, November, February, May). $10.00. Fayette County Genealogical Society, PO Box 342, Washington Court House OH 43160. **Tel** (614)335-0266. **ED** Sandy Fackler. **LC** F497.F2; F39A. **DD** 929/.1/0720771813. **UDC** 929.5(771). **Bk Rev**. **Ad Acc**. **Circ:** 310 (ctrl). ***Continues*** *Fayette County Genealogical Society (Ohio). Newsletter, 0739-6872.*
Desc: Contains bible records, court records, cemetery inscriptions, maps, how-to's, and other genealogical information pertaining to Fayette county and surrounding areas.
Ind/Abst Genealogical Period. Annu. Index.

US/0737-1012
FAYETTE FACTS. (FAYETTE FACTS / FAYETTE COUNTY GENEALOGICAL SOCIETY.). [Fayette facts]. **Added/Corp** Fayette County Genealogical Society (Ill.). (March 1972)-. Periodical. English. Four times a year (Mar., June, Sept., Dec.). $15.00 (members); $16.00 (nonmembers). Fayette County Genealogical and Historical Society, Box 177, Vanalia IL 62471. **Tel** (618)423-2315. **ED** Linda Hanabarger (editor's address: Route 2 Box 207, Ramsey, IL 62080, phone: (618)423-2625). **LC** F547.F35; F39. **DD** 929/.3773797. Index available (Each iss.). **Bk Rev**. **Circ:** 350.
Ind/Abst Genealogical Period. Annu. Index (?-?).

US/1040-2276
FERGUSON FILES. [Ferguson files]. (1987)-. Periodical. English. qt. $10.00. Kinseeker Publications, Box 184, Grawn MI 49637. **ED** V. Wilson. **DD** 929. Index available. **Bk Rev**. **Ad Acc**. **Circ:** 50.
Desc: Contains genealogical information on the Ferguson families.

US
FINDING AIDS TO THE MICROFILMED MANUSCRIPT COLLECTION OF THE GENEALOGICAL SOCIETY OF UTAH. (1978)-. Monographic series. English. ir. Price varies per volume. University of Utah Press / Building 50, Salt Lake City UT 84112. **Tel** (801)581-6771. **ED** R.M. Haigh.

US
FISK(E) FAMILY ASSOCIATION : NEWSLETTER. 1980. Newsletter. English. ir. $15.00. Fisk Family Association, 2215 Anderson, Manhattan KS 66502. **ED** L R Wynar. **LC** CS71; .F5374. **DD** 929/.2/0973. **UDC** 929.5. **Bk Rev**. **Ad Acc**. **Circ:** 200.
Desc: Forum for discussion and evaluation of various trends in ethnic studies, organization, communities and press.

CN/0833-1510
FLAGSCAN. (FLAGSCAN : NEWSLETTER OF THE CANADIAN FLAG ASSOCIATION.). [Flagscan]. **Added/Corp** Canadian Flag Association. Vol. 1, No. 1 (Spring 1986)-. Periodical. English (French). qt (Mar., June, Sept., Dec.). $15.00 school, college, and public libraries; $40.00 institutions; $20.00 individuals. Canadian Flag Association, 50 Heathfield Drive, Scarborough Ontario M1M 3B1 Canada. **Tel** (905)267-9618. **ED** Kevin Harrington. **DD** 929.9/2/0971. Index available. cum. index. **Bk Rev**, (Qty: 12-16). **Ad Acc**. **Circ:** 300.
Desc: Illustrated journal of vexillology covering news of flags in Canada and the world; featuring histories of flags, protocol on flags, and heraldic stories.

US
FLEMISH AMERICAN HERITAGE. English. $10.00. Genealogical Society of Flemish Americans, 18740 Thirteen Mile Road, Roseville MI 48066. **Tel** (313)776-9579.
Ind/Abst Genealogical Period. Annu. Index.

CN/0715-4518
FLETCHER-O'LEARY PERIODICAL, THE. [Fletcher-O'Leary period.]. Issue No. 1 (Oct. 1980)-. Periodical. English. sa. $10.00. George Bidlake, South Devon Publishing, 745 Albert Street, Fredericton New Brunswick E3B 2C5 Canada. **Tel** (506)454-5649. **ED** George C Bidlake. **DD** 929/.2. Index available. cum. index. **Bk Rev**. **Circ:** 150 (ctrl).
Desc: Biographies and current events concerning the descendants of Denis O'Leary and Edward Fletcher, settlers in the New Maryland area of central New Brunswick from the 1840's.

US/0748-0113
FLORIDA ARMCHAIR RESEARCHER, THE. Vol. 1, No. 1 (Winter 1984)-. Periodical. English. qt. $15.00. Route 2 Box 895, Hampton GA 30228. **ED** Joel Dixon Wells, Brian E Michaels. **LC** F310; .F46. **DD** 929/.1/0720759. **UDC** 929.5(759).

US/0161-4932
FLORIDA GENEALOGIST, THE. (THE FLORIDA GENEALOGIST / PUBLISHED BY THE FLORIDA STATE GENEALOGICAL SOCIETY.). **Added/Corp** Florida State Genealogical Society. (Fall 1977)-. Periodical. English. qt. $18.00 US; $20.00 Canada; $35.00 other. Florida State Genealogical Society, 606 Nelson Point Road, Niceville FL 32578. **Tel** (904)897-4844. **LC** F310; .F48. **DD** 929/.1/0720759. Index Available in first issue of next volume--attached. cum. index. **Bk Rev**, (Qty: 30). **Circ:** 600.
Desc: Publishes previously unpublished manuscripts and source materials pertaining to the history and genealogy of the territory and state of Florida.
Ind/Abst Genealogical Period. Annu. Index.

US/8756-2316
FLORIDA PARISHES GENEALOGICAL NEWSLETTER. [Fla. parishes geneal. newsl.]. Vol. 1, No. 1 (Jan./Feb. 1979)-. Newsletter. English. Six times a year. $8.00. Florida Parishes Genealogical Society, 1857 Stonewood Drive, Baton Rouge LA 70816. **Tel** (504)293-7394. **LC** F368; .F57. **DD** 929.
Ind/Abst Genealogical Period. Annu. Index.

AT/0815-4112
FLOWER LINK. [Flower link]. (1983)-. Periodical. English. mo. 24.00Aus$ (Australia); 60.00Aus$ (other). Market Link Publishing, Unit B-3 23-25 Windsor Road, Northmead NSW 2152, Australia. **Tel** 11 61 02 630 25541. **DD** 635.90994. ***Absorbed*** *Flower Link (Victorian ed.), 0817-3664; Flower Link (Queensland ed.), 0818-0822.*

US/0738-159X
FLOWER OF THE FOREST BLACK GENEALOGICAL JOURNAL. [Flower for. black geneal. j.]. **VFOAT** Flower of the Forest. (1982)-. Periodical. English. an. $6.05. Agnes Kane Callum Literary Guild, 822 Bonaparte Avenue, Baltimore MD 21218. **Tel** (410)235-6697. **ED** Agnes Kane Callum. **LC** E185.93.M2; F57. **DD** 929/.1/089960730752. cum. index. **Bk Rev**. **Ad Acc**. **Circ:** 300 (ctrl).
Desc: History and genealogy of Maryland. Educational, historical and geography of Maryland as it relates to black people.

US/0190-8189
FOLK AND KINFOLK OF HARRIS COUNTY. **VFOAT** Folk & Kinfolk. V. 1- 1975-. Periodical. English. an. Harris County High School, PO Box 448, Hamilton GA 31811. **LC** F292.H55; F64. **DD** 975.8/466/005. **UDC** 929.5(758)+975.8.

US
FOOT PRINTS PAST AND PRESENT. **Added/Corp** Richland County Genealogical Society (Ill.) Richland County Genealogical and Historical Society (Ill.). Vol. 1, No. 1 (June 1978)-. Periodical. English. Four times a year. $15.00 Comes with Richland County Genealogical & Historical Society membership. Richland County Genealogical Society, PO Box 202, Onley IL 62450. **Tel** (618)869-2425. **LC** F547.R5; F66. **DD** 929/.1/072077377.

US/0748-0970
FOOTHILLS INQUIRER, THE. Added/Corp Foothills Genealogy Society of Colorado. (1981)-. Periodical. English. Four times a year (Mar., June, Sept., Dec.). $10.00. Foothills Genealogy Society of Colorado, PO Box 150382, Lakewood CO 80215. **Tel** (303)642-7262. **ED** Patricia A. Kemper. **LC** F782.J4; I57. **DD** 929/.1/072078884. Index available (Bound in 3rd iss., in Sept.). cum. index. **Ad Acc**. **Circ:** 275. ***Continues*** *Introducing the Foothills Inquirer, 0748-0989.*
Desc: Records and other information for Clear Creek, Gilpin, Jefferson, and Park Counties, Colorado.
Ind/Abst Genealogical Period. Annu. Index.

UK
FOOTPRINTS. English. qt. £7.50. Northamptonshire Family History Society, 19 Ridgway Road, Kettering NO NN15 5AQ England. **Tel** 011 44 0536516626. **Bk Rev**, (Qty: 10). **Ad Acc**. **Circ:** 9,000 (ctrl).
Desc: Topics of interest to family historians. Local history lectures and members' research are published.

US/0426-8261
FOOTPRINTS (FORT WORTH). (FOOTPRINTS.). **Added/Corp** Fort Worth Genealogical Society. (19??)-. Periodical. English. qt. comes with membership. Fort Worth Genealogical Society, PO Box 9767, Fort Worth TX 76147-2767. **ED** Barbara Knox (editor's address: 2616 Sarah Jane Lane, Fort Worth, TX 76119). **LC** CS42; .F66. **DD** 929.1/05. Index available. **Bk Rev**. **Ad Acc**. **Circ:** 830 (ctrl). available on microfilm.
Ind/Abst Genealogical Period. Annu. Index.

US/8755-6928
FOOTPRINTS IN MARION COUNTY. (FOOTPRINTS IN MARION COUNTY : OFFICIAL PUBLICATION OF MARION COUNTY GENEALOGICAL & HISTORICAL SOCIETY.). Founded 1976. Periodical. English. qt. Marion County Genealogical and Historical Society, PO Box 342, Salem IL 62881. **LC** F547.M3; F66. **DD** 929/.1/0720773794. **UDC** 929.5(773). Each issue contains an index to its own contents (no volume index)--loose. available on microfilm from The State Historical Society of Wisconsin.

US/0735-6218
FORGE (JONESVILLE, MICH.). (FORGE : THE BIGELOW SOCIETY QUARTERLY.). [Forge]. Vol. 4, No. 1 (Jan. 1975)-. Periodical. English. qt. Bigelow Society, 9615 Stornoway Circle, South Jordan UT 84065. **LC** CS71; .B5993. **DD** 929/.2/0973. **UDC** 929.5(73). ***Continues*** *Bigelow Society Quarterly, 0735-6706.*

US/0741-8159
FORSYTH COUNTY GENEALOGICAL SOCIETY JOURNAL, THE. Main/Corp Forsyth County Genealogical Society. Vol. 1, No. 1 (Fall 1982)-. Periodical. English. qt. $15.00. Forsyth County Genealogical Society, PO Box 5715, Winston Salem NC 27113. **Tel** (919)724-0714. **LC** F262.F7; F664a. **DD** 929/.1/072075667. Index available (bound). **Bk Rev**, (Qty: 12). **Pr Rev**. **Circ:** 200 (ctrl).
Ind/Abst Genealogical Period. Annu. Index.

US/0749-8381
FORT INDUSTRY REFLECTIONS. (FORT INDUSTRY REFLECTIONS / LUCAS COUNTY CHAPTER, OGS.). **Added/Corp** Ohio Genealogical Society. Lucas County Chapter. Vol. 1, No. 1 (June 1982)-. Periodical. English. Four times a year. $7.00. Lucas County Chapter / Ohio Genealogical Society, 325 North Michigan Street, Toledo OH 43624. **Tel** (419)255-7055. **ED** Beverly Todd Reed. **LC** F497.L9;

F67. **DD** 929/.377112. **Circ:** 250 (ctrl).
Desc: Queries and 5 generation charts in Lucas County.
Ind/Abst Genealogical Period. Annu. Index (?-?).

US/0894-3265
FORUM. **Main/Corp** Federation of Genealogical Societies (U.S.). **VFOAT** FGS. Vol. 1, No. 1 (Spring 1989)-. Periodical. English. qt. Federation of Genealogical Societies, Box 355, West Springs IL 60558. ***Continues*** *Federation of Genealogical Societies (U.S.). Newsletter -Federation of Genealogical Societies (U.S.).*
Ind/Abst Genealogical Period. Annu. Index.

US/1051-5666
FORUM INSIDER, THE. (THE FORUM INSIDER : NEWSLETTER OF THE GENEALOGICAL FORUM OF OREGON, INC.). [Forum insid.]. (1990)-. Newsletter. English. Four times a year. $15.00 (libraries & societies membership), $21.00 (individual membership), $27.00 (family membership), $51.00 (contributing membership), $99.00 (patron membership), $360.00 (single life membership), $480.00 (joint life membership). Genealogical Forum of Oregon, 1410 SW Morrison Street, Suite 812, Portland OR 97205. **Tel** (503)227-2398. **DD** 929.

US/1044-9809
FOX FAMILY FACTS. [Fox fam. facts]. Issue No. 1 (March 1988)-. Periodical. English. ir. $6.00. Sally S Williams, PO Box 1035, North Highlands CA 95660. **ED** Sally Seaman Williams. **DD** 929. Index available. **Bk Rev.** **Ad Acc.** **Circ:** 100.

US/1059-4051
FRANKLINTONIAN (COLUMBUS, OHIO), THE. (THE FRANKLINTONIAN/ THE FRANKLIN COUNTY CHAPTER, THE OHIO GENEALOGICAL SOCIETY.). [Franklintonian]. **Added/Corp** Ohio Genealogical Society. Franklin County Chapter. Began with: Vol. 8, No. 5, May (1980). Periodical. English. mo. Franklin County Chapter of the Ohio Genealogical Society, PO Box 2503, Columbus OH 43216. **LC** F497.F8; F73. **DD** 929/.1/072077156. ***Continues*** *Franklin County Chapter of the Ohio Genealogical Society.*
Ind/Abst Genealogical Period. Annu. Index.

US/0899-4188
FREDERICK FINDINGS. **Added/Corp** Lineage Search Associates. Vol. 1, No. 1 (Winter 1988)-. Periodical. English. Four times a year. $18.00 (institutions), $21.00 (individuals). Lineage Search Associates, 6419 Colts Neck Road, Mechanicsville VA 23111. **Tel** (804)730-7414. **ED** Michael E. Pollock. **DD** 929. **Bk Rev.** **Ad Acc.**
Ind/Abst Genealogical Period. Annu. Index.

US/1050-3668
FREE QUERIES. ***Ceased.*** [Free queries]. (1988)-Ceased Vol. 2, No. 6. Periodical. English. bm. Box 88100, Atlanta GA 30356-8100. **LC** CS1; .F67. **DD** 929/.105.

US
FREEBORN COUNTY TRACER. English. $8.00. Freeborn County Tracer, PO Box 403, Albert Lea MN 56007. **Tel** (507)373-9269.
Ind/Abst Genealogical Period. Annu. Index.

US/0735-3278
FREESTONE FRONTIERS. (FREESTONE FRONTIERS : QUARTERLY OF THE FREESTONE COUNTY GENEALOGY SOCIETY.). **Added/Corp** Freestone County Genealogy Society. Vol. 1, No. 1 (Nov. 1981)-. English. qt (Feb., May, Aug., Nov.). $12.50. Freestone County Genealogy Society, PO Box 14, Fairfield TX 75840. **Tel** (214)389-2822. **ED** Margaret Tolan. **LC** F392.F85; F75. **DD** 929/.1/0720764232. Index available. **Ad Acc.** **Circ:** 150.

US/8756-8446
FREMONT COUNTY NOSTALGIA NEWS. ***Ceased.*** **Added/Corp** Fremont County Genealogical Society. (19??)-(19??). Periodical. English. Four times a year. Fremont County Genealogical Society, c/o Riverton Branch Library, 1330 West Park Avenue, Riverton WY 82501. **Tel** (307)856-3556. **ED** Marlys A. Bias. **LC** F767.F8; F73. **DD** 929/.1/072078763. Index available. **Bk Rev**, (Qty: (varies)). **Ad Acc.** **Circ:** 65 (ctrl).
Desc: Indexes to local Fremont County, Wyoming court records, marriages, cemeteries and research information on genealogy including queries, family histories, ancestry charts, and 'Do You Know'.

US/0730-2495
FRETZLETTER. ***Title Change.*** **Added/Corp** Fretz Family Association. **VAT** Fretz Letter. (1971)-(1992). Newsletter. English. qt. Osmund R Fretz, 48 East Grandview Avenue, Sellersville PA 18960. **LC** CS71; .F8873. **DD** 929/.2/0973. ***Continues*** *Fretz Newsletter.* ***Continued by*** *Fretz Newsletter (1993), 1076-4011.*

CN/1181-9014
FROM SEA TO SEA. ***Title Change.*** (FROM SEA TO SEA / CLAN DONALD OF CANADA, GLENGARRY-STORMONT BRANCH.). [From sea sea]. **Added/Corp** Clan Donald Society of Canada. Glengarry-Stormont Branch. Newsletter No. 1 (Fall 1990)-(1993). Periodical. English. sa. $6.00. Glengarry-Stormont Branch, Clan Donald Society of Canada, c/o D MacDonald, 268 Bartholomew Street, Brockville, Ontario K6V 2S6 Canada. **DD** 929/.2/0971. ***Continued by*** *Clann Domhnaill Canada, 1197-3293.*

US/0749-3541
FUGATE FAMILY NEWSLETTER, THE. (19??)-. Newsletter. English. qt. Mary D Fugate, 1578 Bellmonte Road, Pittsburgh PA 15237. **ED** M. D. Fugate. **LC** CS71; .F94954. **DD** 929/.2/0973.

US/0896-1980
FULTON COUNTY FOLK FINDER. [Fulton Cty. folk finder]. **Added/Corp** Fulton County Historical Society (Ind.). Genealogy Section. (198?)-. Periodical. English. mo. $8.50 family membership; $6.00 individual membership. Fulton County Historical Society, 37 East 375 North, Rochester IN 46975. **Tel** (219)223-4436. **ED** Shirley Willard. **DD** 929.
Ind/Abst Genealogical Period. Annu. Index.

US
FULTON COUNTY HISTORICAL AND GENEALOGICAL SOCIETY NEWSLETTER. **See** History(General)-History of North, South, and Central America.

US/1065-0164
FULTON-HICKMAN GENEALOGICAL JOURNAL. [Fulton Hickman geneal. j.]. **Added/Corp** Fulton County Genealogical Society. **VFOAT** FHGJournal; FHGJ. **VAT** Fulton Hickman Genealogical Journal. Vol. 1, No. 1 (Feb. 1985)-. English. qt. $10.00 (membership). Fulton County Genealogical Society, PO Box 31, Fulton KY 42041. **Tel** (502)479-2696. **ED** M L Gossum, PO Box 1031, Fulton, KY 42041-1031, Tel. (502)472-2454. **LC** F457.F9; F85. **DD** 929/.376998/05. **Bk Rev.** ctrl circ.

US/0734-080X
FUTRAL, FUTRELL, FUTRELLE AND RELATED FAMILIES, WATKINS, CLIFFORD, WOOD. Began with Oct. 1978. Periodical. English. sa. $15.00. Jenny Futral, Route 3 Box 162, Franklin GA 30217. **Tel** (404)675-3082. **ED** Jenny Futral and John H Futral. **LC** CS71; .F9883. **DD** 929/.2/0973. **UDC** 929.52(73). **Bk Rev.**
Desc: Information contributed with written permission of donors.

US/0882-8377
G.A.S. LITES. [G.A.S. lites]. **Added/Corp** Genealogical Association of Sacramento. **VFOAT** GAS Lites; GAS Lights. **VAT** Genealogical Association of Sacramento Lites. (1984)-. English. Four times a year. $10.00. Genealogical Association of Sacramento, PO Box 28297, Sacramento CA 95828. **Tel** (916)446-5715. **ED** Iris Carter Jones. **LC** F869.S12; G4. **DD** 929/.1/072079454. Index available. cum. index. **Bk Rev.** **Ad Acc.** **Circ:** 450 (ctrl). ***Continues*** *Quarterly (Genealogical Association of Sacramento), 0882-8385.*
Desc: Publication of genealogical and historical material to aid researchers in quest of their ancestry.

US
G.R.I. NEWS 'N' NOTES. **Added/Corp** Genealogical Research Institute of Virginia. **VFOAT** G.R.I. News and Notes; News and Notes. **VAT** Genealogical Research Institute News 'n' Notes. Vol. 1, No. 1 (July 1981)-. Periodical. English. Ten times a year (Except June and July). $10.00 Comes with Genealogical Research Institute membership. Genealogical Research, PO Box 29178, Richmond VA 23229.
Ind/Abst Genealogical Period. Annu. Index.

US
G.S.M.C. RECORD. **VFOAT** GSMC Record. Periodical. English. qt. $5.00 individual membership, $2.50 senior membership, $5.50 husband/wife membership, $3.00 student membership. Genealogical Society of Monroe County Michigan, PO Box 1428, Monroe MI 48161. **LC** F572.M7. **DD** 929/.1/072077432. **UDC** 929.5(774).

US/0882-2166
GAELIC GLEANINGS. ***Suspended.*** [Gaelic glean.]. Vol. 1, No. 1 (Nov. 1981)-Vol. 10 No. 1 (1990). Periodical. English. Four times a year. $18.00 US; $19.00 Canada; $20.00 other. Magee Publications, PO Box 26507, Prescott Valley AZ 86312. **Tel** (602)772-7957. **ED** Peggy Magee. **LC** E184.I6; G33. **DD** 929/.3/0899162. **Bk Rev.** **Ad Acc.** **Circ:** 1,000 (ctrl).
Desc: Irish, Scottish and Welsh genealogy and history. Source material from European repositories, queries, lineage charts, passenger lists, articles by writers on both sides of the Atlantic.
Ind/Abst Genealogical Period. Annu. Index (?-?).

●US/1062-7448
GALENA GENEALOGY. [Galena geneal.]. Vol. 1, No. 1 (Mar. 1992)-. Periodical. English. qt. $10.95. Cottonwood Hill Publishing Company, PO Box 82, Benton WI 53803-0082. **DD** 929.

US/0883-1920
GALLATIN TRAILS. [Gallatin trails]. Vol. 1, No. 1 (Oct. 1979)-. Periodical. English. qt. $5.00 membership. Gallatin Genealogy Society, PO Box 1783, Bozeman MT 59771-1783. **Tel** (406)586-2269. **LC** WMLC L 83/509. **DD** 929. **UDC** 929.5(786). **Bk Rev.** **Circ:** 300 (ctrl).

US/0743-9040
GALLEY (HARRISONBURG, VA.), THE. (THE GALLEY : A PUBLICATION OF THE CLAN MACNEIL ASSOCIATION OF AMERICA.). **Main/Corp** Clan MacNeil Association of America. Vol. 3, No. 4 (Dec. 1982)-. Periodical. English. sa. Galley, 1351 Crawford Avenue, Harrisonburg VA 22801. **LC** CS71; .M4756813. **DD** 929/.2/0973. **UDC** 929.52(73). ***Continues*** *Clan MacNeil Association of America Galley, 0163-9951.*

US/0897-7798
GATES GAZETTE. [Gates gaz.]. Vol. 1 (Sept. 1985)-. Periodical. English. Four times a year. $6.00. Pioneer Publications, PO Box 397, Black Eagle MT 59414-0397. **Tel** (406)453-4266. **ED** Shirley Penna Oakes. **LC** CS71; .G2583. **DD** 929/.2/097305. Index available. **Bk Rev.**

US
GATEWAY: THE JOURNAL OF THE BELL COUNTY HISTORICAL SOCIETY. **See** History(General)-History of North, South, and Central America.

US/0893-3162
GATHERING GIBSONS. Vol. 1, No. 1 (May 1987)-. Periodical. English. qt. $10.00. Kinseeker Publications, Box 184, Grawn MI 49637. **ED** V Wilson. **DD** 929. Index available. **Bk Rev.** **Ad Acc.** **Circ:** 50.
Desc: Contains genealogical information on Gibsons families.

US/0898-8331
GEMINI (ELMIRA, N.Y.). (GEMINI.). **Added/Corp** Twin Tiers Genealogical Society. (1971)-. Periodical. English. Four times a year (Mar., June., Sept., Dec.). $5.00. Twin Tiers Genealogical Society, PO Box 763, Elmira NY 14905. **Tel** (607)734-1878. **ED** Shirley Tuthill. **DD** 929. cum. index (Mar. iss.). **Circ:** 400.
Desc: Concentration is on Chemung, Schyyler, Steuben, Tompkins County, N.Y., and Bradford and Tioga counties in P.A.

US/8756-7989
GENEAGRAM. (GENEAGRAM / CHARLOTTE COUNTY GENEALOGICAL SOCIETY.). [Geneagram]. **Added/Corp** Charlotte County Genealogical Society. (19??)-. Newsletter. English. mo. $10.00. Charlotte County Genealogical Society, PO Box 2682, Port Charlotte FL 33949. **ED** Nita Groh and Bob Grumman. **LC** F317.C4; G46. **DD** 929/.1/072075947. **Bk Rev.** **Ad Acc.** **Circ:** 150.
Desc: Source materials for research and personal genealogies of members.

US/0738-5226
GENEALOGICAL AIDS BULLETIN (1978). (GENEALOGICAL AIDS BULLETIN / MIAMI VALLEY GENEALOGICAL SOCIETY.). Vol. 8, No. 2 (Fall 1978)-. Bulletin. English. qt. $9.00 US; $11.00 other. Miami Valley Genealogical Society, Box 1364, Dayton OH 45401-1364. **Tel** (513)890-0925. **ED** Natalie Kobelak (editor's address:7290 East Studebaker Road, Tipp City OH 45371-9705). **LC** F478; .G46. **DD** 929/.1/0720771. **Bk Rev**, (Qty: Varies). **Circ:** 276. ***Continues*** *Genealogical Aids Bulletin of the Miami Valley Genealogical Society, 0738-0836.*
Desc: Miami Valley vital records, wills, marriages, cemetery, early Miami Valley families and how-to's on genealogy.
Ind/Abst Genealogical Period. Annu. Index.

US/0743-5843
GENEALOGICAL AND HISTORICAL MAGAZINE OF THE SOUTH, THE. [Geneal. hist. mag. South]. Vol. 1, No. 1 (Feb. 1984)-. Periodical. English. qt. $25.00. Carroll Ainsworth Enterprises, PO Box 188, Harleyville SC 29448. **ED** Carroll Ainsworth McElligott. **LC** F208; .G46. **DD** 929/.1/072075. Index available. **Bk Rev.**

US/0146-616X
GENEALOGICAL & LOCAL HISTORY BOOKS IN PRINT. **See** Publishing-Books and Bookmaking.

US/0882-0422
GENEALOGICAL CLEARINGHOUSE QUARTERLY, THE. [Geneal. clgh. q.]. Began in 1984. Periodical. English. qt. $14.00 individuals, $16.00 libraries. Stuempges, 693 Orchard Avenue, Pittsburgh PA 15202. **Tel** (412)734-1615. **ED** Richard N Stuempges. **DD** 929. **Bk Rev.** **Ad Acc.** **Circ:** 200 (ctrl).
Desc: A unique publication that lists old photos, fractures, Bibles, samplers, immigrant chests and hundreds of other identified lost heirlooms. A clean and impressive product.
Ind/Abst Genealogical Period. Annu. Index (?-?).

US/0735-0287
GENEALOGICAL COMPUTER PIONEER. [Geneal. comput. pioneer]. (1981)-. Periodical. English. Six times a year. $30.00. Posey International, PO Box 338, Computer Genealogical Service, Orem UT 84057.

Tel (801)377-5504. **ED** Joanna D. Posey. **LC** CS14; .G46. **DD** 929/.1/02854. **Bk Rev. Ad Acc. Circ:** 3,000 (ctrl). available on microfiche (for library use).
Desc: This serial is an extension of the book "Tracing Your Roots by Computer". Records management, word processing, worldwide telecommunications, consumer guides, software reviews, trends, events calendar.
Ind/Abst Genealogical Period. Annu. Index (?-?).

US/0277-5913
GENEALOGICAL COMPUTING. [Geneal. comput.]. No. 1 (July 1981)-. Periodical. English. Four times a year (Jan., Apr., July, Oct.). $25.00 US; $30.00 Canada and Mexico; $35.00 other. Ancestry, Inc., PO Box 476, Salt Lake City UT 84110. **Tel** (800)531-1790. **ED** Dennis Sampson. **LC** CS14; .G465. **DD** 929/.1/028542. Index available ($8.50). cum. index. **Ad Acc, Adv Mgr:** Gary Sagers, **Tel** (801)531-1490. **Pr Rev. Circ:** 4,500.
Desc: A journal for family researchers interested in getting the most out of computers as they apply to genealogy. Every article combines genealogy and computing.
Ind/Abst Genealogical Period. Annu. Index (?-?).

US/0882-1623
GENEALOGICAL GEMS. (GENEALOGICAL GEMS : PUBLICATION OF THE FOX VALLEY GENEALOGICAL SOCIETY.). [Geneal. gems]. Vol. 1, No. 1 (Summer 1982)-. Periodical. English. qt. Genealogical Gems, PO Box 1592, Appleton WI 54913. **LC** F587.F7; G46. **DD** 929/.1/07207756. **UDC** 929.5(775).

US/0738-3770
GENEALOGICAL GOLDMINE. Added/Corp Paradise Genealogical Society. Vol. 1, No. 1 (June 1968)-. Periodical. English. sa. $16.00 (includes Paradise Genealogical Society membership). Paradise Genealogical Society, PO Box 460, Paradise CA 95967. **Tel** (916)877-2330. **ED** Carllene Marek. **LC** F869.P28; G46. **DD** 929/.1/072079432. Index available. **Bk Rev**, (Qty: 12). **Ad Acc. Circ:** 300 (ctrl).
Desc: Cemetery listings, obituaries, voting register, family histories, Butte County vital records and queries.
Ind/Abst Genealogical Period. Annu. Index.

US/0731-9606
GENEALOGICAL JOURNAL (LEXINGTON, N.C.), THE. (THE GENEALOGICAL JOURNAL / COMPILED BY GENEALOGICAL SOCIETY OF DAVIDSON COUNTY, NORTH CAROLINA.). **Added/Corp** Genealogical Society of Davidson County, North Carolina. **VFOAT** Journal of the Genealogical Society of Davidson County, North Carolina. Vol. 1, No. 1 (Spring 1981)-. Periodical. English. qt. $15.00. Genealogical Society of Davidson County, PO Box 1665, Lexington NC 27292. **Tel** (704)249-8745. **ED** Marie Hinson and Kathleen Craver. **LC** F262.D3; G46. **DD** 929/.375668. **Bk Rev. Circ:** 300 (ctrl).
Desc: Bible, census, cemetery, marriage, deed and will records. Any records of Davidson County, North Carolina that would be beneficial to those researching ancestors of this area.

US/1045-8166
GENEALOGICAL JOURNAL OF JEFFERSON COUNTY, NEW YORK. [Geneal. j. Jefferson Cty., N. Y.]. (1989)-. Periodical. English. qt. $15.00. The Family Tree / Idaho, PO Box 4311, Boise ID 83711. **Tel** (208)939-9136. **LC** F127.J4; G46. **DD** 929/.1/072074757.
Ind/Abst Genealogical Period. Annu. Index.

US/0146-2229
GENEALOGICAL JOURNAL (SALT LAKE CITY, UTAH). (GENEALOGICAL JOURNAL.). **Added/Corp** Utah Genealogical Association. Vol. 1, No. 1 (Mar. 1972)-. Periodical. English. Four times a year. $25.00 US; $30.00 other. Utah Genealogical Association, PO Box 1144, Salt Lake City UT 84110. **Tel** (801)240-4196, FAX (801)240-1929. **LC** CS1; .G382. **DD** 929/.1/072073. Index available. cum. index. **Bk Rev**, (Qty: 4y). **Pr Rev. Circ:** 1,000. available on microfilm and microfiche from University Microfilms International (UMI).
Ind/Abst Genealogical Period. Annu. Index.

US/0016-6367
GENEALOGICAL MAGAZINE OF NEW JERSEY, THE. [Geneal. mag. N. J.]. Vol. 1, No. 1 (July 1925)-. Periodical. English. Three times a year. $15.00. Genealogical Society of New Jersey, 132 West Franklin Street, Bound Brook NJ 08805. **Tel** (908)356-6920. **ED** Janet Riemer and Roxanne Carkhuff. **LC** F131; .G32. **DD** 929/.1/09749. **UDC** 929.5(749). cum. index. **Circ:** 900 (ctrl).
Desc: Gathers and publishes genealogical material relative to New Jersey.
Ind/Abst Genealogical Period. Annu. Index.

US/0072-0593
GENEALOGICAL PERIODICAL ANNUAL INDEX. See Genealogy and Heraldry-Abstracting, Bibliographies and Statistics.

US/0433-3209
GENEALOGICAL RECORD (HOUSTON, TEX.), THE. (THE GENEALOGICAL RECORD.). **Added/Corp** Houston Genealogical Forum. Vol. 1, No. 1 (Oct. 1958)-. Periodical. English. qt (Mar., Jun., Sep., Dec.). $18.00. Houston Genealogical Forum, PO Box 271466, Houston TX 77277-1466. **Tel** (713)481-3636. **ED** Rose Weaver. **LC** F385; .G46. **DD** 929/.1/0720764. Index available. **Bk Rev. Ad Acc. Circ:** 1,000 (ctrl).
Desc: Contains information on feature articles, Bible records, church and cemetery records, news paper gleanings, computers in genealogy, and library resources.
Ind/Abst Genealogical Period. Annu. Index.

US/0739-1447
GENEALOGICAL RECORD OF STRAFFORD COUNTY, THE. (THE GENEALOGICAL RECORD OF STRAFFORD COUNTY : OFFICIAL NEWSLETTER OF THE STRAFFORD COUNTY CHAPTER OF N.H.S.O.G.). **Main/Corp** New Hampshire Society of Genealogists. Strafford County Chapter. Vol. 1 No. 1 (Sept. 1977)-. English. Six times a year. $4.00. New Hampshire Society of Genealogists, Stafford County Chapter, 18 Main Street, East Rochester NH 03867. **Tel** (603)332-4366. **LC** F42.S8; N43a. **DD** 929/.1/07207425.
Ind/Abst Genealogical Period. Annu. Index.

US/0533-7275
GENEALOGICAL REFERENCE BUILDERS NEWSLETTER. (1967)-. Newsletter. English. PO Box 248, Post Falls ID 83854. **LC** CS42; .G469. **DD** 929/.1/0973.

AT
GENEALOGICAL RESEARCH DIRECTORY (SYDNEY, N.S.W. : 1989). (GENEALOGICAL RESEARCH DIRECTORY : NATIONAL & INTERNATIONAL.). **VFOAT** GRD; G.R.D. (1989)-. Directory. English. an. 27.00Aus$ plus 5.00Aus$ postage (softcover); 35.00Aus$ plus 5.00Aus$ postage (hardcover). Library of Australian History, 17 Mitchell Street, New South Wales 2060 Australia. **Tel** 011-61-2-9295087. **ED** Keith A Johnson and Malcolm R Sainty. **LC** CS5; .G46. **DD** 929/.1/025. ***Continues*** *Genealogical Research Directory ... & Guide to Genealogical Societies.*

US/1055-2693
GENEALOGICAL SOCIETY OF CHICKASAW COUNTY, THE. (THE GENEALOGICAL SOCIETY OF CHICKASAW COUNTY : [NEWSLETTER].). [Geneal. Soc. Chickasaw Cty.]. **Added/Corp** Genealogical Society of Chickasaw County (Iowa). Vol. 1, No. 1 (Spring 1984)-. Periodical. English. Chickasaw County Genealogical Society, PO Box 434, New Hampton IA 50659-0434. **LC** F627.C5; G46. **DD** 929/.1/06077315.
Ind/Abst Genealogical Period. Annu. Index.

US/0740-5006
GENEALOGICAL SOCIETY OF IREDELL COUNTY, N.C, THE. ***Title Change.*** (THE GENEALOGICAL SOCIETY OF IREDELL COUNTY, N.C. : NEWSLETTER.). **Main/Corp** Genealogical Society of Iredell County, N.C. Vol. 1, No. 1 (March 1978)-?. Newsletter. English. qt. PO Box 946, Statesville NC 28677. **LC** F262.I7; G46A. **DD** 929/.1/0720756793. **UDC** 929.5(786). ***Continued by*** *Iredell County Tracks.*

US/0433-3233
GENEALOGICAL TIPS. Vol. 1, No. 1 (May 1963)-. Periodical. English. Four times a year. $10.00. Tip-O-Texas Genealogical Society, Harlingen Public Library, 502 East Tyler, Harlingen TX 78550. **Tel** (512)565-4945. **ED** Martha Tutt. **LC** F394.H3; G46. **DD** 929/.1/0720764495. **UDC** 929.5. cum. index. **Bk Rev. Circ:** 230 (ctrl).
Desc: Includes articles, local history, family history and recollections, ancestor charts, family group sheets, ideas for research sources and methods, lists of new books added to the library, queries, cemetery records, seminar notices and information.
Ind/Abst Genealogical Period. Annu. Index.

GW/0016-6383
GENEALOGIE. Added/Corp Deutsche Arbeitsgemeinschaft Genealogischer Verbande. Gesamtverein der Deutschen Geschits- und Alterthumsvereine. Abteilung Genealogie und Heraldik. (1962)-. Periodical. German. mo (12 issues). DM57.00. Verlag Degener & Co., Postfach 1340, Nuernberger Strasse 27, W 8530 Neustadt FR Germany. **Tel** 011 49 9161 2028. ***Continues*** *Familie und Volk.*

GW
GENEALOGIE UND LANDESGESCHICHTE. No. 1 (1959)-. Monographic series. German. Price varies per volume. Verlag Degener and Company, Postfach 1340, Neuinberger Street 27, W-8530 Neustadt Germany. **Tel** 09161-1378.

FR/0223-7237
GENEALOGIES BOURBONNAISES ET DU CENTRE / CERCLE GENEALOGIQUE ET HERALDIQUE DU BOURBONNAIS. Periodical. French. qt. 120. Secretariat General / Cercle Genealogique et Heraldique du Bourbannais, 47 Av Meunier, 03000 Moulins France. **Tel** 70.44.54.01. **LC** CS597.B7; G45. **DD** 929/.1/07204457. **UDC** 929.5/.6(44). **Bk Rev.** ctrl circ.

GW
GENEALOGISCHES HANDBUCH DES ADELS. Vol. 1 1951-. Periodical. German. sa. C A Starke Verlag, PO Box 1310 Limburg 1 Germany.

US/0196-4259
GENEALOGIST (MANCHESTER, N.H.), THE. ***Title Change.*** (THE GENEALOGIST : OFFICIAL JOURNAL OF THE AMERICAN-CANADIAN GENEALOGICAL SOCIETY OF NEW HAMPSHIRE.). [Genealogist]. **Added/Corp** American-Canadian Genealogical Society of New Hampshire. (1975)-(199?). Periodical. English (French). sa. American-Canadian Genealogical Society Inc, PO Box 668, Manchester NH 03105. **Tel** (603)622-1554. **ED** Anne-Marie Perrault. **LC** E184.F85; G46. **DD** 929/.1/089114073. Index available. cum. index. **Bk Rev. Ad Acc. Circ:** 1,500 (ctrl). available on microfiche; available on microfilm. ***Continued by*** *American-Canadian Genealogist, 1076-3902.*
Desc: Contains articles covering history, a query section, along with book reviews; add to the contents of this quarterly periodical. Family lines and genealogical oriented subjects.

AT
GENEALOGIST MELBOURNE. [Genealogist Melb.]. (1974)-. English. Four times a year. 30.00Aus$. Australian Institute of Genealogical Studies, PO Box 339, Blackburn 3130 Australia. **Tel** 011 61 03 8773789. **ED** K. Press. **Ad Acc. Circ:** 2,500 (ctrl).
Ind/Abst Genealogical Period. Annu. Index.

US/0197-1468
GENEALOGIST (NEW YORK), THE. (THE GENEALOGIST.). **Added/Corp** Association for the Promotion of Scholarship in Genealogy. Vol. 1 (Spring 1980)-. Periodical. English. Twice a year (Apr. & Oct.). $25.00 (one year); $45.00 (two years); $65.00 (three years). Association for the Promotion of Scholarship in Genealogy - APSG, 255 North Second West, Salt Lake City UT 84103. **Tel** (801)521-4732. **ED** Neil D. Thompson Ph.D. **LC** CS1; .G393. **DD** 929/.1/05. Index available. cum. index. **Bk Rev**, (Qty: 15-20). **Ad Acc. Pr Rev. Circ:** 500 (ctrl).
Desc: Stresses compiled genealogy or single line multigenerational descents from all periods and geographical areas, emphasis on documentation.
Ind/Abst Genealogical Period. Annu. Index.

US/0742-4094
GENEALOGISTS IN THE UNITED STATES AND CANADA. English. $10.00. Dr William D Andersen and Associates, 2616 Kirby, Memphis TN 38119. **LC** CS8.A1; G45. **DD** 929/.1/02573. **UDC** 929.5(91+93).

UK/0016-6391
GENEALOGISTS' MAGAZINE : OFFICIAL ORGAN OF THE SOCIETY OF GENEALOGISTS, THE. Added/Corp Society of Genealogists. (1925)-. Periodical. English. qt. $19.80. Society of Genealogists, 14 Charterhouse Buildings, Goswell Road, London EC1M 7BA England. **Tel** 011 44 71 2518799. **ED** Francis L. Leeson. **LC** CS410; .S61. Index available. cum. index. **Bk Rev. Ad Acc, Adv Mgr:** M. Gandy. **Circ:** 12,500. available on microfilm and microfiche from University Microfilms International (UMI).
Desc: Articles relating to genealogy and family history. Updates on material held in the Society's Library (in London England). Book reviews, readers queries, society and general news items.
Ind/Abst Br. Humanit. Index; Genealogical Period. Annu. Index.

US/0736-5292
GENEALOGY AND LOCAL HISTORY TITLES ON MICROFICHE. [Geneal. local hist. titles microfiche]. **VFOAT** Genealogy and Local History. Sales Catalog No. 1-. Periodical. English. ir. Microfilming Corporation of America, 21 Harristown Road, Glen Rock NJ 07452. **LC** Z5313.U5; G47; CS47. **DD** 016.973. **UDC** 929.5+973(0.035.23).

US
GENEALOGY CLUB OF THE ALBUQUERQUE PUBLIC LIBRARY NEWSLETTER. Added/Corp Genealogy Club of the APL. (198?)-. Newsletter. English. qt (4 issues). comes with Genealogical Club of Albuquerque Public Library membership; $10.00 (membership). Genealogy Club of Albuquerque, 423 Central Avenue Northeast, Albuquerque Library, Albuquerque NM 87102. **Tel** (505)768-5140. **ED** Jone Chappell. **LC** WMLC 91/1359. ***Continues*** *Genealogy Club of the APL.*

US/0882-5106
GENEALOGY GLEANINGS. [Geneal. glean.]. **Added/Corp** Marion County Genealogy Club. (19??)-. Periodical. English. Four times a year. $7.00. Marion County Genealogy Club, 1600 Mary Lou Retton Drive, Fairmont WV 26554. **Tel** (304)363-7757, (304)366-1366. **LC** F247.M26; G46. **DD** 929/.1/072075454.

Genealogy and Heraldry

CN/0821-5359
GENERATIONS (FREDERICTON). (GENERATIONS : NEWSLETTER / NEW BRUNSWICK GENEALOGICAL SOCIETY / SOCIETE GENEALOGIQUE DU NOUVEAU-BRUNSWICK.). [Generations]. **Added/Corp** New Brunswick Genealogical Society. Issue 16 (June 1983)-. Newsletter. English. qt (Mar., June, Sept., Dec.). 20.00Can$ (individuals), 25.00Can$ (institutions) Canada; $20.00 other. New Brunswick Genealogical Society, Box 3235 Station B, Fredericton NB, E3A 5B9 Canada. **ED** Carmen Willistan. **LC** CS88.N43; N49. **DD** 929/.37151. **Circ:** 350 (ctrl). ***Continues*** *Newsletter (New Brunswick Genealogical Society).*

CN/0226-6105
GENERATIONS (WINNIPEG). (GENERATIONS : THE JOURNAL OF THE MANITOBA GENEALOGICAL SOCIETY.). [Generations]. **Added/Corp** Manitoba Genealogical Society. Vol. 1, No. 1 (Fall 1976)-. Periodical. English. qt (Mar., June, Sept., Dec.). 25.00Can$ (comes with membership). Manitoba Genealogical Society, 885 Notre Dame Avenue, Winnipeg Manitoba R3E 0M4 Canada. **Tel** (204)783-9139. **ED** Joyce Elias. **DD** 929/.1/097127. Index available. cum. index. **Bk Rev**, (Qty: 20-50). **Ad Acc. Circ:** 800 (ctrl).
Desc: Articles relating to family history, queries sent in from persons seeking assistance, listings of new library acquisitions, society news and other items of interest.
Ind/Abst Genealogical Period. Annu. Index.

US
GENERATOR. English. Free to members. St. Mary's County Genealogy Society, PO Box 1109, Brenda Wagoner, Leonardtown MD 20650. **Tel** (301)862-4694.
Ind/Abst Genealogical Period. Annu. Index.

US/0534-0020
GENIE, THE. **Added/Corp** Ark-La-Tex Genealogical Association. (1967)-. Periodical. English. qt (Jan., April, July, Oct.). $12.50. Ark-La-Tex Genealogical Association, PO Box 4462, Shreveport LA 71134. **Tel** (318)746-4598. **ED** LeRoy Musselman. Index available in last issue of volume--attached (free). **Bk Rev. Ad Acc. Circ:** 500.
Desc: To collect, preserve, and make available genealogical data and to make sure Shreveport, Louisiana is a major genealogical research center for genealogists and historians.

US/0739-6090
GENIE BUG. (GENIE BUG : NORTH CENTRAL IOWA GENEALOGICAL SOCIETY NEWSLETTER.). **Added/Corp** North Central Iowa Genealogical Society. (19??)-. Periodical. English. Four times a year (Seasonally). $7.00. North Central Iowa Genealogical Society, PO Box 237, Mason City IA 50401. **Tel** (515)423-5930. **ED** Irma Harris. **LC** F620; .G46. **DD** 929/.1/07207772. cum. index. **Ad Acc. Circ:** 250 (ctrl).
Desc: Covers local society activities, new materials and area genealogical information.

FI/0016-6898
GENOS. **Added/Corp** Suomen Sukututkimusseura. Vol. 1 No. 1 (1930)-. Periodical. Finnish (Swedish). Four times a year. Fmk80.00. Academic Bookstore Akateeminen, Postilokero 23, FIN-00371 Helsinki Finland. **Tel** 011 358 0 12141. **(Subscription address:** Bookstore Tiedekirja, Kirkkokatu 14, SF 00170 Helsinki Finland.**) LC** CS884; .G4.

NE/0016-6936
GENS NOSTRA. [Gens nostra]. **VFOAT** Ons Geslacht. (1945)-. Periodical. Dutch. mo. Fl50.00. Nederlandse Geneal Vereniging, PO Box 976, 1000 AZ Amsterdam Netherlands. **UDC** 929.5.

US/0742-0994
GENTRY FAMILY GAZETTE AND GENEALOGY EXCHANGE. **VFOAT** G.F.G. & G.E.; GFG and GE; GFG & GE. (19??)-. Periodical. English. Six times a year. $25.00. Robert Gentry, 6151 Tompkins Drive, McLean VA 22101. **Tel** (703)356-9370. **LC** CS71; .G338. **DD** 929/.2/0973. ***Continues*** *Gentry Family Gazette and Genealogy, 0730-1685.*

US/0882-9209
GEORGIA ARMCHAIR RESEARCHER, THE. [Ga. armchair res.]. **VFOAT** Georgia Armchair Researcher Quarterly; GACR. Vol. 4, No. 1 (Spring 1983)-. Periodical. English. Four times a year. $15.00. Joel Dixon Wells, Route 2 Box 895, Hampton GA 30228. **Tel** (404)478-9263. **LC** F285; .G363. **DD** 929/.1/0720758. ***Continues*** *Armchair Researcher, 0734-7782.*

US/0435-5393
GEORGIA GENEALOGICAL MAGAZINE. No. 1 (July 1961)-. Periodical. English. qt (Mar., June, Sept., Dec.). $25.00. Georgia Genealogical Magazine, PO Box 1267, Easley SC 29602. **Tel** (803)233-2346. **ED** Silas Emmett Lucas, La Bruce Mortimer Seabrook Lucas and Dawn Gollwitzer. **LC** F281; G2967. Index available. cum. index. **Bk Rev. Circ:** 850 (ctrl).
Desc: Contains valuable genealogical source records from various Georgia counties, and bits of helpful information to aid the researcher in his or her work.
Ind/Abst Genealogical Period. Annu. Index (?-?).

US/0435-5393
GEORGIA GENEALOGICAL SOCIETY QUARTERLY, THE. [Ga. Geneal. Soc. q.]. **Added/Corp** Georgia Genealogical Society. Vol. 1, No. 1 (Sept. 1964)-. Periodical. English. qt. $18.00. Georgia Genealogical Society, PO Box 38066, Atlanta GA 30334. **Tel** (404)656-2350. **LC** CS42.G75. **DD** 929.
Ind/Abst Genealogical Period. Annu. Index.

US/1061-0529
GERMAN ANCESTRY. ***Title Change.*** (GERMAN ANCESTRY : NEWSLETTER.). [Ger. ancestry]. **Added/Corp** Crystal Educational Counselors. Vol. 1, No. 1 Winter (1992)-(1992). Newsletter. English. sa. Crystal Educational Counselors, 62 East Boehms Road, Willow Street PA 17584-9721. **Tel** (717)464-4201. **LC** E184.G3; G322. **DD** 929/.1/08931073. ***Continued by*** *Highwayman (Willow Street, Pa.), 1062-7200.*

US/0195-735X
GERMAN AND CENTRAL EUROPEAN EMIGRATION. **See** Emigration and Immigration.

US/8755-1756
GERMAN CONNECTION, THE. [Ger. connect.]. **Added/Corp** Deutsche Forschungsgemeinschaft. Vol. 1, No. 1 (Aug. 1977)-. Periodical. English. qt. comes with Germany Research Association membership. German Research Association, PO Box 711600, San Diego CA 92171-1600. **Tel** (619)453-6198. **ED** Joan Lowrey. **LC** E184.G3; G33. **DD** 929/.1/08931073. Index available. **Bk Rev. Circ:** 600 (ctrl).
Desc: Contains useful information for persons doing research on Germanic ancestry. Offers suggestions on procedures. Provides historical, geographical and cultural data. Offers surname searches.
Ind/Abst Genealogical Period. Annu. Index.

US
GERMAN GENEALOGICAL DIGEST. **VFOAT** Genealogical Digest. Vol. 1, No. 1 (1st Quarter 1985)-. Periodical. English. qt. $24.00 (one year), $45.00 (two year). German Genealogical Digest, 245 North Vine #106, Salt Lake City UT 84103. **Tel** (801)363-0401. **ED** Laraine Ferguson & Larry O. Jensen. Index available (available each issue / $8.00). cum. index. **Bk Rev. Ad Acc.**
Ind/Abst Genealogical Period. Annu. Index.

US/1058-8736
GEST-GUEST QUARTERLY. (GEST-GUEST QUARTERLY : A HISTORICAL & GENEALOGICAL NEWSLETTER FOR GEST, GIST, GUESS & GUEST FAMILIES.). [Gest-Guest q.]. **VFOAT** Gest, Guest Quarterly. Vol. 1, No. 1 (spring 1982)-. Periodical. English. ir. $10.00. Gest-Guest Quarterly, 101 Hayes #1409, Houston TX 77077. **Tel** (713)784-6130. **ED** Henry G. Guest, Jr. **LC** CS71; .G495a. **DD** 929/.2/097305. **Circ:** 150.
Desc: American genealogical and biographical references and abstracts of Gest, Gist, Guess and Guest families.

US/0736-2838
GEURIN GAZETTE. Issue No. 1 (Jan. 1979)-Issue No. 12 (Dec. 1979)-. Periodical. English. mo. Geurin Gazette, 457 A Manzanita Avenue, Santa Cruz CA 95062. **LC** CS71; .G39814. **DD** 929/.2/0973. **UDC** 929.52(73).

US/1053-4946
GIBSON COUNTY LINES. ***Title Change.*** (GIBSON COUNTY LINES / GIBSON COUNTY HISTORICAL SOCIETY.). [Gibson cty. lines]. **Added/Corp** Gibson County Historical Society. **VFOAT** County Lines. (1988)-(199?). Periodical. English. mo. Gibson County Historical Society, PO Box 516, Princeton IN 47670. **Tel** (812)385-3874. **LC** F532.G4; G53. **DD** 929/.1/072077235. ***Continued by*** *County Lines (Princeton, Ind.), 1070-4922.*
Ind/Abst Genealogical Period. Annu. Index (?-?).

CN/0713-3162
GIGUERERIE (EDITION FRANCAISE). (LA GIGUERERIE : BULLETIN DE LIAISON DE LA FONDATION ROBERT GIGUERE INC.). [Giguererie]. Bulletin. French. Free to members. Fondation Robert Giguere, 25 Ouest rue Jarry, Montreal Quebec H2P 1S6 Canada. **Tel** (514)387-2541. **DD** 929/.2. **UDC** 929.52(714). **Bk Rev. Ad Acc. Circ:** 200.
Desc: Covers the history and genealogy of the Giguere family, past and present.

US/0893-7753
GILA HERITAGE. (GILA HERITAGE / NORTHERN GILA COUNTY GENEALOGICAL SOCIETY, INC.). [Gila herit.]. **Added/Corp** Northern Gila County Genealogical Society. Vol. 1, No. 2 (1983)-. Periodical. English. qt. $5.00. Northern Gila County Genealogical Society, PO Box 952, Payson AZ 85547. **Tel** (602)474-2139. **ED** Opal Follin (editor's address: 304 East Pinon Circle, Payson, AZ 85541). **DD** 929. Index available. **Circ:** 81 (ctrl). ***Continues*** *Tonto Trails.*

US
GILES COUNTY HISTORICAL SOCIETY BULLETIN, THE. **Added/Corp** Giles County Historical Society. (Jan. 1991)-. Bulletin. English. qt. Free to members. Giles County Historical Society, PO Box 693, Pulaski TN 38478. **Tel** (615)363-1767. **LC** F443.G4; B84. **DD** 976.8/61/005. ***Continues*** *Bulletin (Giles County Historical Society), 8756-3541.*

US/0883-2765
GLEANINGS (BEAVER FALLS, PA.). (GLEANINGS : JOURNAL OF THE BEAVER COUNTY GENEALOGICAL SOCIETY.). [Gleanings]. **Added/Corp** Beaver County Genealogical Society. (19??)-. Periodical. English. qt. $7.00. Beaver County Genealogical Society, 1301 7th Avenue, Beaver Falls PA 15010. **Tel** (412)846-4340. **LC** F157.B2; G55. **DD** 929/.1/072074892.
Ind/Abst Genealogical Period. Annu. Index.

US
GLEANINGS FROM THE HEART OF THE CORNBELT. English. Free to members. McLean County Genealogical Society, PO Box 488, Normal IL 61761.
Ind/Abst Genealogical Period. Annu. Index.

US
GLEANINGS ... FROM THE WEST FIELDS. **Added/Corp** Genealogical Society of the West Fields (Westfield, N.J.). Vol. 1, Issue 1 (Nov. 1979)-. Periodical. English. bm. $7.00 (membership). Westfield Memorial Library, 550 East Broad Street, Westfield NJ 07090. **LC** F144.W52; G57. **DD** 929/.1/072074936.
Ind/Abst Genealogical Period. Annu. Index.

US
GLEANINGS (KEOKUK). English. qt. $5.00. Lee County Genealogical Society of Iowa, Box 303, Keokuk IA 52632-0303. **Bk Rev.**
Desc: Includes reviews of books and quarterlies, courthouse records, queries, genealogical helps and features articles written by members of the society.

UK/0143-0513
GLOUCESTERSHIRE FAMILY HISTORY SOCIETY JOURNAL. **Added/Corp** Gloucestershire Family History Society. **VFOAT** Journal of the Gloucestershire Family History Society. No. 1 (Summer 1979)-. English. Four times a year (Mar., June, Sept., Dec.). £7.00 UK; £11.00 other. Gloucestershire Family History Society, Stonehatch Oakridge Lynch Strd, Gloucestershre GL6 7NR England. **Tel** 0452 763193. **ED** Mr. D. E. Rayjourn. **LC** CS435.G5; G57. **DD** 929/.1/07204241. Index available. **Bk Rev**, (Qty: 10). **Ad Acc. Circ:** 1,200 (ctrl).
Desc: Contain articles of information and interest to researchers of genealogy, in particular to those with Gloucestershire connections.

US/0882-7559
GOFFS/GOUGHS, THEIR ANCESTORS & DESCENDANTS. **VFOAT** Goffs/Goughs, Their Ancestors and Descendants; Goffs, Goughs, Their Ancestors & Descendants. Vol. 1, No. 3 (Fall 1982)-. Periodical. English. qt. Goff/Gough Family, 5492 St. Mary's Circle, Westminister CA 92683. **LC** CS71; .G5993. **UDC** 929.52(73). ***Continues*** *Goffs of the U.S. and Their Ancestors, 0882-7540.*

US
GOINGSNAKE MESSENGER, THE. **See** History(General)-History of North, South, and Central America.

US/8755-3023
GOLDEN ROOTS OF THE MOTHER LODE, THE. [Gold. roots mother lode]. **Added/Corp** Tuolumne County Genealogical Society. Vol. 1, No. 4 (Winter 1981/Spring 1982)-. Periodical. English. Four times a year. $12.00. Tuolumne County Genealogical Society, PO Box 3956, Sonora CA 95370. **Tel** (209)532-1317. **ED** Clifford R. Knowles. **LC** F868.T9; G64. **DD** 929/.379445. Each issue contains an index to its own contents (no volume index)--loose. **Bk Rev. Circ:** 225 (ctrl). ***Continues*** *Mother Lode-Ore.*
Desc: Family histories, ancestor charts, vital records, census, military pension, burial records, Bible materials, family group sheets, births, death and reviews.

US/8755-5697
GOLDEN ROOTS OF THE MOTHER LODE. NEWSLETTER. **Added/Corp** Tuolumne County Genealogical Society. (19??)-. Newsletter. English. qt. $12.00. Tuolumne County Genealogical Society, PO Box 3956, Sonora CA 95370. **Tel** (209)532-1317. **ED** Clifford R. Knowles. Index available. **Bk Rev. Ad Acc. Circ:** 500 (ctrl).
Desc: Queries, family histories, genealogy, Bible, military, cemetery, census records, burials, historical book reviews, ancestry charts, school records, death records, voter records and vital records.

US/0738-8268
GOODLET FAMILY NEWSLETTER, THE. Vol. 1, Issue 1 (Winter 1982)-. Newsletter. English. sa. $4.00. Thelma Moon Goodlet, 951 East 37th Street, Hialeah FL 33013. **LC** CS71; .G65334. **UDC** 929.52(73).

US/0892-1423
GOODWIN NEWS, THE. (THE GOODWIN NEWS : NEWSLETTER OF THE GOODWIN FAMILY ORGANIZATION.). [Goodwin news]. **Added/Corp** Goodwin Family Organization. (197?)-. Newsletter. English. qt. $11.00 (libraries and genealogical societies), $15.00 (individuals) US; $14.00 (libraries and genealogical societies), $18.00 (individuals) Canada and Mexico; $16.00 (libraries and genealogical societies), $20.00 (individuals) other. Goodwin Family Organization, 39 Lost Trail, Roswell NM 88201. **Tel** (505)625-0961. **ED** Murray H. Sharp, Alice B. Sharp and Marietta Blazek. **LC** IN PROCESS. **DD** 929. Index available. cum. index. **Bk Rev. Circ:** 250 (ctrl).

●US/1062-7219
GOOSE (WILLOW STREET, PA.), THE. (THE GOOSE: THE GANTZ/GANS INTERNATIONAL GENEALOGY.). **Added/Corp** Crystal Educational Counselors. **VFOAT** Gantz/Gans International Genealogy. (1992)-. Periodical. English. sa. $10.00. Crystal Educational Counselors, 62 East Boehms Road, Willow Street PA 17584-9721. **Tel** (717)464-4201. **ED** Peg L. and James D. Raibley Beissel. available in Loose-leaf.

US
GRADY COUNTY GENEALOGICAL SOCIETY QUARTERLY. (19??)-. English. $12.00. Grady County Genealogical Society, PO Box 792, Chickasha OK 73023. **Tel** (405)224-7482.

US
GRANT COUNTY BEACON / GRANT COUNTY GENEALOGY CLUB. Main/Corp Grant County Genealogy Club. (July 1978)-. Periodical. English. qt. Grant County Genealogical Club, 600 South Washington, Marion Public Library, Marion IN 46953. **LC** F532.G7; G72a. **DD** 929/.1/072077269.
Ind/Abst Genealogical Period. Annu. Index.

US
GRASSROOTS CATALOG. (19??)-. Catalog. English. an. $20.00. COMGENES, Box 1581, Silver City NM 88062. **ED** Barbara Holley Rock. **Bk Rev. Ad Acc. Circ:** 150.

US/0146-0269
GRAVES FAMILY NEWSLETTER, THE. [Graves fam. newsl.]. (March 1976)-. Newsletter. English. Six times a year. $15.00 Comes with Graves Family Association Membership. Graves Family Newsletter, 261 South Street, Wrentham MA 02093. **Tel** (617)384-8084. **LC** CS71; .G776a. **DD** 929/.2/0973.

US/0743-2828
GREEN COUNTRY QUARTERLY, THE. Added/Corp Broken Arrow Genealogical Society. Vol. 1, No. 1 (March 1980)-. Periodical. English. Four times a year (Mar., June, Sept., Dec.). $10.00 (one year);. Broken Arrow Genealogical Society, PO Box 1244, Broken Arrow OK 74013. **ED** Marmie Apsley. **LC** F702.T8; G73. **DD** 929/.1/072076686. Index available. cum. index. **Circ:** 65.
Desc: This newsletter contains local area vital records, history, early newspaper abstracts and general genealogical information.

US/1042-4725
GREEN COUNTY REVIEW. [Green Cty. rev.]. **Added/Corp** Green County Historical Society. Vol. 1, No. 1 (Oct. 1977)-. Periodical. English. qt. $10.00 (one year). Green County Review, PO Box 276, Greensburg KY 42743. **LC** F457.G82; G75. **DD** 929/.3769695/05.

US/0898-9974
GREENE GENES. (GREENE GENES : A GENEALOGICAL QUARTERLY ABOUT GREENE COUNTY, NEW YORK.). [Greene genes]. Vol. 1, No. 1 (Spring 1988)-. Periodical. English. qt. $20.00. Greene Genes, c/o Patricia Morrow, PO Box 116, Maplecrest NY 12454. **Tel** (518)734-3254 (answering machine only). **ED** Patrica Morrow. **LC** F127.G7; G74. **DD** 929/.374737. Index available (published each issue). **Bk Rev**, (Qty: 20+). **Circ:** 100 (ctrl).
Desc: A geneaological publication about Greene County, New York - census, church, Bible, probate and vital records taken from newspapers, cemeteries, courthouses, libraries and archives.
Ind/Abst Genealogical Period. Annu. Index.

US/0883-170X
GREENFIELD QUARTERLY. [Greenfield q.]. V. 1, No. 1 (Jan./March 1985)-. Periodical. English. qt. $1.00. Town Hall, Office of Town Historian, Greenfield Center NY 12833. **Tel** (518)893-7432. **ED** Jayne E Lynch. **DD** 929. **UDC** 929.5(747). **Bk Rev. Ad Acc. Circ:** 200 (ctrl).
Desc: Historical newsletter of town of Greenfield NY from town historian office queries on genealogy articles of local persons history and historical architecture.

NZ/0113-2431
GRINZ YEARBOOK. [GRINZ yearb.]. **VFOAT** Genealogical Research Institute of New Zealand Yearbook. (1987)-. English. an. 16.00NZ$. Genealogical Research Institute of New Zealand, PO Box 36-107, Moera, Lower Hutt, New Zealand 6330. **Tel** 011 64 4 528-6843, . **DD** 929.2.

Desc: Each edition contains about ten scholarly articles and reviews of recent books, dealing with all areas of historical research.

US/0731-3179
GUILFORD GENEALOGIST, THE. V. 4, No. 1- No. 4 (Fall 1976)-. Periodical. English. qt. $10.00 individual, $12.50 families and institutions. Guilford County Genealogical Society, PO Box 9693, Greensboro NC 27429. **LC** F262.G9; G88. **DD** 929/.375662. **UDC** 929.5(756). ***Continues*** *Guilford County Genealogist, 0731-3187.*

US/0738-4866
GUNN SALUTE, THE. (THE GUNN SALUTE / CLAN GUNN SOCIETY OF THE UNITED STATES.). Vol. 3, No. 4-. Periodical. English. qt. Donald Bruce Williamson, 1693 Shirley Street SW/Suite B, Atlanta GA 30310. **LC** CS71; .G958916. **DD** 929/.2/0973. **UDC** 929.52(73). ***Continues*** *Newsletter (Clan Gunn Society of the United States), 0738-4815.*

CN/1187-6360
HALTON-PEEL BRANCH NEWSLETTER. [Halton-Peel Branch newsl.]. **Added/Corp** Ontario Genealogical Society. Halton Peel Branch. Vol. 15, Issue 1 (Feb. 1990)-. Newsletter. English. Five times a year (Feb., Apr., June, Sept., Nov.). 8.00Can$ (members); 18.00Can$ (non-members) Comes with Ontario Genealogical Society membership. Ontario Genealogical Society/Halton-Peel Branch, PO Box 70030, Oakville ONT L6L 6M9 Canada. **Tel** (416)827-6512. **ED** Jeanette Pilson. **DD** 929/.1/06071353. **Circ:** 600. ***Continues*** *Branch Newsletter O.G.S., 1182-8331.*
Desc: Genealogical and historical information for members interest.

US/0017-6834
HALVE MAEN, DE. [Halve maen]. **Added/Corp** Holland Society of New York. (1922)-. Periodical. English. qt (Jan., Apr., July, Oct.). $28.50 (US); $32.50 (other). Holland Society of New York, 122 East 58th Street, New York NY 10022. **Tel** (212)758-1675. **ED** David William Voorhees. **LC** F130.D9; H34. **DD** 974.7/004/3931. Index available. **Bk Rev. Circ:** 1,400 (ctrl).
Desc: Presents recent articles by foremost scholars concerned with the Nieuw Netherland Colony, as well as genealogy relating to families arriving in the Colony prior to 1675.
Ind/Abst Am. Hist. Life (1963-).

US
HAMBLEN CONNECTOR. English. qt (Jan., Apr., July, Oct.). $10.00. Hamblen Connector, 4432 Carya Square, Columbus IN 47201. **Tel** (812)342-0017.

CN/0821-5472
HAMBROOK HERALD, THE. [Hambrook her.]. Periodical. English. qt. 12.00Can$ Canada; $12.00 US; 12.00Aus$ Australia; £8.00 UK; R10.00 South Africa. The Hambrook Family History Society, 37 Walden Cresc, Regina Saskatchewan S4N 1L1 Canada. **Tel** 337-4762. **ED** Kenneth G Aitken. **DD** 929/.2. **UDC** 929.52(100=20). **Bk Rev. Circ:** 165 (ctrl).
Desc: Family history and genealogy of the various branches of the Hambrook family in Britain and the English speaking world.

US/0882-4150
HAMERSKY & ALLIED FAMILIES NEWSLETTER. [Hamersky allied fam. newsl.]. **VFOAT** Hamersky and Allied Families Newsletter. Newsletter. English. bm. $6.00 US; $9.00 other. Michael Hamersky, 13505 Frame Road, Poway CA 92064. **ED** Michael D Hamersky. **DD** 929. **UDC** 929.52(100). Index available. **Bk Rev. Ad Acc. Circ:** 95 (ctrl).
Desc: Family newsletter with genealogical, historical, cultural and current events reported on the Hamerski and Hamersky families of the world. Collateral Germanic families included, theme-style.

US/0731-6968
HARBOUR, HARBOR, HARBER, AND WITT, WHITT, WHIT FAMILY ASSOCIATION BULLETIN. Added/Corp Harbour, Harbor, Harber, and Witt, Whitt, Whit Family Association. Vol. 3, No. 1 (Summer 1980)-. Periodical. English. Four times a year. $12.00. Harbour Witt Family Association Inc., 7904 Joliet Avenue, Lubbock TX 79423-1720. **Tel** (806)795-5136. **ED** Bettye Atkins Cartwright. **LC** CS71; .H25664. **DD** 929/.2/0973. **Bk Rev.** ***Continues*** *Harbour, Harbor, Harber Family Association Bulletin, 0731-6976.*

US/0897-5035
HARD TIMES (MERIDEN, CONN.). (HARD TIMES.). [Hard times]. **VFOAT** Hard Times Newsletter. Vol. 1, No. 1 (March 1988)-. Periodical. English. qt. $7.50. Daramish Associates, 17 Boylston Street, Meriden CT 06450. **DD** 929.

US/0748-1888
HARDIN FAMILY COURIER. Vol. 1, No. 1 (July 1984)-. Periodical. English. qt. $15.00. Hardin Family Courier, PO Box 1320, Winnfield LA 71483-1320.
Desc: Contains 'hard core' Hardin data: marriages, wills, cemetery, Bible, tax, land, etc.

US/0741-7802
HARFORD HISTORICAL BULLETIN. (HARFORD HISTORICAL BULLETIN / HISTORICAL SOCIETY OF HARFORD COUNTY.). **Main/Corp** Historical Society of Harford County. No. 1 (Fall 1972)-. Bulletin. English. Four times a year. $20.00 Comes with Historical Society of Harford County Membership. Historical Society of Harford County, 33 Courtland West, Bel Air MD 21014. **Tel** (410)838-7691. **ED** Barclay E. Tucker and Mabel E. Andrews. **LC** F187.H2; H54a. **DD** 929/.1/072075274. **Circ:** 350.

US/0737-4798
HARGROVE NEWSLETTER, THE. Newsletter. English. E Hartgrove, 1678 Buckhorn Drive, Danville VA 24540. **LC** CS71; .H2744. **DD** 929/.2/0973. **UDC** 929.5(73).

US/0894-8925
HARLAN FOOTPRINTS. [Harlan footpr.]. **Added/Corp** Genealogical Society of Harlan County, Kentucky. Foot Prints Publications & Research. **VFOAT** Harlan Foot Prints. Vol. 1, No. 2 (Dec. 1982)-. Periodical. English. ir. $15.00. Footprints Publications Research, PO Box 1498, Harlan KY 40831. **Tel** (606)573-6958. **DD** 929.
Ind/Abst Genealogical Period. Annu. Index.

US/0737-478X
HARRIS FAMILY NEWSLETTER, THE. Vol. 1 (19??)-. Newsletter. English. sa. $3.00. Thelma Moon Goodlet, 951 East 37th Street, Hialeah FL 33013. **LC** CS71; .H3144. **DD** 929/.2/0973.

US/0740-9001
HARRISON HERITAGE. [Harrison herit.]. Began in 1981. Periodical. English. qt. $10.00. Harrison Heritage, 2816 Sloat Road, Pebble Beach CA 93953. **LC** CS71; .H3194. **DD** 929/.2/0973. **UDC** 929.52(73).

US/0898-543X
HASTINGS HERALD (SPOKANE, WASH.). (HASTINGS HERALD.). Vol. 1 (March 1985)-. English. ir. $7.25. Name Game Enterprises, 4204 South Conklin Street, Spokane WA 99203-6235. **Tel** (509)747-4903. **ED** E. Dale Hastin Smith. **LC** CS71; .H358a. **DD** 929/.2/0973. Index available. **Bk Rev.**
Desc: Contains miscellaneous information on Hastings (all spellings) lineages, queries, reviews, every name index.

GW
HAUBENMACHER, DIE. (19??)-. German. H J Haupler, Post Sauerlach/Obb, Ludwig-Thoma-Str 4, 8021 Arget Germany. **LC** CS610; .H38.

US/0440-5234
HAWKEYE HERITAGE. Added/Corp Iowa Genealogical Society. (Winter 1966)-. Periodical. English. Four times a year. $20.00 family membership. Iowa Genealogical Society, PO Box 7735, Des Moines IA 50322. **Tel** (515)276-0287. **ED** June Beals. **LC** F620; .H39. **DD** 929/.3777. cum. index. **Ad Acc. Circ:** 3,000.
Ind/Abst Genealogical Period. Annu. Index.

US/0736-9468
HAYES OF AMERICA HERALD. [Hayes Am. her.]. Vol. 1, No. 3 (Aug., Sept., Oct. 1981)-. Periodical. English. qt. $12.00. Route 3 Box 193, Keys Lane, Hephzibah GA 30815. **LC** CS71; .H4174. **DD** 929/.2/0973. **UDC** 929.52(73). ***Continues*** *Hayes of America, 0736-9557.*

US/0438-8399
HAYNES EAGLE. Added/Corp Haynes Surname Association. (1963)-. English. qt. Haynes Surname Association, PO Box 5038, George WA 98824. **LC** CS71; .H424a. **DD** 929/.2/0973.

US/0093-9854
HEART OF TEXAS RECORDS. Added/Corp Central Texas Genealogical Society. (1958)-. Periodical. English. qt (Mar., June, Sept., Dec.). $12.50. Central Texas Genealogical Society, 1717 Austin Avenue, Waco-Mc Co Library, Waco TX 76701. **ED** Peggy S. Duty (phone:(817)754-5119). **LC** F385; .H37. **DD** 929/.3764. Index available in last issue of volume--attached (Dec.). **Bk Rev. Circ:** 350. ***Continues*** *Family Tree, 0196-2671.*
Desc: Queries, Bible records, cemetery listings, census records, miscellaneous county records for McLennan and surrounding central Texas counties.
Ind/Abst Genealogical Period. Annu. Index.

US/0739-6082
HEIR-LINES (LAKE ORION, MICH.). (HEIR-LINES / NORTH OAKLAND GENEALOGICAL SOCIETY.). [Heir-lines]. **Added/Corp** North Oakland Genealogical Society. **VFOAT** Heir Lines. Vol. 1, No. 1 (Jan. 1978)-. Periodical. English. qt. Free to members ($15.00 membership fee). North Oakland Genealogical Society, 825 Joslyn Road, Lake Orion MI 48362. **Tel** (810)628-4192. **ED** Marie Pearce (Editor's address: 639 Pontiac Road, Oxford MI 48371-4850; Editor's telephone: (810)628-3589). **LC** F572.O2; H44. **DD** 929/.1/072077438. Index available (Published in the Fall). **Bk Rev**, (Qty: 5-6). **Circ:** 100.
Desc: Publishes genealogical and historical information from the northeastern townships of Oakland.

US/0742-4779
HEIR LINES (LEBANON, OHIO). (HEIR LINES / WARREN CO. GENEALOGICAL SOCIETY.). [Heir lines]. **Added/Corp** Warren Co. Genealogical Society. Vol. 1, Issue No. 1 (Sept. 1981)-. Periodical. English. qt (4 issues). $8.00. Warren County Genealogical Society, 300 East Silver Street, Lebanon OH 45036. **Tel** (513)933-1144. **ED** Harriet E. Foley. **LC** F497.W2; H44. **DD** 929/.1/0720771763. Index available. **Circ:** 250.
Desc: Lists and articles on Warren County, Ohio; deed index, civil war discharges, obituary indexes, pedigree charts of first families of Warren County, etc.
Ind/Abst Genealogical Period. Annu. Index.

UK/0260-1753
HEL ACHAU. MICROFORM. : JOURNAL OF THE CLWYD FAMILY HISTORY SOCIETY. **VFOAT** Clwyd Family History Society Journal. Vol. 1 (1980)-. Periodical. English. qt.

US
HEMPSTEAD TRAILS. English. Twice a year (published spring and fall). $10.00. Hempstead County Genealogical Society, PO Box 1158, Hope AR 71801. **Tel** (501)777-4564, (501)777-4228. **Bk Rev**. ctrl circ.

US/0739-6341
HENCKEL GENEALOGICAL BULLETIN. ***Suspended.*** Began in 1970-?. Bulletin. English. sa. $5.00. Rev A J Henckel, Family National Association, 717 E Ridge Village, Miami FL 33157. **Tel** (305)235-0730. **ED** Mrs Bert Harter. **LC** CS71; .H49524. **DD** 929/.2/0973. **UDC** 929.52(73). **Bk Rev**. **Circ:** 300.

US/1057-008X
HENLEIN-HEINLEIN CHANTICLEER : NEWSLETTER OF THE HENLEIN-HEINLEIN FAMILY ASSOCIATION, THE. **Added/Corp** Henlein-Heinlein Family Association. **VFOAT** Henlein Heinlein Chanticleer; Chanticleer. Vol. 1, Issue 1 (Jan. 1991)-. Newsletter. English. qt. $15.00 (membership). Henlein/Henlein, Etc., Family Association, Enid I Beihold, 1301 North Western Avenue, Lake Forest IL 60045. **LC** CS71; .H5182a. **DD** 929/.2/0973.

US/0730-6520
HERALD (CONROE, TEX.), THE. (THE HERALD / MONTGOMERY COUNTY GENEALOGICAL SOCIETY.). **Added/Corp** Montgomery County Genealogical & Historical Society. Montgomery County Genealogical Society (Tex.) Montgomery County Library (Tex.). Vol. 1, No. 1 (Jan. 1978)-. Periodical. English. Four times a year (Mar., June, Sept., Dec.). $18.00. Montgomery County Genealogical & Historical Society Inc, PO Box 867, Conroe TX 77305-0751. **Tel** (409)756-8625. **ED** Vera Meek Wimberly. **LC** F392.M7; H47. **DD** 929/.1/0720764153. Index available. cum. index. **Bk Rev**. **Circ:** 400 (ctrl).
Desc: Specializes in early Montgomery County records.
Ind/Abst Genealogical Period. Annu. Index.

FR/1142-4966
HERALDIQUE ET GENEALOGIE VILLAINE-LA-JUHEL. (1969)-. Periodical. French. bm. Centre d Entraide Genealogique, BP 101 119 rue de Clignancourt, 75018 Paris France. **Tel** 011 33 1 42556432. **UDC** 929.6. ***Formed by the union of*** *France Genealogique, 0046-4929* ***and*** *Heraldique et Genealogie, 1142-4966.*

CN/0441-6619
HERALDRY IN CANADA. **Added/Corp** Heraldry Society of Canada. Vol. 1, (Sept. 1966)-. Periodical. English (French). Four times a year (Mar., June, Sept., Dec.). 40.00Can$ (institutions); 50.00Can$ (individual); 75.00Can$ sustaining. Herald Society of Canada, 185 Stanley Avenue, Ottawa Ontario K1M 1P2 Canada. **Tel** (613)765-4887. **ED** Mr. Daniel Cogne. Index available. cum. index. **Bk Rev**. **Ad Acc**. **Pr Rev. Circ:** 700 (ctrl).
Desc: Articles of drawings, coloured plates on Canadian heraldry in varied forms as well as some international heraldry.

US
HERALDRY, THE ARMIGER'S NEWS. Vol. 1, No. 1 (Spring 1979)-. Periodical. English. qt. $25.00 membership, $10.00 libraries. American College of Heraldry, Drawer CG, Tuscaloosa AL 35486. **ED** Lawrence E McNutt. **LC** CR200; .H47. **DD** 929.6/0973. **UDC** 929.6(73). **Bk Rev**. **Circ:** 300 (ctrl).
Desc: Features the heraldry of America, including the coats-of-arms and biographies of members plus organizational news.
Ind/Abst Genealogical Period. Annu. Index (?-?).

CN
HERITAGE ECHOES. English. 6.00Can$. Saskatchewan Geneaological Society of Weyburn, 23 McKinnon Bay, Weyburn Saskatchewan S4H 1L8 Canada. **Tel** (306)842-7529.

US
HERITAGE NEWSLETTER. Newsletter. English. ir (Publshed 11 months per year.). $15.00. California African American Genalogical Society, 2026 4th Avenue, Los Angeles CA 90018. **Tel** (213)733-1835. **ED** Geralyn Johnson. **Circ:** 200.
Desc: Contains genealogical and historical research information, queries, books, events etc.

US/0886-0262
HERITAGE QUEST. ***Title Change.*** (HERITAGE QUEST : HQ.). [Herit. quest]. **VFOAT** HQ. Issue No. 1 (Sept./Oct. 1985)-(19??). Periodical. English. bm. Heritage Quest, PO Box 329, Bountiful UT 84011. **Tel** (801)298-5446. **LC** WMLC 93/1277. **DD** 929. ***Continued by*** *Herigate Quest Magazine, 1074-5238.*
Ind/Abst Genealogical Period. Annu. Index.

US/1074-5238
HERITAGE QUEST MAGAZINE. [Herit. quest mag.]. **VFOAT** Heritage Quest. (19??)-. Periodical. English. bm. $28.00 US; $40.00 other. Heritage Quest, PO Box 329, Bountiful UT 84011. **Tel** (801)298-5446. **DD** 929. ***Continues*** *Heritage Quest, 0886-0262.*

CN/0707-0780
HERITAGE SEEKERS. (THE HERITAGE SEEKERS.). **Added/Corp** Alberta Genealogical Society. Grande Prairie and District Branch. Vol. 1, No. 2 (June 1978)-. Periodical. English. qt (4 issues). 10.00Can$ (non-member); 7.00Can$ (member of the Alberta Genealogical Society). Grande Prairie and District Branch, Alberta Genealogical Society, PO Box 1257, Grande Prairie T8V 4Z1 Canada. **Tel** (403)532-5277. **ED** Joan Bowman (editor's telephone: (403)532-4697). **DD** 929/.1/06271231. **Bk Rev**, (Qty: varies). ctrl circ. ***Continues*** *Alberta Genealogical Society. Grande Prairie and District Branch. Newsletter - Alberta Genealogical Society. Grande Prairie and District Branch., 0707-0888.*
Desc: Local newsletter with information, stories and articles of interest to the membership.

CN/0709-3365
HERITAGE (TROIS-RIVIERES). (HERITAGE : BULLETIN OFFICIEL DE LA SOCIETE DE GENEALOGIE DE LA MAURICIE ET DES BOIS-FRANCS.). [Heritage]. Bulletin. French. mo. Free to members, $10.00 others. Heritage, C P 901, Trois-Rivieres Quebec G9A 5K2 Canada. **DD** 929/.2/09714465. **UDC** 929.5(714).

UK/0309-913X
HERTFORDSHIRE PEOPLE. [Hertfs. people]. (1977)-. Periodical. English. tq (Mar., July, Nov.). £5.00 UK; £6.00 other. Hertfordshire Family Populatin History Society, 134 Beechwood Avenue, Saint Albans, Herts AL1 4XY England. **ED** Mr. A. Ruston. Index available. cum. index. **Bk Rev**. **Circ:** 900 (ctrl).
Desc: Articles on family history with a Herefordshire bias.

US/0737-7258
HEYDON-HAYDEN-HYDEN FAMILIES, THE. [Heydon-Hayden-Hyden fam.]. Vol. 2, No. 1 (Jan. 1979)-. Periodical. English. qt. $10.00. The Heydon-Hayden-Hyden Families, PO Box 35004, Tulsa OK 74135. **ED** Bill Hyden. **LC** CS71; .H4148. **DD** 929/.2/0973. **UDC** 929.5(794). ***Continues*** *Hyden Families, 0739-3741.*

US/0741-4773
HIDDEN VALLEY JOURNAL. **Added/Corp** Escondido Genealogical Society. Vol. 6, No. 1 (May 1982)-. Periodical. English. an. Free with membership. Escondido Genealogical Society, PO Box 2190, Escondido CA 92025-0380. **Tel** (619)486-2364. **ED** Gwen Love. **LC** F869.E77; H53. **DD** 929/.1/072079498. Index available. **Bk Rev**. **Circ:** 100 (ctrl). ***Continues*** *Hidden Valley Quarterly, 0741-4757.*
Desc: Genealogical and historical material of Escandido, California, San Diego California and family histories of members.

US/0739-3199
HIGDON FAMILY NEWSLETTER. No. 1 (Jan. 1972)-. Newsletter. English. mo. $15.00. Mrs H A Smith, PO Box 30093, Raleigh NC 27622. **Tel** (919)782-6102. **ED** H A Smith. **LC** CS71; .H636594. **DD** 929/.2/0973. **UDC** 929.52(73). **Bk Rev**. **Circ:** 200 (ctrl).
Desc: Primarily information of genealogical nature about the Higdon family. Queries accepted.

CN/0707-2554
HIGHLAND HERITAGE. **Added/Corp** Glengarry Genealogical Society. Vol. 1 (Feb. 1979)-. Periodical. English. ir. 16.00Can$ (latest volume). Alex W. Fraser of Highland, Heritage Rural Route 1, Lancaster Ontario K0C 1N0 Canada. **Tel** (613)347-2363. **ED** Alex W. Fraser. **DD** 929/.1/0971377. **Bk Rev**. **Ad Acc**. **Circ:** 500.

●US/1062-7200
HIGHWAYMAN (WILLOW STREET, PA.), THE. (THE HIGHWAYMAN.). **Added/Corp** Crystal Educational Counselors. (1992)-. Periodical. English. sa (July and January). $10.00. Crystal Educational Counselors, 62 East Boehms Road, Willow Street PA 17584-9721. **Tel** (717)464-4201. **ED** James and Peg Beissel. **Pr Rev. Circ:** 100 (ctrl). available in Loose-leaf. ***Continues*** *German Ancestry, 1061-0529.*
Desc: Information on genealogy, raible, raibley and surnames.

CN/0707-3836
HILBORN FAMILY JOURNAL. ***Ceased.*** No. 1 (Nov. 1978)-Ceased ?. Periodical. English. ir. Hilborn Family Journal, 42 Sources Boulevard, Pointe Claire Quebec H9S 2H9 Canada. **Tel** (514)695-2515. **ED** Robin Hilborn. **DD** 929/.2. **UDC** 929.52(71). **Bk Rev**. **Circ:** 150 (ctrl).
Desc: Traces the history of the Hilborn family, stemming from Thomas Hilborn (1655-1723); ancestor charts, biographies, photographs, trees, news of the family today.

CN/0828-4466
HILBORN'S FAMILY NEWSLETTER DIRECTORY. [Hilborn's fam. newsl. dir.]. **VAT** Family Newsletter Directory (1984). 3rd Ed. (Aug. 1984)-. Directory. English. an. 5.00Can$ per issue. Hilborn Family Journal, 42 Sources Boulevard, Pointe Claire Quebec H9S 2H9 Canada. **Tel** (514)695-2515. **LC** Z5313.U5; H53; CS47. **DD** 016.929/1/0973. ***Continues*** *Family Newsletter Directory, 0227-5317.*
Desc: An alphabetical list, by surname, of 1,509 newsletters, each devoted to the history and genealogy of one family name.

US
HILL COUNTRY GENEALOGICAL SOCIETY QUARTERLY, THE. Periodical. English. qt. $10.00. Hill Country Genealogical Society Quarterly, c/o Mrs Evelyn Wade, Route 7 Box 52, Llano TX 78643. **LC** F392.T47; H54. **DD** 929/.3764. **UDC** 929.5(764).

FR/0984-7677
HISTOIRE & GENEALOGIE PARIS. (HISTOIRE & GENEALOGIE.). [Hist. geneal. Paris]. **VFOAT** Histoire et Genealogie (Paris). (1987)-. Periodical. French. qt. 220.00F France; 260.00F other. Editions Christian, 5 rue Alphonse Baudin, BP 91, 75522 Paris Cedex 11 France. **Tel** 011 33 1 48055361. **UDC** 929. ***Continues*** *Annales de Genealogie et d'Heraldique, 0763-7802.*

US/0886-5272
HISTORICAL FOOTNOTES (STONINGTON, CONN.). **See** History(General)-History of North, South, and Central America.

US/1064-041X
HISTORICAL GENEALOGICAL MAGAZINE SPECIALIZING IN CLINTON AND BOONE COUNTIES. [Hist. geneal. mag. spec. Clint. Boone Cties.]. **VFOAT** Historic Genealogical Magazine. Vol. 1, No. 1 (1991)-. Periodical. English. sa. $20.00. Joan C. Bohm, 1240 South Vineland Road, Winter Garden FL 34787. **Tel** (407)654-1847. **ED** Joan Bohm. **LC** F532.C65; H57. **DD** 929/.377254. **Bk Rev**, (Qty: 1-2). **Circ:** 150. ***Continues*** *Clinton County, Indiana Roots, 0734-2020.*

US/1065-0024
HISTORY NOTES / LAKE CHELAN HISTORICAL SOCIETY. [Hist. notes - Lake Chelan Hist. Soc.]. **Added/Corp** Lake Chelan Historical Society (Wash.). Vol. 1, No. 1 (Spring 1973)-. English. $5.00. Lake Chelan Historical Society, Box 1948, Chelan WA 98816. **Tel** (509)682-5644. **ED** Hobbie Morehead. **DD** 979. **Circ:** 500.

US
HISTORY OF WASHTENAW COUNTY, MICHIGAN. **Main/Corp** Genealogical Society of Washtenaw County, Michigan. English. $85.00. Genealogical Society of Washtenaw County MII, PO Box 7155, Ann Arbor MI 48107-7155.

CN/1183-1766
HOGTOWN HERALDRY. (HOGTOWN HERALDRY : NEWSLETTER OF THE HERALDRY SOCIETY OF CANADA, TORONTO BRANCH.). [Hogtown her.]. **Added/Corp** Heraldry Society of Canada. Toronto Branch. Vol. 2, No. 4 (Dec. 1990)-. Newsletter. English. qt. Free to members. Heraldry Society of Canada, Toronto Branch, c/o J Kennedy, 22 Carey Road, Toronto, Ontario M5S 1N8 Canada. **DD** 929.6. ***Continues*** *The Hogtown Herald., 1184-8413.*

US/0887-3135
HOLSTON PASTFINDER. [Holston pastfinder]. **Added/Corp** Holston Territory Genealogical Society. **VFOAT** Holston Past Finder. (198?)-. Periodical. English. qt (Mar., June, Sept., Dec.). $18.00. Holston Territory Genealogical Society, PO Box 433, Bristol VA 24203. **Tel** (703)669-6839. **ED** Ms. Shelby Ireson Edwards. **DD** 975. **Bk Rev**, (Qty: 8). **Circ:** 400 (ctrl).
Ind/Abst Genealogical Period. Annu. Index.

US/1071-1112
HOOD COUNTY GENEALOGICAL SOCIETY. ***Title Change.*** (HOOD COUNTY GENEALOGICAL SOCIETY : NEWSLETTER.). [Hood Cty. Genealog. Soc.]. **Added/Corp** Hood County Genealogical Society. **VFOAT** Newsletter. No. 28 (Nov. 1990)-(199?). Newsletter. English. qt. Hood County Genealogical Society, PO Box 1623, Granbury TX 76048. **Tel** (817)573-2840. **DD** 929. ***Changed back to***

Newsletter (Hood County Genealogical Society), 1071-3026.
Ind/Abst Genealogical Period. Annu. Index (?-?).

US/0149-1253
HOOSIER FAMILY ARCHIVES. V. 1- 1977-. English. an. Kenma Publishing Company, PO Box 2786, Evansville IN 47714. **LC** F525; .H59. **DD** 929/.2/0973. **UDC** 929.52(73).

US/1054-2175
HOOSIER GENEALOGIST, THE. (THE HOOSIER GENEALOGIST / GENEALOGICAL SECTION OF THE INDIANA HISTORICAL SOCIETY.). [Hoosier geneal.]. **Added/Corp** Indiana Historical Society. Genealogy Section. Indiana Historical Society. Family History Section. Indiana Historical Society. No. 1 (Jan./Feb. 1961)-. Periodical. English. qt. Comes with Indiana Historical Society membership. Indiana Historical Society, 315 West Ohio Street, Indianapolis IN 46202. **Tel** (317)232-1882. **DD** 929.

US/0147-1228
HOOSIER JOURNAL OF ANCESTRY, THE. Vol. 4 (Jan. 1977)-. Periodical. English. Three times a year. $15.00 (one year), $30.00 (two year), $45.00 (three year). Hoosier Journal of Ancestry, PO Box 33, Little York IN 47139. **Tel** (812)752-2051. **ED** Naomi Keith Sexton. **LC** F525; .H63. **DD** 929/.1/09772. Index available (Included in November issue). **Bk Rev. Ad Acc. Circ:** 750 (ctrl).
Desc: Source records and other miscellaneous genealogical records from 30 counties in south eastern Indiana.
Ind/Abst Genealogical Period. Annu. Index.

CN/0714-8275
HOUALLET. (LE HOUALLET : PERIODIQUE DE L'ASSOCIATION DES FAMILLES OUELLET-TE DU QUEBEC.). [Houallet]. **Added/Corp** Association des Familles Ouellet(te) du Quebec. Vol. 14, No 1 (April 1982)-. Periodical. French (English; summaries and/or abstracts in English). qt. 20.00Can$ (comes with membership). Association des Families Ouellet-Te, Casier Postal 28, La Pocatiere Quebec G0R 1Z0 Canada. **Tel** (418)835-1254. **DD** 929/.2/05. **Ad Acc. Circ:** 1,000 (ctrl). ***Continues** Hoelet, 0318-7322.*
Desc: General information about ancestors, present families; and about the genealogy of members.

US/0748-2736
HOUSER HUNTERS NEWSLETTER. **VFOAT** Houser Hunters. Vol. 1, No. 1 (Jan. 1983)-. Newsletter. English. bm. $10.00. E A Houser Jr, 6412 North University Drive/#301, Tamarac FL 33321. **ED** Frances Clayton Knight. **LC** CS71; .H839984. **DD** 929/.2/0973. **UDC** 929.52(73). **Circ:** 610 (ctrl).
Desc: Historical material relating to the Houser family.

US/0749-6176
HOYT'S ISSUE. Vol. 1, No. 1-. Periodical. English. 11 Craig Road, Chelmsford MA 01824. **LC** CS71; .H86894. **DD** 929/.2/0973. **UDC** 929.52(73).

US/0747-5675
HUGHES FAMILY LETTER. [Hughes fam. lett.]. Vol. 1, No. 1 (Summer 1982)-. Periodical. English. qt. $5.00. Hughes Family Letter, 1857 Stonewood Drive, Baton Rouge LA 70816. **LC** CS71; .H89195. **DD** 929/.2/0973. **UDC** 929.52(73).

CN/0441-6910
HUGUENOT TRAILS. **Added/Corp** Huguenot Society of Canada. Huguenot Society of Ontario. Vol. 1 (Spring 1968)-. Periodical. English. qt. $30.00. Huguenot Society of Canada, 10 Adelaide Street East Suite 104, Toronto Ontario M5C 1J3 Canada. **Tel** (416)361-1685. **LC** F1035.H76; H83. **DD** 929/.1/088245. **Circ:** 300.

US/0147-2364
HUNGATE. **Added/Corp** Hungate Family Historical Society. (19??)-. English. an. Universal Publications, 3101 Gillham Plaza, Kansas City MO 64109. **LC** CS71; .H9317a. **DD** 929/.2/0973.

AT/0811-5559
IBIS LINKS. [Ibis links]. (1982)-. English. Four times a year (Mar., June, Sept., Dec.). 15.00Aus$. Griffith Genealogical Historical Society Inc., PO Box 270, Griffith NSW 2680 Australia. **Tel** 011 61 069 625827. **ED** Ann M. Stevens, (phone: (069)623508). **DD** 929.1069448. Index available (July 1992). **Ad Acc. Circ:** 200 (ctrl).
Desc: Aims to promote family history research, record and transcribe the early burials of the pioneers of this area, and assist members in tracing their own family history by discussing research obstacles and providing alternative sources.

US/0445-2127
IDAHO GENEALOGICAL SOCIETY QUARTERLY. **Added/Corp** Idaho Genealogical Society. (1958)-. Periodical. English. qt. $10.00. Idaho Genealogical Society, 4620 Overland Road #204, Boise ID 83705. **Tel** (208)384-0542. **ED** Phillip A. Marsh. **LC** F745; .I273. **DD** 929/.1/0720796. Index available. **Bk Rev. Ad Acc. Circ:** 400 (ctrl).
Desc: Extracted records from vital records and census of the state of Idaho.

US/0737-5239
ILL. IA. MO. SEARCHER, THE. ***Ceased.*** **Added/Corp** Lee County Genealogical Society. **VFOAT** Illinois, Iowa, Missouri Searcher. Vol. 1, No. 1 (1973)-Vol. 20, No. 2 (April 1992). Periodical. English. qt. M A Kay, Rural Route 1 Box 182, Keokuk IA 52632. **Tel** (319)524-5167. **ED** Mary Alma Kay. **LC** F627.L4; I44. **DD** 929/.377799. **Bk Rev. Circ:** 287 (ctrl).
Desc: From the mailbag, vital records; cemetery listings; newspaper clippings; ancestor charts; local history; queries; date to remember; obituaries; biographies; roster of volunteers; and book reviews.

US/0019-1809
ILLIANA GENEALOGIST. **Added/Corp** Illiana Genealogical & Historical Society. (1965)-. Periodical. English. Four times a year (Mar., June, Sept., Dec.). $15.00. Illiana Genealogical & Historical Society, PO Box 207, Danville IL 61832. **Tel** (217)431-8733. Index available. **Bk Rev. Circ:** 450.
Desc: Publishes material of genealogical interest on Vermilion County, Illinois and the surrounding areas; includes original material.
Ind/Abst Genealogical Period. Annu. Index.

US/0890-3719
ILLINOIS HERITAGE ASSOCIATION NEWSLETTER. **Added/Corp** Illinois Heritage Association. **VFOAT** IHA Newsletter. Vol. 1, No. 1 (Jan./Feb. 1983)-. Newsletter. English. bm. $25.00 (includes membership). Illinois Heritage Association, Station A Box C, Champaign IL 61825. **Tel** (217)359-5600. **ED** Carol B. Betts. **Circ:** 500-1,100.
Desc: Provides information about local, state and national history, culture, arts, education, and historical preservation.

US/0046-8622
ILLINOIS STATE GENEALOGICAL SOCIETY QUARTERLY. [Ill. State Geneal. Soc. q.]. **Added/Corp** Illinois State Genealogical Society. **VFOAT** ISGS Quarterly. (1969)-. Periodical. English. qt. $20.00. Illinois State Genealogical Society, Box 10195, Springfield IL 62791. **Tel** (217)789-1968. **DD** 929. Index available. **Bk Rev. Circ:** 2,500 (ctrl).

US/0899-5400
IMMIGRATION DIGEST. [Immigr. dig.]. **Added/Corp** Genealogical Institute (Salt Lake City, Utah). Vol. 1 (Jan. 1987)-. English. Three times a year. $9.00 per issue (includes postage). Family History World, Box 22045, Salt Lake City UT 84122. **Tel** (801)251-6174. **ED** Arlene H. Eakle. **LC** E184.A1; I437. **DD** 929/.1/072073. **Bk Rev. Circ:** 400.
Desc: Contains new sources to link immigrant ancestors with their origins: naming patterns, passenger lists, and boundary maps.
Ind/Abst Genealogical Period. Annu. Index.

US
IMPRINTS : QUARTERLY PUBLICATION OF THE GENEALOGICAL SOCIETY OF BROWARD COUNTY, INC. **Added/Corp** Genealogical Society of Broward County. (1982)-. English. qt. Genealogical Society of Broward County, PO Box 485, Ft. Lauderdale FL 33301.
Ind/Abst Genealogical Period. Annu. Index.

US
INDIAN HISTORY AND GENEALOGY. English. sa. $10.00. Cherokee Family Researcher, 516 North 38th Street, Mesa AZ 85205. **Tel** (602)832-1467. **ED** Jean Williams. Index available. **Ad Acc.** ctrl circ.
Desc: A culmination of research on several families, primarily Cherokee. Includes pictures, family charts and other data.

US
INDIANA COUNTY HERITAGE. Vol. 1 (Fall/Winter 1965)-. Periodical. English. sa. $20.00 non-profit, $150.00 profit (institutions); $15.00 (individuals) Comes with Historical & Genealogical Society of Indiana County membership. Historical & Genealogical Society of Indiana County, 200 South 6th Street, Indiana PA 15701. **Tel** (412)463-9600.
Ind/Abst Genealogical Period. Annu. Index.

US/1044-694X
INDIANA QUERIES. [Indiana queries]. Issue No. 1 (Feb. 1987)-. Periodical. English. ir. $6.00 per issue. Pioneer Publications, PO Box 397, Black Eagle MT 59414-0397. **Tel** (406)453-4266. **ED** Shirley Penna-Oakes. **DD** 929. Index available. **Bk Rev.**

US/8755-2612
INDIANA ROOTS. ***Ceased.*** [Ind. roots]. Vol. 1, No. 1 (Aug. 1983)-Ceased ?. Periodical. English. qt. The Researchers, PO Box 39063, Indianapolis IN 46239. **LC** F525; .I547. **DD** 929/.3772. **UDC** 929.5(772).

CN/1183-0840
INFO-GENEALOGIE (SAINTE-FOY). (INFO-GENEALOGIE : BULLETIN OFFICIEL DE LA FEDERATION QUEBECOISE DES SOCIETES DE GENEALOGIE.). [Info-genealogie]. **Added/Corp** Federation Quebecoise des Societes de Genealogie. Vol. 3, No. 2 (Jan. 1991)-. Bulletin. French. Three times a year. 10.00Can$ Canada; 15.00Can$ other. Federation Quebecoise des Societes de Genealogie, CP 9454, Sainte Foy Quebec G1V 4B8 Canada. **DD** 929/.1/060714. ***Continues** Bulletin de la Federation Quebecoise des Societes de Genealogie., 1186-1304.*
Desc: Lists conferences, subjects and authors, and news publications - general development of genealogy in Quebec.

US/0882-2883
INSCRIPTIONS (STEVENS POINT, WIS.). (INSCRIPTIONS : NEWSLETTER OF THE WISCONSIN STATE OLD CEMETERY SOCIETY.). **Added/Corp** Wisconsin State Old Cemetery Society. (19??)-. Periodical. English. bm (Jan., Mar., May, July, Sept., Dec.). $8.00 member, $20.00 contributing member US; add $2.00 postage Canada; add $1.50 postage other. Wisconsin State Old Cemetery Society, c/o Bernadine Boulia, 3325 South 26th Street, #18, Milwaukee WI 53215. **Tel** (414)771-7781. **ED** Dan Buckman (editor's address: 2036 North 3 Street, Milwaukee, WI 53212; phone: (414)372-1885). **Bk Rev**, (Qty: when received). **Circ:** 750.
Desc: Deals with cemetery records and tracing deceased relatives.

BE/0020-5621
INTERMEDIAIRE DES GENEALOGISTES. [Intermediaire General.]. **VFOAT** De middelaar Tussen de Genealogische Navorsers. (1954)-. Periodical. French (Dutch). bm. 1750.00F. SCGD, Chaussee de Haecht 147, 1030 Brussels Belgium. Index available. cum. index. **Bk Rev.** ***Continues** Intermediaire, 0773-297X.*
Desc: Articles on genealogy.

US/0090-905X
IOWA GENEALOGICAL SOCIETY SURNAME INDEX. (SURNAME INDEX.). **Main/Corp** Iowa Genealogical Society. **VFOAT** Iowa Genealogical Surname Index. Vol. 1 (1972)-. English. $7.50. Iowa Genealogical Society, PO Box 7735, Des Moines IA 50322. **Tel** (515)276-0287. **LC** CS44; .I58A. **DD** 929/.1/09777. **UDC** 929.5(777).

US/1044-6931
IOWA QUERIES. [Iowa queries]. Vol. 1 (1987)-. Periodical. English. Four times a year. $6.00. Pioneer Publications, PO Box 397, Black Eagle MT 59414-0397. **Tel** (406)453-4266. **ED** Shirley Penna-Oakes. **DD** 929. Index available. **Bk Rev.**

IE/0047-1437
IRISH ANCESTOR, THE. (1969)-. Periodical. English. Twice a year. $12.00. Irish Ancestor, The Glebe House, Fethard Co Tipperary Ireland. **ED** Rosemary Folliott. **Bk Rev. Circ:** 500.
Desc: A wide range of topics connected with Irish genealogy and social history-lineages, will abstracts, tombstone inscriptions, church registers, Bible entries and domestic inventories.
Ind/Abst Genealogical Period. Annu. Index (?-?).

UK/0306-8358
IRISH GENEALOGIST, THE. [Ir. geneal.]. **Added/Corp** Irish Genealogical Research Society. (April 1937)-. English. an (Between January and April). £16.00. Irish Genealogical Research Society, c/o The Irish Club, 82 Eaton Square, London SW1W 9AJ England. **Tel** 01 659 8954. **ED** Peter Manning, (editor's address: 18 Stratford Avenue, Rainham Kent ME8 0EP England). **LC** CS480; .I7313. **DD** 929/.3415. Index available (Publish separately). **Bk Rev. Circ:** 1,000 (ctrl).
Desc: Hitherto unpublished source material, general accounts and narrative pedigrees of Irish families, and instructional articles on various aspects of Irish genealogy.

US/8756-1484
IRISH GENEALOGY DIGEST. [Ir. geneal. dig.]. (Summer 1982)-. Periodical. English. qt. $15.00. Irish Genealogy Company, PO Box 8231003, Dallas TX 75231. **Tel** (214)341-6507. **ED** Minnie Champ. **DD** 929. **Bk Rev. Circ:** 300 (ctrl).
Desc: Relating to Irish genealogy research. Includes surname index, book reviews, articles, events, free queries to subscribers.

UK/0957-0837
IRISH HERITAGE LINKS. [Ir. herit. links]. (1989)-. Periodical. English. qt (Jan., Apr., July, Oct.). £15.00 Ireland; $30.00 US; £16.00 other. Irish Heritage Association, 162A Kingsway Dunmurry, Belfast BT17 9AD Northern Ireland. **Tel** 011 44 232 629595. **ED** K Neill. **DD** 929.10720415. Index available. cum. index. **Bk Rev. Ad Acc. Pr Rev. Circ:** 5,000 (ctrl). ***Continues** Irish Family Links, 0268-1668.*
Desc: Genealogy/local history, methods/sources, member's family histories, news of the clans, members letters, book reviews and notices.
Ind/Abst Genealogical Period. Annu. Index.

US/1044-6923
IRISH QUERIES. [Ir. queries]. Vol. 1 (1986)-. Periodical. English. Four times a year. $7.35. Pioneer Publications, PO Box 397, Black Eagle MT 59414-0397. **Tel** (406)453-4266. **ED** Shirley Penna-Oakes. **DD** 929. Index available. **Bk Rev. Ad Acc.**

US/0743-7579
IROQUOIS STALKER, THE. [Iroq. stalk.]. **Added/Corp** Iroquois County Genealogical Society. Vol. 1, No. 1 (Spring 1971)-. Periodical. English. qt. Free to members; $18.00 membership. Iroquois Genealogical Society, Old Court House, Watseka IL 60970-1524. **Tel** (815)432-2215. **ED** Cheryl Gocken. **LC** F547.I7; I76. **DD** 929/.1/072077364. Index available. **Circ:** 450.
Desc: Local history, cemetery inventories, extractions, including obituaries from local, early newspapers, and genealogical resources.
Ind/Abst Am. Hist. Life.

US/0884-9080
ITALIAN GENEALOGIST. [Ital. geneal.]. English. an. $7.00. Augustan Society, Society Headquarters and Library, PO Box P, Torrance CA 90507-0210. **Tel** (310)320-7766. **LC** E184.I8; I82. **UDC** 929.5(45). **Bk Rev. Circ:** 300 (ctrl).
Desc: Primarily genealogy, secondary heraldry and history; serves as an international contact journal for Italian research.

US/0897-7410
ITALIAN QUERIES. [Ital. queries]. Vol. 1 (1988)-. Periodical. English. Four times a year. $6.00. Pioneer Publications, PO Box 397, Black Eagle MT 59414-0397. **Tel** (406)453-4266. **ED** Shirley Penna-Oakes. **DD** 929. Index available. **Bk Rev.**

US/0737-7932
ITAWAMBA SETTLERS. Vol. 1, No. 1 (Mar. 1981)-. Periodical. English. qt. $20.00. Itawamba Historical Society, PO Box 7, Mantachie MS 38855. **Tel** (601)844-1315. **LC** F347.I8; I86. **DD** 929/.3762982. Index available. **Bk Rev**, (Qty: 5-6). **Pr Rev. Circ:** 700.

NE/0922-6702
JAARBOEK VAN HET CENTRAAL BUREAU VOOR GENEALOGIE EN VAN HET ICONOGRAFISCH BUREAU. [Jaarb. Cent. Bur. Geneal. Iconogr. Bur.]. (1972)-. Periodical. Dutch. an (Nov.). F51.88. Central Bureau Genealogie, Postbus 11755, 2502 Hague Netherlands. **Tel** 011 31 70 6814651. **UDC** 929.5(058).
Ind/Abst BHA : Biblio. Hist. Art.

US/0738-6648
JACKSONIANA. [Jacksoniana]. Vol. 1, No. 1 (Jan. 1978)-. Periodical. English. qt. Ernest H Jackson, 730 Parker Woods Drive, Rockford IL 61102. **Tel** (815)962-0818. **ED** Ernest H Jackson. **LC** CS71; .J1294. **DD** 929/.2/0973. **UDC** 929.52(73). **Ad Acc. Circ:** 100.
Desc: Listings of vital statistics and other information. Jacksons in the US from 1607 to 1900. Short biographies (some unpublished) of Jacksons.

US/0749-8314
JASPER COUNTY GLEANER, THE. Vol. 6, No. 1 (Jan. 1983)-. Periodical. English. qt. $7.50. Jasper County Gleaner, PO Box 163, Newton IA 50208. **Tel** (515)792-1522. **ED** Kathleen Webb. **UDC** 929.5(777). **Bk Rev. Circ:** 200 (ctrl). ***Continues*** *Gleaner, 0749-8322.*
Desc: Has query section for those seeking family connections. Contains lists copied from courthouse records. Hints for little-known research sources.

US/0195-7384
JE ME SOUVIENS. Added/Corp American French Genealogical Society. Vol. 1, No. 1 (Sept. 1978)-V. 4, No. 3 (Autumn 1981); Spring 1982-. Periodical. English. sa. $10.00. American-French Genealogical Society, Box 2113, Pawtucket RI 02861. **Tel** (508)285-7736. **ED** Henri LeBlond. **LC** E184.F85; J4. **DD** 929/.1/089114073. Index available. **Bk Rev. Ad Acc. Circ:** 800 (ctrl). available on microfilm.
Desc: Genealogical and historical articles, society news, questions and answers, ancestral charts, all pertaining to researchers of French-Canadian genealogy.
Ind/Abst Genealogical Period. Annu. Index (?-?).

US
JEFFERSON COUNTY LINES. English. $5.00. Ohio Genealogical Society - Jefferson County, 109 Meadows Road, Wintersville OH 43952. **Tel** (614)264-7914.
Ind/Abst Genealogical Period. Annu. Index.

US/0749-6850
JOHNSON COUNTY GENEALOGIST, THE. Added/Corp Johnson County Genealogical Society. (Mar. 1973)-. Periodical. English. Four times a year (Mar., June, Sept., Dec.). $12.50. Johnson County Genealogical Society, PO Box 12666, Shawnee Mission KS 66208. **Tel** (913)383-2458. **ED** Carlene Mischlich. **LC** F687.J6; J64. **DD** 929/.1/0720781675. Index available. **Ad Acc. Circ:** 250.
Desc: Information to assist genealogy research, primarily in Johnson County, Kansas.
Ind/Abst Genealogical Period. Annu. Index.

US/8755-1721
JOHNSON JOURNAL. [Johnson j.]. Vol. 1, No. 1 (Nov. 1982)-. Periodical. English. Three times a year. $15.00. Johnson Journal, PO Box 96, Broderick CA 95605. **Tel** (916)372-4104. **ED** Miz Johnson. **LC** CS71; .J6984. **DD** 929/.2/0973. **Bk Rev. Ad Acc. Circ:** 400 (ctrl).
Desc: Clearinghouse for genealogical data on all families named Johnson/Johnston everywhere, subscription includes free queries.

CN/0731-8979
JOHNSON REPORTER (LINCOLN, NEB.), THE. (THE JOHNSON REPORTER.). [Johnson rep.]. Vol. 1, No. 1 (Winter 1981)-. Periodical. English. qt. 10.00Can$ Canada; $10.00 US. Johnson Reporter, c/o Mr Roy Johnson, 504 Kilman Road, Rural Route 1, Ridgeville Ontario L0S 1M0 Canada. **Tel** (416)892-2390. **ED** David E Johnson and Roy A C Johnson. **DD** 929/.2. **UDC** 929.5(71+73). **Circ:** 250. available on microfilm.

US/0749-1522
JONES JOURNEYS. English. qt. $15.00 US; $20.00 Canada and Mexico; $30.00 other. Frances R. Nelson, 4041 Pedley Road #18, Riverside CA 92509. **Tel** (714)685-8936. **ED** Frances R Nelson and George Ely Russell. **LC** CS71; .J757. **DD** 929/.2/0973. **UDC** 929.52(73). Index available. **Circ:** 200 (ctrl).

US/8756-7970
JORDANS' JOURNEYS. (JORDANS' JOURNEYS : JJ.). [Jordans' journeys]. **VFOAT** JJ. Vol. 1, No. 1 (Fall 1981)-. Periodical. English. qt. $5.00. Southern Family Publications Inc, 1308 South 58th Street, Birmingham AL 35222. **LC** CS71; .J8194. **DD** 929/.2/0973. **UDC** 929.52(73).

US/0277-4909
JOTS FROM THE POINT. VFOAT Jots. (1???)-. English. Ten times a year. $20.00. Western Pennsylvania Genealogical Society, 4338 Bigelow Boulevard, Building of the Historical Society, Pittsburgh PA 15213. **Tel** (412)681-5533.

US
JOURNAL. Added/Corp Berks County Genealogical Society. **VFOAT** Journal of the Berks County Genealogical Society. (19??)-. English. mo. Free to members. Berks County Genealogical Society, PO Box 14774, Reading PA 19612. **Tel** (215)777-5702. **LC** F157.B3; J68. **DD** 929/.1/072074816.
Ind/Abst Genealogical Period. Annu. Index.

UK/0141-7614
JOURNAL / CORNWALL FAMILY HISTORY SOCIETY. Main/Corp Cornwall Family History Society. (19??)-. Periodical. English. qt (4 issues). Comes with Cornwall Family History Society membership. Cornwall Family History Society, 3 Calenick Street, Truro Con TR1 2SF England. **LC** WMLC L 83/1790. Index available. **Bk Rev. Ad Acc. Circ:** 2,500 (ctrl).

US/0735-6420
JOURNAL - FLORIDA GENEALOGICAL SOCIETY (1978). (JOURNAL / FGS.). **Added/Corp** Florida Genealogical Society. Vol. 14, No. 2 (1978)-. Periodical. English. Twice a year. $10.00. Florida Genealogical Society, PO Box 18624, Tampa FL 33679-8624. **Tel** (813)839-0810. **ED** Helen N. Byrd. **LC** F310; .J68. **DD** 929/.1/0720759. Index available. **Bk Rev. Ad Acc. Circ:** 350 (ctrl). ***Continues*** *Florida Genealogical Journal (Florida Genealogical Society : 1978), 0735-6412.*
Desc: Genealogical information for Florida and Southeastern states: queries, ancestor charts, census and court records, family histories and bible records.

US/0736-4261
JOURNAL / FORT SMITH HISTORICAL SOCIETY, THE. See History(General)-History of North, South, and Central America.

US
JOURNAL / GERMAN-TEXAN HERITAGE SOCIETY, THE. Added/Corp German Texan Heritage Society (Tex.). (198?)-. Periodical. English. Three times a year (Apr., Aug., Dec.). $10.00 regular membership; $20.00 Library and contributing membership; $40.00 Patron membership, Comes with German Texan Heritage Society Membership. German Texan Heritage Society, PO Box 684171, Austin TX 78768. **Tel** (512)280-3351. **ED** W. M. von Maszewski (phone: (713)477-2318). **LC** F395.G3; N48. **DD** 976.4/0031/005. cum. index (1st journal of the year on annual basis). **Bk Rev**, (Qty: 3-5). **Pr Rev. Circ:** 1,200. ***Continues*** *Newsletter (German Texan Heritage Society (Tex.)), 0730-3106.*
Desc: Features a genealogical section which includes hints about research in German-speaking countries, Texas and the United States. Brief family histories submitted by the members.

US/0730-6148
JOURNAL OF AMERICAN INDIAN FAMILY RESEARCH, THE. VFOAT JAIFR. Vol. 1, No. 1 (Jan. 1980)-. Periodical. English. qt. $25.00. Histree, 803 South Fifth Street, Yama AZ 85364. **Tel** (602)343-2755. **ED** Larry S. Watson. **LC** WMLC L 83/316. **Bk Rev. Ad Acc. Circ:** 600.
Desc: A medium of exchanging ideas and resources by researchers of the ethnohistory of American Indians North of Mexico; research methods, resources, and original records are presented.

UK/0262-4842
JOURNAL OF ONE-NAME STUDIES, THE. Added/Corp Guild of One-Name Studies. **VFOAT** Journal of One Name Studies. Vol. 1 No. 1 (Winter 1982)-. Periodical. English. Four times a year. £6.00 Comes with Guild of One Name Studies membership. Guild of One-Name Studies, Box G 14 Charterhouse Building, London EC 1M 7BA England. **ED** M. Rumsey. Index available. **Bk Rev.** ctrl circ. ***Continues*** *Newsletter / Guild of One Name Studies.*
Desc: Genealogy, surnames; distribution of names.

US/0363-1656
JOURNAL OF ROCKINGHAM COUNTY HISTORY AND GENEALOGY, THE. **See** History(General)-History of North, South, and Central America.

US/0272-1937
JOURNAL OF THE AFRO-AMERICAN HISTORICAL AND GENEALOGICAL SOCIETY. [J. Afro-Am. Hist. Geneal. Soc.]. **Main/Corp** Afro-American Historical and Genealogical Society (Washington, D.C.). (Summer 1980)-. Academic Scholarly Publication. English. Four times a year. $35.00. Afro-American Historical and Genealogical Society, PO Box 73086, Washington DC 20056-3086. **Tel** (202)234-5350. **ED** Sandra Lawson. **LC** E185.96; .A46a. **DD** 973/.0496073. cum. index (1980-1990). **Bk Rev. Circ:** 500.
Desc: Articles of Afro-American historical research, family genealogies, ancestor tables, and biographies. Methods of scholarly research and source material of obscure and difficult-to-locate records.
Ind/Abst Am. Hist. Life (1980-1985, 1987-); Genealogical Period. Annu. Index.

UK/0308-4183
JOURNAL OF THE BRISTOL AND AVON FAMILY HISTORY SOCIETY. [J.Bristol Avon Fam. Hist. Soc.]. (1975)-. Periodical. English. Four times a year (Mar., June, Sept., Dec.). £8.00 UK; £9.00 other. Bristol Avon Family History Society, 119 Holly Hill Road / Kingswood, Bristol BS15 4DL England. **Tel** 011 44 0272 645411. **ED** G. Tily (editor's address: 22 Presbury, Yate, Bristol, BS17 4LB England). **Ad Acc. Circ:** 1,400.
Desc: Articles and information covering the family history.

IE
JOURNAL OF THE BUTLER SOCIETY. Periodical. English. 3.50 single issue. Melosina Lenox-Conynham, Secretary Levistown, Kilkenny Ireland. **LC** CT867.5.B87; J68. **DD** 929/.2/09415. **UDC** 929.52(415).

UK/0309-5800
JOURNAL OF THE CAMBRIDGESHIRE FAMILY HISTORY SOCIETY. (CAMBRIDGESHIRE FAMILY HISTORY SOCIETY.). [J.Cambs. Fam. Hist. Soc.]. (1977)-. Periodical. English. Four times a year (Feb., May, Aug., Nov.). £7.00 UK; £10.00 other. Cambridgeshire Family History Society, Kings Farm Horningsea, Cambridge CB5 9JG England. **ED** Mrs. J. Hurst, (phone: (0734)-420194. Index Available Published separately--free--upon request. **Bk Rev**, (Qty: 40). **Ad Acc, Adv Mgr:** Mrs. J. Hurst, **Tel** 0734-420194. **Circ:** 1,000 (ctrl).
Desc: For the members of the Cambridgeshire family History Society. Contains articles on genealogy, families of the area, local history, archive sources and help column.

US/0731-955X
JOURNAL OF THE CLAN CAMPBELL SOCIETY (UNITED STATES OF AMERICA). Vol. 5, No. 2 (Spring 1978)-. Periodical. English. qt. $15.00, $3.75 (single issues). The Clan Campbell Journal, PO Box 4428, Denver CO 80204. **Tel** (303)838-4769. **ED** Diarmid A Campbell. **LC** CS71; .C1894. **DD** 929/.2/0973. **UDC** 929.52(73). **Bk Rev. Ad Acc. Circ:** 2,500. ***Continues*** *Clan Campbell Society (United States of America) Newsletter, 0731-8472.*
Desc: Subjects directly related to the Campbell name and associated names and the social/genealogical history of Clan Campbell and Campbell owned lands.

UK
JOURNAL OF THE HERALDRY SOCIETY OF SCOTLAND. Main/Corp Heraldry Society of Scotland. Vol. 1 (1978)-. English. an. **LC** CR510; .H47a. **DD** 929.6/09411.

IE/0790-7060
JOURNAL OF THE IRISH FAMILY HISTORY SOCIETY. Added/Corp Irish Family History Society. (1985)-. Periodical. English. an (September/October). $20.00. Irish Family History Society, PO Box 36, Naas Co Kildare Republic of Ireland. **Tel** 011 353 045 69110, FAX 011 353 045 69393. **ED** Noel Reid. **LC** CS480; .J68. **DD** 929/.1/0720415. cum. index. **Bk Rev. Pr Rev. Circ:** 800 (ctrl).
Desc: A collection of articles and lists of data of interest to persons researching Irish ancestry.

US/0270-4064
JOURNAL OF THE KANAWHA VALLEY GENEALOGICAL SOCIETY, THE.
Main/Corp Kanawha Valley Genealogical Society. **VFOAT** KVGS Journal. **VAT** Kanawha Valley Genealogical Society Journal. Vol. 1 (Oct. 1977)-. Periodical. English. Eleven times a year. $7.50. Kanawha Valley Genealogical Society, PO Box 8555, South Charleston WV 25303. **LC** F247.K3; K36a. **DD** 929/.1/097543.

US/0893-5416
JOURNAL OF THE MAGOFFIN COUNTY HISTORICAL SOCIETY, THE. **Added/Corp** Magoffin County Historical Society (Ky.). (1979)-. Periodical. English. qt (4 issues). $10.00 (includes membership to Society). Magoffin County Historical Society, Box 222, Salyersville KY 41465. **Tel** (606)349-1607. **ED** Connie Arnett Wireman. **DD** 929. **Circ:** 700.
Desc: Family genealogy articles, queries, pictures, court records, church records, cemetery listings, etc., for Magoffin County, Kentucky.

UK/0141-9544
JOURNAL OF THE NORTH MIDDLESEX FAMILY HISTORY SOCIETY. **Added/Corp** North Middlesex Family History Society. **VFOAT** North Middlesex; Journal of the North Middx. Family History Society. Vol. 1, No. 1 (Autumn 1978)-. Periodical. English. Four times a year (Apr., July, Nov. Dec.). London & North Middlesex Family History Society, 2 Canonbury Cottages A Prudames, Enfield Middlesex EN1 3LR England. **ED** Robin Ford. **LC** CS435.M4; J68. **DD** 929/.1/07204218. **Bk Rev. Ad Acc. Circ:** 800.

US
JOURNAL - THE PETER WILLCOCKS SOCIETY. **Main/Corp** Peter Willcocks Society. No. 1 (July 1973)-. English. $25.00 North America; $30.00 other. Laird Wilcox, PO Box 2047, Olathe KS 66061. **Tel** (913)829-0609. **LC** CS71; .W667a. **DD** 929/.2/0973. **Circ:** 85.
Desc: Genealogical history of Wilcox family.

US/0890-6858
JOURNAL - WESTERN NEW YORK GENEALOGICAL SOCIETY. [J. - West. N. Y. Geneal. Soc.]. **Main/Corp** Western New York Genealogical Society. **VFOAT** A.WNYGS journal; Western New York Genealogical Society Journal; W.N.Y.G.S. Journal. Vol. 1 (June 1974)-. Periodical. English. qt. $20.00. Western New York Genealogical Society, PO Box 338, Hamburg NY 14075. **LC** F118; .W46a. **DD** 929/.3747/9. cum. index. **Bk Rev. Circ:** 700 (ctrl).
Desc: Information on towns and villages of Western New York, basic vital record information, sources for Western New York genealogical data, articles of interest for beginner as well as advanced genealogists

US/0899-1693
K.A.R.D. FILES ADAMSON ANCESTRY, THE. **VFOAT** KARD Files Adamson Ancestry; Adamson Ancestry. English. ir. $6.00 (per volume). Abshire Abstracts, 19305 Southeast 243rd Place, Kent WA 98042. **Tel** (206)432-1659. **ED** Judy K Dye. **LC** CS71; .A1984. **DD** 929/.2/0973. Index available. **Bk Rev.** ctrl circ. ***Continues*** *K.A.R.D. Files Adamson.*
Desc: Raw data and uneages regarding the Adamson surname; your queries, lineages, data published free of charge.

US/0899-1723
K.A.R.D. FILES DYE DATA, THE. (DYE DATA.). [KARD Files Dye data]. **Added/Corp** K.A.R.D. Files. Vol. 1 (Sept. 1983)-. Periodical. English. ir. $6.00 (per volume). Abshire Abstracts, 19305 Southeast 243rd Place, Kent WA 98042. **Tel** (206)432-1659. **ED** Judy K Dye. **DD** 929. Index available. **Bk Rev. Circ:** 600 (ctrl).
Desc: Raw data and lineages regarding the Dye surname. Queries and lineages and data published free of charge.

US/0899-1685
K.A.R.D. FILES PRESENTS ABSHIRE ABSTRACTS, THE. **VFOAT** Abshire Abstracts. Vol. 5 (Sept. 1984)-. English. ir. $6.00 (per volume). K.A.R.D. Files, 19305 Southeast 243rd Place, Kent WA 98042. **Tel** (206)432-1659. **ED** Judy K Dye. **LC** CS71; .A16415. **DD** 929/.2/0973. Index available. **Bk Rev.** ctrl circ. available on microfiche (Vols. 1-4). ***Continues*** *Abshire Abstracts.*
Desc: A collection of Abshire (all spelling variations) lineages and raw data plus an every name index. Lineage and queries can be included with no charge.

US/0899-1715
K.A.R.D. FILES PRESENTS BLAKELEY BANDWAGON, THE. [K.A.R.D. Files presents Blakeley bandwag.]. **Added/Corp** K.A.R.D. Files (Firm). **VFOAT** Blakeley Bandwagon; KARD Files Presents Blakeley Bandwagon. Vol. 1 (Jan. 1987)-. English. ir. $6.00. Abshire Abstracts, 19305 Southeast 243rd Place, Kent WA 98042. **Tel** (206)432-1659. **ED** Judy K. Dye. **LC** CS71; .B646215. **DD** 929/.2/0973. Index available. **Bk Rev.** ctrl circ. ***Continues*** *Blakeley Family Journal.*
Desc: Raw data and lineages regarding the Blakeley surname. Queries and lineages and data published free of charge.

US/0899-1731
K.A.R.D. FILES PRESENTS LUTTRELL LINEAGES & DATA, THE. **VFOAT** Luttrell Lineages & Data; Luttrell Lineages and Data. Vol. 1 (July 1986)-. English. ir. $6.00 (per volume). Abshire Abstracts, 19305 Southeast 243rd Place, Kent WA 98042. **Tel** (206)432-1659. **ED** Judy K Dye. **LC** CS71; .L974214. **DD** 929/.2/0973. Index available. **Bk Rev.** ctrl circ.
Desc: Raw data and linages regarding the Rambo surname. Queries, lineages, and data are published free of charge.

US/0899-174X
K.A.R.D. FILES PRESENTS RAMBO REFERENCES, THE. (RAMBO REFERENCES.). [KARD Files presents Rambo ref.]. Vol. 1 (Jan. 1983)-. Periodical. English. $6.00 (per volume). Abshire Abstracts, 19305 Southeast 243rd Place, Kent WA 98042. **Tel** (206)432-1659. **ED** Judy K Dye. **LC** CS71; .R175A. **DD** 929/.2/0973. Index available. **Bk Rev.** ctrl circ.
Desc: Raw data and lineages regarding the Rambo surname. Queries, lineages and data are published free of charge.

US/0888-7861
KALAMAZOO VALLEY FAMILY NEWSLETTER, THE. ***Ceased.*** [Kalamazoo Val. fam. news lett.]. **VFOAT** The Kalamazoo Valley Family News Letter. Vol. 1 (1971)-(1984). Newsletter. English. qt. Clann Cearr Ltd, Library Section, Box 41, Portage MI 49081. **Tel** (616)657-5210. **LC** F572.K22; K34. **DD** 929/.3774/17. **UDC** 929.5(774). **Circ:** 300 (ctrl).
Desc: Each issue concentrates on one county collecting all available material on that county.

US/0451-3991
KANSAS CITY GENEALOGIST, THE. **Added/Corp** Heart of America Genealogical Society. Vol. 1 (March 1960)-. Periodical. English. Four times a year (Jan., Apr., July, Oct.). $15.00. Heart of America Genealogical Society, 311 East 12th Street, Kansas City Public Library, Kansas City MO 64106. **Tel** (816)221-2685 Ext. 171. **ED** Joanne Chiles Eakin (phone: (816)461-5845). **LC** F465; .K3. cum. index (every 4th issue). **Bk Rev**, (Qty: 4). **Ad Acc. Circ:** 485.
Desc: This covers mostly in the areas of Bible records, wills, diaries, church records, cemetery records, vital records, court records, and land records.
Ind/Abst Genealogical Period. Annu. Index.

US/0451-4084
KANSAS KIN. **Added/Corp** Riley County Genealogical Society. Vol. 1, No. 1 (Jan. 1963)-. Periodical. English. Four times a year (Feb., May, Aug., Nov.). $10.00. Riley County Genealogical Society, 2005 Claflin Road, Manhattan KS 66502. **Tel** (913)537-2205. **ED** J. Harvey Littrell. **LC** F687.R5; K36. **DD** 929/.378128. Index available. **Bk Rev. Circ:** 500.
Desc: Genealogical society's publication containing Bible and other family records as well as court and census records are published, gift books are reviewed, ancestor tables of one page are printed.
Ind/Abst Genealogical Period. Annu. Index.

US
KARANKAWA KOUNTRY : A PUBLICATION OF CALHOUN COUNTY GENEALOGICAL SOCIETY. **Added/Corp** Calhoun County Genealogical Society. **VFOAT** Karankawa Kountry Quarterly. (198?)-. English. Twice a year (Jan. & July). $10.00. Calhoun County Genealogical Society, Box 1150, 911 North Ann Street, Port Lavaca TX 77979. **Tel** (512)552-2588. **LC** F392.C22; K37. **DD** 929/.1/0720764121. ***Continues*** *Karankawa Kountry Quarterly.*

US/0741-2045
KATES KIN. [Kates kin]. Vol. 1, No. 1 (1 Mar. 1978)-. Periodical. English. Four times a year. Free on request. Anna Kates Gardner, PO Box 8, Rarden OH 45671. **Tel** (614)372-6705. **ED** Anna Kates Gardner. **LC** CS71; .C35664. **DD** 929/.2/0973. Index available. **Bk Rev. Ad Acc. Circ:** 800.
Desc: Newsletter for those people researching the family history of the spelling variations of Kates and Cates.

US/0884-7525
KAUFMAN KOUNTY KONNECTIONS. (KAUFMAN KOUNTY KONNECTIONS / KAUFMAN COUNTY GENEALOGICAL SOCIETY.). **Added/Corp** Kaufman County Genealogical Society. **VFOAT** Kaufman County Connections. Vol. 1, No. 1 (June 1982)-. Periodical. English. Four times a year. $15.00. Kaufman County Genealogical Society, PO Box 337, Terell TX 75160. **Tel** (214)524-5605. **ED** Lou Hicks Miller, (editor's address: 206 Pecan Street, Terrell, TX 75160-1768; phone:(214)524-5605). **LC** F392.K25; K38. **DD** 929/.3764277. Each issue contains an index to its own contents (no volume index)--loose. **Bk Rev**, (Qty: 25). **Ad Acc. Circ:** 160.
Desc: Contains family group sheets, census, and historical cemetery listings.

UK/0305-9359
KENT FAMILY HISTORY SOCIETY JOURNAL. **Main/Corp** Kent Family History Society. **VFOAT** Journal. Vol. 1 (Dec. 1974)-. English. qt (4 issues). Comes with Kent Family History Society membership, £6.00. Kent Family History Society, Membership Section, 23 Ersham Road, Canterbury Kent CT1 3AR England. **ED** Doreen Perrott. Index available. **Bk Rev. Ad Acc. Circ:** 1,500 (ctrl).

US/0023-0103
KENTUCKY ANCESTORS. [Ky. ancestors]. **Added/Corp** Kentucky Historical Society. Kentucky Historical Society. Genealogical Committee. Vol. 1 (July 1965)-. Periodical. English. qt. Free to members of the Kentucky Historical Society; $35.00 (institutions), $25.00 (individuals) membership. Kentucky Historical Society, Old State Capitol, PO Box H, Frankfort KY 40602. **Tel** (502)564-3016, FAX (502)564-4701. **LC** F450; .K4.
Desc: Devoted to the history of Kentucky and its people.
Ind/Abst Genealogical Period. Annu. Index.

US
KENTUCKY FAMILY RECORDS.
Added/Corp West-Central Kentucky Family Association. Vol. 1 (1969/70)-. English. qt. $12.00. West Central Kentucky Family Research Association, PO Box 1932, Owensboro KY 42302. **Tel** (502)684-4150. **ED** Elizabeth Cox and Diane Morris. Index available. cum. index. **Circ:** 800.
Ind/Abst Genealogical Period. Annu. Index.

US/0748-5565
KENTUCKY PIONEER GENEALOGY AND RECORDS. **VFOAT** Kentucky Pioneer Genealogy & Records. (Jan. 1979)-. Periodical. English. an. $12.00. Society of Kentucky Pioneers, 11129 Pleasant Ridge Road, Utica KY 42376. **Tel** (502)275-4075. **LC** F450; .K459. **DD** 929/.1/0720769.

US/0899-1359
KENTUCKY QUERIES. ***Title Change.*** (KENTUCKY QUERIES / BY RUBY SIMONSON MCNEILL.). [Ky. queries]. (1987)-(199?). Periodical. English. ir. McNeill Enterprises, PO Box 779, Napavine WA 98565. **Tel** (509)922-4521. **ED** Ruby Simonson McNeill. **LC** F450; .K465. **DD** 929/.3769. **Bk Rev. Circ:** 500 (ctrl). ***Merged with*** *Tennessee Queries, 0898-5472* ***to form*** *Tennessee & Kentucky Queries, 1068-0063.*
Ind/Abst Genealogical Period. Annu. Index.

US/0453-7637
KERN-GEN, THE. V. 1- June 1964-. Periodical. English. qt. $6.00, $10.00 (membership). Kern County Genealogy Society, Box 2214, Bakersfield CA 93303. **Tel** (805)831-7527. **ED** Betty Cook. **LC** F868.K3; K4. **UDC** 929.5(794). Index available. **Bk Rev. Circ:** 200.
Desc: Covers Kern County, California primary records, families of society members, and other family records. Queries accepted.

US/0736-0886
KERSHNER KINFOLK. [Kershner kinfolk]. Vol. 1, No. 1 (Jan.-March 1982)-. Periodical. English. Four times a year (Jan., Apr., July, Oct.). $14.00. Kershner Family Association, 1449 Fox Run Drive, Charlotte NC 28212-7125. **Tel** (704)535-6025, (704)365-7681. **ED** William E. Kershner. **LC** CS71; .K397294. **DD** 929/.2/0973. Index available. cum. index. **Bk Rev. Ad Acc. Circ:** 100 (ctrl).
Desc: Genealogical material on the Kershner (Kirschner, Karschner, Kerschner) family, especially descendants of three brothers who arrived from Langenselbold, Hesse in first half of 18th century.

US/0741-5338
KEY FINDER. **Added/Corp** Northwest Oklahoma Genealogical Society. Vol. 1, No. 1 (July 1980)-. Periodical. English. Four times a year. $15.00. Northwest Oklahoma Genealogical Society, PO Box 834, Woodward OK 73802. **Tel** (405)256-4609. **LC** F693; .K49. **DD** 929/.1/0720766.

US
KEYHOLE. **Added/Corp** Genealogical Society of Southwestern Pennsylvania. (19??)-. Periodical. English. Four times a year (Jan., Apr., July, Oct.). $12.00. Genealogical Society of Southwestern PA, PO Box 894, Washington PA 15301. **LC** F148; .K48. **DD** 929/.1/0627488. Index available. **Circ:** 1,000.

US/0737-2868
KEYSTONE SEEKERS GENEALOGICAL QUARTERLY.
(KEYSTONE SEEKERS GENEALOGICAL QUARTERLY / CAPITAL AREA GENEALOGICAL SOCIETY.). Vol. 1, No. 1 (Winter 1983)-. Periodical. English. qt. $10.00. Capital Area Genealogical Society, POB 4502, Harrisburg PA 17111. **ED** Keith and Beth Nonemaker. **LC** F148; .K49. **DD** 929/.1/0720748. **UDC** 929.5(748). Index available. **Circ:** 175 (ctrl).
Desc: Presents cemetery records, pedigree charts, death records, Bible records, will abstracts, naturalization records, deeds, how-to articles and queries.

US/1064-9999
KIN HUNTERS. [Kin hunt.]. Vol. 1, No. 1 (April 1987)-. Periodical. English. qt. $16.00 (one year), $30.00

Genealogy and Heraldry

(two year). Genealogical Publishing and Research, PO Box 151, Attention: M Vanderpool, Russellville KY 42276. **DD** 929.
Ind/Abst Genealogical Period. Annu. Index.

US/0737-6987
KIN IN LINN. [Kin Linn]. **Added/Corp** Linn Co. Genealogical Society. Vol. 1, No. 1 (Fall 1980)-. Periodical. English. qt. $8.00. Linn County Historical & Genealogical Society, PO Box 137, Pleasanton KS 66075. **Tel** (913)352-8739. **LC** F687.L75; K45. **DD** 929/.1/072078169.
Ind/Abst Genealogical Period. Annu. Index (?-?).

US/1069-207X
KIN KOLLECTING. (KIN COLLECTING.). [Kin kollect.]. **Added/Corp** Ashley County Genealogical Society (Ark.). **VFOAT** Kin Kollecting. Vol. 1, No. 1 (Spring 1986)-. Periodical. English. qt. $15.00. Ashley County Genealogical Society, Drawer R, Crossett AR 71635. **Tel** (501)364-2578. **ED** Rebecca Brown. **DD** 929. Index available (Bound in each issue). **Bk Rev**. ctrl circ.
Desc: Covers history and genealogy of Ashley County Arkansas. Composed of source materials, Bible records, family group sheets, and queries.

CN/0822-9201
KIN MAGAZINE. (KIN MAGAZINE : OFFICIAL PUBLICATION OF THE ASSOCIATION OF KINSMEN CLUBS.). [Kin mag.]. Vol. 62, No. 2 (Oct./Nov. 1982)-. Periodical. English. bm. $5.00. Association of Kinsmen Clubs, 1920 Hal Rogers Drive, Box Kin Canada. **DD** 369.5. ***Continues** Kin, 0023-1436.*

CN/0823-3837
KINDRED SPIRITS. (KINDRED SPIRITS / WHITBY-OSHAWA BRANCH--O.G.S.). [Kindred spirits]. **Added/Corp** Ontario Genealogical Society. Whitby-Oshawa Branch. (Aug. 1983)-. English. Four times a year. 12.00Can$. Whitby-Oshawa Branch O G S, PO Box 174, Whitby Ontario L1N 5S1 Canada. **Tel** (416)623-4978. **ED** D Brown, T Gamble, L Wood. **LC** CS88.W49; G46. **DD** 929/.1/072071356. **Circ:** 500. ***Continues** Genealogical Newsletter of the Whitby-Oshawa Branch--O.G.S.*
Desc: Covers genealogical lists, local histories of people and places, research. Tips, members queries, and miscellaneous genealogical information.

US/0556-9796
KINFOLK. **Added/Corp** Rich Family Association. Vol. 1 (Mar 1966)-. Periodical. English. qt. The Rich Family Association, PO Box 142, Wellfleet MA 02667. **LC** CS71; .R5a.

US/0742-7654
KINFOLKS (LAKE CHARLES, LA.). (KINFOLKS / SOUTHWEST LOUISIANA GENEALOGICAL SOCIETY.). [Kinfolks]. **Added/Corp** Southwest Louisiana Genealogical Society. Vol. 1, No. 1 (Apr.28 1977)-. Periodical. English. Four times a year (Mar., June, Sept., Dec.). $10.00. Southwest Louisiana Genealogical Society, Inc. (SWLGS), PO Box 5652, Lake Charles LA 70606-5652. **Tel** (318)477-3087, President's phone. **ED** Betty Rostreet (editor's address: 2801 St. Francis Street, Sulphur, LA 70606, phone: (318)625-4740). **LC** F368; .K56. **DD** 929/.1/0720763. Index available (bound in each issue). **Bk Rev**, (Qty: approx. 20). **Circ:** 400 (ctrl).
Desc: Contains marriage, parish voter, cemetery, immigration records. Articles submitted by our members recounting family history and genealogy. Focused primarily on south Louisiana.
Ind/Abst Genealogical Period. Annu. Index.

CN/1188-1089
KINGSTON RELATIONS. [Kingst. relat.]. (1992)-. Periodical. English. Five times a year. $20.00. Ontario Genealogical Society / Kingston Branch, PO Box 1394, Kingston Ontario K7L 5C6 Canada. **DD** 929.106071372. ctrl circ. ***Continues** Newsletter - Ontario Genealogical Society, Kingston Branch, 0316-5183.*

US/0882-9802
KINSHIP KRONICLE. (KINSHIP KRONICLE / ROCKINGHAM COUNTY CHAPTER OF THE NEW HAMPSHIRE SOCIETY OF GENEALOGISTS.). **Added/Corp** New Hampshire Society of Genealogists. Rockingham County Chapter. **VFOAT** Kinship Chronicle. (19??)-. Periodical. English. Four times a year (Mar. June, Sept., Dec.). $6.50. Kinship Kronicle, PO Box 81, Exeter NH 03833. **Tel** (603)436-5824. **ED** Carl W. Brage. **LC** F42.R7; K56. **DD** 929/.1/07207426. Index available (Bound in 4th issue in December at $1.70.). **Bk Rev**, (Qty: 4+). **Ad Acc. Circ:** 250.
Desc: Publication is to provide genealogical data and queries to the public at-large.

US
KINSMAN COURIER, THE. **Added/Corp** Ohio Genealogical Society. Coshocton County Chapter. Vol. 1, No. 1 (May 1978)-. Periodical. English. qt. $10.00 nonmembers; Free, members. Ohio Genealogical Society / Coshocton County Chapter, PO Box 117, Coshocton OH 43812. **Tel** (614)622-4583. **ED** Vera Salvant Harrison. **LC** F497.C7; K56. **DD** 929/.1/072077165. Index available. cum. index.
Desc: Biographies, queries, "how to" information; information from newspapers containing names of genealogical nature, court records, and cemetery listings.

CN/1183-2312
KINXIONS (RICHMOND). (KINXIONS : LINKING THE DESCENDANTS OF OLIN LOCKE TILLOTSON AND SUSAN ADELLA DAVIS OF EAST MONTPELIER, VERMONT.). [Kinxions]. **VFOAT** Kinxions. (Spring 1991)-. Periodical. English. sa. Olin Tillotson, 9380 Francis Road, Richmond British Columbia V6Y 1B1 Canada. **ED** Olin Tillotson. **DD** 929/.2.

US
KISHWAUKEE GENEALOGISTS. English. Five times a year. $7.00. Kishwaukee Genealogists, PO Box 5503, Rockford IL 61125. **Tel** (815)399-5554.

US/0273-0391
KITH AND KIN OF BOONE COUNTY, WEST VIRGINIA. **Main/Corp** Boone County Genealogical Society. (1977)-. English. an. $11.00 (per volume). Treasurer, Boone County Genealogical Society, Box 306, Madison WV 25108. **Tel** (304)369-2769. **ED** Lenore Ferrell and Janet Hager. **LC** F247.B6; B66a. **DD** 929/.375439.

US/1053-5837
KITH 'N KIN (FREMONT, OHIO). (SANDUSKY COUNTY KIN HUNTERS.). **Added/Corp** Sandusky County Kin Hunters (Ohio). **VFOAT** Kith and Kin. (19??)-. Periodical. English. Six times a year (Feb., Apr., June, Aug., Oct., Dec.). $8.00 individual membership; $10.00 joint membership (or more people in same household). Sandusky County Kin Hunters, 1337 Hayes Avenue, Fremont OH 43420. **Tel** (419)862-2205. **ED** Mary Ann Bulinger. **DD** 929. Index available (In December issue). **Bk Rev**, (Qty: rarely). **Pr Rev. Circ:** 350 (ctrl).
Desc: Genealogical records of Sandusky County, Ohio & Ohio in general. Also in history, members queries, news, meeting summaries, books at the Hayes Centre, publications for sale.

US
KNARR-KNERR-KNORR FAMILY NEWSLETTER. **VAT** Knarr Knerr Knorr Family Newsletter. No. 68 (Dec. 1990)-. Newsletter. English. qt. Larry Knarr, 7657 Squirrel Creek Drive, Cincinnati OH 45247-3614. **Tel** (513)385-3422. **ED** Larry Knarr. **LC** IN PROCESS. ***Continues** Knarr-Knerr-Knorr Family Lines.*

US/0193-886X
KNIGHT LETTER (CHARLOTTESVILLE). (KNIGHT LETTER.). No. 1, (Aug. 1974)-. Periodical. English. ir. $20.00 Comes with Lewis Carroll Society of North America membership. Secretary of Lewis Carroll Society of North America, 617 Rockford Road, c/o Secretary, Silver Spring MD 20902.

US/0454-8973
KNIGHT LETTER (FORT WORTH, TEX.). (KNIGHT LETTER.). Vol. 1, No. 1 (Feb. 1968)-. Periodical. English. Four times a year. $8.00. Merle Ganier, 2108 Grace Street, Fort Worth TX 76111. **Tel** (817)838-5727. **ED** Merle Ganier. **LC** CS71; .K7244. **DD** 929/.2/0973. Index available. **Bk Rev. Circ:** 200 (ctrl). available on microfiche.
Desc: Provides communication for researchers of Knight, Knecht, and Nite families.

US/0741-7284
KNOX COUNTY, ILLINOIS GENEALOGICAL SOCIETY QUARTERLY. **Added/Corp** Knox County, Illinois Genealogical Society. **VFOAT** Quarterly. Vol. 2, No. 1 (Jan. 1974)-. Periodical. English. qt. Comes with Knox County Illinois Genealogical Society membership. Knox County Illinois Genealogical Society, PO Box 13, Galesburg IL 61402-0013. **Tel** (309)343-1466. **ED** Dale Evelyn Effland. **LC** F547.K7; K56. **DD** 929/.377349. Index available. cum. index. **Circ:** 350 (ctrl). ***Continues** Knox County Genealogical Society Quarterly, 0741-7276.*
Desc: Marriage index, court records, cemetery records, gleanings of early newspapers, early church memberships lists, and Bible records.
Ind/Abst Genealogical Period. Annu. Index.

US/0276-4857
KNOX COUNTY, KENTUCKY KINFOLK. (KNOX COUNTY, KENTUCKY KINFOLK : A PUBLICATION OF THE KNOX COUNTY GENEALOGICAL SOCIETY, INC.). **Added/Corp** Knox County Genealogical Society (Ky.). Vol. 3, No. 1 (Jan. 1979)-. Periodical. English. Four times a year. $15.00. Knox County Genealogical Society, 2603 Aintree Way, Louisville KY 40220. **Tel** (502)459-8718. **ED** Maxine Jones, Virginia Logan. **LC** F457.K6; K65. **DD** 929/.3769125. Index available. ctrl circ. ***Continues** Knox County, Kentucky Kinfolk Newsletter, 0161-8393.*

US/0883-7961
KREFELD IMMIGRANTS AND THEIR DESCENDANTS. (1984)-. English. Twice a year (Apr., Sept.). $12.00. Links Genealogy Publications, 7677 Abaline Way, Sacramento CA 95823. **Tel** (916)428-2245. **ED** Iris Carter Jones. **DD** 929. **Bk Rev. Ad Acc. Pr Rev. Circ:** 300 (ctrl).
Desc: Features historical and genealogical material, wills, marriage, Bible, church, death records; queries, source information and book reviews.
Ind/Abst Genealogical Period. Annu. Index.

US/0743-2763
KRIEGBAUM HERITAGE, THE. Periodical. English. qt. $6.00. The Kriegbaum Heritage, 1112 Monroe Street, Quincy IL 62301. **LC** CS71; .K922694. **UDC** 929.52(73).

US/1059-9762
KURIER (ORANGE, VA), DER. (DER KURIER / MID-ATLANTIC GERMANIC SOCIETY.). (1982)-. English. Free to members. Mid-Atlantic Germanic Society, 12 Locust Boulevard, Middletown MD 21769.
Ind/Abst Genealogical Period. Annu. Index.

US/1049-863X
KYOWVA GENEALOGICAL SOCIETY NEWS LETTER. [Kyowva Geneal. Soc. news lett.]. **Added/Corp** Kyowva Genealogical Society. **VFOAT** Kyowva Genealogical Society Newsletter; News Letter. Vol. 9, No. 3 (Fall 1986)-. English. qt. Kyowva Genealogical Society, PO Box 1254, Huntington WV 25715. **LC** F497.L3; N48. **DD** 929/.1/072073. ***Continues** Kyowva Genealogical Society.*

US
LA FAYETTE. Vol. 1, No. 1 (April 1981)-. Periodical. English. qt. $15.00. Southwest Pennsylvania Genealogical Services, PO Box 253, Laughlintown PA 15655. **Tel** (412)238-3176.

●US/1063-889X
LA POINTE, A. (A LA POINTE : QUARTERLY NEWSLETTER OF THE POINTE DE L'EGLISE HISTORICAL AND GENEALOGICAL SOCIETY.). **Added/Corp** Pointe de l'Eglise Historical and Genealogical Society. (1992)-. Newsletter. English. qt. $10.00. A la Pointe, PO Box 160, Church Point LA 70525. ***Continues** Pointe de l'Eglise Historical and Genealogical Society : [Newsletter], 1063-8881.*

US/1064-5527
LAFAYETTE COUNTY HERITAGE NEWS. [Lafayette Cty. herit. news]. **Added/Corp** Skipwith Historical and Genealogical Society. **VFOAT** Lafayette Co., Mississippi Heritage News. (198?)-. Periodical. English. Four times a year (Jan., Apr., July, Oct.). $8.00 Comes with Skipwith Historical and Genealogical Society membership. Skipwith Historical & Genealogical Society, 1150 South 14th Street, Oxford MS 38655. **Tel** (601)234-1074. **ED** Maggie Winters (editor's address: Route 3 Box 470, Oxford MS 38655, phone: (601)234-6877). **DD** 929. **Bk Rev**, (Qty: 1 or 2). **Circ:** 125 (ctrl). ***Continues** Lafayette Heritage News.*
Desc: Various articles of genealogical and historical interest to members. Lists the business of the society, names of speakers, and a summary of his or her speech, announcements of upcoming events and queries of the members.

US/0736-4059
LAKE COUNTY (IL) GENEALOGICAL SOCIETY QUARTERLY. (QUARTERLY / LAKE COUNTY (IL) GENEALOGICAL SOCIETY.). **Main/Corp** Lake County (IL) Genealogical Society. **VFOAT** L.C.I.G.S.Q.; LCIGSQ. Vol. 1, No. 1 (Fall 1980)-. Periodical. English. qt. $10.00 (individuals and libraries), $11.00 (family) US; $15.00 other. Cook Memorial Library, 413 Milwaukee Avenue, Libertyville IL 60048. **LC** F547.L2; L34A. **DD** 929/.1/072077321. **UDC** 929.5(773). **Circ:** 215 (ctrl).
Ind/Abst Genealogical Period. Annu. Index.

US/0883-7708
LAMB'S PASTURES. [Lamb's pasture]. English. qt. $12.00. Stephen A Lamb, 2983 Bayside Court, Wantagh NY 11793. **Tel** (516)826-7273. **ED** Stephen A Lamb. **DD** 929. **UDC** 929.52(73). **Bk Rev. Ad Acc. Circ:** 150 (ctrl).
Desc: Family name association, specializing in surname Lamb.

US/0748-1071
LANCASTER COUNTY CONNECTIONS. Premier Issue (1983)-. Periodical. English. qt. $17.50. Lancaster County Connections, PO Box 207, Hershey PA 17033. **Tel** (717)533-5662. **ED** Gary T. Hawbaker. **LC** F157.L2; L58. **DD** 929/.1/072074815. Index available. **Bk Rev. Ad Acc. Circ:** 600.
Desc: A genealogical publication dedicated to providing information on ancestry on those who lived or passed through Lancaster County, Pa. Pennsylvania. Contains queries, special articles, Bible records, and cemetery records.
Ind/Abst Genealogical Period. Annu. Index.

US/0890-8893
LANCASTER COUNTY HERITAGE. ***Ceased.*** [Lanc. cty. herit.]. Vol. 1, No. 1 (Jan. 1984)-Ceased Vol. 3 (1986). Periodical. English. qt. Lancaster County Heritage, PO Box 7773, Lancaster PA 17604-7773. **LC** F157.L2; L42. **DD** 974.8/15/005. **UDC** 929.5(748).

US/1048-2059
LANDIS' LANDINGS. [Landis' land.]. English. bm. Jo Landers, 3110 Z Street, Vancouver WA 98661. **LC** CS71; .L256494. **DD** 929/.2/0973. ***Continues** Landers' Landings, 0739-134X.*

US/1055-4661
LANDSMEN (WASHINGTON, D.C.). (LANDSMEN : QUARTERLY PUBLICATION OF THE SUWALK-LOMZA INTEREST GROUP FOR JEWISH GENEALOGISTS.). [Landsmen]. **Added/Corp** Suwalk-Lomza Interest Group for Jewish Genealogists. Vol. 1, No. 1 (Summer 1990)-. Periodical. English. qt. Suwalk-Lomza Interest Group, 3701 Connecticut Avenue NW, Suite 228, Washington DC 20008. **LC** DS135.P62; S854. **DD** 929/.1/08992404383.
Ind/Abst Genealogical Period. Annu. Index.

US/0747-6663
LATAH COUNTY GENEALOGICAL SOCIETY. ***Ceased.*** (LATAH COUNTY GENEAOLOGICAL SOCIETY : [NEWSLETTER].). **Added/Corp** Latah County Genealogical Society. **VFOAT** Latah County Genealogical Society Quarterly. Vol. 1, No. 1 (Sept. 1981)-Vol. 13, No. 4. Periodical. English. qt (4 issues). Latah County Genealogical Society, 1108 Easth 7th, Moscow ID 83843. **Tel** (208)882-5943. **ED** Dorothy Schell. **LC** F752.L3; L37. **DD** 929/.1/072079686. Index available. **Circ:** 60.
Desc: Information on and records of Latah, County, Idaho. Offers queries, and helpful hints of genealogical interest.

US/0023-8988
LAUREL MESSENGER. See History(General)-History of North, South, and Central America.

US
LAVENDER LINE, THE. Periodical. English. qt. $15.00. The Lavender Line, 1913 NE 17th Way, Ft Lauderdale FL 33305. **LC** CS71; .L412714. **DD** 929/.2/0973. **UDC** 929.52(73).

US/1064-9743
LEGACY (MONROEVILLE, ALA.). (LEGACY : THE MAGAZINE OF THE MONROE COUNTY HERITAGE MUSEUM.). [Legacy]. **Added/Corp** Monroe County Heritage Museum (Ala.). (Summer 1991)-. Periodical. English. sa (2 issues). $20.00. Monroe County Heritage Museum, PO Box 1637, Monroeville AL 36461. **Tel** (205)575-7433. **DD** 976. ***Continues** Quarterly (Monroe County Museum and Historical Society), 1063-8156.*

US/0883-7406
LENT (VAN LENT) NEWSLETTER. (LENT (VAN LENT) FAMILY NEWSLETTER.). [Lent (van lent) fam. newsl.]. **VFOAT** Newsletter. Vol. 1, #1 (June 1985). Newsletter. English. sa. Ruth E Lent, POB 2183, Clifton Park NY 12065. **DD** 929. **UDC** 929.52(73).

US/8756-5595
LEON HUNTERS DISPATCH, THE. [Leon hunt. dispatch]. **Added/Corp** Leon County Genealogical Society. (198?)-. Periodical. English. bm. $15.00. Leon County Genealogical Society, PO Box 500, Centerville TX 75833. **Tel** (214)536-7203. **ED** Neita Ellis. **LC** F392.L46; N48. **DD** 929. Index available. **Circ:** 268 (ctrl). ***Continues** Newsletter (Leon County Genealogical Society), 0731-8952.*
Desc: Pedigree charts, family Bible records, old records and probates, announcements, queries, list of members, additional cemetery records, and other related articles available at the center.

US
LEXICON. English. Four times a year. $12.00 US; $16.00 other. Jackson County Genealogical Society / Michigan, 244 West Michigan Avenue, Jackson MI 49201. **ED** Diane Jonas.

US/0747-6485
LEXINGTON GENEALOGICAL EXCHANGE. **Added/Corp** Lexington Genealogical Association. (Summer 1981)-. English. qt (Jan., Apr., July, Oct.). comes with Lexington County Genealogical Association Membership. Lexington County Genealogical Association, c/o Marjorie A Lindler, PO Box 1442, Lexington SC 29072. **Tel** (803)987-5620. **LC** F277.L5; L49. **DD** 929/.1/072075773.

US/0162-0851
L'HERITAGE (CHALMETTE). (L'HERITAGE.). **Added/Corp** St. Bernard Genealogical Society. Vol. 1 (Jan. 1978)-. Periodical. English (English). ir. $17.50 Comes with St. Bernard Genealogical Society membership. St Bernard Genealogical Society, PO Box 271, Chalmette LA 70044. **Tel** (504)279-6236. **LC** CS42; .H43. **DD** 929/.2/0973.

US/0748-1012
LICKING LANTERN, THE. **Added/Corp** Licking County Genealogical Society. Vol. 1, No. 2 (Spring 1976)-. Periodical. English. Four times a year (Mar., June, Sept., Dec.). $12.00. Licking County Genealogical Society, PO Box 4037, Newark OH 43055. **Tel** (614)345-3571. **ED** Kathy Dean (phone: (614)745-2834). **LC** F497.L6; F57a. **DD** 929/.377154. Index available. **Ad Acc. Circ:** 600. ***Continues** First Issue (Newark, Ohio), 0748-0857.*
Desc: Counties and families history and genealogies, bible records, court records, and cemetery records.
Ind/Abst Genealogical Period. Annu. Index.

US/0047-4630
LIFELINER. **Added/Corp** Genealogical Society of Riverside. (19??)-. Periodical. English. qt. $10.00. Genealogical Society of Riverside, PO Box 2557, Riverside CA 92516. **Tel** (909)682-4998. **ED** Georgia Harris. **LC** CS42; .L53. **DD** 929/.1/05. Index available. **Bk Rev. Ad Acc. Circ:** 250. ***Continues** Genealogical Society of Riverside. Life-Line.*
Desc: Genealogically related stories and articles with extracts from various local records. Records and items submitted by members queries.
Ind/Abst Genealogical Period. Annu. Index.

US/8755-920X
LIFELINES (PLATTSBURGH, N.Y.). (LIFELINES : OFFICIAL JOURNAL OF THE NORTHERN NEW YORK AMERICAN-CANADIAN GENEALOGICAL SOCIETY.). [Lifelines]. **Added/Corp** Northern New York American-Canadian Genealogical Society. Vol. 1, No. 1 (Spring 1984)-. Periodical. English. Twice a year (May & Oct.). $20.00. North New York American Canadian Genealogical Society, PO Box 1256, Plattsburgh NY 12901. **LC** F118; .L53. **DD** 929/.3747; 929.

US
LINCOLN CO. TENNESSEE PIONEERS. Vol. 1, No. 1 (Sept. 1970)-. Periodical. English. sa. $8.00. Lincoln County Tennessee, 238 Point Clear, Conroe TX 77304. **Tel** (409)856-5624. Index available (bound in the June issue). ctrl circ.

UK/0261-3565
LINCOLNSHIRE FAMILY HISTORIAN. Vol. 1, No. 1 (Oct. 1981)-. English. qt.

US/0899-1871
LINEAGE (COMMACK, N.Y.). (LINEAGE / JGSLI.). **Added/Corp** Jewish Genealogical Society of Long Island. **VFOAT** JGSLI Lineage. **VAT** Jewish Genealogical Society of Long Island Lineage. Vol. 1, No. 1 (Spring 1988)-. Periodical. English. Four times a year. $20.00 Queens, Nassau & Suffolk Counties; $12.00 other. Jewish Genealogical Society of Long Island, 37 Westcliff Drive, Dix Hills NY 11746. **Tel** (516)549-9532, FAX (516)673-0587. **ED** Shelley Lantheaume (editor's address: 32 Holiday Park Drive, Hauppauge, NY 11788; Telephone: (516)979-9779). **DD** 929. **Bk Rev**, (Qty: 2). **Ad Acc. Circ:** 250.
Desc: Quarterly newsletter of the Jewish Genealogy Society of Long Island; contains information of genealogical research sources and techniques, with an emphasis on Jewish and East European research.
Ind/Abst Genealogical Period. Annu. Index.

US
LINES AND BY-LINES. English. Free to members. Louisville Genealogical Society, PO Box 5164, Louisville KY 40205. **Tel** (502)425-2917.
Ind/Abst Genealogical Period. Annu. Index.

CN
LINES OF DESCENT. English. qt (Mar., June, Sept., Dec.). 15.00Can$. Alberta Genealogical Society, PO Box 12015, Fort McMurray BR, Alberta T9H 4W1 Canada. **Tel** (403)791-2913, telex KS4337. **ED** Marilyn Pierson (Editor's telephone: 403-791-9366). **Bk Rev. Circ:** 70 (ctrl).

US/0897-9839
LIVE OAK (OAKLAND, CALIF. 1982), THE. (THE LIVE OAK : NEWLETTER OF THE EAST BAY GENEALOGICAL SOCIETY.). [Live oak]. **Main/Corp** East Bay Genealogical Society (Oakland, Calif.). (1982)-. Periodical. English. bm (Jan., Mar., May, July, Sept., Nov.). $7.00. East Bay Genealogical Society, PO Box 20417, Oakland CA 94620-0417. **Tel** (510)522-7469. **ED** Josef M. Schmitt, (phone: (510)532-5947). **DD** 929. **Bk Rev**, (Qty: 3-6). **Ad Acc. Circ:** 200.
Desc: News, research aids, references and book reviews.

UK/0260-759X
LIVERPOOL FAMILY HISTORIAN. (1981)-. English. Four times a year. £6.50 Europe; £8.50 Canada & US; £9.00 Australia & New Zealand. Liverpool and Southwest Lancashire Family Historical Society, 11 Bushbys Lane, Formby, Merseyside L37 2DX England. **Tel** 011 44 925 723526. Index available. **Bk Rev. Ad Acc. Circ:** 1,400 (ctrl).

US/8755-9714
LIVING TREE NEWS, THE. [Living tree news]. **Added/Corp** Harris County Genealogical Society. Vol. 1, No. 1 (Fall 1974)-. Periodical. English. qt. comes with membership. Harris County Genealogical Society, PO Box 391, Pasadena TX 77501. **Tel** (713)645-1144. **LC** F392.H38; L58. **DD** 929/.3764141.

US/0742-4744
LIVINGSTON FAMILY NEWSLETTER. No. 1-. Newsletter. English. sa. $5.00. Livingston Newsletter, 8726 Mohawk Way, Fair Oaks CA 95628-2929. **LC** CS71; .L78694. **DD** 929/.2/0973. **UDC** 929.52(73).

US/0732-7595
LOGSDON CONNECTIONS. Vol. 1, No. 1-. Periodical. English. qt. $10.00. Gloria A Lucas, 21056 Niagara Drive, Sonora CA 95370. **LC** CS71; .L822. **DD** 929/.2/0973. **UDC** 929.52(73).

CN/0824-5304
LONDON LEAF. [Lond. leaf]. **Added/Corp** Ontario Genealogical Society. London Branch. No. 1 (1974)-. Periodical. English. Four times a year (Feb., May, Aug., Nov.). Free to members. Ontario Genealogical Society London Branch, PO Box 24017, London Ontario N6H 5C4 Canada. **Tel** (514)451-7594. **ED** Dennis Mulligam (editor's phone: (519)657-1569). **DD** 929/.1/06071326. **Circ:** 700.
Desc: Genealogical interest related to Middlesex county, Ontario, Canada.

US
LOS ANGELES WESTSIDE GENEALOGICAL SOCIETY NEWSLETTER. Newsletter. English. mo (except Dec.). $18.00 (comes with membership Los Angeles Westside Genealogical Society). Los Angeles Westside Genealogical Society, PO Box 10447, Marina del Rey CA 90295. **Tel** (310)204-6808. **ED** Marsha Parkhill. **Circ:** 150.
Desc: Contains articles of interest, news of the Society, and genealogical information which members may find useful in their research.

US
LOS BEXARENOS GENEALOGICAL REGISTER. ***Title Change.*** (1987)-. Periodical. English. qt. Los Bexarenos Genealogical Society, c/o F Martinez, 7422 Castle Crown, San Antonio TX 78218. **UDC** 929.5(764). cum. index. ***Continued by** Bexarenos Genealogical Newsletter.*

US/0362-4293
LOST IN CANADA?. ***Ceased.*** (1975)-Vol. 17 No. 3 (19??). Periodical. English. Three times a year. NWTC & FHC, PO Box 29397, Brooklyn Center MN 55429. **Tel** (612)560-9086. **ED** Joy Reisinger. **LC** CS42; .L68. **DD** 929/.1/0973. Index available (Bound in each iss.). **Bk Rev**, (Qty: varies). **Ad Acc. Circ:** 1,000 (ctrl).
Desc: Primary and secondary source material pertaining to Canadian genealogical resource material.
Ind/Abst Genealogical Period. Annu. Index.

US
LOT OF BUNKUM, A. **Added/Corp** Old Buncombe County Genealogical Society. (19??)-. Periodical. English. Eleven times a year. $20.00 (institutions), $15.00 (individuals). Old Buncombe County Genealogical Society, PO Box 2122, Asheville NC 28802. **Tel** (704)253-1894.

US/0882-2425
LOT OF BUNKUM. YEARBOOK, A. Vol. 1 (1980)-. English. an (includes monthly newsletter). $18.00. Old Buncombe County Genealogical Society, PO Box 2122, Asheville NC 28802. **Tel** (704)253-1894. **ED** Doris Cline Ward and Ethal Meadows Kirkpatrick. **LC** F262.B94; L67. **DD** 929/.1/072075688. **UDC** 929.5(058)(756). Index available. **Bk Rev. Ad Acc. Pr Rev. Circ:** 500 (ctrl).
Ind/Abst Genealogical Period. Annu. Index.

US/0740-9389
LOTT FAMILY NEWSLETTER, THE. Vol. 1, No. 1 (Jan.-Feb.-Mar. 1983)-. Newsletter. English. qt. $12.00. C A McElligott, PO Box 13511, El Paso TX 79913. **LC** CS71; .L88246. **DD** 929/.2/0973. **UDC** 929.52(73).

US/0148-7655
LOUISIANA GENEALOGICAL REGISTER, THE. **Added/Corp** Louisiana Genealogical and Historical Society. Vol. 13 (Mar. 1966)-. Periodical. English. qt (Mar., June, Sept., Dec.). $25.00 US; $35.00 Canada; $45.00 other. Louisiana Genealogical and Historical Society, PO Box 3454, Baton Rouge LA 70821. **Tel** (504)766-3018. **ED** Nell T. Boersma. **LC** F366; .L55. **DD** 929/.3762. Index available. cum. index. **Bk Rev. Circ:** 700. ***Continues** Genealogical Register.*
Desc: Contains individual articles, cemetery and census and land listings, historical stories, and queries- all genealogical in nature.

●US/1044-792X
LOUISIANA QUERIES. (1992)-. English. $5.00. Sims Publishing, PO Box 9576, Sacramento CA 95823-0576.

US/0099-1791
LUPTONIAN, THE. (Mar. 1974)-. English. ir. Free. Luptonian, Box 443, Bayboro NC 28515-7037. **Tel** (919)745-7037. **ED** David Walker Lupton. **LC** CS71; .L968a. **DD** 929/.2/0973.

US/0896-4602
LUTHER FAMILY NEWSLETTER, THE. [Luther Fam. newsl.]. Vol. 1, No. 1 (Feb. 1987)-. Newsletter. English. qt. $10.00. Luther Family Association, 2531 Lakeview Street, Lakeland FL 33801. **Tel** (813)664-5788. **ED** George Luther. **DD** 929. Index available. cum. index. **Circ:** 740 (ctrl).

US
LYCOMING COUNTY GENEALOGICAL SOCIETY NEWSLETTER. Newsletter. English. $10.00. Lycoming County Genealogical Society, 858

West Fourth Street, Williamsport PA 17701. **Tel** (717)326-3326.
Ind/Abst Genealogical Period. Annu. Index.

US/0892-418X
LYNN/LINN LINEAGE QUARTERLY.
VFOAT Lynn Linn Lineage Quarterly Linn Lineage Quarterly. Vol. 1, No. 1 (Spring 1987)-. Periodical. English. qt. $18.00 US; $22.00 other. Phyllis J Bauer, 3312 West Fairway Drive, McHenry IL 60050. **Tel** (815)385-9626. **LC** CS71; .L989A. **DD** 929/.2/0973. Index available. **Bk Rev**. **Circ:** 120.
Desc: Presentation and exchange of material and data concerning the Lynn/Linn surname.

US/0740-1531
M.C.G.S. REPORTER. **Added/Corp** Milwaukee County Genealogical Society. **VFOAT** MCGS; Reporter. Vol. 3, No. 1 (Nov. 1971)-. Periodical. English. Four times a year (Feb., May, Aug., Nov.). $8.00. Milwaukee County Genealogical Society Inc, PO Box 27326, Milwaukee WI 53227-0326. **Tel** (414)278-3011. **ED** Richard Rundel. **LC** F587.M6; M39. **DD** 929/.377594. Index available. **Bk Rev**, (Qty: 4). **Circ:** 1,475 (ctrl). ***Continues** MCGS Reporter.*
Desc: This publications is about Milwaukee County and also includes other states, with some international materials.
Ind/Abst Genealogical Period. Annu. Index.

CN/0821-6290
MAC-TALLA - CLAN MACQUARRIE OF ATLANTIC CANADA. (MAC-TALLA / CLAN MACQUARRIE OF ATLANTIC CANADA.). [Mac-talla - Clan Mac-Quarrie Atl. Can.]. V. 2, No. 2 (Nov. 1982)-. Periodical. English. qt. $15.00. Clan MacQuarrie Association of Atlantic Canada, 3274 Isleville Street, Halifax Nova Scotia B3K 3Y6 Canada. **ED** Angus M Macquarrie. **DD** 929/.2. **UDC** 929.52(71). **Circ:** 1,000. ***Continues** Clan MacQuarrie of Atlantic Canada Newsletter, 0821-6282.*
Desc: Articles center around the MacQuarrie Clan and how its people dispersed from the original homeland on the Isle of Ulva Scotland to various parts of the world. Concentrates primarily on those MacQuarries who to Atlantic Canada and records historical accounts of their experiences.

US/8755-7193
MACHEN FAMILY COURIER. [Machen fam. cour.]. Vol. 1, No. 1 (April 1985)-. Periodical. English. qt. $12.50. Courier Publications, PO Box 1320, Winnfield LA 71483. **Tel** (318)628-2019. **DD** 929. **UDC** 929.52(73).

US/0736-8445
MACLAREN STANDARD, THE. (THE MACLAREN STANDARD : NEWSLETTER OF THE CLAN MACLAREN SOCIETY OF AMERICA.). V. 1, No. 1 (Fall/Winter 1982)-. Newsletter. English. sa. Free to members. Maclaren Society of America, PO Drawer 13577, Savannah GA 31406. **UDC** 929.52(73).

US/0883-556X
MADDEN FAMILY NEWSLETTER. [Madden fam. mewsl.]. Newsletter. English. qt. $10.00. Mariam W Schaefer, 1101 Wilmington Avenue/Apartment A, Dayton OH 45420. **Tel** (513)293-0779. **ED** Mariam W Schaefer. **DD** 929. **UDC** 929.52(73). Index available. cum. index. **Bk Rev**. **Ad Acc**. **Circ:** 85 (ctrl).
Desc: Madden researchers submit lineages, queries, share findings printed August, November, February, and May with the hope of contacting "cousins" and acquiring help from fellow researchers.

US/1061-253X
MADERA HERITAGE QUARTERLY.
[Madera herit. q.]. **Added/Corp** Madera Genealogical Society. (1987)-. Periodical. English. Four times a year (Feb., May, Aug., Nov.). $12.00. Madera Genealogical Society, PO Box 495, Madera CA 93639. **Tel** (209)661-1219. **DD** 929.

US/1071-1937
MADISON CO. MUSINGS. [Madison Co. musings]. **Added/Corp** Madison County Genealogical & Historical Society (Ark.). **VFOAT** Madison County Musings; Musings. Vol. 1, No. 1 (Spring 1982)-. Periodical. English. qt (Mar., June, Sept., Dec.). $12.50. Madison County Musings, PO Box 427, Huntsville AR 72740. **Tel** (501)738-6408. **ED** Lucille Simpson. **LC** F417.M3; M33. **DD** 929/.1/072076715. Index available. **Bk Rev**, (Qty: 12). **Circ:** 550.
Desc: Covers genealogical and historical information on people of Madison County, Arkansas. Includes photographs of historical locations.

US/0090-5186
MADISON COUNTY GENEALOGIST, THE. Began with Dec. 1968 issue. Periodical. English. qt. $4.00. Century Enterprises, PO Box 607, Huntsville AK 72740. **LC** CS42; .M25. **DD** 929/.3767/1505. **UDC** 929.5(767).

US/0568-806X
MAGAZINE - ALABAMA GENEALOGICAL SOCIETY, INC. [Mag. - Ala. Geneal. Soc.]. **Main/Corp** Alabama Genealogical Society. **VFOAT** Alabama Genealogical Society, Inc. Magazine; Alabama Genealogical Society Magazine. (196?)-. Periodical. English. Four times a year. $20.00 Comes with Alabama Genealogical Society membership. Alabama Genealogical Society Library, 800 Lakeshore Drive, PO Box 2296, Birmingham AL 35229-0001. **Tel** (205)879-3500. **ED** Peggy Blaxton and Sharon Townsend. **DD** 929. Index available in last issue of volume--attached. **Bk Rev**.
Ind/Abst Genealogical Period. Annu. Index.

US/0747-8445
MAGAZINE / HUXFORD GENEALOGICAL SOCIETY, INC. **Main/Corp** Huxford Genealogical Society. **VFOAT** Huxford Genealogical Society Quarterly. Vol. 4, No. 3 (Sept. 1977)-. Periodical. English. qt. $15.00 (libraries), $20.00 other. Huxford Genealogical Society, PO Box 595, Homerville GA 31634. **Tel** (912)487-2310. **ED** Leola Settle. **LC** F285; .H84A. **DD** 929/.1/0720758. **UDC** 929.5(758). Index Available, published separately, free-automatically sent. **Bk Rev**. **Circ:** 600. available on microfilm; available on microfiche. ***Continues** Huxford Genealogical Society, Inc., 0747-8437.*
Desc: Genealogical research, source material (court records, census, cemeteries, biographical sketches, etc.) of south Georgia and north Florida and some North and South Carolina.

US/0743-8095
MAGAZINE OF VIRGINIA GENEALOGY. [Mag. Va. geneal.]. **Added/Corp** Virginia Genealogical Society. Vol. 22, No. 1 (Feb. 1984)-. Periodical. English. qt. Free to members; $20.00 membership. Virginia Genealogical Society, 5001 West Broad Street, Suite 115, Richmond VA 23230. **ED** Richard Slatten. **LC** F225; .V86b. **DD** 929/.3755. Index available. cum. index. **Bk Rev**. **Circ:** 2,000 (ctrl). ***Continues** Quarterly of the Virginia Genealogical Society, 0884-2965.*
Ind/Abst Genealogical Period. Annu. Index (?-?).

US
MAHONING MEANDERINGS / MAHONING COUNTY CHAPTER OF THE OHIO GENEALOGICAL SOCIETY.
Added/Corp Ohio Genealogical Society. Mahoning County Chapter. (Sept. 1978)-. Periodical. English. mo. Free to members. Ohio Genealogical Society - Mahoning, 3430 Rebecca Drive, Canfield OH 44406. **LC** F497.M18; M36. **DD** 929/.1/072077139.
Ind/Abst Genealogical Period. Annu. Index.

US/0883-7805
MANLEY FAMILY NEWSLETTER. [Manley fam. newsl.]. (198?)-. Newsletter. English. sa. Manley Family Newsletter, Trudi Manley, 171 Nathan Drive, Bohemia NY 11716. **Tel** (516)567-0386. **ED** Trudi Manley. **DD** 929. **Bk Rev**. **Ad Acc**. **Circ:** 250.
Desc: A periodical dedicated to preserving history, informing Manley/Manly descendants of their heritage, and acquainting family members with other living relatives.
Ind/Abst Genealogical Period. Annu. Index (?-?).

US/0277-8718
MARIN KIN TRACER, THE. (THE MARIN KIN TRACER : A QUARTERLY NEWSLETTER OF THE MARIN COUNTY GENEALOGICAL.). **Added/Corp** Marin County Genealogical Society. Vol. 1, No. 1 (Winter 1977-1978)-. Periodical. English. Four times a year. $8.00. Marin Genealogical Society, PO Box 1511, Novato CA 94947. **Tel** (415)461-9342. **LC** F868.M3; M23. **DD** 929/.1/072079462.
Ind/Abst Genealogical Period. Annu. Index (?-?).

US/0748-2795
MARION COUNTY, ALABAMA TRACKS.
Added/Corp Marion Pioneer Territorial Genealogical Society. Vol. 1, No. 1 (Jan. 1982)-. Periodical. English. Four times a year. $15.00. Marion County Genealogical Society, PO Box 360, Winfield AL 35594. **Tel** (205)487-2330. **LC** F332.M37; M33. **DD** 929/.376189.
Ind/Abst Genealogical Period. Annu. Index.

US/0277-8726
MARKERS. **See** The Arts-Art.

CN/0821-3275
MARKWICK MIDDEN. [Markwick midden]. Vol. 1, No. 1 (Nov. 1982)-. Periodical. English. sa. 5.00Can$ Canada; $5.00 US; £3.00 UK; 5.00Aus$ Australia; 5.00NZ$ New Zealand. V A Melanson, 3506 Swansacre, Vancouver British Columbia V5S 4J8 Canada. **Tel** 435-9806. **ED** Valerie Melanson. **DD** 929/.2. **UDC** 929.52(73). **Bk Rev**. **Ad Acc**. **Circ:** 90 (ctrl).
Desc: Family histories, pedigrees, documents, queries, maps plus illustrations all pertinent to Markwick family history.
Ind/Abst Genealogical Period. Annu. Index (?-?).

US/0736-2498
MARS EXCHANGE. [Mars exch.]. English. qt. Miller Families Exchanges, PO Box 31, Napa CA 94559. **LC** CS71; .M6495. **DD** 929/.2/0973. **UDC** 929.52(73). ***Continues** Mars Exchange Newsletter, 0736-2528.*

US/0099-1864
MARTIN FAMILY QUARTERLY. V. 1- May 1975-. Periodical. English. qt. $5.00. Farmer Genealogy Company, PO Box 140880, Dallas TX 75214. **LC** CS71; .M38A. **DD** 929/.2/0973. **UDC** 929.52(73). cum. index.

US/0025-4150
MARYLAND AND DELAWARE GENEALOGIST, THE. ***Ceased.*** V. 1- (No. 1-); Sept. 1959-Ceased ?. Periodical. English. qt. The Maryland and Delaware Genealogist, PO Box 352, St Michaels MD 21663. **Tel** (410)745-9321. **ED** Raymond B Clark. **LC** CS42; .M35. **UDC** 929.5(751/752). Index available. cum. index. **Bk Rev**. **Ad Acc**. **Circ:** 600.
Desc: Contains source records, family lineages, Bible and tombstone records, queries, book reviews, feature articles, heraldry, ethnic groups, surname exchange, step charts, advertising and annual index.

US
MARYLAND GENEALOGICAL SOCIETY BULLETIN. **Main/Corp** Maryland Genealogical Society. Vol. 14 (1973)-. Bulletin. English. qt. Maryland Genealogical Society, 201 West Monument Street, Baltimore MD 21201. **Tel** (410)685-3750. ***Continues** Bulletin of the Maryland Genealogical Society.*
Ind/Abst Genealogical Period. Annu. Index.

US/0025-4258
MARYLAND HISTORICAL MAGAZINE.
See History(General)-History of North, South, and Central America.

●US/1044-7938
MARYLAND QUERIES. (1992)-. English. $5.00. Sims Publishing, PO Box 9576, Sacramento CA 95823-0576.

US/0885-4459
MASON COUNTY GENEALOGICAL SOCIETY NEWSLETTER, THE. [Mason Cty. Geneal. Soc. newsl.]. **Added/Corp** Mason County Genealogical Society (Ky.). Vol. 2, No. 2 (Apr./May/June 1984)-. Newsletter. English. Four times a year (Mar., June, Sept., Dec.). $7.00 individual (membership). Mason County Genealogical Society, PO Box 266, Maysville KY 41056. **Tel** (606)759-7257. **ED** Edith Phillips Ryan. **LC** F457.M4; M37. **DD** 929/.3769323/05. Index available (($7.00)). **Bk Rev**, (Qty: 6-8). **Circ:** 300 (ctrl). ***Continues** Mason County Genealogical Society, 0748-9137.*
Desc: Includes genealogy, local history, cemetery records, military data, genealogical aids, surnames, queries, and others.

US/0895-4496
MASON FAMILY NEWSLETTER. [Mason Fam. newsl.]. Vol. 1, No. 1 (Winter 1987)-. Newsletter. English. qt. $10.00 North America; $15.00 other. Paula Perkins Mortensen, 363 South Park Victoria Drive, Milpitas CA 95035. **Tel** (408)262-1051. **ED** Paula Perkins Mortensen. **DD** 929. Index available. **Circ:** 75 (ctrl).

US/0897-7739
MASSACHUSETTS QUERIES. [Mass. queries]. Vol. 1 (1988)-. Periodical. English. Four times a year. $6.00. Pioneer Publications, PO Box 397, Black Eagle MT 59414-0397. **Tel** (406)453-4266. **ED** Shirley Penna-Oakes. **DD** 929. Index available. **Bk Rev**.

US/0738-1549
MASSOG. **Added/Corp** Massachusetts Society of Genealogists. **VFOAT** M.A.S.S.O.G. Vol. 1, No. 1 (Jan. 1977)-. Periodical. English. Four times a year (Jan., Apr., July, Oct.). $19.00. Massachusetts Society of Genealogists Inc, 74 Beach Point Road, Lancaster MA 01523. **Tel** (508)365-5021. **ED** Ann Dzindalet. **LC** F63; .M37. **DD** 929/.1/0720744. Index available (Bound in 4th issue, in October). **Ad Acc**. **Circ:** 550.
Desc: A genealogical magazine for the Commonwealth of Massachusetts.
Ind/Abst Genealogical Period. Annu. Index.

US/8756-3959
MAYFLOWER DESCENDANT : A MAGAZINE OF PILGRIM GENEALOGY AND HISTORY, THE. [Mayflower descend.]. **Added/Corp** Massachusetts Society of Mayflower Descendants. (1899)-. Periodical. English. sa. $18.00 US; $23.00 Canada; $28.00 UK. Massachusetts Society of Mayflower Descendants, 101 Newbury Street, Boston MA 02116. **Tel** (617)266-1624. **ED** Alicia Crane Williams. **LC** F68; .M46. **DD** 929. Index available. cum. index. **Bk Rev**. **Circ:** 1,000 (ctrl).
Desc: Continuation of George Ernest Bowman's classic Mayflower Descendant, featuring previously unpublished primary material.
Ind/Abst Genealogical Period. Annu. Index (?-?).

US/1066-8446
MCCLAIN CO. OK HISTORICAL AND GENEALOGICAL SOCIETY QUARTERLY NEWSLETTER. (MCCLAIN COUNTY OKLA HISTORICAL AND GENEALOGICAL SOCIETY QUARTERLY.). [McClain Co. OK Hist. Geneal. Soc. q. newsl.]. **Added/Corp** McClain County OK Historical Society. **VFOAT** Quarterly; McClain Co. OK H & G Society Quarterly; McClain Co. OK H & G Scty Qtrly, . Vol. 1, Issue 1 (Nov. 1984)-. Periodical. English. qt. McClain County Historical and Genealogical Society, 203 Washington Street, Purcell OK 73080. **LC** F702.M2; M335. **DD** 929/.1/072076655.
Ind/Abst Genealogical Period. Annu. Index.

US/0147-992X
MCELROY FAMILY NEWSLETTER, THE. March 1976-. Newsletter. English. qt. $6.00. Editor Kenneth Vanve Graves, 261 South Street, Wrentham MA 02093. **LC** CS71; .M141A. **DD** 929/.2/0973. **UDC** 929.52(73).

US/0885-8314
MCHENRY COUNTY ILLINOIS CONNECTION QUARTERLY. Added/Corp McHenry County Illinois Genealogical Society. **VFOAT** McHenry County Illinois Connection; MCIGS Quarterly. Vol. 1, No. 1 (Jan./March 1983)-. Periodical. English. Four times a year. $12.00. McHenry County Illinois Genealogical Society, PO Box 184, Crystal Lake IL 60012-0184. **Tel** (815)455-7150. **ED** Laurie Turner. **LC** F547.M14; M37. **DD** 929/.1/072077322. cum. index. **Bk Rev**. **Circ:** 250.
Desc: Journal of McHenry County Genealogical Society. Contains early records, Bible records, queries, ancestor charts, and articles relating to McHenry County. Also up-to-date genealogical information and hints.
Ind/Abst Genealogical Period. Annu. Index.

US/0736-2420
MCKINNEY MAZE, THE. (THE MCKINNEY MAZE : NEWSLETTER OF THE MCKINNEY FAMILY ASSOCIATION.). [McKinney maze]. **Added/Corp** McKinney Family Association. Vol. 1, No. 1 (Mar. 1982)-. Newsletter. English. qt. $10.00. Mckinney Family Association Library, 6201 Lansbrook Lane, Oklahoma City OK 73132. **ED** Edgar McKinney. **LC** CS71; .M475615. **DD** 929/.2/0973. Index available. cum. index. **Bk Rev**. **Ad Acc**. **Circ:** 160 (ctrl).
Desc: All information, concerning surname and it's variants in the U.S. and Great Britain, including queries, family records, and articles of genealogical interests.

US/0884-8068
MEDINA COUNTY STORY. [Medina Cty. story]. **Added/Corp** Medina County Genealogical Society. Vol. I, Issue I (Spring Ed. 1982)-. Periodical. English. Four times a year (Feb., May, Aug., Nov.). $8.00 (one year) Comes with Medina County Genealogical Society Membership. Medina County Genealogical Society, PO Box 804, Medina OH 44258. **Tel** (216)725-4257. **LC** F497.M5; M43. **DD** 929/.377135.

US
MELTING POT, THE. (THE MELTING POT GENEALOGICAL SOCIETY QUARTERLY.). **Added/Corp** Melting Pot Genealogical Society. (Feb. 1978)-. Periodical. English. sa. $12.00. Melting Pot Genealogical Society, PO Box 936, Hot Springs AR 71902. **Tel** (501)623-5706. **ED** Charles Moffatt. **Bk Rev**. **Circ:** 150.
Desc: Sources of information for both individuals and genealogical libraries; lists marriage records and pedigree charts, as well as deed and mortgage records.
Ind/Abst Genealogical Period. Annu. Index.

US/0741-0565
MEMBERS' COMPUTERIZED DATA EXCHANGE. (MEMBERS' COMPUTERIZED DATA EXCHANGE / LOS ANGELES WESTSIDE GENEALOGICAL SOCIETY.). **Added/Corp** Los Angeles Westside Genealogical Society. Vol. 1 (1983)-. English. Eleven times a year. Los Angeles Westside Genealogical Society, PO Box 10447, Marina del Rey CA 90295. **Tel** (310)204-6808. **ED** Nancy Elwood. **LC** F868.L8; M45. **DD** 929/.379493. Index available. **Circ:** 200 (ctrl).

US/1056-0394
MEMBERSHIP DIRECTORY / MARYLAND GENEALOGICAL SOCIETY. [Membsh. dir. - Md. Geneal. Soc.]. **Main/Corp** Maryland Genealogical Society. (198?)-. Directory. English. qt (Mar., June, Sept., Dec.). $18.00 (active membership); $43.00 (single joint membership); $53.00 (double joint membership); $20.00 (libraries & societies). Maryland Genealogical Society, 201 West Monument Street, Baltimore MD 21201. **Tel** (410)685-3750. **ED** F. Edward Wright (Editor's address: Rear 63 E., Main St., Westminster MD 21157; Editor's telephone: (410)876-6101). **LC** IN PROCESS. **DD** 929. Index available (Each vol.). **Bk Rev**. **Ad Acc**. **Circ:** 1,400 (ctrl).

CN/0714-4458
MEMBERSHIP LIST / THE QUINTE BRANCH, O.G.S. [Membsh. list - Quinte Branch, O.G.S.]. **Main/Corp** Ontario Genealogical Society. Quinte Branch. **VAT** Membership List - Quinte Branch, Ontario Genealogical Society. (Apr. 1981)-. English. an. Free. Ontario Genealogical Society / Quinte Branch, Box 301, Bloomfield Ontario K0K 1G0 Canada. **Tel** (613)393-3146. **DD** 929/.1/06071358.

US/0196-4976
MEMBERSHIP LIST - VIRGINIA GENEALOGICAL SOCIETY. Main/Corp Virginia Genealogical Society. (19??)-. English. bm. $20.00 (one year), $38.00 (two years), $56.00 (three years) institutions and individuals; $22.00 (one year), $42.00 (two years), $60.00 (three years) families. Virginia Genealogical Society, 5001 West Broad Street, Suite 115, Richmond VA 23230. **LC** F225; .V86a. **DD** 929/.1/060755.
Desc: Features a lively assortment of timely information on ideas, announcements, events, queries, and the latest publications in the field.

US/0882-4231
MEMBERSHIP SURNAME LIST. (MEMBERSHIP SURNAME LIST / UPPER SHORE GENEALOGICAL SOCIETY OF MARYLAND.). [Membsh. surname list]. **Main/Corp** Upper Shore Genealogical Society of Maryland. (19??)-. English. Upper Shore Genealogical Society of Maryland, PO Box 275, Easton MD 21601. **Tel** (301)364-5336. **LC** F180; .U67a. **DD** 929/.1/025752.

CN/0037-9387
MEMOIRES DE LA SOCIETE GENEALOGIQUE CANADIENNE-FRANCAISE. [Mem. Soc. geneal. can.-fr.]. **Main/Corp** Societe Genealogique Canadienne-Francaise. Vol. 1 (Jan. 1944)-. Periodical. French. Four times a year (Mar., June, Sept., Dec.). $25.00 (individual); $30.00 (institution). Societe Genealogique Canadienne Francais, CP 335, Place D Armes, Montreal Quebec H2Y 3H1 Canada. **Tel** (514)729-8366. **ED** Marthe Faribault- Beauregard. Index available (Bound in 4th issue, in December). **Bk Rev**. **Ad Acc**. **Circ:** 3,800 (ctrl).
Desc: Family histories and genealogy are the main topics of this publication. It is devoted to help out members with their research.
Ind/Abst Point Repere (1983-).

US/0730-5214
MENNONITE FAMILY HISTORY. [Mennonite fam. hist.]. Vol. 1, No. 1 (Jan. 1982)-. Periodical. English. qt (Jan., Apr., July, Oct.). $17.00 US; $29.00 other. Mennonite Family History, c/o Lois Mast, Main Street, PO Box 171, Elverson PA 19520. **Tel** (215)286-0258. **ED** Lois Ann Mast. **LC** E184.M45; M46. **DD** 929/.1/088287. Index available. cum. index. **Bk Rev**. **Ad Acc**. **Circ:** 1,600 (ctrl).
Desc: Periodical on Mennonite, Amish, and Brethren traced to their beginnings in the 1500s with a special emphasis on genealogy and family history.
Ind/Abst Genealogical Period. Annu. Index.

US
MENNONITE HERITAGE. Added/Corp Illinois Mennonite Historical and Genealogical Society. Illinois Mennonite Historical Society. Vol. 1 No. 1 (June 1974)-. Periodical. English. qt. Illinois Mennonite Historical and Genealogical Society, PO Box 819, Metamora IL 61548. **Tel** (309)367-2551.
Ind/Abst Genealogical Period. Annu. Index.

US/1045-3199
MERIWETHER CONNECTIONS. [Meriwether connect.]. Began with V. 1, No. 1 (Jan. 1982). Periodical. English. qt. $15.00. Meriwether Society, PO Box 19967, San Diego CA 92159-0967. **LC** CS71; .M55615. **DD** 929/.2/0973. **Circ:** 350 (ctrl).
Desc: A small family history and genealogy newsletter for the Meriwether family.

US/0276-4237
MEYER MIRROR, THE. Issue No. 1 (Spring 1980)-. Periodical. English. qt. $3.00. West 628 Augusta 1, Spokane WA 99205. **LC** CS71; .M6125. **DD** 929/.2/0973. **UDC** 929.52(73).

US/0732-3395
MEYER'S DIRECTORY OF GENEALOGICAL SOCIETIES IN THE U.S.A. AND CANADA. [Meyer's dir. geneal. soc. U.S.A. Can.]. **VAT** Meyer's Directory of Genealogical Societies in the United States of America and Canada. 4th Ed, (1982)-. Directory. English. be. $22.75 (two year). Libra Publications, 5179 Perry Road, Mt Airy MD 21771. **Tel** (410)875-2824. **ED** Mary K. Meyer. **LC** CS44; .M44. **DD** 929/.1/02573. **Ad Acc**. **Circ:** 1,400. ***Continues*** *Meyer, Mary Keysor. Directory of Genealogical Societies in the U.S.A. and Canada, 0734-6867.*
Desc: A listing of every known genealogical society and every known independent genealogical periodical in the USA and Canada.

US/0748-8521
MEYSSEL, MIKESELL, MIXSELL FAMILY NEWSLETTER. Vol. 1, Issue 1 (Fall 1982)-. Newsletter. English. sa. Ardella M Rohde, Box 269, Parowan UT 84761. **LC** CS71; .M6395. **DD** 929/.2/0973. **UDC** 929.52(73).

US/0889-3640
MIAMI MEANDERINGS. **See** History(General)-History of North, South, and Central America.

US/0736-5004
MICHIANA SEARCHER. (MICHIANA SEARCHER : QUARTERLY OF ELKHART, INDIANA GENEALOGICAL SOCIETY.). English. qt. $8.00 US; 9.00Can$ Canada. Elkhart County Genealogical Society, 1812 Jeanwood Drive, Elkhart IN 46514. **Tel** (219)264-1980. **LC** F525; .M58. **UDC** 929.5(772). **Bk Rev**. **Ad Acc**. **Circ:** 250 (ctrl).
Desc: Information of Elkhor and surrounding companies of Indiana.
Ind/Abst Genealogical Period. Annu. Index.

US/0462-372X
MICHIGANA. [Michigana]. **Added/Corp** Western Michigan Genealogical Society. Vol. 1 (Mar. 1955)-. Periodical. English. qt. Free to members of the Western Michigan Genealogical Society. Western Michigan Genealogical Society, Grand Rapids Public Library, Grand Rapids MI 49503. **Tel** (616)454-3600. **ED** Kathleen Tabb. **LC** F565; .M64. Index available. cum. index. **Bk Rev**. **Ad Acc**. **Circ:** 650.
Desc: Local historical listings, previously unpublished manuscripts, book reviews, original articles about genealogy. Caters to the West Michigan area.
Ind/Abst Genealogical Period. Annu. Index.

US
MIDDLE TENNESSEE GENEALOGY. English. $18.00. Middle Tennessee Geneaological Society, PO Box 3016, Nashville TN 37219.
Ind/Abst Genealogical Period. Annu. Index.

UK/0307-2851
MIDLAND ANCESTOR : JOURNAL OF THE BIRMINGHAM AND MIDLAND SOCIETY FOR GENEALOGY AND HERALDRY, THE. Added/Corp Birmingham & Midland Society for Genealogy & Heraldry. (1975)-. Periodical. English. qt. £8.00. Birmingham and Midland Society for Genealogy and Heraldry, 14 West Avenue Castle Bromwich, Birmingham B36 0EB England. **ED** J. Gilmore. **LC** CS435.M53; M53. **DD** 929/.1/0720424. Index available. cum. index. **Bk Rev**, (Qty: 40-50). **Circ:** 4,000 - 5,000 (ctrl). ***Continues*** *Birmingham and Midland Society for Genealogy and Heraldry Journal.*

US/0198-9359
MIDWEST ANCESTREE QUARTERLY, THE. VFOAT MAQ. No. 1- Oct./Dec. 1978-. Periodical. English. qt. $8.00. Ancestree House, E Evelyn Cox, 708 South Maple, Ellensburg WA 98926. **LC** F351; .M6. **DD** 929/.377. **UDC** 929.5(77).

US/0271-8685
MIDWEST HISTORICAL AND GENEALOGICAL REGISTER. Added/Corp Midwest Historical and Genealogical Society. Vol. 15 (April/June 1980)-. Periodical. English. qt. Free to members of the Midwest Historical & Genealogical Society; $20.00 membership. Midwest Historical and Genealogical Society, PO Box 1121, Wichita KS 67201. **Tel** (316)264-3611. **ED** Marjorie Morgan. **LC** CS42; .M53. **DD** 929/.1/0977. Index available. cum. index. **Bk Rev**. **Ad Acc**. **Circ:** 740. ***Continues*** *Midwest Genealogical Register.*
Desc: Abstracts primary source records and articles pertaining to Sedgwick, Kansas and surrounding counties.
Ind/Abst Genealogical Period. Annu. Index (?-?).

US
MILLER MONITOR. Vol. 1, No. 1 (Nov. 1979)-. Periodical. English. Four times a year. $17.00. Frances R. Nelson, 4041 Pedley Road #18, Riverside CA 92509. **Tel** (714)685-8936. **LC** CS71; .M65a. ***Continues*** *Miller Index.*

US/0581-0086
MINNESOTA GENEALOGIST. Added/Corp Minnesota Genealogical Society. Vol. 1 (Mar. 1970)-. Periodical. English. qt. $15.00 (individual and library membership, Minnesota Genealogical Society). Minnesota Genealogical Society, PO Box 16069, St. Paul MN 55116-0069. **Tel** (612)222-6929. Index available. cum. index. **Bk Rev**, (Qty: 15). **Ad Acc**. **Circ:** 2,000.
Desc: Items of genealogical interest for research.
Ind/Abst Genealogical Period. Annu. Index.

US
MIO CONNECTION. (19??)-. English. Four times a year (Jan., Apr., June, Oct.). $8.00. Family Researchers, 11061 West Frances Road, Flushing MI 48433-9224. **Tel** (810)639-5094. **ED** Catherine Henry. **Ad Acc**.

US/0091-3189
MISSISSINEWA GENEALOGICAL QUARTERLY. V. 1- Jan./June 1973-. Periodical. English. qt. $4.00. Robert D Smith, Circulation Manager, 559 Tyler Avenue, Peru IN 46970. **LC** CS42; .G4952. **DD** 929/.1/05. **UDC** 929.52(73). ***Supersedes*** *Genealogist.*

US/0743-1856
MISSISSIPPI ARMCHAIR RESEARCHER, THE. Vol. 1, No. 1 (Fall 1983)-. English. qt. $10.00. Armchair Publications, 810 McDonough Road, Hampton GA 30228. **LC** F340; .M47. **DD** 929/.3762. **UDC** 929.5(772).

US/0742-499X
MISSISSIPPI BIBLE AND CEMETERY RECORDS. (MISSISSIPPI BIBLE AND CEMETERY RECORDS : A PUBLICATION OF THE MISSISSIPPI GENEALOGICAL SOCIETY.). **VFOAT** Mississippi Genealogical Society Cemetery and Bible Records;

Genealogy and Heraldry

Cemetery and and Bible Records. Periodical. English. be. Mississippi Genealogical Society, PO Box 5301, Jackson MS 39206. **Tel** (601)373-4407. **LC** F340; .M48. **DD** 929/.3762. **UDC** 929.53(762). Index available. **Circ:** 100 (ctrl). *Continues Mississippi Cemetery and Bible Records, 0544-4802.*

US/1053-8216
MISSISSIPPI COAST HISTORICAL & GENEALOGICAL SOCIETY. (MISSISSIPPI COAST HISTORICAL & GENEALOGICAL SOCIETY : [MAGAZINE].). [Miss. Coast Hist. Geneal. Soc.]. **Added/Corp** Mississippi Coast Historical and Genealogical Society. **VFOAT** Mississippi Coast Historical and Genealogical Society. Vol. 1, (1968)-. English. Three times a year. Mississippi Coast Genealogical Society, PO Box 513, Biloxi MS 39533. **LC** F340; .M49. **DD** 976.2/005.

US/0540-3995
MISSISSIPPI GENEALOGICAL EXCHANGE. (1955)-. Periodical. English. qt. Mississippi Genealogical Society, PO Box 5301, Jackson MS 39206. **Tel** (601)373-4407. **ED** K.P.W. Esker. **LC** F340; .M5. **DD** 929.309762. **Ad Acc. Circ:** 500.
Desc: Genealogical data on early Mississippians.

US/1056-1587
MISSISSIPPI MEMORIES. [Miss. mem.]. Vol. 1, No. 1 First Quarter (1991)-. Periodical. English. qt. $12.50. Mississippi Memories, PO Box 18991, Shreveport LA 71138-0991. **DD** 929.

US/1064-0320
MISSISSIPPI RECORDS. Ceased. [Miss. rec.]. (1989)-Vol. 6. Periodical. English. qt. L.W.Anderson Genealogical Library, P.O.Box 1647, Gulfport MS 39502. **Tel** (601)865-1554. **DD** 929.

US/1041-6552
MISSOURI QUERIES. [Mo. queries]. Vol. 1, No. 1 (March 1987)-. Periodical. English. ir. $6.25 (per issue) US; $6.75 (per issue) Canada. Weidner Words, West 2206 Borden Road, Spokane WA 99204-9668. **Tel** (509)448-9263. **ED** Carolyn Weidner. **LC** F465; .M573. **DD** 929/.1/0720778. **Bk Rev. Circ:** 100.
Desc: Queries accepted pertaining to Missouri (free).

US/0747-5667
MISSOURI STATE GENEALOGICAL ASSOCIATION JOURNAL. Added/Corp Missouri State Genealogical Association. Vol. 1, No. 1 (Winter 1981)-. Periodical. English. qt. $25.00 (membership). Missouri State Genealogical Association, PO Box 833, Columbia MO 65205-0833. **Tel** (314)428-7048. **ED** Bob Doerr. **LC** F465; .M575. **DD** 929/.1/0720778. Index available (bound in Dec. issue). **Bk Rev. Circ:** 800.
Ind/Abst Genealogical Period. Annu. Index.

US/0740-9699
MOHAWK, THE. Vol. 1, No. 1 (Winter 1984)-. English. qt $14.00 US; $16.00 Canada. Kinship, 60 Cedar Heights Road, Rhinebeck NY 12572. **Tel** (914)876-4592. **ED** Arthur Kelly. **LC** F127.M55; M64. **DD** 929/.37476/05. Index available. cum. index. **Bk Rev. Ad Acc. Circ:** 200.
Desc: Contains subscriber's queries and vital records never before published.

FR/0220-6765
MOI AUVERGNE, A. Periodical. French. qt. 85. 45 Quai Carnot, 92210 Saint-Cloud France. **LC** CS580; .A2. **DD** 929/.1/072044. **UDC** 929.5(455.9).

US/0893-5718
MONROE COUNTY GENEALOGICAL SOCIETY NEWS. Added/Corp Monroe County Genealogical Society (Monroe County, Iowa). (1984)-. Periodical. English. Four times a year (Jan., Apr., July, Oct.). $5.00. Monroe County Genealogical Society, 203 Benton Avenue East, Albia IA 52531. **Tel** (515)932-2593. **ED** Vivian Shelquist, (editor's address: Route 3, Albia IA). **DD** 929. **Circ:** 150 (ctrl).
Desc: Local genealogical material.

US/1041-777X
MONTGOMERY COUNTY GENEALOGICAL SOCIETY QUARTERLY. [Montgomery Cty. Geneal. Soc. q.]. **Added/Corp** Montgomery County Genealogical Society (Ill.). **VFOAT** MCGS. (198?)-. Periodical. English. Four times a year. $9.00 (members), $11.00 (nonmembers). Montgomery County Genealogical Society, PO Box 212, Litchfield IL 62056. **Tel** (217)324-5202. **LC** F547.M7; M69. **DD** 929/.1/072077382. Each issue contains an index to its own contents (no volume index)--loose. **Bk Rev. Continues** *Montgomery County Genealogical Society Newsletter.*

US/0738-8276
MOON FAMILY NEWSLETTER, THE. Vol. 1, Issue No. 1 (Winter 1982)-. Newsletter. English. sa. $4.00. Moon Family Newsletter, Thelma Moon Goodlet Ed 951 East 37th Street, Hialeah FL 33013. **LC** CS71; .M81795. **DD** 929/.2/0973. **UDC** 929.52(73).

US/1067-7402
MORE FROM THE SHORE. (MORE FROM THE SHORE / LOWER DELMARVA GENEALOGICAL SOCIETY.). [More shore]. **Added/Corp** Lower Delmarva Genealogical Society. Vol. 1, No. 1 (Spring 1982)-. Periodical. English. sa. $15.00. Lower Delmarva Genealogical Society, PO Box 3602, Salisbury MD 21802. **ED** Betty Murrell. **DD** 975. Index available. cum. index. **Ad Acc. Circ:** 200 (ctrl).

US/0889-7247
MORRELL, MORRILL FAMILIES ASSOCIATION NEWSLETTER. [Morrell Morrill Fam. Assoc. newsl.]. **VFOAT** Morrell, Morrill Newsletter. Newsletter. English. qt $10.00. Morrell, Morrill Families Association, 3312 East Costilla Avenue, Littleton CO 80122. **Tel** (303)770-7164. **ED** Ann Lisa Pearson. **DD** 920. **UDC** 929.52(73). **Bk Rev. Ad Acc. Circ:** 215 (ctrl). **Continues** *Morrell, Morrill Families Association.*
Desc: Includes compiled genealogies, town, county and state records, histories, vital records, obituaries, cemetery inscriptions, census enumerations, and general genealogy information.

US
MORRIS AREA GENEALOGY SOCIETY NEWSLETTER. Added/Corp Morris Area Genealogy Society. Vol. 1, No. 3 (Sept. 1988)-. Newsletter. English. qt. $5.00 (libraries), $10.00 (other). Morris Area Genealogy Society, PO Box 105C, Convent Station NJ 07961. **Tel** (201)538-6161. **LC** IN PROCESS. *Continues Morris Area Genealogy Club Newsletter.*
Ind/Abst Genealogical Period. Annu. Index.

US/8756-0836
MOULTRIE COUNTY HERITAGE. (MOULTRIE COUNTY HERITAGE / MOULTRIE COUNTY HISTORICAL AND GENEALOGICAL SOCIETY.). **Added/Corp** Moultrie County Historical and Genealogical Society. Vol. 1, No. 1 (Nov. 1973)-. Periodical. English. qt $9.00. Moultrie County Historical & Genealogical Society, PO Box MM, Sullivan IL 61951. **Tel** (217)728-7256. **ED** Gertrude Shirey Dixon. **LC** F547.M9; M68. **DD** 929/.1/0720773675. **Bk Rev. Circ:** 365.
Desc: Contains history and genealogy pertaining to Moultrie County, Illinois; also includes queries.

US/0882-4266
MOUNTAIN EMPIRE GENEALOGICAL QUARTERLY, THE. [Mt. Emp. geneal. q.]. Vol. 2, No. 4 (Winter 1983)-. Periodical. English. Four times a year (Jan., Apr., July, Oct.). Mountain Empire, 185 Wankoma Drive, Remington VA 22734. **ED** Gregory L. Vanover. **LC** F217.A65; M68. **DD** 929/.1/072074. **Bk Rev. Ad Acc. Circ:** 1,000. **Continues** *Mountain Empire Quarterly, 8756-0704.*

US/8756-4327
MUDDY ROOTS. [Muddy roots]. **Added/Corp** Mississippi County Genealogical Society. (19??)-. Periodical. English. qt. comes with membership. Mississippi County Genealogical Society, Box 5, Charleston MO 63834. **LC** F472.M55; M83. **DD** 929/.1/0720778983.

US/0148-6683
MULKEY JOURNAL. V. 1- Aug. 1977-. Periodical. English. qt. $10.00. Mulkey Family Association, PO Box 192, Boise ID 83701. **LC** CS71; .M9565A. **DD** 929/.2/0973. **UDC** 929.52(73).

US/1059-3713
MURPHY MATES. [Murphy mates]. **Added/Corp** Kinseeker Publications (Firm). Vol. 1, No. 1 (Jan. 1991)-. Periodical. English. qt. Kinseeker Publications, Box 184, Grawn MI 49637. **DD** 929.

CN/1183-3726
MURRAY MATTERS. (MURRAY MATTERS : [NEWSLETTER].). [Murray matters]. **Added/Corp** Murray Matters (Organization). Vol. 1, No.1 (Spring 1991)-. Periodical. English. qt. Free to members. Murray Matters, 1023 Lakeway Boulevard, Lethbridge Alberta T1K 3E3 Canada. **DD** 929/.2.

US/1042-3419
MUSCOGIANA (COLUMBUS, GA.). (MUSCOGIANA : JOURNAL OF THE MUSCOGEE GENEALOGICAL SOCIETY.). [Muscogiana]. **Added/Corp** Muscogee Genealogical Society. Vol. 1, No. 1 (Spring 1989)-. English. Twice a year (June, Dec.). $18.00 (library), $12.00 (individual). Muscogee Genealogical Society, PO Box 761, Columbus GA 31902. **Tel** (706)649-0780. **ED** John Lassiter. **LC** F292.M9; M87. **DD** 929/.1/0720758473. Index available (Index in each issue). **Bk Rev. Ad Acc. Pr Rev. Circ:** 225 (ctrl).

US
MUSKOGEE COUNTY GENEALOGICAL SOCIETY QUARTERLY. English. qt. Muskogee County Genealogical Society, 801 West Okmulgee, Muskogee OK 74401. **Tel** (918)682-9393.
Ind/Abst Genealogical Period. Annu. Index.

US/0198-9340
MW NEWSLETTER, THE. Vol. 1 (Nov. 1976)-. English. MW Newsletter, 319 North Maple Street, Prospect IL 60056. **LC** CS42; .M18. **DD** 929/.2/0973.

US/0883-2706
MYERS OF AMERICA. [Myers Am.]. Vol. 1, No. 1 (Jan. 1984)-. English. qt $12.00. Clark's Place, 5712 Wilkes Drive, Fort Worth TX 76119. **LC** CS71; .M99495. **DD** 929/.2/0973.

US/0027-7738
NAMES. [Names]. **Added/Corp** American Name Society. **VFOAT** Names / American Name Society. Vol 1 (Mar. 1953)-. Periodical. English (French and Spanish). Four times a year (Mar., June, Sept., Dec.). $35.00 US; $40.00 other. American Name Society, 7 East 14th Street #17U, C/O Wayne H Finke, New York NY 10003. **Tel** (212)387-1584, FAX (212)387-1591. **ED** Edward Callary, (phone: (815)753-6627). **LC** P769; .N3. **DD** 929.405; 910.3. Index Available Received separately--bound from publisher (In December.). cum. index. **Bk Rev,** (Qty: 6-8). **Pr Rev. Circ:** 950.
Desc: Study of personal, place and literary names, as well as trade-names, slang and nicknames.
Ind/Abst Am. Hist. Life (1965-); Am. Bibliogr. Slavic East Europ. Stud.; GeoRef; Linguist. Lang. Behav. Abstr. (1987-) [Full Cov.]; Middle East Abstr. Index; MLA Int. Bibl. Books Artic. Mod. Lang. Lit.; Romant. Move.; Soc. Plann. Policy Dev. Abstr.

US/0745-239X
NASE DEJINY. Ceased. ( )-(Dec. 1989). Periodical. English. bm. Old Homestead Publishing Company, Route 3 Box 7688, Hallettsville TX 77964. **Tel** (512)798-3322. **ED** Doug Kubicek. **UDC** 929.5(73=850). **Bk Rev. Ad Acc. Circ:** 750.
Desc: Contains articles on history, culture, family histories and biographies. Also included are maps, charts, illustrations and lists of information of interest to Czech genealogists. This magazine is a "must" for anyone interested in Czech genealogy in the United States.
Ind/Abst Genealogical Period. Annu. Index (?-?).

US/1045-8190
NASE RODINA (SAINT PAUL, MINN.). (NASE RODINA.). [Nase rodina]. **Added/Corp** Czechoslovak Genealogical Society (Saint Paul, Minn.). **VFOAT** Our Families. (1989)-. Periodical. English. Four times a year. $15.00 US; $20.00 other. Czechoslovak Genealogical Society International, PO Box 16225, St Paul MN 55116. **Tel** (612)946-6605, FAX (612)426-1222. **ED** Pat Reynolds (editor's address: 4980 Oakview Lane North, Plymouth MN 55442; editor's phone: (612)559-0028). **LC** WMLC 93/1444. **DD** 929. **Bk Rev,** (Qty: 8). **Ad Acc. Circ:** 3,000.
Desc: Contains articles relating to the ethnic groups that occupied the country of Czechoslovakia, as defined by the area included in 1919. Includes items from the former Czechoslovakia and settlements in the U.S.

US/8756-4726
NASH NOTATIONS. [Nash]. Periodical. English. qt. $12.00. Nash Notations, 14945 Gale Avenue, Hacienda Heights CA 91745. **Tel** (818)333-5917. **ED** Lois Hayes Culver. **LC** CS71; .N2496. **DD** 929/.2/0973. **UDC** 929.56(73). Index available. **Bk Rev.**
Desc: Genealogical research on Nash families.

US/0739-1412
NATCHEZ TRACE NEWSLETTER. Added/Corp Natchez Trace Genealogical Society. Vol. 1, No. 1 (Feb. 1980)-. Periodical. English. ir. Natchez Trace Genealogical Society, PO Box 420, Florence AL 35631-0420. **Tel** (205)764-4749. **ED** Kitty Futrell Cox. **LC** F325; .N368. **DD** 929/.1/0720761. **Ad Acc. Circ:** 600 (ctrl).
Desc: Contains program announcements and summaries and board actions that affect members. A list of officers and committees, subscription information and general genealogical information of local interest.

US/0738-985X
NATCHEZ TRACE TRAVELER. Added/Corp Natchez Trace Genealogical Society. Vol. 1, No. 1 (May 1981)-. Periodical. English. qt $20.00. Natchez Trace Genealogical Society, PO Box 420, Florence AL 35631-0420. **Tel** (205)764-4749. **ED** Darrell A. Russel. **LC** F325; .N369. **DD** 929/.1/072076. Index available. **Bk Rev. Circ:** 600.
Desc: Contains genealogical records from northwest Alabama (chiefly Colbert, Franklin, and Lauderdale counties), including court records, Bible records, old letters, church minutes, and cemetery surveys; also includes queries.
Ind/Abst Genealogical Period. Annu. Index.

US/0742-5872
NATCHITOCHES GENEALOGIST, THE. Added/Corp Natchitoches Genealogical Association. Natchitoches Genealogical and Historical Association. Vol. 1, No. 1 (Apr. 1977)-. Periodical. English. Twice a year. 10.00 regular membership; $15.00 family membership. Natchitoches Genealogical & Historical Association, PO Box 1349, Natchitoches LA 71458-1349. **Tel** (318)352-2859. **LC** F377.N4; N37. **DD** 929/.1/072076365. Index available. cum. index. **Bk Rev.**
Desc: Covers that area which composed the original Natchitoches Parish. This includes the parishes of

Sabine, Winn, Rapides, Bienville, Red River, Bossier, Caddo, DeSoto, Claiborne, Grant, Lincoln, Vernon and Webster.

US/0742-9045
NATIONAL DIRECTORY OF LOCAL RESEARCHERS. [Natl. dir. local res.]. **VFOAT** Family Tree National Directory of Local Researchers. Directory. English. an. $5.00. The Family Tree / Ohio, 450 Potter Street, Wauseon OH 43567. **Tel** (419)335-6485. **ED** Howard V Fausey. **LC** CS44; .N3. **DD** 909.1/02573. **UDC** 929.5(058)(73). **Bk Rev. Ad Acc.** ctrl circ.
Desc: Names of people doing local genealogical research.

US/0148-8554
NATIONAL GENEALOGICAL INQUIRER. V. 1 (Spring 1977)-. Periodical. English. qt. $8.00. 2236 South 77th West, Allis WI 53219. **LC** CS42; .N28. **DD** 929/.1/0973. **UDC** 929.5(058)(73).

US/0027-934X
NATIONAL GENEALOGICAL SOCIETY QUARTERLY. [Natl. Geneal. Soc. q.]. **Main/Corp** National Genealogical Society. **Added/Corp** National Genealogical Society. Quarterly. Vol. 1, No. 1 (April 1912)-. Academic Scholarly Publication. English. qt. comes with membership. National Genealogical Society, 4527 17th Street North, Arlington VA 22207. **Tel** (703)525-0050. **ED** Gary Mills and Elizabeth S. Mills. **LC** CS42; .N4. **DD** 929. Index available. cum. index. **Bk Rev. Ad Acc. Circ:** 9,000 (ctrl). available on microfiche.
Desc: Previously unpublished scholarly articles on genealogy.
Ind/Abst Am. Hist. Life (1963-); Book Rev. Index; Genealogical Period. Annu. Index.

US/1058-7020
NATIONAL QUERIES FORUM, THE. [Natl. queries forum]. **VFOAT** NQF. (1990)-. Periodical. English. mo. $13.75 (print), $45.00 (diskette). National Queries Forum, PO Box 593, Santa Cruz CA 95061. **Tel** (408)426-2929. **LC** IN PROCESS. **DD** 929. available on diskette.

US/1064-0894
NAVIGATOR (NORFOLK, VA.), THE. (THE NAVIGATOR.). [Navigator]. **Added/Corp** Norfolk Genealogical Society. Vol. 1, No. 1 (Fall 1981)-. Periodical. English. bm. $12.00. Norfolk Genealogical Society, PO Box 12813, Thomas Corner Station, Norfolk VA 23502. **DD** 929.
Ind/Abst Genealogical Period. Annu. Index.

US/0270-4463
NEBRASKA ANCESTREE. **Added/Corp** Nebraska State Genealogical Society. Vol. 1 (Summer 1978)-. Periodical. English. Four times a year. $15.00 (regular); $18.00 (family); $25.00 (sustaining) Comes with Nebraska State Genealogical Society membership. Nebraska State Genealogical Society, 3507 South 116th Avenue, Omaha NE 68144. **Tel** (402)291-1411. **ED** Pam Lindholm. **LC** F665; .N43. **DD** 929/.1/09782. Index available in last issue of volume--attached. **Bk Rev. Ad Acc. Circ:** 1,000 (ctrl).
Desc: Nebraska related genealogical and historical items. "How-to" genealogy aids.
Ind/Abst Genealogical Period. Annu. Index.

NE
NEDERLANDSCHE LEEUW; MAANDBLAD VAN HET KONINKLIJK NEDERLANDSCH GENOOTSCHAP VOOR GESLACHT- EN WAPENKUNDE, DE. **Added/Corp** Nederlandsch Genootschap voor Geslacht- en Wapenkunde. (1933)-. Periodical. Dutch. Eight times a year. Price varies. Penn Kon Ned Gen voor Geslacht en Wapenkunde, Prins Willem Alexanderhof 24, 2595 BE Gravenhage Netherlands. Index Available, published separately, free-automatically sent. **Ad Acc. Pr Rev. Acid Free. Circ:** 1,000. ***Continues*** *Genealogisch-Heraldisch Genootschap: "De Nederlandsche Leeuw", The Hague Maandblad van het Koninklijk Genealogisch-Heraldisch Genootschap: "De Nederlandsche Leeuw".*

US/0747-9891
NEHGS NEXUS. [NEHGS nexus]. **Added/Corp** New England Historic Genealogical Society. **VFOAT** N.E.H.G.S. Nexus. **VAT** New England Historic Genealogical Society Nexus. Vol. 1, No. 2 (April 1984)-. Periodical. English. bm. comes with New England Historic Genealogical Society Membership. Ne England Historic & Genealogical Society, 101 Newbury Street, Boston MA 02116. **Tel** (617)536-5740. **ED** Julie H. Otto and Robert Shaw. **LC** F3; .N52. **DD** 929/.1/072074. Index available. **Ad Acc. Circ:** 11,000 (ctrl). ***Continues*** *New England Historic Genealogical Society (Series).*
Desc: Covers articles and columns on genealogy or local history.

US/0737-7967
NERIM AND ALLIED FAMILIES NEWS. [Nerim allied fam. news]. **VFOAT** Nerim News. Vol. 1, No. 1 (Jan. 1982)-. English. qt. $10.00. Miner, PO Box 17569, Fountain Hill AZ 85268-0110. **LC** CS71; .N465. **DD** 929/.2/0973. **UDC** 929.52(73).

US/0892-4937
NEW BRASS KEY. (NEW BRASS KEY : NEBRASKA STATE GENEALOGICAL SOCIETY NEWSLETTER.). [New brass key]. **Added/Corp** Nebraska State Genealogical Society. **VFOAT** Nebraska State Genealogical Society Newsletter. Vol. 1, No. 1 (May 1977)-. Periodical. English. Six times a year. Nebraska State Genealogical Society, 3507 South 116th Avenue, Omaha NE 68144. **Tel** (402)291-1411. **DD** 929.

US/0028-4785
NEW ENGLAND HISTORICAL AND GENEALOGICAL REGISTER, THE. (THE NEW ENGLAND HISTORICAL AND GENEALOGICAL REGISTER / NEW-ENGLAND HISTORIC GENEALOGICAL SOCIETY.). [N. Engl. hist. geneal. regist.]. **VFOAT** Historical and Genealogical Register. Vol. 28, No. 1 (Jan. 1874)-. Academic Scholarly Publication. English. qt. $36.00. New England Historical & Genealogical Register, 101 Newbury Street, Boston MA 02116. **Tel** (617)536-5740. **ED** Jane Fletcher Fiske and Margaret F Costello. **LC** F1; .N56. **DD** 974/.005. **UDC** 929.5(74)+974. Index available. cum. index. **Bk Rev. Ad Acc. Circ:** 12,000. available on microfilm from University Microfilms International (UMI). ***Continues*** *New-England Historical & Genealogical Register and Antiquarian Journal.*
Desc: Scholarly articles on New England local and family history. Includes source material, genealogies series on methodology and ethnic groups.
Ind/Abst Am. Hist. Life (1975-); Genealogical Period. Annu. Index.

US/1055-0763
NEW HAMPSHIRE GENEALOGICAL RECORD, THE. (THE NEW HAMPSHIRE GENEALOGICAL RECORD : AN ILLUSTRATED QUARTERLY MAGAZINE DEVOTED TO GENEALOGY, HISTORY, AND BIOGRAPHY : OFFICIAL ORGAN OF THE NEW HAMPSHIRE GENEALOGICAL SOCIETY.). [N. H. geneal. rec.]. **Added/Corp** New Hampshire Genealogical Society. New Hampshire Society of Genealogists. Vol. 1, No. 1 (July 1903)-. Periodical. English (French). Four times a year (Jan., April, July, Oct.). $20.00. New Hampshire Society of Genealogists, PO Box 2316, Concord NH 03302. **Tel** (603)269-4371, FAX (603)437-1808. **ED** Ann Theopold Chaplin (editor's address: RFD 2 Box 668, Center Barnstead, NH 03225). **LC** F33; .N54. **DD** 929/.3742/05. Index available. **Bk Rev. Ad Acc. Pr Rev. Circ:** 900 (ctrl).
Ind/Abst Genealogical Period. Annu. Index.

US/0899-1340
NEW JERSEY QUERIES. [N. J. queries]. (1987)-. Periodical. English. ir. $5.50. McNeill Enterprises, PO Box 779, Napavine WA 98565. **Tel** (509)922-4521. **ED** Ruby Simonson McNeill. **DD** 929. **Bk Rev. Circ:** 500 (ctrl).
Ind/Abst Genealogical Period. Annu. Index.

US
NEW MEXICO GENEALOGIST. **Added/Corp** New Mexico Genealogical Society. Vol. 1, No. 1 (Oct. 1962)-. Periodical. English (Spanish). qt (Mar., Jun., Sep., Dec.). $12.00. New Mexico Genealogical Society, PO Box 8283, Albuquerque NM 87198. **Tel** (505)255-6116. **ED** Andres Segura, (editor's address: 2901 Euclid Avenue Northeast, #22-B, Albuquerque, NM 87106). Index available (bound in Dec. issue). **Bk Rev. Ad Acc. Circ:** 400 (ctrl).
Desc: Devoted to New Mexico. Source material of genealogical and historical value.

US/0548-6424
NEW ORLEANS GENESIS, THE. (NEW ORLEANS GENESIS.). [New Orleans genes.]. **Added/Corp** Genealogical Research Society of New Orleans. (1962)-. Periodical. English. Four times a year. $25.00. Genealogical Research Society of New Orleans, PO Box 51791, New Orleans LA 70151. **Tel** (504)488-1660, (504)596-2614. **ED** Patricia Fenerty. **LC** F379.N5; N54. **DD** 929. **Bk Rev**, (Qty: 20). **Circ:** 400 (ctrl).
Desc: Indices, church registers, genealogies cemetery records, wills and successions, civil marriage records, and interment records of Confederate soldiers in various locations.

US/0028-7237
NEW YORK GENEALOGICAL AND BIOGRAPHICAL RECORD, THE. **Added/Corp** New York Genealogical and Biographical Society. (1870)-. Periodical. English. Four times a year (Jan., Apr., July, Oct.). 25.00. New York Genealogical & Biographical Society, 122 East 58th Street, New York NY 10022. **Tel** (212)755-8532, FAX (212)754-4218. **ED** Henry B. Hoff and Harry Macy Jr. **LC** F116; .N28. Index available. **Bk Rev**, (Qty: 120). **Ad Acc, Adv Mgr:** H. Macy. **Circ:** 2,200. available on microfilm from University Microfilms International (UMI). ***Supersedes*** *Bulletin.*
Desc: Articles, abstracts, book reviews, relating to genealogy of New Netherland and New York State families.
Ind/Abst Genealogical Period. Annu. Index.

US/1041-6560
NEW YORK STATE QUERIES. [N. Y. State queries]. Vol. 1, No. 1 (March 1987)-. Periodical. English. ir. $6.25 (single issue). Weidner Words, West 2206 Borden Road, Spokane WA 99204-9668. **Tel** (509)448-9263. **ED** Carolyn Weidner. **LC** F118; .W44. **DD** 929/.1/0720747. Index available. **Bk Rev. Circ:** 100.
Desc: Queries accepted free pertaining to NY state.

CN/0838-049X
NEWFOUNDLAND ANCESTOR. (THE NEWFOUNDLAND ANCESTOR : QUARTERLY NEWSLETTER OF NEWFOUNDLAND AND LABRADOR GENEALOGICAL SOCIETY INC.). [Nfld. ancestor]. **Added/Corp** Newfoundland and Labrador Genealogical Society. Vol. 4, No. 1 (Winter 1987)-. Newsletter. English. Four times a year (Mar., June, Sept., Nov.). 25.00Can$ Comes with Newfoundland & Labrador Genealogical Society Membership. Newfoundland and Labrador Genealogical Society Inc, Colonial Building, Military Road, St John's NFLD A1C 2C9 Canada. **Tel** (709)754-9525. **ED** Ronald J. Fitzpatrick. **DD** 929/.1/09718. cum. index. **Bk Rev. Ad Acc, Adv Mgr:** R. Fitzpatrick. **Circ:** 1,100 (ctrl). ***Continues*** *Newfoundland and Labrador Genealogical Society Newsletter, 0831-568X.*
Desc: To foster interest in Newfoundland ancestry, to help researchers locate information and opportunities to communicates with each other and share their research efforts.
Ind/Abst Genealogical Period. Annu. Index.

US/0882-6773
NEWKIRK NOTES. Periodical. English. qt. $12.00. Mary & Gil Gilford, 1403 Kingsford Drive, Florissant MO 63031. **LC** CS71; .N54996. **DD** 929/.2/0973 #2 19. **UDC** 929.52(73).

US/8755-9854
NEWS AND JOURNAL (RIPLEY, MISS.). (NEWS AND JOURNAL / TIPPAH COUNTY HISTORICAL AND GENEALOGICAL SOCIETY.). **Added/Corp** Tippah County Historical and Genealogical Society. Vol. 3, No. 1 (Mar. 1977)-. Newsletter. English. qt. Comes with membership. Tippah County Historical and Genealogical Society, 308 North Commerce Street, Ripley MS 38663. **Tel** (601)837-7773. **ED** Tommy Covington. **DD** 929. Index available. **Circ:** 200 (ctrl). ***Continues*** *Newsletter (Tippah County Historical and Genealogical Society).*
Desc: Genealogical and historical information on Tippah County Mississippi.

CN/0708-6350
NEWS & VIEWS - ONTARIO GENEALOGICAL SOCIETY, LEEDS & GRENVILLE BRANCH. **Main/Corp** Ontario Genealogical Society. Leeds & Grenville Branch. **VFOAT** News 'n' Views. **VAT** News and Views - Leeds & Grenville Branch of the Ontario Genealogical Society. (March 1979)-. Periodical. English. Nine times a year. $10.00 Canada; $12.00 other. Leeds & Grenville Branch, Ontario Genealogical Society, PO Box 536, Brockville Ontario K6V 5V7 Canada. **Tel** (613)924-2928. **ED** Myrtle Johnston. **DD** 929/.1/06271373. **Bk Rev**, (Qty: 3). **Circ:** 630. ***Continues*** *Leeds & Grenville Genealogical Society. News 'N' Views, 0318-8728.*

US/0747-8739
NEWS FROM THE NORTHWEST. English. Five times a year. $10.00. Northwest Suburban Council of Genealogists, PO Box AC, Mount Prospect IL 60056. **ED** Evelyn Koons. **LC** F548.25; .N48. **DD** 929/.1/072077311. **UDC** 929.5(773). Index available. **Bk Rev. Circ:** 250.
Desc: Bible and cemetery transcripts; vital record extracts from newspapers, research tips, gleaning from other newsletters, announcements, queries, and book reviews.
Ind/Abst Genealogical Period. Annu. Index.

UK/0140-1912
NEWS LETTER - CUMBRIA FAMILY HISTORY SOCIETY. [News lett. - Cumbria Fam. Hist. Soc.]. (1976)-. English. Four times a year. £5.50 (surface mail); £7.50 (airmail). Cumbria Family History Society, Ulpha 32 Granada Road, Denton Manch M34 2LJ England. **ED** R. H. Postle Thwaite. **Bk Rev**, (Qty: varies). ctrl circ.

US/0148-3994
NEWS LETTER OF THE PARKE SOCIETY. **Main/Corp** Parke Society. Vol. 14, No. 2 (Spring 1977)-. Newsletter. English. Three times a year. Parke Society, PO Box 590, Milwaukee WI 53201. **Tel** (414)781-7100. **LC** CS71; .P235a. **DD** 929/.2/0973. ***Continues*** *Park-e-s Family News, 0363-4582.*

US/8756-6923
NEWS QUARTERLY OF THE MCDONOUGH COUNTY GENEALOGICAL SOCIETY. [News q. McDonough Cty. Geneal. Soc.]. **Added/Corp** McDonough County Genealogical Society. (19??)-. Periodical. English. Four times a year (Jan., Apr., July, Oct.). $10.00 Comes with McDonough County Genealogical Society membership. McDonough County Genealogical Society, Box 202, Macomb IL 61455. **LC** F547.M13; N48. **DD** 929/.1/072077342.

CN/0380-1616
NEWSLEAF - ONTARIO GENEALOGICAL SOCIETY. **Main/Corp** Ontario Genealogical Society. Vol. 1 (March 1971)-. Periodical. English. qt. comes with membership. Ontario Genealogical Society / Toronto, 40 Orchard View Boulevard, Suite 251, Toronto Ontario M4R 1B9 Canada. **Tel** (416)489-0734, FAX (416)489-9803. **ED** Dawn Broughton and Heather Ibbottson. **Bk Rev. Circ:** 5,000 (ctrl).
Desc: Contains items of news value to members of a genealogical society.

US/0893-4290
NEWSLETTER - AFRICAN-AMERICAN FAMILY HISTORY ASSOCIATION. [Newsl. - Afr.-Am. Fam. Hist. Assoc.]. **Main/Corp** African-American Family History Association. **VFOAT** AAFHA Newsletter. (Oct. 1977)-. Periodical. English. Four times a year. $25.00 (institutions); $12.00 (individuals). African-American Family History Association, PO Box 115268, Atlanta GA 30310. **Tel** (404)344-7405. **ED** Herman Mason Jr. **DD** 929. **Bk Rev. Ad Acc. Circ:** 500 (ctrl).

US
NEWSLETTER - AMERICAN HISTORICAL SOCIETY OF GERMANS FROM RUSSIA. **Main/Corp** American Historical Society of Germans from Russia. **VFOAT** AHSGR Newsletter. No. 1 (Oct. 1971)-. Newsletter. English. Four times a year. $30.00 (individuals and families), $50.00 (contributing membership), $100.00 (sustaining membership), $500.00 (life membership). American Historical Society of Germans from Russia, 631 D Street, Lincoln NE 68502. **Tel** (402)474-3363, FAX (402)474-7229. **ED** David Bagby. **Circ:** 5,100 (ctrl).

US/1060-3263
NEWSLETTER / AUSTIN FAMILIES ASSOCIATION OF AMERICA. [Newsl. - Austin Fam. Assoc. Am.]. **Added/Corp** Austin Families Association of America. Vol. 1, No. 1 (Jan., Feb., Mar. 1991)-. Newsletter. English. qt. $15.00 (includes membership). **DD** 929. ***Continues*** *Newsletter (Austin Families Association of America), 1060-3263.*

US/1056-6953
NEWSLETTER / BLAIR COUNTY GENEALOGICAL SOCIETY. [Newsl. - Blair Cty. Genealog. Soc.]. **Added/Corp** Blair County Genealogical Society. **VFOAT** BCGS Newsletter. (Sept. 1980)-. Newsletter. English. qt. Blair County Genealogical Society, PO Box 855, Altoona PA 16603-0855. **LC** IN PROCESS. **DD** 929.
Ind/Abst Genealogical Period. Annu. Index.

CN/0229-527X
NEWSLETTER / BRITISH COLUMBIA GENEALOGICAL SOCIETY. [Newsl. - B.C. Geneal. Soc.]. **Added/Corp** British Columbia Genealogical Society. **VFOAT** BCGS Newsletters. **VAT** British Columbia Genealogical Society Newsletter. (1976)-. Newsletter. English. Six times a year. Free to members. British Columbia Society, PO Box 88054, Richmond British Columbia V6X 3T6 Canada. **Tel** (604)270-6025. **ED** Susan Rideout. **DD** 929/.1/060711. **Circ:** 1,100 (ctrl).

US/1047-2770
NEWSLETTER - BUCKS COUNTY GENEALOGICAL SOCIETY. (NEWSLETTER.). [Newsl. - Bucks Cty. Geneal. Soc.]. **Added/Corp** Bucks County Genealogical Society. Vol. 1, No. 1 (Fall 1981)-. Newsletter. English. qt. comes with membership. Bucks County Genealogical Society, PO Box 1092, Doylestown PA 18901. **Tel** (215)345-0210. **DD** 929.
Ind/Abst Genealogical Period. Annu. Index.

US/8756-694X
NEWSLETTER / CALIFORNIA GENEALOGICAL ASSOCIATION. ***Title Change.*** [Newsl. - Calif. Geneal. Soc.]. **Added/Corp** California Genealogical Society. (19??)-(19??). Newsletter. English. bm. California Genealogical Society, 300 Brannan Street, Suite 409, San Francisco CA 94107. **Tel** (415)777-9936. **LC** F865; .N58. **DD** 929/.1/0720794. ***Continued by*** *CGS News (California Genealogical Society), 1058-5133.*

US
NEWSLETTER / CAPITAL DISTRICT GENEALOGICAL SOCIETY. **Added/Corp** Capital District Genealogical Society. Vol. 1, No. 1 (May 1982)-. Periodical. English. Four times a year. Free to members; $10.00 membership. Capital District Genealogical Society, PO Box 2175, Albany NY 12220.
Ind/Abst Genealogical Period. Annu. Index.

US/0749-0631
NEWSLETTER / CLERMONT COUNTY GENEALOGICAL SOCIETY. **Added/Corp** Clermont County Genealogical Society. No. 1 (Feb. 1978)-. Newsletter. English. qt. Comes with membership. Clermont County Genealogical Society, 3rd & Broadway Public Library, Batavia OH 45103. **ED** Helen Johnson. **LC** F497.C53; N48. **DD** 929/.3771794. Index available. cum. index. **Ad Acc. Circ:** 600 (ctrl).
Desc: Covers genealogy and history of Southwestern Ohio, especially Clermont County. Includes copies of early courthouse records, family trees, ancestor charts, etc.

US/0090-6093
NEWSLETTER - COWAN CLAN UNITED. (NEWSLETTER.). **Main/Corp** Cowan Clan United. V. 1-April 1969-. Newsletter. English. qt. $3.00 members. 510 West First Street, Pittsburg KS 66762. **LC** CS71; .C8734. **DD** 929/.2/0973. **UDC** 929.52(73).

US/1072-0359
NEWSLETTER / DUBUQUE COUNTY-KEY CITY GENEALOGICAL SOCIETY. [Newsl. - Dubuque Cty./Key City Geneal. Soc.]. **Added/Corp** Dubuque County/Key City Genealogical Society. (1978)-. Newsletter. English. qt. $8.00 (1 year), $15.00 (2 year) (includes membership). Dubuque County/ Key City Genealogical Society, PO Box 13, Dubuque IA 52004. **Tel** (319)583-0586. **DD** 929.

US/0895-2078
NEWSLETTER - FAIRFAX GENEALOGICAL SOCIETY (FAIRFAX COUNTY, VA.). (NEWSLETTER / FAIRFAX GENEALOGICAL SOCIETY.). **Added/Corp** Fairfax Genealogical Society (Fairfax County, Va.). **VFOAT** Fairfax Genealogical Society Newsletter. (1???)-. Newsletter. English. Five times a year (Jan., Mar., May, Sept., Nov.). $10.00. Fairfax Genealogical Society, PO Box 2290, Merrifield VA 22116. **Tel** (703)978-3773. **ED** Howard Carr (703)451-7293. **DD** 929. **Bk Rev**, (Qty: 3). **Circ:** 350 (ctrl). available on microfilm, microfiche, and CD-ROM. Documents available.

US
NEWSLETTER / FAMILY HISTORY SOCIETY OF ARIZONA. **Added/Corp** Family History Society of Arizona. Vol. 1, No. 1 (Oct./Nov. 1984)-. Newsletter. English. Twelve times a year. $15.00 Comes with Family History Society of Arizona membership. Family History Society Arizona, PO Box 310, Glendale AZ 85311. **Tel** (602)992-4769. **ED** Robert M. Wilbanks IV, (editor's address: 1208 North 85 Place, Scottsdale, AZ 85257, phone: (602)990-7914). Index available.
Desc: Contains some information about Arizona, but the majority issues are about general genealogy, states, and other countries.

US/0739-6007
NEWSLETTER - FLORIDA GENEALOGICAL SOCIETY. **Main/Corp** Florida Genealogical Society. Newsletter. English. bm. $7.00 US; $20.00 other. Florida Genealogical Society, PO Box 18624, Tampa FL 33679-8624. **Tel** (813)839-0810. **ED** Helen N Byrd. **UDC** 929.5(759). **Circ:** 350.

US
NEWSLETTER - GENEALOGICAL SOCIETY OF NEW JERSEY. **Main/Corp** Genealogical Society of New Jersey. **VFOAT** GSNJ Newsletter. Vol. 1 (1976)-. Newsletter. English. sa. Free to members. Genealogical Society of New Jersey, 132 West Franklin Street, Bound Brook NJ 08805. **Tel** (908)356-6920. **(Subscription address:** PO Box 1291, New Brunswick, NJ 08903) **ED** Joseph R. Klett. **UDC** 929.5(749). **Bk Rev. Circ:** 1,000.
Desc: Announcements, news and book notices of interest to persons doing New Jersey genealogy. Contains large query section.
Ind/Abst Genealogical Period. Annu. Index.

US/0742-9258
NEWSLETTER (GENEALOGICAL SOCIETY OF ORIGINAL MUSCOGEE COUNTY). (NEWSLETTER / THE GENEALOGICAL SOCIETY OF ORIGINAL MUSCOGEE COUNTY.). [Newsl. - Geneal. Soc. Orig. Muscogee Cty.]. No. 1 (Sept. 1980)-. Newsletter. English. bm. $8.00 (individuals). Springer-Verlag New York Inc., 175 5th Avenue, New York NY 10010. **Tel** (212)460-1500, telex 232 235 SPB UR. **(Subscription address:** Springer Verlag New York Inc. / for North America, 44 Hartz Way, Secaucus NJ 07096.) **ED** Shirley G Springer. **LC** F292.M9; N48. **DD** 929/.1/0720758473. **UDC** 929.5(758). **Circ:** 350.
Desc: Primary interest to preserve genealogical records of the area. Muscogee was first Creek Indian Land and included Harris, Lee and Marion counties, GA.

UK/0141-8009
NEWSLETTER - GLASGOW & WEST OF SCOTLAND FAMILY HISTORY SOCIETY. [Newsl. - Glasg. West Scotl. Fam. Hist. Soc.]. **VFOAT** Newsletter - Glasgow and West of Scotland Family History Society. (1977)-. Newsletter. English. Three times a year (available with membership). Glasgow and West of Scotland Family History Society, c/o Strathclyde Regional Archives, Mitchell Library, North Street, Glascow G3 7DN Scotland. **ED** Miss Edna M.S. Stark. **Bk Rev**, (Qty: 18-20/year). **Ad Acc. Circ:** 1,000 (ctrl).
Ind/Abst Genealogical Period. Annu. Index.

US
NEWSLETTER (HOOD COUNTY GENEALOGICAL SOCIETY). (199?)-. Newsletter. English. qt. Hood County Genealogical Society, PO Box 1623, Granbury TX 76048. **Tel** (817)573-2840. ***Continues*** *Hood County Genealogical Society : Newsletter, 1071-1112.*

US
NEWSLETTER / HULL FAMILY ASSOCIATION, THE. **Added/Corp** Hull Family Association. (1990)-. Newsletter. English. qt. Hull Family Association, PO Box 12, Lumberville PA 18933. **Tel** (215)297-5497. **LC** CS71; .H91194. **DD** 929/.2/0973. ***Continues*** *Hull Family Newsletter, 8755-2280.*

US/0737-4321
NEWSLETTER / JOHNSTON COUNTY GENEALOGICAL SOCIETY. **Added/Corp** Johnston County Genealogical Society. (19??)-. Newsletter. English. qt. $10.00. Johnston County Genealogical Society, 305 Market Street, Smithfield NC 27577. **Tel** (919)934-8146. **ED** Virginia M. Sanders. **LC** F262.J6; J63. **DD** 929/.1/072075641. **Circ:** 250 (ctrl). ***Continues*** *Johnston County Genealogical Society, 0737-433X.*
Desc: Does research in all phases of Johnston County history and genealogy.
Ind/Abst Genealogical Period. Annu. Index.

US/0892-6182
NEWSLETTER (LINCOLN-LANCASTER COUNTY GENEALOGICAL SOCIETY). (NEWSLETTER / THE LINCOLN-LANCASTER COUNTY GENEALOGICAL SOCIETY.). [Newsl. - Linc.-Lanc. Cty. Geneal. Soc.]. **Added/Corp** Lincoln-Lancaster County Genealogical Society. **VFOAT** LLCGS Newsletter. (19??)-. Periodical. English. Twelve times a year. $3.00. Lincoln-Lancaster County Genealogical Society, PO Box 30055, Lincoln NE 68503-0055. **Tel** (402)466-3239. **DD** 929.

US/8755-173X
NEWSLETTER / NEW HAMPSHIRE SOCIETY OF GENEALOGISTS. [Newsl. - N.H. Soc. Geneal.]. **Added/Corp** New Hampshire Society of Genealogists. **VFOAT** N.H.S.G. Newsletter; NHSG Newsletter. (19??)-. English. Four times a year (Jan., Apr., July, Oct.). $20.00 Comes with New Hampshire Society of Genealogists membership. New Hampshire Society of Genealogists, PO Box 2316, Concord NH 03302. **Tel** (603)269-4371, FAX (603)437-1808. **ED** Carl W. Brage. **LC** F33; .N59. **DD** 929/.1/0720742. Index available. **Bk Rev. Ad Acc. Circ:** 350.
Desc: Data concerning New Hampshire settlers and their descendants.

CN/0820-8379
NEWSLETTER OF THE ALBERTA FAMILY HISTORIES SOCIETY. [Newsl. Alta. Fam. Hist. Soc.]. No. 8 (May 1982)-. Newsletter. English. mo. Alberta Family Histories Society, P.O.Box 30270 Station B, Calgary Alberta T2M 4P1 Canada. **Tel** (403)255-8660. **DD** 929/.1/0607123. **UDC** 929.5(712). ***Continues*** *Newsletter of the Calgary Branch of the Alberta Family Histories Society, 0712-2209.*

US/0193-8770
NEWSLETTER OF THE CHICAGO GENEALOGICAL SOCIETY. **Main/Corp** Chicago Genealogical Society. (19??)-. Newsletter. English. mo (11 issues). Chicago Genealogical Society, PO Box 1160, Chicago IL 60690. **Tel** (312)725-1306.

US/0090-5704
NEWSLETTER OF THE LAMBERT-LAMBERTH ASSOCIATION. ***Title Change.*** (NEWSLETTER.). [Newsl. Lambert-Lamberth Assoc.]. **Main/Corp** Lambert/Lamberth Association. Jan. (1969)-(19??). Newsletter. English. sa. **LC** CS71; .L2187. **DD** 929/.2/0973. ***Continued by*** *Newsletter of the Lambert/Lamberth Family Association.*

UK
NEWSLETTER OF THE NEWTH/NUTH FAMILY HISTORY SOCIETY. Newsletter. English. **LC** CS71; .N56845. **DD** 929/.2/0973.

US/0743-1341
NEWSLETTER OF THE NORTH SUBURBAN GENEALOGICAL SOCIETY. **Added/Corp** North Suburban Genealogical Society (Winnetka, Ill.). Vol. 1, No. 1 (Nov. 1975)-. Newsletter. English. bm. North Suburban Genealogical Society, Winnetka Public Library, 768 Oak Street, Winnetka IL 60093. **LC** F548.25; .N49. **DD** 929/.377311.
Ind/Abst Genealogical Period. Annu. Index.

US/0883-2099
NEWSLETTER OF THE SOUTHWEST VIRGINIA COPENHAVER FAMILY. [Newsl. southwest Va. Copenhaver fam.]. Began with Vol. 1, No. 1 (Feb. 1973). Newsletter. English. Three times a year. Copenhaver, 202 Frazier Court, Joppa MD 21085-4434.

Genealogy and Heraldry

Tel (410)679-2182. ED Mildred M Copenhaver. LC CS71; .C78623. DD 929/.2/0973. UDC 929.52(73). Circ: 650 (ctrl).

US/0747-6728
NEWSLETTER / ROSE FAMILY ASSOCIATION. [Newsl. - Rose Fam. Assoc.]. **Added/Corp** Rose Family Association. **VFOAT** Rose Family Association Newsletter. (19??)-. Newsletter. English. qt. Comes with membership. Rose Family Association, 1474 Montelegre Drive, San Jose CA 95120. **Tel** (408)268-2137. **ED** Christine Rose and Seymour T. Rose. **LC** CS71; .R759516. **DD** 929/.2/0973. **Circ:** 750.
Desc: Devoted to genealogical research of the Rose family, all nationalities.

US/0740-4395
NEWSLETTER / ROSS COUNTY GENEALOGICAL SOCIETY. **Main/Corp** Ross County Genealogical Society. Vol. 1, No. 1 (Nov. 1973)-. Newsletter. English. qt. $6.00. Ross County Genealogical Society, PO Box 6352, Chillicothe OH 45601. **Tel** (614)773-2715. **LC** F497.R8; R67A. **DD** 929/.377182. **UDC** 929.5(771). Index available. **Bk Rev. Circ:** 500.

US/1069-9317
NEWSLETTER - SOUTH BEND AREA GENEALOGICAL SOCIETY. See Population Studies.

US/0882-9527
NEWSLETTER / STANISLAUS COUNTY GENEALOGICAL SOCIETY. ***Title Change.*** **Added/Corp** Stanislaus County Genealogical Society. Vol. 2, No. 10 (Nov. 1981)-(1992). Newsletter. English. mo. SCGS Newsletter Editor, Renee Renee Carver, 5216 Parker Road, Modesto CA 95355. **LC** F868.S8; S83. **DD** 929/.1/072079457. ***Continues*** *Newsletter-Meeting Notice, 0882-9519.* ***Continued by*** *Stanislaus Researcher.*

US
NEWSLETTER / UTAH GENEALOGICAL ASSOCIATION. **Main/Corp** Utah Genealogical Association. (19??)-. Newsletter. English. qt. Utah Genealogical Association, PO Box 1144, Salt Lake City UT 84110. **Tel** (801)240-4196, FAX (801)240-1929.
Ind/Abst Genealogical Period. Annu. Index.

US/1044-5897
NEWSLETTER / VIRGINIA BEACH GENEALOGICAL SOCIETY. [Newsl. - Va. Beach Geneal. Soc.]. **Added/Corp** Virginia Beach Genealogical Society. (Feb. 1984)-. Newsletter. English. qt. Virginia Beach Genealogical Society, PO Box 62901, Virginia Beach VA 23462. **DD** 929.
Ind/Abst Genealogical Period. Annu. Index.

US/0887-6959
NEWSLETTER / WHITMAN COUNTY GENEALOGICAL SOCIETY. [Newsl. - Whitman Cty. Geneal. Soc.]. **VFOAT** Whitman County Genealogical Society Newsletter; News Letter. Vol. 1, No. 1 (Sept. 1984)-. Newsletter. English. mo. Whitman County Genealogical Society, PO Box 393, Pullman WA 99163. **DD** 929.
Ind/Abst Genealogical Period. Annu. Index.

US
NEWSLETTER / WISCONSIN STATE GENEALOGICAL SOCIETY. **Added/Corp** Wisconsin State Genealogical Society. Vol. 1, No. 1 (Oct. 1954)-. Newsletter. English. qt. $14.00 US; $22.00 Canada and UK; $29.00 New Zealand & Australia. Wisconsin State Genealogical Society, 2109 20th Avenue, Monroe WI 53566. **Tel** (608)325-2609. **LC** F580. A1; W63. cum. index. **Circ:** 1600.
Desc: A publication for history and/or antique enthusiasts, cross-word puzzler, and for those who enjoy unravelling a good mystery story. Also invites new members to begin their search for their ancestors.
Ind/Abst Genealogical Period. Annu. Index.

US/1056-1684
NEWSPAPER ABSTRACTS. (NEWSPAPER ABSTRACTS / GENEALOGICAL SOCIETY, GUTHRIE COUNTY, IOWA.). [Newsp. abstr.]. **Added/Corp** Guthrie County Genealogical Society. Vol. 1 (1984)-. English. Guthrie County Genealogical Society, PO Box 96, Jamaica IA 50128. **Tel** (515)429-3362. **LC** IN PROCESS. **DD** 929.

JA
NIHON JOKUNSHA MEIKAN. **Added/Corp** Nihon Jokunsha Kyokai. (19??)-. Japanese. Nihon Jokunsha Kyokai, 15-7 Akasaka 2 Minato-ku, Tokyo Japan. **LC** CR6090.A2; N5.

CN/1180-1883
NIPISSING VOYAGEUR. (THE NIPISSING VOYAGEUR.). [Nipissing voyag.]. **Added/Corp** Ontario Genealogical Society. Nipissing District Branch. Vol. 11, No.2, June (1990)-. Periodical. English. qt (Mar., May, Aug., Nov.). 9.00Can$. Ontario Genealogical Society Nipissing District Branch, District Branch/PO Box 93, North Bay Ontario P1B 8G8 Canada. **DD** 929/.1/0720713147. ***Continues*** *Public Relations Newsletter., 0843-1159.*

FR
NORD GENEALOGIE. **Added/Corp** Groupement Genealogique de la Region du Nord. (Nov. 1971)-. French. bm (6 issues). 265.00F France; 290.00F other. Group Genealogique de la Region du Nord, BP 62, 59118 Wambrechies France. **ED** Edmond Derrevmaux. **LC** CS807.F4; N66. **DD** 929/.1/05. Index available. cum. index. **Bk Rev**, (Qty: 6). **Circ:** 1,200 (ctrl). available on microfiche.
Desc: Publishes ancestry of members, genealogies and research on families.

UK/0140-5403
NORFOLK ANCESTOR : JOURNAL OF THE NORFOLK & NORWICH GENEALOGICAL SOCIETY, THE. **Added/Corp** Norfolk & Norwich Genealogical Society. (197?)-. Periodical. English. qt. £12.00 (comes with membership). Norfolk & Norwich Genealogical Society, Kirby House 38th Street Giles Street, Norwich Norfolk NR2 1LL England. **Tel** 011 44 603 55918. **Bk Rev. Ad Acc. Circ:** 2,000 (ctrl). ***Continues*** *Journal / Norfolk & Norwich Genealogical Society.*
Desc: Publication for members of Norfolk and Norwich Genealogical Society. Articles on Norfolk genealogy, members' interests, events, queries, and sources.

UK
NORFOLK GENEALOGY. Vol. 1- 1969-. English. Norfolk & Norwich Genealogical Society, Kirby House 38th Street Giles Street, Norwich Norfolk NR2 1LL England. **Tel** 011 44 603 55918.

NO/0029-2141
NORSK SLEKTSHISTORISK TIDSSKRIFT. **Added/Corp** Norsk Slektshistorisk Forening. Vol. 1 (1927)-. Periodical. Norwegian. Twice a year (Apr. & Nov.). $50.00. Norsk Slektshistorisk Forening, Postboks 59 Sentrum, 0101 Oslo Norway. **ED** Per Seland and Magnus Mardal. **LC** CS910; .N57. **DD** 929.109481. cum. index. **Bk Rev. Ad Acc.**

US/0360-1056
NORTH CAROLINA GENEALOGICAL SOCIETY JOURNAL, THE. **Main/Corp** North Carolina Genealogical Society. Vol. 1 (Jan. 1975)-. Periodical. English. qt. $25.00 institutions; $22.00 individuals. North Carolina Genealogical Society, PO Box 1492, Raleigh NC 27602. **Tel** (919)733-7442. **ED** Raymond A Winslow Jr. **LC** F253; .N882A. **DD** 929/.1/09756. **UDC** 929.5(756). Index available. **Bk Rev. Circ:** 2,500 (ctrl).
Desc: Emphasis on unpublished primary source documents of North Carolina genealogical significance including public and private records and methodology.
Ind/Abst Genealogical Period. Annu. Index.

US/0897-7755
NORTH CAROLINA QUERIES. [N. C. queries]. (1987)-. Periodical. English. Four times a year. $6.00. Pioneer Publications, PO Box 397, Black Eagle MT 59414-0397. **Tel** (406)453-4266. **ED** Shirley Penna-Oakes. **DD** 929. Index available. **Bk Rev.**

US/0743-961X
NORTH CENTRAL ILLINOIS GENEALOGICAL SOCIETY. (NORTH CENTRAL ILLINOIS GENEALOGICAL SOCIETY : NEWSLETTER.). Newsletter. English. bm. North Central Illinois Genealogical Society, PO Box 1071, Rockford IL 61105. **LC** F540; .N5. **DD** 929/.1/0720773. **UDC** 929.5(773). ***Continues*** *Newsletter of the North Central Illinois Genealogical Society, 0747-4814.*

US/0736-5667
NORTH CENTRAL NORTH DAKOTA GENEALOGICAL RECORD. **Added/Corp** Mouse River Loop Genealogy Society. Vol. 1, Issue 1 (Summer 1978)-. Periodical. English. Four times a year. $19.00 Comes with North Central North Dakota Genealogical Soceity Membership. Mouse River Loop Genealogy, PO Box 1391, Minot ND 58702. **Tel** (701)838-4748. **ED** Edward Bryans. **LC** F635; .N67. **DD** 929/.1/0720784. Index Available in first issue of next volume--attached. **Bk Rev. Circ:** 135 (ctrl).
Ind/Abst Genealogical Period. Annu. Index.

UK/0306-9206
NORTH CHESHIRE FAMILY HISTORIAN 1975. [North Cheshire fam. hist.1975]. (1975)-. Periodical. English. qt (Nov., Feb., May, Aug.). £4.50. North Cheshire Family Historical Society, 50 Melbourne Road, Stockport Ches SK7 1LS England. **Tel** 011 44 061 4395843. **ED** N. Hollins. **Ad Acc. Circ:** 850. ***Continues*** *Cheshire Family Historian, 0305-9057.*

UK/0264-9217
NORTH IRISH ROOTS. (19??)-. English. sa. 5.50p Ireland; 4.50p UK; 6.50p other UK; 7.00p other. North Ireland Family History Society, Department of Education, Queens University Belfast, Belfast BT17 1HL North Ireland. **ED** Arthur McKeown. **Bk Rev**, (Qty: 8-10). **Ad Acc. Circ:** 800.
Desc: Family history journal.

US
NORTH LOUISIANA GENEALOGICAL SOCIETY JOURNAL. **Added/Corp** North Louisiana Genealogical Society. Vol. 1, No. 1 (Fall 1981)-. English. Four times a year. North Louisiana Genealogical Society, PO Box 324, Ruston LA 71270. **Tel** (318)255-7344. **ED** Ron White. **LC** F368; .N67. **DD** 929/.1/0720763. Index available. **Bk Rev. Ad Acc. Circ:** 125 (ctrl).
Desc: Includes genealogical information primarily from north Louisiana and southern Arkansas.

UK
NORTH MIDDLESEX FAMILY HISTORY SOCIETY GENEALOGICAL DIRECTORY, THE. **Main/Corp** North Middlesex Family History Society. **VFOAT** Genealogical Directory. Directory. English. **LC** CS435.M4; N67A. **DD** 929/.34218.

US/0893-2948
NORTH TEXAS TRAIL TRACERS. [North Tex. trail tracers]. **Added/Corp** North Texas Genealogical Association. Vol. 1, No. 1 (Jan. 1985)-. Periodical. English. Four times a year (Mar., June, Sept., Dec.). $10.00. North Texas Genealogical Association, PO Box 4602, Wichita Falls TX 76308-0602. **Tel** (817)692-7089. **ED** Fred Maier. **DD** 929. Index available (Next iss.). **Ad Acc. Circ:** 170.

US/0742-583X
NORTHEAST ALABAMA SETTLERS. [Northeast Ala. settl.]. **Added/Corp** Northeast Alabama Genealogical Society. **VFOAT** Settlers of Northeast Alabama. (19??)-. Periodical. English. qt (Jan., April, July, Oct.). $15.00. Northeast Alabama Genealogical Society Inc, PO Box 674, Gadsden AL 35902. **Tel** (205)546-8260. **ED** Sybil McClusky. **LC** F325; .S47. **DD** 929/.1/0720761. Index available. **Bk Rev. Circ:** 300 (ctrl). ***Continues*** *Settlers of Northeast Alabama, 0743-3174.*
Ind/Abst Genealogical Period. Annu. Index (?-?).

US/1060-5568
NORTHEAST MISSISSIPPI HISTORICAL & GENEALOGICAL SOCIETY QUARTERLY, THE. [Northeast Miss. Hist. Geneal. Soc. q.]. **Added/Corp** Northeast Mississippi Historical & Genealogical Society. **VFOAT** Northeast Mississippi Historical and Genealogical Society Quarterly. Vol. 1, No. 1 (Sept. 1980)-. Periodical. English. Four times a year (Mar., June, Sept., Dec.). $15.00. Northeast Mississippi Historical and Genealogical Society, PO Box 434, Tupelo MS 38802. **Tel** (601)841-9029. **ED** Martis Ramage Jr. (editor's address: 72 Ridgeway Drive, Belden, MS 38826, Phone: (601)840-0508). **LC** IN PROCESS. **DD** 929. Index available. **Bk Rev**, (Qty: 5). **Circ:** 350.
Desc: Historical and genealogical information from the Northeast Mississippi counties. Also, family records, town histories, family bible records, and church records are included.

US/0887-588X
NORTHWEST GEORGIA HISTORICAL & GENEALOGICAL QUARTERLY. [Northwest Ga. hist. geneal. q.]. **Added/Corp** Northwest Georgia Historical and Genealogical Society. **VFOAT** Quarterly. (1985)-. Periodical. English. qt. $15.00 (includes membership). Northwest Georgia Historical and Genealogical Society Incorporated, PO Box 5063, Rome GA 30162-5063. **Tel** (706)234-4201. **ED** Robert W. Anglea. **DD** 929. **Bk Rev**, (Qty: 1-2). **Pr Rev. Circ:** 300 (ctrl). ***Continues*** *Quarterly (Northwest Georgia Historical and Genealogical Society), 0892-4120.*

US/0741-8248
NORTHWEST MISSOURI GENEALOGY SOCIETY JOURNAL. **Added/Corp** Northwest Missouri Genealogy Society. Vol. 1, No. 1 (April 1981)-. Periodical. English. sa. $15.00. Northwest Missouri Genealogy Society Journal, PO Box 382, St Joseph MO 64502. **Tel** (816)233-0524. **LC** F465; .N67. **DD** 929/.1/0720778. **Bk Rev. Circ:** 450.

US/0740-4999
NORTHWEST TRAIL TRACER. **Added/Corp** Northwest Territory Genealogical Society (Knox County, Ind.). Vol. 1, No. 1 (June 1980)-. Periodical. English. Four times a year. $10.00 Comes with Northwest Territory Genealogical Society membership. Northwest Territory Genealogical Society, Lewis History College Library, Vincennes IN 47591. **Tel** (812)885-4330. **ED** Donna Beeson. **LC** F478; .N67. **DD** 929/.377. **Bk Rev**, (Qty: 4). **Circ:** 300.
Desc: Contains information on Knox County, Indiana. Local information on surnames, ancestor charts, written family histories, marriage records, area newspaper items, and funeral home records.
Ind/Abst Genealogical Period. Annu. Index.

CN/0227-0404
NOS SOURCES. (NOS SOURCES : BULLETIN DE LA SOCIETE DE GENEALOGIE DE LANAUDIERE.). [Nos sources]. **Added/Corp** Societe de Genealogie de Lanaudiere. Vol. 1, No. 1 (Feb./March/April 1981)-. Bulletin. French. qt (Mar., Jun., Sep., Dec.). $15.00.

Societe Genealogie Lanaudiere, CP 221, Joliette Quebec J6E CZ6 Canada. **Tel** (514)765-4444. **DD** 929/.1/06071441.

CN/0229-2750
NOTES FROM NIAGARA. (NOTES FROM NIAGARA / NP-OGS.). [Notes Niagara]. **Added/Corp** Ontario Genealogical Society. Niagara Peninsula Branch. Vol. 1, No. 1 (Jan. 1981)-. Periodical. English. Four times a year. 20.00Can$ Canada; $20.00 US. Ontario Genealogical Society / Toronto, 40 Orchard View Boulevard, Suite 251, Toronto Ontario M4R 1B9 Canada. **Tel** (416)489-0734, FAX (416)489-9803. **ED** Doug Robbins. **LC** F1059.N5; N67. **DD** 929/.1/072071339. **Circ:** 1,000 (ctrl).
Desc: A genealogical newsletter of the branch, including members' names and interests, news of new publications, additions to the library, reports of speakers, branch committee reports, and information of interest to genealogists searching in the Niagara area.

UK/0141-3821
NOTTINGHAMSHIRE FAMILY HISTORY SOCIETY : JOURNAL. **Added/Corp** Nottinghamshire Family History Society. (19??)-. Periodical. English. Four times a year (Jan., April, July, Oct.). Comes with Nottinghamshire Family History Society membership. Nottinghamshire Family History Society, 1 The Paddocks, Edwalton Nottinghamshire, NG12 4AR England. **LC** CS435.N8; N674. **DD** 929/.1/07204252. ***Continues*** *Genealogical Society of East Midlands.*

CN/0714-3672
NOVA SCOTIA GENEALOGIST, THE. [N.S. geneal.]. Vol.1 (1983)-. Periodical. English. Three times a year. 15.00Can$. Genealogical Association of Nova Scotia, Box 641 Station M, Halifax Nova Scotia B3J 2T3 Canada. **Tel** (902)424-6060. **ED** Freda Withrow. **LC** CS88.N64; N68. **DD** 929/.1/0720716. **UDC** 929.5(716). Index available. cum. index. **Bk Rev. Circ:** 1,200. ***Continues*** *Genealogical Newsletter of the Royal Nova Scotia Historical Society.*
Desc: Contains articles, book reviews, sources for research, bulletin board, new genealogical acquisitions, queries, etc.
Ind/Abst Genealogical Period. Annu. Index (?-?).

RU
NOVAIA OTECHESTVENNAIA INOSTRANNA. (1991)-. Academic Scholarly Publication. Russian. Izdatelstvo Nauka / Akademiia Nauk, Publishing House of the Russian Academy of Sciences, Leninskii Porspekt 14, 117901 Moscow Russia. **Tel** 011 95 954-21-53, FAX 011 95 938-21-44, telex 411964. ***Continues*** *Novaia Sovetskaia Inostrannaia Literatura po Obshchestvennym Naukam : Problemy Slavianovedeniia i Balkanistiki, 0134-3041.*

US/1045-2427
NUESTRAS RAICES (QUARTERLY). (NUESTRAS RAICES.). **Added/Corp** Genealogical Society of Hispanic America. **VFOAT** Our Roots Quarterly; Nuestras Raices Quarterly; Our Roots; Genealogical Society of Hispanic America Journal. Vol. 1, No. 1 (Jan. 1989)-. Periodical. English (Spanish). qt. $40.00 institutions; $15.00 individuals (comes with membership). Genealogical Society of Hispanic America, PO Box 9606, Denver CO 80209-0606. **Tel** (303)237-0080. **ED** David Salazar. **LC** IN PROCESS. **DD** 929. Index available. cum. index. **Ad Acc. Pr Rev. Circ:** 400 (ctrl).

CU
NUEVA LINEA (HAVANA, CUBA). ***Suspended.*** (NUEVA LINEA.). **Added/Corp** Centro de Diseno y Orientacion de la Moda (Cuba). (19??)-(1990). Spanish. Ediciones Cubanas, Obispo 527, Altos ESQ Bernaza, CP 10100 Havana Cuba. **Tel** 011 632980, 631942, FAX 011 631011, telex 512337, 6540.

US/1059-9711
NUGGET (SAN FRANCISCO, CALIF.), THE. (THE NUGGET / CALIFORNIA GENEALOGICAL SOCIETY.). [Nugget]. **Added/Corp** California Genealogical Society. (19??)-. Periodical. English. sa. Free to members. California Genealogical Society, 300 Brannan Street, Suite 409, San Francisco CA 94107. **Tel** (415)777-9936. **LC** F860; .N84. **DD** 929/.1/0720794.
Ind/Abst Genealogical Period. Annu. Index.

US
O.C.G.S. NEWSLETTER / OLMSTED COUNTY GENEALOGY SOCIETY. **Added/Corp** Olmsted County Genealogy Society. **VFOAT** OCGS Newsletter. **VAT** Olmsted County Genealogy Society Newsletter. Vol. 11, No. 1 (Jan. 1988)-. Newsletter. English. qt. **LC** F612.O5; O45. **DD** 929/.1/0720776155. ***Continues*** *Olmsted County Genealogy Society Newsletter.*

IE
O'MAHONY JOURNAL, THE. **Main/Corp** O'Mahony Records Society. Vol. 1 (1971)-. English. an. 10.00p (individuals), 12.50p (married couples) 6.50p (retired persons over age 65), 20.00p (institutions) memberships. O'Mahony Records Society, 8 Dunedin, Connaught Avenue, Cork Ireland. **Bk Rev.**
Desc: Founded to promote research of O'Mahony and Mahony genealogy and families associated through marriage and blood connection.

US/0740-8013
OAK LEAVES (BAY CITY, TEX.). (OAK LEAVES.). **Added/Corp** Matagorda County Genealogical Society. Vol. 1, No. 1 (Feb. 1982)-. Periodical. English. Four times a year (Feb., May, aug., Nov.). $17.50. Matagorda County Genealogical Society, PO Box 264, Bay City TX 77414. **Tel** (409)245-6931. **ED** Shirley Brown and Carol Sue Gibbs. **LC** F392.M4; O23. **DD** 929/.1/0720764132. Index available. **Bk Rev. Ad Acc. Circ:** 150 (ctrl).
Desc: Genealogy and history of Matagorda County Texas. Church records of the oldest Episcopal church in Texas history, towns, communities, early settlers, war records and cattle brands.

US/0897-7771
OAKES ACORNS. [Oakes acorns]. Vol. 1 (May 1985)-. Periodical. English. Four times a year. $7.35. Pioneer Publications, PO Box 397, Black Eagle MT 59414-0397. **Tel** (406)453-4266. **ED** Shirley Penna-Oakes. **LC** CS71; .O1119a. **DD** 929/.2/097305. Index available. **Bk Rev. Ad Acc.**
Desc: Genealogical: accepts oakes surname material - lineages, queries, misc. oakes information.

US
OBION ORIGINS. Vol. 1, No. 1 (Feb. 1983)-. Periodical. English. qt. $10.00. Obion County Genealogical Society, PO Box 241, Union City TN 38261. **Tel** (901)885-2322. **ED** Mary Ann Overman. **UDC** 929.5(768). Index available. **Bk Rev. Circ:** 125 (ctrl).
Desc: Genealogical information pertaining to Obion County, Tennessee.

US
OGLE GENEALOGIST : A PUBLICATION OF THE OGLE/OGLES FAMILY ASSOCIATION, THE. **Added/Corp** Ogle/Ogles Family Association. Vol. 1, No. 1 (Sept. 1980)-. Periodical. English. an. $7.00 members only. **LC** CS71; .O356. **DD** 929/.2/0973.

US/0362-0743
OHIO GENEALOGICAL HELPER, THE. v. 1- 1975-. Periodical. English. $4.95. Main PO Box 83, Columbus OH 43216. **LC** F490; .O364. **DD** 929/.1/09771. **UDC** 929.5(771).

US/1052-858X
OHIO GENEALOGICAL SOCIETY NEWSLETTER, THE. [Ohio Geneal. Soc. newsl.]. **VFOAT** Newsletter; OGS Newsletter. Vol. 18, No. 9 (Sept. 1987)-. Newsletter. English. mo. Ohio Genealogical Society / Mansfield Ohio Chapter, 34 Sturges Avenue, PO Box 2625, Mansfield OH 44906. **Tel** (419)522-9077. **DD** 929. ***Continues*** *Newsletter (Ohio Genealogical Society), 0736-2080.*

US/0897-7747
OHIO QUERIES. [Ohio queries]. 1987-. Periodical. English. Four times a year. $6.00. Pioneer Publications, PO Box 397, Black Eagle MT 59414-0397. **Tel** (406)453-4266. **ED** Shirley Penna-Oakes. **DD** 929. Index available. **Bk Rev.**

US
OHIO RECORDS & PIONEER FAMILIES/CROSSROADS OF OUR NATION. Periodical. English. Four times a year. $18.00. Ohio Genealogical Society / Mansfield Ohio Chapter, 34 Sturges Avenue, PO Box 2625, Mansfield OH 44906. **Tel** (419)522-9077. **ED** Susan Dunlap Lee. Index available in last issue of volume--attached. cum. index. **Circ:** 1,200 (ctrl).
Desc: Contains genealogical information on antebellum Ohio including court abstracts, gravestone inscriptions, Bible records, and family articles and queries.

US/0474-0742
OKLAHOMA GENEALOGICAL SOCIETY QUARTERLY. **Added/Corp** Oklahoma Genealogical Society. Vol 6, (Mar. 1961)-. Periodical. English. Four times a year (Mar., June, Sept., Dec.). $10.00. Oklahoma Genealogical Society, PO Box 12986, Oklahoma City OK 73157. **ED** Dorothy A. Pavi (phone: (405)752-5606). **Bk Rev**, (Qty: 30). ctrl circ. available on microfilm. ***Continues*** *Bulletin of the Oklahoma Genealogical Society.*
Ind/Abst Genealogical Period. Annu. Index.

US
OKMULGEE COUNTY GENEALOGICAL SOCIETY NEWSLETTER. Newsletter. English. Twice a year (Dec. and June). $8.00. Okmulgee County Genealogical Society, PO Box 805, Okmulgee OK 74447. **ED** Julie Sims and Ire Ha Love (editors' phone: (918)756-5722). **Bk Rev**, (Qty: 3-4 per year). **Circ:** 100 (ctrl).
Desc: Okmulgee County records (marriages, obituaries, newspaper items, etc.), history, queries, family records, etc.

US/1044-1905
OLD LAWRENCE REMINISCENCES. (OLD LAWRENCE REMINISCENCES : A BULLETIN OF THE LAWRENCE COUNTY ALABAMA HISTORICAL COMMISSION.). **Added/Corp** Lawrence County Historical Commission (Lawrence, Ala.). **VFOAT** Lawrence County Historical Commission Bulletin. (198?)-. Periodical. English. qt. Free to members; $15.00 membership. Lawrence County Historical Commission, PO Box 728, Moulton AL 35650. **Tel** (205)974-1757. **DD** 976. Index available. cum. index. **Bk Rev. Circ:** 475 (ctrl).
Desc: Covers genealogy as it pertains to Lawrence County, Alabama.
Ind/Abst Genealogical Period. Annu. Index.

●US/1061-6985
OLD OTOHATCHER DISTRICT REPORTER. [Old Otohatcher Dist. report.]. Vol. 1, No.1 (1992)-. Periodical. English. qt. $3.00. Mazel Spencer, 4013 Byers Street, Capitol Heights MD 20743. **DD** 929.

US/0887-6231
OLD SPARTANBURG DISTRICT GENEALOGY. ***Ceased.*** Vol. 1, No. 1 (March 1986)-(Dec. 1988). Periodical. English. qt. Gainey Research Service, PO Box 8250, Spartanburg SC 29305. **LC** F277.S7; O44. **DD** 929/.1/072075729.

US
OLD WESTMORELAND. Vol. 1, No. 1 (Aug. 1980)-. Periodical. English. qt. $140.00 US; $16.00 Canada. Southwest Pennsylvania Genealogical Services, PO Box 253, Laughlintown PA 15655. **Tel** (412)238-3176. **ED** William L Iscrupe and Shirley G M Iscrupe. **UDC** 929.5(748). Index available.

GW
OLDENBURGISCHE FAMILIENKUNDE. **Added/Corp** Oldenburger Landesverein fuer Geschichte, Natur- und Heimatkunde. (19??)-. Periodical. German. qt. DM25.00. Oldenburgische Familienkunde, Lerigauweg 14, D 26131 Oldenburg Germany. **LC** CS617; .O43. **DD** 929/.2/0943. Index available.

US/0162-0800
OLMSTE(A)D'S GENEALOGY RECORDED. V. 1- Spring 1976-. English. ir. $5.00. Walt Steesy, PO Box 299, Interlaken NY 14847-0299. **Tel** (607)532-4997. **LC** CS71; .O5A. **DD** 929/.2/0973. **UDC** 929.5(776). Index available. **Bk Rev. Ad Acc. Circ:** 500 (ctrl).
Desc: Material about persons with surname Olmsted and Olmstead.

US/1056-0378
O'LOCHLAINNS PERSONAL JOURNAL OF IRISH FAMILIES. [O'Lochlainns pers. j. Irish fam.]. **Added/Corp** Irish Genealogical Foundation (U.S.). **VFOAT** Irish Families; Irish Family Journal; O'Lochlainns Irish Family Journal. (198?)-. Periodical. English. bm. Free to members of the Irish Genealogical Foundation; $49.00 membership. Irish Genealogical Foundation, PO Box 7575, Kansas City MO 64116. **Tel** (816)454-2410, FAX (816)454-2410. **DD** 929. Index available. cum. index. **Bk Rev**, (Qty: 40). **Ad Acc.** ***Continues*** *O'Lochlainns Journal of Irish Families.*
Ind/Abst Genealogical Period. Annu. Index.

US/0882-1933
OLSCHWANGER JOURNAL. [Olschwanger j.]. Issue No. 1 (Fall 1983)-. Periodical. English. $15.00. Anna Olschwanger, 177 North Highland #909, Memphis TN 38111. **Tel** (901)327-4341. **ED** Anna Olswanger. **LC** CS71; .O518A. **DD** 929/.2/0973. **UDC** 929.5(73). **Circ:** 250 (ctrl).
Desc: History of the Olschwanger family.

US/0736-0185
ORANGE COUNTY GENEALOGICAL SOCIETY. (ORANGE COUNTY GENEALOGICAL SOCIETY : NEWSLETTER.). **Added/Corp** Orange County Genealogical Society. Vol. 1, No. 1 (May 1971)-. Newsletter. English. Four times a year (Feb., may, Aug., Nov.). $10.00. Orange County Genealogical Society, 101 Main Street, Goshen NY 10924. **ED** Madelon Newman. **LC** F127.O8; O78. **DD** 929/.1/072074731. Index Available, published separately, free-automatically sent. **Bk Rev. Ad Acc. Circ:** 850 (ctrl).
Desc: We print genealogical information on area families also early records of the area.
Ind/Abst Genealogical Period. Annu. Index.

US
ORANGE COUNTY, NEW YORK, CEMETERIES SERIES. 1-. Monographic series. English. Price varies per volume. Orange County Genealogical Society, 101 Main Street, Goshen NY 10924. **LC** F127.O8; O83. **DD** 929/.3747/31. **UDC** 929.55(747).

US
ORIGINS (GA.). (ORIGINS.). English. Four times a year (Publishes seasonally). $20.00. Thomasville Cultural

Center Library, PO Box 1597, Thomasville GA 31799. **Tel** (912)226-9640. **Bk Rev. Circ:** 250.
Ind/Abst Genealogical Period. Annu. Index.

●RU
OTECHESTVENNAIA ISTORIIA. **Added/Corp** Institut Rossiiskoi Istorii (Rossiiskaia Akademiia Nauk). (Mar/Apr. 1992)-. Academic Scholarly Publication. Russian (table of contents in English). Six times a year. $109.95. Izdatelstvo Nauka / Akademiia Nauk, Publishing House of the Russian Academy of Sciences, Leninskii Porspekt 14, 117901 Moscow Russia. **Tel** 011 95 954-21-53, FAX 011 95 938-21-44, telex 411964. **(Subscription address:** East View Publications Inc., 3020 Harbor Lane North, Suite 110, Minneapolis MN 55447.) **LC** DK1; .A3275. Documents available from The Genuine Article. ***Continues** Istoriia SSSR, 0131-3150.*
Ind/Abst Arts Humanit. Citation Index [Full Cov.]; Res. Alert [Full Cov.]; Soc. Sci. Cit. Index [Select. Cov.].

CN/0708-5583
OTTAWA BRANCH NEWS - ONTARIO GENEALOGICAL SOCIETY. (OTTAWA BRANCH NEWS.). **Added/Corp** Ontario Genealogical Society. Ottawa Branch. (Sept./Oct. 1979)-. Periodical. English. bm. $10.00. Ottawa Genealogical Society, PO Box 8346, Ottawa Ontario K1G 3H8 Canada. **ED** Joan McKay. **LC** CS88.O6; O5. **DD** 929/.1/06071384. **Bk Rev. Ad Acc. Circ:** 1,000 (ctrl). ***Continues** Branch News -Ontario Genealogical Society, Ottawa Branch, 0380-6006.*
Desc: Contains reports, articles, queries, research findings and other such items to help members develop their family trees.
Ind/Abst Genealogical Period. Annu. Index.

US/0091-6447
OUR FAMILY HERITAGE. V. 1- June 1973-. Periodical. English. qt. $5.00. 322 State Street, Fairborn OH 45324. **LC** CS42; .O9. **DD** 929/.373. **UDC** 929.5(73).

US/0731-325X
OUR FAMILY LEGACY. (OUR FAMILY LEGACY : ACORD FAMILY ASSOCIATION NEWSLETTER.). **Added/Corp** Acord Family Association. (19??)-. Newsletter. English. qt. $5.00. Acord Family Association, PO Box 3084, Brooklyn NY 11202. **LC** CS71; .A1855. **DD** 929/.2/0973.

US
OUR HERITAGE. **Added/Corp** Adams County Genealogical Society. (19??)-. Periodical. English. Four times a year. $10.00. Adams County Genealogical Society, PO Box 424, Hastings NE 68902. **Tel** (402)463-5838. **LC** F497.A2; O94. **DD** 929/.1/072077186. Index available in last issue of volume--attached. **Circ:** 100.
Ind/Abst Genealogical Period. Annu. Index.

US/0733-4559
OUR HERITAGE (WILLS POINT, TEX.). (OUR HERITAGE.). [Our herit.]. **Added/Corp** Genealogical Society of Van Zandt Co. Van Zandt County Genealogical Society. V. 1, No. 1 (June 1980)-. Periodical. English. qt. $10.00. Van Zandt County Genealogical Society, PO Drawer 716, Canton TX 75103. **Tel** (214)887-0656. **LC** F392.V2; O93. **DD** 929/.3764276.

US/0738-8306
OUR NAME'S THE GAME. (OUR NAME'S THE GAME / SOUTH CENTRAL PENNSYLVANIA GENEALOGICAL SOCIETY.). **Added/Corp** South Central Pennsylvania Genealogical Society. (19??)-. Periodical. English. Eleven times a year (July/Aug. issues combined). $12.00 (regular), $15.00 (family) Comes with South Central Pennsuylvania Genealogical Society membership. South Central Pennsylvania Genealogical Society Inc., PO Box 1824, York PA 17405. **Tel** (717)843-6169. **LC** F148; .O92. **DD** 929/.1/0720748. ctrl circ.
Desc: Genealogical and historical information of interest to members; publishes free queries from members; announcements of society meetings and programs. Emphasis on south central region of Pennsylvania.

US/0733-6381
OUSLEY NEWSLETTER. **Added/Corp** Ousley Genealogical Society. (1980)-. Periodical. English. qt. $12.00. Ousley Genealogical Society, PO Box 4305, Dallas TX 75208-0305. **Tel** (2140330-1635. **ED** Monty T. D. Weddell. **LC** CS71; .O9166. **DD** 929/.2/0973. **Bk Rev. Ad Acc. Circ:** 207 (ctrl).
Desc: Concentrates on family history, genealogy, history, and current family events.

CN/0707-8137
OUTAOUAIS GENEALOGIQUE. (L'OUTAOUAIS GENEALOGIQUE : BULLETIN OFFICIEL DE LA SOCIETE DE GENEALOGIE DE L'OUTAOUAIS INC.). **VFOAT** Repertoire BMS-St-Paul-d'Aylmer 1840-1900; Repertoire B.M.S.-Saint-Paul-d'Aylmer 1840-1900; Repertoire BMS-Saint-Paul-d'Aylmer 1840-1900; Repertoire B.M.S.-St-Paul-d'Aylmer 1840-1900. Special hors Serie No 1-. Began with Vol. for Jan. 1979. Bulletin. French. bm. 20.00Can$ Canada; 21.00Can$ US. La Societe de Genealogie de l'Outaouais Inc, C P 2025 Succ B, Hull Quebec J8X 3Z2 Canada. **Tel** (514)777-2900. **LC** CS88.H84; O9. **DD** 929/37142. **UDC** 929.5(714). **Bk Rev. Circ:** 300 (ctrl).

●US/1063-7400
OWEN COUNTY HISTORY AND GENEALOGY. [Owen cty. hist. geneal.]. **Added/Corp** Owen County Historical and Genealogical Society (Owen County, Ind.). Vol. 1, No. 1 (Summer 1992)-. Periodical. English. qt. $10.00. Owen County Historical and Genealogical Society, 110 East Market Street, Spencer IN 47460. **Tel** (812)829-3749. **ED** Vivian Zollinger. **LC** F532.O9; O9. **DD** 977.2/43/005. Index available. **Circ:** 250.
Desc: Owen County, Indiana history and genealogy.

UK
OXFORDSHIRE FAMILY HISTORIAN, THE. Vol. 1 (Spring 1977)-. Periodical. English. Three times a year. £7.00 (individuals), £8.00 (institutions) UK; £10.00 others Comes with Oxfordshire Family History Society membership. Oxfordshire Family History Society, 47 Bull Street, Aston Oxford OX18 2DT England. **Tel** 011 44 0865 820493. **ED** Jean Price. **LC** CS435.O9; O9. **Bk Rev. Circ:** 1,000.

US/1053-2765
OZARK HAPPENINGS NEWSLETTER. [Ozark happen. newsl.]. **Added/Corp** Texas County, Missouri Genealogical and Historical Society. Vol. 2, No. 1 (Jan./Feb. 1985)-. Newsletter. English. Four times a year. $10.00. Texas County, Missouri Genealogical Society, PO Box 12, Houston MO 65483. **ED** Helen Stenger (editor's telephone: (417)967-3275). **LC** F482.T4; N48. **DD** 929/.1/072077884. **Circ:** 300. ***Continues** Newsletter (Texas County, Missouri Genealogical and Historical Society.*

US
OZAR'KIN / OZARKS GENEALOGICAL SOCIETY. **Added/Corp** Ozarks Genealogical Society (Springfield, Mo.). (1979)-. Periodical. English. qt. $12.00. Ozarks Genealogical Society, PO Box 3494 GS, Springfield MO 65808. **Tel** (417)869-2223. **LC** F472.O9; O9. **DD** 929/.3778.
Ind/Abst Genealogical Period. Annu. Index.

US/0897-7763
PAGE PEDIGREE. [Page pedigree]. **Added/Corp** Pioneer Publication (Firm). Vol. 1 (Oct. 1985)-. Periodical. English. Four times a year. $7.35. Pioneer Publications, PO Box 397, Black Eagle MT 59414-0397. **Tel** (406)453-4266. **ED** Shirley Penna-Oakes. **LC** CS71; .P133a. **DD** 929/.2/0973. Index available. **Bk Rev. Ad Acc.**

US
PAINTER CLAN, THE. Vol. 1, No. 1 (Summer 1979)-. English. qt. $7.50. James L Douthat, 2504 Kell Road, Signal Mountain TN 37377. **Tel** (615)821-1654. **ED** James L Douthat. **LC** CS71; .P1473. **DD** 929/.2/0973. **UDC** 929.52(73). **Circ:** 100 (ctrl).
Desc: A newsletter for the descendants of Matthias Painter of Wythe county, Virginia.

US/0884-5735
PALATINE IMMIGRANT, THE. **Added/Corp** Palatines to America (Society). (1976)-. Periodical. English. qt (4 issues). $19.00 US; $30.00 Canada and Mexico; $40.00 other (subscription includes membership in the national society and one state chapter, The Palatine Immigrant, The Palatine Patter and newsletter of the state chapter). Palatines to America, Capital University, Box 101, Columbus OH 43209. **Tel** (614)236-8281. **ED** Dr. John Terence Golden, 2609 Summit Street, Columbus, OH 43202-2432; (614)253-5509. **LC** E184.P3; P33. **DD** 929/.1/08931073. **Bk Rev**, (Qty: 80). **Circ:** 2500 (ctrl).
Desc: Articles relating to the life and times of German-speaking immigrants and their European ancestors. Also contains research methods, resources, reviews of current publications, as well as records of members' immigrant ancestors.

US/8755-6014
PALATINE PATTER. **Added/Corp** Palatines to America (Society). (197?)-. Periodical. English. Four times a year. Free to members: $19.00 US; $30.00 Canada & Mexico; $40.00 other. Palatines to America, Capital University, Box 101, Columbus OH 43209. **Tel** (614)236-8281. **LC** E184.P3; P34. **DD** 929/.1/08931073. ***Continues** Palatines to America (Columbus, Ohio).*

US/1047-3173
PAMTECO TRACINGS. (PAMTECO TRACINGS / BEAUFORT COUNTY GENEALOGICAL SOCIETY.). [Pamteco tracings]. **Added/Corp** Beaufort County Genealogical Society. (198?)-. Periodical. English. Twice a year (June and Dec.). $10.00 (individual); $15.00 (family membership). Beaufort County Genealogical Society, PO Box 1089, Washington DC 27889. **ED** Ms. Sybble M. Smithwick. **LC** F262.B37; P35. **DD** 929/.3756186. **Bk Rev. Circ:** 175 (ctrl).
Desc: It contains genealogical information pertaining to Beaufort County, North Carolina surrounding counties.

US/0730-1693
PANOLA STORY, THE. **Added/Corp** Panola County Historical and Genealogical Society. Vol. 1, No. 1 (Jan.-Mar. 1972)-. Periodical. English. qt. $10.00. Panola Historical and Genealogical Society, c/o Mrs Robert Riser, 210 Kyle Street, Batesville MS 38606. **Tel** (601)563-7287. **ED** Robert N. Carlisle (editor's address: 231 Pollard, Batesville, MS 38606). **LC** F347.P2; P36. **DD** 976.2/84/005. **Bk Rev. Circ:** 120.
Desc: Primarily history of Panola County families.
Ind/Abst Genealogical Period. Annu. Index.

BE
PARCHEMIN, LE. **Added/Corp** Office Genealogique et Heraldique de Belgique. No. 1 (April 1936)-. Periodical. French. bm. 1100.00F Belgium; 1600.00F other. Office Genealogique Heraldique Belgique, Parc Cinquantenaire 10, B 1040 Brussels Belgium. **Tel** 011 32 2 7339610. **Ad Acc. Circ:** 2,000.
Desc: Serves as a means of exchanging of data between members. Provides information to assist in studying genealogical history.
Ind/Abst Numis. Lit.

US/0898-5456
PARKER PAPERS. [Parker pap.]. Vol. 1 (Dec. 1985)-. English. ir. $5.50 (add $1.75 postage). Name Game Enterprises, Mrs E Dale Hastin Smith, S 4204 Conklin Street, Spokane WA 99203-6235. **ED** Dale Hastin Smith. **LC** CS71; .P23916. **DD** 929/.2/0973. Index available. **Bk Rev.**
Desc: Includes Parker lineages, queries and miscellaneous information, on every name index.

US/0093-9811
PARROTT TALK. Periodical. English. qt. $5.00. Mrs Evelyn Parrott Scott, Box 446, Sudan TX 79371. **LC** CS71; .P2616. **DD** 929/.2/0973. **UDC** 929.52(73).

CN/0710-5185
PASQUIN, LE. [Pasquin]. V. 13, No. 1 (Jan./Feb./March 1981)-. Periodical. French. qt. $5.00. Le Pasquin, c/o Association des Familles Pasquin, 1400 Boulevard de l'Aeroport, Ancienne-Lorette Quebec G2G 1G6 Canada. **DD** 929/.2/09714. **UDC** 929.52(714). ***Continues** Origine des Familles Paquin au Canada, 0704-0253.*

US
PASSENGER AND IMMIGRATION LISTS BIBLIOGRAPHY, 1538-1900. Bibliography. English. $110.00. Gale Research Inc., 835 Penobscot Building, Detroit MI 48226. **Tel** (800)877-GALE, (313)961-2242, FAX (313)961-6083, telex TWX 810-221-7086. **ED** P William Filby.
Desc: Over 2,500 annotated entries provide essential details on published passenger lists. Researchers will want to make certain to consult these original sources not only for passenger list information, but also other valuable clues to European origin and other crucial bits of genealogical information. Entry numbers for specific lists correspond with source numbers used in the Passenger and Immigration Lists Index.

US/0736-8267
PASSENGER AND IMMIGRATION LISTS INDEX. SUPPLEMENT. [Passeng. immigr. lists index, Suppl.]. **Added/Corp** Gale Research Company. (1982)-. English. an. $177.00. Gale Research Inc., 835 Penobscot Building, Detroit MI 48226. **Tel** (800)877-GALE, (313)961-2242, FAX (313)961-6083, telex TWX 810-221-7086. **ED** P. William Filby and Dorothy M. Lower. **LC** CS68; .P363 Suppl. **DD** 929/.373. Index available.
Desc: Brings together in one alphabetical sequence more than 125,000 immigration citations found in over 185 published passenger and naturalization lists.

US/0888-9163
PASTFINDER. (PASTFINDER : JOURNAL OF THE GENEALOGY GUILD OF THE LA SALLE COUNTY HISTORICAL SOCIETY.). [Pastfinder]. **VFOAT** Past Finder. Periodical. English. sa. $8.00 (included in membership). Genealogy Guild of the La Salle County Historical Society, PO Box 534, Ottawa IL 61350. **DD** 929. **UDC** 929.5(713).

US/0091-6897
PASTFINDER (SAINT JOSEPH, MICH.). (THE PASTFINDER.). [Pastfinder]. **Added/Corp** Genealogical Association of Southwestern Michigan. **VFOAT** Pastfinder Quarterly. Vol. 1 (Feb. 1972)-. Periodical. English. qt. $10.00. Genealogical Association Southwestern Michigan, PO Box 573, St. Joseph MI 49085. **Tel** (616)925-1223. **ED** Norbert Cramer. **LC** F565; .P36. **DD** 929/.3774. **Circ:** 200.
Desc: Association news, "how to" genealogy articles, listings of cemetery, marriage, death records, ancestor charts and queries.
Ind/Abst Genealogical Period. Annu. Index.

US/0882-5912
PATENTS (HADLEY, N.Y.), THE. (THE PATENTS / THE NORTHEASTERN NEW YORK

GENEALOGICAL SOCIETY NEWSLETTER.). [Patents]. **Added/Corp** Northeastern New York Genealogical Society. Vol. 4, No. 2 (March/April 1985)-. Newsletter. English. Six times a year (Jan., Mar., May, July, Sept., Nov.). $10.00. Northeastern New York Genealogical Society, 9 Lyndia Street, C/O Marjorie Sexton, South Glen Falls NY 12801. **Tel** (518)792-0092. **ED** Ton Lynch. **DD** 929. **Circ:** 125. ***Continues*** *Northeastern New York Genealogical Society Newsletter.*
Desc: Consists of 10 pages of cemetary records, vitul records, and any other information valuable to genealogists.

US/0887-8919
PATHWAYS & PASSAGES. (PATHWAYS & PASSAGES : OFFICIAL PUBLICATION OF THE POLISH GENEOLOGICAL SOCIETY OF CONNECTICUT, INC.). **Added/Corp** Polish Genealogical Society of Connecticut. **VFOAT** Pathways and Passages. (198?)-. Periodical. English. sa. $15.00. Polish Genealogical Society - Connecticut, 8 Lyle Road, New Britain CT 06053. **Tel** (203)229-8873. **DD** 929.
Ind/Abst Genealogical Period. Annu. Index.

US/1052-3278
PATTON (TOMS RIVER, N.J.). (PATTON.). [Patton]. **VFOAT** PEL; Patton Exchange Letter. (1989)-. Periodical. English. qt. $15.00. Patton Exchange Letter, 1856 McDade Road, Augusta GA 30906. **Tel** (706)796-7828. **LC** IN PROCESS. **DD** 929. ***Continues*** *Patton Exchange Letter, 0741-0301.*

US/8756-4181
PEA RIVER TRAILS. [Pea River trails]. **Added/Corp** Pea River Historical and Genealogical Society. Vol. 1, No. 1 (Fall 1975)-. Periodical. English. qt. $15.00. Pea River Historical and Genealogical Society, PO Box 628, Enterprise AL 36330. **Tel** (205)393-2901. **ED** Clayton Metcalf. **LC** F332.P37; P4. **DD** 929/.1/0720761483. **Bk Rev**, (Qty: irregularly). **Circ:** 300 (ctrl).
Desc: Varied genealogical and historical data.

US/0736-6442
PECOS TRAILS. ***Title Change. Suspended.*** **Added/Corp** Eddy Co. Genealogical Society (N.M.). V. 1, No. 1 (Jan. 1981)-Vol. 12, No. 2 (1993). English. sa. Eddy County Genealogical Society, PO Box 461, Carlsbad NM 88221. **LC** F802.E2; P42. **DD** 929/.1/072078942.

US/0749-6192
PEDIGREE POINTERS / STEVENS POINT AREA GENEALOGICAL SOCIETY. Periodical. English. qt. $7.00 (single subscriptions), $10.00 (family subscriptions). Stevens Point Area Genealogical Society, Portage County Library, 1325 Church Street, Stevens Point WI 54481. **ED** Donna L Hanson. **LC** F589.S76; P43. **DD** 929/.1/072077553. **UDC** 929.52(775). Index available. cum. index. **Circ:** 125 (ctrl).

US
PEDIGREE SEARCHERS. English. $12.00. Palm Springs Genealogical Society, PO Box 2093, Palm Springs CA 92263. **Tel** (619)325-7875.

US/0736-5594
PELLISSIPPIAN (CLINTON, TENN.). (PELLISSIPPIAN.). [Pellissippian]. **Added/Corp** Pellissippi Genealogical Society. Pellissippi Genealogical and Historical Society (Clinton, Tenn.). Vol. 1, No. 1 (Jan./March 1980)-. Periodical. English. qt (Jan., Apr., July, Oct.). $16.00. Pellissippi Genealogical and Historical Society, 118 Hicks Street, Clinton TN 37716. **Tel** (615)457-1485. **ED** Mary S. Harris. **LC** F442.1; .P44. **DD** 929/.1/0720768. Index available. **Bk Rev**, (Qty: 5). **Circ:** 215 (ctrl).
Desc: Genealogy and historical related topics for Anderson and surrounding counties.
Ind/Abst Genealogical Period. Annu. Index (?-?).

US/8756-811X
PENN PALS. (PENN PALS : NEWSLETTER SPONSORED BY THE PENNSYLVANIA CHAPTER, PALATINES TO AMERICA.). [Penn pals]. Newsletter. English. qt. Free to members. Penn Pals, c/o Mr Gregory Wonders, 341 South Baltimore Street, Dillsburg PA 17019. **DD** 929. **UDC** 929.5(73).

US/0882-3685
PENNSYLVANIA GENEALOGICAL MAGAZINE, THE. [Pa. geneal. mag.]. **Added/Corp** Genealogical Society of Pennsylvania. Vol 16 (Oct. 1948)-. Periodical. English. sa (June, Dec.). $15.00. Genealogical Society of Pennsylvania, 1300 Locust Street, Philadelphia PA 19107. **Tel** (215)545-0391. **ED** Marion Egge. **LC** F146; .G32. **DD** 929.2. Index Available, published separately, free-automatically sent. **Bk Rev. Ad Acc. Circ:** 2,000 (ctrl). ***Continues*** *Publications of the Genealogical Society of Pennsylvania.*
Ind/Abst Genealogical Period. Annu. Index.

US/0148-4036
PENNSYLVANIA MENNONITE HERITAGE. [Pa. Mennon. herit.]. Vol. 1, (Jan. 1978)-. Periodical. English. qt. $20.00 (1 year), $40.00 (2 year), $60.00 (3 year); $25.00 (1 year), $50.00 (2 year), $75.00 (3 year) membership, (includes subscription to both Pennsylvania Mennonite Heritage and Mirror). Lancaster Mennonite Historical Society, 2215 Mill Stream Road, Lancaster PA 17602-1499. **Tel** (717)393-9745. **ED** David J Rempel Smucker. **LC** F160.M45; P46. **DD** 974.8/005. **UDC** 974.8;289.7(09)(748). Index available. cum. index. **Bk Rev. Circ:** 3,000 (ctrl). ***Supersedes*** *Mennonite Research Journal, 0025-9381.*
Desc: Focuses on historical background, religious thought and expression, culture and genealogy of Mennonite and Amish-related groups originating in Pennsylvania, and of European background.
Ind/Abst Am. Hist. Life (1978-); Genealogical Period. Annu. Index.

US/1044-6915
PENNSYLVANIA QUERIES. [Pa. queries]. 1986-. Periodical. English. $6.00. Pioneer Publications, PO Box 397, Black Eagle MT 59414-0397. **Tel** (406)453-4266. **ED** Shirley Penna-Oakes. **DD** 929. Index available. **Bk Rev.**

US/1065-9056
PERIODICAL SOURCE INDEX (FORT WAYNE, IND.). (PERIODICAL SOURCE INDEX / PREPARED BY THE STAFF OF THE ALLEN COUNTY PUBLIC LIBRARY, GENEALOGY DEPARTMENT, FORT WAYNE, INDIANA.). [Periodical source index]. **Added/Corp** Allen County Public Library. Genealogy Dept. **VFOAT** PERSI. (1986)-. Periodical. English. an. $35.00. Allen County Public Library (ACPL), 900 Webster Street, Box 2270, Fort Wayne IN 46801-2270. **Tel** (219)424-7241. **ED** Michael B. Clegg. **LC** CS1; .P47. **DD** 929/.1/016.
Desc: Provides subject access to the wealth of historical and genealogical information published in newsletters, quarterlies, and journals.

US/0898-1574
PERKINS PRESS. [Perkins press]. (1987)-. English. ir. $6.75 (per volume). Jennifer A Perkins Publications, North 5803 Ash, Spokane WA 99205-6807. **Tel** (509)325-5919. **ED** Jennifer Ann Henley Perkins. **DD** 929. Index available. **Bk Rev.** ctrl circ.
Desc: Surname booklet containing records-birth, marriage, military, etc. of Perkins. Branches (lineages) and queries included.

DK/0300-3655
PERSONALHISTORISK TIDSSKRIFT. (PERSONALHISTORISK TIDSSKRIFT, UDGIVET AF SAMFUNDET FOR DANSK GENEALOGI OG PERSONALHISTORIE.). **Added/Corp** Samfundet for Dansk Genealogi og Personalhistorie. (1???)-. Danish. sa (April and November). kr150.00. Samfundet for Dansk Genealogi Og Personalhistorie, Birgit Flemming Larsen, 9000 AAlborg Denmark. **Tel** 011 45 9 66127704. **ED** Tommy Christensen (editor's address: Bulgariensgade 5 St., 2300 Copenhagen S Denmark). Index available. **Bk Rev. Circ:** 1,500 (ctrl).

SW/0031-5699
PERSONHISTORISK TIDSKRIFT. See Biographies.

CN/0828-9735
PERTH COUNTY PROFILES. [Perth Cty. profiles.]. **Added/Corp** Ontario Genealogical Society. Perth County Branch. Vol. 1, No. 1 (Sept. 1983)-. Periodical. English. qt. 22.00Can$. Ontario Genealogical Society / Perth County Branch, PO Box 9, Stratford Ontario N5A 6S8 Canada. **Tel** (416)489-0734. **DD** 929/.1/06071323. Index available. **Circ:** 350.

US/0884-2140
PHELPS COUNTY GENEALOGICAL SOCIETY QUARTERLY. **Added/Corp** Phelps County Genealogical Society (Mo.). Vol. 1, No. 1 (Jan. 1985)-. Periodical. English. qt. $18.00. Phelps County Genealogical Society, Box 571, Rolla MO 65401. **Tel** (314)364-8795, (314)364-4511. **LC** F472.P55; P47. **DD** 929/.1/05. **Bk Rev. Ad Acc. Circ:** 100 (ctrl).
Desc: We publish genealogical information concerning Phelps County, Missouri, and the surrounding area.

US/8755-7029
PIATT COUNTY HISTORICAL AND GENEALOGICAL SOCIETY, THE. (THE PIATT COUNTY HISTORICAL AND GENEALOGICAL SOCIETY : [NEWSLETTER].). [Piatt Cty. Hist. Geneal. Soc.]. **Added/Corp** Piatt County Historical and Genealogical Society. **VFOAT** Newsletter-Quarterly; Newsletter, Quarterly. Vol. 2, No. 4 (1981)-. Periodical. English. qt. Piatt County Historical and Genealogical Society, Box 123, Monticello IL 61856. **LC** F547.P5; N48. **DD** 929/.1/0720773673. **Circ:** 300. ***Continues*** *Quarterly (Piatt County Historical and Genealogical Society), 8755-7010.*

US/0737-7975
PIERRE-FORT - PIERRE GENEALOGICAL SOCIETY, THE. (THE PIERRE-FORT PIERRE GENEALOGICAL SOCIETY : NEWSLETTER.). No. 5 (Sept. 1977)-. Newsletter. English. bm. $5.00. Pierre-Fort Pierre Genealogical Society, Box 925, Pierre SD 57501. **Tel** (605)224-2612. **ED** Joanne Fix. **LC** F659.P6; P53. **DD** 929/.1/072078329. **UDC** 929.5(783). **Bk Rev. Ad Acc. Circ:** 50. ***Continues*** *Pierre-Fort Pierre Genealogical Society Newsletter, 0737-1551.*
Desc: Genealogical newsletter with personal experiences, news items, book reviews, and research helps.

CN/0713-4169
PINARDIERE. (LA PINARDIERE : BULLETIN GENEALOGIQUE DE L'ASSOCIATION LES DESCENDANTS DE LOUIS PINARD, INC..). [Pinardiere]. Vol. 1, No. 1 (1 Jan. 1980)-. Bulletin. French. sa. $2.50 per no. La Pinardiere, c/o Les Descendants de Louis Pinard, 3155 rue Chambois, Trois-Rivieres Quebec G8Y 3M7 Canada. **DD** 929/.2/0971445. **UDC** 929.52(714).

US/1062-7782
PINCKNEY DISTRICT CHAPTER QUARTERLY. (PINCKNEY DISTRICT CHAPTER QUARTERLY : CHEROKEE, SPARTANBURG, UNION COUNTIES / SOUTH CAROLINA GENEALOGICAL SOCIETY.). [Pinckney Dist. Chapter q.]. **Added/Corp** South Carolina Genealogical Society. Pinckney District Chapter. (1991)-. Periodical. English. qt. $13.00. Pinckney District Chapter, South Carolina Genealogical Society, 385 South Spring Street, Spartanburg SC 29301. **DD** 929. ***Continues*** *Pinckney District Chapter Newsletter.*

US/0737-335X
PINON WHISPERS. **Added/Corp** Southeastern Colorado Genealogical Society. Vol. 1, No. 1 (Apr. 1980)-. Periodical. English. qt. $20.00 (includes Southeastern Colorado Genealogical Society membership). Southeastern Colorado Genealogical Society, 2319 Cedar Street, Pueblo CO 81004. **Tel** (719)564-7815. **ED** Betty M. Hanson. **LC** F775; .P55. **DD** 929/.1/0720788. Index available (free). **Bk Rev**, (Qty: 20). **Ad Acc. Circ:** 200.
Desc: Contains census enumeration schedules, cemetery land entries, family histories, marriages, deaths and more.

US
PIONEER BRANCHES. Periodical. English. Four times a year. $12.00. NE Washington Genealogical Society, 195 South Oak Street, Colville Public Library, Colville WA 99114. **Tel** (509)738-6731.
Ind/Abst Genealogical Period. Annu. Index.

US/0739-4101
PIONEER (LAWRENCE, KAN.), THE. (THE PIONEER.). [Pioneer]. Vol. 1, No. 1 (1977)-. Periodical. English. Four times a year (Mar., June, Sept., Dec.). $15.00. Douglas County Kansas Genealogical Society, PO Box 3664, Lawrence KS 66046. **Tel** (913)842-3732. **ED** Donna M. Shogrin. **LC** F687.D7; P56. **DD** 929/.378165. Index available.

US/0736-8208
PIONEER PATHFINDER. (PIONEER PATHFINDER / SIOUX VALLEY GENEALOGICAL SOCIETY.). **Added/Corp** Sioux Valley Genealogical Society. Vol. 1, No. 1 (Sept. 1975)-. English. Four times a year (Jan., Apr., July, Oct.). $10.00. Sioux Valley Genealogical Society, 200 West 6th Street, Sioux Falls SD 57102. **Tel** (605)647-2447. **ED** Dee Krohse. **LC** F657.B5; P56. **DD** 929/.1/07207833. Index available (Bound in 4th iss. in Oct.). **Ad Acc, Adv Mgr:** Dee Krohse, **Tel** 9605)338-3441. **Circ:** 250. available on microfiche; available on microfilm.
Desc: Useful information of interest and to others, who wish to trace their family tree.

US/1043-0458
PIONEER RECORD. [Pioneer rec.]. **Added/Corp** Midland Genealogical Society. Vol. 1, No. 1 (Apr. 1980)-. Periodical. English. Four times a year (Feb., Apr., Sept., Nov.). $4.50. Midland County Historical Society, 1840 West Street Andrews, Dow Library, Midland MI 48640. **ED** Mr. Ora Flaningam. **LC** F572.M6; P56. **DD** 929/.1/06077448. **Circ:** 140.

US/0739-6155
PIONEER TIMES. **Added/Corp** Mid-Missouri Genealogical Society. Vol. 1 (Apr. 1977)-. Periodical. English. qt (4 issues). Comes with Mid-Missouri Genealogical Society membership. Mid-Missouri Genealogical Society, PO Box 715, Jefferson City MO 65102. **LC** F465; .P56. **DD** 929/.1/0720778.

US/0735-309X
PIONEER WAGON, THE. **Added/Corp** Jackson County Genealogical Society (Mo.). Vol. 1, No. 1 (Spring 1980)-. Periodical. English. qt (4 issues). $15.00. Jackson County Genealogical Society / Missouri, PO Box 1133, Independence MO 64051. **Tel** (816)252-8128. **ED** Verna Gail Johnson. **LC** F472.J2; P56. **DD** 929/.377841/05. Index available. **Bk Rev. Circ:** 350 (ctrl).
Desc: Genealogical and historical articles of local and general interest.
Ind/Abst Genealogical Period. Annu. Index.

CU
PIONERO. **Added/Corp** Organizacion de Pioneros Jose Marti. Union de Pioneros de Cuba. (19??)-. Periodical. Spanish. wk. Ediciones Cubanas, Obispo 527, Altos ESQ Bernaza, CP 10100 Havana Cuba. **Tel** 011 632980, 631942, FAX 011 631011, telex 512337, 6540.

CN/1191-1069
PIONNIER (SILLERY). (LE PIONNIER : JOURNAL DE LA FAMILLE CHARRON DIT CABANA.). [Pionnier]. **Added/Corp** Association des Charon dit Cabana. Vol. 1, No 1 (Spring 1991)-. Periodical. French. Three times a year. Free for members. Association des Charon Dit Cabana, A/S la Federation des Familles-Souches Quebecoises, CP 6700, Sillery Quebec G1T 2W2 Canada. **DD** 929/.2/0971.

US
PIPELINE (CAMPBELL, MO.). (THE PIPELINE.). **Added/Corp** Campbell Area Genealogical and Historical Society. (1984)-. Periodical. English. mo. $6.00 membership. Campbell Area Genealogical & Historical Society, PO Box 401, Campbell MO 63933. **Tel** (314)246-2451. **LC** F484.C2; P56. **DD** 929/.1/0720778993. Documents available from Petroleum Abstracts Document Delivery Service.
Ind/Abst Pet. Abstr.

US
PLATTE COUNTY, MISSOURI, HISTORICAL & GENEALOGICAL SOCIETY BULLETIN. **Added/Corp** Platte County Historical Society. **VFOAT** Platte County, Missouri, Historical and Genealogical Society bulletin; Platte County Historical Society Bulletin. Vol. 36, No. 2 (Spring 1983)-. Bulletin. English. qt (Feb., May, Aug., Nov.). $15.00 North America; $17.00 other. Platte County Historical Society, PO Box 103, Platte City MO 64079. **Tel** (816)431-5121. **ED** Betty N. Soper. **LC** F472.P7; P555. **DD** 977.8/135/005. **Bk Rev**, (Qty: 12-16). **Circ:** 800 (ctrl). ***Continues** Platte County Historical & Genealogical Society Bulletin.*
Desc: Provides historical and genealogical information on Platte County, Missouri.

US/0898-5197
PLUM CREEK ALMANAC. [Plum Creek alm.]. **Added/Corp** Genealogical and Historical Society of Caldwell County (Tex.). Vol. 1, No. 1 (Fall 1983)-. English. Twice a year. $15.00 membership. Genealogical and Historical Society of Caldwell County, 215 South Pecan Avenue, Luling TX 78648. **Tel** (512)875-2381. **ED** M. W. Harp, Ph.D. **LC** F392.C2; P58. **DD** 976.4/33/005. Index available. cum. index. **Bk Rev**, (Qty: 6-10). **Ad Acc. Circ:** 500 (ctrl).

US/0271-2644
POLISH FAMILY TREE SURNAMES. V. 1-1975-. English. be. $10.00 US; $11.00 other. Thaddeus J Obal, 739 Hillsdale Avenue, Hillside NJ 07642. **Tel** (201)664-7836. **ED** Thaddeus J Obal. **LC** CS49; .O22A. **DD** 929/.1/02573. **UDC** 929.5(73=84). Index available. **Bk Rev. Circ:** 2,000 (ctrl).
Desc: Primarily a listing of surnames by researchers tracing Polish ancestry. Indexed by surname, by researcher, and geographic location of researcher.

US/0735-9349
POLISH GENEALOGICAL SOCIETY NEWSLETTER. ***Title Change.*** **Added/Corp** Polish Genealogical Society. Vol. 1, No. 1 (Jan. 1979)-(1992). Newsletter. English. sa. Polish Genealogical Society, 984 North Milwaukee Avenue, Chicago IL 60622. **Tel** (312)586-4242. **ED** Edward A. Peckwas. **LC** CS49; .P64. **DD** 929/.1/0899185073. Index available. cum. index. **Bk Rev. Ad Acc. Circ:** 2,000 (ctrl). ***Continued by** Rodziny, 0735-9349.*
Ind/Abst Am. Bibliogr. Slavic East Europ. Stud.; Genealogical Period. Annu. Index.

●US/1062-7855
POLLOCK POTPOURRI. (1992)-. Periodical. English. qt. $10.00 US; $12.50 other. Lineage Search Associates, 6419 Colts Neck Road, Mechanicsville VA 23111. **Tel** (804)730-7414. **ED** Michael E. Pollock. Index available (bound in 4th issue).
Desc: Focuses upon persons of the surname "Pollock" and all variants, including Polk, Paulk, and Pogue, with stress on original records, using predominantly United States sources, but including material (when available) from outside of the United States.

US/0747-6558
POMMERSCHEN LEUTE, DIE. Vol. 1, No. 1 (July, 1982)-. Periodical. English (French). Four times a year (Jan., Apr., July, Oct.). $10.00. Myron Gruenwald, 1260 Westhaven Drive, Oshkosh WI 54904. **Tel** (414)235-7398. **ED** Myron E. Gruenwald. **LC** E184.G3; P66. **DD** 929/.1/08931073. **Circ:** 650.
Desc: Contains articles on genealogy, history, and culture of German Baltic Provence of Pomerania (Pommern).

US
PONTOTOC COUNTY QUARTERLY, OKLAHOMA. **VFOAT** Pontotoc County Quarterly. Periodical. English. qt. $15.00. Pontotoc County Historical & Genealogical Society, 221 West 16th Street, Ada OK 74820. **ED** Patricia A Smith. **LC** F702.P74; O37. **DD** 929/.1/072076669. Index available. **Bk Rev. Circ:** 225 (ctrl). ***Continues** Oklahoma Pontotoc County Quarterly, 0091-1054.*

US
POPE COUNTY HISTORICAL ASSOCIATION QUARTERLY. **See** History(General)-History of North, South, and Central America.

US/0360-9421
POPE FAMILY REGISTER, THE. Periodical. English. qt. $5.00. John Wiley & Sons, Inc., 605 Third Avenue, New York NY 10158-0012. **Tel** (212)850-6000, (212)850-6645, FAX (212)850-6088, telex 12-7063. **(Subscription address:** John Wiley & Sons / England, Baffins Lane, Chichester, West Sussex PO19 1UD England.**) LC** CS71; .P826A. **DD** 929/.2/0973. **UDC** 929.52(410+71+73).
Desc: Contains information about people named Pope in the U.S., Canada, and Great Britain.

US/0882-8687
POPHAM FAMILY NEWSLETTER. [Popham fam. newsl.]. 1st Issue (1983)-. Periodical. English. ir (two or three issues per year). Six issues for $5.00. Popham Family Newsletter, c/o Clarke Popham, 8442 Watervue Way, Blaine WA 98230. **Tel** (206)371-7737. **ED** Clarke Popham. **DD** 929. **Circ:** 300.

US/0739-2478
POWELL PATHS. Vol. 1, No. 1 (Spring 1981)-. Periodical. English. qt. $9.00. Lorraine Cowles Sencevicky, CGRS, 28174 CG-Lorane Road, Cottage Grove OR 97424-9736. **ED** Lorraine C Sencevicky. **LC** CS71; .P88296. **DD** 929/.2/0973. **UDC** 929.52(410+73).
Desc: Genealogical data on Powell, Foster, Harris surname in the U.S., England, Ireland, Scotland, etc. Genealogical data on Foster, Harris surname in Canada.

US
POWESHIEK COUNTY SEARCHER. **Added/Corp** Poweshiek County, Iowa Historical and Genealogical Society. **VFOAT** Poweshiek County Iowa Searcher. (19??)-. Periodical. English. qt. Poweshiek County Historical & Genealogical Society, PO Box 280, Montezuma IA 50171. **LC** F627.P88; P68. **DD** 929/.1/0720777596.
Ind/Abst Genealogical Period. Annu. Index.

US/0032-6623
PRAIRIE GLEANER, THE. [Prairie glean.]. **Added/Corp** st Central Missouri Genealogical Society. West Central Missouri Genealogical Society and Library. Vol. 1 (1969/70)-. Periodical. English. Four times a year (Dec., Mar., June, Sept.,). $12.00. West Central Missouri Genealogical Society and Library Inc., 705 Broad, Warrensburg MD 64093. **Tel** (816)747-6264. **DD** 929. Index available (bound in Dec. issue - $3.00). **Circ:** 400.

US/0197-3037
PRAIRIE ROOTS. V. 1 (Summer 1974)-. Periodical. English. qt. $5.00 nonmembers. Peoria Genealogical Society, PO Box 1489, Peoria IL 61655. **LC** F547.P4; P73. **DD** 929/.377352. **UDC** 929.5(773).
Ind/Abst Genealogical Period. Annu. Index.

US/0892-6131
PRAIRIELAND PIONEER. [Prairieland pioneer]. **Added/Corp** Prairieland Genealogical Society. **VFOAT** Prairie Land Pioneer. Vol. 1, No. 1 (Fall Quarterly, Sept. 8, 1984)-. Periodical. English. Four times a year. $12.00 (includes membership). Prairieland Genealogical Society, Southwest State University, History Center, Marshall MN 56258. **Tel** (507)823-4225. **ED** Gerald Engesser, 687 2nd Street, Tracy, MN 56175 USA; Telephone: (507)629-3750. **DD** 929. Index available (every five years). cum. index. **Bk Rev. Ad Acc. Circ:** 110.
Desc: Contains transactions of public records as a research resource; also stories and articles relating to local history.

US/0740-2805
PRICES OF AMERICA, THE. **VFOAT** Prices of America Exchange. (19??)-. Periodical. English. Armchair Publications, 810 McDonough Road, Hampton GA 30228. **ED** A M de Rossitt. **LC** CS71; .P9455. **DD** 929/.2/0973. ***Continues** Price Family of America, 0740-1736.*

US/1052-1380
PRINCE GEORGE'S COUNTY GENEALOGICAL SOCIETY BULLETIN. [Prince George's Cty. Geneal. Soc. bull.]. **Added/Corp** Prince George's County Genealogical Society. **VFOAT** Prince George's County Genealogical Society Newsletter; Prince George's County Genealogical Society Monthly Bulletin. (July 1970)-. Periodical. English. Ten times a year (except July, Aug.). $12.00. Prince Georges Genealogical Society, PO Box 819, Bowie MD 20718-0819. **Tel** (301)262-7553. **ED** Roberta Pohl (phone: (301)779-1457). **LC** F187.P9; P74. **DD** 929/.1/06075251. Index available. **Bk Rev**, (Qty: 2). **Circ:** 500.
Desc: Contains articles of genealogical interest - Bible records, exchanges, surnames, and wills.
Ind/Abst Genealogical Period. Annu. Index.

US/1040-4430
PROFESSIONAL GENEALOGISTS OF ARKANSAS NEWSLETTER. **Main/Corp** Professional Genealogists of Arkansas. **VFOAT** PGA Newsletter; Professional Genealogists of Arkansas. Vol. 1, No. 1 (Sept. 1988)-. Newsletter. English. Six times a year (Jan., Mar., May, July, Sept., Nov.). $12.00 (Comes with Professional Genealogists of Arkansas membership). Professional Genealogists of Arkansas, PO Box 1807, Conway AR 72032. **Tel** (501)470-1120, FAX (501)470-1120. **ED** Desmond Walls Allen. Index available. **Bk Rev**, (Qty: 20). **Circ:** 700 (ctrl).
Desc: A lot of information exists about how to become a card-carrying Indian. Their information packet describes the process and gives helpful information to those of us attempting to help someone find an a Indian Princess.
Ind/Abst Genealogical Period. Annu. Index.

AT/0725-914X
PROGENITOR. [Progenitor]. (1982)-. Periodical. English. qt (Mar., June, Sept., Dec.). Comes with membership to the Genealogical Society of the Northern Territory. Genealogical Society of the Northern Territory, PO Box 37212, Winnellie NT 5789 Australia. **Tel** 089 321716. **ED** Digger Tomlinson. **DD** 929.10609429. Index available (bound in Dec. issue). **Bk Rev. Ad Acc. Circ:** 275 (ctrl).
Desc: Publication of the Genealogical Society of the Northern Territory.

US
PROSPECTOR (LAS VEGAS, NV). (THE PROSPECTOR / CLARK COUNTY NEVADA GENEALOGICAL SOCIETY.). **Added/Corp** Clark County Nevada Genealogical Society. (19??)-. Periodical. English. qt (Jan., Apr., July, Oct.). $8.50. Clark County Nevada Genealogical Society, PO Box 1929, Las Vegas NV 89125. **Tel** (702)225-5838. **ED** Helen Smith. **LC** F847.C5; P76. **DD** 929/.1/072079313.

FR/0337-6591
PROVENCE GENEALOGIQUE PORT-DE-BOUC. (1973)-. Periodical. French. ir (25-100 times per year). 120.00F France; 150.00F other. Centre Genealogique du Midi Provence, 13110 Port de Bouc France. **UDC** 92.

UK
PUBLICATIONS OF THE HARLEIAN SOCIETY. NEW SERIES, THE. (1979)-. Periodical. English. an. £20.00 individuals; £35.00 institutions. Harleian Society, College of Arms, Queen Victoria Street, London EC4V 4BT England. **Tel** 071-248 0911. **Circ:** 350 (ctrl). Documents available from BLDSC.

UK
PUBLICATIONS / SURREY RECORD SOCIETY. **Added/Corp** Surrey Record Society. Vol. 1 (1914)-. Monographic series. English. ir. Price varies per volume. The Surrey Record Society, 211 Borough High, London SE1 1JA England. **Tel** 011 81 541 8800. **(Subscription address:** Surrey Record Society Office, County Hall Penrhyn Road, Kingston Thame KT1 2DN England.**) LC** CS435; .S87.

UK/0261-118X
PULVERTAFT PAPERS. Vol. 1, No. 1 (Dec. 1981)-. Newsletter. English. sa. £1.00 UK; £5.00 US. Captain D.M. Pulvertaft, Royal Navy Tucketts, Trusham Newton Abbot, Devon TQ13 ONR England. **ED** D.M. Pulvertaft. **LC** CS439; .P9316. **DD** 929/.2/0941. Index available. cum. index. **Circ:** 60 (ctrl).
Desc: A family history newsletter of the Pulvertaft families.

US/0899-1332
QUAKER QUERIES. [Quaker queries]. Issue No. 1 (1986)-. Periodical. English. ir. $5.00 (single issue). Ruby Simonson McNeil, PO Box 779, Napavine WA 98565. **Tel** (509)922-4521. **ED** Ruby Simonson McNeill. **LC** E184.F89; Q28. **DD** 929/.1/088286.
Ind/Abst Genealogical Period. Annu. Index.

US/0737-8246
QUAKER YEOMEN, THE. [Quaker yeom.]. Vol. 1, No. 1 (Apr. 1974)-. Periodical. English. Four times a year. $17.00 US; $22.00 other. James E. Bellarts RG, CG, FACG, 2330 SE Brookwood Avenue, Suite 108, Hillsboro OR 97123. **ED** James E. Bellarts. **LC** E184.F89; Q3. **DD** 929/.1/088286. cum. index. **Bk Rev. Pr Rev.** ctrl circ.
Ind/Abst Genealogical Period. Annu. Index.

US
QUARTERLY. **Added/Corp** Barton County Genealogical Society. (199?)-. Periodical. English. Four times a year. $12.50. Barton County Genealogical Society, PO Box 425, Great Bend KS 67530. **Tel** (316)793-7182. **LC** F687.B2; N49. **DD** 929/.378152/05. ***Continues** Barton County Genealogical Society Quarterly.*

US
QUARTERLY. **Main/Corp** Blackhawk Genealogical Society. Vol. 1 (Mar. 1974)-. Periodical. English. qt. Free to memebers; $10.00 membership fee. Blackhawk Genealogical Society, PO Box 3912, Rock Island IL 61204. **Tel** (309)786-5927.

US/1056-6732
QUARTERLY - ASSOCIATION OF PROFESSIONAL GENEALOGISTS (U.S.). (QUARTERLY / APG, ASSOCIATION OF PROFESSIONAL GENEALOGISTS.). [Q. - Assoc. Prof.

Geneal. (U. S.)]. **Added/Corp** Association of Professional Genealogists (U.S.). **VFOAT** Association of Professional Genealogists Quarterly; APGQ. (1991)-. English. Four times a year (Mar., June, Sept., Dec.). $35.00. Association Professional Genealogists, 4321 M Street Northwest, Suite 236, Washington DC 20007. **Tel** (703)920-2385, (504)766-3018. **ED** Sharon Carmack, (editor's address: PO Box 338, Simka, CO 80835-0338, phone: (719)541-2739). **DD** 929. **Bk Rev. Ad Acc, Adv Mgr:** S. McVetty, **Tel** (516)997-4757. **Circ:** 770. ***Continues*** *APG Quarterly, 0890-3816.*

US/0735-6730
QUARTERLY / BOULDER GENEALOGICAL SOCIETY. [Q. - Boulder Geneal. Soc.]. **Added/Corp** Boulder Genealogical Society. Vol. 1, No. 1 (Aug. 1969)-. Periodical. English. qt. $12.00. Boulder Genealogical Society, PO Box 3246, Boulder CO 80307. **Tel** (303)443-9466. **ED** L T Ostwald. **LC** F784.B66; Q37. **DD** 929/.3788. Index available. **Circ:** 270 (ctrl).
Desc: Society journal for members and exchange, containing genealogical and related historical data, genealogical research how-to articles, emphasizing Colorado and Boulder county.
Ind/Abst Genealogical Period. Annu. Index.

US/0738-8209
QUARTERLY / CENTRAL GEORGIA GENEALOGICAL SOCIETY, INC.
Added/Corp Central Georgia Genealogial Society. Vol. 4, No. 1 (Mar. 1982)-. Periodical. English. qt. Free to members; $20.00 membership fee. Central Georgia Genealogical Society, PO Box 2024, Warner Robins GA 31099. **Tel** (912)953-3114. **ED** William R. Henry (912)923-7662. **LC** F285; .Q3. **DD** 929/.1/0720758. cum. index (4th issue). **Bk Rev**, (Qty: 10). **Circ:** 400 (ctrl). ***Continues*** *Central Georgia Genealogical Society Quarterly, 0738-8195.*
Desc: Provides abstracts, cemetery records, family history, obituaries, special projects, queries, research, pedigrees, book reviews, and general interest articles.

US/1056-8875
QUARTERLY / DUTCH FAMILY HERITAGE SOCIETY. [Q. - (Dutch Fam. Herit. Soc.)]. **Added/Corp** Dutch Family Heritage Society. **VFOAT** DFHS. Vol. 3, No. 2 (2nd Quarter 1989)-. Periodical. English. qt. $20.00. Dutch Family Heritage Society, 2463 Ledgewood Drive, West Jordan UT 84084. **Tel** (801)967-8400. **LC** E184.D9; N49. **DD** 929/.1/0893931073. ***Continues*** *Newsletter (Dutch Family Heritage Society), 1056-8867.*
Ind/Abst Genealogical Period. Annu. Index.

US/0895-4755
QUARTERLY - OLDE MECKLENBURG GENEALOGICAL SOCIETY (N.C.). (QUARTERLY / OLDE MECKLENBURG GENEALOGICAL SOCIETY.). [Q. - Olde Mecklenbg. Geneal. Soc. (N. C.)]. **Added/Corp** Olde Mecklenburg Genealogical Society (N.C.). Vol. 3, No. 4 (Winter 1985)-. Periodical. English. qt. comes with membership. Olde Mecklenburg Genealogical Society, PO Box 32453, Charlotte NC 28232. **LC** F262.M4; Q37. **DD** 929/.1/072075676. ***Continues*** *Quarterly (Mecklenburg (NC) Genealogical Society), 0740-8951.*

US
QUARTERLY / OLYMPIA GENEALOGICAL SOCIETY. Added/Corp Olympia Genealogical Society. (19??)-. Periodical. English. qt. Comes with the Olympia Genealogical Society membership ($10.00). Olympia Genealogical Society, PO Box 1313, Olympia WA 98507. **Tel** (206)754-6508. **ED** Jan Smith. **LC** F897.T5; Q37. **DD** 929/.1/072079779. Index available. cum. index. **Bk Rev. Circ:** 250 (ctrl).
Ind/Abst Genealogical Period. Annu. Index.

US/0030-4263
QUARTERLY - ORANGE COUNTY CALIFORNIA GENEALOGICAL SOCIETY. Main/Corp Orange County California Genealogical Society. Vol. 1 (Dec. 1964)-. Periodical. English. qt. $15.00 (non-members), $12.00 (members). Orange County California, Box 1587, Orange CA 92668. **Tel** (213)624-5700 ext. 2576. **ED** Robert E Brasher Jr (Editor's address: 6855 Driscoll Street Long Beach, CA 90815). **LC** CS1; .O7. **DD** 929.1/05. Index available. cum. index. **Bk Rev**, (Qty: 12-20). **Ad Acc, Adv Mgr:** same as editor. **Circ:** 400+ (ctrl).
Desc: Family genealogies, Bible records, book reviews, queries, old letters, vital statistics, census records, county records, cemetery records, on Orange county California genealogy and local history. Also articles on California, Western, and back East. Articles are solicited.

US/0738-1891
QUARTERLY / OREGON GENEALOGICAL SOCIETY. VFOAT O.G.S.; OAS. Vol. 21, No. 1 (Fall 1982)-. Periodical. English. Four times a year. $18.00. Oregon Genealogical Society, PO Box 10306, Eugene Or 97440-2306. **Tel** (503)341-4122. **ED** Shari Shuster. **LC** F875; .O74a. **DD** 929/.1/0720795. Index available. **Bk Rev**, (Qty: 12-16). **Ad Acc.** ***Continues*** *Oregon Genealogical Society. Bulletin, 0738-1883.*
Desc: Publishes pedigree charts of members, Oregon pioneer listings, cemetery records, marriages, births, deaths, free queries.
Ind/Abst Genealogical Period. Annu. Index.

US/0739-8840
QUARTERLY REVIEW OF THE EASTERN NORTH CAROLINA GENEALOGICAL SOCIETY, THE. ***Ceased.*** **Added/Corp** Eastern North Carolina Genealogical Society. Vol. 1 (Jan. 1974)-(Dec. 1988). Periodical. English. qt. Eastern North Carolina Genealogical Society, PO Box 395, New Bern NC 28560. **LC** F253; .Q33. **DD** 929/.1/0720756. cum. index.

US/0036-2956
QUARTERLY - ST. LOUIS GENEALOGICAL SOCIETY. (QUARTERLY / ST. LOUIS GENEALOGICAL SOCIETY.). [Q. - St. Louis Geneal. Soc.]. **Added/Corp** St. Louis Genealogical Society. Vol. 1, No. 1 (March 1968)-. Periodical. English. qt. comes with membership. St. Louis Genealogical Society, 9011 Manchester Road, Suite 3, St. Louis MO 63144. **Tel** (314)968-2763. **LC** F474.S253; Q37. **DD** 929/.1/072077865. available on microfilm.

AT/0811-3394
QUEENSLAND FAMILY HISTORIAN : JOURNAL OF THE QUEENSLAND FAMILY HISTORY SOCIETY, INC.
Main/Corp Queensland Family History Society. Vol. 4 (1983)-. Periodical. English. Four times a year (Feb., May, Aug., Nov.). 15.00Aus$. Queensland Family History Society, PO Box 171 Indooroopilly, Brisbane Queensland 4068 Australia. **Tel** 011 61 7 276 7135. **ED** Dawn Montgomery. **LC** WMLC 93/1739. Index available. **Bk Rev**, (Qty: 10-15). **Ad Acc. Circ:** 1,200 (ctrl). ***Continues*** *Q.F.H.S. Newsletter.*
Desc: Encourages the preservation of historical records, to acquire and maintain a reference and research library and to collect and preserve material bearing on the families of the people of Queensland.
Ind/Abst Genealogical Period. Annu. Index.

US
RABBIT TRACKS. English. $10.00. Conejo Valley Genealogical Society, PO Box 1228, Thousand Oaks CA 91358. **Tel** (805)492-6004.
Ind/Abst Genealogical Period. Annu. Index.

US/0893-4525
RACONTEUR (BATON ROUGE, LA. ANNUAL ED.), LE. (LE RACONTEUR.). [Raconteur]. **Added/Corp** Comite des Archives de la Louisiane. (19??)-. English. Three times a year (Apr., Aug., Dec.). $10.00 one year; $15.00 other. Le Comite Archives Louisiane, PO Box 44370, 2576 Bartlett, Baton Rouge LA 70805. **Tel** (504)355-9906. **ED** Judy Riffel. **LC** F369; .R33. **DD** 976.3/005. Index available. **Bk Rev**, (Qty: 6-10). **Circ:** 200.
Desc: Genealogical, historical, archival records primarily relating to Louisiana and the American South.

US/8756-9132
RAILSBACK LINES. [Railsback lines]. April 1984-. English. President Dorothy J Cox, Route 1 Box 222, Reagan TX 76680. **LC** CS71; .R15516. **DD** 929/.2/0973. **UDC** 929.52(73). ***Continues*** *Newsletter (Railsback Descendants Association), 8756-9140.*

US/0734-2055
RAINEY TIMES. Vol. 1, No. 1 (July 1981)-. Periodical. English. an. $20.00. Marynell Bryant Editor, Route 4 Box 56, Sulphur Springs TX 75482. **Tel** (214)885-3523. **ED** Marynell Bryant. **LC** CS71; .R1567. **DD** 929/.2/0973. **UDC** 929.52(73). Index available. **Circ:** 350 (ctrl).
Desc: Surname publication for Rainey, Raney, Rain, Rains, Ranney and all spellings, census, histories, court records and much more on family lines, write for details.
Ind/Abst Genealogical Period. Annu. Index (?-?).

US/0737-7711
RATHBUN, RATHBONE, RATHBURN FAMILY HISTORIAN. VFOAT Family Historian; Rathbun-Rathbone-Rathburn Family Historian. Vol. 1, No. 1 (Jan. 1981)-. Periodical. English. qt. $15.00. Rathbun Family Association, 11308 Popes Head Road, Fairfax VA 22030. **Tel** (703)278-8512. **ED** Frank H Rathbun. **LC** CS71; .R233917. **DD** 929/.2/0973. **UDC** 929.52(73). Index available. **Circ:** 580 (ctrl).
Desc: History and genealogy of the Rathbun-Rathburn-Rathbone family in America.

US/1057-185X
RCGS NEWSLETTER. (RCGS NEWSLETTER / ROSS COUNTY GENEALOGICAL SOCIETY.). (19??)-. Newsletter. English. Free to members. Ross County Genealogical Society, PO Box 6352, Chillicothe OH 45601. **Tel** (614)773-2715. **LC** IN PROCESS. ***Continues*** *Ross County Genealogical Society. Newsletter, 0740-4395.*
Ind/Abst Genealogical Period. Annu. Index.

US/1055-2863
RECORD OF WILLS : SURROGATES COURT. STATEN ISLAND, NEW YORK. English. $12.00 (add $2.50 postage). New Game Enterprises, South 4204 Conklin Street, Spokane WA 99203-6235. **Tel** 1-509-747-4903. **ED** Dale Hastin Smith. Index available.
Desc: Transcription of wills from the will books.

US/0890-2968
REDWOOD RESEARCHER. [Redw. res.]. **Added/Corp** Redwood Genealogical Society. **VFOAT** Redwood Researcher, Inc. (Aug. 1968)-. Periodical. English. Four times a year (Feb., May, Aug., Nov.). $12.00. Redwood Genealogical Society, PO Box 645, Fortuna CA 95540. **Tel** (707)725-5583. **ED** Patricia Madsen (editor's address: 620 8th Stree, Fortuna, CA 95540, phone: (707)725-4573). **LC** CS42; .R36. **DD** 929/.1/05. Index Bound in First Issue. **Bk Rev. Circ:** 230.
Desc: Genealogical records of members, any or all of Humboldt County, CA. Listing includes records, statistics, census, school records and many more.
Ind/Abst Genealogical Period. Annu. Index.

US/0732-488X
REFLECTIONS (CORPUS CHRISTI, TEX.). (REFLECTIONS / COASTAL BEND GENEALOGICAL SOCIETY.). **Added/Corp** Coastal Bend Genealogical Society. (19??)-. Periodical. English. Four times a year (Mar., June, Sept., Dec.). $15.00. Coastal Bend Genealogical Society, PO Box 2711, Corpus Christi TX 78403. **Tel** (512)880-7032. **ED** Allen David, (phone: (512)368-7606). **LC** F385; .R43. **DD** 929/.1/07207641. Index available. cum. index (annually). **Bk Rev. Circ:** 300. ***Continues*** *Register (Corpus Christi, Tex.).*
Desc: Covers news of seventeen counties in the Coastal Bend region of Texas.

US/0484-2685
REFLECTOR (AMARILLO, TEX.), THE. (THE REFLECTOR.). **Added/Corp** Amarillo Genealogical Society. (19??)-. Periodical. English. Four times a year (Mar., June, Sept., Dec.). $10.00. Amarillo Genealogical Society, PO Box 2171, Amarillo TX 79189. **Tel** (806)378-3050. **ED** Beverly Wilkerson. **LC** F394.A4; R43. **DD** 929/.1/0720764825. Index available (Bound in 4th iss., in Dec.). **Bk Rev. Circ:** 1,000. ***Continues*** *Bulletin (Amarillo Genealogical Society).*
Desc: Genealogical and local history of Texas and the Southwest.
Ind/Abst Genealogical Period. Annu. Index.

CN/1185-4235
REGISTER OF CANADIAN HONOURS, THE. [Regist. Can. honours]. **VFOAT** Registre des Distinctions Honorifiques Canadiennes. (1991)-. English (French). $65.00, $185.00 (deluxe ed.). Canadian Almanac and Directory Publishing Co., 2775 Matheson Boulevard East, Mississauga Ontario L4W 9Z9 Canada. **Tel** (905)238-6074. **DD** 929.8/171/025.

CN/1185-4235
REGISTER OF CANADIAN HONOURS, THE. [Regist. Can. honours]. **VFOAT** Registre des Ddistinctions Honorifiques Canadiennes. (1991)-. French (English). 65.00Can$, 185.00Can$ deluxe edition. Canadian Almanac and Directory Publishing Co., 2775 Matheson Boulevard East, Mississauga Ontario L4W 9Z9 Canada. **Tel** (905)238-6074. **DD** 929.8/171/025.

US/0747-5624
RELATIVELY SEEKING. (RELATIVELY SEEKING / CHEROKEE COUNTY GENEALOGICAL SOCIETY OF SOUTHEAST KANSAS.). **Added/Corp** Cherokee County Genealogical Society of Southeast Kansas. (19??)-. Periodical. English. sa (Mar., Oct.). $10.00. Cherokee County Kansas Genealogical-Historical Society Inc., PO Box 33, Columbus KS 66725-0033. **Tel** (316)429-2992. **ED** Clione Bieber. **LC** F687.C38; R44. **DD** 929/.1/072078199. Index available (bound in each issue). cum. index. **Circ:** 125. available on microfilm.
Desc: Records and history of Cherokee County Kansas. Marriages, deaths, land records, census and other genealogical information. Free queries published for subscribers.

CN/0701-8878
RELATIVELY SPEAKING (EDMONTON). (RELATIVELY SPEAKING.). [Relat. speak.]. **Added/Corp** Alberta Genealogical Society. (1972)-. Periodical. English. qt. 22.00Can$. Alberta Genealogical Society, PO Box 12015, Fort McMurray BR, Alberta T9H 4W1 Canada. **Tel** (403)791-2913, telex KS4337. **ED** Judy Bradley. **LC** CS80; .R44. **DD** 929/.1/072071. Index available. **Bk Rev. Circ:** 800 (ctrl).
Desc: Articles of genealogical interest, family histories, cemetery recordings, book reviews, library holdings, and members interests.

US/0738-5889
REMAINS TO BE FOUND. (REMAINS TO BE FOUND : SPECIAL PUBLICATION OF GREATER OMAHA GENEALOGICAL SOCIETY.). **Added/Corp** Greater Omaha Genealogical Society. (19??)-. Periodical. English. Twice a year. $20.00 (family), $15.00 (individuals and institutions). Greater Omaha Genealogical Society, PO Box 4011, Omaha NE 68104. **Tel** (402)296-3414. **ED**

Sandy Faust. **LC** F674.O553; A26. **DD** 929/.3782254. Index available. cum. index. **Ad Acc. Circ:** 300 (ctrl).
Desc: Genealogical records of Douglas, Cass, Sarpy Counties, Nebraska and Pottawattamie County Iowa. Includes church, marriage, birth, death and the Bible. Newsletter contains book reviews, queries and research charts.

US
REPORT / THE OHIO GENEALOGICAL SOCIETY. **Added/Corp** Ohio Genealogical Society. **VFOAT** Ohio Genealogical Society Report. Vol. 9, No. 3 (1969)-. Periodical. English. qt. $25.00 US; $33.00 other. Ohio Genealogical Society / Mansfield Ohio Chapter, 34 Sturges Avenue, PO Box 2625, Mansfield OH 44906. **Tel** (419)522-9077. **ED** Carol Willsey Bell. Index available. cum. index. **Bk Rev. Ad Acc. Circ:** 6.
Desc: Genealogical queries, articles on cemeteries, count abstracts, announcements, and legal news.

US/0884-3716
RESEARCH NEWS - FAMILY HISTORY WORLD. ***Ceased.*** (RESEARCH NEWS.). [Res. news - Fam. Hist. World]. Vol. 1, No. 1 (March 1982)-Ceased with December (1990). Periodical. English. qt. Family History World, Box 22045, Salt Lake City UT 84122. **Tel** (801)251-6174. **ED** Arlene H Eakle. **DD** 929. **Bk Rev. Ad Acc. Circ:** 10,000.
Desc: Contains new sources for genealogy research, published and unpublished indexes, book reviews, and professional techniques.
Ind/Abst Biol. Dig.; Genealogical Period. Annu. Index.

US
RESEARCH PAPERS : SERIES C - THE GENEALOGICAL DEPARTMENT OF THE CHURCH OF JESUS CHRIST OF LATTER-DAY SAINTS. **Main/Corp** Church of Jesus Christ of Latter-Day Saints. Genealogical Dept. Monographic series. English. Price varies per volume. The Church of Jesus Christ of Latter-Day Saints, Genealogical Department, 50 East North Temple Street, Salt Lake City UT 84150. **LC** CS1; .G383. **DD** 929/.3. ***Continues*** *Genealogical Society of The Church of Jesus Christ of Latter-Day Saints. Research Paper: Series C.*

US/8756-9817
RESEARCHIN' OUACHITA-CALHOUN COUNTIES, AR. [Res. Ouachita-Calhoun Cties. Ark.]. **Added/Corp** Ouachita-Calhoun Genealogical Society. **VFOAT** Researchin' Ouachita Calhoun Counties, AR. Vol. 1, No. 1 (Mar. 1981)-. English. sa. Free to members of the Ouachita Calhoun Genealogical Society. Ouachita-Calhoun Genealogical Society, PO Box 2092, Camden AR 71701. **Tel** (501)836-6575. **LC** F417.O75; R47. **DD** 929/.1/072076764.

US/1046-5235
REUNIONS (MILWAUKEE, WIS.). (REUNIONS.). [Reunions]. **VFOAT** Reunions, The Magazine. (1990)-. Periodical. English. qt. $24.00. Reunions Inc., PO Box 11727, Milwaukee WI 53211. **Tel** (414)263-4567, FAX (414)263-6331. **ED** Carol Burns. **DD** 390. **Bk Rev. Ad Acc, Adv Mgr:** Lynn Ryan, **Tel** same as publisher. **Circ:** 4,000.
Desc: For people who are planning and/or searching for reunions; including class/school and military. Beginning genealogy and parent searches for adopted individuals, too.

RM/0034-7043
REVISTA ARHIVELOR. **See** Genealogy and Heraldry-Archives.

US
REVISTA. CUBAN GENEALOGICAL SOCIETY. (19??)-. Periodical. English. Four times a year (Jan., Apr., July, Oct.). $20.00 US; $28.00 other. Cuban Genealogical Society, PO Box 2650, Salt Lake City UT 84110. **Tel** (801)968-7312. **ED** Mayra F. Sanchez-Johnson, (editor's address: 2552 Tamra Drive West, Jordan, UT 84084). Index available (Bound in issue (Oct.)). cum. index. **Circ:** 100 (ctrl).
Desc: News and information on families and historical articles in Cuba.

AG
REVISTA DEL CENTRO DE ESTUDIOS GENEALOGICOS DE BUENOS AIRES. **Main/Corp** Centro de Estudios Genealogicos de Buenos Aires. Vol. 1-. Periodical. Spanish. Centro de Estudios Genealogicos de Buenos Aires, Calle Vicente Lopez 1835 2 Piso A, 1018 Buenos Aires Argentina. **LC** CS288.B84; C45A. **DD** 929/.1/0982. **UDC** 929.5(82).

EC
REVISTA DEL CENTRO NACIONAL DE INVESTIGACIONES GENEALOGICAS Y ANTROPOLOGICAS. SECCION GENEALOGIA. **VFOAT** Genealogia. 1 (March 1981)-. Periodical. Spanish. Three times a year. 300. Centro Nacional de Investigaciones Generalogicas y Antropologicas, Apartado 135-B, Quite Ecuador. **LC** CS339.A2; R48. **DD** 929/.1/0720866. **UDC** 929.5(86).

US/8755-3384
REVISTA DEL INSTITUTO GENEALOGICO E HISTORICO LATINOAMERICANO. [Rev. Inst. geneal. hist. latinoam.]. **Added/Corp** Instituto Genealogico e Historico Latino Americano (Highland, Utah). (1982)-. Periodical. English (Spanish). qt. $20.00. Instituto Genealogico e Historico Latino Americano, PO Box 169, Fairview UT 84629. **DD** 929.

BL
REVISTA DO INSTITUTO GENEALOGICO BRASILEIRO. **Main/Corp** Instituto Genealogico Brasileiro. Yearly V. 1- May 1979-. Periodical. Portuguese. Instituto Genealogico Brasileiro, rua Cons Crispiniano 105 60 A CJ 62, CEP 01037 Sao Paulo Brazil. **LC** CS300; .I58A. **DD** 929/.1/0981. **UDC** 929.5(81).

FR
REVUE INTERNATIONALE D'ONOMASTIQUE. ***Ceased.*** Vol. 1 (Mar./June 1949)-Ceased ?. French. an. Editions d'Artrey, 17 rue de la Rochefoucauld, 75009 Paris France. **LC** CS2300. **DD** 929.405. **UDC** 929.53. ***Supersedes*** *Onomastica.*

US/1057-6010
REYNOLDS RECORDS. (REYNOLDS RECORDS : A NEWSLETTER FOR ALL REYNOLDS RESEARCHERS.). [Reynolds rec.]. Vol. 1, No. 1 (Jan. 1991)-. Newsletter. English. qt. Kinseeker Publications, Box 184, Grawn MI 49637. **LC** CS71; .R4637. **DD** 929/.2/0973.

US/0190-3055
RHODE ISLAND GENEALOGICAL REGISTER. Vol. 1 (July 1978)-. Periodical. English. Four times a year. Alden G. Beaman, PO Box 585, East Princeton MA 01517. **Tel** (617)464-5588. **LC** F78; .R53. **DD** 929/.3745.

US/0893-181X
RHODE ISLAND QUERIES. [R.I. queries]. (1987)-. Periodical. English. ir. $5.00. Bette Butcher Topp, West 1304 Cliffwood Court, Spokane WA 99218. **Tel** (509)467-2299. **ED** Bette Butcher Topp. **DD** 929. Index available. **Bk Rev.** ctrl circ.

US/0730-1235
RHODE ISLAND ROOTS. **Added/Corp** Rhode Island Genealogical Society. Vol. 7, No. 1 (Mar. 1981)-. Periodical. English. Four times a year. $12.00. Rhode Island Genealogical Society, 41 Merrimac Road, North Smithfield RI 02895. **Tel** (401)769-8174. **ED** Jane Fletcher Fiske. **LC** F78; .R2. **DD** 929/.1/0720745. Index available. cum. index. **Bk Rev. Circ:** 800 (ctrl). ***Continues*** *R.I. Roots, 0277-1888.*
Desc: Rhode Island subjects; 17th, 18th, 19th century, tax lists, census, early settlers, Bible records and reviews.
Ind/Abst Genealogical Period. Annu. Index.

US
RICE COUNTY HISTORIAN. English. qt. $15.00. Rice County Historical Society, 1814 NW 2nd Ave, Faribault MN 55021. **Tel** (507)332-2121.

US/0147-2488
RICHARDSON FAMILY RESEARCHER AND HISTORICAL NEWS. **Added/Corp** Richardson Heritage Society. **VFOAT** Richardson Family Researcher & Historical News. Vol. 1, No. 1 (Jan. 1975)-. Periodical. English. Four times a year. $7.50. Richardson Heritage Society, PO Box 123, 944 South G Street, Broken Bow NE 68822. **Tel** (308)872-2167. **ED** Harry M. Richardson. **LC** CS71; .R5197. **DD** 929/.2/0973. cum. index. **Ad Acc. Circ:** 600-700. ***Absorbed*** *Moore Family Inquirer.*

US/1058-0263
RICKEY ROOTS & REVELS. [Rickey roots revels]. **VFOAT** Rickey Roots and Revels. No. 1 (Spring 1990)-. Periodical. English. qt. DuMont Buchverlag GmbH & Co. KG, Postfach 100468, D 50441 Cologne Germany. **Tel** 011 49 221 20530. **ED** Stanton M. Rickey. **DD** 929.

US/0737-6758
RIDDELL, RIDDLE, RUDDELL TRAIL, THE. **VFOAT** Riddle, Reddell, Ruddle Trail; Riddel, Reddell, Riddle, Ruddle Trail. Vol. 1, No. 1 (Jan.-Mar. 1974)-. Periodical. English. qt. cost on request only. Nettie Lee Benson, 2834 Shoal Crest, Austin TX 78705. **Tel** (512)472-2735. **ED** Nettie Lee Benson. **LC** CS71; .R54293. **DD** 929/.2/0973. **UDC** 929.52(73). Index available. **Bk Rev. Circ:** 300 (ctrl).
Desc: Traces descendants of this surname in the United States from 1607 to present based on censuses, Bible and family records, historical sources, memoirs and personal accounts.

US/0093-6987
RIDGE RUNNERS, THE. Periodical. English. qt. $3.00. W A Yates, PO Box 237, Ozark MO 65721-0237. **LC** CS42; .R5. **DD** 929/.1/0973.

US/8756-3819
RINGGOLD ROOTS. (RINGGOLD ROOTS / RINGGOLD COUNTY GENEALOGICAL SOCIETY.). [Ringgold roots]. **Main/Corp** Ringgold County Genealogical Society. Vol. 1 (Oct. 1979)-. English. qt. $4.00 membership. Ringgold Roots, 204 West Jefferson, Mount Ayr IA 50854. **LC** F627.R5; R56A. **DD** 929/.1/07220777873.

US/8756-0798
RIVER COUNTIES, THE. ***Suspended.*** [River cties.]. Vol. 1, Jan. (1972)-?. English. an. $10.00. Jill Garrett, 610 Terrace Drive, Columbia TN 38401. **LC** F435; .R56. **DD** 929/.3768.

CN/1180-5714
ROAMING ROOTS. (ROAMING ROOTS : A KENT FAMILY HISTORY.). [Roam. roots]. Vol. 1, No. 1 (Oct. 1990)-. Periodical. English. qt. $10.00 per year. Roaming Roots, Unit 818700 Dyness Road, Burlington, Ontario L7N 3M2 Canada. **DD** 929/.2/09422305.

US/8756-7741
ROBERTS REGISTOR. [Roberts reg.]. Vol. 1, No. 1 (Nov. 1982)-. Periodical. English. Three times a year. $10.00. Roma Publishing, 5560 Gibson Road, Vicksburg MS 39180. **Tel** (601)638-6334. **ED** Maxine Roberts. **DD** 929. **Bk Rev. Ad Acc. Circ:** 450 (ctrl).
Desc: Clearinghouse for genealogical data on all families named 'Roberts.'

US/0898-5448
ROBERTSON REPORT. [Robertson rep.]. Vol. 1 (July 1984)-. English. ir. $5.50 (add $1.75 postage). Name Game Enterprises, Mrs E Dale Hastin Smith, S 4204 Conklin Street, Spokane WA 99203-6235. **ED** E Dale Hastin Smith. **DD** 929.
Desc: Contains Robertson related lineages, miscellaneous information, queries and book reviews.

US/0888-3807
ROBESON COUNTY REGISTER, THE. Vol. 1, No. 1 (Feb. 1986)-. Periodical. English. Four times a year (Feb., May, Aug., Nov.). $25.00. The Robeson County Register, 1012 South Kings Drive, Doctors Building, Suite 901, Charlotte NC 28283. **Tel** (704)333-1443. **ED** Morris F. Britt. **Bk Rev. Ad Acc. Circ:** 100 (ctrl).

US/8755-3589
ROBINSON/ROBISON RESEARCHER, THE. **VFOAT** Robinson Robison Researcher; R./R./R.; R/R/R. Vol. 1, No. 1 (July/Aug./Sept. Quarter 1982)-. Periodical. English. qt. $7.00. Karen Robison, PO Box 661, Waynesville OH 45068. **LC** CS71; .R6597. **DD** 929/.2/0973.

●PL/0735-9349
RODZINY : THE JOURNAL OF THE POLISH GENEALOGICAL SOCIETY OF AMERICA. **Added/Corp** Polish Genealogical Society of America. Vol. 16, No. 1 (May 1993)-. Periodical. Polish. Twice a year (Jan., & June). $20.00 Comes with Polish Genealogical Society membership. Polish Genealogical Society, 984 North Milwaukee Avenue, Chicago IL 60622. **Tel** (312)586-4242. **LC** CS49; .P64. **DD** 929/.1/0899185073. ***Continues*** *Polish Genealogical Society Newsletter, 0735-9349.*

US/0048-8534
ROGUE DIGGER. **Added/Corp** Rogue Valley Genealogical Society. Vol. 6, No. 2 (Summer 1971)-. Periodical. English. qt. $20.00. Rogue Valley Genealogical Society, 133 South Central Avenue, Medford OR 97501. **Tel** (503)770-5848. **ED** Pat Kennedy and Jean Maack. **LC** F882.R6; R63. **DD** 929/.379521. Index available. **Bk Rev. Ad Acc. Circ:** 350. ***Continues*** *Rogue Valley Genealogical Society Quarterly.*
Desc: Vital records, family histories, queries, ship lists, census, ancestor charts, maps, annual index. Not limited to Oregon records.

UK/0306-9958
ROOT AND BRANCH. (WEST SURREY FAMILY HISTORY SOCIETY.). [Root and branch]. (1974)-. Periodical. English. Four times a year (Mar., June, Sept., Dec.). £7.00. West Surrey Family History Society, 5 Blaise Close, Farnborough GU14 7EW England. **ED** Mrs. D. Beavis. **Bk Rev. Circ:** 1,300 (ctrl).

US/0748-6251
ROOT CELLAR PRESERVES. **Added/Corp** Sacramento Genealogical Society. Vol. 5, No. 2 (Jan. 1983)-. English. qt (Jan., Apr., July, Oct.). $12.50. Sacramento Genealogical Society, PO Box 265, Citrus Heights CA 95611. **Tel** (916)725-9281. **ED** Mary Ann McDaniel. **LC** F869.S12; R66. **DD** 929/.1/072079453. Index available. **Bk Rev. Ad Acc. Circ:** 400 (ctrl). ***Continues*** *Root Cellar, 0748-6243.*
Desc: Sacramento County and California history, local records, genealogical research, how-to and hints, society news, family and Bible records, surname listing, queries, some advertising, and book reviews.
Ind/Abst Genealogical Period. Annu. Index.

US
ROOT'S AND BRANCHES. **Added/Corp** Ohio Genealogical Society. Guernsey County Chapter. Vol. 5, no. 1 (198f1)-. Periodical. English. Four times a year. $8.00 (single membership), $10.00 (couple membership), $100.00 (single life membership), $150.00 (couple life membership). Guernsey County Chapter, 836

Steubenville Avenue, Cambridge OH 43725. **Tel** (419)522-9077. **LC** F497; .G93; R66. **DD** 929/.1/072077192. ***Continues*** *Guernsey roots and branches.*

US/0893-4150
ROOTS & BRANCHES. (ROOTS & BRANCHES : TUSCALOOSA GENEALOGICAL SOCIETY NEWSLETTER.). [Roots branches]. **Added/Corp** Tuscaloosa Genealogical Society. **VFOAT** Roots and Branches. (198?)-. Periodical. English. Three times a year (Feb., July, Nov.). $7.00. Tuscaloosa Genealogical Society, 10663 Webb Black Road, c/o M. Snider, Cottondale AL 35453. **DD** 929. **Bk Rev. Circ:** 300 (ctrl).

US/0748-2485
ROOTS AND LEAVES. (ROOTS AND LEAVES / EASTERN NEBRASKA GENEALOGICAL SOCIETY.). **Added/Corp** Eastern Nebraska Genealogical Society. Vol. 1, No. 1 (Spring 1978)-. Periodical. English. Four times a year (Apr., Jul., Sep., Dec.). $6.50. Eastern Nebraska Genealogical Society, PO Box 541, Fremont NE 68025-0541. **Tel** (402)721-9553. **ED** Claire Mares, 1722 East 19, Fremont, NE 68925. **LC** F665; .R66. **DD** 929/.1/0720782. cum. index. **Bk Rev**, (Qty: 1-4). **Circ:** 324 (ctrl).
Desc: A quarterly mimeographed and mailed to our membership plus other genealogical and historical societies across the United States. Covers articles pertaining to five counties, Dodge, Colfax, Cuming, Washington and Saunders all touching Dodge county.

US/0738-2391
ROOTS & SHOOTS QUARTERLY. (ROOTS & SHOOTS QUARTERLY / SOUTHERN OHIO GENEALOGICAL SOCIETY.). **Added/Corp** Southern Ohio Genealogical Society. **VFOAT** Roots and Shoots Quarterly. Vol. 1, No. 1 (Jan./Feb./Mar., 1979)-. English. qt. Southern Ohio Genealogical Society, 229 Crestview Drive, PO Box 414, Hillsboro OH 45133. **ED** Tom and Marie Knott. **LC** F490; .R66. **DD** 929/.1/0720771. **Bk Rev. Circ:** 350.

CN/0831-5930
ROOTS, BRANCHES AND TWIGS (ONTARIO GENEALOGICAL SOCIETY. KENT COUNTY BRANCH). (ROOTS, BRANCHES AND TWIGS.). [Roots branches twigs.]. **Added/Corp** Ontario Genealogical Society. Kent County Branch. **VAT** Roots, Branches & Twigs. Vol. 1, No. 1 (Summer 1978)-. Periodical. English. qt. $10.00. Ontario Genealogical Society / Toronto, 40 Orchard View Boulevard, Suite 251, Toronto Ontario M4R 1B9 Canada. **Tel** (416)489-0734, FAX (416)489-9803. **LC** CS88.K47; R66. **DD** 929/.1/072071333.

US/8755-8343
ROOTS DIGEST. ***Title Change.*** [Roots dig.]. Vol. 1, No. 1 (Jan. 1986)-(Fall 1987). Periodical. English. mo. Ronald A Bremer, PO Box 16422, Salt Lake City UT 84116. **Tel** (801)329-8128. **ED** Ronald A Bremer. **DD** 929. **Bk Rev. Ad Acc. Circ:** 1,000. ***Continued by*** *Genealogy Digest.*
Desc: A valuable tool for the armchair researcher and is written for the amateur and expert. Articles about libraries and archives from every corner of the globe.
Ind/Abst Genealogical Period. Annu. Index (?-?).

US/0736-802X
ROOTS TRACER. **Added/Corp** Livermore-Amador Genealogical Society. (19??)-. Periodical. English. qt. Comes with membership. Livermore-Amador Genealogical Society, PO Box 901, Livermore CA 94551-0901. **Tel** (510)447-1868. **ED** Ella L Newbury. **LC** F869.L64; L58. **DD** 929/.1/072073. **Bk Rev**, (Qty: (no limit)). **Circ:** 150. ***Continues*** *Livermore Roots Tracer, 0736-802X.*
Desc: Local history as it pertains to genealogy, member's genealogy, articles of interest to genealogists, family charts, etc..,

US/0748-7827
ROSE FAMILY BULLETIN. **Added/Corp** Rose Family Association. Whole No. 1 (Mar. 1966)-. English. Four times a year (Mar., June, Sept., Dec.). $13.00. Rose Family Association, 1474 Montelegre Drive, San Jose CA 95120. **Tel** (408)268-2137. **ED** Christine Rose and Seymour T. Rose. **LC** CS71; .R795917. **DD** 929/.2/0973. Index available. cum. index. **Bk Rev. Circ:** 550.
Desc: Research records including probates, deeds, marriages, war files, census, compilations, biographies, Bible records, queries and photos.

US/8756-4351
ROSTER / THE BIRMINGHAM GENEALOGICAL SOCIETY, INC.
Main/Corp Birmingham Genealogical Society. English. qt. $10.00. Birmingham Genealogical Society Inc, PO Box 2432, Birmingham AL 35201. **Tel** (205)841-8788. **ED** Mary Cochran. **LC** F334.B653; A23A. Index available. **Bk Rev. Circ:** 200-210 (ctrl).

US/0730-5168
ROTA-GENE. [Rota-Gene]. **Added/Corp** International Genealogy Fellowship of Rotarians. **VAT** Rota Gene. (19??)-. Periodical. English. Four times a year. $20.00. International Genealogy Fellowship of Rotarians, 5721 Antietam Drive, Sarasota FL 33581. **Tel** (813)924-9170. **ED** Charles D. Townsend. **LC** CS1; .R67. **DD** 929/.1/05. **Bk Rev. Ad Acc. Circ:** 500.
Desc: Genealogy and family history with queries and genealogical clues, book reviews and advertising.
Ind/Abst Genealogical Period. Annu. Index.

US/0885-8454
ROWAN COUNTY REGISTER. [Rowan Cty. regist.]. **VFOAT** Rowan County, North Carolina Register. Vol. 1, No. 1 (Feb. 1986)-. Periodical. English. Four times a year. $25.00. Rowan County Register, Box 1948, Salisbury NC 28144. **Tel** (704)633-3575. **ED** Jo White Linn. **DD** 929. Index available in last issue of volume--attached. **Bk Rev**, (Qty: 30). **Circ:** 800.
Desc: Abstracts of wills, deeds, and court minutes beginning with 1753. Also, early tax lists, cemetery records and historical material.
Ind/Abst Genealogical Period. Annu. Index.

UK
ROYALTY, PEERAGE AND NOBILITY OF THE WORLD, THE. V. 91-. English. an. Observatory House, Observatory Gardens, London W8 7NS England. **LC** CS404; .R68. **DD** 929.7. ***Continues*** *Royalty, Peerage and Aristocracy of the World.*

US/0749-1867
ROYCE QUARTERLY, THE. (THE ROYCE QUARTERLY : THE OFFICIAL NEWSLETTER OF THE ROYCE FAMILY ASSOCIATION.). Vol. 1, No. 2 (Dec. 1979)-. Newsletter. English. qt. Royce Family Association, 6136 Woodthrush Drive, Charlotte NC 28227. **LC** CS71; .R884597. **DD** 929/.2/0973. ***Continues*** *Royce Family Association, 0749-1859.*

US/1058-6148
R'S RELATIVES, THE. [R's relat.]. Vol. 1, No. 1 (Jan. 1990)-. Periodical. English. qt. The R's Relatives, PO Box 447, Bethel Island CA 94511. **LC** IN PROCESS. **DD** 929.

US
RUSSELL REGISTER, THE. Periodical. English. qt. $15.00 US; $20.00 Canada and Mexico; $30.00 other. Frances R. Nelson, 4041 Pedley Road #18, Riverside CA 92509. **Tel** (714)685-8936. **ED** Frances R Nelson and George Ely Russell. **LC** CS71; .R965A. **DD** 929/.2/0973. Index available. **Circ:** 200 (ctrl).

CN/0823-9533
S.C.A.N. : SIMCOE COUNTY ANCESTORS' NEWS. [S.C.A.N. Simcoe Cty. ancestors' news]. **VFOAT** Simcoe County Ancestors News. Vol. 2, No. 1 (Nov. 1983)-. Periodical. English. qt. $8.00 membership. Simcoe County Branch, Ontario Genealogical Society, Box 892 Barrie Ontario L4M 4Y6 Canada. **Tel** (705)835-2821. **ED** Toni Irwin Brown. **DD** 929/.1/06071317. **Bk Rev. Circ:** 450 (ctrl). ***Continues*** *Ontario Genealogical Society. Simcoe County Branch (Newsletter), 0823-9525.*
Desc: Branch news, activities; meeting reports/speakers; book reviews, library acquisitions; county feature article, marriage registers, church/cemetery histories, etc; publications lists updated; maps; BMD extractions, etc.

CN/0229-7205
SAAMIS SEEKER. (SAAMIS SEEKER / MEDICINE HAT AND DISTRICT BRANCH, ALBERTA GENEALOGY SOCIETY.). [Saamis seeker]. **Added/Corp** Alberta Genealogical Society. Medicine Hat & District Branch. Vol. 2, No. 1 (Winter 1981)-. Periodical. English. qt. $7.00. Alberta Genealogical Society / Medicine Hat, PO Box 12015, Medicine Hat Alberta T5J 3L2 Canada. **Tel** (403)424-4429. **ED** Rita Laczkowski. **DD** 929/.1/06071234. **Bk Rev. Circ:** 60. ***Continues*** *Newsletter (Alberta Genealogical Society. Medicine Hat & District Branch).*

US/8756-6907
SACOGE NEWS. (SACOGE NEWS / SAC COUNTY GENEALOGICAL SOCIETY.). [Sacoge news]. Vol. 1, No. 1 (Sept. 1980)-. Periodical. English. SAC County Genealogical Society, c/o Sue McKnight, R R 1, Early IA 50535. **LC** F627.S2; S28. **DD** 929/.1/0720777424.

US/0740-154X
SAGA OF SOUTHERN ILLINOIS. (SAGA OF SOUTHERN ILLINOIS : A QUARTERLY PUBLICATION OF THE GENEALOGY SOCIETY OF SOUTHERN ILLINOIS.). **Added/Corp** Genealogy Society of Southern Illinois. (Jan./March 1974)-. Periodical. English. Four times a year. $16.00 Comes with Genealogy Society of Southern Illinois membership. Genealogy Society of Southern Illinois, John A Logan College, Route 2 Box 145, Carterville IL 62918. **Tel** (708)960-1500. **LC** F540; .S24. **DD** 929/.1/0720773.

US/0893-3057
SALINE, THE. (THE SALINE : THE QUARTERLY PUBLICATION OF THE SALINE COUNTY HISTORY AND HERITAGE SOCIETY.). [Saline]. **Added/Corp** Saline County History and Heritage Society (Ark.). (1986)-. Periodical. English. qt (4 issues). $15.00 (institutions), $15.00 (individuals). Saline County History and Heritage Society, PO Box 221, Bryant AR 72022. **Tel** (501)778-3770. **ED** Leon R. Moore. **DD** 976. Index available. **Bk Rev. Circ:** 250.
Desc: A collection of material of interest to the genealogist, historian and fan of local history: cemetery listings, transcriptions of Civil War letters, biographies of pioneers, transcription of county records, etc. Anything pertaining to Saline County, Arkansas, history and people.
Ind/Abst Genealogical Period. Annu. Index.

US/0740-4417
SAN DIEGO LEAVES & SAPLINGS. (SAN DIEGO LEAVES & SAPLINGS / SAN DIEGO GENEALOGICAL SOCIETY.). **Added/Corp** San Diego Genealogical Society. **VFOAT** San Diego Leaves and Saplings. (1973)-. Periodical. English. qt. $10.00. San Diego Genealogical Society Diego CA 92104-5414, 2925 Kalmia Street, San Diego CA 92104. **Tel** (619)463-1029 (WEBSTER), FAX (619)465-5154. **ED** Karna M Webster. **LC** F868.S15; S23. **DD** 929/.379498. Index available (Included in Dec. issue). **Circ:** 150.
Desc: Publishes public and private records of genealogical value for San Diego County, California.

US/1047-5893
SAN LUIS OBISPO COUNTY GENEALOGICAL SOCIETY, INC. ***Title Change.*** (SAN LUIS OBISPO COUNTY GENEALOGICAL SOCIETY, INC. : BULLETIN.). [San Luis Obispo Cty. Geneal. Soc. Inc.]. **Added/Corp** California Central Coast Genealogical Society. Vol. 21, No. 1 (Spring 1988)-(19??). Periodical. English. Four times a year. San Luis Ohispo County Genealogical Society, PO Box 4, Atascadero CA 93423-0004. **ED** Mary Scrivner. **LC** F860; .C34a. **DD** 929/.1/072079478. Index available (with each issue). **Bk Rev. Circ:** 275. ***Continues*** *Bulletin (California Central Coast Genealogical Society), 8756-2723.* ***Continued by*** *Bulletin (California Central Coast Genealogical Society : 1993), 1077-095X.*
Desc: Publishes genealogical information in the San Luis Obispo County area.
Ind/Abst Genealogical Period. Annu. Index.

US/0895-6103
SANTA CLARA COUNTY CONNECTIONS. [Santa Clara Cty. connect.]. **Added/Corp** Santa Clara County Historical & Genealogical Society. No. 87 (Spring 1987)-. Periodical. English. sa. $5.00. Santa Clara County Historical and Genealogical Society, 2635 Homestead Road, City Library, Santa Clara CA 95051. **Tel** (408)248-3560. **ED** Dorothy Wuss (Editor's Address: 2256 Woodland Avenue, San Jose, CA 95128). **LC** F868.S25; S23. **DD** 929/.1/072079473. **Bk Rev. Ad Acc.** ctrl circ. ***Continues*** *Santa Clara County Historical and Genealogical Society Quarterly, 0036-4517.*
Ind/Abst Genealogical Period. Annu. Index.

US/0740-9702
SARATOGA (RHINEBECK, N.Y.), THE. (THE SARATOGA.). Vol. 1, No. 1 (Winter 1984)-. English. qt. $14.00 US; $16.00 Canada. Kinship, 60 Cedar Heights Road, Rhinebeck NY 12572. **Tel** (914)876-4592. **ED** Arthur Kelly. **LC** F127.S26; S27. **DD** 929/.1/072074748. Index available. cum. index. **Bk Rev. Ad Acc. Circ:** 200.
Desc: Contains subscriber's queries and vital records never before published.

US/0739-6651
SAVAGE FAMILY DEPOSITORY NEWSLETTER. Vol. 1, No. 1 (June 1983)-. Newsletter. English. qt. Jean Savage Lichtenwald, CGRS, 3840 Smiths Crossing, Freeland MI 48623. **LC** CS71; .S26398. **DD** 929/.2/0973.

XR
SBORNIK JEDNOTY STARYCH CESKYCH RODU V PRAZE. **Added/Corp** Jednota Starych Cesk,ych Rodu v Praze. Vol. 4, No. 2 (1933)-. Periodical. Czech. qt. ***Continues*** *Sbornik Jednoty Potomku Pobelohorskych Exulantu-Pokutniku a Pratel Rodopisu v Praze.*

US/0882-5890
SCHARTZER-SCHERTZER CONNECTION, THE. [Schartzer-Schertzer connect.]. **VFOAT** Schartzer Schertzer Connection. Periodical. English. qt. $17.00 (one year), $33.00 (two year). BGM Publications, 28635 Old Hideaway Road, Cary IL 60013. **Tel** (312)639-2400. **ED** Betty G Massman. **DD** 929. Index available. cum. index. **Circ:** 325 (ctrl).
Desc: Family research, genealogical records, church records, wills, land record, Bible records, pedigree charts, queries, etc.

US/0882-5904
SCHNEIDER CONNECTIONS. [Schneider connect.]. Began 1984. Periodical. English. qt. $17.00 one year, $33.00 two years. BGM Publications, 28635 Old Hideaway Road, Cary IL 60013. **Tel** (312)639-2400. **ED** Betty G Massman. **DD** 929. Index available. cum. index. **Circ:** 700 (ctrl).
Desc: Family research - church records, land and estate records, group sheets, pedigree charts, queries, index of names, general information regarding Schneider (et var) ancestors.

US/0271-5031
SCOTTISH-AMERICAN GENEALOGIST. **Added/Corp** Augustan Society. Scottish Genealogy & Research Committee. **VAT** Scottish American

Genealogist. No. 8 (1977)-. Periodical. English. an. $10.00. Augustan Society, Society Headquarters and Library, PO Box P, Torrance CA 90507-0210. **Tel** (310)320-7766. **ED** Scott R MacMillan. **LC** CS460; .S3. **DD** 929/.1/0899163073. **Bk Rev. Circ:** 550 (ctrl). ***Continues*** *Scottish Genealogical Helper, 0360-4500.*
Desc: Primarily genealogy, secondary emphases heraldry and history; serves as an international contact journal for those engaged in Scottish research.

CN/0707-073X
SCOTTISH BANNER, THE. See Ethnic Interests.

UK
SCOTTISH CLANS & THEIR TARTANS, THE. **VAT** Scottish Clans and their Tartans. English. **LC** DA880.H76. **DD** 929.2.

UK/0300-337X
SCOTTISH GENEALOGIST, THE. **Added/Corp** Scottish Genealogy Society. Vol. 1 (Jan. 1954)-. Periodical. English. Four times a year (Jan., Mar., June, Dec.). £12.00 UK. Scottish Genealogy Society, 5 Learmonth Place, Edinburgh EH4 1AX Scotland. **Tel** 011/44/31/2258585, telex 727251. **ED** Ivor R. Guild. **LC** CS460; .S35. **DD** 929/.1/09411. Index available (publish separately). **Bk Rev**, (Qty: 6). **Ad Acc. Circ:** 1,500 (ctrl). available on microfilm.
Desc: Genealogy and family trees.
Ind/Abst Br. Humanit. Index; Genealogical Period. Annu. Index.

UK
SCOTTISH RECORD SOCIETY : PUBLICATIONS. Part I (Mar. 1898)-. Periodical. English. Dr J Kirk, Department of Scottish History, 9 University Gardens, Glasgow G12 9QH Scotland.

US/0277-5727
SEARCH (NILES, ILL.). ***Ceased.*** (SEARCH.). [Search]. Vol. 1, No. 1 (1981)-Vol. 11, No. 4 ( ). Periodical. English. qt. Jewish Genealogical Society of Illinois, 5819 W Keeney, c/o Maslov, Morton Grove IL 60053. **Tel** (312)965-8277. **ED** Alan Spencer. **LC** CS31; .S43. **DD** 929/.1/089924. **Bk Rev. Circ:** 400 (ctrl).
Desc: How-to articles on Jewish genealogy. Each issue focuses on a city and its specific genealogical resources, areas of interest, articles and announcements.
Ind/Abst Genealogical Period. Annu. Index.

US
SEARCHER : OFFICIAL MONTHLY PERIODICAL OF THE SOUTHERN CALIFORNIA GENEALOGICAL SOCIETY, THE. **Added/Corp** Southern California Genealogical Society. (Dec. 1963)-. Periodical. English. qt. Southern California Genealogical Society, PO Box 7665, Bixby Station, Long Beach CA 90807. **LC** CS1; .S38. **DD** 929.1/09794/9.
Ind/Abst Genealogical Period. Annu. Index.

US/0732-2879
SEARCHERS & RESEARCHERS OF ELLIS COUNTY, TEXAS. **Added/Corp** Ellis County Genealogical Society. **VFOAT** Searchers and Researchers of Ellis County, Texas; Searchers and Researchers; Searchers & Researchers. Vol. 1 (1978)-. Periodical. English. Four times a year. $12.00. Ellis County Genealogical Society, Box 479, Waxahachie TX 75165. **Tel** (214)937-3069. **ED** Jean Davis. **LC** F392.E4; S43. **DD** 929/.1/07207642815. Index available. **Bk Rev. Circ:** 300.

CN/0229-2637
SEARCHLIGHT (BLOOMFIELD, ONT.). (THE SEARCHLIGHT.). [Searchlight]. **Added/Corp** Ontario Genealogical Society. Quinte Branch. Vol. 1, No. 1 (Spring 1981)-. Periodical. English. Four times a year. $15.00. Ontario Genealogical Society / Quinte Branch, Box 301, Bloomfield Ontario K0K 1G0 Canada. **Tel** (613)393-3146. **DD** 929/.371358.

US/0274-6441
SECOND BOAT, THE. [Second boat]. Vol. 1, No. 1 (May 1980)-. Periodical. English. Six times a year (Jan., Mar., May, July, Sept., Nov.). $25.00. Second Boat, PO Box 398, Machias ME 04654. **Tel** (207)255-4114. **ED** Rosemary Bachelor. **LC** CS42; .S44. **DD** 929. Index available. **Bk Rev**, (Qty: 6-12). **Ad Acc. Circ:** 3,000 (ctrl).
Desc: Specializes in Colonial American genealogy with emphasis in pre-1650 immigrants and descendants to the Revolutionary War era.
Ind/Abst Genealogical Period. Annu. Index.

US/0363-4590
SEEKER (PITTSBURG), THE. (THE SEEKER.). **Added/Corp** Crawford County Genealogical Society of Southeast Kansas. Vol. 1 (July 1971)-. Periodical. English. Four times a year (Mar., June, Sept., Dec.). $8.00. Crawford County Genealogical Society / Kansas, 211 West 4th Street, Pittsburg KS 66762. **ED** Maxine Barton. **LC** F687.C9; S44. **DD** 929/.2/0973. Index available. **Circ:** 200 - 300.

US
SEEKING N SEARCHING ANCESTORS. English. Free to members. Seeking N Searching Ancestors, Route 1 Box 52, Peggy S Hake, St. Elizabeth MO 65075. **Tel** (314)793-6998.
Ind/Abst Genealogical Period. Annu. Index.

US/0740-2740
SELLERS LETTERS. Oct. 1982-. Periodical. English. Three times a year. $15.00 (per volume). Sims Publishing, PO Box 9576, Sacramento CA 95823-0576. **ED** M Sims. **LC** CS71; .S4667. **DD** 929/.2/0973. **Bk Rev. Circ:** 250.
Desc: Genealogical clearing house for those searching for ancestors with names sounding like Sellers (Zeller, Sollar, Cellar, etc.).

CN/0824-7331
SEMINAR ANNUAL - ONTARIO GENEALOGICAL SOCIETY. (SEMINAR ANNUAL : PAPERS.). [Semin. annu. - Ont. Geneal. Soc.]. **Main/Corp** Ontario Genealogical Society. Seminar. 1983-. English (summaries and/or abstracts in French). an. Ontario Genealogical Society / Bruce & Grey Branch, Box 66, Owen Sound Ontario N4K 5P1 Canada. **DD** 929/.3713.

US/1046-5545
SENECA SEARCHERS. (SENECA SEARCHERS / THE SENECA COUNTY GENEALOGICAL SOCIETY, CHAPTER OF THE OHIO GENEALOGICAL SOCIETY.). [Seneca searchers]. **Added/Corp** Ohio Genealogical Society. Seneca County Chapter. (Sept. 1981)-. Periodical. English. bm. $15.00 (family), $12.00 (individual), $4.50 (student). Seneca County Genealogical Society, Box 157, Tiffin OH 44883-1057. **LC** CS42; .S46. **DD** 929/.1/0720771.
Ind/Abst Genealogical Period. Annu. Index.

CN/0828-9980
SENEY NEWSLETTER. [Seney newsl.]. 1st Issue (1984)-. Newsletter. English. sa. 7.60Can$ UK, Europe, and Australia; 6.00Can$ other. Seney Newsletter, 224 Cornwallis Court, Oshawa Ontario L1H 8E8 Canada. **Tel** (905)725-0829. **DD** 929/.2/0971.

US/1049-1783
SEPTS (SAINT PAUL, MINN.), THE. (THE SEPTS / IRISH GENEALOGICAL SOCIETY.). [Septs]. **Added/Corp** Irish Genealogical Society (Saint Paul, Minn.). Vol. 10, No. 1 (Jan. 1990)-. Periodical. English. qt. Free to members; $15.00 membership. Irish Genealogical Society International, PO Box 16585, St. Paul MN 55116. **Tel** (612)739-1270. **ED** Ida Troye. **DD** 929. **Bk Rev**, (Qty: 6-10). **Ad Acc. Circ:** 1,600. ***Continues*** *Irish Genealogical Society Newsletter.*
Desc: Newsletter of the Irish Genealogical Society International.

US
SEVIER COUNTY HISTORICAL SOCIETY NEWSLETTER. Newsletter. English. qt (4 issues). $5.00. Sevier County Historical Society, PO Box 288, De Queen AR 71832. **Tel** (501)642-6642.
Desc: Covers historical aspects of Sevier County, Arizona.

US/8756-131X
SHELBY COUNTY ANCESTORS. [Shelby Cty. ancestors]. **Added/Corp** Shelby County Historical and Genealogical Society. Vol. 1, No. 1 (Dec. 1978)-. Periodical. English. qt. $15.00. Shelby County Historical and Genealogical Society, PO Box 287, Shelbyville IL 62565. **Tel** (217)774-2260. **LC** F547.S6; S5. **DD** 929/.1/0720773798. **Circ:** 350.
Desc: Genealogical and historical information of Shelby County, Illinois ancestors.

US
SHELBY EXCHANGE. (19??)-. English. Four times a year. $12.50. Carol Peterson, Box 536, Freeman SD 57029. **Tel** (605)925-7186. **ED** Carol Peterson. **Bk Rev. Ad Acc. Circ:** 40.
Desc: Genealogy publication pertaining only to the Shelby's.

CN/0843-6924
SHEM TOV. [Shem tov]. **Added/Corp** Jewish Genealogical Society of Toronto. Jewish Genealogical Society of Canada. Vol. 4, No. 1 (June 1988)-. Periodical. English. qt. $30.00 US; 30.00Can$ Canada. Jewish Genealogical Society of Canada, PO Box 446, Station A, Willowdale ONT M2N 5T1 Canada. **Tel** (416)638-3280. **LC** CS87.J4; S54. **DD** 929/.1/089924071. Index available. cum. index (Vol. X, No. 2). **Bk Rev. Ad Acc. Circ:** 250 (ctrl).
Desc: Provides a forum for the exchange of knowledge and information, and thereby promotes an awareness of genealogy within the Jewish community of Canada.

US/0735-8016
SHIAWASSEE STEPPIN' STONES. Vol. 1 (1972)-. English. qt. $10.00. Shiawassee County Genealogical Society, PO Box 841, Owosso MI 48867. **Tel** (517)725-8549. **LC** F572.S7; S5. **DD** 929/.1/072077425. Index available. **Bk Rev. Circ:** 160 (ctrl).
Ind/Abst Genealogical Period. Annu. Index.

US/0748-5166
SHINTAFFER NEWSLETTER, THE. Vol. 1, #1 (Oct. 15, 1980)-. Newsletter. English. qt. Bergeron, 6035 SW Wilbard Street, Portland OR 97219. **LC** CS71; .S556517. **DD** 929/.2/0973.

UK/0261-135X
SHROPSHIRE FAMILY HISTORY JOURNAL. [Salop. fam. hist. j.]. (1980)-. Periodical. English. Four times a year (Mar., June, Sept., Dec.). £7.00. Shropshire Family History Society, 19 Brooks Road, Bomere Health, Shrewsbury SY4 3PU England. **Tel** 011 44 939 290516. **ED** Shean Bostock (editor's address; 17 Hazlitt Place, WEM, Shropshire, SY4 5JP England, phone: 011 44 939 235470). Index available. cum. index. **Bk Rev. Ad Acc. Circ:** 1,500.
Desc: Articles relating to family history in Shropshire. List of surnames being researched by new members.

US/0146-9649
SIMMONS KINFOLK. Periodical. English. qt. $5.00. Marcia Eisenberg, 15 Edgewood Parkway, Fayetteville NY 13066. **LC** CS71; .S586A. **DD** 929/.2/0973.

US/1045-9987
SIMS SEEKER, THE. [Sims seek.]. Vol. 1, No. 1 (Summer 1989)-. Periodical. English. qt. $17.00. BGM Publications, 28635 Old Hideaway Road, Cary IL 60013. **Tel** (312)639-2400. **ED** Betty G Massman. **LC** CS71; .S58637. **DD** 929/.2/0973. Index available. cum. index. **Circ:** 150 (ctrl).
Desc: General information for Sims family researchers.

SW/0489-1090
SLAKT OCH HAVD. Periodical. Swedish. Genealogiska Foreningen, Box 2029, 30311 Stockholm Sweden. **LC** CS1.

US/0890-1287
SLVGS NEWS, THE. (THE SLVGS NEWS : A PUBLICATION OF THE ST. LAWRENCE VALLEY GENEALOGICAL SOCIETY.). **Added/Corp** Saint Lawrence Valley Genealogical Society. **VFOAT** S.L.V.G.S. News. **VAT** St. Lawrence Valley Genealogical Society News. (1983)-. English. Six times a year (Jan., Mar., May, July, Sept., Nov.). $10.00 Comes with St. Lawrence Valley Genealogical Society membership. The Saint Lawrence Valley Genealogical Society, PO Box 341, Colton NY 13625. **ED** Dennis E. Eickhoff. **LC** IN PROCESS. **Bk Rev**, (Qty: 8). **Circ:** 250 (ctrl).
Ind/Abst Genealogical Period. Annu. Index.

US/1051-9912
SLVGS QUERY QUARTERLY, THE. (THE SLVGS QUERY QUARTERLY / ST. LAWRENCE VALLEY GENEALOGICAL SOCIETY.). [SLVGS query q.]. **Added/Corp** Saint Lawrence Valley Genealogical Society. **VFOAT** Query Quarterly; S.L.V.G.S. Query Quarterly. Vol. 1, No. 1 (Spring 1984)-. English. Four times a year. $10.00 Comes with St. Lawrence Valley Genealogical Society membership. The Saint Lawrence Valley Genealogical Society, PO Box 341, Colton NY 13625. **ED** Dennis E. Eickhoff. **LC** F1050; .S59. **DD** 929/.1/0720714. **Bk Rev**, (Qty: 8). **Circ:** 250 (ctrl).

US/0897-7860
SMALL SIBLINGS. Vol. 1 (1986)-. Periodical. English. Four times a year. $7.35. Pioneer Publications, PO Box 397, Black Eagle MT 59414-0397. **Tel** (406)453-4266. **ED** Shirley Penna-Oakes. **LC** CS71; .S636a. **DD** 929/.2/0973. Index available. **Bk Rev. Ad Acc.**

US
SMITH COUNTY HISTORICAL & GENEALOGICAL SOCIETY. (19??)-. English. Four times a year (Mar., June, Sept., Dec.). $12.50. Smith County Historical Society / Tennessee, PO Box 112, Carthage TN 37030. **Tel** (615)683-8347.

US/0278-3134
SMITH PAPERS. [Smith pap.]. Vol. 1, No. 1 (July 1980)-. English. Three times a year. $15.00. Sims Publishing, PO Box 9576, Sacramento CA 95823-0576. **ED** M Sims. **LC** CS71; .S6426. **DD** 929/.2/0973. Index available. **Bk Rev. Ad Acc. Circ:** 800 (ctrl).
Desc: Genealogical clearinghouse for Smith data for those searching for their Smith ancestors.

US/0748-5034
SMOKE SIGNALS FROM THE ASSINIBOINE GENEALOGICAL SOCIETY. **Added/Corp** Assiniboine Genealogical Society. **VFOAT** Smoke Signals. (19??)-. Periodical. English. Four times a year. $4.00. Ft. Assiniboine Genealogical Society, PO Box 321, Havre MT 59501. **Tel** (406)265-4409. **LC** F730; .S64. **DD** 929/.3786.

US/8756-3517
SMOKE SIGNALS (MARYVILLE, MO.). (SMOKE SIGNALS / NODAWAY COUNTY GENEALOGICAL SOCIETY.). [Smoke signals]. **Added/Corp** Nodaway County Genealogical Society. Vol. 3, No. 2 (June 1982); (Sept. 1982)-. English. qt (Mar., June, Sept., Dec.). $7.50 membership. Smoke Signals, Nodaway County Genealogical Society, Box 214, Maryville MO 64468. **Tel** (816)582-3254. **ED** Vivian Pruitt.

LC F472.N7; S63. **DD** 929/.1/0720778124. (with each issue). **Circ:** 135.
Desc: Presently including: probate index, Nodaway County - 1879, newspapers, queries. Mostly includes information on Nodaway and surrounding counties.

US/0884-6111
SMOKY MOUNTAIN HISTORICAL SOCIETY NEWSLETTER. See History(General)-History of North, South, and Central America.

US/0489-2593
SOCIAL DIRECTORY OF HOUSTON. See General Interest-General Interest-North America.

US/0360-831X
SOCIAL REGISTER NEW ORLEANS. 1975-. English. an. $27.00. Social Register of New Orleans, PO Box 52255, New Orleans LA 70152. **LC** F379.N53; S6. **DD** 920/.0025/76335.

US/1065-1217
SONOMA SEARCHER, THE. (THE SONOMA SEARCHER / SONOMA COUNTY GENEALOGICAL SOCIETY.). [Sonoma search.]. **Added/Corp** Sonoma County Genealogical Society. (1974)-. Periodical. English. Three times a year. $15.00. Sonoma Genealogical Society, PO Box 2273, Santa Rosa CA 95405. **LC** F868.S7; S74. **DD** 929/.1/07279418.
Ind/Abst Genealogical Period. Annu. Index.

US/0584-164X
SOULE NEWSLETTER. [Soule newsl.]. **Added/Corp** Soule Kindred. Vol. 1 (Jan. 1967)-. Periodical. English. Four times a year. $15.00. Soule Kindred in America Inc., 53 New Shaker Road, Albany NY 12205. **Tel** (518)869-8368. **ED** Julia Soule. **LC** CS71; .S717. **DD** 929.2/0973. Index available. **Bk Rev**. **Circ:** 400.
Desc: Publishes genealogy and current news items on any Soule or related person. Mayflower Pilgrim, George Soule started the family in America.

AT/0311-2756
SOUTH AUSTRALIAN GENEALOGIST. [South Aust. geneal.]. (1974)-. Periodical. English. Four times a year (Jan., Apr., July, Oct.). 16.00Aus$. South Australian Genealogy & Heraldry Society, GPO Box 592, Adelaide 5001, Australia. **Tel** 11 61 8 2724222, FAX 011 61 8 2724910. **ED** A. G. Peake (telephone: 011 61 8 2724222). **DD** 929.1099423. **Bk Rev**. **Ad Acc. Circ:** 3,000.
Desc: Contain material of genealogical interest.

US/0737-2973
SOUTH BEND AREA GENEALOGICAL SOCIETY. ***Title Change.*** (SOUTH BEND AREA GENEALOGICAL SOCIETY : NEWSLETTER.). [South Bend Area Geneal. Soc.]. **Added/Corp** South Bend Area Genealogical Society. (19??)-(19??). Newsletter. English. qt. South Bend Area Genealogical Society, 53139 Oakmont Park West, South Bend IN 46637. **ED** Jeanne Denham and Faye Lies. **LC** F534.S7; S685. **DD** 929/.377289. Index available. cum. index. ctrl circ. ***Continued by*** *Newsletter (South Bend Area Genealogical Society), 1069-9317.*
Ind/Abst Genealogical Period. Annu. Index.

US/0190-826X
SOUTH CAROLINA MAGAZINE OF ANCESTRAL RESEARCH, THE. [S.C. mag. ancestral res.]. (Winter 1973)-. English. qt. $25.00. South Carolina Magazine of Ancestral Research, PO Box 21766, Columbia SC 29221. **Tel** (803)772-6919. **ED** Brent H. Holcomb. **LC** CS42; .S64. **DD** 929/.3757. Index available. cum. index. **Bk Rev. Circ:** 1,200 (ctrl).
Desc: Genealogical and local historical information on South Carolina prior to 1865.
Ind/Abst Genealogical Period. Annu. Index (?-?).

US
SOUTH DAKOTA GENEALOGICAL SOCIETY. (SOUTH DAKOTA GENEALOGICAL SOCIETY QUARTERLY.). [S.D. Geneal. Soc.]. **Added/Corp** South Dakota Genealogical Society. (198?)-. Periodical. English. qt. Free to members; $20.00 (institutions), $15.00 (individuals) membership. South Dakota Genealogical Society, Rural Route 2, Box 80, Mina SD 57462. **Tel** (605)226-0707. **LC** F650; .S68. **DD** 929/.1/0720783. ***Continues*** *South Dakota Genealogical Society.*
Ind/Abst Genealogical Period. Annu. Index.

US/8756-2766
SOUTH FLORIDA PIONEERS. [South Fla. pioneers]. Began with July 1974 issue. English. qt. $10.00. Richard M Livingston, PO Box 3749, North Fort Myers FL 33918-3749. **Tel** (813)334-7550. **ED** Richard M Livingston. **LC** F310; .S67. **DD** 929/.1/0720759. Index available. **Bk Rev. Ad Acc. Circ:** 150 (ctrl).
Desc: Contains genealogies and histories of South Florida pioneer families, with research source records: cemeteries, deeds, tax lists, marriages, census reports, etc.

US
SOUTHEAST ALABAMA GENEALOGICAL SOCIETY QUARTERLY. English. qt. $12.00. SE Alabama Genealogical Soc., PO Box 143, Dothan AL 36302. **Tel** (205)794-7480. **Circ:** 200.
Desc: A genealogy quarterly containing abstracted and or compiled genealogical materials of interest for southeast Alabama counties and upper bordering counties of Florida and lower bordering counties of Georgia.

US/0735-6870
SOUTHERN ECHOES. (SOUTHERN ECHOES / AUGUSTA GENEALOGICAL SOCIETY.). [South. echoes]. **Added/Corp** Augusta Genealogical Society. Vol. 1, No. 1 (Aug. 1979)-. Periodical. English. Twelve times a year. $25.00. Augusta Genealogical Society, PO Box 3743, Augusta GA 30914. **Tel** (404)722-4073. **ED** Carrie M. Adamson. **LC** F294.A9; S65. **DD** 929/.1/072075864. Index available. **Bk Rev. Circ:** 1,000.
Desc: Lecture synopses, book reviews, queries, surname area, search files, educational articles of basic genealogical interest. Current news items information, and hints to aid researchers.

US/8755-1748
SOUTHERN GENEALOGICAL INDEX. [South. geneal. index]. Vol. 1, No. 1 (Jan.-March 1984)-. Periodical. English. qt. $10.00. Mountain Press, PO Box 4810, Sevierville TN 37864. **Tel** (615)428-0746. **ED** James L Douthat. **LC** Z1251.S7; S65; F208. **DD** 929/.1/072075. **Bk Rev. Ad Acc.** ctrl circ.
Desc: Index of the journal contents of societies' printed materials for Southern genealogical researchers.

US/0584-4487
SOUTHERN GENEALOGIST'S EXCHANGE QUARTERLY, THE. (1957)-. Periodical. English. qt (Mar., June, Sept., Dec.). $20.00 (includes quarterly) members, $16.00 nonmembers. Southern Genealogist's Exchange Society, PO Box 2801, Jacksonville FL 32203-2801. **Tel** (904)387-9142. **ED** Mary-Louise Howard and Jim Galton. Index available. **Bk Rev. Ad Acc. Circ:** 400.
Desc: Covers the Southern States. Accepts articles of interest from anyone covering these states. Queries are accepted from members and non-members. No charge for same or limit to number that can be submitted. Articles cover a multitude of information on the Southern States.

US/1056-0874
SOUTHERN GLENN GLEANINGS NEWSLETTER. [South. Glenn glean. newsl.]. **VFOAT** Southern Glenn Gleanings. Vol. 1, No. 1 (Mar. 1991)-. Newsletter. English. qt. $16.00. Nall News Publishing Co., PO Box 2186, Willingboro NJ 08046. **DD** 929.

US/0747-8453
SOUTHERN INDIANA GENEALOGICAL SOCIETY QUARTERLY. **Added/Corp** Southern Indiana Genealogical Society. Vol. 1, No. 1 (Jan. 1980)-. Periodical. English. Four times a year. $10.00. Southern Indiana Genealogical Society, PO Box 665, New Albany IN 47150. **Tel** (812)923-9244. **ED** Lonnie Fink, 4717 Buttontown Road, Georgetown, IN 47122-9721. **LC** F525; .S66. **DD** 929/.1/0720772. Index available. **Bk Rev. Circ:** 250.
Ind/Abst Genealogical Period. Annu. Index.

US/1048-8057
SOUTHERN QUERIES : THE CONTACT MAGAZINE FOR PEOPLE SEARCHING FOR THEIR SOUTHERN ANCESTORS. [South. queries]. Vol. 1, No. 1 (May/June 1990)-. Periodical. English. bm. $24.00 (one year), $42.00 (two year) US; $29.00 (one year), $52.00 (two year) other. PerroBlanco Publications, PO Box 726, Durham NC 27702. **Tel** (919)687-4818. **ED** Steve Smith. **LC** F208; .S57. **DD** 929/.1/072075. Index available. **Bk Rev**, (Qty: 20-30). **Ad Acc, Adv Mgr:** Frank Monachelli, **Tel** (205)322-7700.
Desc: Genealogy magazine for researchers of Southern U.S. families. Contains queries, how-to, resources, calendar, book reviews.
Ind/Abst Genealogical Period. Annu. Index.

US/0895-2876
SOUTHERN ROOTS AND SHOOTS. [South. roots shoots]. **Added/Corp** Delta Genealogical Society. **VFOAT** Southern Roots & Shoots. Vol. 1, No. 1 (July 1985)-. Periodical. English. qt. $12.00 (comes with membership). Delta Genealogical Society, 504 McFarland Avenue, Rossville GA 30741. **ED** Jim Couch. **DD** 929. **Bk Rev. Circ:** 150.
Ind/Abst Genealogical Period. Annu. Index.

US/0736-5683
SOUTHSIDE VIRGINIAN, THE. Vol. 1, No. 1 (Oct. 1982)-. Periodical. English. qt. $20.00. The Southside Virginian, PO Box 3684, Richmond VA 23235. **Tel** (804)358-6358. **ED** J. Christian Kolbe and L.H. Hart III. **LC** F225; .S68. **DD** 929/.10720755. **Bk Rev. Ad Acc. Circ:** 500 (ctrl).
Desc: Covers genealogy of southside Virginia.

US/0740-7335
SOUTHWEST VIRGINIAN, THE. (1978)-. Periodical. English. Four times a year. The Southwest Virginian, 1046 Spruce Street, Norton VA 24273. **ED** R. S. Roberson and N. C. Baker. **LC** F225; .S69. **DD** 929/.3755.

US/0561-5445
SPARKS QUARTERLY, THE. [Sparks q.]. **Added/Corp** Sparks Family Association. Vol. 1 No. 1 (Mar 1953)-. Periodical. English. qt. free. Russell Bidlack, 1709 Cherokee Road, Ann Arbor MI 48104. **LC** CS71; .S7364. **DD** 929/.2/0973. cum. index.

US
SPEEGLE FAMILY QUARTERLY. Vol. 1 (June 1990)-. Periodical. English. qt. Giles Roy Compton, Route 1, Box 446, Attalla AL 35954.

CN
SPLITTING HEIRS. (19??)-. English. 15.00Can$. Vernon & District Family History Society, PO Box 1447, Vernon BC V1T 6N7 Canada. **Tel** (604)542-7735, FAX (604)546-9390. **ED** Peter Ward. **Bk Rev. Circ:** under 100 (ctrl).

US/0275-4525
SPUR AND PHOENIX, THE. (THE SPUR AND PHOENIX : THE NEWSLETTER OF CLAN JOHNSTON/E IN AMERICA.). Newsletter. English. qt. Clan Johnston/e in America, Patricia A Johnston, Secretary and Registrar, 5303 Emerson Drive, Raleigh NC 27609. **LC** CS71; .J7297. **DD** 929/.2/0973.

US/0882-6528
ST. CLAIR COUNTY GENEALOGICAL SOCIETY QUARTERLY. [St. Clair Cty. Soc. geneal. q.]. **Added/Corp** St. Clair County Genealogical Society. **VFOAT** Saint Clair County Genealogical Society Quarterly; Quarterly. (1978)-. Periodical. English. Four times a year. $15.00 (comes with membership). St Clair County Genealogical Society, PO Box 431, Belleville IL 62222. **ED** Mardy Eisloeffel, 5108 Concordia Road, Belleville, IL 62223; Telephone: (618)277-7005. **LC** F547.S2; S22. **DD** 929/.1/072077389. Each issue contains an index to its own contents (no volume index)--loose. cum. index (first 10 vols.). **Circ:** 500 (ctrl).
Desc: Family Bible records; queries of members; and records of St. Clair County, Illinois. Articles concern general genealogical research and methods.
Ind/Abst Genealogical Period. Annu. Index.

US/0882-7311
STALKER. (STALKER / MADISON COUNTY GENEALOGICAL SOCIETY.). [Stalker]. **VFOAT** Madison County Genealogical Society Quarterly. Vol. 1, No. 1 (Spring 1981)-. Periodical. English. Four times a year. $15.00 Comes with Madison County Genealogical Society membership. Madison County Genealogical Society, PO Box 631, Edwardsville IL 62025. **Tel** (618)656-2299, (618)656-1789. **ED** Marie Eberle and Beverly White. **LC** F547.M2; S77. **DD** 929/.1/072077386. Bound Index published separately, free upon request. cum. index. **Bk Rev. Circ:** 450.
Desc: Committed to the preservation of genealogical and historical records. Have published extensive volumes of court records, and ancestor charts of members.
Ind/Abst Genealogical Period. Annu. Index.

●US
STANISLAUS RESEARCHER / GENEALOGICAL SOCIETY OF STANISLAUS COUNTY, CA, INC. **Added/Corp** Stanislaus County Genealogical Society. Vol. 14, No. 8 (Sept. 1992)-. English. mo. **LC** F868.S8; S83. ***Continues*** *Newsletter (Stanislaus County Genealogical Society), 0882-9527.*

US/0893-3359
STANLY COUNTY GENEALOGICAL SOCIETY JOURNAL, THE. [Stanly Cty. Geneal. Soc. j.]. **Added/Corp** Stanly County Genealogical Society. **VFOAT** SCGS Journal. Vol. 1, No. 1 (Winter 1981/1982)-. Periodical. English. ir. Comes with Stanly County Genealogical Society Journal membership, $7.00. Stanly County Genealogical Society, PO Box 31, Albermarle NC 28002. **ED** Mrs. Zelma Eudy. **DD** 929. **Circ:** 220.
Ind/Abst Genealogical Period. Annu. Index.

US/0894-8313
STEPPING BACK IN TIME. Vol. 1, No. 1 (1987)-. Periodical. English. qt (March, June, Sept., Dec.). $31.80. Stepping Back in Time, 2263 Mollys Backbone Road, Sherrills Ford NC 28673. **Tel** (704)478-2469, FAX (704)478-2469. **ED** Elizabeth Bray Sherrill. **LC** F262.C28; S74. **DD** 975.6/785/005. Index available (bound in each issue). **Bk Rev**, (Qty: 12). **Ad Acc, Adv Mgr:** E.B. Sherrill, **Tel** same as publisher. **Circ:** 200 (ctrl).
Desc: Covers history and genealogy information and research regarding Eastern Catawba County people from 1842-present. Newspaper transcripts, histories of people and buildings, census, wills, deeds, vitals, photographs, and studies.

US/0039-1522
STIRPES. [Stirpes]. **Added/Corp** Texas State Genealogical Society. (March 1961)-. Periodical. English.

Four times a year. Texas State Genealogical Society, Rt 4 Box 56, Sulphur Springs TX 75482. **Tel** (713)681-5964. **ED** Trevia Wooster Beverly. **LC** CS1; .S74. Index available. cum. index. **Bk Rev**. **Ad Acc**. **Circ:** 1,000 (ctrl).
Desc: Material of Texas-related genealogy and history, as well as items of general "how-to" methods. Queries, book reviews, and meetings notices are also published.
Ind/Abst Am. Hist. Life (1969-1973); Genealogical Period. Annu. Index (?-?).

US/0733-8392
STRICKLAND SCENE. [Strickland scene]. **Added/Corp** Strickland Research, Inc. Vol. 1, No. 1 (Winter 1980)-. Periodical. English. qt. $12.50 included in membership dues. Strickland Research Inc, 1661 Lauranceae Way, Riverdale GA 30296. **Tel** (404)996-8274. **ED** Nancy J Cornell. **LC** CS71; .S91597. **DD** 929/.2/0973. Index available. cum. index. **Bk Rev**. **Circ:** 205 (ctrl).
Desc: Contains genealogical information on Strickland surname throughout the United States.

US
STUDEBAKER FAMILY, THE. Periodical. English. qt. $7.00 individuals; free to libraries, historical societies, genealogical societies and various organizations. Studebaker Family National Association, 6555 South State Route 202, Tipp City OH 45371. **Tel** (513)667-4451. **ED** Emmert Studebaker and Ruth Epler Studebaker. **LC** CS71; .S9325A. **Circ:** 1,900.
Desc: Births, deaths, marriages, stories, queries.

SW/0280-8633
STUDIA ANTHROPONYMICA SCANDINAVICA. **VFOAT** Tidskrift for Nordisk Personnamnsforskning. (1983)-. Swedish (Danish, English and Norwegian). an. Landequistska Bokhandeln, Box 610, S-751 25, Uppsala Sweden.
Ind/Abst MLA Int. Bibl. Books Artic. Mod. Lang. Lit.

UK
SUBSCRIBERS' INTEREST LIST ... / ULSTER GENEALOGICAL & HISTORICAL GUILD. **Main/Corp** Ulster Genealogical & Historical Guild. English. **LC** CS497.U44; U43A. **DD** 929/.3416.

US
SUN CITIES GENEALOGIST, THE. (THE SUN CITIES GENEALOGIST : A PUBLICATION OF THE SUN CITIES GENEALOGICAL SOCIETY.). [Sun City geneal.]. Vol. 12, No. 1 (Spring 1991)-. Periodical. English. qt. $20.00. Sun Cities Genealogical Society, PO Box 1448, Sun City AZ 85351. available on microfilm. ***Continues*** *Sun City Genealogist, 8756-5463.*

US/0270-9856
SURNAME AND PUBLICATION INDEX. **Added/Corp** Northwest Genealogical Society (Alliance, Neb.). (19??)-. English. $5.00. Northwest Genealogical Society, PO Box 6, Alliance NE 69301. **Tel** (308)762-3677. **ED** Patricia Mammen Pinney. **LC** CS2485; .S94. **DD** 929/.1/0973. **Bk Rev**. **Ad Acc**. **Circ:** 200.
Desc: Issued for the Society membership and other interested researchers. Membership open to any person interested in family research/history and to libraries.

CN/0713-780X
SURNAME EXCHANGE / SASKATCHEWAN GENEALOGICAL SOCIETY. [Surname exch. - Sask. Geneal. Soc.]. **Main/Corp** Saskatchewan Genealogical Society. No. 4 (Sept. 1981)-. English. te. $1.00 each number. Surname Exchange, c/o Saskatchewan Genealogical Society, Box 1894, Regina Saskatchewan S4P 3E1 Canada. **DD** 929/.1/097124. ***Continues*** *Saskatchewan Genealogical Society. Surnames Supplement, 0713-7796.*

US/0091-6439
SURNAME INDEX (WICHITA). (SURNAME INDEX.). [Surn. index]. English. Historical and Genealogical Society Inc, PO Box 1121, Wichita KS 67201. **LC** CS42; .S94. **DD** 929/.3/781.

US/0277-366X
SURNAME RESEARCH DIRECTORY. Directory. English. Guilford County Genealogical Society, PO Box 9693, Greensboro NC 27429. **LC** F253; .S95. **DD** 929/.375662.

US
SURNAMES. **Added/Corp** Harris County Genealogical Society. Seminar and Workshop. **VFOAT** Seminar ... Surname Index. English. Harris County Genealogical Society, PO Box 391, Pasadena TX 77501. **Tel** (713)645-1144. **LC** F392.H38; H29a. **DD** 929/.3764141. ***Continues*** *Surname Index.*

UK
SUSSEX FAMILY HISTORIAN. **Added/Corp** Sussex Family History Group. (19??)-. Periodical. English. qt. $9.00 US; $13.00 other. Sussex Family Historian Groups, 45 Park Terrace East B Tayler, Horsham W Sus. RH13 5DJ England. **Tel** 593906. **ED** P. Eversaed. Index available. **Bk Rev**. **Circ:** 2000 (ctrl).

UK
SUSSEX GENEALOGIST AND LOCAL HISTORIAN, THE. Vol. 1, No. 1 (June 1979)-. English. qt. £2.50. **LC** CS435.S9; S93. **DD** 942.2/5.

US/1061-9992
SUTTON SEARCHERS. (SUTTON SEARCHERS : A CENTRALIZED RESOURCE FOR SUTTON SURNAME RESEARCHERS WORLDWIDE.). [Sutton search.]. **VFOAT** Sutton Searchers Newsletter. Issue 1 (Apr. 1991)-. Periodical. English. qt. $12.00. Sutton Searchers Newsletter, 681 Triunfo Canyon Road, Westlake Village CA 91361-2056. **LC** CS71; .S967a. **DD** 929/.2/097305.

●US/1062-3930
SWARTZLANDER DESCENDANTS, THE. [Swartzlander descend.]. **VFOAT** Die Schwartzlander Nachkommen. Vol. 1, No. 1 (Apr. 1992)-. English. Three times a year. $5.00. Ronald E Swartzlander, PO Box 279, West Sunbury PA 16061-0279. **DD** 929.

US/0275-9314
SWEDISH AMERICAN GENEALOGIST. Vol. 1, No. 1 (Mar. 1981)-. Periodical. English. qt. $20.00 US and Canada; $30.00 other. Swenson Swedish Immigration Research Center, Augustana College, Rock Island IL 61201-2273. **Tel** (309)794-7204, FAX (309)794-7443. **ED** Nils William Olsson (editor's address: PO Box 2186, Winter Park, FL 32790; editor's phone: (407)647-4292). **LC** E184.S23; S88. **DD** 929/.1/089397073. **Bk Rev**, (Qty: 1-2). **Ad Acc**, **Adv Mgr:** same as editor. **Circ:** 1,200.
Desc: A journal devoted to Swedish-American genealogy, immigration, and family personal history.
Ind/Abst Am. Hist. Life (1990-); Genealogical Period. Annu. Index.

US/0895-7126
SWENSON CENTER NEWS. (SWENSON CENTER NEWS : PUBLICATION OF THE SWENSON SWEDISH IMMIGRATION RESEARCH CENTER.). [Swenson Cent. news]. **Added/Corp** Swenson Swedish Immigration Research Center. No. 1 (1986)-. Periodical. English. sa. Free. Swenson Swedish Immigrant Center, PO Box 175, Augustana College, Rock Island IL 61201. **DD** 929.
Ind/Abst Genealogical Period. Annu. Index.

US
SWISS AMERICAN HISTORICAL SOCIETY REVIEW. (19??)-. Periodical. English. Three times a year. comes with membership. Swiss American Historical Society, 6440 North Bosworth, Chicago IL 60626. ***Continues*** *Swiss American Historical Society Review.*

CN/0827-2816
TALBOT TIMES. [Talbot times]. **Added/Corp** Ontario Genealogical Society. Elgin County Branch. Vol. 1, Iss. 1, (Mar. 1982)-. Periodical. English. Four times a year (Mar., June, Sept., Dec.). $10.00 (institutions); $8.00 (individuals). Ontario Genealogical Society Elgin, PO Box 20060, St Thomas Ontario N5P 4H4 Canada. **Tel** (519)773-9405. **LC** CS88.O6; T34. **DD** 929/.1/06071334. **Bk Rev**. **Circ:** 325 (ctrl).

UK
TALBOTANIA; THE BULLETIN OF THE TALBOT RESEARCH ORGANISATION. **Main/Corp** Talbot Research Organisation. **VFOAT** Bulletin of the Talbot Research Organisation. V. 1-Christmas 1977-. Bulletin. English. sa. £0.35 each issue. Mary & Mike Talbot, 142 Albemarle Avenue, Elson Gosport, Hants P012 4HY England. **LC** CS71; .T14A. **DD** 929/.2/0973.

US/0147-6432
TAP ROOTS (SHREVEPORT). (TAP ROOTS.). V. 1- Jan./Mar. 1977-. Periodical. English. qt. $6.00. Southern Genealogical Institute, PO Box 324, Shreveport LA 71162. **LC** F206; .T36. **DD** 929/.375.

US/0494-6944
TAP ROOTS (TUSKEGEE). (TAP ROOTS.). **Added/Corp** Genealogical Society of East Alabama. Vol. 1 (July 1963)-. Periodical. English. qt. Genealogical Society of East Alabama, 336 South Gay Street, Auburn AL 36830. **LC** F325; .T36. **DD** 929/.3761.

AT/0159-0677
TASMANIAN ANCESTRY. (1980)-. Periodical. English. Four times a year (Mar., June, Sept., Dec.). $25.00. Genealogical Society of Tasmania, PO Box 60, Tasmanian Ancestry, Prospect TAS 7250 Australia. **Tel** 011 61 2 202101. **ED** A. Bartlett. **Bk Rev**, (Qty: varies). **Ad Acc**. **Circ:** 1,500 (ctrl).

US/0893-309X
TATE TRAILS. [Tate trails]. **Added/Corp** Tate County MS Genealogical and Historical Society. Vol. 1, No. 1 (1983)-. Periodical. English. qt. $15.00. Tate County MS Genealogical & Historical Society, PO Box 974, Senatobia MS 38668. **Tel** (601)562-4632. **ED** Rebecca Haas Smith. **DD** 929. Each issue contains an index to its own contents (no volume index)--loose. **Circ:** 250.
Desc: Contains family histories, US Census information, ancestor charts, queries, etc.

US/0735-9144
TAYLOR QUARTERLY, THE. Vol. 1, No. 1 (Winter 1983)-. Periodical. English. qt. $8.50. Taylor Quarterly, 5911 Brookview Drive, Alexandria VA 22310-1818. **LC** CS71; .T2398. **DD** 929/.2/0973.

US/1071-054X
TAZEWELL GENEALOGICAL MONTHLY (1985). (TAZEWELL GENEALOGICAL MONTHLY.). [Tazewell geneal. mon. (1985)]. **Added/Corp** Tazewell County Genealogical Society. Vol. 7, No. 3 (Mar. 1985)-. Periodical. English. Twelve times a year. $12.00. Tazewell County Genealogical Society, PO Box 312, Pekin IL 61555. **ED** Connie Perkins (phone: (309)346-6660). **DD** 929. **Circ:** 400 (ctrl). ***Continues*** *Tazewell County Genealogical Society Newsletter (Pekin, Ill. : 1984).*

US/0882-0635
TENNESSEE ANCESTORS. (TENNESSEE ANCESTORS : A TRI-ANNUAL PUBLICATION OF THE EAST TENNESSEE HISTORICAL SOCIETY.). [Tenn. ancestors]. **Added/Corp** East Tennessee Historical Society. Vol. 1, No. 1 (April 1985)-. Periodical. English. tq (Apr., Aug., Sept.). $15.00. East Tennessee Historical Society, 500 West Church Avenue, Knoxville TN 37902. **Tel** (615)544-5732. **ED** Dr. Stephen Ash. **LC** F435; .T33. **DD** 929/.1/0720768. Index available in last issue of volume--attached. **Bk Rev**, (Qty: 5). **Circ:** 2,000.
Desc: Genealogical information abstracted from an extensive collection--strong on East Tennessee.

●US/1068-0063
TENNESSEE & KENTUCKY QUERIES. [Tenn. Ky. queries]. **VFOAT** Tennessee and Kentucky Queries. Issue No. 11 (May 1993)-. Periodical. English. ir. $7.25 (single issue). Name Game Enterprises, 4204 South Conklin Street, Spokane WA 99203-6235. **Tel** (509)747-4903. **DD** 929. ***Formed by the union of*** *Kentucky Queries, 0899-1359* ***and*** *Tennessee Queries, 0898-5472.*

US/0898-5472
TENNESSEE QUERIES. ***Title Change.*** [Tenn. queries]. (1987)-(199?)-. Periodical. English. ir. Name Game Enterprises, Mrs E Dale Hastin Smith, S 4204 Conklin Street, Spokane WA 99203-6235. **DD** 929. ***Merged with*** *Kentucky Queries, 0899-1359* ***to form*** *Tennessee & Kentucky Queries, 1068-0063.*
Desc: Contains related queries and book reviews.
Ind/Abst Genealogical Period. Annu. Index.

US/0735-2794
TERREBONNE LIFE LINES. **Added/Corp** Terrebonne Genealogical Society. Vol. 1, No. 1 (Summer 1982)-. Periodical. English. Four times a year. $18.00 libraries and societies; $25.00 contributors; $20.00 individuals. Terrebonne Genealogical Society, Station 2 Box 295, Houma LA 70360. **Tel** (504)868-0370. **ED** Audrey B. Westerman (editor's telephone: (504)633-2367). **LC** F377.T5; T47. **DD** 929/.1/072076341. Each issue contains an index to its own contents (no volume index)--loose. **Bk Rev**, (Qty: 15). **Circ:** 500 (ctrl).
Desc: Records of assumption, Lafourche and Terrebonne parishes, Louisiana. Court records, cemetery listings, queries, and information on/from private collections.

US/0884-2108
TERRELL TRAILS. [Terrell trails]. **Added/Corp** Terrell Society of America. Vol. 1, No. 1 (Spring 1985)-. Periodical. English. Four times a year. $12.00. Terrell Society of America, Route 5 Box 211, Reed Creek Drive, Bassett VA 24055. **Tel** (703)647-9574. **ED** Dan Brinson (phone: (912)371-6458). **DD** 929. **Bk Rev**. ctrl circ.

US/0741-6105
TEXARKANA USA GENEALOGIST'S QUARTERLY, THE. ***Title Change.*** **Added/Corp** Texarkana USA Genealogical Society. **VFOAT** Texarkana U.S.A. Genealogist's Quarterly. Vol. 9, No. 1 (Spring 1982)-(198?). Periodical. English. qt. Texarkana USA Genealogical Society, PO Box 2323, Texarkana TX 75504-2323. **LC** F385; .T45. **DD** 929/.3764. **Circ:** 300 (ctrl). ***Continues*** *Texarkana U.S.A. Quarterly.* ***Continued by*** *Texarkana USA Quarterly (1987), 1067-1412.*
Desc: Records of Arkansas, Louisiana and Texas history, family information, Bibles, court recordings, documents, cemetary records, and Indian data.

US/1067-1412
TEXARKANA USA QUARTERLY (1987). (TEXARKANA U.S.A. QUARTERLY.). [Texarkana USA q.]. **Added/Corp** Texarkana USA Genealogical Society. **VFOAT** Texarkana USA Quarterly; Texarkana United States of America Quarterly. Vol. 14, No. 1 (Spring 1987)-. Periodical. English. Four times a year. $10.00. Texarkana USA Genealogical Society, PO Box 2323, Texarkana TX 75504-2323. **ED** Mimi Lantz, President (editor's address: 306 Wood Street, Texarkana, AK 75502; phone: (501)773-0271). **LC** F385; .T45. **DD** 929/.3764. ctrl circ. ***Continues*** *Texarkana USA Genealogist's Quarterly, 0741-6105.*

Desc: Records of Arkansas, Louisiana and Texas history, family information, Bibles, court recordings, documents, cemetary records, and Indian data.

US/0148-1983
TEXAS HERITAGE (FORT WORTH). (TEXAS HERITAGE.). **Added/Corp** Texas Family Heritage, inc. (19??)-. Periodical. English. qt. $10.00. Texas Family Heritage Inc, PO Box 17007, Fort Worth TX 76102. **LC** F385; .T48. **DD** 929/.3/764.

US/0748-2590
TEXAS KIN. ***Suspended.*** Vol. 2, No. 1 (March 1973)-?. Periodical. English. qt. Texas Kin, PO Box 17704, Dallas TX 75217. **LC** F392.D14; B35. **DD** 929/.37642811. ***Continues*** *Balch Springs Historical and Genealogical Society, 0748-2582.*

US/0147-7048
THEY MULTIPLIED. (THEY MULTIPLIED, A STORY OF MATLOCKS-MEDLOCKS.). V. 1-. English. sm. $10.00. Jess Armstrong, PO Box DD, Diboll TX 75941. **LC** CS71; .M4375A. **DD** 929/.1/0973.

US/0094-0844
THORNY TRAIL, THE. Periodical. English. sa. $12.00. Midland Genealogical Society, PO Box 1191, Midland TX 79701. **Tel** (915)687-2825. **ED** Ann Auberg. **LC** CS42; .T47. **DD** 929/.1/0973. Index available. **Bk Rev.** **Circ:** 200 (ctrl).
Desc: Contains midland genealogical materials.
Ind/Abst Genealogical Period. Annu. Index.

US/0895-8416
THREADS OF LIFE. **Added/Corp** Lamesa Area Genealogical Society. No. 4, (March 1974)-. Periodical. English. Twice a year (Mar., Sept.). $5.00. Lamesa Area Genealogical Society, POB 1264, Lamesa TX 79331. **Tel** (806)872-3190. **ED** Margaret Kinsey. **DD** 929. **Bk Rev**, (Qty: 20-30/yr). **Circ:** 60 (ctrl). ***Continues*** *Bulletin - Lamesa Area Genealogical Society, 0360-3369.*

●US/1061-8678
TIDEWATER VIRGINIA FAMILIES. [Tidewater Va. fam.]. (1992)-. Periodical. English. qt. $20.00 US; $25.00 other. Virginia L.H. Davis, PO Box 876, Urbanna VA 23175. **Tel** (804)758-3606. **ED** Virginia L.H. Davis. **LC** F225; .T53. **DD** 929/.2/0973. Index available. cum. index. **Bk Rev**, (Qty: 35). **Pr Rev. Circ:** 2,000.
Desc: Explores the families of Tidewater Virginia during its Colonial history. Early records, heretofore unpublished, are presented, along with recently researched genealogies of Tidewater families.

US/0735-018X
TIMBER TRAILS. (TIMBER TRAILS / YAMHILL COUNTY GENEALOGICAL SOCIETY.). Vol. 1, No. 1 (July 1980)-. Periodical. English. $2.00 each issue. Yamhill County Genealogical Society, PO Box 568, McMinnville OR 97128. **LC** F882.Y2; T55. **DD** 929/.1/072079539.

CN/1183-9686
TIMBERLINE (PEMBROKE). (TIMBERLINE.). [Timberline]. **Added/Corp** Upper Ottawa Valley Genealogical Group. (Feb. 1990)-. Periodical. English. Six times a year. 11.00Can$ single; 14.00Can$ family. Upper Ottawa Valley Genealogical Group, PO Box 972, Pembroke Ontario K8A 7M5 Canada. **Tel** (613)687-5006. **ED** Mr. Robbie Gorr. **DD** 929/.1/06071381. **Circ:** 350 (ctrl).
Desc: Articles, news and advice for genealogists and local historians working primarily in the Upper Ottawa Valley (Renfrew County, Ontario and Pontiac County, Quebec).

US/0740-5367
TIMBERTOWN LOG. **Added/Corp** Saginaw Genealogical Society. Vol. 1 No. 1 (Fall 1972)-. Periodical. English. Four times a year. $12.00. Saginaw Genealogical Society Inc, Saginaw Public Library, 505 James Avenue, Saginaw MI 48607. **Tel** (517)755-0904. **LC** F572.S17; T55. **DD** 929/.1/072077446. cum. index.
Ind/Abst Genealogical Period. Annu. Index.

US/0271-2830
TITUS TRAIL, THE. [Titus trail]. Vol. 1, No. 1 (Spring 1980)-. Periodical. English. qt. $6.00. Writers Publishing Company, PO Box 309, Goleta CA 93017. **LC** CS71; .T599a. **DD** 929/.2/0973.

US/0146-9568
TOLEDOT. (TOLEDOT : THE JOURNAL OF JEWISH GENEALOGY.). **VFOAT** Journal of Jewish Genealogy. V. 1- Summer 1977-. Periodical. English. ir. Toledot, c/o Steven Siegel, 155 East 93rd Street/Suite 3C, New York NY 10128. **Tel** (212)427-5395. **LC** CS31; .T64. **DD** 929/.1.

US/0893-7664
TOMBSTONE, THE. ***Suspended.*** [Tombstone]. Vol. 1, No. 1 (Sept. 1983)-?. Periodical. English. sa. $5.00. Cochise Genealogical Society, PO Box 68, Pirtleville AZ 85626. **ED** Charles Field. **DD** 929. **Ad Acc. Circ:** 70 (ctrl).
Desc: Articles and queries pertaining to Cochise County, Arizona.

US/0738-1808
TOMBSTONE TRAILS. **VFOAT** Cemeteries, Mower County, Minnesota. Vol. 1-. Periodical. English. Mower County Genealogical Society, PO Box 145, Austin MN 55912. **LC** F612.M9; T65. **DD** 929.5/09776/17.

US/0734-8495
TOPEKA GENEALOGICAL SOCIETY QUARTERLY, THE. **Added/Corp** Topeka Genealogical Society. (19??)-. Periodical. English. qt. $15.00. Topeka Genealogical Society, PO Box 4048, Topeka KS 66604-0048. **Tel** (913)233-5762. **ED** Helen L. King. **LC** F680; .T63. **DD** 929/.1/0720781. Index available. **Bk Rev. Ad Acc. Pr Rev. Circ:** 800 (ctrl).
Ind/Abst Genealogical Period. Annu. Index.

CN/0381-9167
TORONTO TREE. **Added/Corp** Ontario Genealogical Society. Toronto Branch. Periodical. English. Six times a year. 15.00Can$ (institutions), 12.00Can$ (individuals) Canada. Ontario Genealogical Society / Toronto, 40 Orchard View Boulevard, Suite 251, Toronto Ontario M4R 1B9 Canada. **Tel** (416)489-0734, FAX (416)489-9803. **ED** Steven Playter. Index available. **Circ:** 1,200 (ctrl).
Desc: Newsletter for the Toronto Branch of the Ontario Genealogical Society. Contains news and information for researchers in the York Region of Ontario.

US
TOTAH TRACINGS. English. Four times a year (Mar., June, Sept., Dec.). $15.00. Totah Tracings Genealogical Society, PO Box 125, Salmon Ruin, Bloomfield NM 87413. **Tel** (505)327-9451. **ED** Jo Ellithorpe Minert. **Bk Rev**, (Qty: 15). **Ad Acc.**
Desc: Local items of genealogical interest.
Ind/Abst Genealogical Period. Annu. Index.

US/8756-8462
TRACER - OHIO GENEALOGICAL SOCIETY. HAMILTON COUNTY CHAPTER, THE. (THE TRACER / HAMILTON COUNTY CHAPTER, OHIO GENEALOGICAL SOCIETY.). **Added/Corp** Ohio Genealogical Society. Hamilton County Chapter. Vol. 1 No. 1 (Sept. 1979)-. Periodical. English. Four times a year. $10.00 Comes with Ohio Genealogical Society membership. Hamilton County Chapter / Ohio Genealogical Society, PO Box 15851, Cincinnati OH 45215. **ED** Ruth J. Wells. **DD** 977. Index available in last issue of volume--attached. **Bk Rev. Circ:** 600.
Desc: Genealogical data and queries, especially references to Hamilton County Ohio.
Ind/Abst Genealogical Period. Annu. Index.

US/0882-2158
TRACES OF SOUTH CENTRAL KENTUCKY. (TRACES OF SOUTH CENTRAL KENTUCKY : QUARTERLY PUBLICATION OF THE SOUTH CENTRAL KENTUCKY HISTORICAL AND GENEALOGICAL SOCIETY, INCORPORATED.). [Traces south cent. Ky.]. **Added/Corp** South Central Kentucky Historical and Genealogical Society. **VFOAT** Traces. Vol. 10, Issue 1 (Mar. 1982)-. Periodical. English. Four times a year (Jan., Apr., July, Oct.). $10.00. South Central Kentucky Historical Society, PO Box 157, Glasgow KY 42142. **Tel** (502)651-3657. **ED** Martha P. Reneau (editor's telephone: (502)678-3110). **LC** F450; .T8. **DD** 929/.1/0720769. Index available. **Bk Rev. Circ:** 400 (ctrl). ***Continues*** *South Central Kentucky Historical and Genealogical Society Quarterly.*
Desc: Genealogical items, deaths, census, tax records, Bible records family articles, anything on historical and genealogical interest to this area.

US
TRACKS AND TRACES. **Added/Corp** Union County Genealogical Society. Vol. 1, No. 1 (Oct. 1977)-. Periodical. English. Twice a year (May & Nov.). $10.00 Includes Union County Genealogical Society membership. Union County Genealogical Society, Barton Library, East 5th & North Jefferson, El Dorad AR 71730. **Tel** (501)863-5447, FAX (501)862-3944. **ED** Dorathy Boulden. **Circ:** 150.

US/0362-0344
TRAIL BREAKERS. **Added/Corp** Clark County Genealogical Society. (19??)-. Periodical. English. qt. Free to members of the Clark County Genealogical Society; $12.00. Clark County Genealogical Society / Washington, PO Box 2728, Vancouver WA 98668. **Tel** (206)256-0977. **ED** Jane Germann. **LC** F897.C6; T7. **DD** 929/.1/0979786. Index available. **Bk Rev. Circ:** 500.
Desc: Clark County, WA records, ancestor charts, queries, Bible records, book reviews, research articles and addresses.
Ind/Abst Genealogical Period. Annu. Index.

US/0739-6643
TRAIL SEEKERS. **Main/Corp** Rebecca Winters Genealogical Society. Vol. 2, No. 1 (Mar. 1979)-. English. qt. $3.00. Rebecca Winters Genealogical Society, PO Box 323, Scottsbluff NE 69361. **Tel** (308)632-8803. **ED** Mary Anders and Ann Gabel. **LC** CS42; .R3517. **DD** 929/.1/072073. **Bk Rev. Ad Acc. Circ:** 150. ***Continues*** *Rebecca Winters Genealogical Society. Rebecca Winters Genealogical Society, 0739-6635.*
Desc: Publishes society news and local records.

US
TRAIL TALES. English. $10.00. Boone County Historical Society, 602 Stury Street, Boone IA 50036. **Tel** (515)432-1931. **ED** Larry Adams. Index available. cum. index. **Circ:** 1,000.
Desc: Contains articles, reprints, book reviews, photos, family history, and business history about Boone County.

US/0091-6455
TRAILS AND TALES. [Trails tales]. V. 1- Apr. 1973-. English. Upton County Genealogical Society, PO Box 6, Rankin TX 79778. **LC** CS42; .T7. **DD** 929/.373.

CN/1195-4906
TRAILS (WINDSOR). (TRAILS / ESSEX COUNTY BRANCH OF THE ONTARIO GENEALOGICAL SOCIETY.). [Trails]. **Added/Corp** Ontario Genealogical Society. Essex County Branch. Vol. 3, No. 3 (Oct. 1981)-. Periodical. English. qt (Jan., Apr., July, Oct.). $15.00. Essex County Branch of the Ontario Genealogical Society, PO Box 2, Station A, Windsor Ontario, N9A 6J5 Canada. **Tel** (519)253-6351. **DD** 929/.1/06071331. **Bk Rev**, (Qty: 4). **Circ:** 300. available on microfilm. ***Continues*** *Newsletter (Ontario Genealogical Society. Essex County Branch), 1197-6357.*
Desc: Covers genealogy, family history, and local history for Essex County, Ontario, Canada.

US/0882-1178
TREASURE CHEST NEWS. (TREASURE CHEST NEWS / CENTRAL FLORIDA GENEALOGICAL AND HISTORICAL SOCIETY INC.). [Treas. chest news]. Issue No. 28 (April 1983)-. Periodical. English. mo. $15.00 (membership). Central Florida Genealogical and Historical Society Inc., PO Box 177, Orlando FL 32802. **Tel** (407)351-9282. **ED** Ralyne E Westenhofer. **LC** F310; .C4. **DD** 929/.1/0720759. Index available. cum. index. **Circ:** 300 (ctrl). ***Continues*** *Central Florida Genealogical and Historical Society Inc., 0882-1186.*
Desc: Four to six pages in length, includes items of genealogical interest to the members as well as the monthly activities of the Society.

US
TREASURE STATE LINES. **Added/Corp** Great Falls Genealogy Society. Vol. 1 (1976)-. Periodical. English. qt. $20.00 (individual); $25.00 (couple). Great Falls Genealogy Society, Paris Gibson Square, 1400 1st Avenue, North Great Falls MT 59401. **ED** Judith L Knee. **LC** F739.G7; T73. **DD** 929/.2/0973. Index available. cum. index. **Circ:** 225 (ctrl).
Desc: Topics on genealogy, Montana history, queries, baptisms, cemeteries, marriages and book reviews.

US/0737-9226
TREE CLIMBER (SALINA, KAN.). (TREE CLIMBER / SMOKY VALLEY GENEALOGICAL SOCIETY AND LIBRARY, INC.). **Added/Corp** Smoky Valley Genealogical Society and Library. Vol. 1, No. 1 (1982)-. Periodical. English. Four times a year (Jan., Apr., July, Oct.). $15.00 Comes with Smoky Valley Genealogical Society membership. Smoky Valley Genealogical Society, 211 West Iron, Suite 205, Salina KS 67401. **Tel** (913)827-8029. **ED** Mary Clement Douglass. **LC** F680; .T69. **DD** 929/.1/0720781. **Circ:** 250 (ctrl).
Desc: Vital records: birth, death, marriage; school records, cemetery records, diaries, surname index, how-to study, genealogy and family history for Northern Kansas counties, Saline, Ottawa, Lincoln and Ellsworth.
Ind/Abst Genealogical Period. Annu. Index.

US/0893-2069
TREE SHAKER / EASTERN KENTUCKY GENEALOGICAL SOCIETY. [Tree shak.]. **Added/Corp** Eastern Kentucky Genealogical Society. (1977)-. Periodical. English. qt. $6.00 US; $7.00 North America; $7.50 other. Eastern Kentucky Genealogical Society, PO Box 1544, Ashland KY 41105. **Tel** (606)329-0090. **ED** Evelyn S Jackson. **DD** 929. Index available. cum. index. **Bk Rev. Circ:** 1,000 (ctrl).
Ind/Abst Genealogical Period. Annu. Index.

US/0736-7678
TREE TALK (JACKSONVILLE, TEX.). (TREE TALK.). [Tree talk]. Periodical. English. mo. Cherokee County Genealogical Society, PO Box 1332, Jacksonville TX 75766. **LC** F392.C44; T73. **DD** 929/.1/0720764183.

CN/0841-2642
TREE TRACER. (TREE TRACER / PRINCE GEORGE GENEALOGY CLUB.). [Tree tracer]. **Added/Corp** Prince George Family History Society. Prince George Genealogy Club. (Mar. 1982)-. Periodical. English. qt (4 issues). 17.00Can$. Prince George Family History Society, PO Box 1056, Prince George BC V2L 4V2 Canada. **Tel** (604)964-0699. **DD** 929/.1/05. ***Continues*** *Branch Newsletter (British Columbia Genealogical Society. Prince George Branch).*

US/0162-1440
TREE TRACERS, THE. **Added/Corp** Southwest Oklahoma Genealogical Society. (19??)-. Periodical. English. Four times a year (Feb., May, Aug., Nov.). $12.00. Southwest Oklahoma Genealogical Society, PO Box 148, Lawton OK 73502. **Tel** (405)581-3450, FAX (405)248-0243. **ED** Donna Irwin (phone: (405)355-1731). **LC** F693; .T73. **DD** 929/.1/09766. Index available (Bound

in 4th iss. (Aug.).). cum. index. **Bk Rev. Circ:** 450 (ctrl).
Desc: Southwest Oklahoma records relating to family history and other related fields.
Ind/Abst Genealogical Period. Annu. Index.

US/1046-6339
TREES FROM THE GROVE. (TREES FROM THE GROVE : QUARTERLY PUBLICATION OF COTTAGE GROVE GENEALOGICAL SOCIETY.). [Trees grove]. **Added/Corp** Cottage Grove Genealogical Society. Vol. 1, No. 1 (Feb. 1988)-. Periodical. English. qt (Feb., May, Aug., Nov.). $10.00. Cottage Grove Genealogical Society, PO Box 388, Cottage Grove OR 97424. **Tel** (503)942-0346. **ED** Joanne A. Skelton. **LC** F884.C8; T73. **DD** 929/.379531. Index available (Index in each volume). **Bk Rev. Circ:** 150.
Ind/Abst Genealogical Period. Annu. Index.

US
TREESEARCHER, THE. Added/Corp Southwest Kansas Geneological Society. (19??)-. Periodical. English. Four times a year. $12.00 (libraries), $15.00 (other). Kansas Genealogical Society, PO Box 103, Dodge City KS 67801. **ED** Mrs. Bernard Rooney III. **LC** F680; .T7. Index available (bound in the December issue). **Bk Rev. Circ:** 500.
Desc: Prints prime source records submitted by members. Provides research tips and queries.
Ind/Abst Genealogical Period. Annu. Index.

CN/0713-4282
TREMBLAIE. (LA TREMBLAIE.). [Tremblaie]. **Added/Corp** Association des Tremblay d'Amerique. Vol. 1, No. 1, (Aug. 1979)-. Periodical. French (English). bm. $10.00. La Tremblaie, CP 6700, Sillery Quebec G1T 2W2 Canada. **Tel** (418)653-2137. **DD** 929/.2/0607. **Ad Acc. Circ:** 1,500.
Desc: Subjects such as the conservation of bonds within the individuals bearing the same forefathers, same heritage, or keeping of same heritage by restoration, etc.

US/0496-1803
TRI-CITY GENEALOGICAL SOCIETY BULLETIN, THE. (THE TRI-CITY GENEALOGICAL SOCIETY BULLETIN : RICHLAND, KENNEWICK, PASCO, WASHINGTON.). **Main/Corp** Tri-City Genealogical Society. **Added/Corp** Tri-City Genealogical Society. Bulletin. (1961)-. Bulletin. English. Twice a year. $10.00. Tri-City Genealogical Society, PO Box 1410, Richland WA 99352. **Tel** (509)783-4262. **ED** Leona George (editor's address: 824 South Green Street, Kennewick WA 99336). **LC** F897.B4; T75a. **Bk Rev. Ad Acc, Adv Mgr:** same as editor. **Pr Rev. Circ:** 200.
Desc: Aids to research in tracing family history with emphasis on Washington State and the Pacific Northwest.
Ind/Abst Genealogical Period. Annu. Index.

US/0896-419X
TRI-COUNTY GENEALOGY. [Tri-Cty. geneal.]. **Added/Corp** Tri-County Genealogical Society (Ark.). **VFOAT** Tri County Genealogy. Vol. 1, No. 1 (Fall 1986)-. Periodical. English. Three times a year. $15.00. Tri-County Genealogy, PO Box 580, Marvell AR 72366. **Tel** (501)829-2772. **ED** Jo Claire English (editor's address: PO Box 206, Clarendon, AR 72021-0206; editor's phone: (501)747-3963). **LC** F410; .T74. **DD** 929/.1/07207678. Index available (bound in all issue). cum. index. **Bk Rev**, (Qty: 8-10). **Circ:** 350.
Ind/Abst Genealogical Period. Annu. Index.

US
TRI-COUNTY RESEARCHER. (19??)-. English. Four times a year (Jan., Apr., July, Oct.). $15.00. Tri-County Researcher, Route 1 Box 106A, PO Box 196, Proctor WV 26055. **Tel** (304)455-3203. **ED** Linda Goddard Stout.
Desc: News and information of genealogy covering areas of Marshall, Tyler, and Wetzel counties.

US/0742-5015
TRI-COUNTY SEARCHER, THE. Added/Corp Broken Mountains Genealogical Society. Vol. 3, No. 1 (Mar. 1982)-. Periodical. English. sa (Apr., and Nov.). $8.00. Broken Mountains Genealogical Society, Box 261, Chester MT 59522. **Tel** (406)759-5445, (406)759-5337. **ED** Betty L Marshall. **LC** F737.L7; T74. **DD** 929/.1/072078612. Index available. **Bk Rev. Ad Acc. Circ:** 100 (ctrl). ***Continues** Searcher (Chester, Mont.), 0749-6621.*
Desc: Records any old index records found in the counties, cemetery records, tombstone readings, newspaper articles and more.
Ind/Abst Genealogical Period. Annu. Index.

US/0740-896X
TRI-STATE PACKET OF THE TRI-STATE GENEALOGICAL SOCIETY, THE. [Tri-State pack. Tri-State Geneal. Soc.]. **Added/Corp** Tri-State Genealogical Society. Vol. 1, No. 1 (Sept. 1977)-. Periodical. English. qt (Mar., Jun., Sep., Dec.). $12.00. Tri-State Genealogical Society, c/o Willard Library, 21 First Avenue, Evansville IN 47710. **Tel** (502)425-4309. **ED** Glenda Trapp. **LC** F525; .T75. **DD** 929/.1/0720772. Index available. **Bk Rev. Circ:** 600 (ctrl).
Ind/Abst Genealogical Period. Annu. Index (?-?).

US/0899-7462
TRYON TIMES, THE. [Tryon times]. Vol. 1, No. 1 (March/April 1988)-. Periodical. English. bm. $18.00. Howard Research, 13400 NW Germantown Road, Portland OR 97231. **DD** 929.

US/0149-2438
TUFTS KINSMEN. (TUFTS KINSMEN : THE PERIODICAL OF THE TUFTS KINSMEN ASSOCIATION.). **Added/Corp** Tufts Kinsmen Association. Vol. 1, No. 1 (Spring 1975)-. Periodical. English. qt. $6.00. Tufts Kinsmen Project, PO Box 571, Dedham MA 02026. **Tel** (617)296-0997. **LC** CS71; .T9167. **DD** 929/.2/0973.

US/0161-2719
TULL TRACING. Added/Corp Milbourne & Tull Research Center. (19??)-. Periodical. English. qt. $4.00. Milbourne and Tull Research Center, Willis Clayton Tull Jr, 10605 Lakespring Way, Cockeysville MD 21030. **LC** CS71; .T926a. **DD** 929/.2/0973.

US/0564-4437
TULSA ANNALS. [Tulsa ann.]. **Added/Corp** Tulsa Genealogical Society. (Sept. 1966)-. Periodical. English. Three times a year. $15.00. Tulsa Genealogical Society, PO Box 585, Tulsa OK 74101-0585. **Tel** (918)742-3893. **ED** Ken Wade (editor's telephone: (918)234-7427 or (918)357-2030). **LC** F693; .T95. **DD** 929.1/09766. Each issue contains an index to its own contents (no volume index)--loose. **Bk Rev**, (Qty: 7-8). **Ad Acc, Adv Mgr:** same as editor. **Circ:** 400 (ctrl).
Desc: Instructions and help for people tracing their roots.
Ind/Abst Genealogical Period. Annu. Index (?-?).

US/0891-3706
TWIGS MAGAZINE. ***Ceased.*** [Twigs mag.]. Vol. 1, No. 1 (Dec. 1982)-Vol. 5, No. 2 (19??). Periodical. English. qt. The Juniper Tree Press, 4830 Carol Drive, Troy MI 48098. **DD** 929.

US
ULSTER COUNTY GENIE. English. Four times a year (Jan., Apr., July, Oct.). $12.00. Ulster County Genealogical Society, Box 536, Hurley NY 12443. **Tel** (914)338-4618. **ED** Shirley Mearns (editor's address; 79 Dunneman Avenue, Kingston, New York 12401 (phone: (914)338-4618). **Circ:** 400.
Desc: Information concerning Ulster County, New York.

US/0740-4409
UNDER CONSTRUCTION. (UNDER CONSTRUCTION : NEWSLETTER OF THE MENDOCINO COAST GENEALOGICAL SOCIETY.). Vol. 1, No. 1 (Sept. 1977)-. Newsletter. English. qt. Dora Zimmer, PO Box 762, Fort Bragg CA 95437. **LC** F868.M5; U5. **DD** 929/.1/072079415.

US/0099-1473
UNDERWOOD ANNALS. V. 1- Oct. 1974-. Periodical. English. qt. $6.00. 763 Crescent Drive SW, Largo FL 33540. **LC** CS71; .U56A. **DD** 929/.2/0973.

US/0270-465X
UPCHURCH BULLETIN. V. 1 (Jan. 1980)-. Bulletin. English. qt. $15.00. Michael Enterprises, PO Box 35804, Tucson AZ 85740. **Tel** (602)742-2669. **ED** Robert Phillip Upchurch. **LC** CS71; .U65A. **DD** 929/.2/0973. **Bk Rev. Circ:** 200 (ctrl).
Desc: Historical and genealogical records on Upchurch and related families from 1500 to the present with emphasis on the 14 generations of the family in America.

US/0098-8960
UPSHAW FAMILY JOURNAL, THE. V. 1- Winter 1974-. Periodical. English. ir. $10.00. Ted O Brooke, 79 Wagonwheel Court, Marietta GA 30067. **Tel** (404)971-4737. **ED** Ted O Brooke. **LC** CS71; .U68A. **DD** 929/.2/0973. Index available. **Bk Rev. Circ:** 70 (ctrl).
Desc: Will contain historical and genealogical records concerning any persons descended from William Upshaw (ca 1666-1720), Essex County, Virginia.

CN/0837-0672
VABA EESTLANE. (VABA EESTLANE [MICROFORM] = FREE ESTONIAN.). [Vaba eest.]. **VFOAT** Free Estonian. (1952)-. Estonian. 86.00Can$ Canada; 115.00Can$ other. Free Estonian Ltd., 120A Willowdale Avenue, Willowdale Ontario, M2N 4Y2 Canada. **Tel** (416)733-4550. **DD** 971.3/5410049/4545.

US/0507-6544
VALLEY LEAVES. Added/Corp Tennessee Valley Genealogical Society. Vol. 1 (1966-67)-. Periodical. English. qt. $18.00 (Comes with Tennessee Valley Genealogical Society membership). Tennessee Valley Genealogical Society, PO Box 1568, Huntsville AL 35807. **Tel** (205)539-9060. **ED** Lois Robertson. **LC** F217.T3; V342. **DD** 929/.3768. Index available. **Bk Rev. Circ:** 530 (ctrl).
Desc: A publication of marriage records, cemeteries, court records, census, Bible records, etc. prior to 1900 of North Alabama counties. Unpublished source genealogy material.
Ind/Abst Genealogical Period. Annu. Index (19??-).

US/0897-9413
VAN BUREN ECHOES. (VAN BUREN ECHOES : VAN BUREN REGIONAL GENEALOGICAL SOCIETY QUARTERLY.). [Van Buren echoes]. **Added/Corp** Van Buren Regional Genealogical Society (Van Buren County, Mich.). **VFOAT** Echoes. (198?)-. Periodical. English. qt. $10.00 (US); $15.00 (other). Van Buren Region Genealogical Society, PO Box 143, Decatur MI 49045. **Tel** (616) 423-8045. **DD** 929. **Ad Acc. Circ:** 160.
Desc: Newsletter for genealogical/ family & local history research, containing information from primary & secondary sources for the following counties in Michigan: Allegan, Berrien, Cass, Kalamazoo, & Van Buren.

US/0736-3958
VAN ZANDT RECORD, THE. Vol. 1, No. 1 (March 1975)-. Periodical. English. Three times a year. $5.00 membership. Harrigan, 1343 West Baltimore Park, Media PA 19063. **LC** CS71; .V29138. **DD** 929/.2/0973.

US/0042-3491
VENTURA COUNTY HISTORICAL SOCIETY QUARTERLY. [Ventura Cty. Hist. Soc. q.]. **Main/Corp** Ventura County Historical Society. **Added/Corp** Ventura County Historical Society. Quarterly. Vol. 1 (Nov. 1955)-. Monographic series. English. qt. Price varies per volume. Ventura County Historical Society, 100 East Main Street, Ventura CA 93001. **Tel** (805)653-0323. **ED** Charles N. Johnson. **LC** F868.V5; V54. **DD** 794/.92/008. Index available. cum. index. **Circ:** 2,000.
Desc: Presents aspects/studies of county history and life.
Ind/Abst Am. Hist. Life (1971-1972); Genealogical Period. Annu. Index (19??-).

US/0277-4569
VICTORIA, CROSSROADS OF SOUTH TEXAS. Added/Corp Victoria County Genealogical Society. Vol. 1, No. 1 (Jan. 1980)-. Periodical. English. Four times a year (Mar., June, Sept., Dec.). $15.00. Victoria County Genealogical Society, 302 North Main Street, Victoria TX 77901. **Tel** (512)572-2708. **ED** Patsy Hand (phone: (512)575-0049). **LC** F392.V5; V5. **DD** 929/.3764/25. **Circ:** 200.
Ind/Abst Genealogical Period. Annu. Index (?-?).

US/1057-9761
VINCENT VOICES. [Vincent voices]. Vol. 1 (July 1991)-. Periodical. English. sa. $6.00. Patricia Vincent, 1370 Skyline Drive, Tacoma WA 98406. **DD** 929.

US/0739-3482
VIRGINIA APPALACHIAN NOTES. Added/Corp Southwestern Virginia Genealogical Society. Vol. 1, No. 3 (July 1977)-. Periodical. English. Four times a year (Feb., May, Aug., Nov.). $15.00 (individuals); $12.50 (institutions) Comes with Southwestern Virginia Genealogical Society. Southwestern Virginia Genealogical Society / SVGS, PO Box 12485, Roanoke VA 24026. **Tel** (703)345-8709. **ED** Vicie Fowler. **LC** F225; .A66. **DD** 929/.3755. Index available. **Bk Rev. Circ:** 650 (ctrl). ***Continues** Appalachian Notes (Roanoke, Va.).*
Desc: To publish court records, cemeteries, articles on related subjects of interest to the genealogist, early family histories, queries for this section of Virginia.

US/0300-645X
VIRGINIA GENEALOGIST, THE. Vol. 1, No. 1 (Jan./Mar. 1957)-. Periodical. English. qt. $20.00. Virginia Genealogist, PO Box 5860, Falmouth VA 22403. **Tel** (202)265-0663. **ED** John Frederick Dorman. **LC** F221; .V79. **DD** 929.109755. Index available. cum. index. **Bk Rev**, (Qty: 75). **Circ:** 1,200.
Desc: Source material and accounts of early generations of families of Virginia and West Virginia.
Ind/Abst Genealogical Period. Annu. Index.

US/0885-2626
VIRGINIA SETTLERS (QUARTERLY). (VIRGINIA SETTLERS.). (198?)-. Periodical. English. Four times a year. $10.00. A. Maxim Coppage FSA Scot, 653 Pershing Drive, Walnut Creek CA 94596. **Tel** (415)825-9796. **DD** 929. **Bk Rev.**

US/0099-2496
VIRGINIA TIDEWATER GENEALOGY. Added/Corp Hugh S. Watson Jr. Genealogical Society of Tidewater, Virginia. (19??)-. Periodical. English. Four times a year (Mar., June, Sept., Dec.). $15.00 (regular); $36.00 (sustaining). Tidewater Genealogical Society, PO Box 7650, Hampton VA 23666. **Tel** (804)925-2025. **ED** Franklin H. Farmer. **LC** F225; .V89. **DD** 929/.3755. **Bk Rev. Circ:** 460 (ctrl).
Desc: Genealogical information of Tidewater, Virginia.

US/0890-9423
VIRGINIA/WEST VIRGINIA QUERIES. [Va./W. V. queries]. **VFOAT** Va/W Va Queries; Va W Va Queries; Virginia, West Virginia Queries. Vol. 1 (1987)-. Periodical. English. ir. $5.50. Bette Butcher Topp, West 1304 Cliffwood Court, Spokane WA 99218. **Tel** (509)467-2299. **ED** Bette Butcher Topp. **DD** 929. Each issue contains an index to its own contents (no volume index)--loose. **Bk Rev.**
Desc: Queries of genealogical interest regarding ancestors/descendants in Virginia and/or West Virginia.
Ind/Abst Genealogical Period. Annu. Index.

US/0743-1848
VOIX DES PRAIRIES, LA. (LA VOIX DES PRAIRIES / EVANGELINE GENEALOGICAL AND HISTORICAL SOCIETY.). **Added/Corp** Evangeline Genealogical & Historical Society. No. 1 (Spring 1980)-. Periodical. English. qt (Jan., Apr., July, Oct.). $10.00. Evangeline Genealogy Historical Society, PO Box 664, Ville Platte LA 70586. **Tel** (318)363-1369. **ED** John Young. **LC** PAR. Index available (bound in Oct. issue; $2.00). cum. index. **Bk Rev. Circ:** 200.
Desc: Louisiana genealogy covering southwest parish's of old Imperial St. Landry Parish. Acadian genealogy, French, Spanish, British Isles, ancestry.

US/8755-2167
WACONDA ROOTS AND BRANCHES. [Waconda roots branches]. **Added/Corp** North Central Kansas Genealogical Society and Library, Inc. (19??)-. English. qt. $8.00. North Central Kansas Genealogical Society and Library Inc, PO Box 251, Cawker City KS 67430. **ED** Dorothy Reling. **LC** F680; .W33. **DD** 929/.1/0720781. **Bk Rev. Ad Acc. Circ:** 150 (ctrl).
Desc: Family histories and family records.
Ind/Abst Genealogical Period. Annu. Index.

US/0898-5421
WADE WORLD. [Wade world]. (April 1985)-. English. ir. $5.50 (add $1.75 postage). Name Game Enterprises, Mrs E Dale Hastin Smith, S 4204 Conklin Street, Spokane WA 99203-6235. **LC** CS71; .W11898. **DD** 929/.2/0973.

US
WAGONER (JOURNAL). (THE WAGONER.). **VFOAT** Wagoner Semiannual Journal; Wagoner Semi Annual Journal; NWGS Wagoner Journal. Vol. 2, No. 2 (Spring 1979)-. English. sa. $12.50 (membership fee, individuals), $15.00 (membership fee, couples), $5.00 (membership fee, libraries and institutions). Northwest Genealogical Society, PO Box 6, Alliance NE 69301. **Tel** (308)762-3677. **LC** F665; .N67. **DD** 929/.1/0727829. Index Available in first issue of next volume--attached. **Bk Rev. Ad Acc. Circ:** 200. ***Continues*** *Northwest Genealogical Society Quarterly.*
Desc: General genealogy articles; biographies; ancestor charts; cemetery and court house records, church records and other items and records as they are available.
Ind/Abst Genealogical Period. Annu. Index.

US/1048-9150
WAGS RAG. (WAGS RAG / WASECA AREA GENEALOGY SOCIETY.). [Wags rag]. **Added/Corp** Waseca Area Genealogy Society. (1979)-. Periodical. English. mo. $10.00 (will receive Historical Society Newsletter and Waseca Area Genealogy Society Membership). Waseca Area Genealogy Society, PO Box 314, Waseca MN 56093. **Tel** (507)835-7700. **DD** 929.

US/0743-6483
WAHKAW, THE. Vol. 1, No. 1 (Fall 1981)-. Periodical. English. qt. free. Woodbury County Genealogical Society, Box 624, Sioux City IA 51102. **LC** F627.W8; W34. **DD** 929/.1/072077741. Index available. cum. index. **Pr Rev. Circ:** 120 (ctrl).
Desc: Genealogy events, township history, family interviews, and much more pertaining to genealogy and genealogical research.

US/1055-7857
WAKE TREASURES. [Wake treas.]. **Added/Corp** Wake County Genealogical Society. Vol. 1, No. 1 (Spring 1991)-. Periodical. English. qt. $10.00 (institutions). Wake County Genealogical Society, PO Box 17713, Raleigh NC 27619. **LC** F262.W2; W23. **DD** 929/.1/072075655.
Ind/Abst Genealogical Period. Annu. Index.

UK/0307-028X
WALCOT FAMILY BULLETIN. [Walcot fam. bull.]. V. 1- June 1975-. Bulletin. English. qt. M Walcot, 9 Richmond Road, Birkdale, Southport Merseyside England. **LC** CS39; .W3418. **DD** 929/.2/0941.

US
WARD COUNTY HERITAGE. (19??)-. English. sa. $8.50. Ward County Genealogical Society, 400 East Fourth Street, Monahans TX 79756. **Tel** (915)943-6312. **ED** Chera Chemmer. ctrl circ.

US
WAVERLY GENEALOGICAL AND HISTORICAL SOCIETY NEWSLETTER. (19??)-. Newsletter. English. Four times a year. $7.00. Waverly Genealogical and Historical Society, 359 East Tremont, Waverly IL 62692. **Tel** (217)435-4961. **ED** Myra N. Martin. **Circ:** 100 (ctrl).

US/1067-523X
WEBSTER'S WAGON WHEEL. [Webster's wagon wheel]. **Added/Corp** Webster County Historical and Genealogical Society. **VFOAT** Wagon Wheel. (Jan.-Mar. 1980)-. Newsletter. English. Four times a year. $10.00 US; $2.00 other. Webster County Historical and Genealogical Society, PO Box 215, Dixon KY 42409. **Tel** (502)639-5170. **ED** Betty J. Branson (editor's address: 3448 State Route 983, Dixon, KY 42409). **LC** IN PROCESS. **DD** 929. **Bk Rev. Circ:** 90 (ctrl).
Desc: Newsletter of the Webster County Historical and Genealogical Society. Contains society news, historical articles and genealogical material gathered from various sources or contributed by members from Webster County and surrounding counties of Kentucky.

US/1060-4650
WEDGE (WILLOW STREET, PA.), THE. (THE WEDGE: NEWSLETTER.). [Wedge]. Vol. 1, No. 1 (Summer 1980)-. Newsletter. English. sa. $8.73 US; $12.50 other. Crystal Educational Counselors, 62 East Boehms Road, Willow Street PA 17584-9721. **Tel** (717)464-4201. **DD** 929.
Desc: Filled with genealogical and historical ideas to assist you in your search for your family "roots". Grandfather letters, the "Wanted" flyer, chronological events, genealogical references, directories, and many more items will help you complete your family heritage.

US/0883-7791
WEEDMAN NEWSLETTER. [Weedman newsl.]. Began 1968. Newsletter. English. qt. $5.00. Weedman Newsletter, 21522 Sitio Verano, El Toro CA 92630. **Tel** (714)770-7263. **ED** H N Weedman. **DD** 929. Index Available in first issue of next volume--loose--separately paged. **Bk Rev. Circ:** 100 (ctrl). available on microfilm from The State Historical Society of Wisconsin.
Desc: Family history and genealogy of Weedman and related lines.

UK/0142-517X
WEST MIDDLESEX FAMILY HISTORY SOCIETY JOURNAL. **Added/Corp** West Middlesex Family History Society. Vol. 1 No. 1 (Winter 1978)-. Periodical. English. Three times a year. £5.00 (individuals), £7.50 (family), £4.00 (corporate) memberships. Family History Society, 8 6th Avenue, Hayes Middlesex UB3 2ES England. **LC** CS435.M4; W47. **DD** 929/.1/07204218.

US
WESTCHESTER CONNECTIONS : JOURNAL OF THE WESTCHESTER COUNTY GENEALOGICAL SOCIETY. **Added/Corp** Westchester County Genealogical Society. Vol. 1, No. 1 (Sept. 1990)-. English. be. Westchester County Genealogical Society, PO Box 518, White Plains NY 10603. **LC** IN PROCESS.
Ind/Abst Genealogical Period. Annu. Index.

US/0049-7266
WESTCHESTER HISTORIAN, THE. See History(General)-History of North, South, and Central America.

US/0747-7805
WESTERN MARYLAND GENEALOGY. [West. Md. geneal.]. Vol. 1, No. 1 (Jan. 1985)-. Periodical. English. Four times a year. $19.00 US; $30.00 Canada. Western Maryland Genealogy, PO Box 505, New Market MD 21774-0505. **ED** Donna Valley Russell. **LC** F186.9; .W47. **DD** 929/.3752. Index available in last issue of volume--attached (October). **Bk Rev**, (Qty: 15). **Pr Rev. Circ:** 725 (ctrl).
Desc: Previously unpublished source records of Western Maryland, compiled genealogies, book reviews, free queries.
Ind/Abst Genealogical Period. Annu. Index.

US/0748-2515
WESTERN MONTANA GENEALOGICAL SOCIETY BULLETIN. **VFOAT** Bulletin. No. 1 (Winter 1981)-. Bulletin. English. qt. Western Montana Genealogical Society, PO Box 2714, Missoula MT 59806. **LC** F737.M6; W47. **DD** 929/.1/072078685.

US/0278-7431
WESTERN PENNSYLVANIA GENEALOGICAL SOCIETY QUARTERLY. **Added/Corp** Western Pennsylvania Genealogical Society. (19??)-. English. Four times a year. $20.00 US; $27.00 other. Western Pennsylvania Genealogical Society, 4338 Bigelow Boulevard, Building of the Historical Society, Pittsburgh PA 15213. **Tel** (412)681-5533. **ED** Jean S. Morris, PO Box 8530, Pittsburgh, PA 15220; Telephone: (412)734-4563. **LC** F148; .W48. **DD** 929/.3748. Each issue contains an index to its own contents (no volume index)--loose. **Bk Rev**, (Qty: 50-60). **Circ:** 2,000. available on microfilm. ***Continues*** *Western Pennsylvania Genealogical Quarterly, 0095-0866.*
Desc: Articles and lists pertaining to the 26 counties of western Pennsylvania.
Ind/Abst Genealogical Period. Annu. Index.

US
WESTERN TRAILS NEWSLETTER. (1993)-. Newsletter. English. Four times a year (Jan., Apr., July, Oct.). $10.00. Western Trails Genealogical Society, PO Box 70, Altus OK 73521. **Tel** (405)266-3358. **ED** Jodean Martin. Index available (Bound in next iss. ($10.00)). cum. index. **Circ:** 150.
Desc: News and information on the family history and other articles in Old Greer County, Texas and other surrounding areas.
Ind/Abst Genealogical Period. Annu. Index.

US/0738-0380
WESTWARD INTO NEBRASKA. **Added/Corp** Greater Omaha Genealogical Society. Vol. 1, No. 1-2 (Jan/Feb. 1977)-. Periodical. English. Ten times a year. $20.00. Greater Omaha Genealogical Society, PO Box 4011, Omaha NE 68104. **Tel** (402)296-3414. **ED** Jim and Nancy Phillips. **LC** F674.O553; A28. **DD** 929/.1/0720782254. Index available. **Bk Rev**, (Qty: varies). **Ad Acc. Circ:** 300.
Desc: Society's activities, workshops in the area, queries, advertising, research tips and helps, and committee reports.

US/0092-4164
WHERE THE TRAILS CROSS. [Where trails cross]. **Added/Corp** South Cook and North Will Counties Genealogical and Historical Society. South Suburban Genealogical and Historical Society. (197?)-. Periodical. English. qt. $15.00. South Suburban Genealogical and Historical Society, PO Box 96, South Holland IL 60473. **Tel** (708)333-9474. **ED** Jan Helge. **LC** F547.C7; W47. **DD** 929/.1/0627731. Index available (Index in each quaterly issue). **Bk Rev. Circ:** 550 (ctrl).
Desc: Contains information on local history and the genealogy of those residing in the south Cook and east Will county area of Illinois.
Ind/Abst Genealogical Period. Annu. Index.

US/0738-2340
WHERE TO WRITE FOR VITAL RECORDS. May 1982-. English. US Department of Health and Human Services, 200 Independence Avenue Southwest, Washington DC 20201. **LC** HA38. **DD** 929/.1/02573. **NLM** HA 38.A3; W567. ***Formed by the union of*** *Where to Write for Birth and Death Records, United States and Outlying Areas, 0098-8022; Where to Write for Divorce Records, United States and Outlying Areas, 0565-8454* ***and*** *Where to Write for Marriage Records, United States and Outlying Areas, 0162-0916.*

US/8756-6931
WILL-GRUNDY COUNTIES GENEALOGICAL SOCIETY QUARTERLY. [Will-Grundy Cties. Geneal. Soc. q.]. **Added/Corp** Will-Grundy Counties Genealogical Society. Vol. 1, No. 1/2 (Winter 1982/83)-. Periodical. English. qt. $10.00. Will-Grundy Counties Genealogical Society, PO Box 24, Wilmington IL 60481. **Tel** (815)478-3715. **LC** F547.W5; W54. **DD** 929/.1/072077325. Each issue contains an index to its own contents (no volume index)--loose.

US/0043-5627
WILLIAMS' FAMILY BULLETIN, THE. [Williams' fam. bull.]. Began in Jan. 1966. Bulletin. English. qt. $10.00. Williams Family Trails, 208 Chippewa Street, West Lafayette IN 47906. **Tel** (317)463-7828. **ED** Theodore J and Isabel McAnulty Williams. **LC** CS71; .W7198. **DD** 929/.2/0973. Index available. cum. index. **Bk Rev. Circ:** 100.

US/0734-953X
WILSON WAREHOUSE. Periodical. English. qt. $10.50. Charlotte M. Tucker, #18 Doe Run, The Woodlands TX 77380. **LC** CS71; .W7497. **DD** 929/.2/0973.

US
WINDY TIMES. English. $10.00. Liberal Area Genealogical Society, PO Box 1094, Liberal KS 67905. **Tel** (304)624-5389.
Ind/Abst Genealogical Period. Annu. Index.

US/0742-6356
WINEGAR TREE, THE. Vol. 3, No. 1 (Jan. 1980)-. Periodical. English. qt. $12.00. Arthur Goold Editor, 412 North Plum Street, Northfield MN 55057. **Tel** (507)645-6738. **LC** CS71; .W76698. **DD** 929/.2/0973. Index available. **Circ:** 250. ***Continues*** *Wineinger, Winegar, Wininger Newsletter.*

US/0743-7102
WINN PARISH COURIER. [Winn Parish courier]. Vol. 1, No. 1 (Jan. 1984)-. Periodical. English. qt. $10.00. Courier Publications, PO Box 1320, Winnfield LA 71483. **Tel** (318)628-2019. **LC** F377.W6; W56. **DD** 929/.376366.

US/0743-7099
WOMACK COURIER. **VFOAT** Womack Family Courier. Vol. 1, No. 1 (Jan. 1984)-. Periodical. English. qt. $10.00. Courier Publications, PO Box 1320, Winnfield LA 71483. **Tel** (318)628-2019. **LC** CS71; .W8658. **DD** 929/.2/0973.

US/0091-6706
WOOD-WOODS FAMILY MAGAZINE, THE. [Wood-woods fam. mag.]. (197?)-. Periodical. English. qt. $38.00. Wood-Woods Family Magazine, 903 Myers Avenue, Columbia TN 38401. **Tel** (615)388-2368. **LC** CS71; .W8753. **DD** 929/.2/0973.

US/0741-6881
WOODSON WATCHER PLUS ALLIED LINES. Vol. 1, No. 1 (Nov. 1982)-. Periodical. English. qt (Feb., May, Aug., Nov.). $15.00. Lineage Search Associates, 6419 Colts Neck Road, Mechanicsville VA 23111. **Tel** (804)730-7414. **(Subscription address:** 1750

Allegro Drive, Richmond, VA 23231 or 6419 Colts Neck Road, Mechanicsville, VA 23111-4233) **ED** Felix Earle Luck, Mary McCraw Harland. **LC** CS71; .W88897. **DD** 929/.2/0973.
Desc: A publication for researchers with interest of Woodson ancestry.

US/0740-9516
WORDENS PAST. Vol. 1, No. 1 (May 1980)-. Periodical. English. Wordens Past, 1201 Glendale, Midland MI 48640. **LC** CS71; .W26298. **DD** 929/.2/0973.

US/0270-1995
WORLD HERITAGE WORLD. [World herit. world]. (19??)-. Periodical. English. qt. $9.00 US; $11.00 Canada. World Heritage Publishing Company, 352 South 300/Suite 6, Salt Lake City UT 84111. **LC** CS1; .W67. **DD** 929/.1/05.

US/8755-5344
WORTHINGTON DESCENDANTS. [Worthington descend.]. Began in 1982. Periodical. English. qt. $12.00. Worthington Descendants, 6619 Pheasant Road, Route 16, Baltimore MD 21220. **DD** 929.

US/8756-7229
WRIGHT FAMILY WORKBOOK. [Wright fam. workb.]. Vol. 1, No. 1 (Jan. 1984)-. Periodical. English. Three times a year. $12.00. Claudette Maerz, PO Box 37010, Bloomington MN 55431. **Tel** (613)257-5355, (612)881-4864. **LC** CS71; .W9488. **DD** 929/.2/0973.

US/0428-7282
YEAR BOOK - FLORIDA GENEALOGICAL SOCIETY, TAMPA, FLA. **Main/Corp** Florida Genealogical Society, Tampa, Fla. (19??)-. English. an. $7.00. Florida Genealogical Society, PO Box 18624, Tampa FL 33679-8624. **Tel** (813)839-0810. **ED** Helen Norris Byrd. **DD** 929. **Bk Rev. Ad Acc. Circ:** 315 (ctrl).
Desc: Genealogical and historical material, primarily but not restricted to Florida, queries and book reviews.

US/1050-7361
YELLOWED PAGES. [Yellowed pages]. **Added/Corp** Southeast Texas Genealogical and Historical Society. Vol. 1 (1971)-. Periodical. English. qt. $15.00. Southeast Texas Genealogical and Historical Society, P.O.Box 3827, Tyrrell His. Library, Beaumont TX 77704-3827. **Tel** (409)899-3191. **ED** Margie Boyd. **LC** IN PROCESS. **DD** 929. Index available. **Bk Rev**, (Qty: 20). **Circ:** 300.
Desc: Family histories and genealogies of southeast Texas families. Census information, tax lists, five generation charts, queries from members; Bible, cemetery, and marriage records for southeast Texas counties.

US/0277-9668
YELLOWJACKET (QUINCY, ILL.). (THE YELLOWJACKET: A QUARTERLY PUBLICATION OF THE GREAT RIVER GENEALOGICAL SOCIETY / GREAT RIVER GENEALOGICAL SOCIETY.). [Yellowjacket]. **Added/Corp** Great River Genealogical Society. Vol. 3, No. 1 (Mar. 1977)-. Periodical. English. qt. $8.00 libraries & senior citizens; $10.00 other (comes with membership to Great River Genealogical Society). Quincy Public Library, 526 Jersey, Great River Genealogical Society, Quincy IL 62301. **Tel** (217)223-1309. **ED** Kay J Ginther, Frances Schulte and Nancy Zengel. **LC** F540; .Y36. **DD** 929/.377344. Index available. **Bk Rev. Circ:** 325. ***Continues** Yellowjacket of the Great River Genealogical Society, 0277-5603.*
Desc: Items of interest sent to us by members, also queries published. New books on genealogy listed.

US/0278-3924
YESTERDAYS. Vol. 1, No. 1 (Mar. 1981)-. Periodical. English. sa. Nacogdoches Genealogical Society, PO Box 4634 SFA Sta, Nacogdoches TX 75962. **LC** F392.N2; Y47. **DD** 929/.3764182.
Ind/Abst Genealogical Period. Annu. Index.

US
YESTERDAYS (GONZALES ,TX). (YESTERDAYS.). **Added/Corp** South Texas Genealogical & Historical Society. Vol. 14, No. 1 (Sept. 1979)-. Periodical. English. sa. $6.00 members, $3.00 per issue nonmembers. South Texas Genealogical & Historical Society, PO Box 768, Gonzales TX 78629-0768. **LC** F385; .S67a. **DD** 929/.3764. ***Continues** Semi-Annual Publication of the South Texas Genealogical & Historical Society.*

US/0044-037X
YESTERYEARS. [Yesteryears]. (1956)-. Periodical. English. qt. $9.00 (one year), $17.00 (two year). Yesteryears, 3 Seymour Street, Auburn NY 13021. **Tel** (315)253-4058. **ED** Malcolm O. Goodelle. **LC** F116; .Y4. **DD** 974.7/005. **Bk Rev. Ad Acc. Circ:** 400 (ctrl). available on microfilm from Xerox; available on microfilm and microfiche from University Microfilms International (UMI).
Desc: Unpublished articles dealings with histories and genealogies of New York state citizens.

US
YORK COUNTY GENEALOGICAL SOCIETY JOURNAL. (19??)-. Periodical. English. Four times a year. $10.00 members; $15.00 nonmembers. York County Genealogical Society, PO Box 2242, Ogunquit ME 03907. **Tel** (207)646-3753, FAX (207)646-3753. **ED** Theodore S. Bond (editor's address: 72 Damon Avenue, Melrose, MA 02176). Index available. **Circ:** 200.

US/1058-2045
YOUNKIN FAMILY NEWS BULLETIN. [Younkin fam. news bull.]. **VFOAT** YFNB. Vol. 1, No. 1 (Jan., Feb., Mar. 1990)-. Bulletin. English. qt. Donna Younkin Logan, 12109-A Old Frederick Road, Thurmont MD 21788. **LC** IN PROCESS. **DD** 929.

CN/0833-2908
YOUR NEWS. [Your news]. (1985)-. Periodical. English. Ten times a year (monthly except July and Aug.). 12.15Can$. Your News, PO Box 563, Sta Cote St Luc, Montreal Quebec, H4Z 2Z2 Canada. **ED** Frances Phelan (editor's Address: 131 Percival, Montreal West Quebec H4X 1T7 Canada; editor's Phone: (514)487-5797). **DD** 071/.14281. **Bk Rev**, (Qty: 4-5). **Circ:** 7,500.
Desc: A teaching newspaper used in the classroom to teach language arts, ESL, literacy, special education or regular curriculum middle school.

US
YOUR YANKEE HERITAGE. Vol. 1, No. 1 (June 1979)-. Periodical. English. mo. $12.00. Your Yankee Heritage, Box 186, Strong ME 04983. **LC** F3; .Y68. **DD** 929/.374.

US
YUCAIPA VALLEY FAMILY FINDERS QUARTERLY / YUCAIPA VALLEY GENEALOGICAL SOCIETY. ***Title Change.*** **Added/Corp** Yucaipa Valley Genealogical Society. **VFOAT** Family Finders; YVGS Family Finders Quarterly; Yucaipa Valley Genealogical Society Family Finders Quarterly. Vol. 1, No. 1 (Apr. 1983)-(1992). Periodical. English. qt. Yucaipa Valley Genealogical Society, PO Box 32, Yucaipa CA 92399. **LC** F868.S14; Y8. **DD** 929/.1/072079495. ***Continued by** YVGS Family Finders.*

●US/1069-9333
YVGS FAMILY FINDERS. (YVGS FAMILY FINDERS / YUCAIPA VALLEY GENEALOGICAL SOCIETY, INC.). [YVGS fam. finders]. **Added/Corp** Yucaipa Valley Genealogical Society. **VFOAT** Family Finders. **VAT** Yucaipa Valley Genealogical Society Family Finders. Vol. 10, No. 5 (May 1992)-. Periodical. English. mo. Yucaipa Valley Genealogical Society, PO Box 32, Yucaipa CA 92399. **LC** F868.S14; Y8. **DD** 929/.1/072079495. ***Continues** Yucaipa Valley Family Finders Quarterly.*

AU
ZEITSCHRIFT DES VERBANDES DER NAMENSTRAGER. German. Verband der Namenstrager, A-6800 Feldkirch-Tosters, Illstrasse 53 Austria. **LC** CS519; .B8748. **DD** 929/.2/094.

US
ZIEGENFUSS FAMILIES, THE. English. Mark Amanns, 124 Columbia Heights, Brooklyn NY 11201. **LC** CS71; .Z6499. **DD** 929/.2/0973.

US
[PUBLICATIONS] / NORTHAMPTON COUNTY HISTORICAL AND GENEALOGICAL SOCIETY. **Added/Corp** Northampton County Historical and Genealogical Society. Vol. 1 (1926)-. English. qt (Jan., Apr., July, Oct.). $25.00. Northampton County Historical & Genealogical Society, 101 South Fourth Street, Easton PA 18042. **Tel** (215)253-1222. **ED** Paul Schlueter (phone: (610)258-1790). **LC** F157.N7; N85. **Circ:** 850.

ABSTRACTING, BIBLIOGRAPHIES AND STATISTICS

US
AMERICAN GENEALOGICAL-BIOGRAPHICAL INDEX. **Main/Corp** Godfrey Memorial Library. No. 48 (Feb. 1959)-. Periodical. English. qt (published seasonally). $300.00. Godfrey Memorial Library, 134 Newfield Street, Middletown CT 06457. **Tel** (203)346-4375. ctrl circ.
Desc: Indexes genealogical volumes and city and county histories.

FR
DOCUMENTATION, LIBRARIES, AND ARCHIVES : BIBLIOGRAPHIES AND REFERENCE WORKS. **Added/Corp** Unesco. No. 1 (1972)-. Monographic series. English. UNESCO / France, 31 rue Francois Bonvin, 75732 Paris Cedex 15 France. **Tel** 011 33 1 45684564, 011 33 1 45684565, FAX 011 33 1 42733007, telex 204461 Paris. **DD** 020.

US/0894-0487
FAMILY FOOTSTEPS QUARTERLY. **See** Genealogy and Heraldry.

US/0072-0593
GENEALOGICAL PERIODICAL ANNUAL INDEX. Vol. 1 (1962)-. Abstracting/Indexing Service. English. an. $23.00 (includes postage). Heritage Books Inc, 1540E Pointer Ridge Place, Suite 103, Bowie MD 20716. **Tel** (301)390-7708. **ED** Laird C Towle. **LC** CS42; .G467. **DD** 016.929105873. **Circ:** 1,000.
Desc: Surname, locality and topical index to over 340 current English-language genealogical periodicals.

ARCHIVES

US/0276-8291
ABBEY NEWSLETTER, THE. [Abbey newsl.]. **VFOAT** A.N.L.; A.N.; ANL; AN; Abbey Newsletter: Bookbinding and Conservation. No. 1 (Aug. 1975)-No. 15 (July 1978); Vol. 2, No. 1, (Sept. 1978)-. Newsletter. English. Eight times a year. $49.00 (institutions), $40.00 (individuals). Abbey Publications, 7105 Geneva Drive, Austin TX 78723. **Tel** (512)929-3992, FAX (515)929-3995. **ED** Ellen McCrady. Index Available in first issue of next volume--attached. cum. index. **Bk Rev. Circ:** 1,200. available on an online database from DIALOG.
Desc: Technical aspects of preservation of library and archival materials.
Ind/Abst Abstr. Bull. Inst. Pap. Sci. Tech.; Art Archaeol. Tech. Abstr.; Biodeter. Abstr. (1991-); Graph. Arts Bull. Inst. Pap. Sci. Technol. (March, May, Oct., Dec. 1989).

CN/0709-4604
ACA BULLETIN. (A C A BULLETIN : ASSOC. OF CANADIAN ARCHIVISTS.). [ACA bull.]. **Main/Corp** Association of Canadian Archivists. **VAT** Association of Canadian Archivists Bulletin; Bulletin - Association of Canadian Archivists. V. 4, No. 4- Aug. 1979-. Bulletin. English. bm. 70.00Can$ (membership Association of Canadian Archivists). Association of Canadian Archivists, PO Box 2596 Station D, Ottawa ONT K1P 5W6 Canada. **Tel** (613)443-0251. **DD** 025.17/14/0971. ***Continues** Archives Bulletin, 0319-3179.*
Ind/Abst Art Archaeol. Tech. Abstr.

KE
ACCESSIONS LIST / MINISTRY OF HOME AFFAIRS AND NATIONAL HERITAGE, DEPARTMENT OF KENYA NATIONAL ARCHIVES, NATIONAL DOCUMENTATION AND INFORMATION RETRIEVAL SERVICES. **Main/Corp** Kenya National Archives. National Documentation and Information Retrieval Services. (1990)-. English. sa. Kenya National Archives, Chief Archivist, PO Box 49210, Nairobi, Kenya. **LC** IN PROCESS.

BL
ACERVO : REVISTA DO ARQUIVO NACIONAL. Vol. 1, No. 1 (Jan./June 1986)-. Periodical. Portuguese. sa. Acervo - Revista do Arquivo Nacional, Rua Azeredo Coutinho, 77 CEP 20.230 Rio de Janeiro Brasil. **Tel** (021)224-4525. **LC** CD4060; .A34. **Circ:** 1,500.

AT/0815-0494
ACQUISITIONS ULTIMO. **See** Library and Information Sciences.

CN/0382-9197
ADPA. AUTOMATIC DATA PROCESSING AND ARCHIVES. ***Ceased.*** (ADPA.). [ADPA, Autom. data process. arch.]. **VAT** Automatic Data Processing and Archives. V. 1- Aug. (1972)-?. English (French). ir. International Council on Archives, rue de Buissons 65, B 4000 Liege Belgium. **LC** CD1; .A16. **DD** 025.17/1.
Ind/Abst ARTbibliogr. Mod.; Libr. Inf. Sci. Abstr.

CN/0827-0074
AMA NEWSLETTER. ***Title Change.*** (AMA NEWSLETTER / ASSOCIATION OF MANITOBA ARCHIVISTS.). [AMA newsl.]. **Added/Corp** Association of Manitoba Archivists. Association for Manitoba Archives. **VAT** Association of Manitoba Archivists Newsletter. Vol. 1, No. 1 (Summer 1980)-Vol. 12, No. 4 (Summer 1992). Newsletter. English. qt. Association of Manitoba Archivists, c/o Provincial Archives of Manitoba, 200 Vaughn Street, Winnipeg Manitoba R3C 1T5 Canada. **DD** 027.07127. ***Continued by** Communique (Association for Manitoba Archives), 1193-9958.*

US/0360-9081
AMERICAN ARCHIVIST, THE. [Am. arch.]. Vol. 1 (Jan. 1938)-. Periodical. English. qt. $85.00 US, Canada and Mexico; $100.00 other. Society of American Archivists, 600 South Federal, Suite 504, Chicago IL 60605. **Tel** (312)922-0140, FAX (312)347-1452. **ED** Richard J. Cox, (412)624-9438. **LC** CD3020. **DD** 025.17/1. **NLM** W1 AM1752. Index available. **Bk Rev. Ad Acc, Adv Mgr:** T Brinati, **Tel** (312)922-0140. **Pr Rev. Circ:** 4,600 (ctrl). available on magnetic tape, an online database, and CD-ROM; available on microfilm and microfiche from University Microfilms International (UMI).

Documents available from The Genuine Article.
Desc: In-depth articles on archival theory and practice, reviews of relevant literature, and reports on archival activities around the world. Occasional theme issues focus on specialized aspects of the profession.
Ind/Abst Am. Hist. Life (1954-); Am. Bibliogr. Slavic East Europ. Stud.; Art Archaeol. Tech. Abstr.; Arts Humanit. Citation Index [Full Cov.]; Book Rev. Index; Curr. Contents Arts Humanit.; Curr. Contents Soc. Behav. Sci.; Index Period. Artic. Relat. Law; Inf. Instruc. Technol.; Inf. Sci. Abstr.; Libr. Inf. Sci. Abstr.; Libr. Lit.; Middle East Abstr. Index; Res. Alert [Full Cov.]; Soc. Sci. Cit. Index [Full Cov.].

SP
ANEJOS DEL BOLETIN DE LA DIRECCION GENERAL DE ARCHIVOS Y BIBLIOTECAS. **Added/Corp** Spain. Direccion General de Archivos y Bibliotecas. (19??)-. Monographic series. Spanish. Price varies per volume. Asociacion Espanola de Archiveros, Bibliotecarios Museologosy Documentalistas, Apartado 14281, 28001 Madrid Spain. **Tel** 011 34 1 5751727. **LC** CD27.S6; A3.
Ind/Abst Am. Hist. Life (1955-1967).

CN/0821-7157
ANLA BULLETIN / ASSOCIATION OF NEWFOUNDLAND AND LABRADOR ARCHIVISTS. [ANLA bull.]. **VAT** Association of Newfoundland and Labrador Archivists Bulletin. Vol. 1, No. 1 (May 1983)-. Bulletin. English. qt. Free. Association of Newfoundland and Labrador Archivists, Colonial Building Military Road, St John's Newfoundland A1C 2C9 Canada. **DD** 025.17/14/060718. ctrl circ.

CN/0846-7951
ANNUAL REPORT OF THE BOARD OF TRUSTEES FOR THE YEAR - PUBLIC ARCHIVES OF NOVA SCOTIA. (ANNUAL REPORT OF THE BOARD OF TRUSTEES FOR THE YEAR ...). [Annu. rep. Board Trustees year - Public Arch. N.S.]. **Main/Corp** Public Archives of Nova Scotia. (1978)-. English. Public Archives of Nova Scotia, 6016 University Avenue, Halifax Nova Scotia B3H 1W4 Canada. **Tel** (902)423-9115. **DD** 027.5716. ***Continues*** *Report of the Board of Trustees of the Public Archives of Nova Scotia., 0078-2467.*

US/0160-1415
ANNUAL REPORT OF THE MISSISSIPPI DEPARTMENT OF ARCHIVES AND HISTORY. **Main/Corp** Mississippi. Dept. of Archives and History. **Added/Corp** Mississippi State Library. Report. Mississippi Library Commission. Biennial Report. 1st Ed. (1902)-. English. an. Free. Mississippi Department of Archives and History, PO Box 571, Jackson MS 39205. **Tel** (601)359-1424. **LC** CD3320; .A2; F336.M56.
Desc: Report for 1936-37 includes the Biennial report of the State Librarian, 1935-37; and the 6th biennial report of the State Library Commission, 1936-37.

AT
ANNUAL REPORT, YEAR ENDED 30 JUNE ... / PUBLIC RECORD OFFICE.
Main/Corp Victoria. Public Record Office. English. an. Public Record Office, 19th Floor/Nauru House, 80 Collins Street, Melbourne 3000 Australia. **LC** CD2525.V5; V5A. **DD** 354.9450071/4.

MX
ANUARIO DE BIBLIOTECOLOGIA, ARCHIVOLOGIA E INFORMATICA. **See** Library and Information Sciences.

AG/0325-3899
ANUARIO INTERAMERICANO DE ARCHIVOS. **Added/Corp** Universidad Nacional de Cordoba. Centro Interamericano de Desarrollo de Archivos. (1983)-. Spanish. an. Centro Interamericano de Desarrollo de Archivos, Avd. Hipolito Irigoye 174, 5000 Cordoba, Argentina. **Tel** 011 54 5129048. **LC** CD3680; .B63. ***Continues*** *Boletin Interamericana de Archivos.*
Ind/Abst Am. Hist. Life (1978-); HAPI Hisp. Am. Period. Index.

AT/0812-6755
ARCHEION : THE NEWSLETTER OF THE STATE ARCHIVES. **Main/Corp** Archives Authority of New South Wales. (19??)-. Newsletter. English. an (Nov.). 20.00Aus$ (two year). State Archives Australia, 2 Globe Street, The Rocks, Sydney NSW 2000 Australia. **Tel** 61 2 2370200. **Ad Acc**, **Adv Mgr:** Martyn Killion, **Tel** 011 2 2370126.
Ind/Abst Am. Hist. Life (1954-1961, 1965-1976, 1979-); Aust. Educ. Index (June 1986-); Aust. Libr. Inf. Sci. Abstr. (1983, 1985-).

NZ/0303-7940
ARCHIFACTS. [Archifacts]. **Added/Corp** New Zealand Library Association. Archives Committee. No. 1 (Apr. 1974)-. English. qt (Mar., June, Sept., Dec.). comes with Archives and Records Association of New Zealand membership. Bulletin of the Archives and Records Association of New Zealand, PO Box 11-553, Wellington New Zealand. **Tel** 011 64 4 856109. **ED** C. Marr. **LC** CD2560; .A7. **DD** 027/.0931. **[CCC]**. **Bk Rev**. **Ad Acc**. **Circ:** 600 (ctrl).
Desc: Articles, happenings, collections, personalities, ideas, plans, visitors, reviews and other affairs in the New Zealand archives, manuscripts and records world.
Ind/Abst Libr. Inf. Sci. Abstr.

FR/0769-0975
ARCHIMAG VINCENNES. (1986)-. Periodical. French. Ten times a year. 837.41F France; 950.00F other. ENTDA, 9 rue Bleue, F 75009 Paris France. **Tel** 011 33 1 47704141, FAX 48000342. **UDC** 681.3 : 002. **Bk Rev**. **Ad Acc**. **Circ:** 7,500.
Desc: New technologies applied to the information systems: documentation, archives, software, optical disks, description of applications.

US/8756-9663
ARCHIVAL INFORMER, THE. Periodical. English. qt. $4.50, $8.50 (institutions), $12.00 (patrons), $25.00 (life subscription). Archival Services, PO Box 78191, Shreveport LA 71137-8191. **Tel** (318)929-4707. **ED** J A Sibley and Jeff Hughes. **Bk Rev**. **Ad Acc**. **Circ:** 80.
Desc: Complete update information on archival technology and new procedures written for the layperson. Contains a listing of workshops and seminars held by major museum/archive associations and special guest writings.

●US/1067-4993
ARCHIVAL ISSUES : JOURNAL OF THE MIDWEST ARCHIVES CONFERENCE. [Arch. issues]. **Added/Corp** Midwest Archives Conference. (1992)-. Periodical. English. Twice a year (Jan., & July). $48.00 (institutions); $32.00 (individuals). Midwest Archives Conference, 3400 Broadway Indian University Northwest, Gary IN 46408. **Tel** (219)980-6628. **LC** CD3054; .M53. **DD** 025. Index available ($4.00). **Bk Rev**. ***Continues*** *Midwestern Archivist, 0363-888X.*
Ind/Abst Am. Hist. Life; Libr. Lit.

●US
ARCHIVAL OUTLOOK / THE SOCIETY OF AMERICAN ARCHIVISTS. **Added/Corp** Society of American Archivists. (Mar. 1993)-. Periodical. English. bm. Free to members of the Society of American Archivists. Society of American Archivists, 600 South Federal, Suite 504, Chicago IL 60605. **Tel** (312)922-0140, FAX (312)347-1452. **LC** IN PROCESS. ***Continues*** *SAA Newsletter, 0091-5971.*

GW/0003-9497
ARCHIVALISCHE ZEITSCHRIFT. [Arch. Z.]. **Added/Corp** Bavaria (Germany). Hauptstaatsarchiv. (1876)-. German (English and French). ir. DM146.00. Boehlau Verlag GmbH & Cie / Koeln, Theodor Heuss STR 76, D-51149 Cologne Germany. **Tel** 011 49 2203 307021, FAX 011 49 2203 307349. **(Subscription address:** BDK Buecherdienst GmBh, Postfach 900120, D 51111 Cologne Germany.**)** **LC** D111; .A7. cum. index. **Circ:** 500.
Ind/Abst Am. Hist. Life (1954-1957),(1972-1977); BHA : Biblio. Hist. Art.

GW/0003-9500
ARCHIVAR, DER. [Archivar]. **Added/Corp** Verein Deutscher Archivare. North Rhine-Westphalia. Staatsarchiv. Hauptstaatsarchiv Duesseldorf. Vol. 1 (1947)-. Periodical. German. Four times a year. $66.00. Verlag Franz Schmitt, Kaiserstrasse 99-101, D 53721 Siegburg Germany. **Tel** 011 49 2241 64039, FAX 011 49 2241 53891. **ED** Dieter Weber. **LC** CD9; .A73. Index available. cum. index. **Bk Rev**. **Ad Acc**. **Circ:** 2,200.
Desc: Archives reports, archives of firms, libraries and universities and the government.
Ind/Abst Am. Hist. Life (1968-); Bibliogr. Carto.; Libr. Inf. Sci. Abstr.; PAIS Int. Print.

CN/0318-6954
ARCHIVARIA. [Archivaria]. **Added/Corp** Association of Canadian Archivists. Vol. 1, No. 1 (Winter 1975/6)-. Academic Scholarly Publication. English. sa. $35.00 individuals, $45.00 institutions. Association of Canadian Archivists, PO Box 2596 Station D, Ottawa ONT K1P 5W6 Canada. **Tel** (613)443-0251. **ED** Jay Atherton. **LC** CD3620; .A73. **DD** 027.571. Index available. cum. index. **Bk Rev**, (Qty: 20). **Pr Rev**. **Acid Free**. **Circ:** 900. ***Continues*** *Canadian Archivist, 0068-824X.*
Desc: Devoted to scholarly investigation of archives in Canada and internationally. Explores the history, nature and theory of archival activity and equally the use of archives. Aims to be bridge of communication between archivists and users of archives.
Ind/Abst Am. Hist. Life; Art Archaeol. Tech. Abstr.; Can. Index (?-?); Can. Period. Index; Libr. Inf. Sci. Abstr.; Middle East Abstr. Index.

AT
ARCHIVE OF AUSTRALIAN JUDAICA HOLDINGS TO ... . **Added/Corp** University of Sydney. Archive of Australian Judaica. (198?)-. Monographic series. English. ir. Price varies per volume. University of Sydney Fisher Library, Rare Books, Sydney 2006 New South Wales Australia. **Tel** 011 61 2 6924162, FAX 011 61 2 6922890. **ED** Jennifer Alison, A. D. Crown, N. A. Radford and Marianne Dacy. **LC** Z6611.J48; A73; DS135.A88. **DD** 016.994/004924. cum. index. **Bk Rev**. **Circ:** 200 (ctrl).

UK/0955-1034
ARCHIVE SERVICES STATISTICS ... ESTIMATES. **Added/Corp** Chartered Institute of Public Finance and Accountancy. Statistical Information Service. (19??)-. English. Chartered Institute of Public Finance and Accountancy, 2 3 Robert Street, London WC2N 6BH England. **Tel** 011 44 1 895 8823. **LC** CD1040; .A73. **DD** 027.542.

FR
ARCHIVES. English. Edition la Reliure Admin, BP 11, 33320 Le Taillan France.

AT/0157-6895
ARCHIVES AND MANUSCRIPTS. [Arch. manuscr.]. V. 1- Nov. 1955-. Periodical. English. sa. 40.00Aus$. Australian Society of Archivists Inc, PO Box 83, O'Connor Australian Capital Territory 2601 Australia. **Tel** (02)660 7979, FAX (02)552 2034. **ED** C Smith. **LC** CD4; .A75. **Bk Rev**. **Ad Acc**. **Circ:** 800 (ctrl). ***Continues*** *Bulletin for Australian Archivists.*
Desc: Articles and book reviews on all matters concerned with archives and manuscript theory and practice with emphasis on the Australian scene.
Ind/Abst Am. Hist. Life (1963-1977, 1979-); APAIS, Aust. Public Aff. Inf. Ser.; Art Archaeol. Tech. Abstr.; Aust. Educ. Index (1982-); Inf. Sci. Abstr.; Libr. Inf. Sci. Abstr.

US/1042-1467
ARCHIVES & MUSEUM INFORMATICS. **See** Computers-Automation.

US/1042-1459
ARCHIVES AND MUSEUM INFORMATICS TECHNICAL REPORT. [Arch. mus. inform. tech. rep.]. **Added/Corp** Archives & Museum Informatics (Firm). Vol. 3, No. 1 (Spring 1989)-Vol. 3, No. 4 (1990)-No. 9-13 (1991)-. Monographic series. English. ir. Price varies per volume. Archives & Museum Informatics, 5501 Walnut Street, Suite 203, Pittsburgh PA 15232-2311. **Tel** (412)683-9775, FAX (412)683-7366. **ED** David Bearman and Lynn Cox. **DD** 069. **Circ:** 200. ***Continues*** *Archival Informatics Newsletter & Technical Report. Part 2, Archival Informatics Technical Report, 0894-0266.*
Desc: Addresses information management issues facing archives and museums. Reports are designed to provide practical guidance on such issues as selecting and collecting software, determining functional requirements for management systems, and evaluating the impact of new technologies.
Ind/Abst Ei Page One.

CN/0827-018X
ARCHIVES CANADA MICROFICHES. (ARCHIVES CANADA MICROFICHES / PUBLIC ARCHIVES CANADA.). [Arch. Can. microfiches]. **Main/Corp** Public Archives Canada. **Added/Corp** Public Archives Canada. Picture Division. (1976)-. Periodical. English (French). Five times a year. 25.00Can$ Canada; 30.00Can$ other. Canada Communication Group Publishers, Order Processing, Ottawa Ontario K1A 0S9 Canada. **Tel** (819)956-4800, (819)956-4802. **LC** F1013; .P98a.

BE/0003-9748
ARCHIVES ET BIBLIOTHEQUES DE BELGIQUE. [Arch. bibl. Belg.]. **Added/Corp** Association des Archivistes et Bibliothecaires (Belgium) Association des Archivistes et des Bibliothecaires de Belgique. **VFOAT** Archief- en Bibliotheekwezen in Belgie. (1963)-. Periodical. Dutch (English, French, German, Spanish and Italian). qt. $30.00. Archives Bibl. de Belgique, rue de Ruysbroeck 2-6, B1000 Brussels Belgium. **LC** CD1670; .A7. Index available. **Bk Rev**. **Circ:** 400 (ctrl). ***Continues*** *Archives, Bibliotheques, et Musees de Belgique.*
Ind/Abst Am. Hist. Life (1964-1971); Annu. Bibliogr. Engl. Lang. Lit.; BHA : Biblio. Hist. Art.

US
ARCHIVES II RESEARCHER BULLETIN / NATIONAL ARCHIVES AND RECORDS ADMINISTRATION. **Added/Corp** United States. National Archives and Records Administration. **VFOAT** Archives 2 Researcher Bulletin; Archives Two Researcher Bulletin; National Archives and Records Administration Bulletin; NARA Bulletin. No. 1 (Spring 1991)-. Bulletin. English. qt. National Archives and Records Administration, Eighth Street and Pennsylvania Avenue NW, Washington DC 20408. **Tel** (202)523-3220.

US
ARCHIVES INFORMATION BULLETIN. **Added/Corp** Missouri. Record Management and Archives Service. Vol. 1 (Jan. 1979)-. Bulletin. English. qt. Records Management and Archives Service, 100 Industrial Drive, Jefferson City MO 65102. **LC** CD3330; .A7. **DD** 016.9778.

US/0093-9056
ARCHIVES INFORMATION CIRCULAR. English. Varies from $0.15-$0.50. North Carolina Division of Archives and History, 109 East Jones Street, Raleigh NC 27601. **Tel** (919)733-7442. **LC** F251; .N67A. **DD** 975.6. **Bk Rev**. **Ad Acc**. ctrl circ. ***Continues*** *Archives Information Circular.*

Genealogy and Heraldry —Archives

UK/0003-9535
ARCHIVES (LONDON). (ARCHIVES.).
[Archives]. **Added/Corp** British Records Association. Vol. 1, No. 1 (March 25, 1949)-. Periodical. English. sa. £20.00. British Records Association, 18 Padbury Court, London E2 7EH England. **Tel** 011 44 71 7291415. **ED** John Davies. **LC** CD1; .B7. Index available. **Bk Rev. Ad Acc. Circ:** 1,300.
 Desc: Papers on all aspects of exploitation management; and study of archives and records in all forms.
 Ind/Abst Am. Hist. Life (1954-); Art Archaeol. Tech. Abstr.; Br. Humanit. Index; Libr. Inf. Sci. Abstr.

US
ARCHIVES OF APPALACHIA NEWSLETTER / EAST TENNESSEE STATE UNIVERSITY. See Folklore.

FR
ARCHIVES PARLEMENTAIRES DE 1787 A 1860. Added/Corp France. Senat. France. Chambre des Deputes. France. Assemblee Nationale (1871-1942). Series 1, Vol. 1 (1787), 2nd. Ser., Vol. 1 (1800)-. Monographic series. French. ir. Editions du CNRS, 22 rue Saint Armand, F 75015 Paris France. **Tel** 011 33 1 45075050. **(Subscription address:** CNRS Editions, 20-22 rue Saint Amand, c/o Mme. Bodet, 75015 Paris France.) cum. index. **Circ:** 1,500.
 Desc: Complete collection of legislative and political debates in French houses of parliament from 1787 to 1860, with analysis of sessions and minutes of deliberations in chronological order.

FR
ARCHIVES (PERPIGNAN, FRANCE).
(ARCHIVES : LA CINEMATHEQUE DE TOULOUSE.). (197?)-. French. ir. 78.35F France; 97.94F other. Institut Jean Vigo, 21 rue Mailly, 66000 Perpignan France. **Tel** 011 33 68 663000, 663033.

CN/0044-9423
ARCHIVES (QUEBEC). (ARCHIVES.).
[Archives]. **Added/Corp** Association des Archivistes du Quebec. Archives. Vol. 1 (Jan./June 1969)-. Periodical. French. Three times a year. 50.00Can$ Canada; 75.00Can$ US; 90.00Can$ other. Assn des Archivistes du Quebec, CP 423, Sillery Quebec G1T 2R8 Canada. **Tel** (418)652-2357.
 Ind/Abst Point Repere (1982-?, 1983-?).

IT/0394-9044
ARCHIVI PER LA STORIA : RIVISTA DELL'ASSOCIAZIONE NAZIONALE ARCHIVISTICA ITALIANA. Added/Corp Associazione Nazionale Archivistica Italiana. Vol. 1, No. 1/2 (1988)-. Periodical. Italian. Twice a year. L50000 Italy; L85000 other. Editoriale Finanz Le Monnier, PB 202, Via Meucci 2, 50015 Grassina Florence Italy. **Tel** 011 39 55 64910. **LC** CD1400; .A64. **DD** 945/.005. **Continues** Archivi e Cultura, 0044-0045.
 Ind/Abst Am. Hist. Life (1988-).

IT/0518-3499
ARCHIVIO ECONOMICO DELL'UNIFICAZIONE ITALIANA. SERIE I. Ceased. See Economics-Economic History, Conditions.

IT/0391-7770
ARCHIVIO STORICO ITALIANO. [Arch. stor. ital.]. **Added/Corp** Deputazione Toscana di Storia Patria. Vol. 1 (1842)-. Periodical. Italian. qt. L72000 (Italy); L90000 (other). Casa Editrice Leo S. Olschki, Viuzzo del Pozzetto, Casella Postale 66, 50126 Florence Italy. **Tel** 011 39 55 6530684, FAX 011 39 55 6530214. **LC** DG401; .A7. cum. index. Documents available from The Genuine Article.
 Ind/Abst Am. Hist. Life (1954-1958),(1965-?); Arts Humanit. Citation Index [Full Cov.]; BHA : Biblio. Hist. Art; Curr. Contents Arts Humanit.; MLA Int. Bibl. Books Artic. Mod. Lang. Lit.; Res. Alert [Full Cov.].

CN/0705-2855
ARCHIVIST, THE. VFOAT Archiviste. V. 1- July/Aug. 1974-. Periodical. English (French). bm. Free. National Archives of Canada, 395 Wellington/Community Relations, Ottawa Ontario K1A 0N3 Canada. **Tel** (613)996-0394. **ED** Joy McDonell and Marcel Larocque. **LC** CD3623. **DD** 027.571. **Circ:** 8,000.
 Desc: Highlights the activities and holdings of the National Archives of Canada.
 Ind/Abst Am. Hist. Life (1985-); Can. Index (?-?).

IE/0044-8745
ARCHIVIUM HIBERNICUM. (ARCHIVIUM HIBERNICUM; OR IRISH HISTORICAL RECORDS.). [Archiv. hibernicum]. **Added/Corp** Catholic Record Society of Ireland. **VFOAT** Irish Historical Records. Vol. 1 (1912)-. Multiple languages (English, Irish, Italian, Latin and Spanish). an.
 Ind/Abst Am. Hist. Life (1955-).

GW/0004-038X
ARCHIVMITTEILUNGEN. [Archivmitteilungen]. **VAT** Archiv Mitteilungen. Vol. 1 (1951)-. Periodical. German. bm. 36.20F Switzerland; 38.60F other. Deutscher Judo Verband, Redaktion Ippon Segegwaldweg 40, D 12557 Berlin Germany. **Tel** 011 49 711 210770, telex 051 678. **LC** CD1373.A2; A75. cum. index.
 Ind/Abst Am. Hist. Life (1956-); Libr. Inf. Sci. Abstr.

XR/0004-0398
ARCHIVNI CASOPIS. [Arch. cas.]. 1951-. Periodical. Czech. qt. **(Subscription address:** Artia Pegas Press Ltd., Palac Metro Narodni Trida 25, 11210 Prague 1 Czech Republic). **LC** CD15; .A7.
 Ind/Abst Am. Hist. Life (1957-); Libr. Inf. Sci. Abstr.

SP
ARCHIVO DOMINICANO. Added/Corp Instituto Historico Dominicano de San Esteban. Vol. 1 (1980)-. Spanish (summaries and/or abstracts in Latin). an (Sept.). 4000ptas Spain; 5500ptas other. Editorial San Esteban, Apartado 17, 37080 Salamanca Spain. **Tel** 011 34 23 215000.
 Ind/Abst Bibliogr. Mission.

CK
ARCHIVOS (BOGOTA). (ARCHIVOS.). V. 1- Jan./June 1967-. Spanish. **LC** F225L.A7. **DD** 986.1/005.
 Ind/Abst Am. Hist. Life (1968-).

SP/0004-0630
ARCHIVOS LEONESES. Added/Corp Centro de Estudios e Investigacion San Isidoro. Archivo Historico Diocesano de Leon. (1947)-. Periodical. Spanish. sa. 5500ptas (Spain). Ctro Est E Inves San Isidro, Plaza de la Regla 6, Leon Spain. **Tel** 31 87 257921.
 Ind/Abst BHA : Biblio. Hist. Art.

GW
ARCHIVPFLEGE IN WESTFALEN UND LIPPE / IM AUFTRAGE DES LANDSCHAFTSVERBANDES WESTFALEN-LIPPE HERAUSGEGEBEN VOM WESTFALISCHEN LANDESAMT FUR ARCHIVPFLEGE. Periodical. German. sa. Westfalisches Archivamt, Warendorfer Strasse 24, 4400 Munster Germany. **LC** CD1373.N6; A73. **DD** 026.943/55.

FR/0066-6793
ARCHIVUM (MUNCHEN). (ARCHIVUM.). [Archivum]. **Added/Corp** International Council on Archives. Vol. 1 (1951)-. Periodical. French (English). an. $48.00. Verlag Dokumentation, Postfach 711009, W-8000 Muenchen 71 Germany. **Tel** 089/791040, telex 5212067. **LC** CD1; .A18. **DD** 027.5. **NLM** W1 AR754X. cum. index.
 Desc: International review of archives.
 Ind/Abst Int. Labour Doc.

CN/0828-3192
ARCHIVY (WINDSOR). (ARCHIVY / SOUTHWESTERN ONTARIO ARCHIVISTS ASSOCIATION.). [Archivy]. **Added/Corp** Southwestern Ontario Archivists Association. **VFOAT** Newsletter. No. 1 (Sept. 1985)-. Periodical. English. Five times a year. Southwestern Ontario Archivists, 850 Ouellette Avenue, Windsor Ontario N9A 4M9 Canada. **Tel** (519)255-6782. **DD** 025.17/14/0607132.

SA
ARGIEF-JAARBOEK VIR SUID-AFRIKAANSE GESKIEDENIS.
VFOAT Archives Year Book for South African History. 1.- Yearly volume; 1938-. Afrikaans (English and Dutch). ir. Government Printer / South Africa, Bosman Street, Private Bag X85, Pretoria 0001 South Africa. **Tel** 011 27 12 3239731 Ext. 262. **LC** CD2330; .A7.

YU/0350-2856
ARHIVIST. (ARHIVIST / ORGAN GLAVNOG ARHIVSKOG SAVETA FNRJ.). [Arhivist]. **Added/Corp** Savez Drustava Arhivskih Radnika Jugoslavije. Savez Drustava Arhivskih Radnika FNRJ. Glavni Arhivski Savet FNRJ. (1951)-. Serbo-Croatian (Cyrillic) (Serbo-Croatian (Roman); summaries and/or abstracts in French; table of contents in French). **LC** CD15; .S3A2.
 Ind/Abst Am. Hist. Life (1951-); Libr. Inf. Sci. Abstr.

CI/0570-9008
ARHIVSKI VJESNIK. [Arh. vjesn.]. **VFOAT** Bulletin d'Archives. V. 1-. Serbo-Croatian (Roman) (Latin; summaries and/or abstracts in German and French). an. **ED** B Stulli. **LC** CD1187.C8; A7. **Continues** Vjesnik Hrvatskog Drzavnog Arhiva.
 Ind/Abst Am. Hist. Life (1958-1960, 1974-).

●RU
ARKHIV RUSSKOI ISTORII / TSENTRALYI GOSUDARSTVENNYI ARKHIV DREVNYKH AKTOV. Added/Corp Tsentralnyi Gosudarstvennyi Arkhiv Drevnykh Aktov (Russia (Federation)). (1992)-. Russian.

DK/0004-203X
ARKIV. [Arkiv]. 1.- Vol.; April 1966-. Periodical. Danish. sa.
 Ind/Abst Am. Hist. Life (1966-); Libr. Inf. Sci. Abstr.

PO
ARQUIVO DE BEJA. Main/Corp Beja, Portugal (City). Camara Municipal. Vol. 1 (Jan./Mar. 1944)-. Portuguese.
 Ind/Abst BHA : Biblio. Hist. Art.

IT/0409-6037
BIBLIOTECA DELL'ARCHIVIO STORICO ITALIANO. Main/Corp Archivio Storico Italiano. Monographic series. Italian. ir. Price varies per volume. Casa Editrice Leo S. Olschki, Viuzzo del Pozzetto, Casella Postale 66, 50126 Florence Italy. **Tel** 011 39 55 6530684, FAX 011 39 55 6530214.

US
BIENNIAL REPORT OF THE TEXAS STATE LIBRARY AND ARCHIVES COMMISSION. See Library and Information Sciences.

NQ
BOLETIN (ARCHIVO NACIONAL (NICARAGUA)). (BOLETIN / ARCHIVO NACIONAL.). **VFOAT** Boletin Informativo. Periodical. Spanish. Ministerio de Cultura / Nicaragua, Apartado Postal 3514, Managua Nicaragua. **LC** F1521; .B63. **DD** 972.85. **Continues** Boletin del Archivo General de la Nacion (Managua, Nicaragua).
 Ind/Abst Am. Hist. Life (1954-1958,1963-1964).

SP
BOLETIN DE INFORMACION (CENTRO DE INFORMACION DOCUMENTAL (SPAIN)). (BOLETIN DE INFORMACION / CENTRO DE INFORMACION DOCUMENTAL.). Began in 1980. Spanish. bm. Centro de Informacion, Documental de Archivos, Castellana 109, Madrid 16 Spain. **LC** Z5140; .B64; CD921. **DD** 016.02.

SP/0044-9288
BOLETIN DE LA A.N.A.B.A. See Library and Information Sciences.

SP/0210-4164
BOLETIN DE LA ANABAD. [Bol. ANABAD]. **VFOAT** Boletin de la Asociacion Nacional de Archiveros Bibliotecarios, Arqueologos y Documentalistas. (1978)-. Periodical. Spanish. Four times a year. 2884ptas Spain; $118.00 others. Asociacion Espanola de Archiveros, Bibliotecarios Museologosy Documentalistas, Apartado 14281, 28001 Madrid Spain. **Tel** 011 34 1 5751727. **(Subscription address:** Arco/Libros, S. L. Juan Bautista de Toledo, 28. 28002 Madrid, phone: 415 36 87 - 416 13 71 or 413 59 07 Fax) **UDC** 02. **Continues** Boletin de la A.N.A.B.A., 0044-9288.

VE/0042-3378
BOLETIN DEL ARCHIVO GENERAL DE LA NACION (CARACAS). (BOLETIN DEL ARCHIVO GENERAL DE LA NACION.). [Bol. Arch. gen. nac.]. **Main/Corp** Venezuela. Archivo General de la Nacion. Vol. 33, No. 129 (1945)-. Periodical. Spanish. sa. Archivo General de la Nacion / Venezuela, Santa Capilla a Carmelitas, 15 Caracas Venezuela. **LC** CD4260; .A3. **Continues** Venezuela. Archivo Nacional. Boletin del Archivo Nacional.
 Ind/Abst Am. Hist. Life (1954-); HAPI Hisp. Am. Period. Index (19??-).

DR/1012-9472
BOLETIN DEL ARCHIVO GENERAL DE LA NACION (SANTO DOMINGO). (BOLETIN DEL ARCHIVO GENERAL DE LA NACION (DOMINICAN REPUBLIC).). [Bol. Arch. gen. nac.]. **Added/Corp** Archivo General de la Nacion (Dominican Republic) Dominican Republic. Secretaria de Estado de lo Interior y Policia. Vol. 1, No. 1 (March 1938)-. Spanish. bm (irregular). **LC** CD3985.D6; A3. cum. index.
 Ind/Abst Am. Hist. Life (1954-1962).

VE/0042-3386
BOLETIN DEL ARCHIVO HISTORICO DE MIRAFLORES. Main/Corp Archivo Historico de Miraflores (Venezuela). Vol. 1- (No. 1-); July/Aug. 1959-. Spanish. ir. Secretaria de la Presidencia, Palacio Demirflores, Caracas Venezuela. **Tel** 81059. **ED** Nora Bustamante. **LC** F2301; .V4. **Circ:** 8,000 (ctrl).
 Desc: Basically Venezuelan history, its contemporary history from 1900 to 1959, publishes letters and telegrams, etc. sent to Venezuela presidents during these years.

SP/0210-4946
BOLLETIN DE ARCHIVOS. (BA, BOLETIN DE ARCHIVOS.). [Bol. arch.]. Vol. 1- Jan./April 1978-. Periodical. Spanish. Three times a year. Edificio del Archivo Historico Nacional, Serrano 115, Madrid-6 Spain. **LC** CD921; .B13. **DD** 015.17/14/05. **Continues** Boletin (Spain. Direccion General de Archivos y Bibliotecas), 0012-3145.

UK
BORTHWICK TEXTS AND CALENDARS : RECORDS OF THE NORTHERN PROVINCE. Added/Corp Borthwick Institute of Historical Research. (1973)-. Monographic series.

Genealogy and Heraldry —Archives

English. an. £11.00. University of York / St. Anthonys Hall, Borthwick Institute, York Y01 2PW England. **Tel** 011 44 904 642315. Index available. **Circ:** 350 (ctrl).
Desc: Handlists and calendars of the archives in the Bothwick Institute.

BE/0073-8530
BULLETIN DE L'INSTITUT HISTORIQUE BELGE DE ROME. [Bull. Inst. hist. belge Rome]. **Main/Corp** Institut Historique Belge de Rome. Iss. 1. (1919)-. Bulletin. French (English, Dutch and Italian). an (May). 1050.00F. Institut Hist Belge De Rome, 2-6 Rue Ruysbroek, 1000 Brussels Belguim. **(Subscription address:** Brepols Publishers, Baron Frans du Fourstraat, 8 B 2300 Turnhout Belgium.) **LC** D1; .I47. **DD** 906.2. cum. index. **Circ:** 400.
Ind/Abst Am. Hist. Life (1978-); BHA : Biblio. Hist. Art.

FR/0252-9785
BULLETIN - INTERNATIONAL COUNCIL ON ARCHIVES. [Bull. - Int. Counc. Arch.]. **VFOAT** Bulletin - Conseil International des Archives; ICA Bulletin. (19??)-. Periodical. English (French). Twice a year. Comes with Conseil International des Archives membership. Conseil International des Archives, 60 rue des Francs Bourgeoise, F 75003 Paris France. **Tel** 011 33 1 40276000, 011 33 1 40276306, FAX 011 33 1 40276625. **UDC** 093.2. **Circ:** 1,500 (ctrl).
Desc: Summary reports on meetings of ICA bodies (steering bodies of the organization, sections, regional branches and committees) and other international archival events.

GP/0376-7698
CARIBBEAN ARCHIVES. VFOAT Archives Antillaises; Archivos del Caribe. 1- 1973-. Periodical. Multiple languages (English, French and Spanish). Caribbean Archive Association, Boite Postale 74, Basse-Terre Guadeloupe. **LC** CD3860; .C36. **DD** 027.5/09729.

US/0576-808X
CAROLINA COMMENTS. [Carol. comments]. **Added/Corp** North Carolina. State Dept. of Archives and History. North Carolina. Division of Archives and History. Vol. 1, No. 1, (May 1952)-. Periodical. English. bm (Jan., Mar., May, July, Sept., Nov.). $8.00. North Carolina Division Archives & History, 109 East Jones Street, Raleigh NC 27611. **Tel** (919)733-7442. **ED** Robert M. Topkins. **LC** F251; .C38. **DD** 975. Index available (Published in December Issue). **Circ:** 1,800 (ctrl). available on microfilm and microfiche from University Microfilms International (UMI).
Desc: News of historical societies and history departments of North Carolina colleges and universities and activities of North Carolina's Division of Archives and History.
Ind/Abst Am. Hist. Life; West. Hist. Q.

US/0094-629X
CATALOG OF NATIONAL ARCHIVES MICROFILM PUBLICATIONS. Main/Corp United States. National Archives and Records Service. **VFOAT** National Archives Microfilm Publications. (1974)-. Catalog. English. ir. Free on request. National Archives Trust Fund, 8th Street and Pennsylvania Avenue NW, Washington DC 20408. **Tel** (202)501-6065, FAX (202)501-5680. **LC** CD3027; .M514. **DD** 016.026/953. ***Continues*** *List of National Archives Microfilm Publications.*

US
CATALOG OF THE FLORIDA STATE ARCHIVES. Main/Corp Florida. Division of Archives, History, and Records Management. Oct. 1975-. Catalog. English. Department of State Archives / Florida, RA Gray Building, Tallahassee FL 32301. **Tel** (904)487-2073. **LC** CD3174; .F58A. **DD** 016.9759.

PE
CATALOGO DEL ARCHIVO GENERAL DE LA NACION. Main/Corp Peru. Archivo General de la Nacion. Spanish. Jr Manuel Cuadros, s/n Palacio de Justicia, Casilla No 3124, Lima Peru. **LC** CD4226 1974; .A73A.

CN/0706-3431
CHRONIQUE (QUEBEC). (LA CHRONIQUE.). [Chronique]. **Added/Corp** Association des Archivistes du Quebec. Vol. 6, No. 2 (July 30, 1976)-. Periodical. French. Ten times a year (Sept., thru June). 35.00Can$ Comes with Archivistes du Quebec Membership. Assn des Archivistes du Quebec, CP 423, Sillery Quebec G1T 2R8 Canada. **Tel** (418)652-2357. **DD** 025.17/14/060714. ***Continues*** *Chronique de l'AAQ, 0706-344X.*

US
COLONIAL RECORDS OF THE STATE OF GEORGIA / COMPILED AND PUBLISHED UNDER THE AUTHORITY OF THE LEGISLATURE. *Ceased.* Added/Corp Georgia. Legislature. (1904)-Series complete with Vol. 32. Monographic series. English. ir. University of Georgia Press, 330 Research Drive, Suite B 100, Athens GA 60602. **Tel** (706)542-2830.

II
CONSERVATION NEWS. No. 1- 1978-. English. $3.00 US; $5.00 other. Y P Kathpalia, Chairman, International Council on Archives, Conservation Committee, 11-A/37 Western Extension, Karol Bagh, New Delhi-110005 India. **LC** CD921; .C66. **DD** 027.5/05.
Ind/Abst Art Archaeol. Tech. Abstr.

UK/0307-8086
COURTAULD INSTITUTE ILLUSTRATION ARCHIVES. ARCHIVE 4, LATE 18TH & 19TH CENTURY SCULPTURE IN THE BRITISH ISLES. Added/Corp Courtauld Institute of Art. **VFOAT** Late 18th & 19th Century Sculpture in the British Isles; Late Eighteenth and Nineteenth Century Sculpture in the British Isles. (Dec. 1976)-. Periodical. English. ir. price varies per volume. Harvey Miller Publishers, 20 Marryat Road, London SW19 5BD England. **Tel** 011 44 1 9464426, telex 9312130339 (HMG). **ED** Benedict Read and Philip Ward-Jackson.
Desc: Photographic reference library of European sculpture and architecture. Late 18th and 19th Century sculpture in the British Isles.

AU
DAS AUDIOVISUELLE ARCHIV : INFORMATIONSBLATT DER ARBEITSGEMEINSCHAFT AUDIOVISUELLER ARCHIVE OSTERREICHS. Added/Corp Arbeitsgemeinschaft Audiovisueller Archive Osterreichs. (Oct. 1988)-. Periodical. German. sa (May and Oct.). S180.00. Agava, Liebiggase 5, A 1010 Vienna Austria. **Tel** 43 1 401032734. ***Continues*** *Schallarchiv.*

UK/0307-1391
DATA ARCHIVE BULLETIN / SSRC. *Title Change.* Added/Corp SSRC Data Archive. ESRC Data Archive. **VFOAT** SSRC Data Archive Bulletin; ESRC Data Archive Bulletin. No. 21 (Feb. 1982)-(19??). Bulletin. English. Three times a year. University of Essex ESRC Data Archives, Wivenhoe Park, Bulletin Mailing List, Colchester CO4 3SQ England. **Tel** 011 44 206 763333. **ED** Marcia F Taylor. **Bk Rev. Ad Acc. Circ:** 5,000. ***Continues*** *Survey Archive Bulletin / SSRC, 0307-1391.* ***Continued by*** *Bulletin (ESRC Data Archive).*

CN/0711-0413
DIRECTORY OF CANADIAN ARCHIVES. [Dir. Can. arch.]. **Added/Corp** Bureau of Canadian Archivists. Association of Canadian Archivists. Association des Archivistes du Quebec. **VFOAT** Annuaire des Depots d'Archives Canadiens. (1981)-. Periodical. English (French). an. Assn Archivistes du Quebec, CP 423, Sillery Quebec G1T 2R8 Canada. **Tel** (418)652-2357. **LC** CD3620; .D58. **DD** 016.971/0025. **Ad Acc.** ctrl circ. ***Continues*** *Directory of Canadian Records and Manuscript Repositories, 0700-4850.*

CN/0715-1624
DIRECTORY OF LIBRARIES AND ARCHIVAL INSTITUTIONS IN PRINCE EDWARD ISLAND. **See** Library and Information Sciences.

GW
EDITION ARCHIV DER DEUTSCHEN JUGENDBEWEGUNG. VFOAT Archiv der Deutschen Jugendbewegung. Monographic series. German. Price varies per volume. Verlag Wissenschaft & Politik, Salierring 14 16, D 50677 Cologne Germany. **Tel** 011 49 221 312878.

CN/0836-088X
EPILOGUE (HALIFAX, N.S.). **See** Library and Information Sciences.

CN
ESTIMATES. PART III, NATIONAL ARCHIVES OF CANADA. Main/Corp Canada. **VFOAT** Estimates. Part 3, National Archives of Canada; Budget des Depenses. Partie III, Archives Nationales du Canada. (1988/1989)-. English (French). an. Canada Communication Group Publishers, Order Processing, Ottawa Ontario K1A 0S9 Canada. **Tel** (819)956-4800, (819)956-4802. **LC** CD3623; .C35a. **DD** 354.710071/46. ***Continues*** *Canada. Estimates. Part III, Public Archives Canada.*

CN/0844-6237
ETAPE EN ETAPE. (D'ETAPE EN ETAPE : BULLETIN DE LIAISON DES ARCHIVES NATIONALES DU QUEBEC.). [Etape etape]. **Added/Corp** Archives Nationales du Quebec. **VFOAT** Etape en Etape. Vol. 1, No. 1 (Nov. 28, 1984)-. Periodical. French. ir (One or two times per year). Free. Archives Nationales du Quebec, 1210 Avenue du Seminaire, CP 10450, Sainte Foy Quebec G1V 4N1 Canada. **Tel** (418)644-4822, FAX (418)646-0868. **DD** 354.7140071/46.

GW
FINDBUCHER ZU BESTANDEN DES BUNDESARCHIV. Main/Corp Germany (Federal Republic, 1949-) Bundesarchiv. (1970)-. Monographic series. English. Price varies per volume.

US/0891-2653
FOR THE RECORD. (FOR THE RECORD : NEWSLETTER OF THE ILLINOIS STATE ARCHIVES, OFFICE OF SECRETARY OF STATE.). [For rec.]. Vol. 1, No. 1 (April 1975)-. Newsletter. English. sa. Free. Illinois State Archives, Archives Building, Springfield IL 62756. **Tel** (217)782-3674. **ED** Robert E Bailey and Elaine S Evans. **DD** 025. **Circ:** 3,000 (ctrl).

MX/0199-669X
FORO ARCHIVISTICO : REVISTA TECNICA DEL SISTEMA NACIONAL DE ARCHIVOS. Added/Corp Sistema Nacional de Archivos (Mexico). No. 1 (Jan/Jun. 1991)-. Periodical. Spanish. sa.

FR/0016-5522
GAZETTE DES ARCHIVES, LA. [Gaz. arch.]. **Added/Corp** Association Amicale Professionnelle des Archivistes Francais. Association des Archivistes Francais. (Jan. 1933)-. Periodical. French (summaries and/or abstracts in English, German and Spanish). qt. 280.00F France; 280.00F EEC countries; 300.00F other. Association des Archivistes Francais, 60 rue des Francs Bourgeois, 75141 Paris Cedex 03 France. **Tel** 011 33 1 64877315. Index available. cum. index. **Bk Rev. Ad Acc. Circ:** 1,200.
Desc: Reflection and information on all records in France, or in other countries, with reference to international archive records.
Ind/Abst Am. Hist. Life (1969-); Libr. Inf. Sci. Abstr.

US/0897-6775
HERITAGE EDUCATION QUARTERLY. [Herit. educ. q.]. **Added/Corp** Preservation Library and Resource Center. (1986)-. Periodical. English. qt. $12.00. **DD** 363.
Ind/Abst Curr. Index J. Educ.

II/0367-7435
INDIAN ARCHIVES. [Indian arch.]. **Added/Corp** National Archives of India. Vol. 1 (Jan. 1947)-. Periodical. English. sa. $23.40. Government of India / National Archives of India, Jandath New Delhi 110001 India. **Tel** 383436. **(Subscription address:** Prints India, 11 Darya Ganj, New Delhi 110002 India.) **ED** R K Perti. **LC** CD2080; .I5. **Circ:** 300 (ctrl).
Desc: Stimulates interest in and imparts knowledge of archival studies and preservation of manuscripts.
Ind/Abst Am. Hist. Life (1959-); Libr. Inf. Sci. Abstr.

NE
INFORMATION BULLETIN / INTERNATIONAL ASSOCIATION OF SOUND ARCHIVES. Main/Corp International Association of Sound Archives. **VFOAT** Information Bulletin of the International Association of Sound Archives; IASA Information Bulletin. No. 1 (Mar. 1990)-. Bulletin. English. qt. **LC** IN PROCESS.

GW
INVENTARE NICHTSTAATLICHER ARCHIVE. Began in 1941. Monographic series. German. ir. Price varies per volume. Dr. Rudolf Habelt GmbH, Postfach 150104, D 53040 Bonn Germany. **Tel** 011 49 228 232015. **LC** CD1220; .I5.

IE/0332-4303
IRISH ARCHIVES : JOURNAL OF THE IRISH SOCIETY FOR ARCHIVES. Added/Corp Irish Society for Archives. (1989)-. Periodical. English. an. National Archives, Irish Society of Archives, Four Courts, Dublin 7 Ireland. ***Continues*** *Irish Archives Bulletin, 0332-4304.*

BU
IZVESTIIA NA ARKHIVNIIA INSTITUT. Main/Corp Bulgarska Akademiia na Naukite, Sofia. Arkhiven Institut. (1957)-. Academic Scholarly Publication. Bulgarian (table of contents in Russian and French). Bulgarska Akademiia na Naukite, 7 Noemvri 1, Sofia Bulgaria. **LC** CD15; .B8.
Ind/Abst Am. Hist. Life (1957-1968).

BU/0323-9780
IZVESTIIA NA DURZHAVNITE ARKHIVI / MINISTERSTVO NA VUTRESHNITE RABOTI, OTDEL "DURZHAVEN ARKHIV". Added/Corp Bulgaria. Otdel Durzhaven Arkhiv. Bulgaria. Arkhiven Otdel. Bulgaria. Arkhivno Upravlenie. Bulgaria. Upravlenie na Arkhivite. Bulgaria. Sentralno Upravlenie na Arkhivite. Bulgaria. Glavno Upravlenie na Arkhivite. Vol. 1 (1957)-. Periodical. Bulgarian (summaries and/or abstracts in French and Russian; table of contents in German, French and Russian). sa. DM121.00. **(Subscription address:** Kubon & Sagner, ABT Zeitschriftenimport, D 80328 Munich Germany.) **LC** CD1950; .A3.
Ind/Abst Am. Hist. Life (1987-).

BU/0525-0870
IZVESTIIA NA NAUCHNIIA ARKHIV / BULGARSKA AKADEMIIA NA NAUKITE, TSENTRALNA BIBLIOTEKA SUS SLUZHBA ZA NAUCHNA INFORMATSIIA I NAUCHEN ARKHIV. Added/Corp Bulgarska Akademiia na Naukite. TSentralna Biblioteka sus Sluzhba za Nauchna

Genealogy and Heraldry —Archives

Informatsiia i Nauchen Arkhiv. Vol. 1 (1957)-. Academic Scholarly Publication. Bulgarian. ir. Bulgarska Akademiia na Naukite, 7 Noemvri 1, Sofia Bulgaria. **DD** 891.81; 949.75.

NE/0922-6702
JAARBOEK VAN HET CENTRAAL BUREAU VOOR GENEALOGIE EN VAN HET ICONOGRAFISCH BUREAU. See Genealogy and Heraldry.

NE
JAAROVERZICHT / GEMEENTEARCHIEF AMSTERDAM.
Main/Corp Amsterdam (Netherlands). Gemeentearchief. 1986-. Dutch. an. Gemeentearchief Amsterdam, Amsteldijk 67, 1074 HZ Amsterdam The Netherlands. **LC** CD1708.A47; A58A. **Continues in part** Jaarverslag.

NE
JAARVERSLAG / GEMEENTEARCHIEF AMSTERDAM. Main/Corp Amsterdam (Netherlands). Gemeentearchief. 1986-. Dutch. an. **LC** CD1708.A47; A58B. **Continues in part** Jaarverslag.

GW/0075-2215
JAHRBUCH DER BIBLIOTHEKEN, ARCHIVE UND INFORMATIONSSTELLEN DER DEUTSCHEN DEMOKRATISCHEN REPUBLIK. Ceased. See Library and Information Sciences.

UK/0037-9816
JOURNAL OF THE SOCIETY OF ARCHIVISTS. [J. Soc. Arch.]. **Main/Corp** Society of Archivists (Great Britain). Vol. 1 (April 1955)-. Periodical. English. sa. £38.00. Carfax Publishing Company, PO Box 25 Abingdon, Oxfordshire OX14 3UE England. **Tel** 011 44 235 555335, FAX (0279)31067, telex 817484.
(Subscription address: US and Canada/ PO Box 2025, Dunnellon, FL 34430-2025; telephone:(904)489-6996) **ED** Chris Webb. **LC** CD23.S6; A3. **DD** 016.942. **[CCC]**. Index available in last issue of volume--attached. available on microfiche from University Microfilms International (UMI). Documents available from The Genuine Article. **Supersedes** Society of Archivists. Bulletin.
Ind/Abst Am. Hist. Life (1955-); Arts Humanit. Citation Index [Full Cov.]; Br. Archaeol. Bibliogr.; Br. Humanit. Index; Curr. Contents Arts Humanit.; Inf. Sci. Abstr. (?-?); Libr. Inf. Sci. Abstr.; Museum Abstr.; Res. Alert [Full Cov.]; Soc. Sci. Cit. Index [Select. Cov.].

JA
KITANOMARU; KOKURITSU KOBUNSHOKAN HO. Main/Corp Kokuritsu Kobunshokan. **Added/Corp** Kokuritsu Kobunshokan. Journal of the National Archives of Japan. **VFOAT** Kokuritsu Kobunshokanpo; Journal of the National Archives of Japan. (1973)-. Periodical. Japanese. an. Kokuritsu Kobunshokan, 3-2 Kitanomaru Koen Chiyoda-ku, 102 Tokyo Japan. **Tel** 03-214-0621, FAX 03-212-8806. **LC** CD2163; .K64b. **Circ:** 1,000 (ctrl).
Desc: Introduces activities of the national archives in the forms of articles, reports of activities, notes on books, etc.

HU/0024-1512
LEVELTARI KOEZLEMENYEK. See History(General).

HU/0457-6047
LEVELTARI SZEMLE. Added/Corp Hungary. Leveltarak Orszagos Kozpontja. (1951)-. Periodical. Hungarian (table of contents in English, French, German and Russian). qt. **LC** CD1170; .A314. **Continues** Leveltari Hirado.
Ind/Abst Am. Hist. Life (1964-1977).

US/0196-0075
LIBRARY & ARCHIVAL SECURITY. See Library and Information Sciences.

IS
LIBRARY ARCHIVES AND INFORMATION STUDIES. See Library and Information Sciences.

UK
LIST OF MEMBERS - BRITISH RECORDS ASSOCIATION. Main/Corp British Records Association. English. **LC** CD1040; .B795A. **DD** 001.55/06/242.

UK/0520-6790
LOCAL HISTORY RECORDS - BOURNE SOCIETY. (LOCAL HISTORY RECORDS.). **Main/Corp** Bourne Society. (1962)-. English. **LC** DA670.B66; B68a. **DD** 914.22/1. cum. index.
Ind/Abst BHA : Biblio. Hist. Art.

AT/0725-7015
LU REES ARCHIVES. See Library and Information Sciences.

US/0741-0379
M.A.C. (A.M.A.C.-- : NEWSLETTER OF THE MIDWEST ARCHIVES CONFERENCE.). [M.A.C.]. **Main/Corp** Midwest Archives Conference. **VFOAT** MAC; MAC Newsletter. **VAT** Midwest Archives Conference. (19??)-. Newsletter. English. qt. $15.00 institutional membership/including subscription. Midwest Archives Conference, 3400 Broadway Indian University Northwest, Gary IN 46408. **Tel** (219)980-6628. available on microfilm from University Microfilms International (UMI).

CN/1188-3758
MAGAZINE ARCHIMED. Ceased. (LE MAGAZINE ARCHIMED.). [Mag. Archimed]. **VFOAT** Archimed; Archi-Med. Vol. 1, No. 1 (Feb. 1992)-(199?). Periodical. French. Four times a year (Feb., May, Aug., Nov.). Archi-Med, 520 Rue Des Meandres Bur 125, Quebec QUE G2E 5N4 Canada. **Tel** (418)877-5569, FAX (418)877-6028. **ED** Michel Roberge. **DD** 025/.005. **Circ:** 7,000 to 10,000.
Desc: This magazine is dedicated to the records management, archives management and documentation management. Its goal is to reflect the ideas of the many professionals in this field and to become their common contact point.

XN/0350-1728
MAKEDONSKI ARHIVIST. V. 1- 1972-. Macedonian. an. 500.00 Din Yugoslavia; 200.00 Din US. Sojuz na Drustvata na Arhivskite, Rabotnici na Makedonija, Arhiv na Makedonija, P F 496, 91001 Skopje Macedonia. **Tel** 091-234-461. **LC** CD1987.5.M3; M35. **Circ:** 1,000 (ctrl).
Desc: Archivistic practice, archivistic laws, meetings of the archivists, new archivistic books and other publications.

SW/0282-762X
MEDDELANDEN FRAN SVENSKA RIKSARKIVET. [Medd. Sven. Riksark.]. **Main/Corp** Sweden. Riksarkivet. (19??)-. English. an.
Ind/Abst Am. Hist. Life (1959-).

US/0145-6490
MEMBERSHIP DIRECTORY - SOCIETY OF AMERICAN ARCHIVISTS. [Membsh. dir. - Soc. Am. Arch.]. **Main/Corp** Society of American Archivists. (19??)-. English. ir. $10.00 (two year) institutional membership; $50.00 nonmembers. Society of American Archivists, 600 South Federal, Suite 504, Chicago IL 60605. **Tel** (312)922-0140, FAX (312)347-1452. **LC** CD3020; .S6315. **DD** 020/.622/73. **Circ:** 2,800.

SZ
MEMOIRES ET DOCUMENTS PUBLIES PAR LA SOCIETE D'HISTOIRE ET D'ARCHEOLOGIE DE GENEVE. Main/Corp Societe d'Histoire et d'Archeologie de Geneve. (1841)-. French. an. cum. index.
Ind/Abst BHA : Biblio. Hist. Art.

US
MICROFILM LIST. Main/Corp Atlanta Federal Archives & Records Center (Ga.). Archives Branch. No. 3 (Nov. 1978)-. Periodical. English. Chicago Federal Archives & Records Center, General Service Administration, Washington DC 20408. **Continues** National Archives Microfilm Publications Deposited with the Regional Archives Branch, Atlanta Federal Archives and Records Center: Microfilm List.

BE
MISCELLANEA ARCHIVISTICA. 1-. Monographic series. English (Dutch and French). ir. Price varies per volume. Ministere de Education Culture, Brussels Belgium. **LC** CD1670; .M57.

AU
MITTEILUNGEN DES OSTERREICHISCHEN STAATSARCHIVS. Main/Corp Austria. Staatsarchiv. (1948)-. Monographic series. German. ir. Price varies per volume. Verlag Ferdinand Berger & Soehne, Wienerstrasse 21-23, A-3580 Horn Austria. **Tel** 011/43/2982/23170, 41610. **LC** CD1120; .A8. Index available. cum. index. **Bk Rev**
Ind/Abst Am. Hist. Life (1953-).

CN/0824-8907
NATIONAL ARCHIVES NEWSLETTER. (NATIONAL ARCHIVES NEWSLETTER / CANADIAN JEWISH CONGRESS.). [Natl. Arch. newsl.]. **Main/Corp** Canadian Jewish Congress. National Archives. **VFOAT** Bulletin des Archives Nationales. Vol. 1, No. 1 (Winter 1984)-. Periodical. English (French). sa. Canadian Jewish Congress, 1590 Avenue Docteur Penfield, Montreal Quebec H3G 1C5 Canada. **Tel** (514)931-7531. **ED** Janice Rosen. **DD** 026/.971004924. **Circ:** 700 (ctrl).

NE/0028-2049
NEDERLANDSCH ARCHIEVENBLAD. [Ned. arch.bl.]. **Added/Corp** Van Archivarissen in Nederland. Vol. 1 (1893)-. Periodical. Dutch. qt. Fl181.25. Bureau Van Spaendouck, PO Box 90154, 5000 LF Tilburg Netherlands. **Tel** 050-121719. **LC** CD1690; .V4. **DD** 027.5492. cum. index. **Bk Rev. Circ:** 1,100 (ctrl).

Desc: Describing the history of people, buildings, and cultures, from journals, saved by official keepers of the records.
Ind/Abst Am. Hist. Life (1955-1957, 1969-1983).

UK/0142-2278
NEWS LETTER OF THE SOCIETY OF ARCHIVISTS. [News lett. Soc. Arch.]. (1977)-. English. qt. Society of Archivists, Leicestershire Receiving Office, 57 New Walk, Leicester LE1 7JB England.
Ind/Abst Museum Abstr.

IS/0377-1784
NEWSLETTER - CENTRAL ARCHIVES FOR THE HISTORY OF THE JEWISH PEOPLE. Main/Corp Arkhiyon Ha-Merkazi Le-Toldot Ha-Am Ha-Yehudi. **VFOAT** Yediot - Ha-arkhiyon Ha-Merkazi Le-Toldot Ha-Am Ha-Yehudi. Newsletter. English. Hebrew University Campus, Sprinzak Building, POB 1149, Jerusalem Israel. **LC** CD2019.J4; A84A. **DD** 026/.909/04924.

CN/0829-7142
NEWSLETTER / COUNCIL OF NOVA SCOTIA ARCHIVES. [Newsl. - Counc. N.S. Arch.]. **Added/Corp** Council of Nova Scotia Archives. Public Archives of Nova Scotia. **VFOAT** Council of Nova Scotia Archives Newsletter. No. 1 (Winter 1984)-. Newsletter. English. Twice a year (Jan. and July). 25.00Can$. Council of Nova Scotia, 6016 University Avenue, Pub Archives NS, Halifax NS B3H 1W4 Canada. **Tel** (902)424-6060, FAX (902)424-0628. **ED** Margaret McBride. **DD** 025.17/14/060716. **Bk Rev. Ad Acc. Circ:** 200 (ctrl).

NO
NORRONE TEKSTER. Norwegian. ir. National Archives of Norway, Postboks 10, Dept Historical, Kringsja 0807 Oslo 8 Norway.

IT
NUOVI ANNALI DELLA SCUOLA SPECIALE PER ARCHIVISTI E BIBLIOTECARI. Vol. 1 (1987)-. Italian. an. L70000 Italy; L78000 others. Casa Editrice Leo S. Olschki, Viuzzo del Pozzetto, Casella Postale 66, 50126 Florence Italy. **Tel** 011 39 55 6530684, FAX 011 39 55 6530214. **LC** CD1000; .N86. **Continues** Annali della Scuola Speciale per Archivisti e Bibliotecari dell'Universita di Roma.
Ind/Abst BHA : Biblio. Hist. Art.

CN/1182-0055
OFF THE RECORD (TORONTO. 1990). (OFF THE RECORD.). [Off rec.]. **Added/Corp** Ontario Association of Archivists. Vol. 7, No. 1 (Spring 1990)-. Periodical. English. tq. Free to members. Southwestern Ontario Archivists, 850 Ouellette Avenue, Windsor Ontario N9A 4M9 Canada. **Tel** (519)255-6782. **DD** 025.17/14/060713. **Continues** Newsletter (Ontario Association of Archivists)., 0824-5274.

●CN/0844-7594
ORIENTATIONS STRATEGIQUES DES ARCHIVES NATIONALES DU CANADA. [Strateg. approaches Natl. Arch. Can.]. **Main/Corp** Archives Nationales du Canada. **VFOAT** Orientations Strategiques; Strategic Approaches of the National Archives of Canada. (1992)-. French (English). **DD** 354.710071/46/05. **Continues** Orientations Strategiques des Archives Publiques du Canada., 0844-7586.

FR/0755-2076
POSITIONS DES THESES. See Education-Higher Education.

PL/0067-6470
PRACE BIAOSTOCKIEGO TOWARZYSTWA NAUKOWEGO. See Education-Higher Education.

US/0741-6563
PRIMARY SOURCE (JACKSON, MISS.). (THE PRIMARY SOURCE.). **Added/Corp** Society of Mississippi Archivists. Vol. 1, No. 1 (Jan. 1979)-. Periodical. English. qt. comes with membership. Society of Mississippi Archivists, PO Box 1151, Jackson MS 39205. **Tel** (601)359-6868. **ED** Sandra E. Boyd and Earl E. Hennen. **Bk Rev. Circ:** 275.
Desc: Covers news and accessions of Mississippi repositories plus national news and features of interest to Mississippi archivists, librarians and records administrators.

US/1042-8216
PRIMARY SOURCES AND ORIGINAL WORKS. See Library and Information Sciences.

US/0033-1031
PROLOGUE (WASHINGTON). (PROLOGUE : THE JOURNAL OF THE NATIONAL ARCHIVES.). [Prologue]. **Added/Corp** United States. National Archives. United States. National Archives and Records Administration. National Archives Trust Fund Board. United States. National Archives and Records Service. United States. General Services Administration. Vol. 1, No. 1 (Spring 1969)-. Periodical. English. Four times a

year. $12.00 US; $15.00 other. National Archives Trust Fund, 8th Street and Pennsylvania Avenue NW, Washington DC 20408. **Tel** (202)501-6065, FAX (202)501-5680. **ED** Henry Gwiazda. **LC** CD3020; .P75. **Circ:** 4,000. available on microfilm and microfiche from University Microfilms International (UMI). Documents available from The Genuine Article, Documents on Demand. ***Continues*** *United States. National Archives. National Archives Accessions, 0886-0300.*
Desc: Each issue contains informative articles about America's history based on research on the national archives, its regional archives, and the presidential libraries. It also provides the latest information on accessions, openings, and declassification of valuable historical records.
Ind/Abst Am. Hist. Life (1969-); Am. Stat. Index; Arts Humanit. Citation Index [Full Cov.]; Bibliogr. Carto.; Humanit. Index; Res. Alert [Full Cov.]; Soc. Sci. Cit. Index [Select. Cov.]; West. Hist. Q.

US/0739-4241
PROVENANCE. [Proven.]. (1983)-. Periodical. English. sa. $20.00 US; $24.00 other (institutions); $15.00 US; $19.00 other (individual). Society of Georgia Archivists, Box 261, Georgia State University, Atlanta GA 30303. **Tel** (404)651-2477. **ED** Margery Sly. **DD** 025. Index available. **Bk Rev. Circ:** 275. ***Continues*** *Georgia Archive, 0095-6201.*
Ind/Abst Am. Hist. Life (1983-).

IT
QUADERNI / CENTRO DI RICERCHE INFORMATICHE PER I BENI CULTURALI. See Library and Information Sciences.

IT/0579-1316
QUADERNI DELLA RASSEGNA DEGLI ARCHIVI DI STATO. [Quad. Rass. Arch. Stato]. **Added/Corp** Italy. Ufficio Centrale degli Archivi di Stato. (1960)-. Monographic series. Italian. **LC** CD1400; .A28.
Ind/Abst Am. Hist. Life (1960-1987).

US/0893-4525
RACONTEUR (BATON ROUGE, LA. ANNUAL ED.), LE. See Genealogy and Heraldry.

IT/0392-1522
RASSEGNA DEGLI ARCHIVI DI STATO. [Rass. arch. Stato]. Vol. 15 (Jan./April 1955)-. Periodical. Italian. an. Istituto Poligrafico Zecca Stato, Piazza Verdi 10, 00198 Rome Italy. **Tel** 011 39 6 85082307, 011 39 6 85082221. ***Continues*** *Notizie Degli Archivi di Stato.*
Ind/Abst Am. Hist. Life (1954-); BHA : Biblio. Hist. Art.

AT/0310-4729
RECORD SYDNEY. [RecordSyd.]. (1973)-. Newsletter. English. tq. Free. University of Sydney Fisher Library Office of the Registrar, 9th Floor, Sydney NSW 2006 Australia. **Tel** 011 02 692 2684, FAX 011 02 692 0200. **ED** K. Smith. **DD** 025.171074099441. **Circ:** 500 (ctrl).
Ind/Abst Aust. Educ. Index; Aust. Libr. Inf. Sci. Abstr. (1989-).

US/0147-0817
REFERENCE INFORMATION PAPER. [Ref. inf. pap. - U. S., Natl. Arch. Rec. Serv.]. English. National Archives and Records Administration, Eighth Street and Pennsylvania Avenue NW, Washington DC 20408. **Tel** (202)523-3220. **LC** CD3023; .A35. **DD** 027.5/73. ***Continues*** *Reference Information Papers.*

UK
REPORT - GREATER LONDON RECORD OFFICE AND LIBRARY. **Main/Corp** Greater London Record Office. English. an. £0.30. Greater London Council, The County Hall, London SE1 7PB England. **Tel** (01)633-7139. **LC** CD1067.L65; G7A. **DD** 027.5421.

UK
REPORT OF COUNCIL, ACCOUNTS, AND MINUTES OF ANNUAL GENERAL MEETING. **Main/Corp** British Records Association. 41st (1972/1973)-. English. sa. Free to members of the British Records Association; £38.00 (institutions), £18.00 (individuals) membership. British Records Association, 18 Padbury Court, London E2 7EH England. **Tel** 011 44 71 7291415. **LC** CD1040; .B74. **DD** 651.5/06/241. ***Continues*** *British Records Association. Report of Council, Annual Report of the Records Preservation Section, Accounts, Minutes of Annual General Meetings, and Changes in the List of Members.*

RH
REPORT OF THE DIRECTOR OF NATIONAL ARCHIVES. ***Title Change.*** **Main/Corp** National Archives of Rhodesia. (1962)-?. English. OTC Review Inc, 37 East 28th Street/Room 706, New York NY 10016. **Tel** (212)685-6244, FAX (212)685-8882. **LC** CD2433; .N37a. **DD** 027.5689/1. ***Supersedes*** *Report by the Chief Archivist.* ***Continued by*** *Report of the Director of National Archives for the year ... .*

RH/0301-4347
REPORT OF THE DIRECTOR OF NATIONAL ARCHIVES FOR THE YEAR ... . **Main/Corp** Zimbabwe. National Archives. 1978-. English. an. Free. The National Archives, Gun Hill/Borrowdale Road, Private Bag 7729, Causeway Zimbabwe. **Tel** 792741. **ED** R Douglas. **LC** CD2433; .N37A. **DD** 027.56891. **Circ:** 250 (ctrl). ***Continues*** *National Archives of Rhodesia. Report of the Directory of National Archives.*

DK/0034-5806
RESTAURATOR. [Restaurator.]. Vol. 1, (1969)-. English (French and German; summaries and/or abstracts in Russian). qt. kr850.00 US, Canada and Japan; kr840.00 other. Munksgaard International Publishers Ltd, PO Box 2148, DK-1016 Copenhagen K Denmark. **Tel** 011 45 33 12 70 30, FAX 011 45 33 12 93 87, telex 19431 MUNKS DK. **ED** Helmut Bansa. **LC** Z701; .R4. **DD** 025/.84. **NLM** Z 701 R4361. **CODEN** RESTBP. **[CCC].** Index available. **Bk Rev. Ad Acc. Circ:** 1,100 (ctrl). Documents available from CASDDS.
Desc: International journal for the preservation of library and archival material.
Ind/Abst Abstr. Bull. Inst. Pap. Sci. Tech.; Art Archaeol. Tech. Abstr.; Br. Archaeol. Bibliogr. (?-?); Chem. Abstr.; Libr. Inf. Sci. Abstr.; Libr. Lit.; Rev. Agric. Entomol.

RM/0034-7043
REVISTA ARHIVELOR. [Rev. arhiv.]. **Added/Corp** Romania. Arhivele Statului. Vol. 1 (1924/1926)-. Periodical. Romanian. qt. DM193.00. **(Subscription address:** Kubon & Sagner, ABT Zeitschriftenimport, D 80328 Munich Germany.**) LC** CD15.R8; R4.
Desc: Publishes studies on archive, paleography, diplomacy, sigillography, heraldry, genealogy, history and documents.
Ind/Abst Am. Hist. Life (1973-); Numis. Lit.

HO/1013-2163
REVISTA DE LA ACADEMIA HONDURENA DE GEOGRAFIA E HISTORIA. [Rev. Acad. hondur. geogr. hist.]. **Added/Corp** Academia Hondurena de Geografia e Historia. No. 50 (1968)-. Periodical. Spanish. qt. **LC** F1501; .R45. ***Continues*** *Revista de la Sociedad de Geografia e Historia de Honduras.*
Ind/Abst Am. Hist. Life (1958-1965,1971-).

PE/0259-2371
REVISTA DEL ARCHIVO GENERAL DE LA NACION (LIMA). (REVISTA DEL ARCHIVO GENERAL DE LA NACION.). [Rev. Arch. Gen. Nac.]. **Main/Corp** Peru. Archivo General de la Nacion. Vol. 1 (1972)-. Periodical. Spanish. Instituto Nacional de Cultura / Peru, Casilla No 3124, Lima Peru. **LC** CD4223; .P47a. ***Continues*** *Revista del Archivo Nacional del Peru, 1013-7955.*
Ind/Abst Am. Hist. Life (1972-1973, 1977-).

EC
REVISTA DEL ARCHIVO HISTORICO DEL GUAYAS. **Main/Corp** Archivo Historico del Guayas. Yearly V. 1- (No. 1-) 1. Half-Yearly 1972-. Periodical. Spanish (English). sa. S/10,000 Ecuador; $28.00 other. Archivo Historico del Guayas, Casilla 1333, Guayaquil Ecuador. **Tel** 343373. **ED** Julio Estrada Ycaza. **LC** F3741.G9; A73A. Index available. cum. index. **Bk Rev. Ad Acc. Pr Rev. Circ:** 900.
Desc: Articles, transcriptions and documents; lists documents of the historical archive of Guayas.

CR/0034-9003
REVISTA DEL ARCHIVO NACIONAL. **Main/Corp** Costa Rica. Archivo Nacional. Year 1-Nov./Dec. 1936-. Periodical. Spanish. an. $20.00 US and Europe. Archivo Nacional, Apartado Postal 10212, San Jose 1000 Costa Rica. **Tel** 011 506 335754. **ED** Luz Alba Chacon Leon. **Circ:** 900 (ctrl).
Desc: General archivology, transcription of documents; history of Central America.

CK
REVISTA DEL ARCHIVO NACIONAL. **Main/Corp** Colombia. Archivo Nacional. Ano 1, No. 1-2 (Enero y Feb. de 1936)- T. 7, No. 74-75 (Mayo y Jun. de 1947); 2a. Ser., No. 1 (1977)-. Spanish. **DD** 986.
Ind/Abst HAPI Hisp. Am. Period. Index (19??-).

FR/0373-6075
REVUE D'HISTOIRE DES TEXTES. See Linguistics.

FR
REVUE DU TARN. See History(General)-History of Europe.

XR
ROCENKA OKRESNIHO ARCHIVU V OPAVE. Czech. an. Free. Okresni Archiv V Opave, Lidicka 2A, Opava Czech Republic. **Tel** 21 31 91. **ED** Magda Plackova. **LC** CD1167.5.O62; R63. **Circ:** 300.
Desc: Annual report on the activities of the Archives Department of Opava, covering findings in archival research, expanded utilization of archives, public research data, archival contributions to scientific research and technical equipment supply and management. Contains regional and other specialists reports on historical topics related to Opava and its district.

US/1041-6862
ROCKEFELLER ARCHIVE CENTER NEWSLETTER. [Rockefeller Arch. Cent. newsl.]. **Added/Corp** Rockefeller Archive Center. **VFOAT** Newsletter. (19??)-. Newsletter. English. an. Free on request. Rockefeller Archive Center, Pocantico Hills, North Tarrytown NY 10591. **Tel** (914)631-4505. **DD** 025.
Desc: Covering RAC programs and activities. Recent accessions are described, research grants are listed for current year, archival notes and brief reports by researchers are included. Also a bibliography of works published in the past year that are based on RAC collections.

SA/1012-2796
S.A. ARGIEFBLAD. [S.A. argiefblad]. **VFOAT** Suid-Afrikaanse Argiefblad; South African Archives Journal; S.A. Archives Journal. (1959)-. Periodical. English (Afrikaans). an (Dec.). R45.00. South African Society of Archivist, Private Bag X 236, Pretoria 0001 South Africa. **Tel** 011 27 12 3235300, FAX 011 27 12 3235287. **ED** Verne Harris. Index available. cum. index. **Bk Rev**, (Qty: 15). **Ad Acc. Circ:** 320.

US/0091-5971
SAA NEWSLETTER. ***Title Change.*** [SAA newsl.]. **Added/Corp** Society of American Archivists. **VFOAT** S.A.A. Newsletter. **VAT** Society of American Archivists Newsletter. (19??)-(Jan. 1993). Newsletter. English. bm (irregular). Society of American Archivists, 600 South Federal, Suite 504, Chicago IL 60605. **Tel** (312)922-0140, FAX (312)347-1452. **ED** Teresa Brinati. **LC** IN PROCESS. Index available. cum. index. **Ad Acc. Circ:** 4,500 (ctrl). ***Continues*** *SAA Placement Newsletter.* ***Continued by*** *Archival Outlook.*
Desc: Presents news and topical essays of relevance to the archival profession and, in particular, Society of American Archivists members.
Ind/Abst Art Archaeol. Tech. Abstr.

XR/0036-5246
SBORNIK ARCHIVNICH PRACI. [Sb. arch. pr.]. **Added/Corp** Czechoslovakia. Archivni Sprava. (1951)-. Multiple languages (Czech, Latin and German; summaries and/or abstracts in Russian). Twice a year. $37.70. **(Subscription address:** Artia Pegas Press Ltd., Palac Metro Narodni Trida 25, 11210 Prague 1 Czech Republic.**) LC** CD1150; .S33.
Ind/Abst Am. Hist. Life (1955-); Numis. Lit.

XR
SBORNIK PRACI VYCHODOCESKYCH ARCHIVU. Vol. 1- 1970-. Czech. Nakladatelstvi Kruh / Statni Oblastni Archiv v Zamrsku, Dlouha 108, 500 21 Hradec Kralove, Czech Republic. **LC** CD1166.V9.

GW/0584-9993
SCHRIFTENREIHE DES STAATSARCHIVS DRESDEN. **Main/Corp** Staatsarchiv Dresden. **Added/Corp** Germany Sachsisches Landeshauptarchiv. Germany Staatliche Archivverwaltung. Vol. 1 (1955)-. Monographic series. German. ir. Price varies per volume. Verlag Hermann Boehlaus Nachfolger, Postfach 260, D 99403 Weimar Germany. **Tel** 011 49 3643 2071, . **(Subscription address:** BDK Buecherdienst GmBh, Postfach 900120, D 51111 Cologne Germany.**) ED** Reiner Gross.
Desc: Monographs and reference issues that are based on the archives and records existing in the Dresden public-record offices with special regard to the Saxon history in addition to the German and European history.

CN/0709-4027
SCOPE NOTES (EDMONTON). (SCOPE NOTES / ASSOCIATION OF RECORDS MANAGERS AND ADMINISTRATORS, EDMONTON CHAPTER.). **Main/Corp** Association of Records Managers and Administrators. Edmonton Chapter. Periodical. English. qt. Free to Members. Association of Records Managers and Administrators Edmonton Chapter, PO Box 6033 Station C, Edmonton Alberta T5B 4K5 Canada. **DD** 651.5/06/071233. ***Continues*** *Association of Records Managers and Administrators. Edmonton Chapter. Newsletter.*

US
SGA NEWSLETTER. Newsletter. English. qt. $15.00 (individual membership). Society of Georgia Archivists, Box 261, Georgia State University, Atlanta GA 30303. **Tel** (404)651-2477. **Circ:** 275 (ctrl).
Desc: Membership newsletter for Society of Georgia Archivists. Contains organization news and local, state and national news of interest to archivists.

XO/0583-6123
SLOVENSKA ARCHIVISTIKA. **Added/Corp** Slovenska Archivna Sprava. Archivna Sprava Ministerstva Vnutra SSR v Bratislave. Slovak Socialist Republic (Czechoslovakia). Ministerstvo Vnutra a Zivotneho Prostredia. Odbor Archivnictva. (1966)-. Periodical. Czech (summaries and/or abstracts in French, German, Latin and Russian). sa. **LC** CD15.S5; S5.
Ind/Abst Am. Hist. Life (1985-).

MY
SOUTHEAST ASIA MICROFILMS NEWSLETTER. **Added/Corp** Institute of Southeast Asian Studies. No. 1 (Dec. 1972)-. Periodical. English. sa.

Genealogy and Heraldry —Archives

$5.00. National Archives of Malaysia, Bangunan Persekutuan Jalan, 50568 Kuala Lumpur Malaysia. **Tel** 03943244. **ED** Patricia Lim Pui Huen, Hedwig Annuar, Wan Lye Tim, Maidin Hussin. **Bk Rev**. **Circ:** 200 (ctrl). available on microfilm.
Desc: Articles on microform collections of archives institutions, microform news and techniques, and reviews of microform related machines.

MY/0085-6509
SOUTHEAST ASIAN ARCHIVES. [Southeast Asian arch.]. **Added/Corp** International Council on Archives. Southeast Asian Regional Branch. Vol 1 (1968)-. English. an. **LC** CD2001; .S6. **DD** 025.17/1.
Ind/Abst Am. Hist. Life (1968-).

US/1056-1021
SOUTHWESTERN ARCHIVIST. See Library and Information Sciences.

US
STATE ARCHIVES OF ASSYRIA.
Added/Corp Neo-Assyrian Text Corpus Project. Deutsche Orient-Gesellschaft. Vol. 1 (1987)-. Monographic series. English (translations available in Akkadian). ir. Price varies per volume. Eisenbrauns, PO Box 275, Winona Lake IN 46590. **Tel** (219)269-2011.

●CN/0844-7594
STRATEGIC APPROACHES OF THE NATIONAL ARCHIVES OF CANADA.
[Strateg. approaches Natl. Arch. Can.]. **Main/Corp** National Archives of Canada. **VFOAT** Strategic Approaches; Orientations Strategiques des Archives Nationales du Canada. (1992)-. English (French). National Archives of Canada, 395 Wellington/Community Relations, Ottawa Ontario K1A 0N3 Canada. **Tel** (613)996-0394. **LC** CD3623; .P8b. **DD** 354.710071/46/05. ***Continues*** *Strategic Approaches of the Public Archives of Canada., 0844-7586.*

UK
TRANSACTIONS. TRAFODION. Main/Corp Caernarvonshire Historical Society. **VFOAT** Trafodion. (1939)-. Multiple languages (English and Welsh). an (Oct.). £7.50. Gwynedd Archives & Museum Services, Gwynedd County Council, County Office, Caernavron LL55 1SH Wales. **Tel** 011 44 286 672255, 679088, FAX 011 44 286 679637. **ED** Ms. Nia W. Powell. Index available. cum. index. **Bk Rev**, (Qty: 2). **Circ:** 500 (ctrl).
Desc: Essays on the history and archaeology of the old Welsch county of Caernafonshire.

RU
TRUDY ARKHIVA. Added/Corp Akademiia Nauk SSSR. Arkhiv. (1933)-. Monographic series. Russian. ir. Price varies per volume. Izdatelstvo Nauka / Akademiia Nauk, Publishing House of the Russian Academy of Sciences, Leninskii Porspekt 14, 117901 Moscow Russia. **Tel** 011 95 954-21-53, FAX 011 95 938-21-44, telex 411964. **LC** AS262; .A6135.

US/1056-5531
WESTWORDS (SAN MARINO, CALIF.).
(WESTWORDS : A SERIES OF OCCASIONAL PAPERS PUBLISHED BY THE SOCIETY OF CALIFORNIA ARCHIVISTS.). **Added/Corp** Society of California Archivists. No. 1 (June 1991)-. English. $3.00 (non-member), $2.00 (member). Westwords, c/o Chair Publications Committee, Society of California Archivists, Manuscripts Department, Huntington Library, 1151 Oxford Road, San Marino CA 91108. **DD** 026.

GENERAL INTEREST

FR/0997-654X
01 REFERENCES (PARIS). (01 REFERENCES.). **VFOAT** Zero un References. No 1 (Feb 1989)-. Periodical. French. 01 Informatique, 5 Place du Colonel-Fabien, F-75491 Paris Cedex 10 France. **LC** IN PROCESS. ***Continues*** *01 Informatique Magazine, 0985-2999.*
Ind/Abst Point Repere (1989-).

AG
A.R. PRESS BOLETIN. (19??)-. Bulletin. Spanish. Twelve times a year. $90.00. A R Press Srl, Pte Juan Domingo Peron 1547 - P 2B, 1037 Buenos Aires Argentina. **Tel** 382 1002. **ED** Amalia Sobre-Casas. Index available. **Pr Rev. Circ:** 250. available on diskette.
Desc: General Interest publication whose readers are informed by newspapers, periodicals, and radio programs of the region.

IT
A TRAVERSO. Periodical. Italian.

●US/1062-5321
ABILITY MAGAZINE (IRVINE, CALIF.). (ABILITY.). [Ability]. **VFOAT** Ability Magazine. (1992)-. Periodical. English. Six times a year. $29.70. CR Cooper, 1682 Langley, Irvine CA 92714. **Tel** (714)854-8700, (714)752-4121. **DD** 051.

US/0001-334X
ABRIDGED READERS' GUIDE TO PERIODICAL LITERATURE. See General Interest-Abstracting, Bibliographies and Statistics.

US/1056-7496
ACADEMIC ABSTRACTS. See General Interest-Abstracting, Bibliographies and Statistics.

US/1060-6750
ACADEMIC ABSTRACTS FULL TEXT ELITE. See General Interest-Abstracting, Bibliographies and Statistics.

US/1058-0662
ACADEMIC ABSTRACTS FULL TEXT SELECT. ***Ceased.*** [Acad. abstr. full text sel.]. **Added/Corp** EBSCO Publishing (Firm). (July 1991)-(1993). Abstracting/Indexing Service. English. qt (plus monthly and academic year). EBSCO Publishing / Boston, 83 Pine Street, Peabody MA 01960. **Tel** (800)653-2726 North America, (508)535-8500, FAX (508)535-8545. **DD** 051.
Desc: Covers the same magazines found in Academic Abstracts (CD-ROM), plus offers full text on 60 of those magazines. Key word searching is used to access the abstracts and indexing.

US
ACADEMIC INDEX. [COMPUTER FILE]. See General Interest-Abstracting, Bibliographies and Statistics.

US/1071-2720
ACADEMIC SEARCH. See General Interest-Abstracting, Bibliographies and Statistics.

US/0095-5698
ACCESS (SYRACUSE). See General Interest-Abstracting, Bibliographies and Statistics.

FR/0337-9566
ACTUEL CIDJ. [Actuel CIDJ]. **VFOAT** Actuel Centre d'Information et de Documentation Jeunesse. (1975)-. Periodical. French. mo. 2703.23F France; 3100.00F Europe; 3370.00F other. CIDJ, 101 Quai Branly, 75740 Paris Cedex 15 France. **Tel** 011 33 1 45673585, FAX 011 33 1 40650261. **UDC** 37. Index available. **Bk Rev. Circ:** 5,500 (ctrl).
Desc: Information on every subject which could interest young people. Contains synthetic documents on studies, professional training, employment, daily life, leisure time, holidays, sports, and foreign countries.

IT
ADS NOTIZIE. Italian. qt. Free. Accertamenti Diffusione Stamps, Via Larga 15, 20122 Milan Italy. **Tel** 011 39 2 58307192.

US/0889-2148
AFGHANISTAN FORUM. (AFGHANISTAN FORUM : NEWSLETTER.). [Afghan. Forum]. **Added/Corp** Afghanistan Forum. Vol. 12, No. 2, Mar. (1984)-. Periodical. English. Six times a year. $30.00 (individual); $35.00 (institution). Afghanistan Forum Inc, 201 East 71st Street 2K, New York NY 10021. **Tel** (212)861-4272. **ED** Mary Ann Siegfried. **Bk Rev. Circ:** 225. ***Continues*** *Afghanistan Forum Newsletter.*
Desc: Consist of forum papers of original research on Afghanistan or areas affecting Afghanistan.

UK
AFRICAN TIMES (LONDON, ENGLAND : 1984). (AFRICAN TIMES.). Began in 1984. English. wk. £50.00, 25p (per issue). Hansib Publishing Ltd / London, Tower House, 139-149 Fonthill Road, London N4 3HF England. **Tel** 01-281 1191, FAX 263 9656, telex 22294. **ED** Arif Ali. **LC** PAR. **Bk Rev. Ad Acc. Circ:** 9,500.
Desc: Continental African news coverage and UK features.

FR
AFRIQUE MAGAZINE. No. 57 (March 1989)-. Periodical. French. mo (11 issues per year). 215.48F France; 390.00F US. Groupe Jeune Afrique, 57 Bis rue d Auteuil, 75016 Paris France. **Tel** 011 33 1 44301960. **LC** DT1; .A5418. **DD** 960.3/2/05. ***Continues*** *Jeune Afrique Magazine (Paris, France : 1986), 0299-8602.*

JO
AL-YARMUK. No. 1 (Jan. 1982)-. Periodical. Arabic (English). qt. 0.20JD (single issue); 2.00JD Jordan; 3.00JD other. Jamiat Al-Yarmuk Dairat Al-Alaqat, Al-Thaqafiyah Wa-Al-Ammah, Irbid Jordan. **Tel** (02)271100, FAX (02)274725, telex 51533. **ED** Majeed D Ghanma. **LC** AP95.A6; Y37. **Bk Rev. Ad Acc. Circ:** 3,000.

US
ALASKA LAND & HOME MAGAZINE. Periodical. English. Eighteen times a year. $18.00 US; $36.00 other. Alaska Land & Home Magazine, 801 Barnette Street, Fairbanks AK 99701-4508. **Tel** (907)456-1214. Index available. cum. index. **Bk Rev. Ad Acc. Circ:** 10,000.
Desc: Colorful, feature magazine about life in Alaska. Includes information on travel, outdoor recreation and homes.

CN/0315-2898
ALMANACH MODERNE. (1973)-. Periodical. French. an (Nov. (prior year)). 10.99Can$. Publicor Inc, 7 Chemin Bates, Outremont Quebec H2V 1A6 Canada. **Tel** (514)270-1100, (800)463-2100. **ED** Denis Levesque. **DD** 034/.1. **Bk Rev. Ad Acc. Circ:** 150,000 (ctrl). ***Continues*** *Almanach Moderne Eclair, 0569-096X.*
Desc: Most of the subjects covered are the Olympics, sports, theatres, automobiles, house beautiful, health, science, psychology, travel, calendar of events, post scriptum, the universe, business, astrology, small business and motion picture.

US/0003-0937
AMERICAN SCHOLAR, THE. [Am. sch.]. **Added/Corp** Phi Beta Kappa. Vol. 1 (Jan. 1932)-. Periodical. English. qt (Mar., June, Sept., Dec.). $28.00 (1 year), $54.00 (2 year), $78.00 (3 year). Phi Beta Kappa, 1811 Q Street Northwest, Washington DC 20009. **Tel** (202)265-3808. **ED** Joseph Epstein. **LC** AP2; .A4572. **DD** 051; 371.852. **NLM** W1 AM755. **Bk Rev. Ad Acc. Circ:** 26,500. available on microfilm and microfiche from University Microfilms International (UMI). Documents available from The Genuine Article, UMI Article Clearinghouse, Documents on Demand. ***Supersedes*** *Phi Beta Kappa Key.*
Desc: Features critical commentary on diverse aspects of our culture, reappraisals of important literary and scientific figures, a continuing series of articles about great university teachers, and a selection of poetry, memoirs of other places and times, and book reviews.
Ind/Abst Abstr. Engl. Stud.; Acad. Abstr. Full Text Elite (Jan. 1989-) [Full Txt.]; Acad. Abstr. (Jan. 1989-); Acad. Ind. [Computer File] (1985-); Acad. Search (Jan. 1989-); Am. Hist. Life (1963-); Am. Bibliogr. Slavic East Europ. Stud.; Annu. Bibliogr. Engl. Lang. Lit.; ARTbibliogr. Mod.; Arts Humanit. Citation Index [Full Cov.]; Book Rev. Digest; Book Rev. Index; Curr. Contents Arts Humanit.; Curr. Index J. Educ.; Energy Inf. Abstr.; Environ. Abstr.; Expand. Acad. Index (1985-); Film Lit. Index; Gen. Period. Index (1985-); Guide Soc. Sci. Relig.; High. Educ. Abstr. (1965-19??); Humanit. Index; Humanit. Source (Jul. 1993-) [Full Txt.]; Index Am. Period. Verse; Index Period. Artic. Relat. Law; INFO-SOUTH Abstr.; Infobank (1969-); Int. Polit. Sci. Abstr.; Linguist. Lang. Behav. Abstr.; Lit. Crit. Regist.; Mag. Artic. Summar. Elite (Jan. 1989-) [Full Txt.]; Mag. Artic. Summar. Select (Jan. 1989-); Mag. Artic. Summar. CD-ROM (Jan. 1989-); Mag. Index Plus (1989-); Mag. Search; Middle East Abstr. Index; MLA Int. Bibl. Books Artic. Mod. Lang. Lit.; Newsp. Period. Abstr. (1988-); PAIS Int. Print (1991-?); Peace Res. Abstr. J. (1963-1970, 1976-1979); Read. Guide Abstr. Select Ed.; Read. Guide Period. Lit.; Res. Alert [Full Cov.]; Romant. Move.; Soc. Plann. Policy Dev. Abstr.; Soc. Sci. Source (Jan. 1989-) [Full Txt.]; Soc. Sci. Cit. Index [Select. Cov.]; Soc. Work Abstr. [Select. Cov.]; Sociol. Abstr.; Mag. Index (1977-); Vocat. Search (Jan. 1989-) [Full Txt.]; West. Hist. Q.

US/0896-1433
AMERICAN VIET PRESS. [Am. Viet press]. **VFOAT** Viet. (19??)-. Periodical. Vietnamese. Fifty-two times a year. $36.00. Viet Press Corporation, PO Box 2264, Westminster CA 92684. **Tel** (714)898-1018. **DD** 051.

IT/1120-5768
AMICIZIA PALERMO. (AMICIZIA.). (1986)-. Periodical. Italian. mo. Free. Ufficio Ctrl Studenti Esteri, Via Dei Monti Parioli 57/59, 00197 Rome Italy. **Tel** 06 3604491. **UDC** 82. **CODEN** 008.

US/0198-9391
AMIE. V. 1- May 1980-. Periodical. English. mo. $9.00 New Haven County, $11.00 others. Two Elms Inc, 18 Harkness Drive, Madison CT 06443.

US
ANGLOFILE. English. bm. $12.00 US; $15.00 Mexico and Canada; $22.00 other. Goody Press, Box 33515, Decatur GA 30033. **Tel** (404)633-5587. **ED** William P King. **Bk Rev. Ad Acc. Circ:** 3,000.
Desc: Provides news, reviews, updates on British entertainment and popular culture including television, music, video, books, stage, and movies of productions viewed in the U.S. Also includes celebrity interviews.

US/0192-5717
ANN ARBOR OBSERVER. (19??)-. Periodical. English. Twelve times a year. $14.00. Ann Arbor Observer, 201 Catherine Street, Ann Arbor MI 48104. **Tel** (313)769-3175, FAX (313)769-3375. **ED** John Hilton. **Ad Acc, Adv Mgr:** E. Enos, **Tel** (313)769-3175. **Circ:** 56,000 (ctrl).
Desc: It offers in-depth features, profiles, historial articles, items on new businesses, restaurant reviews, and the city's most complete listing of events and exhibits.

IT
ANTIGONE. (March 1985)-. Periodical. Italian. Centro Studi Funerari Antigone, Via Fossato Mortara 80, 44100 Ferrara Italy. **Tel** 011 39 532 210866.

US
AQUI MAGAZINE. English. Free. Impact Communications, Suite 1700, 2600 N Central, Phoenix

AZ 85004. **Tel** (602)230-2424, FAX (602)274-5130. **ED** Bill Meek and T J Tank. **Bk Rev. Ad Acc. Circ:** 15,000 (ctrl).
Desc: Covers current events and issues as they impact the Hispanic community.

US/0748-5271
ARBUTUS TIMES. (THE ARBUTUS TIMES.). Vol. 13, No. 1 (Mar. 28, 1968)-. Periodical. English. wk. $12.60 (1 year), $18.90 (2 year) Howard county; $14.70 (1 year), $22.00 (2 year) Maryland; $22.00 (1 year), $39.00 (2 year) US. Patuxent Publishing Corporation, 10750 Little Patuxent Parkway, Columbia MD 21044. **Tel** (410)730-3620, FAX (410)730-7053. ***Continues*** *Times (Baltimore, Md. : 1956).*

SW
ARET RUNT. (1???)-. Periodical. Swedish. wk. Kr456.00 Scandinavia; Kr803.50 other. Pressdata, Box 3263, 103 65 Stockholm Sweden. **Tel** 011 46 8 7996200.

US/1048-5015
ARMY MAN. [Army man]. Periodical. English. ir. Army Man, PO Box 1620, Boulder CO 80306. **DD** 051.

UK/0264-8490
ASIAN TIMES. English. Fifty-one times per year (Double issue during Christmas). £42.00 UK; £52.00 Europe; £70.00 other. Readers Book Club, 139-149 Fonthill Road, London N4 3HF England. **Tel** 011 44 71 281-1191, FAX 011 44 71 263-9656. **ED** Arif Ali. **Bk Rev. Ad Acc. Circ:** 20,000 (ctrl).

GW
ASIEN, AFRIKA, LATEINAMERIKA. (ASIA, AFRICA, LATIN AMERICA. SPECIAL ISSUE.). (19??)-. English. Akademie-Verlag GmbH, Muehlenstrasse 33 34, D 13162 Berlin Germany. **Tel** 011 49 30 47889300, FAX 011 49 30 47889357. **(Subscription address:** VCH Publishers Inc., 303 Northwest 12th Avenue, Journals Department, Deerfield FL 33442.**) LC** HC59.69; .A75. **DD** 332/.09172/405.

US/0897-4608
ATLANTA SINGLES. [Atlanta singles]. **VFOAT** Atlanta Singles Magazine; Singles Magazine; Singles. Vol. 11, Issue 65 (Feb./March 1988)-. Periodical. English. bm. $10.00. Hudson Brooke Publishing Inc, 1780 Century Circle, PO Box 49286, Atlanta GA 30359. **Tel** (404)636-2260. **ED** Margaret Anthony. **DD** 306. **Bk Rev. Ad Acc. Circ:** 10,000. ***Continues*** *Atlanta Singles Magazine & Data Book, 8750-8435.*
Desc: Covers interests of single adults.

US/0194-9993
ATLANTIC CITY MAGAZINE. (1977)-. Periodical. English. Twelve times a year. $15.00 one year; $26.00 two years; $33.00 three years. Atlantic City Press, PO Box 2100, Pleasantville NJ 08232. **Tel** (609)272-7900. **ED** Ken Weatherford. **Ad Acc, Adv Mgr:** Mr. Senoff, **Tel** (609)272-7903. **Circ:** 40,000 (ctrl).

CN/0708-5400
ATLANTIC INSIGHT. ***Ceased.*** [Atl. insight]. **VFOAT** Insight. **VAT** Insight (Halifax). Vol. 1 (April 1979)-?. Periodical. English. mo. Atlantic Insight, Insight Publishing Ltd, 1668 Barrington Street, Halifax Nova Scotia B3J 2A2 Canada. **Tel** (902)421-1214, FAX (902)423-8352. **ED** Sharon Fraser. **DD** 971.5/005. Index available. **Ad Acc. Circ:** 37,500. available on microfiche from Micromedia Limited.
Desc: Atlantic Canadian magazine of news and views about the people and happenings that influence life in Atlantic Canada; provides a lifestyle component covering such topics as food, travel, crafts, heritage, entertainment, homes and renovations.
Ind/Abst Can. Index (?-?); Can. Period. Index (19??-19??).

●US/1072-7825
ATLANTIC MONTHLY (1993), THE. (THE ATLANTIC MONTHLY.). [Atl. mon.]. Vol. 272, No. 5 (Nov. 1993)-. Periodical. English. Twelve times a year. $17.94 (one year); $29.95 (two years); $39.95 (three years). Atlantic Monthly, 745 Boylston Street, Boston MA 02116. **Tel** (617)536-9500. **(Subscription address:** Neodata / Colorado, PO Box 2606, Boulder Boulder CO 80322.**) LC** IN PROCESS; AP2; .A8. **DD** 051. Index available (back issues). **Ad Acc.** ctrl circ. ***Continues*** *Atlantic (Boston, Mass. : 1981), 0276-9077.*

SZ
AVENEMENT, L'. French. mo. 79.00F Switzerland; $58.00 North America; 85.00F other. Avenement, Case Postale 140, CH-2400 Le Locle Switzerland. **Tel** 039-31-6124, FAX 039-31-5405. **ED** Lucian Vouillanoz. **Ad Acc. Circ:** 10,000.
Desc: News magazine with a Christian influence.

US/0746-990X
BACKSTREETS. (19??)-. Periodical. English. qt. $15.00 (1 year), $25.00 (2 year), $32.00 (3 year) US and Canada; $20.00 (1 year), $35.00 (2 year) other. Backstreets Publishing Inc, PO Box 51225, Seattle WA 98115. **Tel** (206)728-7603, FAX (206)728-8827. **LC** ML420.S77; B22. **DD** 782.42166/092.

US/1050-9712
BACKWOODS HOME MAGAZINE. [Backwoods home mag.]. No. 1 (Oct./Nov. 1989)-. Periodical. English. bm. $17.95 (one year), $29.95 (two years), $44.95 (three years). Backwoods Home Magazine, 1257 Siskiyou Boulevard, #213, Ashland OR 87520. **Tel** (503)488-2053, FAX (503)488-2063. **ED** Christopher Maxwell & Lance Bisaccia. **LC** WMLC 93/2314. **DD** 051. Index available. **Bk Rev**, (Qty: 12). **Ad Acc, Adv Mgr:** Jennifer Hoie, **Tel** (503)488-2053. **Circ:** 33,000.
Desc: Explores topics such as building your own home, photovoltaics and other alternative energy systems, organic gardening and other topics relating to the self sufficient lifestyle.

US/1060-2801
BECKETT FOCUS ON FUTURE STARS. [Beckett focus future stars]. **VFOAT** Focus on Future Stars. Issue #1 (May 1991)-. Periodical. English. mo. $19.95 US; $29.86 Canada; $31.95 other. Beckett Publications, 15850 Dallas Parkway, Dallas TX 75248. **Tel** (214)991-6657, FAX (214)991-8930. **LC** WMLC 91/2266. **DD** 769.

US/1046-1582
BEDROOM MAGAZINE. ***Title Change.*** [Bedroom mag.]. **VFOAT** Bedroom. Vol. 12, No. 9 (July 1989)-. Periodical. English. Six times a year. Bobit Publishing, 2512 Artesia Boulevard, Redondo Beach CA 90278. **Tel** (310)376-8788, (800)334-8152, FAX (213)376-9043. **DD** 338. ***Continues*** *Waterbed, 0273-7469.* ***Continued by*** *Retailing Today (Lafayette, Calif. : 1991).*

US/0896-4920
BEING SINGLE. [Being single]. Periodical. English. bm. $7.95. The Harbon Corporation, PO Box 49402, Chicago IL 60649. **DD** 051.

GW/0585-3044
BERICHT (VOLKSWAGENSTIFTUNG). **Main/Corp** Volkswagenstiftung. German. Vandenhoeck & Ruprecht, Robert Bosch Breite 6, D-37079 Goettingen Germany. **Tel** 011 49 551 695911, FAX 011 49 551 695917, telex 965226 VAN d. **LC** AS182.S79; A18. **DD** 063/.5954/05. ***Continues*** *Bericht - Stiftung Volkswagenwerk.*

GW/0005-9668
BESTE AUS READER'S DIGEST, DAS. Vol. 1 (1948)-. Periodical. German. mo. DM49.90 Germany; DM57.90 other. Verlag das Beste GmbH, Postfach 178, D 70160 Stuttgart 1 F R Germany. **Tel** 011 49 711 6602 738, FAX 011 49 711 6602547, telex 723539. **ED** Renate Wriedt. **Ad Acc. Circ:** 1,450,000 (ctrl). available on audiocassette; available in print.

US
BEST'S WEEKLY NEWS DIGEST. Periodical. English. AM Best Company, Ambest Road, Oldwick NJ 08858. **Tel** (908)439-2200 ext. 5653, telex 837744.

US/0162-3370
BETTER LIVING MAGAZINE (SUNNYVALE). Nov. 1978-. Periodical. English. mo. $9.00. GRT Corporation, 1286 North Lawrence Station Road, Sunnyvale CA 94806.

US/0745-600X
BETTER LIVING TODAY. (BETTER LIVING TODAY : A PUBLICATION OF THE UNIVERSAL FOUNDATION FOR BETTER LIVING, INC.). **Added/Corp** Universal Foundation for Better Living. (198?)-. Periodical. English. qt. Better Living Today, 8435 South Cottage Grove, Chicago IL 60619.

IT/0393-1951
BIELLESE, IL. [Biellese]. (1886)-. Periodical. Italian. ir (100 issues per year). L110000 Italy; L220000 other. Biellese, Via Losana 26, 13051 Biella Italy. **Tel** 011 39 15 28646. **UDC** 070.23(1-32).

US/1047-3831
BIG PICTURE (KNOXVILLE, TENN.). (THE BIG PICTURE POSTER.). [Big pict.]. (1988)-. Periodical. English. mo. Whittle Communications, 333 Main Avenue, Knoxville TN 37902. **Tel** (615)595-5000, FAX (615)595-5877. **DD** 051.

GW/0341-4906
BILD AM SONNTAG. [Bild Sonntag]. (1956)-. Periodical. German. wk. $180.00. Axel Springer Verlag Ag, Brieffach 2460, D 20350 Hamburg Germany. **Tel** 011 49 40 34724503. **(Subscription address:** German Language Publications Inc., 153 South Deanstreet, Englewood, NJ 07631**) UDC** 008.

DK/0006-2537
BILLED BLADET. (1938)-. Periodical. Danish. wk. $91.46. Berlingske Tidende, Pilestraede 34, 1147 Copenhagen K Denmark.

US
BITE ME. English. Four times a year (Mar., Jun., Sept., Dec.). $8.00; $2.00 (single copy). Llevyn Publishing, PO Box 6841, Pico Rivera CA 90661-6841. **ED** Emily Lazalde. **Ad Acc. Circ:** 100.
Desc: Contains comic strips, humorous stories, tidbits and editorials.

●US/1064-0134
BLACK & WHITE (BIRMINGHAM, ALA.). (BLACK & WHITE.). **VFOAT** Black and White. (May 1992)-. Newspaper. English. Twelve times a year. $9.00. Black & White, Inc., PO Box 13215, 1312 Twentieth Street South, Birmingham AL 35202-3215. **Tel** (205)933-0460, FAX (205)933-0467. **ED** Alison Nichols. Index available. cum. index. **Ad Acc, Adv Mgr:** Chuck Geiss. **Circ:** 100,000 (ctrl).
Desc: Provides news, feature articles, a calendar of events, restaurant reviews and more of interest to residents and friends of Birmingham, Alabama.

US/0744-5601
BLUE BERET. [Blue beret]. **Added/Corp** Wally Byam Caravan Club International. (19??)-. Periodical. English. mo (except July). Blue Beret, POB 612, Jackson Center OH 45334.

CU/0523-8579
BOHEMIA. (1911)-. Periodical. Spanish. wk. $86.00 US; $90.00 Central & South America; $100.00 other. Ediciones Cubanas, Obispo 527, Altos ESQ Bernaza, CP 10100 Havana Cuba. **Tel** 011 63 2980, 631942, FAX 011 631011, telex 512337, 6540. **LC** AP63; .B7. **DD** 056/.1. Index available. **Bk Rev. Ad Acc. Circ:** 200,000 (ctrl).
Desc: A general interest magazine with current topics related to politics, culture, the economy and industry; photo features on Cuba's industrial and agricultural development; interviews of outstanding national and international figures; and national and foreign sports activities.

IT/1121-5305
BOLLETTINO UFFICIALE DEL TOTOCALCIO. (1948)-. Italian. ir (40 issues per year). L70000 Italy; L140000 other. Giornale Totocalcio, Foro Italico, 00194 Rome Italy. **Tel** 011 39 6 36851.

CN/0833-9864
BOUT DE PAPIER. [Bout pap.]. **Added/Corp** Professional Association of Foreign Service Officers. (Sept. 1983)-. Periodical. French (English). Four times a year. 16.00Can$ (one year); $30.00 (two years). Bout de Papier, 45 Rideau Street/Suite 600, Ottawa Ontario K1N 5W8 Canada. **Tel** (613)234-1391. **ED** Debra Hulley. **DD** 354.710089/2/05. **Bk Rev**, (Qty: 20). **Ad Acc. Circ:** 2,800 (ctrl).

SA
BRABY'S NATAL DIRECTORY. **VFOAT** Natal Directory. (1902)-. Directory. English. an. R100.00. AC Braby Pty Ltd, PO Box 1426, Pinetown 3600 South Africa. **Tel** 011 27 31 7017021, FAX 011 27 31 7017036, telex 624529. **ED** A Stagg. **LC** DT867; .B7. **Ad Acc.** ***Continues*** *Natal Directory (Durban, South Africa);* ***Absorbed*** *Davis Natal Directory.*
Desc: Contains maps of Natal, post box listings for Natal, alphabetical section and classified section.

US/0741-9880
BRANDYWINE MAGAZINE. Periodical. English. mo. $10.00 US; $11.00 other. Strafford Associates Inc, 100 N Valley Road, Paoli PA 19301.

UK/0267-9965
BRAZIL (LONDON, ENGLAND). (BRAZIL.). **Added/Corp** Latin American Monitor Ltd. (1985)-. English. an (June). £380.00. Business Monitor International, 56 60 St. John Street, London EC1M 4DT England. **Tel** 011 44 71 6083646.

UK/0307-160X
BRAZILIAN GAZETTE, THE. (1973)-. Periodical. English (Portuguese). ir (six issues per year). £10.00 UK; $20.00 other. Brazilian Gazette, Rua Duvivier 43, Ap 501, Rio de Janeiro RJ Brazil. **Bk Rev. Ad Acc. Circ:** 25,000.

US/1066-260X
BREAKTHROUGH STRATEGIES. ***Ceased.*** [Breakthr. strateg.]. **Added/Corp** Alexander Hamilton Institute (U.S.). (1992)-(1994). Periodical. English. Twenty-four times a year. Alexander Hamilton Institute Inc, 70 Hilltop Road, Ramsey NJ 07446-1119. **Tel** (201)825-8161, FAX (201)825-8696. **DD** 658.

FR/0293-7166
BRISES. BULLETIN DE RECHERCHES SUR L'INFORMATION EN SCIENCES ECONOMIQUES HUMAINES ET SOCIALES. [BRISES, Bull. rech. inf. sci. econ. hum. soc.]. **VFOAT** BRISES (Vandoeuvre-les-Nancy); Bulletin de Recherches sur l'Information en Sciences Economiques Humaines et Sociales. (1981)-. Periodical. French. sa. 132.70F France; 161.54F other. CNRS / Institut d'Information Scientifique et Technique, (Centre National de la Recherche Scientifique), 15 Quai Anatole France, Paris 75700 France. **Tel** 011 33 1 47531515, telex 299 356 F. **UDC** 01.

US/0195-2633
BRITISH HERITAGE. [Br. herit.]. Vol. 1 (Dec. 1979/Jan. 1980)-. Periodical. English. bm. $30.00.

Cowles Magazines, PO Box 8200, Harrisburg PA 17105. **Tel** (717)657-9555, (800)435-9610. available on microfilm and microfiche from University Microfilms International (UMI). ***Supersedes*** *British History Illustrated, 0195-2625.* **Ind/Abst** Abstr. Engl. Stud.; Am. Hist. Life (1974-1991-).

IT
BURKE & NOVI NOTIZIE FLASH DELLA SETTIMANA. Burke & Novi Spa, Via D Fiasella 4 /14, 16121 Genoa Italy.

II/0971-2852
BYWORD NEW DELHI. [Byword New Delhi]. (1973)-. Periodical. English. mo. $20.00. **(Subscription address:** Prints India, 11 Darya Ganj, New Delhi 110002 India.) **UDC** 087.6.

CN/0709-2121
CALENDAR OF EVENTS (VICTORIA. 1979). (CALENDAR OF EVENTS.). Spring/Summer 1979-. Periodical. English. sa. Calendar of Events, 1117 Wharf Street, Victoria British Columbia V8W 2Z2 Canada. **Tel** FAX (604)356-8246. ctrl circ. ***Continues*** *Events, 0707-9125.*

IT
CAMPAGNE. (19??)-. Italian. bm (6 issues). L80000.00 Italy; L110000.00 other. Summa Editori SRL, Via V Monti 8, 20123 Milan Italy. **Tel** 011 39 2 4983290.

IT
CAMPUS. (19??)-. Italian. Ten times a year. L28000.00 Italy; L118000.00 The Americas & Asia; L68000.00 Europe; L107000.00 Africa; L156000.00 other. Class Editori CAM, Via Burigozzo 5, 20122 Milan Italy. **Tel** 011 39 2 582191.

US/1042-3281
CANALES (NEW YORK, N.Y.). (CANALES.). [Canales]. (19??)-. Periodical. Spanish (English). mo. $18.00. Canales Publ, 215 West 92nd Street/#8E, New York NY 10025. **Tel** (212)724-8805. **ED** Fernando Campos. **DD** 791.

US/1044-4769
CAPITAL (ALBANY, N.Y.). (CAPITAL.). **VFOAT** Capital Magazine. Vol. 5, No. 4 (April 1989)-. Periodical. English. mo. $15.00 US; $29.00 Canada. Capital Magazine, Circulation Services, Dept CR, Box 3000, Denville NJ 07834-9990. ***Continues*** *Capital Region, 0887-9184.*

IT
CARABINIERE, IL. Periodical. Italian.

US/0745-2608
CARIBBEAN CONNECTIONS. (198?)-. Periodical. English. Twelve times a year. $20.00 (one year); $37.50 (two years); $55.00 (three years). Caribbean Connections Inc, 7600 Georgia Avenue, Suite 406, Washington DC 20012. **Tel** (202)723-8796.

JM/0254-8038
CARIBBEAN QUARTERLY. [Caribb. q.]. **Added/Corp** University College of the West Indies (Mona, Jamaica). Extra Mural Dept. University of the West Indies (Mona, Jamaica). Dept. of Extra-Mural Studies. **VFOAT** CQ; C.Q. Vol. 1, No. 1 (Apr.-May-June 1949)-. Periodical. English. qt. $30.00. University of the West Indies / Kingston, PO Box 42, Mona St. Andrew, Kingston 7 Jamaica. **Tel** 809 977 2659 ext. 2432. **ED** Rex Nettleford and Everton Pryce. **LC** F1601; .C3. **DD** 972.9/005. **Bk Rev. Ad Acc. Circ:** 2,000.
Desc: Interdisciplinary journal on the Caribbean region. Articles devoted to history, literature, industry, sociology, agriculture, ethology/anthropology, religion, creative arts, and politics.
Ind/Abst Abstr. Engl. Stud.; Am. Hist. Life (1955-1962, 1966-); Appl. Soc. Sci. Index Abstr.; HAPI Hisp. Am. Period. Index; Int. Bibliogr. Sociol.; Leis. Recreat. Tour. Abstr.; Rural Dev. Abstr.; World Agric. Econ.

US/0274-7723
CAROLINA BLUE. Vol. 1 (Summer 1980)-. Periodical. English. Forty times a year. $37.00. Carolina Blue Inc, One Julian Price Place, Charlotte NC 28208. **Tel** (704)374-3740.

IT
CENTO COSE. (19??)-. Italian. mo. L31200 Italy; L57000 other. Arnoldo Mondadori Editore, UFF Cont Abbonamenti, 20090 Segrate MI Italy. **Tel** 011 39 2 75422015, telex 320457 MONDMI I.

IT
CENTRO. (19??)-. Italian. da. L325000. Seci Spa, C SO Vittorio Eman 372, 65100 Pescara Italy. **Tel** 011 39 85 20521.

US/0162-2722
CHARLESTON MAGAZINE. Vol 1, (Aug. 1975)-. Periodical. English. Six times a year (Feb., Apr., June, Aug., Oct., Dec.). $12.00. Charleston Magazine Inc., PO Box 21770, Charleston SC 29413. **Tel** (803) 722-8018. **ED** Dawn Leggett. **Ad Acc, Adv Mgr:** S. Faulkenberry, **Tel** (803)722-8018. **Circ:** 20,000.
Desc: The charms and styles of the city and its tri-county area. Covers current happenings, history, and local personalities.
Ind/Abst BHA : Biblio. Hist. Art.

US/0888-0077
CHATTANOOGA LIFE & LEISURE. ***Ceased.*** **VFOAT** Chattanooga Life and Leisure. (19??)-(1990). Periodical. English. mo. Chattanooga Life & Leisure, PO Box 581, Chattanooga TN 37401.

CN/0009-4501
CHINATOWN NEWS. Vol. 4, No. 1 (Sept. 1956)-. Periodical. English. sm (23 issues). 25.00Can$ Canada; 27.00Can$ other. Chinese Publicity Bureau Ltd., 459 East Hastings Street, Vancouver British Columbia V6A 1P5 Canada. **Tel** (604)254-2533. **ED** Roy Mah. Index available (bound in all issues). **Ad Acc. Circ:** 24,000 (ctrl). ***Continues*** *Chinatown., 0319-4698.*
Desc: General news magazine highlighting Asia and the Pacific for North American readers.
Ind/Abst Acad. Abstr. Full Text Elite (July 1993-) [Full Txt.]; Acad. Abstr. (July 1993-); Acad. Search (July 1993-); Mag. Artic. Summar. Elite (July 1993-) [Full Txt.]; Mag. Artic. Summar. CD-ROM (July 1993-).

US/0743-8389
CINEMA BLUE. Periodical. English. mo. $34.95 US; $39.95 Canada. Modernismo Publications, 462 Broadway, New York NY 10013. **Tel** (212)966-8400.

HK
CINEMART. English (Chinese). Twelve times a year. $43.00. Cinemart Publications Co., 10/F Flat 5 Block B Hankow Center, Kowloon Hong Kong Hong Kong. **Tel** 011 852 678232, FAX 011 852 3113996. **ED** H.K. Lau.

US/0747-3826
CLASS (NEW YORK, N.Y.). (CLASS.). [Class]. **VFOAT** Class Magazine. (19??)-. Periodical. English. Nine times a year (Dec/Jan, Mar/Apr, and Jul/Aug issues combined). $15.00. R. E. John-Sandy Comm Ltd, 900 Broadway, 8th Floor, New York NY 10003. **Tel** (212)677-3055, FAX (212)677-3341. **ED** Constance Weaver. **LC** E185.5; .C53. **DD** 973/.0496073/005. **Bk Rev**, (Qty: 40-50). **Ad Acc. Circ:** 250,000 (ctrl).
Desc: The comprehensive black magazine. Its editorial mix incorporates various cultures and interests appealing to a wide readership of people of color.

US/0160-8533
CLEVELAND MAGAZINE. (July 1973)-. Periodical. English. Twelve times a year. $18.00 one year; $28.00 two year; $38.00 three year. Cleveland Magazine, 1422 Euclid Avenue, 730 Hanna Building, Cleveland OH 44115. **Tel** (216)771-2833, FAX (216)781-6318. **ED** Elizabeth Ludlow. **Bk Rev**, (Qty: 12). **Ad Acc, Adv Mgr:** Lute Harmon. **Pr Rev. Circ:** 50,000. available on microfilm and microfiche from University Microfilms International (UMI). ***Continues*** *Cleveland, 0145-2835.*
Desc: Delivers commentary, award winning editorial, dining guide, and profiles on the people in Cleveland.
Ind/Abst Access (1975-).

PE
COMERCIO. Spanish. da. $2,110.00 US & Canada, $2,510.00 others daily & Sunday (surface mail); $1,410.00 US & Canada, $1,810.00 others Sunday. Empresa Editora el Comercio SA, Quesada 300, Lima Peru. **Tel** 51 14 271050, FAX 51 14 321052, telex 20115.
Desc: Articles of international interest, culture, politics, and music.

US
COMMON SENSE; A MONTHLY MAGAZINE DEVOTED TO THE INTERESTS OF THE NORTHWEST. Periodical. English.

FR
CONFORTIQUE MAGAZINE. (19??)-. Periodical. French. mo. 700.00F France; 1100.00F other. Soc de Gestion de Publications, 72 rue du Docteur Decorse, F 94410 Saint Maurice France. **Tel** 011 33 1 43766529.

IT
CONOSCERE I FATTI. 1987-. Monographic series. Italian. Price varies per volume.

UK/0010-7565
CONTEMPORARY REVIEW (LONDON, ENGLAND). (THE CONTEMPORARY REVIEW.). [Contemp. rev.]. Vol. 1 (Jan.-Apr. 1866)-. Periodical. English. mo (12 issues). $160.00 US and Canada; £36.00 other. Contemporary Review Company Ltd, Cheam Business Center, 14 Upper Mulgrave, Cheam Surrey SM2 7AZ England. **Tel** 011 44 438 740074, FAX 011 44 438 741075. **ED** Rosalind Wade (editor's telephone number: 0252-713883). **LC** AP4; .C7. Index available. cum. index. **Bk Rev. Ad Acc.** available on microfilm and microfiche from University Microfilms International (UMI). Documents available from UMI Article Clearinghouse. ***Absorbed*** *International Review (London, England : 1918); Fortnightly (London, England : 1934), 0950-5679.* **Ind/Abst** Acad. Search (July 1993-); Am. Hist. Life (1955-); Book Rev. Index; Br. Humanit. Index; Expand. Acad. Index (1989-); Film Lit. Index; Guide Soc. Sci. Relig.; Humanit. Index; Humanit. Source (Jul. 1993-); INFO-SOUTH Abstr.; Mag. Search; Middle East Abstr. Index; MLA Int. Bibl. Books Artic. Mod. Lang. Lit.; Newsp. Period. Abstr. (1989-); Read. Guide Period. Lit.; SportSearch.

US
CORDIALITY. English. qt. $7.00. Cordiality, 234 Fifth Avenue, Suite 301, New York NY 10001. **Tel** (212)677-2200. **ED** J Joseph Finora, Michael Banka, and Blake Gerard. **Bk Rev. Ad Acc. Circ:** 100,000.
Desc: Magazine for life in the 1990's.

IT
CORRIERE DI CHIERI E DINTORNI. Corriere Di Chieri E Dintorni, Via Rome 4, 10023 Rome Italy.

IT
CORRIERE DI ROMA, IL. Italian. sw. L50000 Italy; L100000 other. Corriere di Roma, Via IV Novembre 152, 00187 Rome Italy. **Tel** 011 39 6 6784964.

IT
CORRIERE DI SALUZZO. Corriere Di Saluzzo, Via Parra 9, 12037 Saluzzo CN Italy.

US
COUNTRY. **VFOAT** Country Magazine. Vol. 1 (Dec. 1977)-. Periodical. English. mo. $12.00. Country Magazine, PO Box 246, Alexandria VA 22313. **LC** F106; .C83.

UK
COUNTRY GENTLEMEN'S MAGAZINE, THE. Vol. 67, No. 1 (Jan. 1967)-. Periodical. English. mo. Country Gentlemens Association Letchworth, Herts SG6 4AP England. ***Continues*** *Country Gentlemen's Estate Magazine.*

US
COUNTRY WORLD. Periodical. English. mo. Country World, PO Box 598, Sulphur Springs TX 75482. **Tel** (214)885-2030. ***Continues*** *Tulsa Sunday World.*

US/1061-6349
COUNTRYSIDE (NEW YORK, N.Y. 1990). ***Ceased.*** (COUNTRYSIDE.). [Countryside]. **VFOAT** Countryside Magazine. (Fall/Winter 1990)-(Summer 1993). Periodical. English. Five times a year. The Hearst Corporation, 250 West 55th Street, New York NY 10019. **Tel** (212)649-4014. **(Subscription address:** PO Box 7021 Red Oak, IA 5159-2021) **DD** 640. **Ad Acc. Circ:** 250,000 (ctrl). ***Continues*** *Country Living's Countryside, 1057-3372.*

AT/0011-0442
COURRIER AUSTRALIEN. (19??)-. French. mo. 44.00Aus$ Australia; 88.00Aus$ other. Le Couriier Australien, 506-149 Castlereagh Street, Sydney New South Wales, 2000 Australia. **Tel** 011 61 2 2676930, FAX 011 61 2 2647952. **ED** J.P. Sourdin. **Bk Rev**, (Qty: 4). **Ad Acc. Circ:** 7,000.
Desc: News of France, the French Pacific, and the French community in Australia.

FR/1154-516X
COURRIER INTERNATIONAL PARIS. (COURRIER INTERNATIONAL.). (1990)-. Periodical. French. wk. 763.96F France; 1244.00F US Canada & Near East. Courrier International, 4 rue Raoul Dufy, 75980 Paris Cedex 20 France. **Tel** 33 1 43584949, FAX 33 1 43584900. **ED** Glioier Postel-Vinay. **UDC** 082. Index available. cum. index. **Ad Acc. Circ:** 100,000 (ctrl).
Desc: International press translated into French.

US
CPR, CAIRO PRESS REVIEW. Periodical. English. da. $685.00. FHB, PO Box 1509, Cairo AR Egypt. **Tel** 761327. **LC** MICROFILM 03070DT; DT107.821. ***Continues*** *Cairo Press Review.*
Desc: Summary of daily news from Middle East and the world.

CU/0011-2593
CUBA INTERNACIONAL. ***Suspended.*** **Added/Corp** Agencia Prensa Latina. Vol. 1 (July 1969)-(Jan. 1993). Periodical. Spanish. mo. 4.00Cub$. Ediciones Cubanas, Obispo 527, Altos ESQ Bernaza, CP 10100 Havana Cuba. **Tel** 011 632980, 631942, FAX 011 631011, telex 512337, 6540. **Circ:** 30,000 (ctrl). ***Supersedes*** *Cuba.*
Desc: A general interest magazine with articles on politics, economics and culture; also contains topics of national and international events and extensive photo features that reflect Cuba's development in all aspects.

IT
CUCINA ITALIANA. Editrice Quadratum Spa, Piazza Aspromonte 13 A, 20131 Milan Italy.

IT/0011-2798
CULTURA NEL MONDO, LA. Vol. 1 (1945)-. Periodical. Italian (English and French). Four times a year. L20000 Italy; L25000 others. Magnino Leo / Cultura Nel Mondo, via Archimede 139, 00197 Rome Italy. **Tel** 011 39 6 8072575. Index available. cum. index. **Ad Acc.** ctrl circ.

UK/0721-5207
CURRENT CONTENTS AFRICA. ***Ceased.***
See General Interest-Abstracting, Bibliographies and Statistics.

US
CURRENT CONTENTS SEARCH. VFOAT
CC Search. English. Magnetic Tape: $19465.00 (academic), $24320.00 (corporate). Institute for Scientific Information, 3501 Market Street, Philadelphia PA 19104. **Tel** (215)386-0100, (800)523-1850, FAX (215)386-6362, telex 84-5305. **(Subscription address:** Institute for Scientific Information, PO Box 71416, Chicago, IL 60694**)** available on magnetic tape.
Desc: The online format of Current Contents. While it provides the same coverage as the other products, it allows searching within and across as many of the seven editions as needed.

US/0011-3131
CURRENT (NEW YORK). (CURRENT.). [Current]. No. 1 (May 1960)-. Periodical. English. mo (10 issues). $60.00. Heldref Publications, 1319 Eighteenth Street Northwest, Washington DC 20036-1802. **Tel** (202)296-6267, (800)365-9753, FAX (202)296-5149. **ED** Jerome J. Hanus. **LC** AP2; .C9259. **Bk Rev**. **Ad Acc. Circ:** 5,032. available on microfilm and microfiche from University Microfilms International (UMI). Documents available from UMI Article Clearinghouse.
Desc: Unique journal compiles the new thinking on today's problems. The timely articles come from unusual sources and are chosen without any particular bias.
Ind/Abst Acad. Abstr. Full Text Elite (Jan. 1989-) [Full Txt.]; Acad. Abstr. (Jan. 1989-); Acad. Ind. [Computer File] (1984-); Acad. Search (Jan. 1989-); Contents Pages Educ.; Curr. Index J. Educ.; Except. Child Educ. Resour. (19??-19??); Expand. Acad. Index (1984-); Gen. Period. Index (1985-); Guide Soc. Sci. Relig.; Humanit. Source (Jul. 1993-) [Full Txt.]; INFO-SOUTH Abstr.; Mag. Artic. Summar. Elite (Jan. 1989-) [Full Txt.]; Mag. Artic. Summar. Select (Jan. 1989-) [Full Txt.]; Mag. Artic. Summar. CD-ROM (Jan. 1989-); Mag. Index Plus (1989-); Mag. Search; Multicult. Educ. Abstr.; Newsp. Period. Abstr. (1988-); Spec. Educ. Needs Abstr.; Mag. Index (1977-); Vocat. Search (Jan. 1989-).

US/1049-4839
CUTTING EDGE, THE. ***Ceased.*** [Cutt. edge]. Vol. 1, No. 1 (March 1990)-(1991). Periodical. English. mo. Agora Incorporated, 824 East Baltimore Street, Baltimore MD 21202. **Tel** (800)433-1528. **DD** 051.

VI
DAILY NEWS. Periodical. English. da. Virgin Islands Daily News, PO Box 7760, St Thomas Virgin Islands 00801. available on microfiche.

US/0418-3789
DARE. Vol. 1 (1963)-. Periodical. English. bm. Cashin Publishing Company, 1626 Magnolia Court, Cleveland OH 44106. **DD** 051.

CN/0317-7076
DECKS AWASH. Added/Corp Memorial University of Newfoundland. Extension Service. Vol. 1, No. 1 (July/Aug. 1968)-. Periodical. English. Six times a year (Feb., Apr., June, Aug., Oct., Dec.). $20.00 one year; $30.00 two years. Aardvark Communications. LTD, PO Box 9548, Station B, St. Johns NFLD A1A 2YA Canada. **Tel** (709)753-8871, FAX (709)722-3335. **ED** Roger Burrows and Andrew Flaser. **DD** 971.8/005. **Bk Rev**, (Qty: 3). **Ad Acc**, **Adv Mgr:** Jeff, **Tel** (709)368-7670. **Circ:** 1,600 (ctrl).
Desc: Covers everyday life of ordinary and extraordinary of the Newfoundlanders, past and present. Fishermen, farmers, businessmen, clergymen, housewives, and students. People in cities, small towns and out ports.

IT/1121-0311
DELFINO ROMA, IL. (IL DELFINO.). [Delfino Roma]. (1976)-. Periodical. Italian. bm (6 issues). L30000.00 Italy; L60000.00 other. Centro Italiano Di Solidarieta, Via Ambrosini 129, 00147 Rome Italy. **Tel** 011 39 6 5405945. **UDC** 613.83. **Bk Rev**, (Qty: 70/yr).

IT
DIALOGO / DIALOGUE. Edis SRL / Ediz Italo Sovietiche, Corso Italia 22, 20122 Milan Italy.

IT
DIALOGUE. (19??)-. Italian. qt. Free on request. Usis, Via Boncompagni 2, 00187 Rome Italy. **Tel** 011 39 6 46742428.

FR
DICTIONNAIRE PERMANENT. CONSTRUCTION. French. ir. Editions Legislatives et Admin, 80 82 Avenue de la Marne, 92546 Montrouge Cedex France. **Tel** 011 33 1 40926868.

US/1059-4027
DONOSY (WASHINGTON, D.C.). (DONOSY [COMPUTER FILE] : LIBERAL DAILY.). [Donosy]. **Added/Corp** North American Study Center for Polish Affairs. Periodical. English. da. Free. Przemik Klosowski, 417 Muddy Br Road, # 203, Gaithersburg MD 20878. **DD** 051.
Desc: Mode of access: Email on PRZEMEK@NDCVX.CC.ND.EDU

IT
DUEMILA. (19??)-. Italian. Thirty-six times a year. L35000. IL Duemila, C So Statuto 26, 12084 Mondovi to Italy. **Tel** 011 39 174 42763.

IT
EAST-WEST. Italian. Three times a year. L50000. Assn Int Tecn Med Tradiz Cinese, Via Carso 5, 48100 Ravenna Italy. **Tel** 011 39 544 401839.

CN/0821-7394
EASY LIVING GUIDE : THE ORIGINAL GUIDE FOR THE COMMUNITIES OF NEW WESTMINSTER, COQUITLAM, PORT MOODY, BURNABY. [Easy living guide]. Vol. 1, No. 9 (March/April 1982)-. Periodical. English. ir (every 28 days). $38.00. Easy Living Promotions Ltd, 13281 Comber Way, Surrey British Columbia V3W 5V8 Canada. **Tel** (604)591-5101, FAX (604)591-3335. **ED** Vivian Rudd Sinclair. **DD** 051. **Bk Rev. Ad Acc. Circ:** 355,000 (ctrl). ***Continues*** *Easy Living Community Guide (New Westminster), 0821-7386.* ***Continued in part by*** *Easy Living Guide (Burnaby), 0826-6077; Easy Living Guide (Coquitlam), 0827-2875.*
Desc: A home and leisure magazine promoting the quality of our British Columbia lifestyle with informative features on local personalities, home improvement, restaurant listings and entertainment.

IT
ECO DEL CHISONE. Eco Del Chisone, Via Buniva 85, 10064 Pinerolo Italy.

US/0013-6395
ELSEVIERS MAGAZINE. MICROFORM. (Jan. 24, 1970)-. Dutch. BV Uitgeversmaatschappij Bonaventura, PO Box 2158, 1000 CD Amsterdam Netherlands. **Tel** 011 31 20 6914111, 011 31 20 5674911. **LC** MICROFILM 02232 AP. ***Continues*** *Elseviers Weekblad.*

SA
ENGLISH ALIVE. (1???)-. English. an. $10.00. English Alive, PO Box 23912, Claremont 7735 South Africa. **Tel** 011 27 21 531-4876. ctrl circ.
Desc: Prose and verse literature submitted by high school students.

UK
ENITHARMON PRESS GISSING SERIES. VFOAT Gissing Series. 1-. Monographic series. English. Price varies per volume.

US
ENTERPRISE. English. Fifty-two times a year (Mon.). $36.00. The Enterprise / Utah, PO Box 11778, Salt Lake City UT 84147. **Tel** (801)533-0556.

CN/0827-3774
EPILOGES (MONTREAL). (EPILOGES.). [Epiloges]. Periodical. Greek, Modern. mo. $1.00 Per No. Epiloges, 5582 Waverly Street, Montreal Quebec H2T 2Y1 Canada. **DD** 059/.89.

IT/0423-4243
ESPRESSO, L'. Vol. 20, No. 10 (Mar. 1974)-. Periodical. Italian. Fifty-one times per year. L104000 Italy; L215800 others. Arnoldo Mondadori Editore, UFF Cont Abbonamenti, 20090 Segrate MI Italy. **Tel** 011 39 2 75422015, telex 320457 MONDMI I. **LC** AP37; .E78. **DD** 05/.1. available on microfilm and microfiche from University Microfilms International (UMI). ***Continues*** *Espresso.*
Ind/Abst Infomat Int. Bus.; PAIS Int. Print.

IT
ETERNAUTA. Comic Art, Via Flavio Domiziano 9, 00145 Rome Italy.

FR/1161-8884
EUROPE PLURILINGUE. Added/Corp Association pour le Rayonnement des Langues Europeennes. (1991)-. Periodical. Multiple languages. Twice a year. 110.00F EEC Countries; 140.00F others. ARLE, 44 rue Perronet, 92200 Neuilly sur Seine France. **Tel** 011 33 1 46241276, FAX 011 33 1 47481341. **ED** Nadine Dormoy. **UDC** 80. Index available. cum. index. **Bk Rev**, (Qty: 2). **Ad Acc**, **Adv Mgr:** N. Dormoy. **Circ:** 1,000 (ctrl).

CN/0701-4686
EVOLUTION (MONTREAL). (L'EVOLUTION.). 1st.- Yearly V.; 1946?-. Periodical. French (English). mo. L'Evolution, 3271 Boulevard Perras, Montreal Quebec Canada.

US
EXPANDED ACADEMIC INDEX [COMPUTER FILE]. **See** General Interest-Abstracting, Bibliographies and Statistics.

US/1062-9572
FACTS ON FILE NEWS DIGEST CD-ROM. ***Ceased.*** (FACTS ON FILE NEWS DIGEST CD-ROM [COMPUTER FILE].). [Facts file news dig. CD-ROM]. (19??)-(19??). English. an. Facts on File Publications, 460 Park Avenue South, New York NY 10016. **Tel** (212)683-2244, (800)322-8755, FAX (212)683-3633, telex 238 552 FACTS UR. **LC** D410. **DD** 905. Index available. cum. index. **Ad Acc.** available on microfiche; available in print.
Desc: The only current events resource that allows instant full text searches of news information from 1980-the present. Over 50,000 articles on specific people, countries, companies, organizations, events and topics in the news. Over 300 detailed maps of the US, Europe, and the world. A comprehensive index with over 700,000 entries. A single disc contains all the information from the leading US and international news sources published in the print version.

US
FACTS ON FILE YEARBOOK [MICROFORM]. **See** History(General).

US/0014-7575
FAR EAST REPORTER. ***Ceased.*** ?. English. Far East Reporter, PO Box 1536, New York NY 10017. available on microfilm and microfiche from University Microfilms International (UMI).

UK/0266-5182
FAST LANE. [Fast lane]. (1984)-. Periodical. English. mo. $148.50 US and Canada (surface airlift); $105.00 other (surface mail); $58.00 other (air mail). Perry Motorpress ltd, 22 Redan Place, Compass House, London W2 4SZ, England. **Tel** 011 44 71 2297799. **(Subscription address:** Tower Publishing, Tower House, Sovereign Park Market Harborough, Leicester LE16 9EF England.**)** available on microfilm from University Microfilms International (UMI).
Ind/Abst SPORT Discus.

US
FISHER REPORTER. English. wk. $6.50. Fisher Reporter, 118 South Third Street, Fisher IL 61843. **Tel** (217)897-1525.

US/1051-4597
FOOTPRINTS (MARIETTA, GA.). ***Ceased.*** (FOOTPRINTS.). [Footprints]. Vol. 1, No. 1 (Aug./Sept. 1990)-(19??). Periodical. English. bm. Discovery Press Inc., PO Box 669815, Marietta GA 30066. **Tel** (800)553-9676, (404)926-2365. **DD** 797.
Desc: Provides an entertaining look at unusual people, places and events with both contemporary and historical subjects. Each issue focuses on a theme and includes interviews with explorers and great Americans, stories about kids, mysteries, trivia and more.

IT
FORZA MILAN. (19??)-. Italian. mo. L29700 Italy. Arnoldo Mondadori Editore, UFF Cont Abbonamenti, 20090 Segrate MI Italy. **Tel** 011 39 2 75422015, telex 320457 MONDMI I.

US/1047-3963
FOX VALLEY LIVING. ***Ceased.*** [Fox Val. living]. Vol. 1, No. 1 (Oct. 1989)-(June 1993). Periodical. English. bm. 707 Kautz Road, St Charles IL 60174. **Tel** (312)377-8000. **ED** Francie Smith. **DD** 051. **Circ:** 25,000 (ctrl).
Desc: A comprehensive lifestyle magazine featuring the people and places of Fox Valley. The magazine will include a comprehensive guide to special events, dining, shopping and recreational activities.

IT
FRANCE ITALIE. French. bm. 270.00F France; 280.00F Europe. Camera Comm Ital Per Francia, 134 rue du FBG Saint Honore, 75008 Paris France. **Tel** 011 33 1 42254188, FAX 011 33 1 42891458.

IT
FREE. Agenzia Italiana di Esportazione, Via Manzoni 12, 20089 Rozzano Milan, Italy. **Tel** 011 39 2 57512575.

IT
FRIGIDAIRE. (Nov. 1980?)-. Italian. mo. L50000 Italy; L80000 other. Primo Carnera Srl, V Daniello Bartoli 11, 00152 Rome Italy. **Tel** 011 39 6 5883142. **LC** AP37; .F78. **DD** 055/.1.

US/0738-9264
FUTURIFIC. [Futurific]. (197?)-. Periodical. English. mo. $70.00 (individual), $140.00 (institution) US; $100.00 (individual), $170.00 (institution) other. **(Subscription address:** PO Box 1831, Birmingham, AL 35201-1831; telephone: (800)633-4931, (205)995-1567 (outside US and Canada); FAX: (205)995-1588**)**

IT
GALASSIA. (Jan. 1961)-. Periodical. Italian. mo. Casa Editrice La Tribuna, Via Don Minzoni 51, 29100 Piacenza Italy. **Tel** 011 39 523 759015, 011 39 523 759020.

US
GENERAL PERIODICALS INDEX [COMPUTER FILE]. **See** General Interest-Abstracting, Bibliographies and Statistics.

US/1064-8380
GENERAL PERIODICALS ONDISC (RESEARCH 1 ED.). **See** General Interest-Abstracting, Bibliographies and Statistics.

UK/0960-7609
GENERAL STUDIES REVIEW. ***Ceased.*** [Gen. stud. rev.]. (1991)-(1992). Periodical. English. qt. Philip Allan Publishers Ltd, Market Place, Deddington Oxford, OX15 0SE England. **Tel** 011 44 869 38652, FAX 011 44 869 38803. **DD** 001.

MX
GENTE. No. 1 (1966)-. Periodical. Spanish. mo. $65.00 US, Canada & Mexico; $80.00 Pan America; $95.00 others. Editorial Gente SA, Avenue Las Palmas 890, 11000 Lomas Mexico DF Mexico. **Tel** 011 52 5 5202414. **(Subscription address:** Editorial Gente SA, 2554 Lincoln Boulevard, Suite 1016, Marina Del Rey CA 90291.**) Bk Rev. Ad Acc, Adv Mgr:** Juan Azcarraga.

FR/0220-8245
GEO (ED. FRANCAISE). (GEO.). [Geo]. (1979)-. Periodical. English. Twelve times a year. 648.00F (airmail), 77.50F, 102.50F (surface mail) US & Canada; 298.00F France, 439.00F others. Prisma Presse, 6 rue Daru, 75379 Paris Cedex 08, France. **Tel** 011 33 1 44153000, FAX 011 33 1 47641042. **(Subscription address:** Ca M Interesse, Service Abbonements B 110, 60732 Ste Geneva Cedex 9 France.**) DD** 054.

US/1049-6432
GEORGIA LIVING. ***Title Change.*** [Ga. living]. (1989)-(199?). Periodical. English. bm. North Florida Publishing Company Inc, 102 Northeast 10th Avenue, Suite 1, Gainesville FL 32601. **Tel** (904)372-8865, FAX (904)372-3453. **ED** John Paul Jones Jr. **DD** 975. Index available. **Bk Rev. Ad Acc. Circ:** 15,000 (ctrl). ***Merged into*** *Georgia Trend, 0882-5971.*

GW/0016-8769
GERMAN INTERNATIONAL. ***Suspended.*** Vol. 1, 1957-Suspended. Periodical. English. Heinz Moeller-Verlag, Provinzialstr 89 95, 53 Bonn Lengsdorf Germany. available on microfilm and microfiche from University Microfilms International (UMI).

IT
GIORNALINO. Italian. wk. L102000 Italy; L153000 other. Societa San Paolo Gruppo Periodici, Via Liberazione 4, 12051 Alba Cuneo Italy. **Tel** 011 39 173 296356, FAX 011 39 173 317423.

US/0890-4987
GLOBAL STUDIES PROGRAM NOTES. [Glob. stud. program notes]. **Added/Corp** Santa Rosa Junior College (Calif.) Global Studies Committee. **VFOAT** Global Studies. Vol. 1, Issue No. 1 (Oct. 1986)-. Periodical. English. ir. Free on request. Santa Rosa Junior College Library, 1501 Mendocina Avenue, Santa Rosa CA 95401. **Tel** (707)527-4552. **ED** Joanne Black. **DD** 900. **Circ:** 1,000 (ctrl).

IT
GRAND GOURMET. (19??)-. Italian. Four times a year. L100000.00. Elemond Arte SRL, Via Trentacoste 7, 20134 Milan Italy. **Tel** 011 39 2 215631.

IT
GRAND HOTEL. Casa Editrice Universo, Via Margherita de Vizzi 35/39, 20092 Cinisello Balsamo Italy. **Tel** 011 39 2 66030285.

US/0892-6611
GRAPEVINE (DOWNERS GROVE, ILL.), THE. (THE GRAPEVINE.). **VFOAT** Grape Vine. (198?)-. Periodical. English. Six times a year. $22.00. Heritabe Arts, 1807 Prairie, Downers Grove IL 60515. **Tel** (708)964-1194, FAX (708)964-0841. **ED** Sue Vinyard.

IT/0017-3436
GRAPHICUS. (1920)-. Periodical. Italian. Ten times a year (monthly with Jun./Jul. and Aug./Sep. issues combined). L70,000 Italy; L150,000 other. Progresso Grafico, V O Morgari 36 B, 10125 Turin Italy. **Tel** 011 39 11 6690577, FAX 011 39 11 6509659. **ED** Grapaicus Servizi Srl. **UDC** 760. **Bk Rev. Ad Acc. *Continues*** *Piemonte grafico.*
Ind/Abst Infomat Int. Bus.

●US/1046-008X
GREAT AMERICAN STORIES. (1992)-. Periodical. English. bm. Equipment Engineering & Sales Inc., 799 Roosevelt Road Building 6, Suite 208, Glen Ellyn IL 60137. **Tel** (708)858-6161, FAX (708)858-8787.

US/0270-7497
GREAT ISSUES OF THE DAY. [Great issues day]. Vol. 1 (Dec. 1981)-. Monographic series. English. ir. Price varies per volume. Borgo Press, PO Box 2845, San Bernardino CA 92406. **Tel** (714)884-5813, (714)885-1161. **ED** Dr. Jeffrey M. Elliot.
Desc: Discussions on the vital topics of the day, by leading academics, professionals, writers, and government officials.

US/0533-2052
GREAT WESTERN SERIES, THE. **Added/Corp** The Westerners, Potomac Corral. (1967)-. Monographic series. English. ir. Price varies per volume. Potomac Westerners, Box 6006, Arlington VA 22206.

US
GREELEY STYLE MAGAZINE. English. Eight times a year. $10.95 (one year); $18.00 (two years); $24.00 (three years). Greeley Style Magazine, Box 5195, Greeley CO 80631. **Tel** (303)353-7895.

US/1072-2432
GREENWICH (GREENWICH, CONN.). (GREENWICH.). [Greenwich]. **VFOAT** Greenwich Magazine. (199?)-. Periodical. English. mo. $24.00 (one year), $42.00 (two year), $53.00 (three year). Greenwich Magazine, PO Box 3000, Subscription Department. **Tel** 800 783-4903. **ED** Donna C. Moffly (Editor's telephone: (203)869-0009). **DD** 051. **Ad Acc, Adv Mgr:** M. McDonnel. **Circ:** 7,000. ***Continues*** *Greenwich Magazine, 1051-0745.*
Desc: Regional general interest magazine with features on the people, events and other subjects of interest to the residents of Greenwich, Connecticut and the surrounding towns of Fairfield and Westchester.

US/1051-0745
GREENWICH MAGAZINE. ***Title Change.*** [Greenwich mag.]. **VFOAT** Greenwich. Vol. 43, No. 4 (May 1990)-(199?). Periodical. English. Eleven times a year (monthly except Aug.). Moffly Publications Inc, 39 Lewis Street, Greenwich CT 06830. **Tel** (203)869-0009, FAX (203)869-2549. **ED** Donna C. Moffly. **DD** 051. **Bk Rev**, (Qty: 5). **Ad Acc. Circ:** 7,000. ***Formed by the union of*** *Greenwich Review, 0895-6979* ***and*** *Nutmegger (Greenwich, Conn. : 1989), 1048-3179.* ***Continued by*** *Greenwich, 1072-2432.*

US
GUIDES TO CONTEMPORARY ISSUES. **VFOAT** Regina Guides to Contemporary Issues. Vol. 1-. Monographic series. English. an. Price varies per volume. Regina Books, PO Box 280, Claremont CA 91711. **Tel** (714)624-8466. **ED** Richard Dean Burns. **Bk Rev. Circ:** 1,500.

CK
GUION. No. 1- Feb. 14/20, 1977-. Periodical. Spanish. wk. $99.00 US. Buion Editores, Carrera 16, 38-89 or Apartado 9390, Bogota Colombia. **Tel** 2322660. **ED** Juan Carlos Pastrana. **LC** AP66; .G84. **DD** 056/.1. **Bk Rev. Ad Acc. Circ:** 25,000 (ctrl).
Desc: Contains political, national, international and cultural general interest information.

US/0533-7127
GYPSY LOU SERIES. Vol. 1 (1963)-. English. Loujon Press, PO Box 2083, Albuquerque NM 87108. **DD** 080.

IT
HARPERS BAZAAR COLLEZIONI. (19??)-. Italian. sa. $80.00. Agenzia Italiana di Esportazione, Via Manzoni 12, 20089 Rozzano Milan, Italy. **Tel** 011 39 2 57512575.

US/0749-6540
HASAD AL-SHAHR. No. 1, (September 1984)-. Periodical. Arabic. mo. $200.00. Asharq Cultural and Public Affairs Inc, 2025 Eye Street NW/Suite 818, Washington DC 20006. **LC** AP95.A6; H266. **DD** 059.

US/0362-630X
HIGH TIMES. (19??)-. Periodical. English. mo. $29.95 US; $37.45 other. Trans High Corporation, 211 East 43rd Street, New York NY 10023. **Tel** (212)972-8484. **(Subscription address:** Kable Publishers Aide, 308 East Hitt Street, Subscription Department, Mt. Morris IL 61054-1473.**) LC** HV5800; .H53a. **DD** 301.2/2.

US/1045-2591
HOBO JUNGLE : A QUARTERLY JOURNAL OF NEW WRITING. Periodical. English. qt. Free. Hobo Jungle, Rucum Road, Roxbury CT 06783. **DD** 810.
Desc: Contains poetry, short stories, essays, excerpts from plays, drawings, cartoons, and even musical scores.

US/1045-361X
HOLLYWOOD MAGAZINE. ***Ceased.*** [Hollywood mag.]. (1988)-Ceased (March 1991). Periodical. English. bm. Roosevelt, 7000 Hollywood Boulevard, Cabana 9, Hollywood CA 90028. **Tel** (310)856-9022, FAX (310)856-0508. **ED** Kim Williamson. **DD** 791. **Bk Rev. Ad Acc.** ctrl circ.
Desc: City magazine of the entertainment industry.

US
HOLLYWOOD SUN. ***Ceased.*** Ceased Dec. 12, 1991. Sun-Tattler Company, Box 1968, Hollywood FL 33022. **Tel** (305)929-8100.

US/1046-8110
HUDSON'S SUBSCRIPTION NEWSLETTER DIRECTORY. [Hudson's subscr. newsl. dir.]. **VFOAT** Subscription Newsletter; Hudson's Newsletter Directory. (1989)-. Directory. English. ir. $118.00, $98.00 (with an subscription to The Newsletter on Newsletters and Libraries) US; (add $15.00 postage) other. Newsletter Clearinghouse, PO Box 311, Rhinebeck NY 12572. **Tel** (914)876-2081, FAX (914)876-2561. **(Subscription address:** 1452**) ED** Margaret Leonard. **LC** PN4784.N5; N48. **DD** 050/.25. Index available. cum. index. **Ad Acc. *Continues*** *Hudson's Newsletter Directory.*
Desc: Lists information on more than 4,200 US, Canadian and foreign newsletters, divided into 46 subject classifications. Provides name of publisher, address, phone editors, frequency of publication, subscription rates, FAX numbers, circulation and much more.

AG
HUMOR INTERIOR. No. 1 (Nov. 1984)-. Periodical. Spanish.
Desc: Intends to provide coverage to events in the provinces outside Buenos Aires.

HU/0238-9932
HUNGARIAN OBSERVER, THE. Vol. 1, No. 1 (1988)-. Periodical. English. Twelve times a year. $84.00. **(Subscription address:** Kultura, PO Box 149, H 1389 Budapest 62 Hungary, (phone: 011 36 1 359370)**) LC** WMLC 93/387; DB901; .H858.
Ind/Abst PROMT.

US/0899-5451
ICUC. [ICUC]. **VFOAT** I See You See. Vol. 1 No. 1 (Summer 1988)-. Periodical. English. Four times a year. $20.00. Looking Glass Publications, PO Box 3604, Quincy IL 62305. **ED** Linda Hughes. **DD** 051.
Desc: Another welcome addition to the growing number of large print magazines and newspapers, offers sixty pages of widely diverse material with a particular emphasis on literature. An abridged version of Moby Dick is in progress under the "classic series." There are excerpts from Mark Twain. One finds recipes, health hints, games and puzzles, and even jokes. Recommended for libraries with such a need.

CN/0823-7956
ILLUSTRATED CATALOG OF FREE CATALOGS AND SOURCES FOR EVERYTHING IMAGINABLE. **VFOAT** Catalog of Free Catalogs and Sources for Everything Imaginable; Master Directory of Free Catalogs. 1983/84-. Catalog. English. an. $3.99 per volume. Catalog of Free Catalogs, PO Box 317 Station A, Ottawa Ontario K1N 8V3 Canada. **DD** 011/.03.

PR/0890-6548
IMAGEN (SAN JUAN, P.R.). (IMAGEN.). [Imagen]. Vol. 1, No. 1 (1986)-. Periodical. Spanish. Twelve times a year. $24.00 one year; $39.90 two years. Casiano Communications, PO Box 12130, Loiza St. Station, San Juan Puerto Rico 00914. **Tel** (809)728-3000. **ED** Mrs. Tere Paniagua. **LC** AP63; .I35. **DD** 056/.1. **Bk Rev. Ad Acc, Adv Mgr:** Arnaldo Jimenez. **Circ:** 85,000.
Desc: You will find articles about the following topics fashion, trips, family health and business. This magazine is complete for the families of the 90's.

US
INDEPENDENT REPUBLICAN, 1812. wk. $20.00 US; $22.00 Canada and Mexico. Orange Offset Corporation, 132 West Main Street, Postal Drawer A, Goshen NY 10924. **Tel** (914)294-6111. **ED** E. Wright. **Bk Rev**, (Qty: 3 or 4). **Ad Acc, Adv Mgr:** E. Wright, **Tel** (914)294-6111 ext.3. **Circ:** 3,800.
Desc: Local news publication.

US/0362-8183
INDEX TO COMMONWEALTH LITTLE MAGAZINES. ***Ceased.*** (1964/1965)-(1990/1992). Periodical. English. ir. Whitston Publishing Company Inc, PO Box 958, Troy NY 12181. **Tel** (518)283-4363. **ED** Sally Gray. **LC** AI3; .I48. **DD** 051. **Circ:** 300.
Desc: Documents little magazine activity throughout the commonwealth; approximately 40 titles.

US/0147-5630
INDEX TO FREE PERIODICALS. ***Title Change.*** **See** General Interest-Abstracting, Bibliographies and Statistics.

US/0896-095X
INDIA CURRENTS. (April 1987)-. Periodical. English. mo. $16.00 other. Arvind Kumar, PO Box 21285, San Jose CA 95151. **Tel** (408)274-6966, FAX (408)274-6966. **Bk Rev. Ad Acc. Circ:** 15,000.
Desc: A magazine pertaining to Indian arts, entertainments, and dining in the San Francisco bay area.

II
INDIA TODAY (INTERNATIONAL ED). ***Title Change.*** (INDIA TODAY.). (1975)-(1992). Periodical. English. sm. Living Media India Ltd., PO Box 706, Faridabad 121007 India. **(Subscription address:** Living Media India Ltd., 404 Park Avenue South, New York, NY 10016; Telephone: (212)986-6666**) ED** Aroon Purie. **Ad Acc. Circ:** 370,000 (ctrl). ***Continued by*** *India Today (North American Special ed.).*
Desc: The leading newsmagazine. Gives an authentic, readable insight into contemporary India from politics to the sciences, economy to the arts, industry to sports.

CN/0831-2052
INFODEX, INDEX DE LA PRESSE. ***Suspended.*** [Infodex index La Presse]. **Added/Corp** Centrale des Bibliotheques (Montreal, Quebec). **VFOAT** Index de la Presse. (Jan. 1986)-Suspended (19??). Periodical. French. mo. Services Documentaires

Multimedia Inc, 75 rue de Port-Royal, Suite 300, Montreal Quebec H3L 3T1 Canada. **Tel** (514)382-0895, FAX (514)384-9139. **DD** 071/.14281.

UK/0263-5372
INFORME LATNOAMERICANO. (198?)-. Periodical. Spanish. wk. $389.00 (business), $258.00 (academic) US; £29.00 (business), £198.00 (academic) other. Lettres UK Ltd, 61 Old Street, London EC1V 9HX England. **Tel** 011 44 71 251-0012, FAX 011 44 71 253-8193. **ED** Raul Fain Binda. **Bk Rev. Circ:** 3,000 (ctrl).
Desc: Comprehensive and timely analysis of news as it breaks in Latin America. This newsletter provides authoritative information and evaluation on the economic and political regional scene together with the basic group information to understand it. Spanish language.

UK
INTERNATIONAL TECHNOLOGY & INNOVATION. English. Twelve times a year. £95.00 UK; £105.00 others. International Technology & Innovation, Tech House, Riscorough Road, Aylesbury Buck HP225UT England. **Tel** 011 44 296 614040, FAX 011 44 296 612174.

US/1047-0476
JOE FRANKLIN'S NOSTALGIA. [Joe Franklin's nostalg.]. **VFOAT** Nostalgia. Vol. 1, No. 1 (March 1990)-. Periodical. English. Six times a year. $9.75 US; $11.80 Canada. Nostalgia Publications, PO Box 2074, Knoxville IA 50138. **Tel** (800)227-7585. **LC** E169.1; .J624. **DD** 973.9/05.
Desc: Targeted to men and women between the ages of 40 and 55 who want to "recall the days gone by when life seemed simpler and consumer products meant quality."

US/1043-4135
JUDGE DREDD. [Judge Dredd]. Vol. 1, No. 1 (Nov. 1983)-. Periodical. English. Twenty-six times a year. £45.00. World Wide Subscription Services, Unit 4, Gibbs Reed Farm, East Sussex TN5 7HE England. **Tel** (0580)200657, FAX (0580)200616. **DD** 741.

MX
JUEVES DE EXCELSIOR. ***Ceased.*** No. 1 (June 22, 1922)-(Oct. 1994). Periodical. Spanish. wk. Excelsior Cia Editorial Scl, Paseo Reforma 10, Subscripciones, Mexico 1 df Mexico. **Tel** 11 52 5 7054444, 5669360. **LC** AP63; .J84. **DD** 056.

CN/0849-5718
JUST BETWEEN FRIENDS. [Just between friends]. **VFOAT** Just Friends. (June 1989)-. Periodical. English. mo. $24.00. Just Between Friends, 134274 Canada Ltd, PO Box 3394 Station D, Edmonton Alberta T5J 3LA Canada. **ED** Y R Urie. **DD** 070.4/44. Index available. **Ad Acc. Circ:** 20,000 (ctrl).

UK/0143-9553
KEYWORD INDEX TO SERIAL TITLES.
Main/Corp British Library. Lending Division. **VFOAT** KIST. (19??)-. Periodical. English. an. £114.00 UK; £119.00 other. British Library / Publications Sale Unit, Boston Spa, Wetherby, West Yorkshire LS23 7BQ England. **Tel** 011 44 937 546546 546543, FAX 011 44 937 546333, telex 557381. **(Subscription address:** Turpin Distribution Services Limited, Blackhorse Road, Letchworth, Hertfordshire SG6 1HN, United Kingdom.)

IT
KING. (19??)-. Italian. mo. L48000.00 Italy; L90000.00 other. Nuova Eri, Edizioni Rai, Via Arsenale 41, 10121 Turin Italy. **Tel** 011 39 11 8102238.

JA
KOREAN DAILY NEWS / KOREAN CENTRAL NEWS AGENCY. ***Title Change.***
Added/Corp Choson Chungang Tongsinsa. (19??)-No. 8312 (June 30, 1992). Periodical. English. da. Korean News, 42-22 27th Street, Long Island City NY 11101. **LC** DS901; .K848. ***Continued by*** *Korean News.*

CN/0832-1922
LANG VAN. [Lang van]. No. 1, (1984)-. Periodical. Vietnamese. mo. $55.00 Canada; $70.00 US; $85.00 others. Lang Van, PO Box 218, Station U, Toronto ONT M8Z 5P1 Canada. **Tel** (905)607-8010, FAX (905)607-8011. **ED** Nguyen Huu Nghia. **LC** PAR. **DD** 059/.95922. Index available. **Bk Rev. Ad Acc. Circ:** 10,000 (ctrl). ***Continues*** *Sai-Gon Thoi-Bao.*

UK/0143-5280
LATIN AMERICAN WEEKLY REPORT.
Added/Corp Latin American Newsletters Ltd. **VFOAT** Weekly Report. WR-86-24 (June 26, 1986)-. Periodical. English. wk (50 per year). $835.00 (business), $499.00 (academic) US; £642.00 (business), £384.00 (academic) other. Lettres UK Ltd, 61 Old Street, London EC1V 9HX England. **Tel** 011 44 71 251-0012, FAX 011 44 71 253-8193. **ED** Eduardo D Crawley. **LC** F1401; .L3256 Suppl. **DD** 980/.005. available on an online database (files 771,772/Full-Text) from DIALOG. ***Continues*** *Weekly Report (Latin America Newsletters Ltd.).*
Desc: The only comprehensive, timely analysis of news as it breaks in Latin America. Provides authoritative information and expert evaluation on the economic and political scene of the continent and the background to understand it.

US/0742-9665
LEBANON NEWS (WASHINGTON, D.C. 1978). (LEBANON NEWS.). [Lebanon news].
Added/Corp Lebanese Information & Research Center (Washington, D.C.). (1978)-. Periodical. English. mo. $30.00. Lebanese Information and Research Center, 1730 M Street Northwest, Suite 807, Washington DC 20036. **Tel** (202)785-6666, FAX (202)785-6628, telex 64427. **ED** Robert Y. Farah and Joseph G. Bou-Saada. **DD** 956. **Bk Rev. Circ:** 7,000.
Desc: Covers current events in Lebanon through a progress report listing daily events. Includes an editorial page which provides for contributing articles and opinions.

US/1051-4724
LEE LIVING. [Lee living]. (Sept./Oct. 1990)-. Periodical. English. Nine times a year. $18.00 US; $30.00 other. City Events Inc, 6719 Winkler Road, Suite 210, Fort Meyers FL 33919. **Tel** (813)278-3464. **DD** 051. ***Continues*** *City Events Magazine.*

US/0024-3019
LIFE (CHICAGO). (LIFE.). [Life]. **VFOAT** Life Magazine. Vol. 1, No. 1, (Oct. 1978)-. Periodical. English. mo. $30.00. Time Inc. / New York, Time & Life Building, Rockefeller Center, New York NY 10020. **(Subscription address:** Time Customer Service, PO Box 60050, Tampa FL 33609.) **ED** Pat Ryan. **LC** AP2; .L54715. **DD** 051. **Ad Acc.** available on microfilm and microfiche from University Microfilms International (UMI). Documents available from UMI Article Clearinghouse. ***Continues*** *Life (Chicago, Ill.), 0024-3019.*
Desc: The original larger-than-life picture monthly that's become an American tradition. Emotions, enigmas, events large and small, are captured in Life's award-winning photographic style.
Ind/Abst Abr. Read. Guide Period. Lit.; Acad. Abstr. Full Text Elite (Jan. 1984-) [Full Txt.]; Acad. Abstr. (Jan. 1984-); Acad. Ind. [Computer File] (1984-); Acad. Search (Jan. 1984-); Can. Period. Index (19??-); Expand. Acad. Index (1984-1988); Gen. Period. Index (1985-); Health Ref. Cent. (1987-) [Select. Cov.]; INFO-SOUTH Abstr.; Infobank (1978-); Mag. Artic. Summar. Elite (Jan. 1984-) [Full Txt.]; Mag. Artic. Summar. Select (Jan. 1984-); Mag. Artic. Summar. CD-ROM (Jan. 1984-); Mag. ASAP Plus [Full Txt.]; Mag. ASAP Sel. [Full Txt.]; Mag. Express (1986-) [Full Txt.]; Mag. Index Plus (1989-); Mag. Index Sel. Microfiche (1990-1991) [Full Txt.]; Mag. Index. Sel. (1986-); Mag. Search; Mid. Search (Jan. 1984-) [Full Txt.]; Newsp. Period. Abstr. (1986-); NEXIS (1982-); Prim. Search (Jan. 1984-) [Full Txt.]; Read. Guide Abstr. Select Ed.; Read. Guide Period. Lit.; Resource/One Ondisc; Mag. Index (Oct. 1978-); TOM Gen. Index (1985-) [Full Txt.]; Vocat. Search (Jan. 1984-) [Full Txt.].

IT
LITO. ***Ceased.*** (19??)-(19??). Newsletter. Italian. Arnoldo Mondadori Editore, UFF Cont Abbonamenti, 20090 Segrate MI Italy. **Tel** 011 39 2 75422015, telex 320457 MONDMI I.

UK/0268-4969
LOOKS LONDON. [Looks Lond.]. (1985)-. Periodical. English. Twelve times a year. £20.00 UK; £32.00 other Europe; £25.00 other. EMAP National Publications Ltd, Farndon Road, Market Harborough, Leicestershire, LE16 9NR England. **Tel** 011 44 733 555161. **ED** Jenny Tucker. **DD** 646.7205. **Ad Acc.**

CN/0382-5280
LUMERA, LA. [Lumera]. Fall 1969-. Periodical. Italian. qt. Club Vallelonga, 292 Rushton Road, Toronto Ontario M6C 2X7 Canada. **DD** 055/.1.

IT
LYDIA. Periodical. Italian. Twice a year. L54.600 (surface mail) US; (add L4.000 airmail) Europe; (add L12.000 airmail) Asia, Africa and America; (add L19.000 airmail) Oceania. A Pieroni SRL, Viale Vittorio Veneto 28, 20124 Milan Italy. **Tel** 39 2 29000282, 29002876.

CN/0024-9262
MACLEAN'S. [Maclean's]. **VFOAT** Maclean's Magazine. (1911)-. Periodical. English. wk. $39.95 Canada; $55.00 US; $98.00 other. MacLean Hunter Publ. Limited / Toronto, 777 Bay Street, 8th Floor Agency Control, Toronto Ontario M5W 1A7 Canada. **Tel** (416)596-5000, (800)268-6811, FAX (416)596-5526. **ED** Address editor correspondence to: Les Editions du Tricycle Inc., 4545 Avenue Pierre-de-Coubertin, PO Box 1000 Station M, Montreal Quebec H1V 3R2 Canada. **LC** AP5; .M2. **[CCC]. Bk Rev. Ad Acc. Circ:** 645,000. available on microfilm and microfiche from University Microfilms International (UMI); available on an online database (files 647,648/Full-Text) from DIALOG. Documents available from UMI Article Clearinghouse. ***Continues*** *Busy Man's Magazine.*
Desc: Newsmagazine in Canada which examines the impact of Canadian and world news events, trends and issues from a Canadian perspective. Network of correspondents and bureaus across Canada and around the world contribute to weekly sections on politics, business, entertainment, sports, leisure, science, health and technology.
Ind/Abst Acad. Abstr. Full Text Elite (Jan. 1984-) [Full Txt.]; Acad. Abstr. (Jan. 1984-); Acad. Ind. [Computer File] (1984-); Acad. Search (Jan. 1984-); AGRICOLA; Book Rev. Index; Can. Index; Can. Period. Index; Expand. Acad. Index (1984-); Gen. Period. Index (1985-); Guide Soc. Sci. Relig.; Health Ref. Cent. (1987-) [Full Txt.] [Select. Cov.]; INFO-SOUTH Abstr.; Mag. Artic. Summar. Elite (Jan. 1984-) [Full Txt.]; Mag. Artic. Summar. Select (Jan. 1984-) [Full Txt.]; Mag. Artic. Summar. CD-ROM (Jan. 1984-); Mag. ASAP Plus [Full Txt.]; Mag. ASAP Sel. [Full Txt.]; Mag. Express (1986-) [Full Txt.]; Mag. Index Plus (1989-); Mag. Index. Sel. (1986-); Mag. Search; Mid. Search (Jan. 1988-) [Full Txt.]; Newsp. Period. Abstr. (1986-); NEXIS (1985-); PAIS Int. Print (1991-); Peace Res. Abstr. J. (1966-1968); Read. Guide Abstr. Select Ed.; Read. Guide Period. Lit.; Resource/One Ondisc; SPORT Discus; Mag. Index (1977-); TOM Gen. Index (1989-) [Full Txt.]; Vocat. Search (Jan. 1984-) [Full Txt.].

US/1058-6601
MACPREPRESS. [MacPrePress]. **VFOAT** Mac Prepress. (1989)-. Periodical. English. Forty-Five times a year. $295.00 US; $400.00 Canada; $600.00 other. Prepress Information Service, 12 Burr Road, Westport CT 06880. **Tel** (203)227-2357, FAX (203)454-4962. **ED** Kathleen Turkel. **DD** 006. cum. index. **Circ:** 400.
Desc: Prepress information and news.

US/1041-1151
MAGAZINE ARTICLE SUMMARIES (CD-ROM ED.). **See** General Interest-Abstracting, Bibliographies and Statistics.

US/1060-6769
MAGAZINE ARTICLE SUMMARIES FULL TEXT ELITE. **See** General Interest-Abstracting, Bibliographies and Statistics.

US/1058-0255
MAGAZINE ARTICLE SUMMARIES FULL TEXT SELECT. **See** General Interest-Abstracting, Bibliographies and Statistics.

US/0895-3376
MAGAZINE ARTICLE SUMMARIES (PRINT ED.). ***Ceased.*** **See** General Interest-Abstracting, Bibliographies and Statistics.

US
MAGAZINE ASAP PLUS [COMPUTER FILE]. **See** General Interest-Abstracting, Bibliographies and Statistics.

US
MAGAZINE ASAP SELECT [COMPUTER FILE]. **See** General Interest-Abstracting, Bibliographies and Statistics.

US
MAGAZINE COLLECTION. (19??)-. English. sm. Information Access Company, 362 Lakeside Drive, Foster City CA 94404. **Tel** (800)227-8431.
Desc: Self-service reference system designed to provide actual document images from hundreds of the most popular magazines.

US
MAGAZINE EXPRESS [COMPUTER FILE]. **See** General Interest-Abstracting, Bibliographies and Statistics.

US
MAGAZINE INDEX, THE. **See** General Interest-Abstracting, Bibliographies and Statistics.

US
MAGAZINE INDEX PLUS [COMPUTER FILE]. **See** General Interest-Abstracting, Bibliographies and Statistics.

US
MAGAZINE INDEX SELECT MICROFICHE. **See** General Interest-Abstracting, Bibliographies and Statistics.

US
MAGAZINE INDEX SELECT [COMPUTER FILE]. **See** General Interest-Abstracting, Bibliographies and Statistics.

US/1071-2739
MAGAZINE SEARCH. **See** General Interest-Abstracting, Bibliographies and Statistics.

US/0094-1484
MAGYAR NAPTAR (NEW YORK). (MAGYAR EVRONYV.). Hungarian. wk. $25.00 North America; $30.00 other. Amerikai Magyar Szo, 130 East 16th Street, New York NY 10003. **Tel** (212)254-0397, FAX (212)254-0397. **LC** AY78.H8; M28. **Bk Rev. Ad Acc. Circ:** 2,500 (ctrl).
Desc: General news of Hungarian interest.

UK/0261-0876
MAJALLA (LONDON), AL. (AL-MAJALLAH.). [Al Majalla]. **VFOAT** Al Majalla; Majalla. No. 1, (1980)-. Periodical. Arabic. wk. $168.00. Attache International, 3050 Broadway, Suite 300, Boulder CO 80304. **Tel** (303)442-8900, FAX (303)442-7979. **ED** Othman Al-Omeir. **LC** AP95.A6; M248. **Ad Acc, Adv Mgr:** Lisa

Cheng. **Circ:** 101,061.
Desc: Arabic-language news magazine covering international political and economic news, science, sports and culture.

US/0898-5642
MANILA TIMES, USA, THE. (1988)-. Periodical. English. wk. $25.00. Nem B Santos Jr, 7188 Sunset Boulevard/Suite 207, Hollywood CA 90046.

IT
MARFY. ***Ceased.*** (19??)-No. 56 (1993). Italian. A Pieroni SRL, Viale Vittorio Veneto 28, 20124 Milan Italy. **Tel** 39 2 29000282, 29002876.

US
MASTER CARD. Spanish. qt. North South Net Inc, 100 Almeria Avenue, Suite 202, Coral Gables FL 33134. **Tel** (305)441-9744, FAX (305)441-9739, telex 803029 VOYAGERMIA. **ED** Gloria Shanahan. **Ad Acc. Circ:** 100,000 (ctrl).
Desc: A general interest non-controversial magazine distributed to Mastercard cardholders in Latin America, with articles on tourist destinations, art, environment, gastronomy, technology and business.

GW
MAYFLOWER DIGEST. **Main/Corp** International Democratic Trust. International Newsletter Association. 1984-. English. mo. Linden Plaza/Suite 311, Great Neck, New York NY 11021. ***Continues*** *Mayflower Pilgrim.*

US
MCLEAN COUNTY JOURNAL AND TURTLE LAKE WAVE, THE. Vol. 11, No. 48 (Oct. 22, 1936)-. English. wk. $15.00 North Dakota; $22.00 other. McLean County Journal and Turtle Lake Wave, PO Box 220, Turtle Lake ND 58575. **Tel** (701)448-2649. **ED** Gerald W Anderon. **Circ:** 1,000 (ctrl). available on microfilm from State Historical Society of North Dakota. ***Formed by the union of*** *Turtle Lake Wave* ***and*** *McLean County Journal.*

GW/0179-5724
MEDIENSPIEGEL. [Medienspiegel]. **VFOAT** Medienspiegel des Instituts der Deutschen Wirtschaft (1986). (1986)-. Periodical. German. wk. DM573.12. Deutscher Instituts Verlag, Postfach 510670, W-5000 Cologne 51 Germany. **Tel** 011 49 221 370801. **UDC** 654.197 :33. ***Continues*** *Medienspiegel des Instituts der Deutschen Wirtschaft, 0171-3930.*

US
MEMPHIS FLYER, THE. (19??)-. English. wk. $52.00. MM Corporation, 460 Tennessee Street, Box 256, Memphis TN 38101. **Tel** (901)521-9000, FAX (901)521-0129. **ED** Dennis Freeland. Index available. cum. index. **Ad Acc. Circ:** 42,000 (ctrl).
Desc: Covers breaking news, politics (local and national), entertainment listings and entertainment news.

US/0891-5318
MERIDIAN SOFTWARE ANALYSIS BULLETIN. [Meridian softw. anal. bull.]. **Added/Corp** Meridian Software Analysis. **VFOAT** Software Analysis Bulletin. (1989)-. Bulletin. English. mo. FAX Communications Inc, 665 Third Street/Suite 340, San Francisco CA 94107. **DD** 005.

US/0899-4927
MERTON SEASONAL OF BELLARMINE COLLEGE, THE. [Merton seas. Bellarmine Coll.]. **VAT** Merton Seasonal. Periodical. English. qt. $8.00. Thomas Merton Center, Newburg Road, Bellarmine College, Louisville KY 40205. **Tel** (502)452-8187. **ED** Robert E Daggy. **DD** 271. Index available. cum. index. **Bk Rev. Circ:** 1,800 (ctrl).
Desc: Publishes short articles dealing with Thomas Merton and/or his concerns, poems, reviews of books by and about Merton, and an updated bibliography of Merton and Merton-related materials.

CN/0380-1373
METU KALENDORIUS - PRISIKELIMO PARAPIJA, EKONOMINE SEKCIJA. **VFOAT** Lithuanian Calendar - Prisikelimo Parapija, Ekonomine Sekcija; Lithuanian Calendar; Kalendorius. 1975-. Lithuanian (English). an. $6.00. Parish of the Resurrection, 1011 College Street, Toronto Ontario M6H 1A8 Canada. **Tel** (416)233-4486. **ED** Stan Prakapas. **DD** 059/.9192. Index available. cum. index. **Bk Rev. Ad Acc. Circ:** 3,000.
Desc: Poetry, jokes, cooking, travel, educational items, and advertising.

UK/0267-9973
MEXICO (LONDON, ENGLAND). (MEXICO.). **Added/Corp** Latin American Monitor Ltd. (1985)-. English. an (June). $380.00. Latin American Monitor Ltd., 56 60 St. John Street, London EC1M 4DT England. **Tel** 011 44 71 6083646.

IT
MILANO MILANO. Italian. mo. L45000 Italy; L75000 other. Edizioni Arcangelo Srl, Piazzetta Bossi 1, 20121 Milan Italy. **Tel** 2/72020067, FAX 2/72023425.

IT/1120-1967
MODA IN. [Moda in]. (1975)-. Periodical. Multiple languages. qt. $55.00. Zanfi Editori SRL, Via Emilia Ovest 954, CP 433, 41100 Modena Italy. **Tel** 011 39 59 891700, FAX 011 39 59 225719, telex 52 22 72. **UDC** 687.

US/0745-7146
MONEYTALK. **VFOAT** Money Talk; Moneytalk Refunding Bulletin. (19??)-. Periodical. English. mo. $25.00 (1 year), $45.00 (2 year). Moneytalk Refunding Magazine, PO Box 1661, Kingston PA 18704. **Tel** (717)287-6498.

IT
MONTAGNA OGGI. Stigra Sas, Cso San Maurizio 14, 10124 Turin Italy.

NE
MOSCOW MAGAZINE. **Added/Corp** Soiuz Zhurnalistov SSSR. Moskovskaia Organizatsiia. **VFOAT** Moscow. (April 1990)-. Periodical. English. bm. $56.00 US and Canada; $45.00 Europe; $30.00 Commonwealth of Independent States; $65.00 other. Moscow Illustrated Press, Bogdana Khmelnitskogo 10 1 ST2, 10100 Moscow Russia. **Tel** 011 7 95 9280995. **LC** DK588; .M67. **DD** 947/.312/005.

US
MOUNTAIN CITIZEN. (1991)-. Newspaper. English. Fifty-two times a year. $15.00. New Wave Communications Inc., PO Box 1029, Inez KY 41224. **Tel** (606)298-7570, FAX (606)298-3711. **ED** Cisa Stayton. cum. index. **Bk Rev. Ad Acc. Circ:** 5,000 (ctrl). available on microfilm from University of Kentucky. ***Continues*** *Martin Countian and the Mercury, 1042-8135.*

IT
MOUSE. Pisoft, Via Raffaello 5, 56020 Casteldelbosco Pi Italy.

UK
MY GUY. (19??)-. English. wk. £66.00. World Wide Subscription Services, Unit 4, Gibbs Reed Farm, East Sussex TN5 7HE England. **Tel** (0580)200657, FAX (0580)200616. ***Absorbed*** *Oh Boy.*

US/1052-4215
NASHVILLE BUSINESS AND LIFESTYLES. [Nashv. bus. lifestyles]. **VFOAT** Nashville Business & Lifestyles. Vol. 13, No. 9 (Sept. 1990)-. Periodical. English. mo. Southeast Magazines Inc, PO Box 24649, 545 Mainstream Road, Suite 101, Nashville TN 37228. **Tel** (615)242-6992, FAX (615)242-2248. **DD** 051. available on an online database (files 635,648/Full-Text) from DIALOG. Documents available from UMI Article Clearinghouse. ***Absorbed*** *Advantage, 0739-5515.*
Ind/Abst Bus. Dateline (Jan. 1985-) [Full Txt.]; Trade Ind. ASAP [Full Txt.]; Trade Ind. Index [Full Txt.].

US
NATURAL HEALTH: THE GUIDE TO WELL-BEING. English.

IT
NEL MESE. (19??)-. Italian. Eleven times a year. L40000. Gedim, Via Suppa 12, 70122 Bari Italy. **Tel** 011 39 80 5232468.

US
NEW AGE, THE. **VFOAT** New Age Magazine. Periodical. English. mo. $4.00. New Age Magazine, 1733 16th Street NW, Washington DC 20009. **Tel** (202)232-3579. **ED** C Fred Kleinknecht and Chris A Powler. Index available. **Bk Rev. Circ:** 650,000 (ctrl).
Desc: Articles relating to freemasonry, patriotism, public education, masonic charities and human interests.

BB
NEW BAJAN, THE. ***Ceased.*** (Oct. 1987)-(1992). Periodical. English. mo. Carib Publicity Company Ltd, PO Box 718C, Bridgetown Barbados West Indies. **LC** F2041; .B125. **DD** 972.98/1/005. ***Continues*** *Bajan.*

US/0147-2720
NEW QUARTERLY (NEW YORK), THE. (THE NEW QUARTERLY.). V. 1- July 1976-. Periodical. English. qt. $10.00 US; $15.00 other. The Weekly Review / Minnesota, PO Box 113, Emmons MN 56029.

US/0277-0989
NEW YORK TIMES CURRENT EVENTS INDEX, THE. **VFOAT** Current Events Index. Vol. 1 (Jan.-Dec. 1979)-. English. an. Microfilming Corporation of America, 21 Harristown Road, Glen Rock NJ 07452. **LC** AI21.N44; N46 SUPPL. **DD** 071.47/1.

US/0028-792X
NEW YORKER (NEW YORK, N.Y. : 1925). (THE NEW YORKER.). [New Yorker]. Vol. 1 (Feb. 21, 1925)-. Periodical. English. wk. $32.00. Conde Nast Publications / New York, 350 Madison Avenue, New York NY 10017. **Tel** (212)880-8800, (800)777-0700. **(Subscription address:** Neodata / Colorado, PO Box 2606, Boulder Boulder CO 80322.**)** **LC** AP2; .N6763. **DD** 051. **Bk Rev. Ad Acc. Circ:** 500,000. available on microfilm and microfiche from University Microfilms International (UMI). Documents available from UMI Article Clearinghouse, Magazine Collection.
Desc: Discusses current ideas, people, events, literature, (with cartoons), poetry, short fiction, sports, and art critiques.
Ind/Abst Abr. Read. Guide Period. Lit.; Abstr. Engl. Stud.; Acad. Abstr. Full Text Elite (Jan. 1984-); Acad. Abstr. (Jan. 1984-); Acad. Ind. [Computer File] (1984-); Acad. Search (Jan. 1984-); Am. Bibliogr. Slavic East Europ. Stud.; Annu. Bibliogr. Engl. Lang. Lit.; Biogr. Index; Book Rev. Digest; Book Rev. Index; Child. Lit. Abstr. (19??-); Expand. Acad. Index (1984-); Film Lit. Index; Garden Lit. (1992-); Gen. Period. Index (1985-); GeoRef; Index Am. Period. Verse; Index Period. Artic. Relat. Law; INFO-SOUTH Abstr.; Infobank (Jan. 1969-); Mag. Artic. Summar. Elite (Jan. 1984-); Mag. Artic. Summar. Select (Jan. 1984-); Mag. Artic. Summar. CD-ROM (Jan. 1984-); Mag. Index Plus (1989-); Mag. Index Sel. Microfiche (1986-) [Full Txt.]; Mag. Index. Sel. (1986-); Mag. Search; Med. Rev. Dig.; Music Index (-19??); Newsp. Period. Abstr. (1986-); Peace Res. Abstr. J. (1961-1976, 1981, 1986-1987); Read. Guide Abstr. Select Ed.; Read. Guide Period. Lit.; Resource/One Ondisc (1986-); Romant. Move.; Mag. Index (1977-); TOM Gen. Index (1985-) [Full Txt.].

CN/0824-3581
NEWFOUNDLAND HERALD, THE. [Nfld. her.]. **VAT** Herald (St. John's). (1959)-. Periodical. English. wk. 46.68 Newfoundland and Labrador; $48.60 other. Sunday Herald Ltd, PO Box 2015, St John's Newfoundland A1C 5R7 NF Canada. **Tel** (709)726-7060, FAX (709)726-8227. **ED** Bob Hallet. **DD** 051. **Bk Rev**, (Qty: 52). **Ad Acc, Adv Mgr:** G. Greene. **Circ:** 45,000 (ctrl). ***Continues*** *Sunday Herald.*
Desc: Informative and entertainment news focus with complete TV listings. Local and international content.

US
NEWS AND NOTES FROM ALL OVER, NEWSLETTER OF THE SOCIETY FOR THE ERADICATION OF TELEVISION. (1982)-. Newsletter. English. qt. $5.00. Society for the Eradication of Television, PO Box 10491, Oakland CA 94610-0491. **Tel** (510)763-8712. **ED** Steve Wagner. **Bk Rev. Ad Acc. Circ:** 1,200.
Desc: New and updates about the role of television in society.

IT
NEWS FROM ITALY. **VFOAT** Notizie Dall'Italia. Periodical. English. qt.

US/0747-136X
NEWS WEEKLY, THE. Vol. 1, No. 1 (June 7, 1983)-. Newspaper. English. TNW Communications Inc, 619 East Grandview Avenue, Zelienople PA 16063.

US
NEWSDAY INDEX TO THE SUFFOLK EDITION. **VFOAT** Newsday Index. 1977-. English. Suffolk Cooperative Library System, 627 North Sunrise Road, Bellport NY 11713. **LC** AI21.N55; N48. **DD** 071/.47/21.

UK/0163-7053
NEWSWEEK (INTERNATIONAL, ATLANTIC EDITION). (NEWSWEEK.). [Newsweek]. **VFOAT** Newsweek International. (19??)-. Periodical. English. wk. $69.00. Newsweek, 251 West 57th Street, New York NY 10019. **Tel** (201)445-4000. **(Subscription address:** Newsweek House / UK, Wellington Street, Slough SL1 1UG England.**)** **LC** AP2; .N67724. **DD** 051. available on microfilm and microfiche from University Microfilms International (UMI).
Desc: Reports on the economy, science, energy, education, newsmakers, the arts, books, entertainment, medicine, travel and lifestyles.
Ind/Abst F&S Index Plus Text, Int. [Select. Cov.].

US/0163-7061
NEWSWEEK (INTERNATIONAL, PACIFIC EDITION). (NEWSWEEK.). (19??)-. Periodical. English. wk. $151.00. Newsweek, 251 West 57th Street, New York NY 10019. **Tel** (201)445-4000. **(Subscription address:** Newsweek Building, PO Box 420, Livingston NJ 07039.**)**

US/0028-9604
NEWSWEEK (U.S. ED.). (NEWSWEEK.). [Newsweek]. Vol. 1, (Feb. 17, 1933)-. Periodical. English. wk. $41.00. Newsweek, 251 West 57th Street, New York NY 10019. **Tel** (201)445-4000. **(Subscription address:** Newsweek Building, PO Box 420, Livingston NJ 07039.**)** **ED** Richard M. Smith. **LC** AP2; .N6772. **DD** 051. **Bk Rev. Ad Acc.** ctrl circ. available on microfilm and microfiche from University Microfilms International (UMI). Documents available from UMI Article Clearinghouse, Documents on Demand, Magazine Collection. ***Absorbed*** *Today (1933).*
Desc: Signed coverage of news developments in the nation and the world. Reports on the economy, science, energy, education, newsmakers, the arts, books, entertainment, medicine, travel and lifestyles.
Ind/Abst ABI/INFORM Glob. Ed.; ABI Inform Ondisc (1975-1977); Abr. Read. Guide Period. Lit.; Acad. Abstr. Full Text Elite (Jan. 1984-) [Full Txt.]; Acad. Abstr. (Jan. 1984-); Acad. Ind. [Computer File] (1984-); Acad. Search (Jan. 1984-); Account. Tax Datab. (Jan. 1986-); Aviat. Tradescan [Select. Cov.]; Biogr. Index; Biol. Dig.; Book

Rev. Digest; Book Rev. Index; Can. Index (?-?); Can. Period. Index (19??-); Chicano Index; Child. Lit. Abstr. (19??-); Consum. Health Nutr. Index; Cumul. Index Nurs. Allied Health Lit.; Curr. Lit. Fam. Plan.; Curr. Thoughts Trends; Environ. Abstr.; Expand. Acad. Index (1984-); Film Lit. Index; Foods Adlibra; Gen. Period. Index (1985-); Health Plan. Adminis.; Health Ref. Cent. (1987-) [Select. Cov.]; Hospit. Health Admin. Index; Index Period. Artic. Relat. Law; INFO-SOUTH Abstr.; Infobank (Jan. 1969-); Infomat Int. Bus.; Mag. Artic. Summar. Elite (Jan. 1984-) [Full Txt.]; Mag. Artic. Summar. Select (Jan. 1984-) [Full Txt.]; Mag. Artic. Summar. CD-ROM (Jan. 1984-); Mag. Index Plus (1989-); Mag. Index Sel. Microfiche (1986-) [Full Txt.]; Mag. Index. Sel. (1986-); Mag. Search; Manage. Market. Abstr.; Med. Rev. Dig.; Middle East Abstr. Index; Mid. Search (Jan. 1984-) [Full Txt.]; Music Index (-19??); Newsp. Period. Abstr. (1986-); NEXIS (Jan. 6, 1975-); Prim. Search (Jan. 1984-); PROMT; Read. Guide Abstr. Select Ed.; Read. Guide Period. Lit.; Resource/One Ondisc (1986-); Sci. Fict. Fantasy Book Rev. Index; Mag. Index (1977-) [Full Txt.]; TOM Gen. Index (1985-) [Full Txt.]; Urban Aff. Abstr.; Vocat. Search (Jan. 1984-) [Full Txt.].

US/1074-0791
NIP (CINCINNATI, OHIO. 1993). (NIP : NEWS, INFORMATION & PICTURES.). **VFOAT** News, Information & Pictures; News, Information and Pictures; NIP Magazine. (19??)-. English. Twelve times a year. $16.00 (one year); $30.00 (two years); $42.00 (three years). NIP News, Information & Picture, 3915 Reading Road, Cincinnati OH 45206. **Tel** (513)281-6414, FAX (513)281-6674. **ED** Ruby L. Bond (phone: (513)281-6416). **Bk Rev**. **Ad Acc**, **Adv Mgr:** H. Bond, **Tel** (513)281-5416. ctrl circ. ***Continues*** *NIP Magazine, 8750-3220.*
Desc: Reporting the news in pictures.

TU
NOKTA. (1983)-. Periodical. Turkish. wk. $140.00 Americas; $100.00 Europe; $180.00 other. Nokta Yayinlari A S, Buyukdere cad ali Kaya Sok 8, 80720 Levent Istanbul Turkey. **Tel** 011 90 1 2696680. **LC** AP95.T8; N64.

FR/0397-3190
NOUVELLE REVUE DU SON PARIS, LA. (1976)-. Periodical. French. mo (10 issues per year). 250.00F France; 340.00F other. Editions Frequences, 1 Boulevard Ney, 75018 Paris France. **Tel** 011 33 1 40360197, FAX 011 33 1 40361196. **ED** Patrick Vercher. **Ad Acc**.
Ind/Abst Point Repere (1979-1980).

US/0892-5003
NOVASCOPE. [Novascope]. (1986)-. Periodical. English. Ten times a year. $25.00. Novascope, PO Box 283, Upperville VA 22176. **Tel** (703)687-3314. **ED** Mark Sadon Smith. **DD** 051. **Bk Rev**. **Ad Acc**. **Circ:** 60,000 (ctrl).

US/1070-9835
NUDE & NATURAL. [Nude nat.]. **Added/Corp** Naturist Society. **VFOAT** Nude and Natural; N & N. Vol. 9, No. 1 (June 14, 1989)-. Periodical. English. qt (Mar., June, Sep., Dec.). $25.00. The Naturist Society, PO Box 132, Oshkosh WI 54902. **Tel** (414)231-9950, FAX (414)231-9977. **ED** L. Baxandall. **LC** GV450; .C59. **DD** 613/.194. **Bk Rev**. **Ad Acc**. **Circ:** 20,000. ***Continues*** *Clothed with the Sun, 0883-4326.*

IT/0029-6147
NUOVA ANTOLOGIA. [Nuova antol.]. Vol. 325 (1926)-. Periodical. Italian. qt. L90000 Italy; L100000 other. Editoriale Finanz Le Monnier, PB 202, Via Meucci 2, 50015 Grassina Florence Italy. **Tel** 011 39 55 64910. **LC** AP37; .N8. **DD** 055. Index available. **Bk Rev**. **Ad Acc**. **Circ:** 8,100. available on microfilm from University Microfilms International (UMI). ***Continues*** *Nuova Antologia de Lettere, Scienze de Arti.*
Desc: Tries to recover the tradition of the Antologia. Meant to be a new opening to foreign culture, ready to start a dialogue with the outside world beyond the limits of provincialism.
Ind/Abst Abstr. Engl. Stud.; Am. Hist. Life (1954-1956, 1965-1974); Annu. Bibliogr. Engl. Lang. Lit.; MLA Int. Bibl. Books Artic. Mod. Lang. Lit.; Romant. Move.

IT
NUOVI STUDI FANESI. Periodical. Italian. ir.

IT/0030-0705
OGGI. [Oggi]. (1945)-. Periodical. Italian. wk (52 issues). $199.00 US. RCS Rizzoli Periodici, Via A Rizzoli 2, 20132 Milan Italy. **Tel** 011 39 2 27200720. **(Subscription address:** Speedimpex USA, Inc., 35 02 48th Avenue, Long Island City NY 11101.) **Ad Acc**. available on microfilm and microfiche from University Microfilms International (UMI).

UK
OH BOY MONTHLY. ***Title Change.*** (19??)-(19??). English. IPC Group, 11th Floor, Kings Reach Tower, Stamford Street, London SE1 9LS England. **Tel** 011 44 71 2615000. ***Absorbed by*** *My Guy.*

US/0886-182X
OSIA NEWS. (OSIA NEWS : NATIONAL PUBLICATION OF THE SUPREME LODGE, ORDER SONS OF ITALY IN AMERICA.). **Added/Corp** Order Sons of Italy in America. **VAT** Order Sons of Italy in America News. (19??)-. Periodical. English. mo. $12.00. OSIA News, 219 E Street Northeast, Washington DC 20002. **Tel** (202)547-2900.

US/0090-2047
OUI. [Oui]. (1972)-. Periodical. English. mo. $9.00. Laurant Publishers Ltd., 300 West 43rd Street, New York NY 10036. **Tel** (212)397-5200. **LC** AP2; .O63. **DD** 051.
Ind/Abst Index Period. Artic. Relat. Law; Med. Rev. Dig.; Mag. Index (1977-Dec. 1983).

GW/0176-4152
P. M. PETER MOOSLEITNERS INTERESSANTES MAGAZIN. [P. M. Peter Moosleitners interess. Mag.]. **VFOAT** Peter Moosleitners Interessantes Magazin. (1978)-. Periodical. German. mo. DM61.20. Gruner und Jahr Ag & Co, Abonnenten Service, D 20080 Hamburg Germany. **Tel** 011 49 40 37030. **UDC** 001.92 :05.

US/0194-5084
PACIFIC NEWS SERVICE. **Added/Corp** Bay Area Institute. (19??)-. Periodical. English. da. $100.00. Bay Area Institute, 450 Mission Street, Room 506, San Francisco CA 94105. **Tel** (412)243-4364.

FR/0152-0741
PAGES DE L'EVENEMENT, LES. [Page even.]. (1977)-. Periodical. French. mo. 288.93F France; 330.00F other. Bayard Presse, Svc Client, 3 rue Bayard/Dept 2, 75393 Paris Cedex 08 France. **Tel** 011 33 1 44356060, 011 33 1 44356262. **(Subscription address:** Bayard Presse Notre Temps, BP2, 99505 Paris Enterprises France.) **UDC** 37.

IT
PANORAMA MODA & ABBIGLIAMENTO. (19??)-. Italian. mo. L60000 Italy; L100000 Europe; L130000 other. Editoriale Alfa Srl, Viale Marelli 19 3, 20099 Sesto S Giovanni Italy. **Tel** 011 39 2 2423566.

US/0892-3809
PAPER (NEW YORK, N.Y.). **See** The Arts.

FR
PARISIEN. French. 1310.00F France; 1715.60F Algeria, Morocco, Tunisia, and Europe; 2526.00F rest of of Africa; 3338.00F Americas and Asia; 4149.20F other. Promogedis, 24 Avenue des Gresillons, 92600 Asnieres Cedex France. **Tel** 011 33 1 47338500.

FR/0764-4663
PELERIN MAGAZINE. **See** Religion and Theology.

US
PEOPLE'S WEEKLY WORLD. **VFOAT** World. Vol. 5, No. 12 (Oct. 6, 1990)-. Periodical. English (Spanish). wk. Long View Publishing Company, 239 West 23rd Street, New York NY 10011. **Tel** (212)924-2523, FAX (212)645-5436, telex 12-7819. ***Continues*** *People's Daily World.*

US/0197-680X
PHANTASMAGORIA (UNIVERSITY HEIGHTS). (PHANTASMAGORIA.). [Phantasmagoria]. V. 1- Spring 1980. Periodical. English. sa. $3.50 US; $4.00 other. Phantasmagoria Roberta Mendel, Editor, 3766 Meadowbrook Boulevard, University Heights OH 44118.

IT
PICCOLA RASSEGNA IL MODELLARIO. (19??)-. Italian. bm (6 issues). L40000.00. Casanova Editore, Via Torrente Cinghio 5, 43100 Parma Italy. **Tel** 011 39 521 54696.

IT
PIEMONTEUROPA. Italian. Four times a year. L50000.00. Movimento Federalista Europeo MFE, Via Schina 26, 10144 Turin Italy. **Tel** 011 39 11 4732843.

US
PLAYBOY INDEX, THE. **See** Men's Interests.

US/0743-6025
POSTHYPE. (POSTHYPE : THE JOURNAL OF HAPPY YOUNG PEOPLE ENTERPRISES (HYPE).). **VFOAT** Post Hype. Periodical. English. qt. Posthype Press, 43 West 27th Street #6F, New York NY 10001.

FR
POUR EN SAVOIR PLUS SUR LE TIERS MONDE ET L'ETAT DU MONDE EN. ***Ceased.*** (1985)-(19??). French (Italian). ir. Editions de la Decouverte, 1 Place Paul Painleve, 75005 Paris France. **ED** Serge Cordellier. **LC** HC27.2; .P68. **DD** 305.8/006. Index available. cum. index. ***Separated from*** *Etat du Monde.*

GE
PRISMA. ***Ceased.*** **Added/Corp** Germany (Democratic Republic, 1949-). (197?-?). Periodical. German (English and French). qt. Verlag Zeit Im Bild, Franklinstr 17 19, D 01069 Dresden Germany. **Tel** 011 49 351 48640. **ED** Lilli Piater.
Desc: A Digest from the German Democratic Republic. medicines, sports, art and literature. It also deals with major aspects of the GDR's home and foreign policies.

IT
PROVINCIA PAVESE. EAG Srl, Via T Tasso 47, 27100 Ravia Italy.

IT
PUBBLICITA ITALIA TODAY. (19??)-. Italian. wk. L3500000.00. Marketing Finanza Italia, Via Stradella 3, 20129 Milan Italy. **Tel** 011 39 2 29400554, FAX 011 39 2 29401816. ***Continues*** *Today Italia.*

IT
QUADERNI ANALITICI / ISTITUTO NAZIONALE PER LO STUDIO DELLA CONGIUNTURA. **Added/Corp** Istituto Nazionale per lo Studio della Congiuntura (Italy). (19??)-. Italian. Free to members. Farmers Union Community Development Association Istituto Nazio Studio Congiuntura, 800 Lake Air Drive, Piazza Indipendenza 4, 00185 Rome Italy, Waco TX 76710. **Tel** , 011 39 6 444821, FAX , , telex , . **LC** WMLC 93/1745.

US/0892-1415
QUALITY LIVING. ***Ceased.*** [Qual. living]. (1987)-No. 22 (1993). Periodical. English. mo. Quality Living, PO Box 1, Valle Crucis NC 28691. **DD** 170.
Desc: Examines values and promotes a vision of reality that sees life as essentially good and possessing beauty, harmony, and meaning. Ethical investing and personal growth features appear regularly.

US/0899-2576
QUE PASA (TEANECK, N.J.). ***Ceased.*** (QUE PASA.). [Que pasa]. Vol. 1, No. 1 (Nov. 1988)-?. Periodical. English (Spanish). bm. DS Magazines, 1086 Teaneck Road, Teaneck NJ 07666. **Tel** (201)833-1800. **ED** Griselle Colon. **DD** 051. **Ad Acc**.
Desc: Catering to hispanic Americans ages 12 to 19.

US
QUOTES & ANECDOTES. English. bm. $59.00. Speakers Digest Inc, PO Box 363, Salisbury CT 06068. **Tel** (203)435-9458, (800)228-5297.

US/0278-7016
RAISE THE STAKES. (RAISE THE STAKES : THE PLANET DRUM REVIEW.). **Added/Corp** Planet Drum Foundation. (19??)-. Periodical. English. Three times a year. $15.00 US; $20.00 other. Planet Drum Foundation, PO Box 31251, San Francisco CA 94131. **Tel** (415)285-6556. **ED** Peter Berg and Marie Dolcini. **LC** Discard. **Circ:** 3,000.
Desc: Information from both urban and rural areas about the relation of ecology to culture: bioregional reports, letters, poems, stories, interviews and art.
Ind/Abst Altern. Press Index (199?-).

US/0034-0375
READER'S DIGEST, THE. [Read. dig.]. **VFOAT** Reader's Digest Service. Vol. 1, No. 1, (1922)-. Periodical. English. mo. Must order direct. Reader's Digest, Reader Digest Road, Pleasantville NY 10570. **Tel** (914)241-5000, (800)234-9000. **ED** D Wallace, L B Acheson. **LC** AP2; .R255. **DD** 051. available on microfilm and microfiche from University Microfilms International (UMI). Documents available from UMI Article Clearinghouse.
Desc: Contains digest and original articles on a wide variety of health-related topics. Also contains short abstracts of current medical progress in section entitled "News from the World of Medicine."
Ind/Abst Abr. Read. Guide Period. Lit.; Acad. Abstr. Full Text Elite (Jan. 1984-); Acad. Abstr. (Jan. 1984-); Acad. Ind. [Computer File] (1984-); Biogr. Index; Can. Period. Index (19??-); Consum. Health Nutr. Index; Cumul. Index Nurs. Allied Health Lit.; Expand. Acad. Index (1984-); Gen. Period. Index (1985-); Health Ref. Cent. (1987-) [Select. Cov.]; Highw. Res. Abstr.; Mag. Artic. Summar. Elite (Jan. 1984-); Mag. Artic. Summar. Select (Jan. 1984-); Mag. Artic. Summar. CD-ROM (Jan. 1984-); Mag. Index Plus (1989-); Mag. Search; Mid. Search (Jan. 1984-); Newsp. Period. Abstr. (1986-); Read. Guide Abstr. Select Ed.; Read. Guide Period. Lit.; Mag. Index (1977-); TOM Gen. Index (1985-).

US
READER'S DIGEST CONDENSED BOOKS. (Spring 1950)-. Periodical. English. ir. Reader's Digest, Reader Digest Road, Pleasantville NY 10570. **Tel** (914)241-5000, (800)234-9000. **LC** AP2; .R2553. **DD** 051.

FI
READERS DIGEST. FINNISH EDITION. (19??)-. Finnish. mo. $21.41. Readers Digest / Valitut Palat, Stnerikuja 5, SS 00440 Helsinki Finland. **Tel** 011 358 0503441.

KO
READERS' DIGEST (KOREAN EDITION). (READERS' DIGEST.). Korean. mo. $25.71 Japan, Philippines, Thailand, Taiwan, Indonesia, Australia, New Zealand, India, Pakistan, Bangladesh, Malaysia, Papaua New Guinea, Sri Lanka; $28.62 other. Dong A Publishing Co. Ltd., PO Box Guro 110, Seoul Korea. **Tel** 011 822 866 0129.

US/0163-6405
READER'S DIGEST. LARGE-TYPE EDITION. (READER'S DIGEST.). **VFOAT** Selections from the Reader's Digest. (19??)-. Periodical. English. Twelve times a year. $15.60 Australia; $9.95 others. Readers Digest / Fund for Blind, PO Box 241, Mount Morris IL 61054. **Tel** (914)241-5278. available in large print. Documents available from UMI Article Clearinghouse.
Ind/Abst Resource/One Ondisc (1986-).

US
READERS' GUIDE ABSTRACTS SELECT EDITION. **See** General Interest-Abstracting, Bibliographies and Statistics.

US/0896-7350
REFUND EXPRESS. [Refund express]. (198?)-. Periodical. English. mo. $3.00 (sample), $14.00 (6 months), $23.00 (1 year). Sandy Ennis, PO Box 10, Allen Park MI 48101. **Tel** (313)381-8686.

US
REFUNDING MAKES CENTS. (19??)-. English. mo. $12.00. Refunding Makes Cents, PO Box R, Farmington UT 84025.

GW
REGIO MAGAZIN. German. ir. DM67.20. Medela Pharma Verlag Gmbh., Otto Lilienthal Str. 3, W 7835 Teningen 3 Germany. **Tel** 011 49 7663 1001.

US/0146-2008
REPLICA (MIAMI, FLA. 1970). (REPLICA.). [Replica]. (Sept. 18, 1970)-. Spanish. mo. $20.00. Replica Main Office, 2994 NW 7th Street, Miami FL 33125. **Tel** (305)643-5481, FAX 541-7410. **ED** Max Lesnick. **LC** AP62; .R48. **Ad Acc. Circ:** 109,000 (ctrl).
Desc: Ideas in the areas of health, fashion, politics, arts, history, tourism, artists, horoscopes, cinema, TV, self-improvement, business.
Ind/Abst Chicano Index.

PL/0860-4592
RES PUBLICA. ***Title Change.*** R. 1, Nr. 1 (Czerw. 1987)-R. 6, Nr. 1-2 (Stycz./Luty 1992). Periodical. Polish. mo. Res Publica, SP Z 0 0, Raszynska 15-3, 02-026 Warsaw Poland. **Tel** 48 22 26 93 43, telex 813991 RP PL. **ED** Marcin Krol. **LC** AP54; .R47. **Bk Rev. Ad Acc. Circ:** 10,000 (ctrl). ***Continued by*** *Res Publica Nowa.*
Desc: Intellectual magazine.

US
RESOURCE/ONE ONDISC [COMPUTER FILE]. **See** General Interest-Abstracting, Bibliographies and Statistics.

MX
REVISTA DE REVISTAS; EL SEMANARIO NACIONAL. Vol. 1 (1910)-. Periodical. Spanish. wk. $106.00 (North America); $120.00 (South America); $200.00 (other). Excelsior Cia Editorial Scl, Paseo Reforma 10, Suscripciones, Mexico 1 df Mexico. **Tel** 11 52 5 7054444, 5669360.

CK/0120-1115
REVISTA UNIVERSIDAD PONTIFICIA BOLIVARIANA. [Univ. Pontif. Bolivar.]. Began with issue for Sept. 1977. Periodical. Spanish. Biblioteca Central, Apartado Aereo 1178, Medellin Colombia. **LC** AP63; .U623. **DD** 056/.1. ***Continues*** *Universidad Pontificia Bolivariana.*
Ind/Abst Am. Hist. Life (1977-); MLA Int. Bibl. Books Artic. Mod. Lang. Lit.

BE/0770-8602
REVUE GENERALE (1985). (REVUE GENERALE.). [Rev. gen.]. No. 1 (1985)-. Periodical. French. Ten times a year. 1900F Belgium; 2300F other. le Revue Generale, Chaussee de Louvain 41, B 1320 Beauvechain, Belgium. **Tel** (010)866629, FAX (010)866691. **(Subscription address:** Editions Imprim dieu Brichart Chausse de la Croix 47, B 1340 Ottignies Belgium, telephone: (010) 415024**) LC** AP22; .R53. **DD** 054/.1. **Circ:** 5,000. ***Continues*** *Revue Generale pour l'Humaniste des Temps Nouveaux, 0777-2297.*

US/1041-9799
RHONDA WHITE-WARNER'S TIDBITS. **VFOAT** Tidbits. (1988)-. Periodical. English. mo. $15.00. Rhonda White-Warner Associates, PO Box 197, 484 Lake Park Avenue, Oakland CA 94610. **Tel** (415)444-0552. **ED** Rhonda White-Warner and Carolyn Alexander. **DD** 909. **Ad Acc. Circ:** 2,500.

GW
RICHARD STRAUSS JAHRBUCH. 1954-. German. an. Boosey & Hawkes, 52 Cooper Square, New York NY 10003-7102. **Tel** (516)752-1122.

US/0895-3139
RIGHT HERE. ***Title Change.*** [Right here]. **VFOAT** Right Here Magazine. (1984)-?. Periodical. English. bm. Right Here Publications, Box 1014, Huntington IN 46750. **Tel** (219)356-4223. **DD** 051. **Bk Rev. Ad Acc.** ***Continued by*** *Write Now!.*

IT
RISPOSTE. (19??)-. Italian. mo. L80000 Italy; L120000 other. Oasi Editrice Srl, Via Conte Ruggero 73, 94018 Troina En Italy. **Tel** 011 39 935 650234.

IT
RIVISTA DI BERGAMO. (19??)-. Italian. Eleven times a year. L10000.00 Italy; L50000.00 other. Rivista di Bergamo, Rotonda Dei Mille 1, 24100 Bergamo Italy. **Tel** 011 39 35 243162.

IT/0393-5914
RIVISTERIA. Vol. 1, No. 1 (May 1984)-. Periodical. Italian. Ten times a year. L90000.00 Italy; L170000.00 other. Strumenti Editoriali Srl, Via Verona 9, 20135 Milan Italy. **Tel** 011 39 2 58301054. **LC** AP37; .R63. **DD** 055/.1.

IT
RIVOLI 15. Rivoli 15, Viale Partigiani Italia 14, 10098 Rivoli Italy.

US/0279-1447
ROBB REPORT, THE. [Robb rep.]. (19??)-. Periodical. English. mo. $65.00 (one year), $100.00 (two year), US and Mexico; $90.00 (one year), $150.00 (two year) other. Robb Report, 1 Acton Place, Acton MA 01720. **Tel** (508)263-7749, (800)229-7622, FAX (508)263-0722, telex 928360. **(Subscription address:** Fulco, 30 Broad Street, Denville NJ 07834.**) ED** Robert Freeman. **DD** 051. **Bk Rev. Ad Acc. Circ:** 55,000. available on microfilm from University Microfilms International (UMI).
Desc: Manual for wealthy living. Covers subjects ranging from automobiles to travel to investments.
Ind/Abst Numis. Lit.

IT/0391-8017
ROMA COMUNE. [Roma Comune]. (1977)-. Periodical. Italian. mo. Free on request. Ufficio Stampa del Comune, Scala dell Arce Capitolina 7, 00186 Rome Italy. **Tel** 06 67103982. **UDC** 352.

IT
ROMACAPITALE. (19??)-. Italian. mo (11 issues). L120000. Edinvest Srl, Via delle Quattro Fontane 15, 00184 Rome Italy. **Tel** 011 39 6 4743178. ***Continues*** *Hi-Tech.*

US/0896-0712
ROUGE (BATON ROUGE, LA.). ***Ceased.*** (ROUGE.). [Rouge]. Vol. 1, No. 1 (Dec. 1987/Jan. 1988)-(1989). Periodical. English. bm. Baton Rouge Magazine, 603 Europe Street, Baton Rouge LA 70802. **Tel** (504)383-2100. **DD** 917. ***Continues*** *Baton Rouge Magazine, 0279-0416.*

US
SAGA. (1950)-(19??). Periodical. English. mo. MacFadden Women's Group, 233 Park Avenue South, New York NY 10003. **Tel** (212)979-4800, (800)666-8783. **LC** AP2; .S127.

IT/1120-5679
SAHARA (SEGRATE). (SAHARA / CENTRO STUDI LUIGI NEGRO.). [Sahara]. **Added/Corp** Centro Studi Luigi Negro. Vol. 1 (Nov. 1988)-. English (French and Italian). an. L25000 Italy; L30000 other. Pyramids SNC, Seconda Strada 2 San Felice, 20090 Segrate Milan Italy. **Tel** 011 39 2 7532635. **LC** DT335; .S24. **DD** 966/.005. **CODEN** SAHAEZ.

US/0898-4875
SALUDOS HISPANOS. [Saludos Hisp.]. **VFOAT** Saludos. (19??)-. Periodical. Spanish (English). Four times a year. $40.00 (institutions), $10.00 (individuals). Saludos Hispanos, 41550 Eclectic Avenue, Suite 260, Palm Desert CA 92260. **Tel** (6190776-1206. **ED** Maureen Hearing. **DD** 051. **Ad Acc. Circ:** 600,000 (ctrl).
Desc: Educational and career opportunities in the fashion and art fields for the Hispanics.

US/0898-3011
SATORI. ***Ceased.*** (1988)-Vol. 3 ( ). Periodical. English. qt. Hands Off the Press Inc, PO Box 318, Tiroli NY 12583. **DD** 810.
Desc: Provides excellent essays and interviews with such people as Ed Sanders and Linda Montano. Also includes photographs that are examples of surrealistic art and poetry and prose that fit the unusual format.

US/0048-9239
SATURDAY EVENING POST (1839), THE. (THE SATURDAY EVENING POST.). [Saturday evening post]. **VFOAT** United States Saturday Post. Vol. 18, No. 954 (Nov. 9, 1839)-. Periodical. English. bm (6 issues). $13.97. Saturday Evening Post Society, 1100 Waterway Boulevard, Indianapolis IN 46202. **Tel** (317)636-8881, FAX (317)637-0126. **(Subscription address:** CDS Agency Hard Copy, PO Box 4966, Des Moines IA 50340.**) ED** Cory SerVaas. **LC** AP2; .S2. **DD** 051. **CODEN** SAEPAR. **Ad Acc. Circ:** 570,000. available on microfilm and microfiche from University Microfilms International (UMI); available on an online database (file 647/Full-Text) from DIALOG. Documents available from UMI Article Clearinghouse, Magazine Collection. ***Continues*** *Atkinson's Evening Post and Philadelphia Saturday News;* ***Absorbed*** *Country Gentleman, 0147-4928.*
Desc: Contains fiction, humor and the latest technological advances in preventive medicine; general interest content makes for fine reading for the whole family.
Ind/Abst Abr. Read. Guide Period. Lit.; Acad. Abstr. Full Text Elite (Jan. 1984-); Acad. Abstr. (Jan. 1984-); Acad. Ind. [Computer File] (1984-); Acad. Search (Jan. 1984-); Book Rev. Index; Cumul. Index Nurs. Allied Health Lit.; Expand. Acad. Index (1984-); Gen. Period. Index (1985-); GeoRef; INFO-SOUTH Abstr.; Mag. Artic. Summar. Elite (Jan. 1984-); Mag. Artic. Summar. Select (Jan. 1984-); Mag. Artic. Summar. CD-ROM (Jan. 1984-); Mag. Express (1986-) [Full Txt.]; Mag. Index Plus (1989-); Mag. Index Sel. Microfiche (1986-) [Full Txt.]; Mag. Index. Sel. (1986-); Mag. Search; Mid. Search (Jan. 1984-); Newsp. Period. Abstr. (1986-); Peace Res. Abstr. J. (1964-1969); Read. Guide Abstr. Select Ed.; Read. Guide Period. Lit.; Resource/One Ondisc; Mag. Index (1977-); TOM Gen. Index (1985-) [Full Txt.]; Vocat. Search (Jan. 1984-).

US/1049-7455
SCAPE (LOS ANGELES, CALIF.). (SCAPE.). ['Scape]. (1990)-. Periodical. English. bm. $100.00. Mav Enterprises, 8929 Exposition Boulevard, Los Angeles CA 90034. **Tel** (310)841-0182. **ED** Tom Byrnes. **DD** 051. **Ad Acc.** ctrl circ.
Desc: Eclectic general interest magazine.

IT/0036-5742
SCENA ILLUSTRATA. Scena Illustrata, Via Cernaia 43, 00185 Rome Italy.

GW/0176-9472
SCHRIFTEN DES ARBEITSKREISES SELBSTANDIGER KULTUR-INSTITUTE. **Added/Corp** Arbeitskreis Selbstandiger Kultur-Institute (Germany). 1984-. Monographic series. German. Price varies per volume. Bouvier GmbH & Co. KG ABT Verlag, AM Hof 28, D 53113 Bonn Germany. **Tel** 011 49 228 7290141.

US/0199-042X
SCREW WEST. (1978)-. Periodical. English. Fifty-two times a year. $56.00. Milky Way Productions Inc, PO Box 432, Old Chelsea Station, New York NY 10113. **Tel** (212)989-8001.

KO
SEGYE (YONHAP TONGSIN (FIRM)). (SEGYE.). **VFOAT** Segye Monthly Photo Journal. Periodical. Korean (Korean). mo. W3,000. Yonhap Tongsin, 85-1 Susong-dong, Chongno-ku, Seoul 110-140 South Korea. **Tel** 3903-601, FAX 738-0820, telex K23618. **LC** AP95.K6; S43.

US/0885-0496
SELECCIONES DEL READER'S DIGEST (UNITED STATES ED.). (SELECCIONES DEL READER'S DIGEST.). [Sel. Read. Dig.]. (19??)-. Periodical. Spanish (translations available in English). mo. $27.11 Dade County, Florida; $26.99 Florida, $25.46 other US; $35.00 Europe; $45.00 other. Readers Digest, Avenida Lomas Sotelo 1102, 11200 Mexico DF Mexico. **Tel** 011 52 5 3951099, 011 52 5 3951108. **(Subscription address:** Fulfillment Corporation of America, PO Box 1962, Marion OH 43305.**) DD** 051. **Ad Acc.** available on microfilm and microfiche from University Microfilms International (UMI).

CN/0037-1378
SELECTION DU READER'S DIGEST (EDITION CANADIENNE). (SELECTION DU READER'S DIGEST.). [Sel. Read. dig.]. Vol. 1 (July 1947)-. Periodical. French. mo. 29.96Can$ Canada; 43.95Can$ other. Readers Digest Association Canada Ltd., 215 Redfern Avenue, Montreal, Quebec H3Z 2V9 Canada. **Tel** (514)934-0751. **(Subscription address:** ICL Interprovincial Circulation Ltd., 251 Lawrence Avenue, Suite 201, Kelowna BC V1Y 6L2 Canada**) ED** Denise Surprenant. Index available. **Ad Acc. Circ:** 343,425. available on microfilm and microfiche from University Microfilms International (UMI).
Desc: Condensation of previously published articles and books as well as original works on a wide range of subjects-consumers, marriage, personal heroism or triumph and drama in real life.
Ind/Abst Can. Period. Index (1987-); Point Repere (1983-).

US
SEM DNEI. **VFOAT** Seven Days. 1 (Nov. 4, 1983)-. Periodical. Russian. wk (Tues.-Sun.). $90.00, $50.00 (six months), $30.00 (Saturday only). Novoye Russkoye Slovo, 111 Fifth Avenue, 5th Floor, New York NY 10003. **Tel** (212)387-0299 ext. 108, FAX (212)387-9050. **LC** AP51; .S45. **Ad Acc. Circ:** 55,000. ***Continues*** *Novoye Russkoye Slovo.*

IT
SENTINELLA DEL CANAVESE. (19??)-. Italian. sw. L90000 Italy; L110000 other. Edizioni Nuova Europa, Piazza Lamarmora 12, 10015 Ivrea Italy. **Tel** 011 39 125 424946.

FR
SERVICES POSTE AERIENNE. French. Sixteen times a year. 285.00F. Indicateur Universel des PTT, 6 rue le Goff, 75005 Paris France. **Tel** 011 33 1 43267942.

IT
SESIA. Italian. sw. L90000 Italy; L150000 other. La Sesia, V C Leone 10, 13100 Vercelli Italy. **Tel** 011 39 161 250748.

IR
SHAHID (TEHRAN, IRAN : 1983). (SHAHEAD.). (1983)-. Periodical. Persian (Persian). sm. 4800.00IR Iran; $70.00 US. Shahead, No 64 Tabandeh Avenue, 7th Tir Sq, Tehran Iran. **Tel** 829201, telex 837245-7. **ED** A Montazeri. Index available. **Bk Rev. Ad Acc. Circ:** 100,000 (ctrl). ***Continues in part*** *Mahnamahi Shahid.*
Desc: Cultural, social, idiological, and political magazine.

US/1054-0695
SHAREDEBATE INTERNATIONAL. (SHAREDEBATE INTERNATIONAL [COMPUTER FILE].). [ShareDebate int.]. (March 1990)-. Periodical. English. qt. $20.00. Applied Foresight Inc, Box 20607, Bloomington MN 55420. **Tel** (612)936-7378. **ED** R H Martin. **DD** 808. **Bk Rev. Ad Acc. Circ:** 10,000. available on CD-ROM; available on diskette.

UK
SHEBA. VFOAT Bilqis. Periodical. Arabic (Arabic). mo. $95.00 US, $100.00 Canada. Sheba Publications Ltd, 16 Henrietta Street, London WC2 8QH England. **LC** AP95.A6; S44. **DD** 059/.927.

US/1071-4480
SHERMAN SENTINEL, THE. (July 19, 1947)-. Newspaper. English. Twenty-four times a year. $20.00. Sherman Sentinel, PO Box 64, Sherman CT 06784. **Tel** (203)354-3428. **ED** Janet Hopkins (editor's address: 10 Route 37 Center, Sherman CT 06784). **Bk Rev**, (Qty: 4). **Ad Acc. Circ:** 850.

BO
SIGNO (LA PAZ, BOLIVIA). (SIGNO.). Vol. 1 (Oct./Nov. 1956)-. Periodical. Spanish.
Ind/Abst HAPI Hisp. Am. Period. Index.

US
SINGLE LIVING MAGAZINE : AN IOWA PERSPECTIVE. English. mo. $12.00 US; $20.00 other. Single Living Magazine, Box 573, Ames IA 50010. **Tel** (515)292-5104. **ED** Marilyn J Kniss. **Bk Rev. Ad Acc. Circ:** 25,000.
Desc: Lifestyle guide edited for the contemporary single male and female. Regular features on self-growth, health, entertainment and other areas.

US/1047-9066
SINGLE TODAY (LAPORTE, IND.). (SINGLE TODAY.). Vol. 1, Issue 1 (Dec. 1989/Jan. 1990)-. Periodical. English. bm (6 issues). $8.00. Single Today, PO Box 2, Laporte IN 46350. **Tel** (219)362-3942. **DD** 646.

US/8756-0380
SINGLELIFE (MILWAUKEE, WIS.). (SINGLELIFE.). **VFOAT** Single Life; SingleLife Magazine. (198?)-. Periodical. English. Six times a year (Jan., Mar., May, July, Sept., Nov.). $15.00 US; $22.00 other. SingleLife, 606 West Wisconsin Avenue, Suite 703, Milwaukee WI 53203. **Tel** (414)271-9700. **ED** Gail Levine. **Bk Rev**, (Qty: 6). **Ad Acc, Adv Mgr:** David Rose. **Pr Rev. Circ:** 10,000 (ctrl). ***Continues*** *SingleLife Milwaukee, 8756-0380.*

US/0731-986X
SIR PRESENTS 2 BY 2. VFOAT Sir Presents Two by Two; 2 by 2. Periodical. English. sa. $3.50 each issue. Histrionic Publishing Company, 23 West 26th Street, New York NY 10010.

KO
SISA CHUNCHU. (Mar. 1991)-. Periodical. Korean. mo. Kwangjewon, Suun Hoegwan 1009-Ho, 88 Kyongun-Dong Chongno-Ku, Seoul Korea. **LC** AP95.K6; S57.

US/0199-6193
SISA NEWS. [Sisa news]. **VFOAT** SISA News Korea Today. (19??)-. Periodical. English (Korean). Twelve times a year. $30.00. SISA News Company, 945 South Western Avenue, Room 207, Los Angeles CA 90010. **Tel** (213)733-6610.

IT
SKILL. Italian. qt. L80000. Skill Enaip Lombardia, Via G Ventura 4, 20134 Milan Italy. **Tel** 011 39 2 26414765.
Desc: Quaderni di Skill included in subscription to Skill.

UK/0955-6915
SKY INTERNATIONAL. (SKY.). [Sky int.]. **VFOAT** Sky Magazine. (1987)-. Periodical. English. mo. £33.00 Europe. World Wide Subscription Services, Unit 4, Gibbs Reed Farm, East Sussex TN5 7HE England. **Tel** (0580)200657, FAX (0580)200616.

IT/0038-156X
SORRISI E CANZONI TV. [Sorrisi canzoni TV]. **VFOAT** TV Sorrisi e Canzoni. (1972)-. Periodical. Italian. wk. L93600 Italy; L205400 other. Arnoldo Mondadori Editore, UFF Cont Abbonamenti, 20090 Segrate MI Italy. **Tel** 011 39 2 75422015, telex 320457 MONDMI I. **UDC** 791. ***Continues*** *Sorrisi e Canzoni d' Italia, 1121-7502.*

US
SOUTH CAROLINA VOTER. English. Four times a year (Mar., June, Sept., Dec.). $5.00. League of Women Voters of South Carolina, 1314 Lincoln Street, Suite 212, Columbia SC 29201. **Tel** (803)771-0063. **ED** Tamela Pinckney. **Ad Acc, Adv Mgr:** Laurel Suggs, **Tel** (803)782-9147.

US/1067-4977
SOUTH DAKOTA HIGH LINER MAGAZINE. Added/Corp South Dakota Rural Electric Association. (19??)-. Periodical. English. Twelve times a year. $11.00. South Dakota Rural Electric Association, PO Box 1138, Pierre SD 57501. **Tel** (605)224-8823, FAX (605)224-4430. **ED** Brian Boyer. **Bk Rev**, (Qty: 6-12). **Ad Acc, Adv Mgr:** Bernie Ripperger, **Tel** (605)224-8823. **Circ:** 80,000.
Desc: General interest magazine about the rural life in South Dakota.

US/1060-9997
STAR GUIDE. [Star guide]. (1988/1989)-. English. an (July). $14.90. Axiom Information Resources, PO Box 8015, Ann Arbor MI 48107. **Tel** (313)761-4842, FAX (313)761-3276. **LC** CT120; .S696. **DD** 920/.02. Index available. cum. index. **Bk Rev. Circ:** 10,000. ***Continues*** *Celebrity Directory.*
Desc: The up-to-date guide available for over 3,200 addresses of major stars from every field; movies, TV, music, sports, politics, literature and other famous people.

US/8750-815X
STAR (TARRYTOWN, N.Y.). (STAR.). [Star]. (19??)-. Periodical. English. wk. $37.44. National Enquirer, 600 South East Coast Avenue, Lantana FL 33464. **Tel** (407)586-1111. **(Subscription address:** CDS / SIFD Agency Control, 1901 Bell Avenue, Des Moines IA 50315.**)**

US/0743-2267
STEAMBOAT SPRINGS MAGAZINE. VFOAT Steamboat Magazine. (19??)-. Periodical. English. sa (July and Nov.). $17.00 (one year), $29.00 (two year), $41.00 (three year). Steamboat Magazine, PO Box 4328, Steamboat Springs CO 80477. **Tel** (303)879-5250, FAX (303)879-4650.
Desc: New and events about Steamboat Springs Colorado.

US/0894-8968
STRANGE MAGAZINE. VFOAT Strange. (1987)-. Periodical. English. Twice a year (Mar., Sept.). $17.95. Strange Magazine, PO Box 2246, Rockville MD 20852. **Tel** (301)460-4789, FAX (301)460-7959. **ED** Mark Chorvinsky. **DD** 001. **Bk Rev**, (Qty: 12). **Ad Acc. Circ:** 15,000.
Desc: A credible exploration of strange phenomena from a skeptical but open-minded viewpoint. Features articles are fully referenced.

IT/0393-3695
STUDI. FATTI. RICERCHE. [Studi, Fatti, Ric.]. (1978)-. Periodical. Italian. qt. L25000.00. Studi Fatti Ricerche, Via Boccaccio 27, 20123 Milan Italy. **UDC** 2. **Bk Rev. Circ:** 1,000 (ctrl).

UK
SUDAN UPDATE. English. bw. £20.00 Sudan; £32.00 other (individuals), £40.00 Sudan; £52.00 (institutions). Sudan Update, BCM Box CPRS, London WC1N 3XX England. **Tel** 011 44 071 8334924. **ED** Peter Verney. **Bk Rev. Circ:** 600 (ctrl).
Desc: Fortnightly review of media coverage of Sudanese current affairs.

US/0893-844X
SYRACUSE NEW TIMES. [Syracuse new times]. **VFOAT** New Times. (19??)-. Periodical. English. wk. $24.95. Syracuse New Times, 1415 West Genesee Street, Syracuse NY 13204. **Tel** (315)422-7011, FAX (315)422-1721. **ED** Mike Greenstein. **DD** 947. **Bk Rev**, (Qty: 13). **Ad Acc, Adv Mgr:** Karen Belgrader. **Pr Rev. Circ:** 45,000 (ctrl). available on microfilm from University Microfilms International (UMI).
Desc: New York's news arts and entertainment magazine. Each issue contains news and features on politics, sports, visual arts, entertainment, food, film, television and music plus the area's most complete events calendar and most interesting classified section.

FR
TABLES DU JOURNAL LE TEMPS. Vol. 1 (1861-1865)-. French. ir. Editions du CNRS, 22 rue Saint Armand, F 75015 Paris France. **Tel** 011 33 1 45075050. **LC** AI21; .T375. **DD** 074/.36.
Desc: Reprints of indices from the famous journal, tracking its defence of colonial expansion, its opposition to radicalism and hostility to socialism, and its mistrust of British imperialism.

GR/0039-8888
TACHYDROMOS. (1953)-. Greek, Modern. wk. Lambrakis Press SA, 3 Christou Lada, 102 37 Athens Greece. **Tel** 011 30 1 3237283, 011 30 1 3230221.

IT
TASCABILE TV. Italian. wk. L47000. Moreno Polidori Editore, Via di Novoli 75/U, 50127 Firenze Italy. **Tel** 011 39 55 431496.

US/1041-3146
TATTOO (AGOURA HILLS, CALIF.). (TATTOO.). (198?)-. Periodical. English. qt. $33.00. Paisano Publications, 28210 Dorothy Drive, Agoura Hills CA 91301-2693. **Tel** (818)889-8740, FAX (818)889-4726. **(Subscription address:** Kable Publishers Aide, 308 East Hitt Street, Subscriptions Department, Mt. Morris, IL 61054**) LC** GT2345; .T36. **DD** 391/.65/05.
Desc: Brings the artistry and history of tattooing to the reader. Contains featured artists and samples of their work.

US/1065-2590
TECHJOURNAL (SANTA CLARA, CALIF.). ***Ceased.*** (TECHJOURNAL.). [TechJournal]. **Added/Corp** Software Publishing Corporation. **VFOAT** Tech Journal. (1991)-Vol. 4 No. 4 (1994). Periodical. English. Six times a year (Jan., Mar., May, July, Sept., Nov.). Software Publishing Corporation, PO Box 54983, Santa Clara CA 95056. **Tel** (408)988-7518, (800)234-2500, FAX (408)980-0729. **DD** 005.

US/0741-0034
TECOLOTE, EL. (1970)-. Periodical. English (Spanish). mo (11 issues). $45.00 (institutions), $23.00 (individuals). El Telecote Newspaper, PO Box 40037, San Francisco CA 94140. **Tel** (415)824-7878. **ED** Juan Gonzales. **Bk Rev. Ad Acc. Circ:** 14,000. ***Absorbed*** *Tenaz Talks Teatro.*
Desc: Completely bilingual publication which deals with issues of concern to Latinos; national and international politics, culture, health, entertainment and more.

IT/1121-1814
TELEPIU MILANO. (1987)-. Periodical. Italian. wk. L60800 Italy; L123200 other. Arnoldo Mondadori Editore, UFF Cont Abbonamenti, 20090 Segrate MI Italy. **Tel** 011 39 2 75422015, telex 320457 MONDMI I. **UDC** 654.1.

US/0040-2869
TEMAS (NEW YORK, N.Y.). (TEMAS.). [Temas]. (19??)-. Periodical. Spanish. Twelve times a year. $19.00 US & Canada & Mexico & Puerto Rico; $36.00 others. Temas Magazines Inc., 1650 Broadway 3rd Floor, Room 508, New York NY 10019. **Tel** (212)582-4750. **ED** Jose de la Vega. **Bk Rev. Ad Acc. Circ:** 114,000 (ctrl).
Desc: Featuring general topics as fashion, beauty, interviews, outstanding and current events for the family.
Ind/Abst Am. Hist. Life.

SZ
TEMPS STRATEGIQUE, LA. No. 1 (1982)-. Periodical. French (summaries and/or abstracts in English). Six times a year (4 regular issues and 2 special issues in Spring & Fall). 140.00F Europe; 155.00F others. Sonor SA, 15 rue des Savoises, Casa Postale 5015, CH 1211 Geneva 11 Switzerland. **Tel** 011 41 22 7085436. **LC** AP24.; T4. **DD** 054/.1. **Ad Acc.**

US/1047-2843
TENNESSEE ILLUSTRATED. ***Ceased.*** [Tenn. illus.]. Vol. 1, No. 1, May/June (1988)-Ceased with July (1990). Periodical. English. bm. Whittle Communications, 333 Main Avenue, Knoxville TN 37902. **Tel** (615)595-5000, FAX (615)595-5877. **DD** 976.

IT
TERZO MONDO INFORMAZIONI. ***Suspended.*** (19??)-(March 1993). Italian. mo. Movimento Sviluppo Pace, via Saluzzo 58, 10125 Turin Italy. **Tel** 011 39 655866.

CN/0381-3746
THIS MAGAZINE. [This mag.]. Vol. 7, (May/June 1973)-. Periodical. English. Eight times a year. 21.50Can$ (individuals); 23.50Can$ (institutions). This Magazine, 16 Skey Lane, Toronto Ontario M6J 3S4 Canada. **Tel** (416)588-6580, FAX (416) 588-6638. **LC** L11; .T735. **DD** 370/.5. **Ad Acc, Adv Mgr:** Gordon. **Pr Rev. Circ:** 8,000. available on microfilm and microfiche from University Microfilms International (UMI); available in print. ***Continues*** *This Magazine is About Schools.*
Desc: Comments on culture, politics, labor and international affairs; filled with wry humor, graphics, fiction, poetry and cartoons. Each issue contains a major investigative article and news and views from across Canada. Lively journalism that attacks the status quo.
Ind/Abst Altern. Press Index; Can. Index; Can. Period. Index; Women Stud. Abstr.

CN
THISTLE, THE. English. qt. $14.95 Canada; $14.95 US. The Thistle, 117 Queen Street E, Toronto Ontario M5C 1S2 Canada. **Tel** (416)361-3400. **ED** Terry Fletcher. **Bk Rev. Ad Acc. Circ:** 15,000.
Desc: A magazine of Scottish heritage.

US/0040-781X
TIME (CHICAGO, ILL.). (TIME.). [Time]. Vol. 1 (Mar. 3, 1923)-. Periodical. English. wk. $61.88. Time Inc. / New York, Time & Life Building, Rockefeller Center, New York NY 10020. **(Subscription address:** Time Customer Service, PO Box 60050, Tampa FL 33609.**) ED** Jason McManus (Editor-in-Chief); James R Gaines (Managing Editor). **LC** AP2; .T37. **DD** 051. **CODEN** TYMEA9. **Bk Rev. Ad Acc.** available on microfilm and microfiche from University Microfilms International (UMI). Documents available from UMI Article Clearinghouse, Documents on

Demand. ***Absorbed*** *Literary Digest (New York, N.Y. : 1937).*
Desc: Its' up-to-the-minute coverage and in-depth analysis of important events gives readers a clear understanding of the world's week, every week.
Ind/Abst ABI/INFORM Glob. Ed.; ABI Inform Ondisc (March 1975-Jan. 1978); Abr. Read. Guide Period. Lit.; Acad. Abstr. Full Text Elite (Jan. 1984-) [Full Txt.]; Acad. Abstr. (Jan. 1984-); Acad. Ind. [Computer File] (1984-); Acad. Search (Jan. 1984-); Account. Tax Datab. (Jan. 1986-); Aviat. Tradescan [Select. Cov.]; Biogr. Index; Biol. Dig.; Book Rev. Digest; Book Rev. Index; Bus. ASAP (1992-) [Full Txt.]; Bus. Index (1988-); Chicano Index; Consum. Health Nutr. Index (Jan. 1990); Cumul. Index Nurs. Allied Health Lit.; Curr. Lit. Fam. Plan.; Curr. Thoughts Trends; Energy Inf. Abstr.; Environ. Abstr.; Expand. Acad. Index (1984-); F&S Index Plus Text, Int. [Select. Cov.]; Film Lit. Index; Gen. BusinessFile (1988-); Gen. Period. Index (1985-); Health Plan. Adminis.; Health Ref. Cent. (1987-) [Select. Cov.]; Hospit. Health Admin. Index; Index Period. Artic. Relat. Law; Infobank (Jan. 1969-); Infomat Int. Bus.; Law Office Inf. Serv.; Mag. Artic. Summar. Elite (Jan. 1984-) [Full Txt.]; Mag. Artic. Summar. Select (Jan. 1984-) [Full Txt.]; Mag. Artic. Summar. CD-ROM (Jan. 1984-); Mag. ASAP Plus [Full Txt.]; Mag. ASAP Sel. [Full Txt.]; Mag. Express (1986-) [Full Txt.]; Mag. Index Plus (1989-); Mag. Index. Sel. (1986-); Mag. Search; Med. Rev. Dig.; Middle East Abstr. Index; Mid. Search (Jan. 1984-) [Full Txt.]; Newsp. Period. Abstr. (1986-); NEXIS (1981-); Prim. Search (Jan. 1984-); PROMT; Read. Guide Abstr. Select Ed.; Read. Guide Period. Lit.; Resource/One Ondisc; Sci. Fict. Fantasy Book Rev. Index; Mag. Index (1977-); TOM Gen. Index (1985-) [Full Txt.]; Urban Aff. Abstr.; Vocat. Search (Jan. 1984-) [Full Txt.].

US
TLC MONTHLY. (19??)-. English. Twelve times a year. $11.97. Learning Channel, 7700 Wisconsin Avenue, Bethesda MD 20814. **Tel** (301)986-1999, (800)326-4275. **(Subscription address:** P. O. Box 632, Mt. Morris, IL 61054, phone: (800)326-4275**)** **Ad Acc. Circ:** 33,000. ***Continues*** *Learning Channel Monthly Program Guide.*

FR
TODAY. (19??)-. English. mo. 79.72Can$ Canada. Bayard Presse, Svc Client, 3 rue Bayard/Dept 2, 75393 Paris Cedex 08 France. **Tel** 011 33 1 44356060, 011 33 1 44356262. **(Subscription address:** Bayard Presse Jeunes IRS, 25 Blvd. Taschereau Bur 201, Greenfield Park Quebec, J4U 2G8 Canada.**)**

IT
TODAY ITALIA. ***Title Change.*** (19??)-(19??). Italian. Marketing Finanza Italia, Via Stradella 3, 20129 Milan Italy. **Tel** 011 39 2 29400554, FAX 011 39 2 29401816. ***Continued by*** *Pubblicita Italia Today.*

US/0748-2256
TODAY'S TRIVIA. **VFOAT** Trivia. Began in 1984?. Periodical. English. bm. Reese Publishing Company Inc, 460 West 34th Street, New York NY 10001. **Tel** (212)947-6500. **DD** 793.

US
TOM GENERAL INDEX. **See** General Interest-Abstracting, Bibliographies and Statistics.

CN
TORONTO ROYALIST. English. Three times a year (Feb., May, Sept.). 2.00Can$. Monarchist League of Canada / Toronto, 3050 Yonge Street / Suite 206, Toronto Ontario M4N 2K4 Canada. **Tel** (416)429-4123. **ED** Elizabeth Campbell. **Ad Acc. Circ:** 1,500 (ctrl).

US/0740-7564
TOTH-MAATIAN REVIEW, THE. [Toth-Maatian rev.]. **VFOAT** Toth Maatian Review. Vol. 1, No. 1 (April 1982)-. Periodical. English (French, German, Italian, Spanish and Russian). Four times a year (Jan. Apr., July, Oct.). $50.00. Toth-Maatian Press, 3101 20th Street, H. W. Milnes, Lubbock TX 79410. **Tel** (806)797-2788. **ED** Harold W. Milnes. Index Bound in First Issue (Bound 92th issued in January). cum. index. **Bk Rev. Circ:** 250.
Desc: Criticism and dissident opinion in science. Also in arts, humanities, religion and philosophy. Contains original learned papers in same subject headings.

US
TOWN SQUIRE. English. Twelve times a year. $21.99 (one year); $27.99 (two years); $34.99 (three years). Squire Publishers Inc., 3840 West 75th Street, Prairie Village KS 66208. **Tel** (913)384-6397, FAX (913)384-6418.

US/0892-0443
TOWNSFOLK. **VFOAT** Towns Folk. Periodical. English. mo. $7.00. Townsfolk, 919 North Michigan Avenue, Chicago IL 60611.

US/1071-3719
TRAVERSE (TRAVERSE CITY, MICH.). (TRAVERSE.). (19??)-. Periodical. English. Twelve times a year. $24.00 (one year), $44.00 (two years), $66.00 (three years). Prism Publication Inc., 121 South Union Street, Traverse City MI 49684. **Tel** (616)941-8174, FAX (616)941-8391. **ED** Deborah Wyatt Fellows. **Ad Acc.** ***Continues*** *Traverse, The Magazine, 0746-2735.*

US/0192-8600
TRI-COUNTY FREE-PRESS, THE. (197?)-. Periodical. English. mo. Tri-County Free-Press, 3537 Spencerville Road, Burtonsville MD 20866. ***Continues*** *Burtonsville Shopper.*

FR
TRIBUNE INTERNATIONALE LA VERITE. (19??)-. French. ir. 150.00F France & Europe; 450.00F other. Tribune Internationale la Verite, 87 rue du Faubourg Saint Denis, 75010 Paris France.

US/0041-3488
TRUE CONFESSIONS (NEW YORK). (TRUE CONFESSIONS.). (19??)-. Periodical. English. mo. $17.97. MacFadden Women's Group, 233 Park Avenue South, New York NY 10003. **Tel** (212)979-4800, (800)666-8783.

US/0199-0012
TRUE EXPERIENCE (NEW YORK). (TRUE EXPERIENCE.). (19??)-. Periodical. English. mo (12 issues). $17.95. True Experience, PO Box 2107, Harlan IA 51593. **Tel** (800)666-8783. **(Subscription address:** CDS Agency Hard Copy, PO Box 4966, Des Moines IA 50340.**)** **Ad Acc.**

UK/0262-4125
TRUE STORY LONDON. (1922)-. English. Twelve times a year. Argus Specialist Publications, Queensway House, 2 Queensway Redhill, Surrey RH1 1QS England. **Tel** 0737 768611, FAX 0737 773993, telex 948669 TOPJNL G.
Desc: True accounts from everyday people who have faced a variety of difficult situations.

FR/0984-1466
TUTTI INSIEME PARIS. (1985)-. Periodical. Italian. Eight times a year. L18,500 Italy; L23,500, $16.95 other. European Language Institute, Casella Postale 6, 62019 Recanati Italy. **Tel** 011 39 71 976465. **(Subscription address:** Midwest European Publishing, 8220 Christiana Ave., Skokie IL 60076.**)** **UDC** 087.5.

IT
TUTTOLAZIO. Italian. ir. L50000. Tuttolazio, Via PO Box 35, 00198 Rome Italy. **Tel** 011 39 6 8452874.

UK
TV GUIDE MONTHLY. English. mo. £12.00 UK; £12.50 EIRE; £25.00 Europe; £50.00 other. Murdoch Magazines (England), Finum House, 48 Leicester Square, London WC2H 7FB England. **Tel** 011 44 71 930-9300.

MX/0188-0683
TV Y NOVELAS. [TV nov.]. **VFOAT** Television y Novelas. (1978)-. Periodical. Spanish. bw (26 issues). $38.70. Editorial America SA, 6355 Northwest 36th Street, Miami FL 33166. **Tel** (305)871-6400. **(Subscription address:** CDS, SIFD Agency Control, 1901 Bell Avenue, Demoine, IA 50315 (Phone: (515)246-6812)**)** **DD** 056.
Desc: Popular guide to the excitement, romance and glitter of Spanish-language soap operas.

US/1071-2895
TWIN TERRITORIES (MUSKOGEE, OKLA. 1990). (TWIN TERRITORIES.). Vol. 1, No. 1 (June 1990)-. Periodical. English. Nine times a year (monthly except Apr., May & Sep.). $12.50 (one year), $24.00 (two years), $34.00 (three years) US; $25.00 (one year), $48.00 (two years), $78.00 (three years) other. Twin Territories Publishing Company, PO Box 1426, Muskogee OK 74402. **Tel** (918)683-6809.

US/0041-5537
U.S. NEWS & WORLD REPORT. [U.S. news world rep.]. **VFOAT** U.S. News and World Report; US News and World Report; United States News-World Report. Vol. 24, No. 12 (March 19, 1948)-. Periodical. English. wk. $39.75. US News & World Report Inc, 2400 N Street Northwest, Washington DC 20037. **Tel** (202)955-2000. **(Subscription address:** Neodata / Colorado, PO Box 2606, Boulder Boulder CO 80322.**)** **ED** Merrill McLoughlim and Michael Ruby. **LC** JK1; .U65. **DD** 051. **CODEN** XNWRAV. **Ad Acc. Circ:** 2,200,000. available on microfilm and microfiche from University Microfilms International (UMI); available on an online database (file 647/Full-Text) from DIALOG. Documents available from UMI Article Clearinghouse, Documents on Demand. ***Formed by the union of*** *United States News and World Report, 0363-115X.*
Desc: Focuses on news you can put to immediate, personal use with practical information on health, personal finance, careers and education. Shows how and why national and world events are important to its readers.
Ind/Abst Abr. Read. Guide Period. Lit.; Acad. Abstr. Full Text Elite (Jan. 1984-) [Full Txt.]; Acad. Abstr. (Jan. 1984-); Acad. Ind. [Computer File] (1984-); Acad. Search (Jan. 1984-); Account. Tax Datab. (Jan. 1986-); Aviat. Tradescan [Select. Cov.]; BioBusiness; Bus. ASAP (1992-) [Full Txt.]; Bus. Index (1988-); Cumul. Index Nurs. Allied Health Lit.; Curr. Lit. Fam. Plan. (19??-199?); Curr. Thoughts Trends; Energy Inf. Abstr.; Environ. Abstr.; Expand. Acad. Index (1984-); F&S Index Plus Text, Int. [Select. Cov.]; Foods Adlibra; Gen. BusinessFile (1988-); Gen. Period. Index (1985-); Health Plan. Adminis.; Health Ref. Cent. (1987-) [Full Txt.] [Select. Cov.]; Highw. Res. Abstr.; Hospit. Health Admin. Index; Index Period. Artic. Relat. Law; INFO-SOUTH Abstr.; Infobank (Jan. 1969-); Mag. Artic. Summar. Elite (Jan. 1984-) [Full Txt.]; Mag. Artic. Summar. Select (Jan. 1984-) [Full Txt.]; Mag. Artic. Summar. CD-ROM (Jan. 1984-); Mag. ASAP Plus [Full Txt.]; Mag. ASAP Sel. [Full Txt.]; Mag. Express (1986-) [Full Txt.]; Mag. Index Plus (1989-); Mag. Index. Sel. (1986-); Mag. Search; Middle East Abstr. Index; Mid. Search (Jan. 1984-) [Full Txt.]; Newsp. Period. Abstr. (1986-); NEXIS (Jan. 6, 1975-); PAIS Int. Print; Peace Res. Abstr. J. (1964-1967); Prim. Search (Jan. 1984-); PROMT; Read. Guide Abstr. Select Ed.; Read. Guide Period. Lit.; Resource/One Ondisc; Mag. Index (1977-); TOM Gen. Index (1985-) [Full Txt.]; Trade Ind. ASAP [Full Txt.]; Urban Aff. Abstr.; Vocat. Search (Jan. 1984-) [Full Txt.].

US
UNIPUB BULLETIN. **Main/Corp** Unipub. (Spring 1980)-. Periodical. English. Six times a year. UNIPUB, 4611-F Assembly Drive, Lanham MD 20706-4391. **Tel** (800)274-4888, FAX (301)459-0056, telex 28787 GATT CH. **Circ:** 7,000.
Desc: Newsletter published by the marketing department of Bernan/Unipub. It contains listings, including abstracts of many of the books distributed. It also contains information on the publishers we represent.

US/0042-0506
UNSER TSAYT. [Unzer tsayt]. **Added/Corp** Ogolny Zydowski Zwiazek Robotniczy "Bund" w Polsce. American Representation. **VFOAT** Unser Tsait. No. 1 (Feb. 1941)-. Periodical. Yiddish. Eight times a year (Mar/Apr. and July/Aug. issues combined). $20.00 US; $21.00 other. Jewish Labor Bund, Atran Center of Jewish Culture Building, 25 East 21st Street, 3rd Floor, New York NY 10010. **Tel** (212)475-0055. **ED** Michel Lokiecz. **LC** AP91; .U58. **DD** 059. **Bk Rev**, (Qty: 4). **Circ:** 2,500 (ctrl).
Desc: Theoretical organ interpreting general and Jewish problems in the light of Bund ideology.
Ind/Abst MLA Int. Bibl. Books Artic. Mod. Lang. Lit.

IT
UOMO LIBERO, L'. (Jan. 1980)-. Periodical. Italian. qt. L50000 Italy; L100000 other. Edizioni dell Uomo Libero, Via Pradaccio 8, 21014 Laveno Mombello Va Italy. **Tel** 011 39 332 667220.

IT
UP & DOWN : MENSILE DELL'ISPES DI POLITICA, ECONOMIA, CULTURA E SOCIETA. **Added/Corp** Istituto di Studi Politici, Economici e Sociali. **VFOAT** Up and Down; U & D. (1988)-. Periodical. Italian. mo. Up and Down, ISPES, Via Terme di Traiano 5-A, 00184 Rome Italy.

CN/0507-6528
VABA EESTLASE TAHTRAAMAT. Began with 1953 issue?. Estonian. an. Free Estonian Ltd., 120A Willowdale Avenue, Willowdale Ontario, M2N 4Y2 Canada. **Tel** (416)733-4550. **DD** 059/.94/545.

IT
VALSUSA, LA. (19??)-. Italian. wk. L55000 Italy; L85000 other. Stampa Diocesana Segusina, Piazza S Giusto 14, 10059 Susa Turin Italy. **Tel** 011 39 122 758464.

PR/0738-7628
VEA (HATO REY, P.R.). (VEA.). [Vea]. (19??)-. Periodical. Spanish. wk. $47.25. Vea, Apartado 240, Hato Rey, Puerto Rico 00919. **Tel** (809)721-0095. **ED** Mr. Rodolfo Garcia (editor's address: 1666 Ponce de Leon Avenue, San Juan, PR 00909). **Ad Acc. Circ:** 85,000 (ctrl).

UK/0267-9957
VENEZUELA (LONDON. 1985). (VENEZUELA.). [Venezuela]. **Added/Corp** Latin American Monitor Ltd. (1985)-. English. an (June). $380.00. Business Monitor International, 56 60 St. John Street, London EC1M 4DT England. **Tel** 011 44 71 6083646.

●US/1070-4701
VIBE (NEW YORK, N.Y.). (VIBE.). [Vibe]. **VFOAT** Vibe Magazine. Vol. 1, No. 1 (Sept. 1993)-. Periodical. English. Ten times a year (Jan./Feb & June/July issues combined). $11.95. Time Publishing Ventures Inc., 205 Lexington Avenue, 3rd Floor, New York NY 10016. **Tel** (212)522-9180, (800)477-3974, FAX (212)522-4578. **ED** Alan Light. **LC** IN PROCESS. **DD** 051. **Ad Acc, Adv Mgr:** Susan Coppa, **Tel** (212)522-7082. **Circ:** 200,000. available on an online database from America Online.

US
VISIONES DE LA RAZA. **Added/Corp** Centro Cultural Chicano. **VFOAT** Visiones. (19??)-. Periodical. English. mo. $7.50. Centro Culture Chicano, 2201 Nicollet Avenue South, Minneapolis MN 55404. **Tel** (612)874-1412.
Desc: Topics such as cultural events, news, and entertainment.

IT/1120-4486
VISTO. [Visto]. (1989)-. Periodical. Italian. wk. $145.00. RCS Rizzoli Periodici, Via A Rizzoli 2, 20132 Milan Italy. **Tel** 011 39 2 27200720. **UDC** 070.6.

IT
VITA DEL POPOLO, LA. (19??)-. Italian. wk. L55000 Italy; L120000 other. La Vita del Popolo, Via Longhin 7, 31100 Treviso Italy. **Tel** 011 422 546871.

IT/0042-7268
VITA E SALUTE. [Vita salute]. (1952)-. Periodical. Italian. Eleven times a year. L50000 Italy; L64500 other. Edizioni Adv, Via Chiantigiana 30 Falciani, 50023 Impruneta Italy. **Tel** 011 39 55 2326291. **ED** E Battistia. **UDC** 613. Index available. **Bk Rev**, (Qty: 30/yr). **Ad Acc**, **Adv Mgr:** Franco Evangelist.

US/0042-742X
VITAL SPEECHES OF THE DAY. [Vital speeches day]. Vol. 1 (Oct. 8, 1934)-. Periodical. English. sm (24 issues). $40.00 US; $45.00 other. City News Publishing Company, PO Box 1247, Mt. Pleasant SC 29465-1247. **Tel** (803)881-8733, FAX (803)881-4007. **ED** Thomas F. Daly III. **LC** PN6121; .V52. **DD** 808.85. Index available. cum. index. **Circ:** 13,000 (ctrl). available on microfilm and microfiche from University Microfilms International (UMI). Documents available from UMI Article Clearinghouse, Documents on Demand.
Desc: Covers education, government, current events, history, economics, business and commerce, social progress, and politics.
Ind/Abst ABI/INFORM Glob. Ed.; ABI Inform Ondisc (Jan. 1975-); Acad. Abstr. Full Text Elite (June 1984-); Acad. Abstr. (June 1984-); Acad. Ind. [Computer File] (1984-); Acad. Search (June 1984-); Biogr. Index; Curr. Lit. Fam. Plan.; Energy Inf. Abstr.; Environ. Abstr.; Expand. Acad. Index (1984-); Fut. Surv.; Gen. Period. Index (1985-); Hospit. Health Admin. Index (1977-1989); INFO-SOUTH Abstr.; Mag. Artic. Summar. Elite (June 1984-); Mag. Artic. Summar. Select (June 1984-); Mag. Artic. Summar. CD-ROM (June 1984-); Mag. Index Plus (1989-); Mag. Index. Sel. (1986-); Mag. Search; Middle East Abstr. Index; Newsp. Period. Abstr. (1986-); Read. Guide Abstr. Select Ed.; Read. Guide Period. Lit.; Soc. Sci. Source (Jun. 1984-); Mag. Index (1977-); TOM Gen. Index (1985-); UMI ABI/Inform--Bus. Period. Ondisc (Dec. 1987-) [Full Txt.]; Vocat. Search (June 1984-); Work Relat. Abstr.

IT
VOCE DEI BERICI, LA. La Voce dei Berici, Contra Vescovado 1, 36100 Vicenza Italy.

IT
VOCE DI MILANO, LA. Italian. mo. L50000. Editoriale Il Carrobbio, Via Pavese 119, 20089 Rozzano Milan Italy. ***Continues*** *Martinella.*

CN/0383-1930
VOLKS-CALENDAR FUR DIE DEUTSCHEN IN WEST-CANADA (MICROFICHE). (VOLKS-CALENDAR FUR DIE DEUTSCHEN IN WEST-CANADA.). First published 18--. German. an. McLaren Micropublishing, PO Box 972 Station F, Toronto Ontario M4Y 2N9 Canada. **DD** 053/.1.

US
VOZ, LA. Vol.1 (Sept. 1971)-. Periodical. English (Spanish). mo. $10.80. La Voz / Minnesota, PO Box 19206, Diamond Lake Station, Minneapolis MN 55419. **Tel** (612)825-1490. **ED** Joan E. Ramirez. Index available. **Bk Rev. Ad Acc.** ctrl circ.
Desc: Contains local and national news of interest, personalities and human interest stories, cultural and historical stories.

US
VOZ (SEATTLE, WASH.). (LA VOZ : THE NEWS MAGAZINE OF THE CONCILIO FOR THE SPANISH SPEAKING.). **Added/Corp** Concilio for the Spanish Speaking (Seattle, Wash.). (1979)-. Newspaper. English (Spanish). Ten times a year (Except Jan. & Aug.). $10.00. La Voz Newsmagazine / Seattle, 157 Yesler Way / Suite 209, Seattle WA 98104. **Tel** (206)461-4891. **ED** Bob Marvel. **Bk Rev. Ad Acc. Circ:** 20,000. ***Continues*** *Concilio Newsletter.*
Desc: A statewide publication which is designed to bring attention to issues important to U.S. Latinos in politics, cultural, education and artistic areas.

BL
VOZES. VFOAT Revista de Cultura Vozes. Vol. 1 (July 1907)-. Periodical. Portuguese. mo. Editora Vozes Ltda, R Frei Luis, 100 CP 90023, 25689 Petropolis RJ Brazil. **Tel** 11 55 242 435112. **LC** AP66; .V68.
Ind/Abst HAPI Hisp. Am. Period. Index.

US
WANT ADVERTISER. See Hobbies.

CN/0843-3356
WESTWORLD MAGAZINE (BRITISH COLUMBIA ED.). (WESTWORLD MAGAZINE.). [Westworld mag.]. **Added/Corp** British Columbia Automobile Association. **VFOAT** B.C. Motorist; Westworld. Vol. 8, No. 10 (Dec. 1982)-. Periodical. English. bm. 6.00Can$ Canada; 12.00Can$ other. Canada Wide Magazines Ltd, 401 4180 Lougheed Highway, Burnaby BC V5C 6A7 Canada. **Tel** (604)299-7311, FAX (604)299-9188. **ED** Robin Roberts. **DD** 051. **Ad Acc.** ***Continues*** *Westworld., 0316-1315.*

US/0749-5056
WHOLE EARTH REVIEW. [Whole earth rev.]. No. 44 (Jan. 1985)-. Periodical. English. qt (Mar., Jun., Sept., Dec.). $35.00 institution, $27.00 individual (surface mail). Whole Earth Review, 27 Gate Five Road, Sausalito CA 94965. **Tel** (415)332-1716, (800)783-4903, FAX (415)332-3110, (201)627-5872. **(Subscription address:** Whole Earth Review, PO Box 3000, c/o C. Scarpone, Denville NJ 07834.**) ED** John Sumner. **LC** AP2; .C636. **DD** 004. **[CCC]**. Index available (bound in March issue). **Bk Rev**, (Qty: 250). **Circ:** 50,000. available on microfilm and microfiche from University Microfilms International (UMI); available on an online database (file 647/Full-Text) from DIALOG. Documents available from UMI Article Clearinghouse. ***Formed by the union of*** *Whole Earth Software Review, 0742-0560* ***and*** *Coevolution Quarterly, 0095-134X.*
Desc: General interest articles and reviews of books, equipment and tools on almost every topic from crafts, climbing, computers to learning, legal self-help, landscaping and beyond.
Ind/Abst Acad. Abstr. Full Text Elite (July 1990-); Acad. Abstr. (Dec. 1990-); Acad. Ind. [Computer File] (1984-); Acad. Search (Dec. 1990-); Access (1978-); Altern. Press Index; Book Rev. Index; Comput. Rev. Index (1986-); Expand. Acad. Index (1984-); Gen. Period. Index (1985-); Health Source (Jul. 1990-); Humanit. Index; INFO-SOUTH Abstr.; Mag. ASAP Plus [Full Txt.]; Mag. Index Plus (1989-); Mag. Search; Microcomput. Index (Jan. 1985-); Newsp. Period. Abstr. (1989-); Mag. Index (1984-)(1985-).

UK/0956-5353
WIDEWORLD OXFORD. (WIDEWORLD.). [Wideworld Oxf.]. (1989)-. Periodical. English. Four times a year. £14.95 UK; £23.00 Europe; £28.50 other (airmail). Philip Allan Publishers Ltd, Market Place, Deddington Oxford, OX15 0SE England. **Tel** 011 44 869 38652, FAX 011 44 869 38803. **DD** 304.2.

GW
WIENER. Wiener Verlag GmbH Munich, Altheimer Eck 13, W8000 Munich 2 Germany.

US/0363-3276
WILSON QUARTERLY (WASHINGTON), THE. (THE WILSON QUARTERLY.). [Wilson q.]. **Added/Corp** Woodrow Wilson International Center for Scholars. **VFOAT** WQ. Vol. 1 (Autumn 1976)-. Periodical. English. qt. $24.00 (one year), $39.00 (two year). Circulation Specialists Inc., 49 Richmondville Avenue, Westport CT 06880. **Tel** (203)454-0344. **(Subscription address:** Palm Coast Data, PO Box 420235, Agency Department, Palm Coast FL 32142.**) LC** AS36.W79; A37. **DD** 051. **Bk Rev. Ad Acc. Circ:** 110,000. available on microfilm and microfiche from University Microfilms International (UMI). Documents available from UMI Article Clearinghouse.
Desc: This Smithsonian newsmagazine summarizes developments in research on politics, environment, foreign affairs, history environment, the arts, television, the press, economics and science.
Ind/Abst Acad. Search (July 1993-); Am. Hist. Life (1979-); Am. Bibliogr. Slavic East Europ. Stud.; Am. Humanit. Index (1991-199?); Book Rev. Index; Expand. Acad. Index (1989-); Index Book Rev. Relig. (1979-); Index Period. Artic. Relat. Law; INFO-SOUTH Abstr.; Int. Polit. Sci. Abstr.; Mag. Search; Middle East Abstr. Index; Newsp. Period. Abstr. (1991-); Read. Guide Abstr. Select Ed.; Read. Guide Period. Lit. (1991-); Soc. Sci. Source (Jul. 1993-); Soc. Sci. Index; Soc. Sci. Index Fulltext (Winter 1988-) [Full Txt.]; Middle East J.; U.S. Polit. Sci. Doc.; Urban Aff. Abstr. (1991-).

GW/0040-1528
WISSENSCHAFTLICHE ZEITSCHRIFT. **Main/Corp** Chemnitz. Technische Hochschule, Karl-Marx-Stadt. Vol. 1- 1958/59-. Periodical. German. 73.20M. Technische Hochschule Karl-Marx-Stadt / Leipzig, Leninstrasse 16, O-701 Leipzig Germany. **Tel** 668536. **ED** Christine Hackel. **Bk Rev.** ctrl circ.
Desc: Covers mathematics, physics, chemistry, information processing, theoretical fundamentals of engineering, process engineering, textile engineering, materials engineering, philosophy, economics, education and linguistics.

US/0887-9346
WORLD & I, THE. [World I]. **VFOAT** World and I. Vol. 1, No. 1 (Jan. 1986)-. Periodical. English. mo. $60.00 US; $90.00 Canada and Mexico; $139.00 Western Europe; $165.00 other. The Washington Times Corporation, 3400 New York Avenue Northeast, Washington DC 20002. **Tel** (202)635-4000, (800)822-2822. **ED** Morton A. Kaplan and Michael Marshall. **LC** CB428; .W67. **DD** 909.82/05. Index available (free). cum. index. **Bk Rev. Ad Acc.** ctrl circ. Documents available from Documents on Demand.
Desc: Each issue offers over one hundred articles under these sections: Current Issues, The Arts, Life, Natural Science, Book World, Currents in Modern Thought, Culture, and Photo Essays.
Ind/Abst Am. Bibliogr. Slavic East Europ. Stud.; Book Rev. Index; Energy Inf. Abstr.; Environ. Abstr.; Mag. Artic. Summar. Elite (Jan. 1993-); Mag. Artic. Summar. CD-ROM (Jan. 1993-); Mag. Search; PAIS Int. Print.

US/1048-0862
WORLD CLASS ENTERTAINMENT. (1990)-. Periodical. English. mo. Duncan Publications, 621 Renken Road, Staunton IL 62088. **Tel** (618)637-2202. **ED** Susan Duncan. **Circ:** 100,000.
Desc: Covers fashion, travel, celebrities and entertainment targeted for women between the ages of 25 and 54.

US/0897-9472
WORLD MONITOR. ***Ceased.*** [World monit.]. (1988)-(May 1993). Periodical. English. mo. The Christian Science Publishing Society, 1 Norway Street, Boston MA 02115. **Tel** (800)225-7090. **LC** AP2; .W74839. **DD** 051. **[CCC]**. **Ad Acc.** available on microfilm and microfiche from University Microfilms International (UMI). Documents available from UMI Article Clearinghouse.
Desc: A news-in-perspective covering world events and issues from a global angle including science, education, finance, investment, and culture.
Ind/Abst Abr. Read. Guide Period. Lit.; Acad. Abstr. Full Text Elite (Jan. 1992-May 1993) [Full Txt.]; Acad. Abstr. (Jan. 1992-May 1993); Acad. Search (Jan. 1992-May 1993); Access (1989-?); Am. Bibliogr. Slavic East Europ. Stud.; Gen. Period. Index (1989-); INFO-SOUTH Abstr.; Mag. Artic. Summar. Elite (Jan. 1992-May 1993) [Full Txt.]; Mag. Artic. Summar. Select (Jan. 1992-) [Full Txt.]; Mag. Artic. Summar. CD-ROM (Jan. 1992-May 1993); Mag. Index Plus (1989-); Mag. Search; Mid. Search (Jan. 1992-); Newsp. Period. Abstr. (1991-); Read. Guide Abstr. Select Ed.; Read. Guide Period. Lit.; Mag. Index (1989-); TOM Gen. Index (1991-); Vocat. Search (Jan. 1992-May 1993).

US
WORLD PAPER. VFOAT WorldPaper. (19??)-. Periodical. English (Bulgarian, Chinese, Japanese, Polish and Russian). Twelve times a year. $18.00. World Times Inc., 210 World Trade Center, Boston MA 02210. **Tel** (617)439-5400, FAX (617)439-5415, telex 6817273. **ED** Daniel Passent. cum. index. **Bk Rev**, (Qty: 5 or 6). **Ad Acc, Adv Mgr:** E. Brown. **Circ:** 1,000,000.
Desc: The writers offer fresh perspectives from their native countries on important social, political and economic global issues.

US/0748-223X
WORLDWIDE DIRECTORY OF EAST INDIANS QUARTERLY. VFOAT World Wide Directory of East Indians Quarterly. Directory. English. Siveast Consultants, PO Box 271, 410 South State Street, Dover DE 19901.

US/1051-4155
X MAGAZINE. [X mag]. (Apr. 1990)-. Periodical. English. Four times a year. $10.00 (individuals) US; $15.00 (individuals) Canada and Mexico. Card House Productions, Inc., PO Box 1077, Royal Oak MI 48068-1077. **ED** Jeff Hansen. **DD** 051. **Circ:** 1,000. ***Continues*** *Seize The Duck.*
Desc: Humor and music magazine.

AA/0513-5486
YLLI. (1960)-. Periodical. Albanian. mo. $14.55. Book Distribution Enterprise, Rruga Kavajes, Tirana, Albania. **Tel** 011 355 42 27246. **DD** 059.

KO
YONHAP (TAEGU, KOREA). (YONHAP.). 1953-. Periodical. Korean. W42000. Yonhap Tongsin, 85-1 Susong-dong, Chongno-ku, Seoul 110-140 South Korea. **Tel** 3903-601, FAX 738-0820, telex K23618. **LC** LH7.S66; Y66. **Ad Acc. Circ:** 30,000.

US/0738-887X
YOUNG PEOPLE TODAY. ***Suspended.*** Suspended with Vol. 7, No. 4 (Oct. 1989). Periodical. English. bm. $9.95 US; $12.95 Canada. Young People Today, PO Box 3141, Culver City CA 90231.

US/1042-0843
YOUR FAVORITE COUNTRY STARS. See Music.

US/0894-1335
YOUR WORLD (WASHINGTON, D.C.). (YOUR WORLD.). [Your world]. (198?)-. Periodical. English. ir. $5.00. Educational Resources International, 7219 Blair Road NW, Washington DC 20012. **DD** 051.

ABSTRACTING, BIBLIOGRAPHIES AND STATISTICS

US/0001-334X
ABRIDGED READERS' GUIDE TO PERIODICAL LITERATURE. [Abr. read. guide period. lit.]. **Added/Corp** H.W. Wilson Company. (1935)-. Abstracting/Indexing Service. English. mo (except June-Aug., with annual cumulations). $95.00 US and Canada; $105.00 other. H W Wilson Company, 950 University Avenue, Bronx NY 10452. **Tel** (800)367-6770, (718)588-8400, FAX (718)590-1617, telex 4990003 HWILSON. **ED** Jean Marra. **DD** 051. available on an online database; available on CD-ROM; available on magnetic tape.
Desc: Indexes 82 of the most popular general interest magazines. Ideal for smaller libraries.

US/1056-7496
ACADEMIC ABSTRACTS. (ACADEMIC ABSTRACTS [COMPUTER FILE] : EBSCO CD-ROM / COMPILED BY EBSCO ABSTRACTING & INDEXING.). [Acad. abstr.]. **Added/Corp** EBSCO Abstracting & Indexing. EBSCO Electronic Information. (Apr. 1991)-. Abstracting/Indexing Service. English. qt. $999.00 (quarterly), $1399.00 (academic year), $1799.00 (monthly). EBSCO Publishing / Boston, 83 Pine Street, Peabody MA 01960. **Tel** (800)653-2726 North America, (508)535-8500, FAX (508)535-8545. **ED** Melissa Kummerer. **DD** 016.
Desc: Provides key word access to indexing and abstracts for articles for 790 periodicals most commonly found in academic libraries, plus The New York Times. The periodicals abstracts and indexed in AA have been selected through analysis of periodical purchases in academic and large public libraries. A journal title list based on analysis of collection statistics means that you can be confident that AA provides your patrons with access to the magazines they actually need.

US/1060-6750
ACADEMIC ABSTRACTS FULL TEXT ELITE. (ACADEMIC ABSTRACTS FULL TEXT ELITE [COMPUTER FILE].). [Acad. abstr. full text elite]. **Added/Corp** EBSCO Publishing (Firm). (Oct. 1991)-. Abstracting/Indexing Service. English. qt (plus monthly and academic year). $2599.00 (quarterly), $2999.00 (academic year), $3399.00 (monthly). EBSCO Publishing / Boston, 83 Pine Street, Peabody MA 01960. **Tel** (800)653-2726 North America, (508)535-8500, FAX (508)535-8545. **ED** Melissa Kummerer. **DD** 051.
Desc: Key word access to indexing and abstracts of approximately 780 magazines that are found in the basic Academic Abstracts (CD-ROM) and Academic Abstracts Select (CD-ROM), full text abstracts on 90 of those magazines.

US
ACADEMIC INDEX. [COMPUTER FILE]. Abstracting/Indexing Service. English. mo. $4200.00 (basic subscription), $3600.00 (school year subscription) with InfoTrac Enhanced Workstation; $2700.00 (basic subscription), $2100.00 (school year subscription) without hardware. Information Access Company, 362 Lakeside Drive, Foster City CA 94404. **Tel** (800)227-8431.
Desc: Designed to meet the needs of undergraduate research. Provides indexing and abstracting to approximately 530 scholarly and general interest periodicals.

US/1071-2720
ACADEMIC SEARCH. (ACADEMIC SEARCH [COMPUTER FILE].). **Added/Corp** EBSCO Publishing (Firm). September (1993)-. Abstracting/Indexing Service. English. mo. $5999.00. EBSCO Publishing / Boston, 83 Pine Street, Peabody MA 01960. **Tel** (800)653-2726 North America, (508)535-8500, FAX (508)535-8545. **ED** Melissa Kummerer. available on magnetic tape from EBSCO Publishing - Peabody.
Desc: Contains comprehensive indexing and abstracts for over 2,000 titles selected for their popularity in large academic libraries, including The New York Times and Wall Street Journal.

US/0095-5698
ACCESS (SYRACUSE). (ACCESS.). [Access]. (Jan./Apr. 1975)-. Abstracting/Indexing Service. English. Three times a year. $177.50. John Gordon Burke Publisher Inc., PO Box 1492, Evanston IL 60204. **Tel** (708)866-8625, FAX (708)866-8625. **(Subscription address:** Access: The Supplementary Index to Periodicals, Subscription Office, PO Box 830430, Birmingham AL 35283-0430.**)** **ED** John Gordon Burke. **LC** AI3; .A23. **DD** 016.051. **Bk Rev.** ctrl circ. available on an online database. ***Absorbed*** *Monthly Periodical Index, 0197-6567.*
Desc: Provides indexing for popular and special interest periodicals not indexed in the Readers' Guide to Periodical Literature. New periodicals are regularly added. It provides indexing for significant new periodicals upon publication, the major city and regional magazines, and the major periodicals in library science. It also can provide library patrons with indexing for a carefully balanced list of popular and special interest U.S. periodicals.

US/0730-8574
ASCATOPICS. ***Title Change.*** [Ascatopics]. **Added/Corp** Institute for Scientific Information. **VFOAT** Ascatopics Weekly Literature Alerting Service; Ascatopics Literature Alerting Service. (19??)-(19??). Abstracting/Indexing Service. English. wk. Institute for Scientific Information, 3501 Market Street, Philadelphia PA 19104. **Tel** (215)386-0100, (800)523-1850, FAX (215)386-6362, telex 84-5305. **(Subscription address:** Institute for Scientific Information, PO Box 71416, Chicago IL 60694.**)** **DD** 051. ***Continued by*** *Research Alert.*
Desc: A computer-produced, weekly information service that alerts subscribers to new journal articles on topics relevant to their interests. Over 350 topics in science, social sciences, the arts and humanities are covered.

AT/0004-9816
AUSTRALIAN NATIONAL BIBLIOGRAPHY. ***Ceased.*** [Aust. natl. bibliogr.]. **Added/Corp** National Library of Australia. (Jan. 1961)-(19??). Bibliography. English. mo. National Library of Australia, Parkes Place, Canberra ACT, 2600 Australia. **Tel** 011 61 6 2621374, FAX 011 61 6 2731084. **LC** Z4015; .A96. **NLM** Z 4011 A938. available on microfiche (from the National Library of Australia). ***Continues*** *Books Published in Australia;* ***Continues in part*** *Annual Catalogue of Australian Publications.*
Desc: Lists books, pamphlets, serials, printed music and microforms published in Australia.
Ind/Abst Annu. Bibliogr. Engl. Lang. Lit.; Popul. Index (?-?).

CN/0829-8777
CANADIAN MAGAZINE INDEX. ***Title Change.*** [Can. mag. index]. Vol. 1 (1985)- Vol. 8 (1992). Abstracting/Indexing Service. English. mo. Micromedia Limited, 20 Victoria Street, Toronto Ontario M5C 2N8 Canada. **Tel** (416)362-5211, (800)387-2689, FAX (416)362-6161, telex 06524668. **DD** 051. ***Merged with*** *Canadian Business Index, 0277-8669* ***and*** *Canadian News Index, 0225-7459* ***to form*** *Canadian Index (Toronto, Ont.), 1192-4160.*

UK/0721-5207
CURRENT CONTENTS AFRICA. ***Ceased.*** [Curr. contents Afr.]. **Added/Corp** Stadt- und Universitatsbibliothek Frankfurt am Main. **VFOAT** CCA. Vol. 4, No. 1 (1978)-(19??). Abstracting/Indexing Service. English (Multiple languages). qt (Jan., Apr., July, Oct.). K.G. Saur Verlag KG, A Reed Reference Publishing Company, Part of Reed International PLC, Ortlerstrasse 8, D 81373 Munich Germany. **Tel** 011 49 89 769020, FAX 011 49 89 76902150, telex 5212067-SAUR-D. **(Subscription address:** Stuttgerter Verlagskontor, Postfatch 106016, D-70049 Stuttgart, Germany.**)** ***Continues*** *CCA, Current Contents Afrika, 0340-7632.*

GW/0342-040X
DOKUMENTATIONSDIENST AFRIKA. AUSGEWAHLTE NEUERE LITERATUR. (AUSGEWAHLTE NEUERE LITERATUR. INSTITUT FUER AFRIKA-KUNDE, DOKUMENTATIONS-LEITSTELLE AFRIKA.). [Dokumentationsd. Afr., Ausgew. neuere Lit.]. **Added/Corp** Dokumentations-Leitstelle Afrika (Institut fuer Afrika-Kunde) Deutsches Ubersee-Institut. Referat Afrika. **VFOAT** A Selected Bibliography of Recent Literature; Selected Bibliography of Recent Literature. (1973)-. Bibliography. German (Multiple languages). qt. DM80.00. Deutsches Ubersee Institut / Uebersee-Dokumentation Referat Afrika, Neuer Jungfernstieg 21, 20354 Hamburg Germany. **Tel** 040 3562598. **LC** Z3509; .A9; DT3. **DD** 016.96. Index available. **Circ:** 100 (ctrl).
Desc: Bibliography of selected recent literature on Africa. Mainly articles from journals, most references with abstracts, about 450 references.

US
EXPANDED ACADEMIC INDEX [COMPUTER FILE]. Abstracting/Indexing Service. English. mo. $6500.00 (one workstation), $11000.00 (two workstations), $12500.00 (three workstations), $14000.00 (four workstations) basic subscription with InfoTrac Enhanced Workstation; $5000.00 (one workstation), $8000.00 (two through four workstations) basic subscription; $5700.00 school year subscription with InfoTrac Enhanced Workstation; $4200.00 school year subscription. Information Access Company, 362 Lakeside Drive, Foster City CA 94404. **Tel** (800)227-8431.
Desc: Designed for undergraduate research. Provides indexing and abstracting to approximately 1,440 scholarly and general interest periodicals.

US
GENERAL PERIODICALS INDEX [COMPUTER FILE]. (19??)-. Abstracting/Indexing Service. $8000.00 (with one workstation), $12000.00 (with two workstations), $13500.00 (with three workstations), $15000.00 (with four workstations) basic subscription with InfoTrac Enhanced Workstation; $6500.00 (with one workstation), $9000.00 (with two to four workstations) basic subscription. Information Access Company, 362 Lakeside Drive, Foster City CA 94404. **Tel** (800)227-8431.
Desc: Indexes approximately 1200 popular magazines covering current events, consumer information, arts, and business and management.

US/1064-8380
GENERAL PERIODICALS ONDISC (RESEARCH 1 ED.). (GENERAL PERIODICALS ONDISC [COMPUTER FILE].). [Gen. period. ondisc]. **Added/Corp** University Microfilms International. **VFOAT** General Periodicals on Disc; ProQuest Periodical Abstracts. Research I; Research I; Research One; Periodical Abstracts. Research I. (19??)-. Abstracting/Indexing Service. English. mo. $2275.00 (annual subscription to PA-Research II 1,500 journals), $1575.00 (950 journals), $1275.00 (500 journals). University Microfilms International, 300 North Zeeb Road, Ann Arbor MI 48106-1346. **Tel** (313)761-4700, (800)521-0600 Exts. 2490, 2491, FAX (313)973-1540. **LC** AI3. **DD** 050. available on magnetic tape and an online database from OCLC EPIC.
Desc: Accompanied by installation diskette, user's guide, keyboard template, and quick reference card. Entire articles or individual pages can be laser-printed in facsimiles of their original publication formats. Searchers can access these images through the ProQuest search software.

US
GOOD READING (CHICAGO, ILL.). ***Suspended.*** (GOOD READING / PREPARED BY THE COMMITTEE ON COLLEGE READING OF THE NATIONAL COUNCIL OF TEACHERS OF ENGLISH.). **Added/Corp** National Council of Teachers of English. Committee on College Reading. National Council of Teachers of English. Committee on College Reading. College English Association. (1934)-Suspended (199?). English. ir. $8.00. The Sunshine Press, PO Box 40, Litchfield IL 62056. **Tel** (217)324-3425. **ED** Peggy Kuethe. **LC** Z1035; .G6. **DD** 011/.7. **Circ:** 8,000. ***Continues*** *Students' Guide to Good Reading (New York, N.Y.).*
Desc: A wide variety of topics including places of interest, household hints, brief sports, current events, humor, poetry and people.

US/0270-8558
HISPANIC AMERICAN PERIODICALS INDEX (LOS ANGELES, CALIF.). (HAPI, HISPANIC AMERICAN PERIODICALS INDEX.). [Hisp. Am. period. index]. **Added/Corp** University of California, Los Angeles. Latin American Center. **VFOAT** Hispanic American Periodicals Index; HAPI. (1974)-. Abstracting/Indexing Service. English (Spanish, Portuguese, French and German). an (May). $385.00. Regents of the University of California at Los Angeles, 405 Hilgard Avenue, Los Angeles CA 90024-1447. **Tel** (310)825-6634. **ED** Barbara G. Valk. **LC** Z1605; .H16; F1408. **DD** 016.98/0005. **Bk Rev. Circ:** 500. available on CD-ROM from National Information Service Corporation (NISC); available on an online database from UCLA Latin American Center; and RLIN. Documents available.
Desc: Reference annual that indexes by subject and author, over 360 scholarly journals in social sciences and the humanities on the subject of Latin America and the Latin Americans in the US.

US/0147-5630
INDEX TO FREE PERIODICALS. ***Title Change.*** [Index free period.]. Vol. 1 (Jan./June 1976)-Vol. 18, No. 2. Abstracting/Indexing Service. English. sa. Pierian Press, PO Box 1808, Ann Arbor MI 48106. **Tel** (313)434-5530, (800)678-2435, FAX (313)434-6409. **ED** Arnold Rzepecki. **LC** AI3; .I53. **DD** 016.051. **Bk Rev. Ad Acc.** ***Merged into*** *Matter of Fact.*
Desc: An author, title, and subject index to approximately 42 free periodicals chosen to provide balanced coverage of subjects in all fields. Publications from governmental agencies, research centers, universities, foundations, major corporations, and other sources are covered.

PH/0073-599X
INDEX TO PHILIPPINE PERIODICALS. **Added/Corp** University of the Philippines. Inter-Departmental Reference Service. University of the Philippines. Library. (Oct. 1955/Sept. 1956)-. Abstracting/Indexing Service. English. qt. $25.00. University of the Philippines Library, Diliman Quezon Philippines. **LC** AI3; .I63. **DD** 052. **NLM** Z 3291 Q51. Index available. cum. index. **Bk Rev. Circ:** 1,000. available in microform; available on microfilm; available on CD-ROM; available on diskette.

US/0276-2676
JOHN M. ECHOLS COLLECTION ON SOUTHEAST ASIA ACCESSIONS LIST, THE. [John M. Echols Collect. Southeast Asia, Access. list]. **Main/Corp** Cornell University. Libraries. **Added/Corp** Cornell University. Southeast Asia Program. Cornell University. Libraries. Echols Collection on Southeast Asia Accessions List. Vol.17, No.8 (Aug. 1977)-. Periodical. English (Multiple languages). mo. $20.00. Southeast Asia Program, East Hill Plaza, Cornell University, Ithaca NY 14850. **Tel** (607)255-8038, FAX (607)277-1904. **(Subscription address:** East Hill Plaza,

Ithaca, NY 14850) **ED** John H Badgley. **LC** Z3221; .C86a; DS520. **DD** 016.959. **Circ:** 190. ***Continues*** *Southeast Asia Accessions List, 0589-7351.*

US/1041-1151
MAGAZINE ARTICLE SUMMARIES (CD-ROM ED.). (MAGAZINE ARTICLE SUMMARIES [COMPUTER FILE] : EBSCO CD-ROM.). [Mag. artic. summ.]. **Added/Corp** EBSCO Abstracting & Indexing. EBSCO Electronic Information. (Jan. 1989)-. Abstracting/Indexing Service. English. Ten times a year. $799.00 (quarterly and school year quarterly), $1199.00 (academic year), $1599.00 (monthly). EBSCO Publishing / Boston, 83 Pine Street, Peabody MA 01960. **Tel** (800)653-2726 North America, (508)535-8500, FAX (508)535-8545. **ED** Melissa Kummerer. **DD** 051.
Desc: Provides key word access to indexing and abstracts from 400 general interest periodicals plus the New York Times and Magill Book Reviews. The magazines abstracted and indexed have been selected through analysis of periodical purchases in school and small public libraries. This means that you can be confident that MAS provides your patrons with access to the magazines in your collection -- the ones they actually need.

US/1060-6769
MAGAZINE ARTICLE SUMMARIES FULL TEXT ELITE. (MAGAZINE ARTICLE SUMMARIES FULL TEXT ELITE [COMPUTER FILE].). [Mag. artic. summ. full text elite]. **Added/Corp** EBSCO Publishing (Firm). (Oct. 1991)-. Abstracting/Indexing Service. English. an (plus quarterly, monthly, and academic year). $2399.00 (quarterly and school year quarterly), $2799.00 (academic year), $3199.00 (monthly). EBSCO Publishing / Boston, 83 Pine Street, Peabody MA 01960. **Tel** (800)653-2726 North America, (508)535-8500, FAX (508)535-8545. **ED** Melissa Kummerer. **DD** 051.
Desc: Provides abstracts and indexing on approximately 400 magazines found in Magazine Article Summaries (CD-ROM), and Magazine Article Summaries/Select (CD-ROM) with full text on 90 of those magazines.

US/1058-0255
MAGAZINE ARTICLE SUMMARIES FULL TEXT SELECT. (MAGAZINE ARTICLE SUMMARIES FULL TEXT SELECT [COMPUTER FILE].). [Mag. artic. summ. full text sel.]. **Added/Corp** EBSCO Publishing (Firm). (July 1991)-. Abstracting/Indexing Service. English. an (also quarterly, monthly, and academic year). $1799.00 (quarterly and school year quarterly), $2199.00 (academic year), $2599.00 (monthly). EBSCO Publishing / Boston, 83 Pine Street, Peabody MA 01960. **Tel** (800)653-2726 North America, (508)535-8500, FAX (508)535-8545. **ED** Melissa Kummerer. **DD** 051.
Desc: Covers the same magazines as Magazine Article Summaries, plus full text abstracts on 60 of the most popular magazines.

US/0895-3376
MAGAZINE ARTICLE SUMMARIES (PRINT ED.). ***Ceased.*** (MAGAZINE ARTICLE SUMMARIES.). [Mag. artic. summ.]. (1987)-Last issue of print edition June 30, (1993). Abstracting/Indexing Service. English. wk. EBSCO Publishing / Boston, 83 Pine Street, Peabody MA 01960. **Tel** (800)653-2726 North America, (508)535-8500, FAX (508)535-8545. **ED** Gerald M Seaman. **LC** AP2; .P79. **DD** 051. cum. index (every two months). available on CD-ROM from EBSCO Publishing - Peabody. ***Continues*** *Popular Magazine Review, 0740-3763.*
Desc: Contains index and abstract articles from approximately 230 magazines and The New York Times. Indexing is based on the Sears List of Subject Headings. This timely reference service is available for middle schools, high schools, colleges, universities and public libraries.

US
MAGAZINE ASAP PLUS [COMPUTER FILE]. Abstracting/Indexing Service. English. mo. $1400.00. Information Access Company, 362 Lakeside Drive, Foster City CA 94404. **Tel** (800)227-8431.
Desc: Provides full text of approximately 97 general interest magazines frequently found in public libraries.

US
MAGAZINE ASAP SELECT [COMPUTER FILE]. Abstracting/Indexing Service. English. mo. Information Access Company, 362 Lakeside Drive, Foster City CA 94404. **Tel** (800)227-8431.
Desc: Provides full text of 50 of the most frequently requested titles indexed in the Magazine Index Select.

US
MAGAZINE EXPRESS [COMPUTER FILE]. (1993)-. Abstracting/Indexing Service. English. ir. $5,650.00. University Microfilms International, 300 North Zeeb Road, Ann Arbor MI 48106-1346. **Tel** (313)761-4700, (800)521-0600 Exts. 2490, 2491, FAX (313)973-1540. available on magnetic tape; available in reprints from Article Clearinghouse.
Desc: Provides access to 85 of the most frequently requested titles in Resource/One. Researchers can access periodicals such as Time and Business Week, as well as more specialized titles like Rolling Stone, Commentary and Sports Illustrated. Full-image coverage begins with 1988 material, and articles are updated with the corresponding records in the Resource/One database.

US
MAGAZINE INDEX, THE. (April 1978)-. Abstracting/Indexing Service. English. ir. $2532.00. Information Access Company, 362 Lakeside Drive, Foster City CA 94404. **Tel** (800)227-8431. **(Subscription address:** Information Access Company, PO Box 61000, Department 1851, San Francisco CA 84161.**)** available on an online database; available on CD-ROM.
Desc: Provides the general public, scholars, and business professionals with a comprehensive resource to keep track of current affairs, business, sports, fashion, performing arts, popular culture, political opinion, contemporary lifestyles, recreation and travel, consumer product evaluations, health, and science and technology.

US
MAGAZINE INDEX PLUS [COMPUTER FILE]. Abstracting/Indexing Service. English. mo. $3880.00 (with InfoTrac workstation), $2880.00 (without hardware) basic subscription; $3100.00 (with InfoTrac workstation), $2100.00 (without hardware) school year subscription; $950.00 add-on backfile. Information Access Company, 362 Lakeside Drive, Foster City CA 94404. **Tel** (800)227-8431.
Desc: Provides complete indexing and abstracting to over 430 general interest periodicals. Provides research on travel and leisure, consumer surveys, computer technology, current issues, arts and entertainment, business, people, health and fitness, world affairs, and personal finance.

US
MAGAZINE INDEX SELECT MICROFICHE. Abstracting/Indexing Service. English. mo. Information Access Company, 362 Lakeside Drive, Foster City CA 94404. **Tel** (800)227-8431.

US
MAGAZINE INDEX SELECT [COMPUTER FILE]. Abstracting/Indexing Service. English. mo. Information Access Company, 362 Lakeside Drive, Foster City CA 94404. **Tel** (800)227-8431. available on microfiche from Information Access Company.
Desc: Provides complete indexing and abstracting to over 220 of the most requested periodicals. Provides information on current issues, business, health and fitness, travel and leisure, arts and entertainment, people, products, world affairs, and personal finance.

US/1071-2739
MAGAZINE SEARCH. (MAGAZINE SEARCH [COMPUTER FILE].). **Added/Corp** EBSCO Publishing (Firm). (September 1993)-. Abstracting/Indexing Service. English. mo. $5999.00. EBSCO Publishing / Boston, 83 Pine Street, Peabody MA 01960. **Tel** (800)653-2726 North America, (508)535-8500, FAX (508)535-8545. **ED** Melissa Kummerer. available on magnetic tape from EBSCO Publishing - Peabody.
Desc: Provides access to abstracts and indexing coverage of approximately 1,970 journals. Journals abstracted have been selected for their applicability to and subscriber volume in large public libraries.

US/0899-1553
READERS' GUIDE ABSTRACTS. CD-ROM. Abstracting/Indexing Service. English. mo. $1995.00. H W Wilson Company, 950 University Avenue, Bronx NY 10452. **Tel** (800)367-6770, (718)588-8400, FAX (718)590-1617, telex 4990003 HWILSON. **ED** Robert Genovesio. Index available. cum. index. **Bk Rev.** ctrl circ. available on diskette from WILSONSEARCH; available on magnetic tape from WILSONTAPE; available in print; available on an online database from WILSONLINE; available on microfiche.
Desc: Cumulative abstracting service covering general interest periodical literature found in Readers' Guide.

US
READERS' GUIDE ABSTRACTS SELECT EDITION. Abstracting/Indexing Service. English. ir (available 4, 9 and 12 times a year). $395.00 quarterly option; $695.00 school year option; $995.00 monthly option. H W Wilson Company, 950 University Avenue, Bronx NY 10452. **Tel** (800)367-6770, (718)588-8400, FAX (718)590-1617, telex 4990003 HWILSON. cum. index. available on CD-ROM from WILSONDISC. ***Continues*** *Readers' Guide Abstracts School and Public Library Edition.*
Desc: Provides indexing and abstracting of selected articles from core periodicals.

US/0034-0464
READERS' GUIDE TO PERIODICAL LITERATURE. [Read. guide period. lit.]. **VFOAT** Cumulative Index to a Selected List of Periodicals. Vol. 1, No. 3 (Apr. 1901)-. Abstracting/Indexing Service. English. Seventeen times a year (including quarterly cumulations and annual cumulation). $190.00 US and Canada; $205.00 other. H W Wilson Company, 950 University Avenue, Bronx NY 10452. **Tel** (800)367-6770, (718)588-8400, FAX (718)590-1617, telex 4990003 HWILSON. **LC** AI3.R4. **DD** 051. **NLM** ZAI 3 R286. cum. index. available on an online database from WILSONLINE; available on CD-ROM from WILSONDISC; available on magnetic tape from WILSONTAPE; available on diskette from WILSONSEARCH. ***Continues*** *Monthly Cumulative Index to ... Important Periodicals;* ***Absorbed*** *Cumulative Index to a Selected List of Periodicals (Annual).*
Desc: Indexes a core list of popular magazines, central to any school, college, or public library collection.

US
RESOURCE/ONE ONDISC [COMPUTER FILE]. Abstracting/Indexing Service. English. University Microfilms International, 300 North Zeeb Road, Ann Arbor MI 48106-1346. **Tel** (313)761-4700, (800)521-0600 Exts. 2490, 2491, FAX (313)973-1540. available in reprints from Article Clearinghouse; available on magnetic tape; available in microform.
Desc: This periodical and newspaper resource features complete bibliographic data, indexing and concise abstracts to about 140 general-reference periodicals, plus citations to information from The New York Times Current Events Edition and USA Today. Coverage begins with 1986 material. Database size ranges from 20 to 30MB per year.

US
TOM GENERAL INDEX. Abstracting/Indexing Service. English. Information Access Company, 362 Lakeside Drive, Foster City CA 94404. **Tel** (800)227-8431. available on CD-ROM from Information Access Company.
Desc: Contains over 150 periodicals high schools subscribe to most.

GENERAL INTEREST-AFRICA

SA
AFRICA ENTERPRISE UPDATE. See Ethnic Interests.

UK/0267-6362
AFRICA EVENTS. ***Ceased.*** [Afr. events]. (Oct. 1984)-(19??). Periodical. English. mo (Plus one double issue). Dar es Salaam Ltd, 55 57 Banner Street, London EC1Y 8PX England. **Tel** 011 44 71 6083454. **LC** DT1; .A2137. **DD** 960/.05.

UK
AFRICA NOW. ***Ceased.*** 1981-?. Periodical. English. mo. Pan African Publishing Ltd, Dilke House, Malet Street, London WC1E 7JA England. **Tel** (01)631-4881, telex 266667 PANAF G. **ED** Peter Enahoro. **LC** DT1; .A2157. **DD** 960/.05. **Bk Rev. Ad Acc. Circ:** 85,000.
Desc: A new analysis magazine specializing on African affairs, personalities and events. It includes a section on business.

BE
AFRICA-TERVUREN. 7- 1961-. Periodical. Dutch (Flemish, French, English and German). qt. $24.51. Amis du Musee Royale du l'Afrique Centrale, 1980 Tervuren, Tervuren Belgium. ***Continues*** *Congo-Tervuren.*
Ind/Abst Anthropol. Lit.; Ethnoarts Index; MLA Int. Bibl. Books Artic. Mod. Lang. Lit.

UK/0261-1562
AFRICA TODAY (LONDON, ENGLAND). (AFRICA TODAY.). 1st Ed. (1981)-. English. qt. $18.00 (individuals), $48.00 (institutions). Africa Journal Ltd, Kirkman House, 54A Tottenham Court Road, London W1P 0BT England. **Tel** 011 44 71 637 9341. **ED** Jendayi Frazer. **LC** DT1; .A2213. **DD** 960/.05. **Circ:** 16,000. ***Continues in part*** *Africa Year Book and Who's Who, 0141-3341.*
Desc: Basic documents on continental organisations and country surveys for each country covering history, geography, politics, economics and statistical tables.

MW/0300-4651
AFRICAN, THE. ***Title Change.*** [African]. (1950)-. Periodical. English. Likuni Press, PO Box 133, Lilongwe Malawi. ***Continued by*** *Odini.*

US/1045-2303
AFRICAN COMMENTARY. ***Ceased.*** (AFRICAN COMMENTARY : A JOURNAL OF PEOPLE OF AFRICAN DESCENT.). [Afr. comment.]. Vol. 1, Issue 1 (Oct. 1989)-(19??). Periodical. English. mo. African Commentary Corp, 29 Pray Street, Amherst MA 01002-9903. **DD** 960. **Bk Rev. Ad Acc. Circ:** 60,000. available on microfilm and microfiche from University Microfilms International (UMI).
Desc: A Pan-African magazine devoted to the analysis of political, economic, social and cultural events and issues in the black world (Africa and the African diaspora).

US
AFRICAN CONTINENT NEWS. Newspaper. English. mo. $28.00. ACN Publishing Co., PO Box 1096, Massillon OH 44648. **Tel** (210)830-1277. **ED** John Misha.
Desc: U.S. based newspaper covering the continent of Africa.

II/0002-0125
AFRICAN RECORDER. Vol. 1 (Jan. 1/14, 1962)-. English. Twenty-six times a year (Every other

Tuesday and Wednesday). $136.00 (surface mail), $201.00 (airmail) includes binder;. Asian Recorder, A 126 Niti Bagh, New Delhi 110049, India. **Tel** 11 91 11 665405. **(Subscription address:** Prints India, 11 Darya Ganj, New Delhi 110002 India.**) ED** A. K. B. Menon. **LC** DT1; .A228. Index Available, published separately, free-automatically sent. cum. index. **Circ:** 1,000 (ctrl).
Desc: A reference journal on African events, with an index. Events in African countries listed under each country with sources of information are recorded.

US/0002-0206
AFRICAN STUDIES REVIEW. [Afr. stud. rev.]. **Added/Corp** African Studies Association. Vol. 13 (Apr. 1970)-. Periodical. English. Three times a year (Apr., Sept., and Dec.). Based on personal income. African Studies Association, Emory University, Credit Union Building, Atlanta GA 30322. **Tel** (404)329-6410, FAX (404)329-6433. **LC** DT1; .A2293. **DD** 916. cum. index. **Bk Rev. Ad Acc.** ctrl circ. available on microfilm and microfiche from University Microfilms International (UMI). Documents available from UMI Article Clearinghouse. ***Continues** African Studies Bulletin, 0568-1537;* ***Absorbed** ASA Review of Books. African Studies Association, 0364-1686.*
Ind/Abst ABC POL SCI; Abstr. Anthropol.; Acad. Abstr. Full Text Elite (Jan. 1992-); Acad. Abstr. (Jan. 1992-); Acad. Search (Jan. 1992-); Am. Hist. Life (1972-); Appl. Soc. Sci. Index Abstr.; Curr. Geogr. Publ. (199?-); Ethnoarts Index; Expand. Acad. Index (1989-); Hist. Source (Jan. 1992-); Hum. Rights Intern. Rep.; INFO-SOUTH Abstr.; Int. Bibliogr. Sociol.; Int. Polit. Sci. Abstr.; Leis. Recreat. Tour. Abstr.; Mag. Search; Middle East Abstr. Index; Newsp. Period. Abstr. (1991-); Rural Dev. Abstr.; Soc. Sci. Source (Jan. 1992-); Soc. Sci. Index; Soc. Sci. Index Fulltext (April 1988-) [Full Txt.]; World Agric. Econ.

JA/0285-1601
AFRICAN STUDY MONOGRAPHS.
Added/Corp Kyoto Daigaku. Research Committee for African Area Studies. Vol. 1 (1981)-. Periodical. English (French). an. Kyoto University / African Studies Centre, 46 Shimoadachi-cho Yoshida Sakyo-ku Kyoto 606 Japan, Sakyo Kyoto 606 Japan. **Tel** 011 81 75 7537803, FAX 011 81 75 7537810. **ED** Y. Takamura, S. Araki, M. Ichikawa, M. Kakeya, T. Kano, H. Kawanabe, N. Koyama, K. Kyuma, I. Ohta, M. Shigeta, J. Tanaka and T. Yoneyama. **LC** DT1; .K9a. **DD** 960/.05. **Circ:** 1,000 (ctrl). ***Continues** Kyoto University African Studies.*
Desc: Aims to contribute to the advancement of researches on the nature of Africa, the people there and their cultures, and interrelations between them.
Ind/Abst Anthropol. Lit.; Rural Dev. Abstr.; World Agric. Econ.

JA/0286-9667
AFRICAN STUDY MONOGRAPHS. SUPPLEMENTARY ISSUE. No. 1 (1982)-. English. ir. Free. Kyoto University / African Studies Centre, 46 Shimoadachi-cho Yoshida Sakyo-ku Kyoto 606 Japan, Sakyo Kyoto 606 Japan. **Tel** 011 81 75 7537803, FAX 011 81 75 7537810. **ED** Y Takamura, S Araki, M Ichikawa, M Kakeya, T Kano, H Kawanabe, N Koyama, K Kyuma, I Ohta, M Shigeta, J Tanaka, T Yoneyama. **LC** DT1; .A2297. **DD** 960/.05. **UDC** 960. **Circ:** 1,000 (ctrl).
Desc: This journal aims to contribute to the advancement of researches on the nature of Africa, the people there and their cultures, and interrelations between them.
Ind/Abst Anthropol. Lit.

US/0747-8879
AFRICAN WORLD NEWS, THE. ***Suspended.*** [Afr. world news]. Suspended. Periodical. English. mo. $22.00. African World News Network Inc, PO Box 4628, Atlanta GA 30302. **Tel** (404)699-7112. **ED** Mohamed Y Sillah. **DD** 960. **Bk Rev. Ad Acc. Circ:** 25,000.
Desc: A news magazine covering continental Africa. It is uniquely qualified to report Africa's economic, political, and social aspirations through the highest standard of journalism.

SA/0002-032X
AFRICANA NOTES AND NEWS.
Suspended. [Afr. notes news]. **VFOAT** Africana Aantekeninge en Nuus. Vol. 1 (Dec. 1943)-Vol. 30, No. 6. Periodical. English (Afrikaans). qt. R20.00. Africana Museum, Johannesburg Public Library, Market Square, Johannesburg South Africa. **Tel** 011 27 11 8363787. **ED** E.B. Nagelgast. **LC** DT911; .A3. **DD** 968.005. Index available. cum. index. **Bk Rev. Ad Acc. Circ:** 450 (ctrl). available in microform from Xerox; available on microfilm and microfiche from University Microfilms International (UMI).
Desc: A journal of scholarship intended for Africana collectors of books, maps, pictures, numismatics, furniture, etc.
Ind/Abst Am. Hist. Life (1963-); Annu. Bibliogr. Engl. Lang. Lit.; ARTbibliogr. Mod. (1985-).

UA
AFRICANIST NEWS AND VIEWS / ISSUED BY THE PAN AFRICANIST CONGRESS OF AZANIA (SOUTH AFRICA). **Added/Corp** Pan Africanist Congress. No. 1 (June 1966)-. Periodical. English. **LC** WMLC L 82/80. ***Continues** Pan Africanist News and Views.*
Ind/Abst Hum. Rights Intern. Rep.

BE/0772-084X
AFRIKA FOCUS : TIJDSCHRIFT VAN DE AVRUG. **Added/Corp** AVRUG (Association). **VFOAT** Afrika-Focus. Vol. 1 (1985)-. Periodical. Dutch (English and French). ***Continues** AVRUG-Bulletin, 0772-0793.*
Ind/Abst MLA Int. Bibl. Books Artic. Mod. Lang. Lit.

FR/0396-6046
AFRIQUE EXPANSION. [Afr. Expans.]. (1976)-. Periodical. French. ir (48 issues). 3900.00F France; 4050.00F other. Publications du Moniteur, 17 rue d'Uzes, 75108 Paris Cedex 02 France. **Tel** 011 33 1 40133030, FAX 011 33 1 40419495 customer service, 40133037 advertising, telex UPRESSE 680876 F. **UDC** 33.

SG/0002-0532
AFRIQUE NOUVELLE. ***Ceased.*** (19??)-(19??). Periodical. French. wk. Alcino Louis DA Costa, 9 rue Paul Holle, BP 283, Dakar Senegal Africa. **LC** AP27; .A58. **DD** 054/.1.

UA
AKHIR SAAH. **VFOAT** Akher Saa. (1934)-. Periodical. Arabic. ir. $90.00. Akhbar EL Youm, 13 Sahafa Street, Cairo Egypt.

GW/0720-5139
AKTUELLER INFORMATIONSDIENST AFRIKA. BEIHEFT / INSTITUT FUER AFRIKA-KUNDE, DOKUMENTATIONS-LEITSTELLE AFRIKA. **Added/Corp** Dokumentations-Leitstelle Afrika (Institut fuer Afrika-Kunde). (1981)-. Monographic series. German (English and French). ir. Price varies per volume. Institut fuer Afrika-Kunde, Neuer Jungfernstieg 21, D 20354 Hamburg Germany. **Tel** 011 49 40 3562523, 011 49 40 3562524.

LY
AL-BAYT. Periodical. Arabic. Al-Muassasah Al-Ammah Lil-Sihafah, PO Box 4814, Tarabulus Al-Gharb Libya. **LC** AP95.A6; B28.

LY
AL-FUSUL AL-ARBAAH. **Added/Corp** Ittihad al-Udaba wa-al-Kuttab bi-al-Jamahiriyah al-Arabiyah al-LÂibiyah al-Shabiyah al-Ishtirakiyah. Vol. 1 No. 1 (Jan. 1978)-. Periodical. Arabic. qt. 1.00LD. Ittihad Al-Udaba Wa-Al-Kuttab Bi-Al-Jamahiriyah Al-Arabiyah, Al-Libiyah Al-Shabiyah Al-Ishtirakiyah, PO Box 1017, Tarabulus Libya. **LC** AP95.A6; F87.

SJ
AL-JIL. No. 1 (May 1975)-. Arabic. £s0.05 single issue. Dar Al-Nashr Al-Tarbawi, PO Box 258, Al-Khartum Sudan. **LC** AP215.A7; J54.

MR
AL-MIHRAJAN. **VFOAT** Mihrajane. Vol. 1, No. 1 (April 1983)-. Periodical. Arabic. mo. 100.00. 307 Shari Al-Aqid Idris Al-Harti, Al-Dar Al-Bayda 04 Morocco. **LC** AP95.A6; M55.

UA
AL-MUSAWWAR. (1924)-. Periodical. Arabic. wk. $28.00. Georges Bookshop, PO Box 220, Cairo Egypt. **Tel** 011 20 2 3551827, 2590104. **ED** George Andrawes Rezk. **LC** AP95.A6; M83.

UA
AL-THAQAFAH AL-USBUIYAH. No. 48 (1974)-. Periodical. Arabic. £E0.30. Wizarat Al-Magafah, 27 Shari Abd Al-Khaliq Tharwat, Al-Qahirah United Arab Republic Egypt. **LC** AP95.A6; T55. ***Continues** Tahrir (Cairo, Egypt : 1973).*

TI
ALIF. No. 1- Dec. 1971-. French (Arabic). 2. Ceres Production, 8 Avenue Montplaisir, Tunis Tunisia. **LC** AP27; .A6. **DD** 050.
Ind/Abst Middle East Abstr. Index.

CG
AMUKA. **Added/Corp** Institut Superieur d'Etudes Sociales de Bukavu. Institut Superieur de Developpement Rural de Bukavu. (19??)-. Periodical. French. CERPRU, ISDR BP 2849, Bukavu Zaire. **LC** AP27; .A63. **DD** 054/.1.

●US/1062-550X
ANALYSIS OF AFRICAN AFFAIRS.
Added/Corp Institute on African Affairs. (1992)-. Periodical. English. qt. $15.00. Institute on African Affairs, 733 15th Street NW, Suite 700, Washington DC 20005.

FR/0066-2607
ANNUAIRE DE L'AFRIQUE DU NORD.
Added/Corp France. Centre National de la Recherche Scientifique. Aix-Marseilles, Universite d'. Centre de Recherches et d'Etudes sur les Societes Mediterraneenes. Aix-Maseilles, Universite d'. Centre de Recherches sur l'Afrique Mediterraneenne. Aix-Marseille, Universite d'. Centre d'Etudes Nord-Africaines. **VFOAT** Annuaire d'Afrique du Nord. Vol. 1 (1962)-. French. ir. 560.00F. Editions du CNRS, 22 rue Saint Armand, F 75015 Paris France. **Tel** 011 33 1 45075050. **(Subscription address:** CNRS Editions, 20-22 rue Saint Amand, c/o Mme. Bodet, 75015 Paris France.**) LC** DT181; .A74. cum. index. **Circ:** 1,500.

Desc: Studies, current issues, columns, chronology, documents and scientific and cultural news, with a bibliography of works relating to North Africa.
Ind/Abst Int. Bibliogr. Sociol.; Int. Polit. Sci. Abstr.; LABORDOC.

US/0278-2219
ASA NEWS (LOS ANGELES, CALIF.). (ASA NEWS : FOR AFRICAN STUDIES ASSOCIATION MEMBERS.). [ASA news]. **Added/Corp** African Studies Association. **VFOAT** A.S.A. News. **VAT** African Studies Association News. Vol. 14, No. 1 (Jan./March 1981)-. Periodical. English. Four times a year. Based on personal income. African Studies Association, Emory University, Credit Union Building, Atlanta GA 30322. **Tel** (404)329-6410, FAX (404)329-6433. **LC** DT19.9.U5; A65. **DD** 960/.006/01. **Ad Acc. Circ:** 2,000 (ctrl). ***Continues** African Studies Newsletter, 0002-0214.*
Desc: Newsletter for the members of the African Studies Association.
Ind/Abst Ethnoarts Index; Hum. Rights Intern. Rep.

SA
AWU. **VFOAT** A.W.U. Began with Winter 1979. Periodical. English. Three times a year. Editor AWU Magazine, PO Box 909, Durban 4000 South Africa. **LC** AP9; .A9. **DD** 052.

FR/0523-6207
BINGO. (Feb. 1953)-. Periodical. French. mo. 72.00F France; 104.00F Black Africa; 168.00F other. SAPEF, 11 rue de Teheran, 75008 Paris France. **Tel** 33/1/45697476, FAX 33/1/45632248, telex 641916F. **Bk Rev. Ad Acc. Circ:** 50,000.
Desc: General information on Black Africa.

BS/0525-5090
BOTSWANA NOTES AND RECORDS. [Botsw. notes rec.]. **Added/Corp** National Museum and Art Gallery (Botswana) Botswana Society. Vol. 1 (1968)-. English. an. $25.00 (includes membership Botswana Society). Botswana Society, PO Box 71, Gaborone Botswana Africa. **Tel** 011 267 31 351500, FAX (267)372095. **ED** Doreen Nteta. **LC** DT790; .B67. Index available. cum. index. **Bk Rev. Circ:** 700.
Desc: Medium for publication of research and articles of scholarship on Botswana in all disciplines, including anthropology, biology, history, law, wildlife, etc.
Ind/Abst Am. Hist. Life (1968-); Anthropol. Index; Field Crop Abstr.; Grasslands For. Abstr.; Int. Bibliogr. Sociol.; Leis. Recreat. Tour. Abstr.; MLA Int. Bibl. Books Artic. Mod. Lang. Lit.; Rural Dev. Abstr.; World Agric. Econ.

SA
BRABY'S CAPE PROVINCE DIRECTORY. **See** Travel and Tourism-Abstracting, Bibliographies and Statistics.

FR/0249-728X
BULLETIN DES ETUDES AFRICAINES.
Added/Corp Institut National des Langues et Civilisations Orientales. **VFOAT** Bulletin des Etudes Africaines de l'Inalco. Vol. 1, No. 1 (1981)-. Bulletin. French (English). Twice a year. 185.00F. Publications Langues O Inalco, 2 rue de Lille, 75343 Paris Cedex 07 France. **Tel** 011 33 1 49264274. **ED** Gerard Philippson. **Bk Rev. Ad Acc. Circ:** 300.
Desc: African studies-linguistics, anthropology, history of Africa, and literature.

FR/0007-5264
BULLETIN QUOTIDIEN D'AFRIQUE.
Added/Corp Agence France-presse. **VFOAT** Bulletin d'Afrique. (19??)-. Periodical. French. da. 13440.00F France; 10320.00F other. Agence France Presse, 13 Place de la Bourse, BP 20, 75061 Paris Cedex 02 France. **Tel** 011 33 1 40414646.

CM
CAMEROON YEAR BOOK. English. United Publishers, PO Box 200, Victoria Cameroon. **LC** DT561; .C33. **DD** 916.7/11/03405.

CX
CENTRAFRIC-PRESS. French (French). 9,500. Boite Postale 1290, Bangui Central African Republic. **LC** AP27; .C45. **DD** 054/.1.

IT/0530-6442
COLLANA DI STUDI DI STORIA E POLITICA AFRICANA. 1- 1955-. Periodical. Italian. Via Giovanni Pascoli 55, 20133 Milan Italy.

TZ/0588-8387
COMMUNITY: EAST AFRICAN COMMUNITY MONTHLY MAGAZINE, THE. **Added/Corp** East African Community. Information Office. **VFOAT** East African Community Monthly Magazine. (19??)-. Periodical. English. mo. $1.75. East African Community, PO Box 1001, Arusha Tanzania.

UK
COUNTRY REPORT. ALGERIA / EIU, THE ECONOMIST INTELLIGENCE UNIT.
VFOAT Algeria. No. 2, (1986)-. Periodical. English. qt. $335.00 (per country), $100.00 (single issue) North America. The Economist Intelligence Unit, 40 Duke

Street, London W1A 1DW England. **Tel** 011 44 71 8301000. **(Subscription address:** Economist Intelligence Unit / North America Subscriptions, 111 West 57th Street, New York NY 10019.) **LC** HC815.A1; C68. **DD** 330.965/005. ***Continues in part*** *Quarterly Economic Review of Algeria, 0142-4130.*

US/0736-9506
CSIS AFRICA NOTES. (CSIS AFRICA NOTES: A PUBLICATION OF THE AFRICAN STUDIES PROGRAM OF THE GEORGETOWN UNIVERSITY CENTER FOR STRATEGIC AND INTERNATIONAL STUDIES.). [CSIS Afr. notes]. **Added/Corp** Georgetown University. Center for Strategic and International Studies. African Studies Program. **VFOAT** Africa Notes; C.S.I.S. Africa Notes. No. 1 (July 1982)-. Periodical. English. mo. $48.00. CSIS Africa Notes, 1800 K Street Northwest, Suite 400, Washington DC 20006. **Tel** (202)775-3219, FAX (202)775-3199, telex 7108229583. **ED** Helen Kitchen. **LC** DT1; .C77. **DD** 960/.05. Index available. cum. index. **Circ:** 500.
Desc: A briefing paper series for decision makers featuring timely analysis of African issues and developments and the role of external factors.

UK
CURRENT AFRICAN DIRECTORIES. **See** Library and Information Sciences.

SA/1019-2530
CURRENT COMMERCIAL CASES. [Curr. commer. cases]. (1992)-. Periodical. English. Six times a year. R295.00. Law Publisher, PO Box 41055, 2024 Craighill South Africa. **Tel** 27 11 3375380, FAX 27 11 3376634. **ED** M Stranex. **UDC** 38. cum. index.

●US/1060-6149
ETHIOPIAN (CHANTILLY, VA.), THE. (THE ETHIOPIAN.). [Ethiopian]. (1992)-. Periodical. English. bw. $54.00. Tamene Asmare, PO Box 221104, Chantilly VA 22022. **DD** 963.

UK/0959-9576
FOCUS ON AFRICA : BBC MAGAZINE. **Added/Corp** BBC African Service. Vol. 1, No. 1 (1990)-. Periodical. English. Four times a year (Jan., Apr., July, Oct.). £12.00 UK and Europe; $32.00 US; £16.00 other. BBC World Service, PO Box 76, Bush House Strand, London WC2B 4PH England. **Tel** 011 44 71 257 2906, FAX 011 44 71 379 0519. **(Subscription address:** TG Scott Subscriber Services, 6 Bourne Enterprise Centre, Kent TN15 8DG United Kingdom.) **ED** Timothy Ecott. **LC** DT1; .F62. **DD** 960/.05. **Ad Acc.** **Pr Rev.** **Circ:** 45,000 (ctrl).
Desc: Pan-African magazine on current affairs, music, sports, and theatre, as well as language, health and farming.

GH
GHANA REVIEW. **Added/Corp** Ghana. Information Services Dept. (19??)-. Periodical. English. mo. NC0.30. Information Services Department, PO Box 745, Accra Ghana. **Tel** 228011. **ED** J. Oppong-Agyare. **LC** DT510.A1; G473. **DD** 966.7/05/05. **Ad Acc.** **Circ:** 18,000. available with illustrations. ***Supersedes*** *Ghana Review.*

●US/1048-6216
GLOBAL AFRICA. **Added/Corp** African Academy of Arts, Sciences, and Technologies. (1992)-. Periodical. English. $6.00. African Academy of Arts, Sciences & Technologies, 12 Petunia Drive/No 1, North Brunswick NJ 08902.

FR/0249-6879
GRAND MAGHREB : REVUE MENSUELLE DU CENTRE D'INFORMATION SUR LE GRAND MAGHREB (CIGMA). ***Ceased.*** **VFOAT** Maghrib Al-Arabi Al-Kabir; Grand-Maghreb. Ceased 1988. Periodical. French. mo. Centre d'Information sur le Grand Maghreb, Institut d'Etudes Politiques de Grenoble II, B P 45, 38402 St-Martin-d'Heres France. **LC** DT181; .G73.

SA/0533-6961
GUYANA YEAR BOOK. 1963-. English. Guyana Graphic, Lama Avenue, Belair Park, East Demerara, Georgetown Guyana South Africa. **LC** WMLC 83/9083.

BE
INFO ZAIRE. **Added/Corp** Comite Zaire. (197?)-. Periodical. French. qt. 500.00F. Comite Zaire, BP 51, 1050 Bruxelles Belgium. **LC** DT658; .I53.
Ind/Abst Hum. Rights Intern. Rep.

PO
INFORMAFRICA. **VFOAT** Informafrica Confidencial. Vol. 1, No. 1 (Feb. 11, 1989)-. Periodical. Portuguese. Eleven times a year (Except Aug.). $280.00. Informafrica Publicacoes Lda, rua das Pedras Negras 61-5, 1100 Lisbon Portugal. **Tel** 011 351 1 8884751, 011 351 1 8883952, FAX 011 351 1 8880122, telex 44330 AFRINF P. ***Continues*** *Africa Confidencial.*

SA
INSIDER / SOUTH AFRICA. Multiple languages. sm. R125.00 (South Africa & Namibia); $135.00 (Botswana, Lesotho, & Swaziland). Varama Publishers, PO Box 17200, 0027 Groenkloof, South Africa. **Tel** 11 27 12 468858, FAX 11 27 12 465722.

MF
INTERNATIONAL MAURITIUS DIRECTORY. Directory. English (French). an. Rs200.00. PO Box 287, Port Louis Mauritius. **Tel** 2.02.88. **LC** DT469.M4; I57. **DD** 969/.8203/025. Index available. cum. index. **Ad Acc.** **Circ:** 10,000.
Desc: Publishes business and management tools describing government and services of Mauritius.

US/0047-1607
ISSUE (WALTHAM, MASS.). (ISSUE.). [Issue]. **Added/Corp** African Studies Association. **VFOAT** Quarterly Journal of Opinion; Quarterly Journal of Africanist Opinion; Journal of Opinion. No. 1 (Fall 1971)-. Periodical. English. Twice a year (Spring & Fall). $90.00 (individuals), $105.00 (institutions) airmail; $55.00 (individuals), $85.00 (institutions) surface mail Africa, Comes with African Studies Association membership. African Studies Association, Emory University, Credit Union Building, Atlanta GA 30322. **Tel** (404)329-6410, FAX (404)329-6433. **LC** DT1; .I75. **DD** 916/.005. **Ad Acc.** **Circ:** 2,000 (ctrl).
Desc: A journal of opinions about events and affairs relating to Africa.
Ind/Abst Abstr. Anthropol.; Am. Hist. Life (1974-); Hum. Rights Intern. Rep.; Int. Bibliogr. Sociol.; MLA Int. Bibl. Books Artic. Mod. Lang. Lit.; Rural Dev. Abstr.

AE
JAYSH AL-SHAB. JAYCH-ACH-CHAAB. **Added/Corp** Syria. Jaysh al-Arabi al-Suri. Idarat al-Shuun al-Ammah wa-al-Tawjih al-Manawi. Syria. Jaysh al-Arabi al-Suri. Idarah al-Siyasiyah. **VFOAT** Jaych-ach-Chaab. (Mar. 7, 1967)-. Periodical. Arabic. wk. **LC** AP95.A6; J86. ***Continues*** *Jundi.*

KE
JOE. **VFOAT** JOE Magazine. Periodical. English. ir. 3 per copy. Victoria House / Kenya, Tom Mboya Street, PO Box 30362, Nairobi Kenya. **LC** AP101; .J54. **DD** 052.

SA
KAGENNA. ***Ceased.*** (19??)-(19??). Afrikaans. ir (Published 3 or 4 times per year). Kagenna Publications, PO Box 15438, Capetown 8018 South Africa. **Tel** 011 27 21 4617924, FAX 011 27 21 4388690. **Pr Rev.**

NR/0567-4840
KANO STUDIES. [Kano stud.]. **Added/Corp** Abdullahi Bayero College. **VFOAT** Dirasat Kanu. Vol. 1, No. 1 (1965)-. English (Arabic). an. $4.68 Africa; $10.00 other. University Press Limited, PMB 5142, Ibadan Nigeria. **Tel** (022)412313, telex 31121. **LC** AP9; .K36. ctrl circ.
Ind/Abst MLA Int. Bibl. Books Artic. Mod. Lang. Lit.

MG
KIANJA. No. 1- June 30, 1972-. Periodical. Multiple languages (French and Malagasy). 200FMG. BP 3153, Tananarive Malagasy Republic. **LC** DT469.M21; K5. **DD** 916.9/1/03505.

GW/0937-7859
LANDERBERICHT. LIBYEN. **Added/Corp** Germany (West). Statistisches Bundesamt. 1989-. German (table of contents in English). W Kohlhammer Verlag GmbH, Postfach 800430, D 70549 Stuttgart Germany. **Tel** 011 49 711 78631, FAX 011 49 711 7863263, telex 7-255820. ***Continues*** *Statistik des Auslandes. Landerbericht. Libyen, 0173-3125.*

GW
LANDERBERICHT. MAROKKO. **Added/Corp** Germany (West). Statistisches Bundesamt. 1990-. German (table of contents in French). W Kohlhammer Verlag GmbH, Postfach 800430, D 70549 Stuttgart Germany. **Tel** 011 49 711 78631, FAX 011 49 711 7863263, telex 7-255820. **LC** HA2185; .S72. ***Continues*** *Statistik des Auslandes. Landerbericht. Marokko.*

GW/0939-3854
LANDERBERICHT. ZAIRE. **Added/Corp** Germany (West). Statistisches Bundesamt. 1990-. German (table of contents in French). Verlag W Kohlhammer GmbH, Abt Veroffentlichungen des Statistischen Bundesamtes, Philipp-Reis-Strasse 3, W-6500 Mainz 42 Germany. **LC** HA4711; .G47a. ***Continues*** *Statistik des Auslandes. Landerbericht. Zaire, 0173-3257.*

SA/0023-8422
LANTERN. **Added/Corp** S.A. Association for Adult Education. S.A. Association for the Advancement of Knowledge and Culture. Foundation for Education, Science, and Technology (South Africa). (1952)-. Periodical. Multiple languages (Afrikaans and English). qt. R26.32 South Africa; R30.00 other. Foundation for Education Science & Technology, PO Box 1758, Pretoria 0001 South Africa. **Tel** 011 27 12 3226404, FAX 011 27 12 3207803. **ED** Riena van Graan and Ena van der Westhuizen. **LC** AP18; .L36. **DD** 052. Index available. cum. index. **Bk Rev.** **Ad Acc.** **Circ:** 10,000.
Desc: History, fine and performing arts, crafts, architecture, etc.
Ind/Abst Annu. Bibliogr. Engl. Lang. Lit.; ARTbibliogr. Mod. (1984-).

LO
LESOTHO INDEX. **Added/Corp** National University of Lesotho. Institute of Southern African Studies. Documentation and Publications Division. (Apr. 1989)-. English. National University of Lesotho, PO Box 180, Roma Lesotho. ***Continues*** *Lesothana.*

●US/1071-7579
MAGHREB REPORT. [Maghreb rep.]. (1992)-. Newsletter. English. bm. $50.00 (individuals), $89.00 (non-profit institutions), $100.00 (corporate businesses). Maghreb Report, PO Box 1593, Princeton NJ 08542. **Tel** (609)924-0182, FAX (609)924-8185. **ED** Susan T. Rivers. **DD** 961. **Bk Rev**, (Qty: 5). **Ad Acc**, **Adv Mgr Tel** (609)258-3392.
Desc: Newsletter about politics and economics in North Africa. Features news from international sources and cogent analysis of developments in the region, especially as they affect business and trade.

FR
MAGHREB SELECTION. French. Forty-Four times a year. 4.900F. IC Publications Ediafric, 10 rue Vineuse, 75116 Paris France. **Tel** 011 33 1 44308100.

MR
MAJALLAT AL-SHABIBAH AL-SAHRAWIYAH. **VFOAT** Jeunesse Sahraoui; Revue la Jeunesse Sahraoui; Shabibah Al-Sahrawiyah. No. 1- December 1977/Jan. 1978-. Periodical. Arabic (French). 2.00 single issue. Al-Dar Al-Bayda, 7 rue de Breteuil, Casablanca Morocco. **LC** AP95.A6; M258.

MW
MALAWI. English. an. Free. Malawi Department of Tourism, Box 402, Blantyre Malawi. **Tel** 620300, telex 4645 TOURISM MI. **LC** DT858.2; .M34. **DD** 916.89/7/044. **Circ:** 50,000.
Desc: Tourism promotional guide and general information publication.

SG/0373-5338
MEMOIRES DE L'INSTITUT FONDAMENTAL D'AFRIQUE NOIRE. [Mem. Inst. fondam. Afr. noire]. **Main/Corp** Institut Fondamental d'Afrique Noire. No. 75- 1966-. Monographic series. French (English). ir. Price varies per volume. Institut Fondamental d'Afrique Noire, Boite Postale 206, Cheikh Anta Diop, Dakar Senegal. **Tel** 011 221 250090. ***Continues*** *Memoires de l'Institut Francais de Afrique Noire.*
Ind/Abst Life Sci. Collect.

SX
NAMIBIAN STRUGGLE, THE. Vol. 1, No. 1 (Jan. 1981)-. Periodical. English. mo. $7.00. DTA Information Department, Leutwein Street, PO Box 173, Windhoek 9000 Namibia South West Africa.

SA
NATIONAL TRADE INDEX OF SOUTH AFRICA AND RHODESIA. (1928)-. English. an. R65.00. AC Braby Pty Ltd, PO Box 1426, Pinetown 3600 South Africa. **Tel** 011 27 31 7017021, FAX 011 27 31 7017036, telex 624529. **ED** Graham Cleveland. **Ad Acc.**
Desc: Instant information is at your fingertips when you have a National Trade Index of South Africa for reference. This publication is invaluable to the businessman.

UK/0142-9345
NEW AFRICAN (LONDON. 1978). (NEW AFRICAN.). [New Afr.]. No. 129, (May 1978)-. Periodical. English. mo. £36.00 UK; $90.00 US; £50.00 other. IC Publications Ltd., 7 Coldbath Square, London EC1R 4LQ England. **Tel** 011 44 71 713-7711, FAX 011 44 71 713-7898, telex 8811757. **ED** Alan Rake. **LC** HC511; .A12. **DD** 960.3/05. **Bk Rev.** **Ad Acc.** **Circ:** 35,000. available on microfilm from University Microfilms International (UMI). ***Continues*** *New African Development.*
Desc: Gives a balanced mix of reporting and comment, economic and financial analysis, plus features on cultural and social affairs.
Ind/Abst Ethnoarts Index; F&S Index Plus Text, Int. [Select. Cov.]; Int. Labour Doc.; PAIS Int. Print (1991-).

UK
NEW AFRICAN YEARBOOK (LONDON, ENGLAND : 1987). (NEW AFRICAN YEARBOOK.). 7th Ed. (1987/1988)-. English. an. ü38.00 UK; $80.00 US; £40.00 other. IC Publications Ltd., 7 Coldbath Square, London EC1R 4LQ England. **Tel** 011 44 71 713-7711, FAX 011 44 71 713-7898, telex 8811757. **ED** Alan Rave. **LC** DT1; .N473. **Ad Acc.** **Circ:** 10,000. ***Formed by the union of*** *New African Yearbook. East, Southern Africa & Nigeria, 0266-2221* ***and*** *New African Yearbook. West & Central Africa, 0264-181X.*
Desc: A comprehensive survey of all African countries with full statistics and sections on the political, economic and cultural development of the Region.

NR/0189-8892
NEWSWATCH (LAGOS). (NEWSWATCH.). [Newswatch]. **VFOAT** News Watch. (198?)-. Periodical. English. wk. N70.00 North Africa and Middle East; N75.00 Europe and EIRE; N60.00 UK; N100.00 Australia; N90.00 Africa; $170.00 North America. Newswatch Communications Ltd, 14th Street Pancras Way, Suite 46, London NW1 0GQ England. **Tel** 011 44 71 387 9291, FAX 011 44 71 383 7576. **ED** Kayode Sojinka. **LC** AP9; .N48. **DD** 052. **Bk Rev. Ad Acc. Circ:** 100,000 (ctrl).

UK
NIGERIA HOMENEWS. English. Alfa Media Ltd, 173 Kilburn High Road, London NW6 7HY England.

NR
NIGERIA ... OFFICIAL HANDBOOK. (1979)-. English. an. Federal Ministry of Information, Malu Road Apapa, Lagos Nigeria. ***Continues** Nigeria Handbook.*

NR/0078-0685
NIGERIA YEAR BOOK. 1952-. English. an. Daily Times of Nigeria Ltd, Publications Division, New Isheri Road Agidingbi, PMB 21340 Ikeja West Africa. **Tel** 900850-900859. **LC** DT515. **DD** 916.69.

US/0749-5145
NIGERIAN NEWS, THE. [Niger. news]. Vol. 1, No. 1 (Feb. 15, 1984)-. Periodical. English. sm. $12.00. PO Box 5663, Providence RI 02903. **DD** 966.

US/0740-9133
NORTHEAST AFRICAN STUDIES. [Northeast Afr. stud.]. **Added/Corp** Michigan State University. African Studies Center. Vol. 1, No. 1 (1979)-. Academic Scholarly Publication. English. Three times a year. $40.00 institutions; $30.00 individuals. Michigan State University Press, 1405 South Harrison Road, Manly Miles 25, East Lansing MI 48823-5202. **Tel** (517)355-9543, FAX (800)678-2120, (517)336-2611. **ED** Harold G. Marcus. **LC** DT367.A2; N67. **DD** 963/.005. **Bk Rev. Circ:** 175 (ctrl). ***Continues** Ethiopianist Notes.*
Desc: Covers the Horn of Africa including Sudan, Ethiopia, Somalia, Djibouti, and Northern Kenya.
Ind/Abst Abstr. Anthropol.; Am. Hist. Life (1980-).

ET
OAU ECHO. **VFOAT** Echo de l'OUA. **VAT** Organization of African Unity Echo. No. 1 (Feb. 1980)-. Periodical. English (French). mo. OAU Echo, PO Box 3243, Addis Ababa Ethiopia. **Tel** 157700, telex 21046 OAU. **ED** I Dagash. **Circ:** 2,000.
Ind/Abst Hum. Rights Intern. Rep.

SA
OAU IN A MONTH. **Added/Corp** Organization of African Unity. Press and Information Division. (19??)-. Periodical. English. mo.
Ind/Abst Hum. Rights Intern. Rep.

SA/0378-9292
ORANJE VRYSTAAT EN NOORD-KAAPSE GIDS / ORANGE FREE STATE AND NORTHERN CAPE DIRECTORY. **Added/Corp** A. C. Braby (Pty) Ltd. **VFOAT** Brabyse ... Oranje Vrystaat en Noord-Kaapse Gids; Braby's ... Orange Free State and Northern Cape Directory; Orange Free State and Northern Cape Directory; Braby's OVS & Noord-Kaapse Gids; Braby's OVS en Noord-Kaapse Gids; Braby's OFS & Northern Cape Directory; Braby's OFS and Northern Cape Directory; Braby's ... O.V.S. en Noord-Kaapse Gids. (198?)-. Directory. English (Afrikaans). an. R38.00 South Africa; R50.00 other. AC Braby Pty Ltd, PO Box 1426, Pinetown 3600 South Africa. **Tel** 011 27 31 7017021, FAX 011 27 31 7017036, telex 624529. **ED** A. Stagg. **LC** DT891; .B73. ***Continues** Braby's Oranje Vrystaat Adresboek.*
Desc: Commercial directory with alphabetical and classified sections. Includes lists of post office box renters for the area.

FR/0014-2816
OUTREMER (PARIS, FRANCE : 1982). ***Suspended.*** (OUTREMER.). (19??)-(19??). Periodical. French. mo. Europe Outremer, 178 Quai, L Bieriot, 75015 Paris France. **Tel** 46.42.78.44. **LC** JV1801; .E65. **DD** 303.4/8244/06. **Ad Acc. Circ:** 18,000. ***Continues** Europe. Outremer.*
Desc: Economics of French speaking Africa (Nughreb and Black Africa).

US
PAPERS PRESENTED AT THE ANNUAL MEETING OF THE AFRICAN STUDIES ASSOCIATION. **Main/Corp** African Studies Association. (19??)-. English. an (Apr. or May). $375.00. African Studies Association, Emory University, Credit Union Building, Atlanta GA 30322. **Tel** (404)329-6410, FAX (404)329-6433. **LC** DT1.5; .A42a. **DD** 960. **Circ:** 100 (ctrl).

SA
PRO-NAT. Periodical. Multiple languages (English and Afrikaans). an. National Party of the Cape Province, PO Box 15020, Vlaeberg Cape Town 8018, Republic of South Africa. **Tel** 234156. **ED** Christian Matthews van der Westhuizen. **LC** DT779.9; P76. **Ad Acc. Circ:** 15,000 (ctrl).
Desc: Appears as the agenda for the provincial congress, includes general political articles concerning topical national issues.

SA/0034-0456
READER'S DIGEST SOUTH AFRICAN ED. [Read. Dig. S. Afr. ed.]. (1861)-. Periodical. English. mo. R77.15. Reader's Digest Association South Africa Pty Ltd, PO Box 2677, Cape Town 8000 South Africa. **Tel** 011 27 21 254460. **(Subscription address:** Reader's Digest / South Africa, PO Box 4116, Cape Town 8000 South Africa.**) UDC** 008.

UK
RHODESIANS WORLDWIDE. Vol. 1, No. 1 (March/May 1985)-. Periodical. English. Four times a year. £10.00. Rhodesians Worldwide, PO Box 260 / West Lavington, Wiltshire SN10 4QZ England. **Tel** 011 44 0380 818381, 812325, FAX 011 44 0380813620. **ED** P.W. Hagelthorn. **Bk Rev**, (Qty: 6/year). **Ad Acc, Adv Mgr:** Mrs. J. Hagelthorn. **Circ:** 60,000.
Desc: A contact magazine featuring news and views from and about former Rhodesian residents.

US/0899-3785
S.S.A. NEWSLETTER : A PUBLICATION OF THE SUDAN STUDIES ASSOCIATION. [S.S.A. newsl.]. **VFOAT** SSA Newsletter. Newsletter. English. qt. $25.00 US; $29.40 other. Newsletter SSA, c/o Dr Ismail Abdalla, 116 Canterbury Place, Williamsburg VA 23185. **Tel** (804)565-3085. **(Subscription address:** Sudan Studies Association, c/o Dr James Hudson, Morgan State University, Department of Political Science, Baltimore, MD 21239-4098**) ED** Ismail Abdalla. **DD** 962. **UDC** 908.624. **Bk Rev. Ad Acc. Circ:** 225.
Desc: Scholarly articles and information on the Sudan.

FR/0581-2976
SAHARIEN, LE. **Added/Corp** La Rahla. (1951)-. Periodical. French. Four times a year. 180.00F France; 220.00F others. Rahla Amis du Sahara, 116 rue Damremont, 75018 Paris France. **Tel** 011 33 44 920503.

KE
SAMACARA. **VFOAT** Samachar. 1980-81-. Periodical. English (Gujarati). an. Industrial Public Relations Ltd, PO Box 41237, Nairobi Kenya. **LC** AP9; .S27. **DD** 052.

SW/0281-0018
SEMINAR PROCEEDINGS FROM THE SCANDINAVIAN INSTITUTE OF AFRICAN STUDIES. **Added/Corp** Nordiska Afrikainstitutet. **VFOAT** Seminar Proceedings. (19??)-. Proceedings. English.
Ind/Abst World Agric. Econ.

LO
SETHALA : THE VOICE OF LESOTHO. English. bm. $9.51 Lesotho; $12.28 South Africa; $25.84 other. Creative Communications Ltd, PO Box 1561, Maseru 100 Lesotho. **Tel** 011 26 1 311539/314066, FAX 011 26 26 310012. **ED** Theresa Muller. **Circ:** 9,000.
Desc: Articles uniquely reflect on life in Lesotho, and include politics, news, business and finance, people profiles, travel and tourism, consumer affairs, women's issues, the arts, culture, history, the natural environment and youth issues.

US/0738-2820
SIRIUS (LOS ANGELES, CALIF.). (SIRIUS : THE WORLD & AFRICA.). [Sirius]. **VFOAT** World & Africa; World and Africa. (1982)-. Periodical. English. bm. $37.50 (institutions), $22.50 (individuals). The World & Africa, PO Box 35215, Los Angeles CA 90035. ***Continues** Sirius Publications, 0730-8477.*

SA/0015-5055
SOUTH AFRICA INTERNATIONAL. ***Ceased.*** **Added/Corp** South Africa Foundation. Vol. 1 (July 1970)-(1993). Periodical. English. qt. South Africa Foundation, Box 7006, Johannesburg South Africa. **Tel** (011)7266105. **ED** Gavin Lewis. **LC** DT751; .S43. **Bk Rev. Ad Acc. Circ:** 12,000.
Desc: Covers domestic and international affairs affecting South Africa.
Ind/Abst Abstr. Anthropol. (19??-); Am. Hist. Life (1984-); Int. Polit. Sci. Abstr.; Middle East Abstr. Index; PAIS Int. Print.

SA
SOUTH AFRICAN MONITOR, THE. **VFOAT** Monitor. No. 1 (Sept./Oct. 1981)-. Periodical. English. bm. Monitor Publications Ltd, PO Box 13197 Homewood, Port Elizabeth KSA 6013 South Africa. **LC** WMLC L 83/605.

SA
SOUTH AFRICAN OBSERVER, THE. **VFOAT** S.A. Observer. (19??)-. Periodical. English. Twelve times a year. R48.00. The South African Observer, PO Box 2401, Pretoria 0001 South Africa. **Tel** 011 27 12 3222950.

SA
SOUTHERN AFRICA REPORT. **Added/Corp** Southern Africa Report Association (Johannesburg, South Africa). **VFOAT** SA Report. Vol. 1, No. 1 (Feb. 18, 1983)-. Periodical. English. wk (50 issues). R790.00 (corporate rate), R460.00 (academic rate) South Africa, Zimbabwe, Malawi, Mozambique, Zambia, Swaziland, Lesotho, Botswana, Namibia; £430.00 (corporate rate), £275.00 (academic rate) UK; $695.00 (corporate rate), $755.00 (academic rate) other. Southern Africa Report Association, 23 Duncombe Road Forest Town, Johannesburg 2193 South Africa. **Tel** 011 27 11 6468790, FAX 011 27 11 6462596, telex 960 486053. **ED** Raymond Louw. **LC** DT751; .S66. **DD** 960/.05. ctrl circ.
Desc: Digest and informed briefing on Southern Africa current affairs, politics, labor, media, the economy and views of black people.

SA/0258-9168
SOUTHERN AFRICAN UPDATE. **Added/Corp** University of the Witwatersrand. Library. Jan Smuts House (Johannesburg, South Africa). Library. Vol. 1, No. 1 (Apr. 1986)-. Periodical. English. sa. University of Witwatersrand Library, Private Bag 31550, Braamfontein 2017, South Africa.
Ind/Abst Hum. Rights Intern. Rep.

●US/1062-0958
SPECTRUM (NEW YORK, N.Y. : 1992). (SPECTRUM : CRITICAL PERSPECTIVES ON ISSUES IN EAST AFRICA.). (1992)-. Periodical. English. bm. $18.00. Spectrum, Inc., 714 Ninth Avenue, Suite 447, New York NY 10019.

MW
STAR. Periodical. English. Blantyre Periodicals Ltd, Private Bag 39, Blantyre Malawi. **LC** AP9; .S82. **DD** 052.

SJ
SUJUN (KHARTOUM, SUDAN). (AL-SUJUN.). Periodical. Arabic. qt. Idarat Al-Alagat Al-Ammah, SB 551, Al-Khartum Sudan. **LC** AP95.A6; S83.

LY
TALIB (MUTAMAR AL-AMM LI-TALABAT AL-JAMAHIRIYAH). (AL-TALIB.). Periodical. Arabic. sm. 50LD each issue. PO Box 12130-10826, Tripoli Libya. **LC** AP95.A6; T32.

MZ
TEMPO. 1971-. Periodical. Portuguese. wk. $83.20. Caixa Postal 2917, Maputo Mozambique. **Tel** 26191/3 30806. **LC** AP68; .T45. **Bk Rev. Ad Acc. Circ:** 35,000 (ctrl).
Desc: Magazine of general reports about Mozambique and opinion about southern Africa.

US/0041-5715
UFAHAMU. (UFAHAMU : JOURNAL OF THE AFRICAN ACTIVIST ASSOCIATION.). [Ufahamu]. **Added/Corp** University of California, Los Angeles. African Activists Association. University of California, Los Angeles. African Studies Center. Vol. 1, No. 1 (Spring 1970)-. Periodical. English. Three times a year (Jan., June, Sept.). $17.00 (individuals); $23.00 (institutions). Regents of University of California Los Angeles, 10244 Bunche Hall African Studies, Los Angeles CA 90024. **Tel** (213)825-6518, (213)825-3686. **ED** P. Godfrey Okoth. **LC** DT1; .U4. **DD** 916/.005. **Bk Rev. Ad Acc. Circ:** 400 (ctrl).
Desc: An interdisciplinary journal of African studies. The journal represents strong and committed views about social issues, addressing both the general reader and the scholar.
Ind/Abst Am. Hist. Life (1988-); Int. Bibliogr. Sociol.; MLA Int. Bibl. Books Artic. Mod. Lang. Lit.

FR
UJAMAA. French. Nubia Presse, 17 rue du Petit Pont, 75005 Paris France.

IV
VOIX D'AFRIQUE. No. 1 (May 1975)-. Periodical. French. Twelve times a year. 120.00CFAF France; 150.00CFAF Europe; 200.00CFAF others. Society Presse Edition Cote d'Ivoire, BP 1503, Abidjan 01 Ivory Coast. **Tel** 011 225 370666. **(Subscription address:** CCC, 43 des Tilleuls, F 92100 Boulogne France.**) LC** AP27; .V64. **DD** 054/.1.
Ind/Abst Bibliogr. Mission.

US/0512-610X
WASHINGTON NOTES ON AFRICA. (WASHINGTON NOTES ON AFRICA / AMERICAN COMMITTEE ON AFRICA.). [Washington notes Afr.]. **Added/Corp** American Committee on Africa. Washington Office on Africa. (19??)-. Periodical. English. tq. $30.00. Washington Office on Africa, 110 Maryland Avenue NE, Washington DC 20002. **Tel** (202)546-7961. **LC** DT1; .W33. **DD** 960/.05. ctrl circ.
Ind/Abst Hum. Rights Intern. Rep. (19??-).

UK/0043-2962
WEST AFRICA (LONDON). (WEST AFRICA.). [West Afr.]. Vol. 1 (Feb. 3, 1917)-. Periodical. English. Fifty-two times a year. $170.00. West Africa Publishing Company Ltd., 43-45 Coldharbour Lane, Camberwell London SE5 9NR England. **Tel** 11 44 71 737 2946, FAX

11 44 71 978 8334, telex 892420 WEST AF-F. **ED** Kaye Whiteman and Ad Obe. **LC** DT491; .W4. **DD** 966/.005. Index available. **Bk Rev. Ad Acc. Circ:** 22,668. available on microfilm and microfiche. ***Supersedes*** *African Mail.*
Desc: Includes politics, arts, sports, books and latest news covering events in 26 West African countries including Nigeria.
Ind/Abst Hum. Rights Intern. Rep.; MLA Int. Bibl. Books Artic. Mod. Lang. Lit.

DK/0902-9621
WORKING PAPERS (KBENHAVNS DEIVERSITET. CENTER FOR AFRIKASTUDIER). (WORKING PAPERS / CENTER FOR AFRICAN STUDIES, UNIVERSITY OF COPENHAGEN.). **Added/Corp** Kbenhavns Universitet. Center for Afrikastudier. (198?)-. Monographic series. English (Danish). Price varies per volume.

ZA
ZAMBIA DIRECTORY, THE. Directory. English. K10.00. Directory Publishers of Zambia, PO Box 30963, Lusaka Zambia. **Tel** 212650/53. **LC** DT963.A2; Z33. **DD** 916.89/4/0025.

ZA
ZIMBABWE NEWS, THE. Periodical. English. bm. Zimbabwe News Letters Publishing Department, Caixa Postal 743, Manputo Peoples Republic of Mozambique.

GENERAL INTEREST-ASIA

KO
2000-YON. **VFOAT** Ichonnyon. V. 1- (1983. 5)-. Periodical. Korean. mo. W8,000. Hyandae Sahoe / 2000-Yon, Yonguso 7-16 Sinchon-dong Kangdong-ku, Seoul 1 Korea. **LC** AP95.K6; A17.

JA
"ABOUT JAPAN" SERIES. **Added/Corp** Foreign Press Center, Japan. 1 (Mar. 1977)-. Monographic series. English. ir. Price varies per volume. Foreign Press Center, 2-1 Uchisaiwaicho 2 chome, Chiyodaku Tokyoto 100 Japan. **LC** UNC.

US/1046-9834
AFGHANISTAN STUDIES JOURNAL. [Afghan. stud. j.]. **Added/Corp** University of Nebraska at Omaha. Center for Afghanistan Studies. Vol. 1, No. 1 (Spring 1988)-. Periodical. English. an. $10.00. University of Nebraska at Omaha / Center for Afghanistan Studies, PO Box 3588, Omaha NE 68103. **Tel** (402)554-3216, FAX (402)554-3242. **ED** Sara E. Pirtle. **LC** DS350; .A378. **DD** 958.1/005. **Bk Rev**, (Qty: 1-2 per year). **Pr Rev. Circ:** 500 (ctrl).
Desc: Presents insights about current as well as historical events regarding Afghanistan.

UK/0961-1142
AFRICA FORUM. **Added/Corp** Africa Leadership Forum. Vol. 1, No. 1 (1991)-. Periodical. English (French). Four times a year (Apr., June, Sept., Dec.). Africa Forum, PO Box 2286, Abeokuta Ogun State Nigera. **Tel** 011 234 39 722430. **ED** A. A. Obe. **LC** JQ1871.A1; A43. **DD** 960.3/2/05. **Bk Rev. Ad Acc. Pr Rev.** ctrl circ.
Desc: Africa forum focuses on issues relating to development and leadership in the African community.

II
AJAKALA. **Added/Corp** India (Republic) Ministry of Information and Broadcasting. (1945)-. Periodical. Hindi (Hindi). mo. $20.00. Ministry of Information and Broadcasting, Government of India, Patiala House, New Delhi 110 001 India. **Tel** 387983. **(Subscription address:** Prints India, 11 Darya Ganj, New Delhi, 110002 India, (Phone: 011 91 11 3268645)) **LC** AP95.H5; A35. ***Absorbed*** *Visva-Darsana.*

IO/0568-7683
AKTUIL. Periodical. Indonesian (Multiple languages). sm. Rp175 per issue. C V Aktuil, Jl Lengkong Kecil 41, Bandung Indonesia. **LC** AP95.I5; A47.

●HK
ALL-ASIA TRAVEL GUIDE / FAR EASTERN ECONOMIC REVIEW. **VFOAT** All Asia Travel Guide. (1993)-. English. be. $29.95 (two years). Review Publishing Company Ltd., 25 F Citicorp Center, 18 Whitfield Road, GPO Box 160, Hong Kong Hong Kong. **Tel** 011 852 25084337, FAX 011 852 25031549, 25031553, telex 66452 REVCD HX. **(Subscription address:** Review Publishing Company Ltd., PO Box 160, Hong Kong Hong Kong.**)** **ED** Bill Cranfield. **LC** DS504; .G76. **Ad Acc. Circ:** 50,000. ***Continues*** *All-Asia Guide.*
Desc: Guide covering hotels, customs and visa formalities, as well as the history, culture and local color of the region.

II/0002-5593
ALL INDIA REPORTER. **VFOAT** A.I.R. Vol. 1 (1914)-. Periodical. English. mo. $120.00. P R Shrma, Maan Bhawan/1st Floor, Ratanada Road, Jodjpur 342 001 India. **(Subscription address:** Prints India, 11 Darya Ganj, New Delhi 110002 India.**)**

IO
ALMANAK ANTARA. **Main/Corp** Antara (News Agency). 1978/79-. Indonesian. Badan Penerbit Non-Buletin LKBN Antara, J1 Antara No 53-57-61, Jakarta Kotak Pos 257 Indonesia. **LC** AY1165.I5; A5A. ***Continues*** *Almanak Pers Antara.*

US
AN-NA-PAO T'UNG HSUN. (19??)-. Periodical. Chinese. bm. $10.00. PO Box 7448, Ann Arbor MI 48107. **LC** AP95.C5; A5.

IR
ARASH. **VFOAT** Mahnamah-I Arash. (19??)-. Periodical. Persian. mo. 2500.00. Fursat-I Shirazi, Chaharrah-I Iskandari-I Shimali, 155 Tehran Iran. **LC** AP95.P3; A72.

FR/0044-8613
ARCHIPEL PARIS. (ARCHIPEL.). [Archipel Paris]. (1971)-. Periodical. French (English and Indonesian). sa. 250.00F. Archipel Ehess Bureau 732, 54 Boulevard Raspail, 75270 Paris Cedex 06 France. **Tel** 011 33 1 49542564, FAX 45 44 93 11. **UDC** 919.10. Index available. **Bk Rev.**
Desc: Man and society in maritime Southeast Asia.

KO
ARIRANG. Periodical. Korean. W7.560. Arirang SA, 273 5-ka Chongno Chongno-ku, Seoul South Korea. **LC** AP95.K6; A75.

US/0004-2366
ARMENIAN REVIEW, THE. [Armen. rev.]. **Added/Corp** Hairenik Association. Vol. 1 No. 1 (Winter 1948)-. Periodical. English. Four times a year (mar., June, Sept., Dec.). $25.00 (individual); $35.00 (institution). Armenian Review Inc, 80 Bigelow Avenue, Watertown MA 02172. **Tel** (617)926-4037. **ED** Tatul Sonetz-Papazian. **LC** AP2; .A7277. **DD** 052. **Bk Rev**, (Qty: 40). **Ad Acc. Pr Rev. Circ:** 1,000. available on microfilm and microfiche from University Microfilms International (UMI).
Desc: The journal of Armenian studies, Turkey studies, the Kurds, Soviet Transcaucasia, and the Georgians.
Ind/Abst Am. Hist. Life (1971-); Am. Bibliogr. Slavic East Europ. Stud.; ARTbibliogr. Mod.; Middle East Abstr. Index; Middle East J.

II/0304-8659
ARUNA. (19??)-. Hindi (Hindi). mo. PO Box 27, Civil Lines, Muradabada India. **LC** AP95.H5; A78.

JA/0917-0332
ASAHI SHIMBUN JAPAN ACCESS. ***Suspended.*** [Asahi shimbun Jpn. access]. **VFOAT** Japan Access. Vol. 1, No. 1 (Sept. 3, 1990)-(?). Periodical. English. wk. $255.00. Asahi Shimbun International Inc., 757 Third Avenue, New York NY 10017. **Tel** (800)666-0170. **LC** DS801; .A82. available on an online database (files 772,799/Full-Text) from DIALOG.

II
ASAR. **VFOAT** Weekly Aasar. (19??)-. Urdu (Urdu). 1.50 single issue. Zahur Al-Husan Dar, Plaza Cinema Building, Lahor India. **ED** Zahur Al-Hasan Dar. **LC** AP95.U7; A75.

HK/0251-2521
ASEAN BRIEFING. [Asean brief.]. (1978)-. Periodical. English. mo. $72.00. Asia Letter Group, GPO Box 10874, Central Hong Kong. **Tel** 011 852 5 262950, FAX 011 852 5 267131, telex 61166. **UDC** 008.

HK
ASIA LINK. bm. $10.00 (all except Asia); $6.00 (Asia except Hong Kong). Center for Progress of Peoples Ltd., 48 Princess Margaret Road, Homantin, Kowloon, Hong Kong.
Ind/Abst Hum. Rights Intern. Rep.

HK/0004-4474
ASIA MAGAZINE, THE. (Oct. 1, 1961)-. Periodical. English. bw. $25.00. Asia Magazine Ltd, Morning Post Building, Tong Chong Street, Hong Kong Hong Kong. **Tel** 11 852 5 5652332. **ED** N Soong and N Cameron. **LC** AP8; .A72.

CN/0834-194X
ASIA PACIFIC REPORT. (ASIA PACIFIC REPORT / INSTITUTE OF ASIAN RESEARCH, THE UNIVERSITY OF BRITISH COLUMBIA.). [Asia Pac. rep.]. **Added/Corp** University of British Columbia. Institute of Asian Research. University of British Columbia. Asian Centre. Friends of the Asian Centre (Vancouver, B.C.). **VFOAT** Asian Centre Newsletter. Vol. 8, No. 1 (Jan. 1984)-. Periodical. English. Twice a year. $10.00. University British Columbia Vancouver, Institute of Asian Research, 1871 West Mall, Vancouver BC V6T 1Z2 Canada. **Tel** (604)228-4688, FAX (604)228-5207. **DD** 950/.07/071133. ***Continues*** *Asian Centre Newsletter.*
Desc: Detailing events and activities on Asia.

US/1040-8231
ASIA TIMES (LOS GATOS, CALIF.). (ASIA TIMES.). (1990)-. Periodical. English. $9.00. Amar Walia, 461 North Santa Cruz Avenue, Los Gatos CA 95030.

●US/1352-2744
ASIAN ART & CULTURE. **See** The Arts-Art.

HK
ASIAN ART NEWS. English. bm. $38.00 Canada; $28.00 US; $60.00 other. Asian Art News, Suite 2A, Glenealy Mansion, 7 Glenealy, Central Hong Kong. **Tel** 011 852 5223443, FAX 011 852 5215268. **ED** Ian Findley-Brown. **Bk Rev**, (Qty: various). **Ad Acc, Adv Mgr:** Amy Schrier. **Circ:** 10,000.
Desc: Focuses on issues surrounding contemporary art in Asia.

UK/0144-9753
ASIAN DIGEST. Periodical. English. mo. Hansib Publishing Ltd / London, Tower House, 139-149 Fonthill Road, London N4 3HF England. **Tel** 01-281 1191, FAX 263 9656, telex 22294. **LC** AP8; .A724. **DD** 052.

US/1050-3706
ASIAN LEASING JOURNAL, THE. ***Suspended.*** [Asian leas. j.]. Vol. 1, No. 1 (June/July 1990)-(19??). Periodical. English. Six times a year (Feb., Apr., June, Aug., Oct., Dec.). $125.00. Amembal Halladay & Isom, 4 Triad Center, Suite 850, Salt Lake City UT 84180-1408. **Tel** (801)484-8555, FAX (801)533-8778. **DD** 382.

JA
ASIAN PACIFIC CULTURE : APC : CROSS-CULTURAL MAGAZINE OF THE ASIAN CULTURAL CENTRE FOR UNESCO. **Added/Corp** Asian Cultural Centre for Unesco. **VFOAT** APC. No. 41 (1988)-. Monographic series. English. ir. $40.00 (one year), $100.00 (three years) Comes with Asian Cultural Centre for Unesco membership. Asia/Pacific Cultural Centre for UNESCO (ACCU), Japan Publishers Building, No. 6 Fukuromachi, Shinjuku-ku Tokyo, 162 Japan. **Tel** 011 81 3 3269 4435, FAX 011 81 3 3269 4510. **LC** DS12; .A73. **DD** 950/.05. ***Continues*** *Asian Culture, 0385-6402.*
Desc: A magazine introducing various aspects of culture and life in Asia and Pacific with articles contributed by native experts and attractive colour photos.

PH/0004-4679
ASIAN STUDIES. [Asian stud.]. **Added/Corp** University of the Philippines. Institute of Asian Studies. University of the Philippines. Asian Center. Philippine Center for Advanced Studies. Vol. 1 (1963)-. Periodical. English. an. $17.00 (latest volume). Asian Center, University of the Phillipine System, Diliman Quezon City 1101 Philippines. **Tel** 011 63 961821. **LC** DS1; .A4915. **Bk Rev. Circ:** 1,000 (ctrl).
Desc: Concerns mainly cultural, sociological, historical, economic and political issues and accounts in Asia.
Ind/Abst Index Philip. Period.; MLA Int. Bibl. Books Artic. Mod. Lang. Lit.

II
ASIAN STUDIES (CALCUTTA, INDIA). (ASIAN STUDIES.). **Added/Corp** Netaji Institute for Asian Studies. Vol. 1, No. 1 (Jan. 1983)-. Periodical. English. qt. Rs50.00 India; $12.00 US; £6.00 other. The Editor Asian Studies, 1 Woodburn Park, Calcutta-700 020 India. **Tel** 44-3145. **ED** R Chakrabarti. **LC** DS1; .A49157. **DD** 950/.05. Index available. **Bk Rev. Ad Acc. Circ:** 500 (ctrl).
Desc: A multidisciplinary journal of Asian affairs. Focuses attention on the social, political, ethnic, and economic developments of current interest.
Ind/Abst Am. Hist. Life (1955-).

HK
ASIAWEEK. **VAT** Asia Week. Dec. 19, 1975-. Periodical. English. wk (51 issues). $153.00 (one year), $280.00 (two year). Asiaweek Ltd., 35F Citicorp Center, 18 Whitfield, Causeway Bay, Hong Kong. **Tel** 011 852 5125688. **ED** Michael O'Neill. **LC** DS1; .A715. **DD** 950/.05. **Bk Rev. Ad Acc. Circ:** 65,000.
Desc: Report accurately and fairly the affairs of Asia and her people in all spheres of activity and the world beyond Asia from an Asian perspective.

GW/0721-5231
ASIEN. No. 1 (Oct. 1981)-. Periodical. German (English). qt. DM50.00 Germany; $30.00 US. Deutsche Gesellschaft fur Asienkunde EV, Rothenbaumchaussee 32, W-2000 Hamburg 13 Germany. **Tel** 040-445891. **ED** B Dahm and H Wiertz Louven. **LC** DS1; .A727. **DD** 950/.05. Index available. **Bk Rev. Ad Acc. Circ:** 1,300.
Desc: Economics, politics, literature, culture, law, etc.
Ind/Abst Asia.-Pac. Econ. Lit.

II/0304-8683
ASIRYADA. (19??)-. Hindi. sa. **LC** AP95.H5; A84.

AT/0156-7365
AUSTRALIAN JOURNAL OF CHINESE AFFAIRS, THE. [Aust. j. Chin. aff.]. **Added/Corp** Australian National University. Contemporary China Centre. **VFOAT** Ao Chung. Issue No. 1 (Jan. 1979)-. Periodical. English. sa. 25.00Aus$ (individuals), $30.00 (institutions) Australia; $25.00 (individuals), $30.00 (institutions) other. Contemporary China Centre, RSPAS, Anutech GPO Box 4, Canberra ACT 2601 Australia. **Tel** (06) 249 4150, FAX (06) 257 3642, telex AA62694 SOPAC. **ED** Jonathan Unger. **LC** DS701; .A93. **DD**

951/.005. Index available. cum. index. **Bk Rev. Ad Acc. Circ:** 580. available on CD-ROM; available on microfilm and microfiche from University Microfilms International (UMI). Documents available from The Genuine Article.
Desc: Academic and general articles and reviews of contemporary Chinese politics, economics, literature and social sciences in general.
Ind/Abst Am. Hist. Life (1979-); APAIS, Aust. Public Aff. Inf. Ser. (1981-); Curr. Contents Soc. Behav. Sci.; Int. Bibliogr. Sociol.; Int. Dev. Abstr.; Int. Polit. Sci. Abstr.; Leis. Recreat. Tour. Abstr.; Res. Alert [Full Cov.]; Rural Dev. Abstr.; Soc. Sci. Cit. Index [Full Cov.]; World Agric. Econ.

RU/0005-2574
AZIIA I AFRIKA SEGODNIA. [Azija Afr. segodnja]. **Added/Corp** Institut Narodov Azii (Akademiia nauk SSSR) Institut Afriki (Akademiia nauk SSSR). **VFOAT** Asia and Africa Today. (1961)-. Academic Scholarly Publication. Russian (summaries and/or abstracts in English; table of contents in English). mo. $99.95. Izdatelstvo Nauka / Akademiia Nauk, Publishing House of the Russian Academy of Sciences, Leninskii Porspekt 14, 117901 Moscow Russia. **Tel** 011 95 954-21-53, FAX 011 95 938-21-44, telex 411964. **(Subscription address:** East View Publications Inc., 3020 Harbor Lane North, Suite 110, Minneapolis MN 55447.**)** Index available. ***Continues** Sovremennyi Vostok.*
Ind/Abst Am. Hist. Life.

VM
BACH KHOA. Vol. 1, No. 1 (1957)-. Vietnamese. sm. Bach Khoa, 8791 Conner Drive, Huntington Beach CA 92647. **LC** AP95.V5; B3.

PH
BANNAWAG. Periodical. Iloko. wk. Liwayway Publishing Inc, 2249 Pasong Tamo, Makati Rizal 3116 Philippines. **LC** AP95.I46; B36.

JA
BESSATSU TAIYO (HEIBONSHA). (BESSATSU TAIYO.). **VFOAT** Sun. Special Issue. No. 1 (Winter '72)-. Monographic series. Japanese. qt. Price varies per volume. Heibonsha Limited Publishers, 5 Sanbancho, Chiyoda-ku Tokyo 102 Japan. **Tel** (03)265-0451, FAX (03)265-0477. **ED** Youji Takahshi. **LC** AP95.J2; B473. **Ad Acc. Circ:** 100,000.

II
BHARATODAYAH. Periodical. Multiple languages (Sanskrit and Hindi). 6.00. Gurukula Mahavidyalaya, Dist Saharanpura U P, Jvalapura India. **LC** AP95.S3; B46.

II
BOMBAY MARKET. Vol. 34 (1970)-. Periodical. English. mo. Bombay Market, 505 Arun Chambers, Tardeo Road, Bombay 34 India. **ED** K. Multani. **Ad Acc.**

UK
BULLETIN OF THE EUROPEAN ASSOCIATION FOR JAPANESE STUDIES. Main/Corp European Association for Japanese Studies. Bulletin. English. sa. £8.00. University of Oxford Oriental Institute, Pusey Lane, Oxford 0X1 2LE United Kingdom. **Tel** 0865 278200. **(Subscription address:** Aston Management Centre, c/o J B Kidd, University of Aston, Birmingham, B4 7ET United Kingdom; telephone: 021-359-3611**) ED** P T Harries. **LC** DS834.95; .E87A. **DD** 952/.007/114. **UDC** 952.0. **Circ:** 300 (ctrl). ***Continues** Newsletter of the European Association for Japanese Studies.*
Desc: Information about affairs of the Association and of interest to its members (e.g. forthcoming conferences); reports of association's own conferences; short learned articles by members.

JA
BUNGAKUKAI. (1947)-. Periodical. Japanese. mo. $144.00. **(Subscription address:** Japan Publications Trading Company, Ltd., PO Box 5030, Tokyo International, Tokyo 100-31 Japan.**)**

JA
BUNGEI SHUNJU. (1923)-. Periodical. Japanese. mo. $179.00. **(Subscription address:** Kyowa Book Company Inc., 1 38 Kanda Jinbocho Chiyoda-ku, Tokyo 101 Japan.**) LC** AP95.J2; B843.

JA/0525-1885
BUNGEI (TOKYO, JAPAN : 1962). (BUNGEI.). (March 1962)-. Periodical. Japanese. qt. $74.00. **(Subscription address:** Kyowa Book Company Inc., 1 38 Kanda Jinbocho Chiyoda-ku, Tokyo 101 Japan.**) LC** AP95.J2; B83. **DD** 895. ***Continues** Bungei.*

TH
CCTD NEWSLETTER. Added/Corp Sapha Khatholik Haeng Prathet Thai Pha Kanphattana. **VAT** Catholic Council of Thailand for Development Newsletter. (19??)-. Newsletter. English. bm.
Ind/Abst Hum. Rights Intern. Rep.

MY
CERMIN MASYARAKAT. Added/Corp Pusat Pembangunan Masyarakat. (19??)-. Periodical. Malay. qt. Pusat Pembangunan Masyarakat, Jalan Sembulan, Peti Surat 1591, Kota Kinabalu Sabah Malaysia. **LC** DS597.33; .C47. **Circ:** 5,000.

CC
CHIANG HAN LUN TAN. VFOAT Jianghan Luntan. Began with May 1979 issue. Periodical. Chinese. mo. RMBY0.35. Science Press, 16 Donghuangchenggen North Street, Beijing 100707, People's Republic of China. **Tel** 011 86 1 4019821, 011 86 1 4010642, FAX 011 86 1 4012180, 011 86 1 4019810, telex 210147. **LC** AP95.C4; C541144. **DD** 059/.951.

SI/0303-0857
CHIEN WEI. [Qian wei]. **VFOAT** Tsyan Wei Monthly; Vanguard Monthly. (May 1973)-. Chinese. mo. $6.00. Teahouse Publisher, 540 North Bridge Road, Singapore 7 Singapore. **LC** AP95.C4; C54118.

US/1044-890X
CHINA AND PACIFIC RIM LETTER. [China Pac. Rim lett.]. (1989)-. Periodical. English. bm. $50.00. Begell House Inc., PO Box 1109, Pearl River NY 10965. **Tel** (212)725-1999. **ED** Marjorie W. Cline. **DD** 950.
Desc: Covers current events in Asia, emphasizing China, Taiwan, Hong Kong and Tibet.

US/0190-602X
CHINA FACTS & FIGURES ANNUAL. VAT China Facts and Figures Annual. Vol. 1 (1978)-. Academic Scholarly Publication. English. an. Academic International Press, Box 1111, Gulf Breeze FL 32561. **ED** Charles E. Greer. **LC** DS779.15; .C48. **DD** 951/.005. **NLM** DS 701 C536. **Bk Rev.** ctrl circ.
Desc: Accumulates annually all available, relevant, public reference-type and statistical information about the PRC. It is based on a mass of the latest available official, private, international and scholarly sources. Revised and updated each year to include the latest data and developments, each volume contains very substantial information not found in previous editions.

CH
CHINA HANDBOOK (TAIPEI, TAIWAN). (CHINA HANDBOOK.). (19??)-. English. an (Published every 2 or 3 years). NT$150.00 (latest volume); $26.00 (latest volume) airmail;. Ta Kung Pao Ltd., E. Comm Center, 393 Hennessy Road, Room 2003, Hong Kong. **Tel** 011 852 5 7571817. **ED** Ta Kung Pao. **NLM** DS 701 C537.
Desc: Covers articles of general interest - new ministries and departments, economic reform, statements from top Chinese leaders, trade, laws, regulations, and list of Hong Kong firms with mainland links.

CH/0009-4404
CHINA NEWS ANALYSIS. No. 1 (Aug. 25, 1953)-. Periodical. English. sm. $195.00 US. China News Analysis, Hsinchuang PO Box 1-002, Taipei Hsien 24205 Taiwan. **LC** DS777.55; .C4469. **DD** 951.05. Index available (included in every 25th issue). cum. index.
Desc: Analysis of People's Republic of China media on current or background political, economic and social questions. One topic in each issue.

UK/0045-6764
CHINA NOW. Added/Corp Society for Anglo-Chinese Understanding (London, England). (May 1970)-. Periodical. English. Four times a year (Jan., Apr., July, Oct.). £12.00 (individual), £25.00 (institution), UK & Ireland; £18.00 (individual), £30.00 (institution) other. Society for Anglo-Chinese Understanding, 109 Promenade, Cheltenham GLOS GL50 INW England. **Tel** 011 44 242 226625. **ED** Angela Knox and Jean Penders. **DD** 951. **Bk Rev**, (Qty: 20). **Ad Acc, Adv Mgr:** Ms. Ryder. **Circ:** 1,000. ***Continues** Society for Anglo-Chinese Understanding (London, England). SACU News.*
Desc: These are reviews, literature and ideas for teaching about China today. This helps the society of the Anglo-Chinese have better understanding of the views on China.

CC/0009-4420
CHINA PICTORIAL. [China pict.]. **VFOAT** Jen Min Hua Pao. (Jan. 1951)-. Periodical. Multiple languages. Twelve times a year. $23.00. China Pictorial, Huayuan cun, Beijing 100044, People's Republic of China. **(Subscription address:** China International Book Trading Corporation, PO Box 399, Library Service Department, Beijing 100044 People's Republic of China.**) ED** Zhang Jiahua. **LC** DS777.55; .C447. **DD** 951/.005. available in microform from University Microfilms International (UMI). Documents available from The UnCover Company.
Desc: Contains attractive photographs and lively articles on China's economic developments, culture, history, life of the Chinese people, etc.
Ind/Abst Acad. Search (July 1993-); GeoRef; INFO-SOUTH Abstr.; Mag. Search.

US
CHINA REPORT. Began in 1984?. Periodical. English. ***Formed by the union of** China Report. Agriculture (Fouo Version); China Report. Economic Affairs (Fouo Version); China Report. Political, Sociological and Military Affairs (Fouo Version) **and** China Report. Science and Technology (Fouo Version).*
Ind/Abst Geogr. Abstr. Human Geogr.

CC
CHINA TODAY. Vol. 39, No. 1 (Jan. 1990)-. Periodical. English (Chinese). mo. $41.00 institution, $26.00 individual. China Welfare Institute. **(Subscription address:** China Books & Periodicals Inc., 2929 24th Street, San Francisco CA 94110.**) *Continues** China Reconstructs (North American Ed.), 1000-2944.*
Desc: Offers lively, on-the-spot reports on China's socialist construction and the life of Chinese people. Also features minority nationalities, tourism, sports, etc.
Ind/Abst Acad. Search (July 1993-); Mag. Search.

BE
CHINA UPDATE (OUD-HEVERLEE, BELGIUM). (CHINA UPDATE : AN OCCASIONAL NEWSLETTER.). (Oct. 1982)-. Periodical. English (French). Four times a year. J. Spae, Dennenlaan 8, B-3031 Oud-Heverlee Belgium. **Tel** 32 16 22 93 16. **ED** Joseph Spae. **Bk Rev. Circ:** 300.
Desc: Subject matter exclusively relates to today's China in politics, economics, quality of life and population problems. Providing the reader with an all-around picture of what is happening today. Special emphasis is put on human rights and religion.
Ind/Abst Bibliogr. Mission.

US
CHINESE AWARENESS. VFOAT Chueh Hua Pao. 1- July 1971-. Periodical. Chinese. mo. PO Box 30440 Terminal Annex, Los Angeles CA 90030.

HK
CHING HSIN. VFOAT Fresh. V. 1- Sept. 1973-. Periodical. Chinese. Ching Hsin Chih Tso Kung SSU Chu Pan Pu Fresh Productions, Room 11 A/11th Floor, 30-32 Queen's Road East, Hong Kong. **LC** AP95.C4; C54323.

KO
CHONGU. Periodical. Korean. W2,500. Kukhoe Uiwon Tonguhoe, 18-131 6-ka Ulchi-ro, Chung-ku Seoul Korea. **LC** AP95.K6; C4667.

KO
CHUBU SAENGHWAL. (19??)-. Periodical. Korean. Twelve times a year. $114.00. **(Subscription address:** Dong A Book Store, 9828 Garden Grove Boulevard #104, Garden Grove, CA 92644 USA**) LC** AP95.K6; .C47. **Circ:** 300,000.

KO
CHUGAN HANGUK. (19??)-. Periodical. Korean. Fifty-two times a year. $32.55. Kang-Jae Chang, 14 Chunghak-dong Chongno-du, Seoul Korea. **LC** AP95.K6; C475.

HK/0578-1175
CHUN CHIU. VFOAT Observation Post. Vol. 1 (July 1957)-. Periodical. Chinese. sm. Shatin New Territories, Hong Kong Hong Kong. **DD** 909.

CC
CHUN CHUNG WEN HUA. VFOAT Qunzhongwenhua. (19??)-. Periodical. Chinese. mo. $17.17. **(Subscription address:** China International Book Trading Corporation, PO Box 399, Library Service Department, Beijing 100044 People's Republic of China.**) LC** AP95.C4; C553. **DD** 059/.951.

CC
CHUNG-KUO JEN WU NIEN CHIEN. Chinese. China National Publishing Import & Export Corporation, 16 Gongti E Rd., Chaoyang Dist., Beijing 100704, People's Republic of China. **Tel** 011 8601 50630169, 5066688, FAX 011 8601 5063101, 5063010, telex 22313.

CC
CHUNG-KUO LI SHIH HSUEH NIEN CHIEN. 1979-. Chinese. an. RMBY2.85. Hsin Hua Shu Tien Peking, Beijing, People's Republic of China. **LC** PAR.

CH
CHUNG-KUO LUN TAN. *Ceased.* VFOAT Chung-Kuo Lun Tan Pan Yueh Kan; China Tribune. (1975)-(1992). Periodical. Chinese. bw. Chung-Kuo Lun Tan She 6F, 557 Chung Hsiao E Road, Section 4, Taipei Taiwan. **LC** AP95.C4; C5684. **DD** 951/.005.

CC
CHUNG-KUO NIEN CHIEN. VFOAT China Year Book. Vol. 1 (1924)-. Chinese. an. $60.00. China National Publishing Import & Export Corporation, 16 Gongti E Rd., Chaoyang Dist., Beijing 100704, People's Republic of China. **Tel** 011 8601 50630169, 5066688, FAX 011 8601 5063101, 5063010, telex 22313. **LC** DS701; .C757.

HK
CHUNG PAO YUEH KAN. VFOAT Chung Pao Monthly. Began with Feb. 1980 issue. Periodical. Chinese. mo. $1.25. Chung Newspapers Ltd, 171-172 Gloucester Road, Wanchai Hong Kong. **LC** AP95.C4; C5725. **DD** 059/.951.

HK/0010-9568
CHUNG WAI HUA PAO. VFOAT The Cosmorama Pictorial; Chung Wai. (July 1956)-. Periodical. Chinese (summaries and/or abstracts in English). mo. HK$100.00 Hong Kong; $16.00 US. Cosmorama Cultural Enterprise Co Ltd, 6-8 Tsing Fung Street, Haven Commercial Building, 12/F Flat B, North Point Hong Kong. **Tel** 5-709942. **ED** Jack Lin. **LC**

General Interest —General Interest-Asia

AP95.C4; C574. **DD** 059/.951.
Desc: Essays on the Republic of China, its society, industry, agriculture, trade, etc. Also covers the activities of Chinese overseas.

JA
CHUO KORON / THE CENTRAL REVIEW. **VFOAT** Tyuokoron; The Central Review. No. 14-32 (1899)-. Periodical. Japanese. mo. ¥9250. Chuokoronsha, 2-8-7 Kyobashi, Chuo-ku Tokyo 101 Japan. **LC** AP95.J2; C562. cum. index. **Continues** *Hansei Zasshi.*

IT/0529-7451
CINA. **Added/Corp** Istituto Italiano per il Medio ed Estremo Oriente, Rome. Vol. 1 (1956)-. Monographic series. Italian. ir. Price varies per volume. Herder Editrice e Libreria SRL, Piazza Montecitorio 117-120, 00186 Rome Italy. **Tel** 011 39 6 679 4628, FAX 011 39 6 678 4751. **ED** Lionello Lanciotti. **DD** 915.1.
Desc: Information on thought, art, science and organization in China at the present time, without neglecting the tradition of the past.

NP/0303-2930
CITRANA. [Citrana]. V. 1- Pausha 2029- Dec. 1972-. Nepali (Nepali). 10.00. PB No 968, Kathamadau Nepal. **LC** AP95.N4; C55.

SI/0084-8956
COMMENTARY (SINGAPORE). (COMMENTARY.). [Commentary]. 1- , 1972-74; New issue, V. 1, No. 1- 1975-. Periodical. English. qt. 2.50Sing$. University of Singapore, 10 Kent Ridge, Singapore 0511 Republic of Singapore. **Tel** 011 65 7723067. **ED** Zaibun Siraj. **LC** DS501; .U533. **DD** 915.9/005. **Ad Acc. Circ:** 5,000 (ctrl).
Desc: The journal consists of articles on economic, social and cultural affairs, comments on current issues in Singapore and elsewhere and literary materials.

●UK/0958-4935
CONTEMPORARY SOUTH ASIA. Vol. 1, No. 1 (1992)-. Periodical. English. tq (Mar., July, Nov.). £108.00. Carfax Publishing Company, PO Box 25 Abingdon, Oxfordshire OX14 3UE England. **Tel** 011 44 235 555335, FAX (0279)31067, telex 817484. **(Subscription address:** US and Canada/ PO Box 2025, Dunnellon, FL 34430-2025; telephone:(904)489-6996) **ED** Gowher Rizvi & Robert Cassen. **[CCC].** Index available. available on microfiche.
Desc: Presents research and analysis on contemporary policy issues in South Asia.

DK/0904-8626
COPENHAGEN DISCUSSION PAPERS. [Cph. discuss. pap.]. (1988)-. Periodical. English.
Ind/Abst World Agric. Econ.

US/1050-2955
CORNELL EAST ASIA SERIES. [Cornell East Asia ser.]. **Added/Corp** Cornell University. East Asia Program. **VFOAT** East Asia Series; Cornell University East Asia Series. (1990)-? Monographic series. English (Japanese, Chinese and Korean). Five times a year. $10.00. East Asia Program, Cornell University, 140 Uris Hall, Ithaca NY 14853-7601. **Tel** (607)255-6222, FAX (607)254-5000. **ED** David McCann. **DD** 950. **Pr Rev. Continues** *Cornell University East Asia Papers, 8756-5293.*
Desc: CEAS is a non-profit book series that publishes manuscripts related to East Asia (China, Japan, and Korea). Manuscripts range from translations to textbooks to sociological and economic studies.

JA
COSMICA: AREA STUDIES. **Added/Corp** Kyoto Gaikokugo Daigaku. Sogo Kenkyujo. (1971)-. Japanese (English, Portuguese and Spanish). an. Kyoto University of Foreign Studies / Tokyo, Saiin Kasamecho, Ukyo-ku 615, Tokyo Japan. **Tel** 075-311-5181. **LC** AS551; .C67. **Circ:** 1,500.

US/0741-2037
CROSSROADS (DE KALB, ILL.). (CROSSROADS). [Crossroads]. **Added/Corp** Northern Illinois University. Center for Southeast Asian Studies. Vol. 1, No. 1 (Feb. 1983)-. Periodical. English. Twice a year. $20.00. Center for Southeast Asian Studies, 410 Adams Hall, NIU, Dekalb IL 60115. **Tel** (815)753-1771, (815)753-0246, FAX (815)753-0198, telex 981417. **ED** Grant Olson. **LC** DS520; .C76. **DD** 959/.005. Index available (published separately). **Bk Rev. Ad Acc. Pr Rev. Circ:** 150 (ctrl).
Desc: An interdisciplinary journal on southeast Asia.
Ind/Abst Acad. Search (July 1993-); Int. Bibliogr. Sociol.

CH
CROWN. (1954)-. Chinese. mo. $77.00. Crown Magazine, No 50 Lane 120 Tun Hua Road, Taipei Taiwan. **Tel** 011 886 2 7168888.

II/0011-3123
CURRENT, THE. (July 18, 1956)-. Periodical. English. Fifty-two times a year. Current Publications Pvt Ltd, 15 Cawasji Patel Street, Bombay 1 India. **(Subscription address:** Prints India, 11 Darya Ganj, New Delhi 110002 India.**) Continues** *Current News Magazine.*
Ind/Abst Peace Res. Abstr. J. (1965-1966); Mag. Index (?-?).

MY
DAIGES MALAYSIA. Aug. 1983-. Periodical. Malay. mo. $30.00 Peninsular Malaysia. Media Intelek SDN Bhd, Tingkat 2 Wisma Fam J1 SS 5A/9 P S, 6640 Petaling Jaya Selangor Malaysia. **LC** AP95.M24; D34.

US/0898-347X
DAILY REPORT. EAST ASIA. [Dly. rep., East Asia]. **VFOAT** FBIS Daily Report. East Asia. **VAT** US Foreign Broadcast Information Service Daily Report. East Asia. (June 1, 1987)-. Periodical. English. da. National Technical Information Service - NTIS, Room 2027S, 5285 Port Royal Road, Springfield VA 22161. **Tel** (703)487-4630, (703)487-4660, (703)487-4650, FAX (703)321-8547, telex 89-9405. **DD** 320. **Continues** *Daily Report. Asia & Pacific.*

IO
DARMA PUTRA. Edition 1-. Periodical. Indonesian. Jl Medan Merdeka Timur No 3, Jakarta Indonesia. **LC** AP95.I5; D33.

TU
DATELINE TURKEY. (19??)-. English. wk (Saturday). $160.00. Bagimsiz Basin Ajansi, Turkocagi Cad No 17 Kat 1, Istanbul, Turkey. **Tel** 528-5067.
Desc: A weekly news round-up of events.

PK
DAWN. **VFOAT** Dawn Overseas Weekly. (19??)-. English. da. $350.00 Pakistan; $1302.50 other. Friends Book House, Government Printing Office, Box 803, Karachi 1 Pakistan. **ED** Ahmad Alii Khan. **Bk Rev. Ad Acc. Circ:** 100,000.
Desc: General non-party newspaper directed at the more educated strata of the public. Read by businessmen, politicians and members of middle class intelligentsia.

II
DEBONAIR. Periodical. English. Rs3.50 single issue. Caxton House, 289 Shahid Bhagat Singh Road, Bombay 400001 India. **LC** AP8; .D4. **DD** 052.

II
DEVA NAGARA. Hindi (Hindi). Rs8.00. **LC** AP95.H5; D47.

BG
DHAKA COURIER. (198?)-. Periodical. English. wk. Dhaka Courier, 62-61 Purana Paltan, Dhaka, Bangladesh. **Tel** 2-238222. **ED** Enayet Ullah Khan. **Circ:** 5,000.

IO
DIALOG. 1- May 22/June 4 1978-. Periodical. Indonesian (Indonesian). Rp400 single issue. Yayasan Karna Jaya, Jl Garuda No 62, Jakarta Indonesia. **LC** AP95.I5; D42.

MY/0302-8887
DIAN (KOTA BHARU). (DIAN.). [Dian]. Periodical. Malay. mo. $14.40. Sharikat Dian Sdn Berhad, 5315-A Jalan Pasir Puteh, Lundang Malaysia. **LC** AP95.M24; D5.

MY/0126-5180
DISKUSI. [Diskusi]. (19??)-. Periodical. Malay. mo. $19.60 Malaysia; $36.25 other. Yayasan Anda Sdn Bhd, A2-Bangunan Uda, J1 Pantai Baru, Kuala Lumpur Malaysia. **LC** AP95.M24; D57.

HK/0301-9489
DOUSOU SHUANGYUEKAN. (TOU SOU SHUANG YUEH KAN.). [Dousou shuangyuekan]. **VFOAT** Dousou. 1- Jan. 1974-. Periodical. Chinese. $20.00. Dousou, Flat 17 Huang Wan Court 12/F, 7 Wu Kwong Street, Hunghom Kowloon Hong Kong. **LC** AP95.C4; T55.

IS
DVADTSAT DVA. See Literature.

US/0066-0957
EAST ASIA SERIES. Vol. 1 (Aug. 1952)-. Periodical. English. ir. Michigan State University / Department of English, 201 Morrill Hall, East Lansing MI 48824-1035. **Tel** (517)355-9571, (517)355-7570. **Bk Rev. Ad Acc. Circ:** 200 (ctrl). available in microform.
Desc: Wide range of topics pertaining to East Asia.

CH
ECHOS DE LA REPUBLIQUE DE CHINE. (19??)-. Periodical. French. Thirty-six times a year. $10.00. Kwang Hwa Publishing Co., 8 FL No 15 Hangchow S Road Sec. 1, Taipei 100 Taiwan. **Tel** 011 886-2 3922245 ext. 15.

IO/0302-8577
EKSPONEN. [Eksponen]. (19??)-. Periodical. Indonesian. wk. Yayasan Tunas Bangsa, JL Pakuningratan No 30, Yogyakarta Indonesia. **LC** AP95.I5; E38.
Ind/Abst Hum. Rights Intern. Rep.

IO/0531-9145
EKSPRES. [Ekspres]. Vol. 1 No. 1 (1970)-. Periodical. Indonesian. wk. Pt Aksi Press, Jalan Panah Abang III No 17, Jakarta Indonesia. **LC** AP95.I5; .

MX/0185-0164
ESTUDIOS DE ASIA & AFRICA. [Estud. Asia Afr.]. **Added/Corp** Colegio de Mexico. Vol. 10 (1975)-. Periodical. Spanish. Three times a year. $32.00 (individual), $50.00 (institution), US & Canada; $26.00 (individual), $34.00 (institution), Latin America; $42.00 (individual), $60.00 (institution), others. Colegio de Mexico AC, Camino Al Ajusco No 20, 10740 Mexico DF Mexico. **Tel** 011 52 5 6455955 Ext. 3133, telex 1777585 COLME. **ED** David N. Lorenzen. **LC** DS1; .E87. **DD** 950/.05. **Bk Rev. Circ:** 1,000. **Continues** *Estudios Orientales, 0185-0156.*
Desc: General interest of literature and social science of Asia and Africa.
Ind/Abst Am. Hist. Life (1979-)(1975-); Int. Bibliogr. Sociol.; MLA Int. Bibl. Books Artic. Mod. Lang. Lit.

PR
EXEGESIS. **Added/Corp** Humacao Regional College. **VFOAT** Revista Exegesis. (1986)-. Periodical. Spanish. Twice a year. $12.00 US; $15.00 Mexico; $18.00 Central America; $20.00 South America and Europe. Universidad de Puerto Rico Humacao, Colegio Universitario Humanacao, Estacion C U H, Humacao Puerto Rico 00791. **Tel** (809)852-2525. **LC** AS74.A1; E9. **DD** 056/.1.

IS
FAJR (JERUSALEM). (JERUSALEM PALESTINIAN WEEKLY / AL FAJR.) **VFOAT** Dawn; Jerusalem Dawn; Fajr. Vol. 4, No. 142 (Jan. 21, 1983)-. Periodical. English. Fifty-two times a year. $50.00. Al Fajr Newspaper, 16 Crowell Street, Hempstead NY 11550. **Tel** (516)485-5736, FAX (516)564-8850, telex TLX 967701 OMARHEM. **(Subscription address:** 16 Crowell Street, Hempstead, NY 11550**) ED** Hanna Siniora. **LC** DS119.7; F33. **Bk Rev. Ad Acc. Circ:** 3,000. available on microfilm. **Continues** *Jerusalem Dawn.*

RU/0235-6813
FAR EAST, STUDIES BY SOVIET SCHOLARS SERIES, THE. **Added/Corp** Institut Dalnego Vostoka (Akademiia Nauk USSR). **VFOAT** "Far East--Studies by Soviet Scholars" Series; Seriia "Dalnii Vostok, Issledovaniia Sovetskikh Uchenykh". (1989)-. Monographic series. English. Price varies per volume. Social Sciences Today Editorial Board, Academy of Sciences, 33/12 Arbat, Moscow 121002 Russia. **Tel** 241-09-06.

CE
FERGUSON'S SRI LANKA DIRECTORY. **VFOAT** Sri Lanka Directory. 121st Edition (1981-1983)-. English. an. $44.00. Associated Newspapers of Ceylon Ltd, Lake House, PO Box 1195, Colombo 10 Sri Lanka. **Tel** 011 94 1 23119, telex 22202 ANCL CE. **ED** T. C. L. Ferdinando. **LC** DS488.9; .C4. DD 954.9/3/0025. Index available. **Bk Rev. Ad Acc. Circ:** 10,000 (ctrl). **Continues** *Ferguson's Ceylon Directory.*
Desc: Geographical description of the island, history, islands elective franchise, staff officers, diplomatic representation, local government, postal information, tourism, banks, business, commerce, finance, institutions, trade, estates, and agriculture.

TU/0300-2314
FIKIR VE SAN'ATTA HAREKET. **VFOAT** Hareket. (19??)-. Turkish. mo. 90.00TL. Divanyolu Ersoy Han, No 148/5, Istanbul Turkey. **LC** AP95.T8; F5.

TH
FOCUS (BANGKOK, THAILAND). (FOCUS.). Periodical. English. mo. Baht 300. Focus Publications Company Ltd, Bangkok 11 Thailand. **LC** AP8; .F64. **DD** 052.

CE
FORWARD (COLOMBO, SRI LANKA). (FORWARD.). Began 1954. Periodical. English. sm. 234/13 Ihala Welikada Road, Colombo Sri Lanka Ceylon. **LC** AP8; .F673. **DD** 079/.549/3.

CH/0304-1204
FREE CHINA TODAY. V. 3- Summer 1974-. English. $15.00. Epoch Publicity Agency, PO Box 3782, Taipei Taiwan. **Tel** 011 886 2 7524425. **LC** DS799.A2; F73. **DD** 951/.249/05. **Continues** *Free China.*

JA
FRONTIER : A VIEW FROM TOKYO, THE. Vol. 1 (Aug. 1990)-. English (Japanese). qt. Tokyo Frontier Association, TDC Building, 9-18 Misaki-cho 2-chome, Chiyoda-ku, Tokyo 101 Japan. **Tel** 03-5275-0111, FAX 03-5275-0959.

CH
FU-CHIEN CHING NIEN. **VFOAT** Fujian Qingnian. Periodical. Chinese. NT$0.20. Fu-Chien Sheng Yu Tien Chu, China. **LC** AP95.C4; F78. **DD** 059/.591.

JA
FUKUOKA DAIGAKU KENKYUJO HO. **Main/Corp** Fukuoka Daigaku. Kenkyujo. **VFOAT** Bulletin of the Institute for Advanced Research of Fukuoka

University. Academic Scholarly Publication. Japanese (Japanese). 11 Nanakuma Nishi-Ku, Fukuoka Japan. **LC** AS552.F95; A27. **CODEN** FDHODM. Documents available from CASDDS.
Ind/Abst Chem. Abstr.

II/0970-0080
FUSION ASIA. [Fusion Asia]. **Added/Corp** Fusion Asia Society. (1983)-. Periodical. English. qt. $20.00. Fusion Asia Society, C-9 Nizamuddin East, New Delhi 110013 India. **Tel** 617109. **(Subscription address:** Prints India, 11 Darya Ganj, New Delhi, 110002 India, (Phone: 011 91 11 3268645)) **ED** Ramtanu Maitra. **LC** TK1078; .F88. **DD** 333/79/24. **Bk Rev. Ad Acc. Circ:** 10,000.
Desc: Committed to providing accurate and comprehensive information on energy and other advanced technologies and frontier science to optimize economic developing nations.

II/0377-9653
GANTAVYA. [Gantavya]. Hindi (Hindi). mo. 11.00. F 10/14 Model Town, New Delhi 110009 India. **LC** AP95.H5; G25.

II/0072-0348
GAZETTEER OF INDIA; INDIAN UNION, THE. (1965)-. English. ir. Government of India, Patiala House, New Delhi India. Index available.

JA
GENDAI. No. 1 (1967)-. Periodical. Japanese. mo. Kodansha Ltd / Japan, 12-21 Otowa 2-chome, 112 Bunkyo-ku, Tokyo Japan. **Tel** 03 5395 3517, FAX 03 9466200, telex 22570. **(Subscription address:** Kinokuniya Company Ltd., 38-1 Sakuragaoka 5, chome Setagaya-ku, Tokyo 156 Japan.**)**

II
GLORY OF INDIA. Vol. 1 (Mar. 1977)-. Periodical. English (Hindi). qt. $22.00. Glory of India, 40UA Bungalow Road, Jawahar Nagar, Delhi 110007 India. **(Subscription address:** Prints India, 11 Darya Ganj, New Delhi, 110002 India, (Phone: 011 91 11 3268645)) **ED** N P Jain. **LC** DS423; .G53. **DD** 954/.005. Index available. **Bk Rev. Ad Acc. Circ:** 1,000. ***Supersedes*** *Glory of India.*
Desc: Articles on indology, book reviews, research in progress, and announcements of publishers.

PH
GRADUATE FORUM (MINDANAO STATE UNIVERSITY. UNIVERSITY RESEARCH CENTER). (GRADUATE FORUM.). Vol. 1, No. 1 (1988)-. Periodical. English. sa. University Research Center, Mindanao State University, PO Box 5594, 9200 Iligan City Philippines. **Bk Rev. Circ:** 500 (ctrl).

II
GUJARATA SAMSODHANA MANDALANUM TRAIMASIKA. (GUJARATA SAMSODHANA MANDALANUM TRAIMASIKA. JOURNAL OF THE GUJARAT RESEARCH SOCIETY.). **Main/Corp** Gujarat Research Society. **Added/Corp** Gujarat Research Society. Journal. **VFOAT** Journal of the Gujarat Research Society. Vol. 1, (1939)-. Periodical. Multiple languages (English and Gujarati). Four times a year. Rs40.00. Gujarat Research Society, Ramkirshna Mission, 16th Road K, Bombay 400-052 India. **ED** M. R. Shah. **LC** AS472; .B52. **Bk Rev. Ad Acc. Circ:** 400.
Desc: Covers psychology, medical science, economics, sociology, history and culture.

KO
HAGWON. VFOAT Hak Won. Periodical. Korean. mo. $78.00. Korean Publication Center, 2605 W Olympic Boulevard, Los Angeles CA 90006-2802. **Tel** (310)383-0526. **LC** AP215.K6; H33.

KO
HAKTUNG. V. 1-. Periodical. Korean. Hyondaesa, 139-11 Ojang-dong Chung-ku, Seoul Korea. **LC** AP95.K6; H35.

CH
HAN HSUEH YEN CHIU TUNG HSUN. VFOAT Newsletter for Research in Chinese Studies. Jan. 1982-. Periodical. Chinese (English). qt. NT$200.00 Taiwan; $20.00 (airmail) US. Newsletter for Research in Chinese Studies, 20 Chung-shan South Road, Taipei Taiwan. **Tel** (02)314-7321, FAX (02)311-0155. **ED** Pei-ling Tsai. **LC** DS734.97.T28; H35. **DD** 951/.007/051249. cum. index. **Bk Rev. Ad Acc. Circ:** 2,500 (ctrl).
Desc: Feature articles, book reviews, meeting reports, news of the academic organizations and scholars, introduction to the newly published symposiums, and selected treaties.

KO
HAN KAREM. V. 1- Nov./Dec. 1977-. Periodical. Korean. W2,500. Han Karam Chulpan Chusik Hoesa, Seoul South Korea. **LC** AP95.K6; H36.

GW/0179-2784
HANNOVERSCHE STUDIEN UBER DEN MITTLEREN OSTEN. (1986)-. Periodical. German. sa. Peter Lang Publishing, 62 West 45th Street, 4th Floor, New York NY 10036. **Tel** (212)764-1471, (800)770-5264, telex 6973364 PLNY. **ED** Ahmad Mahrad. **LC** DS62.4; .H36. **DD** 956/.005. ***Continues*** *Hannoversche Beitrage zur Geschichte des Mittleren Ostens, 0531-7320.*

SU
HARAS AL-WATANI (RIYADH, SAUDI ARABIA). (AL-HARAS AL-WATANI : MAJALLAH.). **VFOAT** National Guards Journal. V. 1, No. 1, (May 1980)-. Periodical. Arabic. mo. $50.00 US. SB 6819, Al-Riyad Saudi Arabia. **Tel** 4828535. **ED** Hassan Abdulla Al-Khalil, Abd-Alkader Hassan Hemeda, Saied Abu-Melha and Sabri Al-Sherbiny Al-Sayed. **LC** AP95.A6; H263. **Bk Rev. Circ:** 3,000 (ctrl).
Desc: Issued by the Saudi National Guard; interested in military research and studies.

IS
HASAD. Periodical. Arabic. IL20.00 single issue. Al-Hasad Publishing House, PO Box 20592, Jerusalem Israel. **LC** AP95.A6; H264.

KU
HAYATUNA. Periodical. Arabic. PO Box 1708, Al-Kuwayt Kuwait. **LC** AP95.A6; H33.

PK
HERALD, THE. Vol. 1 (Jan. 1970)-. Periodical. English. mo. $28.00 Middle East & South Asia; $35.00 Europe, Africa, Far East & Southeast Asia; $40.00 North America & Australia; $42.00 Central & South America. Pakistan Herald Publications Ltd, Haroon House, GPO Box 3740, Karachi 1 Pakistan. **Tel** 011 92 21 520080. **ED** Razia Bhatti. **DD** 052. **Bk Rev. Ad Acc. Circ:** 30,000.
Desc: Aimed at an educated readership with a very high disposal income.

II
HERALD REVIEW (BANGALORE, INDIA). (THE HERALD REVIEW.). (Sept. 2, 1984)-. Periodical. English. wk. Rs117.00. Circulation Department / India, The Printers (Mysore) Ltd, 75 Mahatma Gandhi Road, Bangalore-560001 India. **LC** AP8; .H43. **DD** 052.

JA/0915-9975
HIRAGANA TAIMUZU. VFOAT Hiragana Times. (1988)-. Periodical. English (Japanese and English). mo. $92.00. Yac Planning Inc, K Hasegawa, 4F Kowa Building Shinj 2 3 12, Shinjuku Ku Tokyo Japan 160. **Tel** 011 81 3 3341 8989, FAX 011 81 3 3341-8987. **(Subscription address:** PO Box 11806, Birmingham, AL 35202-1806; Telephone: 800-633-4931**) ED** Nobuaki Nomura. **DD** 059.956 952. **Circ:** 80,000 (ctrl). ***Continues*** *Hiragana Taimuzu Tokyo.*
Desc: Devoted to topics on Japan, the Japanese people, international exchanges, business and current topics.

HK
HONGKONGIANA. Added/Corp Hong Kong Polytechnic. Library. **VFOAT** Hsiang-Kang Chuan Ti Chi Kan Lun Wen So Yin. Vol. 1 (1978)-. English (Chinese). an. Hong Kong Polytechnic Library, Hong Kong Polytechnic Hung Hom, Kowloon Hong Kong. **Tel** (852) 7666854, FAX (852) 7658274, telex 38964 POLYX HX. **ED** Nancy Wong. **LC** Z6958.H6; H65; G155.H63. **DD** 016.951/25005. available on an online database.
Desc: An index to articles about Hong Kong in selected periodicals published in Hong Kong.

CC
HSIN HUA WEN CHAI. VFOAT Xinhua Wenzhai. Vol. 1, No. 25 (1981)-. Periodical. Chinese. mo. $68.21. Chung-Kuo Kuo Chi Shu Tien, PO Box 2820, Beijing, China. **(Subscription address:** China International Book Trading Corporation, PO Box 399, Library Service Department, Beijing 100044 People's Republic of China.**) ED** Chang Hui-Ching. **LC** AP95.C4; H731423. **DD** 089/.951. **Bk Rev. Circ:** 200,000. ***Continues*** *Hsin Hua Yueh Pao. Wen Chai Pan.*
Desc: Abstract journal of Chinese periodical literatures.

HK
HSIN KUAN CHA. V. 1- July; 1973 Year 7 Month-. Periodical. Chinese. $18.00. PO Box 2953, Hong Kong Hong Kong. **LC** AP95.C4; H731425.

HK
HSING HO. 1- May 1975-. Chinese. $50.00. Huan yu Wen Yu Chi Yeh Kung Ssu, PO Box No 13281, General Post Office, Chiu-Lung Hong Kong. **LC** AP95.C4; H7835.

CH
HU-PEI CHING NIEN. VFOAT Hubei Qingnian; Hu Bei Qing Nian. Periodical. Chinese. NT$0.20. Post Office Wu-chang, Wu-chang, People's Republic of China. **LC** AP95.C4; H846 . **DD** 059/.951.

HK
HUA JEN YUEH KAN. VFOAT Hua Jen; Life Overseas. Periodical. Chinese. mo. $15.00. Horizon Publishing Company, 4-B 10-16 Portland Street, Kowloon Hong Kong. **LC** AP95.C4; H849. **DD** 305.8/951.

IR
HUMA (TEHRAN, IRAN). (HUMA.). (19??)-. Periodical. Persian. mo. 65.00Can$. Far Eastern Books, PO Box 846, Adelaide Street Station, Toronto, Ontario, M5C 2K1 Canada. **Tel** (416)477-2900. **LC** AP95.P3; H86.

KO
HYONDAE. V. 1- ; 1957-. Periodical. Korean. mo. $78.00. Korean Publication Center, 2605 W Olympic Boulevard, Los Angeles CA 90006-2802. **Tel** (310)383-0526. **LC** AP95.K6; H927.

KO
HYONDAE PYONGNON. VFOAT The Contemporary Review; Contemporary Review. (1982)-. Periodical. Korean (Korean). Kukhak Charyowon, 15-1 Inhyon-Dong, Chung, Ku, Seoul Korea. **LC** AP95.K6; H9282.

KO
HYONDAE SAENGHWAL. VFOAT Better Life. (1984)-. Periodical. Korean (Korean). mo. 2.400 Per Issue. Hanguk Konsoltontu SA, 730-4 Yongdu 2-dong Tongdaemun-ku, Seoul Korea. **LC** AP95.K6; H929.

US/8755-4771
I. [i]. Periodical. Vietnamese. mo. $22.00. I Magazine, PO Box 4658, Irvine CA 92716. **DD** 059.

JA/0386-765X
IBARAKI DAIGAKU KYOIKUGAKUBU KIYO. JIMBUN, SHAKAI KAGAKU, GEIJUTSU. VFOAT Bulletin of the Faculty of Education, Ibaraki University. Humanities and Social Sciences. Periodical. Japanese (English; summaries and/or abstracts in German and English). Ibaraki Daigaku Kyoikugakubu, 1-1 Bunkyo 2, Mito 310 Japan. **LC** AS552.I2; A26. ***Continues*** *Ibaraki Daigaku Kyoikugakubu Kiyo. Jimbun Shakai Kagaku.*

JA
ICHI. ***Ceased.*** **Added/Corp** Daiichi Seimei Hoken Sogo Kaisha. 1st Ed. (1973)-?. Japanese. sa. Daiichi Seimei Hoken Sogo Kaisha Eigyokikakwai, 13 Yurakucho 1 Chiyoda-ku, Tokyo Japan. **LC** AP95.J2; I27.

II
IDSA NEWS REVIEW ON EAST ASIA. VFOAT News Review on East Asia. **VAT** Institute for Defense Studies and Analyses News Review on East Asia. Vol. 1, No. 1 (Jan. 1987)-. Periodical. English. mo. Rs66.00. Institute for Defence Studies and Analyses, Sapru House, Barakhamba Road, New Delhi 110001 India. **Tel** 011 91 11 3314951. **LC** DS518.1; .I27. **DD** 950/.05. ***Formed by the union of*** *IDSA News Review on China/Koreas/Mongoloia* ***and*** *IDSA News Review on Japan/S.E. Asia/Australasia.*

II
IDSA NEWS REVIEW ON SOUTHEAST ASIA. Added/Corp Institute for Defence Studies and Analyses. **VFOAT** News Review on Southeast Asia. **VAT** Institute for Defence Studies and Analyses News Review on Southeast Asia. Vol. 19, No. 10 (Oct. 1988)-. Periodical. English. mo. Rs66.00. Institute for Defence Studies and Analyses, Sapru House, Barakhamba Road, New Delhi 110001 India. **Tel** 011 91 11 3314951. **LC** UA830; .I34. **DD** 959.05/3/05. ***Continues*** *IDSA News Review on S.E. Asia/Australasia.*

II
ILLUSTRATED WEEKLY OF INDIA, THE. ***Ceased.*** (Feb. 1929)-(Nov. 1993). Periodical. English. wk. Bennett Coleman & Co., Dr D N Road, Bombay 400 001 India. **Tel** 011 91 22 2620271. ***Continues*** *Times of India Illustrated Weekly.*

II/0302-8623
ILLUSTRATED WEEKLY OF INDIA ANNUAL, THE. [Illus. wkly. India, Annu.]. English. an. Rs10.00. Bennett Coleman & Company Ltd, 26 Station Approach, Sudbury Wembley Middx England. **Tel** (01)903-96[illegible]. **LC** DS401; .I23. **DD** 915.4/005.

JA
IMPAKUTO. July 1979 Ed.-. Periodical. Japanese. ¥600. Izara Shobo, c/o Beru Mezon Fasshon, 38-5 Hongo 2 Bunkyo-ku Tokyo 113 Japan. **LC** AP95.J2; I45.

II/0019-3046
IMPRINT. [Imprint]. V. 1- April 1961-. Periodical. English. mo. $15.00. Business Press Private Ltd, Maker Tower E/18th Floor, Cuffe Pd, Bombay 400 005 India. **Tel** 211752 or 217944. **LC** AP8; .I28.
Ind/Abst Energy Res. Abstr. (March 1982-).

PH/0073-599X
INDEX TO PHILIPPINE PERIODICALS. See General Interest-Abstracting, Bibliographies and Statistics.

II
INDIA MAGAZINE OF HER PEOPLE AND CULTURE, THE. See Ethnic Interests.

II
INDIA TODAY. (Dec. 15, 1975)-. Periodical. English. Twenty-six times a year. $70.00. Thomson Living Media India, K-Block Connaught Circus, New Delhi India. **Tel** 3315801-5. **(Subscription address:** Prints India, 11 Darya Ganj, New Delhi, 110002 India, (Phone: 011 91 11 3268645)) **ED** Aroon Purie. **LC** DS401; .I2769. **DD** 954/.05/05. **Bk Rev. Ad Acc. Circ:** 315,000. available on microfilm and microfiche from University Microfilms

International (UMI).
Desc: A general interest newsmagazine that covers current events in politics, business, arts, sports, etc., also personalities.

II/0019-6304
INDIAN REVIEW (MADRAS). (THE INDIAN REVIEW.). [Indian rev.]. Vol. 1 (1900)-. Periodical. English. Twelve times a year. $5.00. GA Natesan, 2-A Cathedral Road, Madras 6 India. **LC** AP8; .I4. **DD** 052. **Ind/Abst** Am. Hist. Life (1964-1965, 1970-1976).

II
INDO-IRANICA. Added/Corp Iran Society, Calcutta. Vol. 1 (July 1946)-. Periodical. Multiple languages (English and Persian). qt. $50.00. Iran Society, 12 Dr M Ishaque Road, Calcutta 700 016 India. **(Subscription address:** Prints India, 11 Darya Ganj, New Delhi 110002 India.**) LC** DS274.2.I4; I53. **DD** 052. **Ind/Abst** Index Islam. Lit.

UK/0306-2848
INDONESIA CIRCLE : [JOURNAL]. Added/Corp Indonesia Circle (University of London. School of Oriental and African Studies). **VFOAT** Journal of the Indonesia Circle; IC. (July 1973)-. Periodical. English (Indonesian). tq. £22.00 UK and Europe; $38.00 other. Oxford University Press, Walton Street, Oxford OX2 6DP England. **Tel** 011 44 865 56767, FAX 011 44 865 267773, telex 837330 OXPRES G. **(Subscription address:** Oxford University Press / USA, Journals Marketing Department, Oxford University Press, 2001 Evans Road, Cary NC 27513.**) ED** Doris Johnson, Ben Arps, Helen Cordell, Annabel Gallop, Angela Hobart, Sarwar Hobohm, Russell Jones, Ulrich Kratz, and Nigel Phillips. **[CCC]. Bk Rev. Ad Acc. Circ:** 275 (ctrl).
Desc: Prints short-to-medium length articles on the languages, literatures, art, archaeology, history, geography, religions, and anthropology of Indonesia.
Ind/Abst Anthropol. Lit.; Int. Bibliogr. Sociol.

US/1044-3665
INDONESIA NEWS SERVICE. [Indones. news serv.]. (198?)-. Periodical. English. da. $227.00 US & Canada; $298.00 others. Indonesia Publications, 7538 Newberry Lane, Lanhan Seabrook MD 20706. **Tel** (301)552-3251, FAX (301)552-4465. **DD** 959.

II
INDRAMA. Periodical. English. qt. Rs40.00 India; $7.00 other. Mr Ghulam Nagshband, Indrama Magazine, F-12 Connaught Place, 110 001 India. **Tel** 331-1133, 31-66663 SITA IN, telex 31-65141. **ED** G Naqshband. **Bk Rev. Ad Acc. Circ:** 7,000.
Desc: All aspects of India except politics.

PK
INDUS. Periodical. English. qt. Hamid Jalal, Lahore Pakistan.

IO
INFORMASI. Added/Corp Institut Keguruan dan Ilmu Pendidikan (Yogyakarta, Indonesia). Fakultas Keguruan Ilmu Sosial. (1971)-. Periodical. English (Indonesian). Three times a year. Yayasan Penerbitan Fkis-Ikip, Karang Malang, Yokyakarta Indonesia. **LC** AP95.I5; I513.

AT/0814-1185
INSIDE INDONESIA. (INSIDE INDONESIA : BULLETIN OF THE INDONESIA RESOURCES AND INFORMATION PROGRAMME (IRIP).). [Inside Indones.]. **Added/Corp** Indonesia Resources and Information Programme. (Nov. 1983)-. Periodical. English. Four times a year. 34.00Aus$ (individual), 58.00Aus$ (institution) Australia & New Zealand; 58.00Aus$ (individuals), 82.00Aus$ (institutions) others. Inside Indonesia, PO Box 190, Northcote Victoria 3070 Australia. **Tel** 011 61 3 4811581, 011 61 3 4177505.
Desc: An illustrated, independent, quality, quarterly which reports from a peoples perspective on politics, human rights, the environment, culture and the movement for change in contemporary indonesia, and assendant Asian superpower.
Ind/Abst Hum. Rights Intern. Rep.

UK/0265-5799
INTERNATIONAL SAUDI-REPORT. VFOAT Saudi-Report; Saudi Report; International Saudi Report. Began in 1980. Periodical. English. wk. $250.00. Saudi Research & Marketing Inc, Washington DC 20004. **Tel** (202)638-7183, telex 897 063. **ED** Talal K Hafiz. **Bk Rev. Ad Acc. Circ:** 20,000.
Desc: Weekly newsletter to educate about Saudi Arabia's policies, current events, etc.

IO/0535-4900
INTISARI. [Intisari]. (Aug. 1963)-. Indonesian. mo. 150 single issue. Jajasan Intisuri, PO Box 615, Dajakarta Indonesia. **LC** AP95.I5; I56.

II
IRAMANATAPURAM PANCANKAM. Tamil (Tamil). an. M Palaniyanti Cervai Son, Putumantapam Madurai 625001 India. **LC** AY1051; .I7.

II
JANARUCI. V. 1- April 1973-. Hindi (Hindi). Vijaya Kumara Gupta, 107/10 Thomson Road 1, Nai Dilli India. **LC** AP95.H5; J337.

US
JAPAN LETTER, THE. No. 1 (Apr. 1973)-. Periodical. English. bw. $120.00. Asia Letter Group, GPO Box 10874, Central Hong Kong. **Tel** 011 852 5 262950, FAX 011 852 5 267131, telex 61166.

IR
JAVANAN-I IMRUZ. VFOAT Javanan. Periodical. Persian. Khiyaban-I, Khayyam-Sakhman, Tehran 11144 Iran. **LC** AP95.P3; J38.

IO
JAYA BAYA. VAT Jaya Surabaya. Vol. 26 No. 50 (1972)-. Periodical. Javanese. wk. Rp125 single issue. J1 Penghela 2 Atas, Surabaya Indonesia. **LC** AP95.J3; D45. ***Continues*** *Djaja Baja.*

HK
JEN JEN TSA CHIH. VFOAT People to People Magazine. V. 1- July; 1973 Year 1 Month-. Periodical. Chinese. $1.00 single issue. 20 Carnavon Road/2nd Floor, Kowloon Hong Kong. **LC** AP95.C4; J36.

CC
JEN WEN TSA CHIH / RENWEN ZAZHI. Added/Corp Shan-Hsi Sheng She Hui Ko Hsueh Hsueh Hui Lien Ho Hui. Shan-Hsi Sheng She Hui Ko Hsueh Yuan (Sian, China). **VFOAT** Renwen Zazhi; Journal of Humanities. (Apr. 1957)-. Periodical. Chinese. Six times a year. $24.20 (surface mail); $49.94 (airmail). **(Subscription address:** China International Book Trading Corporation, PO Box 399, Library Service Department, Beijing 100044 People's Republic of China.**) ED** Yang Zhao and Li Sanhuai. **LC** AP95.C4; J414. **DD** 059/.951. **Bk Rev. Ad Acc. Circ:** 10,000.
Desc: An academic publication of philosophy, history, economics, literature and other social sciences.

CH
JEN YU SHE HUI. VFOAT Man & Society. Vol. 1- Autobiography; Year 62 Year- 1973-. Periodical. Chinese. bm. NT$80.00. 37 O-Mei Street, 4th Floor, 100 Taipei Taiwan. **LC** AP95.C4; J45.

CC/0009-3823
JIEFANGJUN HUABAO. VFOAT PLA Pictorial. (1951)-. Periodical. Chinese. mo. $42.00. **(Subscription address:** China International Book Trading Corporation, PO Box 399, Library Service Department, Beijing 100044 People's Republic of China.**) DD** 355.1.

IR
JIHAD (TEHRAN, IRAN). (AL-JIHAD.). Periodical. Arabic. wk. $30.00. PO Box 616-11365, Tehran Iran. **Tel** 820691. **ED** Salim Al-Hasani. Index available. **Bk Rev. Ad Acc. Circ:** 10,000 (ctrl).
Desc: Newspaper interested in Islamic world affairs, especially Iraq's affairs. Is the voice of the Islamic movement in Iraq.

●UK/1354-7860
JOURNAL OF ASIA PACIFIC ECONOMIES. **See** Economics.

US/0162-6795
JOURNAL OF ASIAN CULTURE. [J. Asian cult.]. **Added/Corp** University of California, Los Angeles. Dept. of Oriental Languages. Graduate Students Association. Graduate Students in Asian Studies at UCLA. Vol. 1 (Spring 1977)-. English. an. $10.00 (institutions), $7.00 (individuals). East Asian Language & Culture at UCLA, 290 Royce Hall, 405 Hilgard Avenue, Los Angeles CA 90024. **Tel** (310)206-8235. **ED** Linda H. Chance. **LC** DS1; .J638. **DD** 950. Index available. cum. index. **Bk Rev. Ad Acc. Circ:** 500.
Desc: Devoted to articles written by graduate students in various fields in Asian studies.
Ind/Abst Acad. Search (July 1993-); Am. Hist. Life (1977-); Humanit. Source (Jul. 1993-); INFO-SOUTH Abstr.; Mag. Search; Soc. Plann. Policy Dev. Abstr.

US/0742-5929
JOURNAL OF CHINESE STUDIES (ALBUQUERQUE, N.M.). (JOURNAL OF CHINESE STUDIES.). [J. Chin. stud.]. **Added/Corp** American Association for Chinese Studies. Vol. 1, No. 1 (Feb. 1984)-. Periodical. English. Twice a year. $12.00. Journal of Chinese Studies, University of New Mexico, 555 Humanities, Albuquerque NM 87131. **Tel** (505)277-6362. **ED** Fred Gillette Sturm. Index available. **Bk Rev. Ad Acc. Circ:** 500 (ctrl).
Desc: A multidisciplinary forum for the discussion of topics from the entire range of China studies.
Ind/Abst MLA Int. Bibl. Books Artic. Mod. Lang. Lit.

II
JOURNAL OF CONTEMPORARY THOUGHT. Added/Corp Forum on Contemporary Theory. (1991)-. English. Prafulla C Kar, C-11 Vrindavan Estate, Pashabhai Patel Park, Race Course Circle, Vadodara 390015, India. **LC** AS471; .J67. **DD** 052.

●US/1059-3152
JOURNAL OF SUNG-YUAN STUDIES. [J. Sung-Yuan stud.]. **Added/Corp** State University of New York at Albany. Dept. of East Asian Studies. **VFOAT** Journal of Sung Yuan Studies; JSYS; Sung Liao Chin Yuan. No. 22 (1992)- Vol. 23 (1993)-. Periodical. English (Chinese). an (March). $15.00 (individual); $25.00 (institution). State University of New York at Albany / Department of East Asian Studies, Humanities 285, Albany NY 12222. **Tel** (518)356-5398, FAX (518)442-4118. **ED** James M. Hargett. **LC** DS751; .S83. **DD** 951. **Bk Rev**, (Qty: 4-5). **Ad Acc. Pr Rev. Circ:** 400. ***Continues*** *Sung Liao Chin Yuan, 0275-4118.*

II/0368-3303
JOURNAL OF THE ASIATIC SOCIETY. [J. Asiat. Soc.]. **Added/Corp** Asiatic Society (Calcutta, India). Vol. 1, No. 1 (1959)-. Periodical. English. qt. $25.00. The Asiatic Society, 1 Park Street, Calcutta 16 India. **(Subscription address:** Prints India, 11 Darya Ganj, New Delhi 110002 India.**) *Formed by the union of*** *Journal of the Asiatic Society. Letters* ***and*** *Journal of the Asiatic Society. Science.*
Ind/Abst Am. Hist. Life (1959-1971-).

II/0030-5324
JOURNAL OF THE ORIENTAL INSTITUTE, M.S. UNIVERSITY OF BARODA. (JOURNAL OF THE ORIENTAL INSTITUTE.). [J. Orient. Inst. M.S. Univ. Baroda]. **Main/Corp** Oriental Institute (Vadodara, India). Vol. 1 (Sept. 1951)-. Periodical. English (Sanskrit). Four times a year (Mar., June, Sept., Dec.). Oriental Institute / India, Opp Sayaji Gunj Tower, Tilak Road, Vadodara 390 002 India. **Tel** 329727. **(Subscription address:** Prints India, 11 Darya Ganj, New Delhi 110002 India.**) ED** R. T. Vyas. **LC** PJ25; .B3. **DD** 891; 930. Index available. cum. index. **Bk Rev. Ad Acc. Circ:** 550. available on microfiche; available on microfilm.
Desc: This indological articles is about the textual and cultural problems of epic studies, notices of MSS, and survey of oriental journals.
Ind/Abst Int. Bibliogr. Sociol.; MLA Int. Bibl. Books Artic. Mod. Lang. Lit.

JA/0916-7781
JPG LETTER. [JPG lett.]. **VFOAT** Japan Publications Guide Letter. (1985)-. Periodical. English. mo. $200.00. Japan Publications Guide Service, PO Box 5056, Tokyo 100-31 Japan. ***Continues*** *Japan Publications Guide, 0387-3927.*

US
JPRS REPORT. Added/Corp United States. Joint Publications Research Service. United States. Foreign Broadcast Information Service. **VFOAT** Near East & South Asia; JPRS Report. Near East and South Asia. **VAT** Joint Publications Research Service Report. Near East and South Asia. English (translations available in Multiple languages). National Technical Information Service - NTIS, Room 2027S, 5285 Port Royal Road, Springfield VA 22161. **Tel** (703)487-4630, (703)487-4660, (703)487-4650, FAX (703)321-8547, telex 89-9405. ***Continues*** *Near East/South Asia Report.*

KO
KAEBYOK UI SORI. VFOAT Voice of Resurgence; Tongbang Ui Pit Kaebyok Ui Sori. Periodical. English (Korean). W700. Chondogyo Chungang Chongbu Chulpanbu, 88 Kyongun-dong Chongno-ku, Seoul Korea. **LC** AP95.K6; K3.

KO
KAJONG CHOSON. First issue (1985, 1)-. Periodical. Korean. mo. W39.000. Choson Ilbosa, 61 Taepyong-no 1-ka, Chung-ku, Seoul South Korea. **LC** AP95.K6; K32.

IR
KASHANAH. Periodical. Persian. 100.00IR single issue. Maydan-I Firdawsi Sakhtman-I Shahd, Tabaqah-I Panjum Tehran Iran. **LC** AP95.P3; K37.

II
KEYNOTE (BOMBAY, INDIA). (KEYNOTE.). Issue No. 1 (Mar. 1982)-. Periodical. English. mo. 50.00. Century Bhavan Ground Floor, Dr Annie Besant Road, Worli Bombay 400 025 India. **LC** AP8; .K48. **DD** 052.

US/0898-1930
KHOSANA : THE BULLETIN OF THE THAILAND/LAOS/CAMBODIA STUDIES GROUP OF THE SOUTHWEST ASIA COUNCIL, ASSOCIATION FOR ASIAN STUDIES. [Khosana]. No. 1 (Oct. 1976)-. Bulletin. English. Twice a year. $8.00. Association Asian Studies Inc, c/o Dr J Hanks, Hill Side Street, North Bennington VT 05257. **Tel** (802)447-2277. **ED** Jacqueline Butler. **LC** DS524.7; .K48. **DD** 016.959/005. **Circ:** 300 (ctrl).
Desc: Contains news items, bibliographies and filmography.

KO
KIROGI. Periodical. Korean. W150.00. Hungsadan, 199-34 2 Ka Ulchiro, Choong ku Seoul Korea. **LC** AP95.K6; K57.

JA
KOKUSHIKAN DAIGAKU KYOYO RON SHU. Main/Corp Kokushikan Daigaku Kyoyo Gakki. **Added/Corp** Kokushikan Daigaku. Kyoyo Ronshu. **VFOAT** Kyoyo Ronshu. 1975 Edition-. Multiple languages

General Interest —General Interest-Asia

(Japanese and English). Kokushikan Daigaku Kyoyo Gakkai, 28-1 Setagaya 4-chome Setagaya-ku, Tokyo 154 Japan. **LC** AS552.K66; A3.

US/1053-4806
KOREA BRIEFING. [Korea brief.]. **Added/Corp** Asia Society. (1990)-. Periodical. English. an. $14.85 (paperback). Westview Press Inc, 5500 Central Avenue, Boulder CO 80301. **Tel** (303)444-3541, FAX (303)449-3356. **LC** DS922.46; .K67. **DD** 951.9504/3/05.

US/0146-9657
KOREA NEWSREVIEW. VAT Korea News Review. (19??)-. Periodical. English. Fifty-two times a year. $108.00. Korea Herald, CPO Box 6479, Seoul Korea 100 771. **(Subscription address:** Korea Herald, PO Box 312, Hartsdale NY 10530.**) ED** Cook-chin Ahn. **LC** DS901; .K715. **DD** 951.9/005. **Bk Rev. Ad Acc. Circ:** 5,000 (ctrl).
Desc: News concerning Korean business, investments, and Korean politics and culture.

KO
KOREA TODAY. V. 1- Feb. 1971-. English. bm. Peace Book Company Ltd, 903 Wing on House, 71 des Voeux Road C, Room 1502, Hong Kong Hong Kong. **Tel** 011 852 5 8046687, FAX 011 852 5 8046409, telex 76929. **LC** DS902.4; .K67. **DD** 915.19/005.

II
KOSA. Hindi (Hindi). Rs9.00. L F 6 Srikrishanpuri, Boring Road -13, Patana India. **LC** AP95.H5; K67.

HK
KUAN CHA CHIA. VFOAT Observers Monthly. V. 1-. Periodical. Chinese. $3.00 single issue. Kuan Cha Chia Chu Pan She, PO Box 2910, Kowloon Hong Kong. **LC** AP95.C4; K8367.

HK
KUANG CHIAO CHING. VFOAT Wide Angle. (1972)-. Periodical. Chinese. Twelve times a year. $32.22 China Taiwan & Macau; $30.31 Hong Kong; $34.95 others. Wide Angle Press Ltd, 195-197 Johnston Road 7/F, Wanchai Hong Kong. **LC** AP95.C4; K838.

CC
KUANG-TUNG HUA PAO. VFOAT Guangdong Pictorial. (19??)-. Periodical. Chinese. mo. $50.40. **(Subscription address:** China International Book Trading Corporation, PO Box 399, Library Service Department, Beijing 100044 People's Republic of China.**)**

JA/0368-5144
KURUME DAIGAKU RONSO. [Kurume Daigaku ronso]. **Main/Corp** Kurume Daigaku. Shogakubu. **VFOAT** Kurume University Journal. Academic Scholarly Publication. Japanese (English and German). Kurume Daigaku Shogakubu, 1635 Miimachi, Kurume Japan. **LC** AS552.K82; A45. **CODEN** KDRSAY. Documents available from BIOSIS Document Express, CASDDS.
Ind/Abst Biocont. News Inf.; Biol. Abstr.; Chem. Abstr. (1958-1981).

JA
KYODO KANKEI SHIMBUN KIJI SAKUIN. Added/Corp Gifu Kenritsu Toshokan. (1968)-. Periodical. Japanese. Gifu Kenritsu Toshokan, 1 Omiyamachi, Gifu Japan. **Tel** (0582)65-9136. **LC** Z3307.G54; K94; DS894.59.G535. ctrl circ.
Desc: An index of local (Gifu district) pages of the newspapers.

KO
KYORE UI KIL. Added/Corp Han Kyore Sahoe Yonguso. (1991)-. Periodical. Korean. mo. Han Kyore Sahoe Yonguso, 47 Chungjogno 2-Ka Sodaemun-Ku, Seoul Korea. **LC** AP95.K6; K96.

JA
KYOTO DAIGAKU TONAN AJIA KENKYU SENTA YORAN. Main/Corp Kyoto Daigaku Tonan Ajia Kenkyu Senta. Japanese. be. Kyoto Daigaku Tonan Ajia Kenkyu Senta, 46 Yoshida Adachicho, Sakyo-ku 606, Kyoto Japan. **Tel** (075)753-7344, FAX (075)753-7350. **LC** DS524.8.J3; K93A. **Circ:** 800.
Desc: Gives general information on the activities of the organization.

JA
KYOTO FURITSU DAIGAKU SEIKATSU BUNKA SENTA NEMPO. Main/Corp Kyoto Furitsu Daigaku. Seikatsu Bunka Senta. No. 1 (1976)-. Japanese. Kyoto Furitsu Daigaku Fuzoku Toshokan, c/o Kyoto Furitsu Daigaku, Fuzoku Toshokan, Shimokamo Hangicho, Sankyo-ku 606 Kyoto Japan. **LC** AS552.K89; A3.

JA
KYOTO GAIKOKUGO DAIGAKU KENKYU RONSO. Main/Corp Kyoto Gaikokugo Daigaku. **Added/Corp** Kyoto Gaikokugo Daigaku. Academic Bulletin, Kyoto University of Foreign Studies. Kyoto Gaikokugo Daigaku. Sogo Kenkyujo. **VFOAT** Academic Bulletin, Kyoto University of Foreign Studies; Bulletin of the Kyoto University of Foreign Studies. Vol. 3 (1959)-. Bulletin. Japanese (English). Kyoto Gaikokugo Daigaku, 6 Saiin Kasamecho, Ukyo-ku Kyoto Japan. **LC** AS552.K92; A25. **Continues** Kyoto Gaikokugo Tanki Daigaku. Kenkyu Ronso.

GW
LANDERBERICHT. BANGLADESCH. Added/Corp Germany (West). Statistisches Bundesamt. 1989-. German (table of contents in English). W Kohlhammer Verlag GmbH, Postfach 800430, D 70549 Stuttgart Germany. **Tel** 011 49 711 78631, FAX 011 49 711 7863263, telex 7-255820. **LC** HA4590.6; .A27. **Continues** Statistik des Auslandes. Landerbericht. Bangladesch, 0930-2379.

GW/0937-7824
LANDERBERICHT. BIRMA. Added/Corp Germany (West). Statistisches Bundesamt. (1989)-. German (table of contents in English). W Kohlhammer Verlag GmbH, Postfach 800430, D 70549 Stuttgart Germany. **Tel** 011 49 711 78631, FAX 011 49 711 7863263, telex 7-255820. **LC** HA1693; .G43. **Continues** Statistik des Auslandes. Landerbericht. Birma, 0175-8551.

GW/0939-3773
LANDERBERICHT. JAPAN. Added/Corp Germany (West). Statistisches Bundesamt. (1990)-. German (table of contents in English). W Kohlhammer Verlag GmbH, Postfach 800430, D 70549 Stuttgart Germany. **Tel** 011 49 711 78631, FAX 011 49 711 7863263, telex 7-255820. **LC** HA4621; .S73. **Continues** Statistik des Auslandes. Landerbericht. Japan, 0176-313X.

GW/0937-7921
LANDERBERICHT. PHILIPPINEN. Added/Corp Germany (West). Statistisches Bundesamt. 1989-. German (table of contents in English). Verlag W Kohlhammer GmbH, Abt Veroffentlichungen des Statistischen Bundesamtes, Philipp-Reis-Strasse 3, W-6500 Mainz 42 Germany. **LC** HA4611; .S7. **Continues** Statistik des Auslandes. Landerbericht. Philippinen, 0173-3117.

GW/0939-6896
LANDERBERICHT. THAILAND. Added/Corp Germany (West). Statistisches Bundesamt. 1990-. German (table of contents in English). Verlag W Kohlhammer GmbH, Abt Veroffentlichungen des Statistischen Bundesamtes, Philipp-Reis-Strasse 3, W-6500 Mainz 42 Germany. **Continues** Statistik des Auslandes. Landerbericht. Thailand, 0723-4538.

GW/0937-7891
LANDERBERICHT. TURKEI. Added/Corp Germany (West). Statistisches Bundesamt. 1989-. German (table of contents in English). W Kohlhammer Verlag GmbH, Postfach 800430, D 70549 Stuttgart Germany. **Tel** 011 49 711 78631, FAX 011 49 711 7863263, telex 7-255820. **LC** HA4556.5; .A29. **Continues** Statistik des Auslandes. Landerbericht. Turkei, 0930-004x.

GW/0938-4707
LANDERBERICHT. VEREINIGTE ARABISCHE EMIRATE. Added/Corp Germany (West). Statistisches Bundesamt. **VFOAT** Vereinigte Arabische Emirate. 1990-. German (table of contents in English). Verlag W Kohlhammer GmbH, Abt Veroffentlichungen des Statistischen Bundesamtes, Philipp-Reis-Strasse 3, W-6500 Mainz 42 Germany. **LC** HA4566; .A268. **Continues** Statistik des Auslandes. Landerbericht. Vereinigte Arabische Emirate, 0931-1297.

CC
LIAO WANG (PEKING, CHINA). (LIAO WANG.). **VFOAT** Outlook Weekly. (April 1981)-. Periodical. Chinese. wk. $57.70. **(Subscription address:** China International Book Trading Corporation, PO Box 399, Library Service Department, Beijing 100044 People's Republic of China.**) LC** AP95.C4; L535. **DD** 951.05/05.

US/8755-9358
LIAOWANG (INTERNATIONAL ED.). (LIAO WANG = OUTLOOK WEEKLY.). [Liaowang]. **VFOAT** Outlook Weekly; Liaowang; Liao Wang Chou Kan Hai Wai Pan. (19??)-. Periodical. Chinese. Fifty-two times a year (No issue on Feb. 1st (chinese new year holiday)). $100.00. Synergy Publishing, 15 Mercer Street, Suite 102, New York NY 10013. **Tel** (212)274-9465, FAX (212)274-9466, telex 426693. **ED** Mu Qing. **LC** AP95.C4; L534. **DD** 059/.951. **Circ:** 5,000.
Desc: A Chinese news magazine that includes news, reports and information from China.

CH
LIEN HO YUEH KAN. First published in (August 1981)-. Periodical. Chinese. mo. NT$600.00. Tai-Wan Ying Wen Tsa Chin She, 66 Chang-Sha Chieh 2nd Sect, Taipei Shin Taiwan. **LC** AP95.C4; L577. **DD** 059/.951.

PH
LIFESTYLE ASIA. English. $200.00 US; $150.00 Asia. Jacobo & Sons, PO Box 1899, Manila Philippines. **Tel** 63 2 711 1020.

II/0459-469X
LINK. Vol. 1 (Aug. 15, 1958)-. Periodical. English. wk. $16.00. United India Periodicals Ltd, PO Box 7046, Link House, New Delhi 110002, India. **Tel** 11 91 11 3311056. **ED** E Narayanan. **LC** AP8; .L47. **DD** 059/.54. **Bk Rev. Ad Acc.** ctrl circ.
Desc: A weekly news magazine. Special coverage of Indian and foreign affairs, science, art, and economy.
Ind/Abst ARTbibliogr. Mod.; Middle East Abstr. Index.

PH
LIWAYWAY. Tagalog. wk. $28.00. Liwayway Publishing Inc, 2249 Pasong Tamo, Makati Rizal 3116 Philippines. **LC** AP95.T27; L58.
Ind/Abst Index Philip. Period.

CE/0458-1725
LOGOS (COLUMBO, SRI LANKA). (LOGOS.). **Added/Corp** Samajaya ha Samayika Kendraya (Colombo, Sri Lanka). Vol. 1 (1960)-. Periodical. English. Four times a year. $18.00 South Asia; $25.00 others. Centre for Society and Education, 281 Deans Road, Colombo Sri Lanka Ceylon. **Tel** 011 94 1 595425. **ED** Tissa Balasuriya Omi, Bernadeen Silva and Douglas de Silva. **Circ:** 1,000 (ctrl).
Desc: Areas of socio-economics, theology, education, aid, human rights, tourism, MNCS, women, third world arms, urbanization, agriculture, village health and children.
Ind/Abst Bibliogr. Mission.; Hum. Rights Intern. Rep.

JA/0456-5339
LOOK JAPAN. (195?)-. Periodical. English (Spanish). mo. $43.00 North, South and Central America; $38.00 Southeast, Far East, Asia and Oceania; $57.00 Japan; $40.00 other. Look Japan Publishing Pte Ltd, 24 Raffles Place #25-01 Clifford Center, Singapore 0104 Singapore. **Tel** 011 65 5330333. **LC** HC461; .L66. **Ad Acc. Circ:** 50,000 (ctrl). available on CD-ROM.
Desc: Economy and industry, science and technology, culture and people, life and history and opinion of Japan.
Ind/Abst Acad. Abstr. (July 1993-); Acad. Search (Jan. 1994-); Coal Abstr.; Energy Res. Abstr. (April 1980-); Mag. Artic. Summar. Elite (July 1994-); Mag. Artic. Summar. CD-ROM (July 1993-); PAIS Int. Print (1991-).

CC
LUNG MEN CHEN. Periodical. Chinese. RMBY0.35. Ssu-Chuan Jen Min Chu Pan She, Hsin Hua Shu Tien, Cheng-tu Ssu-chuan, People's Republic of China. **LC** AP95.C4; L86. **DD** 089/.951.

JA
MACHIKANEYAMA RONSO : NIHONGAKU-HEN. VFOAT Machikaneyama Ronso: Japanology. No. 9- ; 1975-. Japanese (French; summaries and/or abstracts in French, German and English). Osaka Daigaku Bungakubu, 1-1 Machikaneyamacho, Toyonaka Osaka Japan. **Tel** (06)844-1151. **LC** DS820.8; .M3. **Circ:** 400 (ctrl). **Continues in part** Machikaneyaka Ronso: Shigaku; Machikaneyama Ronso: Bungaku.

II
MADHYAHNA. Periodical. Bengali (Bengali). 2.50. Sailendra Natha Bersu, 68 Mahatma Gandhi Road, Calcutta-9 Ludia, Kalidata India. **LC** PK1700; .M3.

II
MAHARASHTRA TAIMSA VARSHIKA. (19??)-. Marathi (Marathi). 301.00 daily, 57.00 Sunday. Beneta Kolamana, Times of India Press, Mumbai India. **Tel** 4150543. **ED** Govind Talwalkar. **LC** AP95.M3; M354. **Bk Rev. Ad Acc.**
Desc: Covers politics, economics, social interest, literature and the arts.

LE
MAJALLAT AL-FIKR AL-MUASIR. VFOAT Fikr Al-Muasir. V. 1- ; 1974-. Arabic. £L1.50. S B 8808, Beirut Lebanon. **LC** AP95.A6; M254. **Supersedes** Ulum.

II
MANTHANA. Periodical. Hindi. qt. Rs30.00 India; £9.00 UK; $15.00 other. Dinadayala Samsthana, 7-E Swami Ramtirth Nagar, New Delhi 110055 India. **Tel** 526735/526792. **ED** K R Malkani. **LC** AP95.H5; M33. **Bk Rev. Ad Acc. Circ:** 2,000.
Desc: This is a thematic magazine. Recent issues dealt with cleaning ganges, new educational policy, national integration, rural uplift in India, Punjab crisis, etc.

NE
MARUNI. Phanko 1- Vaisakha 2029- 1972-. Nepali (Nepali). 2.00 each issue. Narayani Ka La Mandira, Narayanagadha Nepal. **LC** AP95.N4; M38.

MY
MASSA. V. 1 (June 1982)-. Periodical. Malay (Malay). mo. $2.50 Each Issue. Massa Enterprise, 4B-1 Bangunan Uda JI Pantai Baru, Kuala Lumpur Malaysia. **LC** AP95.M24; M37.

IO/0302-9646
MAWAS DIRI. [Mawas diri]. Periodical. Indonesian. mo. Rp80 each issue. P T Mandiri, Djl Kramat Lontar H 7, Djakarta Indonesia. **LC** AP95.I5; M36.

General Interest —General Interest-Asia

IO
MAYAPADA. Periodical. Indonesian. Jajasan Perpustakaan Nasional, Djalan Gunung Sahari III No 4, PO Box 2729 DKT, Jakarta Indonesia. **LC** AP95.I5; M37.

US
MIJU SAENGHWAL. (1981)-. Periodical. Korean. mo. $30.00. Miju Saenghwasa, 7309 Arlington Boulevard, #203, Falls Church VA 22042. **LC** AP95.K6; M53.

II/0026-8380
MODERN REVIEW (CALCUTTA), THE. (THE MODERN REVIEW.). [Mod. rev.]. Vol. 1 (Jan. 1907)-. Periodical. English. mo. $17.00. Prabasi Press Private Ltd, 109C Block F New Alipore, Calcutta 700 053 India. **Tel** 49 1748. **(Subscription address:** Prints India, 11 Darya Ganj, New Delhi 110002 India.) **ED** Ramananda Chatterjee. **LC** AP8; .M6.
Ind/Abst Annu. Bibliogr. Engl. Lang. Lit.

TU
MONDIAL: BULLETIN OF TENDER ANNOUNCEMENTS. Bulletin. English (Turkish). ir (156 issues). $250.00. Mondial, Karanfil Sokak 21 4, Kizilay Ankara Turkey.

IT/0390-2811
MONDO CINESE. [Mondo cin.]. (Jan./March 1973)-. Periodical. Italian. Four times a year (Mar., June, Sept., Dec.). L48000 Italy; L96000 other. Instituto Italo Cinese, Via Carducci 18, 20123 Milan Italy. **Tel** 011 39 2 8057384. **LC** DS701; .M58. **DD** 951/.005. **Bk Rev**. **Ad Acc**. Circ: 1,100.
Desc: Covers various aspects concerning China such as economics, politics and literature.
Ind/Abst Am. Hist. Life (1973-).

II/0537-1848
MONTHLY PUBLIC OPINION SURVEYS. **Main/Corp** Indian Institute of Public Opinion. Vol. 1, No. 1 (Aug. 1955)-. Periodical. English. Twelve times a year. $80.00. Indian Institute of Public Opinion, PO Box 288, New Delhi 1 India. **Tel** 011 91 11 312846, 011 91 11 312742, FAX 011 91 11 310405, telex 31-65156 NEWS IN. **ED** E. P. W. da Costa. **LC** DS401; .I39. **DD** 954.005.
Bk Rev.
Desc: Results of surveys on social, political and cultural affairs conducted by the institute in India. Also special articles and surveys on international images, tourism, family planning and newspaper readership.

JA
MONUMENTA NIPPONICA MONOGRAPHS. Added/Corp Jochi Daigaku. (1940)-. Monographic series. English. ir. Price varies per volume. Sophia University / Japanese Culture, 7-1 Kioi-cho Chiyoda-ku, Tokyo 102 Japan. **Tel** 11 81 3 32383544, FAX 11 81 3 32385056. **ED** Michael Cooper. **Bk Rev**. **Ad Acc**.
Desc: Japanese culture, especially literature, history, and religion.

NP
MULA-DHARA. V. 1, No. 1-. Periodical. Nepali. qt. $75.00. Post Box 2678, Government Printing Office, Kathmandu Nepal. **Tel** 4-14085. **ED** Shyam Joshy. **LC** DS495.5; .M84. **Bk Rev** **Ad Acc** Circ: 10,000.
Desc: Editorials, local news, international news, humour, foreign affairs articles, political features, economic articles, book reviews, health columns, current topics, readers' views and features.

KO
MYONGNANG. Periodical. Korean. W650 single issue. Myengnang SA, 111-1 1-ka Inhyon-dong Chung-ku, Seoul South Korea. **LC** AP95.K6; M93.

NP
NAYAM KADAMA. V. 1- 2029- 1972-. Nepali (Nepali). 1.25 single issue. Mawalpur, Nawal Parashi Lumbini Anchal, Navalpura Nepal. **LC** AP95.N4; N33.

NP/0028-2723
NEPAL PRESS DIGEST. Added/Corp Regmi Research Project. (19??)-. Periodical. English. Fifty-two times a year. Mehesh Chandra Regni, Lazimpat, Kathmandu Nepal. **LC** DS485.N4; N38.
Desc: A digest of news and editorial comments on national developments based on newspapers.

NP/0028-2731
NEPAL PRESS REPORT. VFOAT Press Report. No. 1/67-. Periodical. English. da (except Saturday, Sunday and public holidays). Rs3,600.00 Nepal, Rs2,500.00 India, $250.00 other countries. Regmi Research Pvt Ltd, Regmi Village, Lazimpat, Kathmandu Nepal. **LC** DS485.N4; R45. **DD** 954.9/6/005.
Desc: Summary translations of news reports, editorial comments, and special articles from the non-English-language press.

US/1075-2951
NEW ASIA REVIEW. (19??)-. English. qt. $72.00 US; $95.00 other. Greenwood Press Inc, PO Box 5007, Westport CT 06881-5007. **Tel** (203)226-3571, FAX (203)222-1502.

II
NEW INDIA. V. 1- Dec. 15, 1976/Jan. 15, 1977-. Periodical. English. Rs1.50 single issue. Y Gondal, 12/90 Connaught Circus, New Delhi 110001 India. **LC** HC435.2; .N44. **DD** 954.05/05.

II
NEW TONES. (19??)-. Periodical. English. mo. Rs10.00. Ratna Dhar Jha, C-19 Model Town, Delhi 9 India. **LC** AP8; .N42. **DD** 052. available with illustrations.

II
NEWS FROM ISRAEL. Added/Corp Israel. Consulate, Bombay. Vol. 1 (195?)-. Periodical. English. mo. $15.00. Consulate of Israel, Bombay, India. **(Subscription address:** Prints India, 11 Darya Ganj, New Delhi, 110002 India, (Phone: 011 91 11 3268645))

UK/0142-6567
NEWS FROM XINHUA NEWS AGENCY, CHINA. WEEKLY ISSUE. Ceased. [News Xinhua News Agency China, Wkly. issue]. (1979)-(Jan. 1989). Periodical. English. wk. W Chinque, 76 Chancery Lane, London WC2A 1AA England. **Tel** 011 41 1 242 9217. **Continues** Xinhua Weekly.

HK
NIEN CHING JEN. Ceased. VFOAT Teens. (Oct. 1973)-(19??). Chinese (Chinese). mo. Teens' Magazine Publishing Company, No 1 on Ning Lane, Sai Ying Pun Hong Kong, Hong Kong. **LC** AP95.C4; N53.

JA/0288-3031
NIHON JOSHI DAIGAKU KIYO. BUNGAKUBU. VFOAT Journal. School of Letters. Began in 1951. Periodical. Japanese. an. Nihon Joshi Daigaku 8-1, Mejirodai 2 Bunkyo-ku, Tokyo-to 112 Japan. **LC** AS552.T71515; A33.

JA
NIKKEI : BIMONTHLY FORUM FOR IDEAS AND NEWS FROM NIHON KEIZAI SHIMBUN, INC. Added/Corp Nihon Keizai Shimbun. (19??)-. Periodical. English. bm. Nihon Keizai Shimbun Inc., 9-5 Otemachi 1 Chome, Chiyoda-Ku Tokyo 100 Japan. **Tel** 011 81 3 32700251.

CC
NING-HSIA TA HSUEH HSUEH PAO. SHE HUI KO HSUEH PAN. Added/Corp Ning-Hsia ta Hsueh. (19??)-. Periodical. Chinese. qt. RMB¥0.36. Ning-Hsia Hsueh Hsueh Pao, Post Office, Yin-Chuan Shih, People's Republic of China. **LC** AS452.Y55; A25. **DD** 089/.951.

KO
NONMUNJIP (TONGNAE YOJA CHONMUN TAEHAK). (NONMUNJIP.). VFOAT Journal. Periodical. Korean. Tongnae Yoja Chonmun Taehak, 640 Pansong-dong Haeundae-ku, Pusan Korea. **LC** AS559.P83; A24.

CH
NOTICIAS DE LA REPUBLICA DE CHINA. (19??)-. Periodical. Spanish. Thirty-six times a year. $5.00. Kwang Hwa Publ Co, 8th Floor No. 15 Hangchow, S RD Sec 1, Taipei 100 Taiwan. **Tel** 011 886 2 3122846, 011 886 2 3922245 ext. 15.

IT
NOTIZIARIO - ISTITUTO GIAPPONESE DI CULTURA. **Main/Corp** Istituto Giapponese di Cultura. Italian. an. Free. Istituto Giapponese di Cultura, Via A Gramsci 74, 00197 Rome Italy. **Tel** (06)3609794. **LC** DS834.95; .I87A. **DD** 952/.007/1145632. Circ: 1,000.
Desc: Bulletin of Japan cultural institute informing of its activities and introducing modern Japanese culture.

MY/0076-3373
OFFICIAL YEAR BOOK - MALAYSIA. **Main/Corp** Malaysia. VFOAT Buku Rasmi Tahunan. Official Yearbook. V. 1- 1961-. English. ir. Government Printing Press / Malaysia, Jalan Chan Sow Ling, Kuala Lumpur Malaysia. **LC** DS591. **DD** 915.95/005.

II/0377-7596
OH CALCUTTA. V. 1- Winter 1971-. Periodical. English. qt. $6.00, £3.50. 49/11A Hindustan Park, Calcutta 29 India. **Tel** 46-0028. **ED** A N Roy. **LC** DS486.C2; O36. **DD** 954/.14. **Bk Rev**. **Ad Acc**. Circ: 10,000.
Desc: Includes Indian themes, collection of world writings, and rare texts.

KO
ONUL UI HANGUK (SEOUL, KOREA : 1983). (ONUL UI HANGUK.). VFOAT Korea Today. Vol. 1, (Feb. 1983)-. Periodical. Korean (Korean). mo. W3,000 single issue. Chusik Hoesa Onlu Ui Hanguk, 446-285 Yonhui-dong Sodaemun-ku, Seoul Korea. **LC** DS922; .O575.

CE
OPEN MIND (COLOMBO, SRI LANKA). (OPEN MIND : THE NEWSPAPER OF THE ENGLISH-SPEAKING UNION OF SRI LANKA.). Periodical. English. mo. English Speaking Union of Sri Lanka, 50/16 Sir James Peiris Mawatha, Colombo 2 Sri Lanka. **LC** PAR.

KO
ORINI SAE NONGMIN. V. 1- (May, '84 issue)-. Periodical. Korean. mo. W500 single issue. Nongop Hyoptong Chohap Chunganghoe, 75 Chunjongno 1-ka Chung-ku, Seoul Korea. **LC** AP215.K6; S22. **Continues** Sae Nongmin Purok Orini Pan.

KO
PAEKKWANG. V. 1-Series. Periodical. Korean. W16,000. Hyondaesa, 139-11 Ojang-dong Chung-ku, Seoul Korea. **LC** AP95.K6; P33.

PK
PAIMAN. V. 1- April 10, 1972-. Urdu (Urdu). 50.00. **LC** AP95.U7; P27.

II
PAINJANA. Ceased. (19??)-?. Marathi (Marathi). mo. Ga Va Behere, 458/2 Sadashiv Peth, Talak Road 30, Pune India. **LC** AP95.M3; P325.

JA
PAIPU. VFOAT The Pipe. Periodical. Japanese (Japanese). Nihon Sembai Kosha Kohoka, 2 Akasaka Aoicho Minato-ku, Tokyo 107 Japan. **LC** AP95.J2; P33.

●US/1061-6101
PAKISTAN (BOULDER, COLO.). (PAKISTAN.). [Pakistan]. Added/Corp American Institute of Pakistan Studies (University of Utah). (1992)-. English. an. $31.50 (two years). Westview Press Inc, 5500 Central Avenue, Boulder CO 80301. **Tel** (303)444-3541, FAX (303)449-3356. **LC** IN PROCESS; DS376; .P275. **DD** 954.

PK/0552-9263
PAKISTAN YEAR BOOK. (1969)-. English. an (Dec.). $36.00. East and West Publishing Company, 22 Corner Chambers, I I Chundrigar Road, Karachi 0102 Pakistan. **Tel** 011 92 21 212036. **LC** DS376; .P3488. **DD** 052.

II
PAKSHIKA RUDRAVANI. Marathi (Marathi). 10.00. Jivana Kirloskara, 499 Rasta Peth 11, Pune India. **LC** AP95.M3; P34.

CC
PAN YUEH TAN. VFOAT Ban Yue Tan; Banyuetan. No. 1 (Apr. 25 1980)-. Periodical. Chinese. sm. $26.18. **(Subscription address:** China International Book Trading Corporation, PO Box 399, Library Service Department, Beijing 100044 People's Republic of China.) **LC** AP95.C5; P35. **DD** 059/.951.

JA
PASSION MAGAZINE. (19??)-. English. Four times a year. 33.00Aus$. Dowa Planning, Dairoku Seiko Bldg, 1-31 Arasaka 5 Chome, Minato-ku Tokyo 107 Japan.

IO
PENCA. Indonesian. 1500. Korps Cacad Veteran R I, JL Tambak 11A, Jakarta Indonesia. **LC** AP95.I5; P42. **Continues** Pentja.

IO
PENYULUH SOSIAL REMAJA. V. 1- June 1972-. Indonesian. Direktorat Bimbingant Penyuluhan Sosial, Jl Ir Juanda 36, Jakarta Indonesia. **LC** AP215.I5; P45.

PH
PHILIPPINE ALMANAC & HANDBOOK OF FACTS. (1973)-. English. 1 Makatarungan St, U P Village, Quezon City D505 Philippines. **LC** DS651; .P34. **DD** 915.99/03/4.

PH
PHILIPPINES TODAY. V. 1- Dec. 1972-. Periodical. English. National Media Production Center, National Press Club Building, Magallanes Drive, Intramuros Manila Philippines. **LC** DS651; .P743. **DD** 915.99/03/405.

JA
PHP INTANASHONARU. (19??)-. Periodical. Japanese. qt. Kokusai PHP Kenkyujo, Rai Roppongi Building, Suite 903/5-1 Roppongi 5, Minato-ku 106 Tokyo Japan. **LC** AP95.J2; P14.

US/0886-5507
PPURI. [Ppuri]. VFOAT The Korean Roots; Korean Roots Journal. Began with Jan. 1980 issue. Periodical. English (Korean). mo. $15.00. Korean Pioneer Press, 431 South Western Avenue/Suite 205, Los Angeles CA 90020. **LC** AP95.K6; P68.

II
PRABHA, DIVALI ANKA. Marathi (Marathi). Rs3.00. 22-B Nirmala Niwas Merbanji Road Lower Parel, Bombay-12 India. **LC** AP95.M3; P7.

General Interest —General Interest-Asia

CE
PROGRESS (COLOMBO, SRI LANKA).
(PROGRESS.). Vol. 1, Issue 1 (Mar. 1981)-. Periodical. English. $35.00. Ministry of Plan Implementation, Central Bank Building, Colombo 1 Sri Lanka Ceylon. **Tel** (01)27477. **LC** HC424.A1; P74. **DD** 338.9549/3/005. **Bk Rev. Circ:** 1,500.
 Desc: Development oriented articles with particular relevance to Sri Lanka. Subjects covered vary from economic analysis to social welfare.

IT
PROSPETTIVE SETTANTA. (19??)-. Periodical. Italian. qt. L90000 Italy; L170000 other. Guide Editori SPA, Via D Morelli 16/B, I-80121 Naples Italy. **LC** AP37; .P73.

KO
PYOLGON'GON. Vol. 1 (1926)-. Periodical. Korean. W7,000 each volume. Kyongin Murhwasa, 86-2 Yonhui-dong Sodaemun-ku, Seoul South Korea. **LC** AP95.K6; P962.

IS
QAUMI AVAZ. VFOAT Qaumi Awaz. V. 1, (October 25, 1981)-. Periodical. Urdu (Urdu). wk. 1.00. Associated Journals, 74-B Government Industrial Estate, Kandiwali Bombay 400076 India. **LC** AP95.U7; Q35.

ET
QUARTERLY YEKATIT. Added/Corp Ethiopia. Ministry of Information and National Guidance. (19??)-. Periodical. English. qt. Ministry of Information and National Guidence, Addis Abba, Ethiopia. **LC** DT380.5; .Q37. **DD** 963/.005.

II
RABINDRABHARATI JOURNAL.
Added/Corp Rabindra Bharati University. (19??)-. Periodical. English. Rs2.00. Rabindra Bharati University, 6/4 Dwarkanath Tagore Lane, Calcutta-7 India. **LC** AS471; .R32. **DD** 052.

US/0278-9957
RAH-I ZINDAGI. VFOAT Rah-e-Zendegi. (19??)-. Periodical. Persian (English). Fifty-two times a year. $58.00 US/ $100.00 Canada; $220.00 other. Rah-e-Zendegi, 1015 Gayley Avenue, Suite 1111, Los Angeles CA 90024. **Tel** (213)470-7007, (213)474-1954. **LC** AP95.P3; R34.

II
RANGA CAKALLASA. VFOAT Rang Chakallas. Periodical. Hindi (Hindi). 7.00. Rangayana, 598 Shantinagar Chembur, Bombay 400071 India. **LC** AP115; .R36.

TH/1011-6435
RAPA BULLETIN. VFOAT Regional Office for Asia and the Pacific bulletin. (1??)-. Periodical. English.
 Ind/Abst Agric. Eng. Abstr.

PH/0115-3870
REVIEW, THE. (19??)-. Periodical. English. mo. $48.00. Philippine Education Company, PO Box 706, MCC Makati Philippines. **Tel** 88 44 70. **LC** AP8; .R46. **DD** 050.

PR
REVISTA DE ORIENTE. Title Change. Added/Corp Humacao Regional College. (1977)-(19??)-. Periodical. Spanish. sa. Universidad de Puerto Rico Colegio, Colegio Universitario Humanacao, Estacion C U H, Humacao Puerto Rico 00791. **Tel** (809)852-2525.

●US
RUSSIA & EURASIA DOCUMENTS ANNUAL. VFOAT Russia and Eurasia Documents Annual. (1992)-. English. an. Academic International Press, Box 1111, Gulf Breeze FL 32561. **LC** IN PROCESS; DK293; .R97. **Continues** USSR Documents Annual, 1051-3507.

●US/1062-3574
RUSSIA, EURASIAN STATES, AND EASTERN EUROPE. (1992)-. English. an. Stryker-Post Publications, PO Drawer 1200, Harpers Ferry WV 25425. **Tel** (800)995-1400. **Continues** Soviet Union and Eastern Europe, 0090-3868.

KO
SAE MULGYOL. Periodical. Korean. Not for Sale. Chayu Pyongnensa, CPO Box 6856, Seoul South Korea. **LC** AP95.K6; S23.

KO
SAEM I KIPPUN MUL. V. 1- (Nov. 1984)-. Periodical. Korean. mo. $112.00 Air Mail. Korea Britannica Corporation, PO Box 343, Gwanghwamun Seoul 110-00 Korea. **LC** AP95.K6; S234.

KO
SAEMTO. Periodical. Korean. 2,800. Saemto S A, CPO Box 201, Seoul Korea. **LC** AP95.K6; S235.

TH
SAKUN THAI. (19??)-. Periodical. Thai. Fifty-two times a year. $75.00 South East Africa; $100.00 North East Asia; $130.00 Europe; $158.00 North America;
$175.00 others. Sakun Thai, 50 Sukhumvit 36 Soi Napasap 5, Bangkok 10110 Thailand. **LC** AP95.T48; S24.

II
SAMSKRTA-RATNAKARAH. Periodical. Sanskrit (Sanskrit). 8.00. **LC** AP95.S3; S244.

AT
SAMSKRTASAKETAH. Multiple languages (Hindi and Sanskrit). 6.00. Rajivalochan Mandir UP, Akhilabharatiya Vidvatsamiti, Ayodhya India. **LC** AP95.S3; S25.

II
SANGAT. VFOAT Monthly Sangat. Urdu (Urdu). mo. Rs25.00. Muhammed Ismail Sabri, 5/197 Mari Road, Ravalpindi India. **LC** AP95.U7; S27.

MY/0586-9412
SANTAJIWA. V. 1- Feb. 1973-. Malay. mo. $0.80 single issue. Sharikat Dian Sdn Berhad, 5315-A Jalan Pasir Puteh, Lundang Malaysia. **LC** AP95.M24; S27. **Supersedes** Santajiwa.

JA
SAPPORO-SHI BUNKAZAI CHOSA HOKOKUSHO. Added/Corp Sapporo-Shi Kyoiku Iinkai. (19??)-. Japanese. Sapporo-Shi Kyoiku Iinkai Nishi, 14-chome Minami 1-jo Chuo-ku, Sapporo-shi Japan. **LC** DS897.S2; S247.

II
SAPTAHA. Periodical. Bengali (Bengali). Rs0.50 single issue. Santana Pablikesanas, 47 Shasi Bhushan Dey Street, Calcutta-12 Halkata India. **LC** HX9.B4; S26.

II/0581-734X
SAPTAHIKA HINDUSTANA. Suspended. VFOAT Saptahik Hindustan. (19??)-(1993). Periodical. Hindi (Hindi). Fifty-two times a year. Hindustan Times Ltd, 18-20 Kasturba Gandhi Marg, New Delhi 110001 India. **Tel** 011 91 11 3318201. **LC** AP95.H5; S28.

IO
SELECTA. 1977/78-. Periodical. Indonesian. an. Rp2000. Analisa, Kebon Kacang 29/4, Jakarta Indonesia. **LC** AP95.I5; S383.

IS
SEMANA. 1- 30 Jan. 1973-. Periodical. Spanish. wk. $90.00 Israel; $110.00 US; $135.00 other. La Semana Publishing Company, PO Box 2427, Jerusalem 91023 Israel. **Tel** FAX 972-2-242910. **ED** Salomon Lewinsky. **LC** DS126.5; .S4325. **DD** 956.94/005. Index available. **Bk Rev. Ad Acc. Pr Rev. Circ:** 15,000.
 Desc: News about Israel; also, analysis news about Latin America.

CC
SHAN HAI CHING. Periodical. Chinese. ir. RMBY0.26. Che-Chiang Sheng Hsin Hua Shu Tien, Hang-Chou, People's Republic of China. **LC** AP95.C4; S34. **DD** 059/.951.

CC
SHAN-TUNG HUA PAO. VFOAT Shandong Pictorial; Shandong Huabao. (19??)-. Periodical. Chinese. mo. $40.68. **(Subscription address:** China International Book Trading Corporation, PO Box 399, Library Service Department, Beijing 100044 People's Republic of China.) **LC** AP95.C4; S35. **DD** 059/.951.

US
SHAN YEN WEN CHE. Ceased. (19??)-Ceased Vol. 11 (19??)-. Chinese. an. Scribner Book Companies, 5245 West Diversey Avenue, Chicago IL 60639. **Tel** (201)256-0700. **LC** AP95.C4; S36.
 Ind/Abst Psychol. Abstr. (?-?).

CC
SHANGHAI PICTORIAL. (1982)-. Periodical. English (Chinese). Six times a year. $33.00. **(Subscription address:** China International Book Trading Corporation, PO Box 399, Library Service Department, Beijing 100044 People's Republic of China.) **LC** DS796.S2; S446. **DD** 951.1/32/005.
 Desc: An illustrated, city-oriented magazine with unique local features that serves as a window on Shanghai and China.

CC
SHIH CHIEH LI SHIH TSA CHIH. First published in 1984. Periodical. Chinese. mo. $95.00. Shu Ming Chu Pan Shih Yeh Yu Hsien Kung SSU 222, Sec 1 5F Ho Ping E Rd, Taipei Taiwan. **LC** AP95.C4; S4344. **DD** 059/.951.

CH
SHIH TAI WEN CHAI. VFOAT Current Digest. Vol. 1, (August 1980)-. Periodical. Chinese. mo. $17.50. Chung Wai Tsa Chih She, 7-2 Shin Sheng S Rd Sect 3, Taipei Taiwan. **LC** AP95.C4; S4393. **DD** 059/.951.

JA
SHIKI NO ATORIE. Periodical. Japanese. qt. ¥2100 single issue with supplement. Atoriesha, c/o Shinichi Building, 8 Yotsuya 2 Shinjuku-ku, Tokyo-to 160 Japan.

JA
SHUKAN ASAHI. VFOAT Asahi Weekly Edition. (April 1922)-. Newspaper. Japanese. wk. ¥26,000. Osaka Asahi Shinbunsha, 3 2 Tsukiji 5 Chuo Ku, Tokyo 105 Japan. **(Subscription address:** Overseas Courier Service of America Inc., 5 East 44th Street, New York NY 10017.) **ED** Ahahi Shinbunsha Shuppankyoku. **LC** AP95.J2; S49. **Ad Acc. Circ:** 47,000. **Continues** Junkan Asahi.
 Desc: Asahi newspaper coverage centering on current topics for weekly magazine.

JA/0488-7484
SHUKAN SHINCHO. VFOAT Shincho. No. 1 (1956)-. Periodical. Japanese. wk. **(Subscription address:** Kinokuniya Company Ltd., 38-1 Sakuragaoka 5, chome Setagaya-ku, Tokyo 156 Japan.) **LC** AP95.J2; S54.

KO
SIN YOSONG. (19??)-. Periodical. Korean. Hyondaesa, 139-11 Ojang-dong Chung-ku, Seoul Korea. **LC** AP95.K6; S553.

KO
SINMIN. 1st Vol.-. Periodical. Korean. Hyondaesa, 139-11 Ojang-dong Chung-ku, Seoul Korea. **LC** AP95.K6; S5538. **Continues** Yudo.

JA
SOGO KENKYUJO HO. Main/Corp Momoyama Gakuin Daigaku. Sogo Kenkyujo Ho. **VFOAT** Momoyama Gakuin Daigaku Sogo Kenkyujo Ho. Vol. 1- ; 1975-. Japanese. Momoyama Gakuin Daigaku Sogo Kenkyujo, 237-1 Nishino Sakai-shi, Osaka-fu 588 Japan. **Tel** 0722-36-1181. **LC** AS552.M65; A36. **Supersedes in part** Kokusai Kankei Kenkyu; **Continues** Momoyama Gakuin Daigaku Sangyo Boeki Kenkyujo Ho.

KO
SONDEI SOUL. Periodical. Korean. wk. Soul Sinmunsa, 31 1-ka Taepyong-no, Chung-ku, Seoul South Korea. **LC** AP95.K6; S62.

IR
SOROUSH / SURUSH. VFOAT Surush. No. 1 (March 1981)-. Periodical. English (Arabic and French). mo. The Soroush Building, PO Box 15875-1163, 228 Motahhari Avenue, Teheran Iran. **Tel** 011 98 21 830771, telex 213910 IRIBIR. **ED** Mahdi Firoozan. **LC** DS251; .S65. **DD** 955/.005. Index available. **Bk Rev. Ad Acc. Circ:** 5,000.
 Desc: An artistic and cultural magazine.

UK/0967-828X
SOUTH EAST ASIA RESEARCH. (19??)-. English. Twice a year. $77.00 US; £48.00 other. In Print Publishing Ltd., Distribution Ctr. Blackhorse Rd., Letchworth SG6 1HN England. **Tel** 011 44 462 672555. **(Subscription address:** Turpin Distribution Services Limited, Blackhorse Road, Letchworth, Hertfordshire SG6 1HN, United Kingdom.) **ED** Dr. Ian Brown.
 Desc: Publishes research from archaeology, language and culture to economics, politics and law.

PH/0038-3600
SOUTHEAST ASIA JOURNAL. [Southeast Asia j.]. V. 6- 1972/73-. Periodical. English. sa. $2.50. Central Philippine University, Box 231, Iloilo City Philippines. **LC** AS539.5; .S67. **DD** 052. available in microform from University Microfilms International (UMI).
 Ind/Abst Index Philip. Period.; Rural Dev. Abstr.

CE/0256-808X
SRI LANKA YEAR BOOK. [Sri Lanka year b.]. 1975-. English (Sinhalese). ir. Rs21.00 per issue. Department of Census and Statistics / Sri Lanka, PO Box 563, Colombo 7 Sri Lanka. **Tel** 595291. **LC** DS488. **DD** 315.49/3. **NLM** DS 488; C425. **Circ:** 4,940. **Continues** Ceylon Year Book. The Official Statistical Annual of the Social, Economic and General Conditions of the Island.
 Desc: Contains salient facts on the historical background, geographical features, social and economic conditions of Sri Lanka and the various development activities of the government.

II
SRI VARSHA SAPTAHIKA. VFOAT Shreewarsha; Srivarsha. V. 1, No. 1 (15 Se 22 August 1980)-. Periodical. Hindi. wk. Rs1.25 each issue. Varsha Publications, Sabla Chambers, 5-B Floor 40 Kawasjji India. **LC** AP95.H5; S73.

UK/0142-6028
STUDIES ON ASIAN TOPICS. Added/Corp Scandinavian Institute of Asian Studies. (1980)-. Monographic series. English. ir. Price varies per volume. Curzon Press Ltd, 42 Grays Inn Road, London WC1 England. **Tel** 011 44 71 242 8310.

IO
SULUH PEPABRI. Ed. 1-. Indonesian. Jln Diponegoro 53, Jakarta Pusat Indonesia. **LC** UB445.I5; S84.

II
SURYA INDIA. V. 1- Oct. 1976-. Periodical. English. Rs335.-. Kanchanjunga, 18 Bara Khamba Road, New Delhi 110001 India. **Tel** 3310202. **ED** J K Jain. **LC** DS401; .S837. **DD** 954/.005. **Bk Rev. Ad Acc. Circ:**

General Interest —General Interest-Asia

40,000 (ctrl).
Desc: A periodical dealing with current affairs, it provides an insight into political, economic and social development. It gives you 80 pages of steady reading matter.

CH
TA TI SHENG HUO. **VFOAT** Mother Earth. August 1981-. Periodical. Chinese. mo. NT$650.00. **LC** AP95.C4; T375. **DD** 951/.249/005.

KO
TAEHWA. **VFOAT** Monthly Dialogue. Periodical. Korean. W5,000. Taehwa S A, 26-6 1-ka Changchung-dong Chung-ku, Seoul Korea. **LC** AP95.K6; T34.

US
TAI-WAN SSU CHAO. **VFOAT** Taiwan Tide. (19??)-. Periodical. Chinese. bm. $15.00. Taiwan Tide, PO Box 33215, Los Angeles CA 90033. **LC** AP95.C4; T435. **DD** 059/.951.
Ind/Abst Hum. Rights Intern. Rep.

●US/1074-5599
TAIWAN STUDIES. (TAIWAN STUDIES : A JOURNAL OF TRANSLATIONS.). (1994)-. Periodical. English. qt. $200.00 US; $230.00 other. M. E. Sharpe Inc., 80 Business Park Drive, Armonk NY 10504. **Tel** (914)273-1800, (800)541-6563, FAX (914)273-2106.

JA
TAIYO (HEIBONSHA). (TAIYO.). **VFOAT** The Sun; Sun. (1963)-. Newspaper. Japanese (summaries and/or abstracts in English). Twelve times a year. ¥18,000. Heibonsha Limited Publishers, 5 Sanbancho, Chiyoda-ku Tokyo 102 Japan. **Tel** (03)265-0451, FAX (03)265-0477. **ED** Mitsunori Tanaka. **LC** AP95.J2; T41. cum. index. **Bk Rev**. **Ad Acc**. **Circ:** 250,000.
Desc: High quality graphic magazine featuring culture, art, history, travel, and modern topics on Japan and the rest of the world.
Ind/Abst Numis. Lit.

US/0191-0256
TAM TAY. So 1- Dec. 1976-. Periodical. Vietnamese. Kavyani-Golesorkhi, 9428 Old Courthouse Road, Vienna VA 22180-2051. **LC** AP95.V5; T34.

PK
TAMSIL. V. 1- Jan. 20, 1972-. Urdu (Urdu). 25.00. **LC** AP95.U7; T345.

AT/0082-2116
TASMANIAN YEAR BOOK. **Added/Corp** Australia. Commonwealth Bureau of Census and Statistics. Tasmanian Office. Australian Bureau of Statistics. Tasmanian Office. No. 1 (1967)-. English. an. 31.00Aus$. Australian Government Publishing Service, GPO Box 84, Canberra ACT 2601 Australia. **Tel** 011 61 6 2954411, FAX 011 61 6 2954455. **LC** HA3111; .T3. **DD** 319.4/6.
Desc: Contains information on history and chronology, physical environment, public finance, demography, agriculture, government and administration.

RU
TATARSKAIA ASSR. See The Arts-Crafts and Decorative Arts.

IO
TEMPO. (March 6, 1971)-. Periodical. Indonesian. wk. $279.40 Asia; $414.60 Australia and Japan; $464.00 Europe, Saudi Arabia and Hong Kong; $583.60 other. PT Gramedia/ Export Department, JL Gajah Mada 104/ PO Box 615, Jakarta 11140 Indonesia. **Tel** 011 62 21 6297809 Ext. 4610, FAX 011 62 21 6498475, telex 41216. **LC** AP95.I5; T45.

US
THOI TAP. (19??)-. Vietnamese. mo. 33$00 Europe; 23$00 other. Thoi Tap, 2941 Espana Court, Fairfax VA 22030. **LC** AP95.V5; T454.

II/0040-6708
TIBETAN REVIEW. See Geography.

US
TIC NEWS. **Main/Corp** Thai Information Center. Vol 1 (Sept. 12, 1977)-. Periodical. English. wk.
Ind/Abst Hum. Rights Intern. Rep.

US/0191-2097
TIEN PHONG. Periodical. Vietnamese. sm. $34.00. 3718 North 4th Street, Arlington VA 22203. **LC** AP95.V5; T53.

II
TIMTARIKITA. Vol. 1, No. 1 (January 3, 1982)-. Periodical. Tamil (Tamil). bw. 25.00. **LC** AP95.T3; T43.

CN/0229-7795
TINIG. (TINIG : VOICE OF FILIPINOS.). Vol. 1, No. 1 (June 1978)-. Periodical. English (Tagalog). mo. **DD** 320.9599/05. **Continues** Siklab.
Ind/Abst Philip. Sci. Technol. Abstr.

VM
TO QUOC. Vietnamese. mo. $16.30 US. Xunhasaba Exports and Imports, 7 Nguyen Thi Minh Khai Str, Dit 1 Ho Chi Minh City Vietnam. **Tel** 011 84 8 294893, telex 278 XUNHASABA. **LC** AP95.V5; T6. **Circ**: 20,000.

JA
TOHO GAKUEN DAIGAKU KENKYU KIYO. **Main/Corp** Toho Gakuen Daigaku. **VFOAT** Toho Gakuen School of Music Faculty Bulletin. Japanese. Toho Gakuen Daigaku, 41-1 Wakabacho 1-chome, Chofu Japan. **LC** AS552.T58; A35.

JA
TOKAI DAIGAKU KIYO : KYOYO GAKUBU. **Main/Corp** Tokai Daigaku. Kyoyo Gakubu. **VFOAT** Tokai Daigaku Kyoyo Gakubu Kiyo; Journal of the Faculty of Liberal Arts, Tokai University; Journal of the Faculty of Living and Culture, Tokai University; Journal of the Faculty of Humanities and Culture, Tokai University. No. 1- ; 1971-. Periodical. Multiple languages (Japanese and English). Tokai Daigaku, Sangyo Kagaku Kenkyujo, 1117 Kita-Kaname, Hiratsuka 259-12 Japan. **LC** AS552.T64; A35.

JA
TOKYO KOGYO DAIGAKU JIMBUN RONSO. **Main/Corp** Tokyo Kogyo Daigaku. **Added/Corp** Tokyo Kogyo Daigaku. Tokyo Kogyo Daigaku Humanities Review. Tokyo Kogyo Daigaku Humanities Review. Tokyo Kogyo Daigaku Humanities Review. (19??)-. Periodical. Japanese. Tokyo Kogyo Daigaku Humanities Review, 12-1 Ookayama 2-Meguro-ku, Tokyo 152 Japan. **LC** AS552.T71713; .A34.

JA/0503-8682
TONAN AJIA KENKYU. **Added/Corp** Kyoto Daigaku. Tonan Ajia Kenkyu Senta. **VFOAT** Southeast Asian Studies. Vol. 1 (July 1963)-. Periodical. Japanese (English). qt. $80.00. The Center for Southeast Asian Studies, Kyoto University, 46 Shimoadachi-cho, Yoshida Sakyo-ku, Kyoto 606 Japan. **Tel** 011 81 75 7537344, FAX 011 81 75 7537350. **LC** DS520; .T66. **CODEN** TNAKAQ. Index available. cum. index. **Bk Rev**. **Circ:** 1,100 (ctrl)
Desc: Publishes the results of academic research contributing to the understanding of nature, culture and society in Southeast Asia.
Ind/Abst Am. Hist. Life (1972-); GeoRef; Rice Abstr.

KO
TONGBANG PYONGNON = THE ORIENTAL REVIEW. **VFOAT** The Oriental Review; Oriental Review. (1982)-. Periodical. Korean (Korean). ir. Hyondaesa, 139-11 Ojang-dong Chung-ku, Seoul Korea. **LC** AP95.K6; T64142.

KO
TONGGWANG. **VFOAT** Oriental Light. V. 1- ; 1926-. Periodical. Korean. W50,000 7 volumes. Asea Munhisasa, 48-24 1-Ka Changchung-dong Chunk-ku, Seoul South Korea. **LC** AP95.K6; T642.

JA
TRANSACTIONS OF THE ASIATIC SOCIETY OF JAPAN. **Added/Corp** Asiatic Society of Japan. Vol. 1 (Oct. 30, 1872 to Oct. 9th, 1873)-Vol. 50 (Dec. 1922); 2nd Series, Vol. 1 (Dec. 1924)- 3rd Series, Vol. 1 (Dec. 1948)-Vol. 20 (1985); 4th Series, Vol. 1 (1986)-. English. an. ¥6000. Asiatic Society of Japan Cntrl, PO Box 592, Tokyo Japan. **Tel** 011 81 3 35634591, FAX 011 81 3 35634595. **ED** Roger Finch (editor's address: Azu-shin Mano 176-6, Oaza Kitagawa, Hanno City, Daitama-ken 357-02, phone: 0429-78-2259). **LC** AS552; .Y8. **DD** 915.2. Index available. cum. index.
Ind/Abst MLA Int. Bibl. Books Artic. Mod. Lang. Lit.

KO
TRANSACTIONS OF THE ROYAL ASIATIC SOCIETY, KOREA BRANCH. English. an. $10.00. Royal Asiatic Society Korea Branch, Central POB 255, Seoul Korea. **Tel** 763-9483. **Circ**: 1,000. **Continues** Transactions of the Korea Branch of the Royal Asiatic Society.
Desc: Contains various articles, text of/or from lectures dealing with Korea on a wide range of subjects. Also included are the current events of the society.
Ind/Abst Am. Hist. Life (1975-1976).

IO
TRIBUN. Vol. 3, No. 42- 1973-. Indonesian. 120 each issue. Jalan Duri I/5, Jakarta Indonesia. **LC** AP95.I5; M486. **Continues** Mimbar.

HK
TSUNG HENG YUEH KAN. **VFOAT** Scintilation Monthly. Vol. 1 ; 1976-. Chinese. $2.00 single issue. Hua Na Tu Shu Kung SSU, Kowloon Central, PO Box 405, Hong Kong. **LC** AP95.C4; T683.

HK/0041-3836
TU CHE WEN CHAI. **VFOAT** Reader's Digest. (March 1965)-. Periodical. Chinese (translations available in English). mo. $62.00. Reader's Digest Association Far East, GPO Box 11852, Hong Kong Hong Kong. **Tel** 011 852 5 5681117, FAX 011 852 8853210, telex 74700. **ED** Janie Couch. **LC** AP95.C4; R4. **DD** 059/.951. **Ad Acc**.

GW
TU PO. **VFOAT** Breakthrough Magazine. V. 1- V.; 1974 Year 1 Month-. Periodical. Chinese. $3.00. 2B Tak Shing Street/1st Floor, Chiu-Lung Hong Kong. **LC** AP95.C4; T89.

II
ULAKA ITAYA OLI. **VFOAT** Ulaga Idaya Voli. Multiple languages (English and Tamil). 5.00. T D Tirumalai, 227 South Masi Street, Maturai 1 India. **LC** AP95.T3; U4.

JA/0041-6576
UNDERSTANDING JAPAN. No. 1- Aug. 1960-. English (French, Spanish and Indonesian). ir (two or three issues per year). International Society for Educational Information Inc, Royal Wakaba/Room 504, 22 Wakaba 1-chome, Shinjuku-ku Tokyo 160 Japan. **Tel** 03(358)1138, FAX (03)359-7188, telex J244. **ED** Fumi Miyamoto. Index available. cum. index. **Bk Rev**. **Ad Acc**. **Circ:** 10,000 (ctrl).

US/1051-3507
USSR DOCUMENTS ANNUAL. **Title Change.** [USSR doc. annu.]. **VAT** Union of Soviet Socialist Republics documents annual. (1988)-(19??). English. an. Academic International Press, Box 1111, Gulf Breeze FL 32561. **LC** DK285.5; .U87. **DD** 947.085/4. **Continues** USSR Documents, 1048-1125. **Continued by** Russia & Eurasia Documents Annual.

TI
UTRUHAT. **VFOAT** Outrouhat. Periodical. Arabic (French). mo. PO Box 492 Hashshad 1049, Tunis Tunisia. **LC** AP95.A6; U8.

MY/0506-418X
VARIASARI. Nov. 1968-. Periodical. Malay. $1.00 single issue. Variasari, 66 F Tingkat 7 Wisma Hock Ann, Jln Haji Hussein, Kuala Lumpur Malaysia. **LC** AP95.M24; V37.

II
VARNANA. V. 1- July/August 2030- 1973/1974-. Nepali (Nepali). Rs1.00 single issue. Susila Mani Dikshita, 64 Bhat Bhateni Dixit Niwas 19, Kathamadaum India. **LC** AP95.N4; V36.

NP
VICARA. **VFOAT** Vichar. No. 1- December 1972-. Nepali. Rs8.00. Kisora Nepala, 7/37 Battisputali, Kathamandu Nepal. **LC** AP95.N4; V52.

VM/0506-9696
VIETNAM COURIER. **Suspended.** **VFOAT** Viet Nam Courier. No. 1 (May 1964)- ; New Ser., No. 1 (June 1972)-(19??). Periodical. English. mo. $10.60. Xunhasaba Exports and Imports, 7 Nguyen Thi Minh Khai Str, Dit 1 Ho Chi Minh City Vietnam. **Tel** 011 84 8 294893, telex 278 XUNHASABA. **LC** DS557.A7; A28.

II
VINELAM MOTI. Gujarati (Gujarati). Rs7.50. Vinelam Moti Karyalaya, Palejwala Building Opp, Maganwadi Savajiganj Baroda 5, Vandodara India. **LC** AP95.G8; V56.

PK
VISION (KARACHI, PAKISTAN). (VISION; A MAGAZINE OF ARTS, LIFE AND THOUGHT.). Began with Vol. 1, in 1952. Periodical. English. mo. Vision Magazine, 81 82 Farid Chambers, Vict Road, Karachi Pakistan.

MY
WANITA. (19??)-. Periodical. Malay. mo. $15.00 Malaysia; $91.80 other. Utusan Melayu Malaysia Berhad, 46M Jalan Chan Sow Lin, Kuala Lumpur Malaysia. **Tel** 280060. **LC** AP95.M24; W35.

II
WEST BENGAL INFORMATION DIRECTORY. 1979/80-. Directory. English. an. Rs15.00. Hony Executive Director, Eastern India Centre for Mass Communication Studies, Nicco House, 2 Hare Street, Calcutta 700 001 India. **LC** DS485.B493; W454. **DD** 915.4/14.

MY/0217-1910
WHO'S WHO IN MALAYSIA & SINGAPORE (PETALING JAYA, SELANGOR). See Biographies.

●US/1059-5392
WHO'S WHO OF THE ASIAN PACIFIC RIM. (1992)-. English. an. $175.00. Barons Who's Who, 412 North Coast Highway, Suite B-110, Laguna Beach CA 92651. **Tel** (714)497-8615.

MY
WIDYA. Vol. 1 (April 1973)-. Malay. $0.60 each issue. **LC** AP95.M24; W5.

KO
WOLGAN CHOSON. 1st Vol. (April 1980)-. Periodical. Korean. mo. W18,000. 61 1-ka Taepyongno, Chung-ku, Seoul 100 South Korea. **LC** AP95.K6; W63.

KO
WOLGAN CHUNGANG. **VFOAT** Joong-Ang Monthly. 1st Vol. (April 1968)-. Periodical. Korean. W7.200. Chungang Ilbo Tongyang Pangsong, 58-9 Sosomun-Dong, Chung-Ku 100, Seoul South Korea. **LC** AP95.K6; W64.

KO
WOLGAN SEDAE. **VFOAT** Sedae. (19??)-. Periodical. Korean. mo. W8,000. Sedaesa, 217 1-ka Hankang-no, Yongsan-ku, Seoul South Korea. **LC** AP95.K6; W66.

SI/0303-0881
XING GUANG. (HSING KUANG.). 1- June 1973-. Periodical. Chinese. $0.40 single issue. Blk 127, 114B Bukit Merah View, Singapore 3 Singapore. **LC** AP95.C4; H784.

CH
YA-CHOU JEN. **VFOAT** The Asian; Asian. Vol. 69, (Feb. 1980)-. Periodical. Chinese (Chinese). mo. NT$400.00. Pa Shih Nien Tai Chu Pan She, 2 Hsin Sheng South Road 3 Section, Taipei Taiwan. **LC** AP95.C4; Y3. **DD** 059/.951. ***Continues*** *Pa Shih Nien Tai.*

US/1042-2773
YA MEI SHI BOA/ASIAN AMERICAN TIMES. Chinese. wk. $100.00. Asian American Times, Inc., 135-25A 40 Road/2nd Fl, Flushing NY 11354. **Tel** (718)358-6413, FAX (718)358-6501.

IR
YAVARAN-I INQILAB. Persian. wk. 20.00 each issue. Muassasah-Yi Ittilaat Khiyaban-I Kharram Min Rtaqah-Yi, 11 Pasti, Tehran Iran. **LC** AP95.P3; Y38.

US/0094-0097
YEH TSAO. (19??)-. Chinese. $6.00. Ye-Tsao Magazine, PO Box 55, Shrub Oak NY 10588. **LC** AP95.C5; Y43.

KO
YOLMAE (SEOUL, KOREA). (YOLMAE.). Periodical. Korean. mo. W500 each issue. Chochuk Chujin Chungang Wiwonhoe, 33 Youido-dong Yongdungpo-ku, Seoul 150 Korea. **LC** AP95.K6; Y63.

KO
YONG REIDI. **VFOAT** Young Lady. (Sept. 1981)-. Periodical. Korean (English). mo. W20,400. Chungang Ilbo Tongyang Pangsong, 58-9 Sosomun-Dong, Chung-Ku 100, Seoul South Korea. **LC** AP95.K6; Y64.

KO
YOSONG. 1st Vol. Periodical. Korean. Hyondaesa, 139-11 Ojang-dong Chung-ku, Seoul Korea. **LC** AP95.K6; Y668.

KO
YOSONG CHUNGANG. **VFOAT** Ladies Joong-Ang. (19??)-. Periodical. Korean. Twelve times a year. $108.00. Chungang Ilbo Tongyang Pangsong, 58-9 Sosomun-Dong, Chung-Ku 100, Seoul South Korea. **(Subscription address:** Dong A Book Store, 9828 Garden Grove, Building 104, Garden Grove CA 92644.**)** **LC** AP95.K6; Y67.

NP
YUVA AVAJA. V. 1- 2029- 1972/73-. Nepali. 1.00 each issue. Koshi Pustak Pasal, Dharana-5 Nepal. **LC** AP95.N4; Y85.

II
YUVAKA. Hindi (Hindi). 8.00. Jivanmandi 4, Agara India. **LC** AP95.H5; Y88.

TS
ZAHRAT AL-KHALIJ. **VFOAT** Zharat el Khaleej. Periodical. Arabic. wk. Shari Al-matar Al-Jadid Khalf Mabna Al-Idhaah Wa-Al-Tilifizyun, S B 3342 Dawlat Al-Imarat Al-Arabiyah Al-Muttahidah, Abu Zaby United Arab Republic. **LC** AP95.A6; Z33.

CH/1012-4195
ZHONGYANG YANJIUYUAN LISHI YUYAN YANJIUSUO JIKAN. (LI SHIH YU YEN YEN CHIU SO CHI KAN / KUO LI CHUNG YANG YEN CHIU YUAN.). [Zhongyang yanjiuyuan lishi yuyan yanjiusuo jikan]. **Added/Corp** Chung Yang Yen Chiu Yuan. Li Shih Yu Yen Yen Chiu So. **VFOAT** Chi Kan; Chung Yang Yen Chiu Yuan Li Shih Yu Yen Yen Chiu So Chi Kan; Bulletin of the Institute of History and Philology, Academia Sinica; Bulletin de l'Institut Historique et Philologique; Bulletin of the National Research Institute of History and Philology. (1928)-. Chinese (English). qt. $30.00. Academia Sinica / Institute of History and Philology, Nankang, Taipei 115 Taiwan. **Tel** 886 2 782-9555, FAX 886 2 786-8834. **ED** Kuan Tung-kuei. **LC** AS455.T2575; A33. **Bk Rev. Circ:** 1,500.
Ind/Abst Am. Hist. Life (1954-1957,1965-); Linguist. Lang. Behav. Abstr.; Soc. Plann. Policy Dev. Abstr.; Sociol. Abstr.

GENERAL INTEREST-AUSTRALIA AND OCEANIA

AT/1033-6060
AUSTRALIAN COUNTRY STYLE. [Aust. ctry. style]. (1989)-. Periodical. English. Twelve times a year. 112.00Aus$ US & Canada; 53.00Aus$ Australia; 88.00Aus$ New Zealand & Papua New Guinea; 119.00Aus$ Europe & Africa; 94.00Aus$ Singapore, Malaysia, Taiwan; 103.00Aus$ other. Federal Publishing Co Pty Ltd, PO Box 199, 180 Bourke Road, Alexandria New South Wales, 2015 Australia. **Tel** 011 61 2 693 6666, FAX 011 61 2 693 9935. **(Subscription address:** Federal Publishing Co. Pty Ltd., PO Box 199, Alexandria NSW 2015 Australia.**)** **ED** Susan Hurley. **DD** 052.
Desc: Magazine reflecting Australian living from a rural perspective.

UK/0301-5785
AUSTRALIAN OUTLOOK. LONDON. [Aust. outlook Lond.]. **VFOAT** Australian Outlook (Bexhill-on-Sea). (1970)-. Periodical. English. Twelve times a year. £13.80 Europe; £20.00 other. Consyl Publishing Ltd., 3 Buckhurst Road, Bexhill-on-Sea, East Sussex TN40 1QF England. **Tel** 011 44 424 223111, FAX 011 44 424 224992. **ED** W. Deacon. **DD** 325.2420994. **Ad Acc, Adv Mgr:** S. Melvin. **Circ:** 30,000.
Desc: A general interest newspaper on life in Australia, specifically designed for migrants and visitors. Includes facts on emigration policy, costs of food, houses and cars, education, weather, etc.

AT/0729-8595
AUSTRALIAN SOCIETY. ***Title Change.*** (1982-1992). Periodical. English. mo. Peter Browne/Australian Society, PO Box 274, Fitzroy Victoria 3065 Australia. **Tel** (03)419-6622, FAX (03)416-0903. **ED** Peter Browne. **LC** HN841; .A884. **DD** 301/.0994. Index available. **Bk Rev. Ad Acc. Circ:** 9,000. ***Continued by*** *Modern Times.*
Desc: An independent journal looking at Australian national affairs, including economy, employment, housing, environment, arts, land rights, health, media, political, and women's issues.
Ind/Abst APAIS, Aust. Public Aff. Inf. Ser. (1986-); Aust. Educ. Index (1982-).

AT
AUSTRALIAN WOMEN'S WEEKLY SALUTE TO BEAUTIFUL AUSTRALIA, THE. (19??)-. English. ir.

AT
AUSTRALIANA. Vol. 7, No. 2 (April 1985)-. English. qt (Feb., May, Aug., Nov.). 45.00Aus$. Australiana Society Inc, PO Box 322, Roseville 2069 Sydney, New South Wales Australia. **Tel** 011 61 2 5606022, FAX 011 61 2 5697246. **ED** Kevin Fahy. Index available. **Bk Rev. Ad Acc. Circ:** 350 (ctrl). ***Continues*** *Australiana Society Newsletter.*
Desc: Research and promotion of Australiana.

AT/0819-0739
BLAST MANUKA. [Blast Manuka]. (1987)-. Periodical. English. Four times a year (Mar., June, Sept., Dec.). 12.00Aus$ (individuals), 25.00Aus$ (institutions) Australia; 15.00Aus$ (individuals), 30.00Aus$ (institutions) others. Blast, PO Box 3514, Nugent & Tully, Manuka ACT 2603 Australia. **Tel** 011 61 6 2621502. **ED** Bill Tully and Craig Cormick. **DD** 805. **Bk Rev. Ad Acc, Adv Mgr:** Bill Tully.

AT/0007-4039
BULLETIN (SYDNEY). (THE BULLETIN.). [Bulletin]. (1880)-. Periodical. English. wk. 99.00Aus$ Australia; 130.00Aus$ New Zealand; 210.00Aus$ Papua New Guinea; 215.00Aus$ Singapore, Malaysia, Brunei, Hong Kong; 235.00Aus$ Vanuatu, New Caledonia, Solomon Islands, Fiji, Indonesia, Tonga, Tahiti; 290.00Aus$ Thailand, Philippines, China, Japan; 320.00Aus$ US, Canada, Middle East; 350.00Aus$ UK, Europe, South Africa, South America. Australian Consolidated Press Ltd, GPO Box 5252, Sydney New South Wales 2001 Australia. **Tel** 011 61 2 2600000. **LC** AP7; .B8. ***Absorbed*** *Australian Financial Times, 0567-0667.*
Ind/Abst Energy Res. Abstr. (Sept. 1982-).

AT
COMMON SENSE. Common Sense Publications, POB 60, Sherwood Old 4075 Australia.

US/1043-898X
CONTEMPORARY PACIFIC, THE. [Contemp. Pac.]. **Added/Corp** University of Hawaii at Manoa. Center for Pacific Islands Studies. University of Hawaii (System). Press. Vol. 1, No. 1 & 2 (Spring/Fall 1989)-. Periodical. English. sa (Spring and Fall). $24.00 (one year), $45.00 (two year), institutions, $17.00 (one year), $31.00 (two year), individual, Pacific Islands; $40.00 (one year), $72.00 (two year), institution, $30.00 (one year), $54.00 (two year), individual, other. University of Hawaii Press, 2840 Kolowalu Street, Honolulu HI 96822. **Tel** (808)956-8833, (808)948-8697, FAX (808)988-6052. **ED** David Hanlon. **LC** DU1; .C66. **DD** 995/.005. **CODEN** COPAEV. **Bk Rev. Ad Acc. Pr Rev. Circ:** 600. available on microfilm.
Desc: Dedicated exclusively to current issues in the Pacific Islands. Brings together refereed, readable articles from a wide range of disciplines focusing on current island affairs. Feature articles are supported by political reviews, book reviews, resource articles, and a dialogue section of letters and short items.
Ind/Abst Int. Bibliogr. Sociol.; Linguist. Lang. Behav. Abstr.; Soc. Plann. Policy Dev. Abstr.; Sociol. Abstr.

AT
DATA EXTRACT. (19??)-. Newsletter. English. Six times a year. 7.00Aus$. Doctor Who Fan Club of Australia, PO Box 4, Epping New South Wales 2121 Australia. **Tel** 011 61 2 764 2905. **ED** Kate Orman. **Bk Rev**, (Qty: 24). **Ad Acc.** Full Page (B&W) 135.00Aus$. Half Page (B&W) 67.50Aus$. **Circ:** 700.
Desc: News and information about the UK science fiction of TV series "Doctor Who."

AT/0103-626X
HERITAGE NEWS (CANBERRA, A.C.T.). (HERITAGE NEWS.). **Added/Corp** Australian Heritage Commission. Vol. 11, No. 3 (Nov. 1988)-. Periodical. English. Four times a year. Free on request. Australian Heritage Commission, 53 Blackall Street, Barton ACT 2601 Australia. **Tel** 11 61 6 2712111, FAX 11 61 6 2732395. **ED** James Morrison, Australian Heritage Commission, GPO Box 1567, Canberra Australia; Telephone: 11 61 6 2712170. ctrl circ. ***Continues*** *Heritage Newsletter (Canberra, A.C.T.), 0313-6701.*

AT/1321-9820
HQ MAGAZINE. (1990)-. English. bm. 35.70Aus$ Australia; 38.40Aus$ New Zealand; 63.00Aus$ other. Australian Consolidated Press Ltd, GPO Box 5252, Sydney New South Wales 2001 Australia. **Tel** 011 61 2 2600000. ***Continues*** *GH Magazine, 1321-9855.*

AT/1031-2331
INDIAN OCEAN REVIEW, THE. **Added/Corp** Curtin University of Technology. Centre for Indian Ocean Regional Studies. Vol. 1 No. 1 (March 1988)-. Periodical. English. qt. 20.00Aus$ (individual), 25.00Aus$ (institutional) Australia, New Zealand, and Papua, New Guinea; 30.00Aus$ (individual), 40.00Aus$ (institutional) other. University of Western Australia Indian Ocean / Center Peace Studies, Nedlands WA 6009 Australia. **Tel** 011 61 9 3803993, FAX 011 61 9 3801074. **LC** DS331; .I49. **DD** 909/.09824/005. ***Continues*** *Indian Ocean Newsletter (Nedlands, W.A.).*
Ind/Abst Abstr. Anthropol. (19??-).

IO/0215-2770
JAKARTA JAKARTA. [Jakarta Jakarta]. (1985)-. Periodical. Indonesian. wk. $279.40. PT Gramedia/ Export Department, JL Gajah Mada 104/ PO Box 615, Jakarta 11140 Indonesia. **Tel** 011 62 21 6297809 Ext. 4610, FAX 011 62 21 6498475, telex 41216. **DD** 059.598.

TO/0113-0374
MATANGI TONGA. Vol. 1, No. 1 (Sept./Oct. 1986)-. Periodical. English (Austronesian and Tonga (Tonga Islands)). bm. $21.90 South Pacific, Hawaii, Australia & New Zealand; $28.40 other. Vavau Press Ltd, PO Box 427, Nukualofa South Pacific, Tonga. **Tel** 676-23101, FAX 011 676-23101. **ED** Pesi & Mary Fonua. **LC** DU880; .M36. **Bk Rev. Ad Acc. Circ:** 3,000.

AT/0085-4441
NEW SOUTH WALES YEAR BOOK. **Added/Corp** Australian Bureau of Statistics. New South Wales Office. No. 66 (1981)-. English. an. 31.00Aus$. Australian Bureau of Statistics, PO Box 10, Belconnen Australian Capital Territory, 2616 Australia. **Tel** 011 61 6 2527911, FAX 011 61 6 2516009. **LC** DU150; .A3. **DD** 994.4. **Circ:** 1,500. ***Continues*** *Official Year Book of New South Wales.*
Desc: Provides a comprehensive statistical, legislative and administrative survey of the social, demographic and economic structure and growth of New South Wales.

NZ/0110-0831
NEW ZEALAND ANNUAL. English. Wilson & Horton Ltd, PO Box 32, Auckland New Zealand. **Tel** 011/64/9/795050, FAX 011/64/9/3660146. **LC** DU400; .N32A. **DD** 919.31/03/305.

NZ/0112-9120
NEW ZEALAND MONTHLY REVIEW 1986. (NEW ZEALAND MONTHLY REVIEW.). [N. Z. mon. rev. 1986]. (1986)-. Periodical. English. Six times a year. 35.00NZ$. New Zealand Monthly Review Society, PO Box 13-483, Christchurch, New Zealand. **DD** 052. **Bk Rev. Ad Acc.** ***Continues*** *Monthly Review (Christchurch), 0110-7909.*
Ind/Abst Annu. Bibliogr. Engl. Lang. Lit.

UK/0028-8500
NEW ZEALAND NEWS UK. **See** Newspapers.

NZ/0113-1982
NEW ZEALAND OUTLOOK. [N.Z. outlook]. **VFOAT** Outlook. (1987)-. Periodical. English. mo. £15.00. Consyl Publishing Ltd., 3 Buckhurst Road, Bexhill-on-Sea, East Sussex TN40 1QF England. **Tel** 011 44 424 223111, FAX 011 44 424 224992. **ED** Sandra Melvin. **DD** 052. **Bk Rev. Ad Acc.** ***Continues*** *New*

Outlook (Auckland), 0111-8811.
Desc: A general interest newspaper on life in New Zealand specifically designed for migrants and visitors. Includes facts on emigration policy, costs of food, houses and cars, education, weather, etc.

AT/0030-7416
OVERLAND. [Overland]. No. 1 (1954)-. Periodical. English. qt. 26.00Aus$ Australia,and New Zealand, Papua and New Guinea and Pacific; 50.00Aus$ (surface), 90.00Aus$ (air mail) other. Overland, 361 Pigdon Street, North Carlton 3054 Australia. **Tel** 11 61 3 3801152, 3802586, FAX 011 61 3 8520527. **ED** Dr. John McLaren. **LC** AP7; .O9. Index available. **Bk Rev. Ad Acc. Circ:** 2,500. available on microfilm and microfiche from University Microfilms International (UMI). Documents available from The Genuine Article.
Desc: Literary magazine that encourages new writers, publishes stories, poems, graphics, and articles.
Ind/Abst Annu. Bibliogr. Engl. Lang. Lit.; APAIS, Aust. Public Aff. Inf. Ser. (1963-); Arts Humanit. Citation Index [Full Cov.]; Curr. Contents Arts Humanit.; MLA Int. Bibl. Books Artic. Mod. Lang. Lit.; Res. Alert [Full Cov.]; Soc. Sci. Cit. Index [Select. Cov.].

FJ
PACIFIC ISLANDS YEAR BOOK. 11th Ed. (1972)-. English. ir. $45.00. Fiji Times & Herald Ltd., GPO Box 1167, Suva Fiji Islands. **Tel** 011 679 304111, FAX 011 679 301521, telex FJ 2124. **LC** DU1; .P15. **Ad Acc. Circ:** 10,000 (ctrl). ***Continues** Pacific Islands Year Book and Who's Who.*

US/0744-1754
PACIFIC MAGAZINE (HONOLULU, HAWAII). (PACIFIC MAGAZINE.). [Pac. mag.]. **VFOAT** Pacific. Vol. 7, No. 1 (Jan.-Feb. 1982)-. Periodical. English. bm. $15.00 US; $39.00 other. Pacific Magazine, PO Box 25488, Honolulu HI 96825. **Tel** (808)377-5335, FAX (808)524-1099. **ED** Bruce Jensen. **LC** DU1; .P156. **DD** 995/.005. **Bk Rev. Ad Acc. Circ:** 10,000 (ctrl). ***Continues** New Pacific Magazine.*
Desc: General news and business of Micronesia, Polynesia, and Melanesia. The source of island news.

AT/0818-1624
PACIFIC NEWS BULLETIN. [Pac. news bull.]. (1986)-. Periodical. English. mo. 30.00Aus$ (Australia, Pacific Asia, & Third World), 40.00Aus$ (other)-institutions; 12.00Aus$ (Australia), 15.00Aus$ (Pacific Asia, & Third World), 25.00Aus$ (other)-individuals; $15.00Aus$ (Australia), $20.00 (Pacfic, Asia, Third World), $30.00 (other) non-government organizations. Pacific Concerns Resource Center, PO Box 489, Petersham NSW, 2049 Australia. **Tel** 011 61 2 5509967 5526022, FAX 011 61 2 5603241 5524583. **ED** Ellen Whelan (address: 11 Mansfield Street, Glebe NSW 2037 Australia) (phone: 02 552 6022). **DD** 327.174091823. ***Continues** Pacific News (Sydney), 0815-9114.*
Ind/Abst Hum. Rights Intern. Rep.

AT
PEOPLE (AUSTRALIAN EDITION). (PEOPLE.). (19??)-. Periodical. English. wk. 130.00Aus$ Australia; 136.00Aus$ New Zealand; 271.00Aus$ other. Australian Consolidated Press Ltd, GPO Box 5252, Sydney New South Wales 2001 Australia. **Tel** 011 61 2 2600000.

NR
POLYCOM. V. 1- April 1978-. Periodical. English. sa. $6.27. Victorian Government Printing Office, PO Box 203, North Melbourne Victoria 3051 Australia. **Tel** 011 61 3 320 0217. **LC** AP9; .P64. **DD** 052.
Ind/Abst Aust. Educ. Index (1978-).

AT/0033-5002
QUADRANT. [Quadrant]. **Added/Corp** Australian Committee for Cultural Freedom. Australian Association for Cultural Freedom. Vol. 1, No. 1 (Summer 1957)-. Periodical. English. Ten times a year (Except Jan/Feb. and July/Aug. issues combined). 45.00Aus$ Australia; 54.00NZ$ New Zealand & PNG; 54.00Aus$ surface mail; 69.00Aus$ airmail, other. Quadrant, PO Box 1495, Collingwood Vic, 3066 Australia. **Tel** 11 61 3 4176855, FAX 011 61 3 4162980, telex 25026. **ED** Roger Sandall, Greg Sheridan, Robin Marsden, and Vivian Smith. **LC** AP7; .Q8. **DD** 052. Index available. **Bk Rev**, (Qty: 100). **Ad Acc. Circ:** 6,000 (ctrl). available on microfiche.
Desc: Deals with Australian literature, arts, general ideas as well as with world problems, ideas, literature and history.
Ind/Abst Abstr. Engl. Stud.; Annu. Bibliogr. Engl. Lang. Lit.; APAIS, Aust. Public Aff. Inf. Ser. (1963-); Energy Res. Abstr. (Oct. 1981-); Int. Bibliogr. Sociol.; MLA Int. Bibl. Books Artic. Mod. Lang. Lit.

AT
SEE. English. Eleven times a year (Monthly except Jan.). 15.00 Aus$. Anglican Media, Cathedral Building 209 Flinders Lane, Melbourne VIC 3000 Australia. **Tel** 11 61 3 6534221, FAX 11 61 3 6505237.

AT
SOUTH SEA DIGEST, THE. No. 1 (Apr. 10, 1981)-. Periodical. English. Twenty-five times a year (Every Second Friday). 150.00Aus$ Australia; 175.00Aus$ others. Nationwide News / HE Secretary, GPO 4245, Sydney 2001 Australia. **Tel** 011 61 2 2883540. **LC** DU1; .S589. **DD** 990/.05.
Desc: News and information on Pacific Islands affairs.

AT/1032-2892
SYDNEY REVIEW 1988. **See** The Arts.

AT
TASMANIAN COUNTRY. English. wk. 130.00Aus$. Tasmanian Country, GPO Box 334D, Hobart Tasmania 7001 Australia. **Tel** 011 61 002 300752, FAX 011 61 002 300555. **ED** Tim Upston. **Ad Acc, Adv Mgr:** Ann Brown. **Circ:** 12,200 (ctrl).

AT/1030-5467
THIRD OPINION. [Third opin.]. (1987)-. Periodical. English. Four times a year. 25.00Aus$. Movement Against Uranium Mining, PO Box K133, Haymarket NSW 2000 Australia. **Tel** 61 2 2124538, FAX 61 2 2815216. **ED** Claire Gerson and Steve Broadbat. **DD** 363.73805. **Bk Rev. Ad Acc. Circ:** 500.

AT/0725-4946
THIS AUSTRALIA. ***Ceased.*** [This Australia]. -Ceased with Spring (1988). Periodical. English. qt. Australian Consolidated Press Ltd, GPO Box 5252, Sydney New South Wales 2001 Australia. **Tel** 011 61 2 2600000. **[CCC].**
Ind/Abst APAIS, Aust. Public Aff. Inf. Ser. (1982-).

AT/0818-0628
TIME AUSTRALIA. [Time Aust.]. **VFOAT** Time. (1986)-. Periodical. English. wk. 102.44Aus$. Time Australia Magazine Pty Ltd., GPO Box 3873, Sydney NSW 2001 Australia. **Tel** 011 61 2 9572044. **DD** 052. **Ad Acc. Circ:** 140,000.
Desc: News magazine with Australian cover stories and events.

AT
VERSION (SIDNEY, N.S.W.). (VERSION.). Vol. 1, No. 1, (Oct. 1981)-. Periodical. Spanish. Twelve times a year. 20.00Aus$ (one year); 35.00Aus$ (two years). Cervantes Publishing, 5 Daking Street North, Parramatta NSW 2155 Australia. **Tel** 011 61 2 6305982, FAX 011 61 2 6304099. **(Subscription address:** P. O. Box 282, Randwick, NSW 2031 Australia**) ED** Michael Gawaba. **LC** AP64; .V4. **DD** 056/.1. **Bk Rev**, (Qty: 12). **Ad Acc, Adv Mgr:** P. Jeavons, **Tel** 02 630 5982. **Circ:** 5,000.

PP
WANTOK. (19??)-. Periodical. Creoles and Pidgins, French-based. bw. $45.00 Solomon Islands; $60.00 US & Europe; $65.00 other. Word Publishing Company Pty Limited, Box 1982, Boroku Papua New Guinea. **Tel** 252500, FAX 252579, telex NE 22213. **ED** Ana Solomon. **Ad Acc. Circ:** 15,000 (ctrl).
Desc: General newsletter aimed at urban and rural working class.

AT/0726-0075
WESTIR'S WESTERN SYDNEY LETTER. **VFOAT** Western Sydney Letter. (1981)-. English. Four times a year. 10.00Aus$ (single issue rate). Westir Ltd., PO Box 457, Blacktown, NSW 2148 Australia. **Tel** (02)622-3011, FAX (02)622-3500. **UDC** 361.9944105. **Circ:** 350 (ctrl).
Desc: Covers social and urban issues and community-based activities in Western Sydney.

AT
WETLANDS : JOURNAL OF THE COAST AND WETLANDS SOCIETY. Vol. 1, No. 1 (Aug. 1981)-. English. sa. 20.00Aus$ Australia; 35.00Aus$ other. Coast and Wetlands Society, PO Box A225, Sydney New South Wales 2000 Australia. **Tel** 011 61 2 6972076. cum. index. **Bk Rev. Circ:** 350 (ctrl).
Ind/Abst Aquat. Sci. Fish. Abstr. (Computer File).

AT/1037-812X
WHO WEEKLY. (1992)-. Periodical. English. wk. 102.44Aus$. Time Australia Magazine Pty Ltd., GPO Box 3873, Sydney NSW 2001 Australia. **Tel** 011 61 2 9572044.

GENERAL INTEREST-CENTRAL AMERICA

CR
APORTES. **Added/Corp** Centro Nacional de Accion Pastoral (Costa Rica). **VFOAT** Aportes Para la Educacion Popular; Revista Aportes. No. 1 (Nov. 1980)-. Periodical. Spanish. bm. $30.00. Cenap Aportes, Apdo 7315, San Jose 1000 Costa Rica. **Tel** 21-13-20. **ED** Melvin Jimenez. **Bk Rev. Ad Acc. Circ:** 2,000.
Desc: Analysis, interviews, and reporting on economic, political, educational and cultural developments in Costa Rica and Central America.

NQ/1013-9567
BARRICADA INTERNACIONAL. ENGLISH. (BARRICADA INTERNACIONAL / OFFICIAL VOICE OF THE SANDINISTA NATIONAL LIBERATION FRONT.). [Barricada int.]. English. wk. $45.00 institutions, $35.00 (individuals) Canada; £23.00 (institutions), £18.00 (individuals) Great Britain; £27.00 (institutions), £22.00 (individuals) rest of Western Europe; $40.00 (institutions), $35.00 (individuals) US; $40.00 (institutions), $30.00 (individuals) Mexico, Caribbean, Central and South America; $58.00 (institutions), $48.00 (individuals) other. Barricada Internacional, Box 410150, San Francisco CA 94141. **Tel** (415)621-8981. **(Subscription address:** Can/ PO Box 398, Station E, Toronto Ontario M6H 4E3 Canada; Europe/ C/O NSC 23, Bevenden Street, London N1 6BH England**) ED** Sandra Garcia. **LC** F1528; .B38. **DD** 972.85/005. **Ad Acc. Circ:** 20,000. available on microfilm and microfiche from University Microfilms International (UMI).
Desc: News and analysis on the current situation in Nicaragua and Central America. Economic, political, cultural features and in-depth reports in a monthly supplement.

CR
BOLETIN / CIRCA, CENTRO DE INFORMACION Y REFERENCIA SOBRE CENTROAMERICA Y EL CARIBE. **Added/Corp** Centro de Informacion y Referencia Sobre Centroamerica y el Caribe. **VFOAT** Boletin CIRCA. No. 1 (1991)-. Periodical. Spanish. Three times a year. CIRCA / Faucltad de Letras Office, 121 Ciudad Universitaria Rodrigo Facio, Universidad de Costa Rica, Costa Rica. **Tel** 506 2535323 ext. 4535 y 5433, FAX 506 2535323 ext. 5089, telex UNICORI 2544. **Ad Acc, Adv Mgr:** Ethel Garcia Buchard. Full Page (B&W) $100.00. Half Page (B&W) $60.00. **Circ:** 1500 (ctrl).

BB
BULLETIN OF EASTERN CARIBBEAN AFFAIRS. **Added/Corp** University of the West Indies (Cave Hill, Barbados). Institute of Social and Economic Research. University of West Indies (Cave Hill, Barbados). Vol. 1, No. 1 (March 1975)-. Periodical. English. qt. $16.00 Caribbean; $20.00 other. Institute of Social and Economic Research / Barbados, University of West Indies, PO Box 64 Cave Hill Canpus, Bridgetown Barbados. **Tel** (809)425-1012. **ED** Patrick Emmanuel. **LC** F2001; .B84. **DD** 972.9/005. **Bk Rev. Ad Acc. Pr Rev.** ctrl circ.
Desc: Various aspects of Caribbean society with emphasis on the Windward and Leeward Islands and Barbados.
Ind/Abst Int. Bibliogr. Sociol.; PAIS Int. Print.

NQ
CAMBIO. No. 1 (Nov./Dec. 1991)-. Periodical. Spanish. bm. Publicaciones Cambio, Villa 9 de Junio C-387, Puente 1 c. arriba 5 vrs. sur, Apdo. 1068 Managua Nicaragua. **Tel** 94095. **ED** Clementina Rivas Franco. **LC** AP63.15; .C252. **Circ:** 3,000.

TR/1011-5765
CARIBBEAN AFFAIRS. Vol. 1, No. 1 (Jan./Mar. 1988)-. Periodical. English. qt. $45.00 US; $50.00 Canada; $60.00 Europe, Central America, and South America; $65.00 other. Trinidad Express Newspapers Ltd, 35 Independence Square, Port of Spain Trinidad. **Tel** (809)623-1711, FAX (809)627-1451. **ED** Owen Baptiste. **LC** F2155; .C362. **DD** 972.9/005. **Bk Rev. Ad Acc, Adv Mgr:** Shida Bolai. **Circ:** 10,000.
Desc: The only journal in the region which is written and edited by Caribbean people. It features authentic and authoritative information on issues and events taking place in the Caribbean Basin today-from Brazil, Suriname and the Guinas in the South to Mexico, the Bahamas and Cuba in the North.
Ind/Abst Am. Hist. Life (1988-); U.S. Polit. Sci. Doc. (199?-).

●US/1058-4315
CARIBBEAN INTERNATIONAL (ALBANY, N.Y.). (CARIBBEAN INTERNATIONAL.). (1992)-. Periodical. English. bm. $14.00. The Berdemes Group, 466 Western Avenue, Albany NY 12203-1419.

MX/0185-4275
CASA DEL TIEMPO. **Added/Corp** Universidad Autonoma Metropolitana. Direccion de Difusion Cultural. Vol. 1, No. 1 (Sept. 1980)-. Periodical. Spanish. Twelve times a year. $30.00. Universidad Autonoma Metropolitana Difusion, Medellin 28 Colo Roma, Mexico 7 DF Mexico. **Tel** 011 52 5 528 9241. **ED** Jose Espinasa. **LC** AP63; .C3254. **DD** 056/.1. Index available. cum. index. **Bk Rev. Ad Acc. Pr Rev. Circ:** 1,500 (ctrl).
Desc: Review of humanistic, literary and general interest.

●US/1062-5283
CHAC MOL NEWSLETTER. (CHAC MOL NEWSLETTER: A PUBLICATION OF THE CENTRAL AMERICAN INSTITUTE OF PREHISTORIC AND TRADITIONAL CULTURES AT BELIZE, 1992.). [Chac mol newsl.]. **Added/Corp** Central American Institute of Prehistoric and Traditional Cultures at Belize. Vol. 1, No. 1 (Mar. 1992)-. Periodical. English. qt. Free to members. The Institute, 68-769 First Street, Suite 286, Cathedral City CA 92234-1244. **DD** 972.

HO
COCONUT TELEGRAPH. English. bm. L.5.00 per issue. Coconut Telegraph, Cooper Building, Suite 301 Coxen Hole, Roatan Honduras CA. **Tel** 011 504 451660.

ED Marion Seaman. **Ad Acc.**
Desc: News, features and information from the Bay Islands.

CL
COSAS. **See** Public Administration.

US/0276-4644
COSTA RICA REPORT. [Costa Rica rep.]. (1981)-. Periodical. English. Twelve times a year. $42.00. US International Marketing Company, 17057 Bellflower Boulevard, PO Box 428, Bellflower CA 90706. **Tel** (310)925-2918.

GT
CULTURA DE GUATEMALA. Began with Jan./June 1980 issue. Periodical. Spanish. Three times a year. Direccion de Investigaciones, Universidad Rafael Landivar, Apartado 39 C, Guatemala. **LC** AP63; .C8268. **DD** 056/.1.
Ind/Abst Ethnoarts Index.

CU
DIRECT FROM CUBA. Began with No. 1, Sept. 30, 1969. Periodical. English. sm. Prensa Latina Agencia, Info LatinoAmericana, Calle 23-No 201, Havana 4 Cuba.

US
DIRECT LINE. Periodical. English. ir. $45.00 per vol., $110.00 3 vol. set. Nightingale-Conant Corporation, 7300 North Lehigh Avenue, Chicago IL 60648. **Tel** (800)323-5552.

US/0091-3235
DIRECTORY OF LATIN AMERICANISTS. 1972/73-. Directory. English. an. Free. Arizona State University / Latin Americans, Center for Latin American Studies, Tempe AZ 85281. **Tel** (602)965-5127. **ED** Evelyn Smith de Galvez. **LC** F1409.9; .D57. **DD** 918/.0025/79173. **Circ:** 1,000.
Desc: Covers topics of interest to Latin Americans.

US
GUATEMALA UPDATE. **Added/Corp** Guatemala Solidarity Committee (Seattle, Wash.). (19??)-. Periodical. English. GUASO, PO Box 31903, Seattle WA 98103.
Ind/Abst Hum. Rights Intern. Rep.

CK
HOJAS DE CULTURA POPULAR COLOMBIANA. **Added/Corp** Colombia. Seccion de Cultura Popular. Colombia. Departamento de Cultura Popular y Extension Artistica. Colombia. Direccion de Informacion y Propaganda. No. 1 (1947)-. Periodical. Spanish. mo. cum. index.
Ind/Abst Am. Hist. Life (1955-1956).

US/0741-8167
HONDURAS UPDATE. ***Suspended.*** **Added/Corp** Honduras Information Center (Cambridge, Mass.). Vol. 1 (Aug. 1982)-(July 1989). Periodical. English. mo. $14.00 (individuals), $22.00 (institutions) US; $16.00 (individuals), $24.00 (institutions) Canada and Mexico; $18.00 (individuals), $26.00 (institutions) other. Honduras Information Center, 1 Summer Street, Somerville MA 02143. **Tel** (617)625-7220. **ED** Sandra Avila, Susan Jessop, Eric Schultz and Luis Sierra. **Bk Rev.** **Circ:** 1,200 (ctrl).
Desc: Updated information and analysis of the impact of Honduran economic, social and political life and in the rest of the region.
Ind/Abst Hum. Rights Intern. Rep. (?-?).

GW
LANDERBERICHT. DOMINIKANISCHE REPUBLIK. **Added/Corp** Germany (West). Statistisches Bundesamt. 1990-. German (table of contents in English). W Kohlhammer Verlag GmbH, Postfach 800430, D 70549 Stuttgart Germany. **Tel** 011 49 711 78631, FAX 011 49 711 7863263, telex 7-255820. **LC** HA886; .S8. ***Continues*** *Statistik des Auslandes. Landerbericht. Dominikanische Republik, 1077-1728.*

GW/0937-082X
LANDERBERICHT. HAITI. **Added/Corp** Germany (West). Statistisches Bundesamt. 1990-. German (table of contents in French). W Kohlhammer Verlag GmbH, Postfach 800430, D 70549 Stuttgart Germany. **Tel** 011 49 711 78631, FAX 011 49 711 7863263, telex 7-255820. **LC** HA881; .S72. ***Continues*** *Statistik des Auslandes. Landerbericht. Haiti, 0179-7557.*

GW/0937-7816
LANDERBERICHT. JAMAIKA. **Added/Corp** Germany (West). Statistisches Bundesamt. 1989-. German (table of contents in English). W Kohlhammer Verlag GmbH, Postfach 800430, D 70549 Stuttgart Germany. **Tel** 011 49 711 78631, FAX 011 49 711 7863263, telex 7-255820. **LC** HA891; .S72. ***Continues*** *Statistik des Auslandes. Landerbericht. Jamaika, 0179-7069.*

UK
LATIN AMERICAN NEWSLINE. (1991)-. English. Twelve times a year. $25.00 Central America; $65.00 other. Latin American News Service, PO Box 24, Manchester M70 EX England. **Tel** 011 44 61 8397050, FAX 011 44 61 8397051. **ED** John Warry (phone: (061)228-7071). **Circ:** 500 (ctrl). ***Absorbed*** *Central American Monitor.*
Desc: A news digest of all countries of Latin America, including Dominican Republic, Cuba, and Haiti.

UK/0264-2867
LATIN AMERICAN SPECIAL REPORTS. ***Title Change.*** [Lat. Am. spec. rep.]. **VFOAT** Latin American Special Report. SR-83-01 (Feb. 1983)-SR-83-06 (Dec. 1983)-?. Periodical. English. bm. Lettres UK Ltd, 61 Old Street, London EC1V 9HX England. **Tel** 011 44 71 251-0012, FAX 011 44 71 253-8193. **ED** Eduardo D Crawley. ***Continued by*** *Special Reports (Latin American Newsletters Ltd.).*
Desc: Appearing six times per year, each of the Latin American Special Reports deals with a specific subject in depth providing facts, figures, analysis and forecasts each year. The Latin American Electorial Scene and Banking Industry are covered along with four other topical subjects.

SW
LATINOAMERICANA (STOCKHOLM). (LATINOAMERICANA / LATINAMERIKA-INSTITUTET I STOCKHOLM.). No. 1-. Periodical. Spanish (Swedish). sa. Latinamerika Institutet, Universitetet, 106 91 Stockholm Sweden. **Tel** 08/16 28 82, telex 8105199 UNIVERS. **LC** Z1605; .L33; F1408. **DD** 016.98. **Circ:** 400 (ctrl). ***Continues in part*** *Ibero-Americana (Stockholm, Sweden : 1971).*

CR
MESOAMERICA (INSTITUTE FOR CENTRAL AMERICAN STUDIES (COSTA RICA)). (MESOAMERICA.). **Added/Corp** Institute for Central American Studies (Costa Rica). Vol. 1, No. 1 (Jan. 1982)-. Periodical. English. mo (12 issues per year). $70.00. Institute for Central American Studies, Apdo 1524, 2050 San Pedro Costa Rica. **Tel** 011 506 337112, FAX 011 506 337221. **ED** Linda Holland. Index available in last issue of volume--attached. **Bk Rev.** **Circ:** 1,000 (ctrl).
Desc: News and analysis of the Central American region.
Ind/Abst Am. Hist. Life (1982-); Hum. Rights Intern. Rep.

US/1044-6303
MEXICO SERVICE. (MEXICO SERVICE : MS : A PUBLICATION OF INTERNATIONAL REPORTS.). [Mex. serv.]. **Added/Corp** International Reports (Firm). **VFOAT** MS. (Jan. 1980)-. Periodical. English. Twenty-five times a year. $300.00 (schools & universities); $595.00 others. United Communications Group, 11300 Rockville Pike, Suite 1100, Rockville MD 20852. **Tel** (301)816-8950 ext. 223, FAX (301)816-8945. **LC** HC131; .M587. **DD** 972. **[CCC].** available on an online database (file 636/Full-Text) from DIALOG.
Desc: Accurate, comprehensive information about Mexico's turbulent financial, political and economics climate.
Ind/Abst PTS Newsl. Database [Full Txt.].

PE
NOTICIAS ALIADAS. **VFOAT** NA. (19??)-. Periodical. English (Spanish). wk (except first 2 weeks of Jan. and Aug.). $85.00 institution; $60.00 individual. Noticias Aliadas, Apartado 18-0964, Lima 18 Peru. **Tel** 011 51 14 475210, FAX 011 51 14 454681. **ED** Brian K. Goonan Costello. Index available (Free). cum. index. **Bk Rev**, (Qty: 12). **Pr Rev.** **Circ:** 3,000 (ctrl).
Desc: An alternative news service that covers major trends in church, human rights and development in Latin America. It publishes bulletins, news, analysis and documentation on Latin America and the Caribbean.

FR
ORDINAIRE MEXIQUE, AMERIQUE CENTRALE, L'. **Added/Corp** Groupement de Recherches Coordonnees sur l'Administration Locale (France) Institut Pluridisciplinaire d'Etudes sur l'Amerique Latine de Toulouse. Universite de Toulouse-Le Mirail. No. 118 (Nov./Dec. 1988)-. French (Spanish; summaries and/or abstracts in Spanish). Six times a year. 170.00F. Assn Francaise Mexicanist Gral, 5 Allee Antonio Machado, 31058 Toulouse Cedex France. **Tel** 33 1 61504395. **LC** F1201; .O73. **DD** 972/.005. ***Continues*** *Ordinaire du Mexicaniste.*

•CR
PENSAMIENTO CENTROAMERICANO. **Added/Corp** Centro de Investigaciones y Actividades Culturales (Managua, Nicaragua) Asociacion Libro Libre (San Jose, Costa Rica). Vol. 47, No. 215 (April-June 1992)-. Periodical. Spanish. qt. ***Continues*** *Revista del Pensamiento Centroamericano.*

FR/0765-1333
PROBLEMES D'AMERIQUE LATINE. [Probl. Am. lat.]. Began in 1966. Monographic series. French. qt. Price varies per volume. Documentation Francaise, 29 Quai Voltaire, 75344 Paris Cedex 7 France. **Tel** 011 33 1 40157000, FAX 011 33 1 40157230, telex 204 826 DOCFRAN. **LC** D411; .F67 subser. **DD** 909.8S; 980/.008. Index available. cum. index. **Bk Rev.** **Circ:** 5,000. available in microform.
Desc: Deals with the analysis of political, economical and social problems in Latin American countries.
Ind/Abst Am. Hist. Life (1979-); Int. Bibliogr. Sociol.; Int. Polit. Sci. Abstr.; PAIS Int. Print (1991-?).

NQ/0378-3340
REVISTA DEL PENSAMIENTO CENTROAMERICANO. ***Title Change.*** [Rev. pensam. centroam.]. **Added/Corp** Centro de Investigaciones y Actividades Culturales (Managua, Nicaragua) Asociacion Libro Libre (San Jose, Costa Rica). (1972)-(1992). Periodical. Spanish. qt. Associacion Libro Libre, Apartado 1154 1250, Escazu Costa Rica. **ED** Xavier Zavala Cuadra. **LC** F1421; .R44. **Bk Rev.** **Ad Acc.** **Circ:** 2,000. available on microfilm and microfiche from University Microfilms International (UMI). ***Continues*** *Revista Conservadora del Pensamiento Centroamericano.* ***Continued by*** *Pensamiento Centroamericano.*
Desc: Topics include Central American affairs, art, economics, history, politics, sociology, and religion.
Ind/Abst Am. Hist. Life (1975-); HAPI Hisp. Am. Period. Index.

US/0162-1270
SA. **VFOAT** Magazine of San Antonio. **VAT** San Antonio. Periodical. English. mo. $10.00. SA, 235 E Commerce, San Antonio TX 78205.

AG
SEMANA LATINOAMERICANA. ***Title Change.*** (19??)-(19??). Periodical. Spanish. wk. Latinoamericana De Servicios, Casilla De Correo 3808, Buenos Aires 1000 Argentina. ***Merged with*** *Semana Latinoamericana (Buenos Aires, Argentina). English. Latinamerican Week* ***to form*** *Semana Latinoamericana (Buenos Aires, Argentina : 1987).*

US/1044-1247
SPOTLIGHT (BROOKLYN, N.Y.). (SPOTLIGHT.). [Spotlight]. **VFOAT** CATC Spotlight; CATC-Spotlight. **VAT** Caribbean American Trade Connection Spotlight. April/June (1989)-. Periodical. English. qt. $10.00. Caribbean American Trade Connection, 1601 Nostrand Avenue, Brooklyn NY 11226. **ED** Austin Tuitt. **DD** 972. cum. index. **Ad Acc.**
Desc: A business consumer directory.

GW
STATISTIK DES AUSLANDES. LANDERBERICHT. HONDURAS. **VFOAT** Landerbericht. Honduras. German (table of contents in English). Verlag W Kohlhammer GmbH, Abt Veroffentlichungen des Statistischen Bundesamtes, Philipp-Reis-Strasse 3, W-6500 Mainz 42 Germany. **LC** HA825; .S73. **DD** 317.283/05. ***Formed by the union of*** *Landerberichte. Honduras* ***and*** *Landerkurzberichte. Honduras.*

GT
THIS WEEK IN CENTRAL AMERICA. **VFOAT** This Week; This Week, Central America and Panama. Vol. 13, No. 1 (Jan. 1, 1990)-. Periodical. English. wk. This Week Publications, Edificio Herrera, 12 Calle 4-53 Zona 1, S-E Guatemala City, Guatemala. ***Continues*** *This week. Central America & Panama.*

US
UPDATE NICARAGUA. Periodical. English. 475 l'Enfant Plaza, PO Box 23126, Washington DC 20024. **Tel** (202)755-0738.

MX/0186-9418
VOICES OF MEXICO. ***Ceased.*** **Added/Corp** Universidad Nacional Autonoma de Mexico. **VFOAT** Voices. No. 1 (Sept.-Nov. 1986)-Ceased No. 16 (1991). Periodical. English. qt. Voices of Mexico, Filosofia y Letras No 88, Col Copilco Universidad, 04360 Mexico DF Mexico. **Tel** (905)658-5853. **(Subscription address:** Hispanic Books Distributors, Inc., 1665 West Grant Road, Tucson, AZ 85745; telephone: (602)882-9484) **ED** Sara Alatorre. **LC** F1236; .V65. **DD** 972/.005. Index available. **Bk Rev.** **Ad Acc.** **Circ:** 3,000.
Desc: Covers political and economic analysis, special reports, interviews with Mexican leaders, science and culture, and book reviews.
Ind/Abst Hum. Rights Intern. Rep. (?-?).

MX/0185-1586
VUELTA. [Vuelta]. Vol. 1, (Dec. 1976)-. Periodical. Spanish. mo. $80.00 North & Central America; $95.00 South America & Europe; $105.00 other. Editoriale Vuelta S A de C V, Presidente Carranza 210, Coyoacan 04000 Mexico DF. **Tel** 011 52 5 5548980 or, 5548811, FAX 011 52 5 6580074. **LC** AP63; .V8. **DD** 056/.1. Index available. cum. index. **Bk Rev.** **Ad Acc, Adv Mgr:** Patricia Rodriguez.
Desc: Literary reviews, politics, etc.
Ind/Abst HAPI Hisp. Am. Period. Index; MLA Int. Bibl. Books Artic. Mod. Lang. Lit.

GENERAL INTEREST-EUROPE

US/1058-6105
2 TO 22 DAYS IN GREAT BRITAIN. See Travel and Tourism.

UK
1992 AND AFTER. (1989)-. English. Pergamon Press, An Imprint of Elsevier Science Ltd., The Boulevard, Langford Lane, Kidlington, Oxford OX5 1GB United Kingdom. **Tel** 011 44 865 843000, 011 44 865 843699, FAX 011 44 865 843010. **(Subscription address:** US/ 395 Saw Mill River Road, Elmsford, NY 10523; Can/ 150 Consumers Road/Suite 104, Willowdale Ontario M2J 1P9; Aus-NZ/ POB 544, Potts Point NSW 2011**)**
Desc: Review of the major issues facing European society in the 1980's and 1990's.

US/0738-2707
ABSTRACTS OF SOVIET AND EAST EUROPEAN EMIGRE PERIODICAL LITERATURE. ***Title Change.*** [Abstr. Sov. East Eur. emigr. period. lit.]. **VFOAT** ASEEPL. Vol. 1, No. 1 (1981)- Vol. 8, No. 4 (1992). English. qt. Informatics & Prognostics, 1400 Shattuck Avenue, Suite 7 10, Berkeley CA 94709. **Tel** (510)236-2935. **(Subscription address:** 1400 Shattuck Avenue/Suite 7, No 10, Berkeley, CA 94705**)** **ED** Leonid Khotin. **LC** DK1; .A32. **DD** 057. Index available. **Bk Rev. Ad Acc. Circ:** 600 (ctrl). ***Continued by*** *Zarubezhnaia Periodicheskaia Pechat na Russkom Iazyke, 1066-4858.*
Desc: Containing arts, economics, government, law, politics, history, international relations, language, literature, philosophy, political theory, religion, science and sociology.

US
ACQUERELLO ITALIANO (AUDIOCASSETTE). Italian (English). bm. $89.00 US; $93.00 Canada; $104.00 other. Champs-Elysees Inc, Box 158067, Nashville TN 37215-8067. **Tel** (800)824-0829, (615)383-8534, FAX (615) 297-3138. **ED** Luigi Monga. **Pr Rev.**
Desc: An hour-long magazine on audiocassette accompanied by a printed transcription with an Italian-English glossary. Contains news, features, interviews, and music in Italian that paint a picture of contemporary Italian culture.

CN/0383-8714
ACTUALITE (MONTREAL. 1976). (L'ACTUALITE.). [Actualite]. Vol. 1 (Sept. 1976)-. Periodical. French. Twenty times a year. 25.00Can$ Canada; 52.00Can$ US; 69.00Can$ other. MacLean Hunter Publ. Limited / Toronto, 777 Bay Street, 8th Floor Agency Control, Toronto Ontario M5W 1A7 Canada. **Tel** (416)596-5000, (800)268-6811, FAX (416)596-5526. **ED** Jean Pare. **LC** AP21; .A363. **DD** 054/.1. **Bk Rev. Ad Acc.** available on microfilm and microfiche from University Microfilms International (UMI). ***Formed by the union of*** *MacLean, 0024-9815* ***and*** *Actualite, 0001-7698.*
Ind/Abst Can. Index; Can. Period. Index; Point Repere (1983-).

UK/0954-1063
AKTUELL AUF DEUTSCH. Vol. 1, No. 1 (Sept./Oct. 1988)-. Periodical. German. Six times a year (6 issues). $25.00. Mary Glasgow Publications, Brockhampton Lane, Kineton, Warwickshire CV35 0JB England. **Tel** 011 44 926 640606, FAX 011 44 926 641016. **(Subscription address:** Scholastic Inc, PO Box 3710, Jefferson City MO 65102.**)** ***Continues*** *Der Roller, 0035-7901.*

SP/0214-0381
ALGO 2000. [Algo 2000]. **VFOAT** Algo dos Mil. (1988)-. Periodical. Spanish. mo. Ediciones Hymsa, Diputacion 211, Barcelona Spain. **UDC** 08. ***Continues*** *Algo, 0002-5348.*

FR/0002-5712
ALLEMAGNE D'AUJOURD'HUI. (ALLEMAGNE D'AUJOURD'HUI; REVUE FRANCAISE D'INFORMATION SUR LES DEUX L'ALLEMAGNES.). [Allem. aujourd'hui]. **Added/Corp** Association Pour la Connaissance de l'Allemagne d'Aujourd'Hui. (1953)-. Periodical. French. bm. 220.00F US. Association Pour la Connaissance de l'Allemagne, 8 rue Faraday, 75017 Paris, France. **Tel** 011 33 1 42274155. **DD** 943. ***Formed by the union of*** *Allemagne d'Aujourd'Hui* ***and*** *Realites Allemandes.*
Ind/Abst Foreign Lang. Index.

SZ
ALLTAG, DER. Periodical. German. qt. 64.00F Switzerland; $45.00 US. Verlag der Alltag, Postfach 331, CH-8031 Zurich Switzerland. **Tel** (01)271 81 42. **ED** Walter Keller and Michael Rutschky. **LC** AP32; .A44. Index available. **Bk Rev. Ad Acc. Circ:** 5,000.
Desc: Articles on the culture of everyday life; the sensation of the culture of the normal.

IT
ALMANACCO (MILAN, ITALY). (ALMANACCO.). (1981)-. Italian (English). an. Almanacco, 25 Hollinger Road, Toronto Ontario M4B 3G2 Canada.

AU/0378-8644
ALMANACH - OSTERREICHISCHE AKADEMIE DER WISSENSCHAFTEN. (ALMANACH.). [Alm. - Osterr. Akad. Wiss.]. **Main/Corp** Osterreichische Akademie der Wissenschaften. Vol. 1 (1851)-. German. an. Oesterreichischen Akademie Wissenschaften, Dr. Ignaz Seipel Platz 2, A-1010 Vienna Austria. **Tel** 011 43 1 51581. **LC** AS142; .V34. **CODEN** OAWABT. **Circ:** 600.
Desc: Almanac of the Austrian Academy of Sciences. Contains a list of all members of the academy and institutes.
Ind/Abst GeoRef.

PL
ALMANACH POLONII. **Added/Corp** Towarzystwo lacznosci z Polonia Zagraniczna. (1969)-. Multiple languages (English, French and Spanish). an. Wydawnictwo Interpress, Ul Bagatela 12, PO Box 388, 00-585 Warsaw Poland. **ED** F. Laszkiewicz and E. Trzeciak. **LC** AY1039.P7; K2545. **Ad Acc. Circ:** 30,000. ***Continues*** *Kalendarz Polonii.*
Desc: Illustrated publication for Poles and residents abroad.

CN/0441-1196
ALMANAKH GOMONU UKRAJINY. (ALMANAKH HOMONU UKRAINY.). **VFOAT** Alamac of Homin Ukrainy. **VAT** Almanah Kalendar Gomonu Ukraini. 1956-. Ukrainian. Homin Ukrainy Publishing Company, 140 Bathurst Street, Ontario Toronto M5V 2R3 Canada. **DD** 057/.91.

BL
ALMANAQUE MINO. No. 1- June 1975-. Portuguese. Mino Criacoes, rua Casimiro Montenegro 50 Sao Gerardo, Fortaleza Brazil. **LC** AP111; .A55. **DD** 056/.1.

SZ
ALPEN. **VFOAT** Alpi; Alps; Alpes; Le Alpi; Las Alps; Les Alpes. Vol. 23 (1957)-. Periodical. German (French). qt. 42.00F, 10.00F (per issue) Switzerland; 58.00F other. Staempfli & Cie SA, Postfach 8326, CH-3001 Bern Switzerland. **Tel** 011 41 31 3006666, telex 031 911 515 EDMZ CH. ***Continues in part*** *Alpen.*

FR/0395-2649
ANNALES (PARIS, FRANCE : 1946). ***Title Change.*** (ANNALES.). [Annales]. **VFOAT** Annales, Economies, Societes, Civilisations. Vol. 1, No. 1 (Jan./Mar. 1946)-(1994). Periodical. French. bm. Librairie Armand Colin, BP 22, 41354 Vineuil Cedex France. **Tel** 011 33 54 438994. **ED** Lucien Febvre and others. **LC** AP20; .A58. **DD** 054/.1. ***Continues*** *Annales d' Histoire Sociale Paris, France : 1945).* ***Continued by*** *Annales d'Historie et de Science Sociale.*
Ind/Abst Am. Hist. Life (1954-); BHA : Biblio. Hist. Art; Int. Bibliogr. Sociol.; Linguist. Lang. Behav. Abstr.; Pop. Period. Index; Popul. Index (?-?); Saf. Health Work; Soc. Plann. Policy Dev. Abstr.; Sociol. Abstr.

FI
APU. (1933)-. Periodical. Finnish. Fifty times a year. A-Lehdet Oy, Hitsaajankatu 10, 00810 Helsinki Finland. **Tel** (358)0-782311. **ED** Matti Saari. **LC** AP80; .A66. **Ad Acc. Circ:** 271,138 (ctrl).

SP
ARCHIPIELAGO (BARCELONA, SPAIN). (ARCHIPIELAGO.). Vol. 1 (1988)-. Periodical. Spanish. Four times a year. 5200ptas Spain; 7800ptas others. Edit Archipielago, C Cardener 31 Bajos, 08026 Barcelona Spain. **Tel** 011 34 3 2108503. **LC** AP60; .A615. **DD** 056/.1.

BE
AROUND EUROPE. (19??)-. Newsletter. English. mo. $23.00. Quaker Council of European Affairs, 50 Square Ambiorix, B-1040 Brussels Belgium. **Tel** 011 32 2 2304935. **Bk Rev.**
Desc: News, views, messages, and occasionally reviews.

LV
ATMODA ATPUTAI : LTF NEDELAS LAIKRAKSTS. **Added/Corp** Latvijas Tautas Fronte. (Sept. 11, 1990)-. Periodical. Latin. wk. $169.95. Atmoda Atputai, Basteja Bulvari 16, Riga 226250 Latvia. **(Subscription address:** East View Publications Inc., 3020 Harbor Lane North, Suite 110, Minneapolis MN 55447.**)**.

IT/0004-8143
AUSONIA. [Ausonia]. Yearly Vol. 1- May 1946-. Periodical. Italian. bm. Casa Editrice Maia, Via Cave 5, 34011 Aurisina Italy. **LC** AP37; .A88. **DD** 055.
Ind/Abst MLA Int. Bibl. Books Artic. Mod. Lang. Lit.

AU/0304-8713
AUSTRIA TODAY. No. 1 (1974)-. Periodical. English (Arabic, English and Russian). qt. S330.00. Austria Today, PO Box 47, Schweizertor A 1014, Vienna Austria. **Tel** 11 43 222 5872184, FAX 11 43 222 566159. **ED** Harold Egger. **LC** DB17; .A88. **DD** 994/.005. Index available. **Bk Rev**, (Qty: 6-15/yr). **Ad Acc. Circ:** 16,000 (ctrl). available on microfilm; available on an online database.
Desc: Represents the Republic of Austria in all its aspects in other countries throughout the world.

RU/0005-2574
AZIIA I AFRIKA SEGODNIA. See General Interest-General Interest-Asia.

GW
BALTISCHE BRIEFE. (Jan. 1948)-. Periodical. German. mo (11 issues). $50.40 Europe; $50.65 other. Wolf Von Kleist, Deefkamp 13, D 22927 Grosshansdorf Germany. **LC** AP30; .B2. **DD** 053/.1.

GW
BAYREUTH. (19??)-. Periodical. German (English, French and German). an. Verlag der Festspielleitung, Postfach 100262, D 95402 Bayreuth Germany. **Ad Acc.** ctrl circ.

IT
BELL'ITALIA. Vol. 1, No. 1 (May 1986)-. Periodical. Italian. mo. L62000 Italy; L110000 other. Giorgio Mondadori Intl, Via A Ponti 10, 20143 Milan Italy. **Tel** 011 39 2 891661. **LC** DG401; .B45. **DD** 945/.005. Index available. **Circ:** 115,000 (ctrl).

GW
BERICHT UBER DIE JAHRESTAGUNG ... . (1982)-. German. an. Vereinigung der Stadt Regional und Landesplaner E V Srl, Paulstrasse 9, W-4630 Bochum Germany. **LC** HT169.G3; B48. **DD** 307.1/216/094305. ***Continues*** *Berichte Uber die Tagungen Im Jahr ... .*

GW/0300-1644
BERLIN MAGAZIN. [Berl. Mag.]. Periodical. German. mo. DM2.25 single issue. Druckhaus Tempelhos, 1 Berlin 42, Mariendorfer Damm 1/3, Berlin Germany. **LC** DD851; .B42. **DD** 914.3/155/005.

NE/0005-9692
BESTE UIT READER'S DIGEST, HET. Vol. 1 (1958)-. Periodical. Dutch. mo. Fl66.00 Netherlands; Fl91.00 other. Uitgeversmaatschappij Reader's Digest NV, PO Box 13600, 1100 KA Amsterdam Netherlands. **Tel** 011 31 20 5678911. **Bk Rev. Ad Acc.**

GW/0302-9468
BGS, ZEITSCHRIFT DES BUNDESGRENZSCHUTZES. Yearly V. 24- ; Jan. 1974-. Periodical. German. mo. DM2.40 quarterly. A Bernecker GmbH & Company KG, Postfach 140, D-34212 Melsungen Germany. **Tel** 011 49 5661 7310, FAX 011 49 5661 73189, telex (17)566 1813. **LC** AP30; .P35. **Ad Acc. Circ:** 13,850. ***Continues*** *Parole.*

RU
BIULLETEN INOSTRANNOI KOMMERCHESKOI INFORMATSII. **Added/Corp** Moscow. Nauchno-Issledovatelskii Koniukturnyi Institut. (1948)-. Periodical. Russian. ir. $347.00 domestic airmail; $595.00 international airmail. **(Subscription address:** Victor Kamkin, 4956 Boiling Brook Parkway, Rockville MD 20852.**)**
Ind/Abst Leis. Recreat. Tour. Abstr.; Rural Dev. Abstr.; World Agric. Econ.

UK/0143-3245
BLOCK (EAST BARNET, HERTFORDSHIRE). ***Ceased.*** (BLOCK.). No. 1 (1979)-Ceased ?. English. ir (two issues per year). Middlesex Polytechnic, Cat Hil Cockfosters E Barnet, Herts EN4 8HT England. **Tel** 01-368-1299. **ED** Jon Bird, Barry Curtis, Tim Putnam, Lisa Tickner. **Ad Acc. Circ:** 1,500.
Desc: Includes radical art and design history, media studies, theories of culture, structuralism, politics and psychoanalytic theory, and feminism.
Ind/Abst Altern. Press Index (-19??); ARTbibliogr. Mod. (1983-).

CK/0001-3773
BOLETIN DE LA ACADEMIA COLOMBIANA. [Bol. Acad. Colomb.]. **Main/Corp** Academia Colombiana. Vol. 1 (June 1936)-. Periodical. Spanish. qt. $30.00 (all except Colombia). Academia Colombiana, Apartado 13-922, Bogota 1 Colombia. **Tel** 57 1 2343152 ext 7. **LC** AS82; .B52. **DD** 056/.1. Index available. **Bk Rev**, (Qty: 4). ctrl circ.
Ind/Abst Am. Hist. Life (1965-1971, 1981-); HAPI Hisp. Am. Period. Index (19??-); Linguist. Lang. Behav. Abstr.; MLA Int. Bibl. Books Artic. Mod. Lang. Lit.; Soc. Plann. Policy Dev. Abstr.; Sociol. Abstr.

NE/0168-7298
BOLLETTINO DI ITALIANISTICA. **Added/Corp** Universita Degli Studi di Roma "La Sapienza." Dipartimento di Italianistica. (1983)-. Italian. ir. L95000 Italy; L110000 others. La Nuova Italia Editrice Spa, Via Ernesto Codignola, 50018 Scandicci Florence Italy. **Tel** 011 39 55 75901, FAX 011 39 55 7590208. **ED** Albereto Asor Rosa. **LC** PQ4001; .B6. **DD** 850/.5.
Desc: Provides a regular and rapid flow of information

about Italian studies-5 sections: reviews, congresses, special events, national reports, research and bibliography.

UK
BOOKS IN POLISH OR RELATING TO POLAND. Vol. 1 (1950)-. Periodical. English (Polish). qt. $28.00. Polish Library, 238-246 King Street, London W6 ORF England. **Tel** 011 4 81 7410474. **Circ:** 100 (ctrl).
Desc: A list of books in Polish or relating to Poland added to the collection of the Polish Library in London.

IT/0006-775X
BORGHESE, IL. ***Ceased.*** Vol. 1, (March 15, 1950)-No. 46 (Dec. 1993). Periodical. Italian. Fifty-one times per year. Borghese, Viale Regina Margh 7, 20122 Milan Italy. **Tel** 011 39 2 55010966. **LC** AP37; .B65. **DD** 055/.1.

UK/0068-1075
BRITAIN. (BRITAIN / ISSUED BY THE CENTRAL OFFICE OF INFORMATION.). **Added/Corp** Great Britain. Central Office of Information. (1950)-. English. an (Jan.). £19.50 (latest volume). Her Majesty's Stationery Office, 51 Nine Elms Lane, London SW8 5DR England. **Tel** 011 44 71 873 8459, 011 44 71 873 8499, FAX 011 44 71 873 8499, 011 44 71 873 8456, telex 297138. **(Subscription address:** PO Box 276, Public Centre, London SW8 5DT England**) LC** DA630; .A17. **DD** 941/.005. **[CCC].**

CN/0823-7743
BRITANNIA (TORONTO). (BRITANNIA.). [Britannia]. Vol. 1, No. 1 (Mar. 1983)-. Periodical. English. Twelve times a year. 37.42Can$ Canada: 34.95Can$ US; 39.95Can$ other. Britannia, RR 1, Hillier Ontario K0K 2J0 Canada. **Tel** (613)399-3634. **ED** Terry Fletcher. **DD** 941/.005. **Bk Rev. Ad Acc. Circ:** 30,000.
Desc: Keeping in touch with the British way of life.

US/0196-7517
BRITISH DIGEST ILLUSTRATED. [Br. dig. illus.]. Vol. 1, No. 1 (Winter 1979)-. Periodical. English. Four times a year (Mar., June, Sept., Dec.). $10.00 (one year), $18.00 (two years), $26.00 (three years) (surface mail); $$16.00 (one year), $26.00 (three years) (airmail. Union Jack Publishers, PO Box 1127, Riverview FL 33569. **Tel** (813)677-6311. **ED** June E. Prance. **LC** AP2; .B84233. **DD** 941.085/7/05. **Bk Rev.** ctrl circ.
Desc: Feature stories of the British, commonwealth, royalty, personal interviews, travel, history, recipes, and everything of interest to Britons living aboard or anglophiles in the United States.

FR
BUDESHTE. **VFOAT** L'Avenir. Periodical. Bulgarian (Bulgarian). $60.00. 18 Bis rue Brunel, 75017 Paris France. **Tel** 45-74-71-48. **ED** Ts Barev. **LC** DR51; .B812. **Bk Rev. Ad Acc. Circ:** 6,550 (ctrl).
Desc: Covers politics, economics, ideology, culture, literature, critic, and information from inside Bulgaria.

IE
BULLETIN OF THE IRISH GEORGIAN SOCIETY. **Added/Corp** Irish Georgian Society. Vol. 25 (1982)-. Bulletin. English. an. 4.00p. Irish Georgian Society, Leixlip Castle, Leixlip Kildare Co Ireland. **LC** DA900.I6295; A34. ***Continues*** *Quarterly Bulletin of the Irish Georgian Society.*
Ind/Abst Archit. Period. Index; BHA : Biblio. Hist. Art.

GW
BUNTE ILLUSTRIERTE. (19??)-. Periodical. German. wk. $170.00. Burda GmbH, Postfach 1230, D-7602 Offenburg Germany. **Tel** 011 49 781-8401. **(Subscription address:** US: German Language Publications, Inc., 153 South Deanstreet, Englewood, NJ 07631**)**

FR/0243-1335
CA M'INTERESSE. [Ca m'Interesse]. (1980)-. Periodical. French. mo. 219.39F France, 310.00F other (surface mail); $313.00 US & Canada, 374.00 Seychelles. Prisma Presse, 6 rue Daru, 75379 Paris Cedex 08, France. **Tel** 011 33 1 44153000, FAX 011 33 1 47641042. **(Subscription address:** Ca M Interesse, Service Abbonements B 110, 60732 Ste Geneva Cedex 9 France.**) UDC** 05.
Ind/Abst Point Repere (1991-).

BL
CADERNOS DE OPINAO. No. 1 (1975)-. Portuguese. Inubia, rua Abade Ramos 78, Rio de Janeiro Brazil. **LC** AP66; .C34.

FR/1145-0320
CAHIERS DE L'EXPRESS (PARIS), LES. (LES CAHIERS DE L'EXPRESS.). [Cah. Express Paris]. (1989)-. Periodical. French. bm. 180.00F. L'Express, 61 Avenue Hoche, 75008 Paris Cedex France. **Tel** 011 33 1 44625430. **UDC** 082.

FR/0182-2373
CAHIERS OBSIDIANE, LES. **VFOAT** Obsidiane. 1 -. Periodical. English (French and German). Three times a year. $15.96. Association Loi, 1901 50 rue des Abbesses, 75018 Paris France. **LC** AC5; .C27. **DD** 084/.1.

FR/0526-8443
CAHIERS PERCHERONS. (1957)-. Monographic series. French. qt. 150.00F. Association des Amis du Perche, Maison des Comtes, 8, rue du Portail St., Denis, 61400 Mortagne-au-Perche France. **ED** P.H. Sigurет. **UDC** 908(442.3).
Ind/Abst BHA : Biblio. Hist. Art.

IT
CAPITAL INTERNATIONAL. (Autumn 1985)-. Periodical. English. $5.00. Capital Internationl, 1500 Broadway/Suite 1603, New York NY 10036. **LC** DG441; .C17. **DD** 945/.005.

SP/0576-8233
CARTA DE ESPANA. **Added/Corp** Instituto Espanol de Emigracion. No.1 (1961). Periodical. Spanish. mo. $20.00. Administracion De Carta De Espana, P Pintor Rosales 44-46, 28008 Madrid Spain. **Tel** (011)34 1 2475200, FAX (011)34 1 5413818. **Circ:** 25000.
Desc: For the people of Spain living in other countries; used as reference in some US schools.

SP
CATALONIA CULTURE. **Added/Corp** Centre Unesco de Catalunya. **VAT** Catalonia. (Jan. 1987)-. Periodical. Catalan (English, French and Spanish). bm. $60.00. Centre UNESCO de Catalunya, Mallorca 285, Barcelona 08037 Spain. **Tel** 011 34 3 2071716, , FAX 0011 34 32575851. **LC** DP302.C57; C34. **DD** 946/.7/005. ctrl circ.
Desc: Cultural magazine with different contents of Catalan culture.

GW/0008-9362
CENTRAL EUROPE JOURNAL. (1???)-. Periodical. English.
Ind/Abst Am. Hist. Life (1955-1963, 1970-1972).

XR
CESKOSLOVENSKY SVET. **Added/Corp** Ceskoslovensky Ustav Zahranicni. (1946)-. Periodical. Czech. bw. **(Subscription address:** Artia Pegas Press Ltd., Palac Metro Narodni Trida 25, 11210 Prague 1 Czech Republic.**) LC** AP52; .C394.

US/0886-005X
CHAMPS-ELYSEES. English. mo (except July). $118.00 US; $122.00 Canada and Mexico; $138.00 other. Concord Business, PO Box 2393, Concord NH 03301. **Tel** (603)224-6566. **ED** Terry Lacassin.
Desc: An hour-long program on audiocasette produced in France with interviews , music and conversation about French politics, current events , sports, the arts, and literature. A transcript with a glossary is included.

BU
CHERNO & BIALO : CHB. **VFOAT** Cherno i Bialo. Vol. 1 No. 1 (Apr. 18/25 1991)-. Periodical. Bulgarian. wk. **LC** AP58.B8; C48. ***Continues*** *Suvremenen Pokazatel.*

UK
CHURCH OF ENGLAND NEWSPAPER : CEN. **VFOAT** CEN; C.E.N. (19??)-. Periodical. English. wk. £34.00 UK; £49.00 Europe; £42.00 other. Church of England Newspaper, 10 Little College Street, London SW1P 3SH England. **Tel** 011 44 71 9767760. **ED** John Martin. **Bk Rev. Ad Acc. Pr Rev. Circ:** 12,000 (ctrl). ***Continues*** *Christian Week.*

SP
COLECCION BASICA ARAGONESA. 1-. Monographic series. Spanish. Price varies per volume. Guara Editorial SA, Jose Oto 24, Zaragoza - 14 Spain.

UK/0587-9914
COLECCION TAMESIS. SERIA A : MONOGRAFIAS. 1- 1964-. Periodical. Spanish. 11 Buckingham Street, London WC2N 6DQ England.

RM
CONTEMPORANUL IDEEA EUROPEANA. **Added/Corp** Romania. Ministerul Culturii. (April 1990)-. Periodical. Romanian. wk. DM188.00. **(Subscription address:** Kubon & Sagner, ABT Zeitschriftenimport, D 80328 Munich Germany.**) LC** AP58.R8; C6; AP86; .C66. ***Continues*** *Contemporanul.*
Desc: National culture, politics and science weekly published by the Ministry of Culture.

US
CONTEMPORARY AUSTRIAN STUDIES. English. $30.00 (paper). Transaction Publishers / Rutgers State University, New Brunswick NJ 08903. **Tel** (908)932-2280 Ext. 105, FAX (908)932-3138. **ED** Anton Pelinka and Gunter Bischof.
Desc: An interdisciplinary journal on Austria in the twentieth century dealing with the history, politics, economics, and society of the two Austrian republics concentrating specifically on contemporary studies.

UK/0045-8856
COUNTRY LIFE. Vol. 1 No. 1 (Jan. 18, 1897)-. Periodical. English. wk. $199.00. IPC Magazines Ltd., Perrymount Road, Haywards Heath, West Sussex RH16 3DH England. **Tel** 011 44 444 440421. **LC** S3; .C9. **[CCC].** available on microfilm and microfiche from University Microfilms International (UMI). ***Supersedes*** *Racing Illustrated.*
Ind/Abst Archit. Period. Index; Art Archaeol. Tech. Abstr.; ARTbibliogr. Mod.; Avery Index Archit. Period. Suppl. Colum. Univ. (Jan. 1990-); BHA : Biblio. Hist. Art; Biodeter. Abstr.; Br. Archaeol. Bibliogr.; Br. Humanit. Index; Leis. Recreat. Tour. Abstr.; Rural Dev. Abstr.; World Agric. Econ.

UK/0011-0272
COUNTRYMAN, THE. (THE COUNTRYMAN : A QUARTERLY REVIEW AND MISCELLANY OF RURAL LIFE AND PROGRESS.). [Countryman]. **VAT** Country Man. Vol. 1, No. 1 (Apr. 1927)-. Periodical. English. Six times a year. £12.00 UK; £14.00 other. **(Subscription address:** United Magazine Subscriptions, 1st Floor, Stephenson House, Brunel C, Milton Keynes, MK2 2EW England; telephone: 11 44 908 371981**) ED** Christopher Hall. **Bk Rev. Ad Acc. Circ:** 75,000.
Desc: Past and present country lifestyle in Great Britain. It also includes farming and wildlife.
Ind/Abst Br. Archaeol. Bibliogr. (?-?).

SP/0011-250X
CUADERNOS HISPANOAMERICANOS. [Cuad. hispanoam.]. **Added/Corp** Instituto de Cultura Hispanica (Spain) Seminario de Problemas Hispanoamericanos (Madrid, Spain) Centro Iberoamericano de Cooperacion. Instituto de Cooperacion Iberoamericana (Madrid, Spain). Vol. 1 (Jan./Feb. 1948)-. Periodical. Spanish. Twelve times a year (Plus 2 complimentary issues). 7500ptas Spain; $95.00 Asia; $90.00 other. Agenica Espanola Cooperacion International, Avda Reyes Catolicos 4, 28040 Madrid Spain. **Tel** 011 34 1 5838391. **LC** AP63; .C6697. **DD** 056. Index available in last issue of volume--attached. cum. index. Documents available from The Genuine Article.
Ind/Abst Am. Hist. Life (1956-1963, 1967-); ARTbibliogr. Mod. (1956-); Arts Humanit. Citation Index [Full Cov.]; Bibliogr. Mission.; BHA : Biblio. Hist. Art; Curr. Contents Arts Humanit.; HAPI Hisp. Am. Period. Index; MLA Int. Bibl. Books Artic. Mod. Lang. Lit.; Res. Alert [Full Cov.]; Romant. Move. (1956-); Soc. Sci. Cit. Index [Select. Cov.].

SP/0211-1381
CUENTA Y RAZON. [Cuenta razon]. **Added/Corp** Fundacion de Estudios Sociologicos. No. 1 (Winter 1981)-. Spanish. Nine times a year. 6800ptas. Fundes Club, General Yague 20 4 A, 28020 Madrid Spain. **Tel** 011 34 1 5555855. **LC** AP60; .C794. **DD** 056/.1.

IT/0393-9707
CULTURA & LIBRI. **VFOAT** Cultura e Libri; C & L; C e L. Vol. 1, No. 1 (March/April 1984)-. Periodical. Italian. Twelve times a year. L80000.00 Italy; L10000.00 other. Societa Edit Dante Alighierei, Via Timavo 3/5, 00195 Rome Italy. **Tel** 011 39 6 3725870.

UK/0590-3394
CUMBRIA. (1951)-. Periodical. English. mo. Dalesman Publishing Co., Ltd., Clapman, Lancaster, LA2 8EB England. **Tel** 05242-51225, FAX 05242-51708. **ED** Terry Fletcher. Index available. **Bk Rev. Circ:** 15,856.

UK/0142-1050
CURRENT (LONDON, ENGLAND). (CURRENT.). (19??)-. Periodical. English. mo. £19.99. Mary Glasgow Publications, Brookhampton Lane, Kineton, Warwickshire CV35 0JB England. **Tel** 011 44 926 640606, FAX 011 44 926 641016. **LC** AP4; .C96. **DD** 052. ***Continues*** *Campus (London, England).*

SW/1101-6345
CURRENT SWEDEN / THE SWEDISH INSTITUTE. **Added/Corp** Svenska Institutet. Svenska Institutet for Culturellt Utbyte med Utlandet. (197?)-. Monographic series. English (French, German and Spanish). ir. Free. Swedish Institute, PO Box 7434, Distribution Section, S-103 91 Stockholm Sweden. **Tel** 011 46 8 7892000, FAX 011 46 8 20 7248. **LC** HN571; .C87.
Desc: Presents information on issues featured in the Swedish public debate.

PL
CZAS. Periodical. Polish. 5.00 single issue. Gdanskie Wydawn, Centrala Kolportazu Prasy I Wydawnictw Rsw, Prasa-Ksiada-Ruch, Warszawa Ul Towarowa 28, 00-958 Gdansk Poland. **LC** AP54; .C88.

CS/0011-4634
CZECHOSLOVAK LIFE. ***Title Change.*** (194?)-(1992). Periodical. English (French, German, Spanish and Italian). mo. Orbis, 120 41 Prague 2, Vinohradska 46 Czech Republic. **ED** Czechoslovak Life-E. Meisnerova. **LC** DB191; .C7. **DD** 914.37. **Ad Acc, Adv Mgr:** Mikatova. ***Continues*** *Czechoslovak Weekly;* ***Absorbed*** *Prague News Letter; Im Herzen Europas.* ***Continued by*** *Czech Life Now.*
Desc: Information on cultural, political, and economical life in Czechoslovakia, with many colored photographs.
Ind/Abst Middle East Abstr. Index.

BU/0861-1033
DAIDZHEST. No. 5 (1990)-. Periodical. Bulgarian. mo. **(Subscription address:** Hemus Foreign Trade Organization, 6 Tzar Osvoboditel Boulevard, 1000 Sofia Bulgaria.**)** ***Continues*** *Nasha Rodina.*

General Interest —General Interest-Europe

LU/0423-6394
DAILY BULLETIN - EUROPE, AGENCE INTERNATIONAL D'INFORMATION POUR LA PRESSE. **Main/Corp** Europe, Agence Internationale d'Information Pour la Presse. (1953)-. Periodical. English. da. 47000F. Agence Europe SA, 32 Rue Philippe II, BP 428, 2014 Luxembourg Luxembourg. **Tel** 011 352 20032.
Desc: Covers current events in the European Union. Includes comments and views, detailed news, economic interpretation, and more.

US/0898-3496
DAILY REPORT. WEST EUROPE. (DAILY REPORT. WEST EUROPE / FOREIGN BROADCAST INFORMATION SERVICE.). [Dly. rep. / West Eur.]. **Added/Corp** United States. Foreign Broadcast Information Service. **VFOAT** West Europe. **VAT** Foreign Broadcast Information Service Daily Report. West Europe. (June 1987)-. Periodical. English. da. National Technical Information Service - NTIS, Room 2027S, 5285 Port Royal Road, Springfield VA 22161. **Tel** (703)487-4630, (703)487-4660, (703)487-4650, FAX (703)321-8547, telex 89-9405. **DD** 320. available on microfiche. **Continues** Daily Report. Western Europe.

CI
DANAS (ZAGREB, CROATIA : 1982). (DANAS.). No. 1 (Jan. 23, 1982)-. Periodical. Serbo-Croatian (Roman). Fifty-two times a year. $140.00. Vjesnik Zagreb, Avenija Bratstva I Jedinstva 4, 41000 Zagreb Croatia. **Tel** 011 38 41 515555. **LC** AP56; .D34.

GW/0414-8894
DDR - REVUE; MAGAZINE AUS DER DEUTSCHEN DEMOKRATISCHEN REPUBLIK. **Ceased.** **Added/Corp** Gesellschaft fur Kulturelle Verbindungen mit dem Ausland. Liga fur Volkerfeundschaft der DDR. Vol. 1 (1956)-(Dec. 1990). Periodical. German (Danish, Dutch, English, Finnish, French, Greek, Modern and Italian, Swedish). mo. Liga fur Volkerireundschaft der DDR, Otto-Grotewohl-Str 19 D, Berlin W-1086 Germany. **Tel** 4 86 40, telex 02291.
Desc: A magazine from the German Democratic Republic.

SP
DEBATS (VALENCIA, SPAIN). (DEBATS / INSTITUCIO ALFONS EL MAGNANIM I DIPUTACIO DE VALENCIA.). **Added/Corp** Institucion Alfonso el Magnanimo. Valencia (Spain : Province). Diputacion Provincial. Institucio Valenciana d'Estudis i Investigacio. (1982)-. Periodical. Catalan (Spanish). Four times a year. 3100ptas Spain; 3900ptas Europe; 5800ptas others. Edicions Alfons El Magnanium, Plaza Alfons El Magnanim 10 1A, 46003 Valencia Spain. **Tel** 011 34 1 963527994. **LC** AP60; .D43. **DD** 056/.1.

SW/0005-3856
DET BASTA UR READER'S DIGEST. (19??)-. Periodical. Swedish. mo. $21.41. Readers Digest AB, Swedish Edition, Box 25, 164-93 Kista Sweden. **Tel** 011 46 8 7520360. **ED** Ullashna Oestberg. **[CCC]** **Ad Acc. Circ:** 200,000 (ctrl).
Ind/Abst Read. Guide Period. Lit.; Mag. Index (?-?).

NO
DET BESTA FRA READER'S DIGEST. (1974)-. Periodical. Norwegian. mo. $21.41. Det Beste A/S, Lilleakerveien 19, 0283 Oslo 2 Norway. **Tel** (914)241-5278. **(Subscription address:** US/ Agents Record Department, Pleasantville, NY 10570**)**
Ind/Abst Mag. Index (?-?).

GW/0023-2211
DEUTSCHE MONATSHEFTE (BERG (STARNBERG, GERMANY) : 1982). (DEUTSCHE MONATSHEFTE.). V. 33, No. 1, (Jan. 1982)-. Periodical. German. mo. 50.00. Turmer Verlag, Dr Phil Gert Sudholt, Postfach W-8137, Berg/Starnberger Germany. **LC** AS181; .D48. **DD** 053/.1. **Formed by the union of** Politischer Zeitspiegel **and** Kluter Blatter.

GW/0012-0812
DEUTSCHE STUDIEN (SCHLOSS BLECKEDE). (DEUTSCHE STUDIEN.). [Dtsch. Stud. (Schloss Bleckede)]. **Added/Corp** Ostdeutsches Akademie. Gesamteuropaisches Studienwerk (Germany) Ost-Akademie. (1963)-. Periodical. German. qt. DM30.00. Verlag Ost Akademie E V, Herderstrasse 1-11, W-2120 Lueneburg Germany. **Tel** 011 49 4131 42094. **ED** Bernhard Schalhorn. **DD** 940. Index available. **Bk Rev. Ad Acc. Circ:** 1,200. **Supersedes** Ostbrief.
Desc: Covers the German Democratic Republic, East-West relations, security, economy, literature and German history.
Ind/Abst Am. Hist. Life (1988-); LABORDOC; MLA Int. Bibl. Books Artic. Mod. Lang. Lit.

GW
DEUTSCHE WOCHEN-ZEITUNG. (19??)-. Periodical. German. wk. DM100.00. DSZ Verlagsgesellschaft MbH, Deutscher Buchdienst, D 81238 Munich Germany. **Tel** 011 49 89 8347007. **LC** AP30; .D463.

GW
DEUTSCHLAND. (Oct. 1993)-. English. Six times a year. $16.00 (one year); $31.00 (two year); $44.50 (three year). Frankfurter Societaetsdruckerei, Postfach 100801, D 60008 Frankfurt Germany. **Tel** 011 49 69 75014807, telex 411655. **(Subscription address:** Edelweiss Publishing Company, 110 Main Street, Nuremburg PA 18241.**)** **Continues** Scala.

US
DEUTSCHLAND NACHRICHTEN. **Added/Corp** German Information Center (New York, N.Y.). (19??)-. Newsletter. German. wk. Free on request. German Information Center, 950 Third Avenue, New York NY 10022. **Tel** (212)888-9840, FAX (212)752-6691.
Desc: Geared to the German-speaking reader and to German-Americans who want to maintain their ties to Germany. Features reports on politics, economics, culture, as well as a sports page devoted to the German soccer league.

BL
DOCUMENTO ABRIL. Yearly V. 1- Sept. 1975-. Portuguese. $20.00 single issue. M & Z Representatives, 112 Ferry Street, Newark NJ 07105. **LC** AP66; .D56.

DK
DP, DANSK PRESSE. **VFOAT** Dansk Presse. Periodical. Danish. kr132.00. Danske Dagblades Pressens Hus, Skindergade 7, 1159 Kobenhavn Denmark. **Tel** 01 12 21 15. **ED** Poul Kristensen. .D18. **Bk Rev. Ad Acc. Circ:** 1,983 (ctrl).
Desc: Everything of interest for publishers of daily newspapers.

GW
DROSTE-JAHRBUCH / IM AUFTRAG DER ANNETTE VON DROSTE-GESELLSCHAFT. 1 (1986/87)-. Periodical. German. an. Verlag Regensberg, Postfach 6748, Daimlerweg 58, W-4400 Muenster Germany. **Tel** (0251)717061. **Continues** Jahrbuch der Droste-Gesellschaft.

SZ/0012-6837
DU. [Du]. Vol. 27 (Jan. 1967)-. Periodical. German (summaries and/or abstracts in English). mo. 129.00F Switzerland; 149.00F Europe; 156.00F other. Du-Verlag, Schoentalstrasse 27, 8036 Zurich Switzerland. **Tel** 41 1 2485350. **LC** AP32; .D78. Index available. **Bk Rev. Ad Acc. Circ:** 20,606 (ctrl). Documents available from The Genuine Article. **Continues** Du Atlantis.
Desc: Covers art and culture.
Ind/Abst Archit. Period. Index (1978-); Art Index; ARTbibliogr. Mod.; ARTbibliogr. Curr. Titles; Arts Humanit. Citation Index [Full Cov.]; Avery Index Archit. Period. Suppl. Colum. Univ. (1990-); BHA : Biblio. Hist. Art; Res. Alert [Full Cov.].

SP
DUNIA. (19??)-. Spanish. ir. 3.600ptas (one year), 7.200ptas (two year) Spain; 10.400ptas (one year), 20.800ptas (two year) Europe; 22.500ptas (one year), 45.000ptas (two year) other. G & J Espana SA, Marques de Villamagna 4, 28001 Madrid Spain. **Tel** 011 34 1 4316631, FAX 011 34 1 2767881, telex 43419 ORBSA E.

PL/0867-3608
DZIS WARSZAWA. (DZIS.). (1990)-. Polish. mo. $42.00. **(Subscription address:** ARS Polona, PO Box 1001, 00068 Warsaw Poland.**) UDC** 304. **CODEN** 323(438).

SZ
EADI BULLETIN. **Main/Corp** European Association of Development Research and Training Institutes. (19??)-. Periodical. English. sa. EADI, PO Box 272, 10 rue Richemont, CH-1211 Geneva 21 Switzerland. **Tel** 011 41 22 314648.
Ind/Abst Int. Labour Doc.

UK/0950-7450
EASTERN EUROPE NEWSLETTER. **VFOAT** Eastern Europe. Vol. 1, No. 1 (3 June 1987)-. Periodical. English. Twenty-five times a year. £490.00 UK; £505.00 others. Eastern Europe Newsletter Ltd, 87 Duke Road, London W4 2BW England. **Tel** 011 44 81 995 3860.

UK
EC UPDATE. English. Twelve times a year. £60.00 IPM members; £100.00 non-members. Institute of Personnel Management, IPM House Camp Road, Wimbledon London SW19 4UX England. **Tel** 011 44 81 9469100 Ext. 214, FAX 011 44 81 9472570. **ED** Susan McCarty. ctrl circ.

FR/0013-0710
ECRITS DE PARIS. (ECRITS DE PARIS : REVUE DES QUESTIONS ACTUELLES.). [Ecrits Paris]. (Jan. 1947)-. Periodical. French. mo. 450.00F. Society Parisienne d'Edit Publishing, 9 Passage des Marais 9, 75010 Paris France. **ED** Renee Anthon. **LC** AP20; .E355. **DD** 054. **Circ:** 6500. **Continues** Bulletin Interieur.
Ind/Abst Am. Hist. Life (1955-1964, 1970-1979); Romant. Move.

GR
EFTHINI. Greek, Modern. mo. $20.00. Costas Tsirpoulos, Panepistimiou 10, Athens 10671 Greece. **ED** Costas E. Tsiropoulos. Index available. cum. index. **Bk Rev. Ad Acc. Circ:** 3,000.

US
EINTRACHT / HARMONY. **VFOAT** Harmony. (1923)-. Newspaper. German (English). wk. $25.00. Eintracht, 9456 North Lawler Avenue, Skokie IL 60076-9471. **Tel** (708)677-9456, FAX (708)677-9471. **ED** Walter Juengling and Klaus Juengling. **Bk Rev. Ad Acc.**
Desc: German newspaper with worldwide general news, German / American activities locally, and sports and information.

FR/0424-7175
EKLITRA / ASSOCIATION CULTURELLE PICARDE. **Added/Corp** Eklitra (Association). (1967)-. French. an. 80.00F. Eklitra/Association Culturelle Picarde, Chez M. Pauchet 7 rue Naurile Garet Appr 43, 80080 Amiens France. **Tel** (22) 43 23 60. **LC** WMLC 93/2057. Index available. cum. index. **Bk Rev. Ad Acc. Circ:** 400.
Desc: Folklore, linguistics, literature, history and traditions.

HU/0424-8848
ELET ES IRODALOM. (1957)-. Periodical. Hungarian. Fifty-two times a year. $50.00 Austria & Croatia, Czech & Slovak Republics, Romania, Yugoslavia, Slovenia & Ukraine; $61.00 others. **(Subscription address:** Kultura, PO Box 149, H 1389 Budapest 62 Hungary**) DD** 704; 800.

UK/0260-0420
ENGLISH HERITAGE MONITOR. [Eng. herit. monit.]. (19??)-. English. an.
Ind/Abst Leis. Recreat. Tour. Abstr.

IT/0013-9718
EPOCA (MILANO). (EPOCA.). (1950)-. Periodical. Italian. wk. L78000 Italy; L189800 other. Arnoldo Mondadori Editore, UFF Cont Abbonamenti, 20090 Segrate MI Italy. **Tel** 011 39 2 75422015, telex 320457 MONDMI I.
Ind/Abst MLA Int. Bibl. Books Artic. Mod. Lang. Lit.

GW
EPOCHE. V. 1- ; Jan. 1977-. Periodical. German. mo. DM50.00. 19 Winfriedstrasse 11, 8000 Munchen Germany. **LC** AP30; .E624.

GW
ERMLANDBUCH. **Added/Corp** Bischof Maximilian Kaller-Stiftung. German. Verlag A Fromm GmbH, Postfach 1948, 49009 Osnabrueck Germany. **Tel** 011 49 541 310334, FAX 011 49 541 310440. **LC** AY859.E3; E7. **Continues** Unser Ermlandbuch.

IT
ES. VAT Esempi. Periodical. Italian. 6.000. Italia Guida, C C P 6/11753, Via F Cilea 215, Naples 80127 Italy. **LC** AP37; .E74.

FR/0014-0759
ESPRIT (PARIS, 1932-). (ESPRIT.). Vol. 1 No. 1 (Oct. 1932)-(Dec. 1976); New Series, (Jan. 1977)-. Periodical. French. Ten times a year. 528.89F France, 550.00F others (surface mail); 760.00F (airmail). Revue Esprit, 212 rue Saint-Martin, 75003 Paris France. **Tel** 011-33-1-48040833. **LC** AP20; .E78. **DD** 054. available on microfilm. Documents available from The Genuine Article.
Ind/Abst Am. Hist. Life (1964-); ARTbibliogr. Mod. (1984-); Arts Humanit. Citation Index [Full Cov.]; Curr. Contents Arts Humanit.; Film Lit. Index (1955, 1964, 1985-1991); Int. Bibliogr. Sociol.; Int. Polit. Sci. Abstr.; MLA Int. Bibl. Books Artic. Mod. Lang. Lit.; PAIS Int. Print; Point Repere (1983-); Res. Alert [Full Cov.]; Soc. Sci. Cit. Index [Select. Cov.].

UK/0014-0910
ESSEX COUNTRYSIDE. Vol. 1 (1952)-. Periodical. English. mo. £11.50 UK; £17.50 other. Essex Countryside Ltd, High Street Barley NR Royston, Hertfordshire SG8 8JA England.

FR/0424-2246
ETUDES CHYPRIOTES. **Main/Corp** Ecole Francaise d'Athenes. Vol. 1 (1961)-. Monographic series. French. ir. Price varies per volume. Diffusion de Boccard, 11 rue de Medicis, 75006 Paris France. **Tel** 011 33 1 43260037.

FR/0750-3547
ETUDES INDO-EUROPEENNES. **Added/Corp** Universite Jean Moulin. Institut d'Etudes Indo-Europeennes. No. 1 (Jan. 1982)-. Periodical. French. qt. Institute Etudes Indo-European Lyon III Faculty des Langues, 74 rue Pasteur, 69007 Lyon Cedex 02 France. **Tel** 011 33 72 722080.
Ind/Abst MLA Int. Bibl. Books Artic. Mod. Lang. Lit.

IT
EURO. Year 1- June 1978-. Periodical. Italian (Italian). mo. L8.000. **LC** AP37; .E85. **DD** 055/.1.

FR/1154-5399
EURO POP BOOK PARIS. (EURO POP BOOK.). (1990)-. Multiple languages. an. $60.00. CIR, 211 Avenue J. Jaures Parc Villette, F-75019 Paris France. **Tel** 011 33 1 42001211. **UDC** 78-051(4). **CODEN** 785.16(4).

IT
EUROPA FACILE. 1971-. Italian. Touring Club Italiano, Corso Italia 10, Milan 20122 Italy. **Tel** 011 39 2 85261, FAX 011 39 2 8526299. **LC** D909; .E75. ***Continues*** *Fascicoli di Documentazione Per I Viaggi in Europa.*

BE
EUROPE. English, French, Italian and Spanish. ir. 18500.00F (universities) Belgium; 22500.00F (universities) Europe; 21500.00F (universities) Luxembourg & Netherlands; 26000.00F (universities) other; 19000.00F (institutions) Europe; 40000.00F (universities & institutions) other. Agence Europe SA, 32 Rue Philippe II, BP 428, 2014 Luxembourg Luxembourg. **Tel** 011 352 20032. **(Subscription address:** Agence Europe SA, 10 Blvd. St. Lazare Bte 13, 1210 Brussels Belgium**)**
Ind/Abst Gas Abstr.

BE
EUROPE / AGENCE INTERNATIONALE D'INFORMATION POUR LA PRESSE, AGENCE EUROPE. Added/Corp Agence Europe. **VFOAT** Bulletin Quotidien; Bulletin Quotidien Europe; Agence Europe. (1952)-. Periodical. French (English, Italian and German). Five issues per week (4 supplements published weekly). 20750.00F Universities Belgium; 23500.00F Universities Luxembourg & Netherlands; 24500.00F Universities Europe; 28000.00F Universities all except Europe; 45000.00F others. Agence Europe SA, 32 Rue Philippe II, BP 428, 2014 Luxembourg Luxembourg. **Tel** 011 352 20032. **(Subscription address:** Agence Europe SA, 10 Boulevard Street Lazare BTE 13, 1210 Brussels Belgium, phone: 011 32 2 2190256**)**
Desc: News which covers the preparation and the implementation of the opening of markets and of community policies in the commerical economic, monetary, social, technological sectors at every stage of their development.

BE
EUROPE ENTREPRISES. French. mo. 9.600F (six months), 17.500F (twelve months). Europe Information Service, rue de Geneve 6, 1140 Brussels Belgium. **Tel** 011 32 2 242 6020, FAX 011 32 2 242 9549.
Desc: Provides a monthly update on the coalition of the EEC's market and particularly for firms.

US/0274-8037
EUROPE REPORT, THE. Added/Corp Greater Europe Mission. (19??)-. Periodical. English. bm (6 issues). Free on request. Greater Europe Mission, PO Box 668, Wheaton IL 60189. ***Continues*** *Greater Europe Report.*

FR
EUROPEAN AFFAIRS. Main/Corp France. Ambassade (U.S.). Service de Presse et d'Information. No 3 (195?)-. English. ***Continues*** *France. Ambassade (U.S.). Service de Presse et d'Information. European Affairs. Document.*
Ind/Abst Selec. Coop. Index Manage. Period; World Agric. Econ.

BE/0379-3133
EUROPEAN FILE. ***Ceased.*** [Eur. file]. **Added/Corp** Commission of the European Communities. (Jan. 1979)-(June 1992). Monographic series. English (English, German, Italian, Spanish, Dutch, Danish, Portuguese and Greek, Modern). Fifteen times a year. Commision of the European Communities, Directorate-General for Information Communication & Culture, rue de la Loi 200, B-1049 Brussels Belgium. **Tel** 32-2-235.11.11, FAX 32-2-236.25.69, telex COMEU B 21877. **LC** HC241.2; .E8574. **DD** 330.94/005. Index available. cum. index. **Circ:** 190,000 (ctrl).
Desc: A series of short monographies about the European community, their main aspects and policies.
Ind/Abst Geogr. Abstr. Human Geogr.; Int. Dev. Abstr.; Manage. Market. Abstr.; World Agric. Econ.; World Ceram. Abstr.; World Text. Abstr.

UK
EUROPEAN GAZETTE. (19??)-. Periodical. English. wk. $21.25. European Gazette, 20 Tudor Street, London EC4 Y0JS England. **LC** D1050; .E8879. **DD** 914/.03/5505.

UK/0261-2747
EUROPEAN INFORMATION SERVICE. [Eur. inf. serv.]. (1978)-. English. Ten times a year. £105.00 local government; £210.00 other. Local Government Intl Bureau, 35 Great Smith Street, London SW1P 3BJ England. **Tel** 011 44 71 222-1636. **ED** J Morris. **DD** 341.2422024354. Index available. **Bk Rev. Ad Acc. Pr Rev. Circ:** 1,500.
Desc: FC legislation, publications and coming events linked with Europe.

BE
EUROPEAN INSIGHT. (19??)-. Periodical. English (French). wk. 16200F Belgium; 18500F other Europe; 19200F other. Europe Information Service, rue de Geneve 6, 1140 Brussels Belgium. **Tel** 011 32 2 242 6020, FAX 011 32 2 242 9549.
Desc: Information package covering the week's EEC-related happenings.

FR
EUROPEAN REGIONAL PLANNING STUDY SERIES. VFOAT European Regional Planning. Study No. 1 (1977)-. Monographic series. English. Price varies per volume. Council of Europe / Group Pact ED, Pharmacopoeia BP 907, 67029 Strasbourg Cedex 01 France. **Tel** 011 33 88 412036, FAX 011 33 88 41277181, telex 880388. **(Subscription address:** Manhattan Publishing Company, PO Box 650, Croton-on-Hudson NY 10520**)**
Desc: Covers European public administration (interdisciplinary: agricultural and civil engineering, economics, etc.).

UK/0969-7764
EUROPEAN URBAN AND REGIONAL STUDIES. See Housing and Urban Development.

BE/0531-4631
EUROPEEN, L'. (L'EUROPEEN. DER EUROPAER.). **VFOAT** Der Europaer; Quest Europa; This Europe. (1959)-. Periodical. French. Four times a year. 400F Belgium; 450F others. L'Europeen, Avenue du Cor Chasse 19, 1170 Bruxelles Belgium. **DD** 338.9.

IT/0014-3189
EUROPEO MILANO, L'. [EuropeoMilano]. (1945)-. Periodical. Italian. wk (52 issues). $210.00. RCS Rizzoli Periodici, Via A Rizzoli 2, 20132 Milan Italy. **Tel** 011 39 2 27200720. **(Subscription address:** Speedimpex USA, Inc., 35 02 48th Avenue, Long Island City NY 11101.**) UDC** 05. available on microfilm and microfiche from University Microfilms International (UMI).

GR/0302-1041
EUTHYNE. [Euthune]. No. 1 (Jan. 1972)-. Periodical. Greek, Modern. Twelve times a year. $35.00. Vivliopoleio Hoi Ekdoseis Ton Philon, Panepistimiou 10, T T 122 Athens Greece. **LC** AP85; .E9.

UK
EVERGREEN (CHELTENHAM, ENGLAND). (EVERGREEN.). (Spring 1985)-. Periodical. English. qt (4 issues). £11.00 UK; £12.95 other. This England International, PO Box 52, Cheltenham, Gloucestershr GL50 1YQ England. **Tel** 011 44 242 577775, FAX 011 44 242 22034, telex 43452.

SZ/0014-4932
EXPERIODICA. Periodical. English. mo. 50/60 Mythenquai, PO Box 8022, Zurich Switzerland.

FR
EXPRESS INTERNATIONAL (PARIS, FRANCE). (L'EXPRESS INTERNATIONAL.). **VFOAT** Express. No. 1749 (18 Jan. 1985)-. Periodical. French. wk (52 issues). 998.00F US and Canada. L'Express, 61 Avenue Hoche, 75008 Paris Cedex France. **Tel** 011 33 1 44625430. **LC** AP20; .E926. **DD** 054/.1. ***Continues*** *Express (Ed. Internationale), 0245-9949.*

FR/0014-5270
EXPRESS (PARIS), L'. (L'EXPRESS.). [Express]. **VFOAT** Express Paris; Express Sport; Express Votre Argent; Express Aujourd'Hui; Express Style. No. 1 (May 16, 1953)-. Periodical. French. wk. 713.00F France (French edition). L'Express, 61 Avenue Hoche, 75008 Paris Cedex France. **Tel** 011 33 1 44625430. **(Subscription address:** L'Express Services Abonnements, 4 Rue Andre Boulle, 94942 Creteil CDX 9 France**) LC** AP20; .E926. available on microfilm.
Ind/Abst PAIS Int. Print.

AU
EXTRABLATT. (Sept. 1977)-. Periodical. German. mo. Extrablatt Vertrieb, Spiegelgasse 3/8, A-1010 Vienna Austria. **LC** AP30; .E94. **DD** 053/.1.

UK
FACLIA. Periodical. Romanian. mo. **(Subscription address:** Rompresfilatelia, PO Box 12 201, Bucharest Romania.**) LC** DR201; .F28.

PL
FAKTY. No. 29, (July 21, 1973)-. Periodical. Polish. wk. **(Subscription address:** ARS Polona, PO Box 1001, 00068 Warsaw Poland.**) LC** AP54; .F35. ***Continues*** *Magazyn Pomorze, Fakty I Mysli.*

UK
FEATURES AND NEWS FROM BEHIND THE IRON CURTAIN. Added/Corp Freedom Communications International News Agency. Free Czechoslovak Press Ltd. Free Czechoslovakia Campaign. Independent Information Centre. Latvian News Agency. Tibetan News Agency. Voice of Cuba News Agency. Vol. 1 (Nov. 1964)-. Periodical. English. ir. $10.00. FCI News Agency, 43 Tregunter Road, London SW10 9LG England.

IE
FIELD REPORT EUROPE. (19??)-. mo. Offshore Intelligence Ltd, Marion Hse 3 Lr Fitzwilliam St, Dublin 2 Ireland.

FR
FIGARO MAGAZINE, LE. VFOAT Magazine. No. 1 (Oct. 7, 1978)-. Periodical. French. Forty-eight times a year (Aug.). $930.00 (surface mail); 1900.00F Europe, North & South America; $2260.00F Korea. Socpresse le Figaro, 37 rue du Louvre, 75081 Paris Cedex 02 France. **Tel** 011 33 1 42213445. **LC** AP20; .F348. **DD** 054/.1.

GW
FINANZEN UND STEUERN. REIHE 3.5, RECHNUNGSERGEBNISSE DER OFFENTLICHEN HAUSHALTE FUER SOZIALE SICHERUNG UND FUER GESUNDHEIT, SPORT, ERHOLUNG. VFOAT Rechnungsbegebnisse der Offentlichen Haushalte fur Soziale Sicherung und fur Gesundheit, Sport, Erholung Fashserie 14. German. an. Verlag W Kohlhammer GmbH, Abt Veroffentlichungen des Statistischen Bundesamtes, Philipp-Reis-Strasse 3, W-6500 Mainz 42 Germany. **LC** HD7177; .F56. ***Formed by the union of*** *Finanze und Steuern. Reihe 3.5, Rechnungsergebnisse der Offentlichen Haushalte fur Soziale Sicherung* ***and*** *Finanzen und Steuern. Reihe 3.6, Rechnungsergebnisse der Offentlichen Haushalte fur Gesundheit, Sport und Erholung.*

FI
FINSK TIDSKRIFT. See Literary and Political Reviews.

IT/1120-7248
FIRENZE IERI, OGGI, DOMANI. VFOAT Firenze. Vol. 1, No. 1 (Oct. 1989)-. Periodical. Italian. Eleven times a year (Except Aug.). Newton Periodici, Via Germanico 197, 00192 Rome Italy. **Tel** 011 39 6 3242966. **LC** WMLC 93/393.

BE
FLANDERS. Added/Corp Belgium. Commissariaat-Generaal voor de Internationale Samenwerking. (1989)-. Periodical. French. Four times a year. 600.00F. Min Vlaamse Gemeenschap Boudewijnln, 30 Admin Ext Betre, B 1210 Brussels Belgium. **Tel** 011 32 2 5076040. **LC** PAR.

FR/0252-0958
FORUM - COUNCIL OF EUROPE. (FORUM.). [Forum - Counc. Eur.]. Periodical. French (English, German and Italian). Three times a year. Free. Council of Europe / Group Pact ED, Pharmacopoeia BP 907, 67029 Strasbourg Cedex 01 France. **Tel** 011 33 88 412036, FAX 011 33 88 41277181, telex 880388. **ED** Harold Wendelbo. **LC** D1050; .F58. **DD** 940.55/05. **Bk Rev. Circ:** 80,000. ***Formed by the union of*** *Education and Culture* ***and*** *Forward in Europe, 0015-8631.*
Desc: Information on organizations, activities, human rights, legal and social affairs, sport, education, culture, environment, youth and a section on topical themes.
Ind/Abst Hum. Rights Intern. Rep.; Middle East Abstr. Index.

US/0015-8399
FORUM (SCRANTON, PA.). (FORUM.). [Forum]. **Added/Corp** Ukrainian Workingmen's Association. Ukrainian Fraternal Association. No. 1 (Winter 1967)-. Periodical. English. qt. $10.00. Ukranian Fraternal Association, 440 Wyoming Avenue, Scranton PA 18503. **Tel** (717)342-0937, FAX (717)347-5649. **ED** Andrew Gregorovich. **LC** DK508.A2; F65. **DD** 910.03/91791/005. **Bk Rev. Circ:** 4,400.
Desc: The only English language magazine for the young adult reader interested in Ukraine and Eastern Europe.
Ind/Abst Am. Bibliogr. Slavic East Europ. Stud.; MLA Int. Bibl. Books Artic. Mod. Lang. Lit.

AU
FORUM (VIENNA, AUSTRIA : 1980). (FORUM.). Vol. 27, No. 313/314 (Jan./Feb. 1980)-. Periodical. German. bm. S30.00 per issue. Gerhard Oberschlick, Museumstrasse 5, A-1070 Vienna Austria. **Tel** 011-43-222-930594. **ED** Gerhard Oberschlick, Brigitte Uddin. **LC** AP30; .F525. **DD** 053/.1. **Circ:** 34,000. ***Continues*** *Neues Forum, 0028-3622.*

US
FRANCE. Added/Corp France. Ambassade (U. S.). Service de Presse et d'Information. (Feb. 1971)-. English. mo. French Embassy, 972 5th Avenue, New York NY 10028. **LC** DC1; .F674. **DD** 944/.005.

FR
FRANCE AFRIQUE. VFOAT Annuaire des Societes et Fournisseurs. 37th Edition (1988)-. French. an. 1,567.09F France; 1,600.00F others. Ediafric la Documentation Africaine, 10 rue Vineuse, 75116 Paris France. **Tel** 011 33 1 44308100, FAX 011 33 1 45208174. **LC** HF3921.A48; F73. ***Formed by the union of*** *Annuaire des Exportateurs; Annuaire de l'Afrique du Nord (Ediafric, La Documentation Africaine (Firm))* ***and*** *Annuaire de l'Afrique Noire.*

FR/0046-4910
FRANCE FORUM. [Fr. forum]. (19??)-. French. qt. 120.00F. France-Forum, 133 rue de l'Universite, F-75017 Paris France. **Tel** 011 33 1 45551010.

US/0886-2478
FRANCE MAGAZINE. [France mag.]. Vol. 1 (Summer 1985)-. Periodical. English. Four times a year. Free on request. France Magazine, 4101 Reservoir Road NW, Washington DC 20007. **LC** WMLC L 83/8848. ***Continues*** *France.*

GW/0171-9289
FREIBEUTER. (1979)-. Periodical. German. qt. Berliner Literature, Postfach 150513, W-1000 Berlin 15 FR Germany. **LC** AP30; .F58. **DD** 053.

GW
FREITAG. (Nov. 16, 1990)-. Periodical. German. wk. Volkszeitung Verlag GmbH, Oranienstrasse 25, Postfach 360520 W-1000, Berlin 36 Germany. **LC** AP30; .F788. ***Formed by the union of*** *Sonntag* ***and*** *Deutsche Volkszeitung, die Tat.*

GW/0016-2450
FUER SIE HAMBURG. [Fur SieHambg.]. (1961)-. Periodical. German. bw. DM140.40. Jahreszeiten Verlag GmbH, Postfach 60 12 20, D 22212 Hamburg Germany. **Tel** 011 49 40 27173529. **UDC** 087-055.2. Index Available Published separately--free--upon request.

SZ/0250-8044
FUROR. (Oct. 1980)-. Periodical. French (English). Twice a year (Apr., Oct.). 40.00F Switzerland; 60.00F Europe; 80.00F other. Furor Revue, 67 Bis Rue de Lyon, Ch 1203 Geneva Switzerland. **Tel** 011 41 22 345146. **LC** AP6; .F87. **DD** 054/.1.

AU
GANZE WOCHE, DIE. (19??)-. wk. S806.00 (surface mail). Die Ganze Woche, Odoakergasse 34 36, A-1160 Vienna Austria. **Tel** 011 43 222 462691.

SP
GARBO. (19??)-. Periodical. Spanish. wk. 1560ptas. M. Fernanda G. de Nadal, Tallers 62, Barcelona 1, Spain. **LC** AP60; .G26. **DD** 056/.1. **Bk Rev. Ad Acc. Circ:** 103,000.

IT
GENTE. (19??)-. Periodical. Italian. wk. L112300 (Ialy); L230000 (other). Rusconi Editore Spa, Servicio Abbonements, V Le Sarca 235, 20126 Milan Italy. **Tel** 011 39 2 66192634.

FR/0220-8245
GEO ED. FRANCAISE. [Geo Ed. fr.]. (1979)-. Periodical. French. mo. Prisma Presse, 6 rue Daru, 75379 Paris Cedex 08, France. **Tel** 011 33 1 44153000, FAX 011 33 1 47641042.
Ind/Abst Point Repere (1981-).

UK/0267-7563
GEOFILE. [Geofile]. (1982)-. Periodical. English. an. £36.00. Mary Glasgow Publications, Brookhampton Lane, Kineton, Warwickshire CV35 0JB England. **Tel** 011 44 926 640606, FAX 011 44 926 641016. **DD** 330.9048.

●US/1063-9837
GEOGRAFFITY (BLACKSBURG, VA.). (GEOGRAFFITY : EXPLORATIONS OF PHYSICAL, CULTURAL AND INTELLECTUAL LANDSCAPES.). **Added/Corp** Rossiiskaia Akademiia Nauk. Quantum Bureau. (1993)-. Periodical. English. qt. $60.00 (institutions). GeoGraffity, PO Box 10308, Blacksburg VA 24062-0308. **Tel** (703)951-9465, FAX (703)552-0210. **ED** Alexei Novikov (Moscow), Jerry McDonald (US). Index available (4th issue of each volume). **Bk Rev. Pr Rev. Acid Free. Circ:** 150.

GW/0072-1468
GERMAN OPINION ON PROBLEMS OF TODAY. Vol. 1 (1962)-. English. Max-Hueber-Verlag, Max-Hueber-Strasse 4, D 85737 Ismaning Germany. **Tel** 011 49 89 96020, FAX 011 49 89 9602 358, telex 523613. **DD** 909.

GW/0016-8858
GERMAN TRIBUNE, THE. ***Ceased.*** [Ger. trib.]. No. 1 (April 1962)-Ceased with Vol. 31, No. 48 (Dec. 1992). Periodical. English (French and Spanish). wk. Friedrich Reinecke Verlag GmbH, Hartwicusstrasse 3 4, W-2000 Hamburg 76 F R Germany. **Tel** 011 49 40 2285279, FAX 040/2285260, telex 2-14-733. **LC** AP4; .G43. **Ad Acc. Circ:** 29,000 (ctrl). available on microfiche.
Desc: Review of the German press.

FR
GRANDS REPORTAGES (LOUVECIENNES, FRANCE). (GRANDS REPORTAGES.). (1978)-. French. mo (with combined July/ Aug. and Dec./ Jan. issues). 255.00F France; 343.00F other. Editions Mondiales, 9 11 13 Rue du Col Pierre Avia, 75754 Paris Cedex 15 France. **Tel** 011 33 1 46622162. **(Subscription address:** Serv. Abonnements Grands Report HS, BP 53, F 77932 Perthes Cedex France) **LC** AP20; .G73. **DD** 054/.1.
Desc: Pictures and reports about adventure, facts, and countries with a practical guide.
Ind/Abst Point Repere.

GW/0017-3185
GRANI. [Grani]. Vol. 1, No. 1 (July 1946)-. Periodical. Russian. qt (Jan., Apr., July, Oct.). $69.95. Possev Verlag V Gorachek KG, Flurscheideweg 15, D 65936 Frankfurt Germany. **Tel** 011 49 69 341265. **ED** E Breitbart. **[CCC].** Index available. cum. index. **Bk Rev. Circ:** 1,500 (ctrl).
Desc: Includes poetry, novels, short stories and book reviews.
Ind/Abst MLA Int. Bibl. Books Artic. Mod. Lang. Lit.

GR
GREEK REPORT : MONTHLY INTELLIGENCE NEWSLETTER. Newsletter. Ten times a year. $275.00 US and Canada. Coronakis Press Ltd., 10 Fokidos St, Athens 115 26 Greece. **Tel** 7706922.

GW/0172-9446
GSF-BERICHT. P. [GSF-Ber., P]. **VAT** Gesellschaft fur Strahlen- und Umweltforschung-Bericht. P. (1976)-. Academic Scholarly Publication. German. ir. Price varies per volume. Gesellschaft fur Strahlen- und Umweltforschung, Ingolstadter Landstr 1, W-8042 Neuherberg Germany. **CODEN** GSBPD9. Documents available from CASDDS.
Ind/Abst Chem. Abstr. (1976-1981).

GW
HAMBURGER ZUSTANDE : JAHRBUCH ZUR GESCHICHTE DER REGION HAMBURG / HERAUSGEGEBEN VON "VEREIN HAMBURG-JAHRBUCH" E.V. **Added/Corp** Verein Hamburg-Jahrbuch. Vol. 1, (1988)-. German. an. **LC** DD901.H21; H26. **DD** 943/.515/005.

BE
HARVARD BELGIUM REVIEW. Dutch. qt. 4800.00F. Harvard Belgium Review, R Lauwersstraat 11, B-1990 Hoeilaart Belgium. **Tel** 02 6572222.

US/0017-842X
HAUSFRAU, MONATSSCHRIFT FUR DIE FRAUENWELT AMERIKAS, DIE. Vol. 1, Sept. (1904)-. Periodical. German. mo. $15.00 (one year); $25.25 (two year); $35.00 (three year). Die Hausfrau Inc, 1060 Gaines School Road, Suite B-3, Athens GA 30605. **Tel** (706)548-4382, FAX (706)548-4382. **ED** Roswitha Slapland. **LC** AP31; .H3. **Bk Rev. Ad Acc. Circ:** 18,000. ***Supersedes*** *Modernes Journal.*
Desc: Contains a variety of general interest articles such as, health, travel, short stories, and German recipes.

GW
HEIMATKUNDLICHE HEFTE DES ARCHIVS DER STADT REMSCHEID. **Added/Corp** Stadtarchiv Remscheid. No. 17 1986-. Monographic series. German. Price varies per volume. ***Continues*** *Heimatkundliche Hefte des Stadtarchivs Remscheid, 0484-3835.*

GR
HELLENEWS. wk. Dr75.00. Hellenews Ltd., 39 Halandriou Amaroussion, Athens Greece. **Tel** 6827 582.

UK
HELLO. (1988)-. English. wk. $231.00. Hello Ltd, 69 71 Upper Ground, London SE1 9PQ England. **Tel** 011 44 71 3347404. **(Subscription address:** US & Canada: Families of International Level Inc., 16091 North Kendall Drive, Suite 303A, Miami, FL 33176) **ED** Maggie Koumi. **Ad Acc, Adv Mgr:** Sarah Pearson. **Circ:** 471,952.
Desc: Covers the lives of celebrities, royalties and public figures. Also features articles on fashion, beauty and cooking.

SW
HEM O FRITID. **VFOAT** Hem Och Fritid. No. 1 (Jan. 1981)-. Periodical. Swedish. mo. Kr195.00. Hus & Hem, ICA-Forlaget, Box 6630, S-113 84 Stockholm Sweden. **Tel** 08-728 40 00, FAX 08-30 12 78. **ED** Sverker Abrahamsson. **Ad Acc. Circ:** 100,000 (ctrl).

GW/0930-4878
HIERZULAND NICHT NUR BADISCHES VON RHEIN, NECKAR UND MAIN : ORGAN DES ARBEITSKREISES HEIMATPFLEGE NORDABADEN / REGIERUNGSBEZIRK KARLSRUHE. **Added/Corp** Arbeitskreis Heimatpflege Nordbaden/Regierungsbezirk Karlsruhe. **VFOAT** Hierzuland. 1986-. Periodical. German. sa.

SP
HOLA. **VFOAT** Hello. (19??)-. Periodical. Spanish (English). wk. $273.00 US & Canada. Hola S A, Velazquez 98 Apt 14707, 28006 Madrid Spain. **Tel** 011 34 1 5770687. **(Subscription address:** Dantel Corporation, 10691 North Kendall Drive, Suite 303A, Miami, FL 33176) **LC** AP60; .H72. **DD** 056/.1.
Desc: Covers glamorous events and big news stories. Also covers beauty, fashion, lifestyle and exclusive VIP news. Known for stunning photography.

NE
HOLLAND HERALD. V. 1- Jan./Feb. 1966-. Periodical. English. mo. $19.05. Multi Media International, PO Box 469, 1180 AL Amstelveen, The Netherlands. **Tel** 31 20 5473550, FAX 31 20 6438581, telex 11636. **ED** Ken Wilkie. Index available. **Bk Rev. Ad Acc. Circ:** 3,600,000 (ctrl).
Desc: Total cultural, business, sport, culinary coverage of the Netherlands plus international travel reportages. Plus complete monthly listings.

IE
HOT PRESS. (1977)-. English. Twenty-six times a year. $105.00. Osnovina Ltd, 13 Trinity Street, Dublin 2 Ireland. **Tel** 011 353 1 6795077.

GW/0018-7623
HUMBOLDT (PORTUGIESISCHE AUSGABE). (HUMBOLDT.). (1961)-. German (Portuguese). ir. Free on request. Inter Nationes EV, Postfach 200749, D 53137 Bonn Germany. **Tel** 11 49 2288801, FAX 11 49 228 880355, telex 228308. **LC** AP1; .H86. **DD** 050.

UK/0307-3262
IBERIAN STUDIES. (IBERIAN STUDIES : JOURNAL OF THE IBERIAN SOCIAL STUDIES ASSOCIATION.). [Iber. stud.]. **Added/Corp** Iberian Social Studies Association (Great Britain) University of Keele. Centre for Iberian Studies. Vol. 1, No. 1 (Spring 1972)-. Periodical. English (Spanish and Portuguese). Twice a year (June & Dec.). £30.00. University of Keele Department of Geography, c/o Dr Naylon, Keele Staffs ST5 5BG England. **Tel** 011 44 782 62111, FAX 0782-613847, telex 36113 UNKLIB G. **ED** John Naylon. **LC** DP233; .I23. **DD** 946/.005. Index available. cum. index. **Bk Rev. Pr Rev. Circ:** 1,000.
Desc: Anthropology, economics, geography, history, language, linguistics, politics, and sociology of modern Spain and Portugal educational systems.
Ind/Abst Am. Hist. Life (1972-).

SW/0345-5068
ICA-KURIREN. [Ica-kuriren]. (1942)-. Periodical. Swedish. wk (46 issues per year). Kr199.00. ICA Kuriren, S-721 85 Vasteras, Sweden. **UDC** 64.

IC
ICELAND. Began in 1926. English. ir. Snaebjorn Jonsson and Cohf, Hafnarstraeti 4-9, Reykjavik Iceland. **LC** DL313; .I24. **DD** 949.1/205.

UK/0019-2422
ILLUSTRATED LONDON NEWS, THE. [Illus. Lond. news]. V. 1 (May 14, 1842)-. Periodical. English. bm. $43.00. Illustrated London News, 91-93 Southwark Street, London SE1 0HX England. **Tel** 071-928-2111. **(Subscription address:** 3/4 Hardwick Street, London EC1R 4RY England) **ED** James Bishop. **LC** AP4; .I3. **DD** 052. Index available. **Bk Rev. Ad Acc. Circ:** 55,000. available on microfilm and microfiche from University Microfilms International (UMI).
Desc: Presents a balanced and lively view of British and international current affairs, politics, arts and sciences, fashion and sport.
Ind/Abst Book Rev. Index; Br. Archaeol. Bibliogr.; Br. Humanit. Index; Middle East Abstr. Index; Numis. Lit.

AU
ILLUSTRIERTE NEUE WELT. (19??)-. Periodical. German. ir. S6.00 single issue. I. N. W. Pressedienst, Jundengasse 1a-V-25, A-1010 Vienna, Austria. **Tel** 022 5356301, FAX 022 5355780. **LC** AP93; .I58.

CN/1188-0066
IMPERIAL QUARTERLY MAGAZINE. ***Ceased.*** [Imp. q. mag.]. Vol. 3, No. 1 (Spring 1992)-(199?). Periodical. English. Four times a year. The Imperial Quarterly, PO Box 2396, Station C, Downsview, Ontario, Canada M4Y 1N9. **Tel** (416)920-6558. **ED** Paul Gilbert. **DD** 947/.005. **Bk Rev. Ad Acc. Circ:** 400 (ctrl). ***Continues*** *Imperial Quarterly., 1191-3231.*
Desc: A celebration of pre-revolutionary Russian culture with a special emphasis on the Romanov Dynasty. We cover art, literature, religion, travel and life in czarist Russia.

FR/0754-023X
INFINI, L'. [Infini]. Vol. 1, (Winter 1983)-. Periodical. French. Four times a year (Mar., June, Sept., Dec.). 289.18F France; 344.00F other. Editions Gallimard, 5 rue Sebastien Bottin, 75328 Paris Cedex 7 France. **Tel** 011 33 1 49544200. **LC** AP20; .I44. **DD** 054/.1. Documents available from The Genuine Article. ***Continues*** *Tel Quel.*
Ind/Abst Annu. Bibliogr. Engl. Lang. Lit.; Arts Humanit. Citation Index [Full Cov.]; MLA Int. Bibl. Books Artic. Mod. Lang. Lit.; Res. Alert [Full Cov.]; Romant. Move.

GW
INFORMATION LETTER - FRANKFURTER HEFTE. **Main/Corp** Frankfurter Hefte. No. 1 (Jan. 2, 1950)-. German. **LC** DD3; .F8.
Ind/Abst Am. Hist. Life (1954-1957, 1967-1984).

IT
INFORMER. (19??)-. English. mo (11 issues). L50000. Buroservice SNC, Via Dei Tigli 2, 20020 Arese

MI Italy. **Tel** 011 39 2 9385742. **ED** John Murphy. **Bk Rev**. **Ad Acc**. **Circ:** 5,000.
Desc: Useful information for foreigners living in Italy.

IE/0332-2483
INSIDE IRELAND. [Inside Irel.]. (19??)-. Periodical. English. qt. $40.00 (one year), $70.00 (two year), $105.00 (three year). Inside Ireland, PO Box 1886, Dublin 16 Ireland. **Tel** 011 353 1 931906. **ED** Brenda Weir. **LC** WMLC 93/4227. **Bk Rev**. **Ad Acc**. **Circ:** 7,000.
Desc: A collection of witty and informative tidbits, in-depth articles, humor, services such as restaurants and accommodation reviews, answers to subscriber's queries on costs of an Irish visit, touring advice, etc.

BU/0861-3117
INSIDER, THE. (1991)-. Periodical. English. mo. $50.00 UK; $57.00 other. ELTEX Ltd., 16A Patriarch Evtimii Blvd. 4th Fl, Sofia Bulgaria. **Tel** 359 2 44 15 47, FAX 359 2 44 54 84. **ED** Alexander Daynov. **LC** DR51; .I57. **DD** 949.77/005. Index available (Dec. issue). cum. index. **Bk Rev**, (Qty: 12/yr). **Ad Acc**, **Adv Mgr:** Rossitsa Tsoleva. **Circ:** 7000.
Desc: Wide-profile color glossy monthly magazine which presents Bulgaria- its politics, economy, culture, news, people and places- to the outside world. It also carries occasional supplements on business and legal matters, as well as guides to places of interest.

HU
IPM, INTERPRESS MAGAZIN. **VFOAT** Interpress Magazin. Periodical. Hungarian. mo. 300.00ft Hungary; $32.00 US. Interpress Kiado es Nyomda Vallalat, Postfach 46, 1525 Budapest Hungary. **Tel** 153-883, telex 22-6777. **LC** AP82; .I15. **DD** 059/.945/11. **Ad Acc**. **Circ:** 160,000.

IE/0021-0943
IRELAND OF THE WELCOMES. [Irel. welcomes]. **Added/Corp** Irish Tourist Board. Vol. 1, No. 1 (May/June 1952)-. Periodical. English. bm. $21.00 (one year), $37.00 (two year). Ireland of the Welcomes, 49 Richmondville Avenue, Westport CT 06880. **Tel** (203)454-0344. **(Subscription address:** Neodata / Colorado, PO Box 2606, Boulder Boulder CO 80322.**)** **ED** Peter Harbison. **DD** 914. **Bk Rev**. **Ad Acc**. **Circ:** 120,000. available on microfilm and microfiche from University Microfilms International (UMI).

US/0888-3556
IRISH PEOPLE (NEW YORK, N.Y. : 1972). (THE IRISH PEOPLE.). [Irish people]. Began in 1972. Periodical. English. wk. $18.00. The Irish People Inc, 4951 Broadway, New York NY 10034. **DD** 071.

IE/0790-7850
IRISH REVIEW (CORK, IRELAND). (THE IRISH REVIEW.). No. 1 (1986)-. Periodical. English (Irish). sa. $30.00. Institute Irish Studies, 8 Fitzwilliam Street, Belfast BT9 6AW, North Ireland. **LC** DA925; .I745. **Bk Rev**, (Qty: 30). **Ad Acc**. **Circ:** 500.

UK/0019-073X
IT. No. 1, (Oct. 14/27, 1966)-. Periodical. English. Newspeak Publishing Ltd, 286 Portobello Road, London W11 England. **Tel** 01/9600488. **LC** AP4; .I8.

IE
IT MAGAZINE. **VFOAT** I.T. Magazine. Periodical. English. mo. It Magazine, The Village Center, Ballybrack Company, Dublin Ireland. **LC** AP4; .I757. **DD** 052. ***Continues*** *Irish Tatler.*
Ind/Abst Can. Index.

IT
ITALIA, ORIENTE, MEDITERRANEO. (1982)-. Monographic series. Italian. ir. Price varies per volume. Alinea Editrice, Via da Palestrina 17-19, Rosso 50144 Florence Italy. **Tel** 011 39 55 333428.

IT/0021-3063
ITALY. (ITALY : DOCUMENTS AND NOTES.). [Italy]. **Added/Corp** Italy. Servizi Delle Informazione e Della Proprieta Letteraria, Artistica e Scientifica. No. 1 (Jan./Feb. 1964)-. Periodical. English. Twice a year. L31000.00 Italy; L50000.00 others. Istituto Poligrafico Zecca Stato, Piazza Verdi 10, 00198 Rome Italy. **Tel** 011 39 6 85082307, 011 39 6 85082221. ***Continues*** *Italian Affairs, 0392-8519.*
Ind/Abst Am. Hist. Life (1954, 1963, 1970, 1975)(1970, 1975); Leis. Recreat. Tour. Abstr.; Rural Dev. Abstr.; World Agric. Econ.

IT
ITINERARIO (NAPLES, ITALY). (ITINERARIO.). Vol. 1, No. 1 (Feb. 1985)-. Periodical. Italian. Twelve times a year. L022000.00. Sevip Srl, Via V Colonna 14, 80121 Naples Italy. **Tel** 011 39 81 406811.
Ind/Abst Int. Bibliogr. Sociol.

GW/0932-0377
JAHRBUCH DES RHEIN-SIEG-KREISES. **Added/Corp** Rhein-Sieg-Kreis (Germany). **VAT** Jahrbuch des Rhein Sieg Kreises. 1986-. German. **LC** DD801.R488; J33.

AU/1016-2712
JAHRBUCH FUER LANDESKUNDE VON NIEDEROSTERREICH. **Added/Corp** Verein fur Landeskunde von Niederosterreich und Wien. **VFOAT** Festschrift zum 70. Geburtstage von Karl Lechner. (1902)-. German. cum. index.
Ind/Abst Am. Hist. Life (1961-); BHA : Biblio. Hist. Art.

PL
JANTAR. (19??)-. Periodical. Polish. wk. PL Holdu Pruskrego 8, Skrytka Poizt 542, Szczecin Poland. **LC** AP54; .J35.

UK/0958-9287
JOURNAL OF EUROPEAN SOCIAL POLICY. [J. Eur. soc. policy]. (1991)-. Periodical. English. qt. £87.00 Europe; £94.00 Other (Institutions). Longman Group Ltd., Fourth Avenue, Longman House, Harlow Essex CM19 5SR England. **Tel** 011 44 279 429655, FAX 011 44 279 431059, telex 81259. **DD** 361.61094. **[CCC].**

●UK/1354-571X
JOURNAL OF MODERN ITALIAN STUDIES. **See** Linguistics.

US/0896-1018
JOURNAL OF THE AMERICAN ROMANIAN ACADEMY OF ARTS AND SCIENCES. [J. Am. Rom. Acad. Arts Sci.]. **VFOAT** ARA Journal; A.R.A. Journal. (1984)-. Periodical. English (Romany and French). an. $20.00. Dr Ion Manea, 3328 Monte Vista Avenue, Davis CA 95616. **Tel** (916)752-6442. **(Subscription address:** Miron Butariu, 4310 Finley Avenue, Los Angeles, CA 90027**)** **ED** Ion Manea. **LC** DR201; .J68. **DD** 949.8. cum. index. **Bk Rev**. **Circ:** 500 (ctrl). ***Continues*** *A.R.A. Bulletin.*
Desc: Includes papers presented at previous conventions on topics of a more general interest, such as history, literature, political science, linguistics, and philosophy.
Ind/Abst Am. Bibliogr. Slavic East Europ. Stud.; MLA Int. Bibl. Books Artic. Mod. Lang. Lit.

UK/0075-4390
JOURNAL OF THE WARBURG AND COURTAULD INSTITUTES. [J. Warburg Courtauld Inst.]. **Added/Corp** Warburg Institute. Courtauld Institute of Art. Vol. 3 (1940)-. English. an. Warburg Institute, University of London, Woburn Square, London WC1H OAB England. **Tel** 011 44 71 5809663, FAX (01)580-9663. **ED** D.S. Chambers, P. Kidson and E. McGrath. **LC** AS122; .L8515. **DD** 052. **CODEN** JWCIAH. Index available. cum. index. **Circ:** 1,200 (ctrl). Documents available from The Genuine Article. ***Continues*** *Journal of the Warburg Institute.*
Desc: A journal of cultural history supplying a forum for historians of art, religion, science, literature, social and political life, and for philosophers and anthropologists.
Ind/Abst Annu. Bibliogr. Engl. Lang. Lit.; Archit. Period. Index (1946-); Art Index; ARTbibliogr. Mod.; Arts Humanit. Citation Index [Full Cov.]; Avery Index Archit. Period. Suppl. Colum. Univ. (1989-); BHA : Biblio. Hist. Art; Br. Archaeol. Bibliogr.; Br. Humanit. Index; Curr. Contents Arts Humanit.; Math. Rev.; MLA Int. Bibl. Books Artic. Mod. Lang. Lit.; Res. Alert [Full Cov.]; Romant. Move.

LV/0132-6295
KAROGS (RIGA). (KAROGS; LITERATURAS, MAKSLAS UN SABIEDRISKI POLITISKS ZURNALS.). [Karogs]. **Added/Corp** Latvijas Padomju Rakstnieku Savieniba. (19??)-. Periodical. Latvian. mo. $30.50. **(Subscription address:** Victor Kamkin, 4956 Boiling Brook Parkway, Rockville MD 20852.**)** **LC** AP95.L4; K37.
Ind/Abst MLA Int. Bibl. Books Artic. Mod. Lang. Lit.

SW/0348-9833
KAROLINSKA FORBUNDETS ARSBOK. (ARSBOK.). [Karol. forb. arsb.]. **Main/Corp** Karolinska Forbundet, Stockholm. (1910)-. Swedish. **LC** DL601; .K3.
Ind/Abst Am. Hist. Life (1954-).

HU
KELETKUTATAS. **See** History(General)-History of Europe.

GW/0023-3528
KONKRET. Began in 1955. Periodical. German. mo. German Language Publications Inc, 560 Sylvan Avenue, Englewood Cliffs NJ 07632. **Tel** (201)871-1010. **LC** AP30; .K65.

PL/0137-4680
KONKRETY. [Konkrety]. (1972)-. Periodical. Polish. wk. $52.00. **(Subscription address:** ARS Polona, PO Box 1001, 00068 Warsaw Poland.**)** **UDC** 07.

GW
KONTINENT. ***Ceased.*** (1974)-(19??). Periodical. Russian. qt. Ullstein-Verlag GmbH, Lindenstr 76, W-1000 Berlin 61, B R D Germany. **Tel** 2710534. **LC** AP50; .K637. **Bk Rev**.

NO
KONTRAST; TIDSSKRIFT FOR POLITIKK, KULTUR, KRITIKK. (1???)-. Periodical. Norwegian. Six times a year. Kr145.00 (individuals); Kr185.00 (institutions). Forlagsentralen Tidsskriftavd, PB 150 Furuset, 1001 Oslo 10 Norway. **Tel** 011 47 2 2320995.

GW
KOOPERATION (LIESSEM, WACHTBERG, GERMANY). (KOOPERATION.). **Added/Corp** European Community. Gulf Cooperation Council. **VFOAT** Taawun. (1986)-. Periodical. German (English). ir. DM89.00. Vandenhoeck & Ruprecht, Robert Bosch Breite 6, D-37079 Goettingen Germany. **Tel** 011 49 551 695911, FAX 011 49 551 695917, telex 965226 VAN d. **LC** HF1584.5.Z44; E864.
Ind/Abst Postharvest News Inf.

PL
KRAJ RAD; RADZIECKI TYGODNIK ILUSTROWANY. Vol. 1 (1958)-. Periodical. Polish. Fifty-two times a year. $40.00 (latest volume). **(Subscription address:** ARS Polona, PO Box 1001, 00068 Warsaw Poland.**)** **LC** AP54; .K7.

PL/0867-4248
KUJAWY I POMORZE. (1990)-. Periodical. Polish. wk. $52.00. **(Subscription address:** ARS Polona, PO Box 1001, 00068 Warsaw Poland.**)** **UDC** 323(438). **CODEN** 304(438).
Desc: Cultural and social publications for Wloclawek region.

YU/0023-5164
KULTURA. **Added/Corp** Zavod za Proucavanje Kulturnog Razvitka (Serbia). (1968)-. Periodical. Serbo-Croatian (Roman) (summaries and/or abstracts in English). qt. $8.00 US. **LC** AP56; .K77. **DD** 057/.85.
Ind/Abst Soc. Plann. Policy Dev. Abstr.

SW
KULTURKATALOGEN. (1977)-. Swedish. Statens Kulturrad, Box 7843 S-103, 98 Stockholm Sweden. **LC** DL631; .K845.

LI/0134-3106
KULTUROS BARAI. (KULTUROS BARAI. DOMAINS OF CULTURE.). [Kult. barai]. **Added/Corp** Lithuania. Kulturos Ministerija. **VFOAT** Domains of Culture. (19??)-. Periodical. Lithuanian. mo. $25.00. **(Subscription address:** Victor Kamkin, 4956 Boiling Brook Parkway, Rockville MD 20852.**)** **LC** AP95.L5; K85.
Ind/Abst MLA Int. Bibl. Books Artic. Mod. Lang. Lit.

GW/0023-5652
KURSBUCH. [Kursbuch]. Vol. 1 (June 1965)-. Periodical. German. Four times a year. DM12.00. Rowohlt Taschenbuch Verlag, Postfach 1349, D 21462 Reinbek Germany. **Tel** 011 49 40 72720. **LC** AP30; .K87. cum. index.
Ind/Abst Philos. Index.

XR/0023-5849
KVETY. (Jan. 1951)-. Periodical. Czech. Fifty-two times a year. $168.20. **(Subscription address:** Artia Pegas Press Ltd., Palac Metro Narodni Trida 25, 11210 Prague 1 Czech Republic.**)** **LC** AP52; .K915.

UK/0023-7167
LADY. [Lady]. (1885)-. Periodical. English. wk. Airmail: £72.00 Pacific Islands, Australasia & Far East; £56.00 Middle East & North Africa; £48.00 Europe; £64.00 other. Lady Ltd., 39-40 Bedford Street Strand, London WC2E 9ER England. **Tel** 011 44 71 379 3985, FAX 011 44 71 397 2137. **ED** Arline Usden. **DD** 052. **[CCC]**. **Bk Rev**, (Qty: 12). **Ad Acc**. **Circ:** 58,650.

UK
LANCASHIRE LIFE. (19??)-. Periodical. English. Twelve times a year. £13.00. Opax Publishing Ltd., Oyston Mill Strand Road, Preston Lancashire PR1 England. **Tel** 011 44 772 722022. **ED** William Amos. **Ad Acc**. **Circ:** 15,000.
Desc: Lancashire current events, local history, topography, social events, arts and crafts.

LV
LATVIA - BALTIC STATE. Periodical. Latvian (English). Four times a year. Latvian International Communications, Commercial Center, 8 Tirgonu Street, LV 1933 Riga Latvia. **Tel** 011 371 2 211602, FAX 011 371 9 348836. **ED** Aivars Berzins.

UK
LEGION, THE. V. 1- Mar. 1980-. Periodical. English. **LC** AP4; .L364. **DD** 052.

IT/0024-1504
LEVANTE. **VFOAT** Mashrik. Vol. 1 (1953)-. Periodical. Italian (Arabic). qt. **LC** DS63.2.I8; L4. **DD** 945/.005.
Ind/Abst Middle East J.

NE/0304-0003
LIAS. Vol. 1 (1974)-. English (French, German and Italian). Twice a year. Fl80.00. Holland University Press, APA Acad Publ Assoc, PO Box 122, 3600 AC Maarssen Netherlands. **Tel** 011 31 30 436166. **LC** AS243; .L5. **DD** 050. Documents available from The Genuine Article.
Ind/Abst Arts Humanit. Citation Index [Full Cov.]; Res. Alert [Full Cov.].

LH
LIECHTENSTEIN : PRINCIPALITY IN THE HEART OF EUROPE. German (English, French and Italian). 5.00F. Press and Information Office,

General Interest —General Interest-Europe

Government Palace, FL-9490 Vaduz Liechtenstein. **Tel** (075)2366720, FAX (075)2366460. ctrl circ.
Desc: General overview about the principality of Liechtenstein.

BE/0776-1325
LIMBURG. (1920)-. Periodical. Dutch. bm. Limburg, Parklaan 9, 3590 Diepenbeek Belgium. **Tel** 011 31 11 322398. **UDC** 7.072.
Ind/Abst BHA : Biblio. Hist. Art.

UK
LONDON REGISTER OF REMARKABLE EVENTS, CONTAINING ACCOUNTS OF MURDERS, SUICIDES, INQUESTS, SHIPWRECKS, DESTRUCTIVE FIRES, ACCIDENTS, AND OTHER REMARKABLE OCCURRENCES IN VARIOUS PARTS OF THE GLOBE, THE. Periodical. English. wk.

FI/0024-6379
LOOK AT FINLAND. *Ceased.* (Spring 1964)-(1992). Periodical. English. qt. Look at Finland, PO Box 53, SF-00521 Helsinki Finland. **Tel** (0)144511, telex 122 690 MEK SF. **ED** Vappu Virkkunen. **LC** DK445; .L66. Index available. **Bk Rev**. **Ad Acc**. **Circ**: 32,000.
Desc: General view on events, culture, architecture, tourism and people in Finland.

SP
LOOKOUT, THE. Main/Corp Council of Social and Health Agencies of San Francisco. Periodical. English. mo. 3000ptas Spain; $42.00 (surface mail); $147.00 (airmail) US. Lookout Publications, Puebla Lucia, Fuengirola Malaga Spain. **Tel** 952 460950, FAX 952 461022. **ED** Ken Brown. Index available. **Bk Rev Ad Acc**. **Circ**: 24,000 (ctrl).
Desc: Aimed at Americans and Britons living in Spain, or those living elsewhere who have and interest in Spain. Features include profiles of Americans and Britons in Spain, travel, food, wine, service articles, politics, business and finance, Spanish law for foreigners, history and culture.

HU/0133-9214
LUDAS EVKONYV. **VFOAT** Ludas Matyi Evkonyve. Hungarian. Hirlapkiado Vallalat, Blaha Luiza Ter 3, 1959 Budapest VII Hungary. **Tel** 135-816. **LC** AY814; .L83. *Continues* Ludas Matyi Evkonyve.

HU
LUDAS MATYI. (May 20, 1945)-. Periodical. Hungarian. wk. $40.00 Austria, Croatia, Czech Republic, Slovakia, Romania, Yugoslavia, Slovenia and Ukraine; $52.00 other. (Subscription address: Kultura, PO Box 149, H 1389 Budapest 62 Hungary.) **LC** AP115; .L8.

RM
LUMINITA. *Ceased.* (19??-19??). Romanian. mo. (Subscription address: Ilexim Press Department, PO Box 1, 136-1-137, Bucharest, Romania.) **LC** AP215.R6; L8.
Desc: Magazine for children.

SW
LUNDIAN : AN INTERNATIONAL MAGAZINE, THE. English. Ten times a year. $25.00 (libraries) $18.00 Sweden; $25.00 US; $30.00 other. Modern Media, PO Box 722 S-220 07 Lund Sweden. **Tel** 046-13 82 21, FAX 046 11 13 22. **ED** M Robinson Diakite. **Bk Rev**. **Ad Acc**. **Circ**: 30,000 (ctrl).
Desc: Covers news, tips, writings about Lund, poetry, short stories, short unpublished articles, list of events and letters.

GW
LYNX JAHRBUCH. German. 10.00. Club Lynx, Hallerplatz 14/11, Hamburg Germany. **LC** AY18; .L95.

YU
M; REVIJA. VFOAT Mladina. Periodical. Slovenian. wk. $9.00. Titova 145 Yugoslavia, Titova 145, Yugoslavia. **LC** AP58.S55; M16.

FR/1164-0359
MADAME JOURS DE FRANCE. (1990)-. Periodical. French. wk. 550.00F France, Belgium, Tunisia, French overseas departments and territories; 760.00F other. Soc de Presse Jours de France, 12 Rue du Mail, 75002 Paris France. **Tel** 011 33 1 42216200. **UDC** 082. *Continues* Jours de France, 0022-5681.

PL
MAGAZYN POMORZE, FAKTY I MYSLI. Vol. 1- 7 Jan. 1973-. Periodical. Polish. RSW Prasa Ksiazka Ruch, Warszawa UL Wronia 23, Bydogozcz Poland. **LC** AP54; .M32. *Formed by the union of Pomorze and Fakty I Mysli.*

LI
MAGAZYN WILENSKI. (1990)-. Periodical. Polish. Twenty-four times a year. Price on Request. (Subscription address: ARS Polona, PO Box 1001, 00068 Warsaw Poland.)

IE/0332-1754
MAGILL. [Magill]. (1977)-. Periodical. English. Fourteen times a year. £15.00 Ireland; $50.00 US. Magill, 14 Merrion Row, Dublin 2 Ireland. **Tel** 610133. **ED** Brian Trench. **LC** AP4; .M213. **DD** 052. **Bk Rev**. **Ad Acc**. **Circ**: 33,000.
Desc: Political and current affairs magazine.

US
MAGYAR KEVE. 1978-. Hungarian. an. 1739 Mehoning Avenue, Youngstown OH 44509. **LC** AY78.H8; M26.

YU
MAGYAR SZO NAPTARA, A. Hungarian. 10.00. Forum Nyomda, Novi Sad Vojvode Misica 1, Ujvidek Yugoslavia. **LC** AY1038.Y6; M3.

UK
MAJESTY. (MAJESTY : THE MONTHLY ROYAL REVIEW.). [Majesty]. (1980)-. Periodical. English. Twelve times a year. $49.00 US. (Subscription address: UK/ United Magazine Subscriptions, 1st Floor, Stephenson House, Brunel C, Milton Keynes, MK2 2EW England; telephone: 11 44 908 371981; Outside UK/ Publisher Mini Systems, PO Box 301369, Escondido, CA 92030)

US/0464-8145
MANA (ALEXANDRIA, VA.). (MANA.). [Mana]. V. 1- ; 1957/58-. Periodical. Estonian. ir. $15.00 (single issue). Hellar Grabbi, 3602 Albee La, Alexandria VA 22309. **Tel** (703)780-2318. **ED** Hellar Grabbi. **LC** AP95.E4; M3. **DD** 058/.7. **Bk Rev**. **Circ**: 1,200.
Desc: International review of Estonian literature, art, history and science.
Ind/Abst MLA Int. Bibl. Books Artic. Mod. Lang. Lit.

PL/0867-0064
MAOPOLSKA KRAKOW. (MAOPOLSKA.). (1989)-. Periodical. Polish. wk. $65.00. (Subscription address: ARS Polona, PO Box 1001, 00068 Warsaw Poland.) **UDC** 304(438). **CODEN** 331(438).

NE/0025-2956
MARGRIET. Dutch. wk. Fl317.20. Medianet BV, Postbus 6298, 2001 LN Haarlem Netherlands. **Tel** 011 31 23 173311.

FR/1148-9006
MARIE CLAIRE MAISON PARIS. (MARIE CLAIRE MAISON.). (1990)-. Periodical. French. Ten times a year. 252.00F France; 329.00F other. Societe Marie-Claire, 11 Bis rue Boissy d'Anglas, F-75008 Paris France. **Tel** 011 33 1 42668888. **UDC** 747. *Continues* La Maison de Marie-Claire, 0542-1594.

FR
MARSEILLE INFORMATIONS. VFOAT Marseille-Informations. Periodical. French. mo. 5F. 125 la Canebiere, 13001 Marseille Cedex France. **LC** DC801.M34; M28. **DD** 944/.912.

UK/0025-4118
MARXISM TODAY. *Ceased.* Vol. 1 (Oct. 1957). Ceased (Dec. 1991). Periodical. English. mo. Communist Party of Great Britain, 16 St John Street, London EC1M 4AY England. **Tel** (01)608 0265. **ED** Martin Jacques. **LC** AP4; .M335. **DD** 335.43/05. Index available. cum. index. **Bk Rev**. **Ad Acc**. **Circ**: 17,000. available on audiocassette. *Continues* Marxist Quarterly.
Desc: Current affairs and political strategy with an emphasis on open debate and controversy; contains a major culture and lifestyle section.
Ind/Abst Curr. Mil. Pol. Lit.; Middle East Abstr. Index; Sage Race Relat. Abstr.

DK/0106-1062
MEDDELELSER OM GRNLAND. MAN & SOCIETY. [Meddr Grnland, Man & Soc.]. **VFOAT** Man & Society; Man and Society. Vol. 1 (1980)-. Monographic series. English (French and German). ir. Price varies per volume. Comm Science Research Greenland, Oster Voldgade 10, DK 1350 Kobenhavn K Denmark. **Tel** 45-1-113666, FAX 01 936815, telex 27125. **ED** Bent Harvald, Torben Agersnap and Hans Christian Gullov. **LC** E99.E7; M48. **DD** 998/.200497. Index available. **Bk Rev**. **Ad Acc**. **Circ**: 800. *Continues in part* Meddelelser om Grnland, 0025-6676.
Desc: Papers, monographs and thematic volumes presenting results of studies in, or related to Greenland within the fields of medicine, anthropology, archaeology, law, linguistics, social sciences and etc.
Ind/Abst Geogr. Abstr. Human Geogr. (?-?).

GW/0933-081X
MEINE FAMILIE & ICH. VFOAT Meine Familie und Ich. (1972)-. Periodical. German. mo. $50.00. Burda GmbH, Postfach 1280, D-7602 Offenburg Germany. **Tel** 011 49 781-8401. (Subscription address: US: German Language Publications, Inc., 153 South Deanstreet, Englewood, NJ 07631) **UDC** 087-055.2.

UK
MEN ONLY. V. 1- (No. 1-); Dec. 1935-. Periodical. English. mo. Quadrant Subscription Services Ltd, Oakfield House, Perrymount Road, Haywards Heath, West Sussex RH16 3DH England. **Tel** (01)828-5571. **LC** AP2; .M416. **DD** 052. *Absorbed* Strand (London, England); Lilliput.

GW/0026-0029
MERIAN (HAMBURG, GERMANY). (MERIAN.). [Merian]. (1948)-. Periodical. German. Twelve times a year. DM131.40. Graefe und Unzer Verlag, Isabellastrasse 32, D 80796 Munich Germany. **Tel** 011 49 89 272720. (Subscription address: Verlegerdienst Muenchen, Postfach 1280, D 82197 Gilching Germany; telephone: 011 49 8105 388142) **LC** DD3; .M45. **DD** 946. cum. index.

FR
MINUTES OF THE REGULAR ANNUAL CONGRESS ... / FEDERATION INTERNATIONALE DES SOCIETES D'AVIRON. Main/Corp Federation Internationale des Societes d'Aviron. Congress. (19??)-. English. Four times a year. 160F France; 225F other. Federation Francaise des Socs d'Aviron, 7 Rue La Fayette, 75009 Paris France. **Tel** 011 33 1 48744377, FAX 011 33 1 49959331. **ED** Dominique Roudy. **LC** WMLC L 83/5079.

GW/0941-4193
MITTEILUNGEN DES BAYERISCHEN NOTARVEREINS, DER NOTARKASSE UND DER LANDESNOTARKAMMER BAYERN. [Mitt. Bayer. Notarver. Notarkasse Landesnotarkamm. Bayern]. **VFOAT** MittBayNot. Mitteilungen des Bayerischen Notarvereins, der Notarkasse und der Landesnotarkammer Bayern. (1961)-. Periodical. German. bm. Landesnotarkammer Bayern, Ottostr 10, W-8000 Munich 2 Germany. **UDC** 34. *Continues* Mitteilungen des Bayerischen Notarvereins und der Notarkasse, 0941-7826.

CN/0026-9042
MOLODA UKRAINA. [Moloda Ukr.]. **Added/Corp** Obiednannia Demokratychnoi Ukrainskoi Molodi. Obiednannia Demokratychnoi Ukrainskoi Molodi. Tsentralnyi Komitet. **VFOAT** Moloda Ukraina. Vol. 1 (Fall 1951)-. Periodical. Ukrainian. ir (156 issues per year). $199.95. Ukranian Democratic Youth Association, Postal Station M Box 40, Toronto Ontario M6S 4T2 Canada. **Tel** 1-763-3422. **ED** Leonid Lishchyna. **Bk Rev**. **Ad Acc**. ctrl circ.
Desc: News in the Ukrainian community, the Ukrainian music scene, Ukrainian youth organization (Odum) activities, Ukrainian literature and criticism.

FR/0153-419X
MONDE. DOSSIERS ET DOCUMENTS, LE. [Monde. Doss. doc.]. **VFOAT** Dossiers et Documents. (1???)-. Periodical. French. Eleven times a year. 120.00F EEC countries. Le Monde / Immeuble Sirius, 1 Place Hubert Beuve Mery, 94852 Ivry-sur-Seine CX France. **Tel** 011 33 1 49603000, 011 33 1 49603290. (Subscription address: International Media Service, 3330 Pacific Avenue Suite 404, Virginia Beach VA 23451.)

IT/0391-6855
MONDO, IL. [Mondo]. Yearly Vol. 1- Feb. 19, 1949-. Periodical. Italian. wk. $92.00. RCS Rizzoli Periodici, Via A Rizzoli 2, 20132 Milan Italy. **Tel** 011 39 2 27200720. **LC** AP37; .M68. cum. index. available on an online database (files 771,772,799/Full-Text) from DIALOG.
Ind/Abst Infomat Int. Bus.

●BE/1021-4224
MONTHLY REPORT ON EUROPE. (1993)-. Periodical. English (English and French). mo. 17700.00F Belgium (add 1200.00F postage) Australia; (add 1100.00F postage) Asia; (add 1000.00F postage) North, South, and Central America; (add 900.00F postage) North Africa, Israel, and Turkey; (add 700.00F postage) Europe. Europe Information Service, rue de Geneve 6, 1140 Brussels Belgium. **Tel** 011 32 2 242 6020, FAX 011 32 2 242 9549. **UDC** 33.

FR
MOTS CROISES DE POCHE. French. bm. 60.00F (one year), 110.00F (one year) France; 73.00F (one year), 136.00F (two year) other. Editions Jibena GH Publication, La Petite Monte Senille, 86100 Chatellerault France. **Tel** 011 33 49 854985. **UDC** 79.

AO
N: NOTICIA. Portuguese. 10.00 single issue. Calcada Gregorio Ferreira 26, A 32 Luanda Angola. **LC** AP68; .N13.

PL/0208-6786
NAD WARTA BODZ. (NAD WARTA.). (1980)-. Periodical. Polish. wk. $52.00. (Subscription address: ARS Polona, PO Box 1001, 00068 Warsaw Poland.) **UDC** 304(438). **CODEN** 943.8.

GW
NAHOST JAHRBUCH. **Added/Corp** Deutsches Orient-Institut. (1987)-. German. an. Leske Verlag & Budrich GmbH, Postfach 300551, Gerhart Hauptmann Strasse 27, W-5090 Leverkusen 3 Opladen Germany. **Tel** 011 49 21712079.

US
NARODNA VOLYA. English. qt. $10.00. Ukrainian Fraternal Association, 440 Wyoming Avenue, Scranton PA 18503. **Tel** (717)342-0937, FAX (717)347-5649.

GR/0028-1735
NEA ESTIA. (NEA HESTIA.). [Nea estia]. Vol. 1, Part 1, April (1927)-. Periodical. Greek, Modern (English). mo. $324.00. G. C. Eleftheroudakis SA, 4 Nikis Street, Athens T-126 Greece. **Tel** 0219410. **LC** AP85; .N4. cum. index. ***Continues*** *Hestia (Athens, Greece : 1876).*
Ind/Abst MLA Int. Bibl. Books Artic. Mod. Lang. Lit.

SZ
NEUE, DIE. Vol. 1, No. 1, (Nov. 1981)-. Periodical. German. mo. 40.00F. Spontan AG, Umgasse 15, 8803 Ruschlikon 01 724 19 18 Switzerland. **LC** HQ1103; .N48. **DD** 305.4/2/09494.

AU
NEUE FREIE ZEITUNG. Added/Corp Freiheitliche Partei Osterreichs. Bundesparteileitung. Freiheitliche Partei Osterreichs. **VFOAT** NFZ. (1973)-. Periodical. German. wk. S360.00. Freiheitliche Partei Oesterreichs, Kartner Strasse 28, A-1010 Vienna Austria. **Tel** 5129452, telex 5138858. **LC** AP30; .N442. Index available. **Bk Rev. Ad Acc. Circ:** 50,000. available in microform. ***Supersedes*** *Neue Front.*
Desc: Home policy, foreign policy, economic information, culture commentaries, and general commentaries.

AU
NEUE ORDNUNG. Periodical. German. 190.00. Wappenverlag, Reitschulgasse 25, 8010 Graz Austria. **LC** AP30; .N477.

US
NEUE ZEITALTER (MICROFICHE), DAS. (DAS NEUE ZEITALTER.). Began publication with July 1949 issue. Periodical. German. wk. Annelies Huter Verlag, Pettenkofersstr 24, 8000 Munchen 2 Germany. **LC** MICROFILM 01365AP; AP30.

GW
NEUES HOCHLAND : NH. VFOAT NH. Vol. 64, No.1 (Jan./Feb. 1972)-. Periodical. German. bm. **LC** AP30; .H67. ***Continues*** *Hochland.*

AA
NEW ALBANIA. ***Ceased.*** Periodical. English. bm. Drejtoria Qendrore Perhapjes, Rruga Konferenca e Pezes, Tirana Albania. **LC** AP95.A3; N46.

UK
NEW OUTLOOK. Periodical. English. qt. £1.00. Lord Beaumont of Whitley, 59 W Heath Road NW, 3 London England. **LC** AP4; .N53. **DD** 052.
Ind/Abst Index Period. Artic. Relat. Law.

IC
NEWS FROM ICELAND. No. 1 (July/Aug. 1975)-. Periodical. English. mo. $28.00. Iceland Review, PO Box 12122, 121 Reykjavik Iceland. **Tel** 11 354 1 675700, telex 2121. **ED** Haraldur J Hamar. **LC** DL301; .N48. **DD** 949.1/2005. **Bk Rev. Ad Acc. Circ:** 20,000.
Desc: General news in Iceland: politics, economy, trade, industry (emphasizing fishing), communications, culture, tourism, people, etc.

CN/0381-6133
NEWSLETTER - CANADIAN ASSOCIATION OF SLAVISTS. Main/Corp Canadian Association of Slavists. **VFOAT** C A S Newsletter. Vol. 1 (1961)-. Newsletter. English. Twice a year (May & Oct.). 6.00Can$. Canadian Slavonic Papers, Department of Compartative Literature, 347 Arts Building, University of Alberta, Edmonton, Alberta, Canada T6G 2E6. **Tel** (403)492-2566, FAX (403)492-9112. **ED** Gust Olson. **Ad Acc. Circ:** 380 (ctrl).
Desc: Materials relating to culture, economy, politics of Eastern Europe and the Soviet Union.

BE/0773-3577
NIEUW WERELDTIJDSCHRIFT : NWT. [NWT. Nieuw wereldtijdschr.]. **VFOAT** NWT. Vol. 1, No. 1 (April 1984)-. Periodical. Dutch. bw. 1200F. Transvaalstraat 8, 2600 Antwerpen Belgium. **Tel** 03/239 56 28. **LC** AP15; .N58. **Ad Acc. Circ:** 10,000. ***Continues*** *Nieuw Vlaams Tijdschrift.*
Ind/Abst MLA Int. Bibl. Books Artic. Mod. Lang. Lit.

NE/0169-6777
NIEUWE STEM. (DE NIEUWE STEM.). [Nieuwe stem]. (1946)-. Periodical. Dutch. Ten times a year. Libresso BV, Postbus 878, 7400 GA Deventer Netherlands. **Tel** 011 31 5700 47421. **LC** AP15; .N63.
Ind/Abst Am. Hist. Life (1955-1957).

YU/0027-6685
NIN. NEDELJNE INFORMATIVNE NOVINE. VFOAT Nedeljne Informativne Novine. (1951)-. Periodical. Serbo-Croatian (Cyrillic). Fifty-two times a year. 265.00Can$. Politika, PO Box 124, 11000 Belgrade Yugoslavia. **Tel** 011 38 11 326 191749. **LC** AP56; .N5.

NO
NORDISK FORUM. Added/Corp Universitetet i Oslo. (1966-1973; Vol. 9 1974)-. Periodical. Norwegian. qt. Forlget Medusa, Silkegade 7, DK-1113 KBH K Denmark.

NO/0029-1846
NORSEMAN. (THE NORSEMAN.). [Norseman]. **Added/Corp** Dreyers Forlag. Nordmanns-Forbundet. (1960)-. Periodical. English (Norwegian). Six times a year. $40.00. Nordmanns Forbundet, Raadhusgt 23 B, N-0158 Oslo 1 Norway. **Tel** 42 23 76. **ED** Johan Heyerdahl. **LC** DL401; .N612. **[CCC]. Bk Rev. Ad Acc. Circ:** 14,000 (ctrl). Documents available from Documents on Demand. ***Supersedes*** *Norseman.*
Desc: A Norwegian/English magazine covering contemporary Norwegian art, history, literature, exploration, science, travel, personalities and business.
Ind/Abst Energy Inf. Abstr.; Environ. Abstr.

UK
NORTHUMBRIANA. Periodical. English (Northumbrian). ir. £90.00. Morpeth Northumbrian Gathering Committee, Roland Bibby, Westgate House, Dogger Bank, Morpeth Northumberland NE61 1RF England. **Tel** 513308 (0670 STD). **ED** Roland Bibby. **LC** DA670.N79; N84. **DD** 942.8/8/005. **Bk Rev. Ad Acc. Circ:** 750.
Desc: Devoted to landscape, history, traditions, culture, language, literature and character of Northumberland.

FR/0029-4004
NOTES ET ETUDES DOCUMENTAIRES. [Notes etud. doc.]. No. 1070 (1968)-. Monographic series. French. ir. Price varies per volume. Documentation Francaise, 29 Quai Voltaire, 75344 Paris Cedex 7 France. **Tel** 011 33 1 40157000, FAX 011 33 1 40157230, telex 204 826 DOCFRAN. **(Subscription address:** Documentation Francaise, 124 rue Henri Barbusse, 93308 Aubervilliers Cedex France.**) ED** Isabelle Crucifix. **LC** D411; .F67. Index available. cum. index. **Circ:** 5,000. available on microfiche. ***Continues*** *Notes Documentaires et Etudes.*
Ind/Abst Geogr. Abstr. Human Geogr. (?-?); Int. Labour Doc.; Int. Polit. Sci. Abstr.; LABORDOC; PAIS Int. Print (1991-); Point Repere (1983-).

FR/1158-5803
NOUS DEUX COLLECTION. (NOUS DEUX.). (1988)-. Periodical. French. wk. 299.00F France; 517.00F other. Editions Mondiales, 9 11 13 Rue du Col Pierre Avia, 75754 Paris Cedex 15 France. **Tel** 011 33 1 46622162. **UDC** 82-3.

FR/0029-4713
NOUVEL OBSERVATEUR (PARIS), LE. (LE NOUVEL OBSERVATEUR.). [Nouv. obs.]. No. 1 (Nov. 19, 1964)-. Periodical. French. wk (52 issues). 744.37F France; 825.00F other (surface mail). Le Nouvel Observateur, 23 rue Turbigo, 75002 Paris France. **Tel** 011 33 1 40263100. **LC** AP20; .N74. **DD** 074/.36. available on microfilm and microfiche from University Microfilms International (UMI). ***Continues*** *France Observateur.*
Ind/Abst PAIS Int. Print; Point Repere (1983-); Romant. Move.

FR
NOUVELLES DE PARIS. (19??)-. French. wk. 663.80F. Informations Paul Deheme, 25 rue Jean Dolent, 75014 Paris France. **Tel** 011 33 1 47076146.

FR/0293-6186
NOUVELLES D'ORLEANS, LES. [Nouv. Orleans]. (19??)-. Periodical. French. wk. 240.00F. Nouvelles d'Orleans, BP 1857, 7 rue du Colombier, 45008 Orleans Cedex 1 France. **Tel** 011 33 38 543233. **UDC** 070.2(1-3)(445.2).

SZ
NOVALIS. Vol. 1 (Jan 1991)-. Periodical. German. mo. **LC** AP30; .K64. ***Continues*** *Kommenden.*

PL
NOWA WIES. Added/Corp ZMP (Organization) Powszechna Organizacja "Suzba Polsce.". (Nov. 28, 1948)-. Periodical. Polish. Twenty-six times a year. $44.00. **(Subscription address:** ARS Polona, PO Box 1001, 00068 Warsaw Poland.**) LC** AP54; .N62.

PL
NOWE PRAVO. ***Ceased.*** ( )-?. Polish. mo. **(Subscription address:** ARS Polona, PO Box 1001, 00068 Warsaw Poland.**)**

PL/0208-6883
NOWINY JELENIOGORSKIE. VFOAT NJ. Nowiny Jeleniogorskie. (1958)-. Periodical. Polish. wk. $39.00. **(Subscription address:** ARS Polona, PO Box 1001, 00068 Warsaw Poland.**) UDC** 304(438). **CODEN** 943.8.

IT/0029-6295
NUOVI ARGOMENTI. [Nuovi argom.]. (1953)-. Periodical. Italian. Four times a year. L44800 Italy; L55000 other. Giunti Editore, Via Bolognese 165, 50139 Florence Italy. **Tel** 011 39 55 6679267, FAX 011 39 55 268312, telex 571438. **LC** AP37; .N88.
Ind/Abst Am. Hist. Life (1955-1958); MLA Int. Bibl. Books Artic. Mod. Lang. Lit.; Romant. Move.

IT/0550-3841
NUOVI QUADERNI DEL MERIDIONE. ***Suspended.*** [Nuovi quad. meridione]. **Added/Corp** Banco di Sicilia. Fondazione "Ignazio Mormino". (1963)-(Vol. 100, 1987). Periodical. Italian. qt. Free. Banco di Sicilia, Servizio Segretatiato Generale, 90141 Palermo Italy. **Tel** 011 39 91 274111. cum. index. ***Continues*** *Quaderni del Meridione.*
Ind/Abst Am. Hist. Life (1975, 1987-); MLA Int. Bibl. Books Artic. Mod. Lang. Lit.

DK/0029-6759
NY POLITIK. V. 1, 1970-. Periodical. Danish. mo. kr12.00. Socialdemokratiet Labour Pty, SNT Focketinget, 1240 Christiansborg Denmark. **Tel** 01-11 66 00. **ED** Jimmy Stahr. **LC** AP42; .N84.

NO/0029-6783
NYE BONYTT. (1941)-. Periodical. Norwegian. Nine times a year. Kr425.00. Hjemmet as Fagpresseforlaget, PO Box 1161 Sentrum, N 0107 Oslo 1 Norway. **Tel** 011 47 2 429470.

YU
OBELEZJA. Periodical. Serbo-Croatian (Roman). 30.00. Jedinstvo, Marsala Tita 33, Pristina Yugoslavia. **LC** AP56; .O24.

FR/0221-0703
OBJECTIF EUROPE STRASBOURG. [Object. Eur. Strasbourg]. (1978)-. Periodical. French (English and German). Six times a year. 250.00F. OCIPE, 6 rue Wencker, 67000 Strasbourg France. **Tel** 011 33 1 88356325, FAX 011 33 1 88365528. **UDC** 32. **Ad Acc. Circ:** 1,500. ***Continues*** *Lettre de l'O.C.I.P.E. (1959), 0224-6988.*

PO
OCIDENTE. V. 1- (No. 1-); May 1938-. Periodical. Portuguese. Ocidente, rue de S Felix 41, 1D Lisbon 2 Portugal. **LC** AP65; .O43. **DD** 056.9.

PL/0472-5182
ODRA. [Odra]. (Mar. 1961)-. Periodical. Polish. mo. $39.00. **(Subscription address:** ARS Polona, PO Box 1001, 00068 Warsaw Poland.**) LC** AP54; .O323. ***Supersedes*** *Odra.*
Ind/Abst MLA Int. Bibl. Books Artic. Mod. Lang. Lit.

AU
OESTERREICHISCHES JAHRBUCH. Added/Corp Austria. Bundespressedienst. (19??)-. German. an. S728.00. Verlag der Oesterreichischen Staatsdruckerei, Rennweg 12A, A-1037 Vienna Austria. **Tel** 011 43 1 797893766.

GW/0078-3714
OFFA. Vol. 1 (1936)-. German. an. **LC** DD51.3. **DD** 913.4351.
Ind/Abst Anthropol. Lit.; BHA : Biblio. Hist. Art; GeoRef.

IT
OGGI E DOMANI. Vol. 1 (Nov. 1973)-. Italian. Twelve times a year. L6000 (regular); L250000 (sustaining). Ediars SAS, Via Italica 56, 65127 Pescara Italy. **Tel** 011 39 85 4510812. **LC** AP37; .O34. **DD** 055/.1.
Ind/Abst Romant. Move.

RU/0131-0097
OGONEK. [Ogonek]. (Apr. 1, 1923)-. Periodical. Russian. wk. $139.95. **(Subscription address:** East View Publications Inc., 3020 Harbor Lane North, Suite 110, Minneapolis MN 55447.**) LC** AP50; .O42.
Ind/Abst Int. Aerosp. Abstr.; Curr. Dig. Post Sov. Press.

UK
OLD LADY OF THREADNEEDLE STREET, THE. Added/Corp Bank of England. Library and Literary Association. (Mar. 1921)-. Periodical. English. Four times a year. £5.00. Bank of England Bulletin Group, Threadneedle Street, London EC2R 8AH England. **Tel** 011 44 71 6014139. **LC** AP4; .O33. Index available. **Bk Rev.**

●UK/0965-2507
OLDIE (LONDON). (THE OLDIE.). (1992)-. English. sm. £35.00 UK; £45.00 Europe; £60.00 other. Oldie Publications Ltd, 26 Charlotte Street, London W1P 1HJ England. **Tel** 071-636-3686, FAX 071-636-3685. **ED** Richard Ingrams. **Ad Acc, Adv Mgr:** Hamish Miller. **Circ:** 30,000.

IT
ONDA TV. Italian. wk. L49900 Italy; L105000 other. Rusconi Editore Spa, Servicio Abbonements, V Le Sarca 235, 20126 Milan Italy. **Tel** 011 39 2 66192634.

PO
OPINIAO, A. Portuguese. 270.00. Rua de Serpa Pinto 162, Porto Portugal. **LC** AP65; .O73.

PL/0137-8546
OPOLE OPOLE. (OPOLE.). (1970)-. Periodical. Polish. mo. Price on Request. **(Subscription address:** ARS Polona, PO Box 1001, 00068 Warsaw Poland.**) UDC** 304(438). **CODEN** 338(438).
Desc: Covers the social and cultural life of the Opole region.

HU
ORSZAG VILAG. ***Ceased.*** 1957-?. Academic Scholarly Publication. Hungarian. wk. Akademiai Kiado, Publishing House of the Hungarian Academy of Sciences, Prielle Kornelia u. 19-35, H-1117 Budapest Hungary. **Tel** 011 36 1 1811991, FAX 011 36 1 1811991, telex 22-6228 AKNYO H. **(Subscription address:** Kultura, Hungarian Foreign Trading Company, PO Box 149, H-1389 Budapest Hungary**) LC** AP82; .O67.

General Interest —General Interest-Europe

RU
OTCHIZNA. Added/Corp Komitet "Za Vozvrashchenie na Rodinu." Sovetskii Komitet po Kulturnym Sviaziam s Sootechestvennikami za Rubezhom. (19??)-. Periodical. Russian. mo. $12.50. **(Subscription address:** Victor Kamkin, 4956 Boiling Brook Parkway, Rockville MD 20852.) **LC** AP50; .O83.

UK/0954-1306
OXFORD TODAY. Vol. 1, No. 1 (Michaelmas Issue 1988)-. Academic Scholarly Publication. English. Three times a year. £14.00 UK and Europe; $30.00 North America; £17.00 other. Basil Blackwell Publishers Ltd, 108 Cowley Road, Oxford OX4 1JF England. **Tel** 011 44 865 791100, **FAX** 011 44 865 791347, telex 837022 OXBOOK G. **(Subscription address:** Blackwell Publishers / UK, Marston Book Services, PO Box 87, Oxford OX2 0DT England.) **LC** WMLC L 83/7519. **[CCC]**. **Ind/Abst** Child. Lit. Abstr. (19??-).

LV
PADOMJU LATVIJAS SIEVIETE. Added/Corp Latvijas Komunistiska Partija. Centrala Komiteja. (Sept. 1952)-. Periodical. Latvian. mo. $11.00. Latvijas KP CK Izdevnieciba, Komunaru Bulvari 6 226098, Riga Latvia. **(Subscription address:** Victor Kamkin, 4956 Boiling Brook Parkway, Rockville MD 20852.) **LC** AP95.L4; P3.

IT/0553-1098
PANORAMA. Vol. 1, No. 1 (Oct. 1962)-. Periodical. Italian. wk. L103800 Italy; L215800 other. Arnoldo Mondadori Editore, UFF Cont Abbonamenti, 20090 Segrate MI Italy. **Tel** 011 39 2 75422015, telex 320457 MONDMI I. **LC** AP37; .P32.

PL/0138-0907
PANORAMA LESZCZYNSKA. (1979)-. Periodical. Polish. wk $39.00. **(Subscription address:** ARS Polona, PO Box 1001, 00068 Warsaw Poland.) **UDC** 304(438). **CODEN** 943.8.
Desc: Cultural and social publication for the Leszno region.

FR/1166-2344
PARIS CAPITALE... - PMR ED. FRANCAISE. (PARIS CAPITALE - PMR.). (198?)-. Periodical. French. mo. 165.00F France; 270.00F Europe; 500.00F North & South America; 400.00F Africa; 770.00F other. Paris Capitale, 59 Avenue Marceau, 75116 Paris France. **Tel** 011 33 1 44439540. **UDC** 082(443.611).

FR/0031-2029
PARIS-MATCH. [Paris-Match]. **VFOAT** Paris Match. No. 1, (March 1949)-. Periodical. French. wk. $140.00. Paris Match Inc., 99 rue d'Amsterdam, 75008 Paris France. **Tel** 011 33 1 42806855. **(Subscription address:** Express Magazine, 4011 Boulevard Robert, Montreal Quebec H1Z 4H6 Canada.) **LC** AP20; .P342.
Ind/Abst Point Repere (1983-).

FR/0397-1635
PARIS-MATCH 1976. (PARIS MATCH.). [Paris-Match 1976]. (1976)-. Periodical. French. wk. 580.00F. Publications Filipacchi, 63-65 Champs Elysees, 75008 Paris France. **Tel** 011 33 1 40747000, telex 651-294. **(Subscription address:** France/99 rue d'Amsterdam, 75008 Paris, France; US/Box 0007, Rouses Point, NY 12979) **Continues** Nouveau Paris-Match, 0337-8721.
Ind/Abst Point Repere (1989).

FR
PARIS PASSION : THE MAGAZINE OF THE FRENCH CAPITAL. Periodical. English. mo (eleven issues per year). 210.00F France; $40.00 North America; £18.00 UK; 280.00F Europe; $70.00 other. Robert Sarner, 23 rue Yves Toudic, F-75010 Paris France. **Tel** 42 39 15 80, **FAX** 42 39 01 26. **ED** Robert Sarner, Randy Koral, Mark Honigsbaum. **Bk Rev. Ad Acc. Circ:** 50,000. **Continues** Passion, 0293-0781.
Desc: The only English language city magazine devoted to life in Paris since 1981.

UK
PAX. Vol. 1, No. 1 (Sept. 1904)-. Periodical. English. qt. £2.50. Prinknash Abbey, Cranham Gloucester GL4 8EX England. **Tel** 0452 812455, **FAX** 0452 812529. **ED** Dom Hildebrand Flint. Index available in last issue of volume--attached. cum. index. **Circ:** 300. *Superseded in part by Eastern Churches Quarterly.*
Desc: Community news with excursus on monastic topics.
Ind/Abst Am. Humanit. Index (-19??).

FR/1149-3305
PAYS D'AUGE LISIEUX. 1951, LE. (1951)-. Periodical. French. mo. **UDC** 061.7 (442.2).
Ind/Abst BHA : Biblio. Hist. Art.

FR/0031-4773
PENSEE. (LA PENSEE.). [Pensee]. No. 1-3, (1939)- New Series No. 1 (1944)-. Periodical. French. Six times a year. 391.77F France; 700.00F other. IRM / Institut de Recherches Marxistes, 64 Boulevard Auguste Blanqui, 75013 Paris France. **Tel** 011 33 1 43364534. **LC** AP20; .P36. **DD** 054/.1. **Circ:** 2,000.

Ind/Abst Am. Hist. Life (1954-1974, 1977-1978); Int. Bibliogr. Sociol.; Int. Polit. Sci. Abstr.; MLA Int. Bibl. Books Artic. Mod. Lang. Lit.

PL/0031-6059
PERSPEKTYWY. Vol. 1 No. 1 (1969)-. Periodical. Polish. Fifty-two times a year. $60.00. **(Subscription address:** ARS Polona, PO Box 1001, 00068 Warsaw Poland.) **LC** AP54; .P47.

UN
PIONERIIA. Added/Corp Leninska Komunistychna Spilka Molodi Ukrainy. Tsentralnyi Komitet. (1923)-. Periodical. Ukrainian. mo $13.00. **(Subscription address:** Victor Kamkin, 4956 Boiling Brook Parkway, Rockville MD 20852.) **LC** AP215.U5; P5.

FR/0048-4229
PIROGUE (ISSY-LES-MOULINEAUX, FRANCE). (PIROGUE.). Periodical. French. qt. Editions Saint-Paul, Perolles 42, CH-1700 Fribourg Switzerland. **LC** BX1680.3; .P57. **DD** 282/.67/05.

PL
PLON. Added/Corp Zwiazek Kolek Rolniczych. Periodical. Polish. Twenty-six times a year. $32.00. **(Subscription address:** ARS Polona, PO Box 1001, 00068 Warsaw Poland.)

PL
POBRZEZE. Added/Corp Koszalinskie Towarzystwo Spoeczno-Kulturalne. (19??)-. Periodical. Polish. ir. RSW Prasa-Kriazka-Ruch, Centrala Kolportazu Prasy i Wydawnictw, Towarowa 28, 00-958 Warsaw Poland. **LC** AP54; .P576.

SZ
POLYGON. VFOAT Polygon Reporter. Vol. 8, 1 (Jan. 1991)-. Periodical. Czech. bm. **LC** AP52; .R39. **Continues** Reporter (Zurich, Switzerland).

IT/0394-4247
POPOLI. [Popoli]. (1987)-. Periodical. Italian. mo (except July and Aug.). L35000 Italy; L45000 other. Missioni della Compagnia di, Gesu Piazza S Fedele 4, 20121 Milan, Italy. **Tel** 011 39 2 722711, **FAX** 011 39 2 72023481. **UDC** 266. Index available (bound in Dec. issue). **Bk Rev** (Qty: 50). **Ad Acc. Continues** Popoli e Missioni, 0394-4220.

BL
POR QUE (SAO PAULO, BRAZIL). (POR QUE.). Periodical. Portuguese (Portuguese). qt. $20.00. Centro Brasileiro de Fomento Cultural, rua Riachuelo 326 Conj 143, CEP 01007 Sao Paulo SP Brazil. **LC** AP66; .P618. **DD** 056/.9.

XO
PRAVDA NA VIKEND. Vol. 1- 1. Nov. 1968-. Periodical. Slovak. Ustredry Vybor KSS, Ustredna Expedicia Tlace, Bratislava Slovakia. **LC** AP58.S53; P68.

FR/0750-3253
PRESENT PARIS. [Present Paris]. (1982)-. Periodical. French. Five times a year. 1225.00F France; 1955.00F other. Present, 5 rue d'Amboise, 75002 Paris France. **UDC** 07.

GW
PRESSESEMINAR DER BFA : REFERATE / HERAUSGEBER, BUNDESVERSICHERUNGSANSTALT FUER ANGESTELLTE, DEZERNAT FUER PRESSE UND OFFENTLICHKEITSARBEIT. Main/Conf Presseseminar der BFA. Added/Corp Bundesversicherungsanstalt fur Angestellte. Dezernat fur Presse- und Offentlichkeitsarbeit. (19??)-. German. an. Bundesversicherungsanstalt fur Angestellte, Dezernat fur Presse und Offentlichkeitsarbeit, Postfach, 1000 Berlin 88 Germany. **LC** PAR.

CN/0315-1557
PREVENIR (MONTREAL). (PREVENIR!). [Prevenir (Montr.)]. Added/Corp Mouvement Naturiste Social. **VAT** Prevenir (Montreal); Prevenir (Boucherville). No. 1 (May 1971)-. Periodical. French. Productions Nor, 7102 rue Saint-Denis, Montreal Quebec Canada.

UK
PROCEEDINGS OF THE ... INTERNATIONAL MATADOR CONFERENCE. See Recreation, Leisure-Sports.

AU
PROFIL (VIENNA, AUSTRIA : 1979). (PROFIL.). (19??)-. Periodical. German. wk. S1670.00 Austrai; S1150.00 other. Wirtschafts Trend Zeitschrift Verlagsges, Marc Aurel Strasse 10, A 0101 Vienna, Austria. **Tel** 011 43 1 5347055. **ED** Herbert Ladauer, Josef Votzi. **LC** AP30; .P865. **DD** 053/.1. **Bk Rev. Ad Acc. Circ:** 96,000. available with illustrations. **Continues** Profil Mit Ecco.
Ind/Abst MLA Int. Bibl. Books Artic. Mod. Lang. Lit.

PL/0138-0893
PRZEGLAD KONINSKI. VFOAT PK. Przeglad Koninski. (1980)-. Periodical. Polish. wk. $65.00. **(Subscription address:** ARS Polona, PO Box 1001, 00068 Warsaw Poland.) **UDC** 304(438). **CODEN** 943.8.
Desc: Cultural and social publication for the Konin region.

PL/0867-3772
PRZEGLAD NARODOWY. (1990)-. Periodical. Polish. Twenty-six times a year. Price on Request. **(Subscription address:** ARS Polona, PO Box 1001, 00068 Warsaw Poland.) **UDC** 943.8. **CODEN** 327.

PL/0209-0023
PRZEGLAD TYGODNIOWY. (19??)-. Newspaper. Polish. wk. $78.00. **(Subscription address:** ARS Polona, PO Box 1001, 00068 Warsaw Poland.)
Desc: Review of society, science and culture.

PL
PRZEKROJ. (April 15, 1945)-. Periodical. Polish. wk. $143.00. **(Subscription address:** ARS Polona, PO Box 1001, 00068 Warsaw Poland.) **LC** AP54; .P82.

NE
PYTTERSEN'S NEDERLANDSE ALMANAK. 1963-. Dutch. an. Fl121.00. Postbus 23, 7400 GA Deventer Netherlands. **Tel** 05700-10011. **Bk Rev. Ad Acc. Circ:** 5,000 (ctrl). **Continues** Pyttersen's Nederlandse Almanak voor Iedereen.
Desc: Approximately 850 pages with more than 55,000 names and over 15,000 addresses of the most important social, political and educational institutions in the Netherlands.

IT
QUADERNI CALABRESI : QUADERNI DEL MEZZOGIORNO E DELLE ISOLE. Italian. bm (6 issues). L35000 Italy; L60000 other. Qualecultura Ed., V S Maria Imperio 29, 88018 Vibo Valentia CZ Italy. **Tel** 011 39 963 43685. **Bk Rev. Pr Rev.**
Desc: A cultural, social and political publication.

IT
QUALESOCIETA. Yearly V. 1- May/June 1972-. Italian. $10.00. c/c 1/62053 Intestato A Napoleone Editore, Rome Italy. **LC** AP37; .Q35.

SP
RADIO NACIONAL DE ESPANA. Spanish. $110.00. Radio Nacional de Espana, Prog Coop Cult Intl, Apartad 156.201, Madrid 28080 Spain.

ER/0234-8179
RADUGA. Added/Corp Eesti Kirjanike Liit. Eestimaa Leninlik Kommunistlik Noorsoouning. Keskkomitee. (July 1986)-. Periodical. Russian. mo $109.95. Kirjastus Perioodika, PO Box 107, Parnu Mnt 8, Tallinn EE0090 Estonia. **Tel** 0142 441 262, **FAX** 0142 442 484. **(Subscription address:** East View Publications Inc., 3020 Harbor Lane North, Suite 110, Minneapolis MN 55447.) **LC** AP50; .V55.

RM
RAMURI. Added/Corp Comitetul Pentru Cultura si Arta al Regiunii Oltenia. (19??)-. Periodical. Romanian. mo. DM145.00. **(Subscription address:** Kubon & Sagner, ABT Zeitschriftenimport, D 80328 Munich Germany.) **LC** AP86; .R35.
Desc: Socio-cultural review.
Ind/Abst Annu. Bibliogr. Engl. Lang. Lit.

UN
RANOK. Added/Corp Leninska Komunistychna Spilka Molodi Ukrainy. Tsentralnyi Komitet. (July 1965)-. Periodical. Ukrainian. mo. $17.00. **(Subscription address:** Victor Kamkin, 4956 Boiling Brook Parkway, Rockville MD 20852.) **LC** AP58.U5; Z5. **Continues** Zmina.

PL
RAZEM. Added/Corp Federacja Socjalistycznych Zwiazkow Modziezy Polskiej. (19??)-. Periodical. Polish. wk. **(Subscription address:** ARS Polona, PO Box 1001, 00068 Warsaw Poland.) **LC** AP54; .R32.

AI
REBORN ARMENIA. Ceased. Added/Corp Committee for Cultural Relations with Armenians Abroad (Yerevan, Armenian S.S.R.) Armianskoe Obshchestvo Druzhby i Kulturnoi Sviazi s Zarubezhnymi Stranami. (19??)-(1992). Periodical. Armenian, English, Russian, French, German and Spanish). mo. Reborn Armenia, 37 Alaverdiant Street, Yerevan 375010 Armeniia. **(Subscription address:** Victor Kamkin, 4956 Boiling Brook Parkway, Rockville MD 20852.) **LC** DK680; .V69. **DD** 947/.92/005.
Desc: Covers material dealing with the development of economy, science and technique, social life, culture and art of Armenia.

FR
RECHERCHES INSTITUTIONNELLES. No. 1 (1978?)-. Monographic series. French. Price varies per volume. CERDIC Universite des Sciences Humaines de Strasbourg, Palais Universitaire, 2 rue Goethe, 67000 Strasbourg France. **ED** Marie Zimmermann and Jean

Schlick.
Desc: Covers areas of law and church, institutions and history, culture and religion, and documentary research.

IE
REPORT / JOINT COMMITTEE ON THE SECONDARY LEGISLATION OF THE EUROPEAN COMMUNITIES. **Main/Corp** Ireland. Oireachtas. Joint Committee on the Secondary Legislation of the European Communities. English. Government Publications, 4 5 Harcourt Road, Dublin 2 Ireland. **Tel** 011 353 1 6613111 Ext.4005. **LC** HC241.25.I7; I74A. ***Continues*** *Tuairisc Oifigiuil - An Comhchoiste Ar Reachtaiocht Tanaisteach na Gcomhphobal Eorpach.*

SP
REVISTA DE GEOGRAFIA CANARIA. **VFOAT** Revista Geografia. (1985)-. Periodical. English. **LC** DP302.C39; R38.

AA
REVISTA LETRARO-ARTISTIKE. (19??)-. Periodical. Albanian. mo. $20.00. Book Distribution Enterprise, Rruga Kavajes, Tirana, Albania. **Tel** 011 355 42 27246. ***Continues*** *Nentori.*
Ind/Abst MLA Int. Bibl. Books Artic. Mod. Lang. Lit.

SP
REVISTA MANRESA. Spanish. qt. $25.50. Centro Loyola, Pablo Aranda 3, 28006 Madrid Spain. **Tel** 011 34 1 565-4930, 562-6604, FAX 011 34 1 563-4073.

FR
REVOLUTION. No 1- 7/13 Mar. 1980-. Periodical. French. $93.12. Revolution, 15 rue Montmartre, 75001 Paris France. **Tel** 233 61 26. **LC** AP20; .R2425. **DD** 054/.1. ***Supersedes*** *Nouvelle Critique.*

LI
REVUE BALTIQUE : THE JOURNAL OF COOPERATION OF THE BALTIC STATES. **VFOAT** Balti Revuu; Baltijas Apskats; Baltijos Apzvalga. Vol. 2, No. 1 (Feb. 1991)-. Periodical. English (German). tq. **LC** IN PROCESS. ***Continues*** *Baltic Review (New York, N.Y.), 0005-4445.*

BE/0035-3809
REVUE NOUVELLE, LA. Vol. 1, (Feb. 1945)-. Periodical. French. Ten times a year. 2650F Belgium; 3250F other; 3750F others (airmail). Artel, Place Baudouin IER 2, B-5004 Namur Belgium. **Tel** 011 32 81 213700, FAX 011 32 81 212372. **LC** AP22; .R72. **DD** 054. Index available. cum. index. **Bk Rev. Ad Acc. Circ:** 4,000.
Desc: General interest review survey of international life, economic policy and political life in Belgium, plus main aspects of cultural life in Belgium and Europe.
Ind/Abst Int. Polit. Sci. Abstr.; Romant. Move.

IT
RISCONTRI. Yearly V. 1- Jan./March 1979-. Periodical. Italian. 14000. Sabatia Editrice, V Pugliese, Via S T Iannaccone 6, 83100 Avellino Italy. **LC** AP37; .R45.
Ind/Abst MLA Int. Bibl. Books Artic. Mod. Lang. Lit.

IT/0391-4240
RIVISTA DI STORIA CONTEMPORANEA. [Riv. stor. contemp.]. Began publication with year 1, Issue 1 (1972)?. Periodical. Italian. qt. L55.000. Loescher Editore, Via Vittorio Amedeo 18, 10121 Turin Italy. **Tel** 011 39 11 5624622. Index available. Documents available from The Genuine Article.
Ind/Abst Am. Hist. Life (1991-); Arts Humanit. Citation Index [Full Cov.]; Curr. Contents Arts Humanit.; Res. Alert [Full Cov.]; Soc. Sci. Cit. Index [Select. Cov.].

RM/0048-8658
ROMANIA, DOCUMENTS, EVENTS / ROMANIAN NEWS AGENCY, AGERPRES. **Added/Corp** Agentia Romana de Presa. Agentia Romina de Presa. (Jan. 11, 1971)-. Periodical. English. wk. $50.00. **(Subscription address:** Ilexim Press Department, PO Box 1, 136-1-137, Bucharest, Romania.**)** **LC** DR267; .R63. **DD** 949.8/03. ***Continues*** *Documents, Articles and Information on Romania.*
Desc: Information bulletin of the Romanian press agency.

RM
ROMANIAN NEWS (BUCHAREST, ROMANIA). (ROMANIAN NEWS : RN.). **VFOAT** RN. No. 1 (Mar. 21, 1978)-. Periodical. English. wk. DM150.00. **(Subscription address:** Kubon & Sagner, ABT Zeitschriftenimport, D 80328 Munich Germany.**)**

●UK/0967-5744
ROYALTY DIGEST. [R. dig.]. (1991)-. Periodical. English. Twelve times a year. £20.00 UK; £25.00 Europe; £35.00 others. Piccadilly Rare Books, Old Knolefrant, Kent TN3 9EJ England. **Tel** 011 44 892 750201, FAX 011 44 892 750340. **ED** Paul Minet. **DD** 929.7094. Index available (Published separately loose). cum. index. **Bk Rev. Ad Acc. Circ:** 1,000.

SZ
ROZHLAD ; CASOPIS ZA SERBSKU KULTURU. Periodical. Sorbian languages. mo. Deutscher Judo Verband, Redaktion Ippon Segewaldweg 40, D 12557 Berlin Germany. **Tel** 011 49 711 210770, telex 051 678. **LC** AP58.W4.

PO
RUA, A. Yearly V. 1- April 8, 1976-. Periodical. Portuguese. 1400.00. Distribuidora da Imprensa Geral, rua das Chagas 2, Lisbon 2 Portugal. **LC** DP680; .R73.

●US/1062-3574
RUSSIA, EURASIAN STATES, AND EASTERN EUROPE. **See** General Interest-General Interest-Asia.

●US/1066-999X
RUSSIAN LIFE. [Russ. life]. Vol. 36, No. 1 (Spring 1993)-. Periodical. English. Six times a year. $25.00. Russian Life, 1706 Eighteenth Street Northwest, Washington DC 20009. **Tel** (202)328-3224. **(Subscription address:** Russian Life Magazine, PO Box 7716, Riverton, NJ 08077; Phone: (718)279-2630**)** **LC** DK1; .U67. **DD** 914. ***Continues*** *Soviet Life, 0038-5549.*

FR/0048-9018
SAISONS D'ALSACE STRASBOURG. [Saisons AlsaceStrasbourg]. (1949)-. Periodical. Multiple languages. qt. Dernieres Nouvelles d'Alsace, 17-21 rue de la Nuee-Bleue,, 67000 Strasbourg Cedex, France. **Tel** 88-23-30-83, FAX 88-75-16-21. **ED** Bernard Reumaux. **UDC** 39(443.83). **Bk Rev. Ad Acc.**
Ind/Abst BHA : Biblio. Hist. Art.

NO/0036-3928
SAMTIDEN. [Samtiden]. Vol. 1 (1890)-. Periodical. Norwegian. bm (6 issues). Kr416.67. H. Aschehoug & Company, Sehesteds Plass, Oslo 1 Norway. **Tel** 011 47 2 206395. **(Subscription address:** Forlagsentralen Tidsskriftavd, PO Box 150, Furuset 1001 Oslo 1 Norway; telephone: 011 47 2 200710**)** **LC** AP45; .S22. Index available (bound in last issue). cum. index.
Ind/Abst Am. Hist. Life (1954-); Annu. Bibliogr. Engl. Lang. Lit.; ARTbibliogr. Mod.; MLA Int. Bibl. Books Artic. Mod. Lang. Lit.

GW/0303-4232
SCALA. ***Title Change.*** (19??)-(Oct. 1993). English (German, French, Portuguese and Spanish). bm. Frankfurter Societatsdruckerei, Postfach 100801, D 60008 Frankfurt Germany. **Tel** 011 49 69 75014807, telex 411655. **ED** Werner Wirthle and Gerd Hofmann. **LC** AP4; .S372. **Bk Rev. Ad Acc.** ctrl circ. ***Continues*** *Scala International. English Edition.* ***Continued by*** *Deutschland.*
Desc: This a periodical of the FRG with the main task to convey to readers abroad a true impression of life in present day Germany.
Ind/Abst Ecol. Abstr.; Geogr. Abstr. Phys. Geogr.; Geogr. Abstr. Human Geogr.; Geol. Abstr.; Int. Dev. Abstr. (?-?).

GW/0340-0441
SCALA DEUTSCHE AUSGABE. ***Title Change.*** [Scala Dtsch. Ausg.]. (1974)-(19??). Periodical. German. bm. Frankfurter Societatsdruckerei, Postfach 100801, D 60008 Frankfurt Germany. **Tel** 011 49 69 75014807, telex 411655. **UDC** 008. ***Continues*** *Scala International (Deutsche Ausgabe), 0581-9385.* ***Continued by*** *Deutschland.*

GW/0581-9385
SCALA INTERNATIONAL. ***Title Change.*** (1961)-(19??). Periodical. German (French, Spanish and English). Six times a year. Frankfurter Societatsdruckerei, Postfach 100801, D 60008 Frankfurt Germany. **Tel** 011 49 69 75014807, telex 411655. **ED** Werner Wirthle. Index available. **Ad Acc. Circ:** 13,000 (ctrl). ***Continued by*** *Scala, 0303-4232.*
Desc: Current social, scientific, cultural, and economic achievements in West Germany. Available in four languages in the United States.

US/1041-2018
SCHAU INS LAND. SOUND RECORDING. [Schau Land]. **VFOAT** Schau Ins Land Transcription. Series 1, No. 1 (Spring 1987)-. German (English). Eleven times a year (June/July combined). $118.00 US, $122.00 Canada, $138.00 others (audio); $16.50 (extra transcripts); $162.00 US, $166.00 Canada, $182.00 other (audio plus study supplements). Champs-Elysees Inc, Box 158067, Nashville TN 37215-8067. **Tel** (800)824-0829, (615)383-8534, FAX (615) 297-3138. **ED** Ingrid Sevin. **DD** 053. Index available. cum. index. available on videocassette.
Desc: Recorded periodical intended for college-level foreign language instruction; issues contain current news items, songs, and other information on the subject of modern German culture.

GW
SCHAUPLATZ KOLN. 1987-. German.

SZ
SCHWEIZER ILLUSTRIERTE. SIE + I.E. UND ER. Periodical. German. 99.70. Ringier & Company AG, Florastrasse, CH-4800 Zofingen Switzerland. **Tel** 011 41 62 503110. **LC** AP32; .S448. ***Formed by the union of*** *Schweizer Illustrierte Zeitung* ***and*** *SIE und ER.*

SZ/0036-7362
SCHWEIZER ILLUSTRIERTE ZEITUNG. (19??)-. Periodical. German. Fifty-two times a year. $178.00. Ringier & Company AG, Florastrasse, CH-4800 Zofingen Switzerland. **Tel** 011 41 62 503110.

SZ/0036-7400
SCHWEIZER MONATSHEFTE. [Schweiz. Mon.hefte]. **VFOAT** Schweizer Monatshefte fur Politik, Wirtschaft, Kultur. Vol. 11 (April 1931)-. Periodical. German. mo. 80.00F. Schulthess Polygraphischer Verlag, Zwinglipl atz 2, CH-8022 Zurich Switzerland. **Tel** 011 41 1 2519336. **LC** AP32; .S47. **DD** 053. available on microfilm and microfiche from University Microfilms International (UMI). ***Continues*** *Schweizerische Monatshefte fur Politik und Kultur.*
Ind/Abst Am. Hist. Life (1959-); Annu. Bibliogr. Engl. Lang. Lit.; Int. Polit. Sci. Abstr.; MLA Int. Bibl. Books Artic. Mod. Lang. Lit.

UK
SCOTS MAGAZINE, THE. V. 1- April 1924-. Periodical. English. mo. $48.00. D C Thomson and Company Ltd, 80 Kingsway East, Dundee DD1 8SL Scotland. **Tel** 011 44 382 23131. **ED** Maurice Fleming. **LC** AP4; .S3732. Index available. cum. index. **Bk Rev. Ad Acc. Circ:** 83,000. ***Supersedes*** *Edinburgh Magazine, and Literary Miscellany.*
Desc: World's oldest popular periodical. Feature articles with color photographs on all topics of Scottish interest except religion and politics.
Ind/Abst Br. Humanit. Index.

US
SELECOES DO READER'S DIGEST; ARTIGOS DE INTERESSE PERMANENTE. Vol. 1, No. 1 (Feb. 1942)-. Periodical. Portuguese. mo. Selecoes do Reader's Digest, rua Joaquim Aguiar 43, 1091 Lisbon Portugal. **Tel** 011 351 1 659871. **Bk Rev. Ad Acc.**

FR/0037-1386
SELECTION DU READER'S DIGEST PARIS. [Sel. Read. Dig. Paris]. (1947)-. Periodical. French. Twelve times a year. 175.00F France; 291.00F other. Selection du Readers Digest SA, 1 A 7 Avenue Louis Pasteur, 92220 Bagneux France. **Tel** 011 33 1 46641020. **UDC** 05. available on microfilm and microfiche from University Microfilms International (UMI).

IT/0037-1483
SELEZIONE DAL READER'S DIGEST. (1948)-. Periodical. Italian. Twelve times a year. L59950. Selezione dal Reader's Digest, Via Alserio 10, 20159 Milan Italy. **Tel** 011 39 2 6987555, FAX 011 39 2 6987401, telex 330378. **ED** Pietro Mariano Benni. **Ad Acc. Circ:** 800,000 (ctrl).
Desc: Art of better living, money investment, medicine, science, self-improvement, home improvement, family care, fiction, politics.

FI/0358-8017
SEURA 1979. (SEURA.). [Seura 1979]. (1979)-. Periodical. Finnish. Fifty times a year. Fmk874.00. Yhtyneet Kuvalehdet Oy, Maistraatinportti 1, 00240 Helsinki Finland. **Tel** 011 358 0 15661, FAX 011 358 0 1566505, telex 121364. **UDC** 79. ***Continues*** *Suur-Seura, 0355-189X.*

XR
SEZNAM PREDNASEK LEKARSKE FAKULTY V HRADCI KRALOVE VE STUDIJNIM ROCE ... . **Main/Corp** Universita Karlova. Lekarska Fakulta V Hradci Kralove. (19??)-. Czech. Charles University / Univerzita Karlova, Ovocnytrh 5, 116 36 Prague 1 Czech Republic. **Tel** 228441. **LC** LF1461.C5; U5475.

RU
SIBIRSKIE OGNI. **Added/Corp** Soiuz Pisatelei SSSR. Novosibirskoe Otdelenie. Soiuz Sovetskikh Pisatelei Zapadnoi Sibiri. Soiuz Pisatelei RSFSR. Novosibirskaia Pisatelskaia Organizatsiia. (1922)-. Periodical. Russian. mo. $90.00 domestic airmail; $99.00 international airmail. **(Subscription address:** East View Publications Inc., 3020 Harbor Lane North, Suite 110, Minneapolis MN 55447.**)** cum. index.

GW/0037-5756
SINN UND FORM. [Sinn form]. **Added/Corp** Deutsche Akademie der Kunste zu Berlin. Vol. 1 (1949)-. Periodical. German. Six times a year (Feb., Apr., June, Aug., Oct., Dec.). DM64.20. Aufbau Verlag Berlin & Weimar, Franzoesische Str. 32, D 10117 Berlin Germany. **Tel** 011 49 30 22350, FAX 011 49 30 2298637. **(Subscription address:** Tableau GmBH, Heinrich Roller STR 17, D 10405 Berlin Germany.**)** **LC** AP30; .S535. **DD** 053/.1. Index available (Free). **Ad Acc. Circ:** 3,500. Documents available from The Genuine Article.
Ind/Abst Annu. Bibliogr. Engl. Lang. Lit.; Arts Humanit. Citation Index [Full Cov.]; Curr. Contents Arts Humanit.; MLA Int. Bibl. Books Artic. Mod. Lang. Lit.; Res. Alert [Full Cov.]; Romant. Move.; Soc. Sci. Cit. Index [Select. Cov.].

General Interest —General Interest-Europe

SW/0282-941X
SIP NEWSLETTER FROM SWEDEN (ENGLISH EDITION). (NEWSLETTER FROM SWEDEN / SIP.). [SIP newsl. Swed.]. **Added/Corp** Swedish-International Press Bureau. **VFOAT** Swedish-International Press Bureau Newsletter from Sweden (English Edition). (19??)-. Periodical. English (Turkish). Forty times a year. Free to journalists and news media. Swedish-International Press Bureau, PO Box 5529, S-114 85 Stockholm Sweden. **Tel** 011 46 8 7838080.
Ind/Abst F&S Index Plus Text, Int. [Select. Cov.]; Pap. Board Abstr.; PROMT.

RU
SMENA. **Added/Corp** Vsesoiuznyi Leninskii Kommunisticheskii Soiuz Molodezhi. Tsentralnyi Komitet. Vol. 1, (1924)-. Periodical. Russian. mo. $99.95. Izdatelstvo Pressa, Myasnitskaia 24, 101877 Moscow Russia. **Tel** 011 95 923 2122, FAX 011 95 200 2259. **(Subscription address:** East View Publications Inc., 3020 Harbor Lane North, Suite 110, Minneapolis MN 55447.**) LC** AP215.R9; S6. **Bk Rev.** available on microfilm from University Microfilms International (UMI).
Desc: Includes popular songs (words and music).

XV/0038-0482
SODOBNOST. [Sodobnost]. **Added/Corp** Drzavna Zalozba Slovenije. Vol. 11 (1963)-. Periodical. Slovenian. mo. $12.15 US and Canada; $9.50 other. Drzavna Zalozba Slovenije, 61000 Ljubljana, Mestni TRG 26 Slovenia. **Tel** (61)152040, FAX (61)215675. **ED** Ciril Zlobec. **LC** AP58.S55; S59. Index available. cum. index. **Bk Rev. Circ:** 1,600 (ctrl). ***Continues*** *Nasa Sodobnost.*
Ind/Abst MLA Int. Bibl. Books Artic. Mod. Lang. Lit.

SW
SOME DATA ABOUT SWEDEN. English. an. Kr180.00. Skandinaviska Enskildz Bankey, 10640 Stockholm Sweden. **Tel** +468-7635000. **ED** Carina Norlander. **LC** HC371; .S64. **DD** 330.9/485/05. **Ad Acc. Circ:** 20,000.

US/0094-4467
SOUTHEASTERN EUROPE (PITTSBURGH). (SOUTHEASTERN EUROPE.). [Southeast. Eur.]. **Added/Corp** Arizona State University. University of Pittsburgh. University Center for International Studies. Temple University. **VFOAT** L'Europe du Sud-Est; Europe du Sud-Est. Vol. 1 (1974)-. Periodical. English (French, German and Russian). sa. $20.00. CMTS USC / Charles Schlacks Jr. Publisher, 734 West Adams Boulevard, Kerckhoff Hall, Los Angeles CA 90089. **Tel** (203)743-6510. **ED** Charles Schlacks Jr. **LC** DR2; .S65. **DD** 914.96/03/05. Index available. **Bk Rev. Ad Acc. Circ:** 300 (ctrl). available on microfilm and microfiche from University Microfilms International (UMI).
Desc: Balkan studies in the humanities and social sciences.
Ind/Abst Am. Hist. Life (1974-); Am. Bibliogr. Slavic East Europ. Stud. (19??-19??).

US/0038-5794
SOVIET REVIEW (WHITE PLAINS), THE. ***Title Change.*** (THE SOVIET REVIEW.). [Sov. rev.]. Vol. 1 (Aug. 1960)-Vol. 33, No. 1 (Jan./Feb 1992). Periodical. English (translations available in Russian). bm. M. E. Sharpe Inc., 80 Business Park Drive, Armonk NY 10504. **Tel** (914)273-1800, (800)541-6563, FAX (914)273-2106. **ED** A Joseph Hollander. **LC** AS261; .S6. **DD** 057/.1. **Bk Rev. Ad Acc. Circ:** 700 (ctrl). available on microfilm and microfiche from University Microfilms International (UMI). ***Supersedes*** *Soviet Highlights.* ***Continued by*** *Russian Social Science Review, 1061-1428.*
Desc: A unique survey of current work in economics, archeology, law, education, government, anthropology, literature, history, psychology, philosophy, and sociology drawn from a broad range of Soviet publications.
Ind/Abst Acad. Abstr. Full Text Elite (July 1990-Feb. 1992); Acad. Abstr. (July 1990-Feb. 1992); Acad. Search (July 1990-Feb. 1992); INFO-SOUTH Abstr.; Mag. Search; MLA Int. Bibl. Books Artic. Mod. Lang. Lit.; Soc. Sci. Source (Jul. 1990-Feb. 1992).

UK
SOVIET WEEKLY. ***Ceased.*** Began publication in 1945-Ceased in Dec. (1991). Periodical. English. wk. Soviet Weekly, 3 Rosary Gardens, London SW7 4NW England. **Tel** (01)373-8421. **Ad Acc.** ***Continues*** *Soviet War News Weekly.*
Desc: News, articles, and features on Soviet and international life and events. and social life.

PL/0208-4163
SOWO PODLASIA. (1979)-. Periodical. Polish. wk. $39.00. **(Subscription address:** ARS Polona, PO Box 1001, 00068 Warsaw Poland.**) UDC** 304(438). **CODEN** 943.8.
Desc: Cultural and social publication for the Biala Podlaska region.

BE
SPECTATOR. (19??)-. Periodical. Dutch. Fifty-two times a year. 1250F Belgium; 1520F Netherlands: 1720F others. Het Vokl - P DeBaere / Spectator, Forelstraat 22, 9000 Gent Belgium. **LC** AP15; .S613. **DD** 053.931.
Ind/Abst Appl. Soc. Sci. Index Abstr.

UK/0038-6952
SPECTATOR (LONDON. 1828). (THE SPECTATOR.). [Spectator]. No. 1 (July 5, 1828)-. Periodical. English. Fifty-one times per year. £80.00 UK; $175.00 US; £91.00 Europe; £111.00 other. The Spectator Ltd, PO Box 14 The Business Centre Harold Hill, Romford RM3 8EQ England. **Tel** 44 708 381122, FAX 44 708 381211, telex 927809. **ED** Charles Moore. **LC** AP4; .S7. Index Available, published separately, free-automatically sent. **Bk Rev. Ad Acc. Circ:** 35,000. available on microfilm and microfiche from University Microfilms International (UMI). Documents available from UMI Article Clearinghouse.
Desc: Covers politics, international affairs, literature and the arts.
Ind/Abst Annu. Bibliogr. Engl. Lang. Lit.; Book Rev. Index; Br. Humanit. Index; Newsp. Period. Abstr. (1988-); Peace Res. Abstr. J. (1966-1968, 1973-1975).

GW/0038-7452
SPIEGEL (HAMBURG), DER. (DER SPIEGEL.). [Spiegel (Hambg.)]. Vol. 1, No. 1 (Jan. 4, 1947)-. Periodical. German. wk. $280.00. Rudolf Augstein Verlag KG der Spiegel Verlag, Postfach 110420, W-2000 Hamburg 11 Germany. **Tel** 011 49 40 30071. **(Subscription address:** German Language Publishing Inc., 153 South Deanstreet, Englewood, NJ 07631**) ED** Rudolf Augstein. **LC** AP30; .S66. **DD** 053. Index available. **Bk Rev. Ad Acc.** ***Continues*** *Diese Woche.*
Ind/Abst Energy Res. Abstr. (June 1975-); Infomat Int. Bus.; PAIS Int. Print.

PL
SPRAWY I LUDZIE. Vol. 1, No. 1 (1982)-. Periodical. Polish. wk. 15.00 each issue. Robotnicza Spodzielnia Wydawnicza, Prasa-Ksi Azka-Ruch Wrocawskie Wydawn, Prasowe Podwale 62, 50-010 Wroclaw Poland. **LC** AP54; .S67.

RU/0131-8721
SPUTNIK (ANGL. JAZ.). (SPUTNIK : DIGEST.). [Sputnik]. **VFOAT** Digest. (1967)-. Academic Scholarly Publication. English (French, German, Portuguese, Spanish and Russian). mo. $119.95. Novosti Press Agency Publishing House, 4 Zubovski Boulevard, Moscow Russia. **Tel** 095-201-2424, FAX 095-201-2119, telex 411321. **(Subscription address:** East View Publications Inc., 3020 Harbor Lane North, Suite 110, Minneapolis MN 55447.**) LC** AP50; .S682. **Bk Rev. Ad Acc.**
Desc: Reprints political articles, reports, memoirs, scholarly essays, stories and business information from the Post-Soviet press; includes running fashions, hobbies and humor columns.

GW
STADTGRUPPEN- UND MITGLIEDERVERZEICHNIS / DEUTSCHE GESELLSCHAFT FUER HERPETOLOGIE UND TERRARIENKUNDE E.V., DGHT. ***Title Change.*** **Main/Corp** Deutsche Gesellschaft fur Herpetologie und Terrarienkunde. (198?)-(19??). German. **LC** QL35; .D48a. **DD** 597.6/06/043. ***Continues*** *Deutsche Gesellschaft fur Herpetologie und Terrarienkunde. Mitgliederverzeichnis.* ***Continued by*** *Deutsche Gesellschaft fur Herpetologie und Terrarienkunde. Mitglieder-Verzeichnis mit Ubersicht der Arbeits-, Landes-, Regional- und Stadtgruppen.*

GW
STATISTIK DES AUSLANDES. LANDERBERICHT. FINLAND. **VFOAT** Landerbericht. Finnland. German (table of contents in English). Verlag W Kohlhammer GmbH, Abt Veroffentlichungen des Statistischen Bundesamtes, Philipp-Reis-Strasse 3, W-6500 Mainz 42 Germany. **LC** HA1450.5; .A39. **DD** 314.897/05. ***Continues*** *Landerkurzberichte. Finnland.*

GW
STATISTIK DES AUSLANDES. LANDERBERICHT. SCHWEDEN. **VFOAT** Landerbericht. Schweden. German (table of contents in English). W Kohlhammer Verlag GmbH, Postfach 800430, D 70549 Stuttgart Germany. **Tel** 011 49 711 78631, FAX 011 49 711 7863263, telex 7-255820. **LC** HA1522; .S73. **DD** 314.85/05. ***Formed by the union of*** *Landerberichte. Schweden* ***and*** *Landerkurzberichte. Schweden.*

GW
STERN MAGAZIN. (19??)-. Periodical. German. wk. $230.00. Gruner und Jahr Ag & Co, Abonnenten Service, D 20080 Hamburg Germany. **Tel** 011 49 40 37030. **LC** AP30; .S675. **DD** 053/.1. ***Continues*** *Stern, 0039-1239.*

IT/1121-1288
STOP MILANO. [Stop Milano]. (1963)-. Periodical. Italian. wk. L83200 Italy; L140000 other. Ind Grafiche Cino Del Duca, Via Borgogna 5, 20122 Milan Italy. **Tel** 011 39 2 781051. **UDC** 05.

GW
STRANA I MIR. ***Ceased.*** **VFOAT** Das Land und die Welt; Our Country and the World; Land und die Welt. (1984)-(1992). Periodical. Russian. bm. Das Land und die Welt E V, Schwanthalerstr 73, W-8000 Munich 2 Germany. **Tel** 089-530514, (089)534603, telex 5218017. **ED** C Lubarsky and B Khazanov. **LC** AP50; .S777. **Bk Rev. Circ:** 2,200 (ctrl).
Desc: Political, economical, philosophical and cultural Russian journal, directed to the reader in the USSR.

IE/0039-3495
STUDIES. [Studies]. Vol. 1 No. 1 (Mar. 1912)-. Periodical. English. qt. $30.00 (individual); $35.00 (institution). Studies - An Irish Quarterly, 35 Lower Leeson Street, Dublin 2 Ireland. **Tel** 11 353 1 6766785. **ED** Noel Barber. **LC** AP4; .S78. **DD** 052. Index available. cum. index. **Bk Rev. Ad Acc. Circ:** 3,000 (ctrl). available on microfilm and microfiche from University Microfilms International (UMI).
Desc: Founded in 1912, it analyses social, political, economic, historical, literary and religious questions in modern Ireland and abroad.
Ind/Abst Abstr. Engl. Stud.; Am. Hist. Life (1955-); Annu. Bibliogr. Engl. Lang. Lit.; Geogr. Abstr. Human Geogr. (?-?); MLA Int. Bibl. Books Artic. Mod. Lang. Lit.; Abr. Cathol. Period. Lit. Index; Cathol. Period. Lit. Index.

UK
SUFFOLK REVIEW (1983). (THE SUFFOLK REVIEW.). No. 1 (Sept. 1983)-. Periodical. English. sa. ***Continues*** *Suffolk Review.*

UK
SUNDAY TIMES MAGAZINE, LONDON. (196?)-. Periodical. English. wk. Thomson Newspapers, 16 Brock Street, Woodstock Ontario N4S 8A5 Canada. **Tel** (519)537-2341. ***Continues*** *Sunday Times Colour Section, London.*
Ind/Abst Child. Lit. Abstr. (19??-).

FI/0039-5552
SUOMEN KUVALEHTI. (1917)-. Periodical. Finnish. wk. Fmk580.00 Finland; Fmk680.00 Scandinavia; Fmk 840.00 other. Yhtyneet Kuvalehdet Oy, Maistraatinportti 1, 00240 Helsinki Finland. **Tel** 011 358 0 15661, FAX 011 358 0 1566505, telex 121364. **LC** AP80; .S83.
Desc: Some numbers of vols. for 19 (25)-accompanied by supplementary issues called Kuvalehden Kertomisto.

FI/0359-0607
SUOMEN MATKAILU. **VFOAT** Matkailu. Periodical. Finnish (Swedish). Six times a year. Fmk80.00. Mikonkatu, 25 PL776, 00100 Helsinki 10 Finland. **Tel** (90)170-868. **(Subscription address:** Suomen Matkailuliitto, Box 776, 00101 Helsinki Finland**) ED** Suomen Matkailuliitto. **LC** G149; .M3. **Bk Rev. Ad Acc. Circ:** 35,000 (ctrl). ***Continues*** *Matkailumaailma.*
Desc: Finland hotel industry, recreation, leisure, games and amusements, outdoor life, sports, travel, and literature.

SW
SVERIGEKONTAKT. **Added/Corp** Riksforeningen for Svenskhetens Bevarande i Utlandet. (1972)-. Periodical. Swedish. Four times a year. $10.00. Riksforeningen Sverigekontakt, Teatergatan 4, S 41135 Goteborg Sweden. **Tel** 031 134245. **LC** AP48; .A44. ***Continues*** *Allsvensk Samling.*

NO/0039-7717
SYN OG SEGN. [Syn segn]. **Added/Corp** Norske Samlaget. **VFOAT** Syn & Segn. Vol. 1, (1895)-. Periodical. Norwegian. Four times a year (Jan., Apr., Sept., Nov.). Kr275.00 (institutions), Kr236.00 (individuals) Europe; Kr198.00 (institutions), Kr159.00 (individuals) Scandinavia; Kr285.60 (institutions), Kr246.60 (individuals) other. Forlagsentralen Tidsskriftavd, PB 150 Furuset, 1001 Oslo 10 Norway. **Tel** 011 47 2 2320995. **ED** Ottar Grepstad. **LC** AP45; .S8. **DD** 058/.3982. **Ad Acc.**
Ind/Abst MLA Int. Bibl. Books Artic. Mod. Lang. Lit.; Peace Res. Abstr. J. (1965-1966).

UK
TATLER, THE. Vol. 274, No. 3477 (May 1979)-. English. Ten times a year. $66.00. Tatler Publishing Company Ltd, Vogue House, Hanover Square, London W1R 0AD England. **Tel** 01 499 9080, FAX 409 0451. **ED** Emma Soames. available on microfilm from University Microfilms International (UMI). ***Continues*** *Tatler & Bystander.*

PL/0208-7006
TEMI. TARNOWSKI MAGAZYN INFORMACYJNY. **VFOAT** Tarnowski Magazyn Informacyjny. (1979)-. Periodical. Polish. wk. $39.00. **(Subscription address:** ARS Polona, PO Box 1001, 00068 Warsaw Poland.**) UDC** 304(438). **CODEN** 943.8.
Desc: Cultural and social publication for the Tarnow region.

FR
TERRORICIEL. French. Eleven times a year. Terroriciel, 18 Av des Champs Elysees, F-75008 Paris France.

FR/0395-6601
TEXTES ET DOCUMENTS POUR LA CLASSE. **Added/Corp** Institut Pedagogique National (France). No. 1, (Sept. 14 1967)-. Periodical. French.

Twenty times a year. 350.00F France and French oversease departments and territories; 515.00F other. Centre National Documentation Pedagogique, 21 Square St. Charles, BP 7, 75012 Paris, France. **Tel** 011 33 1 40020333, 011 33 1 46349425. **(Subscription address:** CNDP Abonnements, B 750, 60732 Genevieve Cedex 9 France.**)** **LC** AP20; .T47. ***Continues*** *Documents Pour la Classe.*

GW/0179-3063
THAT'S YUGOSLAVIA. [That's Yugosl.]. (?985)-. Periodical. English.
Ind/Abst Hum. Rights Intern. Rep.

UK/0040-6171
THIS ENGLAND. Vol.1 (Spring 1968)-. Periodical. English. qt (Feb., May, Aug., Nov.). £13.25 UK; £15.00 other. This England International, PO Box 52, Cheltenham, Gloucestershr GL50 1YQ England. **Tel** 011 44 242 577775, FAX 011 44 242 22034, telex 43452.
Desc: A gentle portrayal and proud love of all that is English including memories and poetry of the countryside and times gone by.

CR
TIEMPO ACTUAL / JUNTA DE PENSIONES Y JUBILACIONES DEL MAGISTERIO NACIONAL. Periodical. Spanish. qt. C30.00. Apartado 3974, San Jose Costa Rica. **LC** AP63; .T468. **DD** 056/.1.

UK/0049-3910
TIME OUT. **VFOAT** Time Out in London. (1968)-. English. mo (12 issues). £80.00 UK; £110.00 other Eurioe; £90.00 other. United Magazine Subscriptions, 1st Floor Stephenson House, Brunel C, Milton Keynes MK2 2EW England. **Tel** 011 44 908 747008.
Desc: The living guide to London.

GW
TRANSIT. 1988-. Periodical. Czech. sa. Iter-Verlag, Helmholtzstr 27, 1000 Berlin 10 Germany. **LC** AP52; .T7.

CN/0049-464X
TRIBUNA ITALIANA, LA. Yearly V. 1- Oct. 15, 1963-. Periodical. Italian. mo. La Tribuna Italiana, 257 Dante Street, Montreal Quebec 327 Canada.

GW/0344-9041
TRIBUNE D'ALLEMAGNE, LA. ***Ceased.*** [Trib. Allem.]. (19??)-(1992). Periodical. French. Forty times a year. Friedrich Reinecke Verlag GmbH, Hartwicusstrasse 3 4, W-2000 Hamburg 76 F R Germany. **Tel** 011 49 40 2285279, FAX 040/2285260, telex 2-14-733. **UDC** 07.

PL/0208-6956
TRYBUNA WABRZYSKA. (1956)-. Periodical. Polish. wk. $52.00. **(Subscription address:** ARS Polona, PO Box 1001, 00068 Warsaw Poland.**)** **UDC** 304(438). **CODEN** 943.8.

TU
TURKEY (ANKARA, TURKEY). (TURKEY.). **Added/Corp** Turkey. Basn-Yayn ve Enformasyon Genel Mudurlugu. (198?)-. English (translations available in Turkish). an. General Directorate of Press and Information, Republic of Turkey, Ataturk Boulevard 203 0t, 688 Ankara Turkey. **LC** DR401; .T832. **DD** 956.1/005. ***Continues*** *Turkey Yearbook.*

PL/0239-6807
TYGODNIK CIECHANOWSKI. (1979)-. Periodical. Polish. wk. $39.00. **(Subscription address:** ARS Polona, PO Box 1001, 00068 Warsaw Poland.**)** **UDC** 308.
Desc: Cultural and social publication for the Ciechanow region.

PL/0209-2166
TYGODNIK LUDOWY. (1982)-. Periodical. Polish. wk. $39.00. **(Subscription address:** ARS Polona, PO Box 1001, 00068 Warsaw Poland.**)** **UDC** 308.

PL/0208-8622
TYGODNIK NADWISLANSKI. (1981)-. Periodical. Polish. wk. $39.00. **(Subscription address:** ARS Polona, PO Box 1001, 00068 Warsaw Poland.**)** **UDC** 304(438).
Desc: Cultural and social publication for the Tarnobrzeg region.

PL/0138-0710
TYGODNIK PILSKI. (1979)-. Periodical. Polish. wk. $39.00. **(Subscription address:** ARS Polona, PO Box 1001, 00068 Warsaw Poland.**)** **UDC** 304(438).
Desc: Cultural and social publication for the Pila region.

PL/0208-6980
TYGODNIK PIOTRKOWSKI. (1978)-. Periodical. Polish. wk. $39.00. **(Subscription address:** ARS Polona, PO Box 1001, 00068 Warsaw Poland.**)** **UDC** 304(438). **CODEN** 943.8.
Desc: Cultural and social publication for the Piotrkow region.

PL/0208-6972
TYGODNIK POCKI. (1972)-. Periodical. Polish. wk. $39.00. **(Subscription address:** ARS Polona, PO Box 1001, 00068 Warsaw Poland.**)** **UDC** 304(438). **CODEN** 943.8.
Desc: Cultural and social publication for the Plock region.

PL/0239-684X
TYGODNIK SIEDLECKI. (1980)-. Periodical. Polish. wk. $39.00. **(Subscription address:** ARS Polona, PO Box 1001, 00068 Warsaw Poland.**)** **UDC** 308.
Desc: Cultural and social publication for the Siedlce region.

PL/0138-0729
TZ. TYGODNIK ZAMOJSKI. **VFOAT** Tygodnik Zamojski. (1979)-. Periodical. Polish. wk. $39.00. **(Subscription address:** ARS Polona, PO Box 1001, 00068 Warsaw Poland.**)** **UDC** 304(438). **CODEN** 943.8.
Desc: Cultural and social publication for the Zamosc region.

US/8750-1082
U.K. MAGAZINE. **VFOAT** UK magazine; U.K.; UK. (198?)-. Periodical. English. bm. $16.00 US; $18.50 Canada; $22.00 other. M D Enterprise, P.O.Box 25, Hatboro PA 19040. **Tel** (215)674-3132. **ED** Jules DeSepulveda. **Bk Rev. Ad Acc.**

HU/0866-4749
UJ MAGYAR HIREK. ***Ceased.*** (Jan. 1991)-(199?). Periodical. Hungarian. Twenty-six times a year. Magyarok Vilaglapja Alapitvany, Naphegy U 29, H 1016 Budapest Hungary. **Tel** 011 36 1 1568465. Index available (Back iss.). **Bk Rev. Circ:** 52,000. ***Continues*** *Magyar Hirek, 0133-090X.*
Desc: Provides news about life in Hungary and in Hungarian communities worldwide.

HU
UJ TUKOR. ***Ceased.*** ( )-(Jan. 1990). Periodical. Hungarian. wk. Lapkiado Vallalat, Lenin Korut 9-11, 1073 Budapest 7, Hungary. **Tel** 222-408. **ED** Sandor Fekete, Laszlo Gyurko, Sandor Korospataki Kiss. **LC** AP82; .T8. **Bk Rev. Ad Acc. Circ:** 69,000 (ctrl). ***Continues*** *Tukor.*
Desc: Biggest circulation cultural weekly in Hungarian. Covers new books, films, plays. Reports on social problems, health and environmental issues.

UN
UKRAINE (KIEV, UKRAINE). (UKRAINE.). No. 1 (1970)-. Periodical. English. Twelve times a year. $99.95. **(Subscription address:** East View Publications Inc., 3020 Harbor Lane North, Suite 110, Minneapolis MN 55447.**)** **DD** 914.77/1/0305.
Desc: Carries articles on the latest development in the nation's industry, agriculture, science and education. Poetry and short prose by noted authors, articles about the Ukraine's classical and modern art, stories on everyday life and leisure and sport reviews are some of the publication's permanent features.

UN/0868-9644
UKRAINSKA KULTURA. (1991)-. Periodical. Ukrainian. mo. **LC** AP58.U5; S57. ***Continues*** *Sotsialistychna Kultura, 0132-1544.*

SZ
UNION TEILT MIT. Periodical. German. mo. Deutscher Judo Verband, Redaktion Ippon Segewaldweg 40, D 12557 Berlin Germany. **Tel** 011 49 711 210770, telex 051 678.

RU
URAL. **Added/Corp** Soiuz Pisatelei RSFSR. Sverdlovskoe Otdelenie. (1938)-. Periodical. Russian. mo. $109.95. **(Subscription address:** East View Publications Inc., 3020 Harbor Lane North, Suite 110, Minneapolis MN 55447.**)** **LC** AP50; .U7.

RM
VATRA. **Added/Corp** Comitetul de Cultura si Educatie Socialista al Judetului Mures Uniunea Scriitorilor din Republica Socialista Romania. (19??)-. Periodical. Romanian. mo. DM145.00. **(Subscription address:** Kubon & Sagner, ABT Zeitschriftenimport, D 80328 Munich Germany.**)** **LC** AP86; .V38.
Ind/Abst Annu. Bibliogr. Engl. Lang. Lit.

IT/0042-3254
VELTRO, IL. [Veltro]. **Added/Corp** Presenza italiana (Society) Societa Dante Alighieri. Vol. 1 (Apr. 1957)-. Periodical. Italian (summaries and/or abstracts in English, French, German and Spanish). bm. L140.000 Italy; $120.00 other. Veltro Editrice, Via S Nicola de Cesarini 3, 00186 Rome Italy. **Tel** 39 6 6865410, FAX 39 6 68300103. **ED** Virginia Cappelletti. **LC** AP37; .V38. **DD** 055/.1. Index available. cum. index. **Bk Rev. Ad Acc. Circ:** 6,000.
Desc: Original research in the areas of past and current Italian values and problems, relations between Italy and other countries, cultures and societies.
Ind/Abst Am. Hist. Life (1975-1977, 1979-); BHA : Biblio. Hist. Art; MLA Int. Bibl. Books Artic. Mod. Lang. Lit.

FR/0767-7294
VESTNIK, LE MESSAGER. (VESTNIK RUSSKOGO KHRISTIANSKOGO DVIZHENIIA.). [Ves., Messager]. **Added/Corp** Russkoe Studencheskoe Khristianskoe Dvizhenie. **VFOAT** Messager. (1974)-. Periodical. Russian (French). Twice a year. 200.00F France; 240.00F other. Messager Vestnik, 91 rue Olivier de Serres, 75015 Paris France. **Tel** 011 33 1 42505366, FAX 011 33 1 43253479. **ED** Nikita Struve. Index available. **Bk Rev. Ad Acc. Circ:** 2,000. ***Continues*** *Vestnik Russkogo Studencheskogo Khristianskogo Dvizheniia.*
Desc: Information on Russia and the former USSR. Covers philosophy and religion, literature, and the Russian Church today.

SW/0346-4180
VI. (1914)-. Periodical. Swedish. ir (Forty issues per year). Kr631.00 Sweden; $133.40 US. VI, Box 15210, 10465 Stockholm Sweden. **Tel** 011 46 8 7431860. **ED** Monica Boethius. **LC** AP48; .V5. **Ad Acc. Circ:** 245,000 (ctrl).
Desc: General family magazine. Home and consumer questions culture and politics high quality.

NE
VIENNA CIRCLE COLLECTION. **Added/Corp** Vienna Circle. Vienna Circle. Collection. Vol. 1 (1973)-. Monographic series. English. ir. Price varies per volume. Kluwer Academic Publishers, Postbus 322, 3300 AH Dordrecht, The Netherlands. **Tel** 011 (31) 78 524400, FAX 011 31 78 183273, telex 20083. **(Subscription address:** Kluwer Academic Publishers / US Subscriptions, PO Box 253, Accord Station, Hingham MA 02018.**)**
Ind/Abst Math. Rev.

IT/0507-1712
VITA ITALIANA. **Added/Corp** Italy. Servizi delle Informazioni e della Proprieta Letteraria, Artistica e Scientifica. Italy. Centro di Documentazione. Documenti di Vita Italiana. Italy. Presidenza del Consiglio dei Ministri Documenti di Vita Italiana. Vol. 1 (Dec. 1951)-. Periodical. Italian. mo. $12.47. Vita Italiana, Via Boncompagni 15, Rome Italy. cum. index.
Ind/Abst Bibliogr. Mission.

●LU/1017-2947
VOILA LUXEMBOURG. **Added/Corp** Luxembourg. Ministere d'Etat. Information and Press Dept. No. 1 (Jan. 1991)-. Periodical. English. Information and Press Department, Ministry of State, 10 Boulevard Roosevelt, L-2450 Luxembourg. **LC** DH901; .V65. **DD** 949.35/005.

RU/0507-2573
VOLGA. **Added/Corp** Saratovskaia Pisatelskaia Organizatsiia. Soiuz Pisatelei RSFSR. Soiuz Pisatelei RSFSR. Saratovskoe Otdelenie. Vol. 1 (Jan. 1966)-. Periodical. Russian. mo. $109.95. Saratov N.G. Chernyshevskii State University, Astrakhanskaya Ulitsa 83, 410071 Saratov Russia. **Tel** 24-16-96, FAX 24-04-46, telex 241125. **(Subscription address:** East View Publications Inc., 3020 Harbor Lane North, Suite 110, Minneapolis MN 55447.**)** **LC** AP50; .V6.

GW/0507-4150
VORGANGE. [Vorgange]. **Added/Corp** Humanistische Union. Humanistische Studenten-Union. (1962)-. Periodical. German. qt (4 issues). DM62.80. Leske Verlag & Budrich GmbH, Postfach 300551, Gerhart Hauptmann Strasse 27, W-5090 Leverkusen 3 Opladen Germany. **Tel** 011 49 21712079. **ED** Dieter Hoffmann. **LC** AP30; .V82. **DD** 053/.1. Index available. **Bk Rev. Ad Acc. Circ:** 2,700 (ctrl).
Ind/Abst Energy Res. Abstr. (1979-).

SP
VOZ DE LA VALDERIA, LA. Spanish. Three times a year. 4000ptas Spain; 8000ptas North America; 7000ptas other. Editorial El Paisaje, Entre los Rios 10, 24760 Castrocalbon Leon Spain. **ED** Agustin Garcia Alonso. Index available. cum. index. **Bk Rev. Ad Acc. Pr Rev. Circ:** 2,000 (ctrl).
Desc: Contains biographies, poems and general information.

NE
VRIJ NEDERLAND : VN. **VFOAT** VN; V.N. (1940)-. Periodical. Dutch. wk. Fl100.00 Netherlands; $172.00 other. Vrij Nederland, Raamgracht 4 PB 1050, 1011 KK Amsterdam Netherlands. **Tel** 011 31 20 5518423. **ED** M. D. Ferdinandusse. **LC** AP15; .V68. Index available. **Bk Rev. Ad Acc. Circ:** 90,000. available on microfilm. ***Absorbed*** *J.M. de Stem van Nederland.*

UN/0320-8370
VSESVIT (KIIV). (VSESVIT.). [Vsesvit]. **Added/Corp** Spilka Pysmennykiv Ukrainy. Ukrainske Tovarystvo Druzhby i Kulturnoho Zviazku z Zarubizhnymy Krainamy. Ukrainskyi Respublikanskyi Komitet Zakhystu Myru. (1925)-. Periodical. Ukrainian. ir. $99.95. **(Subscription address:** East View Publications Inc., 3020 Harbor Lane North, Suite 110, Minneapolis MN 55447.**)** **LC** AP58.U5; V8.
Ind/Abst MLA Int. Bibl. Books Artic. Mod. Lang. Lit.

UK
WEEK IN EUROPE, THE. English. European Communities Commission, Case Postale 1003, Luxembourg Luxembourg. **Tel** (352)48 80 41, FAX (352)48 80 40, telex 2181.

HU/0024-8495
WEEKLY BULLETIN - HUNGARIAN NEWS AGENCY (BUDAPEST, 1970). (WEEKLY BULLETIN - HUNGARIAN NEWS AGENCY.). [Wkly. bull. - Hung. News Agency]. **Added/Corp**

General Interest —General Interest-Middle East

Hungarian News Agency. (1970)-. Bulletin. English. wk. $128.00. MTI Hungarian News Agency, PO Box 3, H 1426 Budapest, Hungary. **Tel** 011 36 1 756722, FAX 011 36 1 188297, telex 224373 224374. **(Subscription address:** Kultura, PO Box 149, H 1389 Budapest 62 Hungary**)**
Ind/Abst F&S Index Plus Text, Int. [Select. Cov.].

GW
WELT AM SONNTAG. (19??)-. Periodical. German. wk (52 issues). DM488.00 US. Axel Springer Verlag Ag, Brieffach 2460, D 20350 Hamburg Germany. **Tel** 011 49 40 34724503.

GW/0043-2598
WELTBUHNE, DIE. Ceased. (June 4, 1946)-(1993). Periodical. German. wk. Deutscher Judo Verband, Redaktion Ippon Segewaldweg 40, D 12557 Berlin Germany. **Tel** 011 49 711 210770, telex 051 678. **ED** Maud V Ossietzky. **LC** AP30; .W33. **DD** 053/.1.
Continues Neue Weltbuhne.
Ind/Abst Art Archaeol. Tech. Abstr.

SZ
WELTWOCHE, DIE. Began in 1933. Periodical. German. wk. 106.00F Switzerland; 134.00F other. Jean Frey Druck, Postfach 299, CH-8021 Zurich, Switzerland. **Tel** 011 41 1 2078919. **ED** Tuerg Rauspeck. **LC** AP32; .W4. **Bk Rev. Ad Acc. Circ:** 98,500 (ctrl).
Desc: A general interest journal.

GW
WERTE UNSERER HEIMAT. Added/Corp Akademie der Wissenschaften, Berlin. Arbeitsgruppe Heimatforschaung. (19??)-. Monographic series. German. ir. Price varies per volume. Akademie-Verlag GmbH, Muehlenstrasse 33 34, D 13162 Berlin Germany. **Tel** 011 49 30 47889300, FAX 011 49 30 47889357. **(Subscription address:** VCH Verlagsges Export Books, Postfach 101161, D 69451 Weinheim Germany.**)**
Continues Werte der Deutschen Heimat.

UK/0953-6906
WESTERN EUROPE. Added/Corp Europa Publications Limited. (1989)-. English. an. $335.00. Europa Publications Ltd, 18 Bedford Square, London WC1B 3JN England. **Tel** 011 44 71 5808236, telex 21540 EUROPA G. **(Subscription address:** Gale Research Co., 835 Penobscot Building, Detroit MI 48226.**) LC** IN PROCESS; HC240; .W415.
Desc: Provides well-informed commentaries and the latest statistical and directory information on more than thirty Western European countries and territories.

UK/0143-6619
WESTINDIAN DIGEST. Suspended. (Apr. 1971)-Suspended (March 1989). Periodical. English. mo. 75p (per issue) UK; $36.00 US. Hansib Publishing Ltd / London, Tower House, 139-149 Fonthill Road, London N4 3HF England. **Tel** 01-281 1191, FAX 263 9656, telex 22294. **ED** Ken Campbell. **LC** F1601; .W58. **Bk Rev. Ad Acc. Circ:** 9,750.
Desc: News and features, food, travel, music, arts and culture.

PL
WIEDZA I ZYCIE. Added/Corp Towarzystwo Uniwersytetu Robotniczego i Ludowego. Towarzystwo Wiedzy Powszechnej. (1926)-. Periodical. Polish. mo. Price on Request. **(Subscription address:** ARS Polona, PO Box 1001, 00068 Warsaw Poland.**) LC** AP54; .W52.

AU/0043-5279
WIEN AKTUELL. Title Change. Periodical. German. Presse-und Informationsdienst der Stadt Wien, Presseforum Volksgartenstrasse 3, 1016 Vienna 1 Austria. **LC** DB841; .W5. **DD** 914.36/13/05. **Continued by** Wien.

SZ
WOCHE (ZURICH, SWITZERLAND). (DIE WOCHE.). (19??)-. Periodical. German. $87.47. Ringier & Company AG, Florastrasse, CH-4800 Zofingen Switzerland. **Tel** 011 41 62 503110. **LC** AP32; .W58. **DD** 053/.1.

●PL
WPROST. No. 1 (1992)-. Periodical. Polish. wk. $91.00. **(Subscription address:** ARS Polona, PO Box 1001, 00068 Warsaw Poland.**)**

NE/0920-4792
YEARBOOK OF EUROPEAN STUDIES. VFOAT Annuaire d'Etudes Europeenes. 1988-. English. an. $29.95. Editions Rodopi BV, Keizersgracht 302-304, 1016 Ex Amsterdam Netherlands. **Tel** 011 31 20 6227507, FAX 011 31 20 380948. **ED** J.T. Leerssen. **LC** D901; .Y4. **DD** 940/.05. Index available.
Desc: Aims to provide a forum for the comparative and interactive study of selected topics in European relations.

YU/0512-9907
YUGOSLAV REVIEW [A MONTHLY MAGAZINE OF THE SERBS, CROATS AND SLOVENES], THE. Vol. 1 (March 1922)-. Periodical. English (French, German, Russian and Spanish). mo. Yugoslav Review, Terazije 31, Belgrade Yugoslavia. **ED** Rajko Bobot. **LC** DR364; .Y8. **Ad Acc** available with illustrations.

RU/0514-2210
ZARUBEZHNYE ZAPISKI. Vol. 1 (1963)-. Russian. **(Subscription address:** Victor Kamkin, 4956 Boiling Brook Parkway, Rockville, MD 20852**) DD** 080.

●US/1066-4858
ZARUBEZNAA PERIODICESKAA PECAT NA RUSSKOM AZYKE. (ZARUBEZHNAIA PERIODICHESKAIA PECHAT NA RUSSKOM IAZYKE : EZHEKVARTALNYI ZHURNAL REFERATOV.). [Zarub. period. pecat rus. azyke]. **Added/Corp** Vserossiiskaia Gosudarstvennaia Biblioteka Inostrannoi Literatury Imeni M.I. Rudomino. (1992)-. Periodical. Russian. qt. $40.00 (institutions), $25.00 (individuals). Informatics & Prognostics, 1400 Shattuck Avenue, Suite 7 10, Berkeley CA 94709. **Tel** (510)236-2935. **LC** DK1; .A32. **DD** 057. **Continues** Abstracts of Soviet and East European Emigre Periodical Literature, 0738-2707.

SZ
ZB, ZEIT IM BILD. VFOAT Zeit im Bild. Periodical. German. wk. Deutscher Judo Verband, Redaktion Ippon Segewaldweg 40, D 12557 Berlin Germany. **Tel** 011 49 711 210770, telex 051 678. **LC** AP30; .Z18.

PL/0138-0745
ZBLIZENIA KOSZALIN. (ZBLIZENIA.). (1979)-. Periodical. Polish. wk. Price on Request. **(Subscription address:** ARS Polona, PO Box 1001, 00068 Warsaw Poland.**) UDC** 304(438). **CODEN** 943.8.
Desc: Cultural and social weekly for the Slupsk region.

RU
ZHIZN. No. 1 (1922)-. Periodical. Russian. wk. $89.95. **(Subscription address:** East View Publications Inc., 3020 Harbor Lane North, Suite 110, Minneapolis MN 55447.**) LC** WMLC 1072/91. **Continues** Soiuz.

PL/0137-9399
ZIELONY SZTANDAR. (1931)-. Periodical. Polish. wk. $39.00. **(Subscription address:** ARS Polona, PO Box 1001, 00068 Warsaw Poland.**) UDC** 323(438). **CODEN** 327.

PL/0208-6999
ZIEMIA GORZOWSKA. (1971)-. Periodical. Polish. wk. $78.00. **(Subscription address:** ARS Polona, PO Box 1001, 00068 Warsaw Poland.**) UDC** 304(438). **CODEN** 943.8.
Desc: Cultural and social publication for the Gorzow region.

XR
ZPRAVY CSAV. Main/Corp Ceskoslovenska Akademie Ved. (19??)-. Multiple languages (Czech and Slovak). Ceskoslovenska Akademie Ved, Ustav Teorie a Dejin Vedy, Jilska 1, 110 00, Prague 1, Czech Republic. **LC** AS142; .C465.

RU/0321-1878
ZVEZDA. Ceased. [Zvezda]. Vol. 1 (1924)-(1992). Periodical. Russian. mo. **(Subscription address:** Victor Kamkin, 4956 Boiling Brook Parkway, Rockville MD 20852.**) LC** AP50; .Z93. available on microfilm from University Microfilms International (UMI).
Ind/Abst MLA Int. Bibl. Books Artic. Mod. Lang. Lit.

RU
ZVEZDA VOSTOKA; LITERATURNO-KHUDOZHESTVENNYI I OBSHCHESTVENNO-POLITICHESKII ZHURNAL. Added/Corp Soiuz Pisatelei Uzbekistana. (1946)-. Periodical. Russian. mo. $109.95. Obedinennoe Izdatelstvo Kzyl Uzbekistan, Tashkent, Uzbekistan. **(Subscription address:** East View Publications Inc., 3020 Harbor Lane North, Suite 110, Minneapolis MN 55447.**) LC** AP50; .Z94.

PL/0208-6964
ZYCIE PRZEMYSKIE. (1967)-. Periodical. Polish. wk. $39.00. **(Subscription address:** ARS Polona, PO Box 1001, 00068 Warsaw Poland.**) UDC** 304(438). **CODEN** 943.8.

GENERAL INTEREST-MIDDLE EAST

UK
AL-AALAM. Periodical. Arabic. wk. $2.00 per issue. Proudrose Ltd, 55-57 Banner Street, London EC1Y 8PX United Kingdom. **Tel** (01)253-4726, FAX (01)608-0209, telex 262028. **ED** Saeed Mohamed. **LC** AP95.A6; A48. Index available. cum. index. **Bk Rev. Ad Acc.** ctrl circ.

KU
AL-ARABI. Added/Corp Kuwait. Dairat al-Matbuat wa-al-Nashr. Kuwait. Wizarat al-Irshad wa-al-Anba. Kuwait. Wizarat al-Ilam. **VFOAT** Alaraby; Alarabi; Al-Arabi. No. 1 (Dec. 1958)-. Periodical. Arabic. Twelve times a year. International Media / Research Planning Implement Bureau, Ministry of Information, 193 Safat, 13002 Safat Kuwait. **Tel** 2424375, telex MITR 44041 KT. **ED** Mohamed Al-Rumeihi. **LC** AP95.A6; A68. Index available. cum. index. **Bk Rev. Ad Acc. Circ:** 300,000

(ctrl).
Desc: A magazine on Arabic culture.
Ind/Abst Am. Hist. Life (1973-1978).

IS
AL-AWDAH. VFOAT Alawdah. Vol. 1, No. 1, (Nov. 6, 1982)-. Periodical. Arabic. mo. Alawdah, PO Box 19563, Jerusalem, Israel. **ED** Raymonda Tawil. **LC** DS119.7; .A932 .

IS
AL-BAYADIR AL-SIYASI. VFOAT Bayader. (19??)-. Periodical. Arabic. mo. $150.00. Al-Bayader, PO Box 21445, 91213 Jerusalem Israel. **Tel** 2-820957. **ED** Jack Y. Khazmo. **LC** DS63.1; B39. **Bk Rev. Circ:** 15,000.
Desc: Specializes in reflecting the real situation in Israel and the area and publishes interviews and has many columns of general subjects.

LE
AL-FIKR AL-ARABI. VFOAT Alfikr Al-Arabi. Vol. 1 (1978)-. Periodical. Arabic. Six times a year. £L10.00 (single issue) Lebanon; $60.00 North America; $45.00 Europe and Africa. Mahad Al-Inma Al-Arabi, Bayrut Al-Ramlah Al-Bayda, 77 Shari Alis Farid Al-Naggash, SB 14/5300, Beirut Lebanon. **Tel** 831026, telex 22234 L E EMARAB. **ED** Maan Ziade. **LC** AP95.A6; F53. Index available. cum. index. **Bk Rev** ctrl circ.

LE
AL-FIKR AL-ARABI AL-MUASIR. VFOAT Alfikr-Arabi Almuacer. No. 1 (May 1980)-. Periodical. Arabic. mo. £L350.00. Markaz Al Inma Al Qawmi Lubnan Ras Bayrut, Al-Manarah Binayat Al-Fakhuri, SB Al-Majallah 135072/AL-Markaz 135048, Beirut Lebanon. **LC** AP95.A6; F53. **Continues** Fikr Al-Arabi.

LE
AL-FUSUL AL-LUBNANIYAH. VFOAT Fusul Allubnaniyah; Siasons Libanaises. 1979-. Periodical. Arabic (French). qt. £L150.00. Tasduru Fi Dayr Awkar, SB 220, Beirut Lebanon. **LC** PAR.

SU
AL-KHAFJI. Periodical. Arabic. mo. Dairat Al-Alaqat Al-Ammah Sharikat Al-Zayt Al-Arabiyah Al-Mahdudah, SB 256, Al-Khafji Saudi Arabia. **LC** AP95.A6; K45.

UA/0303-1578
AL-MARIFAH. [Marifa]. **VFOAT** Maarefa. (1931)-. Periodical. Arabic. mo. **LC** AP95.A6; M32.
Ind/Abst Middle East J.

IS
AL-MAWAKIB. (19??)-. Periodical. Arabic. S B 2396, Al-Nasirah Israel. **ED** F Abd Allah. **LC** AP95.A6; M346.

BA
AL-MAWAQIF. VFOAT Mawakef Weekly Magazine. Periodical. Arabic. wk. 10. PO Box 1083, Al-Manamah Bahrain. **LC** DS247.B2; A26. **UDC** 961.1.

FR/0153-3401
AL-MUSTAQBAL. Ceased. [Mostakbal]. **VFOAT** Mostakbal. (1977)-?. Periodical. Arabic. wk. Al-Kalima, 191 Atlantic Avenue, Brooklyn NY 11201. **Tel** (718)852-0292. **LC** DS36; .M74. **Bk Rev. Ad Acc. Circ:** 80,000.
Desc: Provides coverage on all news events and developments in the Middle East.

KU
AL-NAHDAH. VFOAT Majallat Al-Nahdah. (19??)-. Periodical. Arabic. Dar Al-Ray Al-Amm, PO Box 695, Al-Kuwayt Kuwait. **LC** AP95.A6; N33.

KU
AL-NASHRAH AL-IKHBARIIYAH / TASDURU AN WAHDAT AL-MALUMAT AL-TABIAH LIL-NADWAH AL-ALAMIYAH LIL-ANSHITAH AL-ILMIYAH AL-ISLAMIYAH. VFOAT Information Bulletin. Arabic (English). Dar Al-Buhuth Al-Ilmiyah, SB 2857, Al-Safah Kuwait.

IQ
AL-SHABAB. Periodical. Arabic. 3.00ID. Sahat Antar Maktab Al-Ilam Wa-Al-Nashr Al-Markazi, Al-Ittihad Al-Amm Li-Shabab Al-Iraq, Azamiyah Baghdad Iraq. **LC** AP95.A6; S393.

IS
AL-SHIRA. Periodical. Arabic. Dar Al-Shira Lil-Sihafah Wa-Al-Nashr, PO Box 19436, Al-Quds Israel. **LC** AP95.A6; S46.

IQ
AL-THAQAFAH. VFOAT Thakafa. Arabic. 0.100ID. Imarat Faruq Hashim Yahya, Baghdad Iraq. **LC** AP95.A6; T513.

KU
AL-THAQAFAH AL-ALAMIYAH. V. 1, Nos. 0-2 (April 1982)- Journal 1-. Periodical. Arabic. bm. Al-Majlis Al-Watani Lil-Thaqafah Wa-Al-Funun Wa-Al-Adab, SB 23996, Al-Kuwayt Majallat, Al-Thaqafa Al-Alamiyah, Al-Kuwayt Kuwait. **LC** AP95.A6; T517.

QA
AL-URUBAH. AL-OUROBA. VFOAT Al-Ouroba. (19??)-. Periodical. Arabic (Arabic). wk. Dar Al-Urubah Press and Publishing, PO Box 1115, Doha Qatar. **Tel** 325874, telex 4497. **ED** Abdullah Hussain Naama. **LC** DS36; .U75. **Circ:** 25,000.

LE
AL-USBU AL-ARABI. VFOAT Arabweek. Middle East Pictorial. Began in 1959. Periodical. Arabic. wk. Al-Usbua-Al Arabi, PO Box 1404, Beirut Lebanon. **LC** AP95.A6; U75.

FR/0757-648X
ARAB NEWS & REPORTS. [Arab news rep.]. **VFOAT** Arab News and Reports. (1982)-. Periodical. French. sm. Centre Arabe de Documentation, 34 Ave des Champs Elysees, 75008 Paris France. **Tel** 42254100. **UDC** 32 (=927).

UA
FLASH (CAIRO, EGYPT). (FLASH.). No. 1, (Jan. 1983)-. Periodical. Arabic. ir. 24 Shari Zakariya Ahmad, Al-Qahirah Egypt. **LC** AP95.A6; F6.

US/1050-5296
IDISHER KEMFER. (IDISHER KEMFER / YIDDISHER KEMFER.). **Added/Corp** Poale Zion-Zeire Zion of America. Labor Zionist Organization of America - Poale Zion. **VFOAT** Yiddisher Kemfer. (May 2, 1932)-. Periodical. Yiddish. Forty-six times a year. $30.00. Labor Zionist Alliance, 275 7th Avenue, 17th Floor, New York NY 10001. **Tel** (212)675-7808. **ED** Mordecai Strigler. **LC** DS150.L3; Y5. **DD** 956. **Bk Rev. Ad Acc. Circ:** 3,000. **Desc:** Information on Israel, labor, poetry, essays, novels, politics and Jewish affairs.

UK/0578-6967
IRAN (LONDON). (IRAN: JOURNAL OF THE BRITISH INSTITUTE OF PERSIAN STUDIES.). [Iran]. **Added/Corp** British Institute of Persian Studies. **VFOAT** Journal of Persian Studies. Vol. 1 (1963)-. English (French and German). an. $60.00. British Institute of Persian Studies, 42 Thomas More House Barbican, London EC2Y 8BT England. **Tel** 011 44 71 920-0823. **ED** Vesta Curtis and C E Bosworth. **LC** DS251; .I66. Index available. **Circ:** 700.
Desc: Iranian studies, art, archaeology, history, anthropology, literature, linguistics, philosophy, and religion.
Ind/Abst Anthropol. Index; Anthropol. Lit.; Art Archaeol. Tech. Abstr.; Avery Index Archit. Period. Suppl. Colum. Univ. (1989-); MLA Int. Bibl. Books Artic. Mod. Lang. Lit.; Numis. Lit.

IS
JADID (HAIFA, ISRAEL). (AL-JADID.). **VFOAT** Jadid Lil-Adab Wa-Al-Ulum Wa-Al-Funun; Jadeed; Gadid. (1951)-. Periodical. Arabic. mo. $35.00. 9 Al-Hariri Street, PO Box 104, Haifi 31 000 Israel. **ED** I Tuma. **LC** AP95.A6; J3. Index available in last issue of volume--attached.

IS/0792-6049
JERUSALEM REPORT, THE. [Jerus. rep.]. Vol. 1, No. 1 (Oct. 1990)-. Periodical. English. Twenty-six times a year. $59.94 (one year), $99.94 (two years) US & Canada & Mexico; $69.94 (one year), other. Jerusalem Report Publ Ltd, PO Box 1805, 22 Rehov Yosef Rivlin, Jerusalem 91017 Israel. **Tel** 011 972 2 291011, FAX 011 972 2 291037. **(Subscription address:** P.O. Box 2513, Birmingham, AL 35282-2513; telephone: (800)633-4931, FAX: (205)995-1588**) LC** DS101; .J3525. **DD** 909/.04924. **Circ:** 30,000.
Desc: Issues and events about the Middle East, Israel, and the Jewish Community.
Ind/Abst Index Jew. Period. (199?-).

KU
KUWAITI DIGEST, THE. V. 1- Dec. 1972-. Periodical. English. qt. Free. Kuwait Oil Company (K S C) / Community and Information Services Department, PO Box 9758, Ahmadi 61008 Kuwait. **Tel** 3989111, FAX 3983661, telex 44211. **ED** Salem R Al Roomi. **LC** DS247.K8; A253. **DD** 953/.67/005. **UDC** 953.68. **Circ:** 8,500 (ctrl).
Ind/Abst Middle East Abstr. Index.

IS
MEASEF (MEKHON HA-KETAV (JERUSALEM)). (HA-MEASEF.). Vol. 1, No. 1 (Feb. 1979)-. Periodical. Hebrew. ir. $10.00 4 issues. Haktav Institute, PO Box 6040, Jerusalem 91060 Israel. **LC** BM1; .M4.

UK/0961-8724
MIDDLE EAST MONITOR. VFOAT MEM. Vol. 1, No. 1 (Jan. 1991)-. Periodical. English. mo. $450.00. Business Monitor International, 56 60 St. John Street, London EC1M 4DT England. **Tel** 011 44 71 6083646.

US
MIDDLE EAST QUARTERLY. (1992)-. English. qt. $36.00 individuals, $65.00 institutions. Transaction Publishers / Rutgers State University, New Brunswick NJ 08903. **Tel** (908)932-2280 Ext. 105, FAX (908)932-3138. **ED** Adam Garfinkle. **Ad Acc.**
Desc: Deals with the contemporary Middle East, with a focus on questions pertinent to American interests.

US/0899-2851
MIDDLE EAST REPORT (NEW YORK, N.Y. : 1988). (MIDDLE EAST REPORT.). [Middle East rep.]. **Added/Corp** Middle East Research & Information Project. No. 151 (Mar/Apr 1988)-. Periodical. English. Six times a year. $25.00 (individuals), $50.00 (institutions) US; add $5.00 postage Canada and Mexico; add $18.00 (airmail), $5.00 (surface mail) other. Middle East Research and Information Project : MERIP, 1500 Massachusetts Avenue NW/Suite 119, Washington DC 20005. **Tel** (202)223-3677, FAX (202)223-3604. **ED** Joe Stork. **LC** DS42; .M46a. **DD** 956/.04/05. Index available (published separately). cum. index. **Bk Rev. Ad Acc, Adv Mgr:** M. Zanger. **Pr Rev. Circ:** 8,000 (ctrl). available on microfilm and microfiche from University Microfilms International (UMI). ***Continues*** *MERIP Middle East Report, 0888-0328.*
Desc: Aims to educate the public about the contemporary Middle East with particular attention to peace, human rights and social justice issues, as well as gender and political change, democracy, the politics of food, and the arms race. Covers the most pressing and controversial issues--the Gulf War and its aftermath, the Palestinian-Israeli conflict, the rise of Islamic political activism. Each issue includes articles, interviews, photographs, poems, and cartoons.
Ind/Abst Altern. Press Index (-199?); Geogr. Abstr. Human Geogr.; Int. Dev. Abstr.; Int. Labour Doc.; PAIS Int. Print (1991-); Soc. Plann. Policy Dev. Abstr.; Middle East J.

LE
MONDAY MORNING. AL-SHIRA. ACH-CHIRAH. VFOAT Al-Shira; Ach-Chirah. (1972)-. Periodical. English. Fifty-two times a year. Regie Libanaise de Publicite, PO Box 165612, Beirut Lebanon. **Tel** 011 361517. **LC** DS80.A2; M65. **DD** 052.

IS
MONITIN. Vol. 1- Sept. 1978-. Periodical. Hebrew. IL375.00. Monitin Monthly Magazine, 305 Hayarkon Street, Tel Aviv Israel. **LC** AP91; .M65.

UA
NAHNU AL-ARAB. Arabic. an. $88.00. Mussasat dar Al-Hilal, 16 Mohammed Izz el Arab Street, Al-Qahirah United Arab Republic Egypt. **Tel** 3625473. **LC** DS36; .N34. **Bk Rev. Ad Acc. Circ:** 200,000 (ctrl).

KU
RAID (JAMIYAT AL-MUALLIMIN AL-KUWAYTIYAH). (AL-RAID.). Periodical. Arabic. 20. Jamiyat Al-Muallimin Al-Kuwaytiyah, SB 11259, Kuwait. **LC** AP95.A6; R33.

BA
SADA AL-USBU. (19??)-. Newspaper. Arabic. wk (Published and delivered on Tuesdays). 20.00. Sada Al Usbou, PO BOx 549, Manama Arabian Gulf Bahrain. **Tel** 291234, FAX 290507, telex 8880. **LC** AP95.A6; S236. Index available. **Bk Rev. Photos. Ad Acc.** Full Page (B&W) 300 Bahraini Dinars. Half Page (B&W) 160 Bahraini Dinars. **Circ:** 25,000 (ctrl).
Desc: Focus is mainly on regional, political, social, economic, and sports, etc.

SJ
SOUTHERN SUDAN. VFOAT S.S. Review; SS Review; Southern Sudan Magazine. Periodical. English. mo. £S0.50. Regional Ministry of Culture and Information, Editor, Southern Sudan Magazine, PO Box 126, Juba Sudan. **LC** DT159.6.S73; S69. **DD** 962.4/005.

UK/0954-5697
VOICE OF THE ARAB WORLD. INTELLIGENCE REPORT. VFOAT Intelligence Report. (Jan. 1988)-. Periodical. English. qt. £60.00 UK; £70.00 US & Canada; £68.00 other. Morris International Association, 15A Lowndes Street, London SW1X 9EY England. **Tel** 011 44 71 235-5966. **LC** DS63.1; .V65. **DD** 909/.0974927. ***Continues*** *Voice of the Arab World.*

US/8755-4917
WASHINGTON REPORT ON MIDDLE EAST AFFAIRS, THE. [Washington rep. Middle East aff.]. **Added/Corp** American Educational Trust. Vol. 1, No. 1 (Apr. 5, 1982)-. Periodical. English. Eight times a year. $19.00 (individuals), $50.00 (institutions). American Educational Trust, PO Box 53062, Washington DC 20009. **Tel** (202)939-6052, FAX (202)265-4574, (202)232-6754. **ED** Richard H. Curtis. **DD** 327. **Bk Rev. Ad Acc, Adv Mgr:** Greg Noakes, **Tel** 800-368-5788. ctrl circ.

GENERAL INTEREST-NORTH AMERICA

US/1047-451X
24HOURS (SANTA MONICA, CALIF.). (24HOURS : THE MAGAZINE OF LIFE PAST MIDNIGHT.). [24hours]. **VFOAT** 24 Hours; Twenty-Four Hours. Vol. 1, No. 1 (May/June 1989)-. Periodical. English. bm. $15.00. Schneider Publishing, Box 5657, Santa Monica CA 90409-5657. **Tel** (310)458-3777, FAX (310)458-3770. **ED** Timothy Schneider and Greg Granke. **DD** 979. **Bk Rev. Ad Acc. Circ:** 35,000.
Desc: Publication for people with non-conventional work schedules and businesses with extended operating hours.

US
ABC DE LAS AMERICAS. Began with Oct. 12, 1972 issue. Periodical. Spanish. wk. $22.00. Ediciones y Publicaciones Hispanoamericas Inc, 12-12 37th Avenue, Long Island City NY 11101. **LC** AP62; .A18.

CN/1186-9291
ABORIGINAL BUSINESS COURIER. [Aborig. bus. cour.]. **Added/Corp** Canada. Industry, Science and Technology Canada. **VFOAT** Affaires Autochtones. Premier Issue (1991)-. Periodical. English (French).

CN/0712-8606
ABOUT. [About]. **VFOAT** Magazine About; Magazine About the Generation of Ideas. Vol. 1 No. 1 (Apr. 1982)-. Periodical. English. ir. $15.00. YS Communications, 310 Davenport Road, Toronto Ontario M5R 3K2 Canada. **DD** 051.

US/1060-3905
ABOUT ... TIME. (ABOUT TIME.). [About time]. **VFOAT** About Time Magazine. Vol. 1 (Dec. 1970)-. Periodical. English. Twelve times a year. $12.00 US; $25.68 Canada; $29.40 others. About Time Magazine, 283 Genesee Street, Rochester NY 14611. **Tel** (716)235-7150. **LC** E185.5; .A215. **DD** 973/.0496073/005.

CN/0315-1697
ACFO INFO. Main/Corp Association Canadienne-Francaise de l'Ontario. First issued in 1972. Periodical. French. Association Canadienne-Francaise De L'Ontario, Bureau 204, 260, Rue Dalhousie, Ottawa Ontario K1N 7E4 Canada. ***Supersedes*** *Vie Franco-Ontarienne, 0042-5559.*

CN/0714-2579
ACS NEWSLETTER / ASSOCIATION FOR CANADIAN STUDIES. [ACS newsl. - Assoc. Can. Stud.]. **Added/Corp** Association for Canadian Studies. **VFOAT** Bulletin AEC. **VAT** Association of Canadian Studies Newsletter; Bulletin - Association des Etudes Canadiennes. Vol. 4, No. 1 (Spring 1982)-. Periodical. English (French). Four times a year (Jan., apr., July, Oct.). 75.00 Can$ (institutions), 40.00 Can$ (individuals) Canada; 80.00 Can$ (institutions), 45.00 Can$ (individuals) other;. Association for Canadian Studies Fin Svcs, CP 8888, Succursale Centre-Ville, Montreal Quebec H3C 3P8 Canada. **Tel** (514)987-7784, FAX (514)987-8210. **ED** Beatrice Kowaliczko. **DD** 971/.007. **Ad Acc. Circ:** 1,000 (ctrl). available on microfiche. ***Continues*** *Association for Canadian Studies. Association Newsletter, 0225-3054.*
Desc: Provides information on the various aspects of Canadian studies in Canada and abroad, each newsletter features a special report on a specific field of interest.

CN/0001-7469
ACTION NATIONALE. (L'ACTION NATIONALE.). [Action natl.]. **Added/Corp** Ligue d'Action Nationale. Vol. 1, (Jan. 1933)-. Periodical. French. Ten times a year (Except July/Aug.). 35.00Can$ Canada; 50.00Can$ other. Ligue d'Action Nationale, 82 West Sherbrooke Street, Montreal Quebec H2X 1X3 Canada. **Tel** (514)845-8533. **ED** Rosaire Morin (phone: (514)923-5459). **Bk Rev. Ad Acc. Circ:** 2,000.
Desc: Everything describing the French civilization in North America.
Ind/Abst Am. Hist. Life (1963-); Can. Period. Index; MLA Int. Bibl. Books Artic. Mod. Lang. Lit.; Point Repere (1983-).

CN/0824-3468
ACTION (REGINA). (ACTION.). [Action]. **VAT** Action Magazine (Regina, June 1983). Vol. 1, issue 2 (June 1983)-. Periodical. English. mo. $1.00 per issue. Action Publications, PO Box 1037, Regina Saskatchewan S4P 3B2 Canada. **DD** 051. ***Continues*** *Action Magazine, 0824-3476.*

US/0893-0538
ACTIVITIES OF DAILY LIVING UPDATE. [Act. dly. living update]. **VFOAT** ADL Update. Vol. 1, No. 1 (1987)-. Periodical. English. qt (4 issues). $25.00. Activities of Daily Living Update, PO Box 518, Naples FL 33939. **Tel** (813)263-5121. **DD** 615.

CN/0823-9096
ACTUALITE CANADA. [Actual. Can.]. Vol. 4, No. 2 (Feb. 1984)-. Periodical. French. mo. $50.00. News Canada, Suite 2612, 2 Bloor Street East, Toronto Ontario M4W 1A8. **DD** 054/.1. ***Continues*** *Chroniques Gratuites de Power Newspaper Syndicate, 0823-4396.*

CN/0319-3926
ACTUALITE JOLIETTAINE, L'. V. 1- Oct. 1974-. French. mo. $50.00 per no. L'Actualite Joliette, 598 Saint-Viateur, Joliette Quebec J6E 3B7 Canada. **DD** 054/.1.

CN
ADDRESSES. **See** Communication.

US/0001-8252
ADIRONDACK LIFE. [Adirond. life]. Vol. 1 (Winter 1970)-. Periodical. English. Seven times a year. $17.95 (one year), $32.95 (two year). Adirondack Life Inc., PO Box 97, Jay NY 12941. **Tel** (518)946-2191. **(Subscription address:** Kable Publishers Aide, 308 East Hitt Street, Subscriptions Department, Mt. Morris, IL 61054) **ED** Tom Hughes. **LC** F127.A2; A254. **DD** 917.47/53. Index available. **Bk Rev. Ad Acc. Circ:** 40,000.
Desc: Colorful magazine of life in the Adirondacks. Includes people, places, events, nature, wildlife, food, sports, history, and more.
Ind/Abst Am. Hist. Life (1971-1973).

US/0746-8075
ADIRONDACK MOUNTAIN TIMES. (1984)-. Newspaper. English. wk (published Thursday). The Recorder / Mountain Times, Box 640, Amsterdam NY 12010. **Tel** (518)494-4703. ***Continues** Adirondack Times.*

MX
ADVENTURES IN MEXICO. (19??)-. Periodical. English. Six times a year. $12.00. Adventures in Mexico, Apartado Postal 31-70, 45050 Guadalajara Mexico. **ED** Lloyd H. Wilkins. **Circ:** 2,200 (ctrl).
Desc: A newsletter reporting on living costs, recreation, cultural facilities, and other aspects of life in Mexican cities. Attractive foreign retirement and for those considering retirement in Mexico.

US/1047-031X
ALABAMA LIVING (MONTGOMERY, ALA.). (ALABAMA LIVING / ALABAMA RURAL ELECTRIC ASSOCIATION.). [Ala. living]. **Added/Corp** Alabama Rural Electric Association. **VFOAT** AREA Magazine. Vol. 42, No. 5 (May 1989)-. Periodical. English. Twelve times a year. $6.00. Alabama Living / Alabama Rural Electric Association, PO Box 244014, Montgomery AL 36124. **Tel** (205)215-2732. **ED** Darryl Gates. **DD** 334. **Circ:** 260,000. ***Continues** AREA Magazine, 0883-7392.*
Desc: News and features of general interest to members of rural electric cooperatives, rural and suburban.

US/1040-2349
ALABAMA MAGAZINE. [Ala. mag.]. Vol. 47, No. 3 (March 1984)-. Periodical. English. Six times a year. $16.95. PMT Publishing, PO Box 66200, Mobile AL 36660-1200. **Tel** (205)479-8722, (205)473-6269. **DD** 976. ***Continues** Alabama News Magazine.*

US
ALASKA AIRLINES MAGAZINE. **Added/Corp** Alaska Airlines. Vol. 8, No. 10 (Oct. 1984)-. Periodical. English. mo. $20.00 US; $30.00 Canada. Alaska Airlines Magazine, 2701 1st Avenue/Suite 250, Seattle WA 98121. **Tel** (206)682-5871. **ED** Candace Dempsey. **Ad Acc. Circ:** 35,000 (ctrl). ***Continues** Alaska Fest.*
Desc: A regional magazine for the business traveler and the in flight publication of Alaska Airlines.

●US
ALASKA ALMANAC : FACTS ABOUT ALASKA, THE. **VFOAT** Facts About Alaska. 17th Edition (1993)-. English. an (Nov.). $9.95. Graphic Arts Center Publishing Company, PO Box 10306, c/o Ken Rowe, Portland OR 97210. **Tel** (503)226-2402, FAX (503)223-1410. **ED** Ellen Wheat, (editor's address: 2208 Northwest Market Street, Suite 300, Seattle, WA 98107, phone: 206)784-5071). **LC** F902.3; .F3. **DD** 979.8/005. **Bk Rev. Circ:** 11,000. ***Continues** Facts About Alaska (Bothell, Wash.), 1051-5623.*

US/0002-4503
ALASKA JOURNAL (JUNEAU, ALASKA : 1971). ***Ceased.*** (THE ALASKA JOURNAL.). [Alsk. j.]. Vol. 1 (Winter 1971)-Ceased Vol. 15 (?). Periodical. English. qt. Alaska Northwest Publishing Company, 130 Second Avenue South, Edmonds WA 98020-3588. **Tel** (206)774-4111, (800)533-7381. **ED** Terrence Cole. **LC** F901; .A342. **DD** 917.98/03/05. cum. index. **Circ:** 4,438.
Ind/Abst ASTIS Curr. Aware. Bull. (1978-); Am. Hist. Life (1971-1980); ASTIS Bibliogr. (1978-); Ethnoarts Index (1971-1980).

US/0883-8526
ALASKA NATIVE LANGUAGE CENTER RESEARCH PAPERS. See Linguistics.

US/0273-7841
ALBEMARLE MAGAZINE, THE. Vol. 3, No. 4 (June/July 1980)-. Periodical. English. bm (Feb., Apr., Jun., Aug., Oct., Dec.). $16.00 (one year), $28.00 (two year). Kluge, Carden & Jennings, 853 West Main Street, Charlottesville VA 22903. **Tel** (804)979-4913, FAX (804)979-4025. **ED** Jamie Miller. **Ad Acc, Adv Mgr:** William Carden. **Circ:** 10,000 (ctrl). ***Continues** Albemarle Monthly, 0195-0169.*

CN/0225-0519
ALBERTA REPORT. [Alta. rep.]. Vol. 6, No. 40 (Sept. 7, 1979)-. Periodical. English. wk. 73.83Can$ Canada; 144.92Can$ US; 280.12Can$ other (regular delivery). United Western Communications Ltd, 17327-106A Avenue, Edmonton Alberta T5S 1M7 Canada. **Tel** (403)486-2277. **ED** Stephen Hopkins. **DD** 971.23/005. **CODEN** ALRPE9. Index available (bound in all issues). **Bk Rev. Ad Acc. Circ:** 60,000. available on microfiche (from Toronto : Micromedia). ***Formed by the union of** Saint John's Calgary Report, 0704-0695 **and** Saint John's Edmonton Report, 0380-9137.*
Desc: Newsmagazine covering western Canada.
Ind/Abst Acad. Abstr. Full Text Elite (Jan. 1993-) [Full Txt.]; Acad. Abstr. (Jan. 1993-); Acad. Search (Jan. 1993-); Can. Period. Index; Mag. Artic. Summar. Elite (Jan. 1993-); Mag. Artic. Summar. Select [Full Txt.]; Mag. Artic. Summar. CD-ROM (Jan. 1993-); Mag. Search; Vocat. Search (Jan. 1993-) [Full Txt.].

US/1040-4279
ALBUQUERQUE MONTHLY. [Albuq. mon.]. Vol. 6, Issue 8 (Aug. 1988)-. Periodical. English. mo. $12.00. Starlight Publications, Po Box 928, Albuquerque NM 87103. **Tel** (505)255-4648. **DD** 978. ***Continues** Albuquerque Living, 0746-9616.*

US
ALL ABOUT HAWAII. English. an. Star Bulletin Printing Company, PO Box 100, Honolulu HI 96810. ***Continues** Thrum's Hawaiian Annual and Standard Guide, combined with All About Hawaii.*

CN/0838-6579
ALLIANCE REPORT. [Alliance rep.]. **Added/Corp** Alliance Quebec. Vol. 1, No. 1 (Jan. 1987)-. Periodical. English. Alliance Quebec / Montreal, 1411 rue Crescent/Suite 501, Montreal Quebec H3G 2B3 Canada. **DD** 305.7/21/0714. ***Continues** Monthly Report (Alliance Quebec)., 0821-6266.*

US/0739-6961
ALMANAC FOR FARMERS & CITY FOLK, THE. **VFOAT** Almanac for Farmers and City Folk. 1984-. English. an. $1.50. Greentree Marketing Inc, 2014 Western Avenue, Las Vegas NV 89102-4620. **Circ:** 1,000,000.

CN/0228-1422
ALMANACH DU BAS-DU-FLEUVE. 1980-. French. an. $4.00 per no. Enterprises Castelriand Inc, CP 997, Riviere-du-Loup Quebec G5R 3Z5 Canada. **DD** 054/.1. ***Continues** Almanach Castelriand, 0708-9244.*

CN/0065-650X
ALMANACH DU PEUPLE. **VFOAT** Almanach du Peuple Beauchemin. (1857)-. Periodical. French. an (July). 8.33Can$ Canada; 10.99Can$ other (includes postage). Groupe Polygone Editeur Inc., 11450 Boul Albert Hudon, Montreal Quebec H1G 3J9 Canada. **Tel** (514)327-4464. **DD** 034/.1.

PR
ALMANAQUE PUERTORRIQUENO. (19??)-. Spanish. an (June). Editorial Edil, Box 23088 UPR Station, Rio Piedras 00931 Puerto Rico. **Tel** (809)763-2958. **LC** F1951; .A73. **Bk Rev. Ad Acc. Circ:** 15,000 (ctrl).
Desc: General information about PR, relevant news, history, maps, documents, literature, music, origin of sports and others related fields.

US/0742-3624
ALOFT. (ALOFT : THE MAGAZINE OF AIR VIRGINIA.). Vol. 1, No. 1 (Winter 1984)-. Periodical. English. qt. Free. Cygnet Communications, 5660 East Virginia Beach Boulevard/Suite 103, Norfolk VA 23502. **Tel** (804)625-4800.

US/0270-2924
ALTERNATIVES (NEW MARKET). (ALTERNATIVES.). Periodical. English. qt. $12.00 US; $14.00 Canada. C Shank, Route 1 Box 390, New Market VA 22844. **LC** AP2; .A31059. **DD** 051.
Ind/Abst Curr. Aware. Biol. Sci., CABS.

US/1056-4322
AMERICA AT LARGE. ***Suspended.*** (1991)-(199?). Periodical. English. qt. $15.80. Bolinda Press America, 9120 Nieman Road, Shawnee Mission KS 66214.

US/0279-3555
AMERICAN CITIZEN, THE. Periodical. English (Italian). mo. Victor Failla, PO Box 944, Omaha NE 68101.

●US/1065-7622
AMERICAN CITIZENS REVIEW. (1993)-. Periodical. English. qt. $1.50, (single issue, US), $3.00 (single issue, Canada).

US/0196-2086
AMERICAN CLASSICAL LEAGUE NEWSLETTER. **Added/Corp** American Classical League. American Classical League. Newsletter. Vol. 1 (Sept. 1978)-. Periodical. English. sa. comes with Classical Outlook. American Classical League, Miami University / Ohio, Oxford OH 45056. **Tel** (513)529-7741, FAX (513)529-7742.

US/0065-8278
AMERICAN FARM & HOME ALMANAC, THE. [Am. farm home alm.]. **VFOAT** American Farm and Home Almanac. Vol. 1 (1966)-. English. an. $2.50. Almanac Publishing Company, PO Box 1609, Lewiston ME 04240. **ED** Ray Geiger and Richard Doyle. **LC** AY64; .A58. **Circ:** 650,000 (ctrl).

●US/1064-7139
AMERICAN HARPOON, THE. [Am. harpoon]. (1992)-. Periodical. English. mo. $18.00. American Harpoon, 1685 Elmwood Avenue, Suite 208, Buffalo NY 14207. **Tel** (716)875-0751. **DD** 051. ***Continues** Harpoon (Buffalo, N.Y.), 1060-6688.*

US/0092-119X
AMERICAN JOURNAL (NEW YORK). (AMERICAN JOURNAL.). Vol. 1 (Dec. 1972)-. Periodical. English. wk. $22.50 (one year), $39.00 (two year). American Journal, PO Box 310, Westbrook ME 04092. **Tel** (207)854-2577. **ED** Dan McGillvray. **LC** Z1035.A1; A48. **DD** 051. **Bk Rev**, (Qty: 4). **Ad Acc. Circ:** 7,000.
Desc: General news of communities in Crescenteast, south and west of Portland.

US/0002-998X
AMERICAN MERCURY (1951), THE. (THE AMERICAN MERCURY.). **VFOAT** The (New) American Mercury. Vol. 72 No. 327 (Mar. 1951)-. Periodical. English. ir. American Mercury, PO Box 3567, Shreveport LA 71103. **LC** AP2; .A37. **DD** 051. available on microfilm from University Microfilms International (UMI). ***Continues** New American Mercury; **Absorbed** Western Destiny; Washington Observer Newsletter, 0511-3237.*
Ind/Abst Annu. Bibliogr. Engl. Lang. Lit.; Read. Guide Period. Lit.

US/0193-6859
AMERICAN POPULAR CULTURE. See Sociology-Manners and Customs.

US/8750-5878
AMERICAN SURVIVAL GUIDE. **VFOAT** Survival Guide. Vol. 7, No. 1 (Jan. 1985)-. Periodical. English. Twelve times a year. $26.95 (one year), $44.95 (two years). McMullen Publishing Inc, 2145 West La Palma Avenue, PO Box 70015, Anaheim CA 92801-1785. **Tel** (714)572-2255, FAX (714)572-1864. **ED** Jim Benson. **Bk Rev. Ad Acc.** ***Continues** Survival Guide, 0745-1113.*
Desc: Written for people whose chief concern is promotion of life and property in today's turbulent world.

US/0090-9114
AMERICANA. ***Ceased.*** [Americana]. (1977)-(1993). Periodical. English. bm. Americana Subscription Office, 381 West Center Street, Marion OH 43302. **Tel** (212)398-1550. **ED** Sandra Wilmot. **LC** E171; .A444A. **DD** 973/.05. **UDC** 973. **Bk Rev. Ad Acc. Circ:** 330,000 (ctrl). available on microfilm and microfiche from University Microfilms International (UMI). Documents available from UMI Article Clearinghouse, Magazine Collection. ***Continues** American Heritage Society's Americana, 0090-9114.*
Desc: Combines imaginative writing and beautiful photography to show instances around the country where history is being re-created, while offering tips for travel to historic places, traditional recipes, how-to's for old-time crafts, decorating and gardening ideas, and marketplace information for antiques collecting.
Ind/Abst Acad. Abstr. Full Text Elite (Jan. 1984-Feb. 1993); Acad. Abstr. (Jan. 1984-Feb. 1993); Acad. Ind. [Computer File] (1984-); Acad. Search (Jan. 1984-Feb. 1993); Am. Hist. Life (1987-1989); Expand. Acad. Index (1985-); Gen. Period. Index (1985-); Hist. Source (Jan. 1984-); Index Inf. (1977-); INFO-SOUTH Abstr.; Mag. Artic. Summar. Elite (Jan. 1984-Feb. 1993); Mag. Artic. Summar. Select (Jan. 1984-); Mag. Artic. Summar. CD-ROM (Jan. 1984-); Mag. Index Plus (1989-); Mag. Index. Sel. (1986-); Mag. Search; Newsp. Period. Abstr. (1988-); Read. Guide Abstr. Select Ed.; Read. Guide Period. Lit.; Mag. Index (1977-); Vocat. Search (Jan. 1984-Feb. 1993).

GW/0933-8853
AMERICAS (BONN, GERMANY). (DIE AMERICAS.). **Added/Corp** Zentralamerika Gesellschaft. Periodical. German. qt.

RU/1010-5557
AMERIKANSKII EZHEGODNIK. [Am. ezegod.]. **Added/Corp** Institut Vseobshchei Istorii (Akademiia Nauk SSSR). **VFOAT** Annual Studies of America. (1971)-. Academic Scholarly Publication. Russian. Izdatelstvo Nauka / Akademiia Nauk, Publishing House of the Russian Academy of Sciences, Leninskii Porspekt 14, 117901 Moscow Russia. **Tel** 011 95 954-21-53, FAX 011 95 938-21-44, telex 411964.
Ind/Abst Am. Hist. Life (1980-).

PN
ANALISIS (PANAMA, PANAMA). (ANALISIS.). (19??)-. Periodical. Spanish. mo. $32.00 US and Canada; $50.00 China. Revistas Interamericanas SA, Apartado 8038, Panama 5 Panama. **Tel** 69 4218.

CN/0715-7649
ANALYSTE (MONTREAL, QUEBEC). ***Ceased.*** (L'ANALYSTE.). [Analyste]. No. 1, Spring (1983)-No. 38 (1993). Periodical. French. qt. 35.00Can$ (one year), 60.00Can$ (two year) Canada; 60.00Can$ (one year), 100.00Can$ (two year) other. SODEP, 815 rue Ontario Est, Bureau 202, Montreal Quebec H21 1P1 Canada. **Tel** (514)523-7724, (514)525-2606, FAX

(514)523-9401. **ED** Michel Bedard. **DD** 054/.1. **Bk Rev**. **Ad Acc**. **Circ:** 2,500.
Desc: General interest in economics, politics, ethics, and social questions. Dedicated to promote civil liberties.
Ind/Abst Point Repere.

MX
ANGLO-AMERICAN DIRECTORY OF MEXICO. 19 -. Directory. English. $33.00. J E Smith, Barranca del Muerto 472, Col Alpes 01010 Mexico DF Mexico. **Tel** (905)593-8766. **ED** John E Smith Jr. **LC** F1204.5; .A4. **DD** 917.2. **Ad Acc**. **Circ:** 1,500.
Desc: Informative and comprehensive directory of English speaking people residing in the Mexican Republic.

US/0899-2320
ANNAPOLITAN (ANNAPOLIS, MD.). ***Ceased.*** (ANNAPOLITAN.). [Annapolitan]. (198?)-(19??). Periodical. English. Ten times a year. Annapolitan, Inc, 413 4th Street, Annapolis MD 21403. **Tel** (301)263-7400. **ED** Philip Evans. **DD** 973. **Bk Rev**. **Ad Acc**, **Adv Mgr:** Susan Fink. **Circ:** 12,000.
Desc: A general interest, lifestyle magazine for an upscale audience in the greater Annapolis, Maryland area.

CN/0848-2128
ANNUAL REPORT / ALBERTA CULTURE AND MULTICULTURALISM. [Annu. rep. - Alta. Cult. Multicult.]. **Main/Corp** Alberta. Alberta Culture and Multiculturalism. English. an. Free. CN Tower/12th Floor, 10004-104 Avenue, Edmonton Alberta T5J 0K5 Canada. **Tel** (403)427-6530, FAX (403)427-1496. **LC** PAR. ctrl circ.

US/1049-3085
ANNUAL REPORT (COLONIAL WILLIAMSBURG FOUNDATION). (ANNUAL REPORT.). **VFOAT** Report From the President. (1984)-. English. an. Colonial Williamsburg Foundation, PO Box C, Williamsburg VA 23187. **Tel** (804)229-1000. ***Continues*** *President's Report - Colonial Williamsburg Foundation, 0270-3467.*

US/0279-6376
ARIZONA LIVING. ***Ceased.*** Vol. 1 (Jan. 16, 1970)-(Dec. 1988). Periodical. English. mo. Arizona Living, PO Box 7761, Phoenix AZ 85011-7761. **Tel** (602)264-4295. **ED** Ron Cooper. **Bk Rev**. **Ad Acc**. **Circ:** 12,200.
Desc: Presents the latest information on sports, fashion, travel, economics, health and medicine, and other events of statewide interest; includes a statewide events guide.

US/1046-476X
ARIZONA TREND AZ. (ARIZONA TREND AZ : SOPHISTICATED LIVING IN THE VALLEY.). [Ariz. trend AZ]. **VFOAT** AZ. **VAT** Arizona Magazine. (1989)-. Periodical. English. qt. $4.00 (single issue). Arizona Trend Magazine, 3003 North Central Avenue/Suite 2004, Phoenix AZ 85012. **Tel** (602)230-1117. **ED** Thomas Kunkel. **DD** 051. **Ad Acc**. **Circ:** 60,000 (ctrl).
Desc: Targeted for upscale metro Phoenix residents who are enthusiasts of the good life. Departments and features cover travel, fashion, art and culture, recreation, entertainment, food and wine.

US/0273-4001
ARKANSAS GAZETTE INDEX. **Added/Corp** Arkansas Tech University. Library. (1819/1829)-. English. an. $60.00. Arkansas Tech University Library, Russellville AR 72801. **Tel** (501)968-0288. **ED** Shannon J Henderson. **LC** AI21.A83; H46. **DD** 071/.6773. **Circ:** 50 (ctrl).
Desc: Articles on Arkansas people, places and events.

US
ARKANSAS STATISTICAL ABSTRACT / PREPARED BY THE STATE DATA CENTER, UNIVERSITY OF ARKANSAS AT LITTLE ROCK. **Added/Corp** University of Arkansas at Little Rock. State Data Center. (1986)-. Statistical Publication. English. an (Every two years). $25.00. Arkansas State Data Center, University of Arkansas, 2801 South University, Little Rock AR 72204. **Tel** (501)569-8530, FAX (501)569-8538. **ED** Jerry Bell. **LC** HA251; .A74. **DD** 317.67. **Circ:** 400.
Desc: A comprehensive single source reference volume of economic and demographic data pertaining to the state. its basic goal is to bring together data in a format that will be useful to government agencies, business firms, organizations, and individuals.

US
ARTS & BOOKS : CHICAGO'S WEEKLY ARTS AND ENTERTAINMENT MAGAZINE. **VFOAT** Arts and Books : Chicago Tribune Arts & Books. 1980-. Periodical. English. wk. Chicago Tribune, 777 West Chicago Avenue, Department 300, Chicago IL 60610. **Tel** (312)222-5350. ***Continues*** *Arts & Fun/Books.*

US/0730-8574
ASCATOPICS. ***Title Change.*** **See** General Interest-Abstracting, Bibliographies and Statistics.

US/1043-5085
ASPEN MAGAZINE. [Aspen mag.]. (198?)-. Periodical. English. Six times a year. $18.00 (one year); $36.00 (two years). Ridge Publications, Box G-3, Aspen CO 81612. **Tel** (303)920-4040. **DD** 978. ***Continues*** *Aspen (Aspen, Colo.).*
Ind/Abst Access (1975-).

US/0004-4938
ASPEN : THE MAGAZINE IN A BOX. Vol. 1, No. 1 (1965)-. Periodical. English. qt. $18.00 (one year), $36.00 (two year). Ridge Publications Inc, Box G-3, Aspen CO 81612. **LC** AP2; .A7624.

US/1053-668X
ATCHISON MAGAZINE. [Atchison mag.]. Vol. 1, Issue 1 (Jan./Feb. 1991)-. Periodical. English. bm. $6.00. Lost Creek Publications, RR2 Box 373A, Rushville MO 64484. **Tel** (816)688-7454. **DD** 051.

US/0149-0125
ATHELINGS. V. 1- Jan./Feb. 1974-. Periodical. English. bm. Atheling's, 1047 Baseline Road, Claremont CA 91711. **ED** Geraldine Hartshorn Wheeler, Lloyd Franklyn Wheeler. **LC** AP2; .A767. **DD** 051. ctrl circ.

US/1053-623X
ATHENS MAGAZINE (ATHENS, GA. 1989). (ATHENS MAGAZINE.). [Athens mag.]. (1989)-. Periodical. English. Six times a year (Feb., Apr., June, Aug., Oct., Dec.). $12.95. Athens Newspapers, PO Box 912, Athens GA 30613. **Tel** (706)549-0123, FAX (706)543-5234. **ED** Elaine Kalber. **LC** F294.A7; A84. **DD** 051. **Bk Rev**, (Qty: 6). **Ad Acc**, **Adv Mgr:** Kathy Russo, **Tel** (706)208-2329. **Circ:** 6,000.
Desc: Pertinent to northerns in Georgia.

US/0731-9029
ATLANTA JOURNAL, THE ATLANTA CONSTITUTION INDEX (ANNUAL). (THE ATLANTA JOURNAL, THE ATLANTA CONSTITUTION INDEX.). (19??)-. English. an. University Microfilms International, 300 North Zeeb Road, Ann Arbor MI 48106-1346. **Tel** (313)761-4700, (800)521-0600 Exts. 2490, 2491, FAX (313)973-1540. **LC** AI21.A87; A86. **DD** 071/.58/231. available in microform from University Microfilms International (UMI); available on an online database (file 713/Full-Text) from DIALOG. Documents available from UMI Article Clearinghouse.
Ind/Abst Newsp. Abstr.

US/0276-9077
ATLANTIC (BOSTON, MASS. : 1981), THE. ***Title Change.*** (THE ATLANTIC.). [Atlantic]. Vol. 247, No. 4 (Apr. 1981)-(1993). Periodical. English. Twelve times a year. Atlantic Monthly, 745 Boylston Street, Boston MA 02116. **Tel** (617)536-9500. **ED** William Whitworth. **LC** AP2; .A8. **DD** 051. **CODEN** ATLAEO. **Bk Rev**. **Ad Acc**. **Circ:** 450,000 (ctrl). available on microfilm and microfiche from University Microfilms International (UMI). Documents available from UMI Article Clearinghouse, Magazine Collection. ***Continues*** *Atlantic Monthly (Boston, Mass. : 1971), 0004-6795.* ***Continued by*** *The Atlantic Monthly, 1072-7825.*
Desc: Publication for intelligent people who want to know more. Its expert writers speak of the richness of humanity with fresh and profound voices. Its readers enjoy a magazine devoted to the fabric of everyday life: arts, literature, politics, and more.
Ind/Abst Abr. Read. Guide Period. Lit.; Acad. Abstr. Full Text Elite (Feb. 1984-); Acad. Abstr. (Feb. 1984-); Acad. Ind. [Computer File] (1984-); Acad. Search (Feb. 1984-); Am. Bibliogr. Slavic East Europ. Stud.; Annu. Bibliogr. Engl. Lang. Lit.; Book Rev. Digest; Book Rev. Index; Can. Period. Index (19??-); Expand. Acad. Index (1984-); Film Lit. Index (19??-); Fut. Surv.; Gen. Period. Index (1985-); Index Am. Period. Verse; Index Period. Artic. Relat. Law; INFO-SOUTH Abstr.; Infobank (1981-); Mag. Artic. Summar. Elite (Feb. 1984-); Mag. Artic. Summar. Select (Feb. 1984-); Mag. Artic. Summar. CD-ROM (Feb. 1984-); Mag. Express (1986-) [Full Txt.]; Mag. Index Plus (1989-); Mag. Index Sel. Microfiche (1986-) [Full Txt.]; Mag. Index. Sel. (1986-); Mag. Search; Med. Rev. Dig.; Newsp. Period. Abstr. (1986-); Peace Res. Abstr. J. (1981-1988); Read. Guide Abstr. Select Ed.; Read. Guide Period. Lit.; Resource/One Ondisc; Mag. Index (1981-); TOM Gen. Index (1985-) [Full Txt.].

CN/1183-0891
ATTENTE (LONGUEUIL). ***Ceased.*** (L'ATTENTE.). [Attente]. Vol. 1, No 1 (Dec. 1990)-(199?). Periodical. French. mo. L'Attente, Bureau 102, 72 St-Sylvestre, Longueuil, Quebec J4H 2M2 Canada. **DD** 054/.1.

US/1054-5441
AURA (FORT WORTH, TEX.). (AURA.). [Aura]. (198?)-. Periodical. English. bm (6 issues). $16.95. LeWay Aura Inc., 2917 Morton Street, Ft. Worth TX 76107. **Tel** (817)332-3548, FAX (817)336-8409. **ED** John Paschal. **DD** 051. **Bk Rev**. **Ad Acc**, **Adv Mgr:** Kari Metroka. **Circ:** 20,000 (ctrl).

US/1074-0740
AUSTIN CHRONICLE, THE. (1981)-. Newspaper. English. wk. $55.00 US and Canada; $125.00 other. Austin Chronicle Corporation, PO Box 49066, Austin TX 78765. **Tel** (512)473-8955, FAX (512)458-6910, telex XEPHYR@BGA.COM. **ED** Louis Black. **Bk Rev**. **Ad Acc**. **Circ:** 75,000.
Desc: Entertainment, lifestyle and popular culture reviews, listings and cultural analysis.

US/0890-0574
AUSTIN MAGAZINE. ***Ceased.*** [Austin mag.]. Vol. 25, No. 4 (April 1984)-(199?). Periodical. English. mo. Austin Magazine, 701 Brazos Street, Suite 320, Austin TX 73701-3232. **DD** 976. ***Continues*** *Austin, 0739-201X.*
Ind/Abst Index Period. Artic. Relat. Law.

US/0279-1226
AVENUE (NEW YORK, N.Y.). (AVENUE.). [Avenue]. (1976)-. Periodical. English. mo (June and July issue is combined). $100.00 US; $150.00 other. Avenue NY, 145 East 57th Street, New York NY 10022. **Tel** (212)758-9517, FAX (212)421-9186, telex 501329 AVE. **ED** Quinn Halford. **LC** F128.1; .A9. **DD** 974.7/1043/05. Index available. **Ad Acc**, **Adv Mgr:** Susan Harris. **Circ:** 81,000 (ctrl).
Desc: Upscale, consumer oriented. Major focus on New York City affluent population.

US/1051-323X
BACKHOME (MOUNTAIN HOME, N.C.). (BACKHOME.). [BackHome]. **VFOAT** Back Home. Vol. 1, No. 1 (Aug./Sept./Oct. 1990)-. Periodical. English. qt. $16.00 (one year), $28.00 (two years) US; $21.00 (one year), $33.00 (two years) Canada and Mexico; $26.00 (one year), $38.00 (two years) other. Wordsworth Communications, 119 Third Avenue West, Hendersonville NC 28739. **Tel** (704)696-3838, FAX (704)696-3838. **ED** Terry Krautwurst. **LC** AP2; .B16. **DD** 051. **Bk Rev**, (Qty: 12). **Ad Acc**, **Adv Mgr:** W M Janes, **Tel** (704)859-9000. **Circ:** 18,500.

BF/0005-397X
BAHAMIAN REVIEW. **VFOAT** Bahamian Review Magazine. (1980)-. Periodical. English. Eight times a year. $50.00. 21st Century Publishing / Bahamas, Bay Street, PO Box 494, Nassau Bahamas. **ED** William Cartwright. **Bk Rev**. **Ad Acc**. **Circ:** 25,000 (ctrl). ***Continues*** *Bahamian Review and Freeport Magazine.*
Desc: Tourism, banking, finance USA news, Caribbean affairs, women, fashion, government news, personalities, etc.

US/1049-9970
BALLOONS TODAY. [Balloons today]. (1986)-. Periodical. English. mo (12 issues). $29.95 US; $49.90 other. Festivities Publications Inc., 1205 West Forsyth Street, Jacksonville FL 32204. **Tel** (904)634-1902, FAX (904)633-8764. **ED** April Anderson. **DD** 338. **Ad Acc**, **Adv Mgr:** Greg Smith. **Circ:** 15,000 (ctrl).

US/0005-4453
BALTIMORE MAGAZINE. (197?)-. Periodical. English. mo. $15.00 one year; $28.00 two years; $39.00 three years. ESS Ventures Inc, 6401 Golden Triangle Drive, Suite 120, Greenbelt MD 20770. **Tel** (301)220-2300 or, 800 365-2808, FAX (301)220-2304. **ED** Ramsey Flynn (editor's phone: (410)725-7375). **Ad Acc**, **Adv Mgr:** Linda Sciuto. **Circ:** 50,000. ***Continues*** *Baltimore.*
Desc: Features articles on life and people in Baltimore.

CN/0225-6193
BANAR. Began publication with Nov. 1967 issue. Periodical. English. mo. Free. Blackburn Community Association, L Driscoll, 97 Bearbrook Road, Ottawa Ontario K1B 3H5 Canada. **DD** 071/.1383. ctrl circ.

US/0279-7933
BANTHA TRACKS. **See** Societies and Clubs.

US
BEAUFORT MAGAZINE. English. qt (Jan., Apr., Jul., Oct.). $12.00 (1 year), $22.00 (2 years), $30.00 (3 years). Beaufort Magazine, PO Box 1125, Beaufort SC 29901. **Tel** (803)525-0066, FAX (803)525-6529. **ED** Robert G. Armstrong, Sr. **Bk Rev**, (Qty: 2-3). **Ad Acc**, **Adv Mgr:** K. Griffin. **Circ:** 15,000.

●US/1063-7559
BERKSHIRE REVIEW (PITTSFIELD, MASS.), THE. (THE BERKSHIRE REVIEW.). (1992)-. English. $8.50. Berkshire Writers Room, 28 Renne Avenue, Pittsfield MA 01201.

US/0092-5306
BEST OF NATIONAL LAMPOON, THE. First issue published in 1971. English. $2.50 per issue. National Lampoon Inc., 10850 Wilshire Road Boulevard, Suite 1000, Los Angeles CA 90024. **Tel** (310)474-5252. **LC** AP2; .B4598. **DD** 051.

US/0273-6160
BETTER LIVING (NEW YORK. 1981). (BETTER LIVING.). [Better living]. Vol. 1 (Jan. 1981)-. Periodical. English. qt. Better Living, 1775 Broadway, New York NY 10019. **Tel** (212)581-2000.
Ind/Abst Pop. Mag. Rev. (1984-).

US/8750-7331
BETTER TIMES (POMPANO BEACH, FLA. 1985). (BETTER TIMES.). [Better times]. (Jan./Feb. 1985)-. Periodical. English. Six times a year.

Better Times, 1800 South Ocean Boulevard, Pompano Beach FL 33062. **DD** 051. ***Continues*** *More (Fort Worth, Tex.), 8750-0299.*

CN/0319-6887
BHARATI (TORONTO). (BHARATI.). Apr./May 1975-. Periodical. Hindi (English). wk. 43.00Can$. Asia Times, 1429 Dufferin Street, Toronto Ontario M6H 4C7 Canada. **Tel** (416)533-8243. **ED** P Gill. **DD** 059.91431.
Desc: News and reviews regarding South Asia and Hindi-Panjabi speaking citizens around the world.

US/0730-8612
BIBLIOPHILOS (UNION CITY, PA.). (BIBLIOPHILOS.). [Bibliophilos]. Vol. 1, No. 1 (Winter 1982)-. Periodical. English. qt. $8.50. The Bibliophile, 48 North Main Street, Union City PA 16438. **LC** AP2; .B475. **DD** 051.

US/0006-369X
BIRMINGHAM. Added/Corp Birmingham Area Chamber of Commerce. (1961)-. Periodical. English. Twelve times a year. $15.00 US; $25.00 others. Birmingham Magazine, PO Box 10127, Birmingham AL 35202. **Tel** (205)323-5461. **ED** Joe O'Donnell. **Ad Acc. Circ:** 11,000.
Desc: A city magazine informing the public about people and places along with general interest stories in Birmingham.

US/0885-9647
BLACK ELEGANCE. (BLACK ELEGANCE : BE.). [Black elegance]. **VFOAT** BE. (1986)-. Periodical. English. Nine times a year. $16.99 US; $25.99 other. Starlog Press Inc., 475 Park Avenue South, New York NY 10016. **Tel** (212)689-2830, FAX (212)889-7933. **(Subscription address:** Kable Publishers Aide, 308 East Hitt Street, Subscription Department, Mt. Morris IL 61054-1473.**) ED** Sharon Skeeter. **LC** WMLC 93/689; TT500 b .B62. **DD** 051. **Bk Rev. Ad Acc. Circ:** 180,000.
Ind/Abst Acad. Abstr. (July 1993-); Acad. Search (July 1993-); Mag. Artic. Summar. Elite (July 1993-); Mag. Artic. Summar. CD-ROM (July 1993-).

US/0892-9203
BLACK SWAMP HERITAGE. [Black swamp herit.]. Vol. 7, No. 1 (Winter 1987)-. Periodical. English. qt. $16.00. Black Swamp Heritage, 18620 W Moline-Martin Road, Martin OH 43445. **Tel** (419)862-3751. **DD** 917. ***Continues*** *Sandusky County Heritage.*

US/1041-3456
BLUE RIDGE COUNTRY. [Blue Ridge ctry.]. Vol. 1, No. 1 (June/July 1988)-. Periodical. English. Six times a year (Jan., Mar., May, July, Sept, Nov.). $14.95 (one year); $22.95 (two years); $29.95 (three years). Blue Ridge Country, PO Box 21535, Roanoke VA 24018. **Tel** (703)989-6138, (800)877-6026, FAX (703)989-7603. **(Subscription address:** Kable Publishers Aide, 308 East Hitt Street, Subscription Department, Mt. Morris, IL 61054**) ED** Kurt Rheinheimer. **DD** 975. Index available. cum. index. **Bk Rev**, (Qty: 4). **Ad Acc, Adv Mgr:** Jo Dietrich. **Circ:** 75,000.
Desc: Presents the history, beauty, culture and lifestyle of the Southern Appalachian Mountains of West Virginia, Maryland, Virginia, Kentucky, Tennessee, North and South Carolina and Georgia. Compilation of the work of selected regionalgion's writers and photographers, capturing the charm of the region: the traditions and recipes, the country stores and bed-breakfast inns, the backroad drives and recreation, and the legends and lore of the mountains. Everything that encourgaes the reader to "take a trip home," even if he/she never lived in the beautiful Blue Ridge.

US/1058-0654
BLUE RYDER. [Blue ryder]. (1990)-. Periodical. English. bm. $15.00. Blue Ryder, PO Box 587, Olean NY 14760. **DD** 051.

US/0740-2856
BOCA RATON. No. 1 (Oct. 1981)-. Periodical. English. bm (6 issues). $20.00 (one year), $30.00 (two year), $40.00 (three year). Jes Publishing, 6413 Congress Avenue, Suite 100, Boca Raton FL 33487. **Tel** (407)997-8683. **ED** Christina Houlihen. **LC** WMLC 91/3381. Index available. **Ad Acc. Circ:** 16,000.
Desc: Lifestyle magazine of south Florida including travel, people, interior design and food.

US
BOOMER REPORT, THE. (1989)-. Periodical. English. mo. $195.00. Find/SVP, 625 Avenue of Americas, New York NY 10011. **Tel** (212)645-4500. **LC** HN59.2; .B66.

CN/0383-1353
BOOWATT. V. 1- Oct. 1975-. Periodical. English. mo. $2.00. Boowatt Publications, 616-415 Madison Avenue, Winnipeg Manitoba R2G 0M3 Canada. **DD** 051. ***Supersedes*** *Boowatt Weekly, 0383-1345.*

US/8750-7242
BOP. [Bop]. (198?)-. Periodical. English. mo. $22.00 US; $25.00 Canada; $27.00 other. Laufer Publishing Co., 3500 West Olive Avenue, Suite 850, Toluca Lake CA 91505. **Tel** (818)953-7999, FAX (818)953-4107. **DD** 051.

US/0194-732X
BOSTON MONTHLY, THE. V. 1- May 1979-. Periodical. English. mo. $10.00. Boston Monthly, 20 Newbury Street, Boston MA 02116.

CN/0710-7676
BRANDON DIRECTORY, THE. [Brandon dir.]. **Added/Corp** Brandon University. Rural Community Resource Centre. (1978)-. Directory. English. an. $4.00. Rural Community Resource Centre, Brandon University, Brandon Manitoba R7A 6A9 Canada. **DD** 917.127/3.

US/0737-0768
BRAVEAR. Issue 1-. Periodical. English. mo. $10.00. Bravear, PO Box 3877, Berkeley CA 94703. **LC** AP2; .B842243. **DD** 051.

US/0893-391X
BRIDGES (NEW YORK, N.Y. : 1986). ***Ceased.*** (BRIDGES.). [Bridges]. (1986)-Ceased ?. Periodical. English. mo. New Beginnings, 360 East 72nd Street, New York NY 10021. **DD** 051.
Ind/Abst Relig. Theol. Abstr. (?-?).

US/0892-8673
BRIGHT. ***Ceased.*** **VFOAT** Bright Magazine. Ceased (June 1987). Periodical. English. mo. 22968 Victory Boulevard, Suite 114, Woodland Hills CA 91367.

CN/0382-5272
BRITISH COLUMBIA MONTHLY (VANCOUVER. 1972). (THE BRITISH COLUMBIA MONTHLY.). Vol. 1 (June/July 1972)-. Periodical. English. ir. 30.00Can$. BC Monthly, Box 48884, Vancouver British Columbia V7X 1A8 Canada. **Tel** (604)681-9992.

US/0742-8189
BRUCE DAVID COHEN'S THE GOOD LIFE. VFOAT Good Life. (Nov. 1983)-. Newsletter. English. mo. $59.00. Bruce David Cohen, PO Box 934, Malibu CA 90265. **Tel** (213)457-4428.

US/1068-3208
BUBBA MAGAZINE. [Bubba mag.]. **VFOAT** Bubba. (Spring 1993)-. Periodical. English. qt (4 issues). $2.95 per issue (newsstands), $4.20 per issue (direct from publisher -- if no newsstands copies are available). Allison Magazines, Attention: Greg Easley, 535 5th Avenue, 28th Floor, New York NY 10017. **Tel** (212)867-3510. **ED** Dean King. **DD** 351. **Ad Acc, Adv Mgr:** Logan Ward.
Desc: Magazine devoted to covering the lifestyle of "Bubba." Tries to dispel some of the negative stereotypes often associated with "Bubba."

US
BUFFALO EVENING NEWS OFFICE ALMANAC. (1976)-. English. Buffalo Evening News, 1 News Plaza, PO Box 100, Buffalo NY 14240. **Tel** 800 777-8640 ext. 4530, FAX (716)856-5150, telex 916430. ***Continues*** *Buffalo Evening News Almanac and Fact Book.*

US/0300-7499
BUFFALO SPREE. (1967)-. Periodical. English. Four times a year. $8.00. Spree Publishing Company, PO Box 38, Buffalo NY 14226. **Tel** (716)839-3405. **ED** Johanna V. Shotell. **Ad Acc. Circ:** 21,000 (ctrl).
Desc: Edited for the affluent residents of the metropolitan Buffalo area. General interest including contemporary poetry and high-quality prose.

US
BULLETIN (CROZET, VA.). (THE BULLETIN.). **VFOAT** Bulletin of Western Albemarle County. Vol. 1, No. 1 (Oct. 11, 1978)-. Bulletin. English. wk. The Bulletin of Western Albemarle County, PO Box 280, Crozet VA 22932. ***Absorbed*** *Spirit of Scottsville.*

US/0193-5178
BULLSEYE (NORTH LAS VEGAS). (BULLSEYE.). **VFOAT** Nellis Bullseye. Periodical. English. wk. Bullseye, PO Box 3936, North Las Vegas NV 89030. **Tel** (702)649-9514.

US/1053-3605
BUZZ (LOS ANGELES, CALIF.). (BUZZ : THE TALK OF LOS ANGELES.). [Buzz]. Vol. 1, No. 1 (Oct./Nov. 1990)-. Periodical. English. Ten times a year (Jan./Feb. and June/July issues combined). $15.00 (one year); $25.00 (two years); $30.00 (three years). Buzz Magazine, 11835 West Olympic Boulevard, Suite 450, Los Angeles CA 90064. **Tel** (310)473-2721, (800)876-7884, FAX (310)473-2876. **ED** Allan Mayer. **LC** F869.L8; B93. **DD** 979.4/94/053. **Ad Acc. Circ:** 70,000.
Desc: The magazine of and for Los Angeles that appreciates the new reality of this remarkable city--the fact that L. A. is no longer just an entertainment capital, but a bona fide world capital. Through world-class journalism, essays, fiction, and photography, this magazine provides perspective on the personalities, politics, culture, and commerce that make Los Angeles such an exciting place to live.
Ind/Abst Access (1992-).

US
C C C N (CALIFORNIA COMMUNITY CARE NEWS). English. mo. $45.00 per year. Box 163270, Sacramento CA 95816. **Tel** (916)455-0723. **ED** Charles W. Skoien Jr. **Ad Acc. Pr Rev. Circ:** 15,000 (ctrl).
Desc: Information to non-medical community residential care facilities in California.

US/0194-5165
CALIFORNIA COUNTRY. V. 1- Jan. 1979-. Periodical. English. mo. $1.00 members, $2.00 nonmembers. California Country, 1601 Exposition Boulevard, Sacramento CA 94705.

US/0743-0868
CALIFORNIA COUNTY. (CALIFORNIA COUNTY / COUNTY SUPERVISORS ASSOCIATION OF CALIFORNIA.). **Added/Corp** County Supervisors Association of California. (19??)-. Periodical. English. bm (Jan., Mar., May, July, Sept., Nov.). $22.00. California County, 9719 Lincoln Village Drive, Suite 500, Sacramento CA 95827. **Tel** (916)363-5000.

US/0068-5615
CALIFORNIA HANDBOOK, THE. ***Ceased.*** **Added/Corp** Center for California Public Affairs. California Institute of Public Affairs. 1st Ed. (1969)-919??). English. ir. California Institute of Public Affairs, PO Box 189040, Claremont College, Sacramento CA 95818. **Tel** (916)442-2472. **ED** T C Trzyna. **LC** HC107.C2; C253. **DD** 917.94.
Desc: Covers the whole range of California life: government and politics, the environment and natural resources, social issues, the economy, education, history, arts, and literature.

US
CALIFORNIA JOURNAL NEWSFILE. VFOAT California Journal News File; News File. Vol. 1, No. 1 (Jan. 1984)-. Periodical. English. mo. $32.00. California Journal Press, 1714 Capitol Avenue, Sacramento CA 95814. **Tel** (916)444-2840, FAX (916)444-2339.

US/1061-3900
CALIFORNIA REPUBLIC. ***Ceased.*** [Calif. repub.]. **Added/Corp** Daily Journal (Firm). Vol. 1, No. 1 (Feb. 26, 1991)-(19??). Periodical. English. mo. California Republic, 1390 Market Street, Suite 1210, San Francisco CA 94102. **DD** 051.

US/0196-6847
CAMINOS (SAN BERNARDINO). (CAMINOS.). [Caminos]. **VFOAT** Caminos Magazine. Vol. 1 (March 1980)-. Periodical. English (Spanish). mo. $10.00. Caminos Magazine, PO Box 54307, Los Angeles CA 90054. **Tel** (213)222-1349. **ED** Roberto Rodriquez. **Circ:** 45,000.

CN/0705-9485
CANADA GAZETTE. PART 3. (THE CANADA GAZETTE. PART III: STATUTES OF CANADA.). [Can. gaz., 3]. **Main/Corp** Canada. **VFOAT** La Gazette du Canada. Partie III : Statuts du Canada. Vol. 1 (Dec. 13, 1974)-. Periodical. English (French). ir. 28.50Can$. Canada Communication Group Publishers, Order Processing, Ottawa Ontario K1A 0S9 Canada. **Tel** (819)956-4800, (819)956-4802. available on microfilm from Micromedia Limited.

CN/0318-6814
CANADA NORMANDIE. [Can. Normandie]. V. 1- Oct. 1970-. Periodical. French. te. Free. Bureau 1/4689 rue Delaroche, Montreal Quebec H2J 3J5 Canada.

CN/0300-4511
CANADA RIDES. V. 1- March 1972-. Periodical. English. qt. $6.00. Canada Rides Publications Ltd, PO Box 6818 Station D, Calgary Alberta T2P 2E7 Canada.

UK/0306-8145
CANADA TODAY (LONDON). ***Title Change.*** (CANADA TODAY.). **Added/Corp** Canada. Canadain High Commission (Great Britain). **VFOAT** Canada d'Aujourd'Hui. (May/June 1973)-?. Periodical. English. bm. Canada Today, Counsellor Public Affairs, Canadian High Commission, Canada House, Trafalgar Square, London SW1Y 5BJ England. ***Continued by*** *Canada Today Magazine, 0266-6685.*

US/0045-4257
CANADA TODAY (WASHINGTON). ***Ceased.*** (CANADA TODAY. CANADA D'AUJOURD'HUI.). [Can. today]. **Added/Corp** Canada. Embassy (U.S.). **VFOAT** Canada d'Aujourd'Hui. No. 1 (April 1970)-Ceased with Vol. 23, No. 1 (1993). Periodical. English. bm. Canadian Embassy Office of Information, 501 Pennsylvania Avenue Northwest, Washington DC 20001. **Tel** (202)682-1740. **ED** Judith C. Webster. **Circ:** 80,000 (ctrl).
Desc: Concerns Canadian society, politics, culture and environment.
Ind/Abst Index Free Period.; Museum Abstr.

CN/0527-8759
CANADIAN ANALYST, THE. ***Ceased.*** Vol. 1 June/July (1963-(1993). Periodical. English. $6.50. The Canadian Analyst, 312 Avenue P South, Saskatoon Saskatchewan Canada.

CN
CANADIAN AWARDS AND PRIZES. English (French). an. 35.00Can$. Reference Press, PO Box 70, Teeswater Ontario N0G 2S0 Canada. **Tel** (519)392-6634.
Desc: A source of information about Canadian prizes in diverse fields.

CN
CANADIAN (CANADIAN AIRLINES INTERNATIONAL). (CANADIAN.). English. mo. Canadian Airstream Inflight Magazine, 1305 11th Avenue SW, Suite 306, Calgary, Alberta T3C 3P6 Canada.
Ind/Abst Can. Period. Index (19??-).

US/0704-9412
CANADIAN FARM & HOME ALMANAC (1978). (CANADIAN FARM & HOME ALMANAC.). **VFOAT** Canadian Farm and Home Almanac. Began in 1978. English. an. $1.75 single issue. Paperjacks Ltd, 330 Steelcase Road East, Markham Ontario L3R 2M1 Canada. **LC** AY413; .C36. **DD** 051. ***Continues*** *Farm & Home Almanach, 0317-1124.*

CN/0008-3712
CANADIAN GUIDE. ***Ceased.*** **VFOAT** Canada's Gazetteer and Skipper's Directory; Cnroute. (June 1964)-(19??). Periodical. English (French). an. Interguide Publications, PO Box 1040 Station B, Burlington Ontario L7P 3S9 Canada. **Tel** (416)639-4144. **ED** Stan C Newey. **LC** HE2804; .C3. **DD** 385/.2/02571. **Ad Acc. Circ:** 2,000 (ctrl). ***Continues*** *Canadian Official Railway Guide with Airlines, 0319-3365.*

CN/0829-8777
CANADIAN MAGAZINE INDEX. ***Title Change.*** **See** General Interest-Abstracting, Bibliographies and Statistics.

CN/0008-4565
CANADIAN NEWS FACTS. Vol. 1 (Jan. 16, 1967)-. Periodical. English. Twenty-three times a year. $247.00. MPL Communications, 133 Richard Street West, Suite 700, Toronto Ontario M5H 3M8 Canada. **Tel** (416)869-1177, FAX (416)869-0456. **ED** Don Wright.
Desc: Deals with the major issues in Canadian news.

CN/0007-7720
CANADIAN REVIEW OF AMERICAN STUDIES. [Can. rev. Am. stud.]. **Added/Corp** Canadian Association for American Studies. Vol. 1 (Spring 1970)-. Periodical. English (French). tq (Mar., Jul., Oct.). $40.00, $20.00 (student). University of Calgary Press, 2500 University Drive Northwest, Calgary Alberta T2N 1N4 Canada. **Tel** (403)220-7578. **ED** Ernest Redekop and Roger Hall. **[CCC]**. Index available. **Bk Rev. Circ:** 500 (ctrl). Documents available from The Genuine Article. ***Supersedes*** *Canadian Association for American Studies. C A A S Bulletin.*
Desc: Published articles, review articles, and short reviews whose purpose is the multi-and interdisciplinary analysis and understanding of the culture, both past and present, of the United States--and of the relations between the cultures of the United States and Canada.
Ind/Abst Abstr. Engl. Stud.; Acad. Search (July 1993-); Am. Hist. Life (1970-); Am. Humanit. Index; Arts Humanit. Citation Index [Full Cov.]; Curr. Contents Arts Humanit.; INFO-SOUTH Abstr.; Mag. Search; MLA Int. Bibl. Books Artic. Mod. Lang. Lit.; Res. Alert [Full Cov.]; Sage Race Relat. Abstr.; Soc. Sci. Cit. Index [Select. Cov.]; SportSearch.

CN/0319-6577
CANADIAN SCENE (TORONTO. 1951). ***Ceased.*** (CANADIAN SCENE.). (1951)-(1???). Periodical. English (Chinese, German, Greek, Modern, Hindi, Finnish, Hungarian, Italian, Korean, Polish, Portuguese, Spanish, Slovak and Urdu, Ukrainian). bw. Canadian Scene, Suite 305/2 College Street, Toronto Ontario M5G 1K3 Canada. **Tel** (416)921-9424. **ED** Ben Viccari. **Bk Rev.**
Desc: Provides material to give ethnic readers a better understanding of Canada.

US/0576-6478
CANADO-AMERICAIN, LE. [Can.-Am.]. **Added/Corp** Association Canado-Americaine. (1900)-. Periodical. French (English). Four times a year. $10.00. Association Canado-Americaine, 52 Concord Street, PO Box 989, Manchester NH 03105. **Tel** (603)625-8577. **ED** Julien Olivier. **Bk Rev. Ad Acc. Circ:** 22,000 (ctrl).
Desc: Promotes communication and cooperation between members and local chapters in the U.S. and Canada. Articles pertaining to North American French culture.

US/0164-7024
CANYON ECHO. **Added/Corp** Sierra Club. Grand Canyon Chapter. **VFOAT** Sierra Club Canyon Echo. (19??)-. Periodical. English. Ten times a year (monthly with Dec./Jan. & June/July issues combined). $10.00. Canyon Echo, 516 East Portland Street, Phoenix AZ 85004. **Tel** (602)254-9330, (602)253-8633, FAX (602)258-6533. **ED** Wil Passow (editor's address: 8422 East Vernon Ave. Scottsdale AZ 85257; editor's phone: (602)946-5631). **Bk Rev**, (Qty: 4-6). **Ad Acc, Adv Mgr:** Richard L Isetts, **Tel** (602)945-5586. **Circ:** 15,000 (ctrl).

US/0199-7238
CAPE COD LIFE. (1979)-. Periodical. English. bm (Feb., Apr., June, Aug., Oct., Dec.). $19.75 US; $29.75 other. Cape Cod Life, PO Box 767, Cataumet MA 02532. **Tel** (508) 564-4466, FAX (508) 564-4470. **ED** Brian F. Shortsleeve. Index available. cum. index. **Bk Rev**, (Qty: 2). **Ad Acc, Adv Mgr:** Robin Mayer, **Tel** (508)564-4466. **Circ:** 39,173.
Desc: Focuses on the area's lifestyle, history and culture, people and places, business and industry, and issues and answers.

US
CAPE VERDEAN. Vol. 1, No. 1 (April 1969)-. Newspaper. English (Portuguese). Twelve times a year. $4.50. Cape Verdean, 355 Main Street, Plympton MA 02367. **Tel** (617)598-2728. **ED** Manuel T. Neves. **LC** Newspaper.

US/0008-6207
CARAVEL MAGAZINE. Vol. 1 1958-. Periodical. English. Ben Hagglun, 315 Kneale Avenue South, Theif River Falls MN 56701.

US/0738-9604
CAREFREE ENTERPRISE. (19??)-. Periodical. English. Eleven times a year. $13.00 US; $28.00 Canada; $36.00 other. Carefree Enterprise, PO Box 1145, Carefree AZ 85377. **Tel** (602)488-3098, (602)397-8045, FAX (602)488-3098. **ED** Fran Barbano. **Bk Rev**, (Qty: 12). **Ad Acc, Adv Mgr:** Lynn Grant. **Circ:** 3,000 (ctrl).
Desc: An Arizona lifestyle magazine offering positive profiles, interesting local/general history of Arizona, a wide variety of features/columns; "something for everyone". Referred to as "official" publication of Foothills Communities; second oldest magazine in Arizona; 11x17, sepia-tone ink on book weight paper; considered collector's item.

US/1048-5171
CARIBBEAN EVENTS MAGAZINE. **VFOAT** Caribbean Events. (1991)-. Periodical. English. bm. $1.75 (single issue). American International Hispanic Media, 1219 Palo Verde, Carson City NV 89701.

●US/1058-4315
CARIBBEAN INTERNATIONAL (ALBANY, N.Y.). **See** General Interest-General Interest-Central America.

CJ
CARIBBEAN LIFE & TIMES. **VFOAT** Life & Times. **VAT** Caribbean Life and Times; Life and Times. (1979)-. Periodical. English. mo. Caribbean Life and Times, 3900 NW 79th Avenue/Suite 222, Miami FL 33166. **Tel** (305)591-9280.

US
CARIBBEAN NEWS. ***Suspended.*** Periodical. English. mo. $33.00. Caribbean News, PO Box 5241, New York NY 10185.

US/0090-452X
CATSKILLS, THE. V. 1- Winter 1972/73-. Periodical. English. qt. $4.00. Catskills Quarterly Inc, PO Box L, Prattsville NY 12468. **LC** F127.C3; C45. **DD** 917.47/38/005.

US/0163-8378
CELEBRITY. [Celebrity]. V. 1- June 1975-. Periodical. English. mo. $9.00. Celebrity Service International Inc, 1780 Broadway/Suite 300, New York NY 10019. **LC** AP2; .C3565. **DD** 051.

US/8750-2852
CENTRAL FLORIDA MAGAZINE. **VFOAT** Central Florida. Vol. 11, No. 8 (May 1984)-. Periodical. English. mo. $24.95. Central Florida Magazine, 341 North Maitland Avenue, Maitland FL 32751. **Tel** (407)539-3939, (800)669-1002. **(Subscription address:** Fulfillment Corporation of America, 205 West Center Street İMarion, OH 43302) **ED** John R Bathen. Index available. **Bk Rev. Ad Acc. Circ:** 25,000 (ctrl). ***Continues*** *Central Florida Scene Magazine.*

US/1050-1339
CENTRAL NORTH CAROLINA JOURNAL. [Cent. N. C. j.]. **VFOAT** CNCJ. Vol. 1, No. 1 (Mar. 1990)-. Periodical. English. qt. $23.00. James Vann Comer, PO Box 219, Cameron NC 28326-0219. **Tel** (919) 775-5763, (919) 245-7664. **ED** James Vann Comer. **DD** 975. **Bk Rev. Ad Acc. Circ:** 300 (ctrl).
Desc: To serve as a clearinghouse of Central North Carolina genealogical and historical information.

CN/0316-7046
CHANGES (TORONTO). (CHANGES.). V. 1- Aug. 1972-. English. sa. $3.00. Doug Andrews, PO Box 267, Station M, Toronto Ontario M6S 4T9 Canada. **DD** 051.
Ind/Abst Appl. Soc. Sci. Index Abstr.

CN/0228-8206
CHANNEL (ST. CATHARINES). (CHANNEL.). Oct. 1973-. Periodical. English. ir. Free. Channel, 100 Saint Paul Street 3M2 Canada. **DD** 051.

US/0270-8035
CHAPTERS (CAMBRIDGE). (CHAPTERS.). No. 1- June 1980-. Periodical. English. mo. $10.00. Devil's Trident Publications, 4 Brattle Street, Room 304, Cambridge MA 02138.

US
CHARTER OF THE CITY OF NEW YORK. English. ir. $28.00. CityBooks/ City Publishing Center, Department of General Services, 2208 Municipal Building, 22nd Floor, New York NY 10007. **Tel** (212)669-8245, FAX (212)669-3211.

CN/0227-0900
CHASE ALMANAC. CANADIAN EDITION. (THE CHASE ALMANAC.). [Chase alm., Can. ed.]. (1982)-. English. an. Chase Almanac, c/o A W Chase, PO Box 4444, Pointe-Claire Quebec H9R 4R1 Canada. **DD** 051. ***Continues*** *Chase Almanac & Fact Book, 0316-747X.*

US/0362-4595
CHICAGO. **Added/Corp** WFMT (Radio Station : Chicago, Ill.). Vol. 24, No. 1 (Jan. 1975)-. Periodical. English. mo. $19.90 (one year), $35.00 (two year), $45.00 (three year). Chicago, 414 North Orleans Street, Chicago IL 60610. **Tel** (312)222-8999. **(Subscription address:** Neodata / Colorado, PO Box 2606, Boulder Boulder CO 80322.) **LC** F548.1; .C133. **DD** 977.3/11/0405. **Pr Rev. Circ:** 204,072. available on microfilm from University Microfilms International (UMI). Documents available from UMI Article Clearinghouse, Magazine Collection. ***Continues*** *Chicago Guide, 0042-9651.*
Ind/Abst Acad. Search (June 1984-June 1989); Access (1975-); Gen. Period. Index (1985-); INFO-SOUTH Abstr.; Mag. Artic. Summar. Elite (June 1984-June 1989); Mag. Artic. Summar. Select (July 1989-); Mag. Artic. Summar. CD-ROM (June 1984-June 1989); Mag. Index Plus (1989-); Newsp. Period. Abstr. (1988-); Pop. Period. Index; Mag. Index (1977-).

US/0894-5640
CHICAGO TIMES MAGAZINE. [Chic. times mag.]. **VFOAT** Chicago Times. (1987)-. Periodical. English. bm. $19.95. Chicago Times Magazine, 180 North Michigan Avenue, Suite 1440, Chicago IL 60601. **Tel** (312)372-6612. **ED** Flora Johnson Skelly. **DD** 977. **Bk Rev. Ad Acc. Circ:** 55,000 (ctrl).
Desc: Focuses on metropolitan Chicago and its surrounding counties.

CN/0823-1354
CHIMO MAGAZINE. [Chimo mag.]. **VAT** Chimo (1982). V. 5, No. 1 (Feb./Mar. 1982)-. Periodical. English. ir. $18.00. Kirkwood Associates, Suite L-21, 1455 Peel Street, Montreal Quebec H3A 1T5. **DD** 051. ***Continues*** *Chimo, 0705-3770.*

US/1064-9719
CHIP'S CLOSET CLEANER. [Chip's closet cleaner]. **VFOAT** Closet Cleaner. (Fall 1990)-. Periodical. English. Twice a year. $4.00 (per issue). Chip's Closet Cleaner, 826 Aspen Street Northwest, Washington DC 20012-2510. **ED** Chip Rowe. **DD** 051. **Bk Rev. Circ:** 1,200.
Desc: Contains humor, pop culture, trivia. Provides a complete three-month index to the Weekly World News, and contains information on people who collect strange items, dentist characters in the movies, along with book and magazine reviews.

●US/1065-1241
CHRISTIAN SCIENCE SENTINEL (RADIO ED.). (CHRISTIAN SCIENCE SENTINEL [SOUND RECORDING].). [Christian Science sentinel]. **Added/Corp** Christian Science Publishing Society. (Nov. 1992)-. Periodical. English. mo. $96.00. Christian Science Publishing Society, One Norway Street, Boston MA 02115. **Tel** (617)450-2678, (617)450-2504. **DD** 289. ***Continues*** *Herald of Christian Science (Audio Cassette Ed.), 1061-6659.*

US/0009-689X
CINCINNATI. ***Title Change.*** Periodical. English. mo. Cincinnati Monthly, 617 Vine Street/Suite 900, Cincinnati OH 45202. **Tel** (513)421-4300. **ED** Laura Pulfer. **Ad Acc. Circ:** 20,000 (ctrl). ***Continued by*** *Cincinnati Magazine, 0746-8210.*
Desc: Bright, provocative look each month at Cincinnati people, places, and events that make the Queen city one of the most livable cities in America.

US/0147-6270
CITY AND COUNTRY AMERICAN ELSEWHEN ALMANAC, THE. English. Pyramid Books, 919 Third Avenue, New York NY 10022. **LC** AY53; .C5.

US/0897-4926
CITY & COUNTRY CLUB LIFE. **VFOAT** City & Country Club Life Magazine; City and Country Club Life; Club Life. Vol. 1, No. 1 (Nov. 1984)-. Periodical. English. Six times a year. $15.00 one year; $28.00 two

years; $40.00 three years. International Publishing Company of America, 665 La Villa Drive, Miami Springs FL 33166. **Tel** (305)887-1701, FAX (305)885-1923, telex 6811546. **ED** Kipi Martin Marsico. Index available. **Bk Rev. Ad Acc. Circ:** 30,000 (ctrl).
Desc: Extensive photographic coverage of south Florida society. Focus on society, the rich, famous, and powerful. Features cover travel, health and beauty, finance, food and spirits, yachting, fashion, real estate, profiles, interior design, and entertainment.

US/0899-0948
CITY LIVING. Periodical. English. qt. $12.00. William H Rentschler, 909 Montgomery Street/#200, San Francisco CA 94133. ***Continues*** *San Francisco Gentry.*
Ind/Abst Gen. Period. Index (1988-1990); Mag. Index Plus (1989-1990); Mag. Index (?-?).

US/1051-3183
CITY (SAN FRANCISCO, CALIF. 1989), THE. (THE CITY : SAN FRANCISCO'S MAGAZINE.). [City]. (1989)-. Periodical. English. mo. $15.00. The City, 1095 Market Street, Suite 312, San Francisco CA 94103. **Tel** (415)252-1391. **DD** 051.
Ind/Abst Access (1992-).

US/0894-1904
CLAMOR (LAREDO, TEX.). (CLAMOR.). (198?)-. Periodical. English (Spanish). bw. $26.00. Latinboy Corporation, PO Box 2706, Laredo TX 78044. **DD** 305.

US/0736-5632
CLASSICAL RAG (SILVER SPRING, MD.). (CLASSICAL RAG.). (1982)-. Periodical. English. mo. $6.00. Marble City Publications, 10800 Georgia Avenue #205, Silver Spring MD 20902. **LC** PAR.

MX/0009-8515
CLAUDIA. ***Ceased.*** Vol. 1 (1965)-(19??). Periodical. Spanish. mo. Editorial Mex-Ameris Sa, Av Morelos 16/Fourth Floor, Mexico 1 DF Mexico. **Tel** 510-05-81.

●US/1062-1431
CLEVELAND NOW. VFOAT Now; Now Magazine. (1992)-. Periodical. English. qt. $7.95. National Magazine Publishing Company, 11th Floor, 20600 Chagrin Boulevard, Shaker Heights OH 44122. **Tel** (216)991-2403, (800)321-6343.

US/0897-4640
COAST & COUNTRY. ***Ceased.*** [Coast ctry.]. **VFOAT** Coast and Country. Vol. 5, No. 2 (March/April 1988)-(199?). Periodical. English. bm. Coast & Country, 45 Forest Avenue, Swampscott MA 01907. **DD** 051. ***Continues*** *Lynn Magazine, 0749-5889.*

US/0191-9210
COFFEE BREAK. (19??)-. Periodical. English. ir. $7.00 (6 issues). Coffee Break, Box 103, Burley WA 98322. **Tel** (206)857-4329.

US/0745-2810
COLLAGE (WHEELING, ILL.). (COLLAGE.). Periodical. English. bm. $7.50. Collage Inc, 1200 South Willis Avenue, Wheeling IL 60090.

US/0272-6904
COLORADO HOMES & LIFESTYLES. **See** Interior Design-Home Furnishings.

US/0889-2342
COLUMBIA MAGAZINE (COLUMBIA, MD.). (COLUMBIA MAGAZINE.). **Added/Corp** Columbia Association (Md.). (198?)-. Periodical. English. Four times a year (Mar., May, Sept., Dec.). $6.00. Patuxent Publishing Corporation, 10750 Little Patuxent Parkway, Columbia MD 21044. **Tel** (410)730-3620, FAX (410)730-7053. **ED** Susan Connell. **Ad Acc, Adv Mgr:** Susan Econ. **Circ:** 33000. ***Continues*** *CalendaR (Columbia Association (Md.)), 0739-6805.*
Desc: Features people, events and issues of Columbia, Maryland. Regular departments include health, personal finance, puzzle, business, great jobs, events.

US/0893-276X
COLUMBIANA. [Columbiana]. **Added/Corp** Columbia River Bioregional Education Project. Vol. 1 No. 1 (Spring 1987)-. Periodical. English. Twice a year. $10.00. Columbia Bioregional Education Project, Chesaw Route, Box 83F, Oroville WA 98844. **Tel** (509)485-3844. **ED** Geraldine Payton and Rick Gillespie. **DD** 917. Index available. cum. index. **Bk Rev. Ad Acc. Pr Rev. Circ:** 6,000.
Desc: Contains information on the merging culture in the northwest.

US/1042-3966
COMMON CAUSE/COLORADO. [Common Cause/Colo.]. **Added/Corp** Colorado Common Cause. **VFOAT** Common Cause Colorado; Common Cause. (March 1971)-. Periodical. English. Three times a year. $5.00. Common Cause of Colorado, 770 Grant Street, Suite 230, Denver CO 80203. **Tel** (303)861-7670. **DD** 320.

US/0746-5114
COMMON GROUND (DES MOINES, IOWA). **See** Religion and Theology-Catholicism.

US/0010-3330
COMMONWEAL. [Commonweal]. Vol. 1, (Nov. 12, 1924)-. Periodical. English. Twenty-two times a year. $39.00. Commonweal, 15 Dutch Street, 5th Floor, New York NY 10038. **Tel** (212)732-0800. **ED** Margaret O'Brien Steinfels. **LC** AP2; .C6897. **DD** 051. Index available. **Bk Rev. Ad Acc. Circ:** 20,000. available on microfilm and microfiche from University Microfilms International (UMI); available on an online database (file 647/Full-Text) from DIALOG. Documents available from UMI Article Clearinghouse.
Desc: A review of political affairs, religion, literature and the arts.
Ind/Abst Acad. Abstr. Full Text Elite (Jan. 1984-); Acad. Abstr. (Jan. 1984-); Acad. Ind. [Computer File] (1984-); Acad. Search (Jan. 1984-); Am. Hist. Life (1955-1958); Am. Bibliogr. Slavic East Europ. Stud.; Annu. Bibliogr. Engl. Lang. Lit.; Book Rev. Digest; Book Rev. Index; Curr. Lit. Fam. Plan.; Expand. Acad. Index (1984-); Film Lit. Index; Gen. Period. Index (1985-); Guide Soc. Sci. Relig.; Index Am. Period. Verse; Index Book Rev. Relig.; Index Period. Artic. Relat. Law; INFO-SOUTH Abstr.; Infobank (Jan. 1969-); Mag. Artic. Summar. Elite (Jan. 1984-); Mag. Artic. Summar. Select (Jan. 1984-); Mag. Artic. Summar. CD-ROM (Jan. 1984-); Mag. Express (1986-) [Full Txt.]; Mag. Index Plus (1989-); Mag. Index. Sel. (1986-); Mag. Search; Med. Rev. Dig.; Middle East Abstr. Index; MLA Int. Bibl. Books Artic. Mod. Lang. Lit.; Newsp. Period. Abstr. (1986-); Old Testam. Abstr.; Peace Res. Abstr. J. (1966-1967, 1970, 1974); Read. Guide Abstr. Select Ed.; Read. Guide Period. Lit.; Resource/One Ondisc; Romant. Move.; Abr. Cathol. Period. Lit. Index; Cathol. Period. Lit. Index; Mag. Index (1977-); TOM Gen. Index (1992-) [Full Txt.]; Vocat. Search (Jan. 1984-).

US/0010-3349
COMMONWEALTH (SAN FRANCISCO), THE. (THE COMMONWEALTH.). **Added/Corp** Commonwealth Club of California. Vol. 1 (May 1925)-. Periodical. English. Fifty-two times a year (Mon.). $30.00. Commonwealth Club of California, 595 Market Street, San Francisco CA 94105. **Tel** (415)597-6700. **ED** Gail Burns-Wax. **Circ:** 18,000 (ctrl). available on microfilm and microfiche from University Microfilms International (UMI).
Desc: Features important speakers on topics concerning the public and the nation.

CN/0826-4260
COMMUNITY DIGEST (VANCOUVER). (COMMUNITY DIGEST.). [Community dig.]. (May 1983)-. Periodical. English. Six times a year. 25.00Can$. Community Digest Publications, 1755 Robson Street, Unit 216, Vancouver British Columbia V6G 3B7 Canada. **Tel** (604)875-8313, (604)872-4749. **DD** 051. ctrl circ.

US
COMMUNITY ISSUES (LEXINGTON, KY.). (COMMUNITY ISSUES / UNIVERSITY OF KENTUCKY, COLLEGE OF AGRICULTURE, DEPARTMENT OF SOCIOLOGY.). **Added/Corp** University of Kentucky. Dept. of Sociology. Vol. 3, No. 3-4 (1981)-. Periodical. English. Four times a year. Free. University of Kentucky College of Agriculture, S-205 Agricultural Science Center North, Lexington KY 40546. **Tel** (606)257-7582. ***Continues*** *Community Development Issues.*

US
COMUNIDAD. Added/Corp Southwest Regional Office for the Spanish Speaking. (197?)-. Periodical. English (Spanish).
Ind/Abst HAPI Hisp. Am. Period. Index.

CN/0704-5522
CONCERNED CANADIAN. (THE CONCERNED CANADIAN.). Vol. 1 (Nov. 1977)-. Periodical. English. bm. $15.00 per no. The Concerned Canadian, 4660 Elk Lake Drive, Victoria British Columbia V8Z 5M1 Canada. **DD** 051.

US/1055-4149
CONCH REPUBLIC MAGAZINE. VFOAT Conch Republic. (1991)-. Periodical. English. mo. $13.95. Conch Republic Publications, PO Box 1929, Big Pine Key FL 33043.

US/0300-8258
CONNECTICUT FIRESIDE. ***Ceased.*** (1972)-(19??). Periodical. English. qt. Connecticut Fireside Magazine, Box 5293, Hamden CT 06518.

US/0889-7670
CONNECTICUT MAGAZINE (FAIRFIELD, CONN.). (CONNECTICUT MAGAZINE.). [Conn. mag.]. **VFOAT** Connecticut. (19??)-. Periodical. English. mo. $18.00 Connecticut; $23.00 US; $30.00 other. Connecticut Magazine, 789 Reservoir Avenue, Bridgeport CT 06606. **Tel** (203)374-3388. **(Subscription address:** Neodata / Colorado, PO Box 2606, Boulder Boulder CO 80322.) **LC** WMLC 91/9372. **DD** 051. **Ad Acc. Circ:** 90,000. ***Continues Connecticut, 0163-1136.***
Ind/Abst Access (1975-); Pop. Period. Index.

US/0888-7403
CONSERVATIVE CHRONICLE. [Conserv. chron.]. Vol. 1, No. 23 (June 1986)-. Periodical. English. wk (Published on Thurs.). $42.00 US; $72.00 other. Conservative Chronicle, PO Box 29, Hampton IA 50441. **Tel** (515)456-2585, (515)282-8220. **(Subscription address:** CDS SIFD Agency Control, 1901 Bell Avenue, Des Moines, IA 50315**) ED** Joseph P. Roth. **LC** E839.5; .C65. **DD** 973.92/05. **Circ:** 79,800. ***Continues*** *Hampton's Weekly Conservative Chronicle, 0888-1359.*
Desc: Features nationally syndicated conservative columnists and cartoonists.

CN/0821-2341
CONTACT (TEMISCAMING). (CONTACT.). [Contact]. Periodical. English (French). wk. Free. Association Communautaire de Temiscaming, PO Box 757, Temiscaming Quebec J0Z 3R0 Canada. **DD** 071/.14212. ctrl circ.

MX/0010-7581
CONTENIDO. No. 1 (Jun. 1963)-. Periodical. Spanish. mo. $50.00. Editorial Contenido SA, 101 Colonia Anzures, 11590 Mexico DF Mexico. **Tel** 011 52 5 5313162.

US/0898-3747
CONTEST BUSTER. No. 741 (March 1988)-. Periodical. English. mo. $29.00. Contest Enterprises, PO Box 3012, One Contest Plaza, Boca Raton FL 33431. **Tel** (407)241-1800. ***Continues*** *Sheperd Confidential Contest Bulletin, 0897-7909.*

US/1055-1220
COPAINS (NEW YORK, N.Y.). (COPAINS.). [Copains]. Vol. 1 No. 1 (Sept/Oct 1991)-. Periodical. French. bm. $25.00. Scholastic Inc., 2931 East McCarty Street, PO Box 3710, Jefferson City MO 65102-9957. **Tel** (314)636-5271, (800)631-1586. **DD** 054.

CN/0838-2395
COTTAGE LIFE. **See** Recreation, Leisure.

US
COUNTRY DATA FORECASTS. (19??)-. English. sa. $495.00. Bank of America / World Information Service, PO Box 37000, Department 3015, San Francisco CA 94137. **Tel** (800) 645-6667, (415) 622-1446.

US/1052-8849
COUNTRY EXTRA. [Ctry. extra]. **VFOAT** Country. (19??)-. Periodical. English. Six times a year. $16.98 US; $25.98 other. Reiman Publications, 5400 South 60th Street, Greendale WI 53129. **Tel** (414)423-0100 Ext. 421, FAX (414)423-1143. **LC** Discard. **DD** 051.
Desc: Published in the months alternate to Country Magazine; focuses on the qualities of rural American life.

US/0895-0377
COUNTRY (GREENDALE, WIS.). (COUNTRY.). [Country]. Vol. 1, No. 1 (Feb./March 1987)-. Periodical. English. Six times a year. $16.98 US; $25.98 other. Reiman Publications, 5400 South 60th Street, Greendale WI 53129. **Tel** (414)423-0100 Ext. 421, FAX (414)423-1143. **ED** Bob Ottum. **Circ:** 1,000,000. ***Continues*** *Country People, 0273-5903.*
Desc: Celebrates America's beauty with rural photography, fascinating features, recipes, and crafts for those who live in or long for the country.

US/0898-6355
COUNTRY JOURNAL (HARRISBURG, PA.). (COUNTRY JOURNAL.). [Ctry. j.]. Vol. 13, No. 10 (Oct. 1986)-. Periodical. English. bm. $24.00. Cowles Magazines, PO Box 8200, Harrisburg PA 17105. **Tel** (717)657-9555, (800)435-9610. **LC** AP2; .B618. available on microfilm and microfiche from University Microfilms International (UMI). Documents available from UMI Article Clearinghouse, Magazine Collection. ***Continues*** *Blair & Ketchum's Country Journal, 0094-0526.*
Ind/Abst Acad. Abstr. Full Text Elite (Jan. 1984-); Acad. Abstr. (Jan. 1984-); Garden Lit. (1992-); Gen. Period. Index (1986-); Mag. Artic. Summar. Elite (Jan. 1984-); Mag. Artic. Summar. Select (Jan. 1984-); Mag. Artic. Summar. CD-ROM (Jan. 1984-); Mag. Index Plus (1989-); Mag. Index. Sel. (1986-); Mag. Search; Newsp. Period. Abstr. (1988-); Read. Guide Abstr. Select Ed.; Read. Guide Period. Lit.; Mag. Index.

US/0746-3251
COUNTRY NEWS. (198?)-. Periodical. English. mo. $10.00 US; $13.50 other. Country Hotline News, PO Box 674, Mt. Juliet TN 37122. ***Continues*** *Country Hotline News, 0199-6444.*

●US/1061-3560
COUNTRYPLACE (BIRMINGHAM, ALA.). (COUNTRYPLACE.). [Countryplace]. Vol. 1, No. 1 (1992)-. Periodical. English. bm. $18.00. Progressive Farmer, 820 Shades Creek Parkway, PO Box 2581, Birmingham AL 35202. **Tel** (205)877-6000, FAX (205)877-6450. **DD** 051.

US/0164-5927
COUNTY LIFE (READING). (COUNTY LIFE.). V. 1- Jan. 1979-. Periodical. English. mo. $7.50. County Life, Inc., PO Box 1719, Reading PA 19603. ***Supersedes*** *County.*

US/1054-433X
COVER STORY INDEX, THE. [Cover story index]. (1989)-. English. an. $42.00 (index only); $70.00 (index and cumulative supplement combined). Highsmith Press, W 5527 Highway 106, Ft. Akinson WI 53538. **Tel** (800)558-2110, FAX (414)563-7395. **ED** Robert Skapura. **LC** AI3; .C73. **DD** 741.6/52. Index available.
Desc: Fast access to the most important events, people and social issues reported in the cover story articles of some of the most popular magazines.

US/1053-2633
COWBOY MAGAZINE. [Cowboy mag.]. Vol. 1, Issue 1 (Summer 1990)-. Periodical. English. qt. $16.00. Cowboy Magazine, PO Box 126, La Veta CO 81055. **Tel** (719)742-5250. **LC** F596; .C874. **DD** 978/.005.
Desc: Covers cowboys and ranch life.

US/0738-7008
CRAB CREEK REVIEW. Vol. 1, No. 1 (May 1983)-. Periodical. English. an. $10.00. Crab Creek Review Association, 4462 Whitman Avenue North, Seattle WA 98103. **Tel** (206)633-1090.
Ind/Abst Index Am. Period. Verse.

US/0883-6361
CRACKED. [Cracked]. **VFOAT** Cracked Magazine. (19??)-. Periodical. English. mo (except Feb., April, June, and Dec.). $14.40. Larken Communications Inc., PO Box 51, Rouses Point NY 12979. **Tel** (514)849-7733. **DD** 817. ***Continues*** *Cracked Magazine.*

US/0893-3022
CREATIVE LIVING (MILWAUKEE, WIS.). (CREATIVE LIVING.). [Creat. living]. **Added/Corp** Northwestern Mutual Life Insurance Company. (19??)-. Periodical. English. qt (Jan., Apr., Jul., Oct.). $8.00 (one year); $15.00 (two year). Northwestern Mutual Life, 720 East Wisconsin Avenue, Milwaukee WI 53202. **Tel** (414)226-7144. **DD** 051.

US/0749-2871
CRESCENT REVIEW, THE. Vol. 1, No. 1 (1983)-. Periodical. English. sa. $10.00. The Crescent Review, 1445 Old Town Road, Winston-Salem NC 27106. **Tel** (202)364-5939. **ED** Bob Shar.
Ind/Abst Am. Humanit. Index; Index Am. Period. Verse.

CN/0227-0803
CRIEE. (LA CRIEE : JOURNAL LOCAL DE SAINTE-SOPHIE DE LEVRARD.). [Criee]. V. 1, No. 1 (June 1981)-. Periodical. French. mo. Free. La Criee, c/o N Gerard, 163 rue St-Antoine, Sainte-Sophie-de-Levrard Quebec G0X 3C0 Canada. **DD** 071/.1455.

US/8750-6114
CU IN CHICAGO. **VFOAT** See You in Chicago. Periodical. English. wk. $30.00 members. Chicago Unlimited Inc, 619 North Wabash/2nd Floor, Chicago IL 60611-2713. ***Continues*** *CU Digest.*

US/1058-8124
CURRENT NEWS ON FILE. [Current news file]. **Added/Corp** Facts on File, Inc. Vol. 2, No. 1 (Sept. 17, 1991)-. Periodical. English. bw (26 issues). $244.00. Facts on File Publications, 460 Park Avenue South, New York NY 10016. **Tel** (212)683-2244, (800)322-8755, FAX (212)683-3633, telex 238 552 FACTS UR. **LC** AP2; .C935. **DD** 052. Index available. cum. index. ***Continues*** *Current Events on File, 1052-391X.*
Desc: Designed specifically to answer the current events questions of today's students. Provides background information for many stories, enabling students to understand and evaluate the issues in today's news and place them in the context of history.

US/0011-7153
D.C. GAZETTE. **VAT** District of Columbia Gazette. V. 1- Dec. 1969-. Periodical. English. bw. Capital East Gazette, 1739 Connecticut Avenue NW, Washington DC 20009. **LC** F191; .D2. **DD** 071.53. available on microfilm from University Microfilms International (UMI).

US/0164-8292
D (DALLAS. 1978). ***Ceased.*** (D.). [D]. **VFOAT** Dallas/Ft. Worth. **VAT** Dallas; Dallas Fort Worth. (1978)-(199?). Periodical. English. mo. D Magazine, 3988 North Central Expressway/#1200, Dallas TX 75204. **Tel** (214)827-5000, FAX (214)827-8844. **ED** Ruth Fitzgibbons. **Bk Rev. Ad Acc. Pr Rev. Circ:** 102,000. available on microfilm and microfiche from University Microfilms International (UMI). ***Continues*** *D Magazine, 0161-7826.*
Desc: One unique feature covers "Design," which consists of articles on important design personalities such as Frank Lloyd Wright, and practical consumer information on remodeling and home decoration.
Ind/Abst Access (1975-); Index Period. Artic. Relat. Law; Mag. Index (1978-?).

US/0198-9308
D PROJECT. 1-. Periodical. English (Greek, Modern). D Project, 7906 Santa Monica Boulevard, Hollywood CA 90046. **Tel** (310)656-1937.

US
DELAWARE TODAY (WILMINGTON, DEL. : 1983). (DELAWARE TODAY.). (1983)-. Periodical. English. Twelve times a year. $18.00 one year; $30.00 two years; $37.00 three years. Delaware Today, PO Box 2087, Wilmington DE 19899. **Tel** (302)656-1809, FAX (302)656-5843. **ED** Lise Monty. **LC** F161; .D57. **DD** 975.1/005. **Ad Acc. Pr Rev. Circ:** 25,000. ***Continues*** *Delaware Today Magazine (Wilmington, Del. : 1979).*

US/0893-3758
DEMPSEY CANADIAN LETTER, THE. [Dempsey Can. lett.]. **Added/Corp** Hilborn Information Services. **VFOAT** Canadian Letter. Vol. 32, No. 1 (Jan. 17, 1984)-. Periodical. English. sm. $125.00. John B. Dempsey, 1127 Euclid Avenue, Suite 375, Cleveland OH 44115. **Tel** (216)241-1160, FAX (216)566-1536. **DD** 971/.005. **Circ:** Not disclosed. ***Continues*** *The Dempsey Canadian Newsletter, 0011-8354.*

US/0161-4886
DENVER MAGAZINE, THE. ***Suspended.*** (1970)-Suspended (Feb. 1992). Periodical. English. mo. $15.00 (one year), $26.00 (two year), $36.00 (three year) US; $25.00 (one year), $36.00 (two year), $46.00 (three year) other. General Communications Inc, 100 Garfield Street, Denver CO 80206. **Tel** (303)979-6660, FAX (303)973-0974. **(Subscription address:** 10394 W Chatfield Avenue, Suite 108, Littleton, CO 80127**) ED** Tim McGovern. **LC** F784.D43; D46. **DD** 978.8/83/005. **Ad Acc. Circ:** 13,524.
Desc: Covers local people, places, happenings and history. Contains dining guide and events guide.
Ind/Abst Access (1979-?).

●US/1065-1535
DESTINATION DISCOVERY. [Destin. discov.]. Vol. 8, No. 6 (Sept. 1992)-. Periodical. English. mo. $19.97 US; $40.00 Canada; $63.00 other. Discovery Channel, 7700 Wisconsin Avenue, Bethesda MD 20814. **Tel** (301)986-1999. **(Subscription address:** Kable Publishers Aide, 308 East Hitt Street, Subscription Department, Mt. Morris IL 61054-1473.**) LC** PN1992.3.U5; D47. **DD** 791.45/0973/05. ***Continues*** *Discovery Channel, 0890-8540.*

US/0888-0867
DETROIT MONTHLY. Vol. 9, No. 1 (Jan. 1986)-. Periodical. English. mo. $19.00 US and Possessions; $35.00 other. Crain Communications Inc., 1400 Woodbridge, Detroit MI 48207. **Tel** (313)446-6000, (800)992-9970. **(Subscription address:** Crain Communications, 965 East Jefferson Avenue, Detroit, MI 48207 (800-678-9595)**) ED** Jack Lessenberry. **LC** F574.D4; M77. **DD** 977.4/34/005. **Circ:** 78,911. available on microfilm and microfiche from University Microfilms International (UMI). ***Continues*** *Monthly Detroit, 0149-5976.*
Desc: Features include "Modern Living," which consists of articles on current local topics such as "Shop Warn," a review of local shopping malls; "Front Lines," which includes brief articles on city life and events; and a crossword puzzle.
Ind/Abst Access (1978-).

US/0273-5261
DEUTSCHAMERIKANER (CHICAGO), DER. (DER DEUTSCHAMERIKANER.). **VFOAT** D.A.N.K. Periodical. German (English). mo. German-American National Congress, 4740 North Western Avenue, Chicago IL 60625. **Tel** (312)725-1100. **ED** Karl Stocker. **Bk Rev. Ad Acc.**

MX
DIA LATINOAMERICANO, EL. Vol. 1, No. 1 (May 28, 1990)-. Periodical. Spanish. wk.

US/1057-4182
DIRECT (BUFFALO, N.Y.). (DIRECT ... : THE NEWSLETTER THAT THINK'S IT'S A MAGAZINE... THE NEWSLETTER THAT THINK'S IT'S A MIRROR....). [Direct]. Vol. 1, No. 1 (Oct. 1991)-. Newsletter. English. mo. $21.00. Directions, 775 Main Street, Suite 613, Buffalo NY 14203. **DD** 051.
Ind/Abst F&S Index Plus Text, Int. [Select. Cov.]; Trade Ind. ASAP [Full Txt.]; Trade Ind. Index [Full Txt.].

US
DIRECT RESPONSE SPECIALIST. English. mo. $77.00 (1 year), $130.00 (2 year) US; $102.00 (1 year), $180.00 (2 year) other, postage included. The Direct Response Specialist, PO Box 1075, Tarpon Springs FL 34688. **Tel** (813)786-1411. ***Continues*** *Mail Order Connection.*

US
DISCOVER MID-AMERICA. Twelve times a year. $15.00 (one year); $27.00 (two years). Discovery Publications, 400 Grand/Suite B, Kansas City MO 64106. **Tel** (816)474-1516, FAX (816)474-1427.

US/0148-7884
DISCOVER RENO/TAHOE. V. 1- Dec. 1977-. Periodical. English. mo. $10.00. Discover, 318 Town & Country Village, Palo Alto CA 94306.

US/0197-4947
DISCOVERY (AUSTIN). (DISCOVERY.). [Discovery]. **VFOAT** Research and Scholarship at the University of Texas at Austin. V. 1- Sept. 1976-. Academic Scholarly Publication. English. qt. The University of Texas at Austin, Main Building 201, Austin TX 78712. **Tel** (512)471-5056. **ED** Carol S Hatfield. **LC** AS30; .D55. **DD** 051. Index available. cum. index. **Circ:** 10,000 (ctrl).
Desc: A journal of research and scholarly activities at the University of Texas at Austin.

US
DOMINICAN REPUBLIC, THE. V. 1- June 1934-. English (Spanish). mo. **LC** F1931. **DD** 917.293.

US/0891-5741
DOSSIER (WASHINGTON, D.C.). ***Ceased.*** (DOSSIER.). [Dossier]. Vol. 12, No. 2 (Aug. 1986)-Ceased (March 1991). Periodical. English. mo. C Hamilton, 1015 31st Street NW, 5th Floor, Washington DC 20007. **LC** AP2; .W2437. **DD** 917.53. ***Continues*** *Washington Dossier, 0149-7936.*

US/1061-5474
DOWN MEMORY LANE (LAKELAND, FLA.). ***Ceased.*** (DOWN MEMORY LANE.). [Down mem. lane (Lakel. Fla.)]. **VFOAT** Down Memory Lane Magazine. Vol. 1, No. 1 (May 1992)-(Fall 1993). Periodical. English. bm. Dobbs Publications, PO Box 455, Lakeland FL 33807. **Tel** (813)646-5744. **DD** 051.

US/1057-8366
DREAM (SAN DIEGO, CALIF.). (DREAM.). [Dream]. Vol. 1, Issue 1 (Nov. 1991)-. Periodical. English. mo. $70.00 US; $90.00 other. Dream, The Klinger Building, 2801 4th Avenue, San Diego CA 92103. **DD** 051.

US/0887-2155
DUCKBURG TIMES, THE. **VFOAT** TDT. Periodical. English. qt. $5.00. Duckburg Times, 400 Valleyview, Selah WA 98942. **DD** 051.

US/0012-6969
DUDE RANCHER. (19??)-. Periodical. English. an (Jan.). Free to libraries; $5.00 others. Cimarron Communications, 2016 Simsburg Court, Fort Collins CO 80524. **Tel** (303)223-8440, FAX (303)223-8440. **ED** Jim and Bobbi Futterer (editor's address: PO Box 471, LaPorte. CO 80535). **Circ:** 15,000.
Desc: Stories, articles, pictures on ranch life in the West.

US/0070-7554
DUMBARTON OAKS STUDIES. **Added/Corp** Dumbarton Oaks. Vol. 1 (1950)-. Monographic series. English. ir. Price varies per volume. Dumbarton Oaks Publishing / Maryland, PO Box 4866, Hampden Station, Baltimore MD 21211. **Tel** (410)516-6954.

US/0742-4728
E NEW YORKE. ***Title Change.*** (HE NEA YORKE.). **VFOAT** New York. Periodical. English (Greek, Modern). sm (except monthly in July and Aug.). H Nea Yopkh, PO Box 675 Grand Central Station, New York NY 10163. **LC** WMLC L 83/5087. ***Continued by*** *Greek-American Review, 1056-215X.*

US/0745-0494
EAST WEST. ***Suspended.*** Vol. 3, No. 9 (Summer 1982)-?. Periodical. English. qt. $6.00. East West Magazine Company Inc, Honolulu HI 96813. ***Continues*** *East West Photo Journal, 0274-9084.*

CN/1183-5591
EASY LIVING (SURREY-DELTA ED. 1991). (EASY LIVING.). [Easy living]. (Apr. 1991)-. Periodical. English. mo. Easy Living Promotions, #102, 8431 160th Street, Surrey British Columbia V3S 3T9 Canada. **DD** 051. ***Continues*** *Surrey Delta Magazine., 1184-0269.*

US/0148-5822
EGO (SAN FRANCISCO). (EGO.). V. 1- Jan. 1976-. Periodical. English. qt. $8.00. Harrison Fashion Publishing, 254 Brighton Drive, Beaconsfield Quebec H9W 2L4 Canada. **LC** AS30; .E34. **DD** 051.

CN/0715-3902
EKATA. [Ekata]. Vol. 1, No. 1 (Jan. 1979)-. Periodical. Marathi. qt. $15.00. Ekata Publication, 2315 Bridletowne Circle, Scarborough Ontario M1W 2L3 Canada. **Tel** (416)497-3546. **ED** Vinayak Gokhale. **LC** AP95.M3; E38. Index available. **Bk Rev. Ad Acc. Circ:** 1,000.
Desc: Contains topics concerning Marathi Community in North America.

US/0733-5288
ELAN (NEW YORK, N.Y.). (ELAN.). English. bm. $11.95. Elan C O Edna Greenbaum, 545 Fifth Avenue, New York NY 10017. **LC** AP2; .E367. **DD** 051.

US/0736-881X
ELBERT ROGERS' WASHINGTON STATE SCORE. **VFOAT** Washington State Score; State Score; WSS; W.S.S. (19??)-. Periodical. English. Four times a year. $6.00. Elbert Rogers International, 123 Lake Street South/#105, Kirkland WA 98033-6419. **Tel** (206)828-6409. **ED** Danny J. Shedwin. **Bk Rev. Ad Acc. Circ:** 63,000 (ctrl).
Desc: Periodical from perspectives of color. Nonsensational tabloid format concerning the lifestyles of people of color in or from Washington State.

CN/0319-3187
ELITE (MONTREAL). (ELITE.). V. 1- Feb. 1975-. Periodical. English. bm. $7.00. J E M Publications, 300 Decarie Boulevard/#5, Montreal Quebec H4N 2M2 Canada. **DD** 051.

US/0899-1154
EMERGE (NEW YORK, N.Y.). (EMERGE.). [Emerge]. Vol. 1, Issue 1 (Oct. 1989)-. Periodical. English. Ten times a year. $16.97. Emerge Communications Inc., 1700 North Moore Street, Suite 2200, Rosslyn VA 22209. **Tel** (703)875-0430. **(Subscription address:** CDS Agency Hard Copy, PO Box 4966, Des Moines IA 50340.**) ED** Wilmer Ames. **LC** E185.5; .E45. **DD** 973/.0496073/005. **Ad Acc. Circ:** 150,000.
Desc: Features issue-oriented articles, entertainment, art reviews and a piece of fiction showcasing a new young artist.
Ind/Abst Acad. Abstr. (July 1993-); Acad. Search (July 1993-); Mag. Artic. Summar. Elite (July 1993-); Mag. Artic. Summar. CD-ROM (July 1993-).

US/0046-1946
ENCHANTMENT. [Enchantment]. **Added/Corp** New Mexico Rural Electrification Cooperative Association. (19??)-. Periodical. English (Spanish). mo. $1.00. Enchantment, 614 Don Gaspar Avenue, Santa Fe NM 87501. **Tel** (505)982-4671. **ED** John G. Whitomb. **DD** 333. **Bk Rev. Ad Acc. Circ:** 90,000 (ctrl).
Desc: General, historical with editorial base rooted in the rural areas and geared towards interests of those who obtain power from a rural utility.

US/1055-1239
ENCORE! (NEW YORK, N.Y. 1991). (ENCORE!.). [Encore!]. Vol. 1, No 1 (Sept./Oct. 1991)-. Periodical. French. bm. $25.00. Scholastic Inc., 2931 East McCarty Street, PO Box 3710, Jefferson City MO 65102-9957. **Tel** (314)636-5271, (800)631-1586. **DD** 054.

US
ENCOUNTER INDIANAPOLIS. English. mo. $16.95 North America; $25.95 other. Encounter Publications, 2105 North Meridien, Suite 202, Indianapolis IN 46202. **Tel** (317)923-8868, FAX (317)923-8571. **ED** Richard L Schillen. Index available. **Ad Acc.** ctrl circ.
Desc: Description of Indianapolis.

CN/0703-0312
ENROUTE. [EnRoute]. **Added/Corp** Air Canada. **VAT** Air Canada Enroute. (1965)-. Periodical. English (French). Twelve times a year. 44.95Can$. Airmedia, 150 John Street, Suite 900, Toronto Ontario M5V 3E3 Canada. **Tel** (416)591-1551, FAX (416)591-8479. **DD** 051. **Ad Acc. Circ:** 130,000 (ctrl). ***Continues*** *In Flight, 0494-3945.*
Desc: Tailored to the interest of an affluent, highly educated, well travelled audience who fly for business and pleasure and contains regular columns on finance, wines, humour, technology, cars and both cultural and business events listings.
Ind/Abst Can. Period. Index.

CN/0013-8657
ENTERPRISE. (1963)-. Periodical. English (French). wk. $36.00. The Enterprise / Utah, PO Box 11778, Salt Lake City UT 84147. **Tel** (801)533-0556.

US
EPISODES. (1990)-. Periodical. English. bm. $7.95. ABC Inc., 77 West 66th Street, New York NY 10023. **Tel** (212)456-6070, FAX (212)456-6059. **ED** Joanne Berg. **Ad Acc. Circ:** 1,000,000.
Desc: Covers your favorite soap stars that appear on the ABC network.

US/0890-5681
EQUATOR (SAN FRANCISCO, CALIF.). ***Ceased.*** (EQUATOR.). [Equator]. No. 1 (Oct./Nov. 1986)-Ceased (Dec. 1988). Periodical. English. bm. Equator Magazine, Inc., 285 Ninth Street, San Francisco CA 94103. **Tel** (415)554-0243. **DD** 051.

US/0740-9648
ESCAPE TO THE MINNESOTA GOOD TIMES. ***Ceased.*** **Added/Corp** Creative Concepts, Inc. **VFOAT** Escape Magazine; Escape. Vol. 1, Issue 1 (May 1, 1981)-(19??). Periodical. English. mo. Creative Concepts Inc., PO Box 1108, St. Cloud MN 56302-1108. **Tel** (612)252-1220. **ED** Michael G. Lahr. **Ad Acc. Circ:** 8,500.
Desc: Covers general interest, regional events, business, health, home care, outdoors, sports, investments and history.

US/0194-9535
ESQUIRE (1979). (ESQUIRE.). [Esquire]. (Aug. 1979)-. Periodical. English. mo. $15.94. The Hearst Corporation, 250 West 55th Street, New York NY 10019. **Tel** (212)649-4014. **(Subscription address:** CDS Agency Hard Copy, PO Box 4966, Des Moines IA 50340.**) ED** Lee Eisenberg. **LC** AP2; .E845. **DD** 051. **Ad Acc.** available on microfilm and microfiche from University Microfilms International (UMI). Documents available from UMI Article Clearinghouse, Magazine Collection. ***Continues*** *Esquire Fortnightly, 0884-5220.*
Desc: Covers people, ideas, and events that pertain to contemporary culture. Focuses on search for quality in matters relevant to lives of American men.
Ind/Abst Abstr. Engl. Stud.; Acad. Abstr. Full Text Elite (Jan. 1984-); Acad. Abstr. (Jan. 1984-); Acad. Ind. [Computer File] (1984-); Acad. Search (Jan. 1984-); Annu. Bibliogr. Engl. Lang. Lit.; Book Rev. Index; Consum. Index Prod. Eval. Inf. Source; Expand. Acad. Index (1984-); Film Lit. Index; Gen. Period. Index (1985-); Index Period. Artic. Relat. Law; Mag. Artic. Summar. Elite (Jan. 1984-); Mag. Artic. Summar. Select (Jan. 1984-); Mag. Artic. Summar. CD-ROM (Jan. 1984-); Mag. Express (1986-) [Full Txt.]; Mag. Index Plus (1989-); Mag. Index. Sel. (1986-); Mag. Search; Newsp. Period. Abstr. (1986-); Read. Guide Abstr. Select Ed.; Read. Guide Period. Lit.; Resource/One Ondisc; Mag. Index (1977-); TOM Gen. Index (1992-) [Full Txt.]; Vocat. Search (Jan. 1984-).

●US/1064-7953
FACE (MALIBU, CALIF.). (FACE.). [Face]. Vol. 1, No. 2 (Jan/Feb 1993)-. Periodical. English. Six times a year. $29.00 US; $44.00 Canada; $100.00 other. Transpacific Media Incorporated, 23715 West Malibu Road, Suite 390, Malibu CA 90265. **Tel** (310)456-0790 x 112 Kagy, FAX (310)456-3724. **DD** 051. **Bk Rev. Ad Acc. Circ:** 25,000.

US/1051-5623
FACTS ABOUT ALASKA (1990). ***Title Change.*** (FACTS ABOUT ALASKA : THE ALASKA ALMANAC.). [Facts Alsk.]. **VFOAT** Alaska Almanac. 14th Edition (1990)-16th Edition (1992). English. an (Nov.). Graphic Arts Center Publishing Company, PO Box 10306, c/o Ken Rowe, Portland OR 97210. **Tel** (503)226-2402, FAX (503)223-1410. **LC** F902.3; .F3. **DD** 979. ***Continues*** *Alaska Almanac, 0270-5370.* ***Continued by*** *Alaska Almanac (Anchorage, Alaska : 1993).*

US/0885-1999
FAIRFAX. ***Ceased.*** Vol. 1, No. 1 (Oct./Dec. 1985)-Ceased. Periodical. English. qt. Hough Communications, PO Box 866, 4163 Chain Bridge, Fairfax VA 22030.

US/1056-5760
FAMA (TEANECK, N.J.). (FAMA.). **VFOAT** Fama Magazine. Vol. 1, No. 1 (Jan. 1991)-. Periodical. English. Twenty-four times a year. $26.00. Fama, Inc., 222 Cedar Lane, Teaneck NJ 07666. **Tel** (201)836-7998. **LC** WMLC 91/677. **DD** 051.

US/0889-7972
FANATIC READER, THE. ***Suspended.*** Vol. 1, Issue 1 (Oct. 1986)-(Vol. 2, No. 1 (1987). Periodical. English. Six times a year. $30.00 US; $40.00 Canada. The Fanatic Reader, 9513 Southwest Barbur Boulevard, Suite 162, Portland OR 97219. **Tel** (503)235-3607. **DD** 028.

●US/1059-9126
FIDELIO (WASHINGTON, D.C.). (FIDELIO: JOURNAL OF POETRY, SCIENCE AND STATECRAFT.). [Fidelio]. **Added/Corp** Schiller Institute (Washington, D.C.). Vol. 1 No. 1 Winter (1992)-. Periodical. English. qt. $20.00. Schiller Institute, Inc., PO Box 66082, Washington DC 20035-6082. **DD** 051.

US
FINGER LAKES. **VFOAT** Finger Lakes Magazine. Vol. 7, No. 2 (July/Aug. 1991)-. Periodical. English. bm. Grapevine Press, 108 South Albany Street, Box O, Ithaca NY 14850. **Tel** (607)272-3470. ***Continues*** *Finger Lakes Magazine.*

US/0361-9796
FLORIDA ALMANAC. (1972)-. English. an. $15.45. Suwannee River Press, Route 2, Box 380, Branford FL 32008. **Tel** (904)935-2707, FAX (904)935-2707. **ED** Martha J. Marth. **LC** F311; .F65. **DD** 917.59. Index available (bound in issue). **Pr Rev. Circ:** 8,000.
Desc: Comprehensive resource on the state of Florida.

US/0895-8084
FLORIDA FACTS (DALLAS, TEX.). (FLORIDA FACTS.). [Fla. facts]. **VFOAT** Flying the Colors, Florida Facts. (1987)-. Periodical. English. te. $59.50 (single issue). Clements Research II Inc., 16850 Dallas Parkway, Dallas TX 75248. **Tel** (214)931-9956, FAX (214)248-7159. **ED** John Clements. **LC** F306; .F595; F306; .F55. **DD** 975.9/005.
Desc: Book of facts on state, county-by-county.

US/0888-9600
FLORIDA LIVING. Vol. 6, No. 7 (July 1986)-. Periodical. English. mo. $17.95 US; $22.95 other. North Florida Publishing Company Inc, 102 Northeast 10th Avenue, Suite 1, Gainesville FL 32601. **Tel** (904)372-8865, FAX (904)372-3453. **ED** Holly Hays. Index available. cum. index. **Bk Rev**, (Qty: 12). **Ad Acc, Adv Mgr:** Jill Teter. **Circ:** 25,000 (ctrl). ***Continues*** *North Florida Living, 0887-4670.*

US/0148-9143
FLORIDA MONTHLY. Periodical. English. mo. $12.00. Florida Monthly Inc, 15383 Northwest Seventh Avenue, Miami FL 33169.

US
FLORIDA PATRIOT. Vol. 1 (1970)-. English. Four times a year. Free. Florida Sons American Revolution, c/o Mr. May, 500 Northwest 52nd Street, Boca Raton FL 33431. **Tel** (305)994-0072.

CN
FOR A CHANGE. English. For a Change, 251 Bond Street, Suite 405, Ottawa, Ontario K2P 1X3 Canada.
Ind/Abst Can. Period. Index (19??-).

US/0015-8089
FORT WORTH. ***Title Change.*** [Ft. Worth]. **Added/Corp** Fort Worth Chamber of Commerce. **VFOAT** Fort Worth. (1928-19??). Periodical. English. mo. Branch-Smith Publishing, PO Box 1868, Fort Worth TX 76101. **Tel** (817)332-8236, FAX (817)877-1862. **ED** Jim Batts. **Ad Acc. Circ:** 8,000 (ctrl). Documents available from UMI Article Clearinghouse. ***Continued by*** *Fort Worth Magazine, 1056-1919.*
Desc: Community magazine about people, places, and things in Fort Worth, Texas.
Ind/Abst Bus. Dateline.

US/1056-8174
FRANKFORT AREA NEWS. (1991)-. Periodical. English. wk. Fan Publishing Corporation, 200 North Kansas, Frankfort KS 66427-1326.

US/1064-2757
FREE TIME. (FREE TIME : CALENDAR OF MANHATTAN'S FREE MOVIES, FREE CONCERTS, FREE LECTURES, FREE THEATER, ETC.). [Free time]. (19??)-. Periodical. English. mo. $36.00 (institutions), $13.00 (individuals). Free Time, 20 Waterside Plaza, Suite 6 F, New York NY 10010. **Tel** (212)545-8900. **ED** Natella Vaidman. **DD** 917. **Ad Acc.**
Desc: A calendar of free and low budget cultural events in Manhattan.

US
FREEDOM MAGAZINE. **VFOAT** Freedom. English. bm. $18.00 (one year), $27.00 (two year), $2.00 (single issue) US; $24.00 other. Freedom Magazine, 6331 Hollywood Boulevard/Suite 1200, Los Angeles CA 90028-6329. **Tel** (213)960-3500, FAX (213)960-3508. **ED** Tom Whittle and Debbie Rossouw. **Bk Rev. Circ:** 100,000 (ctrl). available on diskette (upon request). ***Continues*** *American Progress.*
Desc: Sets the trend for issues that are important to the American public.

US/1060-5266
FRESH MEN. [Fresh men]. **VFOAT** Freshmen. (1991)-. Periodical. English. mo. $54.00. Liberation Publications, 6922 Holywood Boulevard, 10th Floor, Los Angeles CA 90028. **Tel** (213)871-1225. **DD** 051.

US
FRISKO. English. qt. $12.00. Frisko Magazine Inc, 1736 Stockton Street, San Francisco CA 94133. **Tel** (415)249-3900. **ED** Leslie Crawford. **Bk Rev. Ad Acc. Circ:** 35,000 (ctrl).
Desc: Features profiles, interviews, reviews and commentary. Dedicated to discovering the newest talents and trends in fashion, food, art, design, media, entertainment and technology.

US/0275-0589
GAMUT (CLEVELAND, OHIO), THE. ***Ceased.*** (THE GAMUT.). [Gamut]. **Added/Corp** Cleveland State University. No. 1 (Fall 1980)-(19??). Periodical. English. Three times a year. Cleveland State University / Special Interest, Rhodes Tower, Room 1319, Cleveland OH 44115. **ED** Louis T Milic. **LC** AS30; .G35. **DD** 051. Index available. cum. index. **Circ:** 1,000.
Desc: A general-interest tri-annual journal of ideas and information emphasizing either the region or regional authors.
Ind/Abst BHA : Biblio. Hist. Art.

US/1049-0191
GARFIELD MAGAZINE. ***Ceased.*** [Garfield mag.]. (Winter 1991)-(1993). Periodical. English. qt. Garfield Magazine, PO Box 10797, Des Moines IA 50340. **DD** 051.

CN/0703-5756
GAZETTE OFFICIELLE DU QUEBEC. PARTIE 1. AVIS JURIDIQUE. (GAZETTE OFFICIELLE DU QUEBEC. PARTIE 1. AVIS JURIDIQUE. QUEBEC OFFICIAL GAZETTE. PART 1. JURIDICAL NOTICES.). **Main/Corp** Quebec (Province). **VFOAT** Quebec Official Gazette. Part 1. Juridical Notices. Vol. 105 (Jan. 6, 1973)-. Periodical. French (English). Fifty-two times a year. 64.00Can$. Les Publications du Quebec, CP 1190, Outremont Quebec H2V 4S7 Canada. **Tel** (514)948-1222, (800)463-2100, FAX (514)278-3030. ***Continues in part*** *Quebec (Province) Gazette officielle du Quebec.*

US/0083-2952
GENERAL INFORMATION: THE VIRGIN ISLANDS OF THE UNITED STATES. **Main/Corp** United States. Office of Territories. **VFOAT** General Information on the Virgin Islands of the United States. (19??)-. Government Publication. English. US Department of Interior / Office of Territories, Washington

DC 20241. **LC** F2136; .U87. **DD** 972.97; 917.2972. ***Continues*** *General Information: The Virgin Islands of the United States. United States. Island Possessions.*

US/0730-9082
GEORGETOWNER, THE. (19??)-. Periodical. English. Twenty-six times a year. Georgetowner, PO Box 3528, Washington DC 20007. **Tel** (202)338-4833. **ED** David Roffman and Chandler Hotrel. **Bk Rev. Ad Acc. Circ:** 25,000 (ctrl).
Desc: Topics include the arts, performing arts, commerce, and restaurants.

US/0746-5963
GEORGIA JOURNAL (ATHENS, GA.). (GEORGIA JOURNAL.). Vol. 1 (Nov./Dec. 1980)-. Periodical. English. qt. $10.00. Georgia Journal Magazine, PO Box 27, Athens GA 30603. **Tel** (706)354-0463. **ED** Conoly Hester. Index available ($25.00). cum. index. **Bk Rev. Ad Acc, Adv Mgr:** Ann Shepherd. **Circ:** 14,000.

US
GHOST TOWN QUARTERLY. ***Ceased.*** (19??)-(19??). English. qt. McLean Enterprises, Box 714, Philipsburg MT 59858. **Tel** (406)859-3365.

US
GILCHRIST COUNTY JOURNAL. (1943)-. Periodical. English. Gilchrist County Journal, PO Box 127, Trenton FL 32693.

CN/0316-5965
GLITTER. V. 1- Jan. 1975-. Periodical. English. bm. $4.00 Canada; $5.00 US; $6.00 other. Glitter Magazine, 377 Ridelle Avenue/Suite 1512, Toronto Ontario M6B 1K2 Canada. **DD** 051.

●US/1071-4251
GOLD COAST. (GOLD COAST : THE MAGAZINE OF SOUTH FLORIDA LIFE.). [Gold Coast]. **VFOAT** Gold Coast Magazine. Vol. 28, No. 1 (Nov. 1992)-. Periodical. English. bm. $12.00. Gold Coast Life Magazine, PO Box 1779, Pompano Beach FL 33061-9949. **Tel** (305)564-5950. **DD** 051. ***Continues*** *Gold Coast Life Magazine, 0745-4619.*

●US/1047-7225
GOOD COUNTRY PEOPLE. **See** Folklore.

US/0164-4033
GOOD TIMES. Periodical. English. wk. Good Times, 1110 Pacific Avenue, Santa Cruz CA 95061. **Tel** (408)426-8430. **ED** Jay Shore. **Circ:** 33,075.

US/0191-4995
GOOD TIMES (GREENVILLE, NY.). (GOOD TIMES.). [Good times]. Periodical. English. bw. $15.00. Good Times / NY, Box 33, Westbury NY 11590. **Tel** (516)334-9650. **DD** 791. **Bk Rev. Ad Acc. Circ:** 25,000 (ctrl).
Desc: Covers music, film, theatre, travel, books, sports.

CN/0823-9398
GOODLIFE (TORONTO). (GOODLIFE.). [Goodlife]. Periodical. English. mo. $36.00. Kinderbook Newsletter Selective Media Ventures, PO Box 24624, Suite 700, 1300 Yonge Street, Toronto Ontario M4T 1X3, Edina MN 55424. **Tel** (612)451-9307, , FAX , , telex , . **DD** 051.
Ind/Abst Can. Index (?-?).

US/8750-7412
GRAPEVINE GAZETTE. (198?)-. Periodical. English. Twelve times a year. $10.00. Grapevine Gazette, 4023 East Grant Road, Suite C, Tucson AZ 85712.

●US/1062-5712
GRAY AREAS. [Gray areas]. **Added/Corp** Gray Areas, Inc. Vol. 1, No. 1 (Fall 1992)-. Periodical. English. ir (3 to 4 issues per year). $18.00 (1 year), $50.00 (3 year) North America; $34.00 (1 year) other. Gray Areas, Inc., PO Box 808, Broomall PA 19008. **Tel** (610)353-8238, FAX (610)353-7693. **ED** Netta Gilboa. **LC** IN PROCESS. **DD** 051. **[CCC]. Bk Rev**, (Qty: varies). **Ad Acc. Circ:** 14,000.
Desc: Magazine for those who love looking at the world a bit askew. Makes comments on the passing scene and annotations on out-of-the-way catalogs, magazines, videos, and comics. Also has interviews, features, and editorial notes referring the reader to more exhaustive sources of reading.

US
GREAT METROPOLIS, OR NEW-YORK ALMANAC, THE. ***Title Change.*** **VFOAT** Great Metropolis. (18??)-(19??). English. ir (49 issues). Almanac Publications Inc., 38 Kellog Street, Jersey City NJ 07305. **Tel** (201)433-8644. **ED** Marvin Tabak. **Ad Acc. Circ:** 8,000. ***Continues*** *Great Metropolis, or Guide to New York.* ***Continued by*** *Metropolitan Almanac, 1045-5108.*
Desc: Day-by-day listings of cultural and special events in New York City area.

US
GREATER MADISON. **Added/Corp** Greater Madison Chamber of Commerce. Vol. 1, No. 1 (July 1971)-. Periodical. English. sm. $140.00 nonmember; $60.00 member. Greater Madison Chamber of Commerce, PO Box 71, Madison WI 53701. **Tel** (608)256-8348. ***Supersedes*** *Progress Special.*

US
GREATER SEATTLE. ***Title Change.*** Vol. 1, No. 1 (Apr. 1992)-Vol. 2, No. 1 (Feb. 1993). Periodical. English. bm. Pacific Northwest Media Inc., 701 Dexter Avenue North, Suite 101, Seattle WA 98109. **Tel** (206)284-1750, FAX (206)284-2550. **LC** F899.S4; G74. ***Continues*** *Seattle Home and Garden.* ***Continued by*** *Seattle (1993).*

US
GUIDE TO SPRINGFIELD. English. an. $7.75. Springfield Communications Inc, Springfield MO 65802. **Tel** (417)882-3966. **(Subscription address:** PO Box 4749, Springfield MO 65808) **ED** Robert C Glazier. **Bk Rev. Ad Acc. Circ:** 20,000 (ctrl).
Desc: An encyclopedia of facts and figures on the Queen city of the Ozarks.

CN/0318-7365
GUIDING LIGHT, THE. V. 1- Jan. 1970-. Periodical. English. Northern Regional Development Council, PO Box 5, Bathurst New Brunswick E2A 3Z1 Canada.

US/0745-0079
GULFSHORE LIFE. **VFOAT** Gulfshore Life Magazine. (1970)-. Periodical. English. mo (except June, July, and Aug.). $19.95. Gulfshore Publishing Company, 2900 Horseshoe Drive South, Suite 400, Naples FL 33942. **Tel** (813)643-3933. **ED** Lynne Groth. **Ad Acc. Circ:** 20,000 (ctrl).

CN/0710-5843
GUT (TORONTO). (GUT.). [Gut]. Periodical. English. ir. $5.00. Solplex, 68 Sumach Street, Toronto Ontario M5A 3J7 Canada. **DD** 051.

HT/0304-1220
HAITI-CULTURE. [Haiti-culture]. No. 1 (Oct. 1973)-. French. mo. Haiti Culture, PO Box 260153, Flatbush Station, Brooklyn NY 11226. **LC** F1913; .H33. **DD** 972.94/003.

CN/0822-9724
HAMILTON CUE MAGAZINE. [Hamilt. cue mag.]. **VFOAT** Cue. **VAT** Cue (1983). May 1983-. Periodical. English. mo. $12.00. Hamilton Publishing Inc, 36 Hess Street South, Hamilton Ontario L8P 3N1 Canada. **Tel** (416)523-5566. **DD** 051. ***Continues*** *Hamilton (1983), 0822-9716.*

●US/1064-3397
HAPPENINGS IN SAN DIEGO COUNTY. 1st Ed. (1992)-. English. $10.00. Coda Publications / California, PO Bin 711, San Marcos CA 92079-0711.

CN/0381-6885
HARROWSMITH (CANADIAN ED.). (HARROWSMITH.). [Harrowsmith]. **VFOAT** Harrowsmith Magazine. Vol. 1 (May/June 1976)-. Periodical. English. bm (6 issues). 19.98Can$ Canada; 25.00Can$ US; 29.00Can$ other. Telemedia Publishing Inc., 555 West 12th Avenue, Suite 300, North York Ontario V5Z 4L4 Canada. **Tel** (604)877-7732. **(Subscription address:** Indas, 35 Riviera Drive, Building 17, Markham Ontario L3R 8N4 Canada.) **ED** Wayne Grady. **LC** S522.C2; H37. **DD** 630/.971. **CODEN** HARSEI. **[CCC]. Bk Rev. Ad Acc. Circ:** 155,000. available on microfilm and microfiche from University Microfilms International (UMI). Documents available from Documents on Demand.
Desc: Explores ideas for cooking, landscaping, and outdoor activities for those interested in country life.
Ind/Abst Acad. Abstr. (Jan. 1993-); Acad. Search (Jan. 1993-); Can. Index; Can. Period. Index; Energy Inf. Abstr.; Environ. Abstr.; Index Inf. (1979-); Mag. Artic. Summar. CD-ROM (Jan. 1993-); Mag. Search.

US/1049-4618
HARROWSMITH COUNTRY LIFE. [Harrowsmith ctry. life]. **VFOAT** Country Life. Vol. 5, No. 27 (May/June 1990)-. Periodical. English. bm (6 issues). 21.38Can$ Canada; 24.00Can$ US; 30.00Can$ other. Telemedia Publishing Inc., 555 West 12th Avenue, Suite 300, North York Ontario V5Z 4L4 Canada. **Tel** (604)877-7732. **(Subscription address:** Indas, 35 Riviera Drive, Building 17, Markham Ontario L3R 8N4 Canada.) **ED** Tom Rawls. **LC** S521; .H28. **DD** 640/.5. **Ad Acc. Circ:** 225,000. ***Continues*** *Harrowsmith (American Ed.), 0884-0296.*
Desc: Magazine of gardening, country living, architecture, energy, fine food and thought.
Ind/Abst AGRICOLA [Select. Cov.]; Garden Lit. (1992-); Mag. Artic. Summar. Elite (Jan. 1993-).

US/0897-7534
HARTFORD MONTHLY. ***Title Change.*** [Hartford mon.]. **VFOAT** Hartford. (May 1988)-(1992). Periodical. English. Eleven times a year. Hartford Monthly, 486 New Park Avenue, West Hartford CT 06110. **Tel** (203)236-7272, FAX (203)233-4805. **ED** Kathy Lenane. **LC** WMLC 93/1304. **DD** 051. **Circ:** 30,000. ***Continued by*** *Metropolitan Hartford Magazine, 1067-4381.*
Desc: General consumer focusing on the people and events in metropolitan Hartford, Connecticut.

US/0091-9845
HAWAII OBSERVER. Vol. 1 (Feb. 19, 1973)-. Periodical. English. bw. $9.00. Hawaii Observer, 835 Keeaumoku Street, Room 203, Honolulu HI 96814. **LC** DU620; .H24. **DD** 919.69/03/405.

CN/1183-2290
HEBDO, PUBLI-MAISON. [Hebdo publi-maison]. Vol. 1 No. 1 (Jan 1991)-. Periodical. French. wk. Limited Free Distribution. Publi-Maison, 523 Boulevard LeBeau, St-Laurent Quebec H4N 1S2 Canada. **DD** 054.

US/0018-0483
HERALD OF FREEDOM (MANVILLE), THE. (THE HERALD OF FREEDOM.). **VFOAT** Herald of Freedom and Metropolitan Review. English. bw. $12.00. New Jersey Herald of Freedom, PO Box 3000, Manville NJ 08835. available on microfilm from University Microfilms International (UMI).

CN/0441-6627
HERBES ROUGES. ***Ceased.*** (LES HERBES ROUGES.). 1-202; Oct./Nov. (1968)-Mar. (1993). Monographic series. French. mo. Les Herbes Rouges, CP 81 Bureau E, Montreal Quebec H2T 3A5 Canada.

CN/0715-5948
HI-RISE. [Hi-rise]. Oct./Nov. 1980-. Periodical. English. ir (eleven issues per year). $7.50. Hi-Rise, Unit 121/95 Leeward Glenway, Don Mills Ontario M3C 2Z6 Canada. **Tel** (416)424-1393. **ED** Valerie M Dunn. **DD** 307/.336. **Bk Rev. Ad Acc. Circ:** 40,000 (ctrl). available on diskette.
Desc: Encouraging creative positive approaches to life, serving apartment/townhouse community, general interest, food, travel, psychology, books, films, music, money, etc.

US/0742-6240
HIGH ROADS FOLIO. [High roads folio]. (19??)-. Periodical. English. an. $5.00. High Roads Folio, 3 Riverfront Plaza, Louisville KY 40202. **Tel** (502)585-5347. **LC** AP2; .H174. **DD** 051. ***Continues*** *Hard Scuffle. Folio, 0272-0361.*

●US/1067-0777
HILLARY CLINTON QUARTERLY, THE. [Hillary Clinton q.]. (1993)-. Periodical. English. qt. $15.00. Maracom, 128C North State Street, Concord NH 03301. **Tel** (603)225-8940. **LC** E887.C55; H55.

US/0193-8614
HILLS AND HARBORS. V. 1- Sept./Oct. 1979-. Periodical. English. bm. $12.00 US; $15.00 other. L'Harbour Publishing Company, 1345 US 31 North, Petoskey MI 49770.

US/0735-2387
HILLSDALE REVIEW. **Added/Corp** Cavaliers (Group) Intercollegiate Studies Institute. (19??)-. Periodical. English. qt. $10.00. Hillsdale Review, PO Box 453, Duluth MN 55801. **Tel** (215)525-7501. **LC** AP2; .H5825. **DD** 051.

MX
HISPANO AMERICANO; SEMINARIO DE LA VIDA Y LA VERDAD. Vol. 1 No. 1 (May 8, 1942)-. Periodical. Spanish. Twelve times a year. $72.00 Americas; $96.00 Europe; $108.00 others. Tiempo Sa de Cv, Apartado 1122, Danta Margarita 232, 03100 Mexico DF Mexico. **Tel** 011 52 5 5234660, 011 52 5 5236800. **LC** AP63; .H56.

US/0162-0266
HIT PARADER. [Hit parader]. Periodical. English. mo. $27.50 (one year), $50.00 (two year). Charlton Publications Inc., PO Box 158, 60 Division Street, Derby CT 06418. **Tel** (203)732-4797. **ED** John Shelton Ivany. **DD** 781. **Circ:** 250,000.

US/1064-1742
HOMETOWN PRESS. [Hometown press]. (Nov./Dec. 1986)-. Periodical. English. Six times a year. $14.95. Hometown Press Inc, 2007 Gallatin Street, Huntsville AL 35801. **Tel** (205)539-3320, FAX (205)539-3340. **ED** Jeff or Mary Hindman. **DD** 051. **Bk Rev. Ad Acc, Adv Mgr:** Dana Jenson. **Pr Rev. Circ:** 10,000 (ctrl).
Desc: Art and lifestlye Magazine of Alabama and the Tennessee Valley. Positive, upbeat view of life in the new south.

CN/0228-2399
HONES MUTUAL MONTHLY. [Hones mutual mon.]. V. 1- Jan. 1979-. Periodical. English. mo. Free. K C Hone, PO Box 4624 Station E, Ottawa Ontario K1S 5A9 Canada. **DD** 051. ctrl circ.

US/0441-2044
HONOLULU. Vol. 1, (July 1966)-. Periodical. English. mo. $15.00 (one year), $24.00 (two year), $33.00 (three year) Hawaii; $21.00 (one year), $36.00 (two year), $51.00 (three year) US; $27.00 (one year), $48.00 (two year), $69.00 (three year) other. Honolulu Publishing Company Ltd, 36 Merchant Street, Honolulu HI 96813. **Tel** (800)272-5245, (808)524-7400. **ED** John Heckathorn. **Ad Acc, Adv Mgr:** Mary Meese. **Circ:** 59,800. ***Supersedes*** *Paradise of the Pacific.*

Desc: City/regional interests and issues, including focus on special people and events which could affect issues and environment.
Ind/Abst Access (1976-).

US/0273-4990
HOT TOPICS. [Hot top.]. **Added/Corp** Information Access Corporation. **VFOAT** Hot Topics and Product Evaluations. (19??)-. English. mo. Information Access Company, 362 Lakeside Drive, Foster City CA 94404. **Tel** (800)227-8431. **LC** AI3; .H67. **DD** 051. ***Continues*** *Magazine Index. Hot Topics, 0273-4990.*

US
HOUGHTON STAR, THE. Added/Corp Houghton Seminary. Houghton Seminary. Union Literary Association. Houghton College. Vol. 1, No. 1 (Feb. 1909)-. Periodical. English. wk. Houghton College Press, Houghton NY 14744.

US
HOUR BOOK (MICROFORM), THE. V. 1- Oct. 1895-. Periodical. English. $1.00. The Hour Book Publishing Company, Cumberland MD 21502. **LC** MICROFILM 04107 AP; AP2.

●CN/1192-6708
HOUR (MONTREAL). (HOUR.). [Hour]. (Feb. 4/10 1993)-. Periodical. English. wk. Free in Montral area; $45.00 other. Communications Voir, 4126 Saint Denis Street, Suite 302 Montreal, PQ H2W 2M5 Canada. **Tel** (514)848-0777, FAX (514)848-0360. **DD** 071/.1428. **Ad Acc, Adv Mgr:** Claudia Pharand. **Circ:** 40,000.

US
HOUSE IN THE HAMPTONS. ***Title Change.*** Periodical. English. ir. Sheahan Publications, Suffolk County Airport, Westhampton Beach NY 11978. **Tel** (516)288-5400, FAX (516)288-5420. ***Continued by*** *House Lifestyle of the Island.*

US/0272-8060
HOUSTON MONTHLY. VFOAT Houston Monthly Magazine. (19??)-. Periodical. English. mo. $24.00. Party Line Publishing Co Inc, 6603 Rookin, Houston TX 77074. **Tel** (713)772-1039. **ED** Janet Henke. **Bk Rev. Ad Acc. Circ:** 56,000 (ctrl).
Desc: Entertainment, what's happening in Houston, dining out, travel, calendar of events, and listings of restaurants and clubs.

US/0888-4013
HOUSTONIAN MAGAZINE. VFOAT Houstonian. Vol. 2, No. 6 (April 1986)-. Periodical. English. Houstonian, PO Box 4319, Houston TX 77210-9990. ***Continues*** *Houston Style, 8750-7013.*

US/0278-8926
HOW, WHEN, & WHERE IN TENNESSEE. VFOAT How, When, and Where in Tennessee. 1982-. English. an. $8.95. Marmac Publishing Company Inc., 6303 Barfield Road, Suite 208, Atlanta GA 30328. **Tel** (404)257-1481.

CN/0824-5851
HUA HSIEH HUEI T'UNG HSIN. [Hua xie hui tong xun]. **VFOAT** Revue de l'Amitie Chinoise de Montreal. 1 (Mar. 7, 1981)-. Periodical. Chinese (English and French). Free. Amitie Chinoise de Montreal, 5609 Park Avenue/Suite 6, Montreal Quebec H2V 4H2 Canada. **DD** 059/.951.
Desc: Membership news and community digest.

CN/0714-5810
HUB (HAY RIVER). (THE HUB.). [Hub]. (Feb. 1973)-. Newspaper. English. wk. 35.00Can$ Hay River; 50.00Can$ Canada; 90.00Can$ other. Hub Publications Limited, PO Box 1250, Hay River NWT, Canada XOE ORO. **Tel** (403)874-6577, FAX (403)874-2679. **DD** 071/.193. ctrl circ.

US/0191-9288
HUDSON VALLEY. [Hudson Val.]. **VFOAT** Hudson Valley Magazine. (1972)-. Periodical. English. mo. $14.97 (one year), $25.97 (two year). Suburban Publishing Company, PO Box 429, 297 Main Mall, Poughkeepsie NY 12602. **Tel** (914)485-7844. **ED** Rick Dandes. **DD** 974. Index available. **Bk Rev. Ad Acc. Circ:** 26,000.
Desc: Includes a calendar of events, restaurant guide, real estate, personal finance, gardening, wine, books and cooking, etc.

CN/0828-1289
IDLER (TORONTO). ***Ceased.*** (THE IDLER.). [Idler]. No. 1 (Jan. 1985)-(Nov. 1993). Periodical. English. bm. The Idler, 255 Davenport Road, Toronto Ontario M5R 1J9 Canada. **Tel** (416)962-6001, FAX (416)962-4279. **ED** David Warren. **DD** 051. **Bk Rev. Ad Acc. Circ:** 10,000. available on microfilm from University Microfilms International (UMI).
Desc: A literary magazine in the broadest possible sense, about the things literature is about. Lucid essays on political and moral issues, reports and investigations, rambles and adventures, humorous and satirical sketches.
Ind/Abst Can. Index (1985-1986, 19??-); Can. Period. Index (19??-).

US
ILLINOIS INFORMER, THE. Added/Corp Illinois. Dept. of Labor. (1978)-. Periodical. English. ir. Free. Illinois Informer, 910 South Michigan, 18th Floor, Chicago IL 60605. **Tel** (312)793-3800.

CN/0705-923X
IMAGE LACHINE. V. 1- May 1978-. Periodical. English (French). qt. City of Lachine, City Hall, 1800 Saint Joseph Boulevard, Lachine Quebec H8S 2N4 Canada. **DD** 054/.1.

CN/1187-7162
IMAGES (MONTREAL. 1991). (IMAGES.). [Images]. Vol. 1, No 1 (Nov. 14 1991)-. Periodical. English (French). ir. Free. Images Interculturelles, 275 rue St. Jacques O, Bureau 9, Montreal Quebec H2Y 1M9 Canada. **Tel** (514)842-7127. **DD** 054/.1.

CN/1187-7162
IMAGES (MONTREAL. 1991). (IMAGES.). [Images]. Vol. 1, No. 1 (Nov. 14 1991)-. Periodical. French (English). Ten times a year. 75.00Can$. Images Interculturelles, 275 rue St. Jacques O, Bureau 9, Montreal Quebec H2Y 1M9 Canada. **Tel** (514)842-7127. **DD** 054/.1.

CN/0824-4286
IMPACT (VAL-BELAIR (QUEBEC)). (L'IMPACT / VAL-BELAIR.). [Impact]. Vol. 1, No. 1-. Periodical. French. bm. Free. Hotel de Ville de Val-Belair, 1105 Nord Avenue de l'Eglise, Val-Belair Quebec G0A 1G0 Canada. **DD** 071/.1447.

MX/0019-2880
IMPACTO (MEXICO). (IMPACTO.). [Impacto]. (19??)-. Periodical. Spanish. wk. Pulicaciones l'Lergo, Av Ceylan 517 Col Industrial V, 02300 Mexico DF Mexico. **Tel** 011 52 5 5873855. **LC** AP63; .I43.

US/0743-1503
IN JOPLIN METROPOLITAN. See Travel and Tourism.

US/0272-779X
INDEX TO THE GRAND FORKS HERALD. Jan./June 1980-. English. sa. $10.00. University of North Dakota Chester Fritz Library, c/o Beth Nienow, Grand Folks ND 58201. **Tel** (701)777-2617. **ED** Beth Nienow. **LC** AI21.G74; I53. **DD** 071/.84/16. **Circ:** 10 (ctrl).
Desc: Grand Forks Herald index.

CN/0709-6178
INDIA TODAY. NORTH AMERICAN EDITION. (INDIA TODAY.). Vol. 1- Jan. 1979-. Periodical. English. sm. $2.00. Universal Media Ltd, 203-33 East Broadway, Vancouver British Columbia V5T 1V6 Canada. **DD** 954/.005.

US/0886-330X
INDIANA FACTBOOK (BLOOMINGTON, IND.). (INDIANA FACTBOOK / INDIANA UNIVERSITY, SCHOOL OF BUSINESS, INDIANA BUSINESS RESEARCH CENTER.). [Indiana factbook]. **Added/Corp** Indiana University. Indiana Business Research Center. Indiana Economic Forum. **VFOAT** Indiana Fact Book. (1985)-. Periodical. English. ir (approximately every 4 years). $44.95. Indiana University Press, 601 North Morton Street, Bloomington IN 47404. **Tel** (812)855-3830, (800)842-6796. **LC** HA361; .I59. **DD** 317.72.

US/0893-2298
INDIANA FACTS. [Indiana facts]. **VFOAT** Flying the Colors: Indiana Facts; Indiana Facts--Flying the Colors Series. (1987)-. English. ir (every three to four years). $59.50 (single issue). Clements Research II Inc., 16850 Dallas Parkway, Dallas TX 75248. **Tel** (214)931-9956, FAX (214)248-7159. **ED** John Clements. **LC** F521; .I33. **DD** 977.2.
Desc: Book of facts on Indiana, county-by-county.

US/0899-0328
INDIANAPOLIS MONTHLY. [Indianap. mon.]. Vol. 4, No. 8 (April 1981)-. Periodical. English. Twelve times a year. $19.95 Indiana; $21.95 other. Emmis Publishing Company, 950 North Meridian Street, Suite1200, Indianapolis IN 46204. **Tel** (317)237-9288 or 326-2235. **ED** Deborah Paul. **LC** F534.I3; I45. **DD** 977.2/52. **Bk Rev. Ad Acc. Circ:** 41,927. ***Continues*** *Indianapolis at Home, 0195-2900.*
Desc: Magazine for Indiana life, entertainment, interior decorating, recipes, apparel, nostalgia, business, government and the city/state. It critiques restaurants, theater, vacation areas, TV, cinema, books and art.

US/1062-449X
INDUSTRIAL NATION. [Ind. nation]. (1991)-. Periodical. English. qt. $9.00. Industrial Nation, 114 1/2 East College Street, #16, Iowa City IA 52240. **DD** 051.

CN/0225-5510
INFORMAG. [Informag]. (Nov. 1979)-. Periodical. French. mo. Editis Ltee, Bureau 21 A/4970 Chemin Queen Mary, Montreal Quebec H3W 1X2 Canada. **DD** 054./1.

CN/0823-6879
INFORMATION BELLECOMBE. [Inf. Bellecombe]. Periodical. French. mo. Free to citizens. Information Bellecombe, Ste-Agnes-de-Bellecombe, Quebec J0Z 1K0 Canada. **DD** 071/.14212.

US/0196-3643
INFORMATION CHICAGO. Vol. 1, No. 1 (Fall 1979)-. English. an. $25.00. Information Chicago, 222 West Ontario Street/Suite 502, Chicago IL 60610. **Tel** (312)787-2677. **ED** Arnie Matanky. **LC** F548.18; .I53. **DD** 977.3/11025. **Ad Acc. Circ:** 5,000 (ctrl).
Desc: Most comprehensive listing of names, addresses and telephone numbers of Chicago area government, transportation, media, clubs and other organizations.

CN/0315-2561
INFORMATION NORTH. [Inf. north]. **Added/Corp** Arctic Institute of North America. (Spring 1973)-. Periodical. English. qt. Free to members of the Arctic Institute of North America. Arctic Institute of North America, University of Calgary, 2500 University Drive Northwest, Calgary Alberta T2N 1N4 Canada. **Tel** (403)220-7515, FAX (403)282-4609. **CODEN** IFNRE7. ***Supersedes*** *Arctic Institute of North America. Newsletter., 0066-6963.*
Ind/Abst Anthropol. Lit.; Can. Period. Index; GeoRef.

US/0731-1443
INFORMATION UPDATE / LEAGUE OF OREGON CITIES. Added/Corp League of Oregon Cities. (June 18, 1980)-. Periodical. English. mo. $15.00. League of Oregon Cities, PO Box 928, Salem OR 93708. **Tel** (503)588-6550, FAX (503)588-6554. **ED** Kim Bentley. **Bk Rev. Ad Acc. Circ:** 2,700. ***Continues in part*** *Information Update for Oregon Cities, 0731-1427.*
Desc: Articles of interest to city government in Oregon. Includes section on Energy issues.

US/1056-1064
INIQUITY (SAN DIEGO, CALIF.). (INIQUITY.). [Iniquity]. Vol. 1, No. 1 (June 1991)-. Periodical. English. mo. $70.00 US; $85.00 Canada. Beverly Hills Bluebook, 2801 4th Avenue, San Diego CA 92103. **DD** 051.

US
INSIDE WORCESTER. English. $7.95 (one year), $13.95 (two year). Worcester Publishing Ltd., 172 Shrewsbury Street, Worcester MA 01604. **Tel** (508)755-8004. **ED** Allen Fletcher. **Ad Acc. Circ:** 12,000 (ctrl).

●US/1076-0830
INSTYLE (NEW YORK, N.Y.). (INSTYLE.). [InStyle]. **VFOAT** In Style. Vol. 1, No. 1 (June 1994)-. Periodical. English. mo. Time Inc. / New York, Time & Life Building, Rockefeller Center, New York NY 10020. **DD** 391.

US
INTERDISCIPLINA. Periodical. English (English). qt. $20.00. **LC** AP2; .I643. **DD** 051.
Ind/Abst PsycINFO; PsycLit.

CN/0705-1972
INTERVENTION (QUEBEC). (INTERVENTION.). **VFOAT** Revue Intervention. V. 1- Mar. 1978-. Periodical. French. qt. $1.25 per number. LES Editions Intervention, 345 rue du Pont, Quebec G1K 6M4 Canada. **Tel** (418)529-9680, FAX (418)648-9201. **DD** 054/.1. cum. index. **Bk Rev. Ad Acc.** ctrl circ. available on audiocassette; available on videocassette.

US/0149-8932
INTERVIEW (NEW YORK, N.Y. 1977). (INTERVIEW.). [Interview]. (Mar. 1977)-. Periodical. English. mo. $20.00 (1 year), $36.00 (2 year) US; $40.00 (1 year), $76.00 (2 year) US Possessions & Canada; $50.00 (1 year), $96.00 (2 year) other. Brant Publishing, 575 Broadway, New York NY 10012. **Tel** (212)941-2800. **(Subscription address:** CDS SIFD Agency Control, 1901 Bell Avenue, Des Moines, IA 50315**) ED** Gael Love. **Ad Acc. Circ:** 100,000. available on microfilm and microfiche from University Microfilms International (UMI). Documents available from UMI Article Clearinghouse. ***Continues*** *Andy Warhol's Interview, 0020-5109.*
Desc: Interviews with celebrities and other people prominent in film, music, art, fashion, politics, etc.
Ind/Abst Access (19??-19??); Bibliogr. Mission. (Mar. 1977-); Film Lit. Index; Gen. Period. Index (1985-); Mag. Index Plus (1989-); Newsp. Period. Abstr. (1988-); Read. Guide Period. Lit.; Mag. Index (March 1977-).

US/0091-3200
INTRODUCING BUFFALO TO YOU. (19??)-. English. $3.50. National Headquarters, 114 South Warren Street/Suite 500, Syracuse NY 13202. **LC** F129.B8; I63. **DD** 917.47/97/0025.

US/0091-3197
INTRODUCING COLUMBUS TO YOU. English. $3.50. Civic Survey Inc., 114 South Warren Street, Suite 500, Syracuse NY 13202. **LC** F499.C7; I57. **DD** 917.71/57/0025.

US/0091-2980
INTRODUCING SYRACUSE TO YOU. [Introd. Syracuse you]. English. $3.50. International Credit, 524 North Salina Street, Syracuse NY 13208-2531. **LC** F129.S8; I57. **DD** 917.47/66/0025.

US
IOWA CITY MAGAZINE. English. bm. $14.70. Iowa City Magazine, 111 Wright Street, Iowa City IA 52240. **Tel** (319)351-0466. **ED** Christopher Green and Nina Lentini. **Ad Acc. Circ:** 17,000 (ctrl).
Desc: Fiction, restaurant reviews, features.

US/0895-8092
IOWA FACTS (DALLAS, TEX.). (IOWA FACTS.). [Iowa facts]. 1988 Ed.-. English. te. $59.50 (single issue). Clements Research II Inc., 16850 Dallas Parkway, Dallas TX 75248. **Tel** (214)931-9956, FAX (214)248-7159. **ED** John Clements. **LC** F616; .I37. **DD** 977.7/005.
Desc: Book of facts on a state, county-by-county.

US
IOWA POLL, THE. Added/Corp Des Moines Register and Tribune Company. Research Dept. (1943/1946)-. English. wk. $85.00. IMR Opinion Research, 714 Locust Street, Des Moines IA 50304. **Tel** (515)286-2540. **ED** Glenn Roberts. Each issue contains an index to its own contents (no volume index)--loose.
Desc: Public opinion poll of Iowans, measuring topics of current interest at both state and national levels.

US/0021-0722
IOWAN, THE. (1952)-. Periodical. English. Four times a year (Mar., June, Sept., Dec.). $18.50. The Iowan, Box 10596, Des Moines IA 50340. **Tel** (515)282-8220, FAX (515)282-0125. **ED** Charles Roberts. Index available. **Ad Acc. Circ:** 28,000 (ctrl). available on microfilm from University Microfilms International (UMI).
Ind/Abst Genealogical Period. Annu. Index.

CN/0384-7349
ISAKIMU. No. 1- Jan. 1962-. Periodical. Eskimo. **DD** 059/.971.

US/0732-9806
ISSUES (DALLAS, TEX.). (ISSUES.). [Issues]. Periodical. English. qt.
Ind/Abst Manage. Market. Abstr.

●US
JAB MAGAZINE. Vol. 1, No. 1 (1993)-. English. qt (Feb., May, Aug., Nov.). $8.00 (one year), $14.00 (two year). Cummings Design Group, PO Box 1691, Alabaster AL 35007. **Tel** (205)664-8660. **ED** Frank Cummings, Tim Spinosi, Jon Knowles and Andy Spinosi. **Ad Acc.**
Desc: A satirical look of the Birmingham area and local TV personalities.

US/1070-5163
JACKSONVILLE (JACKSONVILLE, FLA.). (JACKSONVILLE.). [Jacksonville]. (199?)-. Periodical. English. mo (10 issues). $19.95. White Publishing Company / Jacksonville, 1650 Prudentia Drive, Suite 300, Jacksonville FL 32207. **Tel** (904)396-8666, FAX (904)396-0926. **ED** Larry Marscheck. **DD** 976. **Ad Acc, Adv Mgr:** Bruce Beresford. **Circ:** 25,000. ***Continues** Jacksonville Today, 0885-4769.*
Desc: Published for the sophisticated, concerned reader who appreciates and cares about the region and its business, lifestyles and culture. Strives to help readers get the most out of life and business in Florida's "First Coast."

US/0891-1428
JACKSONVILLE MAGAZINE. ***Ceased.*** **Added/Corp** Jacksonville Chamber of Commerce. Vol. 22 No. 5 (Oct. 1985)-(1992). Periodical. English. mo. Jacksonville Chamber of Commerce, 3 Independent Drive, Jacksonville FL 32202. **Tel** (904)353-0313. **ED** Carolyn Carroll. **Circ:** 25,500. ***Continues** Jacksonville, 0021-3861.*
Desc: Covers life and business on Florida's First Coast. Includes regular coverage of business, health, real estate, dining out, arts/entertainment, home and garden, people and topics of concern to residents and newcomers.

US/0885-4769
JACKSONVILLE TODAY. ***Title Change.*** [Jacksonv. today]. (198?)-(199?). Periodical. English. bm. White Publishing Company / Jacksonville, 1650 Prudentia Drive, Suite 300, Jacksonville FL 32207. **Tel** (904)396-8666, FAX (904)396-0926. **ED** Carole Caldwell. **DD** 976. **Ad Acc, Adv Mgr:** Mischelle Grant, **Tel** (904)396-8666. **Circ:** 22,500. ***Continued by** Jacksonsville Magazine, 1070-5163.*
Desc: Features include "Short Takes," brief stories and statistics on Jacksonville; and "Acclaim," a short profile of a Jacksonville personality.

JM/0021-4124
JAMAICA JOURNAL. [Jam. j.]. **Added/Corp** Institute of Jamaica. (Dec. 1967)-. Periodical. English. Three times a year (Jan., May, Aug.). $30.00 (institutions), $25.00 (individuals). Institute of Jamaica Publications Ltd, 2A Suthermere Road, Kingston 10 Jamaica West Indies. **Tel** (809)929-4785, FAX (809)926-8817. **ED** Mrs. Leeta Hearne. **LC** F1861; .J33. **DD** 917.2/92/05. Index available. cum. index. **Bk Rev. Ad Acc. Circ:** 5,000 (ctrl). available on microfilm from University Microfilms International (UMI).
Desc: Covers science, natural history, art, literature, environment, places and cultural topics.
Ind/Abst Am. Hist. Life (1976, 1978-)(1976-); ARTbibliogr. Mod.; HAPI Hisp. Am. Period. Index.

US/0276-0029
JAMAICAN VIEW. [Jam. view]. **VFOAT** Jamaican View Magazine. Vol. 1, No. 1 (Winter 1981-). Periodical. English. bm. $5.99. Bruce Spalding, 3357 Radcliff Avenue, Bronx NY 10469. ***Continues** Common View.*

CN/0701-1083
JANE CORRIDOR, THE. V. 1- Apr. 1974-. Periodical. English (Italian). mo. Free to the area residents. The Jane Corridor, PO Box 2331 Station C, Downsview Ontario M3N 2V8 Canada. **DD** 071/.13/54.

JA/0388-6115
JAPAN PICTORIAL (NORTH AMERICAN EDITION). (JAPAN PICTORIAL.). (1977)-. English. qt (Mar., June, Sept., Dec.). $32.00 (latest issue). Japan Graphic Inc, 1-1-1 Hitotsubashi, Chiyoda ku, Tokyo Japan. **Tel** 03-214-5055. **(Subscription address:** Japan Publications Trading Company, Ltd., PO Box 5030, Tokyo International, Tokyo 100-31 Japan.**) ED** T. Nakamata. **Ad Acc. Circ:** 200,000 (ctrl).
Desc: To introduce Japanese life, arts, customs, economy, sports, etc. To promote interest and understandings among foreign countries by using beautiful photographs.

US/0277-8130
JIVE. (19??)-. Periodical. English. mo (12 issues). $19.00 (one year), $34.00 (two year). Sterling Macfadden, 233 Park Avenue South, New York NY 10003. **Tel** (212)979-4800.

US/0364-2909
JOURNAL-BULLETIN RHODE ISLAND ALMANAC. [J.-bull. R. I. alm.]. **VFOAT** Providence Journal-Bulletin Almanac. **VAT** Journal Bulletin Rhode Island Almanac. 87th Ed. (1973)-. Bulletin. English. an. $4.95. Providence Journal Company, 75 Fountain Street, Providence RI 02903. **Tel** (401)277-7508. **ED** Joseph O Mehr. **LC** AY67.P9; J7. **DD** 051. **Bk Rev. *Continues** Journal-Bulletin Almanac, 0731-5511.*
Desc: Information on Rhode Island and its 39 cities and towns.

CN/0702-5068
JOURNAL DE CLAVIS, LE. V. 1- Sept. 1977-. Periodical. French. qt. $1.25 per no. Journal de Clavis, CP 395, St-Hyacinthe Quebec J2S 7B8 Canada. **DD** 054/.1.

CN/0824-1317
JOURNAL D'OUTREMONT, LE. [J. Outremont]. Vol. 1, No. 1 (May 1983)-. Periodical. French. mo. Free. Journal d'Outremont, CP 727, Montreal Quebec H2V 4N9 Canada. **Tel** 276-6671. **ED** Patrice Dauzet. **DD** 071/.14281. **Bk Rev. Ad Acc.** ctrl circ.

CN/1183-3084
JOURNAL SUPER-MERITAS, LE. [J. super-meritas]. Vol. 1, No 1 (Jan. 1991)-. Periodical. French. mo. .85Can$ per issue. Journal Super-Meritas, Bureau 205, 5960 Est Jean-Talon, Montreal Quebec H1S 1M2 Canada. **DD** 054.

CN/0827-2077
KAHTOU. ***Title Change.*** [Kahtou]. **Added/Corp** Native Communications Society of B.C. (1983-1992). Periodical. English. sm. Kiwatamus Publications Inc., PO Box 192, Sechelt, British Columbia VON 3AO. **Tel** (604)684-7375, FAX (604)684-5375. **DD** 971.1/00497. **Bk Rev. Ad Acc, Adv Mgr:** Garth. **Circ:** 8,000 (ctrl). ***Continued by** Kahtou News, 1193-3372.*
Desc: News directed to the British Columbia region regarding Native issues.
Ind/Abst Can. Index.

●US/1061-351X
KAKO (NEW YORK, N.Y.), LES. (LES KAKO.). [Kako]. **Added/Corp** Hatian-American Student Association. (Jan./Feb. 1992)-. Periodical. English (French). bm. $15.00. Pierceaxiom, PO Box 10-0600, Brooklyn NY 11210. **DD** 050.

CN/0827-9012
KANADAN SUOMALAINEN. [Kanadan suom.]. (July 1982)-. Periodical. Finnish. bm. $11.00. Kanadan Suomalainen, 6303 Yonge Street, Willowdale M2M 3X7 Canada. **Tel** (905)229-4469. **DD** 059/.94541.

US/0022-8435
KANSAS. [Kansas]. **Added/Corp** Kansas. Dept. of Economic Development. Vol. 12, No. 3 (May/June 1957)-. Periodical. English. qt. $10.00 US; $14.00 other. Kansas Department of Commerce, 700 SW Harrison, Suite 1300, Topeka KS 66603. **Tel** (913)296-3479, (913)296-3481. **(Subscription address:** Kansas Magazine / Department of Commerce, PO Box 146, Topeka KS 66601.**) ED** Andrea Glenn. **LC** F676; .K14. **DD** 917.81/03/305. **Circ:** 45,000. ***Continues** To the Stars.*
Desc: Depicting people, places and events in Kansas.
Ind/Abst GeoRef.

US/0022-8745
KANSAS QUARTERLY. [Kansas q.]. **Added/Corp** Kansas State University. Vol. 1 (Winter 1968)-. Periodical. English. Four times a year. $20.00 US; $28.00 other. Kansas State University / English, 122 Denison Hall, English Department, Manhattan KS 66506. **Tel** (913)532-6011 ext 16, FAX (913)532-7004. **ED** Harold Schneider, Will Moses, and Paul McCarthy. **LC** AP2; .K22. **DD** 051. Index available. **Ad Acc. Circ:** 1,300 (ctrl). ***Supersedes** Kansas Magazine.*
Desc: Concerned with the life, culture, history, art, and writing of Kansas and the Great Plains.
Ind/Abst Abstr. Engl. Stud.; Acad. Search (July 1993-); Am. Hist. Life (1968-); Am. Humanit. Index; Annu. Bibliogr. Engl. Lang. Lit.; Index Am. Period. Verse; INFO-SOUTH Abstr.; Lit. Crit. Regist.; MLA Int. Bibl. Books Artic. Mod. Lang. Lit.; Writ. Am. Hist.

US
KANSAS TOO. English. Six times a year. $2.50. Kansas Department of Commerce, 700 SW Harrison, Suite 1300, Topeka KS 66603. **Tel** (913)296-3479, (913)296-3481. **(Subscription address:** Kansas Magazine / Department of Commerce, PO Box 146, Topeka KS 66601.**)**

US/1063-9357
KENTUCKY JOURNAL (LEXINGTON, KY.). (THE KENTUCKY JOURNAL.). [Ky. j.]. **Added/Corp** Kentucky Center for Public Issues. Vol. 1, No. 1 (Mar. 1989)-. Periodical. English. bm (Feb., Apr., Jun., Aug., Oct., Dec.). $24.00. Kentucky Center for Public Issues, 167 West Main Street, Suite 510, Lexington KY 40507. **Tel** (606)255-5361, FAX (606)254-4103. **ED** David G. Mudd. **LC** IN PROCESS. **DD** 051. Index available (published separately). cum. index. **Bk Rev**, (Qty: 20). **Ad Acc. Circ:** 3,000.
Desc: Journal of ideas, opinions and research dealing with public issues in Kentucky and the U.S.

US/1043-853X
KENTUCKY LIVING. Added/Corp Kentucky Association of Electric Cooperatives. (19??)-. Periodical. English. mo. $9.00 (one year); $18.00 (three years). Kentucky Association of Electric Cooperatives, PO Box 32170, Louisville KY 40232. **Tel** (502)451-2430. **ED** Gary W. Luhr. **Ad Acc. *Continues** Rural Kentuckian, 0036-0066.*
Desc: A feature magazine focusing on the people and history of Kentucky.

CN/0715-4437
KINATUINAMOT ILLENGAJUK / LABRADOR INUIT ASSOCIATION. [Kinatuinamot illengajuk]. **Added/Corp** Labrador Inuit Association. OKalaKatiget Society. **VFOAT** To Whom it May Concern; Kinatuinamot Ilengajuk. Vol. 1, No. 1 (Feb. 17, 1975)-. Newspaper. English (Eskimo). qt. 12.75Can$ Canada; 30.00Can$ other. Kinatuinamot Illengajuk, PO Box 70, Nain Labrador A0P 1L0 Canada. **Tel** (709)922-2955, FAX (709)922-2293. **ED** John Goudie. **DD** 971.8/200497. **Ad Acc. Circ:** 1,700.
Desc: Contains news, current affairs, and cultural stories of interest to the North Labrador coast.

US
KNOXVILLE GAZETTE. V. 1- 197?-. Periodical. English. bm. PO Box 3071, Knoxville TN 37917.

CN/0704-4380
KRONIKA (TORONTO). (KRONIKA.). [Kron.]. V. 1- Sept. 1975-. Periodical. Hungarian (English). mo. $25.00 Canada; $35.00 (first class) US; $35.00 (overseas) other. Hungarian Canadian Cultural Centre, 840 Saint Clair Avenue West, Toronto Ontario M6C 1C1 Canada. **Tel** (416)654-4926. **ED** Joseph Berzy. **DD** 059/.94511. Index available. cum. index. **Bk Rev. Ad Acc. Circ:** 2,000 (ctrl).
Desc: Covers literary, historical and art review of the Canadian Hungarian Ethnic Community.

ER/0452-814X
KULTUUR JA ELU. Added/Corp Estonia. Kultuuriministeerium. Eesti NSV Ametiuhingute Noukogu. (June 1958)-. Periodical. Estonian. mo. $19.00. **(Subscription address:** Victor Kamkin, 4956 Boiling Brook Parkway, Rockville MD 20852.**) LC** AP95.L4; K8.

CN/0822-8140
KW MAGAZINE. (KW MAGAZINE : KITCHENER-WATERLOO.). [KW mag.]. **VFOAT** Cityplus. **VAT** Kitchener-Waterloo Magazine. Vol. 1, No 1 (Sept. 1983)-. Periodical. English. ir. 10.00Can$. KW Magazine, 11 Arthur Street North, Guelph Ontario N1E 4T7 Canada. **Tel** (519)821-1830. **ED** Mario Maiocco. **DD** 051. **Bk Rev. Ad Acc. Circ:** 30,000 (ctrl).
Desc: City magazine featuring events listing, fashion notes, restaurant reviews, recipes, people, profiles, entertainment reviews, home decorating, health and fitness--life in the city.

US/0199-347X
LA VERNE MAGAZINE. Added/Corp University of La Verne. (197?)-. Periodical. English. Twice a year. $7.50. La Verne Magazine, 1950 Third Street, La Verne CA 91750. **Tel** (909)593-8492, FAX (909)593-4418. **ED** Ingrid Salamanca. Index available. cum. index. **Circ:**

2,000 (ctrl).
Desc: General interest and local news from La Verne, California.

US/0890-3050
LAKE SUPERIOR MAGAZINE. [Lake Super. mag.]. (Sept./Oct. 1986)-. Periodical. English. Six times a year. $21.00 (one year); $38.00 (two years); $55.00 (three years). Lake Superior Magazine, PO Box 16417, Duluth MN 55816. **Tel** (218)722-5002. **ED** Paul L. Hayden, Hugh Bishop. **DD** 917. Index available. cum. index. **Bk Rev**. **Ad Acc**. **Circ:** 15,000. ***Continues*** *Lake Superior Port Cities, 0199-7173.*
Desc: A magazine of contemporary and historical photographs. Covers events of people and places in and around Lake Superior.

GW/0937-7913
LANDERGBERICHT. VEREINIGTE STAATEN. Added/Corp Germany (West). Statistisches Bundesamt. **VFOAT** Vereinigte Staaten. 1989-. German (table of contents in English). Verlag W Kohlhammer GmbH, Abt Veroffentlichungen des Statistischen Bundesamtes, Philipp-Reis-Strasse 3, W-6500 Mainz 42 Germany. **LC** HA203; .S75. ***Continues*** *Statistik des Auslandes. Landerbericht. Vereinigte Staaten, 0931-9859.*

US/0742-7972
LAPIDUS LETTER, THE. *Ceased.*
(19??)-(1992). Periodical. English. mo. The Lapidus Letter, 2339 North Quantico Street, Arlington VA 22205.

CN/0381-7415
LAPIN AU QUEBEC, LE. V. 1- Jan. 1968-. Periodical. French. 9700 Boul des Forges, Trois Rivieres Quebec G9C 1A7 Canada.

US/0199-7254
LAS VEGAN. *Title Change.* **VFOAT** Las Vegan City Magazine; Las Vegan Magazine. Periodical. English. mo. Las Vegan City Magazine Inc, 2929 South Industrial Road, Las Vegas NV 89109. ***Continued by*** *Las Vegan City Magazine, 1049-0019.*

US
LAS VEGAN CITY MAGAZINE. English. Las Vegan City Magazine Inc, 2929 South Industrial Road, Las Vegas NV 89109.

US/0271-0145
LAS VEGAS INSIDER, THE. (19??)-. Periodical. English. Twelve times a year. Las Vegas Insider, PO Box 370, Henderson NV 89015. **Tel** (702)564-3895.

US/0886-165X
LAS VEGAS INTERNATIONALE. [Las Vegas int.]. **VFOAT** Las Vegas Magazine. Periodical. English. mo. $18.00 US; $24.00 Alaska and Hawaii; $30.00 other. Las Vegas Living Inc., 3355 West Spring Mountain Road, Suite 69, Las Vegas NV 89102. **DD** 051. ***Continues*** *Las Vegas.*

US/0748-3090
LAUGH FACTORY. [Laugh fact.]. **VFOAT** Laugh Factory Magazine. Began with V. 1, No. 1 (Feb. 1983)?. Periodical. English. mo. $16.95. Laugh Factory, Inc., 400 South Beverly Drive, Suite 214, Beverly Hills CA 90212. **DD** 051.

US/0745-5011
LEISURE WORLD NEWS. (19??)-. Periodical. English. wk. Leisure World News, 23522 Paseo de Valencia, Laguna Beach CA 92653. **Tel** (714)768-3631. **ED** David McAdams. **Circ:** 11,261.

CN/0821-5278
LETHBRIDGE MAGAZINE. [Lethbridge mag.]. Vol. 1, No. 4 (Winter 1981)-. Periodical. English. Seven times a year. 10.00Can$ (1 year), 18.00Can$ (2 year), 25.00Can$ (3 year) Canada; 14.00Can$ (1 year) US; 16.00Can$ (1 year) other. Lethbridge Magazine, Box 1203, Lethbridge ALTA T1J 4A4 Canada. **Tel** (404)327-3200, FAX (403)320-6049. **ED** Ruth Buchanan. **DD** 051. **Ad Acc**. **Circ:** 18,000 (ctrl). ***Continues*** *Stages Magazine, 0821-526X.*
Desc: Information pertaining to Southern Alberta, covering human interest, city events, travel, personality profiles, historic, fashion, gardening, and renovations.

CN/1183-7381
LETTRES ET RENCONTRES DU CASIER POSTAL. [Casier post.]. **VFOAT** Casier Postal. Vol. 1, No 1 (Nov. 15, 1991)-. Periodical. French. bm. 5.95Can$ per issue. Communications R.I.C.P., A/S P Bealieu, Apartment 202, 111 Rue de la Barre, Longueuil Quebec J4K 2T8 Canada. **DD** 054.

US/0360-1765
LEVIATHAN & KINNIKINNIK. Vol. 1 (Oct. 1974)-. English. mo. $5.00. Cutler Publications, Box 2258, Colorado Springs CO 80901. **LC** AP2; .L536. **DD** 051. ***Formed by the union of*** *Leviathan* ***and*** *Kinnikinnik.*

CN/0704-6723
LIAISON ST-LOUIS. [Liaison St-Louis]. **VFOAT** Liais-o-n-St-Louis. V. 1 (Mar. 1977)-. Periodical. French (English, Spanish and Greek, Modern). Free. Journal Liaison St-Louis Inc, 3950 Avenue de l'Hotel-de-Ville, Montreal Quebec H2T 1C5 Canada. **DD** 071/.14281.

US/0360-3342
LIBERTY, THEN AND NOW. V. 1- (No. 9-); Summer 1973-. Periodical. English. qt. $2.95. Liberty Library Corporation, 250 W 57th Street, New York NY 10019. **Tel** (212)541-8030. **LC** AP2; .L5412. **DD** 051. ***Continues*** *Liberty.*

US/0095-1013
LIFESTYLE. No. 1- Oct. 1972-. Periodical. English. bm. $6.00. Mother Earth News, PO Box 70, Hendersonville NC 28739. **Tel** (704)693-0211, (800)247-5470. **LC** AP2; .L54822. **DD** 051. available on microfilm from University Microfilms International (UMI).

US/1055-1204
LISTO (NEW YORK, N.Y.). (LISTO.). [Listo]. Vol. 1, No. 1 (Sept./Oct. 1991)-. Periodical. Spanish. bm. $25.00. Scholastic Inc., 2931 East McCarty Street, PO Box 3710, Jefferson City MO 65102-9957. **Tel** (314)636-5271, (800)631-1586. **DD** 056.

US/0741-5508
LIVING (DENVER ED.). (LIVING). **VFOAT** Denver Living. (1983)-. Periodical. English. bm. South Texas Housing Guide Limited, 4242 Medical OR 2175, San Antonio TX 78229. **Tel** (214)239-2399. ***Continues*** *Denver Living, 0192-9100.*

US/0741-546X
LIVING (FLORIDA GULF COAST ED.). (LIVING.). **VFOAT** Florida Gulf Coast Living. (1983)-. Periodical. English. bm. Living Partners Ltd, 5501 LBJ Freeway/Suite 300, Dallas TX 75240. ***Continues*** *Florida Gulf Coast Living, 0194-8857.*

CN/0706-7046
LOCAL EXCHANGE, THE. V. 1- Sept. 7, 1977-. Periodical. English. wk. $8.00. The Local Exchange, PO Box 1400, Fort Quappelle Saskatchewan S0G 1S0 Canada. **DD** 071/.124/4. available on microfilm.

CN/0711-6233
LONDON MAGAZINE (LONDON, ONT.). (LONDON MAGAZINE.). [Lond. mag.]. Vol. 1, No. 1 (Oct./Nov. 1980)-. Periodical. English. mo (except combined Jan./Feb., May/June, and July/Aug.). 16.00Can$. London Magazine, 231 Dundas Street, Suite 203, London, ONT N6A 1H1 Canada. **Tel** (519)679-4901, FAX (519)434-7842. **ED** Jackie Skender. **DD** 917.13/26. **Bk Rev**, (Qty: 6-12). **Ad Acc**. **Circ:** 40,000 (ctrl). available on an online database from Micromedia Limited. ***Absorbed*** *Ontario Living, 0827-1186.*
Desc: Controlled-circulation city magazine distributed to mid to upper income homes in London and selected areas of southwestern Ontario. Also available in newsstands throughout southwestern Ontario. Feature articles and columns focus on the people, politics, events, history and culture of London and the surrounding area. Regular features include fashion, food, travel, homes, gardens and dining.
Ind/Abst Can. Index; Film Lit. Index.

US
LONG ISLAND SOUND STUDY UPDATE. English. $25.00. Oceanic Society, Long Island Sound Taskforce, Stamford Marine Center, Magee Avenue, Stamford CT 06902. **Tel** (203)327-9786. **ED** Richard Schreiner, Kathryn Clarke, Robert Bachand, Jane Bentley, Chester Arnold, Susan Beede, Melissa Beristain. **Circ:** 6,100.

US/1067-2079
LONG ISLAND UPDATE. [Long Island update]. **VFOAT** New York Long Island Update; New York/Long Island Update; A.Update. (1991)-. Periodical. English. Twelve times a year. $20.00. Long Island Update, 990 Motor Parkway, Central Islip NY 11722. **Tel** (516)435-8890. **DD** 051. ***Continues*** *Long Island Nightlife.*

US/1054-0016
LONG ISLAND'S NIGHTLIFE. *Title Change.* [Long Isl. nightlife]. **VFOAT** Nightlife; Long Island Nightlife. (19??)-(19??). Periodical. English. mo. Long Island Update, 990 Motor Parkway, Central Islip NY 11722. **Tel** (516)435-8890. **DD** 790. ***Continues*** *Long Island's Nightlife Magazine, 0744-7590.* ***Continued by*** *Long Island Update.*

US/0024-6522
LOS ANGELES. [Los Angel.]. **VFOAT** Los Angeles Magazine. (19??)-. Periodical. English. mo. $19.00 (1 year) US. ABC Consumer Magazine, 825 7th Avenue, New York NY 10019. **Tel** (212)887-8469. **(Subscription address:** CDS Agency Hard Copy, PO Box 4966, Des Moines IA 50340.**)** **Bk Rev**. **Ad Acc**. **Circ:** 174,000. available on microfilm and microfiche from University Microfilms International (UMI). Documents available from UMI Article Clearinghouse. ***Continues*** *Los Angeles & Southern California Prompter;* ***Absorbed*** *L.A. Magazine.*
Desc: Designed to help its active, involved readers to get the most out of life in southern California...to make their lives here richer, fuller, and more rewarding. It does this through commentary and informed reports on both problem areas and pleasures, trends and provocative new ideas, emerging personalities and life styles, and on the people and events that will reshape or directly affect the lives of readers. It regularly presents useful, knowledgeable guides on subjects of special interest to sophisticated southern Californians and both a monthly calendar and complete listings of all worthwhile events and attractions. In addition to these reports, department editors preview or critique restaurants, entertainment, excursions and travel, movies, sports, TV, theatre, art, books and leisure activities.
Ind/Abst Acad. Search (Sept. 1984-June 1989); Gen. Period. Index; INFO-SOUTH Abstr. (Sept. 1984-Jun. 1989); Mag. Artic. Summar. Elite (Sept. 1984-June 1989); Mag. Artic. Summar. Select (1984-); Mag. Artic. Summar. CD-ROM (Sept. 1984-June 1989); Mag. Index Plus; Newsp. Period. Abstr.; Pop. Mag. Rev. (?-?); Pop. Period. Index; Read. Guide Period. Lit.; Mag. Index.

US/0893-7265
LOS ANGELES (LAPORTE, PA.). (LOS ANGELES.). 1988-. English. an. Fisher's World Inc, Nutmeg Farm, Rt 17, Laporte PA 18626. **ED** R C Fisher. **LC** F869.L83; L65. **DD** 917.94/9304. ***Continues*** *Los Angeles and Vicinity, 0893-9357.*

US
LOS ANGELES NEWS CONSERVANCY. Vol. 5, No. 3 (May/June 1983)-. Periodical. English. bm. $25.00. Los Angeles Conservancy, 433 S Spring Street/Suite 1024, Los Angeles CA 90013-2048. **Tel** (310)623-2489. **ED** Jim Timmermann. **Ad Acc**. **Circ:** 2,600 (ctrl). ***Continues*** *Los Angeles Conservancy News.*
Desc: Dedicated to the recognition, preservation and revitalization of the cultural and historic resources in the Los Angeles area.

US/0890-0949
LOS ANGELES OBSERVER. (19??)-. Periodical. English. Twelve times a year. $15.00. Los Angeles Observer, 10418 Yarmouth Avenue, Granada Hills CA 91344. **Tel** (818)368-9002. **ED** Leonard Shapiro. **Ad Acc**. **Circ:** 2,500 (ctrl).

US/1046-2392
LOS ANGELES READER. (1989)-. Periodical. English. Fifty-two times a year. $39.95 US; $79.95 other. Los Angeles Reader, 5550 Wilshire Boulevard / #30, Los Angeles CA 90036. **Tel** 9213)933-0161. **ED** James Vowell, (213)965-7430. **Circ:** 80,000. ***Continues*** *Reader (Los Angeles, Calif.), 0745-3361.*

US/1042-9980
LOUISIANA LIFE (1989). (LOUISIANA LIFE.). [La. life]. Vol. 8, No. 6 (Jan./Feb. 1989)-. Periodical. English. qt. $16.00. New Orleans Group, 111 Veterans Memorial Boulevard, Suite 1810, Metairie LA 70005. **Tel** (504)834-9292. **DD** 976. ***Continues*** *New Louisiana Life, 0899-0093.*

US/0024-6948
LOUISVILLE. (19??)-. Periodical. English. Twelve times a year. $15.00. Louisville Magazine, 1 Riverfront Plaza, Suite 604, Louisville KY 40202. **Tel** (502)625-0100. **ED** Betty Lou Amster. **Bk Rev**. **Ad Acc**. **Circ:** 25,000 (ctrl). available on an online database from DIALOG. Documents available from UMI Article Clearinghouse.
Desc: Contains metro-area issues, events, personalities, business and industry, lifestyle, history and preservation, arts, and entertainment.
Ind/Abst Acad. Search (July 1993-); Bus. Dateline; Bus. Index (Jan. 1985-Dec. 1985); Gen. BusinessFile (Jan. 1985-Dec. 1985); Gen. Period. Index (Jan. 1985-Dec. 1985).

US/0885-470X
M/R. (M/R : MEN'S REPORT.). [M/r]. **VFOAT** MR; Men's Report; M/R Magazine. Fall 1986-. Periodical. English. qt. $10.00 five issues (U.S.); $15.00 five issues (other). Prometheus Publishing Company, PO Box 40355, Berkeley CA 94704. **DD** 305.

US/1054-8254
MACARONI (MINNEAPOLIS, MINN.). (MACARONI : A SEASONAL REVIEW OF IDEAS AND EVENTS.). [Macaroni]. Winter (1991)-. Periodical. English. bm. $12.00. Herringbone Press, Inc., PO Box 46142, Minneapolis MN 55446. **DD** 051.

US
MACON MAGAZINE. Vol. 1, No. 1 (Winter 1986)-. Periodical. English. bm (Feb., Apr., June, Aug., Oct., Dec.). $11.95 (one year), $17.95 (two year). Macon Magazine, 227 Orange Street, Macon GA 31201. **Tel** (912)746-7779, FAX (912)743-4608. **ED** Joni W. Woolf. **LC** F294.M2; M32. **Bk Rev**, (Qty: 6). **Ad Acc**, **Adv Mgr:** Judy Sherling. **Circ:** 10,000.
Desc: A city publication featuring the people and places of Macon and surrounding middle Georgia counties.

US/0192-7442
MADISON MAGAZINE. [Madison mag.]. **VFOAT** Madison. (1979). Periodical. English. mo. $18.00 (one year), $29.00 (two year), $39.00 (three year). Madison Magazine, PO Box 1604, Madison WI 53701. **Tel** (608)255-9982. **ED** Doug Moe. **DD** 051. **Bk Rev**. **Ad Acc**. **Circ:** 21,000 (ctrl).
Desc: City and regional magazine of non-fiction articles aimed at an upscale audience.

CN/0712-4910
MADOC REVIEW. [Madoc rev.]. (1973)-. Periodical. English. wk. 30.00Can$ (Canada); 65.00Can$ (other). Cembal Publications Ltd., PO Box 250, Marmora Ontario, K0K 2M0 Canada. **Tel** (613)472-2431, FAX (613)472-5026. **DD** 071/.13585. ***Continues** North Hastings Review.*

US/0897-8921
MAGAZETTE (SHREVEPORT, LA.), THE. ***Ceased.*** (THE MAGAZETTE [COMPUTER FILE].). [Magazette]. (1982)-(19??). Periodical. English. qt. $44.00. The Magazette, 401 Market Street, Suite 1104, Shreveport LA 71101. **Tel** (318)222-8088. **DD** 051.

CN/0709-5775
MAGAZINE ILLUSTRE. (LE MAGAZINE ILLUSTRE.). (Dec. 2, 1978)-. Periodical. French. Fifty-two times a year. 50.00Can$ US; 45.00Can$ Canada; 55.00Can$ other. Editions Pop Jeunesse, 9922 Boulevardst Laurent, Montreal Quebec H2P 2S9 Canada. **Tel** (514)382-8443. **DD** 054/.1.

CN/0711-3692
MAGAZINE (NORTH VANCOUVER). (MAGAZINE.). [Magazine]. V. 1, No. 1 (May/June 1983)-. Periodical. English. Free to High Schools and Colleges in British Columbia; $5.00 other. West Coast Youth Publication Society, PO Box 86959, North Vancouver BC V7L 4P6 Canada. **DD** 051. ctrl circ.

●CN/1192-6929
MAGAZINE PROVIGO (ED. FRANCAISE). (LE MAGAZINE PROVIGO.). (1993)-. French. sm. Quebecor Inc, 7 Bates Rd. Outremont, PQ H2V 1A6 Canada. **Tel** (514)270-1100, FAX (514)276-5120. **ED** Denyse Sisto. **Ad Acc. Circ:** 2,150,000.

●CN/1192-6937
MAGAZINE PROVIGO (ENGLISH EDITION). (MAGAZINE PROVIGO.). (1993)-. English. sm. Quebecor Inc, 7 Bates Rd. Outremont, PQ H2V 1A6 Canada. **Tel** (514)270-1100, FAX (514)276-5120. **ED** Denyse Sisto. **Ad Acc. Circ:** 2,150,000.

CN/0705-6869
MAGAZINE STOP. Vol. 1 (March 1978)-. Periodical. French. mo. Free. Corporation Domic, 74 Boul. Greber, Pointe-Gatineau, Quebec J8T 3P8. **DD** 054/.1.

US/0025-0570
MAIN CURRENTS IN MODERN THOUGHT. [Main curr. mod. thought]. V. 1 (Nov. 1940)-. Periodical. English. ir (five numbers a year). $14.50. Main Currents, 12 Church Street, New Rochelle NY 10805. **LC** AP2; .M252. **DD** 051. available on microfilm from University Microfilms International (UMI). **Ind/Abst** Am. Hist. Life (1954-1958); Annu. Bibliogr. Engl. Lang. Lit.

US/0090-2128
MAINE CATALOG, THE. 1st- Ed.; 1972-. Catalog. English. an. $1.95. Eosphonic Institute, PO Box 1770, Portland ME 04104. **LC** F17.3; .M25. **DD** 917.41/0025.

CN/0228-2763
MAQUIGNON DE LEVRARD. (LE MAQUIGNON DE LEVRARD.). [Maquignon Levrard]. (1978)-. Periodical. French. mo. Le Maquignon de l'Evrard, 614 rue Saint-Antoine, Sainte-Sophie-de-l'Evrard Quebec G0X 3C0 Canada. **DD** 071/.1455.

IE/0047-5874
MARATHON BALLINAMORE, CO. LEITRIM. (MARATHON.). [Marathon Ballinamore Co. Leitrim]. **VFOAT** Marathon (Charleville, Co. Cork); Marathon (Portlaoise); Marathon (Killeagh, Co. Cork). (196?)-. Periodical. English. Ten times a year. 10.00p. Marathon Publications, Dromina, Charleville Co Cork Ireland. **DD** 796.4.

US/0274-6115
MARBLEHEAD MAGAZINE. Vol. 1 (Spring 1980)-. Periodical. English. ir. $12.50 (four issues). Marblehead Magazine, PO Box 1091, Marblehead MA 01945. **Tel** (617)631-0008.

CN/0704-058X
MARIE-EVE. V. 1, No. 1 (Feb. 1977)-. Periodical. French. mo. $12.00. Marie-Eve, C.P. 936, Succursale Place D'Armes, Montreal Quebec H2Y 3J4. **DD** 054/.1.

CN/0715-4461
MARKHAM MONTH. [Markham mon.]. Vol. 1, No. 1 (Nov. 1981)-. Periodical. English. mo. $12.00. Markham Month, Box 250, Thornhill Ontario L3T 3N3 Canada. **DD** 051.

US/0360-2192
MASKS (STANFORD). (MASKS.). V. 1- Fall 1975-. English. $5.00. Masks, PO Box 2338, Stanford CA 94305. **Tel** (415)325-0927. **LC** AP2; .M384. **DD** 051.

US/0894-3427
MASSACHUSETTS FACTS. [Mass. facts]. **VFOAT** Flying the Colors, Massachusetts Facts. 1987 Ed.-. English. te. $59.50 (single issue). Clements Research II Inc., 16850 Dallas Parkway, Dallas TX 75248. **Tel** (214)931-9956, FAX (214)248-7159. **ED** John Clements. **LC** F61; .M24. **DD** 974.4/005.
Desc: Book of facts on a state, county-by-county.

US/0025-5017
MASTER DETECTIVE. Vol. 1 (Sept. 1929)-. Periodical. English. bm. RGH Publishing Corporation, 460 West 34th Street, New York NY 10001. **Tel** (212)947-6500. **(Subscription address:** Neodata / Colorado, PO Box 2606, Boulder Boulder CO 80322.**) LC** AP2; .M392.

US/1053-4423
MAWEWI (MAHWAH, N.J.). (MAWEWI.). Vol. 1, No. 4 (April 1990)-. Periodical. English. Adastra West. Inc., PO Box 874, Mahwah NJ 07430. **DD** 051. ***Continues** Mahwah News.*

US/1055-8489
MAXINE'S PAGES. [Maxine's pages]. No. 13 (1991)-. Periodical. English. bm. $5.00. Crystal Rain Research, Box 866, Manchester GA 31816. **DD** 051. ***Continues** Maxine's Two Pages.*

US/0025-6420
MECANICA POPULAR. [Mech. pop.]. (199?)-. Periodical. Spanish. mo (12 issues). $25.50. Editorial America SA, 6355 Northwest 36th Street, Miami FL 33166. **Tel** (305)871-6400. **(Subscription address:** CDS, SIFD Agency Control, 1901 Bell Avenue, Demoine, IA 50315 (Phone: (515)246-6812)**) ED** Santiago J. Villazon. **Circ:** 218,000.
Desc: The Spanish-language version of Popular Mechanics, this magazine instructs its readers about everything from automobiles and airplanes, to electronics and cameras, to audio and video equipment. Geared to the hobbyist and do-it-yourselfer.

CN/0316-1447
MEDIA FREE TIMES. Added/Corp Nada Foundation. **VFOAT** This. Vol. 1 (1974)-. Periodical. English. $5.00. Nada Foundation, Suite 15/1209 Thurlow Street, Vancouver British Columbia V6E 1X4 Canada. **DD** 051.

US/0162-282X
MEMPHIS. Vol. 3, No. 1 (Apr. 1978)-. Periodical. English. Eleven times a year. $15.00 (one year), $28.00 (two year), $36.00 (three year) US; $22.00 (one year), $42.00 (two year), $57.00 (three year) other. M M Corporation, PO Box 256, Memphis TN 38101. **Tel** (901)521-9000. **ED** Tim Sampson. **LC** F444.M5; M55. **DD** 976.8/19. **Bk Rev**, (Qty: 3). **Ad Acc, Adv Mgr:** Jeffrey Goldberg, **Tel** (901)521-9000. ***Continues** City of Memphis.*
Desc: General interest - nearly all its editorial content deals with Memphis and the way it works - personalities, events, activities, and controversies.

US/0279-3911
MESSENGER, THE. Periodical. English. wk. Belleville Messenger, PO Box 327, Belleville IL 62222.

US/0882-4290
METRO (SAN JOSE, CALIF.). (METRO.). **VFOAT** San Jose Metro. Vol. 1, No. 1 (March 1985)-. Periodical. English. wk. $76.00. Metro, 410 South 1st Street, San Jose CA 95113. **Tel** (408)298-0602. **ED** Dan Pulcrano. **Bk Rev. Ad Acc. Circ:** 70,000 (ctrl).
Desc: News, arts and features with a special emphasis on things to do in the San Jose/Santa Clara Valley area.

US/1045-5108
METROPOLITAN ALMANAC (1989). (METROPOLITAN ALMANAC.). (1989)-. Consumer Publication. English. mo (12 issues). $24.00. Almanac Publications Inc., 38 Kellog Street, Jersey City NJ 07305. **Tel** (201)433-8644. **ED** Elliot Brahams, Michael Brandon. **Bk Rev. Ad Acc. Circ:** 28,000 (ctrl). ***Formed by the union of** New York Almanac, 0745-8940 **and** Singles Almanac.*
Desc: Singles and events calendar publication.

CN/0839-0452
METROPOLITAN TORONTO CITY DIRECTORY (1988). (METROPOLITAN TORONTO CITY DIRECTORY.). [Metrop. Tor. city dir.]. **Added/Corp** Might Directories, Ltd. **VFOAT** Might's Metropolitan Toronto City Directory. (1988)-. Directory. English. Leased to subscribers only. Leased price, $345.00. Might Directories, 220 Bartley Drive, Toronto Ontario M4A 2H4 Canada. **Tel** (416)751-2751. **DD** 917.13/541/0025. ***Continues** Metropolitan Toronto (York County, Ontario) City Directory., 0228-9601.*

US/0730-2584
MEXICAN FORUM, THE. [Mex. forum]. **VFOAT** Foro Mexicano. Vol. 1, No. 1 (Jan. 1981)-. Periodical. English. qt. $5.00 individuals; $10.00 institutions. University of Texas at Austin Office for Mexican Studies, Institute of Latin American Studies, Austin TX 78712. **Tel** (512)471-5551. **ED** E V Neimeyer Jr. **Circ:** 400.
Desc: Articles on current economic, political, social, and cultural situation in Mexico. Issues of US-Mexico relationship, notes on Mexico today and significant acquisitions of University of Texas Latin American Collection.

US/0894-4652
MEXICO MAGAZINE (CARBONDALE, COLO.). (MEXICO MAGAZINE.). Vol. 1, No. 1 (1987)-. Periodical. English. Four times a year. Mexico Magazine, PO Box 700, Carbondale CO 81623. **Tel** (303)963-2330. **DD** 972.

US/0273-9372
MIAMI MENSUAL. (Dec. 1980/Jan. 1981)-. Periodical. Spanish (English). Ten times a year. $16.00 US and Canada; $76.00 other. Miami Mensual, 2455 SW 27th Avenue #200, Miami FL 33145. **Tel** (305)444-5678. **ED** Frank Soler. **LC** F319.M6; M637. **DD** 975.9/381. **Bk Rev. Ad Acc, Adv Mgr:** Ana Soler. **Circ:** 25,000 (ctrl).
Desc: City and regional magazine edited in Spanish for residents and visitors of South Florida. Includes lifestyles, in-depth reporting, finance, arts, travel, dining and guide to area activities.

●US/1063-1763
MID-ATLANTIC ALMANACK, THE. (THE MID-ATLANTIC ALMANACK: THE JOURNAL OF THE MID-ATLANTIC POPULAR/AMERICAN CULTURE ASSOCIATION.). **Added/Corp** Mid-Atlantic Popular/American Culture Association. (1992)-. English. $25.00. Mid-Atlantic Popular/ American Culture Association, C/O M Campbell, Mapca Treasurer, Mount Street, Mary's College, Emmitsburg MD 21727.

US/0888-1022
MID-ATLANTIC COUNTRY. VFOAT Country. Vol. 7, No. 1 (Jan. 1986)-. Periodical. English. Twelve times a year. $18.00. Mid-Atlantic Country Magazine, 6401 Golden Triangle Drive, Suite 120, Greenbelt MD 20770. **Tel** (301)220-2300. **ED** Tim Sayles. **LC** E169.02; .C658. **DD** 974/.005. **Bk Rev. Ad Acc. Circ:** 120,000. ***Continues** Country Magazine, 0271-759X.*
Desc: News and information of the home, garden, travel and leisure.

CN
MIDNIGHT. 1st- Ed.; 1976-. Periodical. English. $2.00 each number. Globe International Inc, 1350 Sherbrooke Street W/Suite 600, Montreal Quebec H3G 2T4 Canada. **DD** 051.
Desc: A projected series of Midnight special reports on various issues, events and personalities of the day.

US/0889-8138
MIDWEST LIVING. [Midwest living]. Vol. 1, No. 1 (April 1987)-. Periodical. English. bm (6 issues). $16.97 (one year), $23.97 (two year), $39.97 (three year). Meredith Corporation, Locust at 17th, Des Moines IA 50309. **Tel** (515)284-3000. **(Subscription address:** Neodata / Colorado, PO Box 2606, Boulder Boulder CO 80322.**) LC** F355; .M53. **DD** 978/.005. **Circ:** 570,000.
Desc: A guide for people seeking the Midwest's cultural attractions and recreation, travel, food and entertaining, personalities and contemporary issues.
Ind/Abst Access (1988-).

US/0026-3451
MIDWEST QUARTERLY (PITTSBURG), THE. (THE MIDWEST QUARTERLY.). [Midwest q.]. **Added/Corp** Pittsburg State University. Kansas State College of Pittsburg. Vol. 1 (Autumn 1959)-. Academic Scholarly Publication. English. qt. $12.00 US; $16.00 other. Pittsburg State University, c/o Dr. James B. M. Schick, Deptartment of Economics, Finance & Banking, Pittsburg KS 66762. **Tel** (316)235-4547, , FAX (316) 232-7515. **ED** James B M Schick, (editor's phone: (316)235-4317). **LC** AS30; .M5. **DD** 378.781/98. Index available. **Bk Rev**, (Qty: 8 or more per year). **Pr Rev. Circ:** 950. available on microfilm and microfiche from University Microfilms International (UMI). Documents available from The Genuine Article, UMI Article Clearinghouse. ***Supersedes** Educational Leader.*
Desc: Publishes scholarly articles dealing with a broad range of subjects of current interest. Also seeks discussions of analytical and speculative nature.
Ind/Abst Abstr. Engl. Stud.; Acad. Search (July 1993-); Am. Hist. Life (1963-); Annu. Bibliogr. Engl. Lang. Lit.; ARTbibliogr. Mod.; Arts Humanit. Citation Index [Full Cov.]; Expand. Acad. Index (1989-); Humanit. Index; Humanit. Source (Jul. 1993-); Index Am. Period. Verse; Index Book Rev. Humanit. (1984-); INFO-SOUTH Abstr.; Lit. Crit. Regist.; Mag. Search; MLA Int. Bibl. Books Artic. Mod. Lang. Lit.; Newsp. Period. Abstr. (1991-); Public Aff. Inf. Serv. Bull.; Recent. Publ. Artic.; Res. Alert [Full Cov.]; Romant. Move.; Soc. Plann. Policy Dev. Abstr.; Soc. Sci. Cit. Index [Select. Cov.]; Sociol. Abstr.; SportSearch; Writ. Am. Hist.

US
MIDWEST SHARED NEWSLETTER. Newsletter. English. $120.00 new, $240.00 renew; $180.00 new, $300.00 renew including diskette. Midwest Shared News Service, PO Box 59255, Chicago IL 60659. **Tel** (312)262-9498. available on diskette.

US/0741-1243
MILWAUKEE MAGAZINE. VFOAT Milwaukee. (19??)-. Periodical. English. mo. $17.00 (1 year), $33.00 (2 year), $43.00 (3 year). Milwaukee Magazine, c/o M McGeary, 312 East Buffalo Street, Milwaukee WI

53202-5808. **Tel** (414)273-1101, FAX (414)273-0016. **ED** John Fennell. **Ad Acc, Adv Mgr:** Pat Replia. **Circ:** 50,000. ***Continues*** *Milwaukee (WFMR, Inc. (Radio Station : Milwaukee)), 0746-3790.*
Desc: Focuses on the people and events in Southeastern Wisconsin. Regular features include a monthly calendar of events, restaurant reviews, dining guide and an inside look at area personalities.
Ind/Abst Access (1986-).

US
MINNESOTA CALLS. ***Ceased.*** (19??)-(19??). Periodical. English. bm (6 issues). Stolee Communications, PO Box 640, Duluth MN 55801. **Tel** (218)722-7761, (800)848-4906, FAX (218)722-8233. **ED** Jo Paull. **Bk Rev. Ad Acc.**
Desc: Magazine about life in Minnesota.

US
MINNESOTA COUNTIES. Added/Corp Association of Minnesota Counties. (19??)-. Periodical. English. mo. $30.00. Association of Minnesota Counties, 125 Charles Avenue, St. Paul MN 55103. **Tel** (612)224-3344.

US/0739-8700
MINNESOTA MONTHLY (COLLEGEVILLE, MINN.). (MINNESOTA MONTHLY.). Vol. 10 (Jan. 1976)-. Periodical. English. mo. $14.95 (one year), $21.95 (two year). Minnesota Monthly, 45 East 8th Street, St Paul MN 55101. **Tel** (612)221-1500. **ED** Len Witt. **Bk Rev. Ad Acc, Adv Mgr:** Steve Fox, **Tel** (612)371-5808. **Circ:** 65,000 (ctrl). ***Continues*** *Preview.*
Desc: Regional magazine explores vitality and variety of life, arts, and public affairs of upper Midwest. Also program guide for broadcast services of Minnesota public radio.

CN/0846-9423
MINUTES OF PROCEEDINGS AND EVIDENCE OF THE STANDING COMMITTEE ON MULTICULTURALISM AND CITIZENSHIP. [Minutes proc. evid. Standing Comm. Multicult. Citizsh.]. **Main/Corp** Canada. Parliament. House of Commons. Standing Committee on Multiculturalism and Citizenship. **VFOAT** Proces-Verbaux et Emoignages du Comite du Multiculturalisme et de la Citoyennete. 2nd Session of the 34th Parliament, Issue No. 1 (Oct. 19, Nov. 23, Dec. 12, Dec. 19/20, 1989)-. Proceedings. French (English and French). **LC** IN PROCESS. **DD** 306.4/46/0971/05. ***Continues*** *Canada. Parliament. House of Commons. Standing Committee on Communications, Culture, Citizenship and Multiculturalism. Minutes of Proceedings and Evidence of the Standing Committee on Communication, Culture, Citizenshipand Multiculturalism, 0844-8604.*
Desc: Speaks of Canada and citizenship.

CN/1182-5812
MIRROR MONTREAL. 1990. (MIRROR.). [Mirror Montr., 1990]. (1990)-. Periodical. English. wk. 125.00Can$. Communication Gratte-Ciel Ltee, 400 McGill Street, First and Second Floor, Montreal Quebec H2Y 2G1 Canada. **Tel** (514)393-1010. **ED** Annarosa Sabbadini. **DD** 700.971428. cum. index. **Bk Rev**, (Qty: 51). **Ad Acc, Adv Mgr:** Paul Cassar. **Circ:** 80,000 (ctrl). available on microfiche from University Microfilms International (UMI). ***Continues*** *Montreal Mirror, 0833-8086.*
Desc: Alternative culture and news weekly.

US/1045-1021
MISSISSIPPI COAST. ***Ceased.*** [Miss. coast]. **VFOAT** Coast; Mississippi Coast Magazine. Vol. 1, No. 1 (Oct./Nov. 1988)-Vol. 5, No. 2 (1992). Periodical. English. bm. Mississippi Coast Magazine, PO Box 1209, Gulfport MS 39502. **Tel** (601)868-1182, FAX (601)867-2986. **ED** Karen Bryant. **DD** 976. **Ad Acc, Adv Mgr:** Jeff Bell. **Circ:** 25,000.
Desc: Showcases Southern Mississippi with lively stories and full-color photography. Designed to help readers experience the beauty, humor, grace and splendid scenery of South Mississippi. Articles are selected, written, and edited with the expectations of the audience in mind.

US/0747-1602
MISSISSIPPI (JACKSON, MISS. 1982). ***Title Change.*** (MISSISSIPPI : A VIEW OF THE MAGNOLIA STATE.). [Mississippi]. Vol. 1, No. 1 (Sept./Oct. 1982)-?. Periodical. English. bm. Downhome Publications Inc, PO Box 16445, Jackson MS 39236. **Tel** (601)982-8418, FAX (601)366-4605. **ED** Ann Wilson Day. **LC** F336; .M598. **DD** 976.2/005. **Bk Rev. Ad Acc. Circ:** 25,000. ***Continued by*** *Mississippi Magazine.*
Desc: Presenting the best of Mississippi's people, places, and events in a lively, attractive format featuring color photography and compelling prose.
Ind/Abst Access (1984-).

US/0199-5677
MISSISSIPPI MAGAZINE (JACKSON). (MISSISSIPPI MAGAZINE.). **VFOAT** Mississippi. Vol. 3, No. 4 (Jan. 1980)-. Periodical. English. bm. $16.00 (one year), $27.00 (two year) US; $21.00 (one year), $37.00 (two year) (other). Downhome Publications Inc, PO Box 16445, Jackson MS 39236. **Tel** (601)982-8418, FAX (601)366-4605. **ED** Ann Becker. **Bk Rev**, (Qty: 6). **Ad Acc, Adv Mgr:** Richard Roper, **Tel** (601)982-8418. **Circ:** 25,000. ***Continues*** *Mississippi / A View of the Magnolia State., 0164-6699.*
Desc: A view of the people, lifestyles, history, food, art, homes, and events of Mississippi.

US/0279-3261
MISSOURI ENTERPRISE. Vol. 1, No. 1 (Aug. 1981)-. Periodical. English. Eleven times a year. Free on request. Missouri Enterprise, PO Box 118, Jefferson City MO 65102. **Tel** (314)751-2741.

US/1047-6830
MISSOURI MAGAZINE (SAINT LOUIS, MO.). (MISSOURI MAGAZINE.). [Mo. mag.]. (Fall 1989)-. Periodical. English. Four times a year (Jan., Apr., July, Oct.). $16.95 (one year); $33.00 (two years); $47.88 (three years). EROMDA Publishing Company, 109 West Washington, Milstadt IL 62260. **Tel** (314)621-0176, FAX (618)476-1616. **DD** 917. ***Continues*** *Missouri Life, 0090-760X.*

CN/0380-4372
MLLE-ACTUALITE. V. 1- Summer 1971-. Periodical. French. qt. Mlle-Actualite, 2120 Est, Rue Sherbrooke, Montreal Quebec H2K 1C3. **DD** 054/.1.

US
MOBILE BAY MONTHLY. Vol. 1, No. 1 (Jan. 1986)-. Periodical. English. mo. PMT Publishing, PO Box 66200, Mobile AL 36660. **Tel** (205)479-8722, (205)473-6269, FAX (205)473-6269. **LC** WMLC 91/1474. ***Continues*** *Greater Mobile Magazine.*

US/0026-7457
MODERN AGE (CHICAGO). (MODERN AGE.). [Mod. age]. **Added/Corp** Intercollegiate Studies Institute. Foundation for Foreign Affairs. Vol. 1, No. 1 (Summer 1957)-. English. qt. $15.00 (one year), $25.00 (two year). Intercollegiate Studies Institute, #100 14 South Bryn Mawr Avenue, Bryn Mawr PA 19010. **Tel** (800)526-7022, (215)525-7501. **ED** George A. Panichas. **LC** AP2; .M628. **DD** 051. Index available. **Bk Rev. Ad Acc. Circ:** 3,500. available on microfilm and microfiche from University Microfilms International (UMI). Documents available from UMI Article Clearinghouse. ***Continued in part by*** *Burke Newsletter.*
Desc: The principal publication of intellectual conservatism.
Ind/Abst Abstr. Engl. Stud.; Acad. Abstr. Full Text Elite (July 1990-); Acad. Abstr. (July 1990-); Acad. Ind. [Computer File] (1987-); Acad. Search (July 1990-); Am. Hist. Life (1962-); Annu. Bibliogr. Engl. Lang. Lit.; Book Rev. Index; Expand. Acad. Index (1987-); Hist. Abstr.; Hist. Source (July 1990-); Humanit. Index; Index Book Rev. Humanit.; INFO-SOUTH Abstr.; Int. Polit. Sci. Abstr.; Mag. Search; Middle East Abstr. Index; MLA Int. Bibl. Books Artic. Mod. Lang. Lit.; Newsp. Period. Abstr. (1991-); Public Aff. Inf. Serv. Bull.; Romant. Move. (1962-); Soc. Sci. Index; Writ. Am. Hist.

US/0076-9894
MODERN AMERICA. No. 1- 1964-. Monographic series. English. ir. Price varies per volume. Ohio State University Press, 1070 Carmack Road, 180 Pressey Hall, Columbus OH 43210. **Tel** (614)292-6930, (614)292-1407, FAX (614)292-2065.

US/0883-5438
MONTAGE (ROCKVILLE, MD.). (MONTAGE.). **VFOAT** Washington, D.C. Montage. English. an. $3.95. Montage Publications, 11408 Hollow Tree Lane, Rockville MD 20852. **LC** F192.3; .M58. **DD** 917.53/044.

US/0274-9955
MONTANA MAGAZINE. (19??)-. Periodical. English. bm. Montana Magazine, Box 5630, Helena MT 59604. **Tel** (406)443-2842, FAX (406)443-5480. ***Continues*** *Montana.*

US/0274-8770
MONTEREY LIFE. ***Suspended.*** Periodical. English. mo. $18.00. Monterey Life, PO Box 2107, Monterey CA 93942-2107. **Tel** (408)372-9200. **ED** Suzie Howell. **Bk Rev. Ad Acc. Circ:** 25,000.

US
MONTHLY REVIEW / CT. English. mo. Free on request. Conning & Company, 185 Asylum Street, City Place II, Hartford CT 06103. **Tel** (203) 520-1521, FAX (203) 520-1504.

US/0277-0482
MORE MINNESOTA GUIDE MAGAZINE. **VFOAT** More Minnesota. Vol. 1, No. 1 (June 1981)-. Periodical. English. mo. $8.00. Eagle Publishing Company / Minnesota, PO Box 449, Northfield MN 55057.

US/0027-1535
MOTHER EARTH NEWS, THE. [Mother earth news]. No. 1 (Jan. 1970)-. Periodical. English. bm (6 issues). $18.00. Sussex Publishers Inc., 49 East 21st Street, 11th Floor, New York NY 10010. **Tel** (212) 260-7210. **(Subscription address:** Neodata / Colorado, PO Box 2606, Boulder Boulder CO 80322.**) LC** AP2; .M7919. **DD** 051. available on microfiche from C.M.I.C. Inc.; available on microfilm from Bell & Howell; available on microfilm and microfiche from University Microfilms International (UMI); available on an online database (file 647/Full-Text) from DIALOG. Documents available from UMI Article Clearinghouse, Magazine Collection.
Desc: A country magazine.
Ind/Abst Acad. Abstr. Full Text Elite (Jan. 1984-) [Full Txt.]; Acad. Abstr. (Jan. 1984-); Acad. Ind. [Computer File] (1984-); Acad. Search (Jan. 1984-); Consum. Index Prod. Eval. Inf. Source; Energy Res. Abstr. (Aug. 1976-); Expand. Acad. Index (1984-); Foods Adlibra; Garden Lit. (1992-); Gen. Period. Index (1985-); Health Source (Jan. 1984-); Index Inf.; Mag. Artic. Summar. Elite (Jan. 1984-) [Full Txt.]; Mag. Artic. Summar. Select (Jan. 1984-) [Full Txt.]; Mag. Artic. Summar. CD-ROM (Jan. 1984-); Mag. Express (1986-) [Full Txt.]; Mag. Index Plus (1989-); Mag. Index Sel. Microfiche (1986-) [Full Txt.]; Mag. Index. Sel. (1986-); Mag. Search; Mid. Search (Jan. 1984-); Newsp. Period. Abstr. (1986-); Read. Guide Abstr. Select Ed.; Read. Guide Period. Lit.; Resource/One Ondisc; Mag. Index (1977-); TOM Gen. Index (1985-) [Full Txt.]; Vocat. Search (Jan. 1984-) [Full Txt.].

US/0194-536X
MOUNTAINEER POSTMASTER. Periodical. English. bm. Mountaineer Postmaster, 416 Mansion Street, Hamlin WV 25523.

US/0191-9482
MOUNTAINWEST MAGAZINE. Vol. 1 (1975)-. Periodical. English. mo. $8.00. Mountainwest Magazine, 125 East 300 South, Provo UT 84601.

CN/0833-0026
MTL. MONTREAL. ***Ceased.*** (MTL : MONTREAL.). [MTL, Montr.]. **VFOAT** Montreal. No 1 (Nov. 15 1986/Jan. 15 1987)-(July 1993). Periodical. English (French). Eight times a year. Canam Publications Ltd., 4954 Place de la Savane, Montreal Quebec H4P 2M9 Canada. **Tel** (514)731-9517. **ED** Alastair Sutherland. **DD** 051. **Ad Acc, Adv Mgr:** Sharon Dawe. **Circ:** 115,000.

US/1056-2664
NASHVILLE INDEX. (1991)-. Periodical. English. Nashville Index, 1277 Cheyenne Boulevard, Madison TN 37115-5528.

US/0895-4321
NATIONAL DIRECTORY OF MAGAZINES, THE. [Natl. dir. mag.]. 1st Ed. (1988)-. Directory. English. an. $395.00 (quarterly updates available with standing order). Oxbridge Communications Inc, 150 5th Avenue, Room 636, New York NY 10011. **Tel** (212)741-0231, FAX (212)633-2938. **ED** Lou Hagood. **LC** Z6941; .N28; PN4877. **DD** 051/.025. Index available. **Ad Acc.** available on magnetic tape.
Desc: Directory of US and Canadian magazines, including trade, professional, special interest tabloids, magazine/buyer's guides and magazine printing companies.

US/1056-3482
NATIONAL ENQUIRER (NEW YORK, N.Y. 1957). (NATIONAL ENQUIRER.). [Natl. enq. (N. Y. N. Y., 1957)]. Vol. 31, No. 41 (June 16/22, 1957)-. Newspaper. English. wk. $37.44. National Enquirer, 600 South East Coast Avenue, Lantana FL 33464. **Tel** (407)586-1111. **(Subscription address:** CDS / SIFD Agency Control, 1901 Bell Avenue, Des Moines IA 50315.**) DD** 051. available on microfilm and microfiche from University Microfilms International (UMI). ***Continues*** *New York Enquirer (1950).*
Desc: Contains unusual new items, celebrity gossip and human interest stories.

US/0027-9587
NATIONAL LAMPOON. (1970)-. Periodical. English. bm. $23.70. National Lampoon Inc., 10850 Wilshire Road Boulevard, Suite 1000, Los Angeles CA 90024. **Tel** (310)474-5252. **(Subscription address:** National Lampoon, PO Box 4140, Irvine CA 92716.**) ED** Larry Sloman, Michael Simmons, Matty Simmons. **LC** AP2; .N28. **DD** 051. Index available. **Ad Acc. Circ:** 250,000. available on microfilm and microfiche from University Microfilms International (UMI).
Desc: Contemporary magazine of humor, satire, and parody. Provides advertisers with access to the young male and young adult markets.

US
NATIONAL TIMES, THE. English. mo. $36.00. Krebs Media Corporation, 318 East 84th Street, New York NY 10028.
Desc: Offers a cross section of American opinion. Covers topics such as American values, the media, and politics.

US/0028-0534
NATIVE NEVADAN, THE. ***Ceased.*** Vol. 2, No. 3 (May 1965)-(1992). Periodical. English. mo. Native Nevadan, 98 Colony Road, Reno NV 89502. **Tel** (702)329-2936. **ED** Becky Lemon. **Bk Rev. Ad Acc. Circ:** 4,500. ***Continues*** *Newsletter (Inter-Tribal Council of Nevada).*
Desc: Newsmagazine covering local, state, national news involving Native Americans, hard news, feature stories.

CN/0028-0542
NATIVE VOICE. (THE NATIVE VOICE.). **Added/Corp** Native Brotherhood of British Columbia. Raven Society. Vol. 1, (Dec. 1946)-. Periodical. English. Six times a year (Jan./Feb., Mar./Apr., May/June, July/Aug., Sept./Oct., Nov./Dec.). $22.00 Canada; $27.50 other. Native Voice Publishing Society, 1755 East Hastings Street, Suite 200, Vancouver BC V5L 1T1 Canada. **Tel** (604)255-3137, FAX (604)251-7107, telex DN04 51439. **Bk Rev**, (Qty: 5). **Ad Acc, Adv Mgr:** Robert MacDonald. **Circ:** 2,500 (ctrl). available on microfilm and microfiche from University Microfilms International (UMI).
Desc: These articles are on issues specifically on the West Coast native commerical fishery.

US/0199-1248
NEVADA (CARSON CITY, NEV.). (NEVADA.). [Nevada]. **Added/Corp** Nevada. Dept. of Economic Development. Vol. 37 No. 4 (1977)-. Periodical. English. bm. $14.95 (one year) US; $16.96 (one year) other. Nevada Magazine, Capitol Complex, Carson City NV 89710. **Tel** (702)687-5416, FAX (702)687-6159. **ED** David Moore. **LC** F836; .N43. **DD** 979. Index available. **Ad Acc. Circ:** 80,000. available on microfilm and microfiche from University Microfilms International (UMI). ***Continues** Nevada Magazine, 0885-9566.*
Desc: Covers the history, travel, people and humor of the real West.
Ind/Abst Access (1975-); Am. Hist. Life; GeoRef.

US/0300-8959
NEW ALASKAN. (1965)-. Periodical. English. mo. New Alaskan, 8339 Snug Harbor Lane, Ketchikan AK 99901. **Tel** (907)247-2490.

US
NEW ALBANY (FLOYD COUNTY, IND.), JEFFERSONVILLE (CLARK COUNTY, IND.) AND CITY DIRECTORY. VFOAT Caron's New Albany-Jeffersonville City Directory. (19??)-. Directory. English. Caron Directory Company, 6400 Monroe Boulevard, Box 500, Taylor MI 48186.

US
NEW AMERICAN NATION SERIES. (19??)-. Monographic series. English. ir. Price varies per volume. Harper Collins Publishers, Keystone Industrial Park, Scranton PA 18512. **Tel** (800)242-7737, (800)233-4727, FAX (800)822-4090.

CN/0834-969X
NEW CATALYST. (THE NEW CATALYST.). [New catal.]. **Added/Corp** Catalyst Education Society. **VFOAT** Catalyst. (Nov./Dec. 1985)-. Periodical. English. qt. Free on request. Catalyst Education society, PO Box 189, Gabriola IS BC V0R, 1X0 Canada. **Tel** (604) 247-9737, FAX (604) 247-7471. **ED** Christopher and Judith Plant. **DD** 051. **Bk Rev. Ad Acc. Circ:** 3,000.
Desc: British Columbia's rural-based review of art and opinion covering key issues of the 1980's: the environment, food supplies, watershed protection, local control of local resources and regional arts and cultures. Provides a refreshing, positive view of local and regional initiatives for change in the face of worsening ecological crises.
Ind/Abst Altern. Press Index (1989-).

US
NEW CHARLOTTE, THE. ***Ceased.*** **VFOAT** Charlotte; New Charlotte Magazine. (May 1986)-?. Periodical. English. Six times a year. Fortune Media Inc, PO Box 36639, Charlotte NC 28236-6639. **Tel** (704)332-0148, FAX (704)332-0165. **ED** Andrea Anapol. **LC** F264.C4; C46. **DD** 975.6/76. **Ad Acc. Circ:** 15,000 (ctrl). ***Continues** Charlotte (Charlotte, N.C.), 0746-3642.*
Desc: City/Regional lifestyle.

US/0891-3501
NEW DOMINION (ALEXANDRIA, VA.). ***Ceased.*** (NEW DOMINION.). [New dom.]. Vol. 1, No. 1 (Winter 1987)-(1992). Periodical. English. qt. Dominion Publishing Company, PO Box 19714, Alexandria VA 22320. **DD** 051.

US/0746-6692
NEW ENGLAND COUNTRY FOLKS. **VFOAT** Country Folks. (198?)-. Periodical. English. Fifty-two times a year. $15.00 one year; $27.00 two years. Lee Publisher Inc., PO Box 121, Palatine Bridge NY 13428. **Tel** (518)673-3237.

US/0884-5166
NEW ENGLAND LIVING. [N. Engl. living]. Feb./March 1984-. Periodical. English. bm. $16.50. New England Living, 177 E Industrial Park Drive, Manchester NH 03103-1899. **Tel** (603)668-7330. **ED** Catherine Smith. **DD** 917. **Circ:** 100,000 (ctrl). ***Continues** Piper Street's Cultural Guide to New England.*
Desc: A family-oriented publication targeted to the young New England homeowner.

US/0028-4947
NEW ENGLANDER, THE. Mar. 1927-. Periodical. English. ir. $12.00. The New Englander, Dublin NH 03444. available on microfilm and microfiche from University Microfilms International (UMI).

CN/0842-3024
NEW FEDERATION, THE. [New fed.]. **Added/Corp** New Federation House. **VFOAT** Opinion Canada; Nouvelle Federation. Vol. 1, No. 1 (Oct./Nov. 1988)-. Periodical. English (summaries and/or abstracts in French). qt. 18.00Can$. New Federation, 22 Metcalfe Street, Suite 300, Ottawa Ontario K1P 5L1 Canada. **Tel** (613)230-6017. **DD** 051. available on microfilm and microfiche from Micromedia Limited.
Ind/Abst Can. Index.

US/0740-3577
NEW FROM U.S. ***Ceased.*** [New U.S.]. **VFOAT** New From US; News From United States. (June 1981)-(May 1993). Periodical. English. mo. Prestwick Publications Inc, 390 North Federal Highway, Suite 401A, Deerfield Beach FL 33441-2209. **Tel** (407)427-2924. **ED** Roy H Roecker. **Bk Rev.**
Desc: Covers new products and new technology developments.

US/0895-8114
NEW HAMPSHIRE FACTS. [N. H. facts]. **VFOAT** Flying the Colors, New Hampshire Facts. 1987 Ed.-. English. ir (every three to four years). $59.50 (single issue). Clements Research II Inc., 16850 Dallas Parkway, Dallas TX 75248. **Tel** (214)931-9956, FAX (214)248-7159. **ED** John Clements. **LC** F31; .N47. **DD** 974.
Desc: Book of facts on a state, county-by-county.

US/1050-5512
NEW HAMPSHIRE PREMIER. [N. H. prem.]. (June 1990)-. Periodical. English. mo. $25.00 US; $40.00 Canada; $75.00 other. New Hampshire Premier, Subscriptions Department, PO Box 659, Portsmouth NH 03802. **Tel** (603)427-2850, FAX (603)427-0405. **ED** Simon Semaan. **LC** WMLC 93/1955. **DD** 974. **Bk Rev. Ad Acc. Circ:** 60,000.
Desc: General interest; news, politics, nature, tourism, and law.

US/0898-5405
NEW JERSEY FACTS. [N. J. facts]. **VFOAT** Flying the Colors, New Jersey Facts; New Jersey Facts--Flying the Colors Series. (1988)-. English. ir (every three to four years). $59.50 (single issue). Clements Research II Inc., 16850 Dallas Parkway, Dallas TX 75248. **Tel** (214)931-9956, FAX (214)248-7159. **ED** John Clements. **LC** F131; .N577. **DD** 974.9/005.
Desc: Book of facts on a state, county-by-county.

US
NEW JERSEY GENESIS. Began with: Vol. 1, No. 1 (Oct. 1953). Periodical. English. qt. Carl M Williams, 151 East 81st Street, New York NY 10028. **LC** F131; .N43. **DD** 974.9/005. cum. index. ***Continues** Beaver Log.*

US/0273-270X
NEW JERSEY MONTHLY. Vol. 1 (Nov. 1976)-. Periodical. English. Twelve times a year. $19.95 (1 year), $34.95 (2 year), $49.95 (3 year). New Jersey Monthly, 55 Park Place, Morristown NJ 07963. **Tel** (201)539-8230. **(Subscription address:** Fulfillment Corporation of America, PO Box 1962, Marion OH 43305.**) ED** Larry Marcheck. **LC** F131; .N73. **DD** 974.9/043/05. **Ad Acc. Circ:** 95,000.
Desc: Aims to inform, educate, persuade, and entertain through articles that address statewide issues, explore changing lifestyles, offer self-help information, and provide cultural and leisure activities.
Ind/Abst Acad. Search (Aug. 1993-); Access (1980-); Pop. Period. Index.

US/8750-7196
NEW LIFE (HOLLYWOOD, CALIF.). (NEW LIFE.). [New life]. Periodical. Korean (English). mo. $24.00. Korean Community Service, 650 North Berendo Street, Los Angeles CA 90004. **Tel** (310)668-9007, FAX (213)666-0858, telex 205 702 ASIAN. **ED** Samuel Sohn. **Circ:** 55,000. **Continues** Nyu Raipu.

US/0028-6249
NEW MEXICO MAGAZINE (SANTA FE, N.M. : 1974). (NEW MEXICO MAGAZINE.). **VFOAT** New Mexico. Vol. 52, No. 3/4 (Mar./Apr. 1974)-. Periodical. English. mo. $21.95 (one year), $35.95 (two year). New Mexico Magazine, 495 Old Santa Fe Trail, Santa Fe NM 87503. **Tel** (505)827-7447. **(Subscription address:** Hutchins and Associates, PO Box 12002, Sante Fe, NM 87504**) ED** Emily Drabanski. **LC** F791; .N3. **DD** 978.9/005. Index available. cum. index. **Bk Rev. Ad Acc. Circ:** 100,000. ***Continues** New Mexico (Santa Fe, N.M. : 1970), 0738-5420.*
Desc: Promotes the state of New Mexico through its peoples, lifestyles, culture, history, arts, architecture, and colorful events.
Ind/Abst Access (1975-); Chicano Index.

US/0897-8174
NEW ORLEANS MAGAZINE (1988). (NEW ORLEANS MAGAZINE.). [New Orleans mag.]. (1988)-. Periodical. English. Twelve times a year. $17.00 (one year), $25.00 (two year), $33.00 (three year). Louisiana Business Publishers, 111 Veterans Memorial Boulevard, Suite 1810, Metairie LA 70005. **Tel** (504)834-9292. **ED** David C. Foster. **DD** 976. **Ad Acc, Adv Mgr:** Amy Taylor, **Tel** (504)834-9292. **Circ:** 41,053. available on microfilm and microfiche from University Microfilms International (UMI). Documents available from UMI Article Clearinghouse, Magazine Collection. ***Continues** New Orleans (Metairie, LA. : 1987), 0897-8166.*
Desc: This magazine is about the everyday lives of the natives, history, antiques, health, and about the animals.
Ind/Abst Bus. Dateline (Nov. 1991-) [Full Txt.]; Mag. Index Plus (1989-); Newsp. Period. Abstr. (1988-).

US/1050-3080
NEW PACIFIC (SEATTLE, WASH.), THE. (THE NEW PACIFIC : A JOURNAL OF THE PACIFIC NORTHWEST AND BRITISH COLUMBIA.). [New Pac.]. **Added/Corp** New Pacific Publishing Association. No. 1 (Fall 1989)-. Periodical. English. qt. $40.00 US; 40.00Can$ Canada. New Pacific Communications, 401-1155 Robson Street, Vancouver British Columbia V6E 1B5 Canada. **Tel** (604)688-0753, FAX (604)688-8239. **ED** Carol Berger. **DD** 051. **Bk Rev**, (Qty: 4). **Ad Acc, Adv Mgr:** Bev Scorey. **Circ:** 25,000 (ctrl).
Desc: News magazine with an in-depth look at issues concerning the West.

US/0028-6737
NEW SOLIDARITY. ***Ceased.*** ( )-(April 1987). Periodical. English. sw. Campaigner Publications Inc, PO Box 9063, McLean VA 22102-0063. **Tel** (703)777-9401. **ED** Nancy Spannaus. **Bk Rev. Ad Acc. Circ:** 63,000. ***Supersedes** Solidarity.*
Desc: Nonpartisan national newspaper of the American system.

●US/1062-9378
NEW VIEWS (FORREST CITY, ARK.). (NEW VIEWS.). (1992)-. Periodical. English. mo. $21.60. Henerine Hudson, PO Box 161, Forrest City AR 72335. **(Subscription address:** New Views, 320 North Rosser Suite B, Forrest City, AR 72335**) ED** Diane Burl. Index available. **Ad Acc, Adv Mgr:** H Hunter, **Tel** (501)633-7547.
Desc: Articles on issues that affect the lower Mississippi River Delta.

US/0028-7369
NEW YORK (1968). (NEW YORK.). [New York]. Vol. 1, (April 8, 1968)-. Periodical. English. wk (50 issues). $42.00 (non-trade), $28.00 (trade). K 3 Magazine Corporation, 200 Madison Avenue 8th Floor, New York NY 10016. **Tel** (212)447-4700, (212)447-4732. **(Subscription address:** Neodata / Colorado, PO Box 2606, Boulder Boulder CO 80322.**) ED** Edward Kosner. **LC** F128.1; .N4. **DD** 051. cum. index. **Ad Acc. Circ:** 426,628. available on microfilm and microfiche from University Microfilms International (UMI). Documents available from UMI Article Clearinghouse.
Desc: Critical examination of contemporary ideas. Deals with politics, business, psychology, the fine arts, entertainment, home furnishings, food, wine, fashion, and a range of subjects.
Ind/Abst Acad. Abstr. Full Text Elite (Jan. 1984-); Acad. Abstr. (Jan. 1984-); Acad. Ind. [Computer File] (1984-); Acad. Search (Jan. 1984-); Art Archaeol. Tech. Abstr.; Book Rev. Index; Curr. Lit. Fam. Plan.; Expand. Acad. Index (1984-); Film Lit. Index; Gen. Period. Index (1985-); Guide Soc. Sci. Relig.; INFO-SOUTH Abstr.; Infobank (Jan. 1969-); Mag. Artic. Summar. Elite (Jan. 1984-); Mag. Artic. Summar. Select (Jan. 1984-); Mag. Artic. Summar. CD-ROM (Jan. 1984-); Mag. Express (1988-) [Full Txt.]; Mag. Index Plus (1989-); Mag. Search; Mark. Advert. Ref. Serv.; Med. Rev. Dig.; Newsp. Period. Abstr. (1988-); Read. Guide Abstr. Select Ed.; Read. Guide Period. Lit. (19??-199?); Resource/One Ondisc; Mag. Index (1977-); Vocat. Search (Jan. 1984-).

US
NEW YORK STYLE & DESIGN. English. bm. $17.00. Manso Inc., Po Box 768, Union City NJ 07087-0768. **Tel** (201)866-6500. **Bk Rev. Ad Acc. Circ:** 25,000 (ctrl).
Desc: Covers lifestyles and general interest.

US/0190-1990
NEW YORK TIMES CURRENT EVENTS EDITION, THE. [N.Y. Times curr. events ed.]. Vol. 1 (Jan. 1-28, 1979)-. Periodical. English. mo. $95.00. Microfilming Corporation of America, 21 Harristown Road, Glen Rock NJ 07452. **DD** 071. Documents available from UMI Article Clearinghouse.
Ind/Abst Resource/One Ondisc (1988-).

US/0028-7822
NEW YORK TIMES MAGAZINE, THE. [New York times mag.]. (1986)-. Periodical. English. wk. Free to subscribers of The New York Times. The New York Times, 229 West 43rd Street, New York NY 10036. **Tel** (800)631-2580, (212)556-1234, FAX (212)556-4603. **DD** 051. available on microfilm and microfiche from University Microfilms International (UMI). Documents available from UMI Article Clearinghouse, Documents on Demand.
Ind/Abst Abr. Read. Guide Period. Lit.; Acad. Abstr. Full Text Elite (May 1984-); Acad. Abstr. (May 1984-); Acad. Ind. [Computer File] (1984-); Acad. Search (May 1984-); Am. Hist. Life (1954-1962); Am. Bibliogr. Slavic East Europ. Stud.; Annu. Bibliogr. Engl. Lang. Lit.; Energy Inf. Abstr.; Environ. Abstr.; Expand. Acad. Index (1984-); Gen. Period. Index (1985-); GeoRef; Health Ref. Cent. (1987-) [Select. Cov.]; Index Period. Artic. Relat. Law;

INFO-SOUTH Abstr.; Mag. Artic. Summar. Elite (May 1984-); Mag. Artic. Summar. Select (May 1984-); Mag. Artic. Summar. CD-ROM (May 1984-); Mag. Express (1986-) [Full Txt.]; Mag. Index Plus (1989-); Mag. Index. Sel. (1986-); Mag. Search; Newsp. Period. Abstr. (1986-); Newsp. Abstr.; Peace Res. Abstr. J. (1964-1969, 1974-1976); Read. Guide Abstr. Select Ed.; Read. Guide Period. Lit.; Resource/One Ondisc; Mag. Index (1977-); TOM Gen. Index (1985-); Vocat. Search (May 1984-).

US/0743-7161
NEWPORT BEACH. (NEWPORT BEACH : NB.). **VFOAT** Newport Beach Magazine; NB. (Dec. 1984/Jan. 1985)-. Periodical. English. Twenty-four times a year. $52.00. Baker Communications Ltd., 9465 Wilshire Boulevard, Suite 307, Beverly Hills CA 90212. **Tel** (213)275-8850. **(Subscription address:** Newport Beach, 901 Dover Drive, Suite 231, Newport CA 92660.**)**

US/0276-5241
NEWPORT REVIEW, THE. [Newport rev.]. Vol. 1 No. 1 (Winter 1979)-. Periodical. English. $2.00 (single issue), $1.50 (single issue, members of Art Association). The Newport Review, 68 Benevolent Street Blazer, Providence RI 02906. **LC** AP2; .N67712. **DD** 051.

CN/0823-9118
NEWS CANADA (TORONTO). (NEWS CANADA.). [News Can.]. Vol. 4, No. 2 (Feb. 1984)-. Periodical. English. mo. $50.00. News Canada, Suite 2612, 2 Bloor Street East, Toronto Ontario M4W 1A8. **DD** 051. ***Continues** Power Newspaper Syndicate's Free Columns, 0823-910X.*

CN/0835-9989
NEWS EXTRA. (198?)-. Periodical. English. Fifty-two times a year. Extra Media Inc., 6375 Sherbrook Street West, Montreal Quebec H4B 1N1 Canada. **Tel** (514)486-7777.

CN/0713-4479
NEWSLETTER / ATLANTIC CANADA INSTITUTE. [Newsl. - Atl. Can. Inst.]. **Added/Corp** Atlantic Canada Institute. **VFOAT** Atlantic Canada Institute Newsletter; Bulletin de l'Institut Canadien de l'Atlantique. Vol. 1, No. 1 (Spring 1982)-. Newsletter. English (French; summaries and/or abstracts in French). sa. 5.00Can$. Atlantic Canada Institute, PO Box 1750, Sackville NB E0A 3C0 Canada. **ED** Gwendolyn Davies. **DD** 971.5/005. **Bk Rev. Ad Acc. Circ:** 500.
Desc: Occasional newsletter on the activities of Atlantic Canada Institute. A cultural and historical educational body. Announces conference and provides pertinent news on Atlantic Canadian history, culture, literature, etc.

US/0895-8106
NORTH CAROLINA FACTS (DALLAS, TEX.). (NORTH CAROLINA FACTS.). [N. C. facts]. **VFOAT** Flying the Colors, North Carolina Facts; North Carolina Facts--Flying the Colors Series. 1988 Ed.-. English. ir (every three to four years). $59.50 (single issue). Clements Research II Inc., 16850 Dallas Parkway, Dallas TX 75248. **Tel** (214)931-9956, FAX (214)248-7159. **ED** John Clements. **LC** F251; .N867. **DD** 975.6/005.
Desc: Book of facts on a state, county-by-county.

US
NORTH COUNTRY ANVIL. V. 1- June 1972-. Periodical. English. ir. $12.00 US; $16.00 other. North Country Anvil, PO Box 37, Billville MN 55957. **Tel** (507)798-2366. **ED** Jack Miller. **Bk Rev. Ad Acc. Circ:** 1,000.
Desc: A regional publication of the Upper Midwest encompassing social critique, decentralist philosophy, environmental concerns, literature, poetry and grassroots activism.

US/0164-3665
NORTH COUNTY LIVING. V. 17, No. 9- Jan. 1979-. Periodical. English. mo. $10.00. North County Living, PO Box 33611, San Diego CA 92103. ***Continues** San Diego's North County Living, 0160-5712.*

US/0029-277X
NORTH DAKOTA QUARTERLY, THE. [N.D. q.]. **Added/Corp** University of North Dakota. **VFOAT** NDQ, North Dakota Quarterly. Vol. 24, No. 1 (Winter 1956)-. Periodical. English. qt (Jan., Apr., July, Oct.). $24.00 (institutions), $20.00 (individuals) US; $28.00 (institutions), $23.00 (individuals) other. North Dakota Quarterly, University of North Dakota, Box 8237, Grand Forks ND 58201. **Tel** (701)777-3321, FAX (701)777-3650. **ED** Robert W. Lewis, William Borden, and Jay Meek. **LC** AS36; .N6. cum. index. **Bk Rev**, (Qty: 20/yr). **Pr Rev. Circ:** 700 (ctrl). ***Continues** Quarterly Journal (University of North Dakota).*
Desc: General review emphasizing humanities alternating with special focus issues; e.g. women's studies, American Indian writing, travel, fiction, poetry, essays and reviews.
Ind/Abst Abstr. Engl. Stud.; Am. Hist. Life (1963-); Am. Humanit. Index; Annu. Bibliogr. Engl. Lang. Lit.; Film Lit. Index (19??-); Index Am. Period. Verse; Middle East Abstr. Index (1963-1967); MLA Int. Bibl. Books Artic. Mod. Lang. Lit.; Romant. Move. (1963-1967); West. Hist. Q.

CN/0700-3420
NORTH PEACE PICTORIAL. Oct. 30, 1973-. Periodical. English. Free - distribution limited to residents of North Peace area. Carcajou Graphic, PO Box 1266, Peace River, Alta T0H 2X0 Canada. **DD** 071/.123/1.

US/0164-5366
NORTH SHORE. (197?)-. Periodical. English. Twelve times a year. $12.00 US; $18.00 Canada; $20.00 other. P B Communications, 874 Green Bay Road, Winnetka IL 60093. **Tel** (312)441-7892. **ED** Asher J. Birnbaum. **Ad Acc. Circ:** 47,000.
Desc: Journal of Chicago's northern suburbs.

US
NORTH SHORE (MINEOLA, N.Y.). (NORTH SHORE.). (19??)-. Periodical. English. bm. $15.00. North Shore Magazine, 21 Rock Hollow Road, Manhasset NY 11030. **Tel** (516)627-2682.

CN/0823-7425
NORTH THOMPSON JOURNAL. [North Thompson j.]. Periodical. English. wk. North Thompson Journal, Box 720, Barriere British Columbia V0E 1E0 Canada. **DD** 071/.1141. ***Continues** North Thompson Review and Bulletin, 0823-7417.*

US/0897-8298
NORTHERN CALIFORNIA MONTHLY. **VFOAT** Northern California. Vol. 1 (1988)-. Periodical. English. mo. $25.00. Northern California Monthly, 7660 Morningside Drive, Loomis CA 95650.

US
NORTHERN LIGHTS. **Added/Corp** Northern Lights Research and Education Institute. Vol. 1, No. 1 (Jan. 1985)-. Periodical. English. Four times a year. $25.00 US; $31.00 Canada; $32.00 other Pan-American nations; $35.00 other. Northern Lights Institute, PO Box 8084, Missoula MT 59807-8084. **Tel** (406)721-7415, FAX (406)721-7364. **ED** Don Snow and Deborah Clow. **Ad Acc. Pr Rev. Circ:** 4,100.
Desc: Addresses issues of the West; subjects include art, culture, politics, education, and environment.

US/0271-5147
NORTHERN OHIO LIVE. **VFOAT** Live. Vol. 1, No. 1 (Sept. 22-Oct. 5, 1980)-. Periodical. English. ir. $16.00 (US except Alaska, Hawaii, & possessions), $28.00 (Alaska, Hawaii, & possessions) US; $40.00 (other). Live Cleveland, 11320 Juniper Road, Cleveland OH 44106. **Tel** (216)721-1800, FAX (216) 721-2525. **ED** Michael von Glahn. Index available. **Bk Rev. Ad Acc, Adv Mgr:** Gail Kerzner. **Circ:** 37,000 (ctrl).
Desc: A full-color consumer magazine that spotlights the arts, entertainment, dining out and leisure activity in Northern Ohio.

US/1050-6063
NORTHERN VIRGINIA MAGAZINE. (1990)-. Periodical. English. qt. $10.00. Hough Communications, PO Box 866, 4163 Chain Bridge, Fairfax VA 22030.

US/0164-6710
NORTHERN VIRGINIAN. ***Suspended.*** 1971-?. Periodical. English. bm. $12.00. Northern Virginian, Box 1177, Vienna VA 22180. **Tel** (703)938-0666. **ED** Ethel E Holden. **Bk Rev. Ad Acc. Circ:** 30,000.
Desc: A regional, general interest magazine focussing on the high quality of life in Northern Virginia and the region's heritage, people and unlimited potential.

CN/0820-6724
NORTHWEST EXPLORER (YELLOWKNIFE). (NORTHWEST EXPLORER.). [Northwest explor.]. Vol. 1, No. 1 (June/July 1981)-. Periodical. English. qt. 16.00Can$ Canada; 20.00Can$ other. Northwest Explorer Magazine, 9821-108st, Fort Saskatchewan Alberta T8L 2J2 Canada. **Tel** (403)992-1212, FAX (403)992-1646. **ED** Jake Ootes. **DD** 917.19/2043/05. **Bk Rev. Ad Acc. Circ:** 37,000 (ctrl).
Desc: Articles on Northwest Territories and Arctic Canada.

US/0888-5346
NORTHWEST LIVING. ***Ceased.*** [Northwest living]. Vol. 3, No. 4 (April 1986)-Vol. 9, No. 3 (March/April 1992). Periodical. English. bm. Alaska Northwest Publishing Company, 130 Second Avenue South, Edmonds WA 98020-3588. **Tel** (206)774-4111, (800)533-7381. **ED** Terry W Sheely. **DD** 979. ***Continues** Northwest Edition, 0739-9537.*
Desc: Celebrates life in the Northwest through upbeat copy regarding outdoors, natural resources, and Northwest things. Includes Northwest Mileposts Traveler's Geography.

US/0191-9091
NORWALK WEEKLY TRADER. (19??)-. Periodical. English. wk. $4.00. Norwalk News Trader, 136 Main Street, Westport CT 06880. **Tel** (203)226-6311. **ED** Jonathon Klein. **Circ:** 21,108.

US/0149-9327
NOSTALGIA ILLUSTRATED. V. 1- Nov. 1974-. Periodical. English. mo. $1.00 per copy. Magazine Management Company, 575 Madison Avenue, New York NY 10022. **Tel** (212)838-7900. **LC** AP2; .N87. **DD** 051.

US/0300-6794
NOSTALGIA NEWSLETTER. Vol. 1 (Jan./Feb. 1973)-. Newsletter. English. bm. $6.00. Nostalgia Newsletter, PO Box 7201, Little Rock AR 72207.

CN/0701-113X
NOUVELLE DU HAUT ST-FRANCOIS. (LA NOUVELLE DU HAUT ST-FRANCOIS.). (1976)-. Periodical. French. wk. 7.00Can$. Imprimerie Cormier Inc, 178 St-Pierre, East Angus Quebec J0B 1R0 Canada. **DD** 071/.14/68. ***Continues** Nouvelle, 0382-0858.*

MX
NOVEDADES; REVISTA LITERARIA Y DE INFORMACION GRAFICA. Vol. 1, No. 1 (Dec. 27, 1911)-. Newspaper. Spanish. da. $954.00. Novedades Editores SA, Balderas 87 Colonia Centro, 06040 Mexico 1 DF Mexico. **Tel** 011 52 5 5210082, 011 52 5 5210042. **ED** Pedro Marroquin.

US/0192-5946
OAKLAND. V. 1-. Periodical. English. mo. Golden Bear Communications, 631 Howard Street, San Francisco CA 94105.

US
OBSERVER (PHILADELPHIA (PA.)). (THE OBSERVER.). Vol. 1, No. 1 (June 1891)-. Periodical. English. mo. $15.00. The Observer / Pennsylvania, 226 North 12th Street, Philadelphia PA 19107. **Tel** (215)567-6221. **ED** Anthony West.
Desc: Liquor and hospitality industry (restaurants, etc.) in Pennsylvania. Also state and local politics.

US/0097-8221
OCCASIONAL REVIEW, THE. Began with Feb. 1974 issue. Periodical. English. sa. $3.00 single issue. World Research, Inc., Campus Studies, 11722 Sorento Valley Road, San Diego CA 92111. **LC** AS30; .O26. **DD** 051.

US/1051-2373
OH! IDAHO. (OH! IDAHO : THE IDAHO STATE MAGAZINE.). [Oh Ida.]. (Spring 1989)-. Periodical. English. qt. $16.00. Peak Media Inc, PO Box 925, Hailey ID 83333. **Tel** (208)788-4500, FAX (208)788-5098. **ED** Laurie Sammis. **DD** 979. **Ad Acc. Circ:** 15,000.

US/0279-3504
OHIO. **VFOAT** Ohio Magazine. Vol. 3, No. 1 (Apr. 1980)-. Periodical. English. mo. $18.00 US; $20.00 other. Ohio Magazine, 62 East Broad Street, Columbus OH 43215. **Tel** (614)461-5083. **ED** Ellen Stein Burbach. **Bk Rev. Ad Acc. Circ:** 105,000 (ctrl). available on microfilm and microfiche from University Microfilms International (UMI). Documents available from UMI Article Clearinghouse. ***Continues** Ohio Magazine, 0164-7172.*
Desc: The magazine for and about Ohio.
Ind/Abst Acad. Search (July 1993-); Access (1981-); Bus. Dateline; INFO-SOUTH Abstr.

US/0473-9760
OHIO ALMANAC. [Ohio alm.]. 1st- Ed. English. an. Lorain Journal Company, 1657 Broadway, Lorain OH 44052. **Tel** (216)245-6901, FAX (216)245-5637. **LC** AY271.L6; O5. **DD** 917.71/005.

US/1040-4872
OHIO FACTS (DALLAS, TEX.). (OHIO FACTS.). [Ohio facts]. **VFOAT** Flying the Colors, Ohio Facts. 1988 Ed.-. English. ir (every three to four years). $59.50 (single issue). Clements Research II Inc., 16850 Dallas Parkway, Dallas TX 75248. **Tel** (214)931-9956, FAX (214)248-7159. **ED** John Clements. **LC** F486; .O347. **DD** 977.1/005.
Desc: Book of facts on a state, county-by-county.

US/0163-7819
OHIONETWORK. **Main/Corp** OHIONET. **VAT** Ohio Network. Vol. 1 (Jan. 1979)-. Periodical. English. Twelve times a year. Free. Ohionet Childrens Book Reviews, 1500 West Lane Avenue, Columbus OH 43221. **Tel** (614)486-2966.

CN/0714-6736
OHS BULLETIN. (OHS BULLETIN / THE ONTARIO HISTORICAL SOCIETY, LOCAL SOCIETIES COMMITTEE.). [OHS bull.]. **Added/Corp** Ontario Historical Society. Local Societies Committee. **VAT** Ontario Historical Society bulletin. Issue 20 (Sept. 1978)-. English. ir. Ontario Historical Society, 5151 Yonge Street, Willowdale Ontario M2N 5P5 Canada. **Tel** (905)226-9011, FAX (905)226-2740. **ED** Meribeth Clow and James Clemens. **DD** 971.3/006. **Bk Rev. Ad Acc. Circ:** 3,000 (ctrl). ***Continues** Ontario Historical Society. Local Soieties Committee., Bulletin.*
Desc: Newsletter to membership of the current news of the heritage field in Ontario and North America.

CN/0840-5492
OKANAGAN LIFE (KELOWNA. 1988). (OKANAGAN LIFE.). [Okanagan life]. **VFOAT** Okanagan Life Magazine. (Fall 1988)-. Periodical. English. Six times a year. 10.00Can$ Canada; 19.00Can$ other. Byrne Publishing Group Inc., PO Box 1479, Kelowna BC V1Y 7V8 Canada. **Tel** (604)861-5399, FAX (604)868-3040. **ED** Holly McNeil. **DD** 971.1/42/005. **Ad Acc, Adv Mgr:** Gerry Lee, **Tel** (604)861-5399. **Circ:** 19,000 (ctrl).

Desc: The city and regional magazine for the Okanagan Valley. Covers the diverse elements affecting the lives in our community.

CN/0823-8243
OKANAGAN SEASONS. [Okanagan seas.]. Vol. 1, No. 1 (Winter 1983/84)-. Periodical. English. qt. Okanagan Seasons, 202-2802 30th Street, Vernon British Columbia V1T 8G7 Canada. **DD** 051.

US/1056-1595
OKAY AMERICA. [Okay Am.]. No. 1 (1991)-. Periodical. English. mo. $25.00. Wir Publishing & Advertising Corporation, 628 East 14 Street, New York NY 10009. **DD** 057.

US/1043-4259
OKC ACTION. **VFOAT** OKC Action Update. **VAT** Oklahoma City Action. No. 1 (Jan. 1989)-. Periodical. English. sm. Oklahoma City Chamber of Commerce, One Santa Fe Plaza, Oklahoma City OK 73102. available on microfilm from University Microfilms International (UMI). ***Continues** Oklahoma, 0030-1639.*

US
OKLAHOMA GAZETTE. (19??)-. Periodical. English. Twenty-six times a year. $26.00 (one year), $38.00 (two year). Oklahoma Gazette, 1200 North Shartel, Oklahoma City OK 73103. **Tel** (405)235-0798.

US/0895-1586
OKLAHOMA HOME & LIFE STYLE. ***Ceased.*** [Okla. home lifestyle]. **VFOAT** Oklahoma Home and Lifestyle. Vol. 11, No. 6 (March/April 1987)-(Nov./Dec. 1990). Periodical. English. bm. Oklahoma Home & Life Style, 5272 South Lewis, Tulsa OK 74105. **Tel** (918)747-2529. **ED** Micki Van Deventer. **LC** NA7235.O5; O34. **DD** 747. **Bk Rev. Ad Acc. Circ:** 13,000 (ctrl). ***Continues** Oklahoma Home Garden, 0745-3051.*
Desc: Includes design, fashion, travel, food preparation and gardening.

●US/1064-8968
OKLAHOMA LIVING. **Added/Corp** Oklahoma Association of Electric Cooperatives. (1992)-. Periodical. English. mo. Oklahoma Living, PO Box 11047, Oklahoma City OK 73136-0047. ***Continues** Oklahoma Rural News, 0048-1610.*

US/0030-1892
OKLAHOMA TODAY. Vol. 6, No. 4 (Jan. 1956)-. Periodical. English. bm. $12.00 US; $16.00 other. Oklahoma Today, PO Box 53384, Oklahoma City OK 73152. **Tel** (405)521-2496, (800)652-6552. **ED** Sue Carter and Jeanne Devlin. Index available. **Bk Rev. Circ:** 45,000. ***Continues** Resourceful Oklahoma.*
Desc: Features travel and entertainment in the Sooner State as well as history and tradition, personality profiles and excellent color photography.

US
OLD FARMER'S ALMANACK, THE. **VFOAT** Thomas's Old Farmer's Almanac. No. 1 (1793)-. English. an. Yankee Publishing Inc., Main Street, Dublin NH 03444. **Tel** (603)563-8111, (800)736-1100. **ED** "Established--by Robert B. Thomas.". **LC** AY81.F3; O6. **DD** 051.

US/0149-8711
OMNI (NEW YORK, N.Y.). (OMNI.). [Omni]. Vol. 1, (Oct. 1978)-. Periodical. English. mo. $24.00 (one year), $44.00 (two year). General Media Publishing Company, 1965 Broadway, New York NY 10023. **Tel** (212)496-6100. **(Subscription address:** CDS Agency Hard Copy, PO Box 4966, Des Moines IA 50340.) **LC** AP2; .O452. **DD** 051. **Ad Acc.** available on microfilm and microfiche from University Microfilms International (UMI); available on an online database (file 647/Full-Text) from DIALOG. Documents available from UMI Article Clearinghouse, Documents on Demand, Magazine Collection.
Desc: The only magazine that combines the realms of science, fact, fiction, and fantasy. Every month it presents science fiction and comprehensive articles by world renowned members of the science community. Monthly departments cover areas such as space exploration and the environment.
Ind/Abst Abr. Read. Guide Period. Lit.; Acad. Abstr. Full Text Elite (Jan. 1984-) [Full Txt.]; Acad. Abstr. (Jan. 1984-); Acad. Ind. [Computer File] (1984-); Acad. Search (Jan. 1984-); Can. Index (?-?); Can. Period. Index (19??-); Environ. Abstr.; Expand. Acad. Index (1984-); Foods Adlibra; Gen. Period. Index (1985-); Gen. Sci. Source (Jan. 1988-) [Full Txt.]; GeoRef; Health Source (Jan. 1984-); INFO-SOUTH Abstr.; Mag. Artic. Summar. Elite (Jan. 1984-) [Full Txt.]; Mag. Artic. Summar. Select (Jan. 1984-) [Full Txt.]; Mag. Artic. Summar. CD-ROM (Jan. 1984-); Mag. Express (1986-) [Full Txt.]; Mag. Index Plus (1989-); Mag. Index. Sel. (1986-); Mag. Search; Mid. Search (Jan. 1984-); Newsp. Period. Abstr. (1986-); Prim. Search (Jan. 1984-); Read. Guide Abstr. Select Ed.; Read. Guide Period. Lit.; Resource/One Ondisc; Sci. Fict. Fantasy Book Rev. Index; SCISEARCH; Mag. Index (1978-); TOM Gen. Index (1985-) [Full Txt.]; Vocat. Search (Jan. 1984-) [Full Txt.].

CN/0229-6047
OOMPHALOSKEPSIS. [Oomphaloskepsis!]. No. 1 (June 5, 1980)-. Periodical. English. S. Carton, 7116-81st Street, Edmonton Alta T6C 2T4. **DD** 051.

●US/1061-9046
OP-ED (BELLINGHAM, WASH.). (OP-ED: THE NATIONAL NEWSLETTER OF PUBLIC OPINION.). [Op-ed]. Vol. 1, No. 1 (Apr. 1992)-. Periodical. English. mo. $18.00. New Legends Publishing Group, PO Box 2567, Bellingham WA 98227. **DD** 051.

US/0737-2183
OPERATIVE (NEW YORK, N.Y.). (OPERATIVE.). [Operative]. **VFOAT** Operative Magazine. No. 1 (Fall/Winter 1982)-. Periodical. English. sa. $5.00. Naatsuk Corporation, Box 686, Old Chelsea Station, New York NY 10113. **LC** AP2; .O498. **DD** 051.

US/0279-0483
ORANGE COAST. [Orange coast]. **VFOAT** Orange Coast Magazine. (19??)-. Periodical. English. mo. $19.95 US and Canada; $31.95 other. Orange Coast Kommunications, 245 D Fischer, Suite 8, Costa Mesa CA 92626. **Tel** (714)545-1900. **ED** Lynn Beresford. **DD** 051. **Ad Acc, Adv Mgr:** Linda Goldstein.
Desc: Coverage of local issues, personalities, entertainment and events.
Ind/Abst Calif. Period. Index (19??-).

US/0279-1323
ORLANDO MAGAZINE. ***Title Change.*** [Orlando mag.]. Vol. 35, No. 9 (July 1981)-(19??). Periodical. English. mo. Orlando Media Affiliate, PO Box 2207, Orlando FL 32802. **Tel** (407)539-3939. **ED** Mike Candeleria, 341 N Maitland Ave, Maitland, FL 32751, (phone# (407)539-3939). **DD** 051. cum. index. **Ad Acc, Adv Mgr:** Karen Poulsen, **Tel** (407)539-3939. **Circ:** 24,000. ***Continues** Orlando-Land, 0145-6431.*
***Continued by** Orlando (Orlando, Fla.), 1059-3624.*
Desc: City magazine focusing on growth and development trends and lifestyles of the Orlando metropolitan area. Includes business, lifestyle, civic events and latest trends in the area.

US
OSCAR ISRAELOWITZ'S GUIDE TO THE LOWER EAST SIDE. **VAT** Lower East Side Guide. (19??)-. Periodical. English. $8.95. Israelowitz Publishing, Box 228, Brooklyn NY 11229. **Tel** (718)951-7072, FAX (718)951-7072.

CN/0226-1081
OTTAWA JOURNAL (INDEX). (OTTAWA JOURNAL.). [Ottawa j.]. July 1979-. Periodical. English. mo. $600.00. Commonwealth Microfilm Library, 3395 American Drive, Unit 11, Mississauga, Ontario, L4V 1T5 Canada. **Tel** (905)671-4173. **DD** 071/.1384.

US/0899-1413
OUT WEST (SACRAMENTO, CALIF.). **See** Travel and Tourism.

US/0882-8938
OVERSEAS LIVING. ***Suspended.*** (OVERSEAS LIVING : A PUBLICATION OF THE INTERNATIONAL ORIENTATION SERVICE.). [Overs. living]. (Jan. 1985)-Suspended June 1988. Periodical. English. bm. $36.00. International Orientation Service, PO Box 1611, Cullowhee NC 27323-1611. **ED** Adela Landsman. **DD** 640. **Ad Acc.** ctrl circ.
Desc: Deals with the issues affecting North Americans abroad.

US/1044-8500
OZARKSWATCH (SPRINGFIELD, MO.). (OZARKSWATCH.). [OzarksWatch]. **Added/Corp** Southwest Missouri State University. Center for Ozarks Studies. **VFOAT** Ozarks Watch. Vol. 1, No. 1 (Summer 1987)-. Periodical. English. Four times a year. $15.00. Southwest Missouri State University / OzarksWatch, 901 South National, Springfield MO 65804. **Tel** (417)836-5755, FAX (417)836-6905. **LC** F472.O9; O94. **DD** 976.7/1/005.
Desc: Purpose is to promote understanding of the Ozarks region - history and culture, people and land. Issues are themed.
Ind/Abst Ozark Period. Index.

CN/0228-3492
P.S. POST-SCRIPTUM. (A.P.S., POST-SCRIPTUM.). **VFOAT** PS, Post-Scriptum; Post-Scriptum; Post-Scriptum. (June/July 1980)-. Periodical. French. Ten times a year (Except Jan. & Aug.). $15.00 (one year); $25.00 (two years). Cobaro Inc., 1255 Carre Phillips Bureau 407, Montreal Quebec H3B 3G1 Canada. **LC** AP21; .P18. **DD** 054/.1.

US/0748-3872
PACER (QUINLAN, TEX.), THE. ***Ceased.*** (THE PACER.). [Pacer]. **VFOAT** Hunt County Pacer. Vol. 1, No. 1 (Feb. 1983)-(1986). Periodical. English. qt. Hunt County Publications, Route 4 Box 482, Quinlan TX 75474. **Tel** (214)356-2789.

US/0199-6363
PACIFIC NORTHWEST. [Pac. Northwest]. (1966)-. Periodical. English. mo (10 issues). $18.95. Adams Publishing, 68860 Perez Road, PO Box 2150, Cathedral City CA 92235. **Tel** (619)770-4370, (800)776-1036. **(Subscription address:** Adams Publishing, PO Box 2150, Cathedral City CA 92235.) **ED** Peter Potterfield. **LC** QH1; .P23. **DD** 979. Index available. **Ad Acc. Circ:** 64,000 (ctrl). available on microfilm and microfiche from University Microfilms International (UMI). ***Absorbed** Oregon Magazine, 0164-9930 **and** Search, 0191-0043.*
Desc: General interest regional publication with editorial emphasis on the Northwest, including social and political issues, personality, profiles, travel, fashion, restaurants, calendar events and entertainment.
Ind/Abst Access (1984-); GeoRef.

US/1043-5050
PACIFIC REVIEW (SAN BERNARDINO, CALIF.). (THE PACIFIC REVIEW / A MAGAZINE OF POETRY AND PROSE / DEPARTMENT OF ENGLISH, CALIFORNIA STATE COLLEGE, SAN BERNARDINO.). [Pac. rev.]. No. 1 (Spring 1983)-. English. an. California State College / Department of English, 5500 University Parkway, San Bernardino CA 92407. **DD** 808.
Ind/Abst Index Am. Period. Verse.

US/1075-3133
PAGEANTRY (ALTAMONTE SPRINGS, FLA.). (PAGEANTRY : THE MAGAZINE FOR THE PAGEANT INDUSTRY.). [Pageantry]. **Added/Corp** Pageantry, Talent & Entertainment Services, Inc. World Pageant Association. **VFOAT** Pageantry Magazine. (June 1980)-. Periodical. English. qt (published within the seasons). $16.00 US; $22.00 other. Pageantry Magazine, PO Box 160307, Altamonte Springs FL 32716. **Tel** (407)260-2262, FAX (407)260-2262. **ED** Brian Chambers. **DD** 791. Index available. cum. index. **Bk Rev,** (Qty: 4). **Ad Acc, Adv Mgr:** C. Dunn. **Circ:** 100,000.
Desc: For pageant, talent, modeling participants, also important for directors, judges, teachers, and coaches giving information regarding events, prizes, scholarships awards, career goals, success stories by noted famous people, and inspirational stories to achieve. Fashion, grooming, fitness, photography, modeling and achievement are what Pageantry offers.

US
PAGEANTRY MAGAZINE. (19??)-. English. qt (published within the seasons). $16.00 US, $24.00 Canada, $28.00 other (1 year); $24.00 US, $36.00 Canada, $44.00 other (2 year). Pageantry Magazine, PO Box 160307, Altamonte Springs FL 32716. **Tel** (407)260-2262, FAX (407)260-2262. **ED** Brian Chambers.
Desc: For pageant, talent, modeling participants, also important for directors, judges, teachers, and coaches giving information regarding events, prizes, scholarships awards, career goals, success stories by noted famous people, and inspirational stories to achieve. Fashion, grooming, fitness, photography, modeling and achievement are what Pageantry offers.

US/0031-0417
PALM BEACH LIFE. 1906. Periodical. English. mo. $24.00. Palm Beach Newspapers Inc, PO Box 1151, Palm Beach FL 33480. **Tel** (407)837-4750. **ED** Joyce Harr. **Bk Rev. Ad Acc. Circ:** 30,000.
Desc: Featuring architecture of Palm Beach's most beautiful homes, travel, gardening, interior designs, people, fashion, food and wine.

US/0031-0425
PALM SPRINGS LIFE. (1958)-. Periodical. English. mo (12 issues). $38.00 (one year), $66.00 (two year), $98.00 (three year) US. Palm Springs Life, 303 North Indian Canyon Drive, Palm Springs CA 92262. **Tel** (619)325-2333, FAX (619)325-7008. **(Subscription address:** Circulation Dept., Palm Springs Life, PO Box 2724, Palm Springs, CA 92263-2724) **ED** Stewart Weiner. **Ad Acc, Adv Mgr:** F. Jones, **Tel** (619)325-2333. **Circ:** 20,000 paid. ***Absorbed** Palm Springs Villager.*
Desc: Publication designed as a showcase for photography and features that celebrate the affluent, Palm Springs lifestyle.

US/0745-2462
PALOS VERDES REVIEW. ***Suspended.*** (19??)-Suspended 1994. Periodical. English. Twelve times a year. $12.00. Palos Verdes Review, PO Box 96, Palos Verdes CA 90274. **Tel** (310)378-8697. **ED** Benjamin S. Loughrin. **Ad Acc. Circ:** 4,500. ***Continues** Palos Verdes Social Review.*
Desc: Review of the social, civic and philanthropic activities of the Palos Verdes Peninsula.

CN/1183-3742
PAPERPLATES (TORONTO). (PAPERPLATES.). [Paperplates]. **VFOAT** Paper Plates. No. 1 (Fall 1990)-. Periodical. English. Four times a year. $32.00 (individuals), $42.00 (institutions). Paperplates, 19 Kenwood Avenue, Toronto, Ontario M6C 2R8 Canada. **Tel** (416)651-2551. **DD** 051.

US
PARADE. V. 1- July 13, 1941-. Periodical. English. wk. **LC** AP2. **DD** 051. Documents available from UMI Article Clearinghouse.
Ind/Abst Mag. Artic. Summar. Elite (June 1984-June

1987); Mag. Artic. Summar. Select (June 1984-April 1987); Mag. Artic. Summar. CD-ROM (June 1984-April 1987); Newsp. Period. Abstr. (1992-).

US/1060-9083
PASS CHRISTIAN REVIEW, THE. [Pass Christ. rev.]. Issue No. 1 (Oct. 1991)-. Periodical. English. mo. Pass Communications, Inc., 116 Davis Avenue, Pass Christian MS 39571-0574. **DD** 051.

US/0895-0857
PAST, PRESENT & FUTURE. (PAST, PRESENT, FUTURE : PRESERVING OUR PAST, STRIVING AT PRESENT, FOR OUR FUTURE / LA CROSSE COUNTY HISTORICAL SOCIETY.). [Past present future]. **Added/Corp** La Crosse County Historical Society (La Crosse, Wis.). **VFOAT** Past, Present and Future. Vol. 1, No. 1 (Nov. 1978)-. Periodical. English. bm (6 issues). Free to members; $25.00 (membership). La Crosse County Historical Society, PO Box 1272, La Crosse WI 54602. **Tel** (608)782-1980. **ED** James Arneson. **DD** 977. Index available. cum. index. **Ad Acc. Circ:** 600. ***Absorbed*** *Historical Notes.*
Desc: Newsletter containing information on the history of the Western Wisconsin area.

US/0162-1327
PENINSULA MAGAZINE. (19??)-. Periodical. English. mo. $9.95 (one year), $17.95 (two years). Peninsula Associates, PO Box 2259, Sequim WA 98382.

US/0888-4846
PENINSULA (REDWOOD CITY, CALIF.). ***Ceased.*** (PENINSULA.). Vol. 1, No. 1 (April 1986)-(Jan. 1993). Periodical. English. mo. Westar Media Inc., PO Box 51823, Palo Alto CA 94303. **Tel** (415)368-8800, FAX (415)368-6251. **ED** David Gorn and Dale Conour. **Ad Acc. Circ:** 35,000 (ctrl).
Desc: A city regional magazine of the San Francisco Peninsula. Features people, events, home and garden, health, fashion, and entertaining on the Peninsula.

US/0894-3850
PENNSYLVANIA FACTS. [Pa. facts]. **VFOAT** Flying the Colors, Pennsylvania Facts. (1987)-. Monographic series. English. ir (every three to four years). Price varies per volume. Clements Research II Inc., 16850 Dallas Parkway, Dallas TX 75248. **Tel** (214)931-9956, FAX (214)248-7159. **ED** John Clements. **LC** F146; .P218. **DD** 974.8.
Desc: Book of facts on states, county-by-county.

US/0744-4230
PENNSYLVANIA MAGAZINE (CAMP HILL, PA.). **See** Travel and Tourism.

US/0093-7673
PEOPLE (CHICAGO. 1974). (PEOPLE WEEKLY.). [People]. **VFOAT** People. Vol. 1, No. 1 (Mar. 4, 1974)-. Periodical. English. wk. $87.88. Time Inc. / New York, Time & Life Building, Rockefeller Center, New York NY 10020. **(Subscription address:** Time Customer Service, PO Box 60050, Tampa FL 33609.) **LC** AP2; .P417. **DD** 051. **Bk Rev. Ad Acc.** available on microfilm and microfiche from University Microfilms International (UMI); available on an online database (files 647,648/Full-Text) from DIALOG. Documents available from UMI Article Clearinghouse.
Desc: Presents a glamorous show of non-stop first-class entertainment, week after week.
Ind/Abst Abr. Read. Guide Period. Lit.; Acad. Abstr. Full Text Elite (Jan. 1984-); Acad. Abstr. (Jan. 1984-); Acad. Ind. [Computer File] (1984-1988); Expand. Acad. Index (1984-1988); Gen. Period. Index (1985-); Health Ref. Cent. (1987-) [Select. Cov.]; Mag. Artic. Summar. Elite (Jan. 1984-); Mag. Artic. Summar. Select (Jan. 1984-); Mag. Artic. Summar. CD-ROM (Jan. 1984-); Mag. ASAP Plus [Full Txt.]; Mag. ASAP Sel. [Full Txt.]; Mag. Express (1986-) [Full Txt.]; Mag. Index Plus (1989-); Mag. Index Sel. Microfiche (1986-1991) [Full Txt.]; Mag. Index. Sel. (1986-); Mag. Search; Mid. Search (Jan. 1984-); Newsp. Period. Abstr. (1986-); NEXIS (1981-); Prim. Search (Jan. 1984-); Read. Guide Abstr. Select Ed.; Read. Guide Period. Lit.; Resource/One Ondisc; Mag. Index (1977-); TOM Gen. Index (1985-) [Full Txt.]; Vocat. Search (Jan. 1984-).

US/0745-0540
PHILADELPHIA HOME VIEWER, THE. (19??)-. Periodical. English. Twelve times a year. $5.00. Homer Viewer Publications, 157 North 3rd Street, Philadelphia PA 19106.

US/0031-7233
PHILADELPHIA MAGAZINE (1967). (PHILADELPHIA.). [Philadelphia mag.]. **VFOAT** Philadelphia Magazine. Vol. 58, No. 2 (Feb. 1967)-. Periodical. English. mo. $15.00 (one year), $28.00 (two year). Philadelphia Magazine, 1500 Walnut Street, Philadelphia PA 19102. **Tel** (215)545-3500. **(Subscription address:** CDS Agency Hard Copy, PO Box 4966, Des Moines IA 50340.) **ED** Ron Javers. **LC** HC108.P5; G7. **DD** 974.8/11/005. **Bk Rev. Ad Acc. Circ:** 148,809 (ctrl). available on microfilm. Documents available from UMI Article Clearinghouse. ***Continues*** *Greater Philadelphia.*
Desc: Strives to keep an affluent, educated, informed audience appraised of life in and around Philadelphia.
Ind/Abst Acad. Search (Sept. 1984-June 1989); Access (1975-); Gen. Period. Index (1985-); INFO-SOUTH Abstr.; Mag. Artic. Summar. Elite (Sept. 1984-June 1989); Mag. Artic. Summar. Select (Sept. 1984-June 1989); Mag. Artic. Summar. CD-ROM (Sept. 1984-June 1989); Mag. Index Plus (1989-); Newsp. Period. Abstr. (1988-); Pop. Period. Index; Mag. Index (1977-).

US/0898-2503
PHILLYSPORT (PHILADELPHIA, PA.). ***Ceased.*** (PHILLYSPORT.). [PhillySport]. **VFOAT** Philly Sport. Vol. 1, No. 1 (June/July 1988)-Ceased (19??). Periodical. English. mo. Phillysport Magazine, 15th & Locust, Lewis Tower Building, Philadelphia PA 19102. **DD** 796.

US/1045-1773
PHOENIX (1989). (PHOENIX.). [Phoenix]. **VFOAT** Phoenix Magazine. Vol. 24, No. 6 (June 1989)-. Periodical. English. mo. $14.00 (one year), $25.00 (two year) US; $27.00 (one year), $51.00 (two year) other. Media America Corporation, 5555 North 7th Avenue, Suite B200, Phoenix AZ 85013. **Tel** (602)207-3750, FAX (602)207-3777. **ED** Dick Vonier. **LC** WMLC L 83/6666. **DD** 917. **Ad Acc. Circ:** 45,000. ***Continues*** *Metro Phoenix, 0886-8859.*
Desc: Edited for residents and visitors in Phoenix area. Content emphasis is on Arizona issues--political and quality of life--and business lifestyle and personalities.
Ind/Abst Access (1975-).

US/0192-8716
PIKESTAFF FORUM, THE. No. 1 (Spring 1978)-. Periodical. English. $5.00. Pikestaff Publications Inc, PO Box 127, Normal IL 61761.
Ind/Abst Index Am. Period. Verse.

US/1066-0062
PITTSBURGH CITY PAPER. [Pittsbg. City Paper]. (1990)-. Periodical. English. wk. Pittsburgh City Paper, One Library Place, Suite G-2, Duquesne PA 15110. **Tel** (412)469-3080, FAX (412)469-3099. **ED** Andy March. **DD** _a051. **Circ:** 50,000 (ctrl).
Desc: Devoted to the urban Pittsburgh dweller. Covers politics, local issues, the arts, and entertainment. A restaurant and shopping guide is included as well.

CN/0708-207X
PLACOTEUX. (LE PLACOTEUX / PSP.). [Placoteux]. Vol. 1, No. 1 (12 Sept. 1978)-. Periodical. French. wk. Le Placoteux, CP 181, St-Pascal Quebec G0L 3Y0 Canada. **DD** 071/.1475.

US/0032-1346
PLATEAU (FLAGSTAFF, AZ : 1939). (PLATEAU.). [Plateau]. **Added/Corp** Museum of Northern Arizona. Northern Arizona Society of Science and Art. Museum of Northern Arizona. Annual report of the Director. Vol. 12, No. 1 July (1939)-. Periodical. English. Four times a year (Feb., May, Aug., Nov.). $30.00. Museum of Northern Arizona, Route 4 Box 720, Flagstaff AZ 86001. **Tel** (602)774-5213. **ED** Diana Lubick, (phone: (602)774-5213). **LC** F806; .P58. **CODEN** PLTUAP. Index available. **Circ:** 7,000-10,000 (ctrl). Documents available from BIOSIS Document Express. ***Continues*** *Museum Notes (Museum of Northern Arizona).*
Desc: Quarterly four-color magazine relating to subjects on the Colorado Plateau.
Ind/Abst Abstr. Anthropol.; Am. Hist. Life (1969-); Anthropol. Index; Biol. Abstr.; Ethnoarts Index; Film Lit. Index (19??-); GeoRef; West. Hist. Q.

US/0092-4318
PLATTE VALLEY REVIEW. (THE PLATTE VALLEY REVIEW.). [Platte Val. rev.]. **Added/Corp** Kearney State College. (1973)-. Academic Scholarly Publication. English. sa (Jan., May). $4.00. Platte Valley Review, University of Nebraska at Kearney, Kearney NE 68847. **Tel** (308)236-8441. **ED** Vern Plambeck. **LC** AS36.K36; A26. **DD** 081. **CODEN** PVREE7. **Circ:** 1,000.
Desc: Contains scholarly and creative writings, primarily by the faculty of the University of Nebraska at Kearney.
Ind/Abst MLA Int. Bibl. Books Artic. Mod. Lang. Lit.

US
POINT OF CONTACT. (1982)-. English. ir. Porto de Cantacta, Inc., 110 Bleecker Street, New York NY 10012.

US/0745-3191
POLK COUNTY ELEGANCE. **VFOAT** Elegance. Periodical. English. mo. Polk County Elegance, POB 1438, Winter Haven FL 33880.

US
PONDERING KENTUCKY. English. mo. $60.00 US; $84.00 other. Kentucky Sound, PO Box 43432, Louisville KY 40253. **Tel** (502)245-3628.

US
POOR JOE'S CALIFORNIA ALMANACK. English. $1.25. Crabapple Press, 300 North Street, Meadville PA 16335. **LC** AY121.M4; P66. **DD** 051.

US
POOR JOE'S COLORADO ALMANACK. English. $1.25. Crabapple Press, 300 North Street, Meadville PA 16335. **LC** AY126.M4; P66. **DD** 051.

US/0160-8193
POOR JOE'S INDIANA ALMANACK. **VFOAT** Indiana Almanack. English. an. $1.00. Crabapple Press, 300 North Street, Meadville PA 16335. **LC** AY166.M4; P66.

US
POOR JOE'S MISSOURI ALMANACK. English. an. $1.25. Crabapple Press, 300 North Street, Meadville PA 16335. **LC** AY221.M4; P66. **DD** 051.

US
POOR JOE'S NORTH CAROLINA ALMANACK. English. $1.25. Crabapple Press, 300 North Street, Meadville PA 16335. **LC** AY261.M4; P66. **DD** 051.

US/0160-8185
POOR JOE'S OHIO STATE ALMANACK. **VFOAT** Ohio State Almanack. English. an. $1.00. Crabapple Press, 300 North Street, Meadville PA 16335. **LC** AY271.M4; P66.

US/0362-8523
POOR JOE'S PENNSYLVANIA FARM ALMANACK. **VFOAT** Poor Joe's Pennsylvania Almanack. English. an. $0.75. Crabapple Press, 300 North Street, Meadville PA 16335. **LC** AY81.F3; P68. **DD** 051.

US/0160-8207
POOR JOE'S WASHINGTON ALMANACK. **VFOAT** Washington Almanack. English. an. $1.00. Crabapple Press, 300 North Street, Meadville PA 16335. **LC** AY331.M4; P66. **DD** 051.

US/0890-3840
PORTLAND FAMILY CALENDAR. Periodical. English. mo. $12.00 US; $13.00 Canada. Portland Family Calendar, 1819 NW Everett, Portland OR 97209.

US/0195-2854
PRAIRIE STATER. Vol. 1, No. 1 (Feb. 1988)-. Periodical. English. mo. Prairie Stater / Indiana, Circulation Department, PO Box 1954, Indianapolis IN 46206. ***Continues*** *Prairie Stater, 0195-2854.*

●US/1065-7762
PREFERRED STOCK (DENVER, COLO.). (PREFERRED STOCK.). [Prefer. stock]. Vol. 1, No. 1 (July 15-28, 1992)-. Periodical. English. bw (26 issues). $30.00. Preferred Stock, Inc., PO Box 18515, Denver CO 80218. **Tel** (303)455-1280. **DD** 051.

CN/1182-9931
PRESS INDEPENDENT. [Press indep.]. **Added/Corp** Native Communications Society of the Western Northwest Territories. Vol. 20, Issue 32, Nov. 2 (1990)-. Periodical. English. wk. $30.00 Canada (add GST); $50.00 US; $75.00 other. **ED** John Holman. **DD** 071/.192. **Bk Rev**, (Qty: 12/yr). **Ad Acc, Adv Mgr:** Teresa Sanderson. **Circ:** 5,600 (ctrl). available on microfilm. ***Continues*** *Native Press (Yellowknife, N.W.T.), 0833-093X.*

CN/0711-2963
PRESSE-LIBRE. [Presse-libre]. No. 1 (March 1981)-. Periodical. French. mo. $1.00 each number, $10.00 each issue. Societe Populaire D'Information De Quebec, 356 Est, Rue Ontario Montreal, Quebec H2X 1H8 Canada. **DD** 071/.14.

US
PRIVATE EYE WEEKLY. (19??)-. Newsletter. English. wk. $30.00. Private Eye Newsletter, PO Box 25301, Salt Lake City UT 84125. **Tel** (801)255-3733. **ED** Tom Walsh. **Bk Rev**, (Qty: 12). **Ad Acc, Adv Mgr:** Kim Gregory, **Tel** (801)575-7003. **Circ:** 30,000 (ctrl).
Desc: Provides alternative independent news, and information on the arts and entertainment.

MX
PROCESO. (1976)-. Periodical. Spanish. wk (52 issues). $150.00 US and Canada; $350.00 Central America; $400.00 Europe and all other US; $450.00 other. Cisa, Fresas 13 Col de Valle, 03210 Mexico DF Mexico. **Tel** 011 52 56292080. **LC** AP63; .P736.

●US/1058-3068
PROFILES INTERNATIONAL. **VFOAT** World and African Profiles. (1991)-. English. bm. $2.50 (single issue). TPA Communications, Inc., PO Box 1679, New York NY 10027.

MX/0555-3768
PROGRESO (MEXICO). (PROGRESO.). [Progreso]. (July/Aug. 1967)-. Periodical. Spanish. mo (11 issues). $90.00 (one year), $160.00 (two year), $190.00 (three year). Vision Inc. / Mexico, Arquimedes 199, Pisos 6TO Piso, 11560 Mexico DF Mexico. **Tel** 011 52 5 2036734, 011 52 5 2543097. **LC** HC121; .P755. ***Supersedes*** *Progreso, 0555-3768.*
Ind/Abst HAPI Hisp. Am. Period. Index (19??-).

CN/0715-5646
PUBLIC LETTER (MISSISSAUGA). (THE PUBLIC LETTER.). [Public letter]. 1st Edition (July

1982)-. Periodical. English. mo. $24.00. EM Research Associates, PO Box 1172 Station B, Mississauga Ontario L4Y 3W4 Canada. **DD** 051.

US/0033-4049
PUERTO RICO LIVING. [P.R. living]. (1962)-. Periodical. English. an. $3.50. Martin Wittstein, 54 Caleta de San Juan, Old San Juan PR 00901. **ED** Barbara Dimando. **LC** F1951; .P94. **Bk Rev. Ad Acc. Circ:** 10,000 (ctrl). available on microfilm and microfiche from University Microfilms International (UMI).
Desc: Handbook for English-speaking residents of Puerto Rico.

CN/0226-9449
PURE BEAUTE, LA. V. 1, No. 1, (April 1981)-. Periodical. French. mo. Free. Editions Publi-Maupel, 6507 De Chateaubriand, Montreal Quebec H2S 2N6. **DD** 054/.1.

US/0276-7120
QC (FOREST HILLS, N.Y.). (QC; THE MAGAZINE OF QUEEN'S COUNTY.). **VFOAT** Queens County. **VAT** Queen's County (Forest Hills, N.Y.). Vol. 1, No. 1 (Fall 1981)-. Periodical. English. qt. $5.95. Motivational Communications Inc, 72 5 Austin Street, Forest Hills NY 11375.

CN/0225-5014
QUORUM (OTTAWA). (QUORUM.). [Quorum]. V. 1- Oct. 9, 1979-. Periodical. English (French). da (during parliamentary session, weekly during intersession). Library of Parliament / Information & Technical Services Branch, Ottawa Ontario K1A 0A9 Canada. **Tel** (613)996-3121. **DD** 971.064/5/05. **Circ:** 1,300 (ctrl).
Desc: Compilation of daily press clippings from the major Canadian newspapers. A compendium of current events, analytical articles and commentary from leading journalists and editorialists.

US/0745-4279
RANCHLAND NEWS. Periodical. English. wk. Ranchland News, 115 Sioux Avenue, Simla CO 80835-0307. **Tel** (303)541-2288. **ED** Dolores Gaddy and Monty Gaddy. **Circ:** 3,500. ***Continues*** *Ranchland Farm News.*

CN/0034-0413
READER'S DIGEST (CANADIAN EDITION). (READER'S DIGEST.). [Read. dig.]. (1???)-. Periodical. English. mo. 30.96Can$ Canada. Readers Digest Association Canada Ltd., 215 Redfern Avenue, Montreal, Quebec H3Z 2V9 Canada. **Tel** (514)934-0751. **(Subscription address:** ICL / Interprovincial Circ. Ltd., 251 Lawrence Avenue, Suite 201, Kelowna, BC V1Y 6L2 Canada.**)** available on microfilm and microfiche from University Microfilms International (UMI).
Ind/Abst Can. Period. Index; Gen. Period. Index (1985-); Mag. Index Plus (1989-); Mag. Index. Sel. (1986-); Mag. Index (1977-); TOM Gen. Index (1989-).

US/1040-9335
REAL PEOPLE. [Real people]. Vol. 1, Issue 2 (March/April 1988)-. Periodical. English. bm (6 issues). $24.00. Hochman Associates, 950 Third Avenue, 16th Floor, New York NY 10022. **Tel** (212)371-4932. **(Subscription address:** CDS Agency Hard Copy, PO Box 4966, Des Moines IA 50340.**) DD** 051. **Bk Rev. Ad Acc. Circ:** 150,000. ***Continues*** *Family Digest (New York, N.Y.), 0894-5586.*
Desc: Features articles on celebrities, and interesting people, as well as stories of interest to the entire family.

CN/0821-1728
REFLET DE TADOUSSAC. (LE REFLET : JOURNAL COMMUNAUTAIRE DE TADOUSSAC.). [Reflet Tadoussac]. Periodical. French. bw. $0.50 each number. Reflet, CP 41, Tadoussac Quebec G0T 2A0 Canada. **DD** 071. ***Continues*** *Reflet de Tadoussac, 0821-1728.*

CN/0833-8116
REFLET (EMBRUN, ONT.). (LE REFLET.). [Reflet]. Vol. 1, No. 1 (April 1986)-. Periodical. French (English). mo. Free. Chambre de Commerce d'Embrun, CP 734, Embrun Ontario K0A 1W0 Canada. **DD** 054/.1. ***Continues*** *Embrun (Embrun, Ont.), 0824-6971.*

CN/0315-212X
REGINA. VAT Regina Magazine. Visitor Information Guide. 1972-. English. an. Regina Chamber of Commerce, 2145 Albert Street, Regina Saskatchewan S4P 2V1 Canada. **Tel** (306)757-4658. **ED** Mack McColl. **DD** 917.124/4. **Bk Rev. Ad Acc. Circ:** 6,500 (ctrl).
Desc: Paid advertising tabloid providing news and information pertinent to the business community of Regina, Saskatchewan.

CN/0827-2611
REGIONAL (KENORA). (THE REGIONAL.). [Regional]. Vol. 1, No. 1 (Oct. 26, 1983)-. Periodical. English. wk. $0.25 each number. Regional, c/o Kenora Daily Miner & News, PO Box 1620, 33 Main Street South, Kenora Ontario P9N 3X7 Canada. **DD** 071/.13112.

●US/1069-8957
REMINISCE EXTRA. [Reminisce extra]. **VFOAT** Reminisce. (1993)-. Periodical. English. Six times a year. $16.98 US; $25.98 Canada. Reiman Publications, 5400 South 60th Street, Greendale WI 53129. **Tel** (414)423-0100 Ext. 421, FAX (414)423-1143. **DD** 051.
Desc: Published in alternating months of Reminisce Magazine, aimed at bringing into view the "good old days."

US/1057-2368
REMINISCE (GREENDALE, WIS.). (REMINISCE.). [Reminisces]. (1991)-. Periodical. English. Six times a year. $16.98 US; $25.98 Canada. Reiman Publications, 5400 South 60th Street, Greendale WI 53129. **Tel** (414)423-0100 Ext. 421, FAX (414)423-1143. **DD** 920.
Desc: Colorful, photo-packed pages aim to rekindle memories of life's "good old days." Issues include warm, personal recollections of life in the 1930's, 1940's, etc.

US/0742-9908
RENAISSANCE TOO MAGAZINE. VFOAT Renaissance Too. Vol. 1, Issue 1 (Spring 1984)-. English. Three times a year. $10.00. Renaissance Too Magazine, 1516 5th Avenue, Pittsburgh PA 15219. **Tel** (412)391-8208, FAX (412)391-8006. **ED** Connie Portis. **LC** F159.P69; N465. **Circ:** 10,000. ***Continued in part by*** *Greater Pittsburgh Black Business Directory.*

US/0034-4451
RENFRO VALLEY BUGLE. Vol. 1, No. 1 (Feb. 15, 1944)-. Newspaper. English. mo. $6.00. Renfro Valley Folks Inc., Renfro Valley KY 40473. **Tel** (606)256-2664.

CN/0708-1510
REPERTOIRE DE LA VIE FRANCAISE EN AMERIQUE. (LE REPERTOIRE DE LA VIE FRANCAISE EN AMERIQUE.). **Added/Corp** Conseil de la vie Francaise en Amerique. (1978)-. French. an. 38.00Can$ Canada; 41.50Can$ US; 42.00Can$ other. Conseil de la vie Francaise en Amerique, 56 rue St-Pierre, 1st Floor, Quebec Quebec G1K 4A1 Canada. **Tel** (418)692-1150, FAX (418)692-4578. **ED** Jean-Luc Cotf. **LC** HS1841; .A34. **DD** 061/.1. **Ad Acc. Circ:** 600 (ctrl). ***Continues*** *Bottin des Societes Patriotiques, 0589-4107.*
Desc: Constitutes an interesting source of information on French speaking people.

MX
REVISTA DE REVISTAS : SEMENARIO DE EXCELSIOR. VFOAT RR. Began in 1910. Periodical. Spanish. wk. $5.00 single issue. Excelsior, Reforma 12-505, Mexico 1 DF 06600 Mexico. **Tel** 566-93-60. **LC** AP63; .R18. **DD** 056/.1. ***Continues*** *Revista de Revistas.*

MX
REVISTA TAMAULIPAS. VFOAT Tamaulipas. (1???)-. Periodical. Spanish. mo. $50.00. Revista Tamaulipas, Apartado Postal 460, CP 89000 Tampico, TAM, Mexico.

MX
REVISTA TROHPOS. VFOAT Trohpos. Yearly V. 1, No. 1 (Sept./Oct. 80)-. Periodical. Spanish. bm. $60.00 single issue. Editorial Katun SA, Columbia 7-A, Mexico 1 DF Mexico. **LC** AP63; .R833. **DD** 056/.1.

US/0199-526X
RHODE ISLAND MAGAZINE. ***Ceased.*** **VFOAT** Rhode Island. Periodical. English. mo. Rhode Island Magazine, PO Box 506, Newport RI 02840. **Tel** (401)846-9300.

US/0274-9734
ROANOKER, THE. Vol. 1 (Fall 1974)-. Periodical. English. Twelve times a year. $16.95 (one year), $26.95 (two year). Blue Ridge Country, PO Box 21535, Roanoke VA 24018. **Tel** (703)989-6138, (800)877-6026, FAX (703)989-7603. **ED** Kurt Rheinheimer. **Ad Acc. Circ:** 10,000.
Desc: City magazine for the greater Roanoke area. Emphasis on lifestyles, issues, history and people profiles.

CN/0704-6472
ROBINSON'S FORTNIGHTLY. Vol. 1 No. 10 (July 29, 1977)-. Periodical. English. bw. $12.00. Robinson's Fortnightly, Box 1329 Comox, Point Holmes British Columbia V9N 3Z0 Canada. **DD** 051. ***Continues*** *Robinson's Weekly, 0703-4393.*

US
ROCHESTER LIVING. (19??)-. Periodical. English. Six times a year. $10.00. Living Publications, 1 Fayette Park Hamilton House, Syracuse NY 13202. **Tel** (315)475-0083.

●US/1075-7856
ROCKY MOUNTAIN MAGAZINE (STAMFORD, CONN.). (ROCKY MOUNTAIN MAGAZINE.). (1994)-. English. bm. $18.00. Cowles Magazines, PO Box 8200, Harrisburg PA 17105. **Tel** (717)657-9555, (800)435-9610.

US/1055-1727
ROGER! ROGER!. [Roger! Roger!]. Vol. 1, No. 1 (1991)-. Periodical. English. mo. $17.00. Mach 5 Corporation, PO Box 751693, Memphis TN 38175-1693. **DD** 051.

CN/0035-8908
ROYAL GAZETTE. PRINCE EDWARD ISLAND. (ROYAL GAZETTE.). [R. gaz., P.E.I.]. **Main/Corp** Prince Edward Island. **VAT** Royal Gazette. Province of Prince Edward Island. Vol. 1 (Aug. 24, 1830)-. Periodical. English. wk. 48.15Can$ (includes GST) Canada; 45.00Can$ other. Royal Gazette Charlottetown, PO Box 2000, Charlottetown Prince Edward Island C1A 7N8 Canada. **Tel** (902)894-9976, (902)566-1667. **ED** Gordon Babineau. **Circ:** 1,000 (ctrl). available on microfilm from New York Public Library; and Micromedia Limited; available on microfiche from Micromedia Limited.

●US/1066-1891
ROZEK'S SEATTLE, WASH. (ROZEK'S.). [Rozek's Seattle Wash.]. (1992)-. Periodical. English. Twelve times a year. $78.00 US; $98.00 Canada; $90.00 other. Rozek's, 3424 10th Avenue West, Seattle WA 98119. **Tel** (206)285-1515, FAX (206)282-5908. **ED** Michael Rozek. **DD** 070. **Circ:** 1,600.
Desc: Each issue contains just one article, a single profile.

CN/0705-3444
RUDE. 1st No. 1- Spring 1978-. Periodical. English. Rude, c/o J Thomas, Box 3 Station B, London Ontario N6A 4V3 Canada. **DD** 051.

US/0048-878X
RURAL ARKANSAS. (19??)-. Periodical. English. mo. $4.00. Arkansas Electric Cooperatives, PO Box 510, Little Rock AR 72203. **Tel** (501)562-0220, FAX (501)570-2205.
Ind/Abst Ozark Period. Index (19??-199?).

CN/0703-7724
RURAL DELIVERY. Vol. 1 (June 1976)-. Periodical. English. mo. 12.85Can$ Canada; 16.85Can$ other. DVL Publishing Inc, PO Box 1509, Liverpool Nova Scotia B0T IK0 Canada. **Tel** (902)683-2763. **ED** Dirk van Loon. **DD** 630/.9716. **Bk Rev. Ad Acc. Circ:** 9,000.
Desc: Relates to all aspects of rural living.

US/1054-4801
RURAL LIVING (A&N ELECTRIC COOPERATIVE ED.). See Agriculture.

●US/0743-9962
RURAL LIVING (LANSING, MICH.). **See** Agriculture.

US/0164-8578
RURAL MISSOURI. (1986)-. Periodical. English. mo. $2.50. Rural Electric Missourian, 2722 East McCarty, Jefferson City MO 65101.
Ind/Abst Ozark Period. Index (19??-199?).

US/0747-8712
SACRAMENTO (JONSSON COMMUNICATIONS CORPORATION). (SACRAMENTO.). **Added/Corp** Jonsson Communications Corporation. Vol. 5, No. 1 (Jan. 1979)-. English. mo. $24.95. Sacramento Magazine, 4471 D Street, Sacramento CA 95819. **Tel** (916)452-6200. **LC** F869.S12; S13. **DD** 979.4/54/005. **Bk Rev. Ad Acc. Circ:** 26,000. ***Continues*** *Sacramento (Jonsson Broadcasting Corporation), 0191-8796.*
Desc: Local, general interest publication.

US/1065-3287
SACRAMENTO NEWS & REVIEW. [Sacram. news rev.]. **VFOAT** Sacramento News and Review. (19??)-. Periodical. English. Fifty-two times a year. $25.00. Community Publishing Inc., 2210 21st Street, Sacramento CA 95818. **Tel** (916)737-1234, FAX (916)737-1437. **ED** Melinda Welsh. **DD** 070. **Bk Rev**, (Qty: 26). **Ad Acc, Adv Mgr:** D. Gillen, **Tel** (916)737-1234. **Pr Rev. Circ:** 90,000 (ctrl).

US/0899-5826
SAN ANTONIO. (Nov. 1987)-. Periodical. English. mo. $17.00. Sutherland Media Inc, PO Box 790239, San Antonio TX 78279-01239, San Antonio TX 78279-1239. **ED** John Obercht. ***Continues*** *San Antonio Monthly, 0744-5954;* ***Absorbed*** *San Antonio, 0036-3960.*

US/0193-3183
SAN DIEGO LOG. Periodical. English. sm. Log Newspapers Inc, PO Box 6350, San Diego CA 92106.

US/0036-4045
SAN DIEGO MAGAZINE (1949). ***Title Change.*** (SAN DIEGO MAGAZINE.). Vol. 1 (1949)-(19??). Periodical. English. mo. San Diego Magazine, PO Box 85409, San Diego CA 92186. **Tel** (619)225-8953, FAX (619)222-0773. **(Subscription address:** PO Box 85409, San Diego, CA 92138**) ED** Edwin Self and Gloria Self. **Bk Rev. Ad Acc. Circ:** 70,000. available on microfilm and microfiche from University Microfilms International (UMI). ***Continued by*** *San Diego & Point Magazine.*
Desc: The first city magazine in the United States.

Published to examine critically the cultural, political and civic issues of San Diego County and California.
Ind/Abst Access (1975-); Calif. Period. Index (19??-?); Chicano Index (?-?).

US/0734-6727
SAN DIEGO MAGAZINE (1968). (SAN DIEGO MAGAZINE.). Vol. 21, No. 1 (Oct. 1968)-. Periodical. English. mo. $16.00. San Diego Magazine, PO Box 85409, San Diego CA 92186. **Tel** (619)225-8953, FAX (619)222-0773. available in microform. ***Continues*** *San Diego.*

US/0036-4096
SAN FRANCISCO BAY GUARDIAN, THE. **VFOAT** Bay Guardian. Vol. 3, No. 1 (Aug. 30, 1968)-. Newspaper. English. Fifty-two times a year. $40.00. San Francisco Bay Guardian, 520 Hampshire Street, San Francisco CA 94110. **Tel** (415)255-3100, FAX (415)241-8037, (415)255-8955. **ED** Bruce B. Brugmann. **Bk Rev**, (Qty: 50 per year). **Ad Acc**, **Adv Mgr:** K. Close, **Tel** (415)255-4600. **Circ:** 135,000 (ctrl). available on microfilm and microfiche from University Microfilms International (UMI). ***Continues*** *Bay Guardian.*
Desc: Alternative journalism: investigative reporting, consumer news and reports, political news and endorsements, entertainment news and reviews.

US/0274-5933
SAN FRANCISCO FOCUS. (19??)-. English. ir. $35.00. KQED Inc, 2601 Mariposa Street, San Francisco CA 94110. **Tel** (415)553-2176. **ED** Mark K. Powelson. **LC** WMLC L 83/2627. **Circ:** 197,996. ***Continues*** *Focus.*
Desc: Contains information on up-and-coming business people and regularly includes fiction.

US/0581-5029
SAN FRANCISCO KEEPER'S VOICE, THE. [San Franc. keep. voice]. **VFOAT** Keeper's Voice. V. 1- Jan. 1965-. Periodical. English. qt. San Francisco Keepers Voice, 1263 6th Avenue, San Francisco CA 94122. **DD** 051.

US/0744-5199
SANTA BARBARA MAGAZINE. Vol. 1, No. 1 (Summer 1975)-. Periodical. English. qt. Must order direct. California Press, 123 West Padre, Suite A, Santa Barbara CA 93105. **Tel** (805)962-8877.
Ind/Abst Calif. Period. Index (19??-); Calif. Period. Microfi. (19??-).

US/1046-2708
SANTA FEAN MAGAZINE (SANTA FE, N.M.). (THE SANTA FEAN MAGAZINE.). [St. Fean mag.]. **VFOAT** Santa Fean. Vol. 1, No. 1 (Dec. 1972)-. Periodical. English. mo (11 issues per year). $19.35. The Santa Fean Magazine, 1440 A St Francis Drive, Santa Fe NM 87501. **Tel** (505)983-8914. **ED** Betty Bauer and Marian F Love. **DD** 051. **Ad Acc. Circ:** 10,000.
Desc: Focuses on Santa Fe, New Mexico, history, culture, profiles, homes, gardens, and events.
Ind/Abst Access (1975-).

US/1048-2245
SARASOTA MAGAZINE. [Sarasota mag.]. **VFOAT** Sarasota. (198?)-. Periodical. English. mo (except Aug., Sept.). $19.95 US; $34.95 Canada; $49.00 Other. Clubhouse Publishing Inc., 601 South Osprey, Sarasota FL 34236. **Tel** (813)366-8225, FAX (813)365-7272. **ED** Pam Daniel. **DD** 051. **Ad Acc. Circ:** 15,000 (ctrl). available on an online database (file 648/Full-Text) from DIALOG. ***Continues*** *Sarasota, 0893-5548.*
Desc: Articles about people, issues, homes and living in Sarasota, Florida. Emphasis is on upscale, arts-oriented lifestyles.
Ind/Abst Acad. Search (July 1993-); Trade Ind. ASAP [Full Txt.]; Trade Ind. Index [Full Txt.].

CN/0820-5043
SASK. REPORT. [Sask. rep.]. **VFOAT** Saskatchewan Report Newsmagazine. **VAT** Saskatchewan Report. Vol. 2, Issue 7 (Jan. 1987)-. Periodical. English. Eight times a year. 17.60Can$ (1 year), 33.60Can$ (2 year), 48.00Can$ (3 year) Canada; 25.00Can$ (1 year), 44.00Can$ (2 year), 62.00Can$ (3 year) other. Sask Report Magazine, 218 103rd Street East, Saskatoon SASK S7N 1Y7 Canada. **Tel** (306)373-0404, FAX (306)373-5553. **ED** Brent Lannan and Heather Sterling. **DD** 051. **Ad Acc**, **Adv Mgr:** Bill Clewes. **Circ:** 15,000 (ctrl). ***Continues*** *Saskatchewan Report Newsmagazine, 0827-5734.*
Desc: General interest magazine of issues regarding the province of Saskatchewan, including sports, travel, agriculture, business, health, lifestyles, people, and current issues and events.

CN/0036-4975
SATURDAY NIGHT. **Added/Corp** Canadian National Institute for the Blind. Library Dept. (1977)-. Periodical. English. Ten times a year. 19.95Can$ Canada; 27.45Can$ US; 31.45Can$ other. Saturday Night, 184 Front Street East, Suite 400, Toronto Ontario M5A 4N3 Canada. **Tel** (416)368-7237. **ED** John Fraser. **DD** 050. **Bk Rev. Ad Acc. Circ:** 110,000. available on microfilm and microfiche from University Microfilms International (UMI). Documents available from UMI Article Clearinghouse.
Desc: Features profiles of Canadians making news and shaping history at home and abroad; reporting goes beyond explanations of events, focusing on why things happen, who makes them happen and how they may effect your future.
Ind/Abst Abr. Read. Guide Period. Lit.; Acad. Abstr. Full Text Elite (Jan. 1992-); Acad. Abstr. (Jan. 1992-); Acad. Search (Jan. 1992-); Book Rev. Index; Can. Index; Gen. Period. Index (1985-); Mag. Artic. Summar. Elite (Jan. 1992-); Mag. Artic. Summar. Select (Jan. 1992-); Mag. Artic. Summar. CD-ROM (Jan. 1992-); Mag. Index Plus (1989-); Mag. Search; Newsp. Period. Abstr. (1988-); PAIS Int. Print; Peace Res. Abstr. J. (1963-1968), (1970-1976); Read. Guide Period. Lit.; SPORT Discus; SportSearch; Mag. Index (1983-); TOM Gen. Index (1989-).

CN/1183-2274
SAWT KANADA. **VFOAT** Voice of Canada; Saout Kanada; Sawt Canada. (1991)-. Periodical. Arabic. mo. $2.00 per no. Typo Media, Po Box 9455, Station T, Ottawa Ontario K1G 3V2. **DD** 071/.1384. ***Continues*** *Sawt Utawa, 1186-1126.*

CN/0706-8387
SCHMAGG. [Schmagg]. No. 1, (1977)-. Periodical. English. qt. Schmagg, 8833-92 Street, Edmonton Alberta T6C 3P9 Canada. **DD** 051.

US/0886-4551
SCHOLASTIC UPDATE (TEACHERS' ED.). (SCHOLASTIC UPDATE.). **VFOAT** Update (Teachers' Edition). Vol. 115, No. 15 (April 1, 1983)-. Periodical. English. bw (during school year, 16 issues). $22.00 (grade 8-12, teachers ed) all except Canada. Scholastic Magazines, 730 Broadway, New York NY 10003. **Tel** (212)505-3000. **ED** Lee Kravitz. **LC** AP2; .S477. **DD** 051. Index available. **Ad Acc. Circ:** 310,000. available on microfilm and microfiche from University Microfilms International (UMI). ***Continues*** *Senior Scholastic (Teachers' Edition), 0886-456X.*
Desc: A public affairs magazine for high school students of government, history, economics, sociology, and world affairs. Focuses on contemporary issues, e.g., immigration, arms control, crime, environment, Southern Africa, Central America, Middle East.
Ind/Abst Abr. Read. Guide Period. Lit.; Acad. Abstr. Full Text Elite (Sept. 1984-); Child. Mag. Guide; Mag. Artic. Summar. Elite (Sept. 1984-); Mag. Artic. Summar. Select (Sept. 1984-); Mag. Artic. Summar. CD-ROM (Sept. 1984-); Read. Guide Abstr. Select Ed.; Read. Guide Period. Lit.; Mag. Index (1983-).

CN/0703-1580
SCOTTISH TRADITION. **Added/Corp** Conference on Scottish Studies. Vol. 1 (Summer 1971)-. Periodical. English. an. 20.00Can$. University of Guelph / History, Department of History, Guelph Ontario N1G 2W1 Canada. **Tel** (519)824-4120. **ED** Scott McLean, R. Andrew McDonald, & Andrew D. Nicholls. **Bk Rev. Pr Rev. Circ:** 300.
Desc: Contents include articles about Scottish culture, history, literature, religion, art, law, and its transfer to other parts of the world. Also, includes Scottish migrations to North America.

US
SCOTTSDALE MAGAZINE. (19??)-. English. Four times a year (Mar., June, Sept., Dec.). $18.00. Robert Rinehart, 6006 East Cheney Road, Paradise Valley AZ 85253. **Tel** (602)948-3484. **ED** Margaret Rinehart. **Ad Acc. Circ:** 40,000 (ctrl).
Desc: This is a local features about people, places and events. It includes a business section, food and art section, and fashion columns.

US/1058-0395
SCRAPE (PHOENIX, ARIZ.). (SCRAPE [SOUND RECORDING].). [Scrape]. (1991)-. Periodical. English. $10.00. Plutonium Press, PO Box 61564, Phoenix AZ 85082. **DD** 051. ***Continues*** *Scrap (Scottsdale, Ariz.), 1040-9955.*

US/0270-5524
SEA HERITAGE NEWS. ***Suspended.*** (19??)-. Periodical. English. qt. $12.00. Sea Heritage News, 254-26 75th Avenue, Glen Oaks NY 11004. **Tel** (718)343-9575. **ED** Bernie Klay. **Bk Rev. Ad Acc. Circ:** 50,000 (ctrl).
Desc: For sea buffs that are hungry for history, dotty on dorys, crazy for crafts, steamed up by steamboats and turned on by traditional lore.

US/0885-6435
SEACOAST LIFE. ***Ceased.*** **VFOAT** Seacoast Life Magazine. Vol. 1, No. 1 (1985)-(19??). Periodical. English. ir (5 times per year). American Marketing Systems, PO Box 594, North Hampton NH 03862. **Tel** (603)964-9898. **ED** Kathleen J Hargreaues, Eileen F Marshall, Brenda A Byrne. **DD** 051. **Ad Acc. Circ:** 20,000 (ctrl).
Desc: Regional publication covering such topics as: fashion, home decorating, gourmet and entertainment, people, art, medicine, fiction, commentary, investigative journalism and coming events.

●US
SEATTLE. Vol. 2, No. 2 (Apr. 1993)-. Periodical. English. bm (6 issues). $9.95. Adams Publishing, 68860 Perez Road, PO Box 2150, Cathedral City CA 92235. **Tel** (619)770-4370, (800)776-1036. **(Subscription address:** Adams Publishing, PO Box 2150, Cathedral City CA 92235.) **LC** F899.S4; G74. ***Continues*** *Greater Seattle.*

US/0037-0649
SECRETS (NEW YORK, N.Y.). ***Ceased.*** (SECRETS.). [Secrets]. (1936)-(Jan. 1990). Periodical. English. mo. MacFadden Women's Group, 233 Park Avenue South, New York NY 10003. **Tel** (212)979-4800, (800)666-8783. **(Subscription address:** CDS Agency Hard Copy, PO Box 4966, Des Moines IA 50340.) **LC** AP2; .S444. **DD** 051.

US/0890-4200
SENIOR TIMES (WELLESLEY, MASS.), THE. (THE SENIOR TIMES.). (1977)-. Periodical. English. mo. $9.95. Senior Times, 880 Worcester Street, Wellesley MA 02181.

US/0741-2894
SENIOR VOICE (ANCHORAGE, ALASKA). (SENIOR VOICE / OPAG.). **Added/Corp** Older Persons Action Group (U.S.). (19??)-. Periodical. English. mo. Senior Voice, 325 East 3rd Avenue, Anchorage AK 99501. **Tel** (907)276-1059. **ED** Dave Herndon. **Circ:** 7,000.

US/1059-3217
SEXY LAFFS. [Sexy laffs]. Series 9, Vol. 1 (1991)-. Periodical. English. bm. $24.00. Camille Publications, PO Box 30067, Arlington TX 76010. **DD** 051.

CN/1185-3158
SHAIR INTERNATIONAL FORUM. [SHAIR int. forum]. **Added/Corp** SHAIR International Resource Centre. **VFOAT** Society in the Hamilton Area for International Response-International Forum. (198?)-. Periodical. English. mo (11 issues per year - not published in August). $30.00 individuals; $40.00 institutions. SHAIR International Resource Centre, 255 West Avenue North, Hamilton, Ontario, L8L 5C8 Canada. **Tel** (416)528-9055. **ED** Mary Anne Peters. **DD** 327/.05. **Bk Rev**, (Qty: 5-6). **Ad Acc. Circ:** 300.
Desc: Contains articles on global and local issues and events of current interest.

US/0886-1501
SHARING IDEAS. [Shar. ideas]. **VFOAT** Speakers & Meeting Planners Sharing Ideas; Speakers and Meeting Planners Sharing Ideas. Periodical. English. bm. $35.00 US; $47.00 other. Sharing Ideas, PO Box 1120, Glendora CA 91740. **Tel** (818)335-8069, FAX (818)335-1137. **ED** Dorothy Walters. **DD** 001. **Bk Rev. Ad Acc. Circ:** 4,000 (ctrl).
Desc: Articles by top speakers, meeting planners and bureaus.

US/0192-687X
SHINING MOUNTAIN SENTINEL. (19??)-. Periodical. English. mo. Shining Mountain Sentinel, PO Box 15, Brady MT 59416.

US/0897-8875
SHOWPLACE (GRAND RAPIDS, MICH.). (SHOWPLACE.). **Added/Corp** WGVU/WGVK (Television Station : Grand Rapids, Mich.) West Michigan Public Broadcasting. Vol. 1, No. 1 (Mar. 1988)-. Periodical. English. mo. $35.00 (contributions). West Michigan Magazine, 7 Ionia Street SW, Grand Rapids MI 49503. ***Continues*** *West Michigan Magazine, 0890-4405.*

US/0746-1682
SIERRA NORTH STAR. ***Title Change.*** (SIERRA NORTH STAR / NORTH STAR SECTION, GREAT LAKES CHAPTER, SIERRA CLUB.). **Added/Corp** Sierra Club. North Star Chapter. Sierra Club. North Star Section. Sierra Club. North Star Group. Vol. 1, No. 1 (Dec. 1966)-(199?). Periodical. English. mo. Sierra North Star, 2929 4th Avenue South/Suite N, Minneapolis MN 55408. ***Continued by*** *North Star Journal, 1070-5279.*

CN/0707-1078
SIMERA (QUEBEC). (SIMERA.). **VFOAT** Aujourd'hui. V. 1- Oct. 1978-. Periodical. Greek, Modern. bw. $22.00. Simera, 2688 Des Oiseaux Blvd., St. Rose Laval Quebec, H7L 3W6. **DD** 051.

MX
SINTESIS CULTURAL (ILCE (INSTITUTE)). (SINTESIS CULTURAL / ILCE.). **Added/Corp** ILCE (Institute). (1980)-. Periodical. Spanish. bm. Juan Luis Vives 200-1, Mexico 10 DF.

US/1040-3620
SISKIYOU COUNTY (CA) SERIES. **VFOAT** Siskiyou County California Series. Vol. 1 (1986)-. Monographic series. English. ir. Price varies per volume. Abshire Abstracts, 19305 Southeast 243rd Place, Kent WA 98042. **Tel** (206)432-1659. **ED** Judy K Dye. **DD** 929. Index available. **Bk Rev.** ctrl circ.
Desc: Data regarding Siskiyou County, California (i.e. newspaper abstracts, census information, history, and more) in addition to queries.

●US/1059-1958
SITUATIONS DIGEST. (1992)-. Periodical. English. qt. $29.99. Publishing & Business Consultants, PO Box 75392, Los Angeles CA 90075. **Tel** (213)732-3477, FAX (213)732-9123. **ED** Andeson

Napoleon Atia. **Ad Acc.** Full Page (B&W) $5750.00. Half Page (B&W) $3575.00. Full Page (Color) $8750.00 (2 color). Half Page (Color) $5500.00 (2 color). **Circ:** 169,000 total.
Desc: Of interest to individuals eager to be informed of timely events occuring around them. Features articles on broad social issues, foreign affairs, finance and health.

CN/0318-3114
SIXTY CANADIAN MAGAZINES.
Added/Corp Canadian Periodical Publishers' Association. (Nov. 1974)-. English (summaries and/or abstracts in French and Eskimo). sa. Canadian Periodical Publishers' Association, 56 The Esplanade East/Suite 401, Toronto Ontario M5E 1A8 Canada. **DD** 016.051.

US/0884-4976
SMART LIVING. [Smart living]. (198?)-. Periodical. English. mo. $20.00. Smart Living Corporation, 22 East 29th Street, New York NY 10016. **DD** 051.

US/0899-2347
SMART (NEW YORK, N.Y.). ***Suspended.*** (SMART.). [Smart]. **VFOAT** Smart Magazine. (1988)-?. Periodical. English. qt. $9.95. Smart Magazine, 80 Fifth Avenue/Suite 501, New York NY 10011. **Tel** (212)687-0680. **ED** Terry McDonell. **LC** AP2; .S587. **DD** 051. **Ad Acc.**
Desc: Slick cultural magazine for upscale adults over 25. Articles on food, travel, art and architecture.

●US/1065-402X
SOAP OPERA BOOK, THE. (THE SOAP OPERA BOOK : WHO'S WHO IN DAYTIME DRAMA.). (1992)-. English. be. $19.95. The Soap Opera Book, 18 North Greenbush Road, West Nyack NY 10994.

US/0164-3584
SOAP OPERA DIGEST. [Soap opera dig.]. (Dec. 1975)-. Periodical. English. Twenty-six times a year. $50.00. K 3 Magazine Corporation, 200 Madison Avenue 8th Floor, New York NY 10016. **Tel** (212)447-4700, (212)447-4732. **(Subscription address:** Neodata / Colorado, PO Box 2606, Boulder Boulder CO 80322.**) DD** 791. available on microfilm and microfiche from University Microfilms International (UMI).

●US/1063-9055
SOAP OPERA ILLUSTRATED. (1992)-. Periodical. English. ir. Soap Opera Illustrated, 45 West 25th, New York NY 10010. **Tel** (212)645-2100.

US/0274-7383
SOAP OPERA MAGAZINE. **VFOAT** Soap Opera. Periodical. English. bm. Dynasty Media Publishing Corporation, PO Box 1629, Englewood Cliff NJ 07632. **Tel** (212)371-4932.

US/1057-9192
SOAP OPERA MAGAZINE (LANTANA, FLA.). (SOAP OPERA MAGAZINE.). [Soap opera mag.]. **VFOAT** Soap Opera. Vol. 1, No. 1 (Oct. 8, 1991)-. Periodical. English. wk. $35.88. Soap Opera Magazine, 600 South East Coast Avenue, Lantana FL 33462. **Tel** (800)441-5071, (800)441-5523. **DD** 791.

US/0883-6930
SOAP OPERA NOW. (1985)-. Periodical. English. wk. $110.00. Soap Opera Now, PO Box 234, White Plains NY 10605. **Tel** (718)275-2062, (800)762-7669. **LC** PN1992.8.S4; S62. **Circ:** 10,000 (ctrl).

US/1058-8647
SOAP OPERA PANORAMA. (1991)-. Periodical. English. mo. $15.00. TGF Soaps, PO Box 29, Denver PA 17517.

US/0889-6569
SOAP OPERA PHOTOROMANCE. **VFOAT** Photoromance. 1988-. Periodical. English. mo. $20.00. Serafini, 216 E 75 Street/1W, New York NY 10021.

US/0898-1485
SOAP OPERA UPDATE. [Soap opera update]. **VFOAT** Inside soaps. (1988)-. Periodical. English. Twenty-six times a year. $59.00. Heinrich Bauer North America, PO Box 1649, 270 Sylvan Avenue, Englewood NJ 07631. **Tel** (201)569-0006. **ED** Angela Shapiro (editor's phone: (201)569-6699). **DD** 791. **Ad Acc. Circ:** 350,000.

US/1047-7128
SOAP OPERA WEEKLY. [Soap opera wkly.]. Vol. 1, Issue 1 (Nov. 21, 1989)-. Periodical. English. wk. $56.00. Murdoch Magazines, 200 Madison Avenue, 8th Floor, New York NY 10016. **Tel** (212)447-4700, (212)447-4732. **(Subscription address:** Neodata / Colorado, PO Box 2606, Boulder Boulder CO 80322.**) DD** 791.

US/0746-9381
SOAP OPERA WORLD. Vol. 1, No. 1 (June 1983)-. Periodical. English. mo. Trahan Enterprises Ltd, 1 World Trade Center #7967, New York NY 10048.

US/0489-2593
SOCIAL DIRECTORY OF HOUSTON. (19??)-. Directory. English. an (third week in September). $32.50. The Social Directory of Houston, PO Box 22454, Houston TX 77227. **ED** Patrick J. Nicholson. **DD** 917.64. **Circ:** 1,200 (ctrl).
Desc: A long-established directory of some 2,800 leading families in Houston, with correct addresses, telephone numbers, summer addresses, university and club affiliations, maiden names (married-maiden section), data regarding married children if not listed separately, and names of juniors over 12 plus other children still resident with parents.

US/0896-5005
SOMA (SAN FRANCISCO, CALIF.). (SOMA.). [Soma]. **VFOAT** Soma Magazine. **VAT** South of Market. (198?)-. Periodical. English. bm (6 issues). $14.95 US; $18.95 Canada; $20.95 other. Soma Magazine, 285 Ninth Street, San Francisco CA 94103. **Tel** (415)558-8974. **ED** Cary Tennis (editor's telephone: (415)558-8080). **DD** 051. **Ad Acc, Adv Mgr Tel** same as publisher. **Circ:** 60,000.
Desc: Features news on the arts, entertainment, music and lifestyles of the West Coast.

MX
SONORENSE, EL. Periodical. Spanish. ir. El Nuevo Sonorense, Hermosillo, Sonora Mexico.

US/0192-5180
SOUND OF VIENNA, THE. (19??)-. Periodical. English. mo. $6.00. Sound Publications, 386 Maple Avenue East, Vienna VA 22180. **Tel** (703)281-0474, FAX (703)281-1099. **ED** Donald G Richards. **Bk Rev. Ad Acc, Adv Mgr Tel** (703)281-0474. **Circ:** 41,000 (ctrl).
Desc: Articles on fashion, points of local interest, restaurant reviews, theater reviews, coming events of a local nature, letters to the editor, real estate and financial advice.

●US/1061-4427
SOUTH DAKOTA HALL OF FAME. (SOUTH DAKOTA HALL OF FAME: [MAGAZINE].). [S. D. Hall Fame]. **Added/Corp** South Dakota Hall of Fame. **VFOAT** South Dakota Heritage; Dakota West. Vol. 18, No. 1 (Mar. 1992)-. Periodical. English. Four times a year (Feb., May, Aug., Nov.). $27.50. South Dakota Hall of Fame, PO Box 180, Chamberlin SD 57532. **Tel** (605)734-4216. **ED** Neoma E. Rossow (phone: (800)697-3130). **DD** 973. ***Continues*** *South Dakota Heritage, 0898-2074.*

US/0886-2680
SOUTH DAKOTA MAGAZINE (YANKTON, S.D.). (SOUTH DAKOTA MAGAZINE.). **VFOAT** South Dakota. Vol. 1, No. 1 (May 1985)-. Periodical. English. Six times a year. $14.00 (one year); $26.00 (two years). South Dakota Magazine, PO Box 175, Yankton SD 57078. **Tel** (605)665-6655. **ED** Bernie Hunhoff. **Bk Rev. Ad Acc. Circ:** 25,000 (ctrl). available on audiocassette.

US/0895-5352
SOUTH FLORIDA. [South Fla.]. Vol. 39, No. 11 (Sept. 1987)-. Periodical. English. mo. $14.95 (1 year), $28.00 (2 year), $39.00 (3 year). Florida Media Affiliates Inc, PO Box 019068, Miami FL 33101. **Tel** (305)445-4500, FAX (305)445-4600. **ED** Glenn Albin. **LC** F319.M6; M636. **DD** 975.3/005. **Ad Acc, Adv Mgr:** Muriel Sommers. **Circ:** 40,000. ***Continues*** *Miami South Florida Magazine, 0737-1403.*
Desc: A unique blend of good writing, good art and indispensable information about South Florida from Boca to Key West.
Ind/Abst Access (1975-).

US/0038-352X
SOUTH SHORE RECORD. (1953)-. Newspaper. English. wk. $20.00 New York; $40.00 other. South Shore Record, 990 Railroad Avenue, Woodmere NY 11598. **Tel** (516)374-9200. **ED** Florence B. Schwartzberg. **Bk Rev. Ad Acc. Circ:** 18,801.
Desc: local news, human interest, sports, etc. Also includes reviews on travel, restaurants, and theatre.

US/0038-4305
SOUTHERN LIVING. [South. living]. Vol. 1, (Feb. 1966)-. Periodical. English. mo. $24.95 US; $32.00 other. Southern Progress Corporation, PO Box 1748, Birmingham AL 35201. **Tel** (205)877-6000. **(Subscription address:** Southern Living, Box C 119, Birmingham AL 35283.**) ED** Gary McCalla. **LC** F206; .S855. **Bk Rev. Ad Acc. Circ:** 2,250,000. available on microfilm and microfiche from University Microfilms International (UMI). Documents available from UMI Article Clearinghouse.
Desc: Reflects and influences the lifestyle of families throughout the changing South, providing information and ideas on travel and recreation, homes and gardens, food and entertaining, and interesting personalities.
Ind/Abst Acad. Abstr. Full Text Elite (Jan. 1984-); Acad. Abstr. (Jan. 1984-); Book Rev. Index; Foods Adlibra; Garden Lit. (1992-); Gen. Period. Index (1985-); Mag. Artic. Summar. Elite (Jan. 1984-); Mag. Artic. Summar. Select (Jan. 1984-); Mag. Artic. Summar. CD-ROM (Jan. 1984-); Mag. Index Plus (1989-); Mag. Index. Sel. (1986-); Mag. Search; Newsp. Period. Abstr. (1988-); Read. Guide Abstr. Select Ed.; Read. Guide Period. Lit.; Mag. Index (1978-); Vocat. Search (Jan. 1984-).

US/0892-8789
SOUTHERN VERMONT. ***Ceased.*** [South. Vt.]. Vol. 1, No. 2 Spring (1986)-?. Periodical. English. bm. Southern Vermont Magazine, PO Box 678, Brattleboro VT 05301. ***Continues*** *Southern Vermont Magazine.*

CN/0701-1423
SOUTHSIDE MIRROR, THE. V. 3, No. 5- May 1, 1976-. Periodical. English. bw. Southside Mirror, Suite 1, 8431 Granville Street, Vancouver BC V6P 4Z9 Canada. **DD** 071/.11/33. ***Continues*** *Magpie.*

US
SOUTHWEST NEWSWEEK, THE. Vol. 36, No. 21 (June 2, 1992)-. Periodical. English. wk. ***Continues*** *Newsweek (Shively, Ky.).*

US/0895-6049
SOUTHWEST PROFILE. ***Suspended.*** [Southwest profile]. (197?)-(Aug. 1993). Periodical. English. Ten times a year. $25.00. Whitney Publishing Company Inc, PO Box 1380, Taos NM 87571. **Tel** (505)984-1773. **(Subscription address:** PO Box 8504, Santa Fe NM 87504**) ED** Stephen M Parks. **LC** NX508.6; .S68. **DD** 700/.978. **Bk Rev. Ad Acc. Circ:** 20,000. ***Continues*** *Santa Fe Profile.*
Desc: Views the arts in New Mexico and Arizona, and modern art that transcends the region.

US/0038-4984
SOU'WESTER (RAYMOND, WASH.), THE. (THE SOU'WESTER.). [Sou'wester]. **Added/Corp** Pacific County Historical Society (Washington). Vol. 1 (1966)-. Periodical. English. qt. $8.00. Pacific County Historical Society, PO Box P, South Bend WA 98586. **Tel** (206)875-5224. **ED** Larry J Weathers. **Circ:** 525 (ctrl).
Desc: Prints southwest Washington state history, folklore, biography, photography, genealogy, literature and related materials. Pacific county history is the focus.
Ind/Abst Am. Hist. Life.

●US/1059-5201
SPECIAL REPORT - WHITTLE COMMUNICATIONS. (SPECIAL REPORT.). [Spec. rep. - Whittle Commun.]. Vol. 4, No. 1 (Mar./Apr. 1992)-. Periodical. English. bm. $15.00 (one year). Whittle Communications, 333 Main Avenue, Knoxville TN 37902. **Tel** (615)595-5000, FAX (615)595-5877. **ED** Keith Bellows (615-595-5830), Jim Sexton (615-595-5223), Brooks Clark (615-595-5841). **DD** 051. **Ad Acc, Adv Mgr:** Mike Huddleston, **Tel** (615) 595-5304. **Circ:** 320,000. ***Formed by the union of*** *Special Report, Fiction, 1047-2886; Special Report on Family, 1047-2878; Special Report on Health, 1047-272X; Special Report on Living, 1047-0123; Special Report on Personalities, 1047-286X* ***and*** *Special report on Sports, 1047-2851.*

US/0164-6745
SPRINGFIELD MAGAZINE. **VFOAT** Springfield. (19??)-. Periodical. English. mo. $16.99 (one year), $29.99 (two year), $39.97 (three year). Springfield Magazine, 175 Maple Street, Springfield MA 01105. **ED** HH Glazier. **Bk Rev. Ad Acc.** ctrl circ.
Ind/Abst Ozark Period. Index.

US/0195-0894
SPRINGFIELD MAGAZINE (SPRINGFIELD, MO.). (SPRINGFIELD MAGAZINE.). **VFOAT** Springfield. (197?)-. Periodical. English. Twelve times a year. $16.99 (one year); $29.99 (two years); $39.97 (three years). Springfield Magazine, PO Box 4749, Springfield MO 65808. **Tel** (417)882-3966. Index available. cum. index. **Bk Rev,** (Qty: 12). **Ad Acc, Adv Mgr:** R. C. Glazier, **Tel** (417)831-1640.

US/0748-6405
SPRINGS MAGAZINE (COLORADO SPRINGS, COLO.). (SPRINGS MAGAZINE.). (198?)-. Periodical. English. mo. $8.95. Springs Magazine, PO Box 9166, Colorado Springs CO 80932. **Tel** (719)636-2001, FAX (719)636-1184. **ED** Michael Gardner. Index available. **Bk Rev,** (Qty: 6-8 per year). **Ad Acc. Circ:** 18,000 (ctrl).
Desc: Focused on the region's quality of life, and informs its readers of significant people, places and events that make the Pikes Peak region so special.

US/0890-1759
SPY (NEW YORK, N.Y.). (SPY.). [Spy]. (Oct. 1986)-. Periodical. English. bm (6 issues). $18.00. Sussex Publishers Inc., 49 East 21st Street, 11th Floor, New York NY 10010. **Tel** (212) 260-7210. **(Subscription address:** Neodata / Colorado, PO Box 2606, Boulder Boulder CO 80322.**) ED** George Kalogerakis. **LC** PN4880; .S69. **DD** 817.008/005.
Desc: Every issue has writing, enterprising reporting and sophisticated fun.
Ind/Abst Access (1992-).

US/0272-1279
ST. LOUIS. ***Ceased.*** **VAT** Saint Louis. Vol. 10, (Jan. 1978)-(June 1993). Periodical. English. Twelve times a year. St. Louis Magazine, One Metropolitan Square, Suite 2120, St Louis MO 63102. **Tel** (314)231-7200, FAX

(314)231-6902. **ED** Tom Rami. **LC** F474.S257; S24. **DD** 977.8/66/005. **Ad Acc.** ***Continues*** *St. Louis Magazine.* **Ind/Abst** Access (1975-).

US/0097-725X
STANDARD MAGAZINE. Vol. 1 (Jan. 1975)-. Periodical. English. mo. $12.00. News Log International, 419 South Arch Street, Janesville WI 53545. **LC** AP2; .S88583. **DD** 051.

US
STAR (LOS ANGELES, CALIF.). (THE STAR.). Vol. 1, No. 1 (Jan. 1928)-. Periodical. English. bw. Los Angeles Star, 8444 Wilshire Boulevard, Beverly Hills CA 90211. **Tel** (310)653-6622.

US/0279-9766
STATEN ISLAND MAGAZINE. Vol. 1, No. 1 (Spring 1981)-. Periodical. English. qt. Staten Island Magazine, 207 West 21st Street, New York NY 10011.

US/0190-1737
STREET MAGAZINE. ***Ceased.*** **VFOAT** Street. -Ceased Vol. 4, No. 4. Periodical. English. an. Street Magazine, PO Box 555, Port Jefferson NY 11777. **Tel** (516)928-4958. **Bk Rev.**

US
STREET NEWS. English. sm. $18.00. Street Aid, 1457 Broadway, Suite 305, New York NY 10036. **Tel** (212)768-7290, FAX (212)768-7297. **ED** Rizza Olegario. **Bk Rev. Ad Acc. Circ:** 62,750.
Desc: Articles of general interest to urban readers.

CN/0229-3048
SUBURBAN (LAVAL EDITION). (THE SUBURBAN.). [Suburban, Laval ed.]. (197?)-. Periodical. English (French; summaries and/or abstracts in French). wk. 105.00Can$ (add 7% tax). Michael Publishers, 8170 Walnell Road, Cote-Saint-Luc Quebec H4W 1M3 Canada. **Tel** (514)484-1107, FAX (514)484-7284. **ED** Christy McCormick. **DD** 071/.14271. **Bk Rev. Ad Acc. Circ:** 101,000 (ctrl).

US/8750-7307
SUFFOLK COUNTY LIFE. **See** Newspapers.

US/0049-2507
SUNDANCE. Periodical. English. mo. $8.00. Running Dog Inc, 1913 Fillmore Street, San Francisco CA 94115. **LC** AP2; .S953. **DD** 051.

US/0039-5404
SUNSET (MENLO PARK, CALIF.). (SUNSET.). [Sunset]. **Added/Corp** Southern Pacific Company. Passenger Dept. **VFOAT** Sunset Magazine. Vol. 1, No. 1 (May 1898)-. Periodical. English. mo. $21.00 (one year), $36.00 (two year), $48.00 (three year). Sunset Publishing Corporation, 80 Willow Road, Menlo Park CA 94025. **Tel** (415)321-3600, (800)777-0117. **(Subscription address:** Neodata / Colorado, PO Box 2606, Boulder Boulder CO 80322.**) ED** William Marken. **LC** F851; .S95. **DD** 979.405. Index available. **Bk Rev. Ad Acc. Circ:** 1,442,478. available on an online database from DIALOG; available on microfilm and microfiche from University Microfilms International (UMI). Documents available from UMI Article Clearinghouse. ***Absorbed*** *Pacific Monthly.*
Desc: Edited for the 13 western states. Entirely staff written to provide timely and practical articles on gardening and landscaping, food and entertainment, travel, building and remodeling, and workshop and craft ideas.
Ind/Abst Acad. Abstr. Full Text Elite (Jan. 1984-); Acad. Abstr. (Jan. 1984-); Consum. Index Prod. Eval. Inf. Source; Foods Adlibra; Garden Lit. (1992-); Gen. Period. Index (1985-); Index Inf. (1977-); Mag. Artic. Summar. Elite (Jan. 1984-); Mag. Artic. Summar. Select (Jan. 1984-); Mag. Artic. Summar. CD-ROM (Jan. 1984-); Mag. ASAP Plus [Full Txt.]; Mag. ASAP Sel. [Full Txt.]; Mag. Index Plus (1989-); Mag. Index. Sel. (1986-); Mag. Search; Newsp. Period. Abstr. (1988-); Read. Guide Abstr. Select Ed.; Read. Guide Period. Lit.; Mag. Index (1977-); TOM Gen. Index (1992-) [Full Txt.]; Vocat. Search (Jan. 1984-).

CN/0708-1561
SUPER MAGAZINE. **VFOAT** Supermagazine. **VAT** Collection Supermagazine. No 1- Oct. 1978-. Periodical. French. qt. $1.50 each number. Distributions Eclair, 8320 Place de Lorraine, Anjou Quebec H1J 1E6 Canada. **DD** 054/.1.

CN/1184-0269
SURREY-DELTA MAGAZINE (JUNE 1990). (SURREY DELTA MAGAZINE.). [Surrey-Delta mag.]. **VFOAT** SurreyDelta Magazine; Surrey Magazine. Vol. 12, Issue 5 (June 1990)-. Periodical. English. mo. Surrey Delta Magazine, 214 6th Street, New Westminster, British Columbia V3L 3A2 Canada. **DD** 051. ***Continues*** *Easy Living's Surrey Delta Magazine., 1181-7267.*

US
TAE NYUYOK CHIGU HANILLOK. **Added/Corp** Tonga Ilbosa. Nyuyok Chisa. **VFOAT** The Korean Directory of Greater New York. (1981)-. English (Korean). an. **LC** F128.9.K6; T83.

CN/0821-0160
TAKE FIVE (SASKATOON, SASK.). ***Ceased.*** (TAKE FIVE.). [Take five]. Vol. 1, No. 1 (Jan. 1983)-?. Periodical. English. mo. Turner Warwick Publications Inc, PO Box 1029, North Battleford Saskatchewan S9A 3E6 Canada. **Tel** (306)445-7261. **ED** Jayne Heese. **DD** 790/.097124. **Bk Rev. Ad Acc. Circ:** 3,500. ***Continues*** *Recreation Saskatchewan, 0708-0743.*
Desc: Of general interest to people who live, work and play in rural and urban Saskatchewan. Business features.

US/0049-2914
TALLOW LIGHT, THE. V. 1- Nov. 1966-. Periodical. English. qt. $5.00. 401 Aurora Street, Marietta OH 45750. **LC** F497.W3; T34. **DD** 917.71/98/034.

US/1048-0056
TAMPA BAY LIFE (TAMPA, FLA.). ***Ceased.*** (TAMPA BAY LIFE.). **VFOAT** Tampa Bay Life, The Magazine. Vol. 1, No. 1 (Sept. 1988)-(July 1992). Periodical. English. Twelve times a year. Tampa Bay Media Affiliates, Bayport Plaza/Suite 990, 6200 Courtney Campbell Causeway, Tampa FL 33607. **Tel** (813)281-8855, FAX (813)281-1920. **ED** Larry Marscheck. Index available. **Bk Rev. Ad Acc. Circ:** 25,000. available on microfilm.
Desc: The premier city/regional lifestyle magazine of the Tampa Bay, Clearwater, St. Petersbury region. Covers people, art, sports, health, home and garden, dining out, food, communities and travel.

US/0896-064X
TAMPA REVIEW. [Tampa rev.]. Periodical. English. sa. $7.50 US; (add $2.00 postage) other. Tampa Review, c/o Richard Mathews, University of Tampa, PO Box 19F, Tampa FL 33606-1490. **Tel** (813)253-3333. **(Subscription address:** Box 19F, The University of Tampa, Tampa, FL 33606-1490**) ED** Richard Mathews. **LC** PS501; .T35. **DD** 810 .8/0005. **Circ:** 500. ***Continues*** *Abatis, 0882-9586.*
Desc: A faculty edited literary journal with an international flavor, featuring poetry, fiction, art, interviews and articles.
Ind/Abst Index Am. Period. Verse (1988-).

US/0895-6065
TAOS MAGAZINE. [Taos mag.]. (198?)-. Periodical. English. Eight times a year. $16.00 US; $25.00 other. Whitney Publishing Company Inc, PO Box 1380, Taos NM 87571. **Tel** (505)984-1773. **DD** 977. ***Continues*** *Mystique (Taos, N.M.).*

●US/1071-5878
TASTE OF HOME. [Taste home]. Vol. 1, No. 1 (Feb.-Mar. 1993)-. Periodical. English. Six times a year. $16.98 US; $25.98 other. Reiman Publications, 5400 South 60th Street, Greendale WI 53129. **Tel** (414)423-0100 Ext. 421, FAX (414)423-1143. **LC** WMLC 93/142. **DD** 641.

US/0274-5151
TC. TWIN CITIES. V. 3, No. 5- May 1980-. Periodical. English. mo. $24.00. Dorn Communications, 15 5th Street/Suite 900, Minneapolis MN 55402. **Tel** (612)835-6855. **ED** Marcia Appel. **Bk Rev. Ad Acc. Circ:** 44,000 (ctrl). ***Continues*** *Twin Cities, 0164-6532.*
Desc: We publish articles about life in the twin cities, profiles the arts, issues home style fashion, high-end products, essays, history and fiction.

CN/0300-3159
TEKAWENNAKE. **Added/Corp** Six Nations Reserve, Ont. New Credit Reserve, Ont. Woodland Indian Cultural Educational Centre. **VFOAT** Six Nations-New Credit Reporter. 13th Issue, (Feb. 24/March 1, 1968)-. Periodical. English. Fifty-two times a year. 45.00Can$ Canada; 55.00Can$. Tekawennake Publications, PO Box 130, Ohsweken Ontario N0A 1M0 Canada. **Tel** (519)445-2238, FAX (519)445-2434. **ED** G. Scott Smith. **Bk Rev. Ad Acc. Circ:** 2,500. available on microfiche. ***Continues*** *New Credit-Six Nations Reporter, 0315-5129.*

CN/0705-694X
TEMPS FOU, LE. [Temps fou]. V. 1- Mar./April 1978-. Periodical. French. qt. Temps Fou, CP 306 Succursale de Lorimier, Montreal Quebec H2H 2N7 Canada. **DD** 054/.1.
Ind/Abst Point Repere (1983-).

US/0492-746X
TENNESSEE MAGAZINE. [Tenn. mag.]. (19??)-. Periodical. English. mo. $8.00 (one year), $21.00 (three year). Tennessee Electric Cooperative Assn, PO Box 100912, Nashville TN 37224. **Tel** (615)367-9284, FAX (615)367-2495.
Ind/Abst Energy Res. Abstr. (April 1978-).

US/0890-4235
TERRITORIAL, THE. Vol. 6, No. 1 (Jan.-Feb. 1986)-. Periodical. English. bm. $16.00 (one year), $28.00 (two year), $42.00 (three year). Territorial, PO Box E, Garden City KS 67846. **Tel** (316)276-8793. **ED** Barbara Oringderff. **Bk Rev**, (Qty: 3-4). **Ad Acc. Pr Rev.** ***Continues*** *Kansas Territorial.*
Desc: Features articles pertaining to the cattle feeding, oil trucking, automobile and farm equipment industries plus history, agriculture, business, entertainment, and recreational facilities of this region. Regularly featuring contemporary commentary, book reviews and treasure hunting.

US/0363-4248
TEXAS ALMANAC AND STATE INDUSTRIAL GUIDE (1967). (TEXAS ALMANAC AND STATE INDUSTRIAL GUIDE.). **VFOAT** Texas Almanac. (1967)-. English. an (Oct. in odd number years). Dallas Morning News, PO Box 655237, Dallas TX 75265. **Tel** (214)977-8262, (800)826-4216. **ED** Mike Kingston. **LC** AY311.D3; T5. **DD** 051. Each issue contains an index to its own contents (no volume index)--loose. **Ad Acc. Circ:** 100,000. ***Continues*** *Texas Almanac, 0363-423X.*
Desc: The almanac strives to present an accurate statistical picture of Texas.

US/0148-7736
TEXAS MONTHLY (AUSTIN). (TEXAS MONTHLY.). [Tex. mon.]. Vol. 1, (Feb. 1973)-. Periodical. English. mo. $18.00 Texas; $21.00 US; $40.00 other. Texas Monthly, PO Box 1569, Austin TX 78767. **Tel** (512)320-6900. **(Subscription address:** CDS Agency Hard Copy, PO Box 4966, Des Moines IA 50340.**) ED** Gregory Curtis. **LC** F381; .T363. **DD** 976.4/005. **Ad Acc. Circ:** 280,000. available on microfilm and microfiche from University Microfilms International (UMI). Documents available from UMI Article Clearinghouse.
Desc: The magazine as big as Texas.
Ind/Abst Acad. Abstr. Full Text Elite (July 1984-); Acad. Abstr. (July 1984-); Acad. Search (July 1984-); Access (1975-?); Bus. Dateline (March 1992-) [Full Txt.]; Chicano Index; Gen. Period. Index (1985-); Index Period. Artic. Relat. Law; INFO-SOUTH Abstr.; Mag. Artic. Summar. Elite (July 1984-); Mag. Artic. Summar. Select (July 1984-); Mag. Artic. Summar. CD-ROM (July 1984-); Mag. Index Plus (1989-); Mag. Search; Newsp. Period. Abstr. (1988-); Pop. Period. Index; Read. Guide Period. Lit.; Mag. Index (1983-).

US/0744-9372
THIRD COAST. ***Ceased.*** (THIRD COAST : THE MAGAZINE OF CONTEMPORARY AUSTIN.). Began in 1981-Ceased July (1987). Periodical. English. mo. Third Coast Magazine, 1609 The High Road/#B, Austin TX 78746. **Tel** (512)472-2016.
Ind/Abst Index Period. Artic. Relat. Law.

US/0040-6201
THIS IS WEST TEXAS. ***Ceased.*** **VFOAT** West Texas. V. 1, (1967)-Ceased with Dec./Jan. Iss. (1988). Periodical. English. bm. West Texas Chamber of Commerce, 300 West 15th Street, Suite 875, Austin TX 78701-1649. **Tel** (915)677-4325. **Ad Acc.** ctrl circ. ***Supersedes*** *West Texas Today.*
Desc: Promotion of West Texas area.

US/0193-7510
THIS WEEK IN THE VALLEY OF THE SUN. KEY. **VFOAT** Key. Periodical. English. wk. This Week in the Valley of the Sun, 2500 East Thomas Road, Suite B-7, Phoenix AZ 85016.

CN/0229-7248
THORNHILL MONTH. [Thornhill mon.]. (1979)-. Periodical. English. mo. 20.00Can$. Thornhill Publications Ltd., 3335 14th Avenue, Unionville L3R 2L6 Canada. **Tel** (905)475-1743. **DD** 071/.13547.

US
THREE SISTERS. Vol. 1 (Fall 1971)-. Periodical. English. qt. Georgetown University Intercultural Center, Box 648, East Campus, Washington DC 20057. **LC** AP2; .T334. **DD** 051.

CN/0823-6542
THUNDER BAY MAGAZINE. [Thunder Bay mag.]. Vol. 1, No. 1 (Spring 1983)-. Periodical. English. bm. $16.95. Thunder Bay Magazine, 1184 Roland Street, Thunder Bay Ontario P7B 5M4 Canada. **Tel** (807)623-8545, FAX (807)623-7110. **ED** Michael Thompson. **DD** 971.3/12. Index available. cum. index. **Bk Rev. Ad Acc. Circ:** 40,000 (ctrl).
Desc: City magazine focusing on life and living in Northwestern Ontario. Subjects range from business to art, sports, leisure, entertainment, travel, history, people and much more.

US/0274-6859
TIJUANA MAGAZINE. **VFOAT** Tijuana. (19??)-. Periodical. English. mo. $10.00. Tijuana, 303 3rd Street/Suite B, PO Box 3101, Chula Vista CA 92001. **Tel** (714)422-7763.

US/0097-8833
TIMES MAGAZINE (WASHINGTON), THE. (THE TIMES MAGAZINE.). (Oct. 9 1974)-. Periodical. English. mo. **LC** AP2; .T49. **DD** 051. ***Supersedes*** *Family Magazine, 0427-9662.*

CN/0715-450X
TIMES OF DOWNTOWN LONDON, THE. [Times downtown Lond.]. **VAT** Times (London, Ont.). Vol. 1, No. 1 (Aug. 1981)-. Periodical. English. mo. Free. Times of Downtown London, 110 Dundas Street/Suite 1, London Ontario N6A 1G1 Canada. **DD** 071/.1326.

CN/0823-9452
TO (TORONTO, ONT.). ***Ceased.*** (TO : THE MAGAZINE OF TORONTO.). V. 1, No. 1, Nov./Dec. (1984)-Ceased with Jan./Feb. (1989). Periodical. English. mo (ten issues per year). TO Magazine, 26 Soho Street/Suite 340, Toronto Ontario M5T 1Z7 Canada. **DD** 971.3/541/005.
Desc: Young city magazine of Toronto; each issue focuses on the new people, ideas and trends changing the shape of Toronto. Turns Toronto inside out to find the best and the newest in entertainment, fashion, services and consumer goods.

US/0192-3080
TOPEKA MAGAZINE. Periodical. English. PMFH Inc, 406 West 7th, Topeka KS 66603. **Tel** (913)295-3013.

US/1060-3018
TOPEKA METRO NEWS, THE. (1991)-. Periodical. English. sw. Hall Publications, 630 South Kansas Avenue, Topeka KS 66603. ***Continues*** *Topeka Legal News, 0889-5295.*

US/1051-371X
TOPICS ON THE CULTURE OF THE AMERICAN SOUTH. (CULTURAL PERSPECTIVES ON THE AMERICAN SOUTH.). Periodical. English. Gordon & Breach Science Publishers, Inc., PO Box 786, Cooper Station, New York NY 10276. **Tel** (212)206-8900, FAX (212)645-2459. **(Subscription address:** International Publishers Distributor at one of the following addresses: 820 Town Center Drive, Langhorne, PA 19047; or PO Box 90, Reading Berkshire RG1 8JL UK; or Kent Ridge PO Box 1180, Singapore 9111, Republic of Singapore**)** ***Continues*** *Perspectives on the American South, 0275-584X.*

US/0730-2231
TORCH (WASHINGTON, D.C. : 1980), THE. (THE TORCH.). [Torch]. No. 80-7 (July 1980)-. Periodical. English. mo. Free. Office of Public Affairs, Arts and Industries Building/Room 2410, Washington DC 20560. **Tel** (202)357-2627. **ED** Mary Combs. **LC** Q11.S8; S88. **DD** 069/.09753. **Circ:** 9,100 (ctrl). ***Continues*** *Smithsonian Torch, 0037-7341.*
Desc: Smithsonian-related articles and columns of interest to SI employees.

CN/0821-6312
TORONTO CHRONICLE, THE. [Tor. chron.]. **VFOAT** Chronicle. **VAT** Chronicle (Toronto). Vol. 1, No. 1 (Apr. 1983)-. Periodical. English. mo. $7.74. Toronto Chronicle, 367 Clinton Street, Toronto Ontario M6G 2Z1 Canada. **Tel** (416)534-9069. **DD** 051.

CN/0049-4194
TORONTO LIFE. [Tor. life]. Vol. 1 (Nov. 1966)-. Periodical. English. mo. 24.00Can$ Canada; 44.00Can$ other. Toronto Life, 59 Front Street East, Toronto Ontario M5E 1B3 Canada. **Tel** (416)364-3333. **ED** Marq de Villiers. **DD** 971.3'541'005. **Bk Rev**. **Ad Acc**. **Circ:** 99,000. available on microfiche from University Microfilms International (UMI). ***Absorbed*** *Ontario Homes and Living, 0474-2044.*
Desc: Serves as a guide book on how the city of Toronto works. Examines city politics, the power elite, society, business, commerce, sports and shopping.
Ind/Abst Access (1992-); Can. Index; Can. Period. Index.

US
TORRINGTON VOICE, THE. (1992)-. Periodical. English. sm (24 issues). Free on request. Voice News Inc., PO Box 149, Winsted CT 06098. **Tel** (203)738-4026.

CN/1180-0313
TOURIST GUIDE, LANAUDIERE. **See** Travel and Tourism.

US/0040-9952
TOWN & COUNTRY (NEW YORK, N.Y.). (TOWN & COUNTRY.). [Town ctry.]. **VFOAT** Town and Country. (1901)-. Periodical. English. mo. $24.00. The Hearst Corporation, 250 West 55th Street, New York NY 10019. **Tel** (212)649-4014. **(Subscription address:** CDS Agency Hard Copy, PO Box 4966, Des Moines IA 50340.**)** **LC** AP2; .T6. **DD** 051. **Circ:** 413,000. available on microfilm and microfiche from University Microfilms International (UMI). Documents available from UMI Article Clearinghouse. ***Continues*** *Home Journal (New York, N.Y.).*
Ind/Abst Access (1975-); Gen. Period. Index (1985-); Mag. Artic. Summar. Elite (Jan. 1984-); Mag. Artic. Summar. Select (Jan. 1984-); Mag. Artic. Summar. CD-ROM (Jan. 1984-); Mag. Index Plus (1989-); Mag. Index. Sel. (1986-); Mag. Search; Newsp. Period. Abstr. (1989-); Mag. Index (1977-).

CN/0701-0869
TOWN OF VAUGHAN VANGUARD, THE. **VFOAT** Vaughan Vanguard. Began with Aug. 26, 1976 issue. Periodical. English. wk. 0.10Can$ each number. Vaughan Vanguard Publishing Company, Suite 4, 7784 Martin Grove Road, Woodbridge Ontario L4L 1B1 Canada. **DD** 071/.13/54.

US/1054-7452
TRADE. [Trade]. **VFOAT** Trade Magazine. Vol. 1, Issue 1 (May 1991)-. Periodical. English. ir. $48.00 US; $69.00 Canada. Flynt Distributing Company, 9171 Wilshire Boulevard, Suite 300, Beverly Hills CA 90210. **DD** 051.

US/0749-1352
TRAIL WALKER. (TRAIL WALKER / NJ/NY TRAIL CONFERENCE.). **Added/Corp** New York-New Jersey Trail Conference. (19??)-. Periodical. English. bm. $12.50. NY-NJ Trail Conference Inc, 232 Madison Avenue #908, New York NY 10016. **Tel** (212) 685-9699.

US/1041-3642
TRAVEL SOUTH (1989). ***Title Change.*** (TRAVEL SOUTH.). [Travel South]. Vol. 3 No. 1 (Winter/Spring 1989)-(1992). Periodical. English. qt. Southern Living Inc, 820 Shades Creek Parkway, Birmingham AL 35209. **Tel** (800)633-8628. **ED** Karen Lingo. **DD** 917. available on microfilm and microfiche from University Microfilms International (UMI). ***Continues*** *Southern Travel, 0891-8023.* ***Continued by*** *Southern Living Travel Guide, 1068-056X.*
Desc: Offers a bounty of history, spectacle and fun for Southern travelers. Articles range from the sand and surf of Southern beaches, rustic resorts, grand hotels and intimate restaurants. Our complete magazine for travelling the South.

CN/0380-0954
TRIP (MONTREAL). (TRIP.). Vol. 1 (Nov. 1974)-. Periodical. French. mo. $1.25 each number. Les Editions Beljo, 2135 Est rue Ste-Catherine, Montreal Quebec Canada. **DD** 054/.1.

CN/0383-1086
TROTTEUR DU MAQUIGNON. (LE TROTTEUR DU MAQUIGNON.). **Added/Corp** Association Cooperative Immobiliere d'Abitibi-Temiscamingue. No. 1 (June 20, 1973)-. Periodical. French. 0.50Can$ per no. Association Cooperative Immobiliere d'Aritibi-Temiscaminque, CP 401, Rouyn Quebec J9X 5A9 Canada. **DD** 054/.1.

US/1064-8232
TRUE NEWS (NEW YORK, N.Y.). ***Ceased.*** (TRUE NEWS.). [True news]. Vol. 1, No. 1 (Nov. 1992)-No. 2 (1993). Periodical. English. bw. K III Press Inc., 424 West 33rd Street, New York NY 10001. **Tel** (212)714-3100, (800)221-5488. **DD** 051.

US
TUCSON GUIDE QUARTERLY. English. qt. $12.95 (1 year), $25.00 (2 year) US; $16.95 (1 year), $29.00 (2 year) other. Madden Publishing Incorporated, PO Box 42915, Tucson AZ 85733. **Tel** (602)624-1135. **ED** John Hudak and Lisa Cooper. **Bk Rev**, (Qty: 3). **Ad Acc**, **Adv Mgr:** Mike Levy. **Circ:** 34,000 (ctrl). ***Continues*** *Tucson Guide.*

US/0198-7895
TWIN CITIES EPICURE. Periodical. English. sa. $2.95 each issue. Twin Cities Epicure, 3941 20th Avenue South, Minneapolis MN 55407.

US/0193-2802
TWIN CITIES READER. Vol. 2, Issue 2 (Jan. 14, 1977)-. Newspaper. English. Fifty-two times a year. $20.00. MPC Inc., 5500 Wayzata Boulevard/Suite 800, Minneapolis MN 55416. **Tel** (612)591-2700, FAX (612)591-2639. **ED** D.J. Tice. **Bk Rev**. **Ad Acc**. **Circ:** 115,000. available on microfilm. ***Continues*** *Entertainer (Minneapolis, Minn.).*

US
TYLER TODAY. English. qt. $6.50. Tyler Today, PO Box 208, Tyler TX 75710-0208. **Tel** (903)533-9191, FAX (903)533-8989. **ED** Janet Drake. **Ad Acc**, **Adv Mgr:** Pene Bridges. **Circ:** 66,000.
Desc: Covers topics of local interest in Tyler, Texas.

US/0279-4322
ULTRA (HOUSTON, TEX.). ***Suspended.*** (ULTRA.). [Ultra]. **VFOAT** Ultra Magazine. Vol. 1, No. 1 (Sept. 1981)-Suspended (Feb. 1991). Periodical. English. mo. $15.00. Ultra Magazine Inc, 1400 Post Oak Boulevard, Houston TX 77056. **Tel** (713)622-1967. **ED** Kathryn Casey. **LC** F381; .U47. **DD** 976.4/005. **UDC** 976.4. **Ad Acc**. **Circ:** 95,000.
Desc: The lifestyle magazine for rich and famous Texans.

US/0361-5731
UNCOVER D.C. **Added/Corp** Friends of the Washington Review of the Arts. **VAT** Uncover District of Columbia. (19??)-. English. ir. $2.50. Friends of the Washington Review of the Arts, 404 10th Street, Washington DC 20003. **LC** F192.3; .U52. **DD** 917.53/04/4.

US/0192-0375
UNICORN TIMES. Periodical. English. mo. $8.00. Unicorn Times, 930 F Street/Suite 511 NW, Washington DC 20004. **Tel** (202)783-6363.

US/0098-9525
UNION (CRANFORD). (UNION.). V. 1- Spring 1975-. English. Union College, 1033 Springfield Avenue, Cranford NJ 07016. **LC** AP2; .U48. **DD** 081.

US/0161-9292
UNION LEADER. **Added/Corp** Retail Store Employees Union. Local 400. (19??)-. Periodical. English. Fifty-two times a year (Thurs.). $28.00 Union County; $32.50 others in New Jersey; $36.50 others. Worral Community Newspapers, 1291 Stuyvesant Avenue, Union NJ 07083. **Tel** (201)686-7700, FAX (201)686-4169. **ED** Rae Hutton. **Bk Rev**. **Ad Acc**. **Circ:** 8,500.
Desc: Local news coverage.

US/0197-1212
UNIVERSITAS (ALBANY). (UNIVERSITAS.). **Added/Corp** United University Professions (Association : U.S.). Vol. 1 (Sept. 1978)-. Periodical. English (English). qt. $7.50. United University Proffessions, 1 Park Place, Albany NY 12205. **LC** AP2; .U724. **DD** 051.

US/0041-9923
UNIVERSITY OF PORTLAND REVIEW. [Univ. Portland rev.]. **Main/Corp** Portland, OR. University. **Added/Corp** University of Portland. Review. Vol. 1 (June 1948)-. Periodical. English. sa. $1.00. University of Portland, 5000 North Willamette Boulevard, Portland OR 97203. **Tel** (503)283-7144. **ED** Thompson M. Faller. **LC** AS36; .P86. **DD** 378.795. Index available. cum. index. **Bk Rev**. **Circ:** 1,000 (ctrl).
Desc: All literature which comments on the human condition and presents information on expanding knowledge in different fields, with relevance to the contemporary scene.
Ind/Abst Abstr. Engl. Stud.

CN
UP HERE : LIFE IN CANADA'S NORTH. English. bm. 15.00Can$ (individuals and institutions) Canada; 19.00Can$ other. PO Box 1350, Yellowknife Northwest Territories X1A 2N9 Canada. **Tel** (403)920-4652, FAX (403)873-2844. **ED** Rosemary Allerston. **Bk Rev**. **Ad Acc**. **Circ:** 25,000 (ctrl).
Desc: Provides colourful coverage, focusing on travel, adventure, arts, crafts, wildlife, culture and history in Yukon and Northwest territories.
Ind/Abst Can. Index; Can. Period. Index (19??-).

US/0042-0999
URBAN WEST. V. 1- Sept./Oct. 1967-. Periodical. English. mo. **LC** AP2; .U84. **DD** 301.451/96/073. available on microfilm from University Microfilms International (UMI).

US/0090-158X
US. (US; A PAPERBACK MAGAZINE.). 1- 1969-. English. bw. $23.95. Bantam Books Inc, 666 Fifth Avenue, New York NY 10019. **Tel** (212)340-7500. **LC** AP2; .U845. **DD** 051.

US/0147-510X
US (NEW YORK, N.Y. 1985). (US.). [Us]. Vol. 3, No. 1 (July 1985)-. Periodical. English. mo. $23.95 (one year), $43.95 (two year). Wenner Media Inc., 1290 Avenue of the Americas, 2nd Floor, New York NY 10104. **Tel** (212)484-1616, FAX (212)759-2966. **(Subscription address:** Neodata / Colorado, PO Box 2606, Boulder Boulder CO 80322.**)** **ED** Carol Wallace. **LC** AP2; .U844. **DD** 051. **Ad Acc**. available on microfilm and microfiche from University Microfilms International (UMI). Documents available from UMI Article Clearinghouse. ***Continues*** *Us, 0147-510X.*
Ind/Abst Access (1977-); Newsp. Period. Abstr. (1988-).

US/0161-7389
USA TODAY (NEW YORK, N.Y.). (USA TODAY.). [USA today]. **Added/Corp** Society for the Advancement of Education. **VAT** United States of America Today. Vol. 107, No. 2398, (July 1978)-. Periodical. English. mo. $225.00 (one year), $405.00 (two year), $595.00 (three year). Society for the Advancement of Education, 99 West Hawthorne Avenue/Suite 518, Valley Stream NY 11580. **Tel** (516)568-9191. **ED** Stanley Lehrer. **LC** L11; .S36. **DD** 973/.05. **Bk Rev**. **Ad Acc**. **Circ:** 247,000. available on microfilm and microfiche from University Microfilms International (UMI). Documents available from UMI Article Clearinghouse. ***Continues*** *Intellect, 0149-0095.*
Desc: An open forum of viewpoints by America's leaders of trends and developments in US politics, economics, science, medicine, law, religion, education, sociology and arts.
Ind/Abst Acad. Abstr. Full Text Elite (Jan. 1989-); Acad. Abstr. (Jan. 1989-); Acad. Ind. [Computer File] (1984-); Acad. Search (Jan. 1989-); Am. Bibliogr. Slavic East Europ. Stud.; Curr. Contents Soc. Behav. Sci.; Curr. Index J. Educ.; Educ. Index; Educ. Adm. Abstr. (?-?); Expand. Acad. Index (1984-); F&S Index Plus Text, Int. [Select. Cov.]; Film Lit. Index; Index Period. Artic. Relat. Law; INFO-SOUTH Abstr.; Mag. Artic. Summar. Elite (Jan. 1989-); Mag. Artic. Summar. Select (Jan. 1989-); Mag. Artic. Summar. CD-ROM (Jan. 1989-); Mag. Express (1988-) [Full Txt.]; Mag. Index Plus (1989-); Mag. Index. Sel. (1986-); Mag. Search; Newsp. Period. Abstr. (1988-); Newsp. Abstr.; Read. Guide Abstr. Select Ed.; Read. Guide Period. Lit.; Resource/One Ondisc; Mag. Index (July 1978-); Urban Aff. Abstr.; Vocat. Search (Jan. 1989-); Women Stud. Abstr.

US
UTAH, THE MORMONS AND THE WEST. **Added/Corp** Tanner Trust Fund. (19??)-. Monographic series. English. ir. Price varies per volume. University of Utah Press / Building 50, Salt Lake City UT 84112. **Tel** (801)581-6771.

US/8750-0256
UTNE READER, THE. [Utne read.]. Vol. 1, No. 1 (Feb. 1983)-. Periodical. English. Six times a year (Jan., Mar., May, Jul., Sept., Nov.). $24.00 (one year), $48.00 (two year). The Utne Reader, Fawkes Building, 1624 Harmon Place, Minneapolis MN 55403. **Tel** (612)338-5040, (800)736-8863. **ED** Eric Utne, Jay Walljasper, Helen Cordes and Lynette Lamb. **LC** PN4784.U53; U88. **DD** 051. **Bk Rev. Ad Acc. Circ:** 200,000. available on microfilm and microfiche from University Microfilms International (UMI). Documents available from UMI Article Clearinghouse.
Desc: Presents excerpts and reviews of important articles selected from over 1,000 independent magazines and newsletters. Focuses on emerging issues in politics, the arts, science, education, psychology, economics, the environment.
Ind/Abst Acad. Abstr. Full Text Elite (July 1989-); Acad. Abstr. (July 1989-); Acad. Ind. [Computer File] (1989-); Acad. Search (July 1989-); Altern. Press Index; Book Rev. Index; Curr. Thoughts Trends; Expand. Acad. Index (1989-); Gen. Period. Index (1989-); Hum. Rights Intern. Rep.; INFO-SOUTH Abstr.; Mag. Artic. Summar. Elite (July 1989-); Mag. Artic. Summar. Select (July 1989-); Mag. Artic. Summar. CD-ROM (July 1989-); Mag. Index Plus (1989-); Mag. Search; Newsp. Period. Abstr. (1988-); Read. Guide Abstr. Select Ed.; Read. Guide Period. Lit.; Mag. Index (1989-); Vocat. Search (July 1989-).

●US/1063-7540
VALLEY VOICE (COLD SPRING, N.Y.). (VALLEY VOICE.). (1992)-. Periodical. English. wk. $18.00. Valley Voice, Box 380, Cold Spring NY 10516.

US/0898-641X
VAN WERT AND SURROUNDING COUNTIES, OHIO. [Van Wert surround. cties. Ohio]. **VFOAT** VWSC; V.W.S.C. (1988)-. English. an. $14.50. Van Wert and Surrounding Counties, 19133 Plum Street, Lois Bassett, Venedocia OH 45894. **Tel** (419)667-3151. **ED** Lois Bassett. **LC** F497.V2; V34. **DD** 929/.3771413. Index available (published separately). **Bk Rev**, (Qty: 2). **Ad Acc. Circ:** 150.

US/0733-8899
VANITY FAIR (NEW YORK, N.Y.). (VANITY FAIR.). [Vanity fair]. Vol. 1, No. 5 (Jan. 1914)-. Periodical. English. mo. $15.00. Conde Nast Publications / New York, 350 Madison Avenue, New York NY 10017. **Tel** (212)880-8800, (800)777-0700. **(Subscription address:** Neodata / Colorado, PO Box 2606, Boulder Boulder CO 80322.) **LC** AP2; .V3. **DD** 051. available on microfilm from University Microfilms International (UMI). Documents available from UMI Article Clearinghouse, Magazine Collection. ***Continues*** *Dress & Vanity Fair.* ***Absorbed in part by*** *Vogue, 0042-8000.*
Desc: Covers all that's exciting in contemporary culture: politics, personalities, books, the arts and humor; outspoken and outstanding journalism; art and photography.
Ind/Abst Acad. Abstr. Full Text Elite (Jan. 1992-); Acad. Abstr. (Jan. 1992-); Access (1984-?); Gen. Period. Index (1991-); Mag. Artic. Summar. Elite (Jan. 1992-); Mag. Artic. Summar. Select (Jan. 1992-); Mag. Artic. Summar. CD-ROM (Jan. 1992-); Mag. Index Plus (1991-); Mag. Index Sel. Microfiche (1990-) [Full Txt.]; Mag. Index. Sel. (1991-); Mag. Search; Newsp. Period. Abstr. (1988-); Read. Guide Abstr. Select Ed.; Read. Guide Period. Lit.; Resource/One Ondisc (1988-); Mag. Index (Jan. 1991-); TOM Gen. Index (1991-) [Full Txt.].

US/0888-0689
VARIA (MONTCHANIN, DEL.). (VARIA.). Vol. 1, No. 1 (1987)-. Periodical. English. Six times a year (Jan., Mar., May, July, Sept., Nov.). $24.00. Ardmoor Corporation, PO Box 301, Montchanin DE 19710. **Tel** (215)388-2500. **LC** AP2; .V325. **DD** 051. ***Continues*** *Views (Montchanin, Del.), 0886-151X.*

US/0746-9918
VENTURA COUNTY. **VFOAT** Ventura County Magazine. Jan./Feb. 1984-. Periodical. English. bm. PO Box 4631, Thousand Oaks CA 91360. ***Continues*** *Conejo, 0279-148X.*

CN/0826-113X
VERDIGRIS MAGAZINE. [Verdigris mag.]. (1983)-. Periodical. English. mo. Free. Verdigris Magazine, 12 Forsythe Avenue, Kingston Ontario K7M 2L8 Canada. **DD** 051.

US/0042-417X
VERMONT LIFE. **Added/Corp** Vermont. Agency of Development and Community Affairs. Vermont Development Commission. Vermont. Development Dept. Vol. 1 (Fall 1946)-. Periodical. English. Four times a year. $11.95 US; $15.95 other. Vermont Life, 6 Baldwin Street, Montpelier VT 05602. **Tel** (802)828-3241, (800)284-3243. **ED** Tom Slayton. **LC** F46; .V54. **DD** 917.43. Index available. cum. index (published separately through the product division). **Ad Acc, Adv Mgr:** Gerianne Smart, **Tel** (802)425-2283. **Circ:** 80,000.
Desc: A regional magazine celebrating Vermont as a place to live in or visit, its historical, cultural and recreational wealth.
Ind/Abst Access (1975-).

US/1044-940X
VERMONT MAGAZINE. [Vt. mag.]. Vol. 1, No. 1 (Sept./Oct. 1989)-. Periodical. English. Six times a year (Jan., Mar., May, July, Sept., Nov.). $16.95. North Country Publishers, PO Box 389, Bristol VT 05443. **Tel** (802)453-3200, (800)457-4760. **ED** David Sleeper. **Circ:** 45,000.
Desc: Covers everything from fiction to political issues, and spotlight recreational facilities and activities.

CN/0829-2299
VICE VERSA (MONTREAL, QUEBEC). (VICE VERSA.). [Vice versa]. No. 1 (May/June 1985)-. Periodical. English (French and Italian). ir. 30.00Can$ (institution), 20.00Can$ (individual) Canada; $23.82 (institution), $15.88 (individual) US. Vice Versa, CP 991 Succursale A, Montreal Quebec H3C 2W9 Canada. **Tel** (514)847-1593. **ED** Lamberto Tassinari. **DD** 051. **Bk Rev. Ad Acc, Adv Mgr:** Josee Bellemare. **Circ:** 2000 (ctrl).
Ind/Abst Can. Period. Index (19??-); Point Repere (19??-).

US/0738-8586
VICTOR VALLEY MAGAZINE. **VFOAT** Victor Valley. Began in Oct. 1982-. Periodical. English. bm. $15.00. Victor Valley Magazine, PO Box 618, Victorville CA 92392. **Tel** (619)243-2026. **ED** Grace Hauser. **Bk Rev. Ad Acc. Circ:** 5,000 (ctrl).
Desc: A city magazine covering local interests of the California Mojave Desert with articles of general interest on lifestyles, places, people, for and about the Mojave Desert. Holiday features welcome.

CN/0832-7238
VIE EN ESTRIE. [Vie Estrie]. **VFOAT** Estrie Living. April/May (1986)-. Periodical. English (French). bm. 35.40Can$. Lise Laverdiere, 5104 Boulevard Bourque, Suite 100, Rock Forest Que J1N 2K7 Canada. **Tel** (819)823-7389. **DD** 971.4/6/005.
Desc: A city magazine serving Estrie (the Eastern Townships). Contains features on architecture and design, fashion, personalities, individual sports, collecting, the arts, restaurants and activities as well as the controversial issues that face residents in the region. Dedicated to preserving and celebrating the quality of life in Estrie.

CN/0382-0262
VIE FRANCAISE (QUEBEC). (VIE FRANCAISE.). [Vie fr.]. **Added/Corp** Conseil de la vie Francaise en Amerique. Conseil de la vie Francaise en Amerique. Vol. 1 (Oct. 1946)-. Periodical. French. qt. 15.00Can$. Conseil de la vie Francaise en Amerique, 56 rue St-Pierre, 1st Floor, Quebec Quebec G1K 4A1 Canada. **Tel** (418)692-1150, FAX (418)692-4578. **Bk Rev. Ad Acc. Circ:** 500 (ctrl).
Desc: Constitutes an interesting source of information on French speaking people. Constantly updates documentation of the activities and interests of the French.
Ind/Abst Am. Hist. Life (1980-1984); Point Repere (1983-).

US/0749-0186
VIEWTRON MAGAZINE & GUIDE. ***Ceased.*** **VFOAT** Viewtron Magazine and Guide Viewtron; Viewtron Magazine. Periodical. English. qt. Viewdata Corporation of America Inc, 1 Herald Plaza, Knight Rider I, Miami FL 33132.

US/0042-6180
VILLAGE VOICE (NEW YORK), THE. (THE VILLAGE VOICE.). [Village voice]. **VFOAT** Voice. Vol. 1, No. 1 (Oct. 26, 1955)-. Newspaper. English. wk. $53.00. Village Voice, 36 Cooper Square, New York NY 10003. **Tel** (212)475-3333 ext. 5105. **(Subscription address:** Village Voice SPFF, PO Box 8044, Syracuse NY 13217.) **LC** AP2; .V72. **DD** 071/.471. **Bk Rev. Ad Acc. Circ:** 151,828. available on microfilm and microfiche from University Microfilms International (UMI). Documents available from UMI Article Clearinghouse.
Desc: Covers NYC, national and social issues. Contains in-depth feature articles and editorial columns. Reviews films, plays, book exhibits and TV. Lists movies, plays, galleries and cultural events.
Ind/Abst Acad. Search (July 1993-); Access (1976-); Book Rev. Index; Film Lit. Index; INFO-SOUTH Abstr.; Infobank (Jan. 1969-); Mag. Search; Med. Rev. Dig.; Music Index; Newsp. Period. Abstr. (1988-); Peace Res. Abstr. J. (1971).

US/0042-6199
VILLAGER (BRONXVILLE, N.Y.), THE. (THE VILLAGER.). **Added/Corp** Bronxville Women's Club. Vol. 1 (Oct. 1929)-. Periodical. English. Nine times a year. $2.75. Bronxville Womens Club, 135 Midland Avenue, Bronxville NY 10701. **LC** AP2; .V73.

US/0734-6603
VIRGINIA COUNTRY. ***Title Change.*** [Va. ctry.]. (1979-1992). Periodical. English. qt. The Country Publishers Inc., PO Box 778, Berryville VA 22611. **Tel** (703)955-1298. **ED** Garrison Ellis. **LC** F221; .V745. **DD** 975.5/005. **Bk Rev. Ad Acc. Circ:** 30,000. ***Continues*** *Virginia Hunt Country.* ***Continued by*** *Virginia (Berryville, Va.), 1064-5691.*
Desc: General interest magazine stressing fiction, art, history, dining, book reviews state events and politics.

US/0743-4243
VIRGINIAN (STAUNTON, VA.), THE. (THE VIRGINIAN.). Vol. 6, No. 3 (May-June 1984)-. Periodical. English. bm (6 issues). $14.97. Shenandoah Valley Magazine Corporation, PO Box 7480, Atlantic Station, Virginia Beach VA 23458. **Tel** (804)422-5577. **ED** Jeffrey Wexler. **LC** F232.S5; S59. **DD** 975.5/005. **Bk Rev. Ad Acc. Circ:** 28,000. ***Continues*** *Shenandoah Virginia Town & Country, 0744-9356.*
Desc: Celebrates the population of Virginia for its history, traditions, foods, travel, adventure and the arts.

US/0733-9720
VISTAS (MIAMI, FLA.). (VISTAS / FLORIDA INTERNATIONAL UNIVERSITY, UNIVERSITY RELATIONS & DEVELOPMENT.). Began publication in 1979?. Periodical. English. wk. $311.00. University Relations & Development, Florida International University, Tamiami Trail, Miami FL 33199.

NE/0149-4473
VIVA (NEW YORK). (VIVA.). Vol. 1 (Oct. 1973)-. Periodical. English. wk. Kr130.00 Netherlands; Kr286.00 other. Medianet BV, Postbus 6298, 2001 LN Haarlem Netherlands. **Tel** 011 31 23 173311. **LC** AP2; .V776. **DD** 051. **Ad Acc. Circ:** 150,000.
Ind/Abst Mag. Index (1977-?).

CN/1187-4988
VIVRE A PIERREFONDS. [Vivre Pierrefonds]. **Added/Corp** Pierrefonds (Quebec). **VFOAT** Life in Pierrefonds. Vol. 14, No 2 (1991)-. Periodical. English (French). Free for Residents. Ville de Pierrefonds, CP 2500, Pierrefonds Quebec H9N 4N2 Canada. **DD** 971.4. ***Continues*** *Bulletin (Pierrefonds (Quebec)), 0820-4942.*

US/0746-0279
VOZ DE PORTUGAL. **VFOAT** Voice of Portugal. Periodical. Portuguese. sm. Voz de Portugal, 370 A Street, Hayward CA 94541. **ED** Lourenco Costa Aguiar. **Circ:** 4,300.

US/0277-352X
WALL STREET JOURNAL MAGAZINE, THE. [Wall Str. j. mag.]. **VFOAT** WSJ Magazine. (June 1981)-. Periodical. English. mo. $3.00 each issue. 22 Cortlandt Street, New York NY 10007. **LC** AP2; .W239. **DD** 051.
Ind/Abst Oper. Res./Manag. Sci.; Qual. Control Appl. Stat.

CN/0712-4945
WASAGA BEACH TIMES. [Wasaga Beach times]. (1981)-. Periodical. English. wk. $12.00. Wasaga Beach Times, Box 187 25 Second Street, Collingwood Ontario L9Y 3Z5 Canada. **DD** 071/.1317.

US/0275-0597
WASHINGTON FACT BOOK. English. be. State University of New York Washington Office, 1730 Rhode Island Avenue Northwest, Suite 500, Washington DC 20036.

US/0744-6373
WASHINGTON LIVING. **VFOAT** Washington Living Magazine. Vol. 1, No. 1 (Apr. 1982)-. Periodical. English. Twelve times a year. $16.80. Spears Publishing Co., 6506 McCahill Drive, Laurel MD 20707. **LC** F191; .W33. **DD** 979.7/005.

US/0363-1214
WASHINGTON NEWSLINES. Periodical. English. American Assembly of Collegiate Schools of Business, 600 Emerson Road, Suite 300, St Louis MO 63141-6762. **Tel** (314)872-8481, FAX (314)872-8495.

US/0887-428X
WASHINGTON SPECTATOR (1985), THE. (THE WASHINGTON SPECTATOR.). [Wash. spect.]. **Added/Corp** Public Concern Foundation (U.S.). **VFOAT** Washington Spectator and Between the Lines. Vol. 11, No. 1 (Jan. 1, 1985)-. Periodical. English. sm. $10.00 (one year), $18.00 (two years) US; $20.00 Canada and Mexico; $28.00 other. Public Concern Foundation, PO Box 20065, London Ter Station, New York NY 10011. **Tel** (212)741-2365. **LC** E839.5; .W36. **DD** 973.92/05. available on microfilm and microfiche from University Microfilms International (UMI). ***Continues*** *Washington Spectator and Between the Lines, 0145-160X.*

US/1042-4229
WASHINGTON VIEW. [Wash. view]. **VFOAT** Washington View Magazine. Vol. 1, No. 1 (Summer 1989)-. Periodical. English. Six times a year (Jan., Mar., May, July, Sept., Nov.). $10.00 North America; $15.00 other. Viewcomm Inc., 1101 14th Street Northwest, Suite 1050, Washington DC 20005. **ED** Effie Upshaw and A. Von Legget. **DD** 975. **Bk Rev. Ad Acc. Circ:** 30,000 (ctrl).
Desc: Articles examine local and national politics, business and entertainment. The magazine also covers fashion, travel and the arts.

US/0043-0897
WASHINGTONIAN (WASHINGTON, D.C.), THE. (THE WASHINGTONIAN.). [Washingtonian]. Vol. 1, (Oct. 1965)-. Periodical. English. mo. $24.00 Virginia, Maryland & Washington DC; $34.95 other. Washingtonian, 1828 L Street Northwest, Washington DC 20036. **Tel** (202)296-3600, (202)331-0715. **ED** John A. Limpert. **LC** F191; .W37. **DD** 917.53/005. **Bk Rev. Ad Acc. Circ:** 149,323. available on microfilm and microfiche from University Microfilms International (UMI). Documents available from UMI Article Clearinghouse.
Desc: Magazine about the Washington metropolitan area, covering all aspects of the city's life.
Ind/Abst Acad. Search (Sept. 1984-June 1989); Access (1975-?); INFO-SOUTH Abstr.; Mag. Artic. Summar. Elite (Sept. 1984-June 1989); Mag. Artic. Summar. Select (Sept. 1984-June 1989); Mag. Artic. Summar. CD-ROM (Sept. 1984-June 1989); Mag. Index Plus (1989-); Mag. Search; Newsp. Period. Abstr. (1991-); Pop. Period. Index; Read. Guide Abstr. Select Ed.; Read. Guide Period. Lit.; Mag. Index (1977-).

CN/0823-6011
WEEK-END NATIONAL, LE. [Week-end. natl.]. V. 1, No. 1, (March/April 1983)-. Periodical. French. wk. $1.00 per no. Le Week-End National, Bureau 200, 2121 Est, Rue Sherbrooke, Montreal Quebec H2K 1C3 Canada. **DD** 054/.1.

US/0199-3356
WEST COAST PEDDLAR. (19??)-. Periodical. English. mo. $19.00. West Coast Peddler, PO Box 5134, Whitter CA 90607. **Tel** (213)698-1718.

US/0890-4391
WEST MICHIGAN PROFILE. Vol. 1, No. 1 (June 1986)-. Periodical. English. mo. $10.00. West Michigan Profile, 7 Ionia Street SW, Grand Rapids MI 49503.

US/0043-3373
WESTCHESTER COUNTY PRESS, THE. VFOAT County Press. (19??)-. Newspaper. English. Fifty-two times a year. $25.00 (one year); $45.00 (two years). Westchester County Press, PO Box 1631, White Plains NY 10602. **Tel** (914)684-0006.

CN/0822-7225
WESTCOAST READER, THE. [Westcoast read.]. (1982)-. Periodical. English. Nine times a year. Free. Capilano College, 2055 Purcell Way North, Vancouver BC V7J 3H5 Canada. **Tel** (604)984-1712. **(Subscription address:** Westcoast Reader, 6137 2040th Street, Langely BC V3A 6H4 Canada, (604)986-3945**) DD** 071/.11. ctrl circ. ***Continues** Westcoaster, 0826-0257.*

CN/0829-4046
WESTERN LIVING (CALGARY ED.). (WESTERN LIVING.). [West. living]. (March 1984)-. Periodical. English. mo. Western Living, 2930 Arbutus Street, Vancouver British Columbia V6J 3Y9 Canada. **Tel** (604)669-7525. **DD** 051. ***Continues in part** Western Living, 0821-6908.*

CN/0824-0612
WESTERN LIVING (EDMONTON ED.). (WESTERN LIVING.). [West. living]. Vol. 9, No. 3 (March 1984)-. Periodical. English. mo. 22.50Can$; $32.00 US; $34.00 other. Western Living, 2930 Arbutus Street, Vancouver British Columbia V6J 3Y9 Canada. **Tel** (604)669-7525. **DD** 051. ***Continues in part** Western Living, 0821-6908.*

CN/0829-4038
WESTERN LIVING (VICTORIA ED.). (WESTERN LIVING.). [West. living]. (March 1984)-. Periodical. English. mo. Comac Communications, 504 Davie Street, Vancouver British Columbia V6B 2G4 Canada. **DD** 051. ***Continues in part** Western Living (British Columbia Ed.), 0821-7017.*

●US/1075-8917
WESTERN STYLES. (1993)-. English. bm. $18.00. Cowles Magazines, PO Box 8200, Harrisburg PA 17105. **Tel** (717)657-9555, (800)435-9610.

CN/0701-1571
WESTERN WHEEL. (THE WESTERN WHEEL.). Vol. 1 (Aug. 3, 1976)-. Periodical. English. wk. $30.00. Western Wheel, Box 238, Okotoks Alberta T0L 1T0 Canada. **Tel** (403)938-6397. **ED** Judi Weaver. **DD** 071/.123/4. **Bk Rev. Ad Acc. Circ:** 7,800 (ctrl).
Desc: Local news for towns and rural areas in municipal district of foothills.

CN/0826-2349
WESTIN. [Westin]. Vol. 2, No. 7 (Jan. 1984)-. Periodical. English. mo. $18.00. Skyword Marketing Ltd, 2802 30th Street/Suite 202, Vernon British Columbia V1T 8G7 Canada. **Tel** (604)549-3131. **DD** 051. ***Continues** First-Class Worldwide, 0826-2330.*

CN/0316-5434
WESTON TIMES REVIEW. VFOAT Times Review. Began publication Aug. 29, 1974. Periodical. English. wk. 0.10Can$ per no. Times Review, PO Box 2053 Station B, Rexdale Ontario M9V 2G2 Canada. **DD** 071/.13/541.

US
WEST'S FLORIDA DIGEST 2D. Added/Corp Florida. Courts. United States. Courts. West Publishing Company. **VFOAT** Florida Digest 2D. (1984)-. Periodical. English.

US
WHAT'S NEW IN ARIZONA. (19??)-. English. wk (50 issues). $55.00. Media America Corporation, 5555 North 7th Avenue, Suite B200, Phoenix AZ 85013. **Tel** (602)207-3750, FAX (602)207-3777.

US/8750-4057
WHOOT. Periodical. English. wk. $20.00. Whoot Inc, 214 Verona Avenue, Pleasantville NJ 08232. ***Continues** Whoot. Casino Guide, 0747-4660.*

US
WILLIAMSBURG'S PUBLICK OBSERVER. April 1980-. Periodical. English. Three times a year. $2.00. Virginia Gazette, PO Box 419, Williamsburg VA 23185. **Tel** (804)220-1736. ***Supersedes** Publick Observer.*

US/0888-0832
WINDHAM PHOENIX. [Windham phoenix]. Began in 1985. Periodical. English. mo. $12.00. Phoenix Publishing Company, PO Box 752, Willimantic CT 06226. **DD** 051.

CN/0318-2460
WINDSOR THIS MONTH. ***Suspended.*** **VFOAT** Inside Windsor. (Apr. 1974)-Suspended. English. mo. $10.00. Windsor This Month, PO Box 1029 Station A, Windsor Ontario N9A 6P4 Canada. **Tel** (519)966-7411. **ED** Laura Rosenthal. **DD** 790/.09713/32. **Bk Rev. Ad Acc. Circ:** 22,000 (ctrl).
Desc: Features timely editorial reflecting the latest trends in lifestyles, with interviews with local personalities, sports heroes and special annual features, such as fashion, travel, interior design, landscaping, gourmet foods and entertainment; a magazine for and about the people of Windsor and Essex County.

CN/0707-6185
WINNIPEG MAGAZINE. No. 1- Sept. 1978-. Periodical. English. ir. $19.35. Winnipeg Magazine, 1670 Church Avenue, Winnipeg Manitoba R2X 2W9 Canada. **Tel** (204)632-2724. **ED** Richard Garlick. **DD** 917.127/4. **Ad Acc. Circ:** 40,000. ***Supersedes** Eye on Winnipeg, 0701-0737.*
Desc: A city magazine incorporating a calendar of events, news, and features of interest to Winnipeggers. Also contains fiction, food, and fashion Pieces.

US/8755-9587
WINSTON-SALEM MAGAZINE. VFOAT Winston Salem Magazine; Winston-Salem. (July/Aug. 1984)-. Periodical. English. bm. $12.00. Winston-Salem Magazine, PO Box 10921, Winston Salem NC 27102. **Tel** (919)722-0836. **ED** Luigi Bozzo. **Ad Acc, Adv Mgr:** Jennifer Valentine, **Tel** (910)722-8706. **Circ:** 12,000 (ctrl).
Desc: City magazine for Winston-Salem area.

US/1059-0935
WISCONSIN NEWMONTH. [Wis. newmon.]. **VFOAT** Wisconsin New Month; Newmonth Magazine. (19??)-. Periodical. English. bm. $12.00 (1 year), $21.00 (2 year) US; $17.00 (1 year), $31.00 (2 year) other. Wisconsin Newmonth Magazine, 1043 South Clay Street, Green Bay WI 54301. **Tel** (414)433-0581. **DD** 051. ***Continues** Newmonth, 0192-1142.*

US/0095-4314
WISCONSIN TRAILS. Vol. 12 (Mar. 1971)-. Periodical. English. Six times a year. $34.95 US; $46.95 other. Wisconsin Trails, PO Box 5650, 6225 University Avenue, Madison WI 53705. **Tel** (608)231-2444, (800)236-8088. **(Subscription address:** Kable Publishers Aide, 308 East Hitt Street, Subscription Department, Mt. Morris, IL 61054**) ED** Howard Mead. **LC** F576; .W99. **DD** 977.5/005. **Bk Rev. Ad Acc. Circ:** 33,000 (ctrl). ***Continues** Wisconsin Tales and Trails.*
Desc: For those who enjoy Wisconsin life, its people and places. Features cover the arts, the environment, history, nostalgia, travel, and outdoor adventures.
Ind/Abst Access (1975-).

US/1057-2821
WONDER (SOUND BEACH, N.Y.). (WONDER : OBSERVING AND CONFRONTING THE ENIGMAS THAT SURROUND US.). [Wonder]. No. 1 (1991)-. Periodical. English. an. $8.00 US; $10.00 (includes postage) other. Ziggurat Press, PO Box 394, Sound Beach NY 11789. **ED** Norman Weisberg. **DD** 051. **Pr Rev. Circ:** 500.
Desc: Gives insights in science and how things work, art reviews, what's new in technology, and history reviews.

US/0884-9013
WORKS (LOS ANGELES, CALIF.). (WORKS.). [Works]. (Spring 1985)-. Periodical. English. qt. $11.00. Landford Inc, South Weatherford, 5601 West Washington Boulevard, Los Angeles CA 90016. **DD** 051.

US/0888-157X
WORLD (ASHEVILLE, N.C.). (WORLD.). Vol. 1, No. 1 (Mar. 17, 1986)-. Periodical. English. wk. $32.00 (one year), $44.00 (two year) US; $58.00 (one year), $82.00 (two year) other. God's World Publications, Box 2330, Asheville NC 28802. **Tel** (704)253-8063, (800)951-5437. **ED** Joel Belz. **DD** 051. **Bk Rev**, (Qty: 40). **Ad Acc, Adv Mgr:** Roger Schoffer. **Circ:** 35,000 (ctrl). available on microfilm and microfiche from University Microfilms International (UMI); available on an online database.
Desc: Balances the non-christian worldview of the national media. Reports on current national and international events from a christian perspective. Reporting on todays hottest issues; the economy, education, AIDS, welfare, pro-life issues, politics and more. Alternative to Time and Newsweek.
Ind/Abst Christ. Period. Index; Curr. Thoughts Trends.

US/1060-3816
WORLD AT LARGE, THE. [World large]. (1991)-. Periodical. English. sm (24 issues). $65.00. World at Large, Inc., PO Box 190330, Brooklyn NY 11219. **Tel** (718)972-4000. **DD** 051.

US/0043-8901
WORLD PROGRESS. [World prog.]. (1930)-. Periodical. English. qt. $18.95. Standard Educational Corporation, 200 West Madison Street, Suite 300, Chicago IL 60606. **Tel** (312)346-7440. **ED** Miriam Creeden. Index available. **Bk Rev.** ctrl circ. ***Continues** Standard Quarterly Review.*

US/1056-8506
YANKEE DOODLER MAGAZINE, THE. VFOAT Doodler. Vol. 3, Issue 1 (Fall 1991)-. Periodical. English. qt. $2.95 (single issue). Tisco Publishing, PO Box 28, Walpole NH 03608. **DD** 051. ***Continues** Pennyworth.*

US/0044-0191
YANKEE (DUBLIN, N.H.). (YANKEE.). [Yankee]. Vol. 1 (Sept. 1935)-. Periodical. English. mo. $22.00 (1 year), $39.00 (2 year), $50.00 (3 year). Yankee Publishing Inc., Main Street, Dublin NH 03444. **Tel** (603)563-8111, (800)736-1100. **(Subscription address:** CDS / SIFD Agency Control, 1901 Bell Avenue, Des Moines IA 50315.**) ED** Judson Hale. **LC** AP2; .Y25. **DD** 051. Index available (published Feb.). **Bk Rev. Ad Acc. Circ:** 1,000,000. available on microfilm and microfiche from University Microfilms International (UMI). Documents available from UMI Article Clearinghouse.
Desc: Yankee Magazine brings enchantment, fascination, and down-home, down-to-earth qualities found in New England and its people.
Ind/Abst Acad. Abstr. Full Text Elite (Jan. 1984-); Acad. Abstr. (Jan. 1984-); Acad. Search (Jan. 1984-); Access (1976-?); Annu. Bibliogr. Engl. Lang. Lit.; Gen. Period. Index (1985-); INFO-SOUTH Abstr.; Mag. Artic. Summar. Elite (Jan. 1984-); Mag. Artic. Summar. Select (Jan. 1984-); Mag. Artic. Summar. CD-ROM (Jan. 1984-); Mag. Index Plus (1989-); Mag. Search; Mid. Search (Jan. 1984-); Newsp. Period. Abstr. (1988-); Pop. Period. Index; Read. Guide Period. Lit.; Mag. Index (1977-); TOM Gen. Index (1993-) [Full Txt.]; Vocat. Search (July 1989-).

US/1058-059X
YESTERDAY TODAY IN NEW JERSEY. (Spring 1991)-. Periodical. English. bm. $6.00 (one year), $11.00 (two year), $15.00 (three year). C & S Publications, Inc., PO Box 374, Scotch Plains NJ 07303. **Tel** (201)332-2598, FAX (201)333-3333. **ED** George Point. **Bk Rev**, (Qty: 10). **Ad Acc, Adv Mgr:** Charlene Burke, **Tel** (201)333-4144. **Circ:** 54,000 (ctrl).
Desc: Stories and articles about New Jersey including historical and cultural, current events and entertainment. Sources for children's activities, antiques, performing arts, museums, and parks.

CN/0829-0652
YUKON DATA BOOK. [Yukon data book]. **Added/Corp** Yukon Territory. Dept. of Tourism and Economic Development. (1985)-. English. be. $20.00. NWT Data Book, c/o Outcrop Ltd, Box 1114, Yellowknife Northwest Territories X0E 1H0 Canada. **Tel** (403)873-6152, FAX (403)873-2844. **DD** 971.9/1/005. **Bk Rev.**
Desc: Summary of economic, social, and political influences on life in the Northwest Territories. Community profile includes services, history, and key leaders.

CN/0705-3606
ZONE LIBRE. V. 1- Summer 1977-. Periodical. French. mo. $1.25 each issue. Zone Libre, 1715 rue Panet, Montreal Quebec H2L 2Z7 Canada. **DD** 054/.1.

CN/0701-0109
ZPRAVODAJ - CESKOSLOVENSKE NARODNI SDRUZENI V KANADE, ODBOCKA VANCOUVER. Main/Corp Czechoslovak National Association of Canada. Vancouver Branch. (April 1970)-. Periodical. Czech. mo. 41.50Can$ US and Europe; 39.50Can$ Canada; 42.50Can$ Pan-American nations; 43.50Can$ other. Jiri Svoboda, 3595 Kingston Road, Scarborough Ontario M1M 1R4 Canada. **DD** 057/.86.

General Interest —General Interest-South America

GENERAL INTEREST-SOUTH AMERICA

BL
2001 DOIS MIL E UM. Vol. 1 (1972)-. Periodical. Portuguese. Twelve times a year. $4.00. Alfredo Tedeschini Distribuidora de Revistas Ltda, rua do Senado 320 A, Rio de Janeiro Brazil. **LC** AP66; .D58.

FR
ALIZES LATINO-AMERICANISTE : BULLETIN D'INFORMATION / GRECO 26 [AND] AFSSAL. **Added/Corp** Centre National de la Recherche Scientifique (France). Reseau Documentaire Amerique Latine. Association Francaise des Sciences Sociales sur l'Amerique Latine. **VFOAT** Alizes; Bulletin d'Information Alizes Latino-Americaniste. Vol. 1 (June 1987)-. Periodical. French. Three times a year. 200.00F Comes with Association Francaise des Sciences Sociales sur l Amerique Latine membership. Association Francaise des Sciences Sociales sur l Amerique Latine, 28 rue and Saint and Guillaumo, 75007 Paris France. **Tel** 011 33 1 4222 3593.

BL
ALMANAQUE DA PARAIBA. 1973-. Portuguese. Editora Almanaque da Pariba Ltd, rua Duque de Caixias 400, Joao Pessoa Brazil. **LC** F2591; .A47.

GW/0933-8853
AMERICAS (BONN, GERMANY). See General Interest-General Interest-North America.

US/0379-0940
AMERICAS (ENGLISH EDITION). (AMERICAS.). [Americas]. **Added/Corp** Organization of American States. Vol. 1 (Mar. 1949)-. Periodical. English (Spanish). Six times a year. $21.00 institutions; $18.00 individuals. Organization of American States, 19th Street & Constitution Avenue NW, Suite 300, Washington DC 20006. **Tel** (202)458-6256. (Subscription address: KCMS Fulfillment, 3401 East West Highway, Hyattsville, MD 20785) **ED** Enrique Durand. **LC** F1401; .A57. **DD** 917. Index available. **Bk Rev.** **Circ:** 65,000. available on microfilm and microfiche from University Microfilms International (UMI). Documents available from The Genuine Article, UMI Article Clearinghouse. **Supersedes in part** Bulletin of the Pan American Union.
Desc: Promotes inter-American understanding through articles on the cultures and peoples of Latin America and the Caribbean, accompanied by stunning color photography. Regular columns inform on current art, theater, music and books of the hemisphere.
Ind/Abst Acad. Abstr. Full Text Elite (Jan. 1984-) [Full Txt.]; Acad. Abstr. (Jan. 1984-); Acad. Search (Jan. 1984-); Am. Hist. Life (1969-); ARTbibliogr. Mod.; Arts Humanit. Citation Index [Full Cov.]; Energy Res. Abstr. (Nov. 1977-); HAPI Hisp. Am. Period. Index; Hist. Source (Jan. 1984-); Humanit. Index; Humanit. Source (Jan. 1988-) [Full Txt.]; INFO-SOUTH Abstr.; Mag. Artic. Summar. Elite (Jan. 1984-) [Full Txt.]; Mag. Artic. Summar. Select (Jan. 1984-); Mag. Artic. Summar. CD-ROM (Jan. 1984-); Mag. ASAP Plus [Full Txt.]; Mag. ASAP Sel. [Full Txt.]; Mag. Index Plus (1989-); Mag. Index Sel. Microfiche (1986-) [Full Txt.]; Mag. Index. Sel. (1986-); Mag. Search; Mid. Search (Jan. 1984-) [Full Txt.]; MLA Int. Bibl. Books Artic. Mod. Lang. Lit.; Newsp. Period. Abstr. (1988-); Peace Res. Abstr. J. (1966-1987); Read. Guide Period. Lit.; Res. Alert [Full Cov.]; Soc. Sci. Cit. Index [Select. Cov.]; Mag. Index (1977-); Vocat. Search (Jan. 1984-) [Full Txt.].

US
ANALISIS-CONFIRMADO. Periodical. Spanish. $208.00. S R L, Independencia 2744, Buenos Aires Argentina. **LC** AP63; .A613. **Formed by the union of** Analisis and Confirmado.

BL
ANIMA. Periodical. Portuguese. Nuvem Cigana, Av Epitacio Pessoa 1674 - Apto 7, Rio de Janeiro Brazil. **LC** AP66; .A63.

PE
ARI, KANAN. No. 1-. Periodical. Spanish. S/150.00. Ramon Herrera 289, Lima Peru. **LC** AP63; .A676.

BL
ATENCAO. Periodical. Portuguese. 300. Grafica Editora Ltd, rua Jordania 411, Caixa Postal 1716, 80.000 Curitiba Brazil. **LC** AP66; .A86.

BL/0260-6739
BASES (SAO PAULO, BRAZIL). (BASES.). Portuguese (Portuguese). ir. $300.00. Momento Editorial, Rua Marques De Itu, 837, Cep 01223, San Paulo Brasil. **LC** AP66; .B34. **DD** 056/.9.

BL
BOLETIM DE ARIEL. Vol. 1, (July 1973)-. Bulletin. Portuguese. mo. $18.00. **LC** AP66; .B59. **Supersedes** Boletim de Ariel; Mensario Critico-Bibliographico.

CL/0716-0763
BOLETIN ANTARTICO CHILENO. Vol. 1, No. 1 (Jan./June 1981)-. Periodical. Spanish (English). sa. Luis Thayer Ojeda, 814 Correo Sucursal 21, Santiago Chile. **Tel** 2322617, telex 346261 INACH CK. **ED** Luz Marta Rivera. **Circ:** 1,000 (ctrl). **Continues** Revista de Difusion (Instituto Antartico Chileno).
Desc: Publication which covers the Chilean activities connected to the Antarctic continent.
Ind/Abst Aquat. Sci. Fish. Abstr. (Computer File); GeoRef; Ocean. Abstr.

BO
BOLIVIA BULLETIN. **Added/Corp** Centro de Documentacion e Informacion--Bolivia. Vol. 1, No. 1 (Jan. 1985)-. Bulletin. English. bm. $20.00. Centro Documentacion, Informacion Casilla 20194, la Paz Bolivia. **Tel** 011 591 2 372940. **Circ:** 500.
Ind/Abst Hum. Rights Intern. Rep.

BL
BRASIL ATRAVES DOS TEXTOS. **VFOAT** Colecao Brasil Atraves Dos Textos. V. 1-. Monographic series. Portuguese. Price varies per volume. Editora Cultrix Ltda, rua Conselheiro Furtado 648, 01511 S Paulo Brazil.

BL
BRASIL HOJE (1981). (BRASIL HOJE.). Vol. 1, No. 0 (July 1981)-. Periodical. Portuguese. mo. Rua Dom Joao V 586 Lapa, Sao Paulo SP CEP 05075 Brazil.

BL
BRAZIL HERALD. Periodical. English. da. The Brazil Herald, rua do Resende 65 ZC06, Rio de Janeiro Brazil.

BL
BRAZIL INFORMATION. **Added/Corp** Instituto Brasileiro de Analises Sociais e Economicas. (198?)-. English. Ibase rua Vicente de Souza, 29 Botafogo, 22251 Rio de Janeiro RJ Brazil.
Ind/Abst Hum. Rights Intern. Rep.

BL
BRAZILIAN OVERSEAS NEWSLETTER. Newsletter. $198.00. Overseas Information Services, Caixa Postal 18-139, 04699 Sao Paulo Brazil. **Tel** 011 55 11 548-5388.

BL
BRAZILINFORM NEWS LETTER. English. bw. $300.00. Brazilinform, Caixa Postal 37584, Rio de Janeiro 22642 Brazil.
Desc: The leading English newsletter on Brazil, containing economic and political analyses and projections. Considered the base source of objective analyses on Brazil.

GY
CARICOM PERSPECTIVE. **Added/Corp** Caribbean Community. Secretariat. **VFOAT** Caribbean Community in the 1980's. No. 1 (March 1980)-. Periodical. English. bm. Free on request. Caribbean Community Secretariat, PO Box 10827, Bank of Guyana Building, Georgetown, Guyana. **Tel** 011 592 2 69281-9, **FAX** 011 592 2 67816, 011 592 2 58039, telex 2263 CARISEC GY. **LC** HC151.A1; C375. **DD** 337.1/729/05. **Bk Rev.** **Circ:** 6,000 (ctrl).
Desc: Reports on the work achievements and problems of the 13-nation Caribbean Community.
Ind/Abst LABORDOC.

PE
COPE. **Added/Corp** Petroleos del Peru. Departamento de Relaciones Publicas. (19??)-. Periodical. Spanish. ir. Petroleos del Peru Departamento de Relaciones Publicas, Paseo de la Republica 3361 San Isidro, Aptdos 1081 y 3126, Lima Peru. **LC** AP63; .C52756. **DD** 056/.1.
Ind/Abst Health Index (Jan. 1989-June 1989); Health Ref. Cent. (Jan. 1989-June 1989) [Full Cov.].

CK/0302-3087
CUADERNOS COLOMBIANOS. [Cuad. colomb.]. Yearly V. 1- 1974-. Spanish. Calle 45A No 28-01, Apartado Aereo 30160, Bogota Colombia. **LC** AS82.A1; C8. **DD** 056/.1.

UY
CUADERNOS DE MARCHA. No. 1 (June 1985)-. Periodical. Spanish. mo. $55.00 Latin America; $78.00 other. Ceual AC, Piedras 524, Montevideo Uruguay. **Tel** 011 598 2 957973, 011 598 2 933134. Index available. cum. index. **Bk Rev.** **Ad Acc.** ctrl circ. **Continues** Cuadernos de Marcha (Mexico City, Mexico : 1979).

SW
CURRENT SWEDISH RESEARCH ON LATIN AMERICA. English. an. **LC** F1409.95.S8; C87. **DD** 980/.0071/1485.

AG/0325-0431
DAVID Y GOLIATH : BOLETIN CLACSO. **Suspended.** **Added/Corp** Consejo Latinoamericano de Ciencias Sociales. **VFOAT** Boletin Clacso. Vol. 11, No. 38-39 (Jan./June/July/Dec. 1980)-(19??). Periodical. Spanish. Three times a year. $12.00 Argentina; $18.00 other. CLACSO, Callao 875 3ER, 1023 Buenos Aires Argentina. **Tel** 54 1 811 6588, **FAX** 54 1 812 8954. **ED** Cristina Micieli. **LC** H62.5.L3; C62. **DD** 300/.7208. Index available. cum. index. **Bk Rev.** **Ad Acc.** **Pr Rev.** **Circ:** 1,500 (ctrl). **Continues** Consejo Latinoamericano de Ciencias Sociales. Secretaria Ejecutiva. Boletin Clasco.
Desc: Covers Latin American societies and social sciences issues, culture, social change, policy, abstracts, and council's programs and activities on social sciences.

GW
DEUTSCH - BRASILIANISCHE HEFTE. CADERNOS GERMANO - BRASILEIROS. **Added/Corp** Lateinamerika-Zentrum. **VFOAT** Cadernos Germano - Brasileiros. **VAT** Deutsch-Brasilianische Hefte; Cadernos Germano-Brasileiros. (1967)-. Periodical. German (Portuguese). Six times a year. DM48.00. Latein Amerika Zentrum E V, Schumannstrasse 2B, 5300 Bonn 1 Germany. **Tel** (0228)210788. **ED** Hermann M. Gorgen. **LC** F2501; .D47. **DD** 301.29/43/081. Index available. cum. index. **Bk Rev.** **Ad Acc.** **Circ:** 10,000 (ctrl). **Continues** Deutsch - Brasilianische Nachrichten.
Desc: Culture, politics, economics concerning Brazil and its relationship between Brazil and the Federal German Republic.

PE
ENCUENTRO (LIMA, PERU). (ENCUENTRO.). **Added/Corp** Centro de Proyeccion Cristiana. No. 1 (Jan./Feb. 1980)-. Periodical. Spanish. mo. $166.00. Centro de Proyeccion Cristiana, Jr Aguarico 586, Brena Lima Peru. **LC** F1401; .E49. **DD** 980/.005.

VE
ENTONCES. No. 1- March 1978-. Periodical. Spanish. mo. Bs3.00 single issue. Quinta Helena, Calle los Araguaneyes Urb Chuao, Caracas 106 Venezuela. **LC** AP63; .E565.

CL/0013-9971
ERCILLA. (193?)-. Periodical. Spanish. wk. $334.29 The Americas; $414.29 other. Editorial Ercilla S A, Luis Thayer Ojeda 1626, Providencia Santiago Chile. **Tel** 011 56 2 2516236. **LC** AP63; .E575. **DD** 056/.1.

PL/0137-3080
ESTUDIOS LATINOAMERICANOS / POLSKA AKADEMIA NAUK, INSTYTUT HISTORII. **Added/Corp** Instytut Historii (Polska Akademia Nauk). (1972)-. Spanish (French and Portuguese). sa. Unam Fac Ciencias Politicas, Edif C, 2 Ciudad Univ Serv Pub, 04510 Mexico DF Mexico. **Tel** 5 6656211. **LC** F1401; .E83. **DD** 980.
Ind/Abst HAPI Hisp. Am. Period. Index (19??-).

BL
ESTUDO GERAL. V. 1- 1973-. Portuguese. Faculade de Ciencias e Letras de Avare, Funda Cao Regional Education de Avare, Caixa Postal 124, C E P San Paulo Brazil. **LC** AS80.F26; E83. **DD** 056/.1.

BL
FATOS & I.I. FOTOS. Vol. 1 (1961)-. Periodical. Portuguese. wk. $76.00. Bloch Editoras SA, Rua do Russell 766 804, 22210 Rio de Janeiro Brazil. **Tel** 011 51 21 2652012, 011 51 21 2850033.

AG
GENTE (BUENOS AIRES, ARGENTINA). (GENTE.). (19??)-. Periodical. Spanish. wk. Interamerican Network, PO Box 364, Scarsdale NY 10583. **Tel** (914)793-9764, **FAX** (914)337-1273. **LC** AP63; .G47. **DD** 056/.1. **Continues** Gente y la Actualidad.

US/0270-8558
HISPANIC AMERICAN PERIODICALS INDEX (LOS ANGELES, CALIF.). See General Interest-Abstracting, Bibliographies and Statistics.

AG
HISTONIUM EN SU NUEVA DIMENSION. **VFOAT** Historium Nueva Dimension. Vol. 34, No. 399 (Aug. 1972)-. Periodical. Spanish. mo. $3.00 single issue. Historium, Parana 464, Buenos Aires Argentina. **LC** AP63; .H57. **Continues** Historium.

US/0273-530X
IMPACTO. (IMPACTO : THE LATIN NEWS.). (19??)-. Periodical. Spanish (English). wk. $20.00. Impacto Latin News, 853 Broadway Avenue, Suite 811, New York NY 10003. **Tel** (212)505-0288.

GW/0937-7794
LANDERBERICHT. GUATEMALA / [STATISTISCHES BUNDESAMT]. **Added/Corp** Germany (West). Statistisches Bundesamt. **VFOAT** Guatemala. (1989)-. German (table of contents in English). W Kohlhammer Verlag GmbH, Postfach 800430, D 70549 Stuttgart Germany. **Tel** 011 49 711 78631, **FAX** 011 49 711 7863263, telex 7-255820. **LC** HA811; .S72. **Continues** Statistik des Auslandes. Landerbericht. Guatemala, 0931-5799.

GW/0937-7948
LANDERBERICHT. PARAGUAY / [STATISTISCHES BUNDESAMT]. **Added/Corp** Germany (West). Statistisches Bundesamt.

General Interest —General Interest-South America

(1989)-. German (table of contents in English). Metzler Poeschel Verlag Veroeffen, Statist Bundesamt Kernerstr 43, D 70182 Stuttgart Germany. **Tel** 011 49 7071 935350. **LC** HA1045; .G453a. **Continues** Statistik des Auslandes. Landerbericht. Paraguay, 0179-8243.

GW
LANDERBERICHTE. CHILE. Main/Corp
Germany (West). Statistisches Bundesamt. (19??)-. German. W Kohlhammer Verlag GmbH, Postfach 800430, D 70549 Stuttgart Germany. **Tel** 011 49 711 78631, FAX 011 49 711 7863263, telex 7-255820. **LC** HA1004; .G44.

UK/0264-2867
LATIN AMERICAN SPECIAL REPORTS.
Added/Corp Latin American Newsletters Ltd. **VFOAT** Latin America Special Report; Special Report. (July 1986)-. Periodical. English. bm. $260.00 US; £200.00 other. Lettres UK Ltd, 61 Old Street, London EC1V 9HX England. **Tel** 011 44 71 251-0012, FAX 011 44 71 253-8193. **Continues** Special Reports (Latin American Newsletters Ltd.).

UK
LATIN AMERICAN STUDIES IN THE UNIVERSITIES AND POLYTECHNICS OF THE UNITED KINGDOM. (1967)-. Directory. ir (3 or 4 yearly). £4.50. Institute of Latin American Studies, 31 Tavistock Square, London WC1H 9HA England. **Tel** 071 3871 5671, FAX 071 385 5024. **ED** A. Bell. **Circ**: 500.

BL
LEGENDA. Periodical. Portuguese. Faculdade de Educacao Ciencias e Letras Norte Dame, rua Barao da Torre 308 - Ipanema, Rio de Janeiro Brazil. **LC** AP66; .L38.

CL
LETTER FROM CHILE, A. Added/Corp
Instituto de Estudios Generales. (Dec. 1976)-. English. mo. 10.00Chil$. Instituto de Estudios Generales, Las Bellatas 270, Department 704, Santiago, Chile. **ED** Berta Correa S. **LC** F3100; .L48. **DD** 983/.005. **Circ**: 12,000 (ctrl).
Desc: Provides objective on-the-spot information and comments on developments in Chile.

PE
LIMA TIMES. No. 1 (Jan. 1975)-. Periodical. English. wk. $95.00. Andean Air Mail Peruvuan Times, Apartado Postal 531, Lima 100 Peru. **Tel** 011 51 14 469120, FAX 011 51 14 467888. **ED** Eleanor Griffis Zuniga. **Bk Rev**. **Ad Acc. Circ**: 6,000. **Supersedes in part** Peruvian Times; Andean Times, 0376-5628.
Desc: Politics, economy, business, travel and exploration, general news of English.

VE
LIVING IN VENEZUELA. VFOAT Vivir en Venezuela. English (Spanish). an. Bs1000.00 Venezuela; $30.00 US. Venezuelan-American Chamber of Commerce and Industry, 2 Avenida Campo Alegre Credival 10, Caracas 1010-A Venezuela. **Tel** 011 58 2 2630833, telex 23627 UACCI UC. **ED** Michael E Heggie. **Ad Acc. Circ**: 3,500. **Continues** VenAmCham's Executive Newcomers Guide, Welcome to Venezuela.
Desc: Contains pages of practical information on life in documentation, schools, housing, domestic help, community groups, culture, entertainment and scores of other subjects.

PE
MARGENES. Added/Corp Casa de Estudios del Socialismo Sur. (Mar. 1987)-. Periodical. Spanish. sa (2 issues). $40.00 institutions; $30.00 individuals. Sur Casa Estudios Socialismo, Apartado 14 0098, Lima 14 Peru. **Tel** 011 51 14 724224. **Circ**: 1,000 (ctrl).

PE
MARKA, ACTUALIDAD Y ANALISIS. Vol. 1, No. 1 (May 1, 1975)-. Spanish. $25.00. Editoria y Distribuidora Runamarka, Av Garcilaso de la Vega, Lima 1082 Peru. **LC** AP63; .M245. **DD** 056.1.

MX
MEYIBO. Began in 1979. Periodical. Spanish. ir. UNAM - Universidad Nacional Autonoma de Mexico / Historia, Instituto de Investigaciones Historicas Unam, Torre 1 de Humanidades, Piso 7 / 7th Floor, Ciudad Universitaria, 04510 Mexico DF Mexico. **Tel** 011 52 5 5505215 Ext 3396. **LC** F1246; .M67. **DD** 972/.2.
Ind/Abst Anthropol. Lit.

AG/0029-571X
NUESTRA HISTORIA. [Nuestra hist.].
Added/Corp Centro de Estudios de Historia Argentina. Fundacion Nuestra Historia. No. 1 (1968)-. Spanish. sa. **LC** F2801; .N78. **DD** 982/.005.
Ind/Abst Am. Hist. Life (1968-1974); HAPI Hisp. Am. Period. Index (19??-).

CK
NUEVA FRONTERA. Vol. 1, No. 1 (Oct. 12, 1974)-. Periodical. Spanish. Fifty-two times a year. $60.00 Columbia; $105.00 US & Canada; $111.00 Latin America; $107.00 others. Nueva Frontera, Carrera 7A No 17-02/Piso 5, Apartado 3137IA, Bogota Colombia. **Tel** 011 57 1 2444389. **LC** AP63; .N76. **DD** 056/.1. Index available. cum. index.

AG
OBSERVADOR (BUENOS AIRES, ARGENTINA), EL. (EL OBSERVADOR.). Vol. 1 No. 1 (Dec. 2 1983)-. Periodical. Spanish. wk. Sarmiento, 1113-20 Piso, CP 1041 Buenos Aires Argentina.

PE/0030-1280
OIGA. (1962)-. Periodical. Spanish. wk. $150.00. Oiga, Arda Salaverry 674, Lima 27 Peru. **Tel** 475851. **LC** AP63; .O39.

●AG
PANORAMA. Vol. 1, No. 1 (May 1992)-. Periodical. Spanish. mo. $6.00 per issue. Grupo Editorial Brasil - Argentina S.A., Avda. Cordoba 1345, Piso 12 (12th Floor), 1055 Buenos Aires, C.F. Argentina. **Tel** 42-3275, FAX 054-1-41-8835. **ED** Enrique Szewach.

BL
PERFIL DO MARANHAO. Portuguese. Avenida Mal Castelo Branco, 605 Sala 017, Edif Cidade de Sao Luis San Francisco, Sao Luis Maranhao Brazil.

AG/0326-3061
PUNTO DE VISTA. [Punto vista]. (1978)-. Periodical. Spanish. tq (Apr., July, Nov.). $50.00. Punto de Vista / Beatriz Sarlo, Casilla de Correo 39, Sucursal 49, Buenos Aires, Argentina. **Tel** 011 54 1 8218773. **ED** Beatriz Sarlo. **Bk Rev**, (Qty: 3). **Ad Acc. Circ**: 3,000.

CK
QUIRAMA. V. 1- 1973-. Spanish. an. $8.00 US. Instituto de Integracion Cultural, Apartado Aereo 3180 Conmutador 319166, Medellin Colombia. **Tel** 2513672. **LC** AS82.I56; A27. **DD** 056/.1. cum. index. **Circ**: 1,000.
Desc: This institution employs foreign editorial services.

BL
REPORTER TRES. Yearly V. 1- May 1978-. Periodical. Portuguese. 360. Editora Tres, Rua William Speers, No 1000, 10 Andar, CEP 05065 Sao Paulo Brazil. **LC** AP66; .R44.

BL/0302-0959
REVISTA DA FACULDADE SALESIANA. (REVISTA.). [Rev. Fac. Salesiana]. **Main/Corp** Faculdade Salesiana. Periodical. Portuguese. sa $18.00. Faculdade Salesiana, rua Dom Bosco 284, Lorena Brazil. **LC** F2501; .F33A. **DD** 918.1/03/605. **Continues** Folhas Pedagogicas.

AG
REVISTA DE LA UNIVERSIDAD NACIONAL DEL CENTRO DE LA PROVINCIA DE BUENOS AIRES.
Main/Corp Universidad Nacional del Centro de la Provincia de Buenos Aires. V. 1- Jan./April 1977-. Spanish (summaries and/or abstracts in English, French, German and Italian). $15.00. Universidad Nacional del Centro de la Provincia de Buenos Aires, Gral Pinto 399 Tandil Pcia, Buenos Aires Argentina. **LC** AS78.U54; A4.

BL
REVISTA DO BRASIL (RIO DE JANEIRO, BRAZIL : 1984). (REVISTA DO BRASIL.). Yearly V. 1, No. 1-. Periodical. Portuguese. Revista do Brasil, Travessa Euricles de Matos 17, Rio de Janeiro Brazil. **LC** F2510; .R44. **DD** 981/.005.

BL/0101-4366
REVISTA DO INSTITUTO HISTORICO E GEOGRAFICO BRASILEIRO. [Rev. Inst. Hist. Geogr. Bras.]. Vol. 172 (1937)-. Periodical. Portuguese. Four times a year. $50.00. Instituto Historico Geographic, AV Augusto Severo 8, 2000 Rio de Janeiro Brazil. **Tel** 011 55 21 2321312. **Continues** Revista do Instituto Historico e Geographico Brasileiro (1912).
Ind/Abst Am. Hist. Life (1955-); HAPI Hisp. Am. Period. Index.

BL
REVISTA GUIA REX. Yearly V. 1 (1973)-. Portuguese. Cr$15.00. Rua Dep Soares Filho 137, Tijuca ZC 11, Rio de Janeiro Brazil. **LC** F2651.N5; R48. **UDC** 918.1.

CK/0120-3088
REVISTA JAVERIANA (BOGOTA).
(REVISTA JAVERIANA.). [Rev. javer.]. **Added/Corp** Jesuits. Provincia Colombiana. Vol. 87, No. 434 (May. 1977)-. Periodical. Spanish. Ten times a year (Jan./Feb. & Nov./Dec. issues combined) $50.00 (one year); $95.00 (two years). Revista Javeriana, Carrera 23 #39-69, Apartado Aerei 24773, Bogota Colombia. **Tel** 11 57 1 2699209. **ED** Javier Sanin. Each issue contains an index to its own contents (no volume index)--loose. **Bk Rev**, (Qty: 10/yr). **Ad Acc**, **Adv Mgr**: Estela de Alaran. **Prev. Rev. Circ**: 15,000. **Continues** Javeriana, 0120-3088.
Desc: Publishes articles of general interest on Colombia on politics, history, philosophy, religion, economy and other current topics; always presented in an analytical mode.
Ind/Abst Am. Hist. Life (1977-).

VE
REVISTA M. Spanish. Four times a year. Free. Corimon, Apartado Postal 3654, Caracas Venezuela. **Tel** (02)239-9133, FAX (02)239-0002, telex 25218. **LC** AP63; .R6668. **Circ**: 7,000 (ctrl).
Desc: Publishes articles of general subjects, mainly concerning Venezuela.
Ind/Abst Peace Res. Abstr. J. (1971-1976).

US/0749-9728
RMCLAS REVIEW. (RMCLAS REVIEW / ROCKY MOUNTAIN COUNCIL ON LATIN AMERICAN STUDIES.). [RMCLAS rev.]. **VAT** Rocky Mountain Council on Latin American Studies Review. Periodical. English (Spanish). be. $2.00. Center for Latin American Studies, PO Box 3JBR, New Mexico State University, Las Cruces NM 88003. **Tel** (505)646-3524. **ED** Maria Telles-McGeagh. **DD** 980. Index available. **Bk Rev**. **Ad Acc. Circ**: 300 (ctrl). **Continues** RMCLAS Newsletter.
Desc: Newsletter with information of interest to members.

CK
SEMANA (BOGOTA, COLOMBIA : 1982). (SEMANA.). **VFOAT** Revista Semana. (1982)-. Periodical. Spanish. wk. $200.00. Editorial Caribe SA, Calle 94 No. 21-28, 253459 Bogota, Colombia. **Tel** 218-08-28-218-06-91, FAX 218-32-33. **LC** AP63; .S45. **Continues** Semana (Bogota, Colombia : 1946).

MX
SEMANA LATINOAMERICANA. AGENCIA LATINOAMERICANA DE SERVICIOS. Added/Corp Agencia Latinoamericana de Servicios Especiales de Informacion (Mexico). (Sept. 22, 1986)-. Periodical. Spanish. wk. Latinoamericana De Servicios, Casilla De Correo 3808, Buenos Aires 1000 Argentina.

CK
SEMANARIO ALTERNATIVA. No. 31- April 28/May 5, 1975-. Spanish. $65.00. Carrera 16 No 38-14, Apartado Aereo 25496, Bogota SN Colombia. **LC** AP66; .A48. **Continues** Alternativa.

AG
SIETE DIAS (BUENOS AIRES, ARGENTINA : 1979). (SIETE DIAS.). (1979)-. Periodical. Spanish. wk. Editorial Abril SA, Avenida Leandro N Alem 896, 1001 Buenos Aires Argentina. **LC** AP63; .S497. **DD** 056/.1. **Continues** Siete Dias Ilustrados.

AG
SIETE DIAS ILUSTRADOS. (1???)-. Spanish. Fifty-two times a year. $113.00. Editorial Abril SA, Avenida Leandro N Alem 896, 1001 Buenos Aires Argentina.

MX
SINTESIS. (197?)-. Periodical. Spanish. Six times a year. Sintesis / Mexico, Apartado Postal 22 118, Mexico 22 DF Mexico.

UY
SOBRETODO. VFOAT Sobre Todo. Vol. 1, No. 1 (Aug. 1991)-. Periodical. Spanish. wk. 2000Uru$ per issue. Sobre Todo Srl, Colonia 1465, 11200 Montevideo Uruguay. **Tel** 48-89-30, FAX 48-03-04. **ED** Ope Pasquet. **LC** AP63; .S67. **DD** 056/.1.

AG
SOMOS (BUENOS AIRES, ARGENTINA).
Ceased. (SOMOS.). Vol. 1, No. 1 (Sept. 24, 1976)-(Dec. 1993). Periodical. Spanish. wk. Interamerican Network, PO Box 364, Scarsdale NY 10583. **Tel** (914)793-9764, FAX (914)337-1273. **LC** AP62; .S65. **DD** 056/.1. **Bk Rev**. **Ad Acc. Circ**: 180,000 (ctrl).
Desc: Covering politics, sciences and general information about important news around the world.

AG/0035-0478
SUR (BUENOS AIRES, ARGENTINA).
Ceased. (SUR.). [Sur]. (Summer 1931)-(Winter 1987). Periodical. Spanish. sa (2 issues). Fundacion Sur, Tucuman 677 Piso 3A, 1049 Buenos Aires Argentina. **LC** AP63; .S85. **DD** 056. cum. index.
Ind/Abst HAPI Hisp. Am. Period. Index; MLA Int. Bibl. Books Artic. Mod. Lang. Lit.

BL
TEMAS DE CIENCIAS HUMANAS. 1- 1977-. Periodical. Portuguese. Editorial Grijalbo, rua Sete de Abril, 264 - Subsolo B - Sala 5, Sao Paulo Brazil. **LC** AP66; .T45.

PE
TEXTUAL. Added/Corp Peru. Instituto Nacional de Cultura. (19??)-. Spanish. $5.00. Ancash 390, Lima Peru. **LC** AP63; .T45. **DD** 056/.1.
Ind/Abst HAPI Hisp. Am. Period. Index (19??-).

US/0040-7917
TIMES OF THE AMERICAS, THE. Ceased.
[Times Am.]. Began in (1966)-?. Periodical. English. bw. Times of the Americas, 910 17th Street NW/Suite 523, Washington DC 20006. **Tel** (202)293-2849, FAX (202)429-5570. **ED** Clarence W Moore. **DD** 980/.005. **Bk Rev**. **Ad Acc. Circ**: 2,500. available on microfilm and

microfiche from University Microfilms International (UMI). ***Continues*** *Times of Havana.*
Desc: The only English-language newspaper in the world dedicated exclusively to covering Latin America and Caribbean news.

CU/0041-8420
UNIVERSIDAD DE LA HABANA. [Univ. Habana]. **Main/Corp** Universidad de La Habana. (Jan./Feb. 1934)-. Spanish. bm. **LC** AP63; .U63. **NLM** W1 UN848S.
Ind/Abst MLA Int. Bibl. Books Artic. Mod. Lang. Lit.

SP
UNO (MADRID, SPAIN). ***Ceased.*** (UNO.). Periodical. Spanish. Uno de la Revista de America, Cl Angelita Cavero, 13 Postal, Madrid 28027 Spain. **Tel** 34 1 742 4748. **LC** F1401; .U68.

CL
VEA. (19??)-. Periodical. Spanish. wk. $334.29 the Americas; $414.29 other. Editorial Ercilla S A, Luis Thayer Ojeda 1626, Providencia Santiago Chile. **Tel** 011 56 2 2516236.

BL/0042-3165
VEJA. No. 352 (June 4,1975)-. Periodical. Portuguese. wk. $280.00. Editora Abril SA, Rua do Curtume 769 Lapa, 05066 900 Sao Paulo SP Brazil. **Tel** 011 55 11 8239222, 011 55 11 2623322, FAX 011 55 11 8643796. **LC** AP66; .V37. **DD** 056/.9. available on microfilm and microfiche from University Microfilms International (UMI). ***Continues*** *Veja e Leia.*
Ind/Abst PAIS Int. Print (19??-).

BL/0042-6873
VISAO. ***Suspended.*** (19??)-. Periodical. Portuguese. wk. $325.00. DCI Diario Comercio Industria, rua Alvaro de Carvalho 350, 01050 030 Sao Paula S P Brazil. **Tel** 011 55 11 256 5011. **ED** Henry Maksoud. **LC** AP66; .V58. **Bk Rev. Ad Acc. Circ:** 150,000 (ctrl).
Desc: Information and analysis magazine with an emphasis on politic and economic subjects.
Ind/Abst PAIS Int. Print (?-?).

VE
ZONA TORRIDA. No. 1-. Periodical. Spanish. Universidad de Carabobo, Calle 150 No 100-223, Apartado 1960, Valencia Venezuela. **LC** AP63; .Z58. **DD** 056/.1.

GEOGRAPHY

US/0275-3995
AAG NEWSLETTER. [AAG newsl.]. **Main/Corp** Association of American Geographers. **Added/Corp** Association of American Geographers. Newsletter. **VAT** Association of American Geographers Newsletter. Began publication in (1967)-. Newsletter. English. mo (except for July and September). Comes with membership - $217.00 (institution membership) US. Association of American Geographers, 1710 16th Street Northwest, Washington DC 20009-3198. **Tel** (202)234-1450, FAX (202)234-2744. **ED** Salvatore J Natoli, Kevin J Fitzpatrick. **Circ:** 5,000. available on microfilm from University Microfilms International (UMI).
Desc: Produced for the members of the Association of American Geographers.

BE
AARDRIJKSKUNDE, DE. Added/Corp Vereniging Leraars Aardrijkskunde. (1977)-. Periodical. Dutch (English and French). qt. 896F Belgium; 950F other. Vereniging Leraars Aardrijkskunde, Postbus 88, 2550 Kontich Belgium. **Tel** 011 32 16 286611. **ED** M. Antrop, D. Coolsaet, G. De Brabander, R. Goossens, E. Lammens, H Van Den Bossche. **LC** G1; .A228. Index available. **Bk Rev. Ad Acc. Circ:** 1,300 (ctrl).
Supersedes *Geo, Geographie, Ecologie, Environnement, Organisation de l'Espace; Aardrijkskunde.*

CN/0380-5301
ABBOTSFORD-CLEARBROOK DIRECTORY (BUSINESS EDITION). (ABBOTSFORD-CLEARBROOK DIRECTORY.). **VFOAT** Official City Directory of Abbotsford-Clearbrook. Began with 1970 issue. Directory. English. an. Henderson Directories, 34 West 2nd Avenue, Vancouver, British Columbia, V5Y 1B3 Canada. **DD** 917.11/33.

CN/0843-7815
ABOVE & BEYOND. [Above beyond]. **Added/Corp** First Air. **VFOAT** Above and Beyond. **VAT** Above and Beyond. Vol. 1, No. 1 (Winter 1989)-. Periodical. English (French; summaries and/or abstracts in Danish, Eskimo and French). Four times a year (Jan., Apr., July, Oct.). 14.00Can$ Canada; 17.00Can$ other. Above & Beyond Ltd., Box 2348, Yellow Knife Northwest Territories X1A 2P7 Canada. **Tel** (403)873-2299, FAX (403)873-2295. **ED** Jake Ootes. **DD** 917.19/03/06. **Bk Rev**, (Qty: 8). **Ad Acc, Adv Mgr:** Dennis Huntley, **Tel** (403)873-2296. **Circ:** 30,000 (ctrl).
Desc: The principal purpose is to promote the lifestyle, people in the communities and attraction of Canada's Arctic, Greenland, and Artic Quebec.
Ind/Abst Can. Period. Index (Winter 1990/1991-).

US/0197-1700
ABSTRACTS, ANNUAL MEETING - ASSOCIATION OF AMERICAN GEOGRAPHERS. Main/Corp Association of American Geographers. **VFOAT** Program Abstracts - Association of American Geographers; AAG Program Abstracts; Annual Meeting Abstracts - Association of American Geographers; Association of American Geographers Annual Meeting Abstracts. (1980)-. English. an. $3.00. Association of American Geographers, 1710 16th Street Northwest, Washington DC 20009-3198. **Tel** (202)234-1450, FAX (202)234-2744. **Ad Acc. Circ:** 2,500 (ctrl). ***Continues*** *Program Abstracts, Anniversary Meeting of the Association of American Geographers.*
Desc: Abstracts of annual meeting papers.

UK/0955-4270
ACIS : JOURNAL OF THE ASSOCIATION FOR CONTEMPORARY IBERIAN STUDIES. See Linguistics.

XO/0231-715X
ACTA FACULTATIS RERUM NATURALIUM UNIVERSITATIS COMENIANAE. [Acta Fac. Rerum Natur. Univ. Comen., Geogr.]. **VFOAT** Geographica. V. 15-. Czech (English). an. Slovenske Pedagogicke Nakladetelstvo, Sasinkova 5, 891 12 Bratislava, Slovakia. **LC** G1; .A24. **DD** 910/.5.
Ind/Abst Ecol. Abstr.; Geogr. Abstr. Phys. Geogr. (?-?); Geogr. Abstr. Human Geogr. (?-?); GeoRef; Meteorol. Geoastrophys. Abstr. (-199?); Plant Grow. Reg. Abstr.

PL/0065-1249
ACTA GEOGRAPHICA LODZIENSIA. [Acta geogr. Lodz.]. **Added/Corp** Odzkie Towarzystwo Naukowe. 16 (1963)-. Monographic series. Polish. ir. Price varies per colume. **(Subscription address:** ARS Polona, PO Box 1001, 00068 Warsaw Poland.**) CODEN** LTWMAS. ***Continues*** *Acta Geographica Lodziendzia.*
Ind/Abst GeoRef.

BE/0065-1257
ACTA GEOGRAPHICA LOVANIENSIA. [Acta geogr. lovan.]. **Added/Corp** Universite Catholique de Louvain (1835-1969). Institut de Geographie. Katholieke Universiteit te Leuven (1970-). Geografisch Instituut. **VFOAT** Acta Geographica Louvaniensia. Vol. 1 (1961)-. Monographic series. French (Dutch, Dutch and English). ir. Price varies per volume. Geografisch Institut Kul, W de Croylaan 42, B 3001 Heverlee Belgium. **Tel** 011 32 16 286611, FAX 011 32 16 220761. **LC** UNC. **CODEN** AGHLAA. Index available. **Circ:** 300 (ctrl).
Ind/Abst Ecol. Abstr. (?-?); Geogr. Abstr. Phys. Geogr.; Geogr. Abstr. Human Geogr. (?-?); GeoRef.

FR/0001-5687
ACTA GEOGRAPHICA (PARIS). (ACTA GEOGRAPHICA.). [Acta geogr.]. **Added/Corp** Societe de Geographie (France). (1947)-. Periodical. French. qt (4 issues). 285.00F. Societe de Geographie, 184 Boulevard Saint Germain, F-75006 Paris France. **Tel** 011 33 1 45485462. **LC** G1; .S553. **DD** 910/.5. **CODEN** ACGEAO. cum. index.
Ind/Abst Bibliogr. Carto.; Geogr. Abstr. Phys. Geogr. (?-?); Geogr. Abstr. Human Geogr.; GeoRef; Int. Dev. Abstr.; Middle East J.

CC/0375-5444
ACTA GEOGRAPHICA SINICA. (TI LI HSUEH PAO / CHUNG-KUO TI LI HSUEH HUI PIEN CHI.). [Acta Geogr. Sin.]. **Added/Corp** Chung-kuo ti li Hsueh hui. Chung-kuo ko Hsueh Yuan. Ti li Yen Chiu so. **VFOAT** Journal of the Geographical Society of China; Acta Geographica Sinica. (1934)-. Periodical. Chinese (English). bm. $89.40. Geographical Society of China, Science Press, 16 Donghuangchenggen North Street, Beijing 100707, People's Republic of China. **Tel** 011 86 1 4019821, FAX 011 86 4012180, telex 210147. **CODEN** TLHPAS. **Bk Rev. Ad Acc. Pr Rev. Circ:** 12,000. available on microfilm from University Microfilms International (UMI).
Desc: Contains theses, reports, experimental observations and reports, theories of geographical science and methodology.
Ind/Abst Ecol. Abstr.; Geogr. Abstr. Phys. Geogr.; Geogr. Abstr. Human Geogr.; GeoRef; Int. Dev. Abstr.

XR/0300-5402
ACTA UNIVERSITATIS CAROLINAE. GEOGRAPHICA. [Acta Univ. Carol., Geogr.]. **Main/Corp** Universita Karlova. Vol. 1 (1966)-. Periodical. Czech (English, French, German and Russian). ir. Price varies per volume. Carolinum Press, Ovochny TRH 5, 11636 Prague 1 Czech Republic. **Tel** 011 42 2 228441. **LC** G58; .P68. **DD** 910. **CODEN** AUCGBZ.
Ind/Abst Geogr. Abstr. Phys. Geogr. (?-?); Geogr. Abstr. Human Geogr.; GeoRef; Int. Dev. Abstr. (?-?).

PL
ACTA UNIVERSITATIS LODZIENSIS. FOLIA GEOGRAPHICA. VFOAT Folia Geographica. (1982)-. Monographic series. Polish (summaries and/or abstracts in English). Price varies per volume. **LC** G58; .A28. **DD** 910. ***Continues in part*** *Acta Universitatis Lodziensis. Seria I, Nauki Humanistyczno-Spoeczne.*
Ind/Abst Geogr. Abstr. Human Geogr.

US/0895-6235
AFRICAN-AMERICAN TRAVELER, THE. [Afr.-Am. travel.]. **VFOAT** African American Traveler. Began with Vol. 1, No. 1 (Spring 1987). Periodical. English. qt. $16.00. The Universal Black Writer, PO Box 5 Radio City Station, New York NY 10101. **Tel** (718)774-4379. **ED** Linda Cousins. **DD** 910. **Ad Acc. Circ:** 1,000 (ctrl).
Desc: Focuses primarily on Caribbean and African countries, giving information on black historical and cultural sites; also lists black-owned hotels, restaurants, and other travel-related businesses.

SP/0213-2966
AL-GEZIRA. See History(General).

US/0361-1353
ALASKA GEOGRAPHIC. [Alsk. geogr.]. **Added/Corp** Alaska Geographic Society. Vol. 1 (1972)-. Periodical. English. qt. $39.00 (paperback), $75.00 (hardback) US; $49.00 (paperback), $85.00 (hardback) other. Alaska Geographic, PO Box 93370, Anchorage AK 99509. **Tel** (907)562-0164, FAX (907)562-0479. **ED** Penny Rennick. **LC** F901; .A266. **DD** 917.98/04/505. Index available. cum. index. **Circ:** 7,000 (ctrl).
Desc: Deals with geography and natural history in Alaska and Northwestern Canada. Full color and many issues have pull-out maps.
Ind/Abst ASTIS Curr. Aware. Bull. (1978-); Access (1976-?); ASTIS Bibliogr. (1978-); GeoRef.

GW
ALLGEMEINE VERMESSUNGS-NACHRICHTEN (1985). (ALLGEMEINE VERMESSUNGS-NACHRICHTEN : AVN.). **VFOAT** AVN. (1985)-. Periodical. English. Ten times a year (except combined Aug.-Sept. and Nov.-Dec.). DM166.00 Germany; DM198.60 other. Herbert Wichmann Verlag GmbH, Postfach 4320, D 76028 Karlsruhe Germany. **Tel** 011 49 721 912-2025. cum. index. ***Continues*** *Allgemeine Vermessungs-Nachrichten. International Supplement.*
Ind/Abst Geogr. Abstr. Phys. Geogr.; Geogr. Abstr. Human Geogr.; GeoRef.

FR
ALSACE LE PAYS. French. da. Soc Alsacienne de Publications, BP 1489, 68072 Mulhouse Cedex France. **Tel** 011 33 89 327010.

RM
ANALELE UNIVERSITATII DIN CRAIOVA: SERIA ISTORIE, GEOGRAFIE, FILOLOGIE. See History(General)-History of Europe.

CR/0567-6509
ANALES / ACADEMIA DE GEOGRAFIA E HISTORIA DE COSTA RICA. See History(General)-History of North, South, and Central America.

MX
ANALES DE GEOGRAFIA. Yearly Vol. 1-1975-. Periodical. Spanish. an. UNAM - Universidad Nacional Autonoma de Mexico / Filosofia, Facultad de Filosofia y Letras, Apartado 70 447, 04510 Mexico DF Mexico. **Tel** 011 52 5 5505215. **LC** G1; .A47. **DD** 910/.5.

SP/0211-9803
ANALES DE GEOGRAFIA DE LA UNIVERSIDAD COMPLUTENSE / SECCION DE GEOGRAFIA. Added/Corp Universidad Complutense de Madrid. Seccion de Geografia. (1981)-. Periodical. Spanish. an. $37.00. Editorial Complutense, Donoso Cortes 65 1RA Planta, 28003 Madrid Spain. **Tel** 011 34 1 3946372. **LC** G1; .A473. **DD** 910/.5.

FR/0003-4010
ANNALES DE GEOGRAPHIE. [Ann. geogr.]. **Added/Corp** Societe de Geographie (France). Vol. 1, No. 1 (Oct. 1891)-. Periodical. French. Six times a year. $140.00 (institution), $110.00 (individual). Librairie Armand Colin, BP 22, 41354 Vineuil Cedex France. **Tel** 011 33 54 438994. **(Subscription address:** 7A Boulevard de Perolles, CH-1701 Fribourg Switzerland**) ED** Armand Colin. **CODEN** ANGEAX. cum. index. **Bk Rev. Circ:** 2,500.
Desc: General geography, geomorphology, climatology, urban policy, agriculture, population, land use, ecology, pollution and hydrology.
Ind/Abst Am. Hist. Life (1971-); Bibliogr. Carto.; Curr. Geogr. Publ. (199?-); Geogr. Abstr. Phys. Geogr. (?-?); Geogr. Abstr. Human Geogr. (?-?); GeoRef; Int. Bibliogr. Sociol.; Int. Dev. Abstr. (?-?); Leis. Recreat. Tour. Abstr.; PAIS Int. Print; Point Repere (1983-); Rural Dev. Abstr.; World Agric. Econ.

LE/0250-7668
ANNALES DE GEOGRAPHIE (BEIRUT, LEBANON). (ANNALES DE GEOGRAPHIE.). Began with V. 1 in 1980. French. an. Universite Saint-Joseph, Faculty Lettres Science Humaines, BP 175, 208 Gemayze Lebanon.

IV/0302-0924
ANNALES DE L'UNIVERSITE D'ABIDJAN. SERIE G : GEOGRAPHIE. [Ann. Univ. Abidjan. Ser. G]. **Main/Corp** Abidjan, Ivory Coast. Universite. V. 1-. Monographic series. French. ir. Price varies per volume. Universite Abidjan, Abidjan Ivory Coast West Africa. **Tel** 44 56 49, telex 26138 RECTU-CI. **LC** G58; .A23A. **DD** 916.66/8/005. **CODEN** AASGDB. **Bk Rev. Circ:** 250. available on microfiche.
Desc: Annals of the University of Abidjan.
Ind/Abst GeoRef.

HU/0524-8965
ANNALES UNIVERSITATIS SCIENTIARUM BUDAPESTINENSIS DE ROLANDO EOTVOS NOMINATAE. SECTIO GEOGRAPHICA. [Ann. Univ. Sci. Budap. Rolando Eotvos nom. Sect. geogr.]. **Main/Corp** Eotvos Lorand Tudomanyegyetem. Vol. 1; 1965-. Periodical. English (German and Russian). an. Free. Eotvos Lorand Tudomanyegyetem, Bolcseszettudomanyi Kar, Pesti BUL, H-1052 Budapest Hungary. **Tel** 36 11 180 966. **ED** Z Antal, B Sarfalvi and A Szekely. **LC** G1; .B8. ctrl circ.
Ind/Abst Am. Hist. Life (1976-); Geogr. Abstr. Phys. Geogr. (?-?).

US/0004-5608
ANNALS OF THE ASSOCIATION OF AMERICAN GEOGRAPHERS. [Ann. Assoc. Am. Geogr.]. **Main/Corp** Association of American Geographers. Vol. 1 (1911)-. Academic Scholarly Publication. English. Four times a year. $112.00 US; $129.00 other. Association of American Geographers, 1710 16th Street Northwest, Washington DC 20009-3198. **Tel** (202)234-1450, FAX (202)234-2744. **(Subscription address:** Blackwell Publishers / Cambridge, MA, 238 Main Street, Cambridge MA 02142.**) ED** Susan Hanson. **LC** G3; .A7. **DD** 910/.5. **CODEN** AAAGAK. **[CCC].** cum. index. **Bk Rev. Ad Acc. Pr Rev. Circ:** 7,500. available on microfilm and microfiche from University Microfilms International (UMI). Documents available from The Genuine Article, UMI Article Clearinghouse.
Desc: Publishes major scholarly articles and commentaries.
Ind/Abst ASTIS Curr. Aware. Bull. (1978-); Abstr. Anthropol.; Acad. Abstr. Full Text Elite (July 1990-); Acad. Abstr. (July 1990-); Acad. Ind. [Computer File] (1987-); Acad. Search (July 1990-); AGRICOLA [Select. Cov.]; Am. Hist. Life (1963-); Am. Bibliogr. Slavic East Europ. Stud.; Arts Humanit. Citation Index [Select. Cov.]; ASTIS Bibliogr. (1978-); Bibliogr. Carto.; Curr. Contents Soc. Behav. Sci.; Ecol. Abstr. (?-?); Expand. Acad. Index (1987-); Field Crop Abstr.; Geogr. Abstr. Phys. Geogr.; Geogr. Abstr. Human Geogr.; GeoRef; Grasslands For. Abstr.; INFO-SOUTH Abstr.; Int. Bibliogr. Sociol.; Int. Dev. Abstr.; Int. Polit. Sci. Abstr.; J. Plan. Lit.; Leis. Recreat. Tour. Abstr.; Mag. Search; Middle East Abstr. Index; Newsp. Period. Abstr. (1991-); Res. Alert [Full Cov.]; Rural Dev. Abstr.; Soc. Sci. Source (Jul. 1990-); Soc. Sci. Cit. Index [Full Cov.]; Soc. Sci. Index; Soc. Sci. Index Fulltext (Sept. 1988-) [Full Txt.]; Soils Fert.; Middle East J. (?-?); World Agric. Econ.

II/0970-972X
ANNALS OF THE NATIONAL ASSOCIATION OF GEOGRAPHERS, INDIA. **Added/Corp** National Association of Geographers, India. Vol. 1, No. 1 (June 1981)-. Periodical. English. sa. **LC** G1; .A62. **DD** 910/5.
Ind/Abst Agrofor. Abstr.; For. Abstr.; World Agric. Econ.

CN/0711-4982
ANNUAIRE DE HULL, GATINEAU, AYLMER, QUEBEC. (HULL, GATINEAU, AYLMER, QUEBEC, CITY DIRECTORY.). [Annu. Hull, Gatineau, Aylmer, Que.]. **VFOAT** Annuaire de Hull, Gatineau, Aylmer, Quebec; Annuaire de Hull, Gatineau, Aylmer. (1980)-. English (French). ir. $91.50 (latest edition). R. L. Polk / Hull Gatineau Aylmer City Directory, c/o Dr. Peter Lombard, 220 Bartley Drive, Toronto Ontario M4A 2N4 Canada. **Tel** (416)751-2751. **DD** 917.14/221/0025. ***Continues*** *Polk's Hull City Directory, 0316-7992.*

FR
ANNUAIRE DES GEOGRAPHES DE LA FRANCE ET DE L'AFRIQUE FRANCOPHONE. **VFOAT** Annuaire des Geographes. 1.- Ed.; 1969-. French. Geographers de la France, 1914 Hamilton St, Regina Saskatchewan S4P 4V4 Canada. **LC** G64; .A55. **DD** 910/.25/17541.

CN/0316-8271
ANNUAIRE POLK DE BAIE-COMEAU. **VFOAT** Polk's Baie-Comeau City Directory; Annuaire de Baie Comeau et Hauterive City Directory. Began publication in 1968?. Periodical. English (French). R.L. Polk & Company Ltd., 2485 Ste-Anne Boulevard, Ste-Anne Quebec G1J 1Y3 Canada. **DD** 917.14/17.

CN/0317-1515
ANNUAIRE POLK DE GRANBY QUEBEC. (POLK'S GRANBY, QUEBEC, CITY DIRECTORY.). **VFOAT** Granby City Directory. Began publication with the 1958/59 issue. Directory. English (French). an. $70.00 per no. R.L. Polk & Company Ltd., 2485 Ste-Anne Boulevard, Ste-Anne Quebec G1J 1Y3 Canada. **DD** 917.14/63. ***Supersedes*** *Annuaire Marcotte de Granby, 0317-1531.*

CN/0316-7992
ANNUAIRE POLK DE HULL. (POLK'S HULL CITY DIRECTORY.). **VFOAT** Annuaire de Hull. 1959-. Directory. Multiple languages (English and French). an. R.L. Polk & Company Ltd., 2485 Ste-Anne Boulevard, Ste-Anne Quebec G1J 1Y3 Canada. **DD** 917.14/221. ***Continues*** *Marcotte's Hull City Directory.*

CN/0380-3961
ANNUAIRE POLK DE RIMOUSKI ET MONT-JOLI QUEBEC. (POLK'S RIMOUSKI AND MONT-JOLI, QUEBEC, CITY DIRECTORY.). **VFOAT** Annuaire de Rimouski et Mount-Joli City Directory. 1971-. Directory. Multiple languages (English and French). qt. R.L. Polk & Company Ltd., 2485 Ste-Anne Boulevard, Ste-Anne Quebec G1J 1Y3 Canada. **DD** 917.14/771. ***Continues*** *Polk's Rimouski, Quebec, City Directory, 0380-397X.*

CN/0380-3775
ANNUAIRE POLK DE SEPT-ILES. (POLK'S SEPT-ILES CITY DIRECTORY.). **VFOAT** Annuaire de Sept-Iles City Directory. 1961-. Directory. English (French). an. R.L. Polk & Company Ltd., 2485 Ste-Anne Boulevard, Ste-Anne Quebec G1J 1Y3 Canada. **DD** 917.14/17.

CN/0700-7272
ANNUAIRE POLK DE SOREL TRACY ET ST-JOSEPH. **VFOAT** Polk's Sorel Tracy and St-Joseph City Directory. V. 1- 1965-. French (English). an. R.L. Polk & Company Ltd., 2485 Ste-Anne Boulevard, Ste-Anne Quebec G1J 1Y3 Canada.

AT/1037-4973
ANNUAL REPORT - AUSTRALIAN LAND INFORMATION COUNCIL. ***Title Change.*** (1988)-(1994). Corporate Report. English. an. Australia New Zealand Land Information Council, PO Box 2, Belconnen ACT 2616 Australia. **Tel** 011 61 6 2014299, FAX 011 61 6 2014366. ***Continues*** *Report - Australian Land Information Council, 1032-3058.* ***Continued by*** *Australia New Zealand Land Infomation Council, 1037-9630.*
Desc: Annual report of activities.
Ind/Abst AESIS Q.

II
ANNUAL REPORT - INDIA. NATIONAL REMOTE SENSING AGENCY. **Main/Corp** India. National Remote Sensing Agency. English. an. Free. National Remote Sensing Agency, 4 Sarda Patel Road, Secunderabad-500003, Andhra Pradesh India. **LC** G70.5.I4; I53A. **DD** 354.540087/78.

TZ/0494-6367
ANNUAL REPORT OF THE AIR SURVEY DIVISION. (ANNUAL REPORT OF THE AIR SURVEY DIVISION (TANGANYIKA).). **Main/Corp** Tanganyika. Air Survey Division. (1961)-. Periodical. English. Ministry of Lands/Forests & Wildlife, Dar Es Salaam Tanzania. **LC** TA593; .T35. **DD** 333. ***Continues in part*** *Tanganyika. Ministry of Lands, Surveys and Water. Report of the Land, Survey, Air Survey, Registrar-General's and Valuation Divisions, 0494-6634.*

TZ/0494-6588
ANNUAL REPORT OF THE LAND DIVISION. (ANNUAL REPORT OF THE LAND DIVISION (TANZANIA).). **Main/Corp** Tanganyika. Land Division. (1961)-. Periodical. English. Survey Division / Tanzania, Ministry of Lands, Forests and Wildlife, Dar Es Salaam Tanzania. **DD** 333. ***Continues in part*** *Tanganyika. Ministry of Lands, Surveys and Water. Report of the Land, Survey, Air Survey, Registrar-General's and Valuation Divisions, 0494-6634.*

TZ
ANNUAL REPORT OF THE SURVEY DIVISION (TANZANIA). **Main/Corp** Tanzania. Survey Division. (1964)-. English. an. Survey Division / Tanzania, Ministry of Lands, Forests and Wildlife, Dar Es Salaam Tanzania. **LC** WMLC L 83/4002. ***Continues*** *Annual Report of the Survey Division.*

US/0149-0184
ANNUAL REPORT ON THE GEOTHERMAL RESOURCES ACT OF 1975 (TEXAS). [Annu. rep. Geotherm. resour. act 1975]. **Main/Corp** Texas. General Land Office. **VAT** Annual Report on the Geothermal Resources Act of Nineteen Hundred and Seventy-Five. English. an. General Land Office & Texas Historical Commission, Garry Mauro Commissioner, Austin TX 78701. **LC** GB1199.7.T4; T48A. **DD** 333.8.

IT
ANNUARIO DEL VENETO. Italian. an. Marsilio Editori, Marittima Fabbricato 205, 30135 Venice Italy. **Tel** 011 39 41 5227822. **LC** DG975.V38; A57. **DD** 914.5/3/0025.

US/0003-5335
ANTARCTIC JOURNAL OF THE UNITED STATES. [Antarc. j. U.S.]. **Added/Corp** National Science Foundation (U.S.). Division of Polar Programs. National Science Foundation (U.S.). Office of Polar Programs. (Jan./Feb. 1966)-. Government Publication. English. qt (plus annual review issue in October). $14.00 domestic; $21.00 other. Superintendent of Documents, US Government Printing Office, Washington DC 20402. **Tel** (202)275-3328, FAX (202)786-2377. **LC** G845; .A56. **DD** 998/.9. **CODEN** AJUSAF. available on microfilm and microfiche from University Microfilms International (UMI). Documents available from BIOSIS Document Express. ***Absorbed*** *Antarctic Report; Bulletin of the U.S. Antarctic Projects Officer, 0503-5392.*
Desc: Provides a common outlet for all information on the National United States Antarctic Program to a broad audience of participants and interested observers. Includes scientific and logistic reports on the United States program in Antarctica, accounts of collaborative activities undertaken in the United States, with authoritative discussions on Antarctic matters of current and historical significance.
Ind/Abst Aquat. Sci. Fish. Abstr. (Computer File); Biol. Abstr.; Ecol. Abstr. (?-?); Energy Res. Abstr.; Geogr. Abstr. Phys. Geogr. (?-?); Geol. Abstr.; GeoRef; INIS Atomindex [Micro.]; Meteorol. Geoastrophys. Abstr.; Ocean. Abstr.; Life Sci. Collect.; Soils Fert.

AG/0302-5691
ANTARTIDA (BUENOS AIRES). (ANTARTIDA.). [Antartida]. **Added/Corp** Argentina. Direccion Nacional del Antartico. No. 1, (Dec. 1971)-. Academic Scholarly Publication. Spanish. an. Direccion Nacional del Antartico, Instituto Antartico Argentina, Cerrito 1248, 1010 Buenos Aires Argentina. **Tel** 812 0071 72, FAX 54 1 812 2039. **LC** G845; .A62. **CODEN** ANTDAR. Index available. cum. index. **Circ:** 350 (ctrl).
Ind/Abst Life Sci. Collect.

UK/0066-4812
ANTIPODE. [Antipode]. Vol. 1 (Aug. 1969)-. Periodical. English. Four times a year. $118.00 North America; $147.00 other. Blackwell Publishers, 238 Main Street, Cambridge MA 02142. **Tel** (617)547-7110, (800)835-6770, FAX (617)547-0789. **ED** Joe Doherty and Eric Sheppard. **LC** G1; .A67. **[CCC].** available on microfilm and microfiche from University Microfilms International (UMI). Documents available from The Genuine Article.
Desc: Publishes articles on the radical analysis of spatial and environmental problems.
Ind/Abst Altern. Press Index; Am. Hist. Life (1986-); Curr. Contents Soc. Behav. Sci.; Geogr. Abstr. Human Geogr.; Int. Bibliogr. Sociol.; Int. Dev. Abstr.; Left Index; Linguist. Lang. Behav. Abstr.; Res. Alert [Full Cov.]; Sage Public Adm. Abstr.; Sage Urban Stud. Abstr; Soc. Plann. Policy Dev. Abstr.; Soc. Sci. Cit. Index [Full Cov.]; Sociol. Abstr.

US/0749-4971
ANTIQUE MAPS, SEA CHARTS, CITY VIEWS, CELESTIAL CHARTS & BATTLE PLANS. ***Title Change.*** [Antiq. maps, sea charts, city views, celes. charts battle plans]. **VFOAT** Antique Map Prices. (1983)-(1992). English. an. Jon Kimmel Rosenthal, PO Box 12, Amherst MA 01004. **Tel** (413)256-8900. **ED** David C. Jolly. **LC** GA197.3; .A57. **DD** 912/.075. **Bk Rev.** ***Continued by*** *Antique map Price Record & Handbook for ..., 1070-8421.*
Desc: Record of the antique map market, with a worldwide dealer directory, recommended references, book reviews, glossary of terms, dictionary of mapmakers, etc.

MX/0570-4073
ANUARIO DE GEOGRAFIA. **Added/Corp** Mexico (City). Universidad Nacional. Facultad de Filosofia y Letras. No. 1 (1961)-. Spanish. an. UNAM - Universidad Nacional Autonoma de Mexico / Historia, Instituto de Investigaciones Historicas Unam, Torre 1 de Humanidades, Piso 7 / 7th Floor, Ciudad Universitaria, 04510 Mexico DF Mexico. **Tel** 011 52 5 5505215 Ext 3396. **LC** G1; .A68.
Ind/Abst HAPI Hisp. Am. Period. Index (-19??).

GW/0173-7619
APPLIED GEOGRAPHY AND DEVELOPMENT. [Appl. geogr. dev.]. Vol. 15-. English. be. Institute for Scientific Co-Operation, Landhausstrasse 18, W-7400 Tubingen Germany. **Tel** 07071/5066. **LC** T1; .A653. **DD** 304.2/05. ***Continues*** *Applied Sciences and Development, 0340-1863.*
Ind/Abst Ecol. Abstr.; Geogr. Abstr. Phys. Geogr. (?-?); Geogr. Abstr. Human Geogr. (?-?); GeoRef; Int. Dev. Abstr. (?-?); Irr. Drain. Abstr.; Maize Abstr.; PAIS Int. Print; Rice Abstr.; Rural Dev. Abstr.; Soils Fert.; Soyabean Abstr.; World Agric. Econ.

UK/0143-6228
APPLIED GEOGRAPHY (SEVENOAKS). (APPLIED GEOGRAPHY.). [Appl. geogr.]. **Added/Corp** Butterworths (Firm). Vol. 1, No. 1 (Jan. 1981)-. Periodical. English. qt. $261.00 The Americas; £175.00 other. Butterworth Heinemann Publishers, Linacre House, Jordan Hill, Oxford OX2 8DP England. **Tel** 011 44 865 310366. **(Subscription address:** Elsevier Science Ltd. Oxford Fulfillment Centre, PO Box 800, Kidlington, Oxford OX5 1DX United Kingdom.) **ED** J. Hansom (editor's address: Department of Geography, University of Sheffield, Sheffield, United Kingdom). **LC** G1; .A69. **DD** 910/.5. **[CCC].** Index available. **Ad Acc. Pr Rev.** available on microfilm and microfiche from University Microfilms International (UMI). Documents available from The Genuine Article, Documents on Demand.
Desc: Aim is to draw together results from current studies across the field of resource sciences, and to provide a forum for these studies at a time when the pressure upon the world's resources demands a more rational and farsighted approach to resource management and allocation. The scope encompasses aspects of both human and physical geography as well as parts of agriculture, ecology, planning and politics.
Ind/Abst Curr. Contents Soc. Behav. Sci.; Ecol. Abstr.; Energy Inf. Abstr.; Environ. Abstr.; Environ. Period. Bibliogr. (?-?); Field Crop Abstr.; For. Abstr.; Geogr. Abstr. Phys. Geogr. (?-?); Geogr. Abstr. Human Geogr.; GeoRef; Grasslands For. Abstr.; Int. Dev. Abstr.; J. Plan. Lit.; Leis. Recreat. Tour. Abstr.; Maize Abstr.; Protozoolog. Abstr.; Res. Alert [Full Cov.]; Rev. Med. Vet. Entomol.; Sage Urban Stud. Abstr; Soc. Sci. Cit. Index [Full Cov.]; Soils Fert.

GW
ARBEITEN AUS DER KOMMISSION FUER GEOMORPHOLOGIE DER BAYERISCHEN AKADEMIE DER WISSENSCHAFTEN. Main/Corp Bayerische Akademie der Wissenschaften. Kommission fuer Geomorphologie. (19??)-. Monographic series. German. ir. Price varies per volume. Selbstverlag des Instituts fuer Geographie der Universitat Wurzburg, Wurzburg Am Hubland, Wurzburg 87074 Germany. **Tel** 0931 888 5555, FAX 0931 888 5544. **ED** D. Bohn, H. Hagedorn, H. Jager and H.G. Wagner. **LC** G58; .W8 subser. Index available. cum. index. **Pr Rev. Acid Free.**

US/1064-6108
ARC NEWS (REDLANDS, CALIF.). See Computers-Software.

IO
ARCHIPEL. Vol. 1- 1971-. Periodical. English (French and Indonesian). sa. $9.00. PO Box 215, Bandung Indonesia. **LC** DS501; .A64. **DD** 915.98/03/05.
Ind/Abst Am. Hist. Life (1990-); Int. Polit. Sci. Abstr.

GW/0003-9462
ARCHIV FUER VATERLANDISCHE GESCHICHTE UND TOPOGRAPHIE. HRSG. VON DEM GESCHICHTVEREINE FUER KARNTEN. UNTER VERANTWORTLICHER REDACTION DES VEREINS-AUSSCHUSSES. See History(General)-History of Europe.

CN/0004-0843
ARCTIC. [Arctic]. **Added/Corp** Arctic Institute of North America. Vol. 1, (Spring 1948)-. Academic Scholarly Publication. English. Four times a year (Mar., June, Sept., Dec.). $85.00. The Arctic Institute of North America, University of Calgary, 2500 University Drive Northwest, Calgary Alberta T2N 1N4 Canada. **Tel** (403)220-7515, FAX (403)282-4609. **ED** Dr. Karen McCullough. **LC** G600; .A695. **DD** 919.8. **CODEN** ATICAB. Index available. cum. index. **Bk Rev**, (Qty: 30/yr). **Pr Rev. Acid Free. Circ:** 2,300 (ctrl). available on microfilm and microfiche from University Microfilms International (UMI). Documents available from The Genuine Article, BIOSIS Document Express, Petroleum Abstracts Document Delivery Service, CASDDS, Documents on Demand.
Desc: This multidisciplinary journal deals with circumpolar research. Original scholarly papers in the life, physical, and social sciences, humanities, engineering, and technology are included, as are letters to the editor and profiles of significant northern people, places, or events. The primary purpose is the international dissemination of research results and current thought relevant to the northern areas of the world.
Ind/Abst ASTIS Curr. Aware. Bull. (1978-); AGRICOLA; Am. Hist. Life (1963-); Am. Bibliogr. Slavic East Europ. Stud.; Anthropol. Lit.; AQUAREF; Aquat. Sci. Fish. Abstr. (Computer File); Arts Humanit. Citation Index [Select. Cov.]; ASTIS Bibliogr. (1978-); Biol. Abstr.; Can. Environ.; Can. Index (?-?); Can. Period. Index; Chem. Abstr. (1948-1982); Curr. Aware. Biol. Sci., CABS; Curr. Contents, Agric. Biol. Environ. Sci.; Curr. Geogr. Publ. (199?-); Curr. Ref. Fish Res.; Ecol. Abstr.; Ecology Abstr.; EMBASE; Energy Inf. Abstr.; Environ. Abstr.; Field Crop Abstr.; Fish Rev.; For. Prod. Abstr.; For. Abstr.; Geogr. Abstr. Phys. Geogr.; Geogr. Abstr. Human Geogr.; Geol. Abstr.; GeoRef; Grasslands For. Abstr.; Int. Dev. Abstr.; Key Word Index Wildl. Res.; Leis. Recreat. Tour. Abstr.; Meteorol. Geoastrophys. Abstr.; Nucl. Sci. Abstr.; Nutr. Abstr. Rev., Ser. B, Live Feeds and Feed.; Life Sci. Collect.; Pet. Abstr.; Ref. Sources; Res. Alert [Full Cov.]; Sci. Cit. Index; SCISEARCH; Soc. Sci. Cit. Index [Select. Cov.]; Soils Fert.; Wildl. Rev.

US/0004-0851
ARCTIC AND ALPINE RESEARCH. [Arct. alp. res.]. Vol. 1 (Winter 1969)-. Periodical. English. qt. $75.00 US; $80.00 other. University of Colorado / Boulder, Colorado, Campus Box 450, Boulder CO 80309. **Tel** (303)492-3765, FAX (303)492-6388. **ED** Kathleen A. Salzberg. **LC** GB395. **DD** 500.1/0998. **CODEN** ATLPAV. **[CCC].** Index available. cum. index. **Bk Rev. Ad Acc. Pr Rev. Acid Free. Circ:** 950 (ctrl). available on microfilm and microfiche from University Microfilms International (UMI). Documents available from The Genuine Article, BIOSIS Document Express, CASDDS.
Desc: Publishes original research papers, contributions, symposia proceedings, correspondence dealing with any scientific or cultural aspect of arctic and alpine environments and related topics on subarctic, subalpine, antarctic, subantarctic, and paleoenvironments.
Ind/Abst ASTIS Curr. Aware. Bull. (1978-); Abstr. Anthropol.; AGRICOLA [Select. Cov.]; AQUAREF; ASTIS Bibliogr. (1978-); Biol. Abstr.; Chem. Abstr. (1969-1982); Curr. Aware. Biol. Sci., CABS; Curr. Contents, Agric. Biol. Environ. Sci.; Ecol. Abstr.; Ecology Abstr.; Environ. Period. Bibliogr.; Field Crop Abstr.; Fish Rev.; For. Prod. Abstr.; For. Abstr.; Geogr. Abstr. Phys. Geogr.; Geogr. Abstr. Human Geogr.; Geol. Abstr.; GeoRef; Grasslands For. Abstr.; INIS Atomindex [Micro.]; Int. Aerosp. Abstr.; Irr. Drain. Abstr.; Key Word Index Wildl. Res.; Meteorol. Geoastrophys. Abstr.; Life Sci. Collect.; Plant Breed. Abstr.; Pollut. Abstr. Indexes; Ref. Z.; Res. Alert [Full Cov.]; Sci. Cit. Index; SCISEARCH; Soils Fert.; Wildl. Rev.

NO
ARCTIC NEWS RECORD. Vol. 1 (1982)-. English. ir (6 regular issues and 1 or 2 supplements). Kr710.00. Arctic News-Record, PO Box 124 Sentrum, N 0102 Oslo Norway. **Tel** 011 47 2 385539. **LC** G600; .A74. **DD** 998.

US/1045-4764
ARCTIC RESEARCH OF THE UNITED STATES. [Arct. res. U. S.]. **Added/Corp** Interagency Arctic Research Policy Committee (U.S.). Vol. 1 (Fall 1987)-. Periodical. English. sa. IARPC Staff, Division of Polar Programs, Room 620, National Science Foundation, Washington DC 20550. **LC** G615; .A74. **DD** 508.311/3.
Ind/Abst Ecol. Abstr.; Geogr. Abstr. Phys. Geogr.; GeoRef.

UK/0004-0894
AREA (LONDON 1969). (AREA.). [Area]. **Added/Corp** Institute of British Geographers. No. 1 (1969)-. Periodical. English. qt. £48.00. Institute British Geographers, 1 Kensington Gore, London SW7 2AR England. **Tel** 011 44 71 584 6371, FAX 071 581 9918. **LC** G7; .A742. **DD** 910/.005. **CODEN** AREAB6. **Ad Acc. Circ:** 3,000. Documents available from The Genuine Article. ***Supersedes*** *Institute of British Geographers. Newsletter.*
Desc: Developments in British geography; material relevant to an international audience.
Ind/Abst Energy Res. Abstr. (July 1982-); Geogr. Abstr. Human Geogr.; GeoRef; Int. Bibliogr. Sociol.; Int. Dev. Abstr. (?-?); Leis. Recreat. Tour. Abstr.; Res. Alert [Full Cov.]; Rural Dev. Abstr.; Soc. Sci. Cit. Index [Full Cov.]; World Agric. Econ.

CN/0228-6637
ARPENTEURS & GEOMETRES. (ARPENTEURS & GEOMETRES : REVUE BIMESTRIELLE.). [Arpent. geom.]. **Added/Corp** Ordre des Arpenteurs-Geometres du Quebec. **VFOAT** Arpenteur & Geometre. Vol. 7, No. 1 (Dec. 1979)-. Periodical. French. Five times a year. 40.00Can$. Ordre des Arpenteurs-Geometres, 2954 Boul Laurier Bur 350, Ste Foy Quebec G1V 4T2 Canada. **Tel** (418)656-0730. **DD** 526.9/09714. ***Continues*** *Revue de l'Ordre des Arpenteurs-Geometres du Quebec, 0709-9002.*
Ind/Abst Point Repere (1983-).

NO
ARSBERETNING / NORGES GEOGRAFISKE OPPMALING. Main/Corp Norges Geografiske Oppmaling. 1980-. Norwegian (summaries and/or abstracts in English). an. Norges Geografiske, Oppmaling Monserudveien, 3500 Hnefoss Norway. **LC** GA982; .A3. ***Continues*** *Beretning Om Norges Geografiske Oppmaalings Virksomhet I Tidsrummet.*

HK
ASIAN GEOGRAPHER. Added/Corp Hong Kong Geographical Association. Vol. 1, No. 1, (1982)-. Periodical. English. Twice a year (May, Nov.). $55.00 (institutions), $30.00 (individuals). Hong Kong Geographical Association, Department of Geography & Geology, HK Bapt CLG 224 Waterloo Road, Kowloon Hong Kong. **ED** Lenng Yee and Wong Kwan Ylu. **Circ:** 400. ***Continues*** *Bulletin (Hong Kong Geographical Association).*
Ind/Abst Geogr. Abstr. Phys. Geogr. (?-?); Geogr. Abstr. Human Geogr. (?-?).

IT/0004-6736
ATLANTE. ***Ceased.*** [Atlante]. (1960)-(19??). Italian. Istituto Geografico de Agostini, via G da Verrazano 15, 28100 Novara Italy. **LC** G1; .A775. **DD** 910/.5.
Ind/Abst GeoRef.

GL
ATUAGAGDLIUTIT. VFOAT Grnlandsposten. Periodical. Multiple languages (Danish and Eskimo). 220.00. Atauagagdliutit, Postbox 39 3900, Godhab Greenland. **LC** G725; .A8. ***Continues*** *Atuagagdliutit, Nalinginarnik Tusaruminasassunik Univkat.*

AT/0004-9182
AUSTRALIAN GEOGRAPHER. (THE AUSTRALIAN GEOGRAPHER.). [Aust. geogr.]. **Added/Corp** Geographical Society of New South Wales. Vol. 1 (Aug. 1928)-. Periodical. English. sa (May and Nov.). 35.00Aus$ Australia; 45.00Aus$ other. Geography Teachers Association of New South Wales Inc., PO Box 602, Gladesville 2111 NSW Australia. **Tel** 011 61 2 817 3647, FAX 011 61 2 817 4592. **ED** D. Rich. **CODEN** AUSGBD. Index available. **Bk Rev. Ad Acc. Pr Rev. Circ:** 1,300. Documents available from The Genuine Article, BIOSIS Document Express.
Desc: Presents papers on the geography of Australia and its hemisphere, and people-environment interactions.
Ind/Abst APAIS, Aust. Public Aff. Inf. Ser. (1967-); Asia.-Pac. Econ. Lit.; Biol. Abstr.; Curr. Contents Soc. Behav. Sci. (1988-); Ecol. Abstr.; Field Crop Abstr.; Geogr. Abstr. Phys. Geogr.; Geogr. Abstr. Human Geogr.; Geol. Abstr.; GeoRef; Grasslands For. Abstr.; Int. Bibliogr. Sociol.; Int. Dev. Abstr. (?-?); Irr. Drain. Abstr.; Leis. Recreat. Tour. Abstr.; Pig News Inf.; Res. Alert [Full Cov.]; Soc. Sci. Cit. Index (1988-) [Full Cov.]; Soils Fert.; World Agric. Econ.

AT/0816-1658
AUSTRALIAN GEOGRAPHIC : THE JOURNAL OF THE AUSTRALIAN GEOGRAPHIC SOCIETY. Added/Corp Australian Geographic Society. No. 1 (Jan./Mar. 1986)-. Periodical. English. Four times a year (Jan., Apr., July, Oct.). 37.60Aus$ Australia; 49.60Aus$ other. Australian Geographic, PO Box 321, Terrey Hills 2084 Australia. **Tel** 011 61 2 450 2300, FAX 011 61 2 450 2990, telex 176203. **LC** DU105.2; .A943. **DD** 994.06/3/05. **CODEN** AUGEEI.

AT/0004-9190
AUSTRALIAN GEOGRAPHICAL STUDIES. [Aust. geogr. stud.]. **Added/Corp** Institute of Australian Geographers. Vol. 1 (Apr. 1963)-. Periodical. English. sa (Apr. & Oct.). 62.00Aus$. University of New South Wales / Department of History, Australian Defence Force Academy, CAMBELL, ACT 2601 Australia. **Tel** (06)2688875, FAX (06)2688879. **(Subscription address:** University College of New South Wales, Department of Geography and Oceanography, Australian Defense Force, Cambell ACT 2601 Australia.) **ED** J. Walmsley and J. Hobbs. **LC** DU97; .A943. **CODEN** AUGSBN. **Bk Rev. Ad Acc. Circ:** 1,000.
Desc: Subjects covered include physical and human geography, environmental management, urban and regional planning and development studies. Both theoretical and empirical studies included.
Ind/Abst APAIS, Aust. Public Aff. Inf. Ser. (1963-19??); Bibliogr. Carto.; Curr. Aware. Biol. Sci., CABS; Curr. Geogr. Publ. (199?-); Ecol. Abstr. (?-?); Geogr. Abstr. Phys. Geogr. (?-?); Geogr. Abstr. Human Geogr. (1963-?); GeoRef; Int. Bibliogr. Sociol.; Int. Dev. Abstr. (?-?); Leis. Recreat. Tour. Abstr.; Rural Dev. Abstr.; World Agric. Econ.

AT/0158-149X
AUSTRALIAN HISTORICAL GEOGRAPHY : A BULLETIN OF THE REFERENCE SECTION OF AUSTRALIA 1788-1988 : A BICENTENNIAL HISTORY. Bulletin. English. University of New South Wales / Department of History, c/o Ms. Meagher, PO Box 1, Kensington New South Wales 2033 Australia. **LC** DU96.5; .A96. **DD** 911/.94.

AT/0159-8910
AUSTRALIAN JOURNAL OF GEODESY, PHOTOGRAMMETRY, AND SURVEYING. See Engineering-Civil Engineering.

CN/0068-1571
B.C. GEOGRAPHICAL SERIES. [B.C. geogr. ser.]. **Added/Corp** Canadian Association of Geography. Western Division. University of British Columbia. Dept. of Geography. No. 1 (1965)-. Periodical. English. ir. University of British Columbia Department of Geography, 217 1984 West Mall, Vancouver BC V6T 1Z2 Canada. **Tel** (604)822-2663. **ED** W. G. Hardwick. **CODEN** BCGSDC. **Circ:** 500.
Desc: Various geographical topics.
Ind/Abst GeoRef.

UK/0966-9035
BAOBAB ARID LANDS INFORMATION NETWORK. [Baobab Arid Lands Inf. Netw.]. **Added/Corp** Arid Lands Information Network. **VFOAT** Baobab (Reseau d'Information des Terres Arides).

Geography

(19??)-. English. £20.00 UK and EEC countries; £27.00 Far East; £25.00 other. Oxfam Publications, 274 Banbury Road, Oxford OX2 7DZ England. **Tel** 011 41 865 313196, FAX 011 41 865 313117. Index available. cum. index. **Circ:** 1,000.

SZ/0067-4486
BASLER BEITRAEGE ZUR GEOGRAPHIE. [Basler Beitr. Geogr.]. No. 7 (1968)-. Monographic series. German. ir. Price varies per volume. Wepf and Company, Eisengasse 5, CH-4001 Basel Switzerland. **Tel** 011/41/61 25 75 74, FAX 25 35 97, telex 965532. **CODEN** BBGEBT. **Continues** Basler Beitrage zur Geographie und Ethnologie. Geographische Reihe.
Ind/Abst GeoRef.

GW/0933-9418
BAYREUTHER GEOWISSENSCHAFTLICHE ARBEITEN. (1980)-. Monographic series. German. ir. Price varies per volume. **UDC** 55.
Ind/Abst Ecol. Abstr.; Geogr. Abstr. Human Geogr.

US
BELLEVUE KIRKLAND REDMOND (KING COUNTY WASH.) POLK DIRECTORY. Directory. English. an. $113.50. Polk & Company, 400 East Linwood Boulevard, Kansas City MO 04109. **Ad Acc**. **Continues** Bellevue, Kirkland, Redmond (King County, Wash.) City Directory.

GW/0523-0160
BERLINER GEOGRAPHISCHE ABHANDLUNGEN. [Berl. Geogr. Abh.]. (1964)-. Periodical. German. **DD** 910. **CODEN** BRGABR. **Supersedes** Geographisches Institut. Abhandlungen.
Ind/Abst Geogr. Abstr. Phys. Geogr.; GeoRef.

GW/0341-8537
BERLINER GEOGRAPHISCHE STUDIEN. [Berl. geogr. Stud.]. (1977)-. Monographic series. German. Price varies per volume.
Ind/Abst Int. Dev. Abstr.

US/1043-6553
BEST OF CHINA WITH HONG KONG AND MACAU, THE. See Travel and Tourism.

US/1043-6545
BEST OF HONG KONG, THE. See Travel and Tourism.

US/1043-6537
BEST OF MACAU, THE. See Travel and Tourism.

SP/0214-4441
BIBLIOGRAFIA ESPANOLA. SUPLEMENTO DE CARTOGRAFIA. (1987)-. Periodical. Spanish. an. 1000ptas Spain; 2000ptas other. Bibliolibria Biblioteca Nacion, Paseo de Recoletos 20, 28001 Madrid Spain. **Tel** 011 34 1 5778707. **(Subscription address:** Distribuiodora de Publicaciones del Ministerio de Cultura, C Fernando el Catolico 77, 28015 Madrid Spain) **LC** Z6027.S72; B53; GA1001. **Circ:** 1,000.

US/0197-5889
BIBLIOGRAPHIC GUIDE TO MAPS AND ATLASES. See Geography-Abstracting, Bibliographies and Statistics.

●FR
BIBLIOGRAPHIE NATIONALE FRANCAISE. ATLAS, CARTES ET PLANS : BIBLIOGRAPHIE ETABLIE PAR LA BIBLIOTHEQUE NATIONALE. See Geography-Abstracting, Bibliographies and Statistics.

BL/0100-3526
BIOGEOGRAFIA. [Biogeografia]. No. 1 (1969)-. Periodical. Portuguese. Instituto de Geografia, USP Cidade Universitaria, Edificio de Geografia e Historia, Caixa Postal 20.715, Sao Paulo SP 05508 Brazil. **LC** QH117; .B48.
Ind/Abst GeoRef.

GW/0523-798X
BOCHUMER GEOGRAPHISCHE ARBEITEN. [Bochum. geogr. Arb.]. **Added/Corp** Ruhr-Universitat Bochum. Geographisches Institut. Vol. 1 (1965)-. Monographic series. German. Price varie per volume. **DD** 914.3. **CODEN** BGHAAM.
Ind/Abst Geogr. Abstr. Human Geogr.

US
BOISE (ADA COUNTY, IDAHO) CITY DIRECTORY. **Added/Corp** Polk (R.L.) and Company, Inc. **VFOAT** Boise City Directory; Polk's Boise City Directory. (19??)-. English. an. $109.72. R. L. Polk & Company, 1155 Brewery Park Boulevard, Detroit MI 48207. **Tel** (313)393-0880. **Bk Rev**. **Ad Acc**.
Desc: Cross reference city directory.

BL
BOLETIM DE GEOGRAFIA TEORETICA. **Added/Corp** Associacao de Geografia Teoretica. (19??)-. Bulletin. Portuguese (English; summaries and/or abstracts in English, Spanish and French). sa. $50.00. Associacao de Geografia Teoretica, Caixa Postal 178, Rio Claro 13500 Brazil. **Tel** 011 55 0195 34-0122, FAX 011 55 0195 24-9622. **ED** Lucia Helena de Oliveira Gerardi. **LC** G1; .B52. **Bk Rev**. **Circ:** 1,200 (ctrl)
Desc: Methods and technics in geographical research, case studies in human, economic and physical geography, notes and book reviews.
Ind/Abst Geogr. Abstr. Phys. Geogr.; Geogr. Abstr. Human Geogr.

BL/0006-6079
BOLETIM PAULISTA DE GEOGRAFIA. [Bol. Paul. geogr.]. No. 1 (March 1949)-. Bulletin. Portuguese (summaries and/or abstracts in English and French). ir. Cr$30.00 (individuals), Cr$45.00 (institutions). Associacao dos Geografos Brasileiros, Secao Sao Paulo, Caixa Postal 64 525, 05 497 Sao Paulo SP Brasil. **Tel** (011)210-2122. **LC** G1; .B55. **CODEN** BLPGAD. Index available. cum. index. **Bk Rev**. **Circ:** 3,000 (ctrl). available on diskette. **Continues** Boletim da Associacao dos Geografos Brasileiros.
Desc: Scholarly articles from Brazilian geographers, especially of the state of Sao Paulo. Reports of meetings of the Association of Brazilian Geographers and of its Sao Paulo regional section. Includes notes and reviews.
Ind/Abst Geogr. Abstr. Human Geogr. (?-?); GeoRef; Int. Dev. Abstr. (?-?).

SP
BOLETIN DE LA REAL SOCIEDAD GEOGRAFICA. **Main/Corp** Sociedad Geografica, Madrid. V. 1- 1876-. Spanish. an. 2,000ptas. Boletin Real Sociedad, Valverde 24, Madrid 13 Spain. **Tel** 2323831. cum. index.

CK/0037-8577
BOLETIN DE LA SOCIEDAD GEOGRAFICA DE COLOMBIA. [Bol. Soc. Geogr. Colomb.]. **Main/Corp** Sociedad Geografica de Colombia. (1934)-. Periodical. qt. **LC** G5; .S615. **DD** 910./5. **CODEN** BSGCA5. cum. index.
Ind/Abst Am. Hist. Life (1955-1970).

PE/0037-8585
BOLETIN DE LA SOCIEDAD GEOGRAFICA DE LIMA. [Bol. soc. geogr. Lima]. **Main/Corp** Sociedad Geografica de Lima. **Added/Corp** Sociedad Geografica de Lima. Memoria. Vol. 1 April (1891)-. Spanish. $3.00. Sociedad Geografica Lima, Jiren Pune 450, Lima Peru. **Tel** 273723. **ED** Santiago E Antunez de Mayolo. **LC** G5; .S67. **DD** 910/.5. **CODEN** SGLBAS. Index available. cum. index. **Bk Rev**.
Ind/Abst Am. Hist. Life (1955-1959); GeoRef.

BO/0254-7449
BOLETIN DE LA SOCIEDAD GEOGRAFICA Y DE HISTORIA "SUCRE". (19??)-. Periodical. Spanish. ir.
Ind/Abst Am. Hist. Life (1954-1955).

IT/0037-8763
BOLLETTINO DELLA SOCIETA GEOGRAFICA ITALIANA. [Boll. soc. geogr. ital.]. **Added/Corp** Societa Geografica Italiana. (1868)-. Periodical. Italian (English). Four times a year. L50000. Bardi Editore, Salita de Crescenzi 16, 00186 Rome Italy. **Tel** 011 39 6 4393111. **LC** G17; .S667. cum. index.
Ind/Abst Geogr. Abstr. Phys. Geogr.; Geogr. Abstr. Human Geogr.; GeoRef.

IT/0037-8755
BOLLETTINO DELLA SOCIETA GEOGRAFICA ITALIANA. [Boll. Soc. Geogr. Ital.]. (1868)-. Periodical. Italian. qt. L100000.00 Italy; L150000.00 other. Societa Geografica Italiana, Via della Navicella 12, 00184 Rome Italy. **Tel** 011 39 6 7008279, FAX 011 39 6 7004677. **CODEN** BSGIABSGIA. cum. index. **Bk Rev**. **Ad Acc**. **Pr Rev**. **Circ:** 2,000.

IT/0392-4424
BOLLETTINO DELLA SOCIETA ITALIANA DI TOPOGRAFIA E FOTOGRAMMETRIA. **Added/Corp** Societa Italiana di Topografia e Fotogrammetria. (1975)-. Periodical. Italian. ir. L120000.00 Italy; L150000.00 other. SIFET, Piazzale R Morandi 2, 20121 Milan Italy. **Tel** 011 39 2 23996500, FAX 011 39 2 23992206. **LC** TA590; .S7. **DD** 526.9/8. Index available. **Bk Rev**. **Ad Acc**. ctrl circ. available on microfiche. **Continues** Bollettino Della Societa Italiana di Fotogrammetria e Topografia.

GW/0373-0468
BONNER GEOGRAPHISCHE ABHANDLUNGEN. [Bonn. geogr. Abh.]. **Added/Corp** Universitat Bonn. Geographisches Institut. Issue 1 (1947)-. Monographic series. German. ir. Price varies per volume. Ferdinand Dummler Verlag, Postfach 1480, D 53004 Bonn Germany. **Tel** 011 49 228 223031. **CODEN** BGGAAH. **Supersedes** Beitrage zur Landeskunde der Rheinlande.
Ind/Abst Bibliogr. Carto.; Ecol. Abstr. (?-?); For. Prod. Abstr.; For. Abstr.; Geogr. Abstr. Phys. Geogr. (?-?); Geogr. Abstr. Human Geogr.; GeoRef; Int. Dev. Abstr.; Leis. Recreat. Tour. Abstr.; Rural Dev. Abstr.; Soils Fert.; World Agric. Econ.

JA
BOSAI KAGAKU GIJUTSU. Began with Sept. 1963 issue. Japanese. Kagaku Gijutsucho Kokuritsu Bosai Kagaku Gijutsu Senta, (National Research Center for Disaster Prevention, Scinece & Technology Agency), 3-1, Tennodai, Tsukubashi, Ibarakiken 305 Japan. **LC** GB5008.J3; B67.

SA
BOTSWANA DIRECTORY. Iss. 1 (1977)-. Directory. English. $5.00. B & T Directories Ltd. / South Africa, PO Box 202, Francistown South Africa. **LC** DT790; .B66. **DD** 916.81/1/0025.

CN/1182-8994
BOWER'S DIRECTORY FOR GREATER METROPOLITAN TORONTO. [Bower's dir. gt. Metrop. Tor.]. (1988)-. Directory. English. Metropolitan Cross-Reference Directory, 2 Ripley Avenue, Toronto Ontario M6S 3N9 Canada. **DD** 917.13/5/0025.
Continues Bower's Directory for Metropolitan Toronto., 0836-7531.

US/1056-8050
BPRC TECHNICAL REPORT. [BPRC tech. rep.]. **Added/Corp** Byrd Polar Research Center. **VAT** Byrd Polar Research Center Technical Report. (1991)-. Periodical. English. Free. Byrd Polar Research Center, Ohio State University, 125 South Oval Mall, Columbus OH 43210. **Tel** (614)292-6531, FAX (614)292-4697, telex 4945696 OSUPOLAR. **DD** 919.

GW/0524-2444
BRAUNSCHWEIGER GEOGRAPHISCHE STUDIEN. No. 1 (1964)-. Monographic series. German. ir. Price varies per volume. Verlag Erich Goltze KG, Stresemannstrasse 28, D 37079 Goettingen Germany. **Tel** 011 49 551 63078.

UK
BRAY'S THE DEVON REFERENCE INFORMATION & GAZETTEER. **VFOAT** Devon Reference Information & Gazetteer. 1st Ed.- 1984-. English. £7.50. EXE Publishing Company, 85 Higher Woolbrook Park, Sidmouth Exeter England. **LC** DA670.D49; B73. **DD** 914.23/5/0025.

CN
BRIEFING / NORTH-SOUTH INSTITUTE. **Added/Corp** North-South Institute (Ottawa, Ont.). (198?)-. Periodical. English (French). ir. 150.00Can$. North-South Institute, 55 Murray Street, Suite 200, Ottawa Ontario K1N 5M3 Canada. **Tel** (613)236-3535, FAX (613)237-7435, telex 053-3300.
Ind/Abst Int. Dev. Abstr.

RM
BULETIN DE INFORMARE STIINTIFICA. GEOLOGIE, GEOGRAFIE / ACADEMIA REPUBLICII POPULARE ROMINE, CENTRUL DE DOCUMENTARE STIINTIFICA. See Earth Sciences-Geology.

BE/0037-8925
BULLETIN DE LA SOCIETE BELGE D'ETUDES GEOGRAPHIQUES. [Bull. Soc. belg. etud. geogr.]. **Main/Corp** Societe Belge d'Etudes Geographiques. **Added/Corp** Societe Belge d'Etudes Geographiques. Tijdschrift van de Belgische Vereniging voor Aardrijkskundige studies. **VFOAT** Tijdschrift van de Belgische Vereniging voor Aardrijkskundige Studies. Vol. 1 (May 1931)-. Bulletin. Dutch (French, English and German). Twice a year. 800F Belgium; 1000F other. Bulletin de la Societe Belge Etudes Geographiques, W de Croylaan 42, B 3001 Heverlee Belgium. **Tel** 011 32 16 286211 ext. 2440, FAX 011 32 16 200720. **LC** G19; .S45. **CODEN** BSEGA7. Index available. cum. index (Every ten years). **Bk Rev**. **Circ:** 600 (ctrl).
Desc: Covers geographical studies.
Ind/Abst GeoRef; Leis. Recreat. Tour. Abstr.; Rural Dev. Abstr.; Soils Fert.; World Agric. Econ.

FR
BULLETIN DE LA SOCIETE DE GEOGRAPHIE DE MARSEILLE. **Main/Corp** Societe de Geographie de Marseille. (19??)-. Bulletin. French. **Continues** Bulletin de Geographie d'Aix-Marseille.
Ind/Abst Geogr. Abstr. Human Geogr.; Int. Dev. Abstr.

SZ/0373-3076
BULLETIN DE LA SOCIETE NEUCHATELOISE DE GEOGRAPHIE. [Bull. Soc. neuchatel. geogr.]. **Main/Corp** Societe Neuchateloise de Geographie. V. 1-49, 1885-1943; New Ser., No. 1- 1944-. Bulletin. French. an. 20.00F. Bibliotheque Publique University, 3 Place Numa Droz, CH-2000 Neuchatel Switzerland. **Tel** 038 25 13 58. **CODEN** BSNGAI. cum. index.
Ind/Abst Anthropol. Lit.; GeoRef.

FR/0004-5322
BULLETIN DE L'ASSOCIATION DE GEOGRAPHES FRANCAIS. [Bull. Assoc. geogr. fr.]. **Added/Corp** Association de Geographes Francais. Centre National de la Recherche Scientifique (France). No. 1 (March 1924)-. Bulletin. French (summaries and/or abstracts in English). Five times a year (Jan., Apr., July, Sept., Dec.). $88.00. Association de Geographes Francais, 191 rue Saint-Jacques, F-75005 Paris France. **Tel** 011 33 1 432-90147. **LC** G11; .A8. **DD** 910.62. **CODEN** BAGFAO. Index available in last issue of volume--attached. cum. index. **Circ:** 950 (ctrl).
Ind/Abst Bibliogr. Carto.; Geogr. Abstr. Phys. Geogr.; Geogr. Abstr. Human Geogr.; GeoRef; Int. Dev. Abstr.; Leis. Recreat. Tour. Abstr.; Rural Dev. Abstr.; World Agric. Econ.

CN/0710-0868
BULLETIN DE RECHERCHE - UNIVERSITE DE SHERBROOKE. DEPARTEMENT DE GEOGRAPHIE. (BULLETIN DE RECHERCHE.). [Bull. rech. - Univ. Sherbrooke, Dep. geogr.]. **Added/Corp** Universite de Sherbrooke. Departement de Geographie. (1972)-. French. ir. Price varies. Universite de Sherbrooke / Droit - Law, Faculte de Droit - Faculty of Law, 2500 Boul de Universite, Sherbrooke Quebec J1K 2R1 Canada. **Tel** (819)821-7508. **(Subscription address:** Service a la Recherche, A4 161 FLSH University of Sherbrooke, Sherbrooke Quebec J1K 2R1 Canada.**)** **DD** 307.7/6/05. Index available. **Circ:** 150.
Ind/Abst Geogr. Abstr. Phys. Geogr.; Geol. Abstr.

FR
BULLETIN D'INFORMATION (INSTITUT GEOGRAPHIQUE NATIONAL (FRANCE) : 1981). (BULLETIN D'INFORMATION.). 1981-. Bulletin. French. sa. **LC** GA66.F8; F73A. **DD** 354.440085/5. ***Continues** Bulletin d'Information de l'Institut Geographique National (Paris, France : 1980).*

US/0019-2031
BULLETIN - ILLINOIS GEOGRAPHICAL SOCIETY. [Bull. Ill. Geogr. Soc.]. **Main/Corp** Illinois Geographical Society. **VFOAT** Bulletin of the Illinois Geographical Society. (April 1955)-. Bulletin. English. sa. $20.00. Illinois Geographical Society, 440 Geography, Illinois State University, Normal IL 61790. **Tel** (309)438-7649. **ED** Jill Freund Thomas. **DD** 910. **CODEN** BIGSAH. **Bk Rev. Ad Acc. Pr Rev. Circ:** 375.
Desc: Deals with all aspects of geography. Publishes maps, research articles, teaching ideas, and notes about Illinois geography.
Ind/Abst Geogr. Abstr. Human Geogr.; GeoRef.

IE/0332-1185
BULLETIN - IRISH BIOGEOGRAPHICAL SOCIETY. [Bull. - Ir. Biogeogr. Soc.]. (1977)-. Periodical. English. an. **DD** _a574.9.
Ind/Abst Entomol. Abstr.; Rev. Agric. Entomol.; Weed Abstr.

US/0732-2186
BULLETIN OF ASIAN GEOGRAPHY. (BULLETIN OF ASIAN GEOGRAPHY / COMMITTEE ON ASIAN GEOGRAPHY, ASSOCIATION OF AMERICAN GEOGRAPHERS.). [Bull. Asian geogr.]. **Added/Corp** Association of American Geographers. Asian Geographers Specialty Group. No. 1 (Fall 1976)-No. 12 (Fall 1982); Vol. 8, No. 1 (Spring 1983)-. Bulletin. English. sa (Apr., Oct.). $10.00 US; $15.00 (1 year), $25.00 (2 year), $35.00 (3 year) other. Bulletin of Asian Geography, c/o B L Sukhwal, University of Wisconsin, Platteville WI 53818. **Tel** (608)342-1386. **ED** Bheru Sukhwal. **LC** G1; .B84. **Bk Rev.**
Desc: Short articles on geographical topics related to Asia, notes on conferences, news of Asian Geography Speciality Group/AAG members. Bibliography of recent publications on Asia, short notes on regions of Asia, and news of geographical center on Asia in the United States.

US/0192-4281
BULLETIN OF THE ASSOCIATION OF NORTH DAKOTA GEOGRAPHERS. **Main/Corp** Association of North Dakota Geographers. (19??)-. Bulletin. English. an. $6.00. North Dakota Association of Geographers, University of North Dakota, Department of Geography, Grand Forks ND 58257. **Tel** (701)777-4246. **LC** G1; .A773a. **DD** 910/.5.

JA/0082-478X
BULLETIN OF THE DEPARTMENT OF GEOGRAPHY, UNIVERSITY OF TOKYO. **Main/Corp** Tokyo Daigaku. Rigakubu. Chirigaku Kyoshitsu. No. 1 (1969)-. Bulletin. English (French). an. University of Tokyo Department of Geography, Faculty of Science, 3-1 Hongo 7-chome, Bunkyo-ku, 113 Tokyo Japan. **Tel** 03-812-2111 (JAPAN). **LC** G1; .T64A. **DD** 910/.5. **CODEN** BDGTAJ. **Circ:** 800 (ctrl).
Ind/Abst Ecol. Abstr.; Geogr. Abstr. Phys. Geogr.; GeoRef.

JA
BULLETIN OF THE GEOGRAPHICAL SURVEY INSTITUTE. **Main/Corp** Kokudo Chiriin. **VFOAT** Kokudo Chiriin Hokoku. (19??)-. Bulletin. English. Geographical Survey Institute / Tokyo, 24-13 Higashiyama 3-chome Meguro-ku, Tokyo Japan. **LC** QB296.J3; C483a. **DD** 354/.52/00855. ***Continues** Chiri Chosajo. Bulletin.*
Ind/Abst Curr. Geogr. Publ. (199?-); Geogr. Abstr. Phys. Geogr.

GH/0016-9536
BULLETIN OF THE GHANA GEOGRAPHICAL ASSOCIATION. **Main/Corp** Ghana Geographical Association. **Added/Corp** Gold Coast Geographical Association. Vol. 1 (Jan. 1956)-. Periodical. English. an. $3.00. Ghana Geographical Association, University of Ghana, Legon Accra Ghana. **LC** G41; .G53.

UK
BULLETIN - OXFORD UNIVERSITY EXPLORATION CLUB. **Main/Corp** Oxford. University. Exploration Club. No. 1- 1948-. Bulletin. English. an. $15.33. Oxford University Exploration Club, 13 Bevington Road, Oxford 0X2 6NB England. **Tel** 0865/56747. **LC** G7; .O95. ***Continues** Oxford. University. Exploration Club. Annual Report.*

BE
BULLETIN / SOCIETE GEOGRAPHIQUE DE LIEGE. **Added/Corp** Societe Geographique de Liege. **VFOAT** Bulletin de la Societe Geographique de Liege. No 1 (June 1965)-. Bulletin. French. **LC** QL1; .S695.
Ind/Abst Ecol. Abstr.; Geogr. Abstr. Phys. Geogr.; Geogr. Abstr. Human Geogr.

FR/0373-3297
BULLETIN - SOCIETE LANGUEDOCIENNE DE GEOGRAPHIE. (BULLETIN DE LA SOCIETE LANGUEDOCIENNE DE GEOGRAPHIE.). [Bull. - Soc. languedoc. geogr.]. **Added/Corp** Societe Languedocienne de Geographie. Vol. 17 No. 3/4 (July./Dec. 1983)-. Bulletin. French. qt. Societe de Languedocienne de Geographie, Universite Paul-Valery, BP 5043, 34032 Montpellier Cedex, France. ***Continues** Bulletin Trimestriel (Societe Languedocienne de Geographie), 0373-3297.*
Ind/Abst Geogr. Abstr. Phys. Geogr.; Geogr. Abstr. Human Geogr.; GeoRef.

US/0036-1607
BULLETIN - SPECIAL LIBRARIES ASSOCIATION. GEOGRAPHY AND MAP DIVISION. (BULLETIN / SPECIAL LIBRARIES ASSOCIATION, GEOGRAPHY AND MAP DIVISION.). [Bull. - Spec. Libr. Assoc., Geogr. Map Div.]. **Main/Corp** Special Libraries Association. Geography and Map Division. (1951)-. Bulletin. English. qt (Mar., June, Sept., Dec.). $25.00 US & Canada; $30.00 other. Geography & Map Division, 406 East Smith Street, Topton PA 19562. **Tel** (610)683-4480, FAX (610)683-4483. **ED** Joanne M. Perry, (editor's address: Kerr Library 121, Oregon State University, Corvallis, Oregon 97331, phone: (503)737-2971). **LC** Z673; .S8224. **CODEN** SGBUB2. Index available (Dec. iss.). cum. index. **Bk Rev**, (Qty: 35). **Ad Acc. Circ:** 750 (ctrl). available on microfilm from University Microfilms International (UMI). ***Continues** Special Libraries Association. Geography and Map Group. Bulletin.*
Desc: Medium of exchange of information, news, and research in the field of geographic and cartographic bibliography, literature and map librarianship.
Ind/Abst Bibliogr. Carto.; Geogr. Abstr. Phys. Geogr.; Geogr. Abstr. Human Geogr.; Geol. Abstr.; GeoRef; Libr. Inf. Sci. Abstr.; Libr. Lit.

CN/0007-9766
CAHIERS DE GEOGRAPHIE DU QUEBEC. [Cah. geogr. Que.]. **Added/Corp** Universite Laval. Departement de geographie. Vol. 22, No. 55 (April 1978)-. French (summaries and/or abstracts in English). Three times a year. 62.00Can$ (institutions), 36.00Can$ (individuals) Canada; 67.00Can$ (institutions), 41.00Can$ (individuals) other. Cahiers de Geographie du Quebec, Departement de Geographie, Universite Laval, Quebec G1K 7P4 Canada. **Tel** (418)656-3350. **ED** Rodolphe de Koninck. **DD** 910/5. Index available. cum. index. **Bk Rev. Ad Acc. Circ:** 1,100. available on microfilm and microfiche from University Microfilms International (UMI). ***Continues** Cahiers de Geographie de Quebec, 0007-9766.*
Desc: Articles, notes and book reviews on the human geography of Canada and Quebec. Papers in French and English, with abstracts and key words.
Ind/Abst Am. Hist. Life (1966-); Bibliogr. Carto.; Ecol. Abstr. (?-?); Geogr. Abstr. Phys. Geogr. (?-?); Geogr. Abstr. Human Geogr.; GeoRef; Environ.; Point Repere (1983-).

FR
CAHIERS DE GEOGRAPHIE (PARIS, FRANCE). (CAHIERS DE GEOGRAPHIE.). No. 28 (1985)-. Monographic series. French. Price varies per volume. Les Belles Lettres, 95 Boulevard Raspail, 75006 Paris France. **Tel** (1)45.48.70.55, FAX (1)45.44.92.88, telex 200577 F. **LC** AS161; .B39 subser. ***Continues** Cahiers de Geographie de Besancon.*

FR
CAHIERS DE L'ATLAS DE FRANCHE-COMTE. Began in 1975. French. Institut de Geographie / Faculte des Lettres, 32 rue Megevand, 25030 Besancon Cedex France. **LC** G1841.G1; C3 DATE. **DD** 912/.1/330944083.

FR/0373-5834
CAHIERS D'OUTRE-MER. (LES CAHIERS D'OUTRE-MER.). [Cah. o.-m.]. **Added/Corp** Universite de Bordeaux III. Institut de Geographie et d'Etudes Regionales. Bordeaux. Institut de la France d'Outre-Mer. Bordeaux. Institut d'Outre-Mer. Centre National de la Recherche Scientifique (France). Vol. 1, No.1 (1948)-. French (summaries and/or abstracts in English). Four times a year (Jan., Mar., July, Oct.). 270.00F. Institut de Geographie, Universite de Bordeaux III, 33405 Talence France. **Tel** 011 33 1 56845050 Ext. 1826, FAX 011 33 1 56842851. **ED** N. Guillemot. Index available. cum. index. **Bk Rev. Ad Acc. Pr Rev. Circ:** 1,200 (ctrl). ***Supersedes** Revue de Geographie Commerciale.*
Desc: Tropical geography.
Ind/Abst Cot. Trop. Fibr. Abstr. Bibliogr.; Curr. Geogr. Publ. (199?-); Foreign Lang. Index; Geogr. Abstr. Human Geogr.; GeoRef; Int. Dev. Abstr.; Int. Labour Doc.; Irr. Drain. Abstr.; LABORDOC; Maize Abstr.; Life Sci. Collect.; Recent. Publ. Artic.; Rice Abstr.; Sorghum Mill. Abstr.; World Agric. Econ.

FR/0181-0839
CAHIERS GEOGRAPHIQUES DE ROUEN. [Cah. geogr. Rouen]. (1973)-. Periodical. French. sa. **UDC** 91.
Ind/Abst Geogr. Abstr. Human Geogr.; Int. Dev. Abstr.

FR
CAHIERS NEPALAIS. No. 1- 1969-. Periodical. French. an. Editions du CNRS, 22 rue Saint Armand, F 75015 Paris France. **Tel** 011 33 1 45075050. **Circ:** 1,500.
Desc: Multidisciplinary studies on the Himalayan environment.

FR/0526-8443
CAHIERS PERCHERONS. **See** General Interest-General Interest-Europe.

RM
CAIET DE INFORMARE: GEOGRAFIE. **Added/Corp** Centrul de Informare si Documentare al Invatamintului. (19??)-. Periodical. Romanian. qt. Calea Grivitei NR 64-66 POB 2001, Bucharest Romania. **LC** G1; .C16.

CN/0226-000X
CALGARY, ALBERTA, CITY DIRECTORY. [Calgary, Alta., city dir.]. **VFOAT** Calgary City Directory; Henderson's Calgary City Directory. **VAT** Henderson's Calgary City Directory (1979). 1979-. Directory. English. an. 115.00Can$. Henderson Directories, 34 West 2nd Avenue, Vancouver, British Columbia, V5Y 1B3 Canada. **DD** 917.123/3. ***Continues** Henderson's Calgary, Alberta, City Directory, 0318-5702.*

US/0590-0158
CALIFORNIA COUNTY FACT BOOK. ***Ceased.*** (19??)-(19??). Periodical. English. be. County Supervisors Association of California, 1100 K Street/Suite 101, Sacramento CA 95814. **Tel** (916)327-7500, FAX (916)441-5507. **ED** Allan Burdick. **Bk Rev. Circ:** 1,400.
Desc: Over 200 pages of statistical tables, maps, graphs, and charts relevant to California's 58 counties.

US/0575-5700
CALIFORNIA GEOGRAPHER, THE. [Calif. geogr.]. **Added/Corp** California Council of Geography Teachers. California Council for Geographic Education. Vol. 1 (1960)-. English. an. $12.00. California Geographical Society, 2610 Kansas Avenue, South Gate CA 90280. **Tel** (818)336-1241. **ED** Donald Floyd. **LC** G1; .C24. Index available. cum. index. **Bk Rev. Ad Acc. Circ:** 500 (ctrl).
Desc: A professional publication of the California Geographical Society yearly meeting of papers presented.
Ind/Abst Abstr. J. Earthq. Eng. (?-?); GeoRef.

US/0737-884X
CALIFORNIA ROAD ATLAS AND TRAVEL GUIDE. ZIP CODE EDITION. (CALIFORNIA ROAD ATLAS AND TRAVEL GUIDE.). **Main/Corp** Thomas Bros. Maps. (1983)-. English. an (Apr.). $19.95. Thomas Brothers Maps, Lockbox PO Box 30845, Los Angeles CA 90030. **Tel** (714)863-1984.

UK/0306-9796
CAMBRIA. [Cambria]. **Added/Corp** St. David's University College (Lampeter, Wales). Dept. of Geography. Vol. 1 (Spring 1974)-. Periodical. English (Welsh). Twice a year (June & Dec.). £9.00 (surface mail), £10.00 (airmail). University College of Swansea, Singleton Park Department of Geography, Swansea SA2 8PP W Glam Wales England. **Tel** 0792 205678. **ED** R. P. D. Walsh. **LC** G1; .C25. **DD** 910/.5. **Bk Rev. Ad Acc. Pr Rev. Circ:** 250.
Desc: Geography, with an emphasis on Wales. The content is intended for university use worldwide.

Ind/Abst Br. Archaeol. Bibliogr. (?-?); Geogr. Abstr. Phys. Geogr. (?-?); Geogr. Abstr. Human Geogr. (?-?); Geol. Abstr.; GeoRef.

UK/0068-6654
CAMBRIDGE GEOGRAPHICAL STUDIES. (1971)-. Monographic series. English. ir. Price varies per volume. Cambridge University Press, The Edinburgh Building, Shaftesbury Road, Cambridge CB2 2RU United Kingdom. **Tel** 011 44 223 312393, FAX 011 44 223 325959. **(Subscription address:** Cambridge University Press / North America, 110 Midland Avenue, Port Chester NY 10573.**)** ***Continues*** *Cambridge Geographical Series.*

CN/0319-5058
CAMPBELL RIVER DIRECTORY (BUSINESS EDITION). (CAMPBELL RIVER DIRECTORY.). **VFOAT** Official City Directory of Campbell River; City Directory of Campbell River; Campbell River City Directory. 1965-. Directory. English. an. Home Supplement Ed. Free to homes in Canvass area. British Columbia Directories / Vancouver, 34 West 2nd Avenue, Vancouver British Columbia V5Y 1B3 Canada. **DD** 917.11/34.

CN/0833-0948
CANADIAN CAVER, THE. See Recreation, Leisure-Outdoor Life.

CN/0008-3658
CANADIAN GEOGRAPHER. (THE CANADIAN GEOGRAPHER. GEOGRAPHE CANADIEN.). [Can. geogr.]. **Added/Corp** Canadian Association of Geographers. **VFOAT** Geographe Canadien. Vol. 1 (1950)-. Periodical. English (French). qt (Mar., Jun., Sep., Dec.). 60.00Can$ Canada; 65.00Can$ other. Canadian Association of Geography, McGill University, 805 Sherbrooke Street West, Montreal Quebec H3A 2K6 Canada. **Tel** (514)398-4946. **ED** Brenton M Barr. **LC** G1; .C28. **CODEN** CNGGAR. cum. index. **Bk Rev. Ad Acc. Pr Rev. Circ:** 2,400 (ctrl). available on microfilm and microfiche from University Microfilms International (UMI). Documents available from The Genuine Article, BIOSIS Document Express, UMI Article Clearinghouse.
Desc: Research articles, reviews, and research reports on any topic of geographical interest.
Ind/Abst ASTIS Curr. Aware. Bull. (1978-); Acad. Abstr. Full Text Elite (Jan. 1992-); Acad. Abstr. (Jan. 1992-); Acad. Search (Jan. 1992-); Am. Bibliogr. Slavic East Europ. Stud.; AQUAREF; ASTIS Bibliogr. (1978-); Biol. Abstr.; Can. Index; Can. Period. Index; Curr. Contents Soc. Behav. Sci.; Curr. Geogr. Publ. (199?-); Ecol. Abstr. (?-?); Expand. Acad. Index (1989-); Fish Rev. (Jan. 1989-July 1992); Geogr. Abstr. Phys. Geogr.; Geogr. Abstr. Human Geogr.; Geol. Abstr.; GeoRef; INFO-SOUTH Abstr.; Int. Bibliogr. Sociol.; Int. Dev. Abstr. (?-?); J. Plan. Lit.; Environ.; Leis. Recreat. Tour. Abstr.; Mag. Search; Middle East Abstr. Index; Newsp. Period. Abstr. (1991-); Res. Alert [Full Cov.]; Rural Dev. Abstr.; Soc. Sci. Source (Jan. 1992-); Soc. Sci. Cit. Index [Full Cov.]; Soc. Sci. Index; Soc. Sci. Index Fulltext (Fall 1988-) [Full Txt.]; Soils Fert.; Wildl. Rev. (Jan. 1989-July 1992); World Agric. Econ.

CN/0706-2168
CANADIAN GEOGRAPHIC. [Can. geogr.]. **Added/Corp** Royal Canadian Geographical Society. Vol. 97 (Aug./Sept. 1978)-. Periodical. English. bm (Jan., Mar., May, Jul., Sep., Nov.). 23.50Can$ Canada; 31.00Can$ other. Royal Canadian Geographic Society, 39 McArthur Avenue, Vanier Ontario K1L 8L7 Canada. **Tel** (613)745-4629, (800)267-0824. **ED** Ross Smith. **LC** G1; .C3. **DD** 917.1/04; 971/.005. **CODEN** CGEJAB. **[CCC].** Index available. **Bk Rev. Ad Acc. Circ:** 200,000. available on microfilm and microfiche from University Microfilms International (UMI). Documents available from UMI Article Clearinghouse. ***Continues*** *Canadian Geographical Journal, 0315-1824.*
Desc: Features articles that explore Canada's people and cities, its wildlife and wilderness, and its history and beauty; brings home to Canadians, and people around the world, the remarkable geographical, historical and cultural characteristics of Canada through carefully researched and informative articles and full-color photography and maps.
Ind/Abst ASTIS Curr. Aware. Bull. (1978-); Abr. Read. Guide Period. Lit.; Acad. Abstr. Full Text Elite (Jan. 1990-); Acad. Abstr. (Jan. 1990-); Acad. Search (Jan. 1990-); Am. Hist. Life (1963-1989); Am. Bibliogr. Slavic East Europ. Stud.; AQUAREF; Art Archaeol. Tech. Abstr.; ASTIS Bibliogr. (1978-); Book Rev. Index; Can. Index (?-?); Can. Period. Index; Coal Abstr.; Curr. Geogr. Publ. (199?-); Ecol. Abstr.; Ethnoarts Index; Expand. Acad. Index (1984-); Fish Rev. (Jan. 1989-July 1992); Gen. Period. Index (1985-); Geogr. Abstr. Phys. Geogr.; Geogr. Abstr. Human Geogr.; GeoRef; Hist. Source (Jan. 1990-); INFO-SOUTH Abstr.; Environ.; Mag. Artic. Summar. Elite (Jan. 1990-); Mag. Artic. Summar. Select (Jan. 1990-); Mag. Artic. Summar. CD-ROM (Jan. 1990-); Mag. Index Plus (1989-); Mag. Search; MINPROC; Mintec, Min. Technol. Abstr.; Newsp. Period. Abstr. (1990-); Read. Guide Period. Lit.; Soc. Sci. Source (Jan. 1990-); Soc. Sci. Index; Soc. Sci. Index Fulltext (Oct. 1988-) [Full Txt.]; Mag. Index (1983-); TOM Gen. Index (1989-); Vocat. Search (Jan. 1990-); Wildl. Rev. (Jan. 1989-July 1992).

JM/0252-9939
CARIBBEAN GEOGRAPHY. Vol. 1, No. 1 (May 1983)-. Periodical. English. an. 24.00Jam$ Jamaica; 35.00Jam$ Eastern Caribbean; $10.00 US; £7.00 UK. Longman Jamaica, PO Box 489, 95 Newport Boulevard, Kingston Jamaica. **ED** Mike Morrissey and Dave Barker. **LC** F2155; .C364. **DD** 972.9/005. Index available. cum. index. **Bk Rev. Circ:** 500 (ctrl).
Desc: Each issue includes articles reporting geographical research related to the Caribbean region; reports of conferences concerned with Caribbean geography; a section entitled "The Changing Caribbean" which consists of an up-to-date description of major development within the region; and reviews.
Ind/Abst Geogr. Abstr. Human Geogr.; HAPI Hisp. Am. Period. Index; Int. Dev. Abstr. (?-?).

CN/0319-7360
CARIBOO CALLING. V. 1- June 1968-. English. an. 20.00Can$ Canada, $40.00 other. 100 Mile Free Press, PO Box 878, 100 Mile House British Columbia Canada. **Tel** 604-395-2219. **DD** 917.11/2. Index available. **Ad Acc. Circ:** 15,000 (ctrl).
Desc: Tourism promotion of area attractions.

FR
CARMEL. French. qt. 166.50F France; 185.00F other. Editions du Carmel, Venasque, 84210 Pernes les Fontns France. **Tel** 011 33 90 660366.

HU/0008-7009
CARTACTUAL. ***Ceased.*** [Cartactual]. **VFOAT** Cart Actual. Vol. 1 (1965)-Vol. 29, No. 4. Periodical. English (French, German and Hungarian). bm. Cartographia, PO Box 132, H 1443 Budapest Hungary. **Tel** 011 36 1 1634639, telex 226218 CARTO H. **LC** G1019; .C32. Index available. cum. index. **Bk Rev. Ad Acc. Circ:** 900 (ctrl).
Desc: Map service titles and legends of the maps.
Ind/Abst Bibliogr. Carto.; GeoRef.

US/0894-2595
CARTOMANIA. (CARTOMANIA : NEWSLETTER OF THE ASSOCIATION OF MAP MEMORABILIA COLLECTORS.). [Cartomania]. **Added/Corp** Association of Map Memorabilia Collectors. (1986)-. Newsletter. English. Twice a year (June, Nov.). $12.50 North America; $17.00 other. Association of Map Memorabilia Collectors, C/O S. Feller, 8 Amherst Road, Pelham MA 01002. **Tel** (413)253-3115. **ED** Siegfried Feller. **DD** 912. **Bk Rev**, (Qty: 5-10/yr). **Ad Acc. Circ:** 370.

NE
CATALOGUS VAN NEDERLANDSE ZEEKAARTEN EN ANDERE HYDROGRAFISCHE PUBLIKATICS. **Main/Corp** Netherlands. Hydrografisch Bureau. **VFOAT** Catalogue of Charts and Other Hydrographic Publications. Multiple languages (Dutch and English). **LC** Z6026.H9; N4; GA359. **DD** 016.62389/2/0222. ***Continues*** *Catalogus Van Nederlandse Zeekaarten en Boekwerken.*

CE
CEYLON GEOGRAPHER, THE. Added/Corp Ceylon Geographical Society. Vol. 12 (1958)-. Periodical. English. ir. Ceylon Geographical Society, Geography Department, University of Ceylon, Columbo 3 Ceylon. **LC** DS488; .C42. ***Continues*** *Ceylon Geographical Society Bulletin.*

JA/0022-135X
CHIGAKU ZASSHI. [Chigaku zasshi]. **Added/Corp** Chigakukai (Japan) Tokyo Chigaku Kyokai. **VFOAT** Journal of Geography. (Jan. 1889)-. Academic Scholarly Publication. Japanese (summaries and/or abstracts in English). bm. $250.00. Tokyo Chigaku Kyokai, (Tokyo Geographical Society), 12-2, Nibancho, Chiyodaku, Tokyoto 102 Japan. **(Subscription address:** Kyowa Book Company Inc., 1 38 Kanda Jinbocho Chiyoda-ku, Tokyo 101 Japan.**) LC** G1; .C34. **CODEN** CGZAAL. Documents available from CASDDS.
Ind/Abst Chem. Abstr.; Coal Abstr.; Curr. Geogr. Publ. (199?-); GeoRef.

US
CHIHUAHUAN DESERT DISCOVERY, THE. Added/Corp Chihuahuan Desert Research Institute. (1975)-. Newsletter. English. Twice a year. $25.00 institutions; $15.00 individuals. Chihuahuan Desert Research Institute, PO Box 1334, Alpine TX 79831. **Tel** (915)837-8370. **Circ:** 700.

●US/1061-9534
CHINESE ENVIRONMENT & DEVELOPMENT. [Chin. environ. dev.]. **VFOAT** A.Chinese environment and development. (1993)-. Periodical. English (translations available in Chinese). qt. $242.00 US; $267.00 other. M. E. Sharpe Inc., 80 Business Park Drive, Armonk NY 10504. **Tel** (914)273-1800, (800)541-6563, FAX (914)273-2106. **DD** 915. ***Continues*** *Chinese Geography and Environment, 0896-2979.*

CC
CHINESE GEOGRAPHICAL ABSTRACTS. Added/Corp Chung-Kuo ko Hsueh Yuan. Geographical Information Network. (1985)-. English. qt. $60.00. China National Publishing Import & Export Corporation, 16 Gongti E Rd., Chaoyang Dist., Beijing 100704, People's Republic of China. **Tel** 011 8601 50630169, 5066688, FAX 011 8601 5063101, 5063010, telex 22313. **LC** Z6001; .C47. **DD** 915.1/005.

CH
CHING CHI TI LI / CHUNG-KUO TI LI HEUEH HUI CHING CHI TI LI CHUAN YEH WEI YUAN HUI, HU-NAN SHENG CHING CHI TI LI YEN CHIU SO HO PAN. **VFOAT** Economic Geography. Periodical. Chinese. qt. NT$0.60. Post Office, Chang-sha Shih, People's Republic of China. **LC** HC426; .C514. **DD** 330.951/005.

JA/0016-7444
CHIRIGAKU HYORON. Added/Corp Nihon Chiri Gakkai. **VFOAT** Geographical Review of Japan. (1925)-. Periodical. Japanese (English). mo. $168.00. Nippon Chiri Gakkai, (Association of Japanese Geographers), 2-10, Kanda Surugadai,, Chiyodaku, Tokyoto 101 Japan. **(Subscription address:** Kyowa Book Company Inc., 1 38 Kanda Jinbocho Chiyoda-ku, Tokyo 101 Japan.**) LC** G1; .C366. **CODEN** CRGHAO.
Ind/Abst Curr. Geogr. Publ. (199?-); Ecol. Abstr.; Geogr. Abstr. Phys. Geogr.; Geogr. Abstr. Human Geogr.; GeoRef.

JA
CHIRIGAKUHO. Added/Corp Osaka Kyoiku Daigaku. Chirigaku Kyoshitsu. (19??)-. Periodical. Japanese (English). an. Chirigaku Kyoshitsu, c/o Osaka Kyoiku Daigaku Tennoji Bunko, 4-88 Minamikawaho Ri-cho, Tennoji-ku Osaka Japan. **Tel** (06)771-8131. **LC** G1; .C37. **Circ:** 500.
Desc: Submission of papers is restricted to the academic staff and the graduates of Osaka Kyoiku University.

KO
CHIRIHAK. VFOAT Geography. Periodical. Korean (summaries and/or abstracts in English, French and German). sa. W6000. Korean Geographical Society, c/o Department of Geography, Seoul National University, Seoul 151 Korea. **Tel** (02)877-4171. **ED** Woo-ik Yu. **LC** G1; .C38. **Bk Rev. Ad Acc. Circ:** 1,000.

JA/0009-4897
CHIZU. MAP. VFOAT Map. (1963)-. Periodical. Japanese (summaries and/or abstracts in English). qt. $134.00. **(Subscription address:** Japan Publications Trading Company, Ltd., PO Box 5030, Tokyo International, Tokyo 100-31 Japan.**) DD** 526.8.
Ind/Abst GeoRef.

CN/0318-2339
CITY OF COTE SAINT-LUC HOUSEHOLDER'S DIRECTORY. VFOAT City of Cote Saint-Luc Annuaires des Residents. 1973-. Directory. Multiple languages (English and French). J Lovell, 423 rue St Nicolas, Montreal Quebec H2Y 2P4 Canada. **Tel** (514)849-2578. **DD** 917.14/281.

CN
CITY OF LETHBRIDGE INFORMATION DIRECTORY. Directory. Information Lethbridge, c/o Bill Kergan Centre, 207 13th Street North, Lethbridge Alberta T1H 2R6 Canada. **Tel** (403)320-3841.

UK
CLACKMANNAN DISTRICT OFFICIAL GUIDE. English. Burrow Publishing Ltd, Publicity House, 106A Stafford Road, Wallington Surrey, SM6 9TD England. **Tel** 011 44 81 773 9944, 011 44 81 773 9955, FAX 011 44 81 773 8888. **LC** DA880.C5; C57. **DD** 914.13/1504.

US
CLEVELAND EAST SUBURBAN DIRECTORY (CUYAHOGA COUNTY, OHIO). Directory. English. ir. R. L. Polk & Company, 1155 Brewery Park Boulevard, Detroit MI 48207. **Tel** (313)393-0880.

GW/0588-3253
COLLOQUIUM GEOGRAPHICUM. [Colloq. geogr.]. Vol. 1 (1951)-. Monographic series. German. ir. Price varies per volume. Ferdinand Dummler Verlag, Postfach 1480, D 53004 Bonn Germany. **Tel** 011 49 228 223031. **DD** 910; 551. **CODEN** CLGEA7.
Ind/Abst Geogr. Abstr. Phys. Geogr.; Geogr. Abstr. Human Geogr.; GeoRef.

US
COMPREHENSIVE LISTING OF AERIAL PHOTOGRAPHY. Main/Corp United States. Agricultural Stabilization and Conservation Service. Aerial Photography Field Office. (July 1975)-. Periodical. English.

FR/0037-9018
COMPTE RENDU DES SEANCES DE LA SOCIETE DE BIOGEOGRAPHIE. ***Title Change.*** [C.r. seances Soc. biogeogr.]. **Main/Corp** Societe de Biogeographie. No. 389/394 (Jan./June 1968)-(199?). Periodical. French. Three times a year. Societe de Biogeographie, 45 Bis rue de Buffon, 75005 Paris France. **CODEN** CRSBBX. Documents available from BIOSIS Document Express. ***Continues*** *Societe de*

Biogeographie. Compte Rendu Sommaire des Seances. ***Continued by*** *Biogeographica.*
Ind/Abst Aquat. Sci. Fish. Abstr. (Computer File); Biol. Abstr.; GeoRef; Life Sci. Collect.

PO/0871-1747
COMUNICACOES - INSTITUTO DE INVESTIGACAO CIENTIFICA TROPICAL. SERIE DE CIENCIAS DE ENGENHARIA GEOGRAFICA. (SERIE DE CIENCIAS DA ENGENHARIA GEOGRAFICA.). [Comun. - Inst. Investig. Cient. Trop., Ser. cienc. eng. geogr.]. (1989)-. Monographic series. Multiple languages. ir. Price varis per volume. Instituto de Investigacao Cientifica Tropical, Centro de Documentacao e Informacao, rua Jau 47, 1 300 Lisbon Portugal. **Tel** 645321. **UDC** 91. **Circ:** 1,000 (ctrl).

UK/0306-6142
CONCEPTS AND TECHNIQUES IN MODERN GEOGRAPHY. **Added/Corp** Institute of British Geographers. Quantitative Methods Study Group. **VFOAT** CATMOG. No. 1 (1975)-. Monographic series. English. an. £3.50. Environmental Publication, C Flack School of Environmental Science, Norwich NR4 7TJ United Kingdom. **Tel** 011 44 603 56161. **ED** Tony Gattrell. **Circ:** 350.
Desc: Created to fill a need in the teaching of quantitative methods in undergraduate geography courses.

US/0090-8061
CONGRESSIONAL DISTRICT ATLAS. [Congr. dist. atlas]. **Main/Corp** United States. Bureau of the Census. (1964)-. English. ir. Superintendent of Documents, US Government Printing Office, Washington DC 20402. **Tel** (202)275-3328, FAX (202)786-2377. **LC** G1201.F7; U45. **DD** 912/.13287307345. ***Continues*** *Congressional District Atlas of the United States, 0748-4828.*

CN/0848-7952
CONTOURS (OTTAWA). (CONTOURS : NEWSLETTER DEDICATED TO THE CUSTOMERS OF THE CANADA MAP OFFICE.). [Contours]. **Main/Corp** Canada. Map Office. **VFOAT** Contours. Vol. 1, No. 1 Dec. (1990)-. Newsletter. English (French). Four times a year. Free on request. Canada Map Office, 580 Booth Street, Ottawa Ont K1A 0E4 Canada. **DD** 354.710081/9.
Desc: The maps of Canada.

US/0733-6845
CONTRA COSTA COUNTY POPULAR STREET ATLAS (CENSUS TRACT ED.). (CONTRA COSTA COUNTY POPULAR STREET ATLAS.). English. an. $17.95. Thomas Brothers Maps, Lockbox PO Box 30845, Los Angeles CA 90030. **Tel** (714)863-1984. **Ad Acc.**
Desc: Street maps and index for Contra Costa County in California.

CN/0229-1991
CORNWALL, ONTARIO CITY DIRECTORY. [Cornwall, Ont. city dir.]. **Added/Corp** Might Directories. **VFOAT** Cornwall City Directory. (1980)-. Directory. English. an. $80.00. Might Directories, 220 Bartley Drive, Toronto Ontario M4A 2H4 Canada. **Tel** (416)751-2751. **DD** 917.13/76. ***Continues*** *Might's Cornwall (United Counties, Stormont, Dundas, and Glengarry, Ontario) Ontario City Directory, 0381-744X.*

US/0196-2809
COUNTRIES OF THE WORLD AND THEIR LEADERS YEARBOOK. [Ctries. world their lead. yearb.]. **VFOAT** Countries of the World. (1980)-. English. an. $180.00. Gale Research Inc., 835 Penobscot Building, Detroit MI 48226. **Tel** (800)877-GALE, (313)961-2242, FAX (313)961-6083, telex TWX 810-221-7086. **ED** Frank Bair. **LC** G1; .C88. **DD** 909.82/8. ***Supersedes*** *Countries of the World and their Leaders.*
Desc: Provides quick access to comprehensive information on nearly 170 countries from around the world. Each country profile is introduced with a brief section listing essential facts. Maps and photos complement the essays. A "Travel Notes" section describes customs and immigration requirements, available telephone and telegraphy services, local transportation, and national holidays.

CN/0383-6118
COURTENAY AND COMOX. **VFOAT** Official City Directory of Courtenay and Comox; City Directory of Courtenay and Comox; Courtenay and Comex City Directory. 1965-. English. an. British Columbia Directories / Courtenay, Box 3039, Courtenay British Columbia Canada. **DD** 917.11/34.

SP/0213-4497
CUADERNOS DO LABORATORIO XEOLOXICO DE LAXE. [Cuad. Lab. Xeol. Laxe]. **Added/Corp** Seminario de Estudos Galegos. Area de Xeoloxia e Mineria. Santiago de Compostela (La Coruña). (1980)-. Multiple languages. ir. **UDC** 55.
Ind/Abst Geogr. Abstr. Phys. Geogr.; GeoRef.

CL
CUADERNOS GEOGRAFICOS DEL SUR. Yearly V. 1- (No. 1-). Periodical. Spanish. $2.00. Universidad de Concepcion / Geografia, Departament de Geografia, Casilla 1257, Concepcion Chile. **LC** G1.C9.

US
CULTURGRAMS. (1994)-. English. an. $90.00. David M. Kennedy Center, 280 HRCB, Brigham Young University, Provo UT 84602. **Tel** (801)378-6528, FAX (801)378-7075. **ED** Grant P. Skabelund.
Desc: Briefings on 96 countries or areas of the world. Provides information on social customs and courtesies, lifestyles, the people, and a nation's history and government.

US/0096-879X
CURRENT ANTARCTIC LITERATURE. **See** Geography-Abstracting, Bibliographies and Statistics.

US/0011-3514
CURRENT GEOGRAPHICAL PUBLICATIONS. **See** Geography-Abstracting, Bibliographies and Statistics.

PL/0045-9453
CZASOPISMO GEOGRAFICZNE : KWARTALNIK ZRZESZENIA POL. NAUCZYCIELI GEOGRAFJI, TOWARZYSTWA GEOGRAFICZNEGO WE LWOWIE I TOWARZYSTWA GEOGRAFICZNEGO W POZNANIU. **Added/Corp** Zrzeszenie Polskich Nauczycieli Geografji. Towarzystwo Geograficzne we Lwowie. Towarzystwo Geograficzne w Poznaniu. Polskie Towarzystwo Geograficzne. **VFOAT** Geographical Journal. (192?)-. Periodical. Polish (summaries and/or abstracts in English). qt. $32.00. **(Subscription address:** ARS Polona, PO Box 1001, 00068 Warsaw Poland.**)** **LC** G72; .C9. ***Continues*** *Czasopismo Geograficzne Poswiecone Sprawom Nauczania Geografji.*

II/0011-7269
DECCAN GEOGRAPHER. (THE DECCAN GEOGRAPHER.). [Deccan Geogr.]. (1962)-. Periodical. English. ir (2-3 issues). $30.00 (institution), $25.00 (individual) India; $40.00 (institution), $35.00 (individual) other. Deccan Geographical Society, 808 Bhandarkar Institute Road, Prabhat Lane 15, Pune 411004 India. **Tel** 011 91 212 334720. **(Subscription address:** Prints India, 11 Darya Ganj, New Delhi 110002 India.**)** **ED** Prof. B.G. Tamaskar (chief editor) and Prof. S.A. Todkar (executive editor). **UDC** 91. **Bk Rev**, (Qty: 6). **Ad Acc**, **Adv Mgr:** S.A. Todkar. **Circ:** 1,000.

US/0363-6828
DECISIONS ON GEOGRAPHIC NAMES IN THE UNITED STATES. (DECISIONS ON GEOGRAPHIC NAMES IN THE UNITED STATES / UNITED STATES BOARD ON GEOGRAPHIC NAMES.). **Main/Corp** United States Board on Geographic Names. Decision List No. 6301 (Jan. through April 1963)-. English. qt (4 issues). Free on request. Domestic Graphic Names, 523 National Center, Reston VA 22092. **Tel** (703)648-4546. **LC** E154; .U54a. ***Continues*** *United States. Board on Geographic Names. Decisions on Names in the United States.*

CN/0843-7378
DEPARTMENT OF GEOGRAPHY PUBLICATION SERIES. (DEPARTMENT OF GEOGRAPHY PUBLICATION SERIES / UNIVERSITY OF WATERLOO.). [Dep. Geogr. publ. ser.]. **Added/Corp** University of Waterloo. Dept. of Geography. University of Waterloo. Faculty of Environmental Studies. **VFOAT** Publication Series. No. 1 (1971)-. Monographic series. English. ir. Price varies per volume. University of Waterloo Department of Geography, Waterloo Ontario N2L 3G1 Canada. **Tel** (519)885-1211. **CODEN** DGPWEI.
Ind/Abst Geogr. Abstr. Human Geogr.

US/1049-5517
DEPARTMENT OF STATE PUBLICATION. BACKGROUND NOTES SERIES. [Backgr. notes ser.]. **Added/Corp** United States. Dept. of State. Office of Public Communication. Editorial Division. **VFOAT** Background Notes Series; Background Notes. (Jan. 1980)-. Monographic series. English. ir. $20.00 US; $25.00 other. Superintendent of Documents, US Government Printing Office, Washington DC 20402. **Tel** (202)275-3328, FAX (202)786-2377. **DD** 321. Documents available from Documents on Demand. ***Continues*** *Background Notes (Washington, D.C. : 1954), 0501-9966.*
Desc: These short factual pamphlets about various countries and territories include information on the country's land, people, history, government, political conditions, economy and foreign relations.
Ind/Abst Am. Stat. Index.

FR
DICTIONNAIRE D'HISTOIRE ET GEOGRAPHIE ECCLESIASTIQUES. (1912)-. Periodical. French. ir. Letouzey et Ane, 87 Boulevard Raspail, 75006 Paris France. **Tel** 011 33 1 45488014.

CC/0257-019X
DILI ZHISHI. (TI LI CHIH SHIH.). [Dili zhishi]. **Added/Corp** Chung-kuo Ti Li Hsueh Hui. Chung-kuo ko Hsueh Yuan. Ti Li Yen Chiu So. **VFOAT** Geographical Knowledge; Dili Zhishi. (1950)-. Periodical. Chinese. mo. $21.00. Geographical Society of China, Science Press, 16 Donghuangchenggen North Street, Beijing 100707, People's Republic of China. **Tel** 011 86 1 4019821, FAX 011 86 4012180, telex 210147. **(Subscription address:** China International Book Trading Corporation, PO Box 399, Library Service Department, Beijing 100044 People's Republic of China.**)** **LC** QE1; .T46. **DD** 551.
Desc: Contains information on the geography of China and other countries as well.
Ind/Abst Ecol. Abstr.; Geogr. Abstr. Human Geogr.

US/0094-209X
DIRECTORIES OF HAWAII. English. Hawaii Department of Business and Economic Development, PO Box 2359, Honolulu HI 96804. **Tel** (808)586-2423. **LC** Z7165.U5; D57. **DD** 016.91969/03/4025. ctrl circ.
Desc: A compilation of governmental and commercial publications which list thousands of Hawaii's business, industrial, scientific and other activities.

CN/0707-3844
DIRECTORY - CANADIAN ASSOCIATION OF GEOGRAPHERS. (DIRECTORY - CANADIAN ASSOCIATION OF GEOGRAPHERS. ANNUAIRE -ASSOCIATION CANADIENNE DES GEOGRAPHES.). **Main/Corp** Canadian Association of Geographers. **Added/Corp** Canadian Association of Geographers. Annuaire. **VFOAT** Annuaire - Association Canadienne des Geographes. (1977)-. English (French). an. 15.00Can$. Canadian Association of Geography, McGill University, 805 Sherbrooke Street West, Montreal Quebec H3A 2K6 Canada. **Tel** (514)398-4946. **ED** William Barr. **LC** G4; .C27a. **DD** 910/.25/71; 910/.7/2071. **Circ:** 1,500 (ctrl). ***Continues*** *Newsletter and Membership List - Canadian Association of Geographers, 0068-8312.*
Desc: Directory of the staff, research activities and current publications for canadian departments of geography, and government departments in geography related work.

CN/0070-5217
DIRECTORY OF CANADIAN MAP COLLECTIONS. **VFOAT** Repertoire des Collections de Cartes Canadiennes. 1969-. Directory. English (French). ir. 12.00Can$. Association of Canadian Map Libraries and Archives, 395 Wellington Street, Ottawa Ontario K1A 0N3 Canada. **Tel** (613)996-7619. **ED** Lorraine Dubrevil. **DD** 026/.912/02571. Index available. **Circ:** 300 (ctrl).

US
DIRECTORY OF SUPPLIERS - INTERNATIONAL MAP DEALERS ASSOCIATION. Directory. English. mo (except. Sept. and Dec.). $35.00. International Map Dealers Association, PO Box 1789, Kankakee IL 60901. **Tel** (815)939-4627, FAX (815)933-8320. **ED** Nancy Edwards. **Circ:** Yes.
Desc: Buyers guide listing suppliers of products and services in the map business.

US/0363-6038
DISCUSSION PAPER SERIES - DEPARTMENT OF GEOGRAPHY, SYRACUSE UNIVERSITY. **Main/Corp** Syracuse University. Dept. of Geography. (1975)-. Monographic series. English. ir. Price varies per volume. Syracuse University / Department of Geography, 343 H B Crouse Hall, Syracuse NY 13210. **Tel** (315)423-2605. **LC** UNC. Index available.
Ind/Abst Int. Dev. Abstr. (?-?).

CN/0823-3039
DISCUSSION PAPER - SIMON FRASER UNIVERSITY, DEPARTMENT OF GEOGRAPHY. (DISCUSSION PAPER.). [Discuss. pap. - Simon Fraser Univ. Dep. Geogr.]. **VFOAT** Discussion Paper Series. **VAT** Department of Geography Discussion Paper Series. No. 1 (Feb. 1978)-. Monographic series. English. Price varies per volume. Simon Fraser University Department of Geography, Burnaby British Columbia V5A 1S6 Canada. **DD** 910.

CN/0317-9893
DISCUSSION PAPER - UNIVERSITY OF TORONTO, DEPARTMENT OF GEOGRAPHY. [Discuss. pap. - Univ. Tor., Dep. Geogr.]. **Main/Corp** University of Toronto. Dept. of Geography. Monographic series. English. ir. Price varies per volume. University of Toronto Department of Geography, Toronto Ontario M5S 1A1 Canada. **Tel** (416)978-3376. **ED** J N ID Britton. **DD** 910.

UK/0262-9291
DISCUSSION PAPERS IN GEOLINGUISTICS. **Added/Corp** North Staffordshire Polytechnic. Dept. of Geography and Sociology. North Staffordshire Polytechnic. Dept. of Geography and Recreation Studies. (1980)-.

Monographic series. English. Price varies per volume. **Ind/Abst** Geogr. Abstr. Phys. Geogr.; Geogr. Abstr. Human Geogr.

SP/0212-1573
DOCUMENTS D'ANALISI GEOGRAFICA / [PUBLICACIONS DEL DEPARTAMENT DE GEOGRAFIA, UNIVERSITAT AUTONOMA DE BARCELONA].
Added/Corp Universidad Autonoma de Barcelona. Departament de Geografia. (1982)-. Periodical. Catalan (Spanish; summaries and/or abstracts in English and French). sa. 2,000ptas Spain; $18.00 US. Universitat Autonoma de Barcelona / Publicacions, Servei de Publicacions Edifici Rectorat, Bellaterra 08193 Barcelona Spain. **Tel** 011 34 93 6914061. **ED** M Dolores, Garcia-Ramon. **LC** G1; .D59. **DD** 910/.5. **Bk Rev. Ad Acc. Pr Rev. Circ:** 1,200.
Desc: The journal aims to reflect the varieties of approaches being applied at present in geography research in Spain and more specifically in Catalonia.
Ind/Abst Ecol. Abstr.; Geogr. Abstr. Human Geogr.; GeoRef.

PL/0012-5032
DOKUMENTACJA GEOGRAFICZNA. [Dok. geogr.]. **Added/Corp** Polska Akademia Nauk. Instytut Geografii. Instytut Geografii i Przestrzennego Zagospodarowania (Polska Akademia Nauk). (1954)-. Periodical. Polish (English, French and Russian). **DD** 914.38. **CODEN** PGDGA4. ***Supersedes*** *Biuletyn Geograficzny Polskiego Towarzystwa Geograficznego.*
Ind/Abst Geogr. Abstr. Phys. Geogr.; Geogr. Abstr. Human Geogr.; GeoRef.

GW
DUSSELDORFER GEOGRAPHISCHE SCHRIFTEN. **Added/Corp** Universitat Dusseldorf. Geographisches Institut. (1974)-. Periodical. English.
Ind/Abst Geogr. Abstr. Phys. Geogr.; GeoRef.

US/8750-0183
EARTHWATCH (BELMONT, MASS.). (EARTHWATCH.). **Added/Corp** Earthwatch (Organization) Earthwatch Expeditions, Inc. **VFOAT** Earth Watch. (198?)-. Periodical. English. bm. $25.00 (includes Earthwatch Expeditions membership). Earthwatch Expedition, 680 Mt. Auburn Street, Box 403, Watertown MA 02172. **Tel** (617)926-8200, FAX (617)926-8532, telex 5106006452. **ED** Mark Cherrington. **DD** 910. **Circ:** 60,000.
Ind/Abst Acad. Abstr. (Jan. 1994-); Acad. Search (Jan. 1994-); Environ. Period. Bibliogr.; Gen. Sci. Source (Jan. 1994-); GeoRef; Mag. Artic. Summar. Elite (Jan. 1994-) [Full Txt.]; Mag. Artic. Summar. CD-ROM (Jan. 1994-).

UG/0070-7961
EAST AFRICAN GEOGRAPHICAL REVIEW, THE. **Added/Corp** Uganda Geographical Association. Makerere University. No. 1 (April 1963)-. Periodical. English. an. East African Geographical Review, PO Box 7062, Kampala Uganda Africa. **LC** DT365; .E16.
Ind/Abst Field Crop Abstr.; Grasslands For. Abstr.; Leis. Recreat. Tour. Abstr.; Rural Dev. Abstr.; World Agric. Econ.

US/0070-8127
EAST LAKES GEOGRAPHER, THE. ***Title Change.*** **Added/Corp** Ohio State University. **VFOAT** Common Market. Vol. 1 (Nov. 1964)-Vol. 27, (1992). Periodical. English. an. University of Western Ontario / Department of Geography, Social Sciences Centre, London Ontario N6A 5C2, Canada. **Tel** (519)679-2111 ext. 5025. **LC** G1; .E2. **DD** 910/.5. ***Merged with*** *Ontario Geography* ***to form*** *Great Lakes Geographer.*
Ind/Abst Geogr. Abstr. Human Geogr. (?-?).

UK/0012-8481
EAST MIDLAND GEOGRAPHER. [East Midl. geogr.]. **Added/Corp** University of Nottingham. Dept. of Geography. Vol. 1, No. 1 (June 1954)-. Periodical. English. sa. $16.00. East Midland Geographer, University of Nottingham Geography, Nottingham NG72RD England. **Tel** 011 44 602 506101 ext. 3043. **LC** DA670.M64; E2. **CODEN** EMGEA2. Index available. **Bk Rev. Ad Acc. Circ:** 500. available on microfilm from University Microfilms International (UMI).
Desc: Deals with all aspects of the geography of the East Midlands of England (Derbyshire, Leicestershire, Lincolnshire, Northamptonshire, Nottinghamshire) and their borders.
Ind/Abst Geogr. Abstr. Phys. Geogr.; Geogr. Abstr. Human Geogr.; GeoRef; Leis. Recreat. Tour. Abstr.

US/0013-0095
ECONOMIC GEOGRAPHY. **See** Economics.

●UK/0967-4608
ECUMENE. Vol. 1, No. 1 (Jan. 1994)-. Periodical. English. qt. $198.00 (institution), $70.00 (individual) North America; £102.00 (institution), £37.50 (individual) Europe; £114.00 (institution), £45.00 (individual) Other. Edward Arnold, 338 Euston Road, London NW1 3BH England. **Tel** 011 44 71 873 6000, FAX 011 44 071 873 6325. **(Subscription address:** Edward Arnold, PO Box 386, Avenel NJ 07001-0386.**) ED** Dennis Cosgrove, James Duncan. **Bk Rev**, (Qty: 40). **Ad Acc, Adv Mgr:** Mary Attree, **Tel** 071 873 6336. **Pr Rev. Acid Free.**
Desc: Publishes research, commentary and review on the cultural appropriation, both material and imaginative, of the earth and its environments for human life. Offers a forum for the scholars and practitioners in the arts, humanities and environmental sciences who are interested in the ways that people imagine, interpret and transform their physical and social worlds.
Ind/Abst Geogr. Abstr. Human Geogr.; Int. Dev. Abstr.

TU
EGE COGRAFYA DERGISI / [EGE UNIVERSITESI, EDEBIYAT FAKULTESI, COGRAFYA BOLUMU]. **Added/Corp** Ege Universitesi. Cografya Bolumu. **VFOAT** Aegean Geographical Journal. Vol. 1 (Jan. 1983)-. Periodical. Turkish (English, French and German; summaries and/or abstracts in English, German and French). an. 5,000TL Turkey; $15.00 other. Ege Universitesi / Edibiyat, Edebiyat Fakultesi, Cografya Bolumu, Bornova Izmir Turkey. **Tel** 9-51-180110. **ED** Ahmet Mecdet Sozer, Ilhan Kayan and Asaf Kocman. **LC** PAR. **Bk Rev. Circ:** 1,000 (ctrl).

FR
ELAN RHONE-ALPES. **Added/Corp** Laboratoire de Geographie Rhodanienne. **VFOAT** Elan Rhone Alpes; Elan; Etudes des Localisations et Activities Nouvelles. No 1 (1990)-. Periodical. French. Three times a year.

US/1053-0924
ELECTRONIC ATLAS NEWSLETTER, THE. **See** Computers.

US
ELECTRONIC MAP CABINET. (19??)-. English. ir. $199.95. Highlighted Data Inc., 6628 Medhill Place, Falls Church VA 22043. **Tel** (703)516-9211.

CN/0710-9911
EQUINOX (CAMDEN EAST). (EQUINOX.). [Equinox]. Vol. 1, No. 1 (Jan. 1982)-. Periodical. English. Six times a year. 19.98Can$ Canada; 25.00Can$ US; 29.00Can$ other. Equinox, 50 Holly Street, Toronto ONT M4S 3B3 Canada. **Tel** (416)482-9399. **(Subscription address:** Indas, 35 Riviera Drive, Building 17, Markham Ontario L3R 8N4 Canada.**) ED** James Lawrence. **LC** G1; .E68. **DD** 910/.5. **[CCC]. Bk Rev. Ad Acc. Circ:** 135,000.
Desc: Canadian magazine that ventures around the world and to the far corners of Canada to bring the reader photography, clear writing and fine printing. Lets the reader join daring expeditions, explore new ideas and amazing scientific discoveries and introduces fascinating people throughout Canada.
Ind/Abst Acad. Abstr. (Jan. 1994-); Acad. Search (Jan. 1994-); Can. Index; Can. Period. Index; Fish Rev.; Mag. Artic. Summar. Elite (Jan. 1994-); Mag. Artic. Summar. CD-ROM (Jan. 1994-).

GR/1011-6656
ERATOSTHENES THESSALONIKE. [Eratosthenes Thessalonike]. **VFOAT** Eratosthenes. (1988)-. Periodical. Multiple languages. Three times a year. Eratosthenes Press, PO Box 19504, GR 54006 Thessaloniki Greece. **UDC** 5. ***Continues*** *Geodaitika Tetradia, 0250-6351.*

GW/0013-9998
ERDE. (DIE ERDE; ZEITSCHRIFT DER GESELLSCHAFT FUER ERDKUNDE ZU BERLIN.). [Erde]. **Added/Corp** Gesellschaft fur Erdkunde zu Berlin. Vol. 1 (1949)-. Periodical. German (summaries and/or abstracts in English and French). qt (Feb., May, Aug., Nov.). DM137.00 with postage, Germany; DM139.00 with postage, other. Gesellschaft fuer Erdkunde, Arno Holz Strasse 14 Zeitschriften, D 1265 Berlin Germany. **Tel** 011 49 30 7919001, FAX 011 49 30 7933249. **ED** Dr. K. Gehrenkemper. **CODEN** ERDEAM. Index available. cum. index. **Bk Rev**, (Qty: 30). **Ad Acc. Circ:** 1,200. ***Supersedes*** *Gesellschaft fur Erdkunde zu Berlin. Zeitschrift ... .*
Desc: Geographical subjects: physical geography, human geography, geography of developing countries, urban studies, nomadism, etc.
Ind/Abst Bibliogr. Carto.; Curr. Geogr. Publ. (199?-); Ecol. Abstr.; Geogr. Abstr. Phys. Geogr.; Geogr. Abstr. Human Geogr.; Geol. Abstr.; GeoRef; Int. Dev. Abstr.; Meteorol. Geoastrophys. Abstr.; Rural Dev. Abstr.

GW/0014-0015
ERDKUNDE. **See** Earth Sciences-Geology.

GW/0170-3188
ERDWISSENSCHAFTLICHE FORSCHUNG. [Erdwiss. Forsch.]. **Added/Corp** Akademie der Wissenschaften und der Literatur (Germany). Kommission fuer Erdwissenschaftliche Forschung. (1968)-. Monographic series. German. ir. Price varies per volume. Franz Steiner Verlag GmbH, Postfach 101061, D 70009 Stuttgart Germany. **Tel** 011 49 0711 2582372, FAX 011 49 0711 2582290, telex 723636 daz d. **ED** Wilhelm Lauer. **CODEN** ERFODV.
Ind/Abst GeoRef.

GW
ERGANZUNGSHEFT ZU PETERMANNS GEOGRAPHSCHISCHEN MITTEILUNGEN. (PETERMANNS GEOGRAPHISCHE MITTEILUNGEN. ERGANZUNGSHEFT.). 1- 1860-. Monographic series. German. ir. Price varies per volume. World Amateur Boxing Magazine Editor's Office, P.O.Box 0141, 10321 Berlin/GERMANY. **Tel** (049.30)423 5932, (049.30)423 6766, FAX (049.30)423 5943. **LC** G1; .P44. cum. index. **Bk Rev. Ad Acc.** ctrl circ.
Desc: Communicates the latest knowledge from all branches of geography and cartography. Literary review, geographical statistics, cartography table of contents and summary in English and Russian, illustrated map supplements.

FR/0046-2497
ESPACE GEOGRAPHIQUE. (L'ESPACE GEOGRAPHIQUE.). [Espace geogr.]. Vol. 1, No. 1 (Jan./March 1972)-. Periodical. French (summaries and/or abstracts in English). qt (4 issues). $131.00. Doin Editeurs, 8 Place de l'Odeon, F 75006 Paris France. **Tel** 011 33 1 46332237. **(Subscription address:** Subscription Office, PO Box 830399, Birmingham, AL 35283-0399; telephone: (800)633-4931 or (205)991-6920 (outside US and Canada); FAX: (205)995-1588**) ED** R. Brunet. **LC** GF1; .E86. **DD** 304.2/05. **[CCC].** Index available. **Bk Rev. Ad Acc. Circ:** 900. available on microfilm from University Microfilms International (UMI).
Desc: Oriented toward the development of geographical thought and practice in the fields of ecology and the social sciences of environment and education.
Ind/Abst Bibliogr. Carto.; Ecol. Abstr.; Geogr. Abstr. Phys. Geogr.; Geogr. Abstr. Human Geogr.; GeoRef; Int. Bibliogr. Sociol.; Int. Dev. Abstr.; Leis. Recreat. Tour. Abstr.; Rural Dev. Abstr.; World Agric. Econ.

SP/0014-1496
ESTUDIOS GEOGRAFICOS. [Estud. geogr.]. **Added/Corp** Instituto Juan Sebastian Elcano. No. 1 (Oct. 1940)-. Periodical. Spanish (English and French). qt. 4000ptas Spain; 5500ptas other. Consejo Superior Investigacion Cientificas (CSIC), Vitruvio 8, 28006 Madrid Spain. **Tel** 011 34 1 5612833, FAX 011 34 1 4113077, telex 42182. **LC** G1; .E96. **CODEN** ESGRAF. Index available. cum. index.
Desc: Contains original articles, news, comments, and bibliographical information on geography.
Ind/Abst Am. Hist. Life (1955-1966,1988-); Ecol. Abstr. (?-?); Geogr. Abstr. Phys. Geogr.; Geogr. Abstr. Human Geogr.; Geol. Abstr.; GeoRef; Indice Hist. Esp. (1955-1966); Int. Dev. Abstr.

US/1055-6621
EXPLORER (MERCED, CALIF.), THE. (THE EXPLORER.). [Explorer]. No. 1 (1991)-. Periodical. English. $25.00. Barbara Showalter, 114 Snomass, Merced CA 95348. **DD** 910.
Ind/Abst Except. Hum. Exp.

US/0895-8521
EXPLORER NEWS. (EXPLORER NEWS / FOUNDATION FOR FIELD RESEARCH.). [Explor. news]. **Added/Corp** Foundation for Field Research. (198?)-. Periodical. English. qt. $20.00. Foundation for Field Research, 787 South Grade Road, PO Box 2010, Alpine CA 92001. **Tel** (619)445-9264. **ED** Annie Cody. **DD** 910. **Bk Rev. Circ:** 5,000.
Desc: Contains descriptions on scientific research expeditions which include the earth, marine, and life sciences. Research results are published.

US/0014-5025
EXPLORERS JOURNAL. **See** Science and Technology.

FI/0015-0010
FENNIA. [Fennia]. **Added/Corp** Suomen Maantieteellinen Seura. **VFOAT** Bulletin de la Societe Geographique de Finlande. Vol. 1 (1889)-. Monographic series. English (Finnish, French and Swedish). ir. Price varies per volume. Academic Bookstore Akateeminen, Postilokero 23, FIN-00371 Helsinki Finland. **Tel** 011 358 0 12141. **LC** G23; .G4. **CODEN** FENNAJ. available on microfilm from University Microfilms International (UMI). ***Absorbed*** *Acta Geographica (Helsinki, Finland).*
Ind/Abst Ecol. Abstr.; Geogr. Abstr. Phys. Geogr.; Geogr. Abstr. Human Geogr.; GeoRef; Int. Dev. Abstr.; Leis. Recreat. Tour. Abstr.; Rural Dev. Abstr.; Soils Fert.; World Agric. Econ.

US/0739-0750
FIELDING'S ECONOMY CARIBBEAN. [Fielding's econ. Caribb.]. **VFOAT** Economy Caribbean. 1984-. English. an. $8.95. William Morrow & Company Inc, 1350 Avenue of the Americas, New York NY 10019. **LC** F2171.3; .F54. **DD** 917.29/0452.

US/0278-8942
FLASHMAPS INSTANT GUIDE TO DALLAS, FORT WORTH. **VFOAT** Flashmaps, Dallas/Fort Worth. (1982)-. English. an. Flashmaps Publications Inc, PO Box 13, Chappaqua NY 10514. ***Continues in part*** *Flashmaps Instant Guide to Texas, 0195-6302.*

US/0428-7088
FLORIDA BUSINESS LETTER. SPECIAL MAPS AND GRAPHS OF FLORIDA. **See** Business.

US/0739-0041
FLORIDA GEOGRAPHER, THE. [Fla. geogr.]. **Added/Corp** Florida Society of Geographers. (196?)-. Academic Scholarly Publication. English. an. $10.00. Florida Society of Geographers, Department of Geography, University of Miami, Coral Gables FL 33124. **Tel** (305)284-4087, 284-4375. **ED** Ira M. Sheskin. **LC** F311; .F654. **DD** 975.9/005. Index available. **Bk Rev**. **Ad Acc**. **Circ:** 150 (ctrl). ***Continues*** *Florida Society of Geographers Newsletter.*
Desc: Scholarly articles on all aspects of the geography of Florida and the US South.
Ind/Abst Ecol. Abstr. (?-?); Geogr. Abstr. Human Geogr.

US/0015-5004
FOCUS (NEW YORK, N.Y. 1950). (FOCUS.). [Focus]. **Added/Corp** American Geographical Society of New York. **VFOAT** American Geographical Society's Focus. Vol. 1 (Oct. 15, 1950)-. Periodical. English. Four times a year. $32.00 institution, $24.00 individual. American Geographical Society, 156 Fifth Avenue, Suite 600, New York NY 10010-7002. **Tel** (212)242-0214, FAX (212)989-1583. **ED** Hillary Renwick. **LC** G1; .F6. **DD** 910.5. **CODEN** BLOFA5. **Bk Rev**. **Ad Acc**. **Circ:** 5,000 (ctrl). available on microfilm and microfiche from University Microfilms International (UMI). Documents available from UMI Article Clearinghouse.
Ind/Abst Acad. Abstr. Full Text Elite (Jan. 1989-) [Full Txt.]; Acad. Abstr. (Jan. 1989-); Acad. Search (Jan. 1989-); Curr. Geogr. Publ. (199?-); Gen. Period. Index (1985-); GeoRef; Humanit. Source (Jul. 1993-) [Full Txt.]; INFO-SOUTH Abstr.; Mag. Artic. Summar. Elite (Jan. 1989-) [Full Txt.]; Mag. Artic. Summar. Select (Jan. 1989-) [Full Txt.]; Mag. Artic. Summar. CD-ROM (Jan. 1989-); Mag. Search; Middle East Abstr. Index; Newsp. Period. Abstr. (1988-); Read. Guide Abstr. Select Ed.; Read. Guide Period. Lit.; Soc. Sci. Source (Jan. 1989-) [Full Txt.]; Mag. Index (1977-); Vocat. Search (Jan. 1989-) [Full Txt.].

HU/0015-5403
FOELDRAJZI ERTESITO. [Foeldr. ert.]. **Added/Corp** Magyar Tudomanyos Akademia, Budapest. Foeldrajztudomanyi Kutatocsoport. Vol. 1 (1952)-. Academic Scholarly Publication. Hungarian. qt. Akademiai Kiado, Publishing House of the Hungarian Academy of Sciences, Prielle Kornelia u. 19-35, H-1117 Budapest Hungary. **Tel** 011 36 1 1811991, FAX 011 36 1 1811991, telex 22-6228 AKNYO H. **ED** S. Marosi. **LC** DB901; .F58. **CODEN** FOERAM. **Bk Rev**. **Circ:** 1,200 (ctrl).
Desc: Recent results in geography. The geography of Hungary, natural and economic geography. Regional divisions, settlements and population. Theoretical and methodological issues.
Ind/Abst AGRICOLA; Ecol. Abstr.; Geogr. Abstr. Phys. Geogr.; Geogr. Abstr. Human Geogr.; Geol. Abstr.; GeoRef; Int. Dev. Abstr. (?-?); Leis. Recreat. Tour. Abstr.; Maize Abstr.; Meteorol. Geoastrophys. Abstr. (-199?); Rural Dev. Abstr.; World Agric. Econ.

HU/0015-5411
FOLDRAJZI KOZLEMENYEK. [Foldr. kozl.]. **Main/Corp** Magyar Foldrajzi Tarsasag. **VFOAT** Geographische Mitteilungen; Geographical Review. Vol. 1, (1873)-. Periodical. Hungarian (summaries and/or abstracts in English, French, German and Russian). Four times a year. $26.00. Magyar Foldrajzi Tarsasag, Andrassy Ut 62, 1062 Budapest Hungary. **Tel** (36-1)111-7688. **(Subscription address:** Kultura, PO Box 149, H 1389 Budapest 62 Hungary**) ED** Gy Miklos, Gy Gabris and J. Lerner. **LC** G9; .M18. Index available. cum. index. **Bk Rev**. **Ad Acc**. **Circ:** 1,100 (ctrl).
Ind/Abst Am. Hist. Life (1963-); Bibliogr. Carto.; Geogr. Abstr. Phys. Geogr.; Geogr. Abstr. Human Geogr.; Geol. Abstr.; Leis. Recreat. Tour. Abstr.; Maize Abstr.; Pig News Inf.; Poult. Abstr.; Rural Dev. Abstr.; Soils Fert.; World Agric. Econ.

DK/0071-6693
FOLIA GEOGRAPHICA DANICA. [Folia geogr. Dan.]. **Added/Corp** Kongelige Danske Geografiske Selskab. Vol. 1 (1940)-. Danish. ir. CA Reitzels Forlag AS, Norregade 20, DK-1165 Copenhagen K Denmark. **Tel** 011 45 3 3122400. **CODEN** FOGDBP.
Ind/Abst Geogr. Abstr. Phys. Geogr. (?-?); GeoRef.

PL/0071-8076
FOTOINTERPRETACJA W GEOGRAFII. [Fotointerpret. geogr.]. Periodical. Polish (English and French). ir. Polskie Towarzystwo Geograficzne, Ul Krakowskie Przedmiescie 30, Warszawa Poland. **Tel** 59-69-15, telex 31-5584 USK PL. **(Subscription address:** Wydawnictwo Uniwersytetu Slaskiego, Ul Bankowa 14, 40-007 Katowice Poland**) ED** Andrzej Ciolkosz, Andrzej T Jankowski, Leon Kozacki, Nogdan Ney, Jan R Oledzki, Stanislaw Ostaficzuk, Kazimierz Trafas, Jan Trembaczowski. **Bk Rev**. **Circ:** 300 (ctrl).
Desc: Application of remote sensing, different methods of interpretation of satellite imagery and aerial photos in earth science, geography, geomorphology, hydrology, climatology, land use, water management, environmental monitoring, anthropogenic changes of environment; agriculture, pedology, geology and some problems of photogrammetry.
Ind/Abst Geogr. Abstr. Phys. Geogr. (?-?); GeoRef; Int. Aerosp. Abstr.

FR/1157-3805
FRANCIS BIBLIOGRAPHIE GEOGRAPHIQUE INTERNATIONALE. 531. **Added/Corp** Institut de l'Information Scientifique et Technique (France) Centre National de la Recherche Scientifique (France). Laboratoire d'Information et de Documentation en Geographie. **VFOAT** Bibliographie Geographique Internationale; International Geographical Bibliography; BGI. Vol. 96, No. 1 (1991)-. French (English). qt (4 issues). 625.00F France; 655.00F other. CNRS / Institut d'Information Scientifique et Technique, (Centre National de la Recherche Scientifique), 15 Quai Anatole France, Paris 75700 France. **Tel** 011 33 1 47531515, telex 299 356 F. **(Subscription address:** Institut d'Information Scientifique et Technique Diffusion, 2 Allee du Parc de Brabois, 54514 Vandoeuvre Nancy France.**) LC** Z6001; .B57. Index available (free). available on CD-ROM. ***Continues*** *Bibliographie Geographique Internationale, 0067-6993.*

GW/0071-9234
FRANKFURTER GEOGRAPHISCHE HEFTE. [Frankf. geogr. Hefte]. **Added/Corp** Verein fuer Geographie und Statistik, Eingetragener Verein, zu Frankfurt am Main. Frankfurter Geographische Gesellschaft. (1927)-. Monographic series. German. ir. Price varies per volume. Johann Wolfgang Goethe-Universitat / Geographische Institute, Bibliothek, Postfach 11 19 32, D 60054 Frankfurt-am-Main. **LC** G13; .F8. **CODEN** FGGHBF.
Desc: Human and physical geography.
Ind/Abst Geogr. Abstr. Human Geogr. (?-?); GeoRef.

PO
GARCIA DE ORTA : SERIE DE GEOGRAFIA. **VFOAT** Serie de Geografia. Vol. 1; 1973-. Portuguese (English, French, Spanish, Italian and German). sa. 340$00. Instituto de Investigacao Cientifica Tropical, Centro de Documentacao e Informacao, rua Jau 47, 1 300 Lisbon Portugal. **Tel** 645321. **LC** DT352; .G33. Index available. **Circ:** 1,000 (ctrl). ***Supersedes in part*** *Garcia de Orta.*
Desc: Publishes articles on various aspects of the geographical sciences (mathematical geography, physical geography, human geography, etc.) which may be handled as pure sciences or applied.

US/0498-6415
GAZETTEER - UNITED STATES BOARD ON GEOGRAPHIC NAMES. **Main/Corp** United States. Board on Geographic Names. **VFOAT** United States Board on Geographic Names: Gazetteer. No. 1-1955-. Monographic series. English. Price varies per volume. US Army Topographic Command, Geographic Names Division, Mailstop 523, Reston VA 22092. **DD** 910. ***Continues in part*** *Cumulative Decision List - United States Board on Geographic Names.*

US/1043-1756
GEMUTLICHKEIT (HAYWARD, CALIF.). (GEMUTLICHKEIT.). [Gemutlichkeit]. (198?)-. Periodical. English. Twelve times a year. $57.00. Upcountry Publications, 2892 Chronicle Avenue, Hayward CA 94542. **Tel** (415)538-0628. **DD** 914.

AT/0157-1338
GEO (DEE WHY WEST, A.C.T.). (GEO.). Vol. 1, No. 1 (1979)-. Periodical. English. qt. $39.75 Australia; $55.00 surface mail, $85.00 air mail, other. GEO Productions Party Ltd, PO Box 1390, Chatswood New South Wales, 2057 Australia. **Tel** 011 61 02 4111766, FAX 011 61 02 4132689. **LC** DU1; .G46. **DD** 994/.005.
Desc: Aimed at the regions of Australia, New Zealand, the Pacific, and South-East Asia, covering subjects such as wildlife, flora and fauna, history, anthropology, and travel and adventure.

BE/0379-0452
GEO-ECO-TROP. **See** Environmental Issues-Ecology.

BE
GEO, GEOGRAPHIE, ECOLOGIE, ENVIRONNEMENT, ORGANISATION DE L'ESPACE. **VFOAT** Geographie, Ecologie, Environment, Organisation de l'Espace. Periodical. French. sa. Federation des Professeurs de Geographie, Avenue du Duc Jean 46, B 1080 Bruxelles Belgium. **LC** G1; .G16. **DD** 910/.5. ***Supersedes in part*** *Aardrijkskunde.*

US/1051-9858
GEO INFO SYSTEMS. [Geo info syst.]. (1990)-. Periodical. English. Ten times a year. $59.00 US and possessions; $79.00 Canada; $117.00 other. Advanstar Communications Inc., 131 West First Street, Duluth MN 55802. **Tel** (218)723-9477, (800)346-0085. **ED** Guy Maynard. **LC** G70.2; .G43. **DD** 910/.285. **[CCC].** ctrl circ.
Desc: The magazine targets geographic information systems (GIS) users; editorial covers practical applications of GIS for planning, developing and managing environments ranging from a local utility infrastructure to the North American ecosystem.
Ind/Abst Curr. Geogr. Publ. (199?-).

UK
GEO MAGAZINE. English. Five times a year (Jan., Apr., Sep.). £13.20. Geo Magazine, 90 Tuckingmill Tisbury, Salisbury SP3 6NS England. **Tel** 11 44 0747870107.

UK/0956-0629
GEOACTIVE. English. Three times a year. £32.95. Mary Glasgow Publications, Brookhampton Lane, Kineton, Warwickshire CV35 0JB England. **Tel** 011 44 926 640606, FAX 011 44 926 641016. **(Subscription address:** Mary Glasgow Publications, Brookhampton Lane, Kineton, Warwicks, CV35 0JB**) ED** Simon Ross. **Circ:** 2000.
Desc: Photocopiable case studies on contemporary geographical topics. Prepared mostly for 14-16 year-old age group.

UK
GEOBASE. (19??)-. Abstracting/Indexing Service. English. Usage charges vary. Elsevier Geo Abstracts, An Imprint of Elsevier Science Ltd., The Boulevard, Langford Lane, Kidlington, Oxford OX5 1GB United Kingdom. **Tel** 011 44 865 843000, 011 44 865 843699, FAX 011 44 865 843010. available in print from the publisher; available on CD-ROM from SilverPlatter (US).
Desc: Multidisciplinary database of the international scientific and technical literature, supplying bibliographic information and abstracts for the geographical, environmental and Earth sciences.

HK/1010-6049
GEOCARTO INTERNATIONAL. [Geocarto int.]. **Added/Corp** Geocarto International Centre. **VFOAT** Geocarto. (19??)-. Periodical. English. qt. $85.00 (airmail); $75.00 (surface mail). Geocarto International Centre, GPO Box 4122, Hong Kong Hong Kong. **Tel** 011 852 5 5464262, FAX 011 852 559 3419. **LC** G70.4; .G447. **DD** 621.36/78. **Bk Rev**. **Ad Acc**. **Pr Rev**. Documents available from Ask*IEEE, Documents on Demand.
Desc: A multi-disciplinary forum dealing with remote sensing serving the world-wide scientific and user community in the fields of remote sensing, geoscience and cartography.
Ind/Abst Curr. Geogr. Publ. (199?-); Ecol. Abstr.; Environ. Abstr.; Geogr. Abstr. Phys. Geogr.; Geol. Abstr.; GeoRef; INSPEC (1986-); Int. Aerosp. Abstr.; Int. Dev. Abstr.; Pollut. Abstr. Indexes.

CL/0431-1930
GEOCHILE. [GeoChile]. Spanish. Lord Cochrane, Providencia 711, Santiago Chile. **LC** F3064; .G46. **DD** 983/.064/05. **CODEN** GCHLAE.
Ind/Abst GeoRef.

AT
GEODATE. (19??)-. English. Four times a year (Mar., May, July, Sept.). 45.00Aus$. Warringal Productions, 114 Argyle Street, Fitzroy 3065 Australia. **Tel** 011 61 03 4160200, FAX 011 61 03 4160402. **(Subscription address:** Warringal Publications, PO Box 336, Fitzroy 3065 Australia.**)**

NE
GEODESIA. (Sept. 1959)-. Periodical. Dutch (summaries and/or abstracts in English). ir (11 issues). Fl60.00 Netherlands; Fl73.00 Belgium; Fl102.00 other. JJS Kopaszeuski, A van Schendellaan 16, 5531 TV Bladel Netherlands. **Tel** 011 31 15 7811567. Index available (bound in last issue). **Bk Rev**. **Ad Acc**. **Circ:** 3,100.
Desc: Geodesy mapping and survey land registry.
Ind/Abst Bibliogr. Carto.

XR/0016-7096
GEODETICKY A KARTOGRAFICKY OBZOR. **Added/Corp** Czechoslovakia. Ustredni Sprava Geodezie a Kartografie. Vol. 1, No. 1 (1955)-. Periodical. Czech. Twelve times a year. $88.20. **(Subscription address:** Artia Pegas Press Ltd., Palac Metro Narodni Trida 25, 11210 Prague 1 Czech Republic.**)**
Ind/Abst Bibliogr. Carto.; Geogr. Abstr. Phys. Geogr. (?-?).

FR/0985-3111
GEODINAMICA ACTA. Vol. 1 (1987)-. Periodical. English (French). qt. $246.00. Masson Editeur, Box Postale 22, 41353 Vineuil 16 France. **Tel** 011 33 54 438994. **(Subscription address:** 7A Boulevard de Perolles, CH-1701 Fribourg Switzerland**) LC** G1; .R44. **DD** 551/.05. **CODEN** GACTE3. **[CCC].** Documents available from The Genuine Article, Petroleum Abstracts Document Delivery Service. ***Continues*** *Revue de Geologie Dynamique et de Geographie Physique, 0241-1407.*
Ind/Abst Curr. Contents Phys. Chem. Earth Sci.; Geogr. Abstr. Phys. Geogr.; Geol. Abstr.; GeoRef; Pet. Abstr.; Res. Alert [Full Cov.]; Sci. Cit. Index; SCISEARCH.

BL
GEOGRAFIA. V. 1- (No. 1-); April 1976-. Periodical. Portuguese (summaries and/or abstracts in English, German and French). sa. $25.00. Associacao de Geografia Teoretica, Caixa Postal 178, Rio Claro 13500 Brazil. **Tel** 011 55 0195 34-0122, FAX 011 55 0195 24-9622. **ED** Antonio Christofoletti. **LC** G1.G292. **DD** 910/.5. Index available. **Bk Rev**. **Ad Acc**. **Circ:** 1,000 (ctrl).

Desc: Methods and techniques in geographical research, case and physical geography, notes and book reviews.
Ind/Abst Ecol. Abstr.; Geogr. Abstr. Phys. Geogr.; Geogr. Abstr. Human Geogr.; Int. Dev. Abstr.; Ref. Z.

IT
GEOGRAFIA. (19??)-. Periodical. Italian. Four times a year. L38000. Edigeo, Via G, Carini 2, 00152 Rome, Italy. **ED** Osvaldo Baldacci. Index available (bound in last issue).

IT
GEOGRAFIA NELLE SCUOLE, LA. **Added/Corp** Istituto Geografico De Agostini. Associazione Italiana Degli Insegnanti di Geografia. (19??)-. Periodical. Italian. bm. L40000 Italy; L60000 other. Prof. Donato Carlo, Via Vasari 2, 34129 Trieste Italy. **Tel** 011 39 40 6763635. **LC** WMLC L 83/9587.

PL/0137-7566
GEOGRAFIA W SZKOLE. [Geogr. Szk.]. (1948)-. Periodical. Polish. Five times a year. $35.00. **(Subscription address:** ARS Polona, PO Box 1001, 00068 Warsaw Poland.**)** **UDC** 372.891.
Ind/Abst Bibliogr. Carto.

XO/0016-7193
GEOGRAFICKY CASOPIS. GEOGRAFICHESKII ZHURNAL. GEOGRAPHICAL REVIEW. GEOGRAPHISCHE ZEITSCHRIFT. REVUE DE GEOGRAPHIE. [Geogr. cas.]. **Added/Corp** Slovenska Akademia Vied. **VFOAT** Geograficheskii Zhurnal; Geographical Review; Geographische Zeitschrift; Revue de Geographie. (1949)-. Periodical. Slovak (summaries and/or abstracts in Russian and German; table of contents in English and Multiple languages). qt. $18.00. Veda, Publishing House of the Slovak Academy of Sciences, Klemensova 19, 814 30 Bratislava Slovakia. **Tel** (7)583-15. **(Subscription address:** Kubon & Sagner, ABT Zeitschriftenimport, D 80328 Munich Germany.**)** **ED** Akademik Emil Mazur. **CODEN** GGCAAI. cum. index. **Bk Rev. Ad Acc. Circ:** 1,000 (ctrl).
Desc: Articles and studies on problems of physical, economical, historical, and regional geography, further subjects are soil erosion, speleology, climatology, hydrology, and protection of environment.
Ind/Abst Bibliogr. Carto.; Geogr. Abstr. Phys. Geogr.; Geogr. Abstr. Human Geogr.; GeoRef; Soils Fert.

●NE/0926-3837
GEOGRAFIE. **Added/Corp** Koninklijk Nederlands Aardrijkskundig Genootschap. (Jan. 1992)-. Periodical. Dutch. bm. KNAG, Postbus 80123, 3508 TC Utrecht Netherlands. ***Continues** Geografisch Tijdschrift, 0016-7215.*
Ind/Abst Bibliogr. Carto.

RU/0016-7207
GEOGRAFIIA V SHKOLE / UPRAVLENIE NACHALNOI I SREDNEI SHKOLY NARKOMPROSA RSFSR. **Added/Corp** Upravlenie Nachalnoi i Srednei Shkoly Narkomprosa RSFSR. Russian S.F.S.R. Narodnyi Komissariat Prosveshcheniia. Russian S.F.S.R. Ministerstvo Prosveshcheniia. Soviet Union. Ministerstvo Prosveshcheniia. Soviet Union. Gosudarstvennyi Komitet po Narodnomu Obrazovaniiu. No. 1 (1934)-. Periodical. Russian. bm. $23.00. Izdatelstvo Vysshaia Shkola, Neglinnaya Ulitsa,, Dom 29-14, GSP-4, Moscow 101430 Russia. **(Subscription address:** Victor Kamkin, 4956 Boiling Brook Parkway, Rockville, MD 20852**)** **LC** G1; .G313.

DK
GEOGRAFISK TIDSKRIFT DET KNOGELIGE DANSKI GEOGRAFISKE SELSKAB. English (Danish). ir. kr200.00. CA Reitzels Forlag AS, Norregade 20, DK-1165 Copenhagen K Denmark. **Tel** 011 45 3 3122400.

DK/0016-7223
GEOGRAFISK TIDSSKRIFT. [Geogr. tidsskr.]. **Added/Corp** Kongelige Danske Geografiske Selskab. (1877)-. Danish. ir. **LC** G25; .D19. **CODEN** GGTKAV. cum. index.
Ind/Abst Agrofor. Abstr.; Bibliogr. Carto.; Geogr. Abstr. Human Geogr.; GeoRef.

SW/0435-3676
GEOGRAFISKA ANNALER. SERIES A, PHYSICAL GEOGRAPHY. [Geogr. ann., Ser. A]. **Added/Corp** Svenska Sallskapet for Antropologie och Geografi, Stockholm. Vol. 47A (1965)-. Periodical. Multiple languages (English, French and German). qt (4 issues per year often combined). Kr570.00, $99.00. Scandinavian University Press, PO Box 2959 Toeyen, N 0608 Oslo 6 Norway. **Tel** 011 47 2 2575400, FAX 011 47 2 2575353, telex 71896 UROR N. **(Subscription address:** Scandinavian University Press, 200 Meacham Ave., Elmont NY 11003.**)** **ED** Gunnar Oestrem. **CODEN** GAPGAP. Index available. **Ad Acc. Pr Rev. Acid Free. Circ:** 1,000 (ctrl). Documents available from The Genuine Article. ***Continues in part** Geografiska Annaler.*
Desc: New results in physical geography, glaciology, hydrology and related subjects, with some emphasis on arctic areas. New methods and scientific results within geo-sciences are welcome. Journal of the Swedish Association for Anthropology and Geography.
Ind/Abst ASTIS Curr. Aware. Bull. (1978-); AQUAREF; ASTIS Bibliogr. (1978-); Bibliogr. Carto.; Curr. Geogr. Publ. (199?-); Ecol. Abstr.; Geogr. Abstr. Phys. Geogr.; Geogr. Abstr. Human Geogr.; Geol. Abstr.; GeoRef; Int. Bibliogr. Sociol.; Int. Dev. Abstr.; Irr. Drain. Abstr.; J. Plan. Lit.; Meteorol. Geoastrophys. Abstr.; Res. Alert [Select. Cov.]; SCISEARCH; Soils Fert.

XV/0373-4498
GEOGRAFSKI ZBORNIK. ACTA GEOGRAPHICA. [Geogr. zb.]. **VFOAT** Acta Geographica. Vol. 1 (1952)-. Slovenian (summaries and/or abstracts in English). an. Cankarjeva Zalozba, POB 201-IV, 61000 Ljubljana, Kopitarjeva 2 Slovenia. **Tel** (61)323841, FAX (61)318782, telex 331821. **CODEN** GFZBAR.
Ind/Abst GeoRef.

II/0072-0909
GEOGRAPHER, THE. **Added/Corp** Aligarh, India. Muslim University. Geographical Society. (19??)-. Periodical. English. sa. $30.00. Treasurer Aligarh Muslim University, Department of Geography, Aligarh UP India. **(Subscription address:** Prints India, 11 Darya Ganj, New Delhi, 110002 India, (Phone: 011 91 11 3268645)**)** **LC** G1; .G317.

US
GEOGRAPHERS : BIOBIBLIOGRAPHICAL STUDIES. **Added/Corp** International Geographical Union. Commission on the History of Geographical Thought. Vol. 1 (1977)-. English. an. $80.00. Cassell PLC / New York, 360 West 36th Street, New York NY 10001. **Tel** (201)939-6064, FAX (201)440-5204. **ED** Geoffrey J. Martin. **LC** Z6001; .G425; G67. **DD** 910/.92/2. **Circ:** 600.
Desc: Consists of studies of individuals who have made major contributions to the development of geographical thought and of geography as a scientific subject and academic discipline.

PL
GEOGRAPHIA. (1976)-. Periodical. Polish (summaries and/or abstracts in English and Russian). ir. varies. Wyduwnictwo Uniwersytetu Slaskiego, Ul Bankowa 14, 40-007 Katowice Poland. **Tel** 59-69-15, telex 31-5584 USKTL. **(Subscription address:** Krakowskie Predmiescie 7, Skrportowa 1001, 00-950 Warszawa Poland**)** **ED** Jan Trembaczowski. **LC** G1; .G3197. Index available. **Bk Rev. Ad Acc. Circ:** 300 (ctrl).
Desc: Includes topics on geomorphology, climatology, social and economic geography and anthropogenic impact on geographical environment.

●IT/1121-8940
GEOGRAPHIA ANTIQUA. (1992)-. Periodical. Italian (French and German). an. L80.000. Giunti Editore, Via Bolognese 165, 50139 Florence Italy. **Tel** 011 39 55 6679267, FAX 011 39 55 268312, telex 571438.
Desc: Articles featured mainly focus on geographic and cartographic history, but ample space is also given over to "on-site" historical geography.

PL/0016-7282
GEOGRAPHIA POLONICA. [Geogr. Pol.]. **Added/Corp** Polska Akademia Nauk. Instytut Geografii. Vol. 1 (1964)-. Periodical. English (French). ir. $37.50. **(Subscription address:** ARS Polona, PO Box 1001, 00068 Warsaw Poland.**)** **LC** G1; .G3195. **CODEN** GGPLAE. Index Available, published separately, free-automatically sent. cum. index.
Ind/Abst Ecol. Abstr. (?-?); Geogr. Abstr. Phys. Geogr. (?-?); Geogr. Abstr. Human Geogr.; Geol. Abstr.; GeoRef; Int. Bibliogr. Sociol.; Int. Dev. Abstr.; Soils Fert.

●US/0083-016X
GEOGRAPHIC AND GLOBAL ISSUES QUARTERLY / UNITED STATES DEPARTMENT OF STATE, BUREAU OF INTELLIGENCE AND RESEARCH. **Added/Corp** United States. Dept. of State. Bureau of Intelligence and Research. United States. Dept. of State. Office of the Geographer. Vol. 3, No. 1 (Spring 1993)-. Government Publication. English. qt. $7.00 US; $8.75. Superintendent of Documents, US Government Printing Office, Washington DC 20402. **Tel** (202)275-3328, FAX (202)786-2377. **LC** G109; .U544. **DD** 910/.212. ***Continues** Geographic Notes.*

US/0083-0100
GEOGRAPHIC BULLETIN. ***Ceased.*** [Geogr. bull.]. **Added/Corp** United States. Dept. of State. Bureau of Intelligence and Research. United States. Dept. of State. Office of the Geographer. (1963)-(19??). Bulletin. English. US Department of State, 2201 C Street NW, Room 5819, Washington DC 20520. **Tel** (202)647-9859. **DD** 910.

UK
GEOGRAPHIC INFORMATION : THE YEARBOOK OF THE ASSOCIATION FOR GEOGRAPHIC INFORMATION. **Added/Corp** Association for Geographic Information. **VFOAT** AGI Yearbook; Yearbook of the Association for Geographic Information. (1991)-. English. an. £29.50. Taylor & Francis Ltd., Rankine Road, Basingstoke Hampshire, RG24 8PR United Kingdom. **Tel** 011 44 256 840366, FAX 011 44 256 479438, telex 858540. **(Subscription address:** Taylor & Francis Inc., 1900 Frost Road, Suite 101, Bristol PA 19007-1598.**)** **LC** G70.2; .A84. **DD** 910/.6/041. ***Continues** Association for Geographic Information Yearbook.*

US/0083-016X
GEOGRAPHIC NOTES / DEPARTMENT OF STATE, BUREAU OF INTELLIGENCE AND RESEARCH, THE GEOGRAPHER. ***Title Change.*** **Added/Corp** United States. Dept. of State. Office of the Geographer. **VFOAT** Geographic Note. (198?)-Vol. 2, No. 4 (Winter 1992/1993). English. qt. Superintendent of Documents, US Government Printing Office, Washington DC 20402. **Tel** (202)275-3328, FAX (202)786-2377. **LC** G109; .U544. **DD** 910/.212. ***Absorbed** Status of the World's Nations, 0732-8605.* ***Continued by** Geographic and Global Issues Quarterly.*

US/0894-9190
GEOGRAPHIC THESAURUS. [Geogr. thesaurus]. **Added/Corp** University of Tulsa. Information Services Dept. University of Tulsa. Information Services Division. (19??)-. English. $150.00 (general subscribers), $175.00 (nonsubscribers). Petroleum Abstracts, University of Tulsa, Information Services Division, 600 South College Avenue, Harwell Hall 101, Tulsa OK 74104-3189. **Tel** (800)247-8678, (918)631-2297, FAX (918)599-9361, telex 49 7543. **LC** G105; .G46. **DD** 025.
Desc: An essential guide to searching the TULSA database efficiently and effectively.

FI
GEOGRAPHICA. No. 1- 1974-. Monographic series. English (Finnish). ir. Price varies per volume. Professor Sakari Piha, University of Oulu, 90100 Oulu 10 Finland. **Tel** 358-81-332133. **ED** Sirkka Kupila-Ahvenniemi. **Ad Acc. Circ:** 500 (ctrl).
Desc: Monographs, reviews, and dissertations in the field of general geography.

SZ/0016-7312
GEOGRAPHICA HELVETICA. [Geogr. Helv.]. **Added/Corp** Geographisch-Ethnographische Gesellschaft Zurich. Vol. 1, (Jan. 1946)-. Periodical. Multiple languages (French, German and Italian). Four times a year (Mar., June, Sept., Dec.). 90.00F. Fotorotar AG, Gewerbe Strasse 18, CH-8132 Egg Switzerland. **Tel** 011 41 1 9841777. **LC** G1; .G328. **CODEN** GGHVA4. Index available. cum. index. available on microfilm from University Microfilms International (UMI). Documents available from BIOSIS Document Express. ***Formed by the union of** Geographisch-Ethnographische Gesellschaft, Zurich. Mitteilungen **and** Schweizer Geograph.*
Ind/Abst Bibliogr. Carto.; Biol. Abstr.; Geogr. Abstr. Phys. Geogr.; Geogr. Abstr. Human Geogr.; GeoRef; Int. Dev. Abstr.; Leis. Recreat. Tour. Abstr.; Rural Dev. Abstr.; Soils Fert.; World Agric. Econ.

YU/0351-3238
GEOGRAPHICA IUGOSLAVICA : BILTEN SAVEZA GEOGRAFSKIH DRUSTAVA JUGOSLAVIJE. **Added/Corp** Savez Geografskih Drustava Jugoslavije. (19??)-. Monographic series. English. Price varies per volume.
Ind/Abst Geogr. Abstr. Human Geogr.

MY/0126-6101
GEOGRAPHICA (KUALA LUMPUR). (GEOGRAPHICA.). [Geographica]. **Added/Corp** University of Malaya (Founded 1962). Dept. of Geography. Universiti Malaya. Persatuan Geografi. (1965)-. Periodical. English (English). an. $5.00. Persatuan Geografi Fakulti Sastera, Dan Sains Sosial Universiti, Malaya Lembah Pantai, Kuala Lumpur Malaysia. **Tel** 7555266. **ED** S H Khoo. **LC** G1; .G324. **Bk Rev. Ad Acc. Circ:** 1,000.
Desc: Contains articles of geographical interest pertaining to Malaysia in particular and the tropical region in general.

UK/0953-9611
GEOGRAPHICAL ABSTRACTS. HUMAN GEOGRAPHY. See Geography-Abstracting, Bibliographies and Statistics.

UK/0954-0504
GEOGRAPHICAL ABSTRACTS : PHYSICAL GEOGRAPHY. See Geography-Abstracting, Bibliographies and Statistics.

US/0016-7363
GEOGRAPHICAL ANALYSIS. [Geogr. anal.]. Vol. 1 (Jan. 1969)-. Periodical. English. qt. $90.00 (institutions), $35.00 (individuals) US; $101.65 (institutions), $42.80 (individuals) includes GST, Canada; $95.00 (institutions), $40.00 (individuals) other. Ohio State University Press, 1070 Carmack Road, 180 Pressey Hall, Columbus OH 43210. **Tel** (614)292-6930, (614)292-1407, FAX (614)292-2065. **ED** Emilio Casetti. **LC** G70; .G43. **DD** 910/.001/82. **CODEN** GPHAA4. **[CCC].** Index available. cum. index. **Bk Rev. Ad Acc. Pr Rev.** available on microfilm and microfiche from University Microfilms International (UMI). Documents

available from The Genuine Article.
Desc: Publishes significant advances in geographical theory, model building and quantitative methods.
Ind/Abst Bibliogr. Carto.; Curr. Contents Soc. Behav. Sci.; Curr. Geogr. Publ. (199?-); Geogr. Abstr. Phys. Geogr.; Geogr. Abstr. Human Geogr.; GeoRef; Int. Bibliogr. Sociol.; J. Plan. Lit.; Leis. Recreat. Tour. Abstr.; Middle East Abstr. Index; Popul. Index; Res. Alert [Full Cov.]; Rural Dev. Abstr.; Sage Race Relat. Abstr.; Soc. Sci. Cit. Index [Full Cov.]; World Agric. Econ.

US/0731-3292
GEOGRAPHICAL BULLETIN (YPSILANTI, MICH.), THE. (THE GEOGRAPHICAL BULLETIN.). [Geogr. bull.]. **Added/Corp** Gamma Theta Upsilon. (Aug. 1970)-. Bulletin. English. sa (May and Nov.). $10.00 (insitutions), $4.00 (other). Gamma Theta Upsilon, Eastern Michigan University, Department of Geography and Geology, Ypsilanti MI 48197. **Tel** (313)487-1480. **ED** Dr. C. Nicholas Raphael. **LC** G1; .G3344. **DD** 910/.5. **Pr Rev. Circ:** 1,500 (ctrl).
Desc: Publishes articles pertaining to geographic topics and related research.
Ind/Abst Bibliogr. Carto.; Curr. Geogr. Publ. (199?-); Geogr. Abstr. Phys. Geogr.; Geogr. Abstr. Human Geogr.; Int. Dev. Abstr. (?-?); Middle East Abstr. Index.

AT/0085-0969
GEOGRAPHICAL EDUCATION. [Geogr. educ.]. **Added/Corp** Australian Geography Teachers' Association. Vol. 1 (June 1969)-. Periodical. English. an. 13.00Aus$. Australian Geography Teachers Association, c/o Dr John Lidstone, Social Studies Dept-Brisbane CAE, Kelvin GR-Queensland 4059 Australia.
Ind/Abst APAIS, Aust. Public Aff. Inf. Ser. (1973-); Aust. Educ. Index (1977-); Curr. Index J. Educ. (March 1990); Geogr. Abstr. Human Geogr.; Int. Dev. Abstr.

US/0739-9499
GEOGRAPHICAL INDEX SUPPLEMENT. [Geogr. index suppl.]. **Added/Corp** Victor Valley College (Victorville, Calif.). Library. **VFOAT** Geographical Index. (197?)-. English. Four times a year (Feb., May, Aug., Nov.). $8.00. Victor Valley College, PO Drawer 00 18422, Bear Valley, Victorville CA 92392. **Tel** (619)245-4271 Ext. 262 300.

UK/0016-7398
GEOGRAPHICAL JOURNAL, THE. [Geogr. j.]. **Added/Corp** Royal Geographical Society (Great Britain). Vol. 1 (Jan. 1893)-. Periodical. English. Three times a year (Mar., July, Nov.). $80.00 North America Comes with Royal Geographical Society membership. Royal Geographical Society / England, 1 Kensington Gore, London SW7 2AR England. **Tel** 011 44 71 589 5466, FAX 011 44 71 584 4447, telex 933669. **ED** R. A. M. Gardner. **LC** G7; .R91. **DD** 910.5. **CODEN** GGJOAR. **[CCC].** Index available (bound in Nov. issue). cum. index. **Bk Rev. Ad Acc. Pr Rev. Circ:** 10,600 (ctrl). available on microfilm and microfiche from University Microfilms International (UMI); available on CD-ROM from University Microfilms International (UMI). Documents available from The Genuine Article, UMI Article Clearinghouse. ***Continues** Proceedings of the Royal Geographical Society and Monthly Record of Geography.*
Desc: Covers geography on all parts of the world for general readers as well as professional geographers. Publishes new research and fieldwork.
Ind/Abst Acad. Abstr. Full Text Elite (July 1990-); Acad. Abstr. (July 1990-); Acad. Ind. [Computer File] (1987-); Acad. Search (July 1990-); AGRICOLA; Am. Hist. Life (1954-); Anthropol. Index; Arts Humanit. Citation Index [Select. Cov.]; Bibliogr. Carto.; Book Rev. Index; Br. Archaeol. Bibliogr.; Br. Humanit. Index; Coal Abstr.; Curr. Contents Soc. Behav. Sci.; Curr. Geogr. Publ. (199?-); Ecol. Abstr.; EMBASE; Expand. Acad. Index (1987-); Field Crop Abstr.; For. Abstr.; Gen. Sci. Source (Jul. 1990-); Geogr. Abstr. Phys. Geogr.; Geogr. Abstr. Human Geogr.; Geol. Abstr.; GeoRef; Grasslands For. Abstr.; INFO-SOUTH Abstr.; Int. Bibliogr. Sociol.; Int. Dev. Abstr.; Int. Polit. Sci. Abstr.; J. Plan. Lit.; Leis. Recreat. Tour. Abstr.; Mag. Search; Meteorol. Geoastrophys. Abstr.; Middle East Abstr. Index; Newsp. Period. Abstr. (1989-); Numis. Lit.; Life Sci. Collect.; Res. Alert [Full Cov.]; Rural Dev. Abstr.; Soc. Sci. Source (Jul. 1990-); Soc. Sci. Cit. Index [Full Cov.]; Soc. Sci. Index; Soc. Sci. Index Fulltext (Nov. 1988-) [Full Txt.]; Soils Fert.; Middle East J.; West. Hist. Q.; World Agric. Econ.

US/0148-7000
GEOGRAPHICAL LOCATION CODES (WASHINGTON. 1976). (GEOGRAPHICAL LOCATION CODES / U.S. DEPARTMENT OF HEALTH, EDUCATION, AND WELFARE.). English. an. Division of Financial Operations and Fiscal Procedures, Department of Health and Human Services, 739 D1 Humphrey Building, 200 Independence Avenue SW, Washington DC 20201. **LC** G108.7; .U54A. **DD** 910/.01/48.

CN/0829-7622
GEOGRAPHICAL MONOGRAPHS. [Geogr. monogr.]. **Added/Corp** Atkinson College. Dept. of Geography. **VAT** Geographical Monograph Series. No. 1 (1973)-. Monographic series. English. ir. Price varies per volume. York University / Department of Geography, 4700 Keele Street, North York Ontario M3J 1P3 Canada. **Tel** (905)736-2100, FAX (905)736-5103. **ED** J. M. Cameron. **LC** UNC. **Pr Rev.**
Desc: Provides an outlet for substantial geographical research efforts and to familiarize researchers elsewhere with work being done at York University.
Ind/Abst GeoRef.

II/0072-0925
GEOGRAPHICAL OBSERVER, THE. **Added/Corp** Meerut College Geographical Society. (1965)-. English. an. $30.00. Geographical Observer, Meerut College of Geographical South, Meerut UP India. **(Subscription address:** Prints India, 11 Darya Ganj, New Delhi, 110002 India, (Phone: 011 91 11 3268645)) **LC** G35; .G4.
Ind/Abst Geogr. Abstr. Phys. Geogr.; Geogr. Abstr. Human Geogr.

CI
GEOGRAPHICAL PAPERS. 1-. English (German; summaries and/or abstracts in Serbo-Croatian (Roman)). **LC** G58. **DD** 910.

UK/0305-5914
GEOGRAPHICAL PAPERS. DEPARTMENT OF GEOGRAPHY, UNIVERSITY OF READING. (GEOGRAPHICAL PAPERS.). [Geogr. pap., Dep. Geogr., Univ. Read.]. **VFOAT** Reading Geographical Papers. Monographic series. English. ir (four-five papers a year). Price varies per volume. Geographical Papers, University of Reading, Whiteknights Reading RG6 2AB England. **Tel** 0734-85123 ext. 7861 7826. **CODEN** GPUGDM. **Bk Rev. Ad Acc.**
Ind/Abst Geogr. Abstr. Phys. Geogr. (?-?); Geogr. Abstr. Human Geogr. (?-?); GeoRef; Int. Dev. Abstr. (?-?).

II
GEOGRAPHICAL PERSPECTIVE. **Added/Corp** Patna University. Dept. of Geography. Geographical Society. Vol. 1, No. 1 (Mar. 1987)-. English. qt. $25.00. Patna University, Geographical Society, Department of Geography, Patna, India. **(Subscription address:** Prints India, 11 Darya Ganj, New Delhi, 110002 India, (Phone: 011 91 11 3268645)) **LC** G1; .G4647.

US/0199-994X
GEOGRAPHICAL PERSPECTIVES. ***Ceased.*** [Geogr. perspect.]. No. 33 (Spring 1974)-(1993). Periodical. English. sa. University of Northern Iowa Department of Geography, Cedar Falls IA 50614-0406. **Tel** (319)273-2016. **ED** C Murray Austin. **LC** G1; .G348. **DD** 910/.5. **[CCC]. Bk Rev. Ad Acc. Circ:** 300 (ctrl). Documents available from Documents on Demand. ***Continues** Iowa Geographer.*
Desc: Covers applied, education, public policy, future orientation, Third World issues, general topics, and opinion.
Ind/Abst Ecol. Abstr. (?-?); Environ. Abstr.; Geogr. Abstr. Human Geogr.; Int. Dev. Abstr. (?-?); Middle East Abstr. Index.

UK/0277-2388
GEOGRAPHICAL RESEARCH STUDIES SERIES. [Geogr. res. stud. ser.]. 1-. Monographic series. English. ir. Price varies per volume. John Wiley & Sons Ltd., Baffins Lane, Chichester West Sussex PO19 1UD England. **Tel** 0243 779777, FAX 0243 776128 BTG:JWP001, telex 86290 WIBOOKG. **(Subscription address:** North, South and Central America/ John Wiley & Sons, Inc., Subscription Department, 605 Third Avenue, New York, NY 10158-0012, USA; telephone: (212)850-6645; FAX: (212)850-6021**)**

US/0016-7428
GEOGRAPHICAL REVIEW. [Geogr. rev.]. **Added/Corp** American Geographical Society of New York. Vol. 1 (Jan. 1916)-. Academic Scholarly Publication. English. Four times a year. $68.00 institution, $48.00 individual. American Geographical Society, 156 Fifth Avenue, Suite 600, New York NY 10010-7002. **Tel** (212)242-0214, FAX (212)989-1583. **ED** Douglas R. McManis. **LC** G1; .G35. **DD** 910.5. **CODEN** GEORAD. Index available. cum. index. **Bk Rev. Ad Acc. Pr Rev. Circ:** 3,000 (ctrl). available on microfilm and microfiche from University Microfilms International (UMI). Documents available from The Genuine Article, BIOSIS Document Express, UMI Article Clearinghouse, CASDDS. ***Supersedes** Bulletin of the American Geographical Society, 0190-5929.*
Desc: A long-established quarterly with a large international circulation, containing scholarly articles. Geographical record notes on topics and areas of current interest, and reviews of monographs and atlases in geography and related fields. It is indispensable to scholars, students, teachers, and librarians.
Ind/Abst Abstr. Anthropol.; Acad. Abstr. Full Text Elite (July 1990-); Acad. Abstr. (July 1990-); Acad. Ind. [Computer File] (1987-); Acad. Search (July 1990-); AGRICOLA; Am. Hist. Life (1963-); Am. Hist. Life Part B (1963-); Am. Bibliogr. Slavic East Europ. Stud.; AQUAREF; Arts Humanit. Citation Index [Select. Cov.]; Bibliogr. Carto.; BHA : Biblio. Hist. Art; Biol. Abstr. (-1978); Br. Archaeol. Bibliogr. (?-19??); Chem. Abstr.; Curr. Contents Soc. Behav. Sci.; Curr. Geogr. Publ. (199?-); Ecol. Abstr. (?-?); Expand. Acad. Index (1987-); For. Abstr.; Gen. Sci. Source (Jul. 1990-); Geogr. Abstr. Phys. Geogr.; Geogr. Abstr. Human Geogr.; Geol. Abstr.; GeoRef; Grasslands For. Abstr.; INFO-SOUTH Abstr.; Int. Bibliogr. Sociol.; Int. Dev. Abstr.; Int. Polit. Sci. Abstr.; J. Plan. Lit.; Leis. Recreat. Tour. Abstr.; Mag. Search; Middle East Abstr. Index; Newsp. Period. Abstr. (1991-); PAIS Int. Print (1991-); Life Sci. Collect.; Popul. Index; Res. Alert [Full Cov.]; Rural Dev. Abstr.; Soc. Sci. Source (Jul. 1990-); Soc. Sci. Cit. Index [Full Cov.]; Soc. Sci. Index; Soc. Sci. Index Fulltext (Oct. 1988-) [Full Txt.]; Soils Fert.; West. Hist. Q.; World Agric. Econ.

II
GEOGRAPHICAL REVIEW OF INDIA. **Added/Corp** Geographical Society of India. Vol. 1 (Sept. 1936)-. Periodical. English. qt. $60.00. Geographical Society of India, 35 Ballygunge Circular Road, Calcutta 700 019 India. **Tel** 75-3681. **(Subscription address:** Prints India, 11 Darya Ganj, New Delhi, 110002 India, (Phone: 011 91 11 3268645)) **ED** P K Saha. **LC** G1; .C17. **DD** 910.5. Index available. **Bk Rev. Ad Acc. Circ:** 700 (ctrl).
Desc: Physical geography, regional development, social geography, land use, cultural geography, economic geography, urban geography, demography, cartography and environment.
Ind/Abst Indian Geosci. Abstr.; Int. Bibliogr. Sociol.; Leis. Recreat. Tour. Abstr.; Rural Dev. Abstr.; World Agric. Econ.

JA/0289-6001
GEOGRAPHICAL REVIEW OF JAPAN. SERIES B. (GEOGRAPHICAL REVIEW OF JAPAN.). [Geogr. rev. Jpn., Ser. B]. **Added/Corp** Nihon Chiri Gakkai. **VFOAT** Chirigaku Hyoron. Vol. 57 No. 1 (1984)-. Periodical. English (summaries and/or abstracts in Japanese). sa. Nippon Chiri Gakkai, (Association of Japanese Geographers), 2-10, Kanda Surugadai,, Chiyodaku, Tokyoto 101 Japan. **LC** G1; .G353. **DD** 915.2/005.
Ind/Abst Curr. Geogr. Publ. (199?-); Ecol. Abstr.; Geogr. Abstr. Phys. Geogr.; Geogr. Abstr. Human Geogr.; GeoRef; Int. Bibliogr. Sociol.; Int. Dev. Abstr.

●US/1069-2665
GEOGRAPHICAL SYSTEMS. (1993)-. Periodical. English. qt. Gordon & Breach Science Publishers, Inc., PO Box 786, Cooper Station, New York NY 10276. **Tel** (212)206-8900, FAX (212)645-2459. **(Subscription address:** International Publishers Distributor at one of the following addresses: 820 Town Center Drive, Langhorne, PA 19047; or PO Box 90, Reading Berkshire RG1 8JL UK; or Kent Ridge PO Box 1180, Singapore 9111, Republic of Singapore**)**
Desc: Concerned with the interface between geographical information systems and mathematical modelling and statistical analysis.

UK
GEOGRAPHICAL : THE MONTHLY MAGAZINE OF THE ROYAL GEOGRAPHICAL SOCIETY. **Added/Corp** Royal Geographical Society (Great Britain). **VFOAT** Geographical Magazine. Vol. 60, No. 12 (Dec. 1988)-. Periodical. English. Twelve times a year. £23.50 UK, £29.50 Europe, £35.50 others (regular delivery); $73.98 Southeast Asia & Mexico & Oceania & US & Canada, $70.82 others (airmail). Centurion Publications, 48 George Street, London W1H 5RE England. **Tel** 011 44 71 4874284. **(Subscription address:** Geographical Magazine, PO Box 425, Woking Surrey GU21 1JP England**)** **ED** R. A. M. Gardner. **LC** G1; .G343. **DD** 910/.5. Index available. cum. index. **Bk Rev. Ad Acc. Circ:** 10,600 (ctrl). ***Continues** Geographical Magazine, 0016-741X.*
Desc: Covers the geography of all parts of the world. For general readers as well as professional geographers. Publishes new research and fieldwork.

GW/0178-7810
GEOGRAPHIE AKTUELL. [Geogr. aktuell]. (1985)-. Periodical. German. qt. DM72.00 Germany; DM80.40 other. Aulis Verlag Deubner & Company, Antwerpenerstrasse 6 12, 50672 Koln Germany. **Tel** 011 49 221 518051, FAX 011 49 221 518443. **UDC** 372.891.

GW/0721-8400
GEOGRAPHIE HEUTE. (19??)-. Periodical. German. Ten times a year (Plus one annual). DM112.00 Germany; DM126.48 others. Erhard Friedrich Verlag, Postfach 100150, D 30917 Seelze Germany. **Tel** 011 49 511 4000452. **LC** G72; .G39. **[CCC]. *Continues** Geographie im Unterricht.*

CN/0705-7199
GEOGRAPHIE PHYSIQUE ET QUATERNAIRE. [Geogr. phys. quat.]. Vol. 31; 1977-. Periodical. English (French, Russian, Spanish and German). Three times a year. $20.25 (individuals), $48.50 (institutions) US. Les Presses de l'Universite de Montreal, PO Box 6128 Station A, Montreal Quebec H3C 3J7 Canada. **Tel** (514)343-6321. **ED** Pierre J H Richard. **LC** G1. **DD** 917.102. **CODEN** GPHQEM. **Bk Rev. Ad Acc. Circ:** 700 (ctrl). Documents available from The Genuine Article. ***Continues** Revue de Geographie de Montreal, 0035-1148.*
Desc: Publishes works dealing with the various processes by which are formed the physical features of the earth's surface (geomorphology, climatology, hydrology, pedology and biogeography).
Ind/Abst AQUAREF; Can. Period. Index; Curr. Contents

Phys. Chem. Earth Sci.; Ecol. Abstr.; Geogr. Abstr. Phys. Geogr.; Geol. Abstr.; GeoRef; Environ.; Point Repere (1983-); Res. Alert [Select. Cov.]; SCISEARCH.

GW/0343-7256
GEOGRAPHIE UND IHRE DIDAKTIK. **VFOAT** GD. Geographie und Ihre Didaktik. (1973)-. German.
Ind/Abst Geogr. Abstr. Phys. Geogr.

GW/0171-8649
GEOGRAPHIE UND SCHULE. [Geogr. Sch.]. (1979)-. Periodical. Multiple languages. bm. DM72.00 Germany; DM80.40 other. Aulis Verlag Deubner & Company, Antwerpenerstrasse 6 12, 50672 Koln Germany. **Tel** 011 49 221 518051, FAX 011 49 221 518443. **UDC** 372.891.02. ***Continues*** *Hefte zur Fachdidaktik der Geographie, 0342-8621.*
Ind/Abst Geogr. Abstr. Human Geogr.

US/0275-2514
GEOGRAPHIES FOR ADVANCED STUDIES. [Geogr. adv. stud.]. Monographic series. English. ir. Price varies per volume. Longman Inc, 95 Church Street, White Plains NY 10601. **Tel** (212)764-1233, telex 662266.

GR
GEOGRAPHIKA CHRONIKA. VFOAT Geographical Chronicles. Multiple languages (English and Greek, Modern). $8.00. Geographikos Homilos Kyprov, PO Box 3656, Nicosia Cyprus. **LC** G1; .G363.

GW/0016-7460
GEOGRAPHISCHE RUNDSCHAU. [Geogr. Rundsch.]. Vol. 1 (1949)-. Periodical. German. mo. DM93.60. Georg Westermann Verlag GmbH, GeorgWestermann Allee 66, D 38104 Braunschweig, Germany. **Tel** 0531 708373, FAX 0531 708127. **ED** Klaus Adam. **LC** G1; .G367. **CODEN** GGRUAH. **[CCC].** Index Available, published separately, free-automatically sent. cum. index. **Bk Rev. Ad Acc. Circ:** 20,000 (ctrl).
Desc: Actual serial between geographical research and practice.
Ind/Abst Bibliogr. Carto.; Ecol. Abstr.; EMBASE; Energy Res. Abstr. (Dec. 1981-); Geogr. Abstr. Phys. Geogr.; Geogr. Abstr. Human Geogr.; Geol. Abstr.; GeoRef; Int. Bibliogr. Sociol.; Int. Dev. Abstr.; Leis. Recreat. Tour. Abstr.; Rural Dev. Abstr.; World Agric. Econ.

GW/0016-7479
GEOGRAPHISCHE ZEITSCHRIFT. [Geogr. Z.]. Vol. 1 (June 15, 1895)-. Periodical. German (English). qt. DM108.00. Franz Steiner Verlag GmbH, Postfach 101061, D 70009 Stuttgart Germany. **Tel** 011 49 0711 2582372, FAX 011 49 0711 2582290, telex 723636 daz d. **ED** Eike W. Schamp. **LC** G1; .G37. **CODEN** GEOZA3. **[CCC].** cum. index. **Pr Rev.** Documents available from The Genuine Article.
Ind/Abst Bibliogr. Carto.; Geogr. Abstr. Phys. Geogr.; Geogr. Abstr. Human Geogr.; Geol. Abstr.; GeoRef; Int. Dev. Abstr.; Leis. Recreat. Tour. Abstr.; Res. Alert [Full Cov.]; Rural Dev. Abstr.; Soc. Sci. Cit. Index [Full Cov.]; Soyabean Abstr.; World Agric. Econ.

AU/0376-1738
GEOGRAPHISCHER JAHRESBERICHT AUS OSTERREICH. [Geogr. Jahresber. Osterr.]. Vol. 1-. English. **ED** H Bobek and H Spreitzer. **LC** G1; .G395. **CODEN** GJBOA8.
Ind/Abst GeoRef.

GW
GEOGRAPHISCHES JAHRBUCH. ***Ceased.*** **Added/Corp** Hermann Haack Geographisch-Kartographische Anstalt Gotha. (1866)-Series complete. German. ir. Justus Perthes Verlag Gotha GmbH, Postfach 274, D 99867 Gotha Germany. **Tel** 011 49 3621 385184, FAX 011 49 3621 385103. cum. index. **Bk Rev.**
Desc: Bibliography about geographical literature.

AU
GEOGRAPHISCHES JAHRBUCH BURGENLAND. 1977-. German. an. S150.00. Vereinigung Burgenlandischer Geographen, Hautplata 50, Neusiedl Am See Austria. **Tel** 02167/2516. **ED** Nick Titz. **LC** DB785.B8; G46. **Bk Rev.**

GW/0072-0968
GEOGRAPHISCHES TASCHENBUCH. (1992)-. Periodical. English. DM58.00. Franz Steiner Verlag GmbH, Postfach 101061, D 70009 Stuttgart Germany. **Tel** 011 49 0711 2582372, FAX 011 49 0711 2582290, telex 723636 daz d. **ED** Eckart Ehlers. ***Continues*** *Geographisches Taschenbuch und Jahrweiser fuer Landeskunge.*

UK/0016-7487
GEOGRAPHY. (GEOGRAPHY : JOURNAL OF THE GEOGRAPHICAL ASSOCIATION.). [Geography]. **Added/Corp** Geographical Association. London Geographical Institute. Vol. 14 (1927)-. Periodical. English. qt (Jan., Apr., July, Oct.). £37.25. Geographical Association, 343 Fulwood Road, Sheffield South Yorkshire S10 3BP England. **Tel** 011 44 742 670666, FAX 011 44 742 670688. **ED** Derek Spooner. **LC** G73; .A15. **CODEN** GGHYAD. Index available. **Bk Rev. Ad Acc. Pr Rev. Circ:** 6,000 (ctrl). available on microfilm and microfiche from University Microfilms International (UMI). Documents available from The Genuine Article, UMI Article Clearinghouse. ***Continues*** *Geographical Teacher.*
Desc: Embodies the latest research, world changes and problems. Covers new methods of analysis and carries in-depth reviews.
Ind/Abst Acad. Search (July 1993-); Am. Hist. Life (1971-); Bibliogr. Carto.; Br. Educ. Index; Br. Humanit. Index; Curr. Geogr. Publ. (199?-); Expand. Acad. Index (1989-); Gen. Sci. Source (Jul. 1993-); Geogr. Abstr. Phys. Geogr.; Geogr. Abstr. Human Geogr.; GeoRef; Int. Dev. Abstr.; Newsp. Period. Abstr. (1991-); Life Sci. Collect.; Pollut. Abstr. Indexes; Popul. Index; Ref. Sources; Res. Alert [Full Cov.]; Soc. Sci. Cit. Index [Full Cov.]; Soc. Sci. Index; Soc. Sci. Index Fulltext (Oct. 1988-) [Full Txt.].

AT
GEOGRAPHY BULLETIN. (19??)-. Bulletin. English. ir. 50.00Aus$ Comes with Geography Teachers Association of New South Wales membership. Geography Teachers Association of New South Wales Inc., PO Box 602, Gladesville 2111 NSW Australia. **Tel** 011 61 2 817 3647, FAX 011 61 2 817 4592. **ED** J. P. Harte (editor's address: Moriah College, PO Box 986, Bond Junction, New South Wales 2022 Australia, phone: 02 3873555). **Bk Rev. Ad Acc.** Full Page (B&W) $250.00. Half Page (B&W) $150.00. **Circ:** 750.
Ind/Abst Aust. Educ. Index.

US
GEOGRAPHY (GUILFORD, CONN.). (GEOGRAPHY.). **VFOAT** Annual Editions. Geography. (1987)-. English. an. $12.95. Dushkin Publishing Group Inc., Sluice Dock, Guilford CT 06437. **Tel** (203)453-4351, (800)243-6532, FAX (203)453-6000. **ED** Gerald R. Pitzl. **LC** G1; .G414. **DD** 910/.5.
Desc: Information on a wide variety of topics within the broad spectrum of today's geography.
Ind/Abst Int. Bibliogr. Sociol.; J. Plan. Lit.; Leis. Recreat. Tour. Abstr.; Mag. Search; Middle East Abstr. Index; World Agric. Econ.

US/0333-5275
GEOGRAPHY RESEARCH FORUM. [Geogr. res. forum]. **Added/Corp** Universitat Ben-Guryon Ba-Negev. Mahlakah Le-Geografyah. Universitat Ben-Guryon Ba-Negev. Fakultah Le-Adae Ha-Ruah Veha-Hevrah. Vol. 7 (1984)-. English. an. $12.00. Geography Research Forum, Geography Department, Ben-Gurion University of the Negev, Beer Sheva 84105 Israel. **Tel** 011 972 057 461096. **ED** David Newman and Shaul Krakover. **LC** G1; .G349. **DD** 910/.5. **[CCC].** Index available. cum. index. **Bk Rev**, (Qty: 10). **Ad Acc. Pr Rev. Circ:** 300 (ctrl). available on microfiche; available on microfilm. ***Continues*** *Geographical Research Forum, 0333-5275.*
Desc: Interdisciplinary studies relating geography to numerous areas of social science research: the spatial and locational aspects of economic activity, energy use, urban change, and telecommunication.
Ind/Abst Geogr. Abstr. Phys. Geogr.; Geogr. Abstr. Human Geogr.; Int. Bibliogr. Sociol.; Int. Dev. Abstr.; Int. Polit. Sci. Abstr.

UK
GEOGRAPHY REVIEW. Vol. 1, No. 1 (Sept. 198?)-. Periodical. English. Five times a year. £19.50 UK; £29.00 Europe; £34.00 other. Philip Allan Publishers Ltd, Market Place, Deddington Oxford, OX15 0SE England. **Tel** 011 44 869 38652, FAX 011 44 869 38803. **ED** David Harvey, Tom Burt, Bill Macmillan, and Graham Corney. **Ad Acc. Circ:** 30,000.
Desc: Contains 'A' level geography for students.
Ind/Abst Curr. Geogr. Publ. (199?-); Ecol. Abstr.; Geogr. Abstr. Phys. Geogr.; Geogr. Abstr. Human Geogr.; Int. Dev. Abstr.

II
GEOGRAPHY TEACHER. Added/Corp Association of Geography Teachers of India. Society for the Promotion of Education in India. Vol. 1 (June 1965)-. Periodical. English. Six times a year. Rs38.90. Association of Geographical Teachers of India, 13 Kodambakkam High Road, Madras 60034 India. **LC** G72; .G44.

GE/0343-2521
GEOJOURNAL. [GeoJournal]. **VFOAT** Geo Journal. Vol. 1 (1977)-. Academic Scholarly Publication. English. mo. $1,878.00. Kluwer Academic Publishers, Postbus 322, 3300 AH Dordrecht, The Netherlands. **Tel** 011 (31) 78 524400, FAX 011 31 78 183273, telex 20083. **ED** Wolf Tietze. **LC** HC79.E5; G425. **CODEN** GEOJDQ. **[CCC]. Bk Rev. Ad Acc. Pr Rev. Acid Free. Circ:** 650. available on microfilm and microfiche from University Microfilms International (UMI). Documents available from Article Express International, BIOSIS Document Express, Ask*IEEE.
Desc: Devoted to geography in its classical form as an integrated science, and interlinking it with all related earth sciences whether focused on the solid earth or the hydrosphere, the atmosphere or the biosphere. Man, including his positive and his negative impact on the environment, is likewise of paramount interest.
Ind/Abst AGRICOLA; AQUAREF; Aquat. Sci. Fish. Abstr. (Computer File); Bibliogr. Carto.; Bioeng. Abstr.; Biol. Abstr.; Curr. Aware. Biol. Sci., CABS; Curr. Geogr. Publ. (199?-); Ecol. Abstr.; Ecology Abstr.; Ei Page One; EMBASE; Energy Res. Abstr. (Mar. 1979-); Eng. Index Annu.; Environ. Period. Bibliogr.; Field Crop Abstr.; Geogr. Abstr. Phys. Geogr.; Geogr. Abstr. Human Geogr.; Geol. Abstr.; GeoRef; Grasslands For. Abstr.; Health Saf. Sci. Abstr.; INSPEC (1983-); Int. Dev. Abstr.; Leis. Recreat. Tour. Abstr.; Meteorol. Geoastrophys. Abstr.; Middle East Abstr. Index; Nutr. Abstr. Rev., Ser. A, Hum. Exp.; Life Sci. Collect.; Plant Breed. Abstr.; Plant Genet. Resour. Abstr.; Pollut. Abstr. Indexes; Rice Abstr.; Rural Dev. Abstr.; Soils Fert.; Weed Abstr.; Wheat Barley Trit. Abstr.; World Agric. Econ.

DK/0105-8258
GEOKOMPENDIER. [Geokompendier]. **Added/Corp** Aarhus Universitet. Laboratoriet for Geofysik. (1979)-. Monographic series. English. ir. Price varies per volume. **LC** UNC. ***Continues*** *Kompendier i Fysisk Geografi.*
Ind/Abst GeoRef.

GW
GEOLIT. Periodical. German. Three times a year. Georg Westermann Verlag GmbH, GeorgWestermann Allee 66, D 38104 Braunschweig, Germany. **Tel** 0531 708373, FAX 0531 708127. **ED** K Adam, Karin Taugermann. **LC** G1; .G416. **DD** 910/.5. **Bk Rev. Ad Acc.** ctrl circ.

US/0732-4286
GEOLOGOS. See Earth Sciences-Geology.

SZ
GEOMETHODICA; VEROFFENTLICHUNGEN DES BASLER GEOMETHODISCHEN COLLOQUIUMS. Vol. 3 (1978)-. German (summaries and/or abstracts in English and French). Basler Afrika Bibliographien, Postfach 2037, CH-4001 Basel Switzerland. **Tel** 061/22.33.45. ***Continues*** *Basler Geomethodisches Kolloquium. Veroffentlichungen des Basler Geomethodischen Colloquiums.*
Ind/Abst Geogr. Abstr. Human Geogr.; Int. Dev. Abstr.

RU/0435-4281
GEOMORFOLOGIJA (MOSKVA). (GEOMORFOLOGIIA.). [Geomorfologija]. **Added/Corp** Akademiia Nauk SSSR. **VFOAT** Geomorphology. (1970)-. Periodical. Russian (summaries and/or abstracts in English). qt. $90.00. **(Subscription address:** East View Publications Inc., 3020 Harbor Lane North, Suite 110, Minneapolis MN 55447.**) CODEN** GMFLA6. **[CCC].**
Ind/Abst Ecol. Abstr.

PN/0256-7253
GEOMUNDO. Vol. 1 July (1977)-. Periodical. Spanish. mo (12 issues). $29.90. Editorial America SA, 6355 Northwest 36th Street, Miami FL 33166. **Tel** (305)871-6400. **(Subscription address:** CDS, SIFD Agency Control, 1901 Bell Avenue, Demoine, IA 50315 (Phone: (515)246-6812)**) ED** Elvira Mendoza. **LC** G1; .G42. **Bk Rev. Ad Acc. Circ:** 13,000.
Desc: Covers anthropology, archaeology, general interest, geography, mythology, zoology, ethnic, arts, general astronomy, conservation/natural resources, folklore, history general, museums science, general travel and earth sciences.

US/0360-8492
GEOPUB REVIEW OF GEOGRAPHICAL LITERATURE. V. 1- Sept. 1974-. English. mo. $8.00. Geographic and Area Study Publications, PO Box 391, Tualatin OR 97062. **LC** Z6001; .G45; G115. **DD** 016.91.

US/0072-1395
GEOSCIENCE AND MAN. [Geosci. man]. (1970)-. Monographic series. English. ir. Price varies per volume. Geoscience Publications, PO Box 16010, Baton Rouge LA 70893. **Tel** (504)388-6245. **ED** Kam-biu Liu, Esther Wilcox. **CODEN** GSCMA2. **Pr Rev. Circ:** 200. available on microfiche.
Desc: Scholarly papers published in edited volumes on subjects in geography, anthropology, or occasionally geology.
Ind/Abst Geogr. Abstr. Human Geogr. (?-?); GeoRef.

CN/0317-6029
GEOSCOPE (MONTREAL). (GEOSCOPE.). [Geoscope]. **Added/Corp** Provincial Association of Geography Teachers (Que.). Vol. 1 (Apr. 1966)-. Periodical. English. Free to members, $4.00 nonmembers. Provincial Association of Geography Teachers, PO Box 32 Station NDG, Montreal Quebec H4A 3P4 Canada.
Ind/Abst Geogr. Abstr. Phys. Geogr.; Int. Dev. Abstr.

CN/0046-581X
GEOSCOPE (OTTAWA). (GEOSCOPE.). [Geoscope]. Began publication in 1968. Periodical. English (French). sa. 7.00Can$. University of Ottawa Department of Geography, 165 Waller Street, Ottawa Ontario K1N 6N5 Canada. **Tel** (613)564-2395. **ED** Clement Prevost. Index available. cum. index. **Ad Acc.** ctrl circ.
Desc: A departmental review-periodical of the University of Ottawa dealing with all aspects of geography.
Ind/Abst Geogr. Abstr. Human Geogr.; GeoRef; Environ.

AU
GEOWISSENSCHAFTLICHE MITTEILUNGEN. **Added/Corp** Technische Universitat Wien. Studienrichtung Vermessungswesen. (1973)-. German. ir.

GW/0435-978X
GIESSENER GEOGRAPHISCHE SCHRIFTEN. [Giessen. geogr. Schr.]. **Added/Corp** Justus Liebig-Universitat Giessen. Geographisches Institut. Periodical. German. **CODEN** GSGSB7.
Ind/Abst Geogr. Abstr. Human Geogr.

US/0897-5507
GIS WORLD. [GIS world]. **VAT** Geographic Information Systems World. Vol. 1, No. 1 (July 1988)-. Periodical. English. Twelve times a year. $72.00 US; $89.00 Canada; $108.00 others. Geographic Information Systems World, 155 East Boardwalk Drive, Suite 250, Ft. Collins CO 80525. **Tel** (800)447-9753, (303)223-4848, FAX (303)223-5700. **ED** Derry Eynon. **LC** G70.2; .G575. **DD** 910/.285. cum. index. **Ad Acc.**
Ind/Abst Geogr. Abstr. Phys. Geogr.; Geogr. Abstr. Human Geogr.; Inf. Sci. Abstr.

US/1072-3080
GLOBAL POSITIONING & NAVIGATION NEWS. **See** Naval Science, Navigation.

SZ
GLOBE, LE. **Added/Corp** Societe de Geographie de Geneve. Vol. 1 (1860)-. Periodical. French. an. $9.50. Societe de Geographie de Geneve, 69 Avenue de Champet, CH 1206 Geneva Switzerland. cum. index. **Circ:** 500.
Ind/Abst Point Repere.

AT/0311-3930
GLOBE (MELBOURNE). (THE GLOBE.). [Globe]. **Added/Corp** Australian Map Curators' Circle. No. 1 (Aug. 1974)-. English. sa. $10.00. Australian Map Circle, PO Box E 133, Victoria Terrace, Canberra ACT 2600 Australia. **Tel** 011 61 3 3290055. **LC** GA101; .G58. **DD** 526/.05.
Ind/Abst AESIS Q.; APAIS, Aust. Public Aff. Inf. Ser. (1981-); Aust. Educ. Index; Aust. Libr. Inf. Sci. Abstr. (1982-); Bibliogr. Carto.; Curr. Geogr. Publ. (199?-); Libr. Inf. Sci. Abstr.

GW/0341-3780
GOTTINGER GEOGRAPHISCHE ABHANDLUNGEN. [Gott. geogr. Abh.]. (1948)-. Monographic series. German. ir. Price varies per volume. Erich Goltze GMBH & Company KG, D 37009 Goettingen Germany. **Tel** 011 49 551 5067643. **CODEN** GGABBC.
Ind/Abst Geogr. Abstr. Phys. Geogr. (?-?); Geogr. Abstr. Human Geogr. (?-?); Geol. Abstr.; GeoRef.

US/1048-5104
GPS WORLD. [GPS world]. **VAT** Global Positioning System World. Vol. 1, No. 1 (Jan./Feb. 1990)-. Periodical. English. sm (2 issues per month). $59.00 US and possessions; $79.00 Canada; $117.00 other. Advanstar Communications Inc., 131 West First Street, Duluth MN 55802. **Tel** (218)723-9477, (800)346-0085. **LC** VK562; .G68. **DD** 526/.6. **[CCC].**
Desc: Written for individuals who purchase and use global positioning system equipment. Includes "how-to" articles on new applications or approaches. Also contains news of programs, policies, and people, with features on technological developments and trends. Gives information on new products, services and literature. Schedules of meetings, conferences, exhibitions, and other events are also listed.
Ind/Abst Int. Aerosp. Abstr.

UK
GREAT BRITAIN. DIRECTORATE OF MILITARY SURVEY. MAP LIBRARY. SELECTED ACCESSIONS. (SELECTED ACCESSIONS LIST OF THE MAP LIBRARY / DIRECTORATE OF MILITARY SURVEY, MINISTRY OF DEFENCE.). **Main/Corp** Map Library (Mapping and Charting Establishment re (Great Britain)). English. mo. Mapping and Charting Establishment, Map Research and Library Group, Block A/Government Buildings, Hook Rise South, Tolworth Surbiton Surrey KT6 7N6 Canada. **LC** Z6026.H6; G7; GA300. **DD** 912/.074/02194. ***Continues*** *Selected Accessions (Great Britain. Directorate of Military Survey. Map Library).*

CN
GREAT LAKES GEOGRAPHER. English. sa (Mar., and Sept.). 12.00Can$ (members), 15.00Can$ (non-members) Canada; 20.00Can$ other. The Great Lakes Geographer, University of Western Ontario, Geography Department, London, Ontario N6A 5C2 Canada. **Tel** (519)661-3423, FAX (519)661-3750.
Desc: Covers all fields of geography, particularly the Great Lakes region.

US/0095-1315
GREAT PLAINS-ROCKY MOUNTAIN GEOGRAPHICAL JOURNAL. ***Ceased.*** [Great Plains-Rocky Mt. geogr. j.]. V. 1- 1972-Ceased 1985. English. an. South Dakota State University, Department of Geography, Janet Gritzner, Brookings SD 57007. **LC** F591; .G764. **DD** 917.8/005. **CODEN** GPGJDT.
Ind/Abst GeoRef.

US/0747-7686
GREAT RIVERS. [Great rivers]. **Added/Corp** National Waterways Foundation (U.S.). Vol. 1 No. 1 (Summer 1984)-. Periodical. English. qt. Collegeman Press, 1515 North Courthouse Road, Arlington VA 22201. **DD** 917.

US
GREEN BOOK : OFFICIAL DIRECTORY OF THE CITY OF NEW YORK, THE. **Main/Corp** New York (N.Y.). **Added/Corp** New York (N.Y.). City Record Office. New York (N.Y.). City Publishing Center. **VFOAT** Official Directory of the City of New York. (1985)-. Directory. English. an (June). $14.88 (includes 8.25% sales tax) New York; $13.75 (other). CityBooks/ City Publishing Center, Department of General Services, 2208 Municipal Building, 22nd Floor, New York NY 10007. **Tel** (212)669-8245, FAX (212)669-3211. **LC** JS1222; date c. **DD** 352/.0052/097471. Each issue contains an index to its own contents (no volume index)--loose. ***Continues*** *New York (N.Y.). City of New York Official Directory.*

BL
GUIA, O. Multiple languages (English and Portuguese). 25,00. **LC** G1779.S8; G8.

FR
GUIDE DES VILLES DU MONDE, LE. French. an. 130.00F. Editionapoas 1, 4 rue de Galliera, 75116 Paris France. **LC** G153.4; .G83. **DD** 910/.9173205.

●US
GUIDE TO PROGRAMS OF GEOGRAPHY IN THE UNITED STATES AND CANADA. **Added/Corp** Association of American Geographers. **VFOAT** AAG Directory of Geographers; Guide to Programs of Geography, AAG Directory of Geographers. **VAT** Association of American Geographers Directory of Geographers. (1992)-. English. an. $35.00. Association of American Geographers, 1710 16th Street Northwest, Washington DC 20009-3198. **Tel** (202)234-1450, FAX (202)234-2744. **LC** G76.5.U5; G8. **DD** 910/.7/1173. ***Continues*** *Guide to Departments of Geography in the United States and Canada, 0882-1542.*
Desc: Provides a comprehensive listing of information about requirements, course offerings, financial aid, personnel and departmental specialties for 240 colleges and universities with programs in geography.

GW/0440-1697
HAMBURGER GEOGRAPHISCHE STUDIEN. [Hamb. geogr. Stud.]. **Added/Corp** Universitat Hamburg. Institut fuer Geographie und Wirtschaftsgeographie. Vol. 1 (1952)-. Monographic series. German. Price varie per volume. Ferdinand Schoeningh Verlag, Postfach 2540, D 33055 Paderborn Germany. **Tel** 011 49 5251 127665. **CODEN** HMGSA9.
Ind/Abst Geogr. Abstr. Human Geogr.

US
HAMMOND CITATION WORLD ATLAS. ***Ceased.*** **See** Geography-Cartography.

ZA
HANDBOOK FOR STUDENTS TAKING COURSES IN GEOGRAPHY / UNIVERSITY OF ZAMBIA, SCHOOL OF EDUCATION, DEPARTMENT OF GEOGRAPHY. **Main/Corp** University of Zambia. Dept. of Geography. English. University of Zambia Department of Geography, POB 32379, Lusaka Zambia. **LC** G77.Z33; U54A. **DD** 910/.7/116894.

GW
HANNOVERSCHE GEOGRAPHISCHE ARBEITEN. **Added/Corp** Geographische Gesellschaft zu Hannover. **VFOAT** HGA. Vol. 45 (1991)-. Periodical. German. ***Continues*** *Jahrbuch der Geographischen Gesellschaft zu Hannover, 0435-3838.*

GW/0375-6572
HEIDELBERGER GEOGRAPHISCHE ARBEITEN. [Heidelb. Geogr. Arb.]. **Added/Corp** Universitat Heidelberg. Geographisches Institut. Vol. 1 (1956)-. Monographic series. German. Price varies per volume. **CODEN** HGGAAF.
Ind/Abst Geogr. Abstr. Human Geogr.

FR/0338-487X
HERODOTE. (1976)-. Periodical. French. qt. 210.00F France. Editions La Decouverte, 1 Place Paul Painleve, 75005 Paris France. **Tel** (1)4633 41 16. **ED** Yves Lacoste. **LC** JC319; .H47. **DD** 327.1/01/105. **Bk Rev.** ctrl circ.
Desc: A multi-disciplinary journal focusing on the complexity of geopolitical phenomena of modern times.
Ind/Abst Geogr. Abstr. Human Geogr. (?-?); Int. Polit. Sci. Abstr.

US
HISTORICAL GEOGRAPHY. Vol. 8, No. 1 (Spring 1978)-. Periodical. English. sa. $10.00 (regular), $12.00 (library). Historical Geography, Louisiana State University, Department of Geography, Baton Rouge LA 70803-4105. **Tel** (504)388-5942, FAX (504)388-5942. **ED** Carville Earle, Anne Mosher. **Bk Rev. Ad Acc.**
Continues *Historical Geography Newsletter.*

NE/0167-9775
HISTORISCH GEOGRAFISCH TIJDSCHRIFT. **Added/Corp** Stichting Matrijs. **VFOAT** Historisch-Geografisch Tijdschrift. Vol.1, No. 1 (1983)-. Periodical. Dutch. Three times a year. Fl24.90. Stichting Matrijs, Postbus 670, 3500 Ar Utrecht Netherlands. **Tel** 030 343148, FAX 030 319824. **ED** T. Stol. **Bk Rev**, (Qty: 20-25). **Ad Acc.**
Desc: Concerned with the historical geography of the Netherlands.

US
HISTORY OF GEOGRAPHY JOURNAL. **Added/Corp** Association of American Geographers. Committee on Archives and Association History. No. 6 (Dec. 1988)-. English. Association of American Geographers / New Haven, Southern Connecticut State University, New Haven CT 06515. **Tel** (203)397-4355. ***Continues*** *History of Geography Newsletter.*

FR/0018-439X
HOMMES ET TERRES DU NORD. (1963)-. Periodical. French (English). ir (three or four times per year). 400.00F. Hommes et Terres du Nord, Bat 2, 59655 Villeneuve d ASCQ France. **Tel** 011 33 20 337054. ***Formed by the union of*** *Revue du Nord* ***and*** *Societe de Geographie de Lille. Bulletin.*
Ind/Abst Ecol. Abstr. (?-?); Geogr. Abstr. Phys. Geogr. (?-?); Geogr. Abstr. Human Geogr.; Geol. Abstr.; Int. Dev. Abstr.; Leis. Recreat. Tour. Abstr.; Rural Dev. Abstr.; World Agric. Econ.

CN/0318-5362
HORIZONS (ARMDALE). (HORIZONS.). **Added/Corp** Eastern Provincial Airways (1963) Limited. Marketing Division. **VFOAT** E P A Horizons. (Nov./Dec. 1970)-. Periodical. English. bm. $6.00. EPA Horizons Magazine, PO Box 886, Armdale N.S Canada. **DD** 917.15/04/4.

US
HUDSON'S STATE CAPITALS DIRECTORY. Directory. English. an. $108.00 US, $120.00 others. Newsletter Clearinghouse, PO Box 311, Rhinebeck NY 12572. **Tel** (914)876-2081, FAX (914)876-2561.

US/0538-5318
ICASALS PUBLICATION. **Main/Corp** International Center for Arid and Semi-Arid Land Studies. **VAT** International Center for Arid and Semi-Arid Land Studies Publication. No. 1 (1967)-. Monographic series. English. Three times a year. Price varies per volume. International Center for Arid and Semiarid Land Studies, Texas Tech University, Box 41036, Lubbock TX 79409-1036. **Tel** (806)742-2218, FAX (806)742-1954, telex 9108964398 TTU CID LBK. **ED** Idris Traylor and Robin Lee. **LC** GB841; .I5. **DD** 333.7/3. **CODEN** ICPUD4. **Bk Rev. Circ:** 2,800.
Desc: Relates education, publications, agriculture and research related to problems of arid lands.

II
ICSSR JOURNAL OF ABSTRACTS AND REVIEWS: GEOGRAPHY. **Main/Corp** Indian Council of Social Science Research. **Added/Corp** Indian Council of Social Science Research. Journal of Abstracts and Reviews: Geography. Vol. 1 (Jan./Dec. 1975)-. Periodical. English. sa (2 issues). $8.00. Indian Council of Social Science Research, 35 Ferozshah Road, New Delhi 110 001 India. **Tel** 011 91 11 38959, 011 91 11 381571. **ED** Aijazuddin Ahmed. **LC** G1; .I62a. **DD** 016.91. **Bk Rev. Ad Acc. Circ:** 500.
Desc: Publishes abstracts and reviews of research in geography.

UK/0018-9804
IGU BULLETIN. **Main/Corp** International Geographical Union. **VFOAT** Bulletin de l'UGI. **VAT** International Geographical Union Bulletin; Bulletin de l'Union Geographique Internationale. Vol. 20 (1969)-. Bulletin. English (French). sa. 10.00Can$. Susan M Squires Geography, School of Economics, Houghton Street, London WC2A 2AE England. **Tel** (403)432-3329, telex 037-2979 KOSINSKI. **ED** L A Kosinski. **CODEN** IGUBDY. **Circ:** 5,500. available on microfilm from University Microfilms International (UMI). ***Continues*** *Bulletin de Nouvelles de l'UGI, 0538-7639.*
Desc: The newsletter of the International Geographical Union; the work of IGU's commissions, working groups, and study groups is reported together with news from member countries.
Ind/Abst Bibliogr. Carto.

CN/0251-0464
IGU NEWSLETTER. [IGU newsl.]. **VAT** International Geographical Union Newsletter. No. 7 (1980)-. Newsletter. English (French). sa. $10.00. Professor L A Kosinski, Department of Geography,

University of Alberta, Edmonton Alberta T6G 2H4 Canada. **Tel** (403)492-2979, FAX (403)492-7219, telex 037-2979 GEOGRAPHY. **ED** Leszek A Kosinski. **DD** 304.6/06/01. **Circ:** 5,000 (ctrl). ***Continues*** *Newsletter (International Geographical Union. Commission on Population Geography), 0251-0456.*
Desc: Contains reports of meetings, minutes of executive/general assembly.

II/0019-4824
INDIAN GEOGRAPHICAL JOURNAL, THE. Added/Corp Indian Geographical Society. Vol. 16 (1941)-. Periodical. English. sa. $25.00. Indian Geographical Society, Department of Geography, University of Madras, Chepauk Madras 600005 India. **Tel** 568778, FAX 91-44-944444. **(Subscription address:** Prints India, 11 Darya Ganj, New Delhi, 110002 India, (Phone: 011 91 11 3268645)) **ED** S Subbiah. **LC** DS401; .I36. **DD** 915.4/005. Index available. **Bk Rev. Ad Acc. Circ:** 600. ***Continues*** *Journal of the Madras Geographical Association.*
Desc: Papers on general and applied geography from all over India. Includes papers on geomorphology, climate, agriculture and urban development.
Ind/Abst Int. Bibliogr. Sociol.; Rural Dev. Abstr.; World Agric. Econ.

II
INDIAN GEOGRAPHICAL STUDIES: RESEARCH BULLETIN. Added/Corp Geographical Research Centre. No. 1 (Sept. 1973)-. Bulletin. English. sa. $10.00. Dr V N P Sinha, Department of Geography, Patna University, 800005 Patna India. **(Subscription address:** Prints India, 11 Darya Ganj, New Delhi, 110002 India, (Phone: 011 91 11 3268645)) **DD** 954.

II/0537-2011
INDIAN JOURNAL OF GEOGRAPHY, THE. (THE INDIAN JOURNAL OF GEOGRAPHY : A JOURNAL OF THE ASSOCIATION OF GEOGRAPHERS, DEPARTMENT OF GEOGRAPHY, UNIVERSITY OF JODHPUR.). Vol. 1, No. 1 (1966)-. English. an. Association of Geographers, Department of Geography, University of Jodhpur, Jodhpur Rajasthan India. **LC** G1; .I633. **DD** 910/.005.

II/0970-1095
INDIAN JOURNAL OF MARKETING GEOGRAPHY, THE. Added/Corp Association of Marketing Geographers of India. Vol. 2, Nos. 1 & 2 (Mar.-Sept. 1984)-. Periodical. English. sa. $20.00. Association of Marketing Geographers of India, Gorakhpur, India. **(Subscription address:** Prints India, 11 Darya Ganj, New Delhi, 110002 India, (Phone: 011 91 11 3268645)) **LC** HF5475.I4; I53. **DD** 381/.1/05. ***Continues*** *Market Studies.*

CL/0537-6041
INFORMACIONES GEOGRAFICAS. Added/Corp Universidad de Chile. Instituto de Geografia. Universidad de Chile. Departmento de Geografia. (April 1951)-. Periodical. Spanish. ir. University of Chile Department of Geografia, Casilla Postal 10136, Santiago Chile.

US/0049-7282
INFORMATION BULLETIN / WESTERN ASSOCIATION OF MAP LIBRARIES. See Library and Information Sciences.

FR/0020-0093
INFORMATION GEOGRAPHIQUE, L'. [Inf. geogr.]. (1936)-. Periodical. French. Five times a year. $120.00 institutions; $65.00 individuals. Librairie Armand Colin, BP 22, 41354 Vineuil Cedex France. **Tel** 011 33 54 438994. **(Subscription address:** 7A Boulevard de Perolles, CH-1701 Fribourg Switzerland) **LC** G1; .I65. **DD** 910.5. **CODEN** IFGGB4. **[CCC].** available on microfilm and microfiche from University Microfilms International (UMI).
Ind/Abst Bibliogr. Carto.; Curr. Geogr. Publ. (199?-); Geogr. Abstr. Phys. Geogr. (?-?); Geogr. Abstr. Human Geogr. (?-?); GeoRef; Int. Dev. Abstr. (?-?); Leis. Recreat. Tour. Abstr.; Rural Dev. Abstr.; World Agric. Econ.

GW/0343-494X
INFORMATIONEN UND MATERIALIEN ZUR GEOGRAPHIE DER EUREGIO RHEIN-MAAS. Added/Corp Paedagogische Hochschule Rheinland. Abteilung Aachen. Lehrstuhl fuer Geographie und ihre Didaktik I. Maas-Rhein Institut fuer Angewandte Geographie und Lehrerbildung. No. 1 (Nov. 1977)-. Periodical. Dutch (Dutch and French; summaries and/or abstracts in French and Dutch). Twice a year. DM27.00 Germany; DM30.00 others. Maas-Rhein Institut fuer Angewandte Geographie und Lehrerbildung E V, Templergraben 55, W-5100 Aachen Germany. **Tel** 0241/803642, telex 832704 THAC D. **LC** HC243.A1; I54. cum. index. **Circ:** 500.

VE
INFORME ANUAL - INSTITUTO PANAMERICANO DE GEOGRAFIA E HISTORIA, SECCION NACIONAL. Main/Corp Venezuela. Seccion Nacional del Instituto Panamericano de Geografia e Historia. Spanish. Edificio Camejo, Oficina No 128 Avenida Este 6, Caracas Venezuela. **LC** F2301; .P2814.

AT/0310-7949
INTERACTION MELBOURNE. See Education-Teaching and Curriculum.

●US/1057-3348
INTERNATIONAL GIS SOURCEBOOK. [Int. G I S sourceb.]. **VFOAT** GIS Sourcebook; GIS Source Book; International Geographic Information Systems Sourcebook. **VAT** International Geographic Information Systems Sourcebook. (1992)-. English. an (Nov.). $148.45 US; $157.89 Canada; $161.94 other. Geographic Information Systems World, 155 East Boardwalk Drive, Suite 250, Ft. Collins CO 80525. **Tel** (800)447-9753, (303)223-4848, FAX (303)223-5700. **LC** G70.2; .G5745. **DD** 910. ***Continues*** *GIS Sourcebook, 1046-8412.*

UK/0269-3798
INTERNATIONAL JOURNAL OF GEOGRAPHICAL INFORMATION SYSTEMS. [Int. j. geogr. inf. syst.]. **VFOAT** Geographical Information Systems; IJGIS. Vol. 1, No. 1 (Jan./March 1987)-. Periodical. English. bm. £197.00 UK; $325.00 other. Taylor & Francis Ltd., Rankine Road, Basingstoke Hampshire, RG24 8PR United Kingdom. **Tel** 011 44 256 840366, FAX 011 44 256 479438, telex 858540. **(Subscription address:** Taylor & Francis Inc., 1900 Frost Road, Suite 101, Bristol PA 19007-1598.) **ED** J. T. Coppock (editor's address: University of Edinburgh, Drummond Street, Edinburgh EH8 9XP United Kingdom); Keith Clarke (editor's address: National Mapping Division, US Geological Survey, 519 National Center, Reston, VA 22092). **LC** G70.2; .I59. **DD** 910/.28/5. **CODEN** IJGSE3. **[CCC].** available on microfilm and microfiche from University Microfilms International (UMI). Documents available from The Genuine Article, Ask*IEEE.
Desc: The aim of the journal is to provide a forum for the exchange of ideas, techniques, approaches and experiences in the rapidly growing field of geographical information systems. It is intended to interest those who design and implement such systems and those who use them for planning, making, and monitoring policies. The journal is interdisciplinary and international.
Ind/Abst Curr. Contents Soc. Behav. Sci.; Ecol. Abstr.; Ergon. Abstr.; Geogr. Abstr. Phys. Geogr.; Geogr. Abstr. Human Geogr.; Geol. Abstr.; GeoRef; INSPEC (Jan./March 1988-);(Jan.-Mar. 1988-); Int. Dev. Abstr.; Res. Alert [Full Cov.]; Soc. Sci. Cit. Index [Full Cov.].

US/0160-0176
INTERNATIONAL REGIONAL SCIENCE REVIEW. See Economics.

MX/0188-4611
INVESTIGACIONES GEOGRAFICAS : BOLETIN DEL INSTITUTO DE GEOGRAFIA. Added/Corp Universidad Nacional Autonoma de Mexico. Instituto de Geografia. No. 21 (1990)-. Spanish (summaries and/or abstracts in English). ***Continues*** *Universidad Nacional Autonoma de Mexico. Instituto de Geografia. Boletin del Instituto de Geografia, 0185-1977.*
Ind/Abst Ecol. Abstr.; Geogr. Abstr. Phys. Geogr.; Geogr. Abstr. Human Geogr.; GeoRef; Int. Dev. Abstr.

IE/0075-0778
IRISH GEOGRAPHY. (IRISH GEOGRAPHY : BULLETIN OF THE GEOGRAPHICAL SOCIETY OF IRELAND.). [Ir. geogr.]. **Added/Corp** Geographical Society of Ireland. Vol. 1, No. 4 (1947)-. Bulletin. English. Twice a year (June, Dec.). 18.00p Ireland; $48.00 US. Geographical Society of Ireland, Geography Department, University College, Belfield Dublin 4 Ireland. **Tel** +353 1 7068484, FAX +353 1 2695597. **LC** DA900; .G4. **DD** 914.15. **[CCC].** cum. index. **Bk Rev. Pr Rev. Circ:** 700. ***Continues*** *Bulletin (Geographical Society of Ireland).*
Desc: Articles of Irish geographical interest.
Ind/Abst Am. Hist. Life (1955-); Br. Archaeol. Bibliogr.; Geogr. Abstr. Phys. Geogr.; Geogr. Abstr. Human Geogr.; Geol. Abstr.; Int. Bibliogr. Sociol.; Leis. Recreat. Tour. Abstr.; Rural Dev. Abstr.; Soils Fert.; World Agric. Econ.

RU/0205-9614
ISSLEDOVANIE ZEMLI IZ KOSMOSA. [Issled. zemli kosm.]. **Added/Corp** Akademiia Nauk SSSR. (1980)-. Academic Scholarly Publication. Russian (summaries and/or abstracts in English). Six times a year. $148.00. Izdatelstvo Nauka / Akademiia Nauk, Publishing House of the Russian Academy of Sciences, Leninskii Porspekt 14, 117907 Moscow Russia. **Tel** 011 95 954-21-53, FAX 011 95 938-21-44, telex 411964. **(Subscription address:** Victor Kamkin, 4956 Boiling Brook Parkway, Rockville MD 20852.) **LC** G70.4; .I88. Documents available from Ask*IEEE.
Desc: Information on remote sensing.
Ind/Abst Coal Abstr.; Ei Page One; GeoRef; INSPEC (1982-); Int. Aerosp. Abstr.

HK/1012-8328
IT ASIA. [IT Asia]. (1987)-. Periodical. English. mo. $52.50 North & South America, Europe, West Asia; $43.95 other. Newscom Pte. Ltd., Blk 105 Boon Keng Road 04 17, Singapore 1233 Singapore. **Tel** 011 65 2919861.

NE/0303-2434
ITC JOURNAL, THE. See Earth Sciences.

RU
ITOGI NAUKI I TEKHNIKI: MEDITSINSKAIA GEOGRAFIIA. Added/Corp Vsesoiuznyi Institut Nauchnoi i Tekhnicheskoi Informatsii (Soviet Union). **VFOAT** Itogi Nauki I Tekhniki: Seriia Meditsinskaia Geografiia; Meditsinskaia Geografiia. (19??)-. Russian. 2.81rub. VINITI - Vsesoyuznyi Institut Nauchno-Tekhnicheskoi Informatsii, All-Union Scientific and Technical Information Institute, Baltiiskaia Ulitsa 14, 125219 Moscow Russia. **Tel** 238-46-00, FAX 9430060, telex 411160. **LC** RA791; .I78. ***Continues*** *Itogi Nauki: Meditsinskaia Geografiia.*

US/0360-0432
ITOGI, SUMMARIES OF SCIENTIFIC PROGRESS: THEORETICAL PROBLEMS IN PHYSICAL AND ECONOMIC GEOGRAPHY. VFOAT Theoretical Problems in Physical and Economic Geography; Physical & Economic Geography. Vol. 1 (1974)-. Monographic series. English. ir. Price varies per volume. GK Hall & Co, 100 Front Street, Riverside NJ 08075. **Tel** (800)257-5755 ext. 2223. **LC** G1; .I86. **DD** 910/.02/08.

●RU
IZVESTIIA AKADEMII NAUK. SERIIA GEOGRAFICHESKAIA / ROSSIISKAIA AKADEMIIA NAUK. Added/Corp Rossiiskaia Akademiia Nauk. **VFOAT** Seriia Geograficheskaia; Geographical Series; Proceedings of the Russian Academy of Sciences. Geographical Series. (1992)-. Academic Scholarly Publication. Russian (summaries and/or abstracts in English; table of contents in English). Six times a year. $179.95. Izdatelstvo Nauka / Akademiia Nauk, Publishing House of the Russian Academy of Sciences, Leninskii Porspekt 14, 117901 Moscow Russia. **Tel** 011 95 954-21-53, FAX 011 95 938-21-44, telex 411964. **(Subscription address:** East View Publications Inc., 3020 Harbor Lane North, Suite 110, Minneapolis MN 55447.) **LC** G23; .A35. ***Continues*** *Izvestiia Akademii Nauk SSSR. Seriia Geograficheskaia, 0373-2444.*
Ind/Abst Geogr. Abstr. Human Geogr.; Int. Dev. Abstr.

RU/0373-2444
IZVESTIIA AKADEMII NAUK SSSR. SERIIA GEOGRAFICHESKAIA. *Title Change.* Added/Corp Akademiia Nauk SSSR. **VFOAT** Seriia Geograficheskaia; Geographical Series; Proceedings of the USSR Academy of Sciences. Geographical Series. (1951-1992). Periodical. Russian (English; table of contents in English). bm. **(Subscription address:** Victor Kamkin, 4956 Boiling Brook Parkway, Rockville MD 20852.) **CODEN** IAKGAM. cum. index. ***Continues in part*** *Izvestiia Akademii Nauk SSSR. Seriia Geograficheskaia i Geofizicheskaia.* ***Continued by*** *Izvestiia Akademii Nauk. Seriia Geograficheskaia.*
Ind/Abst AGRICOLA; Ecol. Abstr.; GeoRef.

RU/0373-353X
IZVESTIIA VSESOIUZNOGO GEOGRAFICHESKOGO OBSHCHESTVA. Main/Corp Geograficheskoe Obshchestvo SSSR. **Added/Corp** Russkoe Geograficheskoe Obshchestvo. Gosudarstvennoe Russkoe Geograficheskoe Obshchestvo. Gosudarstvennoe Geograficheskoe Obshchestvo. Geograficheskoe Obshchestvo SSSR. (1865)-. Academic Scholarly Publication. Russian (summaries and/or abstracts in English and French). ir. Izdatelstvo Nauka / Akademiia Nauk, Publishing House of the Russian Academy of Sciences, Leninskii Porspekt 14, 117901 Moscow Russia. **Tel** 011 95 954-21-53, FAX 011 95 938-21-44, telex 411964. **ED** A. F. Tryoshinikov.
Ind/Abst Bibliogr. Carto.; Ecol. Abstr.; Geogr. Abstr. Human Geogr.

AJ/0002-3124
IZVESTIJA AKADEMII NAUK AZERBAJDZANSKOJ SSR. SERIJA NAUK O ZEMLE. See Earth Sciences-Geology.

RU/0536-101X
IZVESTIJA VYSSIH UCEBNYH ZAVEDENIJ. GEODEZIAJA I AEROFOTOSEMKI. (IZVESTIIA VYSSHIKH UCHEBNYKH ZAVEDENII. GEODEZIIA I AEROFOTOSEMKA.). [Izv. vyss. ucebn. zaved., Geod. aerofotos.]. **Added/Corp** Moskovskii Institut Inzhenerov Geodezii, Aerofotosemki i Kartografii. **VFOAT** Geodeziia i Aerofotosemka. (1957)-. Academic Scholarly Publication. Russian. bm. $229.95. **(Subscription address:** East View Publications Inc., 3020 Harbor Lane North, Suite 110, Minneapolis MN 55447.) **LC** QB275; .R83. **CODEN** IVZAAM. Documents available from CASDDS.
Ind/Abst Chem. Abstr. (-1980); GeoRef; Int. Aerosp. Abstr.; Math. Rev.

GW
JAHRBUCH DES KREISES DUREN. 1973-. German. an. DM9.50. Eifelverein, 5160 Duren, Sturtzstrasse Postfach 100532, Duren Germany. **Tel** 02421/13121. **LC** DD491.R51; J33. **DD** 914.3/55. **Circ:** 3,000. ***Formed by the union of*** *Heimatjahrbuch Kreis Duren* ***and*** *Heimatjahrbuch Kreis Julich.*

CC
JE TAI TI LI. **Added/Corp** Kuang-chou Ti Li Yen Chiu So. **VFOAT** Tropical Geography. (1980)-. Periodical. Chinese. qt. Kuang-Chou Ti Li Yen Chiu so Huang Hua Kang, Canton China. **Tel** 765006. **(Subscription address:** China International Book Trading Corporation, PO Box 399, Library Service Department, Beijing 100044 People's Republic of China.**)** **ED** Yang Shigao. **LC** GB398.7; .J4. **DD** 910/.0913. **Bk Rev. Pr Rev.**
Desc: Carries articles on physical geography, human geography, geomorphology, and climatology. Some papers describe water, plant communities, animal kingdoms, and soil in China's tropical zone.

TU
JEOMORFOLOJI DERGISI. Turkish (summaries and/or abstracts in English, French and German). **LC** GB438.T87; J46.
Ind/Abst Geogr. Abstr. Phys. Geogr.; Geol. Abstr.; Int. Dev. Abstr.

JA
JIMBUN CHIRI. **Added/Corp** Jimbun Chiri Gakkai. **VFOAT** Human Geography. (1948)-. Periodical. Japanese. bm.
Ind/Abst Geogr. Abstr. Human Geogr.

UK/0305-0270
JOURNAL OF BIOGEOGRAPHY. [J. biogeogr.]. Vol. 1 (Mar. 1974)-. Academic Scholarly Publication. English. bm (6 issues). $563.00 US & Canada; £330.00 Europe; £363.00 other. Blackwell Scientific Publications Ltd, Marston Book Services, PO Box 87, Oxford OX2 ODT UK. **Tel** 011 44 865 791155, FAX 011 44 865 791927, telex 837 515 MARDIS G. **ED** J. Flenley. **LC** QH84; .J68. **DD** 574.9. **NLM** W1 JO564BM. **CODEN** JBIODN. **[CCC].** Index available (bound in last issue). **Bk Rev. Ad Acc. Pr Rev.** available on microfilm and microfiche from University Microfilms International (UMI). Documents available from The Genuine Article, Documents on Demand.
Desc: Covers all aspects of biogeography.
Ind/Abst AGRICOLA [Select. Cov.]; Agrofor. Abstr. (1991-); Biocont. News Inf.; Br. Archaeol. Bibliogr.; Curr. Aware. Biol. Sci., CABS; Curr. Contents, Agric. Biol. Environ. Sci.; Curr. Geogr. Publ. (199?-); Curr. Ref. Fish Res.; Ecol. Abstr.; Ecology Abstr.; Environ. Abstr. (Feb. 28, 1992-); Environ. Period. Bibliogr.; Field Crop Abstr.; Fish Rev.; For. Prod. Abstr.; For. Abstr.; Geogr. Abstr. Phys. Geogr.; Geogr. Abstr. Human Geogr.; Geol. Abstr.; GeoRef; Grasslands For. Abstr.; Helminthol. Abstr.; Index Vet.; Int. Bibliogr. Sociol.; Int. Dev. Abstr.; Key Word Index Wildl. Res.; Middle East Abstr. Index; Life Sci. Collect.; Plant Breed. Abstr.; Plant Genet. Resour. Abstr.; Potato Abstr.; Res. Alert [Full Cov.]; Rev. Agric. Entomol.; Rev. Med. Vet. Entomol.; Sci. Cit. Index; SCISEARCH; Soc. Sci. Cit. Index [Select. Cov.]; Soils Fert.; Weed Abstr.; Wildl. Rev.

SI/0218-1444
JOURNAL OF CHINESE GEOGRAPHY, THE. **Added/Corp** Chung-Kuo ko Hsueh Yuan. Ti li Yen Chiu So. Chung-Kuo ti li Hsueh Hui. **VFOAT** Chinese Geography. Vol. 1, No. 1 (1990)-. English. qt. $150.00. Guoji Translation & Publishing, 6001 Beach Rd 02-69, Golden Mi, Singapore 0719 Singapore. **Tel** 011 65 2961453. **LC** G1; .J687.
Ind/Abst Geogr. Abstr. Phys. Geogr.; Geogr. Abstr. Human Geogr.; Int. Dev. Abstr.

US/0887-3631
JOURNAL OF CULTURAL GEOGRAPHY. [J. cult. geogr.]. **Added/Corp** Bowling Green State University. Popular Culture Association. American Culture Association. Vol. 1 (Fall/Winter 1980)-. Periodical. English. sa. $15.00 (one year), $28.00 (two year). Popular Press Journals Area, Bowling Green State University, Bowling Green OH 43403. **Tel** (419)372-7866, (419)372-7865. **ED** Alvar Carlson. **DD** 910. **Bk Rev. Ad Acc. Circ:** 700 (ctrl).
Desc: Discusses all aspects of geography except that which is quantitative.
Ind/Abst Am. Hist. Life (1987-); Curr. Geogr. Publ. (199?-); Geogr. Abstr. Human Geogr.; J. Plan. Lit.; Middle East Abstr. Index; MLA Int. Bibl. Books Artic. Mod. Lang. Lit.

US/0022-1341
JOURNAL OF GEOGRAPHY (HOUSTON). (THE JOURNAL OF GEOGRAPHY.). [J. geogr.]. **Added/Corp** National Council for Geographic Education. National Council of Geography Teachers (U.S.) American Geographical Society of New York. Vol. 1 (Jan. 1902)-. Periodical. English. bm (Jan., Mar., May, July, Sep., Nov.). $60.00 (institutions), $100.00 (corporate members). National Council for Geographic Education, Indiana University of Pennsylvania, 16A Leonard Hall, Indiana PA 15705-1087. **Tel** (412)357-6290, FAX (412)357-7708. **ED** Robert S Bednarz (editor's address: Department of Geography, Texas A & M University, College Station TX 77843-3147). **LC** G1; .J87. **DD** 910. **CODEN** JOGGA9. Index available (Dec. issue). cum. index. **Bk Rev. Ad Acc. Pr Rev. Circ:** 3,500 (ctrl). available on microfilm and microfiche from University Microfilms International (UMI). Documents available from The Genuine Article, Documents on Demand. ***Formed by the union of*** *Journal of School Geography, 1041-8938* ***and*** *Bulletin of the American Bureau of Geography, 0196-2841.*
Desc: Publishes articles about geography and the teaching of geography for geographic educators at all levels.
Ind/Abst Bibliogr. Carto.; Contents Pages Educ.; Curr. Contents Soc. Behav. Sci.; Curr. Geogr. Publ. (199?-); Curr. Index J. Educ.; Educ. Index; Educ. Adm. Abstr.; Energy Inf. Abstr.; Environ. Abstr.; GeoRef; Med. Rev. Dig.; Middle East Abstr. Index; Res. Alert [Full Cov.]; Soc. Sci. Cit. Index [Full Cov.]; Soils Fert.; West. Hist. Q.

UK/0309-8265
JOURNAL OF GEOGRAPHY IN HIGHER EDUCATION. [J. geogr. high. educ.]. **VFOAT** JGHE. Vol. 1 (Spring 1977)-. Periodical. English. Three times a year (Mar., Jul., Nov.). £184.00. Carfax Publishing Company, PO Box 25 Abingdon, Oxfordshire OX14 3UE England. **Tel** 011 44 235 555335, FAX (0279)31067, telex 817484. **(Subscription address:** US and Canada/ PO Box 2025, Dunnellon, FL 34430-2025; telephone:(904)489-6996**)** **ED** Mick Healey & Ifan Shepherd. **LC** G72; .J68. **DD** 910/.7/11. **[CCC]. Bk Rev. Ad Acc. Pr Rev.** available on microfiche. Documents available from The Genuine Article.
Desc: A forum for geographers and others to discuss educational practice and philosophy.
Ind/Abst Br. Educ. Index; Curr. Contents Soc. Behav. Sci.; Curr. Index J. Educ.; Educ. Technol. Abstr.; Geogr. Abstr. Phys. Geogr.; Geogr. Abstr. Human Geogr.; Res. Alert [Full Cov.]; Res. High. Educ. Abstr.; Soc. Sci. Cit. Index [Full Cov.]; Spec. Educ. Needs Abstr.; Stud. Women Abstr.; Tech. Educ. Train. Abstr.

UK/0305-7488
JOURNAL OF HISTORICAL GEOGRAPHY. [J. hist. geogr.]. Vol. 1 (Jan. 1975)-. Academic Scholarly Publication. English. qt. $180.00. Academic Press Ltd., A Division of Harcourt Brace & Company Ltd., 24-28 Oval Road, London NW1 7DX England. **Tel** 071 267 4466, FAX 071 482 2293, 071 485 4752, telex 25775 ACPRES G. **(Subscription address:** Harcourt Brace & Company, Ltd., Foots Cray, High Street, Sidcup Kent DA14 5HP England.**)** **ED** A. R. H. Baker and J. P. Radford. **LC** G141; .J68. **DD** 911/.05. **CODEN** JHGEDP. **[CCC]. Bk Rev. Pr Rev.** Documents available from The Genuine Article, UMI Article Clearinghouse.
Desc: Publishes articles on all aspects of historical geography. Aims to interest an international and interdisciplinary readership. In addition to publishing original research papers, this journal contains discussion of methodology, discourse on items of general interest, and debates on subjects covered in earlier issues. Includes a substantial book review section.
Ind/Abst Abstr. Anthropol.; Acad. Search (July 1993-); Am. Hist. Life (1975-); ARTbibliogr. Mod. (1984-); Arts Humanit. Citation Index [Select. Cov.]; Bibliogr. Carto.; Book Rev. Index; Br. Archaeol. Bibliogr.; Chicano Index; Curr. Contents Soc. Behav. Sci.; Curr. Geogr. Publ. (199?-); Expand. Acad. Index (1989-); Gen. Sci. Source (Jul. 1993-); Geogr. Abstr. Human Geogr.; GeoRef; INFO-SOUTH Abstr.; Int. Dev. Abstr. (?-?); J. Plan. Lit.; Mag. Search; Middle East Abstr. Index; Newsp. Period. Abstr. (1991-); Popul. Index (?-?); Res. Alert [Full Cov.]; Soc. Sci. Source (Jul. 1993-); Soc. Sci. Cit. Index [Full Cov.]; Soc. Sci. Index; Soc. Sci. Index Fulltext (Oct. 1988-) [Full Txt.]; West. Hist. Q.

UK/0379-0703
JOURNAL OF OMAN STUDIES : SCIENTIFIC RESULTS OF THE ROYAL GEOGRAPHICAL SOCIETY. (19??)-. English. ir. £40.00. Royal Geographical Society / England, 1 Kensington Gore, London SW7 2AR England. **Tel** 011 44 71 589 5466, FAX 011 44 71 584 4447, telex 933669.
Ind/Abst World Agric. Econ.

US/0022-4146
JOURNAL OF REGIONAL SCIENCE. **See** Economics.

TZ/0016-738X
JOURNAL OF THE GEOGRAPHICAL ASSOCIATION OF TANZANIA. ***Ceased.*** **Main/Corp** Geographical Association of Tanzania. (1967)-?. Periodical. English. sa. Geographical Association of Tanzania, Box 35049, Dar es Salaam Tanzania Africa. **Tel** 49192. **ED** W F Banyikwa. **LC** DT440; .G43. **DD** 916.78/005. **Bk Rev. Ad Acc. Circ:** 100.
Desc: Geography of Tanzania and East Africa, environmental and developmental studies.

●UK/0966-6923
JOURNAL OF TRANSPORT GEOGRAPHY. **Added/Corp** Institute of British Geographers. Transport Geography Study Group. **VFOAT** Transport Geography. Vol. 1, No. 1 (Mar. 1993)-. Periodical. English. Four times a year. $179.00 The Americas; £120.00 other. Butterworth Heinemann Publishers, Linacre House, Jordan Hill, Oxford OX2 8DP England. **Tel** 011 44 865 310366. **(Subscription address:** Elsevier Science Ltd. Oxford Fulfillment Centre, PO Box 800, Kidlington, Oxford OX5 1DX United Kingdom.**)** **LC** HE1; .J599. **DD** 388/.05.
Desc: Focuses on all aspects of transport and spatial change. It provides an international forum for analytical articles with particular emphasis on topical issues - essential reading for anyone engaged in transport studies with an interest in geographical or spatial perspectives.

JA
KAIGAI TOZAN KENKYUKAI SHIRYO. **Main/Corp** Kaigai Tozan Kenkyukai. Japanese. Nihon Sangakukai Tokai Shibu, c/o Hara Byoin, 3-17 Wakatakecho Chigusa-ku, Nagoya 464 Japan. **LC** G505; .K3.

US
KANSAS GEOGRAPHER, THE. ***Suspended.*** **VFOAT** Kansas Geographers. -Suspended 1985. Periodical. English. an. Free. Kansas Council for Geographic Education, Department of Geography/Dikens Hall, Manhattan KS 66506. **Tel** (913)532-6727. **ED** S L Stover. **LC** G1; .K36. **DD** 375.91. **Bk Rev. Ad Acc. Circ:** 600 (ctrl).
Desc: Variety of articles of geographic interest, especially to teachers and others in geographic education.

GW/0344-7073
KARLSRUHER MANUSKRIPTE ZUR MATHEMATISCHEN UND THEORETISCHEN WIRTSCHAFTS- UND SOZIALGEOGRAPHIE. **VFOAT** Karlsruher Manuskript zur Mathematischen und Theoretischen Wirtschafts- und Sozialgeographie. (1974)-. German.
Ind/Abst Geogr. Abstr. Phys. Geogr.; Geogr. Abstr. Human Geogr.

NO/0047-3278
KART OG PLAN. **Added/Corp** Norges Jordskiftedommer- og Landmalersamband. (1970)-. Periodical. Norwegian. Fourteen times a year. Kr420.00, $66.00. Scandinavian University Press, PO Box 2959 Toeyen, N 0608 Oslo 6 Norway. **Tel** 011 47 2 2575400, FAX 011 47 2 2575353, telex 71896 UROR N. **(Subscription address:** Scandinavian University Press, 200 Meacham Ave., Elmont NY 11003.**)** **LC** TA501; .K3. available on microfilm from University Microfilms International (UMI). ***Continues*** *Norsk Tidskrift for Jordskifte og Landmaling.*
Ind/Abst Bibliogr. Carto.; Ei Page One.

CN/0319-0013
KELOWNA CITY DIRECTORY. (1958. BUSINESS EDITION). (KELOWNA CITY DIRECTORY.). **VFOAT** Official City Directory of Kelowna; City Directory of Kelowna; Kelowna Directory. 1958-. Directory. English. an. British Columbia Directories / Kelowna, 287 Bernard Avenue, Kelowna British Columbia V1Y 6N2 Canada. **DD** 917.11/42. ***Supersedes*** *Kelowna City and Central Okanagan Directory, 0319-0021.*

CN/0828-5543
KENT DIRECTORY. [Kent dir.]. **VFOAT** Kent County Directory. (May 1984/85)-. Directory. English. an. $2.00. Kent County Directory, c/o Leader Publications, PO Box 490, Dresden Ontario N0P 1M0 Canada. **DD** 917.13/33/0025.

GW
KIELER GEOGRAPHISCHE SCHRIFTEN. **Added/Corp** Universitat Kiel. Geographisches Institut. (1976)-. Monographic series. German. Price varies per volume. ***Continues*** *Universitaet Kiel. Geographisches Institut. Schriften.*
Ind/Abst Geogr. Abstr. Phys. Geogr.; Geogr. Abstr. Human Geogr.; Int. Dev. Abstr.

US
KINGSTON CITY DIRECTORY. Directory. English. Johnson Publishing Company / Colorado, PO Box 455, 8th and Vanburen, Loveland CO 80537. **Tel** (303)667-0652.

CN/0023-365X
KONTAKT (TORONTO). (KONTAKT.). V. 1- Dec. 1968-. Periodical. German. bm. Kontakt / Toronto, PO Box 1339, Station A, Toronto Ontario M5W 1G7 Canada. **LC** DD1; .K65. **DD** 914.3/005.

PL/0023-3765
KONTYNENTY. (19??)-. Periodical. Polish. mo. **(Subscription address:** ARS Polona, PO Box 1001, 00068 Warsaw Poland.**)** **LC** G464; .K685.

DK/0416-7066
KULTURGEOGRAFISKE SKRIFTER. **Main/Corp** Danske Geografiske Selskab. Periodical. Danish. ir. CA Reitzels Forlag AS, Norregade 20, DK-1165 Copenhagen K Denmark. **Tel** 011 45 3 3122400.
Ind/Abst Geogr. Abstr. Human Geogr. (?-?).

NR
LAGOS CITY DIRECTORY. Began with Vol. for 1967. Directory. English. an. Lagos City Directory, PO Box 603, Lagos Nigeria. **LC** DT515.9.L3; L33. **DD** 916.69/1/0025.

UK/0265-4210
LAND AND MINERALS SURVEYING. ***Ceased.*** **See** Engineering-Civil Engineering.

NE/0922-4939
LANDENDOCUMENTATIEMAPPEN. [Landendocumentatiemappen]. **VFOAT** Landenreeks. (1988)-. Monographic series. Dutch. ir. Price varies per volume. Koninklijk Instituut voor de Tropen, Mauritskade 63, 1092 AD Amsterdam Netherlands. **Tel** 011 31 20 5688272, FAX 011 31 20 5688286. **ED** P.H.J. van den Boorn. **UDC** 339.9. **Circ:** 7,000. available with illustrations. ***Continues*** *Landendocumentatie (Amsterdam), 0023-7841.*
Ind/Abst Geo Abstr.

US/0023-8023
LANDSCAPE (BERKELEY, CALIF.). (LANDSCAPE.). [Landscape]. Vol. 1 (Spring 1951)-. Periodical. English. Three times a year. $22.00 individuals, $42.00 institutions. Landscape, 3101 Telegraph, Berkeley CA 94705. **Tel** (510)549-3233. **ED** Bonnie Loyd. **LC** G1; .L2. **DD** 712. **[CCC]. Bk Rev. Circ:** 3,000. available on microfilm and microfiche from University Microfilms International (UMI). Documents available from The Genuine Article, Documents on Demand.
Desc: Essays, photographs and sketches explore everyday scenes: bungalows, alleys, billboards, and vacant lots. Geographers, architects, historians, and artists rethink the common place. Award-winning writing and format.
Ind/Abst Am. Hist. Life (1979-); Archit. Period. Index (1955-); Art Index; Arts Humanit. Citation Index [Full Cov.]; Avery Index Archit. Period. Suppl. Colum. Univ. (19??-199?); Curr. Contents Arts Humanit.; Environ. Abstr.; Environ. Period. Bibliogr.; Garden Lit.; Geogr. Abstr. Human Geogr.; Res. Alert [Full Cov.]; Soc. Plann. Policy Dev. Abstr.; Urban Aff. Abstr.; West. Hist. Q.

UK/0143-3768
LANDSCAPE HISTORY. See Gardening and Horticulture.

CC
LI SHIH TI LI / CHUNG-KUO TI LI HSUEH HUI LI SHIH TI LI CHUAN YEH WEI YUAN HUI, LI SHIH TI LI PIEN CHI WEI YUAN HUI PIEN. First published in (Nov. 1981)-. Chinese. RMBY1.50. Hsin Hua Shu Tien / Shang-Hai Fa Hsing So, Shanghai, People's Republic of China. **LC** DS706.5; .L53. **DD** 911/.51.

XR/0024-2896
LIDE A ZEME. See Travel and Tourism.

LI/0202-3288
LIETUVOS TSR AUKSTUJU MOKYKLU MOKSLO DARBAI: GEOGRAFIJA. (GEOGRAFIJA.). [Liet. TSR aukst. mokyklu mokslo darb., Geogr.]. **VFOAT** Geografiia. (1980)-. Lithuanian (Russian; summaries and/or abstracts in English and German). Mintis / Idea, Z Sierakausko 15, Vilnius 2600 Lithuania. **Tel** 3702 632 943. **LC** IN PROCESS. **CODEN** LTAGD5. Documents available from CASDDS. ***Continues in part*** *Lietuvos TSR Aukstuju Mokyklu Mokslo Darbai: Geografija ir Geologija, 0459-3448.*
Ind/Abst Chem. Abstr. (1980-1981); Ecol. Abstr.; Geogr. Abstr. Phys. Geogr.; Geogr. Abstr. Human Geogr.; GeoRef; Leis. Recreat. Tour. Abstr.; World Agric. Econ.

CN/0827-6978
LINK. (THE LINK / CORPORATION OF LAND SURVEYORS OF THE PROVINCE OF BRITISH COLUMBIA.). [Link]. **VAT** Link (Victoria 1977). Vol. 1, No. 1 (June 1977)-. Periodical. English. Three times a year. free to members; $20.00 other. Corporation of land Surveyors of the Province of British Columbia, Suite 306, 895 Fort Street, Victoria BC V8W 1H7 Canada. **DD** 526.9/09711.

UK
LIST OF MEMBERS / THE HAKLUYT SOCIETY. Main/Corp Hakluyt Society. (19??)-. Periodical. English. ir. Free to members. Hakluyt Society, c/o The Map Library, British Library, Great Russell Street, London WCIB 3DG England. **Tel** 011 44 986 86359, FAX 011 44 986 868181. **LC** G7; .H297. **DD** 910/.6. **Circ:** 2,300 (ctrl). ***Continues in part*** *Hakluyt Society. Prospectus and List of Members.*

GW
LITERATURINFORMATION TERRITORIALFORSCHUNG, TERRITORIALPLANUNG. German (English, Polish and Russian). bm. 30.00M (inland); Free on exchange. Institut fur Geographie und Geookologie der Akademie der Wissenschafter der DDR, Georgi-Dimitroff-Platz 1/PF 906, O-7010 Leipzig Germany. **Tel** 328003. **ED** Joachim Heinzmann. **LC** Z7164.R33; L584; HT391. **DD** 016.3616. **Bk Rev. Circ:** 200 (ctrl).
Desc: Reviews and partly abstracts geographical journals and monographies on problems of economic and physical geography, cartography, environment and related subjects.

CN/0712-6360
LIVING IN NORTH YORK. [Living North York]. **Main/Corp** North York (Ont.). English. an. Free. City of North York Public Information Office, 5100 Yonge Street, North York Ontario M2N 5V7 Canada. **ED** Anna Di Ruscio. **DD** 917.13/541. **Circ:** 225,000 (ctrl).

UK
LONDON TOPOGRAPHICAL RECORD. Vol. 2 (1903)-. English. ir. cum. index. ***Continues*** *Annual Record of the London Topographical Society.*
Ind/Abst BHA : Biblio. Hist. Art.

US/0733-6918
LOS ANGELES COUNTY POPULAR STREET ATLAS (CENSUS TRACT ED.). (LOS ANGELES COUNTY POPULAR STREET ATLAS.). **Main/Corp** Thomas Bros. Maps. English. an. $17.95. Thomas Brothers Maps, Lockbox PO Box 30845, Los Angeles CA 90030. **Tel** (714)863-1984. **Ad Acc.**
Desc: Street maps and index for Los Angeles County in Southern California.

US
LOS ANGELES MICRO-GEOGRAPHER, THE. Added/Corp Los Angeles (Calif.). Community Analysis and Planning Division. **VFOAT** Los Angeles Micro Geographer. No. 1 (Winter 1988)-. Periodical. English. City of Los Angeles Community Development Department, Community Analysis and Planning Division, Los Angeles CA 90012.

US/0883-5136
LOS ANGELES, ORANGE COUNTIES STREET ATLAS AND DIRECTORY (ZIP CODE EDITION). (LOS ANGELES, ORANGE COUNTIES STREET ATLAS AND DIRECTORY.). **VFOAT** Los Angeles County; Orange County. (1984)-. Directory. English. an. Thomas Brothers Maps, Lockbox PO Box 30845, Los Angeles CA 90030. **Tel** (714)863-1984. ***Continues*** *Los Angeles, Orange Counties Popular Street Atlas, 0733-6977.*
Desc: Includes: Los Angeles County street atlas and directory (Zip code edition); and: Orange county street atlas and directory (Zip code edition).

CH
LU YU WEN HSUEH. VFOAT Luyonwenxue. 1983, 1-. Periodical. Chinese. NT$0.97. Hsin Hua Shu Tien / Cheng-chou, Cheng-chou, People's Republic of China. **LC** G464; .L83. **DD** 910.4.

RM/1015-2172
LUCUARI STIINTIFICE - INSTITUTUL AGRONOMIC "NICOLAE BALESCU", BUCURESTI. SERIA E. IMBUNATATIRI FUNCIARE. (LUCRARI STIINTIFICE. SERIA E. IMBUNATATIRI FUNCIARE.). [Lucr. stiint. - Inst. agron. "Nicolae Balescu" Bucur., Ser. E, Imbun. funciare]. **Added/Corp** Institutul Agronomic "N. Balcescu". **VFOAT** Imbunatatiri Funciare. (19??)-. Romanian.
Ind/Abst Irr. Drain. Abstr.

SW/0076-146X
LUND STUDIES IN GEOGRAPHY. SERIES A. PHYSICAL GEOGRAPHY. [Lund stud. geogr., Ser. A, Phys. geogr.]. **Added/Corp** Lunds Universitet. Geografiska Institutionen. (1950)-. Monographic series. English. ir. Price varies per volume. Lund University Press, Box 141, S-22100 Lund Sweden. **Tel** 011 46 46 312000, FAX 011 46 46 305338, telex 33345 EDUCATE S. **CODEN** LSGPAI.
Ind/Abst GeoRef.

SW/0076-1478
LUND STUDIES IN GEOGRAPHY. SERIES B, HUMAN GEOGRAPHY. Added/Corp Lunds Universitet. Geografiska Institutionen. **VFOAT** Human Geography. No. 1 (1949)-. Monographic series. English (Scandinavian). ir. Price varies per volume. Lund University Press, Box 141, S-22100 Lund Sweden. **Tel** 011 46 46 312000, FAX 011 46 46 305338, telex 33345 EDUCATE S. **ED** B. Lenntorp. Index available. cum. index.
Ind/Abst Geogr. Abstr. Human Geogr. (?-?).

IO
MAJALAH TEKHNIS PARIWISATA. V. 1-. Periodical. Indonesian. Direcktorat Jenderal Pariwisata, J1 Kramat Raya No 81, Jakarta Indonesia. **LC** G155.I5; M33. ***Supersedes*** *Bulletin Tekhnis Pariwisata.*

MW/1010-5549
MALAWIAN GEOGRAPHER, THE. [Malawian geogr.]. English. an. K10.00. Journal of Social Science of Malawi, PO Box 280, Zomba Malawi. **Tel** 522 222, telex 4742 MI. **ED** Z M Kaufulu and M B Dolozi. **LC** G76.5.M3; M34. **DD** 910/.7. **Bk Rev. Ad Acc. Circ:** 300.
Desc: Geographical education with special emphasis on the school certificate examination classes in Malawi in mind.
Ind/Abst GeoRef.

MY/0126-642X
MALAYSIAN GEOGRAPHERS. (MALAYSIAN GEOGRAPHERS / NATIONAL GEOGRAPHICAL ASSOCIATION OF MALAYSIA.). [Malays. geogr.]. V. 1 (1978)-. Periodical. English. an. $4.23. University of Malaya Department of Geography, 59100 Kuala Lumpur Malaysia. **Tel** 011 60 3 7555266, FAX 011 60 3 7573661, telex UNIMAL MA39845. **LC** G1; .M34. **DD** 910/.5.

MY/0127-1474
MALAYSIAN JOURNAL OF TROPICAL GEOGRAPHY. Added/Corp Universiti Malaya. Jabatan Geografi. Vol. 1 (Sept. 1980)-. Periodical. English. sa (June, December). $15.00. University of Malaya Department of Geography, 59100 Kuala Lumpur Malaysia. **Tel** 011 60 3 7555266, FAX 011 60 3 7573661, telex UNIMAL MA39845. **ED** P. K. Voon. **LC** G905; .M34. **DD** 910/.0913. Index available (free). cum. index. **Bk Rev. Pr Rev. Circ:** 500 (ctrl). ***Continues in part*** *Journal of Tropical Geography, 0022-5290.*
Desc: Papers must be based on original research focusing on techniques of data gatherings, processing and interpretation on geographical issues in the tropical areas.
Ind/Abst Ecol. Abstr. (?-?); Geogr. Abstr. Phys. Geogr.; Geogr. Abstr. Human Geogr.; Int. Bibliogr. Sociol.; Int. Dev. Abstr.; Wildl. Rev.

UK/0260-5503
MANCHESTER GEOGRAPHER : JOURNAL OF THE MANCHESTER GEOGRAPHICAL SOCIETY, THE. Vol. 1, No. 1 (Autumn 1980)-. Periodical. English. an. £4.00 (individuals), £5.00 (institutions). Manchester Geographical Society, 274 The Corn Exchange Building, Manchester M4 3EY England. **Tel** (061)834-2965. **ED** H B Rodgers. **LC** G1; .M35. **DD** 914.2/7005. Index available. **Circ:** 200. ***Continues*** *Journal of the Manchester Geographical Society.*
Desc: Concentrates on all aspects of the geography of North-West England.

●US/1062-0141
MANHATTAN USER'S GUIDE. Vol. 1, No. 1 (May 1992)-. Periodical. English. mo. $42.00 (one year), $82.00 (two year). Manhattan User's Guide, PO Box 772, Ansonia Stn. NY 10023. **Tel** 212-724-4692, FAX 212-496-2681. **ED** Charles A. Suisman. Index available (December). cum. index. **Circ:** 1000.
Desc: A mix of what Manhattan has to offer to people living in NY from the best to the offbeat: restaurants, services, coping, sports, spirits, stores, and ways to save money.

GW
MANNHEIMER GEOGRAPHISCHE ARBEITEN. Added/Corp Universitat Mannheim. Geographisches Institut. Vol. 1 (1977)-. Academic Scholarly Publication. German (English). ir (one to two issues per year). Price varies per volume. Geographisches Institut der Universitat, Gebaude L 9 I-2, D-68131 Mannheim Germany. **Tel** (621)2922546, FAX (621)2923321. **ED** Sebastian Lentz. Index available. cum. index. **Circ:** 500 (ctrl).
Desc: Contains dissertations, research reports, and scientific articles.
Ind/Abst Geogr. Abstr. Phys. Geogr. (?-?); Geogr. Abstr. Human Geogr.

GW/0341-9290
MARBURGER GEOGRAPHISCHE SCHRIFTEN. [Marbg. geogr. Schr.]. **Added/Corp** Marburg. Universitat. Geographisches Institut. (1949)-. Monographic series. German. Price varies per volume. **CODEN** MGGSBN.
Ind/Abst Geogr. Abstr. Phys. Geogr.; GeoRef.

US/0736-8119
MARMAC GUIDE TO LOS ANGELES, A. VFOAT Los Angeles. (1983)-. English. an. $9.95. Marmac Publishing Company Inc., 6303 Barfield Road, Suite 208, Atlanta GA 30328. **Tel** (404)257-1481. **LC** F869.L83; M37. **DD** 917.94/940453. ***Continues*** *How When & Where in Los Angeles.*

US/0090-9300
MARYLAND GEOGRAPHER, THE. Periodical. English. sa. $1.50. Morgan State College Department of Geography, Hillen Road and Cold Spring Lane, Baltimore MD 21212. **LC** G1; .M37. **DD** 910/.7/12.

US/0883-3680
MATERIAL CULTURE. See Anthropology.

CN/0076-1982
MCGILL SUB-ARCTIC RESEARCH PAPERS. [McGill Sub-arct. res. pap.]. No. 1 (1956)-. Monographic series. English (French). ir. Price varies per volume. McGill University / Centre for Northern Studies and Research, 550 Sherbrooke Street W, Suite 460/West Wing, Montreal Quebec H3A 1B9 Canada. **Tel** (514)398-6052. **ED** T R Moore. **LC** GB131; .M22. **DD** 551/.09714/17. **CODEN** MGUPAF. Index available. cum.

index. **Circ:** 220.
Ind/Abst ASTIS Curr. Aware. Bull. (1978-); ASTIS Bibliogr. (1978-); Ecol. Abstr. (?-?); Geogr. Abstr. Phys. Geogr. (?-?); GeoRef.

SW/0346-6787
MEDDELANDEN FRAN LUNDS UNIVERSITETS GEOGRAFISKA INSTITUTION. AVHANDLINAR. [Medd. Lunds Univ. geogr. inst., Avh.]. **Main/Corp** Lunds Universitet. Geografiska Institutionen. **Added/Corp** Lunds Universitet. Geografiska Institutionen. Vol. 1 (1929)-. Monographic series. Swedish (Swedish). ir. Price varies per volume. Lund University Press, Box 141, S-22100 Lund Sweden. **Tel** 011 46 46 312000, FAX 011 46 46 305338, telex 33345 EDUCATE S. **ED** Bo Lenntorp and Jan O. Mattsson. **LC** UNC. Index available. cum. index.
Desc: Doctoral dissertations in physical geography and social and economic geography.
Ind/Abst GeoRef.

FR
MEMOIRES ET DOCUMENTS (FRANCE. SERVICE DE DOCUMENTATION ET DE CARTOGRAPHIE GEOGRAPHIQUES). (MEMOIRES ET DOCUMENTS / SERVICE DE DOCUMENTATION ET DE CARTOGRAPHIE GEOGRAPHIQUES.). **Added/Corp** France. Service de Documentation et de Cartographie Geographiques. Centre National de la Recherche Scientifique (France). Vol. 9 (1969)-. French. ir. 209.00F. Editions du CNRS, 22 rue Saint Armand, F 75015 Paris France. **Tel** 011 33 1 45075050. **LC** GA862; .A33. Index available. cum. index. **Bk Rev. Circ:** 2,000. **Continues** Memoires et Documents (France. Centre de Recherches et Documentation Cartographiques et Geographiques).
Desc: Topics include physical geography, geography and economics, vegetation, and population distribution.

IT
MEMORIE DELLA SOCIETA GEOGRAFICA ITALIANA. **Main/Corp** Societa Geografica Italiana. Vol. 1 (1878)-. Italian.
Ind/Abst Geogr. Abstr. Human Geogr.

IT/0505-2009
MEMORIE DI BIOGEOGRAFIA ADRIATICA. [Mem. biogeogr. adriat.]. **Main/Corp** Venice. Istituto di Studi Adriatici. Vol. 1; 1950-. Italian (summaries and/or abstracts in English). ir. Istituto di Studi Adriatic, Riva 7 Martiri, Venice Italy. **CODEN** IAMBBI.
Ind/Abst GeoRef.

US/1040-7421
MERIDIAN - MAP & GEOGRAPHY ROUND TABLE (AMERICAN LIBRARY ASSOCIATION). See Geography-Cartography.

US/0076-7948
MICHIGAN GEOGRAPHICAL PUBLICATION. [Mich. geogr. publ.]. **Added/Corp** University of Michigan. Dept. of Geography. No. 1 (1970)-. Monographic series. English. ir. Price varies per volume. University of Michigan / LSA Building, George Kish, 4530 LSA Building, Ann Arbor MI 48109.
Ind/Abst GeoRef.

CN/0317-6487
MIGHT'S COBOURG, PORT HOPE, ONTARIO, CITY DIRECTORY. VFOAT Cobourg, Port Hope, City Directory. Began with 1973 issue?. Directory. English. Might Directories, 220 Bartley Drive, Toronto Ontario M4A 2H4 Canada. **Tel** (416)751-2751. **DD** 917.13/57.

CN/0381-8578
MIGHT'S OAKVILLE ONTARIO CITY DIRECTORY. VFOAT Oakville Ontario City Directory. 1971-. Directory. English. $70.00. Might Directories, 220 Bartley Drive, Toronto Ontario M4A 2H4 Canada. **Tel** (416)751-2751. **DD** 917.13/533. **Continues** Might's Oakville Directory, 0381-8586.

UK/0441-4004
MISCELLANEOUS SERIES - DEPARTMENT OF GEOGRAPHY, UNIVERSITY OF HULL. (MISCELLANEOUS SERIES.). [Misc. ser. - Dep. Geogr. Univ. Hull]. **Main/Corp** University of Hull. Dept. of Geography. No. 1 (1965)-. Monographic series. English. Price varies per volume. **CODEN** MSUGE8.
Ind/Abst Geogr. Abstr. Phys. Geogr.; GeoRef.

NZ/0078-0022
MISCELLANEOUS SERIES - NEW ZEALAND GEOGRAPHICAL SOCIETY. (MISCELLANEOUS SERIES NO 9. SOUTHERN APPROACHES: GEOGRAPHY IN NEW ZEALAND.). [Misc. ser. - N.Z. Geogr. Soc.]. VFOAT Special Publications Miscellaneous series. (1950)-. Monographic series. English. ir. 152.00NZ$. New Zealand Geographical Society, University of Canterbury, Private Bag, Christchurch New Zealand. **DD** 919.31. **Bk Rev. Pr Rev. Circ:** 600.

Desc: To commemorate 50 years of geography in the New Zealand University syllabus. Seventeen original essays to review the past, present and future of geography and the environmental society in Europe.

US/0196-5239
MISSOURI GEOCODE LIST. English. an. Free. Department of Social Services / Missouri, Broadway State Office Building, Jefferson City MO 65102. **ED** Garland Lane. **LC** G108.7; .M57. **DD** 917.78/00148. **Circ:** 600.
Desc: Zip codes for Missouri counties.

GW/0374-9061
MITTEILUNGEN DER GEOGRAPHISCHEN GESELLSCHAFT IN HAMBURG. [Mitt. Geogr. Ges. Hamb.]. **Added/Corp** Geographische Gesellschaft in Hamburg. (1876)-. Monographic series. German. ir. Price varies per volume. Franz Steiner Verlag GmbH, Postfach 101061, D 70009 Stuttgart Germany. **Tel** 011 49 0711 2582372, FAX 011 49 0711 2582290, telex 723636 daz d. **ED** Frank Norbert Nagel. **LC** G13; .B32. **CODEN** MGGHAN. **Continues** Geographische Gesellschaft in Hamburg. Jahresbericht.
Ind/Abst Geogr. Abstr. Phys. Geogr.; Geogr. Abstr. Human Geogr.; GeoRef.

GW/0072-0941
MITTEILUNGEN DER GEOGRAPHISCHEN GESELLSCHAFT IN MUNCHEN. [Mitt. - Geogr. Ges. Muench.]. **Main/Corp** Geographische Gesellschaft in Munchen. Vol. 1 (1906)-. German. an. DM40.00. Geographische Gesellschaft, Heinrich Voglstr 7, 8 Munchen 7 Germany. **Tel** 089/794008. **ED** H G Zimpel. **LC** G13; .G382. **CODEN** MGGMA4. cum. index. **Bk Rev.** ctrl circ. **Continues in part** Jahresbericht der Geographischen Gesellschaft in Munchen.
Desc: Scientific articles on physical and cultural geography.
Ind/Abst Bibliogr. Carto.; Geogr. Abstr. Phys. Geogr.; Geogr. Abstr. Human Geogr.; GeoRef.

AU
MITTEILUNGEN DER OSTERREICHISCHEN GEOGRAPHISCHEN GESELLSCHAFT. **Main/Corp** Osterreichische Geographische Gesellschaft. Vol. 101 (1959)-. Periodical. German (English and French). an. S600.00. Osterreichische Geographische, Karl Schweighoferg 3, A-1070 Vienna Austria. **Tel** 0222/93 30 325. **ED** Karl Stiglbauer (editor's address: Universitatsstr 7, A-1010 Vienna Austria). **LC** G9; .G3. Index available. cum. index. **Bk Rev. Ad Acc. Circ:** 1,500 (ctrl). Documents available from The Genuine Article. **Continues** Mitteilungen der Geographischen Gesellschaft Wien.
Ind/Abst Curr. Contents Soc. Behav. Sci.; Geogr. Abstr. Phys. Geogr.; Geogr. Abstr. Human Geogr.; Int. Dev. Abstr.; Res. Alert [Full Cov.]; Soc. Sci. Cit. Index [Full Cov.].

US/0899-6806
MOBIL ROAD ATLAS AND TRIP PLANNING GUIDE, UNITED STATES, CANADA, AND MEXICO. [Mobil road atlas trip plan. guide U. S. Can. Mex.]. VFOAT Road Atlas and Trip Planning Guide, United States, Canada, and Mexico; Mobil Road Atlas. (1989)-. English. an. Random House Inc., 400 Hahn Road, Westminster MD 21157. **Tel** (800)726-0600, (800)733-3000, FAX (800)659-2436. **LC** G1105; .M62. **DD** 917.

AT
MONASH PUBLICATIONS IN GEOGRAPHY. **Added/Corp** Monash University. Dept. of Geography. No. 1 (1972)-. Monographic series. English. ir. Price varies per volume. Monash University, Department of Geography, Clayton Victoria 3168 Australia. **Tel** 011 61 3 541 0811 Ext. 2930. **ED** D. C. Mercer. **Pr Rev. Circ:** 100 to 500.
Desc: The publications are all single topic volumes, usually 60-120 pages. Contains maps, diagrams, pictures, and accompaning text.

●CN/1191-9310
MONCTON CITY DIRECTORY (1992). (MONCTON CITY DIRECTORY.). [Moncton city dir.]. VFOAT Might's Moncton City Directory. (1992)-. Directory. English. an. Might Directories, 220 Bartley Drive, Toronto Ontario M4A 2H4 Canada. **Tel** (416)751-2751. **DD** 917.15/235/0025. **Continues** Moncton, New Brunswick, City Directory, Including Dieppe and Riverview., 0229-7302.

US
MONKEYSHINES ON AMERICA. See History(General)-History of North, South, and Central America.

US
MONOGRAPH OF THE DEPARTMENT OF GEOLOGY AND GEOGRAPHY, ST. LAWRENCE UNIVERSITY. See Earth Sciences-Geology.

CN/0048-1793
MONOGRAPH / ONTARIO ASSOCIATION GEOGRAPHIC ENVIRONMENTAL EDUCATION, THE. [Monograph]. **Main/Corp** Ontario Association for Geographic and Environmental Education. **Added/Corp** Ontario Geography Teachers' Association. Ontario Association for Geographic & Environmental Education. Periodical. English. qt. $20.90. Ontario Association Geographic Environmental Education, 30 Lillian Cres, Barrie Ontario L4N 4P6 Canada. **Tel** (416)669-5373. **ED** B Addison. **LC** G76.5.C3; O56A. **Bk Rev. Ad Acc. Circ:** 800 (ctrl).
Desc: Useful materials for secondary and elementary teachers of geography and environmental studies.

AT/0158-8273
MONOGRAPH SERIES (JAMES COOK UNIVERSITY OF NORTH QUEENSLAND. DEPARTMENT OF GEOGRAPHY). (MONOGRAPH SERIES / DEPARTMENT OF GEOGRAPHY, JAMES COOK UNIVERSITY OF NORTH QUEENSLAND.). [Monogr. ser.- Geogr. Dep. James Cook Univ. North Qld.]. **Added/Corp** James Cook University of North Queensland. Dept. of Geography. (1970)-. Monographic series. English. ir. Price varies per volume. James Cook University Bookshop, PO Townsville, Queensland 4811 Australia. **Tel** 011 61 77 814111. **ED** D. Hopley. **LC** UNC. **CODEN** JCGMAB. **Circ:** 300.
Desc: Publication of geographical research from North Queensland and related tropical areas.
Ind/Abst GeoRef.

US/0080-0627
MONOGRAPH SERIES - REGIONAL SCIENCE RESEARCH INSTITUTE. See Economics.

CN/0700-4222
MONTREAL PEOPLE'S YELLOW PAGES. 1973/74-. Periodical. English. Egg Publishing, PO Box 100 Station G, Montreal Quebec H2W 2M9 Canada. **DD** 917.14/281/0025.

FR
MOSELLA. **Added/Corp** Metz. Universite. Departement de Geographie. Centre d'Etudes Geographiques de Metz. Vol. 1 (Jan./Mar. 1971)-. Periodical. French (summaries and/or abstracts in English and German). qt. 50.00F France; 60.00F other. Centre Etudes Geographique Metz des Lettres, Universite de Metz, 57045 Metz Cedex 1 France. **Tel** 011 33 87 31 52 53. **Bk Rev.** ctrl circ.
Desc: Human, economic and physical geography above East of France and German countries.
Ind/Abst Geogr. Abstr. Human Geogr. (?-?).

US
MOUNTAIN COUNTRY : A NEWS MAGAZINE OF THE MOUNTAINS CONSERVANCY. **Added/Corp** Mountains Conservancy Foundation. Spring (1991)-. English. qt. **LC** GB525.5.C2; M686.

GW/0343-706X
MUNCHENER GEOGRAPHISCHE ABHANDLUNGEN. [Munch. geogr. Abh.]. **Added/Corp** Munich. Universitat. Geographisches Institut. (1970)-. Monographic series. German (summaries and/or abstracts in English and French). Price varies per volume. **CODEN** MGABDC.
Ind/Abst Geogr. Abstr. Phys. Geogr.; GeoRef.

GW/0932-3147
MUNCHENER GEOGRAPHISCHE ABHANDLUNGEN REIHE B. [Munch. geogr. Abh., B]. (1985)-. Monographic series. Multiple languages. ir. Price varies per volume. **UDC** 91. **Continues in part** Munchener Geographische Abhandlungen, 0343-706X.
Ind/Abst Geogr. Abstr. Phys. Geogr.; GeoRef.

CN/0077-2542
MUSK-OX, THE. Ceased. [Musk-ox]. No. 1 (1967)-No. 40 (1994). Periodical. English (French). sa. University of Saskatchewan Department of Geology, Saskatoon Saskatchewan S7N 0W0 Canada. **Tel** (306)966-5720. **ED** W O Kupsch. **LC** G600; .M8. **DD** 919.8/005. **CODEN** MUOXD8. Index available. cum. index. **Bk Rev. Circ:** 700 (ctrl). available on microfiche (from Toronto: Micromedia).
Desc: Multidisciplinary scientific and historic journal on Northern Canada, Alaska, and other circumpolar nations.
Ind/Abst ASTIS Curr. Aware. Bull. (1978-); AQUAREF; ASTIS Bibliogr. (1978-); Can. Index; Can. Period. Index; Ecol. Abstr.; Fish Rev.; Geogr. Abstr. Phys. Geogr.; Geogr. Abstr. Human Geogr.; GeoRef; Int. Dev. Abstr.; Wildl. Rev.

GW/0071-920X
NACHRICHTEN AUS DEM KARTEN- UND VERMESSUNGSWESEN. REIHE I. **Main/Corp** Frankfurt am Main. Institut fur Angewandte Geodasie. German.
Ind/Abst Geogr. Abstr. Phys. Geogr.

GW/0344-5879
NACHRICHTEN AUS DEM KARTEN- UND VERMESSUNGSWESEN. SONDERHEFT. [Nachr. Kt.- Vermess.wes., Sonderh.]. (1968)-. Multiple languages. ir. **UDC** 528(063.055.1). ***Continues*** *Nachrichten aus dem Karten- und Vermessungswesen. Reihe 5, 0429-5617.*
Ind/Abst Geogr. Abstr. Phys. Geogr.; GeoRef.

JA
NAGOYA DAIGAKU SUIKEN KAGAKU KENKYUJO NEMPO. Main/Corp Nagoya Daigaku. Suiken Kagaku Kenkyujo. (1974)-. Japanese. Nagoya Daigaku Suiken Kagaku Kenkyujo, Furocho Chigusa-ku, Nagoka Japan. **LC** G77.N3; N33A.

US/0077-2690
NAMES IN SOUTH CAROLINA. *Ceased.* [Names S. C.]. (Fall 1954)-Vol. 3 (Nov. 1983). English. an. University of South Carolina English Department, Columbia SC 29208. **Tel** (803)777-2239, (803)787-6601. **LC** F267; .N3. **DD** 917.57.
Ind/Abst GeoRef; MLA Int. Bibl. Books Artic. Mod. Lang. Lit.

SW/0077-2704
NAMN OCH BYGD. [Namn och bygd]. (1913)-. Periodical. Swedish. an. Kr210.00 Sweden. Swedish Science Press, PO Box 118, S 751 04 Uppsala Sweden. **Tel** 011 46 18 365566, FAX 011 48 18 365277. **LC** DL1; .N25. cum. index.
Desc: Contains geographical names.
Ind/Abst Annu. Bibliogr. Engl. Lang. Lit.; MLA Int. Bibl. Books Artic. Mod. Lang. Lit.

CN/0317-8838
NANAIMO DIRECTORY (BUSINESS EDITION). (NANAIMO DIRECTORY.). **VFOAT** Nanaimo City Directory; Official City Directory of Nanaimo; City Directory of Nanaimo. 1959-. Directory. English. an. British Columbia Directories / Nanaimo, Box 486, Nanaimo British Columbia V9R 5L5 Canada. **DD** 917.11/34.

JA/0085-7289
NANKYOKU SHIRYO. (NANKYOKU SHIRYO : NIHON NANKYOKU CHIIKI KANSOKUTAI NO HOKOKU.). [Nankyoku shiryo]. **Added/Corp** Nihon Nankyoku Chiiki Kansokutai. Japan. Monbusho. Kokuritsu Kagaku Hakubutsukan (Japan) Kyokuchi Kenkyu Senta (Japan) Kokuritsu Kyokuchi Kenkyujo. **VFOAT** Antarctic Record. (1957)-. Japanese (English). ir. National Institute of Polar Research, Kokuritsu Kyokuchi Kenkyujo, 9-10 Kaga 1-Chome, Itabashi-ku Tokyo 173 Japan. **Tel** 81 3 962 4711, FAX 83 3 962-25 29. **LC** G845; .N36. **CODEN** NSHIAO. Documents available from BIOSIS Document Express.
Ind/Abst Aquat. Sci. Fish. Abstr. (Computer File); Biol. Abstr.; GeoRef; Meteorol. Geoastrophys. Abstr. (19??-); Ocean. Abstr.; Life Sci. Collect.

JA
NANTO NO CHIMEI / NANTO CHIMEI KENKYU SENTA. No. 1 (1983-)-. Japanese. Shinsei Tosho Shuppan, 9-12 Tomari 2 Naha-shi, Okinawa-ken 900 Japan. **LC** DS894.99.O372; N36.

II/0470-0929
NATIONAL GEOGRAPHER. Added/Corp Allahabad Geographical Society. (March 1958)-. English. sa. $15.00. Allahabad Geographical Society University of Allahabad, Allahabad 211002 India. **(Subscription address:** Prints India, 11 Darya Ganj, New Delhi, 110002 India, (Phone: 011 91 11 3268645)) **ED** R C Tiwari. **LC** G1; .N26. **DD** 910/.5. **Ad Acc. Circ:** 400 (ctrl).
Desc: Publishes articles on geography and allied disciplines, currently on themes of current interest, i.e. environment, rural development, urbanization, geomorphological processes, etc.
Ind/Abst Potato Abstr.

US/0027-9358
NATIONAL GEOGRAPHIC. [Natl. geogr.]. **Added/Corp** National Geographic Society (U.S.). **VFOAT** National Geographic Magazine. Vol. 116, No. 6 (Dec. 1959)-. Periodical. English. Twelve times a year. $25.50 US; $37.00 other. National Geographic Society, 11555 Darnestown, Gaithersburg MD 20878. **Tel** (202)857-7000, (800)638-4077, FAX (202)429-5727, telex 64194 NATGEO. **(Subscription address:** National Geographic Society, Attention: Agent Desk, PO Box 98035, Washington DC 20090-8035.) **ED** William Greurs. **LC** G1; .N27. **DD** 910. **CODEN** NGGMAF. Index available. cum. index. **Ad Acc. Circ:** 10,200,000. available on microfilm and microfiche from University Microfilms International (UMI). Documents available from UMI Article Clearinghouse, Documents on Demand. ***Continues*** *National Geographic Magazine, 1044-6613.*
Desc: Color-illustrated articles on the world's places and peoples, nature subjects, explorations, travel adventure, science and research. Frequent full-color map supplements.
Ind/Abst ASTIS Curr. Aware. Bull. (1978-); Abr. Read. Guide Period. Lit.; Abstr. Anthropol.; Acad. Abstr. Full Text Elite (Jan. 1984-); Acad. Abstr. (Jan. 1984-); Acad. Ind. [Computer File] (1984-); Acad. Search (Jan. 1984-); Am. Bibliogr. Slavic East Europ. Stud.; Annu. Bibliogr. Engl. Lang. Lit.; Anthropol. Index; Art Archaeol. Tech. Abstr.; ASTIS Bibliogr. (1978-); Bibliogr. Carto.; Biogr. Index; Biol. Dig.; Can. Index (?-?); Can. Period. Index (19??-); Chicano Index; Child. Lit. Abstr. (19??-); Child. Mag. Guide (1981-); Coal Abstr.; Comput. Rev.; Curr. Geogr. Publ. (199?-); Energy Inf. Abstr.; Energy Res. Abstr. (Jan. 1976-); Environ. Abstr.; Ethnoarts Index; Expand. Acad. Index (1984-); Garden Lit. (1992-); Gen. Period. Index (1985-); Gen. Sci. Source (Jan. 1988-); GeoRef; Guide Soc. Sci. Relig.; Hist. Source (Jan. 1984-); INFO-SOUTH Abstr.; Int. Aerosp. Abstr.; Mag. Artic. Summar. Elite (Jan. 1984-); Mag. Artic. Summar. Select (Jan. 1984-); Mag. Artic. Summar. CD-ROM (Jan. 1984-); Mag. Express (1986-) [Full Txt.]; Mag. Index Plus (1989-); Mag. Index. Sel. (1986-); Mag. Search; Middle East Abstr. Index; Mid. Search (Jan. 1984-); Newsp. Period. Abstr. (1986-); Peace Res. Abstr. J. (1969-1970); Prim. Search (Jan. 1984-); Read. Guide Abstr. Select Ed.; Read. Guide Period. Lit.; Resource/One Ondisc; Mag. Index (1977-); TOM Gen. Index (1985-); Vocat. Search (Jan. 1984-); West. Hist. Q.; World Ceram. Abstr.

US
NATIONAL GEOGRAPHIC INDEX.
Added/Corp National Geographic Society (U.S.). (1888)-. English. an. $3.00. National Geographic Society, 11555 Darnestown, Gaithersburg MD 20878. **Tel** (202)857-7000, (800)638-4077, FAX (202)429-5727, telex 64194 NATGEO. **(Subscription address:** National Geographic Society, Attention: Agent Desk, PO Box 98035, Washington DC 20090-8035.)

US/0361-5499
NATIONAL GEOGRAPHIC WORLD. [Natl. geogr. world]. **Added/Corp** National Geographic Society (U.S.). **VFOAT** World. (Sept. 1975)-. Periodical. English. Twelve times a year. $14.95 US; $19.50 Canada; $22.75 other. National Geographic Society, 11555 Darnestown, Gaithersburg MD 20878. **Tel** (202)857-7000, (800)638-4077, FAX (202)429-5727, telex 64194 NATGEO. **(Subscription address:** National Geographic Society, Attention: Agent Desk, PO Box 98035, Washington DC 20090-8035.) **ED** Pat Robbins. **LC** G1; .N325. **DD** 910/.5. cum. index. **Pr Rev. Circ:** 1,300,000 (ctrl). available on microfilm and microfiche from University Microfilms International (UMI). Documents available from UMI Article Clearinghouse. ***Supersedes*** *National Geographic School Bulletin.*
Desc: Features factual stories on outdoor adventure, natural history, geography, sports, science, and history for children ages 8 through 13.
Ind/Abst Abr. Read. Guide Period. Lit.; Acad. Abstr. Full Text Elite (Dec. 1984-); Acad. Abstr. (Dec. 1984-); Can. Index (?-?); Can. Period. Index (19??-); Child. Mag. Guide (1981-); Gen. Period. Index (1985-); Mag. Artic. Summar. Elite (Dec. 1984-); Mag. Artic. Summar. Select (Aug. 1984-); Mag. Artic. Summar. CD-ROM (Dec. 1984-); Mag. Index Plus (1989-); Mag. Index. Sel. (1986-); Mag. Search; Mid. Search (Jan. 1988-); Newsp. Period. Abstr. (1988-); Prim. Search (Aug. 1984-); Read. Guide Abstr. Select Ed.; Read. Guide Period. Lit.; Mag. Index (1977-).

II/0027-9374
NATIONAL GEOGRAPHICAL JOURNAL OF INDIA, THE. [Natl. geogr. j. India]. **Added/Corp** National Geographical Society of India. Vol. 1 (Sept. 1955)-. Periodical. English. Four times a year (Mar., June, Sept., Dec.). $125.00. National Geographical Society of India, Department of Geography, Banaras Hindu University, Varanasi 221005 UP India. **Tel** 011 91 1 64491364. **(Subscription address:** Prints India, 11 Darya Ganj, New Delhi, 110002 India, (Phone: 011 91 11 3268645)) **ED** R. L. Singh and Rana P. B. Singh. **LC** G1; .N3. **DD** 910/.5. **CODEN** NGJIAI. Index available (Bound in 4th iss. (Free)). cum. index. **Bk Rev**, (Qty: 20-25). **Pr Rev. Circ:** 1,000.
Desc: These articles of geographical interest which might deal with originality and critical appraisal with problems, reviews of the relevant & current literature, and enhancement of geoenvironmental knowledge.
Ind/Abst Geogr. Abstr. Phys. Geogr.; Geogr. Abstr. Human Geogr. (?-?); GeoRef; Indian Geosci. Abstr.; Int. Dev. Abstr.; Middle East Abstr. Index.

NE/0169-4839
NEDERLANDSE GEOGRAFISCHE STUDIES. (1985)-. Dutch.
Ind/Abst Curr. Geogr. Publ. (199?-); Ecol. Abstr.; Geogr. Abstr. Phys. Geogr.; Geogr. Abstr. Human Geogr.; Int. Dev. Abstr.; Rural Dev. Abstr.

US/1043-6405
NEW JERSEY LAKE SURVEY MAP GUIDE. *Title Change.* [N. J. lake surv. map guide]. (1989)-?. Periodical. English. an. Comtech Lithographics Inc, POB 536, Building 20, 7300 Rt 130 North, Pennsauken NJ 08110. **Tel** (609)665-8350, FAX (609)665-8656. **DD** 799. ***Continued by*** *New Jersey Lake Survey Fishing Maps Guide, 1054-4623.*

US
NEW ORLEANS SUBURBAN (JEFFERSON AND ST. BERNARD PARISHES, LA.) DIRECTORY. Added/Corp Polk (R. L.) and Company. (1974)-. English. an. R. L. Polk & Company, 1155 Brewery Park Boulevard, Detroit MI 48207. **Tel** (313)393-0880. ***Continues*** *Polk's New Orleans Suburban (Jefferson and St. Bernard Parishes, La.) Directory.*

NZ/0110-5124
NEW ZEALAND ANTARCTIC RECORD. [N.Z. antarct. rec.]. Vol. 1, No. 3; 1978-. English. Three times a year. Free. DSIR Antarctic, PO Box 14-091, Christchurch Airport, New Zealand. **Tel** 0064-3-358-3578, FAX 0064-3-358-2097, telex NZ4432. **ED** Chris Rudge. **LC** G845; .A58. **DD** 919.8/9/005. cum. index. **Bk Rev. Ad Acc. Circ:** 1,000. ***Continues*** *Antarctic Record.*
Desc: Scientific papers outlining results from research activities carried out in the Annual New Zealand Antarctic Research Programme.
Ind/Abst AESIS Q.; Ecol. Abstr. (?-?); Geol. Abstr.; GeoRef; Life Sci. Collect.

NZ/0110-6007
NEW ZEALAND CARTOGRAPHY AND GEOGRAPHIC INFORMATION SYSTEMS : THE JOURNAL OF THE NEW ZEALAND CARTOGRAPHIC SOCIETY. See Geography-Cartography.

NZ/0028-8144
NEW ZEALAND GEOGRAPHER. [N. Z. geog.]. **Added/Corp** New Zealand Geographical Society. Vol. 1 (Apr. 1945)-. Periodical. English (Multiple languages). Twice a year (Apr., Oct.). 61.00NZ$ (individuals, Elementary and Secondary Schools), 145.00NZ$ (institutions) Australia and the Pacific; 71.00NZ$ (individuals, Elementary and Secondary School), 180.00NZ$ (institutions) other. New Zealand Geographical Society, University of Canterbury, Private Bag, Christchurch New Zealand. **ED** R. Le Heron. **LC** G55; .N45. **DD** 919.31. **CODEN** NZGGAS. **[CCC].** Index available. cum. index. **Circ:** 1,200 (ctrl). Documents available from BIOSIS Document Express.
Desc: Publishing research on New Zealand, Australia and South West Pacific Region. Encourages communication among geographers whatever their professional or regional specialisation.
Ind/Abst AQUAREF; Biol. Abstr.; Dairy Sci. Abstr.; Geogr. Abstr. Phys. Geogr.; Geogr. Abstr. Human Geogr.; GeoRef; Middle East Abstr. Index.

NZ/0028-8292
NEW ZEALAND JOURNAL OF GEOGRAPHY. [N.Z. j. geogr.]. **Added/Corp** New Zealand Geographical Society. No. 47 (Nov. 1969)-. Periodical. English. ir. 61.00NZ$ (individuals, Elementary and Secondary Schools), 145.00NZ$ (institutions) Australia and the Pacific; 71.00NZ$ (individuals, Elementary and Secondary School), 180.00NZ$ (institutions) other. New Zealand Geographical Society, University of Canterbury, Private Bag, Christchurch New Zealand. **ED** T. Hearn. **LC** G53; .N48. **DD** 910/.5. **CODEN** NZJGA9. **[CCC].** Index available. **Bk Rev. Ad Acc. Circ:** 1,500 (ctrl). ***Continues*** *New Zealand Geographical Society. Record, 0375-7196.*
Desc: Reviews, research papers, teaching strategies and techniques, school course design, evaluation and assessment all of great assistance to the teaching of geography at all levels.
Ind/Abst Curr. Index J. Educ. (March 1990); Geogr. Abstr. Human Geogr.; GeoRef; Int. Dev. Abstr.; Middle East Abstr. Index.

AT/0811-9511
NEWSLETTER / AUSTRALIAN MAP CIRCLE. Main/Corp Australian Map Circle. No. 28 (June 1983)-. Newsletter. English. ir. comes with membership. Australian Map Circle, PO Box E 133, Victoria Terrace, Canberra ACT 2600 Australia. **Tel** 011 61 3 3290055. **ED** W. Stinson. **LC** GA1681; .A87. **DD** 912/.074/0994. Index available. **Bk Rev**, (Qty: 3-4). **Circ:** 200 (ctrl). ***Continues*** *Newsletter - Australian Map Curators' Circle.*
Ind/Abst AESIS Q.; Aust. Educ. Index (199?-); Aust. Libr. Inf. Sci. Abstr. (1982-1983),(1983-).

UK
NEWSLETTER/ REMOTE SENSING SOCIETY. See Earth Sciences.

SP/0213-3709
NORBA. REVISTA DE GEOGRAFIA. [Norba, Rev. geogr.]. **Added/Corp** Universidad de Extremadura (Caceres, Spain). Facultad de Filosof,ia y Letras. **VFOAT** Norba-Geografia. No. 5 (1984)-. Periodical. Spanish. an. 1700ptas. University Extremadura Service Publishers / Spain, Donoso Cortes 11, 10003 Caceres Spain. **Tel** 011 34 927 247650. ***Continues*** *Norba, 0211-0636.*

FI/0356-1437
NORDIA. [Nordia]. **Added/Corp** Pohjois-Suomen Maantieteellinen Seura. (1967)-. Monographic series. English. Price varies per volume. **LC** G1; .N56. **DD** 914.897/02.
Ind/Abst Geogr. Abstr. Phys. Geogr.; Geogr. Abstr. Human Geogr.

FR/0029-182X
NOROIS. [Norois]. Vol. 1, No. 1 (Jan./March 1954)-. Periodical. French (summaries and/or abstracts in

English). qt (Mar., July, Sept., Dec.). 280.00F France; 340.00F other. Norois, 95 Av Du Recteur Pineau, 86022 Poitiers Cedex France. **Tel** 011 33 49 453239, FAX 011 33 49 453239. **ED** J. Soumagne. **LC** G1; .N57. **CODEN** NOROAU. Index available in last issue of volume--attached. cum. index. **Bk Rev**, (Qty: 4). **Circ:** 1,000. ***Supersedes*** *Group Poitevin d'Etudes Geographiques. Bulletin; Group Poitevin d'Etudes Geographiques. Chronique Geographique des Pays Celtes.*
Desc: Provides research information on the physical, human, and economic geography of France and the Atlantic countries.
Ind/Abst Geogr. Abstr. Phys. Geogr.; Geogr. Abstr. Human Geogr.; GeoRef.

NO/0029-1951
NORSK GEOGRAFISK TIDSSKRIFT. [Nor. geogr. tidsskr.]. **Added/Corp** Norske Geografiske Selskab. **VFOAT** Norwegian Journal of Geography. Vol. 1 (1926)-. Periodical. English. qt. Kr495.00, $86.00. Scandinavian University Press, PO Box 2959 Toeyen, N 0608 Oslo 6 Norway. **Tel** 011 47 2 2575400, FAX 011 47 2 2575353, telex 71896 UROR N. **(Subscription address:** Scandinavian University Press, 200 Meacham Ave., Elmont NY 11003.**) ED** T Klemsdal. **LC** G1; .N6. **DD** 910/.5. **CODEN** NGGTA2. **[CCC]**. cum. index. **Bk Rev. Ad Acc. Circ:** 800 (ctrl). available on microfilm from University Microfilms International (UMI). ***Supersedes*** *Norske Geografiske Selskab. Arbok.*
Desc: Reflects the many facets of geography and tries to take an all-around geographical view, both regionally and thematically, by striking a nearly equal balance between natural and cultural geographic material.
Ind/Abst Curr. Aware. Biol. Sci., CABS; Curr. Geogr. Publ. (199?-); Ecol. Abstr.; Energy Res. Abstr. (Feb. 1980-); Geogr. Abstr. Phys. Geogr.; Geogr. Abstr. Human Geogr.; Geol. Abstr.; GeoRef; Int. Dev. Abstr. (?-?); Rural Dev. Abstr.; World Agric. Econ.

US/1058-7683
NORTE SUR. (NORTE SUR : LA REVISTA DE LAS AMERICAS.). [Norte Sur]. **Added/Corp** University of Miami. North-South Center. Vol. 1, No. 1 (Jun./Jul. 1991)-. Periodical. Spanish. bm. $18.00. University of Miami / GSIS, North-South Center, Publications-Vega, PO Box 248123, Coral Gables FL 33124-3010. **Tel** (305)284-6866, FAX (305)284-6370. **DD** 900.

●US/1065-2973
NORTH CAROLINA GEOGRAPHER, THE. (THE NORTH CAROLINA GEOGRAPHER : JOURNAL OF THE NORTH CAROLINA GEOGRAPHICAL SOCIETY.). [N.C. geogr.]. **Added/Corp** North Carolina Geographical Society. Vol. 1 (1992)-. Periodical. English. an. $8.00 Comes with North Carolina Geographical Society membership. North Carolina Geographical Society, Barton College, Department of History, College Station, Wilson NC 27893. **Tel** (704)262-2070, (704)262-2650. **DD** 910.

US/0898-2031
NORTHWEST (NEW YORK, N.Y.). (NORTHWEST.). [Northwest]. Periodical. English. mo. $36.00. East/West Network Inc, Subscription Department, 5900 Wilshire Boulevard/8th Floor, Los Angeles CA 90036. **DD** 910.

US/1040-1784
NORTHWEST PORTFOLIO. ***Ceased.*** [Northwest portf.]. **VFOAT** Portfolio; Northwest Magazine. (19??)-(19??). Periodical. English. mo. East/West Network Inc, Subscription Department, 5900 Wilshire Boulevard/8th Floor, Los Angeles CA 90036. **DD** 910.

CN/0824-295X
NOTES DE RECHERCHES - GEOGRAPHIE. UNIVERSITE D'OTTAWA. (NOTES DE RECHERCHES / GEOGRAPHIE.). [Notes rech. - Geogr., Univ. Ottawa]. **VFOAT** Research Notes. **VAT** Research Notes - Geography. University of Ottawa. No. 20-. Monographic series. English (French). ir (three-five issues per year). Price varies per volume. University of Ottawa Department of Geography, 165 Waller Street, Ottawa Ontario K1N 6N5 Canada. **Tel** (613)564-2395. **DD** 910. cum. index. **Ad Acc. Circ:** 150. ***Continues*** *Notes de Recherches (University of Ottawa. Dept. of Geography and Regional Planning), 0704-7606.*
Desc: Covers the broad spectrum of geography, but particularly the physical geography of northern areas, the analysis of natural resources, and social - urban - economic geography.

CN/0710-1767
NOTES ET DOCUMENTS - DEPARTEMENT DE GEOGRAPHIE. UNIVERSITE DE MONTREAL. (NOTES ET DOCUMENTS.). [Notes doc. - Dep. geogr., Univ. Montr.]. No. 77/01-. Monographic series. French. Price varies per volume. **DD** 910.

BL/0029-4128
NOTICIA GEOMORFOLOGICA. [Not. geomorfol.]. Yearly V. 1- (No. 1-); April 1958-. Periodical. Portuguese. **LC** GB155; .C35. **CODEN** NGMFBP.
Ind/Abst GeoRef.

US/0734-7634
NUC. CARTOGRAPHIC MATERIALS. (NUC. CARTOGRAPHIC MATERIALS [MICROFORM] / LIBRARY OF CONGRESS.). [NUC, Cartogr. mater.]. **Added/Corp** Library of Congress. **VFOAT** Cartographic Materials. **VAT** National Union Catalog. Cartographic Materials. (1983)-. English (Multiple languages). Four times a year (Jan., Apr., July, Oct.). $200.00 North America; $225.00 others. Advanced Library Systems, PO Box 246, Andover MA 01810. **Tel** (508)470-0610, FAX (508)475-1072. **LC** Microfiche (o) 93/6005. **DD** 912. Index available. cum. index. available on microfiche.
Desc: Contains bibliographic records of single sheet maps, map sets, atlases and maps treated as serials cataloged by the Library of Congress and 1,500 contributing libraries.

SP
NUEVA GEOGRAFIA DE PUERTO RICO. ir. $5.50. Manuel Pareja, Montana 16, Barcelona Spain.

CN/0711-6330
NWT DATA BOOK. ***Suspended.*** [NWT data book]. **VAT** Northwest Territories Data Book. (1981)-(1994). English. an. $14.00 per no. NWT Data Book, c/o Outcrop Ltd, Box 1114, Yellowknife Northwest Territories X0E 1H0 Canada. **Tel** (403)873-6152, FAX (403)873-2844. **LC** F1060.A1; N88. **DD** 917.19/2043.

CN/1180-2863
OBSERVATIONS (OTTAWA). (OBSERVATIONS : SURVEYS, MAPPING AND REMOTE SENSING SECTOR NEWSLETTER.). [Observations]. **Added/Corp** Canada. Surveys, Mapping and Remote Sensing Sector. **VFOAT** Observations. Vol. 1, No. 1 (June 1990)-. Newsletter. English (French). **DD** 526.9/0971/05.

GY
OCCASIONAL PAPER - DEPT. OF GEOGRAPHY, UNIVERSITY OF GUYANA. **Main/Corp** University of Guyana. Dept. of Geography. No. 1- 1970-. Monographic series. English. ir. Price varies per volume. University of Guyana Department of Geography, Box 841, Georgetown Guyana. **Tel** 54841. **ED** J R K Daniel. **LC** G1; .O229. Index available. cum. index. **Circ:** 500 (ctrl).
Desc: Describes the geomorphological, geological, hydrological, vegetational and soil characteristics of Guyana, with a description of the natural environments of Guyana.

UK
OCCASIONAL PAPER / UNIVERSITY OF KEELE, DEPARTMENT OF GEOGRAPHY. **Added/Corp** University of Keele. Dept. of Geography. No. 1 (1982)-. Monographic series. English. Price varies per volume.
Ind/Abst Geogr. Abstr. Phys. Geogr.

UK/0264-3499
OCCASIONAL PAPERS SERIES - DEPARTMENT OF GEOGRAPHY, UNIVERSITY OF GLASGOW. [Occas. pap. ser. - Dep. Geogr. Univ. Glasg.]. **VFOAT** Occasional Papers - Geography Department, Glasgow University. (1979)-. Monographic series. English. ir. Price varies per volume.
Ind/Abst Geogr. Abstr. Human Geogr.; Int. Dev. Abstr.

US/0271-0366
OCCASIONAL PUBLICATIONS OF THE DEPARTMENT OF GEOGRAPHY (URBANA). (OCCASIONAL PUBLICATIONS. PAPER.). [Occas. publ. Dep. Geogr.]. **Main/Corp** University of Illinois at Urbana-Champaign. Dept. of Geography. No. 1 (1972)-. Monographic series. English. ir. Price varies per volume. University of Illinois Department of Geography, Occasional Publications, 607 S Mathews, 220 Davenport Hall, Urbana IL 61801. **Tel** (217)333-1880. **ED** Susan Enscore, Mark Welford. Index available. cum. index. **Pr Rev. Circ:** 100.
Desc: An internally refereed research publication concerned with the whole physical and human geography.
Ind/Abst GeoRef.

UK
O'DELL MEMORIAL MONOGRAPH. (1968)-. Monographic series. English. Price varies per volume. Aberdeen University Press Ltd., Farmers Hall, Aberdeen AB9 2XT Scotland. **Tel** 0224 630724, FAX 0224 643286, telex 739477.
Ind/Abst Geogr. Abstr. Human Geogr.

AU/1013-9966
OESTERREICH IN GESCHICHTE UND LITERATUR MIT GEOGRAPHIE. **See** History(General)-History of Europe.

US
OFFICIAL STANDARD NAMES GAZETTEER. (OFFICIAL STANDARD NAMES APPROVED BY THE UNITED STATES BOARD ON GEOGRAPHIC NAMES.). **Main/Corp** United States. Board on Geographic Names. 1955-. English. US Department of Defense Defense Mapping Agency, 8613 Lee Highway, Fairfax VA 22031. **Tel** (703)285-9290, FAX (703)285-9374. **Circ:** 1,500.
Desc: Gazetteers incorporate geographic names, identification and location of features in foreign countries, on a country-by-country basis.

CN/0078-4656
ONOMASTICA CANADIANA. **See** Linguistics.

CI/0475-0934
ONOMASTICA JUGOSLAVICA. **See** Linguistics.

PL/0078-4648
ONOMASTICA (WROCAW). (ONOMASTICA.). [Onomastica]. **Added/Corp** Polska Akademia Nauk. Komitet Jezykoznawstwa. Vol. 1, No. 1 (1955)-. Periodical. Polish (summaries and/or abstracts in French). an. $38.00. **(Subscription address:** ARS Polona, PO Box 1001, 00068 Warsaw Poland.**) LC** G104; .O57.
Ind/Abst MLA Int. Bibl. Books Artic. Mod. Lang. Lit.

CN/0078-4850
ONTARIO GEOGRAPHY. ***Title Change.*** [Ont. geog.]. **Added/Corp** University of Western Ontario. Dept. of Geography. No. 1 (Jan. 1967)-No. 39, (1992). English. an. Ontario Geography, University of West Ontario, Geography Department, London Ontario N6A 5C2 Canada. **Tel** (519)661-3423, FAX (519)661-3868. **ED** Brian Ceh. **CODEN** OGEOAM. **Pr Rev.** ***Merged with*** *East Lakes Geographer* ***to form*** *Great Lakes Geographer.*
Desc: Invites submission of articles from across the geographic discipline.
Ind/Abst Curr. Geogr. Publ. (199?-); Geogr. Abstr. Phys. Geogr.; Geogr. Abstr. Human Geogr.; GeoRef.

CN/0822-4838
OPERATIONAL GEOGRAPHER, THE. ***Ceased.*** [Oper. geogr.]. **VFOAT** La Geographie Appliquee; T.O.G.; Geographie Appliquee. No. 1 (1983)-Vol. 11, No. 4 (1993). Periodical. English (French). Three times a year. Canadian Association of Geographers, Burnside Hall, McGill University, 805 Sherbrooke Street West, Montreal Quebec H3A 2K6 Canada. **Tel** (514)392-5496. **ED** Anthony Lea and Michael Bardecki. **DD** 910/.5. **CODEN** OPGEEZ. **Ad Acc. Circ:** 1,500 (ctrl). Documents available from Ask*IEEE, Documents on Demand.
Desc: Journal of applied geography in government, business and education, containing articles, commentaries, reviews, analyses of new technology and current news, conferences, etc.
Ind/Abst Environ. Abstr.; Geogr. Abstr. Phys. Geogr.; Geogr. Abstr. Human Geogr.; GeoRef; INSPEC (1985-); Int. Dev. Abstr.

GW/0030-4395
ORBIS GEOGRAPHICUS. ADRESSAR GEOGRAPHIQUE DU MONDE. WORLD DIRECTORY OF GEOGRAPHY. GEOGRAPHISCHES WELTADRESSBUCH. ***Ceased.*** **Added/Corp** International Geographical Union. International Cartographic Association. **VFOAT** Addresar Geographique du Monde; World Directory of Geography; Geographisches Weltadressbuch. (1960)-(1993). Directory. English (French and German). ir. Franz Steiner Verlag GmbH, Postfach 101061, D 70009 Stuttgart Germany. **Tel** 011 49 0711 2582372, FAX 011 49 0711 2582290, telex 723636 daz d. **ED** E Ehlers. **Ad Acc.** ***Continues*** *World Directory of Geographers.*
Desc: A directory of geographic institutions all over the world.

BG/0030-5308
ORIENTAL GEOGRAPHER. [Orient. geogr.]. **Added/Corp** Bangladesh Geographical Society. East Pakistan Geographical Society. Vol. 1 (Jan. 1957)-. Periodical. English. sa (2 issues). $10.00 US and Canada. Bangladesh Geographical Society, Dhaka University, Department of Geography, Dacca 2 Bangladesh. **Tel** 501103. **LC** G35; .E225. **DD** 915.49/2/005. **CODEN** ORGGAH. cum. index.
Ind/Abst GeoRef; Middle East Abstr. Index.

UK
OSD, OS MAP ADDITIONS LIST. **VFOAT** Map Additions List. **VAT** Overseas Surveys Directorate, Ordnance Survey Map Additions List. Periodical. English. mo. **LC** PAR. ***Continues*** *D.O.S. Map Additions List.*

GW
OSTERREICHISCHE ZEITSCHRIFT FUER VERMESSUNGSWESEN UND PHOTOGRAMMETRIE. Vol. 61, No. 3 (19??)-. Periodical. German. Four times a year (Jan., Apr., July, Oct.). DM600.00. Osterreichischer Verein Fuer, Vermessungsw Schiffamtsgasse 1, A 1025 Vienna Austria. **Tel** 011 43 1 211763700. **LC** QB275; .O3. **Bk Rev. Circ:** 1,200. ***Continues*** *Osterreichische Zeitschrift fur Vermessungswesen.*
Desc: Scientific and technical publications concerning surveying, photogrammetry, geodesy and cartography and remote sensing.
Ind/Abst GeoRef.

CN
OTTAWA CITY DIRECTORY (TORONTO, ONT.). (THE OTTAWA CITY DIRECTORY MICROFORM.). **VFOAT** Boyd and M'Donald's Ottawa City Directory; Mitchell & Co's County of Carleton and Ottawa City Directory; Ottawa City and Counties of Carleton and Russell Directory; Sutherland's City of Ottawa Directory; Hunter, Rose and Co's City of Ottawa Directory; Cherrier & Kirwin's Ottawa Directory; City of Ottawa Alphabetical, General Miscellaneous and Subscribers Classified Business Directory; Ottawa Directory. 1861/2-. Directory. English. Ottawa Public Library Business Office, 120 Metcalfe Street, Ottawa Ontario K1P 5M2 Canada. **DD** 917.13/84/0025.

CN/0822-8086
OTTAWA, HULL (NEPEAN). (OTTAWA, HULL.). [Ottawa Hull]. 1983/1984-. Periodical. English. $6.95 Per Vol. Ottawa Hull, c/o McPhells Enterprises, 20-1668 Woodroffe Avenue, Nepean Ontario K2G 1W4 Canada. **DD** 917.13/84/0025.

CN/0705-2820
OTTAWA-HULL : THE KEY. VFOAT Ottawa-Hull : Le Cle; Key; Cle; Key to Ottawa-Hull. **VAT** Key (Ottawa). V. 1- 1977-. Periodical. English (French). qt. Gordon Lundy Ltd, 1921 Innes Road, Ottawa Ontario K1B 4C6 Canada. **DD** 917.13/84/044.

CN/0383-6967
OTTAWA VALLEY PEOPLE'S YELLOW PAGES. VFOAT Le Guide pour Vivre et Survivre a Ottawa, Hull et dans la Region; Ottawa Valley Peoples Yellow Pages. le Bottin. 1976/77-. English (French). Commoner's Pub Society, 432 Rideau Street, Ottawa Ontario K1N 5Z1 Canada. **DD** 917.13/83.

US
OUR EARTH. See Encyclopedias and General Reference Books.

UK
OUTLOOK. English. Three times a year (Sept., Jan., April). £11.85 UK; £17.85 Europe; £20.85 other. Philip Allan Publishers Ltd, Market Place, Deddington Oxford, OX15 0SE England. **Tel** 011 44 869 38652, FAX 011 44 869 38803.

GW/0935-9621
PADERBORNER GEOGRAPHISCHE STUDIEN. [Paderborn. geogr. Stud.]. **VFOAT** PGS. Paderborner Geographische Studien. (1989)-. Monographic series. German. ir. Price varies per volume. **UDC** 91.
Ind/Abst Ecol. Abstr.; Geogr. Abstr. Phys. Geogr.; Geogr. Abstr. Human Geogr.; Int. Dev. Abstr.

US/0747-5160
PAPERS AND PROCEEDINGS OF APPLIED GEOGRAPHY CONFERENCES. [Pap. proc. appl. geogr. conf.]. **Main/Conf** Applied Geography Conference. **Added/Corp** State University of New York at Binghamton. Dept. of Geography. Kent State University. Dept. of Geography. Ryerson Polytechnical Institute. Dept. of Geography. **VFOAT** Applied Geography Conferences. Vol. 6 (1983)-. Proceedings. English. an. $25.00 (institutions), $20.00 (individuals). State University of New York Department of Geography, PO Box 6000, Binghamton NY 13901. **Tel** (607)777-2755, (607)777-6557. **ED** John W Frazier. **LC** G56; .A66. **DD** 910. ctrl circ. ***Continues*** *Proceedings of Applied Geography Conferences, 0747-5209.*
Desc: Collection of papers delivered at annual conference. Topics from environmental to human, including tools such as automated cartography.
Ind/Abst Ecol. Abstr.; For. Prod. Abstr. (1991-); For. Abstr.; Geogr. Abstr. Phys. Geogr.; Geogr. Abstr. Human Geogr.; GeoRef; Grasslands For. Abstr.; Int. Dev. Abstr.

US/0553-5980
PENNSYLVANIA GEOGRAPHER, THE. (THE PENNSYLVANIA GEOGRAPHER / PENNSYLVANIA COUNCIL FOR GEOGRAPHY EDUCATION.). [Pa. geogr.]. **Added/Corp** Pennsylvania Geographical Society. Pennsylvania Council for Geography Education. (1963)-. Periodical. English. Twice a year (May & Dec.). $12.00. Pennsylvania Geographical Society, Shippinsburg University, Department of Geo. Earth, Shippensburg PA 17257. **Tel** (717)532-1685. **ED** William B. Kory. **LC** G72; .P46. **DD** 910/.5. Index available. **Bk Rev. Pr Rev. Circ:** 220 (ctrl).
Desc: Contents vary with each issue, usually current state and national geographic and conservation items.
Ind/Abst Geogr. Abstr. Phys. Geogr. (?-?); Geogr. Abstr. Human Geogr.; Int. Dev. Abstr. (?-?).

GW/0418-968X
PERGAMENISCHE FORSCHUNGEN. **VFOAT** PF. Vol. 1 (1968)-. Monographic series. German. ir. Price varies per volume. Walter de Gruyter Inc., PO Box 303421, D 10728 Berlin Germany. **Tel** 011 49 30 260050, FAX 011 49 30 26005251. **(Subscription address:** US and Canada/ 200 Saw Mill River Road, Hawthorne, NY 10532**)** **LC** DS156.P4; P4. **DD** 913.

CN/0820-8174
PERLY'S BLUEMAP ATLAS, METROPOLITAN TORONTO AND VICINITY. VAT Bluemap Atlas, Metropolitan Toronto and Vicinity. (1981)-. Periodical. English. an. 54.95Can$. Perly's Maps, 1050 Eglinton Avenue West, Toronto Ontario M6C 2C5 Canada. **Tel** (416)785-6277. **DD** 912/.71354. ***Continues*** *Perly's Bluemap Atlas of Greater Toronto, 0711-267X.*
Desc: Contains information on Toronto and its surroundings.

US
PERSPECTIVE / NATIONAL COUNCIL FOR GEOGRAPHIC EDUCATION. **Added/Corp** National Council for Geographic Education. (1969)-. Periodical. English. Five times a year. National Council for Geographic Education, Indiana University of Pennsylvania, 16A Leonard Hall, Indiana PA 15705-1087. **Tel** (412)357-6290, FAX (412)357-7708. **LC** G72; .P47.

GW/0031-6229
PETERMANNS GEOGRAPHISCHE MITTEILUNGEN. [Petermanns geogr. Mitt.]. V. 84, No. 1, (Jan. 1938)-. Academic Scholarly Publication. German (summaries and/or abstracts in English and Russian). Six times a year. DM320.00. Justus Perthes Verlag Gotha GmbH, Postfach 274, D 99867 Gotha Germany. **Tel** 011 49 3621 385184, FAX 011 49 3621 385103. **ED** Otmar Seuffert (editor's address: Mainstrae 50, D 64625 Bensheim Germany; editor's phone: 49 6251 62529). **LC** G1; .P43. **DD** 016.91. **CODEN** PGGMA3. Index available (bound in last issue). **Bk Rev**, (Qty: 100). ctrl circ. ***Continues*** *Petermanns Mitteilungen.*
Ind/Abst AGRICOLA; Bibliogr. Carto.; Ecol. Abstr. (?-?); EMBASE; Geogr. Abstr. Phys. Geogr.; Geogr. Abstr. Human Geogr.; Geol. Abstr.; GeoRef; Int. Dev. Abstr. (?-?); Meteorol. Geoastrophys. Abstr.; Popul. Index.

PH/0031-7551
PHILIPPINE GEOGRAPHICAL JOURNAL. V. 1- 1st Quarter 1953-. Periodical. English. qt. $15.00. PSSC Central Subscription Service, PO Box 205 UP Diliman, Quezon City 1101 Philippines. **Tel** 011 63 2 9229621. **ED** Dominador Z Rosell. **LC** DS651; .P4. **DD** 919.14. Index available in last issue of volume--attached. cum. index. **Bk Rev. Ad Acc. Circ:** 1,000. available on microfilm and microfiche from University Microfilms International (UMI).
Desc: Publishes studies and papers on the status and development of geography and fields related to geography in the Philippines.
Ind/Abst Philip. Sci. Technol. Abstr.

●UK
PHILIP'S GEOGRAPHICAL DIGEST. **VFOAT** Geographical Digest. (1992)-. English. be. ***Continues*** *Geographical Digest (London, England: 1986).*

US/0733-7574
PHOENIX AND VICINITY POPULAR STREET ATLAS, INCLUDING MARICOPA COUNTY (CENSUS TRACT EDITION). (PHOENIX AND VICINITY POPULAR STREET ATLAS, INCLUDING MARICOPA COUNTY / THOMAS BROS. MAPS.). **Added/Corp** Thomas Bros. Maps. (19??)-. English. an. Thomas Brothers Maps, Lockbox PO Box 30845, Los Angeles CA 90030. **Tel** (714)863-1984. **Ad Acc.**
Desc: Street maps and index for Phoenix and Maricopa County in Arizona.

UK/0031-868X
PHOTOGRAMMETRIC RECORD, THE. [Photogramm. rec.]. **Added/Corp** Photogrammetric Society. Vol. 1 (March 1953)-. Periodical. English. sa. £44.00. Photogrammetric Society, University College London, Department of Photogrammetry/ Gower Street, London WCIE 6BT England. **Tel** 011 44 1 44903, telex 296273 UCLENG G. **ED** K B Atkinson. **LC** TA501; .P5. **DD** 526.9/82/05. **CODEN** PGREAY. Index available. cum. index. **Ad Acc. Pr Rev. Circ:** 2,500 (ctrl). Documents available from Ask*IEEE.
Desc: Record of original research both theoretical and empirical contributing to the advancement of photogrammetric knowledge applicable to all problems.
Ind/Abst Bibliogr. Carto.; Curr. Contents Phys. Chem. Earth Sci.; Curr. Technol. Index; Fish Rev.; Geogr. Abstr. Phys. Geogr.; INSPEC (April 1984-); Life Sci. Collect.; SCISEARCH; Wildl. Rev.

US/0272-3646
PHYSICAL GEOGRAPHY. [Phys. geogr.]. Vol. 1, No. 1 (Jan./June 1980)-. Periodical. English. bm. $243.00 US; $266.00 other. V. H. Winston & Sons Inc., 7961 Eastern Avenue, Suite 202A, Silver Spring MD 20910. **Tel** (301)587-3356. **(Subscription address:** Bellwether Publishing, Ltd, 8640 Guilford Road, Suite 200, Columbia MD 21046.**)** **ED** Antony R. Orme. **LC** G1; .P48. **DD** 910/.02/05. **[CCC]. Circ:** 280 (ctrl). Documents available from The Genuine Article.
Desc: Journal in geography publishing research in geomorphology, climatology, biogeography, natural hazards and related earth sciences.
Ind/Abst Ecol. Abstr.; For. Abstr.; Geogr. Abstr. Phys. Geogr.; Geol. Abstr.; GeoRef; Irr. Drain. Abstr.; Meteorol. Geoastrophys. Abstr.; Res. Alert [Select. Cov.]; SCISEARCH; Soils Fert.

US
PICTURE ATLAS OF THE WORLD. See Encyclopedias and General Reference Books.

US/0733-7663
PIERCE COUNTY POPULAR STREET ATLAS (CENSUS TRACT ED.). (PIERCE COUNTY POPULAR STREET ATLAS.). **Main/Corp** Thomas Bros. Maps. English. an. $17.95. Thomas Brothers Maps, Lockbox PO Box 30845, Los Angeles CA 90030. **Tel** (714)863-1984. **Ad Acc.**
Desc: Street maps and index on Pierce County in Washington.

US
PLACE-NAME-INDEX [COMPUTER FILE]. **Added/Corp** Buckmaster Publishing. **VAT** Place Name Index. (1988)-. Periodical. English. ir. $798.00 US; $803.00 other. Buckmaster Publishing - Virginia, Route 4, Box 1630, Mineral VA 23117. **Tel** (703)894-5777.
Desc: Contains place names in the United States collected from the quadrangle maps of the United States Geological Survey.

II
POINT OF VIEW. Periodical. English. Rs0.75 single issue. 20/36 Rohtak Road, New Delhi 5 India. **LC** DS401; .P64. **DD** 915.4/005.

UK/0957-5073
POLAR AND GLACIOLOGICAL ABSTRACTS. **Added/Corp** Scott Polar Research Institute. Library and Information Service. World Data Centre C: Glaciology. Vol. 1, Pt. A (Jan. 1990)-. Academic Scholarly Publication. English. qt. $138.00 US, Canada and Mexico; £76.00 other. Cambridge University Press, The Edinburgh Building, Shaftesbury Road, Cambridge CB2 2RU United Kingdom. **Tel** 011 44 223 312393, FAX 011 44 223 325959. **(Subscription address:** Cambridge University Press / North America, 110 Midland Avenue, Port Chester NY 10573.**)** **ED** William Mills. **LC** Z6005.P7; P58; G587. **DD** 016.9198/005. cum. index. **Ad Acc.** available on microfilm and microfiche from University Microfilms International (UMI). ***Continues*** *Recent Polar and Glaciological Literature, 0263-547X.*
Desc: Offers comprehensive coverage of the literature of the world's polar regions. Produced by the library of the Scott Polar Research Institute, it provides comprehensive and convenient access to the rapidly growing research and scholarship of all relevant disciplines. It scans over 1,000 series plus relevant books, reports and theses. Each issue contains author, subject and geographic indexes which are cumulated annually.

US/0032-2482
POLAR TIMES, THE. **Added/Corp** American Polar Society. No. 1 (June 1935)-. Periodical. English. Twice a year (April and October). $10.00. American Polar Society, PO Box 692, Reedsport OR 97467. **Tel** (503)759-3589, FAX (503)759-3403. **ED** Della Weston, (phone: (503)997-8826). **LC** G575; .P63. **DD** 919.8. **Bk Rev. Ad Acc, Adv Mgr:** Brian, **Tel** (503)759-3589. **Circ:** 1,100.
Desc: News and information about the American Polar Society.

●UK/0962-6298
POLITICAL GEOGRAPHY. **VFOAT** PG. Vol. 11, No. 1 (Jan. 1992)-. Periodical. English. Eight times a year. $336.00 The Americas; £225.00 other. Butterworth Heinemann Publishers, Linacre House, Jordan Hill, Oxford OX2 8DP England. **Tel** 011 44 865 310366. **(Subscription address:** Elsevier Science Ltd. Oxford Fulfillment Centre, PO Box 800, Kidlington, Oxford OX5 1DX United Kingdom.**)** **LC** JC319; .P59. Documents available from The Genuine Article. ***Continues*** *Political Geography Quarterly, 0260-9827.*
Ind/Abst ABC POL SCI (1992-); Am. Hist. Life (1986-); Arts Humanit. Citation Index [Select. Cov.]; Curr. Contents Soc. Behav. Sci.; Int. Bibliogr. Sociol.; PAIS Int. Print; Res. Alert [Full Cov.]; Soc. Sci. Cit. Index [Full Cov.].

US
POLK'S ALBANY (ALBANY COUNTY, N.Y.) CITY DIRECTORY. **VFOAT** Albany City Directory. (19??)-. English. an. $92.00. R. L. Polk & Company, 1155 Brewery Park Boulevard, Detroit MI 48207. **Tel** (313)393-0880.

US
POLK'S MINNEAPOLIS SUBURBAN CITY DIRECTORY. (19??)-. English. an. R. L. Polk & Company, 1155 Brewery Park Boulevard, Detroit MI 48207. **Tel** (313)393-0880. **Bk Rev. Ad Acc.**
Desc: Cross reference city directory.

US
POLK'S ROCHESTER SUBURBAN (MONROE COUNTY, N.Y.) DIRECTORY. (19??)-. Directory. English. an. R. L. Polk & Company, 1155 Brewery Park Boulevard, Detroit MI 48207. **Tel** (313)393-0880. **(Subscription address:** R. L. Polk, 300 Commerical Street, 15 Riverview, Malden, MA 02148**)**

CN/0316-0556
POLK'S SAGUENAY DIRECTORY. **VFOAT** Annuaire Polk du Saguenay; Annuaire du Saguenay City Directory. 1960-. Directory. English (French). R.L. Polk &

Company Ltd., 2485 Ste-Anne Boulevard, Ste-Anne Quebec G1J 1Y3 Canada. **DD** 917.14/16. ***Continues*** *Marcotte's Saguenay City Directory, 0316-0564.*

CN/0318-2940
PORT ALBERNI DIRECTORY (BUSINESS EDITION). (PORT ALBERNI DIRECTORY.). [Port Alberni dir.]. **VFOAT** Official City Directory of Port Alberni; City Directory of Port Alberni. (1968)-. Directory. English. B C Directories / Port Alberni, 4918 Napier Street, Port Alberni British Columbia Canada. **DD** 917.11/34. ***Supersedes*** *Port Alberni and Alberni Directory, 0318-2959.*

US/0887-5340
PORTLAND MONTHLY. [Portland mon.]. (1986)-. Periodical. English. Ten times a year (July/Aug. and Nov./Dec.issues are combined). $20.00 one year; $32.00 two years; $40.00 three years. Portland Monthly, 578 Congress Street, Portland ME 04101. **Tel** (207)775-4339, FAX (207)775-2334. **ED** Colin Sargent. **DD** 917. **Ad Acc.** ctrl circ.
Desc: Publishes short fiction established as well as newly discovered wiriters.

US
PORTOLAN / WASHINGTON MAP SOCIETY, THE. **Added/Corp** Washington Map Society. Vol. 1, No. 1 (Oct. 10, 1984)-. Periodical. English. Three times a year. $22.00. Washington Map Society, 686 College Parkway, Rockville MD 20850. **Tel** (301)340-6859. **ED** Nancy Goddin Miller and Charles Burroughs. **Bk Rev.**

●NO
POSISJON. (1993)-. Trade Publication. Norwegian. Ten times a year. Kr350.00, $65.00. Scandinavian University Press, PO Box 2959 Toeyen, N 0608 Oslo 6 Norway. **Tel** 011 47 2 2575400, FAX 011 47 2 2575353, telex 71896 UROR N. **(Subscription address:** Scandinavian University Press, 200 Meacham Ave., Elmont NY 11003.**) ED** Knut T. Pettersen.
Desc: Mapping, geodata, and information systems.

●US/1060-5851
POST-SOVIET GEOGRAPHY. [Post-Sov. geogr.]. **VFOAT** Post Soviet Geography. Vol. 33, No. 1 (Jan. 1992)-. Academic Scholarly Publication. English. Ten times a year. $349.00 US, $399.00 other, except Japan (surface mail). V. H. Winston & Sons Inc., 7961 Eastern Avenue, Suite 202A, Silver Spring MD 20910. **Tel** (301)587-3356. **(Subscription address:** Bellwether Publishing, Ltd, 8640 Guilford Road, Suite 200, Columbia MD 21046.**) LC** G1; .S65. **DD** 910/.5. Index available (bound in last issue). Documents available from The Genuine Article. ***Continues*** *Soviet Geography, 0038-5417.*
Ind/Abst Acad. Search (July 1993-); Bibliogr. Carto.; Curr. Contents Soc. Behav. Sci.; EMBASE; Expand. Acad. Index (1992-); GeoRef; INFO-SOUTH Abstr.; Popul. Index; Res. Alert [Full Cov.]; Soc. Sci. Source (Jul. 1993-); Soc. Sci. Cit. Index [Full Cov.]; Soc. Sci. Index; Soc. Sci. Index Fulltext (Jan. 1992-) [Full Txt.].

PL/0032-6143
POZNAJ SWIAT. [Poznaj swiat]. **Added/Corp** Polskie Towarzystwo Geograficzne. (Jan. 1948)-. Periodical. Polish. mo. **(Subscription address:** ARS Polona, PO Box 1001, 00068 Warsaw Poland.**) LC** G1; .P65. cum. index.
Ind/Abst GeoRef.

PL/0083-4343
PRACE GEOGRAFICZNE. **VFOAT** Schedae Geographicae. No. 1; 1960-. Monographic series. Polish (English, French, German and Russian; summaries and/or abstracts in English, French and German). Price varies per volume. Panstwowe Wydawn Naukowe, Miodowa 10, PO Box 391, 00251 Warsaw Poland. **LC** G23; .K8 subser. **DD** 910/.5.
Ind/Abst Geogr. Abstr. Human Geogr.

PL/0373-6547
PRACE GEOGRAFICZNE - POLSKA AKADEMIA NAUK. (PRACE GEOGRAFICZNE.). [Pr. geogr. - Pol. Akad. Nauk]. **VFOAT** Geograficheskie Trudy; Geographical Studies. 1954-. Polish (summaries and/or abstracts in English and Russian). ir. Z30.00 (single issue). Zaklad Narodowy im Ossplinskich, Wydawnictwo Bolskiej Akademii Nauk, Ul Szewska 37, Wroclaw Poland. **LC** G23; .P615. **CODEN** PGPZDM. ***Continues*** *Prace Geograficzne.*
Ind/Abst GeoRef.

PL
PRACE I STUDIA GEOGRAFICZNE / UNIWERSYTET WARSZAWSKI, WYDZIA GEOGRAFII I STUDIOW REGIONALNYCH. **VFOAT** Studies in Geography. V. 1-. Polish (summaries and/or abstracts in English). ir. $10.00 to $15.00. Wydzial Geografii I Studiow Regionalnych, Uniwersytetu Warszawskiego, Ul Krakowskie Przedmiescie 30, 00-927 Warszawa Poland. **Tel** 20-03-81. **(Subscription address:** CHZ Ars Polona, Krakowskie Przedmiescie 7, 00-068 Warszawa Poland**) ED** Antoni Kuklinski, Zdzislaw Mikulski, Andrzej Richling, Bogodar Winid, Wladyslaw Zakowski. **LC** G1; .P66. ctrl circ.
Ind/Abst Geol. Abstr.

UK/0956-277X
PRIMARY GEOGRAPHER. [Prim. geogr.]. (1989)-. English. qt (Jan., Apr., July, Oct.). £15.00. Geographical Association, 343 Fulwood Road, Sheffield South Yorkshire S10 3BP England. **Tel** 011 44 742 670666, FAX 011 44 742 670688. **ED** W. Morgan. **Bk Rev.** **Ad Acc.** **Pr Rev.** **Circ:** 4,000.
Desc: Produced to help primary teachers faced with teaching geography in the national curriculum. Designed to provide lively features, stimulating project work backed by full colour illustrations and teaching resource pictures.

●CN/1191-923X
PRINCE GEORGE CITY DIRECTORY (BUSINESS ED.). (PRINCE GEORGE CITY DIRECTORY.). [Prince George city dir.]. (1992)-. Directory. English. British Columbia Directories / Vancouver, 34 West 2nd Avenue, Vancouver British Columbia V5Y 1B3 Canada. **DD** 917.11/82. ***Continues*** *Prince George Directory., 0317-3186.*

GW/0343-7965
PROBLEME DER KUSTENFORSCHUNG IM SUDLICHEN NORDSEEGEBIET. **Added/Corp** Niedersachsisches Landesinstitut fur Marschen- und Wurtenforschung. **VFOAT** Probleme der Kustenforschung im Gebiet der Sudlichen Nordsee. (1940)-. Periodical. German. Verlag August Lax, Kreuzstr 21, Postfach 100865, Hildesheim Germany. **Tel** 5121/38013. **LC** GB457.5; .W5.
Ind/Abst BHA : Biblio. Hist. Art.

BU/0204-7209
PROBLEMI NA GEOGRAFIIATA. [Probl. geogr.]. **Added/Corp** Bulgarska Akademiia na Naukite. **VFOAT** Problems of Geography. (1974)-. Periodical. Bulgarian (summaries and/or abstracts in English). Four times a year. DM81.00. **(Subscription address:** Kubon & Sagner, ABT Zeitschriftenimport, D 80328 Munich Germany.**) LC** G31; .P76. **Bk Rev.** **Circ:** 540 (ctrl). ***Continues*** *Geografski Institut (Bulgarska Akademiia na Naukite) Izvestiia na Geografskiia Institut.*
Desc: Scientific papers on geomorphology, climatology, hydrology, landscape studies, geography of population and settlements, economic branches and complexes, environment protection and most effective usage of natural resources.
Ind/Abst GeoRef.

US/0160-3159
PROCEEDINGS - NEW ENGLAND-ST. LAWRENCE VALLEY GEOGRAPHICAL SOCIETY. **Main/Corp** New England-St. Lawrence Valley Geographical Society. **Added/Corp** Association of American Geographers. Middle States Division. Proceedings. Vol. 1 (1971)-. Proceedings. English. an. **LC** G3; .N4815. **DD** 910/.6/274.

CN/0541-4393
PROCEEDINGS OF THE MUSKEG RESEARCH CONFERENCE. **Main/Conf** Muskeg Research Conference. **Added/Corp** National Research Council, Canada. Associate Committee on Soil and Snow Mechanics. Vol. 1 (1955)-. Periodical. English. ir. Association Committee on Geotechnical Research, c/o Division of Building Research, Ottawa Ontario K1A 0R6 Canada. **Tel** (807)344-8662. **LC** GB628.15; .M85. **Bk Rev.** **Ad Acc.**
Desc: Form part of the series of technical memoranda issued by the Associate Committee on Geotechnical Research, National Research Council of Canada.

NZ/1170-5698
PROCEEDINGS OF THE NEW ZEALAND GEOGRAPHY CONFERENCE. [Proc. N. Z. Geogr. Conf.]. **Main/Conf** New Zealand Geography Conference. **Added/Corp** New Zealand Geographical Society. **Series/Conf** New Zealand Geographical Society. Conference Series. 1st (1955)-. Proceedings. English. be. comes with the New Zealand Geographer. New Zealand Geographical Society, University of Canterbury, Private Bag, Christchurch New Zealand. **Ad Acc.** **Circ:** 1,100 (ctrl).
Desc: Covers the proceedings of New Zealand geography conferences. Contains reports, papers, etc., that relate to each conference.
Ind/Abst EMBASE.

US/0033-0124
PROFESSIONAL GEOGRAPHER, THE. (THE PROFESSIONAL GEOGRAPHER : THE JOURNAL OF THE ASSOCIATION OF AMERICAN GEOGRAPHERS.). [Prof. geogr.]. **Added/Corp** Association of American Geographers. American Society for Professional Geographers. (1946)-. Periodical. English. Four times a year. $94.00 US; $111.50 other. Association of American Geographers, 1710 16th Street Northwest, Washington DC 20009-3198. **Tel** (202)234-1450, FAX (202)234-2744. **(Subscription address:** Blackwell Publishers / Cambridge, MA, 238 Main Street, Cambridge MA 02142.**) ED** Stanley D Brunn. **LC** G3; .P7. **DD** 910/.5. **CODEN** PFGGAC. **[CCC].** cum. index. **Bk Rev.** **Ad Acc.** **Pr Rev.** **Circ:** 6,600. available on microfilm and microfiche from University Microfilms International (UMI). Documents available from The Genuine Article, UMI Article Clearinghouse. ***Continues*** *American Society for Professional Geographers. Bulletin of the American Society for Professional Geographers;* ***Absorbed*** *Association of American Geographers. Joint Newsletter of the Association of American Geographers and the American Society for Professional Geographers.*
Desc: Publishes concise research papers, technical reports, and brief software reviews of academic or applied geography.
Ind/Abst Acad. Search (Jan. 1993-); AGRICOLA; Am. Bibliogr. Slavic East Europ. Stud.; Arts Humanit. Citation Index [Select. Cov.]; Bibliogr. Carto.; Coal Abstr.; Crim. Justice Abstr.; Curr. Contents Soc. Behav. Sci.; Ecol. Abstr.; Expand. Acad. Index (1989-); Geogr. Abstr. Phys. Geogr.; Geogr. Abstr. Human Geogr.; GeoRef; INFO-SOUTH Abstr.; Int. Bibliogr. Sociol.; Int. Dev. Abstr.; J. Plan. Lit.; Mag. Search; Newsp. Period. Abstr. (1991-); Res. Alert [Full Cov.]; Risk Abstr.; Sage Urban Stud. Abstr; Soc. Sci. Source (Jan. 1993-); Soc. Sci. Cit. Index [Full Cov.]; Soc. Sci. Index; Soc. Sci. Index Fulltext (Nov. 1988-) [Full Txt.]; Vocat. Search (Jan. 1993-); West. Hist. Q.

US/0885-775X
PROFESSIONAL PAPER - INDIANA STATE UNIVERSITY. DEPT. OF GEOGRAPHY AND GEOLOGY. (PROFESSIONAL PAPER.). [Prof. pap. - Indiana State Univ., Dep. Geogr. Geol.]. **Main/Corp** Indiana State University. Dept. of Geography and Geology. English. Terre Haute Tribune, Tribune Building, Terre Haute IN 47808. **LC** G58; .I43. **CODEN** IGPPBF.
Ind/Abst Geogr. Abstr. Phys. Geogr. (?-?); GeoRef.

UK/0309-1325
PROGRESS IN HUMAN GEOGRAPHY. [Prog. hum. geogr.]. Vol. 1 (March 1977)-. Periodical. English. qt (March, June, September and December). $185.00 North America; £105.00 Europe; £120.00 Other. Edward Arnold, 338 Euston Road, London NW1 3BH England. **Tel** 011 44 71 873 6000, FAX 011 44 071 873 6325. **(Subscription address:** Edward Arnold, PO Box 386, Avenel NJ 07001-0386.**) ED** Ron Johnston. **LC** GF1; .P76. **DD** 301.31. **[CCC].** **Bk Rev.** **Pr Rev.** available on microfilm and microfiche from University Microfilms International (UMI); available in hardback. Documents available from The Genuine Article. ***Supersedes in part*** *Progress in Geography, 0556-1892.*
Desc: Reports on the traditional as well as the new aspects of the study of human geography, concentrating not only on the progress made by geographers but also on the cross-fertilization of their ideas with those of researchers in economics, mathematics, social history, archaeology and sociology. In addition to major articles, book reviews, progress reports, opinions and debates are featured. A leading source for information on human geography and on related fields.
Ind/Abst Arts Humanit. Citation Index [Select. Cov.]; Br. Archaeol. Bibliogr.; Curr. Contents Soc. Behav. Sci.; Environ. Period. Bibliogr.; Geogr. Abstr. Phys. Geogr. (?-?); Geogr. Abstr. Human Geogr.; Int. Bibliogr. Book Rev.; Int. Bibliogr. Period. Lit.; Int. Bibliogr. Sociol.; Int. Dev. Abstr.; J. Plan. Lit.; Middle East Abstr. Index; Pollut. Abstr. Indexes; Res. Alert [Full Cov.]; Risk Abstr.; Sage Public Adm. Abstr.; Sage Urban Stud. Abstr.; Soc. Plann. Policy Dev. Abstr.; Soc. Sci. Cit. Index [Full Cov.]; Sociol. Abstr.; SportSearch.

UK/0309-1333
PROGRESS IN PHYSICAL GEOGRAPHY. [Prog. phys. geogr.]. Vol. 1 (Mar. 1977)-. Periodical. English. qt (March, June, September and December). $185.00 North America; £105.00 Europe; £120.00 other. Edward Arnold, 338 Euston Road, London NW1 3BH England. **Tel** 011 44 71 873 6000, FAX 011 44 071 873 6325. **ED** B. W. Atkinson. **LC** G1; .P686. **DD** 910/.02. **[CCC].** **Bk Rev.** **Pr Rev.** available on microfilm and microfiche from University Microfilms International (UMI). Documents available from The Genuine Article, Documents on Demand. ***Supersedes in part*** *Progress in Geography, 0556-1892.*
Desc: An international forum for geographical work, in the natural and environmental sciences, publishes reviews of current research and theoretical developments in any aspect of geomorphology, climatology, biogeography and human-environment interaction. Papers include international coverage and consider the relevance of tangential or parallel developments in other fields.
Ind/Abst ASTIS Curr. Aware. Bull. (1978-); Agrofor. Abstr.; AQUAREF; ASTIS Bibliogr. (1978-); Biol. Abstr.; Curr. Contents Phys. Chem. Earth Sci.; Curr. Geogr. Publ. (199?-); Ecol. Abstr.; Ecology Abstr.; Environ. Abstr.; Environ. Period. Bibliogr.; Geogr. Abstr. Phys. Geogr.; Geogr. Abstr. Human Geogr. (?-?); Geol. Abstr.; GeoRef; Grasslands For. Abstr.; Int. Bibliogr. Book Rev.; Int. Bibliogr. Period. Lit.; Irr. Drain. Abstr.; J. Plan. Lit.; Meteorol. Geoastrophys. Abstr. (199?-); Middle East Abstr. Index; Pollut. Abstr. Indexes; Res. Alert [Full Cov.]; Sci. Cit. Index; SCISEARCH; Soils Fert.

FR
PROVENCE-COTE D'AZUR (HACHETTE (FIRM)). (PROVENCE-COTE D'AZUR.). **VFOAT** Provence Cote d'Azur. French. an. 56.00F (each issue). Guide du Routard, 5 rue de l'Arrivee, 92190 Meudon France. **LC** DC611.P956; P76. **DD** 914.4/904838/05.

PL/0033-2143
PRZEGLAD GEOGRAFICZNY. [Prz. geogr.]. **Added/Corp** Polska Akademia Nauk. Instytut Geografii. Instytut Geografii i Przestrzennego Zagospodarowania (Polska Akademia Nauk) Polskie Towarzystwo Geograficzne. **VFOAT** Polskii Geograficheskii Obzor; Polish Geographical Review; Revue Polonaise de Geographie. Vol. 1 (1919)-. Periodical. Polish (summaries and/or abstracts in English and Russian). qt. $56.00. **(Subscription address:** ARS Polona, PO Box 1001, 00068 Warsaw Poland.**) LC** G1; .P7. **DD** 910.5. **CODEN** PRGGAS.
Ind/Abst AGRICOLA; Am. Hist. Life (1963-1973); Bibliogr. Carto.; Ecol. Abstr. (?-?); Geogr. Abstr. Phys. Geogr.; Geogr. Abstr. Human Geogr.; Geol. Abstr.; GeoRef; Int. Dev. Abstr.

AG
PUBLICACION - INSTITUTO ANTARTICO ARGENTINO. Main/Corp Instituto Ant Artico Argentino. No. 1 (1955)-. Periodical. Spanish. Price varies per volume. Instituto Antartico Argentino, Direccion Nacional del Antartico, Cerrito 1248, 1010 Buenos Aires Argentina. **Tel** 812-1689, FAX 541-812-2039.

UK/0071-0636
PUBLICATIONS - ENGLISH PLACE-NAME SOCIETY. Main/Corp English Place-Name Society. **Added/Corp** British Academy Survey of English Place-Names. Vol. 1 (1924)-. English. bm. English Place-Name Society, University of Nottingham, Department English Studies, Nottingham NG7 2RD England. **Tel** 011 44 602 484848.

US/0073-6953
PUBLICATIONS. GEOGRAPHIC MONOGRAPH SERIES. Main/Corp Indiana University. **VFOAT** Geographic Monograph Series. Vol. 1 (1966)-. Monographic series. English. ir. Price varies per volume. University of Indiana, Department of Geography, Bloomington IN 47401. **Tel** (812)335-1153.

FR/0033-474X
PYRENEES LOURDES. 1950. (PYRENEES.). [Pyrenees Lourdes, 1950]. (1950)-. Periodical. French. qt. 200.00F. Pyrenees / Amis du Parc Nat, BP 204, 2 Pl Albert 1er, F-64000 Pau France. **Tel** 011 33 59 274843. **UDC** 398.
Ind/Abst BHA : Biblio. Hist. Art.

CN/0822-6911
Q.A.G.T. NEWSLETTER. [Q.A.G.T. newsl.]. Sept. 1981-. Newsletter. English. Three times a year. Free to Members. QAGT Newsletter, PO Box 32 Station N D G, Montreal Quebec H4A 3P4 Canada. **DD** 910/.7/0714. ***Continues*** *P.A.G.T. Newsletter, 0821-2457.*

PL/0137-477X
QUAESTIONES GEOGRAPHICAE. [Quaest. geogr.]. **Added/Corp** Uniwersytet im. Adama Mickiewicza w Poznaniu. Instytut Geograficzny. Vol. 1 (1974)-. Academic Scholarly Publication. English (English). ir. Z80.00. Adam Mickiewicz University Press, Nowowiejskiego 55, 61734 Poznan Poland. **Tel** 011 48 527-380, FAX 011 48 61-5265425. **(Subscription address:** ARS Polona, PO Box 1001, 00068 Warsaw Poland.**) ED** Stefan Kozarski. **LC** G1; .Q3. **CODEN** QGEODD.
Ind/Abst Ecol. Abstr. (?-?); Geogr. Abstr. Phys. Geogr.; Geol. Abstr.; GeoRef.

AT/0155-400X
QUEENSLAND GEOGRAPHICAL JOURNAL. NEW SERIES. (QUEENSLAND GEOGRAPHICAL JOURNAL.). [Qld. geogr. j., New ser.]. **Added/Corp** Royal Geographical Society of Australasia. Vol. 15 (1900)-. Monographic series. English. ir. Price varies per volume. Royal Geographical Society of Queensland, 112 Brookes Street, Fortitude Valley, Brisbane Queensland, 4006 Australia. **Tel** 011 61 7 2523856. **ED** P. Lloyd. **LC** UNC. **Ad Acc.** ***Continues*** *Proceedings and Transactions of the Royal Geographical Society of Australasia, Queensland.*
Desc: Centenary history of the Royal Geographical Society of Australasia Queensland.
Ind/Abst Ecol. Abstr.; Geogr. Abstr. Phys. Geogr.; Geogr. Abstr. Human Geogr.; GeoRef.

JA
QUESTIONS AND ANSWERS IN GENERAL TOPOLOGY. VFOAT Q & A; Q and A. Vol. 1, No. 1 (1983)-. Periodical. English. Twice a year (Jan., June). $50.00 (all except Japan). Professor J. Nagata, Department of Mathematics, Osaka Dentsu University, 18-8 Hatsu Cho, Neyagawa Osaka 572 Japan. **Tel** FAX 11 81-720-24-0014. **ED** J. Nagata. Index available. **Circ:** 200.
Desc: Features questions raised in the research of general topology and answers to questions raised in the previous edition.
Ind/Abst Math. Rev.; Zentralbl. Math. Ihre Grenzgeb.

SW/0348-3339
RAPPORTER OCH NOTISER - LUNDS UNIVERSITETS NATURGEOGRAFISKA INSTITUTION. (RAPPORTER OCH NOTISER.). [Rapp. not. - Lunds univ. nat.geogr. inst.]. (1967)-. Monographic series. Multiple languages. ir. Price varies per volume. **UDC** 911.52.
Ind/Abst Geogr. Abstr. Phys. Geogr.; GeoRef.

●CN/1191-9302
RED DEER CITY DIRECTORY (1992). (RED DEER CITY DIRECTORY.). [Red Deer city dir.]. **VFOAT** Henderson's Red Deer City Directory. (1992)-. Directory. English. an. $100.00. Henderson Directories, 34 West 2nd Avenue, Vancouver, British Columbia, V5Y 1B3 Canada. **DD** 917.123/3. ***Continues*** *Red Deer, Alberta, City Directory., 0826-4686.*

RU
REFERATIVNYI ZHURNAL. GEOGRAFIIA. D, BIOGEOGRAFIIA. See Biology.

RU/0034-2378
REFERATIVNYJ ZURNAL - VSESOJUZNYJ INSTITUT NAUCNOJ I TEHNICESKOJ INFORMACII, GEOGRAFIJA. (REFERATIVNYI ZHURNAL. GEOGRAFIIA / AKADEMIIA NAUK SOIUZA SOTSIALISTICHESKIKH REPUBLIK, VSESOIUZNYI INSTITUT NAUCHNOI I TEKHNICHESKOI INFORMATSII.). [Ref. z. - Vses. inst. naucn. teh. inf., Geogr.]. **Added/Corp** Vsesoiuznyi Institut Nauchnoi i Tekhnicheskoi Informatsii (Soviet Union) Institut Nauchnoi Informatsii (Akademiia Nauk SSSR). **VFOAT** Abstracts Journal. Geography; Geography; Geografiia. (1956)-. Abstracting/Indexing Service. Russian (summaries and/or abstracts in English; table of contents in English). mo. VINITI - Vsesoyuznyi Institut Nauchno-Tekhnicheskoi Informatsii, All-Union Scientific and Technical Information Institute, Baltiiskaia Ulitsa 14, 125219 Moscow Russia. **Tel** 238-46-00, FAX 9430060, telex 411160. **LC** G1; .R35. ***Continues in part*** *Referativnyi Zhurnal. Geologiia i Geografiia.*
Ind/Abst Bibliogr. Carto.; GeoRef.

CN/0713-5777
REGINA THIS MONTH. [Regina month]. Spring Issue (May 1982)-. Periodical. English. mo. $13.50. Regina This Month, 2049 Lorne Street, Regina Sask. S4P 2M4 Canada. **DD** 917.12/44.

SZ
REISEVERKEHR DER SCHWEIZER IM AUSLAND. Main/Corp Switzerland. Statistisches Amt. **VFOAT** Touristes Suisses a l'Etranger. Multiple languages (French and German). 6.00F. Hallwylstrasse 15, CH-3003 Bern Switzerland. **LC** G155.S8; S93C.

US/0882-2409
REMOTE SENSING QUARTERLY LITERATURE REVIEW. [Remote sens. q. lit. rev.]. **VFOAT** Remote Sensing. Vol. 1, No. 1 (Jan./March 1984)-. Periodical. English. qt. $155.00 US; $175.00 other. Global Resources & Associates, University of New Mexico, Albuquerque NM 87131. **Tel** (505)242-2313. **LC** G70.4; .R465. **DD** 621.36/78/05.

FR/1147-9558
REPERTOIRE DES GEOGRAPHES FRANCAIS PARIS. (REPERTOIRE DES GEOGRAPHES FRANCAIS.). [Repert. geogr. fr. Paris]. (1984)-. Directory. French. ir (two or three issues a year). 1000.00F. CNRS - Intergeo, 191 rue Saint Jacques, 75005 Paris France. **Tel** 011 33 1 46337431, 011 33 1 43297993, FAX 011 33 1 43 29 6529. **UDC** 91. Index available. **Ad Acc, Adv Mgr:** Gerard Jolly. **Pr Rev. Circ:** 500 (ctrl). ***Continues*** *Repertoire des Geographes Francophones, 0752-7586.*
Desc: Information and means of communication for geographers.

CN/0848-2969
REPERTOIRE TOPONYMIQUE DU QUEBEC (1988). (REPERTOIRE TOPONYMIQUE DU QUEBEC.). [Repert. topon. Que.]. **Main/Corp** Quebec (Province). Commission de Toponymie. (198?)-. French. ir. Les Publications du Quebec, CP 1190, Outremont Quebec H2V 4S7 Canada. **Tel** (514)948-1222, (800)463-2100, FAX (514)278-3030. **DD** 917.14/003/41. ***Continues*** *Quebec (Province). Commission de Toponymie. Supplement au Repertoire Toponymique du Quebec (1978)., 0823-2946.*

NE
REPORT / INSTITUTE FOR LAND AND WATER MANAGEMENT RESEARCH (ICW). See Water Resources.

II
RES. PUB. (NATIONAL GEOGRAPHICAL SOCIETY OF INDIA). (RES. PUB.). **VFOAT** National Geographical Society of India Res. Pub.; Research Publication Series. **VAT** Research Publication / National Geographical Society of India. No. 20 (1978)-. Monographic series. English. Twice a year. Price varies per volume. National Geographical Society of India, Department of Geography, Banaras Hindu University, Varanasi 221005 UP India. **Tel** 011 91 1 64491364. **ED** R L Singh and Rana P B Singh. Index available. **Circ:** 500. ***Continues*** *N.G.S.I. Research Publication.*
Desc: Proceedings of conferences and original research monographs mostly on human aspects.

US/1055-9914
RESEARCH IN CONTEMPORARY AND APPLIED GEOGRAPHY. [Res. contemp. appl. geogr.]. **Added/Corp** State University of New York at Binghamton. Dept. of Geography. (1977)-. Monographic series. English. qt. $16.00 institutions; $11.00 individuals. State University of New York Department of Geography, PO Box 6000, Binghamton NY 13901. **Tel** (607)777-2755, (607)777-6557. **LC** G72; .R47. **DD** 910/.72.

US/0160-3094
RESOURCE ATLAS - UNIVERSITY OF NEBRASKA, CONSERVATION AND SURVEY DIVISION. (RESOURCE ATLAS.). [Resour. atlas, Univ. Nebr., Conserv. Surv. Div.]. **Added/Corp** University of Nebraska--Lincoln. Conservation and Survey Division. (1971)-. Monographic series. English. ir. Price varies per volume. University of Nebraska - Lincoln, 901 North 17th Street, 113 Nebraska Hall, Lincoln NE 80517. **Tel** (402)472-3471. **ED** Charles Flowerday. **LC** UNC. **CODEN** NRATBG. Index available. **Pr Rev.**
Desc: Practical information on a wide range of earth sciences topics.

US
RESTORATION OF LOST OR OBLITERATED CORNERS AND SUBDIVISION OF SECTIONS. Main/Corp United States. Bureau of Land Management. Government Publication. English. US Department of the Interior Bureau of Land Management, 1849 C Street NW, Room 5660, Washington DC 20240. **Tel** (202)208-3801, FAX (202)208-5902. **ED** Keith Williams. **LC** TA622; .U577. Index available. **Bk Rev. Circ:** 50,000. ***Continues*** *Restoration of Lost or Obliterated Corners and Subdivision of Sections.*
Desc: A treatise for private surveyors on restoring lost or obliterated government corners.

TU/0535-8361
REVIEW OF THE GEOGRAPHICAL INSTITUTE OF THE UNIVERSITY OF ISTANBUL. [Rev. Geogr. Inst. Univ. Istanb.]. **Main/Corp** Istanbul Universitesi. Cografya Enstitusu. (1954)-. English (French and German). ir. Istanbul University / Geographical Institute, Geographical Institute, Istanbul Turkey. **LC** G31.I8. **CODEN** RGIIAN.
Ind/Abst GeoRef.

BL/0034-723X
REVISTA BRASILEIRA DE GEOGRAFIA. [Rev. bras. geogr.]. **Added/Corp** Fundacao Instituto Brasileiro de Geografia e Estatistica. Departamento de Documentacao e Divulgacao Geografica e Cartografica. Conselho Nacional de Geografia (Brazil). (Jan. 1939)-. Periodical. Portuguese (summaries and/or abstracts in Multiple languages). qt. $120.00. Inst Brasileiro de Geog e Estat-IBGE-CDDI/GECOM, rua General Canabarro 666 An2, 20271 Rio de Janeiro RJ, Brazil. **Tel** 11 55 21 2840402. **LC** F2501; .R49. **DD** 918.1. **CODEN** RBGGA6. Index available. cum. index. **Circ:** 2,200 (ctrl).
Desc: It diffuses high level geographic and socio-economic, knowledge by means of articles, communication, transcriptions and bibliographic comments.
Ind/Abst GeoRef; HAPI Hisp. Am. Period. Index; Hortic. Abstr.; World Agric. Econ.

CL/0716-2812
REVISTA CHILENA DE HISTORIA Y GEOGRAFIA. See History(General)-History of North, South, and Central America.

SP/0048-7708
REVISTA DE GEOGRAFIA. Spanish. Revista de Geografia, Univ Barcelona, Dept Geografia, Attn A Hermida Historia, Barcelona 08028 Spain.
Ind/Abst Geogr. Abstr. Phys. Geogr.; Geogr. Abstr. Human Geogr.; GeoRef.

BL
REVISTA DO INSTITUTO HISTORICO E GEOGRAFICO DE SAO PAULO. See History(General)-History of North, South, and Central America.

CR
REVISTA GEOGRAFICA DE AMERICA CENTRAL / ESCUELA DE GEOGRAFIA, FACULTAD DE CIENCIAS DE LA TIERRA Y EL MAR. Added/Corp Universidad Nacional (Costa Rica). Escuela de Geografia. Universidad Nacional (Costa Rica). Escuela de Ciencias Geograficas. No. 1 (1974)-. Periodical. Spanish. sa. $8.00. **LC** G1; .R4125. **DD** 910/.5.
Ind/Abst Ecol. Abstr.; Geogr. Abstr. Human Geogr.; Int. Dev. Abstr.

CL/0378-8482
REVISTA GEOGRAFICA DE CHILE TERRA AUSTRALIS. **Added/Corp** Chile. Comite Nacional de Geografia, Geodesia y Geofisica. Instituto Geografico Militar (Chile) Chile. Seccion Nacional del Instituto Panamericano de Geografia e Historia. **VFOAT** Terra Australis. Vol. 1, No. 1 (Sept. 1948)-. Periodical. Spanish (summaries and/or abstracts in English; table of contents in English). Secretaria Geografica IGM, Nueva Santa Isabel 1640, Santiago, Chile. **LC** F3051; .R47. ***Supersedes** Memorial-Tecnico del Ejercito de Chile.*
Ind/Abst Ecol. Abstr.; Geogr. Abstr. Phys. Geogr.; Geogr. Abstr. Human Geogr.; GeoRef; Int. Dev. Abstr.

MX/0031-0581
REVISTA GEOGRAFICA DEL INSTITUTO PANAMERICANO DE GEOGRAFIA E HISTORIA. [Rev. geogr. - Inst. panam. geogr. hist.]. **Added/Corp** Pan American Institute of Geography and History. Pan American Institute of Geography and History. Commission on Geography. **VFOAT** Revista Geografica do Instituto Pan-Americano de Geografia e Historia; Revista Geografica. Vol. 1, No. 1 (Jan. 1941)-. Periodical. Spanish (English, French and Portuguese). Twice a year. $36.00 (1 year), $69.00 (2 year) Western Hemisphere; $42.00 (1 year), $81.00 (2 year) other. Pan American Institute of Geography & History, PO Box 66398, Washington DC 20035-6398. **Tel** 011 52 5 2775888, 2775791, FAX 011 52 5 2716172. **LC** G5; .R4. **DD** 910.5. available on microfilm and microfiche from University Microfilms International (UMI).
Ind/Abst AGRICOLA; GeoRef; HAPI Hisp. Am. Period. Index.

AG
REVISTA GEOGRAFICA UNIVERSAL. V. 1- Oct. 1974-. Periodical. Portuguese. Bloch / New York, 680 Fifth Avenue/Room 1302, New York NY 10019. **LC** G1; .R417.

VE/1012-1617
REVISTA GEOGRAFICA VENEZOLANA. (REVISTA GEOGRAFICA VENEZOLANA : REVISTA DEL INSTITUTO DE GEOGRAFIA Y CONSERVACION DE RECURSOS NATURALES DE LA FACULTAD DE CIENCIAS FORESTALES.). [Rev. geogr. venez.]. **Added/Corp** Universidad de los Andes (Merida, Venezuela). Instituto de Geografia y Conservacion de Recursos Naturales. Vol. 22-23 (1981/1982)-. Periodical. Spanish. sa. $19.00 US, Canada & Central America; $21.50 South America & Europe; $24.00 other. Instituto Panamericano de Geographico Historia, APDO 18879 Secretaria General, 11870 Mexico DF Mexico. **Tel** 011 52 5 2775888, 011 52 5 2775791, FAX 011 52 5 2716172. **ED** Marilourdes Lopes Ferreira. **LC** F2314; .R48. **DD** 987/.005. **Circ:** 600. ***Continues** Revista Geografica (Merida, Venezuela), 0556-6630.*
Ind/Abst Geogr. Abstr. Phys. Geogr.; Geogr. Abstr. Human Geogr.; Int. Dev. Abstr.

BE/0035-0796
REVUE BELGE DE GEOGRAPHIE. [Rev. belge geogr.]. **Added/Corp** Societe Royale Belge de Geographie. Vol. 86 Issue 1 (1962)-. Periodical. French (English). Four times a year. 1500F. Societe Royale Belge de Geographie, Campus de la Plaine, CP 246, B-1050 Bruxelles Belgium. **Tel** 011 32 2 6400015 ext. 5073. **LC** G19; .S67. **DD** 910/.5. **CODEN** BSRGA4. Index available. cum. index. **Bk Rev. Circ:** 800 (ctrl). ***Continues** Societe Royale Belge de Geographie. Bulletin de la Societe Royale Belge de Geographie.*
Desc: Geography, mainly human and economic geography, most papers about Belgium, Western Europe and Central Africa and America.
Ind/Abst Ecol. Abstr. (?-?); Geogr. Abstr. Phys. Geogr. (?-?); Geogr. Abstr. Human Geogr.; GeoRef; Int. Dev. Abstr.

FR/0035-1121
REVUE DE GEOGRAPHIE ALPINE. [Rev. geogr. alp.]. Vol. 8, No. 1 (1920)-. Periodical. French (English, German and Italian). qt. 300.00F (institutions), 250.00F (individuals). Revue de Geographie Alpine, rue Maurice-Gignoux, 38031 Grenoble Cedex France. **Tel** 011/33/76/874643. **ED** Alceir Morel. **LC** DC611.A553; R4. **DD** 910/.5. **CODEN** RVGAAQ. Index available. cum. index. **Bk Rev**, (Qty: 4). **Ad Acc. Circ:** 1,000. ***Continues** Recueil des Travaux de l'Institut de Geographie Alpine.*
Desc: Geographical information on the Alpine mountains of Europe and other mountains of the world.
Ind/Abst Bibliogr. Carto.; Ecol. Abstr. (?-?); Geogr. Abstr. Phys. Geogr. (?-?); Geol. Abstr.; GeoRef; Meteorol. Geoastrophys. Abstr.

FR/0035-113X
REVUE DE GEOGRAPHIE DE LYON. **Added/Corp** Lyons. Universite. Institut des Etudes Rhodaniennes. Etudes et Travaux. Lyons. Universite. Institut des Etudes Rhodaniennes. Vol. 1 (1925)-. Periodical. French (summaries and/or abstracts in French and English). Four times a year (Mar., July, Oct., Dec.). $280.00F France; 300.00F other. Association des Amis de la Revue de Geographie de Lyon, 74 rue Pasteur, 69007 Lyon France. **Tel** 011 33 78 724458. **ED** Bethemont Jacque. cum. index. **Bk Rev. Circ:** 500. ***Continues** Societe de Geographie de Lyon. Bulletin.*
Desc: Includes geography, environmental problems, urban studies, water resources management, and fluvial process.
Ind/Abst GeoRef; Middle East J.

MR/0035-1156
REVUE DE GEOGRAPHIE DU MAROC. [Rev. geogr. Maroc]. No. 1/2-23/24 (1962-1973); New Series, No. 1 (1977)-. Periodical. French (Arabic; summaries and/or abstracts in English and Spanish). Twice a year. $40.00. Librarie Internationale, Boite Postal 302, Rabat Morocco. **Tel** 011 212 7 50183. **LC** DT301. **CODEN** RGMCBQ. ***Continues** Notes Marocaines.*
Ind/Abst GeoRef.

MG/0047-5416
REVUE DE GEOGRAPHIE. MADAGASCAR. (MADAGASCAR.). [Rev. geogr., Madagascar]. No. 1 (July./Dec. 1962)-. French. sa. 3000. Universite de Madagascar, BP 907, Tananarive Antananarivo, Madagascar. **LC** DT469.M28; M25. **CODEN** MRVGA2. **Bk Rev. Circ:** 1,500.
Desc: Geography of Madagascar.
Ind/Abst GeoRef; Int. Dev. Abstr.

FR/0556-7432
REVUE DE GEOMORPHOLOGIE DYNAMIQUE. [Rev. geomorphol. dyn.]. Vol. 1; 1950-. Periodical. French. qt. 245.00F. Centre de Documentation Universitaire et Societe D Edition D Enseignement Superieur, 88 Boulevard Saint Germain, 75005 Paris France. **Tel** 011 33 1 43252323. **LC** G1; .R443. **CODEN** RGDYAC. cum. index. **Ad Acc.** Documents available from CASDDS.
Desc: Overall study of natural environment, earth sciences.
Ind/Abst Chem. Abstr. (1950-1983); Ecol. Abstr. (?-?); Geogr. Abstr. Phys. Geogr.; Geol. Abstr.; Life Sci. Collect.

HT
REVUE DE LA SOCIETE HAITIENNE D'HISTOIRE ET DE GEOGRAPHIE (PORT-AU-PRINCE, HAITI : 1981). **See** History(General).

FR/0035-3213
REVUE GEOGRAPHIQUE DE L'EST. [Rev. geogr. Est]. V. 1 (Jan./March 1961)-. Periodical. French. qt. 270.00F France; 310.00F other. Presses Universitaires Nancy, 42 avenue de la Liberation, 54001 Nancy Cedex France. **Tel** 011 33 83 935830, FAX 011 33 83 935839. **ED** Jean-Marie Bonnet. **CODEN** RGGEB2. **Bk Rev. Ad Acc. Circ:** 800.
Desc: Covers geography in Eastern Europe, Europe and the Middle East.
Ind/Abst Ecol. Abstr.; Geogr. Abstr. Phys. Geogr.; Geogr. Abstr. Human Geogr.; GeoRef; Int. Dev. Abstr. (?-?).

FR/0035-3221
REVUE GEOGRAPHIQUE DES PYRENEES ET DU SUD-OUEST. [Rev. geogr. Pyren. Sud-Ouest]. **Added/Corp** Universite de Toulouse-Le Mirail. Institut de geographie. Universite de Bordeaux. Institut de geographie. (1930)-. Periodical. French. Four times a year. 250.00F EEC countries; 270.00F other. Universite de Toulouse--Le Mirail, 56 Rue du Taur, 31000 Toulouse France. **Tel** 011 33 61 225831, FAX 011 33 61 218420. **LC** DC611.P98; R44. **CODEN** RGPSAK. Index available (published separately). cum. index. **Bk Rev. Pr Rev.**
Ind/Abst Bibliogr. Carto.; Ecol. Abstr.; Geogr. Abstr. Phys. Geogr.; Geogr. Abstr. Human Geogr.; GeoRef.

TI
REVUE TUNISIENNE DE GEOGRAPHIE. **Added/Corp** Jamiah al-Tunisiyah. Kulliyat al-Adab wa-al-Ulum al-Insaniyah. **VFOAT** Majallah Al-Jughrafiyah Al-Tunisiyah. (1978)-. Periodical. Arabic (French; summaries and/or abstracts in English). Six times a year. 5000TD Tunisia and Mahgreb; 15000TD France; 10000TD Arab countries; 20000TD other. University of Tunis / Service des Publications et Sciences Humaines, 94 Boulevard du 9 Avril, 1938 / BP 1128, Tunis 1007 Tunisia. **Tel** , . **LC** G1; .R47. **DD** 916.1/1/005.

GW/0080-2662
RHEIN-MAINISCHE FORSCHUNGEN. [Rhein-mainische Forsch.]. **Added/Corp** Universitat Frankfurt am Main. Geographisches Institut. Issue 1 (1927)-. Monographic series. German. ir. Price varies per volume. Institute fuer Kulturgeographie Stadt- und Regionalforschung, Johann Wolfgang Goethe-Universitat, Fachbereich Geographie (18), Senckenberganlage 36, D 60325 Frankfurt am Main Germany. **Tel** 069 798 2416, FAX 069 798-8173. **CODEN** RHFMBS.
Desc: Covers human and physical geography.
Ind/Abst Geogr. Abstr. Phys. Geogr. (?-?); Geogr. Abstr. Human Geogr. (?-?); GeoRef.

US/0883-5225
RIVERSIDE COUNTY STREET ATLAS AND DIRECTORY. **VFOAT** Riverside County. (1984)-. Directory. English. an. Thomas Brothers Maps, Lockbox PO Box 30845, Los Angeles CA 90030. **Tel** (714)863-1984. ***Continues** Riverside County Popular Street Atlas, 0733-2300.*

IT/0035-6697
RIVISTA GEOGRAFICA ITALIANA. [Riv. geogr. ital.]. **Added/Corp** Societa di Studi Geografici di Firenze. Societa di Studi Geografici e Coloniali (Florence, Italy). Vol. 1 (March 1893)-. Periodical. Italian. qt. L50000 Italy; L55000 other. Pacini Editore Srl, Via A Gherardesca 1, 56121 Ospedaletto Pisa Italy. **Tel** 011 39 50 982439. **LC** G1; .R62. **DD** 910/.5. cum. index.
Ind/Abst Bibliogr. Carto.; GeoRef.

US
ROBINSON'S HOWARD COUNTY, INDIANA RURAL DIRECTORY. Directory. English. Robinson Directories Inc, Hillsdale MI 49249.

CN/0710-5754
ROSTER OF DEPARTMENTS OF GEOGRAPHY, CANADIAN UNIVERSITIES AND COLLEGES. [Roster dep. geogr. Can. univ. coll.]. **VFOAT** Repertoire des Departements de Geographie, Universites et Colleges du Canada. English (French). an. Free. Canadian Commerce for Geography, Office of the Science Advisor, Environment Canada, Ottawa Ontario K1A 0H3 Canada. **DD** 910/.7/1171. ctrl circ.

CN/0226-2169
SAGAMIEN. (LE SAGAMIEN.). **Added/Corp** Universite du Quebec a Chicoutimi. Departement des Sciences Humaines. (1980)-. Periodical. French. ir. 4.00Can$. Universite du Quebec a Chicoutimi Laboratoires de Geographie, 555 Boulevard de l'Universite, Chicoutimi Quebec G7H 2B1 Canada. **Tel** (418)545-5330, FAX (418)545-5012. **ED** Majella-J. Gauthier. **DD** 910/.5. **Bk Rev. Circ:** 250 (ctrl). available on microfilm.
Desc: Articles focused on spatial phenomena, especially in Quebec province.

●CN/1191-940X
SAINT JOHN CITY DIRECTORY (1992). (SAINT JOHN CITY DIRECTORY.). [St. John city dir.]. **VFOAT** Might's Saint John City Directory. (1992)-. Directory. English. an. $115.00. Might Directories, 220 Bartley Drive, Toronto Ontario M4A 2H4 Canada. **Tel** (416)751-2751. **DD** 917.15/32. ***Continues** Saint John, New Brunswick, City Directory., 0713-8962.*

GW/0344-6565
SAMMLUNG GEOGRAPHISCHER FUHRER. Monographic series. German. ir. Price varies per volume. Gebruder Borntraeger Verlagsbuchhandlung, Johannesstrasse 3-A, D-70176 Stuttgart Germany. **Tel** 0711/62 50 01, FAX (0711)625005, telex 723363 SCHB D. **ED** A Leidlmair, H Leser, C Schott and E Meymen. **Bk Rev. Ad Acc.**
Ind/Abst GeoRef.

US/0883-0118
SAN BERNARDINO, RIVERSIDE COUNTIES STREET ATLAS AND DIRECTORY (ZIP CODE ED.). (SAN BERNARDINO, RIVERSIDE COUNTIES STREET ATLAS AND DIRECTORY.). **VFOAT** San Bernardino County; Riverside County. Updated 1984 Ed.-. Directory. English. an. $25.00. Thomas Brothers Maps, Lockbox PO Box 30845, Los Angeles CA 90030. **Tel** (714)863-1984. **Ad Acc.** ***Continues** Thomas Bros. Maps. San Bernardino, Riverside Counties Popular Street Atlas, 0733-7183.*
Desc: Street maps and index for San Bernardino and Riverside County in California.

US/0362-3106
SANBORN MANHATTAN LAND BOOK OF THE CITY OF NEW YORK. [Sanborn Manhattan land book City N. Y.]. **VFOAT** Manhattan Land Book of the City of New York. 1975/76-. English. an. Sanborn Map Company, Pelham NY 10803.

US/0733-740X
SANTA CLARA COUNTY POPULAR STREET ATLAS (ZIP CODE ED.). (SANTA CLARA COUNTY POPULAR STREET ATLAS.). English. an. $10.95. Thomas Brothers Maps, Lockbox PO Box 30845, Los Angeles CA 90030. **Tel** (714)863-1984. **Ad Acc.**
Desc: Street maps and index for Santa Clara County in California.

CN/0228-9695
SASKATOON, SASKATCHEWAN, CITY DIRECTORY. [Saskatoon, Sask., city dir.]. **VFOAT** Henderson's Saskatoon Directory. **VAT** Henderson's Saskatoon Directory (1980). 1980-. Directory. English. an. $85.00 per number. Henderson Directories, 34 West 2nd Avenue, Vancouver, British Columbia, V5Y 1B3 Canada. **DD** 917.12/42. ***Continues** Henderson's Saskatoon, Saskatchewan City Directory, 0316-0491.*

CN/0079-7758
SAVANNA RESEARCH SERIES. [Savanna res. ser.]. No. 1- 1964-. Monographic series. English (French). be. Price varies per volume. McGill University / Department of Geography, 805 Sherbrooke Street, Theo

Hills, Montreal Quebec H3A 2K6 Canada. **Tel** 514-671-2367. **DD** 910/.09/153. **CODEN** SMURDU. **Ind/Abst** GeoRef.

XR/1210-115X
SBORNIK CESKE GEOGRAFICKE SPOLECNOSTI. **Added/Corp** Ceska Geograficka Spolecnost. **VFOAT** Izvestiia Cheshskogo Geograficheskogo Obshchestva; Journal of the Czech Geographical Society. (1991)-. Czech (summaries and/or abstracts in English; table of contents in English). qt. DM124.00. Academia, Publishing House of the Czechoslovak Academy of Sciences, Czech AC SCI, Vodickova 40, PO Box 896, 112 29 Prague 1, Czech Republic. **Tel** 011 42 2 245117. **(Subscription address:** Kubon & Sagner, ABT Zeitschriftenimport, D 80328 Munich Germany.**) ED** Vaclav Kral. **LC** G8; .C4. **Bk Rev. Circ:** 1,100. ***Continues*** *Sbornik Ceskoslovenske Geograficke Spolecnosti, 0231-5300.*

CS
SBORNIK PRACI. ***Title Change.*** Monographic series. Czech (English and French). ir. Unigeo Ostrava, Mistecka ul 258, 720 02 Ostrava Czech Republic. **Tel** 69-3624, FAX 69-354 365, telex 052109. **LC** GB205.4; .S25. **Circ:** 300 (ctrl). ***Continued by*** *Unigeo - Sbornik Praci.*
Desc: Contains results of investigation activities.

US/0734-8185
SCHWENDEMAN'S DIRECTORY OF COLLEGE GEOGRAPHY OF THE UNITED STATES. [Schwendeman's dir. coll. geogr. U.S.]. **Added/Corp** Eastern Kentucky University. Geographical Studies and Research Center. **VFOAT** Directory of College Geography of the United States. Vol. 30, No. 1 (Apr. 1979)-. Directory. English. an. $5.00 US; $7.00 other. Geographical Studies and Research Center, Eastern Kentucky University, Richmond KY 40475. **Tel** (606)622-1418, FAX (606)622-1020. **ED** Wilma J Walker. **LC** G77; .C64. **DD** 910/.7/1173. **Ad Acc. Circ:** 1,000. ***Continues*** *Directory of College Geography of the United States.*
Desc: The directory lists over 600 college departments. The listing includes faculty and student enrollments in 69 topical areas in geography.

JA/0375-7854
SCIENCE REPORTS OF THE TOHOKU UNIVERSITY. SERIES 7. GEOGRAPHY. (THE SCIENCE REPORTS OF THE TOHOKU UNIVERSITY. SEVENTH SERIES: (GEOGRAPHY)). [Sci. rep. Tohoku Univ., Ser. 7]. **Main/Corp** Tohoku Daigaku. **Added/Corp** Tohoku Daigaku. Rigakubu. No. 1 (Mar. 1952)-. English. Tohoku Daigaku Rigakubu, (Faculty of Science, Tohoku University), Aoba, Aramaki, Sendaishi, Miyagiken 980 Japan. **LC** G1; .T6. **CODEN** SRTGAO. cum. index.
Ind/Abst Geogr. Abstr. Phys. Geogr.; Geogr. Abstr. Human Geogr.; GeoRef.

UK/0036-9225
SCOTTISH GEOGRAPHICAL MAGAZINE. [Scott. geogr. mag.]. **Added/Corp** Scottish Geographical Society. Royal Scottish Geographical Society. Vol. 1 (Jan. 1885)-. Periodical. English. Three times a year. £27.00 (UK); £33.00 (other). Royal Scottish Geographical Society, 10 Randolph Crescent, Edinburgh EH3 7TU Scotland. **Tel** 11 44 31 2253330. **ED** A S Mather. **LC** G1; .S43. **DD** 910/.5. **CODEN** SGGMA2. cum. index. **Bk Rev. Ad Acc. Pr Rev. Circ:** 3,000 (ctrl). available on microfilm and microfiche from University Microfilms International (UMI). Documents available from The Genuine Article.
Ind/Abst Am. Hist. Life (1972-); Annu. Bibliogr. Engl. Lang. Lit.; Bibliogr. Carto.; Br. Archaeol. Bibliogr.; Br. Humanit. Index; Curr. Contents Soc. Behav. Sci.; Ecol. Abstr.; Geogr. Abstr. Phys. Geogr.; Geogr. Abstr. Human Geogr. (?-?); Geol. Abstr.; GeoRef; Int. Dev. Abstr. (?-?); Leis. Recreat. Tour. Abstr.; Res. Alert [Full Cov.]; Soc. Sci. Cit. Index [Full Cov.]; SportSearch.

XR/0324-6566
SCRIPTA FACULTATIS SCIENTIARUM NATURALIUM UNIVERSITATIS PURKYNIANAE BRUNENSIS. GEOGRAPHIA. [Scr. Fac. sci. nat. Univ. Purkyn. Brun., Geogr.]. **Main/Corp** Universita J. E. Purkyne. Prirodovedecka Fakulta. **VFOAT** Geographia. V. 2, No. 1 (1972)-. Periodical. Czech (English, German and Russian). Univerzita J E Purkyne, Janackovo Nam 2A, Brno Czech Republic. ***Supersedes in part*** *Universita J. E. Purkyne. Prirodovedecka Fakulta. Folia.*
Ind/Abst Field Crop Abstr.; Math. Rev.

JA
SEKAI NO KUNI ICHIRANHYO. Japanese. ¥180. Sekai No Ugoki Sha, 6-14 Nishi Shimbashi 1, Minato-kum Tokyo 105 Japan. **LC** G1; .S47.

US/0749-3207
SELECTED ACQUISITIONS BULLETIN - UNIVERSITY OF KENTUCKY. LIBRARIES. MAP DEPT. (SELECTED ACQUISITIONS BULLETIN / MAP DEPARTMENT, KING LIBRARY, UNIVERSITY OF KENTUCKY.). [Sel. acquis. bull. - Univ. Ky., Libr., Map Dep.]. **Main/Corp** University of Kentucky. Libraries. Map Dept. No. 1 (Sept. 1974)-. Bulletin. English. qt. Free. Map Department, University of Kentucky Libraries, Lexington KY 40506-0039. **Tel** (606)257-1853. **ED** Gwen Curtis. **DD** 912. **Circ:** 80.

UK/0307-3246
SEMINAR PAPERS - DEPARTMENT OF GEOGRAPHY. UNIVERSITY OF NEWCASTLE UPON TYNE. [Semin. pap. - Dep. Geogr., Univ. Ncastle. Tyne]. (1968)-. Monographic series. English. Price varies per volume. University of Newcastle upon Tyne, 22 24 Windsor Terrace, Newcastle Tyne NE1 7RU England. **Tel** 011 44 91 2226000.
Ind/Abst Ecol. Abstr.; Geogr. Abstr. Human Geogr.; Int. Dev. Abstr.

UK
SHEPPARD'S INTERNATIONAL DIRECTORY OF PRINT AND MAP SELLERS. (1987)-. Directory. English. £21.00. Richard Joseph Publishers Ltd, Unit 2 Monks Walk, Farnham, Surrey GU9 8HT England. **Tel** 11 44 252 734347, FAX 11 44 252 734307.
Desc: Directory of print and map sellers worldwide.

TH
SIAM DIRECTORY. ***Ceased.*** (1947)-(19??). Directory. English. Intercontinental Marketing Corporation, IPO Box 5056, Tokyo 100-31 Japan. **Tel** 011 81 3 3661 7458, FAX 011 81 3 3661 9646. **LC** DS563; .S53. **DD** 915.93.

SI/0129-7619
SINGAPORE JOURNAL OF TROPICAL GEOGRAPHY. [Singap. j. trop. geogr.]. **Added/Corp** National University of Singapore. Dept. of Geography. University of Singapore. Dept. of Geography. **VFOAT** Tropical Geography. Vol. 1 No. 1 (June 1980)-. Periodical. English. sa. $40.00 (airmail), $30.00 (surface mail). National University of Singapore / Department of Geography, Kent Ridge, Singapore 0511 Singapore. **Tel** 011 65 7723861. **ED** Ooi Jin Bee. **LC** G515; .J65. **DD** 905. cum. index. **Pr Rev. Circ:** 600. Documents available from The Genuine Article. ***Continues in part*** *Journal of Tropical Geography.*
Desc: Publishes research articles in geography and associated subjects concerning tropical countries.
Ind/Abst Curr. Contents Soc. Behav. Sci.; Ecol. Abstr. (?-?); Field Crop Abstr.; For. Abstr.; Geogr. Abstr. Phys. Geogr.; Geogr. Abstr. Human Geogr.; GeoRef; Int. Bibliogr. Sociol.; Int. Dev. Abstr.; Popul. Index; Res. Alert [Full Cov.]; Rice Abstr.; Soc. Sci. Cit. Index [Full Cov.]; Soils Fert.

VE
SINTESIS GEOGRAFICA : REVISTA DE LA ESCUELA DE GEOGRAFIA, UNIVERSIDAD CENTRAL DE VENEZUELA. No. 1 (June 1977)-. Spanish. sa. $3.00. Escuela de Geografia, Facultad de Humanidades, UCV Ciudad Universitaria, Caracas Venezuela. **LC** G1; .S53. **DD** 918/.005.

JA/0038-0830
SOKUCHI GAKKAISHI. (JOURNAL OF THE GEODETIC SOCIETY OF JAPAN. SOKUCHI GAKKAI SHI.). [Sokuchi Gakkaishi]. **Main/Corp** Nihon Sokuchi Gakkai. **VFOAT** Sokuchi Gakkai Shi. Vol. 1 (1954)-. Periodical. English (Japanese). qt. $149.00. Nihon Sokuchi Gakkai, (Geodetic Soc. of Japan), Kokudo Chiriin, 1, Kitasato, Tsukubashi, Ibarakiken 305 Japan. **(Subscription address:** Japan Publications Trading Company, Ltd., PO Box 5030, Tokyo International, Tokyo 100-31 Japan.**) LC** QB275; .N56.
Ind/Abst GeoRef; Int. Aerosp. Abstr.; SEA Abstr.

US/1059-5325
SOLSTICE (ANN ARBOR, MICH.). (SOLSTICE : AN ELECTRONIC JOURNAL OF GEOGRAPHY AND MATHEMATICS.). [Solstice]. **Added/Corp** Institute of Mathematical Geography. Vol. 1, No. 1 (Summer 1990)-. Periodical. English. sa. Instiue of Mathematical Geography, 2790 Briarcliff, Ann Arbor MI 48105-1429. **LC** G70.23; .S64. **DD** 526.

SA/0373-6245
SOUTH AFRICAN GEOGRAPHICAL JOURNAL. (THE SOUTH AFRICAN GEOGRAPHICAL JOURNAL, BEING A RECORD OF THE PROCEEDINGS OF THE SOUTH AFRICAN GEOGRAPHICAL SOCIETY.). [S. Afr. geogr. j.]. **Added/Corp** Cape Geographical Society. Report. South African Geographical Society. **VFOAT** Suid-Afrikaanse Aardrykskundige Tydskrif. Vol. 1 (1917)-. Periodical. English (Afrikaans). sa. $55.00. South African Geographical Society, PO Box 128, Wits 2050, Transvaal South Africa. **Tel** 011 27 11 3391951, FAX 011 27 11 4037281. **ED** Prof. M. Meadows. **LC** G1; .S6. **DD** 910.5. **CODEN** SGEJAH. **Bk Rev**, (Qty: varies). **Pr Rev. Circ:** 850.
Desc: Papers reporting results of human and physical geography research and discussion papers.
Ind/Abst Bibliogr. Carto.; GeoRef; Int. Bibliogr. Sociol.

SA/0081-2455
SOUTH AFRICAN JOURNAL OF ANTARCTIC RESEARCH. (SOUTH AFRICAN JOURNAL OF ANTARCTIC RESEARCH. SUID-AFRIKAANSE TYDSKRIF VIR ANTARKTIESE NAVORSING.). [S. Afr. j. antarct. res.]. **Added/Corp** International Council of Scientific Unions. Scientific Committee on Antarctic Research. **VFOAT** Suid-Afrikaanse Tydskrif vir Antarktiese Navorsing. No. 1 (1971)-. English (summaries and/or abstracts in Afrikaans). ir (2 issues). Free on request. CSIR Publishing Division, PO Box 395, Pretoria 0001 South Africa. **Tel** 011 27 12 8412911 ext. 3765. **ED** Prof. J.R.E. Lutjeharms. **LC** G845; .S68. **DD** 919.8/9/005. **CODEN** SAARCF. **Circ:** 400. Documents available from BIOSIS Document Express, Ask*IEEE, CASDDS.
Desc: Scientific papers on various research topics with relevance to Subantarctic and Antarctic.
Ind/Abst Aquat. Sci. Fish. Abstr. (Computer File); Biol. Abstr.; Chem. Abstr. (1971-1971); Ecol. Abstr. (?-?); INSPEC (1972-); Life Sci. Collect.

SA/0085-6398
SOUTH AFRICAN JOURNAL OF PHOTOGRAMMETRY, THE. ***Title Change.*** [S. Afr. j. photogramm.]. **Added/Corp** Photogrammetric Society of South Africa. **VFOAT** Die Suid-Afrikaanse Tydskrif vir Fotogrammetrie. (1959)-(19??). Periodical. English. sa. SAPGIS, PO Box 69, 7725 Newlands South Africa. **Tel** 011 27 21 685 4070. **LC** TA593; .S565. **DD** 526.9/82/0968. **CODEN** SAPJBV. ***Continued by*** *South African Journal of Photogrammetry Remote Sensing and Cartography.*
Ind/Abst GeoRef.

AT
SOUTH AUSTRALIAN GEOGRAPHER. English. Geography Teachers Association of South Australia, 163a Greenhill Road, Parkside South Australia 5063 Australia.

AT/1030-0481
SOUTH AUSTRALIAN GEOGRAPHICAL JOURNAL. **Added/Corp** Royal Geographical Society of Australasia. South Australian Branch. Vol. 87 (1987)-. English. an (Nov.). 35.00Aus$ (individuals), 40.00Aus$ (institutions) Comes with Royal Geographical Society of Australasia membership. Royal Geographical Society of Australasia, State Library Building, No Terrace, Adelaide SA 5000 Australia. **Tel** 011 61 8 2077265, FAX 011 61 8 2077247. Index available. cum. index. **Bk Rev. Ad Acc. Circ:** 750. ***Continues*** *Royal Geographical Society of Australasia. South Australian Branch. Proceedings of the Royal Geographical Society of Australasia, South Australian Branch (Incorporated), 0085-570.*
Desc: Papers relating to geography with emphasis on Australian history, exploration and biography.
Ind/Abst APAIS, Aust. Public Aff. Inf. Ser.; Geogr. Abstr. Phys. Geogr.

US
SOUTH BEND (ST. JOSEPH COUNTY, IND.) CITY DIRECTORY. **VFOAT** Polk's South Bend City Directory. 1974-. Directory. English. an. R. L. Polk & Company, 1155 Brewery Park Boulevard, Detroit MI 48207. **Tel** (313)393-0880. ***Continues*** *Polk's South Bend (St. Joseph County, Ind.) City Directory.*

US/0038-366X
SOUTHEASTERN GEOGRAPHER. [Southeast. geogr.]. **Added/Corp** Association of American Geographers. Southeastern Division. Vol. 1 (1961)-. Periodical. English. sa (May, Nov.). $15.00. Southeastern Geographer, University of Georgia, Department of Geography, Athens GA 30602. **Tel** (706)542-2350, FAX (706)542-2388. **ED** James Wheeler, (706)542-2350. **LC** G1; .S62. **DD** 910/.5. **Bk Rev. Ad Acc. Pr Rev. Circ:** 900 (ctrl).
Desc: The journal publishes research papers on all geographical topics, but its focus is upon the American South.
Ind/Abst Ecol. Abstr.; Geogr. Abstr. Phys. Geogr.; Geogr. Abstr. Human Geogr.; Int. Dev. Abstr.

UK/0073-9006
SPECIAL PUBLICATION--INSTITUTE OF BRITISH GEOGRAPHIES. **Main/Corp** Institute of British Geographers. (1968)-. Academic Scholarly Publication. English (summaries and/or abstracts in English, French and German). ir. Academic Press, Inc., 6277 Sea Harbor Drive, Orlando FL 32887. **Tel** (800)543-9534, (407)345-4100, FAX (407)363-9661.

GW
STANDORT - ZEITSCHRIFT FUER ANGEWANDTE GEOGRAPHIE. (19??)-. German. Four times a year. DM118.00. Springer-Verlag GmbH & Company KG, Heidelberger Platz 3, D 14197 Berlin Germany. **Tel** 011 49 30 8207223, FAX 011 49 30 8214091, telex 183 319 SPBLN D. **(Subscription address:** Springer Verlag New York Inc. / for North America, 44 Hartz Way, Secaucus NJ 07096.**)**

US
STATE OF WORLD POPULATION / RAFAEL M. SALAS, EXECUTIVE DIRECTOR OF THE UNITED NATIONS FUND FOR POPULATION ACTIVITIES, THE. **See** Population Studies.

FR
STRATIGRAPHIE GEOLOGIE REGIONALE GEOLOGIE GENERALE. F44. French. 913.80F France; 945.00F other. Institut de l'Information Scientique et Technique (INIST), 2 Allee du Parc de Brabois, 54514 Vandoeuvre Nancy Cedex France. **Tel** 011 33 83 504600, FAX 011 33 83 504650. ***Continues*** *Pascal Folio. F44: Stratigraphie Geologie Regionale Geologie Generale.*

GE
STUDIA GEOGRAPHICA. Added/Corp Ceskoslovenska Akademie ved. Geograficky Ustav, Brunn. (1969)-. Monographic series. German (Czech, English, French and German). Price varies per volume. **LC** G1; .S8. **CODEN** CAVGBC.
Ind/Abst Geogr. Abstr. Phys. Geogr.; Geogr. Abstr. Human Geogr.; GeoRef.

HU/0209-4835
STUDIA GEOGRAPHICA DEBRECEN. [Stud. geogr. Debr.]. (1977)-. Monographic series. Hungarian. Price varie per volume. **UDC** 91.
Ind/Abst Geogr. Abstr. Human Geogr.

PL/0081-6434
STUDIA GEOMORPHOLOGICA CARPATHO-BALCANICA. (STUDIA GEOMORPHOLOGICA CARPATHO-BALCANICA / POLSKA AKADEMIA NAUK, ODDZIA W KRAKOWIE, KOMISJA GEOGRAFICZNA.). [Stud. geomorphol. Carpatho-Balc.]. **Added/Corp** Polska Akademia Nauk. Komisja Geograficzna. Geomorfologiczna Komisja Karpacko-Bakanska (Krakow, Poland). Vol. 1 (1967)-. Periodical. English (French, Polish and Russian). **LC** QE260; .S77. **CODEN** SGCAAE.
Ind/Abst Geogr. Abstr. Phys. Geogr.; GeoRef.

PL/0082-5549
STUDIA SOCIETATIS SCIENTIARUM TORUNENSIS. SECTIO C. GEOGRAPHIA ET GEOLOGIA. Main/Corp Towarzystwo Naukowe w Toruniu. (1953)-. Periodical. Polish (summaries and/or abstracts in English and Russian).
Ind/Abst Geogr. Abstr. Phys. Geogr.

RM
STUDIA UNIVERSITATIS BABES-BOLYAI. GEOGRAPHIA. Added/Corp Universitatea "Babes-Bolyai.". **VFOAT** Geographia. Vol. 35, No. 1 (1990)-. Periodical. Romanian (English, French, German and Romanian). sa. Available on an exchange basis. Universitatis Babes-Bolyai, Biblioteca Centrala Universitara, Str. Clinicilor 2, Cluj Napoca 3400 Romania. **Tel** 95 117092, FAX 95 117633. **(Subscription address:** Rompresfilatelia, PO Box 12 201, Bucharest Romania.**)** **LC** DR210; .S88. ***Continues in part*** *Studia Universitatis Babes-Bolyai. Geologia-Geographia, 0255-6804.*
Desc: Specifically examines physical geography.

II
STUDIES IN INDIAN PLACE NAMES. Added/Corp Place Names Society of India. **VFOAT** Bharatiya Sthalanama Patrika. Vol. 1 (1980)-. English. an. $30.00. Place Names Society, Mysore, India. **(Subscription address:** Prints India, 11 Darya Ganj, New Delhi, 110002 India, (Phone: 011 91 11 3268645)**)** **LC** DS405; .S79. **DD** 915.4/0014.

SW/1100-1283
STUDIES IN INTERNATIONAL ECONOMICS & GEOGRAPHY. See Economics-International Economics.

SA
SUID-AFRIKAANSE GEOGRAAF. *Ceased.* Added/Corp Society for Geography. **VFOAT** South African Geographer. Vol. 4 (Sept. 1972)-Vol. 20, No. 2. Periodical. Multiple languages (Afrikaans and English; summaries and/or abstracts in Afrikaans and English). Twice a year (April and September). Society for Geography, PO Box 2031 Dennesign, Stellenbosch South Africa. **Tel** 02231-77-3218, FAX 011 27 2231 774336. **ED** W.S. Barnard. **LC** G72; .T9. Index available. cum. index. **Bk Rev. Ad Acc. Circ:** 1,400. ***Continues*** *Tydskrif vir Aardrykskunde, 0021-8243.*

US
SUMMARY OF CORRECTIONS : CHARTS. Began with Jan. 1977. Periodical. English. sa. US Department of Defense Defense Mapping Agency, 8613 Lee Highway, Fairfax VA 22031. **Tel** (703)285-9290, FAX (703)285-9374. ***Continues*** *Summary of Chart Corrections.*

SW/0081-9808
SVENSK GEOGRAFISK ARSBOK. VFOAT Swedish Geographical Yearbook. Vol. 1- 1925-. Swedish. ir. 440.00F. Gleerupska University, Bokhandlns Forlag AB Fack, 221 01 Lund 1 Sweden. **CODEN** SGGAAY. cum. index.
Ind/Abst Ecol. Abstr.; Geogr. Abstr. Phys. Geogr.; Geogr. Abstr. Human Geogr.; Geol. Abstr.; GeoRef; Int. Dev. Abstr.

RU
SVODNYI KATALOG INOSTRANNYH KART I ATLASOV, POLUCHENNYKH BIBLIOTEKAMI AKADEMII NAUK SSSR I BIBLIOTEKAMI AKADEMII NAUK SOIUZNYKH RESPUBLIK. Added/Corp Akademiia Nauk SSSR. Biblioteka. **VFOAT** Svodnyi Katalog Inostrannykh Geograficheskikh Kart I Atlasov. (1971)-. Multiple languages (Russian and Multiple languages). 0.46rub. Bibliotekami Akademi Nauk SSSR I Bibliotekami, Birzhevaia 1, 1 St.Petersburg, 199164 Russia. **LC** Z6021; .A4. ***Continues*** *Katalog Inostrannykh Geograficheskikh Atlasov.*

UK/0081-9980
SWANSEA GEOGRAPHER. [Swansea geogr.]. **Added/Corp** University College of Swansea. Dept. of Geography. University College of Swansea. Geographical Society. (1959)-. Academic Scholarly Publication. English. an. University College of Swansea, Singleton Park Department of Geography, Swansea SA2 8PP W Glam Wales England. **Tel** 0792 205678. **ED** R. Kitchin and S. Toole. **Circ:** 200. Documents available from BLDSC.
Desc: Papers range across teaching and research activities carried out by the geography staff, research students and undergraduates at the University College, Swansea.
Ind/Abst Ecol. Abstr. (?-?); Geogr. Abstr. Phys. Geogr.; Geogr. Abstr. Human Geogr.; Geol. Abstr.; GeoRef; Int. Dev. Abstr.

FR/0039-7946
SYRIA. [Syria]. **Added/Corp** France. Haut Commissariat de la Republique Francaise en Syrie et au Liban. Institut Francais d'Archeologie de Beyrouth. Vol. 1 (1920)-. Periodical. French. Twice a year (Published 2 double issue per volume). 450.00F. Librairie Orientaliste Paul Geuthner, 12 rue Vavin, 75006 Paris France. **Tel** 011 33 1 46347130. **LC** DS94.5; .S8. **DD** 913.394.
Ind/Abst Avery Index Archit. Period. Suppl. Colum. Univ. (19??-199?); BHA : Biblio. Hist. Art; Index Book Rev. Relig.; MLA Int. Bibl. Books Artic. Mod. Lang. Lit.; Numis. Lit.; Relig. Index One Period. (1949-).

CH
TAIWAN YELLOW PAGES. *Ceased.* VFOAT Republic of China Business Telephone Directory. -Ceased Dec. 1989. English (Chinese). ir. Croner Publications Inc., 34 Jericho Turnpike, Jericho NY 11753. **Tel** (516)333-9085. **LC** HF3846.8; .T34. **DD** 380.1/029/451249.
Desc: Similar to US yellow pages, it lists manufacturers, traders, agents, exporters, importers, service firms. Includes name, address, executives, telex numbers, products handled.

UK
TEACHING GEOGRAPHY. See Education-Teaching and Curriculum.

SP
TECNICA TOPOGRAFICA : REVISTA DEL COLEGIO OFICIAL DE INGENIEROS TECNICOS EN TOPOGRAFIA. Periodical. Spanish. bm. Paseo de la Castellana 210, Madrid-16 Spain. **LC** TA590; .T43. **DD** 526.9/8/05.

FI/0040-3741
TERRA. [Terra]. Began publication in 1913. Periodical. Finnish (Swedish and English). qt. Fmk250.00. Akakeeminen-Kirjakuppa, PO Box 128, 00101 Helsinki Finland. **Tel** 011/358/0/90/12141, FAX +358 0 121 4441, telex 125080 AKAHE SF. **LC** G23; .G5. **CODEN** TRRAA7. ***Continues*** *Geografiska Foreningen i Finland. Tidskrift.*
Ind/Abst GeoRef.

US/0082-2884
TERRAE INCOGNITAE. [Terr. incogn.]. **Added/Corp** Society for the History of Discoveries. Vol. 1 (1969)-. English. an (Sept.). $20.00. Society of History of Discoveries, 60 West Walton, c/o Newberry Library, Chicago IL 60610. **Tel** (203)432-1868, (312)943-9090. **ED** David Buisseret. **LC** G2; .S6517. **DD** 910/.9. **Bk Rev. Circ:** 500 (ctrl).
Desc: Publishes articles devoted to exploration and geographical discovery between 1400 and 1900.
Ind/Abst Am. Hist. Life (1969-); Geogr. Abstr. Phys. Geogr. (?-?); Geogr. Abstr. Human Geogr. (?-?).

FR/0758-4083
TERRE INFORMATION. (1973)-. Periodical. French. Thirteen times a year. 58.77F (1 year), 107.74 (2 year) other. Addim, 6 rue Saint Charles, 75015 Paris France. **Tel** 011 33 1 45770376. **UDC** 355.

AG/0327-3210
TERRITORIO PARA LA PRODUCCION Y CRITICA EN GEOGRAFIA Y CIENCIAS SOCIALES. VFOAT Territorio (Buenos Aires). (1989)-. Monographic series. Spanish. qt. Price varies per volume. **UDC** 911(82).
Ind/Abst Geogr. Abstr. Human Geogr.; Int. Dev. Abstr.

AT
THESES AND DISSERTATIONS PRESENTED AND CURRENTLY BEING UNDERTAKEN IN GEOGRAPHY. Main/Corp Western Australia. University. Dept. of Geography. (19??)-. English. ir. University of Western Australia Department of Geography, Nedlands 6009 Australia. **Tel** 011 61 9 3802697, FAX 09 381 6427, telex AA92992. **LC** Z6001; .W47a; G116. **DD** 016.9/94.

SI
TI LI CHI KAN. Added/Corp Nan-yang Ta Hsueh Ti Li Hsueh Hui. Nan-yang Ta Hsueh Ti Li Hsueh Hui. Geographical Journal. **VFOAT** The Geographical Journal. (1968)-. Chinese. an. Geographical Society, Jurong Road, Nanyang University, Singapore 22 Singapore.

II/0040-6708
TIBETAN REVIEW. Vol. 1 (Jan./Feb. 1968)-. Periodical. English. mo. $13.00. Tibetan Review Youth Hostel, P SP Area 2 Plot B1 Sec 14, Rohini 85 New Delhi India. **Tel** 011 91 11 6425974. **(Subscription address:** Prints India, 11 Darya Ganj, New Delhi 110002 India.**)** **ED** Tsering Wangyal, Telephone:011 91 11 7272649. **LC** DS785.A1; T52. **DD** 915.15/005. **Bk Rev. Ad Acc. Circ:** 2,500. ***Continues*** *Voice of Tibet.*
Ind/Abst Hum. Rights Intern. Rep.

NE/0040-747X
TIJDSCHRIFT VOOR ECONOMISCHE EN SOCIALE GEOGRAFIE : TESG. See Economics.

CN/0822-7373
TOPONYME, LE. [Toponyme]. **Main/Corp** Quebec (Province). Commission de Toponymie. Service de l'Animation et de la Diffusion. Vol. 1, No. 1 (Nov. 1983)-. Periodical. French. Free upon request. Commission de Toponymie, 1245 Chemin St Foy, Bureau 344, Quebec Quebec G1S 4P2 Canada. **Tel** (418)643-9705. **DD** 917.14/001/4. **Circ:** 5,000 (ctrl).

BL
TRABALHOS TECNICOS - FUNDACAO INSTITUTO BRASILEIRO DE GEOGRAFIA E ESTATISTICA, SUPERINTENDENCIA DE CARTOGRAFIA. Main/Corp Fundacao Instituto Brasileiro de Geografia e Estatistica. Superintendencia de Cartografia. Portuguese. an. Diretoria Tecnica Superintendencia de Cartografia, Av Brasil 15.051, Parade de Lucas, Rio de Janeiro Brazil. **Tel** (021)391-1673, telex 2131929 EBGE-BR. **ED** M P Mello. **LC** GA63.B8; F84A. **Circ:** 1,000.
Desc: Papers and technical reports produced by IBGE/DGC staff the fields of Cartography Geodesy, Geography and environmental analysis.

UK/0020-2754
TRANSACTIONS - INSTITUTE OF BRITISH GEOGRAPHERS (1965). (TRANSACTIONS - INSTITUTE OF BRITISH GEOGRAPHERS.). [Trans. - Inst. Br. Geogr.]. **Main/Corp** Institute of British Geographers. (1965)-. Periodical. English. Four times a year (Mar., June, Sept., Dec.). £85.00. Institute British Geographers, 1 Kensington Gore, London SW7 2AR England. **Tel** 011 44 71 584 6371, FAX 071 581 9918. **ED** M Williams. **LC** G1; .I67a; G7; .I6 subser. **DD** 910/.6/241. **CODEN** IBGTAE. Index available. **Bk Rev. Pr Rev. Circ:** 3,000 (ctrl). Documents available from The Genuine Article. ***Continues*** *Transactions and Papers - Institute of British Geographers.*
Desc: Informed viewpoints on issues ranging from conceptual and theoretical advances to geography's contribution to effective political decision making.
Ind/Abst Agrofor. Abstr.; Bibliogr. Carto.; Curr. Contents Soc. Behav. Sci.; Curr. Geogr. Publ. (199?-); For. Abstr.; Geogr. Abstr. Phys. Geogr.; Geogr. Abstr. Human Geogr.; GeoRef; Int. Bibliogr. Sociol.; Int. Dev. Abstr.; PAIS Int. Print (1991-?); Res. Alert [Full Cov.]; Rural Dev. Abstr.; Soc. Plann. Policy Dev. Abstr.; Soc. Sci. Cit. Index [Full Cov.]; Sociol. Abstr. (?-?); SportSearch.

II
TRANSACTIONS OF THE INSTITUTE OF INDIAN GEOGRAPHERS. Added/Corp Institute of Indian Geographers. Vol. 1, No. 1 (July 1979)-. Periodical. English. sa. $16.00. University of Poona, Department of Geography, Pune, India. **(Subscription address:** Prints India, 11 Darya Ganj, New Delhi, 110002 India, (Phone: 011 91 11 3268645)**)** **LC** G1; .T717. **DD** 910/.5.
Ind/Abst Ecol. Abstr. (?-?); Geogr. Abstr. Phys. Geogr.; Geogr. Abstr. Human Geogr.; Int. Dev. Abstr.

FR/0048-7163
TRAVAUX DE L'INSTITUT DE GEOGRAPHIE DE REIMS. [Trav. Inst. geogr. Reims]. (1969)-. Periodical. French. Twice a year. 150.00F. Erigur, 57 rue P Taittinger, F-51906 Reims France. **Tel** 011 33 26 053681, FAX 011 33 26 05 36 46. **ED** Professor A. Marre, J. Domingo and M. Bazin. **UDC** 91. **Bk Rev**, (Qty: 20). available on diskette.
Desc: News and information in all aspects and techniques used in geography.
Ind/Abst Geogr. Abstr. Human Geogr.; Int. Dev. Abstr.

Geography

US
TRIENNIAL ATLAS & PLAT BOOK, RICE COUNTY, MINNESOTA. Main/Corp Rockford Map Publishers. VFOAT Plat Book, Rice County, Minnesota. (1968)-. English. te. Rockford Map Publishers, Inc., 4525 Forest View Ave., Box 6126, Rockford IL 61125. LC G1428.R6; R6.

CK/0120-8098
TRIMESTRE GEOGRAFICO. [Trimest. geogr.]. Added/Corp Asociacion Colombiana de Geografos. (1982)-. Periodical. Spanish. sa. DD 918.61.
Ind/Abst Geogr. Abstr. Human Geogr.; Int. Dev. Abstr.

RU
TRUDY SOVETSKOI ANTARKTICHESKOI EKSPEDITSII / ARKTICHESKII I ANTARKTICHESKII NAUCHNO-ISSLEDOVATELSKII INSTITUT. Added/Corp Arkticheskii i Antarkticheskii Nauchno-Issledovatelskii Institut (Leningrad, R.S.F.S.R.). (1962)-. Monographic series. Russian. ir. Price varies per volume. LC G860; .S63. Continues Sovetskaia Antarkticheskaia Ekspeditsiia.

CN/0227-8464
TRURO AND DISTRICT, NOVA SCOTIA, CITY DIRECTORY. [Truro dist., N.S., city dir.]. VFOAT Truro and District, Including Bible Hill, Onslow and Salmon River, City Directory. VAT Truro and District Including Bible Hill, Onslow and Salmon River City Directory. 1980-. Directory. English. $55.00 each number. Might Directories, 220 Bartley Drive, Toronto Ontario M4A 2H4 Canada. Tel (416)751-2751. DD 917.16/12. Continues Might's Truro and District, Nova Scotia, City Directory, 0700-4575.

GW/0564-4232
TUBINGER GEOGRAPHISCHE STUDIEN. [Tubing. geogr. Stud.]. Added/Corp Universitat Tubingen. Geographisches Institut. Vol. 1 (1958)-. Monographic series. German. ir. Price varies per volume. Lange and Springer GmbH and Company, Follerstr 2, POB 101610, W-5000 Cologne 1 Germany. Tel (011/49/221)20830, FAX 011/49/221/208323.
(Subscription address: North America/ Journal Fulfillment Services, 44 Hartz Way, Secaucus, NJ 07094) CODEN TUGSBS.
Ind/Abst Geogr. Abstr. Human Geogr. (?-?); GeoRef; Int. Dev. Abstr.; Soyabean Abstr.

FI/0082-6979
TURUN YLIOPISTON JULKAISUJA. SARJA A 2, BIOLOGICA. GEOGRAPHICA. GEOLOGICA. See Biology.

CN/0229-5334
U.S.G. NEWSLETTER. [U.S.G. newsl.]. Main/Corp Union of Socialist Geographers. Vol. 1, No. 1-. Newsletter. English. Free to members, $10.00 institutions. Union of Socialist Geographers Simon Fraser University, Burnaby British Columbia V5A 1S6 Canada.

AT
UBD BUSINESS TO BUSINESS. SOUTH AUSTRALIA COUNTRY BUSINESS & STREET DIRECTORY. See Business.

SW
UNGI RAPPORT. Main/Corp Uppsala Universitet. Naturgeografiska Institutionen. (1969)-. Monographic series. Swedish (English). Price varies per volume.).
Ind/Abst Ecol. Abstr.; Geogr. Abstr. Phys. Geogr.; Int. Dev. Abstr.

US/0094-4033
UNION CATALOG OF MAPS (BERKELEY). (THE UNION CATALOG OF MAPS.). Catalog. English. bm. $25.00. Berkeley Documentation Center, PO Box 361, Berkeley CA 94701. LC Z6028; .U42. DD 016.912.

UK
UNITED KINGDOM GEODESY REPORT. Main/Corp British National Committee for Geodesy and Geophysics. Geodesy Subcommittee. English. Royal Society, 6 Carlton House Terrace, London SW1Y 5AG England. Tel 011 44 71 839 5561, FAX 071-976 1837, telex 917876 ROYAL G. LC QB275; .B73A. DD 526.

US/0068-6441
UNIVERSITY OF CALIFORNIA PUBLICATIONS IN GEOGRAPHY. [Univ. Calif. publ. geogr.]. Main/Corp University of California, Berkeley. VFOAT Publications in Geography. (1913)-. Monographic series. English. ir. Price varies per volume. University of California Press, 2120 Berkeley Way, Berkeley CA 94720. Tel (510)642-4191, (510)642-3907, FAX (510)642-9917. LC G58; .C3. Circ: 900 (ctrl).
Ind/Abst GeoRef.

US/1054-206X
UNIVERSITY OF CHICAGO GEOGRAPHY RESEARCH PAPER. Added/Corp University of Chicago. Committee on Geographical Studies. VFOAT Geography Research Paper. No. 231 (1990)-. Monographic series. English. ir. Price varies per volume. University of Chicago Press / Book Department, 11030 South Langley Avenue, Chicago IL 60628. Tel (800)621-2736, (312)568-1550, FAX (312)753-0811, telex 23933. Continues Geography Research Paper (Chicago, Ill.).
Ind/Abst Geogr. Abstr. Phys. Geogr. (19??-); Geogr. Abstr. Human Geogr. (19??-); Int. Dev. Abstr. (19??-).

IT/0042-0409
UNIVERSO. (L'UNIVERSO.). [Universo]. Added/Corp Istituto Geografico Militare (Italy). Vol. 1, No. 1 (Jan./Feb. 1920)-. Periodical. Italian (summaries and/or abstracts in English, French, German and Spanish). bm. L36000, Italy; L54000 other. Istituto Geografico Militare, Via C Battisi 10 12, 50122 Florence Italy. Tel 011 39 55 27751, FAX (055)4378120, telex 575597 IGM FI I. ED Enrico Borgonni. LC G1; .U6. DD 910/.5. CODEN UNVSAU. Index available. cum. index. Bk Rev. Ad Acc. Circ: 3,000.
Desc: General geography, mainly anthropic history and archaeology, ancient topography, mapping, history of explorations, and environmental sciences.
Ind/Abst Bibliogr. Carto. (19??-); Geogr. Abstr. Phys. Geogr. (19??-); Geogr. Abstr. Human Geogr. (19??-); GeoRef (19??-).

IT/0042-0409
UNIVERSO [MICROFORM], L'. Added/Corp Istituto Geografico Militare (Italy). Vol. 1, No. 1 (Jan./Feb. 1920)-. Periodical. Italian (summaries and/or abstracts in English, French, German and Spanish). Istituto Geografico Militare, Via C Battisi 10 12, 50122 Florence Italy. Tel 011 39 55 27751, FAX (055)4378120, telex 575597 IGM FI I.
Desc: General geography, mainly anthropic history and archaeology, ancient topography, mapping, history of explorations, and environmental sciences.

US/0360-4403
URBAN AREAS OF WASHINGTON. VFOAT Urban Areas, Washington. English. Washington State Highway Commission, Department of Highways, Olympia WA. LC G1489.A1; U7. DD 912/.797.

US/0272-3638
URBAN GEOGRAPHY. [Urban geogr.]. Vol. 1, No. 1 (Jan./Mar. 1980)-. Periodical. English. Eight times a year. $295.00 US; $336.00 other. V. H. Winston & Sons Inc., 7961 Eastern Avenue, Suite 202A, Silver Spring MD 20910. Tel (301)587-3356. (Subscription address: Bellwether Publishing, Ltd, 8640 Guilford Road, Suite 200, Columbia MD 21046.) ED Brian J. L. Berry. LC GF125; .U73. DD 910/.09173/2. [CCC]. Pr Rev. Circ: 400 (ctrl). Documents available from The Genuine Article.
Desc: Publishes research and state-of-the-art progress reports of interest to all social scientists in geography and urban studies.
Ind/Abst Curr. Contents Soc. Behav. Sci.; Curr. Geogr. Publ. (199?-); Int. Bibliogr. Sociol.; Int. Polit. Sci. Abstr.; J. Plan. Lit.; Popul. Index; Res. Alert [Full Cov.]; Sage Public Adm. Abstr.; Sage Urban Stud. Abstr; Soc. Sci. Cit. Index [Full Cov.]; Stud. Women Abstr.

UK/0956-0904
USA AND CANADA. VFOAT USA & Canada. VAT United States of America and Canada. 1st Ed. (1990)-. English. an. $375.00. Europa Publications Ltd, 18 Bedford Square, London WC1B 3JN England. Tel 011 44 71 5808236, telex 21540 EUROPA G. (Subscription address: Gale Research Co., 835 Penobscot Building, Detroit MI 48226.).
Desc: Provides a comprehensive and detailed survey of each country and their states, provinces, and territories. About thirty eminent experts have contributed essays and other material.

●**US**
USA COUNTIES [COMPUTER FILE]. VFOAT USA Counties Statistics; USA Counties on CD-ROM. (1992)-. Government Publication. English. US Department of Commerce / Bureau of the Census, Data User Services Division, Customer Services, Washington DC 20233-0800. Tel (301)763-4100. (Subscription address: Superintendent of Documents, US Government Printing Office, Washington DC 20402.)

●CN/1191-9396
VANCOUVER CITY DIRECTORY (1992). (VANCOUVER CITY DIRECTORY.). [Vanc. city dir.]. (1992)-. Directory. English. British Columbia Directories / Vancouver, 34 West 2nd Avenue, Vancouver British Columbia V5Y 1B3 Canada. DD 917.11/33/0025. Continues Vancouver B.C. City Directory., 0712-1881.

GW
VECHTAER ARBEITEN ZUR GEOGRAPHIE UND REGIONALWISSENSCHAFT. Added/Corp Universitat Osnabruck. Fachbereich Sozial- und Kulturwissenschaften. VFOAT VAG. (1985)-. Monographic series. German. Price varies per volume.
Ind/Abst Geogr. Abstr. Human Geogr.

NE/0922-9558
VELDSTUDIES / FACULTEIT DER RUIMTELIJKE WETENSCHAPPEN. GEOGRAFISCH INSTITUUT. RIJKSUNIVERSITEIT GRONINGEN. [Veldstud. - Fac. Ruimt. Wet., Geogr. Inst., Rijksuniv. Gron.]. VFOAT Veldstudies - Geografisch Instituut. (1979)-. Monographic series. Dutch. ir. UDC 91.
Ind/Abst Leis. Recreat. Tour. Abstr.

GW/0083-5684
VERHANDLUNGEN DES DEUTSCHEN GEOGRAPHENTAGES. Main/Corp Deutscher Geographentag. VFOAT Verhandlungen, Wissenschaftliche Abhandlungen; Verhandlungen und Wissenschaftliche Abhandlungen; Tagungsbericht; Wissenschaftliche Abhandlungen. Vol. 1 (1881)-. Monographic series. German. ir. Price varies per volume. Franz Steiner Verlag GmbH, Postfach 101061, D 70009 Stuttgart Germany. Tel 011 49 0711 2582372, FAX 011 49 0711 2582290, telex 723636 daz d. cum. index.
Desc: Proceedings of the meetings of the German Geography Association.

SZ/0252-9424
VERMESSUNG, PHOTOGRAMMETRIE, KULTURTECHNIK. See Engineering.

US
VERMONT GEOGRAPHIC INFORMATION SYSTEM : ANNUAL REPORT TO THE LEGISLATURE. Main/Corp Vermont. Office of Geographic Information Services. VFOAT VGIS : Helping Vermonters Visual Choice. (Mar. 1990)-. English. Office of Geographic Information Services, State of Vermont, 120 State Street, Montpelier VT 05602.

CN/0848-9203
VERNON'S ... BRANTFORD CITY DIRECTORY. [Vernon's Brantford city dir.]. VFOAT Vernon's Brantford City Directory; Brantford City Directory. (1988)-. Directory. English. an. Vernon Directories Ltd., 111 Fried Street, Hamilton Ontario L8P 4M3 Canada. Tel (416)522-5066. DD 917.13/48/0025. Continues Vernon's City of Brantford (Ontario) Directory, 0317-2880.

CN/0701-8665
VERNON'S BURLINGTON AND HAMILTON SUBURBAN DIRECTORY. Added/Corp Vernon Directories. (1977)-. English. an. Vernon Directories Ltd, 111 Fried Street, Hamilton Ontario L8P 4M3 Canada. Tel (416)522-5066. DD 917.13/53. Continues Vernon's Hamilton Suburban Directory, 0316-1773.

CN/0317-2899
VERNON'S CITY OF CAMBRIDGE (ONTARIO) DIRECTORY. [Vernon's city Camb. Ont. dir.]. Added/Corp Vernon Directories. VFOAT Vernon's Cambridge City Directory. 43 Ed., (1973)-. Periodical. English. an. Sold by subscription only. Vernon Directories Ltd., 111 Fried Street, Hamilton Ontario L8P 4M3 Canada. Tel (416)522-5066. DD 971.3/44. ctrl circ. Continues Vernon's Galt-Preston, Ontario Directory, 0317-2902.

CN/0316-1765
VERNON'S CITY OF HAMILTON (ONTARIO) DIRECTORY. [Vernon's city Hamilt. (Ont.) dir.]. Added/Corp Vernon Directories. VFOAT Vernon's Hamilton Directory; Vernon's Hamilton City Directory. (1958)-. Periodical. English. an. Leased by subscription only. Vernon Directories Ltd., 111 Fried Street, Hamilton Ontario L8P 4M3 Canada. Tel (416)522-5066. DD 917.13/52. ctrl circ. Continues Vernon's ... City of Hamilton Miscellaneous, Business, Alphabetical and Street Directory.

CN/0229-7337
VERNON'S CITY OF KITCHENER-WATERLOO (ONTARIO) DIRECTORY. [Vernon's city Kitchener-Waterloo (Ont.) dir.]. Added/Corp Vernon Directories. VFOAT Vernon's Kitchener and Waterloo City Directory; Kitchener and Waterloo City Directory. (1979)-. Directory. English. an (Published in February). 362.00Can$. Vernon Directories Ltd., 111 Fried Street, Hamilton Ontario L8P 4M3 Canada. Tel (416)522-5066. DD 917.13/45/0025. Continues Vernon's Kitchener Waterloo (Ontario) Directory, 0316-179X.

CN/0706-5035
VERNON'S CITY OF TIMMINS, ONTARIO, DIRECTORY. Added/Corp Vernon Directories. VFOAT Timmins, Ontario, Directory. VAT Timmins City Directory. 1st Edition (1979)-. English. an (Publishes every three years). 230.00Can$. Vernon Directories Ltd., 111 Fried Street, Hamilton Ontario L8P 4M3 Canada. Tel (416)522-5066. DD 917.13/142.

CN/0849-0813
VERNON'S ... NORTH BAY CITY DIRECTORY. [Vernon's North Bay city dir.]. Added/Corp Vernon Directories. VFOAT Vernon's North

Bay City Directory; North Bay City Directory. (1990)-. Directory. English. be. Vernon Directories Ltd., 111 Fried Street, Hamilton Ontario L8P 4M3 Canada. **Tel** (416)522-5066. **DD** 917.13/147. ***Continues*** *Vernon's City of North Bay (Ontario) Directory, 0316-1692.*

RU/0579-9414
VESTNIK MOSKOVSKOGO UNIVERSITETA. SERIIA V, GEOGRAFIIA. [Vestn. Mosk. univ. Ser. V]. **Added/Corp** Moskovskii Gosudarstvennyi Universitet Im. M.V. Lomonosova. (1960)-. Academic Scholarly Publication. Russian (table of contents in English). bm. $109.95. Izdatelstvo Moskovskogo Universiteta, K-9 Ulitsa Gertsena 5/7, Moscow Russia. **Tel** (301)881-5973. **(Subscription address:** East View Publications Inc., 3020 Harbor Lane North, Suite 110, Minneapolis MN 55447.**)** **CODEN** VMOGAV. Documents available from CASDDS. ***Continues in part*** *Vestnik Moskovskogo Universiteta. Seriia Biologii, Pochvovedeniia, Geologii, Geografii.*
Ind/Abst AGRICOLA; Chem. Abstr. (-1976); Ecol. Abstr.; Geogr. Abstr. Phys. Geogr. (?-?); Geogr. Abstr. Human Geogr.; GeoRef; Int. Dev. Abstr.; Leis. Recreat. Tour. Abstr.; Meteorol. Geoastrophys. Abstr.

●RU
VESTNIK SANKT-PETERBURGSKOGO UNIVERSITETA. SERIIA 7, GEOLOGIIA, GEOGRAFIIA. **See** Earth Sciences-Geology.

CN/0227-8626
VILLE DE HAMPSTEAD REPERTOIRE. [Ville Hampstead repert.]. **VFOAT** Hampstead Annuaire des Residents; Hampstead Householder's Directory. V. 9-1980-. English (French). an. J Lovell, 423 rue St Nicolas, Montreal Quebec H2Y 2P4 Canada. **Tel** (514)849-2578. **DD** 917.14/281/0025. ***Continues*** *Town of Hampstead Directory, 0316-7836.*

US/0042-6512
VIRGINIA GEOGRAPHER, THE. [Va. geogr.]. **Added/Corp** Virginia Geographical Society. George Mason University. Dept. of Public Affairs. George Mason University. Graduate School. George Mason University. Division of Continuing Education. Vol. 1 (Nov. 1966)-. Periodical. English. sa. $8.00. Old Dominion University / Political Science and Geography Department, Norfolk VA 23529. **Tel** (804)683-3841. **ED** Donald Zeigler and Justin Friberg. **DD** 917. Index available. cum. index. **Bk Rev. Ad Acc. Pr Rev. Circ:** 200 (ctrl).
Desc: Articles of interest to teachers. Contains academic articles on the geography of Virginia or neighboring states; items of historical geography, environmental issues, Virginia economy and society are included.
Ind/Abst GeoRef.

BU/0324-1114
VISSA GEODEZIJA. (VISSHA GEODEZIIA.). [Vissa geod.]. **Added/Corp** Bulgarska Akademiia na Naukite. **VFOAT** Geodesy. (1975)-. Academic Scholarly Publication. Multiple languages (Bulgarian, French and Russian; summaries and/or abstracts in English and German). ir. 1.10lv per issue. Bulgarska Akademiia na Naukite, 7 Noemvri 1, Sofia Bulgaria. **LC** QB275; .V58. **CODEN** VGEOEZ. **Circ:** 480. ***Supersedes*** *Bulgarska Akademiia na Naukite, Sofia. Tsentralna Laboratoriia po Geodeziia. Izvestiia.*
Ind/Abst Int. Aerosp. Abstr.

BE/0042-7527
VIVANT UNIVERS. [Vivant univers]. No. 262 (May/June 1969)-. Periodical. French. Six times a year (Jan., Mar., May, July, Sept., Nov.). 33.00F. Vivant Univers, Chee de Binant 115, 5000 Namur Belgium. **Tel** 011 32 81 222891, FAX 00 32 81 24 10 24. **ED** BOOM Constant. **LC** G1; .V57. **DD** 910/.5. **Bk Rev. Ad Acc. Circ:** 10,000. ***Continues*** *Vivante Afrique.*
Desc: Monograph of a Third World country giving the geographical, historical, social, economic, cultural and religious background of that country. Articles are mainly written by the local people.
Ind/Abst Bibliogr. Mission.

RU/0321-0669
VOKRUG SVIETA. Added/Corp Vsesoiuznyi Leninskii Kommunisticheskii Soiuz Molodezhi. Tsentralnyi Komitet. **VFOAT** Vokrug Sveta. (Dec. 1860)-. Periodical. Russian. mo. $79.95. **(Subscription address:** East View Publications Inc., 3020 Harbor Lane North, Suite 110, Minneapolis MN 55447.**)** **LC** G1; .V6.

LV
VOPROSY FIZICHESKOI GEOGRAFII LATVIISKOI SSR. Main/Corp Petera Stuckas Lavijas Valsts Universitate. Fizikas Geografijas Katedra. No. 1 (1972)-. Russian. Redaktsionno-Izdatelskii Otdel RPI, Ulitsa Lenina I, Riga 226047 Latvia. **LC** GB239.L3; R53a.
Desc: Information on physical geography.

US/1040-8541
VOYAGER INTERNATIONAL. [Voyag. int.]. **Added/Corp** Argonaut Enterprises. (198?)-. Periodical. English. mo. $38.00. Argonaut Enterprises Inc, PO Box 2777, Westport CT 06880. **Tel** (203)226-1647, FAX (203)846-2796. **DD** 910. Index available. **Bk Rev. Ad Acc.**

GW/0340-5141
VR. VERMESSUNGSWESEN UND RAUMORDNUNG. (VERMESSUNGSWESEN UND RAUMORDNUNG : VR.). [VR, Vermessungswes. Raumordn.]. **VFOAT** VR. Vol. 35, No. 1 (Jan. 1973)-. Academic Scholarly Publication. German. bm. DM104.00. Ferdinand Dummler Verlag, Postfach 1480, D 53004 Bonn Germany. **Tel** 011 49 228 223031. **ED** H. J. Meckenstock. **LC** TA501; .V4. **DD** 526.9. **[CCC]. Bk Rev. Ad Acc. Circ:** 1,500. ***Continues*** *Vermessungstechnische Rundschau.*
Desc: Covers geodesy, cartography, photogrammetric, real estate, cadastre, consolidation, data processing, and instruments for surveying.
Ind/Abst Bibliogr. Carto.; EMBASE.

US/0739-6538
WASHINGTON REMOTE SENSING LETTER. **See** Earth Sciences.

UK
WESSEX GEOGRAPHER. No. 1- 1960-. English. an. Student Union, University of Southampton, Department of Geography, Highfield Southampton S09 2DA England.

AT/0313-8860
WESTERN GEOGRAPHER. ***Ceased.*** Vol. 1 (197)-?. Periodical. English. an. Geographical Association Western Australia, Box 152, Nedlands Western Australia 6009 Australia.

CN/0315-2022
WESTERN GEOGRAPHICAL SERIES. Added/Corp University of Victoria. Dept. of Geography. Vol. 1 (1970)-. Monographic series. English. ir. Price varies per volume. University of Victoria Department of Geography, Box 3050, Victoria British Columbia, V8W 3P5 Canada. **Tel** (604)721-7342, telex 049-7222. **ED** Harold D. Foster. **Pr Rev. Circ:** 1,500 (ctrl).
Desc: Geography with emphasis on resource management, urban studies, and the Pacific rim (including Canada).
Ind/Abst Geogr. Abstr. Human Geogr. (?-?).

CN/1187-1121
WESTERN GEOGRAPHY. [West geogr.]. **Added/Corp** Canadian Association of Geographers. Western Division. Vol. 1, No. 1, Spring (1990)-. Periodical. English. Tantalus Research Ltd, 2405 Pine Street, PO Box 34248, Vancouver British Columbia V6J 4N8 Canada. **Tel** (604)876-6381. **DD** 910/.5. ***Continues*** *Occasional Papers in Geography (Vancouver, B.C.), 0576-4580.*

CN/0849-309X
WHERE ROCKY MOUNTAINS. [Where Rocky Mt.]. Spring/Summer 1990-. Periodical. English. qt. Westfalisches Archivamt, Warendorfer Strasse 24, 4400 Munster Germany. **DD** 917.11. ***Continues*** *Rocky Mountain Visitor, 0821-5146.*

AU/0083-9957
WIENER GEOGRAPHISCHE SCHRIFTEN. (1957)-. German. ir. Verlag Ferdinand Hirt, Widerhofergasse 8, A-1090 Vienna Austria.
Ind/Abst GeoRef.

AU/1017-0510
WIRTSCHAFTS-GEOGRAPHISCHE STUDIEN. (WIRTSCHAFTSGEOGRAPHISCHE STUDIEN.). [Wirtsch.-geogr. Stud.]. **Added/Corp** Osterreichische Gesellschaft fur Wirtschaftsraumforschung. (1977)-. Periodical. German (summaries and/or abstracts in English). sa. **LC** HC10; .W792.
Ind/Abst Geogr. Abstr. Human Geogr.; GeoRef.

US/0892-5224
WISCONSIN GEOGRAPHER. [Wis. geogr.]. **Added/Corp** Wisconsin Council for Geographic Education. Vol. 1 (Spring 1985)-. English. an. $5.00. Wisconsin Geographical Survey, Dept of Geography, University of Wisconsin, La Crosse WI 54601. **Tel** (608)785-8333. **DD** 977. ***Continues*** *Bulletin of the Wisconsin Council for Geographic Education.*

GW/0936-7195
WISSENSCHAFTLICHE MITTEILUNGEN. Added/Corp Akademie der Wissenschaften der DDR. Institut fuer Geographie und Geookologie. (19??)-. Periodical. German. ir ((2 issues)). $70.00. Akademie-Verlag GmbH, Muehlenstrasse 33 34, D 13162 Berlin Germany. **Tel** 011 49 30 47889300, FAX 011 49 30 47889357. **(Subscription address:** VCH Publishers Inc., 303 Northwest 12th Avenue, Journals Department, Deerfield FL 33442.**)** **LC** G1; .W56. **DD** 910.

UK
WORKING PAPER / SCHOOL OF GEOGRAPHY, UNIVERSITY OF LEEDS. Added/Corp University of Leeds. School of Geography. (19??)-. Monographic series. English. Price varies per volume.
Ind/Abst Geogr. Abstr. Phys. Geogr.; Geogr. Abstr. Human Geogr.; Int. Dev. Abstr.

UK/0951-6158
WORKS ISSUED BY THE HAKLUYT SOCIETY. Added/Corp Hakluyt Society. Vol. 1-100; 2nd Series No. 1 (1847)-. Monographic series. English. ir. Price varies per volume. Hakluyt Society, c/o The Map Library, British Library, Great Russell Street, London WCIB 3DG England. **Tel** 011 44 986 86359, FAX 011 44 986 868181. **LC** G161; .H2. **DD** 910.4.

US/0277-1527
WORLD FACTBOOK (WASHINGTON, D.C.). (THE WORLD FACTBOOK.). [World factbook]. 1981-. English. an. F335.00. National Technical Information Service - NTIS, Room 2027S, 5285 Port Royal Road, Springfield VA 22161. **Tel** (703)487-4630, (703)487-4660, (703)487-4650, FAX (703)321-8547, telex 89-9405. **LC** G122; .U56A. **DD** 910/.5. available on CD-ROM. ***Continues*** *National Basic Intelligence Factbook, 0098-2091.*

UK/0951-2195
WORLD MAGAZINE (LONDON, ENGLAND). ***Ceased.*** (WORLD MAGAZINE.). **VFOAT** World Magazine. Ceased with Issue for Jan./Feb. (1993). Periodical. English. mo. BBC Magazines, 5 Westminster Court, Hippley Street, Surrey GU22 9LG England. **Tel** 011 44 483747008. **LC** GF1; .W67. **DD** 910/.5. available on microfilm and microfiche from University Microfilms International (UMI). Documents available from UMI Article Clearinghouse.
Ind/Abst Gen. Period. Index (1989-1991); Mag. Index Plus (1989-); Newsp. Period. Abstr. (1989-); Mag. Index (1989-).

GW/0510-9833
WURZBURGER GEOGRAPHISCHE ARBEITEN. [Wurzbg. geogr. Arb.]. **Added/Corp** Bayerische Julius-Maximilians-Universitat Wurzburg. Geographisches Institut. Geographische Gesellschaft Wurzburg. (1953)-. Monographic series. German. ir. Price varies per volume. Geographisches Institut der Universitat Wurzburg, Am Hubland, D-97074 Wurzburg Germany. **Tel** 09 31 8 88-55-53, FAX 09 31 8 88-55-56. **ED** D. Bohn, H. Hagedorn, H. Jager, and H. G. Wagner. **LC** G58; .W8. **DD** 910. **CODEN** WBGAA9. **Circ:** 450 (ctrl). ***Continues*** *Frankische Studien.*
Desc: Contains topics of human and physical geography, with emphasis on drylands, Africa, and the Federal Republic of Germany.
Ind/Abst GeoRef.

UK/0308-1451
YEAR BOOK - THE ROYAL INSTITUTION OF CHARTERED SURVEYORS. Main/Corp Royal Institution of Chartered Surveyors. 1974/75-. English. an. £9.00. Thomas Skinner Directories, Windsor Court, East Grinstead House, East Grinstead West Sussex RH19 1XE England. **Tel** 0256 840366, telex 858540. **LC** TA501; .R62514. **DD** 624.

US/0066-9628
YEARBOOK - ASSOCIATION OF PACIFIC COAST GEOGRAPHERS. [Yearb., Assoc. Pac. Coast Geogr.]. **Main/Corp** Association of Pacific Coast Geographers. **VFOAT** Yearbook of the Association of Pacific Coast Geographers. Vol. 1 (1935)-. Monographic series. English. an. $15.00. Oregon State University Press, 101 Waldo Hall, Corvallis OR 97331. **Tel** (503)737-3166. **ED** Jo Alexander. **LC** F851; .A79. **DD** 910/.5. **CODEN** YAPGAJ. Index available. cum. index. **Pr Rev. Circ:** 1,000.
Desc: Collection of papers on varied geographical topics.
Ind/Abst Geogr. Abstr. Phys. Geogr.; Geogr. Abstr. Human Geogr.; GeoRef; Int. Dev. Abstr.

JA
YORAN - KOKURITSU BOSAI KAGAKU GIJUTSU SENTA. Main/Corp Kokuritsu Bosai Kagaku Gijutsu Senta, Tokyo. (19??)-. Periodical. Japanese. Kokuritsu Bosai Kagaku Gijutsu Senta, (National Research Center for Disaster Prevention), 3-chome, Tennodai, Sakura-mura, Ibaraki-Ken 305, Japan. **LC** GB5011.77; .K64a.

ZA
ZAMBIAN GEOGRAPHICAL JOURNAL. Added/Corp Zambia Geographical Association. No. 29/30 (1975)-. Periodical. English. ir. $10.00. Zambia Geographical Association, PO Box RW 287, Lusaka Zambia. **Tel** 213221. **ED** E. Shamilypa Kalapula. **LC** DT963.A2; Z35. **DD** 968.94/005. **Bk Rev. Ad Acc. Circ:** 500. ***Continues*** *Zambia Geographical Association. Magazine.*

GW/0044-2461
ZEITSCHRIFT FUER DEN ERDKUNDEUNTERRICHT. [Z. Erdkundeunterr.]. **Added/Corp** Germany (East). Ministerium fur Volksbildung. **VFOAT** Erdkundeunterricht. Vol. 1 (1949)-. Periodical. German. mo. DM44.00. Paedagogischer Zeitschriftenverlag GmbH, Postfach 269, D 10107 Berlin, Germany. **Tel** 011 49 30 20343431. **LC** G13; .Z4. **CODEN** ZERDAP. **Bk Rev.** ctrl circ.
Desc: Special methodic for teachers of geography.
Ind/Abst Bibliogr. Carto.; GeoRef.

GW/0372-8854
ZEITSCHRIFT FUER GEOMORPHOLOGIE. See Earth Sciences-Geology.

GW/0934-0351
ZEITSCHRIFT FUER PHOTOGRAMMETRIE UND FERNERKUNDUNG. **VFOAT** Photogrammetrie und Fernerkundung; BUL; Bildmessung und Luftbildwesen. Vol. 56 (Jan. 1988)-. Periodical. German (summaries and/or abstracts in English and French). bm. Herbert Wichmann Verlag GmbH, Postfach 4320, D 76028 Karlsruhe Germany. **Tel** 011 49 721 912-2025. **LC** TR693.A1; B5. ***Continues*** *Bildmessung und Luftbildwesen, 0006-2421.*

GW/0044-3751
ZEITSCHRIFT FUER WIRTSCHAFTSGEOGRAPHIE. [Z. Wirtsch.geogr.]. (Jan. 1957)-. Periodical. German (English). qt. DM106.00 (institutions), DM79.00 (individuals) Germany; DM107.00 (institutions), DM82.00 (individuals) other Europe; DM127.00 (institutions), DM100.00 (individuals) other. Buchenverlag, Postfach 900126, D-60441 Frankfurt Germany. **Tel** 011 49 611 394033. **LC** HF1021; .Z44. Index available. **Bk Rev. Ad Acc.**
Ind/Abst Coal Abstr.; Curr. Geogr. Publ. (199?-); Foreign Lang. Index; Geogr. Abstr. Human Geogr.; Int. Dev. Abstr.; PAIS Int. Print.

RU/0514-2989
ZEMLIA I LIUDI. (1958)-. Russian. wk. $99.95. B-71 Leninskii Prospekt 15, 117071 Moscow Russia. **(Subscription address:** East View Publications Inc., 3020 Harbor Lane North, Suite 110, Minneapolis MN 55447.**) LC** G1; .Z72.

●RU/0869-3382
ZEMLIA SIBIR. **Added/Corp** Sovet Mezhregionalnoi Assotsiatsii "Sibirskoe Soglashenie.". No. 1 (1992)-. Russian. bm.

XR/0375-6122
ZPRAVY GEOGRAFICKENO USTAVU CSAV. [Zpr. geogr. ust. CSAV]. **Main/Corp** Geograficky Ustav v Brne. (1962)-. Periodical. Czech. **LC** WMLC L 83/900. **CODEN** ZGUCAH. cum. index.
Ind/Abst Geogr. Abstr. Phys. Geogr.; Geogr. Abstr. Human Geogr.; GeoRef.

ABSTRACTING, BIBLIOGRAPHIES AND STATISTICS

BL
BIBLIOGRAFIA BRASILEIRA DO SEMI-ARIDO. Vol. 1-. Portuguese. Universidade Federal da Paraiba, Centro de Informacao do Semi-Arido Av Aprigio Veloso 882 58100, Campina Grande PB Brazil. **LC** Z6004.A7; B52; GB611. **DD** 016.9181/0954.

NE/0377-8975
BIBLIOGRAFIE VAN IN NEDERLAND VERSCHENEN KAARTEN. 1975-. Dutch. an. Koninklijke Bibliotheek, PO Box 90407, 2509 LK The Hague Netherlands. **LC** Z6027.N4; B53; GA921.
Desc: Part of the Dutch National Bibliography listing all cartographic materials published in the Netherlands, separately as well as enclosure or illustration in books and serials.

GW/0340-0409
BIBLIOGRAPHIA CARTOGRAPHICA. [Bibliogr. cartogr.]. **Added/Corp** Staatsbibliothek Preussischer Kulturbesitz. Deutsche Gesellschaft fuer Kartographie. Nr. 1 (1974)-. Abstracting/Indexing Service. German (English and French). an. $100.00. K.G. Saur Verlag KG, A Reed Reference Publishing Company, Part of Reed International PLC, Ortlerstrasse 8, D 81373 Munich Germany. **Tel** 011 49 89 769020, FAX 011 49 89 76902150, telex 5212067-SAUR-D. **LC** Z6021; .B48. ***Supersedes*** *Bibliotheca Cartographica.*
Desc: International documentation of categorized cartographical literature.
Ind/Abst Bibliogr. Carto.

US/0197-5889
BIBLIOGRAPHIC GUIDE TO MAPS AND ATLASES. [Bibliogr. guide maps atlas]. **Added/Corp** New York Public Library. Library of Congress. New York Public Library. Map Division. Dictionary Catalog of the Map Division. **VFOAT** Maps and Atlases. (1979)-. English. an. $335.00. Macmillan Publishing Company, 100 Front Street, Box 500, Riverside NJ 08075-7500. **Tel** (800)257-5755, (609)461-6500, FAX (609)461-7070. **LC** Z6028; .N58 suppl.; GA105.3. **DD** 016.912.

FR/0150-5998
BIBLIOGRAPHIE DE LA FRANCE. SUPPLEMENT 4. ATLAS, CARTES ET PLANS. ***Title Change.*** (BIBLIOGRAPHIE DE LA FRANCE. SUPPLEMENT IV, ATLAS, CARTES ET PLANS : NOTICES ETABLIES PAR LA BIBLIOTHEQUE NATIONALE.). [Bibliogr. Fr., Suppl. 4, Atlas, ct. plans]. **Added/Corp** Bibliotheque Nationale (France) Cercle de la Librairie (France). **VFOAT** Atlas, Cartes et Plans. Notices 77-1 A 77-128 (1977)-(19??). French. an. Cercle de la Librairie, 35 rue Gregoire de Tours, F-75279 Paris Cedex 06 France. **Tel** 011 33 1 43291000, FAX 011 33 1 43296895, telex LIFRAN 270 838. **LC** Z2165; .B573. **DD** 015.44. ***Continues in part*** *Bibliographie de la France. 1RE Partie, Bibliographie Officielle, 0335-5667.* ***Continued by*** *Bibliographie Nationale Francaise. Supplement IV, Atlas, Cartes et Plans.*

●FR
BIBLIOGRAPHIE NATIONALE FRANCAISE. ATLAS, CARTES ET PLANS : BIBLIOGRAPHIE ETABLIE PAR LA BIBLIOTHEQUE NATIONALE. **Added/Corp** Bibliotheque Nationale (France). **VFOAT** Atlas, Cartes et Plans. (1992)-. Bibliography. French. 3390.00F France; 4650.00F Canada; 3860.00F other. Mereau, 175 bd Anatole-France, BP 189, 93208 Saint-Denis Cedex France. **Tel** 011 48 13 38 58, FAX 011 48 13 09 08. **LC** Z2165; .B573. ***Continues*** *Bibliographie Nationale Francaise. Supplement IV, Atlas, Cartes et Plans, 1142-3293.*

US/0096-879X
CURRENT ANTARCTIC LITERATURE. [Curr. Antarct. lit.]. **Added/Corp** Library of Congress. Science and Technology Division. Cold Regions Bibliography Project. National Science Foundation. Office of Polar Programs. National Science Foundation (U.S.). Division of Polar Programs. No. 1 (Sept. 1972)-. Periodical. English. mo (12 issues). Free to qualified applicants (scientists and research libraries). National Science Foundation, 1800 G Street Northwest, Washington DC 20550. **Tel** (202)357-9859, (202)357-9498. **ED** Stuart G. Hibben. **LC** Z6005.P7; C87; G860. **DD** 016.910/09/167. **CODEN** CAALAN. Index available. **Circ:** 800 (ctrl). available on CD-ROM.
Desc: Contains current citations and abstracts of the Antarctic.
Ind/Abst GeoRef.

US/0011-3514
CURRENT GEOGRAPHICAL PUBLICATIONS. [Curr. geogr. publ.]. **Added/Corp** American Geographical Society of New York. University of Wisconsin--Milwaukee. Library. Golda Meir Library. Vol. 1, No. 1 (Jan. 1938)-. Abstracting/Indexing Service. English (French and German). Ten times a year. $70.00. University of Wisconsin at Milwaukee, American Geographical Society Collection, PO Box 399, AGS Collection, Milwaukee WI 53201. **Tel** (414)229-6282, (800)558-8993. **ED** Roman Drazniowsky and Susan Peschel. **LC** Z6009; .A47. **DD** 016.91. Index Available, published separately, free-automatically sent. cum. index. **Bk Rev. Ad Acc. Circ:** 900. available on microfilm and microfiche from University Microfilms International (UMI).
Desc: A bibliography covering the broad field of geography, earth sciences and related disciplines.
Ind/Abst Bibliogr. Carto.; Popul. Index.

UK/0953-9611
GEOGRAPHICAL ABSTRACTS. HUMAN GEOGRAPHY. **VFOAT** Human Geography. Vol. 1 (1989)-. Abstracting/Indexing Service. English. Twelve times a year. $671.00 The Americas; £450.00 other. Elsevier Geo Abstracts, An Imprint of Elsevier Science Ltd., The Boulevard, Langford Lane, Kidlington, Oxford OX5 1GB United Kingdom. **Tel** 011 44 865 843000, 011 44 865 843699, FAX 011 44 865 843010. **(Subscription address:** Elsevier Science Ltd. Oxford Fulfillment Centre, PO Box 800, Kidlington, Oxford OX5 1DX United Kingdom.**) ED** N. Davey, C. Lloyd. **LC** GF1; .G47. **DD** 304.2. **[CCC]**. Index available. **Bk Rev. Ad Acc. Circ:** 700. available on microfilm and microfiche from University Microfilms International (UMI); available on an online database. ***Formed by the union of*** *Geographical Abstracts. C, Economic Geography (1986), 0268-7895; Geographical Abstracts. D, Social and Historical Geography, 0268-7909* ***and*** *Geographical Abstracts. F, Regional and Community Planning, 0268-7925.*
Desc: A current awareness journal to the international literature on social, human and historical geography.
Ind/Abst Popul. Index.

UK/0954-0504
GEOGRAPHICAL ABSTRACTS : PHYSICAL GEOGRAPHY. **VFOAT** Physical Geography. Vol. 1 (1989)-. Abstracting/Indexing Service. English. Twelve times a year. $917.00 The Americas; £615.00 other. Elsevier Geo Abstracts, An Imprint of Elsevier Science Ltd., The Boulevard, Langford Lane, Kidlington, Oxford OX5 1GB United Kingdom. **Tel** 011 44 865 843000, 011 44 865 843699, FAX 011 44 865 843010. **ED** K. Clayton, A. Pitty, P. Davies, J. Cooper, J. Austin, M. Blakemore, D. Fairbairn. **LC** GB54.5; .G46. **DD** 910/.02. **CODEN** GAPGET. **[CCC]**. Index available. **Bk Rev. Ad Acc. Circ:** 750. available on microfilm and microfiche from University Microfilms International (UMI); available on an online database. ***Formed by the union of*** *Geographical Abstracts. A, Landforms and the Quaternary, 0268-7879; Geographical Abstracts. B, Climatology and Hydrology, 0268-7887; Geographical Abstracts. E, Sedimentology, 0268-7917* ***and*** *Geographical Abstracts. G, Remote Sensing, Photogrammetry, and Cartography, 0268-7933.*
Desc: A bibliographic reference journal of the physical earth sciences literature of the world.

NO
KARTKATALOG / NORGES GEOGRAFISKE OPPMALING. **Main/Corp** Norges Geografiske Oppmaling. Norwegian (summaries and/or abstracts in English). Norges Geografiske, Oppmaling Monserudveien, 3500 Hnefoss Norway. **LC** Z6027.N8; N8; GA981. **DD** 016.912/481. ***Continues*** *Norges Geografiske Oppmaling. Katalog Over Landkart.*

CARTOGRAPHY

US
ACSM / ASPRS CONVENTION PROCEEDINGS. (19??)-. Proceedings. English. ir. Price varies per volume. American Society for Photogrammetry and Remote Sensing / Maryland, 5410 Grosvenor Lane, Suite 210, Bethesda MD 20814-2160. **Tel** (301)493-0290, FAX (301)493-0208. **(Subscription address:** ASPRS Publishing, PO Box 1269, Evans City PA 16033.**)**

US/0747-9417
ACSM BULLETIN. [ACSM bull.]. **Added/Corp** American Congress on Surveying and Mapping. **VFOAT** A.C.S.M. Bulletin; Bulletin. **VAT** American Congress on Surveying and Mapping Bulletin. No. 75 (Nov. 1981)-. Bulletin. English. bm (6 issues). $75.00 US; $85.00 other. American Congress on Surveying and Mapping, 5410 Grosvenor Lane/Suite 100, Bethesda MD 20814-2122. **Tel** (301)493-0200, FAX (301)493-8245. **(Subscription address:** Allen Press, 1041 New Hampshire Street, PO Box 368, Lawrence, KS 66044; telephone: (913)843-1235; FAX: (913)843-1274**) ED** Gail Papa. **LC** TA501; .A6352. **DD** 526.9/05. **Bk Rev. Ad Acc. Circ:** 13,000. available on microfilm from University Microfilms International (UMI). ***Continues*** *American Congress on Surveying and Mapping. Bulletin - American Congress on Surveying and Mapping, 0097-6180.*
Desc: A comprehensive technical news magazine that covers the broad spectrum of surveying, mapping, geodesy and geographic and land information systems. Feature articles are written by experts in private practice, government and academia. Back issues are available and rental use of mailing list.
Ind/Abst Bibliogr. Carto.; Geogr. Abstr. Phys. Geogr.; GeoRef.

●US
ACSM TECHNICAL PAPERS / ACSM/ASPRS ANNUAL CONVENTION & EXPOSITION. **Main/Conf** SM/ASPRS Convention & Exposition. **Added/Corp** American Society for Photogrammetry and Remote Sensing. American Congress on Surveying and Mapping. **VFOAT** Technical Papers; ASPRS Technical Papers. (1993)-. English. American Society for Photogrammetry and Remote Sensing / Maryland, 5410 Grosvenor Lane, Suite 210, Bethesda MD 20814-2160. **Tel** (301)493-0290, FAX (301)493-0208. **LC** TA501; .A5122. ***Continues*** *ASPRS-ACSM Annual Convention. Technical Papers.*

●US/1070-8421
ANTIQUE MAP PRICE RECORD & HANDBOOK. (ANTIQUE MAP PRICE RECORD & HANDBOOK FOR ... / COMPILED AND EDITED BY JON K. ROSENTHAL.). [Antiq. map price rec. handb.]. **VFOAT** Antique Map Price Record and Handbook for ...; Antique Map Price Record. Vol. 11 (1993)-. English. an. $38.00. Jon Kimmel Rosenthal, PO Box 12, Amherst MA 01004. **Tel** (413)256-8900. **LC** GA197.3; .A57. **DD** 912/.075. ***Continues*** *Antique Maps, Sea Charts, City Views, Celestial Charts & Battle Plans, 0749-4971.*

US/0272-8532
BASE LINE (GOLDEN, COLO.). (BASE LINE : A NEWSLETTER OF THE MAP & GEOGRAPHY ROUNDTABLE.). [Base line]. **Added/Corp** Map & Geography Round Table (American Library Association). Vol. 1 No. 1 (1981)-. Newsletter. English. Six times a year. $15.00 US and Canada; $20.00 other. American Library Association / Illinois, Illinois State Library, 300 South Second, Springfield IL 62756. **Tel** (217)782-5823, FAX (217)782-4446. **ED** Pat Seavey (Editor's address: Women' Studies, University of Arizona, Douglass Building, Tucson, AZ 85721). **LC** Z692.M3; B28. **DD** 025. **Circ:** 450. ***Continues*** *Information Bulletin (Map & Geography Round Table (American Library Association)), 0272-2402.*
Desc: Contains activities of A.L.A./Map & Geography Round Table and other map librarian organizations as well as notices of new maps and books and other announcements.

GW/0340-0409
BIBLIOGRAPHIA CARTOGRAPHICA. See Geography-Abstracting, Bibliographies and Statistics.

US/0044-7943
BULLETIN / AMERICAN SOCIETY OF CARTOGRAPHERS. [Bull. - Am. Soc. Cartogr.]. **Added/Corp** American Society of Cartographers. (1965)-. Periodical. English. ir. American Society of Cartographers, PO Box 1493, Louisville KY 40201. **DD** 526. **CODEN** ACABBK.
Ind/Abst GeoRef.

CN/0840-9331
BULLETIN / ASSOCIATION OF CANADIAN MAP LIBRARIES AND ARCHIVES. [Bull. - Assoc. Can. Map Libr. Arch.]. **Added/Corp** Association of Canadian Map Libraries and Archives. **VFOAT** ACML Bulletin; Bulletin de l'ACC; ACMLA Bulletin; Bulletin de l'ACACC. **VAT** Bulletin - Association des Cartotheques et Archives Cartographiquesdu Canada. No. 66 (Mar. 1988)-. Bulletin. English (French). qt (Mar., Jun., Sep., Dec.). 50.00Can$ (includes membership). Association of Canadian Map Libraries and Archives, 395 Wellington Street, Ottawa Ontario K1A 0N3 Canada. **Tel** (613)996-7619. **LC** GA193.C3; A93b. **DD** 026.912/0971. ***Continues** Association of Canadian Map Libraries. Bulletin, 0318-2851.*
Ind/Abst Bibliogr. Carto.; Curr. Geogr. Publ. (199?-).

FR/0588-618X
BULLETIN DU COMITE FRANCAIS DE CARTOGRAPHIE. [Bull. Com. fr. cartogr.]. **Main/Corp** Comite Francais de Cartographie. (196?)-. Bulletin. French. qt. 240.00F. Comite Francais Cartographie, 138 Bis rue de Grenelle, F-75007 Paris France. **Tel** 33 1 45518107. **CODEN** CFCBA4. ***Continues** Bulletin du Comite Francaise de Techniques Cartographiques.*
Ind/Abst GeoRef.

UK
BULLETIN OF THE SOCIETY OF CARTOGRAPHERS, THE. **Added/Corp** Society of Cartographers. **VFOAT** SUC Bulletin. Vol. 24, Pt. 1 (1990)-. Bulletin. English. sa. £20.00. Society of Cartographers Geology Department, University of Cambridge Downing Place, Cambridge CB2 3EN England. **Tel** 011 44 223 330200. **LC** GA101.S62; A3. **DD** 526.8/05. ***Continues** Society of University Cartographers. Bulletin of the Society of University Cartographers, 0036-1984.*
Ind/Abst Geogr. Abstr. Phys. Geogr.

US/0036-1607
BULLETIN - SPECIAL LIBRARIES ASSOCIATION. GEOGRAPHY AND MAP DIVISION. See Geography.

UK
CARTOGRAPHIC ACTIVITIES IN THE UNITED KINGDOM, REPORT. **Main/Corp** British National Committee for Geography. Cartography Subcommittee. English. ir (issued every three to four years). Royal Society, 6 Carlton House Terrace, London SW1Y 5AG England. **Tel** 011 44 71 839 5561, FAX 071-976 1837, telex 917876 ROYAL G. **LC** GA791; .N38A. **DD** 526/.0941. ctrl circ. ***Continues** Cartographic Activity in Great Britain Report.*

UK/0008-7041
CARTOGRAPHIC JOURNAL, THE. [Cartogr. j.]. (1964)-. Periodical. English. sa. £25.00. British Cartographic Society, Science Park, Milton Road, Cambridge CB4 4FY England. **Tel** 011 44 223 420414, FAX 011 44 223 420044. **ED** D Fairbairn. **LC** GA101; .C33. **CODEN** CGJLA8. **[CCC]**. Index available. cum. index. **Bk Rev**. **Ad Acc**. **Pr Rev**. **Circ:** 2,000 (ctrl). Documents available from The Genuine Article.
Desc: Covers all cartographic subjects including topographic and thematic mapping and graphics. Automation and computerized mapping is a major subject. New literature and maps are reviewed.
Ind/Abst Bibliogr. Carto.; Curr. Contents Soc. Behav. Sci.; Geogr. Abstr. Phys. Geogr.; Geogr. Abstr. Human Geogr.; GeoRef; Middle East Abstr. Index; Res. Alert [Full Cov.]; Soc. Sci. Cit. Index [Full Cov.].

US/1048-9053
CARTOGRAPHIC PERSPECTIVES. (CARTOGRAPHIC PERSPECTIVES : BULLETIN OF THE NORTH AMERICAN CARTOGRAPHIC INFORMATION SOCIETY.). [Cartogr. perspect.]. **Added/Corp** North American Cartographic Information Society. Vol. 1, No. 1 (March 1989)-. Bulletin. English. Three times a year. $58.00 (institutions), $28.00 (individuals). NACIS Department of Geology, PO Box 413, University of Wisconsin Milwaukee, Milwaukee WI 53201. **Tel** (800)558-8993. **LC** GA101; .C334. **DD** 526/.05. ***Continues** Cartographic Information.*
Ind/Abst Geogr. Abstr. Phys. Geogr.; GeoRef.

CN/0317-7173
CARTOGRAPHICA (1980). (CARTOGRAPHICA.). [Cartographica]. Vol. 17, No. 1 (Spring 1980)-. Periodical. English (summaries and/or abstracts in French, German and Spanish). Four times a year. $90.00. University of Toronto Press, 5201 Dufferin Street, Downsview Ontario M3H 5T8 Canada. **Tel** (416)667-7781, (416)667-7782, FAX (416)667-7803. **ED** Bernard V. Gutsell. **LC** GA101; .C34. **DD** 526. **[CCC]**. Index available. cum. index. **Bk Rev**, (Qty: 30). **Circ:** 1,200 (ctrl). available on microfilm and microfiche from University Microfilms International (UMI). ***Formed by the union of** Canadian Cartographer, 0008-3127 **and** Cartographica, 0317-7173; **Absorbed** Discussion Paper Series.*
Desc: Publishes research papers on the latest development in computer cartography, cartographic communication and perception, and semantic cartography.
Ind/Abst AQUAREF; Bibliogr. Carto.; Can. Index; Geogr. Abstr. Phys. Geogr.; GeoRef; Int. Dev. Abstr.

SZ/1015-8480
CARTOGRAPHICA HELVETICA. **Added/Corp** Schweizerische Gesellschaft fur Kartographie. Arbeitsgruppe fur Kartengeschichte. No. 1 (Jan. 1990)-. Periodical. German. sa. 30.00F Switzerland; 34.00F other. Verlag Cartographica Helvetica, Untere Langmatt 9, CH 3280 Murten Switzerland. **Tel** 011 41 31 9632327. **LC** GA1021; .C37. **DD** 526/.09494. **Circ:** 1,000.
Ind/Abst Curr. Geogr. Publ. (199?-).

AT/0069-0805
CARTOGRAPHY. [Cartography]. **Added/Corp** Australian Institute of Cartographers. Vol. 1 (Dec. 1954)-. Periodical. English. sa (June and Dec.). 30.00Aus$ Australia; 40.00Aus$ other. Australian Institute of Cartography, PO Box 1292, Canberra Australian Capital Territory 2601 Australia. **Tel** 011 61 9 2223201, 011 61 9 2223486. **ED** D. Clarke. **LC** GA101; .C32. Index available (Free). **Bk Rev**. **Ad Acc**. **Pr Rev**. **Circ:** 2,200 (ctrl).
Desc: The art and science of cartography.
Ind/Abst AESIS Q.; Bibliogr. Carto.; Ecol. Abstr. (?-?); Geogr. Abstr. Phys. Geogr.; GeoRef; Middle East Abstr. Index.

US/1050-9844
CARTOGRAPHY AND GEOGRAPHIC INFORMATION SYSTEMS. [Cartogr. geogr. inf. syst.]. **Added/Corp** American Congress on Surveying and Mapping. Vol. 17, No. 1 (Jan. 1990)-. Periodical. English. qt. $85.00 US; $95.00 other. American Congress on Surveying and Mapping, 5410 Grosvenor Lane/Suite 100, Bethesda MD 20814-2122. **Tel** (301)493-0200, FAX (301)493-8245. **ED** Robert McMaster. **LC** GA101; .A49. **DD** 526/.05. **CODEN** CGISES. Index available. **Bk Rev**. **Ad Acc**. **Pr Rev**. **Circ:** 5,000. available on microfilm and microfiche from University Microfilms International (UMI). Documents available from Article Express International, The Genuine Article. ***Continues** American Cartographer, 0094-1689.*
Desc: Publishes articles of international interest on digital mapping and GIS, digital-image processing, interpretation of diverse data, and GIS infrastructure, management, and policy.
Ind/Abst Bibliogr. Carto.; Bioeng. Abstr.; Curr. Contents Soc. Behav. Sci.; Ei Page One; Eng. Index Annu.; Geogr. Abstr. Phys. Geogr.; GeoRef; Res. Alert [Full Cov.]; Soc. Sci. Cit. Index [Full Cov.].

CN/1183-2045
CARTOUCHE ENGLISH EDITION (CALGARY). (CARTOUCHE : THE OPERATIONAL PUBLICATION OF THE CANADIAN CARTOGRAPHIC ASSOCIATION). [Cartouche]. **Added/Corp** Canadian Cartographic Association. Ontario Institute of Chartered Cartographers. No. 1 (Spring 1991)-. Periodical. English (French). Four times a year (Mar., June, Sept., Dec.). 70.00Can$ (regular) Canada; 75.00Can$ (regular) other; 90.00Can$ (institutions) Canada; 95.00Can$ (institutions) others; 175.00Can$ (corporate) Canada; 180.00Can$ (corporate) others, (Comes with the Canadian Cartographic Association Membership). Canadian Cartographic Association, Geography Department, University of Calgary, Calgary Alberta T2N 1N4 Canada. **Tel** (403)220-4892, FAX (403)282-6561. **ED** Jim Britton (phone: (705)324-9144). **DD** 526/.06/071. **Bk Rev**. **Ad Acc**. **Circ:** 500 (ctrl).

CN/1183-2045
CARTOUCHE FRENCH EDITION (CALGARY). (CARTOUCHE : THE OPERATIONAL PUBLICATION OF THE CANADIAN CARTOGRAPHIC ASSOCIATION). [Cartouche]. **Added/Corp** Association Canadienne de Cartographie. Institut de l'Ontario des Cartographes Sous Charte. No. 1 (Spring 1991)-. Periodical. French (English). Four times a year (Mar., June, Sept., Dec.). 70.00Can$ (regular) Canada; 75.00Can$ (regular) other; 90.00Can$ (institutions) Canada; 95.00Can$ (institutions) others; 175.00Can$ (corporate) Canada; 180.00Can$ (corporate) others, (Comes with the Canadian Cartographic Association Membership). Canadian Cartographic Association, Geography Department, University of Calgary, Calgary Alberta T2N 1N4 Canada. **Tel** (403)220-4892, FAX (403)282-6561. **ED** Jim Britton (phone: (705)324-9144). **DD** 526/.06/071. **Bk Rev**. **Ad Acc**. **Circ:** 500 (ctrl).

US/0163-7347
CATALOG OF COPYRIGHT ENTRIES. FOURTH SERIES. PART 6. MAPS. See Copyright, Intellectual Property.

CN/0833-2045
CATALOGUE / MAPS ALBERTA. [Maps Alta. cat.]. **Main/Corp** Maps Alberta. (1986)-. Catalog. English. an. Free. Department of Forestry Lands & Wildlife, Bureau of Surveying and Mapping, Edmonton Alberta T5K 2M4 Canada. **Tel** (403)427-3590. **DD** 016.912/7123. ***Continues** Alberta. Bureau of Surveying and Mapping. Map Catalogue, 0833-2037.*

JA
CHIZU SENTA NYUSU. **Main/Corp** Nihon Chizu Senta. No. 1- Oct. 1972-. Periodical. Japanese. ¥1500. Nihon Chizu Senta, (Japan Map Center), 9-6, Aobadai 4 Chome, Meguroku, Tokyoto 153 Japan. **LC** GA1241; .N54A.

CN/0841-8233
CISM JOURNAL. ***Title Change.*** [CISM j.]. **Added/Corp** Canadian Institute of Surveying and Mapping. **VFOAT** Journal ACSGC; CISM Journal. **VAT** Canadian Institute of Surveying and Mapping Journal; Journal Association Canadienne des Sciences Geodesiques et Cartographiques. Vol. 42, No. 1 (Spring 1988)-Vol. 46, No. 4 (Winter 1992). Periodical. English (French; summaries and/or abstracts in French). qt. Canadian Institute of Surveying, Box 5378 Station F, Ottawa Ontario K2C 3C1 Canada. **LC** TA501; .C3. **DD** 526.9/05. **CODEN** CISJEV. ***Continues** Canadian Surveyor, 0008-5103. **Continued by** Geomatica.*
Ind/Abst Bibliogr. Carto.; Geogr. Abstr. Phys. Geogr.; Geol. Abstr.

AT
COMMONWEALTH OF AUSTRALIA NATIONAL REPORT. **Main/Corp** Australia. Division of National Mapping. English. 14.80Aus$ (per volume), 76.60Aus$ (per set). MAP Sales, Auslig, PO Box 2, Belconnen Australian Capital Territory 2616 Australia. **Tel** 61-62-526385. **ED** G Parkinson. **LC** QB275; .A85. **DD** 526/.05. ctrl circ.
Desc: Atlas of Australian resources in ten volumes. Three have been published others issued on completion; atlas of population and housing based on each quinquennial census and covering each capital city.

US/1074-5696
COMPASS & TAPE. (COMPASS & TAPE / N.S.S. SURVEY & CARTOGRAPHY SECTION.). [Compass tape]. **Added/Corp** National Speleological Society. Survey and Cartography Section. **VFOAT** Compass and Tape. Vol. 1, No. 1 (Summer 1983)-. Periodical. English. qt (seasonal). $4.00. NSS Survey & Cartography Section, 6304 Kaybro Street, Laurel MD 20707. **Tel** (301)725-5877. **ED** Thomas Kaye (phone: (703)379-8794). **DD** 910. **Bk Rev**, (Qty: 1-2). **Circ:** 175.
Desc: Information on cave surveying and mapping. Includes techniques, equipment, helpful hints, mapping standards, publications of interest, and computer applications.

●US
FGDC NEWSLETTER : A PUBLICATION OF THE FEDERAL GEOGRAPHIC DATA COMMITTEE. **Added/Corp** United States. Federal Geographic Data Committee. **VFOAT** Federal Geographic Data Committee Newsletter. Newsletter No. 1 (Spring 1993)-. Periodical. English. ir. Free. US Geological Survey / Virginia, 407 National Center, Reston VA 22092. **Tel** (703)648-4000, (703)648-6856. ***Continues** FGD Newsletter (United States. Federal Geographic Data Committee), 1055-8357.*

●US/1062-8444
FRONTERAS (ARLINGTON, TEX.). (FRONTERAS, CENTER FOR GREATER SOUTHWESTERN STUDIES AND THE HISTORY OF CARTOGRAPHY.). [Fronteras]. **Added/Corp** University of Texas at Arlington. Center for Greater Southwestern Studies and the History of Cartography. (1992)-. Periodical. English. sa. Center for the Greater Southwestern Studies and the History of Cartography, University of Texas at Arlington, PO Box 19497, Arlington TX 76019-0497. **DD** 979.

HU/0016-7118
GEODEZIA ES KARTOGRAFIA. [Geod. kartogr.]. **Added/Corp** Hungary. Allami Foeldmeresi es Terkepeszeti Hivatal. (1955)-. Periodical. Hungarian (table of contents in English, German and Russian). Six times a year. $20.00 Hungary; $40.00 others. Cartographia, PO Box 132, H 1443 Budapest Hungary. **Tel** 011 36 1 1634639, telex 226218 CARTO H. **LC** TA501; .G38. **CODEN** GEKGAS. Index available. **Bk Rev**. **Ad Acc**. **Circ:** 1,000 (ctrl).
Desc: Scientific journal in Hungarian on geodesy, cartography and cadastral records.
Ind/Abst Bibliogr. Carto.; Energy Res. Abstr. (Feb. 1983-); Geogr. Abstr. Phys. Geogr.; GeoRef.

RU/0016-7126
GEODEZIIA I KARTOGRAFIJA. (GEODEZIIA I KARTOGRAFIIA.). [Geod. kartogr.]. **Added/Corp** Soviet Union. Glavnoe Upravlenie Geodezii i Kartografii. (1956)-. Periodical. Russian. mo. $105.00. Izdatelstvo Nedra, 3 Pl Belorusskogo Vakzala, 125047 Moscow Russia. **Tel** 250-52-55. **(Subscription address:** East View Publications Inc., 3020 Harbor Lane North, Suite 110, Minneapolis MN 55447.**)** **LC** QB275; .G45. **CODEN** GZKGA5. Index available.
Ind/Abst Bibliogr. Carto.; GeoRef; Int. Aerosp. Abstr.

PL/0016-7134
GEODEZJA I KARTOGRAFIA. (GEODEZJA I KARTOGRAFIA; KWARTALNIK NAUKOWY.). **Added/Corp** Komitet Geodezji PAN. Vol. 1 (1952)-. Periodical. Polish (summaries and/or abstracts in French and Russian; table of contents in Russian and French). qt. $36.00. **(Subscription address:** ARS Polona, PO Box 1001, 00068 Warsaw Poland.**)** **LC** QB275; .G46. **CODEN** GEJKAZ. available on microfilm.
Ind/Abst Bibliogr. Carto.

AT/0810-6185
GEOLOGICARTOGRAPHY. [Geologicartography]. (1960)-. Periodical. English. Twice a year (Jan. & July). Free. Geologicartography / Department of Mining & Energy, c/o K Sodd Energy, 140 Bourke Street, Melbourne Victoria 3000 Australia. **LC** QE36; .G46. **DD** 550/.2/22.
Ind/Abst GeoRef.

●CN/1195-1036
GEOMATICA. **Added/Corp** Canadian Institute of Geomatics. Vol. 47, No. 1 (Spring 1993)-. Periodical. English. qt. 150.00Can$. Canadian Institute of Geomatics, Box 5378, Station F, Ottawa, Ontario K2C 3J1 Canada. **Tel** (613)224-9851, FAX (613)224-9577. **LC** TA501; .C5. Index available. cum. index. ***Continues*** *CISM Journal, 0841-8233.*
Desc: Covering photogrammetry, cartography, engineering, and mining surveying, photo-interpretation and remote sensing, land surveying, geodesy and control surveying, and hydrography.

US/1045-4918
GREATER LOS ANGELES 3-D MAP. **VFOAT** Greater Los Angeles Three Dimensional Map. (1991)-. Periodical. English. Action Marketing Maps Corporation, 2535 West 237th Street, Torrence CA 90505.

US
HAMMOND CITATION WORLD ATLAS. ***Ceased.*** (19??)-(19??). Hammond Inc, 515 Valley Street, Maplewood NJ 07040. **Tel** (800)526-4953, (201)763-6000, FAX (201)763-7658.

US
HAMMOND ROAD ATLAS AMERICA. English. an. $5.95. Hammond Inc, 515 Valley Street, Maplewood NJ 07040. **Tel** (800)526-4953, (201)763-6000, FAX (201)763-7658.

US
HAMMOND ROAD ATLAS & VACATION GUIDE. English. an. $2.95. Hammond Inc, 515 Valley Street, Maplewood NJ 07040. **Tel** (800)526-4953, (201)763-6000, FAX (201)763-7658.

US
ILLINOIS MAPNOTES. **VFOAT** Illinois Map Notes. Issue No. 1 (June 1981)-. Periodical. English. sa. Laboratory for Cartography and Spatial Analysis, Department of Geography, Northern Illinois University, Dekalb IL 60115.

UK/0308-5694
IMAGO MUNDI (LYMPNE). (IMAGO MUNDI.). [Imago mundi]. **Added/Corp** International Society for the History of Cartography. **VFOAT** Imago Mundi. Vol. 1- (1935)-. English (German and French). an. £40.00. Imago Mundi Ltd, 26 Lucastes Road Haywards Heath, West Sussex PH16 1JW England. **Tel** 44-444-45354. **ED** E M J Campbell. **LC** GA1; .I6. **DD** 912.05. cum. index. **Bk Rev**, (Qty: 20). **Ad Acc. Circ:** 500+.
Desc: Articles and news connected with the study of the history of cartography, including map facsimiles, bibliographies, and reviews.
Ind/Abst Bibliogr. Carto.; Geogr. Abstr. Phys. Geogr.; GeoRef.

FR/0396-5880
INTERGEO BULLETIN. ***Ceased.*** [Intergeo bull.]. Vol. 10 No. 41 (1976)-?. Bulletin. French. qt. CNRS - Intergeo, 191 rue Saint Jacques, 75005 Paris France. **Tel** 011 33 1 46337431, 011 33 1 43297993, FAX 011 33 1 43 29 6529. Index available. cum. index. **Ad Acc. Circ:** 320 (ctrl). ***Continues*** *Intergeo.*
Ind/Abst Bibliogr. Carto.; GeoRef.

UK
INTERNATIONAL MAPS AND ATLASES IN PRINT. (1974)-. English. ir. R R Bowker, A Reed Reference Publishing Company, Part of Reed International PLC, PO Box 31, 121 Chanlon Drive, New Providence NJ 07974. **Tel** (908)464-6800, (800)521-8110, FAX (908)665-6688, telex 138-755.

NE
KARTOGRAFISCH TIJDSCHRIFT. **Added/Corp** Nederlandse Vereninging voor Kartografie. Vol. 1 (1975)-. Periodical. Dutch. Four times a year. Fl94.34 Netherlands; Fl141.51 other. Nederlandse Vereniging voor Kartographie, Postbus 590, 2501 CN Hague Netherlands. **Tel** 011 31 70 339 3361. **LC** GA101; .K33. ***Supersedes*** *Nederlands Aardrijkskundig Genootschap. Kartografische Sectie. Kaartbulletin.*
Ind/Abst Curr. Geogr. Publ. (199?-); Geogr. Abstr. Phys. Geogr.; Geogr. Abstr. Human Geogr.; GeoRef.

GW/0022-9164
KARTOGRAPHISCHE NACHRICHTEN. [Kartogr. Nachr.]. **Added/Corp** Deutsche Gesellschaft fur Kartographie. (March 1951)-. Periodical. German. Six times a year (Feb., Apr., June, Aug., Oct., Dec.). DM68.00. Kirschbaum Verlag, Siegfriedstr 28, Postfach 210209, D 53157 Bonn Germany. **Tel** 011 49 228 954530. **LC** GA101; .K35. **CODEN** KANAA7. **[CCC].**
Ind/Abst Bibliogr. Carto.; GeoRef.

UK/0140-427X
MAP COLLECTOR, THE. [Map collect.]. **VFOAT** M. No. 8 (Sept. 1979)-. Periodical. English. Four times a year (Mar., June, Sept., Dec.). £30.00 UK and Eire; £35.00 other. Map Collector Publications, 48 High Street, Tring Hertfordshire HP23 5AE England. **Tel** 11 44 442824977, FAX 11 44 296623398. **ED** Valerie G. Scott. **LC** GA192; .M18. **DD** 912/.05. Index available. cum. index. **Bk Rev**, (Qty: 4). **Ad Acc**, **Adv Mgr:** Ben Lane. **Circ:** 3,000. ***Continues*** *M.*
Desc: Includes articles by experts on the history of cartography from earliest times to the nineteenth century. Also news, book reviews, auction results and classified advertisements.
Ind/Abst Am. Hist. Life (1989-); Bibliogr. Carto.; Geogr. Abstr. Phys. Geogr.; Geogr. Abstr. Human Geogr.; Ref. Sources.

US/1065-6324
MAP REPORT (KANKAKEE, ILL.), THE. (THE MAP REPORT / INTERNATIONAL MAP DEALERS ASSOCIATION.). [Map rep.]. **Added/Corp** International Map Dealers Association. **VFOAT** IMDA Newsletter. (1989)-. Periodical. English. mo. $75.00 associates & libraries; $150.00 map dealers & manufacturers. International Map Dealers Association, PO Box 1789, Kankakee IL 60901. **Tel** (815)939-4627, FAX (815)933-8320. **LC** Z286.M3; I58. **DD** 912. ***Continues*** *Newsletter (International Map Dealers Association).*

US/0085-0624
MAP SERIES (TALLAHASSEE, FLA.). (MAP SERIES.). [Map ser.]. **Main/Corp** Florida. Bureau of Geology. Vol. 1 (1956)-. Monographic series. English. ir. Price varies per volume. Department of Natural Resources / Tallahassee Florida, 903 West Tennessee Street, Tallahassee FL 32304. **Tel** (904)488-1555. **DD** 557. **CODEN** MSFGDY.
Ind/Abst GeoRef.

US/0196-0881
MAPLINE. **Added/Corp** Hermon Dunlap Smith Center for the History of Cartography. No. 1, (Mar. 1976)-. Periodical. English. qt (Mar., June, Sept., Dec.). $8.00 North America; $10.00 other. Newberry Library, 60 West Walton Street, Chicago IL 60610. **Tel** (312)943-9090 ext. 472. **ED** James Akerman. **LC** GA201; .H46a. **DD** 912/.05. Index available. **Bk Rev. Circ:** 700.
Desc: Journal about the history of cartography and many facets of maps, such as discovery, spatial analysis and history as shown on maps.
Ind/Abst Bibliogr. Carto.; Geogr. Abstr. Phys. Geogr.; Geogr. Abstr. Human Geogr.

US
MAPLINE. SPECIAL NUMBER. **Added/Corp** Hermon Dunlap Smith Center for the History of Cartography. **VFOAT** Mapline. Special No. (Mar. 1978)-. Monographic series. English. qt. Price varies per volume. Newberry Library, 60 West Walton Street, Chicago IL 60610. **Tel** (312)943-9090 ext. 472. Index available. cum. index. **Bk Rev. Pr Rev. Circ:** 1,000 (ctrl).
Desc: Journal about the history of cartography and many facets of maps, such as discovery, spatial analysis and history as shown on maps.

FR/0764-3470
MAPPEMONDE. [Mappemonde]. **VFOAT** Mappe Monde. Vol. 1 (1986)-. Periodical. French (English). qt. 290.00F (institutions), 210.00F (individuals) France; 300.00F (institutions), 220.00F (individuals) other. Groupement d'Interet Public Reclus, 17 rue Abbe' l'Epe'e, Montpellier F3400 France. **Tel** 011 33 67 724610, FAX 011 33 67 726404. **LC** GA101; .M37. **DD** 526/.05.
Ind/Abst Geogr. Abstr. Phys. Geogr.; Geogr. Abstr. Human Geogr.; Int. Dev. Abstr.

UK/0954-7126
MAPPING AWARENESS. **See** Computers.

US/0749-3878
MAPPING SCIENCES AND REMOTE SENSING. [Mapp. sci. remote sens.]. **Added/Corp** American Congress on Surveying and Mapping. American Society of Photogrammetry. American Geophysical Union. Vol. 21, No. 1 (Jan./March 1984)-. Periodical. English (translations available in Russian and Undetermined). qt. $314.00 US; $345.00 other, except Japan. V. H. Winston & Sons Inc., 7961 Eastern Avenue, Suite 202A, Silver Spring MD 20910. **Tel** (301)587-3356. **(Subscription address:** Bellwether Publishing, Ltd, 8640 Guilford Road, Suite 200, Columbia MD 21046.**)** **ED** Joel Morrison. **LC** QB275; .M35. **DD** 526/.05. **Circ:** 200 (ctrl). ***Continues*** *Geodesy, Mapping and Photogrammetry, 0361-4433.*
Desc: Leading journal, publishing up-to-date research papers in remote sensing, cartography, photogrammetry and geodesy by Soviet and European authors. Includes commentaries.
Ind/Abst Bibliogr. Carto.; Ecol. Abstr.; Fish Rev.; For. Abstr.; Geogr. Abstr. Phys. Geogr.; Geogr. Abstr. Human Geogr.; Geol. Abstr.; GeoRef; Int. Dev. Abstr.; J. Plan. Lit.; Soils Fert.; Wildl. Rev.

US/0278-9655
MAPS AND PUBLICATIONS ... PRICE LIST. **VFOAT** Price List, Maps and Publications. English. Kentucky Commerce Cabinet Map Sales, 133 Holmes Street, Frankfort KY 40601. **LC** Z6027.U5; M36; GA426. **DD** 016.912769.

US/0275-8083
MAPS ON FILE. [Maps file]. **Added/Corp** Facts on File, Inc. (1981)-. English. an. $165.00 (basic volume & first year's update); $40.00 (update only). Facts on File Publications, 460 Park Avenue South, New York NY 10016. **Tel** (212)683-2244, (800)322-8755, FAX (212)683-3633, telex 238 552 FACTS UR. **(Subscription address:** CCH Editions Ltd., Tax Business Law Publications, Telford Road Bicester, Oxfordshire OX6 0XD England.**)**

US/1040-7421
MERIDIAN - MAP & GEOGRAPHY ROUND TABLE (AMERICAN LIBRARY ASSOCIATION). (MERIDIAN.). [Meridian - Map Geogr. Round Table (Am. Libr. Assoc.)]. **Added/Corp** Map & Geography Round Table (American Library Association). No. 1 (1989)-. Periodical. English. Twice a year. $25.00 US; $30.00 other. American Library Association / Arizona, University of Arizona, Main Library / c/o C. Kollen, Tucson AZ 85721. **Tel** (602)621-4312, FAX (602)621-9733. **ED** Charles Seavey, University of Arizona, Graduate Library School, 1515 East 1st Street, Tucson, AZ 85721; Telephone: (602)621-3957. **LC** Z692.M3; M47. **DD** 026.91205. **Bk Rev. Ad Acc**, **Adv Mgr:** David Cobb, **Tel** (617) 495-2417. **Pr Rev. Circ:** 700.
Desc: Advances the organization and dissemination of cartographic, geographic, and remote sensing information collections. It also describes and documents the trends and issues in cartographic and geographic librarianship.
Ind/Abst Libr. Lit. (1991-).

GW/0469-4244
NACHRICHTEN AUS DEM KARTEN-UND VERMESSUNGSWESEN. REICHE II. **Added/Corp** Institut fur Angewandte Geodasie (Deutsches Geodatisches Forschungsinstitut). **VFOAT** Contributions to Geodesy, Photogrammetry and Cartography. No. 43 (1985)-. English (summaries and/or abstracts in French and German). Institut fur Angewandte Geodasie, Stuffenbergstrate 7113, W1000 Berlin 30 Germany. ***Continues*** *Informations Relative to Cartography and Geodesy. Series II: Translations.*

GW
NACHRICHTEN DER NIEDERSACHSISCHEN VERMESSUNGS- UND KATASTERVERWALTUNG. **Added/Corp** Saxony, Lower. Ministerium des Innern. Referat Vermessungs- und Katasterwesen. (19??)-. German. qt. DM12.50. Nieders Landesverwaltungsamt, Landesvermessung Warmbuechenkamp 2, D 30159 Hannover Germany. **Tel** 0511 36 73 288, FAX 0511 36 73 540. **LC** LAW. **DD** 346/.4359/0432. Index available. cum. index. **Bk Rev. Circ:** 1,700 (ctrl).
Desc: Informs about practical solutions and further development in the fields of surveying, mapping, cadastre, valuation of property and management.

NZ/0110-6007
NEW ZEALAND CARTOGRAPHY AND GEOGRAPHIC INFORMATION SYSTEMS : THE JOURNAL OF THE NEW ZEALAND CARTOGRAPHIC SOCIETY. **Added/Corp** New Zealand Cartographic Society. **VFOAT** NZ Cartography and GIS. Vol. 21, No. 1 (1991)-. Periodical. English. Twice a year (June & Dec.). 33.00NZ$. New Zealand Cartographic Society, PO Box 12454, Thordon, Wellington New Zealand. **Tel** 011 64 4 4958495, FAX 011 64 4 4958450. **ED** B. K. Bradley. **LC** GA101; .N48. **DD** 526/.05. **[CCC].** Index available. cum. index. **Bk Rev. Circ:** 200. ***Continues*** *New Zealand Cartographic Journal, 0110-6007.*

US/0364-7064
NEWSLETTER / NATIONAL CARTOGRAPHIC INFORMATION CENTER. ***Ceased.*** **Added/Corp** National Cartographic Information Center. Geological Survey (U.S.). No. 6 (Summer 1977)-(19??). Newsletter. English. ir. US Geological Survey / Denver, Federal Center Box 25425, Denver CO 80225. **Tel** (703)648-6896. **LC** GA108.7; .N37a. **DD** 912/.05. **Bk Rev. Circ:** 5,000 (ctrl). ***Continues*** *National Cartographic Information Center Newsletter, 0749-5781.*
Desc: Newsletter on products, services, information on mapping, geographic digital data and remote sensing from USGS National Mapping Division.

US/0278-3835
OCCASIONAL PAPER / WESTERN ASSOCIATION OF MAP LIBRARIES. [Occas. pap. - West. Assoc. Map Libr.]. **Main/Corp** Western Association of Map Libraries. **Added/Corp** Western Association of Map Libraries. No. 1 (1973)-. Monographic series. English. ir. Price varies per volume. Western Association of Map Libraries, c/o Richard E. Soares, PO Box 1667, Provo UT 84603. **Tel** (801)377-1240, FAX (801)378-3221. **ED** Stanley D. Stevens. **Circ:** 350.
Desc: Occasional papers related to map collections in libraries and archives.
Ind/Abst GeoRef.

US/0254-5799
PAPERS PRESENTED AT THE ... TECHNICAL CONFERENCE ON OCEANOGRAPHIC CARTOGRAPHY. See Earth Sciences-Oceanography.

US/1046-9540
PARK CITY MAIN STREET MAP. (1990)-. Periodical. English. mo. $12.00. Modern Media Publishing Inc, 2870 East 3300 South, Salt Lake City UT 84109.

UK/0275-8768
PROGRESS IN CONTEMPORARY CARTOGRAPHY. [Prog. contemp. cartogr.]. Vol. 1-1980-. English. ir. John Wiley & Sons Ltd., Baffins Lane, Chichester West Sussex PO19 1UD England. **Tel** 0243 779777, FAX 0243 776128 BTG:JWP001, telex 86290 WIBOOKG. **(Subscription address:** North, South and Central America/ John Wiley & Sons, Inc., Subscription Department, 605 Third Avenue, New York, NY 10158-0012, USA; telephone: (212)850-6645; FAX: (212)850-6021**)**

US/0095-3776
REPORT - TEXAS MAPPING ADVISORY COMMITTEE. Main/Corp Texas Mapping Advisory Committee. English. PO Box 13087, Capitol Station, Austin TX 78711. **LC** GA452; .T48A. **DD** 526/.09764.

MX/0080-2085
REVISTA CARTOGRAFICA. [Rev. cartogr.]. **Added/Corp** Pan American Institute of Geography and History. Commission on Cartography. No. 1 (1952)-. Spanish (English and French). Twice a year. $36.00 (one year), $69.00 (two years) Western Hemisphere; $42.00 (one year), $81.00 (two years) other. Instituto Panamericano de Geographico Historia, APDO 18879 Secretaria General, 11870 Mexico DF Mexico. **Tel** 011 52 5 2775888, 011 52 5 2775791, FAX 011 52 5 2716172. **LC** GA101; .P323. **CODEN** RECAAN. Index available. **Circ:** 600.
Desc: Cartographic techniques and surveying.
Ind/Abst Geogr. Abstr. Phys. Geogr. (?-?); Geol. Abstr.; GeoRef.

PO/0870-9351
REVISTA (INSTITUTO GEOGRAFICO E CADASTRAL (PORTUGAL)). (REVISTA / INSTITUTO GEOGRAFICO E CADASTRAL.). [Rev. Inst. Geogr. Cadastr.]. **Added/Corp** Instituto Geografico e Cadastral (Portugal). **VFOAT** Revista do Instituto Geografico e Cadastral. No. 1 (Dec. 1981)-. Periodical. Portuguese (summaries and/or abstracts in English). ir. Price varies. Instituto Geografico e Cadastral, Largo da Estrela, 1200 Lisbon Portugal. **Tel** 011 351 1 609925. **LC** G1; .R36. **DD** 910/.5. **Circ:** 1,000 (ctrl).
Desc: Main themes of the articles include geodesy, cartography, photogrammetry, astronomy, rustic cadastre and history.
Ind/Abst GeoRef.

CN/1184-1885
REVUE DE CARTO-QUEBEC. [Rev. Carto-Que.]. **Added/Corp** Association Quebecoise de Cartographie. **VFOAT** Carto-Quebec. Vol. 2, No 1 (1981)-. Periodical. French. sa. Free to members. Carto-Quebec CEGEP de Limoilou dep de Cartographie, CP 1400, Quebec Quebec G1K 7H3 Canada. **DD** 526/.06/0714. ***Continues** Carto-Quebec, 0228-4030.*

●IT
RIVISTA DEL DIPARTIMENTO DEL TERRITORIO. Added/Corp Italy. Dipartimento del Territorio. Vol. 1 No. 1 (1993)-. Periodical. Italian. Three times a year. L56000 Italy; L70000 others. Istituto Poligrafico Zecca Stato, Piazza Verdi 10, 00198 Rome Italy. **Tel** 011 39 6 85082307, 011 39 6 85082221. **LC** HD671; .A47. ***Continues** Rivista del Catasto e dei Servizi Tecnici Erariali, 0373-367x.*

SA
SOUTH AFRICAN JOURNAL OF GEO INFORMATION. (19??)-. English. sa. $18.00. South African Society for Photogrammetry Remote Sensing and Cartography, PO Box 69, Newlands 7725 Republic South Africa. **Tel** 011 27 21 6854070. ***Continues** South African Journal of Photogrammetry, Remote Sensing, and Cartograhpy.*

SA
SOUTH AFRICAN JOURNAL OF PHOTOGRAMMETRY, REMOTE SENSING, AND CARTOGRAPHY. *Title Change.* **Added/Corp** South African Society for Photogrammetry, Remote Sensing, and Cartography. **VFOAT** Suid-Afrikaanse Tydskrif vir Fotogrammetrie, Afstandswaarneming en Kartografie. Vol. 13, No. 1 (Dec. 1981)-(19??). Periodical. English. sa. South African Society for Photogrammetry Remote Sensing and Cartography, PO Box 69, Newlands 7725 Republic South Africa. **Tel** 011 27 21 6854070. ***Continues** South African Journal of Photogrammetry. **Continued by** South African Journal of Geo Information.*
Ind/Abst Geogr. Abstr. Phys. Geogr.

GW/0178-9902
SPECULUM ORBIS. (1985)-. Periodical. German. Twice a year. DM54.00 Europe; DM60.00 others. Verlag Dietrich Pfaehler, Berliner Strasse 37, D 97616 Bad Neustadt Germany. **Tel** 011 49 9771 8142.

US/1052-2905
SURVEYING AND LAND INFORMATION SYSTEMS. [Surv. land inf. syst.]. **Added/Corp** American Congress on Surveying and Mapping. Vol. 50, No. 1 (Mar. 1990)-. Periodical. English. qt. $85.00 US; $95.00 other. American Congress on Surveying and Mapping, 5410 Grosvenor Lane/Suite 100, Bethesda MD 20814-2122. **Tel** (301)493-0200, FAX (301)493-8245. **ED** James K Crossfield. **LC** TA501; .A6436. **DD** 526.9/05. **CODEN** SLISEZ. **Bk Rev. Ad Acc. Pr Rev. Circ:** 10,000. available on microfilm and microfiche from University Microfilms International (UMI). Documents available from Article Express International. ***Continues** Surveying and Mapping, 0039-6273.*
Desc: Deals with technical papers in surveying and related fields of geodesy.
Ind/Abst Appl. Sci. Technol. Index; Bibliogr. Carto.; Curr. Geogr. Publ. (199?-); Ei Page One; Eng. Index Annu.; Geogr. Abstr. Phys. Geogr.; Geogr. Abstr. Human Geogr.; GeoRef; Highw. Res. Abstr.; Int. Aerosp. Abstr.

US
TECHNICAL PAPERS. Main/Conf SM-ASPRS Fall Convention. **Added/Corp** American Congress on Surveying and Mapping. American Society for Photogrammetry and Remote Sensing. **VFOAT** ACSM-ASPRS Fall Convention Technical Papers. (1990)-. English. American Society for Photogrammetry and Remote Sensing / Virginia, 210 Little Falls Street, Falls Church VA 22046-4398. **Tel** (703)534-6617, FAX (703)533-9614. **LC** TA502; .A476. ***Formed by the union of** ACSM Technical Papers **and** ASPRS Technical Papers.*
Ind/Abst Civ. Struct. Eng. Abstr.; Environ. Eng. Abstr.; Manuf. Process Eng. Abstr.; Mater. Sci. Eng. Abstr.

US
TECHNICAL PAPERS / ASPRS-ACSM ANNUAL CONVENTION. *Title Change.* **Main/Conf** PRS-ACSM Annual Convention. **Added/Corp** American Congress on Surveying and Mapping. American Society for Photogrammetry and Remote Sensing. (1986)-(1992). English. an. American Society for Photogrammetry and Remote Sensing / Maryland, 5410 Grosvenor Lane, Suite 210, Bethesda MD 20814-2160. **Tel** (301)493-0290, FAX (301)493-0208. **LC** TR693; .A85a. **DD** 526.9/05. **CODEN** TPACEK. Index available. cum. index. **Circ:** 5,000. Documents available from Article Express International. ***Formed by the union of** American Congress on Surveying and Mapping. Meeting. Technical Papers ... Annual Meeting ACSM **and** American Society of Photogrammetry. Meeting. Technical Papers ... Annual Meeting, ASP. **Continued by** ACSM/ASPRS Convention & Exposition. ACSM Technical Papers.*
Desc: Technical papers presented at meetings. Topics include photogrammetry, remote sensing, cartography and surveying.
Ind/Abst Ei Page One; Eng. Index Annu.; Mech. Eng. Abstr.; Soils Fert.; Solid State Supercond. Abstr.

AT/0314-657X
THEMATIC MAPPING BULLETIN. [Them. mapp. bull.]. **Main/Corp** Australia. Division of National Mapping. Bulletin. English. Map Sales, Division of NATMAP, PO Box 31, Belconnen Australian Capital Territory Australia. **Tel** 011 61 62 527911. **LC** GA1682; .D57B. **DD** 016.912/.94.

CC
TSE HUI HSUEH PAO. Added/Corp Chung-kuo Tse Hui Hsueh Hui. **VFOAT** Acta Geodetica et Cartographica Sinica; Chinese Journal of Geodesy and Cartography. (19??)-. Periodical. Chinese (summaries and/or abstracts in English, German and Russian). qt. $12.96. **(Subscription address:** China International Book Trading Corporation, PO Box 399, Library Service Department, Beijing 100044 People's Republic of China.**)** **LC** QB275; .T74. **CODEN** CEXUER. ***Continues** Tse Liang Chih tu Hsueh Pao.*

US/0084-1471
WORLD CARTOGRAPHY. [World cartogr.]. **Added/Corp** United Nations. Dept. of Technical Cooperation for Development. United Nations. Dept. of Economic and Social Affairs. United Nations. Dept. of Social Affairs. Vol. 1, (1951)-. Government Publication. English. ir. price varies pe volume. United Nations Publications, 2 United Nations Plaza, Room DC2 0853, Department 007C, New York NY 10017. **Tel** (212)963-8303, (800)253-9646. **LC** GA101; .W6. **DD** 526. **CODEN** WCARB4.
Desc: Surveys the status of world topographic and cadastral mapping. Contains statistics, analyses and reports on recent and projected activities in cartography and toponomy.
Ind/Abst Bibliogr. Carto.; GeoRef.

US/1040-1687
WORLD MAP DIRECTORY, THE. [World map dir.]. (1989)-. Directory. English. an. $29.95 (92/93 latest edition). Map Link, 25 East Mason, Santa Barbara CA 93101. **Tel** (805)965-4402. **LC** Z6028; .W67; GA300. **DD** 016.912.

US/0147-9784
YEAR BOOK COLOR ATLAS SERIES. (19??)-. Monographic series. English. ir. Price varies per volume. Mosby Year Book Inc., 11830 Westline Industrial Drive, St Louis MO 63146. **Tel** (800)325-4177, (314)872-8370, FAX (314)432-1380, telex 44-2402. **LC** UNC.

GIFTS, TOYS

US/0148-0243
AMERICAN GO JOURNAL, THE. See Recreation, Leisure-Games and Amusements.

US/0742-0420
ANTIQUE TOY WORLD. (ANTIQUE TOY WORLD : THE MAGAZINE FOR TOY COLLECTORS AROUND THE WORLD.). (1971)-. Periodical. English. mo (12 issues). $20.00 (one year), $35.00 (two year), $50.00 (three year). Antique Toy World Magazine, PO Box 34509, Chicago IL 60634. **Tel** (312)725-0633. **ED** Dale P. Kelley. **LC** NK9509; .A57. **DD** 688.7/2. **Bk Rev. Ad Acc. Circ:** 10,000.
Desc: Articles on all collectible and antique toys.

AT/0312-5327
AUSTRALIAN GIFTGUIDE. [Aust. giftguide]. **VFOAT** Giftguide. (1975)-. Trade Publication. English. Four times a year (Jan., Apr., July, Oct.). 58.00Aus$ Australia; 135.00Aus$ US. Australian Giftguide Product, PO Box 489, Darlinghurst New South Wales, 2010 Australia. **Tel** 011 61 2 3311188. **ED** Vicki Jarvis, (editor's address: PO Box 606, Roxelle, New South Wales, 2039 Australia, phone: 011 61 2 8184111). **DD** _a658.870994. **Ad Acc, Adv Mgr:** Stephanie Goodmanson, **Tel** 011 61 2 8184111. **Circ:** 5,000.
Desc: Trade magazine for gift retailers. Contains "what's new" features, advertising, and general interest articles in the gift industry. Also includes annual directory issue listing suppliers and their products.

US/1040-094X
BARBIE BAZAAR. [Barbie bazaar]. Vol. 1, No. 1 (1988)-. Periodical. English. bm. $25.95 US; $38.95 Canada; $40.95 other. Barbie Bazaar, 5617 6th Avenue, Attention Subs Dept, Kenosha WI 53140. **Tel** (414)658-1004. **LC** NK4894.3.B37; B37. **DD** 688.7/221/0979493.

AT
BEAR FACTS REVIEW. English. Twice a year (June, Dec.). 12.50Aus Australia; 22.50Aus$ others. M.A. Brooks, PO Box 503, Mossvale New South Wales, 2577 Australia. **Tel** 11 61 4 8681338, FAX 11 61 4 4 8691438. **ED** J. M. Brooks. **Bk Rev. Ad Acc.**
Desc: Antique, old, new and artist's bears of every size and shape.

US/1040-7065
BUYER'S GUIDE TO MEDICAL TOYS & BOOKS FOR TODDLERS THROUGH TEENS. *Ceased.* **Added/Corp** Pediatric Projects Inc. **VFOAT** Medical Toys and Books; Medical Toys & Books. Vol. 1, No. 1 (1988)-(1992). Periodical. English. qt. $14.00 (one year), $24.00 (two year), $34.00 (three year) US; $18.00 (one year), $28.00 (two year), $38.00 (three year) other. Pediatric Projects Inc, PO Box 571555, Tarzana CA 91357. **Tel** (818)705-3660, (800)947-0947. **ED** Pat Azarnoff. **DD** 618. Index available. cum. index. **Bk Rev.**
Desc: A buyer's guide to medically oriented toys and books for toddlers and through teens.

CN/0834-2202
CANADIAN TOY & DECORATION FAIR : DIRECTORY. [Can. Toy Decor. Fair]. **Main/Corp** Canadian Toy & Decoration Fair. **VFOAT** Salon Canadien du Jouet et des Decoration : Annuaire. (1983)-. Directory. English (French). an. Canadian Toy Manufacturers Association, PO Box 294, Kleinburg Ontario L0J 1C0 Canada. **DD** 338.4/768872/02571. ***Continues** Directory - Canadian Toy & Decoration Fair, 0317-9443.*

IT/0390-1513
CASA STILE. (1973)-. Periodical. Italian. Six times a year. L60000.00 Italy; $L110000.00 other. Agepe Agenzia Gestione Per SRL, Via Trentacoste 9, 20134 Milan Italy. **Tel** 011 39 2 2640009. **Bk Rev**. **Ad Acc**. **Circ:** 17,500. ***Continues*** *Casalinghi Stile, 0394-9842.*
Desc: A magazine dedicated to the production of giftware and houseware distributed to all operators of the sector in Italy and abroad to those interested in the Italian market.

US
CELEBRITY DOLL PRICE GUIDE & ANNUAL. **VFOAT** Celebrity Doll Price Guide and Annual. 1984-. English. an. $5.95 per copy. Hobby House Press Inc, 900 Frederick Street, Cumberland MD 21502. **Tel** (301)759-3770, FAX (301)759-4940. **LC** NK4894.3.C44; C44. **DD** 688.7/221/075.

●US/1068-347X
COLLECTING TOYS. [Collect. toys]. (Feb. 1993)-. Periodical. English. bm. $19.95 US; $26.00 other. Kalmbach Publishing Company, PO Box 1612, Waukesha WI 53187. **Tel** (414)796-8776 ext.411, FAX (414)796-0126. **LC** NK9509; .C65. **DD** 688.7/2/075.
Desc: Tips, advice, and current market values.

US
CRAFT SUPPLY DIRECTORY. Directory. English. an. $40.00. Gordons Corner Plaza, Box 420, Manalapan NJ 07726. **Tel** (201)446-4900, FAX (201)446-5488. **ED** Tammy Keck. Index available. **Bk Rev**. **Ad Acc**. **Circ:** 10,000.
Desc: Complete sourcebook for professional crafters listing hundreds of wholesale craft supplies.

US/0732-9873
DIRECTORY / TOY TRAIN OPERATING SOCIETY. **Main/Corp** Toy Train Operating Society. Directory. English. bm. $37.00. Toy Train Operating Society Inc, 25 West Walnut Street/Suite 305, Pasadena CA 91103. **Tel** (818)578-0673. **ED** David Otth. **LC** TF197; .T59B. **DD** 625.1/9/02573. **Bk Rev**. **Ad Acc**. **Circ:** 5,000 (ctrl).
Desc: A newsletter of classified toy train advertisements.

UK
DOLL & TOY. **VFOAT** Doll & Toy Collector; Doll and Toy. Issue No. 1 (Sept./Oct. 1983)-. Periodical. English. bm. International Collectors Publications, The Old Exchange Wales.

US/0744-0901
DOLL READER. (DOLL READER; CLEARINGHOUSE FOR INFORMATION ON DOLLS.). [Doll read.]. (19??)-. Periodical. English. ir (9 issues a year). $29.95. Cowles Magazines, PO Box 8200, Harrisburg PA 17105. **Tel** (717)657-9555, (800)435-9610. **DD** 745. **Bk Rev**. **Ad Acc**. **Circ:** 60,000 (ctrl). ***Continued in part by*** *Doll Artistry, 1052-0805.*
Desc: The ultimate authority on dolls. Also includes over 4,000 doll photos plus 250 in-depth articles, 2,000 pages yearly. A treasure trove of information.

US
DOLL TIMES. (19??)-. Periodical. English. mo. $18.00. Doll Times, 218 West Woodin, Dallas TX 75224. **Tel** (214)943-2107. **ED** Mable Richardson. **LC** Discard. **Bk Rev**. **Ad Acc**. available on audiocassette (for vision impaired and handicapped readers).
Desc: Ads and articles concerning dolls, toys, paperdolls, and bears.

US/0072-4505
GIFT AND DECORATIVE ACCESSORY BUYERS DIRECTORY, THE. Directory. English. Geyer-McAllister Publications Inc, 51 Madison Avenue, New York NY 10010. **Tel** (212)689-4411. **LC** T12; .G46. **DD** 338.4/7/745502573. ***Continues*** *Gift and Art Buyers Directory.*

US/0896-4092
GIFT & STATIONERY BUSINESS. (GIFT & STATIONERY BUSINESS : GSB.). [Gift stationery bus.]. **VFOAT** GSB; G S B; Gift and Stationery Business. Vol. 29, No. 10 (Oct. 1987)-. Periodical. English. mo. $45.00 US; $63.00 Canada & Mexico; $240.00 other. Miller Freeman Inc., 600 Harrison Street, San Francisco CA 94107. **Tel** (415)905-2337, FAX (415)905-2240, telex 278273. **(Subscription address:** JCI, PO Box 1766, Riverton NJ 08077.**)** **DD** 338. **[CCC]**. available on microfilm from University Microfilms International (UMI). ***Continues*** *Giftware Business, 0199-4069.*

US
GIFT BASKET IDEA NEWSLETTER. **See** The Arts-Crafts and Decorative Arts.

US/1050-0316
GIFT BASKET REVIEW. (GIFT BASKET REVIEW : THE MAGAZINE OF THE GIFT BASKET INDUSTRY.). [Gift basket rev.]. **VFOAT** GBR. Vol. 1, No. 1 (March 1990)-. Periodical. English. Twelve times a year. $29.95 US; $49.00 other. Festivities Publications Inc., 1205 West Forsyth Street, Jacksonville FL 32204. **Tel** (904)634-1902, FAX (904)633-8764. **DD** 338.

UK
GIFT BUYER INTERNATIONAL. English. mo. $105.00 US; $120.00 Canada. Gift Buyer International, MI Victoria House, Southampton, London WC1B 4EW England. **Tel** 01 242 4995.

US/0894-4113
GIFT REPORTER. (GIFT REPORTER : GR.). [Gift report.]. **VFOAT** GR; GR, Gift Reporter. (Jan. 1986)-. Periodical. English. mo. Free (qualified professionals), $36.00 (other). Gift Reporter, 2 Park Avenue/Suite 1100, New York NY 10016. **DD** 381.

US/0016-9889
GIFTS & DECORATIVE ACCESSORIES. [Gifts decor. accessories]. **VFOAT** Gifts and Decorative Accessories. Vol. 60, No. 12 (Dec. 1964)-. Periodical. English. Twelve times a year. $37.00 US & Canada, $85.00 others (surface mail); $228.00 others (airmail). Geyer-McAllister Publications Inc, 51 Madison Avenue, New York NY 10010. **Tel** (212)689-4411. **LC** HD9999.G49; G54. **DD** 381/.4567/05. **[CCC]**. available on an online database (file 648/Full-Text) from DIALOG. ***Continues*** *Gift and Decorative Accessories Buyer.*
Ind/Abst Bus. ASAP (1990-) [Full Txt.]; Bus. Index (1985-); Gen. BusinessFile (1985-); Gen. Period. Index (1985-); Mag. Search; Trade Ind. ASAP [Full Txt.]; Trade Ind. Index (1981-) [Full Txt.]; Vocat. Search (July 1993-).

HK
GIFTS & HOME PRODUCTS. **See** Interior Design-Home Furnishings.

CH
GIFTS AND HOUSEWARES ACCESSORIES. **See** Household Hardware and Appliances.

CN/0700-9380
GIFTS & TABLEWARES. Vol. 1 (Fall 1976)-. Periodical. English. Seven times a year. 36.00Can$ (one year), 57.00Can$ (two year), 73.00Can$ (three year) Canada; 47.00Can$ (one year), 74.00Can$ (two year) US; 73.00Can$ other. Southam Information and Technology Group Inc., 1450 Don Mills Road, Don Mills Ontario M3B 2X7 Canada. **Tel** (416)445-6641, (800)668-2374, FAX (416)442-2261. **DD** 658.8/2/0971.

CN
GIFTS AND TABLEWARES TRADE DIRECTORY. Directory. an. 25.00Can$. Southam Information and Technology Group Inc., 1450 Don Mills Road, Don Mills Ontario M3B 2X7 Canada. **Tel** (416)445-6641, (800)668-2374, FAX (416)442-2261.

UK
GIFTS TODAY. English. Ten times a year (published monthly with Jan./Feb. and Nov./Dec. issues combined). £45.00 UK; £55.00 (surface mail), £75.00 (air mail). Lema Publishing Company, Unit 1 Queen Mary's Avenue, Waterford W01 7JR England. **Tel** 011 44 603 250909. **ED** Georgina Godwin. **Ad Acc**, **Adv Mgr:** J. Baulch. **Circ:** 6,000 (ctrl).

US/0092-3850
GIFTS YOU CAN MAKE FOR CHRISTMAS. (WOMAN'S DAY GIFTS YOU CAN MAKE FOR CHRISTMAS.). **VFOAT** Gifts You Can Make for Christmas. (19??)-. English. ir. $0.95. Sunset Publishing Corporation, 80 Willow Road, Menlo Park CA 94025. **Tel** (415)321-3600, (800)777-0117. **LC** TT157; .W62. **DD** 745.5/05.

US/0193-2551
GIFTWARE NEWS. (19??)-. Periodical. English. mo. $32.00 US; $135.00 other. Talcott Communications Corporation, 20 North Wacker Drive, Suite 3230, Chicago IL 60606. **Tel** (312)664-4040.
Ind/Abst Trade Ind. Index.

IT
GIRONALE DEI GIOCATTOLI. Italian. bm. L90000 Italy; L110000 other. Pubblieme International SRL, Via Caracciolo 77, 20155 Milan Italy. **Tel** 39-2-3496967, FAX 39-2-313866. **ED** Giorgio Brautigam, Luigi Abbati. **Ad Acc**. **Circ:** 10,000 (ctrl).
Desc: Features on the production of the branch, companies, profiles, model-making, news from fairs, trends of the Italian and foreign market.

●UK
GREETINGS AND GIFT STATIONER. (1993)-. Periodical. English. bm (6 issues). £20.00 UK; £35.00 other. Trade Media Ltd / England, Brookmead House, Two Rivers, Station Lane, Witney Oxon OX8 6BH England. **Tel** 011 44 993 775545, FAX 011 44 993 778884. **Ad Acc**. **Circ:** 8,600.

AT/1036-5915
GREETINGS AND GIFTS. Vol. 4 (May 1991)-. Periodical. English. Six times a year. 24.00Aus$ Australia; 28.00Aus$ New Zealand; 35.00Aus$ Pacific Basin; 38.00Aus$ other. Merrick Publishing Group, PO Box 305, Balgowlah NSW 2093 Australia. **Tel** 011 61 2 9070366, FAX 011 61 2 9079460. **Ad Acc**, **Adv Mgr:** M. Merrick, **Tel** 02 9070366. **Circ:** 7,000 (ctrl).

US/1064-2048
GREETINGS MAGAZINE. (GREETINGS MAGAZINE : THE BUSINESS MAGAZINE FOR CARD AND GIFT RETAILERS.). [Greet. mag.]. (19??)-. Periodical. English. Twelve times a year. $20.00 US, $40.00 Canada and Mexico, $60.00 other (surface mail), $125.00 (airmail). MacKay Publishing Corporation, 307 Fifth Avenue, New York NY 10016. **Tel** (212)679-6677, FAX (212)679-6374. **DD** 338. available on an online database (file 648/Full-Text) from DIALOG. ***Continues*** *Greeting Card Magazine, 0017-4106.*
Ind/Abst Trade Ind. ASAP [Full Txt.]; Trade Ind. Index [Full Txt.].

HK
HONG KONG GIFTS & PREMIUMS. English. be. $40.00. Hong Kong Trade Development Council, 38th Floor/Office Tower, Convention Plaza, 1 Harbour Road, Hong Kong. **Tel** 852 5844333, FAX 852 8240249, telex 7395 CONHK HX. **(Subscription address:** for North America: 219 East 16th Street, New York NY 10017**)** **ED** Saul Lockhart. **Ad Acc**. **Circ:** 30,000 (ctrl).
Desc: Features Hong Kong's gifts and premiums products.

US/0738-7946
HOSPITAL GIFT SHOP MANAGEMENT. ***Ceased.*** **See** Business-General Management.

US/1050-3994
INTERNATIONAL DOLL WORLD. ***Title Change.*** **See** Hobbies.

JA
JAPAN TOY & HOBBY MARKET REPORT. English. mo. $200.00. Nippon Toys Service Co. Ltd., 3-9-5 Kotobuki, Taito-ku Tokyo Japan. **Tel** 011 81 3 38426001. ***Continues*** *Japan Market Trends.*

FR/0754-068X
JEUX & JOUETS MAGAZINE. [Jeux jouets mag.]. **VFOAT** Jeux et Jouets Magazine. (1983)-. Periodical. French. Twelve times a year. 130.00F France; 160.00F others. Jeux et Jouets, 22 rue du PDT Sider, 92532 Levallois Per Cedex France. **Tel** 011 33 1 47393481, FAX 011 33 1 47393479. **UDC** 688.7. ***Continues*** *Jouet Conseil, Ludorama, 0292-9260.*

FR/0075-4056
JOUETS ET JEUX. [Jouets jeux]. (1962)-. Periodical. French. an. 240.00F France; 223.00F other. Creations Editions Prod Publs, 1 Place d Estienne de Orves, 75009 Paris France. **Tel** 011 33 1 42806762, FAX (33)1 42 82 99 30. Index available. cum. index. **Ad Acc**. ctrl circ. ***Continues*** *Jouets et Jeux de France, 0446-9607.*
Desc: Covers the toys and games market in France.

CN/0707-5081
JOUETS (MONTREAL. 1976). (JOUETS.). **Main/Corp** Association des Consommateurs du Quebec. 1980-. French (English). an. 4.00Can$. Association des Consommateurs du Quebec, 7383 de la Roche, Montreal Quebec H2R 2T4 Canada. **Tel** (514)381-8866. **DD** 688.7/2/05. Index available. **Bk Rev**. **Circ:** 200,000 (French). ***Continues*** *Consumers' Association of Canada (Que.). Jouets, 0707-5081.*

SP/0022-6157
JUGUETES Y JUEGOS DE ESPANA. [Juguetes juegos Esp.]. (1962)-. Periodical. Spanish. Six times a year. $98.00. Ediciones Just SL, San German 5, 08004 Barcelona Spain. **Tel** 011 34 93 325 32 87, FAX 011 34 93 424 44 60. **ED** Maria Dolores Just. **UDC** 688. **Ad Acc**.
Desc: Publication of the Spanish Association of Toy Manufacturers.

CN/0068-9041
LLOYD'S CANADIAN JEWELLERY AND GIFTWARE DIRECTORY. **See** Jewelry.

CN/0068-9955
LLOYD'S CANADIAN VARIETY MERCHANDISE DIRECTORY. **VFOAT** Canadian Variety Merchandise Directory. 43rd Ed. (1967)-. Directory. English. an. 30.00Can$ Canada; 50.00Can$ US; 60.00Can$ other. Sentinel Business Publications, 7575 Trans Canada Highway, Suite 500, St. Laurent Quebec H4T 1V6 Canada. **Tel** (514)333-1116, FAX (514)631-8858. **ED** Carol Clifford. **DD** 338.4/7/688. **Ad Acc**. **Circ:** 3,500 (ctrl). ***Continues*** *Lloyd's Canadian Toy, Notion and Stationery Directory, 0381-5757.*
Desc: A directory of product listings and suppliers of general merchandise for retailers.

US/0743-8680
OFFICIAL PRICE GUIDE TO COLLECTIBLE TOYS, THE. (THE OFFICIAL PRICE GUIDE TO COLLECTIBLE TOYS / BY THE HOUSE OF COLLECTIBLES, INC.). [Off. price guide collect. toys]. **Added/Corp** House of Collectibles. **VFOAT** Collectible Toys; Toys. 1st Ed. (1984)-. English. ir. $15.85 (latest edition). Random House Inc., 400 Hahn Road, Westminster MD 21157. **Tel** (800)726-0600, (800)733-3000, FAX (800)659-2436. **LC** NK9509.65.U6; O36. **DD** 688.7/2/0973075.

Glass and Ceramics

US/0747-5756
OFFICIAL PRICE GUIDE TO TOYS, THE. [Off. price guide toys]. **VFOAT** Toys. 1st Ed. (1983)-. English. an. Random House Inc., 400 Hahn Road, Westminster MD 21157. **Tel** (800)726-0600, (800)733-3000, FAX (800)659-2436. **LC** NK9509.65.U6; O37. **DD** 688.7/2/075.

US/1064-4164
OLD TOY SOLDIER. (OLD TOY SOLDIER : THE JOURNAL FOR COLLECTORS.). [Old toy soldier]. Vol. 14, No. 5 (Oct. 1990)-. Periodical. English. Six times a year (Feb., Apr., June, Aug., Oct., Dec.). Old Toy Soldier Newsletter, 209 North Lombard, Oak Park IL 60302. **Tel** (708)383-6525. **ED** Steve and Jo Sommers. **DD** 745. Index available. cum. index. **Bk Rev**, (Qty: 4-5). **Ad Acc. Circ:** 2,000. **Continues** Old Toy Soldier Newsletter, 8756-7652.
Desc: Cover full range of toy soldier manufacturing: Britians, Mignot, Heyde, American dimestore, and many others.

US/1060-6726
PARTY SOURCE. (PARTY SOURCE : PS.). [Party source]. **VFOAT** PS. (1991)-. Periodical. English. Six times a year. $25.00 US; $36.00 Canada & Mexico; $50.00 other. Miller Freeman Inc., 600 Harrison Street, San Francisco CA 94107. **Tel** (415)905-2337, FAX (415)905-2240, telex 278273. **(Subscription address:** Miller Freeman / Aurora, IL, 434 West Downer Place, Aurora IL 60506.**) DD** 338. **[CCC].**

US
PLASTIC FIGURE AND PLAYSET COLLECTOR. English. bm. $18.00 (surface mail); $26.00 (airmail) North America; $27.00 (surface mail), $33.00 (airmail) other. Specialty Publishing Company, PO Box 1355, La Crosse WI 54602. **Tel** (608)781-1894. **ED** Thomas Terry. **Bk Rev**. **Ad Acc. Circ:** 1,200 (ctrl).
Desc: Information on the collection of plastic figure and playsets. Features Marx Toy Company and others.

CN/0835-4014
PLAY AND PARENTING CONNECTIONS. See Library and Information Sciences.

US/0032-1567
PLAYTHINGS. [Playthings]. Vol. 1, (1903)-. Periodical. English. Twelve times a year (2 issues in May). $24.00 US & Canada & Mexico; $45.00 other (includes the Plaything Directory and Toy Fair). Geyer-McAllister Publications Inc, 51 Madison Avenue, New York NY 10010. **Tel** (212)689-4411. **LC** TS2301.T7; A3. **DD** 338.4/76887/05. **[CCC].** available on an online database (file 648/Full-Text) from DIALOG.
Ind/Abst Bus. ASAP (1990-) [Full Txt.]; Bus. Index (1985-); F&S Index Plus Text, Int. [Select. Cov.]; Gen. BusinessFile (1985-); Gen. Period. Index (1985-); Mag. Search; Mark. Advert. Ref. Serv.; PROMT; Trade Ind. ASAP [Full Txt.]; Trade Ind. Index [Full Txt.].

GW/0032-7697
PRESENT BAMBERG. See The Arts-Crafts and Decorative Arts.

US/0033-877X
RAILROAD MODEL CRAFTSMAN. See Hobbies.

FR/0035-2594
REVUE DU JOUET, LA. (1962)-. Periodical. French. Ten times a year. 323.21F France; 495.00F other. Group Cepp Editions Ampere, 25 rue Dagorno, 75012 Paris France. **Tel** 011 33 1 43473020, FAX 011 33 1 43473080. **UDC** 688.7. **[CCC]. Ad Acc.**
Desc: Professional information in the toys field in France.

US/0273-6241
S GAUGIAN. [S gaugian]. (19??)-. Periodical. English. bm (Jan., Mar., May, July, Sept., Nov.). $26.00. Heimburger House Publishing Co, 7236 W Madison Street, Forest Park IL 60130. **Tel** (708)366-1973. **ED** Donald J. Heimburger. **Bk Rev**, (Qty: 50). **Ad Acc. Circ:** 5,000.
Desc: Covers 3/16" equals 1' model railroading (S/scale). Features how-to articles, photos, plans, ads, news.

GW
SCHAULADE, DIE. See Glass and Ceramics.

US/0037-7260
SMALL WORLD (GUILFORD). See Interior Design-Home Furnishings.

US/0038-4968
SOUVENIRS & NOVELTIES. **VFOAT** Souvenirs and Novelties. Vol 1 No. 1 (Spring 1962)-. Periodical. English. ir. $17.00 (one year); $28.00 (two years);. Kane Communications Inc, 7000 Terminal Square, Suite 210, Upper Darby PA 19082. **Tel** (215)734-2420, FAX (215)734-2423. **ED** Sandy Meschow. Index available. **Bk Rev**. **Ad Acc. Circ:** 22,000 (ctrl).
Desc: An publication for the resort - gift and souvenir industry.

GW/0038-7525
SPIELZEUG, DAS. (1949)-. Periodical. German. mo. DM108.41 Germany; DM120.00 other. Meisenbach GmbH, Postfach 2069, D 96011 Bamberg Germany. **Tel** 011 49 951 861135. **UDC** 688.72/.73.

US/0890-4782
STUFFED. Title Change. See Children and Youth Interests.

CH
TAIWAN GIFTS BUYER'S GUIDE. English. an. $30.00. Trade Winds Inc., PO Box 7-179, #7 Lane 75, Yungkang Street, Taipei Taiwan. **Tel** 011 886 2 3932718, FAX 011 886 3964022.

CN/1186-8503
TLRC DIRECTORY. [TLRC dir.]. Added/Corp Canadian Association of Toy Libraries and Parent Resource Centres. **VFOAT** Toy Libraries and Resource Centres Directory. 3rd Ed. (1991)-. Directory. English. Canadian Association of Toy Libraries and Parent-Child Resource Centres, 205-120 Holland Avenue, Ottawa Ontario K1Y 0X6 Canada. **DD** 027.62/5. **Continues** A National Directory of Canadian Toy Libraries and Parent Child resource Centres., 1186-849X.

AT/1035-9176
TOY & HOBBY RETAILER. [Toy hobby retail.]. (1990)-. Periodical. English. mo. 38.00Aus$ Australia; 105.00Aus$ other. Yaffa Publishing Group Pty Ltd., GPO Box 606, Sydney NSW 2001 Australia. **Tel** 011 61 2 2812333, FAX 011 61 2 2812750. **DD** 381.45688720994. **Continues in part** Australasian Sportsgoods and Toy Retailer, 0004-8488.

●US
TOY & HOBBY WORLD (1993). (TOY & HOBBY WORLD.). (1993)-. English. mo. A4 Publications USA, 41 Madison Avenue, New York NY 10010. **Tel** (212)685-0404, FAX (212)685-0483.

US/1069-3254
TOY & HOBBY WORLD INTERNATIONAL. Title Change. [Toy hobby world int.]. **VFOAT** Toy and Hobby World; Toy and Hobby World International; A.Toy & Hobby world. (199?)-(1993). Periodical. English. mo. A4 Publications USA, 41 Madison Avenue, New York NY 10010. **Tel** (212)685-0404, FAX (212)685-0483. **DD** 338. **Continues** Toy & Hobby World, 0041-011X. **Continued by** Toy & Hobby World, 1073-8932.

US
TOY & HOBBY WORLD. WEEKLY MARKET REPORT. Ceased. See Business-Retail.

US/0885-3991
TOY BOOK, THE. [Toy book]. (1985)-. Periodical. English. mo. $36.00 (1 year), $60.00 (2 year), $72.00 (3 year) US and Canada; $200.00 (1 year) other. Adventure Publishing Group Inc, 264 West 40th Street, New York NY 10018. **Tel** (212)575-4510, FAX (212)575-4521, telex 177368 IEBUT. **ED** Beth Kestenbaum. **DD** 688. **Ad Acc. Circ:** 15,000 (ctrl).

●US
TOY COLLECTOR. **VFOAT** Toy Collector Magazine. Vol. 3, No. 2 (Feb. 1992)-. Periodical. English. bm. $14.97. Dobbs Publishing Group, 3816 Industry Boulevard, Lakeland FL 33811. **Tel** (813)646-5743, FAX (813)648-1187. **Continues** Toy Collector Magazine, 1059-5880.

●US/1069-1685
TOY COLLECTOR & PRICE GUIDE. [Toy collect. price guide]. **VFOAT** Toy Collector and Price Guide. (1993)-. Periodical. English. Six times a year. $16.95 US; $21.75 other. Krause Publications, 700 East State Street, Iola WI 54990-0001. **Tel** (715)445-2214, FAX (715)445-4087, telex 55 6461. **LC** NK9509; .T68. **DD** 688.7/2/0973075. **Formed by the union of** Toys & Prices, 1063-3618 **and** Toys Collector Magazine, 1059-5880.

US
TOY REPORT. English. wk. $165.00 (one year) US and Canada; $275.00 (one year) other. Adventure Publishing Group Inc, 264 West 40th Street, New York NY 10018. **Tel** (212)575-4510, FAX (212)575-4521, telex 177368 IEBUT.

CN/0229-8422
TOY REPORT. (THE TOY REPORT / [CANADIAN TOY TESTING COUNCIL]). [Toy rep.]. **Main/Corp** Canadian Toy Testing Council. (Sept. 1979)-. English. an. $5.95 (add $1.00 for postage) Canada, (add $2.50 for postage) other. The Canadian Toy Testing Council, 881 Lady Ellen Place, Ottawa Ontario K1Z 5L3 Canada. **Tel** (613)729-7101. **ED** Leslie Burtch. **DD** 688.7/2/0216. **Circ:** 55,000. **Continues** Canadian Toy Testing Council. Good Toys., 0229-8430.
Desc: A listing of over 1,500 play items currently available in the marketplace. Evaluated for design, function, durability and primarily play value, Assessments is based on the "use-testing" of the toys by children in normal play environments for an extended period of time.

US/0898-5650
TOY SHOP. [Toy shop]. (1988)-. Periodical. English. mo. $23.95 US; $60.00 other. Krause Publications, 700 East State Street, Iola WI 54990-0001. **Tel** (715)445-2214, FAX (715)445-4087, telex 55 6461. **DD** 688. **Ad Acc. Circ:** 15,593.
Desc: Antique and collector toys, models, dolls and related items for sale. Contains classified ads indexed alphabetically by category.

UK
TOY TRADER. (19??)-. Periodical. English. mo. £52.00 UK; £66.00 other. Turret Group, 177 Hagden Lane, Watford Herts WD1 8LN United Kingdom. **Tel** 011 44 923 228577, FAX 011 44 923 221346. **Continues** Toys International & Toy Buyer.

UK
TOY TRADER YEAR BOOK. English. £3.10. 157 Hagden Lane, Watford WD1 8LW England. **LC** HD9999.T7; G77. **DD** 338.4/7/6887202541.

CN/0381-9930
TOYS & GAMES. Vol. 1, Apr. (1973)-. Periodical. English. bm. G P Page, 333 King Street West Canada. **Continued in part by** Electronic Toys & Games, 0822-5761.

US/0041-0829
TRAIN COLLECTORS QUARTERLY, THE. See Hobbies.

US/1044-1344
U.S. TOY COLLECTOR MAGAZINE. [U. S. toy collect. mag.]. **VFOAT** U.S. Toy Collector. (198?)-. Periodical. English. mo. Gordon Rice, 214 South Grove Street, Missoula MT 59801. **DD** 745.

US/8755-3813
WALLACE-HOMESTEAD PRICE GUIDE TO DOLLS. [Wallace-Homestead price guide dolls]. **VFOAT** Wallace Homestead Price Guide to Dolls; Price Guide to Dolls. English. Wallace-Homestead Book Company / Illinois, 850 Waters Edge, Lombard IL 60148. **LC** NK4893; .W35. **DD** 688.7/221/075.

UK
WORLD TOY NEWS. English. Twenty-four times a year. £240.00. World Toy News, 17 Bridge Hunton Bridge, Kings LG Herts W24 8RQ England. **Tel** 011 44 923265874, FAX 011 44 92320945. **ED** Jon Salisbury. Index available. **Bk Rev**. **Circ:** 1,000.
Desc: The world's only international newspaper for the global toy market.

GLASS AND CERAMICS

US
ACORN (SANDWICH, MASS.). (THE ACORN.). Added/Corp Sandwich Historical Society (Mass.). Vol. 1, No. 1 (March 1965)-. Periodical. English. ir. $10.00 (Comes with Sandwich Historical Society Membership). Sandwich Historical Society, Glass Museum, PO Box 103, Sandwich MA 02563. **Tel** (508)888-0251. **ED** Rosemary Cancian. **Circ:** 1,000.
Desc: These are articles concerned with all aspects of glass, its history, art, and technology.

NE/0268-9847
ADVANCED CERAMICS REPORT. **VFOAT** ACR. Vol. 1, No. 1 (Jan. 1986)-. Periodical. English. mo. $446.00 The Americas; £299.00 other. Elsevier Advanced Technology, An Imprint of Elsevier Science Ltd., The Boulevard, Langford Lane, Kidlington, Oxford OX5 1GB United Kingdom. **Tel** 011 44 865 843000, 011 44 865 843699, FAX 011 44 865 843010. **(Subscription address:** Elsevier Science Ltd. Oxford Fulfillment Centre, PO Box 800, Kidlington, Oxford OX5 1DX United Kingdom.**) ED** J. Binner. **[CCC].** available on microfilm from University Microfilms International (UMI); available on an online database (Full-Text) from DIALOG.
Desc: Regularly features and discusses advanced ceramic materials.
Ind/Abst Nonwovens Abstr.; PTS Newsl. Database [Full Txt.].

US/0730-9546
ADVANCES IN CERAMICS. [Adv. ceram.]. Added/Corp American Ceramic Society. Vol. 1 (1981)-. Academic Scholarly Publication. English. ir. Comes with Journal of the American Ceramic Society. American Ceramic Society, 735 Ceramic Place, Westerville OH 43081-8720. **Tel** (614)890-4700, (614)794-5890, FAX (614)899-6109. **CODEN** ADCEDE. **[CCC].** Documents available from Article Express International, CASDDS.
Ind/Abst Bioeng. Abstr.; Ceram. Abstr. (19??-); Chem. Abstr.; Ei Page One; Eng. Index Annu.

JA/0385-6860
AICHI-KEN TOKONAME YOGYO GIJUTSU SENTA HOKOKU. [Aichi-ken Tokoname Yogyo Gijutsu Senta hokoku]. Added/Corp Aichi-Ken Tokoname Yogyo Gijutsu Senta. **VFOAT**

Reports of Tokoname Ceramic Research Institute, Aichi-Prefectural Government. (1973)-. Japanese. an. Aichiken Tokoname Yogyo Gijutsu Senta, (Tokoname Ceramic Research Inst., Aichi Prefectural Government), 4-50 Osocho, Tokonameshi, Aichiken 479 Japan. **CODEN** ATYHD7. Documents available from CASDDS. ***Continues*** *Aichi-Ken Yogyo Gijutsu Senta Hokoku.*
Ind/Abst Chem. Abstr.

US/0899-806X
AMERICAN CERAMIC CIRCLE JOURNAL. [Am. Ceram. Circ. j.]. **Added/Corp** American Ceramic Circle. Vol. 6 (1988)-. Periodical. English. ir (Every eighteen months). $15.00 (single issue). American Ceramic Circle, PO Box 1495, Grand Central Station, New York NY 10163. **Tel** (207)773-6068. **ED** Meredith Chilton. **LC** NK3700; .A58. **DD** 738/.05. **Bk Rev. Circ:** 400 (ctrl). ***Continues*** *American Ceramic Circle Bulletin, 0270-9279.*
Desc: Scholarly articles on ceramics from all periods and nations.

US/0002-7812
AMERICAN CERAMIC SOCIETY BULLETIN. [Am. Ceram. Soc. Bull.]. **Added/Corp** American Ceramic Society. **VFOAT** Ceramic Bulletin. (Jan. 15, 1946)-. Bulletin. English. mo. $50.00 US; $65.00 Canada and Mexico; $100.00 other. American Ceramic Society, 735 Ceramic Place, Westerville OH 43081-8720. **Tel** (614)890-4700, (614)794-5890, FAX (614)899-6109. **ED** W J Smothers, Donald C Snyder, Jon W Hines, and Steve Robb. **DD** 666. **CODEN** ACSBA7. **[CCC].** Index available. cum. index. **Bk Rev. Ad Acc. Pr Rev. Circ:** 13,000 (ctrl). available on microfilm and microfiche from University Microfilms International (UMI). Documents available from Article Express International, The Genuine Article, Ask*IEEE, CASDDS, Documents on Demand. ***Continues*** *Bulletin of the American Ceramic Society, 0885-7040.* ***Continued in part by*** *American Ceramic Society. Roster.*
Desc: An international association dedicated to the dissemination of technical, scientific, and commercial information on ceramic materials and products. Ceramic information can be obtained from many publications, electronic database products (including CD-ROM), or through our custom information service.
Ind/Abst Alum. Ind. Abstr.; Appl. Sci. Technol. Index; Bioeng. Abstr.; Ceram. Abstr.; Chem. Abstr.; Chem. Titles; Coal Abstr.; Concr. Abstr.; Curr. Contents Eng. Tech. Appl. Sci.; Curr. Contents Phys. Chem. Earth Sci.; Ei Page One; EMBASE; Energy Inf. Abstr.; Energy Res. Abstr.; Eng. Mater. Abstr. (1968-); Eng. Index Annu.; Environ. Abstr.; F&S Index Plus Text, Int. [Select. Cov.]; GeoRef; HTFS Dig.; INIS Atomindex [Micro.]; INSPEC (1968-); Int. Aerosp. Abstr.; Leadscan; Met. Abstr.; MINPROC; PROMT (1968-); Res. Alert [Full Cov.]; Sci. Cit. Index; SCISEARCH; Soc. Sci. Cit. Index [Select. Cov.]; Surf. Treat. Technol. Abstr.; World Ceram. Abstr.

US/0278-9507
AMERICAN CERAMICS. [Amer. ceram.]. (Winter 1982)-. Periodical. English. Four times a year. $28.00. American Ceramics, 9 East 45th Street, 6th Floor, New York NY 10017. **Tel** (212)661-4397. **ED** Michael McTwigan. **LC** NK4005; .A46. **DD** 730/.0973. Index available. **Bk Rev. Ad Acc. Circ:** 6,000.
Desc: A forum for leading scholars and critics, where aesthetic, philosophical, and social issues are aired in a unique investigation of ceramic art.
Ind/Abst Art Index; ARTbibliogr. Mod. (1984-); BHA : Biblio. Hist. Art.

US/0739-6546
AMERICAN CLAY EXCHANGE. ***Suspended.*** [Am. clay exch.]. (198?)-Vol. 8/9 (1988). Periodical. English. mo. $15.00. American Clay Exchange, 800 Murray Drive, El Cajon CA 92020. **Tel** (619)697-5922.

US/0002-8649
AMERICAN GLASS REVIEW. Vol. 45, No. 27 (Apr. 3, 1926)-. Academic Scholarly Publication. English. Twelve times a year. Doctorow Communications Inc., 1033 Clifton Avenue, PO Box 2147, Clifton NJ 07013. **Tel** (201)779-1600, FAX (201)779-3242. **ED** Donald Doctorow. **LC** HD6350.G5; A63. **DD** 338.476661. **CODEN** AGLRAE. **[CCC]. Ad Acc. Circ:** 1,400 (ctrl). available on microfilm and microfiche from University Microfilms International (UMI). Documents available from CASDDS. ***Continues*** *Glass Worker (Pittsburgh, Pa.).*
Ind/Abst Ceram. Abstr.; Chem. Abstr.; Eng. Mater. Abstr.; F&S Index Plus Text, Int. [Select. Cov.]; Int. Packag. Abstr.; PROMT.

BL
ANUARIO BRASILEIRO DE CERAMICA. **Added/Corp** Associacao Brasileira de Ceramica. (1978)-. Portuguese. an. Associacao Brasileira de Ceramica, rua Leonardo Nunes 82, 04039 Sao Paulo SP Brazil. **Tel** 11 55 11 5493922, FAX 11 55 11 8841289. **LC** HD9615.B7; A57. **DD** 338.4/7666/0981.

US/1043-3317
ARS CERAMICA. [Ars ceram.]. **Added/Corp** Wedgwood Society of New York. No. 1 (1984)-. English. an. Comes with Wedgewood Society of New York membership; $35.00 membership. Wedgewood Society of New York, 5 Dogwood Court, Glen Head NY 11545. **Tel** (516)626-3427. **ED** Bernard Starr. **LC** WMLC 93/3328. **DD** 738. Index available. **Bk Rev. Ad Acc. Circ:** 500-600 (ctrl).
Ind/Abst BHA : Biblio. Hist. Art.

XR/0231-5890
ARS VITRARIA. **Added/Corp** Muzeum Skla a Bizuterie v Jablonci nad Nisou. (1966)-. Czech (summaries and/or abstracts in English, French, German and Russian). **LC** NK5100; .A7.
Ind/Abst BHA : Biblio. Hist. Art.

JA/0004-4210
ASAHI GARASU KENKYU HOKOKU. **See** Chemistry-Chemical Technology.

JA/0916-7064
ASAHI GARASU ZAIDAN KENKYU HOKOKU. **Added/Corp** Asahi Garasu Zaidan. **VFOAT** Kenkyu Hokoku; Reports of the Asahi Glass Foundation. Vol. 56 (1990)-. Periodical. Japanese (English). sa. Asahi Garazu Zaidan, 1-4-2 Marunouchi, Chiyoda-ku, Tokyo-to 100 Japan. Documents available from CASDDS. ***Continues*** *Asahi Garasu Kogyo Gijutsu Shoreikai Kenkyu Hokoku, 0365-2599.*
Ind/Abst Chem. Abstr.

AT/1035-4611
AUSTRALIAN CLAY JOURNAL AND CERAMIC NEWS. (1990)-. Periodical. English. Six times a year (Jan., Mar., May, July, Sept., Nov.). 30.00Aus$ Australia; 38.00Aus$ surface mail; 48.00Aus$ airmail. Hamilton Press, PO Box 386, Manly 2095 Australia. **Tel** 011 61 2 9776046, FAX 011 61 2 9763190. **ED** Barry MacCrea. **Bk Rev**, (Qty: varies). **Ad Acc. Circ:** 450.

US/0005-0717
AUTO AND FLAT GLASS JOURNAL. [Auto flat glass j.]. (19??)-. Periodical. English. Twelve times a year. $30.00 US; $35.00 Canada; $58.00 others. Auto & Flat Glass Journal, PO Box 12099, Seattle WA 98102. **Tel** (206)322-5120. **ED** Burton Winters. **DD** 666. **Circ:** 5,800.
Desc: Features step-by-step procedures for removal and installation of glass in current model cars. Reports on automotive glass replacement industry news. Includes general financial and business management information.

US/1047-2061
AUTOGLASS (MCLEAN, VA.). (AUTOGLASS.). **Added/Corp** National Glass Association (U.S.). **VFOAT** Auto Glass Magazine. Vol. 1, No. 1 (Jan./Feb. 1990)-. Periodical. English. Seven times a year. $19.95 North America; $34.95 other. National Glass Association, PO Box 754, Peri River NY 10965-9953. **Tel** (703)442-4890, FAX (703)442-0630. **ED** Nicole Harris and Carolyn Brown. **LC** IN PROCESS. **DD** 629. Index available. cum. index. **Ad Acc. Pr Rev. Circ:** 7,000. ***Continues in part*** *Glass Magazine, 0747-4261.*
Desc: Reporting on auto glass business news, the latest products and technology developments, management, company profiles and industry analysis for both the original equipment manufacturers and the after market segments of the industry.

US/1043-5468
BEAUTIFUL GLASS FOR HOME & OFFICE. ***Suspended.*** [Beautiful glass for home off.]. **VFOAT** Beautiful Glass for Home and Office; Beautiful Glass. Vol. 1, No. 1 (Spring 1990)-Suspended. Periodical. English. qt. $15.00 North America; $30.00 other. Edge Publishing Group, Route 6 Dingle Ridge Road, PO Box 69, Brewster NY 10509. **Tel** (914)279-7399, (800)421-8142, FAX (914)279-7361. **ED** Chris Peterson. **DD** 748. **Bk Rev. Ad Acc. Circ:** 25,000 (ctrl).
Desc: Covers uses of art glass in residential and corporate architecture.

SP/0366-3175
BOLETIN DE LA SOCIEDAD ESPANOLA DE CERAMICA Y VIDRIO (1983). (BOLETIN DE LA SOCIEDAD ESPANOLA DE CERAMICA Y VIDRIO.). **Added/Corp** Sociedad Espanola de Ceramica y Vidrio. (19??)-. Periodical. Spanish (summaries and/or abstracts in English, French and German). bm. 10000ptas. Ctra de Madrid-Valencia, KM 24 300 Arganda del Rey, Madrid Spain. **LC** TP785; .B6. **DD** 666/.06. **[CCC].** Documents available from CASDDS. ***Continues*** *Ceramica Y Vidrio.*
Ind/Abst Art Archaeol. Tech. Abstr.; Ceram. Abstr.; Chem. Abstr.; GeoRef.

CC/1000-2871
BOLI YU TANGCI. (PO LI YU TANG TZU.). [Boli yu tangci]. **Added/Corp** Chuan Kuo Po Li Tang Tzu Kung Yeh Ko Chi Ching Pao Chan. Chung-kuo Ching Kung Yeh Pu Po Li Tang Tzu Kung Yeh Ko Hsueh Yen Chiu So. **VFOAT** Glass & Enamel; Glass and Enamel. (19??)-. Academic Scholarly Publication. Chinese. bm. $45.00. Qinggongye Bu / Boli Yu Tangci Gongye Kexue Yanjiusuo, No. 6, Lane 365, Xinhua Lu, Shanghai 200052, People's Republic of China. **Tel** 2403230. **ED** P. Yukun. **CODEN** BYTAE8. **Bk Rev. Ad Acc. Circ:** 5,150. Documents available from BLDSC, CASDDS.
Ind/Abst Ceram. Abstr. (19??-); Chem. Abstr. (1986-).

US/0161-2794
BRADFORD BOOK OF COLLECTOR'S PLATES, THE. ***Ceased.*** **Added/Corp** Bradford Exhange. (19??)-Ceased with 15th Edition. English. an. The Bradford Exchange, 9333 Milwaukee Avenue, Chicago IL 60648. **Tel** (708)966-2770. **LC** NK4695.P55; B7. **DD** 738.

UK/0268-4373
BRITISH CERAMIC PROCEEDINGS. [Br. ceram. pro.]. **Added/Corp** British Ceramic Society. Institute of Ceramics (Great Britain). **VFOAT** Ceramic Proceedings; Proceedings. No. 34 (August 1984)-. Academic Scholarly Publication. English. ir. $150.00. The Institute of Materials, 1 Carlton House Terrace, London SW1Y 5DB England. **Tel** 011 44 71 839 4071, FAX (071)839 2078. **CODEN** BCPREL. Documents available from Ask*IEEE, CASDDS. ***Continues*** *Proceedings of the British Ceramic Society, 0524-5141.*
Ind/Abst Ceram. Abstr.; Chem. Abstr. (1984-); Ei Page One; INSPEC (Sep. 1984-); World Ceram. Abstr.

UK/0306-7076
BRITISH CERAMIC REVIEW. ***Title Change.*** **Added/Corp** British Ceramic Plant and Machinery Manufacturers' Association. (1966)-. Periodical. English (summaries and/or abstracts in French, German, Italian and Spanish). qt. British Ceramic Plant Machinery, Manufacturing Association, 44 Kingsway Staffs ST4 1JH, England. **Tel** 011 44 782 411433, FAX 0782 747061. **(Subscription address:** 44 Kingsway, Stoke-on-Trent Staffordshire ST4 1JH England) **ED** Charles Wallin. Index available. cum. index. **Bk Rev. Ad Acc. Circ:** 7,000 (ctrl). ***Continued by*** *Global Ceramic Review.*
Desc: Centers on all aspects of production technology for all sectors of the ceramic manufacturing industry.
Ind/Abst Ceram. Abstr.; Eng. Mater. Abstr.; World Ceram. Abstr.

●UK/0967-9782
BRITISH CERAMIC TRANSACTIONS. **Added/Corp** Institute of Materials (London, England). Vol. 92, No. 1 (1993)-. Proceedings. English. bm (Feb., Apr., June, Aug., Oct., Dec.). £108.00 UK; £124.00 other. The Institute of Materials, 1 Carlton House Terrace, London SW1Y 5DB England. **Tel** 011 44 71 839 4071, FAX (071)839 2078. ***Continues in part*** *British Ceramic, Transactions and Journal, 0266-7606.*
Ind/Abst Sci. Cit. Index; Soc. Sci. Cit. Index [Select. Cov.].

UK/0266-7606
BRITISH CERAMIC TRANSACTIONS AND JOURNAL. ***Title Change.*** [Br. ceram., Trans. j.]. **Added/Corp** British Ceramic Society. Institute of Ceramics (Great Britain). **VFOAT** Transactions and Journal. Vol. 83, No. 1 (Jan./Feb. 1984)-(19??). Academic Scholarly Publication. English. bm. British Ceramic Society, Shelton House/Stoke Road, Shelton Stoke-on-Trent England. **LC** TP785; .B862a. **DD** 666. **CODEN** BCTJEH. Documents available from The Genuine Article, CASDDS. ***Continues*** *Transactions and Journal of the British Ceramic Society, 0307-7357.* ***Continued in part by*** *British Ceramic Transactions, 0967-9782;* ***Merged with*** *Metals and Materials (London, England : 1985), 0266-7185* ***and*** *Plastics and Rubber International, 0309-4561* ***to form*** *Materials World, 0967-8638.*
Ind/Abst Ceram. Abstr.; Chem. Abstr. (1984-); Curr. Contents Eng. Tech. Appl. Sci.; Res. Alert [Full Cov.]; Sci. Cit. Index (19??-19??); SCISEARCH.

US/0009-0328
BRUSH DECORATION. (19??)-. Periodical. English. ir. $3.95. Professional Publications Inc., PO Box 12448, Columbus OH 43212. **Tel** (614)488-8236, FAX (614)488-4561. **LC** TP785; .C44. **DD** 666/.05.

II
BULLETIN - CENTRAL GLASS AND CERAMIC RESEARCH INSTITUTE. **Main/Corp** Calcutta. Central Glass and Ceramic Research Institute. Vol. 1 (Aug. 1954)-. Academic Scholarly Publication. English. qt. $50.00. Central Glass & Ceramic Research, Jadavpur Calcutta 32 India. **Tel** 46-7857. **(Subscription address:** Prints India, 11 Darya Ganj, New Delhi 110002 India.) **LC** TP785.C2; A13. **DD** 666.072. Documents available from CASDDS.
Desc: Devoted to the cause of the advancement of glass ceramic and allied sciences and industries.
Ind/Abst Ceram. Abstr. (19??-); Chem. Abstr.; SEA Abstr.; World Ceram. Abstr.

BE
BULLETIN DE L'ASSOCIATION INTERNATIONALE POUR L'HISTOIRE DU VERRE. **Added/Corp** International Association for the History of Glass. No. 5 (1967-1970)-. Bulletin. French (English and German). ir. Price varies per volume. Secretariat AIHV Rijksmuseum, PO Box 74888, 1070 DN Amsterdam Netherlands. **Tel** 011 31 20 6732121. **LC** NK5100; .J64. **Bk Rev. Circ:** 800. ***Continues*** *Bulletin des Journees Internationales du Verre.*
Desc: Each volume is devoted to the glass collections of one country.
Ind/Abst BHA : Biblio. Hist. Art; Br. Archaeol. Bibliogr.

HK
BULLETIN OF THE ORIENTAL CERAMIC SOCIETY OF HONG KONG, THE.
Main/Corp Oriental Ceramic Society of Hong Kong. (1975)-. English (summaries and/or abstracts in Chinese). an. Price varies. Oriental Ceramic Society of Hong Kong, c/o Hong Kong University Press, University of Hong Kong, 139 Pokfulam Road, Hong Kong. **Tel** 5-502703, FAX 5-8750734, telex 71919 CEREB HX. **LC** NK3700; .O7513. **DD** 738/.095.

UK/0306-204X
BUYERS' GUIDE. (EUROPEAN GLASS DIRECTORY & BUYERS GUIDE.). **VFOAT** European Glass Directory and Buyers' Guide. (19??)-. Directory. English. an. £98.60 UK; $164.00 other. Argus Press Group, Queensway House, 2 Queensway Redhill, Surrey RH1 1QS England. **Tel** 011 44 737 768611, 011 44 737 761685, FAX 011 44 737 760510, telex 948669 TOPJNL G. **ED** Bob Sanson. **LC** HD9623.E8; E87. **DD** 380.1/45/66610254. **Ad Acc.**
Desc: Information on manufacturers, processors, and users of glass and the companies who supply them with plant equipment and services.

US/1055-9302
BUYER'S GUIDE (NATIONAL GLASS ASSOCIATION (U.S.)). (BUYER'S GUIDE : AN OFFICIAL PUBLICATION OF THE NATIONAL GLASS ASSOCIATION.). [Buy. guide]. **Added/Corp** National Glass Association (U.S.). **VFOAT** Glass Magazine's ... Buyer's Guide. (1990/1991)-. English. National Glass Association, PO Box 754, Peri River NY 10965-9953. **Tel** (703)442-4890, FAX (703)442-0630. **LC** HD9623.U44; B88. **DD** 666.1/029/473.

US/1049-1252
C2C ABSTRACTS JAPAN. CERAMICS.
See Glass and Ceramics-Abstracting, Bibliographies and Statistics.

US/0895-5948
CA SELECTS: CERAMIC MATERIALS (JOURNALS). **See** Chemistry-Abstracting, Bibliographies and Statistics.

●US/1066-1158
CA SELECTS: COMPOSITE MATERIALS (CERAMIC). **See** Chemistry-Abstracting, Bibliographies and Statistics.

FR/0335-1688
CAHIERS DE LA TERRE CUITE, LES. No. 1 (May 1974)-. Periodical. French. sa. 156. Centre Technique Des Tuiles Et Briques, 2 Avenue, Hoche 75008 Paris France. ***Continues*** *Terre Cuite.*

CN/0316-1137
CANADIAN CERAMICS. **VFOAT** Ceramiques Canadiennes. 1963-. Periodical. English (French). be. Canadian Guild of Potters, 100 Avenue Road, Toronto Ontario M5R 2H3. **DD** 738.3. ***Supersedes*** *Canadian Ceramics.*
Desc: Catalogue of the biennial exhibition of the Canadian Guild of Potters.

CN/0831-2974
CANADIAN CERAMICS QUARTERLY.
[Can. ceram. q.]. **Added/Corp** Canadian Ceramic Society. (Summer 1985)-. Academic Scholarly Publication. English. qt. 40.00Can$ Canada; 45.00Can$ US; 50.00Can$ other. Canadian Ceramic Society, 2175 Sheppard Avenue East/Suite 110, Willowdale Ontario M2J 1W8 Canada. **Tel** (905)491-2886, FAX (905)491-1670. **ED** M. Sayer. **LC** TP786; .C35. **DD** 338.4/7666/0971. **CODEN** CCQUEC. **Ad Acc, Adv Mgr:** B.Howell. **Pr Rev. Circ:** 1,000 (ctrl). Documents available from The Genuine Article, CASDDS. ***Formed by the union of*** *Canadian Clay & Ceramics Quarterly, 0824-2658* ***and*** *Ceramic Hobbyist, 0707-5197;* ***Absorbed*** *Canadian Ceramic Society. Journal, 0068-8444.*
Desc: Articles and news regarding structural clay products, pottery and whitewares, glass, refractories, porcelain enamel, abrasives, electronic ceramics and laboratories and research institutions.
Ind/Abst Ceram. Abstr. (19??-); Chem. Abstr.; Curr. Contents Eng. Tech. Appl. Sci.; Res. Alert [Full Cov.]; SCISEARCH.

NE/0168-4841
CEMENT-, KALK- EN OVERIGE MINERALE PRODUKTENINDUSTRIE, GLASINDUSTRIE EN -BEWERKINGSINRICHTINGEN / CENTRAAL BUREAU VOOR DE STATISTIEK, HOOFDAFDELING STATISTIEKEN VAN INDUSTRIE EN BOUWNIJVERHEID. **VFOAT** Manufacture of Cement, Lime, Plaster, and Non-Metallic Mineral Products, Manufacture of Glass and Glass Products Including Further Processed Flat Glass. Dutch (summaries and/or abstracts in English). Fl9.50. Centraal Bureau voor de Statistiek, AFD ALG Zaken, Postbus 959, 2270 AZ Voorburg Netherlands. **Tel** 011 31 70 3373800, FAX 011 31 038 7429, telex 32692 CBS NL. **LC** HD9585.L52; N43.

US/0095-9960
CERAMIC ABSTRACTS. **See** Glass and Ceramics-Abstracting, Bibliographies and Statistics.

US/1056-3490
CERAMIC ABSTRACTS CD-ROM.
(CERAMIC ABSTRACTS CD-ROM [COMPUTER FILE].). [Ceram. abstr. CD-ROM]. **Added/Corp** American Ceramic Society. National Information Services Corporation. (1991)-. English. sa. $710.00 US, Canada and Mexico; $735.00 other (includes print version). American Ceramic Society, 735 Ceramic Place, Westerville OH 43081-8720. **Tel** (614)890-4700, (614)794-5890, FAX (614)899-6109. **DD** 666. available in print; available on an online database (CERAB) from STN International (Math) Database; (CERM) ORBIT; and (File 335) DIALOG; available on magnetic tape.

US/0009-0190
CERAMIC ARTS & CRAFTS. **VAT** Ceramic Arts and Crafts. (1955)-. Periodical. English. Twelve times a year. $18.70. Scott Publications, 30595 West Eight Mile Road, Livonia MI 48152. **Tel** (313)477-6650, (800)458-8237, FAX (810)477-6795. **ED** Bill Thompson. **Bk Rev. Ad Acc. Circ:** 45,000 (ctrl). available on microfilm from University Microfilms International (UMI).
Desc: The number one ceramics featuring step-by-step projects in full color with easy instructions. An array of different techniques, new products, national shows, patterns and worldwide studio listing.

US/0196-6219
CERAMIC ENGINEERING AND SCIENCE PROCEEDINGS. [Ceram. eng. sci. proc.]. **Added/Corp** American Ceramic Society. **VFOAT** Ceramic Engineering & Science Proceedings. Vol. 1 (Jan./Feb. 1980)-. Academic Scholarly Publication. English. Six times a year (Feb., Apr., June, Aug., Oct., Dec.). $85.00 US; $95.00 other. American Ceramic Society, 735 Ceramic Place, Westerville OH 43081-8720. **Tel** (614)890-4700, (614)794-5890, FAX (614)899-6109. **LC** TP785; .C34. **DD** 666/.05. **CODEN** CESPDK. **[CCC].** available on microfilm from University Microfilms International (UMI). Documents available from Article Express International, CASDDS.
Ind/Abst Alum. Ind. Abstr.; Ceram. Abstr.; Chem. Abstr.; Coal Abstr.; Eng. Mater. Abstr.; Eng. Index Annu.; INIS Atomindex [Micro.]; Int. Aerosp. Abstr.; Met. Abstr.; World Ceram. Abstr.

UK
CERAMIC INDUSTRIES INTERNATIONAL. **Added/Corp** British Pottery Managers Association. **VFOAT** Ceramic Industries Journal. Vol. 98, No. 1073 (Feb. 1989)-. Periodical. English. bm. £60.00 UK; £68.00 (surface), £76.00 (air mail) other. Turret Group, 177 Hagden Lane, Watford Herts WD1 8LN United Kingdom. **Tel** 011 44 923 228577, FAX 011 44 923 221346. **LC** TP785; .C435. **DD** 666/.05. **CODEN** CEIIEI. available on microfilm from University Microfilms International (UMI). ***Continues*** *Ceramic Industries Journal, 0305-7623.*
Ind/Abst Ceram. Abstr. (19??-); World Ceram. Abstr.

US/0009-0220
CERAMIC INDUSTRY. [Ceram. ind.]. Vol. 1 (June 1923)-. Trade Publication. English. mo (except 2 issues in Sept.). $59.00 US; $69.00 Canada and Mexico; $129.00 other. Business News Publishing Company, 755 West Big Beaver Road, Suite 1000, Troy MI 48084. **Tel** (810)362-3700, FAX (810)362-0317, telex 230295. **ED** F L Steinhoff. **LC** TP785; .C35. **DD** 666.05. **CODEN** CEINAT. **Ad Acc. Circ:** 9,850 (ctrl). available on microfilm and microfiche from University Microfilms International (UMI); available on an online database (file 648/Full-Text) from DIALOG. ***Absorbed*** *Ceramic Data Book, 0162-5330.*
Desc: Serves manufacturers of advanced ceramics, glass, whiteware, structural clay, refractories and porcelain enamel products.
Ind/Abst Appl. Sci. Technol. Index (-1990); Ceram. Abstr.; EMBASE; F&S Index Plus Text, Int. [Select. Cov.]; PROMT; Surf. Treat. Technol. Abstr.; Trade Ind. ASAP [Full Txt.]; Trade Ind. Index [Full Txt.]; World Ceram. Abstr.

US/0009-0328
CERAMIC PROJECTS. (19??)-. Periodical. English. ir. $2.95. Professional Publications Inc., PO Box 12448, Columbus OH 43212. **Tel** (614)488-8236, FAX (614)488-4561. **LC** TP785; .C44. **DD** 666/.05.

UK/0144-1825
CERAMIC REVIEW. [Ceram. rev.]. **Added/Corp** Craftsmen Potters Association of Great Britain. (19??)-. Periodical. English. bm. £28.50 UK; £32.00 other. Ceramic Review Publishing Limited, 21 Carnaby Street, London W1V 1PH England. **Tel** 011 44 71 4393377, FAX 011 44 71 2879954. **ED** Eileen Lewenstein and Emmanuel Cooper. **LC** TP808; .C47. **DD** 738/.05. **Bk Rev. Ad Acc. Circ:** 9,000 (ctrl).
Desc: Ceramics making history, teaching of ceramics, contributions from well-known potters and what's happening in ceramics today in UK and all over the world.
Ind/Abst Art Index; ARTbibliogr. Mod. (1984-).

US/0009-0247
CERAMIC SCOPE. ***Ceased.*** [Ceram. scope]. (1964)-(June 1993). Periodical. English. an. Ceramic Scope, PO Box 1992, Wilmington DE 19899. **Tel** (302)656-2209, FAX (302)656-4710. **ED** Michael Scott. **DD** 738. Index available. cum. index. **Bk Rev. Ad Acc. Circ:** 14,000 (ctrl).
Desc: A yearly publication listing suppliers and distributors for ceramic hobby industry, serving the ceramic hobby market.

US/8756-8187
CERAMIC SOURCE. [Ceram. source]. **Added/Corp** American Ceramic Society. Vol. 1 (1986)-. English. an (September). $45.00 US; $55.00 other. American Ceramic Society, 735 Ceramic Place, Westerville OH 43081-8720. **Tel** (614)890-4700, (614)794-5890, FAX (614)899-6109. **ED** W J Smothers and Donald C Snyder. **LC** TP785; .C36. **DD** 666/.05. **CODEN** CESOEI. **[CCC].** Index available. **Ad Acc.** Documents available from Ask*IEEE.
Desc: Contains directories on companies, their products, their services, and product tradenames, and exclusive technical data of interest to ceramic engineering and science professionals.
Ind/Abst INSPEC (1986-).

AT
CERAMIC STUDY GROUP NEWSLETTER. **See** Hobbies.

US/1042-1122
CERAMIC TRANSACTIONS. [Ceram. trans.]. **Added/Corp** American Ceramic Society. Vol. 1 (1988)-. Monographic series. English. ir. Price varies per volume. American Ceramic Society, 735 Ceramic Place, Westerville OH 43081-8720. **Tel** (614)890-4700, (614)794-5890, FAX (614)899-6109. **DD** 666. **CODEN** CETREW. Documents available from CASDDS.
Ind/Abst Ceram. Abstr. (19??-); Chem. Abstr.

US/0748-304X
CERAMIC WORLD. [Ceram. world]. Periodical. English. mo. $15.00 US; $19.00 other. Ceramic World, PO Box 67A, Mukilteo WA 98275-0067. **DD** 738.

IT/1121-6093
CERAMICA ACTA. [Ceram. acta]. (1989)-. Periodical. Italian. bm (6 issues). L100000 Italy; L160000 Europe; L250000 other. Centro Ceramico Bologna, Via Martelli 26, 40138 Bologna Italy. **Tel** 011 39 51 534015. **UDC** 666.3. Index available. **Ad Acc.** ctrl circ.
Desc: Technical subjects about ceramics.

IT/0009-0271
CERAMICA INFORMAZIONE. (CERAMICA INFORMAZIONE; PERIODICO TECNICO SPECIALIZZATO.). [Ceram. inf.]. Vol. 1, (1966)-. Academic Scholarly Publication. Italian (English; summaries and/or abstracts in English, French, German and Italian). mo. L77000.00 Italy; L125000.00 others. Faenza Editrice, Via P de Crescenzi 44, 48018 Faenza Italy. **Tel** 011 39 546 663488, FAX 011 39 546 660440, telex 550387. **CODEN** CINFDR. **Bk Rev. Ad Acc. Circ:** 5,000. Documents available from CASDDS.
Desc: Studies of ceramics in building, industry and chemical branches.
Ind/Abst Ceram. Abstr.; Chem. Abstr.; Eng. Mater. Abstr.; World Ceram. Abstr.

SP/0210-010X
CERAMICA MADRID. [CeramicaMadrid]. (1978)-. Periodical. Spanish. qt. 2800ptas. Antonio Vivas, Ceramica, Paseo Acacias 9, 28005 Madrid Spain. **Tel** 011 34 1 517-3239. **ED** Antonio Vivas. **UDC** 738. Index available. cum. index. **Bk Rev. Ad Acc. Circ:** 10,000.
Desc: Modern ceramics in the world. Internationally focused.

AG/0327-0947
CERAMICA MENDOZA. (1987)-. Periodical. Spanish. tq. **UDC** 738. **CODEN** 738 :904(82).
Ind/Abst Ceram. Abstr.

IT
CERAMICA PER L'ARCHITETTURA : CA. **VFOAT** CA; CA, Ceramica per l'Architettura. Periodical. Italian. Three times a year. L40.000. Faenza Editrice, Via P de Crescenzi 44, 48018 Faenza Italy. **Tel** 011 39 546 663488, FAX 011 39 546 660440, telex 550387.

IT
CERAMICA PER L'EDILIZIA INTERNATIONAL. (19??)-. Italian (French, German and English). bm (6 issues). L72000 Italy; L110000 other. Faenza Editrice, Via P de Crescenzi 44, 48018 Faenza Italy. **Tel** 011 39 546 663488, FAX 011 39 546 660440, telex 550387. **ED** Roberto Ferretti. **LC** TH8541; .C47. **DD** 666/.73. **Bk Rev. Ad Acc. Circ:** 20,000. ***Continues*** *Ceramica Italiana Nell'Edilizia.*
Desc: International magazine of ceramic tiles in building and architecture.

BL/0366-6913
CERAMICA (SAO PAULO). (CERAMICA.). [Ceramica]. **Added/Corp** Associacao Brasileiro de Ceramica. Vol. 1, No. 1 (1955)-. Academic Scholarly Publication. Portuguese (Spanish and English). Four times a year (March, June, Sept. and Dec.). $54.00 Brazil, $90.00 other. Associacao Brasileira de Ceramica, rua Leonardo Nunes 82, 04039 Sao Paulo SP Brazil. **Tel** 11

55 11 5493922, FAX 11 55 11 8841289. **ED** Maria Angelica Togni Paiva. **CODEN** CMCAAG. Index available. cum. index. **Bk Rev**, (Qty: 4). **Ad Acc. Circ:** 2,000 (ctrl). Documents available from CASDDS.
Ind/Abst Ceram. Abstr. (19??-); Chem. Abstr.; Coal Abstr.; GeoRef; World Ceram. Abstr.

AG/0325-0229
CERAMICA Y CRISTAL. Added/Corp Asociacion Tecnica Argentina de Ceramica. Vol. 1 (1961)-. Academic Scholarly Publication. Spanish. bm (6 issues). $16.00. Editorial Ciclo Federico, Av. Melian 2208 COD 1430, Buenos Aires Argentina. **Tel** 544 7007, FAX 542 1612. **ED** Arnoldo Alonso Ibanez. **LC** TP785; .C422. Index available. cum. index. **Ad Acc.** Full Page (Color) $1150.00. Half Page (Color) $650.00. **Circ:** 3,000. Documents available from CASDDS.
Ind/Abst Ceram. Abstr. (19??-); Chem. Abstr.

IT/1121-6956
CERAMICANTICA FERRARA. (CERAMICANTICA.). [CeramicAnticaFerrara]. (1991)-. Periodical. Italian. mo (11 issues per year - not published in August). L85000 Italy; L130000 other. Editrice Belriguardo, Via Mashcheraio 29, 44100 Ferrara Italy. **Tel** 0532-202170, FAX 0532-205332. **ED** Romolo Magnani. **UDC** 738.

US/8756-8179
CERAMICS AND CIVILIZATION. [Ceram. civiliz.]. **Added/Corp** American Ceramic Society. Vol. 1 (1985)-. Academic Scholarly Publication. English. an. Price varies per volume. American Ceramic Society, 735 Ceramic Place, Westerville OH 43081-8720. **Tel** (614)890-4700, (614)794-5890, FAX (614)899-6109. **ED** W David Kingery. **DD** 666. **CODEN** CECIEM. Documents available from CASDDS.
Desc: Provides a historical perspective on the impact of ceramics on civilization and what is the future of ceramics.
Ind/Abst Ceram. Abstr. (19??-); Chem. Abstr. (1985-).

IT/0272-8842
CERAMICS INTERNATIONAL. [Ceram. int.]. Vol. 7, No. 1 (Jan./March 1981)-. Academic Scholarly Publication. English. Six times a year. $559.00 The Americas; £375.00 other. Elsevier Applied Science, An Imprint of Elsevier Science Ltd., The Boulevard, Langford Lane, Kidlington, Oxford OX5 1GB United Kingdom. **Tel** 011 44 865 843000, 011 44 865 843699, FAX 011 44 865 843010. **(Subscription address:** Elsevier Science Ltd. Oxford Fulfillment Centre, PO Box 800, Kidlington, Oxford OX5 1DX United Kingdom.**)** **ED** P. Vincenzini. **LC** TP785; .C436. **DD** 666/.05. **CODEN** CINNDH. **[CCC]. Bk Rev. Ad Acc. Pr Rev.** available on microfilm and microfiche from University Microfilms International (UMI). Documents available from Article Express International, The Genuine Article, Ask*IEEE, CASDDS. ***Continues*** *Ceramurgia International, 0390-5519.*
Desc: Deals with the fundamental aspects of ceramic science and its application to the development of improved traditional and non-traditional ceramic products.
Ind/Abst Alum. Ind. Abstr.; Appl. Mech. Rev.; Bioeng. Abstr.; Ceram. Abstr.; Chem. Abstr.; Curr. Contents Eng. Tech. Appl. Sci.; Ei Page One; Eng. Mater. Abstr.; Eng. Index Annu.; INSPEC (1981-); Met. Abstr.; Res. Alert [Full Cov.]; SCISEARCH; World Ceram. Abstr.

US/1041-1305
CERAMICS MAGAZINE. [Ceram. mag.]. **VFOAT** Ceramics. Vol. 24, Issue 1 (Sept. 1988)-. Periodical. English. mo. $19.60. Scott Publications, 30595 West Eight Mile Road, Livonia MI 48152. **Tel** (313)477-6650, (800)458-8237, FAX (810)477-6795. **LC** TT919; .C47. **DD** 738/.05. ***Formed by the union of*** *Ceramics Teaching Projects, 0162-7090* ***and*** *Ceramics (Fresno, Calif.).*
Desc: Variety of informative articles, helpful tips and decorating secrets and shortcuts, decorating techniques from traditional to trendy, lastest product news and profiles of world-famed artists.

US/0009-0328
CERAMICS MONTHLY. [Ceram. mon.]. Vol. 1 (Jan. 1953)-. Periodical. English. mo (10 issues). $22.00 (one year), $40.00 (two year), $55.00 (three year). Professional Publications Inc., PO Box 12448, Columbus OH 43212. **Tel** (614)488-8236, FAX (614)488-4561. **ED** William H. Hunt. **LC** TP785; .C44. **DD** 666/.05. Index available. cum. index. **Bk Rev. Ad Acc. Circ:** 34,000 (ctrl). available on microfilm and microfiche from University Microfilms International (UMI). Documents available from UMI Article Clearinghouse, Magazine Collection.
Desc: Serving ceramic art field both amateur and professional.
Ind/Abst Access (1980-1988); Art Index; ARTbibliogr. Mod.; Ceram. Abstr.; Gen. Period. Index (1985-); Mag. Index Plus (1989-); Newsp. Period. Abstr. (1988-); Mag. Index (1977-).

AT/1035-1841
CERAMICS PADDINGTON. (CERAMICS). [Ceramics Paddington]. **VFOAT** Ceramics : Art and Perception. (1990)-. Periodical. English. qt. 55.00Aus$ Australia; 66.00Aus$ other. Ceramics Art & Perception, 35 William Street, Paddington New South Wales 2021 Australia. **Tel** 011 61 2 361-5286, FAX 011 61 2 361-5402. **ED** Janet Mansfield. **DD** 738.05. **Bk Rev. Ad Acc. Circ:** 10,000 (ctrl).

XR/0862-5468
CERAMICS (PRAHA). (CERAMICS.). [Ceramics]. **Added/Corp** Ceskoslovenska Aakademie Ved. Ustav Chemie Skelnych a Keramickych Materialu CSAV. **VFOAT** Silikaty. (1990)-. Periodical. English (Czech; summaries and/or abstracts in Russian; table of contents in Russian). qt. DM157.00 Germany; DM187.00 other. **(Subscription address:** Kubon & Sagner, ABT Zeitschriftenimport, D 80328 Munich Germany.**)** **LC** TA455.S46; S5. **DD** 666/.05. **CODEN** CERSEP. Documents available from Article Express International, The Genuine Article, Ask*IEEE, CASDDS. ***Continues*** *Silikaty, 0037-5241.*
Ind/Abst Ceram. Abstr. (199?-); Chem. Abstr.; Eng. Index Annu.; INSPEC (1990-); Res. Alert [Full Cov.]; Sci. Cit. Index; SCISEARCH; World Ceram. Abstr.

SZ/0254-4636
CERAMICS TODAY. No. 1 (Apr. 1983)-. Periodical. English. qt. Edizions Olizane, PO Box 1953, New York NY 10185.
Ind/Abst ARTbibliogr. Mod. (1983-).

FR/0009-0336
CERAMIQUE MODERNE, LA. Vol. 1, No. 10 (Oct. 1960)-. Periodical. French. Eleven times a year. 192.10F France; 235.00F other. Editions Techniques et Artistiques, 22 rue le Brun, Paris 75013 France. **Tel** 011 33 1 45871748. **Ad Acc. Circ:** 4,000. ***Continues*** *Ceramique d'Art.*
Desc: Professional news concerning arts and crafts, ceramics and pottery.
Ind/Abst BHA : Biblio. Hist. Art.

CN/0712-8770
CERAMISTE. (LE CERAMISTE.). [Ceramiste]. Vol. 1, No. 1, (Dec./Jan. 1981)-. Periodical. French. bm. $14.00. Le Ceramiste, Bureau 408/1410 rue Stanley, Montreal Quebec H3A 1P8 Canada. **DD** 738/.05.

IT/0045-6152
CERAMURGIA. [Ceramurgia]. **Added/Corp** Laboratorio di Ricerche Tecnologiche per la Ceramica. (1971)-. Academic Scholarly Publication. Italian (summaries and/or abstracts in English, French and German). Six times a year (Feb., Apr., June, Aug., Oct., Dec.). L150000.00 Italy; $185.00 other. Techna SRL, PO Box 174, 48018 Faenza Italy. **Tel** 011 39 546 22461. **ED** P. Vincenzini. **LC** TP785; .C45. **CODEN** CRGIAR. **Bk Rev. Ad Acc, Adv Mgr:** G. Bertoni, **Tel** 0546 22661. **Pr Rev. Circ:** 6,000. Documents available from Article Express International, CASDDS.
Desc: Applied research and technological innovation in the fields of both classical and hi-tech ceramic products.
Ind/Abst Bioeng. Abstr.; Ceram. Abstr.; Chem. Abstr.; Ei Page One; Eng. Mater. Abstr.; Eng. Index Annu. [Select. Cov.]; GeoRef; World Ceram. Abstr.

GW/0173-9913
CFI, CERAMIC FORUM INTERNATIONAL. (CERAMIC FORUM INTERNATIONAL : CFI : BERICHTE DER DKG.). [CFI, Ceram. forum int.]. **Added/Corp** Deutsche Keramische Gesellschaft. **VFOAT** CFI. Vol. 57, No. 9-10 (Sept./Oct. 1980)-. Academic Scholarly Publication. English (German). Ten times a year. DM258.00 Germany; DM303.00 other. Bauverlag GmbH, Postfach 1460, D 65173 Wiesbaden Germany. **Tel** 011 49 6123 7000, FAX 011 49 6123 700122. **LC** TP785; .D23. **DD** 666/.05. **CODEN** CCFDD7. Index available. **Bk Rev. Ad Acc. Circ:** 4,500 (ctrl). Documents available from Article Express International, The Genuine Article, Ask*IEEE, CASDDS. ***Continues*** *Berichte der Deutschen Keramischen Gesellschaft (Bonn, Germany : 1953), 0365-9542.*
Desc: Scientific papers, ceramic engineering and news from the industry.
Ind/Abst Alum. Ind. Abstr.; Bioeng. Abstr.; Ceram. Abstr.; Chem. Abstr.; Coal Abstr.; Ei Page One; EMBASE; Energy Res. Abstr. (Oct. 1981-); Eng. Index Annu.; GeoRef; HTFS Dig.; INSPEC (Sept./Oct. 1980-); Met. Abstr.; Res. Alert [Full Cov.]; Soc. Sci. Cit. Index [Select. Cov.]; World Ceram. Abstr.

US/0009-4382
CHINA GLASS & TABLEWARE. VAT China Glass and Tableware. Vol. 92, No. 12 (Dec. 1974)-. Trade Publication. English. mo. Doctorow Communications Inc., 1033 Clifton Avenue, PO Box 2147, Clifton NJ 07013. **Tel** (201)779-1600, FAX (201)779-3242. **ED** Amy Stavis. **[CCC]. Ad Acc. Circ:** 3,300 (ctrl). ***Continues*** *China, Glass & Tablewares.*
Desc: We are a tabletop trade magazine dealing with stories on specialty stores, department stores and new lines of dinnerware, glassware and flatware.

CN/1194-6377
CONTACT - ALBERTA POTTERS' ASSOCIATION (1992). (CONTACT.). [Contact - Alta. Potters' Assoc.]. **Added/Corp** Alberta Potters' Association. (Autumn 1992)-. Periodical. English. qt. 30.00Can$ Canada; 35.00Can$ other. Alberta Potter's Association, PO Box 5303, Station A, Calgary, Alberta T2H 1X6 Canada. **Tel** (403)255-8658. **DD** 738/.097123/05. ***Continues*** *Contact Magazine (Calgary, Alta.), 0843-1981.*

CN/0843-1981
CONTACT MAGAZINE (CALGARY). ***Title Change.*** (CONTACT MAGAZINE / ALBERTA POTTERS' ASSOCIATION.). [Contact mag.]. **Added/Corp** Alberta Potters' Association. Issue No. 71 (Dec. 1987)-(1992). Periodical. English. qt. Alberta Potter's Association, PO Box 5303, Station A, Calgary, Alberta T2H 1X6 Canada. **Tel** (403)255-8658. **DD** 738/.097123/05. ***Continues*** *Contact., 0705-3584.* ***Continued by*** *Contact (Calgary, Alta. : 1992), 1194-6377.*
Ind/Abst Can. Period. Index (19??-?).

GW
CONTINENTAL HOMEWARES. ***Ceased.*** **VFOAT** Homewares. (Spring 1984)-(Fall 1993). Periodical. English. sa. SDI Journal & Communications GmbH, Postfach 3208, W-4 Duesseldorf 1 Germany.

US/0009-0328
COPPER ENAMELING. (19??)-. Periodical. English. ir. $2.95. Professional Publications Inc., PO Box 12448, Columbus OH 43212. **Tel** (614)488-8236, FAX (614)488-4561. **LC** TP785; .C44. **DD** 666/.05.

US/0589-7483
CORNING RESEARCH. (1961)-. English. ir. Corning Glass Works, Telecommunications Products Division, Corning NY 14830. **Tel** (607)974-7600.
Ind/Abst Ceram. Abstr. (19??-).

IT
CORPUS VASORUM ANTIQUORUM. ITALIA. **See** Museums and Galleries.

PL
CORPUS VASORUM ANTIQUORUM. POLOGNE. Added/Corp Polska Akademia Umiejetnosci, Krakow. International Union of Academies. Issue 1 (1931)-. Monographic series. French. ir. Price varies per volume. **(Subscription address:** ARS Polona, PO Box 1001, 00068 Warsaw Poland.**)** **LC** NK4640.C6; P6.

US
CURRENT INDUSTRIAL REPORTS. MA-32J, GLASS FIBERS. ***Ceased.*** **Added/Corp** United States. Bureau of the Census. **VFOAT** Glass Fibers. (1987)-(19??). Government Publication. English. an. US Department of Commerce, 14th Street & Constitution Avenue NW, Washington DC 20230. **Tel** (202)482-2000, FAX (202)482-3772. ***Continues*** *Current Industrial Reports. MA-32J, Fibrous Glass.*
Desc: Information on the glass fiber industry.

US/0895-3961
DAZE INC, THE. [Daze Inc.]. **VFOAT** Daze. Vol. 14, No. 7 (Oct. 1984)-. Periodical. English. mo. $21.00 (one year), $40.00 (two year) US; $22.00 (one year), $42.00 (two year) other. Depression Glass Daze Inc., Box 57, Otisville MI 48463. **Tel** (810)631-4593, FAX (810)631-4567. **ED** Teresa L. Steele. **DD** 748. **Bk Rev. Ad Acc. Circ:** 20,000 (ctrl). ***Continues*** *Depression Glass Daze, 0270-8485.*
Desc: Marketplace for glass, china, and pottery.

US/0274-5577
DEPRESSION GLASS NATIONAL MARKET APPRAISAL REPORT, THE. [Depress. glass natl. mark. appraisal rep.]. (19??)-. Periodical. English. qt. $9.95 (one year), $17.95 (two year), $34.95 (three year). Treasure Trove Publishing Company, 2943 Realty Court, Gastonia NC 28052. **Tel** (704)867-1288.

UK
DIGEST OF INFORMATION AND PATENT REVIEW. Main/Corp British Glass Industry Research Association. No. 124 (Sept. 1965)-. Periodical. English. Four times a year. $178.30. British Glass Industry Research Association, Northumberland Road, Sheffield S10 2UA England. **Tel** 011 44 742 686201. **ED** T. Green and P. Smith. Index available. cum. index. **Ad Acc, Adv Mgr:** T. Green. **Circ:** 300 (ctrl). ***Continues*** *British Glass Industry Research Association. Digest of Information, 0952-8032.*

JA
ELECTRONIC CERAMICS. (19??)-. Japanese (English). Six times a year. $132.00. Gakkensha, (Gakkensha Co., Ltd.), 1-3, Koishikawa 3 Chome, Bunkyoku, Tokyoto 112 Japan. **(Subscription address:** Kyowa Book Company Inc., 1 38 Kanda Jinbocho Chiyoda-ku, Tokyo 101 Japan.**)**
Ind/Abst Ceram. Abstr. (19??-).

CI/0350-3607
EMAJL-KERAMIKA-STAKLO. [Emajl, Keram., Staklo]. **Added/Corp** Udruzenje Emajliraca Jugoslavije. (19??)-. Periodical. Serbo-Croatian (Roman). Four times a year. $20.00. Udruzenje Emajliraca Jugoslavije, Yugoslavian Enamellers Association, Srebrnjak 169, 41000 Zagreb, Croatia. **ED** Robert Laslo. **CODEN** EKESDN. **Bk Rev. Ad Acc. Circ:** 1,000 (ctrl). Documents available from CASDDS. ***Supersedes*** *Emajl, 0013-6506.*
Ind/Abst Chem. Abstr.

HU/0013-970X
EPITOANYAG. **See** Building and Construction.

UK/0264-5041
EUROPEAN TABLEWARE BUYERS GUIDE. (Jan. 1984)-. Consumer Publication. English. an. £43.00 UK; £53.00, $86.00 other. Argus Press Group, Queensway House, 2 Queensway Redhill, Surrey RH1 1QS England. **Tel** 011 44 737 768611, 011 44 737 761685, FAX 011 44 737 760510, telex 948669 TOPJNL G. Index available. cum. index. **Ad Acc.** available on diskette. ***Continues*** *Tablware Reference Book* ***and*** *Tableware and Pottery Gazette Reference Book.*
Desc: Guide to manufacturing tableware, giftware and household factories and related service industries throughout Europe.

IT/0014-679X
FAENZA. [Faenza]. **Added/Corp** Museo Internazionale delle Ceramiche (Faenza, Italy). Vol. 1 (1913)-. Periodical. Italian. Four times a year. L60000 (Italy); L70000 (other). Museo Internazionale Delle Ceramiche, Via Campidori 2, 48018 Faenza Italy. **Tel** 39 54621240, FAX 39 54627141. **ED** Gian Carlo Botani. Index available (bound in all issues). cum. index. **Bk Rev**, (Qty: Various). **Circ:** 900.
Desc: Offers historical and technical studies of the art of ceramics.
Ind/Abst Art Archaeol. Tech. Abstr.; ARTbibliogr. Mod. (1982-); BHA : Biblio. Hist. Art; Ceram. Abstr.

RU/0132-6651
FIZIKA I HIMIJA STEKLA. (FIZIKA I KHIMIIA STEKLA.). [Fiz. him. stekla]. **Added/Corp** Akademiia Nauk SSSR. (1975)-. Russian. bm. $192.00. **(Subscription address:** East View Publications Inc., 3020 Harbor Lane North, Suite 110, Minneapolis MN 55447.**) LC** TP845; .F58. **CODEN** FKSTD5. Documents available from Article Express International, Ask*IEEE, CASDDS.
Ind/Abst Chem. Abstr.; Ei Page One; Eng. Index Annu.; INSPEC (1975-).

LV/0134-7071
FIZIKA I KHIMIIA STEKLOOBRAZUIUSHCHIKH SISTEM. **See** Chemistry-Analytical Chemistry.

US/0146-566X
FLAT GLASS. ***Title Change.*** (CURRENT INDUSTRIAL REPORTS. MQ-32A, FLAT GLASS / U.S. DEPARTMENT OF COMMERCE, BUREAU OF THE CENSUS.). [Flat glass]. **Added/Corp** United States. Bureau of the Census. **VFOAT** Flat Glass. (19??)-(1992). Government Publication. English. qt (summary issue). US Department of Commerce, 14th Street & Constitution Avenue NW, Washington DC 20230. **Tel** (202)482-2000, FAX (202)482-3772. **LC** HD9623.U44; U54a. **DD** 338.4/76661/0973. **CODEN** CIRMDY. Documents available from CASDDS, Documents on Demand. ***Continued by*** *Current Industrial Reports. MQ32A, Flat Glass (Computer File).*
Desc: Presents data on the production, inventories, and orders of approximately 5,000 products, which represents 40 percent of all US manufacturing.
Ind/Abst Am. Stat. Index (?-?); Chem. Abstr. (1961-1984).

US/0197-2766
FRACTURE MECHANICS OF CERAMICS. [Fract. mech. ceram.]. (1974)-. Academic Scholarly Publication. English. ir. Price varies per volume. Plenum Press, 233 Spring Street, New York NY 10013-1578. **Tel** (212)620-8000, (800)221-9369, FAX (212)463-0742, (212)807-1047, telex 23/421139. **ED** R.C. Bradt, D.P.H. Hasselman, and F.F. Lange. **LC** TA430; .F68. **DD** 620.1/40426. **CODEN** FMCEDU. Documents available from CASDDS.
Ind/Abst Chem. Abstr. (1974-1983).

CN/0832-9656
FUSION MAGAZINE. [Fusion mag.]. **Added/Corp** Fusion, the Ontario Clay and Glass Association. Vol. 10 No. 4 (1986)-. Periodical. English. Four times a yearQuarterly. 50.00Can$ (individual), 70.00Can$ (institution), Canada; 60.00Can$ (individual), 75.00Can$ (institution), other. Ontario Clay and Glass Association, 80 Spadina Avenue, Suite 204, Toronto ONT M5V 2J3 Canada. **Tel** (416)777-9899, FAX (416)777-9905. **DD** 738/.09713. **Bk Rev**, (Qty: few). **Ad Acc.** ***Formed by the union of*** *Fusion (Toronto, Ont.), 0821-0071* ***and*** *Ontario Potter News, 0822-8930.*
Desc: An annual meeting advocay to the government and business. This includes workshops and lectures, and access to our slide collection.
Ind/Abst Can. Period. Index; INFO-SOUTH Abstr.

US/0016-3155
FUSION WILMINGTON, DEL. [Fusion Wilmington, Del]. (1954)-. English. Four times a year (Feb., May, Aug., Nov.). $32.00 (surface mail); $38.00 Canada, $48.00 others (airmail). American Science Glassblowers Society, 1507 Hagley Road, Toledo OH 43612. **Tel** (419)476-5478, FAX (419)478-0636. **ED** Brenda Cloninger, (editor's address: 2816 Arden Way, Smyrna, GA 30080, phone: (404)432-9131). **CODEN** FUSIA5. Index available. cum. index. **Bk Rev. Ad Acc. Circ:** 1,200.

GW/0016-3538
G-I-T. [GIT]. **VFOAT** GIT; GIT Fachz. Lab.; Fachzeitschrift fur das Laboratorium. **VAT** Glas und Instrumenten-Technik. (1960)-. Periodical. German. mo. DM148.00. GIT Verlag GmbH, Roblerstrabe 90, Postfach 110564, D 64220 Darmstadt Germany. **Tel** 011 49 6151 8090-0, FAX 011 49 6151 8090-45. **CODEN** GITEAR. Documents available from CASDDS. ***Continues*** *Glas + [i.e. und] Instrumenten-Technik.* ***Continued in part by*** *GIT Labor-Medizin, 0170-205X.*
Ind/Abst Chem. Abstr.

US/8756-9213
GEISHA GIRL PORCELAIN. **VFOAT** Geisha Girl Porcelain Newsletter. (19??)-. Periodical. English. bm. $12.00. Geisha Girl Porcelain Newsletter, PO Box 394, Morris Plains NJ 07950. **ED** Elyce Litts. **LC** NK4399.G45; G44. **DD** 738.2/7. **Circ:** 100.
Desc: History, descriptions, pricing, photos, reader letters of titled Japanese export porcelain.

SW/0017-078X
GLAS OCH PORSLIN. [Glas och porslin]. (1930)-. Periodical. Swedish (English). Five times a year. $225.00. Publicisterna Vast AB, Norra Kustbanegatan 13, 41664 Goteborg Sweden. **Tel** 11 46 31 158158, FAX 11 46 31 153446. **ED** Tove M. Gjessing. **UDC** 666. **Ad Acc. Circ:** 1,500 (ctrl).

AU
GLAS OSTERREICHISCHE GLASER ZEITUNG. (19??)-. Trade Publication. German. mo. S492.00 Austria; S732.00 other. Osterreichischer Wirtschaftsvg, Nikolsdorfer Gasse 7 11, A 1051 Vienna Austria. **Tel** 011 43 1 555585.

YU
GLAS - SRPSKA AKADEMIJA NAUKA I UMETNOSTI, ODELJENJE PRIRODNO-MATEMATICKIKH NAUKA. **Main/Corp** Srpska Akademija Nauka i Umetnosti. Odeljenje Prirodno-Matematickikh Nauka. **VFOAT** Glas de l'Academie Serbe des Sciences et des Arts, Classe de Sciences Mathematiques et Naturelles. No. 21; 1961-. Periodical. Serbo-Croatian (Cyrillic) (French). ***Continues*** *Belgrade. Srpska Akademija Nauka. Odeljenje Prirodno-Matematickikh Naks. Glas.*
Ind/Abst Ceram. Abstr.; Ecol. Abstr. (?-?); Geol. Abstr.

GW/0036-3065
GLAS UND RAHMEN. **VAT** Glas + Rahmen. (April 5, 1968)-. Periodical. German. sm. DM171.20 Europe; DM272.00 other. Verlag Karl Hofmann, Postfach 1360, D-73603 Schorndorf Germany. **Tel** 011 49 7181 4020. Index Available in first issue of next volume--loose--separately paged. **Bk Rev. Ad Acc.** ctrl circ. ***Continues*** *St. Lucas Allgemeine Glaserzeitung.*
Desc: Journal about glass manufacturing, isolated glass, window making, etc.

GW/0017-0852
GLASFORUM. [Glasforum]. Vol. 1 (Dec. 1950)-. Periodical. German. Six times a year. DM67.40 Europe; DM95.00 other. Verlag Karl Hofmann, Postfach 1360, D-73603 Schorndorf Germany. **Tel** 011 49 7181 4020. **LC** TP845; .G48. **[CCC].** Index available. **Bk Rev. Ad Acc.**
Desc: Journal about glass architecture.
Ind/Abst Archit. Period. Index (1954-).

UK/0017-0992
GLASS AGE. **Added/Corp** National Federation of Constructional Glass Associations. (1958)-. Periodical. English. Twelve times a year. £28.50 UK, £42.00 others (surface mail); £28.50 (airmail). Link House Magazines Ltd., Link House, Dingwall Avenue, Croydon Surrey CR9 2TA England. **Tel** 011 44 81 686 2599, FAX 011 44 81 760 5154, telex 947709. **(Subscription address:** Link House Magazines Ltd., 120 126 Lavendar Avenue, Mitcham Surrey CR4 3HP England.**)** available on microfilm from University Microfilms International (UMI).
Ind/Abst Archit. Period. Index (Nov. 1977-Dec. 1983).

US/0361-7610
GLASS AND CERAMICS. [Glass ceram.]. **Added/Corp** Consultants Bureau. Consultants Bureau Enterprises. (1956)-. Periodical. English (Russian). mo. $1295.00 US; $1515.00 other. Consultants Bureau, A Division of Plenum Publishing Corporation, 233 Spring Street, New York NY 10013. **Tel** (212)620-8000, (212)620-8466, FAX (212)463-0742, telex 23/421139. **ED** N. N. Rokhlin. **LC** TP845; .S7135. **DD** 666.05. **CODEN** GLCEAV. **[CCC].** Index available. available on microfilm and microfiche from University Microfilms International (UMI). Documents available from Article Express International, Ask*IEEE, CASDDS.
Desc: Publishes research reports by leading Soviet scientists on silicate chemistry, mineralogy, metallurgy, crystal chemistry, solid-state reactions, raw materials, phase equilibria, reaction kinetics and physiochemical analysis.
Ind/Abst Acoust. Abstr.; Bioeng. Abstr.; Ceram. Abstr. (199?-); Chem. Abstr.; Coal Abstr.; Ei Page One; EMBASE; Eng. Index Annu.; INSPEC (March-April 1969-); MINPROC.

UK
GLASS & GLAZING. **See** Architecture.

NO/0802-5428
GLASS & PORSELEN. [Glass porselen]. **VFOAT** Glass og Porselen. (1989)-. Periodical. Norwegian. bm. Kr350.00. Ferbundet for Glass & Porselen, Drammonsvoion 30, 0255 Oslo 2 Norway. **Tel** 011 47 2 556010. **(Subscription address:** A. S. Ursus Forlag of Prosssotryr, Odins GT26 0266, Oslo, 2 Norway.**) DD** 666. ***Continues*** *Glassposten, 0046-6018.*

US/1068-2147
GLASS ART (BROOMFIELD, COLO.). (GLASS ART.). [Glass art]. (19??)-. Periodical. English. Six times a year (Jan., Mar., May, July, Sept., Nov.). $24.00 US & Canada & Mexico; $45.00 others. Travin Inc, PO Box 260377, Highlands Ranch CO 80126. **Tel** (303)791-8998, FAX (303)791-7739. **ED** Shawn Waggoner. **DD** 748. **Bk Rev. Ad Acc, Adv Mgr:** Kevin, **Tel** (303)791-8998. ***Continues*** *Glass Art Magazine (Broomfield, Colo.), 0886-8131.*
Desc: Full color publication featuring hot glass, cold glass, technical articles, business articles and artist profiles for the stains and decorative glass industries.

US/0886-8131
GLASS ART MAGAZINE (BROOMFIELD, COLO.). ***Title Change.*** (GLASS ART MAGAZINE.). [Glass art mag.]. **VFOAT** Glass Art. (1985)-(19??). Periodical. English. mo. Travin Inc, PO Box 260377, Highlands Ranch CO 80126. **Tel** (303)791-8998, FAX (303)791-7739. **DD** 748. **Bk Rev. Ad Acc.** ***Continued by*** *Glass Art (Broomfield, Colo.), 1068-2147.*

US/0740-8889
GLASS ART SOCIETY PHOTOGRAPHIC DIRECTORY. [Glass Art Soc. photogr. dir.]. **VFOAT** Photographic Directory. 1983-1984-. Directory. English. ir. $7.50. Glass Art Society, PO Box 1364, Corning NY 14830. **Tel** (607)936-0530. **LC** NK5112; .G49. **DD** 748/.0973. Index available. cum. index. **Bk Rev. Ad Acc.** ctrl circ.

CN/0843-7041
GLASS CANADA. [Glass Can.]. Vol. 1, No. 1 March (1989)-. Periodical. English (French; summaries and/or abstracts in French). Six times a year (Feb., Apr., June, Aug., Oct., Dec.). $54.00 (US); $39.00 (Canada); $62.00 (other). AIS Communications Limited, 145 Thames Road West, Exeter Ontario N0M 1S3 Canada. **Tel** (519)235-2400, FAX (519)235-0798. **DD** 338.4/766619.

UK
GLASS CIRCLE, THE. **Added/Corp** Circle of Glass Collectors. Vol. 1 (1972)-. English. ir. Price varies. Antique Glass Shop, 42 Kingswood Avenue, Sanderstead Surrey CR2 9DQ England. **Tel** 011 44 1 651 5180. **LC** NK5100; .G54. **DD** 748.2/05.
Ind/Abst ARTbibliogr. Mod. (1984-); Br. Archaeol. Bibliogr.

US
GLASS CLUB BULLETIN. Bulletin. English. tq. (Comes with National Early American Glass Club membership). National Early American Glass Club, PO Box 8489, Membership Chairman, Silver Spring MD 20907. **Tel** (703)465-4040.
Ind/Abst BHA : Biblio. Hist. Art.

US/0893-8660
GLASS COLLECTOR'S DIGEST. [Glass collect. dig.]. Vol. 1, No. 1 (June/July 1987)-. Periodical. English. Six times a year. $19.00 US; $24.00 other. Richardson Printing Corporation, PO Box 553, Marietta OH 45750. **Tel** (614)373-9959. **ED** D. Thomas O'Connor. **LC** NK5100; .G56. **DD** 748.2/075. cum. index. **Bk Rev. Ad Acc.** ctrl circ.
Desc: A color magazine devoted to all types of collectible glass.

US/0364-1872
GLASS CONTAINERS (WASHINGTON). ***Title Change.*** (CURRENT INDUSTRIAL REPORTS. M32G, GLASS CONTAINERS.). [Glass contain.]. **Added/Corp** United States. Bureau of the Census. **VFOAT** Glass Containers. (19??)-(1992). Government Publication. English. mo (summary issue). Superintendent of Documents, US Government Printing Office, Washington DC 20402. **Tel** (202)275-3328, FAX (202)786-2377. **LC** HD9624.C663; U63. **DD** 338.4/7666192/0973. ***Continues*** *Facts for Industry. M77C, Glass Containers.* ***Continued by*** *Current Industrial Reports. M32G, Glass Containers (Computer File).*
Desc: Presents data on quantity of shipments, production, and stocks (end of month) by type of container for the current month and the preceding month.
Ind/Abst Predicasts.

US/0017-1018
GLASS DIGEST. [Glass dig.]. (19??)-. Academic Scholarly Publication. English. mo. $40.00 (one year), $50.00 (two year), $60.00 (three year) US; Canada and Mexico; $45.00 (one year), $60.00 (two year), $70.00 (three year) other. Ashlee Publishing Company Inc, 310 Madison Avenue, New York NY 10017. **Tel** (212)682-7681, (800)360-1926, FAX (212)697-8331, telex 62-480. **ED** Charles Cumpston. **LC** TP845; .G56. **DD** 658.9661. **CODEN** GLDIAE. **[CCC].** Index available. cum. index. **Ad Acc. Circ:** 12,000. available on microfilm from University Microfilms International (UMI). Documents available from Article Express International, CASDDS.

Continues *Glaziers Journal.*
Desc: Editorial and advertising covering the flat glass, architectural metal and allied products.
Ind/Abst Ceram. Abstr.; Chem. Abstr.; Chem. Ind. Notes; Ei Page One; Eng. Index Annu. [Select. Cov.].

US
GLASS FACTORY DIRECTORY. ***Title Change.*** **VFOAT** Directory of Glass Factories in the United States and Canada. (1912)-(19??). Directory. English. an. Glass News, PO Box 7138, Pittsburgh PA 15213. **Tel** (412)362-5136. **ED** Liz Scott. Index available. **Ad Acc. Circ:** 1,000 (ctrl). available on diskette (IBM compatible). ***Continued by*** *Glass Factory Directory of North America and U.S. Industry Factbook, 1057-5405.*
Desc: Glass factories by geographic location and product in U.S. and Canada. Includes reports personnel, uses and patents. Directory of US and Canadian glass plants.

US/0017-1026
GLASS INDUSTRY, THE. [Glass ind.]. Vol. 1 (Nov. 1920)-. Periodical. English. Thirteen times a year (monthly plus one annual directory). $40.00 US & Canada; $50.00 others. Ashlee Publishing Company Inc, 310 Madison Avenue, New York NY 10017. **Tel** (212)682-7681, (800)360-1926, FAX (212)697-8331, telex 62-480. **ED** Lowell E. Perrine. **LC** TP845; .G6. **DD** 666.105. **CODEN** GLINAK. **[CCC].** Index available. cum. index. **Bk Rev. Ad Acc. Circ:** 2,700. available on microfilm and microfiche from University Microfilms International (UMI). Documents available from Article Express International, CASDDS.
Desc: Manufacturing and marketing articles and news pertaining to the glass industry.
Ind/Abst Appl. Sci. Technol. Index; Ceram. Abstr.; Chem. Abstr.; Ei Page One; Eng. Index Annu. [Select. Cov.]; F&S Index Plus Text, Int. [Select. Cov.]; Int. Packag. Abstr.; PROMT; World Ceram. Abstr.

US
GLASS INDUSTRY DIRECTORY ISSUE, THE. (19??)-. Directory. English. ir. $30.00 US and Canada; $45.00 other. Glass Industry, 310 Madison Avenue, Suite 1926, New York NY 10017. **Tel** (212)682-7681. **ED** Edited by the staff of the Glass industry magazine. **LC** HD9623.A1; G54. **DD** 338.4/7/666/025. ***Supersedes*** *Glass Industry International Directory, 0436-0494.*
Desc: Information on glass trade and manufacturing.

UK/0143-7836
GLASS INTERNATIONAL. [Glass int.]. (1978)-. Academic Scholarly Publication. English (French, German, Italian and Spanish). qt. £80.35 UK; £112.80, $174.90. Argus Press Group, Queensway House, 2 Queensway Redhill, Surrey RH1 1QS England. **Tel** 011 44 737 768611, 011 44 737 761685, FAX 011 44 737 760510, telex 948669 TOPJNL G. **ED** John Wallis. **CODEN** GLINDN. Index available. cum. index. **Bk Rev. Ad Acc. Circ:** 5,000. available on an online database (file 16/Full-Text) from DIALOG. Documents available from Article Express International, CASDDS.
Desc: A global insight to international glass manufacturing practice and technology.
Ind/Abst Ceram. Abstr.; Chem. Abstr. (-1981); Curr. Technol. Index; Ei Page One; Eng. Index Annu. [Select. Cov.]; F&S Index Plus Text, Int. [Full Txt.] [Select. Cov.]; HTFS Dig.; Int. Packag. Abstr.; PROMT [Full Txt.].

US/0747-4261
GLASS MAGAZINE. [Glass mag.]. **Added/Corp** National Glass Association (U.S.). **VFOAT** Glass. (May 1984)-(19??). Periodical. English. Twelve times a year. $34.95 (one year), $64.95 (two years), $79.95 (three years) US; $44.95 (one year), $74.95 (two years), $89.95 (three years) other. National Glass Association, PO Box 754, Peri River NY 10965-9953. **Tel** (703)442-4890, FAX (703)442-0630. **LC** HD9623.U44; G57. **DD** 381/.456661/0973. Index available. cum. index. **Ad Acc. Circ:** 13,000 (ctrl). ***Continues*** *Glass Dealer, 0094-3746.* ***Continued in part by*** *AutoGlass, 1047-2061.*
Desc: Serves the architectural and automotive glass industries. Award-winning publication.
Ind/Abst Constr. Index; F&S Index Plus Text, Int. [Select. Cov.]; PROMT.

US/0890-3743
GLASS NEWS. ***Ceased.*** [Glass news]. Vol. 1, No. 1 (Jan. 1985)-?. Academic Scholarly Publication. English. mo. Glass News, PO Box 7138, Pittsburgh PA 15213. **Tel** (412)362-5136. **ED** Liz Scott. **DD** 338. **Bk Rev. Ad Acc. Circ:** 1,650 (ctrl). Documents available from CASDDS. ***Continues*** *National Glass Budget, 0027-9390.*
Desc: Contains news of glass manufacturing worldwide, including products, financial and production reports, personnel, uses and patents.
Ind/Abst Chem. Abstr.

US
GLASS ON METAL. THE ENAMELISTS' NEWSLETTER. (19??)-. Newsletter. English. Six times a year (Feb., Apr., June, Aug., Oct., Dec.). $40.00 US; $46.00 Canada and Mexico; $54.00 other. Enamelist Society, PO Box 310, Newport KY 41072. **Tel** (606)291-3800, FAX (606)291-1849. **ED** Tom Ellis. **Bk Rev. Ad Acc. Circ:** 1,600.

US/0147-8427
GLASS (PORTLAND, OR.). (GLASS.). [Glass]. Vol. 5, (Jan. 1977)-. Periodical. English. Four times a year. Publication Development Inc, PO Box 23383, Portland OR 97223. **Tel** (503)620-3917. **LC** NK5100; .G536. **DD** 748/.05. ***Continues*** *Glass Art.*

US/0091-6625
GLASS (PRINCETON). (GLASS.). V. 1- Nov./Dec. 1972-. Periodical. English. bm. $10.00. Special Publications Inc, 5 Lincoln Court, Princeton NJ 08540. **LC** NK5100; .G53. **DD** 748/.05.
Ind/Abst Int. Packag. Abstr.

UK/0959-0838
GLASS PRODUCTION TECHNOLOGY INTERNATIONAL. (1990)-. English. an. Sterling Publications Ltd., PO Box 799, Brunel House, London W2 1XR England. **Tel** 011 44 71 2580066, FAX 011 44 71 4026441, telex 295819 ESPEEL G.
Ind/Abst Ceram. Abstr. (199?-).

UK/0017-0984
GLASS (REDHILL). (GLASS.). [Glass]. Vol. 1 (Dec. 1923)-. Academic Scholarly Publication. English (French, German, Italian and Spanish). mo. £97.65 UK; £116.10, $180.00 other. Argus Press Group, Queensway House, 2 Queensway Redhill, Surrey RH1 1QS England. **Tel** 011 44 737 768611, 011 44 737 761685, FAX 011 44 737 760510, telex 948669 TOPJNL G. **ED** John Wallis. **LC** TP845; .G525. **DD** 666.105. **CODEN** GLASAT. Index available. cum. index. **Bk Rev. Ad Acc. Circ:** 2,000. available on microfilm from University Microfilms International (UMI). Documents available from Article Express International, CASDDS.
Desc: Provides information on the latest glass production related developments, principally in Europe.
Ind/Abst Ceram. Abstr.; Chem. Abstr.; Ei Page One; EMBASE; Eng. Index Annu. [Select. Cov.]; F&S Index Plus Text, Int. [Full Txt.] [Select. Cov.]; Infomat Int. Bus.; PROMT [Full Txt.].

CS/0323-0635
GLASS REVIEW (PRAGUE, CZECHOSLOVAKIA). ***Title Change.*** (GLASS REVIEW.). [Glass rev.]. Vol. 23 (Jan. 1968)-(1992). Periodical. English. mo. **(Subscription address:** Artia Pegas Press Ltd., Palac Metro Narodni Trida 25, 11210 Prague 1 Czech Republic.**) LC** TP485; .G64. **DD** 748.05. ***Continues*** *Czechoslovak Glass Review, 0034-9127.* ***Continued by*** *New Glass Review (Prague, Czech Republic), 1210-2741.*
Ind/Abst BHA : Biblio. Hist. Art.

UK/0017-1050
GLASS TECHNOLOGY. (GLASS TECHNOLOGY / SOCIETY OF GLASS TECHNOLOGY.). [Glass technol.]. **Added/Corp** Society of Glass Technology. Vol. 1, No. 1 (Feb. 1960)-. Academic Scholarly Publication. English. bm. £112.50 UK; £128.00 other. Society of Glass Technology, Thornton 20, Hallam Gate Road, Sheffield S10 5BT England. **Tel** 011 44 742 663168, FAX 011 44 742 665252. **ED** B. E. Moody. **LC** TP845; .G66. **DD** 666/.1/05. **CODEN** GLSTAK. Index available. **Bk Rev. Ad Acc. Circ:** 1,700 (ctrl). Documents available from Article Express International, The Genuine Article, Ask*IEEE, CASDDS. ***Continues*** *Society of Glass Technology. Journal of the Society of Glass Technology.*
Desc: Society news, proceedings and papers concerned with glassmaking, glass fabrication, properties and applications of glasses or glass-ceramics and other related topics.
Ind/Abst Appl. Sci. Technol. Index; Art Archaeol. Tech. Abstr.; Bibliogr. Mission.; Bioeng. Abstr.; Br. Archaeol. Bibliogr. (-?); Ceram. Abstr.; Chem. Abstr.; Coal Abstr.; Curr. Contents Eng. Tech. Appl. Sci.; Curr. Technol. Index; Ei Page One; EMBASE; Eng. Index Annu.; GeoRef; HTFS Dig.; INSPEC (Oct. 1969-); Int. Packag. Abstr.; Leadscan; Ref. Sources; Res. Alert [Full Cov.]; Sci. Cit. Index; SCISEARCH; Stat. Theory Method Abstr. (1968); World Ceram. Abstr.

JA/0916-0388
GLASS TOKYO. 1986, THE. [Glass Tokyo. 1986]. (1986)-. Periodical. Japanese. qt. **DD** 666.1.
Ind/Abst Ceram. Abstr.

II/0379-0460
GLASS UDYOG. (GLASS UDYOG : JOURNAL OF THE ALL INDIA GLASS MANUFACTURERS' FEDERATION.). [Glass UDYOG]. **Added/Corp** All India Glass Manufacturers' Federation. Vol. 1, No. 1 (Mar. 1972)-. Academic Scholarly Publication. English. qt. $15.00. All India Glass Manufacturers' Federation, Barakhamba Road, 1 New Delhi House, 812 New Delhi India. **(Subscription address:** Prints India, 11 Darya Ganj, New Delhi 110002 India.**) LC** TP845; .G67. **DD** 338.4/76661/0954. **CODEN** GLUDDJ. Documents available from CASDDS. ***Continues*** *AIGMF Bulletin.*
Ind/Abst Ceram. Abstr.; Chem. Abstr.

US/0017-1069
GLASS WORKERS NEWS. Began publication Jan. 14, 1938. Periodical. English. bm. U G and C Workers of North America, AFL C10 556 E Town Street, Columbus OH 43215. ***Supersedes*** *Flat Glass Worker.*
Ind/Abst Work Relat. Abstr. (-19??).

JA
GLASSWORK. ***Ceased.*** (19??)-Vol. 16. Japanese. qt. Glasswork, Teramachidori Ebisugawa-Aguru, Nakagyo-ku Kyoto Japan.

GW/0017-1085
GLASTECHNISCHE BERICHTE. [Glastech. ber.]. **Added/Corp** Deutsche Glastechnische Gesellschaft. Vol. 1 (Nov. 1923)-. Periodical. German (English). mo. DM520.00. Verlag der Deutschen Glastechnischen Gesellschaft, Mendelssohnstrasse 75-77, D 60325 Frankfurt am Main Germany. **Tel** 011 49 69 749088, FAX 011 49 69 749719, telex 990131. **ED** H.A. Schaeffer, Dieter Kaboth and Karin Gunther. **LC** TP845; .G68. **DD** 666.105. **CODEN** GLBEAQ. Index available. cum. index. **Bk Rev. Ad Acc. Pr Rev. Circ:** 2,000. Documents available from Article Express International, The Genuine Article, Ask*IEEE, CASDDS.
Desc: Contains original works on the science and technology of glass: standards, norms and patents, and statistics. Original papers, international news and German news.
Ind/Abst Art Archaeol. Tech. Abstr.; Bioeng. Abstr.; Ceram. Abstr.; Chem. Abstr.; Coal Abstr.; Curr. Contents Eng. Tech. Appl. Sci.; Ei Page One; Energy Res. Abstr. (Mar. 1972-); Eng. Mater. Abstr.; Eng. Index Annu.; GeoRef; INSPEC (Dec. 1969-Dec. 1975); Int. Aerosp. Abstr.; Int. Packag. Abstr.; Res. Alert [Full Cov.]; Saf. Health Work; Sci. Cit. Index; SCISEARCH; World Ceram. Abstr.

SW/0017-1093
GLASTEKNISK TIDSKRIFT. [Glastek. tidskr.]. Vol. 1, (1946)-. Academic Scholarly Publication. Swedish (English and German). Three times a year (Mar., June, Nov.). Kr250.00 Scandinavia; Kr275.00 Europe; Kr350.00 other. Glasteknisk Tidskrift, Box 3293, S-350 03 Vaxjo 3 Sweden. **Tel** 470-10090, FAX 470-40063, telex 52171. **ED** Stellan Persson. **CODEN** GLTIAQ. Each issue contains an index to its own contents (no volume index)--loose. **Bk Rev. Ad Acc. Circ:** 250. Documents available from CASDDS.
Desc: Glass technology.
Ind/Abst Ceram. Abstr.; Chem. Abstr.; Energy Res. Abstr. (May 1977-).

GW/0017-1107
GLASWELT. (1957)-. German. mo. DM183.00 Germany; DM223.80 other. AW Gentner Verlag, Postfach 101742, D-70015 Stuttgart Germany. **Tel** 011 49 711 636720, FAX 011 49 711 6367247, telex 841 722244. **UDC** 686.6. **[CCC].**

UK
GLAZING TODAY. English. qt. £47.30 UK; £49.90, $77.30 other. Argus Press Group, Queensway House, 2 Queensway Redhill, Surrey RH1 1QS England. **Tel** 011 44 737 768611, 011 44 737 761685, FAX 011 44 737 760510, telex 948669 TOPJNL G.

UK
GLOBAL CERAMIC REVIEW. English. qt. £35.00. British Ceramic Plant Machinery, Manufacturing Association, 44 Kingsway Staffs ST4 1JH, England. **Tel** 011 44 782 411433, FAX 0782 747061. ***Continues*** *British Ceramic Review., 0306-7076.*

US/1055-4920
GOVERNMENT AFFAIRS UPDATE. ***Title Change.*** (GOVERNMENT AFFAIRS UPDATE : THE LATEST GOVERNMENT & INDUSTRY NEWS FOR GLASS PROFESSIONALS.). [Gov. aff. update]. **Added/Corp** National Glass Association (U.S.). Vol. 1, No. 1 (Feb. 1991)-(199?). Periodical. English. bm. National Glass Association, PO Box 754, Peri River NY 10965-9953. **Tel** (703)442-4890, FAX (703)442-0630. **DD** 338. ***Merged with*** *Illinois Press Association Bulletin, 1057-9176; Illinois Publisher* ***and*** *Editor's Advisory* ***to form*** *Illinois Presslines, 1074-5009.*

US/0731-8014
HEISEY NEWS. (HEISEY NEWS : OFFICIAL PUBLICATION HEISEY COLLECTORS OF AMERICA.). [Heisey news]. **Added/Corp** Heisey Collectors of America. (19??)-. Periodical. English. mo. $18.50 (regular), $31.50 (first class). Heisey Collectors of America, PO Box 4367, 169 West Church Street, Newark OH 43055. **Tel** (614)345-2932, FAX (614)345-9638. **ED** Kelly Thran and Karen D. Kneisley. **LC** NK5198.A23; H45. **DD** 748.29171/54. Index available. cum. index. **Bk Rev. Ad Acc. Circ:** 2,900 (ctrl).
Desc: Information about Heisey Glass and Heisey Collectors of America, Inc.

GE/0439-0377
HERMSDORFER TECHNISCHE MITTEILUNGEN : HTM. **Added/Corp** Kombinate VEB Keramische Werke Hermsdorf. **VFOAT** HTM; H.T.M. (19??)-. Periodical. German. Kombinat Veb Keramische Werke Hermsdorff, Hermsdorrf Germany. **CODEN** HTMTAN. Documents available from Ask*IEEE, CASDDS.
Ind/Abst Chem. Abstr.; INSPEC (Aug. 1970-).

US/1045-2397
HIGH TECH CERAMICS NEWS. [High tech ceram. news]. (1988)-. Periodical. English. mo. $350.00. Business Communications Inc., 25 Van Zant Street, Suite 13, Norwalk CT 06855. **Tel** (203)853-4266. **DD** 666.

available on an online database (file 636/Full-Text) from DIALOG.
Ind/Abst PTS Newsl. Database [Full Txt.].

US/1041-3510
HOMEOWNER'S GUIDE TO GLASS, THE.
(THE HOMEOWNER'S GUIDE TO GLASS : A NATIONAL GLASS ASSOCIATION PUBLICATION.). [Homewown. guide glass]. **Added/Corp** National Glass Association (U.S.). **VFOAT** Home Owner's Guide to Glass. Vol. 1 Iss. 1 (1989)-. English. an. $4.95. 8200 Greensboro Drive, Suite 302, Mclean VA 22102. **LC** HD9623.U44; H65. **DD** 693/.96/0297.

II/0019-4492
INDIAN CERAMICS.
[Indian ceram.]. Vol. 1 (April 1954)-. Periodical. English. Four times a year. $100.00. Indian Ceramics, 10 Sourin Roy Road Behala, Calcutta 700 034 India. **Tel** 011 33 4780651. **ED** Ambar Roy. **LC** NK3700; .I5. **DD** 666/.0954. **CODEN** IDCMAL. **Bk Rev. Ad Acc, Adv Mgr:** Ms. Suchhandadas. **Circ:** 500. Documents available from CASDDS.
Desc: Covers ceramics, glass refractories, cement, electronic ceramics, and enamel allied products.
Ind/Abst Bibliogr. Mission.; Ceram. Abstr.; Chem. Abstr.; Coal Abstr.; Eng. Mater. Abstr.; Fluid Abstr., Civil Eng.; Fluid Abstr. Proc. Eng.; FLUIDEX (19??-); World Ceram. Abstr.

IT
INDUSTRIAL CERAMICS.
Vol. 7, No. 1 (Jan./Mar. 1987)-. Periodical. English (summaries and/or abstracts in Italian, French and Spanish). Four times a year (Mar., June, Sept., Dec.). L90000.00 Italy; $130.00 other. Techna SRL, PO Box 174, 48018 Faenza Italy. **Tel** 011 39 546 22461. **CODEN** INCEE3. **Bk Rev. Ad Acc, Adv Mgr:** G. Bertoni, **Tel** 0546 22661. **Pr Rev. Circ:** 6,000 (ctrl). Documents available from Ask*IEEE, CASDDS. ***Continues*** *CI News, 0392-2960.*
Desc: Applied research and technological innovation in the fields of both chemical and hi-tech ceramics.
Ind/Abst Ceram. Abstr.; Chem. Abstr.; Chem. Ind. Notes (-1991); Coal Abstr.; F&S Index Plus Text, Int. [Select. Cov.]; INSPEC (1987-); PROMT; World Ceram. Abstr.

FR/0019-9044
INDUSTRIE CERAMIQUE, L'.
[Ind. ceram.]. (1947)-. Academic Scholarly Publication. French (English). mo (11 issues per year). 995.00F. Septima, 14 rue Falguiere, 75015 Paris France. **Tel** 011 33 1 42730359, FAX 011 33 1 47834019, telex 205 916 AGOR. **ED** D Lecat. **CODEN** IDCQAX. **[CCC].** Index available. cum. index. **Bk Rev**, (Qty: 3/yr). **Ad Acc. Pr Rev. Circ:** 1800. Documents available from Article Express International, Ask*IEEE, CASDDS.
Desc: Covers all the ceramic fields: refractories, bricks and tiles, sanitary ware, floor and wall tiles, tableware decoration advanced ceramics.
Ind/Abst Bioeng. Abstr.; Ceram. Abstr.; Chem. Abstr.; Coal Abstr.; Ei Page One; EMBASE; Energy Res. Abstr.; Eng. Index Annu.; GeoRef; INSPEC (1981-); Saf. Health Work; Surf. Treat. Technol. Abstr.

GW/0020-5214
INTERCERAM.
[Interceram]. (1952)-. Academic Scholarly Publication. English (summaries and/or abstracts in French, German and Spanish). Seven times a year (Publishes every six weeks with one international buyers guide). DM340.00 (surface mail); DM380.00 others. Verlag Schmid Journals GmbH, Postfach 6609, Hofackerstr 92, D 79042 Freiburg 1 Germany. **Tel** 011 49 761 82057, FAX 011 49 761 84863, telex 761 403 CARNEWS D. **ED** H. Reh. **LC** TP785; .I58. **DD** 666.3058. **CODEN** ITCRAC. Index available. cum. index. **Bk Rev. Ad Acc. Circ:** 12,000. Documents available from Article Express International, CASDDS. ***Continues*** *International Ceramic Review.*
Desc: The leading international journal for tableware, sanitaryware, tiles, technical and advanced ceramics and refractories producers and their suppliers.
Ind/Abst Bioeng. Abstr.; Ceram. Abstr.; Chem. Abstr.; Coal Abstr.; Ei Page One; EMBASE; Eng. Mater. Abstr.; Eng. Index Annu.; GeoRef; Infomat Int. Bus.; World Ceram. Abstr.

US/0147-300X
INTERNATIONAL GLASS/METAL CATALOG.
[Int. glass-met. cat.]. (195?)-. Catalog. English (French). an (Feb.). $30.00. Ashlee Publishing Company Inc, 310 Madison Avenue, New York NY 10017. **Tel** (212)682-7681, (800)360-1926, FAX (212)697-8331, telex 62-480. **ED** Charles B. Cumpston. **Ad Acc. Circ:** 11,000 (ctrl).
Desc: A comprehensive source of product and services information to the glass/metal industry.

II/0250-5304
IRMA JOURNAL.
[IRMA j.]. **Added/Corp** Indian Refractory Makers Association. Vol. 10, No. 1 (1977)-. Academic Scholarly Publication. English. qt. **CODEN** IRJODR. Documents available from CASDDS. ***Continues*** *Indian Refractory Makers Association Journal.*
Ind/Abst Ceram. Abstr. (19??-); Chem. Abstr. (1977-1982).

SP
JAPANESE NEW MATERIALS IACA SERIES. HIGH-PERFORMANCE CERAMICS.
(19??)-. English. qt. £215.00 UK; $370.00 US. Newmedia International Japan, AV Infanta Carlota 123 5 A, 08029 Barcelona Spain. **Tel** 011 34 3 4195690, FAX 414 42 13. available on an online database (files 16,636/Full-Text) from DIALOG.
Ind/Abst PROMT [Full Txt.]; PTS Newsl. Database [Full Txt.].

JA/0916-4553
JFCC REVIEW.
[JFCC rev.]. **VFOAT** Japan Fine Ceramics Center Review; JFCC Rebyu. (1989)-. Periodical. Multiple languages. an. Nagoya Fain Seramikkusu Senta. **DD** 666. Documents available from CASDDS.
Ind/Abst Chem. Abstr.

US/0278-9426
JOURNAL / GLASS ART SOCIETY.
Added/Corp Glass Art Society. **VFOAT** Glass Art Society Journal. (19??)-. Periodical. English. an. $23.00 (member, Glass Art Society), $27.00 (non-member) US, Canada, and Mexico; $28.00 (member, Glass Art Society), $32.00 (non-member) other. The Glass Art Society Inc, 1305 Fourth Avenue, Suite 711, Seattle WA 98101. **Tel** (206)382-1305, FAX (206)382-2630. **ED** Caryl Hansen. **LC** NK5112; .J68. **DD** 730/.05. Index available. **Bk Rev. Ad Acc. Circ:** 1,500 (ctrl). ***Continues*** *Newsletter - Glass Art.*
Desc: Published as a documentation of international developments in the field of contemporary glass.
Ind/Abst ARTbibliogr. Mod.

UK
JOURNAL - NORTHERN CERAMIC SOCIETY.
Main/Corp Northern Ceramic Society. Vol. 1 (1973)-. Periodical. English.
Ind/Abst BHA : Biblio. Hist. Art.

UK/0449-5713
JOURNAL OF CERAMIC HISTORY.
No. 1 (1968)-. Monographic series. English. ir. Price varies per volume. Stoke-on-Trent Museum Art Gallery, Broad Street Hanley, Stoke-on-Trent ST1 4HS England. **LC** NK3700; .J6. **DD** 738 S.
Ind/Abst Br. Archaeol. Bibliogr. (-?).

US/0075-4250
JOURNAL OF GLASS STUDIES.
[J. glass stud.]. **Added/Corp** Corning Museum of Glass, Corning, New York. Vol. 1 (1959)-. English (German, Italian and French). an (Nov.). $32.50 US; $36.00 other. Corning Museum of Glass, One Museum Way, Corning NY 14830-2253. **Tel** (607)937-5371, FAX (607)937-3352, telex 932498. **CODEN** JGLSAE. **Circ:** 2,000. available on microfilm and microfiche from University Microfilms International (UMI). Documents available from The Genuine Article, CASDDS.
Desc: Publication on artistic, historical, and archaeological aspects of glass from classical antiquity through 1945. Includes checklist of articles and books, plus photographs of acquisitions.
Ind/Abst Anthropol. Index; Art Index; ARTbibliogr. Mod.; Arts Humanit. Citation Index (19??-19??) [Full Cov.]; BHA : Biblio. Hist. Art; Br. Archaeol. Bibliogr.; Ceram. Abstr.; Chem. Abstr.; Curr. Contents Arts Humanit.; Res. Alert [Full Cov.].

NE/0022-3093
JOURNAL OF NON-CRYSTALLINE SOLIDS.
[J. non-cryst. solids]. Vol. 1 (Dec. 1968)-. Academic Scholarly Publication. English. Forty-Five times a year (15 volumes). Fl6915.00. Elsevier Science Publishers BV, PO Box 211, 1000 AE Amsterdam Netherlands. **Tel** 011 31 20 5803642, FAX 011 31 20 5862696, telex 15682. **ED** R.A. Weeks. **LC** TP845; .J65. **DD** 666/.1/05. **CODEN** JNCSBJ. **[CCC]. Pr Rev.** available on microfilm and microfiche from University Microfilms International (UMI). Documents available from Article Express International, The Genuine Article, Ask*IEEE, CASDDS.
Desc: Publishes review articles, research papers, and letters to the editor on oxide and non-oxide glasses, non-crystalline films such as those prepared by vapor-deposition, amorphous metals and semiconductors, glass ceramics, and glass-composites.
Ind/Abst Alum. Ind. Abstr.; Bioeng. Abstr.; Ceram. Abstr.; Chem. Abstr.; Chem. Titles; Comput. Inf. Syst. Abstr. J. [Full Cov.]; Curr. Contents Phys. Chem. Earth Sci.; Ei Page One; Eng. Mater. Abstr.; Eng. Index Annu.; GeoRef; INSPEC (Dec. 1968-); Int. Aerosp. Abstr.; Leadscan; Mass Spect. Bull.; Mater. Sci. Eng. Abstr.; Met. Abstr.; Phys. Briefs; Pollut. Abstr. Indexes; Res. Alert [Full Cov.]; Sci. Cit. Index; SCISEARCH; Solid State Supercond. Abstr.

UK
JOURNAL OF STAINED GLASS : THE JOURNAL OF THE BRITISH SOCIETY OF MASTER GLASS PAINTERS, THE.
Added/Corp British Society of Master Glass Painters. Vol. 18, No. 1 (1984)-. Periodical. English. be. British Society of Master Glass Painters, 6 Queen Square, London WC1 England. **Tel** 029-671-2425. **(Subscription address:** P S London, The Ridings, Singleborough, Buckinghamshire MK17 0RF England**) ED** P Cormack, S Brown. **LC** NK5300; .B7. **DD** 748.5/05. **Bk Rev. Ad Acc. Circ:** 600 (ctrl). ***Continues*** *British Society of Master Glass Painters. Journal of the British Society of Master Glass-Painters.*
Ind/Abst BHA : Biblio. Hist. Art; Br. Archaeol. Bibliogr.; Br. Humanit. Index.

US/0002-7820
JOURNAL OF THE AMERICAN CERAMIC SOCIETY.
[J. Am. Ceram. Soc.]. **Main/Corp** American Ceramic Society. **VFOAT** Journal and Ceramic Abstracts. (1918)-. Periodical. English. mo. $340.00 US; $365.00 other. American Ceramic Society, 735 Ceramic Place, Westerville OH 43081-8720. **Tel** (614)890-4700, (614)794-5890, FAX (614)899-6109. **ED** William J Smothers. **LC** TP785; .A62. **DD** 666/.05. **CODEN** JACTAW. **[CCC].** Index available. **Pr Rev. Circ:** 4,800 (ctrl). available on microfilm and microfiche from University Microfilms International (UMI). Documents available from Article Express International, The Genuine Article, Ask*IEEE, CASDDS, Documents on Demand. ***Supersedes*** *Transactions of the American Ceramic Society Containing the Papers and Discussions of the ... Annual Meeting, 0096-7394;* ***Absorbed*** *Advanced Ceramic Materials, 0883-5551.* ***Continued in part by*** *Ceramic Abstracts, 0095-9960.*
Desc: World's most authoritative technical publication on ceramics, reporting original fundamental research on the latest advances. More than 160 peer-reviewed technical papers per year.
Ind/Abst Alum. Ind. Abstr.; Appl. Sci. Technol. Index; Bioeng. Abstr.; Ceram. Abstr.; Chem Inform; Chem. Abstr.; Chem. Titles; Coal Abstr.; Concr. Abstr.; Curr. Contents Eng. Tech. Appl. Sci.; Curr. Contents Phys. Chem. Earth Sci.; Ei Page One; Energy Inf. Abstr.; Energy Res. Abstr.; Eng. Mater. Abstr.; Eng. Index Annu.; Environ. Abstr.; Fluid Abstr., Civil Eng.; Fluid Abstr. Proc. Eng.; FLUIDEX (19??-); Geol. Abstr.; GeoRef; HTFS Dig.; INIS Atomindex [Micro.]; INSPEC (1968-); Int. Aerosp. Abstr. (1984-); Leadscan; Met. Abstr.; MINPROC; Res. Alert [Full Cov.]; Sci. Cit. Index; SCISEARCH; Surf. Treat. Technol. Abstr.; World Ceram. Abstr.

SZ
JOURNAL OF THE AUSTRALASIAN CERAMIC SOCIETY.
Added/Corp Australasian Ceramic Society. Vol. 26, No. 1 (1990)-. Periodical. English. sa. $106.00. Trans Tech Publications Ltd., Hardstr. 13, CH-4714 Aedermannsdorf Switzerland. **Tel** 011 41 62 741379, FAX 011 41 12 72 10 58. **LC** TP785; .A839a. **DD** 666/.05. **CODEN** JAUSEL. Documents available from CASDDS. ***Continues*** *Australian Ceramic Society. Journal of the Australian Ceramic Society, 0004-881X.*
Ind/Abst Ceram. Abstr. (199?-); Chem. Abstr.

CN/0068-8444
JOURNAL OF THE CANADIAN CERAMIC SOCIETY.
Title Change. [J. Can. Ceram. Soc.]. (19??)-(19??). English. an. Canadian Ceramic Society, 2175 Sheppard Avenue East/Suite 110, Willowdale Ontario M2J 1W8 Canada. **Tel** (905)491-2886, FAX (905)491-1670. **DD** 738.206071. **CODEN** JCCSA9. ***Absorbed by*** *Canadian Ceramics Quarterly Journal.*
Ind/Abst Ceram. Abstr. (19??-19??); Ei Page One; Leadscan; World Ceram. Abstr.

JA/0912-9200
JOURNAL OF THE CERAMIC SOCIETY OF JAPAN.
Added/Corp Nihon Seramikkusu Kyokai. **VFOAT** Yogyo Kyokai-shi; Nippon Seramikkusu Kyokai Gakujutsu Ronbunshi. Vol. 96, No. 1 (Jan. 1988)-. Periodical. English (translations available in Japanese). mo. $2110.00. Nippon Seramikkusu Kyokai, (Ceramic Soc. of Japan), 22-17, Hyakunincho 2 Chome, Shinjukuku, Tokyoto 160 Japan. **(Subscription address:** Maruzen Company Ltd., PO Box 5050, Import & Export Department, Tokyo 100 31 Japan.**) LC** TA455.C43; N563. **DD** 620.1/4. Documents available from Article Express International. ***Continues*** *Yogyo Kyokaishi. English. Journal of the Ceramic Society of Japan, 0912-9200.*
Ind/Abst Ceram. Abstr. (19??-); Civ. Struct. Eng. Abstr.; Comput. Inf. Syst. Abstr. J. [Full Cov.]; Ei Page One; Elect. Comm. Abstr.; Eng. Index Annu.; Environ. Eng. Abstr.; Fluid Abstr., Civil Eng.; Fluid Abstr. Proc. Eng.; FLUIDEX (199?-); Manuf. Process Eng. Abstr.; Mater. Sci. Eng. Abstr.; Mech. Eng. Abstr.; Solid State Supercond. Abstr.

UK/0955-2219
JOURNAL OF THE EUROPEAN CERAMIC SOCIETY.
[J. Eur. Ceram. Soc.]. **Added/Corp** European Ceramic Society. Vol. 5 No. 1 (1989)-. Academic Scholarly Publication. English. Twelve times a year. $813.00 The Americas; £545.00 other. Elsevier Applied Science, An Imprint of Elsevier Science Ltd., The Boulevard, Langford Lane, Kidlington, Oxford OX5 1GB United Kingdom. **Tel** 011 44 865 843000, 011 44 865 843699, FAX 011 44 865 843010. **(Subscription address:** Elsevier Science Ltd. Oxford Fulfillment Centre, PO Box 800, Kidlington, Oxford OX5 1DX United Kingdom.**) ED** R.J. Brook. **CODEN** JECSER. **[CCC].** available on microfilm and microfiche from University Microfilms International (UMI). Documents available from Article Express International, The Genuine Article, Ask*IEEE, CASDDS. ***Continues*** *International Journal of High Technology Ceramics, 0267-3762.*
Desc: Publishes the results of original research relating to the structure, properties and processing of ceramic materials.

Ind/Abst Appl. Mech. Rev.; Ceram. Abstr. (19??-); Chem. Abstr. (1989-); Civ. Struct. Eng. Abstr.; Ei Page One; Eng. Index Annu.; Fluid Abstr., Civil Eng.; Fluid Abstr. Proc. Eng.; FLUIDEX (19??-); INSPEC (1989-); Mater. Sci. Eng. Abstr.; Mech. Eng. Abstr.; Res. Alert [Full Cov.]; Solid State Supercond. Abstr.

UK
JOURNAL OF THE GLASS ASSOCIATION, THE. **Added/Corp** Glass Association (Manchester, England). Vol. 1 (1985)-. English. an. £10.00 (individuals), £15.00 (institutions) UK; £20.00 (individuals) other Comes with Glass Association membership. Glass Association, c/o P. Beebe, 50 Worcester Road, Manchester M24 1WZ England. **Tel** 0384-273011. **ED** I. Wolfenden. **LC** NK5143; .J68. **DD** 748.292/05. **Bk Rev. Circ:** 450.

IT/1120-2343
K : INTERNATIONAL CERAMICS MAGAZINE. **VFOAT** Keramikos. (1987)-. Italian (English). bm. $80.00. Alberto Creco Editore, via del Fusaro 8, 20145 Milan Italy. **Tel** 02 4919086, 02 4691895, FAX 02 4819091. **Ad Acc. Circ:** 25,000.

NE
KERAMIEK. (19??)-. Periodical. Dutch. bm. Ned Vakgroep Keramisten, Poeldijk 8, 3646 AW Waverveen Netherlands. **Tel** 011 31 30 319470.

GW/0173-6760
KERAMIK AUGSBURG. [KeramikAugsbg.]. (1977)-. Periodical. Multiple languages. tq. **UDC** 666.3.
Ind/Abst BHA : Biblio. Hist. Art.

GW/0023-0561
KERAMISCHE ZEITSCHRIFT. [Keram. Z.]. Vol. 1 (Oct. 1948)-. Academic Scholarly Publication. German. mo. DM370.00 (airmail), DM310.00 (surface mail). Verlag Schmid Journals GmbH, Postfach 6609, Hofackerstr 92, D 79042 Freiburg 1 Germany. **Tel** 011 49 761 82057, FAX 011 49 761 84863, telex 761 403 CARNEWS D. **ED** H. Reh. **LC** TP785; .K43. **CODEN** KERZAS. Index available. cum. index. **Bk Rev. Ad Acc. Circ:** 3,000. Documents available from Article Express International, CASDDS.
Desc: Journal for tableware, sanitaryware, tiles, technical and advanced ceramics and refractories producers and their suppliers.
Ind/Abst Art Archaeol. Tech. Abstr.; BHA : Biblio. Hist. Art; Bioeng. Abstr.; Ceram. Abstr.; Chem. Abstr.; Coal Abstr.; Ei Page One; EMBASE; Eng. Mater. Abstr.; Eng. Index Annu.; GeoRef; Saf. Health Work; Surf. Treat. Technol. Abstr.; World Ceram. Abstr.

NE/0167-5001
KLEI, GLAS, KERAMIEK. (KLEI GLAS KERAMIEK.). [Klei, glas, keram.]. **Added/Corp** Nederlandse Keramische Federatie. **VFOAT** Kleiglaskeramiek. Vol. 1, No. 1 (Jan./Feb. 1980)-. Academic Scholarly Publication. Dutch. Twelve times a year. F60.00. Pressofoon Drukkerij BV, PO Box 2093, 1960 GB Heemskerk Netherlands. **Tel** 011 31 2510 41424. **CODEN** KLEIDW. Documents available from CASDDS. ***Continues** Klei en Keramiel.*
Ind/Abst Ceram. Abstr.; Chem. Abstr.; Coal Abstr.; EMBASE.

CN/0705-6931
LEADLINE, THE. **VAT** Lead Line. Began with Apr. 1976 issue. Periodical. English. qt. $10.00. Artists in Stained Glass, Suite 525, 69 Sherbourne Street, Toronto Ontario M5A 2P9 Canada. **DD** 748.5/05.

UK
MEDIEVAL AND LATER POTTERY IN WALES : BULLETIN OF THE WELSH MEDIEVAL POTTERY RESEARCH GROUP. **Added/Corp** Welsh Medieval Pottery Research Group. No. 2 (1979)-. Bulletin. English. an. £5.00 Comes with Medieval Pottery Research Group membership. Archaeological Trust Ltd., Glamorgan Gwent Bath Lane, Swansea SA1 1RD England. **Tel** 011 44 792 655208. **LC** NK4093.A1; M43. **DD** 738/.09429. cum. index. ***Continues** Welsh Medieval Pottery Research Group. Bulletin, 0142-7555.*

UK
MEDIEVAL CERAMICS. **Added/Corp** Medieval Pottery Research Group. Vol. 1 (1977)-. English (French; summaries and/or abstracts in German). Medieval Pottery Research Group, Yat 1 Pavement, York YO1 2NA England.
Ind/Abst BHA : Biblio. Hist. Art.

GW/0723-886X
MITTEILUNGEN DES VEREINS DEUTSCHER EMAILFACHLEUTE E.V. UND DES DEUTSCHEN EMAIL ZENTRUSM E.V. [Mitt. Ver. Dtsch. Emailfachleute Dtsch. Email-Zent.]. **Added/Corp** Verein Deutscher Emailfachleute. Deutsche Email-Zentrums. Vol. 29, No. 1 (Jan. 1981)-. Academic Scholarly Publication. German. mo. DM150.00. Verlag des Vereins Deutscher Emailfachleute, Zehlendorfer Strasse 24, W 58097 Hagen Germany. **Tel** 011 49 2331 10880, FAX 011 49 2331 108833. **CODEN** MVDZDY. Index available. **Bk Rev. Ad Acc.** ctrl circ. Documents available from CASDDS. ***Continues** Mitteilungen des Vereins Deutscher Emailfachleute E.V.*
Ind/Abst Art Archaeol. Tech. Abstr.; Ceram. Abstr.; Chem. Abstr.

US/0192-3900
MONTAGUE'S MODERN BOTTLE IDENTIFICATION AND PRICE GUIDE. 1st-Ed.; 1978-. English. ir (issued four or five times a year). $14.95. H F Montague Enterprises, PO Box 4059, 7919 Grant, Overland Park KS 66204. **Tel** (913)722-5020 OR (913)888-3303. **ED** H F Montaguf. **LC** NK5440.B6; M64. **DD** 738. Index available. **Bk Rev. Ad Acc. Circ:** 25,000 (ctrl).

JA
NAGOYA KOGYO DAIGAKU KOGAKUBU FUZOKU YOGYO GIJUTSU KENKYU SHISETSU NEMPO. ***Title Change.*** [Nagoya Kogyo Daigaku Kogakubu fuzoku Yogyo Gijutsu Kenkyu Shisetsu nenpo]. **Main/Corp** Nagoya Kogyo Daigaku. Kogakubu. Yogyo Gijutsu Kenkyu Shisetsu. **Added/Corp** Nagoya Kogyo Daigaku. Yogyo Gijutsu Kenkyu Shisetsu. Annual Report of Ceramic Engineering Research Laboratory, Nagoya Institute of Technology. **VFOAT** Annual Report of Ceramic Engineering Research Laboratory, Nagoya Institute of Technology. Vol. 1 (1974)-(19??). Academic Scholarly Publication. Japanese (English; summaries and/or abstracts in English and Japanese). Gokishocho Showa-ku, Nagoya Japan. **Tel** 0572-27-6811. **LC** TP785; .N125a. **CODEN** NKDNDY. **Circ:** 400 (ctrl). Documents available from CASDDS. ***Continued by** Yogyo Gijutsu Kenkyu Shisetsu Nenpo, 0911-4769.*
Ind/Abst Chem. Abstr. (-1989).

US/0744-3889
NATIONAL JOURNAL (ALLENTOWN, PA.). (NATIONAL JOURNAL.). Periodical. English. mo. The National Journal, 3340 Birch Avenue, Allentown PA 18103. **DD** 748. ***Continues** National Glass, Pottery & Collectables Journal, 0164-6265.*

US/0739-1544
NCECA JOURNAL. (NCECA JOURNAL / NATIONAL COUNCIL ON EDUCATION FOR THE CERAMIC ARTS.). [NCECA j.]. **Added/Corp** National Council on Education for the Ceramic Arts (U.S.). **VFOAT** N.C.E.C.A. Journal. **VAT** National Council on Education for the Ceramic Arts Journal. Vol. 1, No. 1 (1980)-. Periodical. English. an. $40.00 Comes with National Council for Education for the Ceramic Arts membership. National Council on Education for the Ceramic Arts / NCECA, PO Box 1677, Brandon OR 97411. **Tel** (503)347-4394. **ED** Linda Mosley. **LC** NK4005; .N37. **DD** 738/.0973. **Circ:** 3,500 (ctrl).
Desc: Proceedings of annual meeting of teachers of ceramic art and ceramic artists - covering current issues, history, and technical information.
Ind/Abst Ceram. Abstr.

US/0739-1552
NCECA NEWSLETTER. (NCECA NEWSLETTER / NATIONAL COUNCIL ON EDUCATION FOR THE CERAMIC ARTS.). **VFOAT** National Council on Education for the Ceramic Arts Newsletter; N.C.E.C.A. Newsletter. Vol. 1, No. 1-. Newsletter. English. $20.00 membership. Regina Brown, Executive Secretary, PO Box 1677, Brandon OR 97411.

LV/0132-7267
NEORGANICHESKIE STEKLA, POKRYTIIA I MATERIALY. [Neorg. stekla pokrytia mat.]. **Added/Corp** Rigas Politehniskais Instituts. Latvia. Augstakas un Videjas Specialas Izglitibas Ministrija. (1975)-. Academic Scholarly Publication. Russian. 2.00rub (single issue). **LC** TP845; .N46. **CODEN** NSPMDB. Documents available from CASDDS.
Ind/Abst Art Archaeol. Tech. Abstr.; Chem. Abstr.

GW/0933-2367
NEUE KERAMIK. **See** Literature-Poetry.

GW/0723-2454
NEUES GLAS. **VFOAT** New Glass; Verre Nouveau. Vol. 1, No. 1 (Apr. 1980)-. Periodical. English (French and German). qt. $66.00 Germany; $70.00 other Europe; $76.00 other. Verlagsgesellschaft Ritterbach, Postfach 1820, D 50208 Frechen Germany. **Tel** 011 49 2234 18660. **ED** Karl G. Nicols and H. Ricke. **LC** NK5100; .N48. **DD** 730/.09/04. **Bk Rev. Ad Acc. Circ:** 5,200 (ctrl).
Ind/Abst Art Index; ARTbibliogr. Mod.; Ceram. Abstr. (19??-).

US/0275-469X
NEW GLASS REVIEW. [New glass rev.]. **Added/Corp** Corning Museum of Glass. (1980)-. English (German). an (June). $6.00. Corning Museum of Glass, One Museum Way, Corning NY 14830-2253. **Tel** (607)937-5371, FAX (607)937-3352, telex 932498. **ED** Richard Drice. **LC** NK5110; .N48. **DD** 748.29/049. **Circ:** 2,000 (ctrl). available on microfiche. ***Continues** Contemporary Glass, 0735-2816.*
Desc: Contains one hundred of contemporary glass objects. Full-color photographs and record jury choices from over 2,000 slide entries.
Ind/Abst ARTbibliogr. Mod. (1984-).

●XR/1210-2741
NEW GLASS REVIEW (PRAHA). (NEW GLASS REVIEW.). [New glass rev. (Praha)]. Vol. 47 (1992)-. Periodical. English (French and German). mo. $60.60. Efekt Company Limited, Bardounova 2140, 14900 Prague 4, Czech Republic. **Tel** 011 42 2 7940402. **LC** TP485; .G64. **DD** 748.05. cum. index. **Ad Acc. Circ:** 7,700 (ctrl). ***Continues** Glass Review (Prague, Czech Republic), 0323-0635.*

JA
NEWS / JAPAN GLASS ARTCRAFTS ASSOCIATION. **Main/Corp** Nihon Garasu Kogei Kyokai. Periodical. English. Iwata Glass Company, 4-65-4 Horikiri Katsushika-ku, Tokyo Japan.

US
NEWSLETTER / NATIONAL EARLY AMERICAN GLASS CLUB. **Added/Corp** National Early American Glass Club. **VFOAT** National Early American Glass Club Newsletter; NEAGC Newsletter. No. 1 (Summer 1980)-. Newsletter. English. $25.00 (institutions), $15.00 (individuals), $300.00 (life membership), $20.00 (households). National Early American Glass Club, PO Box 8489, Membership Chairman, Silver Spring MD 20907. **Tel** (703)465-4040. cum. index. **Bk Rev. Circ:** 1,200.

JA/0914-5400
NIHON SERAMIKKUSU KYOKAI GAKUJUTSU RONBUNSHI. [J. Ceram. Soc. Jpn.]. **Added/Corp** Nihon Seramikkusu Kyokai. **VFOAT** Journal of the Ceramic Society of Japan. Vol. 96, No. 1 (1988)-. Academic Scholarly Publication. Japanese (English). mo. $284.00. **(Subscription address:** Kyowa Book Company Inc., 1-38 Kanda Jinbo-Cho, Chiyoda-Ku Tokyo 101, Japan**) CODEN** NSKRE2. **[CCC].** Documents available from Article Express International, The Genuine Article, Ask*IEEE, CASDDS. ***Continues** Yogyo Kyokaishi, 0009-0255.*
Ind/Abst Ceram. Abstr. (19??-); Chem. Abstr.; Civ. Struct. Eng. Abstr.; Ei Page One; Elect. Comm. Abstr.; Eng. Index Annu.; Environ. Eng. Abstr.; INSPEC (1988-); Manuf. Process Eng. Abstr.; Mater. Sci. Eng. Abstr.; Mech. Eng. Abstr.; Res. Alert [Full Cov.]; SCISEARCH; Solid State Supercond. Abstr.; World Ceram. Abstr.

JA/0289-6672
NSG TECHNICAL REPORT. [NSG tech. rep.]. **VFOAT** Nippon Sheet Glass Technical Report. (1983)-. Academic Scholarly Publication. Multiple languages. an. Nippon Ita Garasu K.K., (Nippon Sheet Glass Co., Ltd.), 11-3, Shinbashi 5 Chome, Minatoku, Tokyoto 105, Japan. **DD** 666.1. Documents available from CASDDS.
Ind/Abst Chem. Abstr.

AU/0029-9162
OESTERREICHISCHE GLASER-ZEITUNG. **Added/Corp** Bundesinnung der Glaser Osterreichs. **VFOAT** Glas. Vol. 1 (1947)-. Periodical. German. mo. S568.00. Osterreichische Wirtschaftsverlag, Nikolsdorfergasse 7-11, A-1501 Vienna Austria. **Tel** 011 43 222 555585, FAX 0222/55 55 85/215, telex 1-11669. **Ad Acc. Circ:** 1,700.

US/8755-5530
OFFICIAL IDENTIFICATION GUIDE TO GLASSWARE, THE. [Off. identif. guide glassw.]. **VFOAT** Glassware; Identification Glassware; ID Glassware. 1st Ed.-. English. an. $9.95. Random House Inc., 400 Hahn Road, Westminster MD 21157. **Tel** (800)726-0600, (800)733-3000, FAX (800)659-2436. **LC** NK5104; .O46. **DD** 748.2/075.

US/0743-8699
OFFICIAL PRICE GUIDE TO GLASSWARE, THE. (THE OFFICIAL PRICE GUIDE TO GLASSWARE / BY THE HOUSE OF COLLECTIBLES, INC.). **Added/Corp** House of Collectibles. **VFOAT** Glassware. First Ed. (1984)-. English. ir. Random House Inc., 400 Hahn Road, Westminster MD 21157. **Tel** (800)726-0600, (800)733-3000, FAX (800)659-2436. **LC** NK5104; .O47. **DD** 748.2/075.

US/0748-5522
OFFICIAL PRICE GUIDE TO HUMMEL FIGURINES & PLATES, THE. **See** Hobbies.

US/0747-5705
OFFICIAL PRICE GUIDE TO POTTERY & PORCELAIN, THE. (THE OFFICIAL PRICE GUIDE TO POTTERY & PORCELAIN / BY THE HOUSE OF COLLECTIBLES, INC.). [Off. price guide pottery porcelain]. **Added/Corp** House of Collectibles. **VFOAT** Pottery & Porcelain; Pottery and Porcelain; Pottery. (19??)-. English. an. $15.50 (includes postage). Random House Inc., 400 Hahn Road, Westminster MD 21157. **Tel** (800)726-0600, (800)733-3000, FAX (800)659-2436. **LC** NK4005; .O37. **DD** 738/.0973/075.

US/0748-0121
OFFICIAL PRICE GUIDE TO ROYAL DOULTON, THE. [Off. price guide Royal Doulton]. **Added/Corp** House of Collectibles. **VFOAT** Doulton. (1982)-. English. ir. $15.85 (latest volume). Random House Inc., 400 Hahn Road, Westminster MD 21157. **Tel** (800)726-0600, (800)733-3000, FAX (800)659-2436. **LC** NK4660; .O36. **DD** 738.8/2/0942463.

AU/0472-5522
OSTERREICHISCHE KERAMISCHE RUNDSCHAU. [Osterr. Keram. Rundsch.]. Vol. 1 (Jan. 1964)-. Periodical. German. mo. S746.00. Verlag Lorenz, Ebendorferstrasse 10, A-1010 Vienna Austria. **Tel** 011 43 222 426695, FAX 011 43 222 438693. **DD** 738.
Ind/Abst BHA : Biblio. Hist. Art; Ceram. Abstr. (19??-); Coal Abstr.

US/1065-5034
PHASE EQUILIBRIA DIAGRAMS (ANNUAL). ***Ceased.*** (PHASE EQUILIBRIA DIAGRAMS : PHASE DIAGRAMS FOR CERAMISTS / COMPILED IN THE CERAMICS DIVISION, NATIONAL INSTITUTE OF STANDARDS AND TECHNOLOGY.). [Phase equilib. diagr.]. **Added/Corp** National Institute of Standards and Technology (U.S.). Ceramics Division. American Ceramic Society. (1992)-(1993). English. American Ceramic Society, 735 Ceramic Place, Westerville OH 43081-8720. **Tel** (614)890-4700, (614)794-5890, FAX (614)899-6109. **DD** 666. ***Continues*** *Phase Diagrams for Ceramists (Annual), 1064-5160.*

●US/1065-500X
PHASE EQUILIBRIA DIAGRAMS (FINAL COMPILATION). (PHASE EQUILIBRIA DIAGRAMS : PHASE DIAGRAMS FOR CERAMISTS / COMPILED IN THE CERAMICS DIVISION, NATIONAL INSTITUTE OF STANDARDS AND TECHNOLOGY.). [Phase equilib. diagr.]. **Added/Corp** American Ceramic Society. National Institute of Standards and Technology (U.S.). Ceramics Division. Vol. 9 (1992)-. English. Price varies per volume. American Ceramic Society, 735 Ceramic Place, Westerville OH 43081-8720. **Tel** (614)890-4700, (614)794-5890, FAX (614)899-6109. **DD** 666. ***Continues*** *Phase Diagrams for Ceramists (Final compilation), 1064-5179.*

UK/0031-9090
PHYSICS AND CHEMISTRY OF GLASSES. [Phys. chem. glasses]. **Added/Corp** Society of Glass Technology. Vol. 1 (Feb. 1960)-. Periodical. English. bm. £117.50 UK; £133.00 other. Society of Glass Technology, Thornton 20, Hallam Gate Road, Sheffield S10 5BT England. **Tel** 011 44 742 663168, FAX 011 44 742 665252. **ED** A. E. Owen. **LC** TA450; .P5. **DD** 620.144. **CODEN** PCGLA6. **Bk Rev. Pr Rev. Circ:** 1,200 (ctrl). Documents available from Article Express International, The Genuine Article, Ask*IEEE, CASDDS. ***Supersedes in part*** *Journal of the Society of Glass Technology.*
Desc: Contains papers of a purely scientific interest concerned with glasses and their structure or properties.
Ind/Abst Bioeng. Abstr.; Ceram. Abstr.; Chem. Abstr.; Chem. Titles; Curr. Contents Phys. Chem. Earth Sci.; Curr. Technol. Index; Ei Page One; Eng. Index Annu.; GeoRef; INSPEC (1968-); Leadscan; Nucl. Sci. Abstr.; Res. Alert [Full Cov.]; Sci. Cit. Index; SCISEARCH; World Ceram. Abstr.

UK
PILKINGTON GLASS AGE NEWS. VFOAT Glass Age News. Periodical. English (Spanish and French).

US/0195-5780
PLATE WORLD. ***Ceased.*** [Plate world]. Vol. 1, No. 1 (Spring 1979)-(19??). Periodical. English. Four times a year. Plate World Publishing Company, 9200 North Maryland Avenue, Niles IL 60648-1322. **Tel** (312)763-7773, FAX (312)966-3121, telex B6E-NILE 72-4407. **ED** Alyson Sulaski Wyckoff. **LC** NK4695.P55; P58. **DD** 738.2/4. Index available. **Bk Rev. Ad Acc. Circ:** 55,000.
Desc: A showcase magazine of limited-edition collector's plate art. Edited for the collector, articles include full-color features on artists, collectors, and manufacturers. Tips on decorating, marketing information, trends, industry news, and technical advice.

US/0032-4477
POPULAR CERAMICS. [Pop. ceram.]. (1949)-. Periodical. English. Twelve times a year. $23.95. Joe Jones Publishing, PO Box 337, Iola WI 54945. **Tel** (800)331-0038, (715)445-5000, FAX (715)445-4053, . **ED** Terry O'Neill. **LC** TP785; .P65. **DD** 738. Index available. cum. index. **Bk Rev. Ad Acc. Circ:** 56,536. available on microfilm and microfiche from University Microfilms International (UMI). ***Formed by the union of*** *Plastercrafts, 0164-4017.*
Desc: Contains how-to articles, with instructions for ceramic projects. Includes ceramic information, some historical.

US/0888-0336
PORCELAIN ARTIST. [Porcelain artist]. **Added/Corp** International Procelain Art Teachers. Vol. 17, No. 1 (Oct. 1976)-. Periodical. English. bm. $34.00 US; $38.00 other. International Porcelain Artists Inc., 7424 Greenville Avenue, Suite 101, Dallas TX 75231. **Tel** (214)692-5037. **ED** Mary Ellen Haggerty-Richards and Doris Ann Johnson. **DD** 738. **Ad Acc. Circ:** 7,000. ***Continues*** *International China Painting Teachers Organization News, 0538-5504.*

GW
PORZELLAN + GLAS : P + G / ORGAN DES BUNDESVERBANDES DES GLAS-, PORZELLAN- UND KERAMIK-EINZELHANDELS. ***Ceased.*** **Added/Corp** Bundesverband des Glas-, Porzellan- und Keramik Einzenhandels. **VFOAT** P + G. **VAT** Porzellan und Glas. (19??)-(Dec. 1993). Trade Publication. German. mo. Futura-Verlag R Stephan, Postfach 102464, D 40015 Dusseldorf Germany. **Tel** 011 49 211 387030, telex 8586486. **ED** Jutta Stephan-Druckenmuller. **Bk Rev. Ad Acc. Circ:** 7,000 (ctrl).
Desc: Trade magazine for the tabletop, houseware and gourmet professional in the German-speaking areas of Europe.

NZ/0113-583X
POTTER. [Potter Auckl.]. **VFOAT** New Zealand Potter. (1975)-. Periodical. English. Three times a year. 27.50NZ$ New Zealand; 31.50NZ$ other. New Zealand Potter, P.O.Box 881, Auckland, New Zealand. **Tel** 011 64 9 798665, FAX 011 64 9 3093247. **ED** H.S.Williams. **DD** 738.09931. **Circ:** 6,000 (ctrl). ***Continues*** *New Zealand Potter, 0028-8608.*

AT/0048-4954
POTTERY IN AUSTRALIA. Added/Corp Potters' Society of New South Wales. (19??)-. Periodical. English. qt. 48.00Aus$ Australia; 60.00Aus$ other; 55.00Aus$ Comes with Potters Society of Australia Membership. Potters Society of Australia, 2 68 Alexander Street, Crows Nest 2065, Australia. **Tel** 11 61 2 9013353, FAX 11 61 2 4361681. **ED** Suzanne Breckle. **LC** TT919; .P65. Index available. cum. index. **Bk Rev. Ad Acc, Adv Mgr:** Trish Wilkinds. **Circ:** 3,000.
Desc: Contemporary magazine about Australian pottery with an international flavor. Color, articles, technical information, and review of potters' life and work.

US/0738-8020
POTTERY SOUTHWEST. (POTTERY SOUTHWEST : NEWS, QUERIES & VIEWS ON ARCHAEOLOGICAL CERAMICS BY SOUTHWESTERNISTS.). **Added/Corp** Albuquerque Archaeological Society. Museum of New Mexico. Vol. 1, No. 1 (Jan. 1974)-. Periodical. English. qt (Jan., Apr., July, Oct.). $3.00 US; $6.00 other. Pottery Southwest, 6207 Mossman Place Northeast, Albuquerque NM 87110. **Tel** (505)881-1675. **ED** Eric Blinman, OAS, Museum of New Mexico, PO Box 2087, Santa Fe, NM, 87504. Index available. **Bk Rev. Circ:** 175.
Desc: News, queries and views on archaeological ceramics by southwesternists, pottery type descriptions, book notices and reviews, letters, short articles, and illustrations.
Ind/Abst Anthropol. Lit.; Ethnoarts Index.

US/0148-3765
PRICE TRENDS. 1970-. English. an. $9.00 each issue. Box 4444, Springfield MO 65804. **LC** NK5439.D44; W4 SUPPL. **DD** 748.2/913.

UK
PROCEEDINGS. Main/Corp Wedgwood Society. (1956)-. Proceedings. English. ir. £10.00. Wedgwood Society of London, City Museum and Art Gallery, Stoke-on-Trent ST1 3DW England. **Tel** 011 44 923 853063. **ED** Alison Kelly. **LC** NK3700; .W43. ctrl circ.
Desc: Matters of interest relating to Wedgwood ceramics.

US/0362-2991
PROCEEDINGS OF THE ANNUAL SYMPOSIUM ON REDUCTION OF COSTS IN HAND-OPERATED GLASS PLANTS. [Proc. annu. Symp. Reduct. Costs Hand-oper. Glass Plants]. **Main/Conf** Symposium on Reduction of Costs in Hand-Operated Glass Plants. 1st-1970-. Proceedings. English. an. West Virginia University Foundation Department for Languages, Chitwood Hall, Morgantown WV 26506. **Tel** (304)293-5121. **LC** T7; .W29 subser; TP845. **DD** 666/.12/05.

AT/0155-9796
PROCEEDINGS OF THE AUSTRALIAN CERAMIC CONFERENCE. (PROCEEDINGS.). [Proc. Aust. Ceram. Conf.]. **Main/Corp** Australian Ceramic Conference. (1962)-. Academic Scholarly Publication. English. be. **LC** TP785; .A838. **DD** 666. **CODEN** PACRDR. Documents available from CASDDS.
Ind/Abst Bioeng. Abstr.; Chem. Abstr.

US/0743-409X
PROCEEDINGS / SYMPOSIUM AND EXHIBITION ON THE ART OF GLASSBLOWING. Main/Conf Symposium and Exhibition on the Art of Glassblowing. 2nd International and 26th National (June 22-26, 1981)-. Proceedings. English. an. $25.00. The American Scientific Glassblowers Society, 1507 Hagley Road, Toledo OH 43612. **Tel** (419)476-5478. **ED** James E Panczner. **LC** TP859; .S93A. **DD** 666/.122/05. cum. index. **Circ:** 1,200 (ctrl). ***Continues*** *Proceedings, Symposium on the Art of Glassblowing.*
Desc: Educational, scientific, technical information on the art of scientific glassblowing.

US/0885-1808
PROFESSIONAL STAINED GLASS. [Prof. stained glass]. Vol. 5, No. 11 (Nov. 1985)-. Periodical. English. mo. $30.00. Arts and Media Incorporated, 28 South State Street, Newtown PA 18940. **Tel** (215)860-9947. **ED** Albert Lewis and Chris Peterson. **DD** 748. Index available. **Bk Rev. Ad Acc. Circ:** 15,000. ***Formed by the union of*** *Edge (New York, N.Y.)* ***and*** *Glass Craft News, 0742-5392.*
Desc: Contemporary stained glass work and techniques in full color.
Ind/Abst Art Archaeol. Tech. Abstr.

RU
PROIZVODSTVO TEKHNICHESKOGO I STROITELNOGO STEKLA / GOSUDARSTVENNYI NAUCHNO-ISSLEDOVATELSKII INSTITUT STEKLA, SARATOVSKII FILIAL. Added/Corp Gosudarstvennyi Nauchno-Issledovatelskii Institut Stekla (Moscow, R.S.F.S.R.). Saratovskii Filial. (19??-). Periodical. Russian. **LC** TP845; .P76.
Ind/Abst Ceram. Abstr. (19??-).

UK
REAL POTTERY. ***Ceased.*** Vol. 14, No. 56 (1987)-(19??). Periodical. English. ir. Northfield Studio, Northfield Tring, Hertfordshire England. **Tel** ALDBURY COMMON 229. **ED** Murray Fieldhouse. Index available. **Bk Rev. Ad Acc. Circ:** 2,500. ***Continues*** *Pottery Quarterly.*
Desc: For the studio and crafts potter, professional potter and serious amateur.

SZ/0484-3401
REI CRETARIAE ROMANAE FAUTORUM ACTA. Main/Corp Rei Cretariae Romanae Fautores. Vol. 1 (1958)-. Periodical. Latin (English, French, German, Italian and Spanish). ir. Cretariae Romanae Fautorum, Bahnhofplatz 7, CH-4410 Liestal. **Tel** 0041 61 925 5696. **LC** NK3850; .R43A. ***Continues*** *Rei Cretariae Romanae Fautorum Ubique Consistentium Acta.*

CC
RESEARCH IN INORGANIC MATERIALS. Added/Corp Shanghai Institute of Ceramics. (19??)-. Periodical. English. **LC** TP785; .R48. **DD** 666/.028.
Ind/Abst Ceram. Abstr. (19??-).

UK/0379-0002
REVIEWS ON POWDER METALLURGY AND PHYSICAL CERAMICS. ***Ceased.*** **See** Metals and Metallurgy.

FR
REVUE DE LA CERAMIQUE, LA. ***Title Change.*** No. 1 (Oct./Nov. 1981)-(199?). Periodical. French (English). bm. La Revue de la Ceramique, 61 rue Marconi, BP 3, 62880 Vendin-le-Vieil France. **Tel** 011 33 21 794444, FAX 011 33 21 794445. **ED** Silvie Girard. Index available. cum. index. **Bk Rev. Ad Acc. Circ:** 5,000 (ctrl). ***Continued by*** *La Revue de la Ceramique et du Verre, 0294-202X.*
Desc: All aspects of ceramic and glass from archaeology to present.

FR/0294-202X
REVUE DE LA CERAMIQUE ET DU VERRE, LA. VFOAT Ceramique. No. 4 (Apr.-May 1982)-. French (English). bm. 410.00F US and Canada; 350.00F France. La Revue de la Ceramique, 61 rue Marconi, BP 3, 62880 Vendin-le-Vieil France. **Tel** 011 33 21 794444, FAX 011 33 21 794445. **ED** Sylvie Girard. **LC** NK3700; .R48. Index available (free on request). cum. index. **Bk Rev.** (Qty: 20). **Ad Acc, Adv Mgr:** same as editor. **Circ:** 5,800 (ctrl). ***Continues*** *Revue de la Ceramique.*
Desc: All aspects of ceramic and glass from archaeology to present.

IT
RIVISTA DEL VETRO. Italian. mo. L30000 Italy; L100000 Europe; L130000 other. Editas Srl, Via Washington 50, 20146 Milan Italy. **Tel** 011 39 2 4696565.

GW
SCHAULADE, DIE. (Jan. 1925)-. Periodical. German. Twelve times a year. DM122.00 Germany; DM128.00 other. Meisenbach GmbH, Postfach 2069, D 96011 Bamberg Germany. **Tel** 011 49 951 861135. **ED** Beate Schraml. **LC** NK3; .S355. Index available. **Bk Rev. Ad Acc. Circ:** 7,750. available with illustrations. ***Superseded in part by*** *Gesalt* ***and*** *Hausgeraet.*
Desc: Independent international trade magazine for Chinese ceramics, glass, giftware and household articles.

GW/0586-7665
SCHOTT INFORMATION. [Schott inf.]. (1967)-. Periodical. German. **CODEN** SHIFAW. Documents available from CASDDS. ***Continues Schott.***
Ind/Abst Ceram. Abstr. (19??-); Chem. Abstr. (1964-1983); Energy Res. Abstr. (Mar. 1982-).

NE/0080-7575
SCIENCE OF CERAMICS. (SCIENCE OF CERAMICS : PROCEEDINGS OF A CONFERENCE HELD ... UNDER THE AUSPICES OF THE BRITISH CERAMIC SOCIETY AND THE NEDERLANDSE KERAMISCHE VERENIGING.). [Sci. ceram.]. **Added/Corp** British Ceramic Society. Nederlandse Keramische Vereniging. European Ceramic Association. Vol. 1 (1962)-. Proceedings. English (French and German). an. £66.00. MECC, PO Box 1630, 6201 BP Maastricht, Netherlands. **ED** G. H. Stewart. **LC** TP785; .B86. **DD** 666. **CODEN** SCCEAW. Documents available from Article Express International, CASDDS.
Ind/Abst Bioeng. Abstr.; Chem. Abstr.; Ei Page One; Eng. Index Annu.

JA/0009-031X
SERAMIKKUSU. [Seramikkusu]. **Added/Corp** Yogyo Kyokai (Japan). **VFOAT** Ceramics Japan; Ceramics-Japan; Ceramics. (Jan. 1966)-. Academic Scholarly Publication. Japanese (table of contents in English). mo. $282.00. Nippon Seramikkusu Kyokai, (Ceramic Soc. of Japan), 22-17, Hyakunincho 2 Chome, Shinjukuku, Tokyoto 160 Japan. **(Subscription address:** Kyowa Book Company Inc., 1-38 Kanda Jinbo-Cho, Chiyoda-Ku Tokyo 101, Japan) **CODEN** SERAA7. **[CCC].** Documents available from CASDDS.
Ind/Abst Alum. Ind. Abstr.; Ceram. Abstr.; Chem. Abstr.; Met. Abstr.; World Ceram. Abstr.

JA
SERAMIKKUSU KENKYU SHISETSU NENPO / ANNUAL REPORT OF THE CERAMICS RESEARCH LABORATORY, NAGOYA INSTITUTE OF TECHNOLOGY. **Added/Corp** Nagoya Kogyo Daigaku. Seramikkusu Kenkyu Shisetsu. **VFOAT** Annual Report of the Ceramics Research Laboratory, Nagoya Institute of Technology. Vol. 1 (1991)-. Periodical. Japanese (English). Nagoya Kogyo Daigaku Kogakubu Fuzoku, Seramikkusu Kenkyo Shisetsu, 10 6 29 Asahigaoka, Tajimi-shi 507 Japan. **LC** TP785; .N125a. ***Continues*** *Yogyo Gijutsu Kenkyu Shisetsu Nenpo, 0911-4769.*

US/0272-1910
SHARDS NEWSLETTER, THE. (THE SHARDS NEWSLETTER : REVIEW OF PUBLISHED RESOURCES IN THE CERAMIC ARTS.). [Shards newsl.]. V. 1- Spring 1980-. Newsletter. English. sa. $12.00 includes membership. Institute for Ceramic History, 436 West 12th Street, Claremont CA 91711. **ED** Garth Clark.

BE/0037-5225
SILICATES INDUSTRIELS. (19??)-. Academic Scholarly Publication. French (English and German). bm. 4000F Belgium; 5200F other. Silicates Industriels, Avenue Gouverneur Cornez 4, B-7000 Mons Belgium. **Tel** 32 65 348000, FAX 32 65 348005, telex 578656 B. **ED** R Richez. **LC** TP785; .S47. **CODEN** SIINAT. **Bk Rev. Ad Acc. Circ:** 600. Documents available from CASDDS.
Desc: Journal devoted to ceramic materials including cement, glass, traditional and technical ceramics information about books, conferences and other relevant activities in the ceramic field.
Ind/Abst Ceram. Abstr.; Chem. Abstr.; Concr. Abstr.; Eng. Mater. Abstr.; GeoRef; Highw. Res. Abstr.; World Ceram. Abstr.

FR
SILICATES INDUSTRIELS. French. bm. 995.00F France; 1090.00F other. Dawson France SA, BP 40, 91121 Palaiseau Cedex France. **Tel** 011 33 1 69104700, telex 220064F.

GW
SILIKAT JOURNAL. (19??)-. Periodical. German. mo. DM110.00. Verlag Technischer Zeitschriften Aumann Kg, Witterlsbacher-Strasse 23, 8672 Selb Germany. **LC** TP785; .S49. ***Absorbed*** *Glas-Email-Keramo-Technik.*
Ind/Abst Ceram. Abstr. (19??-).

XR/0037-637X
SKLAR A KERAMIK. ***Ceased.*** [Sklar keram.]. (1950)-(19??). Academic Scholarly Publication. Czech (summaries and/or abstracts in German, Spanish, Russian and English; table of contents in English, German, Spanish and Russian). mo. **(Subscription address:** Artia Pegas Press Ltd., Palac Metro Narodni Trida 25, 11210 Prague 1 Czech Republic.) **CODEN** SKKEAQ. Documents available from CASDDS.
Ind/Abst Art Archaeol. Tech. Abstr.; Ceram. Abstr.; Chem. Abstr.; Saf. Health Work; World Ceram. Abstr.

GW/0417-2256
SONDERHEFT - DEUTSCHE KERAMISCHE GESELLSCHAFT. **Main/Corp** Deutsche Keramische Gesellschaft. Vol. 1- 1958-. Periodical. German. DM173.00 Germany; DM180.00 other. Deutsche Keramische Gesellschaft, Menzenberger Str 47, POB 1226, D Honnef Rheine Germany. **Tel** (02224)7103839. **Bk Rev. Ad Acc. Circ:** 2,500 (ctrl).
Desc: Contains scientific papers on ceramic engineering and news of the industry.

UK/0144-2147
SPECIAL PUBLICATION - BRITISH CERAMIC RESEARCH ASSOCIATION. (SPECIAL PUBLICATION.). [Spec. publ. - Br. Ceram. Res. Assoc.]. **Main/Corp** British Ceramic Research Association. (19??)-. Monographic series. English. Price varies per volume. British Ceramic Research Association, Queens Road Penkhull, Stoke on Trent ST4 7LQ England. **Tel** (0865)794141, FAX (0865)750643, telex 83177. **CODEN** SBCRDX. Documents available from CASDDS.
Ind/Abst Bioeng. Abstr.; Ceram. Abstr.; Chem. Abstr.; GeoRef.

GW/0341-0439
SPRECHSAAL. Vol. 109, No. 5 (May 1976)-. Academic Scholarly Publication. German (English). mo. Sprechsaal Publishing Group, PO Box 2962, D-96418 Coburg Germany. **Tel** 011 49 9561 742810, FAX 011 49 9561 90009, telex 179561817. **ED** Eberhard Ftuer and Christoph Muller. **CODEN** SPREAS. **Bk Rev. Ad Acc. Circ:** 7,600. Documents available from CASDDS. ***Continues*** *Sprechsaal fur Keramik, Glas, Baustoffe, 0340-5133.*
Desc: International magazine dealing with refractories, bricks, clay, glass, advanced ceramics, composite and fibers production, technologies and research and development.
Ind/Abst Ceram. Abstr.; Chem. Abstr.; Coal Abstr.; EMBASE; Infomat Int. Bus.

GW/0341-0676
SPRECHSAAL 1976. [Sprechsaal 1976]. **VFOAT** Spechsaal Ceramics, Glass; Sprechsaal International Ceramics + Glass Magazine; Traditional and Advanced Ceramics, Glass, and Materials Technology. (1976)-. Periodical. Multiple languages. Twelve times a year. DM405.00 Germany; DM525.00 others. Sprechsaal Publishing Group, PO Box 2962, D-96418 Coburg Germany. **Tel** 011 49 9561 742810, FAX 011 49 9561 90009, telex 179561817. **UDC** 666. ***Continues*** *Sprechsaal fuer Keramik, Glas, Baustoffe, 0340-5133.*
Ind/Abst Ei Page One; World Ceram. Abstr.

US/0038-9161
STAINED GLASS. **Added/Corp** Stained Glass Association of America. Stained Glass Association of America. Bulletin. Vol. 1 (1907)-. Periodical. English. qt. $8.00. Stained Glass Association of America / St Louis, 1125 Wilmington Avenue, St Louis MO 63111. **LC** NK5300; .S7.
Ind/Abst Art Index; ARTbibliogr. Mod.

US/1067-8867
STAINED GLASS (LEE'S SUMMIT, MO.). (STAINED GLASS : QUARTERLY OF THE STAINED GLASS ASSOCIATION OF AMERICA.). [Stained glass]. **Added/Corp** Stained Glass Association of America. Vol. 85, No. 4 (Winter 1990)-. Periodical. English. qt (Mar., June, Sept., Dec.). $24.00 US; $40.00 other. Stained Glass Association of America, 6 Southwest 2nd Street 7, Lees Summit MO 64063. **Tel** (816)524-9313, (800)438-9581. **LC** NK5300; .S7. **DD** 748. Index available (Additional $22.00). ***Continues*** *Stained Glass Quarterly, 0895-7002.*
Desc: Information on glass painting and staining.

RU/0131-9582
STEKLO I KERAMIKA. (1948)-. Academic Scholarly Publication. Russian. mo. Documents available from Article Express International, Ask*IEEE, CASDDS.
Ind/Abst Ceram. Abstr. (19??-); Chem. Abstr.; Ei Page One; Eng. Index Annu.; INSPEC (Sept. 1969-); World Ceram. Abstr.

US/0091-6641
STUDIO POTTER. [Studio potter]. **Added/Corp** Daniel Clark Foundation. Vol. 1, (Fall 1972)-. Periodical. English. Twice a year (June, Dec.). $20.00 US; $36.00 others. Studio Potter Foundation, PO Box 70, Goffstown NH 03045. **Tel** (603)774-3582. **LC** NK3700; .S86. **DD** 738/.05.
Ind/Abst Art Index; ARTbibliogr. Mod. (1985-).

HU/0237-2169
SZILIKATIPARI ES SZILIKATTUDOMANYI KONFERENCIA. **VFOAT** Konferenz der Silikatindustrie und Silkatwissenschaft; Konferencija Silikatnoj Promyslennosti i Nauki o Silikatah; Conference on Silicate Industry and Silicate Science; Siliconf. (1977)-. Multiple languages. ***Continues*** *Szilikatipari Konferencia, 0369-8653.*
Ind/Abst Ceram. Abstr. (19??-).

PL/0039-8144
SZKO I CERAMIKA. [Szko ceram.]. **Added/Corp** Poland. Centralny Zarzad Przemysu Szklarskiego. Poland. Centralny Zarzad Przemysu Ceramicznego. Stowarzyszenie Naukowo-Techniczne Inzynierow i Technikow Przemysu Chemicznego. Vol. 1 (1935)-. Academic Scholarly Publication. Polish (English; summaries and/or abstracts in English, French, Polish and Russian). bm. $117.00. **(Subscription address:** ARS Polona, PO Box 1001, 00068 Warsaw Poland.) **LC** TP785; .S9. **CODEN** SZKCAN. Documents available from Ask*IEEE, CASDDS.
Ind/Abst Art Archaeol. Tech. Abstr.; Ceram. Abstr.; Chem. Abstr.; Coal Abstr.; INSPEC (1968-1985); World Ceram. Abstr.

FR/0039-8780
TABLE ET CADEAU, L'OBJET POUR LA MAISON. **See** Interior Design-Home Furnishings.

UK/0143-7755
TABLEWARE INTERNATIONAL. [Tableware int.]. Vol. 1, No. 7 (March 1971)-. Periodical. English. Eleven times a year. £71.00 UK; £86.00, $158.00 other. Argus Press Group, Queensway House, 2 Queensway Redhill, Surrey RH1 1QS England. **Tel** 011 44 737 768611, 011 44 737 761685, FAX 011 44 737 760510, telex 948669 TOPJNL G. ***Continues*** *Tableware International & Pottery Gazette.*
Desc: Provides news, reviews and comment on the tableware industry.

UK/0960-6661
TECHNICAL CERAMICS INTERNATIONAL. [Tech. ceram. int.]. (1990)-. Periodical. English. Twelve times a year. £254.00 UK; $445.00 US. World Business Publications Ltd., 960 High Road, Britannia 4th Floor, London N12 9RY England. **Tel** 11 44 81 446 5141, FAX 11 44 81 446 3659, telex 9419208. **DD** 338.47666. ***Continues*** *Technical Ceramics Bulletin, 0268-8123.*

UK/0144-3631
TECHNICAL NOTE BRITISH CERAMIC RESEARCH ASSOCIATION. (1960)-. English. British Ceramic Research Association, Queens Road Penkhull, Stoke on Trent ST4 7LQ England. **Tel** (0865)794141, FAX (0865)750643, telex 83177.
Ind/Abst Ceram. Abstr. (19??-); Ei Page One.

UK/0528-3701
TECHNICAL REPORT - CEMENT AND CONCRETE ASSOCIATION. (TECHNICAL REPORT.). [Tech. rep. - Cem. Concr. Assoc.]. **Main/Corp** Cement and Concrete Association. (1971)-. Monographic series. English. Price varies per volume. **CODEN** TCCADY. Documents available from CASDDS.
Ind/Abst Bioeng. Abstr.; Ceram. Abstr.; Chem. Abstr. (1954-1983).

SP
TECNICA CERAMICA. (1971)-. Periodical. Spanish. Ten times a year. $90.00. Publica SA, Ecuador 75 Entresuelo, 08029 Barcelona Spain. **Tel** 011 34 3 3215046, 4391027.

●US/1077-6974
TILE DESIGN & INSTALLATION. [Tile des. install.]. **VFOAT** Tile Design and Installation; Tile; TDI. Vol. 7, No. 3 (May/June 1994)-. Trade Publication. English. mo (except Aug.). $49.00. Business News Publishing Company, 755 West Big Beaver Road, Suite 1000, Troy MI 48084. **Tel** (810)362-3700, FAX (810)362-0317, telex 230295. **DD** 738. ***Continues*** *Tile World, 1074-455X.*
Desc: Dedicated to professionals who design, specify, distribute, install and buy quality tile products. Topics from design trends and manufacturing techniques to interesting installations, distribution trends and outstanding tile projects keep you abreast of industry trends.

IT/1120-7884
TILE ITALIA. [Tile Ital.]. (1990)-. Periodical. Italian. bm (6 issues). L30000.00 Italy; L50000.00 other. Tile Italia Srl, V Circonvallazione Nord Est 50, 41049 Sassuolo Mo Italy. **Tel** 011 39 536 807121. **UDC** 691.

LH
TKG : FACHZEITSCHRIFT FUR DIE TECHNIK IN DER KERAMIK, GLAS UND EMAIL INDUSTRIE. Vol. 1, No. 1- Jan. 1980-. Periodical. German. 80.00. Verlag Ar Gantner Kg, Beckagassle 4, Postfach 225, FL9490 Vaduz Liechtenstein. ***Supersedes*** *Silikat Journal, 0560-0421.*

GW
TONINDUSTRIE ZEITUNG FACHBERICHTE. **VFOAT** TIZ-Fachberichte. 101. Vol. No. 7/8- July/Aug. 1977-. Periodical. German. mo. $127.83. Sprechsaal Publishing Group, PO Box 2962, D-96418 Coburg Germany. **Tel** 011 49 9561 742810, FAX 011 49 9561 90009, telex 179561817. ***Continues*** *Tonindustrie-Zeitung und Keramische Rundschau.*

UK
TRANSACTIONS / ENGLISH CERAMIC CIRCLE. **Added/Corp** English Ceramic Circle. Vol. 1 (1933)-. Periodical. English. an. £27.00. English Ceramic Circle, 5 The Drive, Beckenham Kent BR3 1EE England. **LC** NK4085; .T7. **DD** 738/.0942/05. ***Continues*** *Transactions (English Porcelain Circle).*
Ind/Abst Art Archaeol. Tech. Abstr.; ARTbibliogr. Mod.; BHA : Biblio. Hist. Art.

II/0371-750X
TRANSACTIONS OF THE INDIAN CERAMIC SOCIETY. (TRANSACTIONS.). [Trans. Indian Ceram. Soc.]. **Main/Corp** Indian Ceramic Society. Vol. 1 (Sept. 1941)-. Academic Scholarly Publication. English. bm. $40.00 or £25.00. Indian Ceramics, 10 Sourin Roy Road Behala, Calcutta 700 034 India. **Tel** 011 33 4780651. **(Subscription address:** Prints India, 11 Darya Ganj, New Delhi 110002 India.**) ED** D Ganguli. **LC** TP785; .I56. **DD** 666.306254. **CODEN** TICSAP. Index available. cum. index. **Bk Rev. Ad Acc. Pr Rev. Circ:** 1,500. Documents available from Article Express International, CASDDS.
Ind/Abst Bioeng. Abstr.; Ceram. Abstr.; Chem. Abstr.; Coal Abstr.; Ei Page One; Eng. Index Annu.; GeoRef; Indian Geosci. Abstr.; World Ceram. Abstr.

UK/0306-0926
TRANSACTIONS OF THE ORIENTAL CERAMIC SOCIETY. Main/Corp Oriental Ceramic Society. (1922)-. Periodical. English. an. Oriental Ceramic Society, 31B Torrington Square, London WC1E 7JL England. **Tel** 011 44 71 6367987. **(Subscription address:** Phillip Wilson Publishers Ltd., 26 Litchfield Street, London WC2H 9NJ England.**) ED** Margaret Medley. **[CCC]. Circ:** 1,200 (ctrl).
Desc: To increase the knowledge and appreciation of Asian ceramics and other arts.
Ind/Abst ARTbibliogr. Mod.

US/0041-7661
U.S. GLASS, METAL & GLAZING. [U.S. glass met. glaz.]. **VFOAT** U.S. Glass. **VAT** United States Glass, Metal and Glazing. (1966)-. Periodical. English. Twelve times a year. $35.00. US Glass Publications Inc., 560 Oakwood Avenue, Suite 202, Lake Forest IL 60045. **Tel** (708)295-2900, FAX (708)295-2903. **ED** Felicia T. Stott. **DD** 338. **Bk Rev. Ad Acc. Circ:** 16,000 (ctrl).
Desc: Contains flat glass, architectural metal markets, case histories, new products, and management articles geared to help run a glass business.
Ind/Abst F&S Index Plus Text, Int. [Select. Cov.]; PROMT.

US/0009-0328
UNDERGLAZE DECORATION. (19??)-. Periodical. English. ir. $3.95. Professional Publications Inc., PO Box 12448, Columbus OH 43212. **Tel** (614)488-8236, FAX (614)488-4561. **LC** TP785; .C44. **DD** 666/.05.

FR/0180-0078
VERRE ACTUALITES. (1976)-. Periodical. French. Seven times a year. 200.78F France; 278.00F other. Publicat Sarl, 17 Boulevard Poissonniere, 75002 Paris France. **Tel** 011 33 1 40265126. **UDC** 66. **CODEN** 68.

FR/0984-7979
VERRE (PARIS, FRANCE). (VERRE.). **Added/Corp** Institut du Verre-Prover. Vol. 1, No. 1 (Feb. 1987)-. Academic Scholarly Publication. French (English). Six times a year (Feb., Apr., June, Sept., Oct., Dec.). 945.00F France; 1050.00F other. Institut du Verre Prover, 41 rue des Chantiers, 78000 Versailles France. **Tel** 011 33 1 39494401, FAX 011 33 1 39023609. **ED** Dominique Dabas. **LC** TP845; .V37. **DD** 666/.1/05. **CODEN** VERRER. **Bk Rev**, (Qty: 6). **Ad Acc, Adv Mgr:** J. N. Cheureau. **Circ:** 400 (ctrl). Documents available from CASDDS. ***Continues** Verres et Refractaires (Paris, France: 1976), 0337-5676.*
Desc: Deals exclusively with glass making and heat resistant ceramics. Up-to-date reviews of the latest publications.
Ind/Abst Ceram. Abstr.; Chem. Abstr.

IT
VETRO INFORMAZIONE. Periodical. Italian. bm. L37000. Faenza Editrice, Via P de Crescenzi 44, 48018 Faenza Italy. **Tel** 011 39 546 663488, FAX 011 39 546 660440, telex 550387.

NE/0927-748X
VORMEN UIT VUUR. [Vormen vuur]. (1992)-. Periodical. Dutch. Four times a year (Mar., June, Oct., Dec.). Fl100.00. Ned Vereniging van Vrienden, Van de Ceramiek, POB 1129, 8001 BC Zwolle Netherlands. **Tel** 011 31 573057654. **UDC** 738 + 748. ***Continues** Mededelingenblad - Nederlandse Vereniging van Vrienden van de Ceramiek, 0920-1009.*
Ind/Abst BHA : Biblio. Hist. Art.

US
WALLACE-HOMESTEAD PRICE GUIDE TO PATTERN GLASS. Added/Corp Wallace-Homestead. **VFOAT** Wallace Homestead Price Guide to Pattern Glass; Pattern Glass; Price Guide to Pattern Glass. English. $12.95 (single issue). Wallace-Homestead Book Company / Illinois, 850 Waters Edge, Lombard IL 60148. **LC** NK1125; .W25. **DD** 748.2913/075. ***Continues** Wallace-Homestead Price Guide to Antiques and Pattern Glass, 0748-9986.*

CN/0826-2098
WILLOW TRANSFER QUARTERLY. (THE WILLOW TRANSFER QUARTERLY : NEWSLETTER OF THE TORONTO WILLOW SOCIETY.). [Willow tranf. q.]. Vol. 1, No. 1 (Jan. 1983)-. Newsletter. English. qt. $15.00. Willow Society, 39 Medhurst Road, Toronto Ontario M4B 1B2 Canada. **Tel** (416)757-0634. **ED** Conrad Biernacki. **DD** 738.2/3. **Bk Rev. Ad Acc. Circ:** 600 (ctrl). ***Continues** Willow Notebook.*
Desc: Informative, entertaining newsletter for willow pattern china collectors, enthusiasts, and dealers. Includes articles, book reviews, special features. Only newsletter of its type in North America.

UK/0263-1784
WINDOW INDUSTRIES. [Window ind.]. (1982)-. Periodical. English. mo. £58.00 UK; £71.00 (surface), £100.00 (air mail) other. Turret Group, 177 Hagden Lane, Watford Herts WD1 8LN United Kingdom. **Tel** 011 44 923 228577, FAX 011 44 923 221346. **DD** 338.47690182305. ***Continues** Double Glazing, 0306-3879.*

UK/0957-8897
WORLD CERAMICS ABSTRACTS. See Glass and Ceramics-Abstracting, Bibliographies and Statistics.

UK/0959-6127
WORLD CERAMICS & REFRACTORIES. VFOAT World Ceramics and Refractories. Vol. 1, No. 1 (March/April 1990)-. Periodical. English. Six times a year. £53.00 Europe; £58.00 other. London & Sheffield Publishing Company Ltd, 5 Pond Street, Hampstead London NW3 2PN England. **Tel** 011 44 71 7940800, FAX 011 44 71 7940411, telex 9312130191 LSG. **LC** TP785; .W67. **DD** 666. **CODEN** WCREEJ. ***Formed by the union of** Euroclay, 0306-1841 **and** Refractories Journal, 0034-3110.*

KO
YOOP HAKHOE CHI. JOURNAL OF THE KOREAN CERAMIC SOCIETY. Main/Corp Han'Guk Yoop Hakhoe. **Added/Corp** Han'guk Yoop Hakhoe. Journal. **VFOAT** Journal of the Korean Ceramic Society. (19??)-. Periodical. Korean (summaries and/or abstracts in English). Hanguk Yoop Hakhoe, 53-20 Daihyun-dong Seodaemun-ku, Seoul Korea. **LC** TP785; .H36a. Documents available from CASDDS.
Ind/Abst Ceram. Abstr. (19??-); Chem. Abstr.

ABSTRACTING, BIBLIOGRAPHIES AND STATISTICS

US/1049-1252
C2C ABSTRACTS JAPAN. CERAMICS. [C2C abstr. Jap., Ceram.]. **VFOAT** Ceramics. Vol. 1, No. 1 (Feb. 1990)-. English. mo. $200.00. SCAN C2C Inc, Attn Carol G Heffernan Marketing Director, 500 E Street Southwest, Suite 800, 8th Floor, Washington DC 20024. **Tel** (202)863-3850, (800)525-3865, FAX (202)863-3855. **DD** 666. Index available. cum. index. available on CD-ROM from DIALOG; available on an online database from ORBIT; DATA-STAR; and DIALOG.
Desc: English abstracts of over 500 Japanese science, technical and business journals in the field of ceramics.
Ind/Abst ARTbibliogr. Mod.

US/0095-9960
CERAMIC ABSTRACTS. [Ceram. abstr.]. **Added/Corp** American Ceramic Society. **VFOAT** Journal and Ceramic Abstracts. (1922)-. Abstracting/Indexing Service. English. Six times a year (Feb., Apr., June, Aug., Oct., Dec.). $150.00 US; $160.00 other. American Ceramic Society, 735 Ceramic Place, Westerville OH 43081-8720. **Tel** (614)890-4700, (614)794-5890, FAX (614)899-6109. **ED** John B Wachtman. **DD** 666. **[CCC].** Index available. cum. index. **Bk Rev. Circ:** 3,800 (ctrl). available on an online database (CERAB) from STN International (Math) Database; (CERM) ORBIT; and (File 335) DIALOG; available on CD-ROM; available on magnetic tape; available on microfilm and microfiche from University Microfilms International (UMI). ***Continues in part** American Ceramic Society. Journal of the American Ceramic Society, 0002-7820.*
Desc: Includes abstracts on technical ceramic literature from more than 800 publications worldwide.
Ind/Abst MINPROC; World Ceram. Abstr.

UK/0957-8897
WORLD CERAMICS ABSTRACTS. Added/Corp CERAM Research (Firm). Vol. 1, No. 1 (Jan. 1989)-. Abstracting/Indexing Service. English. mo. £260.00 Europe; £290.00 other. Ceram Research Ltd., Queens Road, Penkhull, Stoke-On-Trent ST4 7LQ England. **Tel** 44 782 45431, FAX 44 782 412331. **ED** P. Brassington. **[CCC]. Bk Rev**, (Qty: occasionally). available on an online database from ORBIT. ***Continues** British Ceramic Abstracts, 0300-4570.*
Desc: Provides the fast, comprehensive coverage of the world's literature on the manufacture, processing and applications of ceramics. Coverage includes: high-tech ceramics; whitewares and vitreous enamels; refactories; clay-based building materials; glasses; cements and mortars together with raw material processing, plant development, ceramic processing and applications.
Ind/Abst Nonwovens Abstr.

HEALTH AND PERSONAL FITNESS

IT
18 KARATI. See Recreation, Leisure-Sports.

US
AAWH QUARTERLY. English. qt. American Association of World Health, 1129 20th Street NW Suite 400, Washington DC 20036. **Tel** (202)466-5883.

AT
ACHPER NATIONAL JOURNAL, THE. Added/Corp Australian Council for Health, Physical Education and Recreation. **VFOAT** National Journal. **VAT** Australian Council for Health, Physical Education and Recreation National Journal. No. 99 (Autumn 1983)-. Periodical. English. qt (Summer, Autumn, Winter, Spring). 50.00Aus$ (airmail); 28.00Aus$ (surface mail) Australia; 35.00Aus$ (surface mail) other. ACHPER, 214 Port Road, PO Box 304, Hindmarsh 5007 South Australia. **Tel** 011 61 (08)340 3388, FAX 011 61 (08)340 3399. **ED** Ken Dyer. **Bk Rev. Ad Acc. *Continues** Australian Journal for Health, Physical Education and Recreation.*
Ind/Abst Leis. Recreat. Tour. Abstr.; Phys. Educ. Index; SPORT Discus; SportSearch (May 1987-).

US/0813-2283
ACHPER NATIONAL JOURNAL [MICROFORM], THE. Added/Corp Australian Council for Health, Physical Education and Recreation. **VFOAT** National Journal. **VAT** Australian Council for Health, Physical Education and Recreation National Journal. No. 99 (Autumn 1983)-. Periodical. English. qt. ACHPER, 214 Port Road, PO Box 304, Hindmarsh 5007 South Australia. **Tel** 011 61 (08)340 3388, FAX 011 61 (08)340 3399. available on microfilm and microfiche from University Microfilms International (UMI). ***Continues** Australian Journal for Health, Physical Education and Recreation.*
Ind/Abst Aust. Educ. Index.

●CN/1188-620X
ACTIVE LIVING (TORONTO). (ACTIVE LIVING.). [Act. living Particip.]. **Added/Corp** Participaction (Program). **VFOAT** Active Living with Participaction. Vol. 1, No. 1 (Mar. 1992)-. Periodical. English. Six times a year (Jan., Mar., May, July, Sept., Nov.). 35.00Can$ Canada; 40.00Can$ others. Fitness Report, Box 3080, RR3, Collingwood, ON L9Y 3Z2 Canada. **Tel** (705)445-4968, FAX (705)445-4968. **ED** Joe Taylor. **DD** 613.7. **Bk Rev**, (Qty: varies). **Ad Acc, Adv Mgr:** Sharon Doherty, **Tel** (613)264-2722. **Circ:** 600+. ***Continues** The Fitness Report., 0226-7810.*
Desc: Resource information for fitness and health professionals.
Ind/Abst SPORT Discus.

US/0890-7668
AEROBICS NEWS, THE. ***Ceased.*** (THE AEROBICS NEWS : AN OFFICAL PUBLICATION OF THE INSTITUTE FOR AEROBICS RESEARCH.). Vol. 1, No. 1 (May 1986)-Ceased (June 1989). Periodical. English. mo. The Aerobics News, 12330 Preston Road, Dallas TX 75230. **DD** 613. ***Continues** Aerobics, 0739-8611.*

JA/0915-9517
AIKI NEWS ENGLISH ED. [Aiki news Engl. ed.]. (1990)-. Periodical. English. qt. **DD** 796.8154. ***Continues in part** Aiki News.*
Ind/Abst SPORT Discus.

US/1067-4535
ALSA SWIMMERS' GUIDE. See Recreation, Leisure-Sports.

US/0893-5025
ALTERNATIVES (INGRAM, TEX.). (ALTERNATIVES FOR THE HEALTH CONSCIOUS INDIVIDUAL.). **VFOAT** Alternatives for the Health Conscious Individual. (198?)-. Periodical. English. mo (12 issues). $39.00 (one year); $69.00 (two years); $108.00 (three years). Mountain Home Publishing, PO Box 829, Ingram TX 78025. **Tel** (800)527-3044. **ED** Dr. David G. Williams, (phone: (210)367-4492). **DD** 613. Index available. cum. index. **Bk Rev. Circ:** 100,000 (ctrl).
Desc: An newsletter that emphasizes natural therapies and self-help techniques to obtain optimal health without the use of drugs or surgery. It provides clinically proven information regarding specific nutritional supplements, diets, exercises and therapies that are being used successfully in clinics around the world for the prevention and or treatment of various health conditions. Readers include mature individuals who are sincerely interested in improving their own health and quality of life.

US/0893-5238
AMERICAN FITNESS. [Am. fit.]. **Added/Corp** Aerobics and Fitness Association of America. **VFOAT** AFAA'S American Fitness. Vol. 5 No. 2 (Mar./Apr. 1987)-. Periodical. English. Six times a year (Jan., Mar., May, July, Sept., Nov.). $42.00 Canada and Mexico, $27.00

other (one year); $60.00 Canada and Mexico, $45.00 other (two year). American Fitness / California, 15250 Ventura Boulevard, Sherman Oaks CA 91403. **Tel** (818)905-0040. **ED** Peg Jordon. **DD** 613. **CODEN** AAFIEL. cum. index. **Bk Rev. Ad Acc. Circ:** 30,000 (ctrl). ***Continues** Aerobics & Fitness, 0749-8942.*
Desc: Covers aerobic exercise and sports, health and fitness education. Contains timely, in-depth editorial and articles, new products section, personal profiles, motivational pieces, and photo features.
Ind/Abst Acad. Abstr. Full Text Elite (Jan. 1992-) [Full Txt.]; Acad. Abstr. (Jan. 1992-); Acad. Search (Jan. 1992-); Health Index (1990-); Health Period. Database [Full Txt.]; Health Ref. Cent. (Jan. 1989-) [Full Txt.] [Full Cov.]; Health Source (Jan. 1992-); Mag. Artic. Summar. Elite (Jan. 1992-); Mag. Artic. Summar. CD-ROM (Jan. 1992-); Mag. Search; Phys. Educ. Index; SPORT Discus.

US/0889-2121
AMERICAN FITNESS QUARTERLY. [Am. fit. q.]. (19??)-. Periodical. English. qt. $16.00 (one year), $28.00 (two year), $44.00 (three year) US; $36.00 (one year), $68.00 (two year), $104.00 (three year) other. American Fitness, 6065 Fantz Road, Suite 205, Dublin OH 43017. **Tel** (614)766-7736, FAX (614)766-1186. **ED** Garry Benford. **DD** 613. **Ad Acc. Circ:** 25,000.
Ind/Abst Phys. Educ. Index; SPORT Discus.

US/0730-7004
AMERICAN HEALTH (NEW YORK, N.Y.). (AMERICAN HEALTH.). [Am. health]. **VFOAT** Health; AH; A.H. Vol. 1, No. 1 (March/April 1982)-. Periodical. English. mo (except Feb. and Aug.). $18.97. R D Publications, 28 West 23rd Street, New York NY 10010. **Tel** (800)365-5005, (212)366-8630. **(Subscription address:** CDS / SIFD Agency Control, 1901 Bell Avenue, Des Moines IA 50315.**) ED** Joel Gurin. **LC** RA773; .A55. **DD** 613. **NLM** W1; AM416W. **CODEN** AMHEEZ. Index available. cum. index. **Ad Acc. Circ:** 800,000. available on microfilm and microfiche from University Microfilms International (UMI). Documents available from UMI Article Clearinghouse.
Desc: A special interest magazine focused on personal health and well being. Principal features cover the areas of nutrition, medicine, fitness and athletics, prevention and psychology. Shorter items cover stress, new medical technologies, dental care and the economics of health care.
Ind/Abst Abr. Read. Guide Period. Lit.; Acad. Abstr. Full Text Elite (July 1989-); Acad. Abstr. (July 1989-); Acad. Search (July 1989-); BioBusiness (1988-); Biol. Dig.; Consum. Health Nutr. Index; Cumul. Index Nurs. Allied Health Lit.; Dent. Abstr. (1992-); Foods Adlibra; Gen. Period. Index (1988-); Gen. Sci. Index (1992-); Health Index (1989-); Health Period. Database [Full Txt.]; Health Ref. Cent. (Jan. 1989-) [Full Txt.] [Full Cov.]; Health Source (Jul. 1989-); INFO-SOUTH Abstr.; Mag. Artic. Summar. Elite (July 1989-); Mag. Artic. Summar. Select (July 1989-); Mag. Artic. Summar. CD-ROM (July 1989-); Mag. ASAP Plus [Full Txt.]; Mag. ASAP Sel. [Full Txt.]; Mag. Index Plus (1989-); Mag. Index. Sel. (1988-); Mag. Search; Newsp. Period. Abstr. (1988-); Phys. Educ. Index; Read. Guide Abstr. Select Ed.; Read. Guide Period. Lit.; Mag. Index (1988-); Vocat. Search (July 1989-).

US
AMERICAN PRACTICE ADVISOR. English. mo. $125.00. Eagle Associates Inc, PO Box 1356, Ann Arbor MI 48106. **ED** Joseph Suchocki (editor's address: 6360 Jackson Avenue, Suite G, Ann Arbor, MI 48103 (313)662-8002. Index available. **Circ:** 2,300 (ctrl).
Desc: Topics concerning regulatory compliance, guidance i health-care field related to these topics and quality management.

FR/0753-5058
ANIMATEUR D'ENTRAINEMENT PHYSIQUE DANS LE MONDE MODERNE, L'. (1982)-. Periodical. French. qt. 127.33F France; 190.00F other. FFEPMM, 2 Rue du Maire Kuss, 67000 Strasbourg France. **Tel** 011 33 88 321407. **UDC** 79. ***Continues** Entrainement Physique et Sport Pour Tous Dans le Monde Moderne, 0397-1961.*
Ind/Abst SPORT Discus.

GW/0172-9721
ANIMATION HANNOVER. ***Title Change.*** (ANIMATION.). [Animation Hann.]. (1980)-(1994). Periodical. German. Six times a year (Jan., Mar., May, July, Sept., Nov.). Mr. Rolf von der Horst, Alte Schule Bannetze, D 29308 Winsen Aller Germany. **Tel** 011 49 5146 364, FAX 011 49 5146 4961. **UDC** 379.8. **[CCC].** ***Continued by** Spielraum.*

●US/1076-5778
ASPIRE (NASHVILLE, TENN.). (ASPIRE.). (1994)-. Periodical. English. bm (6 issues). $17.95 US. Royal Magazine Group, 404 BNA Drive, Building 200, Suite 600, Nashville TN 37217. **Tel** (615)872-8080, FAX (615)889-0437. **ED** Mary Hopkins (editor's telephone: (615)872-8080 ext. 2666). **Bk Rev. Ad Acc. Circ:** 50,000 (ctrl).
Desc: Magazine for a healthy body, mind and spirit.

●US/1065-5190
AT YOUR BEST. (1992)-. Periodical. English. mo. Rodale Press Inc., 400 South 10th Street, Emmaus PA 18098. **Tel** (215)967-5171, (800)666-2503.

IT/0392-2251
ATLETICA LEGGERA. ***Ceased.*** [Atlet. leggera]. (1959)-(1994). Periodical. Italian. Ten times a year. Coop Dante SRL, VIA G Silva 21, 27029 Vigevano PV Italy. **Tel** 011 39 381 690636, FAX 011 39 381 690638. **UDC** 796/799. **Ad Acc. Circ:** 7,000 (ctrl).

AT/0812-3896
AUSTRALASIAN HEALTH AND HEALING. [Australas.health heal.]. **VFOAT** Health and Healing. (1982)-. Periodical. English. Four times a year. 26.90Aus$ Australia; 32.80Aus$ New Zealand; 37.00Aus$ other. Australasian Health & Healing, 29 Terrace Street, Kingscliff NSW 2487 Australia. **Tel** 011 61 66 742407. **ED** Maurice Finkel. **DD** 615.53. **Bk Rev**, (Qty: 4). **Ad Acc. Circ:** 10,000. ***Continues** Health and Healing, 0812-3888.*
Desc: Deals with alternative approaches to therapy and the prevention of disease.

US/1056-6228
BB'S HEALTH WATCH. [BB's health watch]. **VFOAT** Health Watch. (1991)-. Periodical. English. bm. $24.95. Nutritional Designs, 3379 Shore Parkway, Brooklyn NY 11235. **DD** 613.

IR/0252-5356
BIHADASHT-I JAHAN. [Bihadasht-i jahan]. (1957)-. Academic Scholarly Publication. Persian. Three times a year. £24.00 Middle East; £25.00 Europe & Asia; £30.00 America & Far East. Iran University Press, 85 Park Avenue, PO Box 15875/4748, Tehran Iran. **Tel** 623232, FAX (008921)4661749, telex 213636-8-D5300. **ED** F. Adibzadeh. **UDC** 61. **CODEN** NU054.
Desc: Journal of physical fitness and hygiene related to Iran's public health needs.

US/0275-9101
BODY BULLETIN. [Body bull.]. (April 1981)-. Bulletin. English. mo. $21.00. Rodale Press Inc., 400 South 10th Street, Emmaus PA 18098. **Tel** (215)967-5171, (800)666-2503. **ED** Porter Shimer. **[CCC].**
Ind/Abst Acad. Abstr. Full Text Elite (Jan. 1992-) [Full Txt.]; Acad. Abstr. (Jan. 1992-); Acad. Search (Jan. 1992-); Health Source (Jan. 1992-) [Full Txt.]; Mag. Artic. Summar. Elite (Jan. 1992-) [Full Txt.]; Mag. Artic. Summar. Select [Full Txt.]; Mag. Artic. Summar. CD-ROM (Jan. 1992-); Mag. Search; Vocat. Search (Jan. 1992-) [Full Txt.].

PR/1053-5543
BUENASALUD (ED. NACIONAL). (BUENASALUD.). [BuenaSalud]. **Added/Corp** Interamerican College of Physicians & Surgeons. **VFOAT** Buena Salud. (198?)-. Periodical. Spanish. Twelve times a year. $17.00 one year; $31.00 two year. Casiano Communications, PO Box 12130, Loiza St. Station, San Juan Puerto Rico 00914. **Tel** (809)728-3000. **ED** Ivonne Longueira. **DD** 613. **Bk Rev. Ad Acc, Adv Mgr:** Arnaldo Jimenez. **Circ:** 65,000. ***Continues in part** Buena Salud, 0896-2642.*
Desc: Oriented to health conscious people. Articles about health, fitness and nutrition in each edition.

AU
BULLETIN UNION INTERNATIONALE DE PENTATHLON MODERNE ET BIATHLON. See Recreation, Leisure-Sports.

●US/1066-7814
CANADIAN JOURNAL OF APPLIED PHYSIOLOGY. See Biology-Physiology.

CN/0709-0269
CANADIAN MARATHON ANNUAL. See Recreation, Leisure-Sports.

CN/0827-3502
CHEF DE FORME - RESEAU PARTICIPACTION. (CHEF DE FORME.). [Chef forme - Reseau Participaction]. Vol. 1, No. 2-. Periodical. French. qt. Free to members. Reseau Participaction, Suite 805, 80 Ouest, Rue Richmond, Toronto Ont M5H 2A4. **DD** 613.7/0971.

US/1056-8530
CHIROHEALTH (FULLERTON, CALIF.). (CHIROHEALTH.). **VFOAT** Chiro Health. (1991)-. Periodical. English. mo. $10.00. Chiro Marketing Corporation, 535 South Ratmond Avenue, Fullerton CA 92631-5026.

US/0747-8283
CLUB INDUSTRY. [Club ind.]. Vol. 1, No. 1 (Sept./Oct. 1984)-. Periodical. English. mo (12 issues). $68.00. Club Industry and Rehabilitation Today, 101 Witmer Road, Horsham PA 19044. **Tel** (215)957-4260. **ED** Jon Feld. **DD** 613. **Ad Acc. Circ:** 30,000 (ctrl).
Desc: A business magazine for health and fitness club management.

FR/0335-5306
COEUR ET SANTE PARIS. See Medical Science and Technology.

US/1058-0832
CONSUMER REPORTS ON HEALTH. See Consumer Interests.

NE
COSMOPOLITAN. See Women's Interests.

UK
COSMOPOLITAN. (ENGLAND EDITION). See Women's Interests.

FR/1161-2258
COSMOPOLITAN (PARIS). See Women's Interests.

US/1058-4595
CPNEWS (SACRAMENTO, CALIF.). (CPNEWS.). [CPnews]. **VFOAT** CP News. Vol. 1, No. 1 (Sept. 1991)-. Newsletter. English. mo (10 issues). $46.00 US; $51.00 Canada and Mexico; $57.00 other. ITservices, 3301 Alta Arden, Number 3, Sacramento CA 95825. **Tel** (800)422-9887, (916)483-1085. **ED** Kris Simpson. **DD** 613.

CN/0828-9034
CURLING CANADA. See Recreation, Leisure-Sports.

US/1055-1352
CURRENT ISSUES IN EXERCISE SCIENCE. ***Ceased.*** [Curr. issues exerc. sci.]. **VFOAT** Current Issues in Exercise Science Series. No. 1 (1991)-No. 3 (1993). Monographic series. English. qt. Human Kinetics Publishers Inc, 1607 North Market Street, PO Box 5076, Champaign IL 61825-5076. **Tel** (217)351-5076, FAX (217)351-2674. **DD** 613.

FR/1157-6197
DECISION SANTE NEUILLY-SUR-SEINE. (DECISION SANTE.). **VFOAT** DS (Neuilly-sur-Seine). (1991)-. Periodical. French. Twenty-two times a year. 587.66F other. Groupe Quotidien Sante, 140 rue Jules Guesde, 92593 Levallois Perret France. **Tel** 011 33 1 47307500. **UDC** 362.11/.13.

CN/0848-9068
DEFI-SANTE. [Defi-sante]. Vol. 1, No. 1 (Nov. 1989)-. Periodical. French. Ten times a year (Monthly except July/Aug.). 25.00Can$ (1 year), 46.00Can$ (2 year) Canada; 40.43Can$ (1 year), 73.68Can$ (2 year) US; 58.41Can$ (1 year), 107.83Can$ (2 year) other. Editions Challenge Sante, 3565 Boulevard LaSalle, Verdun H4G 1Z5 Canada. **Tel** (514)766-4400, FAX (514)766-8365. **DD** 613/.05. **Ad Acc. Circ:** 25,000 (ctrl). ***Continues** Bio-apprenti-sage., 0838-6293.*

US
DELICIOUS MAGAZINE. See Food and Food Industry.

US/0163-0334
DIET & EXERCISE. **VFOAT** Diet and Exercise. (19??)-. Periodical. English. an. Available on newsstand only. Meredith Corporation, Locust at 17th, Des Moines IA 50309. **Tel** (515)284-3000. **LC** RA784; .D53. **DD** 613.2/5/05.

US
DIRECTORY OF HEALTH SERVICE ORGANIZATIONS. (19??)-. Directory. English. an. comes with Directory of Tax-Exempt Organizations. Money Market Directories Inc, 320 East Main Street, PO Box 1608, Charlottesville VA 22902. **Tel** (800)446-2810, (804)977-1450.

US
DISCOVERY YMCA. See Recreation, Leisure.

US/1057-9273
DR. JULIAN WHITAKER'S HEALTH & HEALING. [Dr. Julian Whitaker's health heal.]. **VFOAT** Dr. Julian Whitaker's Health and Healing; Health and Healing; Health & Healing. Vol. 1, No. 1 (Aug. 1991)-. Periodical. English. Twelve times a year. $39.95. Phillips Business Information, Inc., 1201 Seven Locks Road, Potomac MD 20854. **Tel** (301)424-3338, (800)777-5006, FAX (301)309-3847. **DD** 613. **[CCC].**

PL/0137-6187
DZIENNIK URZEDOWY GOWNEGO KOMITETU KULTURY FIZYCZNEJ I SPORTU. **Main/Corp** Poland. Gowny Komitet Kultury Fizycznej i Sportu. (19??)-. Polish. ir. $23.00. RSW Prasa-Kriazka-Ruch, Centrala Kolportazu Prasy i Wydawnictw, Towarowa 28, 00-958 Warsaw Poland. **LC** KKP3035.A13; P65. ***Continues** Dziennik Urzedowy Gownego Komitetu Kultury Fizycznej i Turystyki.*

FR/0245-8977
E.P.S. 1. (EDUCATION PHYSIQUE ET SPORTIVE AU 1ER DEGRE.). **VFOAT** Education Physique et Sport un. (1981)-. Periodical. French. Five times a year. 97.94F France; 125.00F other. Etablissements de Joinville, 11 Av de Tremblay, F-75012 Paris France. **Tel** 011 33 1 48083087. **UDC** 796:373.3.

US/1061-4664
EASTWEST NATURAL HEALTH. ***Title Change.*** [EastWest nat. health]. **VFOAT** East West Natural Health; Natural Health. Vol. 22, No. 1 (Jan./Feb. 1992)-Vol. 22, No. 6 (Nov./Dec. 1992). Periodical. English. bm. Natural Health, PO Box 1200, Brookline Village MA 02147. **Tel** (617)232-1000, (800)666-8576. **LC** AP2; .E154. **DD** 613. **NLM** W1; EA869. ***Continues*** *EastWest (Brookline, Mass. : 1986), 0888-1375.* ***Continued by*** *Natural Health, 1067-9588.*
Ind/Abst Health Index (1992-?); Health Period. Database.

US/1064-4121
EATING AWARENESS & SELF ENHANCEMENT NEWSLETTER. ***Title Change.*** [Eat. aware. self enhanc. newsl.]. **VFOAT** Eating Awareness and Self Enhancement Newsletter. (Mar. 1990)-(1993). Newsletter. English. Six times a year (Jan., Mar.,May, July, Sept., Nov.). EASE, PO Box 8032, Minneapolis MN 55408. **Tel** (215)242-3358. **DD** 613. ***Continued by*** *Enlightened Eating Newsletter.*

FR
ECHANGES SANTE SOCIAL. (19??)-. French. qt. $59.00. Masson Editeur, Box Postale 22, 41353 Vineuil 16 France. **Tel** 011 33 54 438994.

US
ENCYCLOPEDIA OF HEALTH INFORMATION SOURCES. English. $165.00. Gale Research Inc., 835 Penobscot Building, Detroit MI 48226. **Tel** (800)877-GALE, (313)961-2242, FAX (313)961-6083, telex TWX 810-221-7086. **ED** Alan M. Rees.
Desc: Guide to print, electronic and live sources of information related to hundreds of health topics.

●US
ENLIGHTENED EATING NEWSLETTER. (1993)-. Newsletter. English. Six times a year (Jan., Mar., May, July, Sept., Nov.). $25.00. EASE, PO Box 8032, Minneapolis MN 55408. **Tel** (215)242-3358.

US/1078-0475
ENVIRONMENTAL HEALTH PERSPECTIVES. SUPPLEMENTS. [Environ. health perspect., Suppl.]. **Added/Corp** National Institute of Environmental Health Sciences. National Institutes of Health (U.S.). **VFOAT** EHP. Supplements. Vol. 101, Suppl. 1 (Apr. 1993)-. Academic Scholarly Publication. English. bm. $47.00 US; $58.75 other. Superintendent of Documents, US Government Printing Office, Washington DC 20402. **Tel** (202)275-3328, FAX (202)786-2377. **DD** 614. **CODEN** EHPSEO. Documents available from CASDDS.
Desc: Presents conference, workshop and symposium proceedings as well as in-depth perspectives reviews.
Ind/Abst Chem. Abstr.

US/1048-2954
EXECUTIVE EDGE. [Exec. edge]. **Added/Corp** Rodale Center for Executive Development. Vol. 24, (Jan. 1993)-. Periodical. English. mo (12 issues). $69.95 US. Select Press, PO Box 37, Corte Madera CA 94976. **Tel** (415)924-1612. **LC** GV201; .E9. **DD** 650. **Bk Rev.** ***Continues*** *Executive Fitness, 0889-6739.*

US/1071-8680
EXECUTIVE HEALTH'S GOOD HEALTH REPORT. English. mo. $34.00 (1 year), $59.00 (2 year) US; $40.00 (1 year), $71.00 (2 year) Canada and Mexico; $58.00 (1 year), $99.00 (2 year), $139.00 (3 year) other. Executive Health Report, 383 Route 46 West, Fairfield NJ 07004-2402. **Tel** (919)929-7519, FAX (919)929-2458. **ED** Ann Buzenberg. available on an online database (file 149/Full-Text) from DIALOG.
Ind/Abst Acad. Abstr. Full Text Elite (Jan. 1992-); Acad. Abstr. (Jan. 1992-); Acad. Search (Jan. 1992-); Health Source (Jan. 1992-); SPORT Discus.

US/0882-4657
EXERCISE FOR MEN ONLY. [Exerc. men only]. **VFOAT** Exercise. Vol. 1, Issue 1 (March/April 1985)-. Periodical. English. bm. $33.15. Chelo Publishing Inc, 350 5th Avenue, Suite 8216, New York NY 10118. **Tel** (212)947-4322, FAX (212)563-4774. **ED** Steve Downs. **DD** 613.

US/0748-3155
EXERCISE PHYSIOLOGY (NEW YORK, N.Y.). **See** Medical Science and Technology-Sports Medicine.

US
FAMILY SYSTEMS MEDICINE NEWSLETTER. (Spring 1991)-. Newsletter. English. qt. Family Process Inc., 70 W Allendale Ave., Suite D, Allendale NJ 07401. **Tel** (201)236-8381.

US/1078-0203
FAST AND HEALTHY MAGAZINE. [Fast heal. mag.]. **VFOAT** Fast and Healthy. (199?)-. Periodical. English. bm. The Pillsbury Co., 200 S 6th St., Minneapolis MN 55402. **Tel** (612)330-5452. **ED** Diane Anderson. **DD** 641. **Ad Acc. Circ:** 100,000. ***Continues*** *Pillsbury Fast and Healthy Magazine.*
Desc: Lifestyle and food publication concentrating on quick and easy to prepare recipes along with articles on well-being.

CN/0826-2594
FEELING FINE. **See** Nutrition and Dietetics.

US/0888-4102
FEMALE BODYBUILDING AND WEIGHT TRAINING. [Female bodybuild. weight train.]. **VFOAT** Female Body Building and Weight Training; Female Bodybuilding; Female Body Building. (1986)-. Periodical. English. Six times a year. $17.99 US; $23.99 other. Starlog Press Inc., 475 Park Avenue South, New York NY 10016. **Tel** (212)689-2830, FAX (212)889-7933. **(Subscription address:** Kable Publishers Aide, 308 East Hitt Street, Subscription Department, Mt. Morris IL 61054-1473.**)** **ED** Rochelle Larkin. **DD** 646. **Bk Rev. Ad Acc. Circ:** 150,000.

AT
FIA JOURNAL. (19??)-. English. Four times a year. 40.00Aus$ Comes with Fitness Industry Association membership. Fitness Industry Association, PO Box 60, Arncliffe 2205 Australia. **Tel** 011 61 2 2649699, 011 61 2 550 9168, FAX 011 61 2 264 6767. **ED** David G. Keir. **Ad Acc.** Full Page (Color) 600.00Aus$. Half Page (Color) 410.00Aus$. **Circ:** 4,000 (ctrl).
Desc: Contains information on exercise science, health and fitness industry issues such as ongoing education workshops, professional assurance and liability and articles on improving your business.
Ind/Abst SPORT Discus.

US/0146-8812
FIGHTING WOMAN NEWS. (1975)-. Periodical. English. qt (4 issues). $10.00. Fighting Woman News, 6741 Tung Avenue West, Theodore AL 36582. **Tel** (205)653-0549. **ED** Valerie Eads. **[CCC]. Bk Rev. Ad Acc. Circ:** 3,000 (ctrl).
Desc: Martial arts, self-defense and combative sports. History, technique, how-to, reviews, etc. Aimed at literate, adult practitioners.

CN/0827-3103
FIT THIRD AGE. **See** Medical Science and Technology-Geriatrics.

CN/0227-7751
FITNESS AND LIFESTYLE RESEARCH REVIEWS. [Fitness lifestyle res. rev.]. Jan. 1980-. Periodical. English. mo. $89.00 per year Canada. Danielson Research Consultants, Ontario P3E 2P3 Canada. **DD** 613/.05.

CN/0820-6163
FITNESS BULLETIN, THE. [Fitness bull.]. **Added/Corp** Fitness Institute (Toronto, Ont.). Vol. 5, No. 1 (Jan. 1982)-. Bulletin. English. Twelve times a year. 30.00Can$. Fitness Institute, 255 Yorkland Blvd., Willowdale Ontario M2J 1S3 Canada. **Tel** (416)491-5830. **ED** David Steen. **DD** 613.7/05. **Bk Rev. Circ:** 3,500 (ctrl). ***Continues*** *Fitness Institute Bulletin, 0826-4341.*
Desc: The bulletin capsulizes breaking news and trends in fitness and health, and offers practical advice and motivation to adopt a more healthy lifestyle.

US/1046-1701
FITNESS CYCLING. ***Ceased.*** [Fit. cycl.]. Vol. 1, No. 1 (Spring 1990)-(Feb. 1992). Periodical. English. qt. Challenge Publications Inc., 7950 Deering Avenue, Canoga Park CA 91304. **Tel** (818)887-0550. **DD** 613.

US/0882-0481
FITNESS MANAGEMENT (SOLANA BEACH, CALIF.). (FITNESS MANAGEMENT.). Vol. 1, No. 1 (March/April 1985)-. Periodical. English. Twelve times a year. $24.00 US; $45.00 other. Leisure Publishing Company, 3923 West 6th Street, Los Angeles CA 90020. **Tel** (213)385-3926, FAX (213)383-1152. **ED** Edward H. Pitts. **DD** 613. cum. index. **Bk Rev. Ad Acc. Circ:** 21,000 (ctrl).
Desc: Directs management and fitness information to owners, managers and program directors of commercial, community and corporate physical fitness facilities.
Ind/Abst SPORT Discus.

●CN/1189-329X
FITNESS, PHYSICAL HEALTH AND RECREATION EDUCATION (EASTERN U.S. ED.). (FITNESS, PHYSICAL HEALTH AND RECREATION EDUCATION.). [Fit. phys. health recreat. educ.]. 1st Ed. (1992)-. English. Richard J. Garneau, M.P.O. Box 1588, Niagara Falls NY 14302. **DD** 796.

●CN/1189-3303
FITNESS, PHYSICAL HEALTH AND RECREATION EDUCATION (WESTERN U.S. ED.). (FITNESS, PHYSICAL HEALTH AND RECREATION EDUCATION.). [Fit. phys. health recreat. educ.]. 1st ed. (1991/92)-. English. Richard J. Garneau, M.P.O. Box 1588, Niagara Falls NY 14302. **DD** 796.

US/1054-674X
FITNESS PLUS. [Fit. plus]. Vol. 1, No. 1 (Oct. 1990)-. English. Four times a year. $29.00 (available on issues basis only (10 issues); $2.95 (single issue). Fitness Plus, PO Box 267, Sussex WI 53089. **Tel** (800)229-2294. **ED** Steve Raimondi. **LC** WMLC L 83/7242. **DD** 613. **Ad Acc.**
Desc: Editorial covers health, nutrition, weight training, exercise, dieting, fitness fashions and celebrity profiles.

CN/1181-6988
FITNESS WORKS!. [Fit. works]. **Added/Corp** Workplace Fitness Office. **VFOAT** Workplace Fitness Office Newsletter; En Forme--Au Travail!. Vol. 1, No. 1 (Summer 1990)-. Periodical. English (French). qt. Limited free distribution. Workplace Fitness Office, Suite 312, 1600 James Naismith Drive, Gloucester, Ontario K1B 5N4 Canada. **DD** 613.7/08/8.

RU
FIZKULTURA I ZDOROVE. (198?)-. Russian. Fizkultura i Sport, Luzhneskaia Nab 8, 119270 Moscow Russia.

US/1048-7891
FLORIDA RUNNING. (FLORIDA RUNNING : OFFICIAL PUBLICATION OF THE FLORIDA ATHLETICS [CONGRESS].). [Fla. runn.]. **Added/Corp** Florida Athletics Congress. (1987)-. Periodical. English. bm. $12.00 US; $20.00 Canada; $22.00 other. Florida Running, 8640 Tansy Drive, Orlando FL 32819. **Tel** (407)352-9131, (407)898-2425. **DD** 796.

US
FOCUS. **Main/Corp** National Center for Health Services Research and Development. (19??)-. Government Publication. English. ir. $8.00 US; $10.00 other. Superintendent of Documents, US Government Printing Office, Washington DC 20402. **Tel** (202)275-3328, FAX (202)786-2377.

US/1057-8048
FODOR'S HEALTHY ESCAPES. **See** Travel and Tourism.

US/8750-8079
GET FIT. [Get fit]. Periodical. English. mo. Get Fit, 1400 Stierlin Road, Mountain View CA 94043. **DD** 613. ***Continues*** *Fit, 0278-9760.*

RU/0016-9900
GIGIENA I SANITARIIA (1943). (GIGIENA I SANITARIIA.). [Gig. sanit.]. **Added/Corp** Soviet Union. Narodnyi Komissariat Zdravookhraneniia. Soviet Union. Ministerstvo Zdravookhraneniia. Vsesoiuznoe Nauchnoe Obshchestvo Gigienistov (Soviet Union). (1943)-. Academic Scholarly Publication. Russian (summaries and/or abstracts in English; table of contents in English). mo. $109.95. **(Subscription address:** East View Publications Inc., 3020 Harbor Lane North, Suite 110, Minneapolis MN 55447.**)** **NLM** W1 GI133. **CODEN** GISAAA. **[CCC].** Index available in last issue of volume--attached. available on microfilm. Documents available from BIOSIS Document Express, CASDDS. ***Continues*** *Gigiena I Zdorove.*
Ind/Abst Anal. Abstr.; Biodeter. Abstr.; Biol. Abstr.; Chem. Abstr.; Chem. Hazards Ind.; Coal Abstr.; CSA Neuro. Abstr. (?-?); Dairy Sci. Abstr.; Food Sci. Technol. Abstr.; Index Med.; Index Vet.; Int. Aerosp. Abstr.; Lab. Hazards Bull.; Maize Abstr.; Nematol. Abstr.; Nutr. Abstr. Rev., Ser. B, Live Feeds and Feed.; Nutr. Abstr. Rev., Ser. A, Hum. Exp.; Potato Abstr.; Rev. Med. Vet. Entomol.; Rev. Med. Vet. Mycology; Rice Abstr.; Risk Abstr.; Saf. Health Work; Soils Fert.; SportSearch; Sug. Indus. Abstr.; Vet. Bull.; Trop. Dis. Bull.

AT/0819-5668
GOOD HEALTH WARBURTON. ***Ceased.*** (1969)-(1993). Periodical. English. Four times a year. Signs Publishing Co., Periodical Department Main Street, Warburton VIC 3799 Australia. **Tel** 011 61 59 669111.
Ind/Abst Acad. Search (Jan. 1992-Aug. 1993).

●US
GOOD HOUSEKEEPING'S LIVING WELL : IN COOPERATION WITH THE AMERICAN MEDICAL ASSOCIATION. **Added/Corp** American Medical Association. **VFOAT** Living Well. (Spring 1992)-. Periodical. English. $5.99. The Hearst Corporation, 250 West 55th Street, New York NY 10019. **Tel** (212)649-4014. **NLM** W1; GO773.

SP
GUIA DE ENTIDADES E INSTALACIONES DEPORTIVAS. **VFOAT** Guia Deportiva de Vizcaya. Spanish. D.N.E.F. y d'Instalaciones Deportivas, Jose Ma Escuza 16, Bilbao Spain. **LC** GV204.S72; V53.

CN/1187-502X
GUIDE RESSOURCES (1991). **See** Psychology.

CN/1191-1123
GUIDE SANTE (SILLERY). (GUIDE SANTE.). [Guide sante]. Vol. 1, No 1 (Jan. 1991)-. Periodical. French. sa. Limited Free Distribution. R. Blais, 2802 Ch. du Foulon, Sillery Quebec G1T 1Y1 Canada. **DD** 613.

UK
HEALTH AND FITNESS MAGAZINE. English. mo. £17.00 UK; £28.00 Europe; £47.00 other. Hudson Brothers Publishers, 40 Bowling Green Lane,

London ECIR ONE England. **Tel** 011 44 71 2780333, FAX 011 44 71 8377612.
Ind/Abst Acad. Abstr. Full Text Elite (Jan. 1992-); Acad. Abstr. (Jan. 1992-); Health Source (Jan. 1992-); Mag. Search.

US/1048-8405
HEALTH & FITNESS MAGAZINE FOR HEALTHY, SOUND LIVING : HF. See Public Health and Safety.

●US/1064-6728
HEALTH & FITNESS TRIAD. VFOAT Health and Fitness TRIAD. (1992)-. Periodical. English. bm. $4.00 (single issue). Triad Publishing Group, PO Box 102, Chadds Ford PA 19317.

US/0898-3569
HEALTH & YOU (CINNAMINSON, N.J.). (HEALTH & YOU.). **VFOAT** Health and You. (198?)-. Periodical. English. qt (Mar., June, Sept., Dec.). $12.25. Health Ink Publishing Group, 1 Executive Drive, Moorestown NJ 08057. **Tel** (609)829-0011. **ED** Jeff Bredenberg. **DD** 613. **Circ:** 800,000 (ctrl).
Ind/Abst Cumul. Index Nurs. Allied Health Lit.

●US/1055-8241
HEALTH DIET & NUTRITION. See Nutrition and Dietetics.

UK
HEALTH EDUCATION INDEX AND GUIDE TO VOLUNTARY SOCIAL WELFARE ORGANISATIONS. Added/Corp Health Visitors' Association (Great Britain). (19??)-. English. B Edsall & Company Ltd, 124 Belgrave Road, London SW1V 2BL England. **Tel** 01-834 0451. **ED** David Webb. **LC** RA440.55.Z9; H4. **DD** 016.613. **Ad Acc. Circ:** 2,000.
Desc: Definitive reference of health education resources available in Britain and exhaustive index of voluntary and other support organizations and self-help groups concerned with health care.

UK/0017-8969
HEALTH EDUCATION JOURNAL, THE. [Health educ. j.]. (1943)-. Academic Scholarly Publication. English. qt. $72.00 (institution), $54.00 (individual) US; £35.00 (institution), £25.00 (individual) UK & Europe; £40.00 (institution), £30.00 (individual) other. Royal Society of Medicine Press, 1 Wimpole Street, London W1M 8AE England. **Tel** 011 44 71 2902928. **ED** Margaret Whitehead. **LC** RA421; .H414. **DD** 613.05. **NLM** W1 HE322. Index available. **Bk Rev. Ad Acc. Circ:** 5,000. available on microfilm and microfiche from University Microfilms International (UMI).
Desc: A lively look at the full spectrum of health education and health promotion in Britain and overseas, through research papers, opinion pieces, letters and reviews.
Ind/Abst Appl. Soc. Sci. Index Abstr.; Br. Educ. Index; Educ. Technol. Abstr.; EMBASE; Health Plan. Adminis.; Health Serv. Abstr.; Hospit. Health Admin. Index; Res. High. Educ. Abstr.; Stud. Women Abstr.; Tech. Educ. Train. Abstr.; Trop. Dis. Bull.

US/0279-5639
HEALTH FACT NEWS. *Ceased.* [Health fact news]. (1981)-Ceased ?. Periodical. English. mo. Health Fact News, PO Box C-100, Colts Neck NJ 07722. **Tel** (201)946-4429. **ED** Lillian Dichter. **DD** 614. **Bk Rev. Ad Acc. Circ:** 100,000.
Desc: New information about health nutrition and fitness collected from over 2,000 daily, weekly, and monthly world wide publications.

US
HEALTH GAZETTE. Added/Corp Alexander Grant, M.D. and Associates. (19??)-. Periodical. English. Ten times a year. $24.95 one year; $38.40 two years. Health Gazette, PO Box 1786, Indianapolis IN 46206. **Tel** (317)253-7104. Index available. cum. index. **Circ:** 40,000. ***Continues** HealthWise, 0740-1086.*

US
HEALTH INDEX [COMPUTER FILE]. See Health and Personal Fitness-Abstracting, Bibliographies and Statistics.

US/1068-770X
HEALTH NEWS & BREAKTHROUGHS. [Health news breakthr.]. **VFOAT** Health News and Breakthroughs. (199?)-. Periodical. English. mo. $39.95. Grace Publishing, 2888 Bluff Street, Suite 461, Boulder CO 80301-9002. **DD** 613. ***Continues** Insider's Guide to Personal Wellness, 1064-6841.*

US
HEALTH PERIODICALS DATABASE [ONLINE DATABASE]. See Health and Personal Fitness-Abstracting, Bibliographies and Statistics.

US/1042-699X
HEALTH SENTRY. [Health sentry]. Winter (1986-1987)-. Periodical. English. qt. $12.00. Performance Resource Press, Inc., 1863 Technology Drive, Suite 200, Troy MI 48083. **Tel** (810)588-7733, (800)453-7733, FAX (810)588-6633. **DD** 613.

US
HEALTH SHORTS. English. mo. $100.00. Healthwire, 435 Park Place, Kalamazoo MI 49001. **Tel** (616)344-1946, FAX (616)344-7170. **ED** Fred McTaggart and Donna Carroll.

●US/1063-9810
HEALTH SOURCE (PEABODY, MASS.). See Health and Personal Fitness-Abstracting, Bibliographies and Statistics.

AT
HEALTH YOURSELF. (19??)-. English. Eleven times a year. 25.00Aus$. Health Promotion Pty Ltd, PO Box 615, North Sydney NSW Australia. **Tel** 011 61 02 9541888, FAX 011 61 02 9565684. **ED** Wendy Camelotti. **Bk Rev**, (Qty: 2-6). **Circ:** 100,000.
Desc: Lifestyle newsletter on health and wellbeing.

AT/1036-1901
HEALTHCOVER SYDNEY. (HEALTHCOVER.). [Healthcover Syd.]. **VFOAT** Health cover. (1991)-. English. bm (Feb., Apr., June, Aug., Oct., Dec.). 320.00Aus$. Healthdata Services, Suite 16, 2nd Floor, 281-287 Sussex Street, GPO Box 5237, Sydney NSW 2001 Australia. **Tel** 011 61 2 2673050, FAX 011 61 2 2613029. **ED** R. J. Lord. ctrl circ.
Desc: Information about policy development for the funding and delivery of health services.

CN/1181-6139
HEALTHIER YOUTH. [Healthier youth]. **Added/Corp** McCreary Centre Society. Vol. 1, No. 1 (July/Aug. 1990)-. Periodical. English. bm. Society for Children and Youth - British Columbia, 3644 Slocan Street, Vancouver, Biritish Columbia V5M 3E8 Canada. **Tel** (604)433-4180. **DD** 613/.0433/05.

US/0736-7929
HEALTHLINE (SAN MATEO, CALIF.). (HEALTHLINE.). [Healthline]. **Added/Corp** Robert A. McNeil Foundation for Health Education. Healthline Publishing. **VFOAT** Health Line. (1981)-. Periodical. English. mo. $24.00 US; $37.68 Canada; $36.00 other. Healthline, 830 Menlo Avenue, Suite 100, Menlo Park CA 94025. **Tel** (415)325-64557. **ED** Paul Insel. **NLM** W1; HE614E. Index available (index bound in all issues). **Pr Rev. Circ:** 5,773.
Desc: Offers readers information on health and wellness. Written and edited for both the health professional and the general public. Covers topics such as weight control, nutrition, exercise, disease and injury prevention, preventive dentistry, medical consumerism, longevity and aging, stress management, sports medicine, child health, and human sexuality.
Ind/Abst Consum. Health Nutr. Index; Health Index (1989-); Health Period. Database; Health Ref. Cent. (Jan. 1989-) [Full Cov.].

US/0898-8560
HEALTHTALK (MERRICK, N.Y.). (HEALTHTALK.). **VFOAT** Health Talk. (1991)-. Periodical. English. qt. Promed Communications, 2897 Wynsum Avenue, Merrick NY 11566.

US/0740-1086
HEALTHWISE. *Title Change.* [Healthwise]. **Added/Corp** Alexander Grant, M.D. and Associates. **VFOAT** Health Wise. (19??)-(19??). Periodical. English. mo. Health Gazette, PO Box 1786, Indianapolis IN 46206. **Tel** (317)253-7104. ***Continued by** Health Gazette.*

CN/1183-4331
HEALTHY EXCHANGE (OTTAWA). (ECHO SANTE.). [Healthy exch.]. **Added/Corp** CUSO. Service Auxiliaire de Sante. **VFOAT** Healthy Exchange. Vol. 1, No 1 (April 1991)-. Periodical. French (English). ir. Limited free distribution. Cuso Forum, 135 Rideau Street, Ottawa Ontario K1N 9K7 Canada. **Tel** (613)563-1242. **DD** 362.1.

US/1062-4236
HEALTHY KIDS. 4-10 YEARS. (HEALTHY KIDS. 4-10 YEARS : THE MAGAZINE FOR PARENTS FROM THE AMERICAN ACADEMY OF PEDIATRICS.). [Healthy kids, 4-10 years]. **Added/Corp** American Academy of Pediatrics. **VFOAT** Healthy Kids. 4-10; Healthy Kids. Four to Ten Years. Vol. 2, No. 2 (Spring/Summer 1991)-. Periodical. English. mo. Cahners Publishing Company, 249 West 17th Street, New York NY 10011. **Tel** (212)645-0067, FAX (212)242-6987. **DD** 613. ***Continues** American Baby's Healthy Kids. 4-10 Years.*

●US/1063-0945
HEALTHY KIDS. BIRTH-3. (HEALTHY KIDS. BIRTH-3 : THE MAGAZINE FOR PARENTS FROM THE AMERICAN ACADEMY OF PEDIATRICS.). [Healthy kids, Birth-3]. **Added/Corp** American Academy of Pediatrics. **VFOAT** Healthy Kids. Birth to Three. Vol. 4, No. 1 (Winter 1992)-. Periodical. English. mo. Cahners Publishing Company, 249 West 17th Street, New York NY 10011. **Tel** (212)645-0067, FAX (212)242-6987. **DD** 613. ***Continues** American Baby's Healthy Kids. Birth-3.*

UK/0017-9167
HEALTHY LIVING LONDON. *Suspended.* [Healthy living Lond.]. (1966)-(19??). Periodical. English. mo. Turret Group, 177 Hagden Lane, Watford Herts WD1 8LN United Kingdom. **Tel** 011 44 923 228577, FAX 011 44 923 221346. **DD** 613. ***Absorbed** Best of Health, 0268-7445.*

CN/1183-1340
HEARTHEALTH. [HeartHealth]. **Added/Corp** Heart and Stroke Foundation of Ontario. **VFOAT** Heart Health; HeartHealth Newsletter. Vol. 1, No. 1 (Winter 1991)-. Periodical. English. qt. Free. Heart and Stroke Foundation of Ontario / Toronto, 4th Floor, 477 Mount Pleasant Road, Toronto Ontario M4S 2L9 Canada. **DD** 616.1/205/05.

US/0748-6855
HOLISTIC MASSAGE. (HOLISTIC MASSAGE : NEWSLETTER OF THE INTERNATIONAL ACADEMY OF MASSAGE SCIENCE.). Vol. 1, No. 1 (June 23, 1984)-. Newsletter. English. mo. $15.00. International Academy of Massage Science, 25 Price's Lane, Rose Valley PA 19063. **Tel** (215)566-6049. **ED** Karen Carlson. **DD** 615. **Bk Rev. Ad Acc. Circ:** 1,000 (ctrl).
Desc: Comprehensively covers scientific Swedish massage and Holistic health-building modalities for persons interested in professional training. Also covers: reflexology, dowsing, exercise, nutrition, and stress-reduction.

US
HOME HEALTH HANDBOOK. English. $28.89. Home Health Handbook, 300 1st Stamford Place, Box 281044, Stamford CT 06914.

●US/1070-2431
HOME HEALTH PRODUCTS. [Home health prod.]. (1993)-. Periodical. English. bm. Free on request. Stevens Publishing Corporation, 225 North New Road, Waco TX 76702-2604. **Tel** (800)727-7573, (817)776-9000. **(Subscription address:** Stevens Publishing Corp., PO Box 2573, Waco TX 76702.**) DD** 649.

US/1055-6052
HOW YOU CAN STOP SMOKING. (1991)-. Periodical. English. mo. $39.00. United States Medical Information Center, 1133 Fifteenth Street NW, Wahington DC 20005.

US/1040-8126
IDEA TODAY. See Dance.

US/0279-9863
INFOAAU. [InfoAAU]. **Main/Corp** Amateur Athletic Union of the United States. **VFOAT** Info A.A.U.; Info AAU. **VAT** Info Amateur Athletic Union. (198?)-. Periodical. English. Six times a year (Jan., Mar., May, July, Sept., Dec.). $12.00. Amateur Athletic Union / AAU, 3400 West 86th Street, PO Box 68207, Indianapolis IN 46268. **Tel** (317)872-2900, FAX (317)875-0548. **ED** Chip Powers. **Ad Acc. Circ:** 8,000 (ctrl). available on microfilm and microfiche from University Microfilms International (UMI). ***Continues** Amateur Athletic Union of the United States. AAU News, 0199-6991.*
Desc: It covers stories about the Union's activities as well as articles on sports and physical fitness.

●CN/1197-4362
INJURY PREVENTION NEWS. [Inj. prev. news]. **Added/Corp** Injury Prevention Centre (Edmonton, Alta.) University of Alberta. Hospitals. **VFOAT** Injury Prevention Centre news; IPC news. Vol. 6, No. 4 (May/June 1993)-. Periodical. English. Ten times a year. 30.00Can$. Injury Prevention Centre, Universtiy of Alberta Hospital, 8440 112th Street, Edmonton, Alberta T6G 2B7 Canada. **Tel** (403)492-6019, FAX (403)492-7154. **ED** Lloyd Dick, BA. **DD** 363.1/0097123. ctrl circ. ***Continues** Injury Awareness and Prevention Centre News., 1183-4943.*

US/0199-8501
INSIDE KUNG-FU. [Inside kung-fu]. (19??)-. Periodical. English. mo. $20.00. CFW Enterprises Inc., 4201 West Van Owen Place, Burbank CA 91505. **Tel** (818)845-2656. **(Subscription address:** Kable Publishers Aide, 308 East Hitt Street, Subscription Department, Mt. Morris IL 61054-1473.**)**
Ind/Abst SPORT Discus; SportSearch (May 1987-).

US/1064-6841
INSIDER'S GUIDE TO PERSONAL WELLNESS. *Title Change.* [Insid. guide pers. wellness]. **VFOAT** Personal Wellness. Vol. 1, No. 1 (July 1992)-(199?). Periodical. English. mo. Grace Publishing, 2888 Bluff Street, Suite 461, Boulder CO 80301-9002. **DD** 613. ***Continued by** Health News & Breakthroughs, 1068-770X.*

UK/0957-0349
INTERNATIONAL MONOGRAPHS ON OBESITY SERIES. [Int. monogr. obes. ser.]. No. 1 (1985)-. Monographic series. English. John Libbey & Company Ltd, 13 Smiths Yard, Summerley Street, London SW18 4HR England. **Tel** 01-947 2777, FAX 01-947 2664, telex 94013503 JOHN G. **NLM** W1; IN8252.
Ind/Abst AGRICOLA [Select. Cov.].

US/0277-092X
INTERNATIONAL YOGA GUIDE. [Int. yoga guide]. **Added/Corp** Yoga Research Foundation. **VFOAT** Yoga Guide. (19??)-. Periodical. English. mo. $15.00

(one year), $27.00 (two year). Yoga Research Foundation, 6111 SW 74th Avenue, Miami FL 33143. **Tel** (305)666-2006.

GW/0178-7764
INTERNATIONALES SAUNA-ARCHIV. (INTERNATIONALES SAUNA-ARCHIV : ORGAN DER VEREINIGUNGEN, INTERNATIONAL SAUNA SOCIETY, HELSINKI, DEUTSCHER SAUNA-BUND E.V., BIELEFELD, SCHWEIZERISCHER SAUNA-VERBAND, ZUERICH.). [Int. Sauna-Archiv]. **Added/Corp** International Sauna Society. Deutscher Sauna-Bund. Schweizerischer Sauna-Verband. **VFOAT** Internationales Sauna Archiv; Sauna Archiv; Sauna-Archiv. Vol. 1, (March 1984)-. Periodical. German (summaries and/or abstracts in English and French). qt. DM30.00. Sauna Matti GmbH, Kavalleriestr. 9, 4800 Bielefeld Germany. **Tel** 0521 178134. **ED** Werner Fritzesche. **NLM** W1; IN959F. **Bk Rev. Ad Acc. Circ:** 3,000. available with charts. ***Continues*** *Sauna Nachrichten Mit Sauna-Archiv, 0340-0506.*

US/0896-8535
IRELAND REPORT, WOMEN'S HEALTH MARKETING, THE. [Irel. rep. women's health mark.]. **Added/Corp** Ireland Corporation. **VFOAT** Women's Health Marketing; Ireland Report. Vol. 1, No. 1 (Sept./Oct. 1987)-. Periodical. English. bm (6 issues). $199.00. Ireland Report, 13348 Roxton Circle, San Diego CA 92130. **Tel** (619)755-5651, FAX (619)755-2436. **ED** Peggy A. Dalton. **DD** 362.

US/1069-7276
IRON GAME HISTORY. [Iron game hist.]. **Added/Corp** University of Texas at Austin. McLean Sport History Fellowship. Vol. 1, No. 1 (1990)-. Periodical. English. bm. $15.00 US; $20.00 Canada. IGH, Room 217, Gregory Gym, The University of Texas, Austin TX 78712. **DD** 796.
Ind/Abst SPORT Discus.

US/0047-1496
IRON MAN. [Iron man]. **VFOAT** Ironman. (1937)-. Periodical. English. Twelve times a year. $29.95 US; $39.95 others. Iron Man, PO Box 10, 1701 Ives Avenue, Oxnard CA 93033. **Tel** (805)385-3500. **Ad Acc.**
Desc: Bodybuilding, power lifting and weightlifting.
Ind/Abst Phys. Educ. Index.

US/1050-1363
IRV'S BODYBUILDING DIGEST. [Irv's bodybuild. dig.]. **VFOAT** Irv's Body Building Digest; Irv's Bodybuilding Digest Newsletter. (1990)-. Periodical. English. mo. $12.00. Irvs Bodybuilding Network, PO Box 1653, Arlington Heights IL 60006. **DD** 613.

●US/1064-8674
ISLAND SCENE. [Isl. scene]. **Added/Corp** Hawaii Medical Service Association. Vol. 1, No. 1 (Summer 1992)-. Periodical. English. qt. Free (members), $10.00 (non-members). Island Scene, PO Box 3850, Honolulu HI 96812-3850. **DD** 613.

US
ISOKINETICS AND EXERCISE SCIENCE. **VFOAT** IES. Vol. 1, No. 1 (1991)-. Periodical. English. qt. $130.00 (institution), $65.00 (individual), US and Canada; $145.00 (institution), $90.00 (individual) other. Butterworth Heinemann / Woburn, MA, 225 Wildwood Avenue, Unit B, Woburn MA 01801. **Tel** (800)366-2665, FAX (617)928-2620, telex 880052. **ED** George Davies, Terry Malone and Kent Timm. **LC** RM727.I76; I86. **DD** 613.7/1. Index available. **Bk Rev. Ad Acc. Pr Rev.**
Desc: Serves professional needs of contemporary exercise scientists, medical practitioners, and allied health clinicians through a consolidating focus upon the field fo isokinetics.
Ind/Abst Soc. Sci. Cit. Index [Select. Cov.].

UK/0021-681X
JEWISH VEGETARIAN. **See** Ethnic Interests.

US/8750-8915
JOE WEIDER'S FLEX. [Joe Weider's flex]. **Added/Corp** IFBB. **VFOAT** Flex. (1983)-. Periodical. English. mo. $29.97 (one year); $49.97 (two year), $69.97 (three year). Weider Health & Fitness, 21100 Erwin Street, Woodland Hills CA 91367. **Tel** (818)884-6800, (818)595-0594. **(Subscription address:** Kable Publishers Aide, 308 East Hitt Street, Subscription Department, Mt. Morris IL 61054-1473.**) ED** Joe Weider.

US/0893-4460
JOE WEIDER'S MEN'S FITNESS. [Joe Weider's men's fit.]. **VFOAT** Men's Fitness. Vol. 3, No. 7 (Aug. 1987)-. Periodical. English. Twelve times a year. $29.97 (one year). Weider Health & Fitness, 21100 Erwin Street, Woodland Hills CA 91367. **Tel** (818)884-6800, (818)595-0594. **(Subscription address:** Kable Publishers Aide, 308 East Hitt Street, Subscription Department, Mt. Morris IL 61054-1473.**) LC** IN PROCESS. **DD** 613. ***Continues*** *Joe Weider's Sports Fitness, 0885-0763.*
Ind/Abst Phys. Educ. Index.

US/0744-5105
JOE WEIDER'S MUSCLE & FITNESS. [Joe Weider's muscle fitness]. **VFOAT** Joe Weider's Muscle and Fitness; Muscle and Fitness; Muscle & Fitness. (198?)-. Periodical. English. Twelve times a year. $34.97 (one year), $59.97 (two year), $79.97 (three year). Weider Health & Fitness, 21100 Erwin Street, Woodland Hills CA 91367. **Tel** (818)884-6800, (818)595-0594. **(Subscription address:** Kable Publishers Aide, 308 East Hitt Street, Subscription Department, Mt. Morris IL 61054-1473.**) ED** Ben Pesa. **LC** GV481; .J64. **DD** 613.7/1/05. Index available (free). **Ad Acc. Circ:** 674,000. Documents available from UMI Article Clearinghouse. ***Continues*** *Joe Weider's Muscle.*
Desc: A comprehensive magazine on bodybuilding and weight training.
Ind/Abst Acad. Abstr. Full Text Elite (Jan. 1992-); Acad. Abstr. (Jan. 1992-); Acad. Search (Jan. 1992-); Gen. Period. Index (1992-); Health Index (1989-); Health Period. Database; Health Ref. Cent. (Jan. 1989-) [Full Cov.]; Health Source (Jan. 1992-); INFO-SOUTH Abstr.; Mag. Index Plus (1992-); Mag. Search; Newsp. Period. Abstr. (1992-); Phys. Educ. Index; SPORT Discus.

AT/1033-8292
JOE WEIDER'S MUSCLE AND FITNESS AUSTRALIAN ED. [Joe Weider's muscle fit. Aust. ed.]. **VFOAT** Muscle and Fitness. (1988)-. Periodical. English. mo. 49.40Aus$ Australia; 113.00Aus$ US & Canada; 60.00Aus$ New Zealaned & Papua New Guinea; 120.00Aus$ Europe & Africa; 85.00Aus$ other. Federal Publishing Co Pty Ltd, PO Box 199, 180 Bourke Road, Alexandria New South Wales, 2015 Australia. **Tel** 011 61 2 693 6666, FAX 011 61 2 693 9935. **(Subscription address:** Federal Publishing Co. Pty Ltd., PO Box 199, Alexandria NSW 2015 Australia.**) DD** 796.41.

●US/1063-8652
JOURNAL OF AGING AND PHYSICAL ACTIVITY. **See** Medical Science and Technology-Geriatrics.

●US/1057-8358
JOURNAL OF ASIAN MARTIAL ARTS. [J. Asian martial arts]. Vol. 1, No. 1 (Jan. 1992)-. Periodical. English. Four times a year. $75.00 (institutions), $32.00 (individuals) US; add $6.00 postage Canada and Pan American nations; add $8.00 postage other. Via Media Publishing Company, 821 West 24th Street, Erie PA 16502. **Tel** (814)455-9517, FAX (814)838-7811. **ED** Michael A. DeMarco. **LC** GV1100.69.A2; J68. **DD** 796.8/05. Index available. cum. index. **Bk Rev**, (Qty: 18/year). **Ad Acc. Pr Rev. Circ:** 6,000 (ctrl).
Desc: Covers all historical aspects of Asian martial arts; focuses on Asia, but includes important related material from all other countries, such as museum collections, interviews, announcements and media reviews.

US/1044-2790
JOURNAL OF HEALTH & HEALING (WILDWOOD, GA.). (JOURNAL OF HEALTH & HEALING.). **Added/Corp** Wildwood Lifestyle Center & Hospital. **VFOAT** Journal of Health and Healing; Health & Healing; Health and Healing. (19??)-. Periodical. English. qt (4 issues). $20.00 (institutions), $10.00 (individuals). Journal of Health & Healing, PO Box 109, Wildwood GA 30757. **Tel** (706)820-1493, FAX (706)820-1474. **DD** 613. ***Continues*** *Wildwood Echoes.*

UK/0963-6757
JOURNAL OF SEXUAL HEALTH. **See** Sexual Life.

●US/1064-8011
JOURNAL OF STRENGTH AND CONDITIONING RESEARCH. **See** Recreation, Leisure-Sports.

UK/0022-5819
JUDO. ***Suspended.*** **See** Recreation, Leisure-Sports.

CN/0383-6517
KARATE KEBEC. **See** Recreation, Leisure-Sports.

CN/0709-8227
KINO-NOUVELLES. [Kino-nouv.]. **Added/Corp** Quebec (Province). Ministere du Loisir, de la Chasse et de la Peche. Kino-Quebec. (1979)-. Periodical. French. bm. Free on request. Ministere du Loisir de la Chasse et de la Peche, 150 Est Boulevard St. Cyrille, Quebec Quebec G1R 4Y1 Canada. **Tel** (418)643-5526. **DD** 613.7/09714.
Ind/Abst SPORT Discus.

GW/0323-4916
KOERPERERZIEHUNG. [Koerpererziehung]. (1951)-. Periodical. German. Eleven times a year. DM71.50. Paedagogischer Zeitschriftenverlag GmbH, Postfach 269, D 10107 Berlin, Germany. **Tel** 011 49 30 20343431. **UDC** 796.

BU/0368-7066
KURORTOLOGIIA I FIZIOTERAPIIA. [Kurortol. fizioter.]. **VFOAT** Kurortologija i Fizioterapija. (1964)-. Periodical. Bulgarian (summaries and/or abstracts in English and Russian; table of contents in English and Russian). qt. 10lv. Izdatelstvo Medicina i Fizkult, PL Slavejkov 11, 1000 Sofia Bulgaria. **ED** St. Bankov. **NLM** W1 KU708R. **CODEN** KUFIAT. **Circ:** 850. Documents available from CASDDS.
Ind/Abst Chem. Abstr. (1964-1984); EMBASE.

US
LEARNING RESOURCES JOURNAL / UNIVERSITY OF MINNESOTA HEALTH SCIENCES. **See** Education-Teaching and Curriculum.

AU
LEIBESUEBUNGEN-LEIBESERZIEHUNG. German. Six times a year. S400.00. OBV Schulbuchzentrum, Postfach 133, 2351 Wiener Neudorf Austria. **Tel** 011 43 2236 63535. **ED** S430.00.
Desc: Covers education as related to sports.

●US/1064-217X
LIFE DESIGNS. (LIFE DESIGNS : DEDICATED TO PROMOTING A HIGH SELF-ESTEEM LIFESTYLE.). [Life des.]. Vol. 1, No. 1 (Sept. 1992)-. Periodical. English. mo. $39.95 (single issue). Life Designs, 1500 Worcester Road, Suite 106, Framingham MA 01701. **DD** 158.

FI/0357-2498
LIIKUNNAN JA KANSANTERVEYDEN JULKAISUJA. [Liik. kansanter. julk.]. **VFOAT** Reports of Physical Culture and Health. (1975)-. Monographic series. Multiple languages. ir. **UDC** 613 796/799.
Ind/Abst Leis. Recreat. Tour. Abstr.

US/0890-4189
LOOKINGFIT. [Lookingfit]. **VFOAT** Looking Fit. (1986)-. Periodical. English. Thirteen times a year. $45.00. Virgo Publishing Inc., 4141 North Scottsdale Road, Suite 316, Scottsdale AZ 85251. **Tel** (602)483-0014, (602)990-1101, FAX (602)990-0819. **ED** Nancy Bercaw. **LC** GV510.U5; L66. **DD** 613.7/0973. **Ad Acc.** ctrl circ.

US/1055-6028
LOWERING YOUR CHOLESTEROL. (1991)-. Periodical. English. mo. $39.00. United States Medical Information Center, 1133 Fifteenth Street NW, Wahington DC 20005.

US/1057-378X
MASSAGE (DAVIS, CALIF.). (MASSAGE.). (1991)-. Periodical. English. Six times a year (Jan., Mar., May, July, Sept., Nov.). $20.00 one year; $36.00 two years. Massage Magazine, P.O Box 1500, Davis CA 95617. **Tel** (916)757-6033, FAX (916)757-6041. **DD** 646. **Bk Rev**, (Qty: 10-18). **Ad Acc, Adv Mgr:** C Driskill, **Tel** (916)757-6033. **Circ:** 12,000. ***Continues*** *Massage Magazine, 1045-4268.*
Desc: Covers the art and science of massage, bodywork, and their related healing arts. Its purpose is to spread the good word about the healing touch needed by people everywhere.

US/1056-1129
MCGRAW-HILL HEALTH LETTER. [McGraw-Hill health lett.]. **VFOAT** Health Letter. (Summer 1991)-. Periodical. English. qt. McGraw Hill Information Systems Company, 1221 Avenue of the Americas, New York NY 10020. **Tel** (212)512-2000, (800)525-5003, FAX (212)512-6111. **DD** 613.

US
MEMBERSHIP DIRECTORY. **Main/Corp** International Dance-Exercise Association. **VFOAT** IDEA ... Membership Directory. Directory. English. International Dance-Exercise Association, 6190 Cornerstone Court East 204, San Diego CA 92121. **Tel** (619)535-8227, (800)999-4332. **LC** RA781.15.; .I57a. **DD** 613.7/1/06073. ***Continues*** *IDEA Annual Directory.*

US/1059-9169
MEN'S EXERCISE. [Men's exerc.]. (Spring 1990)-. Periodical. English. bm. $17.75 (one year), $32.00 (two year) US; $22.75 (one year), $37.00 (two year) other. Pumpkin Press Inc, Empire State Building, 350 5th Avenue, New York NY 10118. **Tel** (212)947-4322, FAX (212)563-4774. **ED** Steve Downs. **DD** 613. **Ad Acc, Adv Mgr:** Bruce Soffer. ctrl circ.

US/1054-4836
MEN'S HEALTH (MAGAZINE). (MEN'S HEALTH.). [Men's health]. (1987)-. Periodical. English. Ten times a year. $20.00 US; $38.00 Canada. Rodale Press Inc., 400 South 10th Street, Emmaus PA 18098. **Tel** (215)967-5171, (800)666-2503. **(Subscription address:** CDS Agency Hard Copy, PO Box 4966, Des Moines IA 50340.**) LC** RA777.8; .M46. **DD** 613. **CODEN** MEHEE9. Documents available from UMI Article Clearinghouse. ***Continues*** *Prevention Magazine's Guide to Men's Health, 0886-2346.*
Ind/Abst Acad. Search (Jan. 1992-); Health Index (1989-); Health Period. Database [Full Txt.]; Health Ref. Cent. (Jan. 1989-) [Full Txt.] [Full Cov.]; Mag. Artic. Summar. Elite (Jan. 1992-) [Full Txt.]; Mag. ASAP Plus [Full Txt.]; Mag. Index Plus (1989-); Newsp. Period. Abstr. (1992-); Read. Guide Abstr. Select Ed.; Read. Guide Period. Lit.

US
MICHIGAN COUNCIL ON PHYSICAL FITNESS AND HEALTH ANNUAL REPORT TO THE MICHIGAN DEPARTMENT OF PUBLIC HEALTH. **Main/Corp** Michigan Council on Physical Fitness and Health. English. an. Michigan Department of Public

Health and Personal Fitness

Health, 3423 North Logan Street, PO Box 30195, Lansing MI 48909. **Tel** (517)335-8216, FAX (517)335-8560. **LC** RA447.M5; M49A. **DD** 353.97740084/1.

US/1048-910X
MIRKIN REPORT. (MIRKIN REPORT : A JOURNAL OF FITNESS, NUTRITION, AND HEALTH BY GABE MIRKIN, M.D.). [Mirkin rep.]. Vol. 1, No. 1 (Feb. 1990)-. Periodical. English. mo. $36.95 US; $44.00 other. Mirkin Report, PO Box 6608, Silver Spring MD 20916. **Tel** (301)587-9100. **ED** Mary Singer. **DD** 613. Index available. cum. index. **Circ**: 10,000.
 Desc: Various articles and tips on fitness, nutrition and health.

US
MONKEYSHINES ON HEALTH AND SCIENCE. See Science and Technology.

FR/0989-1013
MUSCLE & FITNESS. **VFOAT** Muscle and Fitness. (1987)-. Periodical. French. mo. 276.00F France; 320.00F French territories & possessions; 400.00F Algeria; 360.00F Europe; 530.00F Africa; 470.00F other. Mediafit, 72 Quai des Carrieres, 94220 Charenton le Pont France. **Tel** 011 33 1 43964242, FAX 011 33 1 43963851, telex 214813. **UDC** 796.4.

AT
MUSCLE BUILDER. (19??)-. Periodical. English. mo. 53.40Aus$ Australia; 60.00Aus$ New Zealand & Papua New Guinea; 117.00Aus$ US & Canada; 124.00Aus$ Europe & Africa; 89.00Aus$ other. Federal Publishing Co Pty Ltd, PO Box 199, 180 Bourke Road, Alexandria New South Wales, 2015 Australia. **Tel** 011 61 2 693 6666, FAX 011 61 2 693 9935. **(Subscription address**: Federal Publishing Co. Pty Ltd., PO Box 199, Alexandria NSW 2015 Australia.**)**

CN/0317-087X
MUSCLE MAG INTERNATIONAL. Vol. 1 (Fall 1974)-. Periodical. English. mo (12 issues per year). $45.00 (one year), $82.00 (two years) US and Canada; $75.00 (one year), $130.00 (two years) other. Muscle Mag International, Health Culture Inc, 6465 Airport Road, Mississauga Ontario, L4V 1E4 Canada. **Tel** (416)678-7311, FAX (416)678-9236. **ED** Gino Edwards. **DD** 646.7/5. **Ad Acc**, **Adv Mgr**: Gina Logan, **Tel** (416)678-7312. **Circ**: 290,000 (ctrl).

●US
MUSCLE MEDIA 2000. **VFOAT** Muscle Media Two Thousand. No. 28 (Spring 1992)-. Periodical. English. qt. $36.00 (two year). Mile High Publishing, PO Box 277, Golden CO 80402. **Tel** (800)637-1572. **Continues** Anabolic Reference Update.

US/1047-1960
MUSCLE POWER. (1991)-. Periodical. English. qt. $14.75. CPO Publishing, PO Box 1210, Azusa CA 91702.

US/0163-7401
MUSCLE TRAINING ILLUSTRATED ANNUAL WHO'S WHO OF BODYBUILDING. Ceased. **Added/Corp** World Body Building Guild. **VFOAT** Annual Who's Who of Bodybuilding; Who's Who of Bodybuilding. (1979)-(1993). Periodical. English. Nine times a year. Dan Lurie, 219-10 South Conduit Avenue, Queens NY 11413. **Tel** (718)978-4200, FAX (718)978-4201.

CN/0824-4480
MUSCLE WEST. [Muscle West]. **Added/Corp** Canadian Western Amateur Bodybuilding Association. Vol. 1, No. 1 (Summer 1983)-. Periodical. English. qt. $6.00. Muscle West, Suite 1/246 East Broadway, Vancouver British Columbia V5T 1W3 Canada. **DD** 646.7/5.

US/0047-8415
MUSCULAR DEVELOPMENT. [Muscular dev.]. **VFOAT** Muscular Development Magazine. (1964)-. Periodical. English. Twelve times a year. $29.95 US; $46.95 other. Advanced Research Press, 2120 Smithtown Avenue, Ronkonkoma NY 11779. **Tel** (516)467-3140. **ED** May Pro Inc., (editor's address: 5054 Saddle River Road, Saddle Brook N.J. 07662, Phone: (201)368-2140). **DD** 796. **Ad Acc**, **Adv Mgr**: Ann Fortz, **Tel** (516)467-3140 Ext. 161. **Circ**: 211,000.
 Desc: Devoted to the science of bodybuilding and the use of weight training to build bigger and stronger bodies. We also list the who's who in the sport.
 Ind/Abst Phys. Educ. Index.

US/1048-1532
NATURAL BODY & FITNESS. Ceased. [Nat. body fit.]. **VFOAT** Natural Body and Fitness; Body & Fitness; Body and Fitness. (19??)-(19??). Periodical. English. bm. Fitness Lifestyles, PO Box A, New Britain PA 18901. **DD** 613.
 Desc: Covers topics such as diet, health, nutrition, body building and exercise. Each issue looks at fitness facts and fads and what's new in the world of fitness.

●US/1071-555X
NATURAL BODYBUILDING AND FITNESS. See Recreation, Leisure-Sports.

US
NATURAL HEALING NEWSLETTER. English. mo. $18.00. Frank Cawood & Associates / FC & A, 103 clover Green, Peachtree City GA 30296. **Tel** (404)487-6307, 800 226-8024.

●US/1067-9588
NATURAL HEALTH. [Nat. health]. Vol. 23, No. 1 (Jan./Feb. 1993)-. Periodical. English. bm. $24.00 US; $27.00 Canada; $36.00 other. Natural Health, PO Box 1200, Brookline Village MA 02147. **Tel** (617)232-1000, (800)666-8576. **LC** AP2; .E154. **DD** 613. **NLM** W1; NA804H. available on an online database (file 149/Full-Text) from DIALOG. **Continues** EastWest Natural Health, 1061-4664.
 Ind/Abst Health Index; Health Period. Database.

CN/0701-8002
NATURAL LIFE (UNIONVILLE. 1991). (NATURAL LIFE.). [Nat. life]. No. 24 (1991)-. Periodical. English. Twelve times a year. 28.04Can$ Canada; 30.00Can$ others. Alternate Press, 272 Highway 5, Rural Route 1, St. George Ontario N0E 1N0 Canada. **Tel** (519)448-4001, FAX (519)448-4001. **ED** Wendy Priesnitz. **DD** 051. **Bk Rev**, (Qty: 50): 8-10. **Ad Acc**. **Circ**: 2,000. available on an online database from Cyberstore. **Continues** Home Business Advocate, 0832-8595.
 Desc: How-to information and inspiration about self-reliant living. Includes home business, home schooling, the environment, renewable energy, self-built housing and organic gardening.

AT/0815-7006
NATURE AND HEALTH. [Nat. health]. (1984)-. Periodical. English. qt. 27.00Aus$ Australia; 80.00Aus$ other. Yaffa Publishing Group Pty Ltd., GPO Box 606, Sydney NSW 2001 Australia. **Tel** 011 61 2 2812333, FAX 011 61 2 2812750. **DD** 615-53505. **Continues** Nature and Health Australia, 0815-6999.

CN/0825-0324
NETWORK (TORONTO. 1984). (NETWORK.). [Netw.]. Vol. 1, No. 1 (Mar. 1, 1984)-. Periodical. English. qt. Participaction Network, 80 Richmond Street/Suite 805, Toronto Ontario M5H 2A4 Canada. **DD** 613.7/05.
 Ind/Abst Urban Aff. Abstr.

US/0732-4782
NEW BODY. [New body]. Vol. 1, No. 1 (May 1982)-. Periodical. English. New Body, 888 7th Avenue, Carnegie Publishing, New York NY 10106. **Tel** (212)541-7100. **ED** Judy Jones. **LC** WMLC L 83/5720. **DD** 796. **Ad Acc**. **Continued in part by** American Swimwear, 1070-7190.

US
NEW BODY SPECIAL INTEREST PUBLICATIONS. (Jan 1991)-. English. qt. GCR Publishing Group, 1700 Broadway, 34th Floor, New York NY 10019. **Tel** (212)541-7100, (800)435-0715, FAX (212)245-1241. **LC** WMLC L 83/9180.

US/1055-8934
NEW HEALTH STANDARD JOURNAL, THE. [New health stand. j.]. Vol. 1, No. 1 (Sept./Oct. 1991)-. Periodical. English. bm. $18.00. Burgundy Court Publishers, PO Box 8181, Collins CO 80526-8003. **DD** 613.

US
NEW JERSEY TRACK. English. ir. $18.00 (1 year); $27.00 (2 year). Mr. Edward J. Grant, 39 Mill Pond Road, New Providence NJ 07974. **Tel** (908)464-5722. **ED** Edward J. Grant. **Ad Acc**. **Circ**: 300.
 Desc: Covers the sport of track and field in all aspects in the state of New Jersey, as well as activities of New Jersey natives throughout the world.

US/8755-8742
NEWSLETTER / AMERICAN AEROBICS ASSOCIATION. **Added/Corp** American Aerobics Association. (198?)-. Newsletter. English. mo. $15.00. American Aerobics Association, PO Box 401, Durango CO 81301. **Tel** (303)247-4109. **ED** J. Rosenbaum. **DD** 613. **Bk Rev**. **Circ**: 3,000 (ctrl).
 Desc: Contains information on aerobic dance research.

US/0364-8079
NEWSLETTER (PRESIDENT'S COUNCIL ON PHYSICAL FITNESS AND SPORTS (U.S.)). (NEWSLETTER / PRESIDENT'S COUNCIL ON PHYSICAL FITNESS & SPORTS.). **Added/Corp** President's Council on Physical Fitness and Sports (U.S.). (19??)-. Newsletter. English. ir. Free on request. Presidents Council on Physical Fitness and Sports, 400 6th Street Southwest, Washington DC 20024. **Tel** (202)272-3430. **NLM** W1 PR448N. **Circ**: 9,000 (ctrl).
 Ind/Abst SPORT Discus; SportSearch (May 1987-).

AT
NUTIRDATE. (19??)-. English. Four times a year (Mar., May, July, Sept.). 45.00Aus$. Warringal Productions, 114 Argyle Street, Fitzroy 3065 Australia.

Tel 011 61 03 4160200, FAX 011 61 03 4160402. **(Subscription address**: Warringal Publications, PO Box 336, Fitzroy 3065 Australia.**)**

US/1056-120X
NWFN NEWSJOURNAL : A WOMEN'S FITNESS RESOURCE. [NWFN newsj.]. **Added/Corp** National Women's Fitness Network. **VAT** National Women's Fitness Network Newsjournal. Vol. 1, No. 1 (Jan./Feb. 1991)-. Periodical. English. mo. $36.00. National Women's Fitness Network (NWFN) Newsjournal, PO Box 668, Los Angeles CA 90078-0668. **DD** 613.

US/0148-3560
OFFICIAL AAU PHYSIQUE HANDBOOK : OFFICIAL RULES. [Off. AAU phys. handb., Off. rules]. **Main/Corp** Amateur Athletic Union of the United States. **Added/Corp** Amateur Athletic Union of the United States. AAU official Rules : Physique. **VFOAT** AAU Official Rules : Physique. **VAT** Official Amateur Athletic Union Physique Handbook. Official Rules. (1977/78)-. English. Amateur Athletic Union / AAU, 3400 West 86th Street, PO Box 68207, Indianapolis IN 46268. **Tel** (317)872-2900, FAX (317)875-0548. **LC** GV514; .A46a. **DD** 646.7/5.

US/0198-7941
OFFICIAL AAU TAE KWON DO RULES. See Recreation, Leisure-Sports.

US/0279-9634
OHIO RUNNER, THE. See Recreation, Leisure-Sports.

AT/1036-8124
ON THE LEVEL ASHFIELD. (ON THE LEVEL.). [On level Ashfield]. (1991)-. Periodical. English. qt. 43.00Aus$ Australia; 54.00Aus$ other. Healthrites Publications, 328-336 Liverpool Road, Ashfield 2131 Australia. **Tel** 011 61 2 7166099, FAX 011 61 2 7166164. **ED** Victoria Smith. **DD** 306.7099405. Index available. cum. index. **Bk Rev**, (Qty: 8-10). **Circ**: 2,000.

CN/0713-4207
P5. PERSONAL PARTICIPATION IN PURSUIT OF PHYSICAL PROFICIENCY. (P5.). **VFOAT** P5 Development Digest; P 5; Personal Participation in Pursuit of Physical Proficiency. **VAT** PFive. Vol. 1 No. 1 (Feb. 1982)-. Periodical. English. mo. $17.50. P5 Development Digest, 3549 St. Clair Avenue East, Scarborough Ontario M1K 1L6. **DD** 613.7/05.

CN/0832-8196
PERFORMANCE (VANIER). See Recreation, Leisure-Sports.

US
PERSONAL BEST. (19??)-. English. mo. $24.00 (one year), $42.00 (two year). Scott Publishing, 420 5th Avenue South, Suite D, Edmonds WA 98020. **Tel** (206)775-8777, (800)888-7853, FAX (206)775-8250. **Continues** Shape Write Up.

US/0163-2582
PHYSICAL FITNESS/SPORTS MEDICINE. Ceased. (PHYSICAL FITNESS/SPORTS MEDICINE : A PUBLICATION OF THE PRESIDENT'S COUNCIL ON PHYSICAL FITNESS AND SPORTS.). **Added/Corp** President's Council on Physical Fitness and Sports (U.S.) National Library of Medicine (U.S.). **VFOAT** Physical Fitness, Sports Medicine. Vol. 1, No. 1 (Winter 1978)-Vol. 16. Government Publication. English. qt. Superintendent of Documents, US Government Printing Office, Washington DC 20402. **Tel** (202)275-3328, FAX (202)786-2377. **LC** Z6664.6; .P48; RC1200. **DD** 016.617/1027. **NLM** ZQT 255 P578.
 Desc: Bibliographic listings of materials on exercise physiology, sports injuries, physical conditioning, and the medical aspects of exercise.

US/0883-4938
PHYSICIAN'S SPORTSLIFE. **VFOAT** Physician's Sports Life. Began in 1984?. Periodical. English. bm. $19.00. Medical Publishers Enterprises, 15 22 Fair Lawn Avenue, Fair Lawn NJ 07410. **Tel** (201)796-6500. **DD** 796.

US/0199-8536
POWERLIFTING USA. See Recreation, Leisure-Sports.

US/1060-9385
PREVENTION'S LOSE WEIGHT GUIDEBOOK. [Prevention's lose weight guideb.]. **VFOAT** Lose Weight Guidebook. (1991)-. English. $22.95 US; $28.95 Canada. Rodale Press Inc., 400 South 10th Street, Emmaus PA 18098. **Tel** (215)967-5171, (800)666-2503. **DD** 613.

US
PREVENTION'S MEDICAL HEALING YEARBOOK / WRITTEN BY THE STAFF OF RODALE PRESS. **Added/Corp** Rodale Press. **VFOAT** Medical Healing Yearbook. (1991)-. English. Rodale Press Inc., 400 South 10th Street,

Emmaus PA 18098. **Tel** (215)967-5171, (800)666-2503. **LC** RC81.A1; P74. **DD** 613/.05. ***Continues*** *Prevention's Medical Care Yearbook.*

●US/1064-7503
PREVENTION'S QUICK AND HEALTHY LOW-FAT COOKING. **See** Food and Food Industry.

US
PRIORITIES. (19??)-. English. Four times a year. Comes with membership. American Council on Science and Health, 1995 Broadway, 16th Floor, New York NY 10023. **Tel** (212)362-7044, FAX (212)362-4919. **ED** Dr. Elizabeth Whelan. **Ad Acc. Pr Rev. Circ:** 6,000.
Ind/Abst Consum. Health Nutr. Index; Health Index (1989-); Health Period. Database; Health Ref. Cent. (Sept. 1989-) [Full Cov.].

US/0098-0706
PROFESSIONAL KARATE. **See** Recreation, Leisure-Sports.

US/1056-4004
QI (FAIRFAX, VA.). (QI : THE JOURNAL OF TRADITIONAL EASTERN HEALTH & FITNESS.). [Qi]. Vol. 1, No. 1 (Spring 1991)-. Periodical. English. qt. $18.95. Insight Graphics Inc., 13341 Foxhole Drive, Fairfax VA 22033. **DD** 362.

CC/1000-0895
QIGONG YU KEXUE. (CHI KUNG YU KO HSUEH / [KUANG-CHOU CHI KUNG KO HSUEH YEN CHIU HSIEH HUI].). [Qigong yu kexue]. **Added/Corp** Kuang-chou Chi Kung ko Hsueh Yen Chiu Hsieh Hui. **VFOAT** Journal of Qigong and Science; Journal of Qigong & Science. (1982)-. Periodical. Chinese. bm. RMBY12.00. Guangdongsheng Qigong Kexue Yanjiu Xiehui, Guangdong Qigong Science Research Association, Qigong yu Kexue Zazhishe, PO Box 343, Guangzhou, Guangdong 510030, People's Republic of China. **LC** RM727.C54; C446. **DD** 613.7/1/05.

CN/1182-9478
RENAISSANCE (CHICOUTIMI). (LA RENAISSANCE.). [Renaissance]. **Added/Corp** Centre de Sante et de Repos Total. Vol. 1, No. 1 (June/July 1990)-. Periodical. French. qt. Free. Centre de Sante et de Repos Total, 2075 Pl. Belvedere, Chicoutimi, Quebec G7H 5B3 Canada. **DD** 613.2.

AT/1033-5609
REPS BODYBUILDING AUSTRALIA. [Reps bodybuild. Aust.]. (1988)-. Periodical. English. Four times a year. 18.95Aus$. Reps, PO Box 69, Essendon North 3041 Australia. **Tel** 61 3 3661470, FAX 61 3 3640793. **DD** 646.7505.

CN/1188-6641
RESEARCH FILE, THE. [Res. file]. **Added/Corp** Canadian Fitness & Lifestyle Research Institute. **VFOAT** Dossier de la Recherche. (1991)-. Periodical. English (French). Three times a year (Jan., May, Aug.). 25.00Can$. Canadian Fitness Lifestyle Research Institute, 313 1600 James Naismith, Gloucester, Ontario K1B 5N4 Canada. **Tel** (613)748-5791, FAX (613)748-5792. **DD** 613.7. Index available. cum. index. **Pr Rev.**
Ind/Abst SPORT Discus.

CN/0825-0332
RESEAU (TORONTO). (RESEAU.). [Reseau]. Vol. 1, No. 1 (1 March 1984)-. Periodical. French. qt. Reseau Participaction, Suite 805, 80 Ouest, Rue Richmond, Toronto Ont M5H 2A4. **DD** 613.7/05.

FR/0337-730X
REVUE FRANCAISE DU DOMMAGE CORPOREL. **See** Insurance.

PL
ROCZNIKI NAUKOWE. **Main/Corp** Akademia Wychowania Fizycznego W Poznaniu. No. 22- 1973-. Polish (summaries and/or abstracts in English and French). 110.00. **LC** GV201; .P76. ***Continues*** *Roczniki Naukowe (Wyzsza Szkoa Wychowania Fizycznego W Poznaniu).*

US/0199-6983
RUNNER'S GAZETTE. **See** Recreation, Leisure-Sports.

US/0898-5162
RUNNING & FITNEWS. (RUNNING & FITNEWS / C.AMERICAN RUNNING & FITNESS ASSOCIATION.). [Run. fitnews]. **Added/Corp** American Running and Fitness Association. **VFOAT** Running and Fitnews; Fitnews. Vol. 1, No. 1 (July 1983)-. Periodical. English. Twelve times a year. $25.00 (individual), $40.00 (professional) Comes with American Running & Fitness Association membership. American Running & Fitness Association, 4405 East-West Highway #405, Bethesda MD 20814. **Tel** (301)913-9517, FAX (301)913-9520. **ED** Trevor Smith. **DD** 613. Index available. **Bk Rev. Circ:** 15,000.
Desc: Covers the latest research and findings on training, sports medicine, nutrition, exercise, and injury prevention.
Ind/Abst SPORT Discus.

US/0147-2968
RUNNING TIMES. **See** Recreation, Leisure-Sports.

FR/0247-106X
S.T.A.P.S. SCIENCES ET TECHNIQUES DES ACTIVITES PHYSIQUES ET SPORTIVES. (1980)-. Periodical. French. Three times a year. 280.00F (institutions), 210.00F (individuals) France; 280.00F (institutions), 250.00F (individuals) other. Assn Francophone, 22 Ave Montjoly, 63400 Chamalieres, France. **Tel** 011 33 73 376216. **UDC** 378. **Circ:** 1,500.
Ind/Abst SPORT Discus.

SP
SALUD. Spanish. Free. Colegio Ats, C Alcoy No. 21, 08022 Barcelona Spain. **Tel** 011 34 3 2128108.

CN/0832-6770
SANTE. **See** Women's Interests.

UK/0265-5780
SAYYIDATI. [Sayyidati]. **VFOAT** Sayidaty. (19??)-. Periodical. Arabic. Fifty-two times a year. $166.00. Attache International, 3050 Broadway, Suite 300, Boulder CO 80304. **Tel** (303)442-8900, FAX (303)442-7979. **ED** Fawzeya Salama. **LC** AP95.A6; S293. **Ad Acc. Circ:** 96,787.
Desc: Women's/family magazine that features articles on health, education, fashion, beauty, decorating and culture.

US/0149-0699
SELF (NEW YORK). **See** Women's Interests.

US/0744-5121
SHAPE (WOODLAND HILLS, CALIF.). (SHAPE.). [Shape]. **VFOAT** Shape Magazine; Joe Weider's Shape. (19??)-. Periodical. English. Twelve times a year. $19.97 (1 year), $34.97 (2 year), $44.97 (3 year). Weider Health & Fitness, 21100 Erwin Street, Woodland Hills CA 91367. **Tel** (818)884-6800, (818)595-0594. **(Subscription address:** Kable Publishers Aide, 308 East Hitt Street, Subscription Department, Mt. Morris IL 61054-1473.**) ED** Chris MacIntyre. **Bk Rev. Ad Acc. Circ:** 576,481. Documents available from UMI Article Clearinghouse.
Desc: A women's magazine on health, nutrition, fitness and fashion for today's women.
Ind/Abst Acad. Abstr. Full Text Elite (Jan. 1992-); Acad. Abstr. (Jan. 1992-); Consum. Health Nutr. Index (?-?); Gen. Period. Index (1992-); Health Index (1989-); Health Period. Database; Health Ref. Cent. (Jan. 1989-) [Full Cov.]; Health Source (Jan. 1992-); Mag. Index Plus (1992-); Mag. Search; Newsp. Period. Abstr. (1992-); Phys. Educ. Index; SPORT Discus; SportSearch.

US/1056-7488
SLENDER SENSE. (July 1991)-. Periodical. English. mo. $11.00. Monique Bailey, PO Box 795, Oxon Hill MD 20750. **DD** 613.

US/1055-5552
SLIM FAST MAGAZINE. ***Ceased.*** [Slim fast mag.]. **VFOAT** Slim Fast. Issue 1 (1991)-(Summer 1992). Periodical. English. qt. Welsh Publishing Group Inc., 300 Madison Avenue, New York NY 10017. **Tel** (212)687-0680, FAX (212)986-5849. **DD** 613.

US/0736-6280
SOUTHERN BODYBUILDER. **VFOAT** Southern Body Builder. March 1983-. Periodical. English. mo. $17.50. Southern Bodybuilder Inc., PO Box 6322, Macon GA 31201.

GW/0934-4853
SPIELRAUM. [Spielraum]. (1988)-. Periodical. German. Six times a year (Feb., Apr., June, Aug., Oct., Dec.). DM82.00. Mr. Rolf von der Horst, Alte Schule Bannetze, D 29308 Winsen Aller Germany. **Tel** 011 49 5146 364, FAX 011 49 5146 4961. **ED** Rolf van der Korst and Thomas M. Ruthernoum (phone: 011 49 5146 363). **UDC** 796.1. **Bk Rev**, (Qty: 30). **Ad Acc. Circ:** 6,400 (ctrl). ***Continues*** *Animation, 0172-9721.*

FR/1152-9563
SPORT ET VIE DIJON. **See** Recreation, Leisure-Sports.

US/0899-3815
SPORTCARE & FITNESS. ***Ceased.*** **See** Recreation, Leisure-Sports.

US/0039-2308
STRENGTH AND HEALTH. ***Ceased.*** [Strength health]. -Ceased Vol. 54, No. 3, May 1986. Periodical. English. bm. Strength and Health Publishing Company, PO Box 1707, York PA 17405. **Tel** (717)767-6481. **ED** Bob Hoffman. **Bk Rev. Ad Acc.** ctrl circ.
Desc: Features principles of general physical fitness, olympic weightlifting and training for all major sports, also features women's training and articles on nutrition and sportsmedicine.

US/1043-1047
TAEKWONDO WORLD. **Added/Corp** American Taekwondo Association. **VFOAT** ATA Magazine. **VAT** American Taekwondo Association Magazine. (198?)-. Periodical. English. Four times a year (Jan., Apr., July, Oct.). $7.00. Taekwondo World, Box 898, Yankton SD 57078. **Tel** (605)665-9909. **ED** Milo Dailey and Carla Dailey. **DD** 796. **Ad Acc, Adv Mgr:** Carla Dailey. **Circ:** 45,000. ***Continues*** *ATA Magazine (Memphis, Tenn.), 0884-5786.*
Desc: History, philosophy, sociology and physical and tactical concepts of Songahm Taekwondo martial arts.

US/0730-1049
T'AI CHI. [T'ai chi]. (19??)-. Periodical. English (English). Six times a year. $20.00 US; $30.00 other. Wayfarer Publications, PO Box 26156, Los Angeles CA 90026. **Tel** (213)665-7773. **ED** Marvin Smalheiser. **LC** Discard. **Ad Acc. Circ:** 4,000.
Desc: Articles, photos about T'ai Chi Ch'uan, a Chinese exercise for health, self-defense and meditation.

CS/0040-358X
TEORIE A PRAXE TELESNE VYCHOVY. ***Ceased.*** [Teor. praxe teles. vychovy]. **VFOAT** Teorie a Praxe Telesne Vychovy a Sportu. (1953)-(1992). Periodical. Czech. mo. **(Subscription address:** Artia Pegas Press Ltd., Palac Metro Narodni Trida 25, 11210 Prague 1 Czech Republic.**) UDC** 796/799.
Ind/Abst SportSearch (May 1987-).

US/0748-0245
TOPS IDEAS. [TOPS ideas]. **Added/Corp** TOPS Learning Systems. **VFOAT** Ideas; T.O.P.S. ideas. **VAT** Task Oriented Physical Science Ideas. (198?)-. Periodical. English. sa. Free US; $1.00 Canada and Pan-American countries; $2.00 other. TOPS Ideas, 10970 South Mulino Road, Canby OR 97013. **Tel** (503)266-8550. **DD** 371.

US/0745-2365
TRADITIONAL TAEKWON-DO. ***Ceased.*** **See** Recreation, Leisure-Sports.

US/1058-3548
TRAINING & CONDITIONING. (TRAINING & CONDITIONING : T & C.). [Train. cond.]. **VFOAT** Training and Conditioning; T & C; A.T&C. Vol. 1 (June 1991)-. Periodical. English. Four times a year. $12.00. College Athletic Management, PO Box 4806, Ithaca NY 14852-4806. **Tel** (607)272-0265, FAX (607)272-0701. **DD** 613.

US/1056-4780
ULTIMATE FITNESS FOR A LIFETIME. [Ultim. fit. lifetime]. **VFOAT** Ultimate Fitness Letter. Vol. 1, Issue 1 (Mar. 1991)-. Periodical. English. Action Aerobics, 70 East Sunset Way, Suite 272, Issaquah WA 98027. **DD** 613.

AT
ULTRAFIT AUSTRALIA. (199?)-. English. Seven times a year (Plus annual buyers guide in Apr.). 44.00Aus$ Australia; 75.00Aus$ others. Australian Workout Publishing Pty Ltd., PO Box 266, Eltham Victoria 3095 Australia. **Tel** 011 61 3 439 2828, FAX 011 61 3 439 2605. **ED** Mark McKeon. **Bk Rev**, (Qty: 7). **Ad Acc, Adv Mgr:** Karen Fode, **Tel** 03 4392828. **Circ:** 16,000. ***Continues*** *Ultra Fit.*
Desc: The latest news, information and training programmes from the fitness world.
Ind/Abst SPORT Discus.

US/1056-8042
UP FROM DEPRESSION. [Up depress.]. Fall/Winter (1991)-. Periodical. English. qt. $34.00 US; $36.00 Canada. UFD Publishing, Inc., PO Box 16-0831, Miami FL 33116-0831. **DD** 616.

US/0749-3509
VIBRANT LIFE. [Vibrant Life]. Vol. 1, No. 1 (Jan./Feb. 1985)-. Periodical. English. Six times a year. $8.97 US; $14.07 other. Review and Herald Publishing Association, 55 West Oak Ridge Drive, Hagerstown MD 21740. **Tel** (301)791-7000 ext. 2534, FAX (301)790-9734. **ED** Ralph Blodgett. **LC** R773; .V53. **DD** 613/.05. **Circ:** 50,000. available on microfilm and microfiche from University Microfilms International (UMI); available on an online database (file 149/Full-Text) from DIALOG. ***Continues*** *Your Life and Health, 0279-2680.*
Desc: Offers practical articles promoting a happier home, better health, and more fulfilled life. Articles includes human interest stories, family growth, health, nutrition, interviews, with leading personalities on health and the home.
Ind/Abst Consum. Health Nutr. Index (?-?); Cumul. Index Nurs. Allied Health Lit.; Health Index (1989-); Health Period. Database [Full Txt.]; Health Ref. Cent. (Jan. 1989-) [Full Txt.] [Full Cov.]; Seventh-Day Adventist Period. Index (1971-).

US/0886-6554
VIM & VIGOR. (VIM & VIGOR / MANATEE MEMORIAL HOSPITAL.). [Vim vigor]. **Added/Corp** Manatee Memorial Hospital. **VFOAT** Vim and Vigor. Vol. 1, No. 1 (Spring 1985)-. Periodical. English. qt. $11.00. Vim & Vigor, 8805 North 23rd Avenue/Suite 11, Phoenix AZ 85021. **Tel** (602)395-5850, FAX (602)395-5853. **ED** Fred Petrovsky. **DD** 610. **Bk Rev. Ad Acc. Circ:** 950,000 (ctrl).
Desc: Covers medicine, health and fitness.

HT
VISION DU YOGA, LA. Periodical. French. L'Association Haitienne du Kripalu Centre du Yoga, 9 rue Tertulien Guilbaud, Port-Au-Prince Haiti.

US/1043-4194
VISIONS. [Visions]. Periodical. English. bm. $35.00 North America; $60.00 other. Excellence in Exercise Association, 427-3 Amherst Street/Suite 289, Nashua NH 03063. **Tel** (603)595-2384. **ED** Sandra Belknap. **DD** 613. **Bk Rev**. **Ad Acc**. **Circ:** 112,500 (ctrl).
Desc: Geared to aerobic fitness professionals with articles written by CEC Providers.

FR
VITAL. French. mo. 150.00F France; 240.00F other. Vital Service Abonnements, 90 rue de Flandre, 75943 Paris Cedex 19 France. **Tel** 011 33 1 42003500.

CN/0829-6014
VITALITY. ***Ceased.*** (VITALITY : THE WOMEN'S HEALTH EDUCATION NETWORK QUARTERLY.). **Added/Corp** Women's Health Education Network. Vol. 6, No. 4 (Winter 1984)-(19??). Periodical. English. Four times a year. Womens Health Education Network, PO Box 99, Debert NS M0M 1G0, Canada. **Tel** (902)798-5274. **DD** 613/.04244/05. **Bk Rev**. **Ad Acc**. ***Continues*** *Monthly (Women's Health Education Network), 0829-6006.*

US/1074-5831
VITALITY (DALLAS, TEX.). (VITALITY.). [Vitality]. **VFOAT** A.Vitality magazine. (1987)-. Periodical. English. mo. $14.03. Vitality Magazine, 8080 North Central, Suite 1510, Dallas TX 75206. **Tel** (214)691-1480, FAX (214)891-8202. **DD** 613.

CN/1183-3025
VOTRE SANTE (TORONTO), A. (TO YOUR HEALTH.). [A votre sante]. **Added/Corp** Ontario. Ministry of Health. Vol. 1, No. 2 (Summer 1991)-. Periodical. English (French). qt. Ministry of Health / Toronto, Queen's Park, Toronto Ontario M7A 1S2 Canada. **Tel** (800)268-1153, (416)327-4327. **DD** 362.1. ***Continues*** *A Votre Sante (Toronto, Ont.)., 1183-3025.*

US/1042-2102
WALKING MAGAZINE, THE. [Walk. mag.]. (19??)-. Periodical. English. Six times a year. $15.00. Walking Inc., 9 11 Harcourt Street, Boston MA 02116. **Tel** (617)266-3322. **(Subscription address:** Neodata / Colorado, PO Box 2606, Boulder Boulder CO 80322.**) ED** Brad Ketchum. **LC** GV199; .W35. **DD** 796.5/105. **Bk Rev**. **Ad Acc**. **Circ:** 500,000 (ctrl).
Desc: Focuses on walking as a lifestyle activity with features on health, exercise, nutrition, travel and equipment.
Ind/Abst Acad. Abstr. Full Text Elite (Jan. 1992-); Acad. Abstr. (Jan. 1992-); Acad. Search (Jan. 1992-); Health Source (Jan. 1992-); INFO-SOUTH Abstr.; Mag. Search; Phys. Educ. Index (1990-).

US/1062-4368
WBF BODYBUILDING LIFESTYLES : THE OFFICIAL PUBLICATION OF THE WORLD BODYBUILDING FEDERATION. [WBF bodybuild. lifestyles]. **Added/Corp** World Bodybuilding Federation. **VFOAT** WBF Body Building Life Styles; Bodybuilding Lifestyles. Vol. 1, No. 10 (Nov. 1991)-. Periodical. English. mo. $24.95 US; $39.54 Canada. Titansports, Inc., PO Box 420234, Palm Coast FL 32142-0234. **LC** WMLC L 83/9151. **DD** 613. ***Continues*** *Bodybuilding Lifestyles, 1051-2179.*

US/0043-2180
WEIGHT WATCHERS. (WEIGHT WATCHERS MAGAZINE.). [Weight watchers]. **VFOAT** Weight Watchers Magazine. Vol. 1 (Feb. 1968)-. Periodical. English. Twelve times a year. $15.97 (one year); $31.94 (two years); $47.91 (three years). Weight Watchers Magazine, 360 Lexington Avenue, 11th Floor, New York NY 10017. **Tel** (212)370-0644. **(Subscription address:** Neodata / Colorado, PO Box 2606, Boulder Boulder CO 80322.**) ED** Lee Haiken. **LC** RM222.2; .W32. **Ad Acc**. available on microfilm and microfiche from University Microfilms International (UMI). Documents available from UMI Article Clearinghouse.
Desc: Written for people who want to stay trim and fit; about nutrition, exercise, self-discovery and personal health, with fashion, beauty and grooming advice.
Ind/Abst AGRICOLA [Select. Cov.]; Consum. Health Nutr. Index (?-?); Foods Adlibra; Gen. Period. Index (1985-); Health Index (1989-); Health Period. Database; Health Ref. Cent. (Jan. 1989-) [Full Cov.]; Health Source (Jul. 1989-); Mag. Artic. Summar. Elite (July 1989-); Mag. Artic. Summar. Select (July 1989-); Mag. Artic. Summar. CD-ROM (July 1989-); Mag. Index Plus (1989-); Mag. Index. Sel. (1986-); Mag. Search; Newsp. Period. Abstr. (1989-); Mag. Index (1977-); Vocat. Search (July 1989-).

AT
WELLNESS : MAXIMUM PHYSICAL & MENTAL HEALTH. English. mo. 35.00Aus$. Jericho Publishing Pty Ltd, PO Box 572, Wahroonga NSW 2076 Australia. **Tel** 011 61 02 489 7427.

US/8756-5048
WELLNESS NEW MEXICO. **Added/Corp** Wellness New Mexico Association. (1984)-. Periodical. English. qt. $8.00. Wellness New Mexico Association, Box 36634, Albuquerque NM 87176-6634. **Tel** (505)884-2756.

US/0740-8498
WELLNESS NEWSLETTER, THE. [Wellness newsl.]. **Added/Corp** Wellness Institute. (19??)-. Periodical. English. Six times a year. $30.00 US; $35.00 Canada; $40.00 other. The Wellness Newsletter, 3451 Central Avenue, St. Petersburg FL 33713. **Tel** (813)321-0841. **ED** Carolyn Chambers Clark. Index available. cum. index. **Bk Rev**.
Desc: Health promotion/disease prevention focus. Topics include stress, nutrition, fitness, self-care, relationships, environment, current wellness research, events and free resources.

CN/1187-7472
WELLSPRING (EDMONTON). (WELL SPRING.). [WellSpring]. **Added/Corp** Alberta Centre for Well-Being. Vol. 2, No. 4 (Fall 1991)-. Periodical. English. qt. Free to members. Alberta Centre for Well-Being, 12245-131 St., Edmonton Alberta T5L 1M8. **DD** 613. ***Continues*** *Newsletter (Alberta Centre for Well-Being)., 1187-7480.*

UK/0957-1728
WHICH? WAY TO HEALTH. [Which? way health]. (1988)-. Periodical. English. Six times a year (Feb., Apr., June, Aug., Oct., Dec.). $23.00. Consumers Association, Castlemead, Gascoyne Way, Hertford SG14 1LH England. **Tel** 011 44 992 587773. **DD** 613. ***Continues*** *Self Health, 0265-5497.*

UK
WOMEN'S HEALTH. (19??)-. Newsletter. English. Four times a year. £15.00 (institutions), £10.00 (individuals) UK; £20.00 (institutions), £12.00 (individuals) Europe; £25.00 (institutions), £14.00 (individuals) other. Women's Health, 52 Featherstone Street, London EC1Y 8R7 England. **Tel** 011 44 1 2516580, FAX 011 44 71 6080928. ***Continues*** *Newsletter - Women's Health and Reproductive Rights Information Centre, 0954-6677.*
Desc: Covers women's health issues.

US/1049-3867
WOMEN'S HEALTH ISSUES. **See** Women's Interests.

HU/0230-3035
WORLD WEIGHTLIFTING. Vol. 1 (1981)-. Periodical. English. qt. $20.00 US; $15.00 other. Tamas Ajan, General Secretary IWF, 1442 Budapest PF 116 Hungary. **Tel** 36-11-311162, FAX 36-11-311162, telex 227553. **ED** Jeno Boskovics and Aniko Nemeth-Mora. **LC** GV546; .I58A. **Ad Acc**. ctrl circ. ***Continues*** *Bulletin / International Weightlifting Federation.*
Desc: Official publication of the International Weight Lifting Federation and AIPS.
Ind/Abst SPORT Discus.

PL/0043-9630
WYCHOWANIE FIZYCZNE I SPORT. [Wychow. Fiz. Sport]. (1957)-. Periodical. Polish (summaries and/or abstracts in English and Russian). qt. $30.00. **(Subscription address:** ARS Polona, PO Box 1001, 00068 Warsaw Poland.**) UDC** 796.

US
YMCA DIRECTORY. **See** Sociology-Social Services and Welfare.

SZ
YMCA WORLD. **See** Recreation, Leisure.

US/0191-0965
YOGA JOURNAL. (19??)-. Periodical. English. Six times a year. $21.00 US; $27.47 Canada; $26.00 Mexico; $34.00 other. California Yoga Teachers Association, 2054 University Avenue, Berkeley CA 94704. **Tel** (510)841-9200, FAX (510)644-3101. **(Subscription address:** PO Box 469018, Escondido, CA 92046-9018, (800)334-8152**)) ED** Stephan Bodian. Index available. **Bk Rev**. **Ad Acc**. **Circ:** 55,000. available on microfilm and microfiche from University Microfilms International (UMI).
Desc: Body/mind approaches to personal and spiritual development and on people who in their life and work, epitomize these practices.

US/1055-6036
YOUR CHILD'S HEALTH AND DEVELOPMENT. **See** Family and Marriage.

CC/1000-3525
ZHONGHUA WUSHU. (CHUNG-HUA WU SHU.). [Zhonghua wushu]. **Added/Corp** Chung-Kuo Wu Shu Hsieh Hui. (1982)-. Periodical. Chinese. mo. $41.30. Zhongguo Wushu Xiehui, China Wushu Association, Renmin Tiyu Chubanshe, (People's Sports Publishing House), 8 Tiyuguan Lu, Chongwen Qu, Beijing 100061 People's Republic of China. **Tel** 5112466, FAX 7016129. **(Subscription address:** China Books & Periodicals Inc., 2929 24th Street, San Francisco CA 94110.**) LC** GV1100.7.A2; C47. **DD** 796.8/15.

ABSTRACTING, BIBLIOGRAPHIES AND STATISTICS

US
HEALTH INDEX [COMPUTER FILE]. Abstracting/Indexing Service. English. mo. $2600.00 (with InfoTrac Workstation), $1600.00 (without hardware) basic subscription; $2200.00 (with InfoTrac Workstation), $1200.00 (without hardware) school year subscription. Information Access Company, 362 Lakeside Drive, Foster City CA 94404. **Tel** (800)227-8431.
Desc: Designed to provide the most current information available concerning personal health care. Provides indexing and abstracting to health journals, consumer oriented magazines and newsletters covering topics such as diseases and treatments, nutrition guidelines, AIDS, cancer, heart conditions, and coping with chronic disease and disability.

US
HEALTH PERIODICALS DATABASE [ONLINE DATABASE]. Abstracting/Indexing Service. English. Information Access Company, 362 Lakeside Drive, Foster City CA 94404. **Tel** (800)227-8431.
Desc: Contains and comprehensive coverage of publications in the areas of health, medicine, fitness and nutrition.

●US/1063-9810
HEALTH SOURCE (PEABODY, MASS.). (HEALTH SOURCE.). **Added/Corp** EBSCO Publishing (Firm). (1992)-. Abstracting/Indexing Service. English. bm (also available monthly and quarterly). $795.00 (quarterly), $995.00 (bimonthly), $1995.00 (monthly). EBSCO Publishing / Boston, 83 Pine Street, Peabody MA 01960. **Tel** (800)653-2726 North America, (508)535-8500, FAX (508)535-8545. **ED** Melissa Kummerer.
Desc: Consumer health reference product that provides access to abstract and index coverage of over 160 journals in the fields of diet and nutrition, exercise, medical self-care, drugs and alcohol, and consumer products. Full text of 15 important journals is accompanied by tables, charts and selected graphic images on a single disc.

HEATING, PLUMBING, AND REFRIGERATION

US/0360-0793
ACTIVITIES REPORT - U.S. NATIONAL COMMITTEE FOR THE INTERNATIONAL INSTITUTE OF REFRIGERATION. **Main/Corp** United States National Committee for the International Institute of Refrigeration. **VAT** Activities Report - United States National Committee for the International Institute of Refrigeration. Trade Publication. English. US National Committee for the International Institute of Refrigeration, 2101 Constitution Avenue, Washington DC 20418. **LC** TP490; .U5312. **DD** 621.5/6/0621.

UK/0266-6871
AIR CONDITIONING & REFRIGERATION NEWS. [Air cond. refrig. news]. **VFOAT** Air Conditioning and Refrigeration News; ACRN. (1984)-. Trade Publication. English. mo. £26.00 UK; £34.00 other. Faversham House Group Ltd, 111 St. James Road, Croydon, Surrey CR9 2TH England. **Tel** 011 44 81 6844082, , FAX 011 44 81 6849729, telex 266332 HET. **DD** 338.4762156.

US/0002-2276
AIR CONDITIONING, HEATING & REFRIGERATION NEWS. [Air cond. heat. refrig. news]. **VFOAT** Air Conditioning, Heating, and Refrigeration News; Directory Issue; Directory Section. **VAT** Air Conditioning, Heating and Refrigeration News. Vol. 85, No. 14 (Dec. 1, 1958)-. Trade Publication. English. wk. $76.00 US; $96.00 Canada. Business News Publishing Company, 755 West Big Beaver Road, Suite 1000, Troy MI 48084. **Tel** (810)362-3700, FAX (810)362-0317, telex 230295. **ED** Thomas A Mahoney and Wayne C Johnson. **DD** 621. Index available. cum. index. **Bk Rev**. **Ad Acc**. **Circ:** 33,000. available on microfilm and microfiche from University Microfilms International (UMI); available on an online database from DIALOG; and BRS. ***Continues*** *Air Conditioning and Refrigeration News;* ***Absorbed*** *Air Engineering, 0568-3459.*
Desc: Publication of record of the HVAC/R industry since 1926. Only weekly newspaper serving field with news, features, columns, editorials, listings, directories, and special issues.
Ind/Abst Appl. Sci. Technol. Index; Bus. ASAP (1990-) [Full Txt.]; Bus. Index (1985-); Bus. Period. Index; F&S Index Plus Text, Int. [Select. Cov.]; Gas Abstr. (?-?); Gen. BusinessFile (1985-); Gen. Period. Index (1985-); Mag. Search; Predicasts; PROMT; Stat. Ref. Index; Trade Ind. ASAP [Full Txt.]; Trade Ind. Index (1981-) [Full Txt.]; Vocat. Search (Jan. 1993-).

US
AIR CONDITIONING, HEATING & REFRIGERATION NEWS : DIRECTORY SECTIONS. (1963)-. Directory. English. an. $35.00. Business News Publishing Company, 755 West Big

Beaver Road, Suite 1000, Troy MI 48084. **Tel** (810)362-3700, FAX (810)362-0317, telex 230295. ***Continues*** *Air Conditioning, Heating and Refrigeration News; Directory Issue.*
Desc: Contains comprehensive coverage of profiting strategies, service techniques and business management tips that keep contractors, wholesalers, manufacturers and engineers intelligently informed.

CN
ALLPRISER. (19??)-. Trade Publication. English (French). Seventeen times a year (Every 2 or 3 weeks). 75.00Can$ Western Canada; 160.00Can$ US & Eastern Canada; 180.00Can$ others. Allpriser Limited, Box 307 Station D, East Tobicoke Ontario M9A 4X3 Canada. **Tel** (416)247-8219, FAX (416)247-4961. **ED** Keith Ottaway and Bob Fleming. Index available (bound in issues). **Circ:** 8,000 (ctrl). available on diskette from the publisher.
Desc: Plumbing and heating price guide showing suggested resale prices.

BL
ANUARIO BRASILEIRO DO FRIO. 1973-. Trade Publication. Portuguese. Editar Publicacoes Tecnicas Ltda, Av Sao Joao 1113 Lo and CJ 5/6, Sao Paulo Brazil. **LC** TP490; .A65.

US/1041-2344
ASHRAE HANDBOOK. (ASHRAE HANDBOOK. FUNDAMENTALS.). **Added/Corp** American Society of Heating, Refrigerating and Air-Conditioning Engineers. **VFOAT** Fundamentals; Fundamentals Handbook; ASHRAE Handbook ... Fundamentals I-P. (1985)-. Trade Publication. English. ir (every 4 years). $119.00. ASHRAE Publications / American Society of Heating, Refrigerating and Air-Conditioning Engineers, 1791 Tullie Circle Northeast, Atlanta GA 30329. **Tel** (404)636-8400, FAX (404)321-5478, telex 705343 ASHRAE. **LC** TH7201; .A82. ***Continues in part*** *ASHRAE Handbook. Fundamentals, 0732-8591.*

US
ASHRAE HANDBOOK. HEATING, VENTILATING, AND AIR-CONDITIONING APPLICATIONS. **Added/Corp** American Society of Heating, Refrigerating and Air-Conditioning Engineers. **VFOAT** American Society of Heating, Refrigerating and Air-Conditioning Engineers Handbook. Heating, Ventilating, and Air-o; Air Conditioning Applications; Heating, Ventilating, and Air-Conditioning Applications; HVAC Applications; ASHRAE Handbook. HVAC Applications; Applications Handbook. (1991)-. Trade Publication. English. ir (every 4 years). $119.00. ASHRAE Publications / American Society of Heating, Refrigerating and Air-Conditioning Engineers, 1791 Tullie Circle Northeast, Atlanta GA 30329. **Tel** (404)636-8400, FAX (404)321-5478, telex 705343 ASHRAE. **LC** TH7015; .A74. ***Continues in part*** *ASHRAE Handbook. Heating, Ventilating, and Air-Conditioning Systems and Applications, 1041-2344.*

●US/1041-2344
ASHRAE HANDBOOK. HEATING, VENTILATING, AND AIR-CONDITIONING SYSTEMS AND EQUIPMENT. **Added/Corp** American Society of Heating, Refrigerating and Air-Conditioning Engineers. **VFOAT** Heating, Ventilating, and Air-Conditioning Systems and Equipment; ASHRAE Handbook. HVAC Systems and Equipment; Systems and Equipment Handbook (SI); HVAC Systems and Equipment. **VAT** American Society of Heating, Refrigerating and Air-Conditioning Engineers Handbook. Heating, Ventilating, and Air-Conditioning Systems and Equipment. (1992)-. Monographic series. English. ir (every 4 years). $119.00. ASHRAE Publications / American Society of Heating, Refrigerating and Air-Conditioning Engineers, 1791 Tullie Circle Northeast, Atlanta GA 30329. **Tel** (404)636-8400, FAX (404)321-5478, telex 705343 ASHRAE. ***Continues in part*** *ASHRAE Handbook. Equipment* ***and*** *ASHRAE Handbook. Heating, Ventilating, and Air-Conditioning Systems and Applications.*

●US
ASHRAE HANDBOOK. HEATING, VENTILATING, AND AIR-CONDITIONING SYSTEMS AND EQUIPMENT. **Added/Corp** American Society of Heating, Refrigerating and Air-Conditioning Engineers. **VFOAT** American Society of Heating, Refrigerating and Air-Conditioning Engineers Handbook. Heating, Ventilating, and Air-Conditioning Systems and Equipment; Heating, Ventilating, and Air-Conditioning Systems and Equipment; HVAC Systems and Equipment; ASHRAE Handbook. HVAC Systems and Equipment; Systems and Equipment Handbook. (1992)-. Trade Publication. English. ir (every 4 years). $119.00. ASHRAE Publications / American Society of Heating, Refrigerating and Air-Conditioning Engineers, 1791 Tullie Circle Northeast, Atlanta GA 30329. **Tel** (404)636-8400, FAX (404)321-5478, telex 705343 ASHRAE. ***Continues in part*** *ASHRAE Handbook. Heating, Ventilating, and Air-Conditioning Systems and Applications.*

US
ASHRAE HANDBOOK. REFRIGERATION SYSTEMS AND APPLICATIONS. **Added/Corp** American Society of Heating, Refrigerating and Air-Conditioning Engineers. **VFOAT** Refrigeration Systems and Applications; Refrigeration. **VAT** American Society of Heating, Refrigerating and Air Conditioning Engineers handbook. Refrigeration Systems and Applications. (1986)-. Trade Publication. English. ir (every four years). $119.00. ASHRAE Publications / American Society of Heating, Refrigerating and Air-Conditioning Engineers, 1791 Tullie Circle Northeast, Atlanta GA 30329. **Tel** (404)636-8400, FAX (404)321-5478, telex 705343 ASHRAE. **ED** Robert A. Parsons. **LC** TP490; .A75. **DD** 621.56/05. Index available. **Bk Rev. Circ:** 50,000 (ctrl). ***Continues in part*** *ASHRAE Handbook. Applications, 0737-3651* ***and*** *ASHRAE Handbook. Systems, 0742-9126.*
Desc: Describes refrigeration and freezing of foods. Low temperature and other industrial applications are also covered.

US/0891-4249
ASHRAE INSIGHTS. (ASHRAE INSIGHTS : THE NEWSPAPER OF THE AMERICAN SOCIETY OF HEATING, REFRIGERATING AND AIR-CONDITIONING ENGINEERS, INC.). [ASHRAE insights]. **Added/Corp** American Society of Heating, Refrigerating and Air-Conditioning Engineers. **VFOAT** A.S.H.R.A.E. Insights. **VAT** American Society of Heating, Refrigerating and Air-Conditioning Engineers Insights. Vol. 1, No. 1 (Sept. 1986)-. Trade Publication. English. mo. Comes with ASHRAE membership. ASHRAE Publications / American Society of Heating, Refrigerating and Air-Conditioning Engineers, 1791 Tullie Circle Northeast, Atlanta GA 30329. **Tel** (404)636-8400, FAX (404)321-5478, telex 705343 ASHRAE.
Desc: Newsletter that published for ASHRAE members.

US/0001-2491
ASHRAE JOURNAL. [ASHRAE j.]. **Added/Corp** American Society of Heating, Refrigerating and Air-Conditioning Engineers. Vol. 1, No. 3 (March 1959)-. Trade Publication. English. mo. $49.00 US; $69.00 other. ASHRAE Publications / American Society of Heating, Refrigerating and Air-Conditioning Engineers, 1791 Tullie Circle Northeast, Atlanta GA 30329. **Tel** (404)636-8400, FAX (404)321-5478, telex 705343 ASHRAE. **ED** Stephen W. Comstock. **CODEN** ASHRAA. **[CCC].** Index available (bound in Jan. issue). **Bk Rev. Ad Acc. Pr Rev. Circ:** 50,000 (ctrl). available on microfilm and microfiche from University Microfilms International (UMI). Documents available from Article Express International, The Genuine Article, CASDDS. ***Absorbed*** *Refrigerating Engineering, 0096-0470* ***and*** *Journal of the American Society of Heating and Air-Conditioning Engineers, 0402-1185.*
Desc: Official voice of the American Society of Heating, Refrigerating and Air Conditioning Engineers; includes technical articles on heating, refrigeration, air conditioning, etc.
Ind/Abst Appl. Sci. Technol. Index; Bioeng. Abstr.; Chem. Abstr. (1959-1983); Constr. Index (199?-); Curr. Contents Eng. Tech. Appl. Sci.; Ei Page One; EMBASE; Energy Inf. Abstr.; Energy Res. Abstr.; Eng. Index Annu. [Select. Cov.]; Fluid Abstr., Civil Eng.; Fluid Abstr. Proc. Eng.; FLUIDEX (1973-); Gas Abstr.; Hortic. Abstr.; HTFS Dig.; INIS Atomindex [Micro.]; Int. Aerosp. Abstr.; Int. Build. Serv. Abstr.; Int. Civil Eng. Abstr.; Res. Alert [Select. Cov.]; Risk Abstr.; Saf. Health Work; SCISEARCH; Soft. Abstr. Eng. (1973-).

US/0884-0490
ASHRAE TECHNICAL DATA BULLETIN. [ASHRAE tech. data bull.]. **Added/Corp** American Society of Heating, Refrigerating and Air-Conditioning Engineers. **VFOAT** Technical Data Bulletin. Vol. 1, No. 1 (1985)-. Bulletin. English. ir. Price varies per volume. ASHRAE Publications / American Society of Heating, Refrigerating and Air-Conditioning Engineers, 1791 Tullie Circle Northeast, Atlanta GA 30329. **Tel** (404)636-8400, FAX (404)321-5478, telex 705343 ASHRAE. **LC** TH7201; .A84. **DD** 696/.05. **[CCC].**
Ind/Abst Coal Abstr.; Fluid Abstr., Civil Eng.; Fluid Abstr. Proc. Eng.; FLUIDEX.

US/0001-2505
ASHRAE TRANSACTIONS. [ASHRAE trans.]. **Added/Corp** American Society of Heating, Refrigerating and Air-Conditioning Engineers. **VFOAT** A.S.H.R.A.E. Transactions. **VAT** American Society of Heating, Refrigeration and Air-Conditioning Engineers Transactions. Vol. 74, Pt. 2 (1968)-. Trade Publication. English. sa. $340.00 (nonmembers), $230.00 (members). ASHRAE Publications / American Society of Heating, Refrigerating and Air-Conditioning Engineers, 1791 Tullie Circle Northeast, Atlanta GA 30329. **Tel** (404)636-8400, FAX (404)321-5478, telex 705343 ASHRAE. **LC** TH7201; .A5. **DD** 621. **CODEN** ASHTAG. **[CCC].** available on microfilm and microfiche from University Microfilms International (UMI). Documents available from Article Express International, CASDDS. ***Continues*** *American Society of Heating, Refrigerating and Air-Conditioning Engineers. Transactions, 0888-4366.*
Desc: Contains the latest information on environmental control, new applications, design and operating techniques.
Ind/Abst Bioeng. Abstr.; Chem. Abstr. (1968-1981); Ei Page One; Energy Res. Abstr. (April 1975-); Eng. Index Annu.; Food Sci. Technol. Abstr.; Gas Abstr.; HTFS Dig.; INIS Atomindex [Micro.]; Int. Aerosp. Abstr.; Int. Build. Serv. Abstr. (199?-); Int. Civil Eng. Abstr.; Soft. Abstr. Eng.

AT/0817-6337
AUSTRALIAN PLUMBING INDUSTRY MAGAZINE. [Aust. plumb. ind.]. (1986)-. Trade Publication. English. Six times a year (Feb., Apr., June, Aug., Oct., Dec.). 48.00Aus$ Australia; 60.00Aus$ other. Master Plumbers Mechanical Services, 525 King Street, West Melbourne VIC 3003 Australia. **Tel** 011 61 03 3299622, FAX 011 61 03 3295060, telex 34822. **ED** Mr. Ray Herbert. **DD** 338.4769610994. **Ad Acc. Circ:** 6,000. ***Continues*** *Victorian Plumbing Industry Journal, 0816-6722.*

AT
AUSTRALIAN REFRIGERATION, AIR CONDITIONING AND HEATING. **Added/Corp** Australian Institute of Refrigeration, Air Conditioning & Heating. Cold Storage Association of Australia. Commonwealth Associated Ice Industries (Australia) Commonwealth Cold Storage Association (Australia) Institute of Refrigeration and Air Conditioning Service Engineers (Australia). Vol. 17 No. 1 (July 1963)-. Trade Publication. English. Thirteen times a year. 90.00Aus$ Australia; 235.00Aus$ other. Yaffa Publishing Group Pty Ltd., GPO Box 606, Sydney NSW 2001 Australia. **Tel** 011 61 2 2812333, FAX 011 61 2 2812750. **ED** John Bremner. **LC** TP490; .R438. **Bk Rev. Ad Acc. Circ:** 2,900 (ctrl). Documents available from Article Express International. ***Continues*** *Refrigeration, Air Conditioning and Heating.*
Desc: Journal for the climate control industry; concentrates on technical articles for engineers.
Ind/Abst Eng. Index Annu. [Select. Cov.]; Int. Build. Serv. Abstr.

US/0194-0023
AUTOMOTIVE AIR CONDITIONING AND HEATING SERVICE MANUAL : BOOK SUPPLEMENT. **See** Transportation-Automobiles.

CN/0225-9206
BATH & KITCHEN MARKETER. ***Ceased.*** **See** Interior Design.

GW
BERICHT UBER DIE KALTE-KLIMA-TAGUNG ... DES DEUTSCHEN KALTE- UND KLIMATECHNISCHEN VEREINS E.V (DKV). **Added/Corp** Deutscher Kalte- und Klimatechnischer Verein. **VFOAT** DKV-Tagungsbericht. (198?)-. Trade Publication. German. Deutscher Kaelte und Klimatechnischer Verein, Pfaffenwaldring 10, 7000 Stuttgart 80 Germany. **Tel** 0711 685 3200, FAX 0711 685 3242. **LC** TP490; .D4a. **DD** 621.5. Documents available from CASDDS. ***Continues*** *Bericht uber die Jahrestagung ... des Deutschen Kalte- und Klimatechnischen Vereins e.V. (DKV).*
Ind/Abst Chem. Abstr.

US/0897-0092
BOCA NATIONAL MECHANICAL CODE, THE. [BOCA natl. mech. code]. **Main/Corp** Building Officials and Code Administrators International. **VFOAT** National Mechanical Code. **VAT** Building Officials and Code Administrators National Mechanical Code. 6th Edition (1987)-. Trade Publication. English. ir (Every three years). $44.00 building officials, code administrators, nonmembers, soft cover; $29.00 members, soft cover; $48.00 nonmembers, loose-leaf; $33.00 members, loose-leaf. BOCA International, 4051 West Flossmoore Road, Country Club Hills IL 60478. **Tel** (708)799-2300, FAX (708)799-4981. **LC** KF5701.A73; B82. **DD** 343.73/078624; 347.30378624. ***Continues*** *Building Officials and Code Administrators International. BOCA Basic/National Mechanical Code.*

US/1055-6680
BOCA NATIONAL PLUMBING CODE, THE. [BOCA natl. plumb. code]. **Main/Corp** Building Officials and Code Administrators International. **VFOAT** National Plumbing Code. **VAT** Building Officials and Code Administrators National Plumbing Code. 7th. Edition (1987)-. Trade Publication. English. ir (Every three years). $30.00 (members), $45.00 (non-members) soft cover; $34.00 (members), $49.00 (non-members) loose leaf. BOCA International, 4051 West Flossmoore Road, Country Club Hills IL 60478. **Tel** (708)799-2300, FAX (708)799-4981. **LC** KF5709; .B8. **DD** 343. ***Continues*** *Building Officials and Code Administrators International. BOCA Basic/National Plumbing Code.*

US
BOOK OF SUCCESSFUL FIREPLACES. **Added/Corp** Donley Brothers Company, Cleveland. (1917)-. Trade Publication. English. **ED** R. J. Lytle and Marie-Jeanne Lytle. **LC** TH7426.D6; B6. **DD** 697.1.

US
BRADFORD PRICE BOOK. (19??)-. Trade Publication. English. $96.00. Harrison Publishing House, PO Box 29, Quincy MA 02269. **Tel** (617)773-1870, FAX

(603)444-0826.
Desc: Pricing service for the plumbing/heating/mechanical trades.

UK
BUILDING SERVICES : THE CIBSE JOURNAL. See Building and Construction.

FR/0020-6970
BULLETIN DE L'INSTITUT INTERNATIONAL DU FROID. [Bull. Inst. int. froid]. **Added/Corp** International Institute of Refrigeration. **VFOAT** Bulletin of the International Institute of Refrigeration. Vol. 15E No. 1 (Jan/Feb 1934)-. Bulletin. French (English). bm. 590.00F. Intl Inst of Refrigeration, 177 Boulevard Malesherbes, 75017 Paris France. **Tel** 011 33 1 42273235, FAX 011 33 1 4763 1798, telex 643269F ININFRI. **LC** TP490; .I64. **DD** 621.5605. ***Continues*** *Bulletin International de Renseignements Frigorifiques;* ***Absorbed*** *Bulletin of the International Institute of Refrigeration.*
Ind/Abst Dairy Sci. Abstr.; Food Sci. Technol. Abstr.; Hortic. Abstr.

FR/0750-1552
C.F.P. CHAUD FROID PLOMBERIE. (1971)-. Trade Publication. French. mo (except Aug.). 510.00F France; 850.00F other. Editions Parisiennes, 4 rue Charles Divry, 75014 Paris France. **Tel** 011 33 1 45409599, FAX 011 33 1 45410230. **UDC** 696. Index available. **Bk Rev. Ad Acc.**
Desc: Technical articles about heating, ventilating, and air conditioning.

CN/0700-1223
CANADIAN PLUMBING CODE. [Can. plumb. code]. **Added/Corp** National Research Council Canada. Associate Committee on the National Building Code. 1st Ed. (1970)-. English. ir. 25.00Can$. National Research Council of Canada, Receiver General for Canada, Ottawa Ontario K1A 0R6 Canada. **Tel** (613)993-0362, FAX (613)952-7656. **DD** 343.71/0786961/02632.

CN/1184-177X
CANADIAN RESIDENTIAL HEATING SURVEY (1990). (CANADIAN RESIDENTIAL HEATING SURVEY / PREPARED BY ECONOMICS/STATISTICS DEPARTMENT.). [Can. resid. heat. surv.]. **Added/Corp** Canadian Gas Association. Economics/Statistics Dept. (1990)-. English. an (April). $60.00 nonmembers; $30.00 members. Canadian Gas Association, 243 Consumers Road / Suite 1200, North York Ontario M2J 5E3 Canada. **Tel** (416)498-1994, FAX (416)498-7465. **DD** 697/.00971/021. ***Separated from*** *Canadian Gas Facts., 0316-3547.*
Desc: Covers the penetration and expansion of natural gas in the residential heating market. Provides annual estimates of the residential heating market by fuel, by province, and by year for the past five years.

GW/0009-8914
CCI. CLIMA COMMERCE INTERNATIONAL. [CCI, Clima commer. int.]. **VFOAT** Clima Commerce International; Heizung und Klima. (1967)-. Trade Publication. German. ir (14 issues). DM198.00. Promotor, Verlags und Forderungsgesellschaft mbH, Postfach 21 10 53, D-76160 Karlsruhe Germany. **Tel** 011/49/721/5590232, FAX 011/49/721/590525. **ED** Geunther Keller. **UDC** 697. **Ad Acc, Adv Mgr:** Mrs. Finne. **Circ:** 5,500 (ctrl).
Desc: Information and news for qualified employees of heating, air conditioning, refrigeration and climatization.

AT
CELSIUS. (19??)-. Trade Publication. English. Twelve times a year. 60.00Aus$ Australia; 120.00Aus$ other. Secretary Celsius Management, PO Box 118, Flemington Market, 2129 New South Wales Australia. **Tel** 011 61 2 764-3404, FAX 011 61 2 764-2697. **ED** Phillip Ross, (editor's address: 485 Princes Highway, St. Peters, New South Wales, 2044 Australia, phone: 011 61 2 519 8300). **Bk Rev. Ad Acc. Circ:** 2,500.

BE
CHALEUR ET CLIMATS / WARMTE EN KLIMAAT. **Added/Corp** Union Royale Belge des Installateurs en Chauffage Central, Ventilation et Tuyauteries. Association Belge des Bruleurs Automatiques. Association Technique de l'Industrie du Chauffage, de la Ventilation et des Branches Connexes. **VFOAT** Warmte en Klimaat. (1986)-. Trade Publication. Dutch (French). mo. 2100F Belgium; 2400F others. Editions Coppieters, Bld de Smet de Naeyer, 393 BTE5, B-1090 Brussels Belgium. **Tel** 011 32 2 4783300, FAX 011 32 2 4783502. **LC** TH7005; .C47. **DD** 697/.005. ***Continues*** *Installateur.*

FR/0009-2029
CHAUFFAGE, VENTILATION, CONDITIONNEMENT. [Chauff., vent., cond.]. (1937)-. Trade Publication. French. Ten times a year. 480.00F (France); 730.00F (other). PYC Edition, 5 Avenue de Verdun, BP 105, 94208 Ivry S Seine Cedex France. **Tel** 011 33 1 49608636. **ED** Bernard Caroff and Claudie Cabourdin. **LC** TH7201; .C483. **[CCC].** Index available. **Bk Rev. Circ:** 4,000.
Desc: Journal of the Association of French Heating and Ventilation Engineers (AICVF). Including technical articles and information (societies, products manifestations, books, etc.).
Ind/Abst Energy Res. Abstr. (Aug. 1976-); Int. Build. Serv. Abstr.; Saf. Health Work.

II/0009-8930
CLIMATE CONTROL. [Clim. control]. **Added/Corp** All India Air Conditioning and Refrigeration Association. (1968)-. Trade Publication. English. bm. **DD** 621.5. **CODEN** CLCOAH. available on microfilm from University Microfilms International (UMI). Documents available from CASDDS.
Ind/Abst Chem. Abstr.

●US/1066-8683
COGENERATION AND COMPETITIVE POWER JOURNAL. See Engineering-Electricity, Electrical Engineering, Electronics.

US
COLD STORAGE / STATE OF NEW YORK, DEPARTMENT OF AGRICULTURE AND MARKETS. Began in: June 1976. Trade Publication. English. mo (plus annual issue). $21.00 US; $26.50 other. New York Department of Agriculture & Markets, 1 Winners Circle, Capitol Plaza, Albany NY 12235. **Tel** (518)457-4188, FAX (518)457-3087. ***Continues*** *Holdings in Cold Storage, New York State.*

IT/0373-7772
CONDIZIONAMENTO DELL'ARIA, RISCALDAMENTO, REFRIGERAZIONE. **Added/Corp** Associazione Italiana Condizionamento dell'aria, Riscaldamento, Refrigerazione. (1956)-. Trade Publication. Italian (summaries and/or abstracts in English, French and German). mo. $151.00. Editoriale PEG Spa, Via Fratelli Bressan 2, 20126 Milan Italy. **Tel** 011 39 2 2579841, FAX 011 39 2 255-2779, telex 323088 PEGMOS I. **ED** Roberto Sanguineti. **LC** TH7687.A1; C6. **DD** 697/.005. Index available. **Bk Rev. Ad Acc. Circ:** 5,300 (ctrl). ***Continues*** *Condizionamento dell'Aria.*
Desc: High-level reports on technics, studies, existing plants in the fields of air conditioning, heating, refrigeration.

US/1048-3330
CONSUMERS DIRECTORY OF CERTIFIED EFFICIENCY RATINGS FOR RESIDENTIAL HEATING AND WATER HEATING EQUIPMENT. [Consum. dir. certif. effic. rat. resid. heat. water heat. equip.]. **Added/Corp** Gas Appliance Manufacturers Association. ETL Testing Laboratories. (April 1988)-. Directory. English. sa (April, Oct.). $10.00. Gas Appliance Manufacturing Association, 3933 US Route 11, Cortland NY 13045. **Tel** (607)753-6711. **LC** TH7345; .C66. **DD** 697/.00296. ***Formed by the union of*** *Consumers' Directory of Certified Furnace and Boier Efficiency Ratings* ***and*** *Consumers' Directory of Certified Water Heater Efficiency Ratings.*

US/0279-4071
CONTRACTING BUSINESS. [Contract. bus.]. Vol. 38, No. 9 (Sept. 1981)-. Trade Publication. English. Twelve times a year. $50.00 US; $80.00 Canada; $90.00 Mexico; $100.00 other. Penton Publishing, 1100 Superior Avenue, Cleveland OH 44114-2543. **Tel** (216)696-7000, FAX (216)696-0836. **LC** TP490; .A34. **DD** 621. **[CCC].** available on microfilm and microfiche from University Microfilms International (UMI). ***Continues*** *Airconditioning & Refrigeration Business, 0002-2640.*

US/0897-7135
CONTRACTOR (NEWTON, MASS.). (CONTRACTOR.). [Contractor]. (Jan. 1988)-. Trade Publication. English. mo. $70.00 US; $102.00 Canada; $95.00 Mexico; $130.00 (surface mail) other. Cahners Publishing Company, 249 West 17th Street, New York NY 10011. **Tel** (212)645-0067, FAX (212)242-6987. **(Subscription address:** Cahners Publishing Company / Colorado, Paid Subscription Service Center, PO Box 7610, Highlands Ranch CO 80126-7610.**) LC** HD9715.U5; C66. **DD** 338. **[CCC].** ***Continues*** *Contractor Magazine, 0746-2387;* ***Absorbed*** *Plumbing, Heating, Piping, 1055-3231.*
Desc: Features interpretive news and in-depth articles for contractors who install and service air conditioning, heating and plumbing products.
Ind/Abst Bus. Index (1985-); Gen. BusinessFile (1985-); Gen. Period. Index (1985-); Mag. Search; Trade Ind. Index (1981-?).

IT/0393-9723
CORRIERE TERMO IDRO SANITARIO, IL. [Corr. termo idro sanit.]. **VFOAT** TIS. Il Corriere Termo Idro Sanitario; TIS. Termo Idro Sanitario. (1986)-. Trade Publication. Italian. Eleven times a year. L19000.00. Editoriale PEG Spa, Via Fratelli Bressan 2, 20126 Milan Italy. **Tel** 011 39 2 2579841, FAX 011 39 2 255-2779, telex 323088 PEGMOS I. **ED** Robert Sanguineti. **UDC** 628.8. Index available. **Bk Rev. Ad Acc. Circ:** 25,500.
Desc: Technical, practical, and informative matters as to plumbing and sanitary fields.

US
CURRENT INDUSTRIAL REPORTS. MA-34N, SELECTED HEATING EQUIPMENT / U.S. DEPARTMENT OF COMMERCE, BUREAU OF THE CENSUS. **VFOAT** Selected Heating Equipment. Began with 1973. Government Publication. English. an. $1.00. US Department of Commerce / Bureau of the Census, Data User Services Division, Customer Services, Washington DC 20233-0800. **Tel** (301)763-4100. **(Subscription address:** Superintendent of Documents, US Government Printing Office, Washington DC 20402.**) LC** HD9683.U5; S44. **DD** 338.4/76214025/0973. ***Continues*** *Current Industrial Reports. MA-34N, Heating and Cooking Equipment.*
Desc: Presents timely data on the production, inventories, and orders of approximately 5,000 products, which represents 40 percent of all US manufacturing.

US
CURRENT INDUSTRIAL REPORTS. MQ34E PLUMBING FIXTURES (COMPUTER FILE). (1992)-. Government Publication. English. qt. US Department of Commerce, 14th Street & Constitution Avenue NW, Washington DC 20230. **Tel** (202)482-2000, FAX (202)482-3772. ***Continues*** *Current Industrial Reports. MQ34E Plumbing.*

US/1047-7497
DIRECTORY OF CERTIFIED UNITARY AIR-CONDITIONERS, UNITARY AIR-SOURCE HEAT PUMPS, SOUND-RATED OUTDOOR UNITARY EQUIPMENT. **Added/Corp** Air-Conditioning and Refrigeration Institute. **VFOAT** Directory of Certified Unitary Air Conditioners, Unitary Air Source Heat Pumps, Sound Rated Outdoor Unitary Equipment; ARI Unitary Directory. **VAT** Air-Conditioning and Refrigeration Institute Unitary Directory. (19??)-. Directory. English. Twice a year (Feb. & Aug.). $20.00. Air Condition & Refrigeration Institute, 4301 North Fairfax Drive, Arlington VA 22203. **Tel** (703)524-8800. **LC** TH7687.7; .D57. **DD** 697.9/3/0294.

US
DIRECTORY OF COMMERCIAL CENTRAL AIR CONDITIONERS / PREPARED BY THE NEW YORK STATE ENERGY OFFICE ; PREPARED FOR CENTRAL HUDSON GAS & ELECTRIC ... [ET. AL.]. **Added/Corp** New York (State). State Energy Office. Central Hudson Gas and Electric Corporation. (1991)-. Directory. English.

US
DIRECTORY OF RESIDENTIAL CENTRAL AIR CONDITIONERS / PREPARED BY THE NEW YORK STATE ENERGY OFFICE ; PREPARED FOR CENTRAL HUDSON GAS & ELECTRIC ... [ET. AL.]. **Added/Corp** New York (State). State Energy Office. Central Hudson Gas and Electric Corporation. (1991)-. Directory. English.

US
DISTRICT ENERGY. (19??)-. Trade Publication. English. qt. $40.00. International District Heating and Cooling Association, 1200 19th Street Northwest, Washington DC 20036. **Tel** (202)429-5111, FAX (202)429-5113. ***Continues*** *District Heating and Cooling, 0885-6621.*

US/0885-6621
DISTRICT HEATING AND COOLING. ***Title Change.*** [Dist. heat. cool.]. **Added/Corp** International District Heating and Cooling Association. Vol. 70, No. 4 (2nd Quarter 1985)-(19??). Trade Publication. English. qt. International District Heating and Cooling Association, 1200 19th Street Northwest, Washington DC 20036. **Tel** (202)429-5111, FAX (202)429-5113. **ED** Jack Kattner. **LC** TH7201; .N28. **DD** 697/.54/05. cum. index. **Ad Acc, Adv Mgr:** Tammie Jackson. **Circ:** 825. ***Continues*** *District Heating, 0012-401X.* ***Continued by*** *District Energy, 1077-6222.*
Ind/Abst Coal Abstr.; Ei Page One; Urban Aff. Abstr.

GW/0933-6540
DISTRICT HEATING INTERNATIONAL. [Dist. heat. int.]. **VFOAT** Fernwarme International (1987); Chauffage Urbain International; District Heating (1987). (1987)-. Trade Publication. English (German and French). mo. DM248.00. Verlag Wirtschaftsgesellschaft VWEW, Stresemannallee 23, D 60596 Frankfurt Germany. **Tel** 011 49 69 6304325. **UDC** 697.34. Documents available from Article Express International, Ask*IEEE. ***Continues*** *Fernwaerme International, 0340-3572.*
Ind/Abst Ei Page One; Eng. Index Annu.; INSPEC (Jan./Feb. 1992-).

CN/0822-5877
DOSSIER POELES A BOIS. [Doss. poeles bois]. Vol. 1, No. 1-. Trade Publication. French. an. $2.95 per volume. Decormag, 181 Est, Rue St. Paul, Montreal Quebec H2Y 1G8. **DD** 697/.04.

GW/0174-6189
ELEKTROWARME INTERNATIONAL. EDITION A : ELEKTOWARME IM TECHNISCHEN AUSBAU. [Elektrowrm. int., Ed. A, Elektrowrm. tech. Ausbau]. **Added/Corp** Deutsches Komitee fur Elektrowarme. Elektrowarme-Institut Essen. Elektrowarme-Institut Hannover Fachverband Elektrowarmeanlagen. **VFOAT** Electro-Heat International. Electro-Heat and Technical Equipment; Electrothermie International. L'Electrothermie dans l'Equipment Technique. (Jan. 30, 1972)-. Trade Publication. German (English and French; summaries and/or abstracts in English and French). Four times a year. DM142.00. Vulkan-Verlag, Dr. W. Classen, Postfach 103962, D 45039 Essen 1 Germany. **Tel** 011 49 201 8200214, telex 8579008. **ED** W. Classen. **LC** TK4601; .E375. **CODEN** EIEADN. Index available. cum. index. **Bk Rev. Ad Acc. Circ:** 2,450. Documents available from Article Express International, Ask*IEEE, CASDDS. ***Continues in part*** *Elektrowarme International, 0020-9147.*
Desc: Journal for the entire field of electric heat in the industry of manufacturing and houses.
Ind/Abst Alum. Ind. Abstr.; Bioeng. Abstr.; Chem. Abstr.; Ei Page One; EMBASE; Energy Res. Abstr. (Oct. 1977-); Eng. Mater. Abstr.; Eng. Index Annu.; INSPEC (Jan. 1972-); Int. Aerosp. Abstr.; Met. Abstr.

GW/0340-3521
ELEKTROWARME INTERNATIONAL. EDITION B : INDUSTRIELLE ELEKTROWARME. [Elektrowrm. int., Ed. B, Ind. Elektrowrm.]. **Added/Corp** Deutsches Komitee fur Elektrowarme. Elektrowarme-Institut Essen. Elektrowarme-Institut Hannover. Fachverband Elektrowarmeanlagen. **VFOAT** Electro-Heat International. Edition B, Industrial Applications of Electro-Heat; Electrothermie International. Edition B, Applications Industrielles d'Electrothermie. (Jan. 30, 1972)-. Trade Publication. German (French and English; summaries and/or abstracts in English and French). Four times a year. DM142.00. Vulkan-Verlag, Dr. W. Classen, Postfach 103962, D 45039 Essen 1 Germany. **Tel** 011 49 201 8200214, telex 8579008. **ED** W. Classen. **LC** TK4601; .E38. **CODEN** EIEBDQ. **[CCC].** Index available. cum. index. **Bk Rev. Ad Acc. Circ:** 2,500. Documents available from Article Express International, Ask*IEEE, CASDDS. ***Continues in part*** *Elektrowarme Internationale, 0020-9147.*
Desc: Journal of industrial, commercial and domestic applications of Electro-Heat.
Ind/Abst Alum. Ind. Abstr.; Bioeng. Abstr.; Chem. Abstr.; Coal Abstr.; Ei Page One; Energy Res. Abstr. (Oct. 1977-); Eng. Mater. Abstr.; Eng. Index Annu.; INSPEC (Feb. 1972-); Met. Abstr.

BE/0777-6357
ENTREPRISE 1951, L'. [Entreprise 1951]. (1951)-. Trade Publication. French. Eleven times a year. 850F Belgium; 2100F other. Distrigraph, Ave Alexandre Bertrand 50, 1190 Brussels Belgium. **Tel** (02)343-3347, FAX (02)344-3369. **UDC** 697. Index available. **Bk Rev. Ad Acc. Circ:** 5,000.

GW/0340-3572
FERNWAERME INTERNATIONAL. ***Title Change.*** [Fernwaerme int.]. **Added/Corp** Vereinigung Deutscher Elektrizitaetswerke. International Union of Heating Distributors. (19??)-((19??). Trade Publication. German. Six times a year. Verlag Wirtschaftsgesellschaft VWEW, Stresemannallee 23, D 60596 Frankfurt Germany. **Tel** 011 49 69 6304325. **CODEN** FRWMAG. **[CCC].** Documents available from Article Express International, Ask*IEEE, CASDDS. ***Continued by*** *District Heating International.*
Ind/Abst Bioeng. Abstr.; Chem. Abstr.; Coal Abstr.; Ei Page One; Energy Res. Abstr. (July 1976-); Eng. Index Annu.; INSPEC (1972-); Int. Build. Serv. Abstr.; Int. Civil Eng. Abstr.; Soft. Abstr. Eng.

US
FLORIDA CIRCLE, THE. Added/Corp Florida. Board of Plumbing Commissioners. Florida. Hotel and Restaurant Commission. American Institute of Architects. Florida Association. Vol. 1 (April 1924)-. Trade Publication. English. mo.

US/0046-4112
FLORIDA CONTRACTOR. ***Ceased.*** **Added/Corp** Florida Association of Plumbing-Heating-Cooling Contractors. (19??)-(199?). Trade Publication. English. mo. Florida Association of Plumbing Heating Cooling Contractor, PO Box 13089, Tallahassee FL 32308. **Tel** (904)878-3134. **ED** George Strickland. **Bk Rev. Ad Acc. Circ:** 2,900 (ctrl). ***Continues*** *Florida Plumbing and Heating Contractor.*
Desc: Current information for Florida independent contractors in the PHC business; new products, association news, legislative update, etc.

IT/0016-0296
FREDDO. [Freddo]. **Added/Corp** Associazione Frigorifera Italiana. Notiziario. (1951)-. Trade Publication. Italian. bm (6 issues). $76.00. Editoriale Peg Spa, Via Fratelli Bressan 2, Milan 20126 Italy. **Tel** 011 39 2 2579841, FAX 011 39 2 2552779, telex 323088 PEGMOS I. **ED** Roberto Sanguinen. **CODEN** FREDAZ. Index available (free). **Bk Rev. Ad Acc. Circ:** 2,250 (ctrl). Documents available from Ask*IEEE, CASDDS.
Desc: High-level technical articles on refrigeration, existing plants, machinery and components, research, laws and regulations.
Ind/Abst Chem. Abstr. (1951-1988); INSPEC (Jan.-Feb. 1969-).

SP/0210-0665
FRIO, CALOR, AIRE ACONDICIONADO. [Frio, calor, aire acond.]. (1972)-. Trade Publication. Spanish. mo (July/Aug. combined issue). 10000ptas. Vifeca S.L., Antonio Rodriguez Villa 3, 28002 Madrid Spain. **Tel** 011 34 1 2628683. **UDC** 628. **Ad Acc, Adv Mgr:** Senor de la Pezuela. **Circ:** 5,600.

GW/0016-3406
GA. GAS + ARCHITEKTUR. [GA, Gas + Archit.]. **VFOAT** GA. Gas + Architectuur; GA. Gaz + Architecture; Gas en Architectuur; Gaz et Architecture; Gas und Architektur. (1963)-. Trade Publication. Multiple languages. Four times a year (Mar., June, Sept., Dec.). DM36.00. Karl Kramer Verlag GmbH & Company, Schulze-Delitzsch-Strasse 15, PF 800650, W 7000 Stuttgart 80 Germany. **Tel** 011 49 711 620893, FAX 0711-628955, telex 722203 KKBAUD. **UDC** 72 :697.1/.8 : :662.95.

UK/0268-4225
H & V ENGINEER. [H & V eng.]. **VFOAT** H and V Engineer; Heating and Ventilating Engineer. Vol. 58, No. 665 (April/May 1984)-. Trade Publication. English. bm. £64.00 UK; £72.00 other. Turret Group, 177 Hagden Lane, Watford Herts WD1 8LN United Kingdom. **Tel** 011 44 923 228577, FAX 011 44 923 221346. **LC** TH7201; .H24. **DD** 697/.0005. **CODEN** HVENEH. Documents available from Ask*IEEE. ***Continues*** *Heating & Ventilating Engineer, 0260-1338.*
Ind/Abst Coal Abstr.; INSPEC (Vol. 60, No. 683-).

UK/0307-7950
HAC. THE HEATING AND AIR CONDITIONING JOURNAL. (THE HEATING AND AIR CONDITIONING JOURNAL.). [HAC. Heat. air cond. j.]. Vol. 43, No. 509 (April 1974)-. Trade Publication. English. bm. £50.00. Maclean Hunter Ltd. / UK, Chalk Lane Cockfosters Road, Barnet Herts EN4 0BU England. **Tel** 011 44 81 2423000, FAX 011 44 81 9759753, telex 299072. **ED** Len Sanford. **LC** TJ275; .S822. **DD** 697/.00941. **CODEN** HACJBF. **Ad Acc. Circ:** 18,456 (ctrl). available on microfilm from University Microfilms International (UMI). Documents available from Article Express International, Ask*IEEE. ***Continues*** *Steam and Heating Engineer, 0039-0836.*
Desc: Technical information for the design and specification of building services in industrial and commercial buildings.
Ind/Abst Alum. Ind. Abstr.; Bioeng. Abstr.; Coal Abstr.; Ei Page One; Eng. Index Annu.; Fluid Abstr., Civil Eng.; Fluid Abstr. Proc. Eng.; FLUIDEX (1974-); Gas Abstr.; INSPEC (April 1974-); Int. Build. Serv. Abstr.; Met. Abstr.; World Ceram. Abstr.

UK
HANDBOOK OF BRITISH REFRIGERATION MATERIAL AND REFRIGERATION CATALOGUE, BUYERS' REFERENCE GUIDE. VFOAT British Refrigeration Material. (1937)-. Consumer Publication. English. an.

US/0046-7146
HEAT PIPE TECHNOLOGY. [Heat pipe technol.]. **Added/Corp** University of New Mexico. Technology Application Center. University of New Mexico. Heat Pipe Information Office. (1971)-. Trade Publication. English. qt. $155.00. Global Resources & Associates, University of New Mexico, Albuquerque NM 87131. **Tel** (505)242-2313. **LC** Z5853.H29; H42. **DD** 016.6214/025.

US/8750-4774
HEATING, AIR CONDITIONING & PLUMBING PRODUCTS. ***Ceased.*** [Heat. air cond. plumb. prod.]. **VFOAT** Heating, Air Conditioning and Plumbing Products. Trade Publication. English. bm. Gordon Publications Inc, A Subsidiary of Cahners Publishing Company, 301 Gibraltar Drive, Box 650, Morris Plains NJ 07950. **Tel** (201)292-5100. **DD** 697. ***Continues*** *Heating & Plumbing Product News, 0724-7227.*

UK/0017-9396
HEATING & VENTILATING REVIEW. [Heat. vent. rev.]. (1960)-. Trade Publication. English. mo. £36.00 UK; £45.00 other. Faversham House Group Ltd, Faversham House, 111 Saint James Road, Croydon Surrey CR9 2TH England. **Tel** 011 44 81 684 4082. **ED** Monty Burton. **LC** TH7201; .H42. **DD** 338.4/7/69700941. **Ad Acc.** ctrl circ. ***Absorbed*** *Plumber & Heating Engineer, 0032-1648.*
Desc: Air conditioning ancillary products.
Ind/Abst Coal Abstr.; Infomat Int. Bus.

US/0017-940X
HEATING, PIPING, AND AIR CONDITIONING. [Heat. piping air cond.]. **Added/Corp** American Society of Heating and Ventilating Engineers. American Society of Heating and Air-Conditioning Engineers. **VFOAT** Heating, Piping & Air Conditioning; Heating, Piping, Air Conditioning. Vol. 43, No. 5 (May 1971)-. Trade Publication. English. Twelve times a year. $60.00 US; $75.00 Canada; $85.00 Mexico; $95.00 other. Penton Publishing, 1100 Superior Avenue, Cleveland OH 44114-2543. **Tel** (216)696-7000, FAX (216)696-0836. **(Subscription address:** Penton Publishing, PO Box 96732, Chicago IL 60693.**) LC** TH7201; .H45. **DD** 697. **CODEN** HPAOAM. **[CCC].** cum. index. available on microfilm and microfiche from University Microfilms International (UMI); available on an online database (file 648/Full-Text) from DIALOG. Documents available from Article Express International, Ask*IEEE, CASDDS. ***Absorbed*** *Aerologist; Journal of the American Society of Heating and Ventilating Engineers, 0095-9081.* ***Continued in part by*** *Journal of the American Society of Heating and Air-Conditioning Engineers, 0402-1185.*
Ind/Abst Acoust. Abstr.; Appl. Sci. Technol. Index; Bioeng. Abstr.; Chem. Abstr.; Coal Abstr.; Ei Page One; EMBASE; Energy Res. Abstr.; Eng. Index Annu.; Gas Abstr.; Hospit. Health Admin. Index; HTFS Dig.; INIS Atomindex [Micro.]; INSPEC (Dec. 1968); Int. Aerosp. Abstr.; Int. Build. Serv. Abstr.; Int. Civil Eng. Abstr.; Pollut. Abstr. Indexes; Shock Vibr. Dig.; Soft. Abstr. Eng.; Trade Ind. ASAP [Full Txt.]; Trade Ind. Index [Full Txt.].

CN/0017-9418
HEATING-PLUMBING, AIR CONDITIONING. [Hear.-plumb. air cond.]. Vol. 44, No. 2 (Feb. 1965)-. Trade Publication. English. Ten times a year. 35.00Can$ (one year), 44.00Can$ (two year), 55.50Can$ (three year) Canada; 43.00Can$ (one year), 59.00Can$ (two year) US; 65.00Can$ other. Southam Information and Technology Group Inc., 1450 Don Mills Road, Don Mills Ontario M3B 2X7 Canada. **Tel** (416)445-6641, (800)668-2374, FAX (416)442-2261. ***Continues*** *Automatic Heating/Plumbing/Air Conditioning, 0380-3724;* ***Absorbed*** *Mechanical Contracting & Engineering, 0380-3740.*

CN/0382-6996
HEATING, PLUMBING, AIR CONDITIONING. BUYER'S GUIDE. VFOAT Plomberie, Chauffage et Climatisation. Guide de l'Acheteur; H P A C Annual; Annuaire de P C C; Heating, Plumbing, Air Conditioning Annual; Annuaire du Plomberie, Chauffage et Climatisation. (1973)-. Trade Publication. Multiple languages (English and French). an. 30.00Can$. Southam Information and Technology Group Inc., 1450 Don Mills Road, Don Mills Ontario M3B 2X7 Canada. **Tel** (416)445-6641, (800)668-2374, FAX (416)442-2261. **DD** 338.4/7/69602571. ***Supersedes*** *Heating, Plumbing, Air Conditioning. P A C Annual Buyer's Guide.*

SZ
HEIZUNG UND LUFTUNG. Added/Corp Verband Schweizerischer Heizungs- und Luftungsfirmen. **VFOAT** Schweizerische Blatter fuer Heizung und Luftung; Chauffage et Ventilation. Vol. 47, No. 1 (1980)-. Trade Publication. German (French and Multiple languages). Six times a year (Feb., Apr., June, Aug., Oct., Dec.). 45.00F Switzerland; 70.00F Europe; 110.00F others. VSHL, Postfach 73, Ch 8024 Zurich Switzerland. **Tel** 011 41 1 2519569, FAX 01 252.92.31. Index available (Iss. No. 6 in Dec.). ***Continues*** *Schweizerische Blatter fuer Heizung + Luftung.*

GW/0017-9906
HLH. (HLH : ZEITSCHRIFT FUER HEIZUNG, LUFTUNG, KLIMATECHNIK, HAUSTECHNIK.). [HLH]. **Added/Corp** Verein Deutscher Ingenieure. VDI-Fachgruppe Heizung Luftung Klimatechnik (Germany) VDI-Fachgruppe Haustechnik (Germany) VDI-Gesellschaft Technische Gebaudeausrustung. **VFOAT** Zeitschrift fur Heizung, Luftung, Klimatechnik-Haustechnik; Heizung, Luftung/Klima, Haustechnik. Vol. 21 No. 1 (Jan. 1970)-. Trade Publication. German. mo. DM284.00 Germany; DM320.00. VDI Verlag GmbH, Postfach 101054, D 40001 Dusseldorf Germany. **Tel** 011 49 211 6188313, FAX 011 49 211 6188133. **ED** Hans Schiebold and Dieter Volk. **LC** TH7201; .H53. **DD** 697/.05. **CODEN** HLHZAS. **[CCC]. Ad Acc.** Documents available from Article Express International, Ask*IEEE, CASDDS. ***Continues*** *Heizung, Luftung, Haustechnik.*
Desc: The official journal of the Association of German Engineers for Heating, Ventilation, Air Conditioning, and House Building.
Ind/Abst Bibliogr. Mission.; Bioeng. Abstr.; Chem. Abstr.; Coal Abstr.; Ei Page One; EMBASE; Energy Res. Abstr. (Dec. 1976-); Eng. Index Annu.; Fluid Abstr., Civil Eng.; Fluid Abstr. Proc. Eng.; FLUIDEX (1973-); INSPEC (Jan. 1977-); Int. Aerosp. Abstr.; Int. Civil Eng. Abstr.; Saf. Health Work; Soft. Abstr. Eng.

HU/0018-8085
HUTOIPAR. **See** Food and Food Industry.

US/0887-445X
HVAC PRODUCT NEWS. ***Title Change.*** [HVAC prod. news]. **VAT** Heating, Ventilation, Air Conditioning Product News. April (1983)-(19??). Trade Publication. English. mo. HVAC Product News, Subscription Department, 747 Church Road/Suite G-11, Elmhurst IL 60126. **DD** 338. **[CCC].** ***Continued by*** *HVAC, 1069-823X.*

US/0899-9791
HVAC PROFITMAKER. VFOAT HVAC Profit Maker. Issue 1 (April 1988)-. Trade Publication. English. Ten times a year. $285.00. Tom Davies & Associates,

674 Western Drive, Mobile AL 36607. **Tel** (205)471-2001. **ED** Tom Davies. **DD** 332. Index available. cum. index. **Circ:** 100 (ctrl).
Desc: Financial management designed to improve net before tax.

US/0019-2112
ILLINOIS MASTER PLUMBER. **Added/Corp** Illinois Association of Plumbing, Heating Cooling Contractors. Illinois Master Plumbers Association. **VFOAT** IMP. Illinois Master Plumber. 1 (1915)-. Trade Publication. English. mo. $9.00. Illinois Association for Plumbing and Heating, 821 South Grand Avenue West, Springfield IL 62704. **Tel** (217)522-7219, (217)522-7220. **ED** Dorothy Sharpe. **Bk Rev. Ad Acc. Circ:** 2,200 (ctrl).
Desc: Industry news, local association activities, auxiliary news, Department of Public Health articles, legislative update, advertising and marketing, national arbitration news.

US/1040-5313
INDOOR AIR QUALITY UPDATE. [Indoor air qual. update]. **Added/Corp** Cutter Information Corp. Vol. 1, No. 1 (Sept. 1988)-. Trade Publication. English. mo. $297.00 North America; $367.00 other. Cutter Information Corporation, 37 Broadway, Arlington MA 02174-5539. **Tel** (617)648-8700, (800)964-5118, FAX (617)648-8707, (617)648-1950, telex 650 100 9891. **ED** Hal Levin. **DD** 697. **[CCC]. Bk Rev.**
Desc: Guide to the practical control of indoor air problems.

GW/0367-7788
INDUSTRIEFEUERUNG. (DIE INDUSTRIEFEUERUNG : OFFIZIELLES ORGAN DER GRUPPE INDUSTRIEFEUERUNGEN IM BUNDESVERBAND ENERGIE- UUMWELT-FEUERUNGEN E. V.). [Industriefeuerung]. **Added/Corp** Gruppe Industriefeuerungen im Bundesverband Energie-Uumwelt- Feuerungen. (1972)-. Trade Publication. German. Vulkan Verlag, Classen, POB 103962, D-45039 Essen 1 Germany. **Tel** 011 49 201 820020. **CODEN** IFRGAO. Documents available from CASDDS.
Ind/Abst Chem. Abstr.; Coal Abstr.; Energy Res. Abstr. (April 1977-).

SP/0214-4034
INSTALACIONES Y TECNICAS DEL CONFORT. [Instal. tec. confort]. **VFOAT** ITC. (1988)-. Trade Publication. Spanish. Ten times a year. 16000ptas. Instalaciones Tecnicas del Confort, Santisima Trinidad 6 5TO E, 28010 Madrid Spain. **Tel** 011 34 1 4486126, FAX 011 34 1 4468069. **UDC** 628. **Ad Acc, Adv Mgr:** Victorio Redondo Polo. **Circ:** 6,000. ***Continues*** *Clima y Ambiente, 0210-2935.*
Desc: Covers heating and air installation, gas, etc.

FR/0399-9874
INSTALLATEUR EN CHAUFFAGE PLOMBERIE COUVERTURE GENIE CLIMATIQUE ELECTRICITE. (19??)-. Trade Publication. French. ir. $141.00. ESI Publication, 7 rue Laromiguiere, F 75005 Paris France. **Tel** 011 33 1 46342160.

IT/0020-2118
INSTALLATORE ITALIANO. [Install. ital.]. (1950)-. Trade Publication. Italian (summaries and/or abstracts in English and French). mo. L94000.00. Editoriale PEG Spa, Via Fratelli Bressan 2, 20126 Milan Italy. **Tel** 011 39 2 2579841, FAX 011 39 2 255-2779, telex 323088 PEGMOS I. **ED** Roberto Sanguineti. **UDC** 696+697. Index available. **Bk Rev. Ad Acc.** ctrl circ.
Desc: Technical information and topical data addressed to planners, technicians, entrepreneurs of heating, ventilation, air-conditioning, plumbing, sanitary installations, electricity, telephony, and security.
Ind/Abst Int. Build. Serv. Abstr.

US
INTERMEDIATE MINIMUM PROPERTY STANDARDS FOR SOLAR HEATING AND DOMESTIC HOT WATER SYSTEMS. **Main/Corp** United States. Dept. of Housing and Urban Development. **VFOAT** HUD Intermediate Minimum Property Standards Supplement, Solar Heating and Domestic Hot Water Systems. 1977-. Government Publication. English. US Department of Housing and Urban Development, 451 Seventh Street SW, Washington DC 20401. **Tel** (202)708-0980, FAX (202)708-0299.

UK/0140-4237
INTERNATIONAL BUILDING SERVICES ABSTRACTS. **See** Building and Construction-Abstracting, Bibliographies and Statistics.

UK/0140-7007
INTERNATIONAL JOURNAL OF REFRIGERATION. (REVUE INTERNATIONALE DU FROID / INSTITUT INTERNATIONAL DU FROID. / INTERNATIONAL JOURNAL OF REFRIGERATION / INTERNATIONAL INSTITUTE OF REFRIGERATION.). [Int. j. refrig.]. **Added/Corp** International Institute of Refrigeration. **VFOAT** International Journal of Refrigeration. Vol. 1, No. 1 (May 1978)-. Trade Publication. English (French). Eight times a year. $395.00 The Americas; £265.00 other. Butterworth Heinemann Publishers, Linacre House, Jordan Hill, Oxford OX2 8DP England. **Tel** 011 44 865 310366. **(Subscription address:** Elsevier Science Ltd. Oxford Fulfillment Centre, PO Box 800, Kidlington, Oxford OX5 1DX United Kingdom.**) ED** Marija Vukovokac. **LC** TP490; .R48. **DD** 621.5/6/05. **CODEN** IJRFDI. **[CCC].** Index available. **Bk Rev. Ad Acc. Pr Rev.** available on microfilm and microfiche from University Microfilms International (UMI). Documents available from Article Express International, The Genuine Article, BIOSIS Document Express, CASDDS.
Desc: A journal published for the International Institute of Refrigeration. Of interest to all those wishing to keep abreast of research industrial news in refrigeration, air conditioning and associated fields.
Ind/Abst Agric. Eng. Abstr.; Biol. Abstr.; Chem. Abstr.; Ei Page One; EMBASE; Energy Inf. Abstr.; Eng. Index Annu.; Food Sci. Technol. Abstr.; Hortic. Abstr.; Postharvest News Inf.; Res. Alert [Select. Cov.]; Sci. Cit. Index; SCISEARCH.

US/0277-870X
INTERNATIONAL SOLID FUEL BUYER'S GUIDE DIRECTORY. [Int. solid fuel buy. guide dir.]. (1980)-. Directory. English. an. $4.50 US; $19.95 other. Circulation Manager / Virginia, 411 Cedar Road, Chesapeake VA 23320. **LC** HD9971.5.S76; I57. **DD** 697/.02/029473.

NZ/0114-8257
IRHACE JOURNAL. **VFOAT** Institute of Refrigeration, Heating and Air-Conditioning Engineers Journal. (1989)-. Trade Publication. English. bm. ***Formed by the union of*** *Thermonews, 0112-3084* ***and*** *Heating & Ventilating Engineer, 0111-5553.*

JA
JARN : JAPAN AIR CONDITIONING, HEATING & REFRIGERATION NEWS. (19??)-. Trade Publication. English. mo. $120.00 surface mail; $150.00 (airmail) North & South America, Europe, Middle East & Oceania; $140.00 Asia; $160.00 South America & Africa. JARN Ltd, 1-16 1 Chome Akasaka Hosokawa, Minato Ku Tokyo 107 Japan. **Tel** 011 81 3 3584 4704, FAX 011 84 3 3584 4708. **ED** Atsuzo Ishida. **Ad Acc. Circ:** 7,000.
Desc: Covers HVAC and the R trade, heating, ventilation, air conditioning and refrigeration.

US/0148-8287
JOURNAL OF THERMAL INSULATION. ***Title Change.*** [J. therm. insul.]. Vol. 1 (July 1977)-(1992). Trade Publication. English. qt (July). Technomic Publishing Company, Inc., 851 New Holland Avenue, Box 3535, Lancaster PA 17604. **Tel** (717)291-5609, (800)233-9936, FAX (717)295-4538. **ED** Charles F Gilbo. **LC** TH1715.A1; J68. **DD** 693.8/32/05. **CODEN** JTINDA. **[CCC].** cum. index. **Circ:** 300. available on microfilm from University Microfilms International (UMI). Documents available from Article Express International, CASDDS. ***Continued by*** *Journal of Thermal Insulation and Building Envelopes, 1065-2744.*
Desc: Reports on a wide variety of advances that are taking place worldwide in thermal insulation. Most of the contributions deal with technical aspects of the control of thermal energy and the evaluation and measurement of the materials and systems involved. Includes an Information and Technology Transfer section which covers pertinent news, ideas, and discussion items received from readers and other sources.
Ind/Abst Alum. Ind. Abstr.; Bioeng. Abstr.; Chem. Abstr.; Ei Page One; EMBASE; Energy Res. Abstr. (June 1978-); Eng. Mater. Abstr.; Eng. Index Annu.; Int. Civil Eng. Abstr.; Met. Abstr.; Soft. Abstr. Eng.

FR/0337-2693
JOURNAL RPF. [J. RPF]. **VAT** Journal Revue Pratique du Froid. Trade Publication. French. 545.00F (one year), 1040.00F (two year) France; 860.00F (one year), 1570.00F (two year) other. 254 rue de Vaugirard, 75740 Paris Cedex 15 France. **Tel** 45322719, FAX 45322719, telex 202639. **LC** TP490; .F43. **DD** 621.5/6/05. **CODEN** JRPFD7. **Circ:** 4,000. Documents available from Article Express International, CASDDS. ***Continues*** *Revue Pratique du Froid et du Conditionnement de l'Air. Supplement.*
Ind/Abst Chem. Abstr.; Ei Page One; Eng. Index Annu.

GW/0343-2246
KALTE UND KLIMATECHNIK. (KK, DIE KALTE UND KLIMATECHNIK.). [Kalte Klimatech.]. **VFOAT** Die Kalte und Klimatechnik. (1976)-. Trade Publication. German. Twelve times a year. DM190.20 Germany, DM214.20 other (surface mail);. AW Gentner Verlag, Postfach 101742, D-70015 Stuttgart Germany. **Tel** 011 49 711 636720, FAX 011 49 711 6367247, telex 841 722244. **ED** Wolf-Rudiger Pfundtner. **LC** TP490; .K2. **CODEN** KAKLDS. **[CCC].** Index available. **Bk Rev. Ad Acc. Circ:** 7,800. ***Formed by the union of*** *Klima-Technik* ***and*** *Kalte.*
Ind/Abst Energy Res. Abstr. (Sept. 1977-).

JA
KENCHIKU SETSUBI KOGAKU KENKYUJO HO. **Main/Corp** Kanto Gakuin Daigaku. Osawa Kinen Kenchiku Setsubi Kogaku Kenkyjo. **Added/Corp** Kanto Gakuin Daigaku. Osawa Kinen Kenchiku Setsubi Kogaku Kenkyjo. Bulletin of Institute of Architectural Environmental Engineering. **VFOAT** Bulletin of Institute of Architectural Environmental Engineering. No. 1 (1978)-. Bulletin. Japanese. an. Kanto Gakuin Daigaku Osawa Kinen Kenchiku Setsubi Kogaku Kenkyujo, (Institute of Architectural Environmental, Engineering, Kanto Gakuin University), 4834 Mutsuuramachi Kanazawaku, Yokohomashi Kanagawaken 236 Japan. **Tel** 045-781-2001. **ED** Hiroshi Osawa. **LC** TH6014; .K35a. **Circ:** 500 (ctrl).
Desc: Includes information on architectural environment, air-conditioning, heating and ventilation, plumbing, refrigeration, and noise control.

RU
KHOLODILNAIA TEKHNIKA. **Added/Corp** Vsesoiuznyi Nauchno-Issledovatelskii Institut Kholodilnoi Promyshlennosti. (1???)-. Trade Publication. Russian. Six times a year. $119.95. Kholodilnaia Tekhnika, Ulitsa Kostiakova 12, 125422 Moscow Russia. **(Subscription address:** East View Publications Inc., 3020 Harbor Lane North, Suite 110, Minneapolis MN 55447.**)** Index available. **Bk Rev.** Documents available from CASDDS.
Ind/Abst Chem. Abstr.

GW/0172-1984
KLIMA, KALTE, HEIZUNG. ***Title Change.*** (KI KLIMA KALTE HEIZUNG.). [Klima Kalte Heiz.]. **VFOAT** Klima KËalte Heizung. Vol. 7, No. 4 (April 1979)-(Jan. 1994). Trade Publication. German. mo. Verlag CF Mueller, Verlags GS, D-69018 Heidelberg Germany. **Tel** 011 49 6221 4890. **LC** TH7687.A1; K45. **DD** 697/.005. **CODEN** KKHEDS. **[CCC].** Documents available from Article Express International, CASDDS. ***Continues*** *Kl Klima + Kalteingenieur.* ***Merged into*** *Ki Luft und Kaeltetechnik, 0945-0459.*
Ind/Abst Bioeng. Abstr.; Chem. Abstr. (1979-); Ei Page One; EMBASE; Energy Res. Abstr. (June 1980-); Eng. Index Annu.; Fluid Abstr., Civil Eng.; Fluid Abstr. Proc. Eng.; FLUIDEX (1979-); Int. Build. Serv. Abstr.; SportSearch.

NE
KLIMAATBEHEERSING. Trade Publication. Uitgeverij PC Noordervliet BV, Postbus 268, 3700 AG Zeist Netherlands.

JA/0454-1499
KOGYO KANETSU. [Kogyo kanetsu]. **Added/Corp** Nihon Kogyoro Kyokai. **VFOAT** Industrial Heating. (1966)-. Trade Publication. Japanese. bm. Japan Industrial Furnace Manufacturers Association, Tokyo Japan. **CODEN** KOKTAB. Documents available from CASDDS. ***Continues*** *Denkiro.*
Ind/Abst Chem. Abstr.

KO
KONGGI CHOHWA, NAENGDONG NONGHAK. **VFOAT** Journal of the SAREK; Journal of the S.A.R.E.K. Trade Publication. Korean. qt. Konggi Chohwa Naengdong Konghakhoe, San 76-561 Yoksam-dong Kangnam-ku, Seoul Korea. **LC** TP480; .K66.
Ind/Abst Energy Res. Abstr. (Oct. 1981-).

NE/0925-6318
KOUDE MAGAZINE. (April 1990)-. Trade Publication. Dutch. ir. Fl121.00. Keesing Noordervliet Bv, De Molen 82-86, 3995 Ax Houten Netherlands. **Tel** 011 31 3403 58585, FAX 011 31 3403 58500. **(Subscription address:** Keesing Noordervliet BV, Postbus 1118, 1000 BC Amsterdam Netherlands.**) CODEN** KOMAE2. ***Continues*** *Koude & Klimaat, 0923-6554.*

CN/0833-8973
LIST OF CERTIFIED PLUMBING PRODUCTS (1983). (LIST OF CERTIFIED PLUMBING PRODUCTS.). [List certif. plumb. prod.]. **Main/Corp** Canadian Standards Association. (1983)-. English. 20.00Can$. Canadian Standards Association, 178 Rexdale Boulevard, Rexdale Ontario M9W 1R3 Canada. **Tel** (416)747-4000, (416)747-4044, telex 06-989344. **DD** 696/.1/0216. ***Continues*** *Canadian Standards Association. List of CSA Certified Plumbing Products., 0705-7598.*

CN/1200-006X
LIST OF CSA CERTIFIED COMFORT CONDITIONING EQUIPMENT. [List CSA certif. comf. cond. equip.]. **Main/Corp** Canadian Standards Association. **VFOAT** List of Canadian Standards Association Certified Comfort Conditioning Equipment. (199?)-. English. 20.00Can$. Canadian Standards Association, 178 Rexdale Boulevard, Rexdale Ontario M9W 1R3 Canada. **Tel** (416)747-4000, (416)747-4044, telex 06-989344. **DD** 697/.000216. ***Continues*** *Canadian Standards Association. List of Certified Comfort Conditioning Equipment., 1196-1880.*

SP/0210-184X
M.I. MONTAJES E INSTALACIONES. [M.I., Montaje instal.]. **VFOAT** Montajes e Instalaciones. (1971)-. Trade Publication. Spanish. mo (11 issues). $103.00 Europe; $164.00 other. Editorial Alcion SA, Triana 53, 28016 Madrid Spain. **Tel** 011 34 1 345-6400. **UDC** 628.

US/1054-478X
MEANS PLUMBING CHANGE ORDER COST DATA. ***Ceased.*** [Means plumb. change order cost data]. **Added/Corp** Means (Firm). (1991)-(19??). Trade Publication. English. RS Means Company Inc. Trade Sales, 100 Construction Plaza, PO Box 800, Kingston MA 02364. **Tel** (617)585-7880, (800)448-8182, FAX (617)585-7466. **DD** 696.

US/1042-3850
MEANS PLUMBING COST DATA. [Means plumb. cost data]. **Added/Corp** Means (Firm). 12th Annual ed. (1989)-. Trade Publication. English. an. $83.95. RS Means Company Inc. Trade Sales, 100 Construction Plaza, PO Box 800, Kingston MA 02364. **Tel** (617)585-7880, (800)448-8182, FAX (617)585-7466. **LC** TH6235; .M43. **DD** 696/.1/0299. ***Continues in part*** *Means Mechanical Cost Data, 0748-2698.*

CN/1183-9015
MECHANICAL BUYER & SPECIFIER. HVAC/REFRIGERATION. [Mech. buy. specif., HVAC/refrigeration]. **VFOAT** HVAC/Refrigeration. **VAT** Mechanical Buyer and Specifier. HVAC/Refrigeration. Vol. 1, No. 1 (Oct. 1991)-. Trade Publication. English. bm. $24.95 per year; $3.75 single copy. Nytek Publishing Inc., Suite 100, 452 Attwell Drive, Etobicoke Ontario M9W 5C3 Canada. **DD** 338.4.

CN/1183-9007
MECHANICAL BUYER & SPECIFIER. PLUMBING, PIPING & HEATING. [Mech. buy. specif., Plumb. pip. heat.]. **VFOAT** Plumbing, Piping & Heating. **VAT** Mechanical Buyer and Specifier. Plumbing, Piping & Heating. Vol. 1, No. 1 (Oct. 1991)-. Trade Publication. English. bm. $24.95 per year; $3.75 single copy. Nytek Publishing Inc., Suite 100, 452 Attwell Drive, Etobicoke Ontario M9W 5C3 Canada. **DD** 338.4.

US
MEDVIN P-H-C- TRADELETTER. (19??)-. Trade Publication. English. Twelve times a year. $152.00 (one year); $289.00 (two years). P H C Information Services Inc., 5904 Rossmore Drive, Bethesda MD 20814. **Tel** (301)530-4459, FAX (301)530-6052. **ED** Steve Rynas.
Desc: Business news for the plumbing, heating and cooling industries.

AT/0819-1824
N.S.W. MASTER PLUMBER. (MASTER PLUMBER.). [N.S.W. master plumb.]. **VFOAT** New South Wales Master Plumber. (1986)-. Trade Publication. English. bm (Fb., Apr., June, Aug., Oct., Dec.). 30.00Aus$. Master Plumber & Mechanical Contractors, 121-125 Bland Street, Ashfield NSW 2131 Australia. **Tel** 011 61 2 7977055, 008 42 4181, FAX 011 61 2 7995841. **ED** Richard Rolls. **DD** 696.105. **Ad Acc, Adv Mgr:** R. Rolls. **Circ:** 1,600 (ctrl). available on an online database. ***Continues*** *Master Plumber, 0025-5041.*

CN/0825-8260
NATIONAL DIRECTORY, HOME HEATING PRODUCTS. [Natl. dir. home heat. prod.]. **VFOAT** Repertoire National, Produits de Chauffage Residentiel. 1983/84-. Directory. English (French). an. $4.00. Canadian Institute of Energy, 229 640 5th Avenue Southwest, Calgary Alberta Canada. **Tel** (403)262-6969. **DD** 697/.07/0216.

US
NEW ENGLAND PROGRESS MAGAZINE. Trade Publication. English. Eleven times a year (monthly except April). $20.00. New England Progress Magazine, 5 Mountain Road, Framingham MA 01701. **Tel** (508)879-6799, FAX (508)879-3044. **ED** Carolyn Davis. **Ad Acc. Pr Rev. Circ:** 5,000 (ctrl).

DK/0904-9681
NEWS FROM DBDH. [News DBDH]. (1988)-. Trade Publication. English. Four times a year (Feb., May, Aug., Nov.). Free. Danish Board District Heating, Jembanevej 65, DK 5210 Odense NV Denmark. **Tel** 011 45 661777228, FAX 011 45 66177226. **DD** 697.540 948 9. **Bk Rev. Ad Acc. Circ:** 5,500.

GW/0724-7028
NEWSLETTER - IEA HEAT PUMP CENTER. (NEWSLETTER.). [Newsl. - IEA Heat Pump Cent.]. **VFOAT** Newsletter - International Energy Agency Heat Pump Center; IEA Heat Pump Center newsletter. (1983)-. Newsletter. English. qt. Free, Austria, Canada, Italy, Japan, Netherlands, Norway, Sweden, US; F110.00 other (surface mail); F132.50 (air mail). Heat Pump Centre, P.O.Box 17, 6130 AA Sittard Netherlands. **Tel** 011 31 4490 95236, FAX 011 31 4490 28260, telex 36456. **UDC** 62.

JA/0910-0040
NIHON REITO KYOKAI RONBUNSHU. [Nippon Reito Kyokai ronbunshu]. **Added/Corp** Nihon Reito Kyokai. **VFOAT** Transactions of the Japanese Association of Refrigeration. Vol. 1, No. 1 (1984)-. Academic Scholarly Publication. Japanese (summaries and/or abstracts in English). tq. Nihon Reito Kyokai, (Japanese Assoc. of Refrigeration), 8, Saneicho, Shinjukuku, Tokyoto 160 Japan. **LC** TP490; .N53. **CODEN** NRKRET. Documents available from CASDDS.
Ind/Abst Chem. Abstr. (1984-).

US/0739-3830
NORTH CAROLINA PLUMBING-HEATING-COOLING FORUM. (NORTH CAROLINA PLUMBING-HEATING-COOLING FORUM / NORTH CAROLINA ASSOCIATION OF PLUMBING-HEATING-COOLING CONTRACTORS, INC.). **Added/Corp** North Carolina Association of Plumbing-Heating-Cooling Contractors. **VFOAT** North Carolina Plumbing, Heating, Cooling Forum; NC Plumbing-Heating-Cooling Forum; Forum; N.C. Plumbing-Heating-Cooling Forum. (19??)-. Trade Publication. English. Twelve times a year. Free. North Carolina Association Plumbing Heating Contractors, 413 Glenwood Avenue, Raleigh NC 27603. **Tel** (919)833-0372, FAX (919)833-0921. **ED** Belinda S. Hodde. **Ad Acc, Adv Mgr:** Annette Forsythe, **Tel** (919)833-0372.

US/0192-5784
OFFICIAL (LOS ANGELES). (OFFICIAL.). [Official]. **Added/Corp** International Association of Plumbing and Mechanical Officials. Vol. 1 (1979)-. Trade Publication. English. bm. $27.00. International Association of Plumbing and Mechanical Officials, 20001 Walnut Drive South, Walnut CA 91789. **Tel** (714)595-8449. **ED** Tom Higham. **DD** 696. **Ad Acc. Circ:** 3,000 (ctrl).
Desc: Happenings in the plumbing industry which may be of interest to inspectors.

BE/0777-6349
ONDERNEMING, DE. [Onderneming]. **VFOAT** L'Entreprise Mensuel d'Information du Sanitaire du Chauffage et de la Climatisation. (1951)-. Trade Publication. Dutch (French). Eleven times a year. 750F Belgium; 2000F other. Distrigraph, Ave Alexandre Bertrand 50, 1190 Brussels Belgium. **Tel** (02)343-3347, FAX (02)344-3369. Index available. cum. index. **Ad Acc. Circ:** 5,000. ***Continues*** *Entreprise (1947), 0013-905X.*

US/1045-6198
OPERATING PERFORMANCE REPORT FOR THE PHCP WHOLESALE/DISTRIBUTION INDUSTRY. PVF DISTRIBUTING INDUSTRY. [Oper. perform. rep. PHCP wholes./distrib. ind. PVF distrib. ind.]. **Added/Corp** American Supply Association. Industry Insights, Inc. **VFOAT** Operating Performance Report. (1985)-. Trade Publication. English. American Supply Association, 20 North Wacker Drive/Suite 2260, Chicago IL 60606. **DD** 338. ***Continues*** *Operating Performance of the P-H-C-P Wholesaler Industry.*

US/0031-4412
PENNSYLVANIA CONTRACTOR. **VFOAT** PA. PHC Contractor. Trade Publication. English. mo. Pennsylvania Plumbing Heating, 219 Pine Street, Harrisburg PA 17101.

●US/1071-2372
PHC PROFIT REPORT. [PHC profit rep.]. **VAT** Plumbing Heating Cooling Profit Report. (1993)-. Trade Publication. English. sm. $197.50. Business News Publishing Company, 755 West Big Beaver Road, Suite 1000, Troy MI 48084. **Tel** (810)362-3700, FAX (810)362-0317, telex 230295. **DD** 696.
Desc: Focuses on profitability for the success-minded plumbing, heating and piping professional. Each issue is packed with proven money-making tips and ideas.

UK/0032-1656
PLUMBING. (19??)-. Trade Publication. English. bm. £30.00 (surface mail). Institute of Plumbing, 64 Station Lane, Hornchurch Essex RM12 6NB England. **Tel** 011 44 4024 72791. **Bk Rev**, (Qty: 0-10). **Ad Acc, Adv Mgr:** Marilyn Sansom. **Pr Rev.** ctrl circ.
Desc: Official journal of the Institute of Plumbing, New Technology and Regulations.
Ind/Abst Leadscan.

US/8750-6041
PLUMBING & MECHANICAL. [Plumb. mech.]. **VFOAT** Plumbing and Mechanical. (1984)-. Trade Publication. English. mo. $50.00 US; $62.00 other (includes annual PM Directory issue). Business News Publishing Company, 755 West Big Beaver Road, Suite 1000, Troy MI 48084. **Tel** (810)362-3700, FAX (810)362-0317, telex 230295. **[CCC].**
Desc: Provides plumbing-hydronics-piping and mechanical contractors with the latest technologies, industry news and product coverage.

AT/1034-3075
PLUMBING AND MECHANICAL CONNECTION. [Plumb. mech. connect.]. (1989)-. Trade Publication. English. qt. 49.50Aus$ Australia; 65.00Aus$ New Zealand & New Guinea; 75.00Aus$ Singapore, Malaysia, Hong Kong, & Japan; 85.00Aus$ (other). Patchell Publishing Pty Limited, 302 Waverly Road 1st Floor, E Malvern Vic, 3145 Australia. **Tel** 11 61 3 56356655, FAX 11 61 3 5716006. **DD** 338.4769610994. ***Continues*** *Plumbers Connection, 0816-6900.*

US
PLUMBING BUSINESS. (19??)-(199?). Trade Publication. English. bm. Merit Publications Inc, 12 Perimeter Park Drive, Suite 102, Atlanta GA 30341. **Tel** (404)451-4990, FAX (404)451-4880. **Bk Rev. Ad Acc. Circ:** 31,000 (ctrl).
Desc: Business magazine for the licensed plumbing contractor.

US/0192-1711
PLUMBING ENGINEER. [Plumb. eng.]. Trade Publication. English. bm. $50.00. American Society of Plumbing Engineers, 135 Addison Avenue, Elmhurst IL 60126. **Tel** (312)530-6161. **LC** TH6101; .P74. **DD** 696/.1/05. **CODEN** PLENDY. available on microfilm from University Microfilms International (UMI). Documents available from Article Express International.
Ind/Abst Bioeng. Abstr.; Ei Page One; Eng. Index Annu.; Int. Build. Serv. Abstr.

US/0145-4951
PLUMBING FIXTURES. ***Title Change.*** (CURRENT INDUSTRIAL REPORTS. MQ-34E, PLUMBING FIXTURES / U.S. DEPARTMENT OF COMMERCE, BUREAU OF THE CENSUS.). [Plumb. fixt.]. **Added/Corp** United States. Bureau of the Census. **VFOAT** Plumbing Fixtures. (19??)-(1992). Government Publication. English. qt. US Department of Commerce, 14th Street & Constitution Avenue NW, Washington DC 20230. **Tel** (202)482-2000, FAX (202)482-3772. **LC** TH6249; .C87. **DD** 338.4/768388. Documents available from Documents on Demand. ***Continued by*** *Current Industrial Reports. MQ34E, Plumbing Fixtures (Computer File).*
Desc: Presents timely data on the production, inventories, and orders of approximately 5,000 products, which represents 40 percent of all US manufacturing.
Ind/Abst Am. Stat. Index.

US/0278-5722
PLUMBING-HEATING-COOLING CATALOG : PHC. **VFOAT** PHC, The Orange Book. **VAT** Plumbing Heating Cooling Catalog. Catalog. English. $35.00 US, $40.00 Canada. Hutton Publishing Company Inc, 4300 West 62nd Street, Indianapolis IN 46268. **Tel** (516)935-2740. **LC** TH6255; .P59. **DD** 696/.029/473.

US/1055-3231
PLUMBING, HEATING, PIPING. ***Title Change.*** [Plumb. heat. pip.]. Vol. 255, No. 8 (Feb. 1991)-Vol. 257, No. 11 (May 1993). Trade Publication. English. mo. Cahners Publishing Company, 249 West 17th Street, New York NY 10011. **Tel** (212)645-0067, FAX (212)242-6987. **LC** TH6101; .D18. **DD** 696/.05. **[CCC].** available on microfilm and microfiche from University Microfilms International (UMI). ***Continues*** *DE/Domestic Engineering, 0147-6998.* ***Absorbed by*** *Contractor (Newton, Mass.), 0897-7135.*

UK/0073-9677
PROCEEDINGS - INSTITUTE OF REFRIGERATION. [Proc. - Inst. Refrig.]. **VFOAT** Proceedings of the Institute of Refrigeration. (1943)-. Proceedings. English. an. Institute of Refrigeration, Kelvin House, 76 Mill Lane, Carshalton Surrey England. **Tel** 011 44 81 6477033. **CODEN** IRFPA7. **Pr Rev. Circ:** 800. ***Continues*** *Proceedings of the British Association of Refrigeration, 0369-8475.*
Ind/Abst Agric. Eng. Abstr. (1991-); Hortic. Abstr.; Leis. Recreat. Tour. Abstr.; Postharvest News Inf.

GW
PROCEEDINGS OF THE ... INTERNATIONAL CONGRESS OF REFRIGERATION. **Main/Conf** International Congress of Refrigeration. **VFOAT** Comptes Rendus du ... Congres International du Froid; Progress in Refrigeration Science and Technology; Progres dans la Science et la Technique du Froid. 8th (1951)-. Proceedings. English (French). ir. Association Francaise du Froid, France. ***Continues*** *Actes du Congres International du Froid.*

FR/0249-6526
PROMOCLIM A. (PROMOCLIM. A, ACTUALITES EQUIPEMENT TECHNIQUE.). [Promoclim A]. **Added/Corp** Societe d'Etude et de Diffusion des Industries Thermiques et Aerauliques (France). **VFOAT** Actualites Equipement Technique. (1974)-. Trade Publication. French. ir. 135.00F. Sedit, Domaine de St. Paul, 78470 St-Remy-Chevreuse France. **Tel** 011 33 1 30852016. **LC** TH7005; .P763. **DD** 697/.005. ***Continues*** *Promoclim. A. Applications Thermiques et Aerauliques.*
Ind/Abst Energy Res. Abstr. (May 1978-).

UK
RAC, REFRIGERATION AND AIR CONDITIONING. **VFOAT** Refrigeration and Air Conditioning. Vol. 82, No. 970 (Jan. 1979)-. Trade Publication. English. mo. £35.95 UK; £51.95 Europe; £67.95 other. EMAP Readerlink, Audit House, 260 Field End Road, Ruislip Middlesex HA4 9LT England. **Tel** 011 44 081 868 4499, FAX 011 44 081 429 3117. **ED** Andrew

Bailey. **Bk Rev**. **Ad Acc**. **Acid Free. Circ:** 5,000. available on microfilm and microfiche from University Microfilms International (UMI). ***Continues*** *Refrigeration and Air Conditioning.*
Desc: Covers all aspects of refrigeration, air conditioning and heat recovery markets.

GW/0033-6769
RAS; ROHR, ARMATUR, SANITAR, HEIZUNG. Vol. 1 (19??)-. Trade Publication. German. Twelve times a year. DM90.00. Krammer Verlag, Postfach 170235, 40083 Duesseldorf Germany. **Tel** 011 49 211 679720, FAX 011 49 211 6797231.

NE
RCC KOUDE & LUCHTBEHANDELING. Trade Publication. Dutch. mo. Standex Periodieken BV, Postbus 956, 3900 AZ Veenendaal Netherlands. **Tel** 011 31 8385 28008.

US/0048-7066
REEVES JOURNAL. (19??)-. Trade Publication. English. Twelve times a year. $39.00 US; $51.00 other. Business News Publishing Company, 755 West Big Beaver Road, Suite 1000, Troy MI 48084. **Tel** (810)362-3700, FAX (810)362-0317, telex 230295. **ED** Larry Dill. **Ad Acc. Circ:** 20,511 (ctrl).
Desc: Provides comprehensive coverage of the installation, maintenance and distribution of plumbing, heating and cooling systems and components.

US
REFRIGERATION. (1906)-. Trade Publication. English. Thirteen times a year. $25.00 US; $45.00 other. John W Yopp Publications Inc., PO Box 1147, Beaufort SC 29901. **Tel** (803)521-0239, FAX (803)521-1398. **ED** John W Yopp. **Bk Rev**. **Ad Acc. Circ:** 3,300 (ctrl).
Desc: National news, merchandising management and technical publication for ice and allied industries.

UK
REFRIGERATION AND AIR CONDITIONING (CROYDON, ENGLAND : 1988). (REFRIGERATION AND AIR CONDITIONING.). Vol. 91 No. 1084 (July 1988)-. Trade Publication. English. mo. £35.95, $61.90 UK; £51.95, $89.45 Europe; £67.95, $116.99 other. EMAP Readerlink, Audit House, 260 Field End Road, Ruislip Middlesex HA4 9LT England. **Tel** 011 44 081 868 4499, FAX 011 44 081 429 3117. ***Continues*** *Refrigeration, Air Conditioning and Heat Recovery, 0263-5739.*

UK
REFRIGERATION AND AIR CONDITIONING YEAR BOOK. VFOAT Air Conditioning Year Book; Refrigeration and Air Conditioning Yearbook. (1989)-. Trade Publication. English. EMAP Readerlink, Audit House, 260 Field End Road, Ruislip Middlesex HA4 9LT England. **Tel** 011 44 081 868 4499, FAX 011 44 081 429 3117. ***Continues*** *Refrigeration, Air Conditioning and Heat Recovery Year Book.*

US
REFRIGERATION SERVICE & CONTRACTING. Added/Corp Refrigeration Service Engineers Society. **VAT** Refrigeration Service and Contracting. Vol. 60, No. 8 (August 1990)-. Trade Publication. English. mo. $39.00 US; $51.00 other. Business News Publishing Company, 755 West Big Beaver Road, Suite 1000, Troy MI 48084. **Tel** (810)362-3700, FAX (810)362-0317, telex 230295. available on microfilm; available on an online database (file 648/Full-Text) from DIALOG. ***Continues*** *RSC. Refrigeration Service and Contracting, 0148-382X.*
Desc: Brings you the industry's best tips on servicing hvac/r equipment. Provides answers to your toughest field problems and brings you expert advice on refrigerant regulations.

JA/0034-3714
REITO. [Reito]. **Added/Corp** Nihon Reito Kyokai. **VFOAT** Refrigeration. (1926)-. Trade Publication. Japanese (summaries and/or abstracts in English). mo. 250.00. Nihon Reito Kyokai, (Japanese Assoc. of Refrigeration), 8, Saneicho, Shinjukuku, Tokyoto 160 Japan. **(Subscription address:** Maruzen Company Ltd., PO Box 5050, Import & Export Department, Tokyo 100 31 Japan.**) CODEN** RITOA8. ctrl circ. Documents available from Ask*IEEE, CASDDS.
Desc: Technical explanation of refrigeration.
Ind/Abst Chem. Abstr.; INSPEC (Nov. 1979-).

US/0742-731X
RETROFIT OF BUILDING ENERGY SYSTEMS AND PROCESSES. VFOAT Retrofit. 1982 Ed.-. Trade Publication. English. Sheet Metal and Air Conditioning Contractors' National Association Inc, 8224 Old Courthouse Road, Vienna VA 22180. **LC** TJ163.5.B84; R46. **DD** 696.

BL
REVISTA DO FRIO. Trade Publication. Portuguese. Cr$20.00. Editora Marcos Ltda, Av Sao Joao 1113 10 and CJ 7, Sao Paulo Brazil. **LC** TP490; .A78. ***Continues*** *Abrava.*

FR/0035-3205
REVUE GENERALE DU FROID, LA. [Rev. gen. froid]. **Added/Corp** Association Francaise du Froid. Vol. 22 (1945)-. Trade Publication. French. mo (10 issues). 499.51F France; 730.00F other. AGP Editions, 1 Rue du Coq Heron, 75001 Paris France. **Tel** 011 33 1 40265708. Index available. **Bk Rev**. **Ad Acc. Circ:** 4,500. ***Continues*** *Froid.*
Desc: Contains four or five articles about refrigeration and air conditioning, news about professional associations, industries and exhibitions, and analysis of new books.
Ind/Abst Energy Res. Abstr. (Nov. 1971-); Food Sci. Technol. Abstr.

FR/0370-6699
REVUE PRATIQUE DU FROID ET DU CONDITIONNEMENT DE L'AIR. [Rev. prat. froid cond. air]. **Added/Corp** Federation Nationale des Activites Frigorifiques. (1947)-. Trade Publication. French. Twenty-two times a year. 650.00F (France, Algeria, Morocco, & Tunisia); 935.00F (other). PYC Edition, 5 Avenue de Verdun, BP 105, 94208 Ivry S Seine Cedex France. **Tel** 011 33 1 49608636. **ED** Michele Lery. **LC** TP490; .F43. **CODEN** RPFCAJ. **[CCC]. Bk Rev**. **Ad Acc. Circ:** 5,000 (ctrl). Documents available from Article Express International, CASDDS. ***Continues*** *Revue Pratique du Froid.*
Desc: Industrial and commercial refrigeration and air conditioning: technologies, new products, plants, markets, controls, etc. Reports also on firms, manufacturers, exhibitions, meetings in France and Europe.
Ind/Abst Chem. Abstr.; Ei Page One; Energy Res. Abstr. (Aug. 1976-); Eng. Index Annu.; Food Sci. Technol. Abstr.

GW/0036-4401
SANITAR UND HEIZUNGTECHNIK. [Sanit. Heizungtech.]. **VFOAT** Sanitar und Heizungstechnik. Vol. 29, No. 3 (Mar. 1964)-. Trade Publication. German. Twelve times a year. DM96.00. Krammer Verlag, Postfach 170235, 40083 Duesseldorf Germany. **Tel** 011 49 211 679720, FAX 011 49 211 6797231. **LC** TD3; .S35. **NLM** W1 SA653N. Index available. cum. index. **Bk Rev**. **Ad Acc. Circ:** 23,000 (ctrl). ***Continues*** *Sanitare Technik.*
Ind/Abst Coal Abstr.; Energy Res. Abstr. (Oct. 1971-); Int. Build. Serv. Abstr.

FR/0151-1637
SCIENCE ET TECHNIQUE DU FROID / REFRIGERATION SCIENCE AND TECHNOLOGY. [Sci. tech. froid]. **Added/Corp** International Institute of Refrigeration. **VFOAT** Refrigeration Science and Technology. (1965)-. Proceedings. French (English and French). ir. Price varies per volume. Institut International du Froid, Paris France. **LC** UNC. **CODEN** STFRD4. Documents available from CASDDS. ***Absorbed*** *International Institute of Refrigeration. Supplement au Bulletin I.I.F./I.I.R.*
Desc: Discusses recent developments in areas such as thermodynamics, cryobiology, food science and technology, refrigerated storage, and heat pumps and energy recovery.
Ind/Abst Chem. Abstr.

US/0193-2128
SERVICE REPORTER. [Serv. rep.]. **VFOAT** Air Conditioning, Heating, Ventilation & Refrigeration Service Reporter. (19??)-. Trade Publication. English. Twelve times a year. $15.00 (one year); $28.00 (two years); $39.00 (three years). Service Reporter Company, 651 West Washington Street, Suite 300, Chicago IL 60606. **Tel** (312)993-0929, FAX (312)993-0960. **ED** Ed Schwenn. **DD** 338. **Ad Acc, Adv Mgr:** Mike. **Circ:** 50,000 (ctrl).
Desc: Service data, application information, notices and new products for HVAC and R industry dealers, contractors and inplant engineers.

US/0037-7457
SNIPS. (SNIPS, A JOURNAL OF CONSTRUCTIVE HELP TO THE SHEET METAL, WARM AIR HEATING AND AIR CONDITIONING TRADE.). (1932)-. Trade Publication. English. Twelve times a year. $12.00 US; $20.00 other. Snips, 1949 Cornell Avenue, Melrose Park IL 60160. **Tel** (708)544-3870, FAX (312)544-3884. **ED** Nick Carter. **Bk Rev**, (Qty: 24-36 per year). **Ad Acc. Circ:** 28,000 (ctrl).
Desc: Trade magazine directed to air conditioning, warm air heating, sheet metal, ventilation, refrigeration dealer-contractors, wholesalers, manufacturers and manufacturers representatives.

CN/0709-5031
SOLNOTE. 1 (Feb. 1978)-. Trade Publication. English. Four times a year. Free to members, $0.50 each number. Solar Energy Society of Canada Inc, PO Box No. 1353, Winnipeg Man R3C 2Z1. **Tel** (613)596-1067, FAX (613)596-1120. **DD** 697/.78.

US/0038-4461
SOUTHERN PLUMBING, HEATING, COOLING. Trade Publication. English. mo. $10.00. Southern Trade Publications Company, PO Box 18343, Greensboro NC 27419. **Tel** (919)854-3033. **Bk Rev**. **Ad Acc. Circ:** 6,000 (ctrl).

●UK
SPECIFIER'S GUIDE TO HEATING, VENTILATING, AIR CONDITIONING AND REFRIGERATION. Added/Corp Heating and Ventilating Contractors' Association. **VFOAT** Specifier's Guide. 43rd Ed. (1991/1992)-. Trade Publication. English. Faversham House Group Ltd, 111 St. James Road, Croydon, Surrey CR9 2TH England. **Tel** 011 44 81 6844082, , FAX 011 44 81 6849729, telex 266332 HET. **LC** TH7201; .Y42. **DD** 697. ***Continues*** *Heating, Ventilating, Refrigeration and Air Conditioning Year Book and Daily Buyers Guide.*

US
STANDARD MECHANICAL CODE AMENDMENTS. Trade Publication. English. $19.50 (nonmembers), $13.00 (members). Southern Building Code Congress International, 900 Montclair Road, Birmingham AL 35213. **Tel** (205)591-1853.

US
STANDARD PLUMBING CODE AMENDMENTS. Trade Publication. English. $19.50 (nonmembers), $13.00 (members). Southern Building Code Congress International, 900 Montclair Road, Birmingham AL 35213. **Tel** (205)591-1853.

US/0039-5935
SUPPLY HOUSE TIMES. Vol. 1 (Mar. 1958)-. Trade Publication. English. mo. $70.00 US; $102.00 Canada; $95.00 Mexico; $130.00 (surface mail) other. Cahners Publishing Company, 249 West 17th Street, New York NY 10011. **Tel** (212)645-0067, FAX (212)242-6987. **(Subscription address:** Cahners Publishing Company / Colorado, Paid Subscription Service Center, PO Box 7610, Highlands Ranch CO 80126-7610.**) LC** TH6101; .S8. **[CCC].**
Desc: Monthly business magazine for plumbing wholesalers. Features the latest products and market trends in plumbing, kitchen and bath, industrial pvf, heating and air conditioning, plus business and marketing strategies from successful wholesalers. Also includes detailed updates and forecasts on construction, remodeling, and industrial markets.

JA/0081-1610
TRANSACTIONS OF SHASE JAPAN. Main/Corp Kuki Chowa Eisei Kogakkai. (1963)-. Trade Publication. English. qt. $194.00. **(Subscription address:** Maruzen Company Ltd., PO Box 5050, Import & Export Department, Tokyo 100 31 Japan.**) ED** Ikuo Sato. **LC** TH7201; .K85. **Ad Acc. Circ:** 20,000 (ctrl).
Desc: Covers air conditioning systems, water supply and drainage, and hygienic engineering.
Ind/Abst Appl. Mech. Rev.

US/0733-2335
UNIFORM PLUMBING CODE. (UNIFORM PLUMBING CODE / INTERNATIONAL ASSOCIATION OF PLUMBING AND MECHANICAL OFFICIALS.). [Unif. plumb. code]. **Main/Corp** International Association of Plumbing and Mechanical Officials. (19??)-. Trade Publication. English. ir (Published every three years). $38.95 (three years) members of ICBO; $49.90 (three years) non-members. ICBO Evaluation Service Inc., 5360 South Workman Mill Road, Whittier CA 90601. **Tel** (213)699-0541, FAX (213)692-3853. **ED** Beverly J. Eicholtz. **LC** KF5709; .I65. **DD** 343.73/0786961; 347.303786961.
Desc: Covering all aspects of plumbing, including requirements for plumbing materials, and the International Association of Plumbing and Mechanical Officials Installation Standards.

NE/0042-451X
VERWARMING EN VENTILATIE. Added/Corp Algemene Vereniging voor de Centrale Verwarmings-Industrie. (1938)-. Trade Publication. Dutch. mo. Fl70.00 Netherlands; Fl130.00 other. VNI, Postbus 7272, 2701 AG Zoetermeer Netherlands. **Tel** 079-214402, FAX 079-210702. **ED** E. J. Wagenaar. **LC** TH7201; .V4. Index available (Free). cum. index. **Bk Rev**. **Ad Acc. Circ:** 3,500 (ctrl).
Desc: Technical articles concerning the heating, ventilating and air conditioning industry including product information.
Ind/Abst Int. Build. Serv. Abstr. (19??-).

DK/0346-4636
VVS. [VVS]. **Added/Corp** Dansk VVS Teknisk Forening. **VAT** Varme, Ventilation, Sanitet. (1965)-. Trade Publication. Danish. Eleven times a year. kr195.00 Denmark; kr211.50 other. Danish Technical Press, Skelbaekgade 4, DK 1717 Copenhagen 5 Denmark. **Tel** 011 45 31216801.
Ind/Abst Energy Res. Abstr. (Aug. 1976-); Saf. Health Work.

GW/0720-3438
WARMETECHNIK. [Warmetechnik]. Vol. 26, No. 1 (Jan. 1981)-. Trade Publication. German. Twelve times a year. DM157.80 Germany; DM181.80 other. AW Gentner Verlag, Postfach 101742, D-70015 Stuttgart Germany. **Tel** 011 49 711 636720, FAX 011 49 711 6367247, telex 841 722244. **LC** TH7201; .O4. **DD** 697/.005. **CODEN** WTECDW. **[CCC]. *Continues*** *Ol- und Gasfeuerung.*
Ind/Abst Coal Abstr.; Energy Res. Abstr. (May 1982-); Gas Abstr.; Int. Build. Serv. Abstr.

US/0273-5687
WESTERN HVACR NEWS. [West. HVACR news]. **VAT** Western Heating, Ventilating, Air Conditioning, Refrigeration News. Vol. 1, No. 1 (Jan. 1981)-. Trade Publication. English. Twelve times a year. $12.00 one year; $23.00 two years; $34.00 three years. Western HVACRA News, 4215 North Figueroa Street, Los Angeles CA 90065. **Tel** (213)255-8034. **DD** 697. **Ad Acc**, **Adv Mgr Tel** (213)225-8034. **Circ:** 20,000 (ctrl).
Desc: Contains news, feature and technical articles in heating, ventilation, air conditioning, refrigeration, hydronics, sheet metal, solar and allied industries.

US/0032-1680
WHOLESALER (ELMHURST), THE. (THE WHOLESALER.). (19??)-. Trade Publication. English. mo. $75.00 (one year), $130.00 (two year) US and Canada; $175.00 (one year), $275.00 (two year) other. TMB Publications Inc., 1838 Techny Court, Northbrook IL 60062. **Tel** (708)564-1127, FAX (708)564-1264. **ED** John A. Schweizer. **LC** HD9999.P6868; P6. **DD** 381/.45696/0973. **[CCC]**. **Bk Rev**. **Ad Acc**. **Circ:** 25,000 (ctrl). available on microfilm and microfiche from University Microfilms International (UMI). ***Continues*** *Plumbing, Heating, Air Conditioning Wholesaler.*
Desc: Covers the wholesale/distribution side of the plumbing, heating and refrigeration industry.

US/0199-1639
WISCONSIN MASTER PLUMBER. V. 1- Oct. 1979-. Trade Publication. English. qt. $5.00. Target Communications Corporation, 7626 West Donges Bay Road, Mequon WI 53092. **Tel** (414)242-3990. **ED** Glenn Helgaland. **Ad Acc. Circ:** 6,000 (ctrl).
Desc: Business management information for plumbing, heating, cooling contractors.

US/0044-0205
YANKEE OILMAN. **See** Petroleum and Natural Gas.

CC/0253-4339
ZHILENG XUEBAO. (CHIH LENG HSUEH PAO.). [Zhileng xuebao]. **Added/Corp** Chung-Kuo Chih Leng Hsueh Hui. **VFOAT** Zhileng Xuebao; Journal of the Chinese Association of Refrigeration. (1979)-. Academic Scholarly Publication. Chinese (summaries and/or abstracts in English). qt. RMBY0.60. Chinese Association of Refrigeration, 11 Fu Cheng Road, Beijing, People's Republic of China. **LC** TP490; .C42. **DD** 621.5/6/05. **CODEN** CLHPDE. Documents available from CASDDS.
Ind/Abst Chem. Abstr.

CN/0842-9693
ZONE HEATING NEWS. [Zone heat. news]. Vol. 6, No. 1 (April/May 1987)-. Trade Publication. English. bm. Hipper Industries Ltd, PO Box 238 Station D, Scarborough Ontario M1R 5B7 Canada. **DD** 697/.04. ***Continues*** *Home Energy, 0710-2984.*

HISTORY(GENERAL)

AT/1035-6754
21.C. [21.C]. **Added/Corp** Australia. Commission for the Future Australian Broadcasting Commission. **VFOAT** Twenty-First Century. (1990)-. Periodical. English. Four times a year (Seasonally). 40.00Aus$ (individuals), 60.00Aus$ others. Australian Commission Future, PO Box 1612M, Melbourne 3001 Australia. **Tel** 011 61 3 6633281, FAX 011 61 3 6633620. **DD** 363.705.
Desc: What will the world be like in the 21st century? What are the forces shaping society? What are the crucial new development in science and technology? These are the cutting edge in reporting these issues.

GW/0017-9574
ABHANDLUNGEN DER HEIDELBERGER AKADEMIE DER WISSENSCHAFTEN, PHILOSOPHISCH-HISTORISCHE KLASSE. **See** Philosophy.

GW/0065-0323
ABHANDLUNGEN UND MATERIALIEN ZUR PUBLIZISTIK. **Main/Corp** Berlin. Freie Universitat. Institut fur Publizistik. 1- 1962-. Periodical. German. ir. Colloquium Verlag, Unter den Eichen 93, W-1000 Berlin 45 Germany. **Tel** 030-832 8085. **ED** Bernd Sosemann. **UDC** 930.9. **Bk Rev. Circ:** 1,000 (ctrl).
Desc: Extraordinary scientific publications on history and related journalism.

CN/0848-9033
ABORIGINAL VOICE, THE. [Aborig. voice]. **Added/Corp** Ontario Metis and Aboriginal Association. (1989)-. Periodical. English. Six times a year. 9.00Can$ (OMAA members), 15.00Can$ (individual non-members), 24.07Can$ (groups or outside Canada). Ontario Metis Aboriginal Association, 158 Sackville Roade, Sault Ste., Marie Ontario P6B 4T6 Canada. **Tel** (705)949-5161. **ED** Brad Thompson. **DD** 971.3/00497. ***Continues*** *OMAA., 0841-9353.*

●US/1064-6981
ACCENT (MARLBORO, MASS.). **See** Ethnic Interests.

GW/0567-7580
ACTA HUMBOLDTIANA. (1966)-. Monographic series. German. ir. Price varies per volume. Franz Steiner Verlag GmbH, Postfach 101061, D 70009 Stuttgart Germany. **Tel** 011 49 0711 2582372, FAX 011 49 0711 2582290, telex 723636 daz d.

XR/0567-8293
ACTA UNIVERSITATIS CAROLINAE. PHILOSOPHICA ET HISTORICA. **See** Philosophy.

XR/0567-8307
ACTA UNIVERSITATIS CAROLINAE. PHILOSOPHICA ET HISTORICA. MONOGRAPHIA. **Added/Corp** Universita Karlova. **VFOAT** Philosophica et Historica. Monographia; Monographia. (1962)-. Monographic series. Czech (German; summaries and/or abstracts in German and Russian). (price varies with volume). Carolinum Press, Ovochny TRH 5, 11636 Prague 1 Czech Republic. **Tel** 011 42 2 228441. **LC** AS141; .A522.
Ind/Abst BHA : Biblio. Hist. Art.

HU/0324-6523
ACTA UNIVERSITATIS SZEGEDIENSIS. [Acta Univ. Szeged.]. **VFOAT** Acta Universitatis de Attila Jozsef Nominatae; Acta Universitatis Szegediensis de Attila Jozsef Nominatae. (1939)-. Monographic series. Hungarian. ir. **UDC** 378.4.
Ind/Abst MLA Int. Bibl. Books Artic. Mod. Lang. Lit.

FR/0531-0059
ACTES DU ... COLLOQUE INTERNATIONAL D'ETUDES GAULOISES, CELTIQUES ET PROTOCELTIQUES. **Main/Conf** Colloque International d'Etudes Gauloises, Celtiques et Protoceltiques. Vol. 1 (1960)-. Periodical. French. Ogam, BP 574, 35007 Rennes France. **LC** D70.

PO
AFRICANA (PORTO, PORTUGAL). (AFRICANA.). **Added/Corp** Universidade Portucalense. Centro de Estudos Africanos. No. 1 (Sept. 1987)-. Portuguese. Twice a year. 40$00 Portugal; 44$00 others. University of Portugal / African Estudos, Avenue Rodriguez Freitas 349, 4000 Porto Portugal. **Tel** 011 351 2 577823 43. **LC** D1; .A37.

AT/0044-6726
AGORA MELBOURNE. **See** Education-Teaching and Curriculum.

US/1050-3471
AIM (GLENDALE, CALIF.). (AIM : ARMENIAN INTERNATIONAL MAGAZINE.). [AIM]. **Added/Corp** AIM, Inc. (Glendale, Calif.). **VFOAT** Armenian International Magazine. (July 1990)-. Periodical. English. mo. $45.00 (1 year), $80.00 (2 year) US and Canada; $50.00 Middle East and Australia; $30.00 Armenia; $35.00 USSR; $55.00 others. Armenian International Magazine, PO Box 3296, Manhattan Beach CA 90266. **Tel** (818) 546-2246, FAX (818) 546-2283. **LC** DS161; .A54. **DD** 909/.0491992/005.
Desc: Encompasses the civilization and culture of the Armenian people.

GW
AKTEN ZUR DEUTSCHEN AUSWARTIGEN POLITIK, 1918-1945. SER. E : 1941-1945. **Main/Corp** Germany. Auswartiges Amt. German. ir. Vanderhoeck & Ruprecht, Postfach 3753, Theaterstr 13, W-3400 Goettingen Germany. **Tel** 0551/65061. **ED** Ingrid Kruger-Bulcke Und Hans G Lehmann. **Ad Acc.**

GW
AKTUELL. (19??)-. German. **LC** D410; .A45.

SW/0348-503X
AKTUELLT OM HISTORIA. [Aktuellt hist.]. (1978)-. Periodical. Swedish. qt. ***Continues*** *Aktuellt for Historielararen, 0345-0589.*
Ind/Abst Am. Hist. Life (19??-).

SP/0213-2966
AL-GEZIRA. [Gezira]. **Added/Corp** Alzira (Valencia). Ayuntamiento. (1985)-. Periodical. Spanish. an. Ayuntamiento de Alcira, San Roque 6, 46600 Alcira Valencia Spain. **ED** Aureliano Lairon Pla. **UDC** 908. Index available. cum. index. **Pr Rev. Circ:** 1,000 (ctrl).
Desc: Journal of historical studies on the Ribera Alta region of Spain.

LE
AL-MASIR AL-DIMUQRATI. **VFOAT** Almaseer Al-Democrati. V. 1, No. 1, (Dec. 1980)-. Periodical. Arabic. mo. £L50.00. Binayat Al-Kumudur Sintir, Shari Al-Kumudur, Al-Hamra, Al-Tabiq Al-Khamis Shaqqah, Beirut Lebanon. **LC** D839; .M36.

IQ
AL-MUARRIKH AL-ARABI : MAJALLAH FASLIYAH TARIKHIYAH MUHAKKAMAH TUNI BI-SHUUN AL-TURATH WA-AL-TARIKH AL-ARABI WA-AL-ALAMI. **Added/Corp** Ittihad Al-Muarrikhin Al-Arab. Amanah Al-Ammah. **VFOAT** Arab Historian; Journal of Arab Historians. (198?)-. Periodical. Arabic (table of contents in English). Three times a year. $150.00 institutions; $60.00 historians; $30.00 history students. Union of Arab Historians, PO Box 4085, Baghdad Iraq. **Tel** 011 964 1 4434236. **LC** DS37.7; .M3. ***Continues*** *Majallat Al-Muarrikh Al-Arabi.*

FR
ALMANACH - K.K.L. STRASBOURG. **Main/Corp** KKL Strasbourg. **VFOAT** Almanach du K.K.L., Strasbourg. Periodical. French. an. K K L Strasbourg, 1A rue Rene Hirschler, Strasbourg France. **LC** DS101.K17A. **DD** 909/.04924.

US
ALPHABETISCHER KATALOG. NACHTRAGSBAND. **Main/Corp** Institut fur Zeitgeschichte, Munich. Bibliothek. **VFOAT** Alphabetical Catalog. Supplement. 1.- 1973-. German.

US/0002-7065
AMERICA, HISTORY AND LIFE (SANTA BARBARA, CALIF. : 1989). **See** History(General)-Abstracting, Bibliographies and Statistics.

US/0742-8197
AMERICAN EAGLE (ESTERO, FLA.), THE. (AMERICAN EAGLE.). **Added/Corp** Koreshan Unity. Vol. 1 (1906)-. Periodical. English. sa (April and October). $5.00. American Eagle, PO Box 97, Estero FL 33928. **Tel** (813)992-2184. **ED** Jo Bigelow. **Circ:** 650.
Desc: Devoted to the preservation of and education about the Koreshan Unity Communal Colony from 1870's through 1982.

US/0002-8762
AMERICAN HISTORICAL REVIEW. [Am. hist. rev.]. **Added/Corp** American Historical Association. Vol. 1 (Oct. 1895)-. Academic Scholarly Publication. English. Five times a year. $65.00 (Class 1). American Historical Association, 400 A Street Southeast, Washington DC 20003. **Tel** (202)544-2422. **ED** David L Ransel. **LC** E171; .A57. **DD** 973.05. **NLM** E 172 A522. Index available (bound in last issue). cum. index. **Bk Rev. Ad Acc. Circ:** 17,000. available on microfilm and microfiche from University Microfilms International (UMI). Documents available from The Genuine Article, UMI Article Clearinghouse. ***Superseded in part by*** *Recently Published Articles, 0145-5311.*
Desc: The major historical journal in the United States. It includes scholarly articles and critical reviews of current publications in all fields of history.
Ind/Abst Acad. Abstr. Full Text Elite (July 1990-); Acad. Abstr. (July 1990-); Acad. Ind. [Computer File] (1985-); Acad. Search (July 1990-); Am. Hist. Life (1954-); Am. Bibliogr. Slavic East Europ. Stud.; Annu. Bibliogr. Engl. Lang. Lit.; Arts Humanit. Citation Index [Full Cov.]; BHA : Biblio. Hist. Art; Book Rev. Digest; Book Rev. Index; Chicano Index; Curr. Contents Arts Humanit.; Curr. Contents Soc. Behav. Sci.; Curr. Geogr. Publ. (199?-); Curr. Index J. Educ. (March 1990-); Econ. Lit. Index; Expand. Acad. Index (1985-); Gen. Period. Index (1985-); Hist. Source (July 1990-); Humanit. Index; Humanit. Source (Jul. 1990-); Index Book Rev. Relig.; INFO-SOUTH Abstr.; Int. Bibliogr. Sociol.; Int. Polit. Sci. Abstr.; J. Econ. Lit.; Mag. Index Plus (1989-); Mag. Search; Middle East Abstr. Index; Multicult. Educ. Abstr.; Newsp. Period. Abstr. (1986-); Peace Res. Abstr. J. (1964-); Read. Guide Period. Lit.; Relig. Index One Period. (1966-19??); Res. Alert [Full Cov.]; Romant. Move.; Sage Race Relat. Abstr.; Soc. Sci. Source (Jul. 1990-); Soc. Sci. Cit. Index [Full Cov.]; Sociol. Educ. Abstr.; Mag. Index (1977-); Middle East J.; U.S. Polit. Sci. Doc.; West. Hist. Q.; Women Stud. Abstr.

US/0897-2109
AMERICAN IRISH NEWSLETTER, THE. [Am. Irish newsl.]. (19??)-. Newsletter. English. bm. $20.00 (one year), $35.00 (two year). National Political Education Commission, Malloy Building, North Liberty Drive, Stony Point NY 10980. **Tel** (914)947-2726. **ED** John J. Finucane. **DD** 941. ***Continues*** *Political Education Committee National Newsletter.*
Desc: News, views and features concerning American Irish and Irish affairs, Irish history and more.

US/0895-0482
AMERICAN UNIVERSITY STUDIES. SERIES XXI, REGIONAL STUDIES. [Am. univ. stud., XXI Reg. stud.]. **VFOAT** American University Studies. Series 21, Regional Studies; Regional Studies. 1989-. Monographic series. English. ir. Price varies per volume. Peter Lang Publishing, 62 West 45th Street, 4th Floor, New York NY 10036. **Tel** (212)764-1471, (800)770-5264, telex 6973364 PLNY. **DD** 306.

●US/1058-2398
AMS STUDIES IN CULTURAL HISTORY. **VFOAT** Studies in Cultural History. (1992)-. Monographic

History(General)

series. English. Price varies per volume. AMS Press Inc., 56 East 13th Street, New York NY 10003. **Tel** (212)777-4700, FAX (212)995-5413, telex 710 581 2302.

US/0270-6253
AMS STUDIES IN SOCIAL HISTORY.
[AMS stud. soc. hist.]. (198?)-. Monographic series. English. ir. Price varies per volume. AMS Press Inc., 56 East 13th Street, New York NY 10003. **Tel** (212)777-4700, FAX (212)995-5413, telex 710 581 2302. **LC** UNC. **DD** 900.
  Desc: Series covering topics in social history. Past volumes have discussed subjects such as political loyalties and free love.

IT/0003-2476
ANALECTA CISTERCIENSIA. See Religion and Theology.

IT
ANALECTA ORIENTALIA. Added/Corp Pontificio Istituto Biblico. Vol. 1 (1931)-. Monographic series. Multiple languages (English and German). ir. Price varies per volume. Edit Pontif Instituto Biblio, Piazza Della Pilotta 35, 00187 Rome Italy. **Tel** 011 39 6 6781567, FAX 011 39 66985378. **ED** W Mayer. **Supersedes in part** Orientalia.

NE/0169-7447
ANALECTA PRAEHISTORICA LEIDENSIA. (ANALECTA PRAEHISTORICA LEIDENSIA : PUBLICATIONS OF THE INSTITUTE FOR PREHISTORY OF THE UNIVERSITY OF LEIDEN.). [Analecta praehist. leiden.]. **Added/Corp** Rijksuniversiteit te Leiden. Instituut voor Prehistorie. (1964)-. Monographic series. English (Dutch and German). ir. Price varies per volume. Martinus Nijhoff Publishers, Subsidiary of Kluwer Academic Publishers, Koraalrood 50, 2718 SC Zoetermeer Netherlands. **Tel** 011 31 79 684400. **LC** GN700; .A565. **CODEN** APLED7.
  Ind/Abst Anthropol. Lit.; Br. Archaeol. Bibliogr.; GeoRef.

BE
ANALECTA PRAEMONSTRATENSIA. Added/Corp Tongerloo, Belgium (Premonstratensian Abbey). (1925)-. Periodical. Multiple languages (French, German, Italian, Latin, Flemish and Spanish). Twice a year (July, Dec.). $45.00. Analecta Praemonstratensia, Abdijstraat 1 Averbode, B 3271 Averbode Belgium. **Tel** 011 32 13 772901. **LC** BX3901; .A53. Index available. cum. index. ctrl circ.
  Desc: History and biography about the Praemonstratensia.
  Ind/Abst BHA : Biblio. Hist. Art.

FR/1166-9829
ANAMNESES VILLEJUIF. Ceased.
(ANAMNESES.). (1990)-(1994). Periodical. French. qt. Bureau Etudes Coop et Communtr, 79 rue du Moulin du Saquet, 94800 Villejuif France. **Tel** 011 33 1 47262640. **ED** Desroche Heuis. **UDC** 3:001. **Bk Rev**, (Qty: 1-2). **Ad Acc. Circ:** 300. **Continues** Communautes Archives Sciences Sociales de la Cooperation et du Developpement.

AT/0310-5814
ANCIENT HISTORY: RESOURCES FOR TEACHERS. VFOAT Ancient History. Vol. 18, No. 1 (1988)-. Monographic series. English. Three times a year. Price varies per volume. **Continues** Ancient Society.

BE/0066-1619
ANCIENT SOCIETY. Added/Corp Katholieke Universiteit te Leuven. Vol. 1 (1970)-. Multiple languages (English, French, German and Italian). an (published in Nov.). 3000F. Editions Peeters SA, Bondgenotenlaan 153, BP 41, B-3000 Leuven Belgium. **Tel** 32 16 235170, FAX 32 16 228500, telex 65987 PUL B. **ED** H. Verdin and P. Van Dessel. Index available.
  Desc: Journal of ancient history of the Greek, Hellenistic and Roman world.
  Ind/Abst Numis. Lit.

SP/0211-7215
ANGLO AMERICAN STUDIES. Suspended.
Vol. 1, No. 1 (Nov. 1981)-(Nov. 1989). Periodical. English (Spanish). sa. $20.00. Anglo American Studies, Apartado 113, 37080 Salamanca Spain.
  Ind/Abst Annu. Bibliogr. Engl. Lang. Lit.; Linguist. Lang. Behav. Abstr.; Soc. Plann. Policy Dev. Abstr.; Sociol. Abstr.

IT
ANNALI DELLA SOCIETA ITALIANA DI STUDI SUL SECOLO XVIII. Vol. 1 (1984)-. Monographic series. Italian. Price varies per volume. Societa Editrice il Mulino, Strada Maggiore 37, 40125 Bologna Italy. **Tel** 011 39 51 256011, FAX 011 39 51 256034.

IT
ANNALI DELL'ISTITUTO ITALIANO PER GLI STUDI STORICI. Main/Corp Istituto Italiano per Gli Studi Storici. (1967/68)-. Italian. ir. Societa Editrice il Mulino, Strada Maggiore 37, 40125 Bologna Italy. **Tel** 011 39 51 256011, FAX 011 39 51 256034. **LC** D1; .I725a.

IT
ANNALI DELL'ISTITUTO STORICO ITALO-GERMANICO IN TRENTO. JAHRBUCH DES ITALIENISCH-DEUTSCHEN HISTORISCHEN INSTITUTS IN TRIENT. Main/Corp Istituto Storico Italo-Germanico. **VFOAT** Jahrbuch des Italienisch-Deutschen Historischen Instituts in Trient. Vol. 1 (1975)-. Italian (Italian). an. Societa Editrice il Mulino, Strada Maggiore 37, 40125 Bologna Italy. **Tel** 011 39 51 256011, FAX 011 39 51 256034. **LC** DG401; .I64A. **DD** 943/.005.
  Ind/Abst Am. Hist. Life (1984-).

IT
ANNALI / FONDAZIONE LELIO E LISLI BASSO-ISSOCO. Added/Corp Fondazione Lelio e Lisli Basso-ISSOCO. Vol. 1 (1975)-. Italian. ir. L38000. Libreria Laterza, Via Sparano 134, 70121 Bari Italy. **Tel** 011 39 80 5211780, FAX 011 39 80 235228, telex 811253. **LC** D1; .F57a.

FR/0997-0568
ANNUAIRE DE LA SOCIETE DES AMIS DU PALAIS DES PAPES ET DES MONUMENTS D'AVIGNON. (1912)-. Periodical. French. an. **UDC** 944.
  Ind/Abst BHA : Biblio. Hist. Art.

FR
ANNUAIRE / SOCIETE D'HISTOIRE DE MUTZIG ET ENVIRONS. Added/Corp Societe d'Histoire de Mutzig et Environs. (1983)-. Periodical. French. an. **Continues** Societe d'Historire de Mutzig et Environs (Series).

UK/0066-3832
ANNUAL BULLETIN OF HISTORICAL LITERATURE. Main/Corp Historical Association, London. No. 1 (1911)-. Bulletin. English. an. £43.00 UK and Europe; $73.00 North America; £47.00 other. Basil Blackwell Publishers Ltd, 108 Cowley Road, Oxford OX4 1JF England. **Tel** 011 44 865 791100, FAX 011 44 865 791347, telex 837022 OXBOOK G. **(Subscription address:** Blackwell Publishers / UK, Marston Book Services, PO Box 87, Oxford OX2 0DT England.) **ED** M Greengrass. **LC** Z6205; .H65. **DD** 016.9/05. **Ad Acc. Circ:** 1,000. available in microform.
  Desc: Publishes contributions which illuminate problems in very different periods and historical areas. Reviews cover up to 600 titles in each volume.
  Ind/Abst Br. Archaeol. Bibliogr.

UK/0066-4057
ANNUAL REGISTER (LONDON, ENGLAND) : 1964). (THE ANNUAL REGISTER.). Vol. 206 (1964)-. English. an. $165.00. Longman Group Ltd., Fourth Avenue, Longman House, Harlow Essex CM19 5SR England. **Tel** 011 44 279 429655, FAX 011 44 279 431059, telex 81259. **(Subscription address:** US & Canada: Gale Research Co., 835 Penobscot Building, Detroit, MI 48226) **ED** Alan J. Day. **LC** D2; .A7. **DD** 905. **Continues** Annual Register of World Events.
  Desc: Articles written by distinguished contributors give an analysis of international events, social and economic trends, and major developments in all fields. Statistics, texts of important documents, a chronology of events, charts and photographs make this a valuable resource on the year's events.

UK
ANNUAL REPORT. Main/Corp University of London. Institute of Historical Research. (1922)-. English. an. Free on request (add $1.00 for postage). University of London / Institute of Historical Research, Senate House, Malet Street, London WC1E 7HU England. **Tel** 011 44 71 6360272 ext. 225. **LC** D1; .L6. **Circ:** 2,000.
  Desc: Report of the Institute of Historical Research.

SA
ANNUAL REPORT - INSTITUTE FOR CONTEMPORARY HISTORY, UNIVERSITY OF THE ORANGE FREE STATE. Main/Corp University of the Orange Free State. Institute for Contemporary History. **VFOAT** Jaarverslag - Instituut Vir Eietydse Geskiedenis Universiteit Van die Oranje-Vrystaat. Multiple languages (Afrikaans and English). University of the Orange Free State, Institute for Contemporary History, PO Box 2320, Bloemfontein South Africa. **LC** D1; .B5A. **DD** 906/.0685.

US/0065-8561
ANNUAL REPORT OF THE AMERICAN HISTORICAL ASSOCIATION. Main/Corp American Historical Association. **Added/Corp** Smithsonian Institution. Press. American Historical Association. Annual Report. **VFOAT** Annual Report. (1889)-. English. Comes with American Historical Association Institution*Services Program and American Historical Review Classes II. American Historical Association, 400 A Street Southeast, Washington DC 20003. **Tel** (202)544-2422. **LC** E172; .A60. **DD** 973.062. available on microfilm and microfiche from University Microfilms International (UMI).

GW/0003-5157
ANNUARIUM HISTORIAE CONCILIORUM. (ANNUARIUM HISTORIAE CONCILIORUM; INTERNATIONALE ZEITSCHRIFT FUER KONZILIENGESCHICHTSFORSCHUNG.). [Annu. hist. concil.]. **VFOAT** Internationale Zeitschrift fuer Konziliengeschichtsforschung. (1969)-. Periodical. Multiple languages (English, French, German, Italian and Spanish). sa. DM157.00 Germany; DM160.00 other. Ferdinand Schoeningh Verlag, Postfach 2540, D 33055 Paderborn Germany. **Tel** 011 49 5251 127665. **ED** Walter Brandmuller. [CCC]. **Bk Rev. Circ:** 500.
  Desc: History of the ecclesiastical councils throughout the world.
  Ind/Abst Bibliogr. Mission.

GW/0003-570X
ANTIKE WELT. [Antike Welt]. Vol. 1 (1970)-. Periodical. German. Four times a year (4 issues per year and 1 special issue). DM80.50. Verlag Phillipp Von Zabern, Welschninnengasse 13 A, W 6500 Mainz F R Germany. **Tel** 011 49 6131 232214 or 15, FAX 011 49 6131 223710, telex 4187463. **ED** R. Fellmann, Franz Fischer and F. G. Maier. **LC** CB311; .A56. **Circ:** 8,500.
  Ind/Abst Art Index; ARTbibliogr. Mod.; Avery Index Archit. Period. Suppl. Colum. Univ. (1989-); BHA : Biblio. Hist. Art; Br. Archaeol. Bibliogr.; Ethnoarts Index.

GW/1015-9274
ANTIKE WELT SONDERNUMMER. [Antike Welt, Sondernr.]. (1973)-. Monographic series. German. an. **UDC** 902/903.
  Ind/Abst BHA : Biblio. Hist. Art.

GW/0066-4847
ANTIQUITAS. REIHE 2. ABHANDLUNGEN AUS DEM GEBIETE DER VOR UND FRUHGESCHICHTE. Vol. 1 (1955)-. Monographic series. German. ir. Price varies per volume. Dr. Rudolf Habelt GmbH, Postfach 150104, D 53040 Bonn Germany. **Tel** 011 49 228 232015. **ED** A. Alfoldi, K. Tackenberg, and W. Janssen.
  Desc: Essays in the fields of prehistory and early history.

GW/0066-4855
ANTIQUITAS. REIHE 3. ABHANDLUNGEN ZUR VOR-UND FRUHGESCHICHTE, ZUR KLASSISCHEN UND PROVINZIAL-ROMANISC HEN ARCHAEOLOGIE. V. 1- 1960-. Monographic series. German. ir. Price varies per volume. Dr. Rudolf Habelt GmbH, Postfach 150104, D 53040 Bonn Germany. **Tel** 011 49 228 232015. **ED** G A Refoldy, N Himmelmann-Wildschutz, W Janssen, and J Straub. **UDC** 931.
  Desc: Essays in the fields of prehistory and early history, classical archaeology and the archaeology of the Roman provinces and the history of the ancient world.

SW/0066-4863
ANTIQUITAS. REIHE 4. BEITRAEGE ZUR HISTORIA-AUGUSTA-FORSCHUNG. Vol. 1 (1963)-. Monographic series. German. ir. Price varies per volume. Dr. Rudolf Habelt GmbH, Postfach 150104, D 53040 Bonn Germany. **Tel** 011 49 228 232015. **ED** A. Alfoldi, A. Chastagnol, and J. Straub.
  Desc: Articles concerning research on the Roman Empire.

AT/0001-2068
ANU HISTORICAL JOURNAL. [ANU hist. j.]. **Added/Corp** Australian National University. A.N.U. Historical Society. **VFOAT** A.N.U. Historical Journal; Australian National University Historical Journal. (1964)-. English. an. **LC** D1; .A95a.
  Ind/Abst Am. Hist. Life (1970-).

AG/0589-6924
ANUARIO DEL DEPARTAMENTO DE HISTORIA. [Anu. Dep. Hist., Univ. nac. Cordoba]. **Added/Corp** Universidad Nacional de Cordoba. Departamento de Historia. No. 1 (1963)-. Spanish. an. **LC** F2801; .C67.
  Ind/Abst Am. Hist. Life (1963-).

UK/0950-0731
ARAB AFFAIRS. Ceased. Vol. 1, No. 1 (Summer 1986)-(19??). Periodical. English. qt. Routledge, 11 New Fetter Lane, London EC4P 4EE England. **Tel** 071 583 9855, FAX 071 842 2298. **(Subscription address:** Kinokuniya Company Ltd., 38-1 Sakuragaoka 5, chome Setagaya-ku, Tokyo 156 Japan.) **LC** DS36; .A675. **DD** 909/.0974927/005.
  Ind/Abst Int. Bibliogr. Sociol. (?-?); PAIS Int. Print (1991-?); Middle East J. (?-?).

US/1062-189X
ARCHAEOASTRONOMY & ETHNOASTRONOMY NEWS. See Astronomy.

GW/0003-9233
ARCHIV FUER KULTURGESCHICHTE.
[Arch. Kulturgesch.]. Vol. 1 (1903)-. Periodical. German.

History(General)

Twice a year. DM136.00. Boehlau Verlag GmbH & Cie / Koeln, Theodor Heuss STR 76, D-51149 Cologne Germany. **Tel** 011 49 2203 307021, FAX 011 49 2203 307349. **(Subscription address:** BDK Buecherdienst GmBh, Postfach 900120, D 51111 Cologne Germany.**)** **ED** Herbert Grundmann. **LC** CB3; .A6. **[CCC]. *Continues*** *Zeitschrift fuer Kulturgeschichte.*
Ind/Abst Am. Hist. Life (1954-); Annu. Bibliogr. Engl. Lang. Lit.; MLA Int. Bibl. Books Artic. Mod. Lang. Lit.; Romant. Move.

IT
ARCHIVIO DI STORIA DELLA CULTURA. Vol. 1 (1988)-. Italian. an. L40000. Morano Editore Spa, Vico S Domenico Maggiore 9, 80134 Naples Italy. **Tel** 011 39 81 556727. **LC** CB3; .A74. **DD** 905.

IT/0004-0347
ARCHIVIO STORICO LODIGIANO. [Arch. stor. lodigiano]. (1953)-. Periodical. Italian. an. L30000 Italy; L45000 other. Archivio Storico Lodigiano, Via Fissiraga 17, 20075 Lodi Italy. **Tel** 39 371 424128. **UDC** 945. **Bk Rev. *Continues*** *Archivio Storico per la Citta e ei Comuni del Circondario di Lodi.*
Ind/Abst BHA : Biblio. Hist. Art.

SP/0210-3230
ARCHIVO DE PREHISTORIA LEVANTINA. (ARCHIVO DE PREHISTORIA LEVANTINA : ANUARIO DEL SERVICIO DE INVESTIGACION PREHISTORICA DE LA EXCELENTISIMA DIPUTACION PROVINCIAL DE VALENCIA.). [Arch. prehist. levant.]. **Added/Corp** Valencia (Spain : Province). Diputacion Provincial. Servicio de Investigacion Prehistorica. Consejo Superior de Investigaciones Cientificas (Spain). Vol. 1 (1928)-. Spanish (English). ir. Libreria Segura, c/o Jorge Juanrtado, 14-458 28 Valencia 4 Spain. **LC** DP44; .A695.
Ind/Abst Anthropol. Lit.; GeoRef; Numis. Lit.

CN/1180-4629
ARCTIC CIRCLE. ***Ceased.*** [Arct. Circ.]. Vol. 1, No. 1 (July/Aug. 1990)-(Fall 1994). Periodical. English. bm. Nortext Information Design Ltd, 14 Collonade Road, Suite 280, Nepean Ontario K2E 7M6 Canada. **Tel** (613)727-5466. **ED** Roy Vontobel. **DD** 971.9/005. **CODEN** ARCIEN.
Ind/Abst Can. Period. Index (July 1990-).

IS/0334-4916
ARIEL : KETAV ET LI-YEDIAT ERETS-YISRAEL. (1985)-. Periodical. Hebrew. qt. $27.00. Youval Tal Ltd, PO Box 2160, Jerusalem 91021 Israel. **Tel** 011 972 2 248897. **LC** DS108.9; .K36. ***Continues*** *Kardom.*
Ind/Abst MLA Int. Bibl. Books Artic. Mod. Lang. Lit.

SJ
AROUND THE GLOBE. Main/Corp Wakalat Al-Sudan Lil-Anba. 1978-. English. 1.00. Wakalat Al-Sudan Lil-Anba Shari Al-Jumhuriyah, PO Box 1506, Al-Khartum Sudan. **LC** DT157; .W34A. **DD** 962.4/04/05. ***Continues*** *World and Domestic Important Events and News.*

CL/0004-6507
ATENEA (CONCEPCION, CHILE: 1972). (ATENEA.). **Added/Corp** Universidad de Concepcion. (Jan./June 1972)-. Periodical. Spanish (English). sa. 24.00Chil$. Universidad de Concepcion Publicaciones, M Arevalo, Casilla 1557, Concepcion Chile. **Tel** 011 56 41 234985 Ext 2591. **LC** F3051; .N83. **DD** 983/.005. cum. index. **Bk Rev. Ad Acc. Circ:** 2,500 (ctrl). ***Continues*** *Nueva Atenea.*
Desc: Publishes philosophical and historical essays and works about art and literature. Includes writings by foreign authors as well as Chilean collaborators.
Ind/Abst Am. Hist. Life (1972-1974, 1984-); HAPI Hisp. Am. Period. Index; MLA Int. Bibl. Books Artic. Mod. Lang. Lit.

IT/0583-7952
ATTI E MEMORIE DELLA SOCIETA MAGNA GRECIA. Main/Corp Societa Magna Grecia, Rome. (1925)-. Italian.
Ind/Abst Numis. Lit.

IT
ATTI E MEMORIE DELLA SOCIETA TIBURTINA DI STORIA E D'ARTE. Main/Corp Societa Tiburtina di Storia e d'Arte. Vol. 1 (1921)-. Italian. sa. **LC** DG402; .S65.
Ind/Abst Numis. Lit.

NZ/0111-7653
AUCKLAND-WAIKATO HISTORICAL JOURNAL. Added/Corp Auckland Historical Society. **VFOAT** Journal of the Auckland-Waikato Historical Societies. No. 36 (Apr. 1980)-. Periodical. English. Twice a year (April and Sept.). 12.00NZ$. Auckland Historical Society, 14 Ayr Street, Parnell Auckland 1 New Zealand. **Tel** 011 64 9 790202. **[CCC]. Circ:** 5,000. ***Continues*** *Historical Journal. Auckland-Waikato, 0110-3938.*
Ind/Abst Am. Hist. Life (1979-1984).

BE/0004-8003
AUGUSTINIANA. [Augustiniana]. **Added/Corp** Augustijns Historisch Instituut. Vol. 1 (April 1951)-. Periodical. Dutch (English, French, German and Latin). sa. 1450.00F Belgium and Luxembourg; 2050.00 other. Augustijns Historisch Institut, Pakenstraat 109, 3001 Heverlee Belgium. **Tel** 011 32 16 223379, FAX 011 32 16 292733. Index available. **Bk Rev**, (Qty: 2). **Circ:** 350. ***Supersedes*** *Augustiniana Neerlandica.*
Desc: Life and thought of St. Augustine. History of the order of St Augustine history of Augustinianism and Jansenism.
Ind/Abst MLA Int. Bibl. Books Artic. Mod. Lang. Lit.

AT/0813-0523
AUSTRALIAN SEA HERITAGE. [Aust. sea herit.]. (1984)-. Periodical. English. qt. 25.00Aus$. Sydney Maritime Museum, PO Box 140, Pyrmont New South Wales, 2009 Australia. **Tel** 11 61 2 2810266. **ED** Graeme Andrews. **DD** 387.20994. **Bk Rev**, (Qty: 16). **Ad Acc, Adv Mgr:** H. Clements, **Tel** (02 2810266. **Circ:** 6,000.

UK/1350-7532
AUSTRIAN STUDIES. See Literature.

IE/0790-4304
BANDON HISTORICAL JOURNAL. (BANDON HISTORICAL JOURNAL / CUMANN SEANCHAIS NA BANNDAN.). [Bandon hist. j.]. **Added/Corp** Cumann Seanchais na Banndan. No. 1 (1984)-. Periodical. English (Irish). an. $15.00. Bandon Historical Society, Bawnishal/Hare Hill, Bandon Co Cork Ireland. **Tel** 011 353 21 2342143. **Circ:** 1,000 (ctrl).
Desc: Historical articles on local history in Bandon and Co Cork.

US
BARKER TEXAS HISTORY CENTER SERIES. Added/Corp Eugene C. Barker Texas History Center. (1977)-. Monographic series. English. ir. Price varies per volume. University of Texas Press, PO Box 7819, Austin TX 78713. **Tel** (512)471-4531, FAX (512)320-0668, telex 776453 UTEXPRES AUS. **ED** Barbara N. Spielman.

AU/0522-6554
BEITRAEGE ZUR GESCHICHTE DER STADTE MITTELEUROPAS. Added/Corp Linz, Austria. Archiv. (1963)-. Monographic series. German. ir. Price varies per volume. Archiv der Stadt Linz, Linz Austria. **Tel** 0732/2393-2972. **LC** D104; .B37.

GW/0522-6848
BEITRAEGE ZUR KOLONIAL- UND UBERSEEGESCHICHTE. Vol. 1 (1966)-. Monographic series. German (summaries and/or abstracts in English and French). ir. Price varies per volume. Franz Steiner Verlag GmbH, Postfach 101061, D 70009 Stuttgart Germany. **Tel** 011 49 0711 2582372, FAX 011 49 0711 2582290, telex 723646 daz d. **ED** Rudolf von Albertini, Eberhard Schmitt. **DD** 909.

TU/0041-4255
BELLETEN. *Ceased.* Main/Corp Turk Tarih Kurumu. Vol. 1 (May 1937)-?. Periodical. Turkish (English, German and French). Three times a year. Ataturk Bulvari, Kizilay Sok No 1, Ankara Turkey. **Tel** 011 90 41 3102368, telex 42214. **LC** DR401. **Bk Rev.**
Ind/Abst Am. Hist. Life (1963-); Numis. Lit. (?-?); Middle East J. (?-?).

GW
BERICHT (HISTORISCHER VEREIN FUR DIE PFLEGE DER GESCHICHTE DES EHEMALIGEN FURSTBISTUMS ZU BAMBERG : 1979). (BERICHT / HISTORISCHER VEREIN FUER DIE PFLEGE DER GESCHICHTE DES EHEMALIGEN FURSTBISTUMS ZU BAMBERG.). **Added/Corp** Historischer Verein Fur die Pflege der Geschichte des Ehemaligen Furstbistums zu Bamberg. (1979)-. German. ***Continues*** *Bericht des Historischen Vereins Fur die Pflege der Geschichte des Ehemaligen Furstbistums Bamberg.*

US
BERKELEY JOURNAL, THE. Added/Corp Berkeley County Historical Society. Issue 1 (Spring 1968)-. Periodical. English. an. $5.00. Berkeley County Historical Society, PO Box 1624, Martinsburg WV 25401. **Tel** (304)229-3775.

IT
BIBLIOTECA DEI QUADERNI DEL NOVECENTO FRANCESE. (1982)-. Monographic series. Italian. Price varies per volume. Bulzoni Editore Srl, Via dei Liburni 14, 00185 Rome Italy. **Tel** 011 39 6 445-5207, FAX 011 39 6 445-0355.

SW/0519-9700
BIBLIOTHECA HISTORICA LUNDENSIS. Vol. 1 (1955)-. Monographic series. Multiple languages (English, French, German and Swedish). ir. Price varies per volume. Lund University Press, Box 141, S-22100 Lund Sweden. **Tel** 011 46 46 312000, FAX 011 46 46 305338, telex 33345 EDUCATE S.

SZ/0006-1999
BIBLIOTHEQUE D'HUMANISME ET RENAISSANCE. (BIBLIOTHEQUE D'HUMANISME ET RENAISSANCE. TRAVAUX ET DOCUMENTS.). [Bibl. humanisme renaiss.]. **Added/Corp** Association d'Humanisme et Renaissance. Vol. 1 (1941)-. Periodical. French (English, German and Italian). Three times a year (Feb., May, Sept.). Price varies. Librairie Droz SA, 11 rue Massot BP 389, CH 1211 Geneva 12 Switzerland. **Tel** 011 41 22 3466666, FAX 011 41 22 472391. **LC** CB361; .B5. **DD** 901. **NLM** W1 BI451. **[CCC].** Index available. **Bk Rev. Ad Acc. Circ:** 1,000. Documents available from The Genuine Article. ***Supersedes*** *Humanisme et Renaissance.*
Desc: Renaissance and humanism during the 15th and 16th centuries.
Ind/Abst Am. Hist. Life (1973-); Annu. Bibliogr. Engl. Lang. Lit.; Arts Humanit. Citation Index [Full Cov.]; BHA : Biblio. Hist. Art; Curr. Contents Arts Humanit.; MLA Int. Bibl. Books Artic. Mod. Lang. Lit.; Res. Alert [Full Cov.].

US/1042-4199
BLACK HERITAGE UNVEILED NEWSLETTER. [Black herit. unveiled newsl.]. Vol. 1, No. 1 (May 1990)-. Newsletter. English. mo. $96.00 (institutions). Spencer's International Enterprises Corp, 8627-D S Sepulveda Boulevard Box 43822. **DD** 909.
Ind/Abst Acad. Abstr. (July 1993-); Acad. Search (July 1993-199?); Mag. Artic. Summar. CD-ROM (July 1993-).

GW/0006-4408
BLATTER FUER DEUTSCHE LANDESGESCHICHTE. Added/Corp Gesamtverein der Deutschen Geschichts- und Altertumsvereine. Gesamtverein der Deutschen Geschichts- und Altertumsvereine. Korrespondenzblatt. Gesamtverein der Deutschen Geschichts- und Altertumsvereine. Correspondenzblatt. Vol. 1 (1852)-. Periodical. German. an. DM170.50. Blatter fuer Deutsche Landesgeschichte, Postfach 1340, D-5013 Koblenz Germany. **Tel** 011 49 261 33068. **ED** Wilhelm Janssen and Horst Romeyk. Index available. **Bk Rev. Circ:** 800 (ctrl).
Ind/Abst Am. Hist. Life (1967-1976, 1979-); Bibliogr. Carto.; BHA : Biblio. Hist. Art; Numis. Lit.

GW/0006-4416
BLATTER FUER DEUTSCHE UND INTERNATIONALE POLITIK. [Bl. dtsch. int. Polit.]. Volume 1- Nov. 1956-. Periodical. German. mo. $27.51. Pahl Rugenstein Verlag, Gottesweg 54, W-5000 Koln 51 Germany. **Tel** 0221-360020, FAX 0221-3600248. **LC** D839; .B57. **UDC** 323(430); 327(430). **[CCC].**
Ind/Abst Energy Res. Abstr. (Oct. 1979-); Int. Polit. Sci. Abstr.

AU/0006-4459
BLATTER FUER HEIMATKUNDE ... . [Bl Heim. kd.]. **Added/Corp** Historischer Verein fur Steiermark. (1923)-. Periodical. German. bm. Historischer Verein fuer Steiermark, Hamerlinggasse 3, A-8010 Graz, Austria. **ED** Guenter Cerwinka. **LC** DB681; .B5. **DD** 943.65.
Ind/Abst Am. Hist. Life (1963-).

PO/0430-4497
BOLETIM DA FILMOTECA ULTRAMARINA PORTUGUESA. Main/Corp Filmoteca Ultramarina Portuguesa. No. 1, (1954)-. Bulletin. Portuguese. ir. 970$00. Instituto de Investigacao Cientifica Tropical, Centro de Documentacao e Informacao, rua Jau 47, 1 300 Lisbon Portugal. **Tel** 645321. **ED** A da Silva Rego. **LC** WMLC L 83/7445. Index available. **Circ:** 1,000 (ctrl).
Desc: Publication of microfilmed documents of several archives of African countries with the Portuguese language.

PO/0871-3643
BOLETIM DO CENTRO DE DOCUMENTACAO 25 DE ABRIL. See Social Sciences.

PO/0870-466X
BOLETIM / INSTITUTO HISTORICO DA ILHA TERCEIRA. [Bol. Inst. Hist. Ilha Terc.]. **Added/Corp** Instituto Historico da Ilha Terceira. **VFOAT** Boletim do Instituto Historico da Ilha Terceira. (1943)-. Bulletin. Portuguese. an. **LC** DP702.A99; I5. **DD** 946.99.
Ind/Abst Am. Hist. Life.

SP/0520-4100
BOLETIN AMERICANISTA. [Bol. am.]. **Added/Corp** Universidad de Barcelona. Catedra de Historia de America. Universidad de Barcelona. Seccion de Historia de America. (1959)-. Periodical. Spanish. Universitat de Barcelona, Barcelona Spain. **LC** E11; .B64.
Ind/Abst Am. Hist. Life (1959-1964); HAPI Hisp. Am. Period. Index.

SP/0034-0626
BOLETIN DE LA REAL ACADEMIA DE LA HISTORIA (MADRID). (BOLETIN DE LA REAL ACADEMIA DE LA HISTORIA.). [Bol. R. Acad. Hist.]. **Main/Corp** Real Academia de la Historia (Spain). Vol. 1 (1877)-. Periodical. Spanish. ir. 4500ptas Spain; 5465ptas other. Leon Sanchez Cuesta Librero, Apodaca 1, 28004 Madrid Spain. **Tel** 011 34 1 5226465. **LC** DP1.A16. cum. index.
Ind/Abst Am. Hist. Life (1955-1973); BHA : Biblio. Hist. Art; Numis. Lit. (1955-); Romant. Move. (1955-).

SP
BOLETIN DE SUMARIOS. Spanish. sa. Free. Centro de Estudios Historicos, c/ Duque de Medinaceli 6, 28014 Madrid Spain. **Tel** 011 34 1 5856032.
Desc: A review of reviews enlarged with bibliographical articles on historical subjects.

AG/0524-9767
BOLETIN DEL INSTITUTO DE HISTORIA ARGENTINA Y AMERICANA DOCTOR EMILIO RAVIGNANI. (BOLETIN DEL INSTITUTO DE HISTORIA ARGENTINA Y AMERICANA DOCTOR EMILIO RAVIGNANI / FACULTAD DE FILOSOFIA Y LETRAS.). [Bol. Inst. Hist. argent. am. Dr. Emilio Ravignani]. **Added/Corp** Instituto de Historia Argentina y Americana "Doctor Emilio Ravignani.". Vol. 14/15, No. 24/25 (1970/1971)-. Periodical. Spanish. Twice a year. $29.00 Argentina, $37.00 US & Latin America, $39.00 others (institutions); $25.00 Argentina, $33.00 US & Latin America, $35.00 others (individuals). Sec Redaccion Boletin IHAA, 25 de Mayo 217 2 Piso, 1001 Buenos Aires Argentina. **LC** F2801; .B96. **DD** 982. ***Continues*** *Boletin del Instituto de Historia Argentina Doctor Emilio Ravignani.*
Ind/Abst Am. Hist. Life (1971-); ARTbibliogr. Mod. (1984-).

IT/0578-9850
BOLLETTINO DELL'ISTITUTO DI STORIA E DI ARTE DEL LAZIO MERIDIONALE. **VFOAT** Bollettino dell'Istituto di Storia e di Arte del Lazio Meridionale. (1963)-. Periodical. Italian. ir. **UDC** 93(450.62).
Ind/Abst BHA : Biblio. Hist. Art.

IT/0391-8211
BOLLETTINO DELL'ISTITUTO STORICO ARTISTICO ORVIETANO. **Main/Corp** Istituto Storico Artistico Orvietano. **Added/Corp** Istituto Storico Artistico Orvietano. (1945)-. Italian. ir. L10000. Istituto Storico Artistico, Orvietano/Postale 11638053, Piazza Febei 1 Italy. **LC** N15; .I8. **Bk Rev**. **Ad Acc**. **Circ:** 1,000 (ctrl).
Desc: Publishes articles on the history of Orvieto.
Ind/Abst BHA : Biblio. Hist. Art.

IT
BOLLETTINO LIGUSTICO PER LA STORIA E LA CULTURA REGIONALE. **Added/Corp** Societa Ligure di Storia Patria. (1949)-. Periodical. Italian. an. Price varies per volume. Sagep Editrice, Piazza Merani 1, 16145 Genoa Italy. **Tel** 011 39 10 313453. **LC** DG975.L68; B65. **DD** 945/.18/005. ***Continues*** *Giornale Storico e Letterario della Liguria (1925).*

IT/0391-1780
BOLLETTINO STORICO PISANO / SOCIETA STORICA PISANA. **Added/Corp** Societa Storica Pisana. (1932)-. Periodical. Italian. an. Pacini Editore Srl, Via A Gherardesca 1, 56121 Ospedaletto Pisa Italy. **Tel** 011 39 50 982439. **LC** DG975.P59; B67.
Ind/Abst BHA : Biblio. Hist. Art.

GW
BONNER HISTORISCHE FORSCHUNGEN. V. 1- 1952-. Monographic series. German. an. Price varies per volume. L Rohrscheid Verlag, Historische Forschungen, W-5300 Bonn 1 Germany.
Ind/Abst MLA Int. Bibl. Books Artic. Mod. Lang. Lit.

US/0733-6764
BORGO FAMILY HISTORIES. [Borgo fam. hist.]. **VFOAT** F.H.; FH. No. 1 (1983)-. Monographic series. English. ir. Price varies per volume. Borgo Press, PO Box 2845, San Bernardino CA 92406. **Tel** (714)884-5813, (714)885-1161. **UDC** 929.5(73).
Desc: Genealogies, compendia, census indexes, and family records

NE/0920-8607
BRILL'S STUDIES IN INTELLECTUAL HISTORY. [Brill's stud. intellect. hist.]. (1987)-. Monographic series. English. ir. Price varies per volume. E. J. Brill, Postbus 9000, 2300 PA Leiden Netherlands. **Tel** 011 31 71 312624, FAX 011 31 71 317532, telex 39296 BRILL NL. **UDC** 93.
Desc: Series covering the study of intellectual history. Topics have included the Dutch Republic as the center of the European book trade, medieval discussion of eternity, and the Rose Cross and the Age of Reason.

FR/1148-7771
BUGEY, LE. **VFOAT** Bulletin de la Societe Le Bugey; Bulletin Annuel - Societe Le Bugey. (1909)-. Periodical. French. an. **UDC** 908(444.4).
Ind/Abst BHA : Biblio. Hist. Art.

FR/0525-1044
BULLETIN ANALYTIQUE D'HISTOIRE ROMAINE / UNIVERSITE DE STRASBOURG, GROUPE DE RECHERCHE D'HISTOIRE ROMAINE. **Added/Corp** Universite de Strasbourg. Groupe de Recherche d'Histoire Romaine. Universite des Sciences Humaines de Strasbourg. Groupe de Recherche d'Histoire Romaine. Association pour l'Etude de la Civilisation Romaine (Strasbourg, France). Vol. 1 (1962)-. Monographic series. French. ir. Price varies per volume. Universite Sciences Humaines, 22 rue Rene Descantes, 67084 Strassbourg Cedex France. **Tel** 011 33 88 417317. **LC** Z2357; .B93. cum. index.

NE/0165-9367
BULLETIN ANTIEKE BESCHAVING : BABESCH. [Babesch, Bull. antieke beschav.]. **Added/Corp** Vereeniging Antieke Beschaving (Netherlands). **VFOAT** BABESCH. (1970)-. Bulletin. English (French, German and Italian). an. Fl180.00. Stichting Bulletin Antieke BSC, PO Box 9515, 2300 Ra Leiden Netherlands. **Tel** 011 31 71 897479. **LC** DE2; .V4. Index available. **Bk Rev**. **Ad Acc**. ctrl circ. ***Continues*** *Bulletin Antieke Beschaving.*
Desc: Annual papers on classical archaeology.
Ind/Abst Avery Index Archit. Period. Suppl. Colum. Univ. (1988-); BHA : Biblio. Hist. Art.

KE
BULLETIN (CARDINAL OTUNGA HIGH SCHOOL HISTORICAL SOCIETY). (BULLETIN / HISTORICAL SOCIETY.). **Added/Corp** Cardinal Otunga High School. Historical Society. Cardinal Otunga High School. **VFOAT** Bulletin of the C.O.H.S. Historical Society; Bulletin of the COHS Historical Society; Historical Society Bulletin; Bulletin of the Historical Society of Cardinal Otunga High School; Bulletin of the Historical Society; Bulletin of the Cardinal Otunga Historical Society; Cardinal Otunga Historical Society Bulletin; Bulletin of the History of Cardinal Otunga High School. (19??)-. Bulletin. English. Cardinal Otunga High School, PO Box 520, Kisii Kenya. **Tel** (0381)20052. **ED** Anthony Koning. **LC** DT433.5; .B84. **DD** 967.6/2/005. Index available. **Circ:** 300 (ctrl).
Desc: Original study of history and culture of the Kenya tribes members of which are studying at Cardinal Otunga High School based on oral tradition.

FR/0991-1367
BULLETIN DE LA SOCIETE D'HISTOIRE MODERNE. [Bull. Soc. hist. mod.]. **Main/Corp** Societe d'Histoire Moderne (Paris, France). Bulletin. French. mo. 200.00F. **LC** D1; .S54.
Ind/Abst Am. Hist. Life (1954-).

FR/0247-0101
BULLETIN DE L'INSTITUT D'HISTOIRE DU TEMPS PRESENT (PARIS, FRANCE : 1981). (BULLETIN DE L'INSTITUT D'HISTOIRE DU TEMPS PRESENT.). **Added/Corp** Institut d'Histoire du Temps Present (Paris, France) Centre National de la Recherche Scientifique (France). No. 4 (June 1981)-. Bulletin. French. qt. 20F. 80B rue Lecourbe, 75015 Paris France. **LC** D16; .B928. **DD** 907/.2. ***Continues*** *Bulletin Trimestriel de l'Institut d'Histoire du Temps Present.*
Ind/Abst Am. Hist. Life (1987-).

FR
BULLETIN DU XVII SIECLE. **See** Literature.

UK/0954-1179
BULLETIN OF JUDAEO-GREEK STUDIES. **See** Religion and Theology-Judaism.

US/0739-5612
BULLETIN OF THE ARCHAEOLOGICAL SOCIETY OF CONNECTICUT. **See** Archaeology.

AT/0816-6617
BULLETIN OF THE CENTRE FOR TASMANIAN HISTORICAL STUDIES. **Added/Corp** University of Tasmania. Centre for Tasmanian Historical Studies. Vol. 1, No. 1 (1985)-. English. an. 15.00Aus$. The Centre for Tasmania Historical Studies, University of Tasmania, GPO Box 252C, Hobarts Tasmania 7001 Australia. **Tel** 011 61 002 202305. **ED** Peter Chapman.
Desc: Original articles, research, news, events, and information of Tasmania.

FR
BULLETIN QUOTIDIEN (TEXTES DU JOUR ET PRESSE ETRANGERE). **Main/Corp** France. Direction de la Documentation. **Added/Corp** France. Ministere des Affaires Etrangeres. Service d'Information et de Presse. No. 1 (March 1916)-. Bulletin. French. wk. Societe Generale de Presse, 9-11-13-15 Avenue de l'Opera, 75001 Paris France. **Tel** 260-32-00.

NL
BULLETINS DE LA SOCIETE D ETUDES HISTORIQUES DE LA NOUVELLE CALEDONIE. French. Four times a year (Jan., Apr., July, Oct.). $RD385.00. Societe Historiques Nouvelle Caledonia, BP 63, Noumea New Caledonia.

IT
BULLETTINO SENESE DI STORIA PATRIA. **Added/Corp** Accademia dei Rozzi (Siena, Italy). Commissione Senese di Storia Patria. Istituto Comunale di Arte e di Storia. Deputazione Toscana di Storia Patria. Sezione di Siena. Accademia per le Arti e per le Lettere (Siena, Italy) Accademia Senese Degli Intronati. **VFOAT** Bollettino Senese di Storia Patria. Vol. 1 (1894)-. Periodical. Italian. an. L60000. Libreria Senese, Via di Citta 64/66, 53100 Sienna, Italy. **Tel** 011 39 577 280845. **LC** DG975.S49; B8. cum. index. ***Absorbed*** *Rassegna d'Arte.* ***Absorbed in part by*** *Rassegna d'Arte e del Costume.*
Ind/Abst BHA : Biblio. Hist. Art.

JA
BUMMEI. **Added/Corp** Tokai Daigaku. Bummei Kenkyujo. No. 1 (1962)-. Periodical. Japanese. ¥200. Tokai Building, 27-4 Shinjuku 3, Shinjuku-ku 160 Tokyo Japan. **LC** CB3; .B85.

US/0068-4341
BURT FRANKLIN RESEARCH AND SOURCE WORKS SERIES. (1960)-. Monographic series. English. ir. Price varies per volume. Burt Franklin Publishing Company, PO Box 856, New York NY 10014.

CN/0846-5312
CAHIER - SOCIETE D'HISTOIRE DES PAYS-D'EN-HAUT (1989). (CAHIER.). [Cah. - Soc. hist. Pays Haut]. **Added/Corp** Societe d'Histoire des Pays-d'en-Haut. No. 42 (1989)-. Periodical. French. qt. $25.00. Societe d'Histoire des Pays d'En Haut, C P 1209, Saint Sauveur des Monts Quebec J0R 1R0 Canada. **Tel** (514)227-3122. **ED** Victor Lavoiz. **DD** 971.4/4/005. **Bk Rev**, (Qty: 4). **Circ:** 140. ***Continues*** *Cahiers d'Histoire des Pays-d'en-Haut., 0820-9871.*
Desc: Interviews with descedents of settlers in the region, folklore and establishing of families at the beginning of the century, along with genealogical facts about the families.

BE/0771-6435
CAHIERS. **Added/Corp** Centre de Recherches et d'etudes Historiques de la Seconde Guerre Mondiale (Belgium). **VFOAT** Bijdragen. (Oct. 1985)-. French (Dutch; summaries and/or abstracts in Dutch, English and French). Cntr Rech Etudes Hist Sec Guer Mondiale, 4 Place de Louvain, 1000 Brussels Belgium. **Tel** 2/2184527. ***Continues*** *Cahiers d'Histoire de la Seconde Guerre Mondiale.*

FR/0068-5011
CAHIERS DE CIVILISATION MEDIEVALE. SUPPLEMENT. (1960)-. Periodical. French. Regisseur Recettes Publications, CESCM, 24 rue de la Chaine, 86022 Poitiers France. **Tel** 011 33 49 410386. **DD** 940.

FR/0761-7232
CAHIERS DE L'ECOLE SAINT-JEAN. ***Ceased.*** (1983)-(1993). Periodical. French. qt. Ecole Saint Jean, Maison Saint Joseph, 42590 Saint Jodard France. **Tel** 011 33 77634333. **UDC** 23. ***Continues*** *Bulletin du Cercle Thomiste Saint-Nicolas de Caen, 0761-7224.*

FR/0769-4504
CAHIERS DE L'I.H.T.P, LES. [Cah. I.H.T.P.]. **VFOAT** Cahiers de l'Institut d'Histoire du Temps Present. (1985)-. Monographic series. French. 95.00F France; 110.00F other. Institut d'Histoire du Temps Present, 44 rue de l'Amiral France, 75014 Paris France. **Tel** 011 33 1 45809046. **UDC** 940.5.
Ind/Abst Am. Hist. Life (1987-).

FR/0767-6468
CAHIERS DE L'ORIENT, LES. No. 1 (1986)-. Periodical. French (summaries and/or abstracts in English and Spanish). qt. 293.83F France; 353.83F other. Les Cahiers de l'Orient, 60 rue des Cevennes, 75015 Paris France. **Tel** 011 33 1 40607311. **LC** DS36; .C34. **DD** 909/.0974927/09.
Ind/Abst Middle East J.

CN/0317-5065
CAHIERS DES ETUDES ANCIENNES. **Added/Corp** Societe des Etudes Grecques et Latines du Quebec. **VFOAT** Cahier des Etudes Anciennes. (1972)-. Monographic series. French. ir. Price varies per volume. Exportlivre, PO Box 305, St Lambert Quebec J4P 3P8 Canada. **Tel** (514)671-3888. **LC** CB311; .C24. **DD** 913/.38/0305. ***Continues*** *Aurige, 0318-1170.*

FR/0008-008X
CAHIERS D'HISTOIRE. [Cah. hist.]. **Added/Corp** Comite Historique du Centre-est. Centre National de la Recherche Scientifique (France) Universite de Clermont-Ferrand I. Universite des Sciences Sociales de Grenoble. Universite de Lyon II. Universite Jean Moulin. Universite de Saint-Etienne. Centre Universitaire de Savoie. (1956)-. Periodical. French. tq. 176.00F France; 200.00F other. Comite Historique du Centre Est, 86 rue Pasteur, 69007 Lyon France. **Tel** 011 33 78 290173. **LC** D1; .C215. **DD** 905. Index available. cum. index. **Bk Rev**. **Circ:** 550. Documents available from The Genuine Article.
Ind/Abst Am. Hist. Life (1956-); Arts Humanit. Citation Index (19??-19??) [Full Cov.]; BHA : Biblio. Hist. Art; Res. Alert; Romant. Move.

CN/0225-5359
CAHIERS D'HISTOIRE DE LA SOCIETE D'HISTOIRE DE BELOEIL-MONT-SAINT-HILAIRE, LES. [Cah. hist. Soc. hist. Beloeil-Mont-Saint-Hilaire]. **Added/Corp** Societe d'Histoire de Beloeil-Mont-Saint-Hilaire. No. 1 (Feb. 1980)-. Periodical. French. Three times a year. 20.00Can$. Societe d'Histoire de Beloeil-Mont-Saint-Hilaire, CP 12, Beloeil Quebec J3G 4S8 Canada. **Tel** (514)467-0683. **DD** 971.4/36. cum. index. **Circ:** 400 (ctrl).

CN/0712-2330
CAHIERS D'HISTOIRE (MONTREAL). (CAHIERS D'HISTOIRE.). [Cah. hist.]. **Added/Corp** Universite de Montreal. Departement d'Histoire. Vol. 1, No. 1 (Spring 1981)-. Periodical. French. sa. 12.00Can$ (institution), Canada; 24.00Can$ other. Cahiers d'Histoire, Department d'Histoire, CP 6128 Succ A, University of Montreal, Montreal H3C 3J7 Quebec Canada. **Tel** (514)343-6234. **ED** Elaine Mayrand, Robert Arcand, Xavier Gelinas Robert Bouchard. **DD** 905. Index available. cum. index. **Bk Rev**. **Ad Acc. Circ:** 350.

FR/0008-025X
CAHIERS HAUT-MARNAIS, LES. No. 1 (May 1946)-. Periodical. French. qt. 120.00F. Amis des Cahires Haut-Marnais, BP 565, 52012 Chaumont Cedex, France. **Tel** 25 03 33 54. ***Continues*** *Bulletin des Etudes Locales dans l'Enseignement Publie en Haute-Marne.*
Desc: Includes information about the economic and social aspects of the Haut-Marnais region.
Ind/Abst BHA : Biblio. Hist. Art.

FR/0399-1326
CAHIERS IVAN TOURGUENIEV, PAULINE VIARDOT, MARIA MALIBRAN. **Added/Corp** Association des Amis d'Ivan Tourgueniev, Pauline Viardot et Maria Malibran. No. 1 (Oct. 1977)-. French. an. Institut d'Etudes Slaves, 9 rue Michelet, 75006 Paris France. **Tel** 011 33 1 43265089. **LC** PG3428.5; .C33. **DD** 782.1.

IT/1012-0238
CAHIERS LIGURES DE PREHISTOIRE ET DE PROTOHISTOIRE. **Added/Corp** Istituto Internazionale di Studi Liguri. (1984)-. Periodical. French. ir. Istituto Internationale Studi Liguri, Museo Bicknell, via Romana 39, 18012 Bordighera Italy. **Tel** 011 39 184 263601. ***Continues*** *Cahiers Ligures de Prehistoire et d'Archeologie.*
Ind/Abst Anthropol. Index; BHA : Biblio. Hist. Art.

FR/0409-8846
CAHIERS SAINT-SIMON. **Added/Corp** Societe Saint-Simon. No. 1 (1973)-. French. an. 150.00F. Societe Saint-Simon, 11D, Allee d'Honneur, 92330 Sceaux France. **(Subscription address:** M. Alain Duperon, 15 rue Vavin, F 75006 Paris**)** Index available. **Bk Rev. Circ:** 500.
Desc: Studies about the french memorialist Louis de Saint-Simon (1675)-1755), his works and the time of his life (reign of Louis XIV, Regency).

IT/0393-3741
CALENDARIO DEL POPOLO, IL. [Cal. popolo]. (1945)-. Periodical. Italian. mo. L40000.00 Italy; L50000.00 other. Teti Editore, Via Comelico 30, 20135 Milan Italy. **Tel** 011 39 2 55015575. **UDC** 07.

US/1050-7086
CALLIOPE (PETERBOROUGH, N.H.). (CALLIOPE: THE WORLD HISTORY MAGAZINE FOR YOUNG PEOPLE.). [Calliope]. Vol. 1, No. 1 (Sept./Oct. 1990)-. Periodical. English. Five times a year. $17.95 (one year), $31.95 (two year). Cobblestone Publishing Inc, 7 School Street, Peterborough NH 03458. **Tel** (603)924-7209. **DD** 909. **Circ:** 5,000. ***Continues*** *Classical Calliope, 0271-1966.*
Desc: Focuses on themes from world history throught the Renaissance.

UK/0955-7571
CAMBRIDGE REVIEW OF INTERNATIONAL AFFAIRS. **See** Political Science.

UK
CAMBRIDGE STUDIES IN EARLY MODERN HISTORY. Academic Scholarly Publication. English. ir. Price varies per volume. Cambridge University Press, The Edinburgh Building, Shaftesbury Road, Cambridge CB2 2RU United Kingdom. **Tel** 011 44 223 312393, FAX 011 44 223 325959. **(Subscription address:** Cambridge University Press / Outside of North America, Journal Fulfillment Department, The Edinburgh Building, Cambridge CB2 2RU United Kingdom.**)**

US/1042-864X
CAMOES CENTER QUARTERLY. [Camoes Cent. q.]. **Added/Corp** Camoes Center (Columbia University. Research Institute on International Change). Vol 1 No. 1 (Mar. 1989)-. Periodical. English. qt. Free. **LC** DP536.95; .C35. **DD** 909/.097569.
Desc: Speaks of Luso-Brazilianists.
Ind/Abst Am. Hist. Life (1991-).

CN/0008-4107
CANADIAN JOURNAL OF HISTORY. (CANADIAN JOURNAL OF HISTORY. ANNALES CANADIENNES D'HISTOIRE.). [Can. j. hist.]. **VFOAT** Annales Canadiennes d'Histoire. Vol. 1, (March 1966)-. Periodical. English (French). Three times a year (Apr., Aug., & Dec.). 28.00Can$ (individuals); 34.00Can$ (institutions). Annales Canadiennes d'Histoire, Department of History, University of Saskatchewan, Saskatoon Saskatchewan S7N 0W0 Canada. **Tel** (306)966-5792, FAX (306)966-5852. **ED** Bret Fairbairn, (phone: (306)966-5799). **LC** D1; .C27. (every 5 to 10 years). cum. index. **Bk Rev**, (Qty: 12). **Ad Acc**, **Adv Mgr:** J. Fraser, **Tel** (306)966-5794. **Pr Rev. Circ:** 730. available on microfilm and microfiche from University Microfilms International (UMI). Documents available from UMI Article Clearinghouse.
Desc: Publishes contributions in all fields of history other than Canadian.
Ind/Abst Acad. Abstr. Full Text Elite (Jan. 1992-); Acad. Abstr. (Jan. 1992-); Acad. Search (Jan. 1992-); Am. Hist. Life (1966-); Am. Bibliogr. Slavic East Europ. Stud.; Expand. Acad. Index (1989-); Hist. Source (Jan. 1992-); Humanit. Index; Humanit. Source (Jan. 1992-); INFO-SOUTH Abstr.; Mag. Search; Middle East Abstr. Index; MLA Int. Bibl. Books Artic. Mod. Lang. Lit.; Newsp. Period. Abstr. (1991-); Romant. Move.

CN/1180-968X
CANADIAN QUAKER HISTORY JOURNAL. ***Ceased.*** **See** Ethnic Interests.

CN/0317-7904
CANADIAN REVIEW OF STUDIES IN NATIONALISM. **See** History(General)-Abstracting, Bibliographies and Statistics.

US/0897-3423
CANYON LEGACY. [Canyon leg.]. Vol. 1, No. 1 (Spring 1989)-. Periodical. English. qt. $18.00. Dan O Laurie Museum, 118 E Center, Moab UT 84532. **Tel** (801)259-7985. **ED** Jean Akens. **DD** 978. **Bk Rev**, (Qty: 16-20). **Circ:** 300 subscr., 200 sales.
Desc: Established to publish articles on the history, prehistory, and natural history of the Colorado Plateau in Southeastern Utah and the Four Corners region.
Ind/Abst Am. Hist. Life (1989-).

XV/0590-5966
CASOPIS ZA ZGODOVINO IN NARODOPISJE. (CASOPIS ZA ZGODOVINO IN NARODOPISJE. REVIEW FOR HISTORY AND ETHNOGRAPHY.). [Cas. zgod. narodop.]. **Added/Corp** Univerza v Mariboru. Zgodovinsko Drustvo v Mariboru. **VFOAT** Review for History and Ethnography. (1904)-. Periodical. Slovenian (summaries and/or abstracts in English, French and German; table of contents in English). an. **LC** DR381.S6; C3. cum. index.
Ind/Abst Am. Hist. Life (1965-).

US/0733-8058
CATASTROPHISM AND ANCIENT HISTORY. [Catastr. anc. hist.]. (Aug. 1978)-. Periodical. English. Twice a year. $10.00 US and Canada; $15.00 other. Catastrophism and Ancient History, 3431 Club Drive, Los Angeles CA 90064. **Tel** (310)559-1075. **ED** Marvin A Luckerman. **LC** DS62.2; .C34. **DD** 939/.4. **Bk Rev**, (Qty: 4). **Ad Acc. Circ:** 1,000.
Desc: The purpose of this journal is to establish a new chronology for the ancient world based on history and archaeology.
Ind/Abst Old Testam. Abstr.

●US/1074-0252
CAVALRY JOURNAL, THE. (Sept. 1993)-. English. Four times a year (Mar., June, Sept., Dec.). $20.00 (individuals); $35.00 (organizational); $50.00 (corporate) Includes US Horse Cavalry Association Membership. The U. S. Cavalry Association, PO Box 2325, Fort Riley KS 66442-0325. **Tel** (913)784-5797. **Bk Rev.**
Desc: This information is to preserve the history, traditions, uniform and equipment of the United States Cavalry units.

IT
CAVOUR EPISTOLARIO. (19??)-. Monographic series. Italian. ir. Price varies per volume. Casa Editrice Leo S. Olschki, Viuzzo del Pozzetto, Casella Postale 66, 50126 Florence Italy. **Tel** 011 39 55 6530684, FAX 011 39 55 6530214. **Circ:** 1,000.

SP/0528-3647
CELTIBERIA. [Celtiberia]. **Added/Corp** Centro de Estudios Sorianos. Vol. 1 No. 1 (1951)-. Periodical. Spanish. ir. Centro de Estudios Sorianos, Casa de la Culture, Soria Spain. **DD** 946.
Ind/Abst Am. Hist. Life (1955-1973); Indice Hist. Esp.

US/0069-1461
CENTERS OF CIVILIZATION SERIES. (1959)-. Monographic series. English. ir. Price varies per volume. University of Oklahoma Press, PO Box 787, Norman OK 73070. **Tel** (800)627-7377, (405)325-2000. **DD** 900.
Desc: Devoted to the cities that from earliest times to the present have exercised a radiating influence upon the eras in which they flourished.

US/1042-0371
CENTRO DE ESTUDIOS PUERTORRIQUENOS BULLETIN. **Added/Corp** Hunter College. Centro de Estudios Puertorriquenos. **VFOAT** Bulletin; Centro; Boletin del Centro de Estudios Puertorriquenos, Hunter College. Vol. 2, No. 1 (Spring 1987)-. Bulletin. English (Spanish). $20.00 (institutions), $10.00 (individuals). Hunter College Library, 695 Park Avenue, New York NY 10021. **Tel** (212)772-4168. **LC** E184.P85; C46. **DD** 974.7/1004687295. ***Continues*** *Newsletter (Hunter College. Centro de Estudios Puertorriquenos).*

XR/0862-6111
CESKY CASOPIS HISTORICKY / CESKOSLOVENSKA AKADEMIE VED. **Added/Corp** Historicky Ustav (Ceskoslovenska Akademie Ved). Vol. 88, No. 1-2 (1990)-. Periodical. Czech. Four times a year. DM182.00 Germany; DM232.00 other. **(Subscription address;** Kubon & Sagner, ABT Zeitschriftenimport, D 80328 Munich Germany.**)** **LC** DB191; .C35. ***Continues*** *Ceskoslovensky Casopis Historicky, 0045-6187.*
Ind/Abst Am. Hist. Life (1990-).

FR
CHASSE MAREE. **See** Anthropology.

IT
CHEIRON (BRESCIA, ITALY). (CHEIRON.). **Added/Corp** Centro di Ricerche Storiche e Sociali Federico Odorici. Vol. 1, No. 1 (1983)-. Periodical. Italian. sa. L50000 Italy; L70000 other. Edizioni Centro Federico Odorici, Via Sorbana 11, 25126 Brescia Italy. **Tel** 011 39 376 322626. **LC** D1; .C38. **DD** 905.
Ind/Abst Biodeter. Abstr.

US/0277-7223
CHIRICU (BLOOMINGTON, IND. : 1981). (CHIRICU.). (19??)-. Periodical. English (Spanish). an. $5.00 (individuals); $7.00 (institutions). Chiricu, 849 Ballantine Hall, Indiana University, Bloomington IN 47405. **Tel** (812)335-5257, FAX (812)855-8577. **ED** Sean T. Dwyer. **LC** CB226; .C43. **DD** 909/.09756. **Bk Rev**, (Qty: 1-2). **Circ:** 150.
Desc: Dedicated to the development of the young writers and a interest to the latinos issues and culture.
Ind/Abst MLA Int. Bibl. Books Artic. Mod. Lang. Lit.

US
CHRONOLOGY OF AFRICAN-AMERICAN HISTORY. (1991)-. English. an. $49.95. Gale Research Inc., 835 Penobscot Building, Detroit MI 48226. **Tel** (800)877-GALE, (313)961-2242, FAX (313)961-6083, telex TWX 810-221-7086. **ED** Alton Hornsby, Jr.
Desc: Provides an historical overview of American of African descent over the last 400 years. Its focus is on people, places, and events that have had a major impact on African-American life.

US/1063-9454
CIVIL RIGHTS MONITOR. (CIVIL RIGHTS MONITOR / LEADERSHIP CONFERENCE EDUCATION FUND.). [Civ. rights monit.]. **Added/Corp** Leadership Conference Education Fund. Vol. 1, No. 1 (Oct. 1985)-. Periodical. English. Four times a year (Mar., June, Sept., Dec.). $35.00. Leadership Conference Education Fund, 1629 K Street Northwest, Suite 1010, Washington DC 20006. **Tel** (202)466-3311, FAX (202)466-3435. **DD** 323. **Circ:** 3,000.

US
CLINTON COUNTY HISTORICAL SOCIETY. English. ir. $10.00. Clinton County Historical Society, 1091 Franklin Street, Carlyle IL 62231.

US/1064-4954
COHOCTON JOURNAL, THE. (THE COHOCTON JOURNAL : A PUBLICATION OF THE COHOCTON HISTORICAL SOCIETY.). [Cohocton j.]. Vol. 1, No. 1 (1973)-. Periodical. English. Six times a year. $5.00. Cohocton Historical Society, PO Box 177, Cohocton NY 14826. **ED** Geraldine Deusenberg (editor's address: 14 South Main Street, Cohocton NY 14826; editor's phone: (716)384-5349). **DD** 974. cum. index.
Desc: Local history articles, birth, death & marriages for township of Cohocton, genealogy for people living in Cohocton, meeting notices of Cohocton Historical Society.

FR
COLLECTION D'ETUDES ANCIENNES. French. ir. 210.00F. Societe Edition Belles Lettres, 95 Boulevard Raspail, 75006 Paris France. **Tel** 011 33 1 45487055, FAX 011 33 1 45449288, telex 200577.

NO/0801-9282
COLLEGIUM MEDIEVALE. 1- 1988-. Periodical. Norwegian (summaries and/or abstracts in English, French and German).

●US/1067-0580
COMMITTEE ON EAST ASIAN LIBRARIES DIRECTORY. [Comm. East Asian Libr. dir.]. **Main/Corp** Association for Asian Studies. Committee on East Asian Libraries. **VFOAT** CEAL Directory. (1992)-. Directory. English. ir. $10.00

(non-members). Association for Asian Studies / Commitee on East Asian Libraries, Main Library / Room 310, Ohio State University Libraries, 1858 Neil Avenue Mall, Columbus OH 43210-1286. **Tel** (614)292-3502, FAX (614)292-7859. **DD** 950. ***Continues*** *Association for Asian Studies. Committee on East Asian Libraries. CEAL Directory.*

US/0895-0539
CONCORD REVIEW, THE. [Concord rev.]. Vol. 1, No. 1 (Fall 1988)-. Periodical. English. qt (Mar., June, Sept., Dec.). $37.00. Concord Review Business Office, PO Box 476, Canton MA 02121. **Tel** (617)828-8450. **ED** Will Fitzhugh. **LC** D1; .C67. **DD** 905.

US/0734-3671
CONFEDERATE HISTORICAL INSTITUTE JOURNAL. [Confed. Hist. Inst. j.]. **Added/Corp** Confederate Historical Institute (U.S.). **VFOAT** CHI Journal; C.H.I. Journal. Vol. 1, No. 1 (1980)-. Periodical. English. qt. $20.00. The Confederate Historical Institute, PO Box 7388, Little Rock AR 72217. **Tel** (501)225-3996, FAX (501)225-5167. **ED** Jerry Russell. **Bk Rev**.
Desc: Present day activities relating to an interest in the history of the Confederate States of America.

FR/0154-5639
CONFLUENTS. Vol. 1 (1975)-. Monographic series. French. Price varies per volume. Les Belles Lettres, 95 Boulevard Raspail, 75006 Paris France. **Tel** (1)45.48.70.55, FAX (1)45.44.92.88, telex 200577 F.

CN/0709-9347
CONNAISSANCE ET VIE. [Connaiss. vie]. V. 1- Nov. 1979-. Periodical. French. bm. $12.00 Canada, $11.00 others. Societe Promundo de Recherche et de Financement, CP 2086 Succursale Jacques-Cartier, Sherbrooke Quebec J1J 3Y3 Canada. **DD** 909.82/05. **UDC** 980.

US/0277-1446
CONTINUITY. [Continuity]. **Added/Corp** Intercollegiate Studies Institute. Young America's Foundation. No. 1 (Fall 1980)-. Academic Scholarly Publication. English. Twice a year. $25.00. Young Americas Foundation, 110 Eldon Street, Herndon VA 22070. **Tel** (703)318-9608. **ED** Burton W. Folsom. **LC** D1; .C68. **DD** 905. **Bk Rev**. **Ad Acc. Circ:** 500.
Desc: Scholarly essays on historical subjects from a conservative intellectual perspective.
Ind/Abst Am. Hist. Life (1980-).

US
CONTINUUM. **Added/Corp** St. Xavier College (Chicago, Ill.). Vol. 1, No. 1 (Autumn 1990)-. Periodical. English. tq. Crossroad/Continuum Publishing Group, 370 Lexington Avenue, New York NY 10017. **LC** IN PROCESS. ***Continues*** *Continuum, 0010-7786.*
Ind/Abst BHA : Biblio. Hist. Art.

US/0737-6448
CONTRIBUTIONS IN ANTHROPOLOGY AND HISTORY. **See** Anthropology.

BE
CORPUS CHRISTIANORUM. CONTINUATIO MEDIAEVALIS. **See** Religion and Theology.

UK/0590-8876
COSTUME. **See** Clothing Industry and Fashion.

US
COURIER OF HISTORICAL EVENTS. English. Six times a year (Jan., Mar., May, July, Sept., Nov.). $15.00. North Virginia Association of Historians, Box 1366, Fairfax VA 22030. **Tel** (703)250-3512. **Bk Rev**, (Qty: 4). **Circ:** 300 (ctrl).

UK
CROSS & COCKADE GREAT BRITAIN JOURNAL. **See** Military and Defense.

SP/0214-400X
CUADERNOS DE HISTORIA CONTEMPORANEA. (CUADERNOS DE HISTORIA CONTEMPORANEA / DEPARTAMENTO DE HISTORIA CONTEMPORANEA.). [Cuad. hist. contemp.]. **Added/Corp** Universidad Complutense de Madrid. Departamento de Historia Contemporanea. No. 9 (1988)-. Periodical. Spanish. an. Editorial Complutense, Donoso Cortes 65 1RA Planta, 28003 Madrid Spain. **Tel** 011 34 1 3946372. **LC** D355; .C77. **DD** 909.8/05. ***Continues in part*** *Cuadernos de Historia Moderna y Contemporanea, 0211-0849.*
Ind/Abst Am. Hist. Life (1990-).

SP/0214-4018
CUADERNOS DE HISTORIA MODERNA. **Added/Corp** Universidad Complutense de Madrid. Departamento de Historia Moderna. No. 9 (1988)-. Spanish. an. 2000ptas. Editorial Complutense, Donoso Cortes 65 1RA Planta, 28003 Madrid Spain. **Tel** 011 34 1 3946372. **LC** D355; .C79. **DD** 909.82/05. ***Continues in part*** *Cuadernos de Historia Moderna y Contemporanea, 0211-0849.*
Ind/Abst Am. Hist. Life (1980-).

CL
CUADERNOS DE HISTORIA (SANTIAGO, CHILE). (CUADERNOS DE HISTORIA.). No. 1 (Dec. 1981)-. Periodical. Spanish. **LC** D1; .C76. **DD** 905.
Ind/Abst Am. Hist. Life (1988-); HAPI Hisp. Am. Period. Index.

GW
CUADERNOS DE INVESTIGACION HISTORICA. **Added/Corp** Eberbach (Germany) Eberbach (Germany). Kommission Fur Geschichte und Altertumer. German.

SP/0214-4670
CUADERNOS DE INVESTIGACION HISTORICA BROCAR. [Cuad. invest. hist. Brocar]. **VFOAT** Brocar. (1986)-. Periodical. Multiple languages. an. ***Continues*** *Cuadernos de Investigacion. Historia, 0211-6839.*
Ind/Abst Am. Hist. Life (1986-).

●US/1062-0672
CUBA REPORT, THE. [Cuba rep.]. Vol. 1, No. 1 (May 1992)-. Periodical. English. mo. $425.00. Cuba Newsletter, Inc., 501 Brickell Key Drive, Suite 200, Miami FL 33131. **Tel** (305)381-8685. **LC** HC152.5.A1; C82. **DD** 330.97291/005.

DK/0902-7521
CULTURE & HISTORY (COPENHAGEN). (CULTURE & HISTORY.). [Cult. hist.]. **Added/Corp** Center for Comparative Cultural Research (Copenhagen, Denmark) Center for Research in the Humanities (Copenhagen, Denmark). **VFOAT** Culture and History. (1987)-. English. ir. Price varies per volume. Scandinavian University Press, PO Box 2959 Toeyen, N 0608 Oslo 6 Norway. **Tel** 011 47 2 2575400, FAX 011 47 2 2575353, telex 71896 UROR N. **(Subscription address:** Scandinavian University Press, 200 Meacham Ave., Elmont NY 11003.**) ED** Michael Harbsmeier, Mogens Trolle Larsen and Uffe Ostgard. **LC** GN301; .C86. **DD** 301/.05.
Desc: Functions as an international forum for debate in the general field of cultural historical studies. Founded by scholars attached to Danish research concerned with comparative cultural studies, the serial has roots in a Danish or Scandinavian tradition.
Ind/Abst Am. Hist. Life (1989-); Anthropol. Lit.; Linguist. Lang. Behav. Abstr.; Soc. Plann. Policy Dev. Abstr.; Sociol. Abstr.

US/0011-3530
CURRENT HISTORY (1941). (CURRENT HISTORY.). [Curr. hist.]. Vol. 1, No. 1 (Sept. 1941)-. Periodical. English. ir (9 issues). $32.00 (one year), $61.00 (two year), $81.90 (three year) US. Current History Inc., 4225 Main Street, Philadelphia PA 19127. **Tel** (215)482-4464, FAX (215)482-9197. **ED** William Finan Jr. **LC** D410; .C82. **DD** 910.82. Index available (bound in Dec. issue). cum. index. **Bk Rev**. **Pr Rev. Circ:** 23,847. available on microfilm and microfiche from University Microfilms International (UMI); available on CD-ROM. Documents available from The Genuine Article, UMI Article Clearinghouse, Magazine Collection. ***Absorbed*** *Key to Contemporary Affairs* ***and*** *Forum (1945);* ***Formed by the union of*** *Current History and Forum* ***and*** *Events (New York, N.Y.).*
Desc: Every issue is devoted to a single county or an important area of the world. Provides reliable background material and an objective appraisal of current events - a valuable tool for reference and research.
Ind/Abst ABC POL SCI; Abr. Read. Guide Period. Lit.; Acad. Abstr. Full Text Elite (Jan. 1984-); Acad. Abstr. (Jan. 1984-); Acad. Ind. [Computer File] (1984-); Acad. Search (Jan. 1984-); Am. Hist. Life (1955-); Am. Bibliogr. Slavic East Europ. Stud.; Book Rev. Index; Can. Period. Index (19??-); Curr. Contents Soc. Behav. Sci.; Curr. Geogr. Publ. (199?-); Curr. Mil. Pol. Lit.; Expand. Acad. Index (1984-); Gen. Period. Index (1985-); Guide Soc. Sci. Relig.; Hist. Source (Jan. 1984-); Index Islam. Lit.; INFO-SOUTH Abstr.; Int. Bibliogr. Sociol.; Mag. Artic. Summar. Elite (Jan. 1984-); Mag. Artic. Summar. Select (Jan. 1984-); Mag. Artic. Summar. CD-ROM (Jan. 1984-); Mag. Express (1986-) [Full Txt.]; Mag. Index Plus (1989-); Mag. Index Sel. Microfiche (1986-) [Full Txt.]; Mag. Index. Sel. (1986-); Mag. Search; Middle East Abstr. Index; Newsp. Period. Abstr. (1986-); PAIS Int. Print (1991-); Peace Res. Abstr. J. (1964-1968, 1970, 1978-1980); Read. Guide Abstr. Select Ed.; Read. Guide Period. Lit.; Res. Alert [Full Cov.]; Resource/One Ondisc; Soc. Sci. Cit. Index [Full Cov.]; Soc. Work Abstr. (?-?); Mag. Index (1977-); Middle East J.; TOM Gen. Index (1985-) [Full Txt.]; U.S. Polit. Sci. Doc.; West. Hist. Q.; World Agric. Econ.

GR
CYRILLOMETHODIANUM. 1-. Periodical. English (French, German, Italian and Serbo-Croatian (Roman)). an. $30.00. Association Hellenique d Etudes Slaves, B P 10610, Thessalonique 54110 Greece. **Tel** (031)261135. **ED** Anthony-Emil N Tachiaos. **LC** DF503; .C95. **Bk Rev**.
Desc: Studies on Greco-Slavic historical and literary relations.

NE
DAT WAS DE TOESTAND IN DE WERELD. 2.- 1974-. Dutch. an. Annoventura, B V Uitgeversmaatschappij Annoventura, Amsterdam Netherlands. **LC** D410; .T63. ***Continues*** *Toestand in de Wereld.*

IT
DATI STATISTICI SUL COMMERCIO ESTERO : IMPORTAZIONI ED ESPORTAZIONI PER PAESI, TAVOLA 3. Istituto Nazionale Statistica, GBP SEZ4 Via Cesare Balbo 16, 00184 Rome Italy. **Tel** 011 39 6 46735118.

IT
DEDALO. Italian. qt. L40000 Italy; L50000 other. Belpoliti Fiorella, Via Asiago 9, 42100 Reggio Emilia Italy. **Tel** 011 39 522 76179.

XR/0418-5129
DEJINY A SOUCASNOST. **Added/Corp** Ceskoslovenska Spolecnost pro Sireni Politickych a Vedeckych Znalosti. Czechoslovakia. Ministerstvo Skolstvi a Kultury. Socialisticka Akademie (Prague, Czechoslovakia). (1959)-. Periodical. Czech. mo. **DD** 943.7. ***Continues*** *Nase Vlast.*
Ind/Abst Am. Hist. Life (1968-1969).

US/8755-8459
DEKALB COUNTY HERITAGE. **Added/Corp** DeKalb County Historical Society (Mo.). (19??)-. Periodical. English. Four times a year (Jan., Apr., July, Oct.). $7.50. DeKalb City Historical Society, PO Box 477, Maysville MO 64469. **ED** Martha Spiers and Emma Newkirk (phone: (816)449-5842). **LC** F472.D3; D39. **DD** 977.8/153. **Circ:** 300 (ctrl).
Desc: The events, family news, and photographs of DeKalb County residents.
Ind/Abst Am. Hist. Life.

US
DESOTO PLUME. English. Four times a year. $10.00 Louisiana; $13.00 others Comes with Desoto Historical Society membership. Desoto Historical Society, Route 2 Box 260, Logansport LA 71049.

UK/0305-8549
DEVON HISTORIAN, THE. **Added/Corp** Standing Conference for Devon History. Devon History Society. (1970)-. Periodical. English. Twice a year (Apr., Oct.). £5.00 (individuals); £7.00 (institutions). Devon & Exeter Institute, 7 The Close, Exeter Devon England.
Ind/Abst Br. Archaeol. Bibliogr.

PN/0046-0206
DIALOGO SOCIAL. ***Suspended.*** **Added/Corp** Centro de Capacitacion Social (Panama, Panama). No. 86-87 (Feb./March 1977)-. Periodical. Spanish. mo. $15.00 Panama; $35.00 US; $25.00 Latin American and Europe; $40.00 other. Centro de Capacitacion Social, Apartado 9A - 192, Panama R P Panama. **Tel** 26-6971. **LC** HN1; .D17. **DD** 909.82. **Bk Rev**. **Pr Rev. Circ:** 3,000. ***Continues*** *DS: Dialogo Social.*
Desc: Alternative medium in the field of information on the current state of Panama and Latin America. Strives to provide an opportunity for Panamanian authors, instructive proposals and simple publications.
Ind/Abst Hum. Rights Intern. Rep. (?-?).

FR/0755-7256
DIALOGUES D'HISTOIRE ANCIENNE. **Added/Corp** Universite de Besancon. Centre de Recherches d'Histoire Ancienne. (1974)-. Monographic series. French. ir. Price varies per volume. Societe Edition Belles Lettres, 95 Boulevard Raspail, 75006 Paris France. **Tel** 011 33 1 45487055, FAX 011 33 1 45449288, telex 200577. **LC** AS161; .B39 subser; D51. **DD** 084/.1 S; 930/.05.
Ind/Abst Numis. Lit.

FR
DIEN DAN NGUOI VIET. Vietnamese. ir. $20.00. Dien Dan Nguoi Viet, Mr Khanh, 3179 Wilson Blvd, Arlington VA 22001.

GW
DILTHEY-JAHRBUCH FUER PHILOSOPHIE UND GESCHICHTE DER GEISTESWISSENSCHAFTEN. **VFOAT** Dilthey-Jahrbuch; Dilthey Jahrbuch fur Philosophie und Geschichte der Geisteswissenschaften. (1983)-. German (English). an. Vandenhoeck & Ruprecht, Robert Bosch Breite 6, D-37079 Goettingen Germany. **Tel** 011 49 551 695911, FAX 011 49 551 695917, telex 965226 VAN d. **LC** B3216.D84; A13. **DD** 193.

IT
DIMENSIONI E PROBLEMI DELLA RICERCA STORICA : RIVISTA DEL DIPARTIMENTO DI STUDI STORICI DAL MEDIOEVO ALL'ETA CONTEMPORANEA DELL'UNIVERSITA "LA SAPIENZA" DI ROMA. **Added/Corp** Universita Degli Studi di Roma "La Sapienza." Dipartimento di Studi Storici dal Medioevo all'eta Contemporanea. (1988)-. Periodical. Italian. sa. L60000

Italy; L85000 other. Franco Angeli Riviste SRL, Viale Monza 106, 20127 Milan Italy. **Tel** 011 39 2 2827651, 011 39 2 289562. **LC** D1; .D49. **DD** 907/.2.

US
DIRECTORY OF HISTORY DEPARTMENTS AND ORGANIZATIONS IN THE UNITED STATES AND CANADA. **Added/Corp** American Historical Association. Institutional Services Program. **VFOAT** Directory of History Departments and Organizations. 16th Ed. (1990-91)-. Directory. English. $60.00; Also comes with membership. American Historical Association, 400 A Street Southeast, Washington DC 20003. **Tel** (202)544-2422. **LC** D16.3; .G83. ***Continues*** *Guide to Departments of History.*

CN/1184-6070
DIRECTORY OF MUNICIPAL AND PROVINCIAL HERITAGE PROPERTY IN SASKATCHEWAN (1990). (DIRECTORY OF MUNICIPAL AND PROVINCIAL HERITAGE PROPERTY IN SASKATCHEWAN / HERITAGE RESOURCES SECTION, HERITAGE BRANCH, SASKATCHEWAN CULTURE, MULTICULTURALISM & RECREATION.). [Dir. munic. prov. herit. prop. Sask.]. **Added/Corp** Saskatchewan. Heritage Resources Section. (1990)-. Directory. English. **DD** 363.6/9/0257124. ***Continues*** *Municipal and Provincial Heritage Property Directory., 1184-6062.*

US/1048-4418
DIRECTORY OF WOMEN HISTORIANS. [Dir. women hist.]. **VFOAT** Women Historians. 1st (1975)-. Directory. English. $10.00 non-member, $7.00 member. American Historical Association, 400 A Street Southeast, Washington DC 20003. **Tel** (202)544-2422. **ED** J A Justice. **LC** D14; .D57. **DD** 920.72/025/73.

US/0277-2736
DISCUSSIONS ON TEACHING. ***Ceased.*** **Added/Corp** American Historical Association. (1971)-No. 2 (19??). Monographic series. English. ir. American Historical Association, 400 A Street Southeast, Washington DC 20003. **Tel** (202)544-2422. **LC** UNC. **DD** 371.1/02.

FR/0070-6760
DIX-HUITIEME SIECLE. [Dix-huitieme siecle]. **Added/Corp** Societe Francaise d'Etude du XVIIIe Siecle. No. 1 (1969)-. French (summaries and/or abstracts in French and English). an (Sept.). 30.00F France; 54.00F others. Soc Fran d Etude Xville Siecle, 12 Avenue du Stade Nautique, 64000 Pau France. **Tel** 011 33 78 268445. **LC** CB411; .D57. **DD** 840.
Ind/Abst Annu. Bibliogr. Engl. Lang. Lit.; BHA : Biblio. Hist. Art; MLA Int. Bibl. Books Artic. Mod. Lang. Lit.; Romant. Move.

IT
DIZIONARIO EPIGRAFICO DI ANTICHITA ROMANE. (19??)-. Italian. ir. L18000. Licosa Spa, PO Box 552, 50125 Florence Italy. **Tel** 011 39 55 645415.
Desc: Epigraphic dictionary.

AT/0727-971X
DO IT. [Do it]. (1977)-. English. qt. (Comes with Educational Drama Association of NSW membership). Educational Drama Association of New South Wales, PO Box 55, Rozelle NSW 2039 Australia. **Tel** 62 2 8182591. **DD** 371.332.
Ind/Abst Aust. Educ. Index.

US/0145-9929
DOCTORAL DISSERTATIONS IN HISTORY. **Added/Corp** American Historical Association. Institutional Services Program. Vol. 1 (Jan./June 1976)-. English. an. $10.00. American Historical Association, 400 A Street Southeast, Washington DC 20003. **Tel** (202)544-2422. **LC** Z6205; .D6. **DD** 016.9. ***Continues*** *List of Doctoral Dissertations in History in Progress or Recently Completed in the United States.*

FR/0151-0827
DOCUMENTS STRASBOURG. (DOCUMENTS REVUE DES QUESTIONS ALLEMANDES.). **VFOAT** Documents Traduits et Publies par le Centre d'Information et de Documentation Economiques et sociales; Documents (Paris. 1946). (1945)-. Periodical. French. Five times a year. 210.00F France; 230.00F other. Documents Revue des Questions, 50 rue de Laborde, 75008 Paris France. **Tel** 011 33 1 43872550. **UDC** 3 (430.1). Index available.
Ind/Abst Int. Bibliogr. Sociol.

RU/0568-5796
DOKLADY I SOOBSCENIJA INSTITUTA ISTORII. (DOKLADY I SOOBSHCHENIIA INSTITUTA ISTORII / AKADEMIIA NAUK SSSR.). [Dokl. soobsc. Inst. ist.]. **Added/Corp** Institut Istorii (Akademiia nauk SSSR). (1954)-. Periodical. Russian. **LC** DK1; .A3273.
Ind/Abst Am. Hist. Life (1955-1956).

JA/0420-0918
DOSHISHA AMERIKA KENKYU. **Added/Corp** Doshisha Daigaku. Amerika Kenkyujo. **VFOAT** Doshisha American Studies. (19??)-. Periodical. English (Japanese). ¥1000 (per issue). Doshisha Daigaku Amerika Kenkyujo, Karasuma Higashi-iru Kyoto Japan. **Tel** 075-251-3961. **LC** E171; .D67. cum. index (No. 1-20). **Bk Rev. Circ:** 700.

FR/0419-683X
DOSSIERS DE L'HISTOIRE. (19??)-. French. ir. Carbonel, 194 rue Lafayette, F-75010 Paris France. **Tel** 011 33 1 40357641. **DD** 900.

US
DUCKS OLD TIME JOURNAL. English. Twelve times a year. $6.00. Robert B. Davidson, 3351 Oak Ridge Road, Palmyra TN 37142. **Tel** (615)326-5389. **ED** Robert B. Davidson. Index available (Mail with Dec. iss. (Free)). **Circ:** 200 (ctrl).
Desc: Newsletter of news from way back yonder.

PL/0419-8824
DZIEJE NAJNOWSZE. **Added/Corp** Instytut Historii (Polska Akademia Nauk). Vol. 1 (1969)-. Periodical. Polish. qt. Price on Request. **(Subscription address:** ARS Polona, PO Box 1001, 00068 Warsaw Poland.) **LC** D410; .D9. **DD** 943.8. ***Formed by the union of*** *Najnowsze Dzieje Polski. Materiay I Studia Z Okresu 1914-1939; Najnowsze Dzieje Polski. Materiay I Studia Z Okresu II Wojny Swiatowej* ***and*** *Polska Ludowa.*
Ind/Abst Am. Hist. Life (1985-).

US/0070-8089
EAST CAROLINA UNIVERSITY PUBLICATIONS IN HISTORY. 1976-. Monographic series. English. ir. Price varies per volume. East Carolina University / History, Department of History, Greenville NC 27834. **Tel** (919)757-6587. **UDC** 973. **Bk Rev. Ad Acc. Circ:** 500 (ctrl). ***Continues*** *East Carolina College Publications in History.*

NE/0926-6070
EDUCATION AND SOCIETY IN THE MIDDLE AGES AND RENAISSANCE. [Educ. soc. Middle Ages Renaiss.]. (1991)-. Monographic series. English. ir. Price varies per volume. E. J. Brill, Postbus 9000, 2300 PA Leiden Netherlands. **Tel** 011 31 71 312624, FAX 011 31 71 317532, telex 39296 BRILL NL. **UDC** 94/99"5/17".

AT/1038-1775
EDUCATIONAL HISTORIAN, THE. **See** Education.

IS
EDUT. **Added/Corp** Bet Lohame ha-Getaot (Lohame ha-Getaot, Israel). **VFOAT** Testimony. (1987)-. Periodical. Hebrew. an. $25.00. Beit Lochamei Haghetaot, 102 Arlosoroff Street, 62097 Tel Aviv Israel. **Tel** 011 972 03 5249506. **LC** D804.3; .E38. ***Continues*** *Yediot Bet Lohame ha-Getaot al-Shem Yitshak Katsenelson.*

US/0161-0996
EIGHTEENTH CENTURY, THE. **See** History(General)-Abstracting, Bibliographies and Statistics.

US/0013-2586
EIGHTEENTH CENTURY STUDIES NEWS CIRCULAR. English. qt. $52.00 US; $56.00 other. The American Society for Eighteenth-Century Studies, PO Box 1234, Utah State University, Logan UT 84322. **Tel** (801)750-4065.

UK/0013-8266
ENGLISH HISTORICAL REVIEW, THE. [Engl. hist. rev.]. Vol. 1 No. 1 (Jan. 1886)-. Periodical. English. Five times a year. £82.00 Europe; £87.00 Other (Institutions). Longman Group Ltd., Fourth Avenue, Longman House, Harlow Essex CM19 5SR England. **Tel** 011 44 279 429655, FAX 011 44 279 431059, telex 81259. **ED** P. Williams and R. Evans. **LC** DA20; .E58. **DD** 941/.005. **[CCC].** Index available. cum. index. **Bk Rev. Ad Acc. Circ:** 2,500. available on microfilm and microfiche from University Microfilms International (UMI). Documents available from The Genuine Article, UMI Article Clearinghouse.
Desc: Journal of historical scholarship.
Ind/Abst Acad. Abstr. Full Text Elite (July 1990-); Acad. Abstr. (July 1990-); Acad. Ind. [Computer File] (1987-); Acad. Search (July 1990-); Am. Hist. Life (1954-); Annu. Bibliogr. Engl. Lang. Lit.; Arts Humanit. Citation Index [Full Cov.]; BHA : Biblio. Hist. Art; Book Rev. Digest; Book Rev. Index; Br. Humanit. Index; Curr. Contents Arts Humanit.; Expand. Acad. Index (1987-); Hist. Source (July 1990-); Humanit. Index; Humanit. Source (Jul. 1990-); Index Book Rev. Relig.; INFO-SOUTH Abstr.; Mag. Search; Middle East Abstr. Index; Newsp. Period. Abstr. (1991-); Relig. Index One Period. (1980-); Res. Alert ¡Full Cov.]; Romant. Move.; Soc. Sci. Cit. Index [Select. Cov.]; West. Hist. Q.

XE/1061-4435
ENNAANIN ETTO. [Ennaanin etto]. **Added/Corp** Marshall Islands. Historic Preservation Office. **VFOAT** News from the Past. Vol. 1, No. 1 (Nov. 1 1991)-. Periodical. English (Marshall). qt. Free. Historic Preservation Office, Ministry of Interior and Outer Islands Affairs, PO Box 18, Majuro Atoll, Republic of the Marshall Islands, 96960. **DD** 363.

BE/0773-4980
ENQUETES DU MUSEE DE LA VIE WALLONNE. **Main/Corp** Musee de la Vie Wallonne (Liege, Belgium). Vol. 1 No. 1 (1924)-. French.
Ind/Abst BHA : Biblio. Hist. Art.

IT
ENTE OTTAWA MEDIEVALE DI ORTE (SERIES). (ENTE OTTAWA MEDIEVALE DI ORTE.). (1981)-. Monographic series. Italian. Price varies per volume.

CN
ERASMUS STUDIES. (1973)-. Monographic series. English. ir. Price varies per volume. University of Toronto Press, 5201 Dufferin Street, Downsview Ontario M3H 5T8 Canada. **Tel** (416)667-7781, (416)667-7782, FAX (416)667-7803. **Circ:** 1,500.
Desc: A series of monographs and other book-length studies concerned with Erasmus and related subjects.

IT/0394-5618
ERBA D'ARNO. (1980)-. Periodical. Italian. qt. L35000.00 Italy; L50000.00 other Europe; L60000.00 other. Groupe d Etudes Balzaciennes, 47 rue Raynovard, F-75016 Paris France. **UDC** 82. Index available. cum. index. **Bk Rev. Ad Acc.**

US
ESCAMBIA COUNTY HISTORICAL QUARTERLY. English. qt. $7.50. Escambia County Historical Society, PO Box 276, Brewton AL 36427. **Tel** (205)867-4832. **ED** Barbara Jones. Index available.

US/0071-1411
ESSAYS IN HISTORY. ***Ceased.*** **Added/Corp** University of Virginia. History Club. Vol. 12 (1966/67)-(1993). English. an. University of Virginia Corcoran Department of History, Randall Hall, Charlottesville VA 22903. **Tel** (804)977-4498. available on microfilm from University Microfilms International (UMI). ***Continues*** *Annual Collection of Essays in History.*
Ind/Abst Am. Hist. Life (1988-).

US/0272-0337
ESSAYS IN HISTORY (ARLINGTON). (ESSAYS IN HISTORY.). [Essays hist.]. **Added/Corp** Phi Alpha Theta. Omicron Kappa Chapter (University of Texas at Arlington). **VFOAT** E. C. Barksdale Student Lectures. Vol. 3 (1974)-. Periodical. English. ir. $10.00 (two years). Omicron Kappa Phi Alpha Theta / Department of History, University of Texas, PO Box 19529, Arlington TX 76019. **Tel** (817)273-2907. **LC** D1; .E718. **DD** 905. ***Continues*** *Essays on American Civilization.*
Ind/Abst Am. Hist. Life (1981-).

MX/0185-2620
ESTUDIOS DE HISTORIA MODERNA Y CONTEMPORANEA DE MEXICO. [Estud. hist. mod. contemp. Mex.]. **Added/Corp** Universidad Nacional Autonoma de Mexico. Instituto de Investigaciones Historicas. Vol. 1 (1965)-. Spanish. ir. UNAM - Universidad Nacional Autonoma de Mexico / Historia, Instituto de Investigaciones Historicas Unam, Torre 1 de Humanidades, Piso 7 / 7th Floor, Ciudad Universitaria, 04510 Mexico DF Mexico. **Tel** 011 52 5 5505215 Ext 3396. **LC** F1201; .E77.
Ind/Abst Am. Hist. Life (1967, 1980-1983); HAPI Hisp. Am. Period. Index.

SP/0211-3759
ESTUDIOS - DEPARTAMENTO DE HISTORIA MODERNA, UNIVERSIDAD DE ZARAGOZA. (ESTUDIOS DEL DEPARTAMENTO DE HISTORIA MODERNA.). [Estud. - Dep. Hist. Mod. Univ. Zaragoza]. **Main/Corp** Saragossa. Universidad. Departamento de Historia Moderna. **VFOAT** Estudios del Departamento de Historia Moderna (Zaragoza); Estudios - Departamento de Historia Moderna, Facultad de Filosofia y Letras (Zaragoza). (1971)-. Spanish. **LC** D1; .S23a. **DD** 909.08/05.
Ind/Abst Am. Hist. Life (1971-).

MX
ESTUDIOS ECUMENICOS. **Added/Corp** Centro de Estudios Ecumenicos. (19??)-. Periodical. Spanish. Centro de Estudios Ecumenicos, Guty Cardenas No 131, Mexico 20 D F Mexico.
Ind/Abst Econ. Lit. Index (19??-); J. Econ. Lit.

PO/0870-6344
ESTUDOS DE CASTELO BRANCO. [Estud. Castelo Branco]. No. 1 (June 8, 1961)-. Periodical. Portuguese (Spanish). qt.
Ind/Abst MLA Int. Bibl. Books Artic. Mod. Lang. Lit.

PO/0870-5879
ESTUDOS DE HISTORIA E CARTOGRAFIA ANTIGA. MEMORIAS. (ESTUDOS DE HISTORIA E CARTOGRAFIA ANTIGA MEMORIAS). (1983)-. Monographic series. Multiple languages. ir. price varies per volume. Instituto de

History(General)

Investigacao Cientifica Tropical, Centro de Documentacao e Informacao, rua Jau 47, 1 300 Lisbon Portugal. **Tel** 645321. **UDC** 912. **Circ:** 2,000 (ctrl).

CN/1193-199X
ETUDES D'HISTOIRE RELIGIEUSE. [Etud. hist. relig.]. **VFOAT** Historical Studies. (1990)-. Multiple languages. an. **DD** 282.7105. ***Continues*** *Sessions d'Etude - Societe Canadienne d'Histoire de l'Eglise Catholique, 0318-6172.*

IT
EUI WORKING PAPER. HEC / DEPARTMENT OF HISTORY AND CIVILIZATION, EUROPEAN UNIVERSITY INSTITUTE. **Added/Corp** European University Institute. Dept. of History and Civilization. **VFOAT** HEC; EUI Working Papers in History. (1990)-. Monographic series. English (French). Price varies per volume. European University Institute Badia Fiesolana, Via dei Roccettini 5, San Domenico di Fiesole Florence Italy. **LC** IN PROCESS. ***Continues in part*** *EUI Working Paper.*

US/0271-9649
EVENT (NEW YORK), THE. (THE EVENT.). [Event]. V. 1-. Periodical. English. bm. $2.50 single issue. PO Box 1699, Grand Central Station, New York NY 10017. **LC** D839; .E95. **DD** 905. **UDC** 930.9.

BL
EXPEDICIONARIO, O. Periodical. Portuguese. Editora Expedicionario, rua Leandro Martins 20 Grupos 504 506, Rio de Janeiro CEP 20 Brazil. **LC** D732; .A8213. **DD** 355.1/15/06081.

CN/0708-5974
EYE (DOWNSVIEW. 1979). (THE EYE.). V. 5, No. 5/6- Jan./Feb. 1979-. Periodical. English. mo. Free to members, $5.00 nonmembers. Friends of Pioneering Israel, 272 Codsell Avenue, Downsview Ontario M3H 3X2 Canada. **DD** 909/.04/924.

US/0014-6641
FACTS ON FILE. [Facts file]. Vol. 1, No. 1 (Oct. 30/Nov. 5, 1940)-. Periodical. English. wk. $558.50 public college & university libraries; $396.50 elementary, middle, junior high, & high school libraries; $656.50 other. Facts on File Publications, 460 Park Avenue South, New York NY 10016. **Tel** (212)683-2244, (800)322-8755, FAX (212)683-3633, telex 238 552 FACTS UR. **ED** Martin Greenwald. Index Available, published separately, free-automatically sent. cum. index. available on CD-ROM; available on an online database (file 636/Full-Text) from DIALOG. Documents available from UMI Article Clearinghouse.
Desc: A digest of national and international news. Covers politics, foreign affairs, sports, crime, the arts, religion, space, obituaries environment and personalities.
Ind/Abst Acad. Abstr. (Jan. 1992-); Acad. Ind. [Computer File] (1992-); Expand. Acad. Index (1992-); Gen. Period. Index (1992-); Mag. Artic. Summar. Elite (Jan. 1992-); Mag. Artic. Summar. Select (Jan. 1992-); Mag. Artic. Summar. CD-ROM (Jan. 1992-); Mag. Index Plus (1992-); Mag. Index. Sel. (1992-); Mag. Search; Mid. Search (Jan. 1992-); Newsp. Period. Abstr. (1992-); NEXIS (Jan. 11, 1975-); TOM Gen. Index (1992-).

US/0427-9026
FACTS ON FILE FIVE-YEAR INDEX. (1946/1950)-. English. $110.00 each, $745.00 per set. Facts on File Publications, 460 Park Avenue South, New York NY 10016. **Tel** (212)683-2244, (800)322-8755, FAX (212)683-3633, telex 238 552 FACTS UR. Index available. **Acid Free.**

US/0196-2981
FACTS ON FILE YEARBOOK. V. 1- 1941-. English. an. 124.00Can$ Canada; $95.00 other. Facts on File Publications, 460 Park Avenue South, New York NY 10016. **Tel** (212)683-2244, (800)322-8755, FAX (212)683-3633, telex 238 552 FACTS UR. **LC** D410; .F3. **DD** 905. cum. index. available on microfiche.

US
FACTS ON FILE YEARBOOK [MICROFORM]. **VFOAT** Pearson's Index of World Events. Vol. 1 (1941)-. English. an. $90.00 each, $1,650.00 complete set of 1941-1993. Facts on File Publications, 460 Park Avenue South, New York NY 10016. **Tel** (212)683-2244, (800)322-8755, FAX (212)683-3633, telex 238 552 FACTS UR.
Desc: Provides all of the significant U.S. and international news of a given year--from politics and sports to business and culture.

FI/0356-5629
FARAVID. **Added/Corp** Pohjois-Suomen Historiallinen Yhdistys. (1977)-. Finnish (English and Swedish). an. **LC** DK445; .F26.
Ind/Abst Am. Hist. Life (1984-).

PK
FATH (KARACHI, PAKISTAN). (AL-FATAH.). **VFOAT** Fatah. Periodical. Urdu (English). wk. **LC** DS376; .F37.

NE/0015-5676
FIBULA. Dutch. qt. F30.00. NJBG, PR W Alexanderhof 5, 2595 BE Den Haag Netherlands. **Tel** 31 70 3476590, FAX 31 70 3140450. Index available (December issue). **Bk Rev**, (Qty: 15/yr). **Circ:** 2000 (ctrl).
Desc: Fibula contains archaeological and historical articles for young people between 12 and 25 years old.

GW/0164-0933
FIFTEENTH CENTURY STUDIES. [Fifteenth century stud.]. **Added/Corp** Western Michigan University. Medieval Institute. **VFOAT** Fifteenth-Century Studies. (1978)-. Monographic series. English (French and Spanish). ir. Price varies per volume. Akademischer Verlag Stuttgart MR Heinz, Steiermarkerstr 132, D-70469 Stuttgart Germany. **Tel** 011 49 711 812413. **LC** CB367; .F53. **DD** 909/.4.
Ind/Abst MLA Int. Bibl. Books Artic. Mod. Lang. Lit.

US/0015-3370
FLAG BULLETIN, THE. (FLAG BULLETIN.). [Flag bull.]. **Added/Corp** Flag Research Center. (1961)-. Bulletin. English. bm. $25.00 (individuals), $32.00 (institutions). Flag Research Center, 3 Edgehill Road, Winchester MA 01890. **Tel** (617)729-9410, FAX (617)721-4817. **ED** Whitney Smith. Index available. cum. index. **Bk Rev**. **Ad Acc. Circ:** 1,100. available on microfilm.
Desc: Everything on flags: new designs, history, theory, military and naval, book reviews, conferences, bibliography, etc. from all nations, eras; illustrated, indexed, up-to-date, authenticated.
Ind/Abst Am. Hist. Life (1971).

AT/0726-7215
FLINDERS JOURNAL OF HISTORY AND POLITICS. **See** Political Science.

US/0740-798X
FLORIDA STAR (JACKSONVILLE, FLA. : 1951), THE. (THE FLORIDA STAR.). (1951)-. Newspaper. English. wk. $24.00. Florida Star, PO Box 40629, Jacksonville FL 32203. **Tel** (904)766-8834, (904)765-1703, FAX (904)765-1673. **ED** P. Erica Simpson. **Bk Rev**, (Qty: varies). **Ad Acc, Adv Mgr:** T. J. Stafford, **Tel** (904)765-7940. **Circ:** 9,622 (ctrl).

CN/0709-5201
FLORILEGIUM. [Florilegium]. **Added/Corp** Carleton University. Vol. 1 (1979)-. English (French; summaries and/or abstracts in French). an. 20.00Can$. Carleton University Department of English, 1125 Colonel By. Drive, Ottawa Ontario K1S 5B6 Canada. **Tel** (613)788-2317. **ED** D.J. Wurtele. **LC** CB311; .F57. **DD** 905. **Circ:** 200.
Desc: Devoted to late-ancient and medieval cultures stressing continuities and/or cross cultural and multi-disciplinary approaches, also traditional studies.
Ind/Abst BHA : Biblio. Hist. Art; MLA Int. Bibl. Books Artic. Mod. Lang. Lit.

SW/0349-6279
FOLKETS HISTORIA. [Folkets hist.]. **Added/Corp** Arkivet for Folkets Historia (Sweden) Forbundet for Folkets Historia (Sweden). (1980)-. Periodical. Swedish. qt. ***Continues*** *Meddelanden fran Arkivet for Folkets Historia, 0345-7605.*
Ind/Abst Am. Hist. Life (1987,1991-).

IT
FONTI E DOCUMENTI / CENTRO STUDI PER LA STORIA DEL MODERNISMO. ***Title Change.*** **Added/Corp** Universita di Urbino. Centro Studi per la Storia del Modernismo. Vol. 1 (1972)-. Italian. an. **LC** BX1396; .F66. ***Absorbed in part by*** *Collana Storica (Universita di Urbino. Istituto di Storia).*

GE/0532-2243
FORSCHUNGEN ZUR VOR- UND FURGESCHICHTE (LEIPZIG, 1955-). (FORSCHUNGEN ZUR VOR UND FRUHGESCHICHTE.). No. 1 (1955)-. Monographic series. German. ir. Price varies per volume.

DK/0106-4797
FORTID OG NUTID. [Fortid nutid]. (1914)-. Periodical. Danish. kr168.00. Dansk Historisk Faellesforenin 9, DK-1218 Copenhagen K Denmark.
Ind/Abst Am. Hist. Life (1955-1977); Anthropol. Lit.; Numis. Lit.

GW/0937-7735
FRANCIA 1 MITTELALTER. [Francia, 1 Mittelalt.]. **VFOAT** Francia. 1, Moyen Age. (1989)-. Monographic series. Multiple languages. ir. Price varies per volume. Jan Thorbecke Verlag GmbH and Company, Karlstrasse 10, Postfach 546, D 72482 Sigmaringen Germany. **Tel** 011 49 7571 728100, FAX 011 07571-728-280, telex 732534. **UDC** 92/99. ***Continues in part*** *Francia, 0251-3609.*

GW/0937-7743
FRANCIA 2 FRUHE NEUZEIT. [Francia, 2 Fruhe Neuzeit]. **VFOAT** Francia. 2, Revolution, Empire. (1990)-. Monographic series. Multiple languages. ir. Price varies per volume. Jan Thorbecke Verlag GmbH and Company, Karlstrasse 10, Postfach 546, D 72482 Sigmaringen Germany. **Tel** 011 49 7571 728100, FAX 011 07571-728-280, telex 732534. **UDC** 92/99. ***Continues in part*** *Francia, 0251-3609.*

GW/0937-7751
FRANCIA 3 19./20. JAHRHUNDERT. [Francia, 3 19,/20, Jhd.]. **VFOAT** Francia. 3, Neunzehntes/Zwanzigstes Jahrhundert; Francia. 3, Histoire Contemporaine. (1990)-. Monographic series. Multiple languages. ir. Price varies per volume. Jan Thorbecke Verlag GmbH and Company, Karlstrasse 10, Postfach 546, D 72482 Sigmaringen Germany. **Tel** 011 49 7571 728100, FAX 011 07571-728-280, telex 732534. **UDC** 92/99. ***Continues in part*** *Francia, 0251-3609.*

FR
FRANCIS : HISTOIRE DES SCIENCES ET DES RELIGIONS. 527. French. qt. 530.82F France; 550.00F other. Institut de l'Information Scientique et Technique (INIST), 2 Allee du Parc de Brabois, 54514 Vandoeuvre Nancy Cedex France. **Tel** 011 33 83 504600, FAX 011 33 83 504650. ***Continues*** *Bulletin Signaletique: Section 527. Histoire et Sciences des Religions.*

US
FRIENDS' QUARTERLY. **See** Museums and Galleries.

US/1050-3560
FRONTIER CHRONICLES. [Front. chron.]. (Apr. 1990)-. Periodical. English. Twelve times a year. $25.00. Two Guns Publishing Company, PO Box 66, Laughlin NV 89028. **Tel** (702)298-5703. **DD** 973. **Bk Rev**, (Qty: 24). **Ad Acc, Adv Mgr:** Paul Taylor. **Circ:** 15,000.

US/0071-9641
FRONTIER MILITARY SERIES. **See** Military and Defense.

VE/0506-6220
FUENTES HISTORICAS. **Main/Corp** Venezuela. Universidad Central, Caracas. Instituto de Antropologia e Historia. Vol. 1 (1957)-. Spanish. Universidad Central de Venezuela / Instituto de Antropologia e Historia, Instituto de Antropologia e Historia, Caracas Venezuela. **DD** 987.

US/1070-7735
FULTON COUNTY IMAGES. [Fulton Cty. images]. **Added/Corp** Fulton County Historical Society (Ind.). Vol. 1, No. 1 (1991)-. English. qt (Jan., June, Oct., images in Dec.). $15.00. Fulton County Historical Society, 37 East 375 North, Rochester IN 46975. **Tel** (219)223-4436. **ED** Shirley Willard (phone: (219)223-2352). **LC** WMLC 91/4853. **DD** 977. **Bk Rev**, (Qty: 3-4). ***Continues*** *Fulton County Historical Society Quarterly.*
Desc: Publication of the Fulton County Historical Society.

GW
FUN LETSTN HURBN : TSAYTSHRIFT FAR GESHIKHTE FUN YIDISHN LEBN BEYSN NATSI-REZSHIM. **VFOAT** From the Last Extermination. (1946)-. Periodical. Yiddish (table of contents in English). **LC** D804.3.

GW/0173-539X
G. GESCHICHTE MIT PFIFF. [G, Gesch. Pfiff]. **VFOAT** Geschichte mit Pfiff. (1979)-. Periodical. German. Twelve times a year. DM63.60 Germany; DM70.80 other. F. Sailer Verlag GMBH, Aeusserer Lafer Platz 22, D-90327 Nuernberg 1 Germany. **Tel** 011 49 911 5396655, FAX 011 49 911 5396473. **ED** Dr. Franz Metzger. **UDC** 930.9. **Bk Rev**, (Qty: 40/year). **Ad Acc. Circ:** 40,000.
Desc: World history in a single topic; popular presentation.

IT/0393-005X
GARGANOSTUDI : RIVISTA DEL CENTRO STUDI GARGANICI. **VFOAT** Gargano Studi. 1978-. Italian. an.

FR/1155-3219
GENESES. **See** Social Sciences.

AG/0325-2035
GEOPOLITICA (INSTITUTO DE ESTUDIOS GEOPOLITICOS (BUENOS AIRES, ARGENTINA)). (GEOPOLITICA / INSTITUTO DE ESTUDIOS GEOPOLITICOS.). **Added/Corp** Instituto de Estudios Geopoliticos (Buenos Aires, Argentina). No. 1 (Oct. 1975)-. Periodical. Spanish. qt. 7.000Arg$ per issue. Redaccion y Administracion / Argentina, Viamonte 749 Piso 10 OF, 1 Buenos Aires 1053 Argentina. **LC** F2834; .G46. **DD** 327.1/01/1.

SZ
GESCHICHTE. V. 1- ; Nov./Dec. 1974-. Periodical. German. bm. 48.00F Switzerland; $30.00 US. Historiographisches Institut, CH-8700 Kusnacht-Zurich Switzerland. **Tel** 071 29 77 77. **ED** Christian Schmid. **LC** D1; .G656. Index available. cum. index. **Bk Rev. Ad Acc. Circ:** 18,000.
Desc: Illustrated magazine for interested amateur historians. Concentrating primarily on European history.

GW/0016-9056
GESCHICHTE IN WISSENSCHAFT UND UNTERRICHT. [Gesch. Wiss. Unterr.]. **Added/Corp** Verband der Geschichtslehrer Deutschlands. (April 1950)-. Periodical. German. Twelve times a year. DM144.00 Germany; DM156.00 others. Erhard Friedrich Verlag, Postfach 100150, D 30917 Seelze Germany. **Tel** 011 49 511 4000452. **LC** D1; .G66. **[CCC].** cum. index.
Ind/Abst Am. Hist. Life (1954-).

SA
GISTER EN VANDAG. **See** Education-Teaching and Curriculum.

US/0890-5819
GRAPE VINE NEWSLETTER, THE. (THE GRAPE VINE NEWSLETTER / FRESNO CITY & COUNTY HISTORICAL SOCIETY.). [Grape vine newsl.]. **Added/Corp** Fresno City and County Historical Society. **VFOAT** Grapevine Newsletter. (19??)-. Newsletter. English. Four times a year. $6.00. Fresno City & County Historical Society, PO Box 2029, Fresno CA 93718. **Tel** (209)441-0862. **DD** 979.

US/0895-7851
GREAT BARRINGTON HISTORICAL SOCIETY NEWSLETTER. [Gt. Barringt. Hist. Soc. newsl.]. **Added/Corp** Great Barrington Historical Society (Mass.). **VFOAT** Newsletter. (1982)-. Newsletter. English. Twice a year (Summer and Winter). $15.00. Great Barrington Historic Society, 24 Gilmore Avenue, Bernard Drew, Great Barrington MA 01230. **Tel** (413)528-4953. **DD** 974. **Ad Acc. Circ:** 150 (ctrl).
Desc: An newsletter expanded on the stories of our history of the world.

●US/1071-670X
GREAT BATTLES. [Great battles]. **VFOAT** Military History Magazine Presents Great Battles; Military History Magazine's Great Battles. Vol. 6, No. 3 (Mar. 1993)-. Periodical. English. bm. $19.95. Cowles Magazines, PO Box 8200, Harrisburg PA 17105. **Tel** (717)657-9555, (800)435-9610. **LC** D25; .M48. **DD** 904/.7. ***Continues*** *Military History Magazine Presents Great Battles, 1060-9490.*

US/0275-2182
GREAT CONTEMPORARY ISSUES. GROUP 1, UPDATE, THE. Began with 1979. English. an. Arno Press, 3 Park Avenue, New York NY 10016. **Tel** (212)725-2050. **LC** D839; .G74. **DD** 909.82/7. **UDC** 930.9 "19".
Desc: Contains articles from the New York Times.

US/0890-0280
GUANGARA LIBERTARIA. **Added/Corp** Paul Avrich Collection (Library of Congress). **VFOAT** Guangara. (Winter 1980)-. Periodical. Spanish. qt. Free US; $2.75 other. International Society of Historical and Social Studies, PO Box 1516 Riverside Station, Miami FL 33135. **Tel** (305)446-2788. **LC** HX861; .G8. **DD** 335/.83/097291. **Bk Rev. Circ:** 5,000 (ctrl).

FR
GUERRES MONDIALES ET CONFLITS CONTEMPORAINS. **See** Military and Defense.

UK/0080-4398
GUIDES AND HANDBOOKS. **Main/Corp** Royal Historical Society (London, England). (1938)-. Monographic series. English. ir. Price varies per volume. Royal Historical Society, University College of London, Gower Street, London WE1C 6BT England. **Tel** 011 44 71 387 7532, telex 087342 BOYDEL G.
Desc: Reference volumes ranging from handbook of dates for students of history to texts and calendars. An analytical guide to serial publications.

CN/1180-3673
HANDBOOK TO GRADUATE PROGRAMMES IN HISTORY IN CANADA. [Handb. grad. programmes hist. Can.]. **Added/Corp** Societe Historique du Canada. Comite d'Etudiants/es Diplomes/es. Societe Historique du Canada. **VFOAT** Guide des Programmes d'Etudes Superieures en Histoire au Canada. (1990)-. English (French and English). Limited free distribution. Societe Historique du Canada, Secretariat, a/s J Lutz, Archives Nationales, 395 Rue Wellington, Ottawa, Ontario K1A 0N3 Canada. **DD** 907.1/171.

BE/0774-286X
HANDELINGEN DER MAATSCHAPPIJ VOOR GESCHIEDENIS EN OUDHEIDKUNDE TE GENT. [Handel. maatsch. geschied. oudheidkd. Gent]. **Main/Corp** Societe d'Histoire et d'Archeologie de Gand. (1944)-. Dutch. an. ***Continues*** *Societe d'Histoire et d'Archeologie de Gand. Annales.*
Ind/Abst Am. Hist. Life (1960-).

US/0887-5448
HARLOW'S WOODEN MAN. [Harlow's wooden man]. **Added/Corp** Marquette County Historical Society. Vol. 1 No. 1 (Winter 1965)-. Periodical. English. qt (Jan., Apr., July, Oct.). $15.00. Marquette County Historical Society, 213 North Front Street, Marquette MI 49855. **Tel** (906)226-3571. **ED** Rachel Crary. **DD** 973. **Circ:** 600.
Desc: Articles on history and culture of central upper Peninsula of Michigan and upper Great Lakes regions.

US/0073-0521
HARVARD HISTORICAL MONOGRAPHS. **Added/Corp** Harvard University. Dept. of History. Harvard University. Robert Louis Stroock Fund. (1932)-. Monographic series. English. ir. Price varies per volume. Harvard University Press, 79 Garden Street, Cambridge MA 02138. **Tel** (617)496-1344, (800)448-2242.

US/0073-053X
HARVARD HISTORICAL STUDIES. **Added/Corp** Harvard University. Dept. of History. Harvard University. Henry Warren Torrey Fund. Vol. 1 (1896)-. Monographic series. English. ir. Price varies per volume. Harvard University Press, 79 Garden Street, Cambridge MA 02138. **Tel** (617)496-1344, (800)448-2242.

FR
HEBDO DE L'ACTUALITE SOCIALE, L'. **Added/Corp** Confederation Generale du Travail. (Oct. 1993)-. Periodical. French. wk. Editions de la Ouvriere, 33 rue Bouret, 75940 Paris Cedex 19 France. **Tel** 011 33 1 40403636. **LC** D731; .V53. **DD** 940.53/05. ***Continues*** *Vie Ouvriere.*

UK/0073-1714
HELPS FOR STUDENTS OF HISTORY. **Added/Corp** Society for Promoting Christian Knowledge, London. Historical Association (Great Britain). No. 1 (1918)-. Monographic series. English. ir. Price varies per volume. Historical Association, 59A Kennington Park Road, London SE11 4JH England. **Tel** 011 44 71 735 3907, FAX 011 44 71 582 4989.

PL/0239-8818
HEMISPHERES / [POLISH ACADEMY OF SCIENCES, INSTITUTE OF HISTORY, CENTER FOR STUDIES ON NON-EUROPEAN COUNTRIES]. **Added/Corp** Zakad Badania Krajow Pozaeuropejskich (Polska Akademia Nauk). No. 1 (1984)-. English. an. **LC** D880; .H46. **DD** 909/.09724/005.
Ind/Abst Am. Hist. Life (1984-); Int. Bibliogr. Sociol.

US
HERITAGE NEWS / DALLAS COUNTY HISTORICAL SOCIETY. **Added/Corp** Dallas County Historical Society. (19??)-. Periodical. English. Six times a year. $35.00 Basic Membership; $75.00 Settler Membership; $125.00 Pioneer Membership; $500.00 Trailblazer; $1000.00 Explorer Membership. Dallas County Heritage Society, Old City Park 1717 Gano Street, Dallas TX 75215. **Tel** (214) 421-5141. **ED** Dan Baldwin. **Circ:** 1500.
Desc: Newsletter for volunteers and members of this non-profit organization

US/0018-0718
HERITAGE OF VERMILION COUNTY, THE. [Herit. Vermilion Cty.]. **Added/Corp** Vermilion County Museum Society. (19??)-. Periodical. English. qt. $15.00. Vermilion County Museum Society, 116 North Gilbert Street, Danville IL 61832. **Tel** (217)442-2922. **ED** Donald and Susan Richter. Index available (published separately). cum. index. **Ad Acc. Circ:** 1,200.
Desc: Contains articles on the history of Vermilion County, Illinois.
Ind/Abst Am. Hist. Life.

JA
HIKAKU BUNKA ZASSHI. **Added/Corp** Tokyo Kogyo Daigaku. Hikaku Bunka Kenyukai. **VFOAT** Annual of Comparative Culture. Vol. 1 (1982)-. Periodical. Japanese (English). an. ¥2000 (single issues). Tokyo Kogyo Daigaku Hikaku Bunka Kenkyukai, 12-2 Ookayana Meguro-ku, Tokyo-To 152 Japan. **Tel** 03-726-1111. **ED** Eto Jun. **LC** CB251; .H54. Index available. **Ad Acc. Circ:** 800 (ctrl).

UK/0958-3637
HINDSIGHT CAMBRIDGE. [HindsightCamb.]. (1990)-. Periodical. English. Three times a year (Sept., Jan., Apr.). £14.95 UK; £19.00 Europe; £24.00 other. Philip Allan Publishers Ltd, Market Place, Deddington Oxford, OX15 0SE England. **Tel** 011 44 869 38652, FAX 011 44 869 38803. **DD** 909.8205.

FR/0182-2411
HISTOIRE, L'. (May 1978)-. Periodical. French (table of contents in English). Eleven times a year. 318.32F France, 390.00F others (surface mail); 519.10F France, 598.00F others (airmail). Societe Editions Scientifiques, 5 rue Jacques Callot, 75006 Paris France. **Tel** 011 33 1 43548395. **ED** Stephane Khemis. **[CCC]. Bk Rev. Ad Acc. Circ:** 58,875 (ctrl).
Desc: Objective is to make the latest developments in history sciences accessible to non-specialist readers.
Ind/Abst Point Repere; SportSearch.

FR/0982-1783
HISTOIRE & MESURE. **VFOAT** Histoire et Mesure. Vol. 1, No. 1 (1986)-. Periodical. French (summaries and/or abstracts in English). Twice a year. 250.00F France; 310.00F other. Editions du CNRS, 22 rue Saint Armand, F 75015 Paris France. **Tel** 011 33 1 45075050. **(Subscription address:** Centrale des Revues, 11 rue Gossin, 92543 Montrouge Cedex France.) **LC** DC38; .H47. **DD** 944/.001/5195.
Ind/Abst Am. Hist. Life (1988-).

FR/0995-709X
HISTORAMA SPECIAL. (19??)-. Periodical. French. mo. 278.00F France; 355.00F other. Loft International, 1 Rue Lord Byron, 75008 Paris France. **Tel** 011 33 1 42256520. **(Subscription address:** Historama, Service Abonnements B702, 60732 St. Genevieve CX 9 France) ***Absorbed*** *Historama (Paris, France : 1984).*

PO
HISTORIA. No. 1- Nov. 1978-. Periodical. Portuguese (Portuguese). mo. Publicacoes Projornal SA SVC, Assinaturas AV Liberdade 202 2, 1200 Lisbon Portugal. **Tel** 011 351 1 574520, 011 351 1 574593. **LC** D1; .H19. **DD** 905.

IT
HISTORIA. Ind Grafiche Cino Del Duca, Via Borgogna 5, 20122 Milan Italy. **Tel** 011 39 2 781051.

GW/1010-0466
HISTORIA LATINOAMERICANA EN EUROPA. (1986)-. Periodical. Spanish. sa. Historisches Seminar, Universitat Hamburg, Von-Melle-Park 6/IX, W-2000 Hamburg 13 Germany. **UDC** 980=6; 940. ***Continues*** *Boletin Informativo (Asociacion de Historiadores Latinoamericanistas Europeos).*

FR/0018-2281
HISTORIA (PARIS). (HISTORIA.). [Historia]. (June 1955)-. Periodical. French. Twelve times a year. 264.45F France; 320.00 other. Editions Tallandier, 25 Blvd Malesherbes, 75008 Paris France. **Tel** 011 33 1 44510101. **(Subscription address:** Historia Dip, 70 rue Compans, 75940 Paris Cedex 19 France) Documents available from The Genuine Article. ***Continues*** *Lisez-Moi Historia, 1142-9224.*
Ind/Abst Am. Hist. Life (1955-1956, 1965); Arts Humanit. Citation Index [Full Cov.]; Point Repere (1979-); Res. Alert [Full Cov.]; Soc. Sci. Cit. Index [Select. Cov.].

BL
HISTORIA / UNIVERSIDADE ESTADUAL PAULISTA. **Added/Corp** Universidade Estadual Paulista. Vol. 1 (1982)-. Periodical. Portuguese. **LC** F2501; .H57. **DD** 981/.005. ***Formed by the union of*** *Anais de Historia* ***and*** *Estudos Historicos.*
Ind/Abst Am. Hist. Life (1982-).

GW/0018-2311
HISTORIA (WIESBADEN). (HISTORIA; ZETISCHRIFT FUER ALTE GESCHICTE.). Vol. 1 (1950)-. Periodical. English (French, German and Italian). qt. DM198.00. Franz Steiner Verlag GmbH, Postfach 101061, D 70009 Stuttgart Germany. **Tel** 011 49 0711 2582372, FAX 011 49 0711 2582290, telex 723636 daz d. **ED** Francois Paschoud, Kurt Raaflaub, Hildegard Temporini and Gerold Walser. **LC** D51; .H5. **[CCC]. Ad Acc. Circ:** 1,000. Documents available from The Genuine Article.
Desc: History of the ancient world to ancient Greek and Roman history.
Ind/Abst Arts Humanit. Citation Index [Full Cov.]; BHA : Biblio. Hist. Art; Br. Archaeol. Bibliogr.; Res. Alert [Full Cov.]; Soc. Sci. Cit. Index [Select. Cov.].

PE/0073-2486
HISTORIA Y CULTURA (LIMA). (HISTORIA Y CULTURA.). [Hist. cult.]. **Added/Corp** Museo Nacional de Historia (Peru) Instituto Nacional de Cultura (Peru). (1965)-. Spanish. an. $15.00. Museo Nacional Anthropology Arqueo, Plaza Bolivar S N Lima 21, Lima 100 Peru. **Tel** 011 51 14 635070. **ED** Amalin Castelli. **Bk Rev. Ad Acc.** ctrl circ.
Ind/Abst Am. Hist. Life (1965-); HAPI Hisp. Am. Period. Index.

PR
HISTORIA Y SOCIEDAD. **Added/Corp** University of Puerto Rico (Rio Piedras Campus). Departamento de Historia. No 1 (1988)-. Periodical. Spanish (English and French). an. $18.50 (one year), $44.00 (three year) institutions; $8.00 (one year), $19.00 (three year). University de Puerto Rico / Oficina de Publicaciones, Apartado 23322 Estacion UPR, San Juan Puerto Rica 00931-1787. **Tel** (809)250-0615, (809)250-0725, (809)250-0725, FAX (809)753-9116. **LC** F2155; .H57. **DD** 972.9/005.

SP/0018-2354
HISTORIA Y VIDA. [Hist. vida]. (April 1968)-. Periodical. Spanish. Twelve times a year. $42.50 US and Canada; $29.00 other. Redaccion Administracion Publ, Suscripciones Talleres 62 y 64, Barcelona 1 Spain. **Tel** 301 04 04. **LC** D1; .H213.
Ind/Abst Am. Hist. Life (1968-1971, 1983-); ARTbibliogr. Mod.

FI/0018-2362
HISTORIALLINEN AIKAKAUSKIRJA. [Hist. aikak.]. **Added/Corp** Suomen Historiallinen Seura.

Historian Ystavain Liitto. (1903)-. Periodical. Finnish. qt. Academic Bookstore Akateeminen, Postilokero 23, FIN-00371 Helsinki Finland. **Tel** 011 358 0 12141. **Ind/Abst** Am. Hist. Life (1954-).

US/0018-2370
HISTORIAN (KINGSTON), THE. (THE HISTORIAN; A JOURNAL OF HISTORY.). [Historian]. **Added/Corp** Phi Alpha Theta. Vol. 1 (Winter 1938)-. Periodical. English. qt. $22.50 (one year), $42.50 (two years). International Honor Society in History, 2333 Liberty Street, Allentown PA 18104. **Tel** (215)433-4140. **ED** Roger Adelson. **LC** D1; .H22. **DD** 905. Index available. cum. index. **Bk Rev. Ad Acc. Circ:** 12,000. available on microfilm and microfiche from University Microfilms International (UMI). Documents available from UMI Article Clearinghouse.
Desc: Covers all fields of history. Includes news of the Society and other historical activities.
Ind/Abst Acad. Abstr. (July 1992-); Acad. Search (July 1992-); Am. Hist. Life (1954-); Am. Bibliogr. Slavic East Europ. Stud.; Book Rev. Index; Hist. Source (Jan. 1992-); Humanit. Index; Humanit. Source (Jan. 1992-); Index Book Rev. Relig.; INFO-SOUTH Abstr.; Mag. Search; Newsp. Period. Abstr. (1991-); Soc. Sci. Cit. Index [Select. Cov.].

MX
HISTORIAS. No. 1 (July-Sept. 1982)-. Periodical. Spanish. ir. $70.00. Revista Tri Dir Est Hist Institute, Castillo Chabultebec APD 5 119, Mexico DF 06500 Mexico. **LC** D1; .H222. **DD** 980/.005.

US/1056-6309
HISTORIC PRESERVATION FORUM. [Hist. preserv. forum]. **Added/Corp** National Trust for Historic Preservation in the United States. **VFOAT** Forum. Vol. 5, No. 1 (Jan./Feb. 1991)-. Periodical. English. bm. comes with membership. National Trust for Historic Preservation, 1785 Massachusetts Avenue Northwest, Washington DC 20036. **Tel** (202)673-4035. **LC** NA106; .P75. **DD** 363. ***Formed by the union of*** *Preservation Forum, 0893-9403* ***and*** *Forum Newsletter, 0896-8179.*

US/1065-3562
HISTORIC PRESERVATION NEWS. (HISTORIC PRESERVATION NEWS : THE NEWSPAPER OF THE NATIONAL TRUST FOR HISTORIC PRESERVATION.). [Hist. preserv. news]. **Added/Corp** National Trust for Historic Preservation in the United States. **VFOAT** Preservation News. Vol. 30, No. 7 (July 1990)-. Periodical. English. mo. comes with membership. National Trust for Historic Preservation, 1785 Massachusetts Avenue Northwest, Washington DC 20036. **Tel** (202)673-4035. LC E159; .N355. **DD** 363. available on microfilm and microfiche from University Microfilms International (UMI). ***Continues*** *Preservation News, 0032-7735.*
Ind/Abst Avery Index Archit. Period. Suppl. Colum. Univ.

US
HISTORIC PRESERVATION NEWS [MICROFORM] : THE NEWSPAPER OF THE NATIONAL TRUST FOR HISTORIC PRESERVATION. Added/Corp National Trust for Historic Preservation in the United States. Vol. 30, No. 7 (July 1990)-. Periodical. English. National Trust for Historic Preservation, 1785 Massachusetts Avenue Northwest, Washington DC 20036. **Tel** (202)673-4035. **LC** Microfilm 06007. ***Continues*** *Preservation News (Washington, D.C.).*

US/1074-4665
HISTORIC TRAVELER, THE. [Hist. travel.]. (Spring 1988)-. Periodical. English. qt. $14.95. Cowles Magazines, PO Box 8200, Harrisburg PA 17105. **Tel** (717)657-9555, (800)435-9610. **DD** 917.

US/1074-7869
HISTORICAL ABSTRACTS ON DISC [COMPUTER FILE]. [Hist. abstr. disc]. **Added/Corp** ABC-Clio Information Services. **VFOAT** ABC-Clio Electronic Library User's Guide. Vols. 38-41, 42A:1 (1991)-. Abstracting/Indexing Service. English. Three times a year. $4,250.00. ABC Clio Press, PO Box 1911, 130 Cremona, Santa Barbara CA 93117. **Tel** (805)968-1911, (800)422-2546, FAX (805)685-9685. **LC** D299. **DD** 016.
Desc: This bibliographic database covers the world's scholarly literature in history. System requirements: IBM PC, XT, AT or compatible; 512KB memory; 20MB hard disk drive; one floppy disk drive; CD-ROM drive with controller card and interface cable; MS-DOS or PC-DOS 3.0 or higher.

US/0363-2717
HISTORICAL ABSTRACTS. PART A, MODERN HISTORY ABSTRACTS. **See** History(General)-Abstracting, Bibliographies and Statistics.

US/0363-2725
HISTORICAL ABSTRACTS. PART B, TWENTIETH CENTURY ABSTRACTS. **See** History(General)-Abstracting, Bibliographies and Statistics.

US/0275-1968
HISTORICAL BULLETIN (MADISON, WIS.). (HISTORICAL BULLETIN.). **Added/Corp** Lincoln Fellowship of Wisconsin. (1943)-. Bulletin. English. an (Published in April). $12.00. Lincoln Fellowship Wisconsin, 1923 Grange Avenue, Racine WI 53403-2328. **Tel** (414)634-0114. **ED** Steven K. Rogstad. **Pr Rev. Circ:** 200 (ctrl).
Desc: This publication prints the transcript of the lecture that was delieved to the membership of the Lincoln Fellowship of Wisconsin the year previous. It also contains membership rosters and a list of past and available publications for the organization.

US/0360-9030
HISTORICAL FOOTNOTES (ST. LOUIS, MO.). (HISTORICAL FOOTNOTES.). No. 15 (Dec. 7, 1962)-. Periodical. English. qt. $15.00. Concordia Historical Institute, Dept Arch & Hist, 801 De Mun Avenue, St Louis MO 63105. **Tel** (314)721-5934. **ED** August R Suelflow. **UDC** 284.1(09)(73). **Circ:** 2,000. ***Continues*** *Message From Headquarters.*
Desc: A newsletter published for the members of the Concordia Historical Institute providing information on Institute activities and the history of Lutheranism in America.

UK/0018-246X
HISTORICAL JOURNAL (CAMBRIDGE, CAMBRIDGESHIRE). (THE HISTORICAL JOURNAL.). [Hist. j.]. Vol. 1 (1958)-. Academic Scholarly Publication. English. qt (4 issues). $181.00 US, Canada & Mexico; £94.00 other. Cambridge University Press, The Edinburgh Building, Shaftesbury Road, Cambridge CB2 2RU United Kingdom. **Tel** 011 44 223 312393, FAX 011 44 223 325959. **(Subscription address:** Cambridge University Press / North America, 110 Midland Avenue, Port Chester NY 10573.**) ED** J. S. Morrill and J. Steinberg. **LC** D1; .H33. **[CCC]. Bk Rev.** available on microfilm and microfiche from University Microfilms International (UMI). Documents available from The Genuine Article, UMI Article Clearinghouse. ***Continues*** *Cambridge Historical Journal.*
Desc: Publishes papers on British, European and world history since the fifteenth century. Each issue contains approximately ten full length articles, with an abstract at the beginning, several communications, historiographical essays, surveys of trends in particular fields, review articles giving detailed consideration to a recent book or group of books, plus reviews of recent publications.
Ind/Abst Acad. Abstr. Full Text Elite (Jan. 1992-); Acad. Abstr. (Jan. 1992-); Acad. Search (Jan. 1992-); Am. Hist. Life (1954-); ARTbibliogr. Mod. (1984-); Arts Humanit. Citation Index [Full Cov.]; Br. Archaeol. Bibliogr. (?-?); Br. Humanit. Index; Expand. Acad. Index (1989-); Geogr. Abstr. Human Geogr.; Hist. Source (Jan. 1992-); Humanit. Index; Humanit. Source (Jan. 1992-); Index Book Rev. Relig.; INFO-SOUTH Abstr.; Int. Bibliogr. Sociol.; Mag. Search; Middle East Abstr. Index; Newsp. Period. Abstr. (1991-); Relig. Index One Period. (1979-); Res. Alert [Full Cov.]; Soc. Sci. Cit. Index [Select. Cov.].

NZ/0439-2345
HISTORICAL NEWS. [Hist. news]. **Added/Corp** Christchurch, N.Z. University of Canterbury. History Department. No. 1, (Aug. 1960)-. Periodical. English. Twice a year (May, Oct.). 6.00NZ$. University of Canterbury History Department, Private Bag, Christchurch New Zealand. **Tel** 011 64 3 3642277. **ED** I. Calanech, Marie Peters, Graeme Dunstall and Ken Bye. **[CCC]. Bk Rev. Ad Acc. Circ:** 500.
Desc: Primarily concerned with informing teachers in New Zealand secondary schools of new developments in the study of history.
Ind/Abst Am. Hist. Life (1977-); Annu. Bibliogr. Engl. Lang. Lit.

US
HISTORICAL NEWS. MIFFLIN COUNTY HISTORICAL SOCIETY. (19??)-. Newsletter. English. Four times a year (Jan., Apr., Aug., Nov.). $10.00 Comes with Mifflin County Historical Society membership. Mifflin County Historical Society, One West Market Street, Lewistown PA 17044. **Tel** (717)242-1022. **ED** Elaine Siddons. **Circ:** 750 (ctrl).
Desc: Newsletters issues and activities list to the current members of the Mifflin County Historical Society.

US/0895-3058
HISTORICAL NEWSLETTER (O'NEILL, NEB.). (HISTORICAL NEWSLETTER. HOLT COUNTY HISTORICAL SOCIETY). [Hist. news lett.]. **Added/Corp** Holt County Historical Society (Holt County, Neb.). **VFOAT** Historical Newsletter. (19??)-. Newsletter. English. Three times a year. $8.00 one year membership. Holt County Historical Society, 401 East Douglas, O'Neill NE 68763. **DD** 978. **Circ:** 250.

CN/0315-7997
HISTORICAL REFLECTIONS. [Hist. reflect.]. **Added/Corp** University of Waterloo. History Dept. **VFOAT** Reflexions Historiques. Vol. 1, (June 1974)-. Periodical. English (French; summaries and/or abstracts in French). Three times a year (Apr., Aug., Dec.). $24.00 (individual), $42.00 (institution). Alfred University - Department of History, Kanakadea Hall, Alfred NY 14802. **Tel** (607)871-2126, (607)871-2217. **ED** Stuart Campbell (phone: (607)871-2701). **LC** D1; .H37. **DD** 905. **CODEN** HIREEW. **Ad Acc. Pr Rev. Circ:** 350. Documents available from The Genuine Article.
Desc: In all fields of intellectual-cultural history and the histories of religion and mentalities.
Ind/Abst Acad. Search (July 1993-); Am. Hist. Life (1974-); Arts Humanit. Citation Index [Full Cov.]; Curr. Contents Arts Humanit.; Hist. Source (July 1993-); Humanit. Source (Jul. 1993-); INFO-SOUTH Abstr.; Mag. Search; Res. Alert [Full Cov.]; Soc. Plann. Policy Dev. Abstr.; Soc. Sci. Cit. Index [Select. Cov.].

UK/0268-6724
HISTORICAL RESEARCH FOR HIGHER DEGREES IN THE UNITED KINGDOM. PART II, THESES IN PROGRESS. [Hist. res. high. degrees U.K., 2 theses prog.]. **VFOAT** Theses in Progress. List No. 47 (1986)-. English. an. £7.00 UK; $14.00 other. Publications Secretary, Institute of Historical Research, University of London, Senate House, London WC1E 7HU England. **Tel** 01-636-0272. **ED** Joyce M Horn. **LC** Z6201; .H572; D20. **DD** 016.909. Index available. **Circ:** 800. ***Continues*** *Historical Research for University Degrees in the United Kingdom. Part II, Theses in Progress, 0308-7425.*

UK/0950-3471
HISTORICAL RESEARCH : THE BULLETIN OF THE INSTITUTE OF HISTORICAL RESEARCH. Vol. 60, No. 141 (Feb. 1987)-. Bulletin. English. Three times a year. £37.50 UK and Europe; $74.00 North America; £37.50 other. Basil Blackwell Publishers Ltd, 108 Cowley Road, Oxford 0X4 1JF England. **Tel** 011 44 865 791100, FAX 011 44 865 791347, telex 837022 OXBOOK G. **(Subscription address:** Blackwell Publishers / UK, Marston Book Services, PO Box 87, Oxford OX2 0DT England.**) ED** F M L Thompson. **LC** D1; .L65. **DD** 905. **UDC** 940. **[CCC]. Ad Acc. Circ:** 1,500. available on microfilm and microfiche from University Microfilms International (UMI). Documents available from The Genuine Article. ***Continues*** *Bulletin of the Institute of Historical Research.*
Desc: Journal of closely researched historical articles; chiefly British and European.
Ind/Abst Arts Humanit. Citation Index [Full Cov.]; Br. Humanit. Index; Curr. Contents Arts Humanit.; Res. Alert [Full Cov.]; Soc. Sci. Cit. Index [Select. Cov.].

UK
HISTORICAL SERIES / ROLLS-ROYCE HERITAGE TRUST. Added/Corp Rolls-Royce Heritage Trust. Sir Henry Royce Memorial Foundation. **VFOAT** Joint Heritage Trust/Sir Henry Royce Memorial Foundation Series. No. 1 (1982)-. Monographic series. English. Price varies per volume.

CN/1193-1981
HISTORICAL STUDIES OTTAWA. 1990. [Hist. stud. Ott., 1990]. **VFOAT** Etudes d'Histoire Religieuse. (1990)-. English (Multiple languages). Twice a year (Apr., Sept.). 25.00Can$ (individuals), 35.00Can$ (institutions) Canada; 30.00Can$ (individuals), 40.00Can$ (institutions) others. University of Western Ontario Historical Studies, London NG6 1G7 Canada. **Tel** (519)661-2085, FAX (519)661-3383. **DD** 282.7105. ***Continues*** *Canadian Catholic Historical Studies, 0827-1704.*

MX
HISTORICAS : BOLETIN DE INFORMACION DEL INSTITUTO DE INVESTIGACIONES HISTORICAS UNAM. No. 1 (Sept./Dec. 1979)-. Periodical. Spanish. qt. Torre de Humanidades, 8 Piso, Ciudad Universitaria, Mexico 29 DF Mexico. **Tel** 550-5214 (29-48).

XO
HISTORICKE STUDIE. (19??)-. Slovak (Czech). ir. DM25.00. Slovenska Akademia Vied / Slovak Academy of Sciences, PO Box 57, 81005 Bratislava Slovakia. **Tel** 011 42 7 3782715, 011 42 7 3782925, FAX 011 42 7 496849, telex 93261.
Ind/Abst Am. Hist. Life (1977-1982).

SW/0439-2434
HISTORIELARARNAS FORENINGS ARSSKRIFT. [Historiel. foeren. arsskr.]. (1975)-. Periodical. Swedish. an.
Ind/Abst Am. Hist. Life (1975-).

FR/0046-757X
HISTORIENS ET GEOGRAPHES. [Hist. geogr.]. (1965)-. Periodical. French. ir. 350.00F France; 410.00F other. Assn Professeurs d Histoire, BP 49, 75060 Paris Cedex 02 France. ***Continues*** *Bulletin / Society des Professeurs d'Histoire et de Geographie (France).*
Ind/Abst Am. Hist. Life (1954-1976, 1987-).

GW/0018-2605
HISTORISCH-POLITISCHE BUCH, DAS. (DAS HISTORISCH-POLITISCHE BUCH : EIN WEGWEISER DURCH DAS SCHRIFTTUM.). **Added/Corp** Ranke-Gesellschaft, Vereinigung fuer Geschichte im Offtlichen Leben. (1953)-. Periodical. German (English and French). bm. DM298.00. Verlag Muster Schmidt, Postfach 2751, Grunberger Weg 6,

D-37017 Goettingen Germany. **Tel** 011 49 551 71741, telex 96704 GOFAFI. **ED** Michael Salewski, Olshausenstr. 40, 2300 Keil 1 Germany. **LC** Z6205; .H66. **[CCC].** Index available. cum. index. **Bk Rev. Ad Acc. Desc:** A guide through the literature with altogether more than 700 book reviews written by 300 considerable learned and scientific men.

GW
HISTORISCHE FORSCHUNGEN (BERLIN). (HISTORISCHE FORSCHUNGEN.). Vol. 1 (1968)-. Monographic series. German. ir. Price varies per volume. Jan Thorbecke Verlag GmbH and Company, Karlstrasse 10, Postfach 546, D 72482 Sigmaringen Germany. **Tel** 011 49 7571 728100, FAX 011 07571-728-280, telex 732534.

GW/0936-5796
HISTORISCHE MITTEILUNGEN.
Added/Corp Ranke-Gesellschaft, Vereinigung fuer Geschichte im Offentlichen Leben. **VFOAT** HM; HMRG. Vol. 2, No. 1 (1989)-. Periodical. German (English). sa. DM68.00. Franz Steiner Verlag GmbH, Postfach 101061, D 70009 Stuttgart Germany. **Tel** 011 49 0711 2582372, FAX 011 49 0711 2582290, telex 723636 daz d. **ED** Michael Salewski. **LC** DD1; .M57. ***Continues*** *Mitteilungen der Ranke-Gesellschaft, 0934-3156.*

GW/0018-2613
HISTORISCHE ZEITSCHRIFT. [Hist. Z.]. Vol. 1 (1859)-. Academic Scholarly Publication. German. bm (6 issues). DM418.00. R Oldenbourg Verlag, Postfach 801360, D 81613 Munich Germany. **Tel** 011 49 89 450190, FAX 011 49 89 45019305. **ED** Lothar Gall. **LC** D1; .H6. **[CCC].** Index available. cum. index. **Bk Rev. Ad Acc. Pr Rev. Circ:** 2,800. available in reprints (Johnson Reprint Corporation); available on microfilm from University Microfilms International (UMI). Documents available from The Genuine Article.
Desc: One of the leading international scholarly journals for history.
Ind/Abst Am. Hist. Life (1954-); Arts Humanit. Citation Index [Full Cov.]; Bibliogr. Carto.; Curr. Contents Arts Humanit.; Res. Alert [Full Cov.]; Soc. Sci. Cit. Index [Full Cov.].

GW
HISTORISCHE ZEITSCHRIFT. BEIHEFT.
VFOAT Historische Zeitschrift. Beihefte; Beihefte der Historischen Zeitschrift. Vol. 1 (1971)-. Monographic series. German. ir. Price varies per volume. R Oldenbourg Verlag, Postfach 801360, D 81613 Munich Germany. **Tel** 011 49 89 450190, FAX 011 49 89 45019305. **ED** Lothar Gall. **LC** D1; .H645. **Circ:** 3,000 (ctrl).
Desc: Contributions to various problems of Biomedical research.

GW/0440-971X
HISTORISCHE ZEITSCHRIFT. SONDERHEFT. **VFOAT** Sonderheft. Vol. 1 (1962)-. Monographic series. German. ir. Price varies per volume. R Oldenbourg Verlag, Postfach 801360, D 81613 Munich Germany. **Tel** 011 49 89 450190, FAX 011 49 89 45019305. **(Subscription address:** Rosenheimer STR 145, D 81671 Munich Germany**) ED** Lothar Gall. **Bk Rev. Circ:** 2,000 (ctrl).
Desc: Gives a review of literature and research work for special historical persons or subjects.

GW/0018-2621
HISTORISCHES JAHRBUCH. [Hist. Jahrb.].
Added/Corp Goerres-Gesellschaft. Vol. 1 (1880)-. Periodical. German. Twice a year. DM140.00. Verlag Herder Freiburg, Postfach 79080, Frieburg, Germany. **Tel** (0761)27-17-0, FAX (0761)27 17-520, telex 761489. **ED** Laetitia Boehm, Odilo Engels, Erwin Iserloh, Rudolf Morsey, and Konrad Repgen. **LC** D1; .H7. **[CCC].** cum. index. **Bk Rev. Circ:** 800 (ctrl). Documents available from The Genuine Article.
Ind/Abst Am. Hist. Life (1954-); Arts Humanit. Citation Index [Full Cov.]; Curr. Contents Arts Humanit.; Res. Alert [Full Cov.]; Soc. Sci. Cit. Index [Select. Cov.].

DK/0106-0481
HISTORISK-FILOSOFISKE MEDDELELSER. (HISTORISK-FILOSOFISKE MEDDELELSER / UTGIVET AF DET KGL. DANSKE VIDENSKABERNES SELSKAB.). [Hist.-filos. medd.]. **Added/Corp** Kongelige Danske Videnskabernes Selskab. Vol. 37, No. 1 (1957)-. Monographic series. Danish (English, French and German). Munksgaards Boghandel, 6 Norregade, DK-1165 Copenhagen K Denmark. **LC** AS281; .D214. ***Continues*** *Historisk-Filologiske Meddelelser.*
Ind/Abst MLA Int. Bibl. Books Artic. Mod. Lang. Lit.

UK/0957-0144
HISTORY & COMPUTING. **See** Computers.

●US/1062-2306
HISTORY AND LANGUAGE. (1993)-. Monographic series. English. Price varies per volume. Peter Lang Publishing, 62 West 45th Street, 4th Floor, New York NY 10036. **Tel** (212)764-1471, (800)770-5264, telex 6973364 PLNY.

US/0935-560X
HISTORY AND MEMORY. [Hist. mem.]. **Added/Corp** Bet ha-Sefer le-Historyah al shem Zalman Aran. Eva and Marc Besen Institute for the Study of Historical Consciousness. **VFOAT** History & Memory. Vol. 1, No. 1 (Spring/Summer 1989)-. Periodical. English. sa. $30.00. Indiana University Press, 601 North Morton Street, Bloomington IN 47404. **Tel** (812)855-3830, (800)842-6796. **LC** D16.8; .H6243. **DD** 901.
Desc: Studies in representation of the past.
Ind/Abst Am. Hist. Life (1990-).

US/1058-174X
HISTORY (BOCA RATON, FLA.). (HISTORY.). [History]. **Added/Corp** Social Issues Resources Series, inc. **VFOAT** SirS Global Perspectives, History. (1991)-. English. $80.00. Social Issues Resources Series Inc, PO Box 2348, Boca Raton FL 33427. **Tel** (800)327-0513, (407)994-0079. **DD** 900.

AT/1034-7577
HISTORY FORUM BRIDGEWATER. **See** Education-Teaching and Curriculum.

US
HISTORY HIGHLIGHTS : NEWSLETTER OF THE WASHINGTON STATE HISTORICAL SOCIETY. **Added/Corp** Washington State Historical Society. Vol. 1, No. 1 (Jan. 1983)-. Periodical. English. Twice a year. $10.00. Washington State Historical Society, 315 North Stadium Way, Tacoma WA 98403. **Tel** (206)593-2830, FAX (206)597-4186. ***Continues*** *Circuit Rider (Tacoma, Wash. : 1978).*

US/0098-163X
HISTORY IN NEWSPAPER FRONT PAGES, A. (1974)-. English. an. $2.95. Drake Publishers, 801 Second Avenue, New York NY 10017. **Tel** (212)986-5100, FAX (212)692-9297, telex 6711779 DRAKEUW. **LC** D839.3; .H56. **DD** 909.82/7.

UK/0018-2648
HISTORY (LONDON). (HISTORY.). [History]. **Added/Corp** Historical Association (Great Britain). Vol. 1, No. 1 (Jan. 1912)-. Academic Scholarly Publication. English. Three times a year. £43.00 UK and Europe; $74.00 North America; £47.50 other. Basil Blackwell Publishers Ltd, 108 Cowley Road, Oxford 0X4 1JF England. **Tel** 011 44 865 791100, FAX 011 44 865 791347, telex 837022 OXBOOK G. **(Subscription address:** Blackwell Publishers / UK, Marston Book Services, PO Box 87, Oxford OX2 0DT England.**) ED** Bill Speck. **LC** D1; .H815. **[CCC].** Index available. **Bk Rev. Ad Acc. Pr Rev. Circ:** 5,500. available on microfilm and microfiche from University Microfilms International (UMI). Documents available from UMI Article Clearinghouse.
Desc: Aims to illuminate problems in all aspects of history, in different periods and historical areas.
Ind/Abst Acad. Abstr. Full Text Elite (July 1990-); Acad. Abstr. (July 1990-); Acad. Search (July 1990-); Am. Hist. Life (1953-); Annu. Bibliogr. Engl. Lang. Lit.; Arts Humanit. Citation Index [Full Cov.]; BHA : Biblio. Hist. Art; Br. Archaeol. Bibliogr.; Hist. Source (July 1990-); Humanit. Index; Humanit. Source (Jul. 1990-); INFO-SOUTH Abstr.; Mag. Search; Middle East Abstr. Index; Newsp. Period. Abstr. (1991-); Soc. Sci. Cit. Index [Full Cov.]; Women Stud. Abstr.

US/0887-1078
HISTORY MICROCOMPUTER REVIEW. [Hist. microcomput. rev.]. **Added/Corp** Pittsburg State University. Dept. of History. Vol. 1, No. 1 (Spring 1985)-. Periodical. English. sa (Apr., Nov.). $20.00 US; $25.00 other. Pittsburg State University, Department of History, Pittsburgh KA 66762. **Tel** (316)235-4312, FAX (316)232-7515. **ED** James B.M. Schick (Editor's Telephone: (316)235-4317). **LC** D1; .H817355. **DD** 902/.8/553. **Bk Rev. Circ:** 125. Documents available.
Ind/Abst Am. Hist. Life (1988-).

IT
HISTORY OF LOGIC. **See** Philosophy.

US
HISTORY REVIEW. English. Three times a year. $24.00. History Review, 20 Old Compton Street, London W1V 5PE England.

US/1063-9799
HISTORY SOURCE. ***Title Change.*** **See** History(General)-Abstracting, Bibliographies and Statistics.

AT/0729-154X
HISTORY TEACHER BRISBANE. **See** Education-Teaching and Curriculum.

UK/0018-2753
HISTORY TODAY. [Hist. today]. Vol. 1 (Jan. 1951)-. Periodical. English. Twelve times a year. $54.95 US; 73.00Can$ Canada; £28.50 UK, £41.50 Europe & Eire, £45.00 others (surface mail); £55.00 (airmail). History Today Ltd, 20 Old Compton Street, London W1V 5PE England. **Tel** 011 44 71 287 2365. **ED** Gordon Marsden. **LC** D1; .H818. **DD** 905. Index available (ú2.50 UK; ú3.25 other). cum. index. **Bk Rev. Ad Acc. Circ:** 30,000. available on microfilm and microfiche from University Microfilms International (UMI). Documents available from The Genuine Article, UMI Article Clearinghouse, Magazine Collection.
Desc: Essential reading for students, teachers and history-lovers everywhere. Each issue contains - major historians writing, international features from prehistory to the present, reviews of books and events, heritage/archaeology updates and lavish colour illustrations.
Ind/Abst Acad. Abstr. Full Text Elite (Jan. 1989-) [Full Txt.]; Acad. Abstr. (Jan. 1989-); Acad. Ind. [Computer File] (1984-); Acad. Search (Jan. 1989-); Am. Hist. Life (1954-); Annu. Bibliogr. Engl. Lang. Lit.; ARTbibliogr. Mod.; Arts Humanit. Citation Index [Full Cov.]; Book Rev. Digest; Book Rev. Index; Br. Humanit. Index; Curr. Contents Arts Humanit.; Expand. Acad. Index (1984-); Gen. Period. Index (1985-); Hist. Source (Jan. 1989-) [Full Txt.]; Humanit. Index; Humanit. Source (Jan. 1989-) [Full Txt.]; INFO-SOUTH Abstr.; Mag. Artic. Summar. Elite (Jan. 1989-) [Full Txt.]; Mag. Artic. Summar. Select (Jan. 1989-) [Full Txt.]; Mag. Artic. Summar. CD-ROM (Jan. 1989-); Mag. Express (1988-) [Full Txt.]; Mag. Index Plus (1989-); Mag. Index Sel. Microfiche (1986-) [Full Txt.]; Mag. Index. Sel. (1986-); Mag. Search; Middle East Abstr. Index; Mid. Search (Jan. 1989-); Newsp. Period. Abstr. (1988-); Numis. Lit.; Peace Res. Abstr. J. (1971-1976, 1983-1984); Read. Guide Abstr. Select Ed.; Read. Guide Period. Lit.; Res. Alert [Full Cov.]; Resource/One Ondisc; Romant. Move.; Soc. Sci. Source (Jan. 1984-) [Full Txt.]; Soc. Sci. Cit. Index [Select. Cov.]; Soc. Work Abstr. (?-?); SportSearch; Mag. Index (1978-); TOM Gen. Index (1985-) [Full Txt.]; Vocat. Search (Jan. 1989-) [Full Txt.]; West. Hist. Q.; Women Stud. Abstr.

US/0361-2759
HISTORY (WASHINGTON). (HISTORY.). [History]. **Added/Corp** Helen Dwight Reid Educational Foundation. Vol. 1 (Oct. 1972)-. Periodical. English. qt. $46.00 (individual), $92.00 (institutional), add $12.00 (foreign postage). Heldref Publications, 1319 Eighteenth Street Northwest, Washington DC 20036-1802. **Tel** (202)296-6267, (800)365-9753, FAX (202)296-5149. **ED** Jerome J Hanus. **LC** Z6205; .H69. **DD** 905. **Bk Rev. Ad Acc. Circ:** 800. available on microfilm and microfiche from University Microfilms International (UMI).
Desc: Provides informative, authoritative evaluations of books one to twelve months after their publication. Reviews describe the contents of each book, it's major strengths and weaknesses, the author's credentials, and the intended audience.
Ind/Abst Am. Hist. Life (1974-); Am. Bibliogr. Slavic East Europ. Stud.; Book Rev. Digest; Book Rev. Index; Br. Humanit. Index; Middle East Abstr. Index.

UK/0309-2984
HISTORY WORKSHOP. (HISTORY WORKSHOP; A JOURNAL OF SOCIALIST HISTORIANS.). [Hist. workshop]. **Added/Corp** Ruskin College (University of Oxford). No. 1 (Spring 1976)-. Periodical. English. sa. £37.00 UK and Europe; $65.00 other. Oxford University Press, Walton Street, Oxford OX2 6DP England. **Tel** 011 44 865 56767, FAX 011 44 865 267773, telex 837330 OXPRES G. **(Subscription address:** Oxford University Press / USA, Journals Marketing Department, Oxford University Press, 2001 Evans Road, Cary NC 27513.**) ED** Sally Alexander, Guy Boanas, Susan Bullock, Bernard Canavan, Jane Caplan, Anna Davin, Alun Howkins, Andrew Lincoln, Tim Mason, Alex Potts, Lyndal Roper, Raphael Carolyn Steedman, Anne Summers, Barbara Taylor, Jeffrey Weeks, Jerry White. **LC** D1; .H819. **DD** 905. **[CCC]. Bk Rev. Ad Acc. Pr Rev. Circ:** 1,500. available on microfilm and microfiche from University Microfilms International (UMI). Documents available from The Genuine Article.
Desc: A journal of socialist and feminist historians, including oral history on wide ranging topics. It supports the people's history groups who encourage collective construction of history through memory and research.
Ind/Abst Altern. Press Index; Am. Hist. Life (1976-); Arts Humanit. Citation Index [Full Cov.]; BHA : Biblio. Hist. Art; Curr. Contents Arts Humanit.; Curr. Contents Soc. Behav. Sci.; Left Index (19??-); Middle East Abstr. Index; Res. Alert [Full Cov.]; Romant. Move.; Soc. Plann. Policy Dev. Abstr.; Soc. Sci. Cit. Index [Full Cov.]; Sociol. Abstr.; SportSearch.

PL/0073-277X
HISTORYKA. **Added/Corp** Instytut Historii (Polska Akademia Nauk) Panstwowe Wydawnictwo Naukowe. Polska Akademia Nauk. Komisja Nauk Historycznych. (1967)-. Periodical. Polish (summaries and/or abstracts in English, French and Russian). **LC** D16; .H68.
Ind/Abst Am. Hist. Life (1988-).

JA
HISUTORIA. Periodical. English. qt. $69.00. **(Subscription address:** Japan Publications Trading Company, Ltd., PO Box 5030, Tokyo International, Tokyo 100-31 Japan.**)**
Ind/Abst Am. Hist. Life (1954-1989).

US
HOOVER PRESS BIBLIOGRAPHY.
Added/Corp Hoover Institution on War, Revolution, and Peace. (1987)-. Bibliography. English. Price varies per volume. Hoover Institution Press, Stanford University, HHMB Room 28, Stanford CA 94305. **Tel** (415)723-3373. ***Continues*** *Hoover Press Bibliographical Series.*

History(General)

CN/0315-7946
HORIZON SEPHARDI. April 1974-. Periodical. French. qt. Free to members. Federation Sephardie Canadienne, 1310, Av. Greene, 8E Etage, Montreal Quebec H3Z 2B2 Canada. **DD** 909/.04/924.

JA/0386-8893
HOSEI SHIGAKU. [Hosei Shigaku]. **VFOAT** Journal of Hosei Historical Society in Hosei University; Hosei Daigaku Shigakkai Kaiho. (1950)-. Periodical. Japanese. an. **DD** 900.
Ind/Abst Am. Hist. Life (1965-).

CH
HSIN SHIH HSUEH. VFOAT New History. (1990)-. Periodical. Chinese. qt. San Mi Shu Chu, Number 61, 2nd Floor, Chung-Ching S. Road, 1 Sect, Taipei Shih Taiwan. LC IN PROCESS.

GW/0439-884X
HUMANISMUS UND TECHNIK. (HUMANISMUS UND TECHNIK JAHRBUCH.). [Humanismus Tech.]. **Added/Corp** Technische Universitat Berlin. Gesellschaft von Freunden. (1980)-. German. an. **LC** CB478; .H8. **Continues** *Humanismus und Technik.*
Ind/Abst BHA : Biblio. Hist. Art; Energy Res. Abstr. (Mar. 1982-); Zentralbl. Math. Ihre Grenzgeb.

KO
HYONDAESA. Added/Corp Soul Ollon Munhwa Kullop. **VFOAT** Quarterly Journal of Contemporary History. Vol. 1 (1980)-. Periodical. Korean. qt. W2.200 single issue. **LC** D410; .H94.

US/0735-4576
HYST'RY MYST'RY MAGAZINE. [Hyst'ry myst'ry mag.]. Vol. 1, No. 1 (1983)-. Periodical. English. Three times a year. Hystry Mystry Magazine, One Brush Court, Garnerville NY 10923. **Tel** (914)947-3141. **ED** David Allen. **Circ:** 6,000.
Desc: Topics include anomalies, controversies, mysteries, hoaxes, forgeries, fakes, and curiosa of all ages and places.

FR
IBERICA. 1- 1977-. Periodical. French (Spanish). Editions Hispaniques, 31 rue Gay-Lussac, Paris 5E France. **LC** CB226; .I23. **DD** 909/.09756.
Ind/Abst Am. Hist. Life (1967-1972).

IT/0019-1280
IDEA (ROME). (IDEA. RIVISTA MENSILE DI CULTURA E POILITICA). (Jan. 1945)-. Periodical. Italian. Ten times a year. L70000.00 one year; L76000.00 other. Idea 83, Via Panisperna 261, 00184 Rome Italy. **Tel** 011 39 6 6783261, FAX 011 39 6 85097230. **ED** Roma (phone: (06)6783261). **LC** DG576; .I34. **Bk Rev**, (Qty: 30). **Ad Acc. Circ:** 5,000.
Desc: Comments and studies of the political and cultural life of Italy.

US
IDEAS '92: A PUBLICATION OF THE 1992 INSTITUTE. Added/Corp 1992 Institute. **VFOAT** Ideas Ninety-two. Vol. 1, No. 1 (Fall 1987)-. Periodical. Spanish (English). sa. $10.00 (individuals), $15.00 (institutions). University of Miami / GSIS, North-South Center, Publications-Vega, PO Box 248123, Coral Gables FL 33124-3010. **Tel** (305)284-6866, FAX (305)284-6370. **ED** Joaquin Roy. **LC** CB226; .I34. **DD** 909/.097561. **Ad Acc. Circ:** 500 (ctrl).

CN/0843-6657
IICCG BULLETIN. See The Arts.

US
INCIDENTS OF THE WAR. See Photography and Video.

ML/0081-2838
INFORMATION DOCUMENT (SOUTH PACIFIC COMMISSION). (INFORMATION DOCUMENT.). **VFOAT** Cahier d'Information. Monographic series. English (French). ir. Price varies per volume. South Pacific Commission, PO Box D5, Noumea Cedex New Caledonia. **Tel** (687)26 20 00, FAX (687)26 38 18. **LC** DU1; .S57. **DD** 990. **NLM** W1 IN42N. **Circ:** 600 (ctrl). **Continues** *Economic Development Technical Information Paper.*

AU/0253-0899
INNSBRUCKER HISTORISCHE STUDIEN. [Innsbr. hist. Stud.]. **Added/Corp** Universitat Innsbruck. Institut fur Geschichte. (1978)-. German. an. **LC** DB1; .I56. **DD** 940/.05.
Ind/Abst Am. Hist. Life.

FR/0074-1035
INTER-NORD. Vol. 1 (May 1961)-. English (French). an. Editions du CNRS, 22 rue Saint Armand, F 75015 Paris France. **Tel** 011 33 1 45075050. **UDC** 908.98; 908.48; 930(98); 930(48). **Circ:** 1,500.
Desc: International journal for Arctic and Scandinavian studies.
Ind/Abst Am. Hist. Life (1972-1978).

FR/0074-2015
INTERNATIONAL BIBLIOGRAPHY OF HISTORICAL SCIENCES. See History(General)-Abstracting, Bibliographies and Statistics.

CN/0707-5332
INTERNATIONAL HISTORY REVIEW, THE. [Int. hist. rev.]. Vol. 1 (Jan. 1979)-. Periodical. English. qt. $92.00. Simon Fraser University / History, EAA 2015, Burnaby British Columbia, V5A 1S6 Canada. **Tel** (604)291-3561, FAX (604)291-3429. **ED** Edward Ingram. **LC** D1; .I52. **DD** 905. **[CCC].** Index available. cum. index. **Bk Rev Ad Acc. Pr Rev. Circ:** 750 (ctrl). Documents available from The Genuine Article.
Desc: Articles, notes with documents, book reviews on the relations between all states throughout the world and throughout history; trade, warfare, revolution, imperialism, diplomacy and theory.
Ind/Abst Am. Hist. Life (1982-); Am. Bibliogr. Slavic East Europ. Stud.; Arts Humanit. Citation Index [Full Cov.]; Can. Index (?-?); Can. Period. Index (19??-); Curr. Contents Arts Humanit.; Int. Polit. Sci. Abstr.; Middle East Abstr. Index; Res. Alert [Full Cov.]; Soc. Sci. Cit. Index [Select. Cov.].

●US/1061-0324
INTERNATIONAL OBSERVER (WASHINGTON, D.C.). (INTERNATIONAL OBSERVER.). [Int. obs.]. No. 1 (Mar. 10, 1992)-. Periodical. English. Twenty-four times a year. $350.00 US & Canada; $360.00 others. Government Business Worldwide Reports, PO Box 5997, Washington DC 20016. **Tel** (202)244-7050, FAX (202)244-5410. **DD** 909.

●US
INTERNATIONAL YEARBOOK OF ORAL HISTORY AND LIFE STORIES. Vol. 1 (1992)-. Periodical. English. an. £30.00. Oxford University Press, Walton Street, Oxford OX2 6DP England. **Tel** 011 44 865 56767, FAX 011 44 865 267773, telex 837330 OXPRES G. **(Subscription address:** Oxford University Press / USA, Journals Marketing Department, Oxford University Press, 2001 Evans Road, Cary NC 27513.) **ED** Paul Thompson, Daniel Bertaux, Selma Leydesdorff and Luisa Passerini. **LC** D16.14; .I57. **Formed by the union of** *International Annual of Oral History* **and** *Life Stories.*

GW/0074-9834
INTERNATIONALES JAHRBUCH FUER GESCHICHTS- UND GEOGRAPHIE-UNTERRICH. Added/Corp Arbeitsgemeinschaft Deutscher Lehrerverbande. Brunswick (City). Internationales Schulbuchinstitut. Conseil de la Cooperation Culturelle des Europarats. Gewerkschaft Erziehung und Wissenschaft im DGB. Vol. 1 (1951)-. Periodical. German. an.
Ind/Abst Am. Hist. Life (1955-1978).

RU/0130-6685
ISTORICESKIE ZAPISKI. (ISTORICHESKIE ZAPISKI.). [Istor. zap.]. **Added/Corp** Institut Istorii SSSR (Akademiia Nauk SSSR). (1937)-. Academic Scholarly Publication. Russian. 15.15 US; $16.78 other. Izdatelstvo Nauka / Akademiia Nauk, Publishing House of the Russian Academy of Sciences, Leninskii Porspekt 14, 117901 Moscow Russia. **Tel** 011 95 954-21-53, FAX 011 95 938-21-44, telex 411964. **(Subscription address:** Victor Kamkin, 4956 Boiling Brook Parkway, Rockville MD 20852.) **ED** B D Grekov. **LC** DK1; .I8. cum. index.
Ind/Abst Am. Hist. Life (1955-1956, 1969-).

YU/0352-3160
ISTORIJA 20. VEKA : CASOPIS INSTITUTA ZA SAVREMENU ISTORIJU. Added/Corp Institut za Savremenu Istoriju (Belgrade, Serbia). **VFOAT** Istorija Dvadesetog Veka; History of Twentieth Century; History of 20 Century. (1983)-. Periodical. Serbo-Croatian (Roman) (summaries and/or abstracts in English, French and Russian). sa. **Formed by the union of** *Istorija XX Veka* **and** *Prilozi za Istoriju Socijalizma.*
Ind/Abst Am. Hist. Life (1986-1987).

YU/0350-0802
ISTORIJSKI CASOPIS. (ISTORIJSKI CASOPIS : ORGAN ISTORIJSKOG INSTITUTA SRPSKE AKADEMIJE NAUKA I UMETNOSTI.). [Istor. cas.]. **Added/Corp** Srpska Akademija Nauka i Umetnosti. Istorijski Institut. Istorijski Institut u Beogradu. **VFOAT** Revue Historique. (1960)-. Periodical. Serbo-Croatian (Cyrillic). an. **Continues** *Istoriski Casopis.*
Ind/Abst Am. Hist. Life (1960-).

YU/0021-2644
ISTORIJSKI GLASNIK. (ISTORIJSKI GLASNIK : ORGAN DRUSTVA ISTORICARA SR SRBIJE.). [Istor. glas.]. **Added/Corp** Drustvo Istoricara SR Srbije. (19??)-. Periodical. Serbo-Croatian (Cyrillic) (Serbo-Croatian (Roman)). qt. **Continues** *Istoriski Glasnik*, 0021-2644.
Ind/Abst Am. Hist. Life (1953-1962, 1971-).

GR/1105-1663
ISTORIKA, TA. VFOAT Historica. (1983)-. Periodical. Greek, Modern. sa. $20.00. Melissa Publishing Company, Navarinov 10, Athens 106 80 Greece. **UDC** 949.505. **CODEN** 949.507.

BW
ISTORIKO-FILOSOFSKIE ISSLEDOVANIIA. See Philosophy.

UN/0135-2202
ISTORYCHNI DOSLIDZHENNIA. ISTORIIA ZARUBIZHNYKH KRAIN / AKADEMIIA NAUK UKRAINSKOI RSR, INSTYTUT ISTORII. Added/Corp Instytut Istorii (Akademiia nauk Ukrainskoi RSR). **VFOAT** Istoriia Zarubizhnykh Krain. (1975)-. Ukrainian. an. **LC** D410; .I77.
Ind/Abst Am. Hist. Life (1987-).

JA/0289-9582
IWATE SHIGAKU KENKYU. [Iwate shigaku kenkyu]. **VFOAT** Journal of the Iwate Society for Historical Studies. (1948)-. Periodical. Japanese. an. **DD** 952.
Ind/Abst Am. Hist. Life (1954,1970-1971).

GW
JAHRBUCH DER HISTORISCHEN FORSCHUNG IN DER BUNDESREPUBLIK DEUTSCHLAND. Added/Corp Arbeitsgemeinschaft Ausseruniversitarer Historischer Forschungseinrichtungen in der Bundesrepublik Deutschland. (19??)-. Monographic series. German. ir. Price varies per volume. R Oldenbourg Verlag, Postfach 801360, D 81613 Munich Germany. **Tel** 011 49 89 450190, FAX 011 49 89 45019305. **LC** DD86; .J255.
Ind/Abst Am. Hist. Life (1987).

GW/0076-2741
JAHRBUCH DES ROEMISCH-GERMANISCHES ZENTRALMUSEUM MAINZ. Added/Corp Roemisch-Germanisches Zentralmuseum Mainz. Vol. 1 (1954)-. Monographic series. German. ir. Price varies per volume. Dr. Rudolf Habelt GmbH, Postfach 150104, D 53040 Bonn Germany. **Tel** 011 49 228 232015.
Ind/Abst BHA : Biblio. Hist. Art; Br. Archaeol. Bibliogr.

GW/0724-4762
JAHRBUCH DRITTE WELT. 1-. Periodical. German. an. Nenkin Fukushi Jigyodan, 4-1 Kasumigaseki 1-chome, Chiyoda-ku 100 Tokyo Japan. **LC** D880; .J34. **DD** 909/.09724.

SZ/1013-6959
JAHRESBERICHTE / HISTORISCHES MUSEUM BASEL. See Museums and Galleries.

GW
JAHRESBIBLIOGRAPHIE / BIBLIOTHEK FUER ZEITGESCHICHTE, WELTKRIEGSBUCHEREI. Main/Corp Bibliothek fuer Zeitgeschichte (Germany). Vol. 32 (1960)-. Periodical. German. an. DM158.00. Klartext Verlag, Dickmannstrasse 2 4, D 45143 Essen Germany. **Tel** 011 49 201 8620631. **(Subscription address:** Prolit Verlagsauslieferung, Postfach 9, D 35461 Fernwald Germany.) **Continues** *Bibliothek fuer Zeitgeschichte (Germany). Bucherschau der Weltkriegsbucherei.*

AU/0558-3438
JAHRESSCHRIFT / SALZBURGER MUSEUM CAROLINO AUGUSTEUM. See Museums and Galleries.

US/0361-6169
JAMES SPRUNT STUDIES IN HISTORY AND POLITICAL SCIENCE, THE. [James Sprunt stud. hist. polit. sci.]. **Added/Corp** University of North Carolina. Dept. of History. University of North Carolina. Dept. of Political Science. Vol. 23, No. 1 (1939)-. English. ir. price varies per volume. University of North Carolina Press, 116 South Boundary Street, PO Box 2288, Chapel Hill NC 27515-2288. **Tel** (919)966-3561, FAX (919)966-3829. **Continues** *James Sprunt Historical Studies*, 0361-6150.
Desc: Published for the departments of history and political science at the University of North Carolina at Chapel Hill.

US
JEFFERSON COUNTY HISTORICAL QUARTERLY. Added/Corp Jefferson County Historical Society. Jefferson County Restoration and Preservation Commission. Jefferson County History Commission. Vol. 1 (Autumn 1961)-. Periodical. English. Four times a year (Mar., June, Sept., Nov.). $27.00. Currin Nichol, 408 Martin, Pine Bluff AR 71601.

SA
JOERNAAL VIR EIETYDSE : GESKIEDENIS EN INTERNASIONALE VERHOUDINGE. Added/Corp University of the Orange Free State. Institute for Contemporary History. **VFOAT** Journal for Contemporary History and

International Relations. Vol. 1 (March 1977)-. Periodical. Afrikaans (English). ir. R42.00. Inch, PO Box 2320, Bloemfontein 9300 South Africa. **Tel** 011 27 51 4019111. **LC** D410; .J63. **DD** 909.82. **Bk Rev.** **Ad Acc.** **Pr Rev.** **Circ:** 250 (ctrl). ***Continues*** *Joernaal vir die Eietydse Geskiedenis.*
Desc: Articles must deal with contemporary history of the world in general, although it mainly deals with contemporary Africa, European and American history.

US/0075-3874
JOHNS HOPKINS SYMPOSIA IN COMPARATIVE HISTORY, THE.
Added/Corp Johns Hopkins University. Dept. of History. Vol. 3 (1972)-. Monographic series. English. ir. Price varies per volume. Johns Hopkins University Press, 2715 North Charles Street, Baltimore MD 21218-4319. **Tel** (410)516-6987, FAX (410)516-6968. ***Continues*** *Johns Hopkins Symposia in History.*

FR/0449-4733
JOURNAL DE L'ANNEE.
(1967)-. French. an. Larousse Nathan International, 27 rue de la Glaciere, 75013 Paris France. **Tel** 011 33 1 445874300. **LC** D410; .J64. **[CCC].**

UK/0022-0094
JOURNAL OF CONTEMPORARY HISTORY.
[J. contemp. hist.]. **Added/Corp** Institute of Contemporary History. Institute for Advanced Studies in Contemporary History. Vol. 1 (1966)-. Periodical. English. qt. £90.00. Sage Publications Ltd., 6 Bonhill Street, London EC2A 4PU, UK. **Tel** 071 374 0645, FAX 071 374 8741, telex 296207 SAGE G. **ED** Walter Lacquer. **LC** D410; .J66. **DD** 909.82. **CODEN** JCHID7. cum. index. **Bk Rev.** **Ad Acc.** **Acid Free.** available on microfilm and microfiche from University Microfilms International (UMI). Documents available from The Genuine Article, UMI Article Clearinghouse.
Desc: An international forum for the analysis and discussion of 20th Century history.
Ind/Abst ABC POL SCI; Acad. Abstr. Full Text Elite (Oct. 1990-); Acad. Abstr. (Oct. 1990-); Acad. Ind. [Computer File] (1992-); Acad. Search (Oct. 1990-); Am. Hist. Life (1966-); Arts Humanit. Citation Index [Full Cov.]; Br. Humanit. Index; Curr. Contents Arts Humanit.; Expand. Acad. Index (1989-); Hist. Source (July 1990-); Humanit. Index; Humanit. Source (Jul. 1990-); Index Islam. Lit.; INFO-SOUTH Abstr.; Int. Polit. Sci. Abstr.; Mag. Search; Middle East Abstr. Index; Newsp. Period. Abstr. (1988-); Res. Alert [Full Cov.]; Sage Public Adm. Abstr. (?-?); Sage Urban Stud. Abstr (?-?); Soc. Plann. Policy Dev. Abstr.; Soc. Sci. Cit. Index [Select. Cov.]; SportSearch; West. Hist. Q.

NE/0169-796X
JOURNAL OF DEVELOPING SOCIETIES.
Vol. 1, No. 1 (June 1985)-. Academic Scholarly Publication. English. Twice a year. Fl175.00 Netherlands; $100.00 other. E. J. Brill, Postbus 9000, 2300 PA Leiden Netherlands. **Tel** 011 31 71 312624, FAX 011 31 71 317532, telex 39296 BRILL NL. **ED** K. Ishwaran. **LC** DS1; .C58. **DD** 909/.09724. **CODEN** JDSOEK. **[CCC].** **Circ:** 272. ***Continues*** *Contributions to Asian Studies, 0304-2693.*
Desc: Intended as a forum for scholarly analyses of Asian as well as of Latin American societies and cultures, past and contemporary, from the diverse point of view of the international community of scholars in all the social sciences and humanities.
Ind/Abst Am. Hist. Life (1988-); Anthropol. Lit.; Appl. Soc. Sci. Index Abstr.; Geogr. Abstr. Human Geogr. (?-?); Index Book Rev. Relig.; Int. Bibliogr. Sociol.; Int. Dev. Abstr.; Int. Labour Doc.; Int. Polit. Sci. Abstr.; LABORDOC; PAIS Int. Print (1991-); Relig. Index One Period.; Rural Dev. Abstr.; Soc. Plann. Policy Dev. Abstr.; Sug. Indus. Abstr.; World Agric. Econ.

US/0195-6752
JOURNAL OF HISTORICAL REVIEW, THE.
[J. hist. rev.]. **Added/Corp** Institute for Historical Review (U.S.). Vol. 1, No. 1 (Spring 1980)-. Periodical. English. Six times a year. $40.00 (1 year), $65.00 (2 year), $90.00 (3 year). Institute for Historical Review, 1822 1/2 Newport Boulevard, PO Box 191, Costa Mesa CA 92627. **Tel** (213)326-4504. **ED** Theodore O'Keefe. **LC** D1; .J587. **DD** 905. **Bk Rev.** **Circ:** 3,000 (ctrl).
Desc: Upholds and continues the tradition of Historical Revisionism of scholars such as Harry Elmer Barnes, AJP Taylor, William H Chamberlin, Paul Rassinier, and Charles Callan Tansil. Each issues contains several feature length essays of historical analysis, mainly concerning 20th century history, the world wars, their origins, courses and consequences.

PH
JOURNAL OF HISTORY, THE.
Added/Corp Philippine National Historical Society. Journal. (19??)-. Periodical. English. qt. $32.00. PSSC Central Subscription Service, PO Box 205 UP Diliman, Quezon City 1101 Philippines. **Tel** 011 63 2 9229621. **LC** DS651; .P4942.
Ind/Abst Index Philip. Period.

US/0228-6939
JOURNAL OF HISTORY AND POLITICS.
VFOAT Journal d'Histoire et de Politique. Vol. 6 (1988/89)-. English (French). an. $19.95 North America; £9.95 UK. Edwin Mellen Press, PO Box 450, Lewiston NY 14092. **Tel** (716)754-2788. **ED** Andrew F Johnson, Brian Jenkins; telephone: (716)754-8566; FAX (716)254-4335. Index available. **Bk Rev.** **Pr Rev.** ***Continues*** *Studies in History and Politics (Bishop's University), 0228-6939.*
Desc: Essays by noted scholars on clustered themes in history and politics.
Ind/Abst Am. Hist. Life (1989-).

US/0022-1953
JOURNAL OF INTERDISCIPLINARY HISTORY, THE.
[J. interdiscip. hist.]. **Added/Corp** Massachusetts Institute of Technology. School of Humanities and Social Science. **VFOAT** Interdisciplinary History. Vol. 1 (Autumn 1970)-. Periodical. English. qt. $38.00 (individuals), $120.00 (institutions). Massachusetts Institute of Technology (MIT) Press, 55 Hayward Street, Cambridge MA 02142-1399. **Tel** (617)253-2889, (617)625-8481, FAX (617)258-6779. **ED** Robert Rotberg and Theodore Rabb. **LC** D1; .J59. **DD** 901.9/05. **[CCC].** **Bk Rev.** **Ad Acc.** **Pr Rev.** **Circ:** 1,600. available on microfilm and microfiche from University Microfilms International (UMI). Documents available from The Genuine Article, UMI Article Clearinghouse.
Desc: Features articles, research notes, and review essays that relate historical study to applied fields such as economics and demographics. Spanning all geographical areas and periods of history.
Ind/Abst ABC POL SCI (1970-); Acad. Abstr. Full Text Elite (July 1990-); Acad. Abstr. (July 1990-); Acad. Ind. [Computer File] (1987-); Acad. Search (July 1990-); Am. Hist. Life (1970-); Am. Bibliogr. Slavic East Europ. Stud.; Arts Humanit. Citation Index [Full Cov.]; BHA : Biblio. Hist. Art; Book Rev. Index; Curr. Contents Arts Humanit.; Curr. Contents Soc. Behav. Sci.; Expand. Acad. Index (1987-); Hist. Source (July 1990-); Humanit. Index; Humanit. Source (Jul. 1990-); INFO-SOUTH Abstr.; Int. Bibliogr. Sociol.; Mag. Search; Middle East Abstr. Index; Newsp. Period. Abstr. (1991-); Popul. Index; Res. Alert [Full Cov.]; Romant. Move.; Sage Urban Stud. Abstr (?-?); Soc. Plann. Policy Dev. Abstr.; Soc. Sci. Cit. Index [Full Cov.]; Sociol. Abstr. (1970-); West. Hist. Q.; Women Stud. Abstr.

US/0899-3718
JOURNAL OF MILITARY HISTORY, THE.
See Military and Defense.

US/0022-2801
JOURNAL OF MODERN HISTORY, THE.
[J. mod. hist.]. Vol. 1 (March 1929)-. Periodical. English. qt (4 issues). $72.00 institution, $33.00 individual, $25.00 AHA and HA members and students. University of Chicago Press / Journals Division, PO Box 37005, 5720 South Woodlawn, Chicago IL 60637. **Tel** (312)753-3347, FAX (312)753-0811. **(Subscription telephone:** (312)753-8083) **ED** John Boyer and Julius Kirshner. **LC** D1; .J6. **DD** 905. **[CCC].** **Pr Rev.** **Acid Free.** available on microfilm and microfiche from University Microfilms International (UMI). Documents available from The Genuine Article, UMI Article Clearinghouse.
Desc: Contains studies in European intellectual, political and cultural history. Explores not only events and movements in specific countries, but also broader questions that span particular times and places.
Ind/Abst Acad. Abstr. Full Text Elite (July 1990-); Acad. Abstr. (July 1990-); Acad. Ind. [Computer File] (1987-); Acad. Search (July 1990-); Am. Hist. Life (1954-); Am. Bibliogr. Slavic East Europ. Stud.; Annu. Bibliogr. Engl. Lang. Lit.; Arts Humanit. Citation Index [Full Cov.]; BHA : Biblio. Hist. Art; Book Rev. Index; Curr. Contents Arts Humanit.; Curr. Contents Soc. Behav. Sci.; Expand. Acad. Index (1987-); Hist. Source (July 1990-); Humanit. Index; Humanit. Source (Jul. 1990-); INFO-SOUTH Abstr.; Int. Bibliogr. Sociol.; Int. Polit. Sci. Abstr.; Mag. Search; Middle East Abstr. Index; Newsp. Period. Abstr. (1989-); Peace Res. Abstr. J. (1945-1955, 1966-1969, 1983-1984); Res. Alert [Full Cov.]; Romant. Move.; Sage Public Adm. Abstr. (?-?); Soc. Sci. Source (Jul. 1990-); Soc. Sci. Cit. Index [Full Cov.]; U.S. Polit. Sci. Doc.; West. Hist. Q.; Women Stud. Abstr.

US
JOURNAL OF SCOUTING HISTORY.
See Societies and Clubs.

US/0897-6074
JOURNAL OF THE ANCIENT NEAR EASTERN SOCIETY, THE.
[J. Anc. Near East. Soc.]. **Added/Corp** Ancient Near Eastern Society (New York, N.Y.) Jewish Theological Seminary of America. **VFOAT** JANES. Vol. 14 (1982)-. English. an. $25.00 (institutions), $15.00 (individual) US; $26.00 (institutions), $16.00 (individuals) other. Jewish Theological Seminary, 3080 Broadway, New York NY 10027. **Tel** (212)678-8856. **ED** E.L. Greenstem. **LC** DS41; .C65. **DD** 939.4. **Circ:** 500. available on an online database, CD-ROM, magnetic tape, and microfilm; available on microfilm from University Microfilms International (UMI). ***Continues*** *Journal of the Ancient Near Eastern Society of Columbia University, 0010-2016.*
Desc: Specializes in the history, languages, religion and culture of the Ancient Near East.
Ind/Abst Anthropol. Lit.; Index Book Rev. Relig.; Middle East Abstr. Index; Relig. Index One Period.; Relig. Theol. Abstr.

US/0731-955X
JOURNAL OF THE CLAN CAMPBELL SOCIETY (UNITED STATES OF AMERICA).
See Genealogy and Heraldry.

IE/0332-415X
JOURNAL OF THE GALWAY ARCHAEOLOGICAL AND HISTORICAL SOCIETY.
See Archaeology.

SI/0217-913X
JOURNAL OF THE HISTORY SOCIETY (1979).
(JOURNAL OF THE HISTORY SOCIETY.). [J. Hist. Soc.]. **Added/Corp** University of Singapore. History Society. National University of Singapore. History Society. (1977)-. English. an. **LC** DS1; .S55. **DD** 909.82. ***Continues*** *Journal of the Historical Society, 0217-9083.*
Ind/Abst Am. Hist. Life (1977-).

US/0195-8453
JOURNAL OF THE ROCKY MOUNTAIN MEDIEVAL AND RENAISSANCE ASSOCIATION.
[J. Rocky Mt. Mediev. Renaiss. Assoc.]. **Main/Corp** Rocky Mountain Medieval and Renaissance Association. Vol. 1 (1980)-. Periodical. English. an. $20.00. Rocky Mountain Medieval and Renaissance Association, 1102 Brigham Young University, Provo UT 84602. **Tel** (602)523-6270. **(Subscription address:** Journal of the Rocky Mountain Medieval and Renaissance Association, Campus Box 234, Department of History, Boulder CO 80309.) **ED** James Fitzmaurice. **LC** CB351; .R57A. **DD** 909.07. **UDC** 940.1/.2. **Bk Rev.** **Ad Acc.** **Circ:** 200.
Desc: Medieval and Renaissance studies: history, literature, art, philosophy and music.
Ind/Abst Am. Hist. Life (1980-); Annu. Bibliogr. Engl. Lang. Lit.; MLA Int. Bibl. Books Artic. Mod. Lang. Lit.

US
JOURNAL OF UNCONVENTIONAL HISTORY.
(1989)-. Periodical. English. Three times a year. $22.50 US; $25.00 Canada; $30.00 other. Journal of Unconventional History, Box 459, Cardiff CA 92007. **Tel** (619)944-2936. **ED** Ann Elwood and Aline Hornaday (editors' phone: (619)459-0936). Index available. cum. index. **Bk Rev**, (Qty: 6-10 per year). **Ad Acc.** **Circ:** 400.
Desc: A magazine of history with a scholarly, but light, approach.

US/0096-1442
JOURNAL OF URBAN HISTORY.
[J. urban hist.]. Vol. 1 (Nov. 1974)-. Periodical. English. bm (Jan., Mar., May, July, Sept., Nov.). $197.00. SAGE Periodical Press, 2455 Teller Road, Thousand Oaks CA 91320. **Tel** (805)499-0721, FAX (805)499-0871, telex 100799. **ED** David Goldfield. **LC** HT111; .J68. **DD** 301.36/09. **[CCC].** **Pr Rev.** **Acid Free.** available on microfilm and microfiche from University Microfilms International (UMI). Documents available from The Genuine Article, UMI Article Clearinghouse.
Desc: Studies the history of cities and urban societies in all periods of human history and in all geographical areas of the world.
Ind/Abst ABC POL SCI; Acad. Search (July 1993-); Am. Hist. Life (1974-); Am. Bibliogr. Slavic East Europ. Stud.; Arts Humanit. Citation Index [Full Cov.]; Avery Index Archit. Period. Suppl. Colum. Univ.; Bibliogr. Carto.; BHA : Biblio. Hist. Art; Book Rev. Index; Curr. Contents Arts Humanit.; Curr. Contents Soc. Behav. Sci.; Expand. Acad. Index (1989-); Geogr. Abstr. Human Geogr.; Humanit. Index; Humanit. Source (Jul. 1993-); INFO-SOUTH Abstr.; Int. Bibliogr. Sociol.; Mag. Search; Middle East Abstr. Index; Newsp. Period. Abstr. (1991-); Res. Alert [Full Cov.]; Sage Urban Stud. Abstr; Soc. Plann. Policy Dev. Abstr.; Soc. Sci. Cit. Index [Full Cov.]; Sociol. Abstr.; U.S. Polit. Sci. Doc.; Urban Aff. Abstr.; West. Hist. Q.

US/1045-6007
JOURNAL OF WORLD HISTORY.
(JOURNAL OF WORLD HISTORY : OFFICIAL JOURNAL OF THE WORLD HISTORY ASSOCIATION.). [J. world hist.]. **Added/Corp** World History Association. Vol. 1, No. 1 (Spring 1990)-. Periodical. English. sa (Mar., & Aug.). $35.00 one year; $63.00 two year, US and Canada; $40.00 (one year), $72.00 (two year) other. University of Hawaii Press, 2840 Kolowalu Street, Honolulu HI 96822. **Tel** (808)956-8833, (808)948-8697, FAX (808)988-6052. **ED** Jerry H. Bentley. **LC** D1; .J62. **DD** 905. **CODEN** JWHIEC. Index available. **Bk Rev**, (Qty: 15-20). **Ad Acc.** **Pr Rev.** **Circ:** 1,500.
Desc: Devoted to historical analysis from a global point of view. Features articles on comparative and cross-cultural themes and on the historiography and methodology of world history.
Ind/Abst Am. Hist. Life (1990-); Curr. Index J. Educ.; Int. Bibliogr. Sociol.; Soc. Plann. Policy Dev. Abstr.

RU/0130-2051
KALENDAR ZNAMENATELNYKH I PAMIATNYKH DAT.
Added/Corp Gosudarstvennaia Publichnaia Istoricheskaia Biblioteka RSFSR. (1957)-. Periodical. Russian. mo. $10.00. **(Subscription address:** Victor Kamkin, 4956 Boiling Brook Parkway, Rockville MD 20852.) **LC** D11.5; .K3.

JA
KANAZAWA DAIGAKU BUNGAKUBU RONSHU. SHIGAKUKA HEN. **VFOAT** Studies and Essays. History. 1980 Ed.-. Periodical. Japanese. Kanazawa Daigaku Bungakubu, 1-1 Marunouchi, Kanazawa-shi 920 Japan. **LC** D1; .K36.

NE
KEESINGS HISTORISCH ARCHIEF. **VFOAT** Keesings Drie-Maandelijksch Wereldnieuws. No. 158 (June 26-July 1, 1934)-. Dutch. Keesing Uitgeversmaatschappij, Hogehilweg 13, Postbus 1118, 1000 BC Amsterdam Netherlands. **Tel** 011 31 020 5641183, 5641184.

GW/0453-8471
KIELER HISTORISCHE STUDIEN. Vol. 1 (1966)-. Monographic series. German. ir. Price varies per volume. Jan Thorbecke Verlag GmbH and Company, Karlstrasse 10, Postfach 546, D 72482 Sigmaringen Germany. **Tel** 011 49 7571 728100, FAX 011 07571-728-280, telex 732534.

DK/0450-3171
KIRKEHISTORISKE SAMLINGER. [Kirkehist. saml.]. (1849)-. Multiple languages. an. **DD** 274.89. **CODEN** 27.6.
Ind/Abst BHA : Biblio. Hist. Art.

GW/0075-6334
KLIO (LEIPZIG, GERMANY : 1906). (KLIO.). **Added/Corp** Akademie der Wissenschaften der DDR. Zentralinstitut fuer Alte Geschichte und Archaologie. (1906)-. Periodical. German. an. $195.00. Akademie-Verlag GmbH, Muehlenstrasse 33 34, D 13162 Berlin Germany. **Tel** 011 49 30 47889300, FAX 011 49 30 47889357. **(Subscription address:** VCH Publishers Inc., 303 Northwest 12th Avenue, Journals Department, Deerfield FL 33442.**)** **LC** D51; .K6. **DD** 930/.05. ***Continues** Beitrage zur Alten Geschichte.*
Ind/Abst BHA : Biblio. Hist. Art; Numis. Lit.

RU/0134-837X
KNIGA. ISSLEDOVANIA I MATERIALY. [Kniga, Issled. mater.]. (1959)-. Periodical. Russian. Izdatelstvo Kniga, 50 Gorky Ulitsa, 125047 Moscow Russia.
Ind/Abst BHA : Biblio. Hist. Art.

NE
KONINKRIJK DER NEDERLANDEN IN DE TWEEDE WERELDOORLOG. SDU Uitgeverij, Postbus 20014, Christoffel Plan, 2500 EA Den Haag Netherlands. **Tel** 011 31 70 3789911.

DK
KRIGSHISTORISK TIDSSKRIFT. **Added/Corp** Militre Lseselskab Rendsborg. Vol. 1 (June 1965)-. Periodical. Danish. Three times a year. kr135.00. Major J.C. Andreassen, Kastellet 60, DK 2100 Copenhagen Denmark. **ED** J.C. Andreassen. **LC** D25; .K76. Index available. **Pr Rev. Acid Free. Circ:** 600.
Desc: Publishes original works on war and military history. Features authentic texts and illustrations.

GW
KRITISCHE STUDIEN ZUR GESCHICHTSWISSENSCHAFT. Vol. 1 (1972)-. Monographic series. German. ir. Price varies per volume. Vandenhoeck & Ruprecht, Robert Bosch Breite 6, D-37079 Goettingen Germany. **Tel** 011 49 551 695911, FAX 011 49 551 695917, telex 965226 VAN d. **Ad Acc.**

US/0361-6584
KRONOS. V. 1- Spring 1975-. English. qt. $22.00. Kronos Press, PO Box 343, Wynnewood PA 19096. **Tel** (215)642-3866. **ED** Lewis M Greenberg. **LC** AS30; .K76. **DD** 051. **UDC** 930.9. **Bk Rev. Ad Acc. Circ:** 1,500.
Desc: A publication devoted to the works of Immanuel Velikovsky and the general subject of catastrophism and human history.

US/1046-7335
KTB (FOX LAKE, FLA.). (KTB.). [KTB]. **Added/Corp** Cooper Enterprises. Sharkhunters Div. Sharkhunters (Organization). No. 4 (May 25, 1983)-. Periodical. English. Ten times a year. $35.00 Comes with Shark Hunters membership. Sharkhunters, PO Box 1539, Hernando FL 32642. **Tel** (904)637-2917, FAX (904)637-6289. **LC** D780; .S45. **DD** 623. ***Continues** Sharkhunters Div., Cooper Enterprises.*
Desc: Historically accurate view of the operations of submarines, as well as their history from World War II. These facts are brought to life from the first person accounts of the men who actually waged the World War at sea from both sides of the periscope.

KO
KUKCHE CHONGBO CHARYO. Began with Sept. 21, 1977 issue. Periodical. Korean. wk. Kukche Munje Chosa Yonguso, 4-1 Yejang-dong, Chung-ku Seoul Korea. **LC** D839; .K816.

SW/0454-5915
KULTUREN. **Added/Corp** Kulturhistoriska Foreningen for Sodra Sverige. Kulturhistoriska Foreningen for Sodra Sverige. Redogorelse for Kulturhistoriska Foreningens for Sodra Sverige Verksamhet. (19??)-. Swedish. an. **LC** DL621; .K84.
Ind/Abst BHA : Biblio. Hist. Art.

PL/0023-5903
KWARTALNIK HISTORYCZNY. [Kwart. hist.]. **Added/Corp** Towarzystwo Historyczne (Lwow, Poland) Polskie Towarzystwo Historyczne. Instytut Historii (Polska Akademia Nauk). **VFOAT** Revue Trimestrielle d'Histoire. Vol. 1 (1887)-. Periodical. Polish (summaries and/or abstracts in French). qt. $68.00. **(Subscription address:** ARS Polona, PO Box 1001, 00068 Warsaw Poland.**)** **LC** D1; .K85.
Ind/Abst Am. Hist. Life (1954-).

SP/0212-8985
LAIETANIA. **See** Archaeology.

US
LANSING METROPOLITAN QUARTERLY. English. Four times a year. $8.00. Castle Publications, 1521 South Pennsylvania, Lansing MI 48910. **Tel** (517)372-8433. **ED** Manuel Castro. **Bk Rev. Ad Acc, Adv Mgr:** Jeanne Castro, **Tel** (517)372-8433.
Desc: Interest of the greater Lansing areas.

NE
LANTERNU : GUIA PA NOS HISTORIA. **VFOAT** Gids voor Onze Geschiedenis; Guide to History. Vol. 1, No. 1 (Feb. 1983)-. Periodical. Dutch (Dutch). sa. Roodeweg 7A Willemstad, Curacao Netherlands. **LC** F2141; .L36. **UDC** 972.988.1.

HU/0024-1512
LEVELTARI KOEZLEMENYEK. [Leveltari koezl.]. **Added/Corp** Magyar Orszagos Leveltar. Hungary. Leveltarak Orszagos Koezpontja. (1923)-. Hungarian. sa (2 issues). $20.00. **(Subscription address:** Kultura, PO Box 149, H 1389 Budapest 62 Hungary.**)** **ED** Gy Ember. **Bk Rev. Circ:** 550.
Desc: Historical research related to archives.
Ind/Abst Am. Hist. Life (1962-1967, 1976-).

UK/0024-1873
LIBERATION (LONDON). (LIBERATION.). **Added/Corp** Movement for Colonial Freedom. (Apr. 1966)-. Periodical. English. bm. £8.00 UK; £12.00 (surface mail), £14.00 (air mail) other. Liberation News, 490 Kingsland Road, London E8 4AE England. **Tel** 254 6223. **LC** D839; .L53. **DD** 909.82/05. ***Continues** Colonial Freedom News.*
Ind/Abst Peace Res. Abstr. J. (1964-1977).

IT/0390-1009
LIBRI E DOCUMENTI, ARCHIVO STORICO CIVICO E BIBLIOTECA TRIVULZIANA. **Main/Corp** Archivo Storico Civico (Milan, Italy). Vol. 1 (1975)-. Periodical. Italian. Three times a year (Jan., May, Sept.). L15000 (Italy); L20000 (other). Direz Archiv Stor Civico Bibl, Trivulziana Castello Sforzesco, 20121 Milan Italy. **Tel** 39 2 86454638. **ED** Giulia Bologna. **LC** DG655.6; .M54a. **DD** 945/.21. Index available. **Circ:** 500.
Desc: Medieval and modern history, history of the book, history of literature, history of art.
Ind/Abst BHA : Biblio. Hist. Art.

UK/0459-4487
LINCOLNSHIRE HISTORY AND ARCHAEOLOGY. **See** Archaeology.

CC
LISHI YANJIU. **VFOAT** Li shi yan jiu. (19??)-. Periodical. Chinese. Six times a year. $30.86. **(Subscription address:** China International Book Trading Corporation, PO Box 399, Library Service Department, Beijing 100044 People's Republic of China.**)**
Ind/Abst Am. Hist. Life (1954-1958; 1985-).

XR/0862-8424
LITTERARIA PRAGENSIA. **See** Literature.

US/0047-4851
LIVING HISTORICAL FARMS BULLETIN. [Living hist. farms bull.]. **Added/Corp** Association for Living Historical Farms and Agricultural Museums (U.S.). Vol. 1 (Dec. 1970)-. Periodical. English. Four times a year. $15.00 (individual), $40.00 (institution) Comes with Association for Living Historical Farms and Agricultural Museums membership. Association Living Historical Farms & Agricultural, Route 14 Box 214, Santa Fe NM 87505. **Tel** (505)471-2261. **ED** Stephen L. Cox (editor's address: Conner Prairie, 13400 Allisonville Road, Fishers, Indiana, phone: 317)776-6000).
Desc: Articles of interest to those involved in living history.

UK
LIVING HISTORY LOCAL GUIDE. 1973-. Monographic series. English. Price varies per volume.

US/0076-0072
LIVING HISTORY OF THE WORLD; YEARBOOK. English. an. Stravon Educational Press, 845 3rd Avenue, New York NY 10022. **ED** G D Stoddard. **LC** D410; .L58. **DD** 905. **UDC** 930.9.

BL
LIVRO DO ANO, O. **VFOAT** Livro do Ano, Veja e Leia. (19??)-. Portuguese. Editora Abril SA, Rua do Curtume 769 Lapa, 05066 900 Sao Paulo SP Brazil. **Tel** 011 55 11 8239222, 011 55 11 2623322, FAX 011 55 11 8643796. **LC** D410; .L59.

UK/0520-6790
LOCAL HISTORY RECORDS - BOURNE SOCIETY. **See** Genealogy and Heraldry-Archives.

UK/0076-0625
LONDON ORIENTAL SERIES. **Added/Corp** University of London. School of Oriental and African Studies. (1953)-. Monographic series. English. ir. Price varies per volume. Oxford University Press, Walton Street, Oxford OX2 6DP England. **Tel** 011 44 865 56767, FAX 011 44 865 267773, telex 837330 OXPRES G. **(Subscription address:** Oxford University Press / USA, Journals Marketing Department, Oxford University Press, 2001 Evans Road, Cary NC 27513.**)**

GW/0721-3735
LUBECKER SCHRIFTEN ZUR ARCHAOLOGIE UND KULTURGESCHICHTE / AMT FUER VOR- UND FRUHGESCHICHTE (BODENDENKMALPFLEGE) DER HANSESTADT LUBECK. **See** Archaeology.

CN
LUMEN. **See** Literature.

PO/0076-1508
LUSITANIA SACRA. [Lusit. sacra]. **Added/Corp** Centro de Estudos de Historia Eclesiastica. Universidade Catolica Portuguesa. Centro de Estudos de Historia Religiosa. Vol. 1-10, (1956-1978)-New Series., Vol. 1 (1989)-. Portuguese. an. $30.00. University Catlica Portuguesa Center, Estudos History Religion, Palma CIMA, 1600 Libson Portugal. **LC** BR910; .L8.
Ind/Abst Am. Hist. Life (1962-1971,1989-).

US/0882-228X
MAGAZINE OF HISTORY. (MAGAZINE OF HISTORY / ORGANIZATION OF AMERICAN HISTORIANS.). [Mag. hist.]. **Added/Corp** Organization of American Historians. **VFOAT** OAH Magazine of History. Vol. 1, No. 1 (Apr. 1985)-. Periodical. English. Four times a year. $20.00 OAH member, $25.00 non-member, $30.00 institution. Organization of American Historians, 112 North Bryan Street, Bloomington IN 47408. **Tel** (812)855-7311, FAX (812)855-0696. **ED** Michael Regoli. **LC** D16.3; .M33. **DD** 373. Index available. cum. index. **Bk Rev. Ad Acc, Adv Mgr:** Debby J. Davis, **Tel** (812)855-9854. **Circ:** 5,000. available on microfilm and microfiche from University Microfilms International (UMI).
Desc: A national publication designed to address the interests and concerns of secondary history and social studies teachers. Provides information about ongoing scholarship, trends in the teaching of history. It is a forum between high school and university educators.
Ind/Abst Curr. Index J. Educ.

SP/0212-078X
MAINAKE. **See** Archaeology.

●GW/0945-1439
MAJESTAS. (1993)-. German. ir. DM48.00. Boehlau Verlag GmbH & Cie / Koeln, Theodor Heuss STR 76, D-51149 Cologne Germany. **Tel** 011 49 2203 307021, FAX 011 49 2203 307349. **(Subscription address:** BDK Buecherdienst GmBh, Postfach 900120, D 51111 Cologne Germany.**)**

CN/0824-3298
MAN AND NATURE. ***Title Change.*** (MAN AND NATURE : PROCEEDINGS OF THE CANADIAN SOCIETY FOR EIGHTEENTH-CENTURY STUDIES.). [Man nat.]. **Main/Corp** Canadian Society for Eighteenth-Century Studies. **Added/Corp** University of Western Ontario. Faculty of Education. **VFOAT** Homme et la Nature : Actes de la Societe Canadienne d'Etude du Dix-Huiteme Siecle; Proceedings of the Canadian Society for Eighteenth-Century Studies; Actes de la Societe Canadienne d'Etude du Dix-Huitieme Siecle. Vol. 1 (1982)-(1993). Proceedings. English (French). an. Academic Printing and Publishing, PO Box 4218, South Edmonton, Alberta T6E 4T2 Canada. **Tel** (403)435-5898. **LC** CB411; .C36a. **DD** 909.7. ***Continued by** Lumen.*
Ind/Abst MLA Int. Bibl. Books Artic. Mod. Lang. Lit.

US/0195-7813
MANUSCRIPT SOCIETY NEWS, THE. **See** Hobbies.

US/0025-424X
MARYLAND HISTORIAN, THE. [Md. hist.]. **Added/Corp** University of Maryland, College Park. History Dept. Vol. 1, (Spring 1970)-. Academic Scholarly Publication. English. sa. $22.00 (institutions), $12.00 (individuals). University of Maryland Department of History, Francis Scott Key Hall, College Park MD 20742. **Tel** (301)405-4331. **ED** Mark A Tacyn. **LC** E171; .M28. **DD** 917.3/03/05. **Bk Rev,** (Qty: 10-12). **Ad Acc. Circ:** 250. available on microfilm and microfiche from University Microfilms International (UMI).

History(General)

Desc: Offers scholarly articles, book reviews, review essays, and features of historical interest to historians and general readers.
Ind/Abst Am. Hist. Life (1970-).

UN
MATERIALY DO ZVODU PAMIATOK ISTORII TA KULTURY NARODIV SRSR PO UKRAINSKII RSR. Periodical. Ukrainian. **LC** DK508.154; .M38.

FR/0769-3206
MATERIAUX POUR L'HISTOIRE DE NOTRE TEMPS. (MATERIAUX POUR L'HISTOIRE DE NOTRE TEMPS / EDITE PAR L'ASSOCIATION DES AMIS DE LA BDIC ET DU MUSEE.). [Mater. hist. notre temps]. **Added/Corp** Association des Amis de la BDIC et du Musee (France). No. 1 (1985)-. Periodical. French. Four times a year. 280.00F (institution); 210.00F (individual). Association Amis BDIC, 6 Allee de l Universite, 92001 Nanterre, Cedex France. **Tel** 011 33 1 40977905, FAX 011 33 1 40977940. **LC** D410; .M34. **DD** 909.82/05. *Continues* Lettre de l'Association des Amis de la BDIC & du Musee, 0293-2245.
Ind/Abst Am. Hist. Life (1989-).

UK
MATERIAY / INSTYTUT POLSKI I MUZEUM IM. GENERRA SIKORSKIEGO. (1985)-. Monographic series. Polish. Price varies per volume. Polish Institute 7 Sikorski Mus, 20 Prince Gale, London SW 7 England.

SW/0347-8068
MEDDELANDEN / SVENSKA FORSKNINGSINSTITUTET I ISTANBUL. **Added/Corp** Svenska Forskningsinstitutet i Istanbul. (1976)-. Periodical. Swedish (summaries and/or abstracts in English). kr75.00. Kungl. Biblioteket Forvarvsavd, Box 5039, 102 41 Stockholm Sweden. **LC** DS41; .M39.
Ind/Abst BHA : Biblio. Hist. Art.

GW/0934-7453
MEDIAEVISTIK. (1988)-. Periodical. German (English, French and Italian). an (May). $72.80. Verlag Peter Lang GmbH, Eschborner Landstrasse 42-50, D 60489 Frankfurt Germany. **Tel** 011 49 69 7807050. (Subscription address: Peter Lang Publishing Inc., 62 West 45th Street, 4th Floor, New York NY 10036.) **LC** D111; .M45. **DD** 940.1/05.
Desc: Contains information about the Middle Ages.
Ind/Abst Annu. Bibliogr. Engl. Lang. Lit.

●NE/1380-7854
MEDIEVAL ENCOUNTERS. (1995)-. Academic Scholarly Publication. English. Three times a year. Fl160.00 (institutions) Netherlands; $91.50 (institutions) other. E. J. Brill, Postbus 9000, 2300 PA Leiden Netherlands. **Tel** 011 31 71 312624, FAX 011 31 71 317532, telex 39296 BRILL NL. **ED** Gordon Newby. **Bk Rev**.
Desc: Intended to promote discussion and dialogue across cultural, linguistic and disciplinary boundaries about the interactions of Jewish, Christian and Muslim culture during the period from the fourth through to the fifteenth century.

FR/0751-2708
MEDIEVALES. **Added/Corp** Universite de Paris VIII: Vincennes. Centre de Recherche. No 1 (Jan. 1982)-. Periodical. French. sa. Univ de Paris Puv, 2 rue de la Liberte, 93526 Saint-Denis Cedex 02 France. **Tel** 011 33 1 49406750.
Ind/Abst BHA : Biblio. Hist. Art.

IT
MEDIOEVO LATINO. See History(General)-Abstracting, Bibliographies and Statistics.

IT
MELANGES DE L'ECOLE FRANCAISE DE ROME. ITALIE ET MEDITERRANEE. **Added/Corp** Ecole Francaise de Rome. **VFOAT** Italie et Mediterranee; MEFRIM. (1989)-. Periodical. French (English). sa. Ecole Francaise de Rome, Piazza Navona 62, 00186 Rome Italy. **Tel** 011 39 6 6869851. (Subscription address: Aldo Ausilio Editore, Via A da Bassano 70D, 35135 Padua Italy. Tel. 39 49 8642829) *Continues in part* Melanges de l'Ecole Francaise de Rome. Moyen Age, Temps Modernes, 0223-5110.
Ind/Abst Am. Hist. Life; BHA : Biblio. Hist. Art.

FR/0248-6644
MEMOIRES / SOCIETE D'HISTOIRE ET D'ARCHEOLOGIE DE BEAUNE (COTE-D'OR). See Archaeology.

IT/0392-4564
MEMORIA (TURIN, ITALY). *Ceased*. (MEMORIA.). No. 1 (1981)-(1991). Periodical. Italian. Three times a year. Rosenberg & Sellier, Via Andrea Doria 14, 10123 Turin Italy. **Tel** 011 39 11 8127808, telex 224202 ROSSELI. **ED** Boccia Maria Luisa, Bonacchi Gabriella, D'Amelia Marina, De Giorgio Michela, Ergas Yasmine, Groppi Angela, Pelaja Margherita, Piccone Stella Simonetta. **LC** HQ1104; .M46. **DD** 305.4/05. **UDC**

396(09). **Bk Rev**. **Ad Acc**. **Circ:** 2,500.
Desc: Researches on the specific experience and identity of women in history and the contemporary world. All monographic issues.
Ind/Abst Int. Bibliogr. Sociol.

SP
MEMORIAS DE HISTORIA ANTIGUA. **Added/Corp** Universidad de Oviedo. Instituto de Historia Antigua. Vol. 1 (1977)-. Periodical. Spanish. ir. 2800ptas. Universidad de Oviedo, Arguelles 19, 33003 Oviedo Spain. **Tel** 011 34 8 5210160. **LC** D51; .M45. **DD** 930.

RU
METODOLOGICHESKIE I ISTORIOGRAFICHESKIE VOPROSY ISTORICHESKOI NAUKI. **Added/Corp** Tomskii Gosudarstvennyi Universitet Imeni V.V. Kuibysheva. (19??)-. Periodical. Russian. 1.05rub. Izdatelstvo Tomskogo Universiteta / Tomsk State University, Prospekt Lenina 36, 634050 Tomsk Russia. **Tel** 23-44-65, FAX 22-44-66, telex 128258. **LC** D16; .M593.

US/0738-9396
MID-ATLANTIC ARCHIVIST, THE. [Mid-Atl. arch.]. **Added/Corp** Mid-Atlantic Regional Archives Conference. **VFOAT** MAA. Vol. 1 (Oct. 1972)-. Periodical. English. Four times a year. $15.00. Mid-Atlantic Regional Archives, University of Virginia Library, Charlottesville VA 22903. **Tel** (804)924-3025.

US/0047-7338
MIGRANT ECHO. V. 1- Jan./Mar. 1972-. Periodical. Multiple languages (English and Polish). Three times a year. Society of Christ, 127 Starview Way, San Francisco CA 94131. **LC** DK4122; .M53. **DD** 909./04/9185. **UDC** 908.73.

SA/0026-4016
MILITARY HISTORY JOURNAL. See Military and Defense.

UK/0268-8328
MILITARY ILLUSTRATED : PAST & PRESENT. See Military and Defense.

US/1067-7380
MINERVA HISTORICAL SOCIETY QUARTERLY. [Minerva Hist. Soc. q.]. **Added/Corp** Minerva Historical Society. (1971)-. Periodical. English. Four times a year (Jan., Apr., July, Oct.). $5.00. Minerva Historical Society, c/o Noelle Donahue, PO Box 46, Minerva NY 12851. **Tel** (518)251-2146. **ED** Noelle S. Donahue. **DD** 974.

UK
MINIATURE WARGAMES. See Hobbies.

KO
MIRAERUL MUNNUNDA. **VFOAT** Inquiry into the Future. 1- 1970-. Multiple languages (English and Korean). Hanguk Mirae Hakhoe, Room No 22/Seoul National University, 199 Tongsungdong, Seoul Korea. **LC** CB161; .M54.

FR/0988-0321
MIROIR DE L'HISTOIRE. [Miroir hist.]. 1.- Yearly volume (No. 1-); Feb. 1950-. Periodical. French. Librairie Jules Tallandier, 17 rue Remy Dumoncel, 75680 Paris Cedex 14 France. **ED** L H Paris. **LC** D1; .M6. **UDC** 930.9.
Ind/Abst Am. Hist. Life (1954-1959).

CN/0711-5911
MIRROR (LONDON, ONT.). See College and School Publications.

US/0083-5579
MITTEILUNGEN DES VEREINS FUR GESCHICHTE DER STADT NURNBERG. (MITTHEILUNGEN DES VEREINS FUR GESCHICHTE DER STADT NURNBERG [MICROFORM].). [Mitt. Ver. Gesch. Stadt Nurnb.]. **Added/Corp** Verein fur Geschichte der Stadt Nurnberg. **VFOAT** Mitteilungen des Vereins fur Geschichte der Stadt Nurnberg. (1879)-. German.
Ind/Abst BHA : Biblio. Hist. Art.

UK/0956-0726
MODERN HISTORY REVIEW. [Mod. hist. rev.]. (1989)-. Periodical. English. Four times a year (Feb., April, Sept., Nov.). £16.95 UK; £23.00 Europe; £28.50 (airmail) other. Philip Allan Publishers Ltd, Market Place, Deddington Oxford, OX15 0SE England. **Tel** 011 44 869 38652, FAX 011 44 869 38803. **DD** 941.081.
Ind/Abst Am. Hist. Life (1989-).

US/0738-0429
MODERN MASTERS SERIES. See The Arts-Art.

AT/0818-0032
MONASH PUBLICATIONS IN HISTORY. [Monash publ. hist.]. (1986)-. Periodical. English. ir (two to four issues per year). Monash University, History Department, Clayton Victoria 3168 Australia. **Tel** (03)565-2205, FAX (61)-3-565-2210. **ED** Anokew Makkus. **DD** 905. **Pr Rev**.
Desc: Historical monographs.

FR/0077-0310
MONDE D'OUTRE-MER, PASSE ET PRESENT. (MONDE D'OUTRE-MER, PASSE ET PRESENT; SERIE 1 : ETUDES.). 1- 1957-. Monographic series. French. Price varies per volume. Editions Vuibert, 63 Boulevard Saint Germain, 75005 Paris France. **Tel** 011 33 1 43256100, FAX 011 33 1 43257586, telex 201005. **UDC** 325.3.

UK
MONITOR WEEKLY, THE. **VFOAT** Monitor. Periodical. English. wk. **LC** D839; .M59. **DD** 909.82/05. **UDC** 930.9.

GW/0254-9948
MONUMENTA SERICA. **VFOAT** Hua-yi-xue-zhi. (1935)-. Periodical. English (French and German). an. DM158.00 Germany; $82.00 North America; DM146.00 other. Monumenta Serica Institute, Arnold Janssen STR 20, D 53754 Saint Augustin Germany. **Tel** 011 49 2241 2371. **ED** Heinrich Busch, Willheim Muller and Roman Malek. **UDC** 809. **[CCC]**. Index available. cum. index. **Bk Rev**. **Ad Acc**. **Pr Rev**. **Circ:** 400.
Desc: Sinological scholarly journal, publishing articles. Areas of research covered include the humanities, history, philosophy, religion, missionary history, and literature.
Ind/Abst Am. Hist. Life (1976-).

NE
MONUMENTEN. See Building and Construction.

FR/0027-2671
MOUVEMENT SOCIAL, LE. [Mouv. soc.]. No. 33/34 (Oct. 1960/March 1961)-. Periodical. French (summaries and/or abstracts in English). qt. 180.00F (one year), 350.00F (two year) France; 245.00F (one year), 475.00F (two year) other. Editions Ouvrieres, 12 Avenue Soeur Rosalie, Box Postale 50, 75621 Paris Cedex 13 France. **Tel** 011 33 1 44089515, telex 240 435 LIVREST. **ED** Patrick Fridenson. **UDC** 316.3(09)(4). cum. index. **Bk Rev**. **Ad Acc**. **Pr Rev**. **Circ:** 1,500 (ctrl). Documents available from The Genuine Article. *Continues* Actualite de l'Histoire.
Desc: Labor and social history of industrial societies since the 19th century.
Ind/Abst Am. Hist. Life (1961-); Arts Humanit. Citation Index [Full Cov.]; Curr. Contents Arts Humanit.; Curr. Contents Soc. Behav. Sci.; Int. Bibliogr. Sociol.; Int. Polit. Sci. Abstr.; Res. Alert [Full Cov.]; Soc. Sci. Cit. Index [Full Cov.]; Stud. Women Abstr.

CN/0077-2542
MUSK-OX, THE. *Ceased*. See Geography.

US
N.A.V.A. NEWS. bm. $30.00 per year (members only). North American Vexillological Association, 1977 North Olden Avenue, Suite 225, Trenton NJ 08618. **Tel** (214)539-4653, FAX (214)423-8849. **ED** Grace Cooper. **Bk Rev**. **Circ:** 300 (ctrl).
Desc: Current and historical flags and seals with particular interest paid to North America.

GW/0016-9080
NACHRICHTEN DER GESELLSCHAFT FUER NATUR- UND VOLKERKUNDE OSTASIENS/HAMBURG. [Nachr. Ges. Nat. Volkerkd. Ostasiens, Hambg.]. **Added/Corp** Gesellschaft fur Natur- und Volkerkunde Ostasiens. (19??)-. Periodical. German. sa. Universitaet Hamburg, Seminar fuer Sprache und Kultur Japans, Von Melle Park 6-7, 2000 Hamburg 13, Germany. **Bk Rev**. **Circ:** 750. *Continues* Nachrichten (Gesellschaft fur Natur- und Volkerkunde Ostasiens).
Ind/Abst Am. Hist. Life (1954-1975).

CC
NAN KAI SHIH HSUEH / NAN KAI TA HSUEH LI SHIH HSI HSUEH SHU WEI YUAN HUI. Began in 1980. Periodical. Chinese. sa. RMB¥0.80. Nan Kai Ta Hsueh Li Shih Hsi, Tianjin, People's Republic of China. **Tel** 33-1640. **ED** Chen Zhen Jiang. **LC** DS701; .N23. **DD** 951/.0072. **UDC** 930.9; 951;. **Bk Rev**. **Circ:** 2,000.
Desc: Articles related to world history and Chinese history theory of history, translation documents, and other important sources, theses and dissertation.

US/1053-3338
NAVA NEWS / NORTH AMERICAN VEXILLOLOGICAL ASSOCIATION. [NAVA news - North Am. Vexillol. Assoc.]. **Main/Corp** North American Vexillological Association. **VAT** North American Vexillological Association News. Vol. 2, No. 1 (1968)-. Periodical. English. Six times a year (Jan., Mar., May, July, Sept., Nov.). $30.00 (individuals) $45.00 (institutions) membership; $15.00 (associate membership); $25.00 (others) (Comes with North American Vexillological Association Membership and Nava News). North American Vexillological Association, 1977 North Olden Avenue, Suite 225, Trenton NJ 08618. **Tel** (214)539-4653, FAX (214)423-8849. **ED** Grace R. Cooper, (editor's address: HCR 62, Box 43A, Great Cacapon, WV 25422; (304)947-7622). **DD** 929. **Bk Rev**, (Qty: varies). **Circ:** 350. *Continues* NAVA Newsletter.

History(General)

US
NBC NEWS, RAND MCNALLY WORLD ATLAS & ALMANAC. *Ceased.* See Political Science.

US/1053-4733
NESBITT MEMORIAL LIBRARY JOURNAL. [Nesbitt Meml. Libr. j.]. **Added/Corp** Nesbitt Memorial Library. Archives. Vol. 1, No. 1 (Nov. 1989)-. Periodical. English. Three times a year (Jan., May, Sept.). $18.00. Archives Nesbitt Memorial Library, 529 Washington Street, Columbus TX 78934. **Tel** (409)732-5514. **ED** Bill Stein. **DD** 978. Index available. **Circ:** 125.
Desc: Examine the aspects of Colorado County and Texas

GW
NEUE ZEIT. Began in 1971. German. bm. DM18.00. Verlag Neue Zeit, Postfach 928, 8000 Munchen 33 Germany. **LC** D839; .N4815. **DD** 320.9/047. **UDC** 930.9.

US
NEW APPROACHES TO SOCIAL SCIENCE HISTORY. See Social Sciences.

US
NEW JERSEY & NATIONAL REGISTERS OF HISTORIC PLACES AS OF ... . VFOAT New Jersey and National Registers of Historic Places as of ... . English. an. Free. New Jersey Department of Environmental Protection & Energy, 401 East State Street, CN-402, Trenton NJ 08618. **Tel** (609)292-2885, **FAX** (609)984-3962. **LC** F135; .S78. **DD** 974.9/0025. **UDC** 904(749). **Circ:** 1,000.
Desc: Names and addresses of properties listed in, or determined eligible for listing in, historic registers.

JA
NEW MODEL MAGAZINE. (19??)-. Periodical. Japanese. mo. $100.00. **(Subscription address:** Maruzen Company Ltd., PO Box 5050, Import & Export Department, Tokyo 100 31 Japan.**)**

US/0197-8004
NEW YORK TIMES ANNUAL REVIEW, THE. [New York Times annu. rev.]. 1980-. Periodical. English. an. Arno Press, 3 Park Avenue, New York NY 10016. **Tel** (212)725-2050. **LC** D410; .N434. **DD** 905. **UDC** 930.9.

US/0193-8649
NEWSLETTER - BULGARIAN STUDIES ASSOCIATION. Main/Corp Bulgarian Studies Association. (19??)-. Newsletter. English. Indiana University Northwest Department of History, Tamarack Hall F 12, 3400 Broadway, Gary IN 46408. **LC** DR66.95; .B84a. **DD** 949.7/7/0071173. **Continues** Bulgarian Studies Group. Newsletter, 0828-2056.

US/0578-655X
NEWSLETTER - IOWA ARCHEOLOGICAL SOCIETY. *Title Change.* See Archaeology.

US/0474-3253
NEWSLETTER - ORAL HISTORY ASSOCIATION. (ORAL HISTORY ASSOCIATION NEWSLETTER.). **Main/Corp** Oral History Association. **Added/Corp** Oral History Association. Newsletter. Vol. 1 (June 1967)-. Newsletter. English. qt. Oral History Association, PO Box 3968, Albuquerque NM 87190. **Tel** (505)277-8213.
Ind/Abst Acad. Search (July 1993-).

US
NEWSLETTER TO MEMBERS OF THE TEXAS BAPTIST HISTORICAL SOCIETY. **Added/Corp** Texas Baptist Historical Society. (19??)-. Newsletter. English. an. $7.00. Texas Baptist Historical Society, Box 22000-2E, Fort Worth TX 76122. **Tel** (817)923-1921 Ext. 3330. **ED** Dr. William Pitts (phone: (817)755-1011). **Bk Rev**, (Qty: 5-10). **Circ:** 250 (ctrl).
Desc: Texas Baptist History is the journal of the Texas Baptist Historical. Articles in the journal deals with Baptist individuals, movements and their impact on the state.

IT/1121-323X
NICOLAUS. STUDI STORICI. [Nicolaus, Studi stor.]. (1990)-. Periodical. Italian. sa. Levante Editori, Via Napoli 35, 70123 Bari Italy. **UDC** 931.
Ind/Abst BHA : Biblio. Hist. Art.

GW/0078-0561
NIEDERSACHSISCHES JAHRBUCH FUER LANDESGESCHICHTE. [Niedersachs. Jahrb. Landesgesch.]. (1930)-. Periodical. German. an. DM49.10 Germany; DM52.80 other. Hahnsche Bucchandlung Verlag, Leinster 32, D 30159, Hannover, Germany. **Tel** 011 49 511 322294.
Ind/Abst BHA : Biblio. Hist. Art.

UK
NO. ... IN A SERIES OF LOCAL HISTORY MONOGRAPHS. VFOAT Series of Local History; Local History Monographs. No. 1- 1983-. Monographic series. English. Price varies per volume.

NE
NOORDBRABANTS HISTORISCH JAARBOEK. **Added/Corp** Noordbrabants Genootschap. (1984)-. Periodical. Dutch. an. Noordbrabants Genootschap, Postbus 1104, 5200 BD der Bosch Netherlands. **Tel** 011 31 73 139484.
Continues Varia Historica Brabantica.
Ind/Abst BHA : Biblio. Hist. Art.

SP/0213-375X
NORBA. REVISTA DE HISTORIA. [Norba, Rev. hist.]. **Added/Corp** Universidad de Extremadura (Caceres, Spain). Facultad de Filosofia y Letras. VFOAT Norba-Historia. (1980)-. Periodical. Spanish. an. University Extremadura Service Publishers / Spain, Donoso Cortes 11, 10003 Caceres Spain. **Tel** 011 34 927 247650. **Continues in part** Norba, 0211-0636.

GW
NORDHARZER JAHRBUCH. German. ir. LKG Leipziger Kommissions & Grossbuchhandel, Leninstrasse 16, Postfach 520, D 04005 Leipzig, Germany. **Tel** 011 49 341 71370.
Ind/Abst BHA : Biblio. Hist. Art.

US/1053-0010
NORTH SOUTH TRADER'S CIVIL WAR. [North south trader's Civil War]. **VFOAT** Civil War; NSTCW. Vol. 14, No. 3 (March/April 1987)-. Periodical. English. bm. North South Trader, 725 Caroline Street, Fredericksburg VA 22401. **Tel** (301)434-4080. **LC** NK807; .N67. **DD** 973.7. **Continues** North South Trader, 0094-7318.

UK/0078-172X
NORTHERN HISTORY. [North. hist.]. **Added/Corp** University of Leeds. School of History. Vol. 1 (1966)-. Periodical. English. an. £18.00 (individuals), £24.00 (institutions) UK; £20.00 (individuals), £26.00 (institutions) other. University of Leeds School of History, Leeds LS2 9JT England. **Tel** 011 44 532 333616, FAX 0532 342759, telex 556473. **ED** G.C.F. Forster. **LC** DA20; .L415. **DD** 942/.005. Index available. cum. index. **Bk Rev. Circ:** 1,000. Documents available from The Genuine Article.
Desc: A review of the history of the north of England and the borders.
Ind/Abst Am. Hist. Life (1966-); Arts Humanit. Citation Index (19??-19??) [Full Cov.]; BHA : Biblio. Hist. Art; Br. Archaeol. Bibliogr. (1966-); Br. Humanit. Index (1966-); Curr. Contents Arts Humanit.; Res. Alert [Full Cov.].

FR/0298-7902
NOTEBOOKS FOR STUDY AND RESEARCH - INTERNATIONAL INSTITUTE FOR RESEARCH AND EDUCATION. See Political Science.

US/0886-7151
NOTICIAS DEL PUERTO DE MONTEREY. See The Arts.

UK/0078-2122
NOTTINGHAM MEDIEVAL STUDIES. (NOTTINGHAM MEDIAEVAL STUDIES.). [Nottm. mediev. stud.]. **Added/Corp** University of Nottingham. **VFOAT** Nottingham Medieval Studies. Vol. 1 (1957)-. English. an (Sept.). £12.00. University of Nottingham / Department of History, University Park, Nottingham NG7 2RD England. **Tel** 011 44 602 515939, FAX 011 44 602 515948. **ED** Michael Jones. **LC** PN661; .N6. **DD** 809.02. Index available. **Bk Rev**, (Qty: 4). **Circ:** 350.
Desc: All aspects of medieval history: political, economic, intellectual, literary, and cultural, from early Christian times to the early 16th Century.
Ind/Abst Abstr. Engl. Stud.; Annu. Bibliogr. Engl. Lang. Lit.; Br. Archaeol. Bibliogr.; Br. Humanit. Index; MLA Int. Bibl. Books Artic. Mod. Lang. Lit.

CN/0823-6240
NOUVEL ESSOR MARCELLE MALLET. See Religion and Theology.

RU
NOVAIA OTECHESTVENNAIA LITERATURA PO OBSHCHESTVENNYM NAUKAM. ISTORIIA, ARKHEOLOGIIA, ETNOGRAFIIA / ROSSIISKAIA AKADEMIIA NAUK, INSTITUT NAUCHNOI INFORMATSII PO OBSHCHESTVENNYM NAUKAM. *Title Change.* **Added/Corp** Institut Nauchnoi Informatsii po Obshchestvennym Naukam (Rossiiskaia Akademiia Nauk). **VFOAT** Istoriia, Arkheologiia, Etnografiia. (1992)-(1992). Periodical. Russian. mo. Inion An SSSR, Ulitsa Krasikova D 28/45, Moscow Russia. **Tel** 128.89.71. **(Subscription address:** East View Publications Inc., 3020 Harbor Lane North, Suite 110, Minneapolis MN 55447.**)** **LC** Z6205; .N66. **Continues** Novaia Literatura po Obshchestvennym Naukam. Istoriia, Arkheologiia, Etnografiia. **Merged with** Novaia Inostrannaia Literatura po Obshchestvennym Naukam: Istoria, Arkheologiia, Etnografiia **to form** Novaia Literatura po Sotsialnym i Gumanitarnym Naukam. Istoriia, Arkheologiia, Etnologiia.
Desc: Information on history, archaeology and ethnology.

RU/0130-3864
NOVAJA I NOVEJSAKA ISTORIJA (MOSKVA). (NOVAIA I NOVEISHAIA ISTORIIA.). [Nov. i novejsaja istor.]. **Added/Corp** Institut Istorii (Akademiia Nauk SSSR) Institut Vseobshchei Istorii (Akademiia Nauk SSSR). (1957)-. Periodical. Russian (table of contents in English). bm. $132.00. Nauka, 103717 GSP K-62, Podsosenskii Per 21, Moscow Russia. **Tel** 296-472. **(Subscription address:** East View Publications Inc., 3020 Harbor Lane North, Suite 110, Minneapolis MN 55447.**)** **LC** D1; .A3525. available on microfilm from University Microfilms International (UMI).
Ind/Abst Am. Hist. Life (1957-1961, 1964-); Int. Polit. Sci. Abstr.; Recent. Publ. Artic.

IT/0029-6236
NUOVA RIVISTA STORICA. [Nuova riv. stor.]. Vol. 1 (Jan./Mar 1917)-. Periodical. Italian. Three times a year. L138000 Italy; L170000 others. Societa Edit Dante Alighieri, Via Timavo 3 5, 00195 Rome Italy. **Tel** 011 39 6 3725870. **LC** D1; .N8. Index available (Bound in last issue). cum. index. **Bk Rev. Ad Acc. Circ:** 1,000. Documents available from The Genuine Article.
Desc: Articles on ancient, medieval, modern and contemporary history.
Ind/Abst Am. Hist. Life (1954-); Arts Humanit. Citation Index [Full Cov.]; BHA : Biblio. Hist. Art; Curr. Contents Arts Humanit.; MLA Int. Bibl. Books Artic. Mod. Lang. Lit.; Res. Alert [Full Cov.]; Soc. Sci. Cit. Index [Select. Cov.].

IT/0391-8475
NUOVI STUDI STORICI. **Added/Corp** Istituto Storico Italiano per Il Medio Evo. (1988)-. Monographic series. Italian. ir. Price varies per volume. Istituto Storico Italiano Medio Evo e Archivio Muratoriano, Piazza dell Orologio 4, 00186 Rome Italy. **Tel** 011 39 6 68802075. **Continues** Istituto Storico Italiano per Il Medio Evo. Studi Storici.

RU
OBSHCHESTVENNYE NAUKI V ROSSII. SERIIA 5, ISTORIIA / ROSSIISKAIA AKADEMIIA NAUK, INSTITUT NAUCHNOI INFORMATSII PO OBSHCHESTVENNYM NAUKAM. *Title Change.* **Added/Corp** Institut Nauchnoi Informatsii po Obshchestvennym Naukam (Rossiiskaia Akademiia Nau). **VFOAT** Istoriia. (1992)-(1992). Academic Scholarly Publication. Russian (table of contents in English). bm. Izdatelstvo Nauka / Akademiia Nauk, Publishing House of the Russian Academy of Sciences, Leninskii Porspekt 14, 117901 Moscow Russia. **Tel** 011 95 954-21-53, FAX 011 95 938-21-44, telex 411964. **LC** D1; .O14. **Continues** Obshchestvennye Nauki v SSSR. Seriia 5, Istoriia, 0202-2079. **Continued by** Sotsialnye i Gumanitarnye Nauki. Seriia 5, Istoriia. Otechestvannaia Literatura.

RU
OBSHCHESTVENNYE NAUKI ZA RUBEZHOM. SERIIA 5: ISTORIIA. **Added/Corp** Akademiia Nauk SSSR. Institut Nauchnoi Informatsii i Fundamentalnaia Biblioteka po Obshchestvennym Naukam. **VFOAT** Istoriia. **VAT** Obshchestvennye Nauki Za Rubezhom. Seriia Piat : Istoriia. (1972)-. Russian. qt. Izdatelstvo Nauka / Akademiia Nauk, Publishing House of the Russian Academy of Sciences, Leninskii Porspekt 14, 117901 Moscow Russia. **Tel** 011 95 954-21-53, FAX 011 95 938-21-44, telex 411964. **LC** D1; .O15.

US
OCCASIONAL PAPERS - DEPARTMENT OF HISTORY, ARKANSAS TECH UNIVERSITY. **Main/Corp** Arkansas Tech University. Dept. of History. V. 4-. English. $3.00-$5.00. Arkansas Tech University, Department of History, Russelville AR 72801. **Tel** (501)968-0265. **ED** B B McCool. **LC** E171; .A8A. **DD** 973/.05. **UDC** 930.9. **Bk Rev. Circ:** 100 (ctrl). **Continues** Occasional Papers - Department of History, Arkansas Polytechnic College.
Desc: Essays and research covering pertinent topics of US and Europe.

UK
OCCASIONAL PUBLICATIONS SERIES / ANGLO-NORMAN TEXT SOCIETY. No. 1- 1984-. Monographic series. English (Romance). an. Price varies per volume. Anglo Norman Text Society, University of St Andrews, Fife KY16 9PH Scotland. **Tel** 01 631 6233. **ED** Ian Short. **Circ:** 500.
Desc: Anglo-American texts.

YU
ODELJENJE ISTORIJSKIH NAUKA / SRPSKA AKADEMIJA NAUKA I UMETNOSTI. **Added/Corp** Srpska Akademija Nauka i Umetnosti. Srpska Akademija Nauka i Umetnosti. Odeljenje Istorijskih Nauka. (19??)-. Periodical.

History(General)

Serbo-Croatian (Cyrillic). **LC** AS346; .B4 subser.; DR1932.
Ind/Abst Am. Hist. Life.

HU
OIKUMENE.
(1976)-. Academic Scholarly Publication. English (French, German and Russian). ir. $42.00. Akademiai Kiado, Publishing House of the Hungarian Academy of Sciences, Prielle Kornelia u. 19-35, H-1117 Budapest Hungary. **Tel** 011 36 1 1811991, FAX 011 36 1 1811991, telex 22-6228 AKNYO H. **LC** DE1; .O37.

NR
OKHA.
Vol. 1, No. 1-. Periodical. English. Historical Association / Nigeria, University of Benin, Benin City Nigeria. **UDC** 966.82.

US/0472-8637
OLAM HADASH.
(19??)-. Periodical. Hebrew. Nine times a year (Sept.-May). $12.00. Hebrew Publications Children, 110 East 59th Street, New York NY 10022. **Tel** (212)339-6022, FAX (212)826-8959 or (212)318-6176. **ED** Irene S. Wolk. **Circ:** 3,000.
Desc: Original poetry, short stories, and current events, written in beginners's Hebrews with vowel sounds.

US/1047-3068
OLD NEWS (MARIETTA, PA.).
(OLD NEWS.). [Old news]. Vol. 1, No. 1 (Sept. 1989)-. Periodical. English. Eleven times a year (Except Aug.). $15.00. Susquehanna Times & Magazine Inc., 400 Stackstown Road, Marietta PA 17547. **Tel** (717)426-2212. **ED** Rick Bromer. **DD** 909. **Circ:** 30,000.
Desc: Featuring accurate, interesting, entertaining and readable history and biographies.

UK/0268-6554
OLD WEST RIDING.
VFOAT Local History Publications. Began with 1981 issues. Periodical. English. sa.

PR
OP. CIT. : BOLETIN DEL CENTRO DE INVESTIGACIONES HISTORICAS.
Added/Corp University of Puerto Rico (Rio Piedras Campus). Centro de Investigaciones Historicas. **VFOAT** Boletin del Centro de Investigaciones Historicas. **VAT** Opus Citatum Boletin del Centro de Investigaciones Historicas. No. 1 (1985/86)-. Periodical. English. $18.50 institutions; $8.00 individuals. University de Puerto Rico / Oficina de Publicaciones, Apartado 23322 Estacion UPR, San Juan Puerto Rica 00931-1787. **Tel** (809)250-0615, (809)250-0725, (809)250-0725, FAX (809)753-9116. **LC** F1951; .O6. **DD** 972.95/0072. ***Continues*** *Cuadernos de la Facultad de Humanidades.*
Ind/Abst HAPI Hisp. Am. Period. Index.

UK/0143-0955
ORAL HISTORY (COLCHESTER).
(ORAL HISTORY.). [Oral hist.]. **Added/Corp** Oral History Society (Great Britain). Vol. 1 (1972)-. Periodical. English. sa (Feb. and Sept.). £12.00 (individuals), £18.00 (institutions) UK; £15.00 (individuals), £24.00 (institutions) surface mail;. Oral History Society, University of Essex, Sociology Department, Colchester ESS CO4 3SQ England. **Tel** 011 44 206 873333, FAX 011/44/206/873410. **ED** Paul Thompson, Joanna Bornat, Rob Perks and Bob Little. **LC** D16.14; .O7. **DD** 907/.2. cum. index. **Bk Rev. Ad Acc. Circ:** 1,000 (ctrl).
Desc: Provides regular news, reviews, guides to research important articles on wide-ranging topics.
Ind/Abst Br. Humanit. Index; Int. Bibliogr. Sociol.; MLA Int. Bibl. Books Artic. Mod. Lang. Lit.

US/1047-3467
ORAL HISTORY INDEX.
Ceased. (1992)-(19??). English. be. Mecklermedia Corporation, 11 Ferry Lane West, Westport CT 06880. **Tel** (203)226-6967, (800)632-5537, FAX (203)454-5840.

PP/0310-2556
ORAL HISTORY (PORT MORESBY, PAPUA NEW GUINEA).
(ORAL HISTORY.). [Oral hist.]. **Added/Corp** Institute of Papua New Guinea Studies. (Dec. 1972)-. Periodical. English. qt. $14.32. Institute of Papua New Guinea Studies, Box 1432, Boroko PO, Port Moresby Papua New Guinea. **Tel** 254644. **LC** DU740.A2; O73. **DD** 995.3. cum. index.
Ind/Abst Am. Hist. Life (1983); Anthropol. Lit.

US/0094-0798
ORAL HISTORY REVIEW, THE.
[Oral hist. rev.]. (1973)-. Periodical. English. an. $35.00 North America (add $8.00 for postage) other. Oral History Association, PO Box 3968, Albuquerque NM 87190. **Tel** (505)277-8213. **ED** Michael Frisch. **LC** D16; .O68. **DD** 907/.2/05. **UDC** 973. **NLM** W1 OR105H. **Bk Rev. Ad Acc.** ctrl circ. available on microfilm and microfiche from University Microfilms International (UMI). Documents available from UMI Article Clearinghouse.
Ind/Abst Acad. Search (July 1993-); Am. Hist. Life (1974-); Expand. Acad. Index (1989-); Hist. Source (July 1993-); Humanit. Index; Humanit. Source (Jul. 1993-); Index Period. Artic. Relat. Law (19??-19??); INFO-SOUTH Abstr.; Mag. Search; Newsp. Period. Abstr. (1990-); West. Hist. Q.

US
ORIENTAL INSTITUTE RESEARCH ARCHIVES ACQUISITIONS LIST.
Main/Corp University of Chicago. Oriental Institute. Research Archives. **VFOAT** Acquisitions List. No. 1 (Aug., Sept., Oct. 1991)-. English. qt. University of Chicago Oriental Institute, 1155 East 58th Street, Chicago IL 60637. **Tel** (312)702-9537.

HU/0010-3551
ORVOSTORTENETI KOZLEMENYEK.
Added/Corp Magyar Orvostortenelmi Tarsasag. Semmelweis Orvostorteneti Muzeum es Konyvtar. Semmelweis Orvostorteneti Muzeum, Konyvtar es Leveltar. **VFOAT** Communicationes de Historia Artis Medicinae. (1968)-. Periodical. Hungarian (German, Hungarian and Russian). **NLM** W1 OR887. ***Continues*** *Orszagos Orvostorteneti Konyvtar. Communicationes ex Bibliotheca Historiae Medicae Hungarica, 0301-1984.*
Ind/Abst Am. Hist. Life (1985-); BHA : Biblio. Hist. Art.

US
OVER THE YEARS.
Added/Corp Dakota County Historical Society. **VFOAT** Dakota County, The Cradle of Minnesota. Vol. 1, No. 1 (Jan. 1961)-. Periodical. English. Twice a year (Apr., Oct.). $15.00 (sustaining); $20.00 (individual); $25.00 (others). Dakota County Historical Society, 130 3rd Avenue N, South St. Paul MN 55075. **Tel** (612)451-6260. **Circ:** 650 (ctrl).
Desc: A scholar magazine about the history of Dakota County.

SP
PAIS (MADRID, SPAIN : 1976). ANUARIO.
(EL PAIS. ANUARIO.). **VFOAT** Anuario; Anuario El Pais. (1982)-. Spanish. an. Diario el Pais SA, Miguel Yuste 40, 28037 Madrid Spain. **Tel** 011 34 1 3378363, 011 34 1 3378341. **LC** D839; .P26. **DD** 909.08/05.

US/0883-8577
PALESTINE FOCUS.
Ceased. (PALESTINE FOCUS : NATIONAL NEWSLETTER OF THE NOVEMBER 29TH COMMITTEE FOR PALESTINE.). [Palest. focus]. **Added/Corp** November 29th Committee for Palestine. Palestine Solidarity Committee. (198?)-(1992). Newsletter. English. qt. PSC Palestine Solidarity Comm, PO Box 372 Peck Slip Station, New York NY 10272. **Tel** (212)227-1435. **DD** 956.
Ind/Abst Altern. Press Index (199?-).

US
PAMPHLET SERIES / ORAL HISTORY ASSOCIATION.
Added/Corp Oral History Association. (1985)-. Monographic series. English. ir. $75.00 institutions; $50.00 individuals (with membership). Oral History Association, PO Box 3968, Albuquerque NM 87190. **Tel** (505)277-8213.

KO
PANGGONG.
Periodical. Korean. Not for Sale. Chayu Pyongnensa, CPO Box 6856, Seoul South Korea. **LC** D847; .P34.

US/0743-2097
PAPERS OF LEVERETT SALTONSTOLL, THE.
[Pap. Leverett Saltonstall]. Periodical. English. ir. Massachusetts Historical Society, 1154 Boylston Street, Boston MA 02215. **Tel** (617)536-1608. **UDC** 974.4.

IT/0392-4815
PASSATO E PRESENTE (FLORENCE, ITALY).
(PASSATO E PRESENTE.). No. 1 (Jan./June 1982)-. Periodical. Italian. Three times a year. L52000 Italy; L62000 other. Giunti Editore, Via Bolognese 165, 50139 Florence Italy. **Tel** 011 39 55 6679267, FAX 011 39 55 268312, telex 571438. **ED** Il Chiese. **LC** HX7. **DD** 335.43/05. **UDC** 908. **Ad Acc. Circ:** 2,000 (ctrl).
Desc: A history review covering economical, social, political, artistic, and media problems of the contemporary world.
Ind/Abst Am. Hist. Life (1982-).

UK/0031-2746
PAST & PRESENT.
[Past present]. **Added/Corp** Past and Present Society. **VFOAT** Past and Present. No. 1 (Feb. 1952)-. Academic Scholarly Publication. English. qt. £58.00 UK and Europe; $130.00 other. Oxford University Press, Walton Street, Oxford OX2 6DP England. **Tel** 011 44 865 56767, FAX 011 44 865 267773, telex 837330 OXPRES G. **(Subscription address:** Oxford University Press / USA, Journals Marketing Department, Oxford University Press, 2001 Evans Road, Cary NC 27513.**) ED** Paul Slack and C. H. E. Philpin. **LC** D1; .P37. **[CCC]**. Index available. cum. index. **Bk Rev. Ad Acc. Pr Rev. Circ:** 3,750 (ctrl). available on microfilm and microfiche from University Microfilms International (UMI). Documents available from The Genuine Article, UMI Article Clearinghouse.
Desc: Contains a wide variety of scholarly and original historical articles primarily concerned with social, economic and cultural changes, their causes and consequences.
Ind/Abst Acad. Search (July 1993-); Am. Hist. Life (1954-); Arts Humanit. Citation Index [Full Cov.]; BHA : Biblio. Hist. Art; Br. Archaeol. Bibliogr.; Br. Humanit. Index; Curr. Contents Arts Humanit.; Curr. Contents Soc. Behav. Sci.; Expand. Acad. Index (1989-); Geogr. Abstr. Human Geogr.; Humanit. Index; Humanit. Source (Jul. 1993-); INFO-SOUTH Abstr.; Mag. Search; Middle East Abstr. Index; Newsp. Period. Abstr. (1991-); Numis. Lit.; Res. Alert [Full Cov.]; Soc. Plann. Policy Dev. Abstr.; Soc. Sci. Cit. Index [Full Cov.]; SportSearch; West. Hist. Q.

PO/0871-7486
PENELOPE (LISBON, PORTUGAL).
(PENELOPE.). No. 1 (1988)-. Periodical. Portuguese. Three times a year. $35.00. Edicoes Cosmos, Rua da Emenda 111, 1st Floor, 1200 Lisbon Portugal. **Tel** 011 351 1 3468201.
Ind/Abst BHA : Biblio. Hist. Art.

AT
PEOPLING OF THE BRITISH PERIPHERIES IN THE EIGHTEENTH CENTURY, THE.
(19??)-. Monographic series. English. te. 3.00Aus$. Australian Academy of the Humanities, GPO Box 93, Canberra Australian Capital Territory 2601 Australia. **Tel** FAX 062 486287. **Bk Rev.**

US/0889-8448
PERSPECTIVES IN MEXICAN AMERICAN STUDIES.
[Perspect. Mex. Am. stud.]. **Added/Corp** University of Arizona. Mexican American Studies and Research Center. **VFOAT** Mexican American Studies. Vol. 1 (1988)-. Monographic series. English (Spanish). ir. Price varies per volume. American Mexican Studies Research Center, 315 Douglas Building, University of Arizona, Tuscon AZ 85721. **Tel** (602)612)7551. **LC** E184.M5; P42. **DD** 909.
Ind/Abst Am. Hist. Life (1988-).

BL/0101-9619
PESQUISAS. HISTORIA.
[Pesqui., Hist.]. **Added/Corp** Instituto Anchietano de Pesquisas. **VFOAT** Historia. (1960)-. Monographic series. Portuguese (English, French, German and Spanish). ir. Price varies per volume. Sao Leopoldo, Praca Tiradentes, 35 Rio Grande Do Sul Brazil 93010-020. **Tel** 051 5921035. Index available. cum. index. **Circ:** 500 (ctrl). Documents available from FAXON Xpress. ***Continues in part*** *Pesquisas (Instituto Anchietano de Pesquisas), 0480-1873.*
Ind/Abst Am. Hist. Life (1961-).

PH/0031-7837
PHILIPPINE STUDIES.
[Philipp. stud.]. **Added/Corp** Jesuits. Philippine Province. Vol. 1 (June 1953)-. Academic Scholarly Publication. English. Four times a year (Jan., Apr., July, Oct.). $32.00 one year; $60.00 two years. Ateneo de Manila University Press, PO Box 154, Manila 1099 Philippines. **Tel** 011 63 2 9244495, 011 63 2 9244601, FAX 011 63 2 9244690. **ED** Reverend Joseph A. Galdon. **LC** DS651; .P623. **DD** 991.4. Index available. cum. index (From 1953-1977 for $7.00). **Bk Rev**, (Qty: 18). **Circ:** 650 (ctrl).
Desc: Provides a cross section of articles, notes, texts, and reviews on scholarly writing on historical as well as contemporary Philippine problems and issues.
Ind/Abst Am. Hist. Life (1955-); Bibliogr. Mission.; Index Islam. Lit.; Index Philip. Period. (1955-); Int. Bibliogr. Sociol.; Int. Polit. Sci. Abstr. (1955-); Middle East Abstr. Index (1955-); MLA Int. Bibl. Books Artic. Mod. Lang. Lit.

PH/0554-0577
PHILIPPINIANA SACRA.
Added/Corp University of Santo Tomas. Vol. 1, (Jan./Apr. 1966)-. Periodical. English (Spanish and Latin). Three times a year (Jan., May, Sept.). $30.00 one year; $55.00 two years. Philippiniana Sacra Office, U Santo Tomas CP Bermudez, Manila Philippines. **Tel** 011 63 2 7314066. **(Subscription address:** The Business Manager, Philippiniana Sacra, Father's Residence, University of Santo Tomas, Espana Manila Philippines**) ED** Father Javier Gonzalez, O. P. **LC** BR1; .P39. Index available (Bound in 3rd iss. (Dec.).). cum. index. **Bk Rev. Circ:** 600.
Desc: Devoted to serious studies in theology, philosophy and history with special emphasis on Filipino and Asian issues.
Ind/Abst Bibliogr. Mission.; Index Philip. Period.

US/0032-1613
PLOW, THE.
Began 1965. Periodical. English. qt. Delano Historical Society, 330 Lexington, Delano CA 93215. **Tel** (805)725-9887. **LC** 4363. **UDC** 973; 979.4.

US/0094-4998
POINT OF REFERENCE.
Added/Corp Alexandrian Society. Vol. 1 (April 1974)-. English. an. Virginia Commonwealth University, 901 West Franklin Street, Alexander Society, Richmond VA 23284. **LC** D1; .P63. **DD** 905.

UK/0267-5315
PORTUGUESE STUDIES.
Added/Corp King's College (University of London). Dept. of Portuguese. Modern Humanities Research Association. Vol. 1 (1985)-. English (Portuguese). an. $72.00. W. S. Maney and Son Ltd., Hudson Road, Leeds LS9 7DL England. **Tel** 011 44 532 497481, FAX 011 44 532 486983. **(Subscription address:** W.S. Maney & Son Limited, PO Box YR7, Leeds, LS9 7UU England.**) LC** DP532; .P66. **DD** 909/.097561/005. Documents available from The Genuine Article.
Ind/Abst Arts Humanit. Citation Index [Full Cov.]; Curr. Contents Arts Humanit.; MLA Int. Bibl. Books Artic. Mod. Lang. Lit.; Res. Alert [Full Cov.].

US/0895-0865
POTTER COUNTY HISTORICAL SOCIETY QUARTERLY BULLETIN. [Q. bull. - Potter Cty. Hist. Soc.]. **Added/Corp** Potter County Historical Society (Potter County, Pa.). **VFOAT** Potter County Historical Society Quarterly Bulletin. No. 38 (Oct. 1975)-. Bulletin. English. Four times a year (Jan., Apr., July, Oct.). $5.00. Potter County Historical Society, 308 North Main Street, Coudersport PA 16915. **Tel** (814)274-8124. **ED** Robert K. Currin. **DD** 974. **Pr Rev. Circ:** 350. ***Continues*** *Bulletin (Potter County Historical Society).*
Desc: This bulletin consists of stories about the history of Potter County.

PL/0079-466X
PRACE KOMISJI HISTORII SZTUKI. POZNANSKIE TOWARZYSTWO PRZYJACIO NAUK. [Pr. Kom. Hist. Szt., Pozn. Tow. Przyj. Nauk]. (1922)-. Periodical. Polish. tw. **UDC** 7/09/.
Ind/Abst BHA : Biblio. Hist. Art.

GW
PRAHISTORISCHE BRONZEFUNDE. ABTEILUNG VII. (1972)-. Monographic series. German. ir. Price varies per volume. Franz Steiner Verlag GmbH, Postfach 101061, D 70009 Stuttgart Germany. **Tel** 011 49 0711 2582372, FAX 011 49 0711 2582290, telex 723636 daz d.

GW
PRAHISTORISCHE BRONZEFUNDE. ABTEILUNG XX. **VFOAT** PBF. Abteilung XX. (1974)-. Monographic series. German. ir. Price varies per volume. Franz Steiner Verlag GmbH, Postfach 101061, D 70009 Stuttgart Germany. **Tel** 011 49 0711 2582372, FAX 011 49 0711 2582290, telex 723636 daz d.

RU/0132-0696
PREPODAVANIE ISTORII V SHKOLE. [Prepod. ist. sk.]. **Added/Corp** Russian S.F.S.R. Ministerstvo Prosveshcheniia. Soviet Union. Ministerstvo Prosveshcheniia. (1946)-. Periodical. Russian. bm. $69.95. Izdatelstvo Pedagogika, G-34 Smolenskii Boulevard D. 4, 119034 Moscow Russia. **(Subscription address:** East View Publications Inc., 3020 Harbor Lane North, Suite 110, Minneapolis MN 55447.) **LC** D16.2; .P7. Index available. cum. index. **Bk Rev. Ad Acc. Circ:** 135,000.
Ind/Abst Am. Hist. Life (1954-).

IT/1121-7499
PRESENTE E LA STORIA, IL. (1992)-. Italian. sa. L30000.00. Ist Storico Resistenza Cuneo e Provincia, Cas Post 216, 12100 Cuneo Italy. **Tel** 011 39 171 603636. ***Continues*** *Notiziario Istituto Storico in Cuneo e Provincia, 1120-0634.*

US/0275-3863
PROCEEDINGS AND PAPERS OF THE GEORGIA ASSOCIATION OF HISTORIANS, THE. **VFOAT** Proceedings & Papers of the Georgia Association of Historians. (1980)-. English. an. $10.00. Georgia Association of Historians, Kennesaw College, Marietta GA 30061. **Tel** (404)423-6069. **ED** Ann W. Ellis. **LC** D1; .G63a. **DD** 905. **Circ:** 350 (ctrl).
Desc: Articles written by members of Georgia Association of Historians. Most papers included are proceedings of Georgia Association of Historians annual meeting. All areas of history included.
Ind/Abst Am. Hist. Life (1980-).

UK/0309-3603
PROCEEDINGS OF THE CAMBRIDGE ANTIQUARIAN SOCIETY. (PROCEEDINGS OF THE CAMBRIDGE ANTIQUARIAN SOCIETY, WITH COMMUNICATIONS MADE TO THE SOCIETY.). [Proc. Camb. Antiq. Soc.]. **Added/Corp** Cambridge Antiquarian Society (Cambridge, England). **VFOAT** Proceedings of the Cambridge Antiquarian Society. Vol. 7 (1891)-. English. an. Free to members of the Cambridge Antiquarian Society. Cambridge Antiquarian Society, 3 Orchard Estate Cherry Hinton, Cambridge CB1 3JW England. **Tel** 011 44 223 317312. **LC** CC23; .C2. cum. index. ***Continues in part*** *Cambridge Antiquarian Communications **and** Cambridge Antiquarian Society (Cambridge, England). Report Presented to the Cambridge Antiquarian Society at its ... Annual General Meeting.*
Ind/Abst BHA : Biblio. Hist. Art.

UK
PROCEEDINGS OF THE CAMBRIDGE COLLOQUIUM ON MYCENAEAN STUDIES. **Main/Conf** Cambridge Colloquium on Mycenaean Studies. 4th- ; 1965-. Academic Scholarly Publication. English. ir. Cambridge University Press, The Edinburgh Building, Shaftesbury Road, Cambridge CB2 2RU United Kingdom. **Tel** 011 44 223 312393, FAX 011 44 223 325959. **(Subscription address:** US/ 110 Midland Avenue, Port Chester, NY 10573) **ED** L R Palmer and J Chadwick. **UDC** 938(063). ***Continues*** *Mycenaean Studies.*

US/0886-733X
PROCEEDINGS OF THE MICHIANA AREA HISTORIANS. **Main/Corp** Michiana Area Historians. **Added/Corp** Indiana University. Dept. of History. Vol. 1 (Nov. 1972)-. Proceedings. English. **LC** DT1; .M52. **DD** 905.
Ind/Abst Am. Hist. Life (1972-1975).

US/0890-5592
PROCEEDINGS OF THE ... SEMINAR OF CATASTROPHISM AND ANCIENT HISTORY. [Proc. Sem. Catastr. Anc. Hist.]. **Main/Conf** Seminar of Catastrophism and Ancient History. 1st (1982)-. Proceedings. English. ir. $15.00. Catastrophism and Ancient History Press, 3431 Club Drive, Los Angeles CA 90064. **Tel** (310)509-1075. **LC** DS62.2; .S42A. **DD** 930. **UDC** 931. **Bk Rev. Ad Acc.**
Desc: The lectures given at seminars of the Journal Catastrophism and Ancient History.

UK/0081-1564
PROCEEDINGS OF THE SOCIETY OF ANTIQUARIES OF SCOTLAND. **See** Archaeology.

UK/0262-6004
PROCEEDINGS OF THE SUFFOLK INSTITUTE OF ARCHAEOLOGY AND HISTORY. **See** Archaeology.

IT
PROSPETTIVE LIBRI. V. 1, No. 1, (Jan. 1981)-. Periodical. Italian. mo. 22.000. Editrice Prospettive Nel Mondo, Via Delle Carrozze, 16-00187 Rome Italy. **LC** D839; .P689. **DD** 909.82. **UDC** 930.9.

●US/1063-7974
PROVIDENCE (PROVIDENCE, R.I.). (PROVIDENCE : STUDIES IN WESTERN CIVILIZATION.). [Providence]. **Added/Corp** Providence College. **VFOAT** Providence, Studies in Western Civilization. Vol. 1, No. 1 (Fall 1992)-. Periodical. English. qt. $25.00 (institutions), $15.00 (individuals). Providence College, The Priory, Providence RI 02918. **Tel** (401)865-2374. **LC** CB245; .P7. **DD** 909.

US/0363-891X
PSYCHOHISTORY REVIEW, THE. [Psychohist. rev.]. **Added/Corp** Group for the Use of Psychology in History. Sangamon State University. Vol. 5 (June 1976)-. Periodical. English. Three times a year (Fall, Winter and Spring). $22.00 (one year), $42.00 (two years), $63.00 (three years) Individual; $44.00 (one year), $84.00 (two years), $125.00 (three years) Institutions. Sangamon State University, Brookens 385, Springfield IL 62794. **Tel** (217)786-6084, (217)786-7435. **ED** Larry E Shiner. **LC** D16.16; .P86. **DD** 155. **NLM** W1 PS526. **CODEN** PSRVD2. **[CCC].** Index available. cum. index. **Bk Rev. Ad Acc. Circ:** 500 (ctrl). available on microfilm and microfiche from University Microfilms International (UMI). ***Continues*** *Newsletter - Group for the Use of Psychology in History, 0162-9999.*
Desc: Makes systematic use of concepts, principles and theories of psychology to enhance understanding of particular persons and events in the past.
Ind/Abst Am. Hist. Life (1976-); Psychol. Abstr. (1978-); PsycINFO; PsycLit; Soc. Plann. Policy Dev. Abstr.; Soc. Work Abstr. [Select. Cov.]; Sociol. Abstr.

US/0272-3433
PUBLIC HISTORIAN, THE. [Public hist.]. **Added/Corp** University of California, Santa Barbara. Graduate Program in Public Historical Studies. National Council on Public History (U.S.). (Fall 1978)-. Periodical. English. qt. $36.00 (individuals), $58.00 (institutions), $19.00 (students). University of California Press, 2120 Berkeley Way, Berkeley CA 94720. **Tel** (510)642-4191, (510)642-3907, FAX (510)642-9917. **ED** Otis Graham, Jr. **LC** HN1; .P8. **DD** 905. **NLM** W1; PU617. **[CCC]. Bk Rev. Ad Acc. Pr Rev. Circ:** 1,200 (ctrl). available on microfilm and microfiche from University Microfilms International (UMI). Documents available from The Genuine Article.
Desc: The professional application of history and the historical academic environment.
Ind/Abst Am. Hist. Life (1978-); Arts Humanit. Citation Index [Full Cov.]; Curr. Contents Arts Humanit.; Middle East Abstr. Index; Res. Alert [Full Cov.]; Soc. Sci. Cit. Index [Select. Cov.]; West. Hist. Q.

FR/0069-178X
PUBLICATION - CENTRE DE RECHERCHES D'HISTOIRE ANCIENNE. **Main/Corp** Centre de Recherches d'Histoire Ancienne. Vol. 1 (1969)-. Monographic series. French. Price varies per volume. Les Belles Lettres, 95 Boulevard Raspail, 75006 Paris France. **Tel** (1)45.48.70.55, FAX (1)45.44.92.88, telex 200577 F. **LC** AS161.

UK
PUBLICATION / GULLANE LOCAL HISTORY SOCIETY. Periodical. English. ir.

BE
PUBLICATIONS - ASBL CENTRE D'HISTOIRE ET D'ART DE LA THUDINIE. **Main/Corp** Centre d'Histoire et d'Art de la Thudinie. Vol. 1 (1973)-. Bulletin. French. Four times a year. F350. ASBL Centre d'Histoire et d'Art de la Thudine, rue M. des Ombiaux 6, Thuin 6530 Belgium. **LC** DH811.T4; C45a. **DD** 920/.0493/4. **Pr Rev. Circ:** 400 (ctrl).
Desc: Collection of illustrated articles on local history, biographies of natives of the area, and texts from regional authors.

FR/0290-4500
PUBLICATIONS DE LA SORBONNE. HISTOIRE ANCIENNE ET MEDIEVALE. **Added/Corp** Universite de Paris IV: Paris-Sorbonne. **VFOAT** Histoire Ancienne et Medievale; Serie Histoire Ancienne et Medievale; Publications de la Sorbonne. Serie Histoire Ancienne et Medievale. (19??)-. Monographic series. French. Price varies per volume. Publications de la Sorbonne, 14 rue Cujas, 75231 Paris Cedex 05 France.

CN/0384-8825
PUBLICATIONS DE L'INSTITUT D'ETUDES MEDIEVALES. ***Suspended.*** **Main/Corp** Universite de Montreal. Institut d'Etudes Medievales. Monographic series. French. Price varies per volume. Institut D'Etudes Medievales, CP 6128, Succursale A, Montreal H3C 3J7 Canada. **UDC** 940 "04/14". ***Continues*** *Publications de l'Institut d'Etudes Medievales d'Ottawa, 0398-9518.*

US/0897-8352
PUBLICATIONS IN ANTHROPOLOGY AND HISTORY. ***Ceased.*** **See** Anthropology.

FI
PUBLICATIONS OF THE INSTITUTE OF HISTORY, GENERAL HISTORY, UNIVERSITY OF TURKU, FINLAND. **Main/Corp** Turun Yliopisto. Historian Laitos. Yleinen Historia. **VFOAT** Publikationen des Instituts fur Geschichte, Allgemeine Geschichte, Universitat Turku, Finnland. (1976)-. Monographic series. English (German). ***Continues*** *Turun Yliopisto. Yleisen Historian Laitos. Publications of the Institute of General History, University of Turku, Finland,.*
Ind/Abst Am. Hist. Life (1967-1977,1983-).

CN/0700-6896
PUBLICATIONS OF THE MCMASTER UNIVERSITY ASSOCIATION FOR 18TH CENTURY STUDIES. **Main/Corp** McMaster University Association for 18th Century Studies. Vol. 1 (1971)-. English. an. Garland Publishing Inc, 1000A Sherman Avenue, Hamden CT 06514. **Tel** 800-627-6273, (203)281-4487. **ED** Ralph Carlson.
Desc: Comprehensive reference guide to publications in 18th century studies of the McMaster University Association.

GW
PUBLIZISTIK-HISTORISCHE BEITRAGE. V. 1- 1971-. Periodical. German. ir. K.G. Saur Verlag KG, A Reed Reference Publishing Company, Part of Reed International PLC, Ortlerstrasse 8, D 81373 Munich Germany. **Tel** 011 49 89 769020, FAX 011 49 89 76902150, telex 5212067-SAUR-D. **(Subscription address:** 175 Fifth Avenue, New York, NY 10010) **UDC** 930.9.

IT
QUADERNI DI OCCIDENTALE. Monographic series. Italian. Price varies per volume.

IT
QUADERNI DI STORIA. **Added/Corp** Universita di Bari. Istituto di Storia Greca e Romana. Vol. 1, No. 1 (Jan./June 1975)-. Periodical. English (French, German and Italian). Twice a year. L28000 Italy; L42000 other. Edizioni Dedalo Spa, Casella Postale 362, Bari 70100 Italy. **Tel** 011 39 080 5311400, FAX 011 39 080 5311414. **LC** D1; .Q27. **DD** 905. cum. index. **Bk Rev**, (Qty: 10/year). **Ad Acc, Adv Mgr:** R. Coga. ctrl circ.
Desc: Concerned with ancient history and history of classical studies and modern ideologies with reference to the philosophy of history.

IT
QUADERNI DI STORIA ANTICA E DI EPIGRAFIA. **Added/Corp** Universita degli Studi di Trieste. Istituto di Storia Antica. (1973)-. Monographic series. Italian. ir. Price varies per volume. Edizioni Ateneo and Bizzarri Srl, Via Ruggero Bonghi 11 B, 00184 Rome Italy. **Tel** 011 39 6 7593456. **(Subscription address:** Courier SAS, via I a de Bosis 25 27, 50145 Florence Italy.) **LC** DG11; .Q33.

IT
QUADERNI DI STORIA URBANA E RURALE. Monographic series. Italian. Price varies per volume.

IT
QUADERNI PER LA STORIA DI CASTELBOLOGNESE. **VFOAT** Quaderni. Monographic series. Italian. Price varies per volume.

History(General)

IT
QUADERNI SARDI. 1987-. Monographic series. Italian. Price varies per volume.

II/0033-5800
QUARTERLY REVIEW OF HISTORICAL STUDIES, THE. [Q. rev. hist. stud.]. **Added/Corp** Institute of Historical Studies, Calcutta. Vol. 1 (April/June 1961)-. Periodical. English. qt. $15.00. Quarterly Review Historical Studies, 35 Theatre Road, Calcutta 17 India. **Tel** 44-5236. **(Subscription address:** Prints India, 11 Darya Ganj, New Delhi 110002 India.) **ED** N R Ray. **LC** D1; .Q3. **DD** 905. **Bk Rev. Ad Acc. Circ:** 800.
Desc: The journal is of high academic standard and contains research papers in history and book reviews. It is useful to all teachers and researchers in history.
Ind/Abst Am. Hist. Life (1967-).

GW/0481-3545
QUELLEN UND DARSTELLUNGEN ZUR ZEITGESCHICHTE. Vol. 1 (1957)-. Monographic series. German. ir. Price varies per volume. Zenit Pressevertrieb GmbH, Postfach 810640, 7000 Stuttgart 80 Germany. **Tel** 089-773007.

GW/0079-9068
QUELLEN UND FORSCHUNGEN AUS ITALIENISCHEN ARCHIVEN UND BIBLIOTHEKEN. [Qu. Forsch. ital. Arch. Bibl.]. Vol. 1 (1898)-. Periodical. German (Italian, English and French). an. DM218.00. Max Niemeyer Verlag, Postfach 2140, D 72011 Tuebingen Germany. **Tel** 011 49 7071 989494, FAX 011 49 7071 87419. **LC** D5; .Q3. **DD** 905. cum. index. **Bk Rev. Ad Acc.**
Desc: Contributions of Italian and German history.
Ind/Abst Am. Hist. Life (1964-); BHA : Biblio. Hist. Art.

GW
QUELLENSCHRIFTEN ZUR WESTDEUTSCHEN VOR- UND FRUHGESCHICHTE. Vol. 1-. Periodical. German. ir. Dr. Rudolf Habelt GmbH, Postfach 150104, D 53040 Bonn Germany. **Tel** 011 49 228 232015. **UDC** 943.01; 930.22(430.1).

IT
RACCOLTA VINCIANA. See The Arts-Art.

US/1050-9402
RACONTEUR. (RACONTEUR : A JOURNAL OF WORLD HISTORY.). [Raconteur]. Periodical. English. sa. $10.00 (individuals), $18.00 (institutions). Raconteur Publications, 2020 West Pensacola Street, Unit 46, Tallahassee FL 32304. **Tel** (904)222-5029. **DD** 306.
Desc: An independent, scholarly journal founded to publish the in current historical research. It focuses on the world arena and analyzes and explores alternative topics, such as social and gender history.

US/0730-1812
RADICAL HISTORIANS NEWSLETTER. [Radic. hist. newsl.]. **Added/Corp** MARHO (organization). No. 25 (Dec. 1977)-. Periodical. English. Twice a year (May & Nov.). $3.00 (one year), $6.00 (two year), $9.00 (three year) US; $6.00 (one year), $12.00 (two year), $18.00 (three year) other. Radical Historians Newsletter, PO Box 632, North Cambridge MA 02140. **Tel** (617)625-7649. **ED** Jim O'Brien. **Bk Rev,** (Qty: 3). **Circ:** 1,400. **Continues** Newsletter of the Radical Historians Caucus.

IT
RAGIONAMENTI SUI FATTI E LE IMMAGINI DELLA STORIA. VFOAT Ragionamenti Storia. No. 1 (Febr. 1991)-. Periodical. Italian. mo. L30000 Italy; L500000 other. Ragionamenti, Via Nazionale 87, 00184 Rome Italy. **Tel** 011 39 6 4744160.

US
RANGE HISTORY. Vol. 1, No. 1 (Mar. 1976)-. Periodical. English. qt. $35.00. Iron Range Historical Society, PO Box 786, Gilbert MN 55741. Index available. **Ad Acc.** ctrl circ. available on microfilm; available on audiocassette.

US/0882-312X
RANGEL'S REPORTS. [Rangel's rep.]. Vol. 1, No. 1 (Oct. 1984)-. Periodical. English. Free. Rangel's Reports Marc Rangel, Editor PIAB, PO Box 2498, Rockefeller Center Station, New York NY 10185. **DD** 909. **UDC** 930.9.

US/1071-0043
RAVEN (TRENTON, N.J.). See Social Sciences.

US/0885-7741
RECORDER (NEW YORK, N.Y. 1985), THE. (THE RECORDER : A JOURNAL OF THE AMERICAN IRISH HISTORICAL SOCIETY.). [Recorder]. **Added/Corp** American-Irish Historical Society. Vol. 1, No. 1 (Winter 1985)-. Periodical. English. sa. $35.00 (institutions), $22.50 (individuals) US; $37.00 (institutions), $24.50 (individuals) includes postage other. American Irish Historical Society, 991 5th Avenue, New York NY 10028. **Tel** (212)288-2263, FAX (212)628-7927.

ED Peter Quinn. **LC** E184.I6; R22. **DD** 941. **Bk Rev. Continues** Recorder.
Desc: Irish studies and the American Irish community.

US/0080-0287
RECORDS OF CIVILIZATION, SOURCES AND STUDIES. [Rec. civiliz. sources stud.]. **Added/Corp** Columbia University. Dept. of History. No. 1 (1915)-. Monographic series. English. ir. Price varies per volume. W W Norton & Company Inc, 500 Fifth Avenue, New York NY 10110. **Tel** (800)233-4830. **DD** 909.

US/1054-9110
REFERENCE GUIDES TO ARCHIVAL AND MANUSCRIPT SOURCES IN WORLD HISTORY. [Ref. guides arch. manuscr. sources world hist.]. No. 1 (1991)-. Monographic series. English. Greenwood Press Inc., PO Box 5007, Westport CT 06881-5007. **Tel** (203)226-3571, FAX (203)222-1502. **DD** 909.

CN/0226-7586
REGISTER (MONTREAL, 1980). (THE REGISTER.). [Register]. Vol. 1, No. 1 (Mar. 1980)-. Periodical. English (French). sa. 5.00Can$, 9.00Can$ (two year), 12.00Can$ (three year). Mc Gill University / Register, 3655 Drummond Street, Montreal Quebec H3G 1Y6 Canada. **ED** Anne Maclennan and Michael Duckett. **LC** F1022; .R43. **DD** 905. **UDC** 930.9. Index available. **Bk Rev. Ad Acc. Circ:** 500.
Desc: Co-operatively produced student history journal, published since 1980. Gives fresh new student historical research a place to be published in Canada. Includes essays and book reviews on any number of topics of a historical nature, for example, social, economic, women's, regional, international and political history. Publishes in the autumn and spring.

CN/0068-8088
REGISTER OF POST-GRADUATE DISSERTATIONS IN PROGRESS IN HISTORY AND RELATED SUBJECTS. (REGISTER OF POST-GRADUATE DISSERTATIONS IN PROGRESS IN HISTORY AND RELATED SUBJECTS. REPERTOIRE DES THESES EN COURS PORTANT SUR DES SUJETS D'HISTOIRE ET AUTRES SUJETS CONNEXES.). **Main/Corp** Public Archives of Canada. **Added/Corp** Public Archives of Canada. Canadian Historical Association. Public Archives Canada. **VFOAT** Repertoire des Theses en Cours Portant sur des Sujets d'Histoire et Autres Sujets Connexes. No. 1 (1966)-. Periodical. English (French). an. 10.00Can$. Canadian Historical Association, 395 Wellington Street, Ottawa Ontario K1A 0N3 Canada. **Tel** (613)233-7885. **ED** Paul Aubin. **DD** 016.9. **Circ:** 650 (ctrl).
Desc: Lists theses for: political science, economics, geography and literature, if they involve some degree of historical research and are of interest to the field of Canadian studies.

JA/0386-8907
REKISHI HYORON. [Rekishi hyoron]. **Added/Corp** Minshu Shugi Kagakusha Kyokai (Japan) Minshu Shugi Kagakusha Kyokai (Japan). Rekishi Bukai. Rekishi Kagaku Kyogikai. (1946)-. Periodical. English. mo. ¥36.00. **(Subscription address:** Kyowa Book Company Inc., 1 38 Kanda Jinbocho Chiyoda-ku, Tokyo 101 Japan.) **LC** D1; .R2142.
Ind/Abst Am. Hist. Life (1954-1989).

JA
REKISHI TO BUNKA. Added/Corp Tokyo Daigaku. Rekishigaku Kenkyushitsu. **VFOAT** History and Culture. (1952)-. Japanese (summaries and/or abstracts in English). **LC** D1; .R2145.
Ind/Abst Am. Hist. Life (1963-1972).

US/0897-7836
RENAISSANCE AND BAROQUE. [Renaiss. baroque stud. text]. **VFOAT** Renaissance and Baroque, Studies and Text. 1989-. Monographic series. English. ir. Price varies per volume. Peter Lang Publishing, 62 West 45th Street, 4th Floor, New York NY 10036. **Tel** (212)764-1471, (800)770-5264, telex 6973364 PLNY. **DD** 940.

US/0034-4338
RENAISSANCE QUARTERLY. See Literature.

CK/0034-4605
REPERTORIO BOYACENSE. [Repert. boyac.]. **Added/Corp** Academia Boyacense de Historia. (19??)-. Spanish. **LC** F2251; .R43.
Ind/Abst Am. Hist. Life (1960-1975).

IT
REPERTORIUM FONTIUM HISTORIAE MEDII AEVI. (1962)-. Monographic series. Latin. ir. Price varies per volume. Istituto Storico Itl Medio Evo, Piazza del Orologio 4, 00186 Rome Italy. **Tel** 011 39 6 68802075.

US/0411-4094
REPORT - CENTRAL SOYA, INC., FORT WAYNE IND. Main/Corp Central Soya, Inc., Fort Wayne, Ind. Periodical. English. $30.00. Clio, Indiana University Purdue University, 2101 Coliseum Boulevard E, Fort Wayne IN 46805. **Tel** (219)482-5441. **ED** Henry Kozicki, Clark Butler, and Robert Canary. **UDC** 930.1. **Bk Rev. Ad Acc. Circ:** 600.
Desc: Literature, history and the philosophy of history more specifically three interrelated topics: literature as informed by historical understandings; historical writings considered as literature; philosophy of history, speculative and analytic.

US
REPORT / DALLAS HISTORICAL SOCIETY. Main/Corp Dallas Historical Society. Vol. 1 (1976)-. Periodical. English. qt. Dallas Historical Society, PO Box 150038, Dallas TX 75315.

US/0271-5058
RESEARCHER (JACKSON, MISS.). See Education-Higher Education.

US/0147-9032
REVIEW - FERNAND BRAUDEL CENTER FOR THE STUDY OF ECONOMIES, HISTORICAL SYSTEMS, AND CIVILIZATIONS. See Economics.

US
REVIEW / INSTITUTE FOR THE HISTORY OF TECHNOLOGY & INDUSTRIAL ARCHAEOLOGY. Added/Corp West Virginia University. Institute for the History of Technology and Industrial Archaeology. Vol. 1, No. 2 (Summer 1991)-. Periodical. English. sa. **Continues** Institute for the History of Technology and Industrial Archaeology : [review].

US
REVIEW OF THE SOCIETY FOR THE HISTORY OF CZECHOSLOVAK JEWS. Added/Corp Society for the History of Czechoslovak Jews. **VFOAT** Review of SHCJ. Vol. 1 (1987)-. English. an. $6.00 members of the society, $7.00 nonmembers. Society for the History of Czechoslovak Jews, c/o Joseph Abeles, 10230 62nd Road, Forest Hills NY 11375. **LC** DS135.C95; R48. **DD** 943.7/004924.
Ind/Abst Am. Bibliogr. Slavic East Europ. Stud.

US/1045-5299
REVISIONIST LETTERS. Vol. 1, No. 1 (Spring 1989)-. Periodical. English. Three times a year. $28.00. Revisionist Letters, PO Box 931089, Los Angeles CA 90093. **DD** 909.

BL
REVISTA BRASILEIRA DE HISTORIA / ORGAO DA ASSOCIACAO NACIONAL DOS PROFESSORES UNIVERSITARIOS DE HISTORIA, ANPUH. Added/Corp Associacao Nacional dos Professores Universitarios de Historia. No. 1 (Mar 1981)-. Periodical. Portuguese. Four times a year. Price varies. Associacion Nacional Professores, University de Historia, Avenue Linea Prestes 338 Cid Univ, CEP 05508 Sao Paulo Brazil. **Tel** 011 55 21 2102122 X454. **LC** F2501; .R495. **DD** 981/.005.
Ind/Abst Am. Hist. Life (1988-).

BL
REVISTA DA SBPH / SOCIEDADE BRASILEIRA DE PESQUISA HISTORICA. Added/Corp Sociedade Brasileira de Pesquisa Historica. **VFOAT** Revista da S.B.P.H. No. 1 (1983)-. Periodical. Portuguese (English).
Ind/Abst Am. Hist. Life (1983-).

CL/0716-5455
REVISTA DE ESTUDIOS HISTORICO-JURIDICOS. See Law.

SP/0210-038X
REVISTA DE ESTUDIOS HISTORICOS DE LA GUARDIA CIVIL. [Rev. Estud. Hist. Guard. Civ.]. **VFOAT** Revista de Eestudios Historicos. (1968)-. Periodical. Spanish. sa.
Ind/Abst Am. Hist. Life (1968-1975).

BL/0034-8309
REVISTA DE HISTORIA (SAO PAULO). (REVISTA DE HISTORIA.). [Rev. hist.]. Vol. 1, No. 1 (Jan./March 1950)-. Periodical. Portuguese (English and French). qt. $10.00. Faculda de Filosofia, Letras e Ciencias Humanas USP, Secao de Publicacpes, Caixa Postal 8105 Brazil. **Tel** (011)813-3222. **ED** E Simoes de Paula. **LC** D1; .R23. **DD** 905. **UDC** 930.9; 981; 980=6. Index available. cum. index. **Circ:** 500.
Ind/Abst MLA Int. Bibl. Books Artic. Mod. Lang. Lit.

AG
REVISTA DE HISTORIA UNIVERSAL. Added/Corp Universidad Nacional de Cuyo. Facultad de Filosofia y Letras. (1988)-. Periodical. Spanish. **LC** D1; .R233. **DD** 900.
Ind/Abst Am. Hist. Life (1988-).

History(General)

RM
REVISTA ISTORICA / ACADEMIA ROMANA, INSTITUTUL DE ISTORIE "N. IORGA.". **Added/Corp** Institutul de Istorie "N. Iorga.". (Jan. 1990)-. Periodical. Romanian (summaries and/or abstracts in French). mo. DM299.00. **(Subscription address:** Kubon & Sagner, ABT Zeitschriftenimport, D 80328 Munich Germany.) **LC** D1; .A2. **DD** 949.8/005. **Continues** Revista de Istorie, 0251-3099.
Ind/Abst Am. Hist. Life (1955-); BHA : Biblio. Hist. Art.

FR/0758-881X
REVUE DE LA SOCIETE DES AMIS DU MUSEE DE L'ARMEE. See Military and Defense.

HT
REVUE DE LA SOCIETE HAITIENNE D'HISTOIRE ET DE GEOGRAPHIE (PORT-AU-PRINCE, HAITI : 1981). (REVUE DE LA SOCIETE HAITIENNE D'HISTOIRE ET DE GEOGRAPHIE.). Vol. 39, No. 132 (Sept. 1981)-. Periodical. French. qt. Musee National Haut Turgeau, Port-au-Prince Haiti. **LC** F1900; .S64. **UDC** 972.94; 917.294. **Continues** Revue de la Societe Haitienne d'Histoire, de Geographie et de Geologie.

MG
REVUE DE L'OCEAN INDIEN. No. 1 (Sept. 1980)-. Periodical. English (French). mo. 750.00FMG. 3 Cite Bergere, 75009 Paris France. **LC** DS331; .R492. **DD** 909/.09824.

FR/0241-7413
REVUE DE PAU ET DU BEARN. See The Arts-Art.

FR/0035-1776
REVUE DE SYNTHESE. [Rev. synth.]. **Added/Corp** Centre International de Synthese. Vol. 1 (March 1931)-. Periodical. French. Four times a year. Price varies. Editions Albin Michel, 22 rue Huyghens, 75014 Paris, France. **Tel** 011 33 1 42791000, FAX 011 33 1 43272158, telex 203379. **LC** D1; .R42. **DD** 905. **NLM** W1; RE805LK. **Supersedes** Revue de Synthese Historique, 0997-0541.
Ind/Abst Am. Hist. Life (1968-); BHA : Biblio. Hist. Art.

FR/0035-1849
REVUE D'EGYPTOLOGIE. Vol. 1 (1933)-. French (English and German). an (Jan.). 430.00F. Societe Francaise d Egyptologie, PL Marcelin Berthelot/Coll Fr, 75231 Paris Cedex 05 France. **Tel** 40 46 94 31. **LC** PJ1003. **DD** 913.32. **UDC** 932. Index available ((Vols. 1-20)). cum. index.
Ind/Abst BHA : Biblio. Hist. Art.

FR/0048-8003
REVUE D'HISTOIRE MODERNE ET CONTEMPORAINE. [Rev. hist. mod. contemp.]. Vol. 1 (1954)-. Periodical. French. qt. 489.75F European Union; 533.33F other. Societie Historie Moderne Contemporain, 44 rue du Four c/o Others, F 75006 Paris France. **Tel** 011 33 1 45815533. **LC** D1; .R32. **DD** 905. **UDC** 940.2; 930.9. cum. index. **Bk Rev**. available on microfilm from University Microfilms International (UMI). Documents available from The Genuine Article. **Supersedes** Revue d'Histoire Moderne.
Ind/Abst Am. Hist. Life (1954-); Arts Humanit. Citation Index [Full Cov.]; BHA : Biblio. Hist. Art; Curr. Contents Arts Humanit.; Int. Bibliogr. Sociol.; Int. Polit. Sci. Abstr.; Point Repere (1983-); Res. Alert [Full Cov.]; Romant. Move.; Soc. Sci. Cit. Index [Select. Cov.].

FR/0035-3132
REVUE GENERALE DE L'ETANCHEITE ET DE L'ISOLATION. [Rev. Gen. Etanch. Isol.]. French. qt. 176.00F France; 265.00F other. DTSB, 10 rue du Debarcadere, 75852 Paris Cedex 17 France.

FR/0035-3264
REVUE HISTORIQUE. [Rev. hist.]. (1876)-. Periodical. French. qt. 480.00F France; 580.00 other. Presses Universitaires de France, Department des Revues, 14 Avenue du Bois de l'Epine, BP 90, 91003 Evry Cedex France. **Tel** (1)60 77 82 05, FAX (1) 60 79 20 45, telex PUF 600 474 F. **LC** D1; .R6. **[CCC]**. cum. index. **Bk Rev**. available on microfilm and microfiche from University Microfilms International (UMI). Documents available from The Genuine Article.
Desc: Articles include updates on historical research, critical analyses of international convention proceedings and of current historical articles in French and other journals.
Ind/Abst Am. Hist. Life (1954-); Arts Humanit. Citation Index (19??-19??) [Full Cov.]; BHA : Biblio. Hist. Art; Curr. Contents Arts Humanit.; Numis. Lit.; Point Repere; Res. Alert [Full Cov.]; Romant. Move.; Soc. Sci. Cit. Index [Select. Cov.].

GW/0080-2670
RHEINISCHE LEBENSBILDER. Vol. 1- 1961-. German. ir. Dr. Rudolf Habelt GmbH, Postfach 150104, D 53040 Bonn Germany. **Tel** 011 49 228 232015. **UDC** 943.0-316.

FR/0751-2325
RHODANIE. [Rhodanie]. (1982)-. Periodical. French. qt. **UDC** 908 (448.3).
Ind/Abst BHA : Biblio. Hist. Art.

IT
RICERCHE SUL 600 NAPOLETANO. Italian. an. Grafiche Tognolli, Via C del Majno 1, 20086 Motta Visconti Milan Italy. **Tel** 39 2 90000065. **(Subscription address:** Michael Shamansky Bookseller, PO Box 3904, Kingston NY 12401, Tel. (914)331-8519)
Ind/Abst BHA : Biblio. Hist. Art.

US/0556-9931
RIDING LINE. Added/Corp Texas State Historical Association. Vol. 1 (Oct. 1966)-. English. qt. comes with Texas State Historical Society Membership. Texas State Historical Association, 2/306 Richardson Hall, University Street, Austin TX 78712. **Tel** (512)471-1525, FAX (512)471-1551.

US/0271-6925
RIPLEY P. BULLEN MONOGRAPHS IN ANTHROPOLOGY AND HISTORY. See Anthropology.

IT
RIVISTA DI STORIA DELLA STORIOGRAFIA MODERNA. Yearly V. 1, No. 1 (July 1980)-. Periodical. Italian (English, French and German). Three times a year. L40000 Italy; L50000 other. Via di Villa Zingone, 7-00151 Rome Italy. **Tel** 06/5603919. **(Subscription address:** Edizioni dell'Ateneo, Casella Postale 7216, 00100 Roma Italy) **ED** Massimo Mastrogregori. **LC** D13; .R54. **DD** 907/.2. **UDC** 930.21. Index available. cum. index. **Bk Rev**. **Ad Acc**.
Desc: The first scientific publication specialized in history of historical science. Consists in publishing original research works, documents, and critical surveys in the field of history of historiography and historiographical methodology, characterized by scientific exactitude.
Ind/Abst Am. Hist. Life (1983-); Romant. Move.

IT/0557-1367
RIVISTA DI STUDI BIZANTINI E NEOELLENICI. [Riv. studi biz. neoell.]. (1964)-. Italian. an. Libreria Paolo Tombolini, Via IV Novembre 146, 00186 Rome Italy. **Continues** Studi Bizantini e Neoellenici.
Ind/Abst BHA : Biblio. Hist. Art; MLA Int. Bibl. Books Artic. Mod. Lang. Lit.

IT/0300-340X
RIVISTA STORICA DELL'ANTICHITA. Vol. 1, (1971)-. Periodical. Italian (English, French, German and Italian). an. L70000 Italy; L80000 other. Patron Editore SRL, Via Badini 12, 40050 Quarto Inf. Bologna Italy. **Tel** 011 39 51 767003. **ED** Via Badini Patron. **Bk Rev. Circ:** 500.
Desc: The review subject is about the history of the ancient world.

XR/0862-9773
ROCENKA OBECNYCH DEJIN. Added/Corp Historicky Ustav (Ceskoslovenska Akademie Ved). (1991)-. Czech. **LC** D1; .R77.

US
ROCKCASTLE REMINISCENCE. Newsletter. English. Four times a year (Jan., Apr., Aug., Nov.). $5.00. Rockcastle County Historical Society, PO Box 930, Mountain Vernon KY 40456. **Tel** (606)256-2397. **ED** Juanita Witt. **Ad Acc. Circ:** 250 (ctrl).
Desc: News and information about the people and the places of Rockcastle County in Kentucky.

II
ROMA. Vol. 1 (June 1974)-. Periodical. English. Twice a year. Rs2.60 India; $12.00 US & Canada; $14.50 others. Roma Publications, Indian Institute, Romani Studies, 3290 15 D Chandigarh India. **Tel** 27148. **ED** W. R. Rishi. **LC** DX101; .R58. **DD** 909/.04/91497. **Bk Rev. Ad Acc. Circ:** 400 (ctrl).
Desc: Journal on the language, history and culture of Roma and the so called gypsies of Europe, USSR and Americas.

IT
ROMANICA VULGARIA : QUADERNI. Italian. ir. Japadre Editore, C Postale 170, 67100 L Aquila Italy. **Tel** 011 39 86226025.

US
ROMANTIC SHELTERS. English. ir. National Society for the Preservation of Covered Bridges, 1611 Sandcastle Road, Sanibel FL 33957. **Tel** (813)472-3188.
Desc: Listing of covered bridges.

FR/0048-8593
ROMANTISME. See Literature.

●US/1061-1983
RUSSIAN STUDIES IN HISTORY. [Russ. stud. hist.]. Vol. 31, No. 1 (Summer 1992)-. Periodical. English (translations available in Russian). qt. $381.00 US; $421.00 other. M. E. Sharpe Inc., 80 Business Park Drive, Armonk NY 10504. **Tel** (914)273-1800, (800)541-6563, FAX (914)273-2106. **LC** D1; .S67. **DD** 905. **Continues** Soviet Studies in History, 0038-5867.

GW/0080-5319
SAECULUM. [Saeculum]. (1950)-. German. an. DM98.00 (complete yearbook), DM28.50 (single volume). Verlag Karl Alber GmbH, Hermann Herder Strasse 4, W-7800 Freiburg Germany. **LC** D2; .S3. **DD** 905. **[CCC]**. cum. index. Documents available from The Genuine Article.
Desc: The internationally respected yearbook for general history, deals with the culture of the Ancient Orient, India; East Asia, Ancient America, the Greek-Roman antiquity, the peoples of Islam and with the culture of Occident in a way of methodical covered comparison.
Ind/Abst Am. Hist. Life (1954-1957, 1964-); Arts Humanit. Citation Index [Full Cov.]; BHA : Biblio. Hist. Art; Curr. Contents Arts Humanit.; Int. Bibliogr. Sociol.; Res. Alert [Full Cov.]; Soc. Sci. Cit. Index [Select. Cov.].

UK
SAGE STUDIES IN 20TH CENTURY HISTORY. **Ceased**. VFOAT Studies in 20th Century History. Vol. 1 (1974)-Series completed (199?). Monographic series. English. ir. Sage Publications Ltd., 6 Bonhill Street, London EC2A 4PU, UK. **Tel** 071 374 0645, FAX 071 374 8741, telex 296207 SAGE G. **Acid Free**.

II
SAMAKALINA TISARI DUNIYA. VFOAT Samkaleen Teesari Duniya. Periodical. Hindi (Hindi). ir. Rs2.00. A Varma, 48 WZ Ramgarh, New Delhi 110015 India. **LC** D839; .S37.

IT
SANDALION. Added/Corp Universita Degli Studi di Sassari. (1978)-. Periodical. Italian (English, French and German). ir. Herder Editrice e Libreria SRL, Piazza Montecitorio 117-120, 00186 Rome Italy. **Tel** 011 39 6 679 4628, FAX 011 39 6 678 4751. **ED** A. Battegazzorre, F. Bertini and P. Meloni.
Desc: Annual on Classical, Christian and Medieval culture.

US/1046-3267
SANDLAPPER (1990). (SANDLAPPER : THE MAGAZINE OF SOUTH CAROLINA.). [Sandlapper]. Vol. 1, No. 1 (Jan./Feb. 1990)-. Periodical. English. Four times a year (Mar., June, Sept., Dec.). $14.95. RPW Publishing Corporation, PO Box 1108, Lexington SC 29071-0729. **Tel** (803)359-9954, FAX (803)957-8226. **ED** Robert P. Wilkins. **LC** F266; .S36. **DD** 975.7/005. **Bk Rev. Ad Acc. Circ:** 14,000 (ctrl). **Continues** Carolina Lifestyle, 0744-5237.
Desc: South Carolina history, people, places, and events.

UK
SAWT AL-JABHAH : NASHRAT AL-JABHAH AL-WATANIYAH AL-QAWMIYAH AL-DIMUQRATIYAH FI AL-IRAQ, MAKTAB URUBBA AL-GHARBIYAH (LANDAN). No. 1, (Oct. 1983)-. Periodical. Arabic. N D P F, B M Box 6490, London WC1 N3XX England. **LC** DS79.65; S36.

XR/0577-3725
SBORNIK HISTORICKY. 1- 1953-. Czech (French).
Desc: Devoted to printing original monographs and studies in Czechoslovak and world history.
Ind/Abst Am. Hist. Life (1966-).

XR
SBORNIK K DEJINAM 19. A 20. STOLETI. Added/Corp Ustav Ceskoslovenskych a Svetovych Dejin (Ceskoslovenska Akademie Ved). VFOAT Sborník Novovekých Ceskoslovenských Dejin. Sbornik K Dejinam Devatenacteho a Dvacateho Stoleti. (1972)-. Periodical. Czech (summaries and/or abstracts in German and Russian; table of contents in German and Russian). ir. Histoicky ustav CSAV, Vysehradska 49, 128 26 Prague 2 Czech Republic. **Tel** 296451. **ED** Jurij Krizek. **LC** D353; .S27. Index available. **Bk Rev**. **Ad Acc**.

XR/0036-5335
SBORNIK NARODNIHO MUZEA V PRAZE. RADA A, HISTORIE. [Sb. Nar. Muz. Praze, Rada A, Hist.]. **Added/Corp** Narodni Muzeum v Praze. VFOAT Acta Musei Nationalis Pragae. Series A, Historia. Vol. 15, No. 1 (1961)-. Periodical. Czech (summaries and/or abstracts in English, French and Russian). Four times a year. $55.60. **(Subscription address:** Artia Pegas Press Ltd., Palac Metro Narodni Trida 25, 11210 Prague 1 Czech Republic.) **Continues** Sbornik Narodniho Musea v Praze. A, Historicky.
Ind/Abst Am. Hist. Life (1959-); BHA : Biblio. Hist. Art; Numis. Lit.

XR
SBORNIK PEDAGOGICKE FAKULTY UNIVERSITY KARLOVY. HISTORIE. **Added/Corp** Universita Karlova. Pedagogicka Fakulta. VFOAT Historie. (1966)-. Czech (summaries and/or

abstracts in English, German and Russian; table of contents in English, German and Russian).
Ind/Abst Am. Hist. Life (1966-1974,1977-1982).

XR/0231-7710
SBORNIK PRACI FILOSOFICKE FAKULTY BRNENSKE UNIVERSITY. C, RADY HISTORICKA. [Sb. pr. Filoz. fak. Brnen. univ., Rada hist.]. **Added/Corp** Univerzita J.E. Purkyne v Brne. Filozoficka Fakulta. Masarykova Univerzita v Brne. Filozoficka Fakulta. **VFOAT** Rady Historicka; Sbornik Praci Filozoficke Fakulty Brnenske Univerzity. C, Rada Historicka; Rada Historicka; Studia Minora Facultatis Philosophicae Universitatis Brunensis. Series Historica. (1954)-. Czech (summaries and/or abstracts in English, French and German). an. **LC** DB2000; .S26. **DD** 900.
Ind/Abst Am. Hist. Life (1954-).

XR/0231-5025
SBORNIK PRACI FILOZOFICKE FAKULTY BRNENSKE UNIVERZITY. RADA UMENOVEDNA. See The Arts-Art.

GW
SCHRIFTEN ZUR UR- UND FRUEHGESCHICHTE. **Added/Corp** Akademie der Wissenschaften (Berlin, Germany) Zentralinstitut fuer Alte Geschichte und Archaeologie. (19??)-. German. ir. LKG Leipziger Kommissions & Grossbuchhandel, Leninstrasse 16, Postfach 520, D 04005 Leipzig, Germany. **Tel** 011 49 341 71370.

GW/0080-7273
SCHWEIZERISCHE BEITRAGE ZUR ALTERTUMSWISSENSCHAFT. No. 1 (1945)-. Monographic series. German (French). ir. Price varies per volume. Verlag Friedrich Reinhardt AG, Missionsstrasse 36, CH-4012 Basel Switzerland.

CN/0824-6009
SCINTILLA (TORONTO). See Literature.

FI/0358-710X
SCRIPTA HISTORICA. (ACTA SOCIETATIS HISTORICAE OULUENSIS. SCRIPTA HISTORICA.). [Scr. hist.]. **Added/Corp** Oulun Historiaseura. **VFOAT** Scripta Historica; Oulun Historiaseuran Julkaisuja. (1969)-. Monographic series. English (Finnish, German and Swedish). **LC** D1; .A356. **DD** 940/.05. ***Continues*** *Acta Societatis Historicae Ouluensis. Studia Historica, 0081-6493.*

JA/0386-9253
SEIYO SHIGAKU / NIHON SEIYOSHI GAKKAI. [Seiyo shigaku]. **VFOAT** Studies in Western History. Began in 1948. Japanese. ¥650. Hiei Shobo, 28 Karahashi Kadowaki-cho, Minami-ku, Kyoto-shi 601, Osaka-fu Japan. **LC** D1; .S37. **UDC** 940.
Ind/Abst Am. Hist. Life (1954-).

JA/0582-4532
SEKAI. (1946)-. Periodical. Japanese. mo. $165.00 California; $171.00 other US; $198.00 Europe; $222.00 Asia; $174.00 other. **(Subscription address:** Kinokuniya Company Ltd., 38-1 Sakuragaoka 5, chome Setagaya-ku, Tokyo 156 Japan.**)** **LC** AP95.J2; S46.

JA
SEKAI KARA. No. 1- ; 1979-. Periodical. Japanese. ¥2800. Ajia Taiheiyo Shiryo Senta, c/o Seiko Building 4-kai, 30 Kanda Jimbocho 1, Chiyoda-ku, Tokyo Japan. **LC** D839; .S44.

PL/0867-5864
SEKRETY HISTORII. [Sekrety Hist.]. (1991)-. Periodical. Polish. mo. Price on Request. **(Subscription address:** ARS Polona, PO Box 1001, 00068 Warsaw Poland.**)** **UDC** 94.

US
SELECTIONS FROM THE ANNALES, ECONOMIES, SOCIETES, CIVILISATIONS. See Social Sciences.

CN/0711-0510
SEMAINE INTERNATIONALE, LA. [Sem. int.]. Vol. 1, No. 1 19 Sept.-. Periodical. French. wk. $0.75 per no. Semaine Internationale, c/o S D I, 44 Ouest Boulevard, St-Cyrille Quebec G1S 1S3 Canada. **DD** 905. **UDC** 930.9.

DK/0105-7618
SFINX. [Sfinx]. **VFOAT** Tidsskriftet Sfinx. (1977)-. Periodical. Danish. Four times a year. kr160.00. Aarhus University Press, Aarhus University, Building 170, DK-8000 Aarhus C Denmark. **Tel** 011 45 86 197033, FAX 011 45 86 198433, telex 16600. **DD** 930. **CODEN** 90.191.2. **Bk Rev. Ad Acc. Circ:** 8,500.
Ind/Abst BHA : Biblio. Hist. Art.

JA
SHICHO. **Added/Corp** Otsuka Shigakukai. Rekishi Gakkai. **VFOAT** Shicho, the Journal of History; Journal of History. (1931)-. Periodical. Japanese (table of contents in English). sa.
Ind/Abst Am. Hist. Life (1955-1989).

JA/0386-9318
SHIEN (TOKYO. 1928). (SHIEN.). [Shien]. **Added/Corp** Rikkyo Daigaku. Shigakkai. **VFOAT** Journal of Historical Studies; Journal of Historical Studies, Rikkyo University. (1928)-. Periodical. Japanese. sa. **LC** D1; .S4335.
Ind/Abst Am. Hist. Life (1955-1989).

JA
SHIGAKU. **Added/Corp** Mita Shigakkai. **VFOAT** Historical Science. (May/Oct. 1921)-. Academic Scholarly Publication. Japanese (summaries and/or abstracts in English). qt. $84.00. **(Subscription address:** Japan Publications Trading Company, Ltd., PO Box 5030, Tokyo International, Tokyo 100-31 Japan.**)** **LC** D1; .S434. Documents available from CASDDS.
Ind/Abst Am. Hist. Life (1955-1956, 1972-); Chem. Abstr.

CC
SHIH CHIEH KU TAI SHIH LUN TSUNG / PEI-CHING TA HSUEH, TUNG-PEI, SHIH FAN TA HSUEH, LI SHIH HSI SHIH CHIEN KU TAI SHIH CHIAO YEN SHIH PIEN. V. 1, (May 1982)-. Periodical. Chinese. an. RMBY0.83. Hsin Hua Shu Tien, Beijing, People's Republic of China. **Tel** 551253. **LC** D51; .S43. **DD** 930/.05. **UDC** 930.9; 930.8.

CH
SHIH HSUEH. **Added/Corp** Kuo li Cheng-Kung ta Hsueh li Shih Hsueh Hui. Hsueh Shu Ku. (March 1974)-. Chinese. **LC** D1; .S439.

CC/1002-011X
SHIJIE LISHI. (SHIH CHIEH LI SHIH.). [Shijie lishi]. **VFOAT** Shijie Lishi; World History; Shi Jie Li Shi. (Dec. 1978)-. Periodical. Chinese. bm. $12.90. **(Subscription address:** China International Book Trading Corporation, PO Box 399, Library Service Department, Beijing 100044 People's Republic of China.**)** **LC** D1; .S438. **DD** 905.
Desc: Covers world history.
Ind/Abst Am. Hist. Life (1990-).

JA/0386-9350
SHIKAN. **Added/Corp** Waseda Daigaku Shigakkai. **VFOAT** Shikan, The Historical Review; Historical Review. (1908)-. Periodical. Japanese (table of contents in English). sa.
Ind/Abst Am. Hist. Life (1956-1971,1987-1988).

JA/0386-4022
SHIRON (TOKYO. 1953). (SHIRON.). [Shiron]. **Added/Corp** TokyÂo Joshi Daigaku. Shigaku Kenkyushitsu. **VFOAT** Historic. (1953)-. Periodical. Japanese (Japanese). an. Eibei Bungaku ka Bungakubu, Komazawa Univ. 1 23 1 Komazawa, Setagaya Ku Tokyo 154 Japan. **Tel** 011 81 3 34189246. **LC** D1; .S48.
Ind/Abst Am. Hist. Life (1964-); MLA Int. Bibl. Books Artic. Mod. Lang. Lit.

US/0885-8659
SHMATE. ***Ceased.*** [Shmate]. Vol. 1 No. 1 (April/May 1982)-(1992). Periodical. English. qt. Shmate, Box 4228, Berkeley CA 94704. **ED** Steve Fankuchen. **LC** DS101; .S48. **DD** 909/.04924/005. **UDC** 933. **Circ:** 3,500. available on microfilm.
Desc: Political and cultural, with an emphasis on progressing Jewish thought.
Ind/Abst Altern. Press Index (-1992); Am. Hist. Life (1983-).

US
SIDEWINDER STUDIES IN HISTORY AND SOCIOLOGY. (19??)-. English. ir. Price varies per volume. Borgo Press, PO Box 2845, San Bernardino CA 92406. **Tel** (714)884-5813, (714)885-1161. **ED** Allan Adrian.
Desc: Classic histories, social commentaries, bibliographies, and other treatises, newly repackaged for a modern scholarly audience.

MX
SIGLO XIX. CUADERNOS DE HISTORIA. **Added/Corp** Instituto de Investigaciones Dr. Jose Maria Luis Mora. Universidad Autonoma de Nuevo Leon. Facultad de Filosofia y Letras. **VFOAT** Cuadernos de Historia; Siglo Diez y Nueve. Cuadernos de Historia. (1991)-. Periodical. Spanish. Three times a year. Institute de Investigaciones, Dr. Jose Maria Luis Mora and Facultad de Filosofia and Letras, Universidad Autonoma de Nuevo Leon, Monterrey, Mexico.

GW/0138-3957
SITZUNGSBERICHTE DER SACHSISCHEN AKADEMIE DER WISSENSCHAFTEN ZU LEIPZIG, PHILOLOGISCH-HISTORISCHE KLASSE. See Philosophy.

AU/0029-8832
SITZUNGSBERICHTE / OSTERREICHISCHE AKADEMIE DER WISSENSCHAFTEN, PHILOSOPHISCH-HISTORISCHE KLASSE. [Sitz.ber. - Osterr. Akad. Wiss., Philos.-Hist. Kl.]. **Added/Corp** Osterreichische Akademie der Wissenschaften. Philosophisch-Historische Klasse. (194?)-. Monographic series. German. ir. Price varies per volume. Oesterreichischen Akademie Wissenschaften, Dr. Ignaz Seipel Platz 2, A-1010 Vienna Austria. **Tel** 011 43 1 51581. **LC** AS142; .V31. ***Continues*** *Sitzungsberichte (Akademie der Wissenschaften in Wien. Philosophisch-Historische Klasse).*
Ind/Abst BHA : Biblio. Hist. Art.

US/0885-9302
SIXTEENTH CENTURY BIBLIOGRAPHY. See History(General)-Abstracting, Bibliographies and Statistics.

US/0361-0160
SIXTEENTH CENTURY JOURNAL, THE. [Sixt. century j.]. **Added/Corp** Foundation for Reformation Research. Vol. 3 (April 1972)-. Periodical. English. Four times a year (Apr., July, Oct., Dec.). $25.00 US; $50.00 (institutions), $45.00 (individuals) other. R V Schnucker, NMSU LB 115, Kirksville MO 65301. **Tel** (816)785-4665, FAX (816)785-4181. **ED** R. V. Schnucker. **LC** D219; .S55. **DD** 940.2/3; 914/.03/23. **[CCC].** Index available. **Bk Rev**, (Qty: 200). **Ad Acc. Pr Rev. Acid Free. Circ:** 2,500 (ctrl). available on microfiche (from Silver Halide Positive Microfiche). Documents available from The Genuine Article, UMI Article Clearinghouse. ***Continues*** *Sixteenth Century Essays and Studies, 0080-987X.*
Desc: Presents the latest authoritative research in early modern history in readable form, and provides 200 reviews of the latest books. It is inter-disciplinary in scope, international in its reputation and coverage.
Ind/Abst Abstr. Engl. Stud.; Acad. Search (July 1993-); Am. Hist. Life (1973-); Am. Humanit. Index; Annu. Bibliogr. Engl. Lang. Lit.; Arts Humanit. Citation Index [Full Cov.]; BHA : Biblio. Hist. Art; Curr. Contents Arts Humanit.; Expand. Acad. Index (1989-); Humanit. Index; Humanit. Source (Jul. 1993-); Index Book Rev. Relig.; INFO-SOUTH Abstr.; Mag. Search; MLA Int. Bibl. Books Artic. Mod. Lang. Lit.; Newsp. Period. Abstr. (1991-); Relig. Index One Period. (1972-); Relig. Theol. Abstr.; Res. Alert [Full Cov.]; Soc. Sci. Cit. Index [Select. Cov.].

PL/0037-7511
SLASKI KWARTALNIK HISTORYCZNY SOBOTKA / WROCAWSKIE TOWARZYSTWO MIOSNIKOW HISTORII. **Added/Corp** Wrocawskie Towarzystow Miosnikow Historii. **VFOAT** Sobotka. (1957)-. Periodical. Polish. Four times a year. $50.00. **(Subscription address:** ARS Polona, PO Box 1001, 00068 Warsaw Poland.**)** ***Continues*** *Sobotka.*
Ind/Abst Am. Hist. Life (1955-1976,1979-).

US/0037-6795
SLAVONIC AND EAST EUROPEAN REVIEW, THE. [Slav. East Eur. rev.]. **Added/Corp** Modern Humanities Research Association. University of London. School of Slavonic and East European Studies. (1943)-. Periodical. English. qt. $178.00. W. S. Maney and Son Ltd., Hudson Road, Leeds LS9 7DL England. **Tel** 011 44 532 497481, FAX 011 44 532 486983. **(Subscription address:** W.S. Maney & Son Limited, PO Box YR7, Leeds, LS9 7UU England.**)** **LC** D377.A1; S65. **Bk Rev. Circ:** 1,000. Documents available from The Genuine Article, UMI Article Clearinghouse. ***Continues*** *Slavonic Year-Book.*
Ind/Abst Acad. Abstr. Full Text Elite (July 1990-); Acad. Abstr. (July 1990-); Acad. Ind. [Computer File] (1987-); Acad. Search (July 1990-); Am. Hist. Life (1954-); ARTbibliogr. Mod.; Arts Humanit. Citation Index [Full Cov.]; BHA : Biblio. Hist. Art; Br. Humanit. Index; Curr. Contents Arts Humanit.; Expand. Acad. Index (1987-); Humanit. Index; INFO-SOUTH Abstr.; Int. Bibliogr. Sociol.; Lang. Teach.; Mag. Search; MLA Int. Bibl. Books Artic. Mod. Lang. Lit.; Newsp. Period. Abstr. (1991-); Res. Alert [Full Cov.]; Soc. Plann. Policy Dev. Abstr.; Soc. Sci. Source (Jul. 1990-); Soc. Sci. Cit. Index [Select. Cov.]; Sociol. Abstr.; U.S. Polit. Sci. Doc.

XR/0037-6833
SLEZSKY SBORNIK. See Sociology.

US/0897-6619
SMITH COLLEGE STUDIES IN HISTORY. [Smith coll. stud. hist.]. **Added/Corp** Smith College. Dept. of History. Vol. 1, No. 1 (Oct. 1915)-. Periodical. English. ir. Price varies per volume. Smith College / Department of History, Wright Hall, Northampton MA 01063. **Tel** (413)585-3702, FAX (413)585-3389. **DD** 905. Index available.

US/0081-0258
SMITHSONIAN STUDIES IN HISTORY AND TECHNOLOGY. [Smithson. stud. hist. technol.]. **Main/Corp** Smithsonian Institution. No. 1 (1969)-. Monographic series. English. Smithsonian Institution Press, 470 L'Enfant Plaza, Suite 7100, Washington DC 20560. **Tel** (202)287-3738, (800)782-4612, FAX (202)287-3184. **(Subscription address:** Supt of Documents, US Government Printing Office, Washington, DC 20402**)** **DD** 973.
Ind/Abst BHA : Biblio. Hist. Art.

US/0583-6573
SMOKE SIGNAL (TUCSON), THE. (THE SMOKE SIGNAL.). **Added/Corp** The Westerners. Tucson Corral. No. 1 (May 1960)-. Periodical. English. sa. $10.00. Tucson Corral of the Westerner, 633 North

Jasmine Place, Tucson AZ 85710. **Tel** (602)326-7669, FAX (602)745-2830. **ED** Maurice F Guptill. **LC** F811; .S67. cum. index. **Circ:** 2,000 (ctrl).
Desc: Publishes history and scattered facts of the Southwest. Each issue deals with one particular subject.

UK/0307-1022
SOCIAL HISTORY (LONDON). (SOCIAL HISTORY.). [Soc. hist.]. Vol. 1 (Jan. 1976)-. Periodical. English. Three times a year (Jan., May., Oct.). $115.00 (US & Canada); £75.00 (UK); £80.00 (other). Routledge, 11 New Fetter Lane, London EC4P 4EE England. **Tel** 071 583 9855, FAX 071 842 2298. **(Subscription address:** Kinokuniya Company Ltd., 38-1 Sakuragaoka 5, chome Setagaya-ku, Tokyo 156 Japan.**)** **ED** Janet Blackman and Keith Nield. **LC** HN1; .S56. **DD** 309/.05. **CODEN** SOHSEH. **[CCC]**. **Bk Rev**. **Ad Acc. Circ:** 900 (ctrl). Documents available from The Genuine Article, UMI Article Clearinghouse.
Desc: Articles and reviews in social historical writing, especially of a theoretical kind.
Ind/Abst Acad. Search (July 1993-); Am. Hist. Life (1976-); Arts Humanit. Citation Index [Full Cov.]; Br. Humanit. Index; Curr. Contents Arts Humanit.; Expand. Acad. Index (1989-); Humanit. Index; Humanit. Source (Jul. 1993-); INFO-SOUTH Abstr.; Int. Bibliogr. Sociol.; Mag. Search; Newsp. Period. Abstr. (1991-); Res. Alert [Full Cov.]; Soc. Plann. Policy Dev. Abstr.; Soc. Sci. Cit. Index [Select. Cov.]; Soc. Sci. Index.

IT
SOCIETA E STORIA. Vol. 1, No. 1 (1978)-. Periodical. Italian. Four times a year. L120000 Italy; L150000 other. Franco Angeli Riviste SRL, Viale Monza 106, 20127 Milan Italy. **Tel** 011 39 2 2827651, 011 39 2 289562. **Bk Rev**. **Ad Acc. Circ:** 3,000.
Ind/Abst Am. Hist. Life (1986-); BHA : Biblio. Hist. Art.

FR/1251-9103
SOCIETE D'EMULATION DES COTES-D'AMOUR. **VFOAT** Memoires de l'Annee... - Societe d'Emulation des Cotes-d'Amour. (1991)-. Periodical. French. Societe d'Emulation des Cotes du Nord, Saint-Brieuc France. ***Continues*** *Societe d'Emulation des Cotes du Nord, 0336-7290.*

UK
SOMERSET RECORD SOCIETY : [PUBLICATION]. **Added/Corp** Somerset Record Society. (1887)-. Monographic series. English. ir. Price varies per volume. Somerset Record Society, The Castle, Castle Green, Taunton TA1 4AD England. **Tel** 0823 288871, FAX 0823 336236. **LC** DA670.S49; S5. **Circ:** 250.
Desc: Devoted to publishing the text of a single historical source document or collections.

HU/0133-0748
SOPRONI SZEMLE. [Sopr. szle.]. (1937)-. Periodical. Hungarian. qt. **UDC** 943.9.
Ind/Abst BHA : Biblio. Hist. Art.

●RU
SOTSIALNYE I GUMANITARNYE NAUKI. SERIIA 5, ISTORIIA. OTECHESTVENNAIA LITERATURA / ROSSIISKAIA AKADEMIIA NAUK, INSTITUT NAUCHNOI INFORMATSII PO OBSHCHESTVENNYM NAUKAM.
Added/Corp Institut Nauchnoi Informatsii po Obshchestvennym Naukam (Rossiiskaia Akademiia Nauk). **VFOAT** Istoriia. Otechestvennaia Literatura. (1993)-. Academic Scholarly Publication. Russian. qt. Izdatelstvo Nauka / Akademiia Nauk, Publishing House of the Russian Academy of Sciences, Leninskii Porspekt 14, 117901 Moscow Russia. **Tel** 011 95 954-21-53, FAX 011 95 938-21-44, telex 411964. **LC** D1; .O14. ***Continues*** *Obshchestvennye Nauki v Rossii. Seriia 5, Istoriia.*

FR/0765-0124
SOURCES (PARIS). (SOURCES : REVUE DE L'ASSOCIATION "HISTOIRE AU PRESENT".). [Sources]. **Added/Corp** Association "Histoire au Present" (Paris, France). **VFOAT** Sources Travaux Historiques. No 1 (1985)-. Periodical. French (summaries and/or abstracts in English). qt. 200.00F (non members France); 220.00F (non members Europe); 250.00F (non members, other); 160.00F (members). Histoire au Present, 24 Rue de Ecoles, 75005 Paris France. **LC** IN PROCESS.
Ind/Abst Am. Hist. Life (1987-).

SA
SOUTH AFRICAN JOURNAL OF CULTURAL HISTORY. **Added/Corp** South African Society for Cultural History. **VFOAT** Suid-Afrikaanse Tydskrif vir Kultuurgeskiedenis; Cultural History; Kultuurgeskiedenis. Vol. 4, No. 1 (Jan. 1990)-. Periodical. English (Afrikaans). Twice a year (May & Nov.). R100.00. Science Africa, PO Box 40221, Arcadia 0007 South Africa. **Tel** 011 27 12 3486660. **ED** S. Kirksey. ***Continues in part*** *South African Journal of Cultural and Art History.*

FR/0246-1919
SOUVENIR NAPOLEONIEN, LE. (SOUVENIR NAPOLEONIEN.). [Souvenir napoleon.]. **Added/Corp** Societe d'Histoire Napoleoienne, Nice. No. 1 (June 1948)-. Periodical. French. Six times a year. 180.00F Comes with Societe d'Historie Napoleonienne membership. Souvenir Napoleonien, 82 rue de Monceau, 75008 Paris France. **Tel** 011 33 1 45223732. **Bk Rev**. **Ad Acc. Circ:** 2,000 (ctrl). ***Supersedes*** *Societe d'Histoire Napoleonienne, Nice. Bulletin, 0246-1897.*
Ind/Abst Am. Hist. Life (1955-1956).

US
SPECULUM ANNIVERSARY MONOGRAPHS. **Added/Corp** Mediaeval Academy of America. (1977)-. Monographic series. English. ir. Price varies per volume. Staz Sperimentale Combustibili, Viale Alcide De Gasperi 3, 20097 San Donato Milan Italy. **ED** Luke Wenger. **Circ:** 300.
Desc: Short studies on various aspects of the Middle Ages.

BL
SPHAN PRO-MEMORIA / FUNDACAO NACIONAL PRO-MEMORIA, SECRETARIA DO PATRIMONIO HISTORICO E ARTISTICO NACIONAL, MINISTERIO DA EDUCACAO E CULTURA. **VFOAT** S.P.H.A.N. Pro-Memoria. Periodical. Portuguese. bm. Funda Cao Nacional Pro-Memoria 2 Bloco K, CXP 04-0150 70.710, Brasilia DF Brazil. **LC** F2509.7; .S68. **UDC** 908.469.

NE/0038-7487
SPIEGEL HISTORIAEL. [Spieg. hist.]. Periodical. Dutch. mo. Drukkerij Ten Brink Spiegel, Historiael, Postbus 64, 7940 AB Meppel The Netherlands. **Tel** 02940-80480. **LC** D1; .S685. **UDC** 930.9. **Bk Rev. Ad Acc. Circ:** 8,500 (ctrl).
Desc: Articles on Dutch and world history and archaeology for the general reader.
Ind/Abst Am. Hist. Life (1966-); BHA : Biblio. Hist. Art; Br. Archaeol. Bibliogr.

GW
SPRACHSTRUKTUREN. REIHE A: HISTORISCHE SPRACHSTRUKTUREN. **VFOAT** Historische Sprachstrukturen. (1972)-. Monographic series. Multiple languages (English and German). ir. Price varies per volume. Max Niemeyer Verlag, Postfach 2140, D 72011 Tuebingen Germany. **Tel** 011 49 7071 989494, FAX 011 49 7071 87419. **ED** Herbert L. Kufner, Hugo Steger, Otmar Werner.
Ind/Abst MLA Int. Bibl. Books Artic. Mod. Lang. Lit.

PL/0137-5857
SPRAWOZDANIA - POZNANSKIE TOWARZYSTWO PRZYJACIO NAUK. WYDZIA HISTORII I NAUK SPOECZNYCH. (SPRAWOZDANIA. WYDZIA HISTORII I NAUK SPOECZNYCH.). (1973)-. Polish. ir. **UDC** 93/99.
Ind/Abst BHA : Biblio. Hist. Art.

RU
SREDNIE VEKA. (SREDNIE VEKA: SBORNIK.). **Main/Corp** Institut Vseobshchei Istorii (Akademiia Nauk SSSR). **Added/Corp** Institut Istorii (Akademiia Nauk SSSR). Vol. 1 (1942)-. Russian.

GW
STAAT UND KIRCHE IM 19 UND 20 JAHRHUNDERT. Monographic series. German. ir. Price varies per volume. Duncker und Humblot Verlag, Postfach 410329, D-12113 Berlin Germany. **Tel** 011 49 30 79000612, 011 49 30 79000613.

US/0270-5338
STOKVIS STUDIES IN HISTORICAL CHRONOLOGY & THOUGHT. [Stokvis stud. hist. chronol. thought]. No. 1 (1980)-. Monographic series. English. ir. Price varies per volume. Borgo Press, PO Box 2845, San Bernardino CA 92406. **Tel** (714)884-5813, (714)885-1161. **ED** Robert Reginald. **UDC** 930.24. Index available. **Circ:** 1,000.
Desc: Monographs covering a particular movement, event, or group with emphasis on historical and political background and factors leading to events. Contains bibliographies, notes and indexes.

IT/0039-1875
STORIA CONTEMPORANEA. [Stor. contemp.]. **Added/Corp** Societa Editrice il Mulino. Vol. 1 (March 1970)-. Periodical. Italian. bm. L90000.00 Italy; L160000.00 (surface mail), L180000.00 (airmail) other. Societa Editrice il Mulino, Strada Maggiore 37, 40125 Bologna Italy. **Tel** 011 39 51 256011, FAX 011 39 51 256034. **LC** D410; .S75. Documents available from The Genuine Article.
Ind/Abst Am. Hist. Life (1970-); ARTbibliogr. Mod.; Arts Humanit. Citation Index [Full Cov.]; Curr. Contents Arts Humanit.; Int. Bibliogr. Sociol.; Res. Alert [Full Cov.]; Soc. Sci. Cit. Index [Select. Cov.].

IT
STORIA CONTEMPORANEA IN FRIULI / ISTITUTO FRIULANO PER LA STORIA DEL MOVIMENTO DI LIBERAZIONE. **Added/Corp** Istituto Friulano per la Storia del Movimento di Liberazione. **VFOAT** Movimento di Liberazione in Friuli. Vol. 3, No. 4 (1973)-. Italian. an. L20000 Italy; L50000 others. Istituto Friulano per la Storia del Movimento di Liberazione, Biblioteca Comunale, Piazza Marconi 8, 33100 Udine Italy. **Tel** 011 39 432-295475. **LC** DG975.F85; S79. **DD** 945/.3909/05. ***Continues*** *Rassegna di Storia Contemporanea.*

IT
STORIA DELLA STORIOGRAFIA. **VFOAT** Histoire de l'Historiographie; History of Historiography; Storiografia. (1982)-. Periodical. Italian (English and French). sa. L50000 Italy; L65000 US. Editoriale Jaca Book, Via Gioberti 7, 20123 Milan Italy. **Tel** 011 39 2 4699044, FAX 011 39 2 48198361, telex 324267 JACATE. **ED** Valota Bianca. **LC** D13.2; .S85. **DD** 907/.2. **Bk Rev**. **Ad Acc. Circ:** 800.
Desc: Methodology and history of historical research in different ages and all over the world.
Ind/Abst Am. Hist. Life (1982-).

IT/0394-0209
STORIA E DOSSIER. [Stor. dors.]. Vol. 1, No. 1 (Nov. 1986)-. Periodical. Italian. Eleven times a year. L62000 Italy; L88000 other. Giunti Editore, Via Bolognese 165, 50139 Florence Italy. **Tel** 011 39 55 6679267, FAX 011 39 55 268312, telex 571438.

IT/0039-1905
STORIA E POLITICA. **Added/Corp** Universita di Roma. Istituto di Studi Storico-Politici Rome (City) Universita. Istituto di Studi Storici e Politici. (1962)-. Periodical. Italian. qt.
Ind/Abst Am. Hist. Life (1962-1984).

IT
STUDI DI STORIA MEDIOEVALE E DI DIPLOMATICA. **Added/Corp** Universita di Milano. (1976)-. Periodical. Italian. ir. Price varies. IST Storia Medievale, cia Chiaravalle 7 Univers, 20122 Milan Italy. **Tel** 011 39 2 58304553. **(Subscription address:** Vielle SRL, via Delle ALPI 32, 00198 Rome Italy.**)** **LC** DG501; .S87. **DD** 945.

IT
STUDI E FONTI DI STORIA LOMBARDA : QUADERNI MILANESI. Nuova Attivita Editoriale, Via Mercalli 23, 20122 Milan Italy.

IT/0039-2995
STUDI ROMANI. [Studi rom.]. **Added/Corp** Istituto di Studi Romani. Vol. 1 (1953)-. Periodical. Italian. qt. L50000 Italy; L70000 other. Istituto Nazionale Studi Romani, Piazza dei Cavalieri D Malta 2, 00153 Rome Italy. **Tel** 011 39 6 5743422, telex 5743442. **LC** WMLC 93/251. Index available. cum. index. **Bk Rev. Circ:** 2,000 (ctrl). Documents available from The Genuine Article.
Ind/Abst Am. Hist. Life (1973-); ARTbibliogr. Mod. (1983-); Arts Humanit. Citation Index [Full Cov.]; BHA : Biblio. Hist. Art; Curr. Contents Arts Humanit.; MLA Int. Bibl. Books Artic. Mod. Lang. Lit.; Res. Alert [Full Cov.]; Soc. Sci. Cit. Index [Select. Cov.].

IT
STUDI SETTECENTESCHI. Year 1, No. 1-. Periodical. Italian. sa. L24.000. Bibliopolis, Via Arangio Ruiz 83, 80122 Naples Italy. **Tel** 011 39 81 664606. **LC** D286; .S85. **DD** 909/.7/05.

IT
STUDI STORICI LUIGI SIMEONI. **Added/Corp** Istituto per Gli Studi Storici Veronesi (Verona, Italy). Vol. 32 (1982)-. Italian. an (Sept.). L50000 Italy; L60000 other. Instituto Studi Storici Veronesi, Via Leoncino 6, 37100 Verona Italy. **LC** DG401; .S897. **DD** 945. ***Continues*** *Studi Storici Veronesi Luigi Simeoni.*
Ind/Abst BHA : Biblio. Hist. Art.

IT
STUDI STORICI MERIDIONALI. Vol. 1, No. 1/2, (Jan./Aug. 1981)-. Periodical. Italian. Three times a year (April, Aug., Dec.). L41000.00 Italy; L82000.00 other. Capone Editore, Via Provinciale Lecce Cavallino, 73020 Cavallino Italy. **Tel** 011 39 832 612618, FAX 011 39 832 611877. **LC** DG819; .S83. **DD** 945/.7/005. cum. index. **Circ:** 1,000.

PO/0870-0028
STUDIA. Portuguese. ir. Instituto de Investigacao Cientifica Tropical, Centro de Documentacao e Informacao, rua Jau 47, 1 300 Lisbon Portugal. **Tel** 645321. **Circ:** 1,000.
Ind/Abst Bibliogr. Mission.

PL/0239-832X
STUDIA DO DZIEJOW DAWNEGO UZBROJENIA I UNIFORMU WOJSKOWEGO. [Stud. Dziejow Daw. Uzbroj. Unif. Wojsk.]. **VFOAT** Studies in History of Old Arms and Uniforms. (1982)-. Multiple languages. ir. **UDC** 355(091). ***Continues*** *Studia do Dziejow Dawnego Uzbrojenia i Ubioru Wojskowego, 0137-5733.*
Ind/Abst BHA : Biblio. Hist. Art.

SP/0213-2052
STUDIA HISTORICA. HA. ANTIQUA. **VFOAT** Ha. Antiqua; Studia Historica. Historia Antigua; Historia Antigua. Vol. 1 (1983)-. Spanish (summaries and/or abstracts in English). an. 1200ptas. Ediciones

History(General)

Universidad de Salamanca, Apartado Postal 325, 37080 Salamanca Spain. **Tel** 011 34 23 294598, FAX 011 34 23 263046. **LC** DP91; .S78.

SP/0213-2087
STUDIA HISTORICA. HA. CONTEMPORANEA. VFOAT Studia Historica. Historia Contemporanea; Ha. Contemporanea; Historia Contemporanea. Vol. 1 (1983)-. Spanish. an. 1200ptas. Ediciones Universidad de Salamanca, Apartado Postal 325, 37080 Salamanca Spain. **Tel** 011 34 23 294598, FAX 011 34 23 263046.

PL/0025-1429
STUDIA HISTORYCZNE. Added/Corp Polskie Towarzystwo Historyczne. Oddzia w Kielcach. Polska Akademia Nauk. Komisja Nauk Historycznych. Vol. 1, No. 1, (1958)-. Periodical. Polish. qt. $50.00. **(Subscription address:** ARS Polona, PO Box 1001, 00068 Warsaw Poland.**)**
Ind/Abst Am. Hist. Life (1981-).

IT
STUDIA URBANIANA. Monographic series. Italian. Price varies per volume. Urbaniana University Press, Vatican City, 00120 Rome Italy. **Tel** 06 6868640.

PL/0081-7104
STUDIA Z HISTORII SZTUKI. Added/Corp Warsaw. Pantswowy Instytut Historii. (19??)-. Monographic series. Polish.
Ind/Abst BHA : Biblio. Hist. Art.

PL/0081-7147
STUDIA ZRODOZNAWCZE. COMMENTATIONES. Added/Corp Polska Akademia Nauk. Instytut Historii. VFOAT Commentationes. (1957)-. Periodical. Polish (summaries and/or abstracts in English, French and Multiple languages). **LC** D13; S853.
Ind/Abst BHA : Biblio. Hist. Art.

GW
STUDIEN UBER ASIEN, AFRIKA UND LATEINAMERIKA. Added/Corp Zentraler Rat fuer Asien-, Afrika- und Lateinamerika-wissenschaften in der DDR. Vol. 1 (1972)-. Monographic series. German. ir. Price varies per volume. LKG Leipziger Kommissions & Grossbuchhandel, Leninstrasse 16, Postfach 520, D 04005 Leipzig, Germany. **Tel** 011 49 341 71370.

GW
STUDIEN ZUM WANDEL VON GESELLSCHAFT UND BILDUNG IM NEUNZEHNTEN JAHRHUNDERT. Vol. 1 (1971)-. Monographic series. German. ir. Price varies per volume. Vandenhoeck & Ruprecht, Robert Bosch Breite 6, D-37079 Goettingen Germany. **Tel** 011 49 551 695911, FAX 011 49 551 695917, telex 965226 VAN d. **Ad Acc**.

DK/0107-9212
STUDIER FRA SPROG- OG OLDTIDSFORSKNING. See Linguistics.

US
STUDIES AND DOCUMENTS. Vol.1 (1934)-. Monographic series. English. ir. Price varies per volume. Eerdmans Publishing Company, 255 Jefferson Avenue Southeast, Grand Rapids MI 49502. **Tel** (616)459-4591, (800)253-7521.

UK/0952-4975
STUDIES IN ANCIENT CHRONOLOGY. Vol. 1 (1987)-. English. ir. British School of Archaeology, 31-34 Gordon Square, London WC1 England. **Tel** 011 44 81 675 8343.
Ind/Abst Anthropol. Lit.

SW/1055-2464
STUDIES IN ANTHROPOLOGY AND HISTORY. See Anthropology.

US
STUDIES IN CONTEMPORARY HISTORY. Vol. 1 (1979)-. Monographic series. English. ir. Price varies per volume. Kluwer Academic Publishers / Massachusetts, PO Box 358, Accord Station, Hingham MA 02018. **Tel** (617)871-6600. **(Subscription address:** Kluwer Academic Publishers / Netherlands, PO Box 322, 3300 AH Dordrecht Netherlands.**)**

US/0360-2370
STUDIES IN EIGHTEENTH-CENTURY CULTURE. [Stud. eighteenth-century cult.].
Added/Corp American Society for Eighteenth-Century Studies. VFOAT Studies in Eighteenth Century Culture. Vol. 4 (1975)-. Periodical. Multiple languages (English and French). an. $32.00. Johns Hopkins University Press, 2715 North Charles Street, Baltimore MD 21218-4319. **Tel** (410)516-6987, FAX (410)516-6968. **ED** Carla H. Hay. **LC** CB411; .S8. **DD** 081. **Bk Rev**. **Ad Acc**. **Pr Rev**. **Circ:** 1,000. Documents available from The Genuine Article.
Ind/Abst Am. Hist. Life (1979-); Annu. Bibliogr. Engl. Lang. Lit.; Arts Humanit. Citation Index (19??-19??) [Full Cov.]; BHA : Biblio. Hist. Art; MLA Int. Bibl. Books Artic. Mod. Lang. Lit.; Res. Alert [Full Cov.]; Romant. Move.

DK/0078-3307
STUDIES IN HISTORY AND SOCIAL SCIENCES. Main/Corp Odense Universitet. Vol. 1 (1970)-. Monographic series. Danish (English and German). ir. Price varies per volume. Odense University Press, 55 Campusvej, DK-5230 Odense M Denmark. **Tel** 66 15 79 99, FAX 66 15 81 26. **Circ:** 30 (ctrl).

US
STUDIES IN THE HISTORY OF DISCOVERIES. English. ir. University of Chicago Press / Book Department, 11030 South Langley Avenue, Chicago IL 60628. **Tel** (800)621-2736, (312)568-1550, FAX (312)753-0811, telex 23933.

UK/0435-2866
STUDIES ON VOLTAIRE AND THE EIGHTEENTH CENTURY. See Literature.

BE
SUBSIDIA HAGIOGRAPHICA. See Religion and Theology-Catholicism.

CN/0823-2458
SYMPOSIUM / DEUTSCHKANADISCHE STUDIEN. See Literature.

IT
SYNESIS. *Ceased*. **See** Literature.

HU/0039-8098
SZAZADOK. [Szazadok]. Added/Corp Magyar Toertenelmi Tarsulat. Vol. 1 (1867)-. Periodical. Hungarian (summaries and/or abstracts in English, French, German and Russian). bm. $40.00. **(Subscription address:** Kultura, PO Box 149, H 1389 Budapest 62 Hungary.**) ED** S. Konya. **LC** DB901; .S9. cum. index. **Bk Rev**. **Circ:** 2,400 (ctrl).
Desc: Mainly Hungarian history but also studies on universal history. Theoretical and methodological problems. Reports on congresses and conferences at home and abroad.
Ind/Abst Am. Hist. Life (1979-).

US/0496-7607
TALES OF PARADISE RIDGE. Added/Corp Paradise Fact and Folklore (Organization). VFOAT Tales of Paradise Ridge. Vol. 1, No. 1 (June 1960)-. Periodical. English. Twice a year (June and Dec.). $9.00. Paradise Historical Society, and Fact & Folklore Inc, PO Box 1696, Paradise CA 95967. **Tel** (916)872-0359. **ED** Lois McDonald (phone: (916)873-6110). **LC** F869.P28; T3. **DD** 979.4/32. Index available. cum. index. **Circ:** 300 (ctrl).
Desc: History of the Paradise Ridge of Butte County, California. It includes some folklore, families, agriculture, and development in the mining and lumbering industry.
Ind/Abst Am. Hist. Life.

TU/1015-180X
TARIH ENSTITUSU DERGISI. [Tarih Enst. derg.]. Main/Corp Istanbul Universitesi. Tarih Enstitusu. (1970)-. Turkish. ir. Elif Kitabevi, Sahhaflar Carsisi 4, Beyazit Istanbul Turkey. **LC** D1; .I7.
Ind/Abst Am. Hist. Life (1970-).

UK/0085-7114
TEACHERS OF HISTORY IN THE UNIVERSITIES AND POLYTECHNICS OF THE UNITED KINGDOM. See Education-Higher Education.

US/0730-1383
TEACHING HISTORY (EMPORIA, KAN.). (TEACHING HISTORY.). [Teach. hist.]. Added/Corp Emporia Kansas State College. Emporia State University. Vol. 1 (Spring 1976)-. Periodical. English. sa. $10.00 (one year), $24.00 (three year). Division of Social Science, PO Box 4032 ESU, Emporia KS 66801. **Tel** (316)341-5579, FAX (316)343-5997. **ED** Stephen Kneeshaw. **Bk Rev**. **Ad Acc**. **Pr Rev**. **Circ:** 450.
Desc: Articles and reviews by and for those who train history teachers or who teach history at secondary, undergraduate and graduate levels.
Ind/Abst Am. Hist. Life (1976-); Curr. Index J. Educ.

UK/0040-0610
TEACHING HISTORY (LONDON). See Education-Teaching and Curriculum.

AT/0040-0602
TEACHING HISTORY SYDNEY. See Education-Teaching and Curriculum.

US/0516-9216
TECHNICAL LEAFLET / AMERICAN ASSOCIATION FOR STATE AND LOCAL HISTORY. Added/Corp American Association for State and Local History. July (1962)-. Monographic series. English. Price varies per volume. American Association for State and Local History, 530 Church Street, Suite 600, Nashville TN 37219. **Tel** (615)255-2971, FAX (615)255-2979. **LC** E172; .A542a.

PL/0082-5514
TEKA. Main/Corp Towarzystwo Naukowe w Toruniu. Komisja Historii Sztuki. (1959)-. Polish. **LC** N6991; .T65.
Ind/Abst BHA : Biblio. Hist. Art.

UK/0085-4956
TEKI HISTORYCZNE / POLSKIE TOWARZYSTWO HISTORYCZNE W WIELKIEJ BRYTANII. [Teki hist. - Pol. Tow. Hist. Wielkiej Br.]. Added/Corp Polskie Towarzystwo Historyczne w Wielkiej Brytanii. Polskie Towarzystwo Historyczne na Obczyznie. VFOAT Cahiers d'Histoire; Historical Papers. (1947)-. Polish.
Ind/Abst Am. Hist. Life (1954-1971).

US/0082-3759
TEXTS FROM CUNEIFORM SOURCES. Vol. 1 (1966)-. Monographic series. English. ir. Price varies per volume. J J Augustin Inc, PO Box 311, Locust Valley NY 11560. **Tel** (516)676-1510.

GW/0167-8310
THEORETISCHE GESCHIEDENIS. Added/Corp Stichting Theoretische Geschiedenis. VFOAT Historiography and Theory; Tg. (19??)-. Periodical. German. qt.
Ind/Abst Am. Hist. Life (1988-).

GW/0563-4970
THURN UND TAXIS-STUDIEN. Added/Corp Ratisbon. Furstlich Thurn und Taxissches Zentralarchiv. Ratisbon. Furstlich Thurn und Taxissches Hofbibliothek. (1961)-. English. **LC** D107.9.T3; T5.
Ind/Abst BHA : Biblio. Hist. Art.

NE/0040-7518
TIJDSCHRIFT VOOR GESCHIEDENIS (1920). (TIJDSCHRIFT VOOR GESCHIEDENIS.). [Tijdschr. geschied.]. (1920)-. Academic Scholarly Publication. Dutch. qt (Mar., June, Sept., Dec.). F97.50 Netherlands; Fl95.75 other. Wolters Noordhoff BV, Postbus 567, 9700 AN Groningen Netherlands. **Tel** 011 31 50 226886, FAX 011 31 50 264866. **LC** D1; .T5. **Bk Rev**. **Ad Acc**. **Circ:** 3,000 (ctrl). Documents available from The Genuine Article. *Continues* Tijdschrift Voor Geschiedenis, Land- en Volkenkunde.
Desc: Scholarly journal in the field of general history.
Ind/Abst Am. Hist. Life (1954-); Arts Humanit. Citation Index (19??-19??) [Full Cov.]; Curr. Contents Arts Humanit.; Res. Alert [Full Cov.]; Soc. Sci. Cit. Index [Select. Cov.].

US
TIME ANNUAL : THE YEAR IN REVIEW / BY THE EDITORS OF TIME. Added/Corp Time-Life Books. VFOAT Year in Review. (1969)-. English. an. Time-Life Books, Time & Life Building, New York NY 10020. **Tel** (312)329-6800, (800)621-7026. **LC** D1050; .T56. **DD** 917.3/03/92405.

●US/1054-5042
TIME TABLE OF HISTORY. BUSINESS, POLITICS, AND MEDIA. (TIME TABLE OF HISTORY. BUSINESS, POLITICS, AND MEDIA [COMPUTER FILE].). [Time table hist., Bus. polit. media]. **Added/Corp** Xiphias (Firm). VFOAT Timetable of History. Business, Politics, and Media; Business, Politics, and Media. (1992)-. English. ir. $74.95. Xiphias, Helms Hall, 8758 Venice Boulevard, Los Angeles CA 90034. **Tel** (310)841-2790, FAX (310)841-2559. **(Subscription address:** New Media Source, 3830 Valley Centre Drive, Suite 215, San Diego CA 92130.**)**

HU/0040-9634
TOERTENELMI SZEMLE. [Toert. szle.]. **Added/Corp** Magyar Tudomanyos Akademia. Toertenettudomanyi Intezet. Vol. 1 (1958)-. Periodical. Hungarian (summaries and/or abstracts in Russian and French). qt. $27.50. Magyar Tudomanyos Akademia, Tortenettudomanyi Intezet, Uri u. 53, 1014 Budapest, Hungary. **ED** F. Szakaly. **Bk Rev**. **Circ:** 1,600 (ctrl). *Supersedes* Magyar Tudomanyos Akademia Toertenettudomanyi Intezetenek Ertesitoeje.
Desc: Hungarian and world history, especially 20th century history, studies, lectures, congress reports by Hungarian and international contributors.
Ind/Abst Am. Hist. Life (1958-).

JA
TOKAI SHIGAKU. Added/Corp Tokai Daigaku Shigakkai. (19??)-. Periodical. Japanese. Tokai Daigaku Bungakubu, (Tokei University, Faculty of Literature), Shigeku Kenkyushitsu 1117 Kita Kaname, Hiratsuka Japan. **LC** D1; .T65.

UK
TOWN HISTORY SERIES. No. 1- 1983-. Monographic series. English. Price varies per volume.

AG
TRABAJOS Y COMUNICACIONES / FACULTAD DE HUMANIDADES Y CIENCIAS DE EDUCACION, INSTITUTO DE INVESTIGACIONES HISTORICAS.
Added/Corp Universidad Nacional de la Plata. Departamento de Historia. Universidad Nacional de la Plata. Instituto de Investigaciones Historicas. (1949)-. Spanish. an. cum. index.
Ind/Abst Am. Hist. Life (1959-1978).

CN/0841-6397
TRACES (MONTREAL). See Education-Teaching and Curriculum.

FR/0996-5904
TRANSEUPHRATENE PARIS. (TRANSEUPHRATENE.). [Transeuphratene Paris]. (1989)-. Periodical. Multiple languages. ir. 243.50F. J Gabalda & Cie Editeurs, 18 rue Pierre et Marie Curie, 75005 Paris France. **Tel** 011 33 1 43265355. **UDC** 935.5.

SZ/0082-6073
TRAVAUX D'HISTOIRE ETHICO-POLITIQUE. (1963)-. Monographic series. French. ir. Price varies per volume. Librairie Droz SA, 11 rue Massot BP 389, CH 1211 Geneva 12 Switzerland. **Tel** 011 41 22 3466666, FAX 011 41 22 472391. **[CCC]. Circ:** 400.
Desc: Covers all aspects of history.

GW/0041-2716
TRIBUNE. [Tribune]. 1.- Yearly V. (No. 1-); 1962-. Periodical. German. qt. DM36.00. Habsburgerallee 72, 6000 Frankfurt Germany. **LC** DS101; .T7. **DD** 909/.04924. **UDC** 930.9.
Ind/Abst Philos. Index.

US/0564-2744
TRINITY. [Trinity]. **Added/Corp** Trinity County Historical Society. (19??)-. English. an (Dec.). $4.00. Trinity County Historical Society, PO Box 333, 508 Main Street, Weaverville CA 96093. **Tel** (916)623-5211. **LC** F868.T6; T75. **DD** 979.4/14/05.
Desc: History of Trinity County, its people and events.
Ind/Abst Am. Hist. Life.

IS
TSIKLON. Vol. 1- August 1976-. Periodical. Hebrew. Maarakhot Bet Ha-Hotsaah Shel, Tseva Haganah Le-Yisrae, Rehov Gimel No 1 Hakiryah, POB 7026, Tel-Aviv Israel. **LC** D839; .T79.

RU
UCHENYE ZAPISKI PO NOVOI I NOVEISHEI ISTORII. **Added/Corp** Institut Istorii (Akademiia Nauk SSSR). Vol. 1 (1955)-. Russian. an. Izdatelstvo Nauka / Akademiia Nauk, Publishing House of the Russian Academy of Sciences, Leninskii Porspekt 14, 117901 Moscow Russia. **Tel** 011 95 954-21-53, FAX 011 95 938-21-44, telex 411964. **LC** D1; .A353.
Ind/Abst Am. Hist. Life (1955-1958).

US/0276-864X
UCLA HISTORICAL JOURNAL. [UCLA hist. j.]. **Added/Corp** University of California, Los Angeles. History Graduate Students Association. **VFOAT** U.C.L.A. Historical Journal; University of California, Los Angeles Historical Journal. Vol. 1, (1980)-. English. an (Oct.). $10.00 (individuals); $12.00 (institutions). U.C.L.A., Department of History, Los Angeles CA 90024. **Tel** (310)825-3269. **ED** Jo Ann Woodsum, (Editor in Chief, (phone: (310)859-7848). **LC** D1; .U28. **DD** 905. cum. index (Vol. 14). **Bk Rev**, (Qty: 8). **Ad Acc**. **Pr Rev. Circ:** 400.
Desc: This is dedicated to promoting excellence in graduate students research and writings. This journal welcomes submissions from all fields of history and related disciplines.
Ind/Abst Am. Hist. Life (1980-); Writ. Am. Hist.

UN/0130-5247
UKRAINSKIJ ISTORICNIJ ZURNAL. (UKRAINSKYI ISTORYCHNYI ZHURNAL.). [Ukr. istor. z.]. **Added/Corp** Instytut Istorii (Akademiia Nauk Ukrainskoi RSR). (1957)-. Periodical. Ukrainian (English; summaries and/or abstracts in Russian and English; table of contents in Russian and English). mo. $99.95. **(Subscription address:** East View Publications Inc., 3020 Harbor Lane North, Suite 110, Minneapolis MN 55447.**)**
Ind/Abst Am. Hist. Life (1965-); Numis. Lit.

NE/0503-1486
UMBRAE CODICUM OCCIDENTALIUM. No. 1-. Monographic series. Dutch (English). ir. Price varies per volume. Elsevier Science Publishers BV, PO Box 211, 1000 AE Amsterdam Netherlands. **Tel** 011 31 20 5803642, FAX 011 31 20 5862696, telex 15682. **UDC** 950.

BE/0304-3169
UNESCO KOERIER. See The Arts.

FR
UNESCO WORLD REVIEW. **Added/Corp** U.S. National Commission for UNESCO. No. 1 (Feb. 19, 1949)-. Periodical. English. wk. UNESCO / France, 31 rue Francois Bonvin, 75732 Paris Cedex 15 France. **Tel** 011 33 1 45684564, 011 33 1 45684565, FAX 011 33 1 42733007, telex 204461 Paris. **LC** D410; .U55. **DD** 940.55.

FR
UNIFORMES. French. bm. 117.00F. Argout Editions, 138 rue Montmartre, 75002 Paris France. **Tel** 236 1264.

SZ/0566-263X
UNSERE KUNSTDENKMALER. See The Arts-Art.

GW
UNTERSUCHUNGEN ZUR ANTIKEN LITERATUR UND GESCHICHTE. Vol. 1 (1968)-. Monographic series. German. ir. Price varies per volume. Walter de Gruyter Inc., PO Box 303421, D 10728 Berlin Germany. **Tel** 011 49 30 260050, FAX 011 49 30 26005251.

IT
URSS OGGI. ***Ceased.*** **Main/Corp** Soviet Union. Posolstvo (Italy). Ufficio Stampa. Italian. mo. Novostitalia, Via Clitunno 34, 00198 Rome Italy. **Tel** 011 39 6 8552811. **LC** DK274; .R84A. **DD** 947.085/05.

RU
V GODINU VELIKOI VOINY. ***Ceased.*** **Added/Corp** Russia. Upravlenie po Dielam Melkago Kredita. (1916)-(19??). Russian. an.

US/0887-4026
VARIA AEGYPTIACA. [Varia aegypt.]. Vol. 1, No. 1/2 (Aug. 1985)-. Periodical. English (French and German). Three times a year. $32.00 (institutions), $26.00 (individuals). Van Siclen Books, 111 Winnetka Road, San Antonio TX 78229. **Tel** (512)522-1353. **ED** Charles Van Siclen. **LC** WMLC 93/4411. **DD** 932. **Bk Rev. Circ:** 150.
Desc: Covers all aspects of ancient Egypt.

GW/0436-1180
VEROFFENTLICHUNGEN - MAX-PLANCK-INSTITUT FUER GESCHICHTE. **Main/Corp** Max - Planck - Institut fuer Geschichte. Vol. 1 (1950)-. Monographic series. German. ir. Price varies per volume. Vandenhoeck & Ruprecht, Robert Bosch Breite 6, D-37079 Goettingen Germany. **Tel** 011 49 551 695911, FAX 011 49 551 695917, telex 965226 VAN d. **DD** 900. **Ad Acc.**

GW/0083-5846
VERSTANDLICHE WISSENSCHAFT. [VerstËandl. Wiss.]. Vol. 1 (1927)-. Monographic series. German. ir. Price varies per volume. Springer-Verlag New York Inc., 175 5th Avenue, New York NY 10010. **Tel** (212)460-1500, telex 232 235 SPB UR. **(Subscription address:** Springer Verlag New York Inc. / for North America, 44 Hartz Way, Secaucus NJ 07096.**) CODEN** VEWIAL. Documents available from BIOSIS Document Express.
Ind/Abst Biol. Abstr. (-1981).

GW/0506-8010
VESTIGIA. Vol. 1, (1959)-. Monographic series. German. Price varies per volume. Quelle & Meyer, Greenhall, Lawrence KS 66044. **DD** 930.

RU/0321-0391
VESTNIK DREVNEJ ISTORII. (VESTNIK DREVNEI ISTORII. JOURNAL OF ANCIENT HISTORY.). [Vestn. drevnej istor.]. **Added/Corp** Institut Istorii (Akademiia Nauk SSSR) Institut Vseobshchei Istorii (Akademiia Nauk SSSR). **VFOAT** Journal of Ancient History; Revue d'Histoire Ancienne. Vol. 1 (1937)-. Russian (Russian; summaries and/or abstracts in English). qt. $156.00. Izdatelstvo Nauka / Akademiia Nauk, Publishing House of the Russian Academy of Sciences, Leninskii Porspekt 14, 117901 Moscow Russia. **Tel** 011 95 954-21-53, FAX 011 95 938-21-44, telex 411964. **(Subscription address:** Victor Kamkin, 4956 Boiling Brook Parkway, Rockville, MD 20852**) LC** D51; .V47. **[CCC]**. cum. index.
Desc: Emphasis on ancient history.
Ind/Abst Anthropol. Lit.; BHA : Biblio. Hist. Art; Numis. Lit. (?-?).

RU/0505-3862
VESTNIK ISTORII MIROVOI KULTURY. ***Ceased.*** [Vestn. istor. mir. kult.]. **Added/Corp** Akademiia nauk SSSR. Otdelenie Istoricheskikh nauk. Akademiia nauk SSSR. Otdelenie Ekonomicheskikh, Filosofskikh i Pravovykh Nauk. **VFOAT** Revue d'Histoire de la Civilisation Mondiale. (1957)-(19??). Periodical. Russian (English and French; summaries and/or abstracts in German). bm. **LC** CB3; .V45.
Ind/Abst Am. Hist. Life (1957-1961).

RU
VESTNIK MOSKOVSKOGO UNIVERSITETA. SERIIA VIII: ISTORIIA. **Main/Corp** Moskovskii Gosudarstvennyi Universitet Im. M.V. Lomonosova. **VFOAT** Istoriia. (Jan./Feb. 1977)-. Periodical. Russian. Six times a year. $109.95. Izdatelstvo Moskovskogo Universiteta, K-9 Ulitsa Gertsena 5/7, Moscow Russia. **Tel** (301)881-5973. **(Subscription address:** East View Publications Inc., 3020 Harbor Lane North, Suite 110, Minneapolis MN 55447.**) LC** D1; .M63a. ***Supersedes** Vestnik Moskovskogo Universiteta. Seriia IX, Istoriia, 0130-0083 65058189.*
Ind/Abst Am. Hist. Life (1977-).

●RU
VESTNIK SANKT-PETERBURGSKOGO UNIVERSITETA. SERIIA 2, ISTORIIA, IAZYKOZNANIE, LITERATUROVEDENIE. **Added/Corp** Sankt-Peterburgskii Universitet. **VFOAT** Istoriia, Iazykoznanie, Literaturovedenie. (1992)-. Periodical. Russian (summaries and/or abstracts in English). qt. $99.95. St Petersburg State University / Izdatelstvo Leningradskogo Universiteta, Universitetskaia Nab 7/9, 199034 St Petersburg Russia. **Tel** 011 95 218-97-88, FAX 011 95 218-51-52, telex 121481. **(Subscription address:** East View Publications Inc., 3020 Harbor Lane North, Suite 110, Minneapolis MN 55447.**) LC** AS262; .L463 subser. ***Continues** Vestnik Leningradskogo Universiteta. Seriia 2, Istoriia, Iazykoznanie, Literaturovedenie.*

IT
VIAGGI DI ERODOTO. (19??)-. Italian. Three times a year. L50000 Italy; L80000 other. Ed Scolastiche Bruno Mondadori, Via Archimede 23, 20129 Milan Italy. **Tel** 011 39 2 76009881.

US/1040-6972
VICTORIA'S ERA. (VICTORIA'S ERA : OFFICIAL NEWSLETTER OF THE VICTORIAN RECREATION SOCIETY.). [Victoria's era]. Vol. 1, Issue 1 (Sept. 1988)-. Newsletter. English. qt. $5.00 US; $7.50 other. Specialty News Service, PO Box 258, Montville OH 44064. **DD** 909.

FR
VIE OUVRIERE, LA. ***Title Change.*** **Added/Corp** Confederation Generale du Travail. (Oct. 5, 1909)-(1993). Periodical. French. Fifty-two times a year. Editions de la Ouvriere, 33 rue Bouret, 75940 Paris Cedex 19 France. **Tel** 011 33 1 40403636. **LC** D731; .V53. **DD** 940.53/05. ***Continued by** Hebdo de l'Actualite Sociale.*

GW/0042-5702
VIERTELJAHRSHEFTE FUER ZEITGESCHICHTE. [Vierteljahrsh. Zeitgesch.]. **Added/Corp** Institut fuer Zeitgeschichte (Munich, Germany). Vol. 1 (Jan. 1953)-. Periodical. German. qt. DM78.00. R Oldenbourg Verlag, Postfach 801360, D 81613 Munich Germany. **Tel** 011 49 89 450190, FAX 011 49 89 45019305. **ED** K.D. Brachen and H.P. Schwarz. **LC** D410; .V5. **DD** 905. **[CCC]. Ad Acc. Circ:** 5,000. Documents available from The Genuine Article.
Desc: Principle German language forum for studies in contemporary history; for students and teachers of history, politicians, jurists and journalists.
Ind/Abst Am. Hist. Life (1954-); Arts Humanit. Citation Index [Full Cov.]; Curr. Contents Arts Humanit.; Int. Polit. Sci. Abstr.; Res. Alert [Full Cov.]; Soc. Sci. Cit. Index [Select. Cov.].

GW/0506-9408
VIERTELJAHRSHEFTE FUER ZEITGESCHICHTE. SCHRIFTENREIHE. No. 1 (1960)-. Monographic series. German. Twice a year. DM78.00. R Oldenbourg Verlag, Postfach 801360, D 81613 Munich Germany. **Tel** 011 49 89 450190, FAX 011 49 89 45019305. **Bk Rev. Circ:** 1,200.

US/1046-2902
VIETNAM (LEESBURG, VA.). (VIETNAM.). [Vietnam]. Vol. 1, No. 1 (Summer 1988)-. Periodical. English. bm (6 issues). $16.95. Cowles Magazines, PO Box 8200, Harrisburg PA 17105. **Tel** (717)657-9555, (800)435-9610. **(Subscription address:** Kable Publishers Aide, 308 East Hitt Street, Subscription Department, Mt. Morris, IL 61054**) ED** Harry G. Summers, Jr. **LC** WMLC 93/1465. **DD** 973.
Desc: Takes a popular history approach, examining the American experience and lessons of the war, as well as its personalities, weapons and battles.

US/0899-6601
VIETNAM UPDATE. [Vietnam update]. Vol. 1, No. 1 & 2; Winter/Spring 1988-. Periodical. English (Vietnamese and French). qt. $20.00, $5.00 (single issues) issue. Institute for Democracy in Vietnam, 815-15th Street NW/Suite 511, Washington DC 20005. **Tel** (209)435-4962, FAX (202)628-5946. **(Subscription address:** Institute for Democracy in Vietnam, PO Box 9175, Fresco, CA 93790**) ED** Matthews Chanoff and Doan Van Toai. **Bk Rev. Ad Acc.** ctrl circ.

US/1049-9199
VIEWPOINT. (VIEWPOINT / NATIONAL COUNCIL OF YOUNG ISRAEL.). [Viewp.]. (1989)-. Periodical. English. bm. $25.00 (members), $50.00 (nonmembers). National Council of Young Israel, 3 West 16th Street, New York NY 10011. **LC** BM1; .Y68. **DD** 909. ***Continues** Young Israel Viewpoint, 0044-0809.*

HU/0083-6265
VILAGTORTENET. [Vilagtortenet]. **Added/Corp** Magyar Tudomanyos Akademia. Tortenettudomanyi Intezet. (19??)-. Periodical. Hungarian. qt. **LC** WMLC L 83/3845.
Ind/Abst Am. Hist. Life (1967-1974,1979-).

FR/0294-1759
VINGTIEME SIECLE (PARIS, FRANCE : 1984). (VINGTIEME SIECLE.). [Vingtieme siecle]. **VFOAT** 20E Siecle. No. 1 (Jan. 1984)-. Periodical. French. qt. 395.00F (France), 460.00F (other) institution; 270.00F (France), 315.00F (other) individual. Presses de la Fondation, Nationale des Sciences Politiques, 44 Rue du Four, 75006 Paris France. **Tel** 011 33 1 44393960, FAX 011 33 1 45480441. **LC** D410; .V54. **DD** 909.82/05. **UDC** 930.9 "19". **[CCC]**.
Ind/Abst Am. Hist. Life (1987-); Int. Polit. Sci. Abstr.

History(General)

GR
VIVLIO TES CHRONIAS. **VFOAT** Year Book; Biblo Tes Chronias. Vol. 1 (1979)-. Greek, Modern. an. Dr500.00. Amerikes 4, Athens 133 Greece. **LC** DF701; .V58.

RU/0253-2581
VIZANTIJSKIJ VREMENNIK. See The Arts-Art.

RU
VOENNO-ISTORICHESKII ZHURNAL : ORGAN MINISTERSTVA OBORONY SOIUZA SSR. See Military and Defense.

RU
VOPROSY ISTOCHNIKOVEDENIIA I ISTORIOGRAFII. **Added/Corp** Dalnevostochnyi Gosudarstvenyi Universitet (Vladivostik, R.S.F.S.R.) Russian S.F.S.R. Ministerstvo Vysshego i Srednego Spetsialnogo Obrazovaniia. (19??)-. Periodical. Russian. 0.49rub. **LC** D6; .V64.

RU/0042-8779
VOPROSY ISTORII. (VOPROSY ISTORII / AKADEMIIA NAUK SSSR, INSTITUT ISTORII.). [Vopr. istor.]. **Added/Corp** Akademiia Nauk SSSR. Otdelenie Istorii. Institut Istorii (Akademiia Nauk SSSR) Akademiia Nauk SSSR. Otdelenie Istoricheskikh Nauk. Soviet Union. Ministerstvo Vysshego i Srednego Spetsialnogo Obrazovaniia. (1945)-. Periodical. Russian. mo. $119.95. Izdatelstvo Pressa, Myasnitskaia 24, 101877 Moscow Russia. **Tel** 011 95 923 2122, FAX 011 95 200 2259. **(Subscription address:** East View Publications Inc., 3020 Harbor Lane North, Suite 110, Minneapolis MN 55447.**)** **[CCC]**. Index available. **Bk Rev**. available on microfilm from University Microfilms International (UMI). Documents available from The Genuine Article. ***Continues*** *Istoricheskii Zhurnal (Moscow, R.S.F.S.R.).*
Ind/Abst Am. Hist. Life (1954-1961, 1963-); Arts Humanit. Citation Index [Full Cov.]; Curr. Contents Arts Humanit.; Int. Bibliogr. Sociol.; Numis. Lit.; Res. Alert [Full Cov.]; Soc. Plann. Policy Dev. Abstr.; Soc. Welf. Soc. Plan./Policy Soc. Dev.; Sociol. Abstr.; Curr. Dig. Post Sov. Press.

RU
VOSTOK--ZAPAD. (1982)-. Russian. Six times a year. $79.95. **(Subscription address:** East View Publications Inc., 3020 Harbor Lane North, Suite 110, Minneapolis MN 55447.**)** **LC** CB251; .V67.

US/1062-7634
VOYAGEUR (GREEN BAY, WIS.). (VOYAGEUR : HISTORICAL REVIEW OF BROWN COUNTY AND NORTHEAST WISCONSIN.). [Voyageur]. **Added/Corp** University of Wisconsin--Green Bay. Dept. of History. Brown County Historical Society (Wis.). Vol. 1, No. 1 (June 1984)-. Periodical. English. Twice a year (Summer/Fall and Winter/Spring). $9.00 (individual); $10.00 (institution). Brown County Historical Society, PO Box 8085, Green Bay WI 54308. **Tel** (414)465-2446. **ED** Dean O'Brien. **DD** 977. Index available. cum. index. **Bk Rev**, (Qty: 15). **Ad Acc**, **Adv Mgr:** P. Viets, **Tel** (414)465-2446. **Circ:** 5,000.
Desc: It about the history of a 17-county region of Northeast Wisconsin.

RU/0507-5238
VSPOMOGATELNYE ISTORICHESKIE DISTSIPLINY. **Added/Corp** Akademiia Nauk SSSR. Arkheograficheskaia Komissiia. Leningradskoe Otdelenie. (1968)-. Russian. ir. Izdatelstvo Nauka / Akademiia Nauk, Publishing House of the Russian Academy of Sciences, Leninskii Porspekt 14, 117901 Moscow Russia. **Tel** 011 95 954-21-53, FAX 011 95 938-21-44, telex 411964.
Ind/Abst Numis. Lit.

CH
WAI KUO SHIH CHIH SHIH. **VFOAT** Waiguoshi Zhishi. Periodical. Chinese. mo. NT$0.27. Science Press, 16 Donghuangchenggen North Street, Beijing 100707, People's Republic of China. **Tel** 011 86 1 4019821, 011 86 1 4010642, FAX 011 86 1 4012180, 011 86 1 4019810, telex 210147. **LC** D20; .W35. **DD** 905. **UDC** 930.9.

AT/0729-2473
WAR & SOCIETY. **Added/Corp** University of New South Wales. Dept. of History. **VFOAT** War and Society. Vol. 1, No. 1 (May 1983)-. Academic Scholarly Publication. English. sa (May and October). 22.00Aus$ Australia; $22.00 US. University of New South Wales / Department of History, Australian Defence Force Academy, CAMBELL, ACT 2601 Australia. **Tel** (06)2688875, FAX (06)2688879. **ED** J. Grey, R. Prior. **LC** HM36.5; .W35. **DD** 303.6/6/05. **Ad Acc. Circ:** 400.
Desc: Journal is designed to provide a forum for the discussion of the history of war and its impact on society. Publishes scholarly articles on causes, experiences, and impact of war in all periods of history.
Ind/Abst Am. Hist. Life (1984-); Curr. Mil. Pol. Lit.

UK/0968-3445
WAR IN HISTORY. (19??)-. English. Three times a year. $85.00 (institution), $40.00 (individual) US; £56.00 (institution), £25.00 (individual) EC; £60.00 (institution), £30.00 (individual) other. Edward Arnold, 338 Euston Road, London NW1 3BH England. **Tel** 011 44 71 873 6000, FAX 011 44 071 873 6325. **(Subscription address:** Turpin Distribution Services Limited, Blackhorse Road, Letchworth, Hertfordshire SG6 1HN, United Kingdom.**)** **ED** Hew Strachan, Dennis Showalter.
Desc: Based on the premise that military history should be integrated into a broader definition of history, the journal covers war in all its aspects: economic, social, and political as well as purely military. Articles include the study of navies, maritime power, and air forces of all time periods.
Ind/Abst Am. Hist. Life (19??-); Hist. Abstr. (19??-).

GW/0511-4233
WEHRMACHT IM KAMPF, DIE. Vol. 1 (1954)-. Monographic series. German. Price varies per volume. **LC** D757; .W37.

CC
WEI LAI YU FA CHAN / FUTURE AND DEVELOPMENT. **Added/Corp** Chung-Kuo Wei Lai Yen Chiu Hui. **VFOAT** Future and Development. (19??)-. Periodical. Chinese. qt. Post Office Beijing, Beijing, People's Republic of China. **LC** CB161; .W44.

UK/0261-5681
WEST SURREY FAMILY HISTORY SOCIETY RECORD SERIES. **Added/Corp** West Surrey Family History Society. **VFOAT** Record Series. (1981)-. Monographic series. English. ir. Price varies per volume. West Surrey Family History Society, 5 Blaise Close, Farnborough GU14 7EW England. **LC** UNC.

US/0735-0392
WESTERN CIVILIZATION. **VFOAT** Readings in Western Civilization; Annual Editions. Western Civilization. 1st Ed. (1981)-. Periodical. English. be. $10.95. Dushkin Publishing Group Inc., Sluice Dock, Guilford CT 06437. **Tel** (203)453-4351, (800)243-6532, FAX (203)453-6000. **ED** William Hughes. **LC** CB245; .W46. **DD** 909/.09821.
Desc: Collection of public press articles covering civilization. Contains a broad range of thought-provoking articles. Includes topic guide and complete index.

US/0896-2189
WESTERN LEGAL HISTORY. See Law.

US/0512-5804
WHAT THEY SAID. (1969)-. English. an (Summer of the following year). $41.00 (latest volume). Monitor Book Company Inc, PO Box 9078, Palm Springs CA 92263-7078. **Tel** (619)323-2270. **ED** Alan F. Pater and Jason R. Pater. **LC** D410; .W46. **DD** 901.9/4. **Bk Rev. Ad Acc.**
Desc: A collection of quotations from speeches, interviews and by persons in all walks of life categorized by subject.

US/0748-8114
WHITE HOUSE HISTORY. (WHITE HOUSE HISTORY : JOURNAL OF THE WHITE HOUSE HISTORICAL ASSOCIATION.). [White House hist.]. **Added/Corp** White House Historical Association. Vol. 1 No. 1 (1983)-. Periodical. English. ir. $6.00. White House Historical Association, 740 Jackson Place Northwest, Washington DC 20503. **Tel** (202)737-8292. **ED** William Seale. **LC** F204.W5; W64.
Desc: An occasional journal about the history of the White House.
Ind/Abst Am. Hist. Life (1983-); Avery Index Archit. Period. Suppl. Colum. Univ. (1984-199?).

US/1046-1000
WHOM NEWSLETTER / WOMEN HISTORIANS OF THE MIDWEST. [WHOM newsl.]. **VAT** Women Historians of the Midwest Newsletter. Vol. 1, No. 1 (Jan. 25, 1973)-. Newsletter. English. sm. $10.00. Women Historians of Midwest, PO Box 8138 Como Station, St Paul MN 55108. **DD** 305. available on microfilm.

PL/0511-9162
WIADOMOSCI HISTORYCZNE. [Wiad. hist.]. **Added/Corp** Poland. Ministerstwo Oswiaty i Wychowania. Polskie Towarzystwo Historyczne. Poland. Ministerstwo Oswiaty i Szkolnictwa Wyzszego. Poland. Ministerstwo Oswiaty. Vol. 1 No. 1 (1958)-. Periodical. Polish. Five times a year. $38.00. **(Subscription address:** ARS Polona, PO Box 1001, 00068 Warsaw Poland.**)** **LC** D16.4.P6; W49.
Ind/Abst Am. Hist. Life (1962-1967).

AU/0084-0076
WIENER ZEITSCHRIFT FUER DIE KUNDE DES MORGENLANDES. [Wien. Z. Kunde Morgenl.]. **VFOAT** Vienna Oriental Journal. Vol. 1 (1887)-. German (English and French). an (Dec.). Selbstverlag des Orientalischen Instituts, Universitatstrasse 7/V, 1010 Vienna Austria. **Tel** 011 43 1 4361110. **ED** Arne A. Ambros and Anton C. Schaedlinger. **LC** PJ5; .W6. **Bk Rev. Ad Acc. Circ:** 300 (ctrl).
Desc: Information on Egyptology, Assyriology, African studies, Arabian studies, Iranian studies and Turcology.

US/0147-9873
WITTENBERG HISTORY JOURNAL, THE. English. an. 106 Zimmerman Hall, Wittenberg University, Springfield OH 45501. **LC** D1; .W58. **DD** 905. **UDC** 930.9.

KO
WOLGAN TONGSO MUNHWA. **VFOAT** Tongso Munhwa; Monthly East and West. Periodical. English (Korean). 5,500. Tongso Munhwa Yonguwon, 738-35 Hannam-dong, Yongsan-ku 140, Seoul South Korea. **LC** CB3; .W64. **UDC** 930.9.

AT
WORKING PAPERS (UNIVERSITY OF SYDNEY. CENTRE FOR ASIAN STUDIES). (WORKING PAPERS / THE UNIVERSITY OF SYDNEY, CENTRE FOR ASIAN STUDIES.). **Added/Corp** University of Sydney. Centre for Asian Studies. No. 1 (1983)-. Periodical. English. ir. University of Sydney Department of Southeast Asian Studies, Broadway NSW 2006 Australia. **Tel** 011 61 2 6923121, FAX 011 61 2 6923173.

UK/0043-8235
WORLD AND THE SCHOOL, THE. No. 1-Winter 1963/64-. Periodical. English. Three times a year. Atlantic Information Centre for Teachers, 37A High Street, Wimbledon SW19 5BY England. **LC** D839; .W553. **DD** 909.82. **UDC** 930.9. cum. index. available on microfilm from University Microfilms International (UMI).

US/0886-117X
WORLD HISTORY BULLETIN. (WORLD HISTORY BULLETIN : NEWSLETTER OF THE WORLD HISTORY ASSOCIATION.). [World hist. bull.]. **Added/Corp** World History Association. (19??)-. Periodical. English. Twice a year (May & Nov.). $25.00 (one year), $45.00 (two years), $60.00 (three years) Comes with World History Association membership. World History Association, Drexel University, Department of History and Politics, Philadelphia PA 19104. **Tel** (215)895-2471, FAX (215)895-6614. **ED** Raymond M. Lorantas. **DD** 905. **Pr Rev.**

US
WORLD NEWS DIGEST. See Business-Commerce.

US/0091-1852
WORLD PROGRESS YEARBOOK. English. Standard Educational Corporation, 200 West Madison Street, Suite 300, Chicago IL 60606. **Tel** (312)346-7440. **LC** D410; .W625. **DD** 909.82. **UDC** 930.9(058).

US
WORLD TOPICS YEAR BOOK. **Added/Corp** Tangley Oaks Educational Center. (1956)-. English. an. $18.81. World Topics, Publishers House, Lake Bluff IL 60044. **Tel** (312)234-3700. **LC** D410; .W645. **DD** 905.8.

US/0264-0872
WORLD VIEW (NEW YORK, N.Y.). (WORLD VIEW.). [World view]. English. an. Pantheon Books, 201 East 50th Street, New York NY 10022. **LC** D839; .W65. **DD** 909.82. **UDC** 930.9.

US/0898-4204
WORLD WAR II. [World war II]. **VFOAT** World War Two; World War 2. Vol. 1, No. 1 (May 1986)-. Periodical. English. bm. $18.95. Cowles Magazines, PO Box 8200, Harrisburg PA 17105. **Tel** (717)657-9555, (800)435-9610. **LC** D731; .W68. **DD** 940.53/05. available on microfilm and microfiche from University Microfilms International (UMI).

UK/0953-4857
WORLD WAR II INVESTIGATOR. ***Ceased.*** Vol. 1, No. 1 (April 1988)-(1993). Periodical. English. mo. World War II Investigator Ltd, 194 Muswell Hill Broadway, London N10 3SA England. **Tel** (01)883-3252, FAX (01)883-0945. **Bk Rev. Ad Acc.**

US/0084-3342
YALE HISTORICAL PUBLICATIONS. MANUSCRIPTS AND EDITED TEXTS. (1914)-. Monographic series. English. ir. Price varies per volume. Yale University Press, PO Box 209040, New Haven CT 06520. **Tel** (203)432-0940, (800)987-7323, FAX (203)432-0948.

US/0161-7141
YEAR IN PICTURES, THE. (19??)-. Periodical. English. an. $3.00 per issue. Time Inc. / New York, Time & Life Building, Rockefeller Center, New York NY 10020. **LC** D410; .Y44. **DD** 909.8/05.

UK/0309-3743
YORK HISTORIAN. See Architecture.

YU/0352-5716
ZBORNIK MATICE SRPSKE ZA ISTORIJU / MATICA SRPSKA, ODELJENJE ZA DRUSTVENE NAUKE. **Added/Corp** Matica Srpska (Novi Sad, Serbia) Matica Srpska (Novi Sad, Serbia). Odeljenje za Drustvene Nauke. **VFOAT** Proceedings in History. (1984-). Periodical. Serbo-Croatian (Cyrillic) (summaries and/or

History(General)

abstracts in English and German; table of contents in English). sa. **LC** D1; .Z3. **Continues** *Zbornik za Istoriju, 0305-0489.*
Ind/Abst Am. Hist. Life.

YU/0584-9888
ZBORNIK RADOVA VIZANTOLOSKOG INSTITUTA. Added/Corp Vizantoloski Institut (Srpska Akademija Nauka i Umetnosti) Vizantoloski Institut (Srpska Akademija Nauka). **VFOAT** Recueil de Travaux. (19??)-. Multiple languages (English, French, German and Serbian).
Ind/Abst BHA : Biblio. Hist. Art.

AU/0256-5250
ZEITGESCHICHTE. [Zeitgeschichte]. Vol. 1 (Oct. 1973)-. Periodical. German. Twelve times a year. S500.00 Austria; S570.00 other. Buchhandlung Hoelzl, Seilergasse 3, A-1010 Vienna Austria. **Tel** 011 43 1 5122896. **LC** D1; .Z35. **DD** 901.9. Documents available from The Genuine Article.
Ind/Abst Am. Hist. Life (1973-); Arts Humanit. Citation Index [Full Cov.]; Curr. Contents Arts Humanit.; Res. Alert [Full Cov.]; Soc. Sci. Cit. Index [Full Cov.].

GW/0012-1169
ZEITSCHRIFT DES DEUTSCHEN PALASTINA-VEREINS (1953). (ZEITSCHRIFT DES DEUTSCHEN PALASTINA-VEREINS.). [Z. Dtsch. Palast.-Ver.]. **Main/Corp** Deutscher Verein zur Erforschung Palastinas. **Added/Corp** Deutsches Evangelisches Institut fur Altertumswissenschaft des Heiligen Landes. (1953)-. Periodical. German. sa. Otto Harrassowitz Verlag, Taunusstrasse 14, Postfach 2929, D-65019 Wiesbaden Germany. **Tel** 011 49 611 5300, FAX 530570, telex 4186 135 OH D. **[CCC].** Documents available from The Genuine Article. **Continues** *Beitrage zur Biblischen Landes- und Altertumskunde.*
Ind/Abst Arts Humanit. Citation Index [Full Cov.]; BHA : Biblio. Hist. Art; Res. Alert [Full Cov.]; Soc. Sci. Cit. Index [Select. Cov.].

GW/0342-3131
ZEITSCHRIFT DES HISTORISCHEN VEREINS FUER SCHWABEN. [Z. Hist. Ver. Schwab.]. **Main/Corp** Historischer Verein fur Schwaben. (1941)-. German. **Continues** *Historischer Verein fur Schwaben und Neuburg, Augsburg. Zeitschrift des Historischen Vereins fur Schwaben und Neuburg.*
Ind/Abst BHA : Biblio. Hist. Art.

GW/0083-5587
ZEITSCHRIFT DES VEREINS FUER HAMBURGISCHE GESCHICHTE.
Main/Corp Verein fur Hamburgische Geschichte. (1841)-. German. an (Apr.). DM30.00. Verein Hamburgische Geschichte, ABC Strasse 19A Staatsarchiv, W 2000 Hamburg 36 Germany. **Tel** 49 40 344848. cum. index.
Ind/Abst BHA : Biblio. Hist. Art.

GW/0044-2828
ZEITSCHRIFT FUER GESCHICHTSWISSENSCHAFT. [Z. Geschichtswiss.]. Vol. 1, No. 1 (1953)-. Periodical. German. mo. DM262.00. Metropol Verlag, Kurfuerstenstrasse 135, D 10785 Berlin Germany. **Tel** 011 49 30 2618460. **ED** Friedrich Veitl. **LC** D1; .Z37. Index available. cum. index. **Bk Rev.** an (Qty: 300). **Ad Acc.** Documents available from The Genuine Article.
Desc: A scientific journal for historians, political scientists, and historically interested people which deals with european and universal history from the middle ages to the present.
Ind/Abst Am. Hist. Life (1954-); Arts Humanit. Citation Index [Full Cov.]; Bibliogr. Carto.; Curr. Contents Arts Humanit.; Int. Polit. Sci. Abstr.; Res. Alert [Full Cov.]; Soc. Sci. Cit. Index [Select. Cov.].

GW/0340-0174
ZEITSCHRIFT FUER HISTORISCHE FORSCHUNG. [Z. hist. Forsch.]. Vol. 1 (1974)-. Periodical. German. sa. DM112.00. Duncker and Humblot Verlag, Postfach 410329, D-12113 Berlin Germany. **Tel** 011 49 30 79000612, 011 49 30 79000613. **LC** D1; .Z38. **DD** 905. **UDC** 93. **[CCC].** Documents available from The Genuine Article.
Ind/Abst Am. Hist. Life (1989-); Arts Humanit. Citation Index [Full Cov.]; Bibliogr. Carto.; Curr. Contents Arts Humanit.; Res. Alert [Full Cov.]; Soc. Sci. Cit. Index [Select. Cov.].

IS
ZEMANIM. VFOAT Zmanim. 1- Setav 1979-. Periodical. Hebrew. qt. IL380.00. Zemanim, Circulation Department, School of History, Tel-Aviv University, Ramat Aviv Israel. **LC** D1; .Z39. **UDC** 933.

PL/0083-4424
ZESZYTY NAUKOWE UNIWERSYTETU JAGIELLONSKIEGO. PRACE Z HISTORII SZTUKI. [Zesz. Nauk. Uniw. Jagiell., Pr. Hist. Szt.]. **VFOAT** Universitas Iagellonica. Acta Scientiarum Litterarumque. Schedae ad Artis Historiam Pertinentes. (1962)-. Monographic series. Polish. tw. **(Subscription**

address: ARS Polona, PO Box 1001, 00068 Warsaw Poland.) **UDC** 7.0.
Ind/Abst BHA : Biblio. Hist. Art.

NE/0921-142X
ZEVENTIENDE EEUW, DE. Added/Corp Werkgroep Zeventiende Eeuw. (1985)-. Periodical. Dutch. sa. Vitgeverij Verloren, Alexanderlaan 14 Dr Noordegraa, 1012 VB Amsterdam Netherlands. **Tel** 31 20 35859856. **LC** CB401 Z48.
Ind/Abst BHA : Biblio. Hist. Art.

XV/0350-5774
ZGODOVINSKI CASOPIS. (ZGODOVINSKI CASOPIS. ISTORICHESKII ZHURNAL. HISTORICAL REVIEW.). [Zgod. cas.]. **Added/Corp** Zgodovinsko Drustvo za Slovenijo. **VFOAT** Istoricheskii Zhurnal; Historical Review. Vol 1 (1947)-. Periodical. Slovak. qt.
Ind/Abst Am. Hist. Life (1954-1955,1973-); BHA : Biblio. Hist. Art.

CN/0824-2445
Z'HUITRES. [Z'huitres]. **VFOAT** Huitres. French. an. 4.50Can$. Zhuitres, c/o J P Gauthier, Bureau 50 3241 Forest Hill, Montreal Quebec H3V 1C4 Canada. **DD** 905.

ABSTRACTING, BIBLIOGRAPHIES AND STATISTICS

US/0002-7065
AMERICA, HISTORY AND LIFE (SANTA BARBARA, CALIF. : 1989). (AMERICA, HISTORY AND LIFE.). [Am. hist. life]. **Added/Corp** ABC-Clio Information Services. American Bibliographical Center. Vol. 26, No. 1 (1989)-. Abstracting/Indexing Service. English. Five times a year (including an annual index). Price varies. ABC Clio Press, PO Box 1911, 130 Cremona, Santa Barbara CA 93117. **Tel** (805)968-1911, (800)422-2546, FAX (805)685-9685. **ED** Peter S. Quimby. **LC** Z1236; .A482. **DD** 973/.05. Bound Index published separately, free upon request. cum. index. available on CD-ROM (portions) from the publisher; available on an online database (File 38) from DIALOG. Formed by the union of *America, History and Life. Part A, Article Abstracts and Citations, 0002-7065* and *America, History and Life. Part B, Index to Book Reviews, 0002-7065 America, History and Life. Part C, American History Bibliography, Books, Articles and Dissertations, 0002-7065 America, History and Life. Part D, Annual Index, 0002-7065.*
Desc: Covers all aspects of US and Canadian history, culture, and current affairs from prehistoric times to the present.

US/0094-3770
AMERICAN BIBLIOGRAPHY OF SLAVIC AND EAST EUROPEAN STUDIES. [Am. bibl. Slav. East Eur. stud.]. **Added/Corp** American Association for the Advancement of Slavic Studies. Library of Congress. (1967)-. Abstracting/Indexing Service. English. ir. Price varies. American Association for the Advancement of Slavic Studies, 125 Panama Street, Stanford University, Acacia Building, Stanford CA 94305-6029. **Tel** (415)723-9668, FAX (415)725-7737, telex 348402 STANFRD STNU. **ED** Barbara Dash. **LC** Z2483; .A65. **DD** 016.9147. **Circ:** 700. **Continues** *American Bibliography of Russian and East European Studies.*

UK/0308-4558
ANNUAL BIBLIOGRAPHY OF BRITISH AND IRISH HISTORY. PUBLICATIONS OF ... / ROYAL HISTORICAL SOCIETY. (1975)-. Bibliography. English. an. £20.00 Fellows; £8.00 Associates and retired fellows; £35.00 Libraries. Harvester Wheatsheaf Campus 400, Maylands Avenue, Hemel Hempstead, Hertsfordshire HP2 7EZ England. **Tel** 011 44 442 881900, FAX 011 44 422 257115. **LC** Z2016; .A55; DA30. **DD** 016.941/005. **Continues** *Writings on British History, 0084-2753.*
Ind/Abst Br. Archaeol. Bibliogr.

US/1046-8765
BIBLIOGRAPHIC GUIDE TO EAST ASIAN STUDIES. [Bibliogr. guide East Asian stud.]. **VFOAT** East Asian Studies; Bibliographic Guide. East Asian Studies. (1989)-. English (Chinese, Japanese and Korean). an. $185.00. GK Hall & Co, 100 Front Street, Riverside NJ 08075. **Tel** (800)257-5755 ext. 2223. **LC** Z3001; .B484; DS504.5. **DD** 016.95.

US/0162-5314
BIBLIOGRAPHIC GUIDE TO LATIN AMERICAN STUDIES. (1978)-. English. an. $525.00. GK Hall & Co, 100 Front Street, Riverside NJ 08075. **Tel** (800)257-5755 ext. 2223. **LC** Z1610; .B52; F1408. **DD** 015.8. **Continues** *Benson Latin American Collection Catalog of the Nettie Lee Benson Latin American Collection. Supplement.*

US/0147-6491
BIBLIOGRAPHIC GUIDE TO NORTH AMERICAN HISTORY. (1977)-. English. an. $300.00. GK Hall & Co, 100 Front Street, Riverside NJ 08075. **Tel** (800)257-5755 ext. 2223. **LC** Z1236; .B47; E178. **DD** 016.973.

US/0162-5322
BIBLIOGRAPHIC GUIDE TO SOVIET AND EAST EUROPEAN STUDIES. **Added/Corp** New York Public Library. Slavonic Division. Dictionary Catalog of the Slavonic Collection. **VFOAT** Soviet and East European Studies. (1978)-. English. an. $630.00. GK Hall & Co, 100 Front Street, Riverside NJ 08075. **Tel** (800)257-5755 ext. 2223. **LC** Z2483; .B48. **DD** 015/.47.

IT
BIBLIOGRAPHIE ANALYTIQUE DE L'AFRIQUE ANTIQUE. Vol. 1 (1961/62)-. French. an. Diffusion de Boccard, 11 rue de Medicis, 75006 Paris France. **Tel** 011 33 1 43260037. **LC** Z3511; .B5.

FR
BIBLIOGRAPHIE ANNUELLE DE L'HISTOIRE DE FRANCE DU CINQUIEME SIECLE A 1958. VFOAT Bibliographie Annuelle de l'Histoire de France. (1975)-. French. an. Editions du CNRS, 22 rue Saint Armand, F 75015 Paris France. **Tel** 011 33 1 45075050. **ED** C Albert Samuel. **LC** Z2176; .B5; DC38. **DD** 016.944/005. **Bk Rev. Ad Acc. Circ:** 1,500. **Continues** *Bibliographie Annuelle de l'Histoire de France du Cinquieme Siecle A 1945.*
Desc: French books, articles, foreign books and articles on the history of France 400-1958. Approximately 11,000 references 2,000 periodicals, 300 to 400 mixtures and congress.

NE
BIBLIOGRAPHIE DE LA REFORME, 1450-1648; OOUVRAGES PARUS DE 1940 A 1955. Main/Corp International Committee of Historical Sciences. Commission Internationale d'Histoire Ecclesiastique Comparee. (1961)-. Monographic series. French. ir. Price varies per volume. E. J. Brill, Postbus 9000, 2300 PA Leiden Netherlands. **Tel** 011 31 71 312624, FAX 011 31 71 317532, telex 39296 BRILL NL.

US/0742-6828
BIBLIOGRAPHIES AND INDEXES IN AMERICAN HISTORY. [Bibliogr. indexes Am. hist.]. No. 1 (1984)-. Monographic series. English. ir. Price varies per volume. Greenwood Press Inc., PO Box 5007, Westport CT 06881-5007. **Tel** (203)226-3571, FAX (203)222-1502. **DD** 016.
Ind/Abst Math. Rev.

US/0742-6852
BIBLIOGRAPHIES AND INDEXES IN WORLD HISTORY. [Bibliogr. indexes world hist.]. No. 1 (1985)-. Monographic series. English. ir. Price varies per volume. Greenwood Press Inc., PO Box 5007, Westport CT 06881-5007. **Tel** (203)226-3571, FAX (203)222-1502. **LC** UNC. **DD** 016.

US/0067-7159
BIBLIOGRAPHY OF ASIAN STUDIES. [Bibliogr. Asian stud.]. **Added/Corp** Association for Asian Studies. (1956)-. Bibliography. English. an. $70.00. Association for Asian Studies Inc., University of Michigan, 1 Lane Hall, Ann Arbor MI 48109. **Tel** (313)665-2490, FAX (313)665-3801. **ED** Wayne Surdem. **LC** Z3001; .B49; DS5. **DD** 016.95/005. **Circ:** 3,000 (ctrl). available on microfilm and microfiche from University Microfilms International (UMI). **Continues** *Far Eastern Bibliography.*
Desc: A comprehensive list of articles and books written about Asia, in western languages.

SY
BIBLIOGRAPHY OF THE MIDDLE EAST : A COMPLETE AND CLASSIFIED LIST OF ALL THE BOOKS PUBLISHED IN ABOUT TEN MIDDLE EASTERN COUNTRIES, THE. Added/Corp Syrian Documentation Papers. (19??)-. Bibliography. English. an. $50.00. Syrian Documentation Papers, PO Box 2712, Damascus Syria. **Tel** 233116. **ED** Louis Fares. **LC** Z3013; .S93. **NLM** Z 3013 B582. **Circ:** 5,000. **Continues** *Revue Bibliographique du Moyen Orient.*

JA/0524-0654
BOOKS AND ARTICLES ON ORIENTAL SUBJECTS PUBLISHED IN JAPAN. / TOHOGAKU KANKEI CHOSHO RONBUN MOKUROKU. Added/Corp Toho Gakkai. **VFOAT** Tohogaku Kankei Chosho Rombun Mokuroku. (1954)-. Catalog. English. an. $25.00. Institute of Eastern Culture / Tokyo, 4-1 2 Nishikanda Chome, Chiyoda-ku Tokyo Japan. **Tel** 011 81 3 3261 1061. **ED** MORI Masao. **LC** Z3001; .B58; DS5.

DD 016.95. **Circ:** 1,100 (ctrl).
Desc: Catalogue of books and articles published in Japan in the field of Asian studies.

US/0892-4600
BULLETIN (ASSOCIATION FOR THE BIBLIOGRAPHY OF HISTORY (U.S.)). (BULLETIN / ASSOCIATION FOR THE BIBLIOGRAPHY OF HISTORY.). [Bull. - Assoc. Bibliogr. Hist. (U.S.)]. **VFOAT** Association for the Bibliography of History Bulletin; ABH Bulletin. Vol. 10, No. 1 (Spring/Summer 1987)-. Bulletin. English. sa. $10.00. Association for the Bibliography of History, Georgia State University, Department of History, Atlanta GA 30303-3082. **Tel** (313)370-2100 (EDITORIAL), (404)651-3255 (BUSINESS). **ED** Daniel Ring (editor's address: Reference Department, Kresge Library, Oakland University, Rochester MI 48063; Daniel F Harrison, Eshleman Library, Henry Ford Community College, Dearborn MI 48128). **DD** 900. **UDC** 973. **Bk Rev. Ad Acc. Circ:** 300. ***Continues*** *Newsletter / Association for the Bibliography of History (U.S.), 8755-5921.*

FR/0240-8678
CAHIERS DE CIVILISATION MEDIEVALE. BIBLIOGRAPHIE. (1969)-. French. an. Regisseur Recettes Publications, CESCM, 24 rue de la Chaine, 86022 Poitiers France. **Tel** 011 33 49 410386. **UDC** 016.
Ind/Abst BHA : Biblio. Hist. Art.

CN/0068-9165
CANADIAN LOCAL HISTORIES TO 1950: A BIBLIOGRAPHY. VFOAT Histoires Locales et Regionales Canadiennes des Origines a 1950. (1967)-. Monographic series. English. ir. University of Toronto Press, 5201 Dufferin Street, Downsview Ontario M3H 5T8 Canada. **Tel** (416)667-7781, (416)667-7782, FAX (416)667-7803. **DD** 016; 971.

CN/0317-7904
CANADIAN REVIEW OF STUDIES IN NATIONALISM. (CANADIAN REVIEW OF STUDIES IN NATIONALISM. REVUE CANADIENNE DES ETUDES SUR LE NATIONALISME.). [Can. rev. stud. natl.]. **Added/Corp** University of Prince Edward Island. **VFOAT** Revue Canadienne des Etudes sur le Nationalisme. Vol. 1 (Fall 1973)-. English (French and German). an (Dec.). $13.00 US; $14.00 others. CRSN University of Prince Edward Island CRSN, 550 University Avenue, Charlottetown PEI C1A 4P3 Canada. **Tel** (902)566-0527, FAX (902)566-0420. **ED** Thomas Spira. **LC** JC311; .C335. **DD** 320.5/4/05. Index available (Free). cum. index. **Bk Rev. Ad Acc. Pr Rev. Circ:** 600 (ctrl). ***Absorbed*** *Canadian Review of Studies in Nationalism, 0317-7912.*
Desc: Articles, review essay, book reviews, and annotated bibliographies dealing with nationalism, ethnic issues and related topics.
Ind/Abst ABC POL SCI; Am. Hist. Life (1973-); Am. Bibliogr. Slavic East Europ. Stud.; Can. Index; Int. Bibliogr. Sociol.; Int. Polit. Sci. Abstr.; Linguist. Lang. Behav. Abstr.; PAIS Int. Print (1991-?); Peace Res. Abstr. J. (1973-1987); Sage Race Relat. Abstr.; Soc. Plann. Policy Dev. Abstr.; Sociol. Abstr.

US/1044-3487
CHICANO INDEX, THE. [Chicano index]. **Added/Corp** University of California, Berkeley. Chicano Studies Library. Publications Unit. Vol. 7, No. 1 (Jan./March 1989)-. Abstracting/Indexing Service. English. an. $150.00. Chicano Studies Library, University of California at Berkeley, 510 Barrows Hall #2570, Berkeley CA 94720. **Tel** (510)642-3859. **ED** Lillian Castillo-Speed. **DD** 973. available on CD-ROM. ***Continues*** *Chicano Periodical Index, 0891-6985.*
Desc: Allows librarians to point users to articles, books, and other materials about Mexican-Americans in public and academic core collections as well as in academic Chicano Studies collections. Libraries with limited Chicano collections will be able to direct users to information about Chicano topics.

VE
COLLECCION BIBLIOGRAFICA - ACADEMIA NACIONAL DE LA HISTORIA, DEPARTAMENTO DE INVESTIGACIONES. Main/Corp Academia Nacional de la Historia, Caracas. Departamento de Investigaciones. 1- 1973-. Monographic series. Spanish. ir. Price varies per volume. University Catolica Andres Bello, Apartado 29068, Caracas 1021 Venezuela. **Tel** 011 58 2 4429511.

US/0011-3255
CURRENT BIBLIOGRAPHY ON AFRICAN AFFAIRS, A. [Curr. bibliogr. Afr. aff.]. **Added/Corp** African Bibliographic Center. (1962)-. Bibliography. English. qt. $128.00. Baywood Publishing Company Inc., 26 Austin Avenue, PO Box 337, Amityville NY 11701. **Tel** (516)691-1270, (800)638-7819, FAX (516)691-1770. **ED** Paula Boesch. **LC** Z3501; .C87. Index available. **Bk Rev.**
Desc: Original studies, bibliographic essays and contributions, followed by a bibliographic section of listings in general subject and regional sections. Author index.
Ind/Abst Am. Hist. Life (1984-); Middle East Abstr. Index; MLA Int. Bibl. Books Artic. Mod. Lang. Lit.

US/0161-0996
EIGHTEENTH CENTURY, THE. Added/Corp American Society for Eighteenth-Century Studies. Vol. 1 (1975)-. English. an (Nov.). $84.60. AMS Press Inc., 56 East 13th Street, New York NY 10003. **Tel** (212)777-4700, FAX (212)995-5413, telex 710 581 2302. **LC** Z5579.6; .E36; CB411. **DD** 016.909. Index available (free). **Bk Rev.**
Desc: The bible of reference tools for any subject of inquiry concerning anything that happened anywhere in the world during the years 1660-1800.
Ind/Abst Romant. Move.

UK/0140-492X
EUROPEAN BIBLIOGRAPHY OF SOVIET, EAST EUROPEAN AND SLAVONIC STUDIES. VFOAT Bibliographie Europeenne des Travaux sur l'Urss et l'Europe de l'Est; Europaische Bibliographie der Sowjet- und Osteuropastudien. V. 1- 1975-. Bibliography. English (French and German). an. $12.00. Mme M Aymard, Centre d'Etudes sur l'URSS et l'Europe Orientale, Ecole des Hautes Etudes en Sciences Sociales, 54 Boulevard Raspail, 75270 Paris Cedex 06 France. **ED** T Hnik. **LC** Z2483; .E94; DJK9. **DD** 016.947. ***Supersedes*** *Soviet, East European & Slavonic Studies in Britain.*

US/0363-2717
HISTORICAL ABSTRACTS. PART A, MODERN HISTORY ABSTRACTS. (HISTORICAL ABSTRACTS. PART A, MODERN HISTORY ABSTRACTS, 1775-1914.). [Hist. abstr., Part A, Mod. hist. abstr.]. **Added/Corp** American Bibliographical Center. **VFOAT** Historical Abstracts. Part A, Modern History Abstracts, 1450-1914; Modern History Abstracts, 1450-1914; Modern History Abstracts, 1775-1914. Vol. 17, No. 1 (Spring 1971)-. Abstracting/Indexing Service. English. Four times a year (including an annual index). Price varies. ABC Clio Press, PO Box 1911, 130 Cremona, Santa Barbara CA 93117. **Tel** (805)968-1911, (800)422-2546, FAX (805)685-9685. **ED** Jeffery B Serena and Roger W Davis. **LC** D299; .H512. **DD** 016.90982. **NLM** Z 6204 H673. cum. index. available on an online database (file no. 39) from DIALOG; available on CD-ROM (Portions) from the publisher. ***Continues in part*** *Historical Abstracts, 0018-2435.*
Desc: Covers the history of the world 1450-1914 except for the U.S. and Canada. Includes citations and abstracts to the literature published worldwide.

US/0363-2725
HISTORICAL ABSTRACTS. PART B, TWENTIETH CENTURY ABSTRACTS. (HISTORICAL ABSTRACTS. PART B, TWENTIETH CENTURY ABSTRACTS, 1914-.). **Added/Corp** American Bibliographical Center. **VFOAT** Twentieth Century Abstracts, 1914. Vol. 17, No. 1 (Spring 1971)-. Abstracting/Indexing Service. English. Four times a year (Including an annual index). Price varies. ABC Clio Press, PO Box 1911, 130 Cremona, Santa Barbara CA 93117. Tel (805)968-1911, (800)422-2546, FAX (805)685-9685. **ED** Jeffery B Serena and Roger W Davis. **LC** D299; .H513. **DD** 016.90982. **NLM** Z 6204 H673B. cum. index. available on an online database (file no. 39) from DIALOG; available on CD-ROM (Portions) from the publisher. ***Continues in part*** *Historical Abstracts, 0018-2435.*
Desc: Covers the history of the world 1914 to the present except for the U.S. and Canada. Cumulative subject, author, title and reviewer indexing for all abstracts and citations published in the volume.

US/0018-2656
HISTORY AND THEORY. [Hist. theory]. Vol. 1, (1960)-. Periodical. English (French). Four times a year (Feb., May, Oct., Dec.). $40.00 (institutions), $25.00 (individual). History & Theory, Wesleyan Station, Middletown CT 06457. **Tel** (203)347-9411 Ext. 2068 or 69, FAX (203)343-3934. **ED** Richard T. Vann. **LC** D1; .H8173. **DD** 901. cum. index. **Bk Rev. Ad Acc. Circ:** 2,000 (ctrl). available on microfilm and microfiche from University Microfilms International (UMI). Documents available from The Genuine Article, UMI Article Clearinghouse.
Desc: Monographs, reviews, essays, and bibliographies principally in theories of history, historiography method of history, and related disciplines.
Ind/Abst Acad. Abstr. Full Text Elite (Jan. 1992-); Acad. Abstr. (Jan. 1992-); Acad. Search (Jan. 1992-); Am. Hist. Life (1961-); Arts Humanit. Citation Index [Full Cov.]; Book Rev. Index; Curr. Contents Arts Humanit.; Expand. Acad. Index (1989-); Hist. Source (Jan. 1992-); Humanit. Index; Humanit. Source (Jan. 1992-); INFO-SOUTH Abstr.; Int. Bibliogr. Sociol.; Int. Polit. Sci. Abstr.; Mag. Search; Middle East Abstr. Index; Newsp. Period. Abstr. (1991-); Philos. Index; Res. Alert [Full Cov.]; Romant. Move.; Soc. Plann. Policy Dev. Abstr.; Soc. Sci. Cit. Index [Select. Cov.]; Sociol. Abstr.; U.S. Polit. Sci. Doc.; West. Hist. Q.

US/1063-9799
HISTORY SOURCE. ***Title Change.*** (HISTORY SOURCE [COMPUTER FILE] / DATA PREPARED AND COMPILED BY EBSCO PUBLISHING.). [Hist. source]. **Added/Corp** EBSCO Publishing (Firm). (1992)-(1994). Abstracting/Indexing Service. English. Three times a year. EBSCO Publishing / Boston, 83 Pine Street, Peabody MA 01960. **Tel** (800)653-2726 North America, (508)535-8500, FAX (508)535-8545. **ED** Melissa Kummerer. **DD** 900. Index available. **Pr Rev.** ***Merged into*** *Humanities Source CD-ROM, 1073-1962.*
Desc: Provides keyword access to abstract and index coverage of over 100 journals dedicated to historical research. Full text of important journals is accompanied by tables, charts and selected graphic images on a single disc.

SP/0537-3522
INDICE HISTORICO ESPANOL. Added/Corp Centro de Estudios Historicos Internacionales (Barcelona, Spain). Vol. 1, No. 1 (1953)-. Abstracting/Indexing Service. Spanish. ir. $110.00. Libreria Bosch, Ronda Universidad 11, 08007 Barcelona Spain. **Tel** 011 34 3 3175308. **LC** Z2696; .I6. **Circ:** 1,100.

FR/0074-2015
INTERNATIONAL BIBLIOGRAPHY OF HISTORICAL SCIENCES. (INTERNATIONAL BIBLIOGRAPHY OF HISTORICAL SCIENCES. INTERNATIONALE BIBLIOGRAPHIE DER GESCHICHTSWISSENSCHAFTEN.). **Added/Corp** International Committee of Historical Sciences. **VFOAT** Internationale Bibliographie der Geschichtswissenschaften. (1926)-. English. ir. $160.00 (1990 edition). K.G. Saur Verlag KG, A Reed Reference Publishing Company, Part of Reed International PLC, Ortlerstrasse 8, D 81373 Munich Germany. **Tel** 011 49 89 769020, FAX 011 49 89 76902150, telex 5212067-SAUR-D. **(Subscription address:** Reed Reference Publishing Company / New Jersey, 131 Chanlaon Road, PO Box 31, New Providence NJ 07974.**)** **LC** Z6205; .I61. **DD** 016.9. **NLM** Z 6205 I61.
Desc: A selective, descriptive bibliography which lists books and articles in the field of historical sciences.

ET/0459-5009
LIST OF CURRENT PERIODICAL PUBLICATIONS IN ETHIOPIA. Added/Corp Haile Sellassie I University. Institute of Ethiopian Studies. (1964)-. English. be. Institute of Ethiopian Studies, Addis Ababa University, PO Box 1176, Addis Ababa Ethiopia. **Tel** 119469. **ED** Bahru Zewde, Taddese Beyene and Taddesse Tamrat. **LC** Z6960.E8; L57. **DD** 016.9163/005. **Bk Rev. Circ:** 1,000.
Desc: The journal aims at presenting important results of works on Ethiopia and serves as a cross-fertilizing stimulant to the growing field of Ethiopian Studies.

RU
LITERATURA OB ULIANOVSKOI OBLASTI. Added/Corp Ulianovskaia Oblastnaia Biblioteka Dvorets Knigi Imeni V.I. Lenina. (1968)-. Russian. an. 0.20rub. Privolzhskoe Knizhnoe Izdatelstvo, Ulitsa Goncharova 52, Ulianovsk Russia. **LC** Z2514.U55; U6. ***Continues*** *Novaia Literatura Ob Ulianovskoi Oblasti.*

IT
MEDIOEVO LATINO. Added/Corp Centro Italiano di Studi Sull'alto Medioevo. (1979)-. Italian (English, German and French). an (Sept.). L260000. Centro Italiano di Studi Sull'Alto Medioevo, Palazzo Ancaiani, Piazza della Liberta 12, 06049 Spoleto Italy. **Tel** 011 39 743 220485 or 418, FAX 011 39 743 39107. **ED** Claudio Leonardi. Index available. **Bk Rev. Circ:** 500 (ctrl).
Desc: Bibliography based on 300 periodicals in all fields of medieval studies AD 500-1300, which appears every year in September.

US/0162-766X
MIDDLE EAST, ABSTRACTS AND INDEX. [Middle East abstr. index]. **Added/Corp** Library Information and Research Service. Vol. 1 (March 1978)-. Abstracting/Indexing Service. English. qt. $300.00. Aristarchus Knowledge Industries, PO Box 45610, Seattle WA 98105. **Tel** (206)324-3156, (800)435-8221. **ED** Amy C Lowenstein. **LC** DS41; .M44. **DD** 016.956/005. **Bk Rev. Ad Acc.**
Desc: Abstracts and index to English language citations concerning Middle East. Includes books, book reviews, government documents, doctoral dissertations. Over 1,160 journals scanned regularly.

US/0026-3141
MIDDLE EAST JOURNAL, THE. [Middle East j.]. **Added/Corp** Middle East Institute (Washington, D.C.). Vol. 1 (Jan. 1947)-. Abstracting/Indexing Service. English. qt (back issues available). $40.00 (institutions); $30.00 (one year), $57.50 (two year) (individuals). Middle East Institute, 1761 North Street Northwest, Washington DC 20036. **Tel** (202)785-1141. **ED** Jean C. Newsom. **LC** DS1; .M5. **DD** 956. Index available in last issue of volume--attached. cum. index. **Bk Rev. Ad Acc. Pr Rev. Circ:** 5,100. available on microfilm and microfiche from University Microfilms International (UMI). Documents available from The Genuine Article, UMI Article Clearinghouse.
Desc: Focuses on contemporary social, political and economic issues relevant to the area. Includes chronology and index to periodical literature.
Ind/Abst ABC POL SCI; Acad. Abstr. Full Text Elite (July 1990-); Acad. Abstr. (July 1990-); Acad. Ind. [Computer

File] (1987-); Acad. Search (July 1990-); AGRICOLA [Select. Cov.]; Am. Hist. Life (1955-); Am. Bibliogr. Slavic East Europ. Stud.; Anthropol. Index; Book Rev. Digest; Book Rev. Index; Crim. Penol. Police Sci. Abstr.; Curr. Contents Soc. Behav. Sci.; Expand. Acad. Index (1987-); Guide Soc. Sci. Relig.; Index Islam. Lit.; Index Book Rev. Relig. (-19??); INFO-SOUTH Abstr.; Int. Bibliogr. Sociol.; Int. Dev. Abstr. (?-?); Int. Labour Doc.; Int. Polit. Sci. Abstr.; LABORDOC; Mag. Artic. Summar. Select (July 1990-); Mag. Search; Middle East Abstr. Index; Newsp. Period. Abstr. (1988-); PAIS Int. Print (1991-); Peace Res. Abstr. J. (1969-1971, 1974-); Popul. Index (?-?); Res. Alert [Full Cov.]; Soc. Sci. Source (Jul. 1990-); Soc. Sci. Cit. Index [Full Cov.]; Soc. Sci. Index; Soc. Sci. Index Fulltext (Autumn 1988-) [Full Txt.]; Middle East J.; U.S. Polit. Sci. Doc. (-199?).

AU/0067-236X
OSTERREICHISCHE HISTORISCHE BIBLIOGRAPHIE. **VFOAT** Austrian Historical Bibliography. (1964)-. German (English). ir. ABC Clio Press, PO Box 1911, 130 Cremona, Santa Barbara CA 93117. **Tel** (805)968-1911, (800)422-2546, FAX (805)685-9685. **LC** Z2116; .O47. **DD** 016.914/03/005. cum. index.

US/0275-9713
OZARK PERIODICAL INDEX. **Added/Corp** Southwest Missouri Library Network. (1979)-. Abstracting/Indexing Service. English. sa. $25.00. Ozark Periodical Index, Southwest Missouri Library Network, PO Box 760, Springfield MO 65801. **Tel** (417)869-4621, (800)633-4604. **ED** Vickie Cravens (editor's address: 135 Harwood Ave., Lebanon, MO 65536). **LC** Z1251.O9; O92; F417.O9. **DD** 016.9767/1. **Circ:** 100.
Desc: Indexes thirty periodicals which deal with Missouri or Ozark mountain region history, travel, business, recreation, or related issues.

US/0031-4587
PENNSYLVANIA MAGAZINE OF HISTORY AND BIOGRAPHY, THE. **See** History(General)-History of North, South, and Central America.

US/0885-9302
SIXTEENTH CENTURY BIBLIOGRAPHY. [Sixt. century bibliogr.]. **Added/Corp** Center for Reformation Research. **VFOAT** 16th Century Bibliography. (1975)-. Monographic series. English. ir. Price varies per volume. Center for Reformation Research, 6477 San Bonita Avenue, St Louis MO 63105. **Tel** (314)727-6655. **ED** William S. Maltby. **LC** UNC. **DD** 940. **Circ:** 500. ***Continues*** *Foundation for Reformation Research. Library. Bulletin of the Library, 0015-8941.*
Ind/Abst Am. Hist. Life (1975-).

XO
VYCHODOSLOVENSKY KRAJ V TLACI. Slovak. an. kcs100.00 Czechoslovakia; $10.00 US. Statna Vedecka Kniznica V Kosiciah, Leninova 10 042 30, Kosice Slovakia. **Tel** 223-31, telex 77274. **ED** Jozef Sulacek. **LC** Z2137.V88; V93; DB661.4. **UDC** 943.76; 908.437.6. Index available. **Bk Rev. Circ:** 130 (ctrl).
Desc: Universal bibliography containing more than 10,000 entries depicting the life of the Eastern Slovakia.

US/0043-3810
WESTERN HISTORICAL QUARTERLY. [West. hist. q.]. **Added/Corp** Utah State University. Western History Association. Vol. 1 (Jan. 1970)-. Abstracting/Indexing Service. English. qt (Feb., May, Aug., Nov.). $40.00 US; $45.00 other. Western Historical Quarterly, Utah State University, UMC 0740, Logan UT 84322. **Tel** (801)750-1301. **ED** Clyde A Milner II (Editor) and Anne M Butler (Associate Editor). **LC** F591; .W464. **DD** 978/.005. Index available. **Bk Rev**, (Qty: 42 per year average). **Ad Acc, Adv Mgr:** Barbara Stewart, **Tel** (801)750-1301. **Circ:** 2,500. Documents available from The Genuine Article, UMI Article Clearinghouse.
Desc: The official journal of the Western History Society. Presents original articles dealing with the North American West- the westward movement from the Atlantic to the Pacific, twentieth-century regional studies, the Spanish borderlands, and developments in western Canada, northern Mexico, Alaska and Hawaii. Each issue contains reviews and notices of significant books in the field.
Ind/Abst Acad. Search (July 1993-); Am. Hist. Life (1970-); Am. Bibliogr. Slavic East Europ. Stud.; Arts Humanit. Citation Index [Full Cov.]; Book Rev. Index; Chicano Index; Crim. Justice Abstr.; Curr. Contents Arts Humanit.; Expand. Acad. Index (1989-); Hist. Source (July 1993-); Humanit. Index; Humanit. Source (Jul. 1993-); INFO-SOUTH Abstr.; Mag. Search; Newsp. Period. Abstr. (1991-); Res. Alert [Full Cov.]; Soc. Sci. Cit. Index [Select. Cov.]; SportSearch (1970-); Women Stud. Abstr.

HISTORY OF AFRICA

ET/0244-8327
ABBAY. Periodical. English (summaries and/or abstracts in French). an. Editions du CNRS, 22 rue Saint Armand, F 75015 Paris France. **Tel** 011 33 1 45075050. **LC** DT379.5; .A63. **DD** 963/.005. **UDC** 963. **Circ:** 1,500.
Desc: Offers documents of value on the study of Ethiopian civilization, focusing on topics from natural science, paleontology, archaeology and zoology to art.

FR/0760-9736
ADULIS. **Added/Corp** Eritrean People's Liberation Front. Central Bureau of Foreign Relations. Vol. 1, No. 1 (July 1984)-. Periodical. English. mo. Adulis, 42 rue Lebour, 93100 Montreuil, France. **LC** DT391; .A38. ***Continues*** *Liberation (Beirut, Lebanon).*
Ind/Abst Hum. Rights Intern. Rep.

US/0065-3802
AFRICA. 1968-. English. an. Africana Publishing Company, 30 Irving Place, New York NY 10003. **Tel** (212)254-4100. **LC** DT1; .A14. **DD** 915/.005. **UDC** 960. available on microfilm from University Microfilms International (UMI).

US/0065-3845
AFRICA CONTEMPORARY RECORD. (AFRICA CONTEMPORARY RECORD; ANNUAL SURVEY AND DOCUMENTS.). [Afr. contemp. rec.]. **VFOAT** Annual Survey and Documents; Africa Annual Survey and Documents. (1969)-. English. an. $380.50 US; $385.00 others. Holmes and Meier Publishers Inc, 160 Broadway, Suite 900 East Wing, New York NY 10038. **Tel** (212)374-0100. **LC** DT1; .L43. **DD** 960/.05.

TI/0568-1057
AFRICA; FOUILLES, MONUMENTS ET COLLECTIONS ARCHEOLOGIQUES EN TUNISIE. **Added/Corp** Mahad al-Qawmi lil-Athar Wa-al-Funun. **VFOAT** Afriqiyah. (1966)-. Periodical. Arabic (French). **LC** DT251; .A47. **DD** 939/.7/005.
Ind/Abst Numis. Lit.

US/8755-0067
AFRICA INTERNATIONAL. [Afr. int.]. **Added/Corp** Africa-United States Communications E Educational Institute. Africa Institute (Washington D.C.). (1984)-. Periodical. English. mo. $150.00. Africa Communications Institute, 1377 K Street NW/Suite 104, Washington DC 20005. **DD** 960. ***Continues*** *Africa Press International, 0749-4378.*

FR
AFRICA INTERNATIONAL (DAKAR, SENEGAL). (AFRICA INTERNATIONAL.). **VFOAT** Africa. No. 177 (Nov. 1985)-. Periodical. French (French). Eleven times a year. $50.00. Societe Gilletie, 21 rue Jean Pierre Timbaud, 75011 Paris France. **Tel** 011 33 1 47003585. **LC** DT1; .A13. **DD** 960/.05. ***Continues*** *Africa (Dakar, Senegal).*

LB
AFRICA INTERNATIONAL PERSPECTIVE. No. 1- Dec. 1975/Jan. 1976-. Periodical. English. Africa International, Avenue Marc Monnier 1, PO Box 244, 1211 Geneva 12 Switzerland. **LC** DT30; .A355. **DD** 960/.05. **UDC** 960.

SA/1012-9391
AFRICA PERSPECTIVE. [Afr. perspect.]. **Added/Corp** African Studies Group (University of the Witwatersrand) Students' African Studies Society (University of the Witwatersrand) Students' African Studies Association (University of the Witwatersrand). (197?)-. Periodical. English. Twice a year (Jan. & July). R20.00 (individuals), R40.00 (institutions) South Africa; R25.00 (individuals), R45.00 (insitutions) southern Africa. Africa Perspective, RSC Private Bag X3, Wits 2050 South Africa. **Tel** 011 27 11 7162751. **LC** DT1; .A2158. **DD** 960/.05.
Ind/Abst Hum. Rights Intern. Rep.

II/0001-9828
AFRICA QUARTERLY. [Afr. q.]. **Added/Corp** Indian Council for Africa. Indian Centre for Africa. Vol. 1 (April/June 1961)-. Periodical. English. qt. $15.00. Ind Council for Cultural Rel, Azad Bhavan Indraphasta Estate, New Delhi 110002 India. **Tel** 3319310. **(Subscription address:** Prints India, 11 Darya Ganj, New Delhi, 110002 India, (Phone: 011 91 11 3268645)) **ED** Dr. A.R. Basu. **LC** DT1; .A216. Index available. cum. index. **Bk Rev**, (Qty: 1200/yr). **Ad Acc. Pr Rev. Circ:** 650 (ctrl). available on microfilm and microfiche from University Microfilms International (UMI). ***Absorbed*** *Documentation List: Africa.*
Desc: English language quarterly journal of African affairs and Indo-American relations.
Ind/Abst ABC POL SCI; Am. Hist. Life (1976-); Appl. Soc. Sci. Index Abstr.; Int. Bibliogr. Sociol.; Int. Polit. Sci. Abstr.

US/0001-9836
AFRICA REPORT. [Afr. rep.]. **Added/Corp** African-American Institute. Vol. 5, No. 10 (Oct. 1960)-. Periodical. English. bm (6 issues). $37.00 institution, $30.00 individual. Africa Report, 833 United Nations Plaza, New York NY 10017. **Tel** (212)949-5666, FAX (212)682-6421, telex 666565. **(Subscription address:** Africa Report Subscription Service, PO Box 3000, Department AR, Denville, NJ 07834) **ED** Margaret A. Novicki. **LC** DT1; .A217. Index available. **Bk Rev. Ad Acc. Circ:** 10,000. available on microfilm and microfiche from University Microfilms International (UMI). Documents available from UMI Article Clearinghouse. ***Continues*** *Africa Special Report.*
Desc: Reports on political, economic, and cultural developments in Africa.
Ind/Abst ABC POL SCI; Acad. Abstr. Full Text Elite (July 1990-); Acad. Abstr. (July 1990-); Acad. Ind. [Computer File] (1987-); Acad. Search (July 1990-); Am. Hist. Life (1970-1975); Expand. Acad. Index (1987-); Hist. Source (July 1990-); Hum. Rights Intern. Rep.; INFO-SOUTH Abstr.; Int. Dev. Abstr.; Leis. Recreat. Tour. Abstr.; Mag. Search; Middle East Abstr. Index; MLA Int. Bibl. Books Artic. Mod. Lang. Lit.; Newsp. Period. Abstr. (1989-); PAIS Int. Print; Peace Res. Abstr. J. (1965-1980); Rural Dev. Abstr.; Soc. Sci. Source (Jul. 1990-); Soc. Sci. Index; Soc. Sci. Index Fulltext (Nov. 1988-) [Full Txt.]; World Agric. Econ.

IT/0001-9747
AFRICA (ROME, ITALY). (AFRICA.). [Africa]. **Added/Corp** Associazione Fra le Imprese Italiane in Africa. Istituto Italiano per l'Africa. Istituto Italo-Africano. **VFOAT** Africa. (1946)-. Periodical. Italian (English and French). Four times a year (Mar., June, Sept., Dec.). L50000.00 Italy; L60000.00 other. Instituto Italo-Africano, Via Ulisse Aldrovandi 16, 00196 Rome Italy. **Tel** 011 39 6 3216712. **ED** Teobaldo Filesi. **LC** DT1; .A843. **Bk Rev. Ad Acc. Circ:** 1,000. ***Continues*** *Affrica.*
Desc: Various topics relating to Africanistic studies mainly to human sciences and cooperation and underdevelopment problems.
Ind/Abst Am. Hist. Life (1972-); MLA Int. Bibl. Books Artic. Mod. Lang. Lit.; Rural Dev. Abstr.; Middle East J.

US/0084-2281
AFRICA (WASHINGTON, D.C.). (AFRICA.). [Africa]. (1966)-. English. an (Sept.). $9.50. Stryker-Post Publications, PO Drawer 1200, Harpers Ferry WV 25425. **Tel** (800)995-1400. **ED** Pierre E. Dostert. **LC** DT1; .D6. **DD** 916. ctrl circ.
Desc: One of seven titles focusing on current events. This lively reference tool addresses social, economic, political and controversial issues. A must for schools and libraries.

US/0198-9278
AFRICAN AND AFRO-AMERICAN STUDIES AND RESEARCH CENTER REPRINTS. [Afr. Afro-Am. Stud. Res. Cent. repr.]. **Main/Corp** University of Texas at Austin. African and Afro-American Studies Research Center. Series 2, No. 1- May 1980-. Periodical. English. Free. African and Afro-American Studies and Research Center, University of Texas at Austin, Jester Center A232A, Austin TX 78712. ***Continues*** *Reprint from the African and Afro-American Studies and Research Center of the University of Texas at Austin, 0198-9286.*

●US/1054-9781
AFRICAN CHRONICLE, THE. [Afr. chron.]. Vol. 1, No. 1 (Jan./Feb. 1992)-. Periodical. English. bm. $12.00. Zikawuna Publishing Company, PO Box 703, Palo Alto CA 94302-0703. **DD** 960.

UK/0951-0966
AFRICAN CONCORD. ***Suspended.*** [Afr. concord]. **VFOAT** Concord. No. 63 (24 Oct. 1985)-(19??). Periodical. English. wk. Concord Press of Nigeria, 5-15 Cromer Street, London WC1 England. **LC** DT515; .C688. **DD** 960/.05. ***Continues*** *Concord Weekly.*
Desc: Addresses current affairs covering the whole of Africa.
Ind/Abst Ethnoarts Index.

NR
AFRICAN CRUSADER. V. 1- July 1978-. Periodical. English. $1.00 per copy. Pacific Printers Ltd, 38 Commercial Avenue, Yaba Lagos Nigeria. **LC** DT515.A2; A34. **DD** 960/.05. **UDC** 960.

US/0149-4724
AFRICAN DIRECTIONS. Fall 1977-. Periodical. English. qt. $8.00. CD Chindongo, 5505 Selby Lane, Oxon Hill MD 20022. **LC** DT1; .A224. **DD** 960/.3/05. **UDC** 960.

US/8756-4653
AFRICAN ECHO. [Afr. echo]. (198?)-. Periodical. English. bm. African Echo, 117-32 226th Street, Cambria Heights NY 11411. **DD** 960.

SA
AFRICAN FREEDOM ANNUAL. 1st Ed.; 1977-. English. an. Southern African Freedom Foundation, PO Box 781112, Sandton 2146 Republic of South Africa. **ED** F R Metrowich. **LC** DT1; .A2254. **DD** 960/.05. **UDC** 960.

US
AFRICAN HISTORICAL DICTIONARIES. No. 1 (1974)-. Monographic series. English. ir. $55.00. Scarecrow Press Inc., 52 Liberty Street, PO Box 4167, Metuchen NJ 08840. **Tel** (908)548-8600, (800)537-7107.

US/8755-5565
AFRICAN INTELLIGENCE DIGEST. [Afr. intell. dig.]. **VFOAT** AID; A.I.D. Periodical. English. mo. $59.00. Council on Southern Africa, PO Box 39810, Phoenix AZ 85069. **LC** DT1; .A2263. **DD** 960/.05. **UDC** 960.

History(General) —History of Africa

CN/0827-8040
AFRICAN LETTER, THE. See Ethnic Interests.

US/1056-0483
AFRICAN MIRROR (WASHINGTON, D.C.), THE. (THE AFRICAN MIRROR.). [Afr. mirror]. (Nov. 1990)-. Periodical. English. mo. $1.90 (single issue). Success Group Associates, 816 Easley Street, Number 513, Silver Spring MD 20910. **DD** 960.

KE
AFRICAN SPOTLIGHT. No. 1 (Nov. 1968)-. Periodical. English. mo. $4.20. Equatorial Publishing Ltd., Mercury House, PO Box 7973, Nairobi Kenya. **LC** DT1; .A2287. **DD** 960/.05.

SA/0002-0184
AFRICAN STUDIES (JOHANNESBURG). See Anthropology.

GH
AFRICAN STUDIES JOURNAL. V. 1-. Periodical. English. University of Cape Coast, The Editor, Department of Educational Foundations, Faculty of Education, Cape Coast Ghana. **LC** DT1; .A2295. **DD** 960/.05. **UDC** 960.

UK/0065-406X
AFRICAN STUDIES SERIES. Added/Corp African Studies Centre. Vol. 1 (1970)-. Monographic series. English. ir. Price varies per volume. Cambridge University Press, The Edinburgh Building, Shaftesbury Road, Cambridge CB2 2RU United Kingdom. **Tel** 011 44 223 312393, FAX 011 44 223 325959. **(Subscription address:** North America/ Cambridge University Press, 40 West 20th Street, New York, NY 10011-4211; telephone: (212)924-3900**)**

PL/0002-029X
AFRICANA BULLETIN. [Afr. bull.]. **Added/Corp** Uniwersytet Warszawski. Studium Afrykanistyczne. (1964)-. Bulletin. English (French). ir. $5.50. **(Subscription address:** ARS Polona, PO Box 1001, 00068 Warsaw Poland.**) LC** DT19.9.P6; A65.
Ind/Abst Am. Hist. Life (1975-); Anthropol. Index; Geogr. Abstr. Human Geogr. (?-?); Int. Bibliogr. Sociol.; Int. Dev. Abstr.; Int. Labour Doc.; Leis. Recreat. Tour. Abstr. (1975-); MLA Int. Bibl. Books Artic. Mod. Lang. Lit.; Rural Dev. Abstr. (1975-); Soils Fert.; Trop. Dis. Bull.; World Agric. Econ. (1975-).

GW/0002-0311
AFRICANA MARBURGENSIA. [Afr. Marburgen.]. No. 1 (1968)-. Periodical. German (English and German; summaries and/or abstracts in French). sa. **LC** DT1; .A255.
Ind/Abst MLA Int. Bibl. Books Artic. Mod. Lang. Lit.

US/1058-6156
AFRICENTRIC MONITOR, THE. (1991)-. Periodical. English. bm. $89.00. The Africentric Monitor, 9044 Palisades Plaza, Box 9037, North Bergen NJ 07047.

DK
AFRIKA BULLETIN. Main/Corp Forbundet Mod Imperialismen. Afrikakomiteen. (1975)-. Periodical. Danish (Danish). ir. Afrikagrupperna I Sverige, Barnaengsgat 23 116, 41 Stockholm Sweden. **LC** DT30; .F58a.

NO/0332-6241
AFRIKA INFORMASJON. [Afr. inf.]. **Added/Corp** Fellesradet for det Srlige Afrika (Norway). Vol. 1 (1978)-. Periodical. Norwegian. ir. Kr30.00. Forlagsentralen Tidsskriftavd, PB 150 Furuset, 1001 Oslo 10 Norway. **Tel** 011 47 2 2320995. **LC** DT353; .A43.

GW/0568-1715
AFRIKA-STUDIEN. [Afr.-Stud.]. **Added/Corp** Ifo-Institut fuer Wirtschaftsforschung. (1964)-. Monographic series. German. ir. Price varies per volume. Weltforum Verlagsgesellschaft, Marienburger Strasse 22, D 50968 Cologne Germany. **Tel** 011 49 221 376950. **CODEN** IFOAAP.
Ind/Abst GeoRef; Rural Dev. Abstr.; World Agric. Econ.

GW/0721-3107
AFRIKA UND DIE DEUTSCHEN : JAHRBUCH DER DEUTSCHEN AFRIKA-STIFTUNG. 1981-. Periodical. German (French). an. Verlag Gunther Neske, Pfullingen Germany. **LC** DT1; .A287. **DD** 960/.05. **UDC** 960.

CM
AFRIKA ZAMANI. No. 1- Sept. 1973-. Periodical. French. sa. 12.00CFAF. Association des Historiens Africains, BP 309, Yaounde Cameroon. **LC** DT20; .A66. **DD** 960/.05. **UDC** 960.

UK
AFRIQUE. Ceased. No. 1 (May/June 1977)-Ceased ?. Periodical. French. mo. Africa Journal Ltd, Kirkman House, 54A Tottenham Court Road, London W1P 0BT England. **Tel** 011 44 71 637 9341. **LC** DT1; .A4713. **DD** 960/.05. **UDC** 960.

FR/0399-0370
AFRIQUE ET L'ASIE MODERNES, L'. Ceased. [Afr. Asie mod.]. (1974)- Iss. 168 (Feb. 1992). Periodical. French. qt. L'Afrique et l'Asie Modernes, 13 rue du Four, 75006 Paris France. **Tel** 43269690. **LC** DT1; .A85. **DD** 950/.05. **UDC** 950. **Bk Rev Circ:** 3,000 (ctrl).
Continues Afrique et l'Asie.
Desc: Africa and Asia political, economical and sociological subjects.
Ind/Abst Am. Hist. Life (1954-); Geogr. Abstr. Human Geogr.; Int. Dev. Abstr.; Int. Polit. Sci. Abstr.; LABORDOC; PAIS Int. Print; Middle East J.

US/0741-2592
AFRIQUE HISTOIRE U.S. Suspended. VFOAT AH; A.H.; Afrique Histoire US. **VAT** Afrique Histoire United States. Vol. 1, No. 1 (1982)-(1993). Periodical. English (French). qt. Afrique Histoire US, PO Box 88622, Indianapolis IN 46208-0622. **Tel** (317)283-3634. **ED** Amadou Koly Niang. **LC** DT1; .A537. **DD** 960/.05. **Bk Rev. Ad Acc. Circ:** 2,500 (ctrl).
Desc: Topics emphasize African history and the diaspora with their connections with the world; subjects relate to politics, arts, anthropology, archaeology and sociology.
Ind/Abst Ethnoarts Index.

US/1055-7393
AFRO-AMERICAN HISTORY KIT (K-6 ED.). Ceased. (AFRO-AMERICAN HISTORY KIT.). (1989)-(19??). Monographic series. English. Associated Publishers Incorporated, 1407 14th Street NW, Washington DC 20005. **Tel** (202)265-1441. **Separated from** Afro-American History Kit (Washington, D.C. : 1987).

BL/0002-0591
AFRO-ASIA. [Afro-Asia]. No. 1 (Dec. 1965)-. Periodical. Portuguese. Centro dos Estudos Afro-Orientais da Universidade Federal da Bahia, Salvador Brazil. **UDC** 950.
Ind/Abst Am. Hist. Life (1976-).

NR
AFRO IMAGE. (19??)-. Periodical. English. Twelve times a year. $5.80. African Cultures Publishers Ltd, PO Box 20, Mile 2 Ubulunor Road, Ogwashi-Uku Nigeria. **LC** DT1; .A543. **DD** 916/.03/05.

UA
AL-FIKR AL-JADID. Periodical. Arabic. 0.60 single issue. 58 26 July Street, Al-Qahirah United Arab Republic Egypt. **LC** DT43; .F53. **UDC** 962.

UA
AL-ISKANDARIYAH. Periodical. Arabic. £E0.15 single issue. 8 Shari Talat Harb, PO Box 995, Alexandria Egypt. **LC** DT73.A4; I83.

TI/0330-8081
AL-MAJALLAH AL-TARIKHIYAH AL-ARABIYAH LIL-DIRASAT AL-UTHMANIYAH. VFOAT Arab Historical Review for Ottoman Studies. (1990)-. Periodical. Arabic (English and French). qt. $100.00. Arab Historical Review for Ottoman Studies, PO Box 50, 1118 Zaghouan Tunisia. **Tel** 02 76 446. **LC** DS62.4; .M34. **Bk Rev. Circ:** 200 (ctrl).
Desc: Covers modern and contemporary history of Maghreb.
Ind/Abst Am. Hist. Life (1964-1967).

US
AL-MISRI. VFOAT The Egyptian; Egyptian. Periodical. Arabic. $2.00 Single Issue. The Egyptian, PO Box 2736, Hollywood CA 90028. **LC** DT43; .M583.

AE
AL-MUJAHID. VFOAT El-Moudjahid; Moudjahid. Periodical. Arabic. wk. 180.00. Jabhat Al-Tahrir Al-Watani, PO Box 810, Al-Jazair Algeria. **LC** DT271; .M85. **UDC** 965.

UA
AL-RAY AL-JADID. Periodical. Arabic. Dar Al-Fikr, 58 Shari 26 Yuliyu, Al-Qahirah United Arab Republic Egypt. **LC** DT43; .R38. **UDC** 962.

UK
AL-SABAH AL-JADID / LISAN HAL AL-HIZB AL-ITTIHADI AL-DIMUQRATI WA-JABHAT AL-MUARADAH AL-WATANIYAH AL-DIMUQRATIYAH AL-SUDANIYAH. VFOAT Sabah el Gadid. Began in 1956. Periodical. Arabic. El Sabah el Gadid Magazine, Magazine Office, 25 Berkhamsted Avenue, Wembley Park, London England. **LC** DT154.1; .S23.

UA
AL-SALAM; MAJALLAH SHAHRIYAH SIYASIYAH THAQAFIYAH JAMIAH. No. 1 (July/August 1978)-. Periodical. Arabic. Dar Al-Ilam Al-Arabi, 12 Shari Yusuf Al-Jundi Bi-Bab, Al-Luq Cairo Egypt. **LC** DT43; .S23. **UDC** 962.

MR
AL-TAHADDI. VFOAT Jaridat Al-Tahaddi. Periodical. Arabic. sm. 1MD single issue. 2 Zanqat Istanbul SB 80, Al-Rabat Morocco. **LC** DT325; .T33. **UDC** 964.

UA
AL-TAKAMUL. No. 1, (October 1982)-. Periodical. Arabic. qt. 22 B Shari Al-Jumhuriyah, Al-Qahirah Egypt. **LC** DT43; .T34. **UDC** 962.

MU
AL-WAHDAH. Periodical. Arabic. Wizaarat Al-Shabibah Wa-Al-Riyadah, PO Box 172, Nuwakshut Mauritania. **LC** DT553.M2; W28. **UDC** 966.12.

MR
AL-ZAMAN AL-MAGHRIBI. Periodical. Arabic. qt. 70.00. Al-Zaman Al-Maghribi, Al-Hisab Al-Baridi, RAQM 1877-50 B Al-Rabat, Al-Maghrib Morocco. **LC** DT301; .Z35. **UDC** 964.

AE
ALWAN. VFOAT Revue Alouan. Periodical. Arabic. mo. 24.00AD. Wizarat Al-Ilan Wa-Al-Thagafah C C P 390882, Al-Jazair Algeria. **LC** DT271; .A74. **UDC** 965.

MR
AMAZIGH. VFOAT Revue Amazigh; Amazigh. No. 1 (1980)-. French (Arabic and Berber languages). Six times a year. $20.00. Amazigh, 8 Place des Alaouites BP 4413, Rabat Morocco. **LC** DT313.2; .A48.

IV
ANNALES DE L'UNIVERSITE D'ABIDJAN. SERIE I : HISTOIRE. Main/Corp Abidjan, Ivory Coast. Universite. **VFOAT** Histoire. V. 1- 1972-. Periodical. French. an. Universite Abidjan, Abidjan Ivory Coast West Africa. **Tel** 44 56 49, telex 26138 RECTU-CI. **LC** DT545.A2; A87A. **DD** 916.66/8/005. **UDC** 966.68.

FR/0570-1937
ANNEE AFRICAINE. Ceased. [Annee afr.]. **Added/Corp** Centre de Hautes Etudes Administratives sur l'Afrique et l'Asie Modernes (France) Centre d'Etude des Relations Internationales (France) Centre d'Etude d'Afrique Noire (Institut d'Etudes Politiques de Bordeaux). (1965)-(1993). French. ir. Editions A Pedone, 13 rue Soufflot, 75005 Paris France. **Tel** 011 33 1 43540597. **LC** DT30; .A56. **DD** 320.9/6/03.
Ind/Abst Int. Bibliogr. Sociol.; Int. Polit. Sci. Abstr.

FR/0247-400X
ANNUAIRE DES PAYS DE L'OCEAN INDIEN. [Annu. pays ocean indien]. 1- 1974-. French (summaries and/or abstracts in English). an. Editions du CNRS, 22 rue Saint Armand, F 75015 Paris France. **Tel** 011 33 1 45075050. **LC** DT468; .A54. **DD** 969/.005. **UDC** 969(058). **Circ:** 1,500.
Desc: Focuses on the countries to the southwest of the Indian Ocean, studies, columns, chronology and bibliography in related social science fields.
Ind/Abst Int. Bibliogr. Sociol.; Int. Polit. Sci. Abstr.

FR
ANNUAIRE JEUNE AFRIQUE, L'. VFOAT Rapport Annuel sur l'Etat de l'Afrique. (1991)-. French. an. 100.00F French-speaking Africa; 180.00F Europe; 190.00F other. Groupe Jeune Afrique, 57 Bis rue d Auteuil, 75016 Paris France. **Tel** 011 33 1 44301960.
Continues Annuaire de l'Afrique et du Moyen-Orient.

GO
ANNUAIRE NATIONAL DE LA REPUBLIQUE GABONAISE. VFOAT Annuaire National et International; Annuaire National du Gabon; Annuaire Nationale. (1980)-. French. Edition Inf Afrique, B P 3875, Libreville Gabon. **LC** DT546.1; .A6. **DD** 967/.21005.

UK
ANNUAL REPORT / SCHOOL OF ORIENTAL AND AFRICAN STUDIES, UNIVERSITY OF LONDON. See History(General)-History of Asia.

FR/0066-4871
ANTIQUITES AFRICAINES. [Antiqu. afr.]. **Added/Corp** Centre National de la Recherche Scientifique (France). Vol. 1 (1967)-. French. ir. 32.00F. Editions du CNRS, 22 rue Saint Armand, F 75015 Paris France. **Tel** 011 33 1 45075050. **LC** DT191; .A6. **Circ:** 1,500.
Desc: Archaeological and historical studies on North Africa from protohistory to the Arab Conquest.
Ind/Abst Avery Index Archit. Period. Suppl. Colum. Univ. (19??-1997); BHA : Biblio. Hist. Art; Numis. Lit.

FR/0983-1509
ARABIES. [Arabies]. No. 1 Jan. (1987)-. Periodical. French (French; summaries and/or abstracts in Arabic, English and German). mo. 800.00F (all institutions except Europe and North Africa); 600.00F (institutions France, North Africa and Europe);600.00F (individuals all except Europe and North Africa); 300.00F (individuals France); 400.00F (individuals North Africa and Europe (except France)). Groupe de Conseil En Commun, 78 rue

Jouffroy, F-75107 Paris France. **Tel** 011 33 1 46223414. **LC** DS36; .A76.
Ind/Abst PAIS Int. Print (1991-).

SA
ARGIEF-JAARBOEK VIR SUID-AFRIKAANSE GESKIEDENIS. **See** Genealogy and Heraldry-Archives.

AO/0004-2781
ARQUIVOS DE ANGOLA. [Arq. Angola]. **Added/Corp** Museu de Angola. Angola. Reparticao de Estatistica Geral. Angola. Liceu Central de Salvador Correia. Vol. 1-5 (1933)-. Periodical. Portuguese. qt. **LC** DT611; .A3.
Ind/Abst Am. Hist. Life (1957-1966,1968-1969).

XO/0571-2742
ASIAN AND AFRICAN STUDIES (BRATISLAVA, CZECHOSLOVAKIA). **See** History(General)-History of Asia.

IS/0066-8281
ASIAN AND AFRICAN STUDIES (JERUSALEM). (ASIAN AND AFRICAN STUDIES.). [Asian Afr. stud.]. **Added/Corp** Hevrah ha-Mizrahit ha-Yisreelit. Vol. 1, (1965)-. Periodical. English. Three times a year (Mar., July, Nov.). $60.00 (institutions); $40.00 (individual). Institute of Middle East Studies, University of Haifa, C/O Dick Bruggeman, Haifa 31999 Israel. **Tel** 011 972 4 240655, FAX 011 972 4 342104, telex 46660. **ED** Professor G. R. Warrurg. **LC** DS1; .A4734. **DD** 950. **[CCC]. Bk Rev**, (Qty: 10). **Ad Acc. Pr Rev. Circ:** 800 (ctrl). available on microfiche from University Microfilms International (UMI).
Desc: Studies of India's policy toward West Asia, especially on the Palestine/Israel issue. Contains references to Mahatma Gandhi's views.
Ind/Abst Am. Hist. Life (1973-); Index Islam. Lit.; Int. Bibliogr. Sociol.; Middle East Abstr. Index; MLA Int. Bibl. Books Artic. Mod. Lang. Lit.; Middle East J.

MR
BADIL (RABAT, MOROCCO). (AL-BADIL.). Periodical. Arabic. 150.00MD. 4 Zanqat Zahlah, Al-Rabat Morocco. **LC** DT301; .B33. **UDC** 964.

IV/0378-469X
BALAFON. Began with: No. 1 (Jan. 1965). Periodical. French. qt. Air Afrique, 12 Bis, Rue Jean-Jaures, 92807 Puteaux France. **LC** DT470; .B27.
Ind/Abst Ethnoarts Index.

US/0732-6467
BIBLIOTHECA AEGYPTIA. Vol. 1-. Monographic series. English. ir. Price varies per volume. Undena Publications, PO Box 97, Malibu CA 90265. **Tel** (310)649-2612. **ED** D P Silverman. **UDC** 902(32). **Circ:** 200.
Desc: Philology and archaeology of ancient Egypt, from late prehistory to ptolemaic period.

AO/0020-3726
BOLETIM DO INSTITUTO DE ANGOLA. [Bol. Inst. Angola]. **Added/Corp** Instituto de Angola. No. 1 (1953)-. Bulletin. Portuguese. **LC** DT611.A2; A52. cum. index.

UA
BULLETIN DE LA SOCIETE D'ARCHEOLOGIE COPTE. **Added/Corp** Jamiyat Al-Athar Al-Qibtiyah (Egypt). **VFOAT** Majallat Jamiyat Al-Athar Al-Qibtiyah. (1938)-. Bulletin. French (English, German, Arabic and Italian). **LC** DT57; .S6. ***Continues*** *Bulletin de l'Association des Amis de l'Art Copte.*
Ind/Abst BHA : Biblio. Hist. Art.

FR
BULLETIN DE LA SOCIETE FRANCAISE D'EGYPTOLOGIE. **Added/Corp** Societe Francaise d'Egyptologie. **VFOAT** BSFE. No. 1 (June 1949)-. Periodical. French. Three times a year. 180.00F. Societe Francaise d Egyptologie, PL Marcelin Berthelot/Coll Fr, 75231 Paris Cedex 05 France. **Tel** 40 46 94 31. cum. index.
Ind/Abst BHA : Biblio. Hist. Art.

MU
BULLETIN DOCUMENTAIRE MENSUEL - AGENCE MAURITANIENNE DE PRESSE. **Main/Corp** Agence Mauritanienne de Presse. Bulletin. French. Agence Mauritanienne de Presse, Mauritania. **LC** DT553.M2; A22. **DD** 966/.1/005. **UDC** 966.12.

UK/0952-2948
BULLETIN OF TANZANIAN AFFAIRS. No. 1 (Dec. 1975)-. Bulletin. English. Three times a year (Jan., May, Sept.). £3.80 UK; £7.50 Europe; £10.00 others. Britain-Tanzania Society, 14B Westbourne Grove Terrace, London WC2 England. **Tel** 011 44 71 727 1755, 011 44 71 435 4994, telex 081-671-7306(Quote C119). **ED** David Brewin. **Bk Rev. Ad Acc. Circ:** 800.
Desc: All aspects of life in Tanzania including current affairs.
Ind/Abst Int. Bibliogr. Sociol.

UK/0001-3196
BULLETIN OF THE ABERDEEN UNIVERSITY AFRICAN STUDIES GROUP. **Main/Corp** Aberdeen University African Studies Group. **VFOAT** Bulletin of the University of Aberdeen African Studies. No. 1- Feb. 1967-. Bulletin. English. an. £1.00. University of Aberdeen / African Studies Group, Dunbar Street, Aberdeen AB9 2TY Scotland. **Tel** 011 44 224 40241. **ED** J C Stone. **LC** DT19.95.A3; A62. **DD** 916/.03/007204125. **UDC** 916. **Bk Rev. Circ:** 350 (ctrl).
Desc: A record of activities in African studies at Aberdeen University.

US/0270-210X
BULLETIN OF THE EGYPTOLOGICAL SEMINAR. **See** Archaeology.

US/0164-0666
BULLETIN OF THE SOUTHERN ASSOCIATION OF AFRICANISTS, THE. **Main/Corp** Southern Association of Africanists (U.S.). V. 3, No. 3- Oct. 1975-. Bulletin. English. Three times a year. Ruth J Bishop, 2025 Markham Drive, Chapel Hill NC 27514. **LC** DT1; .S7A. **DD** 960/.05. **UDC** 960. ***Continues*** *Newsletter of the Southern Association of Africanists.*

BD
BURUNDI EN IMAGES / REPUBLIQUE DU BURUNDI, MINISTERE DE L'INFORMATION, DIRECTION GENERALE DES PUBLICATIONS DE PRESSE, DEPARTEMENT DE LA PRESSE PERIODIQUE, LE. **Added/Corp** Burundi. Departement de la Presse Periodique. No. 1 (May 30, 1979)-. Periodical. French. ir. Departement de la Presse Periodique, BP 1400, Bujumbura Republique du Burundi. **LC** DT450.5; .B87. **DD** 967/.572/005.

SG
CAAXAAN FAAXEE / JS. Periodical. French. mo. Caaxaan Faaxee, 22 rue du Docteur Guillet, Dakar Senegal. **LC** DT549.8; .C32. **UDC** 968.0.

SA/0379-4830
CABO. [Cabo]. V. 1- Aug. 1972-. Periodical. Multiple languages (Afrikaans and English). R3.00. Historical Society of Cape Town, PO Box 2615, Cape Town South Africa. **LC** DT848.C5; C2. **DD** 916.8/7.

TI/0008-0012
CAHIERS DE TUNISIE. (LES CAHIERS DE TUNISIE.). [Cah. Tunis.]. **Added/Corp** Institut des Hautes Etudes de Tunis. Jamiah al-Tunisiyah. Kulliyat al-Adab wa-al-Ulum al-Insaniyah. Vol. 1 (1953)-. Periodical. French (Arabic). qt. $12.00 Africa, Saudi Arabian Peninsula; $25.00 other. University of Tunis / Service des Publications et Sciences Humaines, 94 Boulevard du 9 Avril, 1938 / BP 1128, Tunis 1007 Tunisia. **Tel** , . **LC** DT241; .C23. cum. index.
Desc: Covers general history, philosophy, literature, archaeology, and sociology.
Ind/Abst Am. Hist. Life (1963-1969, 1979-); Anthropol. Index; Int. Bibliogr. Sociol.; Middle East J.

FR/0008-0055
CAHIERS D'ETUDES AFRICAINES. [Cah. etud. afr.]. **Added/Corp** Ecole Pratique des Hautes Etudes (France). Section des Sciences Economiques et Sociales. Ecole des Hautes Etudes en Sciences Sociales. Vol. 1 (1960)-. Periodical. French (English). Four times a year. 400.00F (France), 460.00F (other) institutions; 270.00F (individuals). Editions EHESS, 131 Boulevard Saint Michel, 75005 Paris France. **Tel** 011 33 43 544715. **(Subscription address:** Centrale des Revues, 11 rue Gossin, 92543 Montrouge Cedex France.**)** Index Available, published separately, free-automatically sent. cum. index.
Ind/Abst ABC POL SCI; Am. Hist. Life (1966-); Anthropol. Lit.; Curr. Geogr. Publ.; Geogr. Abstr. Human Geogr. (1966-); Int. Bibliogr. Sociol.; Linguist. Lang. Behav. Abstr.; MLA Int. Bibl. Books Artic. Mod. Lang. Lit.; Soc. Plann. Policy Dev. Abstr.; Sociol. Abstr. (1966-).

UA
CAHIERS D'HISTOIRE EGYPTIENNE. **VFOAT** Egyptian History Papers. (1948)-. Periodical. Multiple languages. **LC** DT43; .C33. cum. index.
Ind/Abst Am. Hist. Life (1955-1969).

BE/0250-1619
CAHIERS DU CEDAF, LES. **See** Social Sciences.

II/0376-7647
CAIRO. V. 1- Jan. 1972-. Periodical. English. 4.00. Press Bureau, Embassy of the Arab Republic of Egypt, 55-57 Sundar Nagar, New Delhi India. **LC** DT43; .C34. **DD** 962/.005. **UDC** 962.

SP
CALAMO. **Added/Corp** Instituto Hispano-Arabe de Cultura. No. 1 (April/May/June 1984)-. Periodical. Spanish. qt. Agencia Espanola de Cooperacion Internacional, Ins. Coop.Iberoamericana, Desarrollo Y M. Arabe, Avda. Reyes Catolicos 4, 28040 Madrid Spain. **Tel** 5838180, 2830250. **LC** DS35.74.S7; C34.

CN/0008-3968
CANADIAN JOURNAL OF AFRICAN STUDIES. [Can. j. Afr. stud.]. **Added/Corp** Canadian Association of African Studies. Committee on African Studies in Canada. **VFOAT** Journal Canadien des Etudes Africanes; Revue Canadienne des Etudes Africaines. Vol. 1 (Mar. 1967)-. Periodical. English (French). Three times a year (Apr., Aug., Dec.). 75.00Can$ (comes also with Association Canadienne des Etudes Africaines membership). University of Toronto Innis College, 2 Sussex Avenue, Toronto Ontario M5S 1J5 Canada. **Tel** (416)978-3424, FAX (416)978-7162. **ED** Roger Riendeau (editor's telephone: (416)978-7067). **LC** DT19.9.C3; B82. **DD** 916/.005. **[CCC]. Bk Rev. Ad Acc, Adv Mgr:** same as editor. **Pr Rev. Circ:** 1,200. Documents available from The Genuine Article. ***Supersedes*** *Bulletin of African Studies in Canada, 0525-1370.*
Desc: Multi-disciplinary in character, focuses on African studies in the areas of anthropology, education, political science, economics, history, and arts.
Ind/Abst ABC POL SCI (1968-); Abstr. Anthropol.; Am. Hist. Life (1974-); Anthropol. Index; Arts Humanit. Citation Index [Select. Cov.]; Curr. Contents Soc. Behav. Sci.; Curr. Geogr. Publ. (199?-); Ethnoarts Index; Hum. Rights Intern. Rep.; Int. Bibliogr. Sociol.; Int. Dev. Abstr. (?-?); Int. Labour Doc.; Leis. Recreat. Tour. Abstr. (1974-); Middle East Abstr. Index; MLA Int. Bibl. Books Artic. Mod. Lang. Lit.; Res. Alert [Full Cov.]; Rural Dev. Abstr.; Soc. Plann. Policy Dev. Abstr.; Soc. Sci. Cit. Index [Full Cov.]; Sociol. Abstr. (?-?); Sug. Indus. Abstr.; Women Stud. Abstr.; World Agric. Econ.

JM/1015-6879
CARIBBEAN JOURNAL OF AFRICAN STUDIES. [Caribb. j. Afr. stud.]. **VFOAT** CJAS. No. 1 (1978)-. English. ir. African Studies Association of the West Indies, PO Box 222, Kingston 7 Jamaica West Indies. ***Supersedes*** *Bulletin - African Studies Association of the West Indies.*
Ind/Abst MLA Int. Bibl. Books Artic. Mod. Lang. Lit.

SA
CHAIRMAN'S REPORT - AFRICA INSTITUTE OF SOUTH AFRICA. **Main/Corp** Africa Institute of South Africa. **VFOAT** Voorsittersverslag. 1974/75-. Afrikaans (English). an. Africa Institute of South Africa, PO Box 630, Pretoria 0001 South Africa. **Tel** 011 27 12 328-6970, FAX 011 27 12 323-8153. **LC** DT1; .A2147. **DD** 960/.07/11682. **UDC** 968.2(047). ***Continues*** *Annual Report - Africa Institute of South Africa.*

SX/0578-2724
CIMBEBASIA. MEMOIR. [Cimbebasia Mem.]. No. 1- 1967-. Periodical. English. South-West Africa, Box 1203, Windhoek Africa. **CODEN** CMBMBE. ***Supersedes in part*** *Cimbebasia.*

FR/0418-2901
COLLECTION - (DAKAR). **Main/Corp** Dakar. Universite. Centre de Recherches, d'Etudes et de Documentation sur les Institutions et la Legislation Africaines. Began publication with 1, 1961. Monographic series. French. ir. Price varies per volume. Collection, 8 rue Halvey, 75009 Paris France. **UDC** 34+352/354(6).

UK
COLONIALISM IN AFRICA. ***Ceased.*** (19??)-Series complete with Volume 5. Academic Scholarly Publication. English. ir. Cambridge University Press, The Edinburgh Building, Shaftesbury Road, Cambridge CB2 2RU United Kingdom. **Tel** 011 44 223 312393, FAX 011 44 223 325959.

RE
COMBAT NATIONAL, LE. No. 1 (April 1, 1974)-. Periodical. French. bm. 100.00. B P 907, Saint Dennis 97478 Reunion. **LC** DT469.R3; C65. **DD** 969/.81.

SA/0379-9867
CONTREE / RAAD VIR GEESTESWETENSKAPLIKE NAVORSING, INSTITUUT VIR GESKIEDENISNAVORSING, AFDELING STREEKGESKIEDENIS. **Added/Corp** Institute for Historical Research (Human Services Research Council). Section for Regional History. Institute for Historical Research (Human Services Research Council). Division for Research into Regional and Socio-Economic History. Institute for Historical Research (Human Services Research Council). Division for Local and Regional History Research. No. 1 (Jan. 1977)-. Periodical. Afrikaans (English). sa. R15.00. Contree Rau History Department, PO Box 524, 2092 Johannesburg South Africa. **Tel** 011 27 11 4892001. **ED** C.C. Eloff. **LC** DT751; .C66. **DD** 968/.005. Index available. cum. index. **Bk Rev. Ad Acc. Circ:** 1,500 (ctrl).
Desc: Journal for South African Urban and Regional History.
Ind/Abst Am. Hist. Life (1986-).

US/0069-9624
CONTRIBUTIONS IN AFRO-AMERICAN AND AFRICAN STUDIES. (1969)-. Monographic series. English. ir. Price varies per volume.

History(General) — History of Africa

Greenwood Press Inc., PO Box 5007, Westport CT 06881-5007. **Tel** (203)226-3571, FAX (203)222-1502. **LC** UNC.

US/1051-2853
CONTRIBUTIONS TO AFRICAN AMERICAN LITERATURE AND AFRICAN STUDIES. See Literature.

RH/0250-2992
COOKEIA : SERIES OF MISCELLANEOUS PUBLICATIONS IN THE HUMAN SCIENCES BY THE NATIONAL MUSEUMS AND MONUMENTS OF ZIMBABWE. Added/Corp National Museums and Monuments (Zimbabwe). **VFOAT** Cookeia, Zimbabwe. Vol. 1, No. 1 (Sept. 1984)-. Monographic series. English. ir. Price varies per volume. Zimbabwe Museum of Human Sciences, PO Box 8006, Causeway Harare Zimbabwe. **Tel** 011 263 4 7048312. **LC** DT2871; .C66. **DD** 968.9105. *Continues* Occasional Papers of the National Museums and Monuments. Series A, Human Sciences.

SP
CUADERNOS (CENTRO DE INFORMACION Y DOCUMENTACION AFRICANAS (MADRID, SPAIN)). (CUADERNOS.). Spanish. mo. **LC** DT14; .C8. **DD** 960/.05.

IV
DECENNIE 2 [I.E. DEUX]. (Mar. 1971)-. Periodical. French. mo. 25.00CFAF. SARL Inter-Continents Promotion, B P 20.991, Abidjan Ivory Coast. **LC** DT1; .D3.

SA
DECENTRALISATION BOARD ANNUAL REPORT. Main/Corp South Africa. Decentralisation Board. **VFOAT** Desentralisasierand Jaarverslag. (1990/1991)-. English. **LC** WMLC L 83/609. *Continues* Report on the Activities of the Board for the Period... .

FR/0152-2981
DEMAIN L'AFRIQUE. No. 1- Sept. 1977-. Periodical. French. $18.00. Demain l'Afrique, B N P 3 Bvd Gouvion-Saint-Cyr, 75017 Paris France. **LC** DT1; .D34. **DD** 960/.05. **UDC** 960.

CG
DIONGA. (19??)-. Periodical. French. mo. 600K. Dionga, 2 rue Dima Immeuble Amasco, Kinshasa Zaire. **LC** DT641; .D56. **DD** 916.75/1/03305.

UA
DIRASAT AFRIQIYAH. VFOAT African Studies. 1- April 1979-. Periodical. Arabic (English). qt. 0.50 single issue. Al-Jamiyah Al-Afriqiyah Bi-Al-Qahirah, 5 Shari Ahmad Hishmat Al-Zamalik, Al-Qahirah Egypt. **LC** DT1; D47. **DD** 960/.05. **UDC** 960.

ZA
DIRECTORY FOR ZAMBIA, MALAW, BOTSWANA AND ADJACENT TERRITORIES, THE. Directory. English. an. 10.00. Directory Publishers of Zambia, PO Box 30963, Lusaka Zambia. **Tel** 212650/53. **LC** DT729; .D57. **DD** 968.06/025. **UDC** 968(058). **Ad Acc**.

●US
DIRECTORY OF AFRICAN AND AFRICAN-AMERICAN STUDIES IN THE UNITED STATES. See Ethnic Interests.

US/1052-8512
DOCUMENT - AFRIKA BARAZA. (DOCUMENT.). [Document - Afrika Baraza]. **Added/Corp** Afrika Baraza. No. 1 (1982)-. Monographic series. English. **DD** 960.
Ind/Abst Hum. Rights Intern. Rep.

FR/0073-8212
DOCUMENTS, ETUDES ET REPERTOIRES. See Archaeology.

FR/0419-5779
DOCUMENTS POUR SERVIR A L'HISTOIRE DE L'AFRIQUE EQUATORIALE FRANCAISE. DEUXIEME SERIE: BRAZZA ET LA FONDATION DU CONGO FRANCAIS. Added/Corp Brazza et la Foundation du Congo Francais. (1966)-. Monographic series. French. ir. Price varies per volume. Walter de Gruyter Inc. / Hawthorne, 200 Saw Mill River Road, Hawthorne NY 10532. **Tel** (914)747-0110, GERMANY: 011/49/30/260050, FAX (914)747-1326, telex 646677. **(Subscription address:** Germany/ PO Box 110240, 1 Berlin 11 Germany) **DD** 916.72.

TI/0330-2601
ECHANGES (FRANCE. AMBASSADE (TUNISIA). SERVICE CULTUREL). (ECHANGES.). **VFOAT** Tabadul; Revue Echanges. Periodical. Arabic (French). sa. Revue Echanges, Service Culturel de l'Ambassade de France, 87 Avenue de la Liberte, Tunis Tunisia. **LC** DT241; .E26. **DD** 961/.1/005. **UDC** 961.
Ind/Abst Point Repere.

CN/0318-4382
ECHO D'AFRIQUE (QUEBEC). (ECHO D'AFRIQUE.). V. 1- Nov. 1973-. French. $5.00 Canada; $10.00 other. Union Generale des Etudiants Africains a Quebec, 6744 Pavillon Parent, Universite Laval, Quebec Quebec G1K 7P4 Canada. **DD** 960/.3/05. **UDC** 960.

MG
ECLAIR, L'. Periodical. French. 300Mal$ single issue. L'Eclair, BP 4392, Anosimasina a Antananarivo Republique Democratique de Madagascar. **LC** DT469.M21; E26. **DD** 960/.05. **UDC** 969.1.

DM
EGBAKOKU. Periodical. French (French). 200. Journal Egbakoku, 008/39 Banque Commerciale du Benin Agence de Dassa-Zoume, Rep Pop du Benin, Cotonou Dahomey. **LC** DT541.A2; E37. **DD** 966.9/3/005. **UDC** 966.82.

UK
EGYPTIAN BULLETIN, THE. Bulletin. English. Egyptian Education Bureau, 4 Chesterfield Gardens, London W1 England. **LC** DT70; .E396. **DD** 962/.005. **UDC** 962.

BE
ENQUETES ET DOCUMENTS D'HISTOIRE AFRICAINE. Main/Corp Louvain. Universite Catholique. Centre d'Histoire de l'Afrique. **Added/Corp** Universite Catholique de Louvain (1970-). Centre d'Histoire de l'Afrique. Universite de Lubumbashi. Centre d'Etudes et de Recherches Documentaires sur l'Afrique Centrale. Universite Catholique de Louvain (1970-). Centre de Recherches Africaines. Centre d'Etude et de Documentation Africaines. No 1 (1975)-. Periodical. French. Maria-Theresiatraat 21, B-3000 CCP 511-10, Leuven Belgium. **LC** DT641; .L68a. **DD** 967.5/103/05.
Ind/Abst Am. Hist. Life (1985-).

ML
ESSOR, L'. Periodical. French. 5500CFAF. Comite Militaire de Liberation Nationale, l'Essor, CCO 470, Bamako Republique du Mali. **LC** DT551.A2; E77. **DD** 966/.23/005. *Continues* Essor Hebdomadaire.

US/1048-812X
ETHIOPIAN ART AND CULTURE CODEX / THE ETHIOPIAN ART AND CULTURE CHRONICLES SOCIETY, THE. [Ethiop. art cult. codex]. **Added/Corp** Ethiopian Art and Culture Chronicles Society. **VFOAT** TEACC Codex. Vol. 1, Issue 1 (1991)-. Periodical. English. sa. $100.00. The Ethiopian Art and Culture Chronicles Society, TEACCS, 12251 Viejo Camino, Atascadero CA 93422. **DD** 963.

ET
ETHIOPIAN JOURNAL OF AFRICAN STUDIES / YA ITYOPYA YA AFRIQA QAND TENATENA MERMARA MASHET. Added/Corp Asmara Yunivarsiti. Institute of African Studies. Asmara Yunivarsiti. Faculty of Social Science. Asmara Yunivarsiti. Faculty of Economic and Administrative Sciences. Asmara Yunivarsiti. Institute of Language Studies. **VFOAT** Yaityopya Yafriqa Qud Tenatena Mermara Masehet. Vol. 1 No. 1 (June 1981)-. Periodical. English (Amharic and Tigrinya). sa. $5.78 Ethiopia; $23.00 other. Asmara University, PO Box 1220, Asmara Ethiopis. **LC** DT381; .E87.

US/1056-2354
ETHIOPIAN REVIEW. [Ethiop. rev.]. Vol. 1, No. 1 (Jan. 1991)-. Periodical. English (Amharic). mo. $60.00. Ethiopian Review, PO Box 191220, Los Angeles CA 90019. **Tel** (310)670-8513, FAX (310)670-8324. **ED** Elias Kifle. **LC** DT371; .E84. **DD** 305. **Bk Rev**, (Qty: 12). **Ad Acc, Adv Mgr:** Hailu. **Circ:** 16,000.
Desc: News and opinions magazine covering Ethopian political, economic, cultural and social issues.

SG/0850-2005
ETHIOPIQUES. [Ethiopiques]. (1975)-. French. sa. price varies per volume. Foundation Leopold Sedar Senghor, BP 2035, Dakar Senegal. **Tel** 011 221 212028 or, 215355. **LC** DT1; .E8.

ML
ETUDES MALIENNES. No. 1- 1970-. Periodical. French. B P 1596, Bamako Mali. **LC** DT551.A2; E85. **DD** 916.6/23/005. **UDC** 916.62.

FR
ETUDES SUR L'EGYPTE ET LE SOUDAN ANCIENS. Added/Corp Institut de Papyrologie et d'Egyptologie de Lille. (1973)-. French. an. 150.00F France; 180.00F France. Institute Papyrology Egyptology Lille, BP 149 Universite de Lille III, 59653 Villeneuve D-ASCQ France. **Tel** 011 33 20 9192002 ext. 4306. **LC** DT57; .E88. **DD** 932/.005.

TG/0531-2051
ETUDES TOGOLAISES. VFOAT Revue de l'I.N.R.S. Vol. 1, No. 1 (Dec. 1965)-. Periodical. French. qt. Institut National de la Recherche Scientifique / Togo, Lome Togo. **LC** DT582.A2; E84. **DD** 966.81. **UDC** 966.81. **NLM** W1 ET821.

NE/0046-3116
FACTS AND REPORTS. Added/Corp Holland Committee on Southern Africa. Komitee Zuidelijk Africa (Amsterdam, Netherlands). Angola Comite. **VAT** Facts & Reports. Vol. 1 (Nov. 1970)-. Periodical. English (English and French). Twenty-four times a year. Fl183.96. Holland Committee on South Africa, O Z Achterburgwal 173, 1012 DJ Amsterdam Netherlands. **Tel** 011 31 20 6270801, telex 17125 COMSA NL. **ED** Johan van Kesteren. **LC** DT36; .F2. **DD** 916.6/57/005. Index available. cum. index. **Circ:** 1,500.
Desc: Collation of international press clippings on Southern Africa.
Ind/Abst Hum. Rights Intern. Rep.

SA
FIAT LUX. Periodical. English (English). Distribution-Fiat Lux Indian Affairs, Private Bag X54330, Durban 4 South Africa. **LC** DT764.E3; F5. **DD** 968/.004/91411. **UDC** 968.

CN/1193-7351
FOCUS AFRICA. [Focus Afr.]. **Added/Corp** Inter-Church Coalition on Africa. **VFOAT** AfocusAfrica. (1991)-. Periodical. English. Six times a year. 20.00Can$ institutions; 15.00Can$ individuals. Inter-Church Coalition on Africa, 129 St. Clair Avenue, West, Toronto, Ontario, M4V 1N5 Canada. **Tel** (416)927-1124, FAX (416)927-7554. **DD** 968.06/3/05. *Continues* FocusSouth., 0832-543X.

CN/0827-3022
FOCUS ON NIGERIA. [Focus Niger.]. Vol. 1, No. 1 (1983)-. Periodical. an. Free. Information Service of Nigerian High Commission, 295 Metcalfe Street, Ottawa Ontario K2P 1R9 Canada. **DD** 966.9/005. **UDC** 966.9. ctrl circ. *Continues* Periscoping Nigeria, 0827-3014.

FR
GENERAL HISTORY OF AFRICA, THE. Added/Corp Unesco. Vol. 1 (1978)-. Monographic series. English (French and Spanish). ir. Price varies per volume. University of California Press, 2120 Berkeley Way, Berkeley CA 94720. **Tel** (510)642-4191, (510)642-3907, FAX (510)642-9917. **(Subscription address:** California Princeton Fulfillment Service, 1445 Lower Ferry Road, Ewing NJ 08618.) **LC** UNC.

US/0340-6369
GIORGIO LEVI DELLA VIDA CONFERENCES. [Giorgio Levi della Vida conf.]. **Added/Corp** Gustave E. von Grunebaum Center for Near Eastern Studies. (1967)-. English. be. Undena Publications, PO Box 97, Malibu CA 90265. **Tel** (310)649-2612. **Circ:** 200.
Desc: Contributions of Islamic scholars at biennial Levi Della Vida conferences.

US/1055-7636
GLOBAL AFRICA (WASHINGTON, D.C.). (GLOBAL AFRICA.). [Glob. Afr.]. **VFOAT** Global Africa. (1990)-. Periodical. English. bm. $10.50. Reunion Communications, Inc., PO Box 21700, Washington DC 20009. **DD** 960.

IV/1011-016X
GODO GODO. [Godo godo]. **Added/Corp** Universite d'Abidjan. Institut d'Histoire d'Art et d'Archeologie Africains. Universite Nationale de Cote d'Ivoire. Institut d'Histoire d'Art et d'Archeologie Africains. **VFOAT** Godo-Godo; Go Do Go Do. No. 1 (Oct. 1975)-. Periodical. French. ir. Universite d'Abidjan / History, Institut d'Histoire d'Art et d'Archeologie Africans, BP 945, Abidjan 08 Ivory Coast. **LC** DT1; .G6. **DD** 960/.05.

US/0360-9480
HABARI - AFRICAN BIBLIOGRAPHIC CENTER. (HABARI.). V. 1- Oct./Dec. 1973-. English. ir. African Bibliographic Center, PO Box 53398 Temple Heights Station, Washington DC 20009. **LC** DT1; .H22. **DD** 960/.05. **UDC** 960. *Supersedes* Habari (Washington, D.C. : 1969).

KE
HADITH. 1- 1968-. English. East Africa Literature Bureau, PO Box 30022, Nairobi Kenya. **LC** DT434.E2; A25. **DD** 967.6/2/005. **UDC** 967.62.

SA
HANDHAAF. Ceased. Added/Corp Federasie van Afrikaanse Kultuurvereniginge. (19??)-(19??). Periodical. Afrikaans. mo. Postbus 8711, Johannesburg South Africa. **LC** DT751; .H35.

RH
HERITAGE OF ZIMBABWE. Added/Corp History Society of Zimbabwe. (1986)-. English. an. $10.00. *Continues* Heritage (Salisbury, Zimbabwe).
Ind/Abst Am. Hist. Life (1981-); Int. Bibliogr. Sociol.

MR/0018-1005
HESPERIS TAMUDA. [Hesperis, Tamuda]. Vol. 1 (1960)-. Periodical. French. an. Univ Mohammed V, Faculte Lettre, Science Humainesserv Diffusion, Rabat Morocco. **LC** DT301; .H45. ***Continues*** *Hesperis; Tamuda.*
Ind/Abst Am. Hist. Life (1960-1973,1976-); Anthropol. Index; BHA : Biblio. Hist. Art; Int. Bibliogr. Sociol.; Middle East J.

SA/0018-229X
HISTORIA (THREE RIVERS). (HISTORIA.). [His.]. **Added/Corp** Historical Association of South Africa. (June 1956)-. Periodical. Multiple languages (Afrikaans and English). sa. R25.00. Department van Geskiedenis, Universiteit van Pretoria, Pretoria 0002 South Africa. **Tel** 011 27 12 4202323, FAX 011 27 12 431285. **ED** J. S. Bergh. **Bk Rev**, (Qty: 20). **Ad Acc**, **Adv Mgr:** J. Grobler. **Circ:** 350.

US/0361-5413
HISTORY IN AFRICA. [Hist. Afr.]. **Added/Corp** African Studies Association. Vol. 1 (1974)-. English. an (July). $25.00 (individuals), $40.00 (institutions) US; $27.00 (individuals), $42.00 (institutions) others. African Studies Association, Emory University, Credit Union Building, Atlanta GA 30322. **Tel** (404)329-6410, FAX (404)329-6433. **LC** DT19; .H58. **DD** 960/.07/2. Index available. cum. index. **Bk Rev**. **Ad Acc**. **Circ:** 2,000 (ctrl).
Desc: A journal of historical method.
Ind/Abst Am. Hist. Life (1974-); Ethnoarts Index.

US/0161-4703
HORN OF AFRICA. [Horn Afr.]. Vol. 1 (Jan./Mar. 1978)-. Periodical. English. qt. $25.00. Horn of Africa Journal Company, Rutgers University, Conklin Hall 311, Newark NJ 07102. **Tel** (201)273-1515. **ED** Osman S. Ali. **LC** DT367.A2; H67. **DD** 961/.005. **Bk Rev**. **Ad Acc**. **Circ:** 2,500.
Desc: This publication specializes in covering all aspects of the region called The Horn of Africa: Ethiopia, Somalia, Djibouti and Sudan.
Ind/Abst Altern. Press Index (-199?); Hum. Rights Intern. Rep.; PAIS Int. Print.

SW
HORN OF AFRICA BULLETIN. (1989)-. Bulletin. English. bm. R300.00, R30.00 (single copy) South Africa; $50.00, $5.00 (single copy) US. Life & Peace Institute, Box 297, S-75105 Uppsala Sweden. **Tel** 011 46 18 169500, FAX 011 46 18 693059. **ED** Sture Normark, Susanne Lunden.
Desc: Published reports represent a variety of published sources. Readers are always referred to the original sources for complete versions.

US/1056-4659
HORN REVIEW, THE. [Horn rev.]. Vol. 1, No. 1 (Winter 1991)-. Periodical. English. Twice a year (Jan. & July). $30.00 (institutions); $15.00 (individuals). New Dawn Enterprises, PO Box 770, Grambling LA 71245. **Tel** (318)225-3674. **LC** DT367.8; .H663. **DD** 963.

NE
IBIS, DE. **Added/Corp** Egyptologische Vereniging Sjemsoethot. (19??)-. Periodical. Multiple languages (Dutch and English). Egyptologische Vereniging Sjemsoethst, H Cleyndertweg 139, Amsterdam Netherlands. **LC** DT57; .I25.

SG
ICA INFORMATION : BULLETIN DE L'INSTITUT CULTUREL AFRICAIN. **Main/Corp** Institut Culturel Africain. No. 3 (April-May-June 1976)-. Bulletin. English (French). qt. Institut Culturel Africain, 14 Avenue du President Lamine Gueye, Dakar Senegal. **LC** DT1; .I497A. **DD** 960/.05. ***Continues*** *ICAM Information.*

SG/0070-2625
INITIATIONS ET ETUDES AFRICAINES. No. 1 (1948)-. Monographic series. French. Price varies per volume. Institut Fondamental d'Afrique Noire, Boite Postale 206, Cheikh Anta Diop, Dakar Senegal. **Tel** 011 221 250090.

US/0361-7882
INTERNATIONAL JOURNAL OF AFRICAN HISTORICAL STUDIES, THE. [Intern. j. Afr. hist. stud.]. **Added/Corp** Boston University. African Studies Center. Vol. 5 (1972)-. Periodical. English. Three times a year (Late Spring, Summer, and Fall). $35.00 (individuals); $98.00 (institutions). Boston University / African Studies Center, 270 Bay State Road, Boston MA 02215. **Tel** (617)353-7306, FAX (617)353-4975, telex 9103501947. **ED** Norman R. Bennett. **LC** DT1; .A226. **DD** 960/.05. Index available (Bound in 3rd issue, in late Fall.). **Bk Rev**. **Ad Acc**, **Adv Mgr:** Laura Scott, **Tel** (617)353-7306. **Circ:** 700. Documents available from The Genuine Article, UMI Article Clearinghouse. ***Continues*** *African Historical Studies, 0001-9992.*
Desc: African history from prehistoric archaeology to present problems of the continent, including interaction between Africa and Afro-American people of the new world.
Ind/Abst Abstr. Anthropol.; Acad. Search (July 1993-); Am. Hist. Life (1972-); Arts Humanit. Citation Index [Full Cov.]; Bibliogr. Mission. (1972-); Curr. Contents Arts Humanit.; Curr. Geogr. Publ. (199?-); Ethnoarts Index (1972-); Expand. Acad. Index (1989-); Hist. Source (July 1993-); Humanit. Index; Humanit. Source (Jul. 1993-); Index Islam. Lit.; INFO-SOUTH Abstr.; Newsp. Period. Abstr. (1990-); Res. Alert [Full Cov.]; Soc. Sci. Cit. Index [Select. Cov.].

US
IROHIN. **Added/Corp** University of Florida. Center for African Studies.a40. (Feb. 1991)-. Periodical. English. sa. University of Florida, Gainesville FL 32611.

SA
JAARVERSLAG - DEPARTEMENT VAN KLEURLING-, REHOBOTH - EN NAMABETREKKINGE. **Main/Corp** South Africa. Dept. of Coloured Relations and Rehoboth Affairs. Afrikaans. an. Department van Kleurling die Staatsdrukker, Privaatsak X85, Pretoria 0001 South Africa. **LC** DT763; .S574B. **UDC** 968(047).

UK/0260-0358
JAMAHIRIYA REVIEW. **Added/Corp** Libya. People's Bureau (London, England). Issue No. 1 (June 1980)-. Periodical. English. mo. $0.50 single issue. Jamahiriya Review, 13A Hillgate Street, London W8 75P England. **LC** DT211; .J33. **DD** 961/.2/005.
Ind/Abst Hum. Rights Intern. Rep.

UA
JANUB AL-WADI. Periodical. Arabic. mo. £E0.10 single issue. 46 Shari Mansur Bab Al-Luq Sunduq Barid 1352, Al-Qahirah Egypt. **LC** DT43; .J36. **UDC** 962.

FR
JARIDAT AL-MISRIYIN. **VFOAT** Al Massryeen; Massryeen; Misriyin. No. 1, (August 1984). Periodical. Arabic. mo. $1.00 single issue. Al Massryeen Alliance Egyptienne, Boite Postale No 81, 75623 Paris Cedex 13 France. **LC** DT43; .J37. **UDC** 962.

US/0270-2495
JOURNAL OF AFRICAN CIVILIZATIONS. [J. Afr. civiliz.]. Vol. 1 (April 1979)-. Periodical. English. an. $20.00 (paper). Transaction Publishers / Rutgers State University, New Brunswick NJ 08903. **Tel** (908)932-2280 Ext. 105, FAX (908)932-3138. **ED** Ivan Van Sertima. **LC** DT14; .J68. **DD** 960. **UDC** 960. available on microfilm and microfiche from University Microfilms International (UMI).
Desc: The leading publication exploring contributions by African people to the advancement of world civilization.

UK/0021-8537
JOURNAL OF AFRICAN HISTORY. [J. Afr. hist.]. Vol. 1 (1960)-. Academic Scholarly Publication. English. Three times a year. $116.00 US, Canada & Mexico; £64.00 other. Cambridge University Press, The Edinburgh Building, Shaftesbury Road, Cambridge CB2 2RU United Kingdom. **Tel** 011 44 223 312393, FAX 011 44 223 325959. **(Subscription address:** Cambridge University Press / North America, 110 Midland Avenue, Port Chester NY 10573.**) ED** David Anderson, Joseph C. Miller, Robin Law and David Robinson. **LC** DT1; .J65. **[CCC]**. **Bk Rev**. **Pr Rev.** available on microfilm and microfiche from University Microfilms International (UMI). Documents available from The Genuine Article, UMI Article Clearinghouse.
Desc: Publishes articles and reviews ranging widely over the African past, from the late Stone Age to the 1960s. In recent years increasing prominence has been given to economic history and to the colonial period, and several articles have explored themes which are also of growing interest to historians of other regions. Articles on slavery, the slave trade and the interpretation of oral tradition are also included.
Ind/Abst Abstr. Anthropol.; Acad. Abstr. Full Text Elite (July 1990-); Acad. Abstr. (July 1990-); Acad. Ind. [Computer File] (1987-); Acad. Search (July 1990-); Am. Hist. Life (1960-); Anthropol. Index; Anthropol. Lit.; Arts Humanit. Citation Index [Full Cov.]; Bibliogr. Mission.; Br. Humanit. Index; Curr. Contents Arts Humanit.; Curr. Contents Soc. Behav. Sci.; Curr. Geogr. Publ. (199?-); Expand. Acad. Index (1987-); Geogr. Abstr. Human Geogr.; Hist. Source (July 1990-); Humanit. Index; Index Islam. Lit.; Index Book Rev. Relig.; INFO-SOUTH Abstr.; Int. Bibliogr. Sociol.; Int. Dev. Abstr.; Mag. Search; Middle East Abstr. Index; Newsp. Period. Abstr. (1991-); Numis. Lit.; Relig. Index One Period.; Res. Alert [Full Cov.]; Soc. Sci. Source (Jul. 1990-); Soc. Sci. Cit. Index [Full Cov.].

US/1058-5613
JOURNAL OF AFRICAN POLICY STUDIES. (JOURNAL OF AFRICAN POLICY STUDIES / INSTITUTE ON AFRICAN AFFAIRS.). **Added/Corp** Institute on Adfrican Affairs. (1991)-. Periodical. English. qt. $35.00 (institutions). Institute on African Affairs, 733 15th Street NW, Suite 700, Washington DC 20005.

●US/1047-9716
JOURNAL OF AFRICAN RESEARCH. **Added/Corp** African Academy of Arts, Sciences & Technologies. (1992)-. Periodical. English. qt. African Academy of Arts, Sciences & Technologies, 12 Petunia Drive/No 1, North Brunswick NJ 08902.

US/0093-8483
JOURNAL OF CAMEROON AFFAIRS. 1st (Jan./Feb. 1972)-. English. Cameroon Students Association of Arts and Sciences, Juniata College, Huntingdon PA 16652. **LC** DT561; .J68. **DD** 916.7/11. **UDC** 916.711.

BE/1016-5584
JOURNAL OF COPTIC STUDIES. **Added/Corp** International Association for Coptic Studies. Vol. 1 (1990)-. Periodical. English (French, German and Greek, Ancient). an. 1500F. Editions Peeters SA, Bondgenotenlaan 153, BP 41, B-3000 Leuven Belgium. **Tel** 32 16 235170, FAX 32 16 228500, telex 65987 PUL B. **ED** G. M. Browne, S. Emmel, P. Grossmann, R. Kasser, B. Layton, T. Orlandi, P. van Moorsel.
Desc: Publishes articles concerning Coptic language, literature, history, art, archaeology, and related subjects, before the modern period.

KE/0251-0405
JOURNAL OF EASTERN AFRICAN RESEARCH & DEVELOPMENT. [J. East. Afr. res. dev.]. **Added/Corp** University of Nairobi. Faculty of Arts. East African Literature Bureau. **VFOAT** Eastern African Research and Development. (1971)-. Periodical. English (Swahili). an. $34.00. Gideon S Were Press, PO Box 10622, Nairobi Kenya. **Tel** 340866 ext 5 or 6. **ED** Gideon S Were. **LC** DT365.A2; J67. **DD** 916.7/03/05. **Bk Rev**. **Ad Acc**. **Circ:** 200.
Desc: Caters for history, sociology, economics, anthropology, languages, religion, political science, musicology, literature and culture.
Ind/Abst AGRICOLA [Select. Cov.]; Am. Hist. Life (1985-); Cot. Trop. Fibr. Abstr. Bibliogr.; Int. Bibliogr. Sociol.; Int. Dev. Abstr. (?-?); Int. Labour Doc.; LABORDOC.

ET/0304-2243
JOURNAL OF ETHIOPIAN STUDIES. [J. Ethiop. stud.]. Vol. 1 (Jan. 1963)-. Periodical. English (French, Italian and Amharic). sa. Br24.00 Ethiopia; $32.00 other. Institute Ethiopian Studies, Addis Ababa University, PO Box 1176, Addis Ababa Ethiopia. **Tel** 011 251 1 110844. **ED** Bahru Zewdie, Taddese Beyene, and Taddesse Tamrat. **LC** DT371. **UDC** 916.3. Index available. cum. index. **Bk Rev**. **Ad Acc**. **Pr Rev**. **Circ:** 1,000. ***Continues*** *Addis Ababa. University College. College Review.*
Desc: Offers space for articles in the fields of anthropology, archaeology, geography, linguistics, literature, political science, economics and sociology.
Ind/Abst Am. Hist. Life (1976-); Anthropol. Index; Anthropol. Lit.; Numis. Lit.

UK/0022-278X
JOURNAL OF MODERN AFRICAN STUDIES, THE. [J. mod. Afr. stud.]. Vol. 1 (March 1963)-. Academic Scholarly Publication. English. qt (4 issues). $147.00 US, Canada and Mexico; £78.00 other. Cambridge University Press, The Edinburgh Building, Shaftesbury Road, Cambridge CB2 2RU United Kingdom. **Tel** 011 44 223 312393, FAX 011 44 223 325959. **(Subscription address:** Cambridge University Press / North America, 110 Midland Avenue, Port Chester NY 10573.**) ED** David Kimble. **LC** DT1; .J68. **[CCC]**. **Bk Rev**. **Ad Acc**. **Pr Rev. Circ:** 2,500. available on microfilm and microfiche from University Microfilms International (UMI). Documents available from The Genuine Article, UMI Article Clearinghouse.
Desc: Offers a survey of politics, economics and related topics in contemporary Africa. The main emphasis is upon the peoples and policies, the problems and progress of this dynamic and disparate continent, upon the many societies that are evolving rather than the essential characteristics of the old, and upon the present, rather than the past. Editorial policy avoids commitment to any political viewpoint or ideology but aims at a fair examination of controversial issues in order to promote a deeper understanding of what is happening in Africa today.
Ind/Abst ABC POL SCI; Abstr. Anthropol.; Acad. Abstr. Full Text Elite (July 1990-); Acad. Abstr. (July 1990-); Acad. Ind. [Computer File] (1987-); Acad. Search (July 1990-); AGRICOLA; Am. Hist. Life (1963-); ARTbibliogr. Mod. (1984-); Arts Humanit. Citation Index [Select. Cov.]; Br. Humanit. Index; Contents Recent Econ. J.; Curr. Contents Soc. Behav. Sci.; Expand. Acad. Index (1987-); Geogr. Abstr. Human Geogr.; Guide Soc. Sci. Relig.; Humanit. Source (Jul. 1990-); Index Islam. Lit.; INFO-SOUTH Abstr.; Int. Bibliogr. Sociol.; Int. Dev. Abstr.; Int. Labour Doc.; Int. Polit. Sci. Abstr.; Leis. Recreat. Tour. Abstr.; Mag. Search; Middle East Abstr. Index; MLA Int. Bibl. Books Artic. Mod. Lang. Lit.; Newsp. Period. Abstr. (1991-); Peace Res. Abstr. J. (1963-1979); Res. Alert [Full Cov.]; Rural Dev. Abstr.; Soc. Plann. Policy Dev. Abstr.; Soc. Sci. Source (Jul. 1990-); Soc. Sci. Cit. Index [Full Cov.]; Soc. Sci. Index; Soc. Sci. Index Fulltext (June 1988-) [Full Txt.]; Sociol. Abstr.; World Agric. Econ.

SA/0259-0123
JOURNAL OF NATAL AND ZULU HISTORY. Vol 1 (1978)-. Periodical. English. an. **LC** DT873; .J68. **DD** 968.4/005.
Ind/Abst Am. Hist. Life (1987-).

US/1062-5038
JOURNAL OF NORTHEAST-AFRICAN STUDIES, THE. [J. Northeast-Afr. stud.]. **Added/Corp** Center for Notheast-African Studies and Development. Vol. 1, No. 1 (Spring 1991)-. Periodical. English. sa. The Journal of Northeast-African Studies, PO Box 65395, Washington Square, Washington DC 20035. **DD** 960.

UK/0305-7070
JOURNAL OF SOUTHERN AFRICAN STUDIES. [J. south. Afr. stud.]. Vol. 1 (Oct. 1974)-. Academic Scholarly Publication. English. qt (4 issues). £55.00 (individual), £134.00 (institution). Carfax Publishing Company, PO Box 25 Abingdon, Oxfordshire OX14 3UE England. **Tel** 011 44 235 555335, FAX (0279)31067, telex 817484. **ED** Saul Dubow, Liz Gunner & Debby Potts. **LC** DT727; .J68. **DD** 968/.005. **[CCC].** Index available. **Bk Rev. Ad Acc. Pr Rev. Circ:** 600. available on microfilm and microfiche from University Microfilms International (UMI). Documents available from The Genuine Article.
Desc: Scholarly inquiry and exposition in the fields of economics, sociology, geography, demography, social anthropology, administration, law, political science, international relations, history and natural sciences as they relate to human condition.
Ind/Abst ABC POL SCI; Am. Hist. Life (1974-); Appl. Soc. Sci. Index Abstr.; Br. Humanit. Index; Curr. Contents Soc. Behav. Sci.; Geogr. Abstr. Phys. Geogr. (?-?); Geogr. Abstr. Human Geogr.; Int. Bibliogr. Sociol.; Int. Dev. Abstr.; Int. Labour Doc.; Int. Polit. Sci. Abstr.; LABORDOC; Multicult. Educ. Abstr.; Res. Alert [Full Cov.]; Rural Dev. Abstr.; Soc. Plann. Policy Dev. Abstr.; Soc. Sci. Cit. Index [Full Cov.]; Sociol. Educ. Abstr.; Stud. Women Abstr.; World Agric. Econ.

US/0065-9991
JOURNAL OF THE AMERICAN RESEARCH CENTER IN EGYPT. [J. Am. Res. Cent. Egypt]. **Main/Corp** American Research Center in Egypt. Vol. 1 (1962)-. Monographic series. English. ir. Price varies per volume. Eisenbrauns, PO Box 275, Winona Lake IN 46590. **Tel** (219)269-2011. **LC** DT57; .A57.
Ind/Abst Index Islam. Lit.; Numis. Lit.; Middle East J.

NR/0018-2540
JOURNAL OF THE HISTORICAL SOCIETY OF NIGERIA. ***Suspended.*** [J. Hist. Soc. Niger.]. **Added/Corp** Historical Society of Nigeria. Vol. 1 (Dec. 1956)-Suspended with Vol. 14 (1992). Periodical. English. an. $30.00. Historical Society of Nigeria, PO Box 9739, 4 Are Avenue, Ibadan Nigeria. **LC** DT515.A2; H57. **[CCC].**
Ind/Abst Am. Hist. Life (1956-1976, 1985-); Anthropol. Index; Anthropol. Lit.

SA
JOURNAL OF THE JOHANNESBURG HISTORICAL FOUNDATION. **VFOAT** Tydskrif van die Johannesburgse Historiese Stigting. Began with issue for Feb. 1978. Periodical. Afrikaans (English). Johannesburg Historical Foundation, 2 Pasteur Chambers #191 Jeppe Str, Johannesburg 20001 South Africa. **LC** DT944.J6; J68. **DD** 968.2/21/005. **UDC** 968.

TZ
KALE. **Added/Corp** Historical Association of Tanzania. University Branch. No. 1 (Feb. 1972)-. Periodical. English. sa. University Branch, Historical Association of Tanzania, Secretary H A T, Box 35032, Dar es Salaam Tanzania. **LC** DT436; .K34. **DD** 916.78/005.

KE/0378-2158
KENYA. **VFOAT** Kenya Yearbook; Uhuru; Kenya Uhuru Factbook; Kenya ... Factbook. (1978)-. English. an. $40.00. Newspread International, Leader House, Moi Avenue, PO Box 46854, Nairobi Kenya. **Tel** 331402, FAX 333448, telex 22143. **ED** Kul Bhushan. **LC** DT433.5.A2; U36. **DD** 967.6/2/005. **UDC** 967.62. **Circ:** 5,000. ***Continues** Uhuru (Nairobi, Kenya).*

KE/0257-8301
KENYA PAST AND PRESENT. [Kenya past present]. **Added/Corp** Kenya Museum Society. Vol. 1 (Dec. 1971)-. Periodical. English. an. Comes with Kenya Museum Society membership. Kenya Museum Society, National Museum, PO Box 40658, Nairobi Kenya. **Tel** 742131 ext. 289, telex 22892. **ED** C. M. P. Martin. **LC** DT433.5.A2; K46. **DD** 916.76/2/005. **Bk Rev. Ad Acc. Circ:** 1,800 (ctrl).
Desc: Articles on museum highlights, ethnography, prehistory, natural sciences, and general research in Kenya.
Ind/Abst Ethnoarts Index.

KE
KENYA RECORD. Vol. 1, No. 1 (Oct. 1978)-V. 1, No. 5 (May/June 1979). Periodical. English. mo. $12.50 US. Research, Editorial and Design Services Ltd., PO Box 57881, Nairobi Kenya. **LC** DT433.5; .K48. **DD** 960/.05. **UDC** 967.62.

SA/0023-2084
KLEIO. [Kleio]. **Added/Corp** University of South Africa. Dept. of History. Vol. 1 (June 1969)-. Periodical. Afrikaans (English). an. R7.00. University of South Africa, PO Box 392, Pretoria 0001 South Africa. **Tel** 011 27 12 4298468, FAX 011 (27)12 429 3321, telex (59)350068+. **LC** DT766; .K54. **Bk Rev. Circ:** 3,400 (ctrl).
Desc: Articles, book reviews and bibliographical research data on history.
Ind/Abst Am. Hist. Life (1969-).

SA/0259-0190
KRONOS. **Added/Corp** Western Cape Institute for Historical Research. (1979)-. Afrikaans (English). an.
Ind/Abst Am. Hist. Life (1987-).

BS/0023-5733
KUTLWANO. [Kutlwano]. **Added/Corp** Bechuanaland Protectorate. Information Branch. Botswana. Information Services. Botswana. Dept. of Information and Broadcasting. **VFOAT** Mutual Understanding. (1962)-. Periodical. English (Tswana). mo. Department of Information and Broadcasting, Private Bag 0060, Gaborone, Botswana. **Tel** 352541, telex 2409. **LC** DT790; .A25. **Circ:** 24,000.

GH/0024-0540
LEGON OBSERVER, THE. V. 1- July 1966-. Periodical. English. mo. Legon Observer, PO Box 11, Legon Accra Ghana. **ED** E Daniel and J A Dadson. **LC** DT510.A1; L43. **UDC** 966.7. cum. index. **Bk Rev. Ad Acc. Circ:** 30,000. available on videocassette.

FR/0759-6677
LETTRE DE BOURBON, LA. No. 1 (Mar. 15 1983)-. French. sm. 3 rue Amiral Lacaze B P 600, 97473 Saint-Denis de la Reunion. **LC** DT469.R3; L47. **DD** 969/.81/005.

US
LIBERIA ALERT. **Added/Corp** Liberia Research and Publication Project. (1985)-. English. Liberia Research and Information Project, PO Box 708, Glassboro NJ 08028. **LC** JQ3929.A15; L53. **DD** 966.6/203/05.
Ind/Abst Hum. Rights Intern. Rep.

GW/0179-4515
LIBERIA-FORUM. **Added/Corp** Liberia Working Group. **VFOAT** Liberia Forum. Vol. 1, No. 1 (1985)-. Periodical. English (German). Twice a year. $25.00 US; DM50.00 other. Liberia Working Group, Dernburgstasse 59, D 1000 Berlin 19 Germany. **Tel** 011 49 30 3221366. **(Subscription address:** Liberia Research Information Project, PO Box 708, Glassboro NJ 08028.**) ED** Ben Tehen. **LC** DT621; .L517. **DD** 966,6/2/005. **Bk Rev. Circ:** 200 (ctrl).
Ind/Abst Am. Hist. Life (1985-).

LB
LIBERIAN OUTLOOK, THE. **VFOAT** Outlook. V. 1- Sept. 1977-. Periodical. English. mo. $15.00 Liberia; $25.00 other. Outlook Entreprises, 44 Broad Street, PO Box 3665, Monrovia Liberia. **LC** DT621; .L54. **DD** 966.6/2/0305. **UDC** 966.62.

US/0024-1989
LIBERIAN STUDIES JOURNAL. [Liberian stud. j.]. V. 1- Fall 1968-. Periodical. English. sa. $20.00. Liberian Studies Association, Department of Anthropology, University of Delaware, Newark DE 19715. **Tel** (302)451-2802. **LC** DT621; .L525. **DD** 916.6/6/005. **UDC** 916.662.
Ind/Abst Am. Hist. Life (1970-); Int. Bibliogr. Sociol.; MLA Int. Bibl. Books Artic. Mod. Lang. Lit.

US
LIBERIAN STUDIES RESEARCH WORKING PAPER. **VFOAT** Liberian Studies Working Papers. No. 1- 1971-. Monographic series. English. ir. Price varies per volume. Institute for Liberian Studies, Philadelphia PA 19143. **ED** Svend E Holsoe.

UK
LIBYAN STUDIES : ANNUAL REPORT OF THE SOCIETY FOR LIBYAN STUDIES. **Added/Corp** Society for Libyan Studies (London, England). 10th (1978/1979)-. English (summaries and/or abstracts in Arabic). an. £12.00 Comes with Society for Libyan Studies membership. The Society for Libyan Studies, The Institute of Archaeology, 31-34 Gordon Square, London WC1H OPY England. **Tel** 011 44 71 387 6052. **ED** J. A. Lloyd. **LC** DT221; .S68a. **DD** 961/.2005. Index available. cum. index. **Bk Rev. Circ:** 400 (ctrl). ***Continues** Society for Libyan Studies (London, England). Annual Report, 0302-3168.*
Desc: Contains reports on expeditions honored by the society and articles on Libyan Studies plus reviews of books on related studies.
Ind/Abst Geogr. Abstr. Phys. Geogr.

KE
LIFE & LEISURE. **VFOAT** Life and Leisure. Feb. 1985-. Periodical. English. mo. Nation Newspapers Limited, PO Box 49010, Nairobi Kenya East Africa. **Tel** 011 254 2 228831. **LC** DT433.5; .L54. **DD** 967.6/2/005. **UDC** 930.85(676.2).

CG
LIKUNDOLI : ENQUETES D'HISTOIRE ZAIROISE. **VFOAT** Enquetes d'Histoire Zairoise. 1- 1972/73-. French. sa. Presses Universitaires du Zaire, BP 1825, Lubumbashi Zaire. **LC** DT641; .L54. **DD** 967.5/1.

CG
LOKOLE. (19??)-. Multiple languages (French and Niger-Kordofanian). Four times a year. $1.25. Editions Lokole, 1082 Avenue Colonel, Ebeya BP 5085, Kinshasa 10 Zaire. **Tel** 22559. **LC** DT641; .L64. **DD** 967.5/103/05.

MG
MADAGASCAR RENOUVEAU. No 1- 3. Monthly 1976-. Periodical. French. ir. 1 100. Service des Relations Publiques / Madagascar, Direction de la Presse et des Publications, BP 271 rue Rababolahay, Antananarivo Malagasy Madagascar. **LC** DT469.M21; M28. **DD** 969/.1005. **UDC** 969.1.

TU/0330-9266
MAGHREB, LE. [Maghreb]. Periodical. French. wk. 15TL. Maghreb, 54 rue IBN Charaf, BP 62, Tunis Tunisia. **LC** DT181; .M33. **DD** 961/.005. **UDC** 961.
Ind/Abst LABORDOC.

FR
MAGHREB, MACHREK. **Added/Corp** Centre d'Etude des Relations Internationales. Section Monde Arabe. France. Documentation Francaise. **VFOAT** Al-Alam Al-Arabi Al-Maghrib Wa-Al-Mashriq. No. 55 (Jan./Feb. 1973)-. Periodical. French. qt. 235.06F. Documentation Francaise, 29 Quai Voltaire, 75344 Paris Cedex 7 France. **Tel** 011 33 1 40157000, FAX 011 33 1 40157230, telex 204 826 DOCFRAN. **LC** DT181; .M32. **DD** 961/.005. ***Continues** Maghreb. Documents Algerie, Maroc, Tunisie.*
Ind/Abst Am. Hist. Life (1986-); Int. Polit. Sci. Abstr.; PAIS Int. Print (1991-); Middle East J.

UK/0309-457X
MAGHREB REVIEW, THE. **VFOAT** Majallat Al-Maghrib. (June/July 1976)-. Periodical. English (French). qt. £130.00. Maghreb Review, 45 Burton Street, London WC1H 9AL England. **Tel** 011 44 71 388 1840. **ED** Mohamed Ben-Madani. **LC** DT181; .M35. **DD** 961/.03/05. Index available. cum. index. **Bk Rev. Ad Acc. Circ:** 9,000 (ctrl).
Desc: All aspects of North Africa and Islam from A.D. 600 to the present day.
Ind/Abst Am. Hist. Life (1988-); Geogr. Abstr.; Geogr. Abstr. Human Geogr. (?-?); Index Islam.; Index Islam. Lit.; Int. Dev. Abstr. (?-?); Int. Polit. Sci. Abstr.

LY
MAJALLAT AL-BUHUTH ABTARIKHIYAH. **Added/Corp** Jamiat al-Fath. Libyan Studies Centre. (Jan. 1979)-. Periodical. Arabic. Twice a year. $3.30 Libya; $13.00 US, Canada, Australia & Pan American; $10.00 others. Libyan Studies Centre, PO Box 5070, Hay AL Andalus, Tripoli Libya. **Tel** 46987, 46988, 39415, telex 20424. **ED** Mohamed T. Jerary. Index available. **Bk Rev. Ad Acc. Circ:** 5,000 (ctrl).
Desc: Periodical, specialized on Libya, North Africa, Arab world, and Africa in general.

LY
MAJALLAT AL-BUHUTH AL-TARIKHIYAN. Vol. 1 (Jan. 1979)-. Periodical. Arabic. sa. 13.00LD US, Canada, Australia, and Pan-American nations; 3.30LD Libya; 10.00LD other. Markaz Buhuth WA Dirasatalji, Libyan Studies Center, Box 5070, Tripoli Libya. **Tel** 011 218 21 33996, 011 218 21 46987. **LC** DT224; .M25.
Ind/Abst Am. Hist. Life (1979-); Middle East J.

AE
MAJALLAT AWWAL NUFIMBIR. ***Title Change.*** **Added/Corp** Munazzamah al-Wataniyah Lil-Mujahidin (Algeria). (19??)-?. Periodical. Arabic. Al-Munazzamah Al-Wataniyah Lil-Miyahidin, 23 Shari Ahmad Gharmul, Al-Jazair Algeria. **LC** DT271; .M34. ***Continued by** Awwal Nufimbir.*

MR
MAJALLAT DAR AL-NIYABAH. **VFOAT** Revue Dar Al-Niaba. V. 1, No. 1, Jan. 1984)-. Periodical. Arabic. qt. 100.00 individual, 300.00 institution. DR Abud Al-Aziz, Al-Timsamani Khalluq, Tariq Kuk Raqm 2, Tanjan Morocco. **LC** DT314; .M25. **UDC** 964.

MR
MAJALLAT MUSTAQBAL AL-SHABAB AL-MAGHRIBI. **VFOAT** Revue l'Avenir de la Jeunesse Marocaine. Periodical. Arabic (French). qt. 3.00MD single issue. S B 350, Al-Dar Al-Bayda 01 Morocco. **LC** DT301; .M295.

MR
MAJALLAT TARIKH AL-MAGHRIB. **VFOAT** Majallat Tarikh Al Maghreb. V. 1, No. 1 (Feb. 1981)-. Periodical. Arabic. sa. Jamiyat Al-Imtidad Al-Thaqafi, SB 406, Markaz Al-Madinah, Rabat Morocco. **LC** DT314; .M26.

US/0146-8553
MAKTABA AFRIKANA SERIES. Monographic series. English. ir. Price varies per volume.

History(General) —History of Africa

Library of Congress / African and Middle Eastern Division, African Section, Washington DC 20540. **Tel** (202)287-5528. **UDC** 960. **Circ:** 1,500.

MF
MAURICE. 81-. Periodical. French. an. Rs15.00. LeRiviere, c/o Le Mauriciens, 8 rue St Georges, Port Louis Mauritius. **LC** DT469.M4; M35. **DD** 969/.82/005. **UDC** 969.82.

UK/0265-444X
MAURITIAN INTERNATIONAL. No. 1 (Jan. 1984)-. English. qt. Nautilus Publishing, 2025 First Avenue, Number 1010, Seattle WA 98121. **LC** DT469.M4; M36. **DD** 969.8/2/005. *Continues Voice of Mauritians.*

SA
MAYIBUYE : JOURNAL OF THE AFRICAN NATIONAL CONGRESS. Added/Corp African National Congress. Vol. 1, No. 1 (July/Aug. 1990)-. Periodical. English. mo (11 issues) $63.00 North, South and Central America; $54.00 Australia and Asia. Mayibuye Publications, PO Box 61884, Marshalltown 2107 South Africa. **Tel** 011 27 11 3307150, 011 27 11 3307373. **ED** Joel Netshitenzhe. **LC** JQ1998.A4; M29. *Continues Mayibuye (African National Congress : 1975).*
 Desc: Magazine presenting news and information from and about the African National Congress.

FR
MEMNONIA : BULLETIN EDITE PAR L'ASSOCIATION POUR LA SAUVEGARDE DU RAMESSEUM. Added/Corp Association pour la Sauvegarde du Ramesseum. (1991)-. Bulletin. French. University of the State of New York / Education, State Education Department, Education Building, Albany NY 12234. **Tel** (518)474-7082, FAX (518)474-4351. **LC** DT73.T33; M46.

UK
MENAS MONOGRAPH. VFOAT Middle East & North Africa Studies Monograph; Middle East and North Africa Studies Monograph. No. 1-. Monographic series. English. Price varies per volume. Westview Press Inc, 5500 Central Avenue, Boulder CO 80301. **Tel** (303)444-3541, FAX (303)449-3356. **UDC** 961.

US/1052-0481
MONOGRAPHS IN INTERNATIONAL STUDIES. AFRICA SERIES. [Monogr. int. stud., Afr. ser.]. Added/Corp Ohio University. Center for International Studies. VFOAT Africa Series. No. 44 (1985)-. Monographic series. English. Ohio University / Center for International Studies, Burson House, 56 East Union Street, Athens OH 45701. **Tel** (614)593-1155. **LC** UNC. **DD** 960. *Continues Papers in International Studies. Africa Series, 0078-9100.*
 Ind/Abst MLA Int. Bibl. Books Artic. Mod. Lang. Lit.

FR/0764-5562
MOYEN ORIENT & OCEAN INDIEN, XVIE-XIXE. Added/Corp Societe d'Histoire de l'Orient (Paris, France). VFOAT Moyen Orient et Ocean Indien; Middle East & Indian Ocean; Middle East and Indian Ocean. (1984)-. Periodical. French (English). ir. 160.00F France; 171.60F other. Societe d'Histoire de l'Orient, 11 rue de Reims, 75013 Paris France. **(Subscription address:** Editions l'Harmattan, 5 7 rue de l'Ecole Polytechnique, 75005 Paris France.**) LC** DS62.4; .M67. **DD** 956/.005.

MZ
MOZAMBIQUEFILE : A MOZAMBIQUE NEWS AGENCY MONTHLY / AIM. See Political Science.

SX/0259-2010
NAMIBIANA. (NAMIBIANA / SWA SCIENTIFIC SOCIETY.). [Namibiana]. Added/Corp South West Africa Scientific Society. Vol. 1, No. 1 (1979)-. Monographic series. Afrikaans (English and Afrikaans). ir. Namibia Scientific Society, PO Box 67, Windhoek Namibia. **Tel** 011 264 61 225372. **ED** K.F.R. Budack. **LC** DT711; .N35. **DD** 968.8/005. Index available. **Bk Rev**. **Ad Acc**. ctrl circ.
 Ind/Abst Anthropol. Lit.

URR/0027-8041
NARODY AZII I AFRIKI. *Title Change.* Added/Corp Institut Vostokovedeniia (Akademiia nauk SSSR) Institut Kitaevedeniia (Akademiia nauk SSSR) Institut Narodov Azii (Akademiia nauk SSSR) Akademiia nauk SSSR. Institut Afriki. (1959)-(1992). Periodical. Russian (summaries and/or abstracts in English and Chinese). bm. **(Subscription address:** Victor Kamkin, 4956 Boiling Brook Parkway, Rockville MD 20852.**)** [CCC]. *Formed by the union of Sovetskoe Vostokovedenie and Sovetskoe Kitaevedenie. Continued by Vostok Afro Aziatskie Obshchestva Istoriia i Souvremennost.*
 Ind/Abst MLA Int. Bibl. Books Artic. Mod. Lang. Lit.

SA/0085-3674
NATALIA. Added/Corp Natal Society, Pietermaritzburg. Vol. 1, (Sept. 1971)-. English. an (Dec.). $5.89. National Society Library, PO Box 415, Pieter Maritzburg South Africa. **Tel** 011 27 52520 52383. **LC** DT866; .N36.
 Ind/Abst Annu. Bibliogr. Engl. Lang. Lit.

ZA
NDOLA DIRECTORY. Directory. English. Directory Publishers of Zambia, PO Box 30963, Lusaka Zambia. **Tel** 212650/53. **LC** DT963.9.N37; N38. **DD** 968.94. **UDC** 968.94.

GH
NEW GHANA, THE. Added/Corp Ghana. Information Services Dept. (19??)-. Periodical. English. bw. Ghana Information Services Department, PO Box 745, Accra Ghana. **LC** DT510.A1; N45. **DD** 916.67/005.

US/0148-7264
NEW YORK AFRICAN STUDIES ASSOCIATION NEWSLETTER. Main/Corp New York African Studies Association. Added/Corp New York African Studies Association. NYASA Newsletter. VFOAT NYASA Newsletter. No. 1 (Feb. 1974)-. Newsletter. English. tq (3 issues). $10.00. African Studies Department, State University College, New Paltz NY 12561. **Tel** (914)247-2303. **ED** Thomas Nyquist and Corinne Nyquist. **LC** DT19.9.A33; N48a. **DD** 960/.07/10747. **Bk Rev**. **Circ**: 290 (ctrl).
 Desc: Includes articles, conference highlights, news items, book and film reviews, useful lists, etc. of interest to Africanists teaching at all levels.

NG/0550-6891
NIGER. No. 1- 1967-. Periodical. French. qt. Niger, Boite Postale 860, Niamey Niger Africa. **LC** DT547.A2; N52. **DD** 916.6/26/005. **UDC** 916.626.

US/0066-0981
NORTH AFRICA SERIES. English. American Universities Field Staff, 620 Union Drive, Indianapolis IN 46202-2897. **LC** DT181; .A7. **DD** 916/.03/308. **UDC** 916.1. *Continues Reports Service: North Africa Series.*

SG/0029-3954
NOTES AFRICAINES. [Notes afr.]. Began publication in 1939. Periodical. French (English). qt. Institut Fondamental d'Afrique Noire, Boite Postale 206, Cheikh Anta Diop, Dakar Senegal. **Tel** 011 221 250090. **LC** DT1; .I513. **UDC** 930.85(6). available on diskette.
 Ind/Abst Am. Hist. Life (1964-1969); Anthropol. Index; Ethnoarts Index; Life Sci. Collect.

FR
NOTICE D'INFORMATION A L'USAGE DES AGENTS DE LA COOPERATION : REPUBLIQUE DU SENEGAL. Main/Corp Bureau de Liaison des Agents de Cooperation Technique. French. Bureau de Liaison des Agents de Cooperation Technique, 6 rue Mariguan, 75007 Paris France. **LC** DT594.A2; B87A. **DD** 966/.3. **UDC** 966.3.

MU
NOUAKCHOTT-INFORMATION. French. Direction de la Presse Ecrite et des Relations Exterieures etc, Bureau 37 Ilot K, Nouakchott Mauritania. **LC** DT553.M2; A25. **DD** 966/.1/005. **UDC** 966.12.

UA
NOUVELLE REVUE DU CAIRE, LA. V. 1- 1975-. French. an. Livres de France, 36 rue Kasr El-Nil, Le Caire 36 Egypt. **LC** DT43; .N68. **DD** 962/.005. **UDC** 962.

US
NOUVELLES DU CAMEROUN. Main/Corp Cameroon. Embassy (U.S.) Press and Information Service. VFOAT Cameroon News. Jan. 12, 1972-. Periodical. English (English). sm. Cameroon Embassy, 2349 Massachusetts Avenue Northwest. **LC** DT561; .C3A. **DD** 967/.11/005. **UDC** 916.711.

SA
NUUSBRIEF - AFRIKAANS-DUITSE KULTUURUNIE. Main/Corp Afrikaans-Duitse Kultuurunie. VFOAT Mitteilungen - Afrikaans-Deutsche Kulturgemeinschaft. Periodical. Multiple languages. Afrikaans-Duitse Kultuurunie, Postfach 2308, Pretoria South Africa. **LC** DT764.G3; A35A. **UDC** 968.0.

US/0068-6190
OCCASIONAL PAPER (UNIVERSITY OF CALIFORNIA, LOS ANGELES. AFRICAN STUDIES CENTER). *Ceased.* (OCCASIONAL PAPER - AFRICAN STUDIES CENTER, UNIVERSITY OF CALIFORNIA, LOS ANGELES.). No. 1-Ceased ?. Monographic series. English. UCLA African Studies Center, 405 Hilgard Avenue, 10244 Bunche Hall, Los Angeles CA 90024. **Tel** (310)825-1218. **LC** DT1; .C34. **UDC** 916.

NR/0029-8522
ODU. *Suspended.* [Odu]. Added/Corp University of Ife. Institute of African Studies. (1964)-Suspended (1993). Periodical. English. sa. **LC** DT515.A2; O32. *Supersedes Odu (Ibadan, Nigeria : 1955).*
 Ind/Abst Am. Hist. Life (1971-1978,1980-); Anthropol. Index; MLA Int. Bibl. Books Artic. Mod. Lang. Lit.

MG
OMALY SY ANIO. VFOAT Hier et Aujourd'Hui. No. 1/2- ;Jan./Dec. 1975-. Periodical. French. sa. 1,200Mal$. Universite de Madagascar / History, Departement d'Histoire, PB 566, Antananarivo Madagascar. **LC** DT469.M21; 043. **DD** 969/.1/005. **UDC** 969.1.

SG
OUEST AFRICAIN, L'. Periodical. French. 10,000. Societe Nationale de Presse, B P 2047, Dakar Senegal. **LC** DT470; .Q47. **UDC** 966.

NR
OYO STATE YEAR BOOK AND WHO'S WHO. 1981-. English. an. Ayinda Brothers Ltd, N4/815B Yemetu-Agip, Box 7583, Secretariat, Ibadan Nigeria. **LC** DT515.9.O9; O97. **DD** 966.9/2. **UDC** 966.9(058).

SG/0377-2640
PANORAMA AFRICAIN. Periodical. French. bm. 1.700. BP 135, Dakar Senegal. **LC** DT1; .P32. **DD** 309.1/6/03. **UDC** 308(6).

US/1053-1319
PAS (EVANSTON, ILL.). (PAS : NEWS AND EVENTS.). [PAS]. Added/Corp Northwestern University (Evanston, Ill.) Program of African Studies. VFOAT Program of African Studies; PAS News and Events. Vol. 1, No. 1 (Fall 1990)-. Periodical. English. bm. Northwestern University African Studies, Program of African Studies, 620 Library Place, Evanston IL 60201. **Tel** (708)491-7684. **DD** 305.

SE
PEOPLE, THE. English (French). Seychelles People's United Party, PO Box 154, Victoria Mahe Seychelles. **LC** DT469.S4; P46. **DD** 969/.6/005. **UDC** 969.9.
 Ind/Abst Curr. Lit. Fam. Plan.

CM
PISTES CAMEROUNAISES. No 1- Jan./Mar. 1974-. Periodical. French. $8.00. Delegation Generale au Tourisme, BP 266, Yaounde Cameroon. **LC** DT567; .P5. **DD** 967/.11/005. **UDC** 967.11.

US
PUBLICATIONS. AFRICAN SERIES. Main/Corp Indiana University. Added/Corp Indiana. University. Research Center for the Language Sciences. Indiana University African Series. VFOAT African Series. Vol. 1, (1970)-. Monographic series. English. ir. Price varies per volume. Research for Language Sciences, Patton House, 516 East 16th Street, Indiana University, Bloomington IN 47401.

SA/0038-2418
QUARTERLY BULLETIN OF THE SOUTH AFRICAN LIBRARY. See Library and Information Sciences.

SG
RAPPORT ANNUEL - INSTITUT FONDAMENTAL D'AFRIQUE NOIRE. *Title Change.* Main/Corp Institut Fondamental d'Afrique Noire. (19??)-(1992). French. an. Institut Fondamental d'Afrique Noire, Boite Postale 206, Cheikh Anta Diop, Dakar Senegal. **Tel** 011 221 250090. **LC** DT348; .I5515. **DD** 961/.007/11663. *Continued by Institut Fondamental d'Afrique Noire Cheikh Anta Diop; Rapport Annuel.*

IT
RASSEGNA DI STUDI ETIOPICI. Vol. 1 (Jan./April 1941)-. Periodical. Italian. ir. L50000 Italy; L60000 other. Herder Editrice e Libreria SRL, Piazza Montecitorio 117-120, 00186 Rome Italy. **Tel** 011 39 6 679 4628, FAX 011 39 6 678 4751. **LC** DT371.
 Ind/Abst BHA : Biblio. Hist. Art.

TI
REALITES (TUNIS, TUNISIA). (REALITES.). VFOAT Haqaiq. Periodical. French. wk. $6.35. Realites, 22 rue Jebel Bargou, Tunis Tunisia. **LC** DT241; .R42. **DD** 909/.0917/4927. **UDC** 961.1.

RW
RELEVE, LA. Vol. 1- ; Jan. 12/18, 1976-. Periodical. French. mo. 350F Romania; $27.00 US. Office Rwandais d'Information, B P 83, Kigali Rwanda. **Tel** 75665, telex 557 OR RW. **LC** DT449.R9; A25. **UDC** 916.759.8. **Bk Rev**. **Ad Acc**. **Circ:** 1,000. *Formed by the union of Releve and Rwanda, Carrefour d'Afrique.*
 Desc: Rwandan government publication dealing with various subjects such as national policy, culture, agriculture, social items and, at times, scientific issues related to Rwanda.

BE
REMARQUES ARABO-AFRICAINES. *Suspended.* (Mar. 1978)-(1979). Periodical. French. mo. SPRL Sipredi, Ave Albert 208, B-1180 Bruxelles Belgium. **LC** DT1; .R34. **DD** 960/.05. *Continues Remarques Africaines, 0034-4192.*

UK
REPORT - EGYPT EXPLORATION SOCIETY. Main/Corp Egypt Exploration Society. 84th- 1966/67-. English. an. Egypt Exploration Society, 3 Doughty Mews, Longon WC1N 2PG England. **Tel** 011 44 71 242 1880. **LC** DT57; .E322A. **DD** 930/.1/06262. **UDC**

History(General) —History of Africa

932(047). **Continues** Report of the ... Ordinary General Meeting (... Annual General Meeting) Subscription List and Balance Sheets.

SA
REPORT OF THE ADMINISTRATION OF COLOURED AFFAIRS FOR THE PERIOD
... . Main/Corp South Africa. Administration of Coloured Affairs. English. **LC** DT764.C6; S648A. **DD** 968/.004. **UDC** 968.

SA
REPORT OF THE DEPARTMENT OF CO-OPERATION AND DEVELOPMENT.
Main/Corp South Africa. Dept. of Co-operation and Development. **VFOAT** Verslag van die Departement van Samewerking en Ontwikkeling. Afrikaans (English). an. R13.15. Government Printer / South Africa, Bosman Street, Private Bag X85, Pretoria 0001 South Africa. **Tel** 011 27 12 3239731 Ext. 262. **LC** DT763.6; .S667A. **DD** 354.68063.

GH/0020-2703
RESEARCH REVIEW - INSTITUTE OF AFRICAN STUDIES. Main/Corp University of Ghana. Institute of African Studies. Vol. 1-12, No. 2/3, (1965)-(1981); New Series, Vol.1 (1985)-. Periodical. English. Three times a year. NC1,000 Ghana; $20.00 other. Institute of African Studies / Ghana, University of Ghana, Legon Ghana. **ED** M E Kropp Dakubu. **DD** 960. Index available. cum. index. **Bk Rev**. **Ad Acc**. **Circ:** 500 (ctrl).
Desc: A journal of African Studies focusing on West Africa.
Ind/Abst MLA Int. Bibl. Books Artic. Mod. Lang. Lit.

TI
REVUE D'HISTOIRE MAGHREBINE.
VFOAT Al-Majallah Al-Tarikhiyah Al-Maghribiyah; North African Historical Review. No. 1 (Jan. 1974)-. Periodical. Arabic (English and French). qt. $220.00. CEROMDI, Cite des Andalous BP 50, 1118 Zaghouan Tunisia. **Tel** 2162676446, FAX 2162676710. **ED** A. Temimi. **LC** DT181; .R47. Index available. **Bk Rev**. **Ad Acc**. **Circ:** 500 (ctrl).
Desc: Covers modern and contemporary history of Maghreb.
Ind/Abst Am. Hist. Life (1982-).

UA
RISALAT AFRIQIYA. Periodical. Arabic. 1.00.
Setiausaha Agung Kesatuan Pekerja-Perkerja Keretapi Tanah Melayu, 5 Sh Ahmed Hishmat Street, Kuala Lumpur Malaysia. **LC** DT1; .R57. **UDC** 960.

MF
RODRIGUES ALMANACH. Periodical. French (French). an. 15.00. **LC** DT469.M492; R6. **DD** 969/.82. **UDC** 969.82.

MZ
ROTEIRO DA CIDADE DE LOURENCO MARQUES. Portuguese. Papeleira Folques, Av Pinheiro Chagas 2633/39, Lourenco Marques Mozambique. **LC** DT465.L3; R67. **UDC** 967.9.

SA
RSA CALLING. Main/Corp Radio RSA, Johannesburg. Periodical. English (Afrikaans, Dutch, French, German, Portuguese, Swahili, Spanish, Lozi and Tsonga). an. Free. Radio RSA, PO Box 4559, Johannesburg South Africa. **Tel** (011)7142600, FAX (011)7143106, telex 424116 HEX. **LC** DT751; .R3A. **DD** 968/.005. **UDC** 968.0. **Ad Acc**. **Circ:** 200,000 (ctrl).

GW
RUNDBRIEF. Main/Corp Arbeitskreis der Deutschen Afrika-Forschungs- und Dokumentationsstellen. German. Kolner Strasse 149, 53 Bonn-Bad Godesberg Germany. **LC** DT19.9.G3; A7A. **UDC** 960.

FR
SAHARA-INFO. Added/Corp Association des Amis de la Republique Arabe Sahraouie Democratique. **VFOAT** Sahara Info. (1976)-. Periodical. French (French). mo. 60.00F. **LC** DT346.S7; S22. **DD** 964/.8005.

US/0891-9119
SAMNA WARQ. [Semna warq]. **VFOAT** Sem Inna Worq. (1987)-. Periodical. Amharic. ir (3 issues per year). $40.00. Sem Inna Worq, PO Box 30369, Addis Ababa, Ethiopia. **LC** PAR. **DD** 963.

KE
SAUTI YA KERICHO. No. 1 (April 4, 1980)-. Periodical. Swahili. sm. 0.50 single issue. Sauti ya Kericho, PO Box 376, Kericho Kenya. **LC** DT433.5; .S28. **UDC** 967.62.

UA
SAWT AL-SHAB AL-LIBI. Periodical. Arabic. £E0.03 single issue. PO Box 1570, Al-Qahirah United Arab Republic Egypt. **LC** DT236; .S28. **UDC** 962.

US
SAWT AL-TALIAH (PARIS, FRANCE).
(SAWT AL-TALIAH / TUSDIRUHA AL-HARAKAH AL-WATANIYAH AL-LIBIYAH.). **VFOAT** Sawt Attalea; Saut Atalia. V. 1, No. 1, (December 1980)-. Periodical. Arabic. PO Box 53402, New Orleans LA 70153. **LC** DT236; .S283. **UDC** 961.2.

US/0586-7924
SERAPIS. Vol. 1 (1969)-. English. ir (1-2 issues per volume). Price varies per volume. Serapis - The American Journal, 1155 East 58th Street, Chicago IL 60637. **LC** DT56.8; .S47. **DD** 932/.005.

LY
SHAHID (TRIPOLI, LIBYA). (AL-SHAHID.).
Added/Corp Markaz Dirasat Jihad Al-Libiyin Didda Al-Ghazw Al-Itali. (19??)-. Periodical. Arabic. an. $4.00 US. Lybian Studies Center, PO Box 5070 Sidi Munaider, Tripoli Libya. **Tel** 33996, FAX 31616, telex 20424. **LC** DT224; .S5. Index available. **Circ:** 5,000 (ctrl).

●US/1062-0109
SIERRA LEONE REVIEW, THE. (THE SIERRA LEONE REVIEW: A JOURNAL OF POLICY STUDIES & CULTURE.). [Sierra Leone rev.].
Added/Corp Sierra Leone Institute for Policy Studies. **VFOAT** Journal of Policy Studies. (1992)-. Periodical. English. qt. $28.00. Sierra Leone Institute for Policy Studies, PO Box 65231, Washington DC 20035. **ED** Sorie Musa. **LC** DT516; .S64. **DD** 966.4/005. **Continues** Sierra Leone Newsletter (Washington, D.C.).

●US/1066-4947
SIERRA LEONE REVIEW, THE. (THE SIERRA LEONE DIGEST : A HANDBOOK OF FACTS & FIGURES.). [Sierra Leone rev.]. **Added/Corp** Sierra Leone Institute for Policy Studies. (1993)-. English. $15.00. Sierra Leone Institute for Policy Studies, PO Box 65231, Washington DC 20035. **DD** 966.

MW/0037-993X
SOCIETY OF MALAWI JOURNAL, THE.
[Soc. Mala,,wi j.]. **Added/Corp** Society of Malawi. Vol. 18, No. 2 (July, 1965)-. Periodical. English. sa. **LC** DT858; .N9. **CODEN** SMJODY. Documents available from BIOSIS Document Express. **Continues** Nyasaland Journal.
Ind/Abst Am. Hist. Life (1967-1988); Anthropol. Index; Biol. Abstr.

UV
SOLEIL DE HAUTE-VOLTA, LE. Periodical.
French. 50. BP 1095, Avenue de la Liberte, Ouagadougou Burkina Faso. **LC** DT553.U7; A27. **DD** 916.6/25/.005. **UDC** 916.625.

PG
SORONDA. Added/Corp Instituto Nacional de Estudos e Pesquisa (Guinea-Bissau). **VFOAT** Revista de Estudos Guineenses. No. 1 (Jan. 1986)-. Periodical. Portuguese. sa. $20.00. Instituto Nacional de Estudos &Pesquisa, Caixa Postal 112, Bissau Guinea-Bissau. **Bk Rev**, (Qty: 2).

●RU
SOTSIALNYE I GUMANITARNYE NAUKI. SERIIA 9, VOSTOKOVEDENIE I AFRIKANISTIKA. ZARUBEZHNAIA LITERATURA / ROSSIISKAIA AKADEMIIA NAUK, INSTITUT NAUCHNOI INFORMATSII PO OBSHCHESTVENNYM NAUKAM. See
History(General)-History of Asia.

SA/0302-0681
SOUTH AFRICA. Added/Corp South Africa. Dept. of Information. (1974)-. English. an (published in September). R38.50 South Africa; R39.50 other. South African Communication Service, Private Box X 745, Pretoria 0001 South Africa. **Tel** 011 27 12 3142402. **LC** DT751; .S4. **DD** 968/.005. **NLM** DT 751 S726. **Supersedes** South Africa. Bureau of Census and Statistics. Official Yearbook of the Union (of South Africa) and of Basutoland, Bechuanaland Protectorate and Swaziland.

●SA
SOUTH AFRICA / SOUTH AFRICA FOUNDATION. Added/Corp South Africa Foundation. **VFOAT** South Africa Foundation Information Digest; Information Digest. (1992)-. English. **Continues** Information Digest (South Africa Foundation).

SA
SOUTH AFRICAN CULTURAL HISTORY MUSEUM ANNALS. VFOAT Suid-Afrikaans Kultuurhistoriese Museum Annale. Multiple languages (Afrikaans and English). an. R5.00 South Africa; $12.50 other. South African Cultural History Museum, PO Box 645, Kaapstad 8000 South Africa. **Tel** 021 461 8280. **Ad Acc**.
Desc: History and cultural history.

SA
SOUTH AFRICAN HISTORICAL JOURNAL. (SUID-AFRIKAANSE HISTORIESE JOERNAAL / SOUTH AFRICAN HISTORICAL JOURNAL / THE SOUTH AFRICAN HISTORICAL SOCIETY.).
Added/Corp South African Historical Society. University of South Africa. **VFOAT** South African Historical Journal. No. 1 (Nov. 1969)-. Periodical. Afrikaans (English; summaries and/or abstracts in English). Twice a year (May & Nov.). R70.00. South African Historical Society, University of South Africa, Box 392, Pretoria 0001 South Africa. **Tel** 011-27-12-4296427, FAX 011-27-12-4293221. **LC** DT766; .S585. Index available. cum. index. **Bk Rev**, (Qty: 50). **Ad Acc**, **Adv Mgr:** K. Harris. **Circ:** 700 (ctrl). Documents available from The Genuine Article.
Ind/Abst Am. Hist. Life (1979-); Arts Humanit. Citation Index [Full Cov.]; Int. Bibliogr. Sociol.; Res. Alert [Full Cov.]; Soc. Sci. Cit. Index [Select. Cov.].

SA
SOUTH AFRICAN REVIEW (JOHANNESBURG, SOUTH AFRICA: 1983). (SOUTH AFRICAN REVIEW / EDITED AND COMPILED BY SARS (SOUTH AFRICAN RESEARCH SERVICE).). Added/Corp South African Research Service. (1983)-. English. ir. Raven Press Pty Ltd, 23 O'Riley Road, PO Box 31134, Braamfontein, Johannesburg 2017 South Africa. **Tel** 011 27 11 4033925, FAX (011)339-2439 TELEX 640073, telex 640073. (**Subscription address:** US/ 1185 Avenue of the Americas, New York, NY 10036) **LC** HC905.A1; S67. **DD** 968/.005.
Ind/Abst Hum. Rights Intern. Rep.

US/1061-723X
SOUTHERN AFRICA (DENVER, COLO.).
(SOUTHERN AFRICA.). [South. Afr.]. **Added/Corp** National Namibia Concerns (Denver, Colo.). National Namibia/Southern Africa Concerns (Denver, Colo.). Vol. 1, No. 1 (Feb. 1991)-. Periodical. English. National Namibia Concerns, 915 East 9th Avenue, Denver CO 80218. **DD** 968. **Continues** Namibia Newsletter.

CN/0820-5582
SOUTHERN AFRICA REPORT (TORONTO). (SOUTHERN AFRICA REPORT.).
[South. Afr. rep.]. **Added/Corp** Toronto Committee for the Liberation of Southern Africa. Vol. 1, No. 1 (June 1985)-. Periodical. English. qt. 48.00Can$ (institution), 26.00Can$ (individual) all except Canada; 40.00Can$ (institution), 18.00Can$ (individual) Canada. Toronto Committee for the Liberation of Southern Africa, 427 Bloor Street W, Toronto Ontario, M5S 1X7 Canada. **Tel** (416)967-5562. **DD** 968/.005.
Ind/Abst Hum. Rights Intern. Rep.

SA
SOUTHERN AFRICAN STUDIES. Vol. 4; 1986-. Periodical. English. ir. Raven Press Pty Ltd, 23 O'Riley Road, PO Box 31134, Braamfontein, Johannesburg 2017 South Africa. **Tel** 011 27 11 4033925, FAX (011)339-2439 TELEX 640073, telex 640073. (**Subscription address:** US/ 1185 Avenue of the Americas, New York, NY 10036) **Circ:** 1,000. **Continues** Working Papers in Southern African Studies.
Desc: A collection of papers on the history and economy of Southern Africa, originally presented as seminar papers at the African Studies Institute, University of Witwatersrand, Johannesburg.

SZ/0074-6681
SPECIAL REPORT OF THE DIRECTOR-GENERAL ON THE APPLICATION OF THE DECLARATION CONCERNING ACTION AGAINST APARTHEID IN SOUTH AFRICA / INTERNATIONAL LABOUR OFFICE.
Main/Corp International Labour Office. **VFOAT** Special Report on Apartheid; Apartheid in South Africa. (1991)-. English. International Labour Office - ILO, Publications Sales Service, CH-1211 Geneva 22 Switzerland. **Tel** 011 41 22 7996111. **LC** DT763; .I553a. **DD** 305.8/0096805. **Continues** International Labour Office. Special Report of the Director-General on the Application of the Declaration Concerning Action Against Apartheid in South Africa and Namibia, 0074-6681.

IT/0585-4954
STUDI MAGREBINI. Added/Corp Naples. Istituto Orientale. Centro di Studi Magrebini. (1966)-. Monographic series. Italian. ir. Price varies per volume. Herder Editrice e Libreria SRL, Piazza Montecitorio 117-120, 00186 Rome Italy. **Tel** 011 39 6 679 4628, FAX 011 39 6 678 4751. **ED** R. Rubinacci.
Desc: Studies of Northern Africa.
Ind/Abst Am. Hist. Life (1987-); Numis. Lit.

US/0163-2965
STUDIA AFRICANA. V. 1- Spring 1977-.
Periodical. English (English). be. $20.00. African Institute Study of Human Value, PO Box 456, Accra Ghana. **LC** DT1; .S83. **DD** 960/.05. **UDC** 960.

US/0890-4847
STUDIES IN AFRICAN AND AFRO-AMERICAN CULTURE. [Stud. Afr. Afr.-Am. cult.]. (1990)-. English. an. Peter Lang Publishing, 62 West 45th Street, 4th floor, New York NY 10036. **Tel** (212)764-1471, (800)770-5264, telex 6973364 PLNY. **DD** 305.

History(General) —History of Africa

US/0803-0685
SUDANIC AFRICA. Vol. 1 (1990)-. Periodical. English. ir. Northwestern University African Studies, Program of African Studies, 620 Library Place, Evanston IL 60201. **Tel** (708)491-7684. **LC** DT154.32; .S8.

GW/0170-5946
SUGIA, SPRACHE UND GESCHICHTE IN AFRIKA. See Linguistics.

SJ
SUNA. Main/Corp Wakalat Al-Sudan Lil-Anba. **VFOAT** Suna Daily Bulletin. **VAT** Sudan News Agency. Periodical. English. Sudan News Agency, PO Box 1506 Khartoum Sudan. **LC** DT118; .W33A. **UDC** 916.24. **Continues** English Daily Bulletin.

LY
TALAI AL-FATIH. Periodical. Arabic. 10.00. Amanat Al-Shabab, PO Box 12770, Tarabulus Libya. **LC** DT211; .T34. **UDC** 916.12.

UK
TALKING DRUMS (LONDON, ENGLAND). (TALKING DRUMS.). Vol. 1, No. 1 (Sept. 12, 1983)-. Periodical. English. wk. $95.00. Talking Drums Publications, PO Box 888, London W2 1XY England. **LC** DT1; .T34. **DD** 960/.05. **UDC** 960.

MG
TATSINANANA. (19??)-. Periodical. Multiple languages (French and Malagasy). qt. 129 Av Marechal Joffre Antanimena, Tananarive Martinique. **LC** DT469.M21; T37. **DD** 916.91.

GW
TELE-AFRICA REVUE. VFOAT Revue Tele-Africa. 1971, 3/4-. Multiple languages (French and German). 3.00. Robert-Bosch-Strasse 4, 7 Stuttgart Germany. **LC** DT641; .C58. **DD** 916.75/1. **UDC** 916.75. **Continues** Congo-Revue.

TI
THAQAFAH. Arabic. 0.3TD. Dar Al-Thaqafah IBN Khaldun, 16 Nahj IBN Khaldun, Tunis Tunisia. **LC** AP95.A6; T514. **UDC** 961.1.

IT
THAWRAH (ROME, ITALY). (AL-THAWRAH.). Vol. 1 (1985)-. Periodical. Arabic. mo. **LC** DT397; .T53.

NR
TIMES INTERNATIONAL (LAGOS, NIGERIA : 1979). (TIMES INTERNATIONAL.). Periodical. English. wk. $30.00. Daily Times of Nigeria Ltd, Publications Division, New Isheri Road Agidingbi, PMB 21340 Ikeja West Africa. **Tel** 900850-900859. **ED** Dayo Alao. **LC** DT1; .T55. **DD** 960/.05. **Bk Rev**. **Ad Acc**. **Circ:** 20,000. **Continues** Times International (Lagos, Nigeria : 1978).
 Desc: Focuses the world from Nigerian perspective. Its area of coverage is of general interest that ranges from economy to politics, religion and culture.

KE/0251-0391
TRANSAFRICAN JOURNAL OF HISTORY. [Transafr. j. hist.]. **Added/Corp** Makerere University. Dept. of History. University of Nairobi. Dept. of History. Chuo Kikuu cha Dar es Salaam. Dept. of History. University of Zambia. Dept. of History. University of Malawi. Dept. of History. Vol. 1, No. 1 (Jan. 1971)-. Periodical. English. an. $34.00. Gideon S Were Press, PO Box 10622, Nairobi Kenya. **Tel** 340866 ext 5 or 6. **LC** DT1; .T7.
 Ind/Abst Am. Hist. Life (1971-1976,1986-).

FR
TRIBUNE AFRICAINE. No. 1 (10th Quarterly 1983)-. Periodical. French. qt. 80.00F. Siege Social / Poniatowski, 69 Bd Poniatowski, 75012 Paris France. **LC** DT1; .T75. **DD** 960/.05. **UDC** 960. **Continues** Jonction (Paris, France : 1979).

TI
TUNISIAN HIGHLIGHTS. No. 1- Summer 1974-. Periodical. English. $20.00. Tunisian Highlights, 15 rue Kamal Ataturk, Tunis Tunisia. **LC** DT241; .T79. **DD** 961/.105/005. **UDC** 961.1.

UG/0041-574X
UGANDA JOURNAL. Suspended. (THE UGANDA JOURNAL.). [Uganda j.]. **Added/Corp** Uganda Society. Vol 1 (1934)-. Periodical. English. sa. Uganda Society, PO Box 4980, Kampala Uganda. **LC** DT434.U2; U3. cum. index.
 Ind/Abst Am. Hist. Life (1967-1982); Anthropol. Index.

UA
UKTUBIR. VFOAT October Weekly. Vol. 1 (Oct 31, 1976)-. Periodical. Arabic. wk. £E5.20. Muassasat Uktubar Al-Sahafujah Al-Qahirah, United Arab Republic, Egypt. **LC** DT43; .U38.

URR
VOSTOK AFRO AZIATSKIE OBSHCHESTVA ISTORIA I SOVREMENNOST. (19??)-. Periodical. Russian. bm. $89.95 US and Canada; $99.95 Europe; $114.95 other. **(Subscription address:** East View Publications Inc., 3020 Harbor Lane North, Suite 110, Minneapolis MN 55447.**) Continues** Narody Azii I Afriki.

SJ
WAHDAH (JUBA, SUDAN). (AL-WAHDAH / TUSDIRUHA WIZARAT AL-THAQAFAH WA-AL-ILAM AL-IQLIMIYAH-JUBA.). **VFOAT** Al-Wahda. No. 1 (May 1980)-. Periodical. Arabic. mo. Wizarat Al-Thaqafah Wa-Al-Ilam Al-Iqlimiyah, SB 16, Juba Sudan. **LC** DT159.6.S73; W33. **UDC** 962.4.

SJ
WEEKLY REVIEW - SUDAN NEWS AGENCY. Main/Corp Wakalat Al-Sudan Lil-Anba. No. 1- 9 Mar. 1972-. Periodical. English. PO Box 1506, Gamaa Avenue, Khartoum Sudan. **LC** DT118; .W34A. **DD** 962.4/005. **UDC** 962.4.

US/0066-1058
WEST AFRICA SERIES. English. University Field State International, 620 Union Drive, Indianapolis IN 46202-2897. **LC** DT491; .A7. **DD** 916.6/008. **UDC** 916.6. **Continues** Reports Service: West Africa Series, 0272-2305.

SW/0281-6814
WORKING PAPERS IN AFRICAN STUDIES. (1984)-. Monographic series. English (Swedish). ir. Price varies per volume. University of Uppsala, Department of Cultural Anthropology, Tradgardsgatan 18, S-752 20 Uppsala Sweden. **LC** GN643; .W67. **DD** 960/.05.

SA
YEARBOOK - AFRICANA SOCIETY OF PRETORIA. Main/Corp Africana Society of Pretoria. **VFOAT** Jaarboek - Africana Vereiging van Pretoria. 1-1975-. Afrikaans (English). Africana Society of Pretoria, Post Box 3239, Pretoria 0001 South Africa. **LC** DT766; .A37A. **DD** 968/.005. **UDC** 968.0(058).

ZA
Z MAGAZINE. Added/Corp Zambia. Information Services. No. 1 (June 1969)-. Periodical. English. mo. Zambia Information Service, PO Box RW 20, Ridgeway Lusaka Zambia. **Tel** 250747, telex ZA 41350. **LC** DT963.A2; Z2. **DD** 916.89/4/005. **Bk Rev**. **Ad Acc**. **Circ:** 10,000 (ctrl).
 Desc: Political, developmental and educational.
 Ind/Abst MLA Int. Bibl. Books Artic. Mod. Lang. Lit.

CG/0251-298X
ZAIRE-AFRIQUE. [Zaire-Afr.]. **Added/Corp** Centre d'Etudes pour l'Action Sociale (Kinshasa, Zaire). (Dec. 1971)-. Periodical. French. mo. $30.00 Africa; 250.00F Europe; $60.00 US and Asia. Centre D Etudes L Action Sociale, BP 3375, Kinshasa Gombre Zaire. **Tel** 011 243 30066. **LC** DT1; .C598. **DD** 960/.05. Index available. **Bk Rev**. **Ad Acc**. **Circ:** 4,500. **Continues** Congo-Afrique.
 Ind/Abst Am. Hist. Life (1988-); Int. Bibliogr. Sociol.; MLA Int. Bibl. Books Artic. Mod. Lang. Lit.; Rural Dev. Abstr.

ZA
ZIMBABWE PEOPLE'S VOICE : OFFICIAL ORGAN OF THE ZIMBABWE AFRICAN PEOPLE'S UNION (ZAPU), THE. Added/Corp Zimbabwe African People's Union. Patriotic Front (Zimbabwe). (April 30, 1977)-. Periodical. English. wk. Zimbabwe African People's Union, Box 1657, Lusaka Zambia. **LC** DT962.8; .Z55. **DD** 968.91/005.

RH/0250-3018
ZIMBABWEA. Added/Corp National Museums and Monuments (Zimbabwe). No. 1 (May 1984)-. Periodical. English. $21.45. Zimbabwe Museum of Human Sciences, PO Box 8006, Causeway Harare Zimbabwe. **Tel** 011 263 4 7048312. **LC** DT962.3; .Z55. **DD** 968.91/01/05. **Continues** Occasional Papers of the National Museums and Monuments. Series A, Human Sciences.
 Ind/Abst Anthropol. Lit.

RH
ZIMBABWEAN HISTORY : THE JOURNAL OF THE HISTORICAL ASSOCIATION OF ZIMBABWE. Added/Corp Historical Association of Zimbabwe. Vol. 10 (1979)-. English. an. $130.00. Historical Association of Zimbabwe, PO Box 2054, Harare Zimbabwe. **LC** DT946; .R43. **Continues** Rhodesian History, 1015-8588.
 Ind/Abst Am. Hist. Life (1970-).

NE
ZUIDELIJK AFRIKA NIEUWS. Dutch. 0.50 each issue. Anti-Apartheids Beweging Nederland, Lauriellgracht 116, Amsterdam Netherlands. **LC** DT727; .Z84. **UDC** 968.0.

HISTORY OF ASIA

US/0898-6827
AACAR BULLETIN OF THE ASSOCIATION FOR THE ADVANCEMENT OF CENTRAL ASIAN RESEARCH. [AACAR bull. Assoc. Adv. Cent. Asian Res.]. **Added/Corp** Association for the Advancement of Central Asian Research (U.S.). **VFOAT** AACAR Bulletin. (Sept. 1988)-. Periodical. English. sa (Spring and Fall). $25.00. Association for the Advancement of Central Asian Research, Department of History, Herter Hall, University of Massachusetts, Amherst MA 01003. **LC** WMLC 93/324; DS327; .A233. **DD** 958.

FR
ABHATH ARABIYAH. VFOAT Recherches Arabes. Vol. 1 (May/July 1978)-. Periodical. Arabic (French). qt. **LC** DS36; .A22.

PH
ACADEMICREVIEW. VFOAT Academic Review. Periodical. English. sa. PCU/Research and Publications Center, Room 113/1648 Taft Avenue, Manila Philippines. **LC** DS651; .A65. **DD** 959.9/005. **UDC** 959.9.

JA/0567-7254
ACTA ASIATICA. (ACTA ASIATICA : BULLETIN OF THE INSTITUTE OF EASTERN CULTURE.). **Added/Corp** Toho Gakkai. (1960)-. Bulletin. English. Twice a year. $116.00. Institute of Eastern Culture / Tokyo, 4-1 2 Nishikanda Chome, Chiyoda-ku Tokyo Japan. **Tel** 011 81 3 3261 1061. **(Subscription address:** Kyowa Book Company Inc., 1 38 Kanda Jinbocho Chiyoda-ku, Tokyo 101 Japan.**) LC** DS12; .A45. **DD** 950/.05.
 Ind/Abst Anthropol. Lit.; MLA Int. Bibl. Books Artic. Mod. Lang. Lit.

HU/0001-6446
ACTA ORIENTALIA ACADEMIAE SCIENTIARUM HUNGARICAE. [Acta orient. Acad. Sci. Hung.]. **Added/Corp** Magyar Tudomanyos Akademia. Vol. 1 (1951)-. Academic Scholarly Publication. English (French, German and Russian). Three times a year. $96.00. Akademiai Kiado, Publishing House of the Hungarian Academy of Sciences, Prielle Kornelia u. 19-35, H-1117 Budapest Hungary. **Tel** 011 36 1 1811991, FAX 011 36 1 1811991, telex 22-6228 AKNYO H. **ED** Tokei Ferenc (editor's address: PO Box 24, H-1363 Budapest Hungary). **LC** DS1; .A25. **DD** 950/.05. **[CCC]**. **Bk Rev**. **Ad Acc**. **Circ:** 800.
 Desc: Oriental studies.
 Ind/Abst Hist. Life (1987-); Index Islam. Lit.; Linguist. Lang. Behav. Abstr.; MLA Int. Bibl. Books Artic. Mod. Lang. Lit.; Soc. Plann. Policy Dev. Abstr.; Sociol. Abstr.

PO
ACTAS / II SEMINARIO INTERNACIONAL DE HISTORIA INDO-PORTUGUESA. Portuguese. Instituto de Investigacao Cientifica Tropical, Centro de Documentacao e Informacao, rua Jau 47, 1 300 Lisbon Portugal. **Tel** 645321.

IT
ADHYAYANAMALA. 1- May 1973-. Multiple languages (English, Hindi and Sanskrit). Rs10.00. 23/3 Shakti Nagar-7, Dilli India. **LC** DS401; .A544. **UDC** 954.

KO
AESAN HAKPO. Added/Corp Aesan Hakhoe. (1981)-. Periodical. Korean (English). ir. W4,800. Aesan Hakhoe, 58-14 1-ka Sinmun-ro Chongno-ku, Seoul 110 Korea. **LC** DS901; .A57.

LE
AFAQ. No. 1- Jan. 1974-. Arabic. £L50.00. Ghrighiwar Haddad, PO Box 135065, Beirut Lebanon. **LC** DS36; .A3. **UDC** 956.93.

FR/0244-9676
AFGHANISTAN EN LUTTE. (19??)-. Periodical. French.
 Ind/Abst Hum. Rights Intern. Rep.

AF/0001-9682
AFGHANISTAN (KABUL). (AFGHANISTAN.). [Afghanistan]. Vol. 1 (1946)-. Periodical. English (French). qt. Soc Sci Scientific & Research Center, Afghanistan Academy of Science, Da Afghanistan Bank Kabul Afghanistan. **LC** DS350; .A37. **UDC** 958.1.
 Ind/Abst Am. Hist. Life (1972-1975).

US/1046-9834
AFGHANISTAN STUDIES JOURNAL. See General Interest-General Interest-Asia.

FR/0399-0370
AFRIQUE ET L'ASIE MODERNES, L'. Ceased. See History(General)-History of Africa.

History(General) —History of Asia

BL/0002-0591
AFRO-ASIA. See History(General)-History of Africa.

JA
AJIA-AFURIKA BUNKA KENKYUJO KENKYU NEMPO. Main/Corp Toyo Daigaku, Tokyo. Ajia-Afurika Bunka Kenkyujo. **Added/Corp** Toyo Daigaku, Tokyo. Ajia-Afurika Bunka Kenkyujo Annual Journal of the Asia-Africa Cultural Research Institute. **VFOAT** Annual Journal of the Asia-Africa Cultural Research Institute. (19??)-. Periodical. Japanese. Toyo Daigaku, 28-20 Hakusan 5-chome Bunkyu-ku, Tokyo 112 Japan. **LC** DS1; .T6313.

JA
AJIA CHUTO DOKO NENPO. VFOAT Asia Middle East. 1982-. Japanese. an. ¥8800. Ajia Keizai Shuppankai, 42 Ichigaya Honmura-cho, Shinjuku-ku Tokyo 162 Japan. **LC** DS1; .A313. **UDC** 951. Continues Ajia Doko Nenpo.

JA/0044-9237
AJIA KENKYU (AJIA SEIKEI GAKKAI). (AJIA KENKYU / AJIA SEIKEI GAKKI HEN.). **Added/Corp** Ajia Seikei Gakkai. **VFOAT** Aziya Kenkyu; Asiatic Studies; Asian Studies. Vol. 1 (1954)-. Periodical. Japanese (summaries and/or abstracts in English; table of contents in English and Japanese). qt. $119.00. Do Gakkai, Keto Tsushin 19-ban 30-go Mita, 2-chome Minato-ku, Tokyo 108 Japan. **(Subscription address:** Japan Publications Trading Company, Ltd., PO Box 5030, Tokyo International, Tokyo 100-31 Japan.**) LC** DS1; .A315.
Ind/Abst Am. Hist. Life (1955-).

TS
AKHBAR DUBAYY. Periodical. Arabic. Dairat Al-Ilam, PO Box 1420, Dubayy Trucial States United Arab Emirates. **LC** DS247.D7; A22. **UDC** 953.62.

TS
AL-AZMINAH AL-ARABIYAH. VFOAT Azmena Al-Arabia; Al-Azmena Al-Arabia. Periodical. Arabic. wk. S B 5823, Al-Imarat Al-Muttahidah Al-Arabiyah, Al-Shariqah Trucial States. **LC** DS36; .A96. **UDC** 953.62.

PK
AL-BALAGH. VFOAT Balagh. Periodical. Urdu. wk. $16.00. Ghulam Husain Khoklar, Dacca Book Stall, Bank Road, Ravalpindi Pakistan. **LC** DS376; .B3.

MK
AL-USRAH. VFOAT Alusra. Periodical. Arabic. 12. PO Box 144, Mutrah Muscat. **LC** DS247.O6; A27.

LY
AL-WAHDAH AL-ARABIYAH. Periodical. Arabic. wk. 1.00LD. Al-Muassasah Al-Ammah Lil-Sihafah, PO Box 4814, Tarabulus Al-Gharb Libya. **LC** DS36; .W32.

BA
AL-WATHIQAH. Added/Corp Markaz al-Wathaiq al-Tarikhiyah bi-Dawlat al-Bahrayn. **VFOAT** Document; Watheeka. V. 1, No. 1 (July 1982)-. Periodical. Arabic (English). sa. $16.00. Historical Documents Office, S B 28882, Manama Bahrain. **Tel** 011 973 664854, telex 8727 HAPS BN. **ED** Shaikh Abdulla Bin Khalid Al Khalifa. **LC** DS247.B2; A29. **DD** 953/.65/05. **Bk Rev. Circ:** 3,000 (ctrl).
Desc: Devoted to the history of Bahrain in particular and the Persian Gulf in general.

TS
AL-ZAFRAH. Periodical. Arabic. Al-Imarat Al-Arabiyah Al-Muttahidah Muassatal-Zafr, PO Box 2488, Abu Zaby Trucial States. **LC** DS36; .Z32. **UDC** 953.62.

GW
ALTORIENTALISCHE FORSCHUNGEN. Added/Corp Akademie der Wissenschaften der DDR. Zentralinstitut fuer Alte Geschichte und Archaologie. (1974)-. Multiple languages (English, German, Italian and Russian). Twice a year. $150.00. Akademie-Verlag GmbH, Muehlenstrasse 33 34, D 13162 Berlin Germany. **Tel** 011 49 30 47489300, FAX 011 49 30 47889357. **(Subscription address:** VCH Publishers Inc., 303 Northwest 12th Avenue, Journals Department, Deerfield FL 33442.**) LC** DS42; .A43. **DD** 930.

US/0044-7471
AMERASIA JOURNAL. See Ethnic Interests.

US/0737-6650
AMERICAN ASIAN REVIEW, THE. [Am. Asian rev.]. **Added/Corp** St. John's University (New York, N.Y.). Institute of Asian Studies. Vol. 1, No. 1 (Spring 1983)-. Periodical. English. qt. $24.00 US; $29.00 other. St. John's University / Institute of Asian Studies, Sun Yat Sen Hall, Jamaica NY 11439. **Tel** (718)990-6161. **ED** Dr Winston Yang. **LC** DS701; .A35. **DD** 950/.05. **Bk Rev. Ad Acc. Pr Rev. Circ:** 400 (ctrl).
Desc: Covers promotion studies on Asia, free of cultural and partisan bias. The journal's foremost goal is to provide an open forum for a continuing dialog among academic and professional specialists on the experience and historical development of modern East and Southeast Asia.
Ind/Abst Am. Bibliogr. Slavic East Europ. Stud.; PAIS Int. Print.

US/0094-3770
AMERICAN BIBLIOGRAPHY OF SLAVIC AND EAST EUROPEAN STUDIES. See History(General)-Abstracting, Bibliographies and Statistics.

US/0065-9541
AMERICAN ORIENTAL SERIES, ESSAY. Main/Corp American Oriental Society. Monographic series. English. ir. Price varies per volume. American Oriental Society, 111 E Hatcher Graduate Library, University of Michigan, Ann Arbor MI 48109. **Tel** (313)747-4760. **ED** Edwin Gerow.

US/0003-1550
AMERICAN ZIONIST, THE. Suspended. V. 1- Jan. 14, 1921-Suspended. Periodical. English. qt. $5.00 US; $6.00 other. Zionist Organization of America, 4 East 34th Street, New York NY 10016. **Tel** (212)481-1500. **LC** DS101. **DD** 956.9. **UDC** 956.94. cum. index. available on microfilm and microfiche from University Microfilms International (UMI). **Supersedes** Maccabaean; **Absorbed** Zionist Quarterly.
Ind/Abst Index Jew. Period.

●NE/0929-077X
ANCIENT CIVILIZATIONS FROM SCYTHIA TO SIBERIA. See History(General)-History of Europe.

II
ANCIENT INDIA. Added/Corp Archaeological Survey of India. No. 1 (Jan. 1946)-. Periodical. English. ir. Government of India / International Archives, International Archives of India, Janpath New Delhi 11 India. **LC** DS416; .A55. **DD** 913.34.

PK/0066-1600
ANCIENT PAKISTAN. V. 1- 1964-. English. ir. Ancient Pakistan, Peshawar University, Department of Archaeology, Peshawar NWFP Pakistan. **LC** DS378; .A7. **UDC** 934.

LE
ANNALES D'HISTOIRE ET D'ARCHEOLOGIE / UNIVERSITE SAINT-JOSEPH, FACULTE DES LETTRES ET DES SCIENCES HUMAINES. V. 1 (1982)-. Periodical. Arabic (English and French). an. Universite Saint-Joseph Faculte des Lettres et des Sciences Humaines, BP 293, Beirut Lebanon. **LC** DS56; .A68. **DD** 935/.005. **UDC** 930.

US/0883-8909
ANNALS - ASSOCIATION FOR ASIAN STUDIES. SOUTHEAST CONFERENCE. (ANNALS /SOUTHEAST CONFERENCE, ASSOCIATION FOR ASIAN STUDIES.). [Annals - Assoc. Asian Stud., Southeast Conf.]. **Main/Corp** Association for Asian Studies. Southeast Conference. 18th annual meeting Vol. 1 (Jan. 25-27, 1979)-. English. $10.00 plus shipping. Southeast Conference for Asian Studies, Attn: Avinash C. Maheshwary, South Asia Collection, Perkins Library, Duke University, Durham NC 27708-0175. **Tel** (919)684-5073. **ED** Kenneth Berger (editor's phone: (919)684-2373). **LC** DS1; .A782a. **DD** 950.

II
ANNALS OF ORIENTAL RESEARCH / UNIVERSITY OF MADRAS. Added/Corp University of Madras. (19??)-. Periodical. English. sa. $20.00. University of Madras Registrar, University Building Chepauk, Madras 600 005 India. **(Subscription address:** Prints India, 11 Darya Ganj, New Delhi, 110002 India, (Phone: 011 91 11 3268645)**) Continues** Journal of Oriental Research of the University of Madras.
Ind/Abst Index Islam. Lit.

II
ANNUAL BIBLIOGRAPHY OF CHRISTIANITY IN INDIA. See Religion and Theology.

US/0066-0035
ANNUAL OF THE AMERICAN SCHOOLS OF ORIENTAL RESEARCH, THE. See Archaeology.

JO/0449-1564
ANNUAL OF THE DEPARTMENT OF ANTIQUITIES. Main/Corp Jordan. Dairat Al-Athar Al-Ammah. **VFOAT** Hawliyat Dairat al-Athar; Hawliyat Dairat al-Athar al-Ammah. Vol. 1 (1951)-. English (Arabic, French and German). an (Oct.) $40.00. Department of Antiquities / Jordan, Hasemite Kingdom of Jordon, PO Box 88, Amman Jordan. **Tel** 011 962 6 644482. **LC** DS153.3; .A3. **DD** 913.5695. **Supersedes in part** Palestine. Dept. of Antiquities. Quarterly of the Department of Antiquities in Palestine.
Ind/Abst Anthropol. Lit.; BHA : Biblio. Hist. Art; Middle East Abstr. Index; Numis. Lit.

UK
ANNUAL REPORT / SCHOOL OF ORIENTAL AND AFRICAN STUDIES, UNIVERSITY OF LONDON. Main/Corp University of London. School of Oriental and African Studies. (1989/1990)-. English. **Continues** University of London. School of Oriental and African Studies. Report of the Governing Body and Statement of Accounts.

IT/0080-391X
ANNUARIO - INSTITUTO GIAPPONESE DI CULTURA IN ROMA. (ANNUARIO - ISTITUTO GIAPPONESE DI CULTURA.). [Annu.- Ist. gpn. cult. Roma]. **Main/Corp** Japan Cultural Institute in Rome. (1963/64)-. Periodical. Italian (French; summaries and/or abstracts in French and English). an. Instituto Giapponese di Cultura, Via Antonio Gramsci 74, 00197 Rome Italy. **Tel** (06)3609794. **LC** DS834.95; .I87b. **DD** 952/.007/045. **Circ:** 1,000.
Desc: Academic journal to introduce European studies by Japanese scholars.
Ind/Abst BHA : Biblio. Hist. Art.

BL
AONDE VAMOS?. Periodical. Portuguese. 300. Caixa Postal 441 - ZC-00, Rio de Janeiro Brazil. **LC** DS101; .A684.

PH/0303-8564
ARCHIPELAGO. Began in 1974. Periodical. English. mo. $10.00. Bureau of National and Foreign Information, Department of Public Information, Beneficial Life Building, Solana Street, Manila Philippines. **LC** DS651; .A7. **DD** 959.9/005. **UDC** 959.9.

XR/0044-8699
ARCHIV ORIENTALNI. See Linguistics.

UA
ARD AL-SALAM. No. 1 (July 1982)-. Periodical. Arabic. £E0.10 single issue. Sami Fahmi Siraj 8 B Mamarr Khamis, Shari 26 Yuliyu, Al-Qahirah Egypt. **LC** DS110.5; 0.A73.

II
ARITRA. Periodical. Bengali (Bengali). mo. 2.00. Binay Bandopadhyay, 23 Brindavan Basak Street, Calcutta 700012 India. **LC** DS432.B4; A74.

CN/0826-2667
ARMENIAN CAUSE, THE. Added/Corp Armenian National Committee of Canada. **VFOAT** Cause Armenienne. Vol. 1, No. 1 (Apr. 1984)-. Periodical. English (French). Four times a year. Free. Armenian National Committee of Canada, 3401 Olivar Asselin Street, Montreal Quebec H4J 1L5 Canada. **Tel** (514)334-1299. **ED** Guiragos Manoyan. **DD** 956.6/2. **Bk Rev. Circ:** 2,500 (ctrl).
Desc: Articles, news, reviews of new publications, documents relating to the Armenian question. The Armenian minority of Turkey and Armenians and Armenia in general.

LE/0304-8624
ARMENIAN STUDIES. VFOAT Etudes Armeniennes. 1973-. Multiple languages (English and French). Universitaires Armeniens, Association Libanaise, 11, Rue Negib Haddad Lebanon. **LC** DS161; .645. **DD** 956.6/2/005. **UDC** 956.6.

AF
ARYANA, AFGHANISTAN REPUBLIC. Periodical. English (English). 100.00. Kabul Ministry of Information and Culture, Ansari Watt Kabul, Kabul Afghanistan. **LC** DS350; .A79. **DD** 958.1/005. **UDC** 958.1.
Ind/Abst Numis. Lit.

KO/0021-9126
ASEA YONGU. Added/Corp Koryo Taehakkyo. Asea Munje Yonguso. **VFOAT** Journal of Asiatic Studies. Vol. 1 (1958)-. Periodical. Korean (English). sa. $30.00. Asiatic Research Center, Korea University, 1 Anam-Dong Sungbuk-Ku, Seoul 136-701 Korea. **Tel** 011 82 2 9224117. **ED** Sung-Chick Hong. **LC** DS1; .A47117. Index available. cum. index. **Bk Rev. Circ:** 1,000.
Ind/Abst Am. Hist. Life (1958, 1963-).

IO/0215-1618
ASEAN NEWSLETTER / ASSOCIATION OF SOUTHEAST ASIAN NATIONS. Added/Corp ASEAN. Secretariat. Vol. 1, No. 1 (Sept. 1980)-. Periodical. English. Six times a year. Free. Association of South East Asian Nations, PO Box 2072, Jakarta Indonesia. **LC** DS520; .A8713. **DD** 959/.00977. **Continues** Asean Digest.

MY/0126-5245
ASEAN REVIEW. [Asean rev.]. (19??)-. Periodical. English. mo. $2.50 per copy. Wedgewood Sdn Bhd, 1.91 Wisma Central Jalan Ampang, Kuala Lumpur Malaysia. **LC** DS501; .A646. **DD** 959/.005.

RU
ASIA AND AFRICA TODAY. Added/Corp Sovetskii Komitet Solidarnosti Stran Azii i Afriki. Institut Vostokovedeniia (Akademiia nauk SSSR) Institut Afriki (Akademiia nauk SSSR). (19??)-. Periodical. English (French, Portuguese and Arabic). bm. $159.95. Asia &

Africa Today, Moscow Russia. **(Subscription address:** East View Publications Inc., 3020 Harbor Lane North, Suite 110, Minneapolis MN 55447.**) LC** DS1; .A4714. **DD** 950/.42/05.
Desc: Highlighting major events in the political, economic and cultural life of the Afro-Asian peoples. Contributors are Soviet scholars, public figures, writers and journalists. Covers customs and traditions of Afro-Asian peoples and their ancient and contemporary history.
Ind/Abst Hum. Rights Intern. Rep.

US/0004-4431
ASIA CALLING. V. 1- Feb. 1947-. Periodical. English. qt. $3.00. Pan Pacific Centers, 845 Via de la Paz, Pacific Palisades CA 90272. **LC** DS1; .A472. **DD** 950. **UDC** 950. available on microfilm from University Microfilms International (UMI).
Desc: Issues for Dec. 1948-(Jan. 1950) include section in Chinese called America calling.

HK
ASIA LINK. (19??)-. Periodical. English. bm (6 issues). $6.00 Asia; $10.00 other. Center for Progress of Peoples Ltd., 48 Princess Margaret Road, Homantin, Kowloon, Hong Kong.

US/0004-4482
ASIA MAJOR. [Asia major]. Vol. 1-10, (Jan. 1924-1935); New Series, Vol. 1-19, (1949-1975); Third Series, Vol. 1 (1988)-. Periodical. English (German). Twice a year. $45.00 (individuals), $60.00 (institutions), $30.00 (students). Sheridan Press, PO Box 465, Hanover PA 17331. **Tel** (800)352-2210, (717)632-3535, FAX (717)633-8900. **LC** DS501; .A65. **DD** 950.05. **[CCC].**
Ind/Abst Am. Hist. Life (1962-1974); MLA Int. Bibl. Books Artic. Mod. Lang. Lit.

TH/0857-2062
ASIA-PACIFIC NEWSLETTER. [Asia-Pac. newsl.]. **VFOAT** ILO Asia-Pacific Newsletter. (1985)-. Periodical. English. mo. ILO Regional Office for Asia and the Pacific, United Nations Building, Rajdamnern Avenue, PO Box 1759, Bangkok Thailand. **UDC** 331. **CODEN** NU051.
Ind/Abst Int. Labour Doc.

US/1052-987X
ASIA TODAY INTERNATIONAL. [Asia today int.]. **VFOAT** Asia Today. (19??)-. Periodical. English. mo. $20.00 US; $30.00 other. Asia Communications, 2020 National Press Building, Washington DC 20045. **DD** 950. ***Continues** Asia Today (Washington, D.C.), 1045-2230.*

US/1045-2230
ASIA TODAY (WASHINGTON, D.C.). ***Title Change.*** (ASIA TODAY.). [Asia today]. Vol. 1, No. 1 (July 1989)-(19??). Periodical. English. mo. Asia Communications, 2020 National Press Building, Washington DC 20045. **DD** 950. ***Continued by** Asia Today International, 1052-987X.*
Ind/Abst AESIS Q.

II
ASIA WORLD. V. 1- Jan./Feb. 1978-. Periodical. English. Post-Meridian Publishing Company, PO Box 164 - 15, 700 020 Calcutta India. **LC** DS1; .A47299. **DD** 950/.05. **UDC** 950.

UK/0306-8374
ASIAN AFFAIRS (LONDON). (ASIAN AFFAIRS.). [Asian aff.]. Vol. 57 (Feb. 1970)-. Periodical. English. Three times a year. $62.00 (surface mail) US; £31.00 (surface mail) UK. Royal Soc for Asian Affairs, 2 Belgrave Square, London SW1X 8PJ England. **Tel** 011 44 71 2355122, FAX 011 44 71 2596771. **ED** R. A. Longmire. **LC** DS1; .R6. **DD** 950/.05. **UDC** 950. **Bk Rev. Ad Acc. Circ:** 1,900 (ctrl). Documents available from UMI Article Clearinghouse. ***Continues** Journal of the Royal Central Asian Society, 0035-8789.*
Desc: Covers the cultural, political and social affairs of Asian countries from the Middle East to the Far East.
Ind/Abst Acad. Abstr. Full Text Elite (Jan. 1992-) [Full Txt.]; Acad. Abstr. (Jan. 1992-); Acad. Search (Jan. 1992-); Am. Hist. Life (1955-); Br. Humanit. Index; Curr. Geogr. Publ. (199?-); Expand. Acad. Index (1989-); Hist. Source (Jan. 1992-); Humanit. Source (Jul. 1993-) [Full Txt.]; Index Islam. Lit.; Index Book Rev. Relig.; INFO-SOUTH Abstr.; Int. Polit. Sci. Abstr.; Mag. Artic. Summar. Elite (July 1992-) [Full Txt.]; Mag. Artic. Summar. Select (July 1992-); Mag. Artic. Summar. CD-ROM (Jan. 1992-); Mag. Search; Middle East Abstr. Index; Newsp. Period. Abstr. (1991-); PAIS Int. Print; Soc. Sci. Source (Jan. 1992-) [Full Txt.]; Soc. Sci. Index; Soc. Sci. Index Fulltext (Oct. 1988-) [Full Txt.]; Middle East J.

SI/0004-4520
ASIAN ALMANAC. Vol. 1 (July 1/6 1963)-. Periodical. English. wk. $270.00 seamail, $300.00 airmail. Asian Almanac, PO Box 2737, Singapore 9047 Singapore. **Tel** 011 65 4816047. **ED** Mr. Vedagiri T. Sambandan. **LC** DS1; .A4732. **DD** 950/.05. Index available. **Bk Rev.** ctrl circ.

XR
ASIAN AND AFRICAN LINGUISTIC STUDIES. See Linguistics.

XO/0571-2742
ASIAN AND AFRICAN STUDIES (BRATISLAVA, CZECHOSLOVAKIA). (ASIAN AND AFRICAN STUDIES / DEPARTMENT OF ORIENTAL STUDIES OF THE SLOVAK ACADEMY OF SCIENCES BRATISLAVA.). **Added/Corp** Slovenska Akademia Vied. Kabinet Orientalistiky. Vol. 1 (1965)-. English (French, German and Russian). an. Price varies. Humanities Press, 165 1st Avenue, Atlantic Highlands NJ 07716. **Tel** (908)872-1441, (800)221-3845, FAX (908)872-0717, telex 752233. **ED** Josef Genzor and Viktor Krupa. **LC** DS1; .A4733. **DD** 950/.05. **Bk Rev.**
Desc: A well established series providing sources of reference for scholars and students engaging in Asian and African studies. Covers history, language and literature.
Ind/Abst MLA Int. Bibl. Books Artic. Mod. Lang. Lit.

IS/0066-8281
ASIAN AND AFRICAN STUDIES (JERUSALEM). See History(General)-History of Africa.

JA
ASIAN CULTURAL CENTRE FOR UNESCO, ITS ORGANIZATION AND ACTIVITIES. Main/Corp Asian Cultural Centre for Unesco. (19??)-. English. Asian Cultural Centre for UNESCO, Book Publishers Building, No 6 Fukuromachi Shinjuku-ku, Tokyo Japan. **LC** DS1.A47347; A2. **DD** 341.7/67.

CH/0378-8911
ASIAN CULTURE QUARTERLY. Added/Corp Asian Cultural Center. **VFOAT** Ya-chou Wen Hua. Vol. 1 (Autumn 1973)-. Multiple languages (English and Chinese). qt. Free. Asia Pacific Cultural Center, 66 Aikuo East Road 6F, Taipei Taiwan. **Tel** 011 86 2 3222139. **ED** Tai-chu Chen. **LC** DS1; .A4736. **DD** 950/.05. Index available. cum. index. **Bk Rev. Circ:** 1,000 (ctrl).
Desc: Concerns culture in Asian-Pacific regions.
Ind/Abst Int. Bibliogr. Sociol.

II/0004-4644
ASIAN RECORDER. Vol. 1 (Jan. 1/7, 1955)-. Periodical. English. Fifty-two times a year (Published on Mondays). $175.00 (surface mail), $260.00 (airmail) includes binder & supplement; $153.00 (surface mail), $238.00 (airmail) without binder. Asian Recorder, A 126 Niti Bagh, New Delhi 110049, India. **Tel** 11 91 11 665405. **(Subscription address:** Prints India, 11 Darya Ganj, New Delhi 110002 India.**) ED** A. K. B. Menon. **LC** DS1; .A4747. **DD** 950.05. Each issue contains an index to its own contents (no volume index)--loose. cum. index. **Ad Acc. Circ:** 2,000 (ctrl).
Desc: A reference journal with quarterly index and cover binder. Events in Asian countries listed under each country with sources of information are covered.

US/0066-8486
ASIAN STUDIES AT HAWAII. Added/Corp University of Hawaii. Asian Studies Program. (1965)-. Monographic series. English. ir. Price varies per volume. University of Hawaii Press, 2840 Kolowalu Street, Honolulu HI 96822. **Tel** (808)956-8833, (808)948-8697, FAX (808)988-6052.

US/0362-4811
ASIAN STUDIES NEWSLETTER. [Asian stud. newsl.]. **Added/Corp** Association for Asian Studies. Vol. 17, No. 1 (Sept. 1971)-. Newsletter. English. qt. $10.00 US and Canada. Association for Asian Studies Inc., University of Michigan, 1 Lane Hall, Ann Arbor MI 48109. **Tel** (313)665-2490, FAX (313)665-3801. **LC** DS1; .A713. **DD** 950. ***Continues in part** Newsletter / Association for Asian Studies.*

AT/1035-7823
ASIAN STUDIES REVIEW. Added/Corp Asian Studies Association of Australia. Vol. 13, No. 3 (Apr. 1990)-. Periodical. English. Three times a year (Apr., July, Nov.). 50.00Aus$ Australia; 52.50Aus$ others Comes with Asian Studies Association of Australia Membership. Asian Studies Association Australia / Politics Department, La Trobe University, Bundoora Victoria 3083 Australia. **Tel** 011 61 3 4791111, FAX 011 61 3 4710894. **LC** DS32.9.A8; A75a. **Bk Rev. Ad Acc, Adv Mgr:** Wendy Miller. **Circ:** 1,000. ***Continues** Asian Studies Association of Australia. Review, 0314-7533.*
Desc: Reviews to keep up-to-date with major debates and initiatives in Asian studies in Australia.
Ind/Abst APAIS, Aust. Public Aff. Inf. Ser. (1990-).

US
ASIAN STUDIES SERIES. (1976)-. Monographic series. English. ir. Price varies per volume. AMS Press Inc., 56 East 13th Street, New York NY 10003. **Tel** (212)777-4700, FAX (212)995-5413, telex 710 581 2302. ***Continues** Asian Studies (New York, N.Y.), 0748-5476.*
Desc: Series documenting Asian studies. Volumes have covered topics such as Mongolian heroes and education in China.

US/0004-4687
ASIAN SURVEY. See Social Sciences.

US/1055-6095
ASIAPACIFIC BRIEFING PAPER. [AsiaPac. brief. pap.]. **Added/Corp** East-West Center. **VFOAT** Asia Pacific Briefing Paper. No. 1 (Apr. 1991)-. Periodical. English. mo. free. Center for Cultural and Technical Interchange between East and West Inc, 1777 East-West Road, Honolulu HI 96848. **Tel** (808)944-7401, FAX (808)944-7490, telex 230-980-171. **DD** 950.

CN/0228-4138
ASIATHEQUE. (L'ASIATHEQUE : ETUDES SUR L'ASIE DE L'EST, UNIVERSITE DE MONTREAL.). [Asiatheque]. V. 1, No. 1 (Jan. 4, 1978)-. Periodical. French. Free. Asiatheque, Universite de Montreal, CP 6128 Succursale C, Montreal Quebec H3C 3J7 Canada. **DD** 950/.07/11714281. **UDC** 951. ctrl circ.

SZ/0004-4717
ASIATISCHE STUDIEN. (ASIATISCHE STUDIEN : ZEITSCHRIFT DER SCHWEIZERISCHEN GESELLSCHAFT FUER ASIENKUNDE / ETUDES ASIATIQUES : REVUE DE LA SOCIETE SUISSE D'ETUDES ASIATIQUES.). [Asiat. Stud.]. **Added/Corp** Schweizerische Gesellschaft fuer Asienkunde. **VFOAT** Etudes Asiatiques. (1947)-. Periodical. German (English, French, German and Italian). qt. 85.00F. Verlag Peter Lang AG, Jupiterstrasse 15, CH-3000 Bern 15 Switzerland. **Tel** 011 41 31 9411122, FAX 011 41 31 321131. **ED** Peter Lang. **LC** DS1; .A54. **DD** 950/.05. **Bk Rev. Ad Acc. Circ:** 450. ***Continues** Mitteilungen der Schweizerischen Gesellschaft der Freunde Ostasiatischer Kultur.*
Desc: Contains scientific articles referring to important aspects of the Asian culture, such as literature, philosophy, religion, and art.
Ind/Abst MLA Int. Bibl. Books Artic. Mod. Lang. Lit.

FR/0395-2681
ASIE DU SUD-EST ET MONDE INSULINDIEN. ***Title Change.*** [Asie sud-est monde insulindien]. **VFOAT** ASEMI; A.S.E.M.I. Vol. 2, No. 3 (Sept. 1971)-?. Periodical. French (English). ir. Cedrasemi, 44 rue de la Tour, 75016 Paris France. **ED** Georges Condominas and Monique Zaini-Lajoubert. **LC** DS501; .A86. **DD** 915.9/03/05. **UDC** 915.9. Index available. cum. index. **Bk Rev. Ad Acc.** ***Continues** Asie du Sud-Est & Monde Indonesien.* ***Continued by** Atelier ASEMI, 0993-538X.*
Desc: Publishes articles concerning the humanities in Southeast Asia, Indonesia and the Philippines. After study by the Editorial Committee, the manuscripts are either published or returned to the author within a year. One section is generally devoted to reviews of books in the field.

GW
ASIEN, PAZIFIK / OSTASIATISCHER VEREIN E.V. Added/Corp Ostasiatischer Verein. **VFOAT** Wirtschaftshandbuch Asien/Pazifik. (1991)-. German. ***Continues** Jahres-Bericht.*

US/0145-6334
ASSUR. (MONOGRAPHIC JOURNALS OF THE NEAR EAST. ASSUR.). [Assur]. **Added/Corp** International Institute for Mesopotamian Area Studies. **VFOAT** Assur. Vol. 1 (1974)-. Monographic series. English. ir. Price varies per volume. Undena Publications, PO Box 97, Malibu CA 90265. **Tel** (310)649-2612. **(Subscription address:** Crescent Academic Services, 29528 Madera Avenue, Shafter CA 93263.**) ED** K. Deller, P. Garelli, E. Porada, and C. Saporetti. **DD** 915. **Circ:** 200.
Desc: Studies Assyrian as a dialect of Akkadian and history of the Assyrian Empire.
Ind/Abst MLA Int. Bibl. Books Artic. Mod. Lang. Lit.; Old Testam. Abstr.

IS
ATAH. V. 1- November 1977-. Periodical. Hebrew. IL75.00. Agudat Leumat, POB 3421, Tel-Aviv Israel. **LC** DS101; .A74.

UA
ATILYIH. Periodical. Arabic. £E0.15. Atilyih Al-Qahirah Lil-Kuttab Wa-Al-Fannanain, 2 Shari, Karim Al-Dawlah Mutafarri, Min Shari Al-Antikikh, Al-Qahirah United Arab Republic Egypt. **LC** DS36.88; .A86.

SP/0212-5730
AULA ORIENTALIS. Vol. 1, No. 1 (Jan. 1983)-. Periodical. Spanish (English, French and Italian). Twice a year. $63.00. Editorial Ausa, Apdo 101, 08280 Sadadell Spain. **Tel** 011 34 3 7250721. **UDC** 935. **Bk Rev. Circ:** 150 (ctrl).
Desc: Linguistic, archaeological and historical studies on the Hamito-Semitic and Indo-European cultures of the ancient Near East.
Ind/Abst New Testam. Abstr.

UK
AWRAQ (LONDON, ENGLAND). (AWRAQ.). (19??)-. Periodical. Arabic. mo. $3.00 single issue. Latchon Ltd, 104 Homerton High Street, London England. **LC** DS1; .A86.

II
B.R.P.T. BULLETIN. Main/Corp Bureau of Research & Publications on Tripura. V. 1- 1974-. Bulletin. Multiple languages (Bengali and English). 2.50. Bureau of Research & Publication on Tribura, Ramnagar Road No 2, Agartala 799002 India. **LC** DS485.T8; B86A. **DD** 954/.15/005. **UDC** 954.12.

II
BAGCHI INDOLOGICAL SERIES. 1-. Monographic series. English (Sanskrit). Price varies per volume. K P Bagchi, 286 B B Ganguli Street, Calcutta 700012 India. **UDC** 954.0.

IQ
BAGHDAD. **Added/Corp** Iraq. Wizarat al-Thaqafah wa-al-Ilam. Iraq. Wizarat al-Irshad. Iraq. Wizarat al-Thaqafah wa-al-Irshad. (May 1963)-. Periodical. Arabic. ir. University of Baghdad, College of Science, Bahgdad Iraq. **LC** DS69; .B295. **DD** 956.7/005.

BG
BANGLADESH DIRECTORY. (1978)-. Directory. English. an. $10.00. Times Publications / Bangladesh, 42-43 Purana Paltan, Dacca 2, Bangladesh. **LC** DS393.3; .B36. **DD** 954.9/2.

BA
BANURAMA AL-KHALIJ. **VFOAT** Panurama Al-Khalij; Gulf Panorama. Periodical. Arabic. mo. PO Box 1122, Al-Manamah Bahrain. **LC** DS326; .B29. **UDC** 953.65.

TZ
BARA AFRIKA. **Added/Corp** Communication & Business Service. (July 1978)-. Periodical. Swahili. ir. Communication and Business Service, SLP 853, Tanga Tanzania. **LC** DT1; .B36.

IO/0005-6138
BASIS. Vol. 1 (Oct. 1951)-. Periodical. Indonesian. mo. $7.06 Indonesia; $30.00 other. Yayasan Badan Penerbit Basis, PO Box 299, Yogyakarta 55001 Indonesia. **Tel** 62 0274 88283. **ED** Dick Hartoko. **LC** AP95.I5; B37. **Bk Rev. Ad Acc. Circ:** 2,000 (ctrl).
Desc: Culture in general, especially philosophy, literature, anthropology and history.

LE
BAYRUT AL-MASA. Periodical. Arabic. wk. £L75.00. SB 6012/14, Beirut Lebanon. **LC** DS87; .B36. **UDC** 956.93.

LE/1019-0732
BEIRUT REVIEW, THE. **See** Political Science-International Relations.

II/0005-8807
BENGAL PAST AND PRESENT. [Bengal past present]. **Added/Corp** Calcutta Historical Society. **VFOAT** Bengal, Past and Present. Vol. 1, No. 1 (July 1907)-. Periodical. English. sa. $30.00. Calcutta Historical Society, Calcutta, India. **(Subscription address:** Prints India, 11 Darya Ganj, New Delhi, 110002 India, (Phone: 011 91 11 3268645)**)** **LC** DS486.C2; B5. **DD** 954/.14. cum. index.
Ind/Abst Am. Hist. Life (1954).

IO
BERITA KOMUNIKASI MASYARAKAT SEJARAWAN INDONESIA. **Main/Corp** Masyarakat Sejarawan Indonesia. V. 1- June 1973-. Indonesian. Yayasan Masyarakat Sejarawan Indonesia, Jl Pejambon 3, PO Box 165, Jakarta Indonesia. **LC** DS611; .M33A. **UDC** 959.4.

II/0378-1984
BHARATIYA VIDYA. [Bharatiya vidya]. V. 1- Nov. 1939-. English. qt. Rs120.00 India; Rs240.00 (sea mail), Rs410.00 (airmail) other. Bharatiya Vidya Bhavan, Munshi Sadan, Kulapati KM Munshi Marg, Bombay 400 007 India. **Tel** 011 91 22 3634463. **ED** J H Dave and S A Upadhyaya. **LC** DS401; .B48. **DD** 954.005. **UDC** 930.85(540). **Bk Rev. Ad Acc. Circ:** 250.
Desc: Studies in indology, Indian culture, literature, philosophy, religion, art, Sanskrit, etc.
Ind/Abst MLA Int. Bibl. Books Artic. Mod. Lang. Lit.

US/0732-6467
BIBLIOTHECA AEGYPTIA. **See** History(General)-History of Africa.

US/0732-6440
BIBLIOTHECA MESOPOTAMICA. **See** Archaeology.

NE/0006-1913
BIBLIOTHECA ORIENTALIS. [Bibl. orient.]. **Added/Corp** Nederlands Instituut voor het Nabije Oosten. Nederlandsch Archaeologisch-Philologisch Instituut voor het Nabije Oosten. Vol. 1 (April 1943)-. Periodical. Dutch (German and French). qt. Fl225.00; Fl252.50 (includes postage). Nederlands Institution Nabije Oosten, PO Box 9515, 2300 RA Leiden Netherlands. **Tel** 071-27 20 20. **ED** H J A De Meulenaere, M J Mulder, C Nijland, M Stol, E Van Donzel and D J W Meijer. **LC** Z3001; .B58. **DD** 016.9133. Index available. cum. index. **Bk Rev. Circ:** 700 (ctrl).
Desc: Archaeology of the Near East and Assyriology, Hethites, Old Testament, Hebrew and cognate languages: Arabic, Persian, Turkish and Islam.
Ind/Abst Index Book Rev. Relig.; Middle East Abstr. Index; New Testam. Abstr.; Numis. Lit.; Old Testam. Abstr.; Middle East J.

US/0741-9228
BIENNIAL REPORT - AMERICAN INSTITUTE OF INDIAN STUDIES. (BIENNIAL REPORT / AIIS.). [Bienn. rep. - Am. Inst. Indian Stud.]. **Main/Corp** American Institute of Indian Studies. English. be. American Institute of Indian Studies, Foster Hall, 1130 East 59th Street, University of Chicago, Chicago IL 60637. **LC** DS435.8; .A45A. **DD** 954/.006/073. **UDC** 954.0. ***Continues*** *American Institute of Indian Studies. AIIS Annual Report.*

NE/0006-2294
BIJDRAGEN TOT DE TAAL-, LAND- EN VOLKENKUNDE. **See** Anthropology.

SP/0571-3692
BOLETIN DE LA ASOCIACION ESPANOLA DE ORIENTALISTAS. [Bol. Asoc. Esp. Orient.]. **Added/Corp** Asociacion Espanola de Orientalistas. (1965)-. Periodical. Spanish (French and English). an. 3500ptas. Asociacion Espanola de Orientalistas, Universidad Autonoma de Madrid Rectorado, Madrid 28049 Spain. **ED** Octavio Gil Farres. **LC** DS1; .B64. **Bk Rev. Circ:** 500.
Ind/Abst Am. Hist. Life (1966-1975); BHA : Biblio. Hist. Art; Int. Bibliogr. Sociol.

II
BOMBAY. V. 1- Aug. 22/Sept. 6, 1979-. Periodical. English. sm. Living Media India, 28 A & B Jolly Maker Chambers-II Nariman Pt, Bombay 400 021 India. **LC** DS486.B7; B55. **DD** 954/.792. **UDC** 954.0.

US/0006-7806
BORNEO RESEARCH BULLETIN. **Added/Corp** Borneo Research Council. (March 1969)-. Bulletin. English. an. $20.00. Borneo Research Council, College of William & Mary, Williamsburg VA 23185. **Tel** (804)221-1055, FAX (804)221-1066. **ED** Vinson H. Sutlive Jr.(editor's address: Department of Anthropology, College of William and Mary, PO Box 8795, Williamsburg, VA. 23187). **LC** DS646.3; .B69. **DD** 915.98/3/033. **Circ:** 1,000.
Desc: A journal with 200 review condensations of more than 50 software programs and reviews for an interdisciplinary and international community of scholars.
Ind/Abst Anthropol. Index; Anthropol. Lit.; Field Crop Abstr.; Grasslands For. Abstr.; Linguist. Lang. Behav. Abstr.; Soc. Plann. Policy Dev. Abstr.; Sociol. Abstr.

BL
BRAZILYANER IDISHE TSAYTUNG. **VFOAT** Diario Israelita. (19??)-. Periodical. Multiple languages (Portuguese and Yiddish). wk. Editoria Diario Israelita, rua Senhor dos Passos 174, 6. Andar Caixa Postal 2.313, Rio de Janeiro Brazil. **LC** DS101; .B73.

NE/0925-2916
BRILL'S INDOLOGICAL LIBRARY. [Brill's indol. libr.]. (1991)-. Monographic series. English. ir. Price varies per volume. E. J. Brill, Postbus 9000, 2300 PA Leiden Netherlands. **Tel** 011 31 71 312624, FAX 011 31 71 317532, telex 39296 BRILL NL. **UDC** 294.

NE/0925-6512
BRILL'S JAPANESE STUDIES LIBRARY. [Brill's Jpn. stud. libr.]. (1990)-. Monographic series. English. ir. Price varies per volume. E. J. Brill, Postbus 9000, 2300 PA Leiden Netherlands. **Tel** 011 31 71 312624, FAX 011 31 71 317532, telex 39296 BRILL NL. **UDC** 94 (520) + 895.6.
Desc: Monographic series of Japanese studies.

US/1051-9483
BUDAYA (SHOREVIEW, MINN.). (BUDAYA.). [Budaya]. Vol. 1, No. 1 (Oct. 1990)-. Periodical. English. qt. $30.00. Q. E. D. Publishing, Inc., Box 26217, Shoreview MN 55126. **LC** IN PROCESS. **DD** 959.

IO
BUKU TAHUNAN ... PROPINSI SUMATERA UTARA. **VFOAT** Year Book ... Province of North Sumatra; Year Book ... Sumut. 1984-. English (Indonesian). an. **LC** DS646.15.S8; Y4. **DD** 959.8/1. **UDC** 959.4.

CN/0844-3416
BULLETIN / CANADIAN SOCIETY FOR MESOPOTAMIAN STUDIES. **See** Archaeology.

FR/0336-1519
BULLETIN DE L'ECOLE FRANCAISE D'EXTREME-ORIENT. [Bull. Ec. fr. Extreme-Orient]. **Added/Corp** Ecole Francaise d'Extreme-Orient. (Jan. 1901)-. Periodical. French. an. Ecole Francaise d'Extreme-Orient, 22 Ave Pres Wilson, 75016 Paris France. **Tel** 011 33 1 45532135. **(Subscription address:** Adrien Maisonneuve, 11 rue Saint Sulpice, 75005 Paris France.**)** **LC** DS531; .E395. **DD** 950. cum. index.
Ind/Abst Am. Hist. Life (1957-); Anthropol. Lit.

UA/0253-1623
BULLETIN D'ETUDES ORIENTALES. **Added/Corp** Damascus. Institut Francaise. (1931)-. Bulletin. French. an. 215.00F. Librairie d'Amerique et Dorien, 11 rue Saint Sulpice, F 75006 Paris France. **Tel** 011 33 1 43268635.
Ind/Abst BHA : Biblio. Hist. Art; Numis. Lit.; Middle East J.

US/0007-4810
BULLETIN OF CONCERNED ASIAN SCHOLARS. [Bull. concern. Asian sch.]. Vol. 1, No. 4 (May 1969)-. Bulletin. English. Four times a year. $55.00 institutions; $22.00 individuals. Bulletin of Concerned Asian Scholars Inc., 3239 9th Street, Boulder CO 80304. **Tel** (303)449-7439. **ED** Bill Doub. **LC** DS1; .B84. **DD** 950/.05. **UDC** 911.3(5). Index available. cum. index. **Bk Rev. Ad Acc. Pr Rev. Circ:** 1,800 (ctrl). available on microfilm and microfiche from University Microfilms International (UMI); available on photocopies (of out of print back issues from BCAS, CO). Documents available from The Genuine Article. ***Continues*** *CCAS Newsletter.*
Desc: Presents independent leftist views of Asia, mainly in the 20th century. Covers all fields, especially politics, history, economics and literature. Includes illustrated articles, bibliographies, review essays and reviews.
Ind/Abst Altern. Press Index; Am. Hist. Life (1987-); Arts Humanit. Citation Index [Select. Cov.]; Curr. Contents Soc. Behav. Sci.; Geogr. Abstr. Human Geogr.; Hum. Rights Intern. Rep.; Int. Bibliogr. Sociol.; Int. Dev. Abstr.; Int. Labour Doc.; Left Index; Middle East Abstr. Index; Res. Alert [Full Cov.]; Sage Public Adm. Abstr.; Soc. Sci. Cit. Index [Full Cov.].

UK/0301-9330
BULLETIN OF QUANTITATIVE AND COMPUTER METHODS IN SOUTH ASIAN STUDIES. [Bull. quant. comput. meth. S. Asian stud.]. No. 1- June 1973-. Bulletin. English. sa. $7.50. **LC** DS331; .B84. **DD** 915.9/007/20421.

PH/0115-3226
BULLETIN OF THE AMERICAN HISTORICAL COLLECTION. **Added/Corp** American Association of the Philippines. American Historical Committee. Vol. 1 (June 1972)-. Periodical. English. Four times a year. $30.00. American Association of Philippine, Box 1495, 1099 Manila Philippines. **Tel** 011 63 2 8925198. **ED** Lewis E. Gleeck. **LC** DS685; .B78. **DD** 959.9/04/05. **Bk Rev. Circ:** 600.
Desc: Historical and biographical articles and book reviews on the American experience in the Philippines, 1898 to present.

US/0890-4464
BULLETIN OF THE ASIA INSTITUTE. [Bull. Asia Inst.]. Vol. 1 (1987)-. Bulletin. English (German and French). an. $73.00. Bulletin of the Asia Institute, 3287 Bradway Boulevard, Bloomfield Hills MI 48301. **Tel** (313)647-7917, FAX (313)647-9223, (313)258-1439. **ED** Carol Altman Bromberg. **LC** N7280.A1; I72. **DD** 709/.55. **Bk Rev. Pr Rev. Circ:** 290. ***Continues*** *Bulletin of the Asia Institute of Pahlavi University.*
Desc: Examines the cultures of western and central Asia from ancient to Islamic times, with emphasis on the height of the Persian influence.
Ind/Abst Middle East Abstr. Index (-?).

II/0525-1516
BULLETIN OF TIBETOLOGY. [Bull. Tibetol.]. **Added/Corp** Namgyal Institute of Tibetology. Sikkim Research Institute of Tibetology. Vol. 1, No. 1 (May 26, 1964)-. Bulletin. English. Three times a year. $22.50. Sikkim Research Institute of Tibetology, Po Tadong, Gangtok India. **(Subscription address:** UBS Publishers Distributors, 5 Ansari Road, PO Box 7015, New Delhi 110002 India.**)** **LC** DS785.A1; B8.
Ind/Abst Am. Hist. Life (1969-1978, 1984-).

JA
BUNKAZAI NO HOZON. 1-. Periodical. Japanese. Kyushu Rekishi Shiryokan, 1024 Aza Taro Sakon, Oaza Dazaifu Dazaifumachi, Tsukushi-gun, Fukuoka-ken Japan. **LC** DS894.93; .B86. **UDC** 952.0.

JA
BUSHU KYODO SHIRYO. **Added/Corp** Musashino Kyodoshi Kenkyukai. No. 1 (1973)-. Periodical. Japanese. ¥1800. Nagashima Kihei, 1875 Oaza Kumagata, Saitama-ken 355-2 Japan. **LC** DS894.49.M87; A33.

US/0742-1141
BYZANTINA KAI METABYZANTINA. Vol. 1-. Monographic series. English. ir. Price varies per volume. Undena Publications, PO Box 97, Malibu CA 90265. **Tel** (310)649-2612. **ED** Speros Vryonis. **UDC** 939.2. **Circ:** 300.
Desc: Legacy of classical and byzantine Greek, especially in medieval and modern times.

FR
CAHIERS DE L'EUPHRATE / CENTRE NATIONAL DE LA RECHERCHE SCIENTIFIQUE, CENTRE DU RECHERCHES ARCHEOLOGIQUES, CENTRE REGIONAL DE PUBLICATIONS : SOPHIA-ANTIPOLIS. **See** Archaeology.

US/1053-2285
CAKALELE (HONOLULU, HAWAII). (CAKALELE.). [Cakalele]. Vol. 1, No. 1/2 (1990)-. Periodical. English. an. $40.00 (institutions), 25.00 (individuals), $15.00 (students). University of Hawaii, Southeast Asian Studies Program, 1890 E-W Road, Moore 415, Honolulu HI 96822. **Tel** (808)956-2688, FAX (808)956-6345. **ED** James T Collins (editor's phone: (808)956-7574). **LC** IN PROCESS. **DD** 306. **Bk Rev**. **Pr Rev. Circ:** 100.
Desc: Contains articles and book reviews pertaining to Eastern Indonesia.

II
CALCUTTA HISTORICAL JOURNAL, THE. Vol. 1 (July 1976)-. English. sa. $15.00. Calcutta University / Publications Sales Counter, Asutosh Building, Calcutta 700073 India. **(Subscription address:** Prints India, 11 Darya Ganj, New Delhi, 110002 India, (Phone: 011 91 11 3268645)) **LC** DS401; .C34. **DD** 954/.005.
Ind/Abst Am. Hist. Life (1988-).

US
CAMBODIA TODAY. Added/Corp Study Group for Cambodian Affairs. (Mar. 1979)-. Periodical. English.
Ind/Abst Hum. Rights Intern. Rep.

UK
CAMBRIDGE HISTORY OF CHINA. Academic Scholarly Publication. English. ir. price varies per volume. Cambridge University Press, The Edinburgh Building, Shaftesbury Road, Cambridge CB2 2RU United Kingdom. **Tel** 011 44 223 312393, FAX 011 44 223 325959. **(Subscription address:** North America/ Cambridge University Press, 40 West 20th Street, New York, NY 10011-4211; telephone: (212)924-3900**)**

UK
CAMBRIDGE HISTORY OF IRAN. ***Ceased.*** (19??)-Series completed with Volume 7. Academic Scholarly Publication. English. ir. Cambridge University Press, The Edinburgh Building, Shaftesbury Road, Cambridge CB2 2RU United Kingdom. **Tel** 011 44 223 312393, FAX 011 44 223 325959.

UK/0575-6863
CAMBRIDGE SOUTH ASIAN STUDIES. Added/Corp Cambridge. University. Center for South Asian Studies. **VFOAT** South Asian Studies. No. 1 (1965)-. Monographic series. English. ir. Price varies per volume. Cambridge University Press, The Edinburgh Building, Shaftesbury Road, Cambridge CB2 2RU United Kingdom. **Tel** 011 44 223 312393, FAX 011 44 223 325959. **(Subscription address:** Cambridge University Press / North America, 110 Midland Avenue, Port Chester NY 10573.**)**

CN/0319-8715
CANADIAN INDIA STAR, THE. VFOAT India Star. (1???)-. English. sm. 15.00Can$ Canada; 25.00Can$ other. Asia Times, 1429 Dufferin Street, Toronto Ontario M6H 4C7 Canada. **Tel** (416)533-8243. **ED** S. Singh. **DD** 954/.005. **Bk Rev**. **Ad Acc. Circ:** 5,000 (ctrl). ***Supersedes** India Star, 0317-2090.*
Desc: News and views of South Asia and Canada human rights items around the world.

II
CAPITALIST, THE. V. 1- Nov. 1978-. Periodical. English. mo. Rs40.00. Circulation Manager of the Capitalist, D-4 Kalindi, New Delhi 11065 India. **LC** DS486.D3; C36. **DD** 954/.56/005. **UDC** 954.0.

II
CAUMASA. V. 1, No. 1 (Feb. 83)-. Periodical. Hindi (Hindi). Three times a year. Rs12.00. Madhyapradesh Adivasi Lokakala Parishad, R14 Guru Tech Bahadur Complex, Bhopal India. **LC** DS432.A2; C38. **UDC** 958.

US
CEAL DIRECTORY. ***Title Change.*** **Main/Corp** Association for Asian Studies. Committee on East Asian Libraries. (19??)-(19??). Directory. English. be. Maureen H. Donovan, Room 310 Main Library, Ohio State U. Libraries, Columbus OH 43210-1286. **LC** Z688.E25; A76b. **DD** 950/.072073. ***Continues** Association for Asian Studies. Committee on East Asian Libraries. Directory of East Asian Collections in North American Libraries.* ***Continued by** Association for Asian Studies. Committee on East Asian Libraries. Committee on East Asian Libraries Directory, 1067-0580.*

FR/0764-9878
CEMOTI. CAHIERS D'ETUDES SUR LA MEDITERRANEE ORIENTALE ET LE MONDE TURCO-IRANIEN. VFOAT Cahiers d'Etudes sur la Mediterranee Orientale et le Monde Turco-Iranien. (1985)-. Periodical. French. Twice a year. 300.00F. Meles Agnes Evrer, 4 rue de Chevreuse, 75006 Paris France. **Tel** 011 1 44 108475. **UDC** 3(56). **CODEN** 3(495).
Ind/Abst Middle East J.

US/0893-2301
CENTRAL & INNER ASIAN STUDIES. ***Ceased.*** [Cent. inner Asian stud.]. **Added/Corp** China Institute in America. **VFOAT** Central and Inner Asian Studies. Vol. 1 (1987)-(1993). English. an. M. Rossabi, 175 Riverside Drive, New York NY 10024. **Tel** (212)362-3026. **ED** Monnil Rollabi. **LC** DS327; .C47. **DD** 950. **Bk Rev**. **Ad Acc**. **Pr Rev. Circ:** 200 (ctrl).

PK
CENTRAL ASIA. V. 1- Winter 1978-. Periodical. English (Uzbek, Uigur, Turkmen, Kazakh, Kirghiz and Pushto). sa. Rs80.00 Pakistan; $15.00 other. Area Study Centre/Central Asia, Peshawar Pakistan. **Tel** 41327. **ED** Mohammad Anwar Khan. **LC** DS785.A1; C45. **DD** 958/.005. **UDC** 958. **Circ:** 500 (ctrl).
Desc: Contains research articles on constitutions of Afghanistan, China, Afghan, Musahideens, Tarikah, Furkista, etc.

UK/0263-4937
CENTRAL ASIAN SURVEY. [Centr. Asian surv.]. **Added/Corp** Society for Central Asian Studies. Vol. 1, No. 1 (July 1982)-. Periodical. English. qt (Mar., Jun., Sep., Dec.). $284.00 US and Canada; £144.00 other. Carfax Publishing Company, PO Box 25 Abingdon, Oxfordshire OX14 3UE England. **Tel** 011 44 235 555335, FAX (0279)31067, telex 817484. **(Subscription address:** US and Canada/ PO Box 2025, Dunnellon, FL 34430-2025; telephone:(904)489-6996**)** **LC** DS327; .C39. **DD** 958/.005. **[CCC].** available on microfilm and microfiche from University Microfilms International (UMI).
Ind/Abst Am. Hist. Life (1982-); Geogr. Abstr. Phys. Geogr. (1982-?); Geogr. Abstr. Human Geogr. (1982-); Index Islam. Lit.; Int. Dev. Abstr. (?-?); Middle East J.

GW/0008-9192
CENTRAL ASIATIC JOURNAL. [Cent. Asiat. j.]. Vol. 1 (1955)-. Periodical. English (French and German). Twice a year. Otto Harrassowitz Verlag, Taunusstrasse 14, Postfach 2929, D-65019 Wiesbaden Germany. **Tel** 011 49 611 5300, FAX 530570, telex 4186 135 OH D. **ED** Giovanni Stary. **LC** DS785; .C37. **DD** 958.005. **[CCC].** Index available. cum. index. **Bk Rev**. **Ad Acc. Circ:** 500. available on microfilm and microfiche from University Microfilms International (UMI). Documents available from The Genuine Article.
Desc: History, languages and literature of Central Asia.
Ind/Abst Arts Humanit. Citation Index [Full Cov.]; Curr. Contents Arts Humanit.; Int. Bibliogr. Sociol.; Middle East Abstr. Index; MLA Int. Bibl. Books Artic. Mod. Lang. Lit.; Numis. Lit.; Res. Alert [Full Cov.].

CN/0225-2732
CENTRE FOR EAST ASIAN STUDIES OCCASIONAL PAPERS. [Centre for East Asian Stud. Occas. Pap.]. **Main/Corp** McGill University. Centre for East Asian Studies. Began publication in 1977. Periodical. English. qt. Centre for East Asian Studies / Canada, McGill University, 3434 McTavish Street, Montreal Quebec H3A 1X9 Canada. **DD** 950. **UDC** 950.

II
CHARITHRAM. Periodical. English. qt. Rs10.00. C K Kareem, 10 Trivandrum India. **LC** DS485.K4; C47. **DD** 954/.83/005. **UDC** 954.0.

JA
CHARYO MINJOK TONGIL. Added/Corp Minzoku Toitsu Shinpojumu. **VFOAT** Minjok Tongil. (19??)-. Periodical. Japanese (Korean). Minzoku Toitsu Shinpojumu 5-1, Nishiikebukuro 1 Toshima-ku, Tokyo-To 171 Japan. **LC** DS917.25; .C425.

CH
CHE-CHIANG WEN SHIH TZU LIAO HSUAN CHI / CHUNG-KUO JEN MIN CHENG CHIH HSIEH SHANG HUI I CHE-CHIANG SHENG WEI YUAN HUI, WEN SHIH TZU LIAO YEN CHIU WEI YUAN HUI PIEN. Periodical. Chinese. NT$0.68. Hsin Hua Shu Tien / Hang-Chou, Hang-Chou, People's Republic of China. **LC** DS793.C3; C52. **DD** 951/.242. **UDC** 951.

KO
CHEJU HANGJAENG. Added/Corp Cheju 4.3 Yonguso. (1991)-. Periodical. Korean. Silchon Munhaksa, 98-dong 304-ho Panpo Apatu Panpo Pondong Kangnam-ku, Seoul Korea. **LC** DS917.55; .C465.

CH
CHIANG-HSI WEN SHIH TZU LIAO HSUAN CHI / CHENG HSIEH CHIANG-HSI SHENG WEN SHIH TZU LIAN YEN CHIU WEI YUAN HUI. Periodical. Chinese. NT$0.35. Chiang-Hsi Sheng Hsin Hua Shu Tien, Nan-Chang, People's Republic of China. **LC** DS793.K4; C533. **DD** 951/.222. **UDC** 951.

CC
CHIANG SHAN TO CHIAO. VFOAT China, A Land of Beauty. Began with June 1978 issue. Periodical. Chinese (English). 2.50. Hsin Hua Shu Tien / Shang-Hai Fa Hsing So, Shanghai, People's Republic of China. **LC** DS712; .C466. **DD** 915.1/0457. **UDC** 915.1.

US
CHIEN CHIN CHOU KAN. VFOAT Chien Chin. First published in 1983. Periodical. Chinese. wk. $120.00. Jack Chen, 39 Bowery Box 344, New York NY 10002. **LC** AP95.C4; C541177. **DD** 951/.249/005. **UDC** 951.

FR
CHIEN HU (PARIS, FRANCE). (CHIEN HU.). Periodical. Vietnamese. mo. Association Chien Hu, 21 rue Copreaux, 75015 Paris France. **LC** DS559.912; .C47.

US/0740-8005
CHINA BRIEFING. [China brief.]. **Added/Corp** Asia Society. China Council. Asia Society. (1980)-. English. ir. $15.85 softback, $39.85 hardback. Westview Press Inc, 5500 Central Avenue, Boulder CO 80301. **Tel** (303)444-3541, FAX (303)449-3356. **LC** DS779.15; .C476. **DD** 951/.005.

●PH
CHINA CURRENTS : A PHILIPPINE QUARTERLY ON CHINA CONCERNS. Added/Corp Philippine-China Development Resource Center. **VFOAT** Currents. Vol. 3, No. 1 (Jan./Mar. 1992)-. Periodical. English. qt. ***Continues** PDRC Currents.*

US/1055-8047
CHINA INFORMATION BULLETIN (PORTLAND, OR.). (CHINA INFORMATION BULLETIN.). [China inf. bull.]. **Added/Corp** Northwest Regional China Council. (1990)-. Bulletin. English. bm. $20.00 (non-members), $10.00 (members). Northwest Regional China Council, PO Box 751, Portland OR 97207. **DD** 951.

AT/1037-4299
CHINA PAPER. [China pap.]. **Added/Corp** Australian National University. Research School of Pacific Studies. Economics Division. (1991)-. Monographic series. English. ir. Price varies per volume. **DD** 951.005. ***Continues** China Working Paper, 1030-360X.*

UK/0305-7410
CHINA QUARTERLY (LONDON). (THE CHINA QUARTERLY.). [China q.]. **Added/Corp** University of London. Contemporary China Institute. Congress for Cultural Freedom. No. 1 (Jan./Mar. 1960)-. Periodical. English. qt. £38.00 UK and Europe; $73.00 other. Oxford University Press, Walton Street, Oxford OX2 6DP England. **Tel** 011 44 865 56767, FAX 011 44 865 267773, telex 837330 OXPRES G. **(Subscription address:** Oxford University Press / USA, Journals Marketing Department, Oxford University Press, 2001 Evans Road, Cary NC 27513.**)** **ED** Brian Hook. **LC** DS701; .C472. **DD** 951/.005; 951. Index available. cum. index. **Bk Rev**. **Ad Acc**. **Pr Rev. Circ:** 3,000. available on microfiche. Documents available from The Genuine Article, UMI Article Clearinghouse.
Desc: Dealing with modern Chinese studies, it covers arts, politics, economics, agriculture, social structure and developments and popular arts, with continuing documentation of events.
Ind/Abst ABC POL SCI; Acad. Abstr. Full Text Elite (Jan. 1991-); Acad. Abstr. (Jan. 1991-); Acad. Ind. [Computer File] (1987-); Acad. Search (Jan. 1991-); Am. Hist. Life (1969-); Appl. Soc. Sci. Index Abstr.; Arts Humanit. Citation Index [Select. Cov.]; Asia.-Pac. Econ. Lit.; Curr. Contents Soc. Behav. Sci.; Curr. Geogr. Publ. (199?-); Expand. Acad. Index (1987-); INFO-SOUTH Abstr.; Int. Bibliogr. Sociol.; Int. Labour Doc.; Int. Polit. Sci. Abstr.; LABORDOC; Leis. Recreat. Tour. Abstr.; Mag. Search; Middle East Abstr. Index; MLA Int. Bibl. Books Artic. Mod. Lang. Lit.; Newsp. Period. Abstr. (1990-); PAIS Int. Print (1991-); Peace Res. Abstr. J. (1965-1974); Res. Alert [Full Cov.]; Rural Dev. Abstr.; Soc. Sci. Source (Jul. 1990-); Soc. Sci. Cit. Index [Full Cov.]; Soc. Sci. Index; Soc. Sci. Index Fulltext (Sept. 1988-) [Full Txt.]; Women Stud. Abstr.; World Agric. Econ.

II/0009-4455
CHINA REPORT (NEW DELHI). (CHINA REPORT.). [China rep.]. **Added/Corp** China Study Centre (India) Centre for the Study of Developing Societies. **VFOAT** Chung-Kuo Tung Hsun. Vol. 1, No. 1 (Dec. 1964)-. Periodical. English. Four times a year (Feb., May, Aug., Nov.). £60.00 (one year), £120.00 (two year). Sage Publications Ltd., 6 Bonhill Street, London EC2A 4PU, UK. **Tel** 071 374 0645, FAX 071 374 8741, telex 296207 SAGE G. **LC** DS777.55; .C4484. **DD** 951/.005. **Bk Rev**. **Acid Free.** ctrl circ. available in microform (must order direct from university microfilm international) from University Microfilms International (UMI).

US/0069-3693
CHINA RESEARCH MONOGRAPHS / CENTER FOR CHINESE STUDIES, UNIVERSITY OF CALIFORNIA, BERKELEY. Added/Corp University of California, Berkeley. Center for Chinese Studies. **VFOAT** China Research Monograph. (1967)-. Monographic series. English. ir. Price varies per volume. University of California / Institute of East Asian Studies, 2223 Fulton Street, UC 6th Floor, Berkeley CA 94720. **Tel** (510)642-2809, FAX (510)643-7062. **LC** UNC. **DD** 951.

●US/1069-5834
CHINA REVIEW INTERNATIONAL. [China rev. int.]. **Added/Corp** University of Hawaii at Manoa. Center for Chinese Studies. **VFOAT** Chung-kuo yen Chiu Shu Ping. (1994)-. Periodical. English. sa. $30.00 (one year), $54.00 (two year) institution, $25.00 (one year), $45.00 (two year), individual, $15.00 (student); $27.00 (one year), $48.60 (two year), institution, $22.50 (one

year), $40.50 (two year), individual, other. University of Hawaii Press, 2840 Kolowalu Street, Honolulu HI 96822. **Tel** (808)956-8833, (808)948-8697, FAX (808)988-6052. **ED** Roger T. Ames. **LC** IN PROCESS. **DD** 951. **CODEN** CRINEM.
Desc: Dedicated to serving the Sinological community by keeping it abreast of published scholarship in all areas of Chinese studies in a timely way.

US
CHINA, SIGHTS & INSIGHTS. **VFOAT** China, Sights and Insights. Periodical. English. bm. $15.30. China Sights and Insights, 7680 Winston Street, Burnaby British Columbia V5A 2H4 Canada. **LC** DS712; .C48147. **DD** 951/.005. **UDC** 951.

US/1043-643X
CHINESE HISTORIANS. [Chin. hist.]. **Added/Corp** Chinese Historians in the United States, Inc. (1987)-. Periodical. English. sa. $20.00 (institutions), $12.00 (individuals) North America; $24.00 (institutions), $16.00 (individuals) other. Chinese Historians in the United States Inc, SUNY-Geneseo, Prof. Chen Jian, Geneseo NY 14454. **Tel** (716)245-5375, FAX (716)245-5005. **ED** Jian Chen. **LC** D1; .C417. **DD** 905. cum. index. **Bk Rev**, (Qty: 10-15). **Ad Acc. Circ:** 200.
Desc: A forum for the members of the Chinese Historians in the United States to publish their scholarly research.

US/0009-4633
CHINESE STUDIES IN HISTORY. [Chin. stud. hist.]. **Added/Corp** International Arts and Sciences Press. Vol. 3 (Fall 1969)-. Periodical. English (translations available in Chinese). qt. $381.00 US; $421.00 other. M. E. Sharpe Inc., 80 Business Park Drive, Armonk NY 10504. **Tel** (914)273-1800, (800)541-6563, FAX (914)273-2106. **ED** Li Yu-Ning. **Ad Acc. Circ:** 260. available on microfilm from University Microfilms International (UMI). Documents available from The Genuine Article. ***Continues in part*** *Chinese Studies in History and Philosophy.*
Desc: The journal contains translations of articles from Chinese sources to present the more important Chinese studies in this field.
Ind/Abst Am. Hist. Life (1972-); Arts Humanit. Citation Index [Full Cov.]; Curr. Contents Arts Humanit.; Res. Alert [Full Cov.].

KO
CHONGSIN MUNHWA YONGU. **Added/Corp** Hanguk Chongsin Munhwa Yonguwon. (Summer 1983)-. Periodical. English (Korean). Hanguk Chongsin Munhwa Yonguwon, 50 Unjung-dong, Songnam-si Korea. **LC** DS904; .C5447. ***Continues*** *Chongsin Munhwa.*

KO
CHONTONG MUNHWA. (19??)-. Periodical. Korean. mo. Chontong Munhwasa, 1-115 Tongsung-dong, Chongno-ku Seoul Korea. **LC** DS904; .C5453.

JA/0577-9766
CHOSEN GAKUHO. **Added/Corp** Chosen Gakkai (Japan). **VFOAT** Journal of the Academic Association of Koreanology in Japan. (1951)-. Periodical. Japanese (summaries and/or abstracts in English). qt. $135.00. **(Subscription address:** Kyowa Book Company Inc., 1 38 Kanda Jinbocho Chiyoda-ku, Tokyo 101 Japan.**)** **LC** DS901; .C47. **DD** 951.9.
Ind/Abst Am. Hist. Life (1955-1959).

II
CHOWKHAMBA SANSKRIT STUDIES. Monographic series. English. ir. Price varies per volume. Chowkhamba Sanskrit Series Office, K37/00 Gopal Madir Lane, POB 8, Varanasi 1 UP India.

JA/0578-0918
CHUGOKU. Vol. 1 (1963)-. Periodical. English. **(Subscription address:** Japan Publications Trading Company, Ltd., PO Box 5030, Tokyo International, Tokyo 100-31 Japan.**)**

JA
CHUGOKU GEPPO. **Added/Corp** Sekai Seikei Chosakai. Japan. Naikaku Kambo.Naikaku Chosashitsu. Periodical. Japanese. $165.00. **(Subscription address:** Maruzen Company Ltd., PO Box 5050, Import & Export Department, Tokyo 100 31 Japan.**)** **LC** DS779.15; .C5.

CH
CHUNG-HUA HSUEH PAO. **VFOAT** China Forum. Vol. 1 (1974)-. Multiple languages (Chinese and English). $9.00. China Forum Inc, 7 Linsheng North Road, Taipei Taiwan. **LC** DS777.A567; C518. **UDC** 952.9.

CH
CHUNG JIH WEN HUA. **VFOAT** Chu Nichi Bunka. Periodical. Chinese (Japanese). Chung-Kuo Wen Hua Ta Hsueh Tung Fang, Yu Wen Hsueh Hsi Jih Wen Tsu, Taipei Taiwan. **LC** DS721; .C572465.

CH
CHUNG-KUO HSUEH SHU NIEN KAN. **VFOAT** Annual Journal of Chinese Studies. No. 1- 1976-. Chinese (Chinese). Free. Alumni Association of Research Literature, Taiwan Normal University, Taipei Taiwan. **Tel** 02-3414149. **ED** Huang Chin-Hung. **LC** PL1071; .C55. **UDC** 951.
Desc: Makes an academic study of Chinese classics, philosophy, history, and literature. The contributors are either MA or PhD.

CC
CHUNG-KUO LI SHIH TI LI LUN TSUNG / CHIH NIEN-HAI CHU PIEN. V. 1, (July 1981)-. Periodical. Chinese. 1.25. Shen-Hsi Jen Min Chu Pan She, Hsin Hua Shu Tien, Hsi-An Shen-Hsi, People's Republic of China. **LC** DS706.5; .C472. **DD** 911/.51.

CC
CHUNG-KUO NUNG MIN CHAN CHENG SHIH YEN CHIU CHI KAN. **VFOAT** Chung-Kuo Nung Min Chan Cheng Shih Yen Chiu. V. 1, (Nov. 1979)-. Periodical. Chinese. RMBY1.00. Hsin Hua Shu Tien / Shang-Hai Fa Hsing So, Shanghai, People's Republic of China. **LC** DS740.2; .C55. **DD** 951. **UDC** 951.

CC
CHUNG-KUO PAI KO NIEN CHIEN. **VFOAT** Zhongguo Baike Nianjian. 1980-. Chinese. an. RMBY8.40. Hsin Hua Shu Tien / Shang-Hai Fa Hsing So, Shanghai, People's Republic of China. **LC** DS701; .C7585. **DD** 951.05. **UDC** 951.

CH
CHUNG-KUO SHE HUI CHING CHI SHIH YEN CHIU. **VFOAT** Zhongguo Shehui Jingjishi Yanjiu; Chinese Social-Economic History Research; Journal of Chinese Social and Economic History. 1982, 1-. Periodical. Chinese. qt. RMBY0.50. Science Press, 16 Donghuangchenggen North Street, Beijing 100707, People's Republic of China. **Tel** 011 86 1 4019821, 011 86 1 4010642, FAX 011 86 1 4012180, 011 86 1 4019810, telex 210147. **LC** HC426; .C558. **DD** 951/.005. **UDC** 951.

CC
CHUNG-KUO SHIH YEN CHIU. **VFOAT** Zhongguoshi Yanjiu; Chung-Kuo Shih Yen Chiu Chi; Zhong Guo Shi Yan Jiu. Began with March 1979 issue. Periodical. Chinese. qt. Science Press, 16 Donghuangchenggen North Street, Beijing 100707, People's Republic of China. **Tel** 011 86 1 4019821, 011 86 1 4010642, FAX 011 86 1 4012180, 011 86 1 4019810, telex 210147. **LC** DS701; .C7594. **DD** 951/.005.

CC
CHUNG-KUO SHIH YEN CHIU TUNG TAI. No. 1 (Jan. 1979)-. Periodical. Chinese. mo. RMBY0.22. Pei-Ching Pao Kan Fa Hsing Chu, Beijing, People's Republic of China. **Tel** 483531. **LC** DS734.7; .C63. **DD** 951/.0072. **UDC** 951.

CH
CHUNG-KUO YU YIN-NI. **VFOAT** Tiongkok Dan Indonesia. Periodical. Chinese. NT$50.00. Cheng Chung Shu Chu, 20 Heng Yang Road, Taipei Taiwan. **Tel** 011 886 2 3813825. **LC** DS799.63.I5; C49. **DD** 303.4/82598/051249.

CH
CHUNG-SHAN HSUEH SHU LUN TSUNG. **Added/Corp** Kuo li Tai-wan ta Hsueh. San min chu i yen Chiu so. **VFOAT** Journal of Sun Yat-Senism; Tai-Wan Ta Hsueh Chung-Shan Hsueh Shu Lun Tsung; Kuo Li Tai-Wan Ta Hsueh Chung-Shan Hsueh Shu Lun Tsung. (19??)-. Periodical. Chinese (English). an. **LC** DS777.A595; C53. **DD** 951.04/1/0924.
Ind/Abst Am. Hist. Life (1985-).

KO
CHUNG-SO YONGU. **Added/Corp** Hanyang Taehakkyo. Chung-So Yonguso. Hanyang Taehakkyo. Kukche Munje Yonguwon. **VFOAT** Sino-Soviet Affairs. Vol. 1 No. 1 (June 1980)-. Periodical. Korean (English). qt. W15000. The Institute for Sino-Soviet Studies, Hanyang University, 17 Haengdang-dong Seongdong-gu, Seoul 133 Korea. **Tel** (02) 292-2111. **ED** Yoo Se-Hee. **LC** DS777.75; .C53. **DD** 951.05. Index available. cum. index. **Circ:** 1,600 (ctrl). ***Formed by the union of*** *Chungguk Munje* ***and*** *Soryon Yongu.*
Desc: Dedicated to academic research and study on China and the Soviet Union.

CC
CHUNG YANG YEN CHIU YUAN CHIN TAI SHIH YEN CHIU SO CHI KAN. **Main/Corp** Chung Yang Yen Chiu Yuan. Chin Tai Shih Yen Chiu So. **Added/Corp** Chung Yang Yen Chiu Yuan. Chin Tai Shih Yen Chiu So. Bulletin of the Institute of Modern History, Academia Sinica. **VFOAT** Bulletin of the Institute of Modern History, Academia Sinica. (1969)-. Chinese. an. **LC** DS755; .C53.
Ind/Abst Am. Hist. Life (1969-).

CC
CHUNG YUAN WEN WU. **VFOAT** Relics from Central Plain; Zhong Yuan Wen Wu; Zhongyuan Wenwu; Cultural Relics from Central Plains. (Fall 1977)-. Periodical. Chinese (table of contents in English). qt. $29.00 (surface mail), $49.10 (airmail). **(Subscription address:** China International Book Trading Corporation, PO Box 399, Library Service Department, Beijing 100044 People's Republic of China.**)** **LC** DS715; .C5527. **DD** 931. **UDC** 931.5.
Ind/Abst Art Archaeol. Tech. Abstr.

KO
CHUNGBUK YONGAM. 1970-. Korean. W5000. Chungchong Ilbo SA, 81 2-ka Nammunro, Chongju Korea. **LC** DS924.C53; C46.

JA
CHUTO KIHO. **Added/Corp** Showa Keiazi Kenkyujo. Arabu Chosashitsu. (19??)-. Periodical. Japanese. Four times a year. ¥12000. Showa Keiazi Kenkyujo, 8-4 Takatanobaba 4-chome, Shinjuku-ku, Tokyo Japan. **Tel** (03)367-2879, FAX (03)367-8451. **ED** Kenji Atsumi. **LC** DS63.1; .C547. **Circ:** 150 (ctrl).

JA
CHUTO SOGO KENKYU. **Added/Corp** Ajia Keizai Kenkyujo (Japan). **VFOAT** Middle East Review. (Sept. 1975)-. Periodical. Japanese. qt. Ajia Keizai Kenkyujo, 42 Ichigaya Honmura-cho, Shinjuku-ku Tokyo 162 Japan. **LC** DS41; .C49.

US
CMIP PUBLICATIONS. English. ir. price varies. Cornell Modern Indonesia Project, 102 West Avenue, Ithaca NY 14850. **Tel** (607)255-4359, FAX (607)254-5000. **(Subscription telephone:** FAX (607)255-8038**)** **ED** Audrey R Kahin. **Pr Rev.** available on microfilm from University Microfilms International (UMI).
Desc: A series of books of academic interest on the history and culture, and politics of Indonesia.

GW
CODICES ARABICI ANTIQUI. Began with Vol. 1 in 1972?. Monographic series. French (German). ir. Price varies per volume. Otto Harrassowitz Verlag, Taunusstrasse 14, Postfach 2929, D-65019 Wiesbaden Germany. **Tel** 011 49 611 5300, FAX 530570, telex 4186 135 OH D. **ED** Raif Georges Khoury. **Circ:** 400.
Desc: Editorials of old Arabian manuscripts with commentaries.

UK/0141-0156
COLLECTED PAPERS ON SOUTH ASIA. [Collect. pap. South Asia]. No. 1 (1978)-. Monographic series. English. ir. Price varies per volume. Curzon Press Ltd, 42 Grays Inn Road, London WC1 England. **Tel** 011 44 71 242 8310. **ED** Karl R. Haellquist. **LC** UNC.
Desc: Studies in the history and cultures of Asia.

NE
COMPARATIVE ASIAN STUDIES. **Added/Corp** Centre for Asian Studies Amsterdam. **VFOAT** CAS. (1988)-. Monographic series. English. ir. Price varies per volume.

PK
CONCEPT (ISLAMABAD, PAKISTAN). (THE CONCEPT.). Vol. 1, No. 1 (Dec. 1980)-. Periodical. English. mo. $20.00. Raja Mohammad Afsar, House No 27 Street No 18 Shalimar 7/2, Islamabad Pakistan. **LC** DS35.3; .C66. **DD** 909/.097671. **UDC** 954.9.

II/0019-6010
CONGRESS BULLETIN - INDIAN NATIONAL CONGRESS. **Main/Corp** Indian National Congress. Began publication in Mar. 1928. Bulletin. English. mo. All India Congress Committee, 7 Jantar Mantar Road, New Delhi India. **LC** DS401; .I43. **DD** 954. **UDC** 954.0.

II
CONTEMPORARY AFFAIRS. Vol. 1, No. 1 (Oct.-Dec. 1987)-. Periodical. English. qt. $50.00 (air mail) $40 (surface mail). Patriot Publishers, New Delhi, India. **(Subscription address:** Prints India, 11 Darya Ganj, New Delhi, 110002 India, (Phone: 011 91 11 3268645)**)** **LC** DS401; .C59. **DD** 954/.005.

SI/0129-797X
CONTEMPORARY SOUTHEAST ASIA. [Contemp. Southeast Asia]. **Added/Corp** Institute of Southeast Asian Studies. Vol. 1 (May 1979)-. Periodical. English. qt (Mar., Jun., Sep., Dec.). $44.00 (institutions), $35.00 (individuals), Europe, North America; $36.00 (institutions), $29.00 (individuals) other. Institute of Southeast Asian Studies / Singapore, Heng Mui Keng Terrace, Pasir Panjang Road, Singapore 0511 Republic of Singapore. **Tel** (11) 65 8702447, FAX 011 65 7781735, telex 37068. **ED** Chandran Jeshurun. **LC** DS520; .C65. **DD** 959/.005. Index available. cum. index. **Bk Rev. Pr Rev. Circ:** 900. Documents available from UMI Article Clearinghouse.
Desc: Journal dealing analytically with international politics and strategic studies in the region. Essential to decision makers, planners, political analysts, business executives, financiers, scholars and students of Southeast Asian affairs.
Ind/Abst Am. Hist. Life (1988-); Asia.-Pac. Econ. Lit.; Expand. Acad. Index (1992-); Index Islam. Lit.; Int. Polit. Sci. Abstr.; Leis. Recreat. Tour. Abstr.; Middle East Abstr. Index; Newsp. Period. Abstr. (1992-); PAIS Int. Print (1991-); Rural Dev. Abstr.; Sage Public Adm. Abstr.; World Agric. Econ.

US/1053-1866
CONTRIBUTIONS IN ASIAN STUDIES. (1991)-. Monographic series. English. Greenwood Press Inc., PO Box 5007, Westport CT 06881-5007. **Tel** (203)226-3571, FAX (203)222-1502.

NP/0376-7574
CONTRIBUTIONS TO NEPALESE STUDIES. **Added/Corp** Tribhuvana Visvavidyalaya. Nepala ra Esiyali Anusandhana Kendra. Vol. 1 (Dec. 1973)-. Multiple languages (English and Nepali). sa. $30.00. Institute of Nepal and Asian Studies, Kirtipur, Nepal. **(Subscription address:** Prints India, 11 Darya Ganj, New Delhi 110002 India.**) LC** DS493; .C68. **DD** 954.9/6/005.
Ind/Abst Anthropol. Lit.

II/0257-1404
CONTRIBUTIONS TO SOUTH ASIAN STUDIES. [Contrib. South Asian stud.]. (1979)-. English. an. Oxford University Press / India, Delhi India. **(Subscription address:** UBS Publishers Distributors, 5 Ansari Road, PO Box 7015, New Delhi 110002 India.**) LC** DS331; .C66. **DD** 954/.005.
Ind/Abst Am. Hist. Life (1979-1982).

US/0734-449X
CORMOSEA BULLETIN. **See** Library and Information Sciences.

US/1050-2955
CORNELL EAST ASIA SERIES. **See** General Interest-General Interest-Asia.

US
CROSS CURRENTS. V. 1- July/Aug. 1977-. Periodical. English. Three times a year. Asian American Studies Center, University of California, 3230 Campbell Hall, Los Angeles CA 90024. **Tel** (310)825-2968, FAX (310)206-9844.

JA
CROSSCURRENTS. V. 1- Mar. 1979-. Periodical. English. $10.00 (individuals), $15.00 (institutions). Japanese National Commission for UNESCO, 3-2-2 Kasumigaseki Chiyoda-ku, Tokyo Japan. **LC** DS822.5; .C76. **UDC** 372.880.20.
Desc: A journal of language teaching and cross-cultural communications for classroom teachers. Major emphasis is on practical ideas and techniques for teaching English as a foreign/second language.

IO
CURRENT AFFAIRS TRANSLATIONS - ANTARA. **Main/Corp** Antara (Organization). Jan. 1976-. Periodical. English. Antara National News Agency, Jalan Antara 53, Jakarta Indonesia. **LC** DS611; .A78. **DD** 959.8/005. **UDC** 959.4.

IS/0333-9858
CURRENT CONTENTS OF PERIODICALS ON THE MIDDLE EAST. **Added/Corp** Mekhon Shiloah le-heker ha-Mizrah ha-tikhon ve-Afrikah. Merkaz le-meda. No. 1 (June 1980)-. Periodical. English (French and Arabic). bm. $35.00. Dayan Center for Middle East African Studies, Shiloah Institute, Tel Aviv University, Tel Aviv 69978 Israel. **Tel** 11 972 3 6409646, FAX 011 972 3 6415802. **ED** Anat Ruppoport. **Circ:** 1,000 (ctrl).
Desc: Comprehensive bibliography of current literature on the Middle East. Provides lists of the latest articles and analyses on economic, political and social developments in the Middle East, examined from both the Middle Eastern and Western perspectives.

II
CYCLONE. Periodical. English. 1.00 single issue. S Arambam, Bhagyavati Karyalaya, Chudachand Printing Works, Imphal India. **LC** DS483; .C93. **DD** 954/.1/005. **UDC** 954.0.

CY/0045-9429
CYPRUS TO-DAY. **Added/Corp** Cyprus. Hellenike Koinotike Syneleusis. Cyprus. Ministry of Education. Cyprus. Grapheion Demosion Plerophrion. Vol. 1 (Jan./Feb. 1963)-. Periodical. English. **DD** 956.4.

IO
DAFTAR TAMBAHAN KOLEKSI MIKROFIS. **Main/Corp** Pusat Dokumentasi Ilmiah Nasional. **VFOAT** Accession List of Microfiches. No. 1-. Dutch (English and Indonesian). Pusat Dokumentasi Ilmiah Nasl, PO Box 3065 JKT, Djakarta 10002 Indonesia. **Tel** (021)583465, telex 62875 IA. **LC** Z3279; .P87A; DS615. Index available. **Circ:** 500 (ctrl).
Desc: Information of pre-war material on Indonesia.

US/0892-015X
DAILY REPORT. CHINA. [Dly. rep., China]. **VFOAT** FBIS Daily Report. China; F.B.I.S. Daily Report. China. Vol. 1, No. 062 (April 1, 1981)-. Periodical. English. da (Monday-Friday). **DD** 951. **UDC** 951. available on microfiche (Vols. for (Jan. 2, 1987-) distributed to depository libraries). ***Continues*** *United States. Foreign Broadcast Information Service. Daily Report: People's Republic of China, 0892-0141.*
Ind/Abst Int. Labour Doc.

II
DAINIKA AVAJA. Periodical. Nepali (Nepali). an. Rs1.00. Avaj Prakashan, Church Road, Gangtok Sikkim 737101 India. **LC** DS485.S58; D34.

II
DAKSHINESIA. **Added/Corp** Gandhian Institute of Studies. Dept. of Political Science. (19??)-. English. sa. Rs3.00. Gandhian Institute of Studies Department of Political Science, PO Box 116, Varanasi India. **LC** DS383.5.A2; P36. **DD** 320.9/549/1. ***Continues*** *Pakistan Survey.*

CH/0494-4445
DALU ZAZHI TEKAN. **VFOAT** Continent Magazine Special Issue. (1952)-. Periodical. Chinese. Ta lu tsa Chih she, 3rd Floor, 61 Fu Chou Str, Taipei Taiwan. **UDC** 001(31).
Ind/Abst Am. Hist. Life (1955-1957).

II/0376-8090
DAMILICA. **VFOAT** Tamilakan. English (Tamil). Rs18.50. Department of Archaeology / Madras India, Tamil Nadu 28, Madras India. **LC** DS485.M275; D35. **DD** 954/.82. **UDC** 902(540).

CN/0229-673X
DAN-QUYEN. ***Ceased.*** [Dan-Quyen]. (1978)-?. Periodical. Vietnamese. mo. Dan Quyen, PO Box 667 Station N, Montreal Quebec H3X 3T6 Canada. **LC** PAR. **DD** 959.704/405.

PH
DANSALAN QUARTERLY. ***Ceased.*** Vol. 1 Oct. (1979)-(19??). Academic Scholarly Publication. English. qt. Dansalan College Foundation Inc, PO Box 5430, Iligan City 9200 Philippines. **ED** Manuel R Tawagon. **UDC** 959.9. Index available. **Bk Rev. Circ:** 500 (ctrl). available in microform. ***Formed by the union of*** *Dansalan Research Center. Occasional Papers; DRC Reports; Dansalan Research Center. Research Bulletin* ***and*** *Dansalan Research Center. Bibliographical Bulletin.*
Desc: Publishes scholarly articles/essays about Filipino Muslims' history, society and culture to promote better Muslim-Christian relations in the Philippines by understanding each other's cultural heritage.
Ind/Abst Index Islam. Lit.; Index Philip. Period.

II/0377-6832
DATA INDIA. **Added/Corp** Press Institute of India. (1974)-. English. wk. $255.00. Press Institute of India, Sapru House Annexe Barakhamba Road, New Delhi 110001 India. **Tel** 3318066 OR 3318646. **(Subscription address:** Prints India, 11 Darya Ganj, New Delhi 110002 India.**) LC** DS401; .D28. **DD** 954/.005. Index available. cum. index. ctrl circ.

US/0011-7048
DAVKA. V. 1- Nov./Dec. 1970-. Periodical. English (English). qt. $5.00. Los Angeles Hillel Council, 900 Hilgard Avenue, Los Angeles CA 90024. **LC** DS101; .D28. **DD** 909/.04/924082.

II/0377-6948
DIRECTORY OF INSTITUTIONS OF ORIENTAL STUDIES IN OVERSEAS COUNTRIES. 1974-. Directory. English. $3.00. Lord International, 2/6 Canal Road, Vijay Nagar 110009. **LC** DS32.8; .D57. **DD** 915/.03/0711.

CN/0713-8180
DISCUSSION PAPER (JOINT CENTRE ON MODERN EAST ASIA). (DISCUSSION PAPER / UNIVERSITY OF TORONTO-YORK UNIVERSITY, JOINT CENTRE ON MODERN EAST ASIA.). [Discuss. pap. - Univ. Tor.-York Univ., Jt. Cent. Mod. East Asia]. No. 1 (Oct. 1978)-. Monographic series. English. Price varies per volume. Joint Centre on Modern Asia, Room 14213/Robarts Library, University of Toronto, Toronto Ontario M5S 1A5 Canada. **DD** 951. **UDC** 952.

US/0098-4485
DOCTORAL DISSERTATIONS ON ASIA. [Dr. diss. Asia]. **Added/Corp** Association for Asian Studies. Vol. 1 (Winter 1975)-. English. an. $20.00. Association for Asian Studies Inc., University of Michigan, 1 Lane Hall, Ann Arbor MI 48109. **Tel** (313)665-2490, FAX (313)665-3801. **ED** F. J. Shulman. **LC** Z3001; .D63; DS5. **DD** 016.95.
Desc: Designed to provide comprehensive and accurate information about recently accepted doctoral dissertations on Asia. Interdisciplinary, covers research in the humanities and also in the natural sciences.

US/0070-7546
DUMBARTON OAKS PAPERS. [Dumbarton Oaks pap.]. **Added/Corp** Dumbarton Oaks. Dumbarton Oaks. Center for Byzantine Studies. No. 1 (1941)-. English (German, Italian and French). an. Dumbarton Oaks Publishing / Maryland, PO Box 4866, Hampden Station, Baltimore MD 21211. **Tel** (410)516-6954. **ED** Robert Thomson. **LC** DF503; .D84. **DD** 709.495. Index available. cum. index. **Circ:** 800 (ctrl).
Desc: Articles concerning late classical, early medieval, and Byzantine civilization in the fields of art, architecture, history, theology, literature, and law.
Ind/Abst Am. Bibliogr. Slavic East Europ. Stud.; Avery Index Archit. Period. Suppl. Colum. Univ. (19??-199?); BHA : Biblio. Hist. Art; Numis. Lit.

CY
DUNYA AL-ARAB. **VFOAT** Dunia Al Arab. Periodical. Arabic. $60.00. Central Press Distribution Agency, 41 Sofokleous Street, GR-102-10 Athens Greece. **LC** DS63.1; .D86.

LE
DUNYA AL-MUJTAMA. **VFOAT** Al-Mujtama. Periodical. Arabic. £L150.00. PO Box 6251/113, Beirut Lebanon. **LC** DS36; .D86.

US/0362-5028
EARLY CHINA. [Early China]. **Added/Corp** Society for the Study of Early China (Berkeley, Calif.) University of California, Berkeley. Institute of East Asian Studies. **VFOAT** Ku Tai Chung-Kuo. (Fall 1975)-. English (Chinese). an. $30.00 (includes newsletter). University of California / Institute of East Asian Studies, 2223 Fulton Street, UC 6th Floor, Berkeley CA 94720. **Tel** (510)642-2809, FAX (510)643-7062. **ED** Edward L. Shaughnessy (University of Chicago). **LC** DS701; .E17. **DD** 951/.01. Each issue contains an index to its own contents (no volume index)--loose. **Bk Rev. Ad Acc. Pr Rev. Circ:** 300 (ctrl). available on photocopies. ***Continues*** *Society for the Study of Pre-Han China (Berkeley, Calif.) Newsletter - Society for the Study of Pre-Han China, 0361-9613.*
Desc: Research, reviews, translations, bibliography, and news of the field of Chinese studies from Neolithic through Han times.

US/1043-2140
EAST ASIA AND THE WESTERN PACIFIC. [East Asia West. Pac.]. (1984)-. English. an (Sept.). $8.50. Stryker-Post Publications, PO Drawer 1200, Harpers Ferry WV 25425. **Tel** (800)995-1400. **ED** Harold C. Hinton. **LC** DS502; .H53. **DD** 950/.05. ctrl circ. ***Continues*** *Hinton, Harold C. Far East and Western Pacific.*
Desc: Focus on current events. This lively reference tool addresses social, economic, political and controversial issues.

GW
EAST ASIAN CIVILIZATIONS. **VFOAT** E.A.C.; EAC. 1-. Monographic series. English. sa. Price varies per volume. Verlag Simon & Magiera KG, Rubenmarkt 1, W-8860 Nordlingen Germany. **Tel** 09081/3121. **LC** DS12; .E27. **DD** 950/.05. **UDC** 930.85(51/52).

AT/1036-6008
EAST ASIAN HISTORY. **Added/Corp** Australian National University. Institute of Advanced Studies. Vol. 1 (June 1991)-. Periodical. English. Twice a year (June and Dec.). 45.00Aus$. Research School of Pacific Studies, ANU East Asian History, Canberra ACT 0200 Australia. **Tel** 011 61 6 2493140, FAX 011 61 6 2495525. **ED** Dr. Geremie Barme. **LC** DS511; .E27. Index available. cum. index. **Ad Acc. Pr Rev. Circ:** 350. ***Continues*** *Papers on Far Eastern History, 0048-2870.*
Desc: Covers a wide range of themes and represent scholarship from more diverse sources.
Ind/Abst Am. Hist. Life (1970-); APAIS, Aust. Public Aff. Inf. Ser. (1991-).

JA/0012-8295
EAST (TOKYO, JAPAN). (THE EAST.). **VFOAT** Higashi. (May 1964)-. Periodical. English. Six times a year. $38.00 one year, $70.00 two years, $100.00 three years (seamail); $63.20 one year, $120.40 two years, $175.60 three years (airmail). East Publications Inc, 19-7-101 Minami-Azabu 3, Minato-Ku, Tokyo, Japan. **Tel** 011 86 3 3446-7721, , FAX 011 86 3 3441 9793. **(Subscription address:** East Publications Inc, PO Box 591360, San Francisco CA 94159.**) ED** Tohru Morita. **LC** DS801; .E2. **DD** 952/.005. **Ad Acc, Adv Mgr:** Y. Masaki, **Tel** 03 3446-7721. **Circ:** 60,000. available on microfilm and microfiche from University Microfilms International (UMI).
Desc: Covers history, culture, religion, economics, language, travel, and science in Japan.
Ind/Abst Am. Hist. Life (1991-).

UK/0012-8961
EASTERN WORLD. [East. world]. (May 1947)-. Periodical. English. mo. **LC** DS501; .E45. **DD** 950.05. available on microfilm from University Microfilms International (UMI).
Ind/Abst Am. Hist. Life (1955-1971).

JA
EDO JIDAI BUNGAKUSHI / RYUMONSHA HEN. **See** Literature.

IT
EGITTO E VICINO ORIENTE. **Added/Corp** Universita di Pisa. Istituto di Storia Antica. Sezione Orientalistica. 1 (1978)-. Periodical. Italian (French). an. L70000 Italy; L100000 other. Giardini Editori Stampatori, Via Santa Bibbiana 28, 56127 Pisa Italy. **Tel** 011 39 50 934242. **LC** DS57; .E36. **DD** 932/.005.

JA
ENU NO KUNI. **Added/Corp** Enuma Chihoshi Kenkyukai. (1956)-. Periodical. Japanese. Enuma Chihoshi Kenkyukai, c/o Ishikawa Kenritsu Koto Gakko, 633 Daishoj Nagamachi, Kaga Japan. **LC** DS894.59.I839; E584.

History(General) —History of Asia

CY/0071-0954
EPETERIS. [Epet. - Kent. Epistem. Ereun.].
Main/Corp Kentron Epistemonikon Ereunon. 1- 1967/68-. Multiple languages (English, French and Greek, Modern). an. $6.00. Cyprus Research Center, The Secretary, POB 1436, Leukosia Ceylon. **Tel** 30-3202. **LC** DS54.A2; K44A. **Bk Rev. Circ:** 500.
Ind/Abst MLA Int. Bibl. Books Artic. Mod. Lang. Lit.

TU
ERDEM : ATATURK KULTUR MERKEZI DERGISI. (1985)-. Periodical. Turkish. Three times a year. **LC** DS26; .E73.
Ind/Abst Middle East J.

HK/1017-5725
ERH SHIH I SHIH CHI. Added/Corp Chinese University of Hong Kong. Institute of Chinese Studies. **VFOAT** 21 Shih Chi; 21st Century; Twenty-First Century. (Oct. 27, 1990)-. Periodical. Chinese (table of contents in English). bm (6 issues) $45.00 (institutions), $35.00 (individuals). Institute of Chinese Studies, Chinese University of Hong Kong, Shatin NT Hong Kong. **Tel** 011 852 0 6097414, FAX 011 852 0 6035149. **ED** Qingfeng Liu. **LC** AP95.C4; E72. **DD** 059/.951. Index available. cum. index.
Desc: Dedicated to the long-term development of a new, pluralistic Chinese culture.

IS
ET-MOL. Hebrew. bm. IL27.00. Hotsaat Ha-Sefarim Shel Universitat Tel-Aviv, PO Box 23078, Tel-Aviv Israel. **LC** DS101; .E85.

•UK/0966-8136
EUROPE-ASIA STUDIES. Vol. 46, No. 1 (1994)-. English. Eight times a year. £174.00. Carfax Publishing Company, PO Box 25 Abingdon, Oxfordshire OX14 3UE England. **Tel** 011 44 235 555335, FAX (0279)31067, telex 817484. **(Subscription address:** US and Canada/ PO Box 2025, Dunnellon, FL 34430-2025; telephone:(904)489-6996**) [CCC].** available on microfiche. **Continues** Soviet Studies.
Desc: Covers political, economic and social affairs.
Ind/Abst ABC POL SCI; Acad. Abstr.; Am. Hist. Life; Arts Humanit. Citation Index [Select. Cov.]; Br. Humanit. Index; Crim. Justice Abstr.; Curr. Contents Soc. Behav. Sci.; Geogr. Abstr. Human Geogr.; Hist. Abstr., Part B, Twent. Century Abstr.; Int. Polit. Sci. Abstr.; PAIS Int. Print; Res. Alert; SCISEARCH; Soc. Sci. Cit. Index [Full Cov.]; Soc. Sci. Index.

LE/0252-9459
EVENTS (BEIRUT). (EVENTS.). [Events]. Periodical. English. wk. $1.50. Al Ghazira Distribution & Service Company, PO Box 1281, Beirut Lebanon. **LC** DS41; .E8. **DD** 956/.04/0. **UDC** 956.93.

KO
FACTS ABOUT KOREA. Added/Corp Taehan Kongnonsa. Korea (South). Munhwa Kongbobu. Korean Overseas Information Service. (1963)-. English. an. Minister of Culture & Information of the Republic of Korea, 1 Bunji Sejougro Chnongro-Ku, Seoul Korea. **LC** DS902; .F28.

US/0363-6917
FAR EASTERN QUARTERLY, THE. Title Change. Added/Corp Far Eastern Association. Vol. 1-15 (Nov. 1941)-(Sept. 1956). Periodical. English. qt. **LC** DS501; .F274. **DD** 950.05. **Continued by** Journal of Asian Studies, 0021-9118.

IR/0014-7788
FARHANG-I IRAN ZAMIN. VFOAT Farhang-e Iran Zamin. (1953)-. Periodical. Persian. qt. **LC** DS251; .F33. **DD** 955/.005.
Ind/Abst MLA Int. Bibl. Books Artic. Mod. Lang. Lit.

LE
FIKR. (19??)-. Periodical. Arabic. PO Box 4631, Beirut Lebanon. **LC** DS36; .F53.

LE
FILASTIN AL-MUHTALLAH. Periodical. Arabic. £L200.00. PO Box 9005, Beirut Lebanon. **LC** DS119.7; .F53.

LE
FILASTIN AL-THAWRAH. VFOAT Falestine Al-Thawra. V. 1- No. 1- ; 1977-. Periodical. Arabic. wk. Munazzamat Al-Tahrir Al- Filastiniyah, PO Box 8984, Beirut Lebanon. **LC** DS119; .F53.

US/1056-8557
FOCUS, ISRAEL. [Focus Isa.]. (1991)-. Periodical. English. sm. $50.00. Focus Israel, Inc., Suite 304, 1730 K Street NW, Washington DC 20006. **DD** 956.

US/0046-4295
FOCUS ON ASIAN STUDIES. Ceased. New Ser., V. 1, No. 1 (Fall 1981)-Ceased Vol. 6, No. 1 (1987). Periodical. English. Three times a year. The Asia Society Archives, 725 Park Avenue, Department of Gallery, New York NY 10021. **Tel** (212)288-6400 Ext.231, FAX (212)517-8315, telex 224953 ASIA UR. **LC** DS1; .F63. **DD** 950/.05. **UDC** 950. **Bk Rev. Circ:** 2,400 (ctrl).
Desc: Resource journal of Asian studies for educators, professionals, and those interested in Asia.

US/0430-8301
FOCUS ON INDONESIA. Ceased. [Focus Indones.]. Vol. 1 (Aug. 1967)-Ceased ?. Periodical. English. qt. Embassy of Indonesia, 2020 Massachusetts Avenue NW, Washington DC 20036. **LC** DS611; .F6. **UDC** 959.4. **Supersedes** Report on Indonesia.

PL/0015-5675
FOLIA ORIENTALIA. [Fol. orient.]. **Added/Corp** Polska Akademia Nauk. Komisja Orientalistyczna. Vol. 1 (1959)-. Multiple languages (French, English, German and Russian). ir. Z26.50. **(Subscription address:** ARS Polona, PO Box 1001, 00068 Warsaw Poland.**)**
Ind/Abst MLA Int. Bibl. Books Artic. Mod. Lang. Lit.; Numis. Lit.

IS
FOLK, VELT UN MEDINE. VFOAT Am, Olam U-Medinah; Folk, Welt un Medine. Periodical. Yiddish. mo. Folk Welt un Medina, 228 Bnei Ephraim Street, Tel Aviv Israel. **Tel** 22 57 18. **LC** DS101; .A334. **Continues** Am U-Medinah.

IS/0302-8186
FOLQ UN MEDINAH. (AM U-MEDINAH.). [Folq un medinah]. **VFOAT** Folk un Medine. Periodical. Yiddish. mo. Komitet Jar Yidisher Kultur in Yisroel, 228 Bnei Ephraim Street Maoz Aviv, Tel Aviv Israel. **LC** DS101; .A334.

PH
FOOKIEN TIMES PHILIPPINES YEARBOOK, THE. VFOAT Philippines Yearbook. (1975)-. English. an. $60.00 airmail. Fookien Times Yearbook Publishing, PO Box 747, Manila Philippines. **Tel** 011 63 2 401871 to 401874, FAX 011 63 2 492464. **ED** Betty Go Belmonte (editor's address: 13th Street Corner Railroad Street, Port Area, Manila Philippines; telephone: 011 63 2 402531). **LC** DS666.C5; F66. **DD** 959.9/005. Index available (published separately). cum. index. **Bk Rev. Ad Acc. Adv Mgr:** William Velasco. **Circ:** 50,000 (ctrl). **Continues** Fookien Times Yearbook.
Desc: Chronicles the country's progress for the year under review.
Ind/Abst Index Philip. Period.

US
FOREIGN AND COMPARATIVE STUDIES. SOUTH ASIAN SERIES.
Added/Corp Maxwell Graduate School of Citizenship and Public Affairs. No. 1 (1976)-. Monographic series. English. ir. Price varies per volume. Syracuse University, 321 Sims Hall, Syracuse NY 13210. **Tel** (315)443-4667. **ED** Joanna C Giansanti.
Desc: Contains scholarly monographs on: political science, anthropology, history, language and linguistics, and religion in India, Sri Lanka, Pakistan, and Bangladesh.

FR/0533-0866
FRANCE PAYS ARABES. Added/Corp Association de Solidarite Franco-Arabe. **VFOAT** Faransa wa-al-Buldan al-Arabiyah. (19??)-. Periodical. French. Twelve times a year. 150.00F France; 200.00F other. Association de Solidarite Franco-Arabe, 12 et 14 rue Augereau, 75007 Paris France. **Tel** 45 55 27 52. **LC** WMLC L 83/4534. **DD** 909/.0974927.

CH/0016-030X
FREE CHINA REVIEW. [Free China rev.]. Vol. 1, No. 1 (April 1951)-. Periodical. English. Twelve times a year. $18.00 (one year); $30.00 (two years). Kwang Hwa Publishing Co., 8 FL No. 15 Hangchow S Road Sec. 1, Taipei 100 Taiwan. **Tel** 011 886-2 3922245 ext. 15. **(Subscription address:** Kwang Hwa Publishing Inc., 900 North Western Avenue, Suite 101, Los Angeles CA 90029.**) LC** DS701; .F74. **DD** 951.05/05. available on microfilm and microfiche from University Microfilms International (UMI). Documents available from UMI Article Clearinghouse.
Ind/Abst Acad. Search (July 1993-); Bibliogr. Mission.; INFO-SOUTH Abstr.; Int. Bibliogr. Sociol.; Mag. Search; MLA Int. Bibl. Books Artic. Mod. Lang. Lit.; Newsp. Period. Abstr. (1988-).

II
FRONTLINE (MADRAS, INDIA).
(FRONTLINE.). **VFOAT** Front Line. Vol. 1, No. 1 (Dec. 1-14, 1984)-. Periodical. English. Twenty-six times a year. $70.00. S Rangarajan Kasturi Buildings, Madras 600002 India. **(Subscription address:** Prints India, 11 Darya Ganj, New Delhi, 110002 India, (Phone: 011 91 11 3268645)**) LC** DS401; .F76. **DD** 954/.005.

JA/0285-0206
GAIKO TO BUNKA. Japanese. Nihon Gaiko Kyokai, c/o Sugisho Building 4-11, Kojimachi 5 Chiyoda-ku, Tokyo-to 102 Japan. **LC** DS845; .G29.

UK/0533-7224
GANDHI MEMORIAL LECTURE. Vol. 1 (1969)-. English. School of Oriental and African Studies, University of London, Malet Street, London WC1E 7HP England. **Tel** (01)637-2388. **DD** 920.

II
GANDHI PEACE FOUNDATION LECTURE. VFOAT Lecture. Monographic series. English. Price varies per volume. Gandhi Book House, 1 Rajghat Colony, New Delhi 110002 India. **DD** 954.03/5. **UDC** 954.0.

II
GANDHIAN PERSPECTIVES. Added/Corp Gandhian Institute of Studies. Vol. 1 (Oct. 1978)-. Periodical. English. sa. $8.00. Gandhian Institute of Studies, PO Box 116, Varanasi India. **LC** DS481.G3; G273. **DD** 954.03/5/0924.

II
GARUDA. Periodical. Gujarati (Gujarati). 0.75 single issue. Sabaramati Gandhi Ashrama, Jyotirbhavan 13, Garuda India. **LC** DS422.C3; G37. **UDC** 954.0.

JA
GEIBI CHIHOSHI KENKYU / GEIBI CHIHOSHI KENKYUKAI. No. 1 (July 1953)-. Periodical. Japanese. wk (52 issues, bound into 4 vols.). ¥27000. Kokusho Kankokai, 5-18 Sugamo 3 Toshima-ku, Tokyo-to 170 Japan. **LC** DS894.79.H56; A24.

JA
GENDAI KORIA. No. 239 (April 1984)-. Periodical. Japanese. mo. ¥7000 Japan; ¥9800 other. Gendai Koria Kenkyujo, 25-13 Mejirodai 3 Bunkyo-ku, Tokyo-to Japan. **Tel** 03-944-5624, FAX 03-944-5623. **ED** Sato Katsumi. **LC** DS916.6; .C45. Index available. cum. index. **Bk Rev. Ad Acc. Pr Rev. Continues** Chosen Kenkyu.

IT
GIAPPONE, IL. Added/Corp Centro di Cultura Italo-Giapponese. Japan Cultural Institute in Rome. (19??)-. Monographic series. Italian (English). ir. Price varies per volume. Herder Editrice e Libreria SRL, Piazza Montecitorio 117-120, 00186 Rome Italy. **Tel** 011 39 6 679 4628, FAX 011 39 6 678 4751. **ED** Adolfo Tamburello. **LC** DS820.8; .G5. **DD** 952/.005.
Desc: Deals with cultural aspects of Japan in collaboration with the Japanese Institute of Culture at Rome.
Ind/Abst Bibliogr. Mission.

US/0340-6369
GIORGIO LEVI DELLA VIDA CONFERENCES. See History(General)-History of Africa.

US/1059-5988
GLOBAL STUDIES. JAPAN AND THE PACIFIC RIM. [Glob. stud., Jpn. Pac. Rim]. **VFOAT** Japan and the Pacific Rim. 1st Ed. (1991)-. English. Dushkin Publishing Group Inc., Sluice Dock, Guilford CT 06437. **Tel** (203)453-4351, (800)243-6532, FAX (203)453-6000. **LC** DS801; .G56. **DD** 950.

II
GORKHA. Periodical. English (Nepali). mo. Sajha Pustak Bhandar, Motor Stand Barrack, Darjeeling India. **LC** DS432.N46; G67. **UDC** 954.0.

GR
GRAECO-ARABICA / HETAIREIA HELLENOARAVIKON SPOUDON. VFOAT Graeco-Arabica. Vol. 1-. English (Greek, Modern). an. $12.00. V Christides, 37 Solomou St, Kryoneri Attikis Greece. **LC** DS57; .G68. **DD** 956/.005. **UDC** 956.

GW
GRAUE LITERATUR AUS OSTASIEN.
Added/Corp Institut fur Asienkunde. Bibliothek. (19??)-. Chinese (English, German, Japanese and Korean). ir. Institute of Asian Affairs, Rothenbaumchaussee 32, D-20148 Hamburg Germany. **Tel** 011 49 40 443001, FAX 011 49 40 4107945. **LC** Z3001; .G7; DS504.5. **DD** 016.95.

JA
GUMMA KENRITSU REKISHI HAKUBUTSUKAN NEMPO. Main/Corp Gunma Kenritsu Rekishi Hakubutsukan. Japanese. an. Gunma Kenritsu Rekishi Hakubutsukan, 28 Iwahanacho, Takasaki-shi, Gumma-ken 370-12 Japan. **LC** DS894.49.G84; A2945A.

JA
GURAFU KANAGAWA. Added/Corp Kanagawa-ken (Japan). (19??)-. Periodical. Japanese. mo. ¥50. Kanagawa-ken Chijishitsu Kohoka, Yokohama 231 Japan. **LC** DS894.49.K34; A22.

JA
GURAFU TOKYO. Added/Corp Tokyo (Japan). Kohoshitsu. (19??)-. Periodical. Japanese. Tokyo-To Kohoshitsu, 5-1 Marunouchi Chiyoda-ku 100, Tokyo Japan. **LC** DS896; .G86.

US
HAEOE HANMIN. VFOAT Overseas Korean Journal. Korean (Korean). $18.75 6 issues. Haehoe Hanminbosa, 47-48 Springfield Boulevard, Bayside NY 11361. **LC** DS904.7; .H33.

US
HAEOE SASANGGYE. VFOAT Overseas Korean Thoughts. Periodical. Korean (Korean). $2.50 single issue. The New Korea, 1368 West Jefferson Boulevard, Los Angeles CA 90007. **LC** DS922; .H27.

History(General) —History of Asia

KO
HAEOE TONGPO. Periodical. Korean. qt. Haeoe Kyopo Munje Yonguso, 175-87 Anguk-Dong, Chongno-ku Seoul Korea. **LC** DS904.7; .H337.

II
HALF-YEARLY REPORT - INDIAN COUNCIL OF HISTORICAL RESEARCH. **Main/Corp** Indian Council of Historical Research. May/Sept. 1972-. English. 35 FerozeshaH Road, New Delhi India. **LC** DS401; .I29214. **DD** 954/.007/2.

CH/0254-4466
HAN HSUEH YEN CHIU. **Added/Corp** Han Hsueh Yen Chiu Tzu Liao Chi Fu Wu Chung Hsin (China). **VFOAT** Chinese Studies. (1983)-. Periodical. Chinese (English). sa. $40.00. Center Chinese Studies Taiwan, 20 Chungshan South Road, Taipei Taiwan. **Tel** 011 886 2 3147321. **LC** DS701; .H36. **DD** 951/.005.

CH
HAN SHENG (TAIPEI, TAIWAN). (HAN SHENG.) **VFOAT** Han Sheng Tsa Chih; Echo Magazine. Began with Jan. 1978 issue. Periodical. Chinese. qt. $600.00. Tiawan Ying Wen Tsa Chih She, PO Box 313, Taiwan Taiwan. **LC** AP95.C4; H36. **DD** 951/.005.

KO
HANGUK KOJON SIMPOJIUM. V. 1-Series. Periodical. Korean. W5,000. Ilchogak, 9 Kongpyong-dong Chongno-ku, Seoul Korea. **LC** DS901; .H32129.

KO
HANGUK SA YONGU. **VFOAT** Journal of Korean History. Periodical. Korean. W2,500. Hanguk Sa Yonguhoe, 48-24 1-ka Changchung-dong Chung-ku, Seoul Korea. **LC** DS901; .H321362.

KO
HAN'GUK SA YON'GU HWIBO. **VFOAT** Bulletin for Korean Historical Studies. Periodical. Korean. qt. Kuksa Pyonchan Wiwonhoe, 8-20 Yejang-dong Chung-ku, Seoul 100 Korea. **LC** DS905.9; .H36. **UDC** 951.95.

KO
HANGUKHAK NONJIP (SEOUL, KOREA). (HANGUKHAK NONJIP.). Began with Aug. 1982 issue. Periodical. Korean. sa. Hanyang Taehakkyo Hangukhak Yoguso, 17 Hyangdand-dong Songdong-ku, Seoul Korea. **LC** DS901; .H338. **Continues** Kukhak Nonchong.

US/0073-0459
HARVARD ARMENIAN TEXTS AND STUDIES. V. 1-. Monographic series. English. ir. Price varies per volume. Harvard University Press, 79 Garden Street, Cambridge MA 02138. **Tel** (617)496-1344, (800)448-2242. **UDC** 956.6.

US/0073-0483
HARVARD EAST ASIAN MONOGRAPHS. [Harv. East Asian monogr.]. **Added/Corp** Harvard University. Council on East Asian Studies. (1958)-. Monographic series. English. ir. Price varies per volume. Harvard University Press, 79 Garden Street, Cambridge MA 02138. **Tel** (617)496-1344, (800)448-2242. **LC** UNC. **DD** 951.
Ind/Abst MLA Int. Bibl. Books Artic. Mod. Lang. Lit.

US/0073-0491
HARVARD EAST ASIAN SERIES. **Added/Corp** Harvard University. East Asian Research Center. (1962)-. Monographic series. English. ir. Price varies per volume. Harvard University Press, 79 Garden Street, Cambridge MA 02138. **Tel** (617)496-1344, (800)448-2242. **Continues** Harvard East Asian Studies.

US/0073-0548
HARVARD JOURNAL OF ASIATIC STUDIES. [Harv. j. Asiat. stud.]. **Added/Corp** Harvard-Yenching Institute. **VFOAT** Asiatic Studies. Vol. 1 (April 1936)-. Academic Scholarly Publication. English. sa (June, December). $75.00 (institutions), $60.00 (individuals). Harvard Yenching Institute, 2 Divinity Avenue, Cambridge MA 02138. **Tel** (617)495-2758, FAX (617)495-7798. **ED** Howard S. Hibbett. **LC** DS501; .H3. **DD** 950.05. Index available (December issue/every 5 years). cum. index. **Bk Rev**, (Qty: 15). **Circ:** 1,200. available on microfilm and microfiche from University Microfilms International (UMI). Documents available from UMI Article Clearinghouse.
Desc: A scholarly journal primarily concerned with the languages, literatures, cultures and histories of the countries of eastern and central Asia but not with contemporary political or social matters.
Ind/Abst Acad. Search (July 1993-); Am. Hist. Life (1954-); Anthropol. Lit.; Arts Humanit. Citation Index [Full Cov.]; Curr. Contents Arts Humanit.; Expand. Acad. Index (1989-); Humanit. Index; Humanit. Source (Jul. 1993-); Index Book Rev. Humanit.; INFO-SOUTH Abstr.; Mag. Search; Middle East Abstr. Index; MLA Int. Bibl. Books Artic. Mod. Lang. Lit.; Newsp. Period. Abstr. (1991-); Recent. Publ. Artic.; Res. Alert [Full Cov.].

SZ/0073-0947
HAUTES ETUDES ISLAMIQUES ET ORIENTALES D'HISTOIRE COMPAREE. 1- 1971-. Monographic series. French. ir. Price varies per volume. Librairie Droz SA, 11 rue Massot BP 389, CH 1211 Geneva 12 Switzerland. **Tel** 011 41 22 3466666, FAX 011 41 22 472391. **UDC** 950. **Circ:** 300.
Desc: Orientalism.

SZ/0073-0971
HAUTES ETUDES ORIENTALES. 1- 1968-. Monographic series. French. ir. Price varies per volume. Librairie Droz SA, 11 rue Massot BP 389, CH 1211 Geneva 12 Switzerland. **Tel** 011 41 22 3466666, FAX 011 41 22 472391. **UDC** 951. **Circ:** 400.
Desc: Orientalism.

TI
HAWLIYAT AL-JAMIAH AL-TUNISIYAH. **Main/Corp** Tunis. Al-Jamiah Al-Tunisiyah. **VFOAT** Annales de l'Universite de Tunis. Arabic. Al-Jamiah Al-Tunisiyah, 94 9 April 1938 Boulevard, Tunis Tunisia. **LC** DS36; .T85A.

US/1055-9884
HEAVEN EARTH. (HEAVEN EARTH : THE CHINESE ART OF LIVING.). [Heaven earth]. **Added/Corp** China Advocates (Organization). **VFOAT** HeavenEarth. Vol. 1, No. 1 (May 1991)-. Periodical. English. Three times a year. $20.00 (institutions). Heaven Earth, PO Box 22459, San Francisco CA 94122. **LC** DS721; .H42. **DD** 951/.005.

US/0895-0792
HERITAGE (CARSON, CALIF.). See Ethnic Interests.

JA
HIGASHI AJIA NO KODAI BUNKA. **VFOAT** Kodai Bunka. (1974)-. Periodical. Japanese. qt. ¥720. Terakoya Shuppansha, Daiwa Shobo 33-4 Sekiguchi 1 Bunkyo-ku, Tokyo Japan. **LC** DS509.3; .H52.

II
HIMALAYA TODAY. **VFOAT** Himalaya. Vol. 1, No. 1 (June 1988)-. Periodical. English. qt. $20.00. Himalaya Today Publications, New Delhi, India. **(Subscription address:** Prints India, 11 Darya Ganj, New Delhi 110002 India.) **LC** DS485.H6; H5498. **DD** 954.96/005.

NP
HIMALAYAN CULTURE. Vol. 1 (Oct. 1978)-. Periodical. English (Nepali). qt. Rs38.00 Nepal; $6.00 other. Hari Bangsha Kirant, 20/136 Kamal Pikhari, Kathmandu 711000 Nepal. **LC** DS493.7; .H54. **DD** 954.9/6/005.

US/0891-4834
HIMALAYAN RESEARCH BULLETIN. [Himal. res. bull.]. Vol. 1, No. 2 (Spring 1981)-. Bulletin. English. Three times a year. $15.00 (individual membership); $30.00 (institutional membership); $10.00 (student membership). Southern Asian Institute, Columbia University, New York NY 10027. **Tel** (212)280-4662. **ED** Theodore Riccardi, William F Fisher and Bruce McCoy Owers. **DD** 954. **UDC** 954.135. **Bk Rev**. **Ad Acc**. **Circ:** 500. **Continues** Himalayan Research Bulletin of the Nepal Studies Association, 0891-4869.

II
HINDI EKSAPRESA. **VFOAT** Hindi Express. Periodical. Hindi. wk. Rs60.00. Indian Express Newspapers Ltd, Express Towers, PB No 867, Nariman Point Bombay 1 India. **Tel** 294838-8. **LC** DS401; .H425. **UDC** 954.0.

US
HISTORICAL AND CULTURAL DICTIONARIES OF ASIA. No. 1 (1972)-. Monographic series. English. ir. Price varies per volume. Scarecrow Press Inc., 52 Liberty Street, PO Box 4167, Metuchen NJ 08840. **Tel** (908)548-8600, (800)537-7107.

PH/0116-3655
HISTORICAL BULLETIN / PHILIPPINE HISTORICAL ASSOCIATION. [Hist. bull. - Philipp. Hist. Assoc.]. **Added/Corp** Philippine Historical Association. (19??)-. Bulletin. English. qt. **LC** DS651; .P4534. **DD** 959.9/005. **Continues** Buletin ng Kapisanang Pangkasaysayan ng Pilipinas.
Ind/Abst Am. Hist. Life (1959).

IS/0303-1519
HITHADSHUT. [Hithadsut]. No. 733- Nov. 1972-. Hebrew. Ha-Irgum Ha-Artsi Shel Yehude Kurdistan Be-Yisrael, PO Box 1228, Yershalugim Israel. **LC** DS113.8.K9; H56.

CC
HO-NAN WEN SHIH TZU LIAO HSUAN CHI / CHUNG-KUO JEN MIN CHENG CHIH HSIEH SHANG HUI I HO-NAN SHENG WEI YUAN HUI, WEN SHIH TZU LIAO YEN CHIU WEI YUAN HUI PIEN. V. 1, (Oct. 1979)-. Periodical. Chinese. RMBY0.58. Hsin Hua Shu Tien / Cheng-Chou Shih, Ho Nan, People's Republic of China. **LC** DS793.H5; H692. **DD** 951/.18.

CC
HO-PEI HUA PAO. **VFOAT** He Bei Hua Bao. Periodical. Chinese. bm. RMBY0.80. Post Office, Shih-Shia Chuang, People's Republic of China. **LC** DS793.H6; H644. **DD** 951/.15/005. **UDC** 951.

CH
HO-PEI KO MING HUI I LU. Periodical. Chinese. NT$0.74. Hsin Hua Shu Tien / Ho-Pei, Shih-Chia-Chuang, Ho-Pei, People's Republic of China. **LC** DS793.H6; H65.

CC
HO-PEI SHIH FAN TA HSUEH HSUEH PAO. CHE HSUEH SHE HUI KO HSUEH PAN. **Added/Corp** Ho-Pei Shih Fan Ta Hsueh. **VFOAT** Ho-Pei Shih Fan ta Hsueh Hsueh Pao. She Hui ko Hsueh Pan; Journal of Hebei Normal University. Philosophy and Social Science edition; Hebei Shifan Daxue Xuebao. (19??)-. Periodical. Chinese. qt. $4.80. China National Publishing Company, 380 Bei Su Zhou Lu, Shanghai, People's Republic of China. **LC** AS452.S543; A2. **DD** 951/.005.

CH
HO-PEI WEN SHIH TZU LIAO HSUAN CHI / CHUNG-KUO JEN MIN CHENG CHIH HSIEH SHANG HUI I HO-PEI SHENG WEI YUAN HUI, WEN SHIH TZU LIAO YEN CHIU WEI YUAN HUI PIEN. Periodical. Chinese. NT$0.60. Ho-Pei Sheng Hsin Hua Shu Tien Shih-Chia-Chyang China, People's Republic of China. **LC** DS793.H6; H7. **DD** 951/.15. **UDC** 951.

JA
HOKKAIDO KAITAKU KINENKAN CHOSA HOKOKU. **Main/Corp** Hokkaido Kaitaku Kinenkan. **Added/Corp** Hokkaido Kaitaku Kinenkan. Kaitaku Kinenkan Chosa Hokoku. Hokkaido Kaitaku Kinenkan. Memoirs of the Historical Museum of Hokkaido. **VFOAT** Memoirs of the Historical Museum of Hokkaido. (19??)-. Periodical. Japanese (English). an. Hokkaido Kaitaku Kinenkan / Sapporo, (Historical Museum of Hokkaido), Konopporo Atsubetsucho Shiroishiku, Sapporoshi Hokkaido 061-01 Japan. **Tel** 011-898-0456. **LC** DS894.215; .H64a.
Desc: Research papers co-authored with researchers of the museum will be accepted for publication.

JA
HOKKAIDO KAITAKU KINENKAN DAYORI. **Main/Corp** Hokkaido Kaitaku Kinenkan. **VFOAT** Historical Museum of Hokkaido. Japanese (Japanese). Hokkaido Kaitaku Kinenkan, Konoppporo Atsubetsucho, Shiraishi-ku 061-01, Sapporo Japan. **LC** DS894.215; .H64B. **UDC** 952.

JA
HOPPO KAGAKU CHOSA HOKOKU. **Added/Corp** Tsukuba Daigaku. (1980)-. Japanese. Tsukuba Daigaku, 1-1 Tennodai 1-Chome Sakuramura Niihari-gun, Ibaraki-Ken 305 Japan. **LC** DS894.215; .H66.

CH
HSI NAN CHUN FA SHIH YEN CHIU TSUNG KAN / HSI NAN CHUN FA SHIH YEN CHIU HUI. V. 1- (August 1982)-. Periodical. Chinese. NT$1.38. Ssu-Chuan Sheng Hsin Hua Shu Tien, Cheng-tu, People's Republic of China. **LC** DS793.S644; H75. **DD** 951/.3. **UDC** 951.

CC
HSI NAN MIN TSU YEN CHIU / CHUNG-KUO HSI NAN MIN TSU YEN CHIU HUI PIEN. **Added/Corp** Chung-kuo Hsi Nan Min Tsu Yen Chiu Hui. 1 (June 1983)-. Periodical. Chinese. Ssu-Chuan Sheng Hsin Hua Shu Tien, Cheng-tu, People's Republic of China. **LC** DS793.S6445; H67. **DD** 951/.3004.

US
HSI PEI YU. **VFOAT** Sai Pah Ho. Periodical. Chinese. Hsi Pei Yu She, PO Box 463, Seattle WA 98125. **LC** DS799.8; .H68.

CC
HSI-TSANG YEN CHIU. **Added/Corp** Hsi-tsang She Hui Ko Hsueh Yuan. **VFOAT** Bod Ljons Zib Jug; Tibetan Studies. Vol. 1 (1982)-. Periodical. Chinese. qt. RMBY0.45. Hsi-tsang Yen Chiu, Post Office, Cheng-Tu Shih, People's Republic of China. **LC** DS785.A1; H77. **DD** 951/.5/005.

CH
HSIA CHAO LUN TAN. V. 1-. Periodical. Chinese. $30.00. Mr James Ning, 106 Roosevelt Boulevard, Florham Park NJ 07932. **LC** AP95.C4; H731163. **DD** 951/.249/005. **UDC** 951. **Continues** Hsia Chao.

CC
HSIN-CHIANG HUA PAO. Periodical. Chinese. bm. RMBY0.60. Post Office, Wu-Lu-Mu-Chi Shih, People's Republic of China. **LC** DS793.S62; H767. **DD** 951/.6/005. **UDC** 951.

CC
HSING HUO LIAO YUAN. ***Title Change.*** **VFOAT** Xinghuoliaoyuan. (19??)-(198?). Periodical. Chinese. bm. Science Press, 16 Donghuangchenggen North Street, Beijing 100707, People's Republic of China. **Tel** 011 86 1 4019821, 011 86 1 4010642, FAX 011 86 1 4012180, 011 86 1 4019810, telex 210147. **LC** AP95.C4; H7837. **DD** 951/.005. ***Merged with*** *Hsing Huo Liao Yuan (Selections)* ***to form*** *Hsing Huo Liao Yuan (Tsung Shu).*

CC
HSING HUO LIAO YUAN (SELECTIONS). ***Title Change.*** (HSING HUO LIAO YUAN.). Hsuan Pien Chih 1 (1977)-(198?). Periodical. Chinese. sa. Hsin Hua Shu Tien / Beijing, Pei-Ching Fa Hsing So, Beijing, People's Republic of China. **Tel** 657331-565. **LC** UA837; .H7573. **DD** 951.04. ***Merged with*** *Hsing Huo Liao Yuan* ***to form*** *Hsing Huo Liao Yuan (Tsung Shu).*

CC
HU-NAN LI SHIH TZU LIAO / HU-NAN LI SHIH TZU LIAN PIEN CHI SHIH. Periodical. Chinese. 0.68. Hsin Hua Shu Tien / Chang-Sha, Chang-Sha Hunan, People's Republic of China. **LC** DS793.H7; H764. **DD** 951/.215. **UDC** 951.

UK
HULL MONOGRAPHS ON SOUTH-EAST ASIA. No. 1- 1968-. Periodical. English. ir. Probsthain Arthur, 41 Great Russell Street, London WC1 England.

LE
HURRIYAH (BEIRUT, LEBANON : 1981). (AL-HURRIYAH.). Vol. 1, Journal 1 (March-April 1981)-. Periodical. Arabic. mo. £L15.00. Maktab Al-Markazi Lil-Alaqat Al-Kharijiyah Lil-Jabhah Al-Shabiyah Li-Tahrir Iritriya. **LC** DT391; .H87.

CY
HURRIYAH (NICOSIA, CYPRUS). (AL-HURRIYAH.). **VFOAT** Al-Hourriah; Hourriah. Nos. 83/1 (Festival Year Jan. 1983)-. Periodical. Arabic. wk. $80.00. T H O Publishers Company Ltd, 2 Homer Avenue, Nicosia Cyprus. **LC** DS63.1; .H86.

RU
IAPONIIA. **Added/Corp** Nauchnyi Sovet po Koordinatsii Nauchno-Issledovatelskikh Rabot v Oblasti Vostokovedeniia (Akademiia Nauk SSSR). Seksiia po Izucheniiu Iaponii. Institut Mirovoi Ekonomiki i Mezhdunarodnykh Otnoshenii (Akademiia Nauk SSSR) Institut Vostokovedeniia (Akademiia Nauk SSSR) Institut Dalnego Vostoka (Akademiia Nauk SSSR). (1972)-. Russian. 1.70rub. Izdatelstvo Nauka / Akademiia Nauk, Publishing House of the Russian Academy of Sciences, Leninskii Porspekt 14, 117901 Moscow Russia. **Tel** 011 95 954-21-53, FAX 011 95 938-21-44, telex 411964. **LC** DS801; .I18.

BG
IBS SEMINAR. **Added/Corp** Rajasahi Bivabidyalaya. Inastitiuta aba Bamladesa Stadija. **VFOAT** I.B.S. Seminar. (19??)-. Monographic series. English. Price varies per volume. Institute of Bangladesh Studies, University of Rajshahi, Rajshahi Bangladesh.

JA
ICHIOKUNIN NO SHOWA SHI. **Added/Corp** Mainichi Shinbunsha. Vol. 1 (1975)-. Periodical. Japanese. ¥1000. Mainichi Shimbun Sha, (Mainichi Newspapers), 1-1-1 Hitotsubashi Chiyoda-ku, Tokyo 100-51 Japan. **Tel** 03 3212 0321, FAX 03 3216 2574. **LC** DS888.2; .I25.

II/0376-9682
ICHR NEWSLETTER. **Main/Corp** Indian Council of Historical Research. **VAT** Indian Council of Historical Research Newsletter. Newsletter. English. qt. Indian Council of Historical Research, 35 Ferozeshah Road, New Delhi 110001 India. **Tel** 389021. **LC** DS401; .I29215. **DD** 954/.007/2. **UDC** 954.

UK
IDISHE FOLK. THE JEWISH PEOPLE, DOS. ***Ceased.*** **VFOAT** The Jewish People. (19??)-(1994). Periodical. English (Yiddish). The Jewish People, 13 Carysfort Road, London N16 England. **LC** DS101; .I34.

JA
IKEDA KYODO KENKYU. **Added/Corp** Ikeda Kyodoshi Gakkai. (19??)-. Periodical. Japanese. ¥3000. Ikeda-shi Kyoiku, Kenkyujo 1 Sugawaracho 1, Ikeda Japan. **LC** DS897.I43; I43.

LE
ILA AL-AMAM, MIN AJLI TAHRIR AL-ARD WA-AL-INSAN. Periodical. Arabic. £L1.50 single issue. PO Box 3089, Beirut Lebanon. **LC** DS119.7; .I35.

KO
ILBON CHUNCHU. Vol. 3, No. 7 (Aug. 1975)-. Periodical. Korean. mo. W2.500. Ilbon Chunchu Sa, 340-2 ka Taepyongno, Chung-ku, Seoul Korea. **LC** DS801; .I38. ***Continues*** *Ilbon Yongu.*

KO
ILBON WANGNAE. **VFOAT** Monthly Japanese Journal. V. 1- March 1978-. Periodical. Korean. W3.000 members. Chungoe Munhwa Kyoryu Yonguhoe. **LC** DS801; .I5.

MY/0126-7000
ILMU ALAM. [Ilmu Alam]. **Added/Corp** Universiti Kebangsaan Malaysia. Jabatan Ilmu Alam. Universiti Kebangsaan Malaysia. Persatuan Ilmu Alam. No. 1 (May 1972)-. Multiple languages (English and Malayalam; summaries and/or abstracts in English). an (May). $15.00. Jabatan Geofrafi Universiti, Kebangsaan Malaysi, Department of Geography, Selangor Malaysia. **LC** DS591; .I4. **DD** 959.5/05/05.
Ind/Abst Energy Res. Abstr. (June 1977-); Int. Bibliogr. Sociol.

PH/0019-2538
ILOCOS REVIEW, THE. Vol. 1 (1969)-. Periodical. English. sa. Ilocos Review, Divine Word College, Bangued Abra Philippines. **LC** DS666.I37; I45.

KO
IMYONG MUNHWA. Periodical. Korean. Kangnung Munhwawon, 15 Yonggang-dong, Kangung 210 Korea. **LC** DS925.K37; I45.

II/0019-3852
INDEX INDO-ASIATICUS. No. 1 (1968)-. Periodical. English (Sanskrit, Bengali and Hindi). ir. $200.00 India; $230.00 others. Index Indo Asiaticus, PO Box 11215, Calcutta 14 India. **ED** Sibadas Chaudhuri. Index available. cum. index. **Bk Rev. Ad Acc. Circ:** 300 (ctrl).
Desc: An international indexing journal based on current periodical literature on topics relating to the culture of India and ancient Asia.

II/0073-6090
INDIA, A REFERENCE ANNUAL. **Added/Corp** India. Ministry of Information and Broadcasting. Research and Reference Division. **VFOAT** India. (1953)-. English (Hindi). an. $30.00. Ministry of Information and Broadcasting, Government of India, Patiala House, New Delhi 110 001 India. **Tel** 387983. **(Subscription address:** Prints India, 11 Darya Ganj, New Delhi, 110002 India, (Phone: 011 91 11 3268645)) **LC** DS405; .I64. **DD** 915.4. **NLM** DS 405 I36. Index available. **Ad Acc. Circ:** 16,000 English, 3,000 Hindi.

US/0046-8932
INDIA ABROAD. **See** Ethnic Interests.

US/0894-5136
INDIA BRIEFING. [India brief.]. **Added/Corp** Asia Society. (1987)-. English. $15.85 (paper back), $39.85 (hard bound). Westview Press Inc, 5500 Central Avenue, Boulder CO 80301. **Tel** (303)444-3541, FAX (303)449-3356. **LC** DS480.832; .I5. **DD** 954/.005.

II/0376-9771
INDIA INTERNATIONAL CENTRE QUARTERLY. [India Int. Cent. q.]. **Main/Corp** India International Centre. Vol. 1 (1974)-. Periodical. English. qt. $25.00. India International Centre, 40 Lodi Estate, New Delhi 110003 India. **Tel** 619431. **(Subscription address:** Prints India, 11 Darya Ganj, New Delhi, 110002 India, (Phone: 011 91 11 3268645)) **ED** Jeanette Fernandes. **LC** DS401; .I2746a. **DD** 954/.05/05. **Bk Rev. Ad Acc. Circ:** 2,000 (ctrl).
Desc: Emphasis on energy, environment, design, sports, food, images ... Other issues are on subjects of general interest, including lectures, interviews with eminent personalities, short stories; feature articles which review the current situation in economics, foreign policy and internal affairs, literature and the arts.
Ind/Abst Int. Polit. Sci. Abstr.

US/1059-4973
INDIA JOURNAL, THE. (THE INDIA JOURNAL [COMPUTER FILE].). [India j.]. (1990)-. English. da. Free. The India Journal, PO Box 552, Flushing NY 11352-0552. **DD** 954.
Desc: Available through BITNET.

●CN/0254-8399
INDIA TODAY. Vol. 17, No. 10 (May 31, 1992)-. Periodical. English. Twenty-four times a year. $49.00. Living Media India Ltd., PO Box 706, Faridabad 121007 India. **(Subscription address:** Living Media India Ltd., 404 Park Avenue South, Suite 1205, New York NY 10016.) **LC** DS401; .I535. ***Continues*** *India Today (International Ed.).*

US/0895-4283
INDIA WORLDWIDE. [India worldw.]. Vol. 1, No. 1 (Aug. 1987)-. Periodical. English. mo. India Worldwide Inc., 154 West 27th Street, New York NY 10001. **DD** 954.

II/0376-9836
INDIAN HISTORICAL REVIEW, THE. [Indian hist. rev.]. **Added/Corp** Indian Council of Historical Research. Vol. 1 (March 1974)-. Periodical. English. Twice a year. $14.00. Indian Council of Historical Research, 35 Ferozeshah Road, New Delhi 110001 India. **Tel** 389021. **(Subscription address:** Prints India, 11 Darya Ganj, New Delhi, 110002 India, (Phone: 011 91 11 3268645)) **ED** V. Jha. **LC** DS401; .I373. **DD** 954/.005. **Bk Rev. Ad Acc. Circ:** 1,000.
Desc: A research journal with focus on Indian history of all periods with a comprehensive section of reviews of recent publications.
Ind/Abst Am. Hist. Life (1975-1977, 1979-).

II
INDIAN JOURNAL OF ASIAN STUDIES. **Added/Corp** Indian Council of Social Science Research. Vol. 1 (Jan./June 1977)-. Periodical. English. sa. $30.00. Indian Council of Social Science Research, 35 Ferozshah Road, New Delhi 110 001 India. **Tel** 011 91 11 38959, 011 91 11 381571. **(Subscription address:** Prints India, 11 Darya Ganj, New Delhi, 110002 India, (Phone: 011 91 11 3268645)) **LC** DS1; .I46. **DD** 950/.05.

II
INDIAN OUTLOOK. Periodical. English. mo. Rs20.00. 32/1 Chandi Ghose Road, Calcutta 700040 India. **ED** S K Nag. **LC** DS423; .I56. **DD** 954/.005. **UDC** 954.

US/0194-3391
INDIAN REVIEW (CHICAGO), THE. ***Suspended.*** (THE INDIAN REVIEW.). Vol. 1, Autumn 1978-Suspended 1978. Periodical. English. qt. $12.00 North America. India Society, 5500 S Shore Drive/#1708, Chicago IL 60637. **Tel** (312)752-7977. **LC** DS401; .I457. **DD** 954/.005. **UDC** 954.0.

●NE/0924-8986
INDIAN THOUGHT LEIDEN. [Indian thought Leiden]. (1992)-. Monographic series. Dutch. ir. Price varies per volume. E. J. Brill, Postbus 9000, 2300 PA Leiden Netherlands. **Tel** 011 31 71 312624, FAX 011 31 71 317532, telex 39296 BRILL NL. **UDC** 397 :904. ***Continues*** *Indian Thought and Culture, 0926-9703.*

II/0019-686X
INDICA. [Indica]. **Added/Corp** Heras Institute of Indian History and Culture. Vol. 1 (Mar. 1964)-. English. sa (March and September). $10.00. Heras Institute of Indian History and Culture, St Xavier's College, Bombay 400 001 India. **Tel** 011 91 22 262 0661. **(Subscription address:** Prints India, 11 Darya Ganj, New Delhi, 110002 India, (Phone: 011 91 11 3268645)) **ED** J. Correia-Afonso. **LC** DS401; .I53. Index available. **Bk Rev**, (Qty: 5). **Circ:** 250 (ctrl).
Desc: Presents research articles on archaeology, ancient Indian history and culture, and medieval and modern Indian history. Includes documentation, reviews and notes.
Ind/Abst Am. Hist. Life (1964-); Bibliogr. Mission.

GW
INDIEN, FORSCHUNGSPOLITIK UND FORSCHUNGSPRAXIS / BUNDESSTELLE FUER AUSSENHANDELSINFORMATION. Periodical. German. an. DM3.00. Bundesstelle fuer Aussenhandelsinformation, Agrippastr 87 93, D 50676 Cologne Germany. **Tel** 011 49 221 2057316, FAX 011 49 221 2057212. **LC** Q180.I5; I53. **DD** 338.95402. **UDC** 339.5(540).

GW/0019-719X
INDO ASIA. [Indo-Asia]. **Added/Corp** Deutsch-Indische Gesellschaft. (1959)-. Periodical. German. qt. DM60.00 Germany; DM72.00 other. Burg Verlag GmbH, Untere AU 41, D 74343 Sachsenheim Germany. **LC** DS401; .I56.
Ind/Abst Int. Bibliogr. Sociol.; PAIS Int. Print.

US/0897-4519
INDOCHINA CHRONOLOGY. **Added/Corp** University of California, Berkeley. Institute of East Asian Studies. Vol. 1, No. 1 (Jan./March 1982)-. Periodical. English. qt. $25.00 US; $40.00 other. University of California / Institute of East Asian Studies, 2223 Fulton Street, UC 6th Floor, Berkeley CA 94720. **Tel** (510)642-2809, FAX (510)643-7062. **ED** Douglas Pike. **LC** DS550; .I518. **DD** 959/.005. Index available. **Bk Rev. Circ:** 1,500. available on microfiche.
Desc: Designed as a research tool, teaching aid, and source of reliable and complete data about current events related to Indochina.

US/0742-907X
INDOCHINA JOURNAL. ***Title Change.*** **Added/Corp** Indochina Human Rights Group. (19??)-(1992). Periodical. English. ir. Vietnam Journal, PO Box 1163, Burlingame CA 94010. **LC** DS550; .I534. **DD** 959.7. ***Continues*** *Indochina Newsletter (Portland, Or.).* ***Continued by*** *Vietnam Journal (Burlingame, Calif.).*
Ind/Abst Hum. Rights Intern. Rep.

JA/0019-4344
INDOGAKU BUKKYOGAKU KENKYU. **Added/Corp** Nihon Indogaku Bukkyogaku Kai. **VFOAT** Journal of Indian and Buddhist Studies. Vol. 1, No. 1 (July 1952)-. Periodical. Japanese (summaries and/or abstracts in English; table of contents in English). sa. $90.50. **(Subscription address:** Japan Publications Trading Company, Ltd., PO Box 5030, Tokyo International, Tokyo 100-31 Japan.) cum. index.

History(General) —History of Asia

IO
INDONESIA, FOREIGN AFFAIRS. English. ir. Directorate of Information, Department of Foreign Affairs, 6 Taman Pejambon, Jakarta Pusat Indonesia. **LC** DS640.I4; I5. **DD** 327.598/005. **UDC** 327(594).

US/0889-9355
INDONESIA ISSUES. (INDONESIA ISSUES / INDONESIA PUBLICATIONS.). [Indones. issues]. No. 1 (July 1986)-. Periodical. English. ir. $38.00. Indonesia Publications, 7538 Newberry Lane, Lanhan Seabrook MD 20706. **Tel** (301)552-3251, FAX (301)552-4465. **ED** John A. MacDougall. **DD** 959.
Desc: Analysis and documentation of current events in Indonesia.

US/0019-7289
INDONESIA (ITHACA). (INDONESIA.). [Indonesia]. **Added/Corp** Cornell University. Modern Indonesia Project. No. 1 (April 1966)-. Periodical. English. sa (2 issues). $20.00 US; $25.00 other. Southeast Asia Program Publications, East Hill Plaza, Cornell University, Ithaca NY 14850. **Tel** (607)255-8038, FAX (607)277-1904. **LC** DS611; .A334. Index available (sixth issue). cum. index. **Bk Rev. Pr Rev. Circ:** 900. available on microfilm and microfiche from University Microfilms International (UMI).
Desc: Devoted to Indonesia's culture, history and socio-political problems.
Ind/Abst Int. Polit. Sci. Abstr.; MLA Int. Bibl. Books Artic. Mod. Lang. Lit.

US/0889-9347
INDONESIA MIRROR. (INDONESIA MIRROR / INDONESIA PUBLICATIONS.). [Indones. mirror]. No. 1 (July 1986)-. Periodical. English. mo. $76.00 US & Canada; $120.00 other. Indonesia Publications, 7538 Newberry Lane, Lanhan Seabrook MD 20706. **Tel** (301)552-3251, FAX (301)552-4465. **ED** John A. MacDougell. **DD** 959.
Desc: Analysis and documentation of contemporary political and economic developments in Indonesia.

US/0749-5315
INDONESIA REPORTS. [Indones. rep.]. No. 1 (Nov. 15, 1984)-. Periodical. English. mo. $80.00, $240.00 (includes supplements), $88.00, $248.00 (includes supplements) Canada; $120.00, $280.00 (includes supplements) other. Indonesia Publications, 7538 Newberry Lane, Lanhan Seabrook MD 20706. **Tel** (301)552-3251, FAX (301)552-4465. **DD** 959.
Ind/Abst Hum. Rights Intern. Rep.

IO
INDONESIAN QUARTERLY, THE. **Added/Corp** Centre for Strategic and International Studies. (Oct. 1972)-. Periodical. English. Four times a year. $70.00 US, Canada and Central America; $60.00 Europe, South America and Africa; $50.00 other. Centre for Strategic and International Studies, Jalan Tanah Abang III 27 27, Jakarta 10160 Indonesia. **Tel** 011 62 21 356532. **ED** Kirdi Dipoyudo. **LC** DS611; .I525. **DD** 915.98/005. **Bk Rev. Circ:** 3,000.
Desc: A medium for the news, research and evaluation of scholars on the Indonesian situation and its problems.
Ind/Abst Asia.-Pac. Econ. Lit.; PAIS Int. Print; Rural Dev. Abstr.; Soyabean Abstr.; World Agric. Econ.

CN/0712-8045
INFORM ACTION - ACTION LIBAN. (INFORM ACTION.). [Inform action - Action Liban]. V. 1 No. 1 (Mar./Apr. 1980)-. Periodical. French (English). bm. $8.00. Inform Action / Quebec, c/o Action Liban, CP 452 Station Ahuntsic, Montreal Quebec H3L 3P1 Canada. **DD** 956.92/044/05. **UDC** 956.93.

RU/1012-6570
INFORMATION BULLETIN / INTERNATIONAL ASSOCIATION FOR THE STUDY OF THE CULTURES OF CENTRAL ASIA. [Inf. bull. - Int. Assoc. Study Cult. Cent. Asia]. **Added/Corp** International Association for the Study of the Cultures of Central Asia. **VFOAT** Bulletin. Issue 1 (1982)-. Bulletin. English. sa. Institute of Oriental Studies, Russian Academy of Sciences, 12 Zhdanov Street, 103777 Moscow Russia.
Ind/Abst Anthropol. Lit.

MY
INFORMATION MALAYSIA ... YEARBOOK. **VFOAT** Information Malaysia. (19??)-. English. an. Berita Publishing Company, 22 Jalan Liku, 59100 Kuala Lumpur Malaysia. **Tel** 60 3 2825286, FAX 60 3 2821605, telex 30259. **LC** DS591.5; .I53. **DD** 959.5/05/05. ***Continues** Information Malaysia, 0126-6195.*

CN/0711-2157
INFORMATION PROCHE-ORIENT. [Inf. Proche-Orient]. Periodical. French. Six times a year. 12.00Can$ Canada; $10.00 US. Information Proche-Orient, 1310 Avenue Green/Suite 710, Montreal Quebec H3Z 2B2 Canada. **Tel** (514)934-0771, FAX (514)933-8211. **ED** Gilbert Lemieux. **DD** 956/.04/05. **UDC** 327(569.4:71). **Bk Rev. Circ:** 8,000 (ctrl).
Desc: Covers Canada-Israel relations, Quebec-Israel relations, the French language, Quebec, Canada and Israel; includes commentaries, observations and press reports.

KO
INMUN KWAHAK NONCHONG. Periodical. English (Korean). Konguk Taehakkyo Pusol Inmun Kwahak Yonguso, 93-1 Mojin-dong, Songdong-ku, Seoul South Korea. **LC** DS904; .I56.

US/1054-8025
INSIDE JAPAN : HARVARD'S UNDERGRADUATE JAPAN JOURNAL. [Inside Jpn.]. **Added/Corp** Inside Japan (Organization). Vol. 1, No. 1 (Feb. 1991)-. Periodical. English. sa. $7.00 (U.S.). Inside Japan, PO Box 1696, Cambridge MA 02238. **LC** WMLC 90/0735. **DD** 952.

US/1065-1500
INTERNATIONAL EXAMINER (SEATTLE, WASH. 1973). (INTERNATIONAL EXAMINER.). [Int. exam.]. (1973)-. Newspaper. English. Twenty-four times a year. $18.00 one year; $29.00 two year. International Examiner, 622 South Washington Street, Seattle WA 98104. **Tel** (206)624-3925. **ED** Jeff Lin. **DD** 305. **Bk Rev**, (Qty: 20-50). **Ad Acc, Adv Mgr:** Ron Bruan, **Tel** (206)624-3925. **Circ:** 10,000 (ctrl).

KO/0303-3007
INTERNATIONAL JOURNAL OF KOREAN STUDIES. [Int. j. Korean stud.]. **VFOAT** Han-Kuk Yon-Ku. V. 1- 1973-. Periodical. English. sa. $5.00. Yonsei University Press, Korean Studies Institute, 120 Seoul Korea. **LC** DS901; .I56. **DD** 915.19/03/05. **UDC** 951.9.

HK
INTERNATIONAL WHO'S WHO IN ASIAN STUDIES. **See** Biographies.

NE
JAARBERICHT VAN HET VOORAZIATISCH-EGYPTISCH GENOOTSCHAP EX ORIENTE LUX. **Main/Corp** Vooraziatisch-Egyptisch Genootschap ex Oriente Lux. **VFOAT** Annuaire de la Societe Orientale ex Oriente Lux. No. 1- 1933-. English. be. Fl50.00. Ex Oriente Lux, Postbus 9515, 2300 RA Leiden The Netherlands. **ED** K R Veenhof. **Circ:** 700.

IR
JAMIAH-I NAVIN. **Added/Corp** Inqilab-i Shah va Millat (Society). Vol. 1, (Tabistan 1353 Summer 1974)-. Periodical. Persian. qt. 200.00. PO Box 11/1482, Tehran Iran. **LC** DS251; .J34.

JA/0388-0435
JAPAN ECHO. Vol. 1 (1974)-. Periodical. English. qt (5 issues). $97.00. Nihon Faxon Company Ltd, 4th Floor/Kurihara Building, 7-8-13 Nishi Shinjuku-ku, Tokyo 160 Japan. **Tel** 03-367-3081. **(Subscription address:** Maruzen Company Ltd., PO Box 5050, Import & Export Department, Tokyo 100 31 Japan.**)** **LC** DS801; .J256. **DD** 952/.005. Documents available from UMI Article Clearinghouse.
Ind/Abst Expand. Acad. Index (1992-); Geogr. Abstr. Human Geogr.; Int. Dev. Abstr. (?-?); Newsp. Period. Abstr. (1989-).

UK/0955-5803
JAPAN FORUM (OXFORD, ENGLAND). (JAPAN FORUM.). **Added/Corp** British Association for Japanese Studies. Vol. 1, No. 1 (April 1989)-. Periodical. English (summaries and/or abstracts in Japanese). sa. £60.00 UK & Europe; $112.00 other. Oxford University Press, Walton Street, Oxford OX2 6DP England. **Tel** 011 44 865 56767, FAX 011 44 865 267773, telex 837330 OXPRES G. **(Subscription address:** Oxford University Press / USA, Journals Marketing Department, Oxford University Press, 2001 Evans Road, Cary NC 27513.**)** **[CCC].** available on microfilm and microfiche from University Microfilms International (UMI).
Desc: Provides scholarly articles on Japanese culture and history.
Ind/Abst Am. Hist. Life (1991-); Int. Bibliogr. Sociol.

●CN/1183-885X
JAPAN FOUNDATION PROGRAMS AVAILABLE IN CANADA, THE. [Jpn. Found. programs available Can.]. **Main/Corp** Kokusai Koryu Kikin. Toronto Office. **VFOAT** Programs Available in Canada. (1993)-. English. **DD** 952/.0071/171.

US/0446-6241
JAPAN LETTER. Vol. 1 (Jan. 1954)-. English. wk. $175.00. Asia Letter Group, GPO Box 10874, Central Hong Kong. **Tel** 011 852 5 262950, FAX 011 852 5 267131, telex 61166. **(Subscription address:** Asia Letter Group PO Box 88189 Los Angeles, CA 90009**)** **ED** Charles R. Smith. **LC** DS889; .J337. **DD** 952/.005. **Bk Rev.** ctrl circ.
Desc: An analysis of political and economical developments of Japan. Published for people doing business with Japan.
Ind/Abst Text. Technol. Dig.

US/1053-4997
JAPAN NOTEBOOK. ***Suspended.*** [Jpn. noteb.]. **Added/Corp** Japan Research Group. (19??)-Vol. 5 No. 1 (Sept. 1993). Periodical. English. bm. $30.00 (one year), $54.00 (two years), $72.00 (three years) US; $40.00 (one year), $74.00 (two years), $102.00 (three years) includes postage other. Japan Research Group, 9203 Springbreeze Court, Fort Wayne IN 46804. **Tel** (219)436-4406. **ED** KayLynne Isca. **DD** 952. **Bk Rev**, (Qty: 15-20).
Desc: Newsletter for educators, administrators, and executives interested in Japan. Includes reviews, insights, grant/fellowship information, business tips, and editorials.

JA/0021-4590
JAPAN QUARTERLY. **Added/Corp** Asahi Shinbunsha. (Oct. 1954)-. Periodical. English. qt. $39.80. **(Subscription address:** Japan Publications Trading Company, Ltd., PO Box 5030, Tokyo International, Tokyo 100-31 Japan.**)** **LC** DS801; .J274. **DD** 952/.005. **Pr Rev.** available on microfilm and microfiche from University Microfilms International (UMI). Documents available from The Genuine Article, UMI Article Clearinghouse.
Ind/Abst Acad. Abstr. Full Text Elite (July 1990-); Acad. Abstr. (July 1990-); Acad. Search (July 1990-); Am. Hist. Life (1972-); ARTbibliogr. Mod.; Arts Humanit. Citation Index [Full Cov.]; Curr. Contents Arts Humanit.; Curr. Contents Soc. Behav. Sci.; INFO-SOUTH Abstr.; Int. Polit. Sci. Abstr.; Mag. Search; MLA Int. Bibl. Books Artic. Mod. Lang. Lit.; Newsp. Period. Abstr. (1988-); PAIS Int. Print (1991-); Peace Res. Abstr. J. (1964-1967); Res. Alert [Full Cov.]; Soc. Sci. Source (Jul. 1990-); Soc. Sci. Cit. Index [Full Cov.]; Soc. Sci. Index; Soc. Sci. Index Fulltext (July 1988-) [Full Txt.].

II/0377-0370
JAPAN QUARTERLY (NEW DELHI). (JAPAN QUARTERLY.). Vol. 1; Oct. 1974-. Periodical. English. qt. $3.50. India Committee for Studies on Economic Development in India and Japan, Yojana Rhauan Parliament Street, New Delhi India. **LC** DS801; .J2739. **DD** 952/.005. **UDC** 952.0.
Ind/Abst Acad. Ind. [Computer File] (1987-); Expand. Acad. Index (1987-).

US/1070-9363
JAPAN SOCIETY NEWSLETTER. [Jpn. Soc. newsl.]. **Main/Corp** Japan Society (New York, N.Y.). (19??)-. Newsletter. English. mo. $30.00. Japan Society Inc., 333 East 47th Street, New York NY 10017. **Tel** (212)832-1155, FAX (212)755-6752, telex 234450 JSNY. **DD** 952.

PK
JAVIDAN. Periodical. Urdu (Urdu). 30.00. Zahur Alam Shahid, Javidan, Lahaur Pakistan. **LC** DS376; .J38.

MY/0126-5644
JEBAT. [Jebat]. V. 1- 1971/72-. Malay. Persatuan Sejarah Universiti Kebangsaan Malaysia, D/A Jabatan Sejarah, Kuala Lumpur Malaysia. **LC** DS591; .J42.

MY/0126-5172
JERNAL SEJARAH. [J. sejarah]. Began in 1960. Malay (English). $2.50. Historical Society, University of Malaysia, D/A Jabatan Sejarah, Kuala Lumpa Malaysia. **LC** DS591; .J48.

US/0021-6305
JEWISH AFFAIRS (NEW YORK, N.Y.). (JEWISH AFFAIRS.). [Jew. aff.]. **VFOAT** Yidishe Inyonim. Began in 1971?. Periodical. English (Yiddish). bm. $6.00, $1.25 single issue. Communist Party U S A, 235 West 23 Street, New York NY 10011. **Tel** (212)989-4994. **ED** Herbert Aptheker and Lewis M Moroze. **LC** DS101. **DD** 909/.04924/005. **UDC** 933. **Circ:** 1,574.
Desc: Progressive and internationalist publication.

CC
JIH-PEN HSUEH KAN / JAPANESE STUDIES / CHUNG-HUA JIH-PEN HSUEH HUI, CHUNG-KUO SHE HUI KO HSUEH YUAN JIH-PEN YEN CHIU SO CHU PAN. **Added/Corp** Chung-Hua Jih-Pen Hsueh Hui. Chung-Kuo She Hui ko Hsueh Yuan. Jih-Pen Yen Chiu So. **VFOAT** Japanese Studies. (1991)-. Periodical. Chinese. bm. Jih-Pen Hsueh Kan Tsa Chih She, Chung-Kuo Kuo Chi Tu Shu Mao I Tsung Kung Ssu, PO Box 399, Beijing, People's Republic of China. **LC** DS801; .J615. **DD** 952/.005.

II/0377-743X
JIJNASA. V. 1- Jan./Apr. 1974-. Periodical. English. qt. $10.00. University of Rajastha, Department of History and Indian Culture, 2118 Ansari Road, New Delhi 110002 India. **LC** DS423; .J55. **DD** 954/.005. **UDC** 954.

II
JIJNASA (CALCUTTA, INDIA). (JIJNASA.). Periodical. Bengali (Bengali). qt. Rs30.00 India; Rs130.00 (airmail) other. Jijnasa Educational Society, 4 Jagadishnath Roy Lane, Calcutta 70000 India. **Tel** 5 53988. **ED** Sibnarayan Ray. **LC** PK1700; .J55. Index available. **Bk Rev. Ad Acc. Circ:** 2,000.

Desc: A journal of inquiry and ideas. Publishes original and critical essays in history, philosophy, art literature, social theory, East-West relations.

NE/0021-9096
JOURNAL OF ASIAN AND AFRICAN STUDIES (LEIDEN).
(JOURNAL OF ASIAN AND AFRICAN STUDIES.). [J. Asian Afr. stud.]. Vol. 1 (Jan. 1966)-. Academic Scholarly Publication. English. sa. Fl150.00 (institutions) Netherlands; $85.75 other. E. J. Brill, Postbus 9000, 2300 PA Leiden Netherlands. **Tel** 011 31 71 312624, FAX 011 31 71 317532, telex 39296 BRILL NL. **ED** K. Ishwaran and J. W. Burton. **LC** DT1; .J66. **DD** 309.1/5. **[CCC]**. **Pr Rev. Circ:** 256. Documents available from The Genuine Article, UMI Article Clearinghouse.
Desc: Presents a scholarly account of studies on man and society in the developing nations of Asia and Africa. By uniting contributions from anthropology, sociology, history, and related social sciences using knowledge gleaned from pure research, it helps in the reconstruction of societies entering a phase of advanced technology.
Ind/Abst ABC POL SCI; Abstr. Anthropol.; Acad. Search (July 1993-); Am. Hist. Life (1970-); Anthropol. Index; Anthropol. Lit.; Appl. Soc. Sci. Index Abstr.; Arts Humanit. Citation Index [Select. Cov.]; Curr. Contents Soc. Behav. Sci.; Expand. Acad. Index (1989-); Geogr. Abstr. Human Geogr.; Humanit. Source (Jul. 1993-); INFO-SOUTH Abstr.; Int. Bibliogr. Sociol.; Int. Dev. Abstr.; Int. Labour Doc.; Int. Polit. Sci. Abstr.; Mag. Search; Middle East Abstr. Index; Newsp. Period. Abstr. (1991-); Peace Res. Abstr. J. (1969-1975); Res. Alert [Full Cov.]; Soc. Plann. Policy Dev. Abstr.; Soc. Sci. Source (Jul. 1993-); Soc. Sci. Cit. Index [Full Cov.]; Soc. Sci. Index; Soc. Sci. Index Fulltext (July 1988-) [Full Txt.]; Sociol. Abstr.; Women Stud. Abstr.

GW/0021-910X
JOURNAL OF ASIAN HISTORY.
[J. Asian hist.]. Vol. 1 (1967)-. Periodical. English (French, German and Russian). sa. DM88.00. Otto Harrassowitz Verlag, Taunusstrasse 14, Postfach 2929, D-65019 Wiesbaden Germany. **Tel** 011 49 611 5300, FAX 530570, telex 4186 135 OH D. **ED** Denis Sinor. **LC** DS1; .J64. **UDC** 950. **[CCC]**. Index available. **Bk Rev. Ad Acc. Circ:** 660. available on microfilm and microfiche from University Microfilms International (UMI). Documents available from The Genuine Article, UMI Article Clearinghouse.
Ind/Abst Acad. Search (July 1993-); Am. Hist. Life (1967-); Arts Humanit. Citation Index [Full Cov.]; Curr. Contents Arts Humanit.; Expand. Acad. Index (1989-); Hist. Source (July 1993-); Humanit. Index; Humanit. Source (Jul. 1993-); Index Islam. Lit.; INFO-SOUTH Abstr.; Mag. Search; Newsp. Period. Abstr. (1991-); Numis. Lit.; Res. Alert [Full Cov.]; Soc. Sci. Cit. Index [Select. Cov.].

US/0021-9118
JOURNAL OF ASIAN STUDIES, THE.
Added/Corp Association for Asian Studies. Vol. 1 (Nov. 1941)-. Periodical. English. qt. $50.00. Association for Asian Studies Inc., University of Michigan, 1 Lane Hall, Ann Arbor MI 48109. **Tel** (313)665-2490, FAX (313)665-3801. **ED** David Buck. **LC** DS501; .F274. **DD** 950.05. Index available. **Bk Rev. Ad Acc. Pr Rev. Acid Free. Circ:** 8,400 (ctrl). available on microfilm from University Microfilms International (UMI); available on microfiche. Documents available from The Genuine Article, UMI Article Clearinghouse.
Desc: A publication in the field of Asian studies. Contains articles dealing with all disciplines in humanities and social science.
Ind/Abst ABC POL SCI; Abstr. Anthropol.; Acad. Abstr. Full Text Elite (July 1990-); Acad. Abstr. (July 1990-); Acad. Ind. [Computer File] (1987-); Acad. Search (July 1990-); Am. Hist. Life (1956-); Am. Bibliogr. Slavic East Europ. Stud.; Anthropol. Lit.; Arts Humanit. Citation Index [Select. Cov.]; Book Rev. Index; Curr. Contents Soc. Behav. Sci.; Expand. Acad. Index (1987-); Humanit. Index; Index Islam. Lit.; Index Book Rev. Relig.; INFO-SOUTH Abstr.; Int. Bibliogr. Sociol.; Int. Labour Doc.; Int. Polit. Sci. Abstr.; J. Ferrocement; LABORDOC; Mag. Search; Middle East Abstr. Index; MLA Int. Bibl. Books Artic. Mod. Lang. Lit.; Newsp. Period. Abstr. (1986-); Res. Alert [Full Cov.]; Soc. Sci. Source (Jul. 1990-); Soc. Sci. Cit. Index [Full Cov.]; Soc. Sci. Index; Sociol. Educ. Abstr.; Stud. Women Abstr.; U.S. Polit. Sci. Doc.; Women Stud. Abstr.

PK
JOURNAL OF CENTRAL ASIA.
Added/Corp Centre for the Study of the Civilizations of Central Asia (Pakistan). (July 1978)-. Periodical. English. Twice a year. $50.00. Quaid-I-Azam University Centre for the Study of the Civilizations of Central Asia, Islamabad Pakistan. **Tel** 011 92 51 810220. **ED** A.H. Dani. **LC** DS785.A1; J68. **DD** 958/.005. cum. index. **Bk Rev. Circ:** 1,000.
Desc: History, archaeology, and anthropology of the central Asian region.
Ind/Abst Index Islam. Lit.

US/0278-2847
JOURNAL OF CHINESE STUDIES.
[J. Chin. stud.]. **VFOAT** Han Hsueh. No. 1 (Spring 1980)-. Periodical. English. $2.00. Chinese Program, Department of Foreign Languages, San Francisco State University, 1600 Holloway, San Francisco CA 94132. **LC** DS703.4; .J67. **DD** 951. **UDC** 951.

UK/0047-2336
JOURNAL OF CONTEMPORARY ASIA.
[J. contemp. Asia]. **VFOAT** JCA; J.C.A. Vol. 1, No. 1 (Autumn 1970)-. Academic Scholarly Publication. English. qt. $25.00 (individuals); $44.45 (other) (surface mail); $57.00*(airmail). Journal of Contemporary Asia, PO Box 592, Manila Philippines 1099. **ED** Bruce McFarlane and Peter Limqueco. **LC** DS1; .J65. **DD** 950/.05. Index available. **Bk Rev. Ad Acc. Pr Rev. Circ:** 2,800. available on microfilm and microfiche from University Microfilms International (UMI). Documents available from The Genuine Article, UMI Article Clearinghouse.
Desc: A scholarly journal concerned with the nature and theory of social change in contemporary Asia.
Ind/Abst Acad. Search (July 1993-); Am. Hist. Life (1973-); Appl. Soc. Sci. Index Abstr.; Arts Humanit. Citation Index [Select. Cov.]; Asia.-Pac. Econ. Lit.; Curr. Contents Soc. Behav. Sci.; Expand. Acad. Index (1989-); Index Islam. Lit.; INFO-SOUTH Abstr.; Int. Bibliogr. Sociol.; Int. Dev. Abstr. (?-?); Int. Labour Doc.; Int. Polit. Sci. Abstr.; LABORDOC; Leis. Recreat. Tour. Abstr.; Mag. Search; Middle East Abstr. Index; Newsp. Period. Abstr. (1991-); Res. Alert [Full Cov.]; Rev. Plant Pathol.; Rice Abstr.; Rural Dev. Abstr.; Soc. Sci. Source (Jul. 1993-); Soc. Sci. Cit. Index [Full Cov.]; Soc. Sci. Index; Soc. Sci. Index Fulltext (1988-) [Full Txt.]; World Agric. Econ.

KO/1010-1608
JOURNAL OF EAST ASIAN AFFAIRS, THE.
[J. East Asian aff.]. **Added/Corp** Kukche Munje Chosa Yonguso (Seoul, Korea). Vol. 1, No. 1 (Jan. 1981)-. English. sa. $10.00 Korea; $14.00 other. Research Institute for International Affairs, CPO Box 6856, Seoul Korea. **Tel** 011 82 2 2122712. **ED** Chung No-gwan. **LC** DS501; .J64. **DD** 950/.05. **[CCC]. Circ:** 2,000 (ctrl).
Ind/Abst PAIS Int. Print.

II/0022-1562
JOURNAL OF HISTORICAL RESEARCH.
[J. hist. res.]. Periodical. English. sa. Rs50.00 India; $16.00 North America. Ranchi University / History, Department of History, Ranchi India. **Tel** 21276, 22353. **ED** S M Pathak. **LC** DS401; .J68. **DD** 915.4/03/05. **UDC** 954. **Bk Rev.**

II/0022-1775
JOURNAL OF INDIAN HISTORY.
[J. Indian hist.]. **Added/Corp** University of Kerala. Dept. of History. University of Allahabad. Dept. of Modern Indian History. University of Travancore. University of Kerala. Vol. 1, No. 1 (Nov. 1921)-. Periodical. English. an. $15.00. Department of History / Kerala, Kariyavattom Trivandrum, 685001 Kerala India. **(Subscription address:** Prints India, 11 Darya Ganj, New Delhi 110002 India.**) LC** DS401; .J7. cum. index.
Ind/Abst Am. Hist. Life (1965-); Numis. Lit.

US/0095-6848
JOURNAL OF JAPANESE STUDIES, THE.
[J. Jpn. stud.]. V. 1- Autumn 1974-. Academic Scholarly Publication. English. sa. $33.00. Journal of Japanese Studies, Thomson Hall Drive-05, University of Washington, Seattle WA 98197. **Tel** (206)543-9302, FAX (206)685-0668. **ED** Susan B Hanley. **LC** DS801; .J7. **DD** 952/.005. **UDC** 952. Index available. cum. index. **Bk Rev**, (Qty: 35-50). **Ad Acc. Pr Rev. Circ:** 1,800. Documents available from The Genuine Article, UMI Article Clearinghouse.
Desc: Interdisciplinary scholarly journal on Japan containing refereed research articles, translations of essays and opinion from Japanese, and long reviews of the most significant new books.
Ind/Abst Acad. Search (July 1993-); Am. Hist. Life (1974-); Arts Humanit. Citation Index [Full Cov.]; Curr. Contents Arts Humanit.; Expand. Acad. Index (1989-); Humanit. Index; Humanit. Source (Jul. 1993-); INFO-SOUTH Abstr.; Mag. Search; MLA Int. Bibl. Books Artic. Mod. Lang. Lit.; Newsp. Period. Abstr. (1991-); Res. Alert [Full Cov.]; Soc. Sci. Cit. Index [Select. Cov.]; U.S. Polit. Sci. Doc.

II/0377-0443
JOURNAL OF KERALA STUDIES.
[J. Kerala stud.]. **Added/Corp** University of Kerala. (1973)-. Periodical. English. Four times a year. $3.52. University of Kerala Department of Tamil, Kariovattom Trivandrum, 685001 Kerala India. **LC** DS485.K4; J67. **DD** 954/.83/005.

US/0047-2522
JOURNAL OF KOREAN AFFAIRS.
[J. Korean aff.]. **Added/Corp** Research Institute on Korean Affairs. Vol. 1 (Apr. 1971)-. Periodical. English. qt. $6.00. Research Institute on Korean Affairs, 8555 16th Street, Suite 703, Silver Spring MD 20910. **LC** DS901; .J6. **DD** 915.19/03/05. available on microfilm from University Microfilms International (UMI).
Ind/Abst Am. Hist. Life (1973-1977).

US/0731-1613
JOURNAL OF KOREAN STUDIES (SEATTLE, WASH. : 1979), THE.
(THE JOURNAL OF KOREAN STUDIES.). [J. Korean stud.]. **Added/Corp** Society for Korean Studies (U.S.). Vol. 1 (1979)-. Periodical. English. an. $15.00 US, Canada and Mexico; $20.00 other. University of California Department of History, c/o Charlotte Forth, Los Angeles CA 90089. **Tel** (213)740-1668, FAX (213)740-6999. **ED** Michael Robinson. **LC** DS901; .J68. **Bk Rev. Ad Acc. Pr Rev. Circ:** 350 (ctrl). ***Continues*** *Occasional Papers on Korea, 0364-7676.*
Ind/Abst Am. Hist. Life (1979-).

US/8756-2235
JOURNAL OF MODERN KOREAN STUDIES, THE.
(THE JOURNAL OF MODERN KOREAN STUDIES / KUNDAE HANGUK YONGU.). [J. mod. Korean stud.]. **VFOAT** Kundae Hanguk Yongu. Vol. 1 (Apr. 1984)-. Academic Scholarly Publication. English. an. $15.00. Journal of Modern Korean Studies, 209 Monroe Mary Washington College, Fredericksburg VA 22401. **Tel** (703)899-4309. **ED** Key S. Ryang. **LC** DS901; .J64. **DD** 951.9/005. Index available. **Bk Rev. Ad Acc. Circ:** 300 (ctrl).
Desc: A scholarly, nonprofit and academic publication stressing originality in research on Korean history, culture, economy and politics.
Ind/Abst Int. Bibliogr. Sociol.

MK/0378-8180
JOURNAL OF OMAN STUDIES, THE.
[J. Oman stud.]. **Added/Corp** Oman. Ministere de l'Information et de la Culture. Vol. 1 (1975)-. Periodical. English. ir. Price varies per volume. Ministry National Heritage Culture, PO Box 668, c/o Dr. Ali A. Shanfari, Muscat Sultanate of Oman. **Tel** 011 968 602225, 011 968 602555. **ED** Ali Al-Shanfari. **LC** DS247.O6; A24. **DD** 953/.53/005. Index available. cum. index. **Bk Rev. Ad Acc.** ctrl circ.
Ind/Abst Agrofor. Abstr. (1991-); Anthropol. Lit.; Art Archaeol. Tech. Abstr.; For. Abstr.; Grasslands For. Abstr.; Index Vet.; Middle East Abstr. Index; Rev. Agric. Entomol.; Rev. Med. Vet. Entomol.; Rural Dev. Abstr.; Soils Fert.

HK/0022-331X
JOURNAL OF ORIENTAL STUDIES (HONG KONG).
(JOURNAL OF ORIENTAL STUDIES.). [J. orient. stud.]. **Added/Corp** University of Hong Kong. Institute of Oriental Studies. University of Hong Kong. Centre of Asian Studies. (Jan. 1954)-. Periodical. English (Chinese). sa (Jan., Jul.). HK$200.00 (institution), HK$150.00 (individual). University of Hong Kong, Centre of Asian Studies, Hong Kong Hong Kong. **Tel** 011 852 5 8592460, FAX 011 852 5 5595884, telex 71919 CEREB HX. **ED** Leung Chi Keung, P L Chan, D A Levin, C Y Sin, A Y C Lui. **LC** DS501; .H6. **DD** 950/.05. Index available. cum. index. **Bk Rev. Ad Acc. Circ:** 300 (ctrl). available on microfilm and microfiche from University Microfilms International (UMI).
Desc: Includes traditional and contemporary issues in history, geography, fine arts, languages, literature, philosophy, law, architecture, archaeology, economics, political science, sociology and anthropology of China, Japan, Korea and Southeast Asia.
Ind/Abst Am. Hist. Life (1954-).

II
JOURNAL OF REGIONAL HISTORY.
Vol. 1 (1980)-. Periodical. English. an. $6.00. Registrar / Punjab, Guru Nanak Dev University, Amritsar Punjab India. **LC** DS401; .J73. **DD** 954/.005. **UDC** 954.

SI/0022-4634
JOURNAL OF SOUTHEAST ASIAN STUDIES (SINGAPORE).
(JOURNAL OF SOUTHEAST ASIAN STUDIES.). [J. Southeast Asian stud.]. Vol. 1 (Mar. 1970)-. Periodical. English. Twice a year (Mar. & Sept.). $36.00. Singapore University Press Pte Ltd, Yusof Ishak House, National University of Singapore, 10 Kent Ridge Crescent, Singapore 0511 Republic of Singapore. **Tel** 011 65 7761148, FAX 011 65 7740652. **ED** NG Chin-Keong. **LC** DS501; .J652. Index available (bound in first issue). **Bk Rev. Ad Acc. Adv Mgr:** same as editor. **Circ:** 1,000 (ctrl). Documents available from The Genuine Article, UMI Article Clearinghouse, Petroleum Abstracts Document Delivery Service. ***Continues*** *Journal, Southeast Asian History, 0217-7811.*
Desc: Covers all aspects of Southeast Asian studies.
Ind/Abst ABC POL SCI; Acad. Abstr. Full Text Elite (Jan. 1991-); Acad. Abstr. (Jan. 1991-); Acad. Ind. [Computer File] (1987-); Acad. Search (Jan. 1991-); Agrofor. Abstr. (1991-); Am. Hist. Life (1960-1962, 1967-); Arts Humanit. Citation Index [Select. Cov.]; Curr. Contents Soc. Behav. Sci.; Expand. Acad. Index (1987-); Geogr. Abstr. Human Geogr.; Humanit. Index; Humanit. Source (Jul. 1990-); Index Islam. Lit.; INFO-SOUTH Abstr.; Int. Bibliogr. Sociol.; Int. Dev. Abstr.; Int. Polit. Sci. Abstr.; Mag. Search; Newsp. Period. Abstr. (1991-); Pet. Abstr.; Recent. Publ. Artic.; Res. Alert [Full Cov.]; Rural Dev. Abstr.; Soc. Sci. Source (Jul. 1990-); Soc. Sci. Cit. Index [Full Cov.]; World Agric. Econ.

II
JOURNAL OF THE ANDHRA HISTORICAL RESEARCH SOCIETY.
Added/Corp Andhra Historical Research Society. Vol. 4 Pts. 1 & 2 (July/Oct.1929)-. Periodical. English (Sanskrit). mo. Indian Books and Periodicals, 2429 Tilak Street, Pahar Ganj, New Delhi 110005 India. cum. index. ***Continues*** *Quarterly Journal of the Andhra Historical Research Society.*

Desc: Publication of the Andhra Historical Society, includes a list of members.
Ind/Abst Numis. Lit.

BR/0304-2227
JOURNAL OF THE BURMA RESEARCH SOCIETY. (THE JOURNAL OF THE BURMA RESEARCH SOCIETY.). [J. Burma Res. Soc.]. **Main/Corp** Burma Research Society. V. 1- June 1911-. Periodical. English. sa. Burma Research Society, University Estate, Rangoon Burma. **LC** DS527; .B85a. **DD** 959.1. cum. index.
Ind/Abst Am. Hist. Life (1961, 1964); MLA Int. Bibl. Books Artic. Mod. Lang. Lit.

NE/0022-4995
JOURNAL OF THE ECONOMIC AND SOCIAL HISTORY OF THE ORIENT. [J. econ. soc. hist. Orient]. **VFOAT** Journal de l'Histoire Economique et Sociale de l'Orient. Vol. 1, Pt. 2 (Apr. 1958)-. Periodical. English (French and German). qt. Fl165.00 (institutions) Netherlands; $94.50 other. E. J. Brill, Postbus 9000, 2300 PA Leiden Netherlands. **Tel** 011 31 71 312624, FAX 011 31 71 317532, telex 39296 BRILL NL. **ED** H. T. Zurndorfer. **[CCC]. Circ:** 384. ***Continues*** *Journal of Economic and Social History of the Orient.*
Desc: Aims at furthering knowledge of the economic and social history of Asia and North Africa from the earliest times to the beginning of the 19th century. The issues include articles, miscellanea and review sections.
Ind/Abst Am. Hist. Life (1966-); Index Islam. Lit.; Int. Bibliogr. Sociol.; Middle East Abstr. Index; Numis. Lit.

II/0970-2814
JOURNAL OF THE INSTITUTE OF ASIAN STUDIES. Vol. 3, No. 2 (March 1986)-. Periodical. English. sa. $10.00. Director for Administration, Institute of Asian Studies, 10th East Street, Thirubanmiyur, Madras 600 041 India. **LC** DS1; .J643. **DD** 950/.05. ***Continues*** *Journal of Asian Studies (Madras, India).*

BG
JOURNAL OF THE INSTITUTE OF BANGLADESH STUDIES, THE. Main/Corp University of Rajshani Institute of Bangladesh Studies. V. 1-. English. an. Institute of Bangladesh Studies, Rajshaki University, Rajshaki Bangladesh. **LC** DS392.B3; U55A. **DD** 954.9/2/008. **UDC** 954.93.

II
JOURNAL OF THE MADHYA PRADESH ITIHASA PARISHAD. Main/Corp Madhya Pradesh Itihasa Parishad. No. 1- 1959-. Multiple languages (English and Hindi). an. Rs10.00. Itihasa Parishad, The Managing Editor 7, Malviyanager 462003 Bhopal India. **LC** DS485.C3; M315A. **DD** 934/.005. **UDC** 934.

SI/0126-7353
JOURNAL OF THE MALAYSIAN BRANCH OF THE ROYAL ASIATIC SOCIETY. [J. Malays. Branch R. Asiat. Soc.]. **Added/Corp** Royal Asiatic Society of Great Britain and Ireland. Malaysian Branch. Vol. 37, Pt. 1 (1964)-. Periodical. English. Twice a year. $40.00 institutions; $20.00 individuals. Malaysian Branch of the Royal Asiatic Society, 130M Jalan Thamby Abdullah, 50470 Kuala Lumpur Malaysia. **Tel** 011 60 03 2748345. **LC** AS492; .S61. **Bk Rev. Circ:** 1,300. ***Continues*** *Journal of the Malayan Branch of the Royal Asiatic Society.*
Ind/Abst Am. Hist. Life (1969-); Anthropol. Index; Int. Bibliogr. Sociol.; MLA Int. Bibl. Books Artic. Mod. Lang. Lit.

AT/0030-5340
JOURNAL OF THE ORIENTAL SOCIETY OF AUSTRALIA, THE. [J. Orient. Soc. Aust.]. **Main/Corp** Oriental Society of Australia. (1960)-. Periodical. English. ir. 30.00Aus$. School of Asian Studies / Australia, University of Sydney, New South Wales 2006 Australia. **Tel** 011 61 2 692 4306. **ED** A.D. Syrohomla. **LC** DS41; .O77. **DD** 950. **Bk Rev. Ad Acc.** ctrl circ.
Desc: History, literature and thought of Asia.
Ind/Abst Am. Hist. Life (1988-); APAIS, Aust. Public Aff. Inf. Ser. (1963-).

UK/0035-869X
JOURNAL OF THE ROYAL ASIATIC SOCIETY OF GREAT BRITAIN & IRELAND. [J. R. Asiat. Soc. G.B. Irel.]. **Main/Corp** Royal Asiatic Society of Great Britain and Ireland. **VAT** Journal of the Royal Asiatic Society of Great Britain and Ireland. Vol. 1-20, (1834-1863); New Series, Vol. 1-21, (1864-1889); Series 3, (1889)-. Academic Scholarly Publication. English. Three times a year. $85.00 US, Canada and Mexico; £49.00 other. Cambridge University Press, The Edinburgh Building, Shaftesbury Road, Cambridge CB2 2RU United Kingdom. **Tel** 011 44 223 312393, FAX 011 44 223 325959. **(Subscription address:** Cambridge University Press / North America, 110 Midland Avenue, Port Chester NY 10573.) **ED** D. O. Morgan. **LC** AS122; .L72. **DD** 950/.05. cum. index. **Bk Rev. Ad Acc.** available in microform. Documents available from The Genuine Article. ***Supersedes*** *Royal Asiatic Society of Great Britain and Ireland. Transactions of the Royal Asiatic Society of Great Britain and Ireland;* ***Absorbed*** *Society of Biblical Archaeology (London. England) Proceedings of the Society of Biblical Archaeology.*
Desc: Aims to provide a forum for scholarly articles on the Indian Subcontinent, the Middle East, Central Asia, the Far East and South-east Asia. Publishes articles on history, archaeology, literature, language, religion and art, and up to half of each issue is devoted to reviews of books in these fields. Emphasis is on work that is of high quality and importance from a scholarly point of view, yet also accessible and interesting to as wide a range of readers as possible.
Ind/Abst Am. Hist. Life (1955, 1964-); Anthropol. Index; Arts Humanit. Citation Index [Full Cov.]; Br. Humanit. Index; Middle East Abstr. Index; MLA Int. Bibl. Books Artic. Mod. Lang. Lit.; Numis. Lit.; Res. Alert [Full Cov.]; Soc. Sci. Cit. Index [Select. Cov.].

TH
JOURNAL OF THE SIAM SOCIETY, THE. Main/Corp Siam Society. **VFOAT** JSS, Journal of the Siam Society. V. 1- 1904-. Periodical. English (German and French). an. $25.00. Siam Society, PO Box 65, Bangkok Thailand. **Tel** 011 66 2 2583494, 2583491. **ED** Kaset Pitakpaivan. **LC** DS561. **UDC** 959.3. **Bk Rev. Circ:** 1,500 (ctrl).
Desc: On arts and sciences in relation to Thailand and neighbouring countries.
Ind/Abst Am. Hist. Life (1960-); Int. Bibliogr. Sociol.; Leis. Recreat. Tour. Abstr.; MLA Int. Bibl. Books Artic. Mod. Lang. Lit.; Rice Abstr.; Rural Dev. Abstr.; World Agric. Econ.

US/0747-9301
JOURNAL OF THE SOCIETY FOR ARMENIAN STUDIES. (JOURNAL OF THE SOCIETY FOR ARMENIAN STUDIES : JSAS.). [J. Soc. Armen. stud.]. **Added/Corp** Society for Armenian Studies. **VFOAT** JSAS. Vol. 1 (1984)-. English (Armenian). an. $30.00. Society of Armenian Studies, 4901 Evergreen Road, University of Michigan, Dearborn MI 48128. **Tel** (313)593-5181, FAX (313)593-5452. **ED** James Russell. **LC** DS161; .J68. **DD** 956. **Bk Rev. Ad Acc. Pr Rev. Circ:** 500.
Desc: Devoted to many aspects of Armenian culture, but primarily literature, arts, religion, and history.
Ind/Abst Middle East J.

SI
JOURNAL OF THE SOUTH SEAS SOCIETY. (SOUTH SEAS SOCIETY JOURNAL.). **Main/Corp** Nan-Yang Hsueh Hui, Singapore. **VFOAT** Nan Yang Hsueh Pao. Chinese (Chinese and English). South Seas Society Journal, PO Box 709, Singapore Singapore. **UDC** 959. **Bk Rev. Circ:** 700.
Desc: History of southeast Asia with special emphasis on ethnic Chinese in the region. Interdisciplinary in approach.

CE/1013-9818
JOURNAL OF THE SRI LANKA BRANCH OF THE ROYAL ASIATIC SOCIETY. [J. Sri Lanka Branch R. Asiat. Soc.]. **Main/Corp** Royal Asiatic Society of Great Britain and Ireland. Sri Lanka Branch. **Added/Corp** Royal Asiatic Society of Great Britain and Ireland. Sri Lanka Branch. **VFOAT** Journal of the Royal Asiatic Society, Sri Lanka Branch. New Ser. Vol. 16-27 (1972/1982)-. English (Sinhalese). an. $12.00. Royal Asiatic Society of Sri Lanka, 86 Ananda Coomaraswany Maoseli, Colombo 7 Sri Lanka. **Tel** 011 94 699249. **ED** G.P.S.H. de Silva. **LC** AS472; .C5. **DD** 052. Index available. **Bk Rev. Circ:** 600. ***Continues*** *Royal Asiatic Society of Great Britain and Ireland. Ceylon Branch. Journal, 0304-2235.*
Desc: Institutes and promotes inquiries into the history, religions, languages, literature, arts, science and social conditions of the present and former people of the Island of Sri Lanka and connected cultures.
Ind/Abst Am. Hist. Life (1964-1975, 1980-); Anthropol. Index.

AT/1030-6390
JOURNAL OF VIETNAMESE STUDIES. Added/Corp Australian Association of Vietnamese Studies. **VFOAT** Vietnamese Studies. Vol. 1, No. 1 (Jan. 1988)-. Periodical. English. ir (2-4 a year). 20.00Aus$. Australian Association of Vietnamese Studies, GPO Box 2918DD, Melbourne 3001 Victoria Australia. **Tel** 11 61 3 353 9294, FAX 011 61 3 350 1259. **ED** Ngruyerr Xuan Hru. **LC** DS556.42; .J68. **DD** 959.7/005. cum. index. **Ad Acc, Adv Mgr Tel** 03 353 9294.

MY/0126-8988
JURNAL SEJARAH MELAKA. [J. sejarah Melaka]. V. 1- June 1976-. Periodical. English (Malay). $2.00 single issue. Perstuan Sejarah Malaysia Cawangan Melaka, Sekolah Menengah Tun Tuah, Kampung Lapan Bacang, Melaka Malaysia. **LC** DS598.M45; J87.

IS
KAHOL VE-LAVAN. Periodical. Hebrew. Moatsah Ha-Tsiburit Le-Maan, Yehude Berit Ha-Moatsot, Hesin St 4A, Tel-Aviv Israel. **LC** DS135.R92; K33.

MY/0127-4082
KAJIAN MALAYSIA : JOURNAL OF MALAYSIAN STUDIES. Added/Corp Universiti Sains Malaysia. **VFOAT** Journal of Malaysian Studies. Vol. 1, No. 1 (June 1983)-. Academic Scholarly Publication. English (Malay). Twice a year. $12.00 (individuals); $18.00 (institutions). Kajian Malaysia, Universiti Sains Malaysia, Minden 11800 Penang Malaysia. **Tel** 011 60 4 883822 ext. 728, FAX 011 60 4 871526, telex USMLIB MA 40254. **ED** J. Saravanamuttu. **LC** DS591; .K34. **DD** 959.5/005. **Bk Rev. Ad Acc. Circ:** 120.
Desc: Committed to the advancement of scholarly knowledge on Malaysia in several branches of the social sciences and humanities.
Ind/Abst Am. Hist. Life (1983-); Rice Abstr.; Rural Dev. Abstr.; World Agric. Econ.

PH
KALINANGAN. Added/Corp Philippines. Bureau of National and Foreign Information. National Museum (Philippines). Vol. 1 (Jan./Mar. 1975)-. Periodical. English. qt. Department of Public Information / Philippines, Room 210/National Press Club Building, Magallanes Drive, Intramuros Philippines. **LC** DS651; .K35. **DD** 959.9/005.
Ind/Abst Hum. Rights Intern. Rep.; Index Philip. Period.

JA
KAN. VFOAT Han. Yearly Vol. 1- 1972-. Periodical. Japanese (Japanese). mo. ¥5500. Nihon Ika Daigaku, (Nippon Medical School), 1-5, Sendagi 1 Chome, Bunkyoku, Tokyoto 113 Japan. **LC** DS901; .K34.

CC
KAN-SU HUA PAO. VFOAT Gansuhuabao. Periodical. Chinese. RMBY1.00. Post Office, Lan-Chou Shih, People's Republic of China. **Tel** 26492. **LC** DS793.K2; K2875. **DD** 951/.45/005. **UDC** 951.

JA
KANAGAWA KENRITSU MAIZO BUNKAZAI SENTA NENPO. Added/Corp Kanagawa Kenritsu Maizo Bunkazai Senta. (1983)-. Japanese. an. Kanagawa Kenritsu Maizo, Bunkazai Senta 191-1 Nakamura-cho 3 Minami-ku, Yokohama-shi 232 Japan. **LC** DS894.49.K3435; K37.

JA
KANAGAWA KENSHI KENKYU / KANAGAWA KENSHI HENSHU IINKAI HEN. (19??)-. Periodical. Japanese. Kanagawa-ken Kemminbu Kenshi Henshusitsucho, 9-3 Momijigaoka, Nishi-ku, Yokohama-shi Japan. **LC** DS894.49.K34; A237.

CH
KAO SHIH WEN HSIEN. Added/Corp Kao-Hsiung Shih Wen Hsien Wei Yuan Hui. (1988)-. Periodical. Chinese. tq. Kao-Hsiung Shih Wen Hsien Wei Yuan Hui 400, Lien Tan Lu Tso Ying Ch U, Kao-Hsiung Taiwan. **LC** DS799.9.K38; K4. **DD** 951.24/9. ***Continues*** *Kao-Hsiung Wen Hsien.*

CE
KARAI OLI. Periodical. Tamil (Tamil). Rs1.50 single issue. Karai Nagar Development Association, 98 Vivekananda Road, Colombo-13 Kolumpu Ceylon Sri Lanka. **LC** DS489.25.T3; K33.

PH/0116-0923
KASARINLAN. (KASARINLAN : A QUARTERLY PUBLICATION OF THE THIRD WORLD STUDIES CENTER, UNIVERSITY OF THE PHILIPPINES.). [Kasarinlan]. **Added/Corp** University of the Philippines. Third World Studies Center. Vol. 1, No. 1 (3rd Quarter 1985)-. Periodical. English. Four times a year. $40.00 (institutions); $30.00 (individuals). Third World Studies Center, PO Box 210, University of the Philippines, Diliman Quezon City Philippines. **Tel** 011 63 2 976068 Ext. 783. **ED** Alexander Magno. **LC** DS651; .K36. **DD** 959.9/005. **Bk Rev. Ad Acc, Adv Mgr:** Carlites Escueta, **Tel** 995071 loc. 6783. **Circ:** 700.
Desc: It aims to analyze Phillipine and Third world underdevelopment and marginalization. It also includes empirical and theoretical studies on other problem areas, transcripts of the Center's fora, and accomodates documents sent by other institutions and cause oriented groups.
Ind/Abst Hum. Rights Intern. Rep.; Index Philip. Period.; Rural Dev. Abstr.

US/0895-0032
KATIPUNAN (OAKLAND, CALIF. : 1987). ***Ceased.*** (KATIPUNAN.). [Katipunan]. (1987)-(1991). Periodical. English (Tagalog). mo. Katipunan, PO Box 8477, Berkeley CA 94707-8477. **Tel** (510)845-4613. **LC** DS651; .K38. **DD** 959.9/005. cum. index. ***Continues*** *Ang Katipunan.*

JA
KIKAN NIHON SHISO SHI. VFOAT Nihon Shiso Shi. 1976 Edition-. Japanese. Three times a year. ¥1,400 Japan; $40.00 North America; $60.00 other. Perikansha, 24-4 Hongo 2 Bunkyo-ku, Tokyo 113 Japan. **Tel** 03-814-8515, FAX 03-814-3264. **ED** Kenji Miyata. **LC** DS821; .K34435. **Ad Acc. Circ:** 2,000 (ctrl).

PH
KINAADMAN. WISDOM. Added/Corp Xavier University (Cagayan de Oro City, Philippines) Ateneo e Davao University. Ateneo de Zamboanga. **VFOAT** Wisdom; Kina-Adman. Vol. 1 (1979)-. English. Twice a year. Cellar Book Shop, 18090 Wyoming, Detroit MI 48221. **Tel** (313)861-1776. **ED** M.A. Bernad. **LC** DS651;

History(General) —History of Asia

.K54. **DD** 959.9/005. **Bk Rev**. **Ad Acc**. **Circ**: 1,000.
Desc: Carries articles and book reviews of interest to people concerned with the Philippines, primarily in the area of humanities, i.e., folklore, sociology, history, anthropology etc.
Ind/Abst Index Philip. Period.

JA
KINDAI CHUGOKU. Vol. 1 (1977)-. Periodical. Japanese. Twice a year. $80.00. Gannando Shoten, 2 Kanda Jinbocho 2 Chiyoda-ku, Tokyo Japan. **(Subscription address**: Maruzen Company Ltd., PO Box 5050, Import & Export Department, Tokyo 100 31 Japan.) **LC** DS754; .K56.

JA
KINDAI CHUGOKU KENKYU IHO / HENSHUSHA, TOYO BUNKO KINDAI CHUGOKU KENKYU IINKAI. Japanese. an. ¥1500 Japan; $18.00 US. Toyo Bunko, 28-Ban 21-go, Honkomagome 2-chome, Bunkyo-ku, Tokyo-to Japan. **Tel** 03-942-0121. **LC** DS755.2; .K56. **Bk Rev**. **Circ**: 500.

JA
KITA CHOSEN KENKYU. **Added/Corp** Kokusai Kankei Kyodo Kenkyujo. Vol. 1, No. 1 (1974)-. Periodical. Japanese. mo. ¥1000. Kokusai Kankei Kyodo Kenkyujo, c/o Mita Nd Building 3F 5-3, Mita 1-chome, Minato-ku 108 Tokyo Japan. **LC** DS935.5; .K57.

LE
KITAB AL-SANAWI (MUASSASAH AL-ARABIYAN LIL-DIRASAT WA-AL-NASHR). (AL-KITAB AL-SANAWI.). 1981-. Arabic. an. Binayat Burj Al-Kartun, S B 11/546, Beirut Lebanon. **LC** DS126.5; .K56.

JA
KIYO. **Main/Corp** Kiyo (Ishikawa Kenritsu Kyodo Shiryokan). Periodical. Japanese. Ishikawa Kenritsu Kyodo Shiryokan, 2-ban 4-go Hirosaka 2-chome, Kanazawa-shi 920 Japan. **LC** DS894.59.I83; A295A.

CH
KO MING SHIH TZU LIAO / CHUNG-KUO JEN MIN CHENG CHIH HSIEH SHANG HUI I CHUAN KUO WEI YUAN HUI, WEN SHIH TZU LIAO YEN CHIU WEI YUAN HUI PIEN. 1-. Chinese. NT$0.60. Hsin Hua Shu Tien, Beijing, People's Republic of China. **Tel** 551253. **LC** DS773.83; .K62. **DD** 951.04. **UDC** 951.

JA
KOKUSAI KORYU KIKIN BUNKAJIN TANKI SHOHEISHA ICHIRAN. **Main/Corp** Kokusai Koryu Kikin. Japanese. Kokusai Koryu Kikin, c/o Park Building 3-6 Kioicho, Chiyoda-ku, Tokyo 102 Japan. **Tel** 03 2634504, telex J-23424 KIKINTYO. **LC** DS834.95; .K63F.

JA
KOKUSAI KORYU KIKIN FERO ICHIRAN. **Main/Corp** Kokusai Koryu Kikin. (19??)-. Japanese. Kokusai Koryu Kikin, c/o Park Building 3-6 Kioicho, Chiyoda-ku, Tokyo 102 Japan. **Tel** 03 2634504, telex J-23424 KIKINTYO. **LC** DS834.95; .K63a.

JA
KOKUSAI KORYU KIKIN NEMPO. **Main/Corp** Kokusai Koryu Kikin. Japanese (English). an. Free. Kokusai Koryu Kikin, c/o Park Building 3-6 Kioicho, Chiyoda-ku, Tokyo 102 Japan. **Tel** 03 2634504, telex J-23424 KIKINTYO. **LC** DS845; .K575B. ctrl circ.
Desc: Covers activities of the Japan foundation for the previous fiscal year.

JA
KOKUSAI KORYU KIKIN NYUSU / HENSHU, KOKUSAI KORYU KIKIN SOMUBU SOMUKA. Japanese. mo. Japan Foundation, Park Building, Kioicho-3-6, Chiyoda-ku, Tokyo 102 Japan. **Tel** 11 81 3 3263 4505, telex J-23424. **LC** DS801; .K7314. ctrl circ.

JA
KOKUSHIGAKU. VFOAT Journal of Japanese History. Japanese (Japanese). 2500. Kokushi Gakkai, c/o Kokugakuin Daigaku, 10-28 Higashi 4-chome Shibuya-ku, Tokyo Japan. **LC** DS801; .K74. **UDC** 952.

NP
KONAPI. VFOAT Kongpie. V. 1, No. 1 (Nov. 1980)-. Periodical. Nepali. mo. Rs10.00. Konapi Karyalaya, 21/77 Bagbazar, Kathmandu Nepal. **LC** DS493; .K66. **UDC** 954.135.

JA
KONNICHI NO KANKOKU. VFOAT Korea of Today. 1975-. Japanese (Japanese). Ajia Prsenta, 4-7 Akasaka, Minato-ku 107, Tokyo Japan. **LC** DS902; .K52.

KO
KOREA ANNUAL. Began in (1964)-. English. an. $33.00. Yonhap News Agency, PO Box Kwanghawamun 1039, Seoul Korea. **Tel** 82 2 3983114, American Customer Service: (800)821-8312. **LC** DS901; .K67. **DD** 915.9/005.
Desc: Review of Korean affairs, including chronology of year's events, overviews of culture, government, foreign relations, economy, laws and documents, social affairs, etc. Includes directory of government agencies, civic and business associations, and who's who.

US
KOREA BRIEFING. **Added/Corp** Asia Society. (1991)-. Periodical. English. $29.48. Westview Press Inc, 5500 Central Avenue, Boulder CO 80301. **Tel** (303)444-3541, FAX (303)449-3356.

KO
KOREA DIRECTORY, THE. (1968)-. English. an (Mar.). $75.00. Korea Directory Company, CPO Box 3955, 100-639 Seoul Korea. **Tel** 011 82 2 7761370. **LC** DS901; .K68. **DD** 951.9/5. **Continues** Foreign Community Directory.

KO/0023-3900
KOREA JOURNAL. [Korea j.]. **Added/Corp** Yunesuko Hanguk Wiwonhoe. Vol. 1, (Sept. 1961)-. Periodical. English. Four times a year (Mar., June, Sept., Dec.). $40.00. Korean National Commission, PO Box Central 64, Seoul Korea. **Tel** 011 82 2 7762805, FAX 011 82 2 7743956, telex 23231 2 Ext. 6364. **ED** Jeing Soo-Young. **LC** DS901; .K7. **DD** 951.9/005. **CODEN** KOJODS. Index available. **Ad Acc**. **Circ**: 3,000 (ctrl). Documents available from UMI Article Clearinghouse, CASDDS.
Ind/Abst Chem. Abstr.; Expand. Acad. Index (1992-); Int. Bibliogr. Sociol.; Int. Polit. Sci. Abstr.; MLA Int. Bibl. Books Artic. Mod. Lang. Lit.; Newsp. Period. Abstr. (1989-); RILM Abstr.

KO
KOREA PHOTO NEWS. Periodical. English. qt. Korea Photo News Inc, CPO Box 2147, Seoul Korea. **LC** DS901; .K72. **DD** 951.9/5043/05. **UDC** 951.9.

KO
KOREA PICTORIAL. **Added/Corp** Hanguk Kukche Podo Yonmaeng. VFOAT Hanguk Hwabo. (19??)-. English. Twelve times a year. $186.00 (surface mail); $209.14 (airmail). Apollo Book Company Limited, 27 Kimberly Road, Wing Lee Building, Kowloon Hong Kong. **Tel** 011 852 3 678482, FAX 011 852 3 695282. **DD** 915.19.

KN/0454-4072
KOREA TODAY (PYONGYANG). (KOREA TODAY.). [Korea today]. (1959)-. Periodical. English. mo. HK$462.00. Apollo Book Company Limited, 27 Kimberly Road, Wing Lee Building, Kowloon Hong Kong. **Tel** 011 852 3 678482, FAX 011 852 3 695282. **LC** DS930; .K68. **DD** 951.9/3043/05. **Continues** New Korea.
Ind/Abst GeoRef.

US/0023-3951
KOREA WEEK. Began with Apr. 17, 1968 issue. Periodical. English. sm. **LC** DS901; .K775. **DD** 915.19/03/4305. **UDC** 915.19. available on microfilm from University Microfilms International (UMI).

US/0749-7970
KOREAN AND KOREAN-AMERICAN STUDIES BULLETIN. [Korean Korean-Am. stud. bull.]. VFOAT Korean and Korean American Studies Bulletin. Vol. 1, No. 1 (Fall 1984)-. Bulletin. English. Three times a year. $8.00 individuals, $25.00 institutions. Korean and Korean-American Studies Bulletin, c/o Hraf Korea Program, 2054 Yale Station, New Haven CT 06520-2054. **DD** 951. **UDC** 951.9; 327(73:519).

US/0270-1618
KOREAN CULTURE (LOS ANGELES). (KOREAN CULTURE.). [Korean cult.]. **Added/Corp** Korean Cultural Service. VFOAT Hanguk Munhwa. Vol. 1, No. 1 (Winter 1980)-. Academic Scholarly Publication. English. qt. $12.00. Korean Cultural Service, 5505 Wilshire Boulevard, Los Angeles CA 90036. **Tel** (310)936-7141. **ED** Robert Buswell, Walter Lew. **LC** DS904; .K62. **DD** 951.9/005. Index available. cum. index. **Bk Rev**. **Circ**: 3,000 (ctrl).
Desc: Semi-scholarly articles on the traditional and contemporary culture, arts, and history of Korea.
Ind/Abst Index Free Period.

US/0163-0229
KOREAN REVIEW, THE. [Korean rev.]. Periodical. English. bm. $15.00. PO Box 32 Knickerbocker Station, New York NY 10002. **LC** DS922; .K67. **DD** 320.9/519/043. **UDC** 915.19.

US/0145-840X
KOREAN STUDIES. [Korean stud.]. **Added/Corp** University of Hawaii at Manoa. Center for Korean Studies. Vol. 1, (1977)-. Academic Scholarly Publication. English. an (May). $15.00 (one year), $27.00 (two year) US; $17.00 (one year), $31.00 (two year) other. University of Hawaii Press, 2840 Kolowalu Street, Honolulu HI 96822. **Tel** (808)956-8833, (808)948-8697, FAX (808)988-6052. **ED** Edward J. Shultz. **LC** DS901; .K854. **DD** 951.9/005. **CODEN** KOSTEL. **Bk Rev**. **Ad Acc**. **Circ**: 200.
Desc: Publishes a broad range of scholarly articles in the social sciences and humanities. All scholarly articles on Korea and the Korean community abroad are welcomed, including topics of interest to the specialist and nonspecialist alike. Seeks to further scholarship on Korea by providing a forum for discourse on timely subjects and an interdisciplinary foundation for specialists on Korea and for those whose interests touch on areas of importance to Korean studies.
Ind/Abst Am. Hist. Life (1977-); Int. Bibliogr. Sociol.; PAIS Int. Print (1991-?); Soc. Plann. Policy Dev. Abstr.

KO
KOREIA SEGODNIA. No. 319- 1975-. Periodical. Russian. mo. Izdatelstvo Lit-ry Na Inostannykh Iazykakh Kndr, Ul Ekchzhondon, Pkhenian North Korea. **LC** DS901; .N6. **UDC** 951.93; 915.193. **Continues** Novaia Koreia.

II
KOSALA : JOURNAL OF THE INDIAN RESEARCH SOCIETY OF AVADH. Periodical. English (Hindi). sa. $7.50. The Indian Research Society of Avadh, 1222 Delhi Daravaza Faizabad 224001 India. **LC** DS401; .K65. **DD** 954/.005. **UDC** 954.

JA
KOYU. **Added/Corp** Koyukai (Toa Dobun Shoin Daigaku). (19??)-. Periodical. Japanese. Koyukai, c/o Kazan Building, 2-4 Kasumigaseki Chiyoda-ku, Tokyo 100 Japan. **LC** DS796.S2; K68.

MY
KRITIK. 1- 1975-. Periodical. Malay. $5.50. Pustaka Zakry Abadi, 89A Jalan Raja Muda, Kuala Lumpur Malaysia. **LC** DS591.5; .K75.

CH
KU HSIANG JEN. First published in May 1983. Periodical. Chinese. sm. $500.00. Ku Hsiang Jen Tsa Chih She 135-2 Shih Chien Road, Pan-Chiao Shih Taiwan. **LC** DS799.9.T37; K8. **DD** 951/.24905/05. **UDC** 951.

CH
KUAN HUAI. VFOAT Care Magazine; Kuan Huai Tsa Chih. (Oct. 1981)-. Periodical. Chinese. mo. $500.00. Kuan Huai Tsa Chih She, 136 Chung Hsiao East Road, 2nd Section, Taipei Taiwan. **LC** DS799.83; .K83. **DD** 921/.24905/05.
Ind/Abst Hum. Rights Intern. Rep.

CC
KUANG-TUNG WEN SHIH TZU LIAO. Chinese. RMBY1.10. Kuang-Tung Jen Min Chu Pan She. **LC** DS793.K7; K89.

CC
KUEI-CHOU WEN SHIH TZU LIAO HSUAN CHI / CHUNG-KUO JEN MIN CHENG CHIH HSIEH SHANG HUI I KUEI-CHOU SHENG WEI YUAN HUI, WEN SHIH TZU LIAO YEN CHIU WEI YUAN HUI PIEN. V. 1-. Periodical. Chinese. 0.80. Kai Hui, Hsin Hua Shu Tien, Kuei-Yang Shih, Kuei-Chou, People's Republic of China. **LC** DS793.K8; K86. **DD** 951/.34. **UDC** 951.

CH
KUNG LUN. VFOAT Kung Lun Yueh Kan. Began with May 1980 issue. Periodical. Chinese. mo. $1.60. Kung Lun Fa Hsing Pu, 46 Kai Feng Chieh Sect 2, Taiwan. **LC** DS799.83; .K86. **DD** 951/.249/005. **UDC** 951.

HK
KUO SHIH PING LUN. **Added/Corp** Kuo Shih Ping Lun Pien Chi Wei Yuan Hui. VFOAT National Affairs Review; Kuo Shih Ping Lun Tsa Chih. (1991)-. Periodical. Chinese. mo. **LC** DS775.7; .K88. **DD** 951.05/05.

US
KUWAIT (WASHINGTON, D.C.). (KUWAIT.). English. mo. Kuwait Embassy, 2940 Tilden Street NW, Washington DC 20008. **LC** DS247.K8; A2524. **DD** 953/.67/005. **UDC** 953.68.

JA
KYODO SHIRYOKAN DAYORI. **Main/Corp** Ishikawa Kenritsu Kyodo Shiryokan. (19??)-. Periodical. Japanese. Ishikawa Kenritsu Kyodo Shiryokan, 2-ban 4-go Hirosaka 2-chome, Kanazawa-shi 920 Japan. **LC** DS894.59.I83; A2945a.

KO
KYONGGI YONGAM. VFOAT Kyonggi Yoram. Korean. an. Kyongin ILBO 136 Kto-dong, Sumon-si Korea. **LC** DS924.K9; K97.

JA/0910-1349
KYOTO-SHI REKISHI SHIRYOKAN KIYO. (1984)-. Periodical. Japanese. an. Kyoto-Shi Rekishi Shiryokan, 138-1 Matsukage-cho Kamigyo-ku Kyoto-shi Japan. **Tel** 075-241-4312, FAX 075-241-4012. **LC** DS897.K8; K877. **Circ**: 500 (ctrl).
Desc: The history of Kyoto, focusing on the pre-modern age.

BL
L.E.A. **Main/Corp** League of Arab States. Missao No Brasil. (19??)-. Periodical. Portuguese. mo. Missao da

Liga dos Estados Arabes No Brasil, Shis Q1 15 Conj 07 Casa 23, 70.000 Brasilia Brazil. **LC** DS36; .L43a. **DD** 909/.0974927. ***Continues*** *League of Arab States. Missao no Brasil. Revista da L.E.A.*

CE
LANKA GUARDIAN. Vol. 1, No. 1 (May 1, 1978)-. Periodical. English. sm (24 issues). $50.00 US and Canada. Lanka Guardian Publishing Company, Ltd., 246 Union Place, Colombo 2 Sri Lanka. **Tel** 011 94 1 447584. **LC** DS488; .L36. **DD** 954.9/3/005.
Ind/Abst Annu. Bibliogr. Engl. Lang. Lit.; Hum. Rights Intern. Rep.

US/0884-3236
LATE IMPERIAL CHINA. [Late imp. China]. **Added/Corp** Society for Qing Studies (U.S.). **VFOAT** Ching Shih Wen Ti. Vol. 6, No. 1 (June 1985)-. Periodical. English. Twice a year. $36.00 US; $39.00 Canada and Mexico; $39.70 other. Johns Hopkins University Press, 2715 North Charles Street, Baltimore MD 21218-4319. **Tel** (410)516-6987, FAX (410)516-6968. **ED** James Lee, Charlotte Furth. **LC** DS754; .C5332. **DD** 951/.03/05. **[CCC]. Bk Rev. Ad Acc. Circ:** 500. ***Continues*** *Ching-Shih Wen-Ti, 0577-9235.*
Desc: History, arts, literature, and thought of late Imperial China broadly defined from the fourteenth to the present century.
Ind/Abst Am. Hist. Life (1976-).

UK/0075-8914
LEVANT (LONDON). **See** Archaeology.

FR/0992-0757
LEVANT (MONTPELLIER, FRANCE). (LEVANT.). (1988)-. Periodical. French. an. 95.00F France; 120.00F North America. Editions de l'Eclat / Sommieres, Combas, 30250 Sommieres France. **Tel** 011 33 66 778763, FAX 011 33 66 778076. **LC** DS57; .L48. **DD** 956/.005. **Ad Acc.** ctrl circ.

PH/0024-1679
LEYTE-SAMAR STUDIES. [Leyte-Samar stud.]. **Added/Corp** Divine Word University of Tacloban. Graduate School. Vol. 1 (1967)-. Periodical. English (Spanish and Waray). sa. P90.00, P45.00 (per issue) Philippines; $5.00, $3.00 (per issue) US. Divine Word University, Tacloban City 7101, Philippines. **Tel** 321-2310, 321-2370, 321-3600. **ED** Gregorio C Luangco. **LC** DS688.L4; L49. **DD** 959.9/5. cum. index. **Bk Rev. Circ:** 1,000 (ctrl).
Desc: Published by the Graduate School of the Divine Word University of Tacloban. Articles are screened by the editorial board of four members and must be only about the history, language, literature, culture and anthropology of Leyte and Samar.
Ind/Abst Am. Hist. Life (1972-); Index Philip. Period. (1972-199?); MLA Int. Bibl. Books Artic. Mod. Lang. Lit.; Philip. Sci. Technol. Abstr. (1972-).

US/0892-5828
LIAN HE TONG XUN. (LIEN HO T'UNG HSUN / JOINT BULLETIN OF TAIWANESE SOCIETIES IN SOUTHERN CALIFORNIA.). [Lian he tong xun]. **Added/Corp** Taiwanese Societies in Southern California. **VFOAT** Joint Bulletin of Taiwanese Societies in Southern California. (1986)-. Periodical. Chinese (English). mo. $20.00. Joint Bulletin of Taiwanese, PO Box 30795, Los Angeles CA 90030. **Tel** (213)834-2965. **DD** 951.

JA/0286-3553
LIBERAL STAR. ***Suspended.*** (19??)-(1993). Periodical. English. mo. $10.00. Liberal Star, 1-11-23 Nagato-cho Chiyoda-ku, Tokyo 100 Japan. **LC** DS889; .L45. **DD** 952/.005. **UDC** 952.

CN/0714-8038
LIEN HOA. (LIEN HOA : CO'-QUAN HOANG-PHAP VA THONG-TIN / HOI-PHAT-GIAO VIET-NAMTAI CANADA.). [Lien hoa]. **VFOAT** Tap San Lien Hoa; Vietnamese Buddhist Association in Canada. Periodical. Vietnamese. bm. $10.00. Lien Hoa, c/o Vietnamese Buddhist Association in Canada Brossard Quebec J4W 1Y5 Canada. **LC** BQ8.V5; L53. **DD** 959.704/4/05. **UDC** 959.7(71).

US/0024-4007
LINK (NEW YORK), THE. (THE LINK.). [Link]. (Sept. 1968)-. Periodical. English. Five times a year (Jan., May, Aug., Oct., & Dec.). $25.00 (US & Canada); $30.00 (other). American Middle East Understanding, 475 Riverside Drive/Room 241, New York NY 10027. **Tel** (212)870-2053, FAX (212)870-2050. **ED** Laurel Cooley. **LC** DS119.7; .L54. **DD** 956/.005. **UDC** 956. **Bk Rev. Circ:** 50,000 (ctrl).
Desc: Reports on the culture, history and current events of the Middle East. Focuses on Arab-Israeli conflicts.
Ind/Abst Hum. Rights Intern. Rep.

CN/0380-299X
LINK (WINNIPEG. 1974). (THE LINK.). Vol. 2, No. 3 (March 1974)-. Periodical. English. sw. 77.04Can$. Link Communications Ltd., 201-205 East 17th Avenue, Vancouver British Columbia V5V 1A6, Canada. **Tel** (604)876-9300, FAX (604)876-8500. **ED** Promod Puri. **DD** 954/.005. **Bk Rev. Ad Acc, Adv Mgr:** R. Gupta. **Circ:** 10,000 (ctrl). ***Continues*** *India-Canada Link, 0380-2981.*
Desc: Serves the large and linguistically diversified South Asian and Far Asian communities in Canada.

FR/0755-4796
LIVRET DE LA RECHERCHE / INSTITUT NATIONAL DES LANGUES ET CIVILISATIONS ORIENTALES. **Main/Corp** Institut National des Langues et Civilisations Orientales. **VFOAT** Livret de la Recherche a l'INALCO. **VAT** Livret de la Recherche a l'Institut National des Langues et Civilisations Orientales. 1982-. French. ir. Institut National des Langues et Civilisations Orientales, 2 rue de Lille, 75007 Paris France. **LC** PB39.5.I56; I56A. **DD** 409.5/05.

IR
MAHNAMAH-I SHAHID. **VFOAT** Shahid-I Banuvan; Shahid-I Kudakan; Shahid. (19??)-. Periodical. Persian. Maydan-I Haftum-I Tir Khiyaban-I, Tabandah Plak-I 64 Iran. **LC** DS251; .M34. ***Continued in part by*** *Shahid (Tehran, Iran : 1983); Shahid-i Banuvan.*

IO
MAJALAH KEBUDAYAAN MINANGKABAU. **VFOAT** Kebudayaan Minangkabau. V. 1- Jan. 1974-. Periodical. Indonesian. 200 single issue. Yayasan Kebudayaan Minangkabau, Jakarta Indonesia. **LC** DS632.M4; M34.

PH
MALAYANG PILIPINO / FREE FILIPINO. **Added/Corp** Philippines. Ministry of National Defense. **VFOAT** Free Filipino. Vol. 1, No. 1 (Nov. 1979)-. English (English). qt. Ministry of National Defense Building/Room 203, Camp General Emilio Aguinaldo, Quezon City 3002 Philippines. **LC** DS686.5; .M24. **DD** 959.9/005.

MY
MALAYSIA MASA KINI. 1984-. Periodical. Malay. an. $8.00. Persatuan Sejarah Malaysia, 958 Jl Hose, Kuala Lumpur Malaysia. **LC** DS591; .M355. **UDC** 959.5.

LE
MARAYA. V. 1, No. 1 (Feb. 1983)-. Periodical. Arabic. $50.00. Shari Sami, Al Sulh Bihayat Al Shami, S B 90018, Beirut Lebanon. **LC** DS80.A2; M37.

GW
MARDOM NAMEH. JAHRBUCH ZUR GESCHICHTE UND GESELLSCHAFT DES MITTLEREN ORIENTS. **VFOAT** Jahrbuch zur Geschichte und Gesellschaft des Mittleren Orients. 1980-. Periodical. German. an. Syndikat Autoren und Verlagsgesellschaft, Frankfurt AM Main Germany. **LC** DS41; .M36. **DD** 956/.005. **UDC** 956.

MY
MASTIKA. (19??)-. Periodical. Malay. mo. 99.00Mal$. Utusan Melayu Malaysia Berhad, 46M Jalan Chan Sow Lin, Kuala Lumpur Malaysia. **Tel** 280060. **LC** DS591; .M36.

GW
MATERIALIA TURCICA. Vol. 1 (1975)-. Monographic series. English (German). ir. Price varies per volume. Universitaetsverlag, Brockmeyer PF 100428, D 44704 Bochum Germany. **Tel** 011 49 234 9706122. **LC** DS26; .M28. **DD** 950/.049435.

AJ/0408-2621
MATERIALY PO ISTORII AZERBAIDZHANA. **Main/Corp** Baku. Muzei Istorii Azerbaidzhana. **Added/Corp** Akademiia Nauk Azerbaidzhanskoi SSR, Baku. Muzei Istorii Azerbidzhana. Materialy po Istorii Azerbaidzhana. (1956)-. Multiple languages (Russian and Azerbaijani). **(Subscription address:** Victor Kamkin, 4956 Boiling Brook Parkway, Rockville MD 20852.) **DD** 069; 947.91. ***Continues*** *Materialnaia Kultura Azerbaidzhana.*

US/0076-5279
MATERIAUX POUR L'ETUDE DE L'EXTREME-ORIENT MODERNE ET CONTEMPORAIN. TRAVAUX. **Main/Corp** Maison des Sciences de l'Homme (Paris, France). Vol. 1 (1964)-. Monographic series. French. ir. Price varies per volume. Walter de Gruyter Inc. / Hawthorne, 200 Saw Mill River Road, Hawthorne NY 10532. **Tel** (914)747-0110, GERMANY: 011/49/30/260050, FAX (914)747-1326, telex 646677. **(Subscription address:** Germany/ PO Box 110240, 1 Berlin 11**)** **UDC** 950.

CY
MAWQIF AL-ARABI (NICOSIA, CYPRUS). (AL-MAWQIF AL-ARABI.). **VFOAT** Al-Moukif Al-Arabi; Moukif Al-Arabi. Periodical. Arabic. wk. $3.00 each issue. 3531 North Delaware, Arlington VA 22207. **LC** DS36; .M29.

II
MEETING INVITATION, ANNUAL REPORT, HISTORICAL NOTES / INSTITUTE FOR REWRITING INDIAN HISTORY. **Main/Corp** Institute for Rewriting Indian History. **VFOAT** Annual Report and Historical Notes; Annual Report & Historical Notes. May 1, 1980-. English. an. Institute for Rewriting Indian and World History, 9-B Vrindavan Society, Thane 400601 India. **LC** DS401; .I566A. **DD** 954/.005. **UDC** 954. ***Continues*** *Institute for Rewriting Indian History. General Meeting Invitation, Annual Report, and Historical Notes.*

II/0377-127X
MEGHALAYA YEAR BOOK, THE. English. an. Rs5.00. Northeast India News and Feature Service, Jaiaw Langsning, 793002 Shillong India. **LC** DS485.M58; M43. **DD** 954/.16. **UDC** 954.

US
MICHIGAN MONOGRAPHS IN CHINESE STUDIES. **Added/Corp** University of Michigan. Center for Chinese Studies. No. 45 (1982)-. Monographic series. English. ir. Price varies per volume. Center for Chinese Studies University of Michigan, 104 Lane Hall, Ann Arbor MI 48109. **Tel** (313)764-6308. ***Continues*** *Michigan Papers in Chinese Studies, 0076-8065.*

US/0160-354X
MICHIGAN PAPERS ON SOUTH AND SOUTHEAST ASIA. [Mich. pap. South Southeast Asia]. **Added/Corp** University of Michigan. Center for South and Southeast Asian Studies. University of Michigan. Center for Population Planning. No. 1 (1971)-. Monographic series. English. ir. Price varies per volume. Center for South and Southeast Asian Studies, University of Michigan, 130 Lane Hall, Ann Arbor MI 48109. **Tel** (313)763-5790. **ED** Jan Opdyke. **LC** UNC. **Circ:** 1,000.
Desc: A series of scholarly monographs and conference papers on the history, culture, politics, economy, and languages of South and Southeast Asia.

US/8750-7145
MILLAT-I BIDAR. **VFOAT** Mellat-e-Bidar. Periodical. Persian. bw. $11.00. Melli Publishing House Inc, 8720 Woodley Avenue No 209, Sepulveda CA 91343. **LC** DS318.72; .M55.

JA
MIMPO SARON; ZUIHITSU. **Added/Corp** Fukushima Mimpo. Fukushima Mimpo Sha. No. 1 (1974)-. Periodical. Japanese. ¥1100. Fukushima Mompo Sha, 11-1 Sakaecho, Fukushima 960 Japan. **LC** DS894.39.F83; A25.

US
MIN CHU TAI-WAN. **VFOAT** Tai-Wan Min Chu Yun Tung Chih Yuan Hui Tung Hsun. Periodical. Chinese. bm. $10.00. OSDMT, PO Box 53551, Chicago IL 60653. **LC** DS799.83; .M562.

CC
MIN CHU YU FA CHIH. **VFOAT** Minzhu Yu Fazhi. Periodical. Chinese. mo. RMBY0.26. Science Press, 16 Donghuangchenggen North Street, Beijing 100707, People's Republic of China. **Tel** 011 86 1 4019821, 011 86 1 4010642, FAX 011 86 1 4012180, 011 86 1 4019810, telex 210147. **LC** DS779.15; .M56.

CC
MIN TSU WEN HUA. **VFOAT** Minzuwenhua. Periodical. Chinese. bm. RMBY0.30. Science Press, 16 Donghuangchenggen North Street, Beijing 100707, People's Republic of China. **Tel** 011 86 1 4019821, 011 86 1 4010642, FAX 011 86 1 4012180, 011 86 1 4019810, telex 210147. **LC** DS730; .M523. **DD** 951/.004.

PH/0115-2742
MINDANAO JOURNAL. **Added/Corp** Mindanao State University. University Research Center. Vol. 1 (July/Sept. 1974)-. Periodical. English. Four times a year. P143.00. Mindanao Journal, University Research Center, Mindanao State University, PO Box 5594, 9200 Marawi City Philippines. **LC** DS688.S9; M55. **DD** 959.9/7/0405.

CH
MING JEN. **VFOAT** Newsmakers. First published in 1982. Periodical. Chinese. mo. $30.00. Ming Jen Tsa Chi She 2, Lane 357 100 Nung, San Min Lu 3 Section, Tai-Chung Shih Taiwan. **LC** DS799.83; .M565. **DD** 951/.249057/05. **UDC** 951.

CC
MING SHIH TZU LIAO TSUNG KAN / CHUNG-KUO SHE HUI KO HSUEH YUAN LI SHIH YEN CHIU SO MING SHIH SHIH PIEN. V. 1 (May 1981)-. Periodical. Chinese. RMBY0.78. Chaing-su Sheng Hsin Hua Shu Tien, Nan-Ching, People's Republic of China. **LC** DS753; .M593. **DD** 951/.026. **UDC** 951.

CH
MING SHIH YEN CHIU LUN TSUNG / CHUNG-KUO SHE HUI KO HSUEH YUAN LI SHIH YEN CHIU SO MING SHIH YEN CHIU SHIH PIEN. V. 1, (April 1982)-. Periodical. Chinese. NT$1.35. Hsin Hua Shu Tien / Chiang-Su, Chiang-Su Sheng, People's Republic of China. **LC** DS753; .M5933. **DD** 951/.026. **UDC** 951.

US/0147-037X
MING STUDIES. ***Suspended.*** [Ming stud.]. No. 1 (Fall 1975)-(19??). Periodical. English. Twice a year. $15.00 (individual), $20.00 (institution). Hobart and William Smith Colleges Press, Box 115, Geneva NY 14456. **Tel** (315)781-3349, FAX (315)781-3348. **ED**

William S. Atwell. **LC** DS753; .M594. **DD** 951/.026/05. Index available. cum. index. **Bk Rev. Circ:** 300 (ctrl).
Desc: Reports and reviews of early modern Chinese history, Ming Dynasty, 1368-1644.
Ind/Abst Am. Hist. Life (1978-).

KO
MINJOK MUNHWA (MINJOK MUNHWA CHUJINHOE). (MINJOK MUNHWA.). Periodical. Korean. Minjok Munhwa Chujinhoe, San 1-157 Chongnyangni-dong, Tongdaemun-ku, Seoul Korea. **LC** DS904; .M544.

GW
MITGLIEDER-VERZEICHNIS / DEUTSCHE ORIENT-GESELLSCHAFT. **Main/Corp** Deutsche Orient-Gesellschaft. **VFOAT** Mitglieder Verzeichnis. German. Deutsche Orient-Gesellschaft, Bitterstrabe 8-12, D 14195 Berlin 33 Germany. **Tel** (030)838-3347. **LC** DS43; .D46A. **DD** 956/.0025. **UDC** 956(060.21).

IS
MITSPEH. Hebrew. 5.00. Hazanovits St 1, Jerusalem Israel. **LC** DS150.R3; M46.

GW/0342-118X
MITTEILUNGEN DER DEUTSCHEN ORIENT-GESELLSCHAFT ZU BERLIN. [Mitt. Dtsch. Orient-Ges. Berl.]. **Main/Corp** Deutsche Orient-Gesellschaft. No. 1 (March/May 1899)-. Monographic series. German. ir. Price varies per volume. Deutsche Orient-Gesellschaft, Bitterstrabe 8-12, D 14195 Berlin 33 Germany. **Tel** (030)838-3347. **LC** DS41; .D43. Index available. cum. index. **Circ:** 800.
Desc: Research into the history and culture of the Near Orient up to the Middle Ages. Publishes research findings and stirs public interest in these cultures.
Ind/Abst BHA : Biblio. Hist. Art; MLA Int. Bibl. Books Artic. Mod. Lang. Lit.

UK/0026-749X
MODERN ASIAN STUDIES. [Mod. Asian stud.]. Vol. 1 (Jan. 1967)-. Academic Scholarly Publication. English. qt. $175.00 US, Canada & Mexico; £98.00 other. Cambridge University Press, The Edinburgh Building, Shaftesbury Road, Cambridge CB2 2RU United Kingdom. **Tel** 011 44 223 312393, FAX 011 44 223 325959. **(Subscription address:** Cambridge University Press / North America, 110 Midland Avenue, Port Chester NY 10573.**) ED** Gordon Johnson. **LC** DS1; .M58. **DD** 950/.05. **[CCC]. Pr Rev.** available on microfilm and microfiche from University Microfilms International (UMI). Documents available from The Genuine Article, UMI Article Clearinghouse.
Desc: Covers South Asia, South-east Asia, China and Japan. Publishes original research articles concerned with history, geography, politics, sociology, literature, economics and social anthropology.
Ind/Abst ABC POL SCI; Acad. Search (Jan. 1994-); Am. Hist. Life (1967-); Arts Humanit. Citation Index [Select. Cov.]; Curr. Contents Soc. Behav. Sci.; Curr. Geogr. Publ. (199?-); Expand. Acad. Index (1989-); Geogr. Abstr. Human Geogr.; Index Islam. Lit.; Index Period. Artic. Relat. Law (19??-19??); INFO-SOUTH Abstr.; Int. Bibliogr. Sociol.; Int. Dev. Abstr.; Int. Polit. Sci. Abstr.; Mag. Search; Middle East Abstr. Index; Newsp. Period. Abstr. (1991-); Res. Alert [Full Cov.]; Rice Abstr.; Rural Dev. Abstr.; Soc. Plann. Policy Dev. Abstr.; Soc. Sci. Source (Jul. 1993-); Soc. Sci. Cit. Index [Full Cov.]; Soc. Sci. Index; Soc. Sci. Index Fulltext (Oct. 1988-) [Full Txt.]; World Agric. Econ.

US/0097-7004
MODERN CHINA. [Mod. China]. Vol. 1 (Jan. 1975)-. Periodical. English. qt (Jan., Apr., July, Oct.). $172.00. SAGE Periodical Press, 2455 Teller Road, Thousand Oaks CA 91320. **Tel** (805)499-0721, FAX (805)499-0871, telex 100799. **ED** Philip C. C. Huang (UCLA). **LC** DS701; .M575. **DD** 951/.005. **[CCC]. Pr Rev. Acid Free.** available on microfilm and microfiche from University Microfilms International (UMI). Documents available from The Genuine Article, UMI Article Clearinghouse.
Desc: Encourages a new interdisciplinary scholarship and dialogue on China's ongoing revolutionary experience.
Ind/Abst ABC POL SCI; Acad. Abstr. Full Text Elite (Jan. 1992-); Acad. Abstr. (Jan. 1992-); Acad. Search (Jan. 1992-); Am. Hist. Life (1975-); Arts Humanit. Citation Index [Select. Cov.]; Curr. Contents Soc. Behav. Sci.; Educ. Adm. Abstr. (?-?); Expand. Acad. Index (1989-); Geogr. Abstr. Human Geogr.; Hist. Source (Jan. 1992-); Hum. Resour. Abstr.; INFO-SOUTH Abstr.; Int. Bibliogr. Sociol.; Int. Dev. Abstr.; Int. Labour Doc.; Int. Polit. Sci. Abstr.; Mag. Search; Middle East Abstr. Index; Newsp. Period. Abstr. (1991-); PAIS Int. Print (1991-); Res. Alert [Full Cov.]; Sage Public Adm. Abstr.; Soc. Sci. Source (Jan. 1992-); Soc. Sci. Cit. Index [Full Cov.]; Soc. Sci. Index; Soc. Sci. Index Fulltext (Oct. 1988-) [Full Txt.]; U.S. Polit. Sci. Doc.

AT
MONASH PAPERS ON SOUTHEAST ASIA. **Added/Corp** Monash University. Centre of Southeast Asian Studies. **VFOAT** Papers on Southeast Asia. No. 1 (1972)-. Monographic series. English. ir. Price varies per volume. Monash University, Centre for Southeast Asian Studies, Clayton Victoria 3168 Australia. **Tel** 011 61 3 541 2135. Index available. **Bk Rev. Circ:** 200.

US/0894-6523
MONGOLIA SOCIETY NEWSLETTER (1985), THE. (THE MONGOLIA SOCIETY NEWSLETTER.). [Mong. Soc. newsl.]. **Added/Corp** Mongolia Society. No. 1 (Dec. 1985)-. Periodical. English. ir. $30.00 (regular), $100.00 (corporate) Comes with Mongolia Society Membership. The Mongolia Society Inc. / Indiana, 321-322 Goodbody Hall, Indiana University, Bloomington IN 47405. **Tel** (812)855-4078, FAX (812)855-7500. **ED** John R. Krueger. **LC** DS798.A2; M645. **DD** 951.7/3/005. Index available (Bound in 16th iss. ($20.00)). cum. index (In Vol. 16). **Bk Rev. Ad Acc.**
Desc: Contains material on a wide range of topics related to Mongolia, including travel accounts, information on activities of members and programs, both in the United States and abroad, and cultural news from Mongolia and Mongol communities.

US/0077-0396
MONGOLIA SOCIETY OCCASIONAL PAPERS, THE. (OCCASIONAL PAPERS.). **Added/Corp** Mongolia Society. **VFOAT** Occasional Paper. No. 1 (1964)-. Monographic series. English. ir. Price varies per volume. The Mongolia Society Inc. / Indiana, 321-322 Goodbody Hall, Indiana University, Bloomington IN 47405. **Tel** (812)855-4078, FAX (812)855-7500. **ED** John R. Krueger. **LC** DS798; .M575. **DD** 915.17. **Bk Rev. Ad Acc.**

US/0896-0925
MONGOLIA SOCIETY SPECIAL PAPERS, THE. (SPECIAL PAPERS.). [Mongolia Society spec. pap.]. **Added/Corp** Mongolia Society. **VFOAT** Mongolia Society Special Papers. Issue 1 (1965)-. Monographic series. English (Mongolian and English). ir. Price varies per volume. The Mongolia Society Inc. / Indiana, 321-322 Goodbody Hall, Indiana University, Bloomington IN 47405. **Tel** (812)855-4078, FAX (812)855-7500. **ED** John R. Krueger. **LC** DS798.A3; S67. **DD** 951/.7. **Bk Rev. Ad Acc. Circ:** 400. ***Continues*** *Mongolia Society Special Papers, 0896-0925.*

US/0190-3667
MONGOLIAN STUDIES. [Mong. stud.]. **Added/Corp** Mongolia Society. Vol. 1 (1974)-. Academic Scholarly Publication. English (French and German). an. $30.00 (regular), $100.00 (corporate) Comes with Mongolia Society membership. The Mongolia Society Inc. / Indiana, 321-322 Goodbody Hall, Indiana University, Bloomington IN 47405. **Tel** (812)855-4078, FAX (812)855-7500. **ED** John R. Krueger. **LC** DS793.M7; .M62. **DD** 951/.7/005. **Bk Rev. Ad Acc, Adv Mgr:** Susie Drost. **Circ:** 400. ***Continues*** *Mongolia Society Bulletin.*
Desc: Contains scholarly research articles, reviews, and embraces cross-Asian and multi-disciplinary approaches to Mongolia past and present.
Ind/Abst Am. Hist. Life (1977-); MLA Int. Bibl. Books Artic. Mod. Lang. Lit.

US/1040-9599
MONOGRAPHS IN INTERNATIONAL STUDIES. SOUTHEAST ASIA SERIES. (MONOGRAPHS IN INTERNATIONAL STUDIES. SOUTHEAST ASIA SERIES / OHIO UNIVERSITY, CENTER FOR INTERNATIONAL STUDIES.). [Monogr. int. stud., Southeast Asia ser.]. **Added/Corp** Ohio University. Center for International Studies. **VFOAT** Southeast Asia Series. (198?)-. Monographic series. English. Ohio University Press, Scott Quadrangle 220, Athens OH 45701. **LC** UNC. **DD** 959. ***Continues*** *Papers in International Studies. Southeast Asia Series, 0078-9119.*
Ind/Abst MLA Int. Bibl. Books Artic. Mod. Lang. Lit.

US
MONOGRAPHS OF THE ASSOCIATION FOR ASIAN STUDIES. **Main/Corp** Association for Asian Studies. No. 28- 1975-. Monographic series. English. ir. Price varies per volume. University of Arizona Press, 1230 North Park Avenue, Suite 102, Tucson AZ 85719. **Tel** (602)882-3065, (800)426-3797. **UDC** 950. ***Continues*** *Association for Asian Studies. Monographs and Papers.*

US/0732-6491
MONOGRAPHS ON THE ANCIENT NEAR EAST. (SOURCES AND MONOGRAPHS. MONOGRAPHS ON THE ANCIENT NEAR EAST.). [Monogr. anc. Near East]. **Added/Corp** International Institute for Mesopotamian Area Studies. **VFOAT** Sources and Monographs. Monographs of the Ancient Near East; Monographs on the Ancient Near East; Monographs of the Ancient Near East; MANE. Vol. 1 (1974)-. Monographic series. English. ir. Price varies per volume. Undena Publications, PO Box 97, Malibu CA 90265. **Tel** (310)649-2612. **(Subscription address:** Crescent Academic Services, 29528 Madera Avenue, Shafter CA 93263.**) ED** G. Buccellati and M. Kelly-Buccellati. **LC** UNC. **Circ:** 200. ***Continues*** *Sources and Monographs. Monographs in History. Ancient Near East.*
Desc: Monographs by modern scholars on history, art, literature, and archaeology of ancient Near East.
Ind/Abst Old Testam. Abstr.

SI/0557-384X
MONOGRAPHS - ROYAL ASIATIC SOCIETY OF GREAT BRITAIN AND FINLAND. MALAYSIAN BRANCH. **Main/Corp** Royal Asiatic Society of Great Britain and Finland. Malaysian Branch. 1 (1964)-. Monographic series. English. ir. Price varies per volume. Malaysian Branch of Royal Asiatic Society, 130M Jalan Thamby Abdullah, Off Jalan Tun Sambanthan, Brickfields 50470 Kuala Lumpur Malaysia. **Tel** 560044. **ED** Tan Sri Mubin Sheppard.

JA/0027-0741
MONUMENTA NIPPONICA. **Added/Corp** Jochi Daigaku. **VFOAT** Nihon Bunka Shiso. Vol. 1, No. 1 (Jan. 1938)-. Periodical. English (French and German). Four times a year (Feb., May, Aug., Nov.). $36.00. Sophia University / Japanese Culture, 7-1 Kioi-cho Chiyoda-ku, Tokyo 102 Japan. **Tel** 11 81 3 32383544, FAX 11 81 3 32385056. **ED** Michael Cooper. **LC** DS821.A1; M6. **DD** 952.005. Index available in last issue of volume--attached. cum. index. **Bk Rev**, (Qty: 60). **Ad Acc. Pr Rev. Circ:** 1,200. available on microfilm and microfiche from University Microfilms International (UMI). Documents available from The Genuine Article.
Desc: An academic journal dealing with all aspects of Japanese culture--especially literature, history, religion, and art.
Ind/Abst Am. Hist. Life (1954-)(1976-); Arts Humanit. Citation Index [Full Cov.]; Bibliogr. Mission. (1976-); Curr. Contents Arts Humanit.; Index Book Rev. Humanit.; Int. Bibliogr. Sociol.; MLA Int. Bibl. Books Artic. Mod. Lang. Lit.; Recent. Publ. Artic.; Res. Alert [Full Cov.]; Soc. Sci. Cit. Index [Select. Cov.].

CN/0820-7976
MOREHA LE-MOREH. [Mwreh mwreh]. **VFOAT** Teacher to Teacher; Mwreh Mwreh. Periodical. Hebrew. mo. Free. Canadian Zionist Federation, 1310 Greene Avenue, Montreal Quebec H3Z 2B2 Canada. **DD** 956.94/007/071. **UDC** 956.94(71). ctrl circ.

II
MUNAIVAN. Periodical. Tamil (Tamil). qt. Rs0.60 per issue. V M Pothiyaverpan, 20 R Kodhandapani Street, Kumbakonam 612001 India. **LC** DS432.T3; M86.

JA
MURORAN CHIHOSHI KENKYU. **Added/Corp** Muroran Chihoshi Kenkyukai. (19??)-. Periodical. Japanese. ¥500. Muroran Shiritsu Toshokan, 2-5 Hommachi 2-chome 051, Muroran Japan. **LC** DS897.M8; M76.

BR
MYANMA NAING NGAN THUTEITHANA ATHIN GYANE. THE JOURNAL OF THE BURMA RESEARCH SOCIETY. **Main/Corp** Mran Ma Nuin Nam Sutesana A Sn. **VFOAT** Journal of the Burma Research Society. (19??)-. Periodical. Multiple languages (Burmese and English). sa. Burma Research Society, University Estate, Rangoon Burma. **LC** DS527; .B85a. ***Continues*** *Burma Research Society. Journal of the Burma Research Society.*
Ind/Abst MLA Int. Bibl. Books Artic. Mod. Lang. Lit.

NZ/0110-0343
N.Z.A.S.I.A.N. **Main/Corp** New Zealand Asian Studies Society. No. 1- Dec. 1974-. English. an. $2.26. University of Waikato, c/o Dr D Bing, Department of Politics, Private Bag, Hamilton New Zealand.

JA
NAGASAKI BUNKEN SOSHO. (1973)-. Periodical. Japanese. ¥5000. Nagasaki Bunkensha, 11-1 Kaikokumachi, Nagasaki Japan. **LC** DS897.N29; N28.

JA
NAIKAI BUNKA KENKYU KIYO. **Added/Corp** Hiroshima Daigaku. Bungakubu. Naikai Bunka Kenkyushitsu. Hiroshima Daigaku. Bungakubu. Naikai Bunka Kenkyushitsu. Bulletin of the Institute for the Culture of Seto Inland Sea. **VFOAT** Bulletin of the Institute for the Culture of Seto Inland Sea. Vol. 1 (1973)-. Japanese (Japanese). Higashi Sendacho, Hiroshima Japan. **LC** DS894.79.I542; N34.

KO
NAM YANGJU MUNHWA. Vol. 1 (1982)-. Periodical. Korean. Nam Yangju Munhwawon, c/o Kunnip Tosogwan Sutaek-ri, Kuri-up Nam Yangju-gun, Kyonggi-do Korea. **LC** DS924.N27; N35.

JA
NARITA: NARITASAN REIKOKAN SHIRYOKAN HO. **Added/Corp** Naritasan Reikokan. (19??)-. Periodical. Japanese. Naritasan Reikokan Shiryokan, Naritasan Koen, Narita Japan. **LC** DS894.49.C45; A2953.

PH/0116-2470
NATIONAL MIDWEEK. ***Suspended.*** [Natl. midweek]. **VFOAT** Midweek. Vol. 1, No. 1 (Nov. 6, 1985)- Vol. 7, No. 17 (Apr. 29, 1992). Periodical. English (Tagalog). wk. $70.00 (airmail), $37.00 (surface mail). Lagda Publishing, 4443 Old Sta. Mesa, Manilla Philippines. **LC** DS651; .N25. **DD** 959.9/005.
Ind/Abst Index Philip. Period.

History(General) —History of Asia

US/0196-3562
NEAR EAST SERIES. [Near East ser.]. **Main/Corp** Library of Congress. (1980)-. Monographic series. English. ir. Price varies per volume. Library of Congress, 101 Independence Avenue SE, Washington DC 20540. **Tel** (202)287-5000.

CC
NEI MENG-KU SHE HUI KO HSUEH. Periodical. Chinese. bm. 0.40. Post Office Nei Meng-ku, People's Republic of China. **LC** AP95.C4; N44. **DD** 951/.77/005. **UDC** 951.

JA
NEMPO - SHIMBUN GEPPO SHA. **Main/Corp** Shimbun Geppo Sha. **Added/Corp** Shimbun Geppo. Bessatsu. (1971)-. Periodical. Japanese. ¥1000. Nihon Gakujutsu Kaigi Jimukyoku Chosaka Kokugai Chosagakari, 22-34 Roppongi 7 Minato-ku, Tokyo 106 Japan. **LC** DS889; .S528a.

GW
NEUE CHINA, DAS. **Added/Corp** Gesellschaft fuer Deutsch-Chinesische Freundschaft. Vol. 1 (Sept. 1974)-. Periodical. German. bm. DM30.00 Germany; DM40.00 other. Gesellschaft fuer Deutsch-Chinesische Freundschaft, China Studien-Und Verlagsgesellschaft GmbH, Eschenheimer Anlage 28, D 6000 Frankfurt 1 Germany. **Tel** 069 5970206. **LC** DS701; .N36. **DD** 951/.005. **Bk Rev**. **Ad Acc**. **Circ:** 5,000.

II
NEW DELHI. V. 1- Sept. 1978-. Periodical. English. Rs5.00. Bappaditya Roy PTI Building, Parliament Street, New Delhi India. **LC** DS401; .N44. **DD** 954/.005.

SI/0377-175X
NEW DIRECTIONS (SINGAPORE). (NEW DIRECTIONS.). Began with Oct. 1973 issue. Periodical. English. ir. $3.00. Times Publishers SDN BHD, 422 Shompson Road, 11 Singapore Singapore. **LC** DS598.S7; N48. **DD** 959.5/2/005. **UDC** 959.13.

JA/0077-8591
NEW OFFICIAL GUIDE: JAPAN, THE. **Added/Corp** Nihon Kotsu Kosha. Kokusai Kanko Shinkokai. **VFOAT** Japan. (1966)-. Periodical. English. ir. ¥12000. Japan National Tourist Organization, Japan Travel Bureau Publishing Division, Shibuya Nomura Building, 7F 1-10-8 Dogenzaka Shibuya-ku, Tokyo 150 Japan. **Tel** 03 3477 9529, FAX 03 3477 9587. **(Subscription address:** Japan Publications Trading Company, Ltd., PO Box 5030, Tokyo International, Tokyo 100-31 Japan.) **LC** DS805.2; .N47. **Continues** Japan (Nihon Kotsu Kosha).

MY
NEW STRAITS TIMES ANNUAL, THE. English. an. $7.75. New Straits Times Press, Balai Berita 31 Jalan Riong, 59100 Kuala Lumpur Malaysia. **Tel** 011 60 3 2823131, 011 60 3 2823322, FAX 011 60 3 2825502. **LC** DS591; .S83. **DD** 959.5/05/05. **UDC** 959.5.

US
NEWS DIGEST / CHINESE INFORMATION AND CULTURE CENTER. **Added/Corp** China (Republic : 1949-). Chinese Information and Culture Center (New York, N.Y.). Vol. 1, No. 1 (Jan. 17, 1991). Periodical. English. wk. **Continues** News Roundup (China (Republic : 1949-). Coordination Council for North American Affairs. Information Division in New York : 1990).

US/0402-0731
NEWSLETTER - AMERICAN RESEARCH CENTER IN EGYPT. **See** Archaeology.

US
NEWSLETTER / CENTER FOR SOUTH ASIA STUDIES, UNIVERSITY OF CALIFORNIA AT BERKELEY. **Main/Corp** University of California, Berkeley. Center for South Asia Studies. Vol. 1, No. 1 (Fall 1990)-. Newsletter. English. Center for South and Southeast Asia Studies, Building T-9, Room 116, University of California, Berkeley CA 94720. **LC** DS339.9.U6; U56. **Continues in part** University of California, Berkeley. Center for South Asia Studies. Newsletter.

IT
NEWSLETTER OF BALUCHISTAN STUDIES. **Added/Corp** Istituto Universitario Orientale (Naples, Italy). Seminario di Studi Asiatici. Istituto Universitario Orientale (Naples, Italy). Dipartimento di Studi Asiatici. **VFOAT** NBS. No. 1 (Winter 1982/83)-. Newsletter. English. ir. L30000. Istituto Universitario Orientale di Napoli, Piazza S Giovanni, Maggiore 30, 80134 Naples Italy. **LC** DS392.B2; N48. **DD** 954.9/15.
Ind/Abst Anthropol. Lit.

US/0145-7861
NEWSLETTER OF THE SSIS. **Main/Corp** Society for South India Studies. **VAT** Newsletter of the Society for South India Studies. Newsletter. English. $3.00 member. Glenn Yocum, Department of Philosophy and Religion, Whittier College, Whittier CA 90608. **UDC** 954.8.

US/0740-5510
NEWSLETTER / SOCIETY FOR ARMENIAN STUDIES. [Newsl. - Soc. Armen. Stud.]. **Added/Corp** Society for Armenian Studies. **VFOAT** S.A.S. Newsletter; Society for Armenian Studies Newsletter; SAS Newsletter. (19??)-. Newsletter. English. Three times a year. $5.00. Society for Armenian Studies, 6 Divinity Avenue, Room 103, Cambridge MA 02138. **Tel** (909)593-3511. **ED** Rouben Adalian. **LC** DS161; .N48. **Bk Rev**. **Ad Acc**. **Circ:** 500 (ctrl).
Desc: News of the society and of the Armenological field.

US
NEWSLETTER / THE CENTER FOR SOUTHEAST ASIA STUDIES, UNIVERSITY OF CALIFORNIA AT BERKELEY. **Main/Corp** University of California, Berkeley. Center for Southeast Asia Studies. Vol. 1, No. 1 (Fall 1990)-. Newsletter. English. Free. Center for South and Southeast Asia Studies, Building T-9, Room 116, University of California, Berkeley CA 94720. **LC** DS524.8.U6; U55. **Continues in part** University of California, Berkeley. Center for South Asia Studies. Newsletter.

VM/0866-7497
NGHIEN CUU LICH SU. **Added/Corp** Vien s‡hoc (Vietnam). **VFOAT** Issledovanie Istorii B.(215)-. Vol. 1, April (1959)-. Periodical. Vietnamese (table of contents in French and Russian). bm. Xunhasaba Exports and Imports, 7 Nguyen Thi Minh Khai Str, Dit 1 Ho Chi Minh City Vietnam. **Tel** 011 84 8 294893, telex 278 XUNHASABA. **LC** DS556; .N47. **Continues** Tap San Nghien Cuu Lich Su.
Ind/Abst Am. Hist. Life (1981-1986, 1991-); World Agric. Econ.

DK
NIAS REPORT. **Added/Corp** Nordic Institute of Asian Studies. **VFOAT** NIAS Reports. No. 1 (1991)-. Monographic series. English. Eight times a year. kr250.00 Denmark; kr260.00 Scandinavia; kr265.00 Europe; kr270.00 other. Nordic Institute of Asian Studies / Denmark, Njalsgade 84, DK-2300 Copenhagen S Denmark. **Tel** 011 45 3154 8844.

US/1045-666X
NIF REPORT. (NIF REPORT : THE NEWSLETTER OF THE NEW ISRAEL FUND.). [NIF rep.]. **VAT** New Israel Fund Report. (198?)-. Newsletter. English. qt. Free. New Israel Fund, 111 West 40th Street, Suite 2300, New York NY 10018. **DD** 956. **Continues** New Israel Fund Bulletin.
Ind/Abst Hum. Rights Intern. Rep.

JA
NIHON CHUTO GAKKAI NENPO. **VFOAT** Annals of Japan Association for Middle East Studies. No. 1 (1986)-. Periodical. Japanese (English). an. **LC** DS41; .N63.
Ind/Abst Middle East J.

JA
NIHON GAKUHO / HENSHUSHA, OSAKA DAIGAKU BUNGAKUBU NIHONGAKU KENKYUSHITSU. **VFOAT** Journal of Japanese Studies. No. 1- (1982)-. Japanese (summaries and/or abstracts in French and English). Osaka Daigaku Bungakubu, 1-1 Machikaneyamacho, Toyonaka Osaka Japan. **Tel** (06)844-1151. **LC** DS821; .N658. **DD** 952. **UDC** 952.

JA
NIHON JOMIN BUNKA KIYO. **Added/Corp** Seijo Daigaku. Daigakuin. Bungaku Kenkyuka. No. 1 (March 1973)-. Periodical. Japanese. an. ¥1000. Seijo Daigaku Daigakuin Kenkyuka, 6-1-20 Seijo Setagaya-ku, Tokyo 157 Japan. **ED** Nihon Jomin Bunka. **LC** DS821; .N6734. **Circ:** 500.

JA
NIHON KOKUSEI ZUE. (NIPPON, A CHARTED SURVEY OF JAPAN / BY TSUNETA YANO AND KYOICHI SHIRASAKI.). **Added/Corp** Yano Tsuneta Kinenkai. **VFOAT** Nippon. (1936)-. Periodical. English (translations available in Japanese). an. $45.00. **(Subscription address:** Maruzen Company Ltd., PO Box 5050, Import & Export Department, Tokyo 100 31 Japan.) **LC** DS801; .N43. **DD** 952/.005.

JA/0288-4623
NIHON NO TEIRYU. **VFOAT** Undercurrent. Periodical. Japanese. sa. ¥6000. Nihon No Teiryu 11-5, Funabashi 1-chome Setagaya-ku, Tokyo 156 Japan. **LC** DS801.

JA/0386-9164
NIHON REKISHI. [Nihon rekishi]. **Added/Corp** Nihon Rekishi Gakkai. **VFOAT** Nippon Rekishi; Nippon-Rekishi. (April 1946)-. Periodical. Japanese. mo. $120.00. **(Subscription address:** Kyowa Book Company Inc., 1 38 Kanda Jinbocho Chiyoda-ku, Tokyo 101 Japan.) **LC** DS801; .N417. cum. index.
Ind/Abst Am. Hist. Life (1954-).

JA
NIHONGAKU. **VFOAT** The Quarterly of Japanology; Quarterly of Japanology. 1st Ed. (1983)-. Periodical. Japanese (Japanese). qt. ¥1000 single issue. Meicho Kankokai, 20 Kanda Jinbocho 2 Chiyoda-ku, Tokyo-to Japan. **LC** DS821; .N68393. **UDC** 952.

CC
NING-HSIA HUA PAO. (1983)-. Periodical. Chinese. Pub. by: Ning-Hsia ta Hsueh Hsueh Pao, Post Office, Yin-Chuan Shih, People's Republic of China. **LC** DS793.N5; N56. **DD** 951/.75/005.

JA
NIPPON NANDEMO JIKKETSU. 1979-. Japanese. ¥780. Daiyamondo Sha, (Diamond Inc.), 4-2 1-chome Kasumigaseki, Chiyoda-ku Tokyoto 100 Japan. **LC** DS801; .N53.

JA
NITCHU KANKEI. Japanese. Nitchu Keizai Kyokai, c/o Aoyama Building, 2-3 Kita Aoyama 1-chome Minato-ku, Tokyo 107 Japan. **LC** DS849.C6; N53.

II
NORTH-EAST QUARTERLY. **VFOAT** North East Quarterly. Vol. 1 No. 1 (Aug. 1982)-. Periodical. English. qt. $10.00 individual, $20.00 other. North-East Quarterly, Dibrugarh University, 786004 Assam India. **LC** DS483; .N664. **DD** 954/.1/005.
Ind/Abst Anthropol. Lit.

II/0301-6404
NORTH EASTERN AFFAIRS. [North East. aff.]. V. 1- April/June 1972-. English. qt. $14.00. S Sarin, Purabi Jowai Road, 793003 Shillong India. **LC** DS401; .N68. **DD** 954.05/05. **UDC** 954.

KO
NORTH KOREA SEEN FROM ABROAD. English. an. Kwangwamun, PO Box 523, Seoul Korea. **LC** DS930; .N58. **DD** 951.9/3/04305.

PH/0115-2009
NORTHWESTERN MINDANAO RESEARCH JOURNAL. **Added/Corp** Immaculate Conception College. Graduate School. Vol. 1 (1974/75)-. Periodical. English. an. $5.00. Northwestern Mindanao Research Journal, Graduate School, Immaculate Conception College, Ozamiz City Philippines. **ED** Ramon N. Daomilas. **LC** DS688.M2; N67. **DD** 959.9/7/005. **Bk Rev**. **Circ:** 250.

FR/0550-1350
NOUVEAUX CAHIERS, LES. **See** Religion and Theology-Judaism.

UK/0143-3563
NOVA HRVATSKA. **Ceased.** [Nova Hrvat.]. (1958)-(Dec. 1990). Periodical. Serbo-Croatian (Roman). sm. Nova Hrvatska Ltd, PO Box 190, 30 Fleet Street, London SW19 8DL England. **Tel** (01)947-0498, telex 8811204 NOVA G. **ED** J Kusan. **LC** DB361; .N68. **UDC** 930.85(497.1). **Bk Rev**. **Ad Acc**. **Circ:** 15,000.
Desc: Critically appraising contemporary Yugoslav political, economic, social, cultural and religious life.

●RU
NOVAIA OTECHESTVENNAIA I INOSTRANNAIA LITERATURA PO OBSHCHESTVENNYM NAUKAM. IUZHNAIA I IUGO-VOSTOCHNAIA AZIIA, DALNYI VOSTOK / ROSSIISKAIA AKADEMIIA NAUK, INSTITUT NAUCHNOI INFORMATSII PO OBSHCHESTVENNYM NAUKAM. **Added/Corp** Institut Nauchnoi Informatsii po Obshchestvennym Naukam (Rossiiskaia Akademiia Nauk). **VFOAT** Iuzhnaia i Iugo-Vostochnaia Aziia, Dalnyi Vostok. (1992)-. Periodical. Russian. mo. Inion An SSSR, Ulitsa Krasikova D 28/45, Moscow Russia. **Tel** 128.89.71. **Continues** Novaia Sovetskaia i Inostrannaia Literatura po Obshchestvennym Naukam. Iuzhnaia i Iugo-Vostochnaia Aziia, Dalnyi Vostok, 0134-2959.

RU
NOVAIA SOVETSKAIA I INOSTRANNAIA LITERATURA PO OBSHCHESTVENNYM NAUKAM. STRANY AZII I AFRIKI. OBSHCHIE PROBLEMY. **Added/Corp** Institut Nauchnoi Informatsii po Obshchestvennym Naukam (Akademiia Nauk SSSR). **VFOAT** Strany Azii i Afriki. Obshchie Problemy; Obshchie Problemy; Obshchie Raboty po Stranam Azii i Afriki. (1976)-. Russian. mo. 0.10rub (single issue). Izdatelstvo Nauka / Akademiia Nauk, Publishing House of the Russian Academy of Sciences, Leninskii Porspekt 14, 117901 Moscow Russia. **Tel** 011 95 954-21-53, FAX 011 95 938-21-44, telex 411964. **ED** V A Makarenko and Z A Suprunenko. **LC** Z3001; .N63. **Continues** Novaia Literatura Po Stranam Azii I Afriki: Obshchie Raboty.

XR/0029-5302
NOVY ORIENT. [Novy orient]. Vol. 1-. Periodical. Czech. Ten times a year. DM99.00. **(Subscription address:** Artia Pegas Press Ltd., Palac Metro Narodni

Trida 25, 11210 Prague 1 Czech Republic.) **LC** DS1; .N6. **UDC** 950.
Ind/Abst Am. Hist. Life (1983-).

CH
NUAN LIU. **VFOAT** Current Monthly. V. 1, (Aug. 1980)-. Periodical. Chinese. mo. $28.00 US. Current Monthly-America, 8064 North 62nd Street, Milwaukee WI 53223. **LC** DS799.83; .N83. **DD** 951/.249057/05. **UDC** 951.

RU
OBSHCHESTVENNYE NAUKI ZA RUBEZHOM. SERIIA 9 : VOSTOKOVEDENIE I AFRIKANISTIKA. ***Title Change.*** **Added/Corp** Institut Nauchnoi Informatsii i Fundamentalnaia Biblioteka po Obshchestvennym Naukam (Akademiia Nauk SSSR). **VFOAT** Vostokovedenie I Afrikanistika. **VAT** Obshchestvennye Nauki za Rubezhom: Seriia Deviat: Vostokovedenie i Afrikanistika. (1972)-(1992). Russian. qt. Izdatelstvo Nauka / Akademiia Nauk, Publishing House of the Russian Academy of Sciences, Leninskii Porspekt 14, 117901 Moscow Russia. **Tel** 011 95 954-21-53, FAX 011 95 938-21-44, telex 411964. **LC** DS1; .O24. ***Continued by*** *Sotsialnye i GumanitarnyeNnauki. Seriia 9, Vostokovedenie i Afrikanistika. Zarubezhnaia Literatura.*

US/0732-6475
OCCASIONAL PAPERS ON THE NEAR EAST. ***Ceased.*** (MONOGRAPHIC JOURNALS OF THE NEAR EAST. OCCASIONAL PAPERS ON THE NEAR EAST.). [Occas. pap. Near East]. **Added/Corp** International Institute for Mesopotamian Area Studies. **VFOAT** Occasional Papers on the Near East; OP. Vol. 1, Issue 1 (Oct. 1979)-Completed series. Monographic series. English. ir. Undena Publications, PO Box 97, Malibu CA 90265. **Tel** (310)649-2612. **ED** G. Buccellati. **LC** UNC. **Circ:** 200.
Desc: Archaeology, philology, linguistics, and history from ancient to modern times, from Caucasus to the Gulf, and from Indus to the Nile.
Ind/Abst Old Testam. Abstr.

US/0730-0107
OCCASIONAL PAPERS / REPRINTS SERIES IN CONTEMPORARY ASIAN STUDIES. **Added/Corp** University of Maryland at Baltimore. School of Law. Maryland International Law Society. **VFOAT** Contemporary Asian Studies Series; Reprints Series in Contemporary Asian Studies. No. 1 (1977)-. Monographic series. English. Six times a year. Price varies per volume. University of Maryland School of Law, 500 West Baltimore Street, Baltimore MD 21201. **Tel** (410)706-6744. **ED** Hungdah Chih-yu. **Circ:** 800.
Desc: Publication on East Asia, with emphasis on Chinese law, politics, economics, and international relations.
Ind/Abst Int. Polit. Sci. Abstr.

UK/0266-206X
OCCASIONAL PAPERS / SCANDINAVIAN INSTITUTE OF ASIAN STUDIES. **Main/Corp** Scandinavian Institute of Asian Studies. No. 1 (1988)-. English. ir. Curzon Press Ltd, 42 Grays Inn Road, London WC1 England. **Tel** 011 44 71 242 8310.

US/0076-812X
OCCASIONAL PAPERS. SOUTH ASIA SERIES. **Main/Corp** Michigan. State University, East Lansing. Asian Studies Center. **VFOAT** South Asia Series. No. 1 (1965)-. Monographic series. English. ir. Price varies per volume. Michigan State University / Department of English, 201 Morrill Hall, East Lansing MI 48824-1035. **Tel** (517)355-9571, (517)355-7570. **Bk Rev.** **Ad Acc.** **Circ:** 200 (ctrl). available in microform.
Desc: Wide range of topics pertaining to South Asia, including publication of Bengal Studies Conference Papers.

KO
ONUL UI CHAEK. First issue (Spring 1984)-. Periodical. Korean. qt. W10,000. Hangilsa, 101-21 5-ka Anam-dong Songbuk-ku, Seoul 132 Korea. **LC** DS904; .O58.

JA
ONUL UI HANGUK. Periodical. Korean. mo. Calm 3A 8-4-7, Akasaka Minato-ku, Tokyo Japan. **LC** DS922; .O57.

II
ORACLE, THE. V. 1- Jan. 1979-. Periodical. English. qt. Netaji Bhawan, 38/2 Lala Lajpat Rai Road, Calcutta 700 020 India. **LC** DS481.B6; O7. **DD** 954/.005. **UDC** 954.

NE/0078-6527
ORIENS. [Oriens]. **Added/Corp** International Society for Oriental Research. Vol. 1 (1948)-. Periodical. English (French and German). ir. $108.75. E. J. Brill, Postbus 9000, 2300 PA Leiden Netherlands. **Tel** 011 31 71 312624, FAX 011 31 71 317532, telex 39296 BRILL NL. **ED** R. Sellheim. **LC** DS1; .I623. **DD** 950/.05. **[CCC].** cum. index.
Ind/Abst Am. Hist. Life (1963-); Middle East J.

IT/0030-5189
ORIENS ANTIQUUS. **Added/Corp** Centro per le Antichita e la Storia dell'Arte del Vicino Oriente (Italy). Vol. 1 (1962)-. Periodical. Italian (English, French and Italian). Four times a year. L50000.00. Herder Editrice e Libreria SRL, Piazza Montecitorio 117-120, 00186 Rome Italy. **Tel** 011 39 6 679 4628, FAX 011 39 6 678 4751. **ED** Giovanni Pettinato. **LC** DS56; .O7. **DD** 939/.4/005. **Bk Rev.**
Ind/Abst Numis. Lit.

JA
ORIENT. See Archaeology.

II
ORIENT, THE. Began with June/Aug. 1972 issue. English. $2.50. 10-A Himalaya 41-A Sahar Road, 400 069 Bombay India. **LC** DS1; .O435. **DD** 954. **UDC** 954.

GW/0030-5227
ORIENT (DEUTSCHES ORIENT-INSTITUT). (ORIENT.). [Orient]. **Added/Corp** Deutsches Orient-Institut. Nah- und Mittelost-Verein (Germany). (Oct. 1960)-. Periodical. English (German). Four times a year. DM128.00 Germany; DM131.60 others. Leske Verlag & Budrich GmbH, Postfach 300551, Gerhart Hauptmann Strasse 27, W-5090 Leverkusen 3 Opladen Germany. **Tel** 011 49 21712079. **LC** DS41; .O733. **DD** 956/.005. **[CCC].** Index available. cum. index. **Bk Rev.** **Ad Acc.** ctrl circ.
Desc: Political, economical and social essays, abstracts, book reviews on Near and Middle East.
Ind/Abst Int. Bibliogr. Sociol.; PAIS Int. Print (1991-); Middle East J.; World Agric. Econ.

AT/0474-6546
ORIENTAL MONOGRAPH SERIES. **Added/Corp** Australian National University, Canberra. Centre of Oriental Studies. Monograph. Australian National University, Canberra. Centre of Oriental Studies. Australian National University, Canberra. Faculty of Asian Studies. No. 1 (1965)-. Monographic series. English. ir. Price varies per volume. Bibliotech, GPO Box 4, Canberra Australian Capital Territories 2601, Australia.

UK/0068-6891
ORIENTAL PUBLICATIONS. **Main/Corp** University of Cambridge. **Added/Corp** Cambridge. University. Board of the Faculty of Oriental Languages. No. 1 (1956)-. Monographic series. English. ir. Price varies per volume. Cambridge University Press, The Edinburgh Building, Shaftesbury Road, Cambridge CB2 2RU United Kingdom. **Tel** 011 44 223 312393, FAX 011 44 223 325959. **(Subscription address:** North America/ 110 Midland Avenue, Port Chester, NY 10573; telephone: (800)431-1580, (914)937-9600**)**

US/0474-6589
ORIENTAL STUDIES. (1962)-. Monographic series. English. ir. Price varies per volume. Harvard University Press, 79 Garden Street, Cambridge MA 02138. **Tel** (617)496-1344, (800)448-2242.

RU/0235-6740
ORIENTAL STUDIES IN THE USSR. **Added/Corp** Institut Vostokovedeniia (Akademiia Nauk SSSR). **VFOAT** Vostokovednye Issledovaniia v SSSR; Sovetskie Vostokovednye Issledovaniia. (1987)-. English (translations available in Russian). an. Izdatelstvo Nauka / Akademiia Nauk, Publishing House of the Russian Academy of Sciences, Leninskii Porspekt 14, 117901 Moscow Russia. **Tel** 011 95 954-21-53, FAX 011 95 938-21-44, telex 411964. **LC** DS1; .S66. **DD** 950/.05. ***Continues*** *Soviet Oriental Studies.*

RU
ORIENTAL STUDIES IN THE USSR SERIES / USSR ACADEMY OF SCIENCES, INSTITUTE OF ORIENTAL STUDIES. **Added/Corp** Institut Vostokovedeniia (Akademiia Nauk SSSR). (1987)-. Monographic series. English. Price varies per volume. Social Sciences Today Editorial Board, Academy of Sciences, 33/12 Arbat, Moscow 121002 Russia. **Tel** 241-09-06. **LC** UNC. ***Continues*** *Oriental Studies in the USSR.*

IT/0030-5367
ORIENTALIA; COMMENTARI PERIODICI DE REBUS ORIENTIS ANTIQUI. (1932)-. Periodical. Italian (English, French and German). qt (4 issues). L110000 Italy; $100.00 US. Editrice Pontificio Istituto Biblico, Piazza della Pilotta 35, 00187 Rome Italy. **Tel** 011 39 6 6781567, FAX 011 39 6 6780588. **ED** Richard I. Caplice. Index available (bound in last issue). **Circ:** 600. ***Continues*** *Orientalia (1920-1930).*
Desc: We accept articles and reviews on the languages, literatures and history of the ancient near east, excluding Israel and Biblical history.
Ind/Abst BHA : Biblio. Hist. Art; Index Book Rev. Relig.; MLA Int. Bibl. Books Artic. Mod. Lang. Lit.; Relig. Index One Period.

BE
ORIENTALIA LOVANIENSIA ANALECTA. **Added/Corp** Katholieke Universiteit te Leuven. Departement Orientalistiek. (1975)-. Monographic series. English (English and French). ir. Price varies per volume. Editions Peeters SA, Bondgenotenlaan 153, BP 41, B-3000 Leuven Belgium. **Tel** 32 16 235170, FAX 32 16 228500, telex 65987 PUL B.

BE/0085-4522
ORIENTALIA LOVANIENSIA PERIODICA. See Linguistics.

NE
ORIENTALIA RHENO-TRAIECTINA. Vol. 1 (1949)-. Monographic series. Multiple languages (English and French). ir. Price varies per volume. E. J. Brill, Postbus 9000, 2300 PA Leiden Netherlands. **Tel** 011 31 71 312624, FAX 011 31 71 317532, telex 39296 BRILL NL. **ED** J. Gonda.

SW/0078-6578
ORIENTALIA SUECANA. [Orient. Suec.]. Vol. 1 (1952)-. Periodical. English. an. Price varies. Almqvist & Wiksell International, PO Box 4627, S-11691 Stockholm Sweden. **Tel** 011-46-8-6408800. **ED** E. Gren. **LC** DS1; .O65. **DD** 950/.05.
Ind/Abst MLA Int. Bibl. Books Artic. Mod. Lang. Lit.; Numis. Lit.

HK/0030-5448
ORIENTATIONS (HONG KONG). (ORIENTATIONS.). [Orientations]. (Jan. 1970)-. Periodical. English. mo. $60.00 (one year), $110.00 (two year), $145.00 (three year) US; $55.00 (one year), $100.00 (two year), $132.00 (three year) other. Orientations, c/o Shambhala Publications Inc, PO Box 271, Boulder CO 80306-0271. **Tel** 852 5 8921368, telex 62107 IPLPM HX. **ED** Elizabeth Knight. **LC** DS501; .O73. **DD** 950/.01. cum. index. **Bk Rev.** **Ad Acc.** **Circ:** 12,000.
Desc: Magazine dedicated to Asian art. Authoritative articles on painting, calligraphy, bronzes, ceramics, decorative arts and crafts with quality colour reproduction on luxury art paper.
Ind/Abst ARTbibliogr. Mod.

IT/0030-5472
ORIENTE MODERNO. **Added/Corp** Istituto per l'Oriente (Italy). Vol. 1-61, (June 1921-Jan./Dec. 1981)-. Periodical. Italian. mo. L5000.00. Herder Editrice e Libreria SRL, Piazza Montecitorio 117-120, 00186 Rome Italy. **Tel** 011 39 6 679 4628, FAX 011 39 6 678 4751. **LC** D461; .O7. **DD** 909/.097671. **Bk Rev.** **Circ:** 800.
Desc: Information and studies for promoting acquaintance with the East, especially the Islamic Orient.
Ind/Abst Am. Hist. Life (1955-1978); Bibliogr. Mission.; Int. Polit. Sci. Abstr.; Middle East J.

JA
ORIENTO. ***Title Change.*** **Added/Corp** Nihon Oriento Gakkai. Nippon Orient Gakkai. Bulletin of the Society for Near Eastern Studies in Japan. **VFOAT** Bulletin of the Society for Near Eastern Studies in Japan. (19??)-(1992). Japanese (English). sa. Nippon Orient Gakkai, 1-9 Kanda Nishikicho, Chiyoda-ku 101 Tokyo Japan. **Tel** 03-291-7519. **ED** Katumasa Itakura and San-eki Nakaoka. **LC** DS41; .O78. cum. index. **Bk Rev.** **Ad Acc.** **Circ:** 1,200 (ctrl). ***Continued by*** *Orient (Tokyo, Japan).*

JA
ORYO SHIGAKU. **Added/Corp** Bukkyo Daigaku, Kyoto, Japan. Rekishi Kenkyujo. **VFOAT** Journal of Historical Studies. (1975)-. Japanese (Japanese). Bykkyo Daigaku Rekishi Kenkyujo, 96 Murasakino Kita Hanaobocho, Kita-ku, Kyoto Japan. **LC** DS510.7; .O79.

JA
OSAKA NO REKISHI / OSAKA SHISHI HENSANJO. **Added/Corp** Osaka Shishi Shiryo. (March 1980)-. Periodical. Japanese. Osaka-Shi Shiryo Chosakai, c/o Osaka Shiritsu Chuo Toshokan, 3-3 Kita Horie 4-chome, Nichi-kum Osaka Japan. **LC** DS897.O8; O954.

TU
OSMANL ARASTRMALAR. **Added/Corp** Enderun Kitabevi. **VFOAT** The Journal of Ottoman Studies. (1980)-. Periodical. Turkish (English, French and German). an. 3750.00TL (one year), 6900.00TL (two years), 10250.00TL (three years). Enderun Kitabevi, Beyaz Saray/Beyazit, Istanbul Turkey. **LC** DR401; .O83. **DD** 956.1/005.

KO
PACIFIC FOCUS. **Added/Corp** Inha Taehakkyo. Kukche Kwangye Yonguso. Vol. 1 No. 1 (Spring 1986)-. Periodical. English. sa. $30.00 institutions, $20.00 individuals. INHA University, Center of International Studies, 253 Young Hyun Dong Nam-Ku, Inchon 402-751 Korea. **Tel** 011 82 32 8631336. **LC** DU1; .P13326. **DD** 950/.42/05.

JA
PACIFIC FRIEND. (19??)-. Periodical. English. mo. $54.00. **(Subscription address:** Japan Publications Trading Company, Ltd., PO Box 5030, Tokyo International, Tokyo 100-31 Japan.**)** **LC** DS820.8; .P33. **DD** 915.2/03/4.

FR/0153-9345
PALEORIENT. [Paleorient]. **Added/Corp** Association Paleorient. Vol. 1 (1973)-. Periodical. English (French and German). ir. Price varies. Editions du CNRS, 22 rue Saint Armand, F 75015 Paris France. **Tel** 011 33 1

History(General) —History of Asia

45075050. **(Subscription address:** CNRS Editions, 20-22 rue Saint Amand, c/o Mme. Bodet, 75015 Paris France.) **LC** GN855.M628; P35. **CODEN** PALEDX. **Circ:** 1,500.
Desc: Multi-disciplinary journal of prehistory and protohistory of Southwest Asia.
Ind/Abst Anthropol. Lit.; Art Archaeol. Tech. Abstr.; GeoRef; Middle East Abstr. Index.

CN/0228-8230
PANJAB AFFAIRS. Vol. 1, No. 1 (Feb. 1979)-. Periodical. English. Six times a year. 6.00Can$. Panjab Affairs, PO Box 222 Station H, Toronto Ontario M4C 5J5 Canada. **Tel** (416)752-6867. **DD** 954/.5/055.

IO/0377-2632
PANJI MASYARAKAT. (1972)-. Periodical. Indonesian. ir (36 issues). $174.60. PT Gramedia/ Export Department, JL Gajah Mada 104/ PO Box 615, Jakarta 11140 Indonesia. **Tel** 011 62 21 6297809 Ext. 4610, FAX 011 62 21 6498475, telex 41216. **LC** DS611; .P34.
Continues Pandji Masjarakat, 0556-4365.

AT/0725-0177
PAPERS OF THE JAPANESE STUDIES CENTRE. Added/Corp Japanese Studies Centre (Melbourne, Vic.). (1982)-. Monographic series. English. ir. Price varies per volume. Japanese Studies Centre Inc, Wellington Road, Clayton Victoria 3168 Australia. **Tel** (03)565-2260, FAX (03)565-4007, telex MONASH AA 32691. **ED** J. V. Neustupny and Y. Sugimoto. **Circ:** 300.

FR
PARIS-PEKIN. VFOAT Hai Tien Tsa Chin. No. 1 (Sept./Oct. 1979)-. Periodical. French (French). 150F. BP 82, Paris 75662 Cedex 14 France. **LC** DS701; P362. **DD** 951/.005. **UDC** 951.

NP
PARISTHITI. V. 1, No. 1, Purnanka 1 (Asvina 2037 I.E. Sept./Oct. 198?). Periodical. Nepali (Nepali). mo. Rs55.00. Basant Lohani, PB 190, Kathmandu Nepal. **LC** DS493; .P37. **UDC** 954.135.

II
PARLANCE. Periodical. English. mo. Rs22.00. 7-B Everest House 46-C Chowringhee Road, Calcutta 700071 India. **LC** DS401; .P327.

BE
PATROLOGIA ORIENTALIS. Vol. 1 (1904)-. Monographic series. French. ir. Price varies per volume. Brepols Publishers, Steenweg OP Tielen 68, B-2300 Turnhout Belgium. **Tel** 011 32 14 402500. cum. index.
Desc: A collection of oriental texts edited in the original language with a translation into Latin or a modern language.

US
PAYAM-I IMAM. Periodical. Persian. PO Box 32081, Washington DC 20007. **LC** DS318.72; .P39.

FR/0249-3047
PENINSULE. Added/Corp Cercle de Culture et de Recherches Laotiennes. No. 1 (Oct. 1980)-. Periodical. French. sa. $25.00. Cercle De Culture Et De Recherches Laotiennes, 20 rue De Lourmel, 75015 Paris France. **LC** DS520; .P46. **DD** 959/.005. **Continues** Presence Indochinoise.
Ind/Abst Int. Bibliogr. Sociol.

IO
PENUNTUN WISATA. Main/Corp Indonesia. Direktorat Binawisata. **VFOAT** Travel Manual. 1973/74-. Indonesian. Direktorat Binawisata, Jln Krakat Raya No 81, Jakarta Indonesia. **LC** DS614; .I54A.

CC
PEOPLE'S REPUBLIC OF CHINA YEAR-BOOK. VFOAT People's Republic of China Yearbook; Chung-Kuo Nien Chien; P.R.C. Year-Book; PRC Year-Book. (1983)-. English. an. $125.00 (12th edition). **(Subscription address:** International Publications Service, A Division of Taylor & Francis, 1900 Frost Road, Suite 101, Bristol PA 19007-1598.) **LC** DS779.15; .C49. **DD** 951/.005. **Continues** China Official Annual Report, 0257-7232.
Desc: Filled with facts, figures and photographs. Coverage is given to all major events in China in the fields of politics, economy, legislation, military affairs, foreign relations, science and technology, education, and more.

NE/0079-0893
PERSICA. Added/Corp Genootschap Nederland-Iran. No. 1 (1964)-. Dutch (English, French and German). ir. 75.00F. Editions Peeters SA, Bondgenotenlaan 153, BP 41, B-3000 Leuven Belgium. **Tel** 32 16 235170, FAX 32 16 228500, telex 65987 PUL B. **(Subscription address:** KB Kremer, c/o Amsterdam Rotterdam Bank, Rozemarijntuin 67. 2353 PC Leiderdorp Holland.) **LC** DS251; .P47.

PH/0116-5038
PHILIPPINE NEWS & FEATURES. [Philipp. news features]. (1985)-. Periodical. English. **DD** 303.
Ind/Abst Hum. Rights Intern. Rep.

CN/0712-5550
PHILIPPINE NEWS BULLETIN. [Philipp. news bull.]. Bulletin. English. bm. Free. Philippine News Bulletin, c/o Embassy of the Philippines, 130 Albert Street, Ottawa Ontario K1P 5G2 Canada. **DD** 959.9/005. **UDC** 959.9.

US/0147-9555
PHILIPPINE TIMES, THE. Periodical. English. sa. $7.00. Philippine Times Enterprise, PO Box A3006, Chicago IL 60690. **LC** DS651; .P624. **DD** 909/.04/9921082. **UDC** 959.9; 915.99.

VM
PHNG ONG. Vol. 1- April 7, 1971-. Vietnamese. mo. $5.00. Father Andre Gelinas SJ, PO Box 2094, Saigon Vietnam. **LC** DS557.A5; A32. **UDC** 959.7.

JA
PIKA NI YAKARETE, HIBAKU TAIKENKI. VFOAT Hibaku Taikenki. Japanese. ¥480. Seikyo Genbaku Higaisha No Kai Hiroshima Iryo Seikatsu Kyodo Kumiai, 610 Aoikoichi-Machi Nakasu Asa Minami-ku, Hiroshima-shi 731-01 Japan. **LC** D767.25.H6; P55.

US/0889-5244
PILIPINAS. [Pilipinas]. **Added/Corp** Southeast Asia Council. Philippine Study Committee. Southeast Asia Council. Philippine Studies Group. Vol. 3, No. 1 (June 1982)-. Periodical. English. Twice a year. $40.00 institutions, $16.00 individuals. Association for Asian Studies Inc., University of Michigan, 1 Lane Hall, Ann Arbor MI 48109. **Tel** (313)665-2490, FAX (313)665-3801. **(Subscription address:** Association for Asian Studies, 657 East Avenue, Rochester, NY 14603) **LC** DS651; .F493. **DD** 959.9/005. **Continues** Filipinas, 0735-6447.
Ind/Abst Hum. Rights Intern. Rep.; Index Philip. Period.; Int. Dev. Abstr.

US
POLITICAL HISTORY OF RUSSIA. See Political Science-Socialism, Communism, Anarchism, Utopianism.

CC
POPOLA CINIO, EL. Added/Corp Cina Esperanto Ligo. **VFOAT** Chung-Kuo Pao Tao; Jen Min Chung-Kuo Pao Tao. (1953)-. Periodical. Chinese (Esperanto). mo. $41.00 (seamail) $78.40 (airmail). **(Subscription address:** China Books & Periodicals Inc., 2929 24th Street, San Francisco CA 94110.) **LC** DS777.55; .J3617. **Continues** Jen Min Chung-Kuo Pao Tao.
Ind/Abst MLA Int. Bibl. Books Artic. Mod. Lang. Lit.

II
PRACHYA PRATIBHA. VFOAT Pracya Pratibha. V. 1- July 1973-. Periodical. English. sa. Rs100. Birla Institute of Art and Music, Prachya Niketan Birla Museum, Tayminarayan Giri Bhopal India. **Tel** 64387. **ED** Shri K P Narayanan. **LC** DS423; .P73. **UDC** 954. **Bk Rev. Circ:** 150.
Desc: Highlights the ancient history and culture of the subcontinent. It includes articles on religion, epigraphy, numismatics, art, architecture, sculpture etc. to focus on the rich heritage of the country.

NE/0555-0912
PRETORIA ORIENTAL SERIES. (1954)-. Monographic series. English. ir. Price varies per volume. E. J. Brill, Postbus 9000, 2300 PA Leiden Netherlands. **Tel** 011 31 71 312624, FAX 011 31 71 317532, telex 39296 BRILL NL. **ED** A. Van Gelms.

●US/1065-9382
PRINCETON PAPERS IN NEAR EASTERN STUDIES. (1992)-. Periodical. English. $15.00 (single issue). Darwin Press, Inc., Box 2202, Princeton NJ 08543.

II
PRISM. V. 1- May/June 1979-. Periodical. English. mo. $30.00. Kamlesh, 1646 Main Bazar, Paharganj New Delhi 110055 India. **LC** DS401; .P74. **DD** 954.05/05. **UDC** 954.

IO/0301-6269
PRISMA (JAKARTA, INDONESIA). (PRISMA.). [Prisma]. **Added/Corp** Lembaga Penelitian, Pendidikan dan Penerangan Ekonomi dan Sosial. No. 1 (Nov. 1971)-. Indonesian. Periodical. Indonesian. Four times a year. Rp850. Institute for Economic and Social Research Education and Information (LP3ES), Jalan S Parman 81, PO Box 75, Jakarta 11420 Indonesia. **Tel** 011 62 21 5663525. **LC** DS611; .P75.
Ind/Abst Int. Labour Doc.

RU
PROBLEMY DALNEGO VOSTOKA. Added/Corp Institut Dalnego Vostoka (Akademiia Nauk SSSR). (1972)-. Periodical. Russian. bm. $99.95. **(Subscription address:** East View Publications Inc., 3020 Harbor Lane North, Suite 110, Minneapolis MN 55447.) **Bk Rev**

UK
PROCEEDINGS OF THE SEMINAR FOR ARABIAN STUDIES. Main/Conf Seminar for Arabian Studies. Vol. 1 (1971)-. Proceedings. English. an. £22.00. Seminar for Arabian Studies, Institute of Archaeology, 31 34 Gordon Street, London WC1H 0PY England. **LC** DS201; .S45a. **DD** 915.3/008. **Bk Rev**.
Desc: Papers given at the annual conference of seminars for Arabian studies on all of the Arabian Peninsula prior to 1850 AD.
Ind/Abst Anthropol. Lit.

US
PUBLICATIONS ON ASIA. Main/Corp Washington (State). University. Institute for Comparative and Foreign Area Studies. No. 21- 1972-. Monographic series. English. Price varies per volume. University of Washington Press, Box C-50096, Seattle WA 98145-0096. **Tel** (206)543-8870. **UDC** 950. **Continues** Publications on Asia.

CN/0713-7982
PUBLICATIONS SERIES (JOINT CENTRE ON MODERN EAST ASIA). (PUBLICATIONS SERIES / UNIVERSITY OF TORONTO-YORK UNIVERSITY, JOINT CENTRE ON MODERN EAST ASIA). [Publ. ser. - Univ. Tor.-York Univ., Jt. Cent. Mod. East Asia]. Monographic series. English. Price varies per volume. Joint Centre for Asia Pacific Studies, 631 Spadina Avenue, Toronto Ontario M5S 2H6 Canada. **DD** 950/.4. **UDC** 950.

KO
PUKHAN INMYONG SAJON. Korean. be. W12,000. Chungang Ilbo Tongyang Pangsong, 58-9 Sosomun-Dong, Chung-Ku 100, Seoul South Korea. **LC** DS930; .P924.

II
PURABHILEKH-PURATATVA : JOURNAL OF THE DIRECTORATE OF ARCHIVES, ARCHAEOLOGY AND MUSEUM, PANAJI-GOA. See Archaeology.

II
PURATATTVA. No. 1 (1967/68)-. English. **LC** DS416; .P85.
Ind/Abst Anthropol. Lit.

IO/0127-1857
PURBA. V. 1 (1982)-. Periodical. English (Malay). an. $5.00. Persatuan Muzium Malaysia, D/A Muzium Negara Kuala Lumpur. **LC** DS591; .P87. **UDC** 959.5.

IO/0303-5190
PURNAWIRAWAN (JAKARTA). (PURNAWIRAWAN.). Indonesian. Pengurus Besar Pepabri, JL Lap Banteng Barat 34, Jakarta Indonesia. **LC** DS611; .P85.

UK/0144-946X
PURVADESH. Vol. 1, No. 1 (Summer 1980)-. English (English). sa. $16.00. Purvadesh, 125 Harold Road, London E13 0SF England. **LC** DS1; .P87.

KO
PYONGHWA TONGIL YOMWON. Periodical. Korean. Pyonghwa Tongil Chongchaek Chamun Hoeui Samucho, 209 2-ka Changchung-dong Chung-ku, Seoul Korea. **LC** DS917.25; .P88.

CH/0577-9170
QINGHUA XUEBAO. (CHING HUA HSUEH PAO.). [Qinghua xuebao]. **VFOAT** Tsing Hua Journal of Chinese Studies. Vol. 1 (June/July 1956)-. Periodical. Chinese (English; summaries and/or abstracts in English). Twice a year. $29.00 (airmail), $26.00 (surface mail) Hong Kong and Macao; $36.00 (airmail), $31.00 (surface mail) other. National Tsing Hua University, 101 Section II, Kuang Fu Road, Hsinchu Taiwan. **Tel** 011 886 35 715131 4545, FAX 011 886 35 722436. **LC** AS452.C485; A2. **DD** 378; 951. ctrl circ. **Continues** Ching Hua Hsueh Pao.
Ind/Abst Am. Hist. Life (1982-); MLA Int. Bibl. Books Artic. Mod. Lang. Lit.

JA/0285-4406
RAFIDAN. (AL-RAFIDAN.). **Added/Corp** Kokushikan Daigaku. Iraku Kodai Bunka Kenkyujo. **VFOAT** Journal of Western Asiatic Studies. (1980)-. Japanese (English).
Ind/Abst Anthropol. Lit.

US/0742-8014
RAHAVARD : NASHRIYAH-I ANJUMAN-I DUSTDARAN-I FARHANG-I FARSI. [Rahavard]. **Added/Corp** Society of the Friends of the Persian Culture (Beverly Hills, Calif.). **VFOAT** Rah-I Avard. Vol. 1, No. 1 (Apr. 1982)-. Periodical. Persian. qt. $28.00. Rahavard Persian Journal, PO Box 24640, Los Angeles CA 90024. **LC** DS251; .R35 .

PK
RAJPUT. VFOAT Rajpoot. Vol. 1 (Jan. 1973)-. Periodical. Urdu (Urdu). mo. Rs10.00. Muhammad Afzal Khan, Manager Monthly Rajpoot, 4 Temple Road, Lahaur Pakistan. **LC** DS380.R32; R3.

KO/1014-191X
RAPA PUBLICATION. [RAPA publ.]. **VFOAT** Regional Office for Asia and the Pacific Publication. (1986)-. Periodical. English. ir. **CODEN** NU052. **Continues** RAPA Monograph, 1014-1928.
Ind/Abst For. Abstr.; Rev. Plant Pathol.; Weed Abstr.

History(General) —History of Asia

YE
RAYDAN. Vol. 1 (1978)-. Periodical. English (Arabic and French). an. 1500F. Editions Peeters SA, Bondgenotenlaan 153, BP 41, B-3000 Leuven Belgium. **Tel** 32 16 235170, FAX 32 16 228500, telex 65987 PUL B. **ED** M. A. Ghul, M. A. Bafaqih, and A. A. Muheiriz. **Bk Rev.**
Desc: Journal of Yemeni antiquities and epigraphy.

SI/0218-3056
REGIONAL OUTLOOK, SOUTHEAST ASIA. **Added/Corp** Institute of Southeast Asian Studies. (19??)-. English. an. $31.00 US; $42.00 other. Institute of Southeast Asian Studies / Singapore, Heng Mui Keng Terrace, Pasir Panjang Road, Singapore 0511 Republic of Singapore. **Tel** (11) 65 8702447, FAX 011 65 7781735, telex 37068. **LC** DS520; .R4.
Desc: Provides succinct yet substantive and easily readable overviews and insights into the current geo-political and economic situations in the individual countries and the region as a whole, together with the likely trends over the next year or so.

NP
REGMI RESEARCH SERIES. Monographic series. English. Price varies per volume. Regmiville Lazimpat, Kathmandu Nepal. **UDC** 954.135.
Desc: Materials on historical aspects of Nepal's law, government, society, politics, and economics.

JA
REKISHI KORON. (Dec. 1975)-. Periodical. Japanese. mo. ¥9000. Yuzankaku, 6-9 Fujimi 2-chome, Chiyoda-ku 102 Tokyo Japan. **LC** DS801; .R44.

JA/0386-9237
REKISHIGAKU KENKYU. [Rekishigaku kenkyu]. **Added/Corp** Rekishigaku Kenkyukai (Japan). **VFOAT** Journal of the Historical Science Society; Zeitschrift der Gesellschaft fur Geschichtsforschung; Journal of Historical Studies. (Nov. 1933)-. Periodical. Japanese (summaries and/or abstracts in English and German; table of contents in English, German and Japanese). mo (13 issues). $168.00. **(Subscription address:** Kyowa Book Company Inc., 1 38 Kanda Jinbocho Chiyoda-ku, Tokyo 101 Japan.**) LC** D1; .R2178. cum. index. **Circ:** 10,000 (ctrl).
Ind/Abst Am. Hist. Life (1954-1989, 1991-).

UK
REPRINT SERIES / SOCIETY FOR CENTRAL ASIAN STUDIES. **Added/Corp** Society for Central Asian Studies. (1984)-. Monographic series. Russian. Price varies per volume. Society for Central Asian Studies, Unit 8, 92 Lots Road, London SW10 4BQ England. **Tel** 011 44 71 352-0210, FAX 011 44 71 376-8301. **LC** UNC.

CH/1013-0942
REPUBLIC OF CHINA YEARBOOK. (1989)-. English. an. $55.00. Kwang Hwa Publ Co, 8th Floor No. 15 Hangchow, S RD Sec 1, Taipei 100 Taiwan. **Tel** 011 886 2 3122846, 011 886 2 3922245 ext. 15. **(Subscription address:** International Publications Service, A Division of Taylor & Francis, 1900 Frost Road, Suite 101, Bristol PA 19007-1598.**) LC** DS798.92; .R46. **DD** 951.24/905/05. **Continues** Republic of China.
Desc: Includes a chronology of events for the year covered, and a biographical who's who in Taiwan.

US/0893-2344
REPUBLICAN CHINA. **Added/Corp** University of Illinois at Urbana-Champaign. Center for Asian Studies. **VFOAT** Min Kuo. Vol. 9, No. 1 (Oct. 1983)-. Periodical. English. Twice a year (Apr. & Nov.). $18.00. St. Johns University / New York, St. Johns Hall Room 434, c/o J. Bradley, Jamaica NY 11439. **Tel** (718)990-6161 ext. 5113. **ED** Herman Mast. **DD** 951. **Circ:** 230. **Continues** Chinese Republican Studies Newsletter, 0884-4496.
Ind/Abst Am. Hist. Life (1987-).

II
RESARUN. (19??)-. Periodical. English. Twice a year. Free on request. Directorate of Research / India, Government Arunachal Pradesh, Box 129, Itanagar 791111 India. **Circ:** 700.

US
RESEARCH MONOGRAPH - CENTER FOR SOUTH AND SOUTHEAST ASIA STUDIES, UNIVERSITY OF CALIFORNIA. **Main/Corp** University of California, Berkeley. Center for South and Southeast Asia Studies. No. 1-. Monographic series. English. Price varies per volume. Center for South and Southeast Asia Studies, Building T-9, Room 116, University of California, Berkeley CA 94720.

US
RESEARCH PAPERS AND POLICY STUDIES / INSTITUTE OF EAST ASIAN STUDIES, UNIVERSITY OF CALIFORNIA, BERKELEY. No. 1-. Monographic series. English. Price varies per volume. University of California / Institute of East Asian Studies, Director of Publications, Berkeley CA 94720.

US/0577-7127
RESEARCH SERIES. **Main/Corp** Chicago. University. Philippine Studies Program. No. 1- 1959-. Periodical. English. Philippine Studies, PO Box 37005, Chicago IL 60637.

JA
RETTO NO BUNKASHI. (1984)-. Periodical. Japanese. sa. ¥1800 single issue. Nihon Edita Sukuru Shuppanbu, 6 Ichigaya Tamachi 1, Shinjuku-ku Tokyo 162 Japan. **LC** DS820.8; .R47.

JA/0913-4700
REVIEW OF JAPANESE CULTURE AND SOCIETY. [Rev. Jpn. cult. soc.]. **Added/Corp** Josai Daigaku. Kokusai Bunka Kyoiku Senta. Vol. 1, No. 1 (October 1986)-. Periodical. English. an (Dec.). $17.50 North and Central Middle East; $18.00 Europe, South America & Africa; $17.15 other. Josai University, c/o Ms Natta Phisphumivhi, 1-1 Keyaki-Dai Sakado-Shi, Saitama-Ken 350-02, Japan. **Tel** 011 81 492 86 2233. **ED** Noriko Mizuta. **LC** DS820.8; .R48. **DD** 952/.005. **Circ:** 500.
Desc: This journal offers English translations of essays, critiques, and papers originally written for a Japanese readership.

FR/0080-2549
REVUE DES ETUDES ARMENIENNES (PARIS). (REVUE DES ETUDES ARMENIENNES.). [Rev. etud. armen.]. **Added/Corp** Societe des Etudes Armeniennes. Proceedings. Fundacao Calouste Gulbenkian. Association de la Revue des Etudes Armeniennes. Vol. 1 (1920)-. French (English and German). an. 3000F. Editions Peeters SA, Bondgenotenlaan 153, BP 41, B-3000 Leuven Belgium. **Tel** 32 16 235170, FAX 32 16 228500, telex 65987 PUL B. **ED** S. der Nersessian, N.G. Garsoian, J.P. Mahe, Ch. de Lamberterie. **LC** PK8001; .R4. Index available. **Bk Rev. Ad Acc.**
Ind/Abst BHA : Biblio. Hist. Art; MLA Int. Bibl. Books Artic. Mod. Lang. Lit.; Numis. Lit.; RILA, Int. Rep. Lit. Art.

FR/0080-2603
REVUE HITTITE ET ASIANIQUE. **Suspended.** [Rev. hittite asianique]. **Added/Corp** Societe des Etudes Hittites et Asianiques. Vol. 1, No. 1 (Oct. 1930)-Suspended with Vol. 37. French. ir. Editions Klincksieck, 8 rue de la Sorbonne, 75005 Paris France. **Tel** 11 33 1 43545953, FAX 11 33 1 432252553. **LC** DS66; .R4. cum. index.
Ind/Abst MLA Int. Bibl. Books Artic. Mod. Lang. Lit.

JA/0386-8966
RISSHO SHIGAKU. **VFOAT** Historical Reports of Rissho University. Japanese. Rissho Daigaku Shigakkai, c/o Rissho Daigaku Shigaku, Kenkyushitsu 2-16 Osaki 4, Shinagawa-ku Tokyo-to 141 Japan. **LC** D1; .R757.

IT
RIVISTA DI STUDI FENICI. See Archaeology.

PL/0080-3545
ROCZNIK ORIENTALISTYCZNY. [Rocz. oriental.]. **Added/Corp** Polskie Towarzystwo Orientalistyczne. Polska Akademia Nauk. Komitet Orientalistyczny. **VFOAT** Polnisches Archiv fur Orientalistik; Archives Plonaises d'Etudes Orientales; Polish Archives of Oriental Research. (1914)-. Polish (French, English and Multiple languages). ir (2 issues). Price varies. **(Subscription address:** ARS Polona, PO Box 1001, 00068 Warsaw Poland.**) LC** PJ9; .R6.
Desc: Oriental studies.
Ind/Abst Am. Hist. Life (1954-); MLA Int. Bibl. Books Artic. Mod. Lang. Lit.

CY
SABAH (NICOSIA, CYPRUS). (AL-SABAH.). Periodical. Arabic. wk. £10.00 (individuals), £50.00 (institutions). Zenobia 27, Karpenisiou Street, PO Box 512, Nicosia Cyprus. **LC** DS36; .S23.

MY/0036-2131
SABAH SOCIETY JOURNAL. **Main/Corp** Sabah Society. Vol. 1 (Sept. 1961)-. English. an. Sabah Society Journal, Kota Kinabalu, PO Box 547, Sabah E Malaysia. **LC** DS646.33; .S2. **DD** 959.5/3/005.
Ind/Abst Anthropol. Lit.

PK
SADA-YI BALTISTAN. Periodical. Urdu. wk. Malikah-Yi Baltistani, 1/7-15 East Street, Defence Housing Society, Karachi Pakistan. **LC** DS485.B15; S23.

NP
SAGARA. **VFOAT** Nepali Monthly. V. 1, No. 1 (Vaisakha 2038 April/May 1981)-. Periodical. Nepali (Nepali). mo. Rs1.25. Ashok Shreshtha, Madan Printing Press, 9/1212 Asan Balkumari, Kathmandu Nepal. **LC** DS495.5; .S23.

JA
SAISENKAI SHIRYO. No. 1, (1982)-. Japanese. ¥9000. Hokkaido Shuppan Kikaku Senta, Kita-ku North 18, West 6, Sapporo 001 Japan. **LC** DS894.215; .S24.

II
SAJIT. Periodical. English. 1.25 single issue. Sajit Print, 24/5 Karaya Road, Calcutta -17 India. **LC** DS401; .S17. **DD** 954/.005. **UDC** 954.

II
SAMATALA. 1st Year, 1st Issue (Apr. 1983)-. Periodical. Bengali (Bengali). 2.50. Abala Prakashani Yogendranagar Agartala, Tipura India. **LC** DS485.T8; S26.

NP
SANDARBHA. **VFOAT** Sandarva. Vol. 1- April/June 1978. Periodical. English (Nepali). Rs5.00 single issue. M P Khanal, Sandarbha Karyalaya, 11/226 Kamalakshi, Kathmandu Nepal. **LC** DS493; .S25.

IO
SARAN. Periodical. Indonesian. J1 Kiai Tapa, Tomang Plaza, Lantai Dasar Blok B/III-VIII Indonesia. **LC** DS611; .S24.

II
SARASANDHANA : JATIBHEDABIRO- DHISAMITIRAMUKHAPATRA. Vol. 1, (March 1980)-. Bengali. qt. Rs2.00. Jatibheda Birodhi Samiti, 492 Lake Gardens, Calcutta 700045 India. **Tel** 46-7295. **ED** Tridib Chakraborti. **LC** DS422.C3; S218. **UDC** 316.35(540). **Circ:** 500.
Desc: A crusade against the crystallized prejudice structure of the cast system prevalent in the Indian society and encourages publication of anti-caste materials.

IO
SARINAH. **Added/Corp** Koperasi Karyawan Pers Adijaya. No. 1 (Sept. 20-Oct. 3 1982)-. Periodical. Indonesian. sm. 2000 single issue. Jl Garuda No 62, Jakarta Pusat Indonesia. **LC** DS611; .S244.

MY
SARJANA : JURNAL FAKULTI SASTERA DAN SAINS SOSIAL, UNIVERSITI MALAYA. **Added/Corp** Universiti Malaya. Fakulti Sastera dan Sains Sosial. **VFOAT** Jurnal Fakulti Sastera dan Sains Sosial. Vol. 1, No. 1 (Dec. 1981)-. Periodical. English (Malay). sa. 100.00. Chief Editor Sarjana, Faculty of Arts and Social Sciences, University of Malaya, Lembah Pantai, Kuala Lumpur 22-11 Malaysia. **Tel** (03)7555266. **ED** Taib Osman. **LC** DS591; .S27. **DD** 959.5/005. **Bk Rev.** ctrl circ.
Desc: Deals with the basic differences between human legislation and the divine legislation of the Islamic Shariah.
Ind/Abst Rural Dev. Abstr.

US/0278-8772
SAUDI REPORT. [Saudi rep.]. Periodical. English. wk. $250.00. Saudi Research & Marketing Inc, Washington DC 20004. **Tel** (202)638-7183, telex 897 063. **LC** DS201; .S287. **DD** 953/.8053/05. **UDC** 953.2.

TH/0581-8893
SAWADDI. **Added/Corp** American Women's Club of Thailand. (Sept./Oct. 1962)-. Periodical. English. qt. $17.00 Thailand; $25.00 (surface mail), $36.00 (air mail) other. Sawaddi, c/o American Women Club's of Thailand, 33 Rajadamri Road, Bangkok 10500 Thailand. **Tel** 662 2521689. **ED** Joetter Berkompas and Sharmin. **LC** DS561; .S28. Index available. **Bk Rev. Ad Acc. Circ:** 1,500. **Supersedes** American.
Desc: Cultural magazine on Thailand and Southeast Asia.

LE
SAWT AL-ASIFAH. Periodical. Arabic. sm. PO Box 155183, Beirut Lebanon. **LC** DS119.7; .S3517.

CY
SAWT AL-BILAD. **VFOAT** Bilad; Home Land. Periodical. Arabic. wk. $300.00 Institutions, $150.00 Individuals. A-Diyar Press & Publishing Company, Digenis Akritas Avenue No 60/Flat 502, PO Box 629, Nicosia Cyprus. **LC** DS36; .S2943.

IR
SAWT AL-SHAHADAH. Periodical. Arabic. $16.00 Individuals, $21.00 Associations. S B 2165, Tehran Iran. **LC** DS63.1; .S385.

IQ
SAWT AL-SIRYANI. **VFOAT** Qala Suryaya. Periodical. Arabic (Syriac). mo. 1.51ID. Shari Husam Al-Din, Raqam 154 B 2/12 Alawiyah, Baghdad Iraq. **LC** DS70.8.A89; S28.

UA
SAWT FILASTIN. **Added/Corp** Tajammu Al-Watani Al-Filastini (Egypt). (19??)-. Periodical. Arabic. 12 Shari Yusuf Al-Jundi Bab Al-Luq, PO Box 2206, Al-Qahira Egypt. **LC** DS101; .S28.

JA
SAYAMA-SHI BUNKAZAI CHOSA HOKOKU. **Added/Corp** Sayama, Japan. Kyoiku linkai. (19??)-. Periodical. Japanese. Sayama-shi Kyoiku linkai, 2-25 Irumagawa 2, Sayama Japan. **LC** DS897.S28; S28.

History(General) —History of Asia

SZ
SCHWEIZER ASIATISCHE STUDIEN. STUDIENHEFTE. **VFOAT** Swiss Asian Studies; Etudes Asiatiques Suisses. (1978)-. Monographic series. English. Price varies per volume. Verlag Peter Lang AG, Jupiterstrasse 15, CH-3000 Bern 15 Switzerland. **Tel** 011 41 31 9411122, FAX 011 41 31 321131.

US/0272-5827
SEARCH (MIAMI), THE. Ceased. (THE SEARCH.). [Search]. Vol. 1 (1980)-Vol. 9 ( ). Periodical. English. an. Center for Arab Islamic Studies, PO Box 543, Brattleboro VT 05301. **Tel** (802)257-0872, FAX (802)254-5123. **ED** Samir Abed-Rabbo. **LC** DS36; .S38. **DD** 909/.0974927. **UDC** 930.85(927). **Bk Rev**. **Ad Acc**. **Circ**: 1,000 (ctrl).
Desc: Focuses on social, cultural, economic and political events in Arab Islamic countries.
Ind/Abst Am. Hist. Life (1980-).

JA
SEKAI NI HIRAKU MADO. Added/Corp Nihon Tampa Hoso. (19??)-. Periodical. Japanese. mo. ¥150. Nihon Tampa Hoso, 9-15 Akasaka 1-chome Minato-ku, Tokyo 107 Japan. **LC** DS845; .S35.

FR/0248-8515
SEKSA KHMER. VFOAT Etudes Khmeres; Khmer Studies. No. 1-2 (Dec. 1980)-. Periodical. Khmer (English and French). an. 218 rue Saint-Jacques, 75005 Paris France. **LC** DS554.42; .S44. **DD** 959.6/005. **UDC** 959.6.

TU
SELCUKLU ARASTRMALAR DERGISI. Added/Corp Selcuklu Tarih ve Medeniyeti Enstitusu (Ankara, Turkey). **VFOAT** Journal of Seljuk Studies. (1969)-. Multiple languages (Turkish). an. Selcuklu Tarih Ve Medeniyeti Enstitusu, Posta Kutusu 244, Yenisehir-Ankara Turkey. **LC** DS27; .S44.

JA
SENTA TSUSHIN. VFOAT Center News. Periodical. English (Japanese). Kokusai Koryu Kikin, c/o Park Building 3-6 Kioicho, Chiyoda-ku, Tokyo 102 Japan. **Tel** 03 2634504, telex J-23424 KIKINTYO. **LC** DS834.95; .S4.

IT/0582-7906
SERIE ORIENTALE ROMA. Added/Corp Istituto Italiano per il Medio ed Estremo Oriente. **VFOAT** Rome Orientale Series. (1950)-. Monographic series. Italian (Italian). Price varies per volume. Herder Editrice e Libreria SRL, Piazza Montecitorio 117-120, 00186 Rome Italy. **Tel** 011 39 6 679 4628, FAX 011 39 6 678 4751. **ED** Giuseppe Tucci.
Desc: Far East and Middle Eastern studies.

JA
SETO NAIKAI REKISHI MINZOKU SHIRYOKAN NEMPO. Japanese. an. Seto Naikai Rekishi Minzoku Shiryokan, 1412-2 Tarumicho, Takamatsu-shi 761 Japan. **LC** DS894.79.I54; A27.

LY
SHABAB AL-ARAB. VFOAT Majallat Shabab Al-Arab. Periodical. Arabic. mo. $3.00 single issue. PO Box 12130-10826, Tripoli Libya. **LC** DS36; .S42.

CC
SHANG-HAI HUA PAO. VFOAT Shanghai Huabao. (1982)-. Periodical. Chinese. bm. RMBY1.20. Hsin Hua Shu Tien / Shang-Hai Fa Hsing So, Shanghai, People's Republic of China. **LC** DS796.S2; S445. **DD** 951/.132/005.

CC
SHANG-HAI PO WU KUAN CHI KAN. **VFOAT** Shang-Hai Museum Journal. 1982-. Chinese. RMBY3.50. Hsin Hua Shu Tien / Shang-Hai Fa Hsing So, Shanghai, People's Republic of China. **LC** DS715; .K78. **DD** 931. **UDC** 931. **Continues** Kuan Kan.
Ind/Abst Art Archaeol. Tech. Abstr.

UA/0582-9615
SHARQ (CAIRO, EGYPT). (AL-SHARQ.). **VFOAT** Majallat Al-Sharq. Began with: No 1 (April 1957). Periodical. Arabic. mo. FH, PO Box 1509, Cairo A R Egypt. **ED** Muhammad Mandur. **LC** DS36; .S47.

CH/0582-9860
SHENG LI CHIH KUANG. VFOAT Torch of Victory. Began with July 1953 issue. Periodical. Chinese. mo. $30.00 US. The New China Publication Service, 170 Hsin Sheng North Road Sec 3, Taipei Taiwan. **LC** AP95.C4; S432. **DD** 951/.249/005. **UDC** 952.91.

JA
SHIBORUTO KENKYU : HOSEI DAIGAKU FON SHIBORUTO KENKYUKAI KAISHI. VFOAT Hosei Daigaku Fon Shiboruto Kenkyukai Kaishi; Siebold Kenkyu; Bulletin of the Von Siebold Society of Hosie University. July 1982 Edition-. Japanese (summaries and/or abstracts in English). Hosei Daigaku, 17-1 Fujimi 2 Chiyoda-ku, Tokyo-To 102 Japan. **LC** DS834.9.S55; S53 . **UDC** 952.

JA/0386-9342
SHIGAKU KENKYU (HIROSHIMA. 1929). (SHIGAKU KENKYU.). [Shigaku kenkyu]. **Added/Corp** Hiroshima Shigaku Kenkyukai. **VFOAT** Review of Historical Studies. (Oct. 1929)-. Periodical. Japanese (summaries and/or abstracts in English; table of contents in English and Japanese). ir. **(Subscription address**: Maruzen Company Ltd., PO Box 5050, Import & Export Department, Tokyo 100 31 Japan.) ctrl circ.
Desc: Organ papers of the Hiroshima Historical Study Club.
Ind/Abst Am. Hist. Life (1955-1959).

JA
SHIGAKU ZASSHI. Added/Corp Shigakkai (Japan). **VFOAT** Zeitschrift fur Geschichtswissenschaft; Journal of Historical Science; Historical Journal of Japan. (1892)-. Periodical. Japanese (summaries and/or abstracts in English). mo. $196.00. **(Subscription address**: Kyowa Book Company Inc., 1 38 Kanda Jinbocho Chiyoda-ku, Tokyo 101 Japan.) **LC** D1; .S4338. cum. index. **Continues** Shigakukai Zasshi.
Ind/Abst Am. Hist. Life (1954-).

CH
SHIH CHI KAN KAO / KUO LI CHENG-KUNG TA HSUEH LI SHIH HSUEH HSI SHIH CHI YEN CHIU SHIH PIEN. VFOAT Bulletin of Taiwan Historical Studies. Periodical. Chinese. National Chengkung University, Department of History, Tainan Taiwan. **LC** DS799.3; .S45. **DD** 951/.249. **UDC** 952.91.

CC
SHIH HSUEH CHING PAO / CHUNG-KUO SHIH HSUEH HUI, CHUNG-KUO LI SHIH HSUEH NIEN CHIEN PIEN CHI PU PIEN. Began in 1982 with No. 1. Periodical. Chinese. qt. RMBY0.50. Hsin Hua Shu Tien, Beijing, People's Republic of China. **Tel** 551253. **LC** DS701; .S44. **DD** 951/.0072. **UDC** 951. **Bk Rev**. **Circ**: 12,000.
Desc: Presents new achievements in the history and research in China.

CC
SHIH HSUEH SHIH YEN CHIU. Added/Corp Pei-Ching Shih fan ta Hsueh. Shih Hsueh yen Chiu so. Pei-Ching Shih fan ta Hsueh. Ku chi yen Chiu so. **VFOAT** Journal of Historiography. (19??)-. Periodical. Chinese. qt. **LC** DS734.7; .S497. **DD** 951/.0072.
Ind/Abst Am. Hist. Life (1990-).

HK
SHIH TAI PI PING. VFOAT Modern Critique. Began with June 15, 1938 issue. Periodical. Chinese. qt. HK$2.00. Modern Critique, Government Printing Office, Box 5699, Hong Kong. **LC** AP95.C4; S43915. **DD** 951.05/05. **UDC** 951.

JA/0386-9369
SHIRIN (KYOTO. 1916). (SHIRIN / SHIGAKU KENKYUKAI.). [Shirin]. **Added/Corp** Shigakukai (Japan). **VFOAT** Shirin (Journal of History); Shirin, or, The Journal of History, 1930; Journal of History. (Jan. 1916)-. Periodical. Japanese. bm. $100.00. **(Subscription address**: Maruzen Company Ltd., PO Box 5050, Import & Export Department, Tokyo 100 31 Japan.) **LC** D1; .S478. cum. index. ctrl circ.
Desc: Organ papers of Shigaku-Kenkyu-Kai.
Ind/Abst Am. Hist. Life (1955-).

JA
SHIRYO HENSHUSHITSU KIYO. 1987-. Periodical. Japanese. Okinawa Library Association, Okinawa Prefectural Library, 2-16 Yorimiya 1-chome, Naha Okinawa Japan. **LC** DS894.99.O37; O36A. **Continues** Okinawa Shiryo Henshujo Kiyo.

JA
SHOHO. Main/Corp Saitama Kenritsu Minzoku Bunka Senta. **VFOAT** Saitama Kenritsu Minzoku Bunka Senta Shoho. 1-. Academic Scholarly Publication. Japanese. Saitama Kenritsu Minzoku Bunka Senta, 10068-2 Aza Nakajima, Oaaz Kakura, Iwatsuki-shi 339 Japan. **LC** DS894.49.S244; S27A. Documents available from CASDDS.
Ind/Abst Chem. Abstr.

JA
SHUKAN TOYOGAKU. VFOAT Chinese and Oriental Studies; Toyogaku. (19??)-. Periodical. Japanese (Japanese). Twice a year. $30.00 US. Chugoku Bunsh Ken, Tohoko University, Society for Chinese Literature/History and Philosophy, Sendai Japan. **(Subscription address**: Kyowa Book Company Inc., 1 38 Kanda Jinbocho Chiyoda-ku, Tokyo 101 Japan.) **LC** DS701; .S46.

UK
SHUUN AL-SAAH. VFOAT Shun As-Saa. Periodical. Arabic. **LC** DS36; .S497.

TI
SHUUN ARABIYAH. VFOAT Journal of Arab Affairs; Shoun Arabiyya. No. 1 (Festival Year 1981)-. Periodical. Arabic. mo. Jamit Al-Duwal, Al-Arabiyah 37 Nahj Khayr Al-Don Basha, 1002 Tunis Tunisia. **LC** DS36; .S5.
Ind/Abst Middle East J.

●UK
SIBIRICA : THE JOURNAL OF SIBERIAN STUDIES. VFOAT Sibirica. Vol. 1, No. 1 (1994)-. Periodical. English. sa. £14.00 (individuals), £18.00 (institutions) UK; £18.00 (individuals), £22.00 (institutions) other. Lancaster University Department of History, Professor Alan Wood, Lancaster LA1 4YG England. **(Subscription address**: Ryburn Distribution, Keele University Press, Keele University, Staffordshire ST5 5BG England.) **LC** DK751; .S532. **Continues** Siberia.

MY
SINAR ZAMAN. V. 1- Ogos 1972-. Malay. Jabatan Penerangan Malaysia, Kementerian Penerangan, Jalan Tun Perak, Kuala Lumpur Malaysia. **LC** DS591; .S48.

PK
SINDHOLOGICAL STUDIES. Summer 1977-. Periodical. English. qt. Rs15.00. University of Sind / Institute of Sindhology, Jamshoro Pakistan. **LC** DS392.S5; S56. **DD** 954.9/18/005. **UDC** 954.9.

NE/0169-9563
SINICA LEIDENSIA. Added/Corp Rijksuniversiteit te Leiden. Sinologisch Instituut. Vol. 1 (1931)-. Monographic series. English (Dutch and English). ir. Price varies per volume. E. J. Brill, Postbus 9000, 2300 PA Leiden Netherlands. **Tel** 011 31 71 312624, FAX 011 31 71 317532, telex 39296 BRILL NL. **LC** DS701; .S48.

US
SINO-JAPANESE STUDIES. Added/Corp Sino-Japanese Studies Group (U.S.). **VFOAT** Chung Jih yen Chiu; Chu-Nichi Kenkyu. **VAT** Chu Nichi Kenkyu; Sino Japanese Studies. Vol. 2, No. 1 (Dec. 1989)-. Periodical. English. Twice a year (May & Nov.). $15.00 (individual), $25.00 (institution). University of California - Santa Barbara, Department of History, Santa Barbara CA 93106. **Tel** (805)893-4065, FAX (805)893-8975. **ED** Joshua Fogel. **LC** DS740.5.J3; S56. **DD** 303.48/251052. **Bk Rev**, (Qty: varies). **Ad Acc**. **Pr Rev. Circ**: 135. **Continues** Sino-Japanese Studies Newsletter, 1041-8830.

JA
SOKA-SHI SHI KENKYU. 1981 Ed.-. Japanese. Soka-shi, 1-1 Yakasago 1, Saitama-ken 340, Shoka-shi Japan. **LC** DS897.S65; S64.

●RU
SOTSIALNYE I GUMANITARNYE NAUKI. SERIIA 9, VOSTOKOVEDENIE I AFRIKANISTIKA. ZARUBEZHNAIA LITERATURA / ROSSIISKAIA AKADEMIIA NAUK, INSTITUT NAUCHNOI INFORMATSII PO OBSHCHESTVENNYM NAUKAM. Added/Corp Institut Nauchnoi Informatsii po Obshchestvennym Naukam (Rossiiskaia Akademiia Nauk). **VFOAT** Vostokovedenie i Afrikanistika. Zarubezhnaia Literatura; Zarubzhnaia Literatura. (1993)-. Periodical. Russian. qt. Inion An SSSR, Ulitsa Krasikova D 28/45, Moscow Russia. **Tel** 128.89.71. **LC** DS1; .O24. **Continues** Obshchestvennye Nauki za Rubezhom. Seriia 9, Vostokovedenie i Afrikanistika.

US/0732-6424
SOURCES FROM THE ANCIENT NEAR EAST. (SOURCES AND MONOGRAPHS. SOURCES FROM THE ANCIENT NEAR EAST.). [Sources anc. Near East]. **VFOAT** Sources from the Ancient Near East; SANE. Vol. 1 (1974)-. Monographic series. English. ir. Price varies per volume. Undena Publications, PO Box 97, Malibu CA 90265. **Tel** (310)649-2612. **(Subscription address**: Crescent Academic Services, 29528 Madera Avenue, Shafter CA 93263.) **ED** G. Buccellati and M. Kelly-Buccellati. **LC** UNC. **Circ**: 300.
Desc: Original documents on history, religion, art and archaeology of Ancient Near East.
Ind/Abst Old Testam. Abstr.

US
SOURCES OF ORIENTAL LANGUAGES AND LITERATURES / DOGU DILLERI VE EDEBIYATLARNN KAYNAKLAR. Added/Corp Harvard University. Dept. of Near Eastern Languages and Civilizations. **VFOAT** Dogu Dilleri Ve Edebiyatlarinin Kaynaklari. Vol. 1 (1970)-. Monographic series. English (Turkish, French and German). ir. Price varies per volume. Tekin / Journal of Turkish Studies, PO Box 1447, Duxbury MA 02331. **Tel** (617)585-8796. **ED** Sinasi Tekin and Gonul Alpay Tekin. **Ad Acc**.
Desc: Original research material on Islam, Central Asia, and medieval Middle East. Turkish, Arabic, and Persian original manuscripts in facsimile forms with English translations and annotations.

AT/0085-6401
SOUTH ASIA. [South Asia]. **Added/Corp** South Asian Studies Association. No. 1 (Aug. 1971)-. Periodical. English. tq (3 issues). 80.00Aus$ Australia; 112.55Aus$

other. South Asian Studies Association, University of New England, Department of History, Armidale New South Wales 2351 Australia. **Tel** 011 61 67 732067, 011 61 67 732479, FAX 011 61 67 733520, telex 166050. **ED** Dr. Howard Brasted (editor's telephone: 011 61 67 732081). **LC** DS331; .S65. **DD** 309.1/54. Index available ($15.00). cum. index. **Bk Rev**, (Qty: 35). **Ad Acc. Pr Rev. Circ:** 330.
Desc: Journal of South Asian history, politics and culture.
Ind/Abst Am. Hist. Life (1971-); APAIS, Aust. Public Aff. Inf. Ser. (1973-); Rural Dev. Abstr.

US/0732-3867
SOUTH ASIA BULLETIN. [South Asia bull.]. **Added/Corp** South Asia Association (University of California, Los Angeles) University of California, Los Angeles. Vol. 1 (Winter 1981)-. Bulletin. English. sa (2 issues). $40.00 (institutions), $20.00 (individuals) US; $46.00 (institutions), $26.00 (individuals) other. Duke University Press, PO Box 90660, Durham NC 27708-0660. **Tel** (919)687-3600, (919)688-5134 (orders), FAX (919)688-4574, telex 802829. **ED** Vasant Kaiwar and Sucheta Mazumdar. **LC** DS335; .S58. **DD** 954/.005. **Bk Rev. Ad Acc. Circ:** 700 (ctrl).
Desc: The journal examines current trends in South Asian society, as well as the colonial period.
Ind/Abst Altern. Press Index; Am. Hist. Life (1986-); Geogr. Abstr. Human Geogr. (?-?); Hum. Rights Intern. Rep.; Int. Bibliogr. Sociol.; Int. Dev. Abstr.; Int. Labour Doc.; LABORDOC; PAIS Int. Print; Soc. Plann. Policy Dev. Abstr.

US/1059-4981
SOUTH ASIA CURRENTS [COMPUTER FILE]. [South Asia curr.]. (1991)-. English. da. Free. The India Journal, PO Box 552, Flushing NY 11352-0552. **DD** 954.
Desc: Email on BITNET.

US/0889-8650
SOUTH ASIA IN REVIEW. ***Ceased.*** [South Asia rev.]. Vol. 1 (Oct. 1976)-(199?). Periodical. English. qt. South Asia Books, PO Box 502, Columbia MO 65205. **Tel** (314)474-0116. **ED** B David Burke. **LC** DS331; .S6525. **DD** 954/.005. **Bk Rev. Ad Acc. Circ:** 1,000 (ctrl).
Desc: Reviews recent monographs and books on South Asia. Covers all disciplines.

UK/0038-2841
SOUTH ASIAN REVIEW. [South Asian rev.]. Periodical. English. qt. £6.40. Royal Society for India, Pakistan and Ceylon, Victoria Hall, SE10 ORF. **LC** DS331; .A85. **DD** 954/.005. **UDC** 954. ***Continues*** *Asian Review (London, England).*
Ind/Abst Am. Hist. Life (1971-1975).

II/0038-285X
SOUTH ASIAN STUDIES (JAIPUR). (SOUTH ASIAN STUDIES.). [South Asian stud.]. **Added/Corp** University of Rajasthan. South Asia Studies Centre. Vol. 1 (1966)-. Periodical. English. sa (June, Dec.). $24.00. University of Rajasthan South Asia Studies Centre, Gandhi Nagar, Jaipur 302004 India. **Tel** 011 91 511175. **(Subscription address:** Prints India, 11 Darya Ganj, New Delhi 110002 India.**) ED** Prof. Ramakant. **LC** DS335; .S62. **Bk Rev. Circ:** 350.
Ind/Abst Am. Hist. Life (1971-1974, 1980-); Int. Polit. Sci. Abstr.; World Agric. Econ.

UK/0266-6030
SOUTH ASIAN STUDIES (SOCIETY FOR SOUTH ASIAN STUDIES). (SOUTH ASIAN STUDIES : JOURNAL OF THE SOCIETY FOR SOUTH ASIAN STUDIES (INCORPORATING THE SOCIETY FOR AFGHAN STUDIES).). [South Asian stud.]. **Added/Corp** Society for South Asian Studies, Incorporating the Society for Afghan Studies. Vol. 1 (1985)-. Monographic series. English. an. £30.00. British Museum, Great Russell Street, London WC1B 3DG England. **Tel** 011 44 71 3238274. ***Continues*** *Afghan Studies, 0265-4822.*
Ind/Abst Int. Bibliogr. Sociol.

II
SOUTH ASIAN SURVEY. (1976)-. Periodical. English. sa. $72.00. SAGE Periodical Press, 2455 Teller Road, Thousand Oaks CA 91320. **Tel** (805)499-0721, FAX (805)499-0871, telex 100799. **LC** DS331; .S66. **DD** 954.05/05.

II
SOUTH EAST ASIAN REVIEW, THE. **Added/Corp** Institute of South East Asian Studies, Gaya, India. Vol. 1 (Aug. 1976)-. Periodical. English. sa. $34.00. Centre for South East Asian Studies, Ramsagar Road, Gaya 823001 Bihar India. **(Subscription address:** Prints India, 11 Darya Ganj, New Delhi 110002 India.**) ED** Sachchidanand Sahai. **LC** DS501; .S756. **DD** 959/.005. **Bk Rev. Ad Acc. Circ:** 1,000 (ctrl).
Desc: Covers Southeast Asian social sciences and humanities.

US
SOUTHEAST ASIA PAPER. Added/Corp University of Hawaii (Honolulu). Southeast Asian Studies Program. No. 12 (1979)-. Monographic series. English. ir. Price varies per volume. University of Hawaii, Southeast Asian Studies Program, 1890 E-W Road, Moore 415, Honolulu HI 96822. **Tel** (808)956-2688, FAX (808)956-6345. ***Continues*** *Southeast Asian Studies Working Paper.*

US
SOUTHEAST ASIA PROGRAM SERIES. English. price varies. Southeast Asia Program Publications, East Hill Plaza, Cornell University, Ithaca NY 14850. **Tel** (607)255-8038, FAX (607)277-1904. **(Subscription telephone:** (607)255-8038**) ED** Audrey R. Kahin; telephone: (607)255-4359. **Pr Rev.**
Desc: Occasional paper series that includes books of academic interest on the modern history of Southeast Asia.

US/0073-4934
SPECIAL REPORT (NORTHERN ILLINOIS UNIVERSITY. CENTER FOR SOUTHEAST ASIAN STUDIES). (SPECIAL REPORT - CENTER FOR SOUTHEAST ASIAN STUDIES, NORTHERN ILLINOIS UNIVERSITY.). **Added/Corp** Northern Illinois University. Center for Southeast Asian Studies. No. 1 (1969)-. Monographic series. English. ir. Price varies per volume. Center for Southeast Asian Studies, 410 Adams Hall, NIU, Dekalb IL 60115. **Tel** (815)753-1771, (815)753-0246, FAX (815)753-0198, telex 981417. **LC** UNC.

US/0273-4532
SPRING-AUTUMN PAPERS. [Spring-autumn pap.]. **VFOAT** Chun Chiu Chi Kan. English. sa. Center for Chinese Studies University of Michigan, 104 Lane Hall, Ann Arbor MI 48109. **Tel** (313)764-6308. **LC** DS510.7; .S69. **DD** 951/.005. **UDC** 951.

II
SRIRANGA. VFOAT Sri Ranga. Periodical. Gujarati (Gujarati). 22.00. Prajabandhu Presa, Gujarat Samachar Bhavan Khanpur, Amadavada India. **LC** DS485.G8; S7.

CC
SSU-CHUAN HUA PAO. Periodical. Chinese. RMBY1.00. Post Office, Cheng-Tu, People's Republic of China. **LC** D793.S8; S685. **DD** 951/.38/005. **UDC** 951.

CC
SSU-CHUAN SHIH YUAN HSUEH PAO. SHE HUI KO HSUEH PAN / SICHUANSHI YUANXUEBAO. Added/Corp Ssu-chuan Shih Fan Hsueh Yuan. **VFOAT** Sichuanshi Yuanxuebao; Journal of Sichuan Teachers College. Social Sciences Edition. (19??)-. Periodical. Chinese. qt. RMBY0.35. Ssu-Chuan Shih Yuan Hsueh Pao, Post Office, Cheng-Tu Shih, People's Republic of China. **LC** AS452.C4617; A35. **DD** 951/.005.

IT/0081-6124
STUDI CLASSICI E ORIENTALI. See Classical Studies.

IT
STUDI EBLAITI / MISSIONE ARCHEOLOGICA ITALIANA IN SIRIA. See Archaeology.

FR/0221-5004
STUDIA IRANICA. [Stud. iran.]. Vol. 1- 1972-. Periodical. Multiple languages (English and French). sa. 51.00F. Librairie Orientaliste Paul Geuthner, 12 rue Vavin, 75006 Paris France. **Tel** 011 33 1 46347130. **LC** DS251; .S78. **UDC** 955.
Ind/Abst Index Islam. Lit.; MLA Int. Bibl. Books Artic. Mod. Lang. Lit.; Numis. Lit.

NE/0772-7852
STUDIA IRANICA. (19??)-. French. sa (2 issues). 2000F. Editions Peeters SA, Bondgenotenlaan 153, BP 41, B-3000 Leuven Belgium. **Tel** 32 16 235170, FAX 32 16 228500, telex 65987 PUL B. **ED** M.Ph. Gignoux and R. Gyselen. **Bk Rev. Ad Acc.**

GW/0341-4191
STUDIEN ZUR INDOLOGIE UND IRANISTIK. [Stud. Indol. Iran.]. No. 1- 1975-. Multiple languages. AUI Wezler Verlag, Langenhege 62B, W-2057 Reinbek Germany. **LC** DS423; .S8. **UDC** 954/955.
Ind/Abst MLA Int. Bibl. Books Artic. Mod. Lang. Lit.

US/0081-7554
STUDIES IN ANCIENT ORIENTAL CIVILIZATION. See Archaeology.

II/0257-6430
STUDIES IN HISTORY NEW DELHI. [Stud. Hist.New Delhi]. (1985)-. Periodical. English. sa. $72.00. SAGE Periodical Press, 2455 Teller Road, Thousand Oaks CA 91320. **Tel** (805)499-0721, FAX (805)499-0871, telex 100799. **UDC** 93.

US/0258-1698
STUDIES IN HISTORY (SAHIBABAD). (STUDIES IN HISTORY.). [Stud. hist.]. Vol. 1 (Jan./June 1979)-. Periodical. English. sa. $65.00. Sage India, Sage Publications, Inc., India Private Limited, PO Box 4215, New Delhi 110 048 India). **(Subscription address:** US/ PO Box 5096, Thousand Oaks, CA 91359; India, Malaysia, Pakistan, Sri Lanka, Nepal, Bangladesh and Bhutan/ PO Box 4215, New Delhi 110 048 India**) ED** S Gopal. **LC** DS401; .S834. **DD** 954/.005. **UDC** 954. Index available. **Ad Acc.** available on microfilm and microfiche from University Microfilms International (UMI).
Desc: Reflects the expansion and diversification of research in India in recent years.
Ind/Abst Am. Hist. Life (1979-); Geogr. Abstr. Human Geogr. (?-?); Int. Bibliogr. Sociol.

II
STUDIES IN MODERN INDIAN HISTORY. No. 1- 1972-. English. 30.00. Orient Longman Ltd, 3-6-272 Himayatnagar, Hyderabad 500 029 India. **Tel** 011 91 842 240305, telex 4256803. **LC** DS480.45; .S73. **DD** 954/.008. **UDC** 954.

US/0081-8291
STUDIES IN NEAR EASTERN CIVILIZATION. V. 1- 1968-. Monographic series. English. ir. Price varies per volume. Columbia University Press, 136 South Broadway, Irvington NY 10533. **Tel** (914)591-9111. **UDC** 95-011.

US/0081-8321
STUDIES IN ORIENTAL CULTURE. No. 1 (1967)-. Monographic series. English. ir. Price varies per volume. Columbia University Press, 136 South Broadway, Irvington NY 10533. **Tel** (914)591-9111.

NE/0169-9865
STUDIES IN SOUTH ASIAN CULTURE. ***Title Change.*** **Added/Corp** Universiteit van Amsterdam. Instituut voor Zuid-Aziatische Archeologie. Vol. 1 (1969)-(199?). Monographic series. English. ir. E. J. Brill, Postbus 9000, 2300 PA Leiden Netherlands. **Tel** 011 31 71 312624, FAX 011 31 71 317532, telex 39296 BRILL NL. **LC** DS503; .S77. ***Continued by*** *Studies in Asian Art and Archaeology.*

US
STUDIES ON EAST ASIA. Added/Corp Western Washington University. Center for East Asian Studies. Vol. 13 (1979)-. Monographic series. English. ir. Price varies per volume. Center for East Asian Studies / Western Washington University, Bellingham WA 98225. **Tel** (206)676-3041. ***Continues*** *Western Washington University. Program in East Asian Studies. Occasional Papers.*
Desc: Focuses on both the individual countries and cultures of East Asia and on the region itself, covering a wide range of topics and periods.

US
STUDIES ON SOUTHEAST ASIA. English. ir. price varies. Southeast Asia Program Publications, East Hill Plaza, Cornell University, Ithaca NY 14850. **Tel** (607)255-8038, FAX (607)277-1904. **(Subscription telephone:** (607)255-8038**) ED** Audrey R Kahin; telephone: (607)255-4359. **Pr Rev.**
Desc: Ocassional papers of academic interest on Southeast Asia.

RM/0585-511X
STVDIA ET ACTA ORIENTALIA. (STUDIA ET ACTA ORIENTALIA / SOCIETE DES SCIENCES HISTORIQUES ET PHILOLOGIQUES DE LA R.P.R., SECTION D'ETUDES ORIENTALES.). [Stvd. acta orient.]. **Added/Corp** Societatea de Stiinte Istorice si Filologice din R.P.R. Section d'Etudes Orientales. Asociatia de Studii Orientale din R.S. Romania. (1957)-. Periodical. French. sa. **LC** DS1; .S784. **DD** 950/.05.
Ind/Abst Am. Hist. Life (1962-1971); Numis. Lit.

FR
SUDESTASIE MAGAZINE. ***Suspended.*** **VFOAT** Sudestasie. (19??)-(19??). Periodical. French. bm. Sudestasie Magazine, 17 rue Cardinale Lemoine, 75005 Paris France. **LC** DS520; .S84. **DD** 959/.005.

GW/0722-8821
SUDOSTASIEN AKTUELL. Added/Corp Institut fuer Asienkunde (Hamburg, Germany) Dokumentations-Leitstelle Asien (Institut fuer Asienkunde). Vol. 1, No. 1 (Sept. 1982)-. Periodical. German (English). Six times a year. DM108.00 Germany; DM120.00 others. Institute of Asian Affairs, Rothenbaumchaussee 32, D-20148 Hamburg Germany. **Tel** 011 49 40 443001, FAX 011 49 40 4107945.
Ind/Abst PAIS Int. Print.

US
SUVANNABHUMI. Added/Corp Arizona State University. Program for Southeast Asian Studies. **VFOAT** Southeast Asia, Land of Gold. Vol. 1, No. 1 (Feb. 1990)-. Periodical. English. sa. Arizona State University / Program for Southeast Asian Studies, Tempe AZ 85287-3101. **LC** DS524.8.U6; S98.

II
SWARAJYA. Began publication with issue for July 14, 1956. Periodical. English. mo. Bharathan Publications Private Ltd, Kalki Buildings, Kilpauk Madras 10 India. **LC** DS401.S9.

US/0732-6483
SYRO-MESOPOTAMIAN STUDIES. [Syro-Mesop. stud.]. **Added/Corp** International Institute for Mesopotamian Area Studies. **VFOAT** SMS. **VAT** Syro Mesopotamian Studies. (1977)-. Monographic series. English (French and German). ir. Price varies per volume.

Undena Publications, PO Box 97, Malibu CA 90265. **Tel** (310)649-2612. **(Subscription address:** Crescent Academic Services, 29528 Madera Avenue, Shafter, CA 93263; telephone: (805)746-5870**) ED** M. Kelly-Buccellati. **Circ:** 300.
Desc: Primary sources and analyses on civilizations of ancient Iraq and Syria from late prehistory to first millennium B.C.
Ind/Abst Old Testam. Abstr.

CH
TA LU TSA CHIH. **VFOAT** Continent Magazine. Vol. 1 (July 1950)-. Periodical. Chinese (English). Twelve times a year. $45.60. Ta lu tsa Chih she, 3rd Floor, 61 Fu Chou Str, Taipei Taiwan. **LC** AP95.C4; T3554. **DD** 951/.24905/05. cum. index.
Ind/Abst Am. Hist. Life.

YE
TAAWUN (SANA, YEMEN). (AL-TA AWUN.). Periodical. Arabic. mo. $60.00. S B 2198, Sana Yemen. **LC** DS247.Y48; T28. **UDC** 953.3.

CC
TAI I SHIH / PARLIAMENTARIAN MAGAZINE. **VFOAT** Parliamentarian Magazine; Tai I Shih Tsa Chih. (Oct. 10th 1981)-. Periodical. Chinese. **LC** DS799.83; .T3. **DD** 951/.249057.

CC
TAI SHENG. **Added/Corp** Chung-hua Chuan kuo Tai-Wwan Tung Pao Lien i Hui. (1983)-. Periodical. Chinese. mo. $21.49. Science Press, 16 Donghuangchenggen North Street, Beijing 100707, People's Republic of China. **Tel** 011 86 1 4019821, 011 86 1 4010642, FAX 011 86 1 4012180, 011 86 1 4019810, telex 210147. **(Subscription address:** China International Book Trading Corporation, PO Box 399, Library Service Department, Beijing 100044 People's Republic of China.**) LC** DS777.75; .T36. **DD** 451.05/05.

JA
TAISHO OYOBI TAISHOJIN. (Sept. 1977)-. Periodical. Japanese. bm. ¥5000. Naqushima Building, 3P 9-8 Shinbashi 5, Minato-ku 105 Tokyo Japan. **LC** DS885.8; .T34.

US/1048-2342
TAIWAN STUDIES NEWSLETTER. [Taiwan stud. newsl.]. **Added/Corp** Association for Asian Studies. Committee on Taiwan Studies. Association for Asian Studies. Taiwan Studies Group. Vol. 1, No. 1 (Jan. 1974)-. Newsletter. English. Twice a year (May, Nov.). $10.00 (one year); $18.00 (two years). Association for Asian Studies Inc., University of Michigan, 1 Lane Hall, Ann Arbor MI 48109. **Tel** (313)665-2490, FAX (313)665-3801. **ED** Jack F. Williams. **DD** 951. **Bk Rev. Circ:** 300 (ctrl). ***Continued in part by*** *Directory of Taiwan Scholars, 1048-2350.*
Desc: Dissemination of information of interest to Taiwan scholars.

US/0737-6197
TAIWAN YU SHIJIE. (TAI-WAN YU SHIH CHIEH.). [Taiwan yu shijie]. **VFOAT** Taiwan and World Monthly; Taiwan and World; Taiwan & World. 1 (June 1983)-. Periodical. English. mo (except Aug. and Jan.). $20.00 (individuals), $40.00 (libraries and institutions) US; $30.00 (individuals), $40.00 (libraries and institutions) other. T & W Enterprises, 415 West 13th Street, New York NY 10012. **LC** DS798.92; .T34. **DD** 951/.249/005. **UDC** 952.91. ***Continues*** *Taiwan Review.*

FR
TALIAH (PARIS, FRANCE). (AL-TALIAH.). **VFOAT** At-Taliaa; Taliaa. Periodical. Arabic. wk. Arabia Presse S A R L, 11 rue de la Boetie, 75008 Paris France. **LC** DS63.1; .T34.

II
TAMIL STUDIES (MADIRAI, INDIA). (TAMIL STUDIES.). Vol. 1, No. 1 (Oct. 1981)-. Periodical. English. qt. Rs40.00. 96 N G O Colony, Madurai Tamil Nadu 625019 India. **LC** DS432.T3; T36. **DD** 306/.089948. **UDC** 954.8.

UK/0266-4488
TAMIL TIMES. **Added/Corp** Society for Ethnic Amity (Sri Lanka). (198?)-. Periodical. English. Twelve times a year. £15.00 UK; £20.00 others. Tamil Times Limited, PO Box 121, Sutton Surrey SM1 3TD, England. **Tel** 011 44 81 6440972. **ED** P. Rajanayagam (editor's address: 13 Arbuthnot Lane, Bexley, Kent DA5 1EH England, phone: (0322-550191). Index available. cum. index. **Circ:** 3,500 (ctrl).
Ind/Abst Hum. Rights Intern. Rep.

US/0737-5034
TANG STUDIES. [Tang stud.]. **Added/Corp** Tang Studies Society. No. 1 (1982)-. English (Chinese). an. $15.00 (institutions), $10.00 (individuals). Tang Studies Society / Department of History, Rhodes College, 2000 North Parkway, Memphis TN 38112. **Tel** (901)726-3655, FAX (901)726-3718. **ED** Paul W. Kroll (editor's address: Department of Oriental Languages and Literatures, Campus Box 279, University of Colorado, Boulder CO 80309; telephone: (303)492-7060). **DD** 950. **Pr Rev. Circ:** 215.
Desc: Devoted to the Tang period (618-906 A.D.), especially in China. Includes articles, reviews and bibliographies on art, literature, history, music, etc.

US/1065-6871
TAP CHI NGI DAN. [Tap chi ngi dan]. **VFOAT** Nguoidan Magazine; Ngi Dan Magazine; Ngi Dan. (1990)-. Periodical. Vietnamese. Twelve times a year. $18.00 US; $34.00 Canada & Mexico & Europe; $40.00 others. Tap Chi Ngoui Dan, PO Box 2674, Costa Mesa CA 92628. **Tel** (714)241-1665, FAX (310)402-3070. **ED** Nhiem Tong. **DD** 959. **Circ:** 1,000.
Desc: An attempt to reflect or represent the voices of the silent majority of overseas vietnamese people.

US
TAP HOP. (19??)-. Periodical. Vietnamese. mo. $12.00. Tap Hop, PO Box 4108, Huntington Beach CA 92605.

LE
TARIKH AL-ARAB WA-AL-ALAM. **VFOAT** History of the Arabs and the World. Vol. 1 (Nov. 1978)-. Periodical. Arabic. £L50.00. Dar Al-Siyasah Lil-Sihhafah Wa-Al-Nashr, PO Box 5905, Beirut Lebanon. **LC** DS37.7; .T37.

LE
TARIKHUNA. Began in 1980/1981. Periodical. Arabic. mo. £L100.00. Dar Al-Shura Binayat Al-Tajir Shari Kliminsu, SB 4251, Beirut Lebanon. **LC** DS38.3; .T37.

TH/0125-6637
THAI LIFE. Vol. 1, No. 1 (Oct. 1981)-. Periodical. English. qt. National Identity Board, Phitsanulok Road, Bangkok 10300 Thailand. **Tel** 281-1226. **LC** DS561; .T46. **DD** 959.3/005. **UDC** 930.85(593). **Circ:** 3,000 (ctrl).
Desc: All series show the way of Thai Life style.

II
THINK INDIA. Vol. 1, No. 1 (Aug.-Oct. 1989)-. Periodical. English. qt. $100.00. **(Subscription address:** Prints India, 11 Darya Ganj, New Delhi, 110002 India, (Phone: 011 91 11 3268645)**) LC** DS401; .T47. **DD** 954/.005.

II
TIBET JOURNAL, THE. **Added/Corp** Library of Tibetan Works & Archives. Vol. 1 (July/Sept. 1975)-. Periodical. English. qt. $15.00. Library of Tibetan Works & Archives, Dharamsala, India. **(Subscription address:** Prints India, 11 Darya Ganj, New Delhi 110002 India.**) ED** K Dhonkup. **LC** DS785.A1; T5. **DD** 951/.5/005. **Bk Rev. Ad Acc.**
Desc: An international journal for the study of Tibet and Tibetians.

US/1049-2666
TIBET PRESS WATCH. (TIBET PRESS WATCH : AN INTERNATIONAL SELECTION OF NOTEWORTHY ARTICLES.). [Tibet press watch]. **Added/Corp** International Campaign for Tibet. **VFOAT** TPW. No. 12 (Sept. 1989)-. Periodical. English. bm. International Campaign for Tibet, 1518 K Street NW, Suite 410, Washington DC 20005. **Tel** (202) 628-4123. **LC** DS785.A1; T513. **DD** 951/.5/005.
Ind/Abst Hum. Rights Intern. Rep.

II
TIBETAN BULLETIN (DHARMSALA, INDIA : 1981). (TIBETAN BULLETIN.). (19??)-. Bulletin. English. bm. $10.00. **(Subscription address:** Prints India, 11 Darya Ganj, New Delhi, 110002 India, (Phone: 011 91 11 3268645)**) LC** DS785.A1; T515. **DD** 951/.5/005. ***Continues*** *Tibetan Review.*

CC
TIEN-CHIN WEN SHIH TZU LIAO HSUAN CHI. V. 1, (Dec. 1978)-. Periodical. Chinese. RMBY0.77. Hsin Hua Shu Tien / Tien-Chin, Tien-Chin Shih, People's Republic of China. **LC** DS796.T5; T523. **DD** 951/.15. **UDC** 951.

CE
TIMES DIGEST, THE. V. 1- Sept. 1973-. Periodical. English. 1.50 each issue. Times of Ceylon Ltd, Times Building 2 Bristol Street Fort, Colombo Ceylon. **LC** DS488; .T55. **DD** 954.9/3/005. **UDC** 948.7.

II
TIRUNILAKANTAN. **VFOAT** Thiruneelakandan. (19??)-. Periodical. Tamil. mo. K Baghyam 1, Puthu Theru Salem 646001 India. **LC** DS432.K758; T57.

KO
TOBAGI. Vol. 1 (Spring 1984)-. Periodical. Korean. W2800 each issue. Tongbo Sojok, 165-5 Pujon 2-dong Pusanjin-ku, Pusan Korea. **LC** DS924.K93; T6.

JA
TODA SHISHI KENKYU. **Added/Corp** Toda-shi (Japan). Shishi Hensanshitsu. No. 1 (1977)-. Monographic series. Japanese. Price varies per volume. Toda-Shi, 18-1 Kami Toda 1, Toda Japan. **LC** DS897.T467; T6.

JA/0495-7199
TOHOGAKU. **Added/Corp** Toho Gakkai. **VFOAT** Eastern Studies. Vol. 1, No. 1 (March 1951)-. Periodical. Japanese (summaries and/or abstracts in English). sa. $58.00. Institute of Eastern Culture / Tokyo, 4-1 2 Nishikanda Chome, Chiyoda-ku Tokyo Japan. **Tel** 011 81 3 3261 1061. **(Subscription address:** Maruzen Company Ltd., PO Box 5050, Import & Export Department, Tokyo 100 31 Japan.**) ED** Mori Masao. **Bk Rev. Circ:** 2,200 (ctrl).
Desc: Covers the field of Asian studies.
Ind/Abst MLA Int. Bibl. Books Artic. Mod. Lang. Lit.

MY
TOKOH P2 S POLITIK MALAYSIA. V. 1 (March 1981)-. Periodical. Malay. bm. $2.50. Golongan Penerbit Malaysian, 9 Tingkat 1, Bangunan Data Nazir, Kajang Selangor Malaysia. **LC** DS595.5.

JA
TOKYO YESTERDAY, TODAY AND TOMORROW. (1989)-. English. Liaison and Protocol Section, International Communication Division, Bureau of Citizens and Cultural Affairs, Tokyo Metropolitan Government, 5-1 Marunouchi, 3-chome Chiyoda-ku, Tokyo Japan.
Desc: Gives a brief account of Tokyo's history and current state and an overview of Tokyo's Projects for the future.

KO
TONGA YONGU. **VFOAT** East Asian Studies. Vol. 1-Chip-. Periodical. Korean (summaries and/or abstracts in English). qt. W10000 South Korea; $13.00 other. Sogang Taehakkyo Tonga Yonguso. **Tel** (822)718-4353. **ED** Sang - Woo Rhee. **LC** DS501; .T4355. **UDC** 95-012. Index available. **Bk Rev. Ad Acc. Circ:** 800.

KO
TONGBANG HAKCHI. **VFOAT** Dong Bang Hak Chi; Journal of Far Eastern Studies. Periodical. Korean. Yonse Taehakkyo Kukhak Yonguwon, 134 Sinchon-dong, Sodaemun-ku, Seoul South Korea. **LC** DS501; .T436. **UDC** 95-012.

KO
TONGIL MUNJE YONGU (CHOSON TAEHAKKYO. TONGIL MUNJE YONGUSO). (TONGIL MUNJE YONGU.). **VFOAT** National Unification Research. Periodical. Korean (Korean). Choson Taehakkyo Tongil Munje Yonguso, 17 Pullo-dong, Tong-ku Kwangju-si Korea. **LC** DS917.25; .T6627. **UDC** 951.9.

KO
TONGIL (SEOUL, KOREA). (TONGIL.). V. 1 (August 1981)-. Periodical. Korean. mo. Minjok Tongil Chungang Hyobuihoe, 5-1 2-ka Changchung-dong, Chung-ku 100, Seoul South Korea. **LC** DS917; .T63.

NE/0082-5433
TOUNG PAO. (TUNG PAO. TOUNG PAO.). [Toung pao]. **Added/Corp** Demieville, Paul. **VFOAT** Toung Pao. Vol. 1-10 (April 1890)-(1899); Ser. 2, Vol. 1 (March 1900)-. Periodical. French (English and German). Five times a year. Fl160.00 Netherlands; $91.50 other. E. J. Brill, Postbus 9000, 2300 PA Leiden Netherlands. **Tel** 011 31 71 312624, FAX 011 31 71 317532, telex 39296 BRILL NL. **ED** P.E. Will, W.L. Idema. **LC** DS501; .T45. **DD** 950/.05. **[CCC]. Bk Rev. Ad Acc. Circ:** 550 (ctrl). Documents available from The Genuine Article.
Desc: Aims at furthering our knowledge of traditional Chinese civilization. It covers history, literature, art, history of science, in fact almost anything that concerns China.
Ind/Abst Am. Hist. Life (1955-); Arts Humanit. Citation Index [Full Cov.]; Curr. Contents Arts Humanit.; MLA Int. Bibl. Books Artic. Mod. Lang. Lit.; Res. Alert [Full Cov.].

JA/0564-0202
TOYO BUNKA. **Added/Corp** Toyo Gakkai. Tokyo Daigaku. Toyo Bunka Kenkyujo. **VFOAT** Oriental Culture. (1950)-. Japanese (table of contents in English). an. **LC** DS501; .T5; DS501; .T69.
Ind/Abst Am. Hist. Life (1955-1966,1987-1989).

JA/0563-8089
TOYO BUNKA KENKYUJO KIYO. **Added/Corp** Tokyo Teikoku Daigaku. Toyo Bunka Kenkyujo. Tokyo Daigaku. Toyo Bunka Kenkyujo. **VFOAT** Memoirs of the Institute for Oriental Culture; Memoirs of the Institute of Oriental Culture. (1943)-. Periodical. Japanese (table of contents in Chinese, English and French). tq. **LC** DS509.3; .T695.
Ind/Abst Am. Hist. Life (1955-1965).

JA
TOYO BUNKA KENKYUJO SHOHO. No. 1-. Japanese. Gakushuin Daigaku Toyo Bunka Kenkyujo, 5-1 Mejiro 1 Toshima-ku, Tokyo-to 171 Japan. **LC** DS509.3; .T696.

JA
TOYO KYOIKUSHI KENKYU. **VFOAT** Researches in Educational History of Asia. Began in 1977, 10th Issue. English (Japanese). ir. 1200 single issue. Toyo Kyoikushi Gakkai, c/o Chuo Daigaku, 3804 go Kenkyushitsu 742-1 Higashi Nakano, Hachioji-shi Tokyo-to 192-03 Japan. **LC** LA1050; .T69. **UDC** 37(09)(5).

History(General) —History of Asia

JA
TOYOGAKU BUNKEN RUIMOKU.
Main/Corp Kyoto Daigaku. Jimbun Kagaku Kenkyujo. **VFOAT** Annual Bibliography of Oriental Studies. (1963)-. Bibliography. Japanese (English). an. Research Institute Humanistic Study, 47 Higashi-Oguracho Kitashirak, Kyoto Sakyo Japan. **Tel** (075)751-2111. ctrl circ. **Supersedes** Toyogaku Kenkyu Bunken Ruimoku.
Desc: Bibliography of oriental studies (articles and books) in the order of classification.

GH/0073-2648
TRANSACTIONS OF THE HISTORICAL SOCIETY OF GHANA. Main/Corp Historical Society of Ghana. Vol. 1 (1952)-. Periodical. English. ir. Historical Society of Ghana, PO Bow 12, Legon Ghana. **LC** DT510.A1; H55.
Ind/Abst Am. Hist. Life (1959-1962).

US/0577-7135
TRANSCRIPT. Main/Corp Chicago. University. Philippine Studies Program. 1- 1954-). Periodical. English. Philippine Studies, PO Box 37005, Chicago IL 60637.

US/0196-8386
TRANSLATIONS ON NORTH KOREA.
[Transl. North Korea]. No. 1- July 1, 1966-. English (Korean). National Technical Information Service - NTIS, Room 2027S, 5285 Port Royal Road, Springfield VA 22161. **Tel** (703)487-4630, (703)487-4660, (703)487-4650, FAX (703)321-8547, telex 89-9405. **UDC** 951.93.

II
TREND. Periodical. English. qt. Rs20.00. Pathikrit 88-B Bipin Behari Ganguli Street, Calcutta 7000012 India. **ED** Sri Manik Mukherjee. **LC** DS401; .T67. **UDC** 954. Index available. cum. index. **Bk Rev. Ad Acc. Circ:** 2,100.

BA
TRIBUTE TO BAHRAIN. 1978-. English. an. Al Hilal Group, Media Representation Division, PO Box 224, Manama Bahrain Arabia. **LC** DS247.B2; A28. **DD** 953/.65/005. **UDC** 953.65.

CC/1000-4106
TUN-HUANG YEN CHIU / TUN-HUANG WEN WU YEN CHIU SO PIEN. Added/Corp Tun-Huang Wen Wu Yen Chiu So. Tun-Huang Yen Chiu Yuan (China). **VFOAT** Dunhuan Yanjiu; Dunhuang Research; Research on Dunhuang; Dun Huang Yan Jiu. Vol. 1, (1983)-. Periodical. Chinese (table of contents in English). Hsin Hua Shu Tien / Lan-Chou, People's Republic of China. **LC** DS793.T8; T857. **DD** 951/.45.

TU
TURKISH REVIEW QUARTERLY DIGEST. Added/Corp Turkey. Basn-Yayn ve Enformasyon Genel Mudurlugu. **VFOAT** Turkish Review. 1st Issue (Nov. 1985)-. Periodical. English. qt. General Directorate of Press and Information, Republic of Turkey, Ataturk Boulevard 203 0t, 688 Ankara Turkey. **LC** DR401; .T834. **DD** 956.1/03/05.
Ind/Abst PAIS Int. Print; Middle East J.

TU
TURQUOISE. (198?)-. Periodical. English. qt. A N Graphics Kibris Ltd., 12 A B Hasne Ilgaz Sok, Kosklucifltik Mersin 10 Turkey. **LC** DR401; .T88. **DD** 956.1/005.

KO
UIJONG. Periodical. Korean. W600 each issue. Kukhoe Uiwon Tonguhoe, 18-131 6-ka Ulchi-ro, Chung-ku Seoul Korea. **LC** DS922.35; .U38.

II
UNARVU (MADRAS, INDIA). (UNARVU.). Periodical. Tamil. bw. Rs10.00. Dr A Seppan, 14 Aziz Mulk 5th Street, Madras 600006 India. **LC** DS480.853; .U52.

●US/1070-5198
UNDERSTANDING JAPAN (DENVER, COLO.). (UNDERSTANDING JAPAN.). [Underst. Jpn.]. **Added/Corp** Inter-Pacific Institute for Communication. Vol. 1, No. 1 (Apr. 1992)-. Periodical. English. Ten times a year. $30.00 US; $35.00 Canada & Mexico; $45.00 other. IPIC, 1200 17th Street, Suite 1410, Denver CO 80202. **Tel** (303)629-5811, FAX (303)629-5224. **ED** Machiko Sogo. Index available. cum. index. **Circ:** 3,000.

II/0041-7173
UNITED ASIA (BOMBAY). (UNITED ASIA.). [United Asia]. Vol. 1, No. 1 (May/June 1948)-. Periodical. English. bm. **LC** DS1; .U55. **DD** 950.
Ind/Abst Am. Hist. Life (1954-1960,1963-1971).

US/0068-6514
UNIVERSITY OF CALIFORNIA PUBLICATIONS. NEAR EASTERN STUDIES. [Univ. Calif. publ., Near East. stud.]. **Added/Corp** University of California. **VFOAT** Near Eastern Studies. (1963)-. Monographic series. English. ir. Price varies per volume. University of California Press, 2120 Berkeley Way, Berkeley CA 94720. **Tel** (510)642-4191, (510)642-3907, FAX (510)642-9917. **DD** 956. **Circ:** 650 (ctrl).

II
UTTARAKHANDA BHARATI. V. 1- Jan./March 1973-. Periodical. Hindi (Hindi). qt. Rs10.00. Uttarakhanda Sevanidhi, Badri Niwas 2, Nainitala India. **LC** DS423; .U87.

MY
UTUSAN (KUALA LUMPUR, MALAYSIA). (UTUSAN.). V. 1 (1981)-. Malay. an. $8.00. Kumpulan Syarikat Utusan Melay Bhd, No 46 M Jl Lima Dif Jl, Chan Saw Lin, Kuala Lumpur Malaysia. **LC** DS591; .U88.

KO
VANTAGE POINT. V. 1- May 1978-. Periodical. English. mo. The Editor Vantage Point, Naewoe Press, 42-2 Chuja-dong, Box 9708, Chung-gu Seoul 100 South Korea. **LC** DS930; .V35. **DD** 951.9/3043/05. **UDC** 951.93. **Supersedes** North Korea Newsletter.
Ind/Abst Int. Polit. Sci. Abstr.

GW/0506-7936
VERZEICHNIS DER ORIENTALISCHEN HANDSCHRIFTEN IN DEUTSCHLAND.
Added/Corp Deutsche Morgenlandische Gesellschaft. Vol. 1 (1961)-. Monographic series. German. ir. Price varies per volume. Franz Steiner Verlag GmbH, Postfach 101061, D 70009 Stuttgart Germany. **Tel** 011 49 0711 2582372, FAX 011 49 0711 2582290, telex 723636 daz d.

RU
VESTNIK MOSKOVSKOGO UNIVERSITETA. SERIIA XIII: VOSTOKOVEDENIE. Main/Corp Moskovskii Gosudarstvennyi Universitet Im. M.V. Lomonosova. (Jan./Mar. 1977)-. Periodical. Russian. Four times a year. $69.95. Izdatelstvo Moskovskogo Universiteta, K-9 Ulitsa Gertsena 5/7, Moscow Russia. **Tel** (301)881-5973. **(Subscription address:** East View Publications Inc., 3020 Harbor Lane North, Suite 110, Minneapolis MN 55447.) **LC** DS1; .M632a. **Supersedes** Vestnik. Seriia XIV: Vostokovedenie.

BL
VIDAS SECAS. Year 1, No. 1 (June 1980)-. Periodical. Portuguese. qt. $500. Revista Vidas Secas Ltda, rua Luiz Guimaraes 111, Casa Forte - Recife - 50.000 Pernambuco PE Brazil. **LC** AP66; .V53. **DD** 956/.9. **UDC** 956.9.

VM/0042-5710
VIETNAM. Title Change. (19??)-(19??). Periodical. Vietnamese (English, French, Spanish, Russian and Chinese). mo. 32 Haiba Truna, Hanoi DRV North Vietnam. **Tel** 52323. **LC** DS556; .V514. **DD** 959.7/005. **UDC** 959.7. available on microfilm from University Microfilms International (UMI). **Continued by** Vietnam Illustrated.

NE/0506-9661
VIETNAM BULLETIN. Vol. 1- June 1966-. Bulletin. Dutch (Dutch). ir. Vietnam Bulletin, Postbus 715, 1000 AS Amsterdam Netherlands. **UDC** 959.7.

SI/0218-1169
VIETNAM COMMENTARY / INFORMATION & RESOURCE CENTER.
Suspended. Added/Corp Information & Resource Center (Singapore). No. 1 (March 1988)-. Periodical. English. Six times a year. Information & Resource Center, 6 Nassim Road, Singapore 1025 Singapore. **Tel** 011 65 7349600. **(Subscription address:** Information & Resource Center, PO Box 79 Orchard Point, Singapore 9123 Singapore) **LC** DS556; .V543. **DD** 959.7/005.

US/0272-3344
VIETNAM DIGEST (BERKELEY). (VIETNAM DIGEST.). (Jan. 1979)-. Periodical. English. bm. $6.00. Vietnam Digest, PO Box 2244, Berkeley CA 94702. **Tel** (510)548-1742.

US/0735-3855
VIETNAM FORUM, THE. (THE VIETNAM FORUM / YALE UNIVERSITY SOUTHEAST ASIA STUDIES.). 1 (Winter-Spring 1983)-. Periodical. English (Vietnamese and French). ir. $10.00 US; $11.00 other. Yale Southeast Asia Studies, PO Box 13A Yale Station, New Haven CT 06520. **Tel** (203)436-8897. **LC** DS556; .V553. **DD** 959.7/005. **UDC** 959.7.

VM
VIETNAM ILLUSTRATED. (19??)-. English. mo. Xunhasaba Exports and Imports, 7 Nguyen Thi Minh Khai Str, Dit 1 Ho Chi Minh City Vietnam. **Tel** 011 84 8 294893, telex 278 XUNHASABA. **Continues** Vietnam, 0042-5710.

FR
VIETNAM (IVRY, FRANCE). (VIETNAM.). No. 1 (Dec. 1980)-. Periodical. French. qt. 100F. Madame Diep Bletzacker, BP 48, 94200 Ivry France. **LC** DS556; .V555. **DD** 959.7/005. **UDC** 959.7.

●US
VIETNAM JOURNAL : PROJECT OF THE VIETNAM HUMAN RIGHTS GROUP. See Political Science-Civil Rights.

US/0506-9777
VIETNAM MAGAZINE. Title Change.
Added/Corp Vietnam Council on Foreign Relations. Vol. 1 (1968?)-(19??). Periodical. Vietnamese. mo. Tap Hop, PO Box 4108, Huntington Beach CA 92605. **LC** DS557.A5; A487. available on microfilm from University Microfilms International (UMI). **Continued by** Tap Hop.

US/0364-9407
VIETNAM QUARTERLY. No. 1- Winter 1976-. Periodical. English. qt. $10.00. Vietnam Resource Center, 108 North Mole Street, Philadelphia PA 19102. **LC** DS556; .V57. **DD** 959.704/05. **UDC** 959.7. **Supersedes** Thbao Q, 0193-5577.

US/1047-3475
VIETNAM STUDIES BULLETIN. [Vietnam stud. bull.]. **Added/Corp** Vietnam Studies Group. (Fall 1977)-. Periodical. English. an. Free on request. Association for Asian Studies Inc., University of Michigan, 1 Lane Hall, Ann Arbor MI 48109. **Tel** (313)665-2490, FAX (313)665-3801. **(Subscription address:** Association for Asian Studies / Massachusetts, c/o D. Hunt, University of Massachusetts, Harbor Campus, Boston MA 02125.) **LC** DS556; .V84. **DD** 959. **Continues** Vietnam Studies Newsletter.

VM/0085-7823
VIETNAMESE STUDIES. HANOI, VIETNAM (1966). (VIETNAMESE STUDIES.). No. 8 (1966)-. Periodical. English (French). qt. 4$00 Vietnam; 5$70 US. Xunhasaba Exports and Imports, 7 Nguyen Thi Minh Khai Str, Dit 1 Ho Chi Minh City Vietnam. **Tel** 011 84 8 294893, telex 278 XUNHASABA. **LC** DS556; .V59. Index available. **Bk Rev. Ad Acc. Circ:** 50,000. **Continues** Vietnamese Advances.

PK
VIEWPOINT. V. 1- Aug. 14, 1975-. Periodical. English. wk. M A Kahn, Lawrence Road, Lahore Pakistan. **LC** DS376; .V52. **DD** 954.9/105/05. **UDC** 954.9.

II
VITUTALAIPPULIKAL : TAMILILA VITUTALAIPPULUKALIN ATIKARAPURVAMANA ETU. Kural 1 (15.3.84)-. Periodical. Tamil. ir. Rs2.00 each issue. Post Box 928 Adyar, Madras 600020 India. **Tel** 41 77 77. **LC** DS489.25.T3; V57. ctrl circ.

KE
VOICE OF EGYPT. Added/Corp Egypt. Safarah (Kenya). Press Office. (Jan. 1972)-. English (Swahili). bm. League of Arab States, Uchumi House, 10th Floor, Box 30770, Nairobi Kenya. **LC** DS119.7; .V63. **DD** 956/.005. available with illustrations.

RU/0869-1908
VOSTOK / AKADEMIIA NAUK SSSR, INSTITUT VOSTOKOVEDENIIA [I] INSTITUT AFRIKI. Added/Corp Institut Vostokovedeniia (Akademiia Nauk SSSR) Institut Afriki (Akademiia Nauk SSSR). **VFOAT** Oriens. (1991)-. Academic Scholarly Publication. Russian (summaries and/or abstracts in English; table of contents in English, French and German). bm. Izdatelstvo Nauka / Akademiia Nauk, Publishing House of the Russian Academy of Sciences, Leninskii Porspekt 14, 117901 Moscow Russia. **Tel** 011 95 954-21-53, FAX 011 95 938-21-44, telex 411964. **LC** DS1; .P7. **Continues** Narody Azii i Afriki, 0027-8041.
Ind/Abst Middle East J.

UA
WADI AL-NIL. V. 1, No. 1 (Feb. 1985)-. Periodical. Arabic. mo. £E0.25 single issue. 1119 Shari Kurnish Al-Nil, Al-Qahirah Egypt. **ED** A Mansur. **LC** DT43; .W33.

UA
WAHDAH (CAIRO, EGYPT). (AL-WAHDAH.). Periodical. Arabic. mo. 60 Shari Muhyi Al-Din, Abu Al-Izz, Al-Duqqi Al-Qahirah Egypt. **Tel** 717040. **ED** Mohamed Abdel Wahab Showdery. **LC** DS247.A28; W34. **UDC** 953.4. **Bk Rev. Circ:** 10,000 (ctrl).
Desc: Issued by the opposition of south Yemen. Its policy is anti-Communist against the present Regime and believes in Human Rights Real Democracy.

YE
WATAN (SANA, YEMEN). (AL-WATAN / YUSDIRUHA AL-ITTIHAD AL-AMM LIL-MUGHTARIBIN, AL-JUMHURIYAH AL-ARABIYAH AL-YAMANIYAH.). Periodical. Arabic. mo. $50.00. Al-Ittihad Al-Amm Lil-Mughtaribin, Al-Jumhuriyah Al-Arabiyan Al-Yamaniyah, SB 1299, Sana Yemen. **LC** DS247.Y4; A273.

IO
WAWASAN. Periodical. Indonesian. Rp500 each issue. Lembaga Studi Pembangunan, Gedung Arthaloka Lantai 17, JL Jenderal Sudirman 2, Jakarta Indonesia. **LC** DS611; .W38.

CC
WEN HUA CHIH SHIH. Vol. 1, (Oct. 1981)-. Periodical. Chinese. Hei-Lung-Chiang Sheng Hsin Hua Shu Tien, Ha-Erh-Pin Shih, People's Republic of China. **LC** DS721; .W3693. **DD** 951.

CC
WEN HUA YU SHENG HUO. **VFOAT** Wenhua yu Shenghuo; Culture and Life. (19??)-. Periodical. Chinese. Six times a year. $9.91. Science Press, 16 Donghuangchenggen North Street, Beijing 100707, People's Republic of China. **Tel** 011 86 1 4019821, 011 86 1 4010642, FAX 011 86 1 4012180, 011 86 1 4019810, telex 210147. **(Subscription address:** China International Book Trading Corporation, PO Box 399, Library Service Department, Beijing 100044 People's Republic of China.**)** **ED** Shao De-Xin. **LC** AP95.C4; W42. **DD** 951.05/05. **Ad Acc. Circ:** 120,000.
Desc: Magazine of advocating spirit civilization of the socialism and guiding home life, with cultural appreciating and practical items for daily life.

CC
WEN SHIH TZU LIAO HSUAN CHI (SHANTUNG PROVINCE, CHINA). (WEN SHIH TZU LIAO HSUAN CHI / CHUNG-KUO JEN MIN CHENG CHIH HSIEH SHANG HUI I SHAN-TUNG SHENG WEI YUAN HUI, WEN SHIH TZU LIAO YEN CHIU WEI YUAN HUI PIEN.). Periodical. Chinese. RMBY0.63. Hsin Hua Shu Tien / Chi-Nan, Chi-Nan Shih, People's Republic of China. **LC** DS793.S4; W45. **DD** 951/.14. **UDC** 951.

CC
WEN WU TIEN TI. **See** Archaeology.

CH/0043-3047
WEST & EAST. **Added/Corp** Chung Mei Wen Hua Ching Chi Hsieh Hui. **VFOAT** West and East; Chung Mei Yueh Kan. Vol. 1, No. 1 (Oct. 1956)-. Periodical. English (Chinese). Twelve times a year. $10.00. Sino-American Cultural and Economic Association, 23 Hung Chow South Road Section, Taipei Taiwan. **LC** DS895.F7; W45. **DD** 909.

KO
WOLGAN MUNHWAJAE. **VFOAT** Munhwajae. Periodical. Korean. W5,000. Wolgan Munhwajae S A, 13-13 Kwanchol-dong Chong-ku, Seoul Korea. **LC** DS903; .W64.

AT/0813-9733
WORKING PAPERS OF THE JAPANESE STUDIES CENTRE. Monographic series. English. Price varies per volume. Japanese Studies Centre Inc, Wellington Road, Clayton Victoria 3168 Australia. **Tel** (03)565-2260, FAX (03)565-4007, telex MONASH AA 32691.

PK
WUFA. **VFOAT** W.U.F.A. Vol. 1, No. 1 (1985)-. Periodical. English. Writers Union of Free Afghanistan, PO Box 867, Peshawar University, Peshawar Pakistan. **LC** DS371.2; .W83. **DD** 958/.1044/05. **UDC** 958.1.
Ind/Abst Rural Dev. Abstr.; World Agric. Econ.

CH/1000-4076
XIBEI SHI-DI. (HSI PEI SHIH TI.). [Xibei shi-di]. **Added/Corp** Lan-chou ta Hsueh. **VFOAT** Historical and Geographical Review of Northwest China. (1980)-. Periodical. Chinese. qt. NT$20.00. Lan-Chou ta Hsueh, li Shih Hsi Chung-O Kuan Hsi Shih Yen Chih Shih, Lan-Chou, People's Republic of China. **Tel** 22991. **ED** Yang Jianxin. **LC** DS793.N6; H667. **DD** 951/.4/005. **Bk Rev. Ad Acc. Circ:** 5,000.
Desc: Concerned with problems about Northwest China, history, geography, minorities, religion, the Silk Road and international relationship. It is knowledgeable and academic.
Ind/Abst Am. Hist. Life (1990-).

LY
YAWMIYAT WA-WATHAIQ AL-WAHDAH AL-ARABIYAH / MARKAZ DIRASAT AL-WAHDAH AL-ARABIYAH. 1979-. Arabic. an. SB 113-6001, Beirut Lebanon. **LC** DS63.1; .Y38.

QA
YEAR BOOK (QATAR. WIZARAT AL-ILAM). (YEAR BOOK / STATE OF QATAR, MINISTRY OF INFORMATION.). **Added/Corp** Qatar. Wizarat al-Ilam. Qatar. Wizarat al-Ilam. Far al-Matbuat Wa-al-Nashr. **VFOAT** Qatar, Year Book. (19??)-. English. an. Free on request. Qatar Ministry of Information, PO Box 1836, Doha Qatar. **LC** DS247.Q3; A28. **DD** 953/.63/005. ***Continues** Qatar Year Book.*

KO
YOKSA MINSOKHAK / HANGUK YOKSA MINSOK HAKHOE. **Added/Corp** Hanguk Yoksa Minsok Hakhoe. (1991)-. Periodical. Korean. **LC** DS904; .Y638.

KO
YONHAP YONGAM. Periodical. Korean. an. W25,000. Yonhap Tongsin / Korea, 98-5 Unni-dong Korea. **LC** DS922; .Y6.

JA/0513-5974
YOUNG EAST. ***Ceased.*** **See** Religion and Theology-Buddhism.

II/0049-8378
YOUNG INDIAN. Periodical. English. $5.00. Young Indian, 9-B, Theatre Communication Building, Connaught Place, New Delhi India. **LC** DS401; .Y63. **DD** 954.05/05. **UDC** 954.

CH
YUAN MING YUAN / CHUNG-KUO YUAN MING YUAN HSUEH HUI CHOU PEI WEI YUAN HUI. 1 (Nov. 1981)-. Periodical. Chinese. NT$1.95. Hsin-Hua Shu Tien Pei-Ching Fa Hsing So, Beijing, People's Republic of China. **LC** DS795.6.Y8; Y8. **DD** 915.1/156. **UDC** 915.1.

JA
ZAINICHI CHOSENJIN SHI KENKYU. **Added/Corp** Zainichi Chosenjin Undoshi Kenkyukai. (Dec. 1977)-. Periodical. Japanese. Zainichi Chosenjin Undoshi Kenkyukai, 4249 Ikuta, Tama-ku Zainichi Japan. **LC** DS832.7.K6; Z313.

GW/0934-0696
ZEITSCHRIFT FUER TURKEISTUDIEN : ZFTS. **Added/Corp** Zentrum fur Turkeistudien (Bonn, Germany). **VFOAT** ZfTS. Vol. 1 (1988)-. Periodical. German. sa. Leske Verlag & Budrich GmbH, Postfach 300551, Gerhart Hauptmann Strasse 27, W-5090 Leverkusen 3 Opladen Germany. **Tel** 011 49 21712079. **ED** Heidrun Czock. **LC** HC491; .A284.
Desc: Scholarly articles on social, economic and cultural development of modern Turkey and the Turkish peoples. Explores the relationship of Turkey and immigrant Turks currently living in Germany.
Ind/Abst World Agric. Econ.

GW/0514-857X
ZENTRALASIATISCHE STUDIEN DES SEMINARS FUER SPRACH- UND KULTURWISSENSCHAFT ZENTRALASIENS DER UNIVERSITAT BONN. (ZENTRALASIATISCHE STUDIEN.). [Zentralasiat. Stud. Semin. Sprach- Kulturwiss. Zentralasiens Univ. Bonn]. **Added/Corp** Universitat Bonn. Seminar fuer Sprach- und Kulturwissenschaft Zentralasiens. Vol. 1 (1967)-. German (English). an. Otto Harrassowitz Verlag, Taunusstrasse 14, Postfach 2929, D-65019 Wiesbaden Germany. **Tel** 011 49 611 5300, FAX 530570, telex 4186 135 OH D. **ED** Walther Heissig and Michael Weiers. **LC** DS785.A1; Z45. **Bk Rev. Ad Acc. Circ:** 500.
Desc: Covers cultures and languages of central Asia.

US/0892-7456
ZHONG XI LIAO WANG TAI. (CHUNG HSI LIAO WANG TAI : NEWSLETTER OF THE CHINESE AND CHINESE AMERICAN HISTORY ASSOCIATION (CCAHA).). [Zhong xi liao wang tai]. V. 1, N. 1 (May 1986)-. Newsletter. English. Three times a year. $5.00 individuals, $3.00 senior citizens over 60, $10.00 institutions. Chinese and Chinese American Association, 1355 Arlington, El Cerrito CA 94530. **DD** 951. **UDC** 951.

US/0735-8237
ZHONGGUO ZHI CHUN. ***Title Change.*** (CHUNG-KUO CHIH CHUN.). [Zhongguo zhi chun]. **VFOAT** China Spring. Vol. 1, No. 1 (Dec. 1982)-(May 1994). Periodical. Chinese (summaries and/or abstracts in English). mo. Evergreen Publishing and Stationery, 136 South Atlantic Boulevard, Monterey Park CA 91754. **Tel** (818)284-9066, FAX (818)284-1571. **ED** Hu Ping. **LC** DS779.20; .C523. **DD** 951.05/05. **Ad Acc. Circ:** 10,000 (ctrl). ***Merged into** Pei Ching Chin Chun.*
Desc: Dealing with major social, ideological, economical and political issues concerning contemporary Mainland China.

US/0748-464X
ZORYAN BULLETIN, THE. (THE ZORYAN BULLETIN : A PUBLICATION OF THE ZORYAN INSTITUTE FOR CONTEMPORARY ARMENIAN RESEARCH AND DOCUMENTATION.). [Zoryan bull.]. **Added/Corp** Zoryan Institute for Contemorary Armenian Research and Documentation. Vol. 1, No. 1, (Summer 1983)-. Periodical. English. qt. Zoryan Institute, 19 Day Street, Cambridge MA 02140-1203. **Tel** (617)497-6713. **ED** Lynne Kassabian. **DD** 956.

HISTORY OF AUSTRALIA AND OCEANIA

AT
A TO Z OF WHO IS WHO IN AUSTRALIA'S HISTORY, THE. **VFOAT** Who is Who in Australia's History. (1987)-. Periodical. English. Child & Associates Publishing Pty Ltd, 9 Clearview Place, Brookvale New South Wales 2100 Australia. **Tel** (02)9751700, FAX (02)9751711. **ED** Bruce Elder. Index available. **Bk Rev. Ad Acc.** ctrl circ.
Desc: Over 1,000 short biographies of people who have shaped the history of Australia.

AT
ANNUAL BIBLIOGRAPHY / AUSTRALIAN INSTITUTE OF ABORIGINAL AND TORRES STRAIT ISLANDER STUDIES. **See** Ethnic Interests-Abstracting, Bibliographies and Statistics.

AT/0045-0197
AUSTRALIA NOW. ***Ceased.*** [Aust. now]. Vol. 1 (May 1971)-(1993). Periodical. English. qt. Australian Bureau of Statistics, PO Box 10, Belconnen Australian Capital Territory, 2616 Australia. **Tel** 011 61 6 2527911, FAX 011 61 6 2516009. **LC** DU80; .A946. **DD** 994.06/05. **UDC** 919.4; 994.
Desc: Gives a broad picture of Australia as it is today and covers nearly every aspect of contemporary Australian society-from cultural life, science and technology, to Aboriginals, sport, industries, tourism and the environment.
Ind/Abst APAIS, Aust. Public Aff. Inf. Ser. (1973-); Index Free Period.

AT/0729-4352
AUSTRALIAN ABORIGINAL STUDIES (CANBERRA, A.C.T. : 1983). (AUSTRALIAN ABORIGINAL STUDIES : JOURNAL OF THE AUSTRALIAN INSTITUTE OF ABORIGINAL STUDIES.). **Added/Corp** Australian Institute of Aboriginal Studies. Australian Institute of Aboriginal and Torres Strait Islander Studies. No. 1 (1983)-. Periodical. English. Twice a year. 25.00Aus$. Australian Institute of Aboriginal and Torres Strait Island Studies, PO Box 553, Canberra ACT 2601 Australia. **Tel** 011 061 6 2461111, FAX 011 061 6 2497310. **LC** IN PROCESS; DU120; .A792. cum. index. **Bk Rev. Pr Rev. Circ:** 1,200. ***Continues** Australian Institute of Aboriginal Studies. Newsletter - Australian Institute of Aboriginal Studies, 0004-9344.*
Ind/Abst Abstr. Anthropol.; Anthropol. Lit.; APAIS, Aust. Public Aff. Inf. Ser.; Aust. Educ. Index (199?-); Bibliogr. Mission.; Ethnoarts Index; Int. Bibliogr. Sociol.

AT/0728-8433
AUSTRALIAN CULTURAL HISTORY. **Added/Corp** Australian Academy of the Humanities. Australian National University. History of Ideas Unit. **VFOAT** Papers on Australian Cultural History. (1981)-. English. an (July). 13.00Aus$ one year; 35.00Aus$ three years. Deakin University Australia Cultral History, Faculty of Humanities, Geelong Victoria 3217 Australia. **Tel** 011 61 52 471335, FAX 011 61 52 442777. **ED** David Walker, (phone: (052)271364). **Ad Acc. Pr Rev. Circ:** 1300.
Ind/Abst Am. Hist. Life (1985-); Annu. Bibliogr. Engl. Lang. Lit.; APAIS, Aust. Public Aff. Inf. Ser.; Int. Bibliogr. Sociol.

US/1064-010X
AUSTRALIAN EXPATRIATE, THE. [Aust. expatr.]. (1989)-. Periodical. English. bm. Australian Expatriate, 143 South Credos Avenue, Suite B202, Solana Beach CA 92075. **Tel** (619)793-3694, FAX (619)793-7736. **ED** E.J. Kemmis. **LC** WMLC 93/921. **DD** 994. **Bk Rev**, (Qty: 12-14). **Ad Acc. Circ:** 6,000.

AT
AUSTRALIAN HISTORICAL ASSOCIATION BULLETIN. **Main/Corp** Australian Historical Association. Bulletin. English. Australian Historical Association, Department of History, Canberra ACT 0200 Australia. **Tel** 011 61 06 2492715. **UDC** 994.

AT/0810-5340
AUSTRALIAN HISTORICAL BIBLIOGRAPHY. BROADSHEET. [Aust. hist. bibliogr., Broadsh.]. **Added/Corp** Australia 1788-1988: A Bicentennial History. Reference Section. (1983)-. Bibliography. English. ir. **DD** 010.44.
Ind/Abst Annu. Bibliogr. Engl. Lang. Lit.

AT/1031-461X
AUSTRALIAN HISTORICAL STUDIES. **Added/Corp** University of Melbourne. History Dept. Vol. 23, No. 90 (April 1988)-. Periodical. English. Twice a year (Apr. & Oct.). $36.00. University of Melbourne / Department of History, Parkville Victoria 3052 Australia. **Tel** 011 61 3 3445977. **ED** John Rickard (editor's address: History Department, Monash University, phone: (03)5654000). **LC** DU80; .A943. **DD** 994/.005. Index available (included in issue). cum. index (published by volume). **Bk Rev. Ad Acc. Pr Rev. Circ:** 1,300. Documents available from The Genuine Article. ***Continues** Historical Studies (Melbourne, Vic.), 0018-2559.*
Ind/Abst Am. Hist. Life (1954-); APAIS, Aust. Public Aff. Inf. Ser.; Arts Humanit. Citation Index [Full Cov.]; Br. Humanit. Index; Curr. Contents Arts Humanit.; Int. Bibliogr. Sociol.; Int. Polit. Sci. Abstr.; Res. Alert [Full Cov.].

AT/0005-0091
AUSTRALIAN QUARTERLY. (AQ, THE AUSTRALIAN QUARTERLY.). [Aust. q.]. **VFOAT** Australian Quarterly. Vol. 39, No. 3 (Sept. 1967)-. Periodical. English. qt. 43.00Aus$ (individuals),

47.00Aus$ (institutions) Australia; 54.00Aus$ (individuals), 57.00Aus$ (institutions) other. Australian Institute of Political Science, 72 Bathurst Street, Wea House/Level 4, Sydney New South Wales 2000 Australia. **Tel** 011 61 2 264-8923. **ED** Hugh Pritchard, Elaine Thompson and Geraldine Walsh. Index available. **Bk Rev**. **Ad Acc**. **Circ:** 3,000. ***Continues*** *Australian Quarterly.*
Desc: Political, social and economic issues within Australia for the general reader.
Ind/Abst ABC POL SCI; Am. Hist. Life (1967-1972, 1976-); Annu. Bibliogr. Engl. Lang. Lit.; APAIS, Aust. Public Aff. Inf. Ser. (1967-); Appl. Soc. Sci. Index Abstr.; Aust. Educ. Index (1979-); Int. Bibliogr. Sociol.; Int. Polit. Sci. Abstr.; Middle East Abstr. Index; Res. High. Educ. Abstr.; SportSearch.

UK/0954-0954
AUSTRALIAN STUDIES. Added/Corp British Australian Studies Association. No. 1 (June 1988)-. English. ir (1-2 per year). £21.00 UK; £25.00 other. British Australian Studies Association, University of Strathclyde, Deptartment of English, Stirling FK9 4LA Scotland. **Tel** 011 44 786 73171 ext. 7504. ***Continues*** *BASA Magazine, 0265-9328.*
Ind/Abst APAIS, Aust. Public Aff. Inf. Ser. (1992-); Int. Bibliogr. Sociol.

AT
AUSTRALIAN STUDIES (AUSTRALIAN STUDIES ASSOCIATION). ***Title Change.*** (AUSTRALIAN STUDIES.). **Added/Corp** Australian Studies Association. No. 9 (Apr. 1988)-(19??). Periodical. English. sa. Australian Studies Association Educ Development, Unit Footscray Inst Tech, Footscray Victoria 3011 Australia. ***Continued by*** *Australian Studies Bulletin, 0815-2500.*

FP
BULLETIN DE LA SOCIETE DES ETUDES OCEANIENNES. Added/Corp Societe des Etudes Oceaniennes (Tahiti). (1917)-. Bulletin. French.
Ind/Abst Am. Hist. Life (1988-); Int. Bibliogr. Sociol.

FP
BULLETIN DE LA SOCIETE DES ETUDES OCEANIENNES (POLYNESIE ORIENTALE). Added/Corp Societe des Etudes Oceaniennes (Tahiti). (1922)-. French. qt (Mar., June, Sept., Dec.). $30.00 US. Societe ou au Bibliotecaire, BP 110, Papeete Tahiti French Polynesia. **Tel** 011 689 419603. **LC** DU510.A1; S6. **DD** 920/.05. Index available. cum. index. **Bk Rev**. **Ad Acc**. **Circ:** 600 (ctrl). ***Continues*** *Bulletin de la Societe d'Etudes Oceaniennes (Polynesie Oriental).*
Desc: Information on the anthropology, ethnography, archaeology and history of Polynesia and Polynesie Orientale.
Ind/Abst Anthropol. Lit.; Ethnoarts Index.

AT
BULLETIN / NEWCASTLE AND HUNTER DISTRICT HISTORICAL SOCIETY. ***Ceased.*** **Added/Corp** Newcastle and Hunter District Historical Society. Vol. 1, No. 1 (Sept. 1972)-(19??). Bulletin. English. qt. Newcastle & Hunter District Historical Society, PO Box 22, Broadmeadow New South Wales 2292 Australia.

NL
BULLETIN (SOCIETE D'ETUDES HISTORIQUES DE LA NOUVELLE CALEDONIE). (BULLETIN / SOCIETE D'ETUDES HISTORIQUES DE LA NOUVELLE-CALEDONIE.). **VFOAT** Bulletin ... de la Societe d'Historie de Noumea. Bulletin. French (English). qt. 2000CFPF New Caledonia. These-Pac, 3 rue E Le Grand, BP 920, Noumea Caledonia. **Tel** 26 21 67. **ED** Angleviel Frederic. **LC** DU720; .B9. **DD** 993/.2/005. **UDC** 993.2. Index available. cum. index. **Bk Rev**. **Ad Acc**. **Circ:** 500. available on microfilm. ***Continues*** *Bulletin de la Societe d'Etudes Historiques de la Nouvelle-Caledonie.*
Ind/Abst Am. Hist. Life (1988-).

AT/0310-1584
CABBAGES AND KINGS. [Cabbages & kings]. Vol. 1 (1973)-. Periodical. English. Department of History & Australian Studies, 15 Lorne Avenue, S A C A E, Magill SA 5072 Australia.
Ind/Abst APAIS, Aust. Public Aff. Inf. Ser. (1982-).

AT/0313-5977
CANBERRA HISTORICAL JOURNAL. [Canb. hist. j.]. **Added/Corp** Canberra & District Historical Society. (1973)-New Series No. 1 (March 1978)-. Periodical. English. sa (Mar., Sep.). 16.00Aus$ Australian Capital Territories and New South Wales; 20.00Aus$ (seamail), 24.00Aus$ (airmail) other. Canberra & District Historical Society, PO Box 970, Civic Square Australian Capital Territory 2608 Australia. **Tel** 011 61 062 488401. **ED** Patricia Blarke (phone: (06)2812315). **LC** DU145; .C3. **DD** 994.7/005. Index available. cum. index. **Bk Rev**, (Qty: 1,000). **Circ:** 600 (ctrl). ***Continues*** *Canberra & District Historical Society. Journal.*
Desc: Articles on historic people, places and events particularly of Canberra, the Australian Capital Territory and surrounding region.
Ind/Abst APAIS, Aust. Public Aff. Inf. Ser. (1973-).

PP/0253-2921
CATALYST (GOROKA, PAPUA NEW GUINEA). (CATALYST.). **Added/Corp** Melanesian Institute for Pastoral & Socio-Economic Service. (March 1971)-. Periodical. English. sa. k13.00 US, UK, Europe & Canada; k10.00 Australia & New Zealand; k8.00 Pacific and Asia. Melanesian Institute, PO Box 571, Goroka EHP, Papua New Guinea. **Tel** 675 72 1777, FAX 675 72 1214. **ED** Alphonse Aime. Index available. cum. index. **Bk Rev**. **Ad Acc**. **Circ:** 750 (ctrl).
Desc: Deals with the social and pastoral concerns of Melanesia and covers topics in anthropology, religions, history of Oceania, ethics, folklore, etc.

AT
CHRISTIAN DEFENCE LEAGUE. (19??)-. English. Four times a year (Mar., June, Sept., Dec.). News Digest International, PO Box 535, Parramatta New South Wales, 2155 Australia. **Tel** 011 61 02 6302309. **(Subscription address:** News Digest International, PO Box 449, Arabi LA 70032.**)** ***Continues*** *News Digest International.*

AT/0312-6145
EARLY DAYS. [Early days]. **Added/Corp** Royal Western Australian Historical Society. **VFOAT** Early Days Journal. Vol. 7, Pt. 2 (1970)-. English. an. 25.00Aus$ Australia; 20.00Aus$ other; $50.00 Comes with Royal Western Australian Historical Society membership. Royal Western Australian Historical Society, 49 Broadway, Stirling House, Nedlands Western Australia 6009 Australia. **Tel** 09 386 3841, FAX 09 386 3309. **LC** DU80; .R68. **DD** 994/.005. Index available (published separately). cum. index. **Circ:** 1,000 (ctrl). ***Continues*** *Royal Western Australian Historical Society. Journal and Proceedings.*
Desc: Research papers on Western Australia history.
Ind/Abst APAIS, Aust. Public Aff. Inf. Ser. (1970-).

AT/0815-032X
FEDERAL GOVERNMENT, THE. Added/Corp Canberra College of Advanced Education. Library. (1983)-. English. 45.00Aus$. University of Canberra, PO Box 1, Belconnen ACT 2616 Australia. **Tel** 011/61/6/2015111, FAX 011/61/6/2015999. **LC** DU117.17; .F4. **DD** 994.06/3/05.

AT/0815-4902
FOCUS AUSTRALIA. [Focus Aust.]. (1984)-. Periodical. English. mo. 395.00Aus$ Australia; 418.00Aus$ New Zealand, Papua New Guinea; 422.00Aus$ Indonesia, Malaysia, Singapore, 426.00Aus$ Japan, India; 432.00Aus$ US & Canada; 436.00Aus$ Europe. International Public Relations Pty Ltd., 33 Walsh Street, West Melbourne Victoria 3003 Australia. **Tel** 011 61 03 329 9333, FAX 011 61 03 329 7996. **DD** 320.94.

AT
GASCOYNE, REGIONAL PROFILE. VFOAT Gascoyne. English. an. Department of Regional Development & the North West, Carnarvon Western Australia. **LC** HC607.G37; G36. **DD** 994.1/3.

GU/0889-2938
GUAM & MICRONESIA GLIMPSES. ***Ceased.*** [Guam Micronesia glimpses]. **VFOAT** Guam and Micronesia Glimpses; Guam & Micronesia; Glimpses of Guam & Micronesia; Guam and Micronesia. (1986)-(1992). Periodical. English. qt. Sanchez Publishing House, PO Box 8066, Tamuning, Guam 96931. **Tel** 011 671 649 6128. **DD** 996. ***Continues*** *Glimpses of Micronesia, 0883-9964.*

US/0440-5145
HAWAIIAN JOURNAL OF HISTORY, THE. [Hawaii. j. hist.]. **Added/Corp** Hawaiian Historical Society. Vol. 1 (1967)-. Periodical. English. an. $15.00. Hawaiian Historical Society, 560 Kawaiahao Street, Honolulu HI 96813. **Tel** (808)537-6271. **ED** Helen G. Chapin. **LC** DU1; .H4. **DD** 996/.005. cum. index. **Bk Rev**. **Ad Acc**. **Circ:** 1,000 (ctrl).
Desc: Devoted to the history of Hawaii, Polynesia, and the Pacific area.
Ind/Abst Am. Hist. Life (1967-); West. Hist. Q.

AT
HISTORIAN, THE. Vol. 1, (June 1972)-. Bulletin. English. qt. 45.00Aus$ Australia; Also comes with Kuring Gai Historical Society membership. Ku-Ring-Gai Historical Society, PO Box 109, Gordon New South Wales 2072 Australia. **Tel** 011 61 2 4163635, 011 61 2 4982487. **ED** F. Richardson. **Circ:** 250 (ctrl). Documents available from The Genuine Article.
Ind/Abst Acad. Abstr. Full Text Elite (July 1992-); Arts Humanit. Citation Index [Full Cov.]; Expand. Acad. Index (1988-); Res. Alert [Full Cov.]; Romant. Move.; West. Hist. Q.

AT/0726-6715
HISTORIC ENVIRONMENT. (1981)-. Periodical. English. Four times a year (Mar., June, Sept., Dec.). 35.00Au$. Australia ICOMOS, PO Box N77, Grosvenor Place, Syndey 2000 Australia. **Tel** 011 61 2 357 4811, FAX 011 61 2 357 4603. **Pr Rev**. **Circ:** 400 (ctrl).
Desc: Contain articles on cultural heritage, conservation, architecture and archaeology.
Ind/Abst APAIS, Aust. Public Aff. Inf. Ser. (1984-); Archit. Period. Index (1986-).

NZ/0110-5647
HISTORICAL JOURNAL / OTAKI HISTORICAL SOCIETY. Added/Corp Otaki Historical Society. (1978)-. English. an (Dec.). 32.00NZ$. Otaki Historical Society Inc., PO Box 50, Otaki New Zealand. **Tel** 011 64 6 3648507. **ED** Margaret Long. Index available. **Circ:** 500 (ctrl).
Desc: Journal to record history of Otaki and district.
Ind/Abst Humanit. Index.

AT
HISTORICAL MONOGRAPH / RANDWICK & DISTRICT HISTORICAL SOCIETY. Added/Corp Randwick & District Historical Society. **VFOAT** Randwick and District Historical Society Monographs. No. 1 (1985)-. Monographic series. English. Price varies per volume. Randwick & District Historical Society, Randwick NSW Australia.

NZ/0018-2516
HISTORICAL REVIEW. Added/Corp Whakatane and District Historical Society Inc. Whakatane and District Historical Society Inc. Journal. (1953)-. Periodical. English. Twice a year (May & Nov.). 30.00NZ$. Whakatane and District Historical Society Inc., PO Box 203, Whakatane New Zealand. **ED** E.J. Westgate and T. Jordan. **[CCC]**. Index available in last issue of volume--attached. **Bk Rev**, (Qty: varies). **Circ:** 1,000. ***Supersedes*** *Whakatane and District Historical Society Inc. Newsletter; Whakatane Journal.*
Desc: New Zealand history journal.

AT
HISTORY (SYDNEY, N.S.W.). (HISTORY : MAGAZINE OF THE ROYAL AUSTRALIAN HISTORICAL SOCIETY AND AFFILIATED SOCIETIES.). **Added/Corp** Royal Australian Historical Society. **VFOAT** Magazine of the Royal Australian Historical Society. No. 1 (Oct. 1988)-. Periodical. English. Six times a year. 42.00Aus$ (individuals); 75.00Aus$ (institutions) Comes with Royal Australian Historical Society membership. Royal Australian Historical Society, History House, 133 Macquarie Street, Sydney New South Wales 2000 Australia. **Tel** 011 61 2 2478001, FAX 011 61 2 2477854. **LC** DU80; .H55. **DD** 994/.005. ***Continues*** *Newsletter / Royal Australian Historical Society.*

AT/0021-0013
INVESTIGATOR. Added/Corp Geelong Historical Society. Vol. 1 (Sept. 1965)-. Periodical. English. qt. 10.00Aus$ Australia; 12.00Aus$ other. Geelong Historical Society, 23 Cook Street, Newton Victoria 3220 Australia. **Tel** (052)21-3894. **Bk Rev**. **Circ:** 800 (ctrl).
Desc: Historical subjects pertaining to Geelong and districts in particular, and to Victoria as a secondary consideration.

AT/0314-769X
JOURNAL OF AUSTRALIAN STUDIES. [J. Aust. stud.]. No.1 (June 1977)-. Periodical. English. qt. 55.00Aus$ (institutions), 42.00Aus$ (individuals) Australia; 59.00Aus$ (institutions), 46.00Aus$ (individuals) other. La Trobe University Bookshop, La Trobe University, Bundoora Victoria 3083 Australia. **Tel** (03)479-2969, FAX (03)470-2011, telex AA 33143. **ED** B Bessant. **UDC** 994. **Bk Rev**. **Circ:** 600 (ctrl).
Desc: Academic journal on Australian history, politics, education, economics, literature in Australian studies.
Ind/Abst APAIS, Aust. Public Aff. Inf. Ser. (1978); Aust. Educ. Index (1981-1987).

AT/0022-3344
JOURNAL OF PACIFIC HISTORY, THE. [J. Pac. hist.]. Vol. 1 (1966)-. Academic Scholarly Publication. English (French). sa. 30.00Aus$ Australia, New Zealand, & Pacific Islands; $35.00 other. National Center for Development Studies, Australian National University, Canberra ACT 0200 Australia. **Tel** 011 61 6 2492760, FAX 011 61 6 2495525. **ED** Donald Denoon, Dorothy Shineberg. **LC** DU1; .J66. **DD** 990/.05. **Bk Rev**. **Ad Acc**. **Circ:** 850. Documents available from The Genuine Article, UMI Article Clearinghouse. ***Absorbed*** *Journal of Pacific History Bibliography, 0022-3344.*
Desc: Top scholarly research on history and development of people of Pacific Islands.
Ind/Abst Abstr. Anthropol.; Acad. Search (July 1993-); Am. Hist. Life (1966-); Annu. Bibliogr. Engl. Lang. Lit.; Anthropol. Index; APAIS, Aust. Public Aff. Inf. Ser. (1967-); Arts Humanit. Citation Index [Full Cov.]; Curr. Contents Arts Humanit.; Expand. Acad. Index (1989-); Hist. Source (July 1993-); Humanit. Index; Humanit. Source (Jul. 1993-); INFO-SOUTH Abstr.; Mag. Search; Newsp. Period. Abstr. (1991-); Res. Alert [Full Cov.].

FJ/1011-3029
JOURNAL OF PACIFIC STUDIES. Added/Corp University of the South Pacific. School of Social and Economic Development. Vol. 1 (1975)-. English. an. 9.00Fij$. Journal of Pacific Studies, Univeristy of the South Pacific, PO Box 1168, Suva Fiji Islands. **Tel** 011 679 313900, FAX 011 679 301305. **LC** DU1; .J67. **DD** 990/.05.
Ind/Abst Int. Bibliogr. Sociol.

AT/0312-9640
JOURNAL OF THE HISTORICAL SOCIETY OF SOUTH AUSTRALIA. [J. Hist. Soc. South Aust.]. **Main/Corp** Historical Society of South Australia. No. 1 (1975)-. Periodical. English. an. 15.00Aus$ Australia; 20.00Aus$ other. Historical Society of South Australia, Institute Building, 122 Kintore Avenue, Adelaide 5000 South Australia. **Tel** 011 61 8 2979844. **ED** J. Playford. **Bk Rev. Circ:** 500 (ctrl).
Desc: Papers on a variety of topics dealing with Australian history.
Ind/Abst APAIS, Aust. Public Aff. Inf. Ser. (1976-).

AT/0035-8762
JOURNAL OF THE ROYAL AUSTRALIAN HISTORICAL SOCIETY. [J. Royal Aust. Hist. Soc.]. **Added/Corp** Royal Australian Historical Society. Vol. 51 (March 1965)-. Periodical. English. Four times a year. 45.00Aus$ (individuals); 75.00Aus$ (institutions) Comes with Royal Australian Historical Society memebership. Royal Australian Historical Society, History House, 133 Macquarie Street, Sydney New South Wales 2000 Australia. **Tel** 011 61 2 2478001, FAX 011 61 2 2477854. **ED** Hazel King, Brian Fletcher and Geoffrey Sherington. **LC** DU80; .R6. **DD** 994/.005. cum. index. **Bk Rev. Ad Acc. Circ:** 3,000. ***Continues*** *Journal and Proceedings (Royal Australian Historical Society).*
Desc: Articles on all aspects of Australian history.
Ind/Abst Am. Hist. Life (1965-); APAIS, Aust. Public Aff. Inf. Ser.; SportSearch.

AT
JOURNAL (ROYAL HISTORICAL SOCIETY OF QUEENSLAND : 1985). (JOURNAL / ROYAL HISTORICAL SOCIETY OF QUEENSLAND.). **Added/Corp** Royal Historical Society of Queensland. **VFOAT** Journal of the Royal Historical Society of Queensland. Vol. 12, No. 2 (Sept. 1985)-. Periodical. English. qt (Feb., May, Aug., Nov.). 20.00Aus$. Royal Historical Society of Queensland, PO Box 57, North Quay, Brisbane QLD 4002 Australia. **Tel** 61 7 2214198. **ED** John Kerr. Index available. **Circ:** 650 (ctrl). ***Continues*** *Historical Papers (Brisbane, Qld.), 0815-9653.*
Desc: Historical papers either delivered at society monthly meetings or submitted to editor for publication. Primarily dealing with the history of the state of Queensland.
Ind/Abst APAIS, Aust. Public Aff. Inf. Ser. (1985-).

AT/0041-3151
LA TROBE LIBRARY JOURNAL. See Library and Information Sciences.

AT
LEICHHARDT HISTORICAL JOURNAL. **Added/Corp** Annandale Association. Balmain Association. Glebe Society. Leichhardt-Lilyfield Association. **VFOAT** LHJ, Leichhardt Historical Journal. (197?)-. Periodical. English. an. 15.00Aus$. Leichhardt Historical Journal, 9 the Avenue, Balmain E NSW 2041 Australia. **Tel** 011 61 2 8108560, FAX 011 61 2 5559277. Index available. cum. index. **Bk Rev.**

AT/0076-6232
MELBOURNE HISTORICAL JOURNAL. [Melb. hist. j.]. Vol. 1 (1961)-. English. an. University of Melbourne / Department of History, Parkville Victoria 3052 Australia. **Tel** 011 61 3 3445977. **LC** D1; .M38. **DD** 909/.005.
Ind/Abst Am. Hist. Life (1965-); Int. Bibliogr. Sociol.

AU
MITTEILUNGEN DER GESELLSCHAFT FUER SALZBURGER LANDESKUNDE. **Added/Corp** Gesellschaft fur Salzburger Landeskunde. (19??)-. German. an. **LC** DB601; .G47. cum. index.
Ind/Abst Am. Hist. Life (1964-1977,1980-1983).

JA/0389-5351
NANKAIKEN KIYO. **VFOAT** Memoirs of the Kagoshima University Research Center for the South Pacific. Vol. 2, No. 1-. Periodical. English (Japanese). Kagoshima Daigaku Nanpo Kaiiki Kenkyu Senta, c/o Kagoshima Daigaku, Jimukyoku 21-24 Korimoto 1-chome, Kagoshima-shi 890 Japan. **LC** DU1; .N35. **UDC** 990. ***Continues*** *Nansoken Kiyo.*

NZ
NEW ZEALAND HISTORIC PLACES. **Added/Corp** New Zealand Historic Places Trust. **VFOAT** Historic Places. (1990)-. Periodical. English (Maori). qt. $14.00 New Zealand; $26.00 other. New Zealand Historic Places Trust, PO Box 2629, Wellington New Zealand. **Tel** 011 64 4 724341. **ED** J. Wilson. **LC** IN PROCESS. **Bk Rev**, (Qty: 10/yr). **Ad Acc, Adv Mgr:** T. Reeves. **Circ:** 19,000 (ctrl). ***Continues*** *Historic Places in New Zealand, 0112-0743.*
Desc: Informative articles on historic places in New Zealand.
Ind/Abst Archit. Period. Index (June 1990-).

NZ/0028-8322
NEW ZEALAND JOURNAL OF HISTORY, THE. [N. Z. j. hist.]. **Added/Corp** University of Auckland. Vol. 1 (April 1967)-. Periodical. English. sa. 24.00NZ$ New Zealand; 35.00NZ$ other. University of Auckland, Private Bag 92019, Auckland New Zealand. **Tel** 011 64 9 3737999, telex NZ 21480. **ED** Judith Binney, M.P.K. Sorrenson. **LC** DU420; .N48. **[CCC].** Index available. cum. index. **Bk Rev. Ad Acc. Circ:** 800. Documents available from The Genuine Article.
Desc: History of New Zealand and associated countries.
Ind/Abst Am. Hist. Life (1967-); Annu. Bibliogr. Engl. Lang. Lit.; Arts Humanit. Citation Index [Full Cov.]; Bibliogr. Mission.; Br. Humanit. Index; Curr. Contents Arts Humanit.; Int. Bibliogr. Sociol.; Res. Alert [Full Cov.]; Soc. Sci. Cit. Index [Select. Cov.].

NZ/0114-4189
NEW ZEALAND LEGACY : JOURNAL OF THE NEW ZEALAND FEDERATION OF HISTORICAL SOCIETIES. **Added/Corp** New Zealand Federation of Historical Societies. **VFOAT** NZ Legacy. Vol. 1, No. 1 (1989)-. Periodical. English. Four times a year (Feb., May, Sept., Nov.). $25.00. Legacy Press, PO Box 120, Otaki New Zealand. **Tel** 011 64 69 46243. **LC** DU419; .N49. **DD** 993/.005.

AT
NEWS DIGEST INTERNATIONAL. ***Title Change.*** **Added/Corp** International Information Centre. (19??)-(19??). Periodical. English. qt. News Digest International, PO Box 535, Parramatta New South Wales, 2155 Australia. **Tel** 011 61 02 6302309. **ED** J. P. Kedys. **LC** D839; .N488. Index available. **Bk Rev. Ad Acc. Circ:** 3,000. ***Merged into*** *Christian Defence League.*
Desc: Study and information on politics, history, the economy and the military.

US/0095-1234
NEWSLETTER - FRIENDS OF MICRONESIA. **Main/Corp** Friends of Micronesia (Association). Newsletter. English. qt. $5.00. 2325 McKinley Avenue, Berkeley CA 94703. **LC** DU500; .F73A. **DD** 919.6/5/005.

AT
NEWSLETTER (HISTORICAL SOCIETY OF SOUTH AUSTRALIA). (NEWSLETTER / THE HISTORICAL SOCIETY OF SOUTH AUSTRALIA INC.). **Added/Corp** Historical Society of South Australia. (19??)-. Newsletter. English. ir. Comes with Historical Society of South Australia Membership. Historical Society of South Australia, Institute Building, 122 Kintore Avenue, Adelaide 5000 South Australia. **Tel** 011 61 8 2979844.

GU
NEWSLETTER - PACIFIC STUDIES INSTITUTE. **Main/Corp** Pacific Studies Institute. (197?)-. Periodical. English. qt. Pacific Studies Institute, PO Box 20820, GMF 96921 Guam.

●AT/1037-1176
NORTHERN TERRITORY IN FOCUS. **Added/Corp** Australian Bureau of Statistics. Northern Territory Office. (1992)-. English. ***Continues*** *Northern Territory Statistical Summary, 0067-0855.*

AT/0029-8077
OCEANIA. [Oceania]. **Added/Corp** University of Sydney. Australian National Research Council. Vol. 1 (April 1930)-. Periodical. English. qt (March, June, Sept., Dec.). 50.00Aus$ (institutions) Australia; $50.00 (institutions) other. University of Sydney, 116 Darlington Road / H42, Sydney NSW 2006 Australia. **Tel** 011 61 2 6922666. **ED** J.R. Beckett, G. Cowlishaw A. Ramsey and F. Merlan. **LC** DU28; .O3. **DD** 919. **NLM** W1 OC608. Index available. cum. index (to Vol. 60). **Bk Rev**, (Qty: 50). **Ad Acc, Adv Mgr:** D. Koller, **Tel** (02)692-2666. **Pr Rev. Circ:** 1,200. available on microfilm and microfiche from University Microfilms International (UMI). Documents available from The Genuine Article, UMI Article Clearinghouse, Documents on Demand.
Desc: A journal devoted to the study of the indigenous peoples of Australia, Melanesic, Micronesia and Southeast Asia.
Ind/Abst Abstr. Anthropol.; Acad. Ind. [Computer File] (1992-); Acad. Search (July 1993-); Anthropol. Index; Anthropol. Lit. (1963-); APAIS, Aust. Public Aff. Inf. Ser. (1963-); Appl. Soc. Sci. Index Abstr.; Arts Humanit. Citation Index [Select. Cov.]; Curr. Contents Soc. Behav. Sci.; Environ. Abstr.; Ethnoarts Index; Expand. Acad. Index (1989-); Gen. Sci. Source (Jul. 1993-); INFO-SOUTH Abstr.; Int. Bibliogr. Sociol.; Mag. Search; MLA Int. Bibl. Books Artic. Mod. Lang. Lit.; Newsp. Period. Abstr. (1991-); Res. Alert [Full Cov.]; Soc. Sci. Source (Jul. 1993-); Soc. Sci. Cit. Index [Full Cov.]; Soc. Sci. Index; Soc. Sci. Index Fulltext (June 1988-) [Full Txt.]; Wildl. Rev.

AT/0158-7366
ORAL HISTORY ASSOCIATION OF AUSTRALIA JOURNAL. [Oral Hist. Assoc. Aust. j.]. (1979)-. English. an (Oct.). 30.00Aus$ (individuals), 37.00Aus$ (institutions) Comes with Oral History Association of Australia Membership and includes State Branch Membership. Oral History Association of Australia, 122 Kintore Avenue, Adelaide 5000 Australia. **Tel** 08 2077349. **ED** Rosemary Block. **DD** 994.006. cum. index (No. 1-10). **Bk Rev**, (Qty: varies). **Ad Acc. Circ:** 500.
Desc: This journal includes conference papers and or articles as well as work in progress reports concerning the theory and practice of oral history.
Ind/Abst APAIS, Aust. Public Aff. Inf. Ser. (1992-).

NZ/0113-5376
ORAL HISTORY IN NEW ZEALAND. Vol. 1 (1988)-. Periodical. English. an.
Ind/Abst RILM Abstr.

GU
PACIFIC ASIAN STUDIES. **Added/Corp** Pacific Asian Studies Association. Vol. 1 (Jan. 1975)-. Periodical. English. sa. $5.00. Dr Benjamin F Bast, University of Guam, PO Box EK, Agana 96910 Guam. **LC** DU1; .P133. **DD** 990/.05.

AT/0030-8722
PACIFIC ISLANDS MONTHLY. (PACIFIC ISLANDS MONTHLY : PIM.). [Pac. Isl. mon.]. **VFOAT** PIM; P.I.M. (Aug. 1930)-. Periodical. English. Twelve times a year. 30.00Aus$ Australia; $45.00 US and Canada; £28.00 UK; 63.00Aus$, $50.85 other. Fiji Times & Herald Ltd., GPO Box 1167, Suva Fiji Islands. **Tel** 011 679 304111, FAX 011 679 301521, telex FJ 2124. **LC** DU1; .P145. **DD** 990. cum. index. **Bk Rev. Ad Acc.**
Desc: Current views and news of Pacific Islands and surrounding countries.
Ind/Abst PAIS Int. Print.

US/0085-459X
PACIFIC ISLANDS STUDIES AND NOTES. No. 1-. Monographic series. English. ir. Price varies per volume. N L H Krauss, 2437 Parker Place, Honolulu HI 96822. **Tel** 988-4304. **ED** N L H Krauss. **UDC** 990. **Circ:** 500.

FJ/0377-2543
PACIFIC PERSPECTIVE. ***Ceased.*** [Pac. perspect.]. Vol. 1 (1972)-Vol. 14 (?). Periodical. English. sa. Pacific Perspective, PO Box 5083, Suva Fiji Islands. **Tel** 313900. **ED** A Ravuvu, U Neemia, and R G Cracombe. **LC** DU1; .P16. **DD** 919/.005. **UDC** 919. **Bk Rev. Ad Acc. Circ:** 500.
Ind/Abst Int. Labour Doc. (?-?).

AT/0155-9060
PACIFIC RESEARCH MONOGRAPH. **Added/Corp** Australian National University. (1977)-. Monographic series. English. Price varies per volume. Anutech Pty Limited, GPO Box 4, Canberra Act, 2601 Australia. **Tel** 011 61 6 2492479, FAX 011 61 6 2575088. **LC** UNC.
Ind/Abst Geogr. Abstr. Human Geogr.; Int. Dev. Abstr.

US/0275-3596
PACIFIC STUDIES. [Pac. stud.]. **Added/Corp** Polynesian Cultural Center (Laie, Honolulu, Hawaii) Brigham Young University--Hawaii Campus. Institute for Polynesian Studies. (1977)-. Periodical. English. Four times a year (Mar., June, Sept., Dec.). $30.00. Brigham Young University of Hawaii, PO Box 1979, Polynesian Studies, Laie HI 96762-1294. **Tel** (808)243-3665, FAX (808)293-3645. **ED** Dale B. Robertson. **LC** DU1; .P17. **DD** 990/.05. Index Bound in First Issue. cum. index. **Bk Rev**, (Qty: 20). **Ad Acc. Pr Rev. Circ:** 500 (ctrl).
Desc: An interdisciplinary journal devoted to the study of the Pacific and its islands and adjacent countries.
Ind/Abst Abstr. Anthropol.; Am. Hist. Life (1987-); Anthropol. Lit.; Book Rev. Index; Ethnoarts Index; Int. Bibliogr. Sociol.; Int. Labour Doc.; Int. Polit. Sci. Abstr.; LABORDOC; Linguist. Lang. Behav. Abstr.; PAIS Int. Print (1991-); Soc. Plann. Policy Dev. Abstr.; Sociol. Abstr.

AT/0039-9809
PAPERS AND PROCEEDINGS - TASMANIAN HISTORICAL RESEARCH ASSOCIATION. [Pap. proc. - Tasman. Hist. Res. Assoc.]. **Main/Corp** Tasmanian Historical Research Association. Vol. 1 (Dec. 1951)-. Proceedings. English. qt. 25.00Aus$ Australia; 35.00Aus$ other. Tasmanian Historical Research Association Inc, Box 441 Sandy Bay, Tasmania 7005 Australia. **Tel** 011 61 2 285851. **ED** M.D.Dilger. **LC** DU80; .T28. cum. index. **Bk Rev. Circ:** 400.
Desc: Original research of Australian and Tasmanian history using primary sources located mainly though not exclusively in Tasmania, Australia.
Ind/Abst Am. Hist. Life; APAIS, Aust. Public Aff. Inf. Ser. (1963-).

AT
PAPUA NEW GUINEA HANDBOOK. ***Title Change.*** **Main/Corp** Pacific Publications (Firm). 7th- Ed. English. Fiji Times & Herald Ltd., GPO Box 1167, Suva Fiji Islands. **Tel** 011 679 304111, FAX 011 679 301521, telex FJ 2124. **LC** DU740.A2; P32A. **DD** 945/.3/005. **UDC** 995.4. ***Continues*** *Handbook of Papua and New Guinea.* ***Continued by*** *Papua New Guinea Handbook and Travel Guide, 0155-4743.*

US/0272-3441
PROCEEDINGS OF THE ANNUAL PACIFIC ISLANDS STUDIES CONFERENCE, UNIVERSITY OF HAWAII, THE. [Proc. annu. Pac. Isl. Stud. Conf. Univ. Hawaii]. **Main/Conf** Pacific Islands Studies Conference. **Added/Corp** Pacific Islands Studies Center,

University of Hawaii at Manoa. 1st (1976)-. English. an. University of Hawaii Press, 2840 Kolowalu Street, Honolulu HI 96822. **Tel** (808)956-8833, (808)948-8697, FAX (808)988-6052. **LC** DU29; .P23a. **DD** 990.

AT
PUSH, THE. ***Suspended.*** No. 27 (1989)-(19??). English. an. 10.00Aus$. University of New England Department of History, The Push, Armidale New South Wales 2351 Australia. **Tel** 011 61 67 732107. **ED** Alan Atkinson. ***Continues*** *Push From the Bush, 0155-8633.*
Desc: Social history of the Australian colonies.

FR
QUINOLONEWS INTERNATIONAL.
Ceased. (1993)-(1994). French. qt. ADIS International Ltd, 41 Centorian Drive, Private Bag 65901, Mairangi Bay, Auckland 10 New Zealand. **Tel** 011 64 9 4798100, FAX 011 64 9 4791418.

AT/0557-4242
ROYAL WESTERN AUSTRALIAN HISTORICAL SOCIETY'S NEWSLETTER.
Main/Corp Royal Western Australian Historical Society. **Added/Corp** Royal Western Australian Historical Society. Newsletter. (19??)-. Newsletter. English. Eleven times a year. $50.00 Comes with Royal Western Australian Historical Society membership. Royal Western Australian Historical Society, 49 Broadway, Stirling House, Nedlands Western Australia 6009 Australia. **Tel** 09 386 3841, FAX 09 386 3309.

AT/0048-8879
RYDE RECORDER, THE. **Added/Corp** Ryde District Historical Society. Vol. 1 (Mar. 1967)-. Periodical. English. bm. 3.00Aus$. Mrs E. Benson, Ryde Historical Society, 57 DeLange Road, Putney New South Wales 2112 Australia. **Tel** 02/807-1931.

AT/1030-0481
SOUTH AUSTRALIAN GEOGRAPHICAL JOURNAL. **See** Geography.

NZ/1170-4616
STOUT CENTRE REVIEW : JOURNAL OF THE STOUT RESEARCH CENTRE FOR THE STUDY OF NEW ZEALAND HISTORY AND CULTURE. **Added/Corp** Stout Research Centre for the Study of New Zealand Society, History, and Culture. (19??)-. Periodical. English. Three times a year (Feb., June, Oct.). 35.00NZ$. Victorian University of Wellington, PO Box 600, Sout Research Centre, Wellington New Zealand. **Tel** 011 64 4 715305, FAX 011 64 4 712070. **ED** Dr. J.M. Thomson. **Circ:** 350 (ctrl).
Desc: Covers the ethnic and religious interests of New Zealand as well as native poetry, photography, folklore, and games.

AT
STUDIES IN WESTERN AUSTRALIAN HISTORY. **Added/Corp** University of Western Australia. Dept. of History. (June 1977)-. Periodical. English. an. Price varies per volume. Studies in Western Australian History, University of Western Australia, Department of History, Nedlands Western Australia 6009. **Tel** 011 61 9 2803838. **LC** DU350; .S78. **DD** 994.1/005. **Bk Rev. Circ:** 700.
Ind/Abst APAIS, Aust. Public Aff. Inf. Ser.

MG
TANTARA. **Added/Corp** Societe d'Histoire de Madagascar. (1973)-. Malagasy (French). Societe d'Histoire de Madagascar, BP 3384, Antananarivo Madagascar. **Tel** 235-34. **LC** DT469.M21; T35. **DD** 969/.1/005. Index available. **Bk Rev.**

NZ/0570-4499
TE AO HOU; THE MAORI MAGAZINE.
VFOAT The New World. No. 1- Winter 1952-. Periodical. Multiple languages (English and Maori). **UDC** 930.85(992.32).

AT
TECHNICAL INFORMATION SERVICE / ROYAL AUSTRALIAN HISTORICAL SOCIETY. ***Ceased.*** **Added/Corp** Royal Australian Historical Society. (198?)-(1992). Monographic series. English. bm. Royal Australian Historical Society, History House, 133 Macquarie Street, Sydney New South Wales 2000 Australia. **Tel** 011 61 2 2478001, FAX 011 61 2 2477854.

NL/0081-2862
TECHNICAL PAPER - SOUTH PACIFIC COMMISSION. **Main/Corp** South Pacific Commission. No. 1 (1949)-. Monographic series. English. Price varies per volume. South Pacific Commission, PO Box D5, Noumea Cedex New Caledonia. **Tel** (687)26 20 00, FAX (687)26 38 18. **LC** DU1; .S586. **DD** 338.99. Documents available from BIOSIS Document Express.
Ind/Abst AGRICOLA; Biol. Abstr.

AT
TERRITORY DIGEST. ***Ceased.*** Vol. 3, No. 3, Apr. (1981)-?. Periodical. English. bm. Territory Digest of the Northern Territory Information Service, PO Box 4396, Darwin 5794 Australia. **LC** DU392; .N68. **DD** 994.29/005. **UDC** 994.8. ***Continues*** *Northern Territory Digest.*

CN
TOK BLONG PASIFIK. (199?)-. English. qt. $40.00 institution, $25.00 individual. South Pacific Peoples Foundation, 415-620 View Street, Victoria BC V8W 1J6 Canada. **Tel** (604)381-4131, FAX (604)388-5258. **ED** Stuart Wulff. **Bk Rev**, (Qty: varies). **Ad Acc. Circ:** 1,000. ***Continues*** *Tok Blong SPPF, 0829-9670.*
Desc: News and views on the Pacific Islands.

AT
TRUST : A QUARTERLY FROM THE NATIONAL TRUST OF AUSTRALIA (VICTORIA). **Main/Corp** National Trust of Australia (Victoria). (19??)-. Periodical. English. ir (5 issues). National Trust of Australia, 39 Paterson Street, Launceton Tasmania 7250 Australia. **Tel** 003-319077. **LC** WMLC L 83/1899.

NZ/0111-5871
TU TANGATA. **Added/Corp** New Zealand. Dept. of Maori Affairs. New Zealand Maori Council. Maori Women's Welfare League. No. 1 (Aug./Sept. 1981)-. Periodical. English (Maori). Six times a year. Ministry of Maori Development, Communications Unit, PO Box 3943, Wellington New Zealand. **Tel** 04 499 0055, FAX 04 495 0800. **LC** DU423.A1; T78. **DD** 993.1/0049916. **Circ:** 6,000 (ctrl). ***Formed by the union of*** *Kaea, 0111-0594* ***and*** *Maori.*

AT/1033-1891
UNESCO AUSTRALIA / AUSTRALIAN NATIONAL COMMISSION FOR UNESCO.
See Law-International Law.

AU/1017-2696
UNSERE HEIMAT. **Added/Corp** Verein fur Landeskunde von Niederosterreich und Wien. (19??)-. Periodical. German. mo. S200.00 Austria; $20.02 US. Verein F Landeskunde V Noe, Herrensgasse 11, A 1014 Vienna Austria. **Tel** 011 43 1 53110 6255. **LC** DB111; .U58. ***Continues*** *Verein fur Landeskunde von Niederosterreich und Wien. Monatsblatt.*
Ind/Abst Am. Hist. Life (1963-1985).

AT
VICTORIAN HISTORICAL JOURNAL.
Added/Corp Royal Historical Society of Victoria. Vol. 58, No. 1 (Mar. 1987)-. Periodical. English. qt. Royal Historical Society of Victoria, 1 City Road, South Melbourne Victoria 3205 Australia. **LC** DU200; .J68. **DD** 994.5/005. ***Continues*** *Journal (Royal Historical Society of Victoria), 0813-1295.*
Ind/Abst Am. Hist. Life (19??-19??); APAIS, Aust. Public Aff. Inf. Ser. (1987-).

AU
ZEITSCHRIFT DES HISTORISCHEN VEREINES FUER STEIERMARK. **Main/Corp** Historischer Verein fur Steiermark. (1903)-. German. an. ***Continues*** *Historischer Verein fur Steiermark, Graz. Mitteilungen.*
Ind/Abst Am. Hist. Life (1964-); BHA : Biblio. Hist. Art.

HISTORY OF EUROPE

UK/0955-2359
20 CENTURY BRITISH HISTORY.
Added/Corp Institute of Contemporary British History. **VFOAT** Twentieth Century British History. Vol. 1, No. 1 (1990)-. Periodical. English. Three times a year. £45.00 UK and Europe; $85.00 other. Oxford University Press, Walton Street, Oxford OX2 6DP England. **Tel** 011 44 865 56767, FAX 011 44 865 267773, telex 837330 OXPRES G. **(Subscription address:** Oxford University Press / USA, Journals Marketing Department, Oxford University Press, 2001 Evans Road, Cary NC 27513.**)** **ED** Ross McKibbin and John Rowett. **LC** DA566; .A15. **DD** 941.082/05. **NLM** W1; TW453. **[CCC].** available on microfilm and microfiche from University Microfilms International (UMI).
Desc: Covers all aspects of British history in the 20th century, drawing together the different branches of historical scholarship and work in all related disciplines.
Ind/Abst Am. Hist. Life (1990-); Int. Bibliogr. Sociol.

CN/0707-8544
25-1-1. **VAT** Twenty-Five-One-One. V. 1- Nov. 1978-. Periodical. English. qt. Camp X Military Museum Society, PO Box 2355, Oshawa Ontario L1H 7V5. **DD** 940.54/86/41.

US/0580-4760
A MAGYAR TALALKOZO KRONIKAJA.
Main/Corp Magyar Talalkozo. Vol. 1 (1962)-. Hungarian. an. **LC** DB919.5; .M36.
Ind/Abst Am. Bibliogr. Slavic East Europ. Stud. (19??-19??).

FR
A.S.F. DOCUMENTATION. **Main/Corp** International Association for Francophone Solidarity. **VAT** Association de Solidarite Francophone Documentation. No. 1- Winter 1972-. Periodical. French. 5.00F. **LC** DC33.9; .I56A. **DD** 909 S; 440.

US/0883-9549
AAASS NEWSLETTER. ***Title Change.*** [AAASS newsl.]. **Main/Corp** American Association for the Advancement of Slavic Studies. **VAT** American Association for the Advancement of Slavic Studies Newsletter. Vol. 33, No. 3 (197?)-(May 1993). Periodical. English. Five times a year. American Association for the Advancement of Slavic Studies, 125 Panama Street, Stanford University, Acacia Building, Stanford CA 94305-6029. **Tel** (415)723-9668, FAX (415)725-7737, telex 348402 STANFRD STNU. **ED** Mary Keller. **LC** DK1; .A3814. **DD** 947/.0005. **Ad Acc. Circ:** 4,200. ***Continues*** *American Association for the Advancement of Slavic Studies. Newsletter.* ***Continued by*** *American Association for the Advancement of Slavic Studies. NewsNet, 1074-3057.*
Desc: The newsletter carries news of the profession, opportunities for employment, sources of support for research, and other material of general interest.

DK
AARBGER FOR NORDISK OLDKYNDIGHED OG HISTORIE / UDGIVNE AF DET KONGELIGE NORDISKE OLDSKRIFT-SELSKAB.
Added/Corp Kongelige Nordiske Oldskriftselskab (Copenhagen, Denmark). (1866)-. Danish (summaries and/or abstracts in English and German). an. kr200.00. Lynge & Soen, Silkegade 11 Postboks 2041, DK 1113 Copenhagen K Denmark. **ED** Ulla Lund Hansen. **LC** DL1; .N6. Index available. cum. index. ctrl circ. ***Formed by the union of*** *Annaler for Nordisk Oldkyndighed Og Historie* ***and*** *Antiquarisk Tidsskrift.*
Desc: The culture, literature, and religion of Scandinavia from prehistory to the early Middle Ages.
Ind/Abst Anthropol. Lit.; Br. Archaeol. Bibliogr.

DK/0105-9254
AARBOG / KOEBSTADMUSEET "DEN GAMLE BY". **Main/Corp** Koebstadmuseet "Den Gamle By" (Aarhus, Denmark). **VFOAT** Aarbog. (1927)-. Danish. an. Koebstadmuseet Den Gamle By, DK 8000 Aarhus C, Denmark. **Tel** 011 45 86 1231488, FAX 011 45 86 760687. cum. index.
Ind/Abst BHA : Biblio. Hist. Art.

GW/0080-5297
ABHANDLUNGEN DER SACHSISCHEN AKADEMIE DER WISSENSCHAFTEN ZU LEIPZIG, PHILOLOGISCH-HISTORISCHE KLASSE. **Main/Corp** Sachsische Akademie der Wissenschaften, Leipzig. Philogogische-Historische Klasse. **Added/Corp** Sachsische Akademie der Wissenschaften zu Leipzig. Philologisch-Historische Klasse. Vol. 1 (1950)-. Monographic series. German. ir. Price varies per volume. Akademie-Verlag GmbH, Muehlenstrasse 33 34, D 13162 Berlin Germany. **Tel** 011 49 30 47889300, FAX 011 49 30 47889357. **(Subscription address:** VCH Publishers Inc., 303 Northwest 12th Avenue, Journals Department, Deerfield FL 33442.**)** Index Available, published separately, free-automatically sent.

UK/0044-5622
ABSEES. ***Title Change.*** [ABSEES]. **Added/Corp** National Association for Soviet and East European Studies (Great Britain) University of Birmingham. Centre for Russian and East European Studies. British Association for Soviet, Slavonic, and East European Studies. British Association of Slavonic and East European Studies. **VFOAT** Soviet and East European Abstracts Series; Abstracts, Soviet and East European Series; Abstracts, Russian and East European Series. Vol. 1, No. 27 (July 1970)-Vol. 22, No. 100 (Dec. 1992). English. Three times a year. ABREES Ltd., 77 Roupell Street, London SE1 8SS United Kingdom. **Tel** 011 44 071 2619710. **ED** R. Hutchings (editor's address: 168 Turnpike Link, Croydon CRO 5NZ United Kingdom). **LC** DJK1; .A2; Z2483; .A2. **[CCC].** Index Available, published separately, free-automatically sent. available on microfilm and microfiche from University Microfilms International (UMI). ***Continues*** *Soviet Studies. Information Supplement.* ***Continued by*** *Abstracts, Russian and East European Series.*
Desc: This journal is very useful to people who are concerned with social and economic development in Eastern Europe.

US/0147-3387
ABSTRACTS OF PAPERS - BYZANTINE STUDIES CONFERENCE. 1st Edition (1975)-. Monographic series. English. ir. Price varies per volume. Dumbarton Oaks Publishing, 1703 32nd Street Northwest, Washington DC 20007. **Tel** (202)342-3270. **LC** DF501.5; .B9a. **DD** 949.5.
Ind/Abst BHA : Biblio. Hist. Art.

●US
ABSTRACTS, RUSSIAN AND EAST EUROPEAN SERIES : ABREES. **Added/Corp** British Association of Slavonic and East European Studies. **VFOAT** ABREES; Journal of Russian & East European Economic Affairs. (1993)-. English. Four times a year. £317.00 UK; £319.00 Europe. ABREES Ltd., 77 Roupell Street, London SE1 8SS United Kingdom. **Tel** 011 44 071 2619710. **LC** DJK1; .A2; Z2483; .A2. ***Continues*** *ABSEES, 0044-5622.*

GW
ACHTZEHNTE JAHRHUNDERT, DAS. **Added/Corp** Deutsche Gesellschaft fuer die Erforschung des Achtzehnten Jahrhunderts. Vol. 1 (1977)-. German. sa. DM36.00. Wallstein Verlag GmbH, Planckstr. 23, D 37073 Gottingen Germany. **Bk Rev**. **Ad Acc. Circ:** 800 (ctrl).
Desc: A newsletter for the membership of the German 18th Century Society, containing pertinent articles, a cumulative bibliography and book reviews.

UK/0955-4270
ACIS : JOURNAL OF THE ASSOCIATION FOR CONTEMPORARY IBERIAN STUDIES. **See** Linguistics.

GW/0567-7289
ACTA BALTICA. [Acta Balt.]. **Added/Corp** Albertus-Magnus-Kolleg. Institutum Balticum. Vol. 1 (1960/1961)-. German. an. DM49.50. Albertus Magnus Kolleg / Intitutum Balticum, Postfach 12 29, Bischof-Kindermann-Str 1, 61462 Konigstein Ts Germany. **Tel** 06174/299123, FAX 06174/299135. **LC** DK511.B25; A5. Index available. cum. index. **Bk Rev**, (Qty: 3-5). **Circ:** 700.
Ind/Abst Am. Hist. Life (1966-); Aquat. Sci. Fish. Abstr. (Computer File); MLA Int. Bibl. Books Artic. Mod. Lang. Lit.

PL/0065-1044
ACTA BALTICO-SLAVICA. [Acta Balt.-Slav.]. **Added/Corp** Biaostockie Towarzystwo Naukowe. Vol. 1 (1964)-. Polish (summaries and/or abstracts in English). an. $20.60. **(Subscription address:** ARS Polona, PO Box 1001, 00068 Warsaw Poland.**)** **LC** DK511.B25; A612.
Ind/Abst Anthropol. Index; BHA : Biblio. Hist. Art; MLA Int. Bibl. Books Artic. Mod. Lang. Lit.; Numis. Lit.

US/0361-7491
ACTA - CENTER FOR MEDIEVAL AND EARLY RENAISSANCE STUDIES, STATE UNIVERSITY OF NEW YORK AT BINGHAMTON. (ACTA.). [Acta - Cent. Mediev. Early Renaiss. Stud. State Univ. N. Y. Binghamt.]. **Added/Corp** State University of New York at Binghamton. Center for Medieval and Early Renaissance Studies. Vol. 1 (1974)-. Monographic series. English. ir. Price varies per volume. State University of New York Press, State University Plaza, Albany NY 12246. **Tel** (518)472-5000, FAX (518)472-5038. **(Subscription address:** Cup Service, PO Box 6525, Ithaca, NY 14851, Tel. (800)666-2211**)** **LC** CB351; .A15. **DD** 909.07.
Ind/Abst MLA Int. Bibl. Books Artic. Mod. Lang. Lit.

XV/0351-2789
ACTA ECCLESIASTICA SLOVENIAE. 1-. Slovenian (English, German, Italian and Latin). an. Teoloska Fakulteta v Ljubljana, Institut za Zgodovino Cerkve, Ljubljana Slovenia. **Tel** 061/312-593. **ED** Metod Benedik. **Ad Acc.**
Ind/Abst Am. Hist. Life (1979-); Bibliogr. Mission.

HU/0001-5849
ACTA HISTORICA ACADEMIAE SCIENTIARUM HUNGARICAE. [Acta hist. Acad. Sci. Hung.]. **Added/Corp** Magyar Tudomanyos Akademia. **VFOAT** Acta Historica. Vol. 1 (1951)-. Academic Scholarly Publication. English (French, German and Russian). qt. $92.00. Akademiai Kiado, Publishing House of the Hungarian Academy of Sciences, Prielle Kornelia u. 19-35, H-1117 Budapest Hungary. **Tel** 011 36 1 1811991, FAX 011 36 1 1811991, telex 22-6228 AKNYO H. **ED** Zsigmond Pal Pach (editor's address: Acta Historica, H-1014 Budapest Uri u53 Hungary). **LC** DB901; .M245. **[CCC]**. cum. index. **Bk Rev**. **Ad Acc.**
Desc: Studies on medieval, modern, and contemporary universal and Hungarian history. Reports on the international historical conferences held in Hungary and abroad are given. Also contains selected bibliography of the Hungarian works on history each year.
Ind/Abst Am. Hist. Life (1953-).

RM/0578-5391
ACTA MUSEI NAPOCENSIS. **Main/Corp** Muzeul de Istorie al Transilvaniei. (1964)-. Periodical. Romanian (summaries and/or abstracts in English, French, German and Russian). an. DM212.00. **(Subscription address:** Kubon & Sagner, ABT Zeitschriftenimport, D 80328 Munich Germany.**)** **LC** DR201; .C63.
Ind/Abst BHA : Biblio. Hist. Art; Numis. Lit.

PL/0001-6829
ACTA POLONIAE HISTORICA. [Acta Pol. hist.]. **Added/Corp** Instytut Historii (Polska Akademia Nauk). Vol. 1 (1958)-. English (French, German and Polish). sa. $64.00. **(Subscription address:** ARS Polona, PO Box 1001, 00068 Warsaw Poland.**)** **LC** DK401; .A25. Documents available from The Genuine Article.
Ind/Abst Am. Hist. Life (1958-); Arts Humanit. Citation Index [Full Cov.]; BHA : Biblio. Hist. Art; Curr. Contents Arts Humanit.; Res. Alert [Full Cov.]; Soc. Sci. Cit. Index [Select. Cov.].

JA/0288-3503
ACTA SLAVICA IAPONICA. Vol. 1 (1983)-. English (Russian). an. Slavic Research Center, Hokkaido University Kita 9, Nishi 7 Kita-ku, Sapporo 060 Japan. **Tel** (011)716-2111, FAX 709-9283. **ED** Hiroshi Kimura. **LC** DJK1; .A28. **DD** 940/.0975918. **UDC** 947; 952. **Bk Rev**. **Circ:** 500 (ctrl).
Desc: Interdisciplinary journal in European languages devoted to Russian/Soviet and East European studies.

XR/0472-8947
ACTA UNIVERSITATIS PALACKIANAE OLOMUCENSIS. FACULTAS PHILOSOPHICA. HISTORICA. [Acta Univ. Palacki. Olomuc. Fac. Philos., Hist.]. **Main/Corp** Olomouc, Moravia. Palackeho Universita. Filosoficka Fakulta. **Added/Corp** Univerzita Palackeho v Olomouci. Filozoficka Fakulta. (1960)-. Monographic series. Czech (summaries and/or abstracts in German and Russian). Price varies per volume. **(Subscription address:** Artia Pegas Press Ltd., Palac Metro Narodni Trida 25, 11210 Prague 1 Czech Republic.**)** **LC** D1.O28; A35. ***Continues*** *tSbornik Vysoke Skole Pedagogicke v Olomouci. Historie.*
Ind/Abst Am. Hist. Life (1963-).

HU/0324-6965
ACTA UNIVERSITATIS SZEGEDIENSIS DE ATTILA JOZSEF NOMINATAE ACTA HISTORICA. [Acta hist.]. V. 12-. Monographic series. Hungarian (summaries and/or abstracts in French and Russian). ir. Price varies per volume. Szegedi Jozsef Attila, Tudomanyegyetem Bolcseszettudom Anyi Kar, Szeged Hungary. **UDC** 943.9. ***Continues*** *Acta Universitatis Szegediensis. Acta Historica.*
Ind/Abst Am. Hist. Life (1971-).

IT/0391-9994
ACTUM LUCE. **Added/Corp** Compagnia Balestrieri Lucca. Commissione Storica. Istituto Storico Lucchese. Vol. 1 (Apr. 1972)-. Periodical. Italian. sa.
Ind/Abst BHA : Biblio. Hist. Art.

GW
ADRESSBUCH DER GOLDSTADT PFORZHEIM, DER GROSSEN KREISSTADT MUHLACKER, SOWIE STADTEN UND GEMEINDEN DES ENZKREISES. **VFOAT** Adressbuch Goldstadt Pforzheim, Grosse Kreisstadt Muhlacker, Stadte und Gemeinden des Enzkreises; Adressbuch von Pforzheim, Muhlacker, Enzkreis. German. DM45.00. Pforzheimer Adressbuch-Verlag Neumayer, Friedenstrasse 111, Pforzheimer Germany. **LC** DD901.P5; A66.

GW
ADRESSBUCH DER STADT FURTH. German. DM49.00. Adressbuchverlagsgesellschaft Ruf, Haydnstrasse 1, 8000 Munchen 15 Germany. **LC** DD901.F8943; A6.

GW
ADRESSBUCH DER STADT HANAU. (19??)-. Periodical. German. Verlag Beleke Kg, Kronprinzenstr 13, 4300 Essen Germany. **LC** DD901.H35; A37. **DD** 914.3/41.

GW
ADRESSBUCH PFORZHEIM UND UMGEBUNG. German. Pforzheimer Adressbuch-Verlag Neumayer, Friedenstrasse 111, Pforzheimer Germany. **LC** DD901.P5; A68. **DD** 943/.46.

GW
ADRESSBUCH STADT UND KREIS ESSLINGEN. German. Verlag Bechtle, Zeppelinstrasse 116, 73 Esslingen Germany. **LC** DD801.E78; A63.

FR
ADUK, ADRESAR UKRAINTSIV U VILNOMU SVITI. **VFOAT** Adresar Ukrainstsiv u Vilnomu Sviti. 1- 1973-. Ukrainian. Premiere Improv Ukrainienne en France, 3 rue du Sabot, Paris 75006 France. **ED** V Lazovinskyi. **LC** DK508.44; .A13.

SA
AFRICA SUD. Periodical. Italian. 5.00. Italo-South African Publishers Park, Transvaal South Africa. **LC** DG577; .A47. **UDC** 968.0.

SP
AGENDA - OBRA SINDICAL EDUCACION Y DESCANSO, BARCELONA. **Main/Corp** Obra Sindical Educacion y Descanso, Barcelona. Spanish. Via Layetana 16-18, Planta 8A, Barcelona Spain. **LC** DP402.B2; O22.

US/0899-1146
AGORA (PHILADELPHIA, PA.). (AGORA.). [Agora]. Periodical. Romanian. ir. $17.00. Foreign Policy Research Institute, 3615 Chestnut Street, Philadelphia PA 19104. **Tel** (215)382-0685, FAX (215)382-0131. **LC** PC800; .A36. **DD** 949.

UK
AGRARIAN HISTORY OF ENGLAND & WALES. Academic Scholarly Publication. English. ir. price varies per volume. Cambridge University Press, The Edinburgh Building, Shaftesbury Road, Cambridge CB2 2RU United Kingdom. **Tel** 011 44 223 312393, FAX 011 44 223 325959. **(Subscription address:** North America/ Cambridge University Press, 40 West 20th Street, New York, NY 10011-4211; telephone: (212)924-3900**)**

BE
AKKADICA. **Added/Corp** Fondation Assyriologique Georges Dossin. Vol. 1 (Jan./Feb. 1977)-. Periodical. French (Dutch). Five times a year. 950.00F Belgium; 1500.00F other. Musees Royaux d'Art & Histoire, 10 Parc du Cinquantenaire, 1040 Brussels Belgium. **Tel** 011 32 2 7339610. **LC** WMLC 93/2342.

RU
AL-MADAR. (19??)-. Periodical. Arabic. Bulifar 4, Moscow 11 9021 Russia. **LC** DK1; .M27 .

SP/0211-3589
AL-QANTARA (MADRID). (AL-QANTARA.). [Al-Qantara]. **Added/Corp** Instituto "Miguel Asin.". Vol. 1, No. 1/2 (1980)-. Periodical. English (Spanish). Twice a year. 5000ptas. Consejo Superior Investigacion Cientificas (CSIC), Vitruvio 8, 28006 Madrid Spain. **Tel** 011 34 1 5612833, FAX 011 34 1 4113077, telex 42182. **LC** DP102; .A6. **DD** 946.02/05. Index available. cum. index. **Bk Rev**. ***Continues*** *Andalus, 0304-4335.*
Ind/Abst BHA : Biblio. Hist. Art; MLA Int. Bibl. Books Artic. Mod. Lang. Lit.; Middle East J.

US/0095-1390
ALBION (BOONE). (ALBION.). [Albion]. **Added/Corp** Conference on British Studies. Vol. 1 (1969)-. Periodical. English. Four times a year (Jan., Apr., July, Oct.). $45.00 (individuals); $70.00 (institutions) US & US Posessions; $80.00 (institutions) others. Albion, Department of History, Appalachian State University, Boone NC 28608. **Tel** (704)262-6004, FAX (704)262-2592. **ED** Michael J. Moore. **LC** DA20; .A42. **DD** 941/.005. Index available (Back issues). **Bk Rev**, (Qty: 200-250 per year). **Ad Acc, Adv Mgr:** Michael Moore. **Circ:** 1,400 (ctrl). available on microfilm and microfiche from University Microfilms International (UMI). Documents available from The Genuine Article.
Desc: A journal concerned with the whole of British history. It publishes articles in all fields of British, imperial, and Celtic history, and through its research notes provides the only outlet in North America for such notes over the range of British studies. Its historiographical review essays survey the scholarship of various themes in British history. Its reviews are concerned with the range of British studies, not just in the discipline of history, and are widely respected as thorough critiques of the latest scholarship.
Ind/Abst Am. Hist. Life (1976-); Arts Humanit. Citation Index [Full Cov.]; Res. Alert [Full Cov.]; Soc. Sci. Cit. Index [Select. Cov.].

US
ALERT (MERION, PA.). (ALERT.). **Added/Corp** Union of Councils for Soviet Jews. Vol. 1, No. 1 (Jan. 1977)-. English. ir. $45.00 US; $55.00 other. Union of Councils for Soviet Jews, 1819 H Street NW/Suite 410, Washington DC 20008. **Tel** (202)775-9770. **LC** DS135.R92; A7. **DD** 947/.004924/005.
Desc: Updated news about the UCSJ and its member councils, and actions undertaken across the U.S. in support of Soviet Jewry.
Ind/Abst Hum. Rights Intern. Rep.

RU
ALL MOSCOW. (1991)-. English (translations available in Russian). Joint Venture All Moscow, Chistoprudnyi Boulevard South, Moscow Russia. **LC** DK595; .V783. **DD** 947/.3120854/05. **CODEN** VSMOEN.

IT
ALMANACCO PIEMONTESE. **VFOAT** Armanach Piemonteis. Italian. an. L2.500. A Viglongo, Conto Corrente Postale N 2-31467, Casella Postale 412, Turin 10100 Italy. **LC** DG610; .A44. **UDC** 945.021.

PO/0870-0249
ALMANSOR. **Added/Corp** Biblioteca Municipal de Montemor-o-Novo. **VFOAT** Revista de Cultura Almansor. No. 1 (1983)-. Periodical. Portuguese. **LC** DP802.M67; A57. **DD** 946.9/5.
Ind/Abst BHA : Biblio. Hist. Art.

FR
ALPES : SAVOIE, DAUPHINE. **Main/Corp** Pneu Michelin (Firm). 1st Ed. (1978)-. French. $8.95. Michelin Guides and Maps, PO Box 3305, Spartanburg SC 29304. **Tel** (803)599-0850. **LC** DC611.S363; M34A. **DD** 914.4/4804837. **UDC** 914.444.993/.994. Each issue contains an index to its own contents (no volume index)--loose.

GW/0344-1873
ALT-HILDESHEIM. **Added/Corp** Stadtarchiv und Stadtbibliothek Hildesheim. (1919)-. German. **LC** DD901.H66; A65. **DD** 943/.59.
Ind/Abst BHA : Biblio. Hist. Art.

GW/0065-6585
ALT-THURINGEN. **Added/Corp** Museum fuer Ur- und Fruhgeschichte Thuringens. Vol. 1 (1954)-. Monographic series. German. ir. Price varies per volume. Thueringer Landesamt fuer Arch, Humboldtstrasse 11, O 99423 Weimar Germany. **(Subscription address:** Konrad Theiss Verlag Gmbh & Company, Villastrabe 11, D 70190 Stuttgart Germany.**)** **ED** Rudolf Feustel. **LC** DD801.T46; A7.
Desc: This series presents results of research work on the history of Hanseatic League, Hanse towns, the League's interior organization, its political, economic and cultural history from the 12th up to the 17th century.
Ind/Abst Anthropol. Index; Anthropol. Lit.; Art Archaeol. Tech. Abstr.; BHA : Biblio. Hist. Art; Br. Archaeol. Bibliogr.; Numis. Lit.

SP/0211-4003
ALTAMIRA. (ALTAMIRA : REVISTA DEL CENTRO DE ESTUDIOS MONTANESES.). [Altamira]. (1934)-. Periodical. Spanish. ir. **LC** DP302.S31; A7.
Ind/Abst Am. Hist. Life (1964-1977).

GW/0170-9364
ALTE STADT, DIE. [Alte Stadt]. (1978)-. Periodical. German. Four times a year. DM146.00. W Kohlhammer Verlag GmbH, Postfach 800430, D 70549 Stuttgart Germany. **Tel** 011 49 711 78631, FAX 011 49 711 7863263, telex 7-255820. **LC** HT101; .Z4. **[CCC].** ***Continues*** *Zeitschrift fuer Stadtgeschichte, Stadtsoziologie und Denkmalpflege, 0340-3688.*
Desc: Covers town history, sociology and monument preservation.
Ind/Abst Avery Index Archit. Period. Suppl. Colum. Univ. (1989-); BHA : Biblio. Hist. Art.

GW/0002-6646
ALTERTUM, DAS. **Added/Corp** Deutsche Akademie der Wissenschaften zu Berlin. Sektion fuer Altertumswissenschaft. Akademie der Wissenschaften der DDR. Zentralinstitut fuer Alte Geschichte und Archaologie. Vol. 1 (1955)-. Periodical. German. qt. $68.00 (academic institutions), $106.00 (corporate institutions). Harwood Academic Publishers, PO Box 90, Reading RG1 8JL England. **Tel** 011 44 734 560080. **LC** DE1; .A35. **DD** 930/.0. **[CCC].**
Ind/Abst BHA : Biblio. Hist. Art.

AT/0727-0046
ALTRO POLO. [Altro polo]. **Added/Corp** Frederick May Foundation for Italian Studies. (1978)-. English. an. **LC** DG401; .A543.
Ind/Abst MLA Int. Bibl. Books Artic. Mod. Lang. Lit.

GW/0569-1613
ALZEYER GESCHICHTSBLATTER. **Added/Corp** Altertumsverein Alzey und Umgebung. Museum Alzey. Kuratorium. (1964)-. German. **LC** DD801.H652; A68.
Ind/Abst BHA : Biblio. Hist. Art.

US/0094-3770
AMERICAN BIBLIOGRAPHY OF SLAVIC AND EAST EUROPEAN STUDIES. **See** History(General)-Abstracting, Bibliographies and Statistics.

●US/1054-4607
AMERIKAI MAGYAR LEVELESTAR. [Am. Magy. levtar.]. **VFOAT** Hungarian Archives in America. (1992)-. Monographic series. Hungarian. Price varies per volume. Euroliga, PO Box 101, Bloomington IN 47402-0101. **DD** 947.

US/0270-6261
AMS STUDIES IN THE MIDDLE AGES. [AMS stud. Middle Ages]. **Added/Corp** AMS Press. (19??)-. Monographic series. English. bm. Price varies per volume. AMS Press Inc., 56 East 13th Street, New York NY 10003. **Tel** (212)777-4700, FAX (212)995-5413, telex 710 581 2302.
Desc: Provides accurate and fluent access to the early Middle Ages.
Ind/Abst MLA Int. Bibl. Books Artic. Mod. Lang. Lit.

US/0195-8011
AMS STUDIES IN THE RENAISSANCE. No. 3 (1979)-. Monographic series. English. ir. Price varies per volume. AMS Press Inc., 56 East 13th Street, New York NY 10003. **Tel** (212)777-4700, FAX (212)995-5413, telex 710 581 2302. **LC** UNC.
Desc: Series covering the various aspects of the Renaissance. Contains volumes on subjects such as the literary works of Christopher Marlowe and William Shakespeare, drama in the Renaissance, and the life of Prince Henry Stuart.
Ind/Abst MLA Int. Bibl. Books Artic. Mod. Lang. Lit.

US/0731-2342
AMS STUDIES IN THE SEVENTEENTH CENTURY. [AMS stud. seventeenth century]. **VFOAT** AMS Studies in the 17th Century. No. 1 (1986)-. Monographic series. English. ir. Price varies per volume. AMS Press Inc., 56 East 13th Street, New York NY 10003. **Tel** (212)777-4700, FAX (212)995-5413, telex 710 581 2302. **LC** UNC. **DD** 409.
Desc: Covers all aspects of the seventeenth century. Contains volumes on the French stage and playhouse, the philology in Britain, and John Dryden.
Ind/Abst MLA Int. Bibl. Books Artic. Mod. Lang. Lit.

PO/0870-077X
ANAIS - ACADEMIA PORTUGUESA DA HISTORIA. [An. Acad. Port. Hist.]. **Main/Corp** Academia Portuguesa da Historia. (1940)-. Portuguese. ir. Price varies per volume. Livraria Portugal, Apartado 2681, 1117 Lisbon Codex Portugal. **Tel** 011/351/1/3474982, 011/351/1/3474985. **LC** DP501; .A3.
Ind/Abst Am. Hist. Life (1963-).

RM/0068-3205
ANALELE UNIVERSITATII BUCURESTI : ISTORIE. [An. Univ. Bucur., Ist.]. **Main/Corp** Universitatea din Bucuresti. (19??)-. Periodical. Romanian (summaries and/or abstracts in French and Russian). an. DM164.00. Universitatea din Bucuresti / University of Bucharest, Soseaua Panduri No 90, Bucharest Romania. **(Subscription address:** Kubon & Sagner, ABT Zeitschriftenimport, D 80328 Munich Germany.**)** **LC** DR201; .B82a.
Ind/Abst Am. Hist. Life (1959-); BHA : Biblio. Hist. Art.

RM
ANALELE UNIVERSITATII DIN CRAIOVA: SERIA ISTORIE, GEOGRAFIE, FILOLOGIE. **Main/Corp** Universitatea din Craiova. Vol. 1 (1972)-. Romanian (summaries and/or abstracts in English, French, German, Italian and Russian). Annals of the University of Craiova, Al I Cuza Street Number 13, Craiova Romania. **LC** AS345.U53; A15.
Ind/Abst Numis. Lit.

SP
ANALES DE HISTORIA CONTEMPORANEA. **Added/Corp** Universidad de Murcia. Catedra de Historia Contemporanea. Patronato "Angel Garcia Rogel.". (1982)-. Periodical. Spanish. an. Patronato Angel Garcia Rogel, Pl/Marques de Rafal 1 Y 3, Orihuela (Alicante) Spain. **LC** DP160.9; .A63. **DD** 946/.054/05.
Ind/Abst Am. Hist. Life.

SP
ANALES DE LA UNIVERSIDAD DE ALICANTE. HISTORIA CONTEMPORANEA. **Added/Corp** Universidad de Alicante. Departamento de Historia Contemporanea. **VFOAT** Historia Contemporanea. No. 1 (1982)-. Periodical. Spanish. Universidad de Alicante, Ctra San Vicente Raspeig S N, 03690 Alicante Spain. **Tel** 011 34 6 5903480.

SP/0211-2329
ANALES DEL INSTITUTO DE ESTUDIOS GERUNDENSES. [An. Inst. Estud. Gerund.]. **Main/Corp** Instituto de Estudios Gerundenses. (1946)-. Periodical. Spanish. ir. Consejo Superior Investigacion Cientificas (CSIC), Vitruvio 8, 28006 Madrid Spain. **Tel** 011 34 1 5612833, FAX 011 34 1 4113077, telex 42182. **LC** DP402.G4; A32.
Ind/Abst Am. Hist. Life (1959-1973); Indice Hist. Esp. (1959-1973).

SP/0584-6374
ANALES DEL INSTITUTO DE ESTUDIOS MADRILENOS. [An. Inst. Estud. Madr.]. **Main/Corp** Instituto de Estudios Madrilenos (Consejo Superior de Investigaciones Cientificas). Vol. 1 (1966)-. Spanish. an. 4500ptas. Instituto de Estudios Madrilenos, Duque de Medinaceli 4, Madrid 28014 Spain. **Tel** 011 34 1 4292017 ext. 178. **LC** DP302.M1; S6a. **DD** 946/.41/005. **UDC** 908946. cum. index. **Ad Acc.** ctrl circ.
Desc: Publishes research studies.
Ind/Abst Am. Hist. Life (1966-1977); BHA : Biblio. Hist. Art; Indice Hist. Esp. (1966-1977).

SP/0538-1983
ANALES TOLEDANOS. **Added/Corp** Instituto Provincial de Investigaciones y Estudios Toledanos. (1967)-. Periodical. Spanish. ir. Instituto Provincial de Investigaciones y Estudios Toledanos, Plaza de la Merced 4, 45002 Toledo Spain. **Tel** 1 34 1 25259300. **(Subscription address:** Pedro Alcantarilla, Conchas 1, 28009 Madrid Spain.**)**
Ind/Abst BHA : Biblio. Hist. Art.

BN/0350-1418
ANALI GAZI HASREV-BEGOVE BIBLIOTHEKE. [An. Gazi Husrev-begove bibl.]. **Main/Corp** Sarajevo. Gazi Husrev-Begova Biblioteka. Vol. 1-. Serbo-Croatian (Roman) (summaries and/or abstracts in English). an. Gazi Husrev-Begova Biblioteka, Pariske Komune 4, 71000 Sarajevo, Bosnia and Hercegovina. **LC** DB240.5; .S27A. **Circ:** 1,500.
Ind/Abst Am. Hist. Life (1972-).

SP
ANALISIS E INVESTIGACIONES CULTURALES. **VFOAT** AIC. Vol. 1 (Oct./Dec. 1979)-. Spanish. Bibliolibria Biblioteca Nacion, Paseo de Recoletos 20, 28001 Madrid Spain. **Tel** 011 34 1 5778707. **LC** DP48; .A56. **DD** 306/.0946.

●NE/0929-077X
ANCIENT CIVILIZATIONS FROM SCYTHIA TO SIBERIA. (1994)-. English. Three times a year. Fl190.00 (institutions), Fl120.00 (individuals). E. J. Brill, Postbus 9000, 2300 PA Leiden Netherlands. **Tel** 011 31 71 312624, FAX 011 31 71 317532, telex 39296 BRILL NL. **ED** G. Bongard-Levin.
Desc: Includes scholarly articles in the disciplines of history, intercultural history, comparative history, archaeology, numismatics, epigraphy, papyrology and the history of material culture. Particular emphasis will be given to the Black Sea area, the Caucasus, Asia Minor, Siberia and Central Asia, and the littoral of the Indian Ocean.

AN
ANDORRA 7. **VFOAT** Andorra Set. Periodical. Catalan. wk. 2600. Edinter Carrer Lew Canals, Xalet Forne, Andorra La Vella. **LC** DC921; .A53. **DD** 946/.79/005.

UK/0345-0295
ANEKS. ***Ceased.*** [Aneks]. (1973)-?. Polish. qt. Aneks Press, 61 Dorset Road, London W5 4HX England. **Tel** 01 567-9584. **ED** Aleksander Smolar (editor's address: 56 rue de la Division Leclerc, 94 110 Arcueil France). **LC** DR1; .A82. Index available. cum. index. **Bk Rev. Ad Acc. Circ:** 5,000.
Desc: Selection of uncensored material concerning the communist society and development of modern political thought.

UK/0954-9927
ANGLO-NORMAN STUDIES ... : PROCEEDINGS OF THE BATTLE CONFERENCE. **Main/Conf** Battle Conference on Anglo-Norman Studies. **VFOAT** Proceedings of the Battle Conference. 5 (1982)-. Proceedings. English. an. Boydell and Brewer Limited, PO Box 9, Woodbridge Suffolk, 1P12 3DF England. **Tel** 011 44 394 411320, FAX 011 44 394 411477. **LC** DA195; .B33A. ***Continues*** *Proceedings of the Battle Conference on Anglo-Norman Studies.*

UK/0066-183X
ANGLO-NORMAN TEXTS. **Main/Corp** Anglo-Norman Text Society. (1939)-. Monographic series. Multiple languages (English and French). Price varies per volume. Basil Blackwell Publishers Ltd, 108 Cowley Road, Oxford 0X4 1JF England. **Tel** 011 44 865 791100, FAX 011 44 865 791347, telex 837022 OXBOOK G. **(Subscription address:** Blackwell Publishers / UK, Marston Book Services, PO Box 87, Oxford OX2 0DT England.**)**
Ind/Abst MLA Int. Bibl. Books Artic. Mod. Lang. Lit.

UK/0263-6751
ANGLO-SAXON ENGLAND. [Anglo-Saxon Engl.]. (1972)-. Academic Scholarly Publication. English. an (December). $107.00 US, Canada & Mexico; £63.00 other. Cambridge University Press, The Edinburgh Building, Shaftesbury Road, Cambridge CB2 2RU United Kingdom. **Tel** 011 44 223 312393, FAX 011 44 223 325959. **(Subscription address:** Cambridge University Press / North America, 110 Midland Avenue, Port Chester NY 10573.**)** **ED** Malcolm Godden, Simon Keynes, Michael Lapidge. **LC** DA152.2; .A75. **DD** 942.01/05. **[CCC].** available on microfilm from University Microfilms International (UMI).
Desc: Embraces all the main aspects of study of Anglo-Saxon history and culture - linguistic, literary, textual, palaeographic, religious, intellectual, historical, archaeological, and artistic - and which promotes the more unusual interests, for example, in music, medicine or education. Especially seeks to exploit the advantages of a broadly based, interdisciplinary approach. Provides a systematic bibliography of all the works published in each branch of Anglo-Saxon studies during the preceding twelve months. Regularly publishes a selection of the papers read at the biennial conference of the International Society of Anglo-Saxonists.
Ind/Abst Annu. Bibliogr. Engl. Lang. Lit.; Arts Humanit. Citation Index (19??-19??) [Full Cov.]; BHA : Biblio. Hist. Art; Br. Archaeol. Bibliogr.; MLA Int. Bibl. Books Artic. Mod. Lang. Lit.

UK/0264-5254
ANGLO-SAXON STUDIES IN ARCHAEOLOGY AND HISTORY. **See** Archaeology.

UK/0044-8265
ANGLO-SOVIET JOURNAL, THE. ***Title Change.*** Vol. 1 (Jan. 1940)-Vol. 51 (April 1992). Periodical. English. Three times a year. Society for Cultural Relations with USSR, 320 Brixton Road, London SW9 6AB England. **Tel** (071)274-2282, (071)489-0391, telex 888 941 LCCI A. **ED** Pamela Barlow, Dennis Cunninham, Peter Grant Ross, Arnold Hinchliffe, William Pomeroy, Professor Riordon, Jean Turner. **LC** DK1; .A58.

History(General)—History of Europe

DD 914.7. **Bk Rev. Ad Acc. Circ:** 1,000 (ctrl). *Absorbed Arts in the USSR.*
Desc: Covers soviet cultural affairs.

SZ
ANNALAS DALA SOCIETAD RHAETO-ROMANSCHA. NSS. **Main/Corp** Societa Reto-Romantscha. **Added/Corp** Societa Retorumantscha. **VFOAT** Annalas Della Societa Reto-Romantscha; Annalas da la Societa Retorumantscha; Annalas Della Societad Retorumantscha. (1886)-. Raeto-Romance (German). an. 24.00F (latest volume). Societa Retorumantscha, Rohanstrasse 5, 7000 Cuera Chur Switzerland. **Tel** 011 41 81 223435. **LC** PC901; .S7. Index available. cum. index. **Ad Acc. Circ:** 1,000.
Desc: History of the Grisons region of Switzerland. Also its language and literature.

IT
ANNALE (ISTITUTO REGIONALE PER LA STORIA DELLA RESISTENZA E DELLA GUERRA DI LIBERAZIONE IN EMILIA ROMAGNA). (ANNALE / INSTITUTO REGIONALE PER LA STORIA DELLA RESISTENZA E DELLA GUERRA DI LIBERAZIONE IN EMILIA ROMAGNA.). 1 (1980)-. Periodical. Italian. an. L10000. Cooperative Libraria Universitaria Editrice Bologna, Via Marsala 24, Bologna 40126 Itlay. **LC** DG975.E53; A56. **DD** 945/.4.

GW/0341-289X
ANNALEN DES HISTORISCHEN VEREINS FUER DEN NIEDERRHEIN, INSBESONDERE DAS ALTE ERZBISTUM KOLN. **Added/Corp** Historischer Verein fur den Niederrhein Insbesondere das alte Erzbistum Koln. (1929)-. German. ir. DM45.00. Rheinland Verlag & Betriebsges, PF 2140 Abtei Brauweiler, D 50250 Pulheim Germany. **Tel** 011 49 2234 8051. cum. index. *Continues* Annalen des Historischen Vereins fur den Niederrhein, Insbesondere die alte Erzdiozese Koln.
Ind/Abst BHA : Biblio. Hist. Art.

BE/0775-7506
ANNALEN VAN DE KONINKLIJKE OUDHEIDKUNDIGE KRING VAN HET LAND VAN WAAS. [Ann. K. oudheidkd. kring land Waas]. (1975)-. Periodical. Dutch. an. **UDC** 908. *Continues* Annalen van den Oudheidskundigen Kring van het Land van Waas, 0775-7492.
Ind/Abst BHA : Biblio. Hist. Art.

SZ/0263-7383
ANNALES BENJAMIN CONSTANT. See Literature.

FR/0003-3901
ANNALES DE BOURGOGNE. (ANNALES DE BOURGOGNE : REVUE HISTORIQUE.). [Ann. Bourgogne]. **Added/Corp** Centre d'Etudes Bourguignonnes (Dijon, France). Vol. 1 (1929)-. Periodical. French. qt. 130.00F France; 180.00F other. Societe des Annales Bourgogne, 36 rue Chabot Charny, Dijon 21000 France. **ED** Jean Richard. cum. index. **Bk Rev. Circ:** 550 (ctrl).
Desc: Leading articles, minutes, documents, reviews, criticism, Burgundy bibliography, and summaries of university proceedings.
Ind/Abst Am. Hist. Life (1983-); BHA : Biblio. Hist. Art; Romant. Move.

FR/0399-0826
ANNALES DE BRETAGNE ET DES PAYS DE L'OUEST. (ANNALES DE BRETAGNE ET DES PAYS DE L'OUEST, ANJOU, MAINE, TOURAINE.). [Ann. Bretagne pays Ouest]. **Added/Corp** Universit,e d'Angers. (1974)-. Periodical. French. Four times a year (Mar., June, Sept., Dec.). 165.87F France; 240.00F others. Annales de Bretagne et des Pays de l'Ouest, University de Rennes II, 6 Avenue Gaston Berger, 35043 Rennes France. **Tel** 9954-6635, FAX 9933-0795. **LC** DC611.B841; A54. **DD** 944/.1/08305. Index available. **Bk Rev. Pr Rev.** Documents available from The Genuine Article. *Continues* Annales de Bretagne.
Ind/Abst Arts Humanit. Citation Index [Full Cov.]; BHA : Biblio. Hist. Art; Br. Archaeol. Bibliogr.; Curr. Contents Arts Humanit.; MLA Int. Bibl. Books Artic. Mod. Lang. Lit.; Res. Alert [Full Cov.]; Soc. Sci. Cit. Index [Select. Cov.].

FR/0240-4672
ANNALES DE HAUTE-PROVENCE. [Ann. Ht. Provence]. (1978)-. Periodical. Multiple languages. qt. **UDC** 061.22 (449.5). *Continues* Bulletin de la Societe Scientifique et Litteraire des Alpes-de-Haute-Provence, 0240-4664.
Ind/Abst BHA : Biblio. Hist. Art.

BE
ANNALES DE LA SOCIETE ARCHEOLOGIQUE DE NAMUR. **Main/Corp** Societe Archeologique de Namur. (1849)-. French. **LC** DH801.N2; S6. **DD** 949.3/4.
Ind/Abst BHA : Biblio. Hist. Art; Numis. Lit.

FR/0365-2017
ANNALES DE L'EST. [Ann. Est]. **Added/Corp** Federation Historique Lorraine. Universite de Nancy. Faculte des Lettres. Universite de Nancy. Faculte des Lettres et Sciences Humaines. Universite de Nancy II. (1910)-. Periodical. French. Four times a year. 254.65F France; $320.00F others. Presses Universitaires Nancy, 42 avenue de la Liberation, 54001 Nancy Cedex France. **Tel** 011 33 83 935830, FAX 011 33 83 935839. **ED** F. Roth. **LC** DC603.1; .A6. **Bk Rev. Ad Acc. Circ:** 800 (ctrl). *Continues* Annales de l'Est et du Nord.
Desc: History, genealogy, local history, ideas, literature and history of eastern France.
Ind/Abst Am. Hist. Life; BHA : Biblio. Hist. Art; Romant. Move.

FR/0373-7462
ANNALES DE L'EST; MEMOIRE. No. 1 (1933)-. Monographic series. French. Price varies per volume. Presses Universitaires Nancy, 42 avenue de la Liberation, 54001 Nancy Cedex France. **Tel** 011 33 83 935830, FAX 011 33 83 935839. *Continues in part* Annales de l'Est.

FR/0003-4134
ANNALES DE NORMANDIE. [Ann. Normandie]. Vol. 1, No. 1 (1951)-. Periodical. French (English). ir. 180.00F. Les Annales de Normandie, Logis des Gouverneurs Chateau, 14000 Caen France. **Tel** 11 33 31 860624, FAX 11 33 31 852794. **LC** DC611.N841; A74. cum. index. **Bk Rev. Circ:** 1,000.
Desc: Studies of the history of the Normandie in France and its influence on Europe.
Ind/Abst Am. Hist. Life (1980-); BHA : Biblio. Hist. Art; Br. Archaeol. Bibliogr.; Numis. Lit.

FR/0153-7121
ANNALES DES PAYS NIVERNAIS. **Added/Corp** Caisse Departementale des Monuments et des Sites de la Nievre. (1971)-. Periodical. French. qt. **UDC** 397 (445.6).
Ind/Abst BHA : Biblio. Hist. Art.

FR
ANNALES D'HISTORIE ET DE SCIENCE SOCIALE. French. Six times a year. $103.00. Librairie Armand Colin, BP 22, 41354 Vineuil Cedex France. **Tel** 011 33 54 438994.

SZ/1013-3534
ANNALES FRIBOURGEOISES. **Added/Corp** Societe d'Histoire du Canton de Fribourg, Fribourg. Societe des Aamis des Beaux-Arts, Fribourg. (1913)-. Periodical. French. be. **LC** DQ421; .S65.
Ind/Abst BHA : Biblio. Hist. Art.

FR/0003-4436
ANNALES HISTORIQUES DE LA REVOLUTION FRANCAISE. [Ann. hist. Revolut. fr.]. **Added/Corp** Societe des Etudes Robespierristes. Universite de Paris I: Pantheon-Sorbonne. Institut d'Histoire de la Revolution Francaise. Vol. 1 (Jan./Feb. 1924)-. Periodical. French. qt. 310.00F. Societe des Etudes Robespierristes, 17 rue de la Sorbonne, 75231 Paris Cedex 05 France. **LC** DC139; .A62. **DD** 944.04. cum. index. Documents available from The Genuine Article. *Formed by the union of* Annales Revolutionnaires *and* Revue Historique de la Revolution Francaise.
Ind/Abst Am. Hist. Life (1954-); Arts Humanit. Citation Index [Full Cov.]; Curr. Contents Arts Humanit.; Res. Alert [Full Cov.]; Romant. Move.

MC/0257-960X
ANNALES MONEGASQUES. **Added/Corp** Archives du Palais Princier (Monaco). No 1 (1977)-. Periodical. French. 30F. **LC** DC941; .A56. **DD** 944/.945/005.
Ind/Abst BHA : Biblio. Hist. Art.

PL/0066-2224
ANNALES SILESIAE. (ANNALES SILESIAE / WROCAWSKIE TOWARZYSTWO NAUKOWE.). **Added/Corp** Wrocawskie Towarzystwo Naukowe. (1960)-. Polish (English and Polish). **LC** DD491.S4; A75.
Ind/Abst BHA : Biblio. Hist. Art.

BE
ANNALES - SOCIETE D'ARCHEOLOGIE D'HISTOIRE ET DE FOLKLORE DE NIVELLES ET DU BRABANT WALLON. **Main/Corp** Societe d'Archeologie d'Histoire et de Folklore de Nivelles et du Brabant Wallon. V. 22 (1973)-. French. an. 800F Belgium; $25.00 North America; 950F other. Societe d'Archeologie d'Histoire et de Folklore, de Nivelles et du Brabant Wallon, 27 rue de Bruxelles, B-1400 Nivelles Bruxelles Belgium. **Tel** 067/21 21 61. **LC** DH811.N73; S63A. **DD** 949.3/3. Index available. cum. index. **Bk Rev.**

SZ/1013-3488
ANNALES VALAISANNES. **Added/Corp** Societe d'Histoire du Valais Romand. Vol.1 (1916) Vol. 7 (1929); 2nd Ser. (1930)-. French.
Ind/Abst BHA : Biblio. Hist. Art; Numis. Lit.

IT
ANNALI DELL'ISTITUTO STORIA. **Main/Corp** Universita di Firenze. Istituto di Storia. 1.-. Periodical. Italian. Casa Editrice Leo S. Olschki, Viuzzo del Pozzetto, Casella Postale 66, 50126 Florence Italy. **Tel** 011 39 55 6530684, FAX 011 39 55 6530214. **LC** DG467; .F58A. **DD** 945/.005.

IT
ANNALI DELL'ISTITUTO STORICO ITALO GERMANICO. (1977)-. Monographic series. Italian. Price varies per volume. Societa Editrice il Mulino, Strada Maggiore 37, 40125 Bologna Italy. **Tel** 011 39 51 256011, FAX 011 39 51 256034.

SP/0213-6228
ANNLAS DE L'INSTITUT D'ESTUDIS GIRONINS. [Ann. Inst. Estud. Gironins]. **Added/Corp** Institut de Estudios Gerundenses. **VFOAT** Annals - Institut d'Estudis Gironins. (1979)-. Periodical. Multiple languages. ir. **UDC** 908. *Continues* Anales del Instituto de Estudios Gerundenses, 0211-2329.
Ind/Abst BHA : Biblio. Hist. Art.

FR/0765-1252
ANNUAIRE - 4 SOCIETES D'HISTOIRE DE LA VALLEE DE LA WEISS. **VFOAT** Annuaire - Quatre Societes d'Histoire de la Vallee de la Weiss. (1985)-. an.
Ind/Abst BHA : Biblio. Hist. Art.

FR/0986-9042
ANNUAIRE - ASSOCIATION D'ALSACE POUR LA CONSERVATION DES MONUMENTS NAPOLEONIENS. (ANNUAIRE.). (1987)-. Periodical. French. an. **UDC** 9418 (443.83).
Ind/Abst BHA : Biblio. Hist. Art.

FR/0399-1350
ANNUAIRE-BULLETIN DE LA SOCIETE DE L'HISTOIRE DE FRANCE. [Annu., Bull. Soc. hist. Fr.]. **Added/Corp** Societe de l'Histoire de France. (1863)-. Bulletin. French. **LC** DC2; .S67. *Formed by the union of* Bulletin de la Societe de l'Histoire de France *and* Annuaire Historique pour l'Annee ... .
Ind/Abst Am. Hist. Life (1960-1965).

FR/0986-2684
ANNUAIRE DE LA SOCIETE DES AMIS DU VIEUX STRASBOURG. [Annu. Soc. amis Vieux Strasbourg]. (1970)-. Periodical. French. an. **UDC** 379.8.
Ind/Abst BHA : Biblio. Hist. Art.

FR/0761-8654
ANNUAIRE DE LA SOCIETE D'HISTOIRE DES QUATRE CANTONS. [Annu. Soc. hist. quatre cant.]. **VFOAT** Annuaire - Societe d'Histoire des Quatre Cantons. (1983)-. Periodical. French. **UDC** 908 (443.831).
Ind/Abst BHA : Biblio. Hist. Art.

FR/1146-7371
ANNUAIRE DE LA SOCIETE D'HISTOIRE DES REGIONS DE THANN-GUEBWILLER. **Added/Corp** Societe d'Histoire des Regions de Thann-Guebwiller. (1950)-. French (German). *Continues* Geschichts- und Altertumsverein fur die Sudvogesen. Jahrbuch.
Ind/Abst BHA : Biblio. Hist. Art.

FR/0399-2330
ANNUAIRE DE LA SOCIETE D'HISTOIRE DU VAL DE VILLE. [Annu. Soc. hist. Val Ville]. (1976)-. Periodical. French. an. **UDC** 908.
Ind/Abst BHA : Biblio. Hist. Art.

FR/1146-7363
ANNUAIRE DE LA SOCIETE D'HISTOIRE DU VAL ET DE LA VILLE DE MUNSTER. **Main/Corp** Societe d'Histoire du Val et de la Ville de Munster. (1927)-. Multiple languages (French and German). an.
Ind/Abst BHA : Biblio. Hist. Art.

FR/0990-2473
ANNUAIRE DE LA SOCIETE D'HISTOIRE ET D'ARCHEOLOGIE DE DAMBACH-LA-VILLE, BARR, OBERNAI. **Main/Corp** Societe d'Histoire et d'Archeologie de Dambach-la-Ville, Barr, Obernai. (1967)-. French. an.
Ind/Abst BHA : Biblio. Hist. Art.

FR
ANNUAIRE DE LA SOCIETE D'HISTOIRE SUNDGAUVIENNE. **Added/Corp** Societe d'Histoire Sundgauvienne. **VFOAT** Jahrbuch des Sundgauvereins; Annuaire de la Societe d'Histoire Sundgovienne. (1933)-. French (German). an. cum. index.
Ind/Abst BHA : Biblio. Hist. Art.

History(General) —History of Europe

FR/0996-5750
ANNUAIRE HISTORIQUE DE LA VILLE DE MULHOUSE. **Added/Corp** Mulhouse (France). Vol. 1 (1988)-. French. an. **Continues** Bulletin Historique, Ville de Mulhouse.
Ind/Abst BHA : Biblio. Hist. Art.

FR/0766-5911
ANNUAIRE - SOCIETE D'HISTOIRE ET D'ARCHEOLOGIE DE COLMAR. **Main/Corp** Societe d'Histoire et d'Archeologie de Colmar. **VFOAT** Annuaire de Colmar. (1973)-. Periodical. French. **Continues** Societe Historique et Litteraire de Colmar. Annuaire de la Societe Historique et Litteraire de Colmar.
Ind/Abst BHA : Biblio. Hist. Art.

FR
ANNUAIRE / SOCIETE D'HISTOIRE ET D'ARCHEOLOGIE DE MOLSHEIM ET ENVIRONS. **Added/Corp** Societe d'Histoire et d'Archeologie de Molsheim et Environs. (1967)-. French.
Ind/Abst BHA : Biblio. Hist. Art.

UK/0141-1942
ANNUAL BULLETIN - SOCIETE JERSIAISE. [Annu. bull. - Soc. Jersiaise]. (1957)-. Bulletin. Multiple languages. an. **Continues** Bulletin Annuel de la Societe Jersiaise.
Ind/Abst BHA : Biblio. Hist. Art.

UK
ANNUAL LECTURE SERIES (GERMAN HISTORICAL INSTITUTE (WASHINGTON, D.C.)). (ANNUAL LECTURE SERIES / GERMAN HISTORICAL INSTITUTE.). English. an.

UK/0068-2454
ANNUAL OF THE BRITISH SCHOOL AT ATHENS, THE. [Annu. Br. Sch. Athens]. **Added/Corp** British School at Athens. British School at Athens. Managing Committee. No. 1 (1895)-. English. an. £50.00. British School at Athens, 31-34 Gordon Square, London WCIH 0PY England. **Tel** 071 387 8029. **ED** R A Tomlinson (editor's telephone number: 021 414 5497). **LC** DF11; .B6. **DD** 938/.005. Index available. cum. index. **Circ:** 900.
Ind/Abst Anthropol. Index; Archit. Period. Index (1977-); Art Archaeol. Tech. Abstr. (1894/1895-); Avery Index Archit. Period. Suppl. Colum. Univ. (1989/1990-); BHA : Biblio. Hist. Art; Br. Archaeol. Bibliogr.; Numis. Lit.

UK
ANNUAL REPORT (MEDIEVAL SETTLEMENT RESEARCH GROUP). (ANNUAL REPORT.). **Added/Corp** Medieval Settlement Research Group. (1986)-. English. an. £5.00. Medieval Settlement Research Group, National Monuments Record, Fortress House, 23 Savile Row, London W1X 2HE England. **ED** N Higham. **LC** DA90; .A615. **DD** 941. **Bk Rev. Circ:** 500. *Formed by the union of* Annual Report (Medieval Village Research Group), 0260-5384 *and* Report / Moated Sites Research Group.

UK
ANNUAL REPORT / NATIONAL TRUST FOR SCOTLAND. **Main/Corp** National Trust for Scotland. (1985)-. English. an. National Trust for Scotland, 5 Charlotte Square, Edinburgh EH2 40U Scotland. **Tel** 011 44 31 2265922. **LC** DA873; .N374b. **DD** 354.4110085/9. **Continues** Yearbook / National Trust for Scotland.

●UK
ANNUAL REPORT / ROYAL COMMISSION ON THE HISTORICAL MONUMENTS OF ENGLAND. **Main/Corp** Royal Commission on Historical Monuments (England). (1991/92)-. English. **Continues** Royal Commission on Historical Monuments (England). Annual Review.
Desc: Official journal of the historic buildings and sites of England.

IT/0391-7010
ANNUARIO DELL'ISTITUTO STORICO ITALIANO PER L'ETA MODERNA E CONTEMPORANEA. [Annu. Ist. stor. ital. eta mod. contemp.]. Began publication with V. 5 (1940?). Italian. L40000. Istituto Storico Italiana per l'Eta, Via M Caetani 32, 00186 Rome Italy. **Continues** Annuario del R. Istituto Storico Italiano per l'Eta Moderna e Contemporanea.
Ind/Abst Am. Hist. Life (1975-).

IT
ANNUARIO STORICO DELLA VALPOLICELLA. **Added/Corp** Centro di Documentazione per la Storia della Valpolicella. (1983)-. Italian. an.
Ind/Abst BHA : Biblio. Hist. Art.

IT/0390-0584
ANTICHITA PISANE. Vol. 1 (Mar. 1974)-. Periodical. Italian. qt. **LC** DG975.P6; A57. **DD** 945/.55/005.
Ind/Abst BHA : Biblio. Hist. Art.

GW
ANTIQUITAS. REIHE 4, SERIE 3, BEITRAEGE ZUR HISTORIA-AUGUSTA-FORSCHUNG. KOMMENTARE. **VFOAT** Beitraege zur Historia-Augusta-Forschung. Serie 3, Kommentare; Kommentar zur Historia Augusta. (1991)-. Monographic series. German. Dr. Rudolf Habelt GmBH, Postfach 150104, D 53040 Bonn Germany. **Tel** 011 49 228 232015.

SP/0570-4065
ANUARIO DE ESTUDIOS ATLANTICOS. [Anu. estud. Atl.]. **Added/Corp** Casa de Colon de Las Palmas. No. 1 (1955)-. Spanish. an. Consejo Superior Investigacion Cientificas (CSIC), Vitruvio 8, 28006 Madrid Spain. **Tel** 011 34 1 5612833, FAX 011 34 1 4113077, telex 42182. **LC** DP302.C39; A7. **UDC** 008964.9970/980. cum. index.
Ind/Abst Am. Hist. Life (1955-1974).

SP/0066-5061
ANUARIO DE ESTUDIOS MEDIEVALES. [Anu. estud. mediev.]. **Added/Corp** Universidad de Barcelona. Instituto de Historia Medieval de Espana. Vol. 1 (1964)-. Spanish (French and English). be. 3398ptas. Consejo Superior Investigacion Cientificas (CSIC), Vitruvio 8, 28006 Madrid Spain. **Tel** 011 34 1 5612833, FAX 011 34 1 4113077, telex 42182. **LC** WMLC L 82/272. **Bk Rev.**
Desc: Articles on all aspects of the Middle Ages (primarily in Spain) such as political and economic history, art, religion, and philosophy, and history of institutions. Contains bibliography, biographical sketches, study center up-date.
Ind/Abst Am. Hist. Life (1966-1969); BHA : Biblio. Hist. Art.

SP
ANUARIO DE ESTUDIOS MEDIEVALES. ANEJO. **Added/Corp** Barcelona. Universidad. Instituto de Historia Medieval. (1972)-. Monographic series. Spanish. ir. Price varies per volume. Consejo Superior Investigacion Cientificas (CSIC), Vitruvio 8, 28006 Madrid Spain. **Tel** 011 34 1 5612833, FAX 011 34 1 4113077, telex 42182.

SP/0210-9603
ANUARIO DE HISTORIA CONTEMPORANEA. **Added/Corp** Universidad de Granada. Departamento de Historia Contemporanea. Universidad de Granada. Boletin. 8 (1981)-. Periodical. Spanish. an. Universidad de Granada / Campus de Cartuja, 18071 Granada Spain. **Tel** 011 34 58 243930, 243931. **LC** DP160.9; .A68. **DD** 946/.005. **Continues** Anuario de Historia Moderna y Contemporanea.
Ind/Abst Am. Hist. Life (1981-); GeoRef.

PO
ANUARIO GERAL DE PORTUGAL. Began with Vol. for 1977. Portuguese. 700. Av da Liberadade 266, Lisbon Portugal. **LC** DP501; .A53. **DD** 946.9/005.

SP
ANUARIO GUIA DE SANTA CRUZ DE TENERIFE Y SU PROVINCIA. Spanish. J I M de Gardoqui, Santiago Beyro 12-1 A, Santa Cruz Spain. **LC** DP302.C36; A55.

RM/0253-1550
ANUARUL INSTITUTULUI DE ISTORIE SI ARHEOLOGIE CLUJ-NAPOCA. [Anu. Inst. ist. arheol. Cluj-Napoca]. (19??)-. Periodical. Romanian. Universitatis Babes-Bolyai, Biblioteca Centrala Universitara, Str. Clinicilor 2, Cluj Napoca 3400 Romania. **Tel** 95 117092, FAX 95 117633. **UDC** 930.26.
Ind/Abst BHA : Biblio. Hist. Art.

AU/0378-8652
ANZEIGER / OSTERREICHISCHE AKADEMIE DER WISSENSCHAFTEN, PHILOSOPHISCH-HISTORISCHE KLASSE. [Anz. - Osterr. Akad. Wiss., Philos.-Hist. Klasse]. **Added/Corp** Osterreichische Akademie der Wissenschaften. Philosophisch-Historische Klasse. (1947)-. Periodical. German. in. Oesterreichischen Akademie Wissenschaften, Dr. Ignaz Seipel Platz 2, A-1010 Vienna Austria. **Tel** 011 43 1 51581. **LC** AS142; .V317. cum. index. **Continues** Anzeiger (Akademie der Wissenschaften in Wien. Philosophisch-Historische Klasse).
Ind/Abst Am. Hist. Life (1955-); BHA : Biblio. Hist. Art; MLA Int. Bibl. Books Artic. Mod. Lang. Lit.

SP
APLEC DE TREBALLS - CENTRE D'ESTUDIS DE LA CONCA DE BARBERA. **Main/Corp** Centre d'Estudis de la Conca de Barbera. No. 1-. Periodical. Catalan. Centre d'Estudis de la Conca de Barbera, C Josa 4-6, Montblanc Spain. **LC** DP302.C754; C45A.

RM
APULUM : ACTA MUSEI APULENSIS. **Main/Corp** Muzeul Regional Alba Iulia. **Added/Corp** Muzeul Regional Alba Iulia. Muzeul de Istorie si Alba Iulia. Muzeul Unirii Alba Iulia (Romania). **VFOAT** Acta Musei Apulensis. Vol. 1 (1939/1942)-. Periodical. Romanian (French and German; summaries and/or abstracts in French and German). an. Muzeul de Istorie si Arheologie Alba Julia, Str. Mihai Vieazul Nr. 12-14, Alba Iulia Romania. **LC** DR201; .M88a. available with illustrations.
Ind/Abst Anthropol. Lit.; BHA : Biblio. Hist. Art; Numis. Lit.

FR/0758-9670
AQUITANIA. Vol. 1 (1983)-. Periodical. French (French). an. 185.00F France; 200.00F other. Federation Aquitania, 6 BIS Cours de gourgue, 33074 Bordeaux Cedex France. **Tel** 33 1 56513906, FAX 33 1 56448273. **ED** Louis Maurin (editor's address: Cote Rouge, 33360 Latresne France; editor's phone: 33 1 56207455). **LC** DC611.A652; A57. **DD** 936.4. **Circ:** 800 (ctrl).
Ind/Abst BHA : Biblio. Hist. Art.

NE
ARBEITEN ZUR LITERATUR UND GESCHICHTE DES HELLENISTISCHEN JUDENTUMS. (19??)-. Monographic series. German. ir. Price varies per volume. E. J. Brill, Postbus 9000, 2300 PA Leiden Netherlands. **Tel** 011 31 71 312624, FAX 011 31 71 317532, telex 39296 BRILL NL.

GW
ARBEITEN ZUR SCHLESISCHEN KIRCHENGESCHICHTE. Vol. 1 (1988)-. Monographic series. German. Price varies per volume. Jan Thorbecke Verlag GmbH and Company, Karlstrasse 10, Postfach 546, D 72482 Sigmaringen Germany. **Tel** 011 49 7571 728100, FAX 011 07571-728-280, telex 732534.

GW
ARBEITSMATERIALIEN ZUR GEISTESGESCHICHTE. Vol. 1 (1983)-. Monographic series. German. Price varies per volume. E J Brill, Antwerpener Str 6 12, W-5000 Koeln 1 Germany. **Tel** (221)516488, telex 22 14 304-ORBRI.

DK/0903-2738
ARBOG (HISTORISK-TOPOGRAFISK SELSKAB FOR GLADSAXE KOMMUNE). (ARBOG.). Vol. 18 (1985/86)-. Danish. be. Danmarks Statistik, Sejrgade 11, DK-2100 Copenhagen Denmark. **Tel** 011 45 3 9173917, FAX 011 45 31 18 48 01, telex 1 62 36. **LC** DL291.G56; A77. **Continues** Arsskrift (Historisk-Topografisk Selskab for Gladsaxe Kommune), 0440-9809.

XR
ARCHAEOLOGICA PRAGENSIA : ARCHEOLOGICKY SBORNIK MUZEA HLAVNIHO MESTA PRAHY. See Archaeology.

GR
ARCHEION EUVOIKON MELETON. **Added/Corp** Hetaireia Euvoikon Spoudon. **VFOAT** Archives of Euboean Studies. (1936)-. Greek, Modern (English).
Ind/Abst MLA Int. Bibl. Books Artic. Mod. Lang. Lit.

GR/0518-2867
ARCHEION PONTOU. [Arh. pontou]. **Added/Corp** Epitrope Pontiakon Meleton. (1928)-. Greek, Modern.
Ind/Abst BHA : Biblio. Hist. Art; MLA Int. Bibl. Books Artic. Mod. Lang. Lit.

IT
ARCHEOGRAFO TRIESTINO. **Added/Corp** Societa di Minerva Deputazione di Storia Patria per le Venezie. Sezione di Trieste. Vol. 1 (1829)- Vol. 4 (1837); 2nd Ser., Vol. 1 (1869)- Vol. 24 (1902); 3rd Ser., Vol. 1 (1903)- Vol. 21 (1936); 4th Ser., Vol. 1/2 (1937)-. Periodical. Italian. an. L40000. Societa di Minerva, Bibl. Civica Piazza Hortis 4, 34123 Triest Italy. **Tel** 011 39 40 301214. **LC** DB321; .A6. cum. index.
Ind/Abst BHA : Biblio. Hist. Art; Numis. Lit.

GW/0066-6297
ARCHIV FUER DIPLOMATIK : SCHRIFTGESCHICHTE, SIEGEL, UND WAPPENKUNDE. Vol. 1 (1955)-. German. ir. DM126.00. Boehlau Verlag GmbH & Cie / Koeln, Theodor Heuss STR 76, D-51149 Cologne Germany. **Tel** 011 49 2203 307021, FAX 011 49 2203 307349. (**Subscription address:** BDK Buecherdienst GmBh, Postfach 900120, D 51111 Cologne Germany.)

GW/0341-8324
ARCHIV FUER FRANKFUERTS GESCHICHTE UND KUNST. **Added/Corp** Gesellschaft fur Frankfurts Geschichte und Kunst. Verein fur Geschichte und Altertumskunde, Frankfurt am Main. Frankfurter Verein fur Geschichte und Landeskunde. (1839)-. German. ir. Verlag Waldemar Kramer, Postfach 600445, D 60334 Frankfurt, Germany. **Tel** 011 49 69 449045. **ED** W. Kloetzer. **LC** DD901.F71; A7.
Ind/Abst BHA : Biblio. Hist. Art; Numis. Lit.

History(General) —History of Europe

GW/0066-6335
ARCHIV FUER GESCHICHTE VON OBERFRANKEN. Added/Corp Historischer Verein fur Oberfranken zu Bayreuth. (1838)-. German. Continues Archiv fur Geschichte und Alterthumskunde des Ober-Main-Kreises.
 Ind/Abst BHA : Biblio. Hist. Art.

AU/0003-9322
ARCHIV FUER OSTERREICHISCHE GESCHICHTE. Vol. 1 (1848)-. German. ir. Oesterreichischen Akademie Wissenschaften, Dr. Ignaz Seipel Platz 2, A-1010 Vienna Austria. **Tel** 011 43 1 51581. **LC** DB1. **Circ:** 500.
 Desc: Covers Austrian history.
 Ind/Abst Am. Hist. Life (1953-).

GW/0003-9381
ARCHIV FUER REFORMATIONSGESCHICHTE. (ARCHIV FUER REFORMATIONSGESCHICHTE. ARCHIVE FOR REFORMATION HISTORY.). [Arch. Reformationsgesch.]. **Added/Corp** Verein fuer Reformationsgeschichte. American Society for Reformation Research. **VFOAT** Archive for Reformation History. Vol. 1 (1904)-. Academic Scholarly Publication. English (German). an (Sept., or Nov.). Gutersloher Verlagshaus, Postfach 450, D 33311 Guetersloh Germany. **Tel** 011 49 5241 74050. **ED** Gottfried Krodel. **LC** BR300; .A5. **DD** 270.6/05. **Circ:** 500. Documents available from The Genuine Article.
 Desc: Scholarly articles on the history of the reformation era.
 Ind/Abst Am. Hist. Life (1973-); Annu. Bibliogr. Engl. Lang. Lit.; Arts Humanit. Citation Index [Full Cov.]; BHA : Biblio. Hist. Art; Curr. Contents Arts Humanit.; Index Book Rev. Relig.; MLA Int. Bibl. Books Artic. Mod. Lang. Lit.; Relig. Index One Period. (1948-); Relig. Theol. Abstr.; Res. Alert [Full Cov.].

GW/0341-8375
ARCHIV FUER REFORMATIONSGESCHICHTE. BEIHEFT, LITERATURBERICHT.
Added/Corp Verein fur Reformationsgeschichte. American Society for Reformation Research. **VFOAT** Archive for Reformation History Supplement, Literature Review. Vol. 1 (1972)-. English (French, German and Italian). an. $52.76 US. Gutersloher Verlagshaus, Postfach 450, D 33311 Guetersloh Germany. **Tel** 011 49 5241 74050. **ED** C Augustyn. **LC** Z7830; .A7; BR305.2. **DD** 016.2706. **Bk Rev. Circ:** 1,000.
 Desc: For research on the history of the Protestant reformation and its consequences.
 Ind/Abst BHA : Biblio. Hist. Art.

GW/0066-6505
ARCHIV FUER SOZIALGESCHICHTE. [Arch. Sozialgesch.]. Vol. 1 (1961)-. German. an. DM188.00 (plus DM5.00 postage) Germany; add DM7.00 (postage) other. Verlag Neue Gesellschaft GmbH, Godesberger Allee 143, W-5300 Bonn 2 Germany. **Tel** 0288/37 80 21. **ED** Dieter Dowe. **LC** HN1; .A7. **Bk Rev. Circ:** 1,300. Documents available from The Genuine Article.
 Desc: Social history, labour history, emancipation movements, modern history, history of ideas, history of the working class, methodology, book reviews; Germany and Western Europe.
 Ind/Abst Am. Hist. Life (1975-); Arts Humanit. Citation Index (19??-19??) [Full Cov.]; Res. Alert [Full Cov.]; Soc. Sci. Cit. Index [Select. Cov.].

GW/0003-9462
ARCHIV FUER VATERLANDISCHE GESCHICHTE UND TOPOGRAPHIE. HRSG. VON DEM GESCHICHTVEREINE FUER KARNTEN. UNTER VERANTWORTLICHER REDACTION DES VEREINS-AUSSCHUSSES.
Added/Corp Geschichtverein fuer Karnten, Klagenfurt. Vol. 1 (1849)-. German. ir. DM32.55 Germany; DM35.00 other. Dr. Rudolf Habelt GmbH, Postfach 150104, D 53040 Bonn Germany. **Tel** 011 49 228 232015. **LC** DB281; .A67.

FR
ARCHIVES HISTORIQUES DU POITOU.
Added/Corp Societe des Archives Historiques du Poitou. Vol. 1 (1872)-. French. ir. Societe Archives Historiques, 14 rue Edouard Grimaux, 86000 Poitiers France. **LC** DC611.P732; A6.

FR
ARCHIVES JUIVES. Periodical. French. qt. 75.00F France; 80.00F other. Commission Francaise des Archives Juives, BP 200, F-75023 Paris Cedex 01 France. **Tel** (1)42 33 96 98. **ED** Bernhard Blumenkranz. **LC** DS135.F8; A25. **DD** 914.4/06/924. Index available. cum. index. **Circ:** 600 (ctrl).
 Desc: Covers all the aspects of the history of Jews in France, from the first centuries to present, in the fields of political history, religion, history of the thought and of the culture, demography, etc.
 Ind/Abst Numis. Lit.

FR
ARCHIVES PARLEMENTAIRES DE 1787 A 1860. See Genealogy and Heraldry-Archives.

IT
ARCHIVIO PIOMBINESE DI STUDI STORICI. 1 (Jan./June 1971)-. Periodical. Italian. sa. L3.000. Giardini Editori Stampatori, Via Santa Bibbiana 28, 56127 Pisa Italy. **Tel** 011 39 50 934242. **LC** DG975.P58; A73.

IT
ARCHIVIO STORICO BERGAMASCO.
Suspended. **Added/Corp** Archivio Bergamasco. Vol. 1, No. 1 (1981)-(19??). Periodical. Italian. sa. Pier Luigi Lubrina Editore, V Le Vittorio Emanuele 19, 24100 Bergamo Italy. **Tel** 011 39 35 223050. **LC** DG975.B48; A7. **DD** 945/.24/005.
 Ind/Abst BHA : Biblio. Hist. Art.

IT/0392-2065
ARCHIVIO STORICO DI BELLUNO, FELTRE E CADORE. Vol. 1 No. 1 (Jan./Feb. 1929)-. Periodical. Italian. qt. cum. index.
 Ind/Abst BHA : Biblio. Hist. Art; MLA Int. Bibl. Books Artic. Mod. Lang. Lit.

IT/0392-0232
ARCHIVIO STORICO LOMBARDO. [Arch. stor. lomb.]. **Added/Corp** R. Deputazione di Storia Patria per la Lombardia. Societa Storica Lombarda. Vol. 1 (1874)-. Italian. an. L70000. Cisalpino IST Edit Universitar, via Ferrarese 119 2, 40128 Bologna Italy. **Tel** 011 39 51 370337. **(Subscription address:** Licosa Spa, PO Box 552, 50125 Florence Italy.) **LC** DG651; .A6.
 Ind/Abst BHA : Biblio. Hist. Art; MLA Int. Bibl. Books Artic. Mod. Lang. Lit.

IT/0392-0240
ARCHIVIO STORICO MESSINESE.
Added/Corp Societa Messinese di Storia Patria. Vol. 1 (1900)-. Italian. an.
 Ind/Abst BHA : Biblio. Hist. Art; Numis. Lit.

IT/0004-0355
ARCHIVIO STORICO PER LA CALABRIA E LA LUCANIA. [Arch. stor. Calabria Lucania]. Vol. 1 (1931)-. Periodical. Italian. cum. index.
 Ind/Abst Avery Index Archit. Period. Suppl. Colum. Univ. (1984-); BHA : Biblio. Hist. Art.

IT/0004-0363
ARCHIVIO STORICO PER LA SICILIA ORIENTALE. Added/Corp Societa di Storia Patria per la Sicilia Orientale, Catania. Societa Siciliana per la Storia Patria, Palermo. Sezione de Catania. Vol. 1 (1904)-. Italian. **LC** DG861; .A58. cum. index.
 Ind/Abst BHA : Biblio. Hist. Art; Numis. Lit.

IT/0392-0283
ARCHIVIO STORICO PER LE PROVINCE PARMENSI. [Arch. stor. prov. Parm.]. **Added/Corp** Deputazione di Storia Patria per le Province Parmensi. Deputazione di Storia Patria per l'Emilia e la Romagna. Sezione Parmensi. Vol. 1 (1892)- Vol. 8 (1900); 2nd Ser. Vol. 1 (1901)- Vol. 35 (1935); 3rd Ser. Vol. 1 (1936)- Vol. 8 (1943); 4th Ser. Vol. 1 (1945)-. Italian. an. **LC** DG975.P25; A2. cum. index.
 Ind/Abst Am. Hist. Life (1979-); BHA : Biblio. Hist. Art.

IT/0392-0259
ARCHIVIO STORICO PRATESE.
Added/Corp Societa Pratese di Storia Patria. Vol. 1 (Nov. 1916)-. Periodical. Italian. qt.
 Ind/Abst BHA : Biblio. Hist. Art.

IT/0392-0054
ARCHIVIO STORICO PUGLIESE.
Added/Corp Societa di Storia Patria per la Puglia. Vol.1 (1948)-. Periodical. Italian. sa.
 Ind/Abst BHA : Biblio. Hist. Art.

IT
ARCHIVIO STORICO SICILIANO.
Added/Corp Societa Siciliana per la Storia Patria (Palermo, Italy). (1946)-. Periodical. Italian. an. L50000. Societa Siciliana Storia Patria, Piazza San Domenico 1, 90133 Palermo Italy. **Tel** 011 39 91 582774. cum. index. *Continues Archivio Storico per la Sicilia.*
 Ind/Abst BHA : Biblio. Hist. Art.

IT/0044-8737
ARCHIVIO STORICO SIRACUSANO.
Added/Corp Societa Siracusana di Storia Patria. Vol. 1 (1955)-. Italian. an. L24000. Ediprint SRL, Via della Maestranza 58, 96100 Siracusa Italy. **Tel** 011 39 931 461904. **LC** WMLC L 83/2160.
 Ind/Abst BHA : Biblio. Hist. Art.

IT/0392-0291
ARCHIVIO VENETO. Added/Corp Deputazione de Storia Patria per le Venezie. Vol. 1 (1927)-. Periodical. Italian. sa. L30.0000. Deputazione di Storia Patria per le Venezie, Santa Croce 1583, 30125 Venice Italy. **Tel** 041/5241009. **(Subscription address:** Libreria Al Frari, San Polo 2599 AB, 30125 Venice, Italy.) *Continues Archivio Veneto-Tridentino.*
 Ind/Abst BHA : Biblio. Hist. Art.

IT
ARCHIVIO VENETO, A CURA DELLA R. DEPUTAZIONE DI STORIA PATRIA PER LE VENEZIE. V. 1-39, 1871-90. Periodical. Italian. Six times a year. L20000 Italy; L24000 other. Deputazione di Storia Patria per le Venezie, Santa Croce 1583, 30125 Venice Italy. **Tel** 041/5241009. **LC** DG670. **DD** 945.3. Index available. cum. index. **Bk Rev.**
 Ind/Abst Numis. Lit.

SP/0210-4067
ARCHIVO HISPALENSE. [Arch. hisp.]. Vol. 1, No. 1 (1943)-. Periodical. Spanish. Three times a year. 3000ptas. Diputacion Provincial Sevilla, Plaza del Triunfo 1, 41071 Seville Spain. **LC** DP302.S56; A7. **DD** 946/.86/005. Index available in last issue of volume--attached. Documents available from The Genuine Article. *Continues Archivo Hispalense.*
 Ind/Abst Am. Hist. Life (1955-1973); Annu. Bibliogr. Engl. Lang. Lit.; Arts Humanit. Citation Index [Full Cov.]; BHA : Biblio. Hist. Art; Curr. Contents Arts Humanit.; Indice Hist. Esp.; MLA Int. Bibl. Books Artic. Mod. Lang. Lit.; Res. Alert [Full Cov.]; Romant. Move.

SP/0004-0452
ARCHIVO IBERO-AMERICANO. See History(General)-History of North, South, and Central America.

IT/0392-0305
ARCHIVUM BOBIENSE : RIVISTA DEGLI ARCHIVI STORICI BOBIENSI. Added/Corp Archivi Storici Bobiensi. Vol. 1, No. 1 (1979)-. Italian (French and Latin). an.
 Ind/Abst BHA : Biblio. Hist. Art.

GW/0724-8822
ARCHIVUM EURASIAE MEDII AEIVI.
VFOAT Archivum Eurasiae Medii Aeivi. Vol. 1 (1975)-. English (French). an. Otto Harrassowitz Verlag, Taunusstrasse 14, Postfach 2929, D-65019 Wiesbaden Germany. **Tel** 011 49 611 5300, FAX 530570, telex 4186 135 OH D. **LC** DS327; .A73. **DD** 958/.005.
 Ind/Abst Numis. Lit.

SP/0214-0055
ARDI. [Ardi]. (1988)-. Periodical. Spanish. bm. 9000ptas Spain; 15000ptas Europe; 24000ptas other. Editorial Formentera SA, Bailen 84, 08009 Barcelona Spain. **Tel** 011 34 3 484-6600, FAX 011 34 3 424-0413. **UDC** 7.05.

RU/0204-0476
ARGUMENTY I FAKTY : BIULLETEN ORDENA LENINA VSESOIUZNOGO OBSHCHESTVA "ZNANIE," LEKTORAM, PROPAGANDISTAM, POLITINFORMATORAM, AGITATORAM. Added/Corp Vsesoiuznoe Obshchestvo "Znanie.". (1982)-. Periodical. Russian. wk. $103.95. **(Subscription address:** East View Publications Inc., 3020 Harbor Lane North, Suite 110, Minneapolis MN 55447.) **LC** DK266.A2; A75. **CODEN** ARFAEE.
 Ind/Abst F&S Index Plus Text, Int. [Select. Cov.]; PROMT.

RM
ARHIVELE OLTENIEI / ACADEMIA DE STIINTE SOCIALE SI POLITICE A REPUBLICII SOCIALISTE ROMANIA, CENTRUL DE STIINTE SOCIALE, CRAIOVA. Added/Corp Centrul de Stiinte Sociale Craiova. (Jan. 1922)-. Romanian (summaries and/or abstracts in English and French). Editura Academia Republicii Socialiste Romania, Calea Victoriei Nr 125, R-79717 Bucuresti Romania. **Tel** telex 10376 PRSFI R. **LC** DR281.O45; A73. cum. index.
 Ind/Abst Numis. Lit.

BE
ARMARIUM CODICUM INSIGNIUM. Vol 1 (1980)-. Monographic series. French (English). ir. Price varies per volume. Brepols Publishers, Steenweg OP Tielen 68, B-2300 Turnhout Belgium. **Tel** 011 32 14 402500. **ED** Board.
 Desc: Graeco-Roman manuscripts of Christian inspiration.

FR/0590-966X
ARQUIVOS DO CENTRO CULTURAL PORTUGUES. [Arq. Cent. cult. port.]. **Main/Corp** Centre Culturel Portugais. (1969)-. Monographic series. English (French, Italian, Portuguese and Spanish). an. Price varies per volume. Jean Touzot, 38 rue Saint-Sulpice, 75278 Paris Cedex 06 France. **Tel** 011 33 1 43260388. **LC** DP501; .C45a. **DD** 946.9.
 Ind/Abst BHA : Biblio. Hist. Art; MLA Int. Bibl. Books Artic. Mod. Lang. Lit.

NO
ARSSKRIFT / BIRKENES HISTORIELAG.
Added/Corp Birkenes Historielag. 1 (1982)-. Periodical. Norwegian. an. Birkenes Historielag, 4760 Birkeland Norway. **LC** DL596.B47; A77.

History(General)—History of Europe

DK
ARSSKRIFT - LOKALHISTORISK FORENING FOR SONDERHALD KOMMUNE. **Main/Corp** Lokalhistorisk Forening for Sonderhald Kommune. (1977)-. Periodical. Danish. an. kr50.00. Den Gamle Inspektrbolig, Norregade 5B, 8963 Auning Denmark. **LC** DL291.S637; L64a. ctrl circ.
Desc: News and information on the history of Denmark.

UK
ARTHURIAN STUDIES. See Literature.

IT
ASPRENAS. **Added/Corp** Accademia Ecclesiastica Napolentana. Vol. 1 (1954)-. Periodical. Italian. qt. L38000 (Italy); L45000 (other). Edizioni Dehoniane, Via Casale S Pio V20, 00165 Rome Italy. **Tel** 39 6 6624996, or 6638869.

GW
ATHENAUMS MONOGRAFIEN. ALFERTUMSWISSENSCHAFT. **VFOAT** Athenaum Monografien. Altertumswissenschaft; Beitrage zur Klassischen Philologie. (1988)-. Monographic series. German. Price varies per volume. Verlag Anton Hain Athenaeum, Wormer Strasse 99, D 55294 Bodenheim Germany. **Tel** 011 49 6135 3057. *Continues* Beitrage zur Klassischen Philologie.

CI
ATTI. **Main/Corp** Centro di Ricerche Storiche (Rovinj, Croatia). Vol. 1 (1970)-. Periodical. Italian. an. L40000. Centro Ricerche Storiche, Piazza Matteotti 13, Rovigno Croatia. **Tel** 011 38 52 811133. **LC** DB329; .C45a.
Ind/Abst BHA : Biblio. Hist. Art.

IT
ATTI DELLA SOCIETA LIGURE DI STORIA PATRIA. **Main/Corp** Societa Ligure di Storia Patria. Vol. 1 (1858)-. Periodical. Italian. sa. L150000. Societa Ligure Storia Patria, Via Albaro 11, 16145 Genoa Italy. **Tel** 39 10 308683. **LC** DG631; .S6. cum. index.
Ind/Abst BHA : Biblio. Hist. Art; Numis. Lit.

IT/0393-5566
ATTI E MEMORIE DELLA SOCIETA DALMATA DI STORIA PATRIA. [Atti mem. Soc. dalm. stor. patria]. (1926)-. Periodical. Italian. an. **UDC** 945.
Ind/Abst BHA : Biblio. Hist. Art.

IT/0418-7296
ATTI E MEMORIE - DEPUTAZIONE DI STORIA PATRIA PER LE ANTICHE PROVINCIE MODENESI. [Atti mem. - Deput. stor. patria antiche prov. modenesi]. **Main/Corp** Deputazione di Storia Patria per le Antiche Provincie Modenesi. (19??)-. Italian. an. Deputazione di Storia Patria, Sez R Emilia Pza S Giovanni 4, 42100 Reggio Emilia Italy. **Tel** 011 39 522 435384. **LC** DG975.M62; D46a. **DD** 945/.42/005.
Ind/Abst Am. Hist. Life; BHA : Biblio. Hist. Art; MLA Int. Bibl. Books Artic. Mod. Lang. Lit.; Numis. Lit.

IT/0393-7240
ATTI E MEMORIE - DEPUTAZIONE DI STORIA PATRIA PER LE PROVINCIE DI ROMAGNA. (ATTI E MEMORIE.). [Atti mem. - Deput. stor. patria prov. Romagna]. (1945)-. Periodical. Italian. an. Deputazione Storia Patria / Bologna, Largo Trombetti 1, 40126 Bologna Italy. **Tel** 011 39 51 236230. **(Subscription address:** Forni Arnaldo Editore, Via A Gramsci 164, 40010 Sala Bolognese Italy, Tel. 39 51 6814198) **UDC** 945. *Continues* Atti e Memorie - Deputazione di Storia Patria per l'Emilia e la Romagna, 0393-7232.
Ind/Abst BHA : Biblio. Hist. Art.

IT/0392-033X
ATTI E MEMORIE / SOCIETA SAVONESE DI STORIA PATRIA. **Added/Corp** Societa Savonese di Storia Patria. **VFOAT** Atti e Memorie della Societa Savonese di Storia Patria. Vol. 1 (1967)-. Italian. an. **LC** DG975.S36; A13. **DD** 945/.184/05. *Continues* Atti (Societa Savonese di Storia Patria).
Ind/Abst BHA : Biblio. Hist. Art.

GW/0178-7128
AUFKLARUNG. Vol. 1, No. 1 (1986)-. German. sa (Spring and fall). DM96.00. Felix Meiner Verlag, Postfach 760742, D 22057 Hamburg Germany. **Tel** 011 49 40 294870, FAX 011 49 40 2993614. **LC** B2621; .A78. **DD** 943/.05/05.
Ind/Abst Am. Hist. Life (1990-).

GW
AUFSTIEG UND NIEDERGANG DER ROEMISCHEN WELT. (19??)-. German. ir. Price varies per volume. Walter de Gruyter Inc. / Hawthorne, 200 Saw Mill River Road, Hawthorne NY 10532. **Tel** (914)747-0110, GERMANY: 011/49/30/260050, FAX (914)747-1326, telex 646677.

GW/0341-8499
AUSGRABUNGEN IN BERLIN. (1970)-. German. an. **LC** DD864; .A86. *Supersedes in part* Berliner Jahrbuch fur Vor- und Fruhgeschichte.
Ind/Abst Anthropol. Lit.; BHA : Biblio. Hist. Art.

GW/0175-6133
AUSGRABUNGEN UND FUNDE IN WESTFALEN-LIPPE / IM AUFTRAG DES LANDSCHAFTSVERBANDES WESTFALEN-LIPPE HERAUSGEGEBEN VON WESTFALISCHES MUSEUM FUER ARCHAOLOGIE, AMT FUER BODENDENKMALPFLEGE. **Added/Corp** Landschaftsverband Westfalen-Lippe. Westfalisches Museum fur Archaeologie--Amt fur Bodendenkmalpflege. Vol. 1 (1983)-. Academic Scholarly Publication. German. an. DM73.00. Westfalisches Museum fur Archaologie Amt fur Bodendenkmalpflege, Rothenburg 30, D 48143 Munster I W Germany. **Tel** 0251/590702, FAX 0251/5907211, telex 892835. **ED** Bendix Trier. **LC** DD801.W5445; A87. **DD** 936.3. Index available. **Ad Acc.** Acid Free. Circ: 500 (ctrl).
Desc: Covers archaeology, numismatics, and paleontology. Contains documentation and investigation of excavations of other archaeological sites. Survey of Rhine-Weser region and neighboring areas.
Ind/Abst BHA : Biblio. Hist. Art; Curr. Contents Arts Humanit.

AU
AUSLANDSOSTERREICHER, DER. **Added/Corp** Auslandsosterreicherwerk. (1974)-. Periodical. German. sa. 120.00. **LC** DB1; .S75. **DD** 909/.04/36. *Continues* Stimme Ostereichs.

FR/0396-4590
AUSTRIACA. [Austriaca]. **Added/Corp** Universite de Rouen. Centre d Etudes et de Recherches Autrichiennes. Vol. 1 No. 1 (Dec. 1975)-. Periodical. French (German). Twice a year. 130.00F France; 150.00F others. Centre d'Etudes et de Recherches Autrichiennes, Fac Lettre de Rouen BP 138, 76134 Mt St Aignan CDX France. **Tel** 011 33 35 146343, 146344, FAX 011 33 35 146348, telex 770127. **ED** Gilbert Ravy and Gerald Stieg. **LC** IN PROCESS. cum. index. **Ad Acc.** ctrl circ.
Ind/Abst Am. Hist. Life (1983-); Int. Polit. Sci. Abstr.

US/0067-2378
AUSTRIAN HISTORY YEARBOOK. [Austrian hist. yearb.]. **Added/Corp** Rice University. American Historical Association. Conference Group for Central European History. University of Minnesota. Center for Austrian Studies. Vol. 1 (1965)-. English. ir. $19.50. Austrian History Yearbook, University of Minnesota, 715 Social Science Building, Minneapolis MN 55455. **Tel** (612)624-9811. **ED** William E Wright. **LC** DB1; .A772. **DD** 943. **Bk Rev**. Circ: 1,200. *Continues* Austrian History News Letter.
Desc: Features book reviews, lists of recent books, articles, dissertations and research in progress from North America and Europe on the Hapsburg monarchy and on Austria and Hungary since 1918.
Ind/Abst Am. Hist. Life (1965-).

FR/0759-2345
AUTRE EUROPE, L'. [Autre Eur.]. (1984)-. Periodical. French. qt. 235.06F France; 280.00F other. Editions L'Age d'Homme / France, 5 rue Ferou, 75006 Paris France. **Tel** 011 33 1 46341851, FAX 011 33 1 40517102. **LC** D1; .A96. **DD** 940/.05.

SP/0210-0150
AVENC, L'. [Avenc]. (1977)-. Periodical. Catalan. Twelve times a year. 6600.00ptas. L Avance S A, Consell de Cent 278 1E 2A, 08007 Barcelona Spain. **Tel** 011 34 3 4883482. **LC** DP302.C57; A93. **UDC** 946.71.

UK/0143-1315
AVON CONSERVATION NEWS. (1977)-. English. qt.
Ind/Abst Archit. Period. Index (July 1977-Apr. 1982).

SP/0213-6635
AWRAQ : ESTUDIOS SOBRE EL MUNDO ARABE E ISLAMICO CONTEMPORANEO. **Added/Corp** Instituto Hispano-Arabe de Cultura. Instituto de Cooperacion con el Mundo Arabe (Spain). Vol. 9 (1988)-. Spanish (French, English and Arabic). ir. 2000ptas. Agencia Espanola de Cooperacion Internacional, Ins. Coop.Iberoamericana, Desarrollo Y M. Arabe, Avda. Reyes Catolicos 4, 28040 Madrid Spain. **Tel** 5838180, 2830250. **LC** DS36; .A94. *Continues* Awraq Jadidah.

GW/0404-6307
BADEN-WURTTEMBERG. Vol. 1, (Aug. 1951)-. Periodical. German. Four times a year. DM39.60. G Braun Verlag, Postfach 1709, D 76000 Karlsruhe Germany. **Tel** 011 49 721 165392. **ED** Monika Bachmayer. **Bk Rev**. **Ad Acc**. Circ: 6,000. *Absorbed* Welt am Oberrhein.
Desc: Journal about life in Southwest Germany.

SP
BAETICA. 1- 1978-. Periodical. Spanish. an. 800ptas. Facultad de Filosofia Letras, Universidad de Malaga, c/o S Agustin 4, Malaga Spain. **LC** DP302.A41; B33. **DD** 946/.8/005.

SP
BAJO ARAGON, PREHISTORIA. See Anthropology.

XN/0350-0179
BALCANOSLAVICA. **Added/Corp** Centar za Istrazuvanje na Staroslovenskata Kultura. Savez Arheoloskih Drustava Jugoslavije. Narodni Muzej Krajine--Negotin. (1972)-. Multiple languages (English, French, German and Macedonian). an. **LC** DR20; .B34.
Ind/Abst BHA : Biblio. Hist. Art.

GR/0005-4313
BALKAN STUDIES. (BALKAN STUDIES : BIANNUAL PUBLICATION OF THE INSTITUTE FOR BALKAN STUDIES.). [Balk. stud.]. **Added/Corp** Hidryma Meleton Cheresonesou tou Haimou (Thessalonike, Greece). Vol. 1 (1960)-. Periodical. English (French and German). Twice a year (Jan. & July). Dr20.00. Institute for Balkan Studies, PO Box 10611, GR 54110 Thessaloniki Greece. **LC** DR1; .B32. Index available. cum. index. **Bk Rev**. ctrl circ.
Ind/Abst Am. Hist. Life (1961-); Annu. Bibliogr. Engl. Lang. Lit.; BHA : Biblio. Hist. Art; MLA Int. Bibl. Books Artic. Mod. Lang. Lit.; Numis. Lit.

BU/0205-2512
BALKANISTIKA / BULGARSKA AKADEMIIA NA NAUKITE, INSTITUT PO BALKANISTIKA. **Added/Corp** Institut za Balkanistika (Bulgarska Akademiia na Naukite). (1986)-. Bulgarian. an. 3.58lv (single issue). Izd-vo na BAN, Sofiia Bulgaria. **LC** DR23; .B28.
Ind/Abst Am. Hist. Life (1986-).

GW/0067-3099
BALTISCHE STUDIEN. **Added/Corp** Gesellschaft fur Pommersche Geschichte, Altertumskunde und Kunst. Historische Kommission fur Pommern. Gesellschaft fur Pommersche Geschichte und Alterthumskunde, Stettin. Vol.1(1832)- Vol.46 (1896); New. Ser., Vol. 1 (1897)-. German. an. **LC** DD491.P7; G4. cum. index.
Ind/Abst BHA : Biblio. Hist. Art.

RM
BANATICA / COMITETUL DE CULTURA SI EDUCATIE SOCIALISTA AL JUDETULUI CARAS-SEVERIN, MUZEUL JUDETEAN RESITA. **Added/Corp** Comitetul de Cultura si Educatie Socialista al Judetului Caras-Severin. Muzeul Judetean Resita. Muzeul de Istorie al Judetului Caras-Severin. (1971)-. Periodical. Romanian (summaries and/or abstracts in French and German). be. Muzeul de Istorie al Judetului Caras-Severin, Resita, COD 1700, B-Dul Republicii Nr. 10 Romania. **LC** DR281.B25; B37.
Ind/Abst Numis. Lit.

JA
BARUKAN SHO AJIA KENKYU. **Added/Corp** Tokai Daigaku. Bummei Kenkyujo. **VFOAT** Balkan and Asia Minor Studies. (1975)-. Periodical. Japanese (English). ¥1000. Tokai University Press, Tokai Building 9F, 3-27-4 Shinjuku, Shinjukuku Tokyo 160 Japan. **Tel** 03 3561541, FAX 03 3411833. **LC** DR23; .B35.

SP
BASIT. AL-BASIT. **VFOAT** Basit. Vol. 1 (1975)-. Periodical. Spanish (Spanish). ir. **LC** DP302.A05; .B38. **DD** 946/.771/005.

SZ/0067-4540
BASLER ZEITSCHRIFT FUER GESCHICHTE UND ALTERTUMSKUNDE. (BASLER ZEITSCHRIFT FUER GESCHICHTE UND ALTERTUMSKUNDE / HERAUSGEGEBEN VON DER HISTORISCHEN UND ANTIQUARISCHEN GESELLECHAFT ZU BASEL.). [Basler Z. Gesch. Altert.kd.]. **Added/Corp** Historische und Antiquarische Gesellschaft zu Basel. Stiftung Pro Augusta Raurica. (1901)-. Periodical. German. an. **LC** DQ361; .H44. *Formed by the union of* Beitrage zur Vaterlandischen Geschichte (Basel, Switzerland) *and* Mitteilungen der Historischen und Antiquarischen Gesellschaft zu Basel. *Continued in part by* Jahresberichte aus Augst und Kaiseraugst.
Ind/Abst BHA : Biblio. Hist. Art.

UK
BATH HISTORY. (1985)-. English. an. Alan Sutton Publishing Limited, 30 Brunswick Road, Gloucester GL1 1JJ England.

GW/0341-3918
BAYERISCHE VORGESCHICHTSBLATTER. [Bayer. Vorgeschichtsbl.]. (1932)-. Periodical. German. an. DM80.00. CH Beck Verlagsbuchhandlung, D 80791 Munich Germany. **Tel** 011 49 89 381891. **UDC** 571.

History (General) — History of Europe

Continues *Der Bayerische Vorgeschichtsfreund*, 0932-7150.
Ind/Abst BHA : Biblio. Hist. Art.

UK/0005-7592
BEDFORDSHIRE MAGAZINE, THE. Vol. 1, No. 1 (Summer 1947)-. Periodical. English. Eight times a year. £18.00 (plus postage). White Crescent Press Ltd, Crescent Road, Luton LU2 0AG England. **Tel** 011 44 582 23122, FAX 011 44 582 23126. **ED** Betty Chambers. Index available. cum. index. **Bk Rev. Ad Acc. Circ:** 2,000.
Desc: Records Bedfordshire life and history.
Ind/Abst Archit. Period. Index; BHA : Biblio. Hist. Art.

PO
BEIRA ALTA. **Added/Corp** Assembleia Distrital de Viseu. Junta de Provincia da Beira Alta. Arquivo Provincial (Beira Alta, Portugal) Junta Distrital de Viseu. Arquivo Distrital (Viseu, Portugal). Vol. 1 (1942)-. Periodical. Portuguese. qt. **LC** DP702.B22; B4.
Ind/Abst BHA : Biblio. Hist. Art.

GW
BEITRAEGE ZUR ALTBAYERISCHEN KIRCHENGESCHICHTE. **Added/Corp** Verein fur Diozesangeschichte von Munchen und Freising. **VFOAT** Deutingers Beitraege. Vol. 14 (1929)-. Periodical. German. **Continues** *Beytrage zur Geschichte, Topographie und Statistik der Erzbisthums Munchen und Freysing*.

GW/0005-8068
BEITRAEGE ZUR GESCHICHTE DER ARBEITERBEWEGUNG (BERLIN, DDR). (BEITRAEGE ZUR GESCHICHTE DER ARBEITERBEWEGUNG : BZG.). [Beitr. Gesch. Arb.beweg.]. **Added/Corp** Institut fur Marxismus-Leninismus beim ZK der SED. **VFOAT** BZG. (1969)-. Periodical. German. qt. DM42.00. 3-K Verlag, Klosterasse 5, W 8073 Koesching Germany. **Tel** 011 49 8456 6477, FAX 011 49 8456 6307. **DD** 331. **UDC** 331.88. **Bk Rev. Circ:** 7,000 (ctrl). Documents available from The Genuine Article. **Continues** *Beitrage zur Geschichte der Deutschen Arbeiterbewegung*, 0323-7672.
Desc: Contains scientific contributions and documents. From a scientific point of view takes issue with falsifications of the history of the German and the international working-class movements.
Ind/Abst Am. Hist. Life (1959-);(1969-); ARTbibliogr. Mod.; Arts Humanit. Citation Index [Full Cov.]; Curr. Contents Arts Humanit.; Recent. Publ. Artic.; Res. Alert [Full Cov.]; Soc. Sci. Cit. Index [Select. Cov.]; Writ. Am. Hist.

GW/0405-2021
BEITRAEGE ZUR GESCHICHTE DORTMUNDS UND DER GRAFSCHAFT MARK. **Added/Corp** Historischer Verein fur Dortmund und die Grafschaft Mark. (1875)-. German. **LC** DD901.D6; .B4.
Ind/Abst BHA : Biblio. Hist. Art.

GW
BEITRAEGE ZUR GESCHICHTE KISSLEGGS. **Added/Corp** Heimat und Trachtenverein D'Schellenberger. Arbeitsgruppe Heimatforschung. (1988)-. Monographic series. German. Price varies per volume.

GW
BEITRAEGE ZUR UNIVERSITAETSGESCHICHTE. **Added/Corp** Ernst-Moritz-Arndt-Universitaat Greifswald. No. 1 (1977)-. Monographic series. German. ir. Price varies per volume. Manzsche Verlagsbuchhandlung, Kohlmarkt 16 Postfach 163, A 1014 Vienna Austria. **Tel** 011 43 222 5316171.

GW
BEITRAGE UND MITTEILUNGEN (VEREIN FUER KATHOLISCHE KIRCHENGESCHICHTE IN HAMBURG UND SCHLESWIG-HOLSTEIN). (BEITRAEGE UND MITTEILUNGEN / VEREIN FUER KATHOLISCHE KIRCHENGESCHICHTE IN HAMBURG UND SCHLESWIG-HOLESTIN E.V.). (1987)-. Monographic series. German. Price varies per volume.

HU/0139-0090
BEKES MEGYEI MUZEUMOK KOZLEMENYEI. **Added/Corp** Bekes Megyei Muzeumok Igazgatosaga. (1971)-. Hungarian (summaries and/or abstracts in English). **LC** DB975.B4; B44.
Ind/Abst BHA : Biblio. Hist. Art.

SP/0210-8550
BERCEO. (BERCEO : BOLETIN DEL INSTITUTO DE ESTUDIOS RIOJANOS.). [Berceo]. **Added/Corp** Instituto de Estudios Riojanos. Vol. 1, No. 1 (1946); Vol. 25, No. 82 (1971); No. 82 (1972)-. Periodical. Spanish. sa. 1500ptas. Instituto Estudios Riojanos, Calvo Sotelo 15 Entre Suelo, 26071 Logrono Spain. **Tel** 011 34 41 291305. **LC** DP302.L18; B4. cum. index.
Ind/Abst Am. Hist. Life (1958-1965); BHA : Biblio. Hist. Art; GeoRef.

IT/0005-8955
BERGAMUM. (BERGOMUM : BOLLETTINO DELLA CIVICA BIBLIOTECA.). [Bergamum]. **Added/Corp** Biblioteca Civica A. Mai di Bergamo. Vol. 1, No. 1 (Jan./March 1926)-. Periodical. Italian. Four times a year. L80000.00 Italy; L100000.00 other. Biblioteca Civica Angelo Mai, Piazza Vecchia 15, 24100 Bergamo Italy. **Tel** 011 39 35 240655, FAX 011 3935 240655. **LC** DG975.B48; B4. cum. index. **Continues** *Bollettino della Biblioteca Civica di Bergamo*.
Ind/Abst Am. Hist. Life (1972-1974); BHA : Biblio. Hist. Art; MLA Int. Bibl. Books Artic. Mod. Lang. Lit.

GW
BERICHT DER BAYERISCHEN BODENDENKMALPFLEGE / BAYERISCHES LANDESAMT FUER DENKMALPFLEGE. **Title Change.** **Added/Corp** Bayerisches Landesamt Fur Denkmalpflege. Vol. 22-23 (1982)-(19??). Periodical. German. be. Dr. Rudolf Habelt GmbH, Postfach 150104, D 53040 Bonn Germany. **Tel** 011 49 228 232015. **Continued by** *Jahresbericht der Bayerischen Bodendenkmalpflege*.
Ind/Abst BHA : Biblio. Hist. Art (-19??).

AU
BERICHT UBER DEN ... OSTERREICHISCHEN HISTORIKERTAG IN ... / VERANSTALTET VOM VERBAND OSTERREICHISCHER GESCHICHTSVEREINE IN DER ZEIT VOM ... . **Added/Corp** Verband Osterreichischer Geschichtsvereine. (195?)-. German. an. **LC** DB1; .V375 subser. **Continues** *Osterreichischer Historikertag. Bericht Uber die Konstituierende Versammlung des Verbandes EOsterreichischer Geschichtsvereine*.
Ind/Abst Am. Hist. Life (1963-1971).

GW/0005-9099
BERICHTE ZUR DEUTSCHEN LANDESKUNDE. [Ber. dtsch. Landeskd.]. **Added/Corp** Zentralausschuss fuer Deutsche Landeskunde. Germany. Reichsamt fuer Landesaufnahme. Abteilung fuer Landeskunde. Bavaria. Amt fuer Landeskunde. Germany (Federal Republic, 1949-). Bundesanstalt fuer Landeskunde. Germany (Federal Republic, 1949-). Amt fuer Landeskunde. Vol. 1 (Oct. 1941)-. German. sa (2 issues). DM91.59. Zentralaussch F Deutschen Landeskunde, Universite Universitaetsring, D-54286 Trier Germany. **Tel** 011 49 651 2014526. **LC** DD14; .B4. **DD** 016.9143. **CODEN** BDLKAH. cum. index.
Ind/Abst Bibliogr. Carto.; Ecol. Abstr.; Geogr. Abstr. Phys. Geogr. (?-?); Geogr. Abstr. Human Geogr.; Geol. Abstr.

GW/0175-8446
BERLIN IN GESCHICHTE UND GEGENWART. **Added/Corp** Landesarchiv Berlin. (1982)-. German. an. DM48.00. Siedler Verlag, Postfach 800360, W 8000 Munich 80 F R Germany. **(Subscription address:** VVA Bertelsmann Dist GMBH, Postfach 7777, W 4830 Guetersloh 100 Germany, Tel. 49 5241 800) **LC** DD851; .B415. **DD** 943.1/55/005.
Ind/Abst BHA : Biblio. Hist. Art.

GE/0572-6263
BERLINER BEITRAEGE ZUR NAMENFORSCHUNG. See *Linguistics*.

GW/0067-6055
BERLINER BYZANTINISTISCHE ARBEITEN. [Berl. byz. Arb.]. **Added/Corp** Deutsche Akademie der Wissenschaften zu Berlin. Institut fuer Griechisch-Raomische Altertumskunde. Akademie der Wissenschaften der DDR. Zentralinstitut fuer Alte Geschichte und Archaaologie. Deutsche Akademie der Wissenschaften zu Berlin. Zentralinstitut fuer Alte Geschichte und Archaaologie. Martin-Luther-Universitaat Halle-Wittenberg. Sektion Orient- und Altertumswissenschaften. Vol. 1 (195?)-. Monographic series. German. ir. Price varies per volume. Akademie-Verlag GmbH, Muehlenstrasse 33 34, D 13162 Berlin Germany. **Tel** 011 49 30 47889300, FAX 011 49 30 47889357. **(Subscription address:** VCH Publishers Inc., 303 Northwest 12th Avenue, Journals Department, Deerfield FL 33442.) **LC** UNC.
Ind/Abst MLA Int. Bibl. Books Artic. Mod. Lang. Lit.

SZ
BERNER BRANCHEN- UND ADRESSBUCH. Began with Vol. for 1979. German. an. Hallwag AG, Nordring 4, CH-3001 Bern Switzerland. **Tel** 011 41 31 3323131, FAX 031/414133, telex 912661 HAWA CH. **LC** DQ409.2; .A4. **DD** 949.4/5. **Continues** *Berner Adressbuch*.

GW
BESKIDEN-KALENDER. **Added/Corp** Heimatbund Beskidenland. (19??)-. Periodical. German. **LC** DK4600.B4; B47. **DD** 943.7/3.

●US/1051-1504
BEST OF ANDORRA, THE. (THE BEST OF ANDORRA: WITH SPECIAL FEATURE BARCELONA / INTERNATIONAL DESTINATIONS.). [Best Andorra]. **Added/Corp** International Destinations (Firm). (1992)-. English. te. $8.95. International Destinations Inc, 205 Arizona Avenue, Santa Monica CA 90401. **DD** 946.

HU
BESZELO. (1981)-. Periodical. Hungarian. wk. **LC** DB956; .B47.
Ind/Abst Hum. Rights Intern. Rep.

PL
BIBLIOGRAFIA HISTORII POLSKI XIX WIEKU. Polish. **(Subscription address:** ARS Polona, PO Box 1001, 00068 Warsaw Poland.)

BU/0523-2376
BIBLIOGRAPHIE D'ETUDES BALKANIQUES. (BIBLIOGRAPHIE D'ETUDES BALKANIQUES / ACADEMIE BULGARE DES SCIENCES, INSTITUT D'ETUDES BALKANIQUES, CENTRE INTERNATIONAL DE RECHERCHES SCIENTIFIQUES ET DE DOCUMENTATION.). **Added/Corp** Mezhdunareden Tsentur za Nauchni Izsledvaniia i Dokumentatsiia (Institut za Balkanistika) TSentur za Informatsiia i Dokumentatsiia po Balkanistika (Institut za Balkanistika "Liudmila Zhivkova"). Vol. 1 (1966)-. French. an. **(Subscription address:** Kubon & Sagner, ABT Zeitschriftenimport, D 80328 Munich Germany.)
Ind/Abst Numis. Lit. (?-?).

SP/0409-5308
BIBLIOTECA DE ESTUDIOS MADRILENOS. Vol. 1; 1952-. Monographic series. Spanish. Price varies per volume. Instituto Estudios Madrilenos, Duque Medinaceli, 6 PL4/D50, 28014 Madrid Spain. **LC** AC70.

PL/0067-8031
BIBLIOTHECA LATINA MEDII ET RECENTIORIS AEVI. **Added/Corp** Polska Akademia Nauk. Komitet Nauk o Kulturze Antycznej. Vol. 1 (1960)-. Monographic series. Multiple languages (Latin and Polish). ir. Price varies per volume. **(Subscription address:** ARS Polona, PO Box 1001, 00068 Warsaw Poland.) **DD** 940.

FR
BICENTENAIRE DE LA REVOLUTION FRANCAISE : BULLET DE LA COMMISSION NATIONALE DE RECHERCHE HISTORIQUE POUR LE BICENTENAIRE DE LA REVOLUTION FRANCAISE. No. 1 (Nov. 1983)-. French. an. Editions du CNRS, 22 rue Saint Armand, F 75015 Paris France. **Tel** 011 33 1 45075050. **LC** Z2178; .B53; DC139. **DD** 016.94404. **Circ:** 1,500.
Desc: Indicates the degree of progress in projects initiated by national and regional authorities and analyses international projects relating to the bicentennial of the French Revolution. It also furnishes a detailed calendar of seminars taking place between Fall 1987 and Fall 1988 on this subject.

NE/0165-0505
BIJDRAGEN EN MEDEDELINGEN BETREFFENDE DE GESCHIEDENIS DER NEDERLANDEN. [Bijdr. meded. betreffende geschied. Ned.]. Vol. 83 (1969)-. Periodical. Dutch. Four times a year. Fl98.50. Ned Historisch Genootschap, Postbus 90406, 2509 LK Den Haag Netherlands. **Tel** 070-3140363. **ED** W Blockmans, R C van Caenegem, C Fasseur, P M M Kley, E Lamberts, H K K van Nierop, M de Keuning and G N van der Plaat. Index available. **Bk Rev. Ad Acc.** **Formed by the union of** *Bijdragen Voor de Geschiedenis der Nederlanden* **and** *Bijdragen en Mededelingen*.
Ind/Abst Am. Hist. Life (1958-); BHA : Biblio. Hist. Art.

UK/0006-4335
BLACKCOUNTRYMAN. (THE BLACK COUNTRY MAN.). **Added/Corp** Black Country Society. Vol. 1 (Feb. 1968)-. English. Four times a year (Feb., Apr., July, Oct.). £10.00. Black Country Society, 32 Lawnswood Avenue, Stourbridge DY8 5LP England. **Tel** 011 44 295606. **ED** Stan Hill. **LC** DA670.B55; B53. **DD** 914.24/6. **Circ:** 3,000.
Desc: The aim of the Society is to foster interest in the past, present and future of the black country. That area now covers by black country metropolitian Boroughs of Dudlen, Sandwell, Walsall and many more.

GW/0341-9479
BLATTER FUER WURTTEMBERGISCHE KIRCHENGESCHICHTE. See *Religion and Theology*.

NE/0927-2720
BLIKOPENER DEN BOSCH. See *Sociology*.

History(General)—History of Europe

GW/0523-8587
BOHEMIA (MUNCHEN). (BOHEMIA : JAHRBUCH DES COLLEGIUM CAROLINUM.). [Bohemia]. **Added/Corp** Collegium Carolinum (Munich, Germany). Vol. 1 (1960)-. German (summaries and/or abstracts in English, French and Czech). sa. DM76.00. R Oldenbourg Verlag, Postfach 801360, D 81613 Munich Germany. **Tel** 011 49 89 450190, FAX 011 49 89 45019305. **ED** Gerhard Hanke. **LC** DB193; .B63. **[CCC]. Bk Rev. Continues** Jahrbuch des Vereins fur Geschichte der Deutschen in Bohmen.
Desc: Central scholarly forum for all historical and contemporary topics of East Central Europe; includes essays, book reviews and a comprehensive notated bibliography.
Ind/Abst Am. Hist. Life (1964-); BHA : Biblio. Hist. Art.

PO/0870-0761
BOLETIM CULTURAL - ASSEMBLEIA DISTRITAL DE LISBOA. See Sociology-Manners and Customs.

PO/0870-0478
BOLETIM CULTURAL / CAMARA MUNICIPAL DO PORTO. See Sociology-Manners and Customs.

SP/0020-384X
BOLETIN DEL INSTITUTO DE ESTUDIOS ASTURIANOS. [Bol. Inst. Estud. Ast.]. **Main/Corp** Instituto de Estudios Asturianos (Oviedo, Spain). Vol. 1, No. 1 (July 1947)-. Periodical. Spanish. Three times a year. **LC** DP302.A78; A34.
Ind/Abst Am. Hist. Life (1956-1970); BHA : Biblio. Hist. Art; MLA Int. Bibl. Books Artic. Mod. Lang. Lit.

GW
BOLETIN / INSTITUTO DE ESTUDIOS IBEROAMERICANOS. Added/Corp Institut Fuer Iberomerika-Kunde. No. 1 (Apr. 1990)-. Spanish. Three times a year.

IT/0012-5385
BOLLETTINO DELLA DOMUS MAZZINIANA. [Boll. Domus Mazziniana]. **Main/Corp** Domus Mazziniana. Vol. 1 (1955)-. Periodical. Italian (French and English). sa. L20000 Italy; L30000 other. Bollettino Della Domus, Via Mazzini 71, 56100 Pisa Italy. **ED** Giacomo P Adami. **Bk Rev. Circ:** 500 (ctrl).
Desc: History of Mazzini's philosophy; general bibliography of the history of Italian risorgimento.
Ind/Abst Am. Hist. Life (1975-1976, 1979-); MLA Int. Bibl. Books Artic. Mod. Lang. Lit.

IT
BOLLETTINO DELLA SOCIETA PAVESE DI STORIA PATRIA. Main/Corp Societa Pavese di Storia Patria. Vol. 1 (1901)-. Periodical. Italian. an. **LC** DG975.P29; S6. cum. index.
Ind/Abst BHA : Biblio. Hist. Art.

IT
BOLLETTINO DELLA SOCIETA PER GLI STUDI STORICI, ARCHEOLOGICI ED ARTISTICI NELLA PROVINCIA DI CUNEO. Added/Corp Societa per gli Studi Storici Archeologici e Artistici Della Provincia di Cuneo. (July 1935)-. Periodical. Italian. sa (May & Oct.). (Comes with Societa Studi Storici Archeologici Provincia Cuneo membership). Societa Studi Storici Archeologici Artisitici Provinicia Cuneo, Cas Postale 91, 12100 Cuneo Italy. **Tel** 39 171 54367. cum. index. **Continues** Comunicazioni della Societa per gli Studi Storici Archeologici ed Artistici per la Provincia di Cuneo.
Ind/Abst BHA : Biblio. Hist. Art.

IT/0583-8002
BOLLETTINO DELLA SOCIETA STORICA MAREMMANA. Main/Corp Societa Storica Maremmana. (19??)-. Italian. sa.
Ind/Abst BHA : Biblio. Hist. Art.

IT
BOLLETTINO DELLA SOCIETA STORICA VALTELLINESE. Added/Corp Societa Storica Valtellinese. (19??)-. Italian. an. (Comes with Societa Storica Valtellinese membership). Societa Storica Valtellinese, Villa Quadrio V IV Novembre 20, 23100 Sondrio Italy. **Tel** 39 342 216038.
Ind/Abst BHA : Biblio. Hist. Art.

IT/0391-6715
BOLLETTINO STORICO-BIBLIOGRAFICO SUBALPINO. [Boll. stor. bibliogr. subalp.]. **Added/Corp** Deputazione Subalpina di Storia Patria. Vol. 1 (1896)-. Periodical. Italian. sa (June & Dec.). L65000 (Italy); L75000 (other). Deputazione Subalpina Storia Patria, Via P Amedeo 5, 10123 Turin Italy. **Tel** 39 11 537226. **LC** DG610; .B6. Index available. cum. index. **Bk Rev** (Qty: Varies). ctrl circ.
Ind/Abst Am. Hist. Life (1980-); BHA : Biblio. Hist. Art.

IT
BOLLETTINO STORICO CREMONESE. Added/Corp Cremona. Archivio Storico Comunale. Commissione Conservatrice. Istituto Fascista di Cultura di Cremona. Deputazione di Storia Patria per la Lombardia. Sezione di Cremona. Vol. 1 (1931)-. Italian.
Ind/Abst BHA : Biblio. Hist. Art.

IT/0394-1841
BOLLETTINO STORICO DELLA BASILICATA / A CURA DELLA DEPUTAZIONE DI STORIA PATRIA DELLA LUCANIA. Added/Corp Deputazione di Storia Patria della Lucania. Vol. 1, No. 1 (Dec. 1985)-. Italian. an. **LC** DG975.B3; B65. **DD** 945/.77.
Ind/Abst BHA : Biblio. Hist. Art.

IT/1121-6425
BOLLETTINO STORICO DELLA CITTA DI FOLIGNO / ACCADEMIA FULGINIA DI LETTERE, SCIENZE E ARTI. Added/Corp Accademia Fulginia di Lettere, Scienze e Arti. (1969)-. Italian. an. **LC** DG975.F65; B65. **DD** 945/.651/005.
Ind/Abst BHA : Biblio. Hist. Art.

IT
BOLLETTINO STORICO DI TERRA D'OTRANTO / SOCIETA DI STORIA PATRIA PER LA PUGLIA, SEZIONE DI GALATINA. Added/Corp Societa di Storia Patria per la Puglia. Sezione di Galatina. (1991)-. Periodical. Italian. Congedo Editore Via Marche, 24 73013 Galatina Leece Italy.

IT/0392-1107
BOLLETTINO STORICO PER LA PROVINCIA DI NOVARA 1947. (BOLLETTINO STORICO PER LA PROVINCI DI NOVARA.). [Boll. stor. prov. Novara1947]. (1947)-. Periodical. Italian. sa. **UDC** 930 (450.214). **Continues** R. Deputazione Subalpina di Storia Patria. Bollettino della Sezione di Novara.
Ind/Abst BHA : Biblio. Hist. Art.

IT/0006-6591
BOLLETTINO STORICO PIACENTINO. Vol. 1 (1906)-. Periodical. Italian. sa. L30000.00. TIP Le Co. Sne, Via S Salotti N 37, S Bonico 29100 Piacenza Italy. **Tel** 0523-380102, FAX 0523-380520. **LC** WMLC L 83/7404. cum. index.
Desc: Essays of history, literature and art of Piacenza.
Ind/Abst BHA : Biblio. Hist. Art.

IT/0392-1255
BOLLETTINO STORICO REGGIANO. [Boll. Stor. Reggiano]. (1968)-. Periodical. Italian. tq. (Comes with Deputazione di Storia Patria per le Antiche Provincie Modenesi membership). Deputazione Storia Patria, Sez R Emilia Pza S Giovanni 4, 42100 Reggio Emilia Italy. **Tel** 011 39 522 435384. **UDC** 930.25 (450.453).
Ind/Abst BHA : Biblio. Hist. Art.

IT
BOLLETTINO STORICO VERCELLESE. Added/Corp Societa Storica Vercellese. Vol. 1, No. 1 (1972)-. Periodical. Italian.
Ind/Abst BHA : Biblio. Hist. Art.

GW/0068-0052
BONNER GESCHICHTSBLATTER. (BONNER GESCHICHTSBLATTER / IM AUFTRAGE DES VEREINS ALT-BONN HERAUSGEGEBEN VON STADTARCHIVAR.). [Bonn. Geschichtsbl.]. **Added/Corp** Verein Alt-Bonn. Stadtarchiv Bonn. Bonner Heimat- und Geschichtsverein. **VFOAT** Jahrbuch des Vereins Alt-Bonn; Jahrbuch des Bonner Heimat- und Geschichtsvereins. (1937)-. Monographic series. German. an. **LC** DD901.B6; B6.
Ind/Abst BHA : Biblio. Hist. Art.

GW
BONNER HEFTE ZUR VORGESCHICHTE. Added/Corp Bonn. Universitat. Institut fur Vor- und Fruhgeschichte. No. 1 (1971)-. Monographic series. German.
Ind/Abst BHA : Biblio. Hist. Art.

GW/0938-9334
BONNER JAHRBUCHER DES RHEINISCHEN LANDESMUSEUMS IN BONN UND DES RHEINISCHEN AMTES FUER BODENDENKMALPFLEGE IM LANDSCHAFTSVERBAND RHEINLAND UND DES VEREINS VON ALTERTUMSFREUNDEN IM RHEINLANDE. [Bonn. Jahrb. Rhein. Landesmus. Bonn Rhein. Amtes Bodendenkmalpfl. Landsch.verb. Rheinl. Ver. Altert.freunden Rheinl.]. **VFOAT** Bonner Jahrbucher (1987). (1987)-. Periodical. Multiple languages. an. **UDC** D7/76. **Continues** Bonner Jahrbucher des Rheinischen Landesmuseums in Bonn (im Landschaftsverband Rheinland) und des Vereins von Altertumsfreunden im Rheinlande, 0067-9976.
Ind/Abst BHA : Biblio. Hist. Art.

UK/0524-0913
BORTHWICK PAPERS / UNIVERSITY OF YORK, BORTHWICK INSTITUTE OF HISTORICAL RESEARCH. Added/Corp Borthwick Institue of Historical Research. University of York. **VFOAT** Borthwick Paper. No. 27 (1965)-. Monographic series. English. sa. £3.50. University of York / St. Anthonys Hall, Borthwick Institute, York Y01 2PW England. **Tel** 011 44 904 642315. **ED** W. J. Sheils. **Bk Rev. Circ:** 400 (ctrl). **Continues** Saint Anthony's Hall Publications.

NE
BRABANTS HEEM. [Brabants heem]. (1949)-. Periodical. Dutch. Four times a year. Fl23.11. St. Brabants Heem, Postbus 1104, 2500 BD Den Bosch Netherlands. **Tel** 011 31 08866-1982.
Ind/Abst BHA : Biblio. Hist. Art.

PO
BRACARA AUGUSTA. Added/Corp Braga, Portugal. Camara Municipal. Vol. 2, No. 14 (Apr. 1950)-. Periodical. Portuguese. **LC** DP802.B7; B7.
Ind/Abst BHA : Biblio. Hist. Art.

●UK/1354-7739
BRADFORD STUDIES ON SOUTH EASTERN EUROPE. (1994)-. Academic Scholarly Publication. English. ir. Price varies. The Secretary / England, Research Unit in South East European Studies, University of Bradford, Bradford BD7 1DP West Yorkshire England. Index available. ctrl circ.
Continues Bradford Studies on Yugoslavia, 0143-5043.
Desc: Information on the studies and history of the South Eastern Europe.

UK/0143-5043
BRADFORD STUDIES ON YUGOSLAVIA. Title Change. Added/Corp University of Bradford. Postgraduate School of Yugoslav Studies. No. 1 (1979)-(19??). Monographic series. English. ir. The Secretary / England, Research Unit in South East European Studies, University of Bradford, Bradford BD7 1DP West Yorkshire England. **LC** UNC.
Continued by Bradford Studies on South Eastern Europe, 1354-7739.

GW/0068-0745
BRAUNSCHWEIGISCHES JAHRBUCH. Added/Corp Braunschweiger Geschichtsverein. Braunschweiger Geschichtsverein. Jahrbuch. (1902)-. German. an.
Ind/Abst Bibliogr. Carto.; BHA : Biblio. Hist. Art.

FR
BREIZH. Periodical. Multiple languages (Breton and French). mo. 25.00F. C C P 14467, Rennes France. **LC** DC611.B851; B69. **DD** 944/.1/005.

GW/0341-9622
BREMISCHES JAHRBUCH. Added/Corp Kunstlerverein (Bremen, Germany). Historische Gesellschaft. Historische Gesellschaft zu Bremen. Staatsarchiv Bremen. (1864)-. German. **LC** DD901.B71; B6. cum. index.
Ind/Abst Bibliogr. Carto.; BHA : Biblio. Hist. Art.

PO/0870-8339
BRIGANTIA. Added/Corp Braganca (Portugal : District). Assembleia Distrital. Secretaria. Vol. 1, (Jan./Mar. 1981)-. Periodical. Portuguese. qt. **LC** DP702.B61; B74.
Ind/Abst BHA : Biblio. Hist. Art.

UK
BRITAIN AND EUROPE. (1973)-. English. an. £25.75. Research Publications Ltd., PO Box 45, Reading RG1 8HF England. **Tel** 011 44 734 583247, 011 44 734 583248, FAX 011 44 734 591325, telex 848336 RPLG. **(Subscription address:** Research Publications Inc. / Microfilm, 12 Lunar Drive Drawer AB, Woodbridge CT 06525.**)**

UK/0141-867X
BRITISH JOURNAL FOR EIGHTEENTH-CENTURY STUDIES, THE. See Literature.

●UK/0966-095X
BRITISH JOURNAL OF HOLOCAUST EDUCATION. (THE BRITISH JOURNAL OF HOLOCAUST EDUCATION.). [Br. j. holocaust educ.]. (1992)-. Periodical. English. sa (Summer and Winter). $65.00. Frank Cass & Company Ltd, Newbury House, 890-900 Eastern Avenue, Newbury Park, Ilford, Essex IG7 7HH United Kingdom. **Tel** 011 44 81 599 8866, FAX 011 44 81 599 0984, telex 897719. **DD** 940.5318. **Ad Acc, Adv Mgr:** Anne Kidson.

IT/0392-1158
BRIXIA SACRA 1966. (BRIXIA SACRA.). [Brixia Sacra1966]. (1966)-. Periodical. Multiple languages. bm. **UDC** 930.25 (450.256). **Continues** Memorie Storiche della Diocesi di Brescia.
Ind/Abst BHA : Biblio. Hist. Art.

History(General) —History of Europe

AU
BRUCKE, DIE. Added/Corp Carinthia, Austria. Kulturreferat. Vol. 1 (Spring 1975)-. Periodical. German. sa. S230.00. Amt der Karntner Landesregierung, Abteilung 5, Kultur Paradeisergasse, A-9021 Klagenfurt Austria. **LC** DB290.5; .B78.

IT/0392-3894
BRUTIUM. [Brutium]. (1922)-. Periodical. Italian. qt. **UDC** 908.
Ind/Abst BHA : Biblio. Hist. Art.

GW/0562-5270
BUCHREIHE DER SUDOSTDEUTSCHEN HISTORISCHEN KOMMISSION. Main/Corp Sudostdeutsche Historische Kommission. Vol. 1- 1958-. Monographic series. German. ir. Price varies per volume. R Oldenbourg Verlag, Postfach 801360, D 81613 Munich Germany. **Tel** 011 49 89 450190, FAX 011 49 89 45019305. **ED** Adam Wandruszka. **Circ**: 1,000 (ctrl).

UK
BUCKS AND BERKS COUNTRYSIDE. **VFOAT** Berks and Bucks Countryside. Vol. 16, No. 106 (June 1976)-. Periodical. English. mo. $21.50. Countryside Magazine Group, Connoisseur House, Sawmill Lane, Helmsly York England. **LC** DA670.T2; T45. **DD** 942.2/9/005. Continues Buckinghamshire and Berkshire Countryside, 0306-6614.

HU/0133-1892
BUDAPEST REGISEGEI. Added/Corp Budapesti Torteneti Muzeum. (1889)-. Hungarian. ir. **LC** DB867; .B8.
Ind/Abst BHA : Biblio. Hist. Art; Numis. Lit.

FI
BUDKAVLEN. Swedish. an. FMK8.00. **LC** DL30; .B78.
Ind/Abst Anthropol. Lit.

GW
BULETINUL BIBLIOTECII ROMANE. Added/Corp Biblioteca Romana (Institutul Roman de Cercetari). (19??)-. Romanian (French, German and English). an. DM35.00 Germany; $20.00 other. Institutul Roman-Biblioteca Romana, Uhlandstrasse 7, 78 Freiburg I Br Germany. **Tel** 0761/73551. **LC** DR201; .I5473. **DD** 949.8/005. **Circ**: 300 (ctrl). Continues Buletinul (Biblioteca Romana. Institutul Roman de Cercetari).

BU/0324-0207
BULGARIAN HISTORICAL REVIEW. [Bulg. hist. rev.]. Added/Corp United Center for Research and Training in History. **VFOAT** Revue Bulgare d'Histoire. (1973)-. Periodical. Multiple languages (English, French, German and Russian). qt. DM198.00. Bulgarian Academy of Sciences, 1 rue 15 Noemvri, 1040 Sofia Bulgaria. **Tel** 011 359 2 803127. **(Subscription address:** Kubon & Sagner, ABT Zeitschriftenimport, D 80328 Munich Germany.) **ED** V. Hadshinikolov. **LC** DR51; .B845. **DD** 949.77/005. **Bk Rev. Ad Acc. Circ**: 2,300. Documents available from The Genuine Article.
Desc: Bulgarian and Balkan history. Biographies of noted historical persons, papers and scientific reviews.
Ind/Abst Am. Hist. Life (1973-); Arts Humanit. Citation Index [Full Cov.]; Curr. Contents Arts Humanit.; Res. Alert [Full Cov.]; Soc. Sci. Cit. Index [Select. Cov.].

BU/0205-3209
BULGARISTIKA. Added/Corp TSentur za Bulgaristika (Bulgarska Akademiia na Naukite) Bulgaria. Komitet za Kultura. (1987)-. Periodical. Bulgarian. **LC** DR51; .B8638. Continues Zveno (Sofia, Bulgaria).
Ind/Abst Soc. Plann. Policy Dev. Abstr.

CN/0823-9487
BULLETIN - ASSOCIATION CANADIENNE POUR L'AVANCEMENT DES ETUDES NEERLANDAISES. (BULLETIN / ACAEN, ASSOCIATION CANADIENNE POUR L'ADVANCEMENT DES ETUDES NEERLANDAISES.). [Bull. - Assoc. can. av. etud. neerl.]. **VFOAT** Newsletter. **VAT** Newsletter - Canadian Association for the Advancement of Netherlandic Studies; CAANS Newsletter (1983); ACAEN Bulletin. Jan. 1983-. Bulletin. English (French). sa. 15.00Can$. Canadian Association for the Advancement of Netherlandic Studies, c/o Basil D Kingstone University of Windsor, Windsor Ontario N9B 3P4 Canada. **Tel** (519)253-4232. **ED** Basil D Kingstone. **DD** 949.2/007/071. **Bk Rev. Ad Acc. Pr Rev. Circ**: 300 (ctrl). Continues CAANS Newsletter, 0315-0127.
Desc: Articles on all aspects of life in the Netherlands and Flanders. Mostly scholarly (university level), some general interest.

RM/0004-5551
BULLETIN - ASSOCIATION INTERNATIONALE D'ETUDES DU SUD-EST EUROPEEN. (AIESEE BULLETIN / ASSOCIATION INTERNATIONALE D'ETUDES DU SUD-EST EUROPEEN.). [Bull. Assoc. int. etud. sud-est eur.]. Added/Corp Association Internationale d'Etudes du Sud-Est Europeen. **VFOAT** Bulletin; Bulletin AIESEE.

Vol. 1 (1963)-. Bulletin. English (French and Romanian). sa. **LC** DR1; .I53A14.
Ind/Abst Am. Hist. Life (1966-); Numis. Lit. (?-?).

UK
BULLETIN (ASSOCIATION OF CONTEMPORARY HISTORIANS (GREAT BRITAIN)). (BULLETIN / THE ASSOCIATION OF CONTEMPORARY HISTORIANS.). Added/Corp Association of Contemporary Historians (Great Britain). (19??)-. Bulletin. English. ir. Association of Comtemporary Historians, London School of Economics, London WC2A 2AE England. **LC** D1; .B84a. **DD** 905.

CN/0319-1095
BULLETIN - CENTRE INTERUNIVERSITAIRE D'ETUDES EUROPEENNES. (NEWSLETTER - INTERUNIVERSITY CENTRE FOR EUROPEAN STUDIES.). Main/Corp Centre Interuniversitaire d'Etudes Europeennes. Began with Sept. 15, 1973 issue. Newsletter. French (English). Six times a year. 15.00Can$ (add $3.00 postage for Canada and US, $10.00 postage for Europe). Interuniversity Centre for European Studies, PO Box 8892 Station A, Montreal Quebec H3C 3P8 Canada. **Tel** (514)282-6193. **ED** Odile Civitello. **DD** 940/.007/20714. circ circ.
Desc: Newsletter distributed to Europeanists in Montreal.

FR
BULLETIN - COMITE DU FOLKLORE CHAMPENOIS. Main/Corp Comite du Folklore Champenois. Bulletin. French. Comite du Folklore Champenois, 2 rue Joseph-Servas, 51000 Chalons-Sur-Marne France. **LC** DC611.C44; C64A. **DD** 914.4/3/0305.

FR
BULLETIN COMMISSION HISTORIQUE DU NORD. (19??)-. Bulletin. French. ir (every 2-3 years). 157.14F. Commission Historique du Nord, 22 rue St. Bernard, F-59045 Lille Cedex France. **Tel** 011 33 20 938717.

FR/0246-5825
BULLETIN DE LA COMMISSION DEPARTEMENTALE DES ANTIQUITES DE LA SEINE-MARITIME. [Bull. Comm. dep. antiq. Seine-Marit]. Added/Corp Seine-Maritime. Commission Departementale des Antiquites. (1978)-. Bulletin. French. an. **UDC** 908(442.1/.5-18). Continues Bulletin de la Commission des Antiquites de la Seine-Maritime, 0246-5817.
Ind/Abst BHA : Biblio. Hist. Art.

FR/0750-1331
BULLETIN DE LA COMMISSION DEPARTEMENTALE D'HISTOIRE ET D'ARCHEOLOGIE DU PAS-DE-CALAIS. See Archaeology.

FR/1140-7387
BULLETIN DE LA COMMISSION HISTORIQUE DU DEPARTEMENT DU NORD. (1843)-. Periodical. French. **UDC** 908(442.8).
Ind/Abst BHA : Biblio. Hist. Art.

BE/0522-7496
BULLETIN DE LA COMMISSION ROYALE DES MONUMENTS ET DES SITES (BELGIUM). [Bull. comm. r. monum. sites]. Main/Corp Belgium. Commission Royale des Monuments et des Sites. **VFOAT** Bulletin van de Koninklijke Commissie voor Monumenten en Landschappen. (1949)-. Bulletin. French (Dutch). ir. Commission Royale des Monuments et des Sites, rue Joseph II 30, 1040 Bruxelles Belgium. Supersedes Belgium. Commission Royales d'Art et d'Archeologie. Bulletin.
Ind/Abst Avery Index Archit. Period. Suppl. Colum. Univ. (19??-199?); BHA : Biblio. Hist. Art; Br. Archaeol. Bibliogr.

BE
BULLETIN DE LA COMMISSION ROYALE D'HISTOIRE. (BULLETIN DE LA COMMISSION ROYALE D'HISTOIRE (BELGIUM).). Main/Corp Academic Royale des Sciences, des lettres et des Beaux-Arts de Belgique. Commission Royale d'Histoire. Added/Corp Academie Royale des Sciences, des Lettres et des Beaux Arts de Belgique. Commission Royale d'Histoire. Handelingen. Academie Royale des Sciences, des Lettres et des Beaux Arts de Belgique. Commission Royale d'Histoire. Compte Rendu des Seances. **VFOAT** Handelingen van de Koninklijke Commissie voor Geschiedenis. (1834)-. Bulletin. Multiple languages (Flemish and French). tq. 1000F. Academie Royal de Belgique, rue Ducale 1, 1000 Bruxelles Belgium. **Tel** 02/538.69.17. **(Subscription address:** Le Libraire, Alain Ferraton, Chaussee de Charleroi 162, 1060 Bruxelles Belgium) cum. index. **Circ**: 500 (ctrl).
Ind/Abst Am. Hist. Life (1963-).

FR/1148-7860
BULLETIN DE LA DIANA MONTBRISON. [Bull. DianaMontbrison]. (1876)-. Periodical. French. qt. **UDC** 908(449.98).
Ind/Abst BHA : Biblio. Hist. Art.

FR/0337-579X
BULLETIN DE LA SOCIETE ARCHEOLOGIQUE ET HISTORIQUE DE L'ORLEANAIS 1959. See Archaeology.

FR/0182-3876
BULLETIN DE LA SOCIETE ARCHEOLOGIQUE ET HISTORIQUE DES HAUTS CANTONS DE L'HERAULT. See Archaeology.

FR/1145-7325
BULLETIN DE LA SOCIETE ARCHEOLOGIQUE, HISTORIQUE ET ARTISTIQUE, LE VIEUX PAPIER, POUR L'ETUDE DE LA VIE ET DES MRS D'AUTREFOIS. See Archaeology.

FR/0037-8895
BULLETIN DE LA SOCIETE ARCHEOLOGIQUE HISTORIQUE LITTERAIRE & SCIENTIFIQUE DU GERS. See Archaeology.

FR
BULLETIN DE LA SOCIETE BELFORTAINE D'EMULATION. 1.- Yearly volume; 1872/73-. Bulletin. French. **LC** DC611.B425; S4.
Ind/Abst BHA : Biblio. Hist. Art.

FR/0337-0267
BULLETIN DE LA SOCIETE DE BORDA. [Bull. Soc. Borda]. **VFOAT** Bulletin de la Societe de Borda a Dax; Bulletin Trimestriel de la Societe de Borda. (1876)-. Periodical. French. qt. Societe de Borda, Dax France. **UDC** 908.
Ind/Abst BHA : Biblio. Hist. Art.

FR/1148-7968
BULLETIN DE LA SOCIETE DE L'HISTOIRE DE PARIS ET DE L'ILE-DE-FRANCE. Main/Corp Societe de l'Histoire de Paris et de l'Ile-de-France, Paris. (1874)-. Bulletin. French. an. **LC** DC701; .S65.
Ind/Abst BHA : Biblio. Hist. Art.

FR/0339-0195
BULLETIN DE LA SOCIETE DES AMIS DU CHATEAU DE PAU. (1975)-. Periodical. French. qt. **UDC** 908. Continues Bulletin des Amis du Chateau de Pau, 0339-0187.
Ind/Abst BHA : Biblio. Hist. Art.

FR/0988-1875
BULLETIN DE LA SOCIETE DES AMIS DU VIEUX CHINON. (1972)-. Periodical. French. an. **UDC** 908 (445.4). Continues Bulletin - Les Amis du Vieux Chinon, 0988-1867.
Ind/Abst BHA : Biblio. Hist. Art.

FR/0164-3940
BULLETIN DE LA SOCIETE DES SCIENCES HISTORIQUES ET NATURELLES DE L'YONNE. Added/Corp Societe des Sciences Historiques et Naturelles de l'Yonne. (1847)-. Bulletin. French. qt.
Ind/Abst BHA : Biblio. Hist. Art.

FR/0243-7686
BULLETIN DE LA SOCIETE D'ETUDES DES HAUTES-ALPES. Main/Corp Societe d'Etudes des Hautes-Alpes. (1882)-. Bulletin. French. qt. **LC** DC611.A553; S7. cum. index.
Ind/Abst BHA : Biblio. Hist. Art.

FR/0294-3484
BULLETIN DE LA SOCIETE D'ETUDES ET DE RECHERCHES HISTORIQUES DU PAYS DE RETZ. [Bull. Soc. etud. rech. hist. Pays Retz]. (1982)-. Periodical. French. **UDC** 908 (441.4). Continues Revue du Bas-Poitou et des Provinces de l'Ouest, 0556-767X.
Ind/Abst BHA : Biblio. Hist. Art.

SZ/1017-849X
BULLETIN DE LA SOCIETE D'HISTOIRE ET D'ARCHEOLOGIE DE GENEVE. (1892)-. Periodical. French. **UDC** 930.2. **CODEN** 908.
Ind/Abst BHA : Biblio. Hist. Art.

FR/1153-3277
BULLETIN DE LA SOCIETE D'HISTOIRE ET D'ARCHEOLOGIE DE VICHY ET DE SES ENVIRONS. [Bull. Soc. hist. archeol. Vichy env.]. (1938)-. Periodical. French. **UDC** 061.22(445.7).
Ind/Abst BHA : Biblio. Hist. Art.

FR
BULLETIN DE LA SOCIETE FRANCAISE D'ETUDE DU DIX-HUITIEME SIECLE. Main/Corp Societe Francaise d'Etude du XVIIIE Siecle. No. 1- April 1972-. Bulletin. French. qt. 270.00F France;

History(General)—History of Europe

320.00F other. Societe d'Etude du XVII Siecle, 11 place Marcelin Berthelot, 75005 Paris France. **Tel** 011 33 1 44271211, FAX 011 33 1 44271109. **Supersedes** Bulletin Interieur de la Societe Francaise d'Etude du Dix-Huitieme Siecle,.

CN/0384-0158
BULLETIN DE LA SOCIETE HISTORIQUE DE SAINT-BONIFACE. (BULLETIN.). [Bull. Soc. hist. St.-Boniface]. **Main/Corp** Societe Historique de Saint-Boniface. **VFOAT** Bulletin de la Societ Historique de Saint-Boniface. Vol. 1-5, Pt. 3 (1911)-. Periodical. French. qt (Jan., May, Jul., Nov.). 40.00Can$ institutional member; 25.00Can$ regular member; 35.00Can$ support member; 10.00Can$ student member; 200.00Can$ lifetime member. Societe Historique de Saint Boniface, CP 125, Saint Boniface Manitoba R2H 3D4 Canada. **Tel** (204)233-4888.

FR/1154-368X
BULLETIN DE LA SOCIETE HISTORIQUE ET ARCHELOGIQUE DE CORBEIL, DE L'ESSONNE ET DU HUREPOIX. **Added/Corp** Societe Historique et Archeologique de Corbeil, de l'Essonne et du Hurepoix. (1987)-. Bulletin. French. an. **Continues** Bulletin de la Societe Historique et Archeologique de Corbeil, d'Etampes et du Hurepoix.
Ind/Abst BHA : Biblio. Hist. Art.

FR/1148-859X
BULLETIN DE LA SOCIETE HISTORIQUE ET ARCHEOLOGIQUE DE LANGRES. **Main/Corp** Societe Historique et Archeologique de Langres. (1880)-. Bulletin. French. qt. **LC** DC611.L27; S7.
Ind/Abst BHA : Biblio. Hist. Art.

FR/1141-135X
BULLETIN DE LA SOCIETE HISTORIQUE ET ARCHEOLOGIQUE DU PERIGORD. [Bull. Soc. hist. archeol. Perigord]. (1874)-. Periodical. French. qt. **UDC** 06.055(447.2).
Ind/Abst BHA : Biblio. Hist. Art.

FR/0751-5294
BULLETIN DE LA SOCIETE HISTORIQUE ET SCIENTIFIQUE DES DEUX-SEVRES. **Main/Corp** Societe Historique et Scientifique des Deux-Sevres, Niort. Vol. 1(1912)- Vol. 13 (1967); 2nd Ser. Vol. 1 (1968)-. Bulletin. French. qt. **LC** DC611.S51; S65.
Ind/Abst BHA : Biblio. Hist. Art.

FR
BULLETIN DE LA SOCIETE NATIONALE DES ANTIQUAIRES DE FRANCE. **Added/Corp** Societe Nationale des Antiquaires de France. (1871)-. French. an. Diffusion de Boccard, 11 rue de Medicis, 75006 Paris France. **Tel** 011 33 1 43260037. **LC** DC2; .S73. **Continues** Bulletin de la Societe Imperiale des Antiquaires de France.
Ind/Abst BHA : Biblio. Hist. Art.

FR
BULLETIN DE LA SOCIETE RAMOND. Bulletin. French. an. **LC** DC611.P981; S6. **Continues** Explorations Pyreneennes.

BE/0776-1309
BULLETIN DE LA SOCIETE ROYALE LE VIEUX-LIEGE. [Bull. Soc. r. Vieux-Liege]. **Added/Corp** Societe Royale Le Vieux Liege. **VFOAT** Vieux-Liege. Vol.1 No. 1 (Jan,/Feb. 1932)-. Bulletin. French. qt. **Continues** Vieux-Liege Arch,eologie, Histoire, Folklore & Protection des Sites au Pays de Liege.
Ind/Abst BHA : Biblio. Hist. Art; MLA Int. Bibl. Books Artic. Mod. Lang. Lit.

FR/1148-8298
BULLETIN DE LA SOCIETE SCHONGAUER DE COLMAR. VFOAT Mittheilungen der Schongauer Gesellschaft; Societe Schongauer de Colmar; Bulletin de la Societe Schongauer a Colmar. (1902)-. Periodical. French. ir. **UDC** 061.22(443.83).
Ind/Abst BHA : Biblio. Hist. Art.

FR
BULLETIN DE L'ECOLE ANTIQUE DE NIMES. **Added/Corp** Ecole Antique de Nimes. Musee Archeologique (Nimes, France). No 21 (1990)-. Bulletin. French. **Continues** Bulletin Annual (Ecole Antique de Nimes), 0755-916X.
Ind/Abst BHA : Biblio. Hist. Art.

FR/1140-7425
BULLETIN DES AMIS DE MONTLUCON. **VFOAT** Bulletin Regional - Amis de Montlucon; Bulletin - Amis de Montlucon. (1912)-. Periodical. French. **UDC** 944.
Ind/Abst BHA : Biblio. Hist. Art.

FR/0337-7113
BULLETIN DES AMIS DES MONUMENTS ROUENNAIS. **VFOAT** Les Amis des Monuments Rouennais; Monuments Rouennais; Bulletin - Amis des Monuments Rouennais. (1901)-. Periodical. French. an. **UDC** 908.
Ind/Abst BHA : Biblio. Hist. Art.

LU/1016-961X
BULLETIN DES ANTIQUITES LUXEMBOURGEOISES. [Bull. antiqu. luxemb.]. (1972)-. Periodical. French. an. **UDC** 930.26(435.9). **Continues** Bulletin d'Archeologie Luxembourgeoise.
Ind/Abst BHA : Biblio. Hist. Art.

FR/0525-1249
BULLETIN DES SOCIETES D'HISTOIRE ET D'ARCHEOLOGIE DE LA MEUSE. **Added/Corp** Societe Philomathique de Verdun. Societe des Lettres, Sciences et Arts de Bard-le-Duc. Societe des Naturalistes et Archeologues du Nord de la Meuse. No. 1 (1964)-. Bulletin. French. an.
Ind/Abst BHA : Biblio. Hist. Art.

BE
BULLETIN D'HISTOIRE CISTERCIENNE / BULLETIN OF CISTERICAN HISTORY. See Religion and Theology-Abstracting, Bibliographies and Statistics.

FR/0766-4516
BULLETIN D'HISTOIRE DE LA REVOLUTION FRANCAISE. [Bull. hist. Revolut. fr.]. (1982)-. Periodical. French. **Continues** Bulletin d'Histoire Economique et Sociale de la Revolution Francaise, 0068-4058.
Ind/Abst Am. Hist. Life (1982-).

GR
BULLETIN D'INFORMATION ET DE COORDINATION - ASSOCIATION INTERNATIONALE DES ETUDES BYZANTINES. **Main/Corp** Association Internationale des Etudes Byzantines. Began with 1964 issue. Bulletin. French. Association Internationale des Etudes Byzantines, Centre de Recherches Byzantines, Av Vassileo Konstantinou 48, 501 Athens Greece. **LC** DF501; .A85A. **DD** 949.5.

BE
BULLETIN DU CANGE / UNION ACADEMIQUE INTERNATIONALE. See Linguistics.

FR/0988-9477
BULLETIN DU GROUPE D'HISTOIRE ET D'ARCHEOLOGIE DE BUZANCAIS. [Bull. Group. hist. archeol. Buzancais]. (1969)-. Bulletin. French. an. **UDC** 930 (445.51).
Ind/Abst BHA : Biblio. Hist. Art.

FR
BULLETIN DU MUSEE BASQUE. Bulletin. French. sa (June and Oct.). 50.00F France; 80.00F other. Societe des Amis Musee Basque, 1 rue Marengo, 64100 Bayonne France. **Tel** 011 33 59 590898. **Bk Rev**, (Qty: 1). **Circ:** 1,600. available on an online database.

FR/1162-8774
BULLETIN ET MEMOIRES - SOCIETE D'EMULATION DE MONTBELIARD. (BULLETIN ET MEMOIRES.). [Bull. mem. - Soc. emul. Montbeliard]. (1961)-. Bulletin. French. **UDC** 061.22. **Continues** Memoires de la Societe d'Emulation de Montbeliard, 1162-8898.
Ind/Abst BHA : Biblio. Hist. Art.

GW
BULLETIN, FASCHISMUS/ZWEITER WELTKRIEG. **Added/Corp** Institut fuer Deutsche Geschichte (Berlin, Germany). Arbeitskreis "Faschismus/Zweiter Weltkrieg.". **VFOAT** Bulletin, Faschismus Zweiter Weltkrieg; Bulletin. (19??)-. Bulletin. German. qt. **LC** DD256.5; .A56. **Continues** Bulletin des Arbeitskreises "Zweiter Weltkrieg", 0302-6329.

FR/0521-713X
BULLETIN HISTORIQUE ET ARTISTIQUE DU CALAISIS. (1960)-. Periodical. French. **UDC** 944.
Ind/Abst BHA : Biblio. Hist. Art.

US/0047-7702
BULLETIN OF THE MODERN GREEK STUDIES ASSOCIATION. [Bull. Mod. Greek Stud. Assoc.]. **Main/Corp** Modern Greek Studies Association. **VFOAT** MGSA Bulletin. (1976)-. Periodical. English. sa. $50.00 (individuals); $65.00 (institutions) Comes with Modern Greek Studies Association membership. Modern Greek Studies Association, PO Box 1826, New Haven CT 06508. **Tel** (203)392-5668, FAX (203)3925670. **Continues** Modern Greek Studies Association. Bulletin, 0047-7702.

BE
BULLETIN PERIODIQUE DE LA PRESSE TCHCOSLOVAQUE ... . **Main/Corp** France. Ministere des Affaires Etrangeres. **Added/Corp** France. Minist·ere de la Guerre. Nos. 1-3 (June 1, 1919)-. Bulletin. French. Ministere Affaires Etrangeres, rue des Quatre Bras, D-4000 Liege Belgium. **LC** DB215.A2; F7. **DD** 943.7.

FR/0997-1734
BULLETIN - SOCIETE D'HISTOIRE DE HUNINGUE ET DE SA REGION. (BULLETIN.). (1988)-. Bulletin. French. an. **UDC** 908(443.832). **Continues** Bulletin - Societe d'Histoire et du Musee de la Ville et du Canton de Huningue, 0560-5148.

FR/0753-8413
BULLETIN - SOCIETE D'HISTOIRE DU CANTON DE LAPOUTROIE VAL D'ORBEY. (BULLETIN DE LA SOCIETE D'HISTOIRE DU CANTON DE LAPOUTROIE VAL D'ORBEY.). [Bull. - Soc. hist. canton Lapoutroie Val d'Orbey]. **Added/Corp** Societe d'Histoire du Canton de Lapoutroie Val d'Orbey. (1982)-. Bulletin. French. an.
Ind/Abst BHA : Biblio. Hist. Art.

US/0739-1824
BULLETIN - SOCIETY FOR SPANISH AND PORTUGUESE HISTORICAL STUDIES (U.S.). (BULLETIN - SOCIETY FOR SPANISH AND PORTUGUESE HISTORICAL STUDIES.). **Main/Corp** Society for Spanish and Portuguese Historical Studies. Vol. 4 (Dec. 1977)-. Bulletin. English (Portuguese and Spanish). Three times a year (Jan., July, Oct.). $7.00 (students), $23.00 (institutions), $20.00 (individuals). Central Missouri State University / SSPHS Bulletin, History Department, Daniel A. Crews, Warrensburg MO 64093. **Tel** (816)543-8695. **ED** Benjamin F. Taggie, Daniel A. Crews, & Richard W. Clement. Index Available in first issue of next volume--attached. **Bk Rev**, (Qty: 5). **Ad Acc, Adv Mgr:** Paul Freedman. **Circ:** 500 (ctrl). available on microfilm and microfiche. **Continues** Newsletter (Society for Spanish and Portuguese Historical Studies). **Desc:** News of works in Iberian history, including notes on research, recent publications, archival notes, bibliographical essays, notice of honors and meetings.

CN/0317-4018
BULLETIN - SVETOVY KONGRES SLOVAKOV. **Main/Conf** Svetovy Kongres Slovakov. V. 1- Feb. 1971-. Bulletin. Slovak. qt. Svetovy Kongress Slovakov, 4 King Street West, Toronto Ontario M5H 1B6 Canada. **LC** DB670.7; .S83A.

BE/0772-6961
BULLETIN TRIMESTRIEL DE LA FONDATION AUSCHWITZ. VFOAT Driemaandelijks Tijdschrift van de Auschwitz Stichting; Bulletin de la Fondation Auschwitz; Bulletin van de Stichting Auschwitz. No. 5 (May 1984)-. Bulletin. French (Dutch). Four times a year. 3,000F. Fondation Auschwitz, 65 rue des Tanneurs, B-1000 Brussels Belgium. Index available. **Bk Rev**. ctrl circ. **Continues** Auschwitz.

FR/0037-9204
BULLETIN TRIMESTRIEL DE LA SOCIETE DES ANTIQUAIRES DE PICARDIE. [Bull. trimest. Soc. antiq. Picardie]. **VFOAT** Bulletins de la Societe des Antiquaires de Picardie (1906). (1906)-. Periodical. French. qt. **UDC** 9. **Continues** Bulletins de la Societe des Antiquaires de Picardie (1844), 0755-2157.
Ind/Abst BHA : Biblio. Hist. Art.

BE/0020-2177
BULLETIN TRIMESTRIEL DI L'INSTITUT ARCHEOLOGIQUE DU LUXEMBOURG. See Archaeology.

FR/0397-579X
BULLETINS ET MEMOIRES (SOCIETE ARCHEOLOGIQUE ET HISTORIQUE DE LA CHARENTE : 1983). (BULLETINS ET MEMOIRES - SOCIETE ARCHEOLOGIQUE ET HISTORIQUE DE LA CHARENTE.). Periodical. French. qt. 170.00F France; 185.00F other. 44 rue de Montmoreau, Angouleme France. **Tel** 45-38-45-17. **LC** DC611.C51; B84A. **DD** 944./65/005. Index available. **Bk Rev.**
Ind/Abst BHA : Biblio. Hist. Art.

IT/0394-5006
BULLETTINO DELLA DEPUTAZIONE ABRUZZESE DI STORIA PATRIA. [Bull. Deput. abruzzese stor. patria]. (1953)-. Periodical. Italian. an. **UDC** 945. **Continues** Bullettino della Regia Deputazione Abruzzese di Storia Patria, 0394-4514.
Ind/Abst BHA : Biblio. Hist. Art.

IT
BULLETTINO DELL'ISTITUTO STORICO ITALIANO PER IL MEDIO EVO E ARCHIVIO MURATORIANO. **Main/Corp** Istituto Storico Italiano per il Medio Evo. No. 1 (1886)-.

Italian. ir. Price varies per volume. Istituto Storico Italiano Medio Evo e Archivio Muratoriano, Piazza dell Orologio 4, 00186 Rome Italy. **Tel** 011 39 6 68802075. **LC** DG402; .I6. **DD** 945.005. **Bk Rev.** ctrl circ. ***Continues*** *Archivio Muratoriano.*
Desc: Researches on medieval sources.

IT/0007-5795
BULLETTINO STORICO EMPOLESE.
Added/Corp Associazione Turistica pro Empoli. Vol. 1 (1957)-. Italian.
Ind/Abst BHA : Biblio. Hist. Art.

IT/0007-5809
BULLETTINO STORICO PISTOIESE.
Added/Corp Societa Pistoiese di Storia Patria. Deputazione di Storia Patria per la Toscana, Florence. Sezione di Pistoia. Vol. 1 (1899)-Vol. 60 (1958); New Series Vol. 1 (1959)- Vol. 7, (1965); 3rd Series Vol. 1 (1966)-. Periodical. Italian. an. L30000 Italy; L34000 other. Societa Pistoiese di Storia Patria, Cas Postale 339, 51100 Pistoia Italy. **LC** DG975.P65; A5. cum. index.
Ind/Abst BHA : Biblio. Hist. Art; Numis. Lit.

GW/0007-6201
BURGEN UND SCHLOSSER. [Burgen Schlosser]. **VFOAT** Burgwart. Vol. 1 (1960)-. Periodical. German. sa. DM30.00. Deutsche Burgenvereinigung e V, D 56338 Braubach Germany. **Tel** 011 49 2627 536. **DD** 940. Index available. cum. index. **Ad Acc.** ctrl circ.
Ind/Abst BHA : Biblio. Hist. Art.

GR/1105-0772
BUZANTINA (THESSALONIKE).
(VYZANTINA : EPISTEMONIKON ORGANON KENTROU VYZANTINON EREUNON PHILOSOPHIKES SCHOLES ARISTOTELEIOU PANEPISTEMIOU.). **Added/Corp** Aristoteleio Panepistemio Thessalonikes. Kentro Vyzantinon Ereunon. **VFOAT** Byzantina. (1969)-. English (French, German and Greek, Modern). be. Library Grigoris, Solonos Strasse 71, Athens 106 79 Greece. **Tel** 01-3629684. **LC** DF503; .V97. Index available. **Bk Rev.**
Ind/Abst BHA : Biblio. Hist. Art.

US/0736-2625
BYELORUSSIAN YOUTH. VFOAT Belaruskaia Moladz. Vol. 1, No. 1 (Fall 1972)-. Periodical. Byelorussian (English). qt. $4.00. Byelorussian Youth, PO Box 309, Jamaica NY 11431. **LC** E184.W6; B45. **DD** 973/.0491799/05. **UDC** 973(=82). ***Continues*** *Belaruskaia Moladz.*

US/0742-1141
BYZANTINA KAI METABYZANTINA. See History(General)-History of Asia.

NE/0525-4507
BYZANTINA NEERLANDICA. No. 3 (1972)-. Monographic series. English. ir. Price varies per volume. E. J. Brill, Postbus 9000, 2300 PA Leiden Netherlands. **Tel** 011 31 71 312624, FAX 011 31 71 317532, telex 39296 BRILL NL. ***Formed by the union of*** *Byzantina Neerlandica. Series A: Textus* ***and*** *Byzantina Neerlandica. Series B: Studia.*

AU/0525-3292
BYZANTINA VINDOBONENSIA.
Added/Corp Universitat Wien. Kunsthistorisches Institut. Universitat Wien. Institut fuer Byzantinistik. Osterreichische Akademie der Wissenschaften. Kommission fuer Fruhchristliche und Ostkirchliche Kunst. Universitat Wien. Institut fuer Byzantinistik und Neograzistik. Vol. 1 (1966)-. Monographic series. German (English). ir. Price varies per volume. Oesterreichischen Akademie Wissenschaften, Dr. Ignaz Seipel Platz 2, A-1010 Vienna Austria. **Tel** 011 43 1 51581. **ED** H. Hunger. **LC** UNC. **DD** 949.5. **Ad Acc. Circ:** 600.
Desc: Byzantine art, philology, history, medieval prosopography, sigillography, linguistics and icons are featured.

UK/0307-0131
BYZANTINE AND MODERN GREEK STUDIES. [Byz. mod. Greek stud.]. Vol. 1 (1975)-. Academic Scholarly Publication. English (Greek, Modern). an (Sept.). £40.00 (institutions), £25.00 (individuals) UK; £85.00 (institutions), £55.00 (individuals). University of Birmingham / England, Edgbaston, Center for Byzantine Ottoman, Greek Street, Birmingham B15 2TT England. **Tel** 011 44 21 414 5733, FAX 011 44 21 414 5726. **ED** Dr. J F Haldon. **LC** DF541; .B9. **DD** 949.5/005. **Ad Acc. Pr Rev. Circ:** 400. Documents available from The Genuine Article.
Desc: Scholarly journal which discusses all aspects of its field, including theory and method, in articles, studies and notes.
Ind/Abst Am. Hist. Life (1975-); Arts Humanit. Citation Index (19??-19??) [Full Cov.]; BHA : Biblio. Hist. Art; Curr. Contents Arts Humanit.; Res. Alert [Full Cov.].

US/0095-4608
BYZANTINE STUDIES. [Byz. stud.].
Added/Corp University of Pittsburgh. University Center for International Studies. Temple University. Arizona State University. **VFOAT** Etudes Byzantines. Vol. 1 (1974)-. Periodical. English (French, German and Russian). sa. $20.00 (institutions), $15.00 (individuals). Shepherd College Department of History, c/o Walter K. Hanak, Shepherdstown WV 25443. **LC** DF503; .B86. **DD** 949.5/005. Index available. **Bk Rev. Ad Acc. Pr Rev.** ctrl circ.
Desc: Contains articles concerning the history, literature, and art of the Byzantine Empire.
Ind/Abst BHA : Biblio. Hist. Art.

NE
BYZANTINISCHE FORSCHUNGEN. Vol. 1 (1966)-. Monographic series. German. an. Price varies per volume. J C Gieben Uitgeverij, Nieuwe Herengracht 35, 1011 Rm Amsterdam The Netherlands. **Tel** 011 33 20 6275170. **LC** DF503; .B87.
Ind/Abst BHA : Biblio. Hist. Art; Numis. Lit.

GW/0007-7704
BYZANTINISCHE ZEITSCHRIFT. [Byz. Z.]. Vol. 1 (1892)-. Periodical. German. Twice a year (May & Nov.). DM198.00. BG Teubner GmbH, Postfach 80 10 69, D 75010 Stuttgart Germany. **Tel** 011 49 711 789010, FAX 011 49 711 7890110. **[CCC]**. Documents available from The Genuine Article.
Ind/Abst Arts Humanit. Citation Index [Full Cov.]; BHA : Biblio. Hist. Art; Curr. Contents Arts Humanit.; MLA Int. Bibl. Books Artic. Mod. Lang. Lit.; Numis. Lit.; Res. Alert [Full Cov.].

BU/0204-9864
BYZANTINO BULGARICA.
(BYZANTINOBULGARICA.). [Byz. Bulg.]. **Added/Corp** Institut za Istoriia (Bulgarska Akademiia na Naukite) Sofiiski Universitet "Kliment Okhridski". Filosofsko-Istoricheski Fakulet. (1962)-. Academic Scholarly Publication. French (English and Russian). ir. Bulgarska Akademiia na Naukite, 7 Noemvri 1, Sofia Bulgaria. **LC** DR75; .B95.
Ind/Abst BHA : Biblio. Hist. Art.

BE/0378-2506
BYZANTION (BRUXELLES). See Literature.

SW
CADMOS. ***Title Change.* Added/Corp** European Cultural Centre. Institut Universitaire d'Etudes Europeennes. Vol. 1, No. 1 (1978)-(19??). Monographic series. French. qt. Centre Europeen de la Culture, 120B rue de Lausanne, CH 1202 Geneva 21 Switzerland. **Tel** 011 41 22 732.28.03, FAX 011 41 22 738.40.12, telex (41)(22)289.917. **LC** D1050; .C3. **DD** 940/.08. **Bk Rev. Ad Acc. Circ:** 1,200-5,000. ***Supersedes*** *European Cultural Centre. Bulletin.* ***Continued by*** *Transeuropeennes.*
Ind/Abst Int. Polit. Sci. Abstr.

FR/0292-1979
CAHIER - CENTRE DE RECHERCHES SUR L'ANTIQUITE TARDIVE ET LE HAUT MOYEN-AGE. VFOAT Publication du Centre de Recherches sur l'Antiquite Tardive et le Haut Moyen-Age. (1975)-. Monographic series. French. **UDC** 93.
Ind/Abst BHA : Biblio. Hist. Art.

FR/0575-0385
CAHIERS ALSACIENS D'ARCHEOLOGIE, D'ART ET D'HISTOIRE. See Archaeology.

BE/0007-9626
CAHIERS BRUXELLOIS. (Jan./Mar. 1956)-. Periodical. French. qt. **LC** DH802.A2; C2. **DD** 949.3/3.
Ind/Abst BHA : Biblio. Hist. Art.

FR
CAHIERS CHARLES V. Added/Corp Institut d'Anglais Charles V. **VFOAT** Cahiers Charles-Quint; Cahiers Charles 5. No 1 (Feb. 1979)-. French (English).
Ind/Abst MLA Int. Bibl. Books Artic. Mod. Lang. Lit.

FR/0007-9731
CAHIERS DE CIVILISATION MEDIEVALE. [Cah. civilis. mediev.]. **Added/Corp** Universite de Poitiers. Centre d'Etudes Superieures de Civilisation Medievale. Vol. 1 (Jan./March 1958)-. Periodical. French. Four times a year (Jan., Apr., June, Sept.). 391.71F France; 440.00F others. Regisseur Recettes Publications, CESCM, 24 rue de la Chaine, 86022 Poitiers France. **Tel** 011 33 49 410386. **LC** CB3; .C3. **Bk Rev. Ad Acc.** ctrl circ. Documents available from The Genuine Article.
Ind/Abst Arts Humanit. Citation Index [Full Cov.]; BHA : Biblio. Hist. Art; Br. Archaeol. Bibliogr.; Curr. Contents Arts Humanit.; Educ. Index; MLA Int. Bibl. Books Artic. Mod. Lang. Lit.; Numis. Lit.; Res. Alert [Full Cov.]; Soc. Sci. Cit. Index [Select. Cov.].

FR/0575-0717
CAHIERS DE LA HAUTE-LOIRE LE PUY. (1965)-. Periodical. French. an. **UDC** 944.
Ind/Abst BHA : Biblio. Hist. Art.

FR/0575-0512
CAHIERS D'ETUDES COMTOISES. No. 1 (1960)-. French. ir. Association Franc Comtoise d'Audiophonologie, Faculte de Medecine & de Pharmacie, 25030 Besancon France. **Tel** 011 33 1 81665566, FAX 011 33 1 81665573. **LC** AS161; .B39 subser. **DD** 944.

FR
CAHIERS D'ETUDES MEDIEVALES. No. 1-. French. Librairie Hondre Champion, 7 Quaimalaquais, 75006 Paris France. **LC** CB351; .C2. **DD** 940.1/05.

FR/0221-5047
CAHIERS D'HISTOIRE DE L'INSTITUT DE RECHERCHES MARXISTES.
Added/Corp Institut de Recherches Marxistes (Paris, France). **VFOAT** CH,IRM. No. 1 (3rd Quarter 1980)-. Periodical. French. qt. 244.86F France; 500.00F other. IRM / Institut de Recherches Marxistes, 64 Boulevard Auguste Blanqui, 75013 Paris France. **Tel** 011 33 1 43364534. **ED** R Bourderon. **LC** HX5; .C24. **Bk Rev. Ad Acc. Circ:** 2,000. ***Continues*** *Cahiers d'Histoire de l'Institut Maurice Thorez.*
Desc: Marxist journal of history. Topics include class, and politics in contemporary France.
Ind/Abst Am. Hist. Life (1987-); Int. Bibliogr. Sociol.

FR/0336-5042
CAHIERS DU C.R.E.S.M, LES. Added/Corp Centre de Recherches et d'Etudes sur les Societes Mediterraneennes. **VFOAT** Cahiers du CRESM. Began with 1, (1974)-. Monographic series. French. Price varies per volume. Editions du CNRS, 22 rue Saint Armand, F 75015 Paris France. **Tel** 011 33 1 45075050. **LC** UNC. **Circ:** 1,500.

FR
CAHIERS DU GROUPE DE RECHERCHES SUR L'ARMEE ROMAINE ET LES PROVINCES. Main/Corp Centre National de la Recherche Scientifique (France). Groupe de Recherches sur l'Armee Romaine et les Provinces. **VFOAT** Armee Romaine et Provinces. 1-. Periodical. French. Presses de l'Ecole Normale Superieure, 45 rue d'Ulm, 75230 Paris France. **Tel** 011 33 1 43291225. **(Subscription address:** 48 Boulevard Jourdan, F-75690 Paris Cedex 14 France) **LC** DG89; .F66A. **DD** 937/.005.

●FR
CAHIERS DU MONDE RUSSE. Added/Corp Ecole des Hautes Etudes en Sciences Sociales. Centre d'Etudes sur la Russie, l'Europe Orientale et le Domaine Turc. (1994)-. Periodical. French (English, German and Russian). qt. 391.77F (institution), 264.45F (individual) France; 460.00F (institution), 270.00F France (individual) other. Editions EHESS, 131 Boulevard Saint Michel, 75005 Paris France. **Tel** 011 33 43 544715. **LC** DK1; .C2. ***Continues*** *Cahiers du Monde Russe et Sovietique, 0008-0160.*

FR/0008-0160
CAHIERS DU MONDE RUSSE ET SOVIETIQUE. ***Title Change.*** [Cah. monde russe sov.]. **Added/Corp** Ecole Pratique des Hautes Etudes (France). Section des Sciences Economiques et sociales. Ecole des Hautes ,Studes en Sciences Sociales. Vol. 1 (May 1959)-(1993). Periodical. French (Russian, English and German). qt. Editions EHESS, 131 Boulevard Saint Michel, 75005 Paris France. **Tel** 011 33 43 544715. **(Subscription address:** Centrale des Revues, 11 rue Gossin, 92543 Montrouge Cedex France.) **LC** DK1; .C2. **DD** 947/.005. Index available. cum. index. **Bk Rev. Ad Acc. Circ:** 550 (ctrl). Documents available from The Genuine Article. ***Continued by*** *Cahiers du Monde Russe.*
Desc: All aspects of the Russian past or of the Soviet world: a general view of the history of ideas in Russia. A large space reserved to bibliographical works.
Ind/Abst Am. Hist. Life (1962-); ARTbibliogr. Mod. (1984-); Arts Humanit. Citation Index; BHA : Biblio. Hist. Art; Curr. Contents Arts Humanit.; Int. Polit. Sci. Abstr.; MLA Int. Bibl. Books Artic. Mod. Lang. Lit.; Res. Alert; Soc. Sci. Cit. Index [Select. Cov.].

FR/0008-0217
CAHIERS FRANCAIS, LES. [Cah. fr.]. Began with: No 1 (Jan. 1956). Periodical. French. qt. 168.00F France; 195.00F other. Documentation Francaise, 29 Quai Voltaire, 75344 Paris Cedex 7 France. **Tel** 011 33 1 40157000, FAX 011 33 1 40157230, telex 204 826 DOCFRAN. **LC** DC1; .C32. **DD** 9544/.005. ***Continues*** *Cahiers Francaise d'Information.*
Ind/Abst PAIS Int. Print (1991-); Point Repere (1983-).

FR/0399-1415
CAHIERS LEOPOLD DELISLE. Added/Corp Societe Parisienne d'Histoire et d'Archeologie Normandes. (1947)-. Periodical. French. qt.
Ind/Abst BHA : Biblio. Hist. Art.

FR/0758-6760
CAHIERS LORRAINS, LES. Added/Corp Academie Nationale de Metz. Universite de Metz. Societe d'Histoire et d'Archeologie de la Lorraine. Archives Departementales. **VFOAT** Cahier Lorrain. (1922)-. Periodical. French. qt.
Ind/Abst BHA : Biblio. Hist. Art.

CN/0827-2255
CALABRIA MIA (DOWNSVIEW, ONT.). (CALABRIA MIA.). [Calabr. mia]. **VFOAT** Calabriamia. V. 1, No. 1, (Jan. 1984)-. Periodical. Italian. qt. $8.00. Calabria Mia, 2708 Jane Street Canada. **DD** 945/.78/005.

IT
CALABRIA SCONOSCIUTA. Vol. 1- (N. 1-); Jan./Mar. 1978-. Periodical. Italian. qt. L12000. Frama Sud, c/c Postale N 21, 891000 Reggio, Calabria Italy. **LC** DG975.C13; C34. **DD** 945/.78/005.

US/0068-5798
CALIFORNIA SLAVIC STUDIES. ***Ceased.*** [Calif. slav. stud.]. V. 1-12; 1960-84. English. ir. University of California Press, 2120 Berkeley Way, Berkeley CA 94720. **Tel** (510)642-4191, (510)642-3907, FAX (510)642-9917. **ED** William McCluny. **LC** DK4; .C33. **DD** 947/.005. ***Supersedes*** *University of California Publications. Slavic Studies.*
Desc: Books touch on all aspects of Slavic life.
Ind/Abst MLA Int. Bibl. Books Artic. Mod. Lang. Lit.

UK
CAMBRIDGE HISTORY OF MODERN FRANCE, THE. (1983)-. Monographic series. English. ir. Price varies per volume. Cambridge University Press, The Edinburgh Building, Shaftesbury Road, Cambridge CB2 2RU United Kingdom. **Tel** 011 44 223 312393, FAX 011 44 223 325959. **(Subscription address:** Cambridge University Press / North America, 110 Midland Avenue, Port Chester NY 10573.**)**

UK
CAMBRIDGE STUDIES IN ANGLO-SAXON ENGLAND. VFOAT Cambridge Studies in Anglo Saxton England. (1990)-. Monographic series. English. Price varies per volume. Cambridge University Press, The Edinburgh Building, Shaftesbury Road, Cambridge CB2 2RU United Kingdom. **Tel** 011 44 223 312393, FAX 011 44 223 325959.

UK/0305-4756
CAMDEN HISTORY REVIEW. [Camden hist. rev.]. **Added/Corp** Camden History Society. No. 1 (1973)-. English.
Ind/Abst Archit. Period. Index (No. 5, 1977-).

IT
CAMPANIA SACRA / PONTIFICIA FACOLTA TEOLOGICA DELL'ITALIA MERIDIONALE, SEZIONE DI CAPODIMONTE. Added/Corp Pontificia Facolta Teologica dell'Italia Meridionale. Sezione "S. Tommaso d'Aquino.". Vol. 1 (1970)-. Italian. sa. L60000 (Italy); L65000 (other). Edizioni Dehoniane, Via Casale S Pio V20, 00165 Rome Italy. **Tel** 39 6 6624996, or 6638869. **LC** WMLC L 83/9590.

US/0090-8290
CANADIAN-AMERICAN SLAVIC STUDIES. (CANADIAN-AMERICAN SLAVIC STUDIES. REVUE CANADIENNE-AMERICAINE D'ETUDES SLAVES.). [Can.-Am. Slav. stud.]. **Added/Corp** University of Pittsburgh. University Center for International Studies. **VFOAT** Revue Canadienne-Americaine d'Etudes Slaves. Vol. 6 (Spring 1972)-. Periodical. English (French, German and Russian). Four times a year. $23.00 (individuals), $43.00 (institutions). CMTS USC / Charles Schlacks Jr. Publisher, 734 West Adams Boulevard, Kerckhoff Hall, Los Angeles CA 90089. **Tel** (203)743-6510. **ED** Charles Schlacks Jr. **LC** DK1; .C23. **DD** 914.7/03/05. Index available. **Bk Rev. Ad Acc. Circ:** 700 (ctrl). available on microfilm and microfiche from University Microfilms International (UMI). ***Continues*** *Canadian Slavic Studies, 0008-4999.*
Desc: Studies on Russia and Eastern Europe in the humanities and social sciences.
Ind/Abst Am. Hist. Life (1967-); Am. Bibliogr. Slavic East Europ. Stud. (19??-); Arts Humanit. Citation Index (19??-19??) [Full Cov.]; BHA : Biblio. Hist. Art; MLA Int. Bibl. Books Artic. Mod. Lang. Lit.

CN/0225-0500
CANADIAN JOURNAL OF NETHERLANDIC STUDIES. [Can. j. Neth. stud.]. **Added/Corp** Association for the Advancement of Netherlandic Studies. **VFOAT** Revue Canadienne d'Etudes Neerlandaises. Vol. 1 (Fall 1979)-. Periodical. English (summaries and/or abstracts in French). sa. 15.00Can$ (comes with membership). University of Windsor Department of French, Windsor Ontario N9B 3P4 Canada. **Tel** (604)943-4793. **ED** Basil D. Kingstone. **DD** 949.2/005. **Bk Rev. Ad Acc. Circ:** 350 (ctrl).
Desc: Promotes the study of Netherlands (Dutch and Flemish) language, literature, arts, history, etc.
Ind/Abst Am. Hist. Life (1984-); BHA : Biblio. Hist. Art; MLA Int. Bibl. Books Artic. Mod. Lang. Lit.

CN/0703-1599
CANADIANA GERMANICA. No. 13/14- Nov. 1977-. German (English). qt. $2.00, Free to qualified subscribers. German-Canadian Historical Association, PO Box 406 Station K, Toronto Ontario M4P 2G7 Canada. **DD** 971/.004/31. ctrl circ. ***Continues*** *Mitteilungsblatt der Historical Society of Mecklenburg Upper Canada, 0703-1424.*

AU/0008-6606
CARINTHIA I. (CARINTHIA I. ZEITSCHRIFT FUER GESCHICHTLICHE LANDESKUNDE VON KARTEN.). [Carinthia I]. Vol. 81 (1891)-. Periodical. German. qt. Museumgasse 2, 9020 Klagenfurt Austria. ***Continues in part*** *Carinthia. Zeitschrift fur Vaterlanskunde, Belehrung und Unterhaltung.*
Ind/Abst Am. Hist. Life (1963-); BHA : Biblio. Hist. Art.

UK/0142-1867
CARMARTHENSHIRE ANTIQUARY, THE. Added/Corp Carmarthenshire Antiquarian Society. Vol. 6 (1970)-. Periodical. English (Welsh). an. ***Continues*** *Carmarthen Antiquary.*
Ind/Abst BHA : Biblio. Hist. Art.

RM
CARPICA. Main/Corp Muzeul Judetean de Istorie si Arta Bacau. (1968)-. Romanian. Muzeul de Istorie Siarta Bacau Str, Karl Marx NR 23, Bacau Romania. **LC** DR201; .M86a.
Ind/Abst BHA : Biblio. Hist. Art; Numis. Lit.

IT
CARROBBIO, IL. V. 1- 1975-. Periodical. Italian. an. L16000. Edizoni L Parma, Via Collamarini 23, 40138 Bologna Italy. **LC** DG975.B57; C37. **DD** 945/.41.
Ind/Abst Art Archaeol. Tech. Abstr.; BHA : Biblio. Hist. Art.

UK/0961-4532
CARRYING STREAM, THE. [Carr. stream]. (1991)-. Newsletter. English. ir. Free. University Edinburgh School Scottish Studies, 27 George Square, Edinburgh EH14 1HD Scotland. **Tel** 011 44 31 6503060. **ED** Donald MacQueen. **DD** 378.411. **Pr Rev. Circ:** 1,500 (ctrl).
Ind/Abst Museum Abstr.

XR/0323-052X
CASOPIS MATICE MORAVSKE (1968). (CASOPIS MATICE MORAVSKE.). [Cas. Matice morav.]. **VFOAT** CMM; C.M.M. Vol. 87, Vol. 1-2-. Periodical. Czech (summaries and/or abstracts in English and Russian). qt. **(Subscription address:** Artia Pegas Press Ltd., Palac Metro Narodni Trida 25, 11210 Prague 1 Czech Republic.**) LC** DB541; .M3. ***Continues*** *Sbornik Matice Moravske.*
Ind/Abst Am. Hist. Life (1958-).

IE/0332-4117
CATHAIR NO MART. (CATHAIR NA MART : JOURNAL OF THE WESTPORT HISTORICAL SOCIETY.). [Cathair Mart]. **Added/Corp** Westport Historical Society (Westport, Mayo). (1981)-. Periodical. English. an (Dec.). IL10.00 Ireland; $25.00 other. Westport Historical Society of Ireland, c/o Jarlath Duffy, Carrowholly, Westport Mayo Republic of Ireland. **Tel** 353 098-26492. **ED** Sheila Mulloy. Index available. cum. index. **Ad Acc. Circ:** 1,000 (ctrl).
Desc: History of Ireland with particular emphasis on history of Mayo.

AU/0376-7795
CDPRESS. (CD PRESS.). **VAT** Corps Diplomatique Press. (Sept. 1971)-. Periodical. Multiple languages (English, French and German). mo. 400.00. CD Press Nachrichtenmagazin, A-7332 Kobersdork Austria. **LC** DB1; .C23. **DD** 943.6/05/05.

XV/0576-9760
CELJSKI ZBORNIK. (1951)-. Periodical. Slovenian (summaries and/or abstracts in English and German). be. **LC** WMLC L 83/9857. **DD** #B 949.7.
Ind/Abst BHA : Biblio. Hist. Art.

US/0008-9389
CENTRAL EUROPEAN HISTORY. [Cent. Eur. hist.]. **Added/Corp** Emory University. American Historical Association. Conference Group for Central European History. Vol. 1 (March 1968)-. Periodical. English. Four times a year (Mar., June, Sept., Dec.). $58.00 (institutions); $36.00 (individual) $19.95 (Back Issue Volume price on request). Humanities Press, 165 1st Avenue, Atlantic Highlands NJ 07716. **Tel** (908)872-1441, (800)221-3845, FAX (908)872-0717, telex 752233. **ED** Kenneth Barkin, University of California, Riverside CA. **LC** D901; .C34. **DD** 943/.0005; 940. Index available. **Bk Rev. Ad Acc, Adv Mgr:** J. Camlin, **Tel** (908)872-1441. **Pr Rev. Circ:** 1,200. Documents available from The Genuine Article.
Desc: Covers the whole area historically of the Holy Roman Empire, contains a selection of articles and book reviews, with special attention being paid to issues that are the focus of contemporary debate in Germany among German scholars.
Ind/Abst Am. Hist. Life (1968-); Am. Bibliogr. Slavic East Europ. Stud. (19??-19??); Arts Humanit. Citation Index [Full Cov.]; BHA : Biblio. Hist. Art; Book Rev. Index (1968-); Curr. Contents Arts Humanit.; Curr. Contents Soc. Behav. Sci. (1968-); Expand. Acad. Index (1989-); Humanit. Index; Int. Bibliogr. Zeitschriftenliteratur Allen Gebieten Wissens; Res. Alert [Full Cov.]; Soc. Sci. Cit. Index.

FR/0398-6772
CENTRE DE RECHERCHES SUR LA RENAISSANCE (SERIES). (CENTRE DE RECHERCHES SUR LA RENAISSANCE.). **Added/Corp** Centre de Recherches sur la Renaisance. (1976)-. Monographic series. French. Price varies per volume. Jean Touzot, 38 rue Saint-Sulpice, 75278 Paris Cedex 06 France. **Tel** 011 33 1 43260388. **LC** UNC.

RM
CERCETARI ISTORICE / MUZEUL DE ISTORIE A MOLDOVEI. Added/Corp Muzeul de Istorie a Moldovei. **VFOAT** Das Recherches Historiques. (1970)-. Periodical. Romanian (summaries and/or abstracts in French). an. **LC** DR201; .C48.
Ind/Abst Numis. Lit.

UK/0069-2263
CEREDIGION. V. 1 (1950)-. Periodical. English (Welsh). an. £5.00. Ceredigion Antiquarian Society, c/o The Sec Tal-Y-Werydd Aberarth, Aberaeron Wales United Kingdom. **Tel** 570449. **ED** Geraint H Jenkins. Index available. **Bk Rev. Circ:** 800. ***Continues*** *Cardiganshire Antiquarian Society. Transactions.*
Desc: History, folklore and archaeology of Ceredigion (formerly Cardiganshire) Wales, United Kingdom.
Ind/Abst BHA : Biblio. Hist. Art; Br. Archaeol. Bibliogr.; Br. Humanit. Index.

CN/0820-7488
CESKOSLOVENSKA CESTA ... . [Cesk. cesta]. V. 1, No. 1 (April 1981). Periodical. Czech. ir. $18.00. Ceskoslovenska Cesta, PO Box 13250, Kanata Ontario K2K 1X4 Canada. **DD** 943.7/005.

XR/0009-0794
CESKY LID. [Cesky lid]. Vol. 1 (1892)-. Periodical. Czech (summaries and/or abstracts in German, English and French). qt. DM152.00. Academia, Publishing House of the Czechoslovak Academy of Sciences, Czech AC SCI, Vodickova 40, PO Box 896, 112 29 Prague 1, Czech Republic. **Tel** 011 42 2 245117. **(Subscription address:** Kubon & Sagner, PO Box 34 01 08, 8000 Munchen 34 Germany**) LC** DB191; .C45. **Bk Rev. Circ:** 1,000.
Desc: Devoted to European ethnology and social anthropology, especially of the Czech people and Czech minorities in foreign countries; every volume contains a Czech ethnological bibliography.
Ind/Abst Am. Hist. Life (1969-1973); Anthropol. Index; BHA : Biblio. Hist. Art; MLA Int. Bibl. Books Artic. Mod. Lang. Lit.; Numis. Lit.

US/0009-5931
CHRONICA (DAVIS). See Literature.

CC/1002-6800
CHUNG-KUO PIEN CHIANG SHIH TI YEN CHIU. Added/Corp Chung-Kuo Pien Chiang Shih Ti Yen Chiu Chung Hsin. **VFOAT** Zhongguo Bianjiang Shidi Yanjiu; China's Borderland History and Geography Studies. (1991)-. Periodical. Chinese. qt. **LC** IN PROCESS.
Ind/Abst Am. Hist. Life (1991-).

GW
CIS HILINCIWEG. Brochure 1-. German (German). Geschichtsvehein Heiligenhaus, 5628 Heiligenhaus Rathaus, Heilihenhaus Germany. **LC** DD901.H632; C58. **DD** 943/.55.

BE/0774-4919
CITEAUX, COMMENTARII CISTERCIENSES. See Religion and Theology-Catholicism.

IT/0578-4034
CIVILTA VENEZIANA. FONTI E TESTI. SERIE TERZA : LETTERE, MUSICA E TEATRO. V. 1- 1962-. Periodical. Italian. ir. Cosella Postale, PO Box 66, 50100 Firenze Italy. **Tel** FAX 39/55/6530214.
Desc: A series of books dealing with the history of Venice in the broadest sense.

IT
CIVILTA DELLA CAMPANIA. Yearly Vol. 1- Dec. 1974-. Periodical. Italian. bm. L5.000. Salerno, Ente Provinciale Per Il Turismo di Salerno, Via Velia 15, 84.100, CCPN 12/24770, Salerno Italy. **LC** DG975.C173; C58.

IT/0391-7479
CIVILTA MANTOVANA. ***Ceased.*** [Civ. mantov.]. (1960)-(1990). Periodical. Italian. Publi Paolini, Strada Circonvallazione Sud, 46100 Mantova Italy. **LC** DG975.M27; C58.
Ind/Abst BHA : Biblio. Hist. Art.

IT
CIVILTA PADANA. (1988)-. Periodical. Italian. ir. L35000. Libreria Esente, via Farini 73, 41100 Modena Italy. **Tel** 011 39 59 214031. **LC** DG975.P7; C58. **DD** 937/.2/005.

IT/0069-438X
CIVILTA VENEZIANA. STUDI. 1- 1954-. Periodical. Italian. ir. Casa Editrice Leo S. Olschki, Viuzzo del Pozzetto, Casella Postale 66, 50126 Florence Italy. **Tel** 011 39 55 6530684, FAX 011 39 55 6530214.

BE
CLAIRLIEU : TIJDSCHRIFT GEWIJD ANN DE GESCHIEDENIS DER KRUISHEREN. (1943)-. Periodical. Dutch (English, French and German). an (Published in October). Fl24.00 Netherlands; $10.00 North America; DM25.00 other.

History(General) —History of Europe

Clairlieu, Daam Fockemalaan 10, 3818 KG Amersfoort Netherlands. **Tel** 033-631424. Index available. cum. index. **Bk Rev. Ad Acc.**
Desc: History of the Order of the Holy Cross (Crosier Fathers).
Ind/Abst Am. Hist. Life (1955-1979).

BN
CLANCI I GRADA ZA KULTURNU ISTORIJU ISTOCNE BOSNE. Added/Corp Muzej Istocne Bosne u Tuzli. Tuzla, Yugoslavia (City) Zavicajni Muzej. **VFOAT** Artikel und Materialen zur Kulturgeschichte Ostbosniens. (1957)-. Serbo-Croatian (Roman) (English and French; summaries and/or abstracts in German).
Ind/Abst BHA : Biblio. Hist. Art.

DK
CLASSICA ET MEDIAEVALIA. See Classical Studies.

IE
CLOGHER RECORD. Added/Corp Cloger Diocesan Historical Society (Monaghan, County) Clogher Historical Society (Monaghan, County). Vol. 1, No. 1 (1953)-. Periodical. English. an. Comes with membership to Clogher Historical Society. Clogher Historical Society, 15 Glenview Heights, Monaghan Co Monaghan Ireland. **Tel** 011 353 81365. **LC** DA995.C56; C54. **DD** 941.6/4/005.

SP
COLECCIO HISTORICA. (COLECCION HISTORICA.). **Main/Corp** Universidad de Navarra. Facultad de Filosofia y Letras. **Added/Corp** Universidad de Navarra. (1963)-. Monographic series. Spanish. ir. Price varies per volume. Ediciones Universidad de Navarra, Plaza de Los Sauces 1Y2, Baranain-Pamplona Spain. **Tel** (48)25 68 50, telex 37917 UNAV-E.
(Subscription address: Plaza de los Sauces 1 y 2, Baranain Pamplona Spain) **Pr Rev.**
Desc: This monographic series of books deals with key events of Spanish and Latin American history with special emphasis on the eighteenth century.

IT/0588-0750
COLLANA DI STUDI CICERONIANI. 1-. Monographic series. Italian (German and English). Price varies per volume. Centro di Studi Ciceroniani Editori, Plaza dei Cavalteri di Malta, Rome Italy.

IT/0418-727X
COLLANA STORICA. Main/Corp Deputazione di Storia Patria per la Calabria. Vol. 1 (1959)-. Periodical. Italian. **DD** 945. cum. index.

IE/0530-7058
COLLECTANEA HIBERNICA. No. 1 (1958)-. English. an. C O Dun Mhuire, Seafield Road, Killiney Co Dublin Ireland.
Ind/Abst Bibliogr. Mission.

BE
COLLECTANEA MARITIMA. See Earth Sciences-Oceanography.

FR/0588-1773
COLLECTION DE DOCUMENTS INEDITS SUR L'HISTOIRE DE FRANCE. SERIE IN-8. Added/Corp France. Bibliotheque Nationale France. Comite de Travaux Historiques et Scientifiques. Section de Philologie et d'Histoire, Jusqu'a 1610. (1???)-. Monographic series. French. ir. Price varies per volume. Bibliotheque Nationale, 58 rue de Richelieu, 75084 Paris Cedex 02 France. **Tel** 011 33 1 47038385. **(Subscription address:** CID, 131 Boulevard Saint Michel, 75005 Paris France.) **LC** DC3; .C64. **DD** 944.

FR
COLLECTION DU BICENTENAIRE DE LA REVOLUTION FRANCAISE. *Ceased.* (1983)-(19??). Monographic series. French. Les Belles Lettres, 95 Boulevard Raspail, 75006 Paris France. **Tel** (1)45.48.70.55, FAX (1)45.44.92.88, telex 200577 F. **LC** AS161; .B39 subser. **DD** 084/.1 S; 944.04.

FR
COLLECTION LETTRES MEDIEVALES. VFOAT Lettres Medievales. Vol. 1- 1984-. Monographic series. French. Price varies per volume. A G Nizet, 3 Bix Place de la Sorbonne, 75 Paris VE France.

UK
COLLECTIONS FOR A HISTORY OF STAFFORDSHIRE. Main/Corp Staffordshire Record Society. Vol. 1-18, (1880-1897); New Series. Vol. 1-12, (1898-1909); 3rd Series, (1910-1950/51); 4th Series, Vol. 1 (1956)-. English. ir. £5.00. Staffordshire Record Society, Eastgate St, Wm Salt Library, Stafford STFS ST16 2LZ England. **Tel** 011 44 785 52276. **ED** M. W. Greenslade. cum. index. **Bk Rev. Ad Acc.** available on microfiche from Chadwyck-Healey, Inc.
Desc: Documents and articles relating to the history of Staffordshire.

IT
COLUMBUS 92. VFOAT Columbus Novantadue. Vol. 1, No. 1 (Jan. 1985)-. Periodical. Italian (summaries and/or abstracts in English and Spanish). mo. L50.000. Columbus 92, Via Varese 2, 16122 Genova Italy. **ED** Mario Bottaro.

FR
COMPTES RENDUS, PROCES-VERBAUX, MEMOIRES - MEMOIRES - ASSOCIATION BRETONNE ET UNION REGIONALISTE BRETONNE. Main/Corp Association Bretonne, Saint-Brieuc. **VFOAT** Bulletin Agricole et Archeologique de l'Association Bretonne; Bulletin de l'Association Bretonne. French. Association Bretonne, CCP 179-84 Rennes, Saint-Bretonne France. **LC** DC611.B841; A63A. **DD** 944/.1/005.

PO
CONIMBRIGA. Added/Corp Universidade de Coimbra. Instituto de Arqueologia. Vol. 1, (1959)-. Portuguese (summaries and/or abstracts in English). an. $7.00. Casa do Castelo, rua da Sofia 47-49, Coimbra 3000 Portugal. **Tel** 011 351 39 24686. **DD** 913.

RM
CONSPECT, ROMANIA IN 30 DE ZILE. Added/Corp Fundatia Culturala Romana. **VFOAT** Conspect, Romania in Treizeci de Zile; Revista Conspect. No. 1 (1991)-. Periodical. Romanian. mo. Revista Conspect, Aleea Alexandru, Nr. 38 Sect. 1, Bucuresti Romania. **(Subscription address:** Kubon & Sagner, ABT Zeitschriftenimport, D 80328 Munich Germany.**) LC** DR201; .C64.

NO
CONTEMPORARY APPROACHES TO IBSEN : PROCEEDINGS OF THE INTERNATIONAL IBSEN SEMINARY. See Literary and Political Reviews.

UK/0957-5960
CONTEMPORARY BRITAIN : AN ANNUAL REVIEW. Added/Corp Institute of Contemporary British History. (1990)-. English. an. $74.95. Basil Blackwell Publishers Ltd, 108 Cowley Road, Oxford 0X4 1JF England. **Tel** 011 44 865 791100, FAX 011 44 865 791347, telex 837022 OXBOOK G.
(Subscription address: Blackwell Publishers / UK, Marston Book Services, PO Box 87, Oxford OX2 0DT England.) **ED** Peter Catterall. **LC** IN PROCESS; DA20; .C65.

●UK/0960-7773
CONTEMPORARY EUROPEAN HISTORY. Vol. 1, Pt. 1 (Mar. 1992)-. Academic Scholarly Publication. English. Three times a year. $75.00 US, Canada & Mexico; £47.00 other. Cambridge University Press, The Edinburgh Building, Shaftesbury Road, Cambridge CB2 2RU United Kingdom. **Tel** 011 44 223 312393, FAX 011 44 223 325959. **(Subscription address:** Cambridge University Press / North America, 110 Midland Avenue, Port Chester NY 10573.) **ED** Kathleen Burk and Dick Geary. **LC** D1050; .C65. **DD** 940/.05. **Bk Rev**.
Desc: Focuses on twentieth century European history since 1918 encompassing continental Western and Eastern Europe as well as the United Kingdom and Ireland. A comparative approach to political, diplomatic, social and economic history will be encouraged with a special emphasis on the continuity of pre- and post-war Europe.

US/0147-9156
CONTEMPORARY FRENCH CIVILIZATION. [Contemp. Fr. civiliz.]. **VFOAT** CFC. Contemporary French Civilization. Vol. 1 (Fall 1976)-. Periodical. English (French). sa. $35.00 (institutions), $18.00 (individuals). Montana State University / Department of Modern Languages, c/o Douglas Daniels, Bozeman MT 59171. **Tel** (406)994-6447. **ED** Bernard Quinn. **LC** DC33.9; .C66. **DD** 905. Index available in last issue of volume/-attached. **Bk Rev. Ad Acc. Pr Rev. Circ:** 800. available on microfiche.
Desc: Publishes articles, essays and notes, interviews with notable personalities on subjects relating to the French-speaking world, reviews and bibliographies.
Ind/Abst Am. Hist. Life (1979-); Curr. Index J. Educ.; Int. Polit. Sci. Abstr.; Romant. Move.

UK/0950-9224
CONTEMPORARY RECORD : THE JOURNAL OF THE INSTITUTE OF CONTEMPORARY BRITISH HISTORY. Added/Corp Institute of Contemporary British History. Vol. 1, No. 1 (Spring 1987)-. Periodical. English. Three times a year. $95.00. Frank Cass & Company Ltd, Newbury House, 890-900 Eastern Avenue, Newbury Park, Ilford, Essex IG2 7HH United Kingdom. **Tel** 011 44 81 599 8866, FAX 011 44 81 599 0984, telex 897719. **ED** Anthony Seldon and Peter Catterall. **LC** IN PROCESS. **Bk Rev. Ad Acc, Adv Mgr:** Anne Kidson. **Circ:** 3,000.
Ind/Abst Am. Hist. Life (1987-); Br. Humanit. Index.

SP/0211-2078
CORDUBA / MUSEO ARQUEOLOGICO PROVINCIAL. [Corduba]. V. 1, No. 1- = No. 1-. Periodical. Spanish (Spanish). Servicio De Publicaciones De La Excma, Plaza De Jeronimo Paez 7 Cordoba, Spain. **LC** DP302.C76; C67. **DD** 946/.84/005.

GW/0589-8048
CORPUS FONTIUM HISTORIAE BYZANTINAE. Added/Corp Association Internationale des Etudes Byzantines. (1967)-. Monographic series. English. ir. Price varies per volume. Walter de Gruyter Inc., PO Box 303421, D 10728 Berlin Germany. **Tel** 011 49 30 260050, FAX 011 49 30 26005251.

UK
CORPUS VASORUM ANTIQUORUM. GREAT BRITAIN. Issue 1-. Monographic series. English. ir. Price varies per volume. British Academy, 20-21 Cornwall Terrace, London NW1 4QP United Kingdom. **Tel** 011 44 71 487 5966, FAX 011 44 71 224 3807, telex 263194.

FR
COTE DE L'ATLANTIQUE. Main/Corp Pneu Michelin (Firm). French. Michelin Guides and Maps, PO Box 3305, Spartanburg SC 29304. **Tel** (803)599-0850. **LC** DC611.A863; M36A. **DD** 914.4. *Continues Cote de l'Atlantique de la Loire Aux Pyrenees.*

MG
COURRIER DIPLOMATIQUE DE L'OCEAN INDIEN. No. 1- Nov. 1975/Jan. 1976-. French. Societe de Presse de Madagascar, Banque Commerciale de Madagascar, Compte No 420-1352, Tannanarive Madagascar. **LC** DT468; .C68.

SP/0590-1626
CUADERNOS DE ARAGON. (1966)-. Periodical. Spanish. **LC** WMLC L 83/98.
Ind/Abst Am. Hist. Life (1987-).

SP
CUADERNOS DE ESTUDIOS BORJANOS. 1- Jan. 1978-. Periodical. Spanish. sa (usually 2 numbers in one annual volume). 1200ptas Spain; 1600ptas US; 1600ptas other. Centro de Estudios Borjanos, Institucion Fernando el Catolico, Plaza del Mercado, Borja Zaragoza Spain. **Tel** 976-86 74 02. **LC** DP402.B65; C8. **DD** 946/.553/005. Index available. cum. index. **Pr Rev. Circ:** 1,000.
Desc: Miscellaneous works concerning historical and humanistic aspects of Borja and its region.

SP/0211-7649
CUADERNOS DE ESTUDIOS CASPOLINOS / GRUPO CULTURAL CASPOLINO, INSTITUCION FERNANDO EL CATOLICO. Added/Corp Grupo Cultural Caspolino. (1979)-. Periodical. Spanish. Grupo Cultural Caspino, Apartado de Correos 2, Caspe Spain. **LC** DP402.C428; C8. **DD** 946/.553.

SP/0210-847X
CUADERNOS DE ESTUDIOS GALLEGOS. *Ceased.* [Cuad. estud. gallegos]. No. 1 (1944)-Vol. 40, No. 105 (1992). Periodical. Spanish. Three times a year. Consejo Superior Investigacion Cientificas (CSIC), Vitruvio 8, 28006 Madrid Spain. **Tel** 011 34 1 5612833, FAX 011 34 1 4113077, telex 42182. **LC** DP302.G11; C3.
Ind/Abst Am. Hist. Life (1957,1967); BHA : Biblio. Hist. Art; MLA Int. Bibl. Books Artic. Mod. Lang. Lit.

AG/0325-1195
CUADERNOS DE HISTORIA DE ESPANA. (CUADERNOS DE HISTORIA DE ESPANA / INSTITUTO DE HISTORIA DE LA CULTURA ESPANOLA, MEDIOEVAL Y MODERNA.). [Cuad. hist. Esp.]. **Added/Corp** Universidad de Buenos Aires. Instituto de Historia de la Cultura Espanola, Medioeval y Moderna. Universidad de Buenos Aires. Instituto de Investigaciones Historicas. Universidad de Buenos Aires. Instituto de Investigaciones Historicas. Seccion Espanola. Universidad de Buenos Aires. Instituto de Historia de Espana. (1944)-. Periodical. Spanish. ir. Universidad de Buenos Aires / Argentina, Facultdad Filosofia Letras Puan 470, Buenos Aires 1406, Argentina. **Tel** 011 54 1 4320537, 011 54 1 4328696. **LC** DP1; .C8.
Ind/Abst Am. Hist. Life (1954-1968, 1980-); BHA : Biblio. Hist. Art.

SP/0210-6272
CUADERNOS DE INVESTIGACION HISTORICA. [Cuad. invest. hist.]. **Added/Corp** Seminario Cisneros. (1977)-. Periodical. Spanish. Three times a year. 795ptas Spain; 1000ptas other. Fund Univ Esp Sem Cisneros, Alcala 93, 28009 Madrid Spain. **Tel** 011 34 1 4311193. **(Subscription address:** Pedro Alcantarilla, Conchas 1, 28009 Madrid Spain.) **LC** DP1; .C82.
Ind/Abst Am. Hist. Life (1977-).

FR
CULTURE KHMERE. See Anthropology.

NE/0920-1327
CULTUREN. 1st Vol. Periodical. Dutch. bm. Fl65.00. Openbaar Kunstbezit, Vondelstraat 120, Postbus 5555, 1007 AN Amsterdam the Netherlands. **Tel** 020-854511. **LC** GN1; .C79. *Continues Verre Naasten Naderbij.*

History(General) —History of Europe

HU/0133-6088
CUMANIA. Added/Corp Bacs-Kiskun, Hungary. Bacs-Kiskun Megyei Muzeumok Igazgatosaga. (1972)-. Multiple languages (English, German and Hungarian; summaries and/or abstracts in French and Russian). **LC** DB975 .B16; C85.
 Ind/Abst BHA : Biblio. Hist. Art.

TU
CURRENT TURKISH THOUGHT.
Monographic series. English. qt. Price varies per volume. Redhouse Press Post, Box 142, Istanbul Turkey. **LC** DR401; .C87. **DD** 946.1/05/05.

US/1056-005X
CZECHOSLOVAK AND CENTRAL EUROPEAN JOURNAL. [Czech. cent. Eur. j.]. Added/Corp Czechoslovak Society of Arts and Sciences. **VFOAT** CCEJ. Vol. 8, No. 1/2 (Summer/Winter 1989)-. Periodical. English. Twice a year (varies). $23.00. Czechoslovak Society of Arts and Science, 2 Fordham Hill Oval-9G, New York NY 10468. **Tel** (212)365-5094. **ED** Paul Trensky. **LC** D1; .K67. **DD** 943/.0005. cum. index. **Bk Rev**, (Qty: 10). **Pr Rev. Circ:** 500 (ctrl). *Continues Kosmas, 0731-5430.*
 Desc: Covers social sciences and humanities. Czechoslovakia is usually the main subject.
 Ind/Abst Am. Hist. Life (1982-).

GW/0257-9472
DACHAUER HEFTE. [Dachauer Hefte]. Added/Corp International Dachau Committee. Vol. 1, No. 1 (Dec. 1985)-. Periodical. German. an. DM21.60. Dachauer Hefte, Alte Roemerstrasse 75, D 85221 Dachau Germany. **Tel** 011 49 8131 1741. **ED** Wolfgang Benz And Barbara Distel. **LC** D805.G3; D23. **DD** 940.53/15/03924. **Ad Acc. Circ:** 5,000. available on CD-ROM; available on an online database; available in microform.
 Desc: History of Nazi Concentration Camps; studies, reports and documents.

GW/0934-361X
DACHAUER HEFTER. (DACHAU REVIEW.). Vol. 1, (1988)-. Periodical. English. an (Nov.). DM20.56. Dachauer Hefte, Alte Roemerstrasse 75, D 85221 Dachau Germany. **Tel** 011 49 8131 1741. **ED** Wolfgang Benz and Barbara Distel. **Bk Rev. Ad Acc. Circ:** 5,000 (ctrl).

RM/0070-251X
DACIA. See Archaeology.

GW
DACOROMANIA. (1973)-. Multiple languages (English, French, German and Italian). ir. Verlag Herder Freiburg, Postfach 79080, Frieburg, Germany. **Tel** (0761)27-17-0, FAX (0761)27 17-520, telex 761489. **ED** Dr. P. Miron. **LC** DR212; .D33.

DK/0011-6084
DANISH JOURNAL. [Dan. j.]. V. 65- 1969-. Periodical. English. kr24.00. J H Schultz Boghandel, 19 Montergade, DK-1057 K Copenhagen Denmark. **LC** HF211; .A3. **DD** 948.9/05. *Continues Danish Foreign Office Journal.*
 Ind/Abst ASTIS Curr. Aware. Bull. (1978-); ASTIS Bibliogr. (1978-).

DK/0106-4622
DANSK UDSYN. [Dan. udsyn]. Added/Corp Askov Hoejskole. Askov Hoejskole. Askov Laerlinge. (1920)-. Periodical. Danish. Four times a year. kr190.00. Askov Hoejskole, Dansk Udsyns Kontor,, Askov, DK6600 Vejen, Denmark. **Bk Rev. Ad Acc.**
 Ind/Abst MLA Int. Bibl. Books Artic. Mod. Lang. Lit.

GW/0418-3886
DARSTELLUNGEN UND QUELLEN ZUR GESCHICHTE DER DEUTSCHEN EINHEITSBEWEGUNG IM NEUNZEHNTEN UND ZWANZIGSTEN JAHRHUNDERT. Added/Corp Gesellschaft fuer Burschenschaftliche Geschichtsforschung. Vol. 1 (1957)-. Monographic series. German. ir. Price varies per volume. Universitatsverlag Carl Winter, POB 106140, D 69051 Heidelberg Germany. **Tel** 011 49 6221 770260. **DD** 943. **Circ:** 800. *Supersedes Quellen und Darstellungen zur Geschichte der Burschenschaft und der Deutschen Einheitsbewegung.*

US
DAVID CHANDLER'S AGE OF NAPOLEON. *Ceased.* **VFOAT** Age of Napoleon. Vol. 1, No. 1 (Oct. 1987)-?. Periodical. English. bm. Empire Press, 602 South King Street, Suite 300, Leesburg VA 22075. **Tel** (703)771-9400, FAX (703)777-4627. **LC** DC203.9; .D34. **DD** 944.05/05.

US/0882-7095
DDR-STUDIEN. [DDR-Stud.]. **VFOAT** East German Studies; DDR Studien. English (German). an. Peter Lang Publishing, 62 West 45th Street, 4th Floor, New York NY 10036. **Tel** (212)764-1471, (800)770-5264, telex 6973364 PLNY. **DD** 943.

UK/0046-0079
DESPATCH. See Military and Defense.

GW/0012-1223
DEUTSCHES ARCHIV FUER ERFORSCHUNG DES MITTELALTERS. Added/Corp Reichsinstitut fuer Altere Deutsche Geschichtskunde. Monumeta Germaniae Historica (Deutsches Institut fuer Erforschung des Mittelalters). Vol. 1 (1937)-. Periodical. German. Twice a year. DM160.00 Germany; DM176.00 other. Boehlau Verlag GmbH & Cie / Koeln, Theodor Heuss STR 76, D-51149 Cologne Germany. **Tel** 011 49 2203 307021, FAX 011 49 2203 307349. **(Subscription address:** BDK Buecherdienst GmBh, Postfach 900120, D 51111 Cologne Germany.) **LC** DD126.A1; D4. **DD** 943.01. **[CCC].** *Supersedes Gesellschaft fuer Altere Deutsche Geschichtskunde zur Beforderung Einer Gesamtausgabe der Quellenschriften Deutscher Geschichten des Mittelalters. Neues Archiv.*
 Ind/Abst Annu. Bibliogr. Engl. Lang. Lit.; Bibliogr. Carto.; BHA : Biblio. Hist. Art; MLA Int. Bibl. Books Artic. Mod. Lang. Lit.

GW
DEUTSCHLAND. Main/Corp Michelin Reifenwerke. Multiple languages (English, French, German and Italian). Michelin Reifenwerke, Bannwaldallee 60-62, W-7500 Karlsruhe 21 Germany. **LC** DD16; .M53A.

GW
DEUTSCHLAND IN GESCHICHTE UND GEGENWART. Periodical. German. 16.80. Postfach 1303, Tubingen Germany. **LC** DD1; .D473. **DD** 914.3/03/05. *Continues Deutsche Nation in Geschichte und Gegenwart.*

UK/0012-1681
DEVON & CORNWALL NOTES & QUERIES. (1900)-. Periodical. English. sa (Spring & Fall). £8.00. Devon & Cornall Notes, 3 Johnstone Drive, Tiverton EX16 5BU England. **Tel** 011 44 884 256644. **ED** J. Draisey. Index available (last of volume). **Bk Rev Ad Acc. Circ:** 350.
 Desc: Local history of Devon and Cornwall.
 Ind/Abst BHA : Biblio. Hist. Art; Br. Archaeol. Bibliogr.

US/0882-1240
DIMENSIONS (NEW YORK, N.Y.). (DIMENSIONS.). [Dimensions]. Added/Corp Center for Holocaust Studies (New York, N.Y.) International Center for Holocaust Studies (U.S.). Vol. 1, No. 1 (Spring 1985)-. Periodical. English. Three times a year. $15.00 (one year), $25.00 (two years). Braun Center for Holocaust Studies, 823 United Nations Plaza, New York NY 10017. **Tel** (212)490-2525, FAX (212)867-0779. **ED** Dr. Dennis B. Klein. **DD** 943. **Bk Rev**, (Qty: 30). **Ad Acc, Adv Mgr:** C. Perkins, **Tel**, (212)255-7951. **Circ:** 5,000-10,000.
 Desc: Explores the roots and branches of the holocaust. Written for the students and educators of the holocaust.
 Ind/Abst Hum. Rights Intern. Rep.

CN/0822-6369
DIRECTORY / CANADIAN SOCIETY FOR RENAISSANCE STUDIES. [Dir. - Can. Soc. Renaiss. Stud.]. Main/Corp Canadian Society for Renaissance Studies. **VFOAT** Repertoire. 1983-. Directory. English (French). be. Free. University of Windsor Office of the Dean of Arts, Windsor Ontario N9B 3P4 Canada. **Tel** (519)253-4232 ext. 2332. **ED** W H Herendeen. **LC** CB361; .C28A. **DD** 940.2/1/071171. **Circ:** 2,000 (ctrl).
 Desc: Biographical and bibliographical directory of renaissance scholars and members of Canadian Society for Renaissance Studies and interdisciplinary in scope.

US
DIRECTORY OF PROGRAMS IN RUSSIAN, EURASIAN, AND EAST EUROPEAN STUDIES. (19??)-. Directory. English. ir (every 3 years). American Association for the Advancement of Slavic Studies, 125 Panama Street, Stanford University, Acacia Building, Stanford CA 94305-6029. **Tel** (415)723-9668, FAX (415)725-7737, telex 348402 STANFRD STNU. *Continues Directory of Programs in Soviet and East European Studies.*

US/0889-9487
DIRECTORY OF PROGRAMS IN SOVIET & EAST EUROPEAN STUDIES. *Title Change.* [Dir. programs Sov. East Eur. Stud.]. Added/Corp American Association for the Advancement of Slavic Studies. **VFOAT** AAASS Directory of Programs, Soviet & East European Studies; Directory of Programs, Soviet & East European Studies. **VAT** Directory of Programs in Soviet and East European Studies. (1989)-(1992). Directory. English. ir. American Association for the Advancement of Slavic Studies, 125 Panama St, Stanford University, Acacia Building, Stanford CA 94305-6029. **Tel** (415)723-9668, FAX (415)725-7737, telex 348402 STANFRD STNU. **LC** DJK36.U6; D47. **DD** 947/.0007/1173. **Circ:** 500. *Continued by Directory of Programs, Russian, Eurasian, and East European Studies.*

FR/0012-4273
DIX-SEPTIEME SIECLE. (XVII [DIX-SEPTIEME] SIECLE.). [17 siecle]. Added/Corp Societe d'Etude du XVIIe Siecle (France). No. 1 (1949)-. Periodical. French. qt (4 issues). 310.00F EEC countries; 360.00F other. Societe d'Etude du XVII Siecle, 11 place Marcelin Berthelot, 75005 Paris France. **Tel** 011 33 1 44271211, FAX 011 33 1 44271109. Documents available from The Genuine Article.
 Desc: Seventeenth century.
 Ind/Abst Am. Hist. Life (1974-); Arts Humanit. Citation Index [Full Cov.]; BHA : Biblio. Hist. Art; MLA Int. Bibl. Books Artic. Mod. Lang. Lit.; Res. Alert [Full Cov.]; Soc. Sci. Cit. Index [Select. Cov.].

SP/1130-4936
DOCUMENTOS A. **VFOAT** Documentos Anthropos. No. 1 (Jan. 1991)-. Periodical. Spanish (Gallegan). Twice a year. $43.65. Anthropos Editorial, Apartado 387, 08190 Sant Cugat del Valles Barcelona Spain. **Tel** 011 34 3 5894884. **LC** DP48; .D63. **DD** 946.

FR
DOCUMENTS D'HISTOIRE MAGHREBINE. Began with 1, 1972. Monographic series. French. Price varies per volume. Librairies Paul Geuthner, 12 rue Vanin, Paris 6E France.

UK
DOD'S HISTORY OF PARLIAMENT. 1st issue (Jan. 1991)-. English. **LC** JN500; .D62.

GW/0340-3297
DOKUMENTATION OSTMITTELEUROPA. [Dok. Ostmitteleur.]. Vol. 1- Feb. 1975-. Periodical. German. bm. DM39.00. Johann Gottfried Herder Institut, Gisonenweg 5-7, H-35037 Marburg, Lahn Germany. **Tel** 011 49 6421 1840, FAX 011 49 6421 184139. **ED** Csaba Janos Kenez. **LC** AS181; .D64. **Circ:** 500. *Supersedes in part Wissenschaftlicher Dienst fur Ost-Mitteleuropa.*
 Desc: Research on countries and peoples of eastern central Europe.
 Ind/Abst PAIS Int. Print (1991-).

GW
DOKUMENTATION WESTEUROPA. Added/Corp Deutsches Historisches Institut (Paris, France). (1976)-. Monographic series. German.
 Ind/Abst Am. Hist. Life (1976-1977).

GW/0070-7031
DOKUMENTE ZUR DEUTSCHLANDPOLITIK. Added/Corp Germany (West). Bundesministerium fur Gesamtdeutsche Fragen. Germany (West). Bundesministerium fur Innerdeutsche Beziehungen. Vol. 1, No. 1 (Sept. 3, 1939-Dec. 1941)-. Monographic series. German (English). ir. varies per volume. Bundeszentrale Polit Bildung, Berliner Freiheit 7, D-53111 Bonn Germany. **LC** DD257.4; .D66. **DD** 943.086.

GW
DONAUSCHWABISCHE FORSCHUNGS- UND LEHRERBLATTER. Added/Corp Arbeitsgemeinschaft Donauschwabischer Lehrer. Vol. 23 (March 1977)-. Periodical. German. qt. Arbeitsgemeinschaft Donauschwabischer Lehrer, 844 Straubing Germany. **LC** DJK28.G4; D65. **DD** 949.6/005.

IE/0416-2773
DONEGAL ANNUAL. Added/Corp County Donegal Historical Society. County Donegal Historical Society. Journal. **VFOAT** Bliainiris Thir Chonaill. (1947)-. English. an (February). $18.00. Donegal Historical Society, 61 Cluain Barron, Ballyshannon Donegal Ireland. **Tel** 072 51267. **ED** Vincent O'Donnell. cum. index. **Ad Acc. Circ:** 900 (ctrl).

FR/0150-0104
DOSSIERS ARCHEOLOGIQUES, HISTORIQUES ET CULTURELS DU NORD ET DU PAS-DE-CALAIS. [Doss. archeol. hist. cult. Nord Pas-de-Calais]. (1976)-. Periodical. French. qt. UDC 908. *Continues Dossiers Historiques et Archeologiques (Berck), 0151-3257.*
 Ind/Abst BHA : Biblio. Hist. Art.

GW
DSF JOURNAL. Periodical. German. qt. DSF Journal, Kur Fuerstendamm 72, 1 Berlin 31 Germany. **LC** DK1; .D17.

IE/0012-6861
DUBLIN HISTORICAL RECORD. Vol 1 (March 1938)-. English. qt. £8.00 Ireland; £10.00 other. The Old Dublin Society, 58 South William Street, Dublin 2 Ireland.

GW/0419-8026
DUISBURGER FORSCHUNGEN. Added/Corp Duisburg. Stadtarchiv. Mercatorgesellschaft, Duisburg. (1957)-. German. **DD** 943.
 Ind/Abst BHA : Biblio. Hist. Art.

US/0197-9159
DUMBARTON OAKS. (DUMBARTON OAKS : REPORT.). Main/Corp Dumbarton Oaks. Began with issue for July 1, 1977-June 30, 1979. English. be. Trustees for Harvard University, 1703-32nd Street NW,

History(General) —History of Europe

Washington DC 20007. **LC** DF501; .D8. **DD** 949.5. **Continues** Dumbarton Oaks. Report for the Academic Year.

NE/0376-8686
DUTCH STUDIES. V. 1- 1974-. English. an. Martinus Nijhoff Publishers, Subsidiary of Kluwer Academic Publishers, Koraalrood 50, 2718 SC Zoetermeer Netherlands. **Tel** 011 31 79 684400. **LC** PF1; .D85. **DD** 914.92/03.

US/1048-9401
EARLY DRAMA, ART, AND MUSIC REVIEW, THE. See The Arts.

UK/0963-9462
EARLY MEDIEVAL EUROPE. (19??)-. English. sa (Mar., Sept.). £51.00 qt Europe; £54.00 Other (Institutions). Longman Group Ltd., Fourth Avenue, Longman House, Harlow Essex CM19 5SR England. **Tel** 011 44 279 429655, FAX 011 44 279 431059, telex 81259.

UK/0962-0648
EARLY MODERN HISTORY. [Early mod. hist.]. (1991)-. Periodical. English. Three times a year. £12.50 UK; £15.00 within Europe; £20.00 other. Philip Allan Publishers Ltd, Market Place, Deddington Oxford, OX15 0SE England. **Tel** 011 44 869 38652, FAX 011 44 869 38803. **DD** 940.2.

SW
EARLY NORRLAND. (19??)-. English. ir. Scandinavian University Press, PO Box 2959 Toeyen, N 0608 Oslo 6 Norway. **Tel** 011 47 2 2575400, FAX 011 47 2 2575353, telex 71896 UROR N. **(Subscription address:** Scandinavian University Press, 200 Meacham Ave., Elmont NY 11003.)

US/0012-8430
EAST EUROPE. Suspended. [East Eur.]. **Added/Corp** Free Europe. Free Europe Committee. (Jan. 1957)-(1991). Periodical. English. Four times a year. $126.00. East Europe, PO Box 411, Madison Square Station, New York NY 10159. **Tel** (212)473-0333. **LC** DR1; .N363. **DD** 914.7. available on microfilm from University Microfilms International (UMI). **Continues** News from Behind the Iron Curtain.
Desc: Situation reports, tables and rare information from the USSR and other east European countries.
Ind/Abst Am. Hist. Life (1963-1975); Peace Res. Abstr. J. (1969-1971).

US/0012-8449
EAST EUROPEAN QUARTERLY. [East Eur. q.]. **Added/Corp** University of Colorado (Boulder Campus). Vol. 1 (March 1967)-. Periodical. English (French, German, Italian and Russian). qt (Mar., June, Sept., Dec.). $27.00 (one year), $31.00 (two year). East European Quarterly, PO Box 10039, Bradenton FL 34282. **Tel** (813)753-4782, FAX (813)753-4782. **ED** Stephen Fischer-Galati. **LC** DR1; .E33. **DD** 949.6/005. **Bk Rev. Ad Acc. Pr Rev. Circ:** 900 (ctrl). available on microfilm and microfiche from University Microfilms International (UMI). Documents available from The Genuine Article, UMI Article Clearinghouse.
Desc: History, economics, politics and social sciences of Eastern Europe included, all by scholars throughout the world.
Ind/Abst Acad. Abstr. Full Text Elite (Jan. 1992-); Acad. Abstr. (Jan. 1992-); Acad. Search (Jan. 1992-); Am. Hist. Life (1967-); Am. Bibliogr. Slavic Eaup Europ. Stud.; BHA : Biblio. Hist. Art; Curr. Contents Soc. Behav. Sci.; Expand. Acad. Index (1989-); INFO-SOUTH Abstr.; Int. Bibliogr. Sociol.; Int. Exec.; Int. Polit. Sci. Abstr.; Mag. Search; Middle East Abstr. Index; Newsp. Period. Abstr. (1991-); PAIS Int. Print (1991-); Res. Alert [Full Cov.]; Soc. Sci. Source (Jan. 1992-); Soc. Sci. Cit. Index [Full Cov.]; Soc. Sci. Index; Soc. Sci. Index Fulltext (Sept. 1988-) [Full Txt.]; U.S. Polit. Sci. Doc.

UK/0267-808X
EAST EUROPEAN REPORTER. [East Eur. report.]. **Added/Corp** East European Cultural Foundation. Vol. 1 No. 1 (Spring 1985)-. Periodical. English. bm $40.00 (individuals), $70.00 (libraries and institutions). East European Reporter, 6 10 Csalogany Utea III 118, Budapest 1015 Hungary. **Tel** 36 1 2011056. **LC** DJK50; .E152. **DD** 947/.0005.
Ind/Abst Altern. Press Index (199?-); Hum. Rights Intern. Rep.; Left Index (19??-); PAIS Int. Print (1991-).

UK/0141-6286
EAST LONDON RECORD. No. 1 (1978)-. Periodical. English. an. East London History Society, D Kendall, 20 Puteaux House, Cranbrook Est, London E2 OMF England. **Tel** 01-981-7680. **ED** Colm Kerrigan. **LC** DA685.E1; E17. **DD** 942.1/5/005. Index available. **Bk Rev. Ad Acc. Circ:** 2,000 (ctrl).

US/1053-4679
EASTERN EUROPE ON FILE. Added/Corp Facts on File, Inc. (1991)-. English. bw. $155.00 (loose-leaf). Facts on File Publications, 460 Park Avenue South, New York NY 10016. **Tel** (212)683-2244, (800)322-8755, FAX (212)683-3633, telex 238 552 FACTS UR. available with illustrations; available with charts.
Desc: Visually documents the crucial developments in the former Soviet Union and the Eastern European nations, as well as the complex historical forces at play. Also provides a profile on each individual nation.

GW
EASTERN GERMANY; A HANDBOOK.
Main/Corp Gottinger Arbeitskreis. Vol. 1 (1960/1961)-. English. Holzner Verlag der Gottinger Arbeitskreis EV, Calsowstrasse 54, W-3400 Goettingen Germany. **ED** Goettinger Research Committee. **LC** DD801.O35; G59. **DD** 943.1087.

FR/0154-5280
ECHOS DU CENTRE INTERNATIONAL D'ETUDES PEDAGOGIQUES DE SEVRES. [Echos Cent. int. etud. pedagog. Sevres]. (1976)-. Periodical. French. qt. 130.00F. Centre International D'Etudes Pedagogiques, 1 Avenue Leon Journault, BP 75, 92311 Sevres Cedex France. **Tel** 011 33 1 45347527. **UDC** 37. **Ad Acc. Pr Rev.**
Desc: Information on French civilization for teachers of French as a foreign language.

GW
EICHSFELDER HEIMATHEFTE. Periodical. German. ir. 8.50M. Padagogisches Kreiskabinett Worbis, 5700 Muhlhausen Thomas-Muntzer-Stadt, AM Neuen Ufer 29 Germany. **LC** DD491.S391; E333. **DD** 943/.22.

IE
EIGHTEENTH-CENTURY IRELAND.
Added/Corp Eighteenth-Century Ireland Society. **VFOAT** 18th Century Ireland. **VAT** Eighteenth Century Ireland. Vol. 1 (1986)-. Periodical. English (Irish). 10.00p (membership), 14.00p (general). **LC** DA947.3; .E53. **DD** 941.507/05.
Ind/Abst Am. Hist. Life (1986-1987); Annu. Bibliogr. Engl. Lang. Lit.

US/0193-5380
EIGHTEENTH CENTURY (LUBBOCK), THE. (THE EIGHTEENTH CENTURY.). [Eighteenth century]. Vol. 20, No. 1 (Winter 1979)-. Periodical. English. Three times a year. $19.00 (individuals), $33.00 (institutions). Texas Tech University Press, Administrative Education Room 43, West Basement, Lubbock TX 79409-1037. **Tel** (800)832-4042, (806)742-2982. **ED** Bruce Clarke, Robert M. Markley and John Samson. **LC** DA506.B9; B86. **DD** 909.7. **Bk Rev. Ad Acc. Pr Rev. Circ:** 750 (ctrl). Documents available from The Genuine Article. **Continues** Studies in Burke and His Time, 0039-3584.
Desc: Essays on all aspects of British, American and Continental culture, including literature, history, fine arts, science, history of ideas and popular culture.
Ind/Abst Abstr. Engl. Stud.; Am. Hist. Life (1979-); Arts Humanit. Citation Index [Full Cov.]; BHA : Biblio. Hist. Art; Curr. Contents Arts Humanit.; MLA Int. Bibl. Books Artic. Mod. Lang. Lit.; Res. Alert [Full Cov.].

GW/0934-7887
EINBECKER JAHRBUCH. [Einbeck. Jahrb.]. (1964)-. German. an. **UDC** 908.
Ind/Abst BHA : Biblio. Hist. Art.

GW
EINWOHNER-ADRESSBUCH DES LANDKREISES BREISGAU-HOCHSCHWARZWALD. BD. 3, TITISEE-NEUSTADT UND HOCHSCHWARZWALD. VFOAT Einwohner Adressbuch des Landkreises Breisgau Hochschwarzwald. Bd. 3, Titisee Neustadt und Hochschwarzwald; **EAB** Titisee Neustadt; Titisee-Neustadt und Hochschwarzwald; Titisee Neustadt und Hochschwarzwald; **EAB** Titisee-Neustadt. (19??)-. German. an. Rombach, PO Box 1349, 7800 Freiburg Germany. **LC** DD901.T613; E46. **DD** 943/.46/0025.

GW
EINWOHNERBUCH DER STADTE LORRACH UND WEIL AM RHEIN. VFOAT Lorrach und Weil Am Rhein. (19??)-. German. Rombach, PO Box 1349, 7800 Freiburg Germany. **LC** DD901.L7886; E47. **DD** 914.3/46.

GW
EINWOHNERBUCH OBERNDORF AM NECKAR, EPFENDORF, FLUORN-WINZELN. (19??)-. German. KBK-Druckerei und Verlag, Nowackanlage 13, W-7500 Karlsruhe Germany. **LC** DD901.O2353; E35.

GW
EINWOHNERBUCH RAVENSBURG, WEINGARTEN, AULENDORF, BAD WALDSEE, BAIENFURT, BAINDT, BERG, BERGATREUTE, FRONREUTE, GRUNKRAUT, SCHLIER, VOGT, WOLPERTSWENDE. German. KBK-Druckerei und Verlag, Nowackanlage 13, W-7500 Karlsruhe Germany. **LC** DD801.W99; R3853.

UN
EKONOMIKA SOVESTKOI UKRAINY. (1966)-. Periodical. Russian. mo. $85.95.
Ind/Abst Agric. Eng. Abstr.; Am. Hist. Life (1972-1980); Dairy Sci. Abstr.; Irr. Drain. Abstr.; Nutr. Abstr. Rev., Ser. B, Live Feeds and Feed.; World Agric. Econ.

IT/0070-9972
ELEMENTA AD FONTIUM EDITIONES.
Vol. 1-. Monographic series. Latin. an. Price varies per volume. Institutum Historicum Polonic, Via Virginio Orsini 19, 00192 Rome Italy. **Tel** 6/350831. **LC** DK402. cum. index. **Circ:** 500.

●US/1064-6663
ELEMENTA (YVERDON, SWITZERLAND). See Linguistics.

●US/1064-5020
EMF, STUDIES IN EARLY MODERN FRANCE. VFOAT EMF; Studies in Early Modern France. (1993)-. Monographic series. English. $22.50. Rookwood Press, Serials Department, 520 Rookwood Pl., Charlottesville VA 22903-4734.

UK/0260-0420
ENGLISH HERITAGE MONITOR. See General Interest-General Interest-Europe.

FR/0983-2424
ENQUETES ET DOCUMENTS / CENTRE DE RECHERCHES SUR L'HISTOIRE DU MONDE ATLANTIQUE, UNIVERSITE DE NANTES. (1984)-. Monographic series. French. ir. Price varies per volume. Universite de Nantes, 2 Chemin de la Houssiniere, 44072 Nantes France. **Tel** 011 33 40 373037, 373004. **LC** DC603.1; .C45A. **DD** 944/.009821. **Continues** Enquetes et Documents.

GR/0253-391X
EPETERIS ETAIREIAS BUZANTINON SPOUDON. (EPETERIS.). [Epet. etair. buz. spoudon]. **Main/Corp** Hetaireia Byzantinon Spoudon. **VFOAT** Annuaire de l'Association d'Etudes Byzantines. (1924)-. Greek, Modern. ir. Hetaireia Vyzantinon Spoudon, 8 Aristeidou St 8th Fl, 10559 Athens Greece. **LC** DF501; .H47.
Ind/Abst Am. Hist. Life (1953-1959); BHA : Biblio. Hist. Art; MLA Int. Bibl. Books Artic. Mod. Lang. Lit.

GR
EPETERIS TES HETAIREIAS ELEIAKON MELETON. Added/Corp Hetaireia Eleiakon Meleton. (1982)-. Periodical. Greek, Modern (English). **LC** DF901.E44; E63.

FR/0992-4922
EPHEMERA NANCY. (EPHEMERA (NANCY, FRANCE).). (1984)-. Periodical. French.
Ind/Abst Annu. Bibliogr. Engl. Lang. Lit.

NE/0927-3026
ERFGOED VAN INDUSTRIE EN TECHNIEK. [Erfgoed ind. tech.]. (1992)-. Periodical. Dutch. qt. **UDC** 902. **Formed by the union of** Histechnicon (Delft), 0923-3482 and Industriele Archeologie, 0167-9619.
Ind/Abst BHA : Biblio. Hist. Art.

DK/0071-1152
ERHVERVSHISTORISK AARBOG; MEDDELELSER FRA ERHVERVSARKIVET. (19??)-. Danish. Rosenkilde and Bagger, 3 Kron-Prinsens-Gade, PO Box 2184, DK 1017 Copenhagen K Denmark. **Tel** 011 45 1 157044.
Ind/Abst Am. Hist. Life (1955-1964).

UK/0308-3462
ESSEX ARCHAEOLOGY AND HISTORY : THE TRANSACTIONS OF THE ESSEX ARCHAEOLOGICAL SOCIETY. Added/Corp Essex Archaeological Society. Essex Society for Archaeology and History. 3rd Ser. Vol. 4 (1972)-. Academic Scholarly Publication. English. an. Essex Society for Archaeology and History, Hollytrees Library, High Street Colchester England. Index available. **Bk Rev,** (Qty: 5). **Pr Rev. Acid Free. Circ:** 550 (ctrl). **Continues** Essex Archaeological Society. Transactions of the Essex Archaeology Society.
Desc: Publishes academic articles on the history and archaeology of Essex.
Ind/Abst BHA : Biblio. Hist. Art.

UK/0014-0961
ESSEX JOURNAL. Added/Corp Essex Archaeological & Historical Congress. (Jan. 1966)-. Periodical. English. qt. **Continues** Essex Review.
Ind/Abst BHA : Biblio. Hist. Art.

FR/0014-1097
EST EUROPEEN, L'. Added/Corp Union des Ukrainiens de France. (1962)-. Periodical. French. Four times a year (Feb., May, Aug., Oct.). $20.00. L'Est Europeen, B P 51-06, 75261 Paris Cedex 06 France. **ED**

History(General) —History of Europe

M. Bublinskyi. **LC** DK508.A2; E8. **Bk Rev. Circ:** 900 (ctrl).
Desc: Articles on present situation, history, national and civil rights on East-European countries, particularly of Ukraine.

SP/0212-9515
ESTUDIOS DE HISTORIA Y DE ARQUEOLOGIA MEDIEVALES. Spanish. an. **LC** DP99; .E868. **DD** 946/.02/05.
Ind/Abst BHA : Biblio. Hist. Art; Numis. Lit.

SP
ESTUDIOS DE RONDA Y SU SERRANIA. Periodical. Spanish. **LC** DP402.R65; E84. **DD** 946/.85.

SP/0210-7260
ESTUDIOS SEGOVIANOS. [Estud. segov.].
Added/Corp Spain. Consejo Superior de Investigaciones Cientificas. Instituto Diego de Colomenares, Segovia. Vol. 1 No. 1 (1949)-. Periodical. Spanish. Three times a year. Consejo Superior Investigacion Cientificas (CSIC), Vitruvio 8, 28006 Madrid Spain. **Tel** 011 34 1 5612833, FAX 011 34 1 4113077, telex 42182. **LC** DP402.S35; E8.
Ind/Abst Am. Hist. Life (1958-1959, 1968-1974).

SP
ESTUDIS BALEARICS. Vol. 1, No. 1 (June 1981)-. Periodical. Catalan (Spanish). qt. **LC** DP302.B16; E84.

SP/0210-8704
ESTUDIS D'HISTORIA CONTEMPORANIA DEL PAIS VALENCIA. Catalan (Spanish). Universitat de Valencia, Valencia Spain.

BL/0101-4064
ESTUDOS IBERO-AMERICANOS. [Estud. ibero-am.]. **Added/Corp** Pontificia Universidade Catolica do Rio Grande do Sul. Departamento de Historia. Vol. 1 (July 1975)-. Periodical. English (Portuguese and Spanish). sa (June and Nov.). $20.00 US. Editoria Pontificia da Universidade Catolica, Caixa Postal 1429, 90001 Porto Alegre Brazil. **Tel** 011 55 51 339-1511. **LC** DP48; .E83. Documents available from The Genuine Article.
Ind/Abst Arts Humanit. Citation Index [Full Cov.]; Curr. Contents Arts Humanit.; HAPI Hisp. Am. Period. Index; MLA Int. Bibl. Books Artic. Mod. Lang. Lit.; Res. Alert [Full Cov.].

PO/0870-8584
ESTUDOS ITALIANOS EM PORTUGAL.
Added/Corp Istituto di Cultura Italiana em Portugal. (1939)-. Portuguese (Italian and French). an. **LC** DG401; .E8. **DD** 945.005. cum. index.
Ind/Abst Am. Hist. Life (1982-); BHA : Biblio. Hist. Art.

FR/0520-0121
ETUDES. **Main/Corp** Bibliotheque Byzantine. (1951)-. Monographic series. French.
Ind/Abst Am. Hist. Life (1964-1988).

BU/0324-1645
ETUDES BALKANIQUES. (ETUDES BALKANIQUES / ACADEMIE BULGARE DES SCIENCES, INSTITUT D'ETUDES BALKANIQUES.). [Etud. balk.]. **Added/Corp** Institut za Balkanistika (Bulgarska Akademiia na Naukite). (1964)-. Periodical. French (German and Russian). qt. DM176.00. Institut d'Etudes Balkaniques, rue Acad G. Bonchev Bl 6, Sofia 1113 Bulgaria. **(Subscription address:** Kubon & Sagner, ABT Zeitschriftenimport, D 80328 Munich Germany.**) LC** DR1; .E7. **Bk Rev. Circ:** 700 (ctrl).
Desc: Covers Balkan history.
Ind/Abst Am. Hist. Life (1964-).

RM
ETUDES BYZANTINES ET POST-BYZANTINES. **Added/Corp** Institutul de Studii Sud-Est Europene (Academia de Stiinte Sociale si Politice a Republicii Socialiste Romania). (1979)-. Monographic series. French (English). Editura Academia Republicii Socialiste Romania, Calea Victoriei Nr 125, R-79717 Bucuresti Romania. **Tel** telex 10376 PRSFI R. **LC** IN PROCESS.
Ind/Abst BHA : Biblio. Hist. Art.

FR
ETUDES CRETOISES. **Main/Corp** Ecole Francaise d'Athenes. Vol. 1 (1928)-. Monographic series. French. Price varies per volume. Librairie Orientaliste Paul Geuthner, 12 rue Vavin, 75006 Paris France. **Tel** 011 33 1 46347130. **LC** DF221.C8; E4. **DD** 913.3918.

FR/0769-3656
ETUDES DANUBIENNES. [Etud. danub.].
Added/Corp Institut des Hautes Etudes Europeennes de Strasbourg. Groupe d'Etudes de la Monarchie des Habsbourg. Vol. 1, No. 1 (1985)-. Periodical. French. sa. 140.00F France; 170.00F other. Groupe d'Etudes de la Monarch des Habsbourg, 8 rue des Ecrivains, 67000 Strasbourg France. **Tel** 011 33 88 350269.
Ind/Abst Am. Hist. Life (1989-).

BE/0771-5692
ETUDES ET DOCUMENTS DU CERCLE ROYAL D'HISTOIRE ET D'ARCHEOLOGIE D'ATH ET DE LA REGION. [Etud. Doc. Cercle r. hist. archeol. Ath reg.]. (1979)-. Periodical. French. an. **UDC** 930.26.
Ind/Abst BHA : Biblio. Hist. Art.

FR/0085-0322
ETUDES HAGUENOVIENNES. **Added/Corp** Societe d'Histoire et d'Archeologie de Haguenau. VFOAT Etudes Haguenauiennes. (1955)-. Periodical. French. **Supersedes** Societe d'Histoire et d'Archeologie de Haguenau. Bulletin.
Ind/Abst BHA : Biblio. Hist. Art.

CN/0824-8621
ETUDES HELLENIQUES. [Etud. hell.]. VFOAT Hellenic Studies. Vol. 1, No. 1 (Spring 1983)-. Periodical. English (French). sa. Centre of Hellenic Research, 5582 Waverley Street, Montreal Quebec H2T 2Y1 Canada. **DD** 305.8/89/005.

HU/0237-0301
ETUDES HISTORIQUES HONGROISES.
[Etud. hist. hong.]. (1975)-. Multiple languages. ir.
Continues Etudes Historiques, 0071-2108.
Ind/Abst Am. Hist. Life (1970-).

FR/0183-973X
ETUDES IRLANDAISES. [Etud. irl.].
Added/Corp Universite de Lille III. Centre d'Etudes et de Recherches Irlandaises. No. 1 (1972)-. Monographic series. Multiple languages (English and French). sa. Price varies per volume. Universite Charles de Gaulle, Lille III, BP 149, 59653 Villeneuve D ASCQ Cedex France. **Tel** 011 33 20919202. **ED** P. Joannon, D. Jacquin, J. Brihault, and J. Genet. **LC** DA925; .E86. **DD** 941.50824/05. **Bk Rev. Ad Acc. Circ:** 400. Documents available from The Genuine Article. **Absorbed** Gaeliana, 0243-1106; Cahiers du Centre d'Etudes Irlandaises. Universite de Haute Bretagne. Centre d'Etudes Irlandaises., 0181-561X.
Desc: Contains Irish writings, literary studies, studies in history, civilization, bibliographies, and activities of Irish interest.
Ind/Abst Annu. Bibliogr. Engl. Lang. Lit.; Arts Humanit. Citation Index [Full Cov.]; Curr. Contents Arts Humanit.; MLA Int. Bibl. Books Artic. Mod. Lang. Lit.; Res. Alert [Full Cov.].

FR/0994-5490
ETUDES LAWRENCIENNES NANTERRE. See Literature.

FR/0766-5075
ETUDES MONGOLES ET SIBERIENNES. **Added/Corp** Universite de Paris X: Nanterre. Centre d'Etudes Mongoles. VFOAT Etudes Mongoles. (1976)-. Periodical. French. an. **LC** DS798.A2; E88. **Continues** Etudes Mongoles, 0150-3014.
Ind/Abst Am. Hist. Life (1974-); Anthropol. Lit.; MLA Int. Bibl. Books Artic. Mod. Lang. Lit.

FR
ETUDES NAPOLEONIENNES : BULLETIN HISTORIQUE DE LA SOCIETE DE SAUVEGARDE DU CHATEAU IMPERIAL DE PONT-DE-BRIQUES. **Added/Corp** Societe de Sauvegarde du Chateau Imperial de Pont-de-Briques. (1983)-. Periodical. French. 180.00F. Soc Sauvegarde Chateau Imper, 12 rue Pasteur, 92 300 Levalois France. **Continues** Bulletin Historique de la Societe de Sauvegarde du Chateau Imperial de Pont-de-Briques, 0765-1813.
Ind/Abst Am. Hist. Life (1970-).

FR/0014-2158
ETUDES NORMANDES. **Added/Corp** Association d'Etudes Normandes. (1951)-. Periodical. French. Four times a year. 180.00F France; 200.00F other. Association d' Études Normandes, 7 rue Thomas Becket, 76130 Mon Saint Aignan France. **Tel** 11 33 35 894092, FAX 11 33 35 146940. **Continues** Information Economique et Sociale de Basse-Normandie.
Ind/Abst BHA : Biblio. Hist. Art; Geogr. Abstr. Phys. Geogr.; Geogr. Abstr. Human Geogr.

CN/0318-0808
ETUDES SLAVES (QUEBEC). (ETUDES SLAVES.). **Added/Corp** Association Quebecoise d'Etudes Slaves et est-Europeennes. Vol. 1, (Dec. 1974)-. Periodical. French. qt. M Serge Fleury, 349 rue Jeanne d'Arc, Quebec Quebec G1S 2R8 Canada. **DD** 947/.005.

BE
ETUDES SUR LE XVIIIE SIECLE.
Added/Corp Universite Libre de Bruxelles. Groupe d'Etude du XVIIIe Siecle. (1974)-. Monographic series. French. ir. Price varies per volume. Editions University de Bruxelles, Avenue Paul Heger 26, B-1050 Bruxelles Belgium. **Tel** 32 2 642 3789, 3799, FAX 32 2 642 3794, telex 23069 UNILIB. **ED** Roland Mortier.
Ind/Abst Annu. Bibliogr. Engl. Lang. Lit.; BHA : Biblio. Hist. Art.

FR/0395-238X
ETUDES TOULOISES. [Etud. touloises]. (1974)-. Periodical. French. an. **UDC** 908.
Ind/Abst BHA : Biblio. Hist. Art.

US/0277-0423
EUROPA (NEW YORK, N.Y.). (EUROPA.). [Europa]. Vol. 1, No. 1 (June 1981)-. Periodical. English. qt. $40.00. Karz-Segil Publishers, 320 West 105th Street, New York NY 10025. **LC** D1050; .E874. **DD** 940/.05.
Ind/Abst Am. Hist. Life (1977-1982).

GW
EUROPAISCHE IDEEN. Monographic series. German. Price varies per volume. Verlag Europaische Ideen, Postfach 246, 1 Berlin 37 Germany. **LC** CB203; .E87. **DD** 940/.05.

UK/0959-9584
EUROPE 2000 YEOVIL. (EUROPE 2000.). [Eur. 2000 Yeovil]. (1989)-. Periodical. English. Ten times a year. £297.00. Europe 2000 Ltd., 7A Westminster Street Yeovil, Somerset BA20 1AF England. **Tel** 011 44 935 29489. **DD** _b337.142. available on an online database from DIALOG.
Ind/Abst Mark. Advert. Ref. Serv. [Full Txt.]; PROMT [Full Txt.]; PTS Newsl. Database [Full Txt.]; Trade Ind. ASAP [Full Txt.]; Trade Ind. Index [Full Txt.].

●UK/0966-8136
EUROPE-ASIA STUDIES. See History(General)-History of Asia.

UK/0265-6914
EUROPEAN HISTORY QUARTERLY. [Eur. hist. q.]. Vol. 14, No. 1 (Jan. 1984)-. Periodical. English. qt. £85.00. Sage Publications Ltd., 6 Bonhill Street, London EC2A 4PU, UK. **Tel** 071 374 0645, FAX 071 374 8741, telex 296207 SAGE G. **ED** R. M. Blinkhorn. **LC** D1; .E76. **DD** 940/.05. **CODEN** EHIQEH. Acid Free. Documents available from The Genuine Article, UMI Article Clearinghouse. **Continues** European Studies Review, 0014-3111.
Desc: Focuses on European history since the later middle ages and social and political thought placed squarely within an historical perspective.
Ind/Abst ABC POL SCI (19??-19??); Acad. Search (July 1993-); Am. Hist. Life (1971-); Arts Humanit. Citation Index [Full Cov.]; Curr. Contents Arts Humanit.; Expand. Acad. Index (1989-); Hist. Source (July 1993-); Humanit. Index; Humanit. Source (Jul. 1993-); INFO-SOUTH Abstr.; Int. Polit. Sci. Abstr.; Mag. Search; Middle East Abstr. Index; Newsp. Period. Abstr. (1991-); Res. Alert [Full Cov.]; Romant. Move.; Soc. Plann. Policy Dev. Abstr.; Soc. Sci. Cit. Index [Select. Cov.].

●UK/1350-7486
EUROPEAN REVIEW OF HISTORY. Vol. 1 (1994)-. English. sa (June and December). £48.00. Carfax Publishing Company, PO Box 25 Abingdon, Oxfordshire OX14 3UE England. **Tel** 011 44 235 555335, FAX (0279)31067, telex 817484. **(Subscription address:** US and Canada/ PO Box 2025, Dunnellon, FL 34430-2025; telephone:(904)489-6996) Index available. available on microfiche.

DK/0906-0308
EUROPEAN STUDIES. **Added/Corp** Aalborg Universitetscenter. Institut for Sprog og Internationale Kulturstudier. VFOAT Europaeiske Studien; Etudes Europeennes. (1990)-. Monographic series. English. Price varies per volume.

US/0894-6337
EUROPEAN STUDIES JOURNAL, THE.
[Eur. stud. j.]. Vol. 1, No. 1-2 (1984)-. Periodical. English. sa. $30.00 (institution); $20.00 (individual). European Studies Journal, University of North Iowa, Modern Language Department, Cedar Falls IA 50614. **Tel** (319) 273-3887. **DD** 940.
Ind/Abst Am. Hist. Life (1988-); MLA Int. Bibl. Books Artic. Mod. Lang. Lit.

US/0046-2802
EUROPEAN STUDIES NEWSLETTER.
[Eur. stud. newsl.]. **Added/Corp** Council for European Studies. Vol. 1 (Apr. 1972)-. Newsletter. English. bm. $25.00 (North America), $35.00 (other) institution; $20.00 (North America), $30.00 (other) individual. Columbia University / International Affairs, Box 4, International Affairs Building, New York NY 10027. **Tel** (212) 854-4775. **ED** Marion Kaplan. **LC** D1050.82.U6; E93. **DD** 309.1/4/055. **Bk Rev. Ad Acc. Circ:** 1,300 (ctrl).
Desc: Newsletter publishes announcements of grants

fellowships conferences research resources and books on modern Europe in all social sciences including history, six issues per year.

SP
EUROPEAN TIMES. Spanish. mo. $30.00. European Times, Edificio Online, Oficina One Nueva Andalucia, Marbella 29660 Spain. **Tel** 011 34 52 811818.

•US
EUROWATCH: ECONOMICS, POLICY, AND LAW IN THE NEW EUROPE. Vol. 3, No. 21 (Feb. 10, 1992)-. Newspaper. English. ir (24 issues). $797.00 US, Canada and Mexico; $819.00 other. Buraff Publications Inc., 714 Church Street, Alexandria VA 22314. **Tel** (800)333-1291, (703)739-8500. **LC** HF1532.92; .A18. **DD** 337.1/42/05. ***Continues*** *1992, The External Impact of European Unification, 1043-4380.*

FR/1149-2031
EVOCATIONS CREMIEU. (EVOCATIONS.). (1945)-. Periodical. French. mo. **UDC** 061.22 (449.91).
Ind/Abst BHA : Biblio. Hist. Art.

DK/0106-3324
FABRIK OG BOLIG. [Fabr. bolig]. (1979)-. Periodical. Multiple languages. Twice a year. kr100.00. Koebenhavns Stadsarkiv, Raadhuset, DK 1599 Copenhagen V, Denmark. **DD** 725.409 489 728.310 948 9. **Bk Rev**. ***Continues*** *Industrialismens Bygninger og Boliger, 0106-4975.*
Ind/Abst BHA : Biblio. Hist. Art.

US/0882-3715
FINEST HOUR. (FINEST HOUR : QUARTERLY JOURNAL OF THE INTERNATIONAL CHURCHILL SOCIETY.). **Added/Corp** International Churchill Society. (1968)-. Periodical. English. qt. $25.00 US; $30.00 Canada; £15.00 UK; 30.00Aus$ Australia. International Churchill Society, 1847 Stonewood Drive, Baton Rouge LA 70816-2861. **Tel** (603)746-4433, FAX (603)746-4260. **ED** Richard M. Langworth. **DD** 941. Index available. cum. index. **Bk Rev**. **Ad Acc. Circ:** 2,000 (ctrl).
Desc: Biographic, bibliographic, and historical articles and departments related to Sir Winston S. Churchill's life and times.

IT
FIRENZE. Periodical. Italian. mo. Assessorato Alla Gioventu, Palazzo Vecchio, Firenze Italy. **LC** DG731; .F42.

DK
FOGTDALS MAGASIN OM DANMARK. Periodical. Danish. qt. Fogtdals Service-Kontor, Norre Farimagsgade 49, 1364 Kobenhavn K Denmark. **LC** DL101; .F57.

US/0428-8203
FOLGER DOCUMENTS OF TUDOR AND STUART CIVILIZATION. [Folger doc. Tudor Stuart civiliz.]. Monographic series. English. ir. Price varies per volume. Associated University Press, 440 Forsgate Drive, Cranbury NJ 08512. **Tel** (609)655-4770. **DD** 942.
Ind/Abst MLA Int. Bibl. Books Artic. Mod. Lang. Lit.

US
FOLGER MONOGRAPHS ON TUDOR AND STUART CIVILIZATION. **Added/Corp** Folger Shakespeare Library. No. 1 (1966)-. Monographic series. English. ir. Price varies per volume. Associated University Press, 440 Forsgate Drive, Cranbury NJ 08512. **Tel** (609)655-4770.

HU/0133-6622
FOLIA HISTORICA. **Added/Corp** Budapest. Magyar Nemzeti Muzeum. (1972)-. Hungarian. **LC** DB903.5; .F64.
Ind/Abst BHA : Biblio. Hist. Art.

BE/0015-590X
FOLKLORE BRABANCON. **See** Folklore.

SP/0210-2366
FONAMENTS. 1978-. Periodical. Catalan. an. 2125ptas. Curial Ediciones Catalanes S A, Bruc 144 Baixos, 08037 Barcelona Spain. **Tel** 011 34 3 2588101, FAX 207 74 27. **ED** Miquel Tarradell, Nuria Rafel I Fontanals and Joan Sanmarti. **LC** DP302.C615; F64. **DD** 936.6. cum. index.
Desc: Review devoted to prehistoric and ancient world studies, with the cooperation of specialists in ancient history, epigraphy, numismatics, toponymy, etc., comprising the whole of the history of the Catalan countries, from Palaeolithic to the coming of Islam.
Ind/Abst Anthropol. Lit.

IT
FONDAZIONE GIORGIO CINI, VENICE. CENTRO DI CULTURA E CIVILTA. ISTITUTO DI STORIA DELLA SOCIETA E DELLO STATO. BOLLETTINO. (STUDI VENEZIANI.). (1965)-. Periodical. English (Italian). L50000, L30000 (per issue) Italy; L90000, L50000 (per issue) other. Giardini Editori Stampatori, Via Santa Bibbiana 28, 56127 Pisa Italy. **Tel** 011 39 50 934242. **LC** DG676; .S936. **DD** 945/.31. ***Continues*** *Bollettino dell'Istituto di Storia Della Societa e Dello Stato Veneziano.*
Ind/Abst BHA : Biblio. Hist. Art; Numis. Lit.

AU/0071-6871
FONTES RERUM AUSTRIACARUM. OSTERREICHISCHE GESCHICHTS-QUELLEN. 1. ABTEILUNG. SCRIPTORES. **VFOAT** Osterreichische Geschichts-Quellen. V. 1- 1855-. Monographic series. German. ir. Price varies per volume. Oesterreichischen Akademie Wissenschaften, Dr. Ignaz Seipel Platz 2, A-1010 Vienna Austria. **Tel** 011 43 1 51581. **Circ:** 400.
Desc: Sources of Austrian history.

IT
FONTI ORALI-STUDI E RICERCHE. **VAT** Fonti Orali Studi e Ricerche. Vol. 1, No. 1 (Sept. 1981)-. Periodical. Italian. Three times a year. Istituto Piemontese A Gramsci, Via Vanchiglia 3 Bis, 10124 Turin Italy. **Tel** 011 39 11 8395404. **ED** Daniele Jalla. **Bk Rev**. **Ad Acc. Circ:** 1,000.
Desc: Includes news, book and journal reviews, discussions concerning the research with oral sources in Italy.

IT
FONTI PER LA STORIA D'ITALIA. No. 1- 1887-. Monographic series. Italian. ir. Price varies per volume. Istituto Storico Italiano Medio Evo e Archivio Muratoriano, Piazza dell Orologio 4, 00186 Rome Italy. **Tel** 011 39 6 68802075. ctrl circ.
Desc: Studies of history of Italy by the Institute for Italian Medieval Studies in Rome.

US/1062-614X
FORMER U.S.S.R. MONITOR. ***Ceased.*** [Former U.S.S.R. monit.]. **Added/Corp** Heritage Foundation (Washington, D.C.). **VFOAT** Former USSR Monitor; U.S.S.R. Monitor. No. 28 (Jan. 1992)-(1992). Periodical. English. mo. Heritage Foundation, 214 Massachusetts Avenue Northeast, Washington DC 20002. **Tel** (202)546-4400. **DD** 947. ***Continues*** *U.S.S.R. Monitor, 1050-5059.*

SW/0015-7813
FORNVANNEN. **Added/Corp** Kungl. Vitterhets, Historie och Antikvitets Akademien. Svenska Fornminnesforeningen. (1906)-. Periodical. English (Swedish and German). Four times a year. Kr108.00. Bibliotekstjanst AB, Box 200, S-221 00 Lund Sweden. **Tel** 011 46 46 180000. **LC** DL601; .V82. **DD** 948.5/005. ***Continues in part*** *Kungl. Vitterhets, Historie och Antikvitets Akademien. Manadsblad.*
Ind/Abst Anthropol. Index; Anthropol. Lit.; BHA : Biblio. Hist. Art.

AU
FORSCHUNGEN ZUR GESCHICHTE DER STAEDTE UND MAERKTE OESTERREICHS. **Added/Corp** Oesterreichischer Arbeitskreis fuer Stadtgeschichtsforschung. Ludwig-Boltzmann-Institut fuer Stadtgeschichtsforschung. Vol. 1 (1978)-. Periodical. German. ir. Oesterreichischen Arbeitskreis Staedtgeschichtsforschung, PF 320, A 4010 Linz Austria. **LC** HT145.A8; F67.

AU/0429-1565
FORSCHUNGEN ZUR GESCHICHTE OBEROSTERREICHS. [Forsch. Gesch. Oberoesterr.]. Vol. 1 (1952)-. German. ir. DM68.00. Oberoesterreichisches Landesarchiv, Anzengruberstrasse 19, A-4020 Linz Donau Austria. **Tel** 0732-6555230, FAX 0732655523-4619. **ED** Siegfried Haider and Georg Heilingsetzer. **Circ:** 700.
Desc: History and culture of upper Austria.
Ind/Abst MLA Int. Bibl. Books Artic. Mod. Lang. Lit.

GW/0071-7673
FORSCHUNGEN ZUR MITTELALTERLICHEN GESCHICHTE. Vol. 1 (1956)-. Monographic series. German. ir. Price varies per volume. Verlag Hermann Boehlaus Nachfolger, Postfach 260, D 99403 Weimar Germany. **Tel** 011 49 3643 2071, . **ED** E Heitz, E Muller-Mertens, B Topfer and E Werner.
Desc: Monographs dealing with the German and European history from the early Middle Ages up to the ending Middle Ages (500 to 1500) based on an intensive study of sources.

GW/0532-2197
FORSCHUNGEN ZUR OBERRHEINISCHEN LANDESGESCHICHTE. V. 1- 1954-. Monographic series. German. ir. Price varies per volume. Verlag Karl Alber GmbH, Hermann Herder Strasse 4, D 79104 Freiburg Germany. **Tel** 011 49 761 273495.

GW/0067-5903
FORSCHUNGEN ZUR OSTEUROPAISCHEN GESCHICHTE. (HISTORISCHE VEROFFENTLICHUNGEN. FORSCHUNGEN ZUR OSTEUROPAISCHEN GESCHICHTE / OSTEUROPA-INSTITUT AN DER FREIEN UNIVERSITAT BERLIN.). [Forsch. osteur. Gesch.]. **Added/Corp** Freie Universitat Berlin. Osteuropa-Institut. **VFOAT** Forschungen zur Osteuropaischen Geschichte. (1954)-. Monographic series. German. ir. Otto Harrassowitz Verlag, Taunusstrasse 14, Postfach 2929, D-65019 Wiesbaden Germany. **Tel** 011 49 611 5300, FAX 530570, telex 4186 135 OH D. **LC** DR1; .B45.
Ind/Abst Am. Hist. Life (1963-).

US/0895-3651
FRANCE TODAY (SAN FRANCISCO, CALIF. 1987). (FRANCE TODAY.). [Fr. today]. (May 1987)-. Periodical. English. mo. $35.00 school; $37.00 other. Francepress Inc., 1051 Divisadero Street, San Francisco CA 94115. **Tel** (415)921-5100, 800 851-7785, FAX (415)921-0213. **DD** 944. **Bk Rev**, (Qty: 10). **Ad Acc. Circ:** 10,000. ***Continues*** *En France.*
Desc: Travel publication on France.

RU/0532-6060
FRANCUZSKIJ EZEGODNIK. (FRANTSUZSKII EZHEGODNIK : STATI I MATERIALY PO ISTORII FRANTSII.). [Fr. ezegod.]. **Added/Corp** Institut Istorii (Akademiia Nauk SSSR). **VFOAT** Annuaire d'Etudes Francaises. (1958)-. Academic Scholarly Publication. Russian (summaries and/or abstracts in French; table of contents in French). an. Izdatelstvo Nauka / Akademiia Nauk, Publishing House of the Russian Academy of Sciences, Leninskii Porspekt 14, 117901 Moscow Russia. **Tel** 011 95 954-21-53, FAX 011 95 938-21-44, telex 411964. **LC** DC1; .F68.
Ind/Abst Am. Hist. Life (1981-).

GW
FRANKFURTER HISTORISCHE ABHANDLUNGEN. Vol. 1 (1972)-. Monographic series. German. ir. Price varies per volume. Franz Steiner Verlag GmbH, Postfach 101061, D 70009 Stuttgart Germany. **Tel** 011 49 0711 2582372, FAX 011 49 0711 2582290, telex 723636 daz d. **LC** UNC.
Desc: Monographs dedicated to medieval and modern European history.

BE
FRANSE NEDERLANDEN: JAARBOEK. LES PAYS-BAS FRANCAIS: ANNALES, DE. **Added/Corp** Stichting Ons Erfdeel. **VFOAT** Franse Nederlanden; Pays-Bas Francais; Pays-Bas Francais: Annales. (1976)-. Dutch (French; summaries and/or abstracts in Multiple languages). an. 1200.00F Belgium; 200.00F France; Fl70.00 Netherlands; 1250.00F other. Stichting ons Erfdeel, Murissonstraat 260, B-8931 Rekkem Belgium. **Tel** (056)411201, FAX (056)414707. **LC** DC611.N821; F7. **DD** 944/.28. Index available. **Bk Rev**. **Circ:** 2,000 (ctrl).
Desc: Covers all aspects of the French-speaking Netherlands and its relationship with Dutch-speaking Belgium and the Netherlands. Contains articles on regional history, philology, literature and sociology.

DK/0108-8777
FREDERIKSBERG GENNEM TIDERNE. **Main/Corp** Historisk-Topografisk Selskab for Frederiksberg. (1946)-. Danish.
Ind/Abst BHA : Biblio. Hist. Art.

UK
FREEDOM : A DOCUMENTARY HISTORY OF EMANCIPATION 1861-1867. Academic Scholarly Publication. English. ir. price varies per volume. Cambridge University Press, The Edinburgh Building, Shaftesbury Road, Cambridge CB2 2RU United Kingdom. **Tel** 011 44 223 312393, FAX 011 44 223 325959. **(Subscription address:** North America/ Cambridge University Press, 40 West 20th Street, New York, NY 10011-4211; telephone: (212)924-3900**)**

US/1052-3952
FRENCH AMERICAN REVIEW. [French Am. rev.]. **Added/Corp** American Society of the French Legion of Honor. Vol. 61, No. 2 Winter (1990)-. Periodical. English. sa. $15.00. American Society of the French Legion of Honor, 22 East 60th Street, New York NY 10022. **LC** CR5061.U6; A3. **DD** 944. ***Continues*** *Laurels, 0270-3793.*
Ind/Abst Am. Hist. Life (1976-1983).

US/0016-1071
FRENCH HISTORICAL STUDIES. [Fr. hist. stud.]. **Added/Corp** Society for French Historical Studies. Vol. 1 (1958)-. Periodical. English (French). sa (2 issues). $40.00 (institution), $24.00 (individual) includes membership in the Society for French Historical Studies. Duke University Press, PO Box 90660, Durham NC 27708-0660. **Tel** (919)687-3600, (919)688-5134 (orders), FAX (919)688-4574, telex 802829. **ED** James R. Farr and John J. Contreni. **LC** DC1; .F69. **DD** 944.0058. cum. index. **Circ:** 1,425. available on microfilm and microfiche from University Microfilms International (UMI). Documents available from The Genuine Article, UMI Article Clearinghouse.
Desc: History of France from Middle Ages to the present.
Ind/Abst Acad. Search (July 1993-); Am. Hist. Life (1958-); Arts Humanit. Citation Index [Full Cov.]; BHA : Biblio. Hist. Art; Curr. Contents Arts Humanit.; Expand. Acad. Index (1989-); Hist. Source (July 1993-); Humanit.

History(General) —History of Europe

Index; INFO-SOUTH Abstr.; Middle East Abstr. Index (1958-); Newsp. Period. Abstr. (1991-); Res. Alert [Full Cov.]; Romant. Move. (1958-); Soc. Sci. Cit. Index [Select. Cov.]; Women Stud. Abstr.

UK/0269-1191
FRENCH HISTORY. [Fr. hist.]. **Added/Corp** Society for the Study of French History. Vol. 1, No. 1 (Mar. 1987)-. Periodical. English. qt. £62.00 UK and Europe; $112.00 other. Oxford University Press, Walton Street, Oxford OX2 6DP England. **Tel** 011 44 865 56767, FAX 011 44 865 267773, telex 837330 OXPRES G. **(Subscription address:** Oxford University Press / USA, Journals Marketing Department, Oxford University Press, 2001 Evans Road, Cary NC 27513.) **LC** WMLC 93/1750. **[CCC].** available on microfilm and microfiche from University Microfilms International (UMI).
Ind/Abst Am. Hist. Life (1987-); BHA : Biblio. Hist. Art.

GW/0071-9706
FRUHMITTELALTERLICHE STUDIEN. [Fruhmittelalterl. Stud.]. **Added/Corp** Westfalische Wilhelms-Universitat Munster. Institut fuer Fruhmittelalterforschung. Vol. 1 (1967)-. German. an. DM140.00. Walter de Gruyter Inc., PO Box 303421, D 10728 Berlin Germany. **Tel** 011 49 30 260050, FAX 011 49 30 26005251. **LC** D121; .F88.
Ind/Abst Avery Index Archit. Period. Suppl. Colum. Univ.; BHA : Biblio. Hist. Art; MLA Int. Bibl. Books Artic. Mod. Lang. Lit.; RILA, Int. Rep. Lit. Art.

SP
FUENTES HISTORICAS ARAGONESAS.
Added/Corp Institucion "Fernando el Catolico." Vol. 1 (1962)-. Monographic series. Spanish. ir. Price varies per volume. Institut Fernando el Catolico, Plaza de Espana 2, Zaragoza 50004 Spain. **Tel** 011 34 76 229652. **LC** DP124; .F8.

GW/0016-2612
FULDAER GESCHICHTSBLATTER. [Fulda. Gesch.bl.]. (1902)-. Periodical. Multiple languages. an. **UDC** 908.
Ind/Abst BHA : Biblio. Hist. Art.

DK/0427-7945
FYNSKE MINDER. [Fynske minder]. (1951)-. Periodical. Danish. an. kr90.00. Odense Bys Museer / City of Odense Museums, Jernbanegade 13,, 5000 Odense C Denmark. **Tel** FAX 011 45 65 918900. **DD** 948.94. Index available. **Circ:** 3,000.
Ind/Abst BHA : Biblio. Hist. Art.

FR/0016-4119
GALLIA. *Title Change.* [Gallia]. Vol. 1 (1943)-?. Periodical. French. sa. Editions du CNRS, 22 rue Saint Armand, F 75015 Paris France. **Tel** 011 33 1 45075050. **LC** DC30; .G3. cum. index. **Circ:** 1,500. *Continued by Gallia Informations : Prehistoire et Histoire.*
Desc: Excavations and archaeological discoveries in France from classical antiquity to the 8th Century A.D.
Ind/Abst BHA : Biblio. Hist. Art; Br. Archaeol. Bibliogr.

FR/0994-8899
GALLIA INFORMATIONS : PREHISTORIE ET HISTORIE. **Added/Corp** Centre National de la Recherche Scientifique (France). (1988)-. Periodical. French. sa. Editions du CNRS, 22 rue Saint Armand, F 75015 Paris France. **Tel** 011 33 1 45075050. **LC** DC30; .G32. **DD** 936.4/005. *Continues Gallia.*
Ind/Abst BHA : Biblio. Hist. Art.

FR/0072-0119
GALLIA, SUPPLEMENT. (SUPPLEMENT A GALLIA.). [Gallia, Suppl.]. **Added/Corp** Centre National de la Recherche Scientifique (France). Vol. 1 (1946)-. French. ir. Editions du CNRS, 22 rue Saint Armand, F 75015 Paris France. **Tel** 011 33 1 45075050. **Circ:** 1,500.
Ind/Abst Avery Index Archit. Period. Suppl. Colum. Univ. (1989-); BHA : Biblio. Hist. Art.

NO
GAMMALT FRA STANGE OG ROMEDAL. Norwegian. an. Kr20.00. Stange Historielag, PO Box 108, 2310 Stange Norway. **Tel** 065-72778. **LC** DL596.S78; G35.

US
GARLAND LIBRARY OF MEDIEVAL LITERATURE. See Literature.

US
GARLAND MEDIEVAL TEXTS. See Literature.

US
GAZETTE OF THE AMERICAN FRIENDS OF LAFAYETTE. **Added/Corp** American Friends of Lafayette. Vol. 1, No. 1 (Feb. 1942)-. English. ir (Published every two or three years). $20.00. American Friends of Lafayette, Lafayette College, Skillman Library, Easton PA 18042. **Tel** (215)250-5151. **ED** Leonard Panaggio. **Circ:** 200 (ctrl).
Desc: This historical and patriotic society dedicated to the memory of the Marquis de Lafayette and to the study of his life and times.

GW
GDR : FACTS AND FIGURES. **VAT** German Democratic Republic: Facts and Figures. English. Verlag Zeit Im Bild, Franklinstr 17 19, D 01069 Dresden Germany. **Tel** 011 49 351 48640. **LC** DD261; .G18. **DD** 309.1/43/1.

US/0433-5082
GEORGE MACAULAY TREVELYN LECTURES. Vol. 1 (1961)-. English. Macmillan Publishing Company, 866 3rd Avenue, New York NY 10022. **Tel** (212)702-2000, (800)257-5755. **DD** 900.

SP
GERION / DEPARTAMENTO DE HISTORIA ANTIGUA. 1 (1983)-. Spanish (English, French, German and Italian). an. Editorial Complutense, Donoso Cortes 65 1RA Planta, 28003 Madrid Spain. **Tel** 011 34 1 3946372.

UK/0266-3554
GERMAN HISTORY : THE JOURNAL OF THE GERMAN HISTORY SOCIETY.
Added/Corp German History Society (Great Britain). No. 1 (Autumn 1984)-. English. Three times a year. £49.00 UK and Europe; $88.00 other. Oxford University Press, Walton Street, Oxford OX2 6DP England. **Tel** 011 44 865 56767, FAX 011 44 865 267773, telex 837330 OXPRES G. **(Subscription address:** Oxford University Press / USA, Journals Marketing Department, Oxford University Press, 2001 Evans Road, Cary NC 27513.) **ED** Mary Fulbrook and Jill Stephenson. **LC** WMLC L 83/9325. **[CCC].** **Bk Rev**. **Ad Acc**. available on microfilm and microfiche from University Microfilms International (UMI).
Desc: Principally the history of Germany and other German-speaking areas, but also other aspects of German life and culture which have a clear historical relevance.
Ind/Abst Am. Hist. Life (1989-).

US/0899-9899
GERMAN LIFE AND CIVILIZATION. [Ger. life civiliz.]. English. Peter Lang Publishing, 62 West 45th Street, 4th Floor, New York NY 10036. **Tel** (212)764-1471, (800)770-5264, telex 6973364 PLNY. **DD** 943.

US/0149-7952
GERMAN STUDIES REVIEW. [Ger. stud. rev.]. **Added/Corp** Western Association for German Studies. Vol. 1 (Feb. 1978)-. Periodical. English (German). tq (Feb., May, Oct.). $25.00 US; $27.00 Canada; $30.00 other. German Studies Review, Arizona State University, Tempe AZ 85287. **Tel** (602)965-4839, FAX (602)965-8989. **ED** Gerald R. Kleinfeld. **LC** DD1; .G382. **DD** 943/.005. Index available (every five years). **Bk Rev**. **Ad Acc**: **Pr Rev**. **Circ:** 1,400. Documents available from The Genuine Article.
Desc: Covers library needs in German history, political science, and literature. With six articles and sixty book reviews each issue, GSR covers Germany from medieval times to the present. A major resource for research libraries, and for general libraries needing a comprehensive journal.
Ind/Abst Am. Hist. Life (1978-); Am. Bibliogr. Slavic East Europ. Stud. (1978-); Arts Humanit. Citation Index [Full Cov.]; Child. Lit. Abstr. (19??-); Curr. Contents Arts Humanit.; Middle East Abstr. Index; MLA Int. Bibl. Books Artic. Mod. Lang. Lit.; Res. Alert [Full Cov.]; Romant. Move.; Soc. Sci. Cit. Index [Select. Cov.].

GW
GERMANIA SLAVICA. V. 1 (1980)-. Periodical. German. ir. Duncker und Humblot Verlag, Postfach 410329, D-12113 Berlin Germany. **Tel** 011 49 30 79000612, 011 49 30 79000613. **LC** DD4; .G37. **DD** 943.

●US
GERMANIC NOTES AND REVIEWS. See Humanities.

GW
GERMANY REPORTS. **Main/Corp** Germany (West). Presse- und Informationsamt. Vol. 1 (1953)-. English. Deutscher Bundes-Verlag GmbH, Postfach 12 03 80, W-5300 Bonn 1 Germany. **LC** DD259; .A52. **DD** 914.3.

GW
GESAMMELTE AUFSATZE ZUR KULTURGESCHICHTE SPANIENS. **VFOAT** Spanische Forschungen der Gorres-Gesellschaft. (1928)-. Periodical. German (Spanish). ir. Aschendorffsche Verlagsbuchhandlung, Postfach 1124, D-48135 Muenster Germany. **Tel** 011 49 251 690132, telex 08-92 830 WN MS D. **ED** Odilo Engels.
Desc: Spanish cultural history. German and Spanish scholars publish the results of their research in different fields of Spanish life and culture.

GW/0930-3286
GESCHICHTE IM WESTEN. Vol. 1, No. 1 (1986)-. Periodical. German. sa. Rheinland-Verlag GMBH, Koln, Abtei Brauweiler, 5024 Pulheim 2, Koln. **LC** DD258; .G47. **DD** 943/.005.

GW/0720-3659
GESCHICHTE IN KOLN. **Added/Corp** Universitat zu Koln. Historisches Seminar. **VFOAT** GIK; G.I.K. (19??)-. Periodical. German. bm.
Ind/Abst BHA : Biblio. Hist. Art.

GW/0433-8413
GESCHICHTLICHE ARBEITEN ZUR WESTFAELISCHEN LANDESFORSCHUNG. Vol. 1. German. ir. Aschendorffsche Verlagsbuchhandlung, Postfach 1124, D-48135 Muenster Germany. **Tel** 011 49 251 690132, telex 08-92 830 WN MS D. **DD** 943.
Desc: Monographs about the history of the West German area Westphalia.

GW/0072-4203
GESCHICHTLICHE LANDESKUNDE.
Added/Corp Mainz. Universitat. Institut fuer Geschichtliche Landeskunde. Vol. 1 (1964)-. Monographic series. German. ir. Price varies per volume. Franz Steiner Verlag GmbH, Postfach 101061, D 70009 Stuttgart Germany. **Tel** 011 49 0711 2582372, FAX 011 49 0711 2582290, telex 723263 daz d. **ED** Alois Gerlich.
Desc: Articles about South West German history.

AU
GESCHICHTSBLATTER / ARBEITSKREIS WINDEGG IM SCHWERTBERGER KULTURRING.
Added/Corp Arbeitskreis Windegg im Schwertberger Kulturring. Vol. 1 (1987)-. Monographic series. German. ir. Price varies per volume.

US/0016-920X
GESTA (FORT TRYON PARK, N.Y.). See The Arts-Art.

GW
GEWUSST WO? IN OFFENBACH. (19??)-. German. Beleke Verlag, Kronprinzenstrasse 15, 4300 Essen 1 Germany. **LC** DD901.O29; G4. **DD** 943/.41.

IT/0017-050X
GIORNALE STORICO DELLA LUNIGIANA. See Archaeology.

YU/0583-4961
GLASNIK - INSTITUT ZA NACIONALNA ISTORIJA SKOPJE. (GLASNIK.). [Glas. - Inst. nac. istor.Skopje]. **VFOAT** Revue - Institut d'Histoire Nationale. (1957)-. Periodical. Macedonian. tq. **UDC** 949.717.
Ind/Abst BHA : Biblio. Hist. Art.

CN/0836-7124
GLASNIK (NORTH BURNABY). (GLASNIK HRVATSKE SELJACKE STRANKE.). [Glasnik]. **Added/Corp** Hrvatska Seljacka Stranka. **VFOAT** Messenger of the Croatian Peasant Movement; Glasnik HSS. (1985)-. Newspaper. Serbo-Croatian (Roman) (summaries and/or abstracts in English). mo. 35.00Can$. Glasnik Hrvatske Seljacke Stranke, PO Box 82187, North Burnaby, BC V5C 5P2 Canada. **Tel** (604)524-2813, FAX (604)521-0030. **DD** 949.7/01. *Continues Hrvatski Glas (Winnipeg, Man.).*

UK
GLOUCESTERSHIRE RECORD SERIES.
Vol. 1 (1988)-. Monographic series. English. an. Price varies per volume. Bristol and Gloucestershire Archaeological Society, 22 Beaumont Road, Gloucester GL2 0EJ England. **Tel** 011 44 1452 302610. **ED** D J H Smith. **Circ:** 300 (ctrl).

BN/0350-1981
GODISNJAK DRUSTVA ISTORICARA BOSNE I HERCEGOVINE. (GODISNJAK DRUSTVA ISTORICARA BOSNE I HERCEGOVINE. ANNUAIRE DE LA SOCIETE HISTORIQUE DE BOSNIE ET HERZEGOVINE.). [God. Drus. istor. Bosne Herceg.]. **Main/Corp** Drustvo Istoricara Bosne i Hercegovine. **VFOAT** Annuaire de la Societe Historique de Bosnie et Herzegovine. (1960)-. Periodical. Serbo-Croatian (Roman). be. *Continues Istoricno Drustvo Bosne i Hercegovine. Godisnjak Istoriskog Drustva Bosne i Hercegovine, 0352-8669.*
Ind/Abst Am. Hist. Life (1960-); BHA : Biblio. Hist. Art.

UK
GREATER LONDON LOCAL HISTORY DIRECTORY AND BIBLIOGRAPHY.
Directory. English. Three times a year. £15.00. Peter Marcan Publications, 31 Rowliff Road, High Wycombe Becks HP12 3LD England. **ED** P Marcan. **Ad Acc**. **Circ:** 350.
Desc: Borough by borough guide to local history organisations, their activities and publications.

US/0279-1234
GREEK ACCENT. *Ceased.* [Greek accent]. Vol. 1, No. 1 (July-Aug. 1980)-?. Periodical. English. bm. Greek Accent Publishing Corporation, 41-17 Crescent Street, Long Island NY 11101. **Tel** (718)784-2986. **ED** Anthony H Diamataris. **LC** DF701; .G816. **Bk Rev**. **Ad Acc**.

Desc: Magazine for and about Greek Americans with particular focus on all aspects of Greek history, heritage and culture.

GW
GUBENER HEIMATKALENDER. German. 2.00. Kaltenborner Strasse 2, 756 Wilhelm-Pieck-Stadt Guben Germany. **LC** DD491.B94; G84. **DD** 914.3/15.

UK
GUIDE TO OVER 100 PROPERTIES / NATIONAL TRUST FOR SCOTLAND. **Main/Corp** National Trust for Scotland. **Added/Corp** National Trust for Scotland. **VFOAT** Guide to Over One Hundred Properties. (1985)-. English. an (Apr.). £1.50 Scotland; £2.00 others. National Trust for Scotland, 5 Charlotte Square, Edinburgh EH2 40U Scotland. **Tel** 011 44 31 2265922. **LC** DA875; .G84. **DD** 914.11/04858. ***Continues in part** National Trust for Scotland. Yearbook, 0077-5916.*

HU/0017-6540
HADTORTENELMI KOZLEMENYEK. [Hadtort. kozl.]. **Added/Corp** Hadtorteneti Intezet es Muzeum (Hungary). Vol. 1-44, (1888-1943); Vol. 1, (1954)-. Academic Scholarly Publication. Hungarian. Four times a year. $21.50. Akademiai Kiado, Publishing House of the Hungarian Academy of Sciences, Prielle Kornelia u. 19-35, H-1117 Budapest Hungary. **Tel** 011 36 1 1811991, FAX 011 36 1 1811991, telex 22-6228 AKNYO H. **(Subscription address:** Kultura, Hungarian Foreign Trading Company, PO Box 149, H-1389 Budapest Hungary**)** **LC** DB925.5; .H3.
Ind/Abst Am. Hist. Life (1954-).

HU
HAJDUSAGI MUZEUM EVKOENYVE, A. **Main/Corp** Hajduboeszoermeny, Hungary. Hajdusagi Muzeum. (1973)-. Hungarian (summaries and/or abstracts in English and German). an. Hajdusagi Muzeum, Hajduboeszoermeny, Hungary. **LC** DB975.H3; H344a.
Ind/Abst BHA : Biblio. Hist. Art.

GW/0931-0185
HAMBURGISCHE GESCHICHTS- UND HEIMATBLATTER. **Added/Corp** Verein fur Hamburgische Geschichte. (Feb. 1926)-. German. sa.
Ind/Abst BHA : Biblio. Hist. Art.

GW/0173-0886
HAMMABURG : VOR- U. FRUHGESCHICHTLICHE FORSCHUNGEN AUS DEM NIEDERELBISCHEN RAUM. **Added/Corp** Museum fur Hamburgische Geschichte. Hamburger Vorgeschichtsverein. Helms-Museum. Hamburger Museum fEur Archaologie und die Geschichte Harburgs (Helms-Museum). (1948)-. Periodical. German. **LC** DD901.H245; H3.
Ind/Abst Anthropol. Lit.; BHA : Biblio. Hist. Art.

GW
HANDBUCH SCHLESWIG-HOLSTEIN. German. be. Fotosatz Nord Druck-und Verlagsgesellschaft, Zeyestrasse 24, 2300 Kiel Germany. **LC** DD491.S633; H34. **DD** 943/.5120025.

BE/0770-0822
HANDELINGEN VAN HET GENOOTSCHAP VOOR GESCHIEDENIS. [Handel. genoot. geschied.]. (1979)-. Periodical. Dutch. qt. **UDC** 93/99. ***Continues** Annales de la Societe d'Emulation de Bruges, 0772-4020.*
Ind/Abst BHA : Biblio. Hist. Art.

GW/0073-0327
HANSISCHE GESCHICHTSBLATTER. **Added/Corp** Hansischer Geschichtsverein (Lubeck, Germany). Vol. 1 (1871)-. Monographic series. German. ir. Price varies per volume. Boehlau Verlag GmbH & Cie / Koeln, Theodor Heuss STR 76, D-51149 Cologne Germany. **Tel** 011 49 2203 307021, FAX 011 49 2203 307349. **(Subscription address:** BDK Buecherdienst GmBh, Postfach 900120, D 51111 Cologne Germany.**)** **LC** DD801.H17; H3. cum. index.
Ind/Abst Bibliogr. Carto.; BHA : Biblio. Hist. Art.

US/0896-114X
HARRIMAN INSTITUTE FORUM, THE. ***Title Change.*** [Harriman Inst. forum]. **Added/Corp** Averell Harriman Institute for Advanced Study of the Soviet Union. Vol. 1, No. 1 (Jan. 1988)-(199?). Periodical. English. mo. Harriman Institute Forum, Columbia Univeristy, Advanced Study of the Soviet Union, 420 West 118th Street, New York NY 10027. **Tel** (212)854-6218. **ED** Paul Lerner. **LC** IN PROCESS. **DD** 947. **Circ:** 1,000 (ctrl). ***Continued by** Harriman Review.*
Ind/Abst Am. Bibliogr. Slavic East Europ. Stud.; PAIS Int. Print (1991-).

US/0363-5570
HARVARD UKRAINIAN STUDIES. [Harv. Ukr. stud.]. **Added/Corp** Harvard Ukrainian Research Institute. Vol. 1, No. 1 (March 1977)-. Periodical. English. sa. $28.00 US and Canada; $32.00 other. Harvard Ukrainian Research Institute, 1583 Massachusetts Avenue, Cambridge MA 02138. **Tel** (617)495-4243, (617)495-4053. **ED** Omeljan Pritsak and Ihor Sevcenko. **LC** DK508.A2; H33. **DD** 947/.71/005. Index available. **Bk Rev. Circ:** 450.
Desc: Original scholarship (articles and documents) on topics of Ukrainian and Slavic history, language and literature; also, reviews of new publications relating to Ukranian studies.
Ind/Abst Am. Hist. Life (1985-); Am. Bibliogr. Slavic East Europ. Stud.; Middle East Abstr. Index; MLA Int. Bibl. Books Artic. Mod. Lang. Lit.

UK
HASKINS SOCIETY JOURNAL, THE. **Added/Corp** Haskins Society. **VFOAT** HSJ. Vol. 1 (1989)-. English. an. £25.00, $40.00 North America. Boydell and Brewer Limited, PO Box 9, Woodbridge Suffolk, 1P12 3DF England. **Tel** 011 44 394 411320, FAX 011 44 394 411477. **(Subscription address:** Boydell & Brewer, PO Box 41026, Rochester NY 14604.**)** **LC** D111; .H38.
Desc: Scholarly articles on medieval European history by leading historians; especially covers English and Norman history.

UK/0309-5118
HATCHER REVIEW, THE. **Added/Corp** Hatcher Society. (Spring 1976)-. Periodical. English. sa. $15.00. Hatcher Review Trust, Fairfield House, Godsfield, Alresford Hamp SO249RQ England. **Tel** 011 44 962 733245. **LC** DA690.S16; H37. **DD** 942.3/19/005.

SZ/0073-0955
HAUTES ETUDES MEDIEVALES ET MODERNES. 1- 1964-. Monographic series. French. ir. Price varies per volume. Librairie Droz SA, 11 rue Massot BP 389, CH 1211 Geneva 12 Switzerland. **Tel** 011 41 22 3466666, FAX 011 41 22 472391. **Circ:** 500.
Desc: History of medieval and modern Europe.

SZ
HEFTE DES ARCHAOLOGISCHEN SEMINARS DER UNIVERSITAT BERN. **Main/Corp** Universitat Bern. Archaologisches Seminar. (1975)-. French (German). an. Archaeologisches Seminar der Universitat Bern, Schwanengasse 7, CH-3011 Bern Switzerland. **Tel** 0041/31/65 89 91. **LC** DE1; .B47a. **DD** 938/.005. **Circ:** 400.

GW
HEIMATKALENDER (HANNOVER, GERMANY). (HEIMATKALENDER : JAHRBUCH DER DEUTSCHEN AUS BESSARABIEN.). Vol. 40 (1989)-. German. an. Hilfskomitee der Evangelisch-Lutherischen Kirche aus Bessarabien, Konigsworther Strasse 2, W-3000 Hannover 1 Germany. **LC** DK511.B4; H4. **DD** 947/.7500431/005. ***Continues** Heimatkalender der Bessarabiendeutschen.*

NO/0017-9841
HEIMEN. [Heimen]. **Added/Corp** Landslaget for Bygde og Byhistorie. (1922)-. Monographic series. Norwegian (Swedish and Danish). qt. $33.00. Landslaget for Lokalhistorie, Historisk Institutt, N-7055 Dragvoll Norway. **Tel** 011 47 7 3596433, FAX 011 47 7 3596441. **LC** DL401; .H43. **[CCC].** Index available. cum. index. **Bk Rev. Ad Acc. Circ:** 1,200.
Desc: Local and regional history of Norway.
Ind/Abst Am. Hist. Life (1969-).

BE/0018-0009
HELINIUM. 1- 1961-. Periodical. Multiple languages (French, Dutch, German and English). sa. 1,040F Belgium; 1,270 other. Universa, rue Hoender 24, 9200 Wetteren Belgium. **Tel** 011/32/91/691563. **LC** DH51; .H4. **UDC** 913. **Bk Rev.** ctrl circ.
Ind/Abst Anthropol. Index; Anthropol. Lit.; BHA : Biblio. Hist. Art; Br. Archaeol. Bibliogr.; Numis. Lit.

BN/0351-4552
HERCEGOVINA (MOSTAR, BOSNIA AND HERCEGOVINA: 1981). (HERCEGOVINA.). **Added/Corp** Arhiv Hercegovine Mostar. (1981)-. Serbo-Croatian (Cyrillic).

UK/0950-5245
HERITAGE (BURNHAM-ON-CROUCH, ENG.). (HERITAGE.). [Heritage]. (19??)-. Periodical. English. bm. £21.00. Bulldog Ltd., 2 Courtyard Denmark Street, Wokingham BRKS RG1 12LW England. **Tel** 011 44 734 771677.

UK/0265-3664
HERITAGE INTERPRETATION. **Added/Corp** Society for the Interpretation of Britain's Heritage. **VFOAT** Interpretation. (19??)-. Periodical. English. Three times a year. £25.00 Comes with Society for the Interpretation of Britians Heritage membership. Society for the Interpretation of Britain Heritage, 36 Westhaven Crescent Aughton, Ormskirk Lanc L39 5BW England. **Tel** 011 44 1695 422369.
Ind/Abst Museum Abstr.

CN/0820-2893
HERITAGE LINK. [Herit. link]. July (1986)-. Periodical. English (French, German and Ukrainian). qt. 12.00Can$ Canada; 25.00Can$ other. Heritage Link, 10110-82 Avenue/Suite 205, Edmonton Alberta T6E 1Z4 Canada. **Tel** (403)432-1510. **ED** Mike Pawlus. **DD** 971.23/004. **Circ:** 8,000-10,000.
Desc: Cultural, educational and informative.

US/0162-8267
HERITAGE REVIEW. (HERITAGE REVIEW / NORTH DAKOTA HISTORICAL SOCIETY OF GERMANS FROM RUSSIA.). **Added/Corp** North Dakota Historical Society of Germans from Russia. Germans from Russia Heritage Society. No. 5/6 (June 1973)-. English. qt. $25.00 US; $27.50 other. Germans from Russia Heritage Society, 1008 East Central Avenue, Bismarck ND 58501. **Tel** (701)223-6167. **ED** Armand Bauer. **LC** F645.R85; N67a. **DD** 978.4/004/31. Index available. **Bk Rev. Circ:** 2,000. ***Continues** Work Paper - North Dakota Historical Society of Germans from Russia, 0149-841X.*
Desc: Contains articles of historical and cultural value about the Germans from Russia.
Ind/Abst Am. Hist. Life (1973-).

UK/0264-9144
HERITAGE SCOTLAND : THE MAGAZINE OF THE NATIONAL TRUST FOR SCOTLAND. **Added/Corp** National Trust for Scotland. (198?)-. Periodical. English. qt. $33.00. National Trust for Scotland, 5 Charlotte Square, Edinburgh EH2 40U Scotland. **Tel** 011 44 31 2265922. **(Subscription address:** PO Box 457, Pinehurst, NC 28374; telephone: (919)295-4448**)** **ED** Peter Reeuie. **Bk Rev. Ad Acc.** ctrl circ.
Desc: A journal covering conservation and heritage matters in Scotland.
Ind/Abst Archit. Period. Index; Museum Abstr.

FR/0018-0998
HESPERIDE, L'. (L'HESPERIDE; RENAISSANCE CELTIQUE.). No. 1- Fall 1966-. Periodical. French.

GW/0073-2001
HESSISCHES JAHRBUCH FUER LANDESGESCHICHTE. [Hess. Jahrb. Landesgesch.]. **Added/Corp** Arbeitsgemeinschaft der Historischen Kommissionen in Darmstadt, Frankfurt, Marburg und Wiesbaden. Hessisches Landesamt fur Geschichtliche Landeskunde. (1951)-. German. an. **LC** DD801.H5; H25. cum. index.
Ind/Abst Bibliogr. Carto.; BHA : Biblio. Hist. Art.

SP/0018-1285
HIDALGUIA. [Hidalguia]. V. 1- (No. 1-); April/June 1953-. Periodical. Spanish. bm. $26.16. Hidalguia, Calle de Atocha 91, Madrid 12 Spain.
Ind/Abst Am. Hist. Life (1955-1973); Indice Hist. Esp. (1955-1973).

DK
HIKUIN. **Added/Corp** Forhistorisk Museum. (1974)-. Danish (Swedish, Norwegian, English and German). an. Kr150.00. Forlaget Hikuin, Moesgard, DK-8270 Hojbjerg Denmark. **Tel** 86-27 24 33. **ED** Jens Vellev. **LC** DL121; .H45.
Ind/Abst Anthropol. Lit.; BHA : Biblio. Hist. Art; Numis. Lit.

SP/0018-2141
HISPANIA (MADRID). (HISPANIA : REVISTA ESPANOLA DE HISTORIA / CONSEJO SUPERIOR DE INVESTIGACIONES CIENTIFICAS, INSTITUTO JERONIMO ZURITA.). [Hispania]. **Added/Corp** Instituto de Historia "Jeronimo Zurita". Centro de Estudios Historicos (Spain). Vol. 1, No. 1 (Oct./Dec. 1940)-. Monographic series. Spanish. Three times a year. Price varies per volume. Consejo Superior Investigacion Cientificas (CSIC), Vitruvio 8, 28006 Madrid Spain. **Tel** 011 34 1 5612833, FAX 011 34 1 4113077, telex 42182. **LC** DP1; .H5. **DD** 946.005. **Bk Rev.** Documents available from The Genuine Article.
Desc: Publishes original articles on medieval, modern and contemporary Spain, focusing primarily on history. Authors are specialists on Spanish history, based in Spain and other countries. Includes bibliographic notes.
Ind/Abst Am. Hist. Life (1954-); Arts Humanit. Citation Index [Full Cov.]; Curr. Contents Arts Humanit.; Res. Alert [Full Cov.]; Soc. Sci. Cit. Index [Select. Cov.].

FR
HISTOIRE EN SAVOIE MAGAZINE, L'. **Added/Corp** Societe Savoisienne d'Histoire et d'Archeologie. No 1 (Sept. 1991)-. Periodical. French. qt.

FR
HISTOIRE : H. **VFOAT** H. No. 1 (Mar. 1979)-. Periodical. French. qt. **LC** UNC. Documents available from The Genuine Article.
Ind/Abst Archit. Period. Index (Oct. 1979-June 1983); Arts Humanit. Citation Index [Full Cov.]; Res. Alert [Full Cov.]; Soc. Sci. Cit. Index [Select. Cov.].

FR/0752-3408
HISTORAMA (PARIS, FRANCE : 1984). ***Title Change.*** (HISTORAMA : HISTOIRE MAGAZINE.). **VFOAT** Historama-Histoire Magazine. No. 1 (Mar. 1984)-No 107 (Jan. 1993). Periodical. French (French). mo. Loft International, 1 Rue Lord Byron, 75008 Paris France. **Tel** 011 33 1 42256520. **LC** DC1; .H49. **DD** 944/.005. ***Continues** Histoire Magazine, 0223-4173.* ***Absorbed by** Historama Special.*

Desc: The greatest historians tell their discoveries and reveal the secrets of the past.
Ind/Abst Point Repere (1983-).

SP/0210-6353
HISTORIA 16. (HISTORIA 16 I.E. DIECISEIS.). [Historia 16]. V. 1 (May 1976)-. Periodical. Spanish. mo. 5100ptas Spain; 9720ptas Europe; 11640ptas North America; 15720ptas other. Historia 16, Hermanos Garcia Noblejas 41, 28037 Madrid Spain. **Tel** 011 34 1 4072700. **LC** DP1; .H56. **DD** 946/.005.

SP
HISTORIA 16 I.E. DIECISEIS. EXTRA. Spanish. 100ptas single issue. Historia 16, Hermanos Garcia Noblejas 41, 28037 Madrid Spain. **Tel** 011 34 1 4072700. **LC** DP1; .H562. **DD** 946/.005.

GW/0440-8969
HISTORIA. EINZELSCHRIFTEN. VFOAT Historia-Einzelschriften. (1956)-. Monographic series. German (English). ir. Price varies per volume. Franz Steiner Verlag GmbH, Postfach 101061, D 70009 Stuttgart Germany. **Tel** 011 49 0711 2582372, FAX 011 49 0711 2582290, telex 723636 daz d. **ED** Heinz Heinen, Francois Paschoud, Kurt Raaflaub, Hildegard Temporini, Gerold Walser.
Ind/Abst BHA : Biblio. Hist. Art.

SP
HISTORIA GRAFICA DE CATALUNYA DIA A DIA. (1978)-. Catalan. an. Ediciones 62, Provenca 278, Barcelona-8 Italy. **Tel** 216 00 62. **ED** Marisa Trigo, Joaquim Sabria and Enric Mir. **LC** DP302.C57; H57. Index available. **Circ:** 7,000 (ctrl).
Desc: Contains the most important events which have happened in Catalunya during the past year, explained through photographs and texts. It also contains articles about music, art, theatre, cinema, literature, etc., apart from statistical facts of Catalunya.

SP/0210-7716
HISTORIA, INSTITUCIONES, DOCUMENTOS. [Hist., Inst., Doc.]. **Main/Corp** Universidad de Sevilla. (1974)-. Spanish. an. Universidad de Sevilla / Secretariado de Publicaciones, Valparaiso 5, 41013 Seville Spain. **Tel** 011 34 5 4231958, 011 34 5 4235976. **LC** D1; .S433a. **UDC** 946.
Ind/Abst Am. Hist. Life (1974-1980).

SP
HISTORIA Y FUENTE ORAL. Added/Corp Seminario de Historia Oral del Departamento de Historia Contemporanea de la Universidad de Barcelona y del Institut Municipal d'Historia. No. 1 (1989)-. Periodical. Spanish. Twice a year. $34.00. Instituto Municipal Historia, Santa Llucia 1, 08002 Barcelona Spain. **Tel** 011 34 93 3178327. **LC** DP233; .H57. **DD** 946.08/05.

FI/0073-2540
HISTORIALLINEN ARKISTO. [Hist. ark.]. **Main/Corp** Suomen Historiallinen Seura. **Added/Corp** Suomalaisen Kirjallisuuden Seura. Historiallinen Osakunta. (1866)-. Periodical. Finnish. **LC** DK445; .S583. cum. index.
Ind/Abst Am. Hist. Life (1953-).

US/0883-3559
HISTORIANS OF EARLY MODERN EUROPE. ***Title Change.*** [Hist. early mod. Eur.]. **Added/Corp** American Society for Reformation Research. (19??)-(199?). English. an. NMSU, LB 115, Kirksville MO 63501. **Tel** (816)785-4665. **ED** R V Schnucker. **DD** 907. Index available. cum. index. **Ad Acc. Circ:** 1,500 (ctrl). ***Continued by*** *Scholars of Early Modern Studies, 1059-9185.*
Desc: Provides information on the latest research over 1,500 scholars in the field of early modern studies.

UK/0073-2567
HISTORIC HOUSES, CASTLES, AND GARDENS IN GREAT BRITAIN AND IRELAND. [Hist. houses, castles gard. G.B. Irel.]. (1965)-. English. an. $17.95. Hunter Publishing Inc, 300 Raritan Center Parkway, Edison NJ 08818. **Tel** (908) 225-1900, FAX (908) 225-0812. **ED** Sheila Alcock. **LC** DA660; .H57. **DD** 914.1/04/85. **Bk Rev. Ad Acc. Circ:** 80,000. ***Continues*** *Historic Houses and Castles in Great Britain and Ireland.*

XR/0440-9205
HISTORICA (CESKOSLOVENSKA AKADEMIE VED. SEKCE HISTORICKA). ***Ceased.*** (HISTORICA.). **Added/Corp** Ceskoslovenska Akademie Ved. Sekce Historicka. (1959)-Vol. 30 (19??). English (French, German, Italian and Russian). Academia, Publishing House of the Czechoslovak Academy of Sciences, Czech AC SCI, Vodickova 40, PO Box 896, 112 29 Prague 1, Czech Republic. **Tel** 011 42 2 245117. Documents available from The Genuine Article.
Desc: Informs foreign scholars on major results of historical research in Czechoslovakia. Besides main features there are also book reviews and a news column.
Ind/Abst Arts Humanit. Citation Index [Full Cov.]; Curr. Contents Arts Humanit.; Res. Alert [Full Cov.].

XO/0018-2575
HISTORICKY CASOPIS. [Hist. cas.]. Vol. 1 (1953)-. Periodical. Slovak (summaries and/or abstracts in German, English, French and Russian). bm. kcs120.00. VYD-VO, Slovenskej, Akademic Vied, V Bratislave Slovakia. **Tel** (089)52 20 27. **LC** DB661; .H52. Index available. **Bk Rev. Circ:** 1,350 (ctrl). Documents available from The Genuine Article. ***Continues*** *Historicky Sbornik.*
Desc: Main topics are Slovak history, including history of economy, and that of other nations closely connected with the events in Slovakia.
Ind/Abst Am. Hist. Life (1954-); Arts Humanit. Citation Index [Full Cov.]; Curr. Contents Arts Humanit.; Res. Alert [Full Cov.]; Soc. Sci. Cit. Index [Select. Cov.].

XR/0018-2583
HISTORIE A VOJENSTVI. [Hist. vojenstvi]. 1952, 1-. Periodical. Czech. bm. $58.60. **(Subscription address:** Artia Pegas Press Ltd., Palac Metro Narodni Trida 25, 11210 Prague 1 Czech Republic.**)** **LC** DB2070; .H58.
Ind/Abst Am. Hist. Life (1963-1968, 1974-); Curr. Mil. Pol. Lit.

DK
HISTORIE; JYSKE SAMLINGER. (19??)-. Periodical. Danish. Twice a year. kr160.00 Denmark; $23.00 other. JYSK Selskab Historie, Frhvervs Vester Allee, 12 DK 8000 Aarhus C Denmark. **Tel** 6-12 85 33. **ED** Jorgen Fink, Vagn Dybdahl and Knud J. V. Jespersen. Index available. **Bk Rev. Ad Acc. Circ:** 1,600. ***Continues*** *Samlinger til Jydsk Historie og Topografi (1866-1930) Jyske Samlinger (1932-1965).*
Desc: Economic, social and scientific history, concerning Denmark.
Ind/Abst Am. Hist. Life; Numis. Lit. (?-?).

CI/0351-2193
HISTORIJSKI ZBORNIK. [Hist. zb.]. **Added/Corp** Povijesno Drustvo Hrvatske. Savez Povijesnih Drustava Hrvatske. (1948)-. Periodical. Serbo-Croatian (Roman). an. **LC** DR301; .H5. cum. index.
Ind/Abst Am. Hist. Life (1953-).

AU/0440-9736
HISTORISCHES JAHRBUCH DER STADT LINZ. [Hist. Jahr. Stadt Linz]. **Added/Corp** Archiv der Stadt Linz. Stadtische Sammlungen Linz. (1955)-. German. an. S350.00. Archiv der Stadt Linz, Linz Austria. **Tel** 0732/2393-2972. **Bk Rev.** ctrl circ.
Desc: Local history of Linz.
Ind/Abst Am. Hist. Life (1963-1988); ARTbibliogr. Mod.; Bibliogr. Carto.; BHA : Biblio. Hist. Art.

SZ
HISTORISCHES MUSEUM SCHLOSS THUN. Main/Corp Historisches Museum Schloss Thun. (1971)-. German. an. **LC** DQ851.T5; A2. **DD** 949.4/5. ***Continues*** *Historisches Museum Schloss Thun. Jahresbericht des Historischen Museums im Schloss Thun fur das Jahr ... .*
Ind/Abst BHA : Biblio. Hist. Art.

FI/0046-7596
HISTORISK TIDSKRIFT FOR FINLAND. [Hist. tidskr. Finl.]. **Added/Corp** Svenska Litteratursallskapet i Finland. Vol. 1 (1916)-. Periodical. Multiple languages (English, Finnish, German and Swedish). Four times a year. Fmk90.00. Historisk Tidskrift for Finland, Berggatan 6 A 4 3 van, 00100 Helsingfors Finland. **Tel** 1912985. **ED** Max Engman. **LC** DK445; .H58. **Bk Rev. Ad Acc. Circ:** 1,000 (ctrl).
Desc: Articles, review articles, book reviews, bibliography, short notices in Swedish concerning the history of Finland and Northern Europe.
Ind/Abst Am. Hist. Life (1954-); Numis. Lit.

SW/0345-469X
HISTORISK TIDSKRIFT (STOCKHOLM). (HISTORISK TIDSKRIFT.). [Hist. tidskr.]. **Added/Corp** Svenska Historiska Foreningen. Vol. 1, (1881)-. Periodical. Swedish. qt (Mar., June, Sept., Dec.). Kr210.00 other. Svenska Historiska Foreningen, Box 5405, 11484 Stockholm Sweden. **Tel** 011-46-8-7832502, FAX 011-46-8-7832515. **ED** Arne Jarrick. **LC** DL601; .H6. **Bk Rev**, (Qty: 50). **Circ:** 2,200.
Ind/Abst Am. Hist. Life (1954-); MLA Int. Bibl. Books Artic. Mod. Lang. Lit.; Recent. Publ. Artic.; Selec. Coop. Index Manage. Period; Writ. Am. Hist.

NO/0018-263x
HISTORISK TIDSSKRIFT. Added/Corp Norske Historiske Forening. Vol. 1 (1871)-. Periodical. Norwegian. qt. Kr525.00, $89.00. Scandinavian University Press, PO Box 2959 Toeyen, N 0608 Oslo 6 Norway. **Tel** 011 47 2 2575400, FAX 011 47 2 2575353, telex 71896 UROR N. **(Subscription address:** Scandinavian University Press, 200 Meacham Ave., Elmont NY 11003.**)** **ED** Ole Kristian Grimnes, Soelvi Sogner and Haakon Hovstad. **LC** DL401; .H63. cum. index. **Bk Rev. Circ:** 1,500. Documents available from The Genuine Article.
Desc: Historical research in all the Nordic countries.
Ind/Abst Am. Hist. Life (1954-); Arts Humanit. Citation Index [Full Cov.]; Curr. Contents Arts Humanit.; Res. Alert [Full Cov.]; Soc. Sci. Cit. Index [Select. Cov.].

DK
HISTORISK TIDSSKRIFT. Added/Corp Danske Historiske Forening. Vol. 1 (1840)-. Periodical. Danish. sa. kr340.00 Scandinavia; kr398.00 Europe; kr444.00 other. Danske Historiske Forening, Njalsgade 102 Trappe 15, 2300 Copenhagen South Denmark. **Tel** 011 31 1 542211. **ED** Esben Albrectsen and Hans Kirchhoff. **LC** DL101; .H6. Index available (Published separately). cum. index. **Bk Rev. Circ:** 1,600 (ctrl).
Desc: Danish history from the earliest to the present time.
Ind/Abst Am. Hist. Life (1954-).

DK/0439-2620
HISTORISKE MEDDELELSER OM KBENHAVN. ARBOG. Added/Corp Selskab for Staden Kbenhavn Historie. (1960)-. Danish. an. ***Continues*** *Historiske Meddelelser om Kbenhavn.*
Ind/Abst BHA : Biblio. Hist. Art.

UK/0191-6599
HISTORY OF EUROPEAN IDEAS. [Hist. Eur. ideas]. **Added/Corp** International Society for the Study of European Ideas. Vol. 1, No. 1 (1980)-. Periodical. English (French). mo. $634.00 The Americas; £425.00 other. Pergamon Press, An Imprint of Elsevier Science Ltd., The Boulevard, Langford Lane, Kidlington, Oxford OX5 1GB United Kingdom. **Tel** 011 44 865 843000, 011 44 865 843699, FAX 011 44 865 843010. **(Subscription address:** Elsevier Science Ltd. Oxford Fulfillment Centre, PO Box 800, Kidlington, Oxford OX5 1DX United Kingdom.**)** **ED** Ezra Talmor and Sascha Talmor. **LC** D1; .H81736. **DD** 940/.05. **[CCC].** available on microfilm and microfiche from University Microfilms International (UMI). Documents available from The Genuine Article.
Ind/Abst Acad. Search (July 1993-); Am. Hist. Life (1980-); Appl. Soc. Sci. Index Abstr.; Arts Humanit. Citation Index [Full Cov.]; BHA : Biblio. Hist. Art; Br. Humanit. Index; Curr. Contents Arts Humanit.; Hist. Source (July 1993-); Humanit. Source (Jul. 1993-); INFO-SOUTH Abstr.; Int. Polit. Sci. Abstr.; Mag. Search; MLA Int. Bibl. Books Artic. Mod. Lang. Lit.; Philos. Index; Res. Alert [Full Cov.]; Romant. Move.; Soc. Plann. Policy Dev. Abstr.; Soc. Sci. Cit. Index [Select. Cov.]; Sociol. Abstr.

UK
HISTORY OF LINCOLNSHIRE. ***Ceased.*** (19??)-Series complete with Vol. 12 (19??). English. ir. Society of Lincolnshire History & Archaeology, Jews Court Steep Hill, Lincoln LN2 1L5 England. **Tel** 011 44 0522 21337.

CI/0350-6320
HISTRIA ARCHAEOLOGICA. See Archaeology.

HU
HITEL. 1988-. Periodical. Hungarian. bw. 251 East 82nd Street, New York NY 10028. **LC** DB901; .H58.

JA
HOKKAIDO DAIGAKU SURABU KENKYU SHISETSU BENRAN. Main/Corp Hokkaido Daigaku, Sapporo, Japan. Surabu Kenkyu Shisetsu. **VFOAT** Bulletin of the Slavic Institute of Hakkaido University; Surabu Kenkyu Shisetsu Benran. Multiple languages (Japanese and English). Hokkaido Daigaku Hogakubu Fuzoku Suralde Kenkyo Shisetsu, 060 Sapporo Japan. **LC** DK1; .H64A.

FR
HOLLANDE. Main/Corp Pneu Michelin (Firm). 1.- Ed. French. $9.95. Michelin Guides and Maps, PO Box 3305, Spartanburg SC 29304. **Tel** (803)599-0850. **LC** DJ16; .M28A. **DD** 914.92/0472.

UK/8756-6583
HOLOCAUST AND GENOCIDE STUDIES. Added/Corp United States Holocaust Memorial Council. Yad Va-Shem, Rashut Ha-Zikaron La-Shoah Vela-Gevurah. Vol. 1, No. 1 (1986)-. Periodical. English. tq (3 issues). $148.00 institutions, $39.00 individuals US; $158.00 institutions, $49.00 individuals other. Oxford University Press / New York, 200 Madison Avenue, New York NY 10016. **Tel** (212)679-7300, (919)677-0977, (800)451-7556, (800)445-9714, FAX (919)677-1303. **(Subscription address:** Oxford University Press / USA, Journals Marketing Department, Oxford University Press, 2001 Evans Road, Cary NC 27513.**)** **LC** D810.J4; H6428. **DD** 940.53/15/03924005. **[CCC].** available on microfilm and microfiche from University Microfilms International (UMI). Documents available from The Genuine Article.
Ind/Abst Am. Hist. Life (1987-); Arts Humanit. Citation Index [Full Cov.]; Curr. Contents Arts Humanit.; Index Book Rev. Relig.; Relig. Index One Period.; Res. Alert [Full Cov.]; Soc. Sci. Cit. Index [Select. Cov.].

US/0738-0739
HOLOCAUST STUDIES ANNUAL. ***Ceased.*** [Holocaust stud. annu.]. Vol. 1 (1983)-Vol. 3 (19??). English. an. Holocaust Studies Annual, Penkevill Publishing Company, Box 212, Greenwood FL 32443. **Tel** (904)569-2811. **ED** Sanford Pinsker and Jack Fischel. **LC** D804.3; .H65. **DD** 940.53/15/03924. **Ad Acc. Circ:** 500.
Desc: Collections of essays surrounding the Jewish

Holocaust by professional scholars with similar interests. **Ind/Abst** Am. Bibliogr. Slavic East Europ. Stud. (19??-1992).

SP
HRVATSKO PRAVO : VJESTNIK HOB-A I PRAVASKOG HOP-A ZA DOMOVINU I INOZEMSTVO. Periodical. English (French and Serbo-Croatian (Roman)). mo. $18.00. Hrvatsko Pravo, Apartado 705, Valencia Spain. **LC** DR1593; .H78. **DD** 949.7/2.

DK
HUGIN, LOKALHISTORISK TIDSSKRIFT FOR EGEBJERG KOMMUNE. V. 1-. Danish. Lokalhistorisk Forening for Egebjerg Kommune, Folmer Riss Alpevej 13 Egebjerg 5771, Stenstrup Denmark. **LC** DL291.E32; H84.

HU/0236-6568
HUNGARIAN STUDIES : HS. **Added/Corp** Nemzetkozi Magyar Filologiai Tarsasag. **VFOAT** HS. Vol. 1, No. 1 (1985)-. Academic Scholarly Publication. English (French and German). sa. $64.00. Akademiai Kiado, Publishing House of the Hungarian Academy of Sciences, Prielle Kornelia u. 19-35, H-1117 Budapest Hungary. **Tel** 011 36 1 1811991, FAX 011 36 1 1811991, telex 22-6228 AKNYO H. **ED** Denis Sinor and Vilmos Voigt. **LC** DB901; .H8457. **DD** 943.9/005. **[CCC].**
Desc: Publishes original essays on all aspects of the Hungarian past and present. Multidisciplinary in approach, it is envisaged as an international forum of literary, philological, historical and related studies. Each issue contains about 160 pages.
Ind/Abst Am. Hist. Life (1985-).

US/0194-164X
HUNGARIAN STUDIES NEWSLETTER. [Hung. stud. newsl.]. **Added/Corp** American Hungarian Studies Foundation. Hungarian Research Center. American Hungarian Foundation. Hungarian Research Center. No. 1 (Spring 1973)-. Periodical. English. Four times a year (Seasonally). $10.00. American Hungarian Foundation, 300 Somerset Street, PO Box 1084, New Brunswick NJ 08903. **Tel** (908)846-5777, FAX (908)249-7033. **ED** August J. Molnar. **LC** DB901; .H846. **DD** 943.9/007/073. Index available ($10.00). cum. index. **Bk Rev. Ad Acc. Pr Rev. Circ:** 1,500 (ctrl).
Desc: Reports on English language books, dissertations, journals and other publications relevant to Hungary and Hungarians from the world over.

CN/0713-8083
HUNGARIAN STUDIES REVIEW. [Hung. stud. rev.]. **Added/Corp** Hungarian Readers' Service. **VFOAT** HSR : Hungarian Studies Review. Vol. 8, No. 1 (Spring 1981)-. Academic Scholarly Publication. English. sa. 12.00Can$ (individuals), 15.00Can$ (institutions). Hungarian Studies Review, University of Toronto, 21 Sussex Avenue, Toronto ONT M5S 1A1 Canada. **Tel** (416)978-4157. **ED** George Bisztray and Nandor Dreisziger. **DD** 943.9/005. Index available. **Bk Rev. Circ:** 260 (ctrl). available on microfilm from University Microfilms International (UMI). ***Continues*** *Canadian-American Review of Hungarian Studies, 0317-204X.*
Desc: A scholarly, interdisciplinary journal devoted to the publication of innovative articles, critical reviews, and the analysis of issues related to Hungarian history, politics, and cultural affairs.
Ind/Abst Am. Hist. Life (1976-); Am. Bibliogr. Slavic East Europ. Stud.; MLA Int. Bibl. Books Artic. Mod. Lang. Lit.

HU
HUNGARIKA IRODALMI SZEMLE. V. 7, No. 1- ; Jan./March 1977-. Periodical. Hungarian. qt. 60.00ft. Orszagos Szechenyi Konyvtar, Budavari Palota F Epulet, 1827 Budapest Hungary. **Tel** 757-533/475, FAX (361)156-8731, telex 224226. **ED** Judit Szerb. **LC** Z2143; .H84; DB906. Index available. **Circ:** 520 (ctrl). ***Continues*** *Hungarica Kulfoldi Folyoiratszemle.*
Desc: Selected bibliography of books and articles.

US
HUNGARY UNDER SOVIET RULE. **Added/Corp** ACEN (Organization) Hungarian Freedom Fighters Federation. Hungarian National Council. National Representation of Free Hungary. Hungarian Committee. American Friends of the Captive Nations. **VFOAT** Second Thaw. (1957)-. English. an. **DD** 943.91.

IC/0019-1094
ICELAND REVIEW (REYKJAVIK, ICELAND : 1984). (ICELAND REVIEW.). **VFOAT** Atlantica and Iceland Review. (1984)-. Periodical. English. qt. $30.00. Iceland Review, PO Box 12122, 121 Reykjavik Iceland. **Tel** 11 354 1 675700, telex 2121. **ED** Haraldur J Hamar. **LC** DL301; .I25. **DD** 949.1/2/005. **Bk Rev. Ad Acc. Circ:** 34,000 (ctrl). ***Continues*** *Atlantica & Iceland Review, 0304-1263.*
Desc: Feature articles on Iceland's present life, culture, society, history, industry, physical nature, presented in attractive design with full colour photographs throughout each issue.

IT
ICHNUSA. Began in 1949. Periodical. Italian (Italian). 5.000 single issue. Via Regina Margherita 66, 09100 Cagliari Italy. **LC** DG975.S29; I3. **DD** 945/.9005.

FR
ICOMOS BULLETIN. **Main/Corp** International Council of Monuments and Sites. Bulletin. English (French and German). an. ICOMOS, 75 rue du Temple, 75003 Paris France.
Ind/Abst BHA : Biblio. Hist. Art.

BU
IDC : INFORMATION, DOCUMENTS, COMMENTARIES. **Added/Corp** Sofia Press Agency. **VFOAT** I.D.C.; Information, Documents, Commentaries; IDC, Information, Documents, Commentaries. (19??)-. Periodical. English. 29 Slavyanska Str, Sofia 1000 Bulgaria. **LC** DR51; .I33. **DD** 949.7/7/005.

AA
ILIRIA. **Added/Corp** Universiteti Shteteror i Tiranes. Sektori i Arkeologjise. **VFOAT** Illyrie. Vol. 1 (1971)-. Albanian (summaries and/or abstracts in French). sa (2 issues). $21.21. The Archaeological Research Centre, The People's Socialist Republic of Albania. **(Subscription address:** Book Distribution Enterprise, Rruga Konferenca E Pezes, Tirana, Albania**) LC** DR701.S49; I4. **DD** 913.39/5.
Ind/Abst BHA : Biblio. Hist. Art.

PO
INDEPENDENICA. **Added/Corp** Sociedade Historica da Independencia de Portugal (Lisbon, Portugal). (1940)-. Portuguese. an.
Ind/Abst Am. Hist. Life (1979-1981,1986-1987).

SP/0537-3522
INDICE HISTORICO ESPANOL. **See** History(General)-Abstracting, Bibliographies and Statistics.

II/0019-7211
INDO-BRITISH REVIEW. [Indo-Br. rev.]. **Added/Corp** Indo-British Historical Society. Vol. 1 (June/Aug. 1968)-. Periodical. English. sa. $30.00. Indo British Historical Society, 21 Rajaram Mehta Avenue, Madras 600 029 India. **Tel** 011 91 11 422404. **(Subscription address:** Prints India, 11 Darya Ganj, New Delhi, 110002 India, (Phone: 011 91 11 3268645)**) LC** AP8; .I43.
Ind/Abst Am. Hist. Life (1983-).

AU
INDUSTRIE, ZWANGSARBEIT UND KONZENTRATIONSLAGER IN OSTERREICH WIEN. **Added/Corp** Verein Kritische Sozialwissenschaft und Politische Bildung (Austria). (1987)-. Monographic series. German. ir. Price varies per volume. Verlag fur Gesellschaftskritik, A-1070 Vienna Austria. **Tel** 011 43 222 526 3582. **LC** UNC.

SZ
INFORMACIO - CASA NOSTRA DE GINEBRA. **Main/Corp** Casa Nostra de Ginebra. Vol. 1, No. 1 (Feb. 1972)-. Catalan. Universal Postal Union, Case Postale, CH 3000 Bern 15 Switzerland. **Tel** 011 41 31 3503111. **LC** DQ49.C38; C37a.

FR/0046-9351
INFORMATION HISTORIQUE, L'. [Inf. hist.]. (1938)-. Periodical. French. Five times a year. $120.00 institutions; $65.00 individuals. Librairie Armand Colin, BP 22, 41354 Vineuil Cedex France. **Tel** 011 33 54 438994. **ED** H. Dessain. **LC** D1; .I45. **[CCC].** available on microfilm and microfiche from University Microfilms International (UMI).
Ind/Abst Am. Hist. Life (1955-).

GW
INSELFUHRER. **VFOAT** Borkumer Inselfuhrer. 1.-First Edition; 1976-. German. Frisia-Verlag, 6301 Stufenberg 1 Germany. **LC** DD901.B619; I57.

SP
INSTITUT D'ESTUDIS ILERDENCS. **Main/Corp** Institut d'Estudis Ilerdencs. (1987)-. Catalan. an. Institut d'Estudis Ilerdencs, Antic Hospital de Santa Maria, Lleida Spain. **LC** DP302.L46; I57A.

FR
INTER DITS. No. 1-. Periodical. French. 23 rue Gosselet, Lille Cedex France. **LC** DC611.N821; I57. **DD** 944/.28/005.

UK
INTERNATIONAL DIRECTORY OF EIGHTEENTH-CENTURY STUDIES. **VFOAT** Repertoire International des Dix-Huitiemistes; International Directory of 18th-Century Studies; International Directory of XVIII-Century Studies. (1987)-. Directory. English (French). ir. ***Continues*** *Annuaire International des Dix-Huitiemistes.*

CN/0020-7020
INTERNATIONAL JOURNAL. [Int. j.]. Vol. 1 (Jan. 1946)-. Periodical. English. qt. 63.30Can$ (airmail), 30.00Can$ (surface mail) Canada; 33.00Can$ other. Canadian Institute of International Affairs, 31 Wellesley Street East, Toronto Ontario M4Y 1G9 Canada. **Tel** (416)979-1851. **ED** Robert Matthews and Charles. **LC** D839; .I5. **DD** 940.55. **[CCC]. Bk Rev. Ad Acc. Pr Rev. Circ:** 2,900. available on microfilm and microfiche from University Microfilms International (UMI). Documents available from The Genuine Article.
Desc: A selection of articles on post 1945 international affairs. Each issue has a theme.
Ind/Abst ABC POL SCI; Am. Hist. Life (1955-); Am. Bibliogr. Slavic East Europ. Stud.; Can. Index (?-?); Can. Period. Index; Curr. Contents Soc. Behav. Sci.; Index Period. Artic. Relat. Law (19??-19??); Int. Labour Doc.; Int. Polit. Sci. Abstr.; Middle East Abstr. Index; Peace Res. Abstr. J. (1964-1967, 1970-1985); Res. Alert [Full Cov.]; Soc. Sci. Cit. Index [Full Cov.]; Middle East J.

US/0272-7919
INTERNATIONAL JOURNAL OF TURKISH STUDIES. [Int. j. Turk. stud.]. **Added/Corp** University of Wisconsin--Madison. Vol. 1 (Winter 1979/80)-. Periodical. English. ir (2 issues). $27.00 institution, $21.00 individual. University of Wisconsin / International Journal of Turkish Studies, 4255 Humanities Building, Madison WI 53706. **Tel** (608)263-1825, (608)263-1800. **ED** Kemal H. Karpat. **LC** DR401; .I58. **DD** 909/.0975943. Index available (bound in last issue). **Bk Rev. Ad Acc. Circ:** 1,200 (ctrl).
Ind/Abst Index Islam. Lit.; Middle East J.

SW/0308-762X
INTERNATIONAL NEWSLETTER. ***Suspended.*** **Added/Corp** International Committee for Soviet and East European Studies. International Council for Soviet and East European Studies. (July 1976)-(1993). Newsletter. English. sa. ICSEES / International Information Centre for Soviet and East European Studies, ST Olofsgatan 18, S75225 Uppsala Sweden. **Tel** 011 46 18 181695. **LC** DJK35; .I58. **DD** 947/.0007.

UK/0964-6337
INTERPRETATION NEWSLETTER. [Interpret. newsl.]. (1991)-. Periodical. English. bm. **DD** 333.70941.
Ind/Abst Museum Abstr.

SP
INVESTIGACIONES HISTORICAS (UNIVERSIDAD DE VALLADOLID. DEPARTAMENTO DO HISTORIA MODERNA). (INVESTIGACIONES HISTORICAS / DEPARTAMENTOS DE HISTORIA MODERNA Y CONTEMPORANEA.). **Added/Corp** Universidad de Valladolid. Departamento de Historia Moderna. Universidad de Valladolid. Departamento de Historia Contempornea. (1979)-. Periodical. Spanish. an. 3000ptas. Universidad de Valladolid / Publicaciones, Secretariado de Publicaciones, Calle Juan Mambrilla 7, 47003 Valladolid Spain. **Tel** 011 34 83 294144, 011 34 83 294499, FAX 011 34 83 302095, telex 26357 EDUCI E. **(Subscription address:** l'Estaquirot S A, Nuestra Senora dell Coll 53, 08023 Barcelona Spain.**) ED** Celso Almuina Fernandez. **LC** DP160.9; .I58. **DD** 909.08. Index available. cum. index. **Circ:** 500.

IE/0332-4893
IRISH ECONOMIC AND SOCIAL HISTORY. (IRISH ECONOMIC AND SOCIAL HISTORY : JOURNAL OF THE ECONOMIC AND SOCIAL HISTORY SOCIETY OF IRELAND.). [Ir. econ. soc. hist.]. **Added/Corp** Economic and Social History Society of Ireland. Vol. 1 (1974)-. English. an. $17.00. Economic Social History of Ireland, Clonliffe Road Library, Dublin 3 Ireland. **ED** S J Connolly and T Bartlett. cum. index. **Bk Rev. Ad Acc. Circ:** 450.
Desc: Articles and reviews, select bibliography, and abstracts of recently completed theses on all aspects of Irish social and economic history.
Ind/Abst Am. Hist. Life (1974-).

IE/0021-1214
IRISH HISTORICAL STUDIES. (IRISH HISTORICAL STUDIES : JOINT JOURNAL OF THE IRISH HISTORICAL SOCIETY AND THE ULSTER SOCIETY FOR IRISH HISTORICAL STUDIES.). [Ir. hist. stud.]. **Added/Corp** Irish Historical Society. Ulster Society for Irish Historical Studies. (1938)-. Periodical. English. sa (2 issues). $44.00. Irish Historical Society, Department of Modern History, Art Building, Dublin 2 Ireland. **Tel** 011 353 1 772941, FAX 011 353 1 772694. **ED** J. L. McQuire and K. Jeffrey. **LC** DA900; .I63. **DD** 941.005. Index available (bound in last issue). **Bk Rev. Ad Acc. Circ:** 800 (ctrl). Documents available from The Genuine Article.
Desc: Irish history.
Ind/Abst Am. Hist. Life (1954-1959, 1962-); Arts Humanit. Citation Index (19??-19??) [Full Cov.]; Br. Archaeol. Bibliogr.; Br. Humanit. Index; Curr. Contents Arts Humanit.; MLA Int. Bibl. Books Artic. Mod. Lang. Lit.; Res. Alert [Full Cov.]; Soc. Sci. Cit. Index [Select. Cov.].

UK/0260-2067
IRISH SLAVONIC STUDIES. [Ir. Slavonic stud.]. **Added/Corp** Irish Slavists' Association. **VFOAT** ISS; I.S.S. No. 1 (1980)-. Periodical. English. an (Dec.). $10.00 individual; $15.00 institution. Trinity College / University of Dublin, Department of Russian, Dublin 2 Ireland. **Tel** 011 353 1 7021651, FAX 011 353 1 6770546. **ED** Ronald J. Hill. **LC** DJK1; .I74. **DD** 947/.0005. **Bk Rev**, (Qty: 30-40). **Ad Acc, Adv Mgr:** same as editor. **Pr Rev. Circ:** 250.
Desc: Literature, language, history, politics of Soviet

Union and Eastern Europe with full review section and literary translations by international contributors.
Ind/Abst MLA Int. Bibl. Books Artic. Mod. Lang. Lit.

US/1043-5743
IRISH STUDIES (NEW YORK, N.Y.). (IRISH STUDIES.). [Irish stud.]. (1990)-. Monographic series. English. ir. Price varies per volume. Peter Lang Publishing, 62 West 45th Street, 4th Floor, New York NY 10036. **Tel** (212)764-1471, (800)770-5264, telex 6973364 PLNY. **DD** 941.
Ind/Abst Am. Hist. Life (1981-1986); MLA Int. Bibl. Books Artic. Mod. Lang. Lit.

IE/0021-1389
IRISH SWORD, THE. (THE IRISH SWORD : THE JOURNAL OF THE MILITARY HISTORY SOCIETY OF IRELAND.). [Ir. sword]. **Added/Corp** Military History Society of Ireland. Vol. 1, No. 1 (1949/1950)-. Periodical. English. sa. Free to members of the Military History Society of Ireland. Military History Society of Ireland, Newman House, 86 St Stephens Gre, Dublin 2 Ireland. **Tel** 011 353 1 751752. **ED** Harman Murtagh and M. A. M. Litt. **DD** 941.5. Index available. **Bk Rev. Circ:** 1,200 (ctrl).
Desc: Studies war in Ireland and Irishmen at war.
Ind/Abst Am. Hist. Life (1955-).

US/0894-3494
ISLAND (OAKLAND, CALIF.). (THE ISLAND.). [Island]. March 1987-. Periodical. English. qt. $15.00 (libraries), $25.00 other. Island House, 731 Treat Avenue, San Francisco CA 94110. **ED** Edward Stacio. **DD** 941. cum. index. **Bk Rev. Ad Acc. Circ:** 2,000.

UK
ISLE OF MAN OFFICIAL YEAR BOOK. **VFOAT** Official Isle of Man Year Book. English. an. Motor-In-Mann Publications Ltd, Concorde House/Westbourne Road, Ramsey Isle of Man, British Isles United Kingdom. **Tel** (0624) 813464, FAX (0624) 815822. **ED** Noel J Q Howarth. **LC** JN1174; .I8. **DD** 942.7/9/0025. Index available. **Ad Acc.**
Desc: Articles on all aspects of working and living in the Isle of Man.

RU/0321-2858
ISTOCNIKOVEDENIC OTECESTVENNOJ ISTORII. (ISTOCHNIKOVEDENIE OTECHESTVENNOI ISTORII.). [Istocn. otecestv. istor.]. **Added/Corp** Akademiia Nauk SSSR. Sektor Istochnikovedeniia i Vspomogatelnykh Istoricheskikh Distsiplin. Institut Istorii SSSR (Akademiia Nauk SSSR). Vol. 1 (1973)-. Academic Scholarly Publication. Russian. Izdatelstvo Nauka / Akademiia Nauk, Publishing House of the Russian Academy of Sciences, Leninskii Porspekt 14, 117901 Moscow Russia. **Tel** 011 95 954-21-53, FAX 011 95 938-21-44, telex 411964. **LC** DK38.8; .I82. available on microfiche.

BU/0021-2636
ISTORICHESKI PREGLED. [Istor. pregl.]. **Added/Corp** Bulgarsko Istorichesko Druzhestvo. Institut za Istoriia (Bulgarska Akademiia na Naukite). (1945)-. Periodical. Bulgarian (table of contents in English and French). mo. DM162.00. Bulgarian Academy of Sciences, 1 rue 15 Noemvri, 1040 Sofia Bulgaria. **Tel** 011 359 2 803127. **(Subscription address:** Kubon & Sagner, ABT Zeitschriftenimport, D 80328 Munich Germany.**) LC** DR51; .B883. cum. index. **Ad Acc.**
Desc: Considers the problems of Bulgarian history and the historical relation between Bulgaria and other nations. Scientific reports, using rich sources. Research work and basic methodological problems are included.
Ind/Abst Am. Hist. Life (1960-); BHA : Biblio. Hist. Art.

XN/0579-0263
ISTORIJA (SKOPJE). (ISTORIJA : SPISANIE NA SOJUZOT NA ISTORISKITE DRUSTVA NA SR MAKEDONIJA.). [Istorija]. **Added/Corp** Sojuz na Istoriskite Drustva na SR Makedonija. Sojuz na Drustvata na Istoricarite na Makedonija. (1965)-. Periodical. Macedonian. sa.
Ind/Abst Am. Hist. Life (1977-).

RU/0131-3150
ISTORIJA SSSR. ***Title Change.*** (ISTORIIA SSSR / AKADEMIIA NAUK SSSR, INSTITUT ISTORII.). [Ist. SSSR]. **Added/Corp** Institut Istorii (Akademiia Nauk SSSR) Institut Istorii SSSR (Akademiia Nauk SSSR) Institut Rossiiskoi Istorii (Rossiiskaia Akademiia Nauk). (Mar./Apr. 1957)-(Jan./Febr. 1992). Periodical. Russian. bm. **(Subscription address:** Victor Kamkin, 4956 Boiling Brook Parkway, Rockville MD 20852.**) LC** DK1; .A3275. available on microfilm from University Microfilms International (UMI). ***Continued by*** *Otechestvennaia Istoriia.*
Ind/Abst Am. Hist. Life (1957-); Arts Humanit. Citation Index (19??-19??) [Full Cov.]; Curr. Dig. Post Sov. Press.

UN/0135-2210
ISTORYCHNI DOSLIDZHENNIA : VITCHYZNIANA ISTORIIA. [Ist. dosl., Vitc. ist.]. **VFOAT** Vitchyzniana Istoriia. Vol. 1-. Ukrainian. 1.51rub. Izdatelstvo Naukova Dumka / Ukrainian Academy of Sciences, Vladimirskaia Ulitsa 54, 252601 Kiev Ukraine. **Tel** 225-63-66, telex 131376. **LC** DK508.A3; I77. **UDC** 93.

IS
ITALIA. **VFOAT** Italyah. V. 1-. Periodical. Hebrew (Italian; summaries and/or abstracts in English). an. $12.00. Istituto di Lingue e Letterature, Departimento d' Italiano, Universita Ebraica, PO Box 1255, Gerusalemme Israel. **Tel** 02-660341, FAX 972-2-666804, telex 25391. **(Subscription address:** The Magnes Press, PO Box 7695, Jerusalem 91076 Israel**) ED** R Bonfil and J Sermoneta. **LC** DS135.I8; I85 HEBR. **Bk Rev. Circ:** 500.

IT/0392-3568
ITALIA CONTEMPORANEA. [Ital. contemp.]. **Added/Corp** Istituto Nazionale per la Storia del Movimento di Liberazione in Italia. No. 114, (Jan./Mar. 1974)-. Periodical. Italian (English). Four times a year. L60000 Italy; L80000.00 other. Italia Contemporanea, Piazza Duomo 14, 20122 Milan Italy. **Tel** 011 39 2 86463233. **ED** Massimo Legnani. **LC** DG572; .M65. Index available. cum. index (1949-1965). **Bk Rev. Pr Rev. Circ:** 1,000. ***Continues*** *Movimento di Liberazione in Italia.*
Desc: Italian contemporary history, with particular regard to fascism, antifascism, World War II resistance, the post-war period, political, social and cultural life.
Ind/Abst Am. Hist. Life (1954-); ARTbibliogr. Mod.

IT
ITALIA NOSTRA. **Main/Corp** Italia Nostra (Association). (1957)-. Periodical. Italian. Nine times a year. L48076.00. Italia Nostra, via N Porpora 22, 00198 Rome Italy. **Tel** 011 39 6 8416765. **LC** DG420.5; .I85a.

US/0894-1793
ITALIAN JOURNAL. [Ital. j.]. **Added/Corp** Italian Academy Foundation. No. 1 (1987)-. Periodical. English. Five times a year (Jan., Mar., May, Sept., Nov.). $36.00. Italian Academy Foundation, PO Box 420, 278 Clinton Avenue, Dobbs Ferry NY 10522. **Tel** (914)693-5329, FAX (914)693-7399. **DD** 945. **CODEN** ITJAEY.

US/0021-2954
ITALIAN QUARTERLY. [Ital. q.]. V. 1- (No. 1-); Spring 1957-. Periodical. English. qt. $20.00. Rutgers University / Department of Italian, 18 Seminary Place, New Brunswick NJ 08903. **Tel** (908)932-7031. **ED** C L Golino. **LC** DG401; .I725. **DD** 914.5. cum. index. **Bk Rev. Ad Acc. Circ:** 1,050.
Desc: Italian literature and culture including film, history, art, music, etc. Artistic translations of works of merit; and original work of poetry or prose in Italian.
Ind/Abst Am. Hist. Life (1973-1976, 1980-); Annu. Bibliogr. Engl. Lang. Lit.; MLA Int. Bibl. Books Artic. Mod. Lang. Lit.; Romant. Move.

CN/0700-3234
ITALIANA VITA. Began with March 1967 issue. Periodical. Italian. sm. $7.74. Vita Italiana-Italian Life, PO Box 163 Station L, Toronto Ontario M6E 4Y5 Canada. **Tel** (416)656-2050. **ED** Mario C Varano. **DD** 945.092. **Bk Rev. Ad Acc. Circ:** 25,000 (ctrl).

US/0883-086X
ITALIANO (NEW YORK, N.Y.), L'. (L'ITALIANO.). [Italiano]. Periodical. Italian. mo. L'Italiano, 5 Monroe Street, New York NY 10002. **DD** 945.

AU
ITALIENISCHE STUDIEN. **Added/Corp** Italienisches Kulturinstitut Wien. Vol. 1, (1978)-. Periodical. German (Italian). an. DM1300.00. Instituto Italiano di Cultura, Ungargasse 43, A 1030 Vienna Austria. **Tel** 011 43 1 7133454.

IT
ITINERARI DI RICERCA STORICA : PUBBLICAZIONE PERIODICA DEL DIPARTIMENTO DI STUDI STORICI DAL MEDIOEVO ALL'ETA CONTEMPORANEA / UNIVERSITA DEGLI STUDI DI LECCE. **Added/Corp** Universita degli Studi di Lecce. Dipartimento di Studi Storici dal Medioevo all'Eta Contemporanea. (1987)-. Periodical. Italian.
Ind/Abst BHA : Biblio. Hist. Art.

NE/0165-1153
ITINERARIO. [Itinerario]. **Added/Corp** Rijksuniversiteit te Leiden. Werkgroep voor de Geschiedenis van de Europese Expansie. (1977)-. Periodical. English. qt. $60.00 (institutions), $40.00 (individuals). Leiden University, PO Box 9515, Center History Europe Ex, 2300 Ra Leiden, The Netherlands. **Tel** 011 31 79272768. ***Continues*** *Newsletter - Centre for the History of European Expansion, 0165-1102.*
Ind/Abst Am. Hist. Life (1989-); Bibliogr. Mission.

BU
IZVESTIIA NA INSTITUTA ZA ISTORIIA / BULGARSKA AKADEMIIA NA NAUKITE, OTDELENIE ZA ISTORICHESKI I PEDAGOGICHESKI NAUKI. **Added/Corp** Institut za Istoriia (Bulgarska Akademiia na Naukite). (1960)-. Bulgarian (summaries and/or abstracts in French and Russian; table of contents in French and Russian). ***Continues*** *Izvestiia na Instituta za Bulgarska Istoriia.*
Ind/Abst Am. Hist. Life (1960-1974, 1979-).

NE/0925-7845
JAARBOEK MONUMENTENZORG. **See** Architecture.

BE/0774-5435
JAARBOEK VAN DE GESCHIED- EN OUDHEIDKUNDIGE KRING VOOR LEUVEN EN OMGEVING. (1976)-. Periodical. Dutch. an. 750F. Editions Peeters SA, Bondgenotenlaan 153, BP 41, B-3000 Leuven Belgium. **Tel** 32 16 235170, FAX 32 16 228500, telex 65987 PUL B. **UDC** 930.26.
Ind/Abst BHA : Biblio. Hist. Art.

NE
JAARVERSLAG (NETHERLANDS. KONINKLIJKE LANDMACHT. SECTIE MILITAIRE GESCHIEDENIS). (JAARVERSLAG / SECTIE MILITAIRE GESCHIEDENIS VAN DE LANDMACHTSTAF.). No. 75 (1981)-. Dutch. an. Free. Sectie Militaire Geschiedenis van de Landmachtstaf Frederikkazerne, van der Burchlaan 31, S-Gravenhage The Netherlands. **Tel** 070-165836. **LC** Z2451.M5; J3; DJ124. **Circ:** 500 (ctrl). ***Continues*** *Nasporingen en Studien op Het Gebied der Krijgsgeschiedenis.*
Desc: Report of the Military History Section Royal Netherlands Army.

NE
JAARVERSLAG - RIJKSDIENST VOOR DE MONUMENTENZORG. **Main/Corp** Netherlands. Rijksdienst voor de Monumentenzorg. Dutch. an. Fl15.00. Rijksdienst voor Broederplein 41, PO Box 1001, 3700 BA Zeist The Netherlands. **Tel** (03404)83211. **LC** DJ25; .N48A.

NE
JAARVERSLAG VAN DE NEDERLANDS-ZUIDAFRIKAANSE VERENIGING. Dutch. an. Nederlands-Zuidafrikaanse Vereniging, Keizersgracht 141, 1015 CK Amsterdam Netherlands. **LC** DJ149.S6; J33.

SP/0210-8496
JABEGA : REVISTA DE LA DIPUTACION PROVINCIAL DE MALAGA. Periodical. Spanish. qt. **LC** DP302.M21; J3. **DD** 946/.85.
Ind/Abst BHA : Biblio. Hist. Art.

GW/0084-8808
JAHRBUCH DER COBURGER LANDESSTIFTUNG. [Jahrb. Cobg. Landesstift.]. **Main/Corp** Coburger Landesstiftung. (1956)-. German. an. **LC** DD801.A201; C6.
Ind/Abst BHA : Biblio. Hist. Art.

GW/0072-4238
JAHRBUCH DER GESELLSCHAFT FUER NIEDERSACHSISCHE KIRCHENGESCHICHTE. **See** Religion and Theology.

GW
JAHRBUCH DER SCHLESIER. V. 1- (1979)-. German. an. Helmut Preussler Heimatverlag, Rothernburger Strasse 25, 85 Nuernberg Germany. **LC** DK4600.S42; A237. **DD** 943.8/5/005.

GW
JAHRBUCH DES HISTORISCHEN VEREINS DILLINGEN AN DER DONAU. **Main/Corp** Historischer Verein Dillingen an der Donau. (1896)-. Periodical. German. an. DM30.00. Historischer Verein Dillingen, Abholfach der Studienbibliothek, D 89407 Dillingen Germany. **ED** Rudolf Poppa. **LC** DD901.D485; H57a. **DD** 943/.37. **Bk Rev**, (Qty: 5-10). **Circ:** 900. ***Continues*** *Historischer Verein Dillingen an der Donau. Jahresbericht.*
Ind/Abst BHA : Biblio. Hist. Art.

LH
JAHRBUCH DES HISTORISCHEN VEREINS FUER DAS FURSTENTUM LIECHTENSTEIN. **Main/Corp** Historischer Verein fuer das Furstentum Liechtenstein. (19??)-. German. an (July). Price varies. Historischer Verein, Postfach 626, FL 9495 Triesen Liechtenstein. **Tel** 011 41 75 3921747. **LC** DB540.5; .H57.
Ind/Abst Am. Hist. Life (1954-).

GW/0341-9339
JAHRBUCH DES HISTORISCHEN VEREINS FUER MITTELFRANKEN. [Jahrb. Hist. Ver. Mittelfrank.]. **VFOAT** Jahrbuch - Historischer Verein fuer Mittelfranken. (1956)-. Periodical. German. an. **UDC** 943.01-35.646.
Ind/Abst BHA : Biblio. Hist. Art.

AU
JAHRBUCH DES MUSEALVEREINES WELS. **Added/Corp** Musealverein Wels. (1954)-. German. **LC** DB879.W4; M8.
Ind/Abst BHA : Biblio. Hist. Art.

AU
JAHRBUCH DES OO. MUSEALVEREINES GESELLSCHAFT FUER LANDESKUNDE. **VFOAT** Jahrbuch des O.O. Musealvereines Gesellschaft fur Laneskund; Jahrbuch des Oberosterreichischen Musealvereines Gesellschaft fur Landeskund. Vol. 123-. Periodical. German. an. S270.00. Verlag Oberosterreichischer Musealverein, Linz Austria. **LC** DB151; .L6. cum. index. **Circ:** 800. ***Continues*** *Jahrbuch des Oberosterreichischen Musealvereines.*
Ind/Abst Am. Hist. Life (1978-).

AU/1011-4726
JAHRBUCH DES VEREINS FUER GESCHICHTE DER STADT WIEN. [Jahrb. Ver. Gesch. Stadt Wien]. **Main/Corp** Verein fur Geschichte der Stadt Wien. Vol. 1.-; 1939-. German. an. Verein fur Geschichte der Stadt Wien, A-1082 Vienna Rathaus Austria. **Tel** 0222/4000/84811. **ED** Fertinand Opll. **LC** DB843; .V38. **DD** 943.6/13. **Ad Acc.** ***Continues*** *Verein fur Geschichte der Stadt Wien. Mitteilungen.*
Ind/Abst Am. Hist. Life (1955-); BHA : Biblio. Hist. Art.

GW
JAHRBUCH (FREUNDESKREIS LEBENDIGE GRAFSCHAFT). (JAHRBUCH / HERAUSGEGEBEN VOM FREUNDESKREIS LEBENDIGE GRAFSCHAFT E.V..). **Added/Corp** Freundeskreis Lebendige Grafschaft. **VFOAT** Jahrbuch Fur Rheinhausen und Umgebung. 1985/86-. German. ***Continues*** *Jahrbuch Fur Rheinhausen und Umgebung.*

GW/0075-2614
JAHRBUCH FUER DIE GESCHICHTE MITTEL- UND OSTDEUTSCHLANDS. ***Ceased.*** [Jahrb. Gesch. Mittel- Ostdtschl.]. **Added/Corp** Historische Kommission zu Berlin. Freie Universitat Berlin. Friedrich-Meinecke-Institut. Vol. 2 (1953)-(19??). German. an. Walter de Gruyter Inc., PO Box 303421, D 10728 Berlin Germany. **Tel** 011 49 30 260050, FAX 011 49 30 26005251. **(Subscription address:** US and Canada/ 200 Saw Mill River Road, Hawthorne, NY 10532, phone: (914)747-0110**)** **LC** DD731; .J3. cum. index. ***Continues*** *Jahrbuch fur Geschichte des Deutschen Ostens.*
Ind/Abst Am. Hist. Life (1955-).

GW/0446-3943
JAHRBUCH FUER FRANKISCHE LANDESFORSCHUNG. [Jahrb. frank. Landesforsch.]. Vol. 1 (1935)-. German. an. Verlag Degener and Company, Postfach 1340, Neuinberger Street 27, W-8530 Neustadt Germany. **Tel** 09161-1378. **LC** DD801.B465; E73. **DD** 943/.3. cum. index.
Ind/Abst BHA : Biblio. Hist. Art; MLA Int. Bibl. Books Artic. Mod. Lang. Lit.

GW
JAHRBUCH FUER REGIONALGESCHICHTE UND LANDESKUNDE. **Added/Corp** Sachsische Akademie der Wissenschaften zu Leipzig. Historische Kommission. 17, 2. T. (1990)-. German. ir. DM68.00. Verlag Hermann Boehlaus Nachfolger, Postfach 260, D 99403 Weimar Germany. **Tel** 011 49 3643 2071, . **LC** DD280; .J33. ***Continues*** *Jahrbuch fuer Regionalgeschichte, 0085-2341.*

GW/0173-7600
JAHRBUCH FUER REGIONALWISSENSCHAFT / HERAUSGEGEBEN VOM VORSTAND DER GESELLSCHAFT FUER REGIONALFORSCHUNG E. V. (DEUTSCHSPRACHIGE GRUPPE DER REGIONAL SCIENCE ASSOCIATION). **Added/Corp** Gesellschaft fuer Regionalforschung. Vol. 1 (1980)-. German (English). an. DM66.00. Vandenhoeck & Ruprecht, Robert Bosch Breite 6, D-37079 Goettingen Germany. **Tel** 011 49 551 695911, FAX 011 49 551 695917, telex 965226 VAN d. **[CCC].**

GW
JAHRBUCH FUER WESTDEUTSCHE LANDESGESCHICHTE. **Added/Corp** Landesarchivverwaltung Rheinland-Pfalz. Volume 1 (1975)-. Bibliography. German. an. DM42.00 Germany; DM114.00 others. Selbstverlag der Landesarchivverwaltung Rheinland-Pfalz, Karmeliterstr 1/3, D- 56068 Koblenz Germany. **Tel** 0261/33068, FAX 0261/33086. **ED** H. W. Herrmann and H. G. Borck. **LC** DD259; .J24. **DD** 943. **Circ:** 1,000.
Ind/Abst BHA : Biblio. Hist. Art.

AU/1012-6465
JAHRBUCH FUER ZEITGESCHICHTE. **Added/Corp** Osterreichische Gesellschaft fur Zeitgeschichte. (1978)-. German. an. **LC** DB91; .J26. **DD** 943.6/05/05.
Ind/Abst Am. Hist. Life (1982-).

GW/0448-1607
JAHRBUCH ZUR GESCHICHTE VON STADT UND LANDKREIS KAISERSLAUTERN. **Added/Corp** Historischer Verein der Pfalz. Arbeitsgemeinschaft Kreis Kaiserslautern. (1962)-. German. an. **LC** WMLC L 83/7856.
Ind/Abst BHA : Biblio. Hist. Art.

PL/0021-4019
JAHRBUCHER FUER GESCHICHTE OSTEUROPAS. [Jahrb. Gesch. Osteur.]. **Added/Corp** Osteuropa-Institut Munchen. (1936)-. Periodical. German (English). qt. DM198.00. Franz Steiner Verlag GmbH, Postfach 101061, D 70009 Stuttgart Germany. **Tel** 011 49 0711 2582372, FAX 011 49 0711 2582290, telex 723636 daz d. **ED** Edgar Hosch. **LC** D1; .J3. **DD** 940/.05. **[CCC].** cum. index. **Bk Rev. Ad Acc. Circ:** 600. Documents available from The Genuine Article. ***Supersedes*** *Jahrbucher fuer Kultur und Geschichte der Slaven.*
Desc: Articles and reviews dedicated to East European history, medieval and modern.
Ind/Abst Am. Hist. Life (1954-); Arts Humanit. Citation Index [Full Cov.]; BHA : Biblio. Hist. Art; Curr. Contents Arts Humanit.; Int. Bibliogr. Sociol.; Res. Alert [Full Cov.]; Soc. Sci. Cit. Index [Select. Cov.].

GW
JAHRESBERICHT DES HISTORISCHEN VEREINS FUER STRAUBING UND UMGEBUNG. **Main/Corp** Historischer Verein fur Straubing und Umgebung. German. an. DM54.00 plus postage. Historischer Verein fur Straubing und Umgebung, Fraunhoferstrasse 9, 8440 Straubing Germany. **Tel** 09421/16326. **LC** DD901.S93; H57A. **DD** 943/.34. **Bk Rev. Circ:** 800.
Desc: Themes are folklore, pre-history, ancient history, municipal history.
Ind/Abst BHA : Biblio. Hist. Art.

SZ
JAHRESSCHRIFT DER HISTORISCHEN VEREINIGUNG WYNENTAL. **Main/Corp** Historische Vereinigung Wynental. Periodical. German. be. Historischen Vereinig Wynental 1, 5734 Reinach Switzerland. ***Continues*** *Bericht der Historischen Vereinigung Wynental.*

JA/0389-1186
JAPANESE SLAVIC AND EAST EUROPEAN STUDIES. Vol. 1 (1980)-. Periodical. English (German and Russian; summaries and/or abstracts in Japanese). an. £15.00 UK; $25.00 US and Canada; £17.00 other. Kyoto University / Department of Russian, College of Liberal Arts, Yoshida Nihonmatsu-cho Sakyo-ku, Kyoto 606 Japan. **Tel** (0865)249838. **ED** Iwao Yamaguchi. **LC** DJK1; .J35. **DD** 947/.0005. **Bk Rev. Circ:** 1,000.
Desc: Concerns the societies and cultures of the Slavic world or European socialist countries, studied cooperatively by Society membership.

DK
JDISK ORIENTERING. V. 37- ; Jan. 1966-. Periodical. Danish. 20.00. Mosaisk Troessamfund, Billed-Bladet, G1 Mnt 1 1147 K, Kbenhavn Denmark. **LC** DS133; .J64. ***Continues*** *Jdisk Samfund.*

XR
JIHOCESKY SBORNIK HISTORICKY. **Added/Corp** Jihceske Muzeum Ceske Budejovice. Jihoceska Spolecnost pro Zachovani Husitskych Pamatek v Tabore. **VFOAT** JSH. Vol. 1 (1928)-. Periodical. Czech. qt. **(Subscription address:** Artia Pegas Press Ltd., Palac Metro Narodni Trida 25, 11210 Prague 1 Czech Republic.**)** **LC** DB2500.J553; J54.

CH/1016-0566
JINDAI ZHONGGUO SHI YANJIU TONGXUN. **VFOAT** Newsletter for Modern Chinese History. (1986)-. Periodical. Multiple languages. sa.
Ind/Abst Am. Hist. Life (1986-).

NE
JOURNAAL / UITGAVE STICHTING VOOR CULTURELE SAMENWERKING (STICUSA). **Added/Corp** Stichting voor Culturele Samenwerking (Netherlands). (19??)-. Dutch. Four times a year. Free. Stichting Voor Culturele Samenwerking, J J Violastraat 41, 1071 JP Amsterdam, Postbus 5492 (1007 AL), Amsterdam Netherlands. **Tel** 020-719944, telex 11074 STICU NL. **LC** DJ1; .N34. **DD** 303.4/82492/0.883. **Bk Rev. Circ:** 4,000 (ctrl). ***Continues*** *Sticusa Journaal.*

IE/0790-0090
JOURNAL / ARKLOW HISTORICAL SOCIETY. **Added/Corp** Arklow Historical Society. (1982)-. Periodical. English (Gaelic (Scots)). an (July, (every odd year)). 3p (two years). Arklow Historical Society, Upper Tinahask P Kelly, Arklow County Wicklow Ireland.

UK
JOURNAL / FLINTSHIRE HISTORICAL SOCIETY. **Added/Corp** Flintshire Historical Society. **VFOAT** Publications of the Flintshire Historical Society Journal. Vol. 28 (1977/1978)-. English. ir (published approximately every two years). £5.00. Flintshire Historical Society, 12 Stable Close Greasby Wirral, Merseyside L4N 2RW England. **Tel** 51 605 1147. **ED** A G Veysey and J Gwynn Williams. Index available. **Bk Rev. Circ:** 400 (ctrl). ***Continues*** *Flintshire Historical Society Publications, 0140-8429.*
Desc: Contains facts on the archaeology, history, and architectural history of the county of Flint, North Wales.
Ind/Abst BHA : Biblio. Hist. Art.

US/0162-9778
JOURNAL OF BALTIC STUDIES. [J. Balt. stud.]. **Added/Corp** Association for the Advancement of Baltic Studies. Vol. 3 No. 1 (Spring 1972)-. Periodical. English (German and French). Four times a year. $60.00. Association for the Advancement of Baltic Studies, 111 Knob Hill Road, Hackettstown NJ 07840. **Tel** (908)852-5258. **ED** Laurence Kitching. **LC** DK511.B25; B78. **DD** 309.1/47/4. Index available. **Bk Rev. Ad Acc. Circ:** 1,300 (ctrl). available on microfilm and microfiche from University Microfilms International (UMI). Documents available from The Genuine Article. ***Continues*** *Bulletin of Baltic Studies.*
Desc: Articles by Western and Soviet scholars in all disciplines which focus on Estonia, Latvia and Lithuania and their contemporary and historical relationships.
Ind/Abst Acad. Search (July 1993-); Am. Hist. Life (1972-); Am. Bibliogr. Slavic East Europ. Stud.; Arts Humanit. Citation Index [Full Cov.]; BHA : Biblio. Hist. Art; Curr. Contents Arts Humanit.; INFO-SOUTH Abstr.; Mag. Search; MLA Int. Bibl. Books Artic. Mod. Lang. Lit.; Numis. Lit.; Res. Alert [Full Cov.].

US/0747-6256
JOURNAL OF BASQUE STUDIES. ***Title Change.*** [J. Basque stud.]. Vol. 3-1, Spring 1982)-(1989). Periodical. English (Basque, French and Spanish). sa. Basque American Foundation, PO Box 13212, Fresno CA 93705. **Tel** (209)431-7745. **ED** Juan Cruz Mendizabal. **LC** DP302.B41; B29. **DD** 946/.6. Index available. cum. index. **Bk Rev. Ad Acc. Circ:** 550. ***Continues*** *Basque Artistic Expression, 0748-6545.* ***Continued by*** *Journal of Basque Studies in America.*
Desc: Compendium of articles covering literature, linguistics, history, anthropology, art and folklore of the Basques.
Ind/Abst MLA Int. Bibl. Books Artic. Mod. Lang. Lit.

US/0021-9371
JOURNAL OF BRITISH STUDIES, THE. [J. Br. stud.]. **Added/Corp** North American Conference on British Studies. Conference on British Studies. (Nov. 1961)-. Academic Scholarly Publication. English. qt (4 issues). $70.00 institution; $43.00 non-member individual; $29.00 NACBS individual member. University of Chicago Press / Journals Division, PO Box 37005, 5720 South Woodlawn, Chicago IL 60637. **Tel** (312)753-3347, FAX (312)753-0811. **(Subscription telephone:** (312)753-8083**)** **ED** Cynthia Herrup. **LC** DA20; .J6. **[CCC]. Acid Free.** available on microfilm and microfiche from University Microfilms International (UMI). Documents available from The Genuine Article, UMI Article Clearinghouse.
Desc: Major outlet for scholarly articles in all fields of British history and culture, ranging chronologically from antiquity to the present and geographically from the British Isles and Commonwealth to Britain's former colonies in America. Serving as a forum for works that open new areas of investigation and pose new questions, this publication defines history to include political, social, intellectual, cultural, literary, legal, economic, demographic and other themes.
Ind/Abst Acad. Search (July 1993-); Am. Hist. Life (1961-); Annu. Bibliogr. Engl. Lang. Lit.; Arts Humanit. Citation Index [Full Cov.]; Br. Archaeol. Bibliogr. (-?); Curr. Contents Arts Humanit.; Expand. Acad. Index (1989-); Humanit. Index; Humanit. Source (Jul. 1993-); INFO-SOUTH Abstr.; Int. Bibliogr. Sociol.; Middle East Abstr. Index; MLA Int. Bibl. Books Artic. Mod. Lang. Lit.; Newsp. Period. Abstr. (1991-); Res. Alert [Full Cov.]; Romant. Move.; Soc. Sci. Cit. Index [Select. Cov.]; U.S. Polit. Sci. Doc.

UK/0047-2441
JOURNAL OF EUROPEAN STUDIES. [J. Eur. stud.]. **VFOAT** European Studies. Vol. 1 (March 1971)-. Periodical. English. Four times a year. £60.00 (institutiosns), £30.00 (individuals) UK; $124.00 (institutions), $64.00 (individuals) North & South America & Japan; £62.00 (institutions), £32.00 (individuals) other. Alpha Academic, Mill Lane, Chalfont St Giles, Buckingham HP8 4NR England. **Tel** 44 494 872509. **ED** J E Flower. **LC** D1; .J58. **DD** 914/.03/05. **CODEN** JEUSEF. **[CCC].** Index available. cum. index. **Bk Rev. Ad Acc. Circ:** 600. available on microfilm and microfiche from University Microfilms International (UMI). Documents available from The Genuine Article, UMI Article Clearinghouse.
Desc: Research articles on all aspects of European culture.
Ind/Abst Acad. Search (July 1993-); Am. Hist. Life (1971-); Annu. Bibliogr. Engl. Lang. Lit.; ARTbibliogr. Mod.; Arts Humanit. Citation Index [Full Cov.]; BHA : Biblio. Hist. Art; Child. Lit. Abstr. (19??-); Curr. Contents Arts Humanit.; Expand. Acad. Index (1989-); Humanit. Index; Humanit. Source (Jul. 1993-); INFO-SOUTH Abstr.; Int. Polit. Sci. Abstr.; Mag. Search; MLA Int. Bibl. Books Artic. Mod. Lang. Lit.; Newsp. Period. Abstr. (1991-); Res. Alert [Full Cov.]; Soc. Sci. Cit. Index [Select. Cov.].

PK/0258-9680
JOURNAL OF EUROPEAN STUDIES (KARACHI). (JOURNAL OF EUROPEAN STUDIES.). [J. eur. stud.]. **Added/Corp** University of Karachi. Area Study Centre for Europe. Vol. 1 No. 1 (Jan. 1985)-. Periodical. English. sa. **LC** D1; .J583. **DD** 940/.05. **UDC** 008 (4).
Ind/Abst Am. Hist. Life (1986-).

UK/0308-6534
JOURNAL OF IMPERIAL AND COMMONWEALTH HISTORY, THE. [J. imp. Commw. hist.]. Vol. 1, No. 1 (Oct. 1972)-. Periodical. English. Three times a year. $145.00. Frank Cass & Company Ltd, Newbury House, 890-900 Eastern Avenue, Newbury Park, Ilford, Essex IG2 7HH United Kingdom. **Tel** 011 44 81 599 8866, FAX 011 44 81 599 0984, telex 897719. **ED** Andrew Porter and R.F. Holland. **LC** DA10; .J68. **DD** 909/.0971241. Index available in last issue of volume--attached. **Bk Rev. Ad Acc, Adv Mgr:** Anne Kidson. **Circ:** 850. available on microfilm and microfiche from University Microfilms International (UMI). Documents available from The Genuine Article.
Desc: The journal presents and discusses recent research in the history of the British Empire and Commonwealth, with particular emphasis on imperial policy, the rise of nationalism and transfer of power.
Ind/Abst Am. Hist. Life (1972-); Arts Humanit. Citation Index [Full Cov.]; Br. Humanit. Index; Curr. Contents Arts Humanit.; Res. Alert [Full Cov.]; Soc. Plann. Policy Dev. Abstr.; Soc. Sci. Cit. Index [Select. Cov.]; Sociol. Abstr. (1972-).

US/0047-2573
JOURNAL OF MEDIEVAL AND RENAISSANCE STUDIES, THE. [J. mediev. Renaiss. stud.]. Vol. 1 (Spring 1971)-. Periodical. English. tq (3 issues). $78.00 (institutions), $32.00 (individuals) US; $87.00 (institutions), $41.00 (individuals) other. Duke University Press, PO Box 90660, Durham NC 27708-0660. **Tel** (919)687-3600, (919)688-5134 (orders), FAX (919)688-4574, telex 802829. **ED** Annabel Patterson and Marcel Tetel. **LC** CB351; .J78. **DD** 940.1/05. **[CCC]. Bk Rev. Ad Acc. Circ:** 700 (ctrl). available on microfilm and microfiche from University Microfilms International (UMI). Documents available from The Genuine Article, UMI Article Clearinghouse.
Desc: Focuses on the transition from the Middle Ages to the Renaissance. Examines general problems, specific issues and accomplishments in art, history, literature, music, philosophy, and theology of the two periods.
Ind/Abst Acad. Search (July 1993-); Am. Hist. Life (1973-); Annu. Bibliogr. Engl. Lang. Lit.; Arts Humanit. Citation Index [Full Cov.]; BHA : Biblio. Hist. Art; Curr. Contents Arts Humanit.; Expand. Acad. Index (1989-); Hist. Source (July 1993-); Humanit. Index; Humanit. Source (Jul. 1993-); INFO-SOUTH Abstr.; Mag. Search; MLA Int. Bibl. Books Artic. Mod. Lang. Lit.; Newsp. Period. Abstr. (1991-); Res. Alert [Full Cov.]; Romant. Move.; Soc. Sci. Cit. Index [Select. Cov.].

NE/0304-4181
JOURNAL OF MEDIEVAL HISTORY. [J. mediev. hist.]. Vol. 1 (April 1975)-. Academic Scholarly Publication. Multiple languages (English, French and German). qt (1 volume). Fl425.00. Elsevier Science Publishers BV, PO Box 211, 1000 AE Amsterdam Netherlands. **Tel** 011 31 20 5803642, FAX 011 31 20 5862696, telex 15682. **ED** R Vaughan. **LC** D111; .J67. **DD** 940.1/05. **[CCC].** available on microfilm and microfiche from University Microfilms International (UMI). Documents available from The Genuine Article.
Desc: Aims at meeting the need for a major publication devoted exclusively to the history of Europe in the middle ages.
Ind/Abst Arts Humanit. Citation Index [Full Cov.]; BHA : Biblio. Hist. Art; Br. Archaeol. Bibliogr.; Curr. Contents Arts Humanit.; Res. Alert [Full Cov.]; Soc. Sci. Cit. Index [Select. Cov.].

SZ/0304-4181
JOURNAL OF MEDIEVAL HISTORY MICROFORM. Vol. 1, No. 1 (April 1975)-. Periodical. Multiple languages (English, French and German). North-Holland Publishing Company, PO Box 211, Amsterdam The Netherlands. **LC** Microfilm. **[CCC].**

US/0738-1727
JOURNAL OF MODERN GREEK STUDIES. [J. mod. Greek stud.]. **Added/Corp** Modern Greek Studies Association. Vol. 1, No. 1 (May 1983)-. Periodical. English (Greek, Modern). Twice a year (May, October). $47.50 US; $50.40 Canada and Mexico; $51.70 other. Johns Hopkins University Press, 2715 North Charles Street, Baltimore MD 21218-4319. **Tel** (410)516-6987, FAX (410)516-6968. **ED** Ernestine Friedl. **LC** DF741; .J68. **DD** 949.5/005. **[CCC]. Bk Rev. Ad Acc. Circ:** 600. available on microfilm and microfiche from University Microfilms International (UMI). Documents available from The Genuine Article.
Desc: Publishes critical analyses of Greek social, cultural, and political affairs, covering the period from late Byzantine Empire to the present.
Ind/Abst Am. Hist. Life (1985-); Arts Humanit. Citation Index [Full Cov.]; Curr. Contents Arts Humanit.; Int. Polit. Sci. Abstr.; MLA Int. Bibl. Books Artic. Mod. Lang. Lit.; Res. Alert [Full Cov.].

UK
JOURNAL OF ROMAN STUDIES MONOGRAPHS. Monographic series. English. Price varies per volume. Society of Promotion Roman Studies, 31 34 Gordon Square, London WC1H 0PP England. **Tel** 011 44 1 387 8157.

US/0162-8283
JOURNAL OF THE AMERICAN HISTORICAL SOCIETY OF GERMANS FROM RUSSIA. [J. Am. Hist. Soc. Ger. Russ.]. **Main/Corp** American Historical Society of Germans from Russia. Vol. 1 (Spring 1978)-. Periodical. English. Four times a year. $30.00 (membership). American Historical Society of Germans from Russia, 631 D Street, Lincoln NE 68502. **Tel** (402)474-3363, FAX (402)474-7229. **ED** Richard R Rye. **LC** E184.R85; A53b. **DD** 973/.04/31. **Bk Rev.** ***Supersedes*** *Work Paper - American Historical Society of Germans from Russia, 0145-6105.*
Desc: Historical journal on the culture, folklore, and current activities of Germans from Russia. It carries book reviews and annotates new books on the subject.
Ind/Abst Am. Hist. Life (1977-1979, 1982-).

US/0098-4981
JOURNAL OF THE AMERICAN PORTUGUESE SOCIETY, THE. ***Suspended.*** [J. Am. Port. Soc.]. **Main/Corp** American Portuguese Society. Vol. 8 (Spring/Summer 1974)-. Periodical. English. qt. Free. American Portuguese Society, American Asian Education Exchange, PO Box 174, Saint James NY 11780. **Tel** (212)751-1992. **LC** DP501; .A5. **DD** 946.9/005. ***Continues*** *Journal of the American Portuguese Cultural Society.*
Ind/Abst MLA Int. Bibl. Books Artic. Mod. Lang. Lit.

IE/0010-8731
JOURNAL OF THE CORK HISTORICAL AND ARCHAEOLOGICAL SOCIETY. [J. Cork Hist. Archaeol. Soc.]. **Added/Corp** Cork Historical and Archaeological Society. (1892)-. Periodical. English (Gaelic (Scots)). an (Oct.). $22.00 US and Canada. Cork Historical and Archaeological Society, Sonas Farranlea Park, Cork Ireland. **ED** Diarmaio O. Murchadha. Index available. cum. index. **Bk Rev. Ad Acc. Circ:** 500.
Desc: Every aspect of the history, archaeology, genealogy, folklore, architecture and art of Ireland; especially concerned with the Cork and Munster regions.
Ind/Abst Am. Hist. Life (1955-1957); BHA : Biblio. Hist. Art; Br. Archaeol. Bibliogr.; MLA Int. Bibl. Books Artic. Mod. Lang. Lit.

US/0364-2976
JOURNAL OF THE HELLENIC DIASPORA. [J. Hell. diaspora]. **Added/Corp** Hellenic American Society. Vol. 1, No. 4 (1974)-. Academic Scholarly Publication. English (Greek, Modern). sa (March & Sept.). $20.00 (individual), $30.00 (institutional) US; $25.00 (individual), $35.00 (institutional) other. Pella Publishing Company, 337 West 36th Street, New York NY 10018-6402. **Tel** (212)279-9586. **ED** Alexander Kitroeff & Kostas Myrsiades. **LC** DF701; .J68. **DD** 949.5/005. Index available. **Bk Rev. Ad Acc. Circ:** 1,000. ***Continues*** *Journal of the Hellenic American Society, 0195-4342.*
Desc: The magazine is concerned with the entire spectrum of scholarly, critical, and artistic work that is based on contemporary Greece. Publishes critical, theoretical, and historical studies, review articles, and translations keyed to the Greek experience of the nineteenth and twentieth centuries.
Ind/Abst Am. Hist. Life (1975-); Am. Bibliogr. Slavic East Europ. Stud.; Int. Polit. Sci. Abstr.; MLA Int. Bibl. Books Artic. Mod. Lang. Lit.; Psychol. Abstr.; Soc. Plann. Policy Dev. Abstr.; Sociol. Abstr.; Sociol. Educ. Abstr.

US/8755-3805
JOURNAL OF THE JOHANNES SCHWALM HISTORICAL ASSOCIATION, INC. **See** History(General)-History of North, South, and Central America.

UK
JOURNAL OF THE LANCASHIRE & CHESHIRE BRANCH OF THE WESLEY HISTORICAL SOCIETY. **VFOAT** Journal. **VAT** Journal of the Lancashire and Cheshire Branch of the Wesley Historical Society. (19??)-. Periodical. English. sa. Record Society of Lancashire, PO Box 147, University of Liverpool, Liverpool L69 3BX England. **Tel** 011 44 51 7942000.

GW
JOURNAL OF THE NEPAL RESEARCH CENTRE : NJRC. **Added/Corp** Nepal Research Centre. **VFOAT** JNRC. Vol. 1 (1977)-. Periodical. English. ir. Price varies. Franz Steiner Verlag GmbH, Postfach 101061, D 70009 Stuttgart Germany. **Tel** 011 49 0711 2582372, FAX 011 49 0711 2582290, telex 723636 daz d. **LC** DS493; .N47a. **DD** 954.9/6/05.

UK
JOURNAL OF THE ROYAL INSTITUTION OF CORNWALL. **Main/Corp** Royal Institution of Cornwall. Vol. 1 (Mar. 1864)- Vol.24 (1942); New Ser., Vol. 1 (1951)-. English. **LC** DA670; .C79. **DD** 936.2/37.
Ind/Abst BHA : Biblio. Hist. Art.

IE/0035-9106
JOURNAL OF THE ROYAL SOCIETY OF ANTIQUARIES OF IRELAND, THE. [J. R. Soc. Atiq. Irel.]. **Main/Corp** Royal Society of Antiquaries of Ireland. 5th Series, Vol. 2 (1892)-Vol. 20 (1910); 6th Series, Vol. 1 (1911)-Vol. 20 (1930); 7th Series, Vol. 1 (1931)-Vol. 13 (1943); Vol. 74 (1944)-. English. an. 20.00p. Royal Society Antiquaries of Ireland, 63 Merrion Square, Dublin 2 Ireland. **Tel** 011 353 1 6761749. **ED** Professor Michael Herity. **LC** DA900; .R88. **DD** 936.1/5/005. cum. index. **Bk Rev,** (Qty: varies). **Circ:** 2,000. ***Continues*** *Royal Society of Antiquaries of Ireland. Proceedings and Papers of the Royal Society of Antiquaries of Ireland.*
Desc: The aim is to preserve, examine and illustrate the material culture of Ireland.
Ind/Abst Anthropol. Index; BHA : Biblio. Hist. Art; Br. Archaeol. Bibliogr.; MLA Int. Bibl. Books Artic. Mod. Lang. Lit.; Numis. Lit.; RILA, Int. Rep. Lit. Art.

US/1042-3834
JOURNAL OF THE SOCIETY OF BASQUE STUDIES IN AMERICA. (JOURNAL OF THE SOCIETY OF BASQUE STUDIES IN AMERICA / SOCIETY OF BASQUE STUDIES IN AMERICA.). [J. Soc. Basque Stud. Am.]. **Added/Corp** Society of Basque Studies in America. Vol. 8 (1988)-. English (Spanish). an. University of Bridgeport, 303 University Avenue, Bridgeport CT 06602. **Tel** (203)576-4068. **LC** DP302.B41; J68. **DD** 946/.6/005. ***Continues*** *Journal of Basque Studies in America.*
Ind/Abst MLA Int. Bibl. Books Artic. Mod. Lang. Lit.

CN/0701-1792
JOURNAL OF UKRAINIAN GRADUATE STUDIES. **VFOAT** Zhurnal Vyshchyky Ukrainoznaychykh Studii. V. 1- Fall 1976-. Periodical. English (Ukrainian). sa. $15.00, Individual rate $10.00. Canadian Institute of Ukrainian Studies, University of Alberta, 352 Athabasca Hall, Edmonton Alberta T6G 2E8 Canada. **Tel** (403)492-2972, FAX (403)492-4967, telex 037-2023. **ED** David R Marples. **DD** 947/.71/005. **Bk Rev. Ad Acc. Pr Rev. Circ:** 3,000 (ctrl).
Desc: Publishes articles in the field of Ukrainian-related subjects in both the social sciences and humanities.

UK
JOURNAL - THE ENGLISH PLACE-NAME SOCIETY. **Main/Corp** English Place-Name Society. **Added/Corp** English Place-Name Society. Annual Report. English Place-Name Society. Journal ... & ... Annual Report. English Place-Name Society. Journal ... and ... Annual Report. **VFOAT** Journal ... & ... Annual Report. (1968/69)-. English. an. £25.00 Comes with English Place Name Society membership. English Place-Name Society, University of Nottingham, Department English Studies, Nottingham NG7 2RD England. **Tel** 011 44 602 484848. **LC** DA645; .E57a. **DD** 914.2/001/4. ***Continues*** *English Place-Name Society. Annual Report.*
Desc: Includes the society annual reports.
Ind/Abst Annu. Bibliogr. Engl. Lang. Lit.

●GW
JUDISCHER ALMANACH. (JUDISCHER ALMANACH ... DES LEO BAECK INSTITUTS.). (1993)-. German. an. DM28.00. Juedischer Verlag, Lindenstrasse 29 35, 60325 Frankfurt Germany. **Tel** 011 49 69 75601300. ***Absorbed*** *Leo Baeck Institut Bulletin.*

YU/0350-2902
JUGOSLOVENSKI ISTORIJSKI CASOPIS. [Jugosl. ist. cas.]. **Added/Corp** Savez Drustava Istoricara Jugoslavije. (1962)-. Periodical. Multiple languages (Serbo-Croatian (Roman), Macedonian and Slovenian; summaries and/or abstracts in English, French, German and Russian). qt. **LC** DR301; .J867.
Ind/Abst Am. Hist. Life (1976-).

CN/0410-935X
KALENDAR KANADSKEJ SLOVENSKEJ LIGY. ***Title Change.*** **Added/Corp** Canadian Slovak League. **VFOAT** Kalendar KSL. **VAT** Kalendar KSL. Vol. 1 (1953)-. Slovak. an. Kalendar Kanadskej Ligy, c/o The Canadian Slovak, 400 Queen Street, Toronto Ontario M5V 2A6 Canada. **DD** 943.7/3/005. ***Continued by*** *Kalendar KSL, 0229-6152.*

CN/0229-6152
KALENDAR KSL (1980). (KALENDAR KSL.). [Kal. KSL]. **VAT** Kalendar Kanadskej Slovenskej Ligy (1980). 1979/1980-. Slovak (English). be. 10.00Can$. Kalendar KSL, c/o Canadian Slovak, 1736 Dundas Street West, Toronto Ontario M6K 1V5 Canada. **Tel** (416)531-2055. **ED** Marian Jankovsky. **DD** 943.7/3/005. **Circ:** 1,000. available on diskette. ***Continues*** *Kalendar Kanadskej Slovenskej Ligy, 0410-935X.*

HU/0238-888X
KAPU. (1988)-. Periodical. Hungarian. mo. $35.00. **(Subscription address:** Kultura, PO Box 149, H 1389 Budapest 62 Hungary**) LC** DB920.5; .K27.

GW/0721-4979
KARLSRUHER BEITRAEGE. **Added/Corp** Karlsruhe (Germany). No. 1 (May 1981)-. Periodical. German. **LC** DD901.K3; K376. **DD** 943/.4643/005.
Ind/Abst BHA : Biblio. Hist. Art.

History(General) —History of Europe

AU/0022-7560
KARNTNER HEIMATLEBEN. Added/Corp
Geschichtsverein fuer Karnten. (1959)-. German. ir. Dr. Rudolf Habelt GmbH, Postfach 150104, D 53040 Bonn Germany. **Tel** 011 49 228 232015. **LC** DB283; .K26.

UN
KARPATALJA : A KARPATALJAI MAGYAR KULTURALIS SZOVETSEG LAPJA. Added/Corp Karpataljai Magyar Kulturalis Szovetseg. (1991)-. Periodical. Hungarian. bw. **LC** DK508.9.Z35; K37.

IT
KATUNDI YNE. Added/Corp Circolo di Cultura Gennaro Placco. (19??)-. Multiple languages (Albanian and Italian). $5.00. Circolo di Cultura Gennaro Placco, Conto Corrente Postale N 21/819, Civita Italy. **LC** DG457.A7; K37.

AI/0203-4883
KAVKAZ I VIZANTIIA. Added/Corp
Arevelagitutyan Institut (Haykakan SSH Gitutyunneri Akademia). **VFOAT** Kovkas ev Byuzandia. Vol. 1 (1979)-. Russian (summaries and/or abstracts in Armenian). 2.35rub (single issue). Akademiia Nauk Armianskoi / Armenian Academy of Sciences, Prospekt Marshala Bagramyana 24, 375019 Yerevan Armenia. **Tel** 52 45 80, telex 243344. **LC** DK511.C1; K358.

HU
KELETKUTATAS. Hungarian. **LC** DS12; .K44.

US/0192-1207
KELTICA. [Keltica]. Vol. 1, No. 1 (Winter 1979-80)-. Periodical. English. qt. $18.95. Society for International Celtic Arts and Culture, 96 Marguerite Avenue, Waltham MA 02154. **Tel** (617)899-2204. **ED** Kevin Dixon Gilligan. **LC** CB206; .K44. **DD** 936.4. **Bk Rev**. **Ad Acc**. **Circ:** 2,000.
Desc: 100-page illustrated, journal of Celtic culture (Ireland, Scotland, Wales, Brittany, Man, Cornwall, Galicia). All topics, fiction, and poetry included.

YU
KEPES IFJUSAG. Began with March 7, 1945 issue. Periodical. Hungarian. Forum / Yugoslavia, Vojvode Misica 1/III, Novi Sad Yugoslavia. **LC** DR381.V642; K46.

GW
KLEINE HEFTE ZUR STADTGESCHICHTE. Added/Corp Archiv der Hansestadt Lubeck. 1985-. Monographic series. German. Price varies per volume.

JA
KODAI ROSHIA KENKYU. See Linguistics.

YU
KOHA. Began witH 1978 issue. Periodical. Albanian. ir. 120.00. OGB Pobjeda, 81 000 Titograd Bulevar, Revolucije BR 11, Titograd Yugoslavia. **LC** DR1230.A4; K64.

GW/0075-6512
KOLNER JAHRBUCH FUER VOR- UND FRUHGESCHICHTE. Added/Corp
Romisch-Germanisches Museum (Cologne, Germany) Archaeologische Gesellschaft Koln. Vol. 1 (1955)-. German. ir. DM120.00. Gebrueder Mann Verlag, Lindenstrasse 76, D-10969 Berlin Germany. **Tel** 011 49 30 25913589, telex 183723. **LC** DD901.C745; K6. Index available. **Circ:** 800.
Desc: Contributions to the prehistoric period and early history.
Ind/Abst Anthropol. Lit.; BHA : Biblio. Hist. Art; Br. Archaeol. Bibliogr. (?-); Numis. Lit. (?-?).

US
KONFEDERACJA 76 I.E. SIEDEMDZIESIAT SZESC. VFOAT
Confederation 76. Periodical. Polish. mo. Free (donations). Confederation 76, 90-66 179 Street, Jamaica NY 11423. **LC** DK4010; .K65. **DD** 943.8/005.

FR
KONTAKT (PARIS, FRANCE). (KONTAKT : MIESIECZNIK REDAGOWANY PRZEZ CZONKOW I WSPOPRACOWNIKOW NSZZ SOLIDARNOSC.). **Added/Corp** NSZZ "Solidarnosc" (Labor Organization). (April 1982)-. Periodical. Polish (summaries and/or abstracts in English and French). Ten times a year. $52.00. Kontakt, 42 rue Raymond Marcheron, 92170 Vanves France. **LC** DK4442; .K66.

CN/0226-8566
KRAGOZORI. (KRUGOZORI.). [Kragozori]. **VFOAT** Horizons. **VAT** Horizons (Toronto. 1978). V. 1- Mar. 1978-. Periodical. Bulgarian (English). mo. $6.00 Canada; $7.00 US; $9.00 other. **DD** 949.7/7/005.

RU
KRAI NASH IUZHNOURALSKII.
Added/Corp Cheliabinskaia Oblastnaia Publichnaia Biblioteka. Otdel Bibliografii i Kraevedeniia. (19??)-. Russian. 454000 G Cheliabinsk Pr Im V I Lenina, 60 Cheliabinskaia Oblastnaia Publichnaia Biblioteka, Otdel Bibliografii I Kraevedeniia, Cheliabinsk Russia. **LC** Z2514.C47; K7; DK511.C4.

GW/0935-9060
KRIEG UND LITERATUR. VFOAT War and Literature. Vol. 1, No. 1 (1989)-. Periodical. German (English). sa. DM55.00. H Th Wenner Verlag, Hegestr 2-3, D-4500 Osnabruck Germany. Index available. **Bk Rev**. **Circ:** 400 (ctrl).

PL
KRONIKA. (19??)-. Periodical. Polish. wk. $78.00. Warszawskii Wydawn Prasowe RSW Prasa-Ksiazka-Ruch, Ul Wiejska 12, Warszawa Poland. **(Subscription address:** ARS Polona, PO Box 1001, 00068 Warsaw Poland.) **LC** Al15; .D6.
Ind/Abst Am. Hist. Life (1968-); BHA : Biblio. Hist. Art.

XV/0023-4923
KRONIKA; CASOPIS ZA SLOVENSKO KRAJENO ZGODOVINO. VFOAT Casopis za Slovensko Krajevno Zgodovino: Kronika. Began publication in 1953. Periodical. Slovenian (English). Three times a year. 120.00 Din Yugoslavia; 210.00 Din other. Narodni Muzej, Presernova 20, Ljubljana Slovenia. **Tel** 061-218-886. **(Subscription address:** Filozofska Fakulteta, Askerceva 12, Ljubljana Yugoslavia) **LC** DR381.S6; K68. cum. index. **Ad Acc**. **Circ:** 1,000.
Continues Kronika Slovenskih Mest.
Ind/Abst Am. Hist. Life (1968-).

PL/0867-5244
KRYTYKA. Added/Corp Niezalezna Oficyna Wydawnicza (Poland) Wydawnictwo Krag (Warsaw, Poland). No. 1 (1978)-. Periodical. Polish. qt. £3.50 (per issue) UK; $7.00 (per issue) US. Aneks Press, 61 Dorset Road, London W5 4HX England. **Tel** 01 567-9584. **LC** DK4436; .K79. **DD** 943.8/005. **Bk Rev**. **Ad Acc**. **Circ:** 3,000.
Desc: Polish underground periodical, original edition with essays on social and political scientists, current affairs and social and political analysis.
Ind/Abst Int. Bibliogr. Sociol.

XV
KULTURA, UMETNOST, INFORMACIJE / ZAVOD SR SLOVENIJE ZA STATISTIKO. 1978-. Slovenian. Zavod Sr Slovenije za Statistiko, Vozarski Pot 12, Ljubljana Slovenia. **LC** DR381.S64; S55A. **Continues** Kulturno-Umetniska in Znanstveno-Raziskovalna Dejavnost.

SW/0282-5902
KULTURENS VARLD. 1985-. Periodical. Swedish. Three times a year.
Ind/Abst BHA : Biblio. Hist. Art.

SW/0283-1899
KULTURRADET : STATENS KULTURRAD INFORMERAR. Added/Corp
Kulturradet (Sweden). **VFOAT** Statens Kulturrad Informerar. No. 1 (1988)-. Periodical. Swedish. bm. Free. **LC** DL631; .K85. **Continues** Statens Kulturrad Informerar.
Ind/Abst Leis. Recreat. Tour. Abstr.

DK/0454-6245
KUML. Vol. 1 (1951)-. Danish (summaries and/or abstracts in English and German). an. **LC** DL271.J8.
Ind/Abst Anthropol. Lit.

SW/0560-2416
KUNGL. SKYTTEANSKA SAMFUNDETS HANDLINGAR. VFOAT Acta Regiae Societatis Skytteanae. No. 1 (1961)-. Monographic series. Swedish. ir. Price varies per volume. Scandinavian University Press, PO Box 2959 Toeyen, N 0608 Oslo 6 Norway. **Tel** 011 47 2 2575400, FAX 011 47 2 2575353, telex 71896 UROR N. **(Subscription address:** Scandinavian University Press, 200 Meacham Ave., Elmont NY 11003.) **LC** DL601; .S54.

CY/0081-1580
KUPRIAKAI SPOUDAI. (KYPRIAKAI SPOUDAI : DELTION TES HETAIREIAS KYPRIAKON SPOUDON.). [Kupr. spoud.]. **Added/Corp** Hetaireia Kypriakon Spoudon (Nicosia, Cyprus). (19??)-. Greek, Modern (English, French and Greek, Modern). an. $23.00. Society of Cypriot Studies, Box 1436, Nicosia Cyprus. **Bk Rev**. **Ad Acc**. **Circ:** 500.
Ind/Abst Am. Hist. Life (1966-1989); BHA : Biblio. Hist. Art; MLA Int. Bibl. Books Artic. Mod. Lang. Lit.

GW/0452-9081
KURTRIERISCHES JAHRBUCH.
Added/Corp Verein Kurtrierisches Jahrbuch. Stadtbibliothek Trier. Gesellschaft fur Nutzliche Forschungen (Trier, Germany). (1961)-. German. an. **LC** DD901.T8; T732. **DD** 943/.43/005. **Supersedes in part** Trierisches Jahrbuch, 0452-9081. **Continued in part by** Funde und Ausgrabungen im Bezirk Trier, 0723-8630.
Ind/Abst BHA : Biblio. Hist. Art.

PL/0023-5881
KWARTALNIK HISTORII KULTURY MATERIALNEJ. [Kwart. hist. kult. mater.].
Added/Corp Instytut Historii Kultury Materialnej (Polska Akademia Nauk). Vol. 1 (1953)-. Polish (Latin; summaries and/or abstracts in English, French and Russian). qt. Price on Request. **(Subscription address:** ARS Polona, PO Box 1001, 00068 Warsaw Poland.) **LC** DK401; .K9.
Ind/Abst Am. Hist. Life (1955-1967, 1972-1976, 1979-); BHA : Biblio. Hist. Art; Int. Bibliogr. Sociol.; Numis. Lit.

PL/0023-592X
KWARTALNIK OPOLSKI. Added/Corp
Opolskie Towarzystwo Przyjacio Nauk. (1955)-. Periodical. Polish (summaries and/or abstracts in English and German). qt. $20.00. **(Subscription address:** ARS Polona, PO Box 1001, 00068 Warsaw Poland.) **LC** DK4600.O66; A24. **DD** 943.8/5.
Ind/Abst Numis. Lit.

SP/0214-3038
LA ESPANA MEDIEVAL, EN. Added/Corp
Universidad Complutense de Madrid. Universidad Complutense de Madrid. Facultad de Geografia e Historia. Universidad Complutense de Madrid. Departamento de Historia Medieval. No. 1 (1980)-. Periodical. Spanish. an. 2200ptas. Editorial Complutense, Donoso Cortes 65 1RA Planta, 28003 Madrid Spain. **Tel** 011 34 1 3946372. **LC** DP99; .E5. **DD** 946/.02/05.

UK
LABOUR FOCUS ON EASTERN EUROPE. See Economics-Labor.

US/0094-498X
LAISVE, I. Lithuanian. Three times a year. $5.00. Lietuviu Fronto Biciuliai, 3 Silver Eagle Road, Rolling Hills Estates CA 90274. **LC** DK511.L2; A2325.

LV
LATVIA. (19??)-. English. an. 0.61rub. Liesma / Flame Publishing House, Aspazijas Bulv 24, Riga Latvia 1455. **Tel** 3712 223 063. **LC** DK511.L15; L29. **DD** 947/.43/005.

●SP
LAZARILLO. Added/Corp Asociacion Internacional de Traductores, Interpretes y Profesores de Espanol. No. 1 (1992)-. Periodical. Spanish. Three times a year. 1800ptas. Collegio de Espana, Calle Compania 65 Aitipe, 37008 Salamanca Spain. **Tel** 011 34 23 214788. **LC** PQ6001; .L39. **DD** 860.9/0005.

US/0023-625X
LBI NEWS (NEW YORK, N.Y.). (LBI NEWS.). [LBI news]. **Main/Corp** Leo Baeck Institute of Jews from Germany. **Added/Corp** Leo Baeck Institute. News. **VAT** Leo Baeck Institute News. Vol. 1 (June 1960)-. Periodical. English. Twice a year. $5.00. Leo Baeck Institute, 129 East 73rd Street, New York NY 10021. **Tel** (212)744-6400. **LC** DS135.G3; L12. **DD** 943.

GW
LEBENSBILDER ZUR GESCHICHTE DER BOHMISCHEN LANDER / HERAUSGEGEBEN IM AUFTRAG DEG COLLEGIUM CAROLINUM. See Biographies.

US/0888-2436
LEMKIVSCINA. (LEMKIVSHCHYNA.). [Lemkivscina]. **VFOAT** Lemkivshchyna. V. 1, No. 1 (Spring 1979)-. Periodical. Ukrainian (English). qt. $10.00 US; $16.00 other. Lemkivshchyna, PO Box 7, Clifton NJ 07011-0007. **ED** Marie Duplak. **LC** DJK28.L4; L46. **DD** 947. **Bk Rev**. **Circ:** 1,000.

PO
LER HISTORIA. Added/Corp Centro de Estudos de Historia Contemporˌanea Portuguesa. No. 1 (Jan./April 1983)-. Periodical. Portuguese. Three times a year. Centro de Estudos de Historia Contemporanea Portuguesa, Iscte Av da Forcas Armadas, 1600 Lisbon Portugal. **LC** DP501; .L47. **DD** 946.9/005.

YU/0459-1070
LESKOVACKI ZBORNIK. Added/Corp Narodni Muzej u Leskovcu. (1961)-. Periodical. Serbo-Croatian (Cyrillic) (summaries and/or abstracts in French). **LC** DR381.L4; L4.
Ind/Abst BHA : Biblio. Hist. Art.

RU
LETOPISI I KHRONIKI. Added/Corp Institut Istorii SSSR (Akademiia Nauk SSSR). (1973)-. Academic Scholarly Publication. Russian. 1.83rub. Izdatelstvo Nauka / Akademiia Nauk, Publishing House of the Russian Academy of Sciences, Leninskii Porspekt 14, 117901 Moscow Russia. **Tel** 011 95 954-21-53, FAX 011 95 938-21-44, telex 411964. **LC** DK38; .L44.

YU
LETUNK. Vol. 1- ; Dec. 1971-. Hungarian (summaries and/or abstracts in Serbo-Croatian (Roman), English, French, German and Russian). **LC** DR381.V642.

LV
LIESMA. Added/Corp Latvijas LKJS Centrala Komiteja. (19??)-. Periodical. Latvian. mo. $18.00. Latvijas KP CK Izdevnieciba, Komunaru Bulvari 6 226098, Riga Latvia. **(Subscription address:** Victor Kamkin, 4956 Boiling Brook Parkway, Rockville MD 20852.) **LC** DK511.L15; L5.

US/0091-4347
LIETUVIU TAUTOS PRAEITIS. (LIETUVIU TAUTOS PRAEITIS. LITHUANIAN HISTORICAL REVIEW.). **Added/Corp** Lietuviu Istorijos Draugija. **VFOAT** Lithuanian Historical Review. (1971)-. Lithuanian (summaries and/or abstracts in English). ir. Lithuanian Historical Society, 10425 S Kenton, Oak Lawn IL 60453. **Tel** (312)434-4545. **LC** DK511.L2; A276. ***Continues*** *Tautos Praeitis.*
Ind/Abst Am. Hist. Life (1981-).

LI/0202-3342
LIETUVOS ISTORIJOS METRASTIS. **Added/Corp** Istorijos Institutas (Lietuvos TSR Mokslu Akademija). (19??)-. Lithuanian (summaries and/or abstracts in Russian). an. 1,12rb. **LC** DK511.L2; A247.
Ind/Abst Am. Hist. Life (1979-).

LI/0459-3456
LIETUVOS TSR AUKSTUJU MOKYKLU MOKSLO DARBAI: ISTORIJA. **Added/Corp** Lithuania. Aukstojo ir Specialiojo Vidurinio Mokslo Ministerija. **VFOAT** Nauchnye Trudy Vysshykh Uchebnykh Zavedenii Litovskoi SSR. Istoriia. (1962)-. Lithuanian (Polish and Russian; summaries and/or abstracts in Russian and Lithuanian). an. Mintis / Idea, Z Sierakausko 15, Vilnius 2600 Lithuania. **Tel** 3702 632 943. ***Continues*** *Istorija (Vilnius, Lithuania).*
Ind/Abst Am. Hist. Life (1980-).

UK/0960-9555
LINCOLNSHIRE PAST & PRESENT. **Added/Corp** Society for Lincolnshire History and Archaeology. **VFOAT** Lincolnshire Past and Present. No. 1 (Autumn 1990)-. Periodical. English. Four times a year. Society of Lincolnshire History & Archaeology, Jews Court Steep Hill, Lincoln LN2 1L5 England. **Tel** 011 44 0522 21337.

SW
LISANDUSI MOTETE JA UUDISTE VABALE LEVIKULE EESTIS (LAANE VALJAANNE). (LISANDUSI MOTETE JA UUDISTE VABALE LEVIKULE EESTIS.). 1978/80-. Estonian. ir. **LC** DK503.75; .L57.

IT
LISTY. Czech. $21.00. **LC** DB215.6; .L56.

UK/0306-1973
LITERATURE & HISTORY. **See** Literature.

US
LITOPYS BOIKIVSHCHYNY. Began in 1931. Ukrainian. $4.00. Boykiwschyna, 2222 Brandywine Street, Philadelphia PA 19130. **LC** DK511.B57; L56.

LI/0235-716X
LITUANISTICA / LIETUVOS MOKSLU AKADEMIJA. **Added/Corp** Lietuvos Mokslu Akademija. (1990)-. Periodical. Lithuanian (French and German; summaries and/or abstracts in English and Russian). qt. **LC** DK505; .L57. ***Continues in part*** *Lietuvos TSR Mokslu Akademijos Darbai. Serija A.*
Ind/Abst Am. Hist. Life (1990-).

US/0459-5947
LITUANISTIKOS DARBAI. (LITUANISTIKOS DARBAI. LITHUANIAN STUDIES.). [Litu. darb.]. **Added/Corp** Lituanistikos Institutas (U.S.). **VFOAT** Lithuanian Studies. (1966)-. Lithuanian (English; summaries and/or abstracts in English). **LC** DK511.L2; A264.
Ind/Abst MLA Int. Bibl. Books Artic. Mod. Lang. Lit.

US/0024-5089
LITUANUS. [Lituanus]. **Added/Corp** Lithuanian Student Association (U.S.). Secretariate for External Relations. Lithuanian Student Association (U.S.) Lithuanian Students Association (U.S.) Lituanus Foundation. No. 1 (Nov. 1954)-13 (Dec. 1957); Vol. 4, No. 1 (Mar. 1958)-. Periodical. English. qt. $15.00 (one year), $27.00 (two years), $40.00 (three years). Lituanus Foundation Inc., 6621 South Troy Street, Chicago IL 60629-2913. **Tel** (312)434-0706. **ED** Antanas Klimas. **LC** DK511.L2; A265. Index available. cum. index. **Bk Rev**, (Qty: 7). **Pr Rev. Circ:** 4,000 (ctrl). available on microfilm and microfiche from University Microfilms International (UMI).
Desc: Organizes, sponsors and publishes research material pertaining to the Baltic states, particularly Lithuania. Invites contributions concerning the Baltic countries and general problems of Eastern Europe and the former Soviet Union.
Ind/Abst Am. Hist. Life (1957-); Am. Bibliogr. Slavic East Europ. Stud.; Bibliogr. Mission.; BHA : Biblio. Hist. Art; Hum. Rights Intern. Rep.; Int. Polit. Sci. Abstr.; MLA Int. Bibl. Books Artic. Mod. Lang. Lit.; PAIS Int. Print (1991-).

UK/0024-5585
LOCAL HISTORIAN (LONDON. 1968). (THE LOCAL HISTORIAN.). [Local hist.]. **Added/Corp** Standing Conference for Local History. National Council of Social Service. Vol. 8 (1968)-. Periodical. English. Four times a year. £19.00 UK; £26.00 other. British Association of Local History, Shopwyke Hall, Chichester PO20 6BQ England. **Tel** 011/44/243/787639. **ED** Dr. Margaret Bonney, (editor's address: 7 Carisbrooke Park, Knighton, Leicester LE2 3PQ England). Index available (published separately). cum. index. **Bk Rev**, (Qty: 50). **Ad Acc. Circ:** 2,300 (ctrl). ***Continues*** *Amateur Historian.*
Desc: Covers local history in Britain.
Ind/Abst Am. Hist. Life (1968-); BHA : Biblio. Hist. Art; Br. Archaeol. Bibliogr. (1968-); Br. Humanit. Index (1968-).

UK/0266-2698
LOCAL HISTORY. [Local hist.]. (1984)-. Periodical. English. bm (6 issues). £13.50 UK; £20.00 other. Local History, 3 Devonshire Promenade Lenton, Nottingham NG7 2DS England. **Tel** 011 44 602 700369. **ED** Susan & Robert Howard. **Bk Rev**, (Qty: 300). **Ad Acc. Circ:** 1,100.

UK/0143-2974
LOCAL POPULATION STUDIES. **See** Population Studies.

UK/0305-8034
LONDON JOURNAL, THE. [Lond. j.]. Vol. 1 (May 1975)-. English. Twice a year (July & Dec.). £15.00 (individuals); £30.00 (institutions). London Journal Trust, Museum of London, London Wall, London EC2Y 5HN England. **Tel** 011 44 81 975 5017, FAX 011 44 81 981 7517. **ED** Dr. P. Garside. **LC** DA688; .L63. **DD** 942.1/005. **Bk Rev. Circ:** 370.
Desc: Studies of aspects of the history of London as a metropolitan city.
Ind/Abst Am. Hist. Life (1975-); Archit. Period. Index (1975/1977-); Avery Index Archit. Period. Suppl. Colum. Univ. (1990-); BHA : Biblio. Hist. Art; Br. Archaeol. Bibliogr.; Br. Humanit. Index; Geogr. Abstr. Human Geogr.

FR/0293-373X
LOU TERRAIRE. **VFOAT** Le Terroir; Terroir. Periodical. French. qt. 40F. Centre Culturel Provencal, 15 rue de la Mottee, 83300 Draguignan France. **LC** DC611.P961; L68. **DD** 944/.9/005.

FI/0782-050X
LUTUKKA. [Lutukka]. Periodical. Multiple languages. qt. Fmk134.00 Scandanavia; $Fmk142.00 other. Finnish Museum of Natural History, Botaical Museum, PO Box 7. **Tel** 011 358 0 1911, FAX 011 358 0 1918656. **UDC** 58.

NE/0166-0314
MAASGOUW, DE. [Maasgouw]. **Added/Corp** Provinciaal Geschied- en Oudheidkundig Genootschap in Limburg. Limburgs Geschied- en Oudheidkundig Genootschap. (Jan. 2, 1879)-. Periodical. Dutch. Four times a year. comes with membership. Societe Historique et Archaeologique, Bureau LGOG, PO Box 83, Maastricht 6200 AB Netherlands. **Tel** 011 31 43 212586. **LC** DJ401.L6; L62.
Ind/Abst BHA : Biblio. Hist. Art.

RM/0541-881X
MAGAZIN ISTORIC. [Mag. ist.]. **Added/Corp** Societatea de Stiinte Istorice si Filologice din Republica Socialista Romania. Societatea de Stiinte Istorice din Republica Socialista Romania. Vol. 1, No. 1 (April 1967)-. Periodical. Romanian. mo. DM182.00. **(Subscription address:** Kubon & Sagner, ABT Zeitschriftenimport, D 80328 Munich Germany.**)** **LC** DR201; .M34. cum. index.
Desc: Magazine of information and historical analysis.
Ind/Abst Am. Hist. Life (1967, 1975-); Numis. Lit.

PL/0580-0943
MAGAZYN HISTORYCZNY. **Added/Corp** Polskie Towarzystwo Historyczne. Poland. Ministerstwo Edukacji Narodowej. "Nasza Ksiegarnia" (Firm). (1990)-. Periodical. Polish. mo. ***Continues*** *Mowia Wieki.*

GW/0076-2725
MAINFRANKISCHES JAHRBUCH FUER GESCHICHTE UND KUNST. **See** The Arts-Art.

GR/0076-289X
MAKEDONIKA (THESSALONIKA). **See** Humanities.

UK
MANCHESTER REGION HISTORY REVIEW. (19??)-. Periodical. English. an. £12.00 (institutions), £7.00 (individuals) UK; £18.00 (institutions), £10.00 (individuals) other. Manchester Metropolitan University / Ormond Building, Lower Ormond Street, Manchester M15 6BX England. **Tel** 011 44 61 2471753.

SP/0213-2397
MANUSCRITS. **Added/Corp** Universidad Autonoma de Barcelona. Departament d'Historia Moderna i Contemporania. (1985)-. Periodical. Catalan. an (Jan.). 2700ptas. Departament d'Historia Moderna i Contemporania Fac Letr, University of Autonoma Barcelona, Bellaterra Barcelona Spain. **Tel** 011 34 3 5811285. **(Subscription address:** L'Escaquirot S A, Nuestra Senora del Coll 53, 08023 Barcelona Spain.**)** **LC** DP160.9; .M36. **DD** 946/.05.

RM
MARISIA / COMITETUL DE CULTURA SI EDUCATIE SOCIALISTA AL JUDETULUI MURES, MUSEUL JUDETEAN MURES. **Added/Corp** Muzeul Judetean Mures. (1975)-. Romanian (summaries and/or abstracts in English, French and German). an. **LC** DR281.M78; M38. ***Continues*** *Studii si Materiale.*
Ind/Abst BHA : Biblio. Hist. Art.

RU
MATERIALY I ISSLEDOVANIIA - GOSUDARSTVENNYE MUZEI MOSKOVSKOGO KREMLIA. **Main/Corp** Moscow. Muzei Moskovskogo Kremlia. (1973)-. Russian. 1.65rub each issue. Izdatelstvo Iskusstvo, Vorotnikovskii Pereulok 11, 103009 Moscow Russia. **LC** DK602.3; .M63a.

RU/0302-9107
MATERIALY PO ISTORII KIRGIZOV I KIRGIZII. [Mater. istor. kirg. Kirg.]. **Added/Corp** Institut Vostokovedeniia (Akademiia Nauk SSSR) Tarykh Institutu (Kyrgyz SSR Ilimder Akademiiasy). Vol. 1, (1973)-. Academic Scholarly Publication. Russian. ir. 1.58rub each issue. Izdatelstvo Nauka / Akademiia Nauk, Publishing House of the Russian Academy of Sciences, Leninskii Porspekt 14, 117901 Moscow Russia. **Tel** 011 95 954-21-53, FAX 011 95 938-21-44, telex 411964. **LC** DK911; .M37.

PL/0076-5236
MATERIAY ZACHODNIO POMORSKIE. v. 1- 1955-. Periodical. Polish (table of contents in German and English). ir. **(Subscription address:** ARS Polona, PO Box 1001, 00068 Warsaw Poland.**)** **LC** DD491.P745.
Ind/Abst BHA : Biblio. Hist. Art; Numis. Lit.

SP/0301-8296
MAYURQA. [Mayurqa]. **Added/Corp** Barcelona. Universidad. Facultad de Filosofia y Letras, Palma de Mallorca. (1968)-. Spanish (Catalan). **LC** DP302.B27; M38. **DD** 914.6/75.
Ind/Abst Am. Hist. Life (1968-1974).

US
MBROJTJA KOMBETARE. Periodical. Albanian. Balli Kombetar, PO Box 273 Times Square, New York NY 10036. **LC** DR901; .M39.

NO
MED BIL I EUROPA. **Main/Corp** Norges Automobil-Fordund. Norwegian. 20.00. Norges Automobil-Forbund, Storgaten 2, Oslo 1 Norway. **LC** D909; .N58A.

BE
MEDEDELINGEN VAN DE GESCHIED-EN OUDHEIDKUNDIGE KRING VOOR LEUVEN EN OMGEVING. **Main/Corp** Geschied- en Oudheidkundige Kring voor Leuven en Omgeving. **Added/Corp** Geschied- en Oudheidkundige Kring voor Leuven en Omgeving. Jaarboek. Geschied- en Oudheidkundige Kring voor Leuven en Omgeving. Bulletin. **VFOAT** Jaarboek van de Geschied- en Oudheidkundige Kring voor Leuven en Omgeving; Bulletin de la Societe d'Histoire et d'Archeologie de Louvain et Environs. Vol. 1 (1961)-. Periodical. Dutch (French). an. 750F. Editions Peeters SA, Bondgenotenlaan 153, BP 41, B-3000 Leuven Belgium. **Tel** 32 16 235170, FAX 32 16 228500, telex 65987 PUL B.

DK/0076-5864
MEDIAEVAL SCANDINAVIA. [Mediaev. Scand.]. Vol. 1 (1968)-. English (French and German). ir. Kr200.00. Odense University Press, 55 Campusvej, DK-5230 Odense M Denmark. **Tel** 66 15 79 99, FAX 66 15 81 26. **LC** WMLC L 83/2289.
Ind/Abst BHA : Biblio. Hist. Art; MLA Int. Bibl. Books Artic. Mod. Lang. Lit.

DK/0106-102X
MEDIAEVAL SCANDINAVIA SUPPLEMENTS. Vol. 1, (1980)-. Monographic series. English. ir. Price varies per volume. Odense University Press, 55 Campusvej, DK-5230 Odense M Denmark. **Tel** 66 15 79 99, FAX 66 15 81 26. **ED** Hans Bekker-Nielsen. **Bk Rev. Ad Acc. Circ:** 200.

CN/0076-5872
MEDIAEVAL STUDIES. [Mediaev. stud.]. (1939)-. Periodical. English (French and Latin). an. $57.00. Pontifical Institute of Mediaeval Studies, 59 Queens Park Crescent East, Toronto Ontario M5S 2C4 Canada. **Tel** (416)926-7144, FAX (416)926-7276. **ED** J Black, (416)926-1300, ext 3287. **DD** 901.92. **[CCC]**. Index available. **Pr Rev. Circ:** 1,200. Documents available from The Genuine Article.
Desc: Articles covering all aspects of the Middle Ages including history, literature, philosophy, theology, language, law, and etc.
Ind/Abst Abstr. Engl. Stud.; Annu. Bibliogr. Engl. Lang. Lit.; Arts Humanit. Citation Index [Full Cov.]; BHA : Biblio. Hist. Art; Curr. Contents Arts Humanit.; Middle East Abstr. Index; MLA Int. Bibl. Books Artic. Mod. Lang. Lit.; Philos. Index; Res. Alert [Full Cov.]; Abr. Cathol. Period. Lit. Index; Cathol. Period. Lit. Index.

US/0361-946X
MEDIAEVALIA (BINGHAMTON). (MEDIAEVALIA.). [Mediaevalia]. **Added/Corp** State University of New York at Binghamton. Center for Medieval and Early Renaissance Studies. (Spring 1975)-.

History(General) — History of Europe

Periodical. English (French, German and Latin). an. $27.50. State University of New York Press, State University Plaza, Albany NY 12246. **Tel** (518)472-5000, FAX (518)472-5038. **(Subscription address:** Cup Service, PO Box 6525, Ithaca NY 14851.**) ED** Bernard Levy and Sandro Sticca. **LC** CB351; .M38. **DD** 940.1/05. **Ad Acc. Circ:** 250.
Desc: Pertains to the history of Medieval Europe.
Ind/Abst BHA : Biblio. Hist. Art; MLA Int. Bibl. Books Artic. Mod. Lang. Lit.

XR/0862-979X
MEDIAEVALIA HISTORICA BOHEMICA.
Added/Corp Historicky Ustav (Ceskoslovenska Akademie Ved). (1991)-. Czech. **Continues** *Mediaevalia Bohemica.*

US/0892-9718
MEDIEVAL AND RENAISSANCE MONOGRAPH SERIES.
[Mediev. Renaiss. monogr. ser.]. **Added/Corp** Michigan Consortium for Medieval and Early Modern Studies. (1981)-. Monographic series. English. **(Subscription address:** Fifteen Century Symposium, Marygrove College, Detroit, MI 48221**) DD** 940.
Ind/Abst MLA Int. Bibl. Books Artic. Mod. Lang. Lit.

US/0584-4150
MEDIEVAL AND RENAISSANCE STUDIES (DURHAM).
(MEDIEVAL AND RENAISSANCE STUDIES.). [Mediev. Renaiss. stud.]. **Main/Corp** Southeastern Institute of Medieval and Renaissance Studies. 1st- Session; 1965-. English. ir. $19.00. University North Carolina Press, Box 2288, Chapel Hill NC 27514. **Tel** (919)966-3561. **LC** CB361; .M42 subser. **DD** 914/.03/21.

US
MEDIEVAL & RENAISSANCE TEXTS AND STUDIES.
Added/Corp State University of New York at Binghamton. Center for Medieval and Early Renaissance Studies. **VFOAT** Medieval and Renaissance Texts and Studies. Vol. 1 (1981)-. Monographic series. English (French, Italian, Latin and Spanish). Price varies per volume. **LC** UNC.
Ind/Abst MLA Int. Bibl. Books Artic. Mod. Lang. Lit.

UK/0076-6097
MEDIEVAL ARCHAEOLOGY. See Archaeology.

UK/0960-0752
MEDIEVAL HISTORY.
Vol. 1, No. 1 (1991)-. Periodical. English. Three times a year. £16.00 Europe; £18.00 North America; £20.00 Scandanaiva & South Africa; £25.00 Japan & Australia. Headstart History, PO Box 41, Bangor Gwynedd LL571SB England. **Tel** 011 44 248351816.

NE/0076-6100
MEDIEVAL IBERIAN PENINSULA. TEXTS AND STUDIES.
Vol. 1 (1961)-. Monographic series. English (Arabic, French, Latin and Spanish). ir. Price varies per volume. E. J. Brill, Postbus 9000, 2300 PA Leiden Netherlands. **Tel** 011 31 71 312624, FAX 011 31 71 317532, telex 39296 BRILL NL.

US/0198-9405
MEDIEVAL PROSOPOGRAPHY.
[Mediev. prosopogr.]. Vol. 1, No. 1 (Spring 1980)-. Periodical. English (German and French). sa. $20.00. Western Michigan University Medieval Institute, Kalamazoo MI 49008-3851. **Tel** (616)387-8755, FAX (616)387-8750. **ED** Candance Porath. **LC** D115; .M4. **DD** 920/.009/02. Index available. cum. index. **Bk Rev. Ad Acc. Pr Rev. Circ:** 250.
Desc: Covers any subject pertaining to life in the medieval period, such as warfare, family structure, business, agriculture, land transfer, government, religion and law.
Ind/Abst Annu. Bibliogr. Engl. Lang. Lit.

US/0076-6127
MEDIEVALIA ET HUMANISTICA.
[Mediev. humanist.]. Vol. 1 Jan. (1943)- New Ser. No. 1 (1970)-. Academic Scholarly Publication. English. an. $59.00. Rowman & Littlefield Publishing Inc., 8705 Bollman Place, Savage MD 20763. **Tel** (301)306-6400. **ED** Paul Clogan. **LC** D111; .M5. **DD** 940.105. Index available. cum. index. **Circ:** 2,000 (ctrl). available on microfiche.
Ind/Abst Annu. Bibliogr. Engl. Lang. Lit.; BHA : Biblio. Hist. Art; MLA Int. Bibl. Books Artic. Mod. Lang. Lit.

SP/0211-3473
MEDIEVALIA / INSTITUTO UNIVERSITARIO DE ESTUDIOS MEDIEVALES.
(1980)-. Spanish (French and Catalan). an. Universitat Autonoma de Barcelona / Publicacions, Servei de Publicacions Edifici Rectorat, Bellaterra 08193 Barcelona Spain. **Tel** 011 34 93 6914061. **LC** CB351; .M395. **DD** 909.07.

IT/0394-7858
MEDIOEVO E RINASCIMENTO : ANNUARIO DEL DIPARTIMENTO DI STUDI SUL MEDIOEVO E IL RINASCIMENTO DELL'UNIVERSITA DI FIRENZE.
Added/Corp Universita di Firenze. Dipartimento di Studi sul Medioevo e il Rinascimento.

(1987)-. Italian (German). an. L100000. Centro Italiano di Studi Sull'Alto Medioevo, Palazzo Ancaiani, Piazza della Liberta 12, 06049 Spoleto Italy. **Tel** 011 39 743 220485 or 418, FAX 011 39 743 39107. **LC** CB351; .M3955. **DD** 940.1/05.
Desc: Covers medieval civilization and the Renaissance.
Ind/Abst BHA : Biblio. Hist. Art.

UK
MEDITERRANEAN HISTORICAL REVIEW.
Vol. 1, No. 1 (June 1986)-. Periodical. English. Twice a year. $95.00. Frank Cass & Company Ltd, Newbury House, 890-900 Eastern Avenue, Newbury Park, Ilford, Essex IG2 7HH United Kingdom. **Tel** 011 44 81 599 8866, FAX 011 44 81 599 0984, telex 897719. **ED** Benjamin Arbel and Sylvia Haim. **LC** WMLC 93/430. Index available. cum. index. **Bk Rev. Ad Acc, Adv Mgr:** Anne Kidson. available on microfilm and microfiche from University Microfilms International (UMI). **Continues** *Journal of Mediterranean Studies.*
Desc: Covers the history of the mediterranean basin in ancient, medieval and modern times.
Ind/Abst Am. Hist. Life (1986-); Br. Humanit. Index.

FR/0025-8296
MEDITERRANEE.
(MEDITERRANEE, REVUE GEOGRAPHIQUE DES PAYS MEDITERRANEENS.). [Mediterranee]. **Added/Corp** Universite d'Aix-Marseille. Institut de Geographie. Universite de Nice. Institut de Geographie. Universite d'Alger. Institut de Geographie. Jamiat al-Jazair. Institut de Geographie. Universite de Montpellier. Institut de Geographie. Universite d'Aix-Marseille II. Institut de Geographie. Laboratoire de Geographie Raoul Blanchard. Laboratoire de Geographie d'Avignon. (Jan./March 1960)-. Periodical. French. Four times a year. 270.00F France; 361.80F other. Dawson France SA, BP 40, 91121 Palaiseau Cedex France. **Tel** 011 33 1 69104700, telex 220064F. **LC** D973.A1; M38. **CODEN** MERRBR.
Ind/Abst AGRICOLA ; Ecol. Abstr.; Geogr. Abstr. Phys. Geogr.; Geogr. Abstr. Human Geogr.; Geol. Abstr.; GeoRef; Int. Dev. Abstr. (?-?).

UK/0025-8385
MEDIUM AEVUM. See Linguistics.

FR/0076-230X
MELANGES DE LA CASA DE VELAZQUEZ.
[Melanges Casa Velazquez]. **Main/Corp** Casa de Velazquez. **Added/Corp** Casa de Velazquez. Vol. 1 (1965)-. Monographic series. French. ir. Price varies per volume. Diffusion de Boccard, 11 rue de Medicis, 75006 Paris France. **Tel** 011 33 1 43260037. **LC** DP1; .M3a. **DD** 946.
Ind/Abst Am. Hist. Life (1969-1973); BHA : Biblio. Hist. Art; Br. Archaeol. Bibliogr. -?; Indice Hist. Esp. (1969-1973).

IT/0223-5102
MELANGES DE L'ECOLE FRANCAISE DE ROME. ANTIQUITE.
[Melanges Ec. fr. Rome. Antiq.]. **VFOAT** MEFRA. Vol. 83 (1971)-. Periodical. French (Italian). sa. 500.00F. Diffusion de Boccard, 11 rue de Medicis, 75006 Paris France. **Tel** 011 33 1 43260037. **LC** D111; .E4. **DD** 937/.005. **Continues in part** *Melanges d'Archeologie et d'Histoire.*
Ind/Abst Avery Index Archit. Period. Suppl. Colum. Univ. (19??-199?); BHA : Biblio. Hist. Art; Numis. Lit.

US/0276-7228
MEMBERS IN GOOD STANDING AS OF ... / SOCIETY FOR ITALIAN HISTORICAL STUDIES.
Main/Corp Society for Italian Historical Studies (U.S.). English. Boston College History Department, Chestnut Hill MA 02167. **LC** DG402; .S7618. **DD** 973/.0451/02573.

GW/0539-2896
MEMMINGER GESCHICHTSBLATTER.
Added/Corp Heimatpflege Memmingen. (19??)-. Periodical. German. an. **LC** DD901.M522; M47. **DD** 943/.37. cum. index.
Ind/Abst BHA : Biblio. Hist. Art.

FR/0240-8260
MEMOIRES DE LA SOCIETE ARCHEOLOGIQUE ET HISTORIQUE DE NANTES ET DE LOIRE-ATLANTIQUE. See Archaeology.

FR/0750-1420
MEMOIRES DE LA SOCIETE D'HISTOIRE ET D'ARCHEOLOGIE DE BRETAGNE. See Archaeology.

FR/1149-8080
MEMOIRES DE LA SOCIETE D'HISTOIRE ET D'ARCHEOLOGIE DE CHALON-SUR-SAONE. See Archaeology.

FR
MEMOIRES DE LA SOCIETE HISTORIQUE ET ARCHEOLOGIQUE DE PONTOISE, DU VAL-D'OISE ET DU VEXIN.
Main/Corp Societe Historique et Archeologique de Pontoise, du Val-d'Oise et du Vexin. Periodical. French. Bureaux de la Societe Historique, 43 rue de la Roche, Pontoise France. **LC** DC801.P88; S6.

DD 944/.36. **Continues** *Memoires de la Societe Historique et Archeologique de l'Arrondissement de Pontoise et du Vexin.*

FR
MEMOIRES DE LA SOCIETE NATIONALE DES ANTIQUAIRES DE FRANCE.
VFOAT Bulletin et Memoires de la Societe Nationale des Antiquaires de France. Vol. 32 (1871)- 4th series, Vol. 2E-. French. an. **LC** DC2; .S72. **Continues** *Memoires de la Societe Imperiale des Antiquaires de France.*
Ind/Abst Numis. Lit. (?-?).

BE/1148-8093
MEMOIRES DE LA SOCIETE ROYALE D'HISTOIRE ET D'ARCHEOLOGIE DE TOURNAI. See Archaeology.

IT
MEMOIRES ET DOCUMENTS SUR ROME ET L'ITALIE MERIDIONALE.
VFOAT Memorie e Documenti su Roma e l'Italia Meridionale. (1982)-. Monographic series. French. Price varies per volume. **Continues** *Memoires et Documents sur l'Italie Meridionale.*

FR
MEMOIRES - FEDERATION DES SOCIETES D'HISTOIRE ET D'ARCHEOLOGIE DE L'AISNE. See Archaeology.

● IT
MEMORIA STORICA : RIVISTA DEL CENTRO DI STUDI STORICI TERNI.
Added/Corp Centro di Studi Storici Terni. No. 1 (Mar. 1992)-. Periodical. Italian. qt. Centro Studi Storici Terni, Via degli Artieri 13, 05100 Terni, Italy. **Tel** 0744-417308. **ED** Vincenzo Pirro. **LC** IN PROCESS.

IT
MEMORIE DOMENICANE (PISTOIA : 1970).
(MEMORIE DOMENICANE.). **Added/Corp** Dominicans. Provincia Romana. (1970)-. Monographic series. Italian (English and Latin). an. Price varies per volume. Prov Romana Frati Predicatori, Piazza S Domenico 1, 51100 Pistoia Italy. **Tel** 011 39 573 28158. Index available. cum. index. **Bk Rev. Circ:** 300. **Continues** *Memorie Domenicane (Pistoia : 1926).*
Desc: Covers medieval and Renaissance culture, their impact on theology and religious consciousness, and Dominican contributions.
Ind/Abst Bibliogr. Mission.; BHA : Biblio. Hist. Art.

IT/0392-1496
MEMORIE STORICHE FOROGIULIESI.
Added/Corp Deputazione di Storia Patria per il Friuli. Cividale del Friuli. Museo. Vol. 1 (1905)-. Italian. an.
Ind/Abst BHA : Biblio. Hist. Art.

RM/0256-5293
MEMORIILE SECTIEI DE STIINTE ISTORICE.
[Mem. sect. stiinte ist.]. (1975)-. Periodical. Romanian. an. **UDC** 93. **Continues** *Memoriile Sectiunii Literare, 1015-7786.*
Ind/Abst Numis. Lit.

FR
MESSAGER EUROPEEN, LE.
Added/Corp Fondation Saint-Simon. No. 1 (1987)-. French. an. 132.70F France; 146.00F others. Editions Gallimard, 5 rue Sebastien Bottin, 75328 Paris Cedex 7 France. **Tel** 011 33 1 49544200. **(Subscription address:** Sodis, 128 Avenue Mal Lattre Tass, BP 149, 77043 Lagny France.**)** **LC** D1055; .M49. **DD** 940/.05.

IT/0394-6460
METODI & RICERCHE.
VFOAT Metodi e Ricerche. (1980)-. Periodical. Italian. sa. Via Baldasseria Bassa 353, 33100 Udine Italy. **LC** DG441; .M48. cum. index.

UK/0047-729X
MIDLAND HISTORY.
[Midl. hist.]. **Added/Corp** University of Birmingham. Vol. 1, (Spring 1971)-. Periodical. English. an (Sept.). £10.00 (individuals), £15.00 (institutions) UK; £20.00 other. University of Birmingham / England, Edgbaston, Center for Byzantine Ottoman, Greek Street, Birmingham B15 2TT England. **Tel** 011 44 21 414 5733, FAX 011 44 21 414 5726. **ED** R. P. Cust. **LC** DA670.M64; M48. **DD** 914.24/03/05. **Bk Rev. Ad Acc. Circ:** 500 (ctrl). **Continues** *Historical Journal (University of Birmingham), 0261-2984.*
Desc: All aspects of the history relating to the Midland regions in England.
Ind/Abst Am. Hist. Life (1955-); Annu. Bibliogr. Engl. Lang. Lit.; BHA : Biblio. Hist. Art; Br. Archaeol. Bibliogr.; Br. Humanit. Index.

GW/0026-3826
MILITARGESCHICHTLICHE MITTEILUNGEN.
[Militargesch. Mitt.]. **Added/Corp** Germany (West). Militargeschichtliches Forschungsamt. (1967)-. Periodical. German. Twice a year. DM50.00. R Oldenbourg Verlag, Postfach 801360, D 81613 Munich

History(General) —History of Europe

Germany. **Tel** 011 49 89 450190, FAX 011 49 89 45019305. **LC** DD101; .M54. Documents available from The Genuine Article.
Ind/Abst Am. Hist. Life (1975-); Arts Humanit. Citation Index [Full Cov.]; Res. Alert [Full Cov.].

UK
MINTIS. No. 1- 1971-. Lithuanian (summaries and/or abstracts in English). $2.00. Leit Socialdenokratu, Landbroke Gardens, WII 2PU London England. **LC** DK511.L2; A266.

US/0110-0068
MIORITA. [Miorita]. Vol. 1 (Dec. 1973)-. Periodical. English (Romanian and French). sa (2 issues). $8.00 institutions, $6.00 individuals. University of Rochester / Department of Foreign Language, Rochester NY 14627. **Tel** (716)275-4258. **ED** Norman Simms. **LC** DR201; .M54. **DD** 949.8/005. **Bk Rev. Circ:** 200.
Desc: A general survey of Romanian civilization; art, history, culture, language, politics, and linguistics with essays, translations, book reviews and reports.
Ind/Abst MLA Int. Bibl. Books Artic. Mod. Lang. Lit.

SP/0210-4903
MISCELANEA MEDIEVAL MURCIANA. [Misc. mediev. murc.]. **Added/Corp** Universidad de Murcia. Departamento de Historia Medieval. Universidad de Murcia. Departamento de Historia de Espana. (1973)-. Periodical. Spanish. Departamento de Historia Medieval, Universidad de Murcia, Murcia Spain. **LC** DP302.M8; M58. **DD** 946/.773. **UDC** 946.

GW/0581-0124
MISCELLANEA BAVARICA MONACENSIA. No. 1- 1967-. Monographic series. German. ir. Price varies per volume. R Wolfle, Amalienstrafe 65, W-8000 Muenchen 40 Germany. **ED** Karl Bosl, Michael Schattenhofer and Richard Bauer.
Desc: A numbered monograph series on Bavarian and Munich political and cultural history, including biographical studies. Of interest to institutions and students as a source from official Munich archives.

GW/0544-4128
MISCELLANEA MEDIAEVALIA. [Misc. mediaev.]. **Added/Corp** Universitat zu Koln. Thomas-Institut. Vol. 1 (1962)-. Monographic series. German. ir. Price varies per volume. Walter de Gruyter Inc., PO Box 303421, D 10728 Berlin Germany. **Tel** 011 49 30 260050, FAX 011 49 30 26005251. **(Subscription address:** US and Canada/ 200 Saw Mill River Road, Hawthorne, NY 10532)
Ind/Abst MLA Int. Bibl. Books Artic. Mod. Lang. Lit.

IT/0026-5888
MISCELLANEA STORICA DELLA VALDELSA. **Added/Corp** Societa Storica della Valdelsa. Vol. 1 No. 1 (1893)-. Italian. cum. index.
Ind/Abst BHA : Biblio. Hist. Art.

UK
MISCELLANY OF THE SCOTTISH HISTORY SOCIETY. **Added/Corp** Scottish History Society. Vol. 1 (1893)-. English. **LC** DA755; .M63.
Ind/Abst BHA : Biblio. Hist. Art.

CN/0820-6309
MISE A JOUR DE LA LISTE DES MEMBRES DU CIEE AU ... . **Main/Corp** Interuniversity Centre for European Studies. **VFOAT** Updated List of ICES Members as of ...; Updated List of ICES Members as of. **VAT** Mise a Jour de la Liste des Membres du Centre Interuniversitaire d'Etudes Europeennes; Updated List of Interuniversity Centre for European Studies Members. (April 15, 1980)-. English (French). ir. Free. Interuniversity Centre for European Studies, PO Box 8892 Station A, Montreal Quebec H3C 3P8 Canada. **Tel** (514)282-6193. **DD** 940/.07/20714. **Ad Acc. Circ:** 500 (ctrl). **Continues** Interuniversity Centre for European Studies. Liste des Membres en Regle du CIEE.

CN/0462-792X
MISIJA UKRAJINY. (MISIIA UKRAINY.). **VFOAT** Misiia; Mission of Ukraine. Periodical. Ukrainian. Mission of Ukraine, PO Box 1051 Postal Station C, Toronto Ontario Canada. **DD** 947/.71/005.

SZ
MITTEILUNGEN DER ANTIQUARISCHEN GESELLSCHAFT IN ZURICH. **Main/Corp** Antiquarische Gesellschaft in Zurich. (1837/1841)-. Monographic series. German. Price varies per volume.
Ind/Abst Avery Index Archit. Period. Suppl. Colum. Univ. (1989); BHA : Biblio. Hist. Art.

GW/0073-2680
MITTEILUNGEN DES HISTORISCHEN VEREINS DER PFALZ. **Main/Corp** Historischer Verein der Pfalz. **Added/Corp** Historisches Museum der Pfalz. (1870)-. German. an. **LC** DD801.B5; H3. **DD** 943/.34.
Ind/Abst BHA : Biblio. Hist. Art.

AU
MITTEILUNGEN DES INSTITUTS FUER OESTERREICHISCHE GESCHICHTSFORSCHUNG. ERGAENZUNGSBAND. Main/Corp Institut fuer Oesterreichische Geschichtsforschung (1947-). (1947)-. Monographic series. German. ir. Price varies per volume. Boehlau Verlag GmbH & Co KG, Sachsenplatz 4 6 PF 87, A 1201 Vienna Austria. **Tel** 011 43 222 3302427. **(Subscription address:** Minerva Wissenschaftl Buchhdlg, Sachsenplatz 4 6, Postfach 88, A 1201 Vienna Austria.) **Continues** Oesterreichisches Institut fuer Geschichtsforschung. Mitteilungen des Oesterreichischen Instituts fuer Geschichtsforschung. Ergaenzungsband.

AU/0073-8484
MITTEILUNGEN DES INSTITUTS FUER OSTERREICHISCHE GESCHICHTSFORSCHUNG. **Added/Corp** Universitat Wien. Institut fuer Osterreichische Geschichtsforschung. Vol. 56 (1948)-. Periodical. German. qt. DM168.00. R Oldenbourg Verlag, Postfach 801360, D 81613 Munich Germany. **Tel** 011 49 89 450190, FAX 011 49 89 45019305. **LC** DB1; .V66. Documents available from The Genuine Article.
Continues Mitteilungen des Instituts fur Geschichtsforschung und Archivwissenschaft in Wien.
Ind/Abst Arts Humanit. Citation Index [19??-19??) [Full Cov.]; Curr. Contents Arts Humanit.; Res. Alert [Full Cov.]; Soc. Sci. Cit. Index [Select. Cov.].

AU/0452-7070
MITTEILUNGEN DES KREMSER STADTARCHIVS. Main/Corp Krems an der Donau, Austria (City) Stadtarchiv. (1961)-. Monographic series. German. ir. Price varies per volume. Kulturamt der Stadt Krems, Koernermarkt 13, 3500 Krems an der Donau, Austria.
Ind/Abst Am. Hist. Life (1965-).

AU/0259-4137
MITTEILUNGEN DES OBEROSTERREICHISCHEN LANDESARCHIVS. [Mitt. Oberosterr. Landesarch.]. **Added/Corp** Oberosterreichisches Landesarchiv. (1950)-. Monographic series. German. an. Price varies per volume. **LC** DB153; .A3.
Ind/Abst Am. Hist. Life (1957-).

GW
MITTEILUNGEN DES SUDETENDEUTSCHEN ARCHIVS.
Main/Corp Sudetendeutsches Archiv. (July 1971)-. German. Sudetendeutsches, ARCHIV, Hochstrasse 8/11, 8000 Munchen 80 Germany. **Tel** 089/416003-0. **LC** DB2042.G4; S9a. **DD** 943.7/00431. Index available. cum. index. **Bk Rev. Circ:** 350 (ctrl).

DK/0107-9328
MIV: MUSEERNE I VIBORG AMT.
Main/Corp Viborg Stiftsmuseum. **Added/Corp** Viborg Amt (Denmark) Museerne i Viborg Amt. **VFOAT** Museerne i Viborg Amt. (1971)-. Danish. **LC** DL271.V5; V49a.
Ind/Abst BHA : Biblio. Hist. Art.

NO
MJSA ARBOK. Added/Corp Mjssamlingene ved Minnesund. (19??)-. Norwegian. an. Totens Bokhandel, 2850 Lena, Minnesund Norway. **LC** DL576.M52; M58.

US/0884-8432
MODERN GREEK STUDIES YEARBOOK. [Mod. Greek stud. yearb.]. **Added/Corp** University of Minnesota. Modern Greek Studies Program. Vol. 1 (1985)-. Academic Scholarly Publication. English (German and Italian). an. $30.00 US; $33.00 other. Modern Greek Studies Yearbook, University of Minnesota, 325 Social Sciences Building, 267 19th Avenue South, Minneapolis MN 55455. **Tel** (612)624-4526, FAX (612)626-2242. **ED** Theofanis G Stavrou. **LC** DF701; .M62. **DD** 949.5. cum. index. **Bk Rev.** (Qty: 30-40). **Pr Rev. Circ:** 500.
Desc: The journal's objective is the dissemination of scholarly information in the field of Greek studies (social sciences and humanities). Concentrates on the last three centuries, but Byzantine and classical studies will be considered. Special attention will be paid to subjects dealing with Greek-Slavic relations or Eastern Orthodox history and culture.
Ind/Abst Am. Hist. Life (1975-).

FR/0026-9425
MONDE JUIF, LE. [Monde juif]. **Added/Corp** Centre de Documentation Juive Contemporaine. Vol. 1, No. 1 (Aug 1946)-. Periodical. French. qt. 180.00F, France; 290.00F other. Le Monde Juif, 17 rue Geoffroy l'Asnier IV Arr, Paris 75004 France. **Tel** 011 33 1 42774472. **LC** DS101; .M63. **DD** 296. Index available. cum. index. **Bk Rev. Ad Acc. Circ:** 1,500 (ctrl).
Supersedes Bulletin du Centre de Documentation Juice Contemporaine.
Desc: Specialized review in history of World War II and more specifically dedicated to the study of the genocide of the Jewish people.
Ind/Abst Am. Hist. Life.

GW/0026-9832
MONOGRAPHIEN ZUR GESCHICHTE DES MITTELALTERS. Vol. 1 (1970)-. Monographic series. German. Price varies per volume. Anton Hiersemann Verlag, Rosenbergstrasse 113, D 70193 Stuttgart Germany. **Tel** 011 49 711 638264 5. **Ad Acc. Circ:** 1,200.
Desc: About years 400 to 1400 PC (Medieval).

SZ/0581-0353
MONOGRAPHIEN ZUR SCHWEIZER GESCHICHTE. 1- 1968-. Monographic series. German. ir. Price varies per volume. Francke Verlag, Neuengasse 43, Postfach 1445, CH-3001 Bern Switzerland. **Tel** 011/41/31/221715, FAX 011/41/31/221723, telex 911822.

VE/0252-9076
MONTALBAN. [Montalban]. No. 1- 1972-. Periodical. Spanish. Universidad Catolica Andres Bello, Escuela de Comunicacion Social, Caracas, Venezuela. **LC** AS90.C47; A3.
Ind/Abst Am. Hist. Life (1973-); Anthropol. Index; Anthropol. Index; HAPI Hisp. Am. Period. Index; Soc. Plann. Policy Dev. Abstr.; Sociol. Abstr.

UK/0144-0071
MONTGOMERYSHIRE COLLECTIONS. (THE MONTGOMERYSHIRE COLLECTIONS.). [Montgomeryshire collect.]. **Added/Corp** Powys-Land Club. (1944)-. English. an. **LC** DA740.M7; P8. **DD** 942.9/51. **Continues** Powys-Land Club, Welshpool, Wales. Collections Historical & Archaeological Relating to Montgomeryshire and its Borders.
Ind/Abst BHA : Biblio. Hist. Art.

GW
MONUMENTA GERMANIAE HISTORICA. (1976)-. Monographic series. German. ir. Price varies per volume. Hahnsche Bucchandlung Verlag, Leinster 32, D 30159, Hannover, Germany. **Tel** 011 49 511 322294. **Bk Rev.** ctrl circ. available on microfilm from University Microfilms International (UMI). **Continues** Monumenta Germaniae Historica.

PO
MONUMENTA HENRICINA. V. 1- 1960-. Periodical. Portuguese. ir. Coimbra Editora Ltd, rua Fepreira Borges 77, Coimbra Portugal.

IT/0391-8084
MONUMENTI ANTICHI. SERIE MISCELLANEA. See Architecture.

IT/0391-8092
MONUMENTI ANTICHI. SERIE MONOGRAFICA / ACCADEMIA NAZIONALE DEI LINCEI. See Architecture.

IT/0545-008X
MONUMENTI ETRUSCHI. 1- 1967-. Monographic series. Italian. ir. Price varies per volume. Casa Editrice Leo S. Olschki, Viuzzo del Pozzetto, Casella Postale 66, 50126 Florence Italy. **Tel** 011 39 55 6530684, FAX 011 39 55 6530214. **LC** DG223; .M65.

FR
MONUMENTS ET SITES DE SEINE-ET-MARNE : REVUE DES AMIS DES MONUMENTS ET SITES DE SEINE-ET-MARNE. Began with vol. for 1970. Periodical. French. an. 55 Alle Bleriot, 77350 le Mee-sur-Seine France. **LC** DC611.S451; M65. **DD** 944/.37.
Ind/Abst BHA : Biblio. Hist. Art.

FR/0540-8539
MONUMENTS HISTORIQUES DE SEINE ET MARNE. See Architecture.

PL/1230-4018
MOWIA WIEKI 1992. (MOWIA WIEKI.). (1992)-. Periodical. Polish. mo. $60.00. **(Subscription address:** ARS Polona, PO Box 1001, 00068 Warsaw Poland.) **UDC** 943.8. **CODEN** 931.

GW/0170-8929
MUNCHNER ZEITSCHRIFT FUER BALKANKUNDE. (1978)-. French (German). an. DM98.00. Slavica Buchhandel, Elisabethstrasse 18, W-8000 Munich 40 Germany. **Tel** 011 49 89 271-7041. **ED** Rudolf Trofenik. **LC** DR1; .M79. **DD** 949.6. **Bk Rev.**
Ind/Abst BHA : Biblio. Hist. Art.

SZ
MUSEE NEUCHATELOIS. Added/Corp Societe d'Histoire et d'Archeologie du Canton de Neuchatel. Vol. 1 (1864)- Vol. 50 (1913); New Ser., Vol. 1 (1914)-. Periodical. French. qt. **LC** DQ521; .M8. cum. index.
Ind/Abst BHA : Biblio. Hist. Art.

BN/0547-3136
NASE STARINE. See Architecture.

●RU
NASH DAGESTAN. **Added/Corp** Postoiannoe Predstavitelstvo Po Severnomu Kavkazu i Zakavkaziu. (1992)-. Periodical. Russian. mo. ***Continues*** *Sovetskii Dagestan.*

BU
NASLEDSTVO. **Added/Corp** Otechestven Suiuz. (1991)-. Periodical. Bulgarian. DF Abagar, V. Turnovo Bulgaria. **LC** DR69.5; .N37.

GW/0077-2887
NASSAUISCHE ANNALEN. 42- 1913-. German (Latin). an. DM66.00. Verein F Nassauische Altertumskunde, Mosbacher Strasse 55, W-62 Wiesbaden Germany. **Tel** 06121/881-0. **ED** Hans-Joachim Habel. Index available. **Bk Rev.** **Ad Acc.** **Circ:** 2,000 (ctrl). ***Continues*** *Annalen des Vereins fuer Nassauische Altertumskunde und Geschichtsforschung.*
Desc: Reviews of books concerning the region of Hessen-Nassau in Germany; historical essays concerning the regions of Nassau and Mittelrhein (Middle-Rhine).
Ind/Abst BHA : Biblio. Hist. Art.

NO
NES OG HELGYA. 1977-. Norwegian. an. Kr25.00. Cand Mag Kare Sveen, Ekebergvn 292-21 A, Oslo 11 Norway. **LC** DL596.N447; N47.

GW
NEUBURGER KOLLEKTANEENBLATT. German. A D Donau, Schloss, 8858 Neuburg Germany. **LC** DD801.B52; N47. **DD** 914.3/37.

GW/0548-2682
NEUE AUSGRABUNGEN UND FORSCHUNGEN IN NIEDERSACHSEN. **Added/Corp** Arbeitsgemeinschaft der Ur- und Fruhgeschichsforscher in Niedersachsen. Archaologische Kommission fur Niedersachsen. (1963)-. German. Verlag August Lax, Kreuzstr 21, Postfach 100865, Hildesheim Germany. **Tel** 5121/38013. **LC** DD491.H245; N4. **DD** 943/.59.
Ind/Abst BHA : Biblio. Hist. Art.

UK
NEW EUROPE. ***Ceased.*** Vol. 1 (Sept. 1972)-(March 1993). Periodical. English. Europe House Publishing Ltd, La Whitehall Place, London SW1A 2HA England. **LC** D901; .N48. **DD** 914/.03/5505.
Ind/Abst ARTbibliogr. Mod.

HU
NEW HUNGARIAN QUARTERLY, THE. ***Title Change.*** (NHQ; THE NEW HUNGARIAN QUARTERLY.). [New Hung. q.]. **VFOAT** New Hungarian Quarterly. Vol. 9-33 No. 29-128 (Spring 1968)-(Winter 1992). Periodical. English. qt. MTI Hungarian News Agency, PO Box 3, H 1426 Budapest, Hungary. **Tel** 011 36 1 756722, FAX 011 36 1 188297, telex 224373 224374. **ED** I. Boldizsar. **LC** DB901; .N476. cum. index. **Circ:** 5,400. Documents available from The Genuine Article. ***Continues*** *New Hungarian Quarterly.* ***Continued by*** *Hungarian Quarterly (Budapest, Hungary : 1993).*
Desc: Review of political, cultural, social and economic life in Hungary. fine arts year.
Ind/Abst Am. Hist. Life (1971-); Appl. Soc. Sci. Index Abstr.; ARTbibliogr. Mod. (1984-); Arts Humanit. Citation Index (19??-19??) [Full Cov.]; Curr. Contents Arts Humanit.; Middle East Abstr. Index; MLA Int. Bibl. Books Artic. Mod. Lang. Lit.; Music Index; Res. Alert [Full Cov.]; Soc. Sci. Cit. Index [Select. Cov.].

US/0381-9140
NEW REVIEW OF EAST-EUROPEAN HISTORY. Vol. 14 (Dec. 1974)-. Periodical. English. qt. $100.00. New Review / New York, 811 Broadway Suite 842, New York NY 10012. **DD** 947/.0005. ***Continues*** *New Review, 0028-6605.*
Ind/Abst Am. Hist. Life (1971-1977).

US/1073-8339
NEW YORK IRISH HISTORY. (NEW YORK IRISH HISTORY : JOURNAL OF THE NEW YORK IRISH HISTORY ROUNDTABLE.). (19??)-. English. an. $7.00. New York Irish History Roundtable, PO Box 2087 Church Street Station, New York NY 10008. **Tel** (212)962-4237.

GW
NEWS (INTERNATIONAL FRIENDSHIP LEAGUE OF THE GDR). (NEWS.). Vol. 8 (1985)-. Periodical. English. mo. Verlag Zeit im Bild, O-8012 Dresden, Julian-Grimau-Allee, Postfach 61, Dresden Germany. **LC** DD280; .N48. **DD** 943.1087/05. ***Continues*** *News (GDR-Africa Friendship Society).*

US/0028-9272
NEWS OF NORWAY. [News Nor.]. **Added/Corp** Norway. Aambassaden (U.S.) Norske Informasjonstjeneste i Amerika. (Jan. 17, 1941)-. Periodical. English. Thirteen times a year. Free on request. Royal Norwegian Embassy, 2720 34th Street NW, Washington DC 20008. **Tel** (202)333-6000. **ED** Biarue Flolo. **LC** D731; .N43. **DD** 940.53/.05. Index available. cum. index. **Bk Rev.** **Circ:** 14,000 (ctrl).
Ind/Abst Predicasts F&S Index, U. S. Annu. Ed.

US/0883-9549
NEWSLETTER - AMERICAN ASSOCIATION FOR THE ADVANCEMENT OF SLAVIC STUDIES. **Main/Corp** American Association for the Advancement of Slavic Studies. **VFOAT** AAASS Newsletter. Vol. 1 No. 1 (Fall 1960)-. Newsletter. English. bm. $15.00. American Association for the Advancement of Slavic Studies, 125 Panama Street, Stanford University, Acacia Building, Stanford CA 94305-6029. **Tel** (415)723-9668, FAX (415)725-7737, telex 348402 STANFRD STNU. **ED** Denise J Youngblood. **Ad Acc.** **Circ:** 3,200.
Ind/Abst Am. Bibliogr. Slavic East Europ. Stud. (19??-).

CN/0702-8474
NEWSLETTER - CANADIAN INSTITUTE OF UKRAINIAN STUDIES. (NEWSLETTER.). **Added/Corp** Canadian Institute of Ukrainian Studies. **VFOAT** Biuleten / Kanadskyi Instytut Ukrainskykh Studii. Vol. 1, No. 1 (Nov. 1976)-. Newsletter. English (Ukrainian). sa. Free on request. Canadian Institute of Ukrainian Studies, University of Alberta, 352 Athabasca Hall, Edmonton Alberta T6G 2E8 Canada. **Tel** (403)492-2972, FAX (403)492-4967, telex 037-2023. **ED** David Marbles. **LC** DK508.48; .N48. **DD** 947/.71/0071171233. **Bk Rev.** **Ad Acc.** **Circ:** 4,000 (ctrl).
Desc: Summary of institute publications, seminars and other activities.

US/0737-8092
NEWSLETTER - CENTER FOR HOLOCAUST STUDIES (BROOKLYN, NEW YORK, N.Y.). (NEWSLETTER / CENTER FOR HOLOCAUST STUDIES.). [Newsl. - Cent. Holocaust Stud. (Brooklyn N.Y. N.Y.)]. Began with issue for Spring 1976. Newsletter. English. ir. $25.00 membership. Center for Holocaust Studies Documentation and Research, 1610 Avenue J, Brooklyn NY 11230. **Tel** (718)338-6494. **ED** Yaffa Eliach, Bonnie Gurewitsch. **LC** D810.J4; N46. **DD** 940.53/15/03924. **Bk Rev.** **Ad Acc.** **Circ:** 3,000 (ctrl).
Desc: Records the activities and events of the Center for Holocaust Studies; reflects research projects and archival holdings; reports events relevant to Holocaust studies and commemoration.

UK/0957-0241
NEWSLETTER / ROYAL COMMISSION ON THE HISTORICAL MONUMENTS OF ENGLAND. **Added/Corp** Royal Commission on Historical Monuments (England). (19??)-. Newsletter. English. tq. RCHME, Kate Owen, Publications Section, Newlands House, 37-40 Berners Street, London W1P 4BP England.
Ind/Abst Museum Abstr.

UK/0969-1200
NEWSLETTER - SCOTTISH CIVIC TRUST. (NEWSLETTER.). [Newsl. - Scott. Civic Trust]. (1991)-. Newsletter. English. sa. Scottish Civic Trust, 24 George Square, Glasgow G2 1EF Scotland. **Tel** 041-221-1466. **DD** 333.7209411. ***Continues*** *New Grapevine.*
Ind/Abst Museum Abstr.

UK/0306-8455
NEWSLETTER - STUDY GROUP ON EIGHTEENTH-CENTURY RUSSIA. [Newsl. - Study Group Eighteenth Century Russ.]. **Main/Corp** Study Group on Eighteenth-Century Russia. No. 1 (1973)-. Newsletter. English (Russian). an. £7.50 (individual); £12.00 (institutions). Convener and Editor of Newsletter, Professor A G Cross, Department of Slavonic Studies, University of Cambridge, Sidgwick Avenue, Cambridge CB3 9DA England. **Tel** (0223)335020, FAX (0223)335062. **ED** A. G. Cross. **LC** DK127; .S77a. **DD** 947/.005. cum. index (Vols. 1-10). **Bk Rev**, (Qty: 5-8). **Circ:** 200 (ctrl).
Desc: Eighteenth-century Russian history and culture.
Ind/Abst Annu. Bibliogr. Engl. Lang. Lit.

●US/1074-3057
NEWSNET (STANFORD, CALIF.). (NEWSNET / AMERICAN ASSOCIATION FOR THE ADVANCEMENT OF SLAVIC STUDIES.). [NewsNet]. **Main/Corp** American Association for the Advancement of Slavic Studies. **VFOAT** AAASS Newsnet. Vol. 33, No. 4 (Sept. 1993)-. Periodical. English. Six times a year. $20.00. American Association for the Advancement of Slavic Studies, 125 Panama Street, Stanford University, Acacia Building, Stanford CA 94305-6029. **Tel** (415)723-9668, FAX (415)725-7737, telex 348402 STANFRD STNU. **LC** DK1; .A3814. **DD** 947/.0005. ***Continues*** *American Association for the Advancement of Slavic Studies. AAASS Newsletter, 0883-9549.*

FR/1141-1791
NICE HISTORIQUE. **Added/Corp** Academia Nissarda. (19??)-. Periodical. French. bm. **LC** DC977; .N5. **DD** 944.94.
Ind/Abst BHA : Biblio. Hist. Art.

US/0272-0280
NIEPODLEGOSC. [Niepodlegosc]. **Added/Corp** Instytut Badania Najnowszej Historji Polski (Warsaw, Poland) Instytut Jozefa Pisudskiego Poswiecony Badaniu Najnowszej Historii Polski (Warsaw, Poland) Instytut Jozefa Pisudskiego Poswiecony Badaniu Najnowszej Historii Polski (London, England) Pilsudski Institute of America. (1929)-. Periodical. Polish (summaries and/or abstracts in English). an. $16.50. Pilsudski Institute of America, 381 Park Avenue South, New York NY 10016. **Tel** (212)683-4342. **LC** DK401; .N48.
Ind/Abst Am. Hist. Life (1955-1962).

NE
NIEUWE DRENTSE VOLKSALMANAK. (1883)-. Dutch. an. Van Gorcum & Company BV, PO Box 43, NL 9400 AA Assen Netherlands. **Tel** 011 31 5920 46846, FAX 011 31 5920 72064. **LC** DJ401.D7; N5.
Ind/Abst BHA : Biblio. Hist. Art.

IT/0029-1080
NONCELLO, IL. **See** The Arts.

IT/0029-1188
NORD E SUD. Vol. 1, No. 1 (Dec. 1954)-. Periodical. Italian. Four times a year. L85000.00 (individuals), L110000.00 (institutions) others; L140000.00 others. Edizioni Scientifiche Italiane, Via Chiatamone 7, 80121 Naples Italy. **Tel** 011 39 81 7645768, 011 39 81 7645443, FAX 011 39 81 7646477. **ED** Biagio Grasso. **LC** DG401; .N65. **DD** 945/.005. **Bk Rev.** **Ad Acc.**
Desc: Covers economics, sociology, and cultural studies.
Ind/Abst Int. Polit. Sci. Abstr.

GW
NORDEUROPA STUDIEN. **Added/Corp** Ernst-Moritz-Arndt-Universitaet Greifswald. (1966)-. Academic Scholarly Publication. German. ir. DM10.00. Nordeuropa Institut der Ernst-Moritz-Arndt-Universitat, Domstrasse, D-17487 Greifswald Germany. **Tel** FAX 011 49 3834 63222. **LC** DL1; .N29. **Bk Rev.** **Circ:** 500.

GW/0078-1045
NORDFRIESISCHES JAHRBUCH. [Nordfries. Jahrb.]. **Added/Corp** Nordfrisk Institut. (1965)-. Multiple languages (Friesian and German). **LC** DD491.S695; N672. ***Supersedes*** *Nordfriesisches Institut. Jahrbuch.*
Ind/Abst MLA Int. Bibl. Books Artic. Mod. Lang. Lit.

GW
NORDFRIESLAND CHRONIK. German. Flensburger Zeitungsuerlag, Nikolaistrasse 7 239, Flensburg Germany. **LC** DD491.S695; N673.

SW/0281-8353
NORDIC JOURNAL OF SOVIET AND EAST EUROPEAN STUDIES. ***Ceased.*** [Nord. j. Sov. East Eur. stud.]. Vol. 1 (1984)-?. Academic Scholarly Publication. English. qt. Scandinavian University Press, PO Box 2959 Toeyen, N 0608 Oslo 6 Norway. **Tel** 011 47 2 2575400, FAX 011 47 2 2575353, telex 71896 UROR N. **(Subscription address:** Scandinavian University Press, 200 Meacham Ave., Elmont NY 11003.**)** **ED** Kristian Gerner, Svein Monnesland, Pekka Sutela, Jens-Jorgen Jensen and Orjan Sjoberg. **LC** DJK1; .B53. **Ad Acc.** **Circ:** 600. ***Continues*** *Bidrag Till Oststatsforskningen, 0345-1100.*
Desc: Publishes scholarly works on Soviet and Eastern European politics and society. Includes articles relevant to post-1917/45 developments.
Ind/Abst Am. Hist. Life (1984-).

UK
NORTHAMPTONSHIRE PAST & PRESENT. **VAT** Northamptonshire Past and Present. V. 1- 1948-. English. an. £10.00 (individual members), £12.00 (family memberships), £15.00 (institutions). Northamptonshire Record Society, Delapre Abbey, Northampton NN4 9AW England. **Tel** (0604)762297. **ED** R L Greenall. **LC** DA670.N7; N83. **DD** 942.55. Index available. cum. index. **Bk Rev.** **Ad Acc.** **Circ:** 2,000 (ctrl).
Desc: Covers articles on Northamptonshire local history.
Ind/Abst BHA : Biblio. Hist. Art; Br. Archaeol. Bibliogr.; Br. Humanit. Index.

UK/0307-4455
NORTHERN CATHOLIC HISTORY. **See** Religion and Theology-Catholicism.

UK/0306-5278
NORTHERN SCOTLAND. [North. Scotl.]. **Added/Corp** Centre for Scottish Studies. Vol. 1 (1972)-. English. an. £7.00. University of Aberdeen / Centre for Scottish Studies, King's College, Old Aberdeen AB9 2UB Scotland. **Tel** 272474. **ED** P. Payne. **LC** DA750; .N67. **DD** 941.1/005. **Bk Rev**, (Qty: 12-15). **Circ:** 345.
Desc: Articles, mainly historical, relating to the North of Scotland.
Ind/Abst Am. Hist. Life (1972-); Br. Archaeol. Bibliogr.

PL
NOTATKI POCKIE. **Added/Corp** Towarzystwo Naukowe Pockie. Komisja Badan nad Powstaniem i Rozwojem Pocka. No. 1 (1956)-. Polish. qt. Price on Request. **(Subscription address:** ARS Polona, PO Box 1001, 00068 Warsaw Poland.**)** **LC** DK651.P59; N57.
Ind/Abst Numis. Lit.

History(General) —History of Europe

UK/0029-3989
NOTES & QUERIES FOR SOMERSET AND DORSET. VAT Notes and Queries for Somerset and Dorset. Vol. 1 (March 1888)-. Periodical. English. sa. £2.00 UK; $6.00 US. Hugh Jaques, 18 Louise Road, Dorchester Dorset DT1 2LU England. **Tel** 0305-66286. **ED** D. M. M. Shorrocks and G. J. Davies. **LC** DA670.S49; N8. **DD** 942.3/3/005. Index Available, published separately, free-automatically sent. cum. index. **Bk Rev. Ad Acc. Circ:** 450 (ctrl).
Desc: Includes archaeology, architecture, antiquities, genealogy, heraldry, industries, literature, dialect, and folklore.

US/1044-8853
NOTICIERO ALFONSI. Added/Corp Wichita State University. Vol. 1 (1982)-. Periodical. English (Spanish). an. $5.00 (institutions); $3.00 (individuals). AJ Cardenas, Wichita State University, Box 11, Wichita KS 67208. **Tel** (316)689-3180. **DD** 946.

US
NOTRE DAME CONFERENCES IN MEDIEVAL STUDIES. (1990)-. English (Latin). ir. University of Notre Dame Press, PO Box 635, South Bend IN 46624. **Tel** (219)239-6349, (800)677-3232, FAX (219)239-8148.

FR
NOTRE HISTOIRE. French. mo (July/Aug. issue combined). 280.00F France; 40.00Can$ Canada; 330.00F other. Malesherbes Publications, 163 Boulevard Malesherbes, 75859 Paris France. **Tel** 011 33 1 48884600, FAX 011 33 1 48884601.

UK
NOTTINGHAM QUARTERLY. English. qt. £3.00. J Sheffield, 44 Pyatt Street, Meadows Nottingham England. **LC** DA690.N92; N955. **DD** 942.5/27/005.

UK
NOTTINGHAMSHIRE HISTORIAN, THE. English. sa. Nottinghamshire Local History Council, Shire Hall, High Pavement, Nottingham NG1 1HR England. **LC** DA670.N89; N87. **DD** 942.5/2/005. **Continues** Newsletter - Nottinghamshire Local History Council.

FR
NOUVELLE CLIO (PARIS, FRANCE). (NOUVELLE CLIO : L'HISTOIRE ET SES PROBLEMES.). No. 1, (1966)-. Monographic series. French. ir. Price varies per volume. Presses Universitaires de France, Department des Revues, 14 Avenue du Bois de l'Epine, BP 90, 91003 Evry Cedex France. **Tel** (1)60 77 82 05, FAX (1) 60 79 20 45, telex PUF 600 474 F.

RU
NOVAIA OTECHESTVENNAIA INOSTRANNA. See Genealogy and Heraldry.

RU
NOVAIA SOVETSKAIA I INOSTRANNAIA LITERATURA PO OBSCHESTVENNYM NAUKAM: GERMANSKAIA DEMOKRATICHESKAIA RESPUBLIKA. **Added/Corp** Akademiia Nauk SSSR. Institut Nauchnoi Informatsii po Obschestvennym Naukam. **VFOAT** Germanskaia Demokraticheskaia Respublika. (1976)-. Russian (Multiple languages). mo. 0.20rub (single issue). Izdatelstvo Nauka / Akademiia Nauk, Publishing House of the Russian Academy of Sciences, Leninskii Porspekt 14, 117901 Moscow Russia. **Tel** 011 95 954-21-53, FAX 011 95 938-21-44, telex 411964. **LC** Z2250; .N63; DD261. **Continues** Novaia Literatura po Germanskoi Demokraticheskoi Respublika.

RU
NOVAIA SOVETSKAIA I INOSTRANNAIA LITERATURA PO OBSHCHESTVENNYM NAUKAM: CHEKHOSLOVATSKAIA SOTSIALISTICHESKAIA RESPUBLIKA. **Added/Corp** Institut Nauchnoi Informatsii po Obshchestvennym Naukam (Akademiia Nauk SSSR). (1976)-. Multiple languages (Russian and Multiple languages). mo. 0.20rub (single issue). Izdatelstvo Nauka / Akademiia Nauk, Publishing House of the Russian Academy of Sciences, Leninskii Porspekt 14, 117901 Moscow Russia. **Tel** 011 95 954-21-53, FAX 011 95 938-21-44, telex 411964. **LC** Z2133; .N6; DB196. **Continues** Novaia Literatura Po Chekhoslovakii.

RU/0134-2924
NOVAIA SOVETSKAIA I INOSTRANNAIA LITERATURA PO OBSHCHESTVENNYM NAUKAM. POLSKAIA NARODNAIA RESPUBLIKA. **Added/Corp** Institut Nauchnoi Informatsii po Obshchestvennym Naukam (Akademiia Nauk SSSR). **VFOAT** Novaia Sovetskaia i Inostrannaia Literatura po Obshchestvennym Naukam. Polskaia Narodnaia Respublika; Novaia Sovetskaia i Inostrannaia Literatura po Obshchestvennym Naukam. Polsha; Polskaia Narodnaia Respublika; Polsha. (1976)-. Russian. mo.

0.35rub (single issue). Izdatelstvo Nauka / Akademiia Nauk, Publishing House of the Russian Academy of Sciences, Leninskii Porspekt 14, 117901 Moscow Russia. **Tel** 011 95 954-21-53, FAX 011 95 938-21-44, telex 411964. **LC** Z2523; .N58. **Continues** Novaia Literatura po Polshe.

IT
NOVI MATAJUR. Periodical. Multiple languages (Slovenian and Italian). 3000. **LC** DG457.S5; N67. **Supersedes** Matajur.

AT/0311-6166
NUOVO PAESE. [Nuovo paese]. (1974)-. Newspaper. Italian (English). Eleven times a year (Except Jan.). 25.00Aus$ Australia; 45.00Aus$ other. Nuovo Paese, PO Box 10026, Adelaide SA 5000 Australia. **Tel** 011 61 8 2118842, FAX 011 61 8 4100148. **ED** Mario Bianco. **Bk Rev**, (Qty: 6-11). **Ad Acc. Circ:** 7,000.
Desc: Current affairs concentrating on Italian, Australian and overseas political, social, and work related cultured issues.

GW/0078-2653
NURNBERGER FORSCHUNGEN. Monographic series. German. ir. Price varies per volume. Verein Geschichte Stadt Nurnbg, Nuernberg Germany. **Tel** (0911)162771. Index available. **Circ:** 1,000 (ctrl).
Desc: Covers history, arts, and crafts of Nuremberg.

SW
NY I SVERIGE. V. 1- Feb. 1972-. Swedish. qt. Kr25.00. Statens Invandrarverk, Vikboplan 7, Box 6113, 600 06 Norrkoping Sweden. **LC** DL639; .N9.

DK
NYT FRA ISLAND. 1.- Aug. 1959-. Periodical. Danish. ir (one-two issues per year). kr50.00. Dansk-Islandsk Samfund, Lungtoftevej 5, 2800 Kgs Lyngby Denmark. **Tel** +45-2-882511. **ED** Bent A Koch. **LC** DL326; .N95. **Ad Acc. Circ:** 1,300 (ctrl).

GW/0342-1686
OBERBAYERISCHES ARCHIV. (OBERBAYERISCHES ARCHIV / HERAUSGEGEBEN VOM HISTORISCHEN VEREIN VON OBERBAYERN.). [Oberbayer. Arch.]. **Added/Corp** Historischer Verein von Oberbayern. (1963)-. German. **LC** DD801.B45; H8. **DD** 943/.36. **Continues** Oberbayerisches Archiv fur Vaterlandische Geschichte.
Ind/Abst BHA : Biblio. Hist. Art.

AU/0029-7550
OBEROSTERREICHISCHE HEIMATBLATTER. [Oberosterr. Heimatbl.]. **Added/Corp** Oberosterreichisches Landesmuseum. Institut fur Landeskunde. Institut fur Landeskunde von Oberosterreich. Vol. 1, No. 1 (Jan./Mar. 1947)-. Periodical. German. qt. **LC** DB151; .L58.
Ind/Abst Am. Hist. Life (1963-1964); BHA : Biblio. Hist. Art.

GW/0342-9873
OBERPFALZ, DIE. [Oberpfalz]. (1907)-. Periodical. German. Two issues per month. DM32.00. Verlag Michael Lassleben, Lange Gasse 19, W-8411 Kallmuenz Germany. **Tel** 094731205, FAX 094738357. **ED** Erich Lassleben. **UDC** 908.430.1-35.65. Index available. cum. index. **Bk Rev**, (Qty: 10-15). **Acid Free. Circ:** 2,000.

GW/0930-522X
OBERRHEINISCHE STUDIEN KARLSRUHE. [Oberrh. Stud.Karlsr.]. (1970)-. Monographic series. German. ir. **UDC** 908.
Ind/Abst BHA : Biblio. Hist. Art.

UK/0953-7155
OCCASIONAL PAPER / SOCIETY OF ANTIQUARIES OF LONDON. Added/Corp Society of Antiquaries of London. **VFOAT** Occasional Papers; Occasional Papers from the Society of Antiquaries of London. (1943)-. Monographic series. English. ir. Price varies per volume. The Society of Antiquaries of London, Burlington House, Piccadilly, London W1V 0HS England. **Tel** 011 44 71 734 0193. **(Subscription address:** Oxbow Books, Park End Place, Oxford OX1 1HN England.) **LC** DA20; .S53. **Pr Rev. Circ:** 500.

UK/0078-303X
OCCASIONAL PAPERS - DEPT. OF ENGLISH LOCAL HISTORY, LEICESTER UNIVERSITY. Main/Corp Leicester, England. University. Dept. of English Local History. **Added/Corp** Leicester, Eng. University College. Dept. of English Local History. (1952)-. Monographic series. English. ir. Price varies per volume. Leicester University Press, Fielding Johnson Building, University Road, Leicester LE1 7RH England. **ED** C. Phythian-Adams and H. Fox. **Pr Rev.**
Desc: Specialized topics in English local history.

UK
OCCASIONAL SERIES - HISTORIC SOCIETY OF LANCASHIRE AND CHESHIRE. Main/Corp Historic Society of Lancashire and Cheshire. Vol. 1- 1974-. Monographic series. English. Price varies per volume. Record Society of Lancashire, PO Box 147, University of Liverpool, Liverpool L69 3BX England. **Tel** 011 44 51 7942000.

PO
OCEANOS. Added/Corp Comissao Nacional para as Comemoracoes dos Descobrimentos Portugueses. No. 1 (June 1989)-. Periodical. Portuguese. qt. **LC** DP583; .O25. **DD** 946.9/02.
Ind/Abst BHA : Biblio. Hist. Art.

PL/0029-8247
OCHRONA ZABYTKOW. [Ochr. zabyt.]. **Added/Corp** Poland. Zarzad Ochrony i Konserwacji Zabytkow. Poland. Centralny Zarzad Muxeow. Vol. 1 (1948)-. Periodical. Polish. qt. $35.00. **(Subscription address:** ARS Polona, PO Box 1001, 00068 Warsaw Poland.) **LC** DK409; .O25.
Ind/Abst Art Archaeol. Tech. Abstr.; Avery Index Archit. Period. Suppl. Colum. Univ. (19??-199?); BHA : Biblio. Hist. Art.

PL/0029-8514
ODRODZENIE I REFORMACJA W POLSCE. Added/Corp Instytut Historii (Polska Akademia Nauk). (1956)-. Polish (summaries and/or abstracts in French and Russian). an.
Ind/Abst Am. Hist. Life (1986-).

FI/0357-9956
OESTERBOTTEN. Title Change. [Oesterbotten]. **Added/Corp** Svensk-Oesterbottniska Samfundet. **VFOAT** Oesterbottnisk Aarsbok. (1962)-(1992). Swedish. an. **LC** DL1170.P6; O85. **DD** 948.9/75. **Continues** Oesterbottnisk Aarsbok. **Continued by** Svensk-Oesterbottniska Samfundets Aarsbok.
Ind/Abst MLA Int. Bibl. Books Artic. Mod. Lang. Lit.

AU/1013-9966
OESTERREICH IN GESCHICHTE UND LITERATUR MIT GEOGRAPHIE. [Oesterr. Gesch. Lit. Geogr.]. **Added/Corp** Institut fuer Oesterreichkunde. Vol. 1, No. 16 (1972)-. Periodical. German. bm. S460.00, (add S60.00 for postage). Wilhelm Braumueller, Servitengasse 5, A 1092 Vienna, Austria. **Tel** 011 43 1 3191482, 3191159. **LC** DB1; .O23. **DD** 943.6/005. **Continues** Oesterreich in Geschichte und Literatur, 0029-8743.
Ind/Abst Am. Hist. Life (1957-); MLA Int. Bibl. Books Artic. Mod. Lang. Lit.

FR
OEUVRES COMPLETES OF JULES MICHELOT. French. ir. Price varies. UD Union Distr, Za Delta 29 31 Ave Guynemer, Chev Larue, BP 403, 94152 Rungis Cedex France. **Tel** 011 33 1 46872636.

FR/0030-0691
OGAM. [Ogam]. **Added/Corp** Amis de la Tradition Celtique. No. 1 (1948)-. Periodical. French. Four times a year. Ogam, BP 574, 35007 Rennes France. **LC** IN PROCESS.
Ind/Abst MLA Int. Bibl. Books Artic. Mod. Lang. Lit.; Numis. Lit.

US/1048-6615
OHIO SLAVIC & EAST EUROPEAN NEWSLETTER. [Ohio Slav. East Eur. newsl.]. **Added/Corp** Ohio State University. Center for Slavic and East European Studies. **VFOAT** Ohio Slavic and East European Newsletter. (19??)-. Newsletter. English. **DD** 947.
Ind/Abst Hum. Rights Intern. Rep.

NE/0166-1809
ONS AMSTERDAM. [Ons Amst.]. Vol. 1; Jan. 1949-. Periodical. Dutch. mo. $38.00. Stadshikgeverij, Voormalige Stadstimmertuin 4-6, 1018 ET Amsterdam Netherlands. **Tel** 20-5511735, FAX 020-5511711. **ED** H Heuff. **LC** DJ411.A53; O57. Index available. cum. index. **Bk Rev. Ad Acc. Circ:** 25,000.
Desc: History of the city of Amsterdam Netherlands.

PL/0474-2885
OPOLSKI ROCZNIK MUZEALNY. **Added/Corp** Muzeum Slaska Opolskiego w Opolu. (1963)-. Polish (summaries and/or abstracts in English and German). an. **LC** DD491.S53; O59.
Ind/Abst BHA : Biblio. Hist. Art.

GW
OSNABRUCKER LAND HEIMAT-JAHRBUCH. German. Heimatbund Osnabrucker Land, V-Steuben-Allee 2, 4570 Quakenbruck Germany. **Tel** 05431-3183. **ED** Heinrich Boning. **LC** DD491.H3446; O85. Index available. cum. index. **Bk Rev. Ad Acc. Circ:** 7,000.
Desc: History, culture, biology, Low German, art in Osnabruck.

AU/0029-9308
OSTERREICHISCHE MONATSHEFTE. (OSTERREICHISCHE MONATSHEFTE; ZEITSCHRIFT FUER POLITIK.). [Osterr. Monatsh.]. 1.- Yearly volume; Oct. 1945-. Periodical. German. ir. Ostterrichische Monatshefte, Karntnerstrasse 51, 1010 Vienna Austria. **LC** DB99.1; .O4. **DD** 943.6.
Ind/Abst Am. Hist. Life (1955-1959, 1964-).

History(General) —History of Europe

AU/0029-9375
OSTERREICHISCHE OSTHEFTE. [Osterr. Osth.]. **Added/Corp** Osterreichisches Ost- und Sudosteuropa-Institut. Arbeitsgemeinschaft Ost. Vol. 1 (Sept. 1959)-. Periodical. German. qt (4 issues). S848.45 (includes postage). Minerva, Sachsenplatz 4 6, A 1201 Vienna Austria. **LC** DR1; .O4. **DD** 947/.0005.
Ind/Abst Am. Hist. Life (1960-); MLA Int. Bibl. Books Artic. Mod. Lang. Lit.

● RU
OTECHESTVENNAIA ISTORIIA. See Genealogy and Heraldry.

IE/0332-088X
OTHER CLARE. [Other Clare]. (1977)-. Periodical. English. an. $25.00. Shannon Archaeological Historical Society, 14 Springfield, Clare Republic of Ireland. **Tel** 065 20119. **DD** _a941.54193.

NE/0165-6465
OVERIJSSELSE HISTORISCHE BIJDRAGEN : VERSLAGEN EN MEDEDELINGEN VAN DE VEREENIGING TOT BEOEFENING VAN OVERIJSSELSCH REGT EN GESCHIEDENIS. Added/Corp Vereeniging tot Beoefening van Overijsselsch Regt en Geschiedenis. (1977)-. Dutch. an. Waanders Uitgevers, Postbus 1129, 8001 BC Zwolle Netherlands. **Tel** 011 31 38 658628, FAX 038-655989. **Continues** Vereeniging tot Beoefening van Overijsselsch Regt en Geschiedenis. Verslagen en Mededelingen.
Ind/Abst BHA : Biblio. Hist. Art.

UK/0141-8149
OXFORD GERMAN STUDIES : BOOK SUPPLEMENT. 1-. English. ir. £15.00. Holdan Books Ltd, 11 Broad Street, Oxford OX1 3AR England. **Tel** (0865)242939. **ED** P F Ganz and T J Reed. **Circ:** 500 (ctrl).
Desc: German culture, history, and literature.

UK
OXFORD HISTORY OF ENGLAND, THE. (1936)-. Monographic series. English. ir. Price varies per volume. Oxford University Press / New York, 200 Madison Avenue, New York NY 10016. **Tel** (212)679-7300, (919)677-0977, (800)451-7556, (800)445-9714, FAX (919)677-1303.

UK
OXFORD HISTORY OF MODERN EUROPE. (19??)-. English. ir. Price varies per volume. Oxford University Press, Walton Street, Oxford OX2 6DP England. **Tel** 011 44 865 56767, FAX 011 44 865 267773, telex 837330 OXPRES G. **(Subscription address:** Oxford University Press / USA, Journals Marketing Department, Oxford University Press, 2001 Evans Road, Cary NC 27513.**) ED** Alan Bullock, F.W.D. Deaking.

UK/0474-974X
OXFORD MEDIEVAL TEXTS. (1967)-. Monographic series. English (Latin). ir. Price varies per volume. Oxford University Press, Walton Street, Oxford OX2 6DP England. **Tel** 011 44 865 56767, FAX 011 44 865 267773, telex 837330 OXPRES G. **(Subscription address:** Oxford University Press / USA, Journals Marketing Department, Oxford University Press, 2001 Evans Road, Cary NC 27513.**) ED** D.E. Greenaway, B.F. Harvey and M. Lapidge.

UK/0078-7256
OXFORD SLAVONIC PAPERS. See Linguistics-Abstracting, Bibliographies and Statistics.

UK
OXFORDSHIRE RECORD SOCIETY; [ANNUAL REPORT]. Main/Corp Oxfordshire Record Society. (194?)-. English. be. £8.00. Oxfordshire Record Society, c/o Bodleian Library, Oxford OX1 3BG England. **Circ:** 300. **Continues** Annual Report, Statement of Account, List of Officers and Members.
Desc: Edited texts of historical documents relating to the county of Oxfordshire, England.
Ind/Abst Br. Archaeol. Bibliogr. (?-?).

IT
PADOVA E IL SUO TERRITORIO. (1986)-. Periodical. Italian. bm (Jan., Mar., May, July, Sept., Nov.). L3000000. La Garangula, Via Montona 4, 35137 Padua Italy. **Tel** 011 39 49 8750550, FAX 011 39 49 8751743. **Continues** Padova e la sua Provincia.
Ind/Abst BHA : Biblio. Hist. Art.

BU
PALAEOBULGARICA. STAROBULGARISTIKA. Added/Corp TSentur za Bulgaristika (Bulgarska Akademiia na Naukite). **VFOAT** Starobulgaristika. Vol. 1 (1977)-. Academic Scholarly Publication. Bulgarian (English, French, German and Russian). Four times a year. DM145.00. Bulgarska Akademiia na Naukite, 7 Noemvri 1, Sofia Bulgaria. **(Subscription address:** Kubon & Sagner, ABT Zeitschriftenimport, D 80328 Munich Germany.**) LC** DR63; .P34. Index available. cum. index. **Bk Rev. Circ:** 1,200 (ctrl).
Desc: A scientific journal devoted to the problems of the Old Bulgarian language, history, literature, arts, and culture. Also covers relations between Bulgaria and the other European cultures during the Middle Ages.

SP
PALMAS DE GRAN CANARIA: AGENDA, LAS. Added/Corp Organizacion Sindical. Delegacion Provincial de Sindicatos (Las Palmas). (19??)-. Periodical. Spanish. Servicio de Informacion Y Publicaciones Sindicales, General Franco 21, Las Palmas Spain. **LC** DP302.L193; P3.

XR/0139-9853
PAMATKY A PRIRODA. [Pamat. prir.]. **Added/Corp** Statni Ustav Pamatkove Pece a Ochrany Prirody v Praze. (1976)-. Periodical. Czech (summaries and/or abstracts in English, French, German and Russian). Ten times a year. $83.10. **(Subscription address:** Artia Pegas Press Ltd., Palac Metro Narodni Trida 25, 11210 Prague 1 Czech Republic.**) LC** DB200.5; .P326. **Formed by the union of** Pamatkova Pece and Ochrana Prirody (Prague, Czechoslovakia).
Ind/Abst AGRICOLA; Archit. Period. Index (1981-); Art Archaeol. Tech. Abstr.; BHA : Biblio. Hist. Art; GeoRef.

TK/0131-2677
PAMIATNIKI TURKMENISTANA. [Pamjat. Turkm.]. **Added/Corp** Turkmenistan SSR-ning tarykhy ve Medeni Iadygarliklerini Goramak Baradaky Respublikan Meiletin Jemgyet. (1966)-. Russian (summaries and/or abstracts in English). sa. 0.50rub single issue. Turkmenistan Publishing House, Ulitsa Gogolya 17A, Ashkhabad Turkmenistan. **LC** DK931; .P35.

PL
PANORAMA POLSKA. Ceased. VFOAT Panorama of Poland. No. 186 (Jan. 1972)-(July 1991). Periodical. Polish (English). mo. **(Subscription address:** ARS Polona, PO Box 1001, 00068 Warsaw Poland.**) LC** DK401. **Continues** Nasza Ojczyzna.

GW/0078-9410
PAPYROLOGICA COLONIENSIA. VFOAT Wissenschaftliche Abhandlungen der Arbeitsgemeinschaft fur Forschung des Landes Nordrhein-Westfalen. Papyrologica Coloniensia; Abhandlungen der Rheinisch-Westfalischen Akademie der Wissenschaften. Papyrologica Coloniensia. V. 1-. Monographic series. Multiple languages (German and English). ir. Price varies per volume. Westdeutscher Verlag GmbH, Postfach 5829, D 65048 Wiesbaden Germany. **Tel** 011 49 611 160220.

FR/0428-1551
PARIS ET ILE-DE-FRANCE / PUBLIES PAR LA FEDERATION DES SOCIETES ET ARCHEOLOGIQUES DE PARIS ET DE L'ILE DE FRANCE. Added/Corp Federation des Societes Historiques et Archeologiques de Paris et de l'Ile-de-France. Vol. 5/6 (1953/54)-. French. an. 331.75F. Editions Klincksieck, 8 rue de la Sorbonne, 75005 Paris France. **Tel** 11 33 1 43545953, FAX 11 33 1 432252553. **LC** DC701; .P37. **DD** 944/.36/005. Index available. cum. index. **Continues** Federation des Societes Historiques et Archeologiques de Paris et de l'Ile de France. Memoires.
Ind/Abst BHA : Biblio. Hist. Art.

US/0737-738X
PATRISTIC AND BYZANTINE REVIEW, THE. See Religion and Theology.

US
PAYAM-I IMAM. See History(General)-History of Asia.

FR/0031-3386
PAYS BAS-NORMAND, LE. [Pays Bas-Normand]. (1908)-. Periodical. French. qt. **UDC** 944.23.
Ind/Abst BHA : Biblio. Hist. Art.

FR/1169-2421
PAYS D'ALBE, LE. (1974)-. Periodical. French. an. **UDC** 908(443.831).
Ind/Abst BHA : Biblio. Hist. Art.

FR/0245-8411
PAYS D'ALSACE. Added/Corp Societe d'Histoire et d'Archeologie de Saverne et Environs. (19??)-. Periodical. French. qt.
Ind/Abst BHA : Biblio. Hist. Art.

FR
PAYS D'EUROPE OCCIDENTALE EN ..., LES. French. an. 47.00F. Documentation Francaise, 29 Quai Voltaire, 75344 Paris Cedex 7 France. **Tel** 011 33 1 40157000, FAX 011 33 1 40157230, telex 204 826 DOCFRAN. **ED** Alfred Grosser. **LC** D411; .F67 subser; D1058. **DD** 909.8 S; 940.55/05. **Bk Rev. Ad Acc.**
Desc: Presents for each of the countries studied, general data which aid understanding of that country's development and which pinpoint significant items.

BE/0776-3689
PAYS GAUMAIS, LE. See The Arts.

FR/0031-3394
PAYS LORRAIN, LE. Added/Corp Societe d'Archeologie Lorraine et du Musee Historique Lorrain. **VFOAT** Pays Lorrain et le Pays Messin. Vol. 1 (1904)-. Periodical. French. mo. cum. index.
Ind/Abst BHA : Biblio. Hist. Art.

FR/0338-4659
PAYS SEDANAIS, LE. (1975)-. Periodical. French. **UDC** 908.
Ind/Abst BHA : Biblio. Hist. Art.

SP
PEDRALBES. Added/Corp Universidad de Barcelona. Departament d'Historia Moderna. Vol. 1, No. 1 (1981)-. Periodical. Catalan (French and Spanish). ir. Departament d'Historia Moderna, Faculte Geografia e Historia, Barcelona Spain. **Tel** 011 34 3 5811092. **(Subscription address:** Estakirot, Madre del Deu Dell Coll 53, 08023 Barcelona Spain.**) LC** DP302.C57; P43. **DD** 946/.7/005. **Bk Rev. Ad Acc. Circ:** 300 (ctrl).
Ind/Abst Am. Hist. Life (1987-).

GR/0553-478X
PELOPONNESIAKA. [Peloponnesiaka]. **Added/Corp** Hetaireia Peloponnesiakon Spoudon (Athens, Greece). **VFOAT** Peloponnesiaca. (1956)-. Greek, Modern (summaries and/or abstracts in English). an. **LC** DF901.P4; P4.
Ind/Abst Am. Hist. Life (1956-1957).

IE/0332-1592
PERITIA. [Peritia]. **Added/Corp** Medieval Academy of Ireland. Vol. 1 (1982)-. English (German and French). an. Brepols Publishers / Baron Frans du Fourstraat 8, B2300 Turnhout Belgium.
Ind/Abst MLA Int. Bibl. Books Artic. Mod. Lang. Lit.

US
PERVOPOKHODNIK. V. 1-. (No. 1-); 1971-. Russian. bm. $6.00. T H Puchalsky, 1315 Chelton Way So, Pasadena CA 91030. **LC** DK265; .A14.

FR/0399-1253
PEUPLES MEDITERRANEENS. [Peuples mediterr.]. **VFOAT** Mediterranean Peoples. No. 1, (Oct/Dec. 1977)-. Periodical. French (English). Four times a year (Mar., June, Oct., Dec.). 380.00F one year. Inst d'Etudes Mediterraneenes, BP 188 07, 75326 Paris Cedex 07 France. **Tel** 011 33 1 45670191. **ED** Paul Vieille. **LC** DE1; .P48. **DD** 909/.09822. **Ad Acc. Circ:** 2,000.
Desc: Brings critical thought to bear upon contemporary societies and renew scientific debate concerning past and present of the Mediterranean.
Ind/Abst Am. Hist. Life (1977-); Geogr. Abstr. Human Geogr.; Int. Bibliogr. Sociol.; Int. Dev. Abstr. (?-?); Int. Polit. Sci. Abstr.; PAIS Int. Print (1991-); Recent. Publ. Artic.; Soc. Plann. Policy Dev. Abstr.; Soc. Welf. Soc. Plan./Policy Soc. Dev.; Sociol. Abstr.; Middle East J.

GW/0031-6679
PFALZER HEIMAT. Added/Corp Pfalzische Gesellschaft zur Forderung der Wissenschaften. Historischer Verein der Pfalz. Verein fur Naturforschung und Landespflege "Pollichia". Pfalzischen Verein fuer Naturkunde und Naturschutz "Pollichia". (1950)-. Periodical. German. qt. **LC** DD801.P422; P4. **DD** 943/.43/005. **Supersedes** Pfalzisches Museum-Pfalzische Heimatkunde.
Ind/Abst BHA : Biblio. Hist. Art.

FR/0151-6086
PICTON, LE. (1976)-. Periodical. French. bm. 150.00F France; 200.00F other. Le Picton, 129 Boulevard du Grand Cerf, 86000 Poitiers Cedex France. **Tel** 33 49586414. **ED** Michel Granger. **UDC** 908. Index available. **Bk Rev,** (Qty: 6). **Ad Acc. Circ:** 4000.

LV
PILSETU VESTURES PROBLEMAS. See Housing and Urban Development.

UK/0959-5805
PLANNING HISTORY. [Plann. hist.]. **VFOAT** Bulletin of the Planning History Group. (1988)-. Periodical. English. Three times a year. £10.00. International Planning History Society, Department of Civic Design, University of Liverpool, PO Box 747, Liverpool L69 3BX England. **Tel** (051)794-3112, FAX (051)794-3125. **ED** Dr. S.V. Ward. **DD** 711.09. **Bk Rev. Ad Acc. Circ:** 300. **Continues** PHB. Planning History Bulletin, 0267-0542.
Desc: The prime aim of this magazine is to increase awareness of developments and ideas in planning history in all parts of the world.
Ind/Abst Am. Hist. Life (1991-).

GW
PLESSE-ARCHIV. Added/Corp Bovenden. Issue 1 (1966)-. Monographic series. German. ir. Price varies per volume. Verlag Erich Goltze KG, Stresemannstrasse 28, D 37079 Goettingen Germany. **Tel** 011 49 551 63078.

CN/0227-4361
POLAND TODAY. [Pol. today]. **VFOAT** La Pologne Aujourd'Hui. No. 1 (Nov. 1977)-. Periodical.

English (French). Three times a year. $2.50. Poland Today, c/o SSML, Faculty of Arts, University of Ottawa, Ottawa Ontario K1N 6N5 Canada. **DD** 943.8/005.

GR
POLITIKA THEMATA. **VFOAT** Themata. (1973)-. Periodical. Greek, Modern. wk. Hypsylantou, 25 Athens Greece. **LC** DF853; .P65. available on microfilm from New York Public Library.

GW
POLITISCHER BERICHT DES ZENTRALEN KOMITEES DES KOMMUNISTISCHEN BUNDES WESTDEUTSCHLAND AN DIE ORDENTLICHE DELEGIERTENKONFERENZ. **Main/Corp** Kommunistischer Bund Westdeutschland. Zentrales Komitee. 1.- 1974-. German. Kommunistischer Bundes Westdeutschland an die, Sandhefer Str 29, W-6800 Mannheim Germany. **LC** JN3971.A98; K76.

NO
POLSK KULTUR. 1982/Nr. 1-. Periodical. Norwegian (Polish). Polsk-Norsk Kulturforening Kultura, Postboks 174 Sentrum, Oslo 1 Norway. **LC** DK4110; .P65. **DD** 943.8/005.

PL/0079-3620
POLSKA 2000 / KOMITET BADAN I PROGNOZ "POLSKA 2000" POLSKIEJ AKADEMII NAUK. **Added/Corp** Polska Akademia Nauk. Komitet Badan i Prognoz Polska 2000. **VFOAT** Polska Dwutysieczna. (1970)-. Monographic series. Polish (English). ir. Price varies per volume. Zaklad Narodowy Im Ossolinskch, Ul Szewska 37, Wroclaw Poland. **LC** CB161; .P6.

US/0747-6558
POMMERSCHEN LEUTE, DIE. **See** Genealogy and Heraldry.

US/0884-0172
POMOST. (POMOST : KWARTALNIK.). [Pomost]. Began in 1978. Periodical. Polish. qt. $6.00. Pomost, PO Box 34223, Chicago IL 60634. **LC** DK4442.

CN/0082-5328
PONTIFICAL INSTITUTE OF MEDIAEVAL STUDIES. STUDIES AND TEXTS. (STUDIES AND TEXTS - PONTIFICAL INSTITUTE OF MEDIAEVAL STUDIES.). [Pontif. Inst. Mediaev. Stud., Stud. texts]. **Main/Corp** Pontifical Institute of Mediaeval Studies. Vol. 1 (1955)-. Monographic series. English (French and Latin). ir. Price varies per volume. Pontifical Institute of Mediaeval Studies, 59 Queens Park Crescent East, Toronto Ontario M5S 2C4 Canada. **Tel** (416)926-7144, FAX (416)926-7276. **Circ:** 500.
Desc: Monograph series of studies and critical editions covering a variety of subjects pertaining to the Middle Ages such as history, literature, philosophy, theology, law, and etc.
Ind/Abst MLA Int. Bibl. Books Artic. Mod. Lang. Lit.

SW/1102-0822
POPULAR HISTORIA. [Pop. hist.]. (1991)-. Periodical. Swedish. bm. Kr250 Sweden; Kr275 other Nordic countries; Kr280 other. Historika Media, PO Box 935, S-220 09 Lund Sweden. **(Subscription address:** PROGEK, PO Box 31003, S-400 32 Goeteborg Sweden (telephone 46-31-24-34-25)) **UDC** 93.

GW/0079-421X
PORTUGIESISCHE FORSCHUNGEN DER GORRESGESELLSCHAFT. ERSTE REIHE, AUFSATZE. (PORTUGIESISCHE FORSCHUNGEN. 1. REIHE, AUFSATZE ZUR PORTUGIESISCHEN KULTURGESCHICHTE.). [Port. Forsch. Gorresges., Erste Reihe, Aufs.]. **Added/Corp** Gorres-Gesellschaft. **VFOAT** Aufsatze zur Portugiesischen Kulturgeschichte. (1960)-. German (Portuguese). **LC** DP501; .P85.
Ind/Abst MLA Int. Bibl. Books Artic. Mod. Lang. Lit.

US/1057-1515
PORTUGUESE STUDIES REVIEW. [Port. stud. rev.]. **Added/Corp** International Conference Group on Portugal. Vol. 1, No. 1 (Spring/Summer 1991)-. Periodical. English. Twice a year (Jan. & July). $47.00 (institutions); $24.00 (individuals). International Conference Group on Portugal, Department of History, University of New Hampshire, Durham NH 03824. **Tel** (603)862-1234. **LC** DP532; .P67. **DD** 909/.0917/5691. ***Continues*** *Portuguese Studies Newsletter, 0738-9841.*

SP
POSIBLE. Spanish. 35ptas each issue. Publicaciones 33, Constancia 25, Madrid Spain. **LC** DP1; .P67. **DD** 946/.005.

YU
POSLOVNI VODIC SR SRBIJE SA REGISTROM ORGANIZACIJA OSTALIH REPUBLIKA. **VFOAT** Poslovni Vodic S.R. Srbije sa Registrom Organizacija Ostalih Republika; Poslovni Vodic S.R. Srbije; Poslovni Vodic SR Srbije. Serbo-Croatian (Roman). an. Novinsko-Izdavacka Radna, Organizacija Knjizevne Novine, Belgrad Francuska 7 Yugoslavia. **LC** DR1938.5; .P67.

RU
POVOLZHSKII KRAI. Vol. 1 (1972)-. Russian. 0.75rub each issue. Izdatelstvo Saratovskogo Universiteta, Universitetskaia 42, Saratov Russia. **LC** DK511.V65; P66.

PL
POZNAJ SWOJ KRAJ. **Added/Corp** Poland. Ministerstwo Oswiaty. (19??)-. Periodical. Polish. mo. $51.00. **(Subscription address:** ARS Polona, PO Box 1001, 00068 Warsaw Poland.**)** **LC** DK401; .P8946.

UZ
PRAVDA VOSTOKA. (19??)-. Russian. ir (156 issues per year). $349.95. **(Subscription address:** East View Publications Inc., 3020 Harbor Lane North, Suite 110, Minneapolis MN 55447.**)** **LC** DK861.U8; A26.

RU
PRAVITELSTVENNYI VESTNIK (MOSCOW, R.S.F.S.R.). (PRAVITELSTVENNYI VESTNIK : ORGAN SOVETA MINISTROV SSSR.). **Added/Corp** Soviet Union. Sovet Ministrov. Soviet Union. Komitet po Operativnomu Upravleniiu Narodnym Khoziaistvom. No. 1 (Jan. 1989)-. Periodical. Russian. bw. **LC** DK285.5; .P73. **CODEN** PRVEEX.

XR/0079-4929
PRAVNEHISTORICKE STUDIE. [Pravnehist. stud.]. 1955-. Academic Scholarly Publication. Czech (Slovak; summaries and/or abstracts in German and Russian). an. **(Subscription address:** Artia Pegas Press Ltd., Palac Metro Narodni Trida 25, 11210 Prague 1 Czech Republic.**)**
Desc: Prints original scholarly studies in the history of state and law, both Czechoslovak and foreign; supplemented with book reviews, recent bibliography and personal columns.
Ind/Abst Am. Hist. Life (1963-).

GW
PRESSE-INFORMATIONEN. **Main/Corp** Germany (Democratic Republic, 1949-). Presseamt Beim Vorsitzenden des Ministerrates. German. Thalmannplatz 8/9 108, Berlin Germany. **LC** DD261; .A27. **DD** 943/.1/005. ***Continues*** *Presse-Informationen.*
Ind/Abst AgBiotech News Inf.; Index Vet.; Vet. Bull.

GW/0032-7972
PREUSSENLAND : MITTEILUNGEN DER HISTORISCHEN KOMMISSION FUR OST- UND WESTPREUSSISCHE LANDESFORSCHUNG. **Added/Corp** Historische Kommission fur Ost- und Westpreussische Landesforschung. Stiftung Preussischer Kulturbesitz. Vol. 1, No. 1/2 (1963)-. Periodical. German. Twice a year. DM16.00. N G Elwert Verlag, Postfach 1128, Reitgasse 7+9, W-3550 Marburg Germany. **Tel** 06421 25023, FAX 06421 15487. **[CCC].**
Ind/Abst Am. Hist. Life (1989-).

SP/0032-8472
PRINCIPE DE VIANA. (PRINCIPE DE VIANA / DIPUTACION FORAL, INSTITUCION PRINCIPE DE VIANA, CONSEJO DE CULTURA DE NAVARRA.). [Princ. Viana]. **Added/Corp** Institucion Principe de Viana. No 1 (Dec. 3 1940)-. Periodical. Spanish. Three times a year. 2621ptas. Gobierno de Navarra, Navas de Tolosa 21, 31002 Pamplona Spain. **Tel** 34 948 107121, FAX 34 948 227673. **ED** Fernando Perez Ollo. **DD** 946.5. Index available. cum. index. **Circ:** 1,000 (ctrl).
Ind/Abst Am. Hist. Life (1959-1970); BHA : Biblio. Hist. Art; Indice Hist. Esp. (1959-1970).

US/0196-9730
PROCEEDINGS AND REPORTS - FLORIDA STATE UNIVERSITY, CENTER FOR YUGOSLAV-AMERICAN STUDIES, RESEARCH AND EXCHANGES. ***Ceased.*** (PROCEEDINGS AND REPORTS - CENTER FOR YUGOSLAV-AMERICAN STUDIES, RESEARCH AND EXCHANGES.). [Proc. rep. - Fla. State Univ. Cent. Yugosl.-Am. Stud. Res. Exch.]. **Main/Corp** Florida State University. Center for Yugoslav-American Studies, Research, and Exchanges. **Added/Corp** Florida State University. Center for Yugoslav-American Studies, Research, and Exchanges. Proceedings & Reports of Seminars and Research Conducted Within the Center for Yugoslav-American Studies, Research and Exchanges. **VFOAT** Proceedings & Reports of Seminars and Research Conducted Within the Center for Yugoslav-American Studies, Research and Exchanges. Vol. 8 (1974)-(19??). Proceedings. English. an. 930 West Park Avenue, Tallahassee FL 32306. **Tel** (904)644-5465. **ED** Esther Glenn. **LC** DR1; .F58. **DD** 949.7/02. **Bk Rev. Ad Acc. Circ:** 800 (ctrl). ***Continues*** *Florida State University. Center for Slavic and East European Studies. Slavic Papers.*
Desc: Contains summaries and proceedings generated through the centers in comparative research in monetary financial policy, technology transfer, and science policy, business, international law and relations, physics, chemistry, mathematics, engineering, and geology.

US/0093-2574
PROCEEDINGS - CONSORTIUM ON REVOLUTIONARY EUROPE. ***Title Change.*** (PROCEEDINGS.). [Proc. - Consort. Revolut. Eur.]. **Main/Corp** Consortium on Revolutionary Europe, 1750-1850. (1972)-(19??). English. an. Consortium Revolutionary Europe, PO Box 9561, Samford University, Savannah GA 31412. **LC** D299; .C625a. **DD** 940.2. ***Continued by*** *Selected Papers.*
Ind/Abst Am. Hist. Life (1972-).

US/0099-0329
PROCEEDINGS OF THE ANNUAL MEETING OF THE WESTERN SOCIETY FOR FRENCH HISTORY. [Proc. annu. meet. West. Soc. Fr. Hist.]. **Main/Corp** Western Society for French History. (1974)-. Proceedings. English (French). an (around October). $35.00 US; $40.00 other. Western Society of French History, Department of History, University of Nevado - Reno, Reno NV 89557. **Tel** (702)784-1964. **(Subscription address:** All correspondence should be directed to Dr. M.L. Hildreth of the University of Nevada - Reno.**)** **ED** Norman Ratvich, University of California - Riverside. **LC** DC1; .W48a. **DD** 944/.006/2. Index available (price is $10.00). cum. index (up to Vol. 13). **Pr Rev. Circ:** 250.
Desc: Articles, commentaries and abstracts on French history, literature and topics relating to the French-speaking cultures; selected from papers presented at the society's annual meeting.
Ind/Abst Am. Hist. Life (1973-); MLA Int. Bibl. Books Artic. Mod. Lang. Lit.

●US/0899-3106
PROCEEDINGS OF THE CONFERENCE ON MEDIEVALISM. **Added/Corp** Conference on Medievalism. (1992)-. Proceedings. English. The Conference on Medievalism, 520 Colleve Avenue, Harlem MI 49423.

US/0362-7055
PROCEEDINGS OF THE ... MEETING OF THE FRENCH COLONIAL HISTORICAL SOCIETY. [Proc. Meet. Fr. Colon. Hist. Soc.]. **Main/Corp** French Colonial Historical Society. Meeting. **Added/Corp** French Colonial Historical Society. University Press of America. **VFOAT** Proceedings of the ... Annual Meeting of the French Colonial Historical Society; Actes du ... Colloque de la French Colonial Historical Society. (1975)-. Proceedings. English (French). an. $28.50 (U.S.) per issue. University Press of America, 4720 A Boston Way, Lanham MD 20706. **Tel** (301)459-3366, (800)462-6420. **LC** JV1803; .F74a. **DD** 325/.344.

FR/0033-1856
PROVENCE HISTORIQUE; REVUE TRIMESTRIELLE. [Provence hist.]. Vol. 1 Issue 1 (July/Sept. 1950)-. Periodical. French. qt. 210.00F. Federation Historique Provence, 66 B rue Saint Sebastien. **LC** DC611.P951; P68. cum. index. ***Supersedes*** *Memories de l'Academie de Vaculise; Institut Historique de Provence, Marseilles. Memoires.*
Ind/Abst Am. Hist. Life (1988-); BHA : Biblio. Hist. Art; Geogr. Abstr. Human Geogr.

PL/0033-2186
PRZEGLAD HISTORYCZNY. [Prz. hist.]. **Added/Corp** Towarzystwo Miosnikow Historii w Warszawie. Vol. 1 (1905)-. Periodical. French (Latin and Polish; summaries and/or abstracts in Russian). qt. Price on Request. **(Subscription address:** ARS Polona, PO Box 1001, 00068 Warsaw Poland.**)** **LC** DK4010; .P79. **DD** 943.8/005. cum. index.
Ind/Abst Am. Hist. Life (1954-1962, 1965-); Numis. Lit.

PL/0033-2437
PRZEGLAD ZACHODNI. [Prz. zach.]. **Added/Corp** Instytut Zachodni. Vol. 1 (July 1945)-. Periodical. Polish. qt. $58.00. **(Subscription address:** ARS Polona, PO Box 1001, 00068 Warsaw Poland.**)** **LC** DK4010; .P794. Index Available, published separately, free-automatically sent. cum. index.
Ind/Abst Am. Hist. Life (1954-1973, 1975-).

PL/0552-4245
PRZEGLAD ZACHODNIOPOMORSKI / INSTYTUT ZACHODNIOPOMORSKI. **Added/Corp** Instytut Zachodnio-Pomorski (Szczecin, Poland) Towarzystwo Rozwoju Ziem Zachodnich (Poland). Prezydium Rady Okregu. Szczecinskie Towarzystwo Naukowe. Towarzystwo Rozwoju Ziem Zachodnich (Poland). Zarzad Wojewodski. **VFOAT** PZ, Przeglad Zachodniopomorski. (Oct. 1957)-. Periodical. Polish (table of contents in English). qt. $58.00. **(Subscription address:** ARS Polona, PO Box 1001, 00068 Warsaw Poland.**)** ***Continues*** *Szczecin.*

UK
PUBLICATIONS. **Main/Corp** Buckinghamshire Record Society. Vol. 7 (1943)-. Monographic series. English (Latin). ir. Price varies per volume. Buckinghamshire Record Society, Walton House Walton

History(General) —History of Europe

Street, Aylesbury BKS HP21 7QQ England. **Tel** 011 44 296 382586. **ED** Eileen Scarff. Each issue contains an index to its own contents (no volume index)--loose. available on microfiche. *Continues* Architectural and Archaeological Society for the County of Buckingham. Records Branch. Publications.
 Desc: Historical texts relating to Buckinghamshire.

US/0885-7954
PUBLICATIONS / AUGUSTAN REPRINT SOCIETY. See Literature.

FR
PUBLICATIONS DE LA SORBONNE. SERIE FRANCE XIXE-XXE SIECLES.
VFOAT "France XIXe-XXe Siecles"; Serie "France XIXe-XXe Siecles"; Serie "France Dix-neuvieme-vingtieme Siecles"; Serie "France 19e-20e Siecles"; Publications de la Sorbonne. "Serie France XIXe-XXe". (19??)-. Monographic series. French. ir. Price varies per volume. Publications de la Sorbonne, 14 rue Cujas, 75231 Paris Cedex 05 France.

US
PUBLICATIONS IN MEDIEVAL SCIENCE. Main/Corp University of Wisconsin.
Monographic series. English. ir. Price varies per volume. University of Wisconsin Press, Journal Division, 114 North Murray Street, Madison WI 53715. **Tel** (608)262-4952, FAX (608)262-8909.

UK/0085-2848
PUBLICATIONS / LONDON RECORD SOCIETY. Added/Corp London Record Society.
(1965)-. Monographic series. English. an. $35.00 institutions; $22.00 individuals. London Record Society, Institute of Historical Research, Senate House, London, WC1E 7HU England. **Tel** 011 44 81 636 0272, FAX 011 44 81 436 2183. **ED** V. Harding. **Circ:** 360.

UK/0067-4826
PUBLICATIONS OF THE BEDFORDSHIRE HISTORICAL RECORD SOCIETY. Main/Corp Bedfordshire
Historical Record Society. **Added/Corp** Bedfordshire Historical Record Society. Vol. 1 (1913)-. Monographic series. English. ir. Price varies per volume. Bedfordshire Historical Record Society, County Record Office County Hall, Bedford MK42 9AP England. **Tel** 011 44 234 228833. **LC** DA670.B29; B4.

UK/0267-2634
PUBLICATIONS OF THE LINCOLN RECORD SOCIETY, THE. Added/Corp Lincoln
Record Society. Vol. 1 (1910/1911)-. Monographic series. English (Latin). an. Free to members; £12.00 membership. Lincoln Record Society, Lincoln Cathedral Library, Lincoln LN2 1PZ England. **Tel** 011 44 522 544544. **ED** D.M. Owen. **LC** DA670.L69; R5. **DD** 942.5/3. Index available. **Circ:** 350 (ctrl).
 Desc: Historical documents relating to the county of Lincolnshire and to the ancient diocese of Lincoln.

GW
PUNTO Y HORA DE EUSKAL HERRIA.
VFOAT Punto y Hora. Periodical. Basque (Spanish). wk. 12 single issue. Apartado 1397, San Sebastian Spain. **LC** DP302.B41; P85. **DD** 946/.6. **UDC** 946.6.

IT
PUTEOLI, STUDI DI STORIA ANTICA.
Added/Corp Azienda Autonoma di Soggiorno, Cura e Turismo di Pozzuoli. (1977)-. Italian (English, French and Italian). an. L65000. Azienda Autonoma di Soggiorno e Turismo di Pozzuoli, Via Campi Flegrei 3, (ss. Domitiana), 15477805 Pozzuoli, Naples Italy. **Tel** 011 81 8672419. **ED** Giuseppe Camodeca. **LC** DG70.P9; P87. **DD** 937/.7.

IT
QUADERNI DEL CIRCOLO ROSSELLI.
Added/Corp Circolo Rosselli. **VFOAT** Q/CR. (1981)-. Periodical. Italian. Three times a year. L70000 Italy; L110000 other. Franco Angeli Riviste SRL, Viale Monza 106, 20127 Milan Italy. **Tel** 011 39 2 2827651, 011 39 2 289562. **LC** JN5201; .Q35. **DD** 945/.005.
 Ind/Abst PAIS Foreign Lang. Index (1988-).

IT
QUADERNI DELLA BRIANZA, I. V. 1-
Oct./Nov. 1978-. Periodical. Italian. 10000. Piazza Carrobiolo 5, 10052 Monza Italy. **LC** DG975.B86; Q33. **DD** 945/.21. **UDC** 945.

IT/0393-6821
QUADERNI DELL'ISTITUTO DI ARCHEOLOGIA E STORIA ANTICA / LIBERA UNIVERSITA ABRUZZESE DEGLI STUDI "G. D'ANNUNZIO", CHIETI. See Archaeology.

IT
QUADERNI MEDIEVALI. (June 1976)-.
Periodical. Italian. Twice a year. L30000 Italy; L45000 other. Edizioni Dedalo Spa, Casella Postale 362, Bari 70100 Italy. **Tel** 011 39 080 5311400, FAX 011 39 080 5311414. **ED** Prof. Giosue Musca (editor's address: Che Guevara 37/D, Bari 70100 Italy; phone: 011 39 080 5510445). **LC** D111; .Q32. cum. index. **Bk Rev**, (Qty: 10/yr). **Ad Acc, Adv Mgr:** R. Coga. ctrl circ. Documents available from The Genuine Article.
 Desc: Covers historical research.
 Ind/Abst Arts Humanit. Citation Index [Full Cov.]; BHA : Biblio. Hist. Art; Curr. Contents Arts Humanit.; Numis. Lit.; Res. Alert [Full Cov.]; Soc. Sci. Cit. Index [Select. Cov.].

IT
QUADERNI SICILIANI. 1- May 1973-. Italian. 300
single issue. Di Modica, Via XX Settembre 69, Palermo Italy. **LC** DG861; .Q33.

IT/0301-6307
QUADERNI STORICI. [Quad. stor.]. Added/Corp
Universita di Urbino. Istituto di Storia e Sociologia. (1970)-. Periodical. Italian (summaries and/or abstracts in English). tq. L100000.00 Italy; L130000.00 (surface mail), L150000.00 (airmail) other. Societa Editrice il Mulino, Strada Maggiore 37, 40125 Bologna Italy. **Tel** 011 39 51 256011, FAX 011 39 51 256034. Documents available from The Genuine Article. *Continues* Quaderni Storici Delle Marche.
 Ind/Abst Am. Hist. Life (1974-); Arts Humanit. Citation Index [Full Cov.]; BHA : Biblio. Hist. Art; Curr. Contents Arts Humanit.; Res. Alert [Full Cov.].

IT/0392-873X
QUADERNI UTINENSI. See Literature.

SP/0211-478X
QUADERNS D'ARQUEOLOGIA I HISTORIA DE LA CIUTAT / AJUNTAMENT DE BARCELONA, MUSEU D'HISTORIA DE LA CIUTAT, SEMINARI D'INVESTIGACIO "A. DURAN I SANPERE.". See Archaeology.

SP
QUADERNS D'HISTORIA TARRACONENSE. Added/Corp Instituto de
Estudios Tarraconenses Ramon Berenguer IV. Seccion de Arqueologia e Historia. (1977)-. Periodical. Catalan (Spanish). **LC** DP302.T11; I5 subser.

US
QUARTERLY. Main/Corp Polish Western
Association of America. Vol. 1 (1960)-. Periodical. English. qt. Polish Western Association of America, 1130 North Ashland, Chicago IL 60622. **LC** DK401; .P835a.
 Ind/Abst Am. Bibliogr. Slavic East Europ. Stud.

CN/0822-9902
QUEBEC-URSS INFORMATION.
[Que.-URSS inf.]. **VAT** Quebec-Union des Republiques Socialistes Sovietiques Information. Fall 1983-. Periodical. French. Societe Culturelle Quebec/URSS, Quebec H2J 2L3 Canada. **DD** 947/.005. **UDC** 947; 908.47. *Continues* Quebec-URSS (1982), 0823-003X.

GW
QUELLEN UND BEITRAEGE ZUR GESCHICHTE DER STADT STADTLOHN. (1988)-. Monographic series.
German. ir. Price varies per volume.

GW/0930-9292
QUELLEN UND FORSCHUNGEN ZUR GESCHICHTE DER STADT MUNSTER.
(1960)-. German.
 Ind/Abst BHA : Biblio. Hist. Art.

GW
QUELLEN UND STUDIEN ZUR GESCHICHTE DES OSTLICHEN EUROPA. Vol. 1 (1968)-. Monographic series.
German. ir. Price varies per volume. Franz Steiner Verlag GmbH, Postfach 101061, D 70009 Stuttgart Germany. **Tel** 011 49 0711 2582372, FAX 011 49 0711 2582290, telex 723636 daz d. **ED** Helmut Altrichter.
 Desc: Articles, reports and reviews about East European history.

GW/0079-9114
QUELLEN UND STUDIEN ZUR GESCHICHTE OSTEUROPAS. Vol. 1 (1958)-.
Monographic series. German. ir. Price varies per volume. Akademie-Verlag GmbH, Muehlenstrasse 33 34, D 13162 Berlin Germany. **Tel** 011 49 30 47889300, FAX 011 49 30 47889357. **(Subscription address:** VCH Publishers Inc., 303 Northwest 12th Avenue, Journals Department, Deerfield FL 33442.) **ED** Eduard Winter, Heinz Lemke.
 Desc: Series covering the history of Eastern Europe.

GW
QUELLEN UND STUDIEN ZUR VERFASSUNGSGESCHICHTE DES DEUTSCHEN REICHES IN MITTELALTER UND NEUZEIT, HRSG. VON KARL ZEUMER. German. ir.

AU
QUELLEN ZUR GESCHICHTE OBEROESTERREICHS. Added/Corp
Oberoesterreichisches Landesarchiv. **VFOAT** QGOO. (1991)-. Monographic series. German. ir. Price varies per volume. Oberoesterreichisches Landesarchiv, Anzengruberstrasse 19, A-4020 Linz Donau Austria. **Tel** 0732-6555230, FAX 0732655523-4619.

UN
RADIANSKA UKRAINA. Added/Corp Ukraine.
Tsentralnyi Ispolnitelnyi Komitet. Ukraine. Verkhovna Rada. Prezydiia. (19??)-. Periodical. Ukrainian. mo. $45.00. **(Subscription address:** Victor Kamkin, 4956 Boiling Brook Parkway, Rockville MD 20852.) **LC** DK508.A2; R28.

CI/0351-6709
RADOVI ZAVODA JUGOSLAVENSKE AKADEMIJE ZNANOSTI I UMJETNOSTI U ZADRU. [Rad. Zavoda Jugosl. akad. znan. umjet.
Zadru]. **Added/Corp** Jugoslavenska Akademija Znanosti i Umjetnosti. Zavod za Povijesne Znanosti u Zadru. (1979)-. Periodical. Serbo-Croatian (Roman) (summaries and/or abstracts in English). an. **LC** DB401; .J83. **DD** 949.7/2. *Continues* Radovi Centra Jugoslavenske Akademije Znanosti i Umjetnosti u Zadru, 0350-1299.
 Ind/Abst BHA : Biblio. Hist. Art.

IT
RASSEGNA GALLARATESE DI STORIA E D'ARTE. Periodical. Italian. 10.000. Rassegna
Gallaratese di Storia e d'Arte, c/c Postale N 27-31917, Gallarate Italy. **LC** DG975.G18; R35. **DD** 914.5/22. **UDC** 908.45.

IT/0033-9873
RASSEGNA STORICA DEL RISORGIMENTO. (RASSEGNA STORICA DEL
RISORGIMENTO : ORGANO DELLA SOCIETA NAZIONALE PER LA STORIA DEL RISORGIMENTO ITALIANO.). [Rass. stor. risorgim.]. **Added/Corp** Societa Nazionale per la Storia del Risorgimento Italiano. Regio Istituto per la Storia del Risorgimento Italiano. Istituto per la Storia del Risorgimento Italiano. Vol. 1 (Jan./Feb. 1914)-. Periodical. Italian. qt. L50000 Italy; L65000 other. Istituto Storia Risargimenta, Vittoviano PZA Venezia, 00186 Rome Italy. **Tel** 39 6 6793526. **LC** DG552.A15; I63. Index available (bound in fourth issue). cum. index. **Bk Rev**. **Circ:** 3,000 (ctrl). Documents available from The Genuine Article.
 Ind/Abst Am. Hist. Life (1954-); Arts Humanit. Citation Index [Full Cov.]; Curr. Contents Arts Humanit.; MLA Int. Bibl. Books Artic. Mod. Lang. Lit.; Res. Alert [Full Cov.]; Soc. Sci. Cit. Index [Select. Cov.].

IT/0033-9881
RASSEGNA STORICA TOSCANA. [Rass.
stor. toscana]. **Added/Corp** Comitato Permanente per Gli Studi Storici Della Toscana. Societa Toscana per la Storia del Risorgimento. Vol. 1 (1955)-. Periodical. Italian. sa. L57000 (Italy); L76000 (other). Casa Editrice Leo S. Olschki, Viuzzo del Pozzetto, Casella Postale 66, 50126 Florence Italy. **Tel** 011 39 55 6530684, FAX 011 39 55 6530214. cum. index.
 Ind/Abst Am. Hist. Life (1982-); BHA : Biblio. Hist. Art.

UK
READING MEDIEVAL STUDIES : ANNUAL PROCEEDINGS OF THE GRADUATE CENTRE FOR MEDIEVAL STUDIES IN THE UNIVERSITY OF READING. Added/Corp University of Reading.
Graduate Centre for Medieval Studies. **VFOAT** Annual Proceedings of the Graduate Centre for Medieval Studies in the University of Reading. Vol. 5 (1979)-. Proceedings. English. an (Nov. or Dec.). £12.40. University of Reading / Department of History, Reading RG6 2AA England. **Tel** 011 44 0734 318143. **ED** Mr. A. K. Bate and Mrs. J. Hunter. **LC** CB351; .R4a. **DD** 909.07. **Bk Rev**, (Qty: 4-6). **Ad Acc**. **Circ:** 150. *Continues* Annual Proceedings of the Graduate Centre for Medieval Studies in the University of Reading, 0306-6223.
 Desc: Articles and aspects of the medieval history, literature, philology, and history of art archaeology.
 Ind/Abst BHA : Biblio. Hist. Art; MLA Int. Bibl. Books Artic. Mod. Lang. Lit.

FR/0996-3634
RECHERCHES REGIONALES: COTE D'AZUR ET CONTREES LIMITROPHES.
Added/Corp Alpes-Maritimes, France (Dept.) Archives Departementales. (19??)-. Periodical. French. qt.
 Ind/Abst BHA : Biblio. Hist. Art.

FR
RECHERCHES SUR TOURS. Vol. 1-.
Periodical. French. **LC** DC801.T74; R43. **DD** 936.4. **UDC** 944.54.
 Ind/Abst BHA : Biblio. Hist. Art.

GW/0179-2938
RECHTSRHEINISCHES KOLN. [Rechtsrhein.
Koln]. V. 1-. German. an. DM20.00. Geschichts-und Heimatverein, Rechtsrheinisches Koln, Friedrich-Ebert-Ufer 64-70, 5000 Koln 90 Porz Germany. **ED** Gebhard Aders and Wilhelm Bockn. **LC** DD491.R49568; R42. **DD** 943/.55. **UDC** 943.42. **Bk Rev**. **Ad Acc**.

History(General) —History of Europe

UK
RECORD SOCIETY FOR THE PUBLICATION OF ORIGINAL DOCUMENTS RELATING TO LANCASHIRE AND CHESHIRE : PUBLICATIONS. Added/Corp Record Society for the Publication of Original Documents Relating to Lancashire and Cheshire. Vol. 1, (1879)-. Monographic series. English. ir. Price varies per volume. Record Society of Lancashire, PO Box 147, University of Liverpool, Liverpool L69 3BX England. **Tel** 011 44 51 7942000. **LC** DA670.L19; R3. **DD** 942.71.

UK/0034-1738
RECORDS OF HUNTINGDONSHIRE. V. 1-1965-. Periodical. English. an. Huntingdonshire Local History Society, 7 Post St Godnaschester, Huntingdon PE 18 8BA England. **UDC** 942.562.
Ind/Abst Br. Archaeol. Bibliogr.

FR/1149-767X
RECUEIL DE L'ASSOCIATION DES AMIS DU VIEUX HAVRE. (1922)-. Periodical. French. an. **UDC** 908(442.5).
Ind/Abst BHA : Biblio. Hist. Art.

FR/0515-1864
RECUEIL DES HISTORIENS DE LA FRANCE. DOCUMENTS FINANCIERS.
Main/Corp Academie des Inscriptions et Belles-Lettres, Paris. Vol. 1 (1899)-. Monographic series. French. ir. Price varies per volume. Diffusion de Boccard, 11 rue de Medicis, 75006 Paris France. **Tel** 011 33 1 43260037.

FR/0080-0325
RECUEIL DES HISTORIENS DE LA FRANCE. OBITUAIRES. See Biographies.

UK/0034-1932
RECUSANT HISTORY. [Recusant hist.]. Vol.4 (Jan. 1957)-. Periodical. English. sa. $40.00. Catholic Record Society, 12 Melbourne Place, Wolsingham Company, CO Durham DL13 3EH England. Index available in last issue of volume--attached. available on microfilm from University Microfilms International (UMI). **Continues** Biographical Studies, 1534-1829.
Ind/Abst Am. Hist. Life (1973-); BHA : Biblio. Hist. Art; Br. Humanit. Index.

NE/0927-2704
REFLECTOR DEN BOSCH. See Sociology.

BE
REGARDS (CENTRE COMMUNAUTAIRE LAIC JUIF, BRUSSELS, BELGIUM). (REGARDS : CAHIERS DU CCLJ.). Periodical. French. wk. 30F. Regards, 52 rue Hotel des Monnaies, B-1060 Brussels Belgium. **LC** DS101; .R42A. **DD** 909/.04924.

GW
REICHSMINISTERIALBLATT : ZENTRALBLATT FUER DAS DEUTSCHE REICH / HERAUSSEGEBEN IM REICHSMINISTERIUM DES INNERN.
Main/Corp Germany. Reichsministerium des Innern. Vol. 51 1923-. German. **Continues** Zentralblatt fur das Deutsche Reich.

UK/0269-9656
REMNANTS. [Remnants]. (1986)-. Periodical. English. sa. **DD** 942.
Ind/Abst Museum Abstr.

CN/0034-429X
RENAISSANCE AND REFORMATION.
[Renaiss. reform]. **Added/Corp** Canadian Society for Renaissance Studies. Renaissance Society of America. North Central Conference. Toronto Renaissance and Reformation Colloquium. Victoria University (Toronto, Ont.). Centre for Reformation and Renaissance Studies. **VFOAT** Renaissance et Reforme. Vol. 1-12, No 2 (Oct. 1964-Winter 1976); New Series, Vol. 1 (Spring 1977)-. Periodical. French (English). qt (Feb., May, Aug., Nov.). 37.00Can$ (institutions), 28.00Can$ (individuals). University of Guelph / French Studies, Department of French Studies, Guelph Ontario, N1G 2W1 Canada. **Tel** (519)824-4120 Ext 3884. **ED** Francois Pare (editor's phone: (519)576-8029). **DD** 940.2. **Bk Rev. Pr Rev. Circ:** 800. Documents available from The Genuine Article.
Desc: An interdisciplinary journal printing original substantive contributions to scholarship in all areas of Renaissance and Reformation studies in both English and French.
Ind/Abst Abstr. Engl. Stud.; Am. Hist. Life (1976-); Annu. Bibliogr. Engl. Lang. Lit.; Arts Humanit. Citation Index [Full Cov.]; BHA : Biblio. Hist. Art; Book Rev. Index; Curr. Contents Arts Humanit.; Index Book Rev. Relig.; Index Book Rev. Humanit.; MLA Int. Bibl. Books Artic. Mod. Lang. Lit.; Res. Alert [Full Cov.]; Soc. Sci. Cit. Index [Select. Cov.].

CN/0034-429X
RENAISSANCE AND REFORMATION.
[Renaiss. Reform.]. **Added/Corp** Toronto Renaissance and Reformation Colloquium. Victoria University (Toronto, Ont.). Centre for Reformation and Renaissance Studies. Canadian Society for Renaissance Studies. Renaissance Society of America. North Central Conference. Pacific Northwest Renaissance Conference. **VFOAT** Renaissance et Reforme. Vol. 1, No. 1 (Oct. 1964)-Vol. 12, No. 2 (Winter 1976); New Series, Vol. 1, No. 1 (Spring 1977)-. Periodical. English (French). Four times a year. 28.00Can$ (individuals), 37.00 (institutions). University of Guelph / French Studies, Department of French Studies, Guelph Ontario, N1G 2W1 Canada. **Tel** (519)824-4120 Ext 3884. **LC** CB359; .R45. **DD** 940.2/1.
Ind/Abst Abstr. Engl. Stud.; Am. Hist. Life (1976-); Book Rev. Index; Index Book Rev. Humanit.; MLA Int. Bibl. Books Artic. Mod. Lang. Lit.

UK/0269-1213
RENAISSANCE STUDIES. (RENAISSANCE STUDIES : JOURNAL OF THE SOCIETY FOR RENAISSANCE STUDIES.). [Renaiss. stud.].
Added/Corp Society for Renaissance Studies (Great Britain). Vol. 1, No. 1 (March 1987)-. Periodical. English (Latin). Four times a year. £62.00 UK and Europe; $112.00 other. Oxford University Press, Walton Street, Oxford OX2 6DP England. **Tel** 011 44 865 56767, FAX 011 44 865 267773, telex 837330 OXPRES G. **(Subscription address:** Oxford University Press / USA, Journals Marketing Department, Oxford University Press, 2001 Evans Road, Cary NC 27513.) **ED** Gordon Campbell. **LC** CB361; .R474. **DD** 940.2/1/05. **[CCC]**. **Bk Rev. Ad Acc.** available on microfilm and microfiche from University Microfilms International (UMI).
Desc: Covers all aspects of Renaissance history and culture. It is multi-disciplinary papers on the history, art, architecture, religion, literature and language of any European country or any country influenced by Europe during the Renaissance.
Ind/Abst Am. Hist. Life (1987-); BHA : Biblio. Hist. Art; Br. Humanit. Index; MLA Int. Bibl. Books Artic. Mod. Lang. Lit.

FR
REPERTOIRE DES RECHERCHES LATINO-AMERICANISTES EN FRANCE.
Began in 1979. French. 120.00F France; 150.00F other. Centre National de la Recherche Scientifique, Informascience, 26 rue Boyer, 75971 Paris France. **Tel** 61.41.11.05, telex CNRSDOC 220880 F. **LC** F1409.95.F8; R46. **DD** 980/.0072044.
Desc: Repertory containing 50 research centers, specialized or having an axis of research on Latin America and 716 research workers attached to these institutions or individuals.

NE
REPERTORIUM VAN BOEKEN EN TIJDSCHRIFTARTIKELEN BETREFFENDE DE GESCHIEDENIS VAN NEDERLAND. Added/Corp Nederlands Comite voor Geschiedkundige Wetenschappen. Nederlands Historisch Genootschap. Netherlands. Rijkscommissie voor Vaterlandse Geschiedenis. Netherlands. Ministerie van Onderwijs en Wetenschappen. (1941)-. Dutch. an. Fl60.00. Inst. Nederlandse Geschiedenis, Postbus 90755, 2509LT Sgravenhage Netherlands. **Tel** 011 31 70 3814771. **ED** A. Gast. **Continues** Repertorium van Boeken en Tijdschriftartikelen op Het Gebied van de Geschiedenis van Nederland.

UK
REPORT FOR THE YEAR ... / THE LINCOLN RECORD SOCIETY. Main/Corp Lincoln Record Society. English. an. Lincoln Record Society, Lincoln Cathedral Library, Lincoln LN2 1PZ England. **Tel** 011 44 522 544544. **Continues** Report and List of Subscriber / Lincoln Record Society.

IE
REPORT OF PROCEEDINGS / NEW IRELAND FORUM. Title Change. Main/Corp New Ireland Forum. No. 1 (30 May 1983)-. Proceedings. English (Irish). ir. Government Publications, 4 5 Harcourt Road, Dublin 2 Ireland. **Tel** 011 353 1 6613111 Ext.4005. **LC** DA990.U45. **DD** 941.508/05. **UDC** 941.5. **Circ:** 1,000. **Continued by** New Ireland Forum. Report.

UK
REPORTS OF THE RESEARCH COMMITTEE OF THE SOCIETY OF ANTIQUARIES OF LONDON. Main/Corp Society of Antiquaries of London. Research Committee. (1913)-. Monographic series. English. ir. Price varies per volume. The Society of Antiquaries of London, Burlington House, Piccadilly, London W1V 0HS England. **Tel** 011 44 71 734 0193. **(Subscription address:** Oxbow Books, Park End Place, Oxford OX1 1HN England.) **Circ:** 250.

PO
RESISTENCIA. Periodical. Portuguese. 400.00. Editorial Resistencia, rua Nova de Sao Mamede 2, Lisbon Portugal. **LC** DP501; .R38.

US/0162-9905
RESTORATION (KNOXVILLE). See Literature.

UK/0267-6834
REVIEW OF SCOTTISH CULTURE.
Added/Corp National Museum of Antiquities of Scotland. **VFOAT** ROSC. No. 1 (1984)-. Periodical. English. an. £12.00. Cannongate Press, Frederick Street, Edinburgh Scotland. **Tel** 011 44 31 2203800.
Ind/Abst BHA : Biblio. Hist. Art.

CI
REVIJA. Periodical. Serbo-Croatian (Roman). Centar Za Kulturi I Unjetnost Radnickog Sveucilista, Vukovarska 31, Osijek Croatia. **LC** DB370.5; .R47. **UDC** 949.71; 908.497.1.

SP
REVISTA CATALANA DE GEOGRAFIA.
Added/Corp Societat Catalana de Geografia. (19??)-. Periodical. Catalan (summaries and/or abstracts in English and Spanish). Three times a year. 2000ptas Spain; 3075ptas other. Institut Cartografico Catalunya, Calle Balmes 209, 08006 Barcelona Spain. **Tel** 011 34 3 2188758. **LC** DP302.C57; R36. **DD** 914.6/7.

PO/0871-2352
REVISTA DE CIENCIAS HISTORICAS : [PUBLICACAO DO DEPARTAMENTO DE CIENCIAS HISTORICAS DA UNIVERSIDADE PORTUCALENSE].
Added/Corp Universidade Portucalense. Departamento de Ciencias Historicas. Vol. 1 (1986)-. Periodical. Portuguese. **LC** DP501; .R435. **DD** 946.9.
Ind/Abst BHA : Biblio. Hist. Art.

SP/0210-2854
REVISTA DE ESTUDIOS EXTREMENOS.
[Rev. estud. extrem.]. Periodical. Spanish. Three times a year. **LC** DP302.E83; R4.
Ind/Abst Am. Hist. Life (1958-1974); BHA : Biblio. Hist. Art; MLA Int. Bibl. Books Artic. Mod. Lang. Lit.

SP/0211-2663
REVISTA DE GIRONA. (REVISTA DE GIRONA : PUBLICACION TRIMESTRAL DE LA EXCMA DIPUTACION PROVINCIAL.). [Rev. Girona]. **Added/Corp** Gerona (Spain : Province). Diputacion Provincial. Vol. 22 (1976)-. Catalan. qt. **LC** DP302.G21; R48. **DD** 946/.71005. **Continues** Revista de Gerona.
Ind/Abst Am. Hist. Life (1976-).

PO/0871-0759
REVISTA DE GUIMARAES. [Rev. Guimaraes]. **Added/Corp** Sociedade Martins Sarmento. Vol 1 (1884)-. Periodical. Portuguese. an. $10.00. Soc Martins Sarmento, rua Paio Galvao, 4800 Guimaraes Portugal. **Tel** 415969. **ED** Soc Martins Sarmento. **LC** DP501; .R44. **Circ:** 1,000 (ctrl).
Ind/Abst Am. Hist. Life (1955-1959, 1965-1973); BHA : Biblio. Hist. Art; Br. Archaeol. Bibliogr. (?-?).

SP
REVISTA DE HISTORIA CANARIA.
Added/Corp Universidad de La Laguna. Facultad de Filosofia y Letras. Universidad de La Laguna. Facultad de Geografia e Historia. (1957)-. Periodical. Spanish. **LC** DP302.C36; R4. **Continues** Revista de Historia (Tenerife, Canary Islands).

SP
REVISTA DE HISTORIA JERONIMO ZURITA. VFOAT Jeronimo Zurita; Rev. Zurita; RHJZ. Periodical. Spanish. Centro de Estudios Borjanos, Institucion Fernando el Catolico, Plaza del Mercado, Borja Zaragoza Spain. **Tel** 976-86 74 02. **Continues** Jeronimo Zurita Cuadernos de Historia.
Ind/Abst Am. Hist. Life (1955-).

SP
REVISTA DE HISTORIA MODERNA : ANALES DE LA UNIVERSIDAD DE ALICANTE. Added/Corp Universidad de Alicante. (1983)-. Spanish. ir. 2615ptas. Universidad de Alicante, Ctra San Vicente Raspeig S N, 03690 Alicante Spain. **Tel** 011 34 6 5903480. **(Subscription address:** l'Estaquirot S A, Nuestra Senora dell Coll 53, 08023 Barcelona Spain.**)** **Continues** Anales de la Universidad de Alicante. Historia Moderna.

SP/0541-8585
REVISTA DEL INSTITUTO EGIPCIO DE ESTUDIOS ISLAMICOS EN MADRID. [Rev. Inst. Egip. Estud. Islam. Madr.]. Vol. 17 (1972/73)-. Periodical. Spanish (Arabic). be. **Continues** Revista del Instituto de Estudios Islamicos en Madrid.
Ind/Abst Am. Hist. Life (1972); BHA : Biblio. Hist. Art.

RM
REVISTA MONUMENTELOR ISTORICE / COMISIA NATIONALA A MONUMENTELOR, ASAMBLURILOR SI SITURILOR ISTORICE. Added/Corp Romania. Comisia Nationala a Monumentelor, Asamblurilor si Siturilor Istorice. **VFOAT** RMI. (1990)-. Periodical. Romanian. sa. **(Subscription address:** Rompresfilatelia, PO Box 12 201, Bucharest Romania.) **LC** N9037; .R48.

Continues *Revista Muzeelor si Monumentelor. Monumente Istorice si de Arta.*
Ind/Abst BHA : Biblio. Hist. Art.

PO/0253-1658
REVISTA PORTUGUESA DE HISTORIA. [Rev. port. hist.]. (1940)-. Monographic series. Portuguese. ir. Price varies per volume. Casa do Castelo, rua da Sofia 47-49, Coimbra 3000 Portugal. **Tel** 011 351 39 24686. **LC** DP501; .R49. **DD** 946.9005.
Ind/Abst Am. Hist. Life (1962-).

UK/0954-6545
REVOLUTIONARY RUSSIA. Added/Corp Study Group on the Russian Revolution. Vol. 1, No. 1 (June 1988)-. Periodical. English. Twice a year. $95.00. Frank Cass & Company Ltd, Newbury House, 890-900 Eastern Avenue, Newbury Park, Ilford, Essex IG2 7HH United Kingdom. **Tel** 011 44 81 599 8866, FAX 011 44 81 599 0984, telex 897719. **ED** John Slatter. **LC** DK265; .A175a. **DD** 947.084/1/05. **Ad Acc, Adv Mgr:** Anne Kidson. ***Continues*** *Sbornik - Study Group on the Russian Revolution, 0308-1346.*
Desc: One of the first journals to concentrate on the history of Russia in the Revolutionary period. The journal is interdisciplinary in approach, with contributions from historians, economists, political scientists, literary experts and sociologists.
Ind/Abst Am. Hist. Life (1989-).

BE
REVUE BELGE D'HISTOIRE CONTEMPORAINE. VFOAT Belgisch Tijdschrift voor Nieuwste Geschiedenis. Vol. 1. (1969)-. Periodical. Dutch (French and English; summaries and/or abstracts in English and Russian). sa (May and December). 1200F Belgium; 1400F other. Revue Belge d'Histoire, Blandijnberg 2, B-9000 Gent Belgium. **Tel** 091/25.75.71. **ED** Jan Dhondt Stichting. **LC** DH401; .R44. Index available. cum. index. **Bk Rev. Ad Acc. Circ:** 500 (ctrl).
Desc: Belgian contemporary history.
Ind/Abst Am. Hist. Life (1985-).

FR/0035-0974
REVUE D'ALLEMAGNE. [Rev. Allem.]. **VFOAT** Revue d'Allemagne et des Pays de Langue Allemande. Vol.1 (Jan./Mar. 1969). Periodical. French (French and German). qt. 240.00F France; 290.00F other. Centre d'Etudes Germaniques, 8 rue des Ecrivains, 67081 Strasbourg Cedex France. **Tel** 88 36 45 14. **LC** DD1; .R45. **UDC** 908.430. Index available. cum. index. **Bk Rev**, (Qty: 3/yr). **Ad Acc. Circ:** 700 (ctrl). ***Supersedes*** *Allemagne.*
Desc: Scientific review on political, economical and social as well as cultural problems concerning both Germanys.
Ind/Abst Am. Hist. Life (1969-); Romant. Move.

FR/0181-0448
REVUE D'ALSACE. Vol. 1 (1850)-. Periodical. French (summaries and/or abstracts in German and English). an. 100.00F France; 120.00F other. Federation Societes d'Histoire et d'Archeologie d'Alsace, Siege Social, 8 Place Hospital, 67000 Strasbourg France. **Tel** 88.60.76 40. **UDC** 944.383; 943.44. ***Absorbed*** *Bibliographie Alsacienne.*
Ind/Abst Am. Hist. Life (1979-); BHA : Biblio. Hist. Art.

FR/0035-1008
REVUE D'AUVERGNE. [Rev. Auvergne]. **Added/Corp** Societe des amis de l'Universite de Clermont. Societe d'Emulation de l'Auvergne. (1884)-. Periodical. French. qt. $30.00. Societe des Amis des Universites, 3 Avenue Vercingetorix, 63000 Clermont Ferrand France. **LC** DC611.A94; R. **DD** 944/.59005. **CODEN** RVAUAM. Index available. **Bk Rev.**
Desc: Regional development and planning in the Auvergne (France).
Ind/Abst Am. Hist. Life (1963-); BHA : Biblio. Hist. Art; GeoRef.

FR/0035-1059
REVUE DE COMMINGES. (REVUE DE COMMINGES (PYRENEES CENTRALES).). **Added/Corp** Societe des Etudes de Comminges. Academie Julien-Sacaze. (1885)-. Periodical. French. qt. Societe des Etudes du Comminges, 5 rue de la Republique,, BP 15, 31801 Saint Gaudens Cedex, France. **Bk Rev. Circ:** 1,200.
Ind/Abst BHA : Biblio. Hist. Art.

FR/0338-5256
REVUE DE LA SOCIETE D'HISTOIRE ET D'ART DE LA BRIE ET DU PAYS DE MEAUX. Main/Corp Societe d'Histoire et d'Art de la Brie et du Pays de Meaux. No 26 (1975)-. French. an. ***Continues*** *Societe d'Histoire et d'Art du Diocese de Meaux. Bulletin de la Societe d'Histoire et d'Art du Diocese de Meaux.*
Ind/Abst BHA : Biblio. Hist. Art.

FR/0243-8410
REVUE DE L'ACADEMIE DU CENTRE. [Rev. Acad. Cent.]. (1937)-. Periodical. French. qt. **UDC** 908. ***Formed by the union of*** *Revue du Berry et du Centre, 1144-1429* ***and*** *Bulletin Trimestriel - Academie du Centre, 1144-1402.*
Ind/Abst BHA : Biblio. Hist. Art.

FR
REVUE DE L'AGENAIS. Added/Corp Societe des Sciences, Lettres et Arts d'Agen. Societe Academique d'Agen. Vol. 1 (Jan. 1874)-. Periodical. French. Four times a year. 200.00F France; 250.00F others. Societe Academique d'Agen, 9 Boulevard de la Republique, 47000 Agen France. **Tel** 011 33 53 471804. **LC** DC611.A16; R4.
Ind/Abst BHA : Biblio. Hist. Art.

FR/0395-921X
REVUE DE L'INSTITUT NAPOLEON (1954). (REVUE DE L'INSTITUT NAPOLEON.). **Added/Corp** Institut Napoleon (France). No. 50 (Jan. 1954)-. Periodical. French. qt. 240.94F France; 281.00F other. SPM, 14 rue Charles V, 75004 Paris France. **Tel** 011 33 1 42729227. cum. index. ***Continues*** *Bulletin (Institut Napoleon France).*
Ind/Abst Am. Hist. Life (1964-1981).

FR/0557-773X
REVUE DE MORET ET DE SA REGION, LA. (1959)-. Periodical. French. qt. **UDC** 908 (443.63).
Ind/Abst BHA : Biblio. Hist. Art.

FR/0373-5729
REVUE DES ETUDES BYZANTINES. [Rev. etud. byz.]. Vol. 4 (1946)-. French (English). an. 350.00F. Institut Francais d'Etudes Byzantines, 14 rue Seguier, 75006 Paris France. **Tel** 11 33 1 43261236. **LC** DF501; .E8. **DD** 949.5/005. **UDC** 949.5. Index available. cum. index. **Bk Rev. Ad Acc. Circ:** 600. ***Continues*** *Etudes Byzantines.*
Desc: Byzantine history (religion, literature) reviews of publications about Byzantine topics.
Ind/Abst Bibliogr. Mission.; BHA : Biblio. Hist. Art; Index Book Rev. Relig.; Relig. Index One Period. (1973-).

FR
REVUE DES ETUDES ROUMAINES. Added/Corp Institut Universitaire Roumaine Charles 1er. Vol 1 (1953)-. French. **LC** DR201; .R47.
Ind/Abst Am. Hist. Life (1953-1981).

FR/0080-2557
REVUE DES ETUDES SLAVES. [Rev. etud. slaves]. **Added/Corp** Universite de Paris. Institut d'Etudes Slaves. Vol. 1 (1921)-. French (Russian). Four times a year. 426.54F. Institut d'Etudes Slaves, 9 rue Michelet, 75006 Paris France. **Tel** 011 33 1 43265089. **ED** Jacques Catteau. **LC** PG1; .R4. **DD** 491.805. Index available. **Bk Rev. Circ:** 600.
Desc: A publication which covers the fields of literature, linguistics, history, social sciences in the Soviet Union and East European countries, including Hungary and Rumania.
Ind/Abst Am. Hist. Life (1983-); BHA : Biblio. Hist. Art; Romant. Move.

RM/0035-2063
REVUE DES ETUDES SUD-EST EUROPEENNES. [Rev. etud. sud-est eur.]. **Added/Corp** Institutul de Studii Sud-Est Europene (Academia de Stiinte Sociale Si Politice a Republicii Socialiste Romania) Academia Republicii Socialiste Romania. Academia Republicii Populare Romine. Vol. 1, (1963)-. Periodical. English (French, German and Russian). Four times a year. DM305.00. **(Subscription address:** Kubon & Sagner, ABT Zeitschriftenimport, D 80328 Munich Germany.) **LC** DR1; .R42. **DD** 947/.0005.
Desc: Contains original studies on archeology, and the history of language concerning the south eastern area of Europe.
Ind/Abst Am. Hist. Life (1963-); BHA : Biblio. Hist. Art; Numis. Lit.; Recent. Publ. Artic.; Soc. Plann. Policy Dev. Abstr.; Soc. Welf. Soc. Plan./Policy Soc. Dev.; Sociol. Abstr.

FR
REVUE D'HISTOIRE COMPAREE. 1.- Yearly volume; Jan./June 1923-. Periodical. French. Presses Universitaires de France, Department des Revues, 14 Avenue du Bois de l'Epine, BP 90, 91003 Evry Cedex France. **Tel** (1)60 77 82 05, FAX (1) 60 79 20 45, telex PUF 600 474 F. **LC** DB901. **DD** 940.05. **UDC** 940.

FR/0035-2624
REVUE DU NORD. ***Title Change.*** [Rev. Nord]. Vol.1 (1910)-. Periodical. French. qt. Revue du Nord, Universite de Lille III, BP 149, 59653 Villeneuve d'Ascq France. **Tel** 011 33 20 336320, 011 33 20 336364, FAX 011 33 20 919171. **ED** Nadine Malle-Grain. **LC** DC601.1; .R4. **UDC** 944.1/.2. Index available. cum. index. **Bk Rev. Ad Acc. Circ:** 1800. available in microform; available on microfiche. Documents available from The Genuine Article. ***Merged with*** *Bulletin (Societe de Geographie de Lille)* ***to form*** *Hommes et Terres du Nord.*
Desc: History and archeology of North France, Belgium and Netherlands.
Ind/Abst Am. Hist. Life (1955-); Arts Humanit. Citation Index [Full Cov.]; BHA : Biblio. Hist. Art; Br. Archaeol. Bibliogr.; Curr. Contents Arts Humanit.; Numis. Lit.; Res. Alert [Full Cov.].

FR/0035-2667
REVUE DU ROUERGUE. Vol. 1 No. 1 (Jan./Mar. 1947)- Vol. 38 No. 152 (1984); New Ser., No 1 (1985)-. Periodical. French. qt. **LC** AP20; .R458. **DD** 054.
Ind/Abst BHA : Biblio. Hist. Art.

FR
REVUE DU TARN. Added/Corp Federation des Societes Intellectuelles du Tarn. (March 1935)-. Periodical. French. qt (4 issues). 230.00F. Fed Societes Intellectuelles, Archives Departmente du Tarn, 81013 Albi France. **ED** Jean Roques. Index available (published separately). cum. index. **Bk Rev. *Supersedes*** *Revue Historique, Scientifique & Litteraire du Departement du Tarn.*
Desc: Covers local history of the department of Tarn.
Ind/Abst BHA : Biblio. Hist. Art.

FR/0338-2060
REVUE FRANCAISE D'ETUDES POLITIQUES MEDITERRANEENNES. [Rev. fr.etud. polit. mediterr.]. No. 1- Jan. 1975-. Periodical. French. 20.00. Presses Universitaires de France, Department des Revues, 14 Avenue du Bois de l'Epine, BP 90, 91003 Evry Cedex France. **Tel** (1)60 77 82 05, FAX (1) 60 79 20 45, telex PUF 600 474 F. **LC** DE100; .R48.

FR/0300-9513
REVUE FRANCAISE D'HISTOIRE D'OUTRE-MER. [Rev. fr. hist. o.-m.]. **Added/Corp** Societe Francaise d'Histoire d'Outre-mer. Centre National de la Recherche Scientifique (France). Vol. 46, No. 162 (1959)-. Periodical. French. qt. 350.00F France; 375.00F other. Societe Francaise d'Histoire d'Outre-mer, 9 rue Robert de Flers, F 75015 Paris France. **Tel** 33 1 40584848. **ED** Ageron Ch R. Index available. cum. index. **Bk Rev**, (Qty: 4). ***Continues*** *Revue d'Histoire des Colonies.*
Ind/Abst Am. Hist. Life (1955-); Int. Bibliogr. Sociol.

FR/0037-9212
REVUE FRANCAISE D'HISTOIRE DU LIVRE. See Literature.

●FR
REVUE GERMANIQUE INTERNATIONALE. (1993)-. Periodical. French. sa. 350.00F France; 400.00F other. Presses Universitaires de France, Department des Revues, 14 Avenue du Bois de l'Epine, BP 90, 91003 Evry Cedex France. **Tel** (1)60 77 82 05, FAX (1) 60 79 20 45, telex PUF 600 474 F.
Desc: Information on the cultural history of Germany.

FR/0035-3272
REVUE HISTORIQUE ARDENNAISE. Added/Corp Societe d'Etudes Ardennaise. Societe d'Histoire et d'Archeologie du Sedanais. No. 1 (Jan./June 1969)-. French. ***Supersedes*** *Etudes Ardennaises* ***and*** *Annales Sedanaises d'Histoire et d'Archeologie.*
Ind/Abst BHA : Biblio. Hist. Art.

FR
REVUE HISTORIQUE DE BORDEAUX ET DU DEPARTEMENT DE LA GIRONDE. Yearly V. 1-38- 1908-1945. French. qt. Revue Historique de Bordeaux, 71 rue du Loup, 3300 Bordeau France. **LC** DC801.B71; R4. **DD** 944.71005. **UDC** 944.71. cum. index.
Ind/Abst BHA : Biblio. Hist. Art.

FR
REVUE HISTORIQUE ET ARCHEOLOGIQUE DU LIBOURNAIS ET DE LA VALLEE DE LA DORDOGNE. Added/Corp Societe Historique et Archeologique de Libourne. Vol. 50, No 183 (1982)-. Periodical. French. qt. **LC** DC801.L665; S6. ***Continues*** *Revue Historique et Archeologique du Libournais.*
Ind/Abst BHA : Biblio. Hist. Art.

SZ/1013-6924
REVUE HISTORIQUE VAUDOISE. Added/Corp Societe Vaudoise d'Histoire et d'Archeologie. (Jan. 1893)-. French. an. **LC** DQ721; .R4. **DD** 949.4.
Ind/Abst BHA : Biblio. Hist. Art.

BE
REVUE MABILLON: REVUE INTERNATIONAL D'HISTORIE ET DE LITERATURE RELIGIEUSES. French. an. 1700.00F. Brepols Publishers, Steenweg OP Tielen 68, B-2300 Turnhout Belgium. **Tel** 011 32 14 402500.

US/1058-1278
REVUE - NEW YORK UNIVERSITY. INSTITUTE OF FRENCH STUDIES. (REVUE.). [Revue - N.Y. Univ., Inst. Fr. Stud.]. **Added/Corp** New York University. Institute of French Studies. New York University. Center for French Civilization and Culture. Issue No. 1 (Spring 1991)-. Periodical. French (English). Twice a year. $15.00 (individuals); $25.00 (institutions). Institute of French Studies, New York University, 15 Washington Mews, New York NY 10003. **Tel** (212)998-8740. **LC** DC33; .R395. **DD** 944.

RM/0556-8072
REVUE ROUMAINE D'HISTOIRE. [Rev. roum. hist.]. **Added/Corp** Academia Republicii Socialiste

Romania. Vol. 1 (1962)-. Periodical. French. Four times a year. $120.00. **(Subscription address:** Orion Press SRL, SPL Independentei 202-A, Bucharest 6 Romania.**)** Documents available from The Genuine Article.
Desc: Contains articles and studies of the Middle Ages, both modern and contemporary history.
Ind/Abst Am. Hist. Life (1962-); Arts Humanit. Citation Index (19??-19??) [Full Cov.]; BHA : Biblio. Hist. Art; Curr. Contents Arts Humanit.; Numis. Lit.; Res. Alert [Full Cov.]; Soc. Sci. Cit. Index [Select. Cov.]; Writ. Am. Hist.

FR
REVUE SAVOISIENNE. [Rev. savois.]. **Added/Corp** Academie Florimontane, Annecy. (1860)-. French. mo. cum. index. ***Continues*** *Bulletin de l'Association Florimontane d'Annecy et Revue Savoisienne, 1153-6799.*
Ind/Abst BHA : Biblio. Hist. Art.

SZ
RHEINFELDER NEUJAHRSBLATTER. Periodical. German. Buchdruckerei Herzog AG, Rheinfelden Switzerland. **LC** DQ851.R48; R44. **DD** 949.4/5. **UDC** 949.45.

GW/0035-4473
RHEINISCHE VIERTELJAHRSBLATTER. [Rhein. Vierteljahrsbl.]. **Added/Corp** Universitat Bonn. Institut fuer Geschichtliche Landeskunde der Rheinlande. Vol. 1 (1931)-. German. an. DM63.45. Bouvier GmbH & Co. KG ABT Verlag, AM Hof 28, D 53113 Bonn Germany. **Tel** 011 49 228 7290141. **(Subscription address:** VVA Bertelsmann Distributors GmbH, Postfach 7777, D-33310 Guetersloh Germany.**)** **ED** W. Besch, H. L. Cox and G. Dzoege. **LC** DD491.R4; B65. **DD** 943.4. **Bk Rev. Circ:** 2,000 (ctrl). ***Formed by the union of*** *Rheinische Neujahrsblatter* ***and*** *Geschichtliche Landeskunde.*
Ind/Abst Am. Hist. Life (1966-1979,1987-); Bibliogr. Carto.; BHA : Biblio. Hist. Art; MLA Int. Bibl. Books Artic. Mod. Lang. Lit.; Numis. Lit.

IT
RICERCHE STORICHE. **Added/Corp** Centro Piombinese di Studi Storici. (19??)-. Italian. Three times a year. L75000.00 (individuals), L95000.00 (institutions) Italy; L130000.00 others. Edizioni Scientifiche Italiane, Via Chiatamone 7, 80121 Naples Italy. **Tel** 011 39 81 7645768, 011 39 81 7645443, FAX 011 39 81 7646477. **LC** DG975.P58; R5.

IT
RIETI. Yearly V. 1- Jan./Feb. 1973-. Periodical. Italian. bm. L6000. Associazione Culturale Della Provincia di Rieti, Rieti Italy. **LC** DG975.R46; R5. **UDC** 945.625.

SW/0035-5267
RIG. [Rig]. **Added/Corp** Foreningen for Svensk Kulturhistoria. Nordiska Museet (Stockholm, Sweden) Folklivsarkivet i Lund. Foreningen for Svensk Kulturhistoria. Tidskrift. (1918)-. Swedish (summaries and/or abstracts in English, French and German). qt. Rig, Nordiska Museet, Box 27820, S 115 93, Stockholm Sweden. **Tel** 011 46 08 6664200. **LC** DL601; .R5. **DD** 948.5005. cum. index.
Ind/Abst Am. Hist. Life (1963-); BHA : Biblio. Hist. Art.

NE
RIJKSPROGRAMMA WELZIJN MINDERHEDEN / MINISTERIE VAN WELZIJN, VOLKSGEZONDHEID EN CULTUUR, HOOFDAFDELING WELZIJN MINDERHEDEN. Dutch. Fl10.00. Distributiecentrum Overheidspublikaties, Postbus 20014, 2500 EA den Haag The Netherlands. **LC** PAR.

IT/0035-5607
RISORGIMENTO, IL. [Risorgimento]. Vol. 1- 1949-. Italian. Three times a year. L25000 Italy; L40000 other. Il Risorgimento, Via Borgonuovo 23, 20121 Milan Italy. **Tel** 02/8693549, FAX 02/72001483. **ED** Roberto Guerri. **LC** DG552.A15; R37. **UDC** 940. cum. index. **Bk Rev. Pr Rev. Circ:** 400.
Desc: History of modern Europe from the end of the 18th century to present days. Political, social, military points of view.
Ind/Abst Am. Hist. Life (1955-).

BE
RISORGIMENTO (GROUPE EUROPEEN DE RECHERCHE ET D'INFORMATION SUR L'ITALIE CONTEMPORAINE). ***Suspended.*** (RISORGIMENTO.). Vol. 1 No. 1-?. Periodical. English (French, German and Italian). ir. $10.87. Gerisic, Fond University, rue d' Egmont 11, B-1050 Brussels Belgium. **LC** DG551; .R525. **DD** 945/.005. **UDC** 945.08. Documents available from The Genuine Article.
Ind/Abst Am. Hist. Life (1955-); Arts Humanit. Citation Index [Full Cov.]; Curr. Contents Arts Humanit.; Res. Alert [Full Cov.].

IT/0393-4624
RIVISTA DALMATICA, LA. [Riv. dalm.]. (1899)-. Periodical. Italian. qt. L30000 (Italy); L40000 (Europe); L50000 (other). Assn Nazionale Dalmata, Piazza Firenze 27, 00186 Rome Italy. **Tel** 39 6 6873686. **UDC** 908.
Ind/Abst BHA : Biblio. Hist. Art; MLA Int. Bibl. Books Artic. Mod. Lang. Lit.

IT
RIVISTA D'EUROPA. Vol. 1 (Jan./Feb. 1978)-. Periodical. Italian (French, English, Spanish and German). bm. L20000 Italy; L30000 other. Conto Corrente Postale 22778005, Intestando a Cadmo Editore S R 1, Largo dell'Olgiata, 15 00123 Rome Italy. **ED** Lido Chiusano. **LC** D1050; .R58. **DD** 940.55/05. Index available. **Bk Rev. Ad Acc.**

IT/0035-6913
RIVISTA ITALIANA DI STUDI NAPOLENOICI. [Riv. ital. studi napoleon.]. **Added/Corp** Centro Nazionale di Studi Napoleonici e di Storia dell'Elba. (1965)-. Periodical. Italian. sa. L125000 Italy; L175000 other. Giardini Editori Stampatori, Via Santa Bibbiana 28, 56127 Pisa Italy. **Tel** 011 39 50 934242. **LC** DC197; .R58. ***Continues*** *Bollettino Italiano di Studi Napoleonici.*
Ind/Abst Am. Hist. Life (1968-1975, 1978-); BHA : Biblio. Hist. Art.

IT/0393-022X
RIVISTA STORICA CALABRESE. [Riv. stor. calabr.]. **Added/Corp** Deputazione di Storia Patria per la Calabria. (1980)-. Periodical. Italian (English and French). qt.
Ind/Abst BHA : Biblio. Hist. Art.

IT/0035-7073
RIVISTA STORICA ITALIANA. [Riv. stor. ital.]. **Added/Corp** Istituto Fasciste di Coltura di Torino. Guinta Centrale per Gli Studi Storici. Istituto per Gli Studi di Politica Internazionale (Milan, Italy). Vol. 1, (1884)-. Periodical. Italian. Three times a year. L170000 (institutions), L140000 (individuals) Italy; L250000 other. Edizioni Scientifiche Italiane, Via Chiatamone 7, 80121 Naples Italy. **Tel** 011 39 81 7645768, 011 39 81 7645443, FAX 011 39 81 7646477. **ED** Franco Venturi. **LC** DG401; .R7. **DD** 945/.005. **Bk Rev. Ad Acc.** Documents available from The Genuine Article.
Desc: Information pertaining to historical studies.
Ind/Abst Am. Hist. Life (1954-); Arts Humanit. Citation Index [Full Cov.]; BHA : Biblio. Hist. Art; Curr. Contents Arts Humanit.; Int. Bibliogr. Sociol.; MLA Int. Bibl. Books Artic. Mod. Lang. Lit.; Numis. Lit.; Res. Alert [Full Cov.]; Soc. Sci. Cit. Index [Select. Cov.].

XR
ROCENKA - KRAJSKE KULTURNI STREDISKO V BRNE. **Main/Corp** Krajske Kulturni Stredisko V Brne. Czech (English and German). an. KKS BRNO, PO Box 141, 657 41 Brno, 2 Czech Republic. **Tel** 42.5.333247. **LC** DB785.B73; K73A. **UDC** 908.437. **Bk Rev.** ctrl circ.
Desc: Review of the culture centre of South Moravian district.

PL/0080-3421
ROCZNIK BIAOSTOCKI. **Added/Corp** Muzeum w Biaymstoku. (1961)-. Multiple languages (Polish; summaries and/or abstracts in English and Russian). be. **LC** DK401; .R54.
Ind/Abst Anthropol. Index; BHA : Biblio. Hist. Art.

PL/0080-3456
ROCZNIK GDANSKI. **Added/Corp** Gdanskie Towarzystwo Naukowe. Wydzia I. Nauk Spoecznych; Humanistycznych. Gdanskie Towarzystwo Naukowe. Towarzystwo Przyjacio Nauki i Sztuki w Gdansku. (1927)-. Polish. **LC** DD901.D2; R6.
Ind/Abst BHA : Biblio. Hist. Art.

PL/0080-3499
ROCZNIK KRAKOWSKI. **Added/Corp** Towarzystwo Miosnikow Historii i Zabytkow Krakowa. (1898)-. Polish.
Ind/Abst BHA : Biblio. Hist. Art.

PL
ROCZNIK MUZEUM WSI LUBELSKIEJ / MUZEUM WSI LUBELSKIEJ. V. 4 (1981)-. Periodical. Polish. an. Muzeum Wsi Lubelskiej, Al Warszawska 96, 20-833 Lublin Poland. **LC** DK4600.L8242; Z17. ***Continues*** *Z Zagadnien Kultury Ludowej.*

PL/0080-360X
ROCZNIK WARSZAWSKI. **Added/Corp** Warsaw. Archiwum Panstwowe Warszawy i Wojewodztwa Warszawskiego. (1960)-. Polish. **LC** DK651.W2; R6.
Ind/Abst BHA : Biblio. Hist. Art.

BU/0324-1629
RODOLIUBIE. **Added/Corp** Komitet za Bulgarite v Chuzhbina (Sofia, Bulgaria). Vol. 1 (1983)-. Periodical. Bulgarian (English). mo. **(Subscription address:** Hemus Foreign Trade Organization, 6 Tzar Osvoboditel Boulevard, 1000 Sofia Bulgaria.**)** **LC** DR51; .R63. **DD** 949.7/7/005. ***Continues*** *Slaviani.*
Ind/Abst MLA Int. Bibl. Books Artic. Mod. Lang. Lit.

AU
ROETZER HEIMATKUNDLICHE ARBEITEN. **Added/Corp** Volksschule Roetz. Vol. 1 (1989)-. Monographic series. German. ir. Price varies per volume. Volksschule Roetz, Roetz Germany.

US/0045-2351
ROMANIAN NEWS AND WORLD REPORT. (ROMANIAN NEWS AND WORLD REPORT / BOIAN NEWS SERVICE, BNS.). **VFOAT** Romanian News & World Report. Periodical. English (Romanian). wk. BNS, PO Box 713, New York NY 10028-0012. **DD** 949. **UDC** 949.8; 908.498.

US/0098-6054
ROMANIAN SOURCES. [Rom. sources]. Vol. 1 (Jan. 1975)-. Periodical. English. sa. $5.00. Mt Union College, Chapman Hall, 1972 Clark Avenue/Room 346, Alliance OH 44601. **Tel** (216)823-3194. **LC** DR201; .R65. **DD** 949.8/005. **UDC** 949.8.
Desc: Includes translations of Romanian texts.
Ind/Abst Am. Hist. Life (1975-1982).

AU/0080-3790
ROMISCHE HISTORISCHE MITTEILUNGEN. **Added/Corp** Osterreichisches Kulturinstitut in Rom. Abteilung fuer Historische Studien. Osterreichische Akademie der Wissenschaften. (1957)-. German. an. Oesterreichischen Akademie Wissenschaften, Dr. Ignaz Seipel Platz 2, A-1010 Vienna Austria. **Tel** 011 43 1 51581. **ED** Otto Kresten and Adam Wandruszka. **LC** DG404; .R6. **Circ:** 400 (ctrl).
Desc: Deals with the history of art and the church in Rome and Italy.
Ind/Abst Am. Hist. Life (1962-1976, 1979-); BHA : Biblio. Hist. Art; MLA Int. Bibl. Books Artic. Mod. Lang. Lit.

AU/1012-5833
ROMISCHES OSTERREICH. **Added/Corp** Osterreichische Gesellschaft fur Archaologie. (1973)-. German. an. **LC** DB29; .R6.
Ind/Abst BHA : Biblio. Hist. Art.

NE/0923-6287
ROTTERDAMS JAARBOEKJE. [Rotterdams jaarb.]. (1888)-. Periodical. Dutch. an. **UDC** 949.2*3000(058).
Ind/Abst BHA : Biblio. Hist. Art.

UK/0269-2244
ROYAL HISTORICAL SOCIETY STUDIES IN HISTORY. **Added/Corp** Royal Historical Society (Great Britain). **VFOAT** Studies in History; Royal Historical Society Studies in History Series; Studies in History Series. (19??)-. Monographic series. English. ir. Price varies per volume. Boydell and Brewer Limited, PO Box 9, Woodbridge Suffolk, 1P12 3DF England. **Tel** 011 44 394 411320, FAX 011 44 394 411477.

UK/0950-3439
ROYALTY MONTHLY. [R. mon.]. (July 1981)-. Periodical. English. Twelve times a year. $50.00. Royalty Reader Services, 803 2805 Finchley Road, London NW11 8DP England. **Tel** 011 44 81 2019978. **DD** 941.08580922.

PL/0084-2982
ROZPRAWY KOMISJI HISTORII SZTUKI. [Rozpr. Kom. Hist. Szt.]. (1957)-. Polish. tw. **UDC** 7.
Ind/Abst BHA : Biblio. Hist. Art.

●GW
RUSSIA & CIS TODAY / COMPILED BY THE RFE/AL RESEARCH INSTITUTE MONITORING UNIT. **Added/Corp** RFE/RL, Inc. RFE/RL Research Institute. **VFOAT** Russia and CIS Today. No. 296 (Mar. 17. 1992)-. Russian. da. DM1500.00. Radio Free Europe RL Res Publ, Oettingenstrasse 67, D 80538 Munich Germany. **Tel** 011 49 89 21022631. **LC** DK266.A2; U88. ***Continues*** *CIS Today.*

●RU
RUSSIA & CIS TODAY / COMPILED BY WHAT THE PAPERS SAY. **Added/Corp** What the Papers Say (Organization) RFE/RL, Inc. **VFOAT** Russia and CIS Today. No. 1 (June 1, 1992)-. Russian. **LC** DK266.A2; U93. ***Continues in part*** *Russia & CIS Today.*

US/0094-288X
RUSSIAN HISTORY (PITTSBURGH). (RUSSIAN HISTORY / HISTOIRE RUSSE.). [Russ. hist.]. **Added/Corp** University of Pittsburgh. University Center for International Studies. Temple University. **VFOAT** Historie Russe. Vol 1 (1974)-. Periodical. English (French, German and Russian). Four times a year. $43.00 (institutions), $23.00 (individuals). CMTS USC / C. Schlacks Junior Publishing, 734 West Adams Boulevard, Kerckhoff Hall, Los Angeles CA 90089. **Tel** (213)743-1621. **ED** Charles Schlacks Jr. **LC** DK1; .R74. **DD** 947/.005. Index available. **Bk Rev. Ad Acc. Circ:** 500 (ctrl). available on microfilm and microfiche from University Microfilms International (UMI). Documents available from The Genuine Article.

Desc: Devoted exclusively to Russian history: medieval, imperial and Soviet.
Ind/Abst Am. Hist. Life (1974-); Am. Bibliogr. Slavic East Europ. Stud.; Arts Humanit. Citation Index [Full Cov.]; Curr. Contents Arts Humanit.; Res. Alert [Full Cov.]; Soc. Sci. Cit. Index [Select. Cov.].

US/0036-0341
RUSSIAN REVIEW (STANFORD), THE. (THE RUSSIAN REVIEW.). [Russ. rev.]. **Added/Corp** Hoover Institution on War, Revolution, and Peace. Ohio State University. Vol. 1 (Nov. 1941)-. Periodical. English. qt. $55.00 (institutions), $30.00 (individuals) US; $64.20 (institutions), $37.45 (individuals) Canada; $60.00 (institutions), $35.00 (individuals) other. Ohio State University Press, 1070 Carmack Road, 180 Pressey Hall, Columbus OH 43210. **Tel** (614)292-6930, (614)292-1407, FAX (614)292-2065. **ED** Allan Wildman. **LC** DK1; .R82. **DD** 947. cum. index. **Bk Rev**. **Ad Acc. Circ:** 1,300. available on microfilm and microfiche from University Microfilms International (UMI). Documents available from The Genuine Article, UMI Article Clearinghouse.
Desc: A journal of historical and literary studies that serves the considerable number of Americans and other speakers of English with a serious or professional interest in Russia.
Ind/Abst Acad. Abstr. Full Text Elite (July 1990-); Acad. Abstr. (July 1990-); Acad. Ind. [Computer File] (1987-); Acad. Search (July 1990-); Am. Hist. Life (1954-); Am. Bibliogr. Slavic East Europ. Stud.; Annu. Bibliogr. Engl. Lang. Lit.; Arts Humanit. Citation Index [Full Cov.]; BHA : Biblio. Hist. Art; Book Rev. Index; Curr. Contents Arts Humanit.; Expand. Acad. Index (1987-); Hist. Source (July 1990-); Humanit. Index; INFO-SOUTH Abstr.; Mag. Search; MLA Int. Bibl. Books Artic. Mod. Lang. Lit.; Newsp. Period. Abstr. (1991-); PAIS Int. Print (?-?); Res. Alert [Full Cov.]; Soc. Sci. Source (Jul. 1990-); Soc. Sci. Cit. Index [Select. Cov.]; U.S. Polit. Sci. Doc.

RU/0869-1177
RUSSKOE PROSHLOE. (1991)-. Periodical. Russian (table of contents in English and French). qt. $19.00 per issue. **(Subscription address:** Albionic Inc., 1167 Route 22 East, Mountainside, NJ 07092; Telephone: (908)233-2075**)** **LC** DK510; .R87.

UK/0260-3322
RUTLAND RECORD. (RUTLAND RECORD : JOURNAL OF THE RUTLAND RECORD SOCIETY.). [Rutland rec.]. No. 1 (1980)-. Periodical. English. an. £7.50 UK; £8.50 other. Rutland Record Society, Rutland County Museum, Catmos Street, Oakham Rutland LE15 6HW England. **Tel** (0572)723654. **ED** Bryan Waites. **LC** DA670.R89; R954. **DD** 942.5/45. **UDC** 942.545. **Bk Rev. Ad Acc. Circ:** 1,000 (ctrl).
Desc: Major articles, reviews, museum reports, notes, records, bibliography.
Ind/Abst BHA : Biblio. Hist. Art; Geogr. Abstr. Human Geogr. (?-?).

GW/0036-2115
SAARBRUCKER HEFTE. **Added/Corp** Kultur- und Schulamt der Stadt Saarbrucken. Kulturamt der Stadt Saarbrucken. (1955)-. Periodical. German. sa. **LC** DD801.S13; S195.
Ind/Abst BHA : Biblio. Hist. Art.

UK/0305-9219
SAGA-BOOK. **See** Literature.

BE
SAINT-HUBERT D'ARDENNE. Vol. 1-. French. Compte 068-0397349-55, Credit Communal de Belgique, Terre et Abbaye de Saint Hubert, Saint-Hubert Belgium. **LC** DH811.S327; S23. **DD** 949.3/5. **UDC** 949.38.

SP
SAIOAK. Yearly V. 1-. Periodical. Basque (Spanish). C Victor Pradera 3-5, San Sebastian Spain. **LC** DP302.B41; S24. **DD** 946/.6/005.

SP/0210-9980
SAITABI. [Saitabi]. (1940)-. Spanish. an. Universidad de Valencia / Moderna, Dept Moderna, 46080 Valencia Spain. **Tel** 011 34 3 3864100. **LC** DP1; .S3.
Ind/Abst Am. Hist. Life (1969-); GeoRef.

YU/0409-008X
SAOPSTENJA - REPUBLICKI ZAVOD ZA ZASTITU SPOMENIKA KULTURE SR SRBIJE. **See** Architecture.

US/1059-5872
SARMATIAN REVIEW, THE. [Sarmatian rev.]. **Added/Corp** Polish Institute of Arts and Sciences of America. Houston Circle. (1988)-. Periodical. English. Three times a year (Jan., Apr., Sept.). $18.00 US; $24.00 other. Polish Institute Arts and Science, PO Box 79119, Houston Chapter, Houston TX 77279. **Tel** (713)467-5836, FAX (713)467-6348. **ED** E. M. Thompson. **LC** IN PROCESS. **DD** 943. **Bk Rev**, (Qty: 10-15). **Ad Acc, Adv Mgr:** C. Allen. **Circ:** 1,000. ***Continues*** *Houston Sarmatian, 0892-1466.*
Desc: Interviews with and articles about leading Polish political, literary, and economic figures. Lively exchanges in letters. Scholars and educational journal but avoid the abstruse format of some academic publications. This is also for the college educated readers.

HU/0230-1954
SAVARIA. **Added/Corp** Vas Megyei Muzeumok Igazgatosaga. (1963)-. Hungarian (summaries and/or abstracts in German). an. **LC** DB975.V3; S28.
Ind/Abst BHA : Biblio. Hist. Art.

XR/0036-5246
SBORNIK ARCHIVNICH PRACI. **See** Genealogy and Heraldry-Archives.

XR
SBORNIK PRACI HISTORICKYCH. **VFOAT** Studies from History. 1-. Czech (French and German). ir. **(Subscription address:** Artia Pegas Press Ltd., Palac Metro Narodni Trida 25, 11210 Prague 1 Czech Republic.**)** ***Continues*** *Sbornik Vysoke Skoly Pedagogicke v Olomouci. Historie.*

DK/0108-7827
SCANDINAVIAN ATLAS OF HISTORIC TOWNS. No. 1 (1977)-. English. ir. varies. Odense University Press, 55 Campusvej, DK-5230 Odense M Denmark. **Tel** 66 15 79 99, FAX 66 15 81 26.

SW/0346-8755
SCANDINAVIAN JOURNAL OF HISTORY. [Scand. j. hist.]. Vol. 1 (1976)-. English. qt. Kr725.00, $123.00. Scandinavian University Press, PO Box 2959 Toeyen, N 0608 Oslo 6 Norway. **Tel** 011 47 2 2575400, FAX 011 47 2 2575353, telex 71896 UROR N. **(Subscription address:** Scandinavian University Press, 200 Meacham Ave., Elmont NY 11003.**)** **ED** Helge Pharo. **LC** DL1; .S34. **DD** 948/.005. **UDC** 948. Documents available from The Genuine Article.
Desc: Presents articles on Scandinavian history and review essays surveying themes in recent Scandinavian historical research. Concentrates on perspectives of national historical particularities and important long-term and short-term developments.
Ind/Abst Am. Hist. Life (1976-); Arts Humanit. Citation Index [Full Cov.]; Curr. Contents Arts Humanit.; Res. Alert [Full Cov.]; Soc. Sci. Cit. Index [Select. Cov.].

SZ/0259-3599
SCHAFFHAUSER BEITRAGE ZUR GESCHICHTE. (SCHAFFHAUSER BEITRAEGE ZUR GESCHICHTE / HERAUSGEGEBEN VOM HISTORISCHEN VEREIN DES KANTONS SCHAFFHAUSEN.). [Schaffhauser Beitr. Gesch.]. **Added/Corp** Historischer Verein des Kantons Schaffhausen. (1973)-. German. an. **LC** DQ561; .S35. ***Continues*** *Schaffhauser Beitrage zur Vaterlandischen Geschichte.*
Ind/Abst BHA : Biblio. Hist. Art.

IT/0392-5404
SCHEDE MEDIEVALI. **Added/Corp** Officina di Studi Medievali (Palermo, Italy). No. 1 (July-Dec. 1981)-. Periodical. Italian. sa. L60000 Italy; L75000 other. Officina Studi Medievali, Via del Parlamento 32, 90133 Palermo Italy. **Tel** 011 39 91 6161333. **LC** D111; .S33. **DD** 940.1/05.

IT/0036-6145
SCHLERN, DER. (1920)-. Periodical. German. mo. L82000 (Italy). Althesia Druck, Via del Vigneto 7, 39100 Bolzano Italy. **Tel** 39 471 202016. **LC** DB1; .S35. **DD** 053. cum. index.
Ind/Abst BHA : Biblio. Hist. Art.

GW/0036-6153
SCHLESIEN. [Schlesien]. **Added/Corp** Kulturwerk Schlesien. **VFOAT** Schlesien; Niederschlesien, Oberschlesien, Sudetenschlesien, Kunst, Wissenschaft, Volkstum. (1956)-. Periodical. German. qt. **LC** DD491.S4; S27. **DD** 943.8/5/005.
Ind/Abst BHA : Biblio. Hist. Art; MLA Int. Bibl. Books Artic. Mod. Lang. Lit.

GW/0937-7247
SCHLESWIG-HOLSTEIN. **Added/Corp** Schleswig-Holsteinischer Heimatbund. (Jan./Feb. 1990)-. Periodical. German. mo. **LC** DD801.S6331; S34; DD491.S6; S3. **DD** 943/.512/005. ***Continues*** *Logo Schleswig-Holstein, 0935-4786.*

US/1059-9185
SCHOLARS OF EARLY MODERN STUDIES. [Sch. early mod. stud.]. **Added/Corp** American Society for Reformation Research. Northeast Missouri State Univerrsity. Vol. No. 25 (Summer 1991)-. English (German, Spanish, French and Italian). an (July). $20.00 US; $22.00 other. NMSU / Northeas Missouri State University, LB 115, Kirksville MO 63501. **Tel** (816)785-4665, FAX (816)785-4181. **LC** D219; .H5. **DD** 907. **Ad Acc. Circ:** 2,000. ***Continues*** *Historians of Early Modern Europe, 0883-3559.*
Desc: Provides information on the history of the Reformation and sixteenth century.

GW
SCHRIFTEN. **Main/Corp** Akademie der Wissenschaften der DDR. Zentralinstitut fur Geschicht. V. 38- 1974-. Monographic series. German. ir. Price varies per volume. ***Formed by the union of*** *Akademie der Wissenschaften, Berlin. Zentralinstitut fur Geschichte. Schriften. Reihe I: Allgemeine und Deutsche Geschichte.* ***and*** *Akademie der Wissenschaften, Berlin. Zentralinstitut fuer Geschichte. Schriften. Reihe III: Vortraege, Tagungen und Abhandlungen.*
Desc: Single problems, periods or regions from the revolution in France to our time.

GW/0080-6951
SCHRIFTEN DER MONUMENTA GERMANIAE HISTORICA (DEUTSCHES INSTITUT FUR ERFORSCHUNG DES MITTELALTERS). [Schr. Monum. Ger. Hist., Dtsch. Inst. Erforsch. Mittelalt.]. **Main/Corp** Monumenta Germaniae Historica (Deutsches Institut fur Erforschung des Mittelalters). V. 10, No. 1-. Monographic series. German. Price varies per volume. Anton Hiersemann Verlag, Rosenbergstrasse 113, D 70193 Stuttgart Germany. **Tel** 011 49 711 638264 5. **UDC** 940"04/14". **Circ:** 1,200. ***Continues*** *Schriften des Reichsinstituts fur Altere Deutsche Geschichtskunde (Monumenta Germaniae Historica).*
Desc: Monographs, years 400 to 1400.

AU
SCHRIFTEN DES INSTITUTES FUER OESTERREICHKUNDE. **Added/Corp** Institut fuer Oesterreichkunde. **VFOAT** Schriften des Instituts fuer Oesterreichkunde; Schriftenreihe des Instituts fuer Oesterreichkunde. (19??)-. Monographic series. German. ir. Price varies per volume. Oesterreichischer Bundesverlag, Schwarzenbergstr 5, Postfach 79, A-1015 Vienna Austria. **Tel** 011 43 1 51405.

GW
SCHRIFTEN DES VEREINS FUER GESCHICHTE DES BODENSEES UND SEINER UMGEBUNG. **Main/Corp** Verein fur Geschichte des Bodensees und seiner Umgebung. (1869)-. German. an. **LC** DD801.C7; V3. cum. index.
Ind/Abst BHA : Biblio. Hist. Art.

GW/0582-0367
SCHRIFTEN ZUR KIRCHEN- UND RECHTGESCHICHTE. Vol. 1, (1957)-. Monographic series. German. ir. Price varies per volume. Boehlau Verlag GmbH & Cie / Koeln, Theodor Heuss STR 76, D-51149 Cologne Germany. **Tel** 011 49 2203 307021, FAX 011 49 2203 307349. **(Subscription address:** BDK Buecherdienst GmBh, Postfach 900120, D 51111 Cologne Germany.**)**

GW
SCHRIFTENREHE DES STADTARCHIVS ROSTOCK. **Added/Corp** Rostocker Stadtarchiv. 1988-. Monographic series. German. Price varies per volume. ***Continues*** *Kleine Schriftenreihe des Stadtarchivs Rostock.*

GW
SCHRIFTENREIHE DES INSTITUTS FUER DEUTSCHE GESCHICHTE, UNIVERSITAT TEL AVIV. **Added/Corp** Universitat Tel-Aviv. Makhon le Historyah Germanit. 1976-. Monographic series. German. Price varies per volume. Droste Verlag GmbH, Postfach 101135, D 40196 Dusseldorf Germany. **Tel** 011 49 211 505604.

GW/0584-9993
SCHRIFTENREIHE DES STAATSARCHIVS DRESDEN. **See** Genealogy and Heraldry-Archives.

GW
SCHRIFTENREIHE ZUR BAYERISCHEN LANDESGESCHICHTE. **Added/Corp** Akademie der Wissenschaften, Munich. Kommission fuer Bayerische Landesgeschichte. (1929)-. Monographic series. German. ir. Price varies per volume. CH Beck Verlagsbuchhandlung, D 80791 Munich Germany. **Tel** 011 49 89 381891. **LC** DD801.B322; S4. **Circ:** 600.
Desc: Deals with Bavarian history and problems of comparative regional history.

GW
SCHWABISCHE CHRONIKEN DER STAUFERZEIT. **Added/Corp** Kommission fur Geschichtliche Landeskunde in Baden-Wurttemberg. 1978-. Monographic series. German. Price varies per volume. Jan Thorbecke Verlag GmbH and Company, Karlstrasse 10, Postfach 546, D 72482 Sigmaringen Germany. **Tel** 011 49 7571 728100, FAX 011 07571-728-280, telex 732534.

SZ/0036-7834
SCHWEIZERISCHE ZEITSCHRIFT FUER GESCHICHTE. (SCHWEIZERISCHE ZEITSCHRIFT FUER GESCHICHTE. REVUE SUISSE D'HISTOIRE. RIVISTA STORICA SVIZZERA.). [Schweiz. Z. Gesch.]. **Added/Corp** Allgemeine Geschichtforschende Gesellschaft der Schweiz. Vereinigung Schweizerischer Archivare. **VFOAT** Revue Suisse d'Histoire; Rivista Storica Svizzera. Vol. 1 (1951)-. Periodical. German (French and Italian). Four times a year. 95.00F Switzerland; 97.50F others. Schwabe & Company Ltd., Farnsburgerstrasse 8 PF 254, CH-4132 Muttenz 1 Switzerland. **Tel** 011 41 61 4613001, FAX 01 41 61 4612500. **ED** Boris Schneider. **LC** D1; .S34. **DD**

905. **[CCC]. Bk Rev. Ad Acc. Circ:** 1,600 (ctrl). ***Supersedes*** *Zeitschrift fur Schweizerische Geschichte.* **Desc:** Publishes original contributions about Swiss and general history.
Ind/Abst Am. Hist. Life (1954-); Bibliogr. Carto.; BHA : Biblio. Hist. Art.

US/0273-0693
SCOTIA. (SCOTIA.). [Scotia]. **Added/Corp** Old Dominion University. Institute of Scottish Studies. (Apr. 1977)-. Periodical. English. an (Oct.). $10.00. Institute of Scottish Studies, c/o Dr. William S. Rodner, Old Dominion University, History Department, Norfolk VA 23529. **Tel** (804)683-3949. **ED** Dr. William S. Rodner. **LC** DA750; .S126. **DD** 941.1/005. **Pr Rev.** Documents available from The Genuine Article.
Ind/Abst Arts Humanit. Citation Index (19??-19??) [Full Cov.]; Res. Alert [Full Cov.]; Soc. Sci. Cit. Index [Select. Cov.].

UK/0036-9209
SCOTTISH FIELD (GLASGOW). (SCOTTISH FIELD.). [Scott. field]. (1903)-. Periodical. English. Twelve times a year. $22.00 UK; $28.00 other. George Outram & Co Ltd, 195 Albion Street, Glasgow G1 1QP Scotland. **Tel** 011 44 355246444, FAX 011 44 355263013. **(Subscription address:** Caledonian Magazines Ltd., Plaza Towers Plaza E Kilbride, Glasgow G74 1LW Scotland) **LC** DA750; .S207. **DD** 914.1.

UK/0036-9241
SCOTTISH HISTORICAL REVIEW, THE. [Scott. hist. rev.]. **Added/Corp** Company of Scottish History. (1903)-. Periodical. English. sa. £32.00 UK & Europe; $64.00 US; £35.00 other. Edinburgh University Press, 22 George Square, Edinburgh EH8 9LF Scotland. **Tel** 011 44 31 650 6207, FAX 011 44 31 662 0053. **ED** Alexander Grant and Stewart J. Brown. **LC** DA750; .S21. **DD** 941.1/005. **[CCC]**. Index available. cum. index. **Bk Rev. Ad Acc, Adv Mgr:** Kathryn MacLean. **Circ:** 900. available on microfilm and microfiche from University Microfilms International (UMI). Documents available from The Genuine Article. ***Continues*** *Scottish Antiquary, or, Northern Notes and Queries.*
Desc: Covers all periods of Scottish history from the early to the modern, and encourages a variety of historical approaches.
Ind/Abst Am. Hist. Life (1955-); Annu. Bibliogr. Engl. Lang. Lit.; Arts Humanit. Citation Index (19??-19??) [Full Cov.]; BHA : Biblio. Hist. Art; Br. Archaeol. Bibliogr.; Br. Humanit. Index; Curr. Contents Arts Humanit.; Numis. Lit.; Res. Alert [Full Cov.]; Romant. Move.

UK
SCOTTISH HISTORY SOCIETY (SERIES). (SCOTTISH HISTORY SOCIETY.). **Added/Corp** Scottish History Society. (1964)-. Monographic series. English. an. Price varies per volume. University Glasgow, Department of Scottish History, 9 University Gardens, Glasgow G12 8Q4 Scotland. **Tel** 44 41 339 8855 ext. 4148. **LC** UNC. Index available. **Circ:** 800 (ctrl). ***Continues*** *Publications of the Scottish History Society.*
Desc: The Scottish History Society is a publisher of manuscript sources relating to the history of Scotland on a variety of topics covering all periods.

UK/0265-3273
SCOTTISH SLAVONIC REVIEW. See Linguistics.

SW/0582-3234
SCRIPTA ISLANDICA. [Scr. isl.]. **Added/Corp** Islandska Sallskapet. (1950)-. Swedish. **LC** DL301; .S37. cum. index.
Ind/Abst MLA Int. Bibl. Books Artic. Mod. Lang. Lit.

US
SELECTED PAPERS. (19??)-. English. an. Price varies. Consortium Revolutionary Europe, PO Box 9561, Samford University, Savannah GA 31412. ***Continues*** *Consortium on Revolutionary Europe Proceedings, 0093-2574.*

US/8756-5579
SERB WORLD U.S.A. See History(General)-History of North, South, and Central America.

US/0742-3330
SERBIAN STUDIES. [Serb. stud.]. **Added/Corp** North American Society for Serbian Studies. Vol. 1, No. 1 (Spring 1980)-. Academic Scholarly Publication. English. Twice a year. $15.00. University of Illinois in Chicago / Department of Slavic Languages and Literatures, Box 4348/1228 UH, Chicago IL 60680. **Tel** (312)996-4412. **ED** Nicholas Moravcevich. **LC** DR1932; .S47. **DD** 949.7/1. **Bk Rev. Circ:** 500.
Desc: Publishes original scholarly articles on all aspects of the Serbian cultural heritage as well as the scholarly notes and book reviews pertinent to this field of study.
Ind/Abst Am. Hist. Life (1984-).

PO/0870-6735
SERIE SEPARATAS / CENTRO DE ESTUDOS DE HISTORIA E CARTOGRAFIA ANTIGA. Added/Corp Centro de Estudos de Historia e Cartografia Antiga (Instituto de Investigacao Cientifica Tropical). **VFOAT** Separatas. (18??)-. Monographic series. Portuguese (English, French and Spanish). ir. Instituto de Investigacao Cientifica Tropical / Portugal, Centro de Documentacao e Informacao, Rua Jau 47, 1 300 Lisbon Portugal. **Tel** 645327. **LC** DP538; .S45. **DD** 946.9/005. **Circ:** 1,500 (ctrl). ***Continues*** *Serie Separatas (Centro de Estudos de Cartografia Antiga (Portugal)).*
Desc: Separate articles on different magazines about the history and geography of Antiga.

IT/0528-5666
SETTIMANE DI STUDIO DEL CENTRO ITALIANO DI STUDI SULL'ALTO MEDIOEVO. [Settim. stud. Cent. ital. studi alto Medioevo]. **Main/Corp** Centro Italiano di Studi Sull'Alto Medioevo. **Added/Corp** Centro Italiano di Studi Sull'Alto Medioevo. Vol. 1 (1953)-. Monographic series. Multiple languages (French, German, Italian and Spanish). an. Price varies per volume. Centro Italiano di Studi Sull'Alto Medioevo, Palazzo Ancaiani, Piazza della Liberta 12, 06049 Spoleto Italy. **Tel** 011 39 743 220485 or 418, FAX 011 39 743 39107.
Desc: Spotlights key topics of interest from the medieval world including religious rites, symbols, military organization and labor.
Ind/Abst Avery Index Archit. Period. Suppl. Colum. Univ. (19??-199?); BHA : Biblio. Hist. Art.

UK/0268-117X
SEVENTEENTH CENTURY, THE. Added/Corp University of Durham. Centre for Seventeenth-Century Studies. Vol. 1, No. 1 (Jan. 1986)-. Periodical. English. Twice a year. £12.00 (individuals), £18.00 (institutions). University of Durham Centre / UK, Palace Green, Centre for the 17th Century Studies, Durham DH1 3RN England. **Tel** 011 44 91 374 2721. **ED** Richard Maber. Index available. **Ad Acc. Circ:** 400. Documents available from The Genuine Article.
Desc: An interdisciplinary journal concerned with aspects of the 17th century.
Ind/Abst Am. Hist. Life (1986-); Arts Humanit. Citation Index [Full Cov.]; Curr. Contents Arts Humanit.; MLA Int. Bibl. Books Artic. Mod. Lang. Lit.; Res. Alert [Full Cov.]; Soc. Sci. Cit. Index [Select. Cov.].

UK/0265-1068
SEVENTEENTH-CENTURY FRENCH STUDIES. See Literature.

US/0037-3028
SEVENTEENTH CENTURY NEWS. See Literature.

US/0896-1638
SEWANEE MEDIAEVAL STUDIES. [Sewanee mediaev. stud.]. **Added/Corp** University of the South. No. 3 (1988)-. Academic Scholarly Publication. English. ir. Price varies. Sewanee Mediaeval Colloquium, University of the South, Box 1234, Sewanee TN 37375. **(Subscription address:** Editions Peeters SA, Bondgenotenlaan 153, 3000 Leuven, Belgium) **ED** E.B. King and S.J. Ridyard. **LC** CB351; .S48a. **DD** 909.07. ***Continues*** *Sewanee Mediaeval Colloquium. Sewanee Mediaeval Colloquium Occasional Papers, 0734-5704.*

IS
SHEVET ROMANIA. VFOAT Shevet Romanyan. 1- May 1977-. Periodical. Hebrew (Romanian). IL75.00. Hitahdut Olei Romania Din, Israel Eilat St 8, Tel Aviv Israel. **LC** DS135.R7; S43. **UDC** 908.498.

GW/0583-1938
SIEBENBURGISCHES ARCHIV. Added/Corp Arbeitskreis fur Siebenburgische Landeskunde. Verein fur Siebenburgische Landeskunde. Archiv. Dritte Folge. (1962)-. Monographic series. German. **LC** DB735; .S53.
Ind/Abst BHA : Biblio. Hist. Art.

US/0733-0367
SIEGRUNEN. [Siegrunen]. Periodical. English. qt. $35.00. Siegrunen, 624 Rattlesnake Circle Road, Glendale OR 97442. **LC** DD253.65; .S53. **DD** 940.54/13/43. **UDC** 940.53/.54.

PL/0080-9594
SILESIA ANTIQUA. Added/Corp Muzeum Slaskie we Wrocawiu. Dzia Archeologiczny. (1959)-. Polish (summaries and/or abstracts in English, French and German; table of contents in English, French and German). an.
Ind/Abst Anthropol. Index; BHA : Biblio. Hist. Art.

US/0741-8450
SIMON WIESENTHAL CENTER ANNUAL. ***Suspended.*** [Simon Wiesenthal Cent. annu.]. **Added/Corp** Simon Wiesenthal Center. **VFOAT** S.W.C. Annual; SWC Annual. (1984)-Suspended (1990). English. an. Simon Wiesenthal Center, 9760 West Pico Boulevard, Los Angeles CA 90035. **Tel** (310)553-9036. **ED** Henry Freidlander and Sybil Milton. **LC** D810.J4; S537. **DD** 940.53/15/03924.
Desc: Focuses on the scholarly study of the Holocaust.
Ind/Abst Am. Hist. Life (1984-); Am. Bibliogr. Slavic East Europ. Stud.

FR/0489-0280
SITES ET MONUMENTS. [Sites monum.]. **Added/Corp** Societe pour la Protection des Paysages. No. 1 (Jan./March 1958)-. Periodical. French. Four times a year (Jan., Apr., July, Dec.). 190.00F France; 270.00F other. Societe Protection Paysages France, 39 Avenue de la Motte Picquet, 75007 Paris France. **Tel** 011 33 1 47053771. **ED** M. Pierie Joste. **Ad Acc.**
Ind/Abst Avery Index Archit. Period. Suppl. Colum. Univ. (1990-); BHA : Biblio. Hist. Art.

XV/0583-4554
SITULA. Added/Corp Ljubljana. Narodni Muzej. (1960)-. Slovenian (French and German; summaries and/or abstracts in English). **LC** DR311.A1; S37.
Ind/Abst BHA : Biblio. Hist. Art.

NO/0458-7073
SKRIFTER. Main/Corp Landslaget for Bygde- Og Byhistorie. Began in 1965. Norwegian. ir. Universitetsbiblioteket I Oslo, Oslo Norway. **Tel** (02)564980. **LC** DL403.5; .L32. **UDC** 5/6(09). Documents available from Ask*IEEE.
Ind/Abst INSPEC.

●RU/0869-544X
SLAVIANOVEDENIE. Added/Corp Institut Slavianovedeniia i Balkanistiki (Rossiiskaia Akademiia Nauk). (1992)-. Academic Scholarly Publication. Russian. Six times a year. $115.00. Izdatelstvo Nauka / Akademiia Nauk, Publishing House of the Russian Academy of Sciences, Leninskii Porspekt 14, 117901 Moscow Russia. **Tel** 011 95 954-21-53, FAX 011 95 938-21-44, telex 411964. **(Subscription address:** East View Publications Inc., 3020 Harbor Lane North, Suite 110, Minneapolis MN 55447.) **LC** D377.A1; S74. ***Continues*** *Sovetskoe Slavianovedenie (Moscow, R.S.F.S.R. : 1965), 0132-1366.*

IS
SLAVIC AND SOVIET SERIES. V. 1- Sept. 1975-. Monographic series. English. sa. Price varies per volume. Russian and East European Research Center, Tel-Aviv University, Tel-Aviv Israel. **LC** DJK1; .S55. **DD** 947/.0005. **UDC** 947.

GW/0583-5437
SLAVISTISCHE FORSCHUNGEN. (1962)-. Monographic series. German. ir. Price varies per volume. Boehlau Verlag GmbH & Cie / Koeln, Theodor Heuss STR 76, D-51149 Cologne Germany. **Tel** 011 49 2203 307021, FAX 011 49 2203 307349. **(Subscription address:** BDK Buecherdienst GmBh, Postfach 900120, D 51111 Cologne Germany.)

XO
SLOVACI V ZAHRANICI : ZBORNIK USTAVU PRE ZAHRANICNYCH SLOVAKOV MS. 1-. Periodical. Slovak (summaries and/or abstracts in English, German and Russian). ir. kcs29.00. **LC** DB2743; .S57.

US/0583-5623
SLOVAKIA (WEST PATERSON, N.J.). (SLOVAKIA.). [Slovakia]. **Added/Corp** Slovak League of America. Vol. 1, No. 1 (May 1951)-. English. an. $6.00. Slovak League of America, 870 Rifle Camp Road, West Paterson NJ 07424. **Tel** (201)256-1687. **ED** M. Mark Stolarik. **LC** DB661; .S47. **DD** 943.7/3. **Bk Rev. Circ:** 2,000 (ctrl). available on microfilm from University Microfilms International (UMI).
Desc: Devoted to the history, literature and culture of Slovaks.
Ind/Abst Am. Hist. Life (1954-); Am. Bibliogr. Slavic East Europ. Stud.; MLA Int. Bibl. Books Artic. Mod. Lang. Lit.

XR/0081-007X
SLOVANSKE HISTORICKE STUDIE. [Slov. hist. stud.]. **Added/Corp** Slovansky Ustav CSAV. Ceskoslovensko-Sovetsky Institut (Ceskoslovenska Akademie Ved). (1955)-. Slovak (summaries and/or abstracts in French and Russian). ir. kcs40.00 Czechoslovakia; $13.00 US. Academia, Publishing House of the Czechoslovak Academy of Sciences, Czech AC SCI, Vodickova 40, PO Box 896, 112 29 Prague 1, Czech Republic. **Tel** 011 42 2 245117. **ED** Jana Svobodova. **LC** D147; .S56. **Circ:** 600.
Desc: Presents historical studies, mostly by Czech authors, viewing various periods of the Slavonic nations, inhabited areas and subjects of development. In majority, concerned with modern history, political relations and economic contacts between Czechoslovakia and other Slavic countries.
Ind/Abst Am. Hist. Life (1955-).

NE/0583-564X
SLOVANSKE STUDIE. Added/Corp Slovenska Akademia vied. Sekcia Spolocenskych Vied. Ceskoslovenska Akademie Vied. Ceskoslovensko-Sovietsky Institut SAV. Ustav Dejin Europskych Socialistickych Krajin (Slovenska Akademia Vied) Ustav Historickych Vied (Slovenska Akademia Vied) Historicky Ustav SAV. No. 1 (1957)-. Periodical. Slovak (summaries and/or abstracts in German and Russian; table of contents in English and Russian). sa. Fl53.00. Veda, Publishing House of the Slovak Academy of Sciences, Klemensova 19, 814 30 Bratislava Slovakia. **Tel** (7)583-15. **(Subscription address:** John Benjamins

North America, PO Box 27519, Philadelphia PA 19118-0519.) **LC** DR37; .S55.
Ind/Abst Am. Hist. Life (1978-).

US/0193-1075
SLOVENE STUDIES. (SLOVENE STUDIES : JOURNAL OF THE SOCIETY FOR SLOVENE STUDIES.). [Slov. stud.]. **Added/Corp** Society for Slovene Studies. (1979)-. Academic Scholarly Publication. English. Twice a year. $30.00 institutions; $20.00 individuals. Bowling Green State University / Society for Slovene Studies, Bowling Green OH 43403. **Tel** (419)372-8028. **ED** Tom Priestly. **LC** DR1352; .S57. **DD** 949.7/3005. Index available. **Bk Rev. Circ:** 500 (ctrl). ***Formed by the union of*** *Newsletter - Society for Slovene Studies, 0145-6830* ***and*** *Papers in Slovene Studies, 0360-179X.*
Desc: A scholarly multi-discipline journal devoted to Slovene affairs.
Ind/Abst Am. Hist. Life (1975-1977, 1979-); Am. Bibliogr. Slavic East Europ. Stud.; MLA Int. Bibl. Books Artic. Mod. Lang. Lit.

XO
SLOVENSKO; KULTURNO-SPOLECENSK MESACNIK. Began in 1977. Periodical. Slovak (summaries and/or abstracts in English and Russian). mo. kcs60.00. Matica Slovenska, Slovenska Narodna Kniznica Bibliograficke Oddelenie, Novomeskeho 32, 036 52 Martin Slovakia. **Tel** (842)313-71, FAX (842)331-88, telex 75331. **LC** DB2700; .S57. **UDC** 908.437.

FR/0299-8556
SOCIETE D'HISTOIRE DU VAL DE LIEPVRE. [Soc. hist. Val de Liepvre]. (1963)-. Periodical. French. **UDC** 908(443.832).
Ind/Abst BHA : Biblio. Hist. Art.

FR/0154-0505
SOCIETE HISTORIQUE ET ARCHEOLOGIQUE DE L'ORNE. [Soc. hist. archeol. Orne]. (1974)-. Periodical. French. qt. **UDC** 908. ***Continues*** *Bulletin Principal - Societe Historique et Archeologique de l'Orne, 0154-0513.*
Ind/Abst BHA : Biblio. Hist. Art.

UK/0038-0903
SOLANUS. See Library and Information Sciences.

HU/0139-4983
SOMOGYI MUZEUMOK KOZLEMENYEI. Added/Corp Somogy Megyei Muzeumok Igazgatosaga. (1973)-. Hungarian (summaries and/or abstracts in English, French and German). an. **LC** DB975.S65; S654.
Ind/Abst BHA : Biblio. Hist. Art.

US/0038-1462
SONS OF NORWAY VIKING, THE. See Ethnic Interests.

JA
SOREN TOO / SOREN TOO KENKYUKAI HENCHO. Vol. 1 (81-82)-. Japanese. an. ¥3800. Hara Shobo, 25-13 Shinjuku 1, Shinjuku-ku Tokyo-To 160 Japan. **LC** DK274.A2; S64.

FI/0357-816X
SOTAHISTORIALLINEN AIKAKAUSKIRJA. See Military and Defense.

FR/0398-3811
SOURCES D'HISTOIRE MEDIEVALE. [Sources d'hist. mediev.]. **Added/Corp** Institut de Recherche et d'Histoire des Textes (France). 1 (1965)-. Monographic series. French. an. Price varies per volume. Editions du CNRS, 22 rue Saint Armand, F 75015 Paris France. **Tel** 011 33 1 45075050. **Circ:** 1,500.
Desc: Reproduces and analyzes sources of European history of the medieval period.
Ind/Abst Math. Rev.

UK
SOUTH SLAV JOURNAL, THE. Added/Corp Dositey Obradovich Circle. Vol. 1 (April 1978)-. Periodical. English. Four times a year (Feb., May, Aug., Nov.). $26.00 (individuals), $30.00 (institutions). The South Slav Journal, 7 Chesterford Gardens, London NW3 7DD England. **Tel** 011 44 1 435-0094, FAX 011 44 1 435-8597. **ED** N. Marcetic. **LC** DR301; .S58. **DD** 949.7/005. Index available. **Bk Rev. Ad Acc. Circ:** 1,000.

UK/0142-4688
SOUTHERN HISTORY. [South. hist.]. Vol. 1 (1979)-. Academic Scholarly Publication. English. an. £18.00. Dawson UK Ltd, Cannon House, Folkestone Kent CT19 5EE England. **Tel** 011 44 303-850101, FAX 011 44 303-850440, telex 96392. **ED** R. A. E. Wells. **LC** DA20; .S67. **DD** 942/.005. **Bk Rev**, (Qty: 20). **Pr Rev. Circ:** 450. Documents available from FAXON Xpress, BLDSC.
Ind/Abst Am. Hist. Life (1979-); BHA : Biblio. Hist. Art; Br. Archaeol. Bibliogr.

RU/0132-1366
SOVETSKOE SLAVIANOVEDENIE. ***Title Change.*** [Sov. slavanoved.]. **Added/Corp** Institut Slavianovedeniia (Akademiia Nauk SSSR) Institut Slavianovedeniia I Balkanistiki (Akademiia Nauk SSSR). (1965-1992). Periodical. Russian. bm. **(Subscription address:** Victor Kamkin, 4956 Boiling Brook Parkway, Rockville MD 20852.) ***Continued by*** *Slavianovedenie.*
Ind/Abst Am. Hist. Life (1967-); ARTbibliogr. Mod.

US/1060-9474
SOVIET OBSERVER (NEW YORK, N.Y.). ***Ceased.*** (SOVIET OBSERVER / W. AVERELL HARRIMAN INSTITUTE FOR ADVANCED STUDY OF THE SOVIET UNION, COLUMBIA UNIVERSITY.). [Sov. obs.]. **Added/Corp** Averell Harriman Institute for Advanced Study of the Soviet Union. Vol. 1, No. 1 (Apr. 1990)-(1992). Periodical. English. qt. **LC** IN PROCESS. **DD** 947.

CN/0380-0660
SOVIET PANORAMA. Added/Corp Russia (U. S. S. R.) Posolstvo (Canada). No. 7, (July 1975)-. Periodical. English. mo. Ottawa Editorial Board, 400 Stewart Street, Ottawa Ontario K1N 6L2 Canada. **DD** 947/.005. ***Continues*** *Soviet Union Today, 0584-5696.*

US/1055-1042
SOVIET PERSPECTIVES. ***Ceased.*** [Sov. perspect.]. **Added/Corp** International Freedom Foundation. **VFOAT** Soviet Perspectives. Vol. 1, No. 1 (March 1991)-(19??). Periodical. English. mo. International Freedom Foundation, PO Box 15439, Washington DC 20002. **Tel** (301)699-0703. **DD** 947. available on an online database (file 636/Full-Text) from DIALOG.
Ind/Abst PTS Newsl. Database [Full Txt.].

II/0038-5786
SOVIET REVIEW INDIA. Added/Corp Soviet Union. Posolstvo (India). Information Dept. (19??)-. English (Hindi). Sixty times a year. Rs85.00. USSR Embassy in India, Information Department, 25 Barakhamba Road, PO Box 241, New Delhi 110001 India. **Tel** 42527. **LC** DK1; .S5485.

US/0038-5867
SOVIET STUDIES IN HISTORY. ***Title Change.*** [Sov. stud. hist.]. **Added/Corp** International Arts and Sciences Press. Vol. 1-30 (Summer 1962)-(Spring 1992). Periodical. English (translations available in Russian). qt. M. E. Sharpe Inc., 80 Business Park Drive, Armonk NY 10504. **Tel** (914)273-1800, (800)541-6563, FAX (914)273-2106. **ED** Donald J Raleigh. **LC** D1; .S67. **DD** 905. **Bk Rev. Ad Acc. Circ:** 200 (ctrl). available on microfilm from University Microfilms International (UMI). ***Continued by*** *Russian Studies in History, 1061-1983.*
Desc: Major studies by historians and historiographers chosen to reflect the broad range of Soviet interests.
Ind/Abst Am. Hist. Life (1966-); Middle East Abstr. Index.

RU/0584-5688
SOVIET UNION. ***Title Change.*** [Sov. Union]. **VFOAT** VD Voskresenie; Voskresenie. (1950-1992). Periodical. English (German, French, Spanish, Italian, Finnish, Serbo-Croatian (Roman), Japanese, Chinese, Korean, Arabic, Hindi, Bengali, Urdu, Hungarian, Vietnamese, Portuguese and Russian). mo. **(Subscription address:** Victor Kamkin, 4956 Boiling Brook Parkway, Rockville MD 20852.) **LC** DK266.A2; S574. **DD** 914.7. ***Continues*** *USSR in Construction.* ***Continued by*** *New Russia.*
Desc: Investigates all aspects of Soviet life, including the national economy, technology, culture and sports. Features and reports acquaint the reader with the interests and desires of the Soviet people.

US/1057-1531
SOVIET UPDATE. [Sov. update]. (1991)-. English. be. Westview Press Inc, 5500 Central Avenue, Boulder CO 80301. **Tel** (303)444-3541, FAX (303)449-3356. **DD** 947.

GW/0038-5999
SOWJETSTUDIEN. (SOWJET STUDIEN.). [Sowjetstudien]. **Added/Corp** Institut zur Erforschung der UdSSR. (July 1956)-. Periodical. German. **LC** DK266.A2; S78.
Ind/Abst Am. Hist. Life (1956-1970).

GW/0724-5823
SOWJETUNION (MUNCHEN). (SOWJETUNION.). [Sowjetunion]. 1973-. German. an. C Hanser, Lindenbornstrasse 22, W-5000 Koln 1 Germany. **LC** DK274.A2; S67. **UDC** 914.7; 908.47.

GW
SPANISCHE FORSCHUNGEN DER GORRES-GESELLSCHAFT. REIHE 2. Periodical. German. Aschendorffsche Verlagsbuchhan, Postfach 1124, D 48135 Muenster Germany. **Tel** 011 49 251 690132.

UK
SPANISH STUDIES. No. 1 (1979)-. English (Spanish). an. £8.95. c/o Olga Kenyon, 29 Woosyre Sydenham Hill, London SE26 6SS England. **Tel** 011 44 081 6707073. **ED** Olga Kenyon. **LC** DP1; .S66. **DD** 946/.005. **Bk Rev**, (Qty: approx. 3/year). **Ad Acc. Acid Free. Circ:** 800.
Desc: A journal of modern Spanish literature, history, and politics. Offers rapid publication of short articles of interest to teachers and students.

US/0038-7134
SPECULUM. [Speculum]. **Added/Corp** Mediaeval Academy of America. Vol. 1 (Jan. 1926)-. Academic Scholarly Publication. English. qt (4 issues). $70.00 US & Canada; $80.00 other. Medieval Academy of America, 1430 Massachusetts Avenue, Cambridge MA 02138. **Tel** (617)491-1622. **ED** Luke Wenger. **LC** PN661; .S6. **DD** 809. **NLM** W1 SP325T. Index available. cum. index. **Bk Rev. Ad Acc. Circ:** 5,700. available on microfilm and microfiche from University Microfilms International (UMI). Documents available from The Genuine Article, UMI Article Clearinghouse.
Desc: Devoted to the promotion of research in all disciplines of medieval studies. Publishes articles of scholarly importance on all facets of medieval civilization.
Ind/Abst Abstr. Engl. Stud.; Acad. Abstr. Full Text Elite (July 1990-); Acad. Abstr. (July 1990-); Acad. Ind. [Computer File] (1987-); Acad. Search (July 1990-); Annu. Bibliogr. Engl. Lang. Lit.; Art Index; Arts Humanit. Citation Index [Full Cov.]; BHA : Biblio. Hist. Art; Book Rev. Index; Br. Archaeol. Bibliogr.; Curr. Contents Arts Humanit.; Expand. Acad. Index (1987-); Hist. Source (July 1990-); Humanit. Index; Index Book Rev. Relig.; INFO-SOUTH Abstr.; Lit. Crit. Regist.; Mag. Search; MLA Int. Bibl. Books Artic. Mod. Lang. Lit.; Newsp. Period. Abstr. (1991-); Relig. Index One Period.; Res. Alert [Full Cov.]; Soc. Sci. Cit. Index [Select. Cov.].

IT/0490-4788
SPOLETIUM. [Spometium]. (1954)-. Periodical. Italian. an. **UDC** 908.
Ind/Abst BHA : Biblio. Hist. Art.

RU/0131-8780
SREDNIE VEKA. [Srednie veka]. **Main/Corp** Institut Vseobshchei Istorii (Akademiia Nauk SSSR). Vol. 33 (1971)-. Academic Scholarly Publication. Russian (summaries and/or abstracts in English, French and Italian). 2.02rub each issue. Izdatelstvo Nauka / Akademiia Nauk, Publishing House of the Russian Academy of Sciences, Leninskii Porspekt 14, 117901 Moscow Russia. **Tel** 011 95 954-21-53, FAX 011 95 938-21-44, telex 411964. **LC** D111; .A452. ***Continues*** *Institut Istorii (Akademiia Nauk SSSR). Srednie Veka.*
Ind/Abst Am. Hist. Life (1980-); BHA : Biblio. Hist. Art.

PL/0079-3183
SREDNIOWIECZE. VFOAT Etudes sur la Culture Medievale; Middle Ages. (1961)-. Multiple languages. ir. **UDC** 82(438)(091)"09/14". **CODEN** 1(438)(091)"09/14".
Ind/Abst BHA : Biblio. Hist. Art.

GW
STADER JAHRBUCH. Added/Corp Stader Geschichts- und Heimatverein. (1911)-. German. **LC** DD491.H35; S7. ***Supersedes*** *Verein. Archiv des Verein fur Geschichte und Altertumer der Herzogtumer Bremen und Verden und des Landes Hadeln.*
Ind/Abst BHA : Biblio. Hist. Art.

UK/0950-1630
STAFFORDSHIRE STUDIES. Added/Corp University of Keele. Vol. 1 (1988)-. English. an. **CODEN** STSTE8. ***Continues*** *North Staffordshire Journal of Field Studies, 0078-1649.*
Ind/Abst BHA : Biblio. Hist. Art.

YU/0585-0886
STARINE CRNE GORE. Added/Corp Cetinje, Yugoslavia. Zavod za Zastitu Spomenika Kulture Crne Gore. Cetinje, Yugoslavia. Zavod za Zastitu Spomenika Kulture Crne Gore. (1963)-. Serbo-Croatian (Cyrillic) (summaries and/or abstracts in French; table of contents in French). an. **LC** DR101; .S8.
Ind/Abst BHA : Biblio. Hist. Art.

YU/0351-4536
STAROHRVATSKA PROSVJETA. [Starohrv. prosvjeta]. (19??)-. Periodical. Serbo-Croatian (Roman). ir. **UDC** 902.
Ind/Abst BHA : Biblio. Hist. Art.

AU
STICHWORT OESTERREICH. (1975)-. German. S690.00. Internationale Publikationen Gesellschaft MBH, Altmannsdorfer Strasse 154-156, 1232 Vienna Austria. **ED** K. H. Ritschel. **LC** DB17; .S76. **DD** 943.6/0025.

SW/0491-0893
STOCKHOLMER GERMANISTISCHE FORSCHUNGEN. [Stockh. ger. Forsch.]. (1956)-. Monographic series. English. ir. Price varies per volume. Almqvist & Wiksell International, PO Box 4627, S-11691 Stockholm Sweden. **Tel** 011-46-8-6408800.
Ind/Abst MLA Int. Bibl. Books Artic. Mod. Lang. Lit.

PL
STOLICA. Added/Corp Poland. Naczelna Rada Odbudowy Warszawy. (19??)-. Periodical. Polish. wk (52 issues). $47.00. Warszawskii Wydawn Prasowe RSW Prasa-Ksiazka-Ruch, Ul Wiejska 12, Warszawa Poland. **(Subscription address:** ARS Polona, PO Box 1001, 00068 Warsaw Poland.) **LC** DK651.W2; S78.

IT
STORIA IN LOMBARDIA. Added/Corp Istituto Lombardo per la Storia del Movimento di Liberazione in Italia. (19??)-. Periodical. Italian. Three times a year.

L81000 Italy; L110000 other. Franco Angeli Riviste SRL, Viale Monza 106, 20127 Milan Italy. **Tel** 011 39 2 2827651, 011 39 2 289562. **LC** WMLC 93/4155.

IT/0391-7762
STUDI ETRUSCHI. Added/Corp Comitato Permanente per l'Etruria. Istituto di Studi Etruschi ed Italici. Vol. 1, (1927)-. Italian. an. L480000.00. Casa Editrice Leo S. Olschki, Viuzzo del Pozzetto, Casella Postale 66, 50126 Florence Italy. **Tel** 011 39 55 6530684, FAX 011 39 55 6530214. **LC** DG223.A1; S8. **DD** 913.375.

IT/0391-8467
STUDI MEDIEVALI (SPOLETO). See Literature.

IT/0394-5499
STUDI MONTEFELTRANI. [Studi montefeltrani]. (1971)-. Monographic series. Italian. ir. **UDC** 945.
Ind/Abst BHA : Biblio. Hist. Art.

IT
STUDI PIEMONTESI. Added/Corp Centro Studi Piemontesi. Vol.1 (Mar. 1972)-. Periodical. Multiple languages (Italian; summaries and/or abstracts in English). sa. L85000 Italy; L90000 other. Centro Studi Piemontesi Srl, Via Ottavio Revel 15, 10121 Turin Italy. **Tel** 011 39 11 537486, FAX 011 39 11 534777. **LC** DG610; .S77. Index available. **Bk Rev**, (Qty: 120-130/yr). **Ad Acc, Adv Mgr:** Albina Malerba. **Circ:** 1,500. Documents available from The Genuine Article.
Desc: Interdisciplinary journal devoted to the study of the culture and civilization of the Piedmont region of Italy; publishes original articles and studies, research results, regular columns, news, business activity and documents reflecting the history and life of the Piedmont.
Ind/Abst Am. Hist. Life; Arts Humanit. Citation Index [Full Cov.]; BHA : Biblio. Hist. Art; Curr. Contents Arts Humanit.; Res. Alert [Full Cov.]; Romant. Move.; Soc. Sci. Cit. Index [Select. Cov.].

IT/0081-6205
STUDI ROMAGNOLI. Added/Corp Societa di Studi Romagnoli. (1950)-. Italian. an. L30000 (Italy); L50000 (other). Societa Studi Romagnoli, Biblioteca Malatestiana, 47023 Cesena FO Italy. **Tel** 011 39 547 610892.
Ind/Abst BHA : Biblio. Hist. Art.

IT/0039-3002
STUDI SALENTINI. Added/Corp Centro di Studi Salentini, Lecce. (1956)-. Italian. cum. index.
Ind/Abst BHA : Biblio. Hist. Art.

IT
STUDI SARDI. Added/Corp Universita di Cagliari. Istituto di Studi Sardi. (1934)-. Multiple languages (Catalan, English, French, Italian and Spanish). **LC** DG975.S29; S68.
Ind/Abst BHA : Biblio. Hist. Art.

IT/0081-6248
STUDI SECENTESCHI. [Studi secenteschi]. Vol. 1 (1960)-. Periodical. Italian. an. L72000. Casa Editrice Leo S. Olschki, Viuzzo del Pozzetto, Casella Postale 66, 50126 Florence Italy. **Tel** 011 39 55 6530684, FAX 011 39 55 6530214. Documents available from The Genuine Article.
Ind/Abst Am. Hist. Life (1979-); Arts Humanit. Citation Index [Full Cov.]; BHA : Biblio. Hist. Art; Curr. Contents Arts Humanit.; MLA Int. Bibl. Books Artic. Mod. Lang. Lit.; Res. Alert [Full Cov.].

IT/0039-3037
STUDI STORICI. [Stud.stor.]. **Added/Corp** Istituto Gramsci. (Oct./Dec. 1959)-. Periodical. Italian. Four times a year. L60000 Italy; L90000 other. Edizioni Dedalo Spa, Casella Postale 362, Bari 70100 Italy. **Tel** 011 39 080 5311400, FAX 011 39 080 5311414. **LC** DG401; .S89. Index available. cum. index. **Ad Acc. Circ:** 6,000 (ctrl). Documents available from The Genuine Article.
Desc: Research and studies on ancient history and modern history in Italy and internationally.
Ind/Abst Am. Hist. Life (1959-); Arts Humanit. Citation Index [Full Cov.]; Curr. Contents Arts Humanit.; Int. Bibliogr. Sociol.; Res. Alert [Full Cov.]; Soc. Sci. Cit. Index [Select. Cov.].

AA/0585-5047
STUDIA ALBANICA. [Studia Alban.]. **Added/Corp** Universiteti Shteteror i Tiranes. Instituti i Historise dhe i Gjuhesise. Instituti i Historise (Akademia e Shkencave e RPS te Shqiperise) Instituti i Gjuhesise i Letersise (Akademia e Shkencave e RPS te Shqiperise). (1964)-. Periodical. French (German, Italian and Russian). bm. $5.50. Ndermarrja e Perhapjes SE, Rruga Konferenca e Pezes, Tirane Albania. **LC** DR701.S49; S85.
Ind/Abst Am. Hist. Life (1964-); BHA : Biblio. Hist. Art; Geogr. Abstr. Human Geogr.; MLA Int. Bibl. Books Artic. Mod. Lang. Lit.; Numis. Lit.

BE/0081-6345
STUDIA CAUCASICA. [Stud. Cauc.]. (1963)-. Periodical. English. an. 1000F. Editions Peeters SA, Bondgenotenlaan 153, BP 41, B-3000 Leuven Belgium. **Tel** 32 16 235170, FAX 32 16 228500, telex 65987 PUL B. **ED** G. Dumezil, C. L. Ebeling, T. Halasi-Kun, A. H. Kuipers, D. M. Lang, K. H. Schmidt and H. Vogt. **LC** DK511.C1; S75.
Ind/Abst MLA Int. Bibl. Books Artic. Mod. Lang. Lit.

XO/0585-5225
STUDIA HISTORICA SLOVACA. [Stud. hist. Slovaca]. **Added/Corp** Historicky Ustav SAV. (1963)-. English (French and German). **LC** DB661; .S8.
Ind/Abst Am. Hist. Life (1978-).

PL
STUDIA I MATERIAY Z DZIEJOW POLSKI LUDOWEJ. V. 10-. Periodical. Polish (summaries and/or abstracts in Russian and English). Z40.00. Wydawn Slaski Instytut Naukowy, Poland. **LC** DK4600.K37; A27. **UDC** 943.8. ***Continues*** *Studia I Materiay Z Dziejow Wojewodztwa Katowickiego W Polsce Ludowej.*

PL
STUDIA ITALO-POLONICA. 1-. Periodical. English (French and Italian). Z130.00. Panstwowe Wydawn Naukowe, Miodowa 10, PO Box 391, 00251 Warsaw Poland. **LC** DK4010; .K73A subser; DK4185.I8. **DD** 909; 943.8. **UDC** 943.8.

IT
STUDIA PICENA. Added/Corp Fano, Italy. Pontificio Seminario Marchigiano Pio XI. (1925)-. Italian. sa. Istituto Teologico Marchigiano, Via Roma 118, 61032 Fano Italy. **LC** DG975.M4; S8.
Ind/Abst BHA : Biblio. Hist. Art.

RM
STUDIA UNIVERSITATIS BABES-BOLYAI. HISTORIA. Main/Corp Universitatea Babes-Bolyai. Vol. 20 (1975)-. Periodical. English (French, German and Romanian; summaries and/or abstracts in Russian). sa. DM230.00. **(Subscription address:** Kubon & Sagner, ABT Zeitschriftenimport, D 80328 Munich Germany.) **LC** D1; .C63a. **DD** 949.8/005. ***Continues in part*** *Studia Universitatis Babes-Bolyai. Historia Philologia, Oeconomica.*
Ind/Abst Numis. Lit. (?-?).

PL
STUDIA Z DZIEJOW ROSJI I EUROPY SRODKOWO-WSCHODNIEJ / POLSKA AKADEMIA NAUK, INSTYTUT HISTORII, ZAKAD DZIEJOW EUROPY XIX I XX WIEKU. Added/Corp Instytut Historii (Polska Akademia Nauk). Zakad Dziejow Europy XIX i XX Wieku. (1992)-. Polish. an. Polska Akademiia Nauk, Instytut Historii, Rynek Starego Miasta 29-31, 00-272 Warsaw Poland. **Tel** 011 48 22 313642. **LC** D410; .S85. ***Continues*** *Studia z Dziejow ZSRR i Europy Srodkowej, 0081-7082.*

SZ
STUDIEN UND QUELLEN. VFOAT Etudes et Sources; Studi Ponti. 1- 1975-. Multiple languages (French and German; summaries and/or abstracts in French and Italian). Schweizerisches Bundesarchiv, Archivstrasse 24, CH-3003 Bern Switzerland. **LC** DQ54; .S88. **DD** 949.4/005. **UDC** 949.4.

NE/0585-5837
STUDIEN UND TEXTE ZUR GEISTESGESCHICHTE DES MITTELALTERS. Vol. 1 (1950)-. Monographic series. Multiple languages (English and German). ir. Price varies per volume. E. J. Brill, Postbus 9000, 2300 PA Leiden Netherlands. **Tel** 011 31 71 312624, FAX 011 31 71 317532, telex 39296 BRILL NL. **ED** A. Limmermann.

GW/0562-3251
STUDIEN ZUR BAYERISCHEN VERFASSUNGS- UND SOZIALGESCHICHTE. Vol. 1- 1962-. Monographic series. German. ir. Price varies per volume. Kommission fuer Bayerische Landesgeschichte, Marstallplatz 8, W-8000 Muenchen 22 Germany. **Tel** 89-293911. **(Subscription address:** Verlag Michael LaBleben, D-8411 Kallmunz West Germany**) ED** Andreas Kraus. **UDC** 943.3; 930.85(433). Index available. **Circ:** 500.
Desc: Designed to contribute topics of a more fundamental nature or of more general interest to the series 'Historischer Atlas von Bayern' in the fields of history of government and social stratification.

GW
STUDIEN ZUR EUROPAISCHEN GESCHICHTE. Vol. 1- 1955-. Monographic series. German. ir. Price varies per volume. Colloquium Verlag, Unter den Eichen 93, W-1000 Berlin 45 Germany. **Tel** 030-832 8085. **ED** Otto Buesch. **UDC** 940. **Circ:** 1,000.
Desc: Scientific publications on special historical developments in different European countries.

GW
STUDIEN ZUR HEIMATGESCHICHTE DER STADT BAD HONNEF AM RHEIN. Added/Corp Heimat und Geschichtsverein Herrschaft Lowenburg. Monographic series. German. Price varies per volume.

UK
STUDIES IN CELTIC HISTORY. 1-. Monographic series. English. Price varies per volume. Rowman & Littlefield Publishing Inc., 8705 Bollman Place, Savage MD 20763. **Tel** (301)306-0400. **UDC** 936.4.

NE
STUDIES IN EUROPEAN SOCIETY. (1973)-. Periodical. English.

UK/0081-8100
STUDIES IN IRISH HISTORY. *Ceased.* (1???)-(19??). Monographic series. English. ir. Routledge, 11 New Fetter Lane, London EC4P 4EE England. **Tel** 071 583 9855, FAX 071 842 2298. **(Subscription address:** Kinokuniya Company Ltd., 38-1 Sakuragaoka 5, chome Setagaya-ku, Tokyo 156 Japan.**) [CCC].**

US/0081-8224
STUDIES IN MEDIEVAL AND RENAISSANCE HISTORY. [Stud. mediev. renaiss. hist.]. **Added/Corp** University of British Columbia. Committee for Medieval Studies. Vol. 1-10, (1964-1973); [New Ser.] Vol. 1 (Old Ser. Vol. 11-) (1978)-. English. an. $45.00. AMS Press Inc., 56 East 13th Street, New York NY 10003. **Tel** (212)777-4700, FAX (212)995-5413, telex 710 581 2302. **ED** J. A. S. Evans, R. W. Unger. **LC** D119; .S8. **DD** 940.1/05.
Desc: Features works on economic, religious, and social history, the development of labor and technology, research in literature, demography, and law.
Ind/Abst Am. Hist. Life (1973-)(1973).

US/1050-9739
STUDIES IN MEDIEVAL AND RENAISSANCE TEACHING : SMART. [Stud. Mediev. Renaiss. teach.]. **VFOAT** SMART; S.M.A.R.T. Vol. 9, No. 1 (Spring 1982)-. Periodical. English. sa. $10.00 US; $15.00 other. Central Missouri State University, Robert Graybill, Warrensburg MO 64093. **ED** Tom Derrick, Harriet Hudson. **LC** CB351; .S82. **DD** 940. **UDC** 372.894.021; 372.894.0 "04/14". **Bk Rev. *Continues*** *Ralph for Medieval-Renaissance Teaching.*

US/0085-6878
STUDIES IN MEDIEVAL CULTURE. [Stud. mediev. cult.]. (1964)-. English (German, French and Italian). ir. $40.00. Western Michigan University Medieval Institute, Kalamazoo MI 49008-3851. **Tel** (616)387-8755, FAX (616)387-8750. **ED** Thomas Seiler. **LC** CB351; .S83. **DD** 901.921. **UDC** 930.85 "04/14". **Circ:** 700.
Desc: All areas of Medieval studies.
Ind/Abst MLA Int. Bibl. Books Artic. Mod. Lang. Lit.

UK/0738-7164
STUDIES IN MEDIEVALISM. [Stud. mediev.]. **VFOAT** SIM. Vol. 1 (Spring 1979)-. English. an (Apr.). $53.00. Boydell and Brewer Limited, PO Box 9, Woodbridge Suffolk, 1P12 3DF England. **Tel** 011 44 394 411320, FAX 011 44 394 411477. **(Subscription address:** Boydell & Brewer, PO Box 41026, Rochester NY 14604.**) ED** Kathleen Verduin. **LC** CB351; .S78. **DD** 909.07/05.
Ind/Abst Am. Hist. Life (1979-); BHA : Biblio. Hist. Art; MLA Int. Bibl. Books Artic. Mod. Lang. Lit.

US/0098-275X
STUDIES IN MODERN EUROPEAN HISTORY AND CULTURE. [Stud. mod. Eur. hist. cult.]. V. 1- 1975-. English. an. $9.00. Institute for the Study of Nineteenth Century Europe, 188 Lawton Road, Riverside IL 60546. **ED** E T Wilke. **LC** D1; .S868. **DD** 940.2/05. **UDC** 940. **Bk Rev.** available on microfilm from University Microfilms International (UMI).
Ind/Abst Am. Hist. Life (1975-).

US/1054-3120
STUDIES ON THE SHOAH. [Stud. Shoah]. **Added/Corp** Strochlitz Institute of Holocaust Studies (Haifa, Israel). (1991)-. Monographic series. English. ir. Price varies per volume. Verlag Peter Lang AG, Jupiterstrasse 15, CH-3000 Bern 15 Switzerland. **Tel** 011 41 31 9411122, FAX 011 41 31 321131. **DD** 940.

RM/0585-749X
STUDII SI ARTICOLE DE ISTORIE. [Stud. artic. ist.]. **Main/Corp** Societatea de Stiinte Istorice din Republica Socialista Romania. (1968)-. Bulletin. Romanian. an. lei1000.00. Societatea de Stiinte Istorice din Romania, Bdul. Republicii 13, 70031 Bucharest Romania. **Tel** 40 1 613 13 29. **ED** Gheorghe Smarandache. **LC** DR201; .S626. **Bk Rev. Circ:** 500. ***Continues*** *Societatea de Stiinte Istorice si Filologice din Republica Socialista Romania. Studii si Articole de Istorie, 0585-749X.*
Ind/Abst Am. Hist. Life (1968-).

RM
STUDII SI MATERIALE DE ISTORIE CONTEMPORANA. Main/Corp Institutul de Istorie "N. Iorga.". Vol 3 (1978)-. Romanian. Editura Academia Republicii Socialiste Romania, Calea Victoriei Nr 125, R-79717 Bucuresti Romania. **Tel** telex 10376 PRSFI R. **LC** DR264; .A26a. ***Continues*** *Institutul de Istorie*

(Academia Republicii Populare Romine) Studii si Materiale de Istorie Contemporana, 0515-1678.
Ind/Abst Am. Hist. Life (1956-1962).

RM/0567-6312
STUDII SI MATERIALE DE ISTORIE MEDIE. [Stud. mater. ist. medie]. **Main/Corp** Institutul de Istorie "N. Iorga.". (19??)-. Romanian (summaries and/or abstracts in English, French, German and Russian). ir. Editura Academia Republicii Socialiste Romania, Calea Victoriei Nr 125, R-79717 Bucuresti Romania. **Tel** telex 10376 PRSFI R. **LC** DR203; .I58. **Bk Rev. Ad Acc. Circ:** 800. ***Continues*** *Institutul de Istorie (Academia Republicii Populare Romine) Studii si Materiale de Istorie Medie, 0567-6312.*
Ind/Abst Am. Hist. Life (1973-1974); BHA : Biblio. Hist. Art; Numis. Lit.

RM/0567-6320
STUDII SI MATERIALE DE ISTORIE MODERNA. (STUDII SI MATERIALE DE ISTORIE MODERNA / ACADEMIA REPUBLICII POPULARE ROMINE, INSTITUTUL DE ISTORIE.). [Stud. mater. ist. mod.]. **Added/Corp** Institutul de Istorie (Academia Republicii Populare Romine) Institutul de Istorie "N. Iorga.". Vol. 1 (1957)-. Romanian (summaries and/or abstracts in French). ir. Editura Academia Republicii Socialiste Romania, Calea Victoriei Nr 125, R-79717 Bucuresti Romania. **Tel** telex 10376 PRSFI R. **LC** DR242; .S9. **Bk Rev. Ad Acc.**
Ind/Abst Am. Hist. Life (1957-1975).

AA/0563-5799
STUDIME HISTORIKE. [Stud. hist.]. **Added/Corp** Instituti i Historise (Akademia e Shkencave e RPSH). (19??)-. Periodical. Albanian (summaries and/or abstracts in French). qt. $10.91. Book Distribution Enterprise, Rruga Kavajes, Tirana, Albania. **Tel** 011 355 42 27246. **LC** DR901; .S85. ***Continues in part*** *Buletin i Universitetit Shteteror te Tiranes. Seria Shkencat Shogerore.*
Ind/Abst Am. Hist. Life (1955-1956, 1962-); BHA : Biblio. Hist. Art.

RM/1016-460X
SUCEAVA. [Suceava]. (1977)-. Periodical. Romanian. ir. **UDC** 908(498).
Ind/Abst BHA : Biblio. Hist. Art.

GW/0585-8682
SUDETENLAND. [Sudetenland]. (1959)-. Periodical. German (English). Four times a year. DM32.00 (latest volume). Verlagshaus Sudetenland, Hochstrasse 8, D 81669 Munich Germany. **Tel** 011 49 89 41600367. **LC** DB200.5; .S78. Index Available, published separately, free-automatically sent. cum. index.
Ind/Abst Am. Hist. Life; MLA Int. Bibl. Books Artic. Mod. Lang. Lit.

GW/0081-9077
SUDOST-FORSCHUNGEN. [SËudost-Forsch.]. **Added/Corp** Munich. Sudostinstitut. Berlin. Deutsches Auslandswissenschaftliches Institut. (1940)-. Periodical. German (English and French). an. DM136.00. R Oldenbourg Verlag, Postfach 801360, D 81613 Munich Germany. **Tel** 011 49 89 450190, FAX 011 49 89 45019305. **ED** Mathias Bernath and Karl Nehring. Index available. cum. index. **Bk Rev. Circ:** 600 (ctrl). ***Continues*** *Sudostdeutsche Forschungen.*
Desc: History of South-East Europe.
Ind/Abst Am. Hist. Life (1954-); BHA : Biblio. Hist. Art; MLA Int. Bibl. Books Artic. Mod. Lang. Lit.

GW/0081-9085
SUDOSTDEUTSCHES ARCHIV. [Suedostdtsch. Arch.]. **Added/Corp** Sudostdeutsche Historische Kommission. Vol. 1 (1958)-. German. an. DM98.00. R Oldenbourg Verlag, Postfach 801360, D 81613 Munich Germany. **Tel** 011 49 89 450190, FAX 011 49 89 45019305. **ED** Adam Wandruszka. **LC** DR27.G4; S85. **Bk Rev. Circ:** 500 (ctrl).
Desc: History of the Germans in South-East Europe.
Ind/Abst Am. Hist. Life (1963-); MLA Int. Bibl. Books Artic. Mod. Lang. Lit.

GW/0340-174X
SUDOSTEUROPA-MITTEILUNGEN. [Sudosteur.-Mitt.]. **Added/Corp** Suedosteuropa-Gesellschaft (Germany). Vol. 15 (Jan./March 1975)-. Periodical. German. Four times a year. DM40.00. Sudosteuropa-Gesellschaft, EV Widenmayerstr 49, D 80538 Munchen 22 Germany. **Tel** 011 49 89 2285291. **ED** Peter Althammer. **LC** DR1; .S842a. **DD** 949.6/005. **Bk Rev. Circ:** 1,000. ***Continues*** *Suedosteuropa-Gesellschaft (Germany). Mitteilungen der Suedosteuropa-Gesellschaft, 0039-4572.*
Desc: Articles in the field of Southeast European Studies. Covers Albania, Bulgaria, Greece, Yugoslavia, Romania, Turkey and Hungary. Economics, social and political science, language, etc.
Ind/Abst PAIS Int. Print.

GW
SUDOSTEUROPA-STUDIEN. 1- 1962-. Monographic series. German. ir. Price varies per volume. Sudosteuropa-Gesellschaft, EV Widenmayerstr 49, D 80538 Munchen 22 Germany. **Tel** 011 49 89 2285291. **UDC** 940-12; 908.4-12. **Circ:** 1,000-2,000.

UK/0585-878X
SUFFOLK RECORDS SOCIETY (SERIES). (SUFFOLK RECORDS SOCIETY.). **Added/Corp** Suffolk Records Society. (1958)-. Monographic series. English. an. $10.00. Suffolk Records Society, c/o Suffolk County Council, Arts Libraries, St. Andrew House, St. Helen's Street, Ipswich, Suffolk IP4 2JS England. **Tel** 44-93406. **LC** UNC. **DD** 942.6/4.

FI
SUOMEN KULTTUURIRAHASTON VUOSIKATSAUS. **Main/Corp** Suomen Kulttuurirahasto. **VFOAT** Vuosikatsaus; Suomen Kulttuurirahasto ... . Finnish (English). an. Suomen Kulttuurirahasto, Bulevardi 5 A PL203, 00121 Helsinki 12 Finland. **Tel** 0-602144. **LC** DK450.8; .S848. **UDC** 791.6(480). **Circ:** 1,500 (ctrl). ***Continues*** *Suomen Kulttuurirahaston Toimintakertomus.*
Desc: List of grants given by the Finnish Cultural Foundation with reports of annual feasts.

IT
SUPPLEMENTA ITALICA / UNIONE ACCADEMICA NAZIONALE. **Added/Corp** Unione Accademica Nazionale. (1981)-. Monographic series. Italian. ir. Price varies per volume. Edizioni Quasar Severino Togno, Via Quattro Novembre 152, 00187 Rome Italy. **Tel** 011 39 6 6789888, 6796522. **LC** CN530; .S9. **DD** 937.

JA/0562-6579
SURABU KENKYU. **VFOAT** Slavic Studies. No. 1- 1957-. Periodical. English (Japanese and Russian). Counsel of Chalcedon, PO Box 888022, Atlanta GA 30338. **UDC** 947.
Ind/Abst Am. Hist. Life (1959, 1971-).

FI
SVENSK-OESTERBOTTINISKA SAMFUNDETS ASBOK. Swedish. an.

SZ
SWISS PRESS REVIEW AND NEWS REPORT. German. bw. 80.00F. Schweizerisches Ost Institut, Jubilaeumsstr 41, CH-3000 Bern 6 Switzerland. **Tel** 011 41 31 431212.

US/1057-0896
SWITZERLAND, JEWEL OF EUROPE. [Switz. jewel Eur.]. Vol. 1, No. 1 (June 1991)-. Periodical. English. mo. $48.00. European Publishers, Inc., 1308 Rodman Avenue, Portsmouth VA 23707. **DD** 949.

NE/0923-9073
SYMBOLA ET EMBLEMATA. [Symb. embl.]. (1989)-. Monographic series. English. ir. Price varies per volume. E. J. Brill, Postbus 9000, 2300 PA Leiden Netherlands. **Tel** 011 31 71 312624, FAX 011 31 71 317532, telex 39296 BRILL NL. **UDC** 396.6.

GR
SYMMEIKTA / VASILIKON HIDRYMA EREUNON, KENTRON VYZANTINÂON EREUNON. **Added/Corp** Kentron VyzantinÂon Ereunon (Athens, Greece). (1966)-. Greek, Modern (French and English). be. Dr1,500.00. Ethnikon Hidryma Erevnon, Kentron Byzantinon Erevnon, Vas Konstantinou 48, Athens 116 35 Greece. **Tel** 7247959. **LC** DF501; .S93. **Circ:** 1,000 (ctrl).
Desc: Covers Byzantine history, Post-Byzantine history archives, historical geography, Byzantium and the Slavs, and data bank history.

FR/0291-1655
SYNTHESE (EDITIONS RECHERCHE SUR LES CIVILISATIONS). (SYNTHESE.). **VFOAT** Syntheses; Recherche sur les Civilisations. Syntheses. Monographic series. French. Price varies per volume. ***Continues*** *Recherche sur les Grandes Civilisations. Synthese.*

GR
TA HISTORIKA. **VFOAT** Historica. Vol. 1, No. 1 (Sept. 1983)-. Periodical. Greek, Modern. Three times a year. $16.00. Melissa Publishing Company, Navarinov 10, Athens 106 80 Greece. **LC** DF701; .H58.

TU
TARIH INCELEMELERI DERGISI. (1983)-. Periodical. Turkish. an. Ege Universitesi / Edibiyat, Edebiyat Fakultesi, Cografya Bolumu, Bornova Izmir Turkey. **Tel** 9-51-180110. **LC** DR438; .T37.

TU/1019-4681
TARIH VE TOPLUM : AYLK ANSIKLOPEDIK DERGI. (1984)-. Periodical. Turkish. mo. **LC** DR401; .T37.
Ind/Abst Am. Hist. Life (1988-).

IT/0393-5949
TATTI STUDIES, I. [Tatti stud.]. **Added/Corp** Villa I Tatti (Florence, Italy). Vol. 1 (1985)-. Monographic series. English (French, German, Italian and Spanish). ir. Price varies per volume. Casa Editrice Leo S. Olschki, Viuzzo del Pozzetto, Casella Postale 66, 50126 Florence Italy. **Tel** 011 39 55 6530684, FAX 011 39 55 6530214. **LC** DG445; .T29. **DD** 945/.005.
Ind/Abst Am. Hist. Life (1985-); BHA : Biblio. Hist. Art.

SZ
TERRA GRISCHUNA. Periodical. German. bm. 36.70F Switzerland; 52.70F North America; 42.70 other. Terra Grischuna Verlag, Postfach 4103, Bottmingen Switzerland. **Tel** 061 401 00 11, FAX 061 401 50 05. **ED** Terra Grischuna Verlag. **LC** DQ481; .T47. **DD** 949.4/7. **UDC** 949.4; 908.494. Index available. cum. index. **Bk Rev. Ad Acc. Circ:** 24,000 (ctrl).
Desc: Journal on nature, culture, tourism and traffic of the cantons Grisons.

SP/0210-3524
TERUEL. [Teruel]. **Added/Corp** Instituto de Estudios Turolenses. Vol. 1 (1949)-. Periodical. English. sa. Consejo Superior Investigacion Cientificas (CSIC), Vitruvio 8, 28006 Madrid Spain. **Tel** 011 34 1 5612833, FAX 011 34 1 4113077, telex 42182. **LC** DP302.T31; T4.
Ind/Abst Am. Hist. Life (1967-1969); BHA : Biblio. Hist. Art; GeoRef.

IT
THESAURISMATA TOU HELLENIKOU INSTITOUTOU VYZANTINON KAI METAVYZANTINON SPOUDON. **VFOAT** Thesaurismata. Vol. 1, No. 1 (1962)-. Periodical. Greek, Modern. an. **LC** DF501; .T48.
Ind/Abst BHA : Biblio. Hist. Art; MLA Int. Bibl. Books Artic. Mod. Lang. Lit.

GR
THESSALIKE HESTIA. Periodical. Greek, Modern. 25.00. M Staphylas, Mourouzi 18, Larisa Greece. **LC** DF901.T7; T45. **UDC** 949.53.

RM/0259-1081
THRACO-DACIA. (THRACO-DACICA / ACADEMIA DE STIINTE SOCIALE SI POLITICE A REPUBLICII SOCIALISTE ROMANIA, INSTITUTUL DE TRACOLOGIE.). [Thraco-Dacia]. **Added/Corp** Institutul de Tracologie (Romania). (1976)-. Periodical. French (German and Romanian). sa. $44.00. Editura Academia Republicii Socialiste Romania, Calea Victoriei Nr 125, R-79717 Bucuresti Romania. **Tel** telex 10376 PRSFI R. **(Subscription address:** Rompresfilatelia, PO Box 12 201, Bucharest Romania.**) ED** Dumitru Berciu. **LC** DR211; .T5. **DD** 939/.51/05.
Ind/Abst Numis. Lit.

SP/0495-5773
TIERRAS DE LEON. **Added/Corp** Leon (Spain : Province) Diputacion Provincial. (19??)-. Periodical. Spanish. qt. **LC** DP302.L2; A3.
Ind/Abst BHA : Biblio. Hist. Art.

IE
TIPPERARY HISTORICAL JOURNAL. **Added/Corp** County Tipperary Historical Society. **VFOAT** Irisleabhar Staire Thiobraid Arann. (1988)-. Periodical. English. an. £12.00. John Kelly Honorary Treasurer, Hillvies Chadville, Cappawhit Co Tipperary Ireland.

AU/1013-8919
TIROLER HEIMAT. [Tirol. Heim.]. (1921)-. Academic Scholarly Publication. German. an. Price varies. Universitaetsverlag Wagner GmbH, Andreas Hofer Str. 13, Postfach 165, A 6010 Innsbruck Austria. **Tel** 011 43 512 587721, FAX 011 43 512 582209. **Bk Rev.**
Ind/Abst Am. Hist. Life (1963-1978); BHA : Biblio. Hist. Art.

SW
TJUSTBYGDEN. **VFOAT** Arsbok - Tjustbygdens Kulturhistoriska Forening. Swedish. Kr75.00. Kulbackens Museum, Box 257, 593 01 Vastervik Sweden. **Tel** 0490/11177. **ED** Arne Sandelin. **LC** DL991.T56; T56. **UDC** 948.5. cum. index. **Bk Rev. Ad Acc. Pr Rev. Circ:** 1,200 (ctrl).

●JA
TOKYO: THE MAKING OF A METROPOLIS. (Mar. 1993)-. English. ir. Tokyo Metropolitan Government / Liaison and Protocol Section, 8-1 Nishi-Shinjuku 2-chome, Shinjuku-ku Tokyo 163-01, Japan. **Tel** 03-5388-3172. **ED** Yamamoto Kenji,.
Desc: News and information on the history of Tokyo, Japan. Numerous articles on artifacts, government, people, education and other history news.

JA/0386-6904
TOOSHI KENKYU. **VFOAT** Journal of East European Studies. 1st Edition 1978-. Japanese (Japanese). Tooshi Kenkyukai, c/o Tsudajuku Daigaku Kokusai, Kankei Gakka 14-1, Tsudamachi Kodaira 187, Tokyo Japan. **LC** DJK1; .T66. **UDC** 947; 908.47.

SW/0495-8772
TOR. **Added/Corp** Uppsala Universitet. Institutionen for Nordisk Fornkunskap. Uppsala Universitet. Museum for Nordiska Fornsaker. Vol. 1 (1948)-. Swedish (summaries and/or abstracts in English, French and German). an. University Uppsala, Institute of Archaeology, Sarskilt Nord, Gustavianum, S 752 20 Uppsala Sweden. **LC** DL621; .T65. **DD** 936.3.
Ind/Abst Anthropol. Lit.; BHA : Biblio. Hist. Art.

History(General) —History of Europe

CN
TORONTO MEDIEVAL LATIN TEXTS. See Literature.

SP
TORRENS. 1 (1982)-. Periodical. Spanish. an. Only exchange (similar publications). Arxiu Municipal, Ajuntament de Torrent, c/o Sagra 17, 46900 Torrent, Valencia Spain. **Tel** (96)157-10-06. **ED** Josep Ramon Sanchis Alfonso. **LC** DP402.T8243; T67. **DD** 946/.76. **UDC** 946.73. Index available. cum. index. **Pr Rev. Circ:** 1,000 (ctrl).
Desc: Mainly dedicated to the history of Torrent and its region: the fertile area of Valencia and its more varied aspects.

US/0732-6645
TOURNAMENTS ILLUMINATED.
[Tournaments illum.]. **Added/Corp** Society for Creative Anachronism. **VFOAT** Tournaments Illuminated. (19??)-. Periodical. English. qt. comes with membership. Society for Creative Anachronism Inc., PO Box 360743, Milpitas CA 95035. **Tel** (415)428-1181, (408)263-9305. Index available. cum. index. **Bk Rev. Ad Acc. Circ:** 11,000 (ctrl).
Desc: Serves living-history enthusiasts studying the Middle Ages and the Renaissance, providing historical background pieces and construction tips for clothing and artifacts of the period.

US/0362-1529
TRADITIO. [Traditio]. **Added/Corp** Institute of Research and Study in Medieval Canon Law. Bulletin. Vol. 1 (1943)-. Academic Scholarly Publication. English (German, French and Latin). an (fall publication). $52.00. Fordham University Press, Box L, Fordham University, Bronx NY 10458. **Tel** (718)817-4780, FAX (718)817-4785. **ED** Elizabeth Parker (718)817-3130. **LC** D111; .T7. **DD** 940.1058. **[CCC]. Circ:** 800. available on microfilm from University Microfilms International (UMI). Documents available from The Genuine Article.
Desc: A volume of articles, original texts, bibliographical surveys and scholarly studies in classical antiquity and the middle ages.
Ind/Abst Annu. Bibliogr. Engl. Lang. Lit.; Arts Humanit. Citation Index (19??-19??) [Full Cov.]; Index Book Rev. Relig.; MLA Int. Bibl. Books Artic. Mod. Lang. Lit.; New Testam. Abstr.; Relig. Index One Period. (1975-); Res. Alert [Full Cov.]; Soc. Sci. Cit. Index [Select. Cov.].

XV
TRADITIONES. 1- 1972-. Slovenian (summaries and/or abstracts in English, French, German and Italian). an. Biblioteka Slovenske Akademije Znanosti In Umetnosti, Postni Predal 323, 61001 Ljubljana Slovenia. **ED** Tone Cevc. **LC** DR381.S64; T72. **Circ:** 1,000.
Desc: Communications from the Slovenie Academy of Arts and Sciences.
Ind/Abst MLA Int. Bibl. Books Artic. Mod. Lang. Lit.

UK
TRANSACTIONS. Main/Corp Halifax Antiquarian Society, Halifax, Eng. (1901)-. English. cum. index.
Ind/Abst BHA : Biblio. Hist. Art.

UK/0306-5790
TRANSACTIONS - ANGLESEY ANTIQUARIAN SOCIETY AND FIELD CLUB. Main/Corp Anglesey Antiquarian Society. (1914)-. English. an. **LC** DA740.A5; A66a. **DD** 942.9/21/005.
Ind/Abst BHA : Biblio. Hist. Art.

UK/0068-1032
TRANSACTIONS - BRISTOL AND GLOUCESTERSHIRE ARCHAEOLOGICAL SOCIETY. See Archaeology.

UK/0144-0098
TRANSACTIONS - CAERNARVONSHIRE HISTORICAL SOCIETY. [Trans. - Caernarvonshire Hist. Soc.]. **VFOAT** Trafodion - Cymdeithas Hanes Sir Gaernarfon. (1939)-. English. an.
Ind/Abst BHA : Biblio. Hist. Art.

UK/0140-3990
TRANSACTIONS - LEICESTERSHIRE ARCHAEOLOGICAL AND HISTORICAL SOCIETY. See Archaeology.

UK/0309-7986
TRANSACTIONS OF THE CUMBERLAND & WESTMORLAND ANTIQUARIAN & ARCHAEOLOGICAL SOCIETY. [Trans. Cumberl. Westmorl. Antiq. Archaeol. Soc.]. (1866)-. Periodical. English. an.
Ind/Abst BHA : Biblio. Hist. Art.

UK/0140-332X
TRANSACTIONS OF THE HISTORIC SOCIETY OF LANCASHIRE AND CHESHIRE FOR THE YEAR. Began with: Vol. 7 (1854/55). English. an. £17.00 UK; £21.00 other. Historic Society of Lancashire and Cheshire, Liverpool Institute of HE, Stand Park Road, Liverpool L16 9JD England. **ED** C Phillips and C Lewis. **LC** MICROFILM (O) 82/5883 . **UDC** 908.497.1. Index available. cum. index. **Bk Rev. Circ:** 600 (ctrl). **Continues** Proceedings and Papers / Historic Society of Lancashire and Cheshire.
Ind/Abst Br. Archaeol. Bibliogr.; Br. Humanit. Index.

UK/0950-4699
TRANSACTIONS OF THE LANCASHIRE AND CHESHIRE ANTIQUARIAN SOCIETY. [Trans. Lancs. Ches. Antiq. Soc.]. **Main/Corp** Lancashire and Cheshire Antiquarian Society. Vol. 1 (1883)-. English. ir. £8.00. Lancashire and Cheshire Antiquarian Society, 59 Malmesbury Road, M Garratt, Cheadle Cheshire SK8 7QL England. **Tel** 061-643-5228.
Ind/Abst Avery Index Archit. Period. Suppl. Colum. Univ. (1988); BHA : Biblio. Hist. Art.

UK/0306-848X
TRANSACTIONS OF THE RADNORSHIRE SOCIETY, THE.
Added/Corp Radnorshire Society. **VFOAT** Radnorshire Society Transactions. (19??)-. English. an. **LC** WMLC L 83/5943.
Ind/Abst BHA : Biblio. Hist. Art.

UK/0080-4401
TRANSACTIONS OF THE ROYAL HISTORICAL SOCIETY. [Trans. R. Hist. Soc.].
Main/Corp Royal Historical Society (Great Britain). **Added/Corp** Royal Historical Society (Great Britain). (1872)-. Academic Scholarly Publication. English. an. £35.00. Cambridge University Press, The Edinburgh Building, Shaftesbury Road, Cambridge CB2 2RU United Kingdom. **Tel** 011 44 223 312393, FAX 011 44 223 325959. (**Subscription address:** Cambridge University Press / North America, 110 Midland Avenue, Port Chester NY 10573.) **LC** DA20; .R9. **Circ:** 2,500. available on microfilm from University Microfilms International (UMI). Documents available from The Genuine Article.
Desc: Papers on varied topics read to meetings of the fellows of the Royal Historical Society.
Ind/Abst Am. Hist. Life (1954-); Arts Humanit. Citation Index [Full Cov.]; BHA : Biblio. Hist. Art; Br. Archaeol. Bibliogr.; Br. Humanit. Index; Res. Alert [Full Cov.].

UK/0309-9210
TRANSACTIONS OF THE THOROTON SOCIETY OF NOTTINGHAMSHIRE.
Main/Corp Thoroton Society, Nottingham, Eng. **Added/Corp** Thoroton Society. Vol. 1 (1897)-. English. an. Thoroton Society of Nottinghamshire, The Barn Hopyard Lane, Bathley Neward Notts England. **LC** DA670.N89; T5. cum. index.
Desc: List of members in each volume.
Ind/Abst BHA : Biblio. Hist. Art; Numis. Lit.

UK/0457-7817
TRANSACTIONS - SOUTH STAFFORDSHIRE ARCHAEOLOGICAL AND HISTORICAL SOCIETY. See Archaeology.

SZ
TRANSEUROPEENNES. (19??)-. French. Four times a year. 95.00F Switzerland; 100.00F other. Centre Europeen de la Culture, 120B rue de Lausanne, CH 1202 Geneva 21 Switzerland. **Tel** 011 41 22 738.28.03, FAX 011 41 22 738.40.12, telex (41)(22)289.917. (**Subscription address:** Ulysse Diffusion, 5 rue Joseph Serlin, F 69001 Lyon France) **Continues** Cadmos.

RM
TRANSILVANIA. Added/Corp Sibiu (Romania : Judet). Comitetul Judetean de Cultura si Educatie Socialista. (1868)-. Periodical. Romanian (summaries and/or abstracts in German). qt. $40.00 Europe; $50.00 other. Transilvania, Str. Dr. Ion Ratiu Nr. 2, 2400 Sibiu Romania. **ED** Ion Mircea. **LC** DR201; .T7. **Bk Rev Ad Acc. Circ:** 4,000 (ctrl).
Desc: Socio-cultural review.
Ind/Abst Annu. Bibliogr. Engl. Lang. Lit.

FR/0079-0028
TRAVAUX. Main/Corp Paris. Universite. Institut d'Etudes Slaves. (1923)-. French. ir. Institut d'Etudes Slaves, 9 rue Michelet, 75006 Paris France. **Tel** 011 33 1 43265089. **Circ:** 300.
Desc: Series devoted to Slavic studies.

SZ/0082-6081
TRAVAUX D'HUMANISME ET RENAISSANCE. [Trav. humanisme renaiss.]. No. 1 (1950)-. Monographic series. French (English). ir. Price varies per volume. Librairie Droz SA, 11 rue Massot BP 389, CH 1211 Geneva 12 Switzerland. **Tel** 011 41 22 3466666, FAX 011 41 22 472391. **[CCC].**
Desc: Renaissance and humanism.
Ind/Abst MLA Int. Bibl. Books Artic. Mod. Lang. Lit.

FR
TRAVAUX ET MEMOIRES (CENTRE DE RECHERCHE D'HISTOIRE ET CIVILISATION DE BYZANCE (PARIS, FRANCE)). (TRAVAUX ET MEMOIRES / CENTRE DE RECHERCHE D'HISTOIRE ET CIVILISATION DE BYZANCE.). **Added/Corp** Centre de Recherche d'Histoire et Civilisation de Byzance (Paris, France). No. 5 (1973)-. French. ir. Diffusion de Boccard, 11 rue de Medicis, 75006 Paris France. **Tel** 011 33 1 43260037. **LC** DF503; .C45. **DD** 949.5/02. **Continues** Travaux et Memoires (Centre de Recherche d'Histoire et Civilisation Byzantines).
Ind/Abst BHA : Biblio. Hist. Art.

NE
TREFPUNT. Added/Corp Netherlands. Ministerie van Cultuur, Recreatie en Maatschappelijk Werk. (19??)-. Periodical. Dutch. mo (12 issues). Fl55.00. SDU Uitgeverij, Postbus 20014, Christoffel Plan, 2500 EA Den Haag Netherlands. **Tel** 011 31 70 3789911. **LC** DJ1; .T16. **Continues** TP; Trefpunt van Cultuur, Recreatie en Maatschappelijk Werk.

SP
TRIBUNA COSTENA. Year 1- Nov. 1975-. Periodical. Spanish. $12.00. Apartado Aereo 1989, Cartagena Spain. **LC** F2251; .T75.

CN/0228-250X
TRICOLORUL. (TRICOLORUL : ISTORIE-LITERATURA-ARTA-SI-CIVILIZATIE-ROMANEASCA.). [Tricolorul]. Year 1, No. 1, (Aug. 1980)-. Romanian. $15.00 US. Tricolorul, Apt 1018B 103 West Lodge Avenue, Toronto Ontario M6K 2T7 Canada. **ED** Cornelius Dima-Dragan. **DD** 949.8/005. **UDC** 949.8; 908.498.

GW/0041-2953
TRIERER ZEITSCHRIFT FUER GESCHICHTE UND KUNST DES TRIERER LANDES UND SEINER NACHBARGEBIETE. [Trier. Z. Gesch. Kunst Trier. Landes Nachbargeb.]. **Added/Corp** Rheinisches Landesmuseum Trier. **VFOAT** Trierer Zeitschrift. Vol. 11, Issue 1 (1936)-. Academic Scholarly Publication. German. an. DM72.00. Rheinisches Landesmuseun Trier, Ostallee 44, Bibliothek W-55 Trier Germany. **Tel** 011 0651 48368. **Bk Rev**, (Qty: 10). **Acid Free. Circ:** 750. **Continues** Trierer Zeitschrift.
Desc: Archaeology, prehistory, fine arts, numismatics, and history of Trier county.
Ind/Abst BHA : Biblio. Hist. Art; Numis. Lit.

II/0041-3135
TRIVENI (GUNTUR). See The Arts-Art.

NO/0333-2802
TROMURA. KULTURHISTOIRE : TROMS MUSEUMS RAPPORTSERIE.
VFOAT Kulturhistorie. No. 1- 1982-. Monographic series. Norwegian (summaries and/or abstracts in English). Price varies per volume. Universitetet i Troms, Univ. Biblio Tromso Mus Folkepark, N 9000 Tromso, Norway.

RU
TRUDY (CHUVASHSKAIA A.S.S.R. (R.S.F.S.R.)). (TRUDY / NAUCHNO-ISSLEDOVATELSKII INSTITUT IAZYKA, LITERATURY, ISTORII I EKONOMIKI PRI SOVETE MINISTROV CHUVASHSKOI ASSR.). **Added/Corp** Chuvashskaia A.S.S.R. (R.S.F.S.R.). Nauchno-Issledovatelskii Institut Iazyka, Literatury, Istorii i Ekonomiki. Vol. 72 (1977)-. Monographic series. Russian. Price varies per volume. Nauchno-Issl, Moskovskii Prospekt 29, Korpus 1, Cheboksary, Russia. **LC** DK511.C5; C48. **Continues** Uchenye Zapiski.

SW
TUNUM : TUNABYGDENS FORNMINNES- OCH HEMBYGDSFORENINGS ARSSKRIFT.
Periodical. Swedish. an. Kr20.00. Tunabygdens Fornminnes-Och Hembygdsforening Gemmelgarden, 781 00 Borlange Sweden. **LC** DL991.T853; T86.

US/0161-8903
TURKEY YEAR BOOK. VAT Turkey Yearbook. English. an. $10.00. D. Uluc, 18 West 56th Street, New York NY 10019. **LC** DR401; .T833. **DD** 949.6/1/005. **UDC** 949.6(058).

FI/0085-7440
TURUN HISTORIALLINEN ARKISTO.
[Turun hist. ark.]. **VFOAT** Turun Historiallisen Yhdistyksen Julkaisuja. (1924)-. Monographic series. Multiple languages. ir. Price varies per volume. Turun Historiallinen Yhdistys, Turun Yliopisto, SF-20500 Turku 50, Finland. **Tel** 011 358 21 6335385, FAX 011 358 21 6336585. **UDC** 93/99.
Ind/Abst Am. Hist. Life (1955-).

IT
TUSCIA. Added/Corp Inte Provinciale per il Turismo di Viterbo. (19??)-. Periodical. Italian. qt. L500 (single issue). Ente Provinciale Per Il Turismo, Piassa Dei Caduti 16, 01100 Italy. **Tel** 0761/226161. **LC** DG731; .T87. **DD** 945/.5/005.

BE/0775-3381
TYPOLOGIE DES SOURCES DU MOYEN AGE OCCIDENTAL. [Typol. sources M Age. occident.]. (1972)-. Periodical. French (French, English and German). ir. Brepols Publishers, Steenweg OP Tielen

History(General) —History of Europe

68, B-2300 Turnhout Belgium. **Tel** 011 32 14 402500. **UDC** 940.1.
Desc: The objective of this is to facilitate the correct and exhaustive utilization of the extent primary sources.

CN/0824-6238
UKRAINSKE VIDRODZHENNJA.
(UKRAINSKE VIDRODSHENNIA.). V. 1, No. 1 (Dec. 1983)-. Periodical. Ukrainian. qt. Free. Ukrainske Vidrodzhennia, PO Box 323, Grimsby Ontario L3M 4G5 Canada. **DD** 947/.71/005. **UDC** 947.7. ctrl circ.

US/0041-6061
UKRAINSKYI ISTORYK. [Ukr. istor.].
Added/Corp Zarevo (Organization). Istorychna Komisiia. Ukrainske Istorychne Tovarystvo. **VFOAT** Ukrainian Historian. Vol. 1 No. 1 (1963)-. Periodical. Ukrainian (English and German; table of contents in English). Twice a year. $40.00. Ukrainian Historian, PO Box 312, Kent OH 44240. **ED** Lulomyr R. Wynar. **LC** DK508.A2; U685. **DD** 947. **Bk Rev**. **Ad Acc**. ctrl circ.
Desc: Ukrainian and East European history, auxiliary historical sciences biography and a historical bibliography.
Ind/Abst Am. Hist. Life (1964-); Am. Bibliogr. Slavic East Europ. Stud. (19??-19??); MLA Int. Bibl. Books Artic. Mod. Lang. Lit.

GW
UKRAINSKYI SAMOSTIINYK.
UKRAINSKYJ SAMOSTIJNYK. **VFOAT**
Ukrainskyj Samostijnyk. (1950)-. Periodical. Ukrainian. qt. **LC** DK508.A2; U695.
Ind/Abst Am. Hist. Life (1970-1972).

US/0897-9669
UNCAPTIVE MINDS. (UNCAPTIVE MINDS / IDEE.). **Added/Corp** Institute for Democracy in Eastern Europe. Vol. 1, No. 1 (April/May 1988)-. Periodical. English. Four times a year (Published during seasons). $30.00. Institute for Democracy in Eastern Europe, 30 East 20th Street, Suite 201, New York NY 10003. **Tel** (212)677-5801, FAX (212)475-5829. **ED** Eric Chenoweth. **LC** DJK50; .U52. **DD** 947/.0005. **Ad Acc, Adv Mgr:** Eric Chenoweth. **Circ:** 4,000. **Continues** Committee in Support of Solidarity Special Reports.
Desc: Devoted to opposition movements in Eastern Europe.

UK/0264-6501
UNCENSORED POLAND NEWS BULLETIN / INFORMATION CENTRE FOR POLISH AFFAIRS (U.K.), STUDIUM SPRAW POLSKICH (WLK. BRYTANIA).
No. 18/81 (27 Nov. 1981)-. Bulletin. English. bw. £80.00 (individuals), £100.00 (institutions) UK and Europe; $200.00 (individuals), $240.00 (institutions) other. Information Centre for Polish Affairs (UK), 115 Redston Road, London N8 7HG Great Britain. **Tel** 01-340-9225. **LC** DK4442; .U53. **DD** 943.8/005. **UDC** 943.8. **Circ:** 400. **Continues** Information Center for Polish Affairs (U.K.)(Series).
Desc: Apart from the regular Calendarium, UPNB contains translations of news, documents, articles, interviews, etc. appearing in the Polish independent (underground) press.
Ind/Abst Hum. Rights Intern. Rep.

US/0888-3882
UNIVERSITY OF CINCINNATI STUDIES IN HISTORICAL AND CONTEMPORARY EUROPE. [Univ. Cincinnati stud. hist. contemp. Eur.]. **VFOAT** Studies in Historical and Contemporary Europe. Vol. 1 (1988)-. Monographic series. English. ir. Price varies per volume. Peter Lang Publishing, 62 West 45th Street, 4th Floor, New York NY 10036. **Tel** (212)764-1471, (800)770-5264, telex 6973364 PLNY. **ED** Otic C Mitchell. **DD** 940.
Desc: Modern history and contemporary studies of Europe.

CN
UNIVERSITY OF MANITOBA ICELANDIC STUDIES. **VFOAT** Icelandic Studies. V. 1-. Monographic series. English. ir. Price varies per volume. University Manitoba Press, University of Manitoba, Winnipeg Manitoba R3T 2N2 Canada. **Tel** (204)474-9495. **ED** Haraldur Bessason and Robert Glendinning. **UDC** 949.11; 908.491.1. cum. index.

CN
UNIVERSITY OF TORONTO ITALIAN STUDIES. See Literature.

US/0749-4149
UNIVERSITY STUDIES IN MEDIEVAL AND RENAISSANCE LITERATURE. See Literature.

●UK/0967-4764
URBAN FOCUS LONDON. [Urban focus Lond.]. (1992)-. Periodical. English. Six times a year (Jan., Mar., May, July, Sept., Nov.). 10.50 UK; £15.00 Europe; £17.00 other. Heritage Outlook, 17 Carlton House Terrace, London SW1Y 5AW England. **Tel** 011 44 1 930 0914, FAX 011 44 1 321 0180. **Continues** Heritage Outlook, 0261-1988.
Ind/Abst Museum Abstr.

IT
URBE (ROME, ITALY). Suspended. (L'URBE : REVISTA ROMANA DI STORIA, ARTE, LETTERE, COSTUMANZE.). 1st Vol. (Oct. 1936)-(Dec. 1989). Periodical. Italian. bm. L45000 Italy; L60000 other. Organizzazione RAB SRL, Via Crocifisso 51, 00165 Rome Italy. **Tel** 011 39 6 632595, 6381177. **ED** Antonio Munoz. **LC** DG401; .U7.
Ind/Abst Avery Index Archit. Period. Suppl. Colum. Univ. (1988/89-); BHA : Biblio. Hist. Art; MLA Int. Bibl. Books Artic. Mod. Lang. Lit.

SP
URGELLIA / SOCIETAT CULTURAL URGELITANA. 1 (1978)- = Vol. 1-. Periodical. Catalan (Latin). an. 3,400ptas Spain; $30.00 US. Societat Cultural Urgellitana, Pati del Palau 3, 25700 La Sue D'Urgell (LIneida) Spain. **Tel** (973)350054. **LC** DP302.C57; U73. **DD** 946/.7/005. **UDC** 946.71. **Circ:** 800.
Desc: Historical studies on a wide section of Catalonia and the Central Pyrenees, with sources from the 9th century.

RU/0136-7455
USPEKHI SREDNEAZIATSKOI ARKHEOLOGII. **Added/Corp** Akademiia Nauk SSSR. Institut Arkheologii. Nauchnyi Sovet po Problemam Arkheologii Srednei Azii i Kazakhstana (Akademiia Nauk SSSR). (1972)-. Periodical. Russian. 1.80rub single issue. Izdatelstvo Nauka St. Petersburg, Mendeleevskaia Liniia 1, 199034 St. Petersburg, B-34 Russia. **Tel** 218-26-12. **LC** DK855; .U84.

US/1054-6510
USSR NEWS & INFORMATION DIGEST [COMPUTER FILE] : USSR-D / COMPILED & EDITED BY JOHN B HARLAN. [USSR news inf. dig.]. **VFOAT** USSR News and Information Digest; USSR-D. Issue 1 (Jan 1-7 1991)-. Periodical. English. wk. Free. USSR News & Information Digest, 125 West Marion Street, #529, South Bend IN 46601-1096. **DD** 947.
Desc: Available only through electronic mail from ListServe@IndyVAX (CREN) or ListServe@IndyVax.IUPUI.Edu (Internet).

FR/0989-6139
VALENTIANA VALENCIENNES. See Archaeology.

GR/1105-0136
VALKANIKA SYMMEIKTA. **Added/Corp** Hidryma Meleton Chersonesou tou Haimou (Thessalonike, Greece). (1981)-. Periodical. Greek, Modern. an. Dr2000.00, $9.21. Hidryma Meleton Chersonissou, Tu Emu Meg Alexanohou 31A, Thessaloniki 54641 Greece. **Tel** 011 30 31 832143. **LC** DR1; .V34.
Ind/Abst Am. Hist. Life (1981-).

SZ
VALLESIA. **Added/Corp** Valais (Switzerland). Bibliotheque Cantonale. Archives Cantonales du Valais. (1946)-. French (German). an. Archives Cantonales du Valais, Rue des Vergers 7, CH 1950 Sion Switzerland. **Tel** 011 41 27 216341, 011 41 27 215111. **LC** DQ701; .V35. **DD** 949.4.
Ind/Abst BHA : Biblio. Hist. Art (19??-).

HU/0505-0332
VASI SZEMLE SZOMBATHELY. 1958.
[Vasi szle.Szombathely. 1958.] (1958)-. Periodical. Hungarian. qt. **UDC** 908. **Continues** Dunantuli Szemle, 0200-2485.
Ind/Abst BHA : Biblio. Hist. Art.

GW
VECHE (MUNICH, GERMANY). (VECHE.). **Added/Corp** Rossiiskoe Natsionalnoe Obedinenie v FRG. (1981)-. Periodical. Russian. qt (Mar., June, Sept., Dec.). $90.00. Veche, PO Box 68, Flushing Station, Mid Vill NY 11379. **Tel** (719)651-5662, FAX (719)651-5662. **LC** DK510; .V43.

BU/0324-0967
VEKOVE. **Added/Corp** Bulgarsko Istorichesko Druzhestvo. Vol. 1 (1972)-. Periodical. Bulgarian. bm. $28.00. **(Subscription address:** Hemus Foreign Trade Organization, 6 Tzar Osvoboditel Boulevard, 1000 Sofia Bulgaria.) **LC** DR51.V44.
Ind/Abst Numis. Lit. (19??-).

SW
VEM AR DET SVENSK BIOGRAFISK HANDBOK. 1912-. Swedish. be. Norstedt and Soners Forlag AB, PO Box 2052, Stockholm S-10312 Sweden. **ED** E Thyselius and G Linbald. **LC** DL644. **UDC** 929(485). **NLM** CT 1313 V446.

GW
VERHANDLUNGEN DES HISTORISCHEN VEREINS FUER NIEDERBAYERN. **Main/Corp** Historischer Verein fuer Niederbayern. (1846)-. Academic Scholarly Publication. German. an. DM20.00. Historischer Verein fuer Niederbayern, Altstadt 79, D 84026 Landshut Germany. **Tel** 0871 881218. **ED** Georg Spitzlberger. Index available. **Bk Rev**, (Qty: 5). **Circ:** 1,000 (ctrl).
Ind/Abst BHA : Biblio. Hist. Art.

GW/0342-2518
VERHANDLUNGEN DES HISTORISCHEN VEREINES FUER OBERPFALZ UND REGENSBURG.
[Verhandl. Hist. Ver. Oberpf. Regensbg.]. **Added/Corp** Historischer Verein fur Oberpfalz und Regensburg. **VFOAT** Verhandlungen des Historischen Vereins von Oberpfalz und Regensburg. (18??)-. Periodical. German. an. **Continues** Verhandlungen des Historischen Vereines fur den Regenskreis.
Ind/Abst BHA : Biblio. Hist. Art.

GW/0530-9794
VEROFFENTLICHUNGEN. **Main/Corp**
Collegium Carolinum. Vol. 1 1958-. Monographic series. German. Price varies per volume. R Oldenbourg Verlag, Postfach 801360, D 81613 Munich Germany. **Tel** 011 49 89 450190, FAX 011 49 89 45019305. **UDC** 940-191.2.
Desc: Monographs on the history of Central Europe considered politically, socially and culturally.

GW
VEROFFENTLICHUNGEN DER ALTERTUMSKOMMISSION IM PROVINZIALINSTITUT FUER WESTFALISCHE LANDES- UND VOLKSFORSCHUNG, LANDSCHAFTSVERBAND WESTFALEN-LIPPE. Monographic series. German. Price varies per volume. Aschendorffsche Verlagsbuchhandlung, Postfach 1124, D-48135 Muenster Germany. **Tel** 011 49 251 690132, telex 08-92 830 WN MS D. **LC** DD491.W41; M8. **DD** 943/.56. **UDC** 943.0-316. **Continues** Veroffentlichungen der Altertumskommission im Provinzialinstitut fur Westfalische Landes- und Volkskunde.

GW
VEROFFENTLICHUNGEN DER SENATSKOMMISSION FUER HUMANISMUS-FORSCHUNG. **Main/Corp**
Deutsche Forschungsgemeinschaft (Founded 1949). Senatskommission fuer Humanismus-Forschung. (1974)-. Monographic series. German. ir. Price varies per volume. Wilhelm Fink Verlag, Ohmstrasse 5, D 80802 Munich Germany. **Tel** 011 49 89 348017, 348018. **ED** H. Chantraine, M. Schlenke, F. Trautz and F.K. Werner.

GW
VEROFFENTLICHUNGEN DES ARCHIVES DER STADT STUTTGART.
Main/Corp Stuttgart. Archiv der Stadt Stuttgart. (19??)-. Monographic series. German. ir. Price varies per volume. Ernst Klett Verlag, Postfach 106016, D 70049 Stuttgart Germany. **Tel** 011 49 711 667205.

GW
VEROFFENTLICHUNGEN DES DEUTSCHEN HISTORISCHEN INSTITUTS IN LONDON. **Main/Corp** Deutsches Historisches Institut, London. **VFOAT** Veroffentlichungen; Publications of the German Historical Institute in London. Began with 1, 1975. Periodical. German. ir. Klett-Cotta Verlagsgemeinschft, PO Box 106016, D 70049 Stuttgart Germany. **Tel** 011 49 711 66720. **UDC** 940.

GW
VEROFFENTLICHUNGEN DES STAATSARCHIVS POTSDAM. **Added/Corp**
Staatsarchiv Potsdam. (1968)-. Monographic series. German. ir. Price varies per volume. Verlag Hermann Boehlaus Nachfolger, Postfach 260, D 99403 Weimar Germany. **Tel** 011 49 3643 2071, . **ED** Friedrich Bech. **LC** UNC. **Continues** Veroffentlichungen Des Brandenburgischen Landeshauptarchivs.
Desc: Based on the Potsdam public-record offices' archives, refers to the bibliographical data, local lexica, reference issues which pertain to the Brandenburg history to the Prussian and German history.

AU/0379-0231
VEROFFENTLICHUNGEN DES TIROLER LANDESMUSEUM FERDINANDEUM. **Added/Corp** Tiroler Landesmuseum Ferdinandeum. (1965)-. Periodical. German. an. Tiroler Landesmuseum Ferdinand, 15 Museumstrasse, A 6020 Innsbruck Austria. **Tel** 011 43 512 59489. **LC** DB761; .I63. **DD** 934.64. **Continues** Veroffentlichungen des Museum Ferdinandeum in Innsbruck.
Ind/Abst BHA : Biblio. Hist. Art (19??-).

SZ/0505-3668
VERSAILLES PREGNY-CHAMBERY.
[VersaillesPregny-Chambery]. (1959)-. Periodical. French. qt.
Ind/Abst BHA : Biblio. Hist. Art.

History(General) —History of Europe

FR/0563-9786
VIA DOMITIA. *Ceased.* [Via domitia]. Vol. 1 (1954)-Ceased Vol. 30 (1984). French. sa. Faculte des Lettres / Toulouse, 56 rue du Taur, 31000 Toulouse France. **Tel** 23 07 50. **LC** DC607.1; .V5. **DD** 944/.8. **UDC** 944. cum. index.
Ind/Abst MLA Int. Bibl. Books Artic. Mod. Lang. Lit.

UN
VIATKA. Russian. 0.29rub. Volgo-Viatskoe Knizhnoe Izdatelstvo. **LC** DK511.K42; V5.

UK
VICTORIA HISTORY OF THE COUNTY OF GLOUCESTER. **VFOAT** Victoria History of the Counties of England. (19??-). English. ir. price varies per volume. Oxford University Press, Walton Street, Oxford OX2 6DP England. **Tel** 011 44 865 56767, FAX 011 44 865 267773, telex 837330 OXPRES G. **(Subscription address:** Oxford University Press / USA, Journals Marketing Department, Oxford University Press, 2001 Evans Road, Cary NC 27513.**)** Index available. available with illustrations.
Desc: English local history, county by county, place by place.

SP
VIDA VALENCIANA, LA. Spanish. F Domenech, Mar 31, Valencia Spain. **LC** DP302.V11; V5. **DD** 946/.763/082. **UDC** 930.85(467.3); 908.467.3.

BE/0042-5648
VIE WALLONNE. (LA VIE WALLONNE.). [Vie Wallonne]. Vol. 1 (Sept. 1920)-. Periodical. French. qt. 600F. **ED** Jean Servais. **Bk Rev. Ad Acc. Circ:** 500.
Desc: History of Wallonia, ethnography, folklore, French and dialect literature of Wallonia, fine arts, music, criticism, biography, etc.
Ind/Abst BHA : Biblio. Hist. Art; MLA Int. Bibl. Books Artic. Mod. Lang. Lit.; Numis. Lit.

FR/0988-1808
VIEUX MARLY, LE. (1932)-. Periodical. French. an. **UDC** 908 (443.62).
Ind/Abst BHA : Biblio. Hist. Art.

DK/0108-8408
VIKING COLLECTION, THE. (1983)-. Monographic series. English. ir. Price varies per volume. Odense University Press, 55 Campusvej, DK-5230 Odense M Denmark. **Tel** 66 15 79 99, FAX 66 15 81 26.
Desc: Studies in northern civilization.

NO/0332-608X
VIKING (OSLO). (VIKING.). [Viking]. **Added/Corp** Norsk arkeologisk selskap. Vol. 1 (1937)-. Norwegian. an. Norsk Arkeologisk Selskap, Huk Aveny 35, 0287 Oslo 2 Norway. **LC** DL1; .V54.
Ind/Abst Avery Index Archit. Period. Suppl. Colum. Univ. (19??-199?); Br. Archaeol. Bibliogr.

SP/0042-6164
VILLA DE MADRID : REVISTA DEL EXMO. AYUNTAMIENTO. **Added/Corp** Madrid (Spain). Ayuntamiento. Vol. 1, No. 1 (1957)-. Periodical. Spanish. qt. **LC** DP350; .V55. **DD** 946/.4101.
Ind/Abst BHA : Biblio. Hist. Art.

UK/0264-5564
VINAVER STUDIES IN FRENCH. **See** Literature.

SP
VISIONS DE GUERRA I DE RETAGUARDA. **VFOAT** Visiones de Guerra y de Retaguardia. Series A, No. 1 (April 24, 1937)-. Multiple languages (Catalan and Spanish). Les Punxes Peninsular, Escornalbou 12, Barcelona Spain. **LC** DP269.15; .V57. **DD** 946.081/022/2. **UDC** 946.088.2.

XR
VLASTIVEDNE LISTY. Vol. 1-. Czech. sa. 5.00 single issue. Pns, Ustredni Expedice Tisku, Kubanska 1539, 108 72 Ostrava, Opava Czech Republic. **LC** DB2500.S5; V53.

XO/0508-1976
VLASTIVEDNY CASOPIS. **Added/Corp** Slovensky Pamiatkovy Ustav, Bratislava. Vol. 1 (1952)-. Periodical. Czech (German; summaries and/or abstracts in Russian and German; table of contents in Russian and German). ir. kcs31.00. Artia Pegas Press Ltd., Palac Metro Narodni TR 25, 11000 Prague 1 Czech Republic. **Tel** 011 42 2 24196265 or 24196266, 24196266.
Ind/Abst BHA : Biblio. Hist. Art (19??-).

XR
VLASTIVEDNY VESTNIK MORAVSKY. **Added/Corp** Musejni Spolek v Brne. (Moravskii Stranovedcheskii Biulleten; Mahrische Heimatkundliche Mitteilungen.). Vol. 1 (1946)-. Periodical. Czech (summaries and/or abstracts in German and Russian). Three times a year. $61.10. Artia Pegas Press Ltd., Palac Metro Narodni TR 25, 11000 Prague 1 Czech Republic. **Tel** 011 42 2 24196265 or 24196266, 24196266. **LC** DB541; .V53. cum. index.
Ind/Abst BHA : Biblio. Hist. Art (19??-).

RM
VOLK UND KULTUR : ZEITSCHRIFT DES RATES FUER KULTUR UND SOZIALISTISCHE ERZIEHUNG. **Added/Corp** Consiliul Central al Sindicatelor din Republica Populara Romina. Romania. Ministerul Invatamintului si Culturii. (19??)-. Periodical. German. mo. **(Subscription address:** Ilexim Press Department, PO Box 1, 136-1-137, Bucharest, Romania.**) LC** AP33; .V64. **DD** 949.8/005.

GW
VOLKSBOTE; UNABHANGIGE WOCHENZEITUNG DER VERTRIEBENEN (MICROFICHE). (VOLKSBOTE; UNABHANGIGE WOCHENZEITUNG DER VERTRIEBENEN.). Periodical. German. wk. Verlag Athesia, Via Museo 42, I 39100 Bolzano Italy. **LC** MICROFILM 03027DJK; DJK28.G4.

BW
VOPROSY ISTORII. **Added/Corp** Belaruski Dziarzhauny Universitet Imia Ul. I. Lenina Minski Pedahahichny Instytut. (1974)-. Periodical. Russian. Izdatelstvo Bagu Im V I Lenina, Ulitsa Kirova 24, Minsk Byelarus. **LC** DK507.A2; V66.
Ind/Abst Soc. Sci. Cit. Index [Select. Cov.].

GW/0537-7927
VORTRAGE. **Main/Corp** Institut fuer Europaische Geschichte (Mainz, Germany). No. 1 (1954)-. Monographic series. German. ir. Price varies per volume. Franz Steiner Verlag GmbH, Postfach 101061, D 70009 Stuttgart Germany. **Tel** 011 49 0711 2582372, FAX 011 49 0711 2582290, telex 723636 daz d. **ED** Karl Otmar Freiherr von Aretin.
Desc: Publication of papers read at the Mainz Institute for European History at Mainz.

●RU
VOSKRESENIE. **VFOAT** New Russia. (1992)-. Periodical. Russian. mo. $79.95. **(Subscription address:** East View Publications Inc., 3020 Harbor Lane North, Suite 110, Minneapolis MN 55447.**) LC** DK226.A2; S57. **Continues** VD Voskresenie.

YU/0507-4428
VRANJSKI GLASNIK. **Added/Corp** Vranje, Serbia, Narodni Muzej. (1965)-. Serbo-Croatian (Roman) (summaries and/or abstracts in English, French and German). an. **LC** DR381.V69; V7.
Ind/Abst BHA : Biblio. Hist. Art.

GR
VYZANTINOS DOMOS. **VFOAT** Domus Byzantinus. Vol. 1 (1987)-. Periodical. Greek, Modern (English and French). an. Domus Editions, 16 Mavromichali Street, 106 80 Athens Greece. **LC** DF552; .V93.

XR/0862-2930
VYZKUMY V CECHACH. **Added/Corp** Archeologicky Ustav (Ceskoslovenska Akademie ved). (1969)-. Czech. an. **LC** DB200; .V97. **Supersedes** Ceskoslovenska Akademie Ved. Archeologicky Ustav. Zachranne Oddeleni. Bulletin Zachranneho Oddeleni.
Ind/Abst BHA : Biblio. Hist. Art.

XR/0231-956X
VYZKUMY V CECHACH. SUPPLEMENTUM. [Vyzk. Cech., Suppl.]. (1974)-. Multiple languages. ir. **UDC** 902.
Ind/Abst BHA : Biblio. Hist. Art.

GW
WAIBLINGEN IN VERGANGENHEIT UND GEGENWART. **Added/Corp** Heimatverein Waiblingen. (19??)-. German. W Glassner, Postfach 72, Waiblingen 705 Germany. **LC** DD901.W2; W34.
Ind/Abst BHA : Biblio. Hist. Art.

CN/1180-2901
WANDERING VOLHYNIANS. [Wander. Volhynians]. **Added/Corp** Society for Ancestral Research of Germans from Poland and Volhynia. (Mar. 1989)-. Periodical. English. qt. $15.00. Ewald Wuschke, 3492 West 39th Avenue, Vancouver, British Columbia, V6N 3A2 Canada. **Tel** (604)263-3458. **DD** 947.718/00431. Index available. cum. index. **Bk Rev. Circ:** 600 (ctrl) **Continues** Volhynian Newsletter., 1186-7434.

UK
WARWICKSHIRE HISTORY. **Added/Corp** Warwickshire Local History Society. Vol 1 (Spring 1969)-. Periodical. English. sa (Summer & Winter). £1.75. Warwickshire Local History Society, 28 Lillinton Road, Leamington Spa CV35 5YY United Kingdom. **Tel** 011 44 12303 524495. **LC** DA670.W3; W388. **DD** 914.24/8/0305.

UK/0043-2431
WELSH HISTORY REVIEW. (THE WELSH HISTORY REVIEW. CYLCHGRAWN HANES CYMRU.). [Welsh hist. rev.]. **Added/Corp** University of Wales. Board of Celtic Studies. History and Law Committee. **VFOAT** Cylchgrawn Hanes Cymru. Vol. 1 (1960)-. Periodical. English (Welsh). qt (4 issues). Price varies. University of Wales Press, 6 Gwennyth Street, Cathays Cardiff CF2 4YD Wales United Kingdom. **Tel** 011 44 222 231919. **ED** Kenneth O. Morgan. **LC** DA700; .W468. Index available (Free). **Bk Rev. Ad Acc. Circ:** 500. available on microfilm from University Microfilms International (UMI). Documents available from The Genuine Article.
Desc: An invaluable medium for publishing the fruits of the steady upsurge of interest in the history of Wales.
Ind/Abst Am. Hist. Life (1973-); Arts Humanit. Citation Index [Full Cov.]; BHA : Biblio. Hist. Art; Br. Archaeol. Bibliogr.; Br. Humanit. Index; Curr. Contents Arts Humanit.; MLA Int. Bibl. Books Artic. Mod. Lang. Lit.; Res. Alert [Full Cov.]; Soc. Sci. Cit. Index [Select. Cov.].

US/0084-2338
WESTERN EUROPE (WASHINGTON, D.C.: 1982). (WESTERN EUROPE.). [West. Eur.]. (1982)-. Periodical. English. an. $16.50. Stryker-Post Publications, PO Drawer 1200, Harpers Ferry WV 25425. **Tel** (800)995-1400. **ED** Wayne C. Thompson. **LC** D901; .W47. **DD** 940/.05. ctrl circ.
Desc: One of seven titles focusing on current events. A reference addressing social, economic, political, and controversial issues.

GW/0083-9043
WESTFAELISCHE ZEITSCHRIFT. [Westfael. Z.]. **Added/Corp** Verein fuer Geschichte und Altertumskunde Westfaelens. Vol. 87 (1930)-. German. an. DM52.00 Germany; DM56.00 other. Bonifatius GmbH, Karl Schruz Strasse 26, D 33100 Paderborn Germany. **Tel** 011 49 5251 153171. **LC** DD491.W4; V3. **DD** 943/.56/005. **Continues** Zeitschrift fuer Vaterlandische Geschichte und Altertumskunde.
Ind/Abst Bibliogr. Carto.; BHA : Biblio. Hist. Art.

GW/0043-4337
WESTFALEN (MUNSTER). (WESTFALEN; HEFTE FUER GESCHICHTE, KUNST UND VOLKSKUNDE.). [Westfalen]. **Added/Corp** Verein fur Geschichte und Altertumskunde Westfalens. Vol. 1 (1909)-. German. an. DM90.00. Aschendorffsche Verlagsbuchhandlung, Postfach 1124, D-48135 Muenster Germany. **Tel** 011 49 251 690132, telex 08-92 830 WN MS D. **ED** Bernard Korzus. **LC** DD491.W4; V28. **Bk Rev. Ad Acc.**
Desc: History, art and folklore of the West German area of Westphalia. Includes care of monuments, historical finds, many illustrations and maps.
Ind/Abst Art Archaeol. Tech. Abstr.; BHA : Biblio. Hist. Art.

GW/0083-9027
WESTFALISCHE FORSCHUNGEN. [Westfal. Forsch.]. **Added/Corp** Provinzialinstitut fur Westfalische Landes- und Volkskunde. (1938)-. German. an. **LC** DD491.W4; W45.
Ind/Abst Bibliogr. Carto.; BHA : Biblio. Hist. Art.

GW
WESTPREUSSE, DER. Periodical. German. German Language Publications Inc, 560 Sylvan Avenue, Englewood Cliffs NJ 07632. **Tel** (201)871-1010. **LC** DD491.08; W45.

GW/0511-8484
WESTPREUSSEN-JAHRBUCH. **Added/Corp** Landsmannschaft Westpreussen. (1950)-. German. an. DM28.00. Westpreussen-Verlag Muenster, Norbertstr. 29-, 4400 Meunster, Germany. **Tel** 0251-523424, FAX 0251-533830. **ED** Hans-Juergen Schuch. **Ad Acc.** available on an online database.
Ind/Abst BHA : Biblio. Hist. Art.

BE
WETENSCHAPPELIJKE TIJDINGEN. Vol. 1 (1940)-. Academic Scholarly Publication. Dutch. qt. 720.00F. Wetenschappelijke Tydingen, Congreslaan 40, 9000 Gent Belgium. **Tel** 011 32 91 211935. **ED** G. DeSmet. **Bk Rev. Ad Acc. Circ:** 550. Documents available from CASDDS. **Continues** Wetenschap in Vlaanderen.
Desc: History of the Flemish movement.
Ind/Abst Chem. Abstr.; MLA Int. Bibl. Books Artic. Mod. Lang. Lit.

GW/0509-6213
WETTERAUER GESCHICHTSBLAETTER. **Added/Corp** Friedberger Geschichtsverein. Heimatverein Bad Nauheim. Geschichtsverein fur Butzbach und Umgebung. (1909)-. Monographic series. German. an. Bibliothekszentrum Klosterbau, Augustinergasse 8, 01169 Friedberg (Hessen) Germany. **Tel** 06031-88277, FAX 06031-18396. **ED** M. Keller. Index available. **Bk Rev. Circ:** 700.
Ind/Abst BHA : Biblio. Hist. Art.

UK
WHITLOCK'S WESSEX. 1- 1975-. English. an. $2.95. **LC** DA670.W48; W45. **DD** 942.2. **UDC** 942.2.

PL
WIEK OSWIECENIA. **Added/Corp** Uniwersytet Warszawski. (1978)-. Periodical. Polish. **LC** DK4314.5; .W53.

AU
WIENER ARCHIV FUR GESCHICHTE DES SLAWENTUMS UND OSTEUROPAS. **Added/Corp** Vienna. Universitat. Institut fur Osteuropaische Geschichte und Sudostforschung. Vol. 1 (1955)-. Monographic series. German. ir. Price varies per volume. Boehlaus Verlag GmbH & Company KG, Sachsenplatz 4 6 PF 87, A 1201 Vienna Austria. **Tel** 011 43 1 3302427.

AU/0043-5317
WIENER GESCHICHTSBLATTER. [Wien. Gesch.bl.]. Vol. 1 1946-. Periodical. German. qt. S240.00 (add S80.00 for postage). Verein Geschichte Stadt Wien, Stadt und Landesarchiv, 1 Rathaus, A-1082 Vienna Austria. **Tel** 0222/4000/84811. **LC** DB841; .V36. Index available. cum. index. **Bk Rev. Ad Acc.** ***Supersedes*** *Nachrichtenblatt -Verein fur Geschichte der Stadt Wien.*
Ind/Abst Am. Hist. Life (1955-).

AU
WIENER STUDIEN. **Added/Corp** Osterreichische Akademie der Wissenschaften. Vol. 1 (1967)-. Periodical. German (Latin). an. S700.00. Oesterreichischen Akademie Wissenschaften, Dr. Ignaz Seipel Platz 2, A-1010 Vienna Austria. **Tel** 011 43 1 51581. **Bk Rev. Ad Acc. Circ:** 500. ***Supersedes*** *Wiener Studien; Zeitschrift fuer Klassische Philologie.*
Desc: Classical philology, history of the church, history of the ancient world.

UK/0308-6321
WINCHESTER CATHEDRAL RECORD. [Winchester Cathedral rec.]. (1932)-. Periodical. English. an.
Ind/Abst BHA : Biblio. Hist. Art.

NE
WINKLER PRINS JAARBOEK. 1970-. Academic Scholarly Publication. Dutch. ir. $25.60. Elsevier Science Publishing Company Inc, Madison Square Station, PO Box 882, New York NY 10159-0882. **Tel** (212)633-3950, FAX (212)633-3990. ***Continues*** *Winkler Prins Boek van Het Jaar.*

SZ/0508-8410
WINTERTHURER JAHRBUCH. **Added/Corp** Winterthur, Switzerland. Bibliothekamt. Winterthur (Switzerland) Amt fur Kulturelles. (19??)-. Periodical. German. Amt fur Kulturelles der Stadt Winterthur, Sruckerei Winterthur Ag, Winterthur Switzerland. **LC** DQ851.W63; W56. **DD** 949.4/5.
Ind/Abst BHA : Biblio. Hist. Art; Numis. Lit.

PL/0043-7182
WOJSKOWY PRZEGLAD HISTORYCZNY. [Wojs. prz. hist.]. Vol. 1 (Oct./Dec. 1956)-. Periodical. Polish (summaries and/or abstracts in French and Russian; table of contents in Russian and French). qt. $46.00. **(Subscription address:** ARS Polona, PO Box 1001, 00068 Warsaw Poland.) **LC** DK417; .W6. cum. index.
Ind/Abst Am. Hist. Life (1960-1963); Curr. Mil. Pol. Lit.

GW/0724-956X
WOLFENBUTTELER ABHANDLUNGEN ZUR RENAISSANCEFORSCHUNG. **Added/Corp** Herzog August Bibliothek. Wolfenbutteler Arbeitskreis fur Renaissanceforschung. (1981)-. Monographic series. German. Dr. Ernst Hauswedell & Co. Verlag, Rosenbergstrasse 113, D 70193 Stuttgart Germany. **Tel** 011 49 711 638265.
Ind/Abst BHA : Biblio. Hist. Art.

GW/0342-4340
WOLFENBUTTELER RENAISSANCE MITTEILUNGEN. Vol. 1- ; July 1977-. Academic Scholarly Publication. German. Three times a year. DM54.00. Otto Harrassowitz Verlag, Taunusstrasse 14, Postfach 2929, D-65019 Wiesbaden Germany. **Tel** 011 49 611 5300, FAX 530570, telex 4186 135 OH D. **ED** August Buck. **UDC** 940.21. **[CCC]. Bk Rev. Ad Acc. Circ:** 500.
Desc: Brief reviews of important new scholarly publications in the field of international Renaissance research, short articles on research roundtables, reports on institutions and meetings, bibliographic notices, announcements of research projects.

US/0732-2674
WORKING PAPERS IN IRISH STUDIES. (WORKING PAPERS IN IRISH STUDIES / IRISH STUDIES COMMITTEE, NORTHEASTERN UNIVERSITY.). [Work. pap. Ir. stud.]. **VFOAT** Working Papers. 83-1-. Monographic series. English. ir. Price varies per volume. Working Papers in Irish Studies, 236 Huntington Avenue, Northeastern University, Boston MA 02115. **Tel** (617)437-2907. **ED** James E Doan and Ruth-Ann M Harris. **UDC** 908.415. Index available. **Bk Rev. Circ:** 75 (ctrl).
Desc: The series, working papers in Irish studies, encompasses the entire field of Irish and Irish-American studies, including history, literature, folklore, sociology, psychology and politics.

●US/1063-1259
WORLDWIDE GOVERNMENT DIRECTORY, REGIONAL EDITION. THE FORMER SOVIET BLOC. **VFOAT** Former Soviet Bloc; Worldwide Government Directory. (1992)-. Directory. English. $95.00. Belmont Publications, 7979 Old Georgetown Road, Bethesda MS 20814. **Tel** (301)718-8770.

IE
WRITINGS ON IRISH HISTORY (PRINT COPY). (WRITINGS ON IRISH HISTORY.). **Added/Corp** Irish Committee of Historical Sciences. (1984)-. English. an. Irish Historical Studies, Department of Modern History, 265 History Street, Trinity College, Dublin 2 Ireland. **Tel** 011 353 1 7021020. **LC** Z2041; .W75; DA910. **DD** 016.9415. ***Continues*** *Writings on Irish History.*

MX
XALOC. Periodical. Catalan (Catalan). $5.00. Uraguay 40-202, Mexico DF Mexico. **LC** DP302.C57; X35. **UDC** 972.
Ind/Abst Am. Hist. Life (1966-1981).

IS/0084-3296
YAD VASHEM STUDIES. [Yad Vashem stud.]. **Added/Corp** Yad Va-shem, Rashut Ha-zikaron La-Shoah Vela-gevurah. (1976)-. Academic Scholarly Publication. English (Hebrew). an. £45.00 (latest volume). Yad Vashem Publications Department, PO Box 3477, Mount Herzl, Jerusalem 91034 Israel. **Tel** 011-972-2-531202. **(Subscription address:** Rubin Mass Ltd., PO Box 990, Jerusalem 91009 Israel.) **ED** Aharon Weiss. **LC** DS135.E83; Y3. **DD** 940.53/15/03924. **[CCC].** Index available. **Circ:** 1,000. available on microfilm and microfiche from University Microfilms International (UMI). ***Continues*** *Yad Vashem Studies on the European Jewish Catastrophe and Resistance, 0792-3333.*
Desc: A yearbook containing important scholarly contributions to the study of the Holocaust.
Ind/Abst Am. Hist. Life (1967-).

US/0044-0078
YALE FRENCH STUDIES. [Yale Fr. stud.]. (1948)-. Periodical. English. Twice a year (Spring and Fall). $37.00. Yale University Press, PO Box 209040, New Haven CT 06520. **Tel** (203)432-0940, (800)987-7323, FAX (203)432-0948. **LC** DC1; .Y3. **DD** 944/.005. available on microfilm and microfiche from University Microfilms International (UMI). Documents available from The Genuine Article, UMI Article Clearinghouse.
Desc: Provides a conduit for French thought in its most adventurous manifestations.
Ind/Abst Acad. Abstr. Full Text Elite (Jan. 1991-); Acad. Abstr. (Jan. 1991-); Acad. Ind. [Computer File] (1987-); Acad. Search (Jan. 1991-); Annu. Bibliogr. Engl. Lang. Lit.; Arts Humanit. Citation Index (19??-19??) [Full Cov.]; BHA : Biblio. Hist. Art; Curr. Contents Arts Humanit.; Expand. Acad. Index (1987-); Humanit. Index; Humanit. Source (Jul. 1990-); INFO-SOUTH Abstr.; Mag. Search; MLA Int. Bibl. Books Artic. Mod. Lang. Lit.; Newsp. Period. Abstr. (1991-); Res. Alert [Full Cov.]; Romant. Move.; Soc. Plann. Policy Dev. Abstr.; Soc. Sci. Cit. Index [Select. Cov.]; Soc. Sci. Index.

US/0084-3334
YALE GERMANIC STUDIES. ***Ceased.*** [Yale Ger. stud.]. **Added/Corp** Yale University. (1964)-(19??). Monographic series. English. ir. Yale University Press, PO Box 209040, New Haven CT 06520. **Tel** (203)432-0940, (800)987-7323, FAX (203)432-0948. **DD** 943.
Ind/Abst MLA Int. Bibl. Books Artic. Mod. Lang. Lit.

US/0149-7219
YEARBOOK OF ROMANIAN STUDIES. [Yearb. Romanian stud.]. No. 1- 1976-. Periodical. English. an. $5.00. University of South Florida / Department of Foreign Languages, c/o Edward J. Neugaard, Tampa FL 33620. **LC** DR201; .Y4. **DD** 949.8/03/05. **UDC** 949.8; 908.498.
Ind/Abst MLA Int. Bibl. Books Artic. Mod. Lang. Lit.

UK
YETMINSTER LOCAL HISTORY SOCIETY. **Added/Corp** Yetminster Local History Society. No. 1, (1987)-. Monographic series. English. ir. Price varies per volume.

YU/0044-1341
YUGOSLAV SURVEY. Vol. 1 (Apr. 1960)-. Periodical. English (Serbian). Four times a year. $42.00. Promimpro Export and Imports Limited, 66 Makarios 111 Cronos Court, Office 44 Nicosia Cyprus. **Tel** 011 357 21 360411, FAX 011 357 21 365072. **ED** Jugoslovenski Pregled (editor's phone: 38 111 333 610). **LC** DR301; .Y85. Index available in last issue of volume--attached (Nov.). cum. index. **Ad Acc, Adv Mgr:** Gordana Maljkovic. ctrl circ.
Ind/Abst Int. Labour Doc.; LABORDOC; Seed Abstr.; World Agric. Econ.

YU
ZAJEDNICA KULTURE. (19??)-. Serbo-Croatian (Cyrillic). Republicka Zajednica Kulture, Nemanjina 24/III, Belgrad Yugoslavia. **LC** DR370; .R46a.

PL/0044-1791
ZAPISKI HISTORYCZNE. **Main/Corp** Towarzystwo Naukowe w Toruniu. Wydzia nauk Historycznych. **Added/Corp** Towarzystwo Naukowe w Toruniu. Wydzia Nauk Historycznych, Prawniczych i Spoecznych. Towarzystwo Naukowe w Toruniu. Zapiski. (1908)-. Periodical. Polish (English, German and Russian; summaries and/or abstracts in French and English). qt. Price on Request. **(Subscription address:** ARS Polona, PO Box 1001, 00068 Warsaw Poland.) cum. index.
Ind/Abst Am. Hist. Life (1979-).

US/0510-3746
ZAPISY BELARUSKAHA INSTYTUTU NAVUKI I MASTATSVA. **Added/Corp** Byelorussian Institute of Arts and Sciences (New York, N.Y.). **VFOAT** Zapisy. Vol. 1 (1952)-. Periodical. Byelorussian (English; table of contents in German). an. $30.00. Byelorussian Institute Arts Science, 230 Springfield Avenue, Rutherford NJ 07070. **LC** DK507.A2; W5.
Ind/Abst MLA Int. Bibl. Books Artic. Mod. Lang. Lit.

XO/0139-5378
ZBORNIK SLOVENSKEHO NARODNEHO MUZEA. HISTORIA. ANNALES MUSEI NATIONALIS SLOVACI. **Main/Corp** Slovenske Narodne Muzeum. **Added/Corp** Slovenske Narodne Muzeum. Annales. **VFOAT** Historia. (196?)-. English (French, Russian and Slovak; summaries and/or abstracts in German). an. **LC** DB661; .B72. ***Continues*** *Slovenske Narodne Muzeum. Sbornik Slovenskeho Narodne Muzea. Historia.*
Ind/Abst BHA : Biblio. Hist. Art.

XO
ZBORNIK UNIVERZITY KOMENSKEHO. HISTORICA. **Added/Corp** Univerzita Komenskeho v Bratislave. **VFOAT** Historica; Zbornik Filozofickej Fakulty. Historica. Vol. 34 (1983)-. Slovak (summaries and/or abstracts in Russian and German; table of contents in German and Russian). Slovenske Pedagogicke Nakladetelstvo, Sasinkova 5, 891 12 Bratislava, Slovakia. **ED** Jan Hucko. **LC** DB2700; .B7a. **Circ:** 600 (ctrl). ***Continues*** *Zbornik Ustavu Marxizmu-Leninizmu a Filozofickej Fakulty Univerzity Komenskeho. Historica.*

XV/0351-224X
ZBORNIK ZA UMETNOSTNO ZGODOVINO. ARCHIVES D'HISTOIRE DE L'ART. **Added/Corp** Umetnostno Zgodovinsko Drustvo. **VFOAT** Archives d'Histoire de l'Art. (1921)-(1944); New Series (1951)-. Serbo-Croatian (Roman) (French).
Ind/Abst BHA : Biblio. Hist. Art.

YU/0514-616X
ZBORNIK ZASTITE SPOMENIKA KULTURE. RECUEIL DES TRAVAUX SUR LA PROTECTION DES MONUMENTS HISTORIQUES. **See** The Arts-Art.

CI/0351-2681
ZBORNIK ZAVODA ZA POVIJESNE ZNANOSTI ISTRAZIVACKOG CENTRA JUGOSLAVENSKE AKADEMIJE ZNANOSTI I UMJETNOSTI. Vol. 9-. Periodical. Serbo-Croatian (Roman) (summaries and/or abstracts in German). Hrvatska Akademija Znanosti i Umjetnosti / Croatian Academy of Sciences & Arts, Zrinski TRG 11, 41000 Zagreb Croatia. **Tel** 011 38 41 433 661, FAX 011 38 41 433 383. **LC** DR301; .J82. **DD** 949.7/005. **UDC** 949.71. ***Continues*** *Zbornik Historijskog Zavoda Jugoslavenske Akademije Znanosti I Umjetnosti.*
Ind/Abst Am. Hist. Life (1974-).

GW/0065-0137
ZEITSCHRIFT DES AACHENER GESCHICHTSVEREINS. [Z. Aachen. Geschichtsver.]. **Main/Corp** Aachener Geschichtsverein. Vol. 1 (1879)-. German. an. DM30.00. Aachener Geschichtsverein E V, Fischmarkt 3, W-5100 Aachen Germany. **Tel** (0241)4324502-09. **ED** Herbert Lepper. cum. index. **Bk Rev. Circ:** 1,300 (ctrl).
Desc: Journal of the Historic Society of Aachen, West Germany.
Ind/Abst BHA : Biblio. Hist. Art; Numis. Lit.

GW
ZEITSCHRIFT DES BREISGAU-GESCHICHTSVEREINS SCHAUINSLAND. **Main/Corp** Breisgau-Geschichtsverein Schauinsland. (19??)-. Periodical. German. an. Breisgau-Geschichtsverein, Schauinsland, Freiburg Im Breisgau, Grunwalderstrasse 15, D 79098 Freiburg Germany. **LC** DD801.B11; S3. **DD** 943/.46. ***Continues*** *Schau-In's-Land.*

GW
ZEITSCHRIFT DES VEREINS FUER HESSISCHE GESCHICHTE UND LANDESKUNDE. **Main/Corp** Verein fur Hessische Geschichte und Landeskunde. Vol. 1 (1837)-. German. ir. Verein Hess Gesch Landeskunde, Brueder Grimm Pl 4A,

D 34117 Kassel Germany. **Tel** 011 49 561 8047334. **LC** DD491.H6; V3. **DD** 943/.41/005. cum. index.
Ind/Abst Numis. Lit.

GW/0083-5609
ZEITSCHRIFT DES VEREINS FUER LUBECKISCHE GESCHICHTE UND ALTERTUMSKUNDE. **Main/Corp** Verein fur Lubeckische Geschichte und Altertumskunde. Vol. 1 (1855)-. German. an. DM48.00. Max Schmidt Romhild, Mengstr 16, Funfhausen 27-31, 24 Lubeck 1 Germany. **Tel** (0451)1605-1. cum. index. **Bk Rev**.
Desc: A publication of a private club in Luebeck. Activities, studies and remarks about Luebeck.
Ind/Abst BHA : Biblio. Hist. Art; Numis. Lit.

GW/0044-2356
ZEITSCHRIFT FUER BALKANOLOGIE. [Z. Balkanol.]. Vol. 1 (1962)-. German (English, French and Italian). Twice a year. Price varies. Otto Harrassowitz Verlag, Taunusstrasse 14, Postfach 2929, D-65019 Wiesbaden Germany. **Tel** 011 49 611 5300, FAX 530570, telex 4186 135 OH D. **ED** Rudolf Trofenik. **LC** DR1; .Z385. **DD** 949.6/005. **[CCC]**. Index available. **Bk Rev**. **Ad Acc**.
Desc: The study and history of Balkan countries.
Ind/Abst BHA : Biblio. Hist. Art; MLA Int. Bibl. Books Artic. Mod. Lang. Lit.

GW/0044-2364
ZEITSCHRIFT FUER BAYERISCHE LANDESGESCHICHTE. [Z. bayer. Landesgesch.]. **Added/Corp** Gesellschaft fuer Frankische Geschichte. Bayerische Akademie der Wissenschaften. Kommission fuer Bayerische Landesgeschichte. (1928)-. Periodical. German. tq. DM96.00. CH Beck Verlagsbuchhandlung, D 80791 Munich Germany. **Tel** 011 49 89 381891. **LC** DD801.B31; Z4.
Ind/Abst Am. Hist. Life (1988-); Bibliogr. Carto.; BHA : Biblio. Hist. Art.

GW/0513-9058
ZEITSCHRIFT FUER DIE GESCHICHTE DER SAARGEGEND. **Added/Corp** Historischer Verein fur die Saargegend. Saarland (1947-) Landesarchiv. (1951)-. German. an. **LC** DD801.S13; Z4.
Ind/Abst BHA : Biblio. Hist. Art.

GW
ZEITSCHRIFT FUER DIE GESCHICHTE DES OBERRHEINS. **Added/Corp** Landesarchiv zu Karlsruhe. Grossherzogliches General-Landesarchiv zu Karlsruhe. Badische Historische Kommission. Oberrheinische Historische Kommission. Badisches General-Landesarchiv. Kommission fur Geschichtliche Landeskunde in Baden-Wurttemberg. Vol. 1 (1850)-. German. an. W Kohlhammer Verlag GmbH, Postfach 800430, D 70549 Stuttgart Germany. **Tel** 011 49 711 78631, FAX 011 49 711 7863263, telex 7-255820. **LC** DD801.B11; B2. **DD** 943/.4. cum. index.
Desc: Journal for the history of the Upper Rhine region.
Ind/Abst Am. Hist. Life (1989-); BHA : Biblio. Hist. Art; Numis. Lit.

GW/0044-2976
ZEITSCHRIFT FUER KULTURAUSTAUSCH. [Z. Kult.austausch]. **Added/Corp** Institut fuer Auslandsbeziehungen. Vol. 12, No. 2/3 (1962)-. Periodical. German. Four times a year. DM40.00. Institut fuer Auslandsbeziehungen, Postfach 102463, 70020 Stuttgart Germany. **Tel** 011 49 711 2225112. **LC** DD68; .I6. **DD** 943/.005. ***Continues*** *Institut fuer Auslandsbeziehungen. Mitteilungen.*
Ind/Abst Foreign Lang. Index; Writ. Am. Hist.

GW/0044-3239
ZEITSCHRIFT FUER OSTFORSCHUNG. [Z. Ostforsch.]. **Added/Corp** Johann Gottfried Herder-Forschungsrat. Vol. 1 (1952)-. Periodical. German (summaries and/or abstracts in English). qt (Mar., June, Sept., Dec.). DM98.00 Germany; DM110.00 other. Johann Gottfried Herder Institut, Gisonenweg 5-7, H-35037 Marburg, Lahn Germany. **Tel** 011 49 6421 1840, FAX 011 49 6421 184139. **ED** Winfried Irgang. **LC** DR1; .Z4. cum. index. **Bk Rev. Circ:** 750.
Desc: Research on countries and peoples of Eastern Central Europe.
Ind/Abst Am. Hist. Life (1954-); Bibliogr. Carto.; BHA : Biblio. Hist. Art; MLA Int. Bibl. Books Artic. Mod. Lang. Lit.

GW/0344-3418
ZEITSCHRIFT FUER SIEBENBURGISCHE LANDESKUNDE. [Z. Siebenb. Landeskd.]. **Added/Corp** Arbeitskreis fuer Siebenburgische Landeskunde. Vol. 1 (1978)-. Periodical. German. sa. DM42.00. Arbeitskreis fuer Siebenburgische Landeskunde e. V., Schlob Horneck, D-74831 Gundelsheim Neckar Germany. **Tel** 0049 6269 8476, FAX 0049 6269 8397. **ED** Konrad G. Guenoisch and Harald Roth. **LC** DR279.92.G4; Z44. **DD** 949.8/4. Index available (1970-1990). **Bk Rev. Acid Free. Circ:** 850 (ctrl). Documents available from FAXON Xpress. ***Supersedes*** *Arbeitskreis fuer Siebenburgische Landeskunde. Korrespondenzblatt.*

GW/0044-3786
ZEITSCHRIFT FUER WURTTEMBERGISCHE LANDESGESCHICHTE. [Z. Wurttemb. Landesgesch.]. (1937)-. Periodical. German. ir. W Kohlhammer Verlag GmbH, Postfach 800430, D 70549 Stuttgart Germany. **Tel** 011 49 711 78631, FAX 011 49 711 7863263, telex 7-255820. **LC** DD801.W6; Z4. **DD** 943/.47/005. ***Supersedes*** *Wurttembergische Vierteljahrshefte fur Landesgeschichte.*
Desc: Concerns ancient and modern history of the Baden-Wuerttemberg region.
Ind/Abst Am. Hist. Life (1971-); Bibliogr. Carto.; BHA : Biblio. Hist. Art.

GW
ZEITWEISER DER GALIZIENDEUTSCHEN. **Added/Corp** Hilfskomitee der Galiziendeutschen. (19??)-. German. DM10.00. Hilfskomitee der Galiziendeutschen, Stuttgart 50 Germany. **LC** DK4600.G3992; Z43.

FR/0044-4391
ZESZYTY HISTORYCZNE. No. 1- (1962)-. Periodical. Polish. qt. 330.00F Kultura subscribers, 360.00F non subscribers. Institut Litteraire, 91 Avenue de Poissy, Mesnil le Roi, 78600 Maisons Laffitte France. **Tel** 011 33 1 39621904, FAX 011 33 1 39625752. **LC** DK401. **Bk Rev. Circ:** 2,000.
Desc: Publishes articles on the modern history of Poland and East Europe.
Ind/Abst Am. Hist. Life (1970-).

PL/0084-5507
ZIEMIE ZACHODNIE. No. 1- 1957-. Polish. Instytut Zachodni, Poznan Poland.

CN/0227-2423
ZINOTAJS. [Zinotajs]. Began publication 196-. Periodical. Latvian (English and French). mo. 22.50Can$ Canada, (add 12.00Can$ for airmail postage) other. Montrealas Latviesi Biedribas, 291 Lorraine Drive, Baiedurfe Quebec H9X 2R2 Canada. **Tel** (514)457-9832. **ED** Martin Stauvers. **DD** 947/.43/005. **Bk Rev. Ad Acc. Circ:** 1,400 (ctrl).

US/0044-4901
ZNAMJA ROSSII. (ZNAMIA ROSSII.). **VFOAT** The Banner of Russia; Banner of Russia. No. 1- Sept. 1944-. Periodical. Russian. mo. Nicholas Chuhnov Publishing, 3544 Broadway, New York NY 10031. **LC** DK266.A2; Z6.

YU/0514-7867
ZOGRAF : CASOPIS ZA SREDNJOVEKOVNU UMETNOST. **Added/Corp** Galerija Fresaka u Beogradu. **VFOAT** Zographe. Vol. 1 (1966)-. Serbo-Croatian (Cyrillic) (summaries and/or abstracts in French). **LC** N5950; .Z6.
Ind/Abst BHA : Biblio. Hist. Art.

HISTORY OF NORTH, SOUTH, AND CENTRAL AMERICA

US/1046-1671
1992 LECTURE SERIES WORKING PAPERS. [1992 Lect. Ser. work. pap.]. **Added/Corp** University of Maryland, College Park. Dept. of Spanish and Portuguese. **VFOAT** 1992 Lecture Series. No. 1 (1998)-. Monographic series. English (Spanish). Price varies per volume. University of Maryland Department of Spanish and Portuguese, N. Levinson, 2215 Jinenez Hall, College Park MD 20742. **Tel** (301)454-4305. **LC** IN PROCESS. **DD** 970.

PE
ABC. Periodical. Spanish. .70 single issue. Distribucion Prosida SA, G Schereiber 290, Lima Peru. **LC** F3401; .A14. **DD** 985/.005. **UDC** 985.

CN/0044-5851
ACADIENSIS (FREDERICTON). (ACADIENSIS.). [Acadiensis]. **Added/Corp** University of New Brunswick. Dept. of History. Vol. 1 (Autumn 1971)-. Periodical. English (French). Twice a year (June, & Nov.). 21.00Can$ (individuals), 27.50Can$ (institutions) Canada. Acadiensis / University of New Brunswick / Campus House, PO Box 4400, Fredericton New Brunswick E3B 5A3 Canada. **Tel** (506)453-4978, FAX (506)453-4599. **ED** Gail Campbell. **LC** F1035.8; .A26. **[CCC]**. Index available. **Circ:** 900 (ctrl). available on microfilm. Documents available from The Genuine Article.
Desc: History of Atlantic Canada. Each issue includes original research, review articles, documents, notes and a running bibliography compiled by librarians in the four provinces.
Ind/Abst Am. Hist. Life (1971-?, 1973-)(1973-); Arts Humanit. Citation Index [Full Cov.]; Can. Index; Can. Period. Index; Curr. Contents Arts Humanit.; Res. Alert [Full Cov.]; Soc. Sci. Cit. Index [Select. Cov.].

US/0734-4546
ACSUS. CANADIAN STUDIES UPDATE. (CANADIAN STUDIES UPDATE / ACSUS.). [ACSUS, Can. stud. update]. **Added/Corp** Association for Canadian Studies in the United States. **VFOAT** ACSUS Canadian Studies Update. **VAT** Association for Canadian Studies in the United States Canadian Studies Update. Vol. 1, No. 1 (Fall 1982)-. Periodical. English (French). Twice a year. $110.00 (individuals), $200.00 (institutions). Association for Canadian Studies in the United States, One Dupont Circle, Suite 620, Washington DC 20036. **Tel** (202)887-6375, FAX (202)296-8379. **ED** Ellen Reisman Babby. **DD** 971/.007/073. ctrl circ. ***Continues*** *ACSUS Newsletter (1977).*
Desc: Newsletter including a listing of upcoming conferences relating to Canadian studies.

US/0892-7111
ACSUS MEMBERSHIP DIRECTORY. [ACSUS membsh. dir.]. **Main/Corp** Association for Canadian Studies in the United States. **VFOAT** Membership Directory. **VAT** Association for Canadian Studies in the United States Membership Directory. (1985)-. Directory. English. ir. $30.00 (individuals), $50.00 (institutions). Association for Canadian Studies in the United States, One Dupont Circle, Suite 620, Washington DC 20036. **Tel** (202)887-6375, FAX (202)296-8379. **ED** Ellen Reisman Babby. **LC** F1025; .A85a. **DD** 971/.0025/73. **Ad Acc. Circ:** 1,300 (ctrl).
Desc: A listing of ACSUS members by discipline, area of Canadian studies, alphabetically and by state.

US/0191-8664
ADENA. [Adena]. V. 1- Spring 1976-. Periodical. English. sa. $4.00. William E. Grant/Editor, Department of English, University of Louisville, Louisville KY 40208. **LC** F516; .A34. **DD** 977. **UDC** 977.
Ind/Abst Annu. Bibliogr. Engl. Lang. Lit.

US/0882-5297
AFRO-AMERICAN CULTURE SOCIETY MONOGRAPH SERIES. [CAAS monogr. ser.]. Periodical. English. ir. Center for Afro-American Studies, 3111 Campbell Hall, Los Angeles CA 90024. **Tel** (310)825-3528. **ED** Toni Leiteau. **DD** 973. **UDC** 973(96).
Desc: Contains books written by authors on issues reflecting to black people in the Western Hemisphere and the Caribbean.

●US/1055-7385
AFRO-AMERICAN HISTORY KIT (7TH GRADE AND ABOVE ED.). (AFRO-AMERICAN HISTORY KIT.). (1991)-. Periodical. English. Associated Publishers Incorporated, 1407 14th Street NW, Washington DC 20005. **Tel** (202)265-1441. ***Continues in part*** *Afro-American History Kit (Washington, D.C. : 1987).*

US/1055-7393
AFRO-AMERICAN HISTORY KIT (K-6 ED.). ***Ceased.*** **See** History(General)-History of Africa.

CN
AFRO CANADIAN. (19??)-. English. Twelve times a year. 20.00Can$. Negro Community Centre, PO Box 370, Station A, Montreal Quebec H3C 2T1 Canada. **Tel** (514)933-9013.

US/0065-857X
AHA PAMPHLETS. **Main/Corp** American Historical Association. (19??)-. Monographic series. English. ir. Price varies. American Historical Association, 400 A Street Southeast, Washington DC 20003. **Tel** (202)544-2422. ***Continues*** *American Historical Association. Publication.*

●US
AKWE:KON JOURNAL. **Added/Corp** Cornell University. American Indian Program. **VFOAT** Akwekon Journal; All of Us Journal. Vol. 9, No. 1 (Spring 1992)-. Periodical. English. Four times a year. $18.00 (individuals); $35.00 (institutions). AKWE- KON Press Cornell University, 400 Caldwell Hall, Ithaca NY 14853. **Tel** (607)255-4308, FAX (607)255-0185. **ED** Jose Barreiro and Susan Dixon. **LC** E78.E2; A494. **Bk Rev**, (Qty: varies). **Ad Acc, Adv Mgr:** Jennifer Bedell, **Tel** (607)255-4308. **Circ:** 2,500. ***Continues*** *Northeast Indian Quarterly, 0897-2354.*
Desc: Current and interesting topics dealing with Indians of the northeast. It provides in-depth examination of current issues as well as information about native American ideas, history, art, and traditions.
Ind/Abst Curr. Index J. Educ.

BL
AL-MARAHIL. **VFOAT** Etapas. Periodical. Arabic (Portuguese). mo. $100.00. Redacao e Administra Cao, rue Capote Valente No 65 Apt 3, Sao Paulo Brasil. **LC** F2659.L42; M37.

US/1056-2168
ALABAMA FACTS. [Ala. facts]. **VFOAT** Flying the Colors, Alabama Facts; Alabama Facts--Flying the Colors Series. (1991)-. English. ir. Price varies. Clements Research II Inc., 16850 Dallas Parkway, Dallas TX 75248. **Tel** (214)931-9956, FAX (214)248-7159. **LC** F321; .A159. **DD** 976.1.

US/0887-493X
ALABAMA HERITAGE. [Ala. herit.]. **Added/Corp** University of Alabama. No. 1 (Summer

1986)-. Periodical. English. Four times a year (Jan., Apr., July, Oct.). $16.95 one year; $28.95 two years; $38.95 three years. Alabama Heritage, University of Alabama, 24 Bryce Lawn, Tuscaloosa AL 35487-0342. **Tel** (205)348-7467, FAX (205)348-7473. **ED** Suzanne Wolfe. **LC** F326; .A545. **DD** 976.1/005. Index available. cum. index. **Ad Acc. Circ:** 15,000.
Desc: An magazine devoted to Alabama/Southern culture and history. Local, state, art, architecture, music, folklore, and literature are included.
Ind/Abst Am. Hist. Life (1989-); RILM Abstr.

US/0002-4341
ALABAMA REVIEW, THE. [Ala. rev.]. **Added/Corp** Alabama Historical Association. Vol. 1, No. 1 (Jan. 1948)-. Periodical. English. Four times a year. $25.00 (institutions); $20.00 (individuals) US, $25.00 (individuals) other. University of Alabama / School of Law, PO Box 870380, Tuscaloosa AL 35487-0380. **Tel** (205)348-1175. **ED** Sarah W. Wiggins. **LC** F321; .A2535. **DD** 976.1005. **[CCC].** Index available. **Bk Rev. Pr Rev. Circ:** 1,900. available on microfilm and microfiche from University Microfilms International (UMI).
Desc: Covers the civil, economic, political, natural, literary, and ecclesiastical history of the state of Alabama and its people, reviews of books about Alabama and the South, and reports on the activities of the Alabama Historical Association.
Ind/Abst Am. Hist. Life (1963-); Annu. Bibliogr. Engl. Lang. Lit.; GeoRef; Index Book Rev. Humanit.; MLA Int. Bibl. Books Artic. Mod. Lang. Lit.; Recent. Publ. Artic.; Writ. Am. Hist.

CN/0828-1858
ALASKA HISTORY. [Alsk. hist.]. No. 18 (1981)-. Monographic series. English. ir. Price varies per volume. Limestone Press, PO Box 1604, Kingston Ontario K7L 5C8 Canada. **Circ:** 350. ***Continues** Materials for the Study of Alaska History.*
Desc: The history of Alaska before the sale to the United States in 1867.
Ind/Abst Am. Hist. Life (1984-); West. Hist. Q.

US/0890-6149
ALASKA HISTORY (ANCHORAGE, ALASKA). (ALASKA HISTORY : A PUBLICATION OF THE ALASKA HISTORICAL SOCIETY.). [Alsk. hist.]. **Added/Corp** Alaska Historical Society. Vol. 1, No. 1 (Fall 1984)-. Academic Scholarly Publication. English. sa. $8.00 members; $10.00 non-members. Alaska Historical Society, PO Box 100299, Anchorage AK 99510-0299. **Tel** (907)276-1596. **ED** James H Ducker. **LC** F904; .A485. **DD** 979.8/005. **Ad Acc. Circ:** 600.
Desc: Scholarly articles on Alaskan history, photographer essays, book reviews, and book announcements.

US/1040-6964
ALBANY PRESERVATION REPORT. [Albany preserv. rep.]. **Added/Corp** Historic Albany Foundation (N.Y.). (Sept. 1982)-. Periodical. English. **DD** 363. ***Continues** Weathervane (Albany, N.Y.).*
Ind/Abst Avery Index Archit. Period. Suppl. Colum. Univ. (Feb. 1990-).

CN/0319-1737
ALBERTA ECHO. Began publication in 1969. Periodical. Multiple languages (English and German). mo. German-Canadian Association of Alberta, PO Box 637, Edmonton Alberta T5J 2K8 Canada. **DD** 971.23/004/31. **UDC** 971.2.

CN/0316-1552
ALBERTA HISTORY. [Alta. hist.]. **Added/Corp** Historical Society of Alberta. Vol. 23 (Winter 1975)-. Periodical. English. Four times a year. $20.00 (individuals); $100.00 (associate); $45.00 (affiliate) Comes with Historical Society of Alberta membership. Historical Society of Alberta, PO Box 4035, Postal Station C, Calgary Alberta T2T 5M9 Canada. **Tel** (403)261-3662. **ED** Hugh A. Dempsey. **LC** F1075; .A6. **DD** 971.23/005. **CODEN** ALHIE6. Index available. cum. index. **Bk Rev. Circ:** 2,200. available on microfilm and microfiche from University Microfilms International (UMI). ***Continues** Alberta Historical Review, 0002-4783.*
Desc: Illustrated magazine, containing interesting articles on pioneer life, Indians, fur trade, ethnic groups and other topics
Ind/Abst Am. Hist. Life (1975-); BHA : Biblio. Hist. Art; Can. Index (?-?); Can. Period. Index; West. Hist. Q.

CN
ALBERTA PAST. English. Four times a year. Free on request. Historic Sites & Archives Service, 8820-112 Street / Old St. Stephens College, Edmonton Alberta T6G 2P8 Canada. **Tel** (403)427-2022, FAX (403)427-0808. **ED** Erna Dominey. **Ad Acc. Circ:** 20,000 Fall/Winter, 50,000 Spring/Summer.
Desc: Directed towards those with an interest in historic preservation, Alberta history and archaeology, and the heritage resource management activities of the Historical Resources Division.

US/0887-7106
ALERT! (NEW YORK, N.Y. 1984). ***Ceased.*** (ALERT! / COMMITTEE IN SOLIDARITY WITH THE PEOPLE OF EL SALVADOR.). [Alert!]. **Added/Corp** Committee in Solidarity with the People of El Salvador (U.S.). **VFOAT** Alert, Focus on Central America. (July 1984)-(199?). Periodical. English. mo. CISPES, PO Box 12156, Washington DC 20005. **DD** 972. ***Continues** El Salvador Alert, 8755-4984.*
Ind/Abst Altern. Press Index (199?-); Hum. Rights Intern. Rep. (?-?).

US/1041-9381
ALLEN COUNTY-FORT WAYNE HISTORICAL SOCIETY BULLETIN. [Allen Cty.-Fort Wayne Hist. Soc. bull.]. **Added/Corp** Allen County-Fort Wayne Historical Society. **VFOAT** Historical Society Bulletin. (Jan.-Feb. 1987)-. Periodical. English. Six times a year. $25.00 (indivduals), $35.00 (family), $20.00 (senior), $100.00 (contributing), $250.00 (sustaining), $1,000.00 (cornerstone) Comes with Allen County Fort Wayne Historical Society membership. Allen County-Fort Wayne Historical Society, 302 East Berry Street, Ft Wayne IN 46802. **Tel** (219)426-2882. **LC** F534.F7; .O57. **DD** 977.2/74/006. ***Continues** Historical Society Bulletin.*

US/1052-9381
ALLIANCE LETTER. (ALLIANCE LETTER / BOSTON PRESERVATION ALLIANCE.). [Alliance lett.]. **Added/Corp** Boston Preservation Alliance. Vol. 8, No. 5 (May 1987)-. Periodical. English. Ten times a year. $25.00 (individuals), $100.00 (institutions) Comes with Boston Preservation Alliance membership. Boston Preservation Alliance, Old City Hall, 45 School Street, Boston MA 02108. **Tel** (617)367-2458. **DD** 711. ***Continues** Boston Preservation AllianceLetter (1984 July/Aug.).*
Ind/Abst Avery Index Archit. Period. Suppl. Colum. Univ. (1990-).

US
ALLIANCELETTER : MONTHLY NEWSLETTER OF THE BOSTON PRESERVATION ALLIANCE. ***Title Change.*** Vol. 1, No. 1 (Apr. 1980)-V. 5, No. 2 (March 1984). Newsletter. English. mo. Boston Preservation Alliance, Old City Hall, 45 School Street, Boston MA 02108. **Tel** (617)367-2458. ***Continued by** Boston Preservation Alliance Letter (1984 Apr.).*

SZ
AMAZIND BULLETIN. Main/Corp Documentation and Information Center for Indigenous Affairs In the Amazon Region. **VAT** Documentation and Information Center for Indigenous Affairs in the Amazon Region Bulletin. 1- Autumn 1973-. Bulletin. English. 10.00F single issue. Amazind, PO Box 509, 1211 Geneva 3 Switzerland. **LC** F2520; .D6A. **DD** 981/.004/98. **UDC** 981.

PE/0252-886X
AMAZONIA PERUANA. [Amazonia peru.]. **Added/Corp** Centro Amazonico de Antropologia y Aplicacion Practica. (1977)-. Periodical. Spanish (English, French and German). sa. $40.00 Latin America; $45.00 (individuals), $50.00 (institutions) other. Centro Amazonico de Antropologia y Aplicacion Practica, Apartado 140166, Lima 14 Peru. **Tel** 011 51 14 615223, 011 51 14 625811, FAX 011 51 14 638846. **ED** Jaime Regan. **LC** F3429; .A55. **DD** 985/.00498. cum. index. **Bk Rev. Circ:** 1,000. ***Continues** Amazonia.*
Desc: Includes articles on anthropology and social sciences concerning the Amazonian region; written by Peruvian and foreign authors.
Ind/Abst Anthropol. Lit.; HAPI Hisp. Am. Period. Index.

US
AMERICA, HISTORY AND LIFE. FIVE YEAR INDEX. V. 11-15 (1974-1978) & Suppl. (1964-1973)-. English. an. ABC Clio Press, PO Box 1911, 130 Cremona, Santa Barbara CA 93117. **Tel** (805)968-1911, (800)422-2546, FAX (805)685-9685. **ED** Jeffery B Serena. **LC** Z1236; .A483; E171. **DD** 973/.05. **UDC** 973; 908.73.

US/0002-7065
AMERICA, HISTORY AND LIFE ON DISC. COMPUTER FILE. Added/Corp ABC-Clio Information Services. **VFOAT** ABC-Clio Electronic Library User's Guide. Vols. 24-27, 28:1 & 2 (1991)-. Periodical. English. Three times a year. ABC Clio Press, PO Box 1911, 130 Cremona, Santa Barbara CA 93117. **Tel** (805)968-1911, (800)422-2546, FAX (805)685-9685.

US
AMERICA : HISTORY AND LIFE. PART A : ARTICLE ABSTRACTS AND CITATIONS. (1974)-. Periodical. English. Three times a year. ABC Clio Press, PO Box 1911, 130 Cremona, Santa Barbara CA 93117. **Tel** (805)968-1911, (800)422-2546, FAX (805)685-9685. **(Subscription address:** Clio Press, 35A Great Clarendon Street, Oxford OX2 6AT England, telephone: 011 44 865311350**) ED** Jeffery B. Serena.
Desc: Access to recently published articles from nearly 2,000 international periodicals; fully indexed in each issue for rapid access to specific topics, subject classified for productive browsing in broad areas of interest.

US
AMERICA, HISTORY AND LIFE. SUPPLEMENT. 1964/73-. English. ABC Clio Press, PO Box 1911, 130 Cremona, Santa Barbara CA 93117. **Tel** (805)968-1911, (800)422-2546, FAX (805)685-9685. **UDC** 973; 908.73.

MX/0185-1179
AMERICA INDIGENA. **See** Anthropology.

RU
AMERICA LATINA. ***Ceased.*** (1974)-Ceased in Dec. (1992). Periodical. Spanish (Russian). mo. **(Subscription address:** Victor Kamkin, 4956 Boiling Brook Parkway, Rockville MD 20852.**) LC** F1401; .A522.
Desc: Deals with a wide range of social, political and economic problems relating to both individual Latin American countries and the continent as a whole.
Ind/Abst Am. Hist. Life (1976-1978); Anthropol. Index; HAPI Hisp. Am. Period. Index (19??-).

AG
AMERICA LATINA INTERNACIONAL. Spanish. $25.00. Facultad Latinoamerica Ciencia Soc., Av. Lacroze 2097, 1426 Buenos Aires Argentina.
Ind/Abst Int. Labour Doc.

MX
AMERICA LATINA (MEXICO CITY, MEXICO : 1979). (AMERICA LATINA : ESTUDIOS Y PERSPECTIVAS.). **VFOAT** Estudios y Perspectivas. Vol. 1, No. 1 (April 1979)-. Periodical. Spanish. Unidad de Investigacion Latinoamericana, Apartado 20-371, Mexico 20 DF Mexico. **UDC** 9806.

US/0517-032X
AMERICAN BULLETIN, THE. Added/Corp Czechoslovak National Council of America. No. 1 (1957)-. Periodical. English. mo. $5.00. Czechoslovak National Council of America, 2137 South Lombard Avenue, Room 202, Cicero IL 60650. **Tel** (312)656-1117. **LC** E184.B67; A43.
Ind/Abst Hum. Rights Intern. Rep.

US
AMERICAN CULTURAL HERITAGE SERIES. VFOAT American Cultural Heritage. Began in 1979. Monographic series. English. Price varies per volume. Burt Franklin Publishing Company, PO Box 856, New York NY 10014. **UDC** 908.73.

US/1056-2605
AMERICAN CURRENTS (WASHINGTON, D.C.). (AMERICAN CURRENTS.). [Am. curr.]. **Added/Corp** United States Industrial Council. Educational Foundation. No. 1 (May 1991)-. Periodical. English. qt. $12.00. US Industrial Council Educational Foundation, 220 National Press Building, Washington DC 20045. **LC** E839.5; .A66. **DD** 973.

US/0736-9948
AMERICAN EXAMINER (EAST LANSING, MICH.). (AMERICAN EXAMINER.). [Am. exam.]. **Added/Corp** Michigan State University American Studies Association. Vol. 1, No. 1 (Spring 1972)-. Periodical. English. Three times a year. **LC** E169.1.A471982. **DD** 973/.05.
Ind/Abst MLA Int. Bibl. Books Artic. Mod. Lang. Lit.

US/0065-8219
AMERICAN EXPLORATION AND TRAVEL SERIES. Vol. 1 (1937)-. Monographic series. English. ir. Price varies per volume. University of Oklahoma Press, PO Box 787, Norman OK 73070. **Tel** (800)627-7377, (405)325-2000.
Desc: To depict the original condition and gradual recession of the American frontier and present and ongoing picture of the processes of American exploration and settlement.

US/0002-8738
AMERICAN HERITAGE. [Am. herit.]. **Added/Corp** American Association for State and Local History. Society of American Historians. Vol. 1-3, No. 3 (Jan./Feb. 1947)-. Periodical. English. ir (8 issues). $32.00 (one year), $48.75 (two years), $64.00 (three years). American Heritage, Forbes Building, 60 Fifth Avenue, New York NY 10011. **Tel** (212)206-5512, (212)620-1804. **(Subscription address:** CDS Agency Hard Copy, PO Box 4966, Des Moines, IA 50340; (telephone: (515)247-7569)**) LC** E171; .A43. **DD** 973.05. **[CCC].** Index available. cum. index. **Bk Rev. Ad Acc. Circ:** 275,000. available on an online database from DIALOG; available on microfilm and microfiche from University Microfilms International (UMI). Documents available from The Genuine Article, UMI Article Clearinghouse, Magazine Collection.
Desc: The magazine of American history. Includes articles, art portfolios, photographs, diaries and biographies, the story of America with all its contradictions, its drama, its human interest, its historical significance.
Ind/Abst Abr. Read. Guide Period. Lit.; Acad. Abstr. Full Text Elite (Jan. 1984-) [Full Txt.]; Acad. Abstr. (Jan. 1984-); Acad. Ind. [Computer File] (1984-); Acad. Search (Jan. 1984-); Am. Hist. Life (1955-); Annu. Bibliogr. Engl. Lang. Lit.; ARTbibliogr. Mod.; Arts Humanit. Citation Index [Full Cov.]; Biogr. Index; Book Rev. Index; Child. Lit. Abstr. (19??-); Curr. Contents Arts Humanit.; Expand. Acad. Index (1985-); Gen. Period. Index (1985-); Guide Soc. Sci. Relig.; Hist. Source (Jan. 1984-) [Full Txt.]; Humanit. Source (Jan. 1988-) [Full Txt.]; INFO-SOUTH Abstr.; Mag. Artic. Summar. Elite (Jan. 1984-) [Full Txt.]; Mag. Artic. Summar. Select (Jan. 1984-) [Full Txt.]; Mag. Artic. Summar. CD-ROM (Jan. 1984-); Mag. Index Plus

(1989-); Mag. Index Sel. Microfiche (1986-) [Full Txt.]; Mag. Index. Sel. (1986-); Mag. Search; Mid. Search (Jan. 1984-) [Full Txt.]; MLA Int. Bibl. Books Artic. Mod. Lang. Lit.; Newsp. Period. Abstr. (1986-); Read. Guide Abstr. Select Ed.; Read. Guide Period. Lit.; Res. Alert [Full Cov.]; Resource/One Ondisc (1986-); Soc. Sci. Source (Jan. 1984-) [Full Txt.]; Soc. Sci. Cit. Index [Select. Cov.]; SportSearch; Mag. Index (1977-); TOM Gen. Index (1985-) [Full Txt.]; Vocat. Search (Jan. 1984-) [Full Txt.]; West. Hist. Q.

US
AMERICAN HISTORY. (19??)-. Periodical. English. Six times a year. $23.95. Cowles Magazines, PO Box 8200, Harrisburg PA 17105. **Tel** (717)657-9555, (800)435-9610. **(Subscription address:** Kable Publishers Aide, 308 East Hitt Street, Subscriptions Department, Mt. Morris, IL 61054**)** ***Continues** American History Illustrated.*

US/0733-3560
AMERICAN HISTORY. [Am. hist.]. **VFOAT** Annual Editions. American History. 6th Edition (1982)-. Periodical. English. an. $11.95. Dushkin Publishing Group Inc., Sluice Dock, Guilford CT 06437. **Tel** (203)453-4351, (800)243-6532, FAX (203)453-6000. **ED** Robert James Maddox. **LC** E171; .A75. **DD** 973/.05. ***Continues** Readings in American History, 0090-4511.*
Desc: Provides coverage of the complete panorama of America's history. Articles expose students to the thoughts of contemporaries in various historical time periods, as well as to the secondary literature of professional historians.

●US/1076-8866
AMERICAN HISTORY. [Am. hist.]. Vol. 29, No. 2 (June 1994)-. Periodical. English. bm. $23.95. Cowles Magazines, PO Box 8200, Harrisburg PA 17105. **Tel** (717)657-9555, (800)435-9610. **(Subscription address:** Kable Publishers Aide, 308 East Hitt Street, Subscription Department, Mt. Morris IL 61054-1473.**) LC** E171; .A574. **DD** 973. ***Continues** American History Illustrated, 0002-8770.*
Desc: A magazine of cultural, social, political, and military history for a general audience; publishes articles on significant persons, events, issues, and places from America's past.
Ind/Abst Mag. Artic. Summar. Elite (June 1994-) [Full Txt.].

US/0002-8770
AMERICAN HISTORY ILLUSTRATED.
Title Change. [Am. hist. illus.]. Vol. 1 (April 1966)-(19??). Periodical. English. mo (except July and Aug.). Cowles Magazines, PO Box 8200, Harrisburg PA 17105. **Tel** (717)657-9555, (800)435-9610. **ED** Ed Holm, Geneva B Politzer, and Kathleen Doyle. **LC** E171; .A574. **DD** 973.05. **UDC** 973. Index available. **Bk Rev. Ad Acc. Circ:** 135,372. available on microfilm and microfiche from University Microfilms International (UMI). Documents available from The Genuine Article, UMI Article Clearinghouse, Magazine Collection. ***Continued by** American History.*
Desc: A magazine of cultural, social, political, and military history for a general audience; publishes articles on significant persons, events, issues, and places from America's past.
Ind/Abst Abr. Read. Guide Period. Lit.; Acad. Abstr. Full Text Elite (Jan. 1984-) [Full Txt.]; Acad. Abstr. (Jan. 1984-); Acad. Search (Jan. 1984-); Am. Hist. Life (1966-); ARTbibliogr. Mod.; Arts Humanit. Citation Index [Full Cov.]; Curr. Contents Arts Humanit.; Gen. Period. Index (1985-); Hist. Source (Jan. 1984-); Humanit. Source (Jan. 1988-); INFO-SOUTH Abstr.; Mag. Artic. Summar. Elite (Jan. 1984-May 1994) [Full Txt.]; Mag. Artic. Summar. Select (Jan. 1984-); Mag. Artic. Summar. CD-ROM (Jan. 1984-); Mag. Index Plus (1989-); Mag. Index Sel. Microfiche (1986-) [Full Txt.]; Mag. Index. Sel. (1986-); Mag. Search; Mid. Search (Jan. 1984-); Newsp. Period. Abstr. (1988-); Prim. Search (Jan. 1984-); Read. Guide Abstr. Select Ed.; Read. Guide Period. Lit.; Res. Alert [Full Cov.]; Resource/One Ondisc (1988-); Soc. Sci. Cit. Index [Select. Cov.]; Mag. Index (1977-); TOM Gen. Index (1985-) [Full Txt.]; West. Hist. Q.

US/0748-6731
AMERICAN HISTORY (WESTPORT, CONN.). ***Ceased.*** (AMERICAN HISTORY.). Vol. 1 (1985)-(19??). Periodical. English. an. Mecklermedia Corporation, 11 Ferry Lane West, Westport CT 06880. **Tel** (203)226-6967, (800)632-5537, FAX (203)454-5840. **LC** Z1236; .A51357; E178. **DD** 016.973.

US
AMERICAN INDIAN CALENDAR.
Government Publication. English. an. Department of the Interior, 1849 C Street Northwest, Washington DC 20240. **Tel** (202)343-3171, FAX (202)208-5048. **UDC** 973(97)(058.3).

US/0894-4040
AMERICAN INDIAN REPORT. [Am. Indian rep.]. **Added/Corp** Dartmouth Institute (Springfield, Va.) Falmouth Institute. Vol. 1, No. 1 (Oct. 1985)-. Periodical. English. Twelve times a year. $79.00 (individuals), $89.00 (institutions). Falmouth Institute, 3918 Prosperity Avenue, Suite 302, Fairfax VA 22031-3333. **Tel** (703)641-9100, FAX (703)641-1558. **ED** Marquerite Carroll. **DD** 970. **Circ:** 550 (ctrl).
Desc: Covers news, legislation, regulations, law, health and education that affects the American Indian community.

●US/1058-563X
AMERICAN INDIAN STUDIES. **See** Ethnic Interests.

US/0882-5351
AMERICAN MAGAZINE AND HISTORICAL CHRONICLE, THE.
Suspended. [Am. mag. hist. chron.]. **Added/Corp** William L. Clements Library. Clements Library Associates. **VFOAT** American Magazine. Vol. 1, No. 1 (Spring-Summer 1985)-Vol. 4 No. 2 (19??). Periodical. English. Twice a year (May & Dec.). Clements Library Associates, 910 South University, Ann Arbor MI 48109. **Tel** (313)764-2347. **ED** John C. Dann and John C. Harriman. **DD** 973. **Circ:** 1,000 (ctrl).
Desc: Published for the edification and amusement of book collectors, bibliographers and the discriminating general public.
Ind/Abst Am. Hist. Life (1987-).

US/0148-3668
AMERICAN PRESERVATION. [Am. preserv.]. Vol. 1 (Oct./Nov. 1977)-. Periodical. English. bm. $12.00. American Preservation, 1785 Mass Avenue NW, Washington DC 20036. **Tel** (202)673-4000. **LC** E159; .A386. **DD** 069/.53/0993.
Ind/Abst Am. Hist. Life (1977-1981); Archit. Period. Index; Avery Index Archit. Period. Suppl. Colum. Univ. (19??-199?).

US/0003-0678
AMERICAN QUARTERLY. [Am. q.]. **Added/Corp** University of Minnesota. Program in American Studies. University of Pennsylvania. Committee on American Civilization. American Studies Association. **VFOAT** AQ. Vol. 1 (Spring 1949)-. Academic Scholarly Publication. English. Four times a year (March, June, September, December). $62.00 US; $65.40 Canada and Mexico; $78.00 other. Johns Hopkins University Press, 2715 North Charles Street, Baltimore MD 21218-4319. **Tel** (410)516-6987, FAX (410)516-6968. **(Subscription address:** John Hopkins University Press, Journals Publishing Division, PO Box 19966, Baltimore MD 21211.**) ED** Gary Kulik and Mary Corbin Sies. **LC** AP2; .A3985. **DD** 051. **[CCC]. Bk Rev. Ad Acc. Circ:** 4,500. available on microfilm and microfiche from University Microfilms International (UMI). Documents available from The Genuine Article, UMI Article Clearinghouse.
Desc: The official journal of the American Studies Association. It publishes reviews of relevant books in American studies and scholarly articles with an interdisciplinary approach providing an insight into the nature of American culture.
Ind/Abst Abstr. Engl. Stud.; Acad. Abstr. Full Text Elite (July 1990-); Acad. Abstr. (July 1990-); Acad. Ind. [Computer File] (1987-); Acad. Search (July 1990-); Am. Hist. Life (1954-); Annu. Bibliogr. Engl. Lang. Lit.; Arts Humanit. Citation Index (1954-) [Full Cov.]; Book Rev. Digest; Book Rev. Index; Child. Lit. Abstr. (19??-); Curr. Contents Arts Humanit.; Expand. Acad. Index (1987-); Film Lit. Index (19??-); Humanit. Index; Humanit. Source (Jul. 1990-); Index Book Rev. Relig. (1954-); Index Period. Artic. Relat. Law; INFO-SOUTH Abstr.; Lit. Crit. Regist.; Mag. Search; Middle East Abstr. Index; MLA Int. Bibl. Books Artic. Mod. Lang. Lit.; Newsp. Period. Abstr. (1991-); Relig. Index One Period. (1970-); Res. Alert [Full Cov.]; Romant. Move. (1970-); Soc. Sci. Cit. Index [Select. Cov.]; SportSearch (1954-); West. Hist. Q.; Women Stud. Abstr.

US/0272-2011
AMERICAN REVIEW OF CANADIAN STUDIES, THE. [Am. rev. Can. stud.]. **Added/Corp** Association for Canadian Studies in the United States. Vol. 3 (Spring 1973)-. Periodical. English (French). Four times a year (Jan., Apr., July, Oct.). $60.00 (individual), $105.00 (institutions). Association for Canadian Studies in the United States, One Dupont Circle, Suite 620, Washington DC 20036. **Tel** (202)887-6375, FAX (202)296-8379. **ED** Lee Thompson and Robert Thacker. **LC** F1008; .A54. **DD** 971/.005. Index available. cum. index. **Bk Rev. Ad Acc. Circ:** 2,500 (ctrl). available on microfilm and microfiche from University Microfilms International (UMI). ***Continues** ACSUS Newsletter, 0193-6093.* ***Continued in part by** ACSUS Newsletter (1977).*
Desc: This journal is devoted exclusively to Canada and Canadian/US relations. The interdisciplinary journal contains articles in all fields including history, geography, political science and literature.
Ind/Abst Am. Hist. Life (1973-); BHA : Biblio. Hist. Art; Can. Index; Can. Period. Index (19??-); Int. Bibliogr. Sociol.; PAIS Int. Print; U.S. Polit. Sci. Doc.

NO/0044-8060
AMERICAN STUDIES IN SCANDINAVIA.
[Am. stud. Scand.]. **Added/Corp** Nordic Association for American Studies. No. 1 (Summer 1968)-. Periodical. English (Swedish). sa (2 issues). $35.00. The Nordic Association for American Studies, Department of English, University of Copenhagen, Njalsgade 86, DK-2100 Copenhagen S Denmark. **Tel** 011 45 31 542211. **ED** Niels Thorsen. **LC** E11; .A38. **DD** 917.3/03/05. **Bk Rev. Ad Acc. Circ:** 550. Documents available from The Genuine Article.
Desc: Related to American studies, especially by Nordic authors. Studies on history, linguistics, political science, and social anthropology or sociology are covered.
Ind/Abst Am. Hist. Life (1968-); Annu. Bibliogr. Engl. Lang. Lit.; Arts Humanit. Citation Index [Full Cov.]; Curr. Contents Arts Humanit.; Res. Alert [Full Cov.]; Soc. Sci. Cit. Index [Select. Cov.].

US/0883-105X
AMERICAN STUDIES INTERNATIONAL.
[Am. stud. int.]. **Added/Corp** George Washington University. American Studies Program. Vol. 14 (Autumn 1975)-. Periodical. English. Four times a year (two journal issues and two newsletter issues). $25.00 (individual), $35.00 (institution) US; $35.00 other. George Washington University / American Studies Program, 2108 G Street Northwest, Washington DC 20052. **Tel** (202)994-7368. **ED** Lisa Johnson Bedell. **LC** AP2; .A3985 Suppl. **DD** 973/.05. Index available (bound in issue). cum. index. **Bk Rev. Ad Acc. Pr Rev. Circ:** 2,000. available on microfilm. Documents available from The Genuine Article, UMI Article Clearinghouse. ***Continues** American Studies, 0003-1321.*
Desc: Academic journal of international scholarship on American history, literature, philosophy and social and political institutions. Includes bibliographic and thematic essays and book reviews.
Ind/Abst Abstr. Engl. Stud.; Acad. Search (July 1993-); Am. Hist. Life (1975-); Am. Humanit. Index; Annu. Bibliogr. Engl. Lang. Lit.; Arts Humanit. Citation Index [Full Cov.]; Curr. Contents Arts Humanit.; Expand. Acad. Index (1989-); Humanit. Index; Humanit. Source (Jul. 1993-); INFO-SOUTH Abstr.; Lit. Crit. Regist.; Mag. Search; MLA Int. Bibl. Books Artic. Mod. Lang. Lit.; Newsp. Period. Abstr. (1991-); Res. Alert [Full Cov.]; Soc. Sci. Cit. Index [Select. Cov.].

US/0883-1068
AMERICAN STUDIES INTERNATIONAL NEWSLETTER. [Am. stud. int. newsl.]. **Added/Corp** George Washington University. American Studies Program. **VFOAT** ASI Newsletter. (Spring 1983)-. Periodical. English. Twice a year (Jan. & July). $30.00 (institutions & others); $27.00 (individuals) Comes with American Studies International membership. George Washington University / American Studies Program, 2108 G Street Northwest, Washington DC 20052. **Tel** (202)994-7368. **LC** E169.1; .A4943. **DD** 973/.05.
Ind/Abst Humanit. Index.

US/0026-3079
AMERICAN STUDIES (LAWRENCE).
(AMERICAN STUDIES.). [Am. stud.]. **Added/Corp** University of Kansas. Midcontinent American Studies Association. Vol. 12 (Spring 1971)-. Periodical. English. ir (twice per year). $25.00 institutional; $15.00 individual. Mid-American Studies Association, 2120 Wescoe Hall, University of Kansas, Lawrence KS 66045. **Tel** (913)864-4878, . **ED** David Katzman and Norman Yetman. **DD** 917.3/03/05. **[CCC].** Index available. cum. index. **Bk Rev**, (Qty: 30-70 per year). **Ad Acc. Pr Rev. Circ:** 1,600 (ctrl). available on microfilm and microfiche from University Microfilms International (UMI). Documents available from UMI Article Clearinghouse. ***Continues** Midcontinent American Studies Journal, 0544-0335.*
Desc: Interdisciplinary journal focusing on American life and culture in the arts, in history and in popular culture. Articles, reviews, and essays on scholarship and teaching.
Ind/Abst Abstr. Engl. Stud.; Am. Hist. Life (1971-); Am. Humanit. Index (1971-); Child. Lit. Abstr. (19??-); Humanit. Index; Lit. Crit. Regist.; Newsp. Period. Abstr. (1991-); PAIS Int. Print (1991-?); SportSearch (1971-); West. Hist. Q.

US
AMERICAN STUDIES / THE WILLIAM L. BRYANT FOUNDATION. Added/Corp William L. Bryant Foundation. No. 1 (1959)-. Monographic series. English. **LC** E77.8; .U5. **DD** 973.1.

US/0066-0884
AMERICAN TRAIL SERIES. Vol. 1 (1922)-. Monographic series. English. ir. Price varies per volume. Arthur H. Clark Company, PO Box 14707, Spokane WA 99214. **Tel** (509)928-9540, (800)842-9286. **ED** Robert A. Clark. cum. index. **Circ:** 1,000 (ctrl).
Desc: An ongoing series of books on the development of transportation routes in the American West.

US
AMERICAN TRAILS SERIES. NEW YORK. Monographic series. English. ir. Price varies per volume. McGraw Hill Publishing Company, Inc., 1221 Avenue of the Americas, New York NY 10020. **Tel** (212)512-6410, (800)525-5003, FAX (212)512-6111.

US/0895-0490
AMERICAN UNIVERSITY STUDIES. SERIES XXII, LATIN AMERICAN STUDIES. [Am. univ. stud., XXII Lat. Am. stud.]. **VFOAT** American University Studies. Series 22, Latin American Studies; Latin American Studies. Vol. 1 (1988)-. Monographic series. English. ir. Price varies per volume. Peter Lang Publishing, 62 West 45th Street, 4th Floor, New York NY 10036. **Tel** (212)764-1471, (800)770-5264, telex 6973364 PLNY. **ED** Michael Flamini. **DD** 980. Index

available. cum. index. **Bk Rev**. Documents available. **Desc:** Encompasses all areas of Latin American studies; history, literature, political science, etc.

US/0884-9390
AMERICAN VISIONS. [Am. vis.]. **Added/Corp** Visions Foundation (Washington, D.C.). Vol. 1, No. 1 (Jan./Feb. 1986)-. Periodical. English. Six times a year. $22.00 libraries, & institutions); $18.00 (individuals) Comes with American Visions membership. Dialogue Diaspora, 2101 S Street Northwest, Washington DC 20008. **Tel** (202)462-1779, (800)998-0864. **LC** E185.5; .A533. **DD** 973/.0496073/005. available on microfilm and microfiche from University Microfilms International (UMI). Documents available from UMI Article Clearinghouse. **Ind/Abst** Acad. Abstr. Full Text Elite (Oct. 1989-); Acad. Abstr. (Oct. 1989-); Acad. Ind. [Computer File] (1989-); Acad. Search (Oct. 1989-); Am. Hist. Life (1986-); Curr. Lit. Fam. Plan. (19??-199?); Expand. Acad. Index (1989-); Gen. Period. Index (1989-); INFO-SOUTH Abstr.; Mag. Artic. Summar. Elite (Oct. 1989-); Mag. Artic. Summar. Select (July 1989-); Mag. Artic. Summar. CD-ROM (Oct. 1989-); Mag. Index Plus (1989-); Mag. Index. Sel. (1989-); Mag. Search; Mid. Search (Jul. 1989-); Newsp. Period. Abstr. (1988-); Read. Guide Abstr. Select Ed.; Read. Guide Period. Lit.; Soc. Work Abstr. (?-?); Mag. Index (1989-); TOM Gen. Index (1989-) [Full Txt.]; Vocat. Search (Oct. 1989-).

US/0199-8072
AMERICAN WAR MOTHER, THE. **Main/Corp** American War Mothers. Periodical. English. qt. **LC** D570.A15; A815.

US/0066-121X
AMERICANS BEFORE COLUMBUS. **Added/Corp** National Indian Youth Council. Vol. 1 (Oct. 1969)-. Periodical. English. bm. $20.00. National Indian Youth Council, 318 Elm Street SE, Albuquerque NM 87102-3614. **Tel** (505)247-2251, FAX (505) 247-4251. **ED** Neil Singer. **Bk Rev**. **Ad Acc**. **Circ:** 20,000.

US/1046-2899
AMERICA'S CIVIL WAR. [Am. Civ. War]. **VFOAT** Civil War. Vol. 1, No. 1 (May 1988)-. Periodical. English. bm. $19.95. Cowles Magazines, PO Box 8200, Harrisburg PA 17105. **Tel** (717)657-9555, (800)435-9610. **LC** E461; .A47. **DD** 973.7/005.

US/0003-1615
AMERICAS (WASHINGTON. 1944), THE. (THE AMERICAS.). [Americas]. **Added/Corp** Academy of American Franciscan History. Vol. 1 (July 1944)-. Periodical. English. qt. $75.00 (institution), $35.00 (individual) US. Catholic University of America Press, 620 Michigan Avenue Northeast, Administration Building/Room 303, Washington DC 20064. **Tel** (202)319-5052, FAX (202)319-5802. **ED** Vincent Peloso. **LC** E11; .A4. **DD** 970.05. Index available (bound in April issue). cum. index. **Bk Rev. Circ:** 900. Documents available from Magazine Collection. **Desc:** Publishes articles and review articles of inter-American cultural history. **Ind/Abst** Acad. Ind. [Computer File] (1984-); Am. Hist. Life (1954-); Bibliogr. Mission.; Book Rev. Index; Curr. Geogr. Publ. (199?-); Expand. Acad. Index (1985-); Gen. Period. Index (1985-); HAPI Hisp. Am. Period. Index; Index Period. Artic. Relat. Law (19??-19??); Read. Guide Abstr. Select Ed.; Read. Guide Period. Lit.; TOM Gen. Index (1985-) [Full Txt.].

JA
AMERIKA-GAKUKAI KAIHO. **Main/Corp** Amerika Gakkai (Japan). **VFOAT** The American Studies News-Letter. Japanese. ir. Amerika-Gakukai, c/o Tokyo Daigaku Amerika Kenkyu Shiryo Senta, 8-1 Komaba 3 Meguro-ku 153, Tokyo Japan. **LC** E175.8; .A592A.

GW/0340-2827
AMERIKASTUDIEN. [Amerikastudien]. **Added/Corp** Deutsche Gesellschaft fuer Amerikastudien. **VFOAT** American Studies. Vol. 19 (1974)-. Periodical. Multiple languages (English and German; summaries and/or abstracts in English and German). Four times a year (Mar., June, Sept., Dec.). DM134.00 Germany; DM136.00 other. Amerikastudien, Dr. A Hornung, Johann Guten University, Welderweg 18, D 55128 Mainz Germany. **Tel** 11 49 61 31 393535, FAX 11 49 61 31 395100. **(Subscription address:** Ferdinand Schoeningh Verlag, Postfach 2540, D 33055 Paderborn Germany.**)** **ED** Professor Dr. Alfred Hornung (phone: 011 49 6131 39 2146). **LC** E169.1; .J33. **DD** 973.92/05. **[CCC].** Index available in last issue of volume--attached. cum. index. **Bk Rev**, (Qty: 50). **Ad Acc, Adv Mgr:** Korkendick, **Tel** 11 49 89 348017. **Pr Rev. Circ:** 1,000. Documents available from The Genuine Article. ***Continues*** *Jahrbuch fuer Amerikastudien.* **Desc:** Interdisciplinary studies from any field of American studies. **Ind/Abst** Abstr. Engl. Stud.; Am. Hist. Life (1974-); Arts Humanit. Citation Index (19??-19??) [Full Cov.]; Curr. Contents Arts Humanit.; MLA Int. Bibl. Books Artic. Mod. Lang. Lit.; Res. Alert [Full Cov.].

GW
AMERIKASTUDIEN. SCHRIFTENREIHE. AMERICAN STUDIES. **VFOAT** American Studies. Vol. 38 (1974)-. Monographic series. German (English). ir. Price varies per volume. Wilhelm Fink Verlag, Ohmstrasse 5, D 80802 Munich Germany. **Tel** 011 49 89 348017, 348018. ***Continues*** *Jahrbuch fuer Amerikastudien.* **Ind/Abst** Am. Hist. Life (1955-); MLA Int. Bibl. Books Artic. Mod. Lang. Lit.

JA/0069-598X
ANAIS - COLOQUIO DE ESTUDOS LUSO-BRASILEIROS. **Main/Corp** Coloquio de Estudos Luso-Brasileiros. **Added/Corp** Associacao de Professores de Portugues no Japao. Associacao Japonesa de Estudos Luso-Brasileiros. 1 (1967)-. Periodical. Portuguese. an. Associacao Japonesa de Estudos Luso-Brasileiros, Tokyo University of Foreign Studies, Nishigahara 4-51-21 Kita-ku, Tokyo 114 Japan. **LC** F2510; .C656a.

BL
ANAIS DA ... REUNIAO / SOCIEDADE BRASILEIRA DE PESQUISA HISTORICA, SBPH. **Main/Corp** Sociedade Brasileira de Pesquisa Historica. Reuniao. (1981)-. Periodical. Portuguese. **LC** F2501.5; .S63a. **DD** 981. **Ind/Abst** Am. Hist. Life (1982-).

BL
ANAIS DO MUSEU HISTORICO NACIONAL. **Main/Corp** Rio de Janeiro. Museu Historico Nacional. **Added/Corp** Brazil. Ministerio da Educacao e Saude Publica. Brazil. Ministerio da Educacao e Cultura. (1940)-. Portuguese. **LC** F2501; .R63. **DD** 981.0058. **Ind/Abst** HAPI Hisp. Am. Period. Index.

BL
ANAIS DO MUSEU PAULISTA. **Main/Corp** Museu Paulista. (1922)-. Portuguese. an. Museu Paulista da Univ de Sao Paulo, Caixa Postal 42503, 04263 Sao Paulo Brazil. **LC** F2501; .S23. **Ind/Abst** Anthropol. Lit. (-Vol. 12, 1990); HAPI Hisp. Am. Period. Index.

CR/0567-6509
ANALES / ACADEMIA DE GEOGRAFIA E HISTORIA DE COSTA RICA. [An. - Acad. Geogr. Hist. Costa Rica]. **Added/Corp** Academia de Geografia e Historia de Costa Rica. (1962/63)-. Spanish. an. Imprenta Nacional, San Jose, Costa Rica. **LC** F1451; .A332. **DD** 980. ***Continues*** *Anales (Academia Costarricense de la Historia)., 1010-3813.* **Ind/Abst** Am. Hist. Life (1963-1965).

PR
ANALES DE INVESTIGACION HISTORICA. Vol. 1, No. 1 (Jan./March 1974)-. Periodical. Spanish. sa. Universidad de Puerto Rico / Humanidades, Facultad de Humanidades, Rio Piedras 00931 Puerto Rico. **LC** F1951; .A78. **DD** 972.95/005. **Ind/Abst** HAPI Hisp. Am. Period. Index.

AG
ANALES DEL INSTITUTO BELGRANIANO CENTRAL. **Added/Corp** Instituto Belgraniano Central (Buenos Aires, Argentina). (1979)-. Periodical. Spanish. Instituto Belgraniano Central Convento de Santo Domingo, Defensa 422, Buenos Aires Argentina. **LC** F2845.B378; A5. **DD** 982/.03.

AG/0327-1676
ANDES : ANTROPOLOGIA E HISTORIA. **Added/Corp** Universidad Nacional de Salta. Centro Promocional de las Investigaciones en Historia e Antropologia. No. 1 (1990)-. Spanish. **LC** F2831; .A93. ***Continues*** *Avances en Investigacion.*

CN/1182-3178
ANISHINABEK NEWS. [Anishinabek news]. **Added/Corp** Union of Ontario Indians. (1990)-. Periodical. English. mo. $20.00 per year. Anishinabek News, PO Box 711, North Bay, Ontario P1B 8J8 Canada. **DD** 971.3/00497/005. ***Continues*** *Anishinabek., 1182-316X.*

US/0003-4827
ANNALS OF IOWA. [Ann. Iowa]. **Added/Corp** Iowa. Division of Historical Museum and Archives. State Historical Society of Iowa. Iowa. Historical Dept. Iowa. Historical, Memorial, and Art Dept. (1863)-. Academic Scholarly Publication. English. Four times a year (Jan., Apr., July, Oct.). $20.00. State Historical Society of Iowa, 402 Iowa Avenue, Centennial Building, Iwoa City IA 52240. **Tel** (319)335-3916, FAX (319)335-3924. **ED** Marvin Bergman. **LC** F616; .A6. **DD** 977.7/005. **[CCC].** Index available (Bound in 4th iss. (Oct.).). cum. index. **Bk Rev**, (Qty: 70-80). **Pr Rev. Circ:** 1,000 (ctrl). available on microfilm and microfiche from Xerox. **Desc:** A scholarly journal of articles devoted to the history of Iowa and the midwest. **Ind/Abst** Am. Hist. Life (1963-); Recent. Publ. Artic.; Ref. Sources; Writ. Am. Hist.

US/0003-4991
ANNALS OF WYOMING. V. 1- July 1923-. Periodical. English. qt. $20.00 (institutional membership), $7.00 (joint membership), $5.00 (single membership). Wyoming State Historical Society, Barrett Building, Cheyenne WY 82001. **Tel** (307)777-7015. **ED** Rick Ewig. **LC** F756. **DD** 978.7005. **UDC** 978.7. Index available. cum. index. **Bk Rev. Circ:** 2,000. **Desc:** Articles about Wyoming history. **Ind/Abst** Am. Hist. Life (1963-); West. Hist. Q.

US
ANNE BURNETT TANDY LECTURES IN AMERICAN CIVILIZATION, THE. No. 1-. Monographic series. English. ir. Price varies per volume. Amon Carter Museum, Box 2365, Fort Worth TX 76113. **Tel** (817)738-1933. **UDC** 908.73. Index available. **Desc:** A series of books based on an annual lecture series, on various subjects in American history and art.

US/0160-8460
ANNOTATION. (ANNOTATION : THE NEWSLETTER OF THE NATIONAL HISTORICAL PUBLICATIONS AND RECORDS COMMISSION.). **Added/Corp** United States. National Historical Publications Commission. United States. National Historical Publications and Records Commission. (Fall/Winter 1973)-. Newsletter. English. Three times a year. Free. National Historical Publications and Records Commission, National Archives Building/Room 300, Washington DC 20408. **Tel** (202)523-5391. **ED** Donald L Singer. **LC** E171; .A73. **DD** 973/.05. **Circ:** 3,000 (ctrl). **Desc:** Discusses the documentary publications and records programs of the National Historical Publications and Records commission.

US
ANNUAL PRESERVATION PROGRAM - MINNESOTA HISTORICAL SOCIETY. STATE HISTORIC PRESERVATION OFFICE, THE. **Main/Corp** Minnesota Historical Society. State Historic Preservation Office. **VFOAT** Historic Preservation in Minnesota. English. an. Minnesota Historical Society, 345 Kellogg Boulevard West, St. Paul MN 55102. **Tel** (612)297-3243, (800)647-7827, FAX (612)297-3343. **LC** F607; .M53A. **DD** 069/.53/09776. **UDC** 904(776).

US/0888-3165
ANNUAL PROCEEDINGS / DUBLIN SEMINAR FOR NEW ENGLAND FOLKLIFE. **See** Archaeology.

US/0882-035X
ANNUAL REPORT - HISTORICAL SOCIETY OF YORK COUNTY (PA.). (ANNUAL REPORT / THE HISTORICAL SOCIETY OF YORK COUNTY.). **Main/Corp** Historical Society of York County (PA.). **VFOAT** Annual Report of the Historical Society of York County. English. an. Historical Society of York County, 250 East Market Street, York PA 17403. **LC** F157.Y6; H746A. **DD** 974.8/41/006074841. **UDC** 974.8(047).

US/0098-3403
ANNUAL REPORT - MARYLAND HISTORICAL TRUST. **Main/Corp** Maryland Historical Trust. English. an. Maryland Historical Trust, Council for Maryland Archeology, 21 State Circle, Annapolis MD 21401. **Tel** (301)443-5972. **LC** F176; .M386A. **DD** 309.2/5/09752. **UDC** 975.2(047).

US/0091-5467
ANNUAL REPORT / NATIONAL TRUST FOR HISTORIC PRESERVATION. (ANNUAL REPORT.). **Main/Corp** National Trust for Historic Preservation in the United States. (19??)-. Periodical. English. an. National Trust for Historic Preservation, 1785 Massachusetts Avenue Northwest, Washington DC 20036. **Tel** (202)673-4035. **LC** E151.N38; N35a. **DD** 069/.53.

US/0893-9780
ANNUAL REPORT OF THE CONNECTICUT HISTORICAL SOCIETY, THE. [Annu. rep. Conn. Hist. Soc.]. **Main/Corp** Connecticut Historical Society. **VFOAT** Annual Report - Connecticut Historical Society; Connecticut Historical Society Annual Report. (1894)-. English. an. $20.00 Comes with Connecticut Historical Society Bulletin. Connecticut Historical Society, 1 Elizabeth Street, Hartford CT 06105. **Tel** (203)236-5621, FAX (203)236-2664. **LC** F91; .C65. **DD** 974. ***Continues*** *Papers and Reports Presented to the Connecticut Historical Society at the Annual Meeting of the Society.*

US/0099-1287
ANNUAL REPORT OF THE MARYLAND BICENTENNIAL COMMISSION TO THE GOVERNOR, THE GENERAL ASSEMBLY, AND THE SECRETARY, DEPARTMENT OF ECONOMIC AND COMMUNITY DEVELOPMENT. **Main/Corp** Maryland Bicentennial Commission. English. an. Tiedotuspalvelu, PO Box 350, SF-00101 Helsinki 10, Finland. **LC** E285.4.M3; M37A. **DD** 353.9/752/0085. **UDC** 353(047)(752).

CN/0710-8990
ANNUAL REPORT / ONTARIO ADVISORY COUNCIL ON MULTICULTURALISM AND CITIZENSHIP. [Annu. rep. - Ont. Advis. Counc. Multicult. Citizsh.]. **Main/Corp** Ontario Advisory Council

on Multiculturalism and Citizenship. **Added/Corp** Ontario. Ministry of Culture and Recreation. **VFOAT** Rapport Annuel. (1980)-. English (French). an. Ontario Advisory Council on Multiculturalism And Citizenship, 1200 Bay Street/10th Floor, Toronto Ontario M7A 2R9 Canada. **LC** F1059.7.A1; O57a. **DD** 354.7130085. ***Continues*** *Ontario Advisory Council on Multiculturalism. Annual Report of the Ontario Advisory Council on Multiculturalism., 0704-2655.*

CN/0706-0106
ANNUAL REPORT--ONTARIO HERITAGE FOUNDATION. **Main/Corp** Ontario Heritage Foundation. (19??)-. English (French). an. Ontario Heritage Foundation, 77 Bloor Street West, Toronto Ontario M7A 2R9 Canada. **Tel** (416)965-9504, FAX (416)965-4315. **LC** F1057.8; .O65a. **DD** 363.6/9/060713. **Circ:** 1,000 (ctrl).
Desc: Covers the activities of the Ontario Heritage Foundation, an agency of the Ontario Ministry of Culture and Communications, for one fiscal year and includes audited financial statements.

US
ANNUAL REPORT - THE SOUTHERN REGIONAL COUNCIL. **Main/Corp** Southern Regional Council. English. an. Southern Regional Council, 134 Peachtree Street Northwest, Suite 1900, Atlanta GA 30303. **Tel** (404)522-8764, FAX (404)522-8791. **LC** HC107.A13; S768A. **DD** 975/.006. **UDC** 975(047).

US/0270-5303
ANNUAL REPORTS OF THE NORTH CAROLINIANA SOCIETY, INC. AND THE NORTH CAROLINA COLLECTION. **Main/Corp** North Caroliniana Society. 1975-. English. an. North Carolina Collection, University of North Carolina, Library, Chapel Hill NC 27514. **LC** F251; .N955A. **DD** 975.6/006/0756. **UDC** 975.6(047). ***Supersedes*** *University of North Carolina at Chapel Hill. Library. North Carolina Collection. Annual Report.*

US
ANNUAL STATE HISTORIC PRESERVATION PLAN (INDIANA). **Main/Corp** Indiana. Dept. of Natural Resources. English. an. State Office Building, Room 608, Indianapolis IN 46204. **LC** F527; .I5A. **DD** 353.9/772/00853. **UDC** 904(772).

US
ANNUAL STATE HISTORIC PRESERVATION PLAN (WYOMING). **Main/Corp** Wyoming. Recreation Commission. **VFOAT** Wyoming Historic Preservation Plan. English. an. Wyoming Recreation Commission, 604 East 25th Street, Cheyenne WY 82002. **LC** F762; .W96A. **DD** 353.9/787/0085. **UDC** 904(787).

US/0733-5229
ANNUAL WHO'S IN CHARGE HERE YEARBOOK. **VFOAT** Who's In Charge Here Yearbook. 1st (1981)-. English. an. $3.95. G P Putnam's Sons, 200 Madison Avenue, New York NY 10016. **LC** E839; .G37. **DD** 973.92/0207. **UDC** 973(058).

NE
ANTILLEN REVIEW. Vol. 1, No. 1 (Nov./Dec. 1980)-. Periodical. English. PO Box 15, Curacao Antilles Netherlands. **LC** F2141; .A565. **DD** 972.98/6005.

GT/0003-6102
ANTROPOLOGIA E HISTORIA DE GUATEMALA. (ANTROPOLOGIA E HISTORIA DE GUATEMALA / INSTITUTO DE ANTROPOLOGIA E HISTORIA DE GUATEMALA.). [Antropol. hist. Guatem.]. **Added/Corp** Instituto de Antropologia e Historia (Guatemala). Guatemala. Direccion General de Antropologia e Historia. Vol. 1, No. 1 (Jan. 1949)-. Spanish. an. Instituto de Antropologia e Historia de Guatemala, Edificio No 5 de la Aurora, Guatemal City 13 Guatemala. **LC** F1461; .I63. **DD** 913.7281.
Ind/Abst Am. Hist. Life (1953-); Anthropol. Index; Anthropol. Lit. (1953-); Ethnoarts Index (1953-); HAPI Hisp. Am. Period. Index (19??-).

BL
ANUARIO DE DIVULGACAO CIENTIFICA. Yearly V. 1 1974-. Portuguese. an. Gabinete de Arqueologia da Universidade Catolica de Goias Goiania Brazil, Brazil. **LC** F2519.1.G68; A57. **UDC** 902(058)(81).
Ind/Abst Anthropol. Lit.

SP/0210-5810
ANUARIO DE ESTUDIOS AMERICANOS. [Anu. estud. am.]. **Added/Corp** Escuela de Estudios Hispano-Americanos (Consejo Superior de Investigaciones Cientificas). Vol. 1 (1944)-. Spanish. an. 2300ptas Spain; 3450 other. Consejo Superior Investigacion Cientificas (CSIC), Vitruvio 8, 28006 Madrid Spain. **Tel** 011 34 1 5612833, FAX 011 34 1 4113077, telex 42182. **LC** F1401; .A587. **UDC** 970/980. cum. index.
Desc: Research and theoretical articles on various topics of Latin American interest, such as history, literature, and anthropology in general and the colonial history of Latin America in particular.
Ind/Abst Am. Hist. Life (1953-); Bibliogr. Mission.; BHA : Biblio. Hist. Art; HAPI Hisp. Am. Period. Index.

CU
ANUARIO DEL CENTRO DE ESTUDIOS MARTIANOS. **Main/Corp** Centro de Estudios Martianos (1977-). (1978)-. Periodical. Spanish. an. Apartado Postal 6640, Habana 6 Cuba. **LC** F1783.M38; C454a. **DD** 972.91/05/0924. ***Supersedes*** *Anuario Martiano, 0066-524X.*

AG/0326-9671
ANUARIO IEHS. **Added/Corp** Universidad Nacional del Centro de la Provincia de Buenos Aires. IEHS. Universidad Nacional del Centro de la Provincia de Buenos Aires. **VFOAT** Anuario del IEHS. (1986)-. Spanish. an. $25.00. IEHS / Instituto de Estudios Historico - Sociales, Pinto 399 2 Piso, 7000 Tandil Argentina. **Tel** 011 54 293 2 2000, FAX 011 54 293 2 1928. **LC** F2801; .A645. **DD** 982/.005. Index available. cum. index. **Bk Rev.** **Ad Acc.** **Pr Rev. Circ:** 1,000 (ctrl).
Ind/Abst Am. Hist. Life.

MX/0304-2596
ANUARIO INDIGENISTA. See Anthropology.

PY
ANUARIO (INSTITUTO DE INVESTIGACIONES HISTORICAS DR. JOSE GASPAR RODRIGUEZ DE FRANCIA). (ANUARIO / INSTITUTO DE INVESTIGACIONES HISTORICS DR. JOSE GASPAR RODRIGUEZ DE FRANCIA.). V. 1, No. 1 (May 1979)-. Periodical. Spanish. **LC** F2686.F832; A57. **DD** 989.2/05/0924. **UDC** 989.2(058).
Ind/Abst Am. Hist. Life (1957-1969).

US/0736-5357
APALACHEE. [Apalachee]. **Added/Corp** Tallahassee Historical Society. (1944)-. English. ir. $11.70. Tallahassee Trust, 329 North Meridian Street, Tallahassee FL 32301. **Tel** (904)488-3901. **ED** Susan Hamburger. **LC** F306; .A6. **DD** 975.9/88. **Circ:** 300. ***Supersedes*** *Tallahassee Historical Society. Annual.*
Desc: Local history covering North Florida from the Suwannee to Ochlockonee River.

US/0090-3779
APPALACHIAN JOURNAL. [Appalach. j.]. Vol. 1 (Autumn 1972)-. Periodical. English. qt. $18.00 (US); $24.00 (other). Appalachian State University / University Hall ASU, Boone NC 28608. **Tel** (704)262-4072, FAX (704)262-2553. **ED** Jerry W Williamson. **LC** F216.2; .A66. **DD** 917.4/005. **UDC** 908.74. Index available. cum. index. **Bk Rev**, (Qty: 20-30 /yr). **Pr Rev. Circ:** 1,200. Documents available from The Genuine Article.
Desc: Interdisciplinary quarterly devoted to Appalachia, its history, culture, geography, literature, folklore, politics, music, religion, anthropology, sociology, etc. and to the pop culture representation of the mountains and mountain people in the American media.
Ind/Abst Am. Hist. Life (1972-); Am. Humanit. Index; Arts Humanit. Citation Index [Full Cov.]; Curr. Contents Arts Humanit.; Curr. Index J. Educ. (March 1990); MLA Int. Bibl. Books Artic. Mod. Lang. Lit.; Res. Alert [Full Cov.]; Soc. Sci. Cit. Index [Select. Cov.].

US/0883-9336
APPRISE. **Added/Corp** WITF, Inc. (19??)-. Periodical. English. Twelve times a year. $35.00. WITF TV, Box 2954, Harrisburg PA 17105. **Tel** (717)236-6000. **LC** F159.H3; A64. **DD** 974.8/18.

CN/0823-8014
APPUI. (L'APPUI : BULLETIN D'INFORMATION DU COMITE D'APPUI AUX NATIONS AUTOCHTONES DE LA LIGUE DES DROITS ET LIBERTES.). [Appui]. Dec. 1980-. Bulletin. French. ir. Free. Appui, 1825 de Champlain, Montreal Quebec H2L 2S9 Canada. **DD** 971/.00497/05. **UDC** 971(97).

CL
APSI : ACTUALIDAD NACIONAL E INTERNACIONAL. (19??)-. Periodical. Spanish. Twenty-six times a year. $150.00 (Americas); $180.00 (other). Sopel S A, Casilla 9896, Santiago Chile. **Tel** 11 56 2 775450. **LC** F3100; .A664.

PY
APUNTES TRIMESTRALES. **Added/Corp** Comite de Iglesias (Asuncion, Paraguay). Departamento de Estudios. (1983)-. Spanish. qt. **LC** F2689; .A79. **DD** 989.2/073/05.
Ind/Abst Hum. Rights Intern. Rep.

US/0742-9576
ARAB AMERICAN ALMANAC. [Arab Am. alm.]. **VFOAT** Dalil Al-Arab Al-Amrikiyin; Arab Americans' Almanac. 3rd Ed. (1984)-. English. ir (Publishes every 4 to 6 years). $19.95. The News Circle, PO Box 3684, Glendale CA 91201. **Tel** (818)545-0333, FAX (818)242-5039. **ED** Joseph Haiek. **LC** E184.A65; A45. **DD** 973/.04927. **Ad Acc. Circ:** 15,000. ***Continues*** *American Arabic Speaking Community Almanac, 0094-8543.*
Desc: The comprehensive reference book on the Arab-American community. It includes an historical chronology of the Arab-American community and a glimpse of prominent Arabic literary figures.

SP
ARAUCARIA DE CHILE. (1978)-. Periodical. Spanish. qt. $16.00. Peralta Ediciones, Carlos Nahum, San Fermin 65, Pamplona Spain. **LC** F3051; .A67. **DD** 983/.005. cum. index.
Ind/Abst HAPI Hisp. Am. Period. Index.

SP/0004-0452
ARCHIVO IBERO-AMERICANO. [Arch. ibero-am.]. **Added/Corp** Franciscans. Vol. 1, No. 1 (1914)-. Periodical. Spanish. qt. $77.00. Archivo Ibero Americano, Joaquin Costa 36, 28002 Madrid Spain. **Tel** 011 34 1 2619900. **LC** BX3601; .A65. **UDC** 970/980. **Bk Rev.**
Desc: History of the Americas' old missions from its discovery in 1492. Also Philippine and all Far East history, important figures in Spain's history, etc.
Ind/Abst Am. Hist. Life (1955-); Bibliogr. Mission.; BHA : Biblio. Hist. Art; HAPI Hisp. Am. Period. Index.

AG
ARGENTINA. **Added/Corp** Argentine Republic. Secretaria de Informacion Publica. (Dec. 1976)-. Periodical. English (Spanish). bm. Secretaria de Informacion Publica, Av Corrientes 640 - 7 Piso, Buenos Aires Argentina. **LC** F2801; .A654. **DD** 982/.005.

PE
ARINSANA : REVISTA DE LA COOPERACION INTERNACIONAL EN AREAS INDIGENAS DE AMERICA LATINA. No. 1 (April 1986)-. Periodical. Spanish. qt. Revista Arizana, Apartado 129, Cuzco Peru. **ED** Emanuelle Amodio.
Ind/Abst Anthropol. Lit.

US/1043-1659
ARIZONA FACTS. [Ariz. facts]. **VFOAT** Flying the Colors, Arizona Facts; Arizona Facts--Flying the Colors Series. (1989)-. English. te. $59.50 (single issue). Clements Research II Inc., 16850 Dallas Parkway, Dallas TX 75248. **Tel** (214)931-9956, FAX (214)248-7159. **ED** John Clements. **LC** F806; .A697. **DD** 979.1/053/05.
Desc: Narrative description of facts about a state, developed county-by-county.

US
ARIZONA HISTORY. ***Suspended.*** Vol. 15, No. 1 (April/May 1984)-Suspended. Periodical. English. bm. Arizona Historical Society, 949 East 2nd Street, Tucson AZ 85719. **Tel** (602)628-5774, FAX (602)628-5695. **UDC** 979.1. **Circ:** 4,000. ***Continues*** *La Reata.*

US/0004-1823
ARKANSAS HISTORICAL QUARTERLY, THE. [Ark. hist. q.]. **Added/Corp** Arkansas Historical Association. Vol. 1 (March 1942)-. Academic Scholarly Publication. English. qt. Comes with Arkansas Historical Association membership. Arkansas Historical Association, Old Main 416, History Department, University of Arkansas, Fayetteville AR 72701. **Tel** (501)575-5884, FAX (501)575-2642. **ED** Jeannie M. Whayne. **LC** F406; .A6. **DD** 976.70062. Index available (bound in 4th issue). cum. index (volumes 1-35 only). **Bk Rev**, (Qty: 40). **Ad Acc. Pr Rev. Circ:** 1,500. available in reprints ((volumes 1-15)) from Kraus Reprint Co.; available on microfilm from University Microfilms International (UMI). Documents available from The Genuine Article.
Desc: Publishes scholarly articles primarily on the history of Arkansas but including articles on the American South and the state's place in the region. Includes book notes, and a section on historical news and notices.
Ind/Abst Am. Hist. Life (1963-); Annu. Bibliogr. Engl. Lang. Lit.; Arts Humanit. Citation Index [Full Cov.]; Curr. Contents Arts Humanit.; Ozark Period. Index; Recent. Publ. Artic.; Ref. Sources; Res. Alert [Full Cov.]; Soc. Sci. Cit. Index [Select. Cov.]; West. Hist. Q.; Writ. Am. Hist.

US/0066-7684
ARLINGTON HISTORICAL MAGAZINE, THE. [Arlingt. hist. mag.]. **Added/Corp** Arlington Historical Society. Vol. 1 (Oct. 1957)-. English. an (Oct.). $9.25. Arlington Historical Society Inc., PO Box 402, Arlington VA 22210. **Tel** (703)892-4204. **ED** Phyllis W. Johnson. **LC** F232.A4; A7. **DD** 975.5/295. **Circ:** 500.
Desc: The Arlington Historical Society is discovering and preserving the history of Arlington County, Virginia.
Ind/Abst Am. Hist. Life.

BL
ARQUIVOS. Periodical. Portuguese. Secretaria de Educacao e Cultura, Recife Brazil. **LC** F2651.R4; A77. **DD** 981/.3/005. **UDC** 981;908.81.

DK
ARSBERETNING - DENMARK-AMERIKA FONDET. **Main/Corp** Danmark-Amerika Fondet. Danish (summaries and/or abstracts in English). Danmark-Amerika Fondet, Nytorv 9, 1450 K Kbenhavn Denmark. **LC** E183.8.D4; D33A.

US/0160-6034
ARTIFACTS (DAYTON). (ARTIFACTS.). V. 1-July 20, 1971-. Periodical. English. qt. $6.00. Artifact Society, PO Box 947, Tiffin OH 44883. **LC** E77.8; .A77. **DD** 973/.05. **UDC** 973.

CN/0046-1040
ARTZAKANK. (ARTZAKANK. ECHO.). **VFOAT** Echo. No. 1 (March 1968)-. Periodical. Armenian (English; summaries and/or abstracts in English). mo. Echo, 18 Dupont Street, Toronto Ontario M5R 1V2 Canada. **DD** 971/.004/4792.

ES
ASI ES MI TIERRA. Periodical. Spanish. Calle Libertad Oriente, Y 5A Avenida sur Apartado Postal 208, Santa Ana El Salvador. **LC** F1481; .A84. **DD** 972.84/005. **UDC** 972.84.

US/0195-8097
ASIAN VOICE. **Added/Corp** Asian Benevolent Corps. (19??)-. Periodical. English. ir. Free. Asian Benevolent Corp, 2423 Pennsylvania Avenue NW, Washington DC 20037. **Tel** (202)331-0129. **LC** E184.O6; A86. **DD** 973/.0495.

CN/0066-992X
ASTICOU (HULL). (ASTICOU.). [Asticou]. **Added/Corp** Societe Historique de l'Ouest du Quebec. Societe Historique de l'Ouest du Quebec. Cahier. Societe d'Histoire de l'Outaouais. No. 1 (1968)-. Periodical. French. Twice a year. 10.00Can$. Societe Historique de l'Outaouais, CP 1007, Succursale B, Hull Quebec J8X 3X5 Canada. **DD** 971.4/005.
Ind/Abst Am. Hist. Life; Point Repere (1983-).

CN/0714-8801
AT ISSUE (REGINA, SASK.). (AT ISSUE.). [At issue]. Periodical. English. ir. $30.00 per no. At Issue Teachers Guide, c/o L A Weigl Educational Associates Saskatchewan S4P 1C5 Canada. **DD** 971.064/6/07. **UDC** 971.

US/0896-3975
ATLANTA HISTORY. [Atlanta hist.]. **Added/Corp** Atlanta Historical Society. Vol. 31, No. 1-2 (Spring-Summer 1987)-. Periodical. English. Four times a year (Jan., Apr., July, Oct.). $20.00. Atlanta Historical Society, 130 West Paces Ferry Road, Atlanta GA 30305. **Tel** (404)261-1837, FAX (404)238-0670. **ED** Elizabeth Tucker, (phone: (404)814-4084). **LC** F294.A8; A863. **DD** 975.8/231. Index available. cum. index. **Bk Rev**, (Qty: 30). **Ad Acc. Pr Rev. Circ:** 6,500. ***Continues*** *Atlanta Historical Journal, 0162-5721.*
Desc: History of Atlanta, Georgia and the south. It features photos, arts, politics, war, religion, transportation, minorites, personalities and many more.
Ind/Abst Am. Hist. Life.

CN/0004-6744
ATLANTIC ADVOCATE, THE. ***Ceased.*** [Atl. advocate]. Vol. 47 (Sept. 1956)-(Jan. 1992). Periodical. English. mo. Atlantic Advocate, PO Box 3370 E3B 5A2 Canada. **LC** AP5; .M245. **DD** 971.5. **UDC** 971.5. ***Continues*** *Maritime Advocate and Busy East, 0319-2458;* ***Absorbed*** *Atlantic Guardian, 0319-2466.*
Ind/Abst Annu. Bibliogr. Engl. Lang. Lit. (19??-19??); AQUAREF; Can. Index (?-?); Can. Period. Index (19??-19??).

CN/0823-6933
ATLANTIC CANADA RESEARCH LETTER. [Atl. Can. res. lett.]. Vol. 1, No. 1 (1982)-. Periodical. English. Three times a year. Free. Gorsebrook Research Institute, c/o St Mary's University, Halifax Nova Scotia B3H 3C3 Canada. **Tel** (902)420-5668. **DD** 971.5/005. **UDC** 971.5. **Circ:** 400 (ctrl).

US/0571-8236
ATTAKAPAS GAZETTE. V. 1- 1966-. Periodical. English. an. $8.00. University of Southwestern Louisiana, Box 40831, LaFayette LA 70504. **Tel** (318)264-6027. **ED** Gertrude C Taylor. **UDC** 908.763. **Bk Rev. Circ:** 625 (ctrl).
Desc: Articles on history, genealogy, folklore and landmarks of the southwest or Attakapas district of south Louisiana.
Ind/Abst Am. Hist. Life.

CN/0836-3102
AU "PAYS" DE MATANE. (AU "PAYS" DE MATANE : REVUE DE LA SOCIETE D'HISTOIRE ET DE GENEALOGIE DE MATANE.). [Au "pays" Matane]. **Added/Corp** Societe d'Histoire et de Genealogie de Matane. Vol. 22, No. 1 (April 1987)-. Periodical. French. Twice a year. 12.00Can$ institutions; 8.00Can$ individuals. Societe d'Histoire et de Genealogie de Matane, 145 Soucy, Matane Quebec G4W 2E1 Canada. **Tel** (418)562-9466. **DD** 971.4/775/005. **Bk Rev. Circ:** 1,000. ***Continues*** *L'Histoire au "Pays" de Matane., 0046-7499.*
Desc: Reviews treating regional history, folklore, handicraft, parish, monography, family histories, art and museum pieces.
Ind/Abst Point Repere.

US/0091-5483
AUDIT OF THE UNITED STATES CAPITOL HISTORICAL SOCIETY FOR THE YEAR ENDED ... . Began with 1972. English. an. US General Accounting Office / District of Columbia, 441 G Street NW, Room 4528, Washington DC 20548. **Tel** (202)275-2812. **LC** F191.U55; U5. **DD** 353.007/232.

US
AUDIT REPORT, TEXAS HISTORICAL COMMISSION. **Main/Corp** Texas Historical Commission. **Added/Corp** Texas. Office of the State Auditor. **VFOAT** Texas Historical Commission. (19??)-. English. an. State Auditor, John H Reagan, State Office Building, PO Box 12067, Austin TX 78711. **LC** F381; .A93. **DD** 353.97640072/32.

US/1064-038X
AUGUSTA (AUGUSTA, GA.). (AUGUSTA : THE LIFESTYLE MAGAZINE OF METROPOLITAN AUGUSTA.). [Augusta]. **VFOAT** Augusta Magazine. (19??)-. Periodical. English. Six times a year. $12.95 US; $19.95 others. Augusta Magazine, PO Box 47250, Augusta GA 30903. **Tel** (404)722-5833, FAX (404)722-8901. **DD** 975. ***Continues*** *Augusta Magazine, 1040-5879.*

US/0571-8899
AUGUSTA HISTORICAL BULLETIN. [Augusta hist. bull.]. **Added/Corp** Augusta County Historical Society. Vol. 1, No. 1 (1965)-. Bulletin. English. Twice a year (Spring, Fall). $10.00. Augusta County Historical Society, PO Box 686, Staunton VA 24401. **Tel** (703)886-1479. **ED** Katherine G. Bushman, (editor's address: 12 Taylor, Staunton, VA 24401). **DD** 975. Index available. cum. index. **Circ:** 500 (ctrl).
Desc: News and information on the history of Augusta County, Virginia.

AT/0705-7113
AUSTRALASIAN JOURNAL OF AMERICAN STUDIES : AJAS. **Added/Corp** Australian and New Zealand American Studies Association. **VFOAT** AJAS; A.J.A.S. Vol. 1, No. 3 (July 1982)-. Academic Scholarly Publication. English. sa (2 issues). 35.00Aus$. Anzasa, History Arts Anu, Canberra ACT 0200 Australia. **Tel** 011 61 6 2494085. **ED** Peter Bastian. **LC** E169.1; .A443. **DD** 973/.05. **Bk Rev. Ad Acc. Pr Rev. Circ:** 170 (ctrl). ***Continues*** *Australian Journal of American Studies.*
Desc: A scholarly, interdisciplinary journal publishing articles on the history, institutions, geography, literature and other arts of the United States.
Ind/Abst Am. Hist. Life (1987-); Annu. Bibliogr. Engl. Lang. Lit.

AT/0810-1906
AUSTRALIAN-CANADIAN STUDIES. [Aust.-Can. stud.]. **Added/Corp** La Trobe University. Dept. of Social Work. Association for Canadian Studies in Australia and New Zealand. Vol. 1, (Jan. 1983)-. English. Twice a year (Autumn & Spring). 15.00Aus$ (individuals), 30.00Aus$ (institutions), Australia; 18.00Aus$ (individuals), 33.00 (institutions), other. University Wollongong, Dr. Turcotte, Department of English, Locked Bag 8844, Wollongong 2521 Australia. **Tel** 011 61 42 213737, FAX 011 61 42 213179. **ED** Dr. G. Turcotte. **DD** 971/.005. Index Bound in First Issue. **Bk Rev**, (Qty: varies). **Ad Acc. Pr Rev. Circ:** 1,000.
Desc: A refereed journal of both the humanities and the social sciences for intellectual debate and information exchange in Australia, Canada and New Zealand.
Ind/Abst Can. Period. Index (1990-);(Vol. 8, no. 1 (1990)-); MLA Int. Bibl. Books Artic. Mod. Lang. Lit.

US/0567-1744
AUTHOR SERIES. **Main/Corp** Norwegian-American Historical Association. (1963)-. Monographic series. English. ir. Price varies per volume. Norwegian-American Historical Association, St. Olaf College, Northfield MN 55057. **Tel** (507)646-3221. **ED** Odd S. Lovoll. **Bk Rev. Ad Acc. Circ:** 1,500 (ctrl).
Desc: A series of accounts by early Norwegian pioneers in America.

US
AVAILABLE FOR RESTORATION. (1984)-. Periodical. English. qt (4 issues). Comes with membership. Historic Preservation Foundation of North Carolina, PO Box 27644, Raleigh NC 27611. **Tel** (919)832-3652.

BO
AVANCES; REVISTA BOLIVIANA DE ESTUDIOS HISTORICOS Y SOCIALES. Feb. 1978-. Periodical. Spanish. $7.50. Revista Avances, Casilla No 6599, La Paz Bolivia. **LC** F3301; .A82. **DD** 984/.005. **UDC** 984;908.84.

CN/0825-0103
B.C. DIGEST (VICTORIA). (B.C. DIGEST.). [B.C. dig.]. **VAT** British Columbia Digest (Victoria). Issue No. 1/84 (Jan. 4, 1984)-. Periodical. English. sm. $125.00. Arrow Publications, PO Box 1854, Victoria BC V8W 2Y3. **DD** 971.1/04/05. **UDC** 971.1. ***Continues*** *Leading Edge (Victoria, B.C.), 0826-029X.*

US
B.C.H.S. SLICKENS / BUTTE COUNTY HISTORICAL SOCIETY. **Main/Corp** Butte County Historical Society (Calif.). **VFOAT** BCHS Slickens. Vol. 22, No. 3 (March 1985)-. Periodical. English. Twelve times a year. $15.00 Comes with Butte County Historical Society Membership. Butte County Historical Society, PO Box 2195, Oroville CA 95965. **Tel** (916)533-5316. **ED** Lori Adams. Index available. cum. index. **Bk Rev. Circ:** 800. ***Continues*** *Slickens.*

CN/0045-2963
B.C. HISTORICAL NEWS. [B.C. hist. news]. **Added/Corp** British Columbia Historical Association. British Columbia Historical Federation. **V5HOAT** British Columbia Historical News. Vol. 1 (Feb. 1968)-. Periodical. English. qt. 10.00Can$ (individuals), 16.00Can$ (institutions) Canada; 14.00Can$ (individuals), 20.00Can$ (institutions) other. British Columbia Historical Fed, #7 5400 Patterson, Burnaby BC V5H 2M5 Canada. **Tel** (604)422-3594. **ED** Naomi Miller, (604)422-3594. cum. index. **Bk Rev**, (Qty: (12-15)). **Circ:** 1150. available on microfiche from Micromedia Limited.
Ind/Abst Am. Hist. Life; Can. Period. Index.

CN/0701-1288
B C TODAY. V. 1- Apr. 30/May, 7 1976-. Periodical. English. sm. $12.00. Phoenix Publications, PO Box 1390, Victoria BC V8W 3C4 Canada. **DD** 971.1/04. **UDC** 971.1.

US/0199-6290
BACK HOME IN KENTUCKY. **VFOAT** In Kentucky. (1978)-. Periodical. English. bm. $14.00 (one year), $22.00 (two year), $28.00 (three year). Greysmith Publishing Company Inc., PO Box 681629, Franklin TN 37064. **Tel** (615)791-1953, FAX (615)790-6188. **ED** Nanci Gregg. **LC** F446; .B3. **DD** 976.9/005. Index available. cum. index. **Ad Acc, Adv Mgr:** Lori Fisher. **Circ:** 20,000 (ctrl).
Desc: Reflects contemporary Kentucky and maintains its historic traditions.

US/0270-0344
BALTIMORE COUNTY HERITAGE PUBLICATION, A. **Added/Corp** Baltimore County Public Library, Towson. (1980)-. Monographic series. English. ir. Price varies per volume. Baltimore County Public Library, 320 York Road, Towson MD 21204. **Tel** (410)887-6194, FAX (410)296-3139. **ED** Richard Parsons (chairman), Neal Brooks, Charles W. Wagandt II, Jean Walsh and Jacques Kelly. Index available. **Bk Rev.**
Desc: Covers local history, Baltimore County, Maryland history, U.S. economic and industrial history.

US
BAY STATE HISTORY. Vol. 10, No. 1 (Summer 1984)-. Periodical. English. sa. $25.00. Bay State Historical League, The State House, Box 247, Boston MA 02133. **UDC** 974.4. **Bk Rev. Circ:** 350. ***Continues*** *Bay State Historical League. Bulletin.*
Desc: Magazine of Massachusetts history and historical administration.

CN/0005-2949
BC STUDIES. [BC stud.]. **VAT** British Columbia Studies. No. 1 (Winter 1969)-. Periodical. English. qt. 32.71Can$ (Canada), 37.71Can$ (US), 42.71Can$ (other) institution; 28.04Can$ (Canada), 33.04Can$ (US), 38.04Can$ (other) individual. University of British Columbia / West Mall, 2029 West Mall, Rooms 217 and 218, Vancouver British Columbia V6T 1Z2 Canada. **Tel** (604)822-3727, FAX (604)822-9452. **ED** Allan Smith. **LC** F1086; .B13. **DD** 917.11/03. **Bk Rev. Circ:** 800 (ctrl). available on microfilm and microfiche from University Microfilms International (UMI).
Desc: Devoted to all aspects of human history in British Columbia. Each issue is divided into three sections: articles covering a wide range of interests such as anthropology, economics, resource management development, history, sociology and archaeology; reviews of books and publications related to British Columbia; and a bibliography of recently published material on B.C.
Ind/Abst Am. Hist. Life (1974-); BHA : Biblio. Hist. Art; Can. Index; Can. Period. Index; Ethnoarts Index; Int. Bibliogr. Sociol.; West. Hist. Q.

CN/0005-7517
BEAVER, THE. [Beaver]. **Added/Corp** Hudson's Bay Company. Vol. 1 (Oct. 1920)-. Periodical. English. bm (Feb., Apr., Jun., Aug., Oct., Dec.). 25.00Can$ Canada; $25.00 US; $32.00 other. Hudson's Bay Company, 450 Portage Avenue, Winnipeg Manitoba R3C OE7 Canada. **Tel** (204)786-7496, FAX (204)786-7048. **ED** Christopher Dafoe. **LC** F1060.1; .B4. Index available. cum. index. **Bk Rev. Ad Acc. Circ:** 30,000. available on microfilm from Micromedia Limited; available on microfilm and microfiche from University Microfilms International (UMI). Documents available from UMI Article Clearinghouse.
Desc: Researched articles on Canadian social history are regular features; also historic pictures. For instruction of the student of history and the casual reader.
Ind/Abst ASTIS Curr. Aware. Bull. (1978-); Am. Hist. Life (1955-); ARTbibliogr. Mod.; ASTIS Bibliogr. (1978-); BHA : Biblio. Hist. Art; Can. Index; Can. Period. Index; Child. Mag. Guide (1981-); Ethnoarts Index; Gen. Period. Index (1986-); Mag. Index Plus (1989-); Mag. Search; Newsp. Period. Abstr. (1988-); Mag. Index (1977-?); West. Hist. Q.

US/0883-8380
BEEHIVE HISTORY. **Added/Corp** Utah State Historical Society. (1975)-. English. an. $20.00 Comes with Utah State Historical Society membership. Utah

State Historical Society, 300 Rio Grande, Salt Lake City UT 84101. **Tel** (801)533-3500, FAX (801)533-3503. **ED** Miriam B. Murphy. **LC** F826; .B43. **DD** 979.2/005. **Circ:** 3,200 (ctrl).
Desc: Short articles on Utah history topics, including all aspects of the states history from the arts to technology, sports, ethnic heritage, etc.
Ind/Abst West. Hist. Q.

GW
BEITRAEGE ZUR SOZIOLOGIE UND SOZIALKUNDE LATEINAMERIKAS. (1967)-. Monographic series. German (English and Spanish). ir. Price varies per volume. Wilhelm Fink Verlag, Ohmstrasse 5, D 80802 Munich Germany. **Tel** 011 49 89 348017, 348018. **ED** Hanns-Albert Steger.
Desc: Publishes monographic studies on various academic fields about Latin America such as history, literary and political sciences, sociology and economic history.

BH/0250-6831
BELIZEAN STUDIES. [Belizean stud.]. **Added/Corp** Belize Institute of Social Research and Action. Vol. 4, No. 2 (March 1976)-. Periodical. English. Three times a year. $25.00 US, Canada, Central America and Caribbean Islands; $30.00 other. Belize Institute of Social Research and Action, St Johns College, PO Box 548, Belize City Belize. **Tel** 011 501 33732, FAX 011 501 32752. **ED** Herman J. Byrd. **LC** F1441; .N37. **DD** 972.82/005. cum. index. **Bk Rev. Ad Acc. Circ:** 350. ***Continues** National Studies, 0303-8688.*
Desc: A journal of social research and thought. Publishes articles on contemporary Belizean affairs.
Ind/Abst Am. Hist. Life (1978-); Anthropol. Lit. (1978-); Ethnoarts Index (1978-); HAPI Hisp. Am. Period. Index (1978-).

CN/0821-4735
BENRI CHO / BANKUBA IJUSHA NO KAI. **VFOAT** Information & Directory for Greater Vancouver. **VAT** Information and Directory for Greater Vancouver - Japanese Immigrants' Association. 1978-. Japanese (English). Japanese Immigrants' Association, PO Box 69012 Station K, Vancouver British Columbia V5K 4W3 Canada. **DD** 971.1/33. **UDC** 971.1956.

US/0409-0829
BENTON COUNTY PIONEER, THE. **Added/Corp** Benton County Historical Society (Ark.). **VFOAT** Pioneer. Vol. 1 (1955)-. Periodical. English. qt. $15.00 institutions; $10.00 individuals. Benton County Historical Society, PO Box 1034, Bentonville AR 72712. **ED** Bernice Freeze (editor's address: 12 Mindy Lane, Bella Vista AR 72714). **LC** F417.B4; B43. **DD** 976.7/13/005. Index available. **Circ:** 300 (ctrl).

GW
BERICHTE ZUR ENTWICKLUNG IN SPANIEN, PORTUGAL UND LATEINAMERIKA. ***Title Change.*** Periodical. German. bm. 50 Langenpreisinger, Strasse 57, Munchen 8 Germany. **LC** F1401; .B36. **UDC** 9806. ***Continued by** Lateinamerika Berichte.*
Ind/Abst Leis. Recreat. Tour. Abstr.; Rural Dev. Abstr.; World Agric. Econ.

US/1042-587X
BERKSHIRE MAGAZINE. [Berks. mag.]. **VFOAT** Berkshire. (1982)-. Periodical. English. Four times a year (Feb., May, Aug., Nov.). $11.95. Berkshire Magazine, PO Box 97, Route 9N, Jay NY 12941. **Tel** (518)946-2191. **DD** 974. **Ad Acc.**
Desc: General interest magazine of the Berkshire region.

US/0146-4191
BEST OF TRUE WEST, THE. Vol. 1 (1977)-. English. an. Western Publications / Oklahoma, PO Box 2107, Stillwater OK 74076. **Tel** (405)743-3370, (800)749-3369, FAX (405)743-3374. **LC** F591; .B53. **DD** 978/.005.
Desc: Covers the cowboys and Indians of North America.

US/0749-9108
BETHEL COURIER (BETHEL, ME 1976), THE. (THE BETHEL COURIER.). [Bethel cour.]. **Added/Corp** Bethel Historical Society (Bethel, Me.). (1976)-. Periodical. English. qt. Bethel Historical Society, Box 12, 15 Brad Street, Bethel ME 04217-0012.
Ind/Abst Genealogical Period. Annu. Index.

US/0894-8917
BETWEEN THE LAKES. (BETWEEN THE LAKES : A NEWSLETTER OF THE INTERLAKEN HISTORICAL SOCIETY.). **Added/Corp** Interlaken Historical Society. (197?)-. Newsletter. English. qt (Jan., Apr., Jun. Oct.). $5.00. Interlaken Historical Society, c/o Newsletter, Interlaken NY 14847. **Tel** (607)532-4430. **ED** Maurice L Patterson. ***Continues** Interlaken Historical Society Newsletter, 0748-6758.*
Desc: Local historical news and programs.

US/1055-291X
BFLO JOURNAL. [BFLO j.]. (199?)-. Periodical. English. Four times a year. $15.00. BFLO Journal, 2316 Delaware Avenue, Suite 246, Buffalo NY 14216. **DD** 973.

MX/0523-1795
BIBLIOGRAFIA HISTORICA MEXICANA. **Added/Corp** Colegio de Mexico. (1967)-. Spanish. an. Colegio de Mexico AC, Camino Al Ajusco No 20, 10740 Mexico DF Mexico. **Tel** 011 52 5 6455955 Ext. 3133, telex 1777585 COLME. **LC** Z1411; .B5.

US/0742-6828
BIBLIOGRAPHIES AND INDEXES IN AMERICAN HISTORY. **See** History(General)-Abstracting, Bibliographies and Statistics.

US/1054-9102
BIBLIOGRAPHIES AND INDEXES IN LATIN AMERICAN AND CARIBBEAN STUDIES. [Bibliogr. indexes Latin Am. Caribb. stud.]. No. 1 (1991)-. Monographic series. English. Greenwood Press Inc., PO Box 5007, Westport CT 06881-5007. **Tel** (203)226-3571, FAX (203)222-1502. **DD** 972.

US/0360-8530
BIENNIAL REPORT - TEXAS HISTORICAL COMMISSION. **Main/Corp** Texas. Historical Commission. English. be. Free. Historical Commission, PO Box 12276 Capitol Station, Austin TX 78711. **Tel** (512)463-6100. **ED** Roni Morales. **LC** F381.T285; A17. **DD** 976.4/006/1764. **UDC** 976.4(047). **Circ:** 2,500.
Desc: News of historic preservation activities in Texas.

CN/0703-1440
BIG COUNTRY CARIBOO MAGAZINE. No. 1- Fall/Winter 1976-. Periodical. English. qt. $1.50 per no. Big Country Cariboo Magazine, Box 4400, Quesnel British Columbia V2J 3J3 Canada. **DD** 971.1/2. **UDC** 971.1.

BL
BILADI. **VFOAT** Revista Biladi. Began in 1972. Periodical. Arabic (Portuguese). ir. $100.00. Rua J Boemer, 967 Pari, CEP 03018 Saulo Paulo SP Brazil. **LC** F2659.A7; B54.

US
BIRMINGHAM HISTORICAL SOCIETY ANNUAL PUBLICATION. Monographic series. English. an. $30.00 Comes with Birmingham Historical Society membership. Birmingham Historical Society, 1 Sloss Quarters, Birmingham AL 35222. **Tel** (205)551-1880.

US/0890-2801
BISBEE MAGAZINE. (BISBEE MAGAZINE : HISTORY, ARTS & LEISURE IN THE QUEEN OF THE COPPER CAMPS.). Fall 1985-. Periodical. English. qt. $6.00. Bisbee Magazine, 7 Bisbee Road/Suite K, Bisbee AZ 85603. **DD** 979.

US/0198-8670
BITS AND PIECES (DENVER). (BITS AND PIECES.). **Added/Corp** Lincoln County Historical Association (N.C). (19??)-. Periodical. English. qt. $4.00. Bits and Pieces, Lincoln County Historical Association, 2385 Forney Hill Road, Denver NC 28037. **LC** F262.L6; B57. **DD** 975.6/782/005.
Ind/Abst Am. Hist. Life (1970-1972).

CN/0503-1036
BJULETEN' - KOMITETU UKRAJINCIV KANADY. (BIULETEN' - KOMITET' UKRAINTSIV KANADY.). **Main/Corp** Ukrainian Canadian Committee. **VFOAT** Bulletin - Ukrainian Canadian Committee. V. 1- Jan. 1953-. Periodical. Ukrainian (English). qt. 10.00Can$. Byuletin Komitetu Ukraincîv, 456 Main Street, Winnipeg Manitoba R3B 1B6 Canada. **Tel** (204)947-3882. **ED** Oksana Rozumna. **UDC** 971(83). **Bk Rev. Circ:** 7,500.

CN/0701-0605
BLACK DIAL DIRECTORY. 1975/77-. Directory. English. be. Black Dial Directory, 631A Bloor Street West, Toronto Ontario M6G 1K8 Canada. **DD** 971.3/004/96. **UDC** 971.3(96)(036).

US/1064-5489
BLOUNT COUNTY HISTORICAL SOCIETY. (BLOUNT COUNTY HISTORICAL SOCIETY : NEWSLETTER.). [Blount Cty. Hist. Soc.]. **Added/Corp** Blount County Historical Society (Oneonta, Ala.). (19??)-. Newsletter. English. qt (Jan., Apr., July, Oct.). $5.00. Blount County Historical Society, PO Box 45, Oneonta AL 35121. **Tel** (205)274-9111 Ext. 306. **ED** Emma Linder. **DD** 977. **Circ:** 125.
Desc: Covers local history subjects and interests of Blount County, Alabama .

US/1056-6252
BLOUNT JOURNAL, THE. **See** Genealogy and Heraldry.

US/0741-2207
BLUE & GRAY MAGAZINE. [Blue gray mag.]. **VFOAT** Blue & Gray; Blue and Gray Magazine. V. 1, Issue 1 (Aug./Sept. 1983)-. Periodical. English. bm. $19.00. Blue & Gray Enterprises, 522 Norton Road, Columbus OH 43228. **Tel** (614)870-1861. **ED** David E Roth. **LC** E461; .B64. **DD** 973.7/05. **UDC** 973.07. **Bk Rev**, (Qty: 50 or more per year). **Ad Acc, Adv Mgr:** Robin Roth, **Tel** (614)870-1865. **Circ:** 50,000 (ctrl).
Desc: An award winning magazine that offers its readers a modern and colorful adventure back in time. Each issue features a battle or significant Civil War site with modern color photographs, period photos, battle maps and a self-guiding tour.

US/1055-6265
BN HISTORIAN, THE. **Added/Corp** BN Historical Society. (1991)-. Periodical. English. qt. $10.00. BN Historical Society, PO Box 2480, Monrovia CA 91017.

BL
BOLETIM / CEHILA. **Added/Corp** Comision de Estudios de Historia de la Iglesia en Latinoamerica. (19??)-. Bulletin. Portuguese (Spanish). Twice a year (Feb., July). $20.00. Cehila, Rua Prof Sebastiao Soares 57-6, 01317 Sao Paulo SP, Brazil. **ED** Jose Oscar Beozzo (phone: 55 11 284 6299). **LC** WMLC 93/1518. **Bk Rev. Circ:** 1,500 (ctrl).

BL
BOLETIM DO INSTITUTO DE ARQUEOLOGIA BRASILEIRA : SERIE ESPECIAL. **Main/Corp** Instituto de Arqueologia Brasileira. No. 1- 1975-. Bulletin. Portuguese. Centro de Estudios Arqueologicos, Novo End Av Suburbana 4616 del Castillo, 20000 Rio de Janeiro Brazil. **LC** F2519; .I57A. **UDC** 902(81).

AG/0325-6081
BOLETIN - ARCHIVO GENERAL DE LA PROVINCIA DE SANTA FE. **Main/Corp** Archivo General de la Provincia de Santa Fe. (1969)-. Periodical. Spanish. ir. $6.00. Boletin del Archivo General, Avenida General Lopez 2792, Santa Fe Argentina.
Ind/Abst Am. Hist. Life (1970-1976).

CK/0006-6303
BOLETIN DE HISTORIA Y ANTIGUEDADES. [Bol. hist. antig.]. **Added/Corp** Colombia. Comision de Historia Nacional. Academia de Historia Nacional (Colombia). Academia Nacional de Historia (Colombia). Academia Colombiana de Historia. Vol. 1, No. 1 (Sept. 1902)-. Periodical. Spanish. mo. $100.00. Academia de Historia, Apartado Aereo 14428, Bogota de Colombia. **Tel** 011 57 1 2413615. **LC** F2251; .A16. cum. index.
Ind/Abst Am. Hist. Life (1954-); ARTbibliogr. Mod.; BHA : Biblio. Hist. Art; HAPI Hisp. Am. Period. Index.

CL/0716-5439
BOLETIN DE LA ACADEMIA CHILENA DE LA HISTORIA. [Bol. Acad. Chil. Hist.]. **Main/Corp** Academia Chilena de la Historia. Vol. 1, No. 1 (1933)-. Periodical. Spanish. an. 15000.00Chil$. Academia Chilena de la Historia, Clasificador 245 Correo Central, Santiago Chile. **Tel** 011 56 2 6399323, FAX 011 56 2 332129. **LC** F3051; .A24. **DD** 983. cum. index.
Ind/Abst Am. Hist. Life (1955-1970); BHA : Biblio. Hist. Art; HAPI Hisp. Am. Period. Index; Indice Hist. Esp.

CK/0120-9493
BOLETIN DE LA ACADEMIA DE HISTORIA DEL VALLE DEL CAUCA. [Bol. Acad. Hist. Valle Cauca]. **Main/Corp** Academia de Historia del Valle del Cauca. (1952)-. Periodical. Spanish. Academia de Historia del Valle Del Cauca, Apartados Aereos, 2242 Y 10.088, Cali, Columbia. ***Continues** Academia de Historia del Valle. Boletin de la Academia de Historia del Valle.*
Ind/Abst Am. Hist. Life (1960-1973).

AG/0325-0482
BOLETIN DE LA ACADEMIA NACIONAL DE LA HISTORIA. [Bol. Acad. Nac. Hist.]. **Main/Corp** Academia Nacional de la Historia (Argentina). (1938)-. Spanish. an. **LC** F2801; .A22. **DD** 980.062. ***Continues** Boletin de la Junta de Historia y Numismatica Americana.*
Ind/Abst Am. Hist. Life (1959-1972).

VE/0254-7325
BOLETIN DE LA ACADEMIA NACIONAL DE LA HISTORIA (CARACAS). (BOLETIN DE LA ACADEMIA NACIONAL DE LA HISTORIA.). [Bol. Acad. Nac. Hist.]. **Main/Corp** Academia Nacional de la Historia (Venezuela). No. 1 (March 31, 1912)-. Periodical. Spanish. ir. Bs90.00. Libreria Mundal T Forero & Company, Santa Cailla Mijares 26, Edif San Mauricio Venezuela. **LC** F2301; .A15. **DD** 987.005. Index Available, published separately, free-automatically sent. cum. index.
Ind/Abst Am. Hist. Life (1953-); HAPI Hisp. Am. Period. Index (1953-).

PR/0567-6037
BOLETIN DE LA ACADEMIA PUERTORRIQUENA DE LA HISTORIA. [Bol. Acad. Puertorriq. Hist.]. **Main/Corp** Academia Puertorriquena de la Historia. Vol. 1 (Nov. 1968)-. Periodical. Spanish. sa. $12.00. Academia Puertorriquena de la Historia, San Juan PR 00905. **Tel** (801)723-8772. **ED** D Aurelio Tio, Nazario de Figueroa. **LC** F1951; .A63. **DD** 972.95/005. ctrl circ.

History(General) —History of North, South, and Central America

Desc: Historical studies in general, and in particular of Puerto Rico.
Ind/Abst Am. Hist. Life (1971-1972); HAPI Hisp. Am. Period. Index (19??-).

VE/1012-9464
BOLETIN DE LA BIBLIOTECA NACIONAL (CARACAS). (BOLETIN DE LA BIBLIOTECA NACIONAL.). [Bol. Bibl. nac.]. **Main/Corp** Biblioteca Nacional de Venezuela. **VFOAT** Boletin de la Biblioteca Nacional de Caracas. (1923)-. Periodical. Spanish. qt.
Ind/Abst Am. Hist. Life (1959-1965).

PY/0583-7316
BOLETIN DE LA SOCIEDAD BOLIVARIANA DEL PARAGUAY. [Bol. Soc. boliv. Parag.]. **Main/Corp** Sociedad Bolivariana del Paraguay. Vol. 1 (1954)-. Spanish. LC F2235.3; .S87.
Ind/Abst Am. Hist. Life (1957-1970).

VE/0042-3386
BOLETIN DEL ARCHIVO HISTORICO DE MIRAFLORES. See Genealogy and Heraldry-Archives.

PE/0258-8536
BOLETIN DEL INSTITUTO DE ESTUDIOS AYMARAS. [Bol. Inst. Estud. Aymaras]. **Added/Corp** IDEA (Organization : Puno, Puno, Peru). (1978)-. Periodical. Spanish. ir. $6.00 (individuals); $9.00 (institutions). Estudios Aymaras, Apartado 295, Puno Peru.
Ind/Abst Anthropol. Lit.

DR
BOLETIN DEL MUSEO DEL HOMBRE DOMINICANO. **Main/Corp** Museo del Hombre Dominicano. Vol. 1 (1972)-. Periodical. Spanish. sa.
Ind/Abst Anthropol. Lit.; Ethnoarts Index.

CK
BOLETIN HISTORIAL. **Added/Corp** Centro de Historia de Cartagena de Indias. Academia de la Historia de Cartagena de Indias. (1915)-. Periodical. Spanish. mo. LC F2251; .B65.
Ind/Abst Am. Hist. Life (1955-1961, 1968-1971).

VE/0016-2701
BOLETIN HISTORICO (CARACAS). (BOLETIN HISTORICO.). [Bol. hist.]. **Added/Corp** Fundacion John Boulton. Vol. 1 (Dic. 1962)-. Periodical. Spanish. Three times a year. Fundacion John Boulton, Apartado 929, Caracas Venezuela. LC F2301; .B58.
Ind/Abst Am. Hist. Life (1955-1970); HAPI Hisp. Am. Period. Index (19??-).

BO
BOLETIN INDIGENISTA. See Anthropology.

VE/0523-9133
BOLETIN INDIGENISTA VENEZOLANO. See Anthropology.

GW
BOLETIN INFORMATIVO (ASOCIACION DE HISTORIADORES LATINOAMERICANISTAS EUROPEOS). (BOLETIN INFORMATIVO / ASOCIACION DE HISTORIADORES LATINOAMERICANISTAS EUROPEOS AHILA.). Spanish. Iberische und Lateinamerikanische Abteilung des Historischen Seminars, Universitat zu Koln Albertus Magnus Platz, W-5000 Koln 41 Germany. UDC 9806.

PN
BOLETIN INFORMATIVO DEL ARCHIVO NACIONAL DE PANAMA. **Main/Corp** Panama. Archivo Nacional. (19??)-. Periodical. Spanish. sa. Ministerio de Gobierno y Justicia, Apartado 6618, Panama Panama. LC F1561; .P26a. DD 972.87.

CK
BOLETIN / MUSEO DEL ORO, BANCO DE LA REPUBLICA. Jan./April 1978-. Periodical. Spanish. Three times a year. LC F2269; .B69. DD 986.1/01. UDC 986.1.
Ind/Abst Anthropol. Lit.

SP
BOLETIN OFICIAL DEL TERRITORIO HISTORICO DE ALAVA. Spanish. ir. 4335.00ptas. Diputacion Fural de Alava, Plaza de la Provincia, 01001 Vitoria Gasteiz Spain. Tel 011 34 45 135500.

CN/0824-3816
BOLIVIA (MONTREAL). (BOLIVIA / ASSOCIACION SIC. BOLIVIANA DE MONTREAL.). [Bolivia]. Periodical. Spanish. Asociacion Boliviana de Montreal, PO Box 727 Station B Canada. DD 984/.006/0714281. UDC 984.

US/0896-1557
BONANZA BUGLE, THE. (THE BONANZA BUGLE / LAKE ODESSA AREA HISTORICAL SOCIETY.). **Added/Corp** Lake Odessa Area Historical Society. (19??)-. Periodical. English. qt (4 issues). $7.00 (includes membership). Lake Odessa Area Historic Society, Page Memorial Building, Lake Odessa MI 48849. Tel (616)374-8420. DD 977.

CN/0228-2046
BOREAL INSTITUTE VERTICAL FILES ON NORTHERN AFFAIRS, KWIC INDEX TO CLIPPING SERVICE ON MICROFICHE. [Boreal Inst. vert. files north. aff., KWIC index clipp. serv. microfiche]. **VFOAT** KWIC Index to Clipping Service on Microfiche. **VAT** Boreal Institute Library. KWIC Index. News Clippings. 1975-. English. an. Micromedia Limited, 20 Victoria Street, Toronto Ontario M5C 2N8 Canada. Tel (416)362-5211, (800)387-2689, FAX (416)362-6161, telex 06524668. DD 971.9. UDC 971.9.

UK
BRAND BOOK, THE. Vol. 14, No. 2 (Jan. 1972)-. Periodical. English. qt. $4.00. English Westerners Society, 90 Babbacombe Road, Bromley Kent England. LC F592; .E5. DD 978/.02/05. Continues English Westerners' Brand Book.

US/0006-9078
BRANDING IRON, THE. No. 1- Mar. 1948-. Periodical. English. qt. William Escherich, PO Box 2890 Terminal Annex, Los Angeles CA 90051. Continues Westerners. Los Angeles Corral. Brand Book.

US
BRASILIANS, THE. (19??)-. Periodical. Portuguese (English). Twelve times a year. $20.00. Brasilians, PO Box 985, New York NY 10185. Tel (212)382-1630.

US/0741-0298
BRASILIANS, THE. [Brasilians]. (197?)-. Newspaper. English (Portuguese). Twelve times a year. $20.00. The Brasilians, PO Box 985, 20 West 46th Street, New York NY 10036. Tel (212)382-1630. ED Edilberto Mendes, Margaret Kowarick (Managing Editor). DD 981. Bk Rev, (Qty: 20 per year). Photos. Ad Acc, Adv Mgr: Jack Donado. Pub. Size: Standard. Wire Svcs.: AP. Circ: 45,000. available in microform.

US/0741-1200
BRIDGE (SALEM, OR.), THE. (THE BRIDGE : JOURNAL OF THE DANISH AMERICAN HERITAGE SOCIETY.). [Bridge]. **Added/Corp** Danish American Heritage Society. No. 1 (May 1978)-. Periodical. English. sa. $15.00. Danish American Heritage Society, 132 North 132nd Street 301, Seattle WA 98133. Tel (503)588-1331. ED Egon Bodtker. LC E184.S19; B74. DD 973/.043981. Bk Rev. Circ: 700.
Desc: Records the history of Danish immigrants - a history reflecting the ideals, strengths and traditions they brought with them and their contributions to their new homeland. The society is committed to stimulating interest in the Danish cultural contribution and to preserving it for future generations.

CN
BRITISH COLUMBIA HISTORICAL NEWS : JOURNAL OF THE B.C. HISTORICAL FEDERATION. **Added/Corp** British Columbia Historical Federation. **VFOAT** B.C. Historical News. (19??)-. English. qt.
Ind/Abst Can. Index; Can. Period. Index (19??-).

CN
BRITISH COLUMBIA REPORT. (19??)-. English. wk. 89.00Can$ Canada; 152.96Can$ US; 288.16Can$ other. United Western Communications Ltd, 17327-106A Avenue, Edmonton Alberta T5S 1M7 Canada. Tel (403)486-2277.

CN/0847-2998
BRITISH COLUMBIA REPORT (VANCOUVER). (BRITISH COLUMBIA REPORT.). [B.C. rep.]. Vol. 1, No. 1 (Sept. 4, 1989)-. Periodical. English. wk. $2.50 (single issue), $69.00 (per year). BC Report Magazine Ltd., 103-1161 Melville Street, Vancouver, British Columbia V6E 2X7 Canada. LC F1088; .B88. DD 971.1/005.
Ind/Abst Can. Index; Can. Period. Index (19??-).

UK/0269-9222
BRITISH JOURNAL OF CANADIAN STUDIES. [Br. j. Can. stud.]. **Added/Corp** British Association of Canadian Studies. Vol. 1, No. 1 (June 1986)-. English (French; summaries and/or abstracts in French). sa. £25.00. British Association for Canadian Studies / BACS, 21 George Square, Edinburgh EH8 9LD United Kingdom. Tel 011 44 31 662 1117, FAX 011 44 31 662 1118. ED Ged Martin. LC F1021; .B94. DD 971/.005. Index available. Bk Rev. Circ: 700 (ctrl). Continues Bulletin of Canadian Studies, 0141-2639.
Ind/Abst Am. Hist. Life (1986-); Can. Period. Index (June 1989-); Int. Bibliogr. Sociol.

US/0007-2249
BRONX COUNTY HISTORICAL SOCIETY JOURNAL, THE. (JOURNAL / BRONX COUNTY HISTORICAL SOCIETY.). [Bronx County Hist. Soc. j.]. **Main/Corp** Bronx County Historical Society. Vol. 1, No. 1 (Jan. 1964)-. Periodical. English. sa. $12.00. Bronx County Historical Society, 3309 Bainbridge Avenue, Bronx NY 10467. Tel (212)881-8900. ED Gary Hermalyn. Index available. cum. index. Bk Rev. Ad Acc. Circ: 10,000. available on microfilm from University Microfilms International (UMI); available on audiocassette.
Desc: The only regular published compendium on the history and heritage of New York.
Ind/Abst Am. Hist. Life (1986-).

US/0884-8815
BROOKGREEN JOURNAL. See The Arts-Art.

US
BROOKLYN TRIBUNE, THE. Vol. 2, No. 14 (Oct. 2, 1981)-. Periodical. English. $2.00. A&F Newspaper Enterprises, Box 445 Coney Island Station, Brooklyn NY 11224. LC F129.B7; B76. DD 974.7/23043/05. UDC 974.7. Continues Brooklyn Feature.

US/0148-0340
BROWARD LEGACY. **Added/Corp** Broward County Historical Commission. Vol. 1 (Oct. 1976)-. Periodical. English. Twice a year (Mar., Sept.). $6.00. Broward County Historical Commission, 151 Southwest Second Street, Ft Lauderdale FL 33301. Tel (305)765-4670. ED Rodney E. Dillion, Jr. (phone: (305)765-4671). LC F317.B85; B76. DD 975.9/35/005. Index available. cum. index. Circ: 1,500.
Desc: History of Broward County and the surrounding region of southeast Florida.

BH
BRUKDOWN. Vol. 1 No. 1 (Jan. 1977)-. Periodical. English. ir. $15.00. PO Box 679, Belize City Belize. LC F1441; .B78. DD 972.82/005. UDC 972.82.

US/0045-3307
BUCKSKIN BULLETIN. V. 1- 1960-. Bulletin. English. qt. $5.00. Westerners International, 1700 Northeast 63rd Street, Oklahoma City OK 73111. UDC 973-15. Bk Rev. Ad Acc. Circ: 4,500 (ctrl).
Desc: Articles on western history, reprints of awards, papers by members, book reviews, corral activities and member's activities.
Ind/Abst West. Hist. Q.

CN/0318-5486
BULLETIN - ASSOCIATION DES PROFESSEURS D'HISTOIRE LOCALE DU QUEBEC. **Main/Corp** Association des Professeurs d'Histoire Locale du Quebec. First issue in Feb. 1975. Bulletin. French. ir. $5.00. Association des Professeurs d'Histoire Locale du Quebec, CP 112, Quebec Quebec G1T 2P7 Canada. DD 971/.007. UDC 971.4.

CN/0318-9600
BULLETIN - CANADIAN AURAL/ORAL HISTORY ASSOCIATION. Title Change. **Main/Corp** Canadian Aural/Oral History Association. **VFOAT** Bulletin. Vol. 1 (March 1975)-. Bulletin. Multiple languages (English and French). Public Archives Canada Sound Archives Section, 395 Wellington Street, Ottawa Ontario K1A 0N3 Canada. DD 971/.006/271. UDC 971. Continued by Canadian Oral History Association. Bulletin, 0383-6576.

US/0577-9065
BULLETIN - CHINESE HISTORICAL SOCIETY OF AMERICA. (BULLETIN OF THE CHINESE HISTORICAL SOCIETY OF AMERICA.). [Bull. - Chin. Hist. Soc. Am.]. **Main/Corp** Chinese Historical Society of America. **Added/Corp** Chinese Historical Society of America. **VFOAT** Bulletin. (Jan. 15, 1966)-. Bulletin. English. Ten times a year. $35.00 US individuals; $45.00 institutions and foreign institutions. Chinese Historical Society of America, 650 Commercial Street, San Francisco CA 94111. Tel (415)391-1188. ED Eve Armentrout Ma. LC E184.C5; C48a. DD 909. Bk Rev. Circ: 500 (ctrl).
Ind/Abst Am. Hist. Life; West. Hist. Q.

CN/0712-2187
BULLETIN DE L'INSTITUT D'HISTOIRE DE L'AMERIQUE FRANCAISE. [Bull. Inst. hist. Am. fr.]. **Added/Corp** Institut d'Histoire de l'Amerique Francaise. Vol. 1, No. 1 (Oct. 1981)-. Periodical. French. sa. Free to members. Institut d'Histoire de l'Amerique Francaise, 261 Bloomfield Avenue, Montreal Quebec H2V 3R6 Canada. Tel (514)278-2232. DD 971.4/006. Circ: 1,400 (ctrl).

PE/0303-7495
BULLETIN DE L'INSTITUT FRANCAIS D'ETUDES ANDINES. [Bull. Inst. fr. etud. andines]. **Main/Corp** Institut Francais d'Etudes Andines. **VFOAT** Boletin del Instituto Frances de Estudios Andinos. V. 1- 1972-. Bulletin. Multiple languages (English, French and Spanish). sa. $2.00 single issue. Institut Francais d'Etudes Andines, Contralmirante Montero 141, Miraflores, Lima 18 Peru. Tel 476070. LC F2212. DD 918. UDC 985;908.85. CODEN BIFEB5. Bk Rev.
Ind/Abst Anthropol. Index; Anthropol. Lit.; Ecol. Abstr. (?-?); Geogr. Abstr. Human Geogr.; GeoRef; HAPI Hisp. Am. Period. Index; Int. Dev. Abstr.

US/0196-6170
BULLETIN (MICHIGAN HISTORICAL COLLECTIONS). (BULLETIN - MICHIGAN HISTORICAL COLLECTIONS.). [Bull. - Mich. Hist. Collect.]. No. 1-. Bulletin. English. University Michigan Department of History, Ann Arbor MI 48189. **UDC** 930.9. cum. index.
Desc: Comparative study of history and society internationally and from all disciplines.

UK/0261-3050
BULLETIN OF LATIN AMERICAN RESEARCH. [Bull. Lat. Am. res.]. **Added/Corp** Society for Latin American Studies (Great Britain). Vol. 1, No. 1 (Oct. 1981)-. Periodical. English. Three times a year. $157.00 The Americas; £105.00 other. Pergamon Press, An Imprint of Elsevier Science Ltd., The Boulevard, Langford Lane, Kidlington, Oxford OX5 1GB United Kingdom. **Tel** 011 44 865 843000, 011 44 865 843699, FAX 011 44 865 843010. **(Subscription address:** Elsevier Science Ltd. Oxford Fulfillment Centre, PO Box 800, Kidlington, Oxford OX5 1DX United Kingdom.**) ED** Sylvia Chant. **LC** F1401; .B84. **DD** 980/.005. **CODEN** BLARE9. **[CCC].** available on microfilm and microfiche from University Microfilms International (UMI). ***Continues*** *Society for Latin American Studies (Great Britain). Bulletin of the Society for Latin American Studies.*
Ind/Abst ABC POL SCI; Abstr. Anthropol.; Acad. Search (July 1993-); Am. Hist. Life (1981-); Br. Humanit. Index; Curr. Geogr. Publ. (199?-); Geogr. Abstr. Human Geogr.; HAPI Hisp. Am. Period. Index; INFO-SOUTH Abstr.; Int. Bibliogr. Sociol.; Int. Dev. Abstr.; Mag. Search; PAIS Int. Print (1991-).

PH
BULLETIN OF THE AMERICAN HISTORICAL COLLECTION. 1- June 1972-. Bulletin. English. ir. P12.00. American Association of Philippine, Box 1495, 1099 Manila Philippines. **Tel** 011 63 2 8925198. **ED** Lewis E Gleeck. **UDC** 959.9. **Bk Rev. Circ:** 600.
Desc: Historical and biographical articles and book reviews on the American experience in the Philippines, 1898 to present.
Ind/Abst Index Philip. Period.

US
BULLETIN OF THE CORTLAND COUNTY HISTORICAL SOCIETY. Vol. 1, No. 1 (Jan. 1947)-. Bulletin. English. bm. Cortland County Historical Society, 25 Homer Avenue, Cortland NY 13045. **ED** Mary Ann Kane. **UDC** 974.7. Index available. **Circ:** 750.

US/0887-5413
BULLETIN OF THE GLOUCESTER COUNTY HISTORICAL SOCIETY. [Bull. Glos. Cty. Hist. Soc.]. **Added/Corp** Gloucester County Historical Society (N.J.). Vol. 1, No. 1 (Sept. 1947)-. Periodical. English. qt. $8.00. Gloucester County Historical Society, 17 Hunter Street, Woodbury NJ 08096-4605. **Tel** (609)845-4771. **ED** Mr. and Mrs. Joseph Laughlin (Editor's Address: PO Box 321, Swedesboro, NJ 08085; Editor's Phone: (609)467-4418). **DD** 974. Index available. **Bk Rev. Circ:** 1,900 (ctrl).
Desc: Articles on the history and genealogy of the South Jersey area, with emphasis in Gloucester County. Also contains news of the society's activities.
Ind/Abst Am. Hist. Life.

US/0362-8590
BULLETIN OF THE HISTORICAL SOCIETY OF MONTGOMERY COUNTY, PENNSYLVANIA. **Main/Corp** Historical Society of Montgomery County (Pennsylvania). Vol. 1 (Oct. 1936)-. Bulletin. English. sa (Fall and Spring). $15.00. Historical Society of Montgomery County, 1654 Dekalb Street, Norristown PA 19401. **Tel** (610)272-0297. **ED** Suzanne Hilton. **LC** F157.M7; H45. Index available. cum. index. **Circ:** 1,250 (ctrl).
Desc: Articles on the history of Montgomery County and its people.

US/0458-3108
BULLETIN OF THE LOUDOUN COUNTY HISTORICAL SOCIETY, INC. **Main/Corp** Loudoun County Historical Society. Began with Vol. for 1958. Bulletin. English. Loudoun County Historical Society, 9 East Market Street, PO Box 359, Leesburg VA 22075. **LC** F232.L8; L5812. **DD** 975.5/28/005. **UDC** 975.5.

US/0362-1731
BULLETIN - SHAWNEE COUNTY HISTORICAL SOCIETY. (BULLETIN OF THE SHAWNEE COUNTY HISTORICAL SOCIETY.). **Main/Corp** Shawnee County Historical Society. **Added/Corp** Shawnee County Historical Society (Kan.). No. 1 (Dec. 1946)-. Bulletin. English. an (Dec.). $15.00. Shawnee County Historical Society, PO Box 2201, Topeka KS 66601. **Tel** (913)267-0309. **LC** F687.S5; S4.

CN/0845-4493
BULLETIN / UKRAINIAN CANADIAN COMMITTEE, SASKATCHEWAN PROVINCIAL COUNCIL, THE. [Bull. - Ukr. Can. Comm., Sask. Prov. Counc.]. **VFOAT** Biuleten. **VAT** Buleten - Komitet Ukrainciv Kanadi. Provincijna Rada Saskacebanu. Vol. 1, No. 1 (Oct. 1986)-. Bulletin. English (Ukrainian). an. Free. Ukrainian Canadian Committee National, 456 Main Street, Winnipeg Manitoba R3B 1B6 Canada. **DD** 971/.00491791.

US/0501-0918
BULLETIN - UNDERHILL SOCIETY OF AMERICA. (BULLETIN OF THE UNDERHILL SOCIETY OF AMERICA EDUCATION AND PUBLISHING FUND.). **Main/Corp** Underhill Society of America. (19??)-. Periodical. English. ir. Free on request. Underhill Society of America, PO Box 712, Oyster Bay NY 11771. **ED** N. Robert Underhill. **Circ:** 1,000 (ctrl).

US/1070-8243
BUSHWHACKER MUSINGS : VERNON COUNTY HISTORICAL SOCIETY NEWSLETTER. **Added/Corp** Vernon County Historical Society. (19??)-. Newsletter. English. Four times a year. $5.00 US; $6.50 Canada; $10.00 Pan-American nations; $11.00 other. Vernon County Historical Society, 231 North Main Street, Nevada MO 64772. **Tel** (417)667-7108. **ED** Patrick Brophy (editor's address: 411 South Adams Street, Nevada, MO 64772). **DD** 977. **Bk Rev,** (Qty: few). **Ad Acc. Circ:** 700. ***Continues*** *Bushwhacker.*

BL
CADERNOS DO RIO GRANDE DE NORTE. (19??)-. Periodical. Portuguese. bm. Cr$48.00. Calima-Editorial Promocoes e Publicidade, rua Camara Cascudo 231, 10 Andar Sala 106 Natal Brazil. **LC** F2616; .C24.

CN/0705-2944
CAHIER HISTORIQUE. [Cah. hist.]. **VFOAT** Cahiers Historiques de la Petite-Nation. 1- April 1978-. Periodical. French. mo. $5.00. La Societe de Recherches Communautaires, CP 240, Saint-Andre-Avellin Quebec J0V 1W0 Canada. **DD** 971.4/71/4227005. **UDC** 971.4.

CN/0711-0529
CAHIER - SOCIETE HISTORIQUE DU MARIGOT, LONGUEUIL (1980). (CAHIER ... / SOCIETE HISTORIQUE DU MARIGOT, LONGUEUIL.). [Cah. - Soc. hist. Marigot, Longueuil (1980)]. No. 5 (June 1980)-. Periodical. French. $1.00 per number. Societe Historique du Marigot, CP 432 Succursale A, Longueuil Quebec J4H 3Z2 Canada. **DD** 971.4/37/005. **UDC** 971.4. ***Continues*** *Cahiers (Societe Historique du Marigot (Longueuil)), 0711-0375.*

CN/0228-0930
CAHIERS DE LA SEIGNEURIE DE CHAMBLY. **Added/Corp** Societe d'Histoire de la Seigneurie de Chambly. (1979)-. French. Twice a year. Societe d'Histoire de la Seigneurie de Chambly, Case Postale 142, Chambly Quebec J3L 4B1 Canada. **Tel** (514)658-1200. **DD** 971.4/37/005. **Ad Acc. Circ:** 500 (ctrl).
Desc: Local history told by local historians in love with their localities.

FR
CAHIERS DES AMERIQUES LATINES (PARIS, FRANCE : 1985). (CAHIERS DES AMERIQUES LATINES.). Vol. 1 (Spring 1985)-. Periodical. French (English, Portuguese and Spanish). sa. 200.00F. Service Publications IHEAL, 28 rue Saint-Guillaume, 75007 Paris France. **Tel** 011 44 39 86 53, FAX 011 45 48 79 58. **LC** F1401; .C18. **DD** 980/.005. **UDC** 9806. **Bk Rev. Ad Acc. Circ:** 600 (ctrl). ***Continues*** *Serie Sciences de l'Homme, 0008-0020.*
Ind/Abst Am. Hist. Life (1975-); HAPI Hisp. Am. Period. Index; Int. Bibliogr. Sociol.; Int. Polit. Sci. Abstr.

CN/0575-089X
CAHIERS DES DIX. (LES CAHIERS DES DIX.). [Cah. dix]. **Main/Corp** Les Dix. No 1 (1936)-. Periodical. French. ir. $18.00. Les Editions la Liberte, 3020 Chemin Sainte-Foy, Sainte-Foy Quebec G1X 3V6 Canada. **Tel** (418)658-3763. **DD** 971/.005.
Desc: Ten articles by ten authors on the history of Canada.
Ind/Abst Point Repere (1983-19??).

CN/0226-7063
CAHIERS D'HISTOIRE DE DEUX-MONTAGNES. [Cah. hist. Deux-Montagnes]. V. 1- Jan. 1978-. Periodical. French. ir (two to three issues per year). Free to members, membership 20.00Can$. Societe d Histoire de Deux Montagnes, CP 204, Saint-Eustache Quebec J7R 4K6 Canada. **ED** Gilles Boileau. **DD** 971.4/25/05. **UDC** 971.4. Index available. **Bk Rev. Ad Acc. Circ:** 300.
Desc: Articles and reviews concerning the regional history of two mountains county.

CN/0824-796X
CAHIERS D'HISTOIRE DE LA RIVIERE DU NORD, LES. Vol. 1, No. 1 (Mar. 1983)-. Periodical. French. Three times a year. Free to members. Societe d'Histoire de la Riviere du Nord, C P 784, St-Jerome Quebec J7Z 5V4 Canada. **DD** 971.4/24/005. **UDC** 971.4.

CN/0701-4031
CAHIERS D'HISTOIRE DE L'UNIVERSITE LAVAL, LES. [Cah. hist. Univ. Laval]. **Added/Corp** Universite Laval. Institut d'Histoire. (1974)-. Monographic series. French. ir. Price varies per volume. Presses de l'Universite Laval, CP 2447 Avenue de la Medicine, Saint Foy Quebec G1K 7P4 Canada. **Tel** (418)656-5106, (418)656-2590. **DD** 971/.005. ***Continues*** *Cahiers de l'Institut d'Histoire (Universite Laval. Institut d'Histoire)., 0079-8398.*

CN/0704-6952
CAHIERS D'HISTOIRE (QUEBEC). ***Ceased.*** (CAHIERS D'HISTOIRE.). [Cah. hist.]. No. 1 (1947)-Ceased Vol. 35. Monographic series. French (English). ir. Societe Historique de Quebec / Historical Society of Quebec, 43 Cote de la Fabrique, Quebec Quebec G1R 5M1 Canada. **Tel** (418)694-9740, FAX (418)691-7759. **UDC** 971.4. **Bk Rev. Circ:** 600.
Desc: Quebec local history.
Ind/Abst Point Repere (1983-19??).

FR/0008-0152
CAHIERS DU MONDE HISPANIQUE ET LUSO-BRESILIEN. [Cah. monde hisp. luso-bres.]. **Added/Corp** Universite de Toulouse-Le Mirail. Toulouse. Universite. Institut d'Etudes Hispaniques, Hispano-Americaines et Luso-Bresiliennes. **VFOAT** Caravelle. No. 6 (1966)-. Periodical. French. sa. 200.00F. L'Universite de Toulouse- Le Mirail, 56 rue Taur, 31000 Toulouse France. **Tel** 33 61 225831, FAX 33 61 218420. **(Subscription address:** Regisseur SVC des Publications, 56 rue du Taur, U Toulouse Mira, 31000 Toulouse France.**)** **DD** 946; 980. ***Continues*** *Caravelle.*
Ind/Abst MLA Int. Bibl. Books Artic. Mod. Lang. Lit.

MQ
CAHIERS DU PATRIMOINE (FORT-DE-FRANCE, MARTINIQUE). (LES CAHIERS DU PATRIMOINE / CONSEIL REGIONAL DE LA MARTINIQUE, BUREAU DE PATRIMOINE.). No. 1 (July/Aug./Sept. 1988)-. Periodical. French. qt. **LC** F2081.A2; C34. **DD** 972.98/2/005.

CN/0049-1098
CAHIERS--SOCIETE HISTORIQUE ACADIENNE, LES. **Main/Corp** Societe Historique Acadienne. Vol. 1 (1961)-. Periodical. French (English). qt. 25.00Can$ Canada; 30.00Can$ other. Societe Historique Acadienne, Box 632, Moncton NB E1C 8M7 Canada. **Tel** (506)855-5918. **ED** Robert Pichette. Index available (Index bound separately). cum. index. **Circ:** 450.
Desc: History and culture of the Acadians. Also, genealogy of Acadian families.

US
CALIFORNIA CHRONICLE : NEWS FROM THE CALIFORNIA HISTORICAL SOCIETY. **Main/Corp** California Historical Society. Vol. 1, No. 1 (Dec. 1987)-. Periodical. English. Four times a year. $40.00 Comes with California Historical Society Membership. California Historical Society, 2099 Pacific Avenue, San Francisco CA 94109. **Tel** (415)567-1848, FAX (415)567-2394. **Circ:** 5,500. ***Continues*** *California Historical Courier.*

US/0575-5751
CALIFORNIA HISTORIAN. [Calif. hist.]. **Added/Corp** Conference of California Historical Societies. Vol. 6, No. 2 (Dec. 1959)-. Periodical. English. Four times a year (Mar., June, Sept., Dec.). $25.00 museum membership; $20.00 individual membership; $15.00 subscription only. University of the Pacific Conference of the California Historical Society, Stockton CA 95211. **Tel** (209)946-2169. **ED** Lois McDonald (phone: (916)873-6110). **LC** F856; .C462. **DD** 979.4/005. **Bk Rev,** (Qty: 20-24). **Ad Acc, Adv Mgr:** A. Almeida, **Tel** (619)833-2872. **Circ:** 1,600. ***Continues*** *Conference of California Historical Societies. Newsletter of the Conference of California Historical Societies;* ***Absorbed*** *Conference of the California Historical Societies. Meeting. Proceedings of the Annual Meeting of the Conference of California Historical Societies, 0414-3337.* ***Continued in part by*** *Conference of California Historical Societies. Newsletter - Conference of California Historical Societies, 0271-8243.*
Desc: A compilation of articles, photoessays, and news items on state and local history.
Ind/Abst Am. Hist. Life (1963-1981); Calif. Period. Index; Calif. Period. Microfi.

US
CALIFORNIA HISTORICAL LANDMARKS. English. Department of Parks and Recreation, PO Box 2390, Sacramento CA 95811. **Tel** (916)322-7000. **LC** F862; .C156. **DD** 979.4/005. **UDC** 979.4.

US/0882-357X
CALIFORNIA HISTORY ACTION. [Calif. hist. action]. **Added/Corp** California Committee for the Promotion of History. (1983)-. Periodical. English. Four times a year (Jan., Apr., July, Oct.). $30.00 (individual), $35.00 (institutions) Comes with California Council for the Promotion of History membership. California Council Promotion of History, 21250 Stevens Creek Boulevard,

Cupertino CA 95014. **Tel** (408)864-8964. **ED** Jim Williams. **DD** 979. **Bk Rev**. **Ad Acc**. **Circ:** 200 (ctrl).
Desc: Official newsletter of the California Committee for the Promotion of History. Activities of interest to historians and history advocates and legislative reports.

US/0162-2897
CALIFORNIA HISTORY (SAN FRANCISCO). (CALIFORNIA HISTORY.). [Calif. hist.]. **Added/Corp** California Historical Society. Vol. 57 (Spring 1978)-. Periodical. English. qt. $40.00 US; $50.00 other (comes with membership). California Historical Society, 2099 Pacific Avenue, San Francisco CA 94109. **Tel** (415)567-1848, FAX (415)567-2394. **ED** Richard Orsi. **LC** F856; .C24. **DD** 979.4/005. Index available. cum. index. **Bk Rev**. **Circ:** 5,600. Documents available from The Genuine Article. ***Continues*** *California Historical Quarterly, 0097-6059.*
Desc: History of California, past and present, in relation to the diversity of its people and the issues raised due to this diversity.
Ind/Abst Abstr. Engl. Stud.; Am. Hist. Life (1954-); Annu. Bibliogr. Engl. Lang. Lit.; ARTbibliogr. Mod.; Arts Humanit. Citation Index [Full Cov.]; Calif. Period. Index; Curr. Contents Arts Humanit.; Res. Alert [Full Cov.]; Soc. Sci. Cit. Index [Select. Cov.]; West. Hist. Q.

US/0742-5465
CALIFORNIAN (CUPERTINO, CALIF.), THE. (THE CALIFORNIAN.). [Californian]. **Added/Corp** California History Center Foundation. Vol. 1, No. 1 (Jan. 1980)-. Periodical. English. Three times a year (Mar., Sept., Dec.). $25.00 Comes with California History Center Foundation Membership. California Council Promotion of History, 21250 Stevens Creek Boulevard, Cupertino CA 95014. **Tel** (408)864-8964. **ED** Kathi Peregrin. **DD** 979. **Ad Acc**. ***Continues*** *California History Center Foundation Newsletter.*
Desc: Contains feature articles, events calendar, pioneer profiles, and foundation notes.

US/0745-5895
CALIFORNIANS (SAN FRANCISCO, CALIF.), THE. (THE CALIFORNIANS.). [Californians]. **Added/Corp** Grizzly Bear Publishing Company. Vol. 1 No. 1 (Jan./Feb. 1983)-. Periodical. English. Six times a year (Jan., Mar., May, July, Sept., Nov.). $22.50. The Californians, 5720 Ross Branch Road, Sebastopol CA 95472. **Tel** (707)887-9834, FAX (707)887-9834. **LC** F861; .C25. **DD** 979.4/005. Index available (Bound in 6th issue publish in October at regular price). **Bk Rev**, (Qty: 60). **Ad Acc**, **Adv Mgr:** Robin Pendergraft, **Tel** (707)557-5552. **Circ:** 18,000.
Ind/Abst Am. Hist. Life (1987-); West. Hist. Q.

US/0575-6383
CALL OF THE PLATEAU. [Call plateau]. **Added/Corp** Plateau Sciences Society (U.S.). (19??)- Vol. 32 (Sept. 1992)-. Periodical. English. Nine times a year. $12.00. Plateau Sciences Society, PO Box 2433, Gallup NM 87305. **Tel** (505)722-6694. **ED** Martin Link. **DD** 970. **Bk Rev**. **Circ:** 100 (ctrl).
Desc: Articles on physical and social sciences of the Colorado Plateau region.

US
CAMAGUEYANO, EL. Periodical. Spanish. mo. $15.00. 221 NE 26th Terrace, Miami FL 33137. **Tel** (305)573-8155. **ED** Maria A Crespi. **UDC** 972.91. **Ad Acc**. **Circ:** 2,250 (ctrl).
Desc: Data on the history, traditions and culture of the province of Camaguey, Cuba.

UK
CAMBRIDGE HISTORY OF LATIN AMERICA. Academic Scholarly Publication. English. ir. price varies per volume. Cambridge University Press / New York, 40 West 20th Street, New York NY 10011-4211. **Tel** (212)924-3900, (800)221-4512. **(Subscription address:** Cambridge University Press / Outside of North America, Journal Fulfillment Department, The Edinburgh Building, Cambridge CB2 2RU United Kingdom.**)**

UK/0068-6689
CAMBRIDGE LATIN AMERICAN STUDIES. Vol. 1 (1967)-. Monographic series. English. ir. Price varies per volume. Cambridge University Press, The Edinburgh Building, Shaftesbury Road, Cambridge CB2 2RU United Kingdom. **Tel** 011 44 223 312393, FAX 011 44 223 325959. **(Subscription address:** Cambridge University Press / North America, 110 Midland Avenue, Port Chester NY 10573.**)**
Desc: Series covering Latin American studies. Contains volumes on subjects such as the economic history of Latin America and the relationship between Peronism and the Argentine working class.

CN/1183-5672
CAMPANILOIS (SAINTE-FOY). (LE CAMPANILOIS : JOURNAL OFFICIEL DE LA RUE DU CAMPANILE.). [Campanilois]. **Added/Corp** Bureau d'Administration de la rue du Companile. No 1 (Febr. 1991)-. Periodical. French. mo. Limited free distribution. Bureau D'Administration de la Rue du Campanile, 3700 Rue du Campanile, Sainte-Foy Quebec G1X 4G6 Canada. **DD** 971.4.

CN/0704-7991
CANADA NOW. V. 1- Sept. 26, 1977-. Periodical. English (French). ir. $18.00. Canada Now Publishers Ltd, PO Box 91386, West Vancouver British Columbia V7V 3P1 Canada. **DD** 971/.005. **UDC** 971;908.71.

US/0883-8135
CANADA (WASHINGTON, D.C. 1985). (CANADA.). [Canada]. 1985-. English. an. Stryker-Post Publications, PO Drawer 1200, Harpers Ferry WV 25425. **Tel** (800)995-1400. **ED** Wayne C Thompson. **LC** F1001; .C1225. **DD** 971. **UDC** 908.71. ctrl circ.
Desc: One of seven titles focusing on current events. This lively reference tool addresses social, economic, political and controversial issues. A must for schools and libraries.

CN
CANADIAN CENTENARY SERIES, THE. (1963)-. English. ir. 39.95Can$. Longhouse Book Shop, 497 Bloor Street West, Toronto Ontario M5S 1Y2 Canada. **Tel** (416)921-9995.

CN/0008-3755
CANADIAN HISTORICAL REVIEW. [Can. hist. rev.]. Vol. 1 (March 1920)-. Periodical. English (French). qt (Mar., Jun., Sept., Dec.). $60.00 (institutions). University of Toronto Press, 5201 Dufferin Street, Downsview Ontario M3H 5T8 Canada. **Tel** (416)667-7781, (416)667-7782, FAX (416)667-7803. **ED** J. R. Miller and Susan Houston. **LC** F1001; .C27. **[CCC]**. Index available. cum. index. **Bk Rev**. **Ad Acc**. **Circ:** 3,000 (ctrl). available on microfiche from Micromedia Limited; available on microfilm and microfiche from University Microfilms International (UMI). Documents available from The Genuine Article, UMI Article Clearinghouse, Magazine Collection. ***Continues*** *Review of Historical Publications Relating to Canada, 0381-8055.*
Desc: Chronicles Canada's past from a broad and multicultural perspective. A wide range of topics are examined from political and military history to cultural and social studies, from economics and labor analysis to legal and judicial reform.
Ind/Abst Abstr. Anthropol.; Acad. Abstr. Full Text Elite (Jan. 1992-); Acad. Abstr. (Jan. 1992-); Acad. Search (Jan. 1992-); Am. Hist. Life (1954-); Am. Bibliogr. Slavic East Europ. Stud.; Arts Humanit. Citation Index [Full Cov.]; BHA : Biblio. Hist. Art; Book Rev. Digest; Book Rev. Index (1986-); Can. Index; Can. Period. Index; Curr. Contents Arts Humanit.; Expand. Acad. Index (1984-); Gen. Period. Index (1985-); Hist. Source (Jan. 1992-); Humanit. Index; Humanit. Source (Jan. 1992-); INFO-SOUTH Abstr.; Int. Bibliogr. Sociol.; Mag. Index Plus (1989-); Mag. Search; Newsp. Period. Abstr. (1990-); Res. Alert [Full Cov.]; Soc. Sci. Cit. Index [Select. Cov.]; Mag. Index (1983-); TOM Gen. Index (1989-) [Full Txt.]; West. Hist. Q.

CN/0318-8442
CANADIAN ISSUES (ASSOCIATION FOR CANADIAN STUDIES). (CANADIAN ISSUES : A PUBLICATION OF THE ASSOCIATION FOR CANADIAN STUDIES.). [Can. issues - Assoc. Can. Stud.]. **Added/Corp** Association for Canadian Studies. **VFOAT** Themes Canadians. Vol. 1, No. 1 (Spring 1975)-. Academic Scholarly Publication. English (French; summaries and/or abstracts in French). an (June). Free to members: $15.00 non-members. Association for Canadian Studies Fin Svcs, CP 8888, Succursale Centre-Ville, Montreal Quebec H3C 3P8 Canada. **Tel** (514)987-7784, FAX (514)987-8210. **LC** UNC. **DD** 971/.005. **Pr Rev**. **Circ:** 1,000.
Desc: A selection of scholarly papers presented at our annual conference. Topics change every year but there is usually a theme for each volume.
Ind/Abst Int. Polit. Sci. Abstr.

CN/0826-3663
CANADIAN JOURNAL OF LATIN AMERICAN AND CARIBBEAN STUDIES. [Can. j. Lat. Am. Caribb. stud.]. **Added/Corp** Canadian Association of Latin American and Caribbean Studies. **VFOAT** Revue Canadienne des Etudes Latino-Americaines et Caraibes. Vol. 9, No. 17 (1984)-. English (French and Spanish; summaries and/or abstracts in French and Spanish). sa. 55.00Can$ (1 year), 165.00Can$ (3 year) institutions; 45.00Can$ (1 year), 135.00Can$ (3 year) individuals. Calacs-ACELAC, University of Ottawa, 35 Copernicus #120, Ottawa Ontario U1N 6N5 Canada. **Tel** (613)564-5939, FAX (613)564-3891. **LC** F1401; .N18. **DD** 980/.005. **Bk Rev**. ***Continues*** *N S, Northsouth, 0384-1367.*
Ind/Abst Am. Hist. Life (1985-); Geogr. Abstr. Human Geogr.; HAPI Hisp. Am. Period. Index; Int. Dev. Abstr.; PAIS Int. Print; Rural Dev. Abstr.; World Agric. Econ.

CN/0715-3244
CANADIAN JOURNAL OF NATIVE STUDIES, THE. [Can. j. native stud.]. **Added/Corp** Society for the Advancement of Native Studies. Canadian Indian/Native Studies Association. Vol. 1, No. 1 (1981)-. Periodical. English. sa. $30.00. Brandon University / Manitoba, 1229 Lorne Avenue, Brandon Manitoba R7A 6A9 Canada. **Tel** (204)727-9640. **LC** IN PROCESS. **DD** 971/.00497.
Ind/Abst Am. Hist. Life (1982-); Anthropol. Lit.; Can. Index; Can. Period. Index (19??-); Ethnoarts Index.

CN/0316-0343
CANADIAN PLAINS BULLETIN. **Added/Corp** University of Saskatchewan. Regina Campus. Canadian Plains Research Center. University of Regina. Canadian Plains Research Centre. Vol. 2 (April 1974)-. Bulletin. English. sa (March and September). 10.00Can$. University of Regina, Canadian Plains Research Center, Regina Saskatchewan S4S 0A2 Canada. **Tel** (306)585-4758, FAX (306)585-4699. **ED** B. Mlazgar. **DD** 971.2/007/2071244. **Bk Rev**. **Circ:** 4,500 (ctrl). ***Continues*** *Canadian Plains Area Studies Bulletin, 0316-0351.*
Desc: Newsletter of the Canadian Plains Research Center. CPRC news, developments in the prairie region, conferences, and new publications.

CN/0317-6401
CANADIAN PLAINS PROCEEDINGS. **Added/Corp** Canadian Plains Research Center. Vol. 2 (1975)-. Monographic series. English. ir. Price varies per volume. University of Regina, Canadian Plains Research Center, Regina Saskatchewan S4S 0A2 Canada. **Tel** (306)585-4758, FAX (306)585-4699.
Desc: Publication of papers from symposiums dealing with man and nature on the prairies.
Ind/Abst AGRICOLA [Select. Cov.]; Geogr. Abstr. Human Geogr. (?-?).

CN
CANADIAN PLAINS STUDIES. **Added/Corp** University of Saskatchewan. Regina Campus. Canadian Plains Studies Centre. University of Regina. Canadian Plains Research Centre. (1973)-. Monographic series. English. ir. Price varies per volume. University of Regina, Canadian Plains Research Center, Regina Saskatchewan S4S 0A2 Canada. **Tel** (306)585-4758, FAX (306)585-4699.
Desc: Canadian plains studies, historical, ethnic, etc.
Ind/Abst Seed Abstr.; Weed Abstr.

CN/0829-5026
CANADIAN WEST (1985). (CANADIAN WEST.). [Can. West]. **VFOAT** Canadian West Magazine. Issue No. 1 (Aug. 1985)-. Periodical. English. qt. 14.02Can$ Canada; 19.00Can$ other. Sunfire Publications Ltd., PO Box 3399, Langley British Columbia V3A 4R7 Canada. **Tel** (604)534-9378. **ED** Garnet Basque. **LC** F1060.A1; C36. **DD** 971.2/005. Index available. **Bk Rev**. **Ad Acc**. **Circ:** 8,000. available on microfiche from University Microfilms International (UMI). ***Continues*** *History of the Canadian West, 0712-581X.*
Desc: Devoted to the life and times of early pioneer history in British Columbia, Alberta and the Yukon. Printed in full color, topics include almost every aspect of pioneer life that formed the social fabric of western Canada.
Ind/Abst Am. Hist. Life (1987-); Can. Index; Can. Period. Index (19??-).

●PN
CANAL DE PANAMA HOY / CENTRO DE ESTUDIOS LATINOAMERICANOS "JUSTO AROSEMENA.". **Added/Corp** Centro de Estudios Latinoamericanos (Panama). Vol. 1, No. 1 (April 1992)-. Bulletin. Spanish. bm. Centro Estudios Latinoamericanos Cela, Apartado 87-1918, Panama 7 Rep. de Panama. **Tel** 011 507 23-0028, FAX 011 507 69-2032. available with illustrations.

CN/0829-7983
CAP-AUX-DIAMANTS. **Added/Corp** Societe Historique de Quebec. Vol. 1, No. 1 (Spring 1985)-. Periodical. French. qt. 25.00Can$ (institution); 17.00Can$ (individual) Canada; 32.00Can$ (other). Les Editions Cap-Aux-Diamants, 1 Cote de la Fabrique, CP 609, Haute-Ville Quebec G1R 4S2 Canada. **Tel** (418)656-5040, (418)656-5043, FAX (418)656-7282. **DD** 971.4/47/005.
Ind/Abst Point Repere (1987-).

CN/0319-4639
CAPE BRETON'S MAGAZINE. No. 1, (Nov. 1972)-. Periodical. English (French and Gaelic (Scots)). Three times a year (Jan., June, Aug.). 17.00Can$ Canada; 25.00Can$ other. Cape Bretons Magazine, Wreck Cove, Cape Breton Nova Scotia Canada. **Tel** (902)539-3817, (800)929-2001. **ED** Ronald Caplan. **LC** F1039.C2; C25. **DD** 971.6/95. **Bk Rev**. **Ad Acc**. **Circ:** 6,000 (ctrl).
Desc: Oral history, traditional crafts and natural history of Cape Breton Island. Includes many photographs.
Ind/Abst Can. Index.

US/0738-9604
CAREFREE ENTERPRISE. See General Interest-General Interest-North America.

CN/0821-2295
CARIBBEAN FOCUS. [Caribb. focus]. Sept. 1981-. Periodical. English. mo. $1.00 per no. Caribbean Focus, PO Box 6630 Station A, Toronto Ontario M5W 1X4 Canada. **DD** 971.3/541/004969729. **UDC** 908.729.

UK/0142-4742
CARIBBEAN INSIGHT. **Added/Corp** West India Committee. **VFOAT** Insight. (197?)-. Periodical. English. Twelve times a year. $136.00. West India Committee, 819 Northumberland Avenue, London WC2N 5RA

England. **Tel** 011 44 71 936 1493, FAX 011 44 71 976 1541, telex 22911. **ED** Rod Prince. **LC** F2155; .C366. **DD** 972.9/005. **Ad Acc, Adv Mgr:** Jeff, **Tel** 976-1493. **Circ:** 5,000. ***Absorbed** Caribbean & West Indies Chronicle, 0143-1862.*
Desc: Presents political and general commentary on the Caribbean Basin.
Ind/Abst Infomat Int. Bus.

PR/0069-0511
CARIBBEAN MONOGRAPH SERIES. 1- 1964-. Monographic series. English. ir. Price varies per volume. University of Puerto Rico / Institute of Caribbean Studies, PO Box 23361 UPR Station, Rio Piedras 00931 Puerto Rico. **Tel** 809 764 0000 Ext. 3292. **UDC** 972.9.

US/0894-0223
CARIBBEAN NEWSLETTER (NEW YORK, N.Y.). (CARIBBEAN NEWSLETTER / FRIENDS FOR JAMAICA.). [Caribb. newsl.]. **Added/Corp** Friends for Jamaica. (198?)-. Newsletter. English. mo. $8.00 (regular), $10.00 (institutions). Caribbean Newsletter, Box 20392, Cathedral Finance Station, New York NY 10025-9992. **DD** 972. ***Continues** Friends for Jamaica Newsletter.*
Ind/Abst Hum. Rights Intern. Rep.

US/1053-9700
CARIBBEAN PERSPECTIVES. [Caribb. perspect.]. **Added/Corp** University of the Virgin Islands. Vol. 1 (1991)-. Periodical. English. ir. $19.95. Transaction Publishers / Rutgers State University, New Brunswick NJ 08903. **Tel** (908)932-2280 Ext. 105, FAX (908)932-3138. **LC** F2130; .C37. **DD** 972.9/005.

US/0069-0538
CARIBBEAN SERIES. ***Ceased.*** **VFOAT** Yale Caribbean Series. Vol. 1 (1959)-Ceased (Jan. 1982). Monographic series. English. ir. Yale University Press, PO Box 209040, New Haven CT 06520. **Tel** (203)432-0940, (800)987-7323, FAX (203)432-0948.

US/0275-5793
CARIBBEAN STUDIES (NEW YORK N.Y.). (CARIBBEAN STUDIES.). [Caribb. stud.]. Vol. 1-. Monographic series. English. ir. Price varies per volume. Gordon & Breach Science Publishers, Inc., PO Box 786, Cooper Station, New York NY 10276. **Tel** (212)206-8900, FAX (212)645-2459. **(Subscription address:** International Publishers Distributor at one of the following addresses: 820 Town Center Drive, Langhorne, PA 19047; or PO Box 90, Reading Berkshire RG1 8JL UK; or Kent Ridge PO Box 1180, Singapore 9111, Republic of Singapore**)** **ED** Roberta Marx Delson. **UDC** 972.9;908.729.
Ind/Abst Appl. Soc. Sci. Index Abstr.; Int. Dev. Abstr. (?-?).

PR/0271-6577
CARIBBEAN STUDIES NEWSLETTER. [Caribb. stud. newsl.]. V. 1- June 1974-. Newsletter. English. qt. $30.00. Caribbean Studies Association / San Juan, GPO Box 3255, c/o John Zebrowski/Secretary-Treasurer, San Juan 00936 Puerto Rico. **DD** 972.9. **UDC** 972.9.

PR/0008-6533
CARIBBEAN STUDIES (RIO PIEDRAS, SAN JUAN, P.R.). (CARIBBEAN STUDIES.). [Caribb. stud.]. **Added/Corp** University of Puerto Rico (Rio Piedras Campus). Institute of Caribbean Studies. Vol. 1 (April 1961)-. Periodical. English (Spanish). qt. $25.00 (institution), $18.00 (individual) surface mail; $26.50 (institution), $19.50 (individual) airmail. University of Puerto Rico / Institute of Caribbean Studies, PO Box 23361 UPR Station, Rio Piedras 00931 Puerto Rico. **Tel** 809 764 0000 Ext. 3292. **LC** F2161; .C29. Index Available in first issue of next volume--attached.
Ind/Abst Acad. Search (Jan. 1992-); Am. Hist. Life (1961-1967, 1977-); Anthropol. Lit.; HAPI Hisp. Am. Period. Index (-199?); INFO-SOUTH Abstr.; Int. Bibliogr. Sociol.; Int. Labour Doc.; Int. Polit. Sci. Abstr.; PAIS Int. Print.

CN/0705-2731
CARIBBEAN YEAR BOOK, THE. [Caribb. year book]. 48th- Ed.; 1977/78-. English. an. Caribbean LTD, 1255 Yonge Street, Toronto Canada MT4 1W6 Canada. **LC** F2131; .W47. **DD** 972.9/005. **UDC** 972.9(058). **NLM** F 1601 W517. ***Continues** West Indies & Caribbean Year Book, 0083-8233.*

US/0889-4027
CARIBUS. [Caribus]. Vol. 1, No. 1 (Sept. 1986)-. Periodical. English. mo. $12.00. Amalgamated Publishing, 8327 Birdrun Drive, Missouri City TX 77459. **Tel** (713)437-0694. **DD** 972. **UDC** 972.9.

US/0576-808X
CAROLINA COMMENTS. **See** Genealogy and Heraldry-Archives.

US/1062-841X
CARROLL COUNTY HISTORICAL QUARTERLY (1992). (CARROLL COUNTY HISTORICAL QUARTERLY : OFFICIAL JOURNAL OF THE CARROLL COUNTY HISTORICAL SOCIETY.). [Carroll Cty. hist. q.]. **Added/Corp** Carroll County Historical Society (Ark.). (19??)-. Periodical. English. qt. $10.00. Carroll County Historical Society / Arkansas, PO Box 249, Berryville AR 72616. **Tel** (501)423-6312. **DD** 976. ***Continues** Carroll County Historical Society (Ark.) Carroll County Historical Society Quarterly, 0191-6637.*

US/0191-6637
CARROLL COUNTY HISTORICAL SOCIETY QUARTERLY, THE. ***Title Change.*** **Main/Corp** Carroll County Historical Society (Arkansas). (197?)-(19??). Periodical. English. ir (4 times a year). Carroll County Historical Society / Arkansas, PO Box 249, Berryville AR 72616. **Tel** (501)423-6312. **ED** O Klute Braswell. **LC** F417.C4; C37a. **DD** 976.7/17/005. **Circ:** 780 (ctrl). ***Continues** Carroll County Historical Quarterly (Berryville, Ark. : 1966). **Continued by** Carroll County Historical Quarterly (Berryville, Ark. : 1992), 1062-841X.*
Desc: Stories and historical and genealogical information about Carroll County, Arkansas, and the pioneer families who settled in the area.
Ind/Abst Ozark Period. Index (19??-199?).

US
CARROLL COUNTY HISTORY JOURNAL. English. qt. $15.00. Carroll County Historical Society / Maryland, 210 East Main Street, Westminister MD 21157. **Tel** (301)848-6494. **ED** Joseph M. Getty. **Ad Acc. Circ:** 1,200 (ctrl).
Desc: Local history essays and historical society activities in Carroll County Maryland.

BL
CARTA POLITICA. (1991)-. Periodical. Portuguese. wk. **LC** F2538.3; .C37. **DD** 981/.005.

US/0528-2276
CASSELMAN CHRONICLE, THE. [Casselman chron.]. **Added/Corp** Springs Historical Society of the Casselman Valley. Vol. 1 (Winter 1961)-. Periodical. English. sa. $10.00. Springs Historical Society, c/o Verda Yoder, Springs PA 15662. **Tel** (814)662-2625. **DD** 974.8. **Circ:** 300.
Desc: Mainly articles written by local people about their childhood or parents, grandparents, etc.
Ind/Abst Am. Hist. Life.

CN/0824-2062
CATALYST (TORONTO. 1982). (CATALYST.). [Catalyst]. Vol. 5, No. 2 (Sept. 1982)-. Periodical. English. ir (ten times a year). Free to members, $75.00 annual membership, $10.00 nonmembers. Citizens for Public Justice, 229 College Street #311, Toronto Ontario M5T 1R4 Canada. **Tel** (416)979-2443. **DD** 971.064/605. **UDC** 908.71. ***Continues** Catalyst for Public Justice, 0225-0772.*

CL
CAUCE (SANTIAGO, CHILE). (CAUCE.). Yearly V. 1, No. 1 (Nov. 18, 1983)-. Periodical. Spanish. wk. **LC** F3100; .C38.
Ind/Abst Annu. Bibliogr. Engl. Lang. Lit.

US/0576-9736
CEDAR COUNTY HISTORICAL SOCIETY REVIEW, THE. **Added/Corp** Cedar County (Iowa). Historical Society. (19??)-. English. an (July). $6.20 (add $1.20 for postage) Comes with Cedar County Historical Society Membership. Cedar County Historical Society, 210 West 8th Street, Tipton IA 52772. **Tel** (319)886-2740. **ED** Mr. and Mrs. J. Curtis Frymoyer. **LC** F627.C4; C43. Index available. cum. index. **Circ:** 550.

US/0887-0594
CENTRAL AMERICA NEWSPAK. **See** Political Science.

US/0882-8792
CENTRAL NEVADA'S GLORIOUS PAST. (CENTRAL NEVADA'S GLORIOUS PAST : A PUBLICATION OF THE CENTRAL NEVADA HISTORICAL SOCIETY.). **Added/Corp** Central Nevada Historical Society. Vol. 1, No. 1 (May 1978)-. Periodical. English. sa. $25.00. Nevada Historical Society, 1650 North Virginia Street, Reno NV 89502. **Tel** (702)688-1191. **ED** William J Metscher. **LC** F841; .C43. **DD** 979.3/005. **Bk Rev. Circ:** 600.
Desc: Stories and photographs dealing with the history of the Central Nevada area.

US/0577-1099
CENTRE COUNTY HERITAGE. [Cent. cty. herit.]. **Added/Corp** Centre County Historical Society. Vol. 1, No. 1 (Feb. 1956)-. Periodical. English. sa ($6.00). Centre County Historical Society, 1001 East College Avenue, State College PA 16801. **Tel** (814)234-4779. **DD** 974.
Ind/Abst Am. Hist. Life.

US/0749-6834
CHAGRIN VALLEY DIRECTORY. Directory. English. an. Chagrin Valley Chamber of Commerce, 13 1/2 North Franklin Street, PO Box 225, Chagrin Falls OH 44022. **LC** F499.C33; .C45. **DD** 977.1/31/0025. **UDC** 977.1(036).

CN/0823-6186
CHAINON (OTTAWA. 1983). (LE CHAINON / SOCIETE FRANCO-ONTARIENNE D'HISTOIRE ET DE GENEALOGIE.). [Chainon]. **Added/Corp** Societe Franco-Ontarienne d'Histoire et de Genealogie. Vol. 1, No. 1 (April 1983)-. Periodical. French. Twice a year. Societe Franco-Ontarienne d'Histoire et de Genealogie, CP 720 Succursale B, Ottawa Ontario K1P 8M4 Canada. **Tel** (613)744-1740. **DD** 971.3/004114/006. **Circ:** 900 (ctrl).

US/0742-129X
CHARITON COLLECTOR, THE. Periodical. English. $7.00. Kirksville Senior High School, Kirksville MO 65301. **Tel** (816)665-4631. **LC** F474.K49; C47. **DD** 977.8/264. **UDC** 977.8. **Circ:** 1,250 (ctrl).
Desc: The magazine attempts to preserve the history and local folklore of northeast Missouri, in particular Kirksville, Missouri.

CN/0316-6724
CHARLOTTES, THE. ***Suspended.*** Vol. 1 (1971)-?. Periodical. English. an. Queen Charlotte Islands Museum Society, Box 1, Second Beach, Charlotte, British Columbia V0T 1S0 Canada. **DD** 971.1/31/005. **UDC** 971.1.

CN/0319-1249
CHATEAUGUAY VALLEY HISTORICAL SOCIETY ANNUAL JOURNAL. (CHATEAUGUAY VALLEY HISTORICAL SOCIETY ANNUAL JOURNAL. / REVUE ANNUELLE DE LA SOCIETE HISTORIQUE DE LA VALLEE DE LA CHATEAUGUAY.). [Chateauguay Val. Hist. Soc. annu. j.]. **Main/Corp** Chateauguay Valley Historical Society. **VFOAT** Journal Annuel de la Societe Historique de la Vallee de la Chateauguay. Vol. 1 (1968)-. Periodical. English (French). an. 12.00Can$. Chateauguay Valley Historical Society, PO Box 61, Howick Quebec J0S 1G0 Canada. **Tel** (514)825-2276. **DD** 971.4/33/005.

US/0528-9599
CHEMUNG HISTORICAL JOURNAL, THE. **Added/Corp** Chemung County Historical Society. Vol. 1 (Sept. 1955)-. Periodical. English. qt (Mar., June, Sept., Dec.). Comes with Chemung County Historical Society membership. Chemung County Historical Society, 415 East Water Street, Elmira NY 14901. **Tel** (607)734-4167. **ED** Thomas E. Byrne.
Ind/Abst Am. Hist. Life.

US
CHERRY VALLEY HISTORICAL ASSOCIATION. Periodical. English. Cherry Valley Museum, 40 Main Street, Cherry Valley NY 13320. **UDC** 947.7.

US
CHEY-ARAP BULLETIN. V. 1- 1968?-. Bulletin. English. mo. Box 38, Concho OK 73022.

CN/0226-5109
CHIA HUA CH'IAO PAO. [Chia hua ch'iao pao]. **VFOAT** Chinese-Canadian Community News. V. 1- July 1979-. Periodical. Chinese. Free. Chinese-Canadian Community News, 80 Florence State, Ottawa Ontario K1R 7W6. **DD** 971.3/84004951. **UDC** 971.3(951).

US/0195-9638
CHICAGO FACES. V. 1- July/Aug. 1979-. Periodical. English. bm. $7.50. Chicago Faces Publications Inc, 625 N Michigan Avenue/Suite 750, Chicago IL 60611-3103. **LC** F548.1; .C17. **DD** 977.3/11/005. **UDC** 977.3;908.773.

US/0272-8540
CHICAGO HISTORY. [Chicago hist.]. **Added/Corp** Chicago Historical Society. (1945)-. Periodical. English. Three times a year. Comes with Chicago Historical Society membership, $30.00 (membership). Chicago Historical Society, 1601 North Clark Street, Chicago IL 60614. **Tel** (312)642-4600. **ED** Russell Lewis. **LC** F548.1; .C465. **DD** 977.311. **CODEN** CHHIEY. cum. index. **Bk Rev**, (Qty: 1 extended review each year). **Circ:** 9,000 (ctrl). available on microfilm and microfiche from University Microfilms International (UMI). ***Continues** News Review (Chicago Historical Society).*
Desc: Makes the most current research on Chicago history accessible to the general public without sacrificing the integrity of the scholarship. The articles are aimed at a popular general audience rather than professional historians by publishing engaging, creative interpretations of the city's history.
Ind/Abst Am. Hist. Life (1963-); SportSearch (1963-).

US/1044-3487
CHICANO INDEX, THE. **See** History(General)-Abstracting, Bibliographies and Statistics.

CN/0227-874X
CHINESE-CANADIAN BULLETIN (1980). (CHINESE-CANADIAN BULLETIN.). [Chin-Can. bull.]. **VFOAT** Hua Ch'iao Tao Pao. V. 19- (No. 115-); Jan./Feb. 1980-. Bulletin. English (Chinese). $10.00. Chinese-Canadian Press, 3289 Main Street, Vancouver BC V5V 9Z9 Canada. **DD** 971.1/004951. **UDC** 971.1(=951). ***Continues** Chinese-Canadian Bulletin and Vacation Guide, 0708-1650.*

US/0591-1281
CHIPS & SHIPS. **Added/Corp** Bay County Genealogical Society. **VAT** Chips and Ships. Vol. 1 (Fall 1969)-. Periodical. English. qt. $4.00. Bay County Genealogical Society, Box 27, Essexville MI 48732. **LC** F572.B3; C55.

US/0440-9426
CHRONICLE (ANN ARBOR). ***Suspended.*** (CHRONICLE.). [Chronicle]. **Added/Corp** Historical Society of Michigan (1874-). **VFOAT** Historical Society of Michigan Newsletter. Vol. 1 No. 2 (Feb. 1964)-Vol. 27. Periodical. English. bm. Free to members. Historical Society of Michigan, 2117 Washenaw Avenue, Ann Arbor MI 48104. **Tel** (313)769-1828. **LC** F561; .H57. **DD** 977. ***Continues*** *HSM Bulletin.*
Ind/Abst Am. Hist. Life (1979-).

US/0001-3048
CHRONICLE OF THE AARON BURR ASSOCIATION, THE. **Main/Corp** Aaron Burr Association. Vol. 1 (May 1948)-. Periodical. English. Four times a year. $7.50 Comes with Aaron Burr Association membership. Aaron Burr Association, 2064 Faculty Drive, Winston-Salem NC 27106. **Tel** (919)725-0830. **LC** E302.6.B9; A15. **DD** 973.4/6/0924.

US/0009-6024
CHRONICLES OF OKLAHOMA. [Chron. Okla.]. **Added/Corp** Oklahoma Historical Society. Vol. 1 Jan. (1921)-. Periodical. English. Four times a year (seasonally). $25.00 (institution); $15.00 (individual). Oklahoma Historical Society, Historical Building, North Lincoln, Oklahoma City OK 73105. **Tel** (405)521-2491. **(Subscription address:** John Wiley & Sons, Inc., PO Box 7247-8491, Philadelphia, PA 19170-8491**) ED** Bob L Blackburn and Mary Ann Blochowiak. **LC** F691; .C55. Index Available Published separately--free--upon request. cum. index. **Bk Rev. Circ:** 6,000 (ctrl). available on microfilm. ***Continues*** *Historia.*
Desc: Includes a wide variety of subject matter relative to Oklahoma history, from narrative treatment and biography to anthropology and archaeology.
Ind/Abst Am. Hist. Life (1963-); Annu. Bibliogr. Engl. Lang. Lit.; West. Hist. Q.

US/0578-0462
CHRONICLES OF SMITH COUNTY, TEXAS. **Added/Corp** Smith County Historical Society. Vol. 1 (Fall 1962)-. Periodical. English. sa (July and Dec.). $12.50. Smith County Historical Society / Texas, 125 South College Drive, Tyler TX 75702. **Tel** (903)592-5993. **(Subscription address:** Smith County Historical Society, Sam Kidd, 2805 Rockbridge, Tyler TX 75701.**) ED** Andy Leath. ($10.00). cum. index. **Circ:** 400.
Desc: History of Smith County, Texas.

CN/0823-6097
CHRONIQUEUR DE L'ILE, LE. [Chron. l'Ile]. Vol. 1, No. 1 (Nov. 1982)-. Periodical. French. mo. Free to citizens. Chroniqueur de l'Ile, 449 Place Closse, Ile Bizard Quebec H9C 1Y7 Canada. **DD** 971.4/28. **UDC** 971.4.

US/0898-0330
CIRCUIT RIDER (FRANKFORT, KY.), THE. (THE CIRCUIT RIDER.). **Added/Corp** Historical Confederation of Kentucky. Kentucky Historical Society. Field Services Division. (Aug. 1978)-. Periodical. English. qt. $9.50 (general), $7.50 (member). Historical Confederacy of Kentucky, PO Box H, Frankfort KY 40602-2108. **Tel** (502) 564-3016, FAX (502) 564-4701. **ED** Charles R Stapleton. **DD** 973. **Circ:** 400 (ctrl).
Desc: Historical publication detailing activities of history groups across the state.

US/0097-7195
CITYSCAPE. V. 1- Oct. 1974-. English. $2.00. Cityscape Inc, 35th & R Street NW, Washington DC 20007. **LC** F191; .C58. **DD** 975.3/005. **UDC** 975.3.

US/0897-6015
CIVIL WAR (BERRYVILLE, VA.). (CIVIL WAR : THE MAGAZINE OF THE CIVIL WAR SOCIETY.). [Civil War]. **Added/Corp** Civil War Society. Vol. 12 (March 1988)-. Periodical. English. bm (6 issues). $19.97. Civil War Society, PO Box 770, Berryville VA 22611. **Tel** (703)955-1176. **LC** E461; .C53. **DD** 973.7/05. ***Continues*** *Civil War Quarterly, 0897-599X.*
Desc: A scholarly publication that looks at both points of view.

US/1070-3756
CIVIL WAR CHRONICLES. [Civil War chron.]. (1991)-. Periodical. English. qt (4 issues). $10.00. American Heritage, Forbes Building, 60 Fifth Avenue, New York NY 10011. **Tel** (212)206-5512, (212)620-1804. **(Subscription address:** Civil War Chronicles, PO Box 6903, Syracuse NY 13217.**) LC** IN PROCESS. **DD** 973.

US/0009-8078
CIVIL WAR HISTORY. [Civil War hist.]. **Added/Corp** State University of Iowa. Libraries. State University of Iowa. Vol. 1 (Mar. 1955)-. Academic Scholarly Publication. English. qt (March, June, Sept. and Dec.). $28.00 (one year), $54.00 (two year) (institutions), $18.00 (one year), $34.00 (two year) (individuals) US; $34.00 (one year), $66.00 (two year) (institutions), $24.00 (one year), $46.00 (two year) other. Kent State University Press / Journals Manager, Kent OH 44242-0001. **Tel** (216)672-7913, FAX (216)672-3104. **ED** John T. Hubbell. **LC** E461; .C5. **DD** 973.705. **[CCC]**. Index available. cum. index. **Bk Rev. Ad Acc. Pr Rev. Circ:** 1,500. available on microfilm and microfiche from University Microfilms International (UMI). Documents available from The Genuine Article, UMI Article Clearinghouse.
Desc: A scholarly journal featuring studies of mid-19th Century American history. Includes an annual bibliography of articles dealing with the Civil War era.
Ind/Abst Acad. Search (July 1993-); Am. Hist. Life (1955-); Annu. Bibliogr. Engl. Lang. Lit.; Arts Humanit. Citation Index [Full Cov.]; Curr. Contents Arts Humanit.; Expand. Acad. Index (1989-); Hist. Source (July 1993-); Humanit. Index; Humanit. Source (Jul. 1993-); INFO-SOUTH Abstr.; Mag. Search; Newsp. Period. Abstr. (1991-); Ref. Sources; Res. Alert [Full Cov.]; Soc. Sci. Cit. Index [Select. Cov.]; West. Hist. Q.; Writ. Am. Hist.

US/1053-1181
CIVIL WAR NEWS, THE. [Civil War news]. Vol. 15, No. 2 (April 1989)-. Periodical. English. Eleven times a year (Feb./Mar. issues combined). $24.00. Cutter and Locke Publishers, RR 1 Box 36, Tunbridge VT 05077. **Tel** (802)889-3500, FAX (802)889-5627. **ED** Kathryn Jorgensen. **DD** 973. **Bk Rev**, (Qty: 150). **Ad Acc. Circ:** 9,000. ***Continues*** *Civil War Book Exchange and Collector's Newspaper.*
Desc: A current events tabloid newspaper for people with an active interest in the Civil War today - news, features, photos, columns, and events listing.

US/1055-3266
CIVIL WAR REGIMENTS. (CIVIL WAR REGIMENTS : A JOURNAL OF THE AMERICAN CIVIL WAR.). [Civil War regim.]. Vol. 1, No. 1 (1990)-. Periodical. English. qt. $27.00. Regimental Studies, Inc., 1475 South Bascam Avenue, Suite 204, Campbell CA 95008. **Tel** (408)879-9039. **DD** 973.
Ind/Abst Am. Hist. Life (1991-).

US/0009-8086
CIVIL WAR ROUND TABLE DIGEST. **Added/Corp** Civil War Round Table Associates. (1968)-. Periodical. English. mo. $12.50 US; $15.00 Canada; $17.50 other. Civil War Round Table Associates, PO Box 7388, Little Rock AR 72217. **Tel** (501)225-3996, FAX (501)225-5167. **ED** Jerry L Russell. **LC** E461; .C55. **DD** 973.7/05. **Bk Rev. Circ:** 1,200.
Desc: A newsletter devoted to news of contemporary activities, inspired by an interest in Civil War history, historic preservation and history articles.

US/1059-4302
CIVIL WAR SERIALS & BIBLIOGRAPHY. (CIVIL WAR SERIALS & BIBLIOGRAPHY / [EDITED AND PUBLISHED BY DAVID SCOTT MOORE].). [Civ. War ser. bibliogr.]. **VFOAT** Civil War Serials and Bibliography. Vol. 1, No. 1 (Spring 1991)-. Bibliography. English. qt. $15.00 per year. Civil War Serials & Bibliography, c/o David S Moore, 15 Borthwick Avenue, Delmar NY 12054. **DD** 973.

US/0009-8094
CIVIL WAR TIMES ILLUSTRATED. [Civil War times illus.]. Vol. 1 (April 1962)-. Periodical. English. mo (except March and Sept.). $21.00. Cowles Magazines, PO Box 8200, Harrisburg PA 17105. **Tel** (717)657-9555, (800)435-9610. **LC** E461; .C562. **UDC** 973.07. available on microfilm and microfiche from University Microfilms International (UMI). ***Continues*** *Civil War Times;* ***Absorbed*** *Tradition.*
Ind/Abst Acad. Search (July 1993-); Am. Hist. Life (1962-); Hist. Source (July 1993-); Humanit. Source (Jul. 1993-); INFO-SOUTH Abstr.; Mag. Search.

US/0090-449X
CLARK COUNTY HISTORY. **Added/Corp** Fort Vancouver Historical Society. Vol. 1 (1960)-. English. an. $6.50. Fort Vancouver Historical Society of Clark County, PO Box 1834, Vancouver WA 98668. **Tel** (206)695-4681. **LC** F897.C6; C55. **DD** 917.97/86/0305. Index available. cum. index. **Circ:** 800 (ctrl).

MX
CLAUSTRO. 3 (May/June 1980)-. Periodical. Spanish. bm. Claustro Sor Juana, Mexico 1 DF Mexico. **LC** F1201; .C55. **DD** 972/.005. **UDC** 970(=916.3). ***Continues*** *Claustro de Sor Juana.*

US/0163-9943
CLAYMORE (CONVENT STATION), THE. (THE CLAYMORE / COUNCIL OF SCOTTISH CLAN ASSOCIATIONS INC.). **Added/Corp** Council of Scottish Clan Associations. Vol. 1 No. 1 (June 1977)-. Periodical. English. qt. $15.00. Council of Scottish Clan Association, 2805 Legion Avenue, Durham NC 27707. **Tel** (713)664-6033. **LC** DA880.H6; C55. **DD** 970.004/9163.

US/0740-5987
CLEBURNE COUNTY HISTORICAL SOCIETY JOURNAL. **Added/Corp** Cleburne County Historical Society (Ark.). **VFOAT** Cleburne County Historical Journal. Vol. 1 (Fall 1974)-. Periodical. English. Four times a year (Mar., Jun., Sep., Dec.). $8.00. Cleburne County Historical Society, PO Box 794, Heber Springs AR 72543. **Tel** (501)362-6286. **ED** Charlsie B. Little. Index available. cum. index. **Bk Rev. Circ:** 300 (ctrl).

US/0149-1725
CLUES (LINCOLN). (CLUES.). **Added/Corp** American Historical Society of Germans from Russia. (19??)-. English. an. $30.00 (individuals & families); $50.00 (contributing); $100.00 (sustaining); $500.00 (life) Comes with American Historical Society of Germans from Russia membership. American Historical Society of Germans from Russia American Historical Society of Germans from Russia, 631 D Street, 631 D Street, Lincoln Lincoln NE NE 68502 68502. **Tel** (402)474-3363, (402)474-3363, FAX (402)474-7229, (402)474-7229, telex , . **ED** Jo Ann Kuhr and Linda Kahler. **LC** E184.R85; C58. **DD** 973/.04/31.
Desc: Contains articles on genealogical research including publication of passenger lists, cemetery records, and census and church listings. An extensive surname exchange.
Ind/Abst Am. Bibliogr. Slavic East Europ. Stud.

US/0748-6073
COAL PEOPLE. [Coal people]. **VFOAT** Coal People Magazine. (19??)-. Periodical. English. mo. $25.00. Coal People Magazine, PO Box 6247, Charleston WV 25302. **Tel** (304)342-4129, FAX (304)343-3124. **ED** Al Skinner. **DD** 338. Index available. **Bk Rev. Ad Acc. Circ:** 11,000 (ctrl).
Desc: Features stories on coal people and old coal towns.

US
COBWEB : NEWSLETTER OF THE DES PLAINES HISTORICAL SOCIETY. **Added/Corp** Des Plaines Historical Society (Ill.). (19??)-. Newsletter. English. mo. $15.00 institutions; $10.00 individuals. Des Plaines Historical Society, 789 Pearson Street, Des Plaines IL 60016. **Tel** (708)391-5399. **ED** James P. Whitcomb.

●US
COLEGIOS : THE NEWSLETTER ON THE HISTORY OF IDEAS IN COLONIAL LATIN AMERICA. **Added/Corp** Our Lady of the Lake University of San Antonio. Vol. 1, No. 1 (Feb. 1992)-. Newsletter. English.

CN/0710-5002
COLLECTIF PAROLES. [Collect. paroles]. No. 1 (Sept. 1979)-. Periodical. French. bm. $2.50 per number. Collectif Paroles, CP 6 Succursale Outremont, Montreal Quebec H2V 4M6 Canada. **DD** 972.94/06/05.

CN/0828-7597
COLLECTION OF TALKS OF HISTORICAL INTEREST, A. [Collect. talks hist. interest]. **VAT** Pittsburgh Township Historical Society (1979). 1978/1979-. English. an. Pittsburgh Historical Society, PO Box 966, Kingston Ontario K7L 4X8 Canada. **DD** 971.3/71. **UDC** 971.3;929(713). ***Continues*** *Collection of Historical Talks on Pittsburgh Township Families & Homes, 0828-7589.*

US/0733-7760
COLLECTIONS / GEORGIA HISTORICAL SOCIETY. [Collect.- Ga. Hist. Soc.]. **Main/Corp** Georgia Historical Society. (1840)-. Monographic series. English. ir. Price varies per volume. Georgia Historical Society, 501 Whitaker Street, Savannah GA 31499. **Tel** (912)651-2128, FAX (912)651-2831. **LC** F281; .G35. **DD** 975.8/005. available on microfiche.

US/1046-1396
COLLECTIONS OF THE MASSACHUSETTS HISTORICAL SOCIETY. [Collect. Mass. Hist. Soc.]. **Main/Corp** Massachusetts Historical Society. **Added/Corp** Massachusetts Historical Society. **VFOAT** MHS Collections; M.H.S. Collections. Vol. 1 (1792)-. Monographic series. English. ir. Price varies per volume. Northeastern University Press / New York, Box 250, Ithaca NY 14851. **(Subscription address:** Cup Service, PO Box 6525, Ithaca, NY 14851**) ED** Conrad E. Wright. **LC** F61; .M41. **DD** 974. Index available. **Circ:** 400.
Desc: Edited historical documents from the collections of the Massachusetts Historical Society.

CN/1193-9451
COLLECTIONS OF THE ROYAL NOVA SCOTIA HISTORICAL SOCIETY. [Collect. R. N.S. Hist. Soc.]. **Added/Corp** Royal Nova Scotia Historical Society. Vol. 41 (1982)-. English. Free to members. Royal Nova Scotia Historical Society, % Nova Scotia Public Archives, 6016 University Avenue, Halifax, Nova Scotia, B3H 1W4 Canada. **DD** 971.6/005. ***Continues*** *Nova Scotia Historical Society. Collections of the Nova Scotia Historical Society., 0383-8420.*

CN/1186-1193
COLLINGWOOD LIFE & PICTORIAL. [Collingwood life pict.]. (Feb 1991)-. Periodical. English. mo. Free. Collingwood Life & Pictorial, Box 3064, RR 3, Collingwood Ontario L9Y 3Z2 Canada. **DD** 971.318/005.

●US/1063-5769
COLONIAL LATIN AMERICAN HISTORICAL REVIEW. (COLONIAL LATIN AMERICAN HISTORICAL REVIEW : CLAHR.). [Colon.

Latin Am. hist. rev.]. **Added/Corp** Spanish Colonial Research Center (Albuquerque, N.M.). **VFOAT** CLAHR. Vol. 1, No. 1 (Fall 1992)-. Periodical. English (Spanish). Four times a year (Seasonally). $35.00. Spanish Colonial Research Center, University of New Mexico, Zimmerman Library, Albuquerque NM 87131. **Tel** (505)766-8743, FAX (505)277-4603. **ED** Joseph P. Sanchez. **LC** F1412; .C63. **DD** 980/.005. Index available. **Bk Rev**, (Qty: 28 minimum). **Ad Acc**, **Adv Mgr:** Denise Padilla, **Tel** (505)277-1370. **Pr Rev. Circ:** 1,000.
Desc: Covers the era of Spanish colonialism in the Americas. Accepts original research articles in this area.

US/0883-2749
COLONIAL WILLIAMSBURG INTERPRETER, THE. [Colon. Williamsbg. interpret.]. **VFOAT** Interpreter. Vol. 1, No. 1 (July 1980)-. Periodical. English. bm. The Colonial Williamsburg Foundation, Department of Interpretive Education, Williamsburg VA 23187. **LC** F234.W7; C875. **DD** 975.5/4252/005. **UDC** 975.5.

US/0149-9149
COLONY VISITOR. Periodical. English. qt. $2.00 single issue. Old Amherst Colony Museum Park, 500 Smith Road, East Amherst NY 14051. **LC** F119; .C72. **DD** 974.7/96. **UDC** 974.7.

US/0272-9377
COLORADO HERITAGE. (COLORADO HERITAGE : THE JOURNAL OF THE COLORADO HISTORICAL SOCIETY.). [Colo. herit.]. **Added/Corp** State Historical Society of Colorado. Issue 1 (1981)-. English. Four times a year. $35.00 schools, libraries, museums, historians & local historical societies; $100.00 centennial member; $300.00 patron member; $1,000.00 corporate member also comes with Colorado Historical Society membership. Colorado Historical Society, PO Box 480203, Denver CO 80203. **Tel** (303)866-3678. **ED** Judith Gamble. **LC** F771; .C43. **DD** 978.8/005. **Bk Rev. Circ:** 6,500 (ctrl). available on microfiche. ***Continues** Colorado Magazine, 0010-1648.*
Desc: A magazine about the history of Colorado and the American West.
Ind/Abst Am. Hist. Life (1981-); West. Hist. Q.

US/0895-0083
COLORADO HISTORY NEWS. [Colo. hist. news]. **Added/Corp** State Historical Society of Colorado. (Aug. 1987)-. Periodical. English. ir. $35.00 schools, libraries, museums, historians, & local historical societies; $100.00 centennial member; $300.00 patron member; $1,000.00 corporate member, Comes with Colorado Historical Society membership. Colorado Historical Society, PO Box 480203, Denver CO 80203. **Tel** (303)866-3678. **DD** 978. ***Continues** Colorado Heritage News, 0272-8907.*

US/0010-1702
COLORADO PROSPECTOR. (1969)-. Periodical. English. bm (Jan., Mar., May, July, Sept., Nov.). $8.00 (one year), $14.00 (two year) US; $10.00 other. Colorado Prospector, PO Box 6482, Denver CO 80206. **Tel** (303)841-0609. **ED** Alan J. Kania. **Bk Rev. Ad Acc. Circ:** 3,500.
Desc: Colorado history from early day newspapers.

US/0892-3094
COLUMBIA (TACOMA, WASH.). (COLUMBIA.). **Added/Corp** Washington State Historical Society. (Spring 1987)-. Periodical. English. qt (March, June, Sept., Dec.). $26.00 US; $31.00 other. Washington State Historical Society, 315 North Stadium Way, Tacoma WA 98403. **Tel** (206)593-2830, FAX (206)597-4186. **DD** 979.
Desc: The Northwest magazine of history, oriented toward a popular audience.

US/0882-7761
COLUMBUS AND CENTRAL OHIO HISTORIAN. [Columb. Cent. Ohio hist.]. No. 1 (April 1984)-. Periodical. English. sa. Richard E Barrett, 798 Chaffin Ridge, Columbus OH 43214. **LC** F499.C757; C64. **DD** 977.1/57/005. **UDC** 977.1.

US/0740-2171
COLUMBUS MAGAZINE. Began in 1982?. Periodical. English. bm. $15.00 US; $30.00 other. Columbus Magazine Inc, PO Box 12246, Columbus GA 31907. **Tel** (404)563-8252. **LC** F294.C7; C64. **DD** 975.8.473. **UDC** 975.8.

US/0196-1306
COLUMNS (MADISON). (COLUMNS : BIMONTHLY NEWSLETTER OF THE HISTORICAL SOCIETY OF WISCONSIN.). [Columns]. **Added/Corp** State Historical Society of Wisconsin. Vol. 1 (Feb./March 1980)-. Periodical. English. bm (6 issues). Comes with Wisconsin Magazine of History. State Historical Society of Wisconsin, 816 State Street, Madison WI 53706. **Tel** (608)264-6461, FAX (608)264-6404. **Circ:** 5,500 (ctrl). ***Supersedes** Wisconsin Then and Now, 0043-6739.*
Desc: News and information about the activities, programs and staff of the State Historical Society of Wisconsin, a government agency and membership organization.
Ind/Abst West. Hist. Q.

US
COMMEMORATIVE SERIES. Main/Corp University of California, Riverside. Latin American Studies Program. (Oct. 1977)-. Monographic series. English (Spanish). an. Price varies per volume. University of California at Riverside, Latin American Studies Program, Riverside CA 92521. **Tel** (714)787-3863. **ED** William W. Megenney.
Desc: Series commemorating famous Latin American authors and events.

US
COMMUNIQUE / ORDER OF THE INDIAN WARS. (19??)-. Newsletter. English. Free to members; Membership: $20.00 US; $25.00 other. Order of the Indian Wars, PO Box 7401, Little Rock AR 72217. **Tel** (501)225-3996, FAX (501)225-5167. **ED** Jerry L. Russell. **Bk Rev.**
Desc: Contains present day activities relating to interests in Indian Wars History.

CN/0712-5070
COMUNITA (MONTREAL). (LA COMUNITA : BOLLETTINO DELLA FONDAZIONE N.C.I.C. QUEBEC ...). [Comunita]. Periodical. Italian. ir. la Comunita, 505 East rue Jean-Talon, Montreal Quebec H2R 1T6 Canada. **DD** 971.4/00451/05. **UDC** 971.4(=50).

US/0010-5260
CONCORDIA HISTORICAL INSTITUTE QUARTERLY. See Religion and Theology-Protestantism.

US/0895-9455
CONFEDERATE CHRONICLES OF TENNESSEE. [Confed. chron. Tenn.]. **Added/Corp** Society of the Confederate Chronicles. Vol. 1 (June 1986)-. Academic Scholarly Publication. English. an. $12.00. Confederate Chronicles of Tennessee / Tennessee Division Services, 117 West Fayette Street, Somerville TN 38068. **Tel** (901)465-3901. **ED** R. W. Rosser. **LC** E483.4.T2; C66. **DD** 973.7/09768. Index available. **Bk Rev. Ad Acc. Circ:** 1,000 (ctrl).
Desc: Scholarly articles and unpublished photos pertaining to Tennessee and Tennesseans during The War Between States. It is strictly from The Confederate perspective.

US/0890-2216
CONFEDERATE VETERAN (MURFREESBORO, TENN.). (CONFEDERATE VETERAN.). **Added/Corp** Sons of Confederate Veterans (Organization). **VFOAT** Confederate Veteran Magazine. Vol. 32, No. 6 (Sept. 1984)-. Academic Scholarly Publication. English. bm (6 issues). $13.00. Confederate Veteran, 8506 Braesdale, Houston TX 77071. **Tel** (601)268-6100. **ED** James N. Vogler, Jr. (editor's telephone: (713)778-0074). **LC** E482; .C743. **DD** 369/.17. **Bk Rev**, (Qty: 36). **Ad Acc, Adv Mgr:** same as publisher. **Circ:** 20,000 (ctrl).
Desc: Scholarly articles about the war between the states with news of interest to members of Sons of Confederate Veterans.

CN/0705-6885
CONGRESSO (TORONTO). (IL CONGRESSO.). Vol. 1- April 1977-. Periodical. English (Italian). bm. Free. National Congress of Italian Canadians Toronto District, 756 Ossington Avenue, Toronto Ontario M6G 3T9 Canada. **DD** 971.3/541/00451. **UDC** 971.3(50).

HT/0304-5757
CONJONCTION. Added/Corp Institut Francais d'Haiti. No. 1 (Jan. 1946)-. Periodical. French. Four times a year. $40.00. Institut Francais d'Haiti, Po Box 131, Port-Au-Prince Haiti. **Tel** 011 509 1 226060, 011 509 1 226063. **LC** F1912; .C65.
Ind/Abst HAPI Hisp. Am. Period. Index.

US/0010-6054
CONNECTICUT ANTIQUARIAN, THE. ***Ceased.*** (THE CONNECTICUT ANTIQUARIAN : THE BULLETIN OF THE ANTIQUARIAN & LANDMARKS SOCIETY OF CONNECTICUT.). [Conn. antiq.]. Vol. 4, No. 1 (June 1952)-Ceased July 1991. Bulletin. English. Twice a year. Antiquarian and Landmarks Society Inc, 394 Main Street, Hartford CT 06103. **Tel** (203)247-8996. **ED** Mary Beth Baker. **LC** F96; .C65. **DD** 974. **UDC** 974.6. Index available. **Bk Rev. Ad Acc. Circ:** 1,000 (ctrl). available on microfiche. ***Continues** Antiquarian (Antiquarian and Landmarks Society, Connecticut).*
Desc: Articles on Connecticut history and culture.
Ind/Abst Am. Hist. Life (1978-).

US/0885-4831
CONNECTICUT HISTORICAL SOCIETY BULLETIN, THE. [Conn. Hist. Soc. bull.]. **Added/Corp** Connecticut Historical Society. Vol. 47, No. 4 (Winter 1982)-. Bulletin. English. Four times a year (variable). $20.00. Connecticut Historical Society, 1 Elizabeth Street, Hartford CT 06105. **Tel** (203)236-5621, FAX (203)236-2664. **ED** Everett C. Wilkie, (phone: (203)236-5621). **LC** F91; .C67. **DD** 974.6/005. Index Available Received separately--bound from publisher. cum. index. **Bk Rev**, (Qty: 10). **Ad Acc.** ***Continues** Connecticut Historical Society. Bulletin - Connecticut Historical Society, 0883-9220.*
Desc: Today the Bulletin publishes manuscripts that deal with any aspect of Connecticut history and culture or with early New England history and culture. It does not publish commentaries on current events. Scholarly editions of original manuscript sources, such as diaries or documents, are also published.
Ind/Abst Am. Hist. Life (1963-1966); Annu. Bibliogr. Engl. Lang. Lit.; BHA : Biblio. Hist. Art.

US
CONNECTICUT HISTORY. No. 1- Oct. 1967-. Periodical. English. ir. Eastern Connecticut State College, Center for Connecticut Studies, D Roth, Willimantic CT 06226. **UDC** 974.6.
Ind/Abst Am. Hist. Life (1974-).

US/0010-6216
CONNECTICUT REVIEW (NEW BRITAIN). (CONNECTICUT REVIEW.). **Added/Corp** Board of Trustees for Connecticut State Colleges. Connecticut State University (System). Vol. 1 (Oct. 1967)-. Periodical. English. ir. Southern Connecticut State College, 501 Crescent Street, New Haven CT 06515. **LC** AS30; .C62. **DD** 051.
Ind/Abst Am. Hist. Life (1990-); Linguist. Lang. Behav. Abstr.; Soc. Plann. Policy Dev. Abstr.; Sociol. Abstr.

CN/0820-8301
CONTACT-ACADIE. (CONTACT-ACADIE : BULLETIN DU CENTRE D'ETUDES ACADIENNES.). [Contact-Acadie]. **Added/Corp** Universite de Moncton. Centre d'Etudes Acadiennes. **VFOAT** Bulletin du Centre d'Etudes Acadiennes. No. 1 (Dec. 1982)-. Periodical. French. sa (June and Dec.). Free on request. Centre d'Etudes Acadiennes, Universite de Moncton, Moncton New Brunswick E1A 3E9 Canada. **Tel** (506)858-4085, FAX (506)858-4585. **ED** Ronald Labelle. **DD** 971.5/004114/071171523. **Circ:** 600.
Desc: Bulletin of information on Acadian studies at the University of Moncton.

CL
CONTRIBUCION HISTORICA. Periodical. Spanish. Museo Regional de Atacama, Casilla N PO S 134, Copiapo Chile. **LC** F3131. **DD** 983/.14. **UDC** 983.

US/0084-9219
CONTRIBUTIONS IN AMERICAN HISTORY. (1969)-. Monographic series. English. ir. Price varies per volume. Greenwood Press Inc., PO Box 5007, Westport CT 06881-5007. **Tel** (203)226-3571, FAX (203)222-1502. **ED** Jon L. Waklyn. **LC** UNC.

US/0084-9227
CONTRIBUTIONS IN AMERICAN STUDIES. (19??)-. Monographic series. English. ir. Price varies per volume. Greenwood Press Inc., PO Box 5007, Westport CT 06881-5007. **Tel** (203)226-3571, FAX (203)222-1502. **ED** Robert H. Walker. **LC** UNC.

US/0163-3813
CONTRIBUTIONS IN COMPARATIVE COLONIAL STUDIES. [Contrib. comp. colon. stud.]. No. 1 (197?)-. Monographic series. English. ir. Price varies per volume. Greenwood Press Inc., PO Box 5007, Westport CT 06881-5007. **Tel** (203)226-3571, FAX (203)222-1502. **ED** Robin W. Winks.

US/1054-6790
CONTRIBUTIONS IN LATIN AMERICAN STUDIES. (1991)-. Monographic series. English. Price varies per volume. Greenwood Press Inc., PO Box 5007, Westport CT 06881-5007. **Tel** (203)226-3571, FAX (203)222-1502.

SP/0589-8056
CORPUS HISPANORUM DE PACE. Added/Corp Consejo Superior de Investigaciones Cientificas (Spain) Spain. Consejo Superior de Investigaciones Cientificas. Instito Francisco de Vitoria. Vol. 1 (1963)-. Monographic series. Spanish. ir. Price varies per volume. Consejo Superior Investigacion Cientificas (CSIC), Vitruvio 8, 28006 Madrid Spain. **Tel** 011 34 1 5612833, FAX 011 34 1 4113077, telex 42182.

CN/1185-975X
COUNTRY ROADS MAGAZINE (CARP). ***Ceased.*** (COUNTRY ROADS MAGAZINE.). [Ctry. roads mag.]. Vol. 3, Issue 2 (Apr./June 1991)-(1993). Periodical. English. qt. Limited free distribution. Country Roads Publications Ltd., RR2, Carp Ontario K0A 1L0 Canada. **DD** 971.3. ***Continues** Country Roads (Carp, Ont.), 1186-9925.*

US
COUNTRY WAYS. English. sa. $12.50 (one year), $17.50 (two year). Pearl Design Associates, PO Box 1367, Middlebury IN 46540. **Tel** (219)825-2267. ***Continues** Heritage Country.*

US/0590-0107
COUNTY COURIER. (Feb. 1970)-. Newsletter. English. Twelve times a year. $15.00 individual membership; $30.00 institutional membership. Orange County Historical Society, PO Box 10984, Santa Ana CA 92711. **Tel** (714)557-7074. **DD** 979.4.

CN/0826-3035
COUNTY MAGAZINE (BLOOMFIELD. 1983). (COUNTY MAGAZINE.). [Cty. mag.]. Vol. 5, No. 30 (Winter 1983)-. Periodical. English. ir. 15.00Can$. County Magazine Printshop Ltd., Rural Route 1, Bloomfield Ontario K0K 1G0 Canada. **Tel** (613)393-3355. **ED** Ian S. Robertson. **DD** 971.3/587/005. **Ad Acc, Adv Mgr:** Kim Klaver. Full Page (B&W) 210.00Can$. Half Page (B&W) 150.00Can$. **Circ:** 2,500. ***Continues*** *County, 0826-1822.*
Desc: Covers people, places, homes, lifestyle and history of Prince Edward County, Ontario Canada.

CN/0840-9536
COURRIER (SOCIETE D'HISTOIRE DES FRANCO-COLOMBIENS). (LE COURRIER.). [Courr. - Soc. hist. Fr.-Colomb.]. **VFOAT** Courrier de la S.H.F.C. Vol. 1, No. 1 (Dec. 1988)-. Periodical. French. qt. Free to members. Societe d'Histoire des Franco-Colombiens, 9 East Broadway, Vancouver British Columbia V5T 1V4 Canada. **Tel** (504)879-3911. **DD** 971.1/004114/05. **Circ:** 5,000. ***Continues in part*** *Chronographe, 0822-3149.*

US/0574-3680
COVERED WAGON, THE. **Added/Corp** Shasta Historical Society. (19??)-. English. an. $6.00. Shasta Historical Society, PO Box 990277, Redding CA 96099. **Tel** (916)225-4155. **LC** F868.S49; C67. **DD** 979.4/24/005.

US
COW NECK PENINSULA HISTORICAL SOCIETY JOURNAL, THE. **Main/Corp** Cow Neck Peninsula Historical Society. English. an. Cow Neck Peninsula Historical Society, 336 Port Washington Boulevard, Port Washington NY 11050. **Tel** (516)767-2130. **ED** Catherine Sandy. **UDC** 974.7. Index available. **Circ:** 800.
Desc: Articles on Colonial and 19th Century History of Port Washington, Nassau County, and New York.

US/8756-0542
COWLITZ HISTORICAL QUARTERLY. [Cowlitz hist. q.]. **Added/Corp** Cowlitz County Historical Society. (Nov. 1976)-. Periodical. English. qt. $15.00. Cowlitz County Historical Society, 405 Allen Street, Kelso WA 98626. **Tel** (206)577-3119. **ED** Virginia Urrutia, David Freece. **LC** F897.C85; C6. **DD** 979.7/88/005. cum. index. **Circ:** 475. ***Continues*** *Cowlitz County Historical Quarterly.*
Desc: The editors invite manuscripts and articles dealing with the history of Cowlitz County, southwestern Washington or Washington state.
Ind/Abst Am. Hist. Life.

US/0574-377X
CRAIGHEAD COUNTY HISTORICAL QUARTERLY, THE. **Added/Corp** Craighead County Historical Society (Ark.). Vol. 1 (1962)-. Periodical. English. qt (Jan., Apr., July.,Oct.). $10.00 (individuals and libraries), $25.00 (institutions). Craighead County Historical Society, PO Box 1011, Jonesboro AR 72403. **Tel** (501)935-6838. **ED** Mrs. Frank F. Sloan. Index available. **Circ:** 270.
Desc: Devoted entirely to Craighead County. Contains histories, remembrances, photos, genealogies, etc.
Ind/Abst Am. Hist. Life.

AG/0590-1154
CRONICA DE LA GUERRA ESPANOLA. No. 1, (1966)-. Periodical. Undetermined. wk. **DD** 355; 946.

UY
CRONICA GENERAL DEL URUGUAY. Periodical. Spanish. Ediciones de la Banda Oriental, Uruguay. **UDC** 989.9.

●US/1065-9110
CROSSROADS (UNIVERSITY, MISS.). (CROSSROADS : A JOURNAL OF SOUTHERN CULTURE.). [CrossRoads]. **Added/Corp** University of Mississippi. Center for the Study of Southern Culture. **VFOAT** Cross Roads. Vol. 1, No. 1 (Fall 1992)-. Periodical. English. sa. $12.00 (institutions), $9.00 (individuals). University of Mississippi, Sam Hall Room 206, University MS 38677. **Tel** (601)232-5742, FAX (601)232-7842. **DD** 975.

MX/0011-2356
CUADERNOS AMERICANOS. [Cuad. am.]. Vol. 1, (Jan./Feb. 1942)-. Periodical. Spanish. Six times a year (Jan., Mar., May, July, Sept., Dec.). $125.00. Unam Cuadernos Americanos-, Torre Humanidad, Ciudad Universitaria, 04510 Mexico DF Mexico. **Tel** 011 52 5 6221910, or 6221903. **ED** Liliana Weinberg. **LC** AP63; .C669. **DD** 056. Index available in last issue of volume--attached. cum. index. **Bk Rev. Ad Acc. Circ:** 2,500 (ctrl).
Desc: Covers politics, culture, philosophy and literature of Latin America.
Ind/Abst Am. Hist. Life (1954-1965); HAPI Hisp. Am. Period. Index; Int. Bibliogr. Sociol.; Int. Polit. Sci. Abstr.; MLA Int. Bibl. Books Artic. Mod. Lang. Lit.; Romant. Move.

AG/0070-1769
CUADERNOS DEL SUR. [Cuad. sur]. No. 1-. Periodical. Spanish. Universidad Nacional del Sur, Instituto de Humanidades, Argentina Balcarce 257, Bahia Blanca Argentina. **LC** F2810; .C8. **DD** 980/.005. **UDC** 980.
Ind/Abst Am. Hist. Life (1967-1968).

MX
CUADERNOS PREHISPANICOS. v. 1-1973-. Spanish. Seminario Americanista de la Universidad, Calle de Colon SN, Valladolid Mexico. **LC** E65; .C82. **UDC** 972.01.
Ind/Abst Anthropol. Lit.

US/0361-4441
CUBAN STUDIES. [Cuban stud.]. **Added/Corp** University of Pittsburgh. Center for Latin American Studies. University of Pittsburgh. Press. **VFOAT** Estudios Cubanos. Vol. 5 (Jan. 1975)-. Academic Scholarly Publication. English (Spanish). an. $39.95 (Vol. 23). University of Pittsburgh Center for Latin American Studies, 4E04 Forbes Quadrangle, Pittsburgh PA 15260. **Tel** (412)648-7392. **(Subscription address:** Cup Service, PO Box 6525, Ithaca NY 14851.**) ED** Carmelo Mesa-Lago. **LC** F1751; .C986. **DD** 972.91/005. **Bk Rev. Circ:** 600 (ctrl). ***Continues*** *Cuban Studies Newsletter, 0011-2631.*
Desc: Scholarly, multidisciplinary journal devoted entirely to Cuba; includes articles, book reviews and a classified bibliography.
Ind/Abst ABC POL SCI; Am. Hist. Life (1973-); HAPI Hisp. Am. Period. Index (19??-); Int. Dev. Abstr. (?-?); Int. Polit. Sci. Abstr.

AG
CUESTIONARIO. Began with May 1973 issue. Periodical. Spanish. $60.00. Cuestionario Sri, Paraguay 2028/214, Buenos Aires Argentina. **LC** F2849.2; .C83. **UDC** 982.

US/0195-2714
CULTURE & HISTORY. [Cult. hist.]. **VFOAT** Culture and History. -Mar./Apr. 1984; Vol. 1, No. 1 (July-Aug.-Sept. 1984)-. Periodical. English. qt. Free. Culture & History, Department of Culture and History, Capitol Complex, Charleston WV 25305. **Tel** (304)348-0162. **LC** F241; .C9. **DD** 975.4/005. **UDC** 975.4. **Circ:** 15,000 (ctrl).
Desc: Publication reflecting the activities and events of the West Virginia department of culture and history and a three month cultural calendar of upcoming events throughout West Virginia.

CN/0825-2777
CULTURES DU CANADA FRANCAIS. [Cult. Can. fr.]. **Added/Corp** Universite d'Ottawa. Centre de Recherche en Civilisation Canadienne-Francaise. No 1 (1984)-. French. an. 7,00 $ par annee. 19,00 $ pour 3 annees. Centre de Recherche en Civilisation Canadienne-Francaise, de l'Universite d'Ottawa, A/S Editions de l'Universite d'Ottawa, 603 Avenue Cumberland, Ottawa, Ont K1N 6N5. **DD** 971/.004114. ***Continues*** *Universite d'Ottawa. Centre de Recherche en Civilisation Canadienne-Francaise. Bulletin du Centre de recherche en Civilisation Canadienne-Francaise, Universite d'Ottawa., 0045-608X.*
Ind/Abst Am. Hist. Life (1986-).

US
CUMTUX : CLATSOP COUNTY HISTORICAL SOCIETY QUARTERLY. **Added/Corp** Clatsop County Historical Society. **VFOAT** Clatsop County Historical Society Quarterly. Vol. 1, No. 1 (Winter 1980)-. Periodical. English. Four times a year. $25.00 US; $50.00 other. Clatsop County Historical Society, 1618 Exchange Street, Astoria OR 97103. **Tel** (503)325-2203.

US/0739-1145
CURRENT EVENTS SWEEPSTAKES. **Added/Corp** Innovations Associates. (19??)-. Periodical. English. Thirty-six times a year. $140.00. Innovations Associates, Box 311, Sharon MA 02067. **Tel** (617)784-7338. **ED** Marjorie V. Gordon. ctrl circ.
Desc: Game which uses carefully selected news events from the U.S. and around the globe to stimulate awareness of current events. Each week categorized questions concerning the very latest happenings and the personalities involved in them are arranged in an easy-to-play game.

NE
CURRENT INDONESIAN STUDIES IN THE NETHERLANDS. **Added/Corp** Koninklijk Instituut voor Taal-, Land- en Volkenkunde (Netherlands). Modern Indonesian Dept. Instituut voor Maatschappij-Wetenschappelijk Onderzoek in Ontwikkelingslanden (Netherlands). (1978/1979)-. English. Royal Institute of Linguistics and Anthropology, PO Box 9515, 2300 RA Leiden, The Netherlands. **Tel** 011 31 71 272372, FAX 011 31 71 272638. ***Separated from*** *Excerpta Indonesica, 0046-08885.*

US
CURRY COUNTY ECHOES. **Added/Corp** Curry County Historical Society. (19??)-. Periodical. English. bm. Free to members; $7.50 membership fee. Curry County Historical Society, 920 South Ellensburg Avenue, Gold Beach OR 97444. **Tel** (503)247-6113. **ED** Lola Gardner, Marguerite Metzgus. cum. index. **Circ:** 350 (ctrl).

US/0415-0368
DARIEN HISTORICAL SOCIETY ANNUAL, THE. **Main/Corp** Darien Historical Society. **Added/Corp** Darien Historical Society. Annual. Darien Historical Society. Proceedings. Vol. 1 (1954/1955)-. English. an. Free (members); $2.00 (non-members). Darien Historical Society, 45 Old Kings Highway North, Darien CT 06820. **Tel** (203)655-0834.

BO
DATA : REVISTA DEL INSTITUTO DE ESTUDIOS ANDINOS Y AMAZONICOS. **Added/Corp** Instituto de Estudios Andinos y Amazonicos (Bolivia). No. 1 (1991)-. Periodical. Spanish. sa. **LC** F3321; .D37.

US/0011-7013
DAUGHTERS OF THE AMERICAN REVOLUTION MAGAZINE. [Daughters Am. Rev. mag.]. **Main/Corp** Daughters of the American Revolution. **Added/Corp** Daughters of the American Revolution. Magazine. **VFOAT** DAR Magazine. Vol. 80, No. 7 (July 1946)-. Periodical. English. Ten times a year (published monthly except July and Aug.). $12.00. National Society of the Daughters of the American Revolution, 1776 D Street NW, Washington DC 20006. **Tel** (202)879-3285, FAX (202)879-3283. **ED** Mary Rose Hall, (phone: (202)879-3286). Index available in last issue of volume--attached. **Ad Acc, Adv Mgr:** Bob Fones, **Tel** (202)879-3286. **Circ:** 40,000. available on microfilm and microfiche from University Microfilms International (UMI). ***Continues*** *National Historical Magazine.*
Desc: Contains material of interest to the student of the American Revolution and genealogy as well as information and material slated for the DAR.
Ind/Abst Am. Hist. Life (1971-); Genealogical Period. Annu. Index.

US/0882-2395
DAVIESS COUNTY HISTORICAL QUARTERLY, THE. [Daviess Cty. hist. q.]. **Added/Corp** Daviess County Historical Society (Ky.). Vol. 1, No. 1 (Jan. 1983)-. Periodical. English. Four times a year (Jan., Apr., July, Oct.). $10.00 (comes with Daviess County Historical Society membership). Daviess County Historical Society, Kentucky Wesleyan History Dept., Owensboro KY 42301. **Tel** (502)926-3111 Ext. 276. **ED** Lee A. Dew. **LC** F457.D3; D38. **DD** 976.9/864/005. Index available. **Bk Rev. Circ:** 150.
Desc: History of Daviess County, the Green River area of Kentucky, and Kentucky history generally.

US/0199-9214
DAYTON. ***Suspended.*** **VFOAT** Dayton Magazine. Periodical. English. bm. $6.00. Dayton, 1980 Winters Bank Tower, Dayton OH 45423. **LC** F499.D2; D28. **DD** 977.1/73005. **UDC** 977.1. available on microfilm from University Microfilms International (UMI). ***Continues*** *Dayton U.S.A., 0011-7137.*

CN/0823-0080
DECIMA QUARTERLY REPORT. (THE DECIMA QUARTERLY REPORT : PUBLIC AFFAIRS TRENDS.). [Decima q. rep.]. **Added/Corp** Decima Research. Public Affairs International Ltd. **VFOAT** Decima Quarterly Report : Public Affairs Trends. Executive Summary. Vol. 1, No. 1 (Spring 1980)-. Periodical. English. Four times a year. 24,000.00Can$. Public Affairs International Ltd., One Eglinton Avenue E/Suite 800, Toronto Ontario M4P 3A1 Canada. **Tel** (416)481-5123. **DD** 971/.005.

GW/0011-7765
DELAWARE HISTORY. [Del. hist.]. **Added/Corp** Historical Society of Delaware. Vol. 1, No. 1 (Jan. 1946)-. Periodical. English. Four times a year. $15.00. Historical Society of Delaware, 505 Market Street Mall, Wilmington DE 19801. **Tel** (302)655-7161, FAX (302)655-7844. **ED** Constance J. Cooper. **LC** F161; .D37. **DD** 975.1005. Index available. **Pr Rev. Circ:** 1,200 (ctrl).
Desc: Covers all aspects of history, biography, genealogy, and economic development of Delaware from colonial times to the present.
Ind/Abst Am. Hist. Life (1963-); Annu. Bibliogr. Engl. Lang. Lit.; Recent. Publ. Artic.; Writ. Am. Hist.

US/0278-7970
DENVER WESTERNERS ROUNDUP, THE. [Denver West. roundup]. **Added/Corp** Westerners. Denver Posse. (19??)-. Periodical. English. bm. $20.00. Denver Posse of the Westerners, c/o Robert D. Stull, 8206 Adams Way, Denver CO 80221. **Tel** (303)428-1035. **ED** Alan J. Stewart. **LC** F591; .W515. **DD** 979/.005. **Bk Rev**, (Qty: 40-50). **Circ:** 250 (ctrl). ***Continues*** *Denver Westerners Monthly Roundup.*
Desc: History of Western North America.
Ind/Abst Writ. Am. Hist.

CK/0418-7547
DESARROLLO INDOAMERICANO. [Desarro. indoam.]. Vol. 1 (1966)-. Periodical. Spanish. Twelve times a year. $120.00 (one year), $300.00 (three years). Desarrollo Indoamericano, Carrera 68 #80-61 Apart 50122, Barranquilla Colombia. **Tel** 011 57 58

341606. **ED** Universidad Simon Bolivar (address: 341 606 Barranquilla Colombia). **DD** 980.1. cum. index. **Bk Rev. Ad Acc, Adv Mgr:** Ana de Consuegra. ctrl circ.
Desc: Contains economic analysis and theory in particular those of developing countries (Latin America).
Ind/Abst HAPI Hisp. Am. Period. Index.

FR
DIAL : DIFFUSION DE L'INFORMATION SUR L'AMERIQUE LATINE. (19??)-. French. ir (48 per year). 386.88F France; 440.00F other. Dial, 43 Ter rue de la Glaciere, 75013 Paris France. **Tel** 011 33 1 43369313.

CN/0826-2187
DIALOGO. (DIALOGO : REVISTA DE INFORMACION Y OPINION.). [Dialogo]. Periodical. Spanish. ir. $7.00. Dialogo, PO Box 532, Station E, Monteral Quebec H2T 3A9. **DD** 971.4/00461/05. **UDC** 971.4(=60). ***Continues** Correo Espanol, 0826-2071.*

SP
DIALOGO IBEROAMERICANO. (19??)-. Periodical. Spanish. Ed Latinoamericanas y Espanolas, Edilesa, Viriato 2-10 8, Madrid 10 Spain. **LC** F1401; .D497. **DD** 980/.005.

HT
DIALOGUE (PORT-AU-PRINCE, HAITI). (DIALOGUE : ORGANE OFFICIEL DU MINISTERE DE L'INFORMATION ET DES RELATIONS PUBLIQUES.). Periodical. French. mo. Ministere de l'Information et des Relations Publiques, 8 rue Sylvain Salnave, Delmas Haiti. **LC** F1912; .D5. **DD** 972.94/005. **UDC** 972.94.

AG
DINAMIS. (Oct. 1968)-. Periodical. Spanish. mo. Editorial, 2 de Octubre, Defensa 453 90. Piso, Buenos Aires Argentina. **LC** F2801; .D555. **DD** 918.2/03/05.

US/0145-2096
DIPLOMATIC HISTORY. [Dipl. hist.]. **Added/Corp** Society for Historians of American Foreign Relations. Vol. 1 (Winter 1977)-. Periodical. English. qt (Jan., April, July, Oct.). $65.00 US and Canada; $78.00 other. Blackwell Publishers, 238 Main Street, Cambridge MA 02142. **Tel** (617)547-7110, (800)835-6770, FAX (617)547-0789. **ED** Michael Hogan. **LC** E183.7; .D48. **DD** 973.92/05. Index available. cum. index. **Ad Acc, Adv Mgr:** John Paschetto. **Pr Rev. Circ:** 2175. Documents available from The Genuine Article, UMI Article Clearinghouse.
Desc: Focuses of the role of the United States in the world from the American Revolution through the end of the Cold War. With review articles, round-table discussions and book review essays.
Ind/Abst Acad. Search (July 1993-); Am. Hist. Life (1977-); Am. Bibliogr. Slavic East Europ. Stud.; Arts Humanit. Citation Index [Full Cov.]; Curr. Contents Arts Humanit.; Expand. Acad. Index (1989-); Hist. Source (July 1993-); Humanit. Index; Humanit. Source (Jul. 1993-); INFO-SOUTH Abstr.; Mag. Search; Middle East Abstr. Index; Newsp. Period. Abstr. (1991-); Res. Alert [Full Cov.]; Soc. Sci. Cit. Index [Select. Cov.].

US/0747-6434
DIRECTORY - COUNCIL OF SCOTTISH CLAN ASSOCIATIONS. (DIRECTORY.). [Dir. - Counc. Scott. Clan Assoc.]. Directory. English. Council of Scottish Clan Associations, 7 Wyndmoor Drive, Convent Station NJ 07961. **LC** E184.S3; D57. **DD** 973/.049163/025. **UDC** 973(=916.3)(036).

CN/0382-9073
DIRECTORY OF CANADIAN SCHOLARS AND UNIVERSITIES INTERESTED IN LATIN AMERICAN STUDIES. ***Title Change.*** [Dir. Can. sch. univ. interest. Lat. Am. stud.]. **VFOAT** Repertoire des Universitaires et Universites se Specialisant dans les Etudes Latino-Americaines au Canada. (1974/75)-. Directory. English (French). an. Cityscope Publications, PO Box 807, Manly New South Wales 2095 Australia. **Tel** 011 61 2 957 4811, FAX 011 61 2 922 2247. **DD** 980/.0072. **UDC** 9806(036). ***Supersedes** Directory of Scholars in Latin American Teaching and Research in Canada, 0382-9081.* ***Continued by** Canadian Association of Latin American Studies. Newsletter, 0821-624X.*

CN/1185-3417
DIRECTORY OF CANADIANISTS IN ALBERTA. [Dir. Can. Alta.]. **Added/Corp** University of Calgary. Canadian Studies and Communications Research Project. (July 1990)-. Directory. English. University of Calgary / Canadian Studies, Canadian Studies and Communication Research Project, c/o Margaret Cote, 2500 University Drive NW, Calgary, Alberta T2N 1N4 Canada. **DD** 971/.0071/17123.

●US/1074-9667
DIRECTORY OF HISPANIC EXPERTS, THE. **Added/Corp** Arizona State University. Hispanic Research Center. (1995)-. Directory. English. $250.00. Arizona State University / Hispanic Research Center, Tempe AZ 85287-2702. **Tel** (602)965-3867, FAX (602)964-8309.

US
DIRECTORY OF HISTORICAL SOCIETIES OF NEW JERSEY. 1972-. Directory. English. $1.00. League of Historical Societies of New Jersey, 44 East Oak Street, Basking Ridge NJ 07920. **LC** F131; .D57. **DD** 917.49/0025. **UDC** 061.23: 974.9(036).

CN/1183-9260
DIRECTORY OF MEMBERS / THE CANADIAN HISTORICAL ASSOCIATION. [Dir. memb. - Can. Hist. Assoc]. **Main/Corp** Canadian Historical Association. **VFOAT** Repertoire des Membres. **VAT** Repertoire des Membres - Societe Historique du Canada. (1991)-. Directory. English (French). $19.95 (members), $31.95 (non-members). Canadian Historical Association, 395 Wellington Street, Ottawa Ontario K1A 0N3 Canada. **Tel** (613)233-7885. **DD** 971/.006/071.

CN/1183-9260
DIRECTORY OF MEMBERS / THE CANADIAN HISTORICAL ASSOCIATION. [Dir. memb. - Can. Hist. Assoc]. **Main/Corp** Societe Historique du Canada. **VFOAT** Repertoire des Membres. **VAT** Repertoire des Membres - Societe Historique du Canada. (1991)-. Directory. French (English). 19.95Can$ per issue members, 31.95Can$ per issue non-membres. Canadian Historical Association, 395 Wellington Street, Ottawa Ontario K1A 0N3 Canada. **Tel** (613)233-7885. **DD** 971/.006/071.

●US/1064-9018
DIRECTORY OF PANAMANIAN BUSINESSES, ASSOCIATIONS AND ORGANIZATIONS IN THE UNITED STATES. 1st Ed. (1992)-. Directory. English. $10.00. Viaful Dynamics, PO Box 7498, Grand Central Station NY 10163. **DD** 338.

US/0899-8329
DISCOVERY FIVE HUNDRED : NEWSLETTER OF THE INTERNATIONAL COLUMBIAN QUINCENTENARY ALLIANCE LTD. [Discov. five hundred]. (May 1986)-. Newsletter. English. Three times a year. $15.00. PO Box 1492, Columbus NJ 08022. **DD** 970.

●US
DISPATCH. **Added/Corp** American Association for State and Local History. **VFOAT** History News dispatch. Vol. 9, No. 1 (Jan. 1994)-. Periodical. English. mo. Comes with membership. American Association for State and Local History, 530 Church Street, Suite 600, Nashville TN 37219. **Tel** (615)255-2971, FAX (615)255-2979. **LC** E171; .H67. ***Continues** History News Dispatch.*

US/1046-2341
DISPATCH - COLUMBIA UNIVERSITY. CENTER FOR AMERICAN CULTURE STUDIES, THE. (THE DISPATCH : THE NEWSLETTER OF THE CENTER FOR AMERICAN CULTURE STUDIES, COLUMBIA UNIVERSITY.). [Dispatch - Columbia Univ., Cent. Am. Cult. Stud.]. **Added/Corp** Columbia University. Center for American Culture Studies. (19??)-. Newsletter. English. sa. Free on request. Center for American Culture Studies, 603 Lewisohn, Columbia University, New York NY 10027. **Tel** (212)280-8253. **DD** 973. ***Absorbed** Studies in American Indian Literature, 0730-3238.*

US/1065-0636
DISPATCH CONGRESS NEWS. ***Title Change.*** (DISPATCH CONGRESS NEWS / ILLINOIS STATE HISTORICAL SOCIETY, CONGRESS OF ILLINOIS HISTORICAL SOCIETIES AND MUSEUMS.). [Dispatch Congr. news]. **Added/Corp** Illinois State Historical Society. Illinois Historical Societies and Museums. Congress. **VFOAT** Dispatch and Congress News; Dispatch/Congress News. Ser. 15, Vol. 1, No. 1 (Summer 1992)-(1993). Periodical. English. qt. Dispatch/Congress News, Illinois State Historical Society, Old State Capitol, Springfield IL 62701. **LC** F541; .D57. **DD** 977.3/005. ***Formed by the union of** Dispatch from the Illinois State Historical Society, 0419-4187 **and** Congress News (Springfield, Ill.). **Continued by** Dispatch/News (Springfield, Ill.), 1069-451X.*

●US/1069-451X
DISPATCH/NEWS (SPRINGFIELD, ILL.). (DISPATCH/NEWS.). [Dispatch/news]. **Added/Corp** Illinois State Historical Society. Association of Illinois Historical Societies and Museums. **VFOAT** Dispatch News. Ser. 16, Vol. 1 (Summer 1993)-. Periodical. English. qt. Comes with Illinois State Historical Society membership. Illinois State Historical Society, 1 Old Capitol Plaza, Springfield IL 62701. **Tel** (217)782-8160, FAX (217)524-8042. **LC** F451; .D57. **DD** 977. ***Continues** Dispatch Congress News, 1065-0636.*

US/0419-4187
DISPATCH (SPRINGFIELD, ILLINOIS). ***Title Change.*** (DISPATCH FROM THE ILLINOIS STATE HISTORICAL SOCIETY / ILLINOIS STATE HISTORICAL SOCIETY.). [Dispatch]. **Added/Corp** Illinois State Historical Society. **VFOAT** Dispatch From the Illinois State Historical Society. No. 1 (May 1958)-(1992). Periodical. English. bm. Illinois State Historical Society, 1 Old Capitol Plaza, Springfield IL 62701. **Tel** (217)782-8160, FAX (217)524-8042. **LC** F536; .D5. **DD** 977.3. ***Merged with** Dispatch Congress News, 1065-0636 **to form** Congress News (Springfield, Ill.).*

CN/0700-6039
DOCUMENTS HISTORIQUES - SOCIETE HISTORIQUE DU NOUVEL-ONTARIO. [Doc. hist. - Soc. hist. Nouv.-Ont.]. **Added/Corp** Societe Historique du Nouvel-Ontario. No. 1 (1942)-. Monographic series. French. sa. Price varies per volume. Societe Historique du Nouvel Ontario, Universite de Sudbury Canada, Sudbury Ontario P3E 2C6 Canada. **Tel** (705)673-5661. Index available. **Circ:** 1,500.
Desc: History of the New-Ontario region. Covers all aspects including political, economic, social and cultural development of the region.

US
DOCUMENTS IN AMERICAN HISTORY. English. ir. University of Chicago Press / Book Department, 11030 South Langley Avenue, Chicago IL 60628. **Tel** (800)621-2736, (312)568-1550, FAX (312)753-0811, telex 23933. **UDC** 970.

US/0083-6389
DOCUMENTS - VIRGINIA HISTORICAL SOCIETY. **Main/Corp** Virginia Historical Society. Vol. 1 (1961)-. Monographic series. English. ir. Price varies per volume. Virginia Historical Society, PO Box 7311, Richmond VA 23221-0311. **Tel** (804)358-4901, FAX (804)355-2399. **DD** 975.5. ctrl circ.
Desc: Documents related to Virginia history published as monographs or as sub-series of few volumes.

US/0416-3184
DOWN SOUTH. Began with Dec. 1950/Jan. 1951 issue. Periodical. English. bm. $4.50 (two year). Department 256, Box 80-B, West Beach Boulevard, Biloxi MS 39531. **LC** F347.G9; D68. **DD** 917.62/1. **UDC** 917.62.

US/0418-1379
DUKES COUNTY INTELLIGENCER, THE. [Dukes Cty. intell.]. **Added/Corp** Dukes County Historical Society. **VFOAT** Intelligencer. Vol. 1 (Aug. 1959)-. Periodical. English. qt. $30.00. Dukes County Historical Society, Cooke and School Streets, Box 827, Edgartown MA 02539. **Tel** (617)627-4441. **ED** Arthur Railton. **LC** F72.M5; D8. **DD** 917.44/94. **Circ:** 1,200.
Desc: Articles related to the history and legends of Martha's Vineyard and the Elizabeth Islands, including the pre-colonial era.
Ind/Abst Am. Hist. Life (1986-).

US/0891-7159
DUPAGE. ***Suspended.*** [DuPage]. **VFOAT** Dupage Magazine. Vol. 1, No. 1 (Nov. 1986)-?. Periodical. English. mo. $28.00. LFC Publishing Inc, 739 Roosevelt Road, Building 8/Suite 206, Glen Ellyn IL 60137. **DD** 974. **UDC** 977.

US/0739-9618
DURHAM RECORD, THE. Vol. 1 (Fall 1983)-. English. an. $10.00. Historic Preservation Society of Durham, 120 Morris Street/Room 225, Durham NC 27701-3282. **UDC** 975.6.

US/0012-8155
EARLY AMERICAN LIFE. [Early Am. life]. **Added/Corp** Early American Society. (1970)-. Periodical. English. bm. $22.00. Cowles Magazines, PO Box 8200, Harrisburg PA 17105. **Tel** (717)657-9555, (800)435-9610. **LC** E162; .E214. **DD** 917.3/03/05. Index available. **Ad Acc.** available on microfilm and microfiche from University Microfilms International (UMI). Documents available from UMI Article Clearinghouse, Magazine Collection.
Ind/Abst Access (1976-); Am. Hist. Life (1977-1979, 1982-); ARTbibliogr. Mod.; Ceram. Abstr. (19??-); Gen. Period. Index (1985-); Index Inf. (1977-); Mag. Index Plus (1989-); Newsp. Period. Abstr. (1988-); Pop. Period. Index; Mag. Index (1977-).

US/0094-7083
EARLY AMERICAN LIFE. YEARBOOK. English. an. Early American Society, 206 Hanover Street, Gettysburg PA 17325. **LC** E162; .E216. **DD** 917.3/03/2. **UDC** 930.85(058)(73); 973.01(058).

US/0422-0374
EARLY GEORGIA. **See** Archaeology.

CN/0228-572X
EARTH & TIDE. [Earth tide]. Vol. 1, No. 1 (July 1980)-. Periodical. English. ir. $6.00. Fundy Group Publications, PO Box 128, Yarmouth Nova Scotia B5A 4B1 Canada. **Tel** (902)453-2330, FAX (902)455-7162. **DD** 971.6/3/005. **UDC** 971.6. ***Continues** Bluenose Magazine, 0383-7939.*

CN/0710-1279
EAST GEORGIAN BAY HISTORICAL JOURNAL. [East Georgian Bay hist. j.]. Vol. 1 (1981)-. English. an. 13.95Can$ Canada; 13.95Can$ US.

East Georgian Bay Historical, Elmvale Ontario L0L 1P0 Canada. **Tel** (705)322-3000. **DD** 971.3/15/005. **UDC** 971.3.

US/0424-1444
EAST TEXAS HISTORICAL JOURNAL. [East Tex. hist. j.]. **Added/Corp** Stephen F. Austin State College. East Texas Historical Association. Vol. 1 (July 1963)-. Periodical. English. sa (spring and fall). $15.00. East Texas Historical Association, PO Box 6223 SFA Station, Nacogdoches TX 75962. **Tel** (409)568-2407. **ED** Archie P. McDonald. **LC** F381; .E2. **DD** 976.4/1/05. Index available ($20.00). cum. index (through first twenty volumes). **Bk Rev**, (Qty: 30 - 50). **Ad Acc. Pr Rev. Circ:** 575 (ctrl).
Desc: Articles and reviews pertaining to Texas and Eastern Texas history.
Ind/Abst Am. Hist. Life (1986-); West. Hist. Q.

CN/0381-9604
EASTERN STAR. V. 1- Dec. 1975-. Periodical. English. mo. 0.50Can$ per no. I.M. Dewji, Suite 607, 1057 Don Mills Road, Don Mills Ontario M3C 1W9. **DD** 971/.004/91411. **UDC** 971.

CN/0821-9869
ECHO DE MONNOIR. (L'ECHO DE MONNOIR : REVUE DE LA SOCIETE D'HISTOIRE DE LA SEIGNEURIE DE MONNOIR.). [Echos Monnoir]. V. 1, No. 2, (April/May/June 1983)-. Periodical. French. qt. Free to members, $12.00 others. Societe d'Histoire de la Seigneurie de Monnoir, C P 2051, Marieville Quebec J0L 1J0 Canada. **DD** 971.4/53/005. **UDC** 971.4. ***Continues*** *Echos de Monnoir, 0821-9869.*

CN/0706-7402
ECHO DES CANTONS. V. 1- Feb. 1979-. Periodical. French. mo. $1.50 per number. Editions Blm, CP 1086, Sherbrooke Quebec J1H 5L3. **DD** 971.4/6/005. **UDC** 971.4.

CN/0227-5457
ECHO NOTRE-DAME. [Echo Notre-Dame]. Periodical. French. bw. $0.35 per no. Echo Notre-Dame, CP 176, Notre-Dame-de-Lourdes Manitoba R0G 1M0 Canada. **DD** 971.27/3/005. **UDC** 971.2.

US/1043-3341
ECHOES (BLAINE, ME.). (ECHOES : THE VOICE OF AROOSTOOK...THE CROWN OF MAINE.). **Added/Corp** Association of Aroostook Chambers of Commerce. **VFOAT** Echoes Magazine. Vol. 1, No. 1 (Jan. 1988)-. Periodical. English. qt. $15.00 (US), $19.00 (Canada), $23.00 (other). Echoes Press, PO Box 626, Caribou ME 04736. **Tel** (207)498-8564. **ED** Kathryn Olwstead. **DD** 974. Index available. **Bk Rev**, (Qty: 4 /year). **Ad Acc. Circ:** 6,200 (ctrl).
Desc: Rural culture and history, rural America in fraustaration. positive values relevant to the future. Importance in understanding who we are - where we came from.

US/0012-933X
ECHOES (COLUMBUS). (ECHOES.). [Echoes]. **Added/Corp** Ohio Historical Society. Vol. 1 (Jan. 1962)-. Periodical. English. mo. Comes with membership. Ohio Historical Society, 1982 Velma Avenue, Subscription Office, Columbus OH 43211. **Tel** (614)297-2332, (614)297-2360. **ED** Corinne Colbert. **LC** F486; .E25. **Circ:** 8,000. available on microfilm and microfiche from University Microfilms International (UMI). ***Formed by the union of*** *Ohio Local History News* ***and*** *Museum Echoes.*
Desc: A newsletter to the members of the Ohio Historical Society describing society programs, publications, and projects, and containing short features related to Ohio's history.
Ind/Abst Am. Hist. Life.

US/0046-1091
ECHOES OF HISTORY. V. 1- Nov. 1970-. Periodical. English. bm. $3.00. Pioneer Society of America, 626 South Washington Street, Falls Church VA 22046. **LC** E180; .E26. **DD** 975.5. **UDC** 975.5.

MX
ECO. Added/Corp Instituto Jalisciense de Antropologia e Historia. Vol. 1 (Jan. 1960)-. Periodical. Spanish. Three times a year. Instituto Jalisciense de Antropologia e Historia, Biblioteca Lic Jose Parres Arias, Calle de Escorza No 130, Guadalajara Mexico. **LC** F1296; .E26.

CN/1187-3957
EDMONTON FACTS. [Edmont. facts]. **Added/Corp** Edmonton Social Planning Council. Vol 1 (Sept. 1991)-. Periodical. English. Free. Edmonton Social Planning Council, 9912 106th Street, Suite 41, Edmonton Alberta T5K 1C5 Canada. **Tel** (403)423-2031. **DD** 971.23/34/005.

US/0271-9819
EIDOS (CAZENOVIA). (EIDOS.). V. 1- Winter 1977-. English (English). Three times a year. $6.00. Idyllic Foundation, Box 455, Cazenovia NY 13055. **LC** F127.M2; E38. **DD** 974.7/64/005.

ES
EL SALVADOR PROCESO. Added/Corp Universidad Centroamericana Jose Simeon Canas. Centro Universitario de Documentacion e Informacion. **VFOAT** Proceso. (19??)-. Periodical. Spanish. wk. $30.00. Centro Universitario de Documentacion e Informacion (CUDI), Apdo. Posta (01) 575, San Salvador, El Salvador C A. **LC** F1488.3; .E43s.
Ind/Abst Hum. Rights Intern. Rep.

US/1049-5665
ENCOUNTERS (ALBUQUERQUE, N.M.). ***Ceased.*** (ENCOUNTERS.). [Encounters]. **Added/Corp** University of New Mexico. Latin American Institute. Vol. 1 (Winter 1989)-(1992). Periodical. English. qt. Latin American Institute, University of New Mexico, 801 Yale Northeast, Albuquerque NM 87131. **Tel** (505)277-5985, FAX (505)277-5989. **LC** F1408.3; .E53. **DD** 980/.005.

NQ
ENCUENTRO. Periodical. Spanish. Three times a year. C$3,000 Nicaragua; $30.00 US. Universidad Centro Americana Departamento de Culture, Apartado Postal 69, Managua Nicaragua. **Tel** 70352, telex 2296 IHCA. **LC** F1401; .E5. **UDC** 908.728.5; 972.85. Index available. cum. index. **Bk Rev. Circ:** 6,000 (ctrl).
Desc: The magazine of the Central American University; articles basically refer to current events and conditions in Nicaragua, seen from an academic perspective.
Ind/Abst HAPI Hisp. Am. Period. Index.

UK/0013-841X
ENGLISH WESTERNERS' TALLY SHEET. 1958-. Periodical. English. Three times a year. £7.50 UK; $10.00 US. English Westerners Society, 90 Babbacombe Road, Bromley Kent England. **ED** Francis B Taunton. **UDC** 973.071.08. **Bk Rev. Ad Acc. Circ:** 300. ***Supersedes in part*** *English Westerners' Brand Book.*
Desc: Articles on American frontier history - 1860-1900 including Indian wars, law and order etc.

AG/0327-649X
ENTREPASADOS : REVISTA DE HISTORIA. VFOAT Entre Pasados. Vol. 1, No. 1 (1991)-. Periodical. Spanish. sa. $25.00. Revista de Historia Juan Suriano, Arevalo 2240, 1425 Buenos Aires, Capital Federal Argentina. **Tel** 011 54 21 769-9013. **(Subscription address:** Fernando Garcia Cambeiro, 7331 Northwest 35th Street, Box 014, Miami, FL 33122 (telephone 361-0473)) **LC** F2801; .E58. **DD** 982/.005.

NQ/0259-4374
ENVIO. Added/Corp Instituto Historico Centroamericano. Universidad Centroamericana (Nicaragua). Loyola University (New Orleans, La.). Institute of Human Relations. Central American Historical Institute. (19??)-. Periodical. English (table of contents in German and Spanish). mo. CAHI, Intercultural Center, Georgetown University, Washington DC 20057. **Tel** (202)687-5676. **LC** F1521; .E59. ***Absorbed*** *Update (Central American Historical Institute).*
Desc: The premier monthly magazine of analysis on the Central American region. A must for concerned citizens and scholars alike, this magazine provides analytical articles, documents, interviews and news stories on the politics and economics of Nicaragua and Central America.
Ind/Abst Hum. Rights Intern. Rep.

US/0014-0376
ESCRIBANO, EL. (EL ESCRIBANO. SCRIBE.). [Escribano]. **Added/Corp** St. Augustine Historical Society. **VFOAT** Scribe. No. 1 (Jan. 1955)-. English. ir. $20.00. St Augustine Historical Society, 271 Charlotte Street, St Augustine FL 32084. **Tel** (904)824-2872. **ED** Jacqueline K. Fretwell. **LC** F319.S2; E83. **DD** 975.9/18. **Bk Rev. Circ:** 750 (ctrl).
Desc: History of northeast Florida.
Ind/Abst Am. Hist. Life (1972-).

US/0899-0409
ESSAYS AND MONOGRAPHS IN COLORADO HISTORY. [Essays monogr. Colo. hist.]. **Added/Corp** Colorado Historical Society. **VFOAT** Essays in Colorado History; Essays & Monographs; Essays and Monographs. No. 1 (1983)-. Monographic series. English. ir. Free to members of the Colorado Historical Society. Colorado Historical Society, PO Box 480203, Denver CO 80203. **Tel** (303)866-3678. **ED** David N. Wetzel. **LC** UNC. **DD** 978.8. Index available. **Bk Rev.** ctrl circ. ***Continues*** *Colorado Historical Society Monograph Series, 0731-2474.*
Desc: Scholarly historical journal of the Colorado Historical Society containing primary and secondary material on the history of Colorado and the Mountain West.
Ind/Abst West. Hist. Q.

US
ESSEX INSTITUTE HISTORICAL COLLECTIONS. ***Title Change.*** **Main/Corp** Essex Institute. Vol. 1 (1859)-(19??). Periodical. English. qt. Essex Institute, 132 Essex Street, Salem MA 01970. **Tel** (508)744-3390, FAX (508)744-0036. **ED** William T. LaMoy. Index available. cum. index. **Bk Rev. Ad Acc. Pr Rev. Circ:** 1,100. available on microfilm and microfiche from University Microfilms International (UMI). Documents available from The Genuine Article. ***Continues*** *Historical Collections of the Essex Institute.* ***Continued by*** *Peabody Essex Museum Collections.*
Desc: History and life of Essex County, Massachusetts. Covers architecture, decorative arts, economics, maritime trade and social history.
Ind/Abst Am. Hist. Life (1963-); Arts Humanit. Citation Index [Full Cov.]; Curr. Contents Arts Humanit.; MLA Int. Bibl. Books Artic. Mod. Lang. Lit.; Res. Alert [Full Cov.]; West. Hist. Q.

CN
ESTIMATES. PART III, INDIAN AND NORTHERN AFFAIRS CANADA. ***Title Change.*** **Main/Corp** Canada. **VFOAT** Budget des Depenses. Partie III, Affaires Indiennes et du Nord Canada; Canada. Estimates. Part III, Indian and Northern Affairs Canada, Administration Program, Northern Affairs Program, Native Claims Program. (198?)-(1991/1992). English (French). Statistics Canada, Publications Sales & Services, Main Building Room 1710, Ottawa Ontario K1A 0T6 Canada. **Tel** (613)951-5078, (800)267-6677, FAX (613)951-1584, telex 053-3585. **LC** E92; .C213a. ***Continues*** *Estimates. Part III, Indian and Northern Affairs Canada, Administration Program, Northern Affairs Program, Native Claims Program.* ***Continued by*** *Canada. Estimates. Part III, Indian and Northern Affairs Canada and Canadian Polar Commission.*

VE
ESTO ES VENEZUELA. Spanish. Bs0.30. Edif, Malak PH-2 Calle Real de Sabana Grande, Caracas Venezuela. **ED** H Castellon. **LC** F2301; .E8. **UDC** 987.

MX/0185-5271
ESTUDIOS DE CULTURA MAYA. ***Ceased.*** [Estud. cult. maya]. Vol. 1 (1961)-Ceased Vol. 17. Spanish (English). an. Unam Instituto Investiga Filologicas, Ciudad Universitaria, 04510 Mexico DF Mexico. **Tel** 011 52 5 6227487, 011 52 5 6650411. **LC** F1435; .A2.
Ind/Abst Anthropol. Lit. (?-?); Ethnoarts Index (?-?); HAPI Hisp. Am. Period. Index (?-?); MLA Int. Bibl. Books Artic. Mod. Lang. Lit. (?-?).

MX/0071-1675
ESTUDIOS DE CULTURA NAHUATL. [Estud. cult. nahuatl]. **Added/Corp** Universidad Nacional Autonoma de Mexico. Instituto de Investigaciones Historicas. Universidad Nacional Autonoma de Mexico. Seminario de Cultura Nahuatl. Vol. 1 (1959)-. Spanish (English). ir. Estudios de Cultura Nahuatl, 80 Piso Universitaria, Mexico 20 DF Mexico. **LC** F1219; .E8.
Ind/Abst Am. Hist. Life (1969-1972); Anthropol. Index; Anthropol. Lit.; Ethnoarts Index; HAPI Hisp. Am. Period. Index; MLA Int. Bibl. Books Artic. Mod. Lang. Lit.

MX/0185-2523
ESTUDIOS DE HISTORIA NOVOHISPANA. [Estud. hist. novohisp.]. **Added/Corp** Universidad Nacional Autonoma de Mexico. Instituto de Investigaciones Historicas. (1966)-. Spanish. **LC** F1231; .E85.
Ind/Abst Am. Hist. Life (1966-); BHA : Biblio. Hist. Art.

AG/0326-7458
ESTUDIOS MIGRATORIOS LATINOAMERICANOS. Added/Corp Centro de Estudios Migratorios Latinoamericanos. (1985)-. Periodical. Spanish. tq. $33.00. Centro de Estudios Migratorios Latino Americanos, Independencia 20, 1099 Buenos Aires, Argentina. **Tel** 011 54 1 346749. **LC** JV7398; .E8. **DD** 325.8.
Ind/Abst Am. Hist. Life (1987-); Popul. Index; Soc. Plann. Policy Dev. Abstr.

CL/0716-1468
ESTUDIOS NORTEAMERICANOS. Added/Corp Universidad de Chile. Instituto de Ciencia Politica. Vol. 1, No. 1 (Aug 1984)-. Periodical. Spanish. qt.
Ind/Abst Am. Hist. Life (1985-).

PY/0251-2483
ESTUDIOS PARAGUAYOS. [Estud. parag.]. V. 1 (Nov. 1973)-. Periodical. Spanish. sa. $25.00. Universidad Catolica / Estudios Paraguayos, Casilla 1718, Asuncion Paraguay. **Tel** 011 595 21 446251. **LC** F2661; .E85. **UDC** 989.2. **Bk Rev. Ad Acc. Circ:** 1,000.
Desc: Concentrates on Paraguay and Rio de la Plata history and problems of development and theory and practice.
Ind/Abst AGRICOLA; Am. Hist. Life (1980-); HAPI Hisp. Am. Period. Index.

BL/0103-4014
ESTUDOS AVANCADOS. Added/Corp Universidade de Sao Paulo. Instituto de Estudos Avancados. Universidade de Sao Paulo. Coordenadoria de Atividades Culturais. Vol. 1, No. 1 (Oct./Dec. 1987)-. Periodical. Portuguese. tq (3 issues). $90.00. Instituto de Estudos Avancados, Travessa J 374, Ciudade Universitaria, 05508 Sao Paulo Brazil. **Tel** 011 51 11 2129421. **LC** F2510; .E5885. **DD** 981/.005.

BL
ESTUDOS HISTORICOS. (19??)-. Periodical. Portuguese (summaries and/or abstracts in English and French). sa. $40.00. Fundacao Getulio Vargas, Praia de Botafogo, 190 6 Andar, 22253-900 Rio de Janeiro RJ Brazil. **Tel** 011 5521 551 0698, FAX 011 5521 551 1596, 011 5521 551 5755.
Desc: A comprehensive analysis of Brazilian history in relation to the major social science fields, such as Sociology and Literature.

FR/0153-1700
ETUDES CANADIENNES. (ETUDES CANADIENNES. CANADIAN STUDIES.). [Etud. Can.]. **Added/Corp** Association Francaise des Etudes Canadiennes. Centre d'Etudes Canadiennes en Sciences Sociales (Institut d'Etudes Politiques de Bordeaux) Universite de Lille III. Centre d'Etudes et de Recherches Nord-Americaines et Canadiennes. **VFOAT** Canadian Studies. (1975)-. Periodical. English (French). sa (June and Dec.). $43.00. Assn Francaise Canadiennes, 6 rue Jean Racine, Jean Michel Lacroix, 33170 Gradignan France. **Tel** 33 56 846804, FAX 33 56 371726, telex 540127. **ED** Prof. Jacques Portes (editor's address: 85 br. Gallieni, 92130 Issy-Les-Moulineaux France). **DD** 971/.005. **Bk Rev**, (Qty: 1). **Ad Acc**, **Adv Mgr:** Lacroix. **Pr Rev. Circ:** 500.
Desc: Interdisciplinary publication concerning Canada; articles contributed by French and Canadian scholars.
Ind/Abst Am. Hist. Life (1986-); Can. Lit. Index (1985-1986); Int. Bibliogr. Sociol.

FR/0765-412X
EVENEMENT DU JEUDI, L'. (198?)-. Periodical. French. wk (52 issues). 832.52F France; 1296.00F EEC; 1115.00F other. L Evenement du Jeudi, 2 rue Christine, 75280 Paris Cedex 06 France. **Tel** 011 33 1 43548480. **LC** AP20; .E915. **DD** 054/.1.

US/0014-388X
EX-CBI ROUNDUP. Added/Corp China-Burma-India Veterans Association. **VAT** Ex-China--Burma--India Roundup. Vol. 1 (1946/47)-. Periodical. English. mo. $13.00 US; $17.00 other. Ex-CBI Roundup, PO Box 2665, La Habra CA 90631.

BL
EXCELENCIA. Vol. 1 (May 1991)-. Periodical. Portuguese. mo. **LC** F2501; .E95. **DD** 981/.005.

●US/1062-4511
EXEMPLARIA HISPANICA. (EXEMPLARIA HISPANICA : A JOURNAL ON ALFONSO X AND ALFONSINE IBERIA.). [Ex. hisp.]. **Added/Corp** Alfonsine Society of America. (1992)-. Periodical. English (Spanish). an. $20.00 institution. Alfonsine Society of America, c/o Dr. Gonzales, 1115 Patterson Office Tower, Spanish Department, Lexington KY 40506. **LC** IN PROCESS; DP140.3; .E93. **DD** 946.

US
FACT SHEETS / NORTH DAKOTA INDIAN AFFAIRS COMMISSION.
Added/Corp North Dakota Indian Affairs Commission. (19??)-. English. an. North Dakota Indian Affairs Commission, 18th Floor State Capitol, Bismarck ND 58505. **LC** E78.N75; F33. **DD** 978.4/00497.

●CN/1183-4854
FAIT FRANCAIS EN AMERIQUE DU NORD. (REPERTOIRE DESCRIPTIF. LE FAIT FRANCAIS EN AMERIQUE DU NORD.). [Fait fr. Am. Nord]. **Added/Corp** Alliance Champlain. **VFOAT** Fait Francais en Amerique du Nord. (1992)-. French. be. 29.95Can$. Quebec Dans Le Monde, CP 8503, Sainte-Foy Quebec G1V 4N5 Canada. **Tel** (418)659-5540, FAX (418)659-4143. **DD** 970.004/41/0025.

US
FAMOUS FIRST FACTS; A RECORD OF FIRST HAPPENINGS, DISCOVERIES AND INVENTIONS IN THE UNITED STATES. (19??)-. English. ir. 4th Edition: $80.00 US and Canada; $90.00 other. H W Wilson Company, 950 University Avenue, Bronx NY 10452. **Tel** (800)367-6770, (718)588-8400, FAX (718)590-1617, telex 4990003 HWILSON. **ED** Joseph Nathan Kane.
Desc: Lists more than 9,000 inventions, discoveries, and places on the American continent from 1007 to present.

US/0430-0688
FAR-WESTERNER, THE. Added/Corp Stockton Corral of Westerners. **VAT** Far Westerner. Vol. 1 (1960)-. Periodical. English. sa. $24.00. Stockton Corral of Westerners, PO Box 1315, Stockton CA 95201. **Tel** (209)466-0194. **ED** Joe Elliff, (209)478-6599. **Circ:** 60.

US/0430-1188
FAULKNER FACTS AND FIDDLINGS. V. 1- Sept. 1959-. Periodical. English. qt. $10.00. Faulkner County Historical Society, PO Box 731, Conway AR 72032. **Tel** (501)327-7788. **ED** Tyler Treadway. **LC** F417.F3; F3. **DD** 976.7/74/005. **UDC** 976.7. cum. index. **Bk Rev. Circ:** 325.
Desc: Local history.

US/0736-8151
FEDERALIST (WASHINGTON, D.C. : 1980), THE. (THE FEDERALIST : NEWSLETTER OF THE SOCIETY FOR HISTORY IN THE FEDERAL GOVERNMENT.). [Federalist]. **Added/Corp** Society for History in the Federal Government (U.S.). Vol. 1, No. 1 (Summer 1980)-. Newsletter. English. qt. $22.00. Society for History in the Federal Government, Box 14139, Ben Franklin Station, Washington DC 20044. **Tel** (703)351-2621. **ED** Kevin C. Ruffner. **Bk Rev**, (Qty: 2). **Ad Acc. Circ:** 400.
Desc: A professional newsletter dealing with history.

CN/1197-5334
FEDERATION NEWS / FEDERATION OF NOVA SCOTIAN HERITAGE. [Fed. news - Fed. N.S. Herit.]. **Added/Corp** Federation of Nova Scotian Heritage. **VFOAT** Fed. of M. H. & H. News. (Spring 1983)-. Periodical. English. Four times a year. 15.00Can$. Federation of Nova Scotian Heritage, 1809 Barrington Street, Suite 901, Halifax NS B3J 3K8 Canada. **Tel** (902)423-4677, 423-4361, FAX (902)422-0881. **ED** Deanna Almond. **DD** 971.6/006. **Circ:** 250. ***Continues*** *Federation News (Federation of Museums, Heritage and Historical Societies of Nova Scotia), 0715-5190.*
Desc: Covers news (local, national and international), book reviews, special articles of interest to membership representing museum, heritage and historical groups and other related groups around the province.

US/0094-1263
FESTIVAL USA. English. sa. American Revolution Bicentennial Administration, 2401 E Street NW, Washington DC 20276. **LC** E285.3; .F475. **DD** 791. **UDC** 973.04.

UY
FICHAS. Main/Corp Iglesia y Sociedad en America Latina. (19??)-. Periodical. Spanish. mo. $10.00. **LC** F1401; .I36a.

US/0739-4802
FILIPINO DIRECTORY OF CALIFORNIA, THE. Directory. English. Fil-Am Enterprises, 46060 Hollywood Blvd., Los Angeles CA 90027. **LC** F870.F4; F54. **DD** 979.4/053/025. **UDC** 979.4(=992.11).

US/0015-1874
FILSON CLUB HISTORY QUARTERLY, THE. [Filson Club hist. q.]. **Added/Corp** Filson Club. Vol. 4, No. 1 (Jan. 1930)-. Periodical. English. qt (Jan., April, July, Oct.). $24.00. The Filson Club Inc, 1310 South Third Street, Louisville KY 40208-2306. **Tel** (502)635-5083, FAX (502)635-5086. **ED** Nelson L. Dawson. **LC** F446; .F484. **DD** 976. Index available (bound in Oct. issue). **Bk Rev**, (Qty: 25-30). **Ad Acc. Pr Rev. Circ:** 3000 (ctrl). available on microfilm and microfiche from University Microfilms International (UMI). ***Continues*** *History Quarterly (Louisville, Ky.).*
Desc: Deals with the history of Kentucky and its adjacent states.
Ind/Abst Am. Hist. Life (1970-).

US
FINGER LAKES MAGAZINE. English. bm. Grapevine Press, 108 South Albany Street, Box O, Ithaca NY 14850. **Tel** (607)272-3470. ***Continues*** *Grapevines Finger Lakes Magazine, 0892-5658.*

US/0362-2576
FINNISH AMERICAN ANNUAL. VFOAT Amerikansuomalaisten Vuosikirja. 1976-. Multiple languages (English and Finnish). an. $4.00. Finnish American Publishing Company, PO Box 334, Cliffside Park NJ 07010. **LC** E184.F5; F48. **DD** 973/.04/94541. **UDC** 973(=945.47)(058).

US/0162-5462
FINNISH AMERICANA. Vol. 1 (1978)-. Periodical. English. an. $6.00. Finnish Americana, Box 120804, New Brighton MN 55112. **Tel** (612)636-6348. **ED** M.G. Karni. **LC** E184.F5; F493. **DD** 973/.04/94541. Each issue contains an index to its own contents (no volume index)--loose. **Bk Rev. Circ:** 1,500.
Desc: Contains articles, fiction, poetry and reviews dealing with all aspects of the history and culture of Finns in North America.

US/1042-2307
FIRESIDE SENTINEL : THE ALEXANDRIA LIBRARY, LLOYD HOUSE NEWSLETTER, THE. Added/Corp Lloyd House. **VFOAT** Alexandria Library, Lloyd House Newsletter. Vol. 1, No. 1 (Mar. 1987)-. Newsletter. English. bm. $6.00. Alexandria Library, 717 Queen Street, Alexandria VA 22314. **Tel** (703)838-4577. **ED** T. Michael Miller. **LC** F234.A3; F57. **DD** 975.5/296/005. **Circ:** 700.
Desc: Focusing on Alexandria, VA history; covers people, events, neighborhoods, and daily life.

CN/0703-8437
FIRST PEOPLE, THE. V. 1- Spring 1976-. Periodical. English. bm. $4.00, Free to institutions and native organizations. The First People, Kikino Alberta T0A 2B0 Canada. **DD** 970/.004/97. **UDC** 970. ***Supersedes*** *4th World Speaks.*

US/1045-4209
FIVE HUNDRED. (FIVE HUNDRED : OFFICIAL PUBLICATION OF THE CHRISTOPHER COLUMBUS QUINCENTENARY JUBILEE COMMISSION.). [Five hundred]. **Added/Corp** Christopher Columbus Quincentenary Jubilee Commission. **VFOAT** Five Hundred Magazine; 500. Vol. 1, No. 1 (May/June 1989)-. Periodical. English. Six times a year. $22.00. Impressions of Miami, c/o Jose Segrera, 7274 SW 48th Street, Miami FL 33155. **Tel** (305)666-0277. **LC** WMLC 93/1512. **DD** 970.

US/0428-5573
FLASHBACK (FAYETTEVILLE, ARK.). (FLASHBACK, PRESERVING THE PAST FOR THE FUTURE.). **Added/Corp** Washington County Historical Society (Ark.). Vol. 1 (1951)-. Periodical. English. qt. $10.00. Washington County Historical Society / Arkansas, 118 East Dickson Street, Fayetteville AR 72701-5612. **Tel** (501)521-2970. **ED** Keith Newhouse. Index Available Published separately--free--upon request. cum. index. **Bk Rev**, (Qty: 2+ /year). **Circ:** 1,000.
Desc: History of Washington County, Arkansas.
Ind/Abst Ozark Period. Index.

US/0361-9788
FLORIDA HANDBOOK, THE. (1948)-. English. be. $43.82 Florida; $40.95 other. Peninsular Publishing Company, PO Box 5078, Tallahassee FL 32301. **Tel** (904)576-4151. **ED** Allen Morris. **LC** F306; .F597. **DD** 917.59. **Circ:** 21,000.
Desc: Reference Book concerning the history of Florida: latest information about state government, public education, climate chronology, literature and books, forest and trees.

US/0015-4113
FLORIDA HISTORICAL QUARTERLY, THE. [Fla. hist. q.]. **Added/Corp** Florida Historical Society. Vol. 15, No. 4 (Apr. 1937)-. Periodical. English. qt. $25.00 (individuals), $35.00 (institutions). Florida Historical Society, South Florida University Library, Tampa FL 33620. **Tel** (813)974-3815, (800)221-5106, FAX (813)974-3815. **ED** George E. Pozzetta. **LC** F306; .F65. Index available. cum. index. **Bk Rev**, (Qty: 80). **Circ:** 2,000 (ctrl). available on microfiche; available in microform. ***Continues*** *Florida Historical Society Quarterly, 0361-624X.*
Desc: Florida focus, 16th century to present; utilization of primary sources, contribution to knowledge and understanding of the history of the state and region.
Ind/Abst Am. Hist. Life (1954-); Annu. Bibliogr. Engl. Lang. Lit.; Recent. Publ. Artic.; Ref. Sources; West. Hist. Q.; Writ. Am. Hist.

US
FLORIDA HISTORY NEWSLETTER. ***Ceased.*** **Added/Corp** Florida Confederation of Historical Societies. **VFOAT** Florida Historical Newsletter. Vol. 1 (Feb. 1975)-(March 1988). Newsletter. English. Three times a year. Florida Historical Confederation, 4202 Fowler Avenue, University of South Florida, Tampa FL 33620. **Tel** (813)974-3815. **ED** Thomas Greenhaw. **Circ:** 2,500 (ctrl).

US
FLORIDA INDIANS. Vol. 1 (1974)-. English. Garland Publishing Inc, 1000A Sherman Avenue, Hamden CT 06514. **Tel** 800-627-6273, (203)281-4487. **LC** E78.F6; F585. **DD** 970.4/59.

US/0271-6100
FLORIDA KEYS MAGAZINE. V. 1- 1st Quarter 1978-. Periodical. English. qt. $5.50. Magazine, PO Box 818, Marathon FL 33050. **LC** F317.M7; F56. **DD** 975.9/41005. **UDC** 975.9.

US/0887-5235
FLORISSANT VALLEY QUARTERLY. [Florissant Val. q.]. **Added/Corp** Florissant Valley Historical Society (Mo.). Vol. 1, No. 1 (Jan. 1984)-. Periodical. English. Four times a year. $10.00. Florissant Valley Historical Society, PO Box 298, Florissant MO 63032. **Tel** (314)831-8012. **DD** 977. ***Continues*** *Quarterly (Florissant Valley Historical Society).*
Ind/Abst Am. Hist. Life.

US
FLUVANNA COUNTY HISTORICAL SOCIETY BULLETIN. Bulletin. English. sa. $8.00. Fluvanna County Historical Society, PO Box 8, Minny McGehee, Palmyra VA 22963. **Tel** (804)589-8815.
Ind/Abst Am. Hist. Life (1987-).

US/0896-3096
FOLIO (SAINT LOUIS, MO.). (FOLIO : THE QUARTERLY NEWSLETTER OF THE PATRICE PRESS.). [Folio]. **Added/Corp** Patrice Press. (Jan. 1988)-. Newsletter. English. qt. $12.00. Patrice Press, 1810 West Grant Road, Suite 108, Tucson AZ 85745. **Tel** (800)367-9242, FAX (602)882-4161. **ED** Gregory Franzwwa. **DD** 028. **Bk Rev**, (Qty: 10).

CN/0824-3085
FOLKLORE (MOOSE JAW). **See** Folklore.

CN/0847-382X
FOLLOWING CHAIN AND COMPASS : NEWSLETTER OF THE ARCHIVAL AND HISTORY COMMITTEE OF SMITH TOWNSHIP. [Follow. chain compass]. **Added/Corp** Archival and History Society of Smith Township. Archival and History Committee of Smith Township. **VFOAT** Newsletter of the Archival and History Committee of Smith Township; Newsletter of the Archival and History Society of Smith Township. Vol. 1, No. 1 (Oct. 2, 1984)-.

Newsletter. English. qt. $14.40. Smith Township Historical Society, Box 41, Bridgenorth ONT K0L 1H0 Canada. **Tel** (705)745-8139. **DD** 971.3/67.

CN/0015-6957
FORCES (MONTREAL). (FORCES.). [Forces]. **Added/Corp** Hydro-Quebec. Directions des Relations Publiques. Societe d'Edition de la Revue Forces. No. 1 (Winter 1967)-. Periodical. French. Four times a year. $35.00 (one year), $65.00 (two year). Societe Edition Revue Forces, 500 rue Sherbrooke Quest 1270, Montreal Quebec H3A 3C6 Canada. **Tel** (514)286-7600. **LC** F1051; .F6. **DD** 971.4/04.
Ind/Abst Can. Period. Index; Environ. (1983-); Point Repere.

DK
FORENINGER REGISTRERET I. VFOAT Foreninger. Danish. an. **LC** AS281.A7; F67.

US/1049-3239
FORT CONCHO AND THE SOUTH PLAINS JOURNAL. ***Ceased.*** **Added/Corp** Fort Concho National Historic Landmark. Vol. 22, No. 2 (Spring 1990)-(Fall 1992). Periodical. English. qt. Fort Concho Museum Press, 213 East Avenue D, San Angelo TX 76903. **Tel** (915)657-4441, FAX (915)657-4540. **LC** F394.S15; F67. **DD** 976.4/721. ***Continues*** *Fort Concho Report, 1055-3681.*
Ind/Abst Am. Hist. Life (1989-).

US/0899-658X
FORT HENRIETTA NEWSLETTER. No. 1 (Sept. 1985)-. Newsletter. English. Four times a year. $10.00 (US); $11.50 (Mexico); $12.00 (Canada); $17.50 (other). City of Echo, PO Box 9, Echo OR 97876. **Tel** (503)376-8411.

●US/1065-5263
FORT NORFOLK COURIER. [Fort Norfolk cour.]. **Added/Corp** Norfolk Historical Society (Norfolk, VA.). Vol. 1, No. 1 (Sept. 1992)-. Periodical. English. qt. Free. Norfolk Historical Society, PO Box 6367, Norfolk VA 23508. **DD** 977.

US/0046-4651
FRANKLIN COUNTY HISTORICAL REVIEW, THE. [Frankl. Cty. hist. rev.]. **Added/Corp** Franklin County Historical Society (Tenn.). (19??)-. Periodical. English. sa. comes with membership. Franklin County Historical Society / Tennessee, PO Box 130, Winchester TN 37398. **Tel** (615)967-3706. **ED** Virginia McKown Brock and James Waring McCrady. **LC** F443.F7; F7. **DD** 976.8/63/005. cum. index. **Bk Rev.** ctrl circ.
Desc: Collection of historical articles relating to local and area history.
Ind/Abst Am. Hist. Life.

US/0888-6342
FRANKLIN HISTORICAL REVIEW. [Frankl. hist. rev.]. **Added/Corp** Franklin County Historical Society (N.Y.). (Aug. 1964)-. Periodical. English. an. $2.75. Franklin County Historical Society / New York, 51 Milwaukee Street, Malone NY 12953. **Tel** (518)483-2750. **DD** 974. **Circ:** 1,000.
Desc: Contains articles and pictures of historical interest.
Ind/Abst Am. Hist. Life.

US/1064-3591
FRENCH ANCESTORS : HERITAGE OF THE FRENCH SETTLERS IN WESTERN OHIO. [Fr. ancestors]. (1988)-. Periodical. English. Six times a year (Jan., Mar., May, July, Sept., Nov,). $8.00. Marianne R. Doyle, 2923 Tara Trail, Beavercreek OH 45434. **Tel** (513)429-2979. **ED** Marianne R. Doyle. **DD** 929. Index available (Bound in 6th iss., in (Nov).).
Desc: Covers the historical, social, genealogical information of French immigrants to the Western Ohio. Includes record extracts, articles on local french history, customs, and society.

US/0160-0907
FRENCH SETTLEMENT HISTORICAL REGISTER, THE. V. 1 (1976)-. Periodical. English. an. $5.00. French Settlement Historical Society, French Settlement LA 70733. **LC** F379.F73; F7. **DD** 976.3/14. **UDC** 976.3.

AG/0327-4071
FRENTE DE TORMENTA. No. 1 (January, 1991)-. Periodical. Spanish. bm. **LC** F2848; .F74. **DD** 982.06/05.

US/0429-7164
FRESNO PAST AND PRESENT. **Added/Corp** Fresno City and County Historical Society. Fresno County Historical Society. **VFOAT** Fresno--Past & Present; Fresno--Past and Present. **VAT** Fresno-Past and Present. (Jan. 1959)-. Periodical. English. qt. $8.00 (for U.S. and Canada). Fresno City and County Historical Society, PO Box 2029, Fresno CA 93718. **Tel** (209)441-0862. **ED** Doris Hall. **LC** WMLC L 83/4438. **DD** 979. **Circ:** 1,500 (ctrl). ***Absorbed*** *Leaves from the Ash Tree.*

PE/0532-7865
FUENTES E INVESTIGACIONES PARA LA HISTORIA DEL PERU. SERIE : TEXTOS CRITICOS. No. 1 (1966)-. Spanish. IEP Editions, Horacio Urteaga 694, Lima 11 Peru. **Tel** 011 51 14 323070, 011 51 14 244856. **ED** Lucia Cano Correa. **DD** 985.
Desc: Dedicated to research in the fields of the economics, history, anthropology, ethnic history, political science, sociology and linguistics of Peru and Latin America.

UY/0581-1856
FUENTES PARA LA HISTORIA SOCIAL Y ECONOMICA DEL RIO DE LA PLATA. **Main/Corp** Montevideo, Universidad. Facultad de Humanidades y Ciencias. Seccion Historia de la Cultura. No. 1 (1967)-. Monographic series. Spanish. ir. Price varies per volume. Universidad de la Republica / Humanidades, Facultad de Humanidades, Tristan Narvaja 1674, Departamento de Historia Americana, Montevideo Uruguay. **Tel** 42673 MONTEVIDEO. **DD** 989.5. **UDC** 989.5.
Desc: Serial of sources and bibliographic texts related to the seminars given by the department of Latin American history.

US
FULTON COUNTY HISTORICAL AND GENEALOGICAL SOCIETY NEWSLETTER. V. 1, No. 1- Jan., 1970-. Newsletter. English. qt. Spoon River Press / Bushnell, 358 East Main, Bushnell IL 61422. **ED** Charles R DeBusk. **UDC** 977.3; 929.5(773).

US
FULTON COUNTY IMAGES. (19??)-. Periodical. English. qt. comes with membership. Fulton County Historical Society, 37 East 375 North, Rochester IN 46975. **Tel** (219)223-4436.

US/0090-4368
G.H.S. FOOT-NOTES. **Main/Corp** Georgia Historical Society. Vol. 1 (Nov. 1972)-. English. qt. Georgia Historical Society, 501 Whitaker Street, Savannah GA 31499. **Tel** (912)651-2128, FAX (912)651-2831. **ED** Lisa White. **LC** F281; .G353. **DD** 917.58/03/4062. **Circ:** 2,500 (ctrl).
Desc: Provides information on society activities and events.

CN/0227-1370
GASPESIE (GASPE. 1979). (GASPESIE.). [Gaspesie]. **Added/Corp** Societe Historique de la Gaspesie. Vol. 17, No. 65 (Jan./March 1979)-. Periodical. French. qt (4 issues). 22.00Can$ Canada. Societe Historique de la Gaspesie, 80 Boulevard Gaspe, Box 680, Gaspe Quebec G0C 1R0 Canada. **Tel** (418)862-2155. **DD** 971.4/77/005. Index available (bound in separate issue). cum. index. **Ad Acc. Circ:** 1,000 (ctrl). ***Continues*** *Revue d'Historie et de Traditions Populaires de la Gaspesie, 0380-0296.*
Desc: Historical society and museum implication in cultural life of the region, current projects, implication and tourism, etc.
Ind/Abst Am. Hist. Life (1986-); Point Repere (1983-).

US/0198-9375
GATEWAY HERITAGE. (GATEWAY HERITAGE : QUARTERLY JOURNAL OF THE MISSOURI HISTORICAL SOCIETY.). [Gatew. herit.]. **Added/Corp** Missouri Historical Society. Vol. 1, No. 1 (Summer 1980)-. Periodical. English. Four times a year. $20.00. Missouri Historical Society, PO Box 11940, St Louis MO 63112. **Tel** (314)746-4559, FAX (314)454-3162. **ED** Kenneth H. Winn. **LC** F466; .G34. **DD** 977.8/005. cum. index. **Bk Rev. Circ:** 4,400 (ctrl). available on microfilm and microfiche from University Microfilms International (UMI). ***Continues*** *Bulletin (Missouri Historical Society), 0026-6590.*
Desc: Popular history of St Louis, the state of Missouri and the Western United States.
Ind/Abst Am. Hist. Life (1980-); ARTbibliogr. Mod.; Ozark Period. Index; West. Hist. Q.

US
GATEWAY: THE JOURNAL OF THE BELL COUNTY HISTORICAL SOCIETY. **Added/Corp** Bell County Historical Society (Ky.). Vol. 1, No. 1 (Spring 1982)-. Periodical. English. qt. $10.00. Bell County Historical Society, PO Box 1344, Middlesboro KY 40965. **Tel** (606)248-5304. **ED** Allan Green. **LC** WMLC L 83/508. **Bk Rev. Ad Acc. Circ:** 150 (ctrl).
Desc: Local history and genealogy of Bell County, Kentucky.

US/0882-0856
GATHERINGS FROM THE ADIRONDACK FOOTHILLS. VFOAT Gatherings. Vol. 1, Issue 1 (Summer 1983)-. Periodical. English. qt. $10.00 US; $13.00 other. Gatherings from the Adirondack Foothills, 10 Clay Street, Malone NY 12953. **LC** F127.A2; G29. **DD** 974.7/53/005. **UDC** 974.7.

UY
GAZETA DE MONTEVIDEO. Vol. 1 (Oct. 13, 1810)-. Spanish. Universidad de la Republica / Humanidades, Facultad de Humanidades, Tristan Narvaja 1674, Departamento de Historia Americana, Montevideo Uruguay. **Tel** 42673 MONTEVIDEO. **LC** F2701; .G28. **DD** 989.1.

CN/1180-2677
GAZETTE DU GRANIT, LA. [Gaz. granit]. Vol. 2, No 5 (May 1991)-. Periodical. French. mo. Limited Free distribution. La Gazette du Granit, 2946 Rue D'Orsennens, Lac-Megantic Quebec G6B 2R2 Canada. **DD** 971.4. ***Continues*** *L'Informateur Economique., 1186-8473.*

US/0743-5843
GENEALOGICAL AND HISTORICAL MAGAZINE OF THE SOUTH, THE. **See** Genealogy and Heraldry.

US/0736-5292
GENEALOGY AND LOCAL HISTORY TITLES ON MICROFICHE. **See** Genealogy and Heraldry.

US/1055-1921
GEORGIA BYWAYS. [Ga. byways]. **VFOAT** Byways. Vol. 1, No. 1 (Jan./Feb. 1990)-. Periodical. English. Four times a year. $14.00. Byways Publications Inc., PO Box 1289, Alpheretta GA 30239. **Tel** (404)664-6432. **LC** F281; .G47. **DD** 975.

US/1044-9086
GEORGIA FACTS. **VFOAT** Flying the Colors, Georgia Facts; Georgia Facts--Flying the Colors Series. (1989)-. Monographic series. English. ir. Price varies per volume. Clements Research II Inc., 16850 Dallas Parkway, Dallas TX 75248. **Tel** (214)931-9956, FAX (214)248-7159. **ED** John Clements. **LC** F281; .G2965. **DD** 975.8/005.
Desc: Narrative description of facts from the state of Georgia developed county-by-county.

US/0016-8297
GEORGIA HISTORICAL QUARTERLY, THE. [Georgia hist. q.]. **Added/Corp** Georgia Historical Society. Vol. 1 (Mar. 1917)-. Academic Scholarly Publication. English. qt (Apr., July, Oct., Dec.). comes with Georgia Historical Society membership. Georgia Historical Society, 501 Whitaker Street, Savannah GA 31499. **Tel** (912)651-2128, FAX (912)651-2831. **ED** Dr. John Inscoe, (706)542-6300. **LC** F281; .G2975. **DD** 975.8/008. Index available. cum. index. **Bk Rev**, (Qty: 4). **Circ:** 2,200 (ctrl). available on microfilm and microfiche from University Microfilms International (UMI).
Desc: Scholarly journal publishing articles, book reviews, and review essays relating to the history of the South in general and Georgia, in particular.
Ind/Abst Am. Hist. Life (1955-); Annu. Bibliogr. Engl. Lang. Lit.; Sage Race Relat. Abstr.

CN/0316-8603
GERMAN-CANADIAN YEARBOOK. [Ger.-Can. yearb.]. **Added/Corp** Historical Society of Mecklenburg Upper Canada. **VFOAT** German Canadian Yearbook; Deutschkanadisches Jahrbuch. Vol. 1 (1973)-. Periodical. Multiple languages (English and German). ir. 18.00Can$ Canada; 19.00Can$ other. Historical Society of Mecklenburg Upper Canada, PO Box 1251 Station K, Toronto Ontario M4P 3E5 Canada. **Tel** (416)635-6529. **DD** 917.1/06/31.
Ind/Abst MLA Int. Bibl. Books Artic. Mod. Lang. Lit.

US/0742-6631
GERMANTOWN CRIER. [Germant. crier]. **Added/Corp** Germantown Historical Society. Vol. 45 (Jan. 1993)-. Periodical. English. Twice a year (January and July). $16.00 one year; $28.00 two year. Germantown Historical Society, 5501 Germantown Avenue, Philadelphia PA 19144. **Tel** (215)844-0514. **LC** F159.G3; G336. **DD** 974.8/11. Index available. cum. index. **Bk Rev. Ad Acc. Circ:** 1,000. ***Continues*** *Germantowne Crier, 0742-6631.*
Ind/Abst Am. Hist. Life (1989-).

GW/0936-4595
GESELLSCHAFT FUER KANADA-STUDIEN : MITTEILUNGEN. [Mitt. - Ges. Kan.-Stud.]. Periodical. German (English and French). ir. **DD** 971/.007/1143.

US/0730-5036
GILCREASE MAGAZINE OF AMERICAN HISTORY AND ART, THE. ***Title Change.*** **See** Museums and Galleries.

CN/0229-6705
GLENGARRY HISTORICAL SOCIETY. [Glengarry Hist. Soc.]. **Main/Corp** Glengarry Historical Society. (1960)-. Newsletter. English. Seven times a year. comes with membership. The Glengarry Historical Society, PO Box 416, Alexandria Ontario K0C 1A0 Canada. **Tel** (613)525-1934. **ED** G. Arnott (editor's address: 401 Westmoreland, Cornwall ONT K6J 2H1 Canada). **DD** 971.3/77/006. **Circ:** 225.
Desc: A series of usually seven newsletters with updates on local history: genealogies, local books publishes, etc. One small annual volume each year publishes items of local interest.

CN/0703-1556
GLENGARRY LIFE. Added/Corp Glengarry Historical Society. (1977)-. English. an. 3.00Can$. The Glengarry Historical Society, PO Box 416, Alexandria Ontario K0C 1A0 Canada. **Tel** (613)525-1934. **DD** 971.3/77/005. **Circ:** 300 (ctrl). ***Continues*** *Glengarry Historical Society. Annual Volume and Yearbook of Activities, 0703-1548.*

CN/0824-7706
GLUT. [Glut]. V. 1, No. 1 (Summer/Fall 1984)-. Periodical. English. qt. $8.00. Main Street Productions, PO Box 607 Station C, St Johns Newfoundland A1C 5K8 Canada. **DD** 971.8/002/07. **UDC** 974.4.

US
GOINGSNAKE MESSENGER, THE. Added/Corp Goingsnake District Heritage Association. **VFOAT** Goingsnake. Vol. 1, No. 1 (Feb. 1984)-. Periodical. English. Four times a year (Feb., May, Aug., Nov.). $10.00 Comes with Goingsnake District Heritage Association membership. Goingsnake District Heritage Association, PO Box 180, Westville OK 74965. **Tel** (918)597-2700. **ED** Virgil Talbot, (editor's address: Route 4 Box 6, Colcord, OK 74338, phone: (918)326-4532). **LC** E99.C5; G64. **DD** 973/.04975. Index available. cum. index (Ten year index available in 1994). **Bk Rev**, (Qty: 20). **Circ:** 325.
Desc: Historical and genealogical articles of Cherokee & white history and other feature articles.
Ind/Abst Genealogical Period. Annu. Index.

US/0887-5898
GOLDEN BALL GRAPEVINE, THE. [Gold. Ball grapevine]. **Added/Corp** Golden Ball Tavern (Weston, Mass.). Vol. 1, No. 1 (Autumn 1970)-. English. an (Nov.). $10.00. Golden Ball Tavern Museum, PO Box 223, Weston MA 02173. **Tel** (617)894-1751. **DD** 974. ctrl circ.
Desc: Articles about years' events plus articles on related historical events of colonial cooking.
Ind/Abst Am. Hist. Life.

US
GOLDEN NUGGETS. Added/Corp Sacramento County Historical Society. (June 1963)-. Periodical. English. mo (10 issues). comes with membership. Sacramento County Historical Society, PO Box 160065, Fort Sutter Station, Sacramento CA 95816. **Tel** (916)481-4525, (916)443-6265. ***Supersedes*** *Monthly Bulletin.*

US/0278-0208
GOLDFINCH, THE. See Children and Youth Interests.

US/0160-7510
GOOD OLD DAYS. SPECIAL ISSUES. ***Title Change.*** (GOOD OLD DAYS.). (19??)-(19??). Periodical. English. qt. House of White Birches, 306 East Parr Road, Berne IN 46711. **Tel** (219)589-8741, FAX (219)589-8093. **ED** Rebekah Montgomery. **LC** E161; .G55. **DD** 917.3/03/05. **Ad Acc. Circ:** 35,000. ***Continued by*** *Fireside Companion (Berne, Ind.), 1050-480X.*
Desc: Contains more nostalgia, authentic photos, drawings, cartoons, memories, letters, etc.

CN/0316-2702
GRAND MANAN HISTORIAN, THE. Added/Corp Grand Manan Historical Society. No. 1 (1934)-. Monographic series. English. ir. Price varies per volume. The Grand Manan Historical Society, PO Box 60, Grand Harbour New Brunswick E09 1X0 Canada. **Tel** (506)662-3524. **DD** 917.5/33.

US/0739-084X
GRAND RIVER VALLEY REVIEW, THE. ***Title Change.*** **Added/Corp** Grand Rapids Historical Society. Vol. 1 (Fall 1979)-(199?). Periodical. English. sa. Grand Rapids Public Library, 60 Library Plaza NE, Grand Rapids MI 49503. **Tel** (616)456-3629. **ED** Ellen Arlinsky. **Bk Rev. Ad Acc. Circ:** 1,000 (ctrl). ***Continued by*** *Grand River Valley History.*
Desc: Concerned with the history of Grand Rapids, Michigan, the Grand River valley area and Western Michigan.

AG
GRANDES TEMAS ARGENTINOS, LOS. V. 1-. Periodical. Spanish. A N Ramirez, Sarmiento 1142 - Piso 11 Office I, Buenos Aires Argentina. **LC** F2801; .G7. **DD** 982/.005. **UDC** 982; 908.82.

US/0148-771X
GRASS ROOTS PERSPECTIVES ON AMERICAN HISTORY. No. 1 (1978)-. Monographic series. English. ir. Price varies per volume. Greenwood Press Inc., PO Box 5007, Westport CT 06881-5007. **Tel** (203)226-3571, FAX (203)222-1502. **ED** David P. Thelen.

US
GRAVE MATTERS : NEWSLETTER FOR CIVIL WAR NECROLITHOLOGISTS. Added/Corp Society of Civil War Necrolithologists. (July 1985)-. Newsletter. English. qt. **LC** WMLC 91/1183.

US/0017-3673
GREAT PLAINS JOURNAL. [Gt.-Plains j.]. **Added/Corp** Great Plains Historical Association. (Fall 1961)-. English. ir. $15.00 US; $17.00 Canada; $18.00 other. Museum of the Great Plains, PO Box 68, Lawton OK 73502. **Tel** (405)581-3460. **ED** Steve Wilson, (405)581-3460. **LC** F591; .G76. **DD** 978/.005. **Circ:** 1,000 (ctrl). available on microfilm and microfiche from University Microfilms International (UMI).
Desc: An interdisciplinary journal devoted to the Great Plains of North America.
Ind/Abst Am. Hist. Life (1963-); Annu. Bibliogr. Engl. Lang. Lit.; West. Hist. Q.

US/0275-7664
GREAT PLAINS QUARTERLY. [Great plains q.]. **Added/Corp** University of Nebraska--Lincoln. Center for Great Plains Studies. Vol. 1, No. 1 (Winter 1981)-. Academic Scholarly Publication. English. qt. $25.00 (institutions), $20.00 (individuals) US; $28.00 (institutions), $23.00 (individuals) Canada; $31.00 (institutions), $26.00 (individuals) other. Center for Great Plains Studies, University of Nebraska, 1215 Oldfather Hall, Lincoln NE 68588. **Tel** (402)472-3082. **ED** Frances W. Kaye. **LC** F591; .G762. **DD** 978/.005. Index available. **Bk Rev. Ad Acc, Adv Mgr:** Linda Ratcliffe, **Tel** (407)472-3082. **Circ:** 700 (ctrl). available on microfilm and microfiche from University Microfilms International (UMI). Documents available from The Genuine Article.
Desc: A scholarly interdisciplinary journal which publishes studies that illuminate the human and nonhuman aspects of the region. It seeks a readership among scholars and laypersons.
Ind/Abst Am. Hist. Life (1981-); Annu. Bibliogr. Engl. Lang. Lit.; Arts Humanit. Citation Index [Full Cov.]; Curr. Contents Arts Humanit.; Geogr. Abstr. Human Geogr.; Lit. Crit. Regist.; MLA Int. Bibl. Books Artic. Mod. Lang. Lit.; Res. Alert [Full Cov.]; Soc. Sci. Cit. Index [Select. Cov.]; West. Hist. Q.

US/0072-7342
GREAT WEST AND INDIAN SERIES. 1-1943-. Monographic series. English. ir. Price varies per volume. Westernlore Press, PO Box 35305, Tucson AZ 85740. **Tel** (213)255-8685. **UDC** 970(97).

US/0145-8825
GREATER LLANO ESTACADO SOUTHEAST HERITAGE, THE. ***Ceased.*** (THE GREATER LLANO ESTACADO SOUTHWEST HERITAGE / OFFICIAL PUBLICATION OF THE LLANO ESTACADO HERITAGE, INC.). **VFOAT** Southwest Heritage. Periodical. English. qt. Southwest Heritage Magazine Inc, College of Southwest, 6610 Lovington Highway, Hobbs NM 88240. **Tel** (505)392-6561. **ED** Robert E Cates. **LC** F786; .G774. **DD** 979/.005. **UDC** 979; 908.79. **Bk Rev. Ad Acc. Circ:** 1,000. ***Continues*** *LLano Estacado Heritage.*
Desc: History, culture and art of Western America. Blends the accomplishments of the past with those of the present and hopes for the future.

CN/0703-7821
GREENBORO. Added/Corp Greenboro Office of Public Information. Vol. 1 (Fall 1977)-. Periodical. English (French). Greenboro Office of Public Information, 100-71 Bank Street, Ottawa Ontario K1P 5N2 Canada. **DD** 971.3/84.

US/0894-8135
GREENE COUNTY HISTORICAL JOURNAL. [Greene Cty. hist. j.]. Vol. 6, Issue 1 (Spring 1982)-. Periodical. English. qt. $6.00. Greene County Historical Society - New York, PO Box 62, Hannacroix NY 12087. **Tel** (518)731-6822. **ED** Raymond Beecher. **DD** 974. **UDC** 974. Index available. cum. index. **Circ:** 1,200 (ctrl). ***Continues*** *Quarterly Journal (Greene County Historical Society N.Y.).*

US
GREENE COUNTY MAGAZINE. Added/Corp Greene County Historical Society. Vol. 1, (1979)-. English. Greene County Historical Society, PO Box 185, Stanardsville VA 22973.

CN/0715-3783
GRENVILLE SENTINEL. (THE GRENVILLE SENTINEL / GRENVILLE COUNTY HISTORICAL SOCIETY.). [Grenville sentinel]. Periodical. English. ir. Free to members. Grenville County Historical Society, PO Box 982, Prescott Ontario K0E 1T0 Canada. **DD** 971.3/74. **UDC** 971.3.

US/0886-1668
GRIO' (BLACK HISTORY ED.). (GRIO'.). [Grio']. **VFOAT** Grio, The Praise Singer. Vol. 1 (1985)-. English. an (Sept.). $11.90. Enteracom Inc, PO Box 834, Philadelphia PA 19105. **ED** Sara M. Lomax. **DD** 973. **Ad Acc, Adv Mgr:** Al Thomas.

US/0737-0873
GRIOT (HOUSTON, TEX.), THE. (THE GRIOT.). [Griot]. **Added/Corp** Southern Conference on Afro-American Studies. Vol. 1 No. 1 (Summer 1981)-. Periodical. English. sa. $25.00. Southern Conference on Afro-American Studies Inc, PO Box 33163, Houston TX 77233. **ED** Andrew Baskins. **LC** WMLC L 83/507. **Bk Rev**, (Qty: 2/yr). **Ad Acc. Circ:** 500 (ctrl).
Desc: History and culture of Afro-Americans. Also includes information on Caucasian and other non-white groups as they have interacted with black Americans.
Ind/Abst MLA Int. Bibl. Books Artic. Mod. Lang. Lit.

PE/0252-9041
GRUPO ANDINO. ***Ceased.*** (GRUPO ANDINO : CARTA INFORMATIVA OFICIAL DE LA JUNTA DEL ACUERDO DE CARTAGENA.). [Grupo andino]. Periodical. Spanish. mo. Junta del Acuerdo de Cartagena, Casilla Postal 18 1177, Lima 18 Peru. **Tel** 011 51 14 414212. **LC** HC167.A5; .G78. **DD** 343.8/07.

GW
GUATEMALA-NACHRICHTEN / HRSG. SOLIDARITATSBEWEGUNG MIT DEM VOLK VON GUATEMALA. VFOAT Guatemala Nachrichten. German. ir. Informationsstelle Guatemala, Maistr 19, W-8000 Munchen 2 Germany. **LC** F1461; .G8514. **DD** 972.81/005.

CN/0712-2179
GUELPH HISTORICAL SOCIETY NEWSLETTER. [Guelph Hist. Soc. newsl.]. **Added/Corp** Guelph Historical Society. (1977)-. Periodical. English. Six times a year. Free to members. Guelph Historical Society, PO Box 1502, Guelph Ontario N1H 6N9 Canada. **Tel** (905)529-8111. **DD** 971.3/43/006.

BL
GUIA TURISTICO INFORMATIVO DE CURITIBA E DO PARANA. Portuguese. an. Sociedade Comercial e Representacoes Graficas, Caixa Postal 305, Curitibas Brazil. **LC** F2651.C83; G82. **UDC** 918.1; 379.85(81).

CN/1185-3131
GUIDA MENSILE. (LA GUIDA MENSILE). [Guida mens.]. **VFOAT** Guide, Monthly Publication. Vol. 1, No. 1 (1990)-. Periodical. English (Italian and English). mo. Limited free distribution. VQ Creative Advertising, 6095 Dunn Street, Niagara Falls, Ontario L2G 2P1 Canada. **DD** 971.3/380045.

CN/0708-983X
GUIDE CASTELRIAND. 1977-. French. an. $4.00 per number. Entreprises Casterriand, 2 rue de la Cour, Riviere-du-Loup Quebec G5R 1J2 Canada. **DD** 971.4/76/0025. **UDC** 917.14; 971.4.

US/0892-9025
GULF COAST HISTORICAL REVIEW. [Gulf Coast hist. rev.]. **Added/Corp** University of South Alabama. History Dept. **VFOAT** GCHR. Vol. 1, No. 1 (Fall 1985)-. Academic Scholarly Publication. English. sa (April, October). $14.00 (one year), $25.00(two year). Gulf Coast Historical Review, University of South Alabama, Humanities Building #344, Mobile AL 36688. **Tel** (205)460-6210, FAX (205)460-6750. **ED** Michael Thomason. **LC** F296; .G86. **DD** 976/.005. Index available. **Bk Rev**, (Qty: 30-40). **Ad Acc. Pr Rev. Circ:** 550 (ctrl).
Desc: Covers Gulf Coast history, illustrations, book reviews and features general readership. Provides history of the Gulf Coast region, Texas to Florida, for a scholarly and general audience.
Ind/Abst Am. Hist. Life (1985-).

CN/0714-9298
HAI WAI SHU LIN. [Hai wai shu lin]. **VFOAT** The Crossroads; Crossroads (Toronto). **VAT** Crossroads (Toronto). Vol. 1, No. 1 (Jan. 1977)-. Periodical. Chinese (English). mo. **DD** 971/.004951. **UDC** 908.71(=951).

US/0072-9833
HANDBOOK OF LATIN AMERICAN STUDIES. Added/Corp American Council of Learned Societies. Committee on Latin American Studies. Joint Committee on Latin American Studies. Library of Congress. Library of Congress. Hispanic Foundation. Library of Congress. Latin American, Portuguese, and Spanish Division. Library of Congress. Hispanic Division. No. 1 (1935)-. English. an. price varies per volume. University of Texas Press, PO Box 7819, Austin TX 78713. **Tel** (512)471-4531, FAX (512)320-0668, telex 776453 UTEXPRES AUS. **LC** Z1605; .H23.
Desc: Compiled annually by the hispanic division of the Library of Congress and annotated by a corps of more than one hundred specialists in various disciplines, the handbook is the oldest, most comprehensive, and most respected annual bibliography in its field.

US/8755-6073
HARDIN COUNTY HISTORICAL QUARTERLY. [Hardin Cty. hist. q.]. **Added/Corp** Hardin County Historical Society (Tenn.). **VFOAT** HCHS Quarterly; Hardin County Historical Society Newsletter; Hardin County Historical Society Quarterly; Hardin County Historical Genealogical Quarterly. Vol. 1, No. 1 (July/Sept. 1982)-. Periodical. English. qt. $12.00. Hardin County Historical Society, PO Box 630, Savannah TN 38372. **Tel** (901)688-5374. **ED** Ronney R Brewington. **LC** F443.H3; H37. **DD** 976.8/31/005. **Bk Rev. Ad Acc. Circ:** 400 (ctrl).
Desc: Stories of local history, articles on Hardin County families, and genealogy of Hardin County.

US/0732-0396
HARPETH GLEANINGS. Added/Corp Bellevue-Harpeth Historical Society. Vol. 1 (Winter

1981)-. English. Bellevue-Harpeth Historical Society, PO Box 85, Bellevue TN 37221. **LC** F444.B44; H37. **DD** 976.8/55.

US/1064-6043
HARRISONBURG-ROCKINGHAM HISTORICAL SOCIETY NEWSLETTER. [Harrisonburg Rockingham Hist. Soc. newsl.]. **Added/Corp** Harrisonburg-Rockingham Historical Society. **VFOAT** Newsletter; Harrisonburg Rockingham Historical Society Newsletter; Harrisonburg Rockingham Historical Society. Vol. 1, No. 1 (summer 1978)-. Periodical. English. qt (Jan., Apr., July, Oct.). $20.00 (individual), $50.00 (institution). Harrisonburg Rockingham History, 115 Bowman Road, PO Box 716, Dayton VA 22821. **Tel** (703)879-2616. **DD** 929.

US/1062-340X
HAVERSACK (TICONDEROGA, N.Y. 1991), THE. (THE HAVERSACK : A NEWS-LETTER FOR FRIENDS OF FORT TICONDEROGA.). [Haversack]. **Added/Corp** Friends of Fort Ticonderoga. Vol. 1, No. 1 (Autumn 1991)-. Periodical. English. sa. $20.00 (membership). The Haversack, PO Box 390, Ticonderoga NY 12883. **DD** 974.

US/0364-5924
HAYES HISTORICAL JOURNAL: A JOURNAL OF THE GILDED AGE. ***Ceased.*** [Hayes hist. j.]. **Added/Corp** Rutherford B. Hayes Presidential Center (Fremont, Ohio) Hayes Historical Society. Rutherfored B. Hayes Presidential Center. Vol. 1 (Spring 1976-Vol. 2 1992)-Vol. 12 (Aug. 1993). Periodical. English. Four times a year (Fall, Winter, Spring and Summer). Rutherford B Hayes Presidential Center, Speigel Grove, Fremont OH 43420-2796. **Tel** (419)332-2081. **ED** Bruce Bowlus. **LC** E682; .H43. **DD** 973.8/3/0924. Index available (Bound in the 4th issue, publish in Summer.). **Bk Rev**, (Qty: 8). **Circ:** 525 (ctrl).
Desc: Explores matters relating to the Gilded Age, events in life of Rutherford B. Hayes, and topics dealing with historical northwest Ohio.
Ind/Abst Am. Hist. Life (1976-); ARTbibliogr. Mod. (1984-).

US/0149-5046
HEARD HERITAGE. V. 1- May 1976-. Periodical. English. sa. $8.00. PO Box 249, Lanett AL 36863. **LC** F292.H7; H4. **DD** 929/.3758/422.

DR
HELIOS. V. 1- ; July/Sept. 1973-. Periodical. Spanish. Fondo Cultural de la Cuva de America, Jose Reyes 50, Santo Domingo Dominican Republic. **LC** F1931; .H44. **DD** 917.293/03/5405. **UDC** 917.293; 908.729.3.

US
HENNEPIN HISTORY. **Added/Corp** Hennepin County Historical Society (Hennepin County, Minn.). Vol. 49, No. 3 (summer 1990)-. Periodical. English. qt (Jan., Apr., July, Oct.). $25.00. Hennepin History Museum, 2303 3rd Avenue South, Minneapolis MN 55404. **Tel** (612)870-1329, FAX (612)870-1320. **ED** Ellen Green (editor's address: 2303 Third Avenue South, Minneapolis, MN 55404; phone (612)292-0314). **LC** F612 .H5; H4. **DD** 977.657. Index available. ***Continues*** *Hennepin County History, 0361-7890.*

US/1047-5613
HERITAGE (AUSTIN, TEX.). (HERITAGE.). [Heritage]. **Added/Corp** Texas Historical Foundation. (Summer 1985)-. Periodical. English. Four times a year. $30.00 (contributing), $50.00 (patron), $100.00 (preservationist), $250.00 (pioneer), $500.00 (Texan), $1,000.00 (life) Comes with Texas Historical Foundation membershp. Texas Historical Foundation, PO Box 50314, Austin TX 78763. **Tel** (512)453-2154, FAX (512)451-3323. **ED** Gene Krane. **DD** 976. **Bk Rev**. **Ad Acc. Circ:** 3,000. ***Continues*** *Texas Heritage (Texas Historical Foundation : 1983).*
Desc: Articles in relation to Texas' heritage, archaeology, preservation, etc. throughout the state.

US/8755-9064
HERITAGE (COOPERSTOWN, N.Y.). (HERITAGE : THE MAGAZINE OF THE NEW YORK STATE HISTORICAL ASSOCIATION.). **Added/Corp** New York State Historical Association. **VFOAT** Heritage News. Vol. 1, No. 1 (Sept./Oct. 1984)-. Periodical. English. bm. $16.00, $35.00 (includes New York History). New York State Historical Association, PO Box 800 Lake Road, Cooperstown NY 13326. **Tel** (607)547-2533, FAX (607)547-5384. **ED** Paul D'Ambrosia. **LC** F119; .H5. **DD** 974.7/005. **Circ:** 5,800. ***Continues*** *Yorker (1975), 0044-0574.*
Desc: Illustrated magazine of popular history of New York State.

US/1055-9515
HERITAGE COUNTRY. ***Title Change.*** [Herit. ctry.]. **VFOAT** Heritage Country Magazine. (1982)-(19??). Periodical. English. Four times a year. Heritage Country, PO Box 427, Shipshewana IN 46565. **Tel** (219)674-0372. **ED** Julienne Barth (Editor's Address: 14052 Kimberly Lane, Middlebury, IN 46540; Editor's Phone: (219)825-7217). **DD** 977. **Ad Acc.** ***Continued by*** *Country Ways.*
Desc: Covers the Amish lifestyle and the surrounding areas.

CN/1183-5834
HERITAGE NOTES (LOUISBOURG). (HERITAGE NOTES.). [Herit. notes]. No. 1 (July 1991)-. Periodical. English. Free to members. Louisbourg Historical Society, PO Box 396, Louisbourg Nova Scotia B0A 1M0 Canada. **DD** 971.6/955/05.

US/0739-4772
HERITAGE OF THE GREAT PLAINS. [Herit. Gt. Plains]. **Added/Corp** Emporia State University. School of Liberal Arts and Sciences. Vol. 13, No. 1 (Winter 1980)-. Periodical. English. sa. $7.00 US; $7.25 Canada; $8.00 other. Emporia State University / Graduate Office, 1200 Commercial St, Emporia KS 66081. **Tel** (316)341-5574, FAX (316)343-5997. **ED** Roy McCoy & Julie Johnson. **LC** F681; .H47. **DD** 978.1/005. **Pr Rev. Circ:** 350. ***Continues*** *Heritage of Kansas.*
Desc: Strives to be a repository for scholarship on the life and culture of the Great Plains region.
Ind/Abst Am. Hist. Life (1988-); Annu. Bibliogr. Engl. Lang. Lit.; MLA Int. Bibl. Books Artic. Mod. Lang. Lit.; West. Hist. Q.

US/0193-998X
HERITAGE TALES. 1st- 1978-. English. an. $7.50 individual members, $50.00 corporate members. City of San Bernardino Historical Society, PO Box 875, San Bernardino CA 92402. **LC** F869.S18; H47. **DD** 979.4/95. **UDC** 979.4.

US/0883-1513
HERITAGE. THE YORKER SCENE. (HERITAGE. THE YORKER SCENE / NEW YORK STATE HISTORICAL ASSOCIATION.). **Added/Corp** New York State Historical Association. **VFOAT** Yorker Scene. Vol. 1, No. 1 (Sept./Oct. 1984)-. Periodical. English. qt (Jan., April, July, Oct.). $8.00, $25.00 (with New York History). New York State Historical Association, PO Box 800 Lake Road, Cooperstown NY 13326. **Tel** (607)547-2533, FAX (607)547-5384. **ED** Paul S D'Ambrosio.
Desc: Magazine of New York State history and American Culture for general readership and members of the New York State Historical Association.

US/0439-027X
HERITAGE (VAN BUREN), THE. (THE HERITAGE.). **Added/Corp** Crawford County Historical Society (Ark.). Vol. 1 (July 1957)-. Periodical. English. an (July). $10.00. Crawford County Historical Society, PO Box 1317, Van Buren AR 72956. **Tel** (501)474-2218. **ED** Doris West. **LC** F417.C87; H4. **DD** 976.7/35. **Circ:** 200.
Desc: Covers the history of Crawford County including family genealogy.

US
HERITAGE WINDOWS. (19??)-. Newsletter. English. qt (Jan., April, July, Oct.). $9.00. Tyler County Heritage & Historical Society, PO Box 317, Middlebourne WV 26149. **Tel** (304)758-4288.
Desc: Newsletter of the Tyler County Heritage and Historical Society.

US/0018-1420
HIGH COUNTRY, THE. ***Ceased.*** No. 1 (Summer 1967)-Ceased (19??). Periodical. English. qt. High Country, PO Box 178, Temecula CA 92390. **Tel** (909)676-5031. **ED** William A Harker. **LC** F869.T43; H5.
Ind/Abst Am. Hist. Life (1971-1973); Calif. Period. Index (-19??).

PE
HISLA. **See** Economics-Economic History, Conditions.

US/0018-2168
HISPANIC AMERICAN HISTORICAL REVIEW, THE. [Hisp. Am. hist. rev.]. **VFOAT** HAHR. Vol. 1, No. 1 (Feb. 1918)-. Periodical. English (Spanish). qt (Feb., May, Aug., Nov.). $88.00 (institutions), $40.00 (individuals) US; $100.00 (institutions), $52.00 (individuals) other. Duke University Press, PO Box 90660, Durham NC 27708-0660. **Tel** (919)687-3600, (919)688-5134 (orders), FAX (919)688-4574, telex 802829. **ED** Mark D. Szuchman. **LC** F1401; .H66. **DD** 980/.005. **Bk Rev**. **Ad Acc.** available on microfilm and microfiche from University Microfilms International (UMI). Documents available from The Genuine Article, UMI Article Clearinghouse.
Desc: Contains articles, book reviews, and book notes on subjects dealing with Latin American history and culture.
Ind/Abst Acad. Abstr. Full Text Elite (July 1990-); Acad. Abstr. (July 1990-); Acad. Ind. [Computer File] (1987-); Acad. Search (July 1990-); Am. Hist. Life (1954-); Annu. Bibliogr. Engl. Lang. Lit.; Arts Humanit. Citation Index [Full Cov.]; Book Rev. Index (1954-); Curr. Contents Arts Humanit.; Expand. Acad. Index (1987-); Gen. Period. Index (1987-); HAPI Hisp. Am. Period. Index; Hist. Source (July 1990-); Humanit. Index (1954-); INFO-SOUTH Abstr.; Int. Bibliogr. Sociol.; Mag. Search; Newsp. Period. Abstr. (1991-); Numis. Lit.; Res. Alert [Full Cov.]; Romant. Move.; Sage Urban Stud. Abstr; Soc. Sci. Cit. Index [Select. Cov.]; U.S. Polit. Sci. Doc.

US/0018-2168
HISPANIC AMERICAN HISTORICAL REVIEW [MICROFORM], THE. **VFOAT** HAHR. Vol. 1, No. 1 (Feb. 1982)-. Periodical. English (Spanish). Duke University Press, PO Box 90660, Durham NC 27708-0660. **Tel** (919)687-3600, (919)688-5134 (orders), FAX (919)688-4574, telex 802829.

PE
HISTORIA. No. 1-. Spanish. Universidad Nacional de San Agustin, Departamento Academic Academico de Historia, Apartado 23, Arequipa Peru. **LC** F3451.A7; H57. **UDC** 985.

PE
HISTORIA ANDINA. **Added/Corp** Instituto de Estudios Peruanos. (1973)-. Monographic series. Spanish. ir. Price varies per volume. IEP Editions, Horacio Urteaga 694, Lima 11 Peru. **Tel** 011 51 14 323070, 011 51 14 244856. **ED** Lucia Cano Correa.
Desc: Dedicated to research in the fields of the economics, history, anthropology, ethnic history, political science, sociology and linguistics of Peru and Latin America.

AG/0326-1352
HISTORIA (BUENOS AIRES, ARGENTINA : 1981). (HISTORIA.). V. 1, No. 1, (March 1981)-. Periodical. Spanish. qt. Maipu 621 40, 1058 Buenos Aires Argentina. **ED** A Alonso Peneiro. **LC** F2801; .H52. **DD** 982/.005. **UDC** 982.

CK
HISTORIA CRITICA (BOGOTA, COLOMBIA). (HISTORIA CRITICA : REVISTA DEL DEPARTAMENTO DE HITORIA DE LA UNIVERSIDAD DE LOS ANDES.). **Added/Corp** Universidad de Los Andes (Bogota, Colombia). Departamento de Historia. No. 1 (Jan./June 1989)-. Periodical. Spanish. sa. 30.00Col$. Departamento de Historia / Bogota, Facultad de Humanidades y Ciencias Sociales, Universidad de los Andes, Calle 18A No. 0-33 E, Bogota Colombia. **ED** Hugo Fazio. **LC** F2251; .H5. **DD** 986.1/005. **Bk Rev**, (Qty: 6). **Ad Acc, Adv Mgr:** Hugo Fazio, **Tel** 572-2819260. Full Page (B&W) 400.00Col$. Half Page (B&W) 250.00Col$. **Pr Rev. Circ:** 1,500. available on diskette.

MX
HISTORIA DE LA REVOLUCION MEXICANA. Vol. 1-. Monographic series. Spanish. ir. Price varies per volume. Colegio de Mexico AC, Camino Al Ajusco No 20, 10740 Mexico DF Mexico. **Tel** 011 52 5 6455955 Ext. 3133, telex 1777585 COLME. **ED** Luis gonzalez. **UDC** 972.07. Index available. **Pr Rev. Circ:** 4,000.
Desc: Describes all different subjects about the Mexican Revolution from 1910.

MX/0185-0172
HISTORIA MEXICANA. [Hist. mex.]. **Added/Corp** Colegio de Mexico. Centro de Estudios Historicos. Colegio de Mexico. Vol. 1 (July/Sept. 1951)-. Periodical. Spanish. Four times a year. $51.00 US and Canada; $34.00 Latin America; $60.00 other (institutions); $32.00 US and Canada; $26.00 Latin America; $42.00 other (individuals). Colegio de Mexico AC, Camino Al Ajusco No 20, 10740 Mexico DF Mexico. **Tel** 011 52 5 6455955 Ext. 3133, telex 1777585 COLME. **ED** Alfonso Martinez Rosales. **LC** F1201; .H5. Index Available, published separately, free-automatically sent. cum. index. **Bk Rev. Ad Acc. Pr Rev. Circ:** 1,500. Documents available from The Genuine Article.
Desc: Articles, research, and original documents related to Mexican history.
Ind/Abst Am. Hist. Life (1954-); Arts Humanit. Citation Index [Full Cov.]; Curr. Contents Arts Humanit.; HAPI Hisp. Am. Period. Index; Res. Alert [Full Cov.]; Soc. Sci. Cit. Index [Select. Cov.].

PY/0440-9094
HISTORIA PARAGUAYA. (HISTORIA PARAGUAYA : ANUARIO DEL INSTITUTO PARAGUAYO DE INVESTIGACIONES HISTORICAS.). [Hist. parag.]. **Added/Corp** Instituto Paraguayo de Investigaciones Historicas. Academia Paraguaya de la Historia. (1956)-. Spanish. an. **LC** F2661; .H5.
Ind/Abst Am. Hist. Life (1956-1965, 1973-).

BL/0100-6932
HISTORIA, QUESTOES & DEBATES. **VFOAT** Historia, Questoes e Debates. Periodical. Portuguese. sa. Associacao Paranaense de Historia, Caixa Postal 1 538, 80 000 Curitiba PR Brazil. **ED** Sergio Odilon Nadalin. **LC** F2596; .H53. **DD** 981/.62/005. **UDC** 972.87. Index available. cum. index. **Bk Rev. Ad Acc. Circ:** 700.
Desc: Publication concerned with history as knowledge, research and as a means of education.

CL/0073-2435
HISTORIA (SANTIAGO). (HISTORIA.). [Historia]. **Added/Corp** Universidad Catolica de Chile. Instituto de Historia. Vol. 1 (1961)-. Periodical. Spanish. an. $30.00. Instituto de Historia, Casilla 6277, Santiago 22 Chile. **Tel** 011 56 2 744041. **ED** Roberto Hernandez. **LC** F3051; .H5. **DD** 983/.005. Index available. cum. index. **Bk Rev. Ad Acc. Circ:** 600.
Desc: Articles and documents on Chilean and Latin American history plus Chilean historical bibliography.
Ind/Abst Am. Hist. Life (1961-); HAPI Hisp. Am. Period. Index.

CN/0709-5562
HISTORIC GUELPH. **Added/Corp** Guelph Historical Society. Vol. 17 (1978)-. English. ir. Guelph Historical Society, PO Box 1502, Guelph Ontario N1H 6N9 Canada. **Tel** (905)529-8111. **ED** Ruth Pollard and Eber Pollard. **LC** F1059.5.G9; H57. **DD** 971.3/43005. **Circ:** 800. ***Continues*** *Guelph Historical Society. Guelph Historical Society Publications, 0317-0721.*
Desc: Includes articles concerning the history and people of Guelph and Wellington County, Province of Ontario, Canada.

US/0164-5293
HISTORIC ILLINOIS. **Added/Corp** Illinois. Division of Historic Sites. Vol. 1 (June 1978)-. Periodical. English. bm (6 issues). $10.00 (one year), $17.00 (two year). Illinois Historic Preservation Agency, Old State Capitol, Springfield IL 62701. **Tel** (217)782-4836. **ED** Cindy Fuener. **Circ:** 4,200.
Desc: Magazine features historic people and places in Illinois and news of the Federal Historic Preservation Program in Illinois.
Ind/Abst Avery Index Archit. Period. Suppl. Colum. Univ. (Aug. 1989, Feb. 1990-).

CN/0440-9191
HISTORIC KINGSTON. **Added/Corp** Kingston Historical Society. No. 1 (1952)-. Periodical. English. an. $20.00. Kingston Historical Society, Box 54, Kingston Ontario K7L 4V6 Canada. **ED** Donald Redmond. **DD** 971.3/72/005. Index available. **Circ:** 400.
Desc: Transactions of the Kingston Historical Society.

US
HISTORIC LANDMARKS OF BLACK AMERICANS. (1991)-. English. an. $29.95. Gale Research Inc., 835 Penobscot Building, Detroit MI 48226. **Tel** (800)877-GALE, (313)961-2242, FAX (313)961-6083, telex TWX 810-221-7086. **ED** George Cantor.
Desc: This illustrated guide, describes some 300 sites significant to African-American History. Brimming with photos, maps, famous figures, infamous events, and inspiring triumphs, this in-depth guide is a fascinating resource detailing the scope and impact of African-American culture.

US/1065-0016
HISTORIC MAURY. [Hist. Maury]. **Added/Corp** Maury County Historical Society (Maury County, Tenn.). (19??)-. English. qt. $10.00. Maury County Historical Society, Box 147, Columbia TN 38401. **Tel** (615)388-7479. **DD** 976.

US/0439-2248
HISTORIC NANTUCKET. [Hist. Nantucket]. **Added/Corp** Nantucket Historical Association. Vol. 1 (July 1953/1954)-. English. qt. $25.00 membership. Nantucket Historical Association, PO Box 1016, Nantucket MA 02554. **Tel** (508)228-1894. **ED** Helen Winslow Chase and Diane Ucci. **LC** F72.N2; H68. **DD** 974.497. Index available. cum. index. **Circ:** 3,000 (ctrl).
Desc: Articles, poetry and illustrations pertaining to Nantucket and Maritime history.
Ind/Abst Am. Hist. Life.

US/0018-2419
HISTORIC PRESERVATION (WASHINGTON, D.C.). (HISTORIC PRESERVATION.). [Hist. preserv.]. **Added/Corp** National Trust for Historic Preservation in the United States. National Council for Historic Sites and Buildings. Quarterly Report of the National Council for Historic Sites and Buildings. Vol. 1 (Mar. 1949)-. Periodical. English. bm. comes with membership. National Trust for Historic Preservation, 1785 Massachusetts Avenue Northwest, Washington DC 20036. **Tel** (202)673-4035. **LC** E151; .H5. **DD** 363.6/9/097305. **[CCC].** available on microfilm and microfiche from University Microfilms International (UMI). Documents available from The Genuine Article. ***Continues*** *Quarterly Report (National Council for Historic Sites and Buildings).*
Ind/Abst Abstr. Anthropol.; Am. Hist. Life (1964-); Archit. Period. Index; Art Archaeol. Tech. Abstr.; Art Index; Arts Humanit. Citation Index [Full Cov.]; Avery Index Archit. Period. Suppl. Colum. Univ. (Jan. 1990-); Garden Lit. (1992-); J. Plan. Lit.; Res. Alert [Full Cov.]; Soc. Sci. Cit. Index [Select. Cov.].

US/0892-6336
HISTORIC SCHAEFFERSTOWN RECORD. (HISTORIC SCHAEFFERSTOWN RECORD / HISTORIC SCHAEFFERSTOWN, INC.). **Added/Corp** Historic Schaefferstown, Inc. (Pa.). (19??)-. Periodical. English. Four times a year. $50.00. Historic Schaefferstown Inc, Schaefferstown PA 17088. **Tel** (717)949-2244. **DD** 974.

MX
HISTORICA. Periodical. Spanish. $20.00. Universidad Automona del Estado de Mexico, Constituyentes 100, Oriente, Apartado Postal 65-A, Toluca Mexico. **LC** F4201; .H53. **UDC** 972.

PE/0252-8894
HISTORICA (LIMA). (HISTORICA.). [Historica]. Vol. 1 (July 1977)-. Periodical. Spanish. sa. $12.80 US. Pontificia Universidad Catolica del Peru, Fondo Editorial, Apartado 1761, Lima 100 Peru. **Tel** 011 51 14 622540 or, 622220 ext. 220. **ED** Franklin Pease G Y. **LC** F3401; .H54. **DD** 985/.005. **UDC** 985. **Bk Rev. Ad Acc. Pr Rev.** ctrl circ.
Desc: Articles on Peruvian history, ethnohistory and historiography. Also on Latin American history related to Peru.
Ind/Abst Am. Hist. Life (1977-).

CN/0068-886X
HISTORICAL BOOKLETS / THE CANADIAN HISTORICAL ASSOCIATION. [Hist. bookl. - Can. Hist. Assoc.]. **VFOAT** Canadian Historical Association Booklets; Historical Booklet; Canadian Historical Association Booklets. **VAT** Historical Booklets - Canadian Historical Association. No. 1 (1953)-. English (French). ir. $30.00 (series). Canadian Historical Association, 395 Wellington Street, Ottawa Ontario K1A 0N3 Canada. **Tel** (613)233-7885. **ED** Terry Cook and Gabrielle Blais. **[CCC].**

US/0362-000X
HISTORICAL COLLECTIONS OF THE DANVERS HISTORICAL SOCIETY. **Main/Corp** Danvers Historical Society. Vol. 1 (1913)-. English. ir. $10.00. Danvers Historical Society, PO Box 381, Danvers MA 01923. **Tel** (617)774-4195. **LC** F74.D2; D42. **DD** 974.4/5. cum. index.
Desc: Includes "Necrology."

US/0886-5272
HISTORICAL FOOTNOTES (STONINGTON, CONN.). (HISTORICAL FOOTNOTES.). **Added/Corp** Stonington Historical Society. (19??)-. Periodical. English. qt (Feb., May, Aug., Nov.). $10.00. Stonington Historical Society, PO Box 103, Stonington CT 06378. **Tel** (203)572-8441. **ED** Victor Boatwright (editor's telephone: (203)535-0018). **DD** 974. Index available (published separately). cum. index. **Ad Acc. Circ:** 850.
Desc: Publishes material related to the history and genealogy of Stonington, Connecticut.

US/0276-8313
HISTORICAL JOURNAL OF MASSACHUSETTS. [Hist. j. Mass.]. Vol. 8, No. 2 (June 1980)-. Periodical. English. sa. $7.00 (one year), $13.00 (two years), $18.00 (three years) North America; $8.00 (one year), $14.00 (two years), $19.00 (three years) other. Institute for Massachusetts Studies, Westfield State College, Westfield MA 01086. **Tel** (413)568-3311 Ext. 344, FAX (413)562-3613. **ED** Martin Kaufman. **LC** E171; .H635. **DD** 973/.05. Index available. cum. index. **Bk Rev. Ad Acc. Circ:** 1,200. available on microfilm and microfiche from University Microfilms International (UMI). ***Continues*** *Historical Journal of Western Massachusetts, 0163-3929.*
Desc: Articles, reviews and book notes of the history of Massachusetts.
Ind/Abst Am. Hist. Life (1972-).

US/0018-2508
HISTORICAL NEW HAMPSHIRE. [Hist. N.H.]. **Added/Corp** New Hampshire Historical Society. Vol. 1 (Nov. 1944)-. Periodical. English. Four times a year. $30.00 individual membership. New Hampshire Historical Society, 30 Park Street, Concord NH 03301-6384. **Tel** (603)225-3381, FAX (603)224-0463. **ED** David R. Starbuck. **LC** F31; .H57. **DD** 974.2005. Index available. **Bk Rev. Circ:** 2,800 (ctrl).
Desc: The state-wide historical journal for New Hampshire.
Ind/Abst Am. Hist. Life (1963-); Genealogical Period. Annu. Index; SportSearch; West. Hist. Q.

US/0199-9664
HISTORICAL NEWS LETTER. (HISTORICAL NEWSLETTER.). **Main/Corp** Nebraska State Historical Society. Vol. 1 (July 1948)-. Periodical. English. ir. $20.00 Comes with Nebraska State Historical Society membership. Nebraska State Historical Society, 1500 R Street, Box 82554, Lincoln NE 68501. **Tel** (402)471-4746, (800)833-6747. **ED** Jacklin Goldsmith. **LC** F661; .N24. **Circ:** 5,000 (ctrl).
Desc: Keep you up-to-date on what's happening with history and historic preservation around the state.

CN/0846-3190
HISTORICAL PORT HOPE. [Hist. Port Hope]. **Added/Corp** Port Hope & District Chamber of Commerce. **VFOAT** Historic Port Hope. (1990/1991)-. English. Free. Port Hope and District Chamber of Commerce, 84 Ontario Street, Port Hope, Ontario L1A 2T8. **DD** 917.13/56.

CN
HISTORICAL PUBLICATIONS - CANADIAN WAR MUSEUM. **Main/Corp** Canadian War Museum. No. 1-. Monographic series. English. ir. Price varies per volume. Receiver General for Canada, National Museum of Canada, 360 Lisgar Street, Ottawa Ontario K1A 0M8 Canada. **UDC** 971.

US/0018-2524
HISTORICAL REVIEW OF BERKS COUNTY. [Hist.]. **Added/Corp** Historical Society of Berks County, Reading, Pa. Vol. 1 (Oct. 1935)-. Periodical. English. qt (Mar., June, Sept., Dec.). $15.00 US; $20.00 other. Historical Review of Berks County, 940 Center Avenue, Reading PA 19601. **Tel** (215)375-4375. **ED** Paula Flippin. **LC** F157.B3; H48. **DD** 974.816. **Bk Rev. Ad Acc. Circ:** 2,550 (ctrl).
Ind/Abst Am. Hist. Life (1969-1971).

US/0440-940X
HISTORICAL SOCIETY MIRROR. V. 1, No. 1- Jan. 1955-. Periodical. English. bm. Kansas State Historical Society, 120 West 10th Street, Topeka KS 66612. **Tel** (913)296-3251, (913)296 2623, FAX (913)296-1005. **UDC** 973.

US
HISTORICAL SOCIETY OF FAIRFAX COUNTY YEARBOOK. English. be. $5.00 (two year). Historical Society of Fairfax, PO 415, Fairfax VA 22030. **Tel** (703)356-3094.
Ind/Abst Am. Hist. Life (1983-).

US
HISTORICAL WHISPERINGS. **Added/Corp** Washington County Historical Society (Minn.). Vol. 1, No. 1 (April 1974)-. Periodical. English. qt. $10.00. Washington County Historical Society, 1013 South 7th Street, Stillwater MN 55082. **Tel** (612)439-5722. **ED** Jerry Brosious. Index available. cum. index. **Circ:** 600 (ctrl).
Desc: History of people, events, and places primarily in Washington, Minnesota.

US/0275-8385
HISTORICALLY SPEAKING. [Hist. speak.]. Periodical. English. Afro-American Historical Association of the Niagara Frontier, PO Box 1663, Buffalo NY 14216. **UDC** 973.
Desc: A local newsletter which is distributed to members and supporters of the Afro-American Historical Association.

CN/0826-5283
HISTORIEN MUNICIPAL, L'. [Hist. munic.]. Periodical. French. mo. Free. Historien Municipal, 8928 Boulevard St-Michel, Montreal Quebec H1Z 3G4 Canada. **DD** 971.4/005. **UDC** 971.4.

CN/0821-1469
HISTORIGRAM. (HISTORIGRAM / YARMOUTH COUNTY HISTORICAL SOCIETY.). [Historigram]. **Added/Corp** Yarmouth County Historical Society. (19??)-. Periodical. English. mo. $12.00 U.S. Yarmouth County Historical Society, PO Box 39, Yarmouth Nova Scotia B5A 4B1 Canada. **Tel** (902)742-5539. **ED** Ingrid Prosser. **DD** 971.6/31/006. **Bk Rev. Ad Acc. Circ:** 300 (ctrl).
Desc: Newsletter of Yarmouth County Historical Society. Yarmouth, Nova Scotia, Canada.

US/0883-8143
HISTORY LIVES HERE. [His. lives here]. **Added/Corp** Friends of the Amador County Museum and Archives. (198?)-. Periodical. English. qt. $6.00. Friends of the Amador County Museum and Archives, PO Box 913, Jackson CA 95642. **Tel** (209)223-1513. **ED** Leslie McLaughlin. **DD** 979. **Circ:** 500 (ctrl).
Desc: Covers museum collection, acquisitions and news, archives collection and acquisitions, documented Amador County history and genealogy.

US
HISTORY NEWS DISPATCH. ***Title Change.*** **Added/Corp** American Association for State and Local History. **VFOAT** HND. (Jan. 1986)-(1993). Periodical. English. mo. American Association for State and Local History, 530 Church Street, Suite 600, Nashville TN 37219. **Tel** (615)255-2971, FAX (615)255-2979. **LC** E172; .H57. ***Continued by*** *Dispatch (Nashville, Tenn.).*
Ind/Abst Museum Abstr. (?-?).

US/0363-7492
HISTORY NEWS (NASHVILLE, TENN.). (HISTORY NEWS.). [Hist. news]. **Added/Corp** American Association for State and Local History. Vol. 5 (Nov. 1949)-. Periodical. English. Six times a year. $90.00 Comes with American Association for State & Local History membership. American Association for State and Local History, 530 Church Street, Suite 600, Nashville TN 37219. **Tel** (615)255-2971, FAX (615)255-2979. **LC** E172; .A533. **DD** 973. available on microfilm and microfiche from University Microfilms International (UMI). ***Continues*** *State and Local History News, 0364-3042.*
Ind/Abst Am. Hist. Life (1963-1976); Art Archaeol. Tech. Abstr.; Museum Abstr.; West. Hist. Q.

US
HISTORY NOTES : THE NEWSLETTER OF THE VIRGINIA HISTORICAL SOCIETY. **Added/Corp** Virginia Historical Society. **VFOAT** Newsletter of the Virginia Historical Society. No. 1 (Winter 1991)-. Newsletter. English. qt. comes with membership. Virginia Historical Society, PO Box 7311, Richmond VA 23221-0311. **Tel** (804)358-4901, FAX (804)355-2399. **LC** F221; .V823. ***Continues*** *Occasional Bulletin.*

US/0889-6186
HISTORY TRAILS. (HISTORY TRAILS / BALTIMORE COUNTY HISTORICAL SOCIETY.). [Hist. trails]. **Added/Corp** Baltimore County Historical Society.

Vol. 1, No. 1 (Sept. 1966)-. Periodical. English. Four times a year (Seasonally). $15.00. Baltimore County Historical Society, 9811 Van Buren Lane, Cockeyville MD 21030. **Tel** (301)592-7339. **ED** John W. McGrain and William Hollifield. **LC** F187.B2; H57. **DD** 975. **Circ:** 425. available on microfilm.

HO
HONDURAS ... : ORGANO DE LA SECRETARIA DE PRENSA DE LA JUNTA MILITAR DE GOBIERNO. Began in 1961. Periodical. Spanish. mo. Secretaria de Prensa de la Junta Militar de Gobierno, Apartado Postal No 403, Tegucigalpa Honduras. **LC** F1508; .H66. **DD** 972.83/005. **UDC** 972.83.

US/0742-7727
HOOFPRINTS FROM THE YELLOWSTONE CORRAL OF THE WESTERNERS. **Added/Corp** Westerners. Yellowstone Corral. **VFOAT** Hoofprints. Vol. 1, No. 1 (Autumn 1971)-. Periodical. English. sa (2 issues). $10.00 (includes membership). Yellowstone Corral of the Westerners International, Box 355, Billings MT 59103. **Tel** (406)259-1966. **ED** John Willard. **Bk Rev. Circ:** 500 (ctrl).
Desc: Activities of the Yellowstone Corral of Westerners and articles of historical nature pertaining to this area and the West.

US/0884-0628
HOUSTON CITY MAGAZINE. ***Ceased.*** [Houst. city mag.]. **VFOAT** Houston City. April (1978)-(1987). Periodical. English. mo. North Central Expressway, #120, Dallas TX 75204-3005. **LC** F394.H8; H827. **DD** 976.4/1411/005. ***Continues*** *In Houston.*
Ind/Abst Access (1980-1987); Index Period. Artic. Relat. Law.

US/0272-4030
HOUSTON REVIEW, THE. (THE HOUSTON REVIEW: HISTORY AND CULTURE OF THE GULF COAST.). [Houston rev.]. **Added/Corp** Houston Public Library. Houston Metropolitan Research Center. **VFOAT** Houston Review. Vol. 1 (Spring 1979)-. Periodical. English. Three times a year (Fall, Winter & Summer). $12.00 (institutions), $7.50 (individuals). Houston Public Library, 500 McKinney Street, Houston TX 77002. **Tel** (713)247-1661. **ED** Louis J. Marchiafava (editor's telephone (713)247-3562). **LC** F394.H857; H68. **DD** 976/.005. Index available. **Bk Rev. Circ:** 500.
Desc: Publishes historical research: political, social, economic studies of the Houston metropolitan area and the surrounding Gulf Coast region.
Ind/Abst Am. Hist. Life (1987-).

UY
HOY ES HISTORIA. No. 1 (Dic. 1983/Enero 1984)-. Periodical. Spanish. bm.
Ind/Abst HAPI Hisp. Am. Period. Index.

US/0199-9583
HUGUENOT HISTORIAN, THE. 1980/82-. English. be. Huguenot Society of New Jersey, English Villege, Cranford NJ 07016. **LC** E184.H9; H55. **DD** 973/.0441. **UDC** 284.1/.2(44:73); 973.

US/1048-3152
HUNTSVILLE HISTORICAL REVIEW, THE. [Huntsville hist. rev.]. **Added/Corp** Huntsville-Madison County Historical Society (Ala.). (1971)-. Periodical. English. sa. $10.00 (one year), $18.00 (two year). Huntsville-Madison County Historical Society, PO Box 666, Huntsville AL 35804. **Tel** (205)852-7141. **ED** Frances C. Roberts. **LC** F334.H9; H89. **DD** 976.1/97/005. ctrl circ.

CN/0822-9503
HURON HISTORICAL NOTES. [Huron hist. notes]. **Added/Corp** Huron County Historical Society (Ont.). **VFOAT** Huron Historical Society. Vol. 1 (1965)-. Periodical. English. an. 6.50Can$. Huron County Historical Society, RR 1, c/o Rae McFarlane, Bayfield Ontario N0M 1L0 Canada. **Tel** (519)228-6219. **ED** Sandra Orr. **LC** F1059.H92; H85. **DD** 971.3/22/005. **Circ:** 200 (ctrl).
Desc: History pertaining to approximately 17 townships of Huron County in Ontario Canada.

US/0146-9274
IAM (NEW YORK). (I AM.). [IAM]. **VAT** Italian American. (19??)-. Periodical. English. mo. $12.00. I-AM Publishing Corporation, 3 East 54th Street, New York NY 10022. **LC** E184.I8; I18. **DD** 973/.04/51.
Ind/Abst Public Aff. Inf. Serv. Bull.

XR/0536-2520
IBERO-AMERICANA PRAGENSIA. [Ibero-Am. Prag.]. **Added/Corp** Universita Karlova. Stredisko Iberoamerickych Studii. Vol. 1 (1967)-. Spanish. an. **LC** F1401; .I23. **DD** 980/.005.
Ind/Abst Am. Hist. Life (1971-1972); BHA : Biblio. Hist. Art.

GW/0340-3068
IBERO-AMERIKANISCHES ARCHIV. [Ibero-am. Arch.]. **Added/Corp** Universitat Bonn. Ibero-Amerikanisches Forschungs-Institut. Ibero-Amerikanisches Institut (Berlin, Germany). Vol. 1 (1924)-. Periodical. German (English; summaries and/or abstracts in Spanish). Twice a year (Double issues per year). Price varies. Vervuert Verlagsgesellschaft, Wielandstr 40, D 60318 Frankfurt Germany. **Tel** 011 49 69 5974617. **ED** Guenter Vollmer. **LC** F1401; .I24. **DD** 972.005. **[CCC]. Bk Rev. Ad Acc. Circ:** 500 (ctrl).
Desc: Covers the political, social and cultural problems of Latin America and the Spanish-Portuguese civilization in history, present time and future.
Ind/Abst Am. Hist. Life (1987-); Anthropol. Lit.; Bibliogr. Mission.; GeoRef; HAPI Hisp. Am. Period. Index.

GW/0342-1864
IBEROAMERICANA. (1977)-. Periodical. German (Portuguese and Spanish). Four times a year. DM50.00. Vervuert Verlagsgesellschaft, Wielandstr 40, D 60318 Frankfurt Germany. **Tel** 011 49 69 5974617. **ED** Martin Franzbach, Karsten Garscha, Jurgen M Meisel, Klaus Meyer-Minnemann, Dieter Reichardt. **LC** F1408.3; .I24. **DD** 946. cum. index. **Bk Rev. Ad Acc. Circ:** 1,000.
Desc: Publishes articles about literature, language and cultural affairs in Spain, Portugal and Latin America.
Ind/Abst HAPI Hisp. Am. Period. Index.

CN/0046-8452
ICELANDIC CANADIAN. **See** Ethnic Interests.

US/0019-1264
IDAHO YESTERDAYS. [Ida. yesterdays]. **Added/Corp** Idaho State Historical Society. Vol. 1 (Spring 1957)-. Academic Scholarly Publication. English. qt. $15.00. Idaho Historical Society, 210 Main Street, Boise ID 83702. **Tel** (208)334-2120. **ED** Judith Austin (editor's address: 450 N 4th Street, Boise, ID, 83702; phone: (208)334-3428). **LC** F741; .I23. **DD** 979.6/005. **Pr Rev. Circ:** 2,175 (ctrl).
Desc: History of Idaho, the Pacific Northwest, and the West in general. Of scholarly substance, designed for a primarily lay audience.
Ind/Abst Abstr. Anthropol.; Am. Hist. Life (1963-); West. Hist. Q.

II/0301-9101
IDEAS (HYDERABAD). (IDEAS. INDIAN DOCTORAL ENGAGEMENTS IN AMERICAN STUDIES.). [Ideas]. **VFOAT** Indian Doctoral Engagements in American Studies. English. 1.00 single issue. American Studies, Research Center, 500007 Hyderabad India. **LC** E169.1; .I33. **DD** 917.3/03/05.

AG
IDENTIDAD. **Added/Corp** Rafaela (Argentina). Archivo Historico Municipal. 1, No. 1 (Jan./Mar. 1991)-. Periodical. Spanish. qt.

BO/1013-9796
ILLIMANI. [Illimani]. **Added/Corp** Instituto de Investigaciones Historicas y Culturales de La Paz. No. 1 (1972)-. Periodical. Spanish. sa.
Ind/Abst Am. Hist. Life (1972-1978).

US/0748-8149
ILLINOIS HISTORICAL JOURNAL. [Ill. hist. j.]. **Added/Corp** Illinois State Historical Society. Vol. 77, No. 3 (Autumn 1984)-. Periodical. English. qt. Free to members; $20.00 (institutions); $25.00 (individuals) membership. Illinois State Historical Society, 1 Old Capitol Plaza, Springfield IL 62701. **Tel** (217)782-8160, FAX (217)524-8042. **ED** Evelyn Taylor. **LC** F536; .I18. **DD** 977.3/005. Index available. cum. index (Up to Volume 60). **Bk Rev**, (Qty: 100). **Pr Rev. Circ:** 2,400 (ctrl). available on magnetic tape, an online database, and CD-ROM; available on microfilm and microfiche from University Microfilms International (UMI). ***Continues*** *Illinois State Historical Society. Journal of the Illinois State Historical Society, 0019-2287.*
Desc: Illinois history and biography; focuses on Civil War involvement and Abraham Lincoln.
Ind/Abst Am. Hist. Life (1963-); MLA Int. Bibl. Books Artic. Mod. Lang. Lit.; West. Hist. Q.

US/0019-2058
ILLINOIS HISTORY. [Ill. hist.]. **Added/Corp** Illinois State Historical Library Illinois State Historical Society. Vol. 10, No. 4, (Jan. 1957)-. Periodical. English. Three times a year. Free on request to Illinois elementary and secondary schools; $6.00 other. Illinois State Historical Society, 1 Old Capitol Plaza, Springfield IL 62701. **Tel** (217)782-8160, FAX (217)524-8042. **ED** Keith Sculle. Index available. **Circ:** 19,000 (ctrl). ***Continues*** *Illinois Junior Historian.*
Desc: Articles by Illinois 7th to 12th graders on topics related to Illinois history and social studies.

US/0747-9794
ILLINOIS MAGAZINE. ***Suspended.*** [Ill. mag.]. Vol. 22, No. 4 (July/Aug. 1983)-(19??). Periodical. English. bm. $12.50 US; $14.50 other. Illinois Magazine, Henrichs Publications Inc, PO Box 40, Sunshine Park, Litchfield IL 62056. **Tel** (217)324-3425. **ED** Peggy Kuethe. **LC** F536; .I16. **DD** 977.3/005. Index available. cum. index. **Bk Rev. Ad Acc. Circ:** 13,000 (ctrl). ***Continues*** *Illinois, 0148-3390.*
Desc: Concentrates on history, travel, people, points of interest to readers concerned with the state of Illinois.
Ind/Abst Am. Hist. Life; Genealogical Period. Annu. Index.

BL
IMAGEM DO BRASIL E DA AMERICA LATINA. **VFOAT** Brazil and Latin America. 1972-. Portuguese (Portuguese). Editora Banas SA, Av Presidente Castelo Branco 6241, CEP 05038, Sao Paulo Brazil. **LC** F2501; .I48. **DD** 981/.06/05. **UDC** 981; 980=6. ***Continues*** *Imagem do Brasil.*

CN/1180-5579
IMAGES D'OUTREMONT. [Images Outremont]. Vol. 1, No 1 (Autumn 1990)-. Periodical. French. qt. Free. Images d'Outremont, CP 177, Succursale Outremont, Outremont, Quebec H2V 4M8 Canada. **DD** 971.4.

US/0899-1138
IMAGES OF EXCELLENCE. [Images excell.]. **Added/Corp** Images of Excellence Foundation. (1986)-. Monographic series. English. bm. $5.00. Images of Excellence, PO Box 1131, Boiling Springs NC 28017. **Tel** (803)895-1410. **DD** 973.

US/1059-5511
IN CONTEXT (CROWNSVILLE, MD.). (IN CONTEXT. : A NEWSLETTER OF THE DIVISION OF HISTORICAL AND CULTURAL PROGRAMS, MARYLAND DEPTARTMENT OF HOUSING AND COMMUNITY DEVELOPMENT.). [In context]. **Added/Corp** Maryland Historical Trust. Vol. 1, No. 1 (Sept./Oct. 1991)-. Newsletter. English. qt. Free. In Context, 100 Community Place, 3rd Floor, Crownsville MD 21032. **DD** 975. ***Formed by the union of*** *Byways (Annapolis, Md.), 1052-4673; Update (Annapolis, Md. : 1985), 1052-4657* ***and*** *Across the state, 1052-4665.*

SZ
INCOMINDIOS. Periodical. German (German). 10.00. **LC** E51; .I32. **DD** 970.004/97. **UDC** 975.7.

US/0046-8843
INDEPENDENT REPUBLIC QUARTERLY, THE. **Added/Corp** Horry County Historical Society. (1967)-. Periodical. English. Four times a year. $20.00. Horry County Historical Society, PO Box 2025, Conway SC 29526. **Tel** (803)248-4947. **ED** Ben Burroughs. cum. index. **Circ:** 450.

US
INDEX TO THE JOURNALS OF THE NORTH DAKOTA HISTORICAL SOCIETY. **Main/Corp** State Historical Society of North Dakota. English. North Dakota State Library Commission, Bismarck ND 58505. **Tel** 224-2492. **LC** Z732.N9; N925 subser; [F631]. **DD** 021/.009784S; 978.4. **UDC** 978.4(083.86:05).

US/0736-265X
INDIAN-ARTIFACT MAGAZINE. **See** Archaeology.

II/0019-5030
INDIAN JOURNAL OF AMERICAN STUDIES. [Indian j. Am. st.]. **Added/Corp** American Studies Research Centre (Hyderabad, India). Vol. 1 No. 1 (July 1969)-. Periodical. English. sa. $20.00. Osmania University Campus, American Studies Research Center, Hyderabad 500007 India. **Tel** 71546. **(Subscription address:** Prints India, 11 Darya Ganj, New Delhi, 110002 India, (Phone: 011 91 11 3268645)**)** **ED** M Glen Johnson. **LC** E169.12; .I45. **DD** 917.3/03/05. Index available. cum. index. **Bk Rev. Ad Acc. Pr Rev. Circ:** 3,500 (ctrl).
Desc: Publishes work primarily by Indian scholars, but also by specialists of any nationality on the history, institutions, literature and culture of the US.
Ind/Abst Abstr. Engl. Stud.; Am. Hist. Life (1969-); Annu. Bibliogr. Engl. Lang. Lit.; MLA Int. Bibl. Books Artic. Mod. Lang. Lit.

US/0046-9076
INDIAN TRADER, THE. (19??)-. Periodical. English. Twelve times a year. $18.00 (one year), $32.50 (two year), $48.00 (three year). Indian Trader, PO Box 1421, 311 East Aztec Avenue, Gallup NM 87305. **Tel** (505)722-6694. **ED** Bil Donovan. Index available. **Bk Rev. Ad Acc. Circ:** 4,500 (ctrl).
Desc: A newspaper featuring Indian history, culture, arts and crafts, ceremonials and tribal news. Also stories on the early west, pioneers, outlaws, soldiers and explorers.

US/0091-102X
INDIAN VOICE (SANTA CLARA). (INDIAN VOICE.). Periodical. English. mo. $7.50. Native American Publishing Company, PO Box 2033, Santa Clara CA 95051. **LC** E75; .I5. **DD** 970.1/05. **UDC** 973(97).

US/0739-9391
INDIANA ALWAYS. **VFOAT** INDA. Vol. 1, No. 1 (Apr. 1983)-. Periodical. English. sa. Indiana Always, Inc., 871 Sayre Drive, Greenwood IN 46142. **ED** Bobby Hamilton. **LC** F524.3; .I53. **DD** 977.2/0433. **UDC** 977.2.

GW
INDIANA (BERLIN, GERMANY). (INDIANA.). (1973)-. English (German and Spanish). ir. Gebrueder Mann Verlag, Lindenstrasse 76, D-10969 Berlin Germany. **Tel** 011 49 30 25913589, telex 183723. **LC** E51; .I37. **DD** 970/.004/97.
Ind/Abst Anthropol. Lit.

US/0073-6902
INDIANA HISTORICAL SOCIETY PUBLICATIONS. **Added/Corp** Indiana Historical Society. Vol. 1, (1897)-. Monographic series. English. ir. Price varies per volume. Indiana Historical Society, 315 West Ohio Street, Indianapolis IN 46202. **Tel** (317)232-1882. **LC** F521; .I41. **DD** 977.2. **Circ:** 6,000.
Desc: Includes the Society's proceedings and all papers and publications from its organization in 1830 to 1886.

US/0019-6649
INDIANA HISTORY BULLETIN. [Indiana hist. bull.]. **Added/Corp** Indiana Historical Bureau. Indiana Historical Commission. Indiana Historical Society. Vol. 1, (Nov. 1923)-. Periodical. English. Four times a year. $5.00. Indiana Historical Bureau, 140 North Senate Avenue, Room 408, Indianapolis IN 46204. **Tel** (317)232-2537. **ED** Virginia Turpening. **LC** F521; .I367. **DD** 977.2. Index available. cum. index. **Circ:** 4,350 (ctrl).
Desc: News of interest to amateur and professional historians about Indiana state, and local history and Indiana historical organizations' activities.
Ind/Abst Am. Hist. Life (1968-1978); Annu. Bibliogr. Engl. Lang. Lit.; West. Hist. Q.

US/0019-6673
INDIANA MAGAZINE OF HISTORY. [Indiana mag. hist.]. **Added/Corp** Indiana University. Dept. of History. Indiana University, Bloomington. Dept. of History. Indiana State Library. Indiana Historical Society. Vol. 9, No. 2 (June 1913)-. Academic Scholarly Publication. English. Four times a year (Mar., June, Sept., Dec.). $10.00. Indiana Magazine of History, Indiana University, Ballantine Hall 742, Bloomington IN 47401. **Tel** (812)855-4139. **ED** Richard Blackett. **LC** F521; .I52. cum. index. **Bk Rev.** **Pr Rev.** **Circ:** 9,000 (ctrl). available on microfilm. ***Continues*** *Indiana Quarterly Magazine of History, 0147-2259.*
Desc: A scholarly journal featuring articles and book reviews on midwestern and Indiana history.
Ind/Abst Am. Hist. Life (1963-); Annu. Bibliogr. Engl. Lang. Lit.; West. Hist. Q.

US/0737-8602
INDIANA PRESERVATIONIST, THE. **See** Travel and Tourism.

CN/0843-8145
INDO-CANADIAN NATIONAL NEWS. ***Title Change.*** [Indo-Can. natl. news]. **Added/Corp** National Indo-Canadian Council. **VFOAT** Nouvelles Nationales Indo-Canadiennes. Vol. 1, No. 1 (April 1989)-(199?). Periodical. English. qt. National Indo-Canadian Council, Quebec H3A 1R3 Canada. **DD** 971/.00491311/005. ***Continued by*** *News (National Indo-Canadian Council), 1193-6770.*

●CN/1187-8401
INFORMATION AND APPLICATION GUIDE / CANADIAN STUDIES AND SPECIAL PROJECTS DIRECTORATE. [Inf. appl. guide - Can., Can. Stud. Spec. Proj. Dir.]. **Main/Corp** Canada. Canadian Studies and Special Projects Directorate. **VFOAT** Renseignements et Guide du Demandeur. (1993)-. English (French). **DD** 971/.0079. ***Continues*** *Canadian Studies Directorate., 0848-7251.*

US/0748-6502
INFORMATION BULLETIN (ROMANIAN-AMERICAN HERITAGE CENTER (U.S.). (INFORMATION BULLETIN / ROMANIAN-AMERICAN HERITAGE CENTER.). **Added/Corp** Romanian-American Heritage Center (U.S.). (1984)-. Periodical. English. qt. $10.00. Romanian-American Heritage Center, 2450 Grey Tower Road, Jackson MI 49201. **Tel** (517)522-8260. **ED** Traian Lascu. **DD** 973. **Bk Rev.** **Circ:** 1,800 (ctrl).
Desc: Primarily concerned with the history of the Romanian immigration to the US and Canada and with the achievements of those pioneers and of their descendants.

US/1054-6855
INFORMATION SERIES - NATIONAL TRUST FOR HISTORIC PRESERVATION IN THE UNITED STATES. (INFORMATION SERIES.). **Added/Corp** National Trust for Historic Preservation in the United States. **VFOAT** Forum Information; Information. (198?)-. Monographic series. English. ir. Price varies per volume. National Trust for Historic Preservation, 1785 Massachusetts Avenue Northwest, Washington DC 20036. **Tel** (202)673-4035. **LC** E159; .I53. **DD** 363.6/9/0973. ***Continues*** *Information, from the National Trust for Historic Preservation, 0272-6556;* ***Absorbed*** *Private Nonprofit Statewide Preservation Organizations.*

BL
INFORMATIVO FUNAI - FUNDACAO NACIONAL DO INDIO. **Main/Corp** Fundacao Nacional do Indio. **VAT** Informativo Fundacao Nacional do Indio. Vol. 3, No. 11/12 (1974)-. Periodical. Portuguese. Fundacao Nacional do Indio Edificio Alvorado, SCS 2O Andar, Brasilia Brazil. **LC** F2519. **UDC** 981(98); 909.81(98). ***Continues*** *Boletim Informativo Funai.*

SW
INFORME ANUAL / INSTITUTO DE ESTUDIOS LATINOAMERICANOS. UNIVERSIDAD DE ESTOCOLMO. **Main/Corp** Latinamerika-Institutet i Stockholm. (1990)-. Spanish. **LC** F1401.L36; A15. ***Continues*** *Latinamerika-Institutet I Stockholm. Informe de Actividades.*

US/0882-3901
INFORME COLOMBIANO. [Inf. colomb.]. (19??)-. Periodical. English. mo. $20.00 (general), $25.00 (institutions). Informe Colombiano, PO Box 1017, Murray Hill Station, New York NY 10156. **DD** 986.
Ind/Abst Hum. Rights Intern. Rep.

US/0020-1537
INLAND SEAS. [Inland seas]. **Added/Corp** Great Lakes Historical Society. Vol. 1 (Jan. 1945)-. Periodical. English. Four times a year (Jan., Apr., July, Oct.). $35.00 Comes with Great Lakes Historical Society Membership. Great Lakes Historical Society, 480 Main Street, Vermilion OH 44089. **Tel** (216)967-3467, FAX (216)967-1519. **ED** William D. Ellis and Nancy Schneider. **LC** F551; .I46. **DD** 977.005. Index available (published anually). **Bk Rev**, (Qty: 20). **Ad Acc.** **Circ:** 3,000.
Desc: Comprehensive history of the Great Lakes, its ships, people, places, and transportation.
Ind/Abst Am. Hist. Life (1963-).

CN/0713-343X
INSIDE QUEBEC (QUEBEC, QUEBEC). (INSIDE QUEBEC.). [Inside Que.]. Periodical. English. wk. $250.00. Inside Quebec, NDG, PO Box 381 Canada. **DD** 971.4/04/05. **UDC** 971.4.

US/1057-0845
INSIGHT INTO AMERICAN LIFE & OPINIONS REVEALED BY POLLS & SURVEYS. (INSIGHT INTO AMERICAN LIFE & OPINIONS REVEALED BY POLLS & SURVEYS [COMPUTER FILE].). [Insight Am. life opin. reveal. polls surv.]. **VFOAT** Insight; Insight Into American Life and Opinions Revealed by Polls & Surveys. (1990)-. English. $795.00. ORS Pub, 1342 Timberlane Road, Suite 201A, Tallahassee FL 32312. **DD** 973. available in print (American Public Opinion Index); available on microfiche (American Public Opinion Data).
Desc: Contains data compiled from companion publication: American Public Opinion Index and microfiche publication: American Public Opinion Data.

US
INTER-AMERICAN INSTITUTE SERIES. **Main/Corp** University of Florida Institute of Inter-American Affairs. Vol. 1 (June 15, 1930)-. English. **LC** F1401; .F59. **DD** 378.759.

●CN/0846-5495
INTERNATIONAL DIRECTORY TO CANADIAN STUDIES. (REPERTOIRE INTERNATIONAL DES ETUDES CANADIENNES). [Int. dir. Can. stud.]. **Added/Corp** Conseil International d'Etudes Canadiennes. Conseil International d'Etudes Canadiennes. Secretariat. **VFOAT** Repertoire; Directory; International Directory of Canadian Studies. (1992)-. French (English). be. Conseil International d'Etudes Canadiennes, 2 Avenue Daly, Ottawa Ontario K1N 6E2 Canada. **DD** 971/.007. ***Continues*** *International Directory to Canadian Studies., 0846-5495.*

●CN/0846-5495
INTERNATIONAL DIRECTORY TO CANADIAN STUDIES. (REPERTOIRE INTERNATIONAL DES ETUDES CANADIENNES). [Int. dir. Can. stud.]. **Added/Corp** International Council for Canadian Studies. International Council for Canadian Studies. Secretariat. **VFOAT** Directory; Repertoire; International Directory of Canadian Studies. (1992)-. English (French). be. International Council for Canadian Studies, 2 Daly Avenue, Ottawa Ontario K1N 6E2 Canada. **Tel** (613)232-0417, (613)232-0417, FAX (613)232-2495. **DD** 971/.007. ***Continues*** *International Directory to Canadian Studies., 0846-5495.*

CN/1180-3991
INTERNATIONAL JOURNAL OF CANADIAN STUDIES. [Int. j. Can. stud.]. **Added/Corp** International Council for Canadian Studies. **VFOAT** Research on Canada; Recherche sur le Canada; Revue Internationale d'Etudes Canadiennes. 1/2 (Spring/Fall 1990)-. Academic Scholarly Publication. English (French). sa. 30.00Can$ (non-members), 20.00Can$ (members) Canada; 35.00Can$ (non-members), 25.00Can$ (members) other. International Council for Canadian Studies, 2 Daly Avenue, Ottawa Ontario K1N 6E2 Canada. **Tel** (613)232-0417, (613)232-0417, FAX (613)232-2495. **ED** Kenneth McRoberts (editor's address: Robarts Center for Canadian Studies, York University, 4700 Keele Street, North York Ontario M3J 1P3 Canada; editor's phone: (416)736-5499; editor's fax: (416)736-5739). **LC** F1001; .I58. **DD** 971/.0071/1. **Ad Acc**, **Adv Mgr:** Guy Leclair. **Pr Rev.** **Circ:** 650.
Desc: Of interest to anyone doing research or comparative studies on Canada. Recent and forthcoming issues include: ethnicity, Charter of Rights and Freedoms, federalism, parliamentary Government and the Constitution, arts and literature, generations, evolving Canadian landscape, and comparative Canada/Russia-CIS studies.
Ind/Abst Am. Hist. Life (1990-); Can. Period. Index (19??-); Point Repere (1992-).

GL/0108-6898
INUIT. (INUIT / INUIT CIRCUMPOLAR CONFERENCE.). [Inuit]. **Added/Corp** Inuit Circumpolar Conference. (1982)-. Periodical. English (Eskimo). bm. Inuit Circumpolar Conference, PO Box 204, DK-3900 Nuuk, Greenland. **DD** 970.004/97.
Ind/Abst Hum. Rights Intern. Rep.

AG/0539-242X
INVESTIGACIONES Y ENSAYOS. [Invest. ens.]. **Added/Corp** Academia Nacional de la Historia (Argentina). (Oct./Dec. 1966)-. Periodical. Spanish. ir. $25.00 (one year), $47.50 (two year). Librart Department Argent Scientific, Casilla Correo Central 5047, Buenos Aires Argentina. **LC** F2801; .I5. **DD** 982/.005.
Ind/Abst Am. Hist. Life (1968-1974); HAPI Hisp. Am. Period. Index.

US/0884-4240
IRISH AMERICA. [Ir. Am.]. Vol. 1, No. 1 (1985)-. Periodical. English. Six times a year. $19.95. Irish America Magazine, 432 Park Avenue South, Suite 1503, New York NY 10016. **Tel** (212)725-2993, FAX (212)779-1198. **ED** Trish Harty. **LC** E184.I6; I62. **DD** 973/.049162. **Bk Rev.** **Ad Acc**, **Adv Mgr:** Eilleen McMahon.

US/0741-1138
ISLA (OAKLAND, CALIF.). (ISLA / INFORMATION SERVICES ON LATIN AMERICA.). [ISLA - Inf. Serv. Latin Am.]. **Added/Corp** Information Services on Latin America (Oakland, Calif.). **VFOAT** I.S.L.A. (19??)-. Periodical. English. mo. $640.00. Information Service on Latin America, 464 19th Street, Oakland CA 94612. **Tel** (510)835-0678, FAX (510)835-3017. **ED** Carrie Barclay. Index available. **Circ:** 250. available on microfilm.
Desc: Clippings of Latin American political, social and economic news from various English language newspapers.

CN/0384-8175
ISLAND MAGAZINE, THE. **Added/Corp** Prince Edward Island Heritage Foundation. No. 1, (Fall-Winter 1976)-. Periodical. English. Twice a year (May, Nov.,). 8.00Can$ Canada; 10.00Can$ US; $12.00Can$ other. Prince Edward Island Museum and Heritage Foundation, 2 Kent Street, Charlottetown C1A 1M6 Canada. **Tel** (902)892-9127, FAX (902)892-3420. **ED** Dr. Edward MacDonald. **LC** F1048; .I84. **DD** 971.7/005. Index available (Published separately). cum. index. **Bk Rev.** **Circ:** 3,000 (ctrl).
Desc: Explores the province's rich human and natural heritage. All articles are profusely illustrated with a mixture of maps, drawings, photographs, and original artwork.

CN/0849-6056
ISLANDSIDE MAGAZINE. [Isl.Side mag.]. **VFOAT** Island Side Magazine. Vol. 1, No. 1 (Jan. 1989)-. Periodical. English. mo. $12.00 per year, PEI; $18.00 per year Canada. Crossed Keys Publishing, PO Box 1330, Montague, Prince Edward Island C0A 1R0 Canada. **DD** 971.7/005.
Ind/Abst Can. Period. Index (Vol. 3, No. 3, Apr. 1991-).

●BL
ISTOE. **VFOAT** Isto E. No. 1174 (April 1, 1992)-. Periodical. Portuguese. Fifty-two times a year. $350.00. Empresa de Communicacao Tres Editorial Ltda., Rua William Speers, No. 1000, 1o Andar, Conj. 39, CEP 05067, Sao Paulo, SP, Brazil. **LC** F2501; .I88. **DD** 981/.005. ***Continues in part*** *Isto E Senhor.*

US/0163-0423
ITALIAN-AMERICAN IDENTITY. **Added/Corp** Identity Enterprises for the American-Italian. **VFOAT** Identity. Vol. 1, (Jan. 1977)-. Periodical. English. Identity Enterprises for the American-Italian, 420 Madison Avenue, New York NY 10017. **LC** E184.I8; I68. **DD** 973/.04/51.

US/0164-7539
IZARD COUNTY HISTORIAN, THE. ***Suspended.*** Vol. 1, Jan. 1970-Suspended Jan. 1990. Periodical. English. qt. $12.00. Izard County Historical Society, PO Box 84, Dolph AR 72528. **Tel** (501)297-3751. **UDC** 979.1. Index available. **Bk Rev.** **Circ:** 600 (ctrl).

US/1071-2348
JACKSON COUNTY CHRONICLES. [Jackson Cty. chron.]. **Added/Corp** Jackson County Historical Association (Jackson County, Ala.). (197?)-. Periodical. English. qt. Free to members; $10.00 membership. Jackson County Historical Association, PO Box 1494, Scottsboro AL 35768. **Tel** (205)259-5286. **DD** 976. ***Continues*** *Jackson County Historical Association Newsletter.*

US
JACKSON COUNTY HISTORY. (19??)-. English. Four times a year. $10.00. Jackson County Historical Society / West Virginia, PO Box 22, Ripley WV 25271. **Tel** (304)372-2541. **ED** Carolyn Miihlbach.

GW/0075-2673
JAHRBUCH FUER GESCHICHTE VON STAAT, WIRTSCHAFT UND GESELLSCHAFT LATEINAMERIKAS. [Jahrb. Gesch. Staat, Wirtsch. Ges. Lateinam.]. Vol. 1 (1964)-. Multiple languages (German, French and Spanish). ir. DM118.00. Boehlau Verlag GmbH & Cie / Koeln, Theodor Heuss STR 76, D-51149 Cologne Germany. **Tel** 011 49 2203 307021, FAX 011 49 2203 307349. **(Subscription address:** BDK Buecherdienst GmBh, Postfach 900120, D 51111 Cologne Germany.**)** **ED** R. Konetzke and H. Kellenbenz. **LC** F1401; .J3.
Ind/Abst Am. Hist. Life (1975-); Bibliogr. Mission.; HAPI Hisp. Am. Period. Index; Int. Bibliogr. Sociol.

JM/1010-6367
JAMAICAN HISTORICAL REVIEW, THE. **Added/Corp** Jamaica Historical Society. Vol. 1 (June 1945)-. Periodical. English. be (every eighteen months). $15.00 (two year). Jamaican Historical Society, 12-16 East Street, Institute of Jamaica, Kingston Jamaica. **Tel** (509)926-2217, FAX (509)926-2217. **ED** Dr. Carl Campbell. **LC** F1861; .J32. **DD** 972.92005. **Bk Rev**. **Ad Acc, Adv Mgr:** Anthont Gambrill, **Tel** (509)965-7280. **Circ:** 1,000.
Desc: An academic journal focusing on historical research in the Caribbean and Jamaica.
Ind/Abst Am. Hist. Life (1991-).

US/1046-2279
JAMES BURNSIDE BULLETIN OF RESEARCH, THE. ***Suspended.*** [James Burnside bull. res.]. **Added/Corp** Burnside Plantation (Bethlehem, Pa.). Vol. 1, No. 1 (1988)-Suspended. Periodical. English. sa. $12.00. Burnside Plantation Inc., Box 0559, Bethlehem PA 18016. **Tel** (215)868-5044. **ED** Valerie Livingston. **DD** 974. Index available. **Bk Rev**. **Pr Rev. Circ:** 400 (ctrl).

JA
JAPANESE JOURNAL OF AMERICAN STUDIES, THE. **Added/Corp** Amerika Gakkai (Japan). No. 1 (1981)-. Periodical. English. an (April). Y4500. University of Tokyo Center American Studies, Komaba Meguro-KU, Tokyo Japan. **ED** Yasuo Okada. **LC** E169.1; .J36. **DD** 973/.05. **Circ:** 1,200.

CN/0841-9787
JAVELIER (LA POCATI'ERE). (LE JAVELIER : BULLETIN DE LA SOCIETE HISTORIQUE DE LA COTE-DU-SUD.). [Javelier]. **Added/Corp** Societe Historique de la Cote-du-Sud. Vol. 1, No 1 (Jan. 1985)-. Periodical. French. ir (Published 3 or 4 times a yr.). 15.00Can$ (individual); 25.00Can$ (institutions). Societe Historique Cote du Sud, CP 937, La Pocatiere Quebec G0R 1Z0 Canada. **Tel** (418)856-2104. **DD** 971.4/7/005. **Ad Acc, Adv Mgr:** Michael D., **Tel** (418)856-2104. **Circ:** 350.
Desc: Questions and answers for genealogy and historical articles.

US/0449-4873
JEDNOTA ANNUAL FURDEK. English. an. First Catholic Slovak Union, 6611 Rockside Road, Cleveland OH 44131-2398. **LC** E184.S64; J39. ***Continues*** *Jednota Almanac Furdek, 0191-1929.*
Ind/Abst Am. Hist. Life (1975-1987).

CN/0700-916X
JERAGEH. Began publication in 197-. Periodical. Iranian. Progressive Iranian Study Group, PO Box 185, Station Outremont, Montreal Quebec H2V 4M8 Canada. **DD** 971/.004/915.

US
JERSEY JOURNEYS. English. Eight times a year. $25.00 institutions. New Jersey Historical Society, 230 Broadway, Newark NJ 07104. **Tel** (201)483-3939, FAX (201)483-1988.

US/0747-6876
JOHNSON COUNTY HISTORICAL SOCIETY JOURNAL. [Johnson Cty. Hist. Soc. j.]. **Added/Corp** Johnson County Historical Society (Ark.). Vol. 1, No. 1 (Jan. 1975)-. Periodical. English. Twice a year (April and October). $15.00. Johnson County Historical Society, PO Box 505, Clarksville AR 72830. **Tel** (501)754-2824. **ED** Marion Carter. **LC** F417.J6; J63. **DD** 976.7/33/005. **Circ:** 250 (ctrl).
Desc: History and genealogy of places, things and peoples of Johnson County, Arkansas.

GP
JOUGWA. Periodical. Creoles and Pidgins, French-based (French). mo. Jougwa, B P 1252, Pointe a Pitre Guadeloupe. **LC** F2066; .J68. **DD** 972.97/6/005. **UDC** 972.974.

CN/0383-6894
JOURNAL - CANADIAN ORAL HISTORY ASSOCIATION. [J. - Can. Oral Hist. Assoc.]. **Main/Corp** Canadian Oral History Association. Vol. 1 (1975/76)-. Periodical. English (French). sa. 25.00Can$ (institutions), 15.00Can$ (individuals); comes with membership. Canadian Oral History Association, PO Box 2064 Station D, Ottawa Ontario K1P 5W3 Canada. **Tel** (613)996-6996, FAX (613)995-6575. **ED** James Morrison. **LC** F1021; .C33. **DD** 971/.007/2. **Bk Rev. Circ:** 150 (ctrl). ***Absorbed*** *Canadian Oral History Association. Bulletin - Canadian Oral History Association., 0318-9600.*
Ind/Abst Am. Hist. Life (1975-); MLA Int. Bibl. Books Artic. Mod. Lang. Lit.

US/0736-4261
JOURNAL / FORT SMITH HISTORICAL SOCIETY, THE. **Main/Corp** Fort Smith Historical Society. Vol. 1, No. 1 (Sept. 1977)-. Periodical. English. sa (Apr. and Sept.). $15.00. Fort Smith Historical Society, 61 South 8th Street, Fort Smith Public Library, Fort Smith AR 72901. **Tel** (501)783-0229, FAX (501)782-8571. **ED** Amelia Martin. **LC** F419.F7; F725a. **DD** 976.7/36. Each issue contains an index to its own contents (no volume index)--loose. cum. index. **Bk Rev. Circ:** 500 (ctrl). available on an online database.
Desc: Local history articles, primary records, 100 year old news and inquiries.

US/0895-500X
JOURNAL - LEWIS COUNTY HISTORICAL SOCIETY. [J. - Lewis Cty. Hist. Soc.]. **Main/Corp** Lewis County Historical Society. **VFOAT** Journal of the Lewis County Historical Society. Vol. 1 (June 1966)-. English. an. $5.00. Lewis County Historical Society, PO Box 277, Lyons Falls NY 13368. **Tel** (315)348-8089. **DD** 974. ctrl circ.

US/0739-8069
JOURNAL - MIDDLE STATES COUNCIL FOR THE SOCIAL STUDIES (U.S.). **See** Social Sciences.

US/0739-005X
JOURNAL / NORTH LA. HIST. ASSOC. [J. - North La. Hist. Assoc.]. **Added/Corp** North Louisiana Historical Association. **VFOAT** North Louisiana Historical Association Journal. Vol. 1, No. 1 (Fall 1969)-. Periodical. English. Three times a year. $10.00. North Louisiana Historical Association, PO Box 6701, Shreveport LA 71136. **Tel** (318)797-5355, (318)797-5337. **ED** Dr. Alan Thompson. **LC** F369.N67a. ***Continues*** *Newsletter (North Louisiana Historical Association).*
Ind/Abst Am. Hist. Life (1970-).

JA/0914-8035
JOURNAL OF AMERICAN AND CANADIAN STUDIES, THE. **Added/Corp** Jochi Daigaku. Amerika Kanada Kenkyujo. **VFOAT** Amerika Kanada Kenkyu. No. 1 (Spring 1988)-. Periodical. English (Japanese). sa. Institute of American and Canadian Studies, Sophia University, 7-1 Kioicho, Chiyoda-ku, Tokyo 102 Japan. **LC** E169.1; J69. **DD** 973/.05.
Ind/Abst Am. Hist. Life (1988-); Can. Period. Index (19??-).

US/0191-1813
JOURNAL OF AMERICAN CULTURE. [J. Am. cult.]. **Added/Corp** Bowling Green State University. Popular Culture Association. Vol. 1 (Spring 1978)-. Periodical. English. qt. $45.00 (one year), $88.00 (two year). Popular Press Journals Area, Bowling Green State University, Bowling Green OH 43403. **Tel** (419)372-7866, (419)372-7865. **ED** Ray Browne, Russel Nye, and Tom Towers. **LC** E169.1; .J7. **DD** 973/.05. **Bk Rev. Ad Acc. Pr Rev. Circ:** 1,300 (ctrl). available on CD-ROM; available on microfilm and microfiche from University Microfilms International (UMI). Documents available from The Genuine Article, UMI Article Clearinghouse.
Desc: Discusses all aspects of American culture, including literature, television, film, and material culture.
Ind/Abst Abstr. Anthropol.; Acad. Search (July 1993-); Am. Hist. Life (1983-); Am. Bibliogr. Slavic East Europ. Stud.; Annu. Bibliogr. Engl. Lang. Lit.; Arts Humanit. Citation Index [Full Cov.]; Curr. Contents Arts Humanit.; Expand. Acad. Index (1989-); Film Lit. Index; Humanit. Index; Humanit. Source (Jul. 1993-); INFO-SOUTH Abstr.; Leis. Recreat. Tour. Abstr.; Mag. Search; MLA Int. Bibl. Books Artic. Mod. Lang. Lit.; Newsp. Period. Abstr. (1991-); Res. Alert [Full Cov.]; Soc. Plann. Policy Dev. Abstr.; Sociol. Abstr.; SportSearch.

US/0021-8723
JOURNAL OF AMERICAN HISTORY, THE. [J. Am. hist.]. **Added/Corp** Organization of American Historians. Mississippi Valley Historical Association. Vol. 51, No. 1 (June 1964)-. Periodical. English. Four times a year. $140.00 US; $155.00 other. Organization of American Historians, 112 North Bryan Street, Bloomington IN 47408. **Tel** (812)855-7311, FAX (812)855-0696. **ED** David Thelen. **LC** E171; .J87. Index available (annual index issue 4 of each volume). cum. index. **Bk Rev. Ad Acc. Pr Rev. Circ:** 12,000 (ctrl). available on microfilm and microfiche from University Microfilms International (UMI). Documents available from The Genuine Article, UMI Article Clearinghouse, UMI Article Clearinghouse. ***Continues*** *Mississippi Valley Historical Review, 0161-391X.*
Desc: All subscribers receive four issues each of the Journal, the OAH Newsletter, the OAH Magazine of History, and one copy of the Annual Meeting Program.
Ind/Abst Acad. Abstr. Full Text Elite (July 1990-); Acad. Abstr. (July 1990-); Acad. Ind. [Computer File] (1984-); Acad. Search (July 1990-); Am. Hist. Life (1954-); Am. Bibliogr. Slavic East Europ. Stud.; Annu. Bibliogr. Engl. Lang. Lit.; Arts Humanit. Citation Index [Full Cov.]; Book Rev. Digest; Book Rev. Index; Crim. Justice Abstr.; Curr. Index J. Educ. (March 1990); Expand. Acad. Index (1984-); Hist. Source (July 1990-); Humanit. Index; Index Period. Artic. Relat. Law; INFO-SOUTH Abstr.; Mag. Artic. Summar. Elite (July 1990-); Mag. Artic. Summar. Select (July 1990-); Mag. Artic. Summar. CD-ROM (July 1990-); Mag. Express (1986-) [Full Txt.]; Mag. Index Plus (1977-), (1964-); Mag. Search; Middle East Abstr. Index; MLA Int. Bibl. Books Artic. Mod. Lang. Lit.; Newsp. Period. Abstr. (1986-); Res. Alert [Full Cov.]; Resource/One Ondisc; Risk Abstr. (19??-19??); Sage Race Relat. Abstr.; Soc. Plann. Policy Dev. Abstr.; Soc. Sci. Source (Jul. 1990-); Soc. Sci. Cit. Index [Full Cov.]; Mag. Index (1977-)(1964-); U.S. Polit. Sci. Doc.; Vocat. Search (July 1990-); West. Hist. Q.; Women Stud. Abstr.

US/0271-5139
JOURNAL OF AMERICAN ROMANIAN CHRISTIAN LITERARY STUDIES. [J. Am. Rom. Christ. lit. stud.]. **Added/Corp** American Romanian Christian and Educational Corporation. Vol. 1 (1980)-. Periodical. English. an. $5.00 (includes Journal and newsletters). American Romanian Christian and Educational Corporation, Box 514, Buies Creek NC 27506. **LC** E184.R8; J68. **DD** 973/.0459.

UK/0021-8758
JOURNAL OF AMERICAN STUDIES. [J. Am. stud.]. **Added/Corp** British Association for American Studies. Vol. 1 (April 1967)-. Academic Scholarly Publication. English. Three times a year. $107.00 US, Canada & Mexico; £61.00 other. Cambridge University Press, The Edinburgh Building, Shaftesbury Road, Cambridge CB2 2RU United Kingdom. **Tel** 011 44 223 312393, FAX 011 44 223 325959. **(Subscription address:** Cambridge University Press / North America, 110 Midland Avenue, Port Chester NY 10573.**)** **ED** Michael Heale and Richard Gray. **LC** E151; .J6. **DD** 973/.05. **Bk Rev**. available on microfilm and microfiche from University Microfilms International (UMI). Documents available from The Genuine Article, UMI Article Clearinghouse. ***Supersedes*** *British Association for American Studies. Bulletin, 0524-5001.*
Desc: Publishes works by scholars from all over the world on American literature, history, institutions, politics, economics, geography and related subjects. A 'Notes and Comments' section provides a forum for shorter pieces and responses from readers to points made in articles or reviews. Also includes review essays, book reviews and biennially, a list of theses on American topics in progress at completed British universities.
Ind/Abst Abstr. Engl. Stud.; Acad. Abstr. Full Text Elite (July 1990-); Acad. Abstr. (July 1990-); Acad. Search (July 1990-); Am. Hist. Life (1960-); Annu. Bibliogr. Engl. Lang. Lit.; Arts Humanit. Citation Index [Full Cov.]; Book Rev. Index; Br. Humanit. Index; Curr. Contents Arts Humanit.; Expand. Acad. Index (1989-); Film Lit. Index; Humanit. Index; Humanit. Source (Jul. 1990-); INFO-SOUTH Abstr.; Int. Bibliogr. Sociol.; Int. Polit. Sci. Abstr.; Mag. Search; Middle East Abstr. Index; MLA Int. Bibl. Books Artic. Mod. Lang. Lit.; Newsp. Period. Abstr. (1989-); Res. Alert [Full Cov.]; Sage Race Relat. Abstr.; Soc. Sci. Cit. Index [Select. Cov.]; SportSearch; West. Hist. Q.; Women Stud. Abstr.

US/0021-9053
JOURNAL OF ARIZONA HISTORY, THE. [J. Ariz. hist.]. **Added/Corp** Arizona Historical Society. Arizona Pioneer's Historical Society. Vol. 6, No. 1 (Spring 1965)-. Periodical. English. Four times a year (Jan., Apr., July, Nov.). $25.00 US; $50.00 other. Arizona Historical Society, 949 East 2nd Street, Tucson AZ 85719. **Tel** (602)628-5774, FAX (602)628-5695. **ED** Bruce J. Dinges. **LC** F806; .A762. **DD** 979. Index available. **Bk Rev. Pr Rev. Circ:** 4,000. available on microfilm and microfiche from University Microfilms International (UMI). ***Continues*** *Arizoniana, 0883-346X.*
Desc: Focuses on the history of Southwest Arizona.
Ind/Abst Am. Hist. Life (1965-); West. Hist. Q.

US/1058-4617
JOURNAL OF BIG BEND STUDIES. [J. Big Bend stud.]. **Added/Corp** Sul Ross State University. Center for Big Bend Studies. Vol. 1 (Jan. 1989)-. Periodical. English. an. $15.00. Center for Big Bend Studies, Box C 71 / Sul Ross State University, Alpine TX 79832. **Tel** (915)837-8179, (915)837-8149. **ED** Earl H. Elam. **LC** WMLC 93/4314. **DD** 976. **CODEN** JBBSEZ. Index available. **Circ:** 500.

US/0886-5655
JOURNAL OF BORDERLANDS STUDIES. [J. borderl. stud.]. **Added/Corp** New Mexico State University. Dept. of Economics. Association of Borderlands Scholars. Vol. 1, No. 1 (Spring 1986)-. Periodical. English. Twice a year (May & Nov.). $25.00. Journal of Borderlands Studies, New Mexico State University, Economics Department, Box 30001, Las Cruces NM 88003. **Tel** (505)646-3113, FAX (505)646-6155. **ED** James T. Peach. **LC** F787; .J68; F1225.5; .J687. **DD** 303.48/273072. **Bk Rev**, (Qty: (10)). **Ad Acc. Circ:** 500.
Ind/Abst HAPI Hisp. Am. Period. Index.

CN/0021-9495
JOURNAL OF CANADIAN STUDIES. [J. Can. stud.]. **Added/Corp** Trent University. **VFOAT** Revue d'Etudes Canadiennes. Vol. 1 (May 1966)-. Academic Scholarly Publication. English (French). Four times a year. 28.00Can$ (individuals), 45.00Can$ (institutions) Canada; 32.00Can$ (individuals), 49.00Can$ (institutions) others. Journal of Canadian Studies, Trent University, Champlain College/ Nassau Campus, Peterborough Ontario K9J 7B8 Canada. **Tel** (705)748-1655, FAX (705)748-1246. **ED** Michele Lacombe (phone: (705)748-1279). **LC** F1001; .J68. **DD** 971/.005. **[CCC].** Index available (Spring). cum. index. **Bk Rev**, (Qty: 8-10). **Ad Acc**, **Adv Mgr:** J. Manson, **Tel** (709)748-1279. **Pr Rev. Circ:** 1,450. available on microfilm and microfiche from University Microfilms International (UMI); and Micromedia Limited. Documents available from The Genuine Article, UMI Article Clearinghouse.
Desc: Publishes a lively variety of scholarly articles, critical comments and book reviews on Canadian history, politics, economics, education, literature and the arts, public policy, communication, anthropology and sociology. Devoted to interdisciplinary Canadian studies and has established a solid international reputation for excellence since its founding in 1966.
Ind/Abst Abstr. Engl. Stud.; Acad. Abstr. Full Text Elite (Jan. 1992-); Acad. Abstr. (Jan. 1992-); Acad. Search (Jan. 1992-); Am. Hist. Life (1968-); Annu. Bibliogr. Engl. Lang. Lit.; ARTbibliogr. Mod. (1984-); Arts Humanit. Citation Index [Full Cov.]; Can. Index; Can. Legal Lit.; Can. Period. Index; Curr. Contents Arts Humanit.; Expand. Acad. Index (1989-); Humanit. Index; INFO-SOUTH Abstr.; Int. Bibliogr. Sociol.; Middle East Abstr. Index; MLA Int. Bibl. Books Artic. Mod. Lang. Lit.; Newsp. Period. Abstr. (1991-); Res. Alert [Full Cov.]; Romant. Move.; Sage Race Relat. Abstr.; Soc. Sci. Source (Jan. 1992-); Soc. Sci. Cit. Index [Select. Cov.]; West. Hist. Q.

BB/0047-2263
JOURNAL OF CARIBBEAN HISTORY, THE. [J. Caribb. hist.]. **Added/Corp** University of the West Indies (Cave Hill, Barbados). Dept. of History. University of the West Indies (Mona, Jamaica). Dept. of History. Vol. 1 (Nov. 1970)-. Periodical. English. sa (May and Nov). $12.50 Caribbean; $18.00 other. Journal of Caribbean History, Department of History, Cave Hill Barbados. **Tel** (809)425-1310, FAX (809)425-1327. **ED** Dr. Bridget Brereton (809)663-2060. **LC** F2155; .J68. **DD** 972.9/005. cum. index. **Bk Rev. Ad Acc. Circ:** 500. Documents available from The Genuine Article.
Desc: Publishes articles on aspects of Caribbean history, including the history of mainland territories in North, Central and South America as it relates to the Caribbean.
Ind/Abst Am. Hist. Life (1970-); Arts Humanit. Citation Index (19??-19??) [Full Cov.]; Curr. Contents Arts Humanit.; Res. Alert [Full Cov.].

US/0190-2008
JOURNAL OF CARIBBEAN STUDIES. [J. caribb. stud.]. **Added/Corp** Association of Caribbean Studies. Vol. 1 (Winter 1980)-. Academic Scholarly Publication. English (French, Spanish, Dutch and Portuguese). Three times a year. $200.00 Comes with Association of Caribbean Studies membership. Association of Caribbean Studies / Lexington, Kentucky, PO Box 22202, Lexington KY 40522. **Tel** (606)257-6966. **ED** O. R. Dathorne. **LC** F2155; .J72. **DD** 972.9/005. **[CCC].** Index available. cum. index. **Bk Rev. Circ:** 1,000.
Desc: Devoted to the inter-disciplinary scholarly study of the Caribbean.
Ind/Abst HAPI Hisp. Am. Period. Index; MLA Int. Bibl. Books Artic. Mod. Lang. Lit.

US/0146-2962
JOURNAL OF CHEROKEE STUDIES. See Ethnic Interests.

●US/1065-4690
JOURNAL OF CHICANA STUDIES. **VFOAT** Revista de Estudios Chicanas. (1992)-. Periodical. English. $10.00. Chicano Studies, Hart Hall, University of California, Davis CA 95616.

●US
JOURNAL OF CONFEDERATE HISTORY SERIES. Vol. 8 (1992)-. Monographic series. English. Price varies per volume. ***Continues*** *Journal of Confederate History.*

US/0091-9640
JOURNAL OF CURRITUCK COUNTY HISTORICAL SOCIETY, THE. **Main/Corp** Currituck County Historical Society. Yearbook Committee. Vol. 1 (1973)-. English. an (Publishes every four to five years). $25.00 US; $28.00 others. Currituck County Historical Society, PO Box 134, Currituck NC 27929. **Tel** (919)232-2311. **LC** F262.C95; C87a. **DD** 917.56/132/0305.

US
JOURNAL OF EAST TENNESSEE HISTORY. English. an (published in Jan.). $15.00. East Tennessee Historical Society, 500 West Church Avenue, Knoxville TN 37902. **Tel** (615)544-5732. **ED** Dr. Stephen Ash. **Bk Rev**, (Qty: 5). ctrl circ.

US/1058-2126
JOURNAL OF EAST TENNESSEE HISTORY, THE. [J. East Tenn. hist.]. **Added/Corp** East Tennessee Historical Society. No. 62 (1990)-. Periodical. English. an. $15.00. East Tennessee Historical Society, 500 West Church Avenue, Knoxville TN 37902. **Tel** (615)544-5732. **ED** R B Rosenburg, (615)974-2441. **LC** F442.1; .E14. **DD** 976. Each issue contains an index to its own contents (no volume index)--loose. **Bk Rev**, (Qty: 1). ***Continues*** *East Tennessee Historical Society. East Tennessee Historical Society's Publications, 0361-6193.*
Desc: Contains articles relating to all aspects of Tennessee history, as well as edited historical documents.
Ind/Abst Am. Hist. Life (1976-).

US/0090-1938
JOURNAL OF ERIE STUDIES. (THE JOURNAL OF ERIE STUDIES.). [J. Erie stud.]. **Added/Corp** Mercyhurst College. Erie County Historical Society. Vol. 1 (Spring 1972)-. Periodical. English. sa (Spring and Fall). $10.00. Erie County Historical Society, 417 State Street, Erie PA 16501. **Tel** (814)454-1813. **ED** Carl Lechnes. **LC** F159.E7; J6. **DD** 917.48/99/0305. Index available. cum. index. **Bk Rev**, (Qty: 2-4). **Circ:** 1,000.
Desc: This publication examines the culture of northwestern Pennsylvania area and those living in the Ohio, New York and Ontario sections, bordering on Lake Erie.

US/0273-4966
JOURNAL OF EVERETT & SNOHOMISH COUNTY HISTORY. ***Ceased.*** **VFOAT** Journal of Everett and Snohomish County History. No. 1 (Winter 1980-81)-(19??). Periodical. English. sa. Everett Public Library, 2702 Hoyt, Everett WA 98201. **UDC** 979.7.

US/0361-574X
JOURNAL OF HISTORIC MADISON, INC. OF WISCONSIN, THE. **Main/Corp** Historic Madison, Inc. V. 1- 1975-. English. an. $1.50. PO Box 4004, Madison WI 53711-4004. **LC** F589.M1; H55A. **DD** 977.5/84/005. **UDC** 977.5.

CN/0838-4711
JOURNAL OF INDIGENOUS STUDIES, THE. [J. indig. stud.]. **Added/Corp** Gabriel Dumont Institute of Native Studies and Applied Research. **VFOAT** Revue des Etudes Indigenes. Vol. 1, No. 1 (Winter 1989)-. Periodical. English (French). Twice a year (Jan., July). 33.00Can$ (institutions); 23.00Can$ (individuals). Dumont Institute of Native Studies, 121 Broadway Avenue East, Regina Saskatchewan S4N 0Z6 Canada. **Tel** (306)522-5691, FAX (306)565-0809. **ED** R. James McNinch (Editor's Address: 505 23rd Street East, Saskatoon, Saskatchewan S7K 4K7 Canada, phone: (306)934-4941). **DD** 971/.00497/00711. **Bk Rev. Pr Rev. Circ:** 300 (ctrl).
Desc: Provides the academic world with a voice on Indigenous issues which comes from the Indigenous community itself.
Ind/Abst Can. Period. Index (Winter 1991-).

US/0738-2030
JOURNAL OF INTERMOUNTAIN ARCHEOLOGY. See Archaeology.

UK/0022-216X
JOURNAL OF LATIN AMERICAN STUDIES. [J. Lat. Am. stud.]. Vol. 1 (May 1969)-. Academic Scholarly Publication. English. Three times a year. $129.00 US, Canada & Mexico; £74.00 other. Cambridge University Press, The Edinburgh Building, Shaftesbury Road, Cambridge CB2 2RU United Kingdom. **Tel** 011 44 223 312393, FAX 011 44 223 325959. **(Subscription address:** Cambridge University Press / North America, 110 Midland Avenue, Port Chester NY 10573.**) ED** Victor Bulmer-Thomas and Laurence Whitehead. **LC** F1401; .J69. **DD** 918/.005. **[CCC]. Pr Rev.** available on microfilm and microfiche from University Microfilms International (UMI). Documents available from The Genuine Article, UMI Article Clearinghouse.
Desc: Presents recent research in the field of Latin American studies in history, politics, international relations, sociology and social anthropology. Regular features include articles on contemporary themes, specially commissioned commentaries and an extensive section of book reviews. There is no commitment to any political viewpoint or ideology.
Ind/Abst ABC POL SCI; Abstr. Anthropol.; Acad. Abstr. Full Text Elite (July 1990-); Acad. Abstr. (July 1990-); Acad. Search (July 1990-); Am. Hist. Life (1969-); Anthropol. Lit.; Arts Humanit. Citation Index [Full Cov.]; Br. Humanit. Index; Curr. Contents Arts Humanit.; Curr. Contents Soc. Behav. Sci.; Curr. Geogr. Publ. (199?-); Expand. Acad. Index (1989-); Geogr. Abstr. Human Geogr.; HAPI Hisp. Am. Period. Index; Humanit. Source (Jul. 1990-); INFO-SOUTH Abstr.; Int. Bibliogr. Sociol.; Int. Dev. Abstr.; Int. Labour Doc.; Int. Polit. Sci. Abstr.; Mag. Search; Newsp. Period. Abstr. (1986-); PAIS Int. Print (1991-); Res. Alert [Full Cov.]; Rural Dev. Abstr.; Soc. Plann. Policy Dev. Abstr.; Soc. Sci. Source (Jul. 1990-); Soc. Sci. Cit. Index [Full Cov.]; Soc. Sci. Index; Soc. Sci. Index Fulltext (Nov. 1988-) [Full Txt.]; Sociol. Abstr. (?-?); West. Hist. Q.; World Agric. Econ.

US/0047-2581
JOURNAL OF MEXICAN AMERICAN HISTORY, THE. ***Ceased.*** [J. Mex. Am. hist.]. Vol. 1 (1970)-(1975). Periodical. English. an. Journal of Mexican American History, Box 13861, Santa Barbara CA 93107. **LC** E184.M5; J6. **DD** 917.3/06/6872. **UDC** 973.06; 972.
Ind/Abst Am. Hist. Life (1970-); Humanit. Index.

US/0022-2771
JOURNAL OF MISSISSIPPI HISTORY, THE. [J. Miss. hist.]. **Added/Corp** Mississippi. Dept. of Archives and History. Mississippi Historical Society. Vol. 1 (Jan. 1939)-. Periodical. English. Four times a year (Feb., May, Aug., Nov.). $15.00 (Comes with membership in the Mississippi Historical Society). Mississippi Historical Society, Box 571, Jackson MS 39205-0571. **Tel** (601)359-6850, FAX (601)359-6905. **ED** Kenneth McCarthy (editor's address: P. O. Box 5047, University of Mississippi, Hattiesburg, MS 39406, phone: (601)266-5170). **LC** F336; .J68. **DD** 976.2005. cum. index. **Bk Rev**, (Qty: 50). **Ad Acc**, **Adv Mgr:** Chrissy Wilson, **Tel** (601)359-6850. **Pr Rev.** available on microfilm and microfiche from University Microfilms International (UMI).
Desc: Articles and history of the Mississippi.
Ind/Abst Am. Hist. Life (1963-); Am. Humanit. Index; Annu. Bibliogr. Engl. Lang. Lit.; GeoRef.

US/0094-8039
JOURNAL OF MUSCLE SHOALS HISTORY, THE. **Added/Corp** Tennessee Valley Historical Society. (19??)-. Monographic series. English. ir. Price varies per volume. Tennessee Valley Historic Society, PO Box 149, Sheffield AL 35660. **Tel** (205)383-4409. **LC** F334.M85; J67. **DD** 976.1/9/005.

US/0022-2992
JOURNAL OF NEGRO HISTORY, THE. [J. Negro hist.]. **Added/Corp** Association for the Study of Negro Life and History, Inc. Vol. 1 (Jan. 1916)-. Academic Scholarly Publication. English. qt. $30.00 US and Canada; $32.00 other. Morehouse College Journal of Negro History, Box 20, Atlanta GA 30314. **Tel** (404)681-2800 ext. 2508, FAX (404)681-2650. **ED** Alton Hornsby Jr. **LC** E185; .J86. **DD** 325.260973; 301.451*. available on microfilm and microfiche from University Microfilms International (UMI).
Desc: A scholarly journal of African, Afro-American and Diasporan history and culture. Interdisciplinary, with history focus. Suitable for high school and collegiate levels and general readers.
Ind/Abst Acad. Abstr. Full Text Elite (July 1990-); Acad. Abstr. (July 1990-); Acad. Ind. [Computer File] (1987-); Acad. Search (July 1990-); Am. Hist. Life (1954-); Expand. Acad. Index (1987-); Gen. Period. Index (1987-); Hist. Source (July 1990-); Humanit. Index; Humanit. Source (Jul. 1990-); INFO-SOUTH Abstr.; Mag. Search; MLA Int. Bibl. Books Artic. Mod. Lang. Lit.; Romant. Move.; West. Hist. Q.

US
JOURNAL OF ORANGE COUNTY STUDIES. ***Suspended.*** **Added/Corp** University of California, Irvine. Department of History. California State University, Fullerton. Department of History. No. 1 (Fall 1988)-(1992). Periodical. English. Four times a year. Journal of Orange County Studies, History Department, California State University, Fullerton CA 92634. **Tel** (714)773-3474, (714)773-3170.
Ind/Abst Am. Hist. Life (1988-).

US/0022-3840
JOURNAL OF POPULAR CULTURE. [J. pop. cult.]. **Added/Corp** Modern Language Association of America. Popular Literature Section. Popular Culture Association. Midwest Modern Language Association. Popular Culture Section. Midwest Modern Language Association. Folklore Section. Vol. 1 (Summer 1967)-. Periodical. English. qt. $45.00 (one year), $88.00 (two year). Popular Press Journals Area, Bowling Green State University, Bowling Green OH 43403. **Tel** (419)372-7866, (419)372-7865. **LC** AP2; .J8325. **Bk Rev. Ad Acc. Circ:** 5,000. available on microfilm and microfiche from University Microfilms International (UMI); available on microfilm from Kraus Microform. Documents available from The Genuine Article, UMI Article Clearinghouse.
Ind/Abst Abstr. Engl. Stud.; Acad. Abstr. Full Text Elite (July 1990-); Acad. Abstr. (July 1990-); Acad. Ind. [Computer File] (1987-); Acad. Search (July 1990-); Am. Hist. Life (1967-); Am. Bibliogr. Slavic East Europ. Stud.; Annu. Bibliogr. Engl. Lang. Lit.; Appl. Soc. Sci. Index Abstr.; ARTbibliogr. Mod. (1984-); Arts Humanit. Citation Index [Full Cov.]; BHA : Biblio. Hist. Art; Book Rev. Index; Child. Lit. Abstr. (19??-); Commun. Abstr.; Curr. Contents Arts Humanit.; Curr. Geogr. Publ. (199?-); Expand. Acad. Index (1987-); Film Lit. Index; Humanit. Index; Humanit. Source (Jul. 1990-); Index Am. Period. Verse; INFO-SOUTH Abstr.; Int. Bibliogr. Sociol.; Lit. Crit. Regist.; Mag. Search; Middle East Abstr. Index; MLA Int. Bibl. Books Artic. Mod. Lang. Lit.; Music Index; Newsp. Period. Abstr. (1986-); Res. Alert [Full Cov.]; Romant. Move.; Sci. Fict. Fantasy Book Rev. Index; Soc. Sci. Cit. Index [Select. Cov.]; SportSearch; West. Hist. Q.; Women Stud. Abstr.

US/0363-1656
JOURNAL OF ROCKINGHAM COUNTY HISTORY AND GENEALOGY, THE. **Added/Corp** Rockingham County Historical Society. Vol.

1 (April 1976)-. Periodical. English. Twice a year (June, & Dec.). $10.00. Rockingham County Historical Society, Box 84, Wenworth NC 27375. **Tel** (919)951-2595. **ED** Robert W. Carter Jr. **LC** F262.R7; J67. **DD** 975.6/63/005. Index available. cum. index. **Circ:** 350 (ctrl).
Desc: Contains history and genealogical source materials of Rockingham County, North Carolina and adjacent areas.

US/0022-4383
JOURNAL OF SAN DIEGO HISTORY, THE. [J. S. Diego hist.]. **Added/Corp** San Diego Historical Society. Vol. 12, No. 1 (Jan. 1966)-. Periodical. English. qt (Jan., April, July, Dec.). $35.00 (basic membership), $60.00 (business membership). San Diego Historical Society, PO Box 81825, San Diego CA 92138. **Tel** (619)237-6203. **ED** Thomas L Scharf. **LC** F868.S15; J6. **DD** 979.4/98. Index available. cum. index. **Bk Rev. Circ:** 3,000 (ctrl). available on microfilm and microfiche from University Microfilms International (UMI). ***Continues*** *Times Gone By.*
Desc: Articles and photos relating to the history of San Diego and Baja, California from 1542 to the present time.
Ind/Abst Am. Hist. Life (1972-); Calif. Period. Index; Chicano Index; West. Hist. Q.

US/0022-4642
JOURNAL OF SOUTHERN HISTORY, THE. [J. south. hist.]. **Added/Corp** Southern Historical Association. Vol. 1 (Feb. 1935)-. Periodical. English. qt (4 issues). $35.00 institution; $25.00 individual; (includes Southern Historical Association membership). Southern Historical Association, Department of History, University of Georgia, Athens GA 30602. **Tel** (706)542-8848. **ED** John B. Boles. **LC** F206; .J68. **DD** 975.005. Index available (bound in Nov. issue). cum. index. **Bk Rev. Ad Acc. Circ:** 4,200 (ctrl). available on microfilm and microfiche from University Microfilms International (UMI). Documents available from The Genuine Article, UMI Article Clearinghouse.
Desc: Contains four research articles, edited documents or historical notes. Also, book reviews and news of historical interest to Southern history.
Ind/Abst Acad. Abstr. Full Text Elite (July 1990-); Acad. Abstr. (July 1990-); Acad. Ind. [Computer File] (1987-); Acad. Search (July 1990-); Am. Hist. Life (1954-); Annu. Bibliogr. Engl. Lang. Lit.; Arts Humanit. Citation Index [Full Cov.]; Book Rev. Index; Curr. Contents Arts Humanit.; Expand. Acad. Index (1987-); Hist. Source (July 1990-); Humanit. Index; Humanit. Source (Jul. 1990-); INFO-SOUTH Abstr.; Mag. Search; Newsp. Period. Abstr. (1991-); Ref. Sources; Res. Alert [Full Cov.]; Soc. Sci. Cit. Index [Select. Cov.]; West. Hist. Q.; Writ. Am. Hist.

US/0739-1943
JOURNAL OF SOUTHWEST GEORGIA HISTORY, THE. [J. southwest Ga. hist.]. **Added/Corp** Thronateeska Heritage Foundation. Vol. 1 (Fall 1983)-. Periodical. English. an (Dec.). $20.00. Thronateeska Heritage Foundation, 100 Roosevelt Avenue, Albany State College, Albany GA 31701. **Tel** (912)430-4870. **ED** Lee W. Formwalt. **LC** F286; .J8. **DD** 975.8/005. Index available (bound in all issues). **Bk Rev. Ad Acc. Pr Rev. Circ:** 400.
Desc: A continuous look at the history and culture of southwest Georgia, from the native American past through the present.
Ind/Abst Am. Hist. Life (1983-).

US/1048-2431
JOURNAL OF TEXAS CATHOLIC HISTORY AND CULTURE / TEXAS CATHOLIC HISTORICAL SOCIETY, THE.
See Religion and Theology-Catholicism.

US/0898-4212
JOURNAL OF THE ABRAHAM LINCOLN ASSOCIATION. [J. Abraham Lincoln Assoc.]. **Added/Corp** Abraham Lincoln Association (Springfield, Ill.). Vol. 9 (1987)-. Periodical. English. sa (2 issues). $25.00 (one year), $45.00 (two year). University of Illinois Press, 1325 South Oak Street, Champaign IL 61820. **Tel** (217)333-0950, FAX (217)244-8082. **ED** Thomas F. Schwartz. **LC** E457.1; .A27a. **DD** 973.7/092/4. **[CCC].** Index available. cum. index. **Ad Acc. Circ:** 450. available on microfilm from University Microfilms International (UMI). ***Continues*** *Abraham Lincoln Association (Springfield, Ill.). Papers of the Abraham Lincoln Association, 0195-914X.*
Desc: Devoted to Lincoln scholarship.
Ind/Abst Am. Hist. Life (1979-).

US/0276-7449
JOURNAL OF THE ALLEGHENIES. **Added/Corp** Institute of Allegheny Life and Culture. Council of the Alleghenies. (Spring 1963)-. Periodical. English. an (June). $10.00 (individuals); $25.00 (supporting); $50.00 (sustaining). Council of the Alleghenies, PO Box 514, Frostburg MD 21532. **Tel** (301)689-8907. **ED** Mrs. Harold J. Cordts. **LC** F217.A3; J68. **DD** 974.8/7/005. Index available. cum. index. **Bk Rev. Circ:** 200.
Desc: Reflects purposes of the Council of the Alleghenies to preserve, develop, and share the rich traditions, history and folk culture of the Alleghenies.

US/0587-5064
JOURNAL OF THE AMERICAN STUDIES ASSOCIATION OF TEXAS. [J. Am. Stud. Assoc. Tex.]. **Main/Corp** American Studies Association of Texas. **Added/Corp** Wayland Baptist College. Vol. 1 (1970)-. Academic Scholarly Publication. English. an (Nov.). $15.00 US college and university libraries; $17.00 other. American Studies Association of Texas, Box 97240, Baylor University, Waco TX 76798. **Tel** (817)755-2710, FAX (817)755-1571. **ED** J. R. LeMaster, (phone: (817)755-1768). **LC** E169.1; .A493. **DD** 917.3/03/05. **Bk Rev**, (Qty: 25). **Ad Acc, Adv Mgr:** Lois E. Myers, **Tel** (817)755-3437. **Pr Rev. Circ:** 400 (ctrl).
Desc: Scholarly articles on American life and literature, both applied and theoretical.
Ind/Abst Am. Hist. Life (1988-); Am. Humanit. Index (-199?); Annu. Bibliogr. Engl. Lang. Lit.; MLA Int. Bibl. Books Artic. Mod. Lang. Lit.

US/1064-2595
JOURNAL OF THE BRAXTON HISTORICAL SOCIETY. **Added/Corp** Braxton Historical Society (W. Va.). Vol. 1, No. 1 (Mar. 1973)-. Periodical. English. qt. $3.00. Braxton Historical Society, Rt 1 Box 14, Exchange WV 26619. **Tel** (304)765-2415.

CN/0847-4478
JOURNAL OF THE CANADIAN HISTORICAL ASSOCIATION. [J. Can. Hist. Assoc.]. **Added/Corp** Canadian Historical Association. Canadian Historical Association. Meeting. **VFOAT** Revue de la Societe Historique du Canada. New Series Vol. 1 (1990)-. English (French). Free to members. Canadian Historical Association, 395 Wellington Street, Ottawa Ontario K1A 0N3 Canada. **Tel** (613)233-7885. Documents available from The Genuine Article. ***Continues*** *Canadian Historical Association. Meeting. Historical Papers, 0068-8878.*
Ind/Abst Am. Hist. Life (1990-); Arts Humanit. Citation Index [Full Cov.]; Can. Period. Index (19??-); Curr. Contents Arts Humanit.; Res. Alert [Full Cov.].

US
JOURNAL OF THE CHEROKEE STRIP. **Added/Corp** Association of Sons and Daughters of the Cherokee Strip Pioneers. (Sept. 1959)-. Periodical. English. an (Sept.). $7.00. Journal of the Cherokee Strip, PO Box 465, Enid OK 73701. **LC** F702.C42; J68a. **DD** 976.6.

US/0731-3020
JOURNAL OF THE CHESTERFIELD HISTORICAL SOCIETY OF VIRGINIA. **Added/Corp** Chesterfield Historical Society of Virginia. (1988)-. English. be. Chesterfield Historical Society of Virginia, PO Box 40, Courthouse Square, Chesterfield County VA 23832.

US/0275-1275
JOURNAL OF THE EARLY REPUBLIC. [J. early Repub.]. **Added/Corp** Society for Historians of the Early American Republic. Vol. 1, No. 1 (Spring 1981)-. Periodical. English. Four times a year. $40.00. Purdue University / Department of History, 1358 University Hall, West Lafayette IN 17907. **Tel** (317)494-4135. **ED** Ralph D. Gray. **LC** E164; .J68. **DD** 973/.05. Index available. **Bk Rev. Ad Acc. Pr Rev. Circ:** 1,200. available on microfilm and microfiche from University Microfilms International (UMI). Documents available from UMI Article Clearinghouse.
Desc: Devoted to the history and culture of the US during the early National Period, 1789-1848.
Ind/Abst Acad. Search (July 1993-); Am. Hist. Life (1981-); Expand. Acad. Index (1989-); Hist. Source (July 1993-); Humanit. Index; Humanit. Source (Jul. 1993-); INFO-SOUTH Abstr.; Mag. Search; Newsp. Period. Abstr. (1990-); West. Hist. Q.

US/8755-3805
JOURNAL OF THE JOHANNES SCHWALM HISTORICAL ASSOCIATION, INC. **Added/Corp** Johannes Schwalm Historical Association. Vol. 2, No. 1 (1981)-. Periodical. English. an. Free to members; $20.00 membership. Johannes Schwalm Historical Association, PO Box 99, Pennsauken NJ 08110. **Tel** (609)663-8292. **ED** R. Carl Barth. **LC** F160.G3; J63. **DD** 929/.1/08931073. **Bk Rev. Circ:** 5-800 (ctrl). ***Continues*** *Johannes Schwalm, The Hessian, 8755-3791.*

US/0023-7477
JOURNAL OF THE LANCASTER COUNTY HISTORICAL SOCIETY. [J. Lanc. Cty. Hist. Soc.]. **Main/Corp** Lancaster County (PA.) Historical Society. (1956)-. Periodical. English. Four times a year. $30.00 (regular); $40.00 (family); $75.00 (contributing); $100.00 (benefactor). Lancaster County Historical Society, 230 North President Avenue, Lancaster PA 17603-3125. **Tel** (717)392-4633. **ED** John W. W. Loose. **LC** F157.L2; L5. **DD** 974. Index available. cum. index. **Bk Rev. Ad Acc, Adv Mgr:** Denise Baer, **Tel** (717)393-8880. **Circ:** 1,400. ***Continues*** *Historical Papers and Addresses of the Lancaster County Historical Society, 0364-2399.*
Ind/Abst Am. Hist. Life (1963-); ARTbibliogr. Mod.; Recent. Publ. Artic.; Writ. Am. Hist.

US
JOURNAL OF THE LINCOLN ASSASSINATION. (19??)-. Periodical. English. Three times a year. $10.00 US; $11.00 other. Autograph Press, PO Box 241579, Los Angeles CA 90024. **Tel** (310)673-1908. **ED** Frederick Hatch. Index available. **Bk Rev**, (Qty: 3). **Ad Acc. Circ:** 100.
Desc: Publishes new and reprint articles on subject, reviews books and films, lists current event notices, and includes short biographies of participants.

US/0887-543X
JOURNAL OF THE LYCOMING COUNTY HISTORICAL SOCIETY, THE. **Added/Corp** Lycoming County Historical Society (Lycoming County, Pa.). (19??)-. Periodical. English. an. $3.25 US; $3.36 Canada; $3.60 Pan America; $3.70 other. Lycoming County Historical Society, 858 West 4th Street, Williamsport PA 17701. **Tel** (717)326-3326, FAX (717)326-3689. **ED** Stephanie R. Zebrowski. **DD** 974. Index available. cum. index. **Ad Acc. Circ:** 1,100. ***Continues*** *Lycoming Historical Society. Journal.*
Desc: Articles relating to the history of Lycoming County, Pennsylvania.
Ind/Abst Am. Hist. Life.

●CN/1188-164X
JOURNAL OF THE MILITARY HISTORY SOCIETY OF MANITOBA. See Military and Defense.

US/0196-2019
JOURNAL OF THE MODOC COUNTY HISTORICAL SOCIETY. **Main/Corp** Modoc County Historical Society. No. 1 (1979)-. Periodical. English. an. $9.50. Modoc County Historical Society, 600 South Main Street, Museum, Alturas CA 96101. **Tel** (916)233-2944. **LC** F868.M6; M6a. **DD** 979.4/23/005. Index available. cum. index. **Circ:** 2,500.
Desc: Deals with various aspects of Modoc County's history.

US/0548-4987
JOURNAL OF THE NEW HAVEN COLONY HISTORICAL SOCIETY. [J. New Haven Colony Hist. Soc.]. **Main/Corp** New Haven Colony Historical Society, New Haven. Vol.1 (Mar. 1952)-. Periodical. English. ir (Spring, Fall). $15.00. New Haven Colony Historical Society, 114 Whitney Avenue, New Haven CT 06510. **Tel** (203)562-4183. **ED** John O.C. McCrillis. **LC** F91; .N4. **DD** 974.6/2/0062. **Circ:** 800 (ctrl). ***Supersedes*** *New Haven Colony Historical Society. News Sheet.*
Desc: Various articles of and about New Haven and the colony New Haven, historical and present.

US/0894-8410
JOURNAL OF THE SOUTHWEST. [J. Southwest]. **Added/Corp** University of Arizona. Southwest Center. Vol. 29, No. 1 (Spring 1987)-. Periodical. English. Four times a year (Mar., June, Sept., Dec.). $18.00 individuals; $24.00 institutions. University of Arizona / Tucson, 1052 North Highland Avenue, Tucson AZ 85721. **Tel** (602)621-2484, FAX (602)621-9424. **ED** Joseph C. Wilder. **LC** F806; .A69. **DD** 979/.005. Index available (4th iss. in Dec.). **Bk Rev**, (Qty: 40). **Ad Acc. Pr Rev. Circ:** 1,200 (ctrl). available on microfilm and microfiche from University Microfilms International (UMI). Documents available from The Genuine Article. ***Continues*** *Arizona and the West, 0004-1408.*
Desc: Multidisciplinary journal of American Southwest and Mexican northwest.
Ind/Abst Am. Hist. Life (1963-);(1987-); Annu. Bibliogr. Engl. Lang. Lit. (1987-); Arts Humanit. Citation Index [Full Cov.]; Chicano Index; MLA Int. Bibl. Books Artic. Mod. Lang. Lit.; Recent. Publ. Artic. (1987-); Res. Alert [Full Cov.]; Soc. Sci. Cit. Index [Select. Cov.]; West. Hist. Q.; Women Stud. Abstr. (1987-); Writ. Am. Hist. (1987-).

US/0095-3911
JOURNAL OF THE ST. CLAIR COUNTY HISTORICAL SOCIETY. **Main/Corp** Saint Clair County (Ill.). (19??)-. English. an. Price varies. St Clair County Historical Society, 20 Sherwood Forest, Belleville IL 62223. **Tel** (618)234-0600. **LC** F547.S2; S23a. **DD** 977.3.

US/0022-5169
JOURNAL OF THE WEST. [J. West]. Vol. 1 (July 1962)-. Periodical. English. qt. $48.00 (institutions), $38.00 (individuals) US; $56.00 (institutions), $46.00 (institutions) other. Journal of the West Inc., PO Box 1009, 1531 Yuma, Manhattan KS 66502. **Tel** (913)539-1888. **ED** Robin Higham. **LC** F591; .J65. **CODEN** JNLWA7. Index available. cum. index. **Bk Rev**, (Qty: 200). **Ad Acc, Adv Mgr:** Carol Williams. **Pr Rev. Circ:** 4,500 (ctrl). Documents available from The Genuine Article, UMI Article Clearinghouse.
Desc: An illustrated journal devoted to topics of interest in Western American history. Issues examine in-depth factors critical to the growth and development of the United States.
Ind/Abst Acad. Abstr. Full Text Elite (July 1990-); Acad. Abstr. (July 1990-); Acad. Ind. [Computer File] (1987-); Acad. Search (July 1990-); Am. Hist. Life (1963-); Annu. Bibliogr. Engl. Lang. Lit.; Arts Humanit. Citation Index

[Full Cov.]; Expand. Acad. Index (1987-); GeoRef; Humanit. Index; INFO-SOUTH Abstr.; Mag. Artic. Summar. Elite (July 1990-); Mag. Artic. Summar. Select (July 1990-); Mag. Artic. Summar. CD-ROM (July 1990-); Mag. Search; Newsp. Period. Abstr. (1991-); Ref. Sources; Res. Alert [Full Cov.]; Soc. Sci. Cit. Index [Select. Cov.]; SportSearch; West. Hist. Q.; Women Stud. Abstr.; Writ. Am. Hist.

US/0270-4765
JOURNAL OF THE WEST VIRGINIA HISTORICAL ASSOCIATION, THE. [J. W. Va. Hist. Assoc.]. **Main/Corp** West Virginia Historical Association. (19??)-. Periodical. English. an. $2.00. Marshall University / Historical Association, West Virginia Historical Association, Huntington WV 25101. **Tel** (304)696-2725. **LC** F241; .W643a. **DD** 975.4/005.
Ind/Abst Am. Hist. Life (1977-).

US/0092-9549
JOURNAL - OSWEGO COUNTY HISTORICAL SOCIETY. (JOURNAL.). **Main/Corp** Oswego County Historical Society. 33rd-1972-. English. an. Oswego County Historical Society, Richardson-Bates House, 135 East 3rd Street, Oswego NY 13126. **LC** F127.O91; O88A. **DD** 917.47/67/0305. **UDC** 974.7. ***Continues*** *Oswego County Historical Society. Yearbook.*
Ind/Abst Am. Hist. Life.

CN/0081-4369
JOURNAL - STANSTEAD COUNTY HISTORICAL SOCIETY. **Main/Corp** Stanstead Historical Society. V. 1- 1965-. Periodical. English. be. $15.00. Stanstead Historical Society, Stanstead Quebec J0B 3E0 Canada. **Tel** (819)876-7322. **ED** Liz Getty. **LC** F1054.S7; S73A. **DD** 971.4/67/005. **UDC** 971.4. **Circ:** 300 (ctrl).
Desc: Primarily a history of the county of Stanstead Quebec and the villages and towns around it. Also serves as a record of the past two years of the activities of the Society.

IO
JURNAL STUDI AMERIKA / UNIVERSITAS INDONESIA, PROGRAM PASCASARJANA KAJIAN WILAYAH AMERIKA. **Added/Corp** Universitas Indonesia. Program Pascasarjana Kajian Wilayah Amerika. Vol. 1, No. 1 (Jan. 1991)-. Periodical. English (Indonesian). sa. $20.00. Jurnal Studi Amerika, American Studies Graduate Program, UI, JL Salemba Raya 4, Jakarta 10430 Indonesia.

CN/0820-8417
KALFOU. [Kalfou]. V. 1, No. 1, (Dec. 1982)-. Periodical. French. mo. $10.00 Canada, $15.00 others. Kalfou, C P 475 Succursale A Boul St-Joseph, Hull Quebec J8Y 6P2 Canada. **DD** 972.94/06/05. **UDC** 972.94.

US/0738-9736
KANHISTIQUE. (KANHISTIQUE : KANSAS HISTORY AND ANTIQUES.). [Kanhistique]. Vol. 1, No. 1 (May 1975)-. Periodical. English. mo. $15.89 (includes tax) Kansas; $15.00 other. Kanhistique, Box 7, Ellsworth KS 67439. **Tel** (913)472-3103, FAX (913)472-3268. **ED** Edna Marie Lee. **Ad Acc. Circ:** 2,800.
Desc: Covers Kansas history and antiques.
Ind/Abst Am. Hist. Life.

US/0896-8292
KANSAS CITY MAGAZINE & THE TOWN SQUIRE. **VFOAT** Kansas City Magazine and the Town Squire; Kansas City; Kansas City Magazine. Vol. 12, No. 9 (Sept. 1987)-. Periodical. English. mo. Sutherland Magazines Inc, 13750 San Pedro Avenue, San Antonio TX 78232-4353. **DD** 917. ***Formed by the union of*** *Kansas City Town Squire* ***and*** *Kansas City Magazine, 0745-1830.*

●US
KANSAS HERITAGE. (1993)-. English. qt. Free to members; $25.00 (membership). Kansas State Historical Society, 120 West 10th Street, Topeka KS 66612. **Tel** (913)296-3251, (913)296 2623, FAX (913)296-1005. **ED** Bobbie Pray. ***Continues*** *Kansas State Historical Society Mirror.*

US/0149-9114
KANSAS HISTORY. [Kansas hist.]. **Added/Corp** Kansas State Historical Society. Vol. 1 (Spring 1978)-. Periodical. English. qt. Free to members; $25.00 (membership). Kansas State Historical Society, 120 West 10th Street, Topeka KS 66612. **Tel** (913)296-3251, (913)296 2623, FAX (913)296-1005. **ED** Virgil Dean. **LC** F681; .K177. **DD** 978.1/005. Index available. cum. index. **Bk Rev. Pr Rev. Circ:** 5,000. available on microfilm and microfiche from University Microfilms International (UMI). ***Supersedes*** *Kansas Historical Quarterly, 0022-8621.*
Desc: History and prehistory of Kansas and the Central Plains.
Ind/Abst Am. Hist. Life (1978-); Annu. Bibliogr. Engl. Lang. Lit.; Soc. Work Abstr. (?-?); West. Hist. Q.

CK
KATXA-TA. No. 1 (July/Sept. 1976)-. Periodical. Spanish. qt. Apartado Aereo 92099, Bogota Colombia. **LC** F2269; .K37. **DD** 986.1/004/98. **UDC** 986.1.

BL
KENKYU REPOTO - SAN PAURO JIMBUN KAGAKU KENKYUJO. **Main/Corp** Centro de Estudos Nipo-Brasileiros. Japanese (Japanese). Centro de Estudos Nipo-Brasileiros, rua Sao Joaquim 381, C Postal, 30023 Sao Paulo Brasil. **LC** F2501; .C4A. **UDC** 981(=956).

US/0890-8362
KENTUCKY EXPLORER, THE. [Ky. explor.]. (198?)-. Periodical. English. Ten times a year. $15.00. The Kentucky Explorer, PO Box 227, Jackson KY 41339. **Tel** (606)666-5060. **ED** Charles Hayes. **DD** 976. Index available. **Ad Acc. Circ:** 9,500.
Desc: History magazine for the "Bluegrass State."

US
KEPI, THE. 1st Issue (Apr. 1983)-. Periodical. English. bm. $18.00. Kepi, 12115 Magnolia Boulevard, PO Box 107, North Hollywood CA 91600. **LC** E461; .K46. **DD** 973.7/05. **UDC** 973.7.

US/0451-9949
KIRKWOOD HISTORICAL REVIEW. [Kirkw. hist. rev.]. Vol. 1 (March 1962)-. Periodical. English. qt. Kirkwood Historical Society, PO Box 3702, Kirkwood MO 63122. **DD** 977. **UDC** 977.8.

CN/0824-4650
KONGRES POLONII KANADYJSKIEJ. (KONGRES POLONII KANADYJSKIEJ : REPORT.). **Main/Corp** Canadian Polish Congress. Meeting. 1980/1982-. Polish (English). be. Canadian Polish Congress, 288 Roncesvalles Avenue, Toronto Ontario M6R 2L7 Canada. **DD** 971/.0049185. **UDC** 971(=84); 908.71(=84). ***Continues*** *Canadian Polish Congress. Meeting. Biuletyn Informacyjny, 0824-4642.*

CN/0318-9678
KONGRES UKRAJINCIV KANADY. (KONGRES UKAINTSIV KANADY.). [Kongr. ukr. kan.]. **Main/Corp** Ukrainian Canadian Congress. Began with 1943 issue. Periodical. Ukrainian (English). te. Ukrainian Canadian Committee, 456 Main Street, Winnipeg Manitoba R3B 1B6 Canada. **Tel** (204)947-3882. **DD** 971/.004/91791. **UDC** 971(=83).
Desc: Minutes of congress, speeches at banquets, etc.

US/0732-7250
KORIAN-OMERIKAN. **VFOAT** Korean-American. V. 1- No. 1- (1982)-. Periodical. Korean (English). qt. $6.00. Korean-American Community Services, 4300 North California, Chicago IL 60618. **LC** E184.K6; K656. **UDC** 973(=957); 908.73(=957).

PE
KOTOSH / INSTITUTO NACIONAL DE CULTURA - FILIAL HUANUCO. V. 1, No. 1, (August 1976)-. Periodical. Spanish (Spanish). an. $2.00. Institute Nacional de Cultura, Apartado 201, Huanuco Huanuco Peru. **LC** F3451.H8; K67. **DD** 985/.2201/05. **UDC** 930.85(85); 908.85.

US/0271-5414
LANDMARK (EL MONTE), THE. (THE LANDMARK.). **Added/Corp** El Monte Historical Society. (19??)-. Periodical. English. Four times a year. $10.00. El Monte Historical Society, 3150 North Tyler Avenue, El Monte CA 91731. **Tel** (818)444-3813. **ED** Alvin Fickewirth and Elizabeth Van Note. **Circ:** 475. available on diskette.

US/0272-1384
LANDMARKS OBSERVER. [Landmarks obs.]. **Added/Corp** Greater Portland Landmarks, Inc. (19??)-. Periodical. English. Six times a year. $25.00 Comes with Greater Portland Landmarks membership. Greater Portland Landmarks Inc, 165 State Street, Portland ME 04101. **Tel** (207)774-5561. **ED** Tom Verde and Deborah Andrews. **Bk Rev. Ad Acc. Circ:** 1,500 (ctrl).
Desc: Publication of non-profit historic preservation organization serving greater Portland area.
Ind/Abst Am. Hist. Life; Avery Index Archit. Period. Suppl. Colum. Univ.

US/0734-4007
LANDMARKS (SEATTLE, WASH.). ***Suspended.*** (LANDMARKS.). Vol. 1, No. 1 (Summer 1981)-Suspended with Vol. 4, No. 4. Periodical. English. qt. $10.00. 835 Securities Building, Seattle WA 98108. **Tel** (206)622-3538. **ED** Barbara Krohn. **UDC** 979. **Bk Rev. Ad Acc. Circ:** 13,000 (ctrl). ***Continues*** *Washington Landmarks.*
Desc: Articles on history of Pacific Northwest and historical buildings; also humanities in general.
Ind/Abst Key Word Index Wildl. Res.

US/0458-7227
LANE COUNTY HISTORIAN. [Lane Cty. hist.]. **Added/Corp** Lane County Pioneer Historical Society (Or.) Lane County Historical Society (Or.). (Feb. 1956)-. Periodical. English. Three times a year. comes with membership. Lane County Historical Society, Box 11532, Eugene OR 97440. **Tel** (503)343-4496. **ED** Kenneth T. Metzler. **LC** F882.L2; L34. **DD** 979.5/31/005. cum. index. **Bk Rev. Circ:** 485 (ctrl).
Desc: Lane County, Oregon history, personal, family, business and community information.
Ind/Abst Am. Hist. Life.

US/1045-1013
LAS AMERICAS. [Am.]. Vol. 1, No. 1 (May 26, 1989)-. Periodical. English. bw. Free. Constance Freeman, 670 Glebe Road/Suite B-3, Arlington VA 23203. **DD** 975.

US/0890-7218
LASA FORUM / LATIN AMERICAN STUDIES ASSOCIATION. [LASA forum]. **Added/Corp** Latin American Studies Association. **VAT** Latin American Studies Association Forum. Vol. 14, No. 2 (Summer 1983)-. Periodical. English (Spanish). qt. $30.00 surface mail; $45.00 air mail. Latin American Studies Association, 946 William Pitt Union, University of Pittsburgh, Pittsburgh PA 15260. **Tel** (412)648-7929, FAX (412)624-7145. **ED** Reid Reading. **LC** F1401; .L318. **DD** 980/.005. **Ad Acc. Circ:** 2,500. ***Continues*** *LASA Newsletter.*
Desc: Official news organ of LASA. Also publishes articles of interest to Latin American studies specialists.

GW/0176-2818
LATEINAMERIKA. **Added/Corp** Institut fuer Iberoamerika-Kunde. No. 1 (May 1984)-. Periodical. German (summaries and/or abstracts in Spanish). tq. Institut Iberoamerika-Kunde, Alsterglacis 8, 2000 Hamburg 36 Germany.
Ind/Abst PAIS Int. Print.

GW/0343-3781
LATEINAMERIKA STUDIEN. [Lateinam.-Stud.]. 1-. Periodical. German (summaries and/or abstracts in Spanish and Portuguese). Wilhelm Fink Verlag, Ohmstrasse 5, D 80802 Munich Germany. **Tel** 011 49 89 348017, 348018. **LC** F1401; .L3215. **UDC** 980=6; 908.8=6.

US/0736-9700
LATIN AMERICA AND CARIBBEAN CONTEMPORARY RECORD. [Lat. Am. Caribb. contemp. rec.]. Vol. 1 (1982)-. English. an. $380.00. Holmes and Meier Publishers Inc, 160 Broadway, Suite 900 East Wing, New York NY 10038. **Tel** (212)374-0100. **LC** F1401; .L3253. **DD** 980/.03. **Ad Acc.**

US
LATIN AMERICA COMMENTARY. (1990)-. Periodical. English. mo. $20.00 (individual), $40.00 (institution). Latin America Commentary, Box 227, Malta IL 60150.

US/0092-4148
LATIN AMERICA (WASHINGTON). (LATIN AMERICA.). [Lat. Am.]. (1967)-. English. an. $4.50. Stryker-Post Publications, PO Drawer 1200, Harpers Ferry WV 25425. **Tel** (800)995-1400. **ED** Luis E. Aguilar. **LC** F1401; .L3252. **DD** 980. ctrl circ.
Desc: One of seven titles focusing on current events. This lively reference tool addresses social, economic, political and controversial issues.

US
LATIN AMERICAN HISTORICAL DICTIONARIES. (1967)-. Monographic series. English. ir. Price varies per volume. Scarecrow Press Inc., 52 Liberty Street, PO Box 4167, Metuchen NJ 08840. **Tel** (908)548-8600, (800)537-7107.

US/0741-3378
LATIN AMERICAN ISSUES. [Lat. Am. issues]. **Added/Corp** Allegheny College (Meadville, Pa.) University of Akron. Dept. of Urban Studies. Vol. 1, No. 1 (1984)-. Monographic series. English (Spanish). ir. Price varies per volume. Latin American Issues, Allegheny College, PO Box 63, Meadville PA 16335. **Tel** (814)332-3349. **ED** Frank Cajka, Frank Kendrick, Sheldon Liss, and Giles Wayland-Smith. **LC** F1401; .L328. **DD** 980/.005. ctrl circ.
Desc: A monograph series for works in the social sciences and the humanities, with Latin America and the Caribbean as the central focus.

US/1050-2351
LATIN AMERICAN POPULATION HISTORY BULLETIN. [Lat. Am. popul. hist. bull.]. **Added/Corp** University of Minnesota. Dept. of History. Conference on Latin American History. Committee on Demographic History. International Union for the Scientific Study of Population. Committee on Historical Demography. **VFOAT** LAPH Bulletin. No. 16 (Fall 1989)-. Bulletin. English (French, Portuguese and Spanish). University of Minnesota Department of History, Prof. Kim Mulholland, Minneapolis MN 55455. **Tel** (612)373-2700. **DD** 980. ***Continues*** *Latin American Population History Newsletter, 0887-6002.*
Ind/Abst Popul. Index.

US/0023-8791
LATIN AMERICAN RESEARCH REVIEW. [Lat. Am. res. rev.]. **Added/Corp** Latin American Studies Association. Vol. 1 (Fall 1965)-. Periodical. English (Spanish and Portuguese). tq (3 issues). $27.00 (institutions), $20.00 (individuals) Latin

America; $42.00 (institutions), $27.00 (individuals) other; $20.00 US; $18.00 Latin America (students). Latin American Institute, University of New Mexico, 801 Yale Northeast, Albuquerque NM 87131. **Tel** (505)277-5985, FAX (505)277-5989. **ED** Gilbert W. Merkx, Enylton de Sa Rego, Karen L. Remmer and Sharon Kellum. **LC** F1401; .L345. Index available (bound in last issue). **Bk Rev**, (Qty: 25-35). **Ad Acc. Pr Rev. Circ:** 4,500 (ctrl). available on microfilm and microfiche from University Microfilms International (UMI); available on CD-ROM. Documents available from The Genuine Article, UMI Article Clearinghouse.
Desc: Articles, research notes, book reviews and essays of an interdisciplinary nature relating to Latin America.
Ind/Abst ABC POL SCI; Acad. Abstr. Full Text Elite (July 1990-); Acad. Abstr. (July 1990-); Acad. Ind. [Computer File] (1987-); Acad. Search (July 1990-); Am. Hist. Life (1965-); Anthropol. Lit.; Arts Humanit. Citation Index [Select. Cov.]; Chicano Index; Curr. Contents Soc. Behav. Sci.; Expand. Acad. Index (1987-); Film Lit. Index (19??-); Geogr. Abstr. Human Geogr.; HAPI Hisp. Am. Period. Index; INFO-SOUTH Abstr.; Int. Bibliogr. Sociol.; Int. Dev. Abstr.; Int. Labour Doc.; Int. Polit. Sci. Abstr.; LABORDOC; Mag. Search; Newsp. Period. Abstr. (1991-); PAIS Int. Print (1991-); Res. Alert [Full Cov.]; Rural Dev. Abstr.; Soc. Sci. Source (Jul. 1990-); Soc. Sci. Cit. Index [Full Cov.]; Soc. Sci. Index; Soc. Sci. Index Fulltext (1989-) [Full Txt.]; West. Hist. Q.; World Agric. Econ.

FR
LATIN AMERICAN ROUNDUP. Periodical. English (Spanish). sw. **LC** F1401; .L346A. **DD** 980/.037/05. **UDC** 980=6; 908.8=6.

US/0076-8189
LATIN AMERICAN STUDIES CENTER MONOGRAPH SERIES. Added/Corp Michigan State University. Latin American Studies Center. No. 1 (1967)-. Monographic series. English. ir. Price varies per volume. Michigan State University / 103 International Building, East Lansing MI 48824. **LC** UNC.

JA/0285-3582
LATIN AMERICAN STUDIES (SAKURA-MURA, IBARAKI-KEN, JAPAN). (LATIN AMERICAN STUDIES.). **VFOAT** Raten Amerika Kenkyu. 1-. English (Japanese). Tsukuba Daigaku Raten Amerika Tokubetsu Purojekuto Kenkyu Soshiki, 1-1-1 Sakura-mura Tennodai, Niihari-gun 305, Ibaraki-ken Japan. **LC** F1401; .L3465. **UDC** 908.8=6.

US
LATIN AMERICAN STUDIES WORKING PAPERS. English. ir. Indiana University / Comparative Literature Program, Ballantine Hall 402, Bloomington IN 47405. **Tel** (812)855-2140, FAX (812)855-7070, telex 272279 INDIANA U BLOM. **UDC** 980.8=6.

US/0265-0886
LATIN AMERICAN TIMES (BOGOTA). (THE LATIN AMERICAN TIMES.). [Lat. Am. times]. Vol. 1, No. 1 (April 1979)-. Periodical. English. Ten times a year. £150.00 UK and Ireland. World Reports Ltd., 108 Horse Ferry Road, Westminster, London SW1P 2EF United Kingdom. **Tel** 011 44 71 222 3836, FAX 11 44 71 233 0185. **LC** F1401; .L348. **DD** 980/.005.
Desc: An intelligence service for the international financial community providing exclusive coverage of financial, economic, political and social developments in Central and South America, and the Caribbean.

PE
LATINAMERICA PRESS. VFOAT Latin America Press. (1969)-. Periodical. English (Spanish). wk. $60.00 (one year), $108.00 (two year), $162.00 (three year) institutions, $40.00 (one year), $72.00 (two year), $108.00 (three year) individuals. Noticias Alidas, Apartado 5594, Lima 100 Peru. **Tel** 011 51 14 475210. **(Subscription address:** Communication Data Services, 112 Tenth Street, Des Moines, IA 50309**) ED** David Molineaux. **LC** F1414.2; .L344. **DD** 980/.005. **Bk Rev. Circ:** 1,500.
Desc: A news and analysis bulletin that focuses on human rights, church and people's movements throughout the region.
Ind/Abst Hum. Rights Intern. Rep.

RU/0044-748X
LATINSKAIA AMERIKA. Added/Corp Institut Latinskoi Ameriki (Akademiia Nauk SSR) Rossiisko-Iberoamerikanskaia Palata Sodeistviia Progressu. Sovetskii Komitet Solidarnosti s Narodami Latinskoi Ameriki. **VFOAT** LA, Latinskaia Amerika. (1991)-. Academic Scholarly Publication. Russian. mo. Izdatelstvo Nauka / Akademiia Nauk, Publishing House of the Russian Academy of Sciences, Leninskii Porspekt 14, 117901 Moscow Russia. **Tel** 011 95 954-21-53, FAX 011 95 938-21-44, telex 411964. **LC** F1401; .L37. ***Continues*** *Evropa + Amerika.*

US/0023-8988
LAUREL MESSENGER. Added/Corp Historical and Genealogical Society of Somerset County. (Feb. 1960)-. Periodical. English. Four times a year. $15.00. Historical and Genealogical Society of Somerset County, RD 2 Box 238, Somerset PA 15501. **Tel** (814)445-6077. **ED** Marguerite Cockley and Jeanne Coleman. **LC** F157.S6; L3. **Bk Rev. Circ:** 1,100 (ctrl).
Desc: Facts about people and places.
Ind/Abst Genealogical Period. Annu. Index.

US
LAWRENCE COUNTY HISTORICAL SOCIETY BULLETIN. Bulletin. English. Lawrence County Historical Society Bulletin, PO Box 406, Mt Vernon MO 65712. **Tel** (417)466-2743, (417)466-2670.
Ind/Abst Ozark Period. Index.

US
LEAGUE BULLETIN. Main/Corp Connecticut League of Historical Societies, Inc. (1957)-. Periodical. English. Three times a year. Free to members; $15.00 (individuals & libraries), $25.00 (historical societies) membership. Connecticut League of Historical Societies, 37 Parker Road, Meriden CT 06405. **ED** Louise Pittaway. **Bk Rev. Ad Acc. Circ:** 2,000 (ctrl).
Desc: Articles of local historic interest, reports member/society activities and quarterly programs, book reviews, membership recruitment, etc.

US/1045-3423
LEGACY. (LEGACY : THE JOURNAL OF THE RENO COUNTY HISTORICAL SOCIETY.). 1989-. Periodical. English. qt. $20.00 (individuals), $100.00 (institutions) member. Reno County Historical Society 67504-0664. **DD** 978.

CN/0317-2910
LEMKIVSKYJ KALENDAR. (LEMKIVS'KYI KALENDAR.). **VFOAT** Lemko Almanac. 1965-. Periodical. Ukrainian. an. Baxter Publishing Company, 310 Dupont Street, Toronto Ontario M5R 1V9 Canada. **Tel** (416)968-7252, FAX (416)968-2377. **DD** 971/.004/91791. **UDC** 971(=83).

US/0731-8960
LEON COUNTY HISTORICAL COLLECTIONS. Vol. 1-. Periodical. English. an. $9.50 Vol. 1, $7.00 Vol. 2, $7.00 Vol. 3. Leon County Genealogical Society, PO Box 500, Centerville TX 75833. **Tel** (214)536-7203. **LC** F392.L46; L47. **DD** 976.4/233. **UDC** 976.4; 929.5(764). Index available.
Desc: Includes: Newspaper clippings, pictures, family stories, early schools, teachers, students, Masonic Lodge abstracts and membership rolls, early newspaper abstracts, early marriage journal, Cedar Creek Ledger of James P Parker, 1868 voter list, Alliance records, WOW Keechi Lodge Ledger, Mt Pisgah Church records from the beginning, and maps.

CN/0713-3448
LETTRE DE QUEBEC, LA. [Lett. Que.]. Periodical. French. wk. $250.00. Communications CCDD, CP 1696, Quebec, Quebec G1K 7K6 Canada. **DD** 971.4/04/05. **UDC** 971.4.

US/0024-3671
LINCOLN HERALD. [Linc. her.]. **Added/Corp** Lincoln Memorial University. Vol. 40, No. 2 (Feb. 1938)-. Periodical. English. qt. $20.00 US; $25.00 other. Lincoln Memorial University, c/o The Lincoln Museum, Harrogate TN 37752. **Tel** (615)869-6235, FAX (615)869-6350. **ED** Stephen Hague, Tom Turner, Gary Planck. **LC** E457; .M887. **DD** 973. Index available. cum. index. **Bk Rev**, (Qty: 30). **Ad Acc. Circ:** 1,200 (ctrl). available on microfilm and microfiche from University Microfilms International (UMI). ***Continues*** *Mountain Herald (Harrogate, Tenn.).*
Desc: Incorporates historical research and scholarship on the War between the States and Abraham Lincoln.
Ind/Abst Am. Hist. Life (1955-); Annu. Bibliogr. Engl. Lang. Lit.

US/0162-8615
LINCOLN LORE. Added/Corp Lincoln National Life Insurance Company. Lincoln Historical Research Foundation. Lincoln National Life Foundation. No. 1 (Apr. 15, 1929)-. Periodical. English. mo. Free on request. Lincoln Life Insurance Co., 1301 South Harrison Street, Fort Wayne IN 46802. **Tel** (219)427-2000. **ED** Mark E. Neely. **LC** E457; .L74. **DD** 973.7/092/4 [B]. Index available. cum. index. ctrl circ.
Desc: Information relating to Abraham Lincoln, his contemporaries, the Civil War, and his era.

US/0192-5083
LINCOLN REVIEW. [Lincoln rev.]. **Added/Corp** Lincoln Institute for Research and Education. Vol. 1 (Spring 1979)-. Periodical. English. Four times a year (Jan., Apr., July, Oct.). $12.00 one year; $22.00 two years; $30.00 three years. Lincoln Institute of Research & Education, 1001 Connecticut Avenue Northwest, Washington DC 20036. **Tel** (202)223-5112. **ED** J. A. Parker. **LC** E185.5; .L55. **DD** 973/.04/96073. Index available. cum. index. **Bk Rev**, (Qty: 30). **Ad Acc, Adv Mgr:** Lori Saxon. **Circ:** 7,000.
Desc: Studies public policy issues that impact on the lives of black middle Americans. Makes its findings available to elected officials and the public.

CN/0715-3015
LIVYERE, THE. [Livyere]. Vol. 1, No. 1 (Summer 1981)-. Periodical. English. sa. $6.00. Livyere, c/o Leeward Publishing, PO Box 1205 Station C, St John's Newfoundland A1C 5M9 Canada. **LC** F1121; .L58. **DD** 971.8/005. **UDC** 971.8.

US/0361-3577
LOBLOLLY. ***Ceased.*** (19??)-(19??). Periodical. English. Twice a year. Loblolly Inc., PO Box 189, Gary TX 75643. **LC** F392.P17; L62. **DD** 976.4/187/005.

US/0893-3340
LOCAL HISTORIAN (COLUMBUS, OHIO). ***Title Change.*** (THE LOCAL HISTORIAN.). [Local hist.]. V. 1, No. 1 (March/April 1985)-. Periodical. English. bm. Ohio Historical Society, 1982 Velma Avenue, Subscription Office, Columbus OH 43211. **Tel** (614)297-2332, (614)297-2360. **ED** E L Langer. **DD** 977. **UDC** 977.1. **Bk Rev.** ***Continues*** *Gazetteer.* ***Continued by*** *Gazetteer.*
Desc: A newsletter of the Ohio Association of Historical Association of Historical Societies and museums.

US/0276-4105
LOCAL HISTORY STUDIES. Added/Corp De Anza College. California History Center. Vol. 1 (1968)-. Periodical. English. an. $25.00 Comes with California History Center Foundation Membership. California Council Promotion of History, 21250 Stevens Creek Boulevard, Cupertino CA 95014. **Tel** (408)864-8964. **LC** UNC.

US/0898-8056
LOCUS (DENTON, TEX.). (LOCUS. AN HISTORICAL JOURNAL OF REGIONAL PERSPECTIVES.). [Locus]. **Added/Corp** University of North Texas. College of Arts and Sciences. University of North Texas. Center for Studies in Local History. Vol. 1, No. 1 (Fall 1988)- Vol. 5 (Fall 1992)- Vol. 6 No. 1 (Fall 1993)-. Periodical. English. Twice a year (Spring and Fall). $8.00 (individual), $12.00 (institution) US & Canada; $20.00 other. University of North Texas Press, PO Box 13856, Denton TX 76203. **Tel** (817)565-2124, FAX (817)369-8770. **ED** Donald E Chipman and Mike Campbell, (817)565-2288. **LC** IN PROCESS. **DD** 973. **Bk Rev**, (Qty: 50). **Ad Acc, Adv Mgr:** Jane Tanner, **Tel** (817)565-2124. **Pr Rev. Circ:** 350.
Desc: A journal of local history with regional, national or international significance.
Ind/Abst Am. Hist. Life (1988-); Book Rev. Index; Sci. Fict. Fantasy Book Rev. Index; West. Hist. Q.

US/0024-5828
LOG OF MYSTIC SEAPORT, THE. V. 1- Oct. 1948-. Academic Scholarly Publication. English. qt. $25.00. Mystic Seaport Museum, 50 Greenmanville Avenue, Mystic CT 06355. **Tel** (203)572-0711. **ED** Gerald E Morris and Andrew W German. **LC** F104.M99; L6. **DD** 974.65. **UDC** 974.6. **Bk Rev. Circ:** 18,300. available on microfilm and microfiche from University Microfilms International (UMI).
Desc: Publishes scholarly articles, no fiction, on American non-naval maritime history, especially 19th century. Includes biography and social, economic and artistic studies.
Ind/Abst Am. Hist. Life (1980-).

CN/0700-8147
LOK AWAZ (PANJABI EDITION). (LOK AWAZ.). Began publication in 1974?. Periodical. Panjabi. wk. 25.00Can$ per no. Lok Awaz, PO Box 67617 Station O, Vancouver British Columbia V5W 3V1 Canada. **DD** 971.1/004/9142. **UDC** 971.1(=911).

CN/0316-1986
LONDON BROADSIDE. No. 1- 1975-. Periodical. English. 0.50Can$ per no. Applegarth Follies, PO Box 40, Station B, London Ontario N6A 4V3 Canada. **ED** D J Brock. **DD** 971.3/26/005. **UDC** 971.3.

US/0024-628X
LONG ISLAND FORUM. [Long Isl. forum]. (Jan. 1938)-. Periodical. English. qt. $8.00 (members); $20.00 (non-members). Friends of the Long Island Heritage, 1864 Muttontown Road, Muttontown LI NY 11791. **Tel** (516)364-1050, FAX (516)364-2946. **ED** Richard Welch. **LC** F127.L8; L73. **DD** 974.721. **Ad Acc.** available on microfilm and microfiche from University Microfilms International (UMI).
Ind/Abst Am. Hist. Life (1970-1973).

US
LONG ISLAND HERITAGE : A GUIDE TO AND A JOURNAL OF THE ISLAND'S HISTORY, ANTIQUES AND ARTS. ***Ceased.*** -Ceased April 1986. Periodical. English. ir. Long Island Heritage, Box 471, Glen Cove NY 11542. **Tel** (516)676-1200. **UDC** 974.7.

US/0898-7084
LONG ISLAND HISTORICAL JOURNAL, THE. [Long Isl. hist. j.]. **Added/Corp** State University of New York at Stony Brook. Dept. of History. Vol. 1, No. 1 (Fall 1988)-. Periodical. English. Twice a year. $15.00. Long Island Historical Journal, Department of History, SUNY Stony Brook, Stony Brook NY 11794. **Tel** (516)632-7500, FAX (516)632-7367. **ED** Roger Wunderlich. **DD** 974. Index available. cum. index (For the years 1983-1988). **Bk Rev**, (Qty: 12). **Ad Acc. Pr Rev. Circ:** 1,000.
Desc: Presents studies of Long Island as America, reflecting as well as contributing to the major phases of national life from colonial times to the present. Encourages articles and reviews of the political,

economic, ethnic, social, and cultural history of Long Island.
Ind/Abst Am. Hist. Life (1988-).

US
LOUDOUN COUNTY HANDBOOK. 1st Ed. (1984)-. English. an. LC F232.L8; L56. DD 975.5/28/005.

US
LOUISA COUNTY HISTORICAL MAGAZINE. **Added/Corp** Louisa County Historical Society. Vol. 1 (June 1969)-. Periodical. English. sa. $10.00. Louisa County Historical Society, PO Box 1172, Louisa VA 23093. **Tel** (703)894-4441. **ED** Jane W Woolfolk and Kate R Besley. **LC** F232.L85; L68. Index available. **Circ:** 425.
Desc: Documented materials of old homes, public places, cemeteries, and events of the past.

US/0741-0867
LOUISIANA DIRECTORY OF CITIES, TOWNS, AND VILLAGES. **VFOAT** Directory of Cities, Towns, and Villages. Directory. English. Office of Public Works, Internal Services Section, PO Box 44155, Baton Rouge LA 70804. **LC** F379.A15; D57. **DD** 976.3/0025. **UDC** 976.3(036); 911.37(763). ***Continues*** *Directory of Louisiana Cities, Towns and Villages, 0092-0614.*

US/0095-5949
LOUISIANA HISTORICAL QUARTERLY. (THE LOUISIANA HISTORICAL QUARTERLY.). [La. hist. q.]. **Added/Corp** Louisiana Historical Society. Vol. 1 (Jan. 8, 1917)-. Periodical. English. qt. Louisiana Historical, 921 Canal Street, 630 Maison Building, New Orleans LA 70112. **LC** F366; .L79. ***Supersedes*** *Louisiana Historical Society, New Orleans. Publications.*
Ind/Abst Am. Hist. Life (1955-1957).

US/0024-6816
LOUISIANA HISTORY. [La. hist.]. **Added/Corp** Louisiana Historical Association. Vol. 1, (Winter 1960)-. Periodical. English. Four times a year (Feb., May, Aug., Nov.). $15.00 (individuals) active; $20.00 (individuals) contributing; $25.00 associate organizations active including libraries and schools; $200.00 associate organizations sustaining including libraries and schools. Louisiana Historical Association, PO Box 42808, Lafayette LA 70504. **Tel** (318)231-6871. **ED** Carl A. Brasseaux (phone: (318)231-6871). **LC** F366; .L6238. Index available (Bound in 4th iss.). cum. index. **Bk Rev. Ad Acc, Adv Mgr:** G. R. Conrad, **Tel** (318)231-6871. **Pr Rev. Circ:** 1,200.
Desc: History of Louisiana and the lower Mississippi Valley.
Ind/Abst Am. Hist. Life (1961-); Annu. Bibliogr. Engl. Lang. Lit.; Recent. Publ. Artic.; West. Hist. Q.; Writ. Am. Hist.

CN/0228-2380
LOUSAVORITCH. [Lousavoritch]. **VFOAT** Loussavoritch; Loosavoritch. V. 1- May 1978-. Periodical. Armenian. mo. Free to members of St. Gregory's Armenian Parish. Armenian Canadians, PO Box 1211, Station A, Montreal Quebec H3C 2Z1. **DD** 971.4/28100491992. **UDC** 971.4.

CN/0047-5149
LOYALIST GAZETTE, THE. [Loyalist gaz.]. **Added/Corp** United Empire Loyalists' Association of Canada. Dominion Council. Vol. 1 (April 1963)-. Periodical. English. sa. 12.50Can$ Canada; $12.50 US; $15.00 other. United Empire Loyalist Association, 50 Baldwin George Brown House, Toronto ONT M5T 1L4 Canada. **Tel** (416)591-1783. **ED** David K. Dorward. **LC** F1058; .L83. **DD** 369/.271. Index available. **Bk Rev. Ad Acc. Circ:** 3,500 (ctrl). available on microfiche.
Desc: Related to the Loyalist Period in history (1776 to about 1800) and the American Revolution. Deals with researched articles, book reviews, book notices (free) and family histories.
Ind/Abst Am. Hist. Life; Can. Period. Index (19??-);.

US
LURE OF THE LITCHFIELD HILLS, THE. **Added/Corp** Litchfield Hills Federation. Vol. 1, (May 1929)-. Periodical. English. Four times a year. $3.00 (two years). Lure of Litchfield Hills, Box 907, West Cornwall CT 06976.

US/0464-2910
MADERA COUNTY HISTORIAN, THE. [Madera Cty. hist.]. **Added/Corp** Madera County Historical Society. Vol. 1, (Jan. 1961)-. Periodical. English. ir. Madera County Historical Society, PO Box 478, Madera CA 93639. **LC** F868.M2; M3. **DD** 979. Index available. **Circ:** 600.
Ind/Abst Am. Hist. Life.

US/0197-498X
MADISON COUNTY HERITAGE. [Madison Cty. herit.]. **Added/Corp** Madison County Historical Society (N.Y.). No. 1 (August 1977)-. Periodical. English. an. $5.00. Madison County Historical Society, 435 Main Street, PO Box 415, Oneida NY 13421. **Tel** (315)363-4136. **ED** Russell Grills. **LC** F127.M2; M24. **DD** 974.7/64/005. cum. index.

GW/0170-2513
MAGAZIN FUER AMERIKANISTIK. (1977)-. Periodical. German. qt. DM27.00 Germany; $6.00 US. Verlag Fuer Amerikanistik D Kuegler, Rebbelstieg 37, PO Box 1332, W-2270 Wyk auf Foehr Germany. **Tel** 04681/3112, FAX 04681/3258. **ED** Dietmar Kuegler. **LC** F596; .M18. **DD** 978/.008. **Bk Rev. Ad Acc. Circ:** 2,000 (ctrl).
Desc: Contains information of the history and ethnology of the North American Indian, the development of the Great Plains and the American Civil War.

US/0076-2342
MAGAZINE OF ALBEMARLE COUNTY HISTORY, THE. **Added/Corp** Albemarle County Historical Society (Va.). Vol. 12 (1951/52)-. Periodical. English. an. **LC** F232; .A3A5. **DD** 975. ***Continues*** *Papers of the Albemarle County Historical Society.*
Ind/Abst Am. Hist. Life (1985-).

US
MAGAZINE OF THE JEFFERSON COUNTY HISTORICAL SOCIETY. **Main/Corp** Jefferson County Historical Society (W. VA.). (1935)-. English. an. $5.00. Jefferson County Historic Society, PO Box 485, Charles Town WV 25414. **Tel** (304)725-5191. **LC** F236; .M25.

CN/0824-6300
MAGYAR HIRMONDO (CALGARY). (MAGYAR HIRMONDO.). **VFOAT** Calgary Hungarian Courier. Periodical. Hungarian. mo. Hungarian-Canadian Cultural Association of Calgary, PO Box 1903, Calgary Alberta T2P 2M2 Canada. **DD** 971/.00494511. **UDC** 971(=945.11).

US/1046-6053
MAINE (AUBURN, ME.). (MAINE.). [Maine]. Vol. 1, No. 1 (Sept./Oct. 1989)-. Periodical. English. Six times a year. $12.00. New England Publishing Company, PO Box 172, Leeds ME 04263-0172. **Tel** (207)777-1777, FAX (207)783-1563. **DD** 974. ***Continues*** *New Maine Life Magazine, 1044-5978.*

US/0163-1152
MAINE HISTORICAL SOCIETY QUARTERLY. [Me. Hist. Soc. q.]. **Added/Corp** Maine Historical Society. (Summer 1973)-. Academic Scholarly Publication. English. qt. $20.00. Maine Historical Society, 485 Congress Street, Portland ME 04101. **Tel** (207)774-1822. **LC** F19; .M253. **DD** 974.1/005. **Bk Rev. Circ:** 2,000. ***Continues*** *Maine Historical Society. Maine Historical Society Newsletter.*
Desc: Publishes scholarly writings on Maine history.
Ind/Abst Am. Hist. Life (1973-).

CN/0229-012X
MAL-I-MIC (1979). (MAL-I-MIC NEWS.). [Mal-i-mic news]. Periodical. English. mo. $3.50. Mal-I-Mic News, 320 St Marys Street, Fredericton New Brunswick E3A 2S4 Canada. **Tel** (506)472-0982. **DD** 971.5/00497. **UDC** 971.5(=97). ***Continues*** *Nouvelles Mal-I-Mic, 0708-9708.*

CN/0317-6983
MALTESE DIRECTORY : CANADA, UNITED STATES. 1974-. Directory. English (Maltese). be. Malta Service Bureau, PO Box 826 Station B, Ottawa Ontario K1P 5P9 Canada. **Tel** (613)521-5285. **ED** G Bonavia. **LC** E184.M34; M35. **DD** 971/.004/9277. **UDC** 945.82; 971. **Bk Rev.** ctrl circ.
Desc: Listing of information about Maltese organizations in Canada and other information on Malta and the Maltese.

CN/0226-5036
MANITOBA HISTORICAL SOCIETY NEWSLETTER. [Manit. Hist. Soc. newsl.]. **Added/Corp** Manitoba Historical Society. **VAT** Newsletter - Manitoba Historical Society. (1968)-. Newsletter. English. bm (6 issues). 33.00Can$ individuals, 38.00Can$ institutions (comes with membership to Manitoba Historical Society). Manitoba Historical Society, 470-167 Lombard Avenue, Winnipeg Manitoba R3B OT6 Canada. **Tel** (204)947-0559. **ED** Lily Stearns. **DD** 971.27/006. **Circ:** 1,100 (ctrl).
Desc: Source of information on Manitoba Historical Society's events, programs, lecture series, dinners, field trips, etc.

CN/0226-5044
MANITOBA HISTORY. [Man. hist.]. **Added/Corp** Historical and Scientific Society of Manitoba. Manitoba. Dept. of Cultural Affairs and Historical Resources. Manitoba. Manitoba Culture, Heritage, and Recreation. 1st Ed. (1980)-. Periodical. English. sa. 18.50Can$ Canada; 20.50Can$ US; 22.50Can$ other. Manitoba Historical Society, 470-167 Lombard Avenue, Winnipeg Manitoba R3B OT6 Canada. **Tel** (204)947-0559. **ED** Morris Mott. **LC** F1063; .M3. **DD** 971.27/005; 971.27/005. **Bk Rev. Circ:** 1,000 (ctrl). ***Continues*** *Manitoba Pageant, 0025-2263.*
Desc: History in North America, Canada, Western Canada and the Northern Great Plains.
Ind/Abst Am. Hist. Life (1980-); Can. Index (1980-?); Can. Period. Index (19??-); SportSearch (1980-); West. Hist. Q. (1980-).

US/0892-7820
MARIEL (MIAMI, FLA. : 1986). (MARIEL.). [Mariel]. **VFOAT** Mariel Magazine. Vol. 1, No. 1 (1986)-. Periodical. Spanish (English). qt. $10.00 (individuals), $15.00 (institutions) US; $20.00 other. Mariel Magazine Inc, PO Box 452304 Shanandoah Station, Miami FL 33245. **LC** E184.C97; M36. **DD** 973/.04687291.

US/0738-7571
MARSHALL COUNTY HISTORICAL QUARTERLY. **Added/Corp** Marshall County Historical Society (Tenn.). Vol. 1, No. 1 (Aug. 1970)-. Periodical. English. qt (Feb., May, Aug., Nov.). $10.00. Marshall County Historical Society, 224 3rd Avenue, North Knox Bigham, Lewisburg TN 37091. **Tel** (615)359-2283. **ED** Charlene Nicholas. Index available (annually). **Bk Rev. Circ:** 250-275.

US
MARYLAND BICENTENNIAL STUDIES. (19??)-. Monographic series. English. ir. Price varies per volume. Johns Hopkins University Press, 2715 North Charles Street, Baltimore MD 21218-4319. **Tel** (410)516-6987, FAX (410)516-6968.

US/0025-4258
MARYLAND HISTORICAL MAGAZINE. [Md. hist. mag.]. **Added/Corp** Maryland Historical Society. (Mar. 1906)-. Periodical. English. Four times a year. $20.00 US. Maryland Historical Society, 201 West Monument Street, Baltimore MD 21201. **Tel** (410)685-3750. **ED** Robert J. Brugger. **LC** F176; .M18. **Bk Rev. Ad Acc. Circ:** 6,100.
Desc: Maryland history, genealogy, biography, decorative arts, fine arts, politics and culture.
Ind/Abst Am. Hist. Life (1963-); Annu. Bibliogr. Engl. Lang. Lit.; Genealogical Period. Annu. Index.

US/1040-7936
MARYLAND MAGAZINE (1988). (MARYLAND MAGAZINE.). [Md. mag.]. **Added/Corp** Maryland. Dept. of Economic and Employment Development. Vol. 21, No. 2 (Winter 1988)-. Periodical. English. bm. $12.50 US; $16.50 other. Maryland Magazine, 100 South Charles Street, 13th Floor, Baltimore MD 21201. **Tel** (410) 539-3100, FAX (301)333-6643. **ED** Michelle Burke. **DD** 975. **Bk Rev**, (Qty: 6 /yr). **Ad Acc. Circ:** 25,000. ***Continues*** *Maryland (Annapolis, MD.), 1040-7944.*
Desc: Editorial & photography on Maryland's history, culture, people, & places.

US/0735-4754
MASON MEMORIES. ***Ceased.*** Periodical. English. qt. Mason County Historical Society, 115 Loomis, Ludington MI 49431. **UDC** 977.4.

CN/1183-1073
MATERIAL HISTORY REVIEW. [Mater. hist. rev.]. **Added/Corp** National Museum of Science and Technology (Canada). **VFOAT** Revue d'Histoire de la Culture Materielle. (Spring 1991)-. Periodical. English (French). sa. $30.00 (institutions), $18.00 (individuals). National Museum of Science and Technology, PO Box 9724, Ottawa Terminal, Ottawa, Ontario K1G 5A3 Canada. **Tel** (613)991-2986. **LC** F1021; .N37a. **DD** 971/.005. ***Continues*** *Material History Bulletin, 0703-489X.*
Ind/Abst Am. Hist. Life (1977-); BHA : Biblio. Hist. Art; Can. Period. Index (19??-).

CN
MATERIALS FOR THE STUDY OF ALASKA HISTORY. No. 1-. Monographic series. English. ir. Price varies per volume. Limestone Press, PO Box 1604, Kingston Ontario K7L 5C8 Canada. **UDC** 979.8.

US/8756-3959
MAYFLOWER DESCENDANT : A MAGAZINE OF PILGRIM GENEALOGY AND HISTORY, THE. See Genealogy and Heraldry.

US/0148-5032
MAYFLOWER QUARTERLY, THE. **Added/Corp** General Society of Mayflower Descendants. Vol. 1 (Oct. 1935)-. Periodical. English. Four times a year. Mayflower Quarterly, 3800 Montrose Avenue, Richmond VA 23222. **LC** F68; .S64. **DD** 369.124.
Ind/Abst Genealogical Period. Annu. Index.

US/1060-1309
MEASURE OF EXCELLENCE / LAURANCE D. LINFORD, A. [Meas. excell.]. **Added/Corp** Inter-Tribal Indian Ceremonial Association. 1st Annual Ed. (1991)-. English. $16.95. Inter-Tribal Indian Ceremonial Association, PO Box 1, Church Rock NM 87311. **DD** 970.

US/0890-7595
MEDALLION (AUSTIN, TEX.). (THE MEDALLION / TEXAS HISTORICAL COMMISSION.). [Medallion]. **Added/Corp** Texas Historical Commission. Texas Historical Survey Committee. Texas State Historical Survey Committee. (19??)-. Periodical. English. Six times a year (Jan., Mar., May, July, Sept., Nov.). $7.00 (one year), $13.00 (two years). Texas Historical

Commission, PO Box 12276 Capitol Station, Austin TX 78711. **Tel** (512)463-6100, FAX (512)463-6095. **ED** Roni Morales (phone: (512)463-8886). **DD** 976. **Circ:** 2,500.
Desc: News of historic preservation activities in Texas.

US/0543-3754
MEET THE PRESS : AMERICA'S PRESS CONFERENCE OF THE AIR. VFOAT America's Press Conference of the Air. (Jan. 6, 1957)-. Periodical. English. Fifty-two times a year. $260.00. Meet the Press, 4001 Nebraska Avenue NW, Washington DC 20016. **Tel** (202)885-4361. **LC** E743. Documents available from UMI Article Clearinghouse.
Ind/Abst Gen. Period. Index (1985-); Mag. Index Plus (1989-); Newsp. Period. Abstr. (1988-); Mag. Index (1977-).

US
MEIE TEE, AMEERIKA EESTLASTE AJAKIRI. ***Ceased.*** Vol. 1, No. 1 (1931)-(1988). Periodical. Estonian. bm. World Association of Estonians Inc, 243 East 34th Street, New York NY 10016. **LC** E184.E7; M5. **UDC** 973.

●US/1064-5675
MEMBER NEWS / MINNESOTA HISTORICAL SOCIETY. [Memb. news - Minn. Hist. Soc.]. **Added/Corp** Minnesota Historical Society. Vol. 1, No. 2 (Aug. 1992)-. Periodical. English. mo. Minnesota Historical Society, 345 Kellogg Boulevard West, St. Paul MN 55102. **Tel** (612)297-3243, (800)647-7827, FAX (612)297-3343. **DD** 977. ***Continues*** *Minnesota History News, 0544-358X.*

US
MEMBERSHIP DIRECTORY / EL PASO COUNTY HISTORICAL SOCIETY. **Main/Corp** El Paso County Historical Society (El Paso Co., Tex.). Directory. English. $2.50. El Paso County Historical Society, Box 28, El Paso TX 79940. **Tel** (915)584-1026. **Bk Rev**. **Pr Rev. Circ:** 900 (ctrl).
Desc: Original articles of items of historical interest in Southwest, primarily El Paso area.

MX
MEMORIA - REUNION LATINOAMERICANA DE PRODUCCION ANIMAL. Main/Corp Reunion Latinoamericana de Produccion Animal. 1st- 1966-. Periodical. Spanish. an. $16.25. Assn Latinoamericana Prod Anim, Apdo 4579 Fac Agronomia UCV, Maracay Venezuela. **UDC** 636(8=6).

MX/0378-0724
MEMORIAS DE LA ACADEMIA MEXICANA DE LA HISTORIA. (MEMORIAS.). [Mem. Acad. Mex. Hist.]. **Main/Corp** Academia Mexicana de la Historia. Vol. 1 (Jan./March 1942)-. Monographic series. Spanish. an. Price varies per volume. Academia Mexicana Historia, Plaza Carlos Pacheco No 21, Mexico 1 DF Mexico. **Tel** 521-96-53. **ED** Juan A Ortega y Medina. **LC** F1201; .A14. **DD** 972.0062. cum. index. **Circ:** 2,000.
Ind/Abst Am. Hist. Life (1956-1965).

US/1040-5712
MENSAJERO (SAN FRANCISCO, CALIF.), EL. (EL MENSAJERO.). [Mensajero]. (1987-. Newspaper. Spanish (English). Fifty-two times a year (Wednesday). $100.00 one year. El Mensajero, 385 Eighth Street, San Francisco CA 94103. **Tel** (415)864-7612, FAX (415)864-8076. **ED** Carlos Vargas. **DD** 071. **Bk Rev**, (Qty: 3). **Ad Acc. Circ:** 30,000.
Desc: Local, state and international news and information pertaining to the Latino Community.

GT/0252-9963
MESOAMERICA (ANTIGUA, GUATEMALA). (MESOAMERICA : REVISTA DEL CENTRO DE INVESTIGACIONES REGIONALES DE MESOAMERICA.). [Mesoamerica]. **Added/Corp** Centro de Investigaciones Regionales de Mesoamerica. Vol. 1, No. 1 (Jan./June 1980)-. Periodical. Spanish (summaries and/or abstracts in English). sa. $20.00 US; $11.50 Latin America; $24.00 other. Centro Invest Regionale Mesoamerica, Apartado Postal 336, Antigua Guatemala. **(Subscription address:** Centro de Investigaciones Regionales Mesoamerica, PO Box 38, South Woodstock VT 05071.) **ED** Christopher H. Lutz. **LC** F1421; .M47. **DD** 972/.0005. **Bk Rev**.
Ind/Abst Anthropol. Index; Anthropol. Lit.; HAPI Hisp. Am. Period. Index; Int. Bibliogr. Sociol.

US
MESOAMERICAN STUDY GROUP NEWSLETTER, THE. Added/Corp Mesoamerican Study Group. Vol. 1, No. 1 (1991)-. Newsletter. English.

US/0731-3012
MESSENGER OF THE CHESTERFIELD HISTORICAL SOCIETY OF VIRGINIA, THE. VFOAT Messenger. No. 1 (Feb. 1982)-. Periodical. English. sa. $10.00. Chesterfield Historical Society of Virginia, PO Box 40, Courthouse Square, Chesterfield County VA 23832. **ED** Jeanette Hartter Ortiz. **UDC** 975.5; 929.5(755). **Circ:** 700.
Desc: Publication sent to members of the historical society as part of their membership benefits. In general, all articles pertain to Chesterfield County history, or other information of interest to members such as genealogy requests, trip schedules and donations.

US/0272-6890
MEXICAN REVOLUTION REPORTER, THE. [Mex. Revolut. rep.]. Periodical. English. qt. Revmex, Rural Route 2 Box 90, Ozawkie KS 66070-9417. **UDC** 972.

US/1062-5615
MEXICAN WAR QUARTERLY. [Mex. war q.]. **Added/Corp** Descendants of Mexican War Veterans. Vol. 1, No. 1 (Fall 1991)-. Periodical. English. qt. $15.00. Mexican War Quarterly, 1114 Pacific, Richardson TX 75081. **DD** 973.

MX
MEXICO GEOGRAFICO. Yearly V. 1- Sept. 1978-. Periodical. Spanish. $2.00. Salvat Y Asociados, Insurgentes Sur 300-801, Mexico D F Mexico. **LC** F1201; .M5934. **DD** 972/.005. **UDC** 917.72.

GW/0720-5988
MEXICON. [Mexicon]. **Added/Corp** Internationale Gesellschaft Fur Mesoamerika-Forschung. Vol. 1, No. 1 (March 15, 1979)-. Periodical. English (German and Spanish). bm. $35.00. Verlag von Flemming, Anton Saurwein, Schlossberg 20, 74219 Moeckmuehl, Germany. **Tel** 011/49/40/41235900. **ED** Gordon Whittaker. **LC** F1219; .M748. cum. index. **Ad Acc. Circ:** 600.
Desc: News and studies on Mesoamerican research, featuring news on archaeology, ethnohistory, and ethnology.
Ind/Abst Anthropol. Lit.; Ethnoarts Index.

GW/0418-842X
MEXIKO-PROJEKT DER DEUTSCHEN FORSCHUNGSGEMEINSCHAFT, DAS. **Main/Corp** Deutsche Forschungsgemeinschaft (1951-). **Added/Corp** Deutsche Forschungsgemeinschaft. **VFOAT** Proyecto Mexico de la Fundacion Alemana para la Investigacion Cientifica. Vol. 1 (1968)-. Monographic series. German (Spanish). ir. Price varies per volume. Franz Steiner Verlag GmbH, Postfach 101061, D 70009 Stuttgart Germany. **Tel** 011 49 0711 2582372, FAX 011 49 0711 2582290, telex 723636 daz d. **ED** Wilhelm Lauer.

US/0024-8185
MHS MISCELLANY. Main/Corp Massachusetts Historical Society. **Added/Corp** Massachusetts Historical Society. Miscellany. **VAT** Massachusetts Historical Society Miscellany. No. 1 (Feb. 1955)-. Periodical. English. Four times a year. Published for membership only. Massachusetts Historical Society, 1154 Boylston Street, Boston MA 02215. **Tel** (617)536-1608. **ED** Conrad E. Wright. **LC** F61; .M15. **DD** 974.4/006/074461. **Circ:** 1,800 (ctrl).
Desc: News and events concerning the Massachusetts Historical Society, its library and collections.

US/0889-3640
MIAMI MEANDERINGS. (MIAMI MEANDERINGS : VOICE OF THE MIAMI COUNTY HISTORICAL SOCIETY.). Vol. 1, Issue 1 (Sept./Oct. 1986)-. Periodical. English. bm. $5.00 (individual memberships). Miami County Historical & Genealogical Society, PO Box 305, Troy OH 45373. **UDC** 975.9.

US/0890-1686
MICHIGAN HISTORICAL REVIEW, THE. [Mich. hist. rev.]. **Added/Corp** Clarke Historical Library. Historical Society of Michigan (1874-). Vol. 12, No. 1 (Spring 1986)-. Periodical. English. sa. $14.50 US; $17.50 other. Central Michigan University / Michigan Historical Review, Clarke Historical Library, Mt Pleasant MI 48859. **Tel** (517)774-6567, FAX (517)774-4499. **ED** Carol Green. **LC** PS273; .G73. **DD** 977.4/005. **Bk Rev**, (Qty: 50). **Ad Acc, Adv Mgr:** Carol Riddle. **Pr Rev. Circ:** 4,000. Documents available from The Genuine Article, Documents on Demand. ***Continues*** *Great Lakes Review, 0360-1846.*
Desc: An academic history journal which publishes articles that deal with Michigan history and the history of the Midwest.
Ind/Abst Am. Hist. Life (1986-); Arts Humanit. Citation Index [Full Cov.]; Curr. Contents Arts Humanit.; Environ. Abstr.; Res. Alert [Full Cov.]; Soc. Sci. Cit. Index [Select. Cov.]; West. Hist. Q.

US/0026-2196
MICHIGAN HISTORY. [Mich. hist.]. **Added/Corp** Michigan. History Division. Michigan Historical Commission. Vol. 31 (1947)-. Periodical. English. Six times a year. $12.95 one year; $23.95 two year. State of Michigan, 717 West Allegan, Lansing MI 48918. **Tel** (517)373-1645, FAX (517)373-0851. **ED** Roger Rosentreter (editor's telephone: (517)373-3704). Index available (published separately). **Bk Rev. Circ:** 36,000. ***Continues Michigan History Magazine.***
Desc: Dedicated to preserving and informing people of the heritage of Michigan.

US/0026-2927
MID-AMERICA (CHICAGO). See Religion and Theology-Catholicism.

US
MIDLAND LOG. V. 1, No. 1- Spring, 1970-. Periodical. English. qt. Midland County Historical Society, 1840 West Street Andrews, Dow Library, Midland MI 48640. **UDC** 977.4.

US/0740-3208
MIDWEST REVIEW (WAYNE, NEB. : 1975). (THE MIDWEST REVIEW.). [Midwest rev.]. **Added/Corp** Wayne State College. Vol. 1 (Spring 1975)-Second Series, Vol. 1 (Spring 1979)-. Periodical. English. an. Free. Wayne State College / Nebraska, Department of Social Science, Wayne NE 68787. **Tel** (402)375-2200. **ED** Kent Blaser. **LC** WMLC L 83/516. **Bk Rev**. **Ad Acc. Circ:** 900 (ctrl).
Desc: History and Culture of the Northern Great Plains-Missouri Valley region.
Ind/Abst Am. Hist. Life (1979-); West. Hist. Q.

KO
MIGUK PYONGNON. (1971)-. Multiple languages (Korean and English; summaries and/or abstracts in English). 1300. Ilchogak, 9 Kongpyong-dong Chongno-ku, Seoul Korea. **LC** E855; .K64.

KO
MIGUKHAK / AMERICAN STUDIES. **Added/Corp** Soul Taehakkyo. Migukhak Yonguso. **VFOAT** American Studies. (1978)-. Periodical. Korean (English and Korean). **LC** E151; .M48.

US
MIJU AN UI HAN'GUKIN. VFOAT The Koreans in America; Hangukin. V. 1- ; 1979-. Periodical. English (Korean). mo. 42-22 27th Street, Long Island City NY 11101. **LC** E184.K6; M54. **DD** 973/.04957. **UDC** 973(=957).

US/0163-7622
MILWAUKEE HISTORY. [Milwaukee hist.]. **Added/Corp** Milwaukee County Historical Society. Vol. 1 (Spring/Summer 1978)-. Periodical. English. qt. $20.00 individual; $25.00 family. Milwaukee County Historical Society, 910 North Third Street, Milwaukee WI 53203. **Tel** (414)273-8288. **ED** Ralph M. Aderman. **LC** F587.M6; M69. **DD** 977.5/95/005. Index available. cum. index. **Circ:** 1,250. ***Supersedes*** *Historical Messenger of the Milwaukee County Historical Society, 0361-1671.*
Ind/Abst Am. Hist. Life (1978-); West. Hist. Q.

US/0363-289X
MINNESOTA ALMANAC, THE. 1977-. English. $4.95. R.A. Jones, 2409 West 66th Street, Minneapolis MN 55423. **LC** F606; .M662. **DD** 977.6. **UDC** 977.6.

US/0544-3571
MINNESOTA HISTORIC SITES PAMPHLET SERIES. No. 1- 1966-. Monographic series. English. ir. Price varies per volume. Minnesota Historical Society, 345 Kellogg Boulevard West, St. Paul MN 55102. **Tel** (612)297-3243, (800)647-7827, FAX (612)297-3343. **UDC** 904(776).

US/0076-9193
MINNESOTA HISTORICAL ARCHAEOLOGY SERIES. Added/Corp Minnesota Historical Society. No. 1 (1969)-. Monographic series. English. ir. Price varies per volume. Minnesota Historical Society, 345 Kellogg Boulevard West, St. Paul MN 55102. **Tel** (612)297-3243, (800)647-7827, FAX (612)297-3343. **LC** F612.R42; M5. **DD** 977.6/005.

US/0026-5497
MINNESOTA HISTORY. [Minn. hist.]. **Added/Corp** Minnesota Historical Society. Vol. 6, No. 1 (Mar. 1925)-. Periodical. English. qt (Mar., June, Sept., Oct.). $15.00. Minnesota Historical Society, 345 Kellogg Boulevard West, St Paul MN 55102. **Tel** (612)297-3243, (800)647-7827, FAX (612)297-1345. **ED** Anne Kaplan and Marilyn Ziebarth. **LC** F601; .M72. **DD** 977.6/005. **[CCC]**. **Bk Rev**, (Qty: 20-25). **Pr Rev. Circ:** 8,000 (ctrl). available on microfilm and microfiche from University Microfilms International (UMI). ***Continues*** *Minnesota History Bulletin, 0190-6348.*
Desc: History magazine focusing on people, issues, and events from presettlement to recent past in Minnesota and the region. Illustrated and annotated.
Ind/Abst Am. Hist. Life (1963-); Annu. Bibliogr. Engl. Lang. Lit.; SportSearch; West. Hist. Q.

●CN/1189-3672
MINUTES OF PROCEEDINGS AND EVIDENCE OF THE ABORIGINAL LIAISON COMMITTEE OF THE SPECIAL JOINT COMMITTEE ON A RENEWED CANADA (ENGLISH EDITION). [Minutes proc. evid. Aborig. Liaison Comm. Spec. Jt. Comm. Renew. Can.]. **Main/Corp** Canada. Parliament. Aboriginal Liaison Committee. **VFOAT** Aboriginal Liaison Committee; Proces-Verbaux et Temoignages du Comite de Liaison avec les Autochtones du Comite Mixte Special

sur le Renouvellement du Canada. 3rd Session of the 34th Parliament, Issue No. 1 (1992)-. Proceedings. English (French). **DD** 323.1/197071.

●CN/1189-3672
MINUTES OF PROCEEDINGS AND EVIDENCE OF THE ABORIGINAL LIAISON COMMITTEE OF THE SPECIAL JOINT COMMITTEE ON A RENEWED CANADA (FRENCH EDITION). [Minutes proc. evid. Aborig. Liaison Comm. Spec. Jt. Comm. Renew. Can.]. **Main/Corp** Canada. Parlement. Comite de Liaison avec les Autochtones. **VFOAT** Comite de Liaison avec les Autochtones; Proces-Verbaux et Temoignages du Comite de Liaison avec les Autochtones du Comite Mixte Special sur le Renouvellement du Canada. 3rd Session of the 34th Parliament, Issue No. 1 (1992)-. Proceedings. French (English). **DD** 323.1/197071.

US/0275-6145
MINUTES OF THE ANNUAL MEETING OF THE FIRST CATHOLIC SLOVAK UNION OF THE UNITED STATES OF AMERICA AND CANADA. [Minutes annu. meet. First Cathol. Slovak Union U. S. A. Can.]. **Main/Corp** First Catholic Slovak Union of America. English. an. First Catholic Slovak Union, 6611 Rockside Road, Cleveland OH 44131-2398. **LC** E184.S64; F57B. **DD** 973/.049187.

AG
MIRADA, LA. **Added/Corp** Fundacion del Sur. **VFOAT** Mira. Vol. 1, No. 1 (Spring 1990)-. Periodical. Spanish. Fundacion del Sur, Buenos Aires Argentina. **LC** F2849.2; .M56. **DD** 982/.005.

US/0738-7237
MIRROR, THE. See Religion and Theology.

US/1056-9596
MISSOURI FACTS. [Mo. facts]. **VFOAT** Flying the Colors, Missouri Facts; Missouri Facts--Flying the Colors Series. (1991)-. English. te. $59.50 (single issue). Clements Research II Inc., 16850 Dallas Parkway, Dallas TX 75248. **Tel** (214)931-9956, FAX (214)248-7159. **LC** F461; .M57. **DD** 977.

US/0026-6582
MISSOURI HISTORICAL REVIEW. [Mo. hist. rev.]. **Added/Corp** State Historical Society of Missouri. Vol. 1, (Oct. 1906)-. Periodical. English. Four times a year (Jan., Apr., July, Oct.). $10.00 (regular), $25.00 (contributing), $50.00 (supporting) Comes with State Historical Society of Missouri membership. State Historical Society of Missouri, 1020 Lowry Street, Columbia MO 65201. **Tel** (314)882-7083, FAX (314)884-4950. **ED** Dr. James W. Goodrich and Lynn Wolf Gentzler. **LC** F461; .M59. **DD** 977.8005. Index available (July iss.). cum. index. **Bk Rev**, (Qty: 16). **Circ:** 8,000 (ctrl). available on microfilm and microfiche from University Microfilms International (UMI).
Desc: Articles and documents relating to the history of Missouri.
Ind/Abst Am. Hist. Life (1962-); Annu. Bibliogr. Engl. Lang. Lit.; Ozark Period. Index; Recent. Publ. Artic.; West. Hist. Q.; Writ. Am. Hist.

US
MISTLETOE LEAVES. (MISTLETOE LEAVES; A NEWSLETTER OF THE OKLAHOMA HISTORICAL SOCIETY.). **Added/Corp** Oklahoma Historical Society. Vol. 4 (1973)-. Periodical. English. mo. Comes with subscription to Chronicles of Oklahoma. Oklahoma Historical Society, Historical Building, North Lincoln, Oklahoma City OK 73105. **Tel** (405)521-2491. **ED** Bob L. Blackburn and Mary Ann Blocholiak. **Bk Rev. Circ:** 6,000 (ctrl). ***Continues** Mistletoe Leaves.*
Desc: State and local history news and features of Oklahoma, the West and the Southwest.

US
MONKEYSHINES ON AMERICA. Periodical. English. Five times a year. $22.00. North Carolina Learning Institute for Fitness & Education, PO Box 10245, Greensboro NC 27404. **Tel** (919)292-6999.
Desc: History and geography of a different state in each issue.

US/0146-5651
MONOGRAPH SERIES - UNITED STATES HISTORICAL SOCIETY. **Main/Corp** United States Catholic Historical Society. 1-. Monographic series. English. ir. Price varies per volume. US Catholic Historical Society, Dunwoodie NY 10704. **LC** E184.C3; U6. **UDC** 282(09)(73).

US
MONOGRAPH SERIES (UNIVERSITY OF CALIFORNIA, SAN DIEGO. CENTER FOR U.S.-MEXICAN STUDIES). (MONOGRAPH SERIES / CENTER FOR U.S.-MEXICAN STUDIES, UNIVERSITY OF CALIFORNIA, SAN DIEGO.). **Added/Corp** University of California, San Diego. Center for U.S.-Mexican Studies. **VFOAT** Monographs in U.S.-Mexican Studies; Monograph in U.S.-Mexican Studies. (1982)-. Monographic series. English. ir. Price varies per volume. Center for United States-Mexican Studies, University of California at San Diego, 9500 Gillman Drive, 0510, La Jolla CA 92093. **Tel** (619)534-4503. **ED** Sandra Del Castillo and Wayne Cornelius. Index available. cum. index. **Bk Rev**. ***Continues** Monographs in U.S.-Mexican Studies.*
Desc: Contains reports of recent academic research on the politics, society, economy, and history of the 20th century.

US
MONOGRAPH - UNIVERSITY OF CALIFORNIA, LOS ANGELES. CHICANO STUDIES CENTER. **Main/Corp** University of California, Los Angeles. Chicano Studies Center. No. 1 (1970)-. Periodical. English. Chicano Studies Center, UCLA, 405 Hilgard Avenue, Los Angeles CA 90024. **Tel** (310)825-2642.

US/0026-9891
MONTANA. (MONTANA : THE MAGAZINE OF WESTERN HISTORY.). [Montana]. **Added/Corp** Historical Society of Montana. Montana Historical Society. Vol. 5, No. 2 (1955)-. Periodical. English. qt. $20.00 (one year), $38.00 (two year) US; $28.00 (one year), $56.00 (two year) other. Montana Historical Society, 225 North Roberts Street, Helena MT 59620. **Tel** (406)44-4708, FAX (406)444-2696. **ED** Charles E. Rankin. **LC** F726; .M74. **DD** 978.6005. Index available. cum. index. **Bk Rev. Ad Acc. Circ:** 10,000. available on microfilm and microfiche from University Microfilms International (UMI). Documents available from The Genuine Article. ***Continues** Montana Magazine of History.*
Desc: History of Montana and the trans-Mississippi west.
Ind/Abst Am. Hist. Life (1955-); Annu. Bibliogr. Engl. Lang. Lit.; Arts Humanit. Citation Index [Full Cov.]; Curr. Contents Arts Humanit.; Res. Alert [Full Cov.]; Soc. Sci. Cit. Index [Select. Cov.]; Women Stud. Abstr.

US
MONTGOMERY COUNTY STORY, THE. **Added/Corp** Montgomery County Historical Society (Md.). Vol. 1, No. 1 (Nov. 1957)-. Periodical. English. qt. $15.00. Montgomery County Historical Society Inc., 111 West Montgomery Avenue, Rockville MD 20850. **Tel** (310)762-1492. **LC** F187.M7; M74.
Ind/Abst Am. Hist. Life.

CN/1183-2142
MONTREAL PASSIONS. [Montr. passions]. Vol. 1, No 1 (Jan. 1991)-. Periodical. French (English). bm. Editions M. P., Inc., Suite 100, 203 Place D'Youville, Montreal Quebec H2Y 2B3 Canada. **DD** 971.4/28/005.

CN/0707-9656
MONTREAL REVIEW. [Montreal rev.]. V. 1-Spring/Summer 1979-. Periodical. English. qt. $7.50. Deluge Press, CP 190/Suite Anne De Belleuve, Montreal Quebec H9X 3L9 Canada. **Tel** (514)457-6542. **DD** 971.4/281/005. **UDC** 971.4.

US/1059-8197
MOSAIC (BLOOMINGTON, IND.). (MOSAIC : THE NEWSLETTER OF THE CENTER ON HISTORY-MAKING IN AMERICA.). [Mosaic]. **Added/Corp** Center on History-Making in America. Vol. 1, No. 1 (Fall 1991)-. Newsletter. English. Three times a year. Center on History-Making in America, Indiana University, 1503 East 3rd Street, Suite 201-202, Bloomington IN 47405. **DD** 970.
Ind/Abst Acad. Abstr. (Jan. 1992-Sept. 1992).

US/0146-8855
MOUNTAIN DIGGINGS. English. an. $3.00. Lake County Civic Center Association, Box 962, Leadville CO 80461. **Tel** (303)486-1878. **ED** Sherrill Warford. **LC** F784.L4; M68. **DD** 978.8/46. **UDC** 978.8. Index available. cum. index. **Circ:** 250 (ctrl).
Desc: History of Leadville and Lake County, Colorado. 1860 to present.

US/0162-6655
MPLS. ST. PAUL. [Minneap. St. Paul]. **VFOAT** Mpls.-St. Paul Magazine. **VAT** Minneapolis Saint Paul. Vol. 6, No. 5 (May 1978)-. Periodical. English. mo. $18.00 Minnesota & Wisconsin; $22.00 US; $28.00 other. MSP Communication, 220 South 6th Street, Suite 500, Minneapolis MN 55402. **Tel** (612)339-7571, FAX (612)339-5806. **LC** F614.M6; M56. **DD** 977.6/579/0505. available on microfilm and microfiche from University Microfilms International (UMI). Documents available from UMI Article Clearinghouse, Magazine Collection. ***Continues** Mpls., 0162-3516.*
Ind/Abst Access (1975-); Bus. Dateline (March 1992-) [Full Txt.]; Gen. Period. Index (1985-); Mag. Index Plus (1989-); Newsp. Period. Abstr. (1988-); Mag. Index (1978-).

EC
MUNDO SHUAR. SERIE C. **VFOAT** Serie C, Proceso de Elaboracion de Artesanias; Proceso de Elaboracion Artesanias. 1-. Monographic series. Multiple languages (Spanish and South American Indian). ir. Price varies per volume. **LC** F3722.1.J5; M794. **UDC** 977.4.

EC/0378-2018
MUSEO HISTORICO. (MUSEO HISTORICO : ORGANO DEL MUSEO DE HISTORIA DE LA CIUDAD DE QUITO.). [Mus. hist.]. **Added/Corp** Museo de Historia de la Ciudad de Quito (Ecuador) Archivo Historico Municipal de la Ciudad de Quito. No. 1 (1949)-. Periodical. Spanish. qt. **LC** F3781; .M8. **DD** 986.
Ind/Abst Am. Hist. Life (1955-1972).

US/0580-3772
MY COUNTRY. V. 1- Jan. 1967-. English. ir. $5.00. My Country Society, PO Box 1123, Litchfield CT 06759. **ED** Edwin Wigglesworth. **LC** E171; .M9. **DD** 973/.05. **UDC** 980=6; 908.8=6. Index available. cum. index. **Circ:** 1,800.
Desc: Contains little known facts of history.

US/1056-2265
NANTUCKET JOURNAL (NANTUCKET, MASS. 1987). (NANTUCKET JOURNAL.). (1987)-. Periodical. English. Four times a year (Apr., June, Aug., Nov.). $15.95 (one year); $29.95 (two years); $44.95 (three years). Nantucket Journal Inc., 7 Sea Street, Nantucket MA 02554. **Tel** (508)228-8700, FAX (508)228-9063. **ED** Mary. S. Parker. **DD** 051. **Bk Rev**, (Qty: 3). **Ad Acc. Circ:** 8,000.
Desc: Articles, features, fiction, reviews, and photography focus on the traditions, history, environment, and life styles of this unique island community.

US/0027-8246
NASH SVIT. [Nas svit]. **VFOAT** Our World. Began with Oct. 1959 issue. Periodical. Ukrainian (Ukrainian). bm. Self Reliance Association of American Ukrainians, 98 Second Avenue, New York NY 10003. **LC** AP58.U5; N34. **DD** 970. **UDC** 745/749(8)(=98). ***Formed by the union of** Novyi Svit and Nash Kontakt.*

US/0278-6036
NASHVILLE CITY GUIDE. Periodical. English. Plusmedia, 230 Great Circle Road, Nashville TN 37228. **LC** F444.N2; N33. **DD** 976.8/55. **UDC** 976.8.

US/0094-9450
NASSAU COUNTY HISTORICAL SOCIETY JOURNAL, THE. **Main/Conf** Nassau County Historical Society. **Main/Corp** Nassau County Historical Society. **Added/Corp** Nassau County Historical Society. Journal. (19??)-. English. an. $10.00. Nassau County Historical Society, Box 207, Garden City NY 11530. **ED** Myron H. Luke. **LC** F127.N2; N3. **DD** 974.7/245/005. Index available. cum. index. **Circ:** 550. ***Continues** Nassau County Historical Journal.*
Desc: Articles on Long Island history, particularly Nassau County.

US
NATIONAL AFRO AMERICAN HISTORY KIT. English. an (Oct.). $45.00 (k-9th grade); $75.00 (other). Associated Publishers Incorporated, 1407 14th Street NW, Washington DC 20005. **Tel** (202)265-1441.

US
NATIONAL REGISTER OF HISTORIC PLACES INDEX ON CD-ROM. English. $298.00 US; $303.00 other. Wayzata Technolog Inc., PO Box 807, Grand Rapids MN 55744. **Tel** (218)326-0597, (800)735-7321.
Desc: Provides access to over 52,000 places on the US National Register. All US states and territories are included. Each record contains place, name, state, country, street address, city, type of place, certification date, criteria indicators, national historic landmark indicator, and reference number.

US/0890-068X
NATIONAL TOMBSTONE EPITAPH, THE. **VFOAT** Tombstone Epitaph. Vol. 9, No. 4 (April 1982)-. Periodical. English. mo. $8.00 (libraries) US; $9.00 (libraries) other. National Tombstone Epitaph, Box 1880, Tombstone AZ 85638. **Tel** (602)457-2211. **ED** Wallace E. Clayton. **DD** 978. **Bk Rev. Ad Acc. Circ:** 8,000. ***Continues** Tombstone Epitaph. National Ed.*
Desc: Articles by contemporary historians and archival material on all factual aspects of the development of, and life in, the American West.

US/1061-7884
NATIVE MONTHLY READER. [Native mon. read.]. **Added/Corp** International Traditional Education Systems. RedSun Institute (Crestone, Colo.). Vol. 1, No. 1 (1990)-. Periodical. English. mo. $15.00. RedSun Institute, PO Box 122, Crestone CO 81131. **Tel** (719)256-4848, FAX (719)256-4849. **DD** 305.
Desc: Dedicated to promoting cross-cultural understanding and excellence in education.

US/0895-7606
NATIVE PEOPLES. (NATIVE PEOPLES : THE JOURNAL OF THE HEARD MUSEUM.). [Native peoples]. **Added/Corp** Heard Museum of Anthropology and Primitive Art. Heard Museum. (Fall 1987)-. Periodical. English. qt (Jan., Apr., July, Oct.). $18.00 US & Canada; $29.00 other. Native Peoples, PO Box 36820, Phoenix AZ 85067-6820. **Tel** (602)252-2236, FAX (602)277-7857. **ED** Gary M. Avey. **LC** IN PROCESS. **DD** 970. **Bk Rev**, (Qty: 10). **Ad Acc, Adv Mgr:** J. Sixkiller. **Circ:** 112,000 (ctrl).
Desc: Focuses on personal stories of native American individuals and families. Intentions are to make the magazine more personal than other cultural magazines.
Ind/Abst Ethnoarts Index.

CN/0831-585X
NATIVE STUDIES REVIEW. See Ethnic Interests.

CN/0703-4733
NATOTAWIN. Began with Feb. 15, 1976 issue. Periodical. English. sm. Free. Regional Communication Centre, PO Box 70, Beauval Sask S0M 0G0 Canada. **DD** 971.24/1/00497. **UDC** 971.2. ctrl circ.

US/0149-2551
NEARA JOURNAL. **Main/Corp** New England Antiquities Research Association. **Added/Corp** New England Antiquities Research Association. Journal. **VAT** New England Antiquities Research Association Journal. Vol. 10, No. 36 (Spring 1975)-. Periodical. English. qt. $25.00 US; $30.00 other. New England Antiquities Research Association, 3 Whitney Drive, Paxton MA 01612. **Tel** (617)753-3992. **ED** Katherine Stannard (editor's phone: (508)753-3992). **LC** F6; .N48a. **DD** 974/.004/97. Index available. **Bk Rev**, (Qty: 3). **Ad Acc, Adv Mgr:** Suzanne, **Tel** (508)752-3490. **Circ:** 600 (ctrl). ***Continues*** *NEARA Newsletter, 0149-256X.*
Ind/Abst Abstr. Anthropol.

US/0028-1859
NEBRASKA HISTORY. [Neb. hist.]. **Added/Corp** Nebraska State Historical Society. Vol. 19, (Jan./Mar. 1938)-. Periodical. English. Four times a year (Mar., June, Sept., Dec.). $20.00. Nebraska State Historical Society, 1500 R Street, Box 82554, Lincoln NE 68501. **Tel** (402)471-4746, (800)833-6747. **ED** James E. Potter. **DD** 978. Index available. cum. index. **Bk Rev. Circ:** 5,000 (ctrl). available on microfilm and microfiche from University Microfilms International (UMI). ***Continues*** *Nebraska History Magazine, 0196-0733.*
Desc: Devoted to the story of Nebraska's past.
Ind/Abst Am. Hist. Life (1963-); Annu. Bibliogr. Engl. Lang. Lit.; West. Hist. Q.

US/0028-2529
NEGRO HISTORY BULLETIN. [Negro hist. bull.]. **Added/Corp** Association for the Study of Negro Life and History, Inc. Vol. 1 (Oct. 1937)-. Periodical. English. Four times a year (Jan., Apr., July, Oct.). $16.00 (individuals), $25.00 (institutions). Association for the Study of Afro-American Life & History, 1407 14th Street Northwest, Washington DC 20005. **Tel** (202)667-2822, FAX (202)387-9802. **ED** Dr. Neverdon-Morton (phone: (410)383-5638 or (410)521-4924). **LC** E185.5; .N383. **DD** 325.260973. Index available. **Bk Rev. Ad Acc, Adv Mgr:** Dr. J. Harris, **Tel** (202)667-2822. **Circ:** 2,300 (ctrl). available on microfilm and microfiche from University Microfilms International (UMI). Documents available from Magazine Collection.
Desc: Covers the history of African Americans in the United States, then some of the issues dealt with are slavery, colonization, abolition, music, drama, arts, and others. It also aims at the youth as well as scholars, teachers, churches, and professionals.
Ind/Abst Abr. Read. Guide Period. Lit.; Acad. Ind. [Computer File] (1984-); Acad. Search (July 1993-); Am. Hist. Life (1954-1977); Curr. Index J. Educ.; Expand. Acad. Index (1984-); Gen. Period. Index (1985-); Index Am. Period. Verse; Mag. Index Plus (1989-); Mag. Search; Read. Guide Period. Lit.; SportSearch; Mag. Index (1977-); TOM Gen. Index (1993-) [Full Txt.]; West. Hist. Q.

US/0273-0359
NEU-BRAUNFELSER JAHRBUCH. English (English). an. **LC** F395.G3; S347. **DD** 976.4/00431. **UDC** 976.4.

US/0099-0892
NEVADA HISTORICAL REVIEW. [Nev. hist. rev.]. Began with summer 1973 issue. Periodical. English. qt. $5.00. Dave's Print and Publishing, PO Box 1431, Sparks NV 89431. **LC** F841; .N514. **DD** 979.3/005. **UDC** 979.3.
Ind/Abst Am. Hist. Life (1974-1975).

US/0047-9462
NEVADA HISTORICAL SOCIETY QUARTERLY (1961). (NEVADA HISTORICAL SOCIETY QUARTERLY.). [Nev. Hist. Soc. q.]. **Added/Corp** Nevada Historical Society. **VFOAT** Back Number. Vol. 4, No. 1 (Jan.-Mar. 1961)-. Periodical. English. qt (4 issues). Comes with Nevada Historical Society membership ($25.00-regular membership, $50.00 sustaining membership). Nevada Historical Society, 1650 North Virginia Street, Reno NV 89502. **Tel** (702)688-1191. **ED** Cheryl A. Fox and William D. Rowley. **LC** F836; .N45. **DD** 979.3/005. Index available (free published in Aug.). cum. index. **Bk Rev. Ad Acc. Circ:** 1,600 (ctrl). available on microfilm and microfiche from University Microfilms International (UMI). ***Continues*** *Back Number.*
Ind/Abst Am. Hist. Life (1963-); West. Hist. Q.

US/0091-4959
NEW BOOKS QUARTERLY CHECKLIST SERIES : AFRO-AMERICAN HISTORY AND CULTURE. **VFOAT** Afro-American History and Culture. V. 1- Feb. 1973-. English. qt. $15.00. 7139 Hopkins Road, PO Box 138, Mentor OH 44060. **LC** Z1361.N39; N43. **DD** 016.9173/06/96073. **UDC** 973(=96); 908.73(=96).

US/0734-2802
NEW CANAAN HISTORICAL SOCIETY ANNUAL, THE. **Added/Corp** New Canaan Historical Society. New Canaan Historical Society. Annual. (19??)-. English. an. $8.00. New Canaan Historical Society, 13 Oenoke Ridge, New Canaan CT 06840. **Tel** (203)966-1776.

US/0028-4785
NEW ENGLAND HISTORICAL AND GENEALOGICAL REGISTER, THE. See Genealogy and Heraldry.

US/0028-4866
NEW ENGLAND QUARTERLY, THE. [New Engl. q.]. **Added/Corp** Colonial Society of Massachusetts. Northeastern University (Boston, Mass.). Vol. 1, (Jan. 1928)-. Periodical. English. qt (4 issues). $25.00 (institutions), $20.00 (individuals) US; $30.00 (institutions), $25.00 (individuals) other. The New England Quarterly, 243 Meserve Hall, Northeastern University, Boston MA 02115. **Tel** (617)373-2734, (617)373-2660, FAX (617)373-2661. **ED** William M. Fowler Jr and Linda Smith Rhoads. **LC** F1; .N62. **DD** 974.005. cum. index. **Bk Rev. Ad Acc. Circ:** 2,300. available on microfilm and microfiche from University Microfilms International (UMI). Documents available from The Genuine Article, UMI Article Clearinghouse.
Desc: Historical review of New England life and letters. Contains major essays, book reviews, memoranda and documents.
Ind/Abst Abstr. Engl. Stud.; Acad. Abstr. Full Text Elite (July 1990-); Acad. Abstr. (July 1990-); Acad. Ind. [Computer File] (1987-); Acad. Search (July 1990-); Am. Hist. Life (1954-); Annu. Bibliogr. Engl. Lang. Lit.; Arts Humanit. Citation Index [Full Cov.]; Book Rev. Digest; Book Rev. Index; Child. Lit. Abstr. (19??-); Curr. Contents Arts Humanit.; Expand. Acad. Index (1987-); Humanit. Index; INFO-SOUTH Abstr.; Lit. Crit. Regist.; Mag. Search; MLA Int. Bibl. Books Artic. Mod. Lang. Lit.; Newsp. Period. Abstr. (1991-); Relig. Theol. Abstr. (199?-); Res. Alert [Full Cov.]; Romant. Move.; Soc. Sci. Cit. Index [Select. Cov.]; SportSearch; West. Hist. Q.

US/0193-3108
NEW FLORIDA. Began with Vol. 1, No. 1 (July 1981). Periodical. English. mo. $15.00 (Florida residents), $18.00 (other states) US; $24.00 other. Fleet Street Corporation, 656 Quince Orchard Road, Gaithersburg MD 20878. **Tel** (301)977-3900. **LC** F306; .N48. **DD** 975.9/005. **UDC** 975.9.

US
NEW HAMPSHIRE HISTORICAL SOCIETY NEWSLETTER. **Main/Corp** New Hampshire Historical Society, Concord. Vol. 14, No. 1 (Jan. 1976)-. Newsletter. English. Four times a year. $30.00 Comes with New Hampshire Historical Society membership. New Hampshire Historical Society, 30 Park Street, Concord NH 03301-6384. **Tel** (603)225-3381, FAX (603)224-0463. **ED** Joan E. Desmarais. ***Continues*** *Newsletter - New Hampshire Historical Society, 0548-4944.*
Desc: News and information about the members and the society.

US/0028-5307
NEW HAMPSHIRE PROFILES. ***Ceased.*** Vol. 1 (Dec. 1951)-(Dec. 1991). Periodical. English. mo. New Hampshire Profiles Publishing, PO Box A40, Hanover NH 03755. **Tel** (603)772-5252. **(Subscription address:** PO Box 870, Farmingdale, NY 11737**) ED** Lynn Harnett. **LC** F31; .N76. **DD** 917.42. **UDC** 908.742; 974.2. ***Absorbed*** *Shoreliner.*
Desc: The only magazine dedicated solely to people who live in or love New Hampshire. It's the showcase of life in New Hampshire. A general interest, four-color magazine focusing on the people, places, events, history, nature, and food of New Hampshire.
Ind/Abst Access (1975-?).

US/0364-8184
NEW HORIZON (JERSEY CITY). See Ethnic Interests.

US/0047-9772
NEW JERSEY HISTORICAL COMMISSION NEWSLETTER. **Main/Corp** New Jersey Historical Commission. **Added/Corp** New Jersey Historical Commission. Newsletter. **VFOAT** NJ Historical Commission Newsletter. Vol. 1 (Sept. 1970)-. Periodical. English. mo (except July, Aug.). $10.00. New Jersey Historical Commission, 4 North Broad Street, CN 305, Trenton NJ 08625. **Tel** (609)292-6062, FAX (609)633-8168. **ED** Lee Parks (Phone: (609)984-3459). **LC** WMLC L 82/104. **Bk Rev**, (Qty: 20-30). **Circ:** 3,000 (ctrl).

US/0028-5757
NEW JERSEY HISTORY. [N.J. hist.]. **Added/Corp** New Jersey Historical Society. Vol. 85,No. 328, (Spring 1967)-. Periodical. English. qt. $20.00. New Jersey Historical Society, 230 Broadway, Newark NJ 07104. **Tel** (201)483-3939, FAX (201)483-1988. **LC** F131; .N58. **DD** 974.9/006/2. Index Available, published separately, free-automatically sent. available on microfilm and microfiche from University Microfilms International (UMI); available in machine readable format; available on labels. ***Continues*** *Proceedings of the New Jersey Historical Society, 0096-8935.*
Ind/Abst Am. Hist. Life (1963-); Annu. Bibliogr. Engl. Lang. Lit.

US/0890-8346
NEW JERSEY STATE LIBRARY IMPRESSIONS. ***Suspended.*** [N.J. State Libr. impress.]. **Added/Corp** New Jersey State Library. **VFOAT** Impressions; NJ State Library Impressions. Vol. 1, No. 1 (Oct. 1979)-Suspended. Periodical. English. Four times a year. Free on request. New Jersey State Library, 185 West State Street, Trenton NJ 08625. **Tel** (609)292-7306. **DD** 974.

CN/0824-6076
NEW LINK. (THE NEW LINK / ASSOCIATION OF POLISH ENGINEERS IN CANADA.). [New link]. **Added/Corp** Association of Polish Engineers in Canada. Vol. 37 (Oct. 1983)-. Periodical. English (Polish). bm. $1.50 per no. Association of Polish Engineers in Canada, 206 Beverley Street, Toronto Ontario M5T 1Z3 Canada. **DD** 971/.0049185. **Circ:** 1,000. ***Continues*** *Bulletin (Association of Polish Engineers in Canada), 0044-9644.*

US/0028-6206
NEW MEXICO HISTORICAL REVIEW. [N.M. hist. rev.]. **Added/Corp** University of New Mexico. Historical Society of New Mexico. School of American Research. (Santa Fe, N. M.). Dept. of History. (1926)-. Periodical. English. Four times a year. $28.00 (institutions), $24.00 (individuals) US; $35.00 (institutions), $30.00 (individuals) other. University of New Mexico, 1013 Mesa Vista Hall, Albuquerque NM 87131-1186. **Tel** (505)277-5839, FAX (505)277-6023. **ED** Robert Himmerich y Valencia (editor's phone: (505)277-7847). **LC** F791; .N65. **DD** 978.9/005. Index available. cum. index (4 vols. 1926-1985; $5 each). **Bk Rev. Ad Acc, Adv Mgr:** Bill Broughton, **Tel** (505)277-0991. **Circ:** 1,000. available on microfilm and microfiche from University Microfilms International (UMI); available on CD-ROM. Documents available from The Genuine Article.
Desc: Emphasizes Spanish, Mexican, territorial and statehood periods of New Mexico and relevant materials. Features manuscripts, documents, state history news, book reviews and notes.
Ind/Abst Am. Hist. Life (1954-); Anthropol. Index; Arts Humanit. Citation Index [Full Cov.]; Curr. Contents Arts Humanit.; Res. Alert [Full Cov.]; West. Hist. Q.

US/0272-6394
NEW WORLD JOURNAL. [New world j]. **Added/Corp** Netzahaulcoyotl Historical Society. Vol. 1 (1975)-. Periodical. English. an. New World Journal, 2845 Buena Vista Way, Berkeley CA 94708.

US/0146-437X
NEW YORK HISTORY. (NEW YORK HISTORY: QUARTERLY JOURNAL OF THE NEW YORK STATE HISTORICAL ASSOCIATION.). [N.Y. hist.]. **Added/Corp** New York State Historical Association. New York State Historical Association. Meeting. **VFOAT** Proceedings of the New York State Historical Association. Vol. 13, No. 1 (Jan. 1932)-. Periodical. English. qt. $20.00, $35.00 (includes Heritage). New York State Historical Association, PO Box 800 Lake Road, Cooperstown NY 13326. **Tel** (607)547-2533, FAX (607)547-5384. **ED** Wendell Tripp. **LC** F116; .N865. **DD** 974. Index available. cum. index. **Circ:** 2,500. available on microfilm and microfiche from University Microfilms International (UMI). Documents available from The Genuine Article. ***Continues*** *Quarterly Journal of the New York State Historical Association, 0146-3519.*
Desc: Publishes articles relating to the history and culture of New York State from the colonial period to the present.
Ind/Abst Am. Hist. Life (1955-); Annu. Bibliogr. Engl. Lang. Lit.; Arts Humanit. Citation Index [Full Cov.]; BHA : Biblio. Hist. Art; MLA Int. Bibl. Books Artic. Mod. Lang. Lit.; Res. Alert [Full Cov.]; Soc. Sci. Cit. Index [Select. Cov.]; West. Hist. Q. (1955-).

CN/0827-3960
NEWFOUNDLAND LIFESTYLE. **VFOAT** Lifestyle. Vol. 1, No. 1 (Aug./Sept. 1983)-. Periodical. English. Four times a year. 12.00Can$ (one year), 20.00Can$ (two year) Canada; 18.00Can$ (one year), 30.00Can$ (two year) US; 25.00Can$ (one year), 43.00Can$ (two year) other. Newfoundland Lifestyle Magazine, PO Box 2356 Station C, St John's Newfoundland, A1C 6E7 Canada. **Tel** (709)726-9300, FAX (709)726-3013. **ED** Adrian Smith. **DD** 971.8/005. **Ad Acc, Adv Mgr:** Hubert Hutton. **Circ:** 17,500 (ctrl).
Desc: An entertaining provincial magazine compatible with the social and cultural history found in the old world charm of Newfoundland.

CN/0380-5832
NEWFOUNDLAND QUARTERLY (1971). (NEWFOUNDLAND QUARTERLY.). [Nfld. q. (1971)]. **Added/Corp** Newfoundland Historical Society. Aspects. Vol. 68 (Spring 1971)-. Periodical. English. qt. 12.00Can$ Canada, 15.00Can$ other. Newfoundland Quarterly, PO Box 13486 Stn A Kenmount Rd, St Johns A1B 4B8 Newfoundland Canada. **Tel** (709)726-6590. **ED** Harry A. Cuff (editor's address: 94 LeMarchant Rd, St. John's, Newfoundland). **Bk Rev. Circ:** 5,000. ***Continues*** *New Newfoundland Quarterly, 0380-5824.*

Desc: Publishes fiction, poetry, and articles dealing with Newfoundland culture, also historical articles, and news highlights.
Ind/Abst Am. Hist. Life (1963-1964); Can. Index (?-?); Can. Period. Index (19??-).

CN/0823-1737
NEWFOUNDLAND STUDIES. [Nfld. stud.]. **Added/Corp** Memorial University of Newfoundland. Dept. of English Language and Literature. Vol. 1, No. 1 (Spring 1985)-. Periodical. English. sa. $25.00 (institutions), $18.00 (individuals). Newfoundland Studies, Memorial University of Newfoundland, Department of English, St John's Newfoundland A1C 5S7 Canada. **Tel** (709)737-2144, FAX (709)737-2164, telex 016-4101. **ED** Patrick O'Flaherty (editor's phone: (709)737-2600). **DD** 971.8/005. Index available (bound in 2nd issue). **Bk Rev**, (Qty: 6). **Circ:** 500.
Desc: Publishes essays in the arts and sciences about the society and culture of Newfoundland.
Ind/Abst Am. Hist. Life (1985-); Can. Index (?-?).

US/0028-8918
NEWPORT HISTORY. (NEWPORT HISTORY : BULLETIN OF THE NEWPORT HISTORICAL SOCIETY.). [Newport hist.]. **Added/Corp** Newport Historical Society. No. 113 (Jan. 1964)-. Bulletin. English. Four times a year. $25.00. Newport Historical Society, 82 Touro Street, Newport RI 02840. **Tel** (401)846-0813. **ED** Ron Potvin. **LC** F89.N5; N615. Index available. cum. index. **Ad Acc. Circ:** 1,500 (ctrl). available on microfilm from University Microfilms International (UMI). ***Continues*** *Bulletin of the Newport Historical Society.*
Ind/Abst Am. Hist. Life (1969-); Writ. Am. Hist.

US/8755-9854
NEWS AND JOURNAL (RIPLEY, MISS.). **See** Genealogy and Heraldry.

CN/0700-4427
NEWS AND VIEWS - SIMCOE COUNTY HISTORICAL ASSOCIATION. (NEWS AND VIEWS.). Periodical. English. mo. $3.00. Simcoe County Historical Association, PO Box 144, Barrie Ontario L4M 4T6 Canada. **DD** 971.3/17. **UDC** 971.3.

US/1040-5437
NEWS FROM NATIVE CALIFORNIA. [News native Calif.]. Vol. 1, No. 1 (March/April 1987)-. Periodical. English. qt (Feb., May, Aug., Nov.). $17.50 (1 year), $35.00 (2 year), $44.00 (3 year) US; $25.00 other. Heyday Books, PO Box 9145, Berkeley CA 94709. **Tel** (510)549-3564, FAX (510)549-1889. **ED** Malcolm Margolin and Jeannine Geudar. **LC** E78.C15; N45. **DD** 979.4/00497/005. Index available. **Bk Rev**, (Qty: 15-20). **Ad Acc, Adv Mgr:** Yolanda Montijo. **Circ:** 4,800.
Desc: Devoted to cultural, political, and historic concerns of California Indians.
Ind/Abst West. Hist. Q.

US/1047-708X
NEWS / INDIANA HISTORICAL SOCIETY. [News - Ind. Hist. Soc.]. **Added/Corp** Indiana Historical Society. Vol. 1, No. 1 (Jan./Feb. 1986)-. Periodical. English. bm. Comes with membership. Indiana Historical Society, 315 West Ohio Street, Indianapolis IN 46202. **Tel** (317)232-1882. **ED** Kent Calder. **DD** 977; 2 11. **Circ:** 6,000. ***Continues*** *Newsletter (Indiana Historical Society).*

US/0020-2843
NEWS LETTER FROM THE INSTITUTE OF EARLY AMERICAN HISTORY & CULTURE, A. **Main/Corp** Institute of Early American History and Culture, Williamsburg, VA. **Added/Corp** College of William and Mary. Colonial Williamsburg Foundation. No. 1 (Sept. 1952)-. Academic Scholarly Publication. English. sa. free on request. Institute of Early American History and Culture, PO Box 8781, Williamsburg VA 23187-8781. **Tel** (804)221-1120, FAX (804)221-1047. **ED** Michael McGiffert. **Circ:** 2,100 (ctrl).
Desc: A collection of information of scholarly conferences, the coming and going of visiting scholars, and other matters useful to specialists in the field.

US/0271-7522
NEWS-LETTER - NATIONAL SOCIETY OF UNITED STATES DAUGHTERS OF 1812. **See** Societies and Clubs.

US/0277-5263
NEWS MONITORING SERVICE. (NEWS MONITORING SERVICE / COMITE DE MEXICO Y AZTLAN.). **Added/Corp** Comite de Mexico y Aztlan. **VFOAT** COMEXAZ News Monitoring Service. (May 1972)-. Periodical. English. mo. Comite Mexico y Aztlan, Box 12062, Oakland CA 94604. **LC** E184.M5; N44. **DD** 973/.046872/005.

US/0474-4535
NEWS - OREGON HISTORICAL SOCIETY. ***Title Change.*** [News - Or. Hist. Soc.]. **Main/Corp** Oregon Historical Society. (19??)-(Vol. 35, 19??). Periodical. English. bm. Oregon Historical Society, 1200 Southwest Park Avenue, Portland OR 97205. **Tel** (503)222-1741 ext.28, FAX (503)221-2035. **ED** Marguerite W. Wright. **LC** F871; .O436. **DD** 979.5/006/279549. **Circ:** 9,000 (ctrl). ***Continues*** *Newsletter (Oregon Historical Society).* ***Continued by*** *Oregon History.*
Desc: Activities and programs at the Oregon Historical Society.

US/0882-3154
NEWS / WESTERN RESERVE HISTORICAL SOCIETY. **Added/Corp** Western Reserve Historical Society. Vol. 37, No. 2 (March-April 1983)-. Periodical. English. qt. Included in membership. Western Reserve Historical Society, 10825 East Boulevard, Cleveland OH 44106. **Tel** (216)721-5722. **ED** Eric Johannesen. **LC** F486; .W55. **DD** 977.1/005. **Circ:** 5,000. ***Continues*** *Western Reserve Historical Society News, 0882-3146.*
Desc: Current events at regional historical society with museum, library and historic properties, plus articles on Northeast Ohio history.

CN/0225-1248
NEWSCALL NEWSLETTER, THE. [Newscall newsl.]. Began publication in June 1978?. Newsletter. English. Free. Native Brotherhood Society, PO Box 160, Prince Albert Saskatchewan S6V 5R6 Canada. **DD** 971/.00497. **UDC** 971. ***Continues*** *Native Brotherhood Newscall, 0700-690X.*

US/0882-8474
NEWSLETTER (AFRO-AMERICAN HISTORICAL AND GENEALOGICAL SOCIETY (WASHINGTON, D.C.) : 1983). (NEWSLETTER / AFRO-AMERICAN HISTORICAL AND GENEALOGICAL SOCIETY, INC.). [Newsl. - Afro-Am. Hist. Geneal. Soc. (Wash., D.C.)]. **Added/Corp** Afro-American Historical and Genealogical Society (Washington, D.C.). Vol. 6, No. 3 (Dec. 1983)-. Periodical. English. ir. $35.00 Comes with Journal of the Afro-American Historical and Genealogical Society. Afro-American Historical and Genealogical Society, PO Box 73086, Washington DC 20056-3086. **Tel** (202)234-5350. **LC** E185.5; .A2. **DD** 973/.0496/005. ***Continues*** *AAHGS News.*

US/0521-5722
NEWSLETTER - BUFFALO AND ERIE COUNTY HISTORICAL SOCIETY. **Main/Corp** Buffalo and Erie County Historical Society. (1978)-. Newsletter. English. Four times a year. $20.00 Comes with Buffalo & Erie County Historical Society Membership;. Buffalo and Erie County Historical Society, 25 Nottingham Court, Buffalo NY 14216. **Tel** (716)874-0670. ***Continues*** *Buffalo and Erie County Historical Society Broadside.*

CN/0703-959X
NEWSLETTER - CARIBBEAN ASSOCIATION OF NOVA SCOTIA. **Main/Corp** Caribbean Association of Nova Scotia. V. 1-1977-. Newsletter. English. Caribbean Association of Nova Scotia, PO Box 3603, Halifax South Postal Station, Halifax NS B3J 3K6 Canada. **DD** 971.6/004/969729. **UDC** 971.6.

CN/0821-2430
NEWSLETTER - COLCHESTER HISTORICAL SOCIETY. (NEWSLETTER.). [Newsletter - Colchester Historical Museum]. Newsletter. English. mo (except for July and August). Free to members. Colchester Historical Society, PO Box 412, Truro Nova Scotia B2N 5C5 Canada. **Tel** (902)895-6284. **ED** Ira E Creelman. **DD** 971.6/12. **UDC** 971.6. **Bk Rev. Circ:** 250 (ctrl).
Desc: Newsletter for members of Colchester Historical Society. Provides information on society, museum, archives, and genealogy activities.

US/0197-9027
NEWSLETTER - CUBA HISTORICAL SOCIETY, THE. [Newsl. - Cuba Hist. Soc.]. **Main/Corp** Cuba Historical Society (N.Y.). Vol. 1 (May 1970)-. Periodical. English. Four times a year. $3.00 Comes with Cuba Historical Society membership. Cuba Historical Society, PO Box 71, Cuba NY 14727. **Tel** (716)968-1492.
Ind/Abst Am. Hist. Life.

US
NEWSLETTER FOR THE ROCKY MOUNT HISTORICAL ASSOCIATION. ***Title Change.*** **Added/Corp** Rocky Mount Historical Association. **VFOAT** Rocky Mount Newsletter. (19??)-(19??). Newsletter. English. Rocky Mount Historical Association, 200 Hyder Hills, Piney Flats TN 37686. **Tel** (615)538-7396. ***Continued by*** *Rocky Mount Gazette, 1065-3813.*

US/0882-3774
NEWSLETTER / FREMONT-CUSTER HISTORICAL SOCIETY. **Added/Corp** Fremont-Custer Historical Society. (19??)-. Newsletter. English. bm. Comes with membership. Fremont-Custer Historical Society, PO Box 965, Canon City CO 81212.

CN/0381-0119
NEWSLETTER - FRONTENAC HISTORIC FOUNDATION. **See** Architecture.

CN/0821-0373
NEWSLETTER - HERITAGE ST. CATHARINES. (NEWSLETTER.). [Newsl. - Herit. St. Catharines]. 1st issue (Autumn 1982)-. Newsletter. English. sa. Free. Heritage St Catharines, PO Box 1692, St Catharines Ontario L2R 7K1 Canada. **DD** 971.3/51. **UDC** 971.3. ctrl circ.

CN/0711-3803
NEWSLETTER (HISTORICAL SOCIETY OF OTTAWA). (NEWSLETTER.). [Newsl. - Hist. Soc. Ottawa]. **Added/Corp** Historical Society of Ottawa. (1977)-. Periodical. English. Four times a year (Jan., Apr., Sept., Nov.). 4.00Can$. Historical Society of Ottawa, PO Box 523 Station B, Ottawa Ontario K1P 5P6 Canada. **Tel** (613)820-6717. **ED** June Graig. **DD** 971.3/84/06. **Circ:** 400 (ctrl).

US
NEWSLETTER / INDIANA COVERED BRIDGE SOCIETY. **Added/Corp** Indiana Covered Bridge Society. Vol. 1, No. 1 (Jan. 1964)-. Periodical. English. qt. $5.00. Indiana Covered Bridge Society, 725 Sanders Street, Indianapolis IN 46203. **ED** George E. Gould. **Bk Rev. Ad Acc.** ctrl circ.
Desc: Information relating to covered bridges in Indiana, their history and current status.

CN/0713-8806
NEWSLETTER / INNISFIL HISTORICAL SOCIETY. [News. - Innisfil Hist. Soc.]. Aug. 1981-. Newsletter. English. Ten times a year. 10.00Can$. Innisfil Historical Society, PO Box 381, Stroud Ontario L0L 1M0 Canada. **ED** P Weber. **DD** 971.3/17. **UDC** 971.3. **Bk Rev. Circ:** 125 (ctrl). ***Continues*** *Innisfil Historical and Archaeological Society. Newsletter, 0228-0884.*

CN/0709-7794
NEWSLETTER - INUIT CULTURAL INSTITUTE. [Newsl. -Inuit Cult. Inst.]. **Main/Corp** Inuit Cultural Institute. Began with Spring 1978 issue?. Newsletter. English. Inuit Cultural Institute, Eskimo Point Northwest Territories X0C 0E0 Canada. **Tel** (819)857-2803. **DD** 971/.004/97. **UDC** 971.2(=947.5); 930.85(=947.5) (712).

CN/1180-081X
NEWSLETTER / KEMPTVILLE & DISTRICT HISTORICAL SOCIETY. [Newsl. - Kemptv. Dist. Hist. Soc.]. **Added/Corp** Kemptville and District Historical Society. Vol. 1, No. 1 (Jan./Feb. 1990)-. Newsletter. English. bm. Limited free distribution. Kemptville and District Historical Society, PO Box 1269, Kemptville, Ontario K0G 1J0 Canada. **DD** 971.3/73.

CN/0713-6285
NEWSLETTER - KITCHENER WATERLOO REGIONAL FOLK ARTS MULTICULTURAL CENTRE. (NEWSLETTER.). [Newsl. - Kitchener Waterloo Reg. Folk Arts Multicult. Cent.]. **Added/Corp** Kitchener Waterloo Regional Folk Arts Multicultural Centre. No. 36 (Mar. 1980)-. Newsletter. English. Limited free distribution. Languages and Multicultural Centre, 139 Grote Street, Adelaide SA 5000 Australia. **DD** 971.3/45004/05. ctrl circ. ***Continues*** *Newsletter (K-W Regional Folk Arts Council. Multi Cultural Centre), 0713-6277.*

CN/0838-7249
NEWSLETTER / LETHBRIDGE HISTORICAL SOCIETY. [Newsl. - Lethbridge Hist. Soc.]. **Added/Corp** Lethbridge Historical Society. No. 5 (Sept. 1987)-. Newsletter. English. Six times a year (Jan., Mar., May, July, Sept., Nov.). 8.50Can$. Lethbridge Historical Society, PO Box 974, Lethbridge Alberta T1J 4A2 Canada. **Tel** (403)320-3957. **ED** Erma Doglerom. **DD** 971.23/4. ***Continues*** *Newsletter - Historical Society of Alberta, Whoop-Up Country Chapter., 0382-9812.*

US/0459-5866
NEWSLETTER - LITTLE BIG HORN ASSOCIATES. **Main/Corp** Little Big Horn Associates. (1967)-. Newsletter. English. mo (10 issues). comes with membership. Little Big Horn Associates, PO Box 640286, El Paso TX 79904. **Tel** (915)755-6676. **ED** Lowell Smith. **LC** E83.876; .L77a. **DD** 973.8/2. **Bk Rev**, (Qty: 10). **Pr Rev. Circ:** 1100 (ctrl).
Desc: Study of the Battle of Little Big Horn and life and times of George Armstrong Custer.

CN/0824-5614
NEWSLETTER / LONDON AND MIDDLESEX COUNTY HISTORICAL SOCIETY. [Newsl. - Lond. Middlx. Hist. Soc.]. **Main/Corp** London and Middlesex Historical Society (Ont.). Feb. 1979-. Newsletter. English. Eight times a year. London and Middlesex Historical Society, PO Box 303 Station B, London Ontario N6A 4W1 Canada. **Tel** (519)686-1239. **ED** Wilfred Farrell. **DD** 971.3/25/006. **UDC** 971.3. Index available. cum. index. **Circ:** 200 (ctrl). available on audiocassette.

US/0882-4223
NEWSLETTER / MAINE HISTORICAL SOCIETY. **Main/Corp** Maine Historical Society. (19??)-. Newsletter. English. qt. comes with membership. Maine Historical Society, 485 Congress Street, Portland

ME 04101. **Tel** (207)774-1822. **ED** Michael Donahue. **LC** F16; .M29. **DD** 974.1/006/0741. **Ad Acc. Circ:** 2,500 (ctrl).

US
NEWSLETTER - MICHIGAN STATE UNIVERSITY, LATIN AMERICAN STUDIES CENTER. **Main/Corp** Michigan State University. Latin American Studies Center. No. 1 (19??)-. Newsletter. English. qt. Free on request. Michigan State University / Latin American Studies, 206 Center for International Programs, East Lansing MI 48824. **Tel** (517)353-1690.

US/0740-8781
NEWSLETTER / MONMOUTH COUNTY HISTORICAL ASSOCIATION. **Added/Corp** Monmouth County Historical Association (N.J.). (19??)-. Newsletter. English. Four times a year. comes with membership. Monmouth County Historical Association, 70 Court Street, Freehold NJ 07728. **Tel** (908)462-1466. **Bk Rev. Circ:** 1,300 (ctrl).
Desc: An article on a subject of local historical significance and articles and calendar of events relating to the Association's programs and activities.

US/1075-248X
NEWSLETTER - MONROE COUNTY HISTORICAL SOCIETY (WIS.). (NEWSLETTER / MONROE COUNTY HISTORICAL SOCIETY.). [Newsl. - Monroe Cty. Hist. Soc. (Wis.)]. **Added/Corp** Monroe County Historical Society (Wis.). (19??)-. Newsletter. English. qt. $5.00 US; $7.00 other. Monroe County Historical Society, Box 422, Sparta WI 54656. **Tel** (608)378-4388, FAX (608)378-3006. **ED** Jim Schlosser. **DD** 977. Index available. cum. index. **Bk Rev**, (Qty: 12). **Circ:** 210.
Desc: Prints Monroe County historical stories, club events and business, state meetings, etc.

US/0889-6178
NEWSLETTER OF THE AFRO-AMERICAN RELIGIOUS HISTORY GROUP OF THE AMERICAN ACADEMY OF RELIGION. [Newsl. Afro.-Am. Relig. Hist. Group Am. Acad. Relig.]. **Main/Corp** American Academy of Religion. Afro-American Religious History Group. (Fall 1976)-. Periodical. English. Twice a year. $4.00 US; $10.00 other. WEB DuBois Institute, Harvard University, 44 Brattle Street, Cambridge MA 02138. **Tel** (617)495-4192, FAX (617)495-8547. **ED** Randall K. Burkett (editor's phone: (617)495-4965). **DD** 280. **Bk Rev. Circ:** 400.

CN/0831-9871
NEWSLETTER OF THE GANANOQUE HISTORICAL SOCIETY. [Newsl. Gananoque Hist. Soc.]. **Added/Corp** Gananoque Historical Society. No. 1 (Sept. 1984)-. Newsletter. English. sa. 35.00Can$ (organizations); 12.00Can$ Canada; 13.00Can$ US (individuals). Gananoque Historical Society, PO Box 511, Gananoque Ontario, K7G 2V1 Canada. **Tel** (613)382-2282. **DD** 971.3/73.

CN/0824-1732
NEWSLETTER OF THE KINGS COUNTY HISTORICAL AND ARCHIVAL SOCIETY, INC. [Newsl. Kings Cty. Hist. Arch. Soc. Inc.]. **Added/Corp** Kings County Historical and Archival Society (N.B.). (Sept. 1983)-. Periodical. English. Seven times a year. Free to members; 20.00Can$ membership. Kings County Historical and Archival Society, Sussex Corner NB E0E 1R0 Canada. **Tel** (506)832-6009. **DD** 971.5/41/005. ***Continues*** *Kings County Historical Society (N.B.). Newsletter of the Kings County Historical Society, 0380-3384.*

CN/0822-8353
NEWSLETTER / SCARBOROUGH HISTORICAL SOCIETY. See Societies and Clubs.

US/0895-0822
NEWSLETTER / THE CROW WING COUNTY HISTORICAL SOCIETY. [Newsl. - Crow Wing Cty. Hist. Soc.]. **Added/Corp** Crow Wing County Historical Society. (198?)-. Newsletter. English. qt. $10.00. Crow Wing County Historical Society, PO Box 722, Brainerd MN 56401. **Tel** (218)829-3268. **ED** Mary Lou Moudry. **DD** 977. **Bk Rev**, (Qty: 4). **Ad Acc. Circ:** 900.
Desc: Highlighting past, present and future activities of the Crow Wing County Historical Society and its museum.

US/0078-1967
NEWSLETTER - THE NORWEGIAN-AMERICAN HISTORICAL ASSOCIATION. **Main/Corp** Norwegian-American Historical Association. No. 1 (1934)-. Periodical. English. ir (2 issues). Free on request. Norwegian-American Historical Association, St. Olaf College, Northfield MN 55057. **Tel** (507)646-3221. **ED** Lloyd Hustvedt. **Bk Rev. Ad Acc. Circ:** 1,400 (ctrl).
Desc: News about the activities of the Association. Directed mainly to the members.

CN/0823-6275
NEWSLETTER / UNITED NATIVE FRIENDSHIP CENTRE. [Newsl. - United Native Friendsh. Cent.]. **Added/Corp** United Native Friendship Centre. (1982)-. Newsletter. English. mo. Free to members. United Native Friendship Centre, PO Box 752, Fort Frances Ontario P9A 3N1 Canada. **DD** 971.3/11700497/06.

CN/0823-0161
NEWSLETTER - VANCOUVER HISTORICAL SOCIETY (1980). (NEWSLETTER / VANCOUVER HISTORICAL SOCIETY.). [Newsl. - Vanc. Hist. Soc.]. Vol. 20, No. 1 (Sept. 1980)-. Newsletter. English. Nine times a year. 20.00Can$. Vancouver Historical Society, PO Box 3071, Vancouver British Columbia V6B 3X6 Canada. **Tel** (604)254-0221. **ED** Christine Mullins. **DD** 971.11/33. **UDC** 971.1. **Bk Rev. Circ:** 250 (ctrl). ***Continues*** *Vancouver History, 0706-747X.*
Desc: History of city of Vancouver and British Columbia. Short articles, book reviews, book lists, and local events of historical interest. Activities of society.

CN/0382-0831
NEWSLETTER - WESTMORLAND HISTORICAL SOCIETY. (NEWSLETTER - WESTMORLAND HISTORICAL SOCIETY.). **Main/Corp** Westmorland Historical Society (N.B.). (1965)-. Newsletter. English. Three times a year. Westmorland Historical Society, Route 1, College Bridge, New Brunswick E0A 1L0 Canada. **Tel** (506)758-9355. **ED** Edith Gillcash. cum. index. **Bk Rev. Circ:** 225 (ctrl).
Desc: History and historic events surrounding Westmorland County, New Brunswick.

US
NEWSLINE. **Main/Corp** East Tennessee Historical Society. Vol. 1, No. 1 (March 1985)-. Periodical. English. Four times a year. $20.00 Comes with East Tennessee Historical Society membership. East Tennessee Historical Society, 500 West Church Avenue, Knoxville TN 37902. **Tel** (615)544-5732. **ED** Mark V. Wetherington. **Circ:** 2,000 (ctrl). ***Continues*** *East Tennessee Historical Society. Echoes from the East Tennessee Historical Society, 0422-2482.*
Desc: News and information about the society and it's members.

CN/1182-6649
NIAGARA'S HISTORICAL MUSEUMS ... DIRECTORY. [Niagara's hist. mus. dir.]. **Added/Corp** Museums of Niagara Association. (1990)-. Directory. English. Region Niagara Tourist Council, 2201 St. David's Road, PO Box 1042, Thorold Ontario L2V 4T7 Canada. **Tel** (416)685-1571. **DD** 971.3/38/0074. ***Continues*** *Directory to Niagara's Historical Museums., 0836-5296.*

NQ
NICARAGUA THROUGH OUR EYES. ***Ceased.*** **Added/Corp** Committee of US Citizens Living in Nicaragua. (1985)-(1993). Periodical. English. mo. Committe of US Citizens Living in Nicaragua, Cusclin Apartado 4110-Z5, Managua, Nicaragua.
Ind/Abst Hum. Rights Intern. Rep.

US
NICARAGUA UPDATE. **Added/Corp** Nicaragua Interfaith Committee for Action. Vol. 1, No. 1 (Sept. 1979)-. Periodical. English. qt. $10.00. Nicaragua Interfaith Committee for Action, 942 Market Street, Room 706, San Francisco CA 94102.
Ind/Abst Hum. Rights Intern. Rep.

US/8755-4968
NICARAGUA (WASHINGTON, D.C. 1982). (NICARAGUA.). [Nicaragua]. (1982)-. Periodical. English. $10.00. National Network in Solidarity with Nicaraguan People, 930 F Street NW, Room 720, Washington DC 20004. **DD** 972. **UDC** 972.85; 908.728.5.
Ind/Abst Hum. Rights Intern. Rep.

CN/0708-8132
NICOLA VALLEY HISTORICAL QUARTERLY. [Nicola Val. hist. q.]. **Added/Corp** Nicola Valley Archives Association. Vol. 2 (Jan. 1979)-. Periodical. English. Four times a year. 15.00Can$ (individual), 25.00Can$ (institutions) Comes with Nicola Valley Archives Association membership. Nicola Valley Archives Association, PO Box 1262, 2201 Jackson Avenue, Merritt British Columbia, V0K 2BO Canada. **Tel** (604)378-4145. **ED** Pat Lean. **DD** 971.1/41/006. Index available. cum. index. **Bk Rev. Ad Acc. Circ:** 1,000. ***Continues*** *Nicola Valley Archives Association. News Letter, Historical Work Paper, 0706-5531.*
Desc: Publishes historical material on the history of the Nicola Water Shed of South Central British Columbia.

CN/0712-5054
NIEN GIAM VIET-NAM, MONTREAL. [Nien giam Viet-nam Montr.]. **VFOAT** Repertoire Vietnamienne, Montreal; Vietnamese Directory, Montreal. 1982-. Vietnamese. an. Free. Nien Giam Vietnam (Vietnamese Directory), c/o Vietnam Canada Foundation, PO Box 75 Station H, Montreal Quebec H3G 2M7 Canada. **Tel** (514)527-6640. **ED** Van Tan Ngo. **DD** 971.24/0049592/025. **Ad Acc. Circ:** 5,000 (ctrl).

JA
NIHON TO BURAJIRU. **Added/Corp** Japan. Gaimusho. Joho Bunkakyoku. (19??)-. Periodical. Japanese. Gaimusho Joho Bunkakyoku, 2-1 Kasumigaseki 2, Chiyoda-ku Tokyo-to 100 Japan. **LC** F2501; .N53.

US
NIKKEI PAIONIYA AYUMI NO ATO. **Added/Corp** Japanese Community Pioneer Center (Los Angeles, Calif.). (1980)-. Japanese. **LC** F870.J3; A98. ***Continues*** *Ayumi No Ato.*

CN/0844-5869
NIKKEI VOICE. [Nikkei voice]. **Added/Corp** Nikkei Research & Education Project of Ontario. Vol. 1, No. 1 (Dec. 1987)-. Periodical. English (Japanese). Twelve times a year. Free. Nikkei Voice, 192 Spadina, Suite 401, Toronto ONT M5T 2C2 Canada. **Tel** (416)365-3343. **DD** 971/.004956/05.

US/0890-0485
NINNAU : THE NORTH AMERICAN WELSH NEWSLETTER. See Ethnic Interests.

BL
NITEROI. Yearly V. 1- 1969-. Portuguese. Rua Coronel Gomes Machado, 38/304 Niteroi Brazil. **LC** F2651.N55; N55.

US
NORTH AMERICA INDIANS. CD-ROM. English. $74.95. Quanta Press, Inc., 1313 Fifth Street Southeast, Suite 208C, Minneapolis MN 55414. **Tel** (612)379-3956, FAX (612)623-4570.
Desc: Database on the history of Native Americans. Included are leadership, tribal heritage, religion, family life, and customs. Available in DOS and MAC formats.

US/0029-2494
NORTH CAROLINA HISTORICAL REVIEW, THE. [N.C. hist. rev.]. **Added/Corp** North Carolina Historical Commission. North Carolina. State Dept. of Archives and History. North Carolina. Office of Archives and History. North Carolina. Division of Archives and History. Vol. 1, No. 1 (Jan. 1924)-. Academic Scholarly Publication. English. qt (Jan., Apr., July, Oct.). $25.00. North Carolina Division of Archives and History, 109 East Jones Street, Raleigh NC 27601. **Tel** (919)733-7442. **ED** Kathleen Wyche. **LC** F251; .N892. Index available. cum. index. **Bk Rev. Pr Rev. Circ:** 1,700 (ctrl). available on microfilm and microfiche from University Microfilms International (UMI).
Desc: State's journal of history containing scholarly articles, documentary materials, and book reviews.
Ind/Abst Am. Hist. Life (1963-); Annu. Bibliogr. Engl. Lang. Lit.; BHA : Biblio. Hist. Art; MLA Int. Bibl. Books Artic. Mod. Lang. Lit.; West. Hist. Q.

US/0193-547X
NORTH CAROLINA INFORMATION AND FACT BOOK, THE. **VFOAT** Tar Heel Almanac. 1979-. English. an. $3.25. C R Cannon, PO Box 1961, Greenville NC 27843. **LC** F251; .N8947. **DD** 975.6/005. **UDC** 975.6.

US/0029-2710
NORTH DAKOTA HISTORY. [N.D. hist.]. **Added/Corp** State Historical Society of North Dakota. Vol. 12, No. 1-2 (Jan./April 1945)-. Academic Scholarly Publication. English. qt. comes with membership. State Historical Society of North Dakota, North Dakota Heritage Center, Bismarck ND 58505. **Tel** (701)224-2799. **(Subscription address:** North Dakota Heritage Foundation, PO Box 1976, Bismarck ND 58502.**) ED** Virginia Heidenreich. **LC** F631; .N862. **DD** 978. **Bk Rev. Circ:** 1,600 (ctrl). available on microfilm and microfiche from University Microfilms International (UMI). ***Continues*** *North Dakota Historical Quarterly, 0361-6231.*
Desc: Publishes scholarly, illustrated articles and features about the history and culture of North Dakota and the Northern Great Plains.
Ind/Abst Am. Hist. Life (1963-); Annu. Bibliogr. Engl. Lang. Lit.; West. Hist. Q.

US
NORTH DAKOTA HORIZONS. (1970)-. Periodical. English. Four times a year (Mar., June, Sept., Dec.). $15.00 (one year), $28.00 (two years). Greater North Dakota Association, 2000 Schafer Street, PO Box 2639, Bismarck ND 58502. **Tel** (701)222-0929, (800)382-1405. **ED** Sheldon Green. **Circ:** 17,000.

US/8756-9256
NORTH GEORGIA JOURNAL. [North Ga. j.]. **Added/Corp** Northeast Georgia Historical and Genealogical Society. (1984)-. Academic Scholarly Publication. English. qt (Mar., June, Sept., Dec.). $17.50 (one year), $30.00 (two year). North Georgia Journal, PO Box 127, Roswell GA 30077. **Tel** (404)642-5569. **ED** Olin Jackson. **LC** WMLC 93/1953; F291.7; .N67. **DD** 975. **Ad Acc, Adv Mgr:** Carole Webster, **Tel** (404)642-5569. **Circ:** 16,000.
Desc: Specializes in scholarly research of historical nature indigenous to the North Georgia region.

US/0029-2850
NORTH JERSEY HIGHLANDER, THE.
Added/Corp North Jersey Highlands Historical Society. (19??)-. Periodical. English. an (Published in August). $6.00. North Jersey Highlands Historical Society, PO Box 248, Ringwood NJ 07456. **Tel** (201)839-2389. **ED** Ralph Colfax. **LC** F134; .N67. **DD** 974.9.
Ind/Abst Am. Hist. Life (1971-1973).

●US
NORTH-SOUTH ISSUES. **Added/Corp** University of Miami. North-South Center. **VFOAT** North South Issues. (Feb. 1992)-. Periodical. English. mo. University of Miami / North-South Center, PO Box 248205, Mercy Vega, Coral Gables FL 33124-3027. **Tel** (305)284-8914.

US/0048-0738
NORTHEAST HISTORICAL ARCHAEOLOGY. **Added/Corp** Council for Northeast Historical Archaeology. (Spring 1971)-. Periodical. English. an. $12.00. Boston University Center Archaeological, 675 Commonwealth Avenue, Boston MA 02215. **Tel** (617)353-3415. **LC** F106; .N67. **DD** 974/.04/05.

CN/0703-8364
NORTHERN BREED, THE. V. 1- Dec. 1976-. Periodical. English. mo. $15.00 Northwest Territory and Yukon, $17.00 others. Northern Breed, Box 1614, Yellowknife NWT X0E 1H0, Canada. **DD** 971.9/2/00497. **UDC** 971.2.

US/0549-9186
NORTHERN NECK OF VIRGINIA HISTORICAL MAGAZINE. **Added/Corp** Northern Neck of Virginia Historical Society. Vol. 3, No. 1 (1953)-. Periodical. English. an. $14.00. Northern Neck of Virginia Historical Society, PO Box 716, Montross VA 22520. **Tel** (804)224-9251, (804)224-0161. **LC** F232.N86; N6. **Ad Acc. Circ:** 700 (ctrl). ***Continues*** *Northern Neck Historical Magazine.*
Desc: Articles dealing with the history, genealogy, and antiquities of six counties of Virginia known as the Northern Neck.
Ind/Abst Am. Hist. Life (1986-).

CN/1183-0875
NORTHERN RESEARCH AND EDUCATION AT YUKON COLLEGE.
[North. res. educ. Yukon Coll.]. **Added/Corp** Yukon College. Yukon College. Northern Research Centre. **VFOAT** Northern Research and Education. (Fall 1990)-. Periodical. English. sa. Free. Yukon College Northern Review, PO Box 2799, Whitehorse, Yukon Y1A 5K4 Canada. **Tel** (403)668-8736, FAX (403)668-8828. **DD** 971.9/0071/17191.

US/0078-1789
NORTHWEST HISTORICAL SERIES. No. 1 (1923)-. Monographic series. English. ir. Price varies per volume. Arthur H. Clark Company, PO Box 14707, Spokane WA 99214. **Tel** (509)928-9540, (800)842-9286. **ED** Robert A. Clark. cum. index. **Circ:** 1,000 (ctrl).
Desc: An ongoing series of books on the history of the Pacific Northwestern United States.

US/0029-3407
NORTHWEST OHIO QUARTERLY.
[Northwest Ohio q.]. **Added/Corp** Maumee Valley Historical Society. Historical Society of Northwestern Ohio. Vol. 16, (1944)-. Periodical. English. qt. $29.00 US; $33.00 others. Maumee Valley Historical Society, 1031 River Road, Maumee OH 43537. **Tel** (419)893-9602. **ED** David C. Skaggs. Index available (free). cum. index. **Bk Rev. Circ:** 500. ***Continues*** *Quarterly Bulletin - The Northwest Ohio Historical Society.*
Desc: A selection of articles, book reviews and archival collection listings on the local history, archaeology, architecture, culture, and natural history of the Maumee Valley.
Ind/Abst Am. Hist. Life (1963-); Annu. Bibliogr. Engl. Lang. Lit.; MLA Int. Bibl. Books Artic. Mod. Lang. Lit.

US/0885-7628
NORTHWEST PASSAGES HISTORICAL NEWSLETTER. **VFOAT** Northwest Passages. Vol. 1, No. 1 (Sept. 1985)-. Newsletter. English. Six times a year. $14.00. Calapooia Publications, PO Box 160, Brownsville OR 97327. **Tel** (503)369-2439. **ED** Patricia Hainline and Margaret Carey. **Bk Rev**, (Qty: 6-10).
Desc: Historical articles and tidbits, original writings about early Northwest days from diaries, journals, scrapbooks, letters and newspapers.

US/0078-1983
NORWEGIAN-AMERICAN STUDIES.
[Nor.-Am. stud.]. **Added/Corp** Norwegian-American Historical Association. **VAT** Norwegian American Studies. Vol. 21 (1962)-. Periodical. English. ir. Price varies. Norwegian-American Historical Association, St. Olaf College, Northfield MN 55057. **Tel** (507)646-3221. **LC** E184.S2; N85. ***Continues*** *Norwegian-American Studies and Records, 0885-5900.*
Ind/Abst Am. Hist. Life; MLA Int. Bibl. Books Artic. Mod. Lang. Lit.

US/0163-1632
NOTES ON VIRGINIA. See Architecture.

US/0581-5916
NOTICIAS - SANTA BARBARA HISTORICAL SOCIETY. [Noticias - St. Barbara Hist. Soc.]. **Main/Corp** Santa Barbara Historical Society. **VAT** Quarterly Bulletin of the Santa Barbara Historical Society. Vol. 1 (1955)-. Periodical. English. qt. $35.00. Santa Barbara Historical Society, 136 East de la Guerra Street, Santa Barbara CA 93102. **Tel** (805)966-1601. **(Subscription address:** Santa Barbara Historical Society, PO Box 578, Santa Barbara CA 93102**) ED** Michael Redmon. **DD** 979. Index available. **Circ:** 1,000.
Desc: History of Santa Barbara county; including architecture, natural history, and biography.

CN/0226-1278
NOUVELLES / CONSEIL DES MONUMENTS ET SITES DU QUEBEC.
[Nouv. - Cons. monuments sites Que.]. **Added/Corp** Conseil des Monuments et Sites du Quebec. (March 9, 1979)-. Periodical. French. Free to members, $12.00 others. Conseil Des Monuments Et Sites Du Quebec, CP 465, Sillery Quebec G1T 2R8. **DD** 971.4/006. ***Continues*** *Nouvelles du CMSQ, 0227-678X.*

CN/0715-7541
NOUVELLES D'ICITTE. ***Title Change.*** Periodical. French. mo. Nouvelles d'Icitte, CP 40, Riviere Portneuf Quebec G0T 1P0 Canada. **DD** 971.4/17. **UDC** 979.4(=924). ***Continued by*** *Nouvelles d'ICI.*

CN/0829-2612
NOUVELLES / LA FEDERATION DES SOCIETES D'HISTOIRE DU QUEBEC.
[Nouv. - Fed. soc. hist. Que.]. **Added/Corp** Federation des Societes d'Histoire du Quebec. Vol. 1, No. 1 (April 1985)-. Periodical. French. bm. 17.33Can$. Federation des Societes d'Histoire du Quebec, CP 1000 Succursale M, Montreal Quebec H1V 3R2 Canada. **Tel** (514)252-3031, FAX (514)251-8038. **ED** Louis Cabral. **DD** 971.4/006. **Bk Rev**, (Qty: 20). **Ad Acc. Circ:** 2,000 (ctrl).
Desc: Contains specialized information about history, genealogy, toponymy and heritage in Quebec.

CN/0227-4752
NOVA SCOTIA HISTORICAL REVIEW.
[N.S. hist. rev.]. **Added/Corp** Public Archives of Nova Scotia. Vol. 1, No. 1 (1981)-. Academic Scholarly Publication. English. Twice a year (June & Dec.). 20.00Can$. Nova Scotia Historical Review, Public Archives of Nova Scotia, 6016 University Avenue, Halifax, Nova Scotia B3H 1W4 Canada. **Tel** (902)424-6085, FAX (902)424-0628. **ED** Barry Cahill. **LC** F1036; .N928. **DD** 971.6/005. Index available (back issues). **Bk Rev**, (Qty: 20). **Ad Acc. Circ:** 700. available on microfiche from Micromedia Limited. ***Continues*** *Nova Scotia Historical Quarterly., 0300-3728.*
Desc: Publishes scholarly articles on every aspect and period of Nova Scotia history.
Ind/Abst Am. Hist. Life (1971-); Can. Index; Can. Period. Index (19??-).

US/0896-2693
NOW AND THEN (JOHNSON CITY, TENN.). (NOW AND THEN.). [Now then]. **Added/Corp** East Tennessee State University. Center for Appalachian Studies and Services. Vol. 1, No. 1 (Fall 1984)-. Periodical. English. Three times a year. $10.00 (subscribing members), $25.00 (supporting members), $50.00 (contributing members), $100.00 (sustaining members) $12.00 (institutional members). Center for Appalachian Studies, Tennessee State University, PO Box 70556, Johnson City TN 37614. **Tel** (615)929-5348, FAX (615)929-5348. **ED** Pat Arnow. **LC** F217.A65; N68. **DD** 976/.005. cum. index. **Bk Rev. Circ:** 1000.
Desc: Contains articles, interviews, photos, poetry, short stories and essays about Appalachian life past and present.

US/0029-5361
NOW AND THEN (MUNCY). (NOW AND THEN.). [Now then]. **Added/Corp** Muncy Historical Society and Museum of History, Muncy, Pa. Vol. 1 (June 1868)-. Periodical. English. Three times a year (Apr., Aug., Dec.). 410.00. Muncy Historical Society & Museum, PO Box 11, Muncy PA 17756. **ED** Jane Jackson, (phone: (717)546-3470). **LC** F159.M95; N6. **DD** 974.851. Index available. cum. index. **Ad Acc, Adv Mgr:** Bill Ritter, **Tel** (717)546-2211. **Circ:** 500.
Desc: Recorded history from and before Indian occupation, superb architecture of every period, local artists, heroes, and death and marriage records.
Ind/Abst Am. Hist. Life (1962-1974).

CN/1184-9754
NS TRAILS. [NS trails]. **Added/Corp** Nova Scotia Trails Federation. **VFOAT** Nova Scotia Trails. Vol. 1, No. 3 (Jan. 1991)-. Periodical. English. qt. Free to members. Nova Scotia Trails Federation, PO Box 310 S, Halifax Nova Scotia B3J 3G6 Canada. **DD** 971.6. ***Continues*** *Newsletter (Nova Scotia Trails Federation)., 1180-5196.*

US
NUEVA BANDERA, LA. (19??)-. English. La Nueva Bandera, 30-08 Broadway No. 159, Queens NY 11106. **ED** Luis Quispe.
Desc: Strives to educate Americans on the developments of the civil war in Peru.

VE/0251-3552
NUEVA SOCIEDAD. [Nueva soc.]. (July/Aug. 1972)-. Periodical. Spanish. Six times a year (Feb., Apr., June, Aug., Oct., Dec.). Bs30.00 Latin America; Bs60.00 other. Nueva Sociedad, Apartado 61712 Chacao, Caracas 1060 A Venezuela. **Tel** 011 58 2 321849 329975. **LC** F1401; .N76.
Ind/Abst HAPI Hisp. Am. Period. Index; Int. Bibliogr. Sociol.; Int. Labour Doc.; LABORDOC; PAIS Int. Print.

CN/0715-5840
NYUGATI MAGYARSAG (CALGARY).
Title Change. (NYUGATI MAGYARSAG.). [Nyugati magy.]. **VFOAT** Hungarians of the West. Vol. 1, No. 1, (Jan. 1982)-?. Periodical. Hungarian (English). mo. Corwin Publishing, 44 Deerview Way SE, Calgary Alta T2J 6K2 Canada. **DD** 971.2/00494511/05. ***Continued by*** *Montreali Magyarsag, 0849-1429.*

BL
O PODER. Portuguese. 10.00. Empresa Jornalistica O Poder, Caixa Postal 3491, Rio de Janeiro Brazil. **LC** F2538.2; .P57. **UDC** 908.81(054).

US/1071-5622
OAH COUNCIL OF CHAIRS NEWSLETTER. [OAH Counc. Chairs newsl.]. **Added/Corp** Organization of American Historians. **VFOAT** Council of Chairs Newsletter. (19??)-. Newsletter. English. Six times a year. $10.00. Organization of American Historians, 112 North Bryan Street, Bloomington IN 47408. **Tel** (812)855-7311, FAX (812)855-0696. **DD** 378.

US/1059-1125
OAH NEWSLETTER. (OAH NEWSLETTER / ORGANIZATION OF AMERICAN HISTORIANS.). [OAH newsl.]. **Added/Corp** Organization of American Historians. **VFOAT** Organization of American Historians Newsletter. Vol. 9, No. 3, Oct. (1981)-. Newsletter. English. Four times a year. Included with subscription to Journal of American History: $140.00 US; $155.00 other (also includes Connections). Organization of American Historians, 112 North Bryan Street, Bloomington IN 47408. **Tel** (812)855-7311, FAX (812)855-0696. **ED** Howard McMains. **LC** E172; .O15. **DD** 973/.05. Index available. **Ad Acc. Circ:** 12,000 (ctrl). available on microfilm and microfiche from University Microfilms International (UMI). ***Continues*** *Newsletter - Organization of American Historians, 0196-3341.*
Desc: Includes historical essays, regular columns, and articles on current trends in the historical profession. Published job announcements and notices of meetings, grants, and calls for papers within the historical profession.
Ind/Abst Am. Hist. Life (1983-).

CN/0227-1540
OBLIGATION, L'. [Obligation]. V. 1- June 1979-. Periodical. French. mo. Free. J J Roy, l'Obligation, 5692 Av Jeanne d'Arc, Montreal Quebec H1X 2G3 Canada. **DD** 971.4/04. **UDC** 976. ctrl circ.

CN/0048-1343
OBZORJE PACIFIKA. ***Title Change.*** 1968-. Periodical. Serbo-Croatian (Roman). sa. Obzorje Pacifika, Box 2622, Vancouver British Columbia Canada. **DD** 971/.004/91823. **UDC** 979. ***Continued by*** *Vrijeme, 0384-1421.*

US/0083-5234
OCCASIONAL PAPER - GRADUATE CENTER FOR LATIN AMERICAN STUDIES (VANDERBILT UNIVERSITY).
Main/Corp Vanderbilt University, Nashville. Graduate Center for Latin American Studies. No. 1- 1964-. English. Vanderbilt University Graduate Center for Latin American Studies, PO Box 6309 Station B, Nashville TN 37203. **UDC** 979.5/.7.

CN/0068-0303
OCCASIONAL PUBLICATION - BOREAL INSTITUTE FOR NORTHERN STUDIES.
(OCCASIONAL PUBLICATION.). [Occas. publ. - Boreal Inst. North. Stud.]. **Main/Corp** Boreal Institute for Northern Studies. **Added/Corp** Boreal Institute for Northern Studies. Occasional Papers. University of Alberta. **VFOAT** Occasional Paper. (19??)-. Monographic series. English. ir. Price varies per volume. University of Alberta / Boreal Institute of Northern Studies, Edmonton Alberta T6G 2E9 Canada. **Tel** (403)432-4999, (403)432-4512. **Bk Rev. Ad Acc.** ctrl circ.
Desc: All publications are northern related.
Ind/Abst ASTIS Curr. Aware. Bull. (1978-); ASTIS Bibliogr. (1978-); GeoRef.

US
OCHS JOURNAL : PUBLICATION OF THE ORANGE COUNTY HISTORICAL SOCIETY. **Added/Corp** Orange County Historical Society (N.Y.). **VFOAT** Orange County Historical Society Journal. Vol. 14 (Nov. 1, 1985)-. English. an. $15.00.

Orange County Historical Society, Clove Furnace Historic Site, Arden NY 10910. **Tel** (914)351-4696. ***Continues*** *Orange County Historical Society Journal.*

CN/0823-8596
OFFICIAL HELLENIC YEAR BOOK (1984). (OFFICIAL HELLENIC YEAR BOOK.). [Off. Hellenic year book]. **Added/Corp** Hellenic Canadian Community of Ottawa and District. **VFOAT** Hellenic Community of Ottawa. **VAT** Hellenic Community of Ottawa (1984). (1984)-. English (Greek, Modern). an. Free. Hellenic Canadian Community of Ottawa and District, 1315 Prince of Wales Drive, Ottawa Ontario K2C 1N2 Canada. **DD** 971.3/8400489. ctrl circ. ***Continues*** *Year Book (Hellenic Canadian Community of Ottawa and District), 0822-5958.*

US
OHIO CUES. English. Eight times a year. $15.00. Maumee Valley Historical Society, 1031 River Road, Maumee OH 43537. **Tel** (419)893-9602. Index available (free).

US/0149-2934
OHIO FARMER COUNTY LINE RURAL DIRECTORY : CRAWFORD COUNTY, THE. **VFOAT** County Line Rural Directory: Crawford County. 1976-. Directory. English. 9800 Detroit Avenue, Cleveland OH 44102. **LC** F497.C8; O36. **DD** 977.1/27/04025.

US/0148-981X
OHIO FARMER COUNTY LINE RURAL DIRECTORY : HURON COUNTY, THE. **VFOAT** County Line Rural Directory. Huron County. 1976-. Directory. English. 9800 Detroit Avenue, Cleveland OH 44102. **LC** F497.H8; O36. **DD** 977.1/25/04025. **UDC** 976.4/.6; 978.9.

US/0030-0934
OHIO HISTORY. (OHIO HISTORY / OHIO HISTORICAL SOCIETY.). [Ohio hist.]. **Added/Corp** Ohio Historical Society. Vol. 71, No. 1 (Jan. 1962)-. English. Twice a year (Apr. & Oct.). $5.00 (members) Ohio Historical Society; Free to Ohio Main Branch Public Libraries; $15.00 (individuals), $25.00 (institutions) non-members. Ohio Historical Society, 1982 Velma Avenue, Subscription Office, Columbus OH 43211. **Tel** (614)297-2332, (614)297-2360. **ED** Robert L. Daugherty. **LC** F486; .O51. **DD** 977.1/005. Index available. cum. index. **Bk Rev. Circ:** 4,000 (ctrl). available on microfilm and microfiche from University Microfilms International (UMI). ***Continues*** *Ohio Historical Quarterly.*
Desc: Articles, notes, and reviews concerning political social and cultural history of Ohio and the midwest.
Ind/Abst Am. Hist. Life (1958-); Annu. Bibliogr. Engl. Lang. Lit.; BHA : Biblio. Hist. Art; West. Hist. Q.

CN/0835-5770
OKAMI : JOURNAL DE LA SOCIETE D'HISTOIRE D'OKA. **Added/Corp** Societe d'Histoire d'Oka. (1986)-. Periodical. French. qt. 18.00Can$. Societe d' Histoire d' Oka Inc., CP 999, OKA J0N 1E0 Canada. **Tel** (514)479-8974. **ED** Pere Louis-Marie Turcotte. **LC** F1054.5.O4; O38. **DD** 971.4/25. Index available. **Circ:** 400.

CN/0830-0739
OKANAGAN HISTORY. (OKANAGAN HISTORY : REPORT OF THE OKANAGAN HISTORICAL SOCIETY.). [Okanagan hist.]. **Added/Corp** Okanagan Historical Society. **VFOAT** Report of the Okanagan Historical Society. 49th Edition (1985)-. English. an (Oct.). $14.95. Okanagan Historical Society, PO Box 313, Vernon British Columbia V1T 6M3 Canada. **Tel** (604)495-7672. **ED** Robert Cowan. **DD** 971.1/42/005. Index available. **Bk Rev. Circ:** 2,000 (ctrl). ***Continues*** *Okanagan Historical Society. Annual Report of the Okanagan Historical Society., 0317-0691.*
Desc: Contains information on the local history, economic, environmental, political and cultural of the Okanangan, Similkameen and Shuswap areas of British Columbia.

US/0271-6941
OKLAHOMA SERIES, THE. V. 1-. Monographic series. English. ir. Price varies per volume. Oklahoma Historical Society, Historical Building, North Lincoln, Oklahoma City OK 73105. **Tel** (405)521-2491. **ED** Bob Blackburn. **Circ:** 1,500 (ctrl).
Desc: Each volume focuses on a different aspect of Oklahoma history, ranging from Indians and ethnic groups to railroads and architecture.

US/0030-1892
OKLAHOMA TODAY. **Added/Corp** Oklahoma. State Department of Commerce and Industry. Oklahoma. Planning and Resources Board. Oklahoma. Tourism and Recreation Dept. (1950)-. Periodical. English. bm. $13.50 (1 year), $23.00 (2 year). Oklahoma Today, PO Box 53384, Oklahoma City OK 73152. **Tel** (405)521-2496, (800)652-6552. **ED** Jeanne Devlin. **Ad Acc. Circ:** 50,000.
Desc: Consumer publication oriented to the history and culture of Oklahoma, published by the state of Oklahoma.

US/0098-4760
OLD FORT LOG. **Added/Corp** Old Fort Genealogical Society of Southeastern Kansas. Vol. 1 (Dec. 1974)-. Periodical. English. qt. $7.00. Old Fort Genealogical Society, 201 South National, Fort Scott KS 66701. **Tel** (316)223-2933. **ED** Ken Lyon. **LC** F680; .O4. **DD** 929/.3781.
Desc: Contains information about people and places of Southeastern Kansas, with emphasis on Bourbon County, Kansas.

US/0196-7045
OLD FORT NEWS. [Old Fort news]. **Added/Corp** Allen County-Fort Wayne Historical Society. **VFOAT** Old-Fort News. Vol. 1 (Mar. 1936)-. Periodical. English. Twice a year. $25.00 Comes with Allen County Fort Wayne Historical Society membership. Allen County-Fort Wayne Historical Society, 302 East Berry Street, Ft Wayne IN 46802. **Tel** (219)426-2882. **ED** Walter Font. **LC** F534.F7; O6. **DD** 977.274. Index available. cum. index. **Circ:** 2,000 (ctrl). ***Supersedes*** *Allen County-Fort Wayne Historical Society. Bulletin.*
Desc: Contains articles that pertain to the history of Allen County, Fort Wayne and Northeastern Indiana.
Ind/Abst Am. Hist. Life.

US/0360-5531
OLD NORTHWEST, THE. ***Ceased.*** [Old Northwest]. **Added/Corp** Miami University (Oxford, Ohio). Vol. 1 (March 1975)-Vol. 16, No. 4 (1992). Periodical. English. ir. $15.00 (US); $16.00 (other). Miami University, 302 Bachelor Hall, Oxford OH 45056. **Tel** (513)529-5253. **ED** Robert Kettler. **LC** F351; .O44. **[CCC].** Index available. cum. index. **Bk Rev. Pr Rev. Circ:** 600 (ctrl). available on microfilm and microfiche from University Microfilms International (UMI).
Desc: Interdisciplinary publication examining culture of old NW territory and states developed from it: Ohio, Indiana, Illinois, Michigan, Wisconsin, and other midwestern states.
Ind/Abst Abstr. Engl. Stud.; Am. Hist. Life (1975-); Annu. Bibliogr. Engl. Lang. Lit.; MLA Int. Bibl. Books Artic. Mod. Lang. Lit.

US
OLD SOUTH LEAFLETS. Vol. 1, No. 1 (1896)-. English. ir. Burt Franklin Publishing Company, PO Box 856, New York NY 10014.

US/0147-2089
OLD TIMER. 1st-. English. $30.00 each issue. PO Box 278, Albany TX 76430. **LC** F394.A35; O43. **DD** 976.4/734. **UDC** 976.8.

US/0148-575X
OLD TRAILS. [Old trails]. Spring 1977-. Periodical. English. qt. $1.00 each issue. 16001 Ventura Boulevard, Encino CA 91436. **LC** F591; .O59. **DD** 978/.03/05. **UDC** 971.3; 929.5(713). ***Supersedes*** *Westerner, 0511-8328.*

US/0030-2058
OLD WEST. [Old West]. Vol. 1, No. 1 (Fall 1964)-. Periodical. English. bm. $10.95 (1 1/2 year), $19.95 (3 year) US; $15.95 (1 1/2 year), $29.95 (three year) includes postage other. Western Publications / Oklahoma, PO Box 2107, Stillwater OK 74076. **Tel** (405)743-3370, (800)749-3369, FAX (405)743-3374. **ED** John Joerschke. **LC** F591; .O6. **DD** 978/.005. Index available. **Bk Rev. Ad Acc. Circ:** 100,000 (ctrl).
Desc: Covers a broad range of western American history and culture from pre-Civil War days to the present.

US/0883-6442
OLDE TIMES. **VFOAT** Old Times. Vol. 1, No. 1 (July/Aug. 1985)-. Periodical. English. ir (Publishes three to four issues per year). $18.50. Olde Towne Ventures Inc., 417 Middle Street, Portsmouth VA 23704. **Tel** (804)397-4300. **ED** Louise A. DeVere. **Bk Rev. Ad Acc. Circ:** 2,000.
Desc: Features the history and culture of Virginia's Tidewater area. Nautical history, family recipes and never before published photos enliven this unique regional publication.

CN/0030-2953
ONTARIO HISTORY. [Ont. hist.]. **Added/Corp** Ontario Historical Society. Vol. 39 (1947)-. Periodical. English. qt. 15.00Can$ (members of the Ontario Historical Society), 35.00Can$ (institutions or organizations not affiliated) Canada; $45.00 US. Ontario Historical Society, 5151 Yonge Street, Willowdale Ontario M2N 5P5 Canada. **Tel** (905)226-9011, FAX (905)226-2740. **ED** Jean Burnet. **LC** F1056; .O58. Index available. **Bk Rev. Ad Acc. Pr Rev. Circ:** 1,400. ***Continues*** *Papers and Records - Ontario Historical Society, 0380-6022;* ***Absorbed*** *Ontario Historical Society. News Letter.*
Desc: Publishes articles, book reviews, and historical notes and comments on the history of Ontario. Includes material from many eras and regions and publishes articles on a variety of themes and issues.
Ind/Abst Am. Hist. Life (1963-); Can. Index (?-?); Can. Period. Index; Curr. Geogr. Publ. (199?-); West. Hist. Q.

US
OPPORTUNITY STILL KNOCKS : FREEDOM'S LIVING PROOF OF THE OPPORTUNITIES IN OUR AMERICAN WAY OF LIFE / HORATIO ALGER AWARDS COMMITTEE OF THE AMERICAN SCHOOLS AND COLLEGES ASSOCIATION. Began publication with 1st in 1956?. English. an. Horatio Alger Society, 4907 Allison Drive, Lansing MI 48910-5682. **Tel** (517)882-3203. **LC** E747. **DD** 920.073. **UDC** 971.6.

CN/1183-3092
OPTIONS - CENTRALE DE L'ENSEIGNEMENT DU QUEBEC. (OPTIONS.). [Options - Centr. enseign. Que.]. **Added/Corp** Centrale de l'Enseignement du Quebec. **VFOAT** Options CEQ. No. 1 (Spring 1991)-. Periodical. French. Twice a year. 16.00Can$. Centrale de L'Enseignement du Quebec, 9405 Est Rue Sherbrooke, Montreal Quebec H1L 6P3 Canada. **Tel** (418)627-8888. **DD** 971.4.

US/0030-4727
OREGON HISTORICAL QUARTERLY. **Main/Corp** Oregon Historical Society. Vol. 1 (March 1900)-. Periodical. English. Four times a year. $25.00. Oregon Historical Society, 1200 Southwest Park Avenue, Portland OR 97205. **Tel** (503)222-1741 ext.28, FAX (503)221-2035. **ED** Rick Harmon. **LC** F871; .O47. **UDC** 971.4. Index available. cum. index. **Bk Rev. Circ:** 8,400. available in microform; available on microfilm. Documents available from The Genuine Article. ***Supersedes*** *Sources of the History of Ohio.*
Desc: Articles on the history of the Oregon country. Contains book reviews, news items of historical interest and a listing of historical resources.
Ind/Abst Am. Hist. Life (1955-); Arts Humanit. Citation Index [Full Cov.]; Curr. Contents Arts Humanit.; Res. Alert [Full Cov.]; Soc. Sci. Cit. Index [Select. Cov.]; West. Hist. Q.

US
OREGON HISTORY. (19??)-. Periodical. English. qt. Oregon Historical Society, 1200 Southwest Park Avenue, Portland OR 97205. **Tel** (503)222-1741 ext.28, FAX (503)221-2035.

US/0899-1960
ORGAN MOUNTAIN TRAILBLAZER. Vol. 1 Iss. 1 (July 1988)-. Periodical. English. mo. $22.20. Organ Mountain Publishing Company, 210 W Fleming, Las Cruces NM 88005. **DD** 978.

US/0272-4650
ORGANO OFICIAL DE LA JUNTA CIVICO-MILITAR CUBANA. Began with Jan./Feb. 1978 issue?. Periodical. Spanish. bm. $12.00 US; $18.00 other. Junta Civico-Militar Cubana, PO Box 795, Huntington Park CA 90255. **Tel** (310)666-5000. **LC** F1751; .O73. **DD** 972.91/005. **UDC** 971.6. **Bk Rev. Ad Acc.** ctrl circ.
Desc: Conservative, pro-democracy journal

US/0889-0501
ORIGINS (GRAND RAPIDS, MICH.). (ORIGINS : HISTORICAL MAGAZINE OF CALVIN COLLEGE AND SEMINARY ARCHIVES.). [Origins]. **Added/Corp** Calvin College and Seminary. Archives. **VFOAT** Historical Magazine of Calvin College and Seminary Archives. (1983)-. Periodical. English. Twice a year (Spring and Fall). $10.00. Origins MI, Archives of Calvin College and Seminary Library, 3233 Burton, Grand Rapids MI 49506. **Tel** (616)957-6313. **LC** F574.G7; O75. **DD** 977.4/56/005.

CN/0228-2119
OSEILLEUR, L'. [Oseilleur]. V. 1- June 1976-. Periodical. French. ir. $2.00 per no. Secretariat de CPPB, 15 rue Lestang, Beaumont Quebec G0R 1C0 Canada. **DD** 971.4/733/005. **UDC** 974.8.

US
OUACHITA COUNTY HISTORICAL QUARTERLY. **Added/Corp** Ouachita County Historical Society (Ark.). (Sept. 1969)-. Periodical. English. Four times a year. $15.00. Ouachita County Historical Society, 926 Washington Street, Camden AR 71701. **Tel** (501)836-9243, 836-8548. **ED** Edward Parham, (501)836-8590. **Circ:** 500.
Desc: Covers local history of Ouachita County - its people, places and events.

US
OUR HERITAGE. **Added/Corp** San Antonio Genealogical and Historical Society. Vol. 1 (Oct. 1959)-. Periodical. English. Four times a year (Jan., Apr., July, Oct.). $15.00 (one year); $20.00 Comes with San Antonio Genealogical and Historical Society membership. San Antonio Genealogical & Historical Society, PO Box 17461, San Antonio TX 78217-0461. **Tel** (512)821-5735. **LC** F385; .O9.

CN
OUTLOOK / OUTLOOK SASK CANADA. English. wk. $17.29Can$ (40 mile radius of Outlook); 25.23Can$ (Canada); 75.00Can$ (other). Outlook Printers, Outlook Sask, S0L 2N0 Canada. **Tel** (306) 867-8262.

UK
OVER HERE : REVIEWS IN AMERICAN STUDIES. **Added/Corp** University of Nottingham. Dept. of American Studies. (1980)-. Periodical. English. sa. £5.00 (individuals) £8.00 (institutions) UK; £8.00 (individuals) other; £10.00 (institutions) other. University of Nottingham, Dept. of American and Canadian Studies, Nottingham NG7 2RD England. **Tel** 0602 484848.

US/0738-1093
OVERLAND JOURNAL. (OVERLAND JOURNAL : THE OFFICIAL JOURNAL OF THE OREGON-CALIFORNIA TRAILS ASSOCIATION.). **Added/Corp** Oregon-California Trails Association. Vol. 1, No. 1 (July 1983)-. Periodical. English. Four times a year (Mar., June, Sept., Dec.). $30.00 (one year), Overland Journal; $30.00 libraries & individuals, $1,000.00 corporations, $100.00 other, Oregon-California trails association membership. Oregon-California Trails Association, PO Box 1019, Independence MO 64051-0519. **Tel** (816)252-2276, FAX (816)252-2276. **ED** Lois Daniel (editor's address: 3533 Wyandotte, Kansas City, MO 64111, phone: (816)561-9062). **LC** F593; .O93. **DD** 978/.005. Index available (1st iss. (Mar.).). **Bk Rev**, (Qty: 12 per year). **Ad Acc**, **Adv Mgr Tel** (816)252-2276. **Pr Rev. Circ:** 2,400 (ctrl).
Desc: Original research concerning the trans-Mississippi western emigrant trails. Articles exmaines traveling, perparation, personalities, remnants of the trail today. It also list the graves sites, identifications and preservations.
Ind/Abst Am. Hist. Life (1986-); West. Hist. Q.

US/0889-6380
OWYHEE OUTPOST. **Added/Corp** Owyhee County Historical Society. No. 1 (Apr. 1970)-. English. an (May). $10.25. Owyhee City Historical Museum & Library, PO Box 67, Murphy ID 83650. **Tel** (208)495-2319. **ED** Glenda Bean. **DD** 979. **Circ:** 500 (ctrl). available on diskette.
Ind/Abst Am. Hist. Life.

US/0275-9713
OZARK PERIODICAL INDEX. **See** History(General)-Abstracting, Bibliographies and Statistics.

US/0743-9032
OZARK SOCIETY JOURNAL. ***Ceased.*** [Ozark Soc. j.]. Vol. 16, No. 2 (Autumn 1982)-(19??). Periodical. English. qt. Ozark Society Journal, PO Box 2914, Little Rock AR 72203. **LC** F417.O9; O95. **DD** 976.7/1. **UDC** 973(069). ***Continues*** *Ozark Society Bulletin, 0475-0837.*

US/0030-7769
OZARKS MOUNTAINEER, THE. (1952)-. Periodical. English. Six times a year (Feb., Apr., June, Aug., Oct., Dec.). $11.50 (one year); $21.00 (two years); $30.00 (three years). The Ozarks Mountaineer, Star Route 3, Box 868, Kirbyville MO 65679. **Tel** (417)546-5390. **ED** Clay M. Anderson and Kathleen Van Buskirk. **LC** F417.O9; O96. **DD** 976.7/1005. **Bk Rev. Ad Acc. Circ:** 35,000.
Desc: Articles and information relative to the Ozarks. No fiction.
Ind/Abst Ozark Period. Index.

US/0030-8684
PACIFIC HISTORICAL REVIEW. [Pac. hist. rev.]. **Added/Corp** American Historical Association. Pacific Coast Branch. American Historical Association. Pacific Coast Branch. Proceedings of the Pacific Coast Branch of the American Historical Association. Vol. 1, (Mar. 1932)-. Periodical. English. qt (Feb., May, Aug., Nov.). $49.00 (institutions), $24.00 (individual). University of California Press, 2120 Berkeley Way, Berkeley CA 94720. **Tel** (510)642-4191, (510)642-3907, FAX (510)642-9917. **ED** Norris Hundley Jr. **LC** F851; .P18. **[CCC]**. Index available (published in Nov.). **Bk Rev. Pr Rev. Circ:** 1,700 (ctrl). available on microfilm and microfiche from University Microfilms International (UMI). Documents available from The Genuine Article, UMI Article Clearinghouse.
Desc: Articles on the history of American expansionism to the Pacific and beyond, and on the development of the 20th Century American West.
Ind/Abst Acad. Abstr. Full Text Elite (July 1990-); Acad. Abstr. (July 1990-); Acad. Ind. [Computer File] (1987-); Acad. Search (July 1990-); Am. Hist. Life (1954-); Am. Bibliogr. Slavic East Europ. Stud.; Annu. Bibliogr. Engl. Lang. Lit.; Arts Humanit. Citation Index [Full Cov.]; Book Rev. Index; Chicano Index; Curr. Contents Arts Humanit.; Expand. Acad. Index (1987-); Hist. Source (July 1990-); Humanit. Index; Humanit. Source (Jul. 1990-); INFO-SOUTH Abstr.; Int. Bibliogr. Sociol.; Mag. Search; Middle East Abstr. Index; Newsp. Period. Abstr. (1991-); Res. Alert [Full Cov.]; Soc. Sci. Source (Jul. 1990-); Soc. Sci. Cit. Index [Select. Cov.]; West. Hist. Q.

US
PACIFIC NORTHWEST FORUM, THE. v. 1- Jan. 1976-. Periodical. English. Three times a year. $5.00 one year, $9.00 two years, $12.00 three year. Eastern Washington University / Pacific Northwest Forum, Cheney WA 99004. **Tel** (509)359-7951. **(Subscription address:** The Pacific North West Forum, EWU-MS 27, Cheney WA 99004) **ED** J William T Youngs. **UDC** 973(=96). **Bk Rev. Circ:** 250 (ctrl).
Desc: Devoted to promoting historical, literary and environmental knowledge, featuring historical articles, stories, biographical sketches and documents; designed for anyone interested in learning more about the Northwest.

US/0030-8803
PACIFIC NORTHWEST QUARTERLY. [Pac. Northwest q.]. **Added/Corp** Washington State Historical Society. University of Washington. Vol. 27 (1936)-. Periodical. English. Four times a year (Jan., Apr., July, Oct.). $22.00 US; $28.00 other. University of Washington / Seattle, Washington, 4045 Brooklyn Avenue Northeast, JA-15, Seattle WA 98105. **Tel** (206)543-5900, (206)543-2992, FAX (206)685-3234. **ED** John M. Findlay. **LC** F886; .W28. **Bk Rev**, (Qty: varies). **Pr Rev. Circ:** 1,200. Documents available from The Genuine Article. ***Continues*** *Washington Historical Quarterly, 0361-6223.*
Desc: History articles on the Pacific Northwest, western Canada and Alaska and book reviews on American history and bibliographies of region history.
Ind/Abst Am. Hist. Life (1955-1957, 1961-); Am. Bibliogr. Slavic East Europ. Stud.; Annu. Bibliogr. Engl. Lang. Lit.; ARTbibliogr. Mod.; Arts Humanit. Citation Index [Full Cov.]; Curr. Contents Arts Humanit.; Hist. Abstr.; Recent. Publ. Artic.; Ref. Sources; Res. Alert [Full Cov.]; Soc. Sci. Cit. Index [Select. Cov.]; Soc. Work Abstr.; West. Hist. Q.; Women Stud. Abstr.; Writ. Am. Hist.

US/0030-882X
PACIFIC NORTHWESTERNER, THE. [Pac. northwest.]. **Added/Corp** Westerners. Spokane Corral. Westerners. Spokane Posse. Vol. 1 (Winter 1956/1957)-. Periodical. English. Four times a year. $10.00. Spokane Corral of the Westerners, PO Box 1717, Spokane WA 99210. **Tel** (509)353-3539. **ED** Terry D. Russell. **LC** F852; .P25. **DD** 979.5. Index available. cum. index. **Pr Rev. Circ:** 600 (ctrl).
Desc: Emphasis is on history of the Pacific Northwest.
Ind/Abst Am. Hist. Life (1973-); GeoRef.

PK
PAKISTAN JOURNAL OF AMERICAN STUDIES. **Added/Corp** Quaid-i-Azam University. Area Study Centre for Africa, North & South America. Vol. 1, No. 1 & 2 (1983)-. Periodical. English. sa. **LC** E169.1; .P16. **DD** 973/.072.
Ind/Abst Annu. Bibliogr. Engl. Lang. Lit.

US/0031-0158
PALACIO, EL. [Palacio]. **Added/Corp** Museum of New Mexico. Archaeological Society of New Mexico. School of American Research (Santa Fe, N.M.). Vol. 1 (Nov. 1913)-. Periodical. English (Indonesian and Spanish). Three times a year. $13.50. Museum of New Mexico Foundation, PO Box 2087, Santa Fe NM 87504-2087. **Tel** (505)827-6476. **LC** F791; .P15. **DD** 978.9/005. **Bk Rev. Circ:** 4,000 (ctrl).
Desc: Covers interests ranging from history, fine arts, folk arts, geography, exploration and natural history.
Ind/Abst Am. Hist. Life (1965-); Anthropol. Index; ARTbibliogr. Mod.; Ethnoarts Index; MLA Int. Bibl. Books Artic. Mod. Lang. Lit.; West. Hist. Q.

US/0031-0360
PALIMPSEST (IOWA CITY), THE. (THE PALIMPSEST.). [Palimpsest]. **Added/Corp** Iowa. Division of the State Historical Society. State Historical Society of Iowa. (1920)-. Periodical. English. Four times a year (Mar., June, Sept., Dec.). $14.95. State Historical Society of Iowa, 402 Iowa Avenue, Centennial Building, Iwoa City IA 52240. **Tel** (319)335-3916, FAX (319)335-3924. **ED** Ginalie Swaim (editor's telephone: (319)335-3932). **LC** F616; .P16. **DD** 977.7005. **[CCC]**. Index available. cum. index. **Ad Acc, Adv Mgr:** Debi Meyers, **Tel** (815)242-4861. **Circ:** 3,500. available on microfilm from University Microfilms International (UMI). ***Continues*** *Iowa. Division of the State Historical Society. News for Members.*
Desc: Popular history magazine of Iowa and the Midwest. Highly illustrated with a general readership.
Ind/Abst Am. Hist. Life (1965-); Annu. Bibliogr. Engl. Lang. Lit.; MLA Int. Bibl. Books Artic. Mod. Lang. Lit.; West. Hist. Q.

US/0148-7795
PANHANDLE-PLAINS HISTORICAL REVIEW. V. 1- 1928-. English. an. $20.00 US; $22.50 other. Panhandle Plains Historical Museum, Box 967 West Texas Station, Canyon TX 79016. **Tel** (806)656-2244. **ED** Dianna Everett. **LC** F381; .P2. **UDC** 977.1(036). Index available. **Circ:** 950 (ctrl).
Desc: History, art, and archeology of the High Plains of Texas, New Mexico, Oklahoma and Texas.
Ind/Abst Am. Hist. Life (1974-).

CN/0701-0508
PANJAB. URDU. (PANJAB.). Vol. 1; May/June 1975-. Periodical. Panjabi (English). mo. 11.00Can$ Canada; $18.00 other. Asia Publications, 1433 Bloor Street West, Toronto Ontario M6P 3L6 Canada. **Tel** (416)533-8243. **ED** G Gill and M Yusif. **DD** 971/.004/9143. **UDC** 977.1. **Bk Rev.**
Desc: Contains news and views of Panjabi speaking people around the world. Also includes, literature and human rights issues.

BL
PANORAMA. Portuguese. $100.00. Pan, S M Distribuidora de Veiculos GB, Curitiba Brazil. **LC** F2596; .P17. **UDC** 971.1; 908.711.

MX
PANTOC : PUBLICACIONES ANTROPOLOGICAS DE OCCIDENTE. **VFOAT** P.A.N.T.O.C.; Publicaciones Antropologicas de Occidente. No. 1 (July 1981)-. Periodical. English (Spanish). sa. **LC** F1219; .P224. **UDC** 976.6; 908.766.
Ind/Abst Anthropol. Lit.

CN/0703-7058
PAPERS AND RECORDS - THUNDER BAY HISTORICAL MUSEUM SOCIETY. **See** Museums and Galleries.

US
PAPERS DELIVERED AT THE ANNUAL CONFERENCE ON THE CARIBBEAN. **Main/Corp** University of Florida. No. 1 (1950)-. English. University of Florida Press, 15 Northwest 15th Street, Gainesville FL 32611. **Tel** (904)392-5717, (800)226-3822. **LC** F2171. **DD** 972.9. **UDC** 908.781; 929.5(781).
Desc: Each vol. has also a distinctive title: Vol. 1 1950, The Caribbean at mid-century. Vol. 2, 1951, The Caribbean: peoples, problems, and prospects. Vol. 3, 1952, The Caribbean: contemporary trends.

US/0149-4880
PAPERS IN INTERNATIONAL STUDIES : LATIN AMERICAN SERIES. No. 1-. Monographic series. English. Price varies per volume. Center for International Studies, Ohio University Press University, Athens OH 45701. **UDC** 977.2.

US/0361-6215
PAPERS - WEST TENNESSEE HISTORICAL SOCIETY. (THE WEST TENNESSEE HISTORICAL SOCIETY PAPERS.). [Pap. - West Tenn. Hist. Soc.]. **Main/Corp** West Tennessee Historical Society, Memphis. **Added/Corp** West Tennessee Historical Society. Papers. No. 1 (1947)-. English. an (Dec.). $15.00 Comes with West Tennessee Historical Society membership. West Tennessee Historical Society, Box 111046, Memphis TN 38111. **Tel** (901)372-7495. **ED** Marius M. Carriere. **LC** F442.3; .W42. **DD** 976.80082. Index available. cum. index. **Bk Rev. Circ:** 500 (ctrl).
Desc: A journal focusing on the history and culture of West Tennessee. Also studies the state as a whole as well as neighbouring states.
Ind/Abst Am. Hist. Life (1963-).

CN/0711-0758
PAR-DELA LE RIDEAU. [dela Rideau]. Vol. 1, No. 1 (Spring 1981)-. Periodical. French. Soc History and Genealogy Ottawa, 53 Queen Street, Ottawa Ontario K1P 5C5 Canada. **DD** 971.3/84/005. **UDC** 978; 325.2(09) (78/79).

PY
PARAGUAY NOTICIAS. **VFOAT** Noticias Paraguay; Paraguay News. (198?)-. Periodical. Spanish. mo.
Ind/Abst Hum. Rights Intern. Rep.

US/0890-6939
PARKER'S GAZETTE. ***Ceased.*** [Parker's gaz.]. (1985)-Vol. 3, No. 6 (?). Periodical. English. bm. Parkers Gazette, PO Box 28444, Santa Ana CA 92799. **DD** 973. **UDC** 973-15.

US/0889-5864
PASADENA HERITAGE. [Pasadena herit.]. Vol. 1, No. 1 (Spring 1977)-. Periodical. English. ir (4 to 6 times per year). $35.00 includes Pasadena Heritage membership. Pasadena Heritage, 80 West Dayton Street, Pasadena CA 91105. **Tel** (818)793-0617. **ED** Sue Mossman and Harlean Tobin. **DD** 979. **Ad Acc, Adv Mgr:** H. Tobin, **Tel** (818)793-0617. **Pr Rev. Circ:** 1,550 (ctrl).
Desc: Contains upcoming events, activities and interest of Pasadena.

US/0031-2738
PASSWORD (EL PASO). (PASSWORD.). **Added/Corp** El Paso County Historical Society. Vol. 1, (Feb. 1956)-. Periodical. English. Four times a year (Mar., Jun., Sep., Dec.). $2.50 membership, $25.00 other one year. El Paso County Historical Society, Box 28, El Paso TX 79940. **Tel** (915)584-1026. **ED** Lillian Collingwood. **LC** F786; .P28. Index available. cum. index. **Bk Rev. Circ:** 1,200 (ctrl).
Desc: History of the Southwest.
Ind/Abst Am. Hist. Life (1985-).

US/8755-4747
PATHWAYS (MAYNARDVILLE, TENN.). (PATHWAYS.). **Added/Corp** Union County Historical Society (Tenn.). Vol. 1, No. 1 (Jan./Mar. 1982)-. Periodical. English. qt. $15.00 (membership). Union County Historical Society, PO Box 95, Maynardville TN 37807. **Tel** (615)689-4694. **ED** William G Tharpe (editor's address: 3615 Essary Drive, Knoxville Tn 37918). **LC** F443.U6; P38. **DD** 929/.3768935. **Bk Rev. Circ:** 500 members; 40 states (ctrl).
Desc: Focused on genealogy, history and related aspects of Union County, Tennessee.

US/1074-0457
PEABODY ESSEX MUSEUM COLLECTIONS. [Peabody Essex Mus. collect.]. **Added/Corp** Peabody Essex Museum. Vol. 129, No.4 (Oct. 1993)-. Periodical. English. sa. $25.00. Peabody Museum of Salem, East India Square W, Salem MA 01970. **Tel** (508)745-1876. **LC** IN PROCESS; F72.E7; E81. **DD** 974. ***Continues*** *Essex Institute Historical Collections, 0014-0953.*

CN/0710-3670
PEMMICAN JOURNAL, THE. [Pemmican j.]. Autumn 1981-. Periodical. English. qt. $2.50 per number. Pemmican Publications Inc., 34 Carlton Street, Winnipeg Manitoba R3C 1N9. **DD** 971.2/00497. **UDC** 971.2.

US/0197-2197
PENINSULA (SAN MATEO), LA. (LA PENINSULA.). Periodical. English. Three times a year. $25.00 membership. San Mateo Historical Association and Museum, 1700 West Hilldale Boulevard, San Mateo CA 94402. **Tel** (415)574-6441. **ED** Sandi Tatman. **UDC** 979.4. Index available. **Bk Rev. Ad Acc. Circ:** 1,400 (ctrl).
Desc: Publication deals with all facets of the history of San Mateo County.

US/0894-3850
PENNSYLVANIA FACTS. **See** General Interest-General Interest-North America.

US/0031-4498
PENNSYLVANIA FOLKLIFE. [Pa. folklife]. **Added/Corp** Pennsylvania Folklife Society. (1958)-. Periodical. English. Three times a year. $15.00. Pennsylvania Folklife Society, PO Box 92, Collegeville PA 19426. **Tel** (215)489-4111 ext 2388. **ED** Nancy K. Gaugler. **LC** F146; .P2227. Index available. cum. index. **Pr Rev.** ***Continues*** *Pennsylvania Dutchman (Bethal, Pa.).*
Desc: The history and folklore of Pennsylvania with special emphasis on the Pennsylvania Dutch (Germans).
Ind/Abst Am. Hist. Life (1964-); BHA : Biblio. Hist. Art; MLA Int. Bibl. Books Artic. Mod. Lang. Lit.

US/0270-7500
PENNSYLVANIA HERITAGE (1974). (PENNSYLVANIA HERITAGE.). [Pa. herit.]. **Added/Corp** Pennsylvania Historical and Museum Commission. Vol. 1, No. 1 (Dec. 1974)-. Periodical. English. qt (Mar., June, Sept., Dec.). $15.00 US; $20.00 other. Pennsylvania Historical and Museum Commission, Box 1026, Harrisburg PA 17108. **Tel** (717)787-9123, FAX (717)783-1073. **ED** Michael J. O'Malley. **Bk Rev. Circ:** 10,000. ***Continues*** *Pennsylvania Heritage (1967).*
Desc: Contains articles on fine and decorative arts, architecture, archaeology, oral history, industry and technology, natural history, historic sites, exhibits, travel and folklore, and state and local history.
Ind/Abst Am. Hist. Life (1980-).

US/0031-4528
PENNSYLVANIA HISTORY. [Pa. hist.]. **Added/Corp** Pennsylvania Historical Association. Vol. 1, (Jan. 1934)-. Periodical. English. qt (Jan., Apr., July, Oct.). $30.00 (comes with Pennsylvania Historical Association Membership). Pennsylvania Historical Association, 777 West Harrisburg Pike, Crags Buildings, Middleton PA 17057. **Tel** (717)948-6416. **ED** William A. Pencack (editor's address:Penn State, Ogantz, Abington, PA 19001; phone (215)887-9217. **LC** F146; .P597. **DD** 974.8005. Index available. **Bk Rev**, (Qty: 40). **Ad Acc. Pr Rev. Circ:** 800 (ctrl). available on microfilm and microfiche from University Microfilms International (UMI).
Desc: Articles dealing with the social, intellectual, economic, political, and cultural history of Pennsylvania and the Middle Atlantic region. Articles may reflect investigation of new areas of research or may reflect on past scholarship.
Ind/Abst Am. Hist. Life (1963-).

US/0031-4587
PENNSYLVANIA MAGAZINE OF HISTORY AND BIOGRAPHY, THE. [PA. mag. hist. biogr.]. Vol. 1, (1877)-. Periodical. English. Four times a year (Jan., Apr., July, Oct.). $30.00 (individuals); $35.00 (institutions). Historical Society of Pennsylvania, 1300 Locust Street, Philadelphia PA 19107. **Tel** (215)732-6201, FAX (215)732-2680. **ED** Randall M. Miller. **LC** F146; .P65. **DD** 974.8/005. **UDC** 974.8. Index available. cum. index. **Bk Rev. Ad Acc. Pr Rev. Circ:** 3,200 (ctrl). available on microfilm from University Microfilms International (UMI). Documents available from The Genuine Article.
Desc: It carries articles on the history, literature, and culture of the mid-Atlantic states from settlement to the present.
Ind/Abst Am. Hist. Life (1955-); Annu. Bibliogr. Engl. Lang. Lit.; Arts Humanit. Citation Index [Full Cov.]; BHA : Biblio. Hist. Art; Curr. Contents Arts Humanit.; MLA Int. Bibl. Books Artic. Mod. Lang. Lit.; Res. Alert [Full Cov.]; Romant. Move.; Soc. Sci. Cit. Index [Select. Cov.]; West. Hist. Q.

US/0148-4036
PENNSYLVANIA MENNONITE HERITAGE. **See** Genealogy and Heraldry.

US
PENSACOLA HISTORY ILLUSTRATED. **Added/Corp** Pensacola Historical Society. Vol. 1, No. 1 (Summer 1983)-. Periodical. English. sa. **LC** F319.P4; E35. **DD** 975.9/99. ***Continues*** *Echo (Pensacola, Fla.), 0275-3669.*
Ind/Abst Am. Hist. Life (1986-).

US/0553-6901
PERMIAN HISTORICAL ANNUAL. [Permian hist. annu.]. **Added/Corp** Permian Historical Society. Vol. 5 (1965)-. English. an. Comes with Permian Historical Society membership. Permian Historical Society, 3610 South County Road 1187, c/o E. Welch, Midland TX 79701. **Tel** (915)367-2128. **LC** F381; .P4. **DD** 976. ***Continues*** *Texas Permian Historical Annual.*
Ind/Abst Am. Hist. Life (1980-).

AG
PERONISMO Y SOCIALISMO. Yearly V. 1-Sept. 1973-. Spanish. $12.00 single issue. Casilla de Correo Num 119, Sucursal 25, Buenos Aires Argentina. **LC** F2849.2; .P49. **UDC** 982.

US
PERSIAN GULF UPDATE. **Added/Corp** Students Against US Intervention in the Middle East. Education Committee. Vol. 1, No. 1 (Jan. 10, 1991)-. Periodical. English. mo.

US/0093-707X
PERSIMMON HILL. **Added/Corp** National Cowboy Hall of Fame and Western Heritage Center. (1970)-. Periodical. English. qt. $20.00. National Cowboy Hall Fame West Her, 1700 NE 63rd Street, Oklahoma City OK 73111. **Tel** (405)478-2250. **ED** M J Van Deventer. **LC** F596; .P465. **DD** 917.8/03/05. **Circ:** 18,000.
Desc: Publication on American West sponsored by National Cowboy Hall of Fame. Features history, art, ranching, biography, environmental issues. Good graphics: color, b/w photography; accurate history.

US/0743-7021
PERSPECTIVES (WASHINGTON, D.C. 1984). (PERSPECTIVES : NEWSLETTER OF THE AMERICAN HISTORICAL ASSOCIATION.). [Perspectives]. Vol. 22, No. 3 (March 1984)-. Newsletter. English. mo (except June-Aug.). Comes with membership. American Historical Association, 400 A Street Southeast, Washington DC 20003. **Tel** (202)544-2422. **LC** E172; .A57. **DD** 905. **UDC** 973. available on microfilm and microfiche from University Microfilms International (UMI). ***Continues*** *AHA Perspectives, 0745-0516.*
Ind/Abst Am. Hist. Life (1976-).

CN/0713-5734
PHARE (ROUYN). (LE PHARE.). [Phare]. Periodical. French. mo. $3.00. Le Phare, Societe Nationale des Quebecois d'Abitibi-Temiscamingue, CP 308, 102 East rue Perreault, Rouyn Quebec J9X 5C3 Canada. **DD** 971.4/13/005. **UDC** 971.4.

US/1046-4204
PHILLIPS COUNTY HISTORICAL REVIEW. [Phillips Cty. hist. rev.]. **Added/Corp** Phillips County Historical Society (Ark.). Vol. 27, No. 1 (Jan. 1989-Apr. 1989)-. Periodical. English. sa. Phillips County Historical Society, 623 Pecan Street, Helena AR 72342. **ED** Ivey S Gladin, (501)338-3271. **LC** F417.P45; P45a. **DD** 976.7/88/005. **Circ:** 350. ***Continues*** *Phillips County Historical Society : [Publication], 1046-4190.*
Desc: East Arkansas history.

US
PIBROCH, THE. Periodical. English. sa. Saint Andrew's Society of the State of New York, 281 Park Avenue South, New York NY 10010. **LC** F130.S3; P5. **UDC** 980.747.

US/0195-5799
PIEGAN STORYTELLER, THE. V. 1 (Jan. 1976)-. Periodical. English. qt. $4.00 US and Canada; $5.00 other. Andrews, 135 Wildwood Drive, New Bern NC 28560-9530. **LC** E99.S54; P53. **DD** 970.004/97. **UDC** 970.

US/0079-2098
PIONEER HERITAGE SERIES, THE. (1959)-. Monographic series. English. ir (3 to 9 issues per year). Price varies per volume. University of Nebraska Press, PO Box 880484, Lincoln NE 68588-0520. **Tel** (402)472-3584, (800)755-1105, FAX (402)472-6214, (800)526-2617. **LC** UNC.

US/1069-4706
PITTSBURGH HISTORY. [Pittsbg. hist.]. **Added/Corp** Historical Society of Western Pennsylvania. Vol. 72, No. 1 (Winter 1989)-. Periodical. English. qt (Jan., Apr., July, Oct.). $30.00 US; $35.00. Historical Society of Western Pennsylvania, 4338 Bigelow Boulevard, Pittsburgh PA 15213. **Tel** (412)681-5533. **ED** Paul Roberts. **LC** F146; .W52. **DD** 974.8/86/05. Index available. cum. index. **Bk Rev**, (Qty: 40). **Ad Acc. Pr Rev. Circ:** 4,200. available on microfilm and microfiche from University Microfilms International (UMI). ***Continues*** *Western Pennsylvania Historical Magazine, 0043-4035.*
Desc: Historical articles and book reviews relating to the Western counties of Pennsylvania and adjacent areas of Ohio and West Virginia.
Ind/Abst Am. Hist. Life (1965-).

US/0032-0447
PLAINS ANTHROPOLOGIST. **See** Ethnic Interests.

US/0554-2375
PLAINS TALK. **Added/Corp** State Historical Society of North Dakota. (1963)-. Newsletter. English. Four times a year. $25.00 basic membership; $30.00 active membership. State Historical Society of North Dakota, North Dakota Heritage Center, Bismarck ND 58505. **Tel** (701)224-2799. **(Subscription address:** North Dakota Heritage Foundation, PO Box 1976, Bismarck ND 58502.**) ED** Larry Remele. **Circ:** 2,000 (ctrl).
Desc: The newsletter of the State Historical Society of North Dakota. Covers the activities of the agency, lists book notes and forthcoming events of historical interest in North Dakota.

US/0894-7589
PLIMOTH PLANTATION JOURNAL : THE NEWSLETTER OF PLIMOTH PLANTATION. [Plimoth Plant. j.]. **VFOAT** Journal. Vol. 1, No. 1 (Summer 1984)-. Newsletter. English. Plimoth Plantation, PO Box 1620, Plymouth MA 02360. **Tel** (617)746-1622. **DD** 974. **UDC** 974.4.

US/0032-2806
POLISH AMERICAN STUDIES (CHICAGO, ILL.). (POLISH AMERICAN STUDIES.). [Pol. Am. stud.]. **Added/Corp** Polish-American Historical Association. Polish Institute of Arts and Sciences in America. Vol. 1 (1944)-. Periodical. English. Twice a year. $35.00. Polish American Historical Association, 1275 Harlem Road, Buffalo NY 14206. **Tel** (716)893-5771. **ED** K. Symonolewicz. **LC** E184.P7; P75. **DD** 973/.049185. Index available. **Bk Rev. Ad Acc. Pr Rev. Circ:** 750 (ctrl).
Desc: Contains articles, reviews and other scholarship on all aspects of history and culture of Poles in America. Also comparative articles with other groups and European immigrant antecedents.
Ind/Abst Am. Hist. Life (1959-); Am. Bibliogr. Slavic East Europ. Stud.; Abr. Cathol. Period. Lit. Index; Cathol. Period. Lit. Index.

US/0735-9209
POLISH HERITAGE. **Added/Corp** American Council of Polish Cultural Clubs. Vol. 32, No. 2 (Summer 1981)-. Periodical. English. Four times a year (Mar., June, Sept., Dec.). $10.00. American Council of Polish Cultural Clubs, 23354 Longview, Dearborn Heights MI 48127. **ED** Wallace West, (editor's address: 6507 107th Terrace No., Pinellas Park, FL 34666). **LC** E184.P7; A42a. **DD** 973/.049185. **Bk Rev**, (Qty: 20-40). **Ad Acc, Adv Mgr:** W. West. **Circ:** 4,000. ***Continues*** *Quarterly Review of Polish Heritage, 0148-6446.*
Desc: News and information on the Polish culture.
Ind/Abst Am. Bibliogr. Slavic East Europ. Stud.

CN/0704-7002
POLYPHONY (TORONTO). (POLYPHONY : BULLETIN OF THE MULTICULTURAL HISTORY SOCIETY OF ONTARIO.). [Polyphony]. **Added/Corp** Multicultural History Society of Ontario. Vol. 1, No. 1 (Fall and Winter 1977)-. Periodical. English. sa. 24.00Can$. Multicultural History Society of Ontario, 43 Queens Park Crescent East, Toronto Ontario M5S 2C3 Canada. **Tel** (416)979-2973. **(Subscription address:** University of Toronto Press, 5201 Dufferin Street, Downsview ONT M3H 5T8 Canada.**) ED** Robert F. Harney. **LC** F1059.7.A1; P65. **DD** 971.3/004. **Circ:** 300.
Desc: Articles, photo essays and oral histories on various aspects of the many cultural communities in the province from their origin to the present day.
Ind/Abst Am. Hist. Life (1987-); Am. Bibliogr. Slavic East Europ. Stud.; Can. Period. Index.

US
POPE COUNTY HISTORICAL ASSOCIATION QUARTERLY. **Added/Corp** Pope County Historical Association. Vol. 1 (Dec. 1966)-. Periodical. English. qt. $10.00. Pope County Historical Association, 4200 A Street, Little Rock AR 72205. **Tel** (501)663-3301. **ED** Elaine Weir Cia. **Bk Rev. Circ:** 300. ***Continues*** *Arkansas Valley Historical Papers.*
Desc: We publish material contributed by our members and Pope County courthouse material.

US
POPULAR CULTURE ASSOCIATION NEWSLETTER : PCAN. **Added/Corp** Popular Culture Association. Bowling Green University. Center for the Study of Popular Culture. **VFOAT** PCAN. Vol. 13, No. 1 (Mar. 1985)-. Newsletter. English. sa. Free to members of the Popular Culture Association. Popular Press Journals Area, Bowling Green State University, Bowling Green OH 43403. **Tel** (419)372-7866, (419)372-7865. ***Continues*** *Popular Culture Association Newsletter and Popular Culture Methods (Bowling Green, Ohio : 1983).*

CR
POR EL RESCATE DEMOCRATICO DE LA REVOLUCION NICARAGUENSE / MOVIMIENTO DEMOCRATICO NICARAGUENSE. ***Title Change.*** **VFOAT** Rescate. Began with July 1982 issue. Periodical. Spanish. wk. El Movimiento, Apartado 348 Pavas, San Jose 1200 Costa Rica. **LC** F1528; .P67. **DD** 972.85/005. **UDC** 972.85. ***Continued by*** *Por el Rescate Democratico de Nicaragua.*

US/0048-5055
POWWOW TRAILS. (Apr. 1964)-. Periodical. English. mo. Powwow Trails, Box 258, South Plainfield NJ 07080. **LC** E75; .P68. **DD** 970/.004/97.

CN/0317-6282
PRAIRIE FORUM. [Prairie forum]. **Added/Corp** University of Regina. Canadian Plains Research Center. Vol. 1 (April 1976)-. Periodical. English (summaries and/or abstracts in French). Twice a year. includes Canadian Plains Bulletin: 28.00Can$ institutions, 23.00Can$ individuals. University of Regina, Canadian Plains Research Center, Regina Saskatchewan S4S 0A2 Canada. **Tel** (306)585-4758, FAX (306)585-4699. **ED** Alvin Finkel. **LC** F1060.A1; P7. **DD** 971.2/005. **CODEN** PFOREL. Index available. cum. index. **Bk Rev. Circ:** 500. available on microfiche.
Desc: Concerns research relating to the Canadian Plains region; drawn from a wide variety of disciplines.
Ind/Abst Am. Hist. Life (1977-); Am. Bibliogr. Slavic East Europ. Stud.; Can. Index; Can. Period. Index; Ecol. Abstr. (?-?); Geogr. Abstr. Human Geogr.; Geol. Abstr.; Sage Race Relat. Abstr.

US/0032-6631
PRAIRIE LORE. [Prairie lore]. **Added/Corp** Southwestern Oklahoma Historical Society. (July 1964)-. Periodical. English. Twice a year. $7.00. Southwest Oklahoma Historical Society, PO Box 628, Lawton OK 73502. **Tel** (405)353-3632. **ED** Barbara Goodin. **DD** 973. Index available ($8.50). cum. index. **Circ:** 500.
Desc: A historical account of early-day southwest Oklahoma.

US/0196-3481
PRAIRIE STATE PATRIOT. Added/Corp Illinois Society of the Sons of the American Revolution. Vol. 1 (Jan. 1980)-. Periodical. English. qt. Free to members. Illinois Society of the Sons of the American Revolution, PO Box 186, Libertyville IL 60048. ***Supersedes*** *Illinois Patriot.*

US/0885-7016
PRESERVATION BRIEFS. [Preserv. briefs]. **Added/Corp** United States. Office of Archeology and Historic Preservation. Technical Preservation Services Division. United States. Interagency Historic Architectural Services Program. (1975)-. Monographic series. English. ir. Price varies per volume. Superintendent of Documents, US Government Printing Office, Washington DC 20402. **Tel** (202)275-3328, FAX (202)786-2377. **DD** 721.
Ind/Abst Avery Index Archit. Period. Suppl. Colum. Univ. (1988-).

US
PRESERVATION PERSPECTIVE.
Added/Corp New Jersey. Office of Cultural and Environmental Services. Preservation New Jersey, Inc. Vol. 1, No. 1 (Fall 1981)-. Periodical. English. bm.
Ind/Abst Avery Index Archit. Period. Suppl. Colum. Univ. (Jan. 1990-).

US
PRESERVATION REPORT. Vol.2, No.2 (Feb. 1971)-. Periodical. English. Six times a year. Free on request. Alabama Historical Association, 725 Monroe Street, Montgomery AL 36130. **Tel** (205)832-6621. **ED** Alta C. Hodgson and Eugene Heritins. **Bk Rev. Circ:** 4,500. ***Continues*** *Alabama. Historical Commission. Newsletter.*
Desc: Promotes preservation of Alabama's historic structures, awareness of historical heritage and its value.

US
PRESIDENTS : IT ALL STARTED WITH GEORGE. (19??)-. English. $69.95. National Geographic Society, 11555 Darnestown, Gaithersburg MD 20878. **Tel** (202)857-7000, (800)638-4077, FAX (202)429-5727, telex 64194 NATGEO. **(Subscription address:** National Geographic Society / CD-ROM Products, 1145 17th Street NW, Educational Media Division, Washington DC 20036.**)**

US/0276-2730
PRINCETON HISTORY. [Princeton hist.]. No. 1-1971-. English. an. History Society Princeton New Jersey, 158 Nassau Street, Bainbridge House, Princeton NJ 08540. **Tel** (609)921-6748. **LC** F144.P9; P93. **DD** 974.9/67. **UDC** 974.9. **Circ:** 850 (ctrl).
Desc: Periodical journal including articles covering various aspects of Princeton history, i.e. great houses, D&R Canal, Terra Cotta Works, medicine, etc.
Ind/Abst Am. Hist. Life (1971-).

US/0196-1136
PRINCETON RECOLLECTOR. ***Ceased.*** (PRINCETON RECOLLECTOR; A MONTHLY JOURNAL OF LOCAL HISTORY.). Vol. 1 (May 1975)-Ceased Vol. 9 No. 9. Periodical. English. mo (ten no. a year). The Princeton Recollector, 158 Nassau Street, Princeton NJ 08542. **Tel** (609)921-8330. **ED** Elric J Endersby and Tari Pantaleo. **LC** F144.P9; P95. **DD** 974.9/67/005. **UDC** 974.9. cum. index. **Bk Rev. Ad Acc. Circ:** 2,500 (ctrl).
Desc: A journal of local history featuring oral history, photographs, letters, and reader-written articles.

RU
PROBLEMY AMERIKANISTIKI.
Added/Corp Moskovskii Gosudarstvennyi Universitet im. M.V. Lomonosova. (1978)-. Periodical. Russian. 2.80rub each issue. Izdatelstvo Moskovskogo Universiteta, K-9 Ulitsa Gertsena 5/7, Moscow Russia. **Tel** (301)881-5973. **LC** E156; .P76.

US/0044-751X
PROCEEDINGS OF THE AMERICAN ANTIQUARIAN SOCIETY. [Proc. Am. Antiq. Soc.]. **Main/Corp** American Antiquarian Society. (1843)-. Proceedings. English. Twice a year (Oct., Apr.). $45.00. American Antiquarian Society, 185 Salisbury Street, Worcester MA 01609. **Tel** (508)752-5813, (508)755-5221. **ED** John B. Hench and Caroline Sloat. **LC** E172; .A35. **DD** 973/.05. Index available (bound in second issue). cum. index. **Ad Acc. Circ:** 1,200 (ctrl). available on microfilm from Xerox; available on microfilm and microfiche from University Microfilms International (UMI). Documents available from The Genuine Article.
Desc: Specializes in the publication of mid-length works, in the publication of tools for scholarship such as bibliographies and primary documents, and in scholarship at the cutting edge of the new interdisciplinary field of the history of the book in American culture.
Ind/Abst Abstr. Engl. Stud.; Am. Hist. Life (1954-); Annu. Bibliogr. Engl. Lang. Lit.; Arts Humanit. Citation Index [Full Cov.]; BHA : Biblio. Hist. Art; Biogr. Index; Curr. Contents Arts Humanit.; MLA Int. Bibl. Books Artic. Mod. Lang. Lit.; Res. Alert [Full Cov.]; Soc. Sci. Cit. Index [Select. Cov.]; Writ. Am. Hist.

US/0162-0053
PROCEEDINGS OF THE ANNUAL CONVENTION OF THE DAUGHTERS OF THE REPUBLIC OF TEXAS. Main/Corp Daughters of the Republic of Texas. Proceedings. English. an. $4.00 each. DRT Museum, 112 East 11th Street, Austin TX 78701. **LC** F381; .D23. **DD** 976.4/006/2. **UDC** 976.4. ***Continues*** *Proceedings of the Annual Meetings of the Daughters of the Republic of Texas.*

US
PROCEEDINGS OF THE ... CONTINENTAL CONGRESS OF THE NATIONAL SOCIETY OF THE DAUGHTERS OF THE AMERICAN REVOLUTION. Main/Corp Daughters of the American Revolution. Continental Congress. (April 1910)-. English. an (Oct.). $12.00. National Society of DAR, 1776 D Street Northwest, Washington DC 20006. **Tel** (202)879-3285. **LC** E202.5; .A164.

US/0273-2912
PROCEEDINGS OF THE LEHIGH COUNTY HISTORICAL SOCIETY.
Main/Corp Lehigh County Historical Society. Vol. 1 (1908)-. Proceedings. English. be (published in even years). $25.00 Comes with LeHigh County Historical Society membership. Lehigh County Historical Society, PO Box 1548, 5th and Hamilton Streets, Allentown PA 18105. **Tel** (215)435-4664. **ED** Dr. Mahlon Hellerich. **LC** F157.L5; L52. **DD** 974. **Bk Rev.** ctrl circ.

US/0076-4981
PROCEEDINGS OF THE MASSACHUSETTS HISTORICAL SOCIETY. [Proc. Mass. Hist. Soc.]. **Main/Corp** Massachusetts Historical Society. V. 1- 1791/1835-. Proceedings. English. an. $31.00 US. Massachusetts Historical Society, 1154 Boylston Street, Boston MA 02215. **Tel** (617)536-1608. **ED** Conrad E Wright. **LC** F61; .M38. **UDC** 974.4. Index available. cum. index. **Circ:** 400. available on microfilm from University Microfilms International (UMI).
Desc: Scholarly journal of New England history and report of activities of the Massachusetts Historical Society.
Ind/Abst Abstr. Engl. Stud.; Am. Hist. Life (1953-); MLA Int. Bibl. Books Artic. Mod. Lang. Lit.

US/0080-3383
PROCEEDINGS OF THE ROCKBRIDGE HISTORICAL SOCIETY. Main/Corp Rockbridge Historical Society. Vol. 1 (1939/41)-. English. ir. $5.00. Rockbridge Historical Society, Box 514, Lexington VA 24450. **Tel** (703)436-5546. **ED** Larry Bland and Joellen Bland. **LC** F232.R68; R6. **DD** 975.585. Index available. cum. index. **Circ:** 1,000 (ctrl).
Desc: Papers presented at regular meetings of society-on various local historical subjects.
Ind/Abst Am. Hist. Life (1975-).

US/0361-6207
PROCEEDINGS OF THE SOUTH CAROLINA HISTORICAL ASSOCIATION, THE. [Proc. S. C. Hist. Assoc.]. **Main/Corp** South Carolina Historical Association. (1931)-. Proceedings. English. an (Spring). $15.00. South Carolina Historical Association, c/o Dr. William S. Brockington, University of South Carolina-Aiken, 171 University Parkway, Aiken SC 29801. **Tel** (803)641-3223. **ED** Peter W. Becker, (phone: (803)777-4495). **LC** F266; .S58. Index available. **Ad Acc, Adv Mgr:** W. S. Brockington, **Tel** (803)648-6851. **Pr Rev. Circ:** 300. available on an online database, CD-ROM, magnetic tape, and microfilm; available on microfilm from University Microfilms International (UMI).
Desc: Presents papers given at the SCHA Annual Meeting. Topics focus on South Carolina and Southern history, but also include a wide variety of other topics.
Ind/Abst Am. Hist. Life (1963-).

US/0197-9884
PROGRAM OF THE ANNUAL MEETING - ORGANIZATION OF AMERICAN HISTORIANS. (PROGRAM / ORGANIZATION OF AMERICAN HISTORIANS ... ANNUAL MEETING.). [Program annu. meet. - Organ. Am. Hist.]. **Main/Corp** Organization of American Historians. Meeting. **Added/Corp** National Council on Public History (U.S.). Meeting. **VFOAT** Program of the ... Annual Meeting; OAH Annual Meeting Program; OAH/NCPH Annual Meeting Program. **VAT** Organization of American Historians Annual Meeting Program. (Apr. 28-30, 1966)-. Periodical. English. an. Included with subscription to the Journal of American History: $140.00 US; $155.00 other. Organization of American Historians, 112 North Bryan Street, Bloomington IN 47408. **Tel** (812)855-7311, FAX (812)855-0696. **LC** F351; .M645. **DD** 973/.06. ***Continues*** *Mississippi Valley Historical Association. Program: Annual Meeting.*

US/0033-1031
PROLOGUE (WASHINGTON). See Genealogy and Heraldry-Archives.

US/0361-2333
PROSPECTS (NEW YORK). (PROSPECTS.). [Prospects]. **Added/Corp** Columbia Universtiy. Center for American Culture Studies. Vol. 1 (1975)-. Academic Scholarly Publication. English. an. $79.00 US, Canada and Mexico; £49.00 other. Cambridge University Press / New York, 40 West 20th Street, New York NY 10011-4211. **Tel** (212)924-3900, (800)221-4512. **(Subscription address:** Cambridge University Press / Outside of North America, Journal Fulfillment Department, The Edinburgh Building, Cambridge CB2 2RU United Kingdom.**) ED** Jack Salzmann. **LC** E169.1; .P898. **DD** 973.925/05. **[CCC].** Index available (free). available on microfilm from University Microfilms International (UMI). Documents available from UMI Article Clearinghouse.
Desc: A multidisciplinary journal that explores all aspects of American civilization. Articles combine sound, creative scholarship with speculative discourse. Publishes in interdisciplinary subject areas ranging over literature, film, humor, satire, photography, music history, art, urban studies, television and sociology, with challenging and stimulating theoretical essays. Each volume is illustrated with line drawings, cartoons, photographs, reproductions of paintings and other graphic art.
Ind/Abst Expand. Acad. Index (1992-); MLA Int. Bibl. Books Artic. Mod. Lang. Lit.; Newsp. Period. Abstr. (1992-).

US/0092-0851
PUBLICATION - HISTORICAL SOCIETY OF WASHINGTON COUNTY, VIRGINIA. ***Ceased.*** **Main/Corp** Historical Society of Washington County, Virginia. (1965)-(19??). English. ir. Historical Society Washington County, VA, PO Box 484, Abingdon VA 24210. **Tel** (703)682-2745. **LC** F232.W3; W38a. **DD** 917.55/725/0305. ***Supersedes*** *Bulletin - Washington County Historical Society of Abingdon, Virginia.*
Ind/Abst Am. Hist. Life (1986-1987).

US
PUBLICATIONS OF THE COLONIAL SOCIETY OF MASSACHUSETTS.
Added/Corp Colonial Society of Massachusetts. Vol. 1 (1895)-. Monographic series. English. ir. Price varies per volume. University Press of Virginia, PO Box 3608, Charlottesville VA 22903. **Tel** (804)924-3469. **ED** Frederick S. Allis Jr. **LC** F61; .C71. Index available (Bound in all issues). **Circ:** 500.
Desc: Scholarly articles and documentary collections on the early history of the Plymouth and Massachusetts Bay colonies in particular and of New England in general.

US/0191-037X
PUBLICATIONS OF THE NEBRASKA STATE HISTORICAL SOCIETY. Main/Corp Nebraska State Historical Society. **Added/Corp** Nebraska State Historical Society. **VFOAT** Publications. Vol. 18 (1917)-. Monographic series. English. ir. Price varies per volume. Nebraska State Historical Society, 1500 R Street, Box 82554, Lincoln NE 68501. **Tel** (402)471-4746, (800)833-6747. **ED** James Potter. **LC** F661; .N3. **Bk Rev.** ctrl circ. ***Continues*** *Collections of the Nebraska State Historical Society.*
Desc: History of Nebraska and the great plains area.

US/0745-8800
QUADERNI SARDI DI ECONOMIA PODPORUJICI JEDMPTA STATU TEXAS. (VESTNIK; SPJST HERALD.). **VFOAT** SPJST Herald. Periodical. English (English). wk. Supreme Lodge SPJST, 520 North Main Street, Temple TX 76503. **LC** F395.S5; S5.

US/0033-5053
QUAKER HISTORY. See Religion and Theology.

US/0895-1152
QUARTERLY BULLETIN - ASHTABULA COUNTY HISTORICAL SOCIETY. (QUARTERLY BULLETIN.). [Q. bull. - Ashtabula Cty. Hist. Soc.]. **Main/Corp** Ashtabula County Historical Society. Vol. 8 (March 1961)-Vol. 20, No. 1 (March

1973)-. Periodical. English. qt. $4.00. Ashtabula County Historical Society, PO Box 36, Jefferson OH 44047. **Tel** (216)466-7337. **ED** Marilyn Aho. **DD** 977. **Circ:** 280 (ctrl).

US/0027-4135
QUARTERLY - MUSEUM OF THE FUR TRADE. **Main/Corp** Museum of the Fur Trade. 1-Spring 1965-. Academic Scholarly Publication. English. qt. $6.00 US; $7.00 other. Museum Fur Trade, HC-74 Box 18, Chadron NE 69337. **Tel** (308)432-3843. **ED** Charles E Hanson Jr. **UDC** 675(09)(7). Index available. cum. index. **Bk Rev. Circ:** 2,000 (ctrl).
Desc: Illustrated and scholarly magazine devoted to the material aspects of the historic fur trade of North America.
Ind/Abst Am. Hist. Life (1986-); EMBASE; West. Hist. Q.

US/0160-9602
QUARTERLY - NORTHEASTERN NEVADA HISTORICAL SOCIETY. [Quarterly - Northeast. Nev. Hist. Soc.]. **Main/Corp** Northeastern Nevada Historical Society. (1970)-. Periodical. English. qt. $10.00 individuals, schools and libraries; $20.00 family; $25.00 contributing members; $50.00 patron and business members; $100.00 sustaining member. Northeastern Nevada Museum, 1515 Idaho Street, Elko NV 89801. **Tel** (702)738-3418. **ED** Howard Hickson. **LC** F841; .N67A. **DD** 979.3/005. **UDC** 979.3. Index available. cum. index. **Bk Rev. Circ:** 1,200.
Desc: Any subject dealing with Northeastern Nevada.
Ind/Abst Am. Hist. Life (1977-); West. Hist. Q.

US/1071-4189
QUARTERLY OF THE NATIONAL ASSOCIATION FOR OUTLAW AND LAWMAN HISTORY, INC. [Q. Natl. Assoc. Outlaw Lawman Hist. Inc.]. **Added/Corp** National Association for Outlaw and Lawman History, Inc. (U.S.). (19??)-. Periodical. English. qt. $35.00 (membership). National Association & Center for Outlaw and Lawman History, 1201 Holly Court, Harker Heights TX 76453. **Tel** (817)698-6518. **ED** Chick Parsons. **DD** 973. **Bk Rev**, (Qty: 12-15). **Ad Acc. Circ:** 400 (ctrl). ***Continues*** *Quarterly of the National Association and Center for Outlaw and Lawman History (Laramie, Wyo.), 0890-3700.*

US/0890-5975
QUARTERLY PUBLICATION OF THE BUTLER COUNTY HISTORICAL SOCIETY, THE. [Q. publ. Butl. Cty. Hist. Soc.]. Vol. 12, No. 3 (Sept. 1976)-. Periodical. English. qt. $8.00 membership. Butler County Historical Society, 101 Adams Street, Greenville AL 36037. **Tel** (205)382-3216. **DD** 976. **UDC** 976.1. ***Continues*** *Publication of the Butler County Historical Society.*

US/0558-1931
QUARTERLY - ST. LAWRENCE COUNTY HISTORICAL ASSOCIATION, THE. [Q. - St. Lawrence Cty. Hist. Assoc.]. **Main/Corp** Saint Lawrence County Historical Association. Vol. 1, (Jan. 1956)-. Periodical. English. Four times a year (Jan., Apr., July, Oct.). $25.00 regular membership; $100.00 sustaining membership. St Lawrence County Historical Association, Box 8, Canton NY 13617. **Tel** (315)386-8133. **ED** Dr. Cornel Reinhart. Index available. **Ad Acc. Circ:** 1,000.
Desc: Articles relating to the history and development of St. Lawrence County New York.
Ind/Abst Am. Hist. Life.

NE
QUATERNARY OF SOUTH AMERICA AND ANTARCTIC PENINSULA. Vol. 1-(1983)-. Periodical. English. Fl65.00 Netherlands; $33.50 US. AA Balkema, Box 1675, 3000 BR Rotterdam Netherlands. **Tel** 011 31 10 4145822, FAX 011 31 10 4135947, telex 41605. **ED** Jorge Rabassa.

●US/1064-9026
QUE PASA PANAMA! NEWSLETTER. [Que pasa Panama newsl.]. **VFOAT** Que Pasa Panama!. Vol. 1, Issue No. 1 (June-Aug. 1992)-. Newsletter. English (Spanish). bm. $10.00. Viaful Dynamics, PO Box 7498, Grand Central Station NY 10163. **DD** 305.

CN/0836-0014
QUEBEC A VOTRE PORTEE, LE. **Added/Corp** Alliance Champlain. (1988/89)-. French. be. 27.95Can$. Quebec Dans Le Monde, CP 8503, Sainte-Foy Quebec G1V 4N5 Canada. **Tel** (418)659-5540, FAX (418)659-4143. **LC** F1051.5; .Q43. **DD** 971.4/0025. **Bk Rev.**
Desc: An alphabetical listing of more than 600 key subjects covering all principal sectors of the social sciences, including culture, education, communications, sports, leisure, tourism and others. There are 2 indexes, one by subject with 200 indicators, and one by region. Appendices cover several hundred additional resources.

US/0737-3759
QUEBEC STUDIES. [Quebec stud.]. **Added/Corp** Northeast Council for Quebec Studies (U.S.) American Council for Quebec Studies. Vol. 1, No. 1 (Spring 1983)-. English (French; summaries and/or abstracts in French). Twice a year (July, & Nov.). $40.00 one year; $50.00 libraries. Quebec Studies, Dartmouth College, Department of French Italian, Hanover NH 03755. **Tel** (207)872-3151. **(Subscription address:** Amercian Council for Quebec Studies, J. Moss Colby College, Mod for Language, Waterville, ME 04901**) ED** William Averyt, (phone: (802)656-0504). **LC** F1051; .Q33. **DD** 971/.005. **Bk Rev. Ad Acc.**
Ind/Abst Am. Hist. Life (1991-); Can. Period. Index (1989-).

CN/0226-210X
QUEBECENSIA. [Quebecensia]. **Added/Corp** Societe Historique de Quebec. Vol. 1 (Jan./Feb. 1980)-. Periodical. French. Five times a year. 40.00Can$ Comes with Societe Historique de Quebec membership. Societe Historique de Quebec / Historical Society of Quebec, 43 Cote de la Fabrique, Quebec Quebec G1R 5M1 Canada. **Tel** (418)694-9740, FAX (418)691-7759. **DD** 971.4/471/005.

US/0746-3472
QUEEN CITY HERITAGE. (QUEEN CITY HERITAGE : THE JOURNAL OF THE CINCINNATI HISTORICAL SOCIETY.). [Queen City herit.]. **Added/Corp** Cincinnati Historical Society. Vol. 41, No. 1 (Spring 1983)-. Periodical. English. Four times a year (Jan., Mar., Aug., Nov.). $20.00. Cincinnati Historical Society, 1301 Western Avenue, Cincinnati OH 45203. **Tel** (513)287-7030, (513)287-7033, FAX (513)241-7653. **ED** Dottie L. Lewis. **LC** F486; .H653. **DD** 977.1/78/005. Index available. **Circ:** 4,500 (ctrl). ***Continues*** *Cincinnati Historical Society Bulletin, 0194-2883.*
Desc: Articles on the cultural, economic, political, and social history of Cincinnati, the Miami Valley, or the Northwest Territory in reference to Ohio and the Ohio River.
Ind/Abst Am. Hist. Life (1964-); Annu. Bibliogr. Engl. Lang. Lit.; ARTbibliogr. Mod. (1983-); West. Hist. Q. (1983-).

CN/0315-2804
RAINCOAST CHRONICLES. ***Suspended.*** Vol. 1 (Spring 1972)-. English. qt. $12.38. Raincoast Chronicles, PO Box 91603, West Vancouver B.C. V7V 3P3. **Tel** (604)883-2730. **ED** Howard White. **UDC** 971.1. **Bk Rev. Circ:** 5,000.
Desc: History and culture of the coast of British Columbia, Canada.

US/0485-9758
RAMSEY COUNTY HISTORY. V. 1 (1964)-. Periodical. English. sa. Free to members, $3.00 single issue, others. Ramsey Co Historical Society, 75 West 5th Street, 323 Landmark, St Paul MN 55102. **Tel** (612)222-0701. **LC** F612.R2; R3. **DD** 977.6/58. **UDC** 977.6.

CN/0225-6959
RAPPORT ET TRAVAUX - GROUPE DE RECHERCHE SUR LA SOCIETE MONTREALAISE AU 19E SIECLE. **Main/Corp** Universite du Quebec a Montreal. Groupe de Recherche sur la Societe Montrealaise au 19E Siecle. 1973/75-. French. an. Universite du Quebec a Montreal d'Histoire Dep, Succursale Centre, Montreal Quebec H3C 3P8 Canada. **DD** 971.4/28102. **UDC** 971.4"18". ***Continues*** *Universite du Quebec a Montreal. Groupe Recherche sur la Societe Montrealaise au 19E Siecle. Rapport, 0317-7149.*

JA/0286-1127
RATEN AMERIKA KENKYU NENPO. [Raten Amerika kenkyu nenpo]. **VFOAT** Annals of Latin American Studies. No. 1 (1981)-. Japanese (English and Portuguese). an. Nihon Raten Amerika Gakkai, c/o Tokyo Daigaku Kyoyo Gakubu Chu-Nanbei Bunka 8-1 Komaba 3 Meguro-ku Tokyo-to-153 Japan. **LC** F1401; .R36. **UDC** 908.8=6.

US/0034-0898
REAL WEST. ***Ceased.*** Ceased (1988). Periodical. English. bm. Charlton Publications Inc., PO Box 158, 60 Division Street, Derby CT 06418. **Tel** (203)732-4797. **ED** Ed Doherty. **LC** F596; .R37. **DD** 978/.005. **UDC** 978. **Bk Rev. Ad Acc. Circ:** 50,000.
Desc: Settlement and early development of the American West (1865-1920).

US/0899-2371
RECENT AMERICAN HISTORY. [Rec. Am. hist.]. Vol. 1 (1989)-. Monographic series. English. ir. Price varies per volume. Peter Lang Publishing, 62 West 45th Street, 4th Floor, New York NY 10036. **Tel** (212)764-1471, (800)770-5264, telex 6973364 PLNY. **ED** Kenneth K. Hendrikson. **DD** 973. **Pr Rev.**
Desc: Covers 20th century US history.

CN/0318-4137
RECHERCHES AMERINDIENNES AU QUEBEC. [Rech. amerindiennes Que.]. **Added/Corp** Recherches Amerindiennes au Quebec (Association). **VFOAT** Bulletin d'Information. Vol. 1 (1971)-. French (English). qt. 53.00Can$ (Canada), 52.00Can$ (other) institution; 40.00Can$ (Canada), 42.00Can$ (other) individual. Recherches Amerindiennes au Quebec, 6742 rue St Denis, Montreal Quebec, H2S 2S2 Canada. **Tel** (514) 277-6178. **DD** 971.4/004/97.

HT
RECHERCHES HAITIENNES. No. 1 (Oct. 1979)-. French. an. Institut Francais d'Haiti, Po Box 131, Port-Au-Prince Haiti. **Tel** 011 509 1 226060, 011 509 1 226063. **LC** F1912; .R43. **DD** 972.94/005. **UDC** 972.94.

US/0163-6820
RECORD - GARLAND COUNTY HISTORICAL SOCIETY, THE. (THE RECORD.). [Rec. - Garland Cty. Hist. Soc.]. **Added/Corp** Hot Springs-Garland County Historical Society. Garland County Historical Society. (19??)-. English. an (Oct.). $14.00. Garland County Historical Society, 222 McMahan Drive, Hot Springs AR 71913. **Tel** (501)623-6766. **ED** Wendy B. Richter and Bobbie J. McLane. **LC** F419.H8; R43. **DD** 917.67/41/0305. **Circ:** 500.
Desc: Articles, information relating to Garland County, City of Hot Springs, and its history.

US/0739-1838
RED RIVER VALLEY HERITAGE PRESS, THE. [Red River Val. herit. press]. **Added/Corp** Red River Valley Heritage Society. Red River Valley Historical Society. **VFOAT** Heritage Press. Vol. 1 (1976)-. Periodical. English. Six times a year. $25.00 Comes with Red River Valley Heritage Society membership. Red River Valley Heritage Society, 202 1st Avenue N, PO Box 157, Moorhead MN 56560. **Tel** (218)233-5604. **ED** Karla Winter. **Bk Rev**, (Qty: 3-4). **Circ:** 800 (ctrl). ***Supersedes*** *Red River Valley History News.*
Desc: Information on the "going on" of two organization and a major historical articles and news.
Ind/Abst Am. Hist. Life.

US/0362-6415
RED RIVER VALLEY HISTORICAL REVIEW. [Red River Val. hist. rev.]. Began with Spring 1974 issue. Periodical. English. qt. $9.00. Museum and Archives of the Red River Valley, 601 North 16th Street, Durant OK 74701. **LC** F591; .R417. **DD** 978/.055. **UDC** 976.6.
Ind/Abst Am. Hist. Life (1974-1982).

US/1071-0515
REFLECTIONS (TAZEWELL, TENN.). (REFLECTIONS : THE QUARTERLY NEWSLETTER OF THE CLAIBORNE COUNTY HISTORICAL SOCIETY.). **Added/Corp** Claiborne County Historical Society (Tenn.). Vol. 1, No. 1 (Aug. 1982)-. Newsletter. English. qt. $10.00 (membership dues). Claiborne County Historical Society, PO Box 32, Tazewell TN 37879. **Tel** (615)626-3872. **ED** Mary England. **DD** 929. **Bk Rev**, (Qty: 4). **Ad Acc. Circ:** 350.

CN/1181-7372
REFLETS DU NORD. [Reflets nord]. **Added/Corp** Comite Recreatif et Communautaire du Quartier Nord. (Sept. 1990)-. Periodical. French. qt. Limited Free Distribution. Comite Recreatif et Communautaire du Quartier Nordde Sherbrooke, 60 Rue Marchand, Sherbrooke Quebec J1J 3V2 Canada. **DD** 971.4/66/005.

US/0034-3269
REGGEBOGE, DER. (DER REGGEBOGE. THE RAINBOW.). **Added/Corp** Pennsylvania-German Society. **VFOAT** Rainbow. (March 1967)-. English (German). Twice a year. $50.00 institutions; $40.00 individuals. Pennsylvania German Society, PO Box 397, Birdsboro PA 19508. **Tel** (215)582-1441. **LC** F160.G3; R43. **DD** 974.8/004/31.

CN/0821-7769
REGINA - CITY OF REGINA. (REGINA.). [Regina - City Regina]. 1982-. English. an. Regina Development and Public Relations Department, PO Box 1790, Regina Saskatchewan S4P 3C8 Canada. **DD** 971.24/4. **UDC** 971.2. ***Continues*** *City of Regina Data Book, 0824-2836.*

US/0023-0243
REGISTER OF THE KENTUCKY HISTORICAL SOCIETY, THE. [Regist. - Ky. Hist. Soc.]. **Added/Corp** Kentucky Historical Society. **VFOAT** Register. Vol. 45, No. 150 (Jan. 1947)-. Periodical. English. qt. $25.00 (individuals), $30.00 (libraries). Kentucky Historical Society, Old State Capitol, PO Box H, Frankfort KY 40602. **Tel** (502)564-3016, FAX (502)564-4701. **ED** J C Klotter and T H Appleton. **LC** F446; .K43. Index available. cum. index. **Bk Rev. Circ:** 6,000 (ctrl). available on microfilm. ***Continues*** *Register of Kentucky State Historical Society.*
Desc: Articles and reviews on the history of the US, with emphasis on Kentucky and neighboring states.
Ind/Abst Am. Hist. Life (1963-); Genealogical Period. Annu. Index.

MX/0185-3929
RELACIONES / COLEGIO DE MICHOACAN. **Added/Corp** Colegio de Michoacan. No. 1 (Winter 1980)-. Periodical. Spanish. qt. $48.00. El Colegio de Michoacan, Avenida de Martinez, de Navarrete 505, 59690 Zamora Michoacan Mexico. **Tel** 011 52 351 26381. **LC** F1201; .R43. **DD** 972/.005. cum. index (issue 1-35). **Circ:** 1,000 (ctrl).

BL
RELATORIO ANUAL - SOCIEDADE BRASILEIRA DE CULTURA JAPONESA. **Main/Corp** Sociedade Brasileira de Cultura Japonesa. Portuguese. Sociedade Brasileira de Cultura Japonesa, rua Sao Joaquim 381, Sao Paulo Brazil. **LC** F2659.J3; S56A. **DD** 981/.004/956. **UDC** 981(=956); 930.85(81)(=956).

US/0034-3897
RELICS. (19??)-. English. Four times a year (March, May, Sept., Nov.). $10.00. Pascack Historical Society, PO Box 285, Park Ridge NJ 07656. **ED** Katharine P. Randall (editor's address: 1 Carlyle Place, Hillsdale, NJ 07642 , phone: 201)664-4934). **Pr Rev. Circ:** 300 (ctrl).

CN/0227-4442
REPERTOIRE DES RESSOURCES FRANCO-ONTARIENNES. **Added/Corp** Francophonie Ontarienne (Association). (1978)-. French. an. $15.00 each number. Francophonie Ontarienne, 70 rue Templeton, Ottawa Ontario K1N 6X3 Canada. **DD** 971.3/004114.

CK
REPERTORIO HISTORICO. **Main/Corp** Academia Antioquena de Historia, Medellin, Colombia. (1905)-. Periodical. Spanish. bm. **LC** F2281.A6; A13. **Ind/Abst** Am. Hist. Life (1967-1975).

US/0098-4035
REPORT - ADVISORY COUNCIL ON HISTORIC PRESERVATION. **Main/Corp** United States. Advisory Council on Historic Preservation. (19??)-. Periodical. English. an. Free on request. Advisory Council on Historic Preservation, 1100 Pennsylvania Avenue NW/ #809, Washington DC 20004. **Tel** (202)786-0503, FAX (202)786-1172. **ED** Elizabeth Moss. **LC** E159; .U5b. **DD** 309.2/0973. ***Continues*** *Newsletter - Advisory Council on Historic Preservation, 0091-9748.*
Desc: The intersection of federal and local historic preservation issues within the context of federal property management. One of a yearly series on preservation activity across the nation. Also summarizes advisory council activities, including casework, litigation under the National Historic Preservation Act of 1966, and preservation legislation.

CN/0846-9253
REPORT OF THE CANADIAN MULTICULTURALISM COUNCIL. **Main/Corp** Canadian Multiculturalism Council. **VFOAT** Rapport du Conseil Canadien du Multiculturalisme. English (French). an. Multiculturalism & Citizenship, Canada Communications Branch, Ottawa Ontario K1A 0M5 Canada. **Tel** (819)994-0055. ***Continues*** *Report of the Canadian Consultative Council on Multiculturalism, 0846-9237.*

CN
REPORT OF THE PRINCE EDWARD ISLAND HERITAGE FOUNDATION. **Main/Corp** Prince Edward Island Heritage Foundation. English. Prince Edward Island Heritage Foundation, 2 Kent Street, PO Box 922, Charlottetown Prince Edward Island Canada. **LC** F1046; .P76A. **DD** 354/.717/0085. **UDC** 971.3.

US
REPORT OF THE VERMONT BICENTENNIAL COMMISSION. **Main/Corp** Vermont Bicentennial Commission. Oct. 1974/Dec. 1976-. English. Box 195, Montpelier VT 05602. **LC** E285.4.V4; V47A. **DD** 353.9/743/0085. **UDC** 974.3. ***Continues*** *Annual Report of the Vermont Bicentennial Commission, 0149-6506.*

US
REPORT OF THE VIRGINIA COUNCIL ON INDIANS TO THE GOVERNOR AND THE GENERAL ASSEMBLY. **Main/Corp** Virginia Council on Indians. English. be. **LC** PAR. ***Continues*** *Report of the Commission on Indians to the Governor and the General Assembly of Virginia.*

US/1058-5397
REPORT ON THE AMERICAS. ***Title Change.*** [Rep. Am.]. **Added/Corp** North American Congress on Latin America. **VFOAT** NACLA Report on the Americas. Vol. 24 No. 5 (Feb. 1991)-(1993). Periodical. English. qt. North American Congress on Latin America, 475 Riverside Drive, Room 454, New York NY 10115. **Tel** (212)870-3146. **LC** F1401; .N58. **DD** 309.1/8/003. ***Continues*** *North American Congress on Latin America. NACLA Report on the Americas, 0149-1598.* ***Continued by*** *NACLA Report on the Americas (New York, N.Y. : 1993), 1071-4839.*
Ind/Abst Altern. Press Index (199?-); Hum. Rights Intern. Rep.; PAIS Int. Print.

US
REPORT - TENNESSEE HISTORICAL COMMISSION. **Main/Corp** Tennessee. State Historical Commission. English. be. Tennessee Historical Commission, 701 Broadway, Nashville TN 37219. **LC** F431.T25; A35. **DD** 353.9/768/0085. **UDC** 976.8.

BO
REPORTAJES; DOCUMENTOS PARA LA HISTORIA. Yearly V. 1- 6/20 July 1970-. Periodical. Spanish. $2.00. Edificio Almaraz 50, Casilla Postal 382, La Paz Bolivia. **LC** F3301; .R43. **DD** 984/.005. **UDC** 984.

AG
RES GESTA. Periodical. Spanish (Spanish). Instituto de Historia / Argentina, Avda Salta 2763, 2000 Rosario Argentina. **LC** F2801; .R4. **DD** 982/.005. **UDC** 982.

CN
RESEARCH BULLETIN (CANADA PARKS). (1986)-. Bulletin. English. Parks Canada, Ottawa Ontario K1A 0H3 Canada. **Tel** (613)993-9800. ***Continues*** *Parks Canada Research Bulletin.*

US/0276-0509
RESEARCH DIGEST - LATINO INSTITUTE (RESTON, VA.). (RESEARCH DIGEST / LATINO INSTITUTE.). [Res. dig. - Lat. Inst. (Reston, Va.)]. **VFOAT** Latino Institute Research Digest. Vol. 1 (1980)-. English. $10.00. Lation Institute Research Division, 1760 Reston Avenue, Suite 101, Reston VA 22090. **LC** E184.S75; R47A. **DD** 016.3058/68/073. **UDC** 973(=4); 908.73(=4).

US/0195-8224
RESEARCH REVIEW - LITTLE BIG HORN ASSOCIATES. **Main/Corp** Little Big Horn Associates. Periodical. English. qt. $17.50, $16.00 (members), $50.00 (donors). Little Big Horn Associates, PO Box 27046, El Paso TX 79926. **UDC** 973.042.
Desc: Covers Indian wars, Indians, army, and Custer.

CN/0710-1287
RESSOURCES CULTURELLES DES FRANCOPHONES HORS QUEBEC. (LES RESSOURCES CULTURELLES DES FRANCOPHONES HORS QUEBEC / UNE PUBLICATION DE LA F.C.C.F. SUBVENTIONNEE PAR LE SECRETARIAT D'ETAT.). [Ressour. cult. francoph. Que.]. **Main/Corp** Federation Culturelle des Canadiens-Francais. 1980 Ed.-. Periodical. French. ir. $15.00 per volume. Federation Culturelle Des Canadiens-Francais, CP 26, Succursale Norwood Grove, Saint Bonifac, Manitoba R2H 3B8. **DD** 971/.004114/025. **UDC** 971(=40); 908.71(=40).

CN/0821-7335
REVIEW - COLE HARBOUR RURAL HERITAGE SOCIETY. (REVIEW OF ... / COLE HARBOUR RURAL HERITAGE SOCIETY.). [Rev. - Cole Harb. Rural Herit. Soc.]. **Added/Corp** Cole Harbour Rural Heritage Society. (1981)-. English. an. Cole Harbour Rural Heritage Society, R R 1, Dartmouth Nova Scotia B2W 3X7 Canada. **DD** 971.6/22. ***Continues*** *Newsletter (Cole Harbour Rural Heritage Society), 0715-5123.*

US
REVIEW OF LATIN AMERICAN STUDIES. ***Suspended.*** Vol. 1, No. 1 (1988)-(199?). Periodical. English (Spanish). sa. $30.00 (institutions), $16.00 (individuals). San Diego State University Press, San Diego State University, San Diego CA 92182. **Tel** (619)594-6220. **ED** Frederick M Nunn. **Circ:** 750. ***Continues*** *Proceedings of the Pacific Coast Council on Latin American Studies.*
Desc: An interdisciplinary journal founded on proceedings of the Pacific Coast Council on Latin American Studies.
Ind/Abst HAPI Hisp. Am. Period. Index.

US
REVIEW, THE MAGAZINE FOR ALABAMIANS. V.1, No. 3- April 1974-. Periodical. English. mo. Brooks Barganir, 919 Greensboro Avenue, PO Box 2044, Tuscaloosa AL 35401. **DD** 976.1. **UDC** 976.1; 908.761. ***Continues*** *Alabama News Review.*

US/0048-7511
REVIEWS IN AMERICAN HISTORY. [Rev. Am. hist.]. Vol. 1 (Mar. 1973)-. Periodical. English. Four times a year (March, June, September, December). $66.00 US; $69.90 Canada & Mexico; $75.40 other. Johns Hopkins University Press, 2715 North Charles Street, Baltimore MD 21218-4319. **Tel** (410)516-6987, FAX (410)516-6968. **(Subscription address:** John Hopkins University Press, Journals Publishing Division, PO Box 19966, Baltimore MD 21211.**)** **ED** Stanley I. Kutler. **LC** Z1236; .R47. **DD** 973. **NLM** Z 1236; R454. **[CCC]. Bk Rev. Ad Acc. Circ:** 3,200. available on microfilm and microfiche from University Microfilms International (UMI). Documents available from The Genuine Article, UMI Article Clearinghouse.
Desc: Provides a means for scholars, instructors, and students of American history to stay up to date in their discipline. Presents comparative and interpretive essays analyzing recent research published in specialties of American history, including economics, military history, women in history, law, political philosophy, and religion.
Ind/Abst Acad. Abstr. Full Text Elite (July 1990-); Acad. Abstr. (July 1990-); Acad. Search (July 1990-); Am. Hist. Life (1974-); Am. Bibliogr. Slavic East Europ. Stud.; Arts Humanit. Citation Index [Full Cov.]; Book Rev. Digest; Book Rev. Index; Curr. Contents Arts Humanit.; Expand. Acad. Index (1989-); Hist. Source (July 1990-); Humanit. Index; Humanit. Source (Jul. 1990-); Index Period. Artic. Relat. Law (19??-19??); INFO-SOUTH Abstr.; Mag. Search; Newsp. Period. Abstr. (1990-); Res. Alert [Full Cov.]; Soc. Sci. Cit. Index [Select. Cov.].

II
REVIEWS IN AMERICAN STUDIES. **Added/Corp** American Studies Research Centre (Hyderabad, India). (19??)-. Periodical. English. qt. **LC** E169.12; .I45 Suppl. **DD** 973/.05.
Ind/Abst Am. Hist. Life (1972-1975).

CL/0716-2812
REVISTA CHILENA DE HISTORIA Y GEOGRAFIA. [Rev. chil. hist. geogr.]. Began in 1911. Periodical. Spanish. sa. 3,500Chil$ Chile; $25.00 US. Sociedad Chilena de Historia y Geografia, Casilla 1386, Santiago Chile. **Tel** 382489. **LC** F3051; .R45. **UDC** 983; 902(83); 918.3. Index available. cum. index. **Circ:** 1,000 (ctrl).
Desc: Covers Chilean history, geography and archaeology.
Ind/Abst Am. Hist. Life (1954-); HAPI Hisp. Am. Period. Index.

MX
REVISTA COAHUILENSE DE HISTORIA. **Added/Corp** Colegio Coahuilense de Investigaciones Historicas. Vol. 1 (May/June 1978)-. Periodical. Spanish. bm. $7.00. Ediciones Recinto de Juarez, Apartado Postal 648, Saltillo Coahuila Mexico. **LC** F1266; .R46. **DD** 972/.14.005.

SP
REVISTA COMPLUTENSE DE HISTORIA DE AMERICA. (1991)-. Spanish. an. ***Continues*** *Quinto Centenario, 0211-6111.*
Ind/Abst Am. Hist. Life (1989-).

SP/0211-6111
REVISTA COMPLUTENSE DE HISTORIA DE AMERICA / DEPARTAMENTO DE HISTORIA DE AMERICA I. **Added/Corp** Universidad Complutense de Madrid. Departamento de Historia de America I. (1991)-. Periodical. Spanish. an. $17.00. Editorial Complutense, Donoso Cortes 65 1RA Planta, 28003 Madrid Spain. **Tel** 011 34 1 3946372. **LC** E18; .Q48. **DD** 980. ***Continues*** *Quinto Centenario.*
Ind/Abst Am. Hist. Life.

PN
REVISTA CULTURAL LOTERIA. **Added/Corp** Loteria Nacional de Beneficencia (Panama). **VFOAT** L. Ano 49, No. 375 (Enero-Feb. 1990)-. Periodical. Spanish. bm. Department Cultural, Apartado 21, Panama, Republica de Panama. **LC** F1561; .L68. ***Continues*** *Revista Loteria, 0024-662X.*
Ind/Abst Am. Hist. Life (1960-1975, 1985-).

BL
REVISTA DA ACADEMIA SOBRALENSE DE ESTUDOS E LETRAS. **Main/Corp** Academia Sobralense de Estudos e Letras. Periodical. Portuguese. Academia Sobralense de Estudos e Letras, rua Floriano Peixota, 154 Sala 2 Altos, CEP Sobral Ceara Brazil. **Tel** (085)224-6039. **ED** Joao Ribeiro Ramos. **LC** F2651.S62; A33A. **DD** 981/.31. **UDC** 908.81. **Bk Rev. Ad Acc. Circ:** 500 (ctrl).
Desc: Poetry, short novels, biographies and articles of general interest by members of the Sobralian Academy of Studies and Letters and by other intellectuals.

BL
REVISTA DE ATUALIDADE INDIGENA. Yearly V. 1- Nov./Dec. 1976-. Periodical. Portuguese. bm. Fundacao Nacional do Indio, Sas Q1 Bloco A Lotes 9 10 7, Andar S270, Brasilia DF Brazil. **LC** F2520; .R45. **DD** 980/.00498. **UDC** 981; 908.81.

CR
REVISTA DE COSTA RICA. **Added/Corp** Costa Rica. Ministerio de Cultura, Juventud y Deportes. (19??)-. Spanish. ir. Universidad de Costa Rica / Editorial, Apartado 75, 2060 Ciudad Universitaria, San Jose Costa Rica. **Tel** 011 506 2247051, 2253133. **LC** F1541; .R47. available on microfilm.

BL
REVISTA DE DIVULGACAO CULTURAL / FURB. **VFOAT** F.U.R.B. Revista de Divulgacao Cultural; FURB Revista de Divulgacao Cultural. Yearly V. 2, No. 6, (May 1979)-. Periodical. Portuguese (English, French and Spanish). qt. Cr$1,337.12 Brazil; $7.15 US. Fundacao Universidade Regional de Blumenau, Caixa Postal 7-E, 89.100 Blumenau, Santa Catarina Brazil. **Tel** (0473) 22-8288. **ED** Anamaria Kovacs. **LC** AP66; .R54. **DD** 056/.9. **UDC** 908.81. Index available. **Bk Rev. Ad Acc. Circ:** 800 (ctrl). ***Continues*** *Abertura (Blumenau, Brazil).*
Desc: Technical and scientific articles written by teachers at the Universidade Regional de Blumenau. Eventually, students and other intellectuals have their articles published.

NQ
REVISTA DE HISTORIA. **Added/Corp** Instituto de Historia de Nicaragua. (1990)-. Periodical. Spanish. sa. **LC** F1521; .R48. **DD** 972.85/005.

AG/0556-5960
REVISTA DE HISTORIA AMERICANA Y ARGENTINA. ***Ceased.*** [Rev. hist. am. argent.]. **Added/Corp** Universidad Nacional de Cuyo. Instituto de Historia y Disciplinas Auxiliares. Seccion Historia Americana y Argentina. (1956)-(19??). Spanish. ir. Editorial Facultad Filosofia, Letras Casilla de Correo 345, 5500 Mendoza Argentina. **Tel** 011 54 61 253010, 234571. **LC** E11; .R38.
Ind/Abst Am. Hist. Life (1956-1971,1978-).

MX/0034-8325
REVISTA DE HISTORIA DE AMERICA. [Rev. hist. Am.]. **Added/Corp** Pan American Institute of Geography and History. Vol. 1 (March 1938)-. Periodical. English (French, Portuguese and Spanish). sa. $21.00 US, Canada & Central America; $23.50 South America & Europe; $26.00 other. Instituto Panamericano de Geographico Historia, APDO 18879 Secretaria General, 11870 Mexico DF Mexico. **Tel** 011 52 5 2775888, 011 52 5 2775791, FAX 011 52 5 2716172. **ED** Laurio H. Destefani. **LC** F1401; .R44. **DD** 980.05. cum. index. **Circ:** 750. available on microfilm and microfiche from University Microfilms International (UMI). Documents available from The Genuine Article.
Desc: Publishes articles, essays and research works related to history, historiography and history of the ideas in Latin America.
Ind/Abst Am. Hist. Life (1955-1975)(1955-); Arts Humanit. Citation Index [Full Cov.]; BHA : Biblio. Hist. Art; Curr. Contents Arts Humanit.; HAPI Hisp. Am. Period. Index; Res. Alert [Full Cov.].

AG/0556-5995
REVISTA DE HISTORIA DE ROSARIO. Vol. 1, No. 1 (1963)-. Periodical. Spanish. an. Sociedad de Historia Rosario, 1 de Mayo 1082, 2000 Rosario Argentina. **Tel** 47225. **ED** Wladimir C. Mikielievich. **Ad Acc. Circ:** 1,000.
Desc: History of Rosario, second city of the Republic Argentine, and its' department. Covers every aspect from its' origin in XVII century until present time.

CR/1012-9790
REVISTA DE HISTORIA (HEREDIA). (REVISTA DE HISTORIA.). [Rev. hist.]. **Added/Corp** Universidad Nacional (Costa Rica). Escuela de Historia. Universidad de Costa Rica. Centro de Investigaciones Historicas. Vol. 1, No. 1 (1975)-. Spanish (summaries and/or abstracts in English). Twice a year (Jan. & July). $20.00. Universidad de Costa Rica / Publicaciones, Apartado 75, 2060 Ciudad Univeridad, San Jose Costa Rica. **Tel** 011 506 2247051, 011 506 2253133, FAX 011 506 342723, telex 2544 UNICORI. **ED** Edwin Gonzales. **LC** F1541; .R49. Index available. **Bk Rev. Pr Rev. Circ:** 1,000 (ctrl).
Desc: Original research articles on the economic, political and cultural history of Costa Rica and Central America. Publishes copies of original documents for the serious scholar. Includes a critical bibliography.
Ind/Abst Am. Hist. Life (1960-1971.

SP/0034-8341
REVISTA DE INDIAS. [Rev. Indias]. **Added/Corp** Instituto Gonzalo Fernandez de Oviedo. Vol. 1 (1940)-. Periodical. Spanish (summaries and/or abstracts in English). tq (Jan., May, Sept.). 5000ptas Spain; 7500ptas other. Consejo Superior Investigacion Cientificas (CSIC), Vitruvio 8, 28006 Madrid Spain. **Tel** 011 34 1 5612833, FAX 011 34 1 4113077, telex 42182. **LC** F1401; .R442. **DD** 980.05. **UDC** 970/980. cum. index. Documents available from The Genuine Article.
Desc: Covers chronologically the pre-Spanish, colonial and modern periods in the history of the Indies, with emphasis on social and economic aspects of history.
Ind/Abst Am. Hist. Life (1955-1971, 1979-); Anthropol. Index; Arts Humanit. Citation Index (19??-19??) [Full Cov.]; Curr. Contents Arts Humanit.; HAPI Hisp. Am. Period. Index; Res. Alert [Full Cov.]; Soc. Sci. Cit. Index [Select. Cov.].

MX
REVISTA DE INVESTIGACIONES HISTORICAS / SEMINARIO DE HISTORIA. V. No. 1, 1979. Periodical. Spanish. Seminario de Historia de la Universidad Veracruzana, Nicolas Bravo, 7 Xalapa Veracruz Mexico. **LC** F1371; .R48. **DD** 972/.62/005. **UDC** 972.

CK/0120-8268
REVISTA DE LA ACADEMIA COLOMBIANA DE HISTORIA ECLESIASTICA. (REVISTA.). [Rev. Acad. Colomb. Hist. Ecles.]. **Main/Corp** Academia Colombiana de Historia Eclesiastica. (1966)-. Periodical. Spanish. qt.
Ind/Abst Am. Hist. Life (1966-1973,1980).

VE/0798-0019
REVISTA DE LA SOCIEDAD BOLIVARIANA. (REVISTA DE LA SOCIEDAD BOLIVARIANA DE VENEZUELA.). [Rev. Soc. Boliv.]. **Main/Corp** Sociedad Bolivariana de Venezuela. Vol. 1 No. 1 (Jul 1939)-. Periodical. Spanish. qt. **LC** F2235.3; .S8.
Ind/Abst Am. Hist. Life (1958-1974,1979-1982).

BL
REVISTA DE PRE-HISTORIA. Added/Corp Universidade de Sao Paulo. Instituto de Pre-Historia. Vol. 1 (Aug. 1979)-. French (Portuguese and Spanish; summaries and/or abstracts in English). an. $10.00 Brazil; $15.00 other. Museu de Arqueologia e Etnologia, Universidade de Sao Paulo, Av. Prof. Almelda Prado 1466, Cidade Universitaria - CEP 05508-900, Sao Paulo SP Brazil. **Tel** 011 818 4978, FAX 011 818 5042. **ED** Jose Jobson de Andrade Arrua and Haiganuch Sarian. **LC** F2519; .R48. **DD** 980/.01/05. Index available. **Bk Rev**, (Qty: 5). **Pr Rev. Acid Free. Circ:** 1,000 (ctrl).
Desc: Information on the Indians of South America.

PE/0590-4609
REVISTA DEL ARCHIVO HISTORICO DEL CUZCO. (REVISTA DEL ARCHIVO HISTORICO / UNIVERSIDAD NACIONAL DEL CUZCO.). [Rev. Arch. hist. Cuzco]. **Added/Corp** Archivo Historico del Cuzco. Universidad Nacional de "San Antonio Abad" del Cusco. **VFOAT** Revista del Archivo Historico del Cuzco. No. 1 (1950)-. Spanish. an. **LC** F3401; .C8.
Ind/Abst Am. Hist. Life (1954-1963).

EC
REVISTA DEL ARCHIVO HISTORICO DEL GUAYAS. See Genealogy and Heraldry-Archives.

CR/0034-9003
REVISTA DEL ARCHIVO NACIONAL. See Genealogy and Heraldry-Archives.

CR/0034-9003
REVISTA DEL ARCHIVO NACIONAL (SAN JOSE). (REVISTA DEL ARCHIVO NACIONAL.). [Rev. Arch. nac.]. **Added/Corp** Costa Rica. Archivo Nacional. (1966)-. Periodical. Spanish. ir. $20.00. Archivo Nacional, Apartado Postal 10212, San Jose 1000 Costa Rica. **Tel** 011 506 335754. **LC** F1541; .C45. ***Continues*** *Revista de los Archivos Nacionales.*
Ind/Abst Am. Hist. Life (1966-).

PR/0020-3815
REVISTA DEL INSTITUTO DE CULTURA PUERTORRIQUENA. [Rev. inst. cult. Puertorriq.]. **Main/Corp** Instituto de Cultura Puertorriquena. (1958)-. Periodical. Spanish. qt. $10.00. Institute de Cultura Puertorriquena, Arpartado 4184, San Juan, Puerto Rico. **Tel** (809)725-1988, 725-7515. **LC** F1951; .I534.
Ind/Abst Am. Hist. Life (1959-1961, 1966-1974, 1987-); HAPI Hisp. Am. Period. Index (19??-).

PE
REVISTA DEL INSTITUTO DE ESTUDIOS HISTORICO-MARITIMOS DEL PERU. No. 1 (Jan./June 1978)-. Spanish. an. $0.50. Instituto de Estudios Historico-Maritimos del Peru, Avenida Nicolas de Aranibar, 744 Lima -14 Peru. **Tel** 710735+712729. **LC** F3432; .R48. **DD** 985/.005. **UDC** 656.61(09)(85). **Ad Acc. Circ:** 1,000.
Desc: Offers cultural topics concerning scientific and historical aspects of naval and maritime sciences, in general, as they occurred in the arena of the Peruvian Sea from ancient times through today.

PO
REVISTA DO BRASIL. Ano 1 (1916)-; (Julho, 1938)-. Periodical. Portuguese. mo.
Ind/Abst HAPI Hisp. Am. Period. Index (19??-).

BL
REVISTA DO INSTITUTO HISTORICO DE OEIRAS. Periodical. Portuguese. Instituto Historico de Oeiras, Praca 24 de Janeiro, 64.500 Oeiras Piaui Brazil. **LC** F2651.O35; R48. **DD** 981/.22. **UDC** 981.

BL
REVISTA DO INSTITUTO HISTORICO E GEOGRAFICO DE SAO PAULO. Main/Corp Instituto Historico e Geografico de Sao Paulo. Vol. 1 (1895)-. Periodical. Portuguese. ir. Instituto Historico Geografico de Sao Paulo, Rua Benjamin Constant 158, 01005 Sao Paulo SP Brazil. **LC** F2631; .I59. **DD** 981.
Ind/Abst MLA Int. Bibl. Books Artic. Mod. Lang. Lit.

DR
REVISTA DOMINICANA DE ANTROPOLOGIA E HISTORIA. Added/Corp Universidad Autonoma de Santo Domingo. Departamento de Historia y Antropologia. Centro Dominicano de Investigaciones Antropologicas. Ano 9, Vol. 6, No. 8/11 (1977/1979)-. Periodical. Spanish. ***Continues*** *Revista Dominicana de Arqueologia, Antropologia e Historia.*
Ind/Abst HAPI Hisp. Am. Period. Index (19??-).

BL
REVISTA GUIA REX. Portuguese. an. Cr$600.00. Revista Revista Guia Rex, rua Dep Soares Filho 326, Tijuca Cep 20540 Rio de Janeiro Brazil. **LC** F2509.5; .R48. **DD** 918.1/530463. ***Continues*** *Revista Guia Rex (Edicao Especial). Revista Guia Rex.*

UY/0252-8983
REVISTA HISTORICA. Added/Corp Archivo Historico Nacional (Uruguay) Archivo y Museo Historico Nacional (Uruguay) Museo Historico Nacional (Uruguay). (1910)-. Periodical. Spanish. qt. ***Continues*** *Revista Historica de la Universidad.*

UY/0252-8983
REVISTA HISTORICA (MONTEVIDEO). (REVISTA HISTORICA.). [Rev. hist.]. (Aug. 1941)-. Periodical. Spanish. Three times a year. Museo Historico Nacional, Casa de Rivera, Rincon 437, Montevideo Uruguay. **LC** F2721; .U85. **DD** 989.5/005. **UDC** 989.5. ***Continues*** *Revista Historica (Archivo y Museo Historico Nacional (Uruguay)).*
Ind/Abst Am. Hist. Life (1955-1962); HAPI Hisp. Am. Period. Index.

AG
REVISTA - JUNTA DE ESTUDIOS HISTORICOS DE ENTRE RIOS. Main/Corp Junta de Estudios Historicos de Entre Rios. No. 1-. Spanish. Juenta de Estudios Historicos de Entre Rios, Buenos Aires 256, Parana Argentina. **LC** F2896; .J76A. **UDC** 982.

MX/0185-6022
REVISTA MEXICANA DE POLITICA EXTERIOR. Vol. 1 (Oct./Dec. 1983)-. Periodical. Spanish. qt. $2,000 Mexico; $25.00 Western Hemisphere; $34.00 other. Av Peralvillo 124 Col Morelos, Delegacion Cuauhtemo, C P 06200 Mexico DF Mexico. **Tel** 5-26-86-65, telex 017725531 SRE ME. **ED** Jose Luis Leon and Rosario Green. **LC** F1236; .R49. Index available. **Bk Rev. Ad Acc. Circ:** 2,000 (ctrl).
Desc: Studies the postwar era, through its changes in world order and diplomatic relations as well as social, economic and cultural developments. Contents include original essays, diplomatic news and documentation.

SZ
REVISTA MUNDIAL. (19??)-. Spanish. **LC** D410; .R44.

PN
REVISTA NACIONAL DE CULTURA. Added/Corp Instituto Nacional de Cultura (Panama). No. 1 (Oct./Dec. 1975)-. Periodical. Spanish. qt. 4.50. Instituto Nacional de Cultura / Panama, Apt Postal 662, Panama. **LC** F1563.8; .R48.

VE
REVISTA VENEZOLANA DE CIENCIA POLITICA. See Political Science.

US/0888-2258
REVOLUTIONARY WAR MAGAZINE. ***Ceased.*** [Revolut. war mag.]. Issue No. 1 (May 1986)-Ceased ?. Periodical. English. bm. Russell Mahan, PO Box 587, Bountiful UT 84010. **DD** 973. **UDC** 973.07.

CN/0820-0793
REVUE DE LA SOCIETE HISTORIQUE DU MADAWASKA (1982). (REVUE DE LA SOCIETE HISTORIQUE DU MADAWASKA.). [Rev. Soc. hist. Madawaska]. **Added/Corp** Societe Historique du Madawaska. Vol. 10, No. 1/2 (Jan./June 1982)-. Periodical. French. Four times a year (Jan., Apr., July, Oct.). 40.00Can$ (institutions), 20.00Can$ (individuals). Madawaska Historical Society, PO Box 474, Edmundston New Brunswick, E3V 3L1 Canada. **Tel** (506)735-8804. **DD** 971.5/54/005. Index available. cum. index. **Ad Acc. Circ:** 500 (ctrl). ***Continues*** *Brayon, 0226-6156.*

CN/0828-9468
REVUE D'HISTOIRE DE LA COTE-NORD. (LA REVUE D'HISTOIRE DE LA COTE-NORD.). [Rev. hist. Cote-Nord]. **Added/Corp** Societe Historique de la Cote-Nord. Societe Historique du Golfe. No. 1 (1984)-. Periodical. French. sa. 12.00Can$ Canada; 14.00Can$ other. Society Historique de La Cote-Nord, CP 258 Baie-Comean Que, G4Z2H1 Canada. **Tel** (418)296-8228. **DD** 971.4/17/005. **Ad Acc. Circ:** 1,200 (ctrl).

CN/0035-2357
REVUE D'HISTOIRE DE L'AMERIQUE FRANCAISE. [Rev. hist. Am. fr.]. **Added/Corp** Institut d'Histoire de l'Amerique Francaise. Vol. 1 (June 1947)-. Periodical. French. qt (4 issues). 50.00Can$. Institution Histoire Amerique Francaise, 261 Bloomfield Avenue, Montreal Quebec H2V 3R6 Canada. **Tel** (514)278-2232. **ED** Louise Dechene. **LC** F1001; .R48. Index available (published in Dec. issue). cum. index. **Bk Rev. Ad Acc. Circ:** 1,400 (ctrl). available on microfilm and microfiche from University Microfilms International (UMI). Documents available from The Genuine Article.
Desc: Presents articles concerning the history of French civilization in America - research notes, review articles, book reviews, bibliography of current publication relating to the history of French America, research information and news of the institute.
Ind/Abst AGRICOLA; Am. Hist. Life (1954-); Arts Humanit. Citation Index [Full Cov.]; Can. Period. Index; Curr. Contents Arts Humanit.; MLA Int. Bibl. Books Artic. Mod. Lang. Lit.; Point Repere (1983-); Res. Alert [Full Cov.]; Soc. Sci. Cit. Index [Select. Cov.]; West. Hist. Q.

CN/0381-8454
REVUE D'HISTOIRE DU BAS ST-LAURENT. Added/Corp Societe d'Histoire du Bas Saint-Laurent. Vol. 1 (Oct. 1973)-. Periodical. French. Twice a year (Summer & Winter). 35.00Can$. Societe

d'Histoire Bas St. Laurent, UQAR 300 des Ursulines, Rimouski Quebec G5L 3A1 Canada. **Tel** (418)724-1649. **LC** F1054.S3; R48. **DD** 917.14/005. cum. index. **Bk Rev**, (Qty: 5). **Ad Acc. Circ:** 350.
Desc: Every aspects of history with the exception of genealogy. Centered on the lower St. Lawrence region of the Province of Quebec.

CN/0713-7958
REVUE D'HISTOIRE LITTERAIRE DU QUEBEC ET DU CANADA FRANCAIS. ***Ceased.*** **See** Literature.

CN/0708-1715
REVUE DU NOUVEL ONTARIO. **Added/Corp** Universite Laurentienne de Sudbury. Institut Franco-Ontarien. No. 1 (1978)-. Monographic series. French. an. Price varies per volume. Laurentienne University of Sudbury / Department of French, Sudbury Ontario P3E 2C6 Canada. **Tel** (705)675-1151. **DD** 971.3/004/114.

FR/0397-7870
REVUE FRANCAISE D'ETUDES AMERICAINES. [Rev. fr. etud. am.]. **Added/Corp** Association Francaise d'Etudes Americaines. No. 1 (April 1976)-. Periodical. English (French). qt. 235.06F France; 285.00F other. Presses Universitaires Nancy, 42 avenue de la Liberation, 54001 Nancy Cedex France. **Tel** 011 33 83 935830, FAX 011 33 83 935839. **ED** J. M. Bonnet and M. Chenetier. **LC** E169.1; .R485. **DD** 973/.05. **Bk Rev. Ad Acc. Circ:** 1,000 (ctrl). Documents available from The Genuine Article.
Desc: American studies.
Ind/Abst Am. Hist. Life (1976-); ARTbibliogr. Mod.; Arts Humanit. Citation Index [Full Cov.]; Curr. Contents Arts Humanit.; MLA Int. Bibl. Books Artic. Mod. Lang. Lit.; PAIS Int. Print (?-?); Res. Alert [Full Cov.]; Soc. Sci. Cit. Index [Select. Cov.].

US/0035-4619
RHODE ISLAND HISTORY. [R.I. hist.]. **Added/Corp** Rhode Island Historical Society. Vol. 1 (Jan. 1942)-. Periodical. English. qt. $20.00. Rhode Island Historical Society, 110 Benevolent Street, Providence RI 02906. **Tel** (401)331-8575, FAX (401)751-7930. **ED** Albert Klyberg. **LC** F76; .R472. **DD** 974.5005. Index available. cum. index. **Ad Acc. Circ:** 3,000 (ctrl). available on microfilm from Xerox; available on microfilm and microfiche from University Microfilms International (UMI). ***Supersedes*** *Rhode Island Historical Society Collections, 0361-0330.*
Desc: Analysis of people, events, and social processes that have shaped the history of Rhode Island and Southern New England.
Ind/Abst Am. Hist. Life (1963-); ARTbibliogr. Mod. (1963-).

US/0035-5119
RICHMOND COUNTY HISTORY. [Richmond Cty. hist.]. **Added/Corp** Richmond County Historical Society (Ga.). Vol. 1 (Winter 1969)-. Periodical. English. Twice a year (Summer & Winter). $15.00. Richmond County Historical Society, 2500 Walton Way, Augusta GA 30910. **Tel** (706)737-1532. **ED** Dr. Helen Callahan. **LC** F292.R5; R52. **DD** 975.8/64/005. cum. index. **Pr Rev. Circ:** 350 (ctrl).
Desc: Research papers presented for print that deals with the history of Augusta and Richmond County in Georgia. Information on the people and events in Georgia.
Ind/Abst Am. Hist. Life (1971-).

US/0360-1978
RICHMOND HISTORIAN, THE. V. 1- Summer 1975-. Periodical. English. sa. Richmond Historian, 130 Stuivesant Place, Staten Island NY 10301. **LC** E171; .R53. **DD** 973. **UDC** 973.

US/0146-1869
RIO GRANDE HISTORY. ***Suspended.*** [Rio Gd. hist.]. Vol. 1 (Jan. 1973)-Suspended (1985). Periodical. English. ir. $10.00 (minimum contribution). Rio Grande Historical Collections, Box 3475, Las Cruces NM 88003. **Tel** (505)646-3839. **ED** Austin Hoover. **UDC** 978.9. **Bk Rev. Circ:** 700 (ctrl).
Desc: Contains articles, photographs, manuscripts, and documents of interest to New Mexico and Southwest history enthusiasts.
Ind/Abst Am. Hist. Life.

BL
RIOTUR. **Main/Corp** RIOTUR (Firm). Vol. 1 (Oct/Dec 1975)-. Portuguese. Empresa de Turismo do Municipio do Rio de Janeiro, rua Sao Jose 90 80 Andar Centro, CEP 20.000 Rio de Janeiro Brazil. **LC** F2646.1; .E46a. **DD** 981/.5.

US/0739-9790
RIVER CIRCULAR, THE. 1st Ed.-. Periodical. English. an. Mississippi River Revival, Box 10281 Main Post Office, Minneapolis MN 55440. **LC** F351; .R6. **DD** 977/.005. **UDC** 977.6.

IT
RIVISTA DI STUDI ANGLO-AMERICANI. **VFOAT** R.S.A.; RSA. Vol. 1 (1981)-. Periodical. Italian. an. L15000. C C P 17/19477, Intestato A Paideia Editrice, Brescia Italy. **LC** E169.1; .R715. **DD** 973/.04. **UDC** 973(=20).

●US/0035-7413
ROCHESTER HISTORY. [Rochester hist.]. **Added/Corp** Rochester Public Library. Vol. 1, (Jan. 1939)-. Periodical. English. qt (Winter, Spring, Summer, Fall). $4.00 library; $6.00 other libraries; $10.00 other. Office of the City Historian, Rochester Public Library, 115 South Avenue, Rochester NY 14604. **Tel** (716)428-7340. **ED** Ruth Rosenberg-Naparsteck. **LC** F129.R7; R59. **DD** 974.789. **Circ:** 900. available on microfilm from University Microfilms International (UMI).
Desc: Concerned with the history of Rochester, New York and the surrounding areas of people, places, ideas and events.
Ind/Abst Am. Hist. Life (1963-); Writ. Am. Hist.

CN/1187-3280
ROCKY MOUNTAIN HOUSE LIEU HISTORIQUE NATIONAL. [Rocky Mt. House lieu hist. natl.]. **Added/Corp** Service Canadien des Parcs. No 1 (Spring 1991)-. French. **DD** 333.78.

CN/1187-3299
ROCKY MOUNTAIN HOUSE NATIONAL HISTORIC SITE. [Rocky Mt. House natl. hist. site]. **Added/Corp** Canadian Parks Service. Spring (1991)-. English. Environment Canada, Department Canada, 351 St. Joseph Blvd., Ottawa Ontario K1A 1C7 Canada. **Tel** (613)997-4191. **DD** 333.78.

US/0148-6659
ROOTS (ST. PAUL, MINN.). ***Ceased.*** (ROOTS.). **Added/Corp** Minnesota Historical Society. Vol. 1 (Fall 1972)-(Spring 1993). Periodical. English. Three times a year. Minnesota Historical Society, 345 Kellogg Boulevard West, St Paul MN 55102. **Tel** (612)297-3243, (800)647-7827, FAX (612)297-1345. **ED** James Smith. **LC** F606.3; .R66. **DD** 477.6/005. **Circ:** 4,000 (ctrl). ***Supersedes*** *Gopher Historian, 0017-2227.*
Desc: Single-theme issues on aspects of Minnesota history.
Ind/Abst Am. Hist. Life.

US/0738-8497
ROUNDUP (WASHINGTON, D.C.), THE. (THE ROUNDUP / NATIVE AMERICAN PHILANTHROPIC NEWS SERVICE.). [Roundup]. Periodical. English. ir. $15.00. American Indian Program, Phelps-Strokes Fund, 1029 Vermont Avenue, Suite 1100, Washington DC 20005. **UDC** 908.73(=97).

IT
RSA JOURNAL. **Added/Corp** Associazione Italiana di Studi Nord-Americani. **VFOAT** RSA. (1990)-. English (Italian). Mozzon Giuntina SPA, Via Mannelli 29R, 50136 Florence, Italy. **Tel** 011 39 55 2476781, FAX 055/2478568. **LC** IN PROCESS.
Ind/Abst Int. Dev. Abstr.

US
RUGBEIAN. English. sa. $18.00 (includes Historic Rugby membership). Historic Rugby Inc., PO Box 8, Rugby TN 37733. **Tel** (615)628-2441.

BL
RUMO PARANAENSE. Periodical. Portuguese. Rua Riachuelo No 305, Curitiba Brazil. **LC** F2596; .R85. **DD** 981/.6. **UDC** 981; 908.81.

US/0748-2493
RUTLAND HISTORICAL SOCIETY QUARTERLY. [Rutl. Histor. Soc. q.]. **Added/Corp** Rutland Historical Society (Vt.). (19??)-. Periodical. English. qt. comes with membership. Rutland Historical Society, 96 Center Street, Rutland VT 05701. **Tel** (802)775-2006. **ED** Jean Ross. **LC** F59.R9; R85. **DD** 974.3/7. **Bk Rev**, (Qty: 1800/yr). **Circ:** 450 (ctrl).
Desc: Articles about the history of the Rutland area.
Ind/Abst Am. Hist. Life.

CN/0581-295X
SAGUENAYENSIA. [Saguenayensia]. **Added/Corp** Societe Historique du Saguenay. Vol. 1 (Jan./Feb. 1959)-. Periodical. French. qt (4 issues). 25.00Can$ Canada; 30.00Can$ other. La Societe Historique du Saguenay, CP 456, Chicoutimi Quebec G7H 5C8 Canada. **Tel** (418)549-2805. ***Supersedes*** *Societe Historique de Saguenay. Bulletin.*
Ind/Abst Am. Hist. Life (1986-); BHA : Biblio. Hist. Art; Point Repere (1983-).

CN/1180-3916
SALUT MONTREAL! (ED. FRANCAISE). (SALUT MONTREAL!.). [Salut Montr.,]. **Added/Corp** Corporation des Celebrations du 350e Anniversaire de Montreal (1642-1992). Vol. 1, No 1 (May/June 1990)-. Periodical. French. bm. Free. Corporation des Celebrations du 350e Anniversaire de Montreal, 329 Commune Street West, Montreal, Quebec H2Y 2E1 Canada. **DD** 971.4/28/005.

US/1040-113X
SAN FRANCISCO/BAY AREA POWER BOOK, THE. [San Franc./Bay Area power book]. **VFOAT** San Francisco Bay Area Power Book. English. an. $50.00. San Francisco Publications and Communications Inc, 45 Belden Place, San Francisco CA 94104. **Tel** (415)987-3232. **LC** F868.S156; S18. **DD** 979.4/6/0025.

US/0092-9719
SANGO (BRONX). (SHANGO.). V. 1- 1973-. Periodical. English. $4.50. West Indian American, 2385 Grand Avenue, Bronx NY 10468. **LC** F2155; .S55. **DD** 917.29/03/505. **UDC** 917.29; 908.729.

EC
SARANCE. **Added/Corp** Instituto Otavaleno de Antropologia. (Oct. 1975)-. Periodical. Spanish. qt. S/9,000 Ecuador; $20.00 US. Instituto Otavaleno de Antropologia, Casilla 1478, Otavalo Ecuador. **Tel** 06 920321, FAX 06 920461. **LC** F3721; .S47. Index available. **Bk Rev. Circ:** 1,000 (ctrl).

CN/0036-4908
SASKATCHEWAN HISTORY. [Sask. hist.]. **Added/Corp** Saskatchewan Archives Board. Vol. 1 (Jan. 1948)-. Periodical. English. Twice a year (Spring & Fall). 15.00Can$. Saskatchewan Archives Board, University of Saskatchewan, Murray Building, Saskatchewan S7N 0W0 Canada. **Tel** (306)933-8326, FAX (306)933-7305. **ED** Ms. Joan Champ. **LC** F1071; .S245. **DD** 971.24. Index available. cum. index. **Bk Rev**, (Qty: 8). **Pr Rev. Circ:** 700 (ctrl).
Desc: Articles, edited documents and news/notes on all aspects of Saskatchewan's history.
Ind/Abst Am. Hist. Life (1963-); Can. Index (?-?); Can. Period. Index; West. Hist. Q.

CN/0828-3907
SASKATCHEWAN INDIAN FEDERATED COLLEGE JOURNAL. ***Suspended.*** [Sask. Indian Fed. Coll. j.]. Vol. 1, No. 1 (1984)-?. Periodical. English. sa. 15.00Can$ individuals, 25.00can$ institutions. Saskatchewan Indian Federated College, 118 College West, University of Regina, Regina Saskatchewan S4S 0A2 Canada. **Tel** (306)584-8333 or 8334, (800)667-8060. **DD** 970.004/97/005. **UDC** 971.24(=97).

CN/0843-6002
SASKATOON HISTORY REVIEW. [Saskat. hist. rev.]. No. 4 (1989)-. English. an. Saskatoon Heritage Society, PO Box 7051, Saskatoon Saskatchewan S7K 4J1 Canada. **Tel** (306)242-0118. **DD** 971.24/2. **Bk Rev. Circ:** 1,500. ***Continues*** *Saskatoon History, 0714-8925.*
Desc: Occasional publication dealing with the history, architecture and archaeology of Saskatoon.

CN/0823-1796
SCANDINAVIAN-CANADIAN STUDIES. [Scand.-Can. stud.]. **Main/Corp** Association for the Advancement of Scandinavian Studies in Canada. Meeting. **Added/Corp** Association for the Advancement of Scandinavian Studies in Canada. **VFOAT** Etudes Scandinaves au Canada. (1982)-. English (French). an (Oct.). 18.00Can$. Association for Advancement of Scandinavian Studies, Carleton University Comparative Literature, Ottawa Ontario K1S 5B6 Canada. **Tel** (613)564-2894. **(Subscription address:** Wolfgang P. Ahrens / Department of Language, Literatures, & Linguistics, York University, North York Ontario, M3J 1P3 Canada.) **ED** Professor W. P. Ahrens. **LC** DL1; .A85a. **DD** 948. **Bk Rev**, (Qty: 10-12). **Pr Rev. Circ:** 250.
Desc: The main aims of the journal is to encourage studies on and promote research in Canada in all aspects of life in the Scandinavian societies, to provide a multi-disciplinary forum for papers on all matters relevant to Scandinavian studies, and to stimulate awareness of and interest in Scandinavian studies in Canada.

CN/0318-014X
SCANNER (TORONTO). (THE SCANNER.). (1968)-. Periodical. English. Nine times a year. 25.00Can$ US & Canada; 37.00Can$ other. Toronto Marine Historical Society, 173 Glenrose Avenue, Toronto Ontario M4T 1K7 Canada. Documents available from Ask*IEEE.
Ind/Abst INSPEC (Summer 1969-).

CN/0712-4961
SCARBOROUGH HISTORICAL NOTES & COMMENTS. [Scarborough hist. notes comments]. **Added/Corp** Scarborough Historical Society. Vol. 1, No. 1 (Nov. 1976)-. Periodical. English. Twice a year. 10.00Can$. Scarborough Historical Society, PO Box 593, Station A, Scarborough Ontario M1K 5C4 Canada. **Tel** (905)282-2710. **ED** D.B. McCowan. **DD** 971.3/541. **Circ:** 300 (ctrl).
Desc: Historical notes, letters, diaries, and comments on various aspects of local Scarborough, Ontario. Includes Canadian history and Scarborough heritage.

US/0361-8528
SCHOHARIE COUNTY HISTORICAL REVIEW. [Schoharie Cty. hist. rev.]. **Added/Corp** Schoharie County Historical Society. (195?)-. Periodical. English. Twice a year (Apr. & Oct.). $15.00 Comes with Schoharie County Historical Society membership. Schoharie County Historical Society, PO Box 69, Schoharie NY 12157. **Tel** (518)295-7192. **ED** Edward A. Hagan (editor's address: 134 Cliff Street, Middleburgh, NY 12122). **LC** NOT in LC. **DD** 974. Index available. **Bk**

Rev. **Circ:** 1,500 (ctrl). ***Continues** County Historical Review.*
Ind/Abst Am. Hist. Life.

US/0745-7065
SCHOLASTIC UPDATE. See Education.

US/1046-1027
SCOTT COUNTY IOWAN. (SCOTT COUNTY IOWAN / SCOTT COUNTY, IOWA, GENEALOGICAL SOCIETY.). [Scott Cty. Iowan]. **Added/Corp** Scott County Iowa Genealogical Society. Vol. 1, No. 1 (May 1977)-. Periodical. English. Four times a year. $10.00 (includes membership). Scott County, Iowa Genealogical Society, PO Box 3132, Davenport IA 52808-3132. **DD** 929. **Circ:** 175 (ctrl).
Desc: Compiles and publishes material relating to Scott County, Iowa and immediate surrounding areas prior to 1932.

US/0890-8281
SCRAPBOOK PAGES. [Scrapb. pages]. Vol. 1, No. 1 (April 1984)-. Periodical. English. Six times a year. $10.50. Scrapbook Pages, PO Box 5583, Arlington VA 22205. **Tel** (703)533-3592. **ED** Jane Cook. **DD** 973. **Circ:** 300.
Desc: Includes news features for reminiscing and discussion, hobby information, puzzles, crafts, quizzes, recipes.

CN/0824-6947
SCRIBE (VANCOUVER). (THE SCRIBE : OFFICIAL NEWSLETTER OF THE JEWISH HISTORICAL SOCIETY OF B.C.). [Scribe]. **Added/Corp** Jewish Historical Society of B.C. Vol. 1, No. 1 (March 1979)-. Newsletter. English. Three times a year. 20.00Can$ (indidivuals), 30.00Can$ (families), 35.00Can$ (institutions). Jewish Historical Society of British Columbia, 950 West 41st Avenue, Vancouver British Columbia V52 2N7 Canada. **Tel** (604)266-3529. **ED** Barry Dunner. **DD** 971.1/004924. **Bk Rev. Circ:** 250 (ctrl).

US/0582-3471
SEA CHEST, THE. Added/Corp Puget Sound Maritime Historical Society. Vol. 1 (Sept. 1967)-. Periodical. English. Four times a year. $50.00 (sustaining), $125.00 (corporate) Comes with Puget Sound Maritime Historical Society membership. Puget Sound Maritime Historical Society Inc, 2700 24th Avenue East, Seattle WA 98112. **Tel** (206)624-3028. **ED** Austen Hemion. Index available. cum. index. **Bk Rev. Circ:** 1,000.
Desc: Historical journal of Pacific Northwest and Alaska Maritime subjects. Includes many photographs that in themselves are historical (many are glass plate) and the members have the benefit of writing and/or coming into the Museum to order photos at a discount.

US/0364-9172
SEA CHEST (BUXTON). (SEA CHEST.). **Added/Corp** Cape Hatteras School. (19??)-. Periodical. English. Three times a year. $6.00. Cape Hatteras School, Buxton NC 27920. **LC** F262.D2; S42. **DD** 975.6/175.

US/0737-9889
SEAFORD HISTORICAL SOCIETY QUARTERLY. ***Suspended.*** **VFOAT** Historical Society Quarterly. Suspended with Vol. 18, No. 1 (1988). Periodical. English. qt. 2234 Jackson Avenue, Seaford NY 11783. **UDC** 974.7.

US/0743-6246
SEAPORT. (SEAPORT : THE MAGAZINE OF THE SOUTH STREET SEAPORT MUSEUM.). [Seaport]. **Added/Corp** South Street Seaport Museum (New York, N.Y.). Vol. 12, No. 3 (Fall 1978)-. Periodical. English. Three times a year. $25.00 library, $35.00 other. South Street Seaport Museum, 207 Front Street, New York NY 10038. **Tel** (212)669-9400. **ED** Madeline Rogers (editor's telephone: (212)748-8750). **Bk Rev**, (Qty: 8-9). **Ad Acc, Adv Mgr:** Ann Wells, **Tel** (203)855-9750. **Circ:** 5,000 (ctrl). ***Continues** South Street Reporter, 0038-3538.*
Desc: New York's history magazine.
Ind/Abst Avery Index Archit. Period. Suppl. Colum. Univ. (19??-199?).

CN/0225-6339
SEASONS NORTH. [Seas. north]. V. 1- Sept. 1978-. Periodical. English. ir. $3.50 per no., $12.00 per year. Saddleback Ridge Productions, Box 730, Geraldton Ontario P0T 1M0. **DD** 971.3/1/005. **UDC** 971.3.

US/0081-2951
SECOLAS ANNALS. (SECOLAS ANNALS : JOURNAL OF THE SOUTHEASTERN COUNCIL ON LATIN AMERICAN STUDIES.). [SECOLAS ann.]. **Main/Conf** Southeastern Council on Latin American Studies. **VFOAT** Southeastern Council on Latin American Studies Annals; S.E.C.O.L.A.S. Annals; SECOLAS. **VAT** Southeastern Council on Latin American Studies Annals. Vol. 12 (March 1981)-. Monographic series. English (Spanish and Portuguese). an (March). $4.00. Georgia Southern College History Department, c/o Ray Shurbutt, Statesboro GA 30460. **Tel** (912)681-5866. **ED** T. Ray Shurbutt; address: L.B. 8054, GSU, Statesboro, GA 30460; telephone:(912)681-5862. **LC** F1408; .S66. **DD** 980/.005. **Pr Rev. Circ:** 550 (ctrl). available on microfilm and microfiche from University Microfilms International (UMI). ***Continues** Southeastern Conference on Latin American Studies. SECOLAS Annals, 0081-2951.*
Desc: All topics dealing with Latin-American studies.
Ind/Abst Am. Hist. Life (1981-); MLA Int. Bibl. Books Artic. Mod. Lang. Lit.

HO
SECTANTE. V. 1- Nov./Dec. 1975-. Periodical. Spanish. ir. Secretaria de Cultura Turismo e Informacion Comision Publicitaria, 2A Avenida y 3A, Calle No 101, Tegucigalpa Honduras. **LC** F1501; .S42. **UDC** 908.728.3; 379.85(728.3).

CN/0229-074X
SEIGNEURIE DE LAUZON. (LA SEIGNEURIE DE LAUZON : BULLETIN DE LA SOCIETE D'HISTOIRE REGIONALE DE LEVIS.). **Added/Corp** Societe d'Histoire Regionale de Levis. (June 1979)-. Periodical. French. Four times a year (Seasonally). 15.84Can$ Canada; 21.08Can$ other. Societe d'Histoire Regionale de Levis, 9 Mgr. Gosselin, Levis Quebec G6V 5K1 Canada. **Tel** (418)833-1249. **DD** 971.4/59/005. Index available. cum. index. **Circ:** 150.

VE
SEMESTRE HISTORICO. Added/Corp Venezuela. Universidad Central, Caracas. Facultad de Humanidades y Educacion. Coordinacion de los Cursos de Postgrado. No. I (Enero/Jun. 1975)-. Periodical. Spanish. sa. $6.00. Los Caobos - Av Bogota Confluencia Con la Av Libertador, Quinta Cantabria Apartado de Correos, 40274 Caracas Venezuela. **LC** F2321; .S44.
Ind/Abst HAPI Hisp. Am. Period. Index.

US
SENATE HISTORY / SENATE HISTORICAL OFFICE, OFFICE OF THE SECRETARY, UNITED STATES SENATE. Main/Corp United States. Congress. Senate. Historical Office. No. 1 (July 1978)-. English. sa. Free. Historical Office, Office of the Secretary, United States Senate, Washington DC 20510. **Tel** (202)224-6900, FAX (202)224-5329. **ED** Richard A Baker. **UDC** 342.531(09)(73). **Circ:** 5,000.
Desc: Includes articles and notices related to the substance and study of the Senate's history.

CL
SEPA. Periodical. Spanish. 624.00. **LC** F3100; .S17. ***Absorbed** Cambalache.*

US/0037-2374
SEPIA (FORT WORTH, TEX.). (SEPIA.). [Sepia]. V. 1- 1952-. Periodical. English. mo. $15.00 US; $18.00 other. Sepia Publishing Corporation, 1220 Harding Street, Fort Worth TX 76102. **Tel** (214)521-9020. **LC** E185.5; .S44. available on microfilm and microfiche from University Microfilms International (UMI).
Ind/Abst Index Black Period.; Mag. Index (1977-1982).

US/8756-5579
SERB WORLD U.S.A. [Serb world U.S.A.]. **VFOAT** Serb World USA. Vol. 1, No. 1 (Sept./Oct. 1984)-. Periodical. English. Six times a year (Jan., Mar., May, July, Sept., Nov.). $18.00 (one year); $33.00 (two years). Serb World USA, 415 East Mabel, Tucson AZ 85705. **Tel** (602)624-4887. **ED** Mary Nicklanovich Hart. **LC** DR1955; .S47. **DD** 973/.0491822. **Bk Rev. Ad Acc. Circ:** 3,500. ***Continues** Serb World.*
Desc: Articles for and about Serbs in America; their history and culture, past and present. Valuable information for all of Serbian heritage. Highly illustrated, national in scope.
Ind/Abst Am. Bibliogr. Slavic East Europ. Stud.

●US/1065-688X
SERIES IN CHICANA CRITICAL ISSUES. Added/Corp University of California, Davis. Chicano Studies Program. Chicano/Latina Research Project. (1992)-. English. $10.00. Chicano Studies, Hart Hall, University of California, Davis CA 95616.

CN/0827-5564
SERVICIO MENSUAL DE INFORMACION Y DOCUMENTACION - AGENCIA LATINOAMERICANA DE INFORMACION. ***Title Change.*** (SERVICIO MENSUAL DE INFORMACION Y DOCUMENTACION / ALAI.). [Serv. mens. inf. doc. - Agencia Latinoam. Inf.]. **Added/Corp** Agence Latino-Americaine d'Information (Montreal, Quebec). **VFOAT** Servicio Informativo. (1984)-(1992). Periodical. Spanish. mo. **DD** 980/.005. ***Continues** Servicio Informativo, 0821-5014. **Continued by** Servicio Informativo (Agence Latino-Americaine d'Information : 1992).*
Ind/Abst Hum. Rights Intern. Rep. (?-?).

CN/1185-3425
SES CANADA FOCUS. ***Ceased.*** (SES CANADA FOCUS / SES CANADA RESEARCH INC.). [SES Can. focus]. (Aug. 1990)-(199?). Periodical. English. qt. SES Canada Research, Suite 212, LaSalle Mews, Kingston, Ontario K7L 1A8 Canada. **DD** 971/.005.

US/0488-4965
SETTLER (TOWANDA, PA. 1952), THE. (THE SETTLER, A QUARTERLY MAGAZINE OF HISTORY AND BIOGRAPHY.). [Settler]. **Added/Corp** Bradford County Historical Society (Pa.). Vol. 1 (April 1952)-. Periodical. English. qt. Free to members of the Bradford County Historical Society; $10.00 membership. Bradford County Historical Society, 21 Main Street, Towanda PA 18848. **Tel** (717)265-2240. **ED** Sylvia L. Wilson. **DD** 974. Index available. **Ad Acc. Circ:** 900.
Desc: Bradford County and Pennsylvania state history covering pioneers, politics, and agricultural development.
Ind/Abst Am. Hist. Life.

US/0270-9368
SHAKER MESSENGER, THE. Vol. 1 (Fall 1978)-. Periodical. English. Four times a year. $14.00 (one year); $28.00 (two years). Shaker Messenger, PO Box 1645, Holland MI 49422. **Tel** (616)396-4588. **ED** Diana L. Van Kolken. **Bk Rev. Ad Acc, Adv Mgr Tel** (616)396-4588. **Circ:** 1,000. ***Supersedes** World of Shaker.*
Desc: Current events at Shaker restorations, museums, libraries; research papers; antique market music; reports from Shaker study groups and articles about persons involved in reproduction of Shaker items...all devoted to the study of the American Shakers.

CN/0822-4080
SHELBURNE HISTORICAL SOCIETY (NEWSLETTER). (NEWSLETTER.). [Shelburne Hist. Soc.]. **VAT** Shelburne Co. Bicentennial Committee (Newsletter). Newsletter. English. Three times a year. Free. Shelburne Historical Society, PO Box 39, Shelburne Nova Scotia B0T 1W0 Canada. **DD** 971.6/25/006. **UDC** 971.6. ctrl circ.

CN
SHURA (EDMONTON, ALTA.). (AL-SHURA.). **VFOAT** Shoura. Periodical. Arabic. Al Shoura, 13536 97 Street, Edmonton Alberta T5E 4E2 Canada. **LC** DT236; .S55.

AG
SIN CENSURA (BUENOS AIRES, ARGENTINA). (SIN CENSURA.). Year 1, No. 1 (August 24-Sept. 7 1982)-. Periodical. Spanish. sm. Selear SA, Alsina 500-1087, Buenos Aires Argentina. **LC** F2849.2; .S55. **DD** 982/.064/05.

US/1060-5525
SIN CENSURA (WASHINGTON, D.C.). (SIN CENSURA.). [Sin censura]. (Feb. 1980)-. Periodical. Spanish. mo. $24.00 (12 issues). Sin Censura, PO Box 2635, Washington DC 20013. **LC** F1401; .S58. **DD** 980/.005.

SP
SINTESIS INFORMATIVA IBEROAMERICANA. Began in 1971. Spanish. an. Centro de Documentacion Iberoamericana, Instituto de Cultura Hispanica, Avenida de los Reyes Catolicos S/N, Madrid Spain. **LC** F1414.2; .S53. **UDC** 980=6.

CN/0227-6550
SKYLINE (HAMILTON). (SKYLINE.). [Skyline]. Vol. 3, Issue 1 (1980)-. English. Skyline, c/o Economic Development Department, Regional Municipality of Hamilton-Wentworth, PO Box 910, Hamilton Ontario L8N 3V9 Canada. **DD** 971.3/52/005. **UDC** 971.3;9 908.713. ***Continues** Hamilton-Wentworth Skyline, 0316-7607.*

US/0884-6111
SMOKY MOUNTAIN HISTORICAL SOCIETY NEWSLETTER. [Smoky Mt. Hist. Soc. newsl.]. **Added/Corp** Smoky Mountain Historical Society. **VFOAT** Newsletter; SMHS Newsletter; S.M.H.S. Newsletter. (19??)-. Newsletter. English. Four times a year. $10.00. Smoky Mountain Historical Society, PO Box 5078, Sevierville TN 37864. **Tel** (615)453-2388. **LC** F443.G7; S65. **DD** 976.8/89. **Bk Rev.** ctrl circ.
Desc: Covers the Tennessee counties of Blount, Cocke and Sevier. Carries articles of interest to historians and genealogists.

US/0584-5025
SMRC-NEWSLETTER. (SMRC NEWSLETTER / SOUTHWESTERN MISSION RESEARCH CENTER.). [SMRC-newsl.]. **Added/Corp** Southwestern Mission Research Center (U.S.). **VFOAT** Southwestern Mission Research Center Newsletter. **VAT** Southwestern Mission Research Center newsletter. Vol.1, No.1 (Feb. 1967)-. Newsletter. English. qt. $10.00. Southwestern Mission Research Center, Arizona State Museum, University of Arizona, Tucson AZ 85721. **Tel** (602)621-4898, FAX (602)621-2976. **ED** Dr. Thomas Sheridan. **DD** 973. **Bk Rev. Pr Rev. Circ:** 800.
Desc: News and reviews of books and articles pertaining to the greater Hispanic southwest (Southwest US and New Mexico) in the colonial period.

US/0882-374X
SNAKE RIVER ECHOES. Vol. 3, No. 2 (Winter 1974)-. Periodical. English. Twice a year. $5.00. Upper Snake River Valley Historical Society, PO Box 244, Rexburg ID 83440. **Tel** (208)356-9101. **ED** Louia Elements (editor's address: 102 West 2000 North, Rexburg ID 83440; editor's phone: (208)356-7030). **DD** 979. Index available. cum. index. **Circ:** 400. ***Continues***

Upper Snake River Valley Historical Society Quarterly.
Desc: History of eastern Idaho. Local.
Ind/Abst Am. Hist. Life.

US
SNAKEROOTS. Periodical. English. sa. $15.00. Indiana Historical Society, 315 West Ohio Street, Indianapolis IN 46202. **Tel** (317)232-1882. **UDC** 977.2. **Circ:** 6,000.

CN/0712-6867
SOCIAL INFOPAC (TORONTO). (SOCIAL INFOPAC.). [Soc. infopac]. **Added/Corp** Social Planning Council of Metropolitan Toronto. Vol. 1, No. 1 (Feb. 1982)-. Periodical. English. ir. Social Planning Council of Metropolitan Toronto, 2 Carlton Street Suite 1001, Toronto Ontario M5B 1J3 Canada. **Tel** (416)351-0095. **DD** 971.3/541/0405.

BL
SOCIEDADE BRASILEIRA. Portuguese. Livraria Sao Jose, rua Sao Jose 70, Rio de Janeiro Brazil. **LC** F2504.5; .S64. **UDC** 908.81.

US/0272-8249
SOMBRAS DEL PASADO. **VFOAT** Shadows of the Past. V. 1- 1979-. Periodical. English. an. Socorro High School, 10150 Almeda, El Paso TX 79927. **LC** F394.E4; S57. **DD** 976.4/96. **UDC** 976.4.

US
SOUNDER NEWSLETTER (SNOQUALMIE, WASH. : 1980). (SOUNDER NEWSLETTER.). Vol. 23, No. 11 (Nov. 1980)-. Newsletter. English. mo. Puget Sound Railway Historical Association, PO Box 459, Snoqualmie WA 98065. **UDC** 979.7. ***Continues*** *Sounder (Snoqualmie, Wash. : 1977).*

US/0888-4072
SOUNDINGS (MILWAUKEE, WIS.). **See** Transportation-Ships and Shipping.

UK/0268-0661
SOUTH AMERICA, CENTRAL AMERICA, AND THE CARIBBEAN. [South Am. Cent. Am. Caribb.]. **Added/Corp** Europa Publications Limited. (1986)-. Directory. English. an. $295.00. Europa Publications Ltd, 18 Bedford Square, London WC1B 3JN England. **Tel** 011 44 71 5808236, telex 21540 EUROPA G. **LC** F1401; .S68. **DD** 980. **NLM** F 1406.5; S726.
Desc: Facts and statistics on people, organizations, economics, and politics in forty-six countries of the region.

US
SOUTH CAROLINA ANTIQUITIES.
Added/Corp Archeological Society of South Carolina. (19??)-. Periodical. English. an. comes with membership. University of South Carolina / Institute of Archeology & Anthropology, Columbia SC 29208. **Tel** (803)777-8170.
Ind/Abst Anthropol. Lit.; Ethnoarts Index.

US/1056-960X
SOUTH CAROLINA FACTS. [S. C. facts]. **VFOAT** Flying the Colors, South Carolina Facts; South Carolina Facts--Flying the Colors Series. (1991)-. English. te. $59.50 (single issue). Clements Research II Inc., 16850 Dallas Parkway, Dallas TX 75248. **Tel** (214)931-9956, FAX (214)248-7159. **LC** F266; .S555. **DD** 975.7/005.

US/0361-1639
SOUTH CAROLINA HISTORIC PRESERVATION PLAN : ANNUAL PRESERVATION PROGRAM. **Main/Corp** South Carolina. Dept. of Archives and History. English. an. PO Box 11669, 1430 Senate Street, Columbia SC 29211. **LC** F270; .S7A. **DD** 069/.53. **UDC** 904(757).

US/0038-3082
SOUTH CAROLINA HISTORICAL MAGAZINE. [S. C. hist. mag.]. **Added/Corp** South Carolina Historical Society. Vol. 53 (Jan. 1952)-. Periodical. English. qt. Free to members of the South Carolina Historical Society. South Carolina Historical Society, Fireproof Building, 100 Meeting Street, Charleston SC 29401. **Tel** (803)723-3225. **ED** Stephen Hoffius. **LC** F266; .S55. Index available (indexes are published in last issue of volume). cum. index. **Bk Rev. Ad Acc. Pr Rev. Circ:** 5,000 (ctrl). available on microfilm and microfiche from University Microfilms International (UMI). ***Continues*** *South Carolina Historical and Genealogical Magazine, 0148-7825.*
Desc: Articles treating all facets of South Carolina history, edited documents from that history, reviews of works in the field, reports on accessions of manuscript.
Ind/Abst Am. Hist. Life (1963-); Sage Race Relat. Abstr. (1963-).

US/0361-8676
SOUTH DAKOTA HISTORY. [S.D. hist.]. **Added/Corp** South Dakota State Historical Society. Vol. 1 (Winter 1970)-. Periodical. English. qt. $30.00. South Dakota State Historical Society, 900 Governors Drive, Pierre SD 57501. **Tel** (605)773-3458. **ED** Nancy Tystad Koupal. **LC** F646; .S8. **DD** 917.83/03. Index available (published separately). cum. index. **Bk Rev. Circ:** 3,000. available on microfilm and microfiche from University Microfilms International (UMI).
Desc: Published by the South Dakota State Historical Society to increase the knowledge of the history of South Dakota and surrounding region.
Ind/Abst Am. Hist. Life (1970-); West. Hist. Q.

US/0049-1527
SOUTH EASTERN LATIN AMERICANIST. (SOUTH EASTERN LATIN AMERICANIST : QUARTERLY REVIEW OF THE SOUTH EASTERN COUNCIL OF LATIN AMERICAN STUDIES.). [South East. Lat. Am.]. **VFOAT** SELA; S.E.L.A. **VAT** Southeastern Latin Americanist. Began with: Vol. 1, No. 1 (Spring 1957). Periodical. English. qt. $12.00 (individuals), $20.00 (institutions). South Eastern Council of Latin American Studies, 580 East Main Street, Spartanburg SC 29302. **Tel** (803)596-9609, FAX (803)596-9158. **ED** Helen Delpar. **UDC** 908.8=8. **Bk Rev. Ad Acc. Circ:** 350. available on microfilm from University Microfilms International (UMI).
Desc: Interdisciplinary journal of Latin American studies. Original research, news, comments and book reviews.

US
SOUTH FLORIDA HISTORY MAGAZINE : QUARTERLY OF THE HISTORICAL MUSEUM OF SOUTHERN FLORIDA.
Ceased. **Added/Corp** Historical Museum of Southern Florida (Miami, Fla.) Historical Association of Southern Florida. (Winter 1989)-Vol. 22, No. 1 (Winter 1994). Periodical. English. Four times a year. Historical Association of Southern Florida, 101 West Flagler Street, Miami FL 33130. **Tel** (305)375-1492. **ED** Natalie Brown. **LC** F311; .S67. **DD** 975.9/005. **Circ:** 2,400 (ctrl). ***Continues*** *Update (Historical Association of Southern Florida), 0735-7699.*
Ind/Abst Am. Hist. Life 91985-).

US/0275-4428
SOUTH JERSEY MAGAZINE. Vol. 1, (Winter 1972)-. Periodical. English. Four times a year (Jan., Apr., July, Oct.). $12.00. South Jersey Magazine, PO Box 847, Millville NJ 08332. **Tel** (609)825-1615. **ED** Shirley R. Bailey. **Bk Rev. Ad Acc, Adv Mgr:** Ella Batchelor, **Tel** (609)455-3286. **Circ:** 6,000 (ctrl).
Desc: Containing history and genealogical information in the South Jersey area. Railroad information in each issue, and topics varying on industry, nautical, etc.

US/0489-9563
SOUTH OF THE MOUNTAINS. [South mt.]. **Added/Corp** Historical Society of Rockland County. Vol. 1 (Jan./Mar. 1957)-. Periodical. English. Four times a year (Jan., Apr., July, Oct.). $20.00 Comes with Historical Society of Rockland County membership. Historical Society of Rockland County, PO Box 495, 20 Zukor Road, New City NY 10956. **Tel** (914)634-9629. **ED** Marianne B. Leese. Index available. cum. index. **Bk Rev. Circ:** 1,900 (ctrl).
Desc: Articles on Rockland County, New York history.
Ind/Abst Am. Hist. Life.

US/0897-3695
SOUTHEAST LOUISIANA HISTORICAL PAPERS. [Southeast La. hist. pap.]. **Added/Corp** Southeast Louisiana Historical Association. Southeastern Louisiana University. Vol. 10 (1984/85)-. English. an. $5.00. Southeastern Louisiana University, PO Box 730, University Station, Hammond LA 70402. **Tel** (504)549-2151. **ED** Dr. Joy Jackson. **DD** 976. ***Continues*** *Papers - Southeast Louisiana Historical Association, 0098-9193.*
Desc: Emphasizes historical topics dealing with southeast Louisiana.

US/0197-5307
SOUTHERN A.R.C. [South. A.R.C.]. **VAT** Southern Appalachian Resource Catalog. 1980-. English. an. $4.60. Southern Appalachian Resource Catalog, Box 71-A, Warne NC 28909. **LC** F217.A65; S68. **DD** 975. **UDC** 975.

US/0038-3929
SOUTHERN CALIFORNIA QUARTERLY. [South. Calif. q.]. **Added/Corp** Historical Society of Southern California. Vol. 44 (1962)-. Academic Scholarly Publication. English. qt (Mar., June, Sept., Dec.). $50.00 (1 year), $90.00 (2 year), $125.00 (3 year) US; $60.00 (1 year), $110.00 (2 year), $155.00 (3 year) other. Historical Society of Southern California, 200 East Avenue 43, Los Angeles CA 90031. **Tel** (213)222-0546. **ED** Doyce B. Nunis Jr. Index available (bound in Jan. issue). **Bk Rev,** (Qty: 15-20). **Circ:** 1,000 (ctrl). Documents available. ***Continues*** *Historical Society of Southern California Quarterly.*
Desc: Scholarly journal devoted to the publication of articles and edited documents relating to the history of the Far West, with special emphasis on California and its neighboring regions.
Ind/Abst Am. Hist. Life (1962-); Soc. Work Abstr. (?-?); SportSearch; West. Hist. Q.

US
SOUTHERN CALIFORNIAN, THE.
Main/Corp Historical Society of Southern California. Vol. 1, No. 1 (Spring 1989)-. Periodical. English. qt. $50.00 (with Historical Society of Southern California). Historical Society of Southern California, 200 East Avenue 43, Los Angeles CA 90031. **Tel** (213)222-0546.

US/0146-809X
SOUTHERN EXPOSURE (DURHAM, N.C.). (SOUTHERN EXPOSURE.). V. 1- Spring 1973-. Periodical. English. qt. $20.00 US; $22.00 other. Institute Southern Studies, PO Box 531, Durham NC 27702. **Tel** (919)688-8167. **ED** Eric Bates. **LC** F206; .S643. **DD** 975/.005. **UDC** 975. **Bk Rev. Ad Acc. Circ:** 9,000 (ctrl). available on microfilm and microfiche from University Microfilms International (UMI).
Desc: Extremely readable..well documented, says Library Journal. 'Well designed for browsing...useful for research, choice. Quarterly journal of southern politics and culture. Investigative journalism, scholarship, interviews, news. Back issues kept in stock, perfect bound 64-128 pages. Recommended by authorities from Washington Post to American Historical Association.
Ind/Abst Access (1977-); Altern. Press Index; Am. Hist. Life (1973-); Am. Humanit. Index; Annu. Bibliogr. Engl. Lang. Lit.; Energy Res. Abstr. (Oct. 1981-); Humanit. Index; Index Period. Artic. Relat. Law; Soc. Plann. Policy Dev. Abstr.; Sociol. Abstr.

US/0738-5102
SOUTHERN HISTORIAN, THE. [South hist.]. **Added/Corp** Alabama Media Planning Board. Phi Alpha Theta. Beta Omicron Chapter (University of Alabama). Vol. 4 (1983)-. Periodical. English. an. $7.50 US; $9.50 other. Southern Historian, University of Alabama, Box 031609, Tuscaloosa AL 35403. **Tel** (205)348-7100. **ED** Robert McFarland (editor's address: University of Alabama History Department, Box 870212, Tuscaloosa, AL 35487-0212). **LC** F206; .A45. **DD** 975/.005. **Bk Rev,** (Qty: 70). **Ad Acc. Pr Rev. Circ:** 500. ***Continues*** *Alabama Historian.*
Desc: A graduate student journal focusing on all aspects and periods of Southern history and culture.
Ind/Abst Am. Hist. Life (1985-).

US/0085-6525
SOUTHERN INDIAN STUDIES. [South. Indian stud.]. **Added/Corp** Archaeological Society of North Carolina. University of North Carolina (1793-1962). Laboratory of Anthropology and Archaeology. University of North Carolina (1793-1962). Research Laboratories of Anthropology. University of North Carolina at Chapel Hill. Research Laboratories of Anthropology. Vol. 1, No. 1 (Apr. 1949)-. Periodical. English. an. $25.00 (institutions), $10.00 (individuals). North Carolina Archaeological Society Inc., 109 E Jones Street, Raleigh NC 27601. **Tel** (919)733-7342. **ED** Steve Davis. **LC** E78.S55; S6. **Circ:** 400 (ctrl).
Desc: Includes information pertaining to the life and customs of the Indians in the southern states, both prehistoric and historic.
Ind/Abst Am. Hist. Life (1959-); Anthropol. Lit.; Ethnoarts Index.

US/0739-1714
SOUTHERN PARTISAN, THE. **See** Political Science.

US/1063-9640
SOUTHERN RE-ENACTING VETERAN, THE. ***Title Change.*** **See** Recreation, Leisure.

US/0895-5573
SOUTHERN REGISTER : THE NEWSLETTER OF THE CENTER FOR THE STUDY OF SOUTHERN CULTURE, THE UNIVERSITY OF MISSISSIPPI, THE. [South. regist.]. Vol. 1, No. 1 (Winter 1981)-. Newsletter. English. Four times a year. Free on request. University of Mississippi, Sam Hall Room 206, University MS 38677. **Tel** (601)232-5742, FAX (601)232-7842. **LC** F209; .S746. **DD** 975/.005.
Ind/Abst Lit. Crit. Regist.

US/0735-8342
SOUTHERN STUDIES. [South. stud.]. **Added/Corp** Northwestern State University of Louisiana. Southern Studies Institute. (Spring 1977)-. Periodical. English. Four times a year (Feb., May, Aug., Nov.). $20.00 US; $35.00 other. Southern Studies Institute, Northwestern State University, Natchitoches LA 71497. **Tel** (318)357-5941. **ED** Dr. Maxine Taylor (phone: (318)357-5507). **LC** F366; .L935. **DD** 975/.005. Index available. cum. index. **Bk Rev. Ad Acc. Pr Rev. Circ:** 400. available on microfilm and microfiche from University Microfilms International (UMI). ***Continues*** *Louisiana Studies, 0024-693X.*
Desc: Original research that contributes to a greater knowledge, understanding and appreciation of the South - its history, its people, its literature, and more.
Ind/Abst Abstr. Engl. Stud.; Am. Hist. Life (1976-); Annu. Bibliogr. Engl. Lang. Lit.; MLA Int. Bibl. Books Artic. Mod. Lang. Lit.; Sage Race Relat. Abstr.

US/0038-478X
SOUTHWESTERN HISTORICAL QUARTERLY. [Southwest. hist. q.]. **Added/Corp** Texas State Historical Association. University of Texas at Austin. Center for Studies in Texas History. Vol. 16, No. 1 (July 1912)-. Periodical. English. qt (Jan., Apr., July, Oct.).

Comes with Texas State Historical Association membership. Texas State Historical Association, 2/306 Richardson Hall, University Street, Austin TX 78712. **Tel** (512)471-1525, FAX (512)471-1551. **ED** Ron Tyler. **LC** F381; .T45. **DD** 976. Index available. cum. index. **Bk Rev. Ad Acc. Circ:** 3,300 (ctrl). available on microfilm and microfiche from University Microfilms International (UMI). Documents available from The Genuine Article, UMI Article Clearinghouse. ***Continues*** *The Quarterly of the Texas State Historical Association.*
Desc: Historical articles concerning Texas and the Southwest.
Ind/Abst Abstr. Anthropol.; Acad. Search (July 1993-); Am. Hist. Life (1955-1958, 1962-); Annu. Bibliogr. Engl. Lang. Lit.; Arts Humanit. Citation Index [Full Cov.]; Chicano Index; Curr. Contents Arts Humanit.; Expand. Acad. Index (1989-); Hist. Source (July 1993-); Humanit. Index; Humanit. Source (Jul. 1993-); Index Period. Artic. Relat. Law; INFO-SOUTH Abstr.; Mag. Search; Newsp. Period. Abstr. (1991-); Res. Alert [Full Cov.]; Soc. Sci. Cit. Index [Select. Cov.]; SportSearch; West. Hist. Q.

US/0081-315X
SOUTHWESTERN STUDIES. [Southwest. stud.]. Monograph No. 1- 1963-. Monographic series. English. ir. Price varies per volume. Texas Western Press, University of Texas at El Paso. **Tel** (915)747-5688. **ED** Dale L Walker and Nancy Hamilton. **DD** 979. **UDC** 973-14; 908.73-14. **Circ:** 700.
Desc: Covers topics related to history, geography, and social issues of the Southwestern United States and Northern Mexico.
Ind/Abst Annu. Bibliogr. Engl. Lang. Lit.

CN/0383-9370
SPEAK UP. ***Ceased.*** [Speak up]. Vol. 1 (June 1975)-(19??). Periodical. English. mo. Speak Up, Box 272 Station B, Toronto Ontario M5T 2W2 Canada. **Tel** 769-0513. **DD** 971.06/44. **Bk Rev. Ad Acc. Circ:** 7,000 (ctrl).

US/0882-3464
SPECULATOR (BUTTE, MONT.), THE. (THE SPECULATOR.). [Speculator]. Vol. 1, No. 1 (Winter 1984)-. Periodical. English. sa. $10.00. The Speculator, PO Box 3918, Butte MT 59702. **DD** 979. **UDC** 978.6.

CN/0229-7655
SPHQ NOUVELLES. [SPHQ nouv.]. **VAT** Societe des Professeurs d'Histoire du Quebec Nouvelles. V. 1, No. 1 (12 Dec. 1980)-. Periodical. French. qt. $27.09. Societe des Professeurs d'Histoire du Quebec, 7E Etage Quebec H2K 4L1 Canada. **DD** 971.4/007. **UDC** 971.4.

US/0730-2657
SPINNER (NEW BEDFORD, MASS.). (SPINNER.). Vol. 1 (1981)-. Periodical. English. an. Price varies. Spinner Publications, PO Box C-801, New Bedford MA 02741. **Tel** (508)994-4564. **ED** Joseph D. Thomas and Marsha McCabe. **LC** F71; .S68. **DD** 974.4/8/005. **Bk Rev. Ad Acc. Circ:** 10,000 (ctrl).
Desc: Cultural anthology concerned with history of the people of Southeastern Massachusetts region, their heritage, ethnicity, workplaces, family life and artistry, history of textile, fishing industries, land use, environment, oral history, photography and illustration.
Ind/Abst Am. Hist. Life (1981-).

US/0161-004X
SPOTLIGHT (NEW YORK). (SPOTLIGHT.). Began with Dec. 1943 issue. Periodical. English. wk. $171.00. The Spotlight / New York, 125 Adams Street, Delmar NY 12054. **Tel** (518)439-4949. **ED** Thomas McPheeters. **LC** E151; .S66. **DD** 973.91/05. **Circ:** 6,400.

BL/0582-1150
STADEN-JAHRBUCH. (STADEN-JAHRBUCH / BEITRAEGE ZUR BRASILKUNDE.). **Added/Corp** Instituto Hans Staden, Sao Paulo, Brazil. **VFOAT** Beitrage zur Brasilkunde. No. 1 (1953)-. German. an. $30.00. Instituto Hans Staden, Rua 7 de Abril 59-4 Andar, 01043-000 Sao Paulo SP Brazil. **Tel** 011 55 11 2558966, FAX 011 55 11 2558391. **ED** Rosemarie Erika Horch. **LC** F2501; .S9. Index available. **Bk Rev**, (Qty: 2-3). **Ad Acc. Circ:** 1,000 (ctrl).

US/0038-9994
STATE (CHARLOTTE, N.C.), THE. (THE STATE.). Vol. 1, (193?)-. Periodical. English. Twelve times a year. $18.00. Shaw Publishing Inc, 128 S Tryon Street, Suite 2200, Charlotte NC 28202. **Tel** (704)375-7404, (407)231-7788. **ED** Scott Smith. **LC** F251; .S77. **DD** 975.6. **Bk Rev**, (Qty: 12). **Ad Acc, Adv Mgr:** S. Rogers, **Tel** (704)371-3269. ctrl circ.

US
STATE OF THE UNION REPORT. Began with Sept. 1978 issue?. Periodical. English. Commercial Division, Canadian Embassy, Melchor Ocampo 463-7, Mexico 5 DF Mexico. **DD** 972.08/33. **UDC** 972.

US/0039-0232
STATEN ISLAND HISTORIAN, THE. [Staten Isl. hist.]. **Added/Corp** Staten Island Historical Society. Vol. 1, No. 1 (Jan. 1938)-. Periodical. English. qt (Jan., Apr., July, Oct.). $9.00. Staten Island Historical Society, 441 Clarke Avenue, Staten Island NY 10306-1125. **Tel** (718)351-1617. **ED** John B. Woodall and Anna Marie Sandecki. **LC** F127.S7; S68. **DD** 974.7/26/005. Index available. **Bk Rev. Ad Acc. Circ:** 1,800.
Desc: Articles on the history of Staten Island and the Mid-Atlantic Region.
Ind/Abst Am. Hist. Life.

US/0039-0844
STEAMBOAT BILL (1958). (STEAMBOAT BILL : JOURNAL OF THE STEAMSHIP HISTORICAL SOCIETY OF AMERICA.). **Added/Corp** Steamship Historical Society of America. **VFOAT** Steamboat Bill. No. 66 (June 1958)-. Periodical. English. Four times a year (Jan., Apr., July, Oct.). $22.00. Steamship Historical Society, 300 Ray Drive, Suite 4, Providence RI 02906. **Tel** (401)274-0805. **ED** William M. Rau, (editor's address: 22 Kings Highway, New City, NY 10956, Telephone: (914)634-5465). **LC** VM1; .S75. **DD** 387. cum. index. **Bk Rev. Ad Acc. Circ:** 4,000 (ctrl). available on microfilm and microfiche from University Microfilms International (UMI). ***Continues Steamboat Bill of Facts.***
Desc: History of and current information relating to self-propelled vessels.
Ind/Abst Am. Hist. Life.

US
STEPPING STONES (WARREN, PA.). (STEPPING STONES.). **Added/Corp** Warren County Historical Society (Pa.). (March 1955)-. Periodical. English. tq (3 issues). $10.00; Comes also with membership. Warren County Historical Society, 210 Fourth Avenue, PO Box 427, Warren PA 16365. **Tel** (814)723-1795.
Ind/Abst Am. Hist. Life.

US/0039-1522
STIRPES. **See** Genealogy and Heraldry.

US/0562-1690
STREAM OF HISTORY, THE. (THE STREAM OF HISTORY / JACKSON COUNTY HISTORICAL SOCIETY.). **Added/Corp** Jackson County Historical Society (Ark.). Vol. 2, No. 4 (Oct. 1964)-. Periodical. English. Four times a year. $10.00 (individual membership) US and Canada. Jackson County Historical Society, c/o J.L. Morgan, 314 Vine Street, Newport AR 72112. **LC** F417.J3; S75. **DD** 976.7/97/005. ***Continues*** *Quarterly of the Jackson County Historical Society.*

US/1055-4831
SUPPRESSED! (PLYMOUTH, MICH.). (SUPPRESSED! : HISTORY AND VIOLENCE IN AMERICA.). [Suppressed!]. Vol. 1, No. 1 (1991)-. Periodical. English. qt. $2.95 (single issue, U.S.), $3.75 (single issue, Canada). Tome Press, G21B South Main Street, Plymouth MI 48170. **DD** 973.

CN/0228-9016
SUR L'EMPREMIER. (SUR L'EMPREMIER : LA GAZETTE DE LA SOCIETE HISTORIQUE DE LA MER ROUGE.). [Sur empremier]. **Added/Corp** Societe Historique de la Mer Rouge. Vol. 1, No. 1 (1981)-. French (English). an. 6.14Can$ Canada & US; 6.76Can$ Pan America; 9.00Can$ other. Societe Historique de la Mer Rouge, Rural Route 1, Robichaud New Brunswick E0A 2S0 Canada. **ED** R. Giues Le Blanc. **DD** 971.5/23004114. **Bk Rev. Circ:** 180.
Desc: Dedicated to the local history of the Acadians.

US/8756-0143
SWAMPFOX. **VFOAT** Swamp Fox. Periodical. English. qt. $8.00. Swampfox, Box 177, Buena Vista GA 31803. **Tel** (912)649-7520. **ED** Harold Grimsley. **LC** F292.M25; S9. **DD** 975.8/482. **UDC** 975.8; 908.758. **Circ:** 300.
Desc: An attempt to preserve "the essence of life" in rural Georgia with emphasis on local personalities, hobbies, and lifestyles. Except printing, work is done entirely by high school students.

US/0730-028X
SWEDISH-AMERICAN HISTORICAL QUARTERLY. (THE SWEDISH-AMERICAN HISTORICAL QUARTERLY / SWEDISH PIONEER HISTORICAL SOCIETY.). [Swed.-Am. hist. q.]. **Added/Corp** Swedish-American Historical Society (1983-). Swedish Pioneer Historical Society. **VFOAT** Swedish American Historical Quarterly. **VAT** Swedish American Historical Quarterly. Vol. 33 No. 1 (Jan. 1982)-. Periodical. English. qt. $25.00. Swedish American Historical Society, 5125 North Spaulding Avenue, Chicago IL 60625. **Tel** (312)583-5722. **ED** H Arnold Barton. **LC** E184.S23; S955. **DD** 973/.04397; 369. Index available. cum. index. **Bk Rev. Ad Acc. Circ:** 2,000. available on microfilm from University Microfilms International (UMI). ***Continues*** *Swedish Pioneer Historical Quarterly, 0039-7326.*
Desc: Contains articles on Swedish American history submitted from numerous sources ranging from original document research to personal reminiscences.
Ind/Abst Am. Hist. Life (1982-); MLA Int. Bibl. Books Artic. Mod. Lang. Lit.; West. Hist. Q.

US
SWISS AMERICAN HISTORICAL SOCIETY REVIEW. English. tq. Swiss American Historical Society, 6440 North Bosworth, Chicago IL 60626.
Ind/Abst Am. Hist. Life (1976-).

CN/0700-5199
SZAMADAS. **VFOAT** Recount. V. 1- Aug. 15, 1975-. Periodical. Hungarian. mo. 0.50Can$ each number. Szamadas, PO Box 42 Station W, Toronto Ontario M6M 4Y9 Canada. **DD** 971.004/94511. **UDC** 971(=945.11); 908.71(=945.11).

US/0894-105X
TAMPA BAY (CLEARWATER, FLA.). (TAMPA BAY.). (1986)-. Periodical. English. bm. $12.00, $15.00 (Alaska, Hawaii, Canada and US possessions). Tampa Bay Publications Inc., 2531 Landmark Drive, Suite 102, Clearwater FL 33519. **Tel** (813)855-1894, FAX (813)796-0527. **DD** 917.

US/0272-1406
TAMPA BAY HISTORY. [Tampa Bay hist.]. **Added/Corp** University of South Florida. Dept. of History. Vol. 1, No. 1 (Spring/Summer 1979)-. Academic Scholarly Publication. English. sa (June & Dec.). $18.00. University of South Florida / Department of History, 4202 East Fowler Avenue, Tampa FL 33620. **Tel** (813)974-2807, FAX (813)974-6228. **ED** Bob Ingalls (editor's phone: (813)974-6233). **LC** F319.T2; T26. **DD** 975.9/65. Index available. **Bk Rev. Circ:** 1,000.
Desc: Covers the history of central and southwest Florida through research articles, documents, interviews and photos. Aimed at both scholarly and interested lay audiences.
Ind/Abst Am. Hist. Life (1979-); SportSearch.

US/0496-8913
TAR HEEL JUNIOR HISTORIAN. **Added/Corp** Tar Heel Junior Historian Association. North Carolina. Museum of History. **VFOAT** Tarheel Junior Historian. (19??)-. Periodical. English. sa. $4.00. Tar Heel Junior Historian Association, 109 East Jones Street, Raleigh NC 27611. **Tel** (919)715-0200. **ED** Lea Marshall. **Pr Rev. Circ:** 8,500. ***Continues*** *Tarheel Historian.*
Desc: Designed to present the history of North Carolina for the state's young people.

BE/0040-1382
TECHNIQUES NOUVELLES. [Tech. nouv.]. Academic Scholarly Publication. Multiple languages. 150F. Techniques Nouvelles / Belgium, rue des Deux Gares 80, 1070 Bruxelles Belgium. **UDC** 54. **CODEN** TENOD9. Documents available from CASDDS.
Ind/Abst Chem. Abstr.

BL
TEMA (RIO DE JANEIRO, BRAZIL). (TEMA.). **Added/Corp** Brazil. Servico Federal de Processamento de Dados. Departamento de Recursos Humanos. Vol. 1 No. 3 (July 1975)-. Periodical. Portuguese. Twelve times a year. Serpro, Ed Sede, Sgan 601/Mod V/Terraco, 70830 Brasilia DF Brazil. **Tel** 216-2566. **LC** F2501; .T45. **DD** 981/.005. ***Continues*** *Revista SERPRO.*

CN/0706-1757
TEMISCOUATA, LE. [Temiscouata]. V. 1- Feb. 1980-. Periodical. French. Three times a year. $7.00. Societe Historique de Cabano, Le Temiscouata, CP 464, Cabano Quebec G0L 1E0 Canada. **DD** 971.4/76/005. **UDC** 971.4.

US
TENNESSEE COUNTY HISTORY SERIES. ***Ceased.*** 1-?. Monographic series. English. ir. Memphis State University Press, Memphis TN 38152. **Tel** (901)678-2752. **ED** Frank B Williams Jr, Robert B Jones and Charles W Crawford. **UDC** 976.8. Index available. cum. index. **Circ:** 300.
Desc: Monograph histories of the 95 counties in Tennessee from Indian times to the present. Includes at least one map and about 25-30 halftones. Authors are contracted with the Press.

US/0040-3261
TENNESSEE HISTORICAL QUARTERLY. [Tenn. hist. q.]. **Added/Corp** Tennessee Historical Society. Tennessee. State Historical Commission. Vol. 1 (Mar. 1942)-. Periodical. English. Four times a year. $35.00 Comes with Tennessee Historical Society membership. Tennessee Historical Society, War Memorial Building, Nashville TN 37219. **Tel** (615)741-8934. **ED** Robert B. Jones. **LC** F431; .T285. **DD** 976.8005. Index available. cum. index. **Circ:** 2,500. available on microfilm and microfiche from University Microfilms International (UMI); available on CD-ROM; available in microform. ***Supersedes*** *Tennessee Historical Magazine.*
Desc: Tennessee civil, political and cultural history.
Ind/Abst Am. Hist. Life (1963-); Annu. Bibliogr. Engl. Lang. Lit.; MLA Int. Bibl. Books Artic. Mod. Lang. Lit.; West. Hist. Q.

US/0097-9708
TENNESSEE VALLEY HISTORICAL REVIEW. Vol. 1 (Spring 1972)-. Periodical. English. Four times a year. $7.00. Historical Review & Digest, 605 Merritt Street, Nashville TN 37203. **LC** F431; .T38. **DD** 976.8/005.

US/0363-3705
TEQUESTA. [Tequesta]. **Added/Corp** Historical Association of Southern Florida. University of Miami. (1941)-. English. an. $35.00. Historical Association of Southern Florida, 101 West Flaglen Street, Miami FL 33130. **Tel** (305)375-1492. **ED** Anna Parks. **LC** F306; .T47. **DD** 975.90062. Index available. **Circ:** 3,500 (ctrl).
Desc: Scholarly journal covering the history of south Florida and the Caribbean.
Ind/Abst Am. Hist. Life (1973-).

IT/0040-375X
TERRA AMERIGA. ***Suspended.*** [Terra Ameriga]. Vol. 1, No. 1 (1964)-Suspended (1988). Periodical. Italian. qt. L12000 Italy. Association Italiana Studi Americanst, Corso Solferino 29, 1-16122 Genoa Italy. **Tel** 814737. **LC** E51; .T47.
Ind/Abst Am. Hist. Life (1972); Anthropol. Lit.; HAPI Hisp. Am. Period. Index.

US/0082-2884
TERRAE INCOGNITAE. **See** Geography.

SP
TESTIMONIO LATINOAMERICANO. Yearly Vol. 1, No. 1 (March/April 1980)-. Periodical. Spanish. bm. Circulo de Estudios Latinoamericanos, Apartado Postal 32.142, Barcelona Spain. **LC** F1401; .T4. **DD** 980/.005. **UDC** 980-6; 908.8-6.

US/0040-411X
TEXANA. V. 1- Winter 1963-. Periodical. English. qt. $5.00. **LC** F381; .T23. **UDC** 908.764. available on microfilm from University Microfilms International (UMI).
Ind/Abst Am. Hist. Life (1964-1974).

US
TEXAS GULF HISTORICAL AND BIOGRAPHICAL RECORD, THE. **Added/Corp** Texas Gulf Historical Society. Vol. 1 (Nov. 1965)-. English. an (Dec.). $10.00. Texas Gulf Historical Society, PO Box 1621, Beaumont TX 77704. **Tel** (409)833-3333. **ED** Ellen Reinstra. **LC** F392.G9; T48. **Bk Rev**. **Ad Acc**. **Circ:** 400.

US/0022-6602
TEXAS HISTORIAN, THE. [Tex. hist.]. **Added/Corp** Texas State Historical Association. (19??)-. Periodical. English. qt (Feb., May, Sep., Nov.). $7.00. Texas State Historical Association, 2/306 Richardson Hall, University Street, Austin TX 78712. **Tel** (512)471-1525, FAX (512)471-1551. **ED** David Deboe. **LC** F381; .J8. **Ad Acc**. **Circ:** 2,000. ***Continues*** *Junior Historian.*
Desc: Written by and for junior high and high school students to further education in Texas history. Journal of the Junior Historians of Texas. All articles deal with local history.
Ind/Abst Am. Hist. Life.

US/1045-764X
TEXAS INDEX. [Tex. index]. (1987)-. Periodical. English. an. Price varies per volume. Texinfo, 2824 Burning Tree Lane, Irving TX 75062. **Tel** (214)255-7098. **ED** Sharon Giles. **DD** 976.

US
TEXAS NOTES ON PRECOLUMBIAN ART, WRITING, AND CULTURE. **Added/Corp** University of Texas at Austin. Center of the History and Art of Ancient American Culture. **VFOAT** Texas Notes. No. 1 (Sept. 1990)-. Periodical. English. University of Texas at Austin / Precolumbian Studies, Center of History and Art of Ancient American Cultures, Austin TX 78712.
Desc: Information on the Indians of Central America and Mexico.

US
TEXAS PAN AMERICAN SERIES. English. ir. University of Texas Press, PO Box 7819, Austin TX 78713. **Tel** (512)471-4531, FAX (512)320-0668, telex 776453 UTEXPRES AUS.
Ind/Abst MLA Int. Bibl. Books Artic. Mod. Lang. Lit.

CN/0081-1130
TEXTES - SOCIETE HISTORIQUE DE QUEBEC. (TEXTES.). **Main/Corp** Societe Historique de Quebec. No. 1 (March 1968)-. Bulletin. French. ir (4 issues). Price varies per volume. Societe Historique de Quebec / Historical Society of Quebec, 43 Cote de la Fabrique, Quebec Quebec G1R 5M1 Canada. **Tel** (418)694-9740, FAX (418)691-7759. Index available. cum. index. **Bk Rev**, (Qty: 3). **Ad Acc**, **Adv Mgr:** Gilles Mathieu. **Circ:** 600 (ctrl).
Desc: Historical guide to Quebec City.

CN/0381-6109
THEM DAYS. [Them days]. **Added/Corp** Labrador Heritage Society. Old Timers League. (Aug. 1975)-. Periodical. English. qt. 14.00Can$ Canada; 16.00Can$ other. Them Days Inc., PO Box 939, Station B, Happy Valley, Labrador A0P 1E0 Canada. **Tel** (709)896-8531. **ED** Doris Saunders. **LC** F1137; .T45. **DD** 971.8/2/005. Index available. cum. index. **Bk Rev**. **Circ:** 1,200 (ctrl).
Desc: Historically documenting old ways and early days of Labrador through interviews, photographs, documents, diaries, poetry, music, crafts, genealogy, archaeology and special interest features.

US/0888-5230
THIRD DECADE, THE. (THE THIRD DECADE : A JOURNAL OF RESEARCH ON THE JOHN F. KENNEDY ASSASSINATION.). Vol. 1, No. 1 (Nov. 1984)-. Periodical. English. Six times a year. $15.00. Third Decade, State University College, Fredonia NY 14063. **Tel** (716)673-3421. **DD** 973.

US
THREE WIRE WINTER. **Added/Corp** Steamboat Springs High School. Vol. 1 (Winter 1976)-. Periodical. English. ir. $3.00 per issue. Three Wire Winter, PO Box 770664, Steamboat Springs CO 80477. **Tel** (303)879-1562. **ED** Bill McKelvie. **LC** AP2; .T3344. **DD** 051. Index available. cum. index. **Ad Acc**. **Circ:** 1,500.
Desc: Magazine is produced by Steamboat Springs high school students about Northwest Colorado local history.

CN/0826-4775
THROUGH THE YEARS. (THROUGH THE YEARS : MANITOULIN DISTRICT HISTORY AND GENEALOGY.). [Through years]. Vol. 1, No. 1 (Nov. 1983)-. Periodical. English. mo. 30.00Can$ Canada; 35.00Can$ other. Through the Years, PO Box 235, Gore Bay Ontario P0P 1H0 Canada. **Tel** (705)282-2695. **ED** W J McQuarrie. **DD** 971.3/135/005. **Circ:** 1,000.
Desc: The publication is of the early years in the District of Manitoulin, Ontario, Canada.

CN/0705-9027
THYME. Nov. 1977-. Periodical. English. 0.50Can$ each no. Sunrise Pavilion, 10341-135th Street, Surrey British Columbia V3T 4C3 Canada. **DD** 971.2/02.

US/0897-0335
TIDINGS (WESTERLY, R.I.). (TIDINGS.). **VFOAT** Tidings Magazine. (1983)-. Periodical. English. Six times a year. Tidings Magazine, Drawer 502, Westerly RI 02891. **DD** 974.

US/0748-9579
TIMELINE. (TIMELINE : A PUBLICATION OF THE OHIO HISTORICAL SOCIETY.). [Timeline]. **Added/Corp** Ohio Historical Society. **VFOAT** Time Line. Vol. 1, No. 1 (Oct. 1984)-. Periodical. English. Six times a year. Free to Ohio Public Main Libraries; $22.50 others. Ohio Historical Society, 1982 Velma Avenue, Subscription Office, Columbus OH 43211. **Tel** (614)297-2332, (614)297-2360. **ED** Christopher S. Duckworth. **LC** F491; .T55. Index available. **Bk Rev**. **Circ:** 12,000.
Desc: A popular magazine featuring authoritative, well-illustrated articles. Its subject matter encompasses history, art, and natural history of Ohio and the Midwest.
Ind/Abst Am. Hist. Life (1984-); West. Hist. Q.

US/0748-8637
TIMEPIECE (NAPLES, FLA.). (THE TIMEPIECE : A QUARTERLY PUBLICATION OF THE COLLIER COUNTY HISTORICAL SOCIETY.). [Timepiece]. **Added/Corp** Collier County Historical Society. Vol. 1, No. 1 (Winter 1973)-. Periodical. English. an. $15.00 (two years). Collier County Historical Society, PO Box 201, Naples FL 33939. **Tel** (813)261-1383. **DD** 975.

CN/1188-0376
TIN TYPE : AMHERSTBURG HISTORIC SITES ASSOCIATION NEWSLETTER. [Tin type]. **Added/Corp** Amherstburg Historic Sites Association. **VFOAT** Amherstburg Historic Sites Association Newsletter. Vol. 1, No. 1 (Oct. 1991)-. Newsletter. English. qt. Free to members. Amherstburg Historic Sites Association, 214 Dalhousie Street, Amherstbur Ontario N9V 1W4 Canada. **DD** 971.3/31/06.

CN/0709-0846
TOBIQUER. (THE TOBIQUER.). **Added/Corp** Southern Victoria Historical Society of Perth-Andover. (Apr. 1978)-. Periodical. English. $2.00 each number. The Tobiquer, PO Box 147, Perth-Andover New Brunswick E0J 1V0 Canada. **DD** 971.5/53/05.

AG/0040-8611
TODO ES HISTORIA. ***Ceased.*** **VFOAT** Historia. (May 1967)-(19??). Periodical. Spanish. mo (irregular). Honegger SA, Mexico 4256, Buenos Aires Argentina. **LC** F2801; .T6. **DD** 982/.005. cum. index.
Ind/Abst HAPI Hisp. Am. Period. Index.

JA
TOKYO DAIGAKU AMERIKA KENKYU SHIRYO SENTA NEMPO. **Main/Corp** Tokyo Daigaku. Amerika Kenkyu Shiryo Senta. **VFOAT** Bulletin of the Center for American Studies of the University of Tokyo. No. 1 (1978)-. Japanese (English, Korean and Russian). Tokyo Daigaku Amerika Kenkyu Shiryo Senta, c/o Tokyo Daigaku Kyoyo, Gakubu 8-1 Komaba 3-chome Meguro-ku, Tokyo Japan. **LC** E175.8; .T73A. **UDC** 908.73.

US/0145-5443
TOLEDO AREA ABORIGINAL RESEARCH BULLETIN. ***Ceased.*** **Added/Corp** Toledo Area Aboriginal Research Club. Vol. 4 (1975)-(19??). Bulletin. English. an. T A A R S Inc, University of Toledo, 2801 West Bancroft Street, Toledo OH 43606. **Tel** (419)537-4650. **ED** David M Stothers. **LC** E78.O3; T63. **DD** 977.1/1/0405. **Circ:** 200. ***Continues*** *Toledo Area Aboriginal Research Club Bulletin.*
Desc: Prehistory of Western Basin region of Lake Erie (Toledo area as defined).

US/0271-0218
TOMLINSON'S LONE STAR BOOK OF TEXAS RECORDS. **VFOAT** Lone Star Book of Texas Records. 1st- Ed.; 1977-. English. an. Lone Star Book of Texas Records, PO box 11406, Fort Worth TX 76109. **LC** F386.5; .T64. **DD** 976.4/005. **UDC** 976.4.

US
TOPICAL STUDIES. **Main/Corp** Norwegian - American Historical Association. **Added/Corp** Norwegian-American Historical Association. Vol. 1 (1971)-. Periodical. English. ir. Norwegian-American Historical Association, St. Olaf College, Northfield MN 55057. **Tel** (507)646-3221. **ED** Odd S. Lovall. **Bk Rev**. **Ad Acc**. **Circ:** 1,500 (ctrl).
Desc: Prints, letters and other historical accounts of Norwegian-Americans in the early 1800's. Subjects include practice of medicine, church history, songs, prairie pioneering, daily life, farming and etc.

CN/0821-2740
TORONTO IRISH NEWS. (TORONTO IRISH NEWS / IRISH-CANADIAN AID AND CULTURAL SOCIETY.). [Tor. Ir. news]. Periodical. English. bm. Free. Toronto Irish News, 1650 Dupont Street, Toronto Ontario M6P 3T2 Canada. **Tel** (416)367-8311, FAX (416)367-8311, telex 065- 24037. **ED** Paul M FArrelly. **DD** 971.3/5410049162. **UDC** 908.713(=916.2). **Bk Rev**. **Ad Acc**. ctrl circ.
Desc: A community newspaper covering Irish cultural, sporting and social activities.

US/0740-8986
TOUCHSTONE (MARSHALL, TEX.). (TOUCHSTONE.). [Touchstone]. **Added/Corp** Walter Prescott Webb Historical Society. Vol. 1 (1982)-. English. an (March). $5.00. Texas State Historical Association, 2/306 Richardson Hall, University Street, Austin TX 78712. **Tel** (512)471-1525, FAX (512)471-1551. **ED** David DeBoe. **LC** F386; .T68. **DD** 976.4/005. **Circ:** 500.
Desc: Publishes undergraduate research in Texas history.
Ind/Abst Am. Humanit. Index.

US/1040-788X
TRACES OF INDIANA AND MIDWESTERN HISTORY. (TRACES OF INDIANA AND MIDWESTERN HISTORY : A PUBLICATION OF THE INDIANA HISTORICAL SOCIETY.). [Traces Indiana midwest. hist.]. **Added/Corp** Indiana Historical Society. **VFOAT** Traces. Vol. 1, No. 1 (Winter 1989)-. Periodical. English. qt. Free to members of the Indiana Historical Society; $20.00 membership. Indiana Historical Society, 315 West Ohio Street, Indianapolis IN 46202. **Tel** (317)232-1882. **ED** Kent Calder. **DD** 977. **Circ:** 6,500 (ctrl).
Desc: Focuses on topics of general historical interest.

US/0884-3309
TRANSACTIONS - PIONEER AMERICA SOCIETY. (PIONEER AMERICA SOCIETY TRANSACTIONS : P.A.S.T.). [Trans. - Pioneer Am. Soc.]. **Main/Corp** Pioneer America Society. **VFOAT** Transactions; P.A.S.T.; PAST. (1978)-. Periodical. English. $5.00, Free to members. Pioneer America Society, 601 South College Road, Wilmington NC 28403. **Tel** (910)395-3493. **LC** E179.5; .P48a. **DD** 973/.05. ***Continues*** *Pioneer America Society. Proceedings, 0092-6582.*
Ind/Abst Avery Index Archit. Period. Suppl. Colum. Univ. (1989).

CN/0079-8339
TRAVAUX ET DOCUMENTS. **Main/Corp** Universite Laval. Centre d'Etudes Nordiques. Vol. 1 (1963)-. Monographic series. French. ir. Price varies per volume. Presses de l'Universite Laval, CP 2447 Avenue de la Medicine, Saint Foy Quebec G1K 7P4 Canada. **Tel** (418)656-5106, (418)656-2590. **LC** F1051; .U56a. **DD** 971.4.
Ind/Abst Ecol. Abstr. (?-?); Geogr. Abstr. Phys. Geogr. (?-?); Int. Dev. Abstr. (?-?).

US
TRAVEL AND DESCRIPTION SERIES. **Added/Corp** Norwegian-American Historical Association. (1926)-. Monographic series. English. ir. Price varies per volume. Norwegian-American Historical Association, St Olaf College, Northfield MN 55057. **Tel** (507)646-3221. **ED** Odd S. Lovoll. **LC** E184.S2; N83. **Bk Rev**. **Ad Acc**. **Circ:** 1,500 (ctrl).
Desc: A series printing original text and translations of old Norwegian books, letters and other historical accounts of Norwegian travel especially in America.

CN/0702-8679
TRIINU. (1953)-. Periodical. Estonian. qt. $14.00. Triinu, 50 Old Kingston Road/#5-209, Scarborough Ontario M1E 4Y1 Canada. **ED** Tanni Kents. **DD** 971/.004/94545. ctrl circ.

TR
TRINIDAD & TOBAGO REVIEW. **Added/Corp** Trinidad and Tobago Institute of the West Indies. **VFOAT** Trinidad and Tobago Review. Vol. 1, No. 1 (July 3, 1977)-. Periodical. English. sm. $321.00. Trinidad Express Newspapers Ltd, 35 Independence Square, Port of Spain Trinidad. **Tel** (809)623-1711, FAX (809)627-1451. **LC** F2122; .T745. **DD** 972.983/005. ***Continues*** *Tapia.*

US/0041-3615
TRUE WEST. [True West]. Vol. 1, No. 1 (Summer 1953)-. English. mo. $19.95 (one year), $37.00 (two year) US; $24.95 (one year), $47.00 (two year) includes postage other. Western Publications / Oklahoma, PO Box 2107, Stillwater OK 74076. **Tel** (405)743-3370, (800)749-3369, FAX (405)743-3374. **ED** John Joerschke. **LC** AP2; .T773. **DD** 917.8. **UDC** 981. Index available. **Bk Rev. Ad Acc. Circ:** 110,000 (ctrl).
Desc: Covers a broad range of western American history and culture from previous Civil War days to the present.
Ind/Abst West. Hist. Q.

BL
TUDO E HISTORIA; CADERNOS DE PESQUISA. 1-. Periodical. Portuguese. Brasiliense, rua Barao de Itapetininga 93, Sao Paulo Brazil. **LC** F2501; .T82. **DD** 981/.005. **UDC** 976.3.

US
U MUT MAYA : AN UNOFFICIAL COLLECTION OF PAPERS, REPORTS, AND READINGS BY ATTENDANTS OF THE ... ADVANCED SEMINAR ON MAYA HIEROGLYPHIC WRITING HELD AT THE UNIVERSITY OF TEXAS AT AUSTIN ... . **Main/Conf** Advanced Seminar on Maya Hieroglyphic Writing (Austin, Tex.). (1988)-. Periodical. English.
Ind/Abst Anthropol. Lit.

US
U S L HISTORY SERIES, THE. **Main/Corp** Louisiana. University of Southwestern Louisiana, Lafayette. Monographic series. English. ir. Price varies per volume. Center for Louisiana Studies, PO Box 4-0831, Lafayette LA 70504.

US/1046-9176
UCLA LATIN AMERICAN STUDIES. [UCLA Lat. Am. stud.]. **Added/Corp** UCLA Latin American Center. **VFOAT** Latin American Studies. **VAT** University of California, Los Angeles Latin American Studies. Vol. 1 (1975)-. Monographic series. English. ir. Price varies per volume. Regents of the University of California at Los Angeles, 405 Hilgard Avenue, Los Angeles CA 90024-1447. **Tel** (310)825-6634. **(Subscription address:** UCLA Latin American Center, Regents of the University of California, Los Angeles CA 90024.) **DD** 980. **Circ:** 250. ***Continues*** *Latin American Studies.*
Desc: Offers theoretical and methodological statements, interpretative essays and monographic research findings of Latin American interest.

US/0733-8686
ULSTER-AMERICAN NEWSLETTER. (ULSTER-AMERICAN NEWSLETTER / ULSTER-AMERICAN HERITAGE FOUNDATION.). [Ulster-Am. newsl.]. **Added/Corp** Ulster-American Heritage Foundation. **VAT** Ulster American Newsletter. No. 1 (Spring 1982)-. Periodical. English. qt. $5.00. Ulster-American Heritage Foundation, PO Box 1271, Torrance CA 90505.

US/0041-6339
UMPQUA TRAPPER, THE. **Added/Corp** Douglas County Historical Society, Oregon. Vol. 1 (Spring 1965)-. Periodical. English. qt. $10.00. Douglas County Historical Society, 733 West Ballf Street, Roseburg OR 97470. **Tel** (503)673-7891. **ED** Doris L. Bacon. Index available. **Circ:** 350.
Desc: Relating to the history of Douglas County, Oregon.

CN/0826-1172
UNION FAIT LA FORCE (MONTREAL, QUEBEC). (L'UNION FAIT LA FORCE.). [Union fait force]. **VFOAT** Eendracht Maakt Macht. Periodical. French (Dutch). mo. Free to Members. Union National Belge, 452 Est rue Notre-Dame, Montreal Quebec H2Y 1C8 Canada. **DD** 971.4/2810043932/06. **UDC** 971.4(=393.2).

US
UNITED DAUGHTERS OF THE CONFEDERACY MAGAZINE. Vol. 1 (1938)-. Periodical. English. mo (except combined June/July). $10.00 US; $17.50 Canada; $22.50 other. United Daughters of the Confederacy Magazine, 328 North Boulevard, Richmond VA 23220. **Tel** (804)355-1636. **ED** Dorothy Edgar. Index available. **Bk Rev. Ad Acc. Circ:** 9,000.
Desc: Covers history and war between the States.

US/0276-4709
UNITED STATES VIEWS ON MEXICO. [U.S. views Mex.]. Periodical. English. qt. $150.00. Banamex Cultural Foundation, 2010 Massachusetts Avenue NW, Washington DC 20036. **LC** F1235; .U55. **DD** 972.08/33. **UDC** 972.

US
UNIVERSITY OF FLORIDA LATINAMERICANIST. **VFOAT** Latinamericanist. V. 1- Feb. 3, 1964-. Periodical. English. bw. Center for Latin American Studies University of Florida, Gainesville FL 32601. **UDC** 980-6; 908.8-6.

US/0085-5227
UNIVERSITY OF UTAH PUBLICATIONS IN THE AMERICAN WEST. **Added/Corp** University of Utah. **VFOAT** Publications in the American West. Vol. 2 (1969)-. Monographic series. English. ir. Price varies per volume. University of Utah Press, 101 University Services Building, Salt Lake City UT 84112. **Tel** (801)581-6771.

CN/0700-933X
UP THE GATINEAU. 1975-. English. an. $1.50 each number. Historical Society of the Gatineau, c/o S Strang Secretary-Treasurer, Old Chelsea Quebec J0X 2N0 Canada. **DD** 971.4/221/005. **UDC** 971.4.

CN/0828-5799
UPDATE - NATIONAL ASSOCIATION OF CANADIANS OF ORIGIN IN INDIA. (UPDATE / NATIONAL ASSOC. OF CANADIANS OF ORIGIN IN INDIA.). [Update - Natl. Assoc. Can. Orig. India]. Vol. 1, No. 1 (Apr. 1984)-. Periodical. English. ir. Association Finance Counsel Planning Education, 1787 Neil Avenue, Columbus OH 43210. **Tel** (614)292-3741, FAX (614)292-7536. **DD** 971/.00491411. **UDC** 971(=914); 908.71(=914).

US
UPPER OHIO VALLEY HISTORICAL REVIEW / [WHEELING AREA HISTORICAL SOCIETY]. **Added/Corp** Wheeling Area Historical Society. (19??)-. Periodical. English. sa. $5.00. Wheeling West Virginia Historical Society, West Liberty State College, West Library WV 26074. **Tel** (305)336-5000.
Ind/Abst Am. Hist. Life (1978-).

CN/0703-0428
URBAN HISTORY REVIEW. (URBAN HISTORY REVIEW. REVUE D'HISTOIRE URBAINE.). [Urban hist. rev.]. **Added/Corp** National Museum of Man (Canada). History Division. **VFOAT** Revue d'Histoire Urbaine. (Feb. 1972)-. Periodical. English (French). Twice a year (Mar. & Oct.). 35.00Can$ (individuals), 40.00Can$ (institutions) US & Canada; 50.00Can$ other. Becker Associates, 36 Bessemer Court, Unit 3, Concord Ontario L4K 3C9 Canada. **Tel** (416)669-5373, FAX (416)669-1927. **ED** Gwenne Becker. **LC** HT127; .U7. **DD** 301.36/3/0971. **Bk Rev. Circ:** 1,000 (ctrl). Documents available from The Genuine Article. ***Absorbed*** *Urbanism Past & Present.*
Desc: Informs and entertains its readers about all aspects of the development of Canadian communities. Regular features include lively articles covering topics such as architecture; heritage and urbanization; research notes; an annual bibliography; comprehensive reviews on Canadian and non-Canadian material, notes, comment on conferences, urban policy and other related publications.
Ind/Abst Am. Hist. Life (1972-); Appl. Soc. Sci. Index Abstr. (1972-); ARTbibliogr. Mod.; Arts Humanit. Citation Index [Full Cov.]; Avery Index Archit. Period. Suppl. Colum. Univ. (199?-); Can. Index (?-?); Can. Period. Index (1972-); Curr. Contents Arts Humanit.; Geogr. Abstr. Phys. Geogr.; Geogr. Abstr. Human Geogr.; J. Plan. Lit.; Res. Alert [Full Cov.]; Sage Public Adm. Abstr. (1972-?); Sage Urban Stud. Abstr; Soc. Sci. Cit. Index [Select. Cov.]; U.S. Polit. Sci. Doc.

US
URUGUAY NEWS. **Added/Corp** Uruguay Information Group. **VFOAT** Noticias del Uruguay. No. 1 (April 1977)-. Periodical. English. Uruguay Information Group, PO Box 1259, GPO New York, New York NY 10001.
Ind/Abst Hum. Rights Intern. Rep.

US
US HISTORY ON CD-ROM. (19??)-. English. $79.95. Bureau of Electronic Publishing Inc., 141 New Road, Parsippany NJ 07054. **Tel** (201)808-2700, FAX (201)808-2676. Index available. cum. index. **Bk Rev.**
Desc: Recounts the story of a young republic's evolution into a world super power; from Columbus' discovery of the New World through today.

US
USA. **Added/Corp** United States. Embassy (Hungary). (1972)-. Periodical. Hungarian (Hungarian). qt. US Information Agency, 301 4th Street SW, Washington DC 20547. **Tel** (202)619-4700. **LC** E169.12; .U77.

US
USA WARS: CIVIL WAR. CD-ROM. **See** Political Science.

US/0042-143X
UTAH HISTORICAL QUARTERLY. [Utah hist. q.]. **Added/Corp** Utah State Historical Society. Vol. 1 (Jan. 1928)-. Periodical. English. Four times a year (Mar., June, Sept., Dec.). $20.00 Comes with Utah State Historical Society membership. Utah State Historical Society, 300 Rio Grande, Salt Lake City UT 84101. **Tel** (801)533-3500, FAX (801)533-3503. **ED** Max J. Evans, Stanford J. Layton and Miriam B. Murphy. **LC** F821; .U92. **DD** 979.2005. Index available. cum. index. **Bk Rev. Circ:** 3,500 (ctrl).
Desc: Journal devoted to the history of Utah and related western history. All aspects of history from art to technology, folklore to politics, included.
Ind/Abst Am. Hist. Life (1963-); Annu. Bibliogr. Engl. Lang. Lit.; SportSearch; West. Hist. Q.

US/0888-4331
UTAH PRESERVATION/RESTORATION. [Utah preserv./restor.]. **Added/Corp** Utah Historic Preservation Office. **VFOAT** Utah Preservation, Restoration. Vol. 1, Issue 1 (1979)-. Periodical. English. an. University Services, 1159 East Second Avenue, Salt Lake City UT 84103. **Tel** (801)532-3361.
Ind/Abst Archit. Period. Index (1979-May 1981).

US
UTAH STATE HISTORICAL SOCIETY NEWSLETTER. **Added/Corp** Utah State Historical Society. **VFOAT** Newsletter. (19??)-. Newsletter. English. Six times a year (Feb., Apr., June, Aug., Oct., Dec.). $20.00 Comes with Utah State Historical Society membership. Utah State Historical Society, 300 Rio Grande, Salt Lake City UT 84101. **Tel** (801)533-3500, FAX (801)533-3503. **LC** WMLC L 83/6538. ***Continues*** *Utah State Historical Society. Newsletter - Utah State Historical Society.*
Desc: Information of the society activities that they can enjoy.

CN/1183-1847
VALLEY (BURNSTOWN). (VALLEY.). [Valley]. Spring (1991)-. Periodical. English. qt. $2.95 per number. General Store Publishing House, 1 Main Street, Burnstown Ontario K0J 1G0 Canada. **DD** 971.3.

US/0734-5712
VALLEY FORGE JOURNAL, THE. [Valley Forge j.]. **Added/Corp** Valley Forge Historical Society. Vol. 1 No. 1 (June 1982)-. Periodical. English. Twice a year (June & Dec.). $10.00 Comes with Valley Forge Historical Society membership. Valley Forge Historical Society, Valley Forge PA 19481. **Tel** (215)884-0129. **ED** Lawrence Currey. **LC** F159.V18; V34. **DD** 973.3/341. **Bk Rev. Ad Acc. Circ:** 500 (ctrl). ***Continues*** *Picket Post, 0031-9619.*
Desc: Articles pertaining to American Revolution and other subjects relating to American history.
Ind/Abst Am. Hist. Life (1988-).

US/0740-4727
VALLEY JOURNAL, THE. Vol. 1 No. 1 (Summer 1983)-. Periodical. English. qt. The Valley Journal, Box 112, Plainfield PA 17081. **LC** F157.F8; V35. **DD** 974.8/44/005. ***Absorbed*** *Rosenberry Newsletter.*

US/0742-1818
VENTANA (NEW YORK, N.Y.), LA. (LA VENTANA / THE WINDOW.). [Ventana]. **VFOAT** Window. (1983-84)-. English (English). an. $15.00. La Ventana, 114 Liberty Street/Suite 204, New York NY 10016. **LC** E184.S75; V45. **DD** 973/.0468/0025.

US/0042-4161
VERMONT HISTORY. **Added/Corp** Vermont Historical Society. Vermont Historical Society. Proceedings. (1860)-. Academic Scholarly Publication. English. qt (4 issues). Comes with membership. Vermont Historical Society, Pavillion Building, 109 State Street, Montpelier VT 05602. **Tel** (802)828-2291. **ED** Gene Sessions. **LC** F46; .V55. **DD** 974.30062. Index available (bound in last issue). cum. index. **Bk Rev. Circ:** 2,500 (ctrl).
Desc: A scholarly journal of Vermont history that is available with Vermont Historical Society membership.
Ind/Abst Am. Hist. Life (1963-); Annu. Bibliogr. Engl. Lang. Lit.; West. Hist. Q.

US/0364-3387
VERMONT HISTORY NEWS. [Vt. hist. news]. **Added/Corp** Vermont Historical Society. (1976)-. Periodical. English. bm. $25.00 includes membership and Vermont History. Vermont Historical Society, Pavillion Building, 109 State Street, Montpelier VT 05602. **Tel** (802)828-2291. **ED** Michael Sherman. **LC** F46; .V5. **DD** 974.3/005. **Circ:** 2,500 (ctrl). ***Continues*** *News and Notes / Vermont Historial Society.*
Desc: A magazine featuring Vermont Historical Society news and articles on various aspects of Vermont history.
Ind/Abst Am. Hist. Life (1985-); West. Hist. Q. (19??-).

CN/0700-8171
VESTNIK CESKOSLOVENSKYCH SPOLKU V MONTREALE. V. 1- 1964-. Periodical. Czech. mo (June and September). Vestnik Ceskoslovenskych Spolku V Montreale, 4605 West Broadway Avenue, Montreal Quebec H4B 2A7 Canada. **Tel** (514)489-7712. **ED** Bohuslav Janicer. **DD** 971.4/281/0049186. **UDC** 971.4(=850). **Ad Acc. Circ:**

580 (ctrl).
Desc: Information bulletin of Czechoslovakia associations of Montreal.

CN/0843-4395
VICTORIA INSIDER. ***Ceased.*** (VICTORIA INSIDER : THE WEEKLY NEWSLETTER ON B.C. GOVERNMENT, POLITICS AND BUSINESS.). [Vic. insid.]. Vol. 1, No. 5 (Feb. 13, 1989)-(May 1994). Newsletter. English. Forty-two times a year. Maitland Publications, 7 Cook Street, Victoria BC V8V 3W6 Canada. **Tel** (604)360-4053, FAX (604)360-0548. **ED** John Twigg. **DD** 971.1/04/05. **Bk Rev**, (Qty: 3). **Ad Acc. Circ:** 75 (ctrl). ***Continues*** *Victoria Legislature Update, 0846-4413.*

US/1042-7597
VIETNAM GENERATION. [Vietnam gener.]. **Added/Corp** Vietnam Generation, Inc. **VFOAT** Viet Nam Generation. Vol. 1, No. 1 (Winter 1989)-. Periodical. English. Four times a year (Jan., Apr., Aug., Oct.). $40.00 (individual), $75.00 (institutions). Vietnam Generation, 18 Center Road, Woodridge CT 06525. **Tel** (203)387-6882, FAX (203)389-6104. **ED** Kali Tal and Dan Duffy. **LC** DS556; .V554. **DD** 959.704/3/05. **Bk Rev**, (Qty: 50+/yr). **Ad Acc. Pr Rev. Circ:** 400 (ctrl).
Desc: Important essays in all disciplines, representing a wide variety of critical methodologies and perspectives.
Ind/Abst Am. Hist. Life (1989-).

CN/0828-6183
VILLE DE JONQUIERE, VILLE A CONGRES ET TOURISTIQUE. [Ville Jonquiere ville congr. tour.]. **Main/Corp** Jonquiere (Quebec). 1983-. French. an. Free. Ville de Jonquiere Ville a Congres et Touristique, 2025 rue Masson, Montreal Quebec H2H 2P7 Canada. **DD** 971.4/16. **UDC** 971.4.

●US/1064-5691
VIRGINIA (BERRYVILLE, VA.). (VIRGINIA.). [Virginia]. **VFOAT** Virginia Magazine. Vol. 15, No. 1 (Summer 1992)-. Periodical. English. qt. The Country Publishers Inc., PO Box 778, Berryville VA 22611. **Tel** (703)955-1298. **DD** 975. ***Continues*** *Virginia Country, 0734-6603.*

US/0042-6474
VIRGINIA CAVALCADE. [Va. cavalcade]. **Added/Corp** Virginia State Library. Virginia State Library. History Division. Vol. 1, (Summer 1951)-. Periodical. English. Four times a year (Jan., Apr., July, Oct.). $6.00 (one year); $10.00 (two years). Virginia State Library and Archives, 11th Street at Capitol Square, Richmond VA 23219-3491. **Tel** (804)786-2329, FAX (804)225-4035. **ED** Edward D. C. Campbell Jr. **LC** F221; .V74. **DD** 975.5005. **Pr Rev. Circ:** 8,500 (ctrl). available on microfilm and microfiche from University Microfilms International (UMI).
Desc: This magazine covers areas of Virginia's history and culture.
Ind/Abst Access (1978-); Am. Hist. Life (1963-); Annu. Bibliogr. Engl. Lang. Lit.; MLA Int. Bibl. Books Artic. Mod. Lang. Lit.

US/1054-8351
VIRGINIA FACTS (DALLAS, TEX.). (VIRGINIA FACTS.). [Va. facts]. **VFOAT** Flying the Colors, Virginia Facts; Virginia Facts--Flying the Colors Series. (1991)-. English. te. $59.50 (single issue), $54.50 (discount if all state books are ordered). Clements Research II Inc., 16850 Dallas Parkway, Dallas TX 75248. **Tel** (214)931-9956, FAX (214)248-7159. **LC** F221; .V77. **DD** 975.5043/05.

US/0734-5089
VIRGINIA HISTORICAL ABSTRACTS. [Va. hist. abstr.]. **Added/Corp** Virginia History Services, Inc. Vol. 1, No. 1 (Jan./June 1982)-. English. ir. $18.00. Virginia History Services Inc, PO Box 3751, Arlington VA 22203. **Tel** (703)671-7189. **LC** F226; .V9. **DD** 016.9755/005.

US/0042-6636
VIRGINIA MAGAZINE OF HISTORY AND BIOGRAPHY, THE. [Va. mag. hist. biogr.]. (1893)-. Periodical. English. qt. $35.00. Virginia Historical Society, PO Box 7311, Richmond VA 23221-0311. **Tel** (804)358-4901, FAX (804)355-2399. **ED** Nelson D Lankford and Sara B Bearss. **LC** F221; .V91. **UDC** 975.5. Index available. **Bk Rev. Ad Acc. Circ:** 3,600 (ctrl). available on microfilm and microfiche from University Microfilms International (UMI). Documents available from The Genuine Article, UMI Article Clearinghouse.
Desc: Virginia History
Ind/Abst Acad. Search (July 1993-); Am. Hist. Life (1955-); Annu. Bibliogr. Engl. Lang. Lit.; Arts Humanit. Citation Index [Full Cov.]; Curr. Contents Arts Humanit.; Expand. Acad. Index (1989-); Hist. Source (July 1993-); Humanit. Index; Humanit. Source (Jul. 1993-); INFO-SOUTH Abstr.; Mag. Search; MLA Int. Bibl. Books Artic. Mod. Lang. Lit.; Newsp. Period. Abstr. (1991-); Res. Alert [Full Cov.]; Soc. Sci. Cit. Index [Select. Cov.]; West. Hist. Q.

US/0083-6524
VIRGINIA STATE LIBRARY PUBLICATIONS. No. 1 (1956)-. Monographic series. English. qt. Price varies per volume. Virginia Cavalcade, Virginia State Library, Richmond VA 23219. **Tel** (804)786-2312. **ED** Edward D C Campbell Jr. **DD** 975.5. **UDC** 975.5. **Circ:** 12,000 (ctrl).
Desc: Magazine of Virginia's history and culture, published by the Publications Branch of the Virginia State Library, Richmond.

BO
VISION BOLIVIANA. (19??)-. Periodical. Spanish. bm. 7.00 per copy. Calle Loayza 420, Casilla 2870, La Paz Bolivia. **LC** F3301; .V56. **DD** 984/.05.

US/1042-2161
VISIONS OF NEW MEXICO. ***Ceased.*** [Vis. N. M.]. **VFOAT** Visions; Visions Magazine. (Winter 1988/89)-?. Periodical. English. qt. Pan-American Publishing Company, PO Box 1505, Las Vegas NM 87701. **DD** 978.

CN/0824-5991
VISTI / (OSEREDOK UKRAINSKOI KULTURY I OSVITY. [Visti - Osered. ukr. kult. osv.]. **Added/Corp** Oseredok Ukrainskoi Kultury i Osvity. **VFOAT** News. **VAT** News - Ukrainian Cultural and Educational Centre. (19??)-. Periodical. Ukrainian (English; summaries and/or abstracts in English). ir. $20.00. Ukrainian Cultural And Educational Centre, 184 Alexander Avenue East, Winnipeg Manitoba R3B 0L6 Canada. **Tel** (204)942-0218. **DD** 971/.00491791/06071274. **Circ:** 2,000 (ctrl).
Desc: Newsletter of the Ukrainian Cultural and Educational Centre in Winnipeg, Canada. Provides information concerning membership, programming, and collections.

CN/1187-4988
VIVRE A PIERREFONDS. (LIFE IN PIERREFONDS.). [Vivre Pierrefonds]. **Added/Corp** Pierrefonds (Quebec). **VFOAT** Vivre a Pierrefonds. Vol. 14, No 2 (1991)-. Periodical. English (French). Free to residents. Ville de Pierrefonds, CP 2500, Pierrefonds Quebec H9N 4N2 Canada. **DD** 971.4. ***Continues*** *Bulletin (Pierrefonds (Quebec))., 0820-4942.*

CN/0713-8040
VOIX FRANCO-ONTARIENNE, LA. [Voix fr.-ont.]. Vol. 1, No. 1 (March 1982)-. Periodical. French. $20.00. Voix Franco-Ontarienne, 273 Chemin McArthur, Vanier Ontario K1L 6P3 Canada. **DD** 971.3/004114.

CN/0227-2067
VOIX MULTICULTURELLE, LA. [Voix multicult.]. V. 1- Spring 1980-. Periodical. French. qt. Confederation Des Associations Linguistiques Et Culturelles, De Quebec, Bureau 312, CP 771, 835 Rue Brown, Haute-Ville, Quebec G1R 4S7 Canada. **DD** 971.4/471004/05. **UDC** 908.714.

US/0042-904X
VOYAGEUR. (1965)-. Periodical. English. ir. Voyageur, Box 7246 Powderhorn Station, Minneapolis MN 55407. **LC** F551; .V6.

US/0198-7496
WAGNER LATIN AMERICAN NEWSLETTER, THE. Newsletter. English. bw. Wagner and Associates, 6405 East Prairie Street, Cottonwood MN 56229. **Tel** (507)537-6116. **ED** W Wagner. **UDC** 980-6; 908.8-6.

PR
WALKING TOURS & RESTAURANT MENU GUIDE. **VFOAT** Walking Tours and Restaurant Menu Guide; Walking Tours of San Juan. (19??)-. Periodical. English. sa. First Federal Building, Office 301, Santurce 00909 Puerto Rico. **Tel** (809)722-1767. **LC** F1981.S2; W34. **DD** 917.29504/53/05. ***Continues*** *Walking Tours of San Juan.*

US/1044-9078
WASHINGTON FACTS. [Wash. facts]. **VFOAT** Flying the Colors, Washington Facts; Washington Facts--Flying the Colors Series. (1989)-. English. te. $59.50. Clements Research II Inc., 16850 Dallas Parkway, Dallas TX 75248. **Tel** (214)931-9956, FAX (214)248-7159. **ED** John Clements. **LC** F886; .W245. **DD** 979.7/005.
Desc: Narrative description of state facts developed county-by-county.

US/1042-9719
WASHINGTON HISTORY. (WASHINGTON HISTORY : MAGAZINE OF THE HISTORICAL SOCIETY OF WASHINGTON, D.C.). [Wash. hist.]. **Added/Corp** Historical Society of Washington, D.C. Vol. 1, No. 1 (Spring 1989)-. Periodical. English. sa. $28.00. Historical Society of Washington DC, 1307 New Hampshire Avenue NW, Washington DC 20036-1507. **Tel** (202)785-2068. **LC** F194; .W36. **DD** 975.3/005. ***Continues*** *Records of the Columbia Historical Society, Washington, D.C., 0897-9049.*
Ind/Abst Am. Hist. Life (1989-).

US/0745-1520
WASSAJA (1982). ***Suspended.*** (WASSAJA.). [Wassaja]. **Added/Corp** American Indian Historical Society. Vol. 9, No. 1 (Sept./Oct. 1982)-(Aug. 1983). Periodical. English. bm. American Indian Historical Society, 1451 Masonic Avenue, San Francisco CA 94117. ***Continues*** *Wassaja. The Indian Historian, 0199-9052.*
Ind/Abst Soc. Work Abstr. (?-?); Mag. Index (Sept./Oct. 1982-?).

CN/0315-5021
WATERLOO HISTORICAL SOCIETY. (WATERLOO HISTORICAL SOCIETY : ANNUAL VOLUME.). **Added/Corp** Waterloo Historical Society (Ont.). Vol. 53 (1965)-. English. an. 15.00Can$. Waterloo Historical Society, c/o Kitchener Public Library, Grace Schmidt Room, 85 Queen Street North, Kitchener Ontario N2H 2H1, Canada. **Tel** FAX (519)570-1360. **LC** F1059.W32; W3. **DD** 971.3/44. Index available. cum. index. **Circ:** 1,000. ***Continues*** *Annual Volume of the Waterloo Historical Society, 0315-503X.*
Desc: History of the Waterloo Ontario area.

CN/0700-8163
WATNO DUR, THE. Vol. 1 (July 1973)-. Periodical. Panjabi. mo. $5.00. Watno Dur Punjabi, Post Box 1041, Coquitlam British Columbia Canada V3J 6Z4. **Tel** (604)734-1413. **DD** 971.1/004/9142.

US
WAVERLY GENEALOGICAL AND HISTORICAL SOCIETY NEWSLETTER.
See Genealogy and Heraldry.

US
WEATHERCOCK, THE. Periodical. English. sa. **LC** F128.1; .S193. **DD** 974.7/10043931. **UDC** 974.7.

CN/0083-8004
WENTWORTH BYGONES. **Added/Corp** Head-of-the-Lake Historical Society. No. 1 (1958)-. Monographic series. English. ir. Price varies per volume. Head of the Lake Historical Society, PO Box 896, Station A, Hamilton Ontario L8N 3P6 Canada. **Tel** (905)336-0317. **DD** 971.3/52/005.

US/0886-6155
WEST TEXAS HISTORICAL ASSOCIATION YEAR BOOK, THE. [West Tex. Hist. Assoc. year b.]. **Main/Corp** West Texas Historical Association, Abilene. **VFOAT** Year Book. V. 1-1925. English. an. $10.00. West Texas Historical Association, Hardin Simmons, University State 152, Abilene TX 79698. **Tel** (915)670-1239. **ED** Ken Jacobs. **LC** F381; .W53. **DD** 976. **UDC** 976.4(058). Index available. cum. index. **Bk Rev. Ad Acc. Circ:** 300. available on microfiche; available on microfilm.
Desc: We print articles that relate to the history of West Texas. They may be on any subject.
Ind/Abst Am. Hist. Life (1978-).

US/0043-325X
WEST VIRGINIA HISTORY. [W. Va. hist.]. **Added/Corp** West Virginia. Dept. of Archives and History. (Oct. 1939)-. Periodical. English. an (June). $12.00. Culture and History Archives / Charleston, History Section, 1900 Kanawha Boulevard East, Charleston WV 25305. **Tel** (304)558-0230. **ED** William T. Doherty. **LC** F236; .W52. **DD** 975.4005. Index available. **Bk Rev. Circ:** 1,000.
Desc: State journal of history, biography, genealogy, bibliography addresses, Appalachian region, economic and political development; Colonial, Civil War, social, cultural and military progress to the present.
Ind/Abst Am. Hist. Life (1962-); Annu. Bibliogr. Engl. Lang. Lit.; West. Hist. Q.

US/0049-7266
WESTCHESTER HISTORIAN, THE. [Westchest. hist.]. **Added/Corp** Westchester County Historical Society. (1955)-. Periodical. English. qt. $25.00 US; $30.00 other. Westchester County Historical Society, 2199 Saw Mill River Road, Elmsford NY 10523. **Tel** (914)592-4323. **ED** Karolyn Wrightson, Elizabeth G Fuller. **DD** 974. Index available. **Bk Rev. Ad Acc. Circ:** 800 (ctrl). ***Continues*** *Quarterly Bulletin of the Westchester County Historical Society.*
Desc: Contains illustrated articles on history of Westchester County. Its towns and villages, and its people. Subjects range from colonial period to the recent past. Also includes genealogical indexes.

US/0511-7445
WESTERN EXPLORER, THE. [West. explor.]. **Added/Corp** Cabrillo Historical Association. Vol 1 (Feb 1961)-. Periodical. English. **LC** F856; .C14. **DD** 917.
Ind/Abst Am. Hist. Life (1964-1966).

US/0083-887X
WESTERN FRONTIER LIBRARY, THE. English. ir. University of Oklahoma Press, PO Box 787, Norman OK 73070. **Tel** (800)627-7377, (405)325-2000. **UDC** 973-15.
Desc: Designed to introduce today's readers to the exciting events of our frontier past and to some of the memorable writings about them.

US/0083-8888
WESTERN FRONTIERSMAN SERIES. Vol. 1 (1937)-. Monographic series. English. ir. Price varies per volume. Arthur H. Clark Company, PO Box 14707, Spokane WA 99214. **Tel** (509)928-9540, (800)842-9286. **ED** Robert A. Clark. **Circ:** 1,000 (ctrl).
Desc: An ongoing series of books on the men and women who helped develop the American West.

US/0043-3810
WESTERN HISTORICAL QUARTERLY.
See History(General)-Abstracting, Bibliographies and Statistics.

US/0192-1355
WESTERN ILLINOIS REGIONAL STUDIES. ***Ceased.*** [West. Ill. reg. stud.]. Vol. 1 (Spring 1978)-Vol. 14 No. 2 (Jan. 1992). Periodical. English. sa. Western Illinois University, 114 Simpkins Hall, Macomb IL 61455. **Tel** (309) 298-2212, FAX (309) 298-2289. **ED** Bill Griffin. **LC** F536; .W47. **DD** 977.3/005. **UDC** 977.3. cum. index. **Bk Rev. Circ:** 300.
Desc: Studies of the history, literature, and culture of Western Illinois and adjacent areas.
Ind/Abst Am. Hist. Life (1978-); Annu. Bibliogr. Engl. Lang. Lit. (19??-19??); MLA Int. Bibl. Books Artic. Mod. Lang. Lit. (?-?).

●US/1072-6756
WESTERN KENTUCKY JOURNAL. [West. Ky. j.]. Vol. 1, No. 1 (Winter 1994)-. Periodical. English. qt. $21.05. Western Kentucky Journal, 300 West Water Street, Newburgh IN 47630. **Tel** (812)853-5562, (812)853-8092. **DD** 929.

US/0083-8934
WESTERN LANDS AND WATER SERIES. **VFOAT** Western Lands and Waters. Vol. 1 (1959)-. Monographic series. English. ir. Price varies per volume. Arthur H. Clark Company, PO Box 14707, Spokane WA 99214. **Tel** (509)928-9540, (800)842-9286. **ED** Robert H. Clark. **LC** UNC. cum. index. **Circ:** 1,000 (ctrl).
Desc: An ongoing series of books on the history of the land and water resources in the American West.

●US/1065-4011
WESTERN OBLATE STUDIES. **VFOAT** Etudes Oblates de l'Ouest. (1992)-. English. $29.95. Edwin Mellen Press, PO Box 450, Lewiston NY 14092. **Tel** (716)754-2788.

CN/0831-8891
WESTERN REPORT. [West. rep.]. Vol. 1, No. 1 (Jan. 27, 1986)-. Periodical. English. Forty-Five times a year. 73.83Can$ Canada; 144.92 US; $280.12 other. United Western Communications Ltd, 17327-106A Avenue, Edmonton Alberta T5S 1M7 Canada. **Tel** (403)486-2277. **DD** 971.2/005. **CODEN** WESRE9. available on microfilm and microfiche from Micromedia Limited.
Ind/Abst Acad. Abstr. (Jan. 1993-); Can. Index; Mag. Artic. Summar. CD-ROM (Jan. 1993-); Mag. Search; Vocat. Search (Jan. 1993-).

CN/0709-0455
WESTERN SIKH SAMACHAR. (THE WESTERN SIKH SAMACHAR.). **Added/Corp** Western Sikh Samachar Society. No. 70 (June 1978)-. Periodical. Panjabi (summaries and/or abstracts in English). mo. The Western Sikh Samachar, PO Box 67669 Station O, Vancouver British Columbia V5W 3V2 Canada. **DD** 971.1/004/91417. ***Continues*** *Canadian Sikh Samachar, 0700-8155.*

US/0300-6565
WHISPERING WIND. **See** Ethnic Interests.

US/0043-4906
WHITE COUNTY HERITAGE. [White Cty. herit.]. Vol.1 (June 1962)-. Periodical. English. an. $10.00. White County Historical Society, Box 537, Searcy AR 72143. **Tel** (501)268-8726. **ED** Cloie Presley. **LC** F417.W4; W48. **DD** 976.7/76/005. **UDC** 973.07. **Circ:** 75.
Desc: Provides information on the Civil War, settlements, customs, social life, business and churches.
Ind/Abst Am. Hist. Life.

US/0737-9218
WHITE HOUSE WEEKLY. [White House wkly.]. Vol. 1, No. 1 (Jan. 23, 1981)-. Periodical. English. Fifty times a year (Every Monday). $495.00. Feistritzer Publications, 4401A Connecticut Avenue Northwest, Suite 212, Washington DC 20008. **Tel** (202)362-3444, FAX (202)362-3493. **LC** E839.5; .W5. **DD** 973/.005.

US/0510-372X
WHITE RIVER VALLEY HISTORICAL QUARTERLY. (WHITE RIVER VALLEY HISTORICAL SOCIETY QUARTERLY.). [White River Val. hist. q.]. **Added/Corp** White River Valley Historical Society. Vol. 1, (Oct. 1961)-. Periodical. English. Four times a year. $16.00 Comes with White River Valley Historical Society Quarterly membership. White River Valley Historical Society, Box 555, Point Lookout MO 65726. **Tel** (417)748-2314. **ED** Lynn Morrow, (phone: (314)636-6041). **LC** F472.W5; W48. **DD** 977. **Circ:** 200.
Ind/Abst Ozark Period. Index.

CN/0700-9534
WHO? (SHERBROOKE). (WHO?). **VFOAT** Qui?. **VAT** Qui? (Sherbrooke). 1975/76-. Periodical. French (summaries and/or abstracts in English). $20.00 each number. Index des Adresses de Sherbrooke, 974 Ouest rue King, Sherbrooke Quebec J1H 1S2 Canada. **DD** 917.14/66. **UDC** 917.14(058.7).

US/0749-6427
WICAZO SA REVIEW. [Wicazo sa rev.]. **Added/Corp** Eastern Washington University. Indian Studies. Eastern Washington University. Native American Study Center. **VFOAT** Wicazo Sa. Vol. 1, No. 1 (Spring 1985)-. Periodical. English. Twice a year (June & Nov.). $20.00. Wicazo SA Review, Route 8 Box 510, Dakotah Meadows, Rapid City SD 57702. **Tel** (605)341-3228. **ED** Elizabeth Cook-Lynn (editor's address: 3755 Blake Court North, Rapid City, South Dakota 57701-4716). **LC** E96; .W5. **DD** 973/.0497/005. **Bk Rev. Ad Acc. Circ:** 600 (ctrl).
Desc: Publishes the scholarship useful to the development of the discipline of Native American studies.
Ind/Abst Am. Hist. Life (1985-); Curr. Index J. Educ. (March 1990); Ethnoarts Index; MLA Int. Bibl. Books Artic. Mod. Lang. Lit.

US/1046-4638
WILD WEST (LEESBURG, VA.). (WILD WEST.). [Wild west]. Vol. 1, No. 1 (June 1988)-. Periodical. English. bm. $18.95. Cowles Magazines, PO Box 8200, Harrisburg PA 17105. **Tel** (717)657-9555, (800)435-9610. **LC** F596; .W579. **DD** 978/.02/05. **Bk Rev.** available on microfilm from University Microfilms International (UMI).
Desc: Contains editorials regarding the old west.

US/0278-1603
WILDROWS. Vol. 1, No. 1 (Spring 1978)-. English. sa. Wildrows, 801 58th, Adel IA 50003. **LC** F629; .A25; W54. **DD** 977.7/57. **UDC** 977.7.

US/0043-5597
WILLIAM AND MARY QUARTERLY, THE. [William Mary q.]. **Added/Corp** Institute of Early American History and Culture (Williamsburg, Va.) College of William and Mary. 3rd Ser., Vol. 1 (Jan. 1944)-. Periodical. English. qt. $30.00 (institutions), $25.00 (individuals) US; $34.00 (institutions), $29.00 (individuals) other. Institute of Early American History and Culture, PO Box 8781, Williamsburg VA 23187-8781. **Tel** (804)221-1120, FAX (804)221-1047. **ED** Michael McGiffert. **LC** F221; .W71. **DD** 973. Index available. cum. index. **Bk Rev. Ad Acc. Circ:** 3,900 (ctrl). available on microfiche from KTO Microform; and Kraus Microform; available on microfilm and microfiche from University Microfilms International (UMI). Documents available from The Genuine Article, UMI Article Clearinghouse. ***Continues*** *William and Mary College Quarterly Historical Magazine.*
Desc: Early American history to 1815 and related history of the British Isles, the European continent and other areas of the New World.
Ind/Abst Abstr. Engl. Stud.; Acad. Abstr. Full Text Elite (July 1990-); Acad. Abstr. (July 1990-); Acad. Ind. [Computer File] (1987-); Acad. Search (July 1990-); Am. Hist. Life (1954-); Annu. Bibliogr. Engl. Lang. Lit.; Arts Humanit. Citation Index [Full Cov.]; Book Rev. Index; Curr. Contents Arts Humanit.; Expand. Acad. Index (1987-); Hist. Source (July 1993-); Humanit. Index; Humanit. Source (Jul. 1990-); Index Book Rev. Relig.; Index Book Rev. Humanit.; INFO-SOUTH Abstr.; Mag. Search; MLA Int. Bibl. Books Artic. Mod. Lang. Lit.; Newsp. Period. Abstr. (1991-); Recent. Publ. Artic.; Relig. Theol. Abstr. (199?-); Res. Alert [Full Cov.]; Romant. Move.; Soc. Sci. Humanit. Index; Soc. Sci. Cit. Index [Select. Cov.]; West. Hist. Q.; Women Stud. Abstr.; Writ. Am. Hist.

US
WILLIAMSBURG RESEARCH STUDIES. English. ir. University Press of Virginia, PO Box 3608, Charlottesville VA 22903. **Tel** (804)924-3469. ctrl circ.
Desc: Regional and local history monograph.

US/0739-232X
WIND RIVER RENDEZVOUS, THE. (WIND RIVER RENDEZVOUS.). **Added/Corp** Wind River Reservation. Saint Stephen's Indian Mission Foundation. **VFOAT** Rendezvous. (19??)-. English. qt. $10.00. St Stephens Indian Mission Foundation, PO Box 278, St Stephens WY 82524. **Tel** (307)856-6730.
Desc: Issues cover history and present activities of the Shoshone and Arapaho tribes and St Stephens Indian Mission as well as Wyoming history.

US/0734-0982
WISCONSIN ALMANAC, THE. Began with 1981. English. an. $6.95. J L Brekke, Route 1 Box 83, Taylors Falls MN 55084. **LC** F576; .W64. **DD** 977.5/005. **UDC** 977.5.

US/0743-7218
WISCONSIN BALTIC STUDIES. [Wis. Balt. stud.]. Monographic series. English. ir. Price varies per volume. University of Wisconsin/Baltic Studies Center, 1168 Van Hise Hall, 1200 Linden Drive, Madison WI 53706. **UDC** 908.474.

US/0043-6534
WISCONSIN MAGAZINE OF HISTORY. [Wis. mag. hist.]. **Added/Corp** State Historical Society of Wisconsin. Vol. 1 (Sept. 1917)-. Periodical. English. qt (4 issues). $30.00. State Historical Society of Wisconsin, 816 State Street, Madison WI 53706. **Tel** (608)264-6461, FAX (608)264-6404. **ED** Paul H. Hass. **LC** F576; .W7. **DD** 977.5005. Index available (free). cum. index. **Bk Rev. Pr Rev. Circ:** 6,000 (ctrl). available on microfilm and microfiche from University Microfilms International (UMI). ***Absorbed*** *State Historical Society of Wisconsin. Proceedings ... of the State Historical Society of Wisconsin, 0893-9632.*
Desc: Articles on the social, political, and economic history of the upper Midwest with emphasis on Wisconsin.
Ind/Abst Am. Hist. Life (1962-); Am. Bibliogr. Slavic East Europ. Stud.; Annu. Bibliogr. Engl. Lang. Lit.; Curr. Geogr. Publ. (199?-); MLA Int. Bibl. Books Artic. Mod. Lang. Lit.; Recent. Publ. Artic.; West. Hist. Q.; Writ. Am. Hist.

US
WRANGLER. **Main/Corp** Westerners. San Diego Corral. Vol. 1 (1968)-. Periodical. English. qt. $12.00. San Diego Corral, PO Box 87307, San Diego CA 92138. **Tel** (619)222-4491. **Bk Rev. Circ:** 300.
Desc: Strives to preserve in permanent form, research material relative to the cultural and historical background throughout the area commonly termed the West.

US/0275-9179
WYTHE COUNTY HISTORICAL REVIEW. (WYTHE COUNTY HISTORICAL REVIEW / WYTHE COUNTY HISTORICAL SOCIETY.). [Wythe Cty. hist. rev.]. **Added/Corp** Wythe County Historical Society. (July 1971)-. Periodical. English. sa. Wythe County Historical Society, 1635 West Main Street, Wytheville VA 24382. **Tel** (703)228-2715. **ED** William R. Grove. **LC** F232.W9; W94. **DD** 975.5/773/005. cum. index. **Circ:** 300.
Desc: Published by and for members of the Wythe County Historical Society, with special emphasis on Wythe County history; some material on southwest Virginia.
Ind/Abst Am. Hist. Life.

NQ
YA VEREMOS. Periodical. Spanish. mo. $15.00. Ediciones Ya Veremos, Apartado Postal 1302, Managua Nicaragua. **LC** F1528; .Y3. **DD** 972.8/005.

US/0084-3563
YALE WESTERN AMERICANA SERIES. No. 1 (1962)-. Monographic series. English. ir. Price varies per volume. Yale University Press, PO Box 209040, New Haven CT 06520. **Tel** (203)432-0940, (800)987-7323, FAX (203)432-0948.

US/0742-7638
YALOBUSHA PIONEER. **Added/Corp** Yalobusha County Historical Society. Vol. 1, No. 1 (Spring 1977)-. Periodical. English. qt. comes with membership. Yalobusha County Historical Society, RR 1, Box 15, Coffeeville MS 38922. **ED** A.C. Tatum. **LC** F347.Y15; Y36. **DD** 929/.1/072076282. Index available. cum. index. **Bk Rev. Circ:** 250.
Desc: Preserves and publishes all historical data relating to the surrounding area in and around Yalobusha County.

HO
YAXKIN. **See** Anthropology.

US/0739-8565
YEAR BOOK / DUTCHESS COUNTY HISTORICAL SOCIETY. **Main/Corp** Dutchess County Historical Society. **VFOAT** Yearbook. (1919)-. English. an. Dutchess County Historical Society, PO Box 88, Poughkeepsie NY 12602. **Tel** (914)471-1630. **Bk Rev. Ad Acc. Circ:** 1,000. ***Continues*** *Year Book of the Dutchess County Historical Society, 0739-8565.*
Desc: Scholarly and folk articles concerning the local history of Dutchess County, New York, from pre-Colonial days through the present.

US/0197-0291
YEAR BOOK - HISTORICAL SOCIETY OF HOPKINS COUNTY. **Main/Corp** Historical Society of Hopkins County (Kentucky). (1975)-. English. an. comes with membership. Historical Society of Hopkins County, 107 Union Street, Madisonville KY 42431. **Tel** (502)821-3986. **LC** F457.H8; H53a. **DD** 976.9/823/005.

US/0196-8866
YEAR BOOK - PERQUIMANS COUNTY HISTORICAL SOCIETY. **Main/Corp** Perquimans County Historical Society. 1958/59-. English. an. Secretary of Perquimans County Historical Society, PO Box 652, Hertford NC 27944. **LC** F262.P4; P47A. **DD** 975.6/144/005. **UDC** 975.6(058). Each issue contains an index to its own contents (no volume index)--loose.

US/0882-2328
YEARBOOK / GENERAL SOCIETY OF COLONIAL WARS. [Yearb. - Soc. Colon. Wars (U.S.)]. **Main/Co:p** General Society of Colonial Wars (U.S.). 1976-. English. an. Society of Colonial Wars / New York, 122 East 58th Street, New York NY 10022. **Tel** (212)755-7082. **LC** E186.3; .A37. **UDC** 973.02(058). ***Continues*** *General Society of Colonial Wars.*

US/0741-2827
YEARBOOK OF GERMAN-AMERICAN STUDIES. [Yearb. Ger.-Am. stud.]. **Added/Corp** Society for German-American Studies (U.S.). Max Kade Document and Research Center. **VFOAT** Yearbook of German American Studies; Year Book of German American Studies. Vol. 16 (1981)-. Academic Scholarly

Publication. English (German). an. $25.00 North America, $30.00 other (institutions); $20.00 North America, $25.00 others (individuals) Comes with Society for German American Studies membership. Society for German-American Studies, 500 Belmont Road, c/o Wiliam Roba, Bettendorf IA 52722. **Tel** (319)359-7531. **ED** Helmut Huelsbergen and William Keel. **LC** E184.G3; G315. **DD** 973/.0431. Index available. cum. index. **Bk Rev. Ad Acc. Circ:** 500 (ctrl). ***Continues*** *Journal of German-American Studies, 0195-5381.*
Desc: Scholarly articles on all aspects of German culture in America.
Ind/Abst Am. Hist. Life (1987-); MLA Int. Bibl. Books Artic. Mod. Lang. Lit.

US/0519-3117
YEARBOOK, WITH HISTORICAL AND GENEALOGICAL JOURNAL. Main/Corp Atlantic County (N.J.) Historical Society. (195?)-. English. an. $10.00. Atlantic County Historical Society, PO Box 301, Somers Point NJ 08244. **Tel** (609)927-5218. **ED** R. Craig Koedel. **LC** F142.A8; A83. **DD** 974.9/84. **Circ:** 500. ***Continues*** *Atlantic County Historical Society. Yearbook, with Historical and Genealogical Data.*
Desc: Covers local history and genealogy.

CN/0318-5494
YESTERDAY'S NEWS. V. 1- Dec. 1974-. Periodical. English. West Hants Historical Society, PO Box 878, Windsor Nova Scotia B0N 2T0 Canada. **DD** 971.6/35. **UDC** 971.6.

US/0513-2673
YONKERS HISTORICAL BULLETIN. Added/Corp Yonkers Historical Society. Vol. 2, No. 1 (April 1954)-. English. an. Yonkers Historical Society, 191 Park Avenue #21, Ms. Glaeser, Yonkers NY 10703. ***Continues*** *Yonkers Historical Society Bulletin.*
Ind/Abst Am. Hist. Life.

CN/0513-2711
YORK PIONEER, THE. Added/Corp York Pioneer and Historical Society. (1955)-. Periodical. English. an. 13.00Can$ US & Canada; 15.00Can$ ordinary, 18.00Can$ family & corporate, 65.00Can$ sustaining 115.00Can$ benefactor, (one year subscription for York Pioneer and Historical Society Membership). York Pioneer & Historical Society, PO Box 45026, Toronto Ontario M4P 3E3 Canada. **Tel** (416)489-4188. **ED** Jeanine C. Avigdor, (editor's address: 61 Thorncrest Road, Etobicoke Ontario, M9A 158, phone: (416)231-1829). **DD** 971.3/54/005. (under preparation). **Circ:** 500.
Desc: A selection of short articles on Ontario history, intended for the interested amateur.

CN/0822-2517
YORKVIEW. [Yorkview]. Nov. 1983-. Periodical. English. bm. Free. Yorkview, c/o Alcoma Communications, 40 McPherson Street, Markham Ontario L3R 3V6 Canada. **DD** 971.3/547. **UDC** 971.3. ctrl circ.

AU
ZEITSCHRIFT FUER LATEINAMERIKA. Added/Corp Osterreichisches Lateinamerika-Institut. (1971)-. German.
Ind/Abst HAPI Hisp. Am. Period. Index (19??-).

CN/0700-5172
ZVAZAJ. (ZVAZHAI.). **VFOAT** Svazhay. Vol. 1- List. 1974-. Periodical. Belorussian (English and Russian). qt. 5.00Can$ Canada; $6.00 US. Liaison Committee of Byelorussian War Veterans, 57 Riverdale Avenue, Toronto Ontario M4K 1C2 Canada. **Tel** (416)461-3992. **ED** Kastus Akula. **DD** 971/.004/91799. **UDC** 947.6. **Bk Rev. Circ:** 500.
Desc: Strives to present Byelorussian general and especially military history in capsule. Present activities of Byelorussian war veterans features as a priority.

HISTORY OF THE MIDDLE EAST

SU
AL-ARAB. Periodical. Arabic. mo. 35 riyals. Al-Arab, King Faysal Street, Al-Riyad Saudi Arabia. **LC** DS161; .A615. **UDC** 953.2.

SY
AL-ARD. Added/Corp Muassasat Al-Ard Lil-Dirasat al-Filastiniyah. (Sept. 21, 1973)-. Periodical. Arabic. bw. PO Box 3392, Dimashq Syria. **LC** DS126.5; .A79.

FR
AL-BAHITH. VFOAT Al-Baheth. Periodical. Arabic. bm. 180.00F. S A R L Sosep, 116 Avenue des Champs Elysees, 75008 Paris France. **LC** DS36; .B33.

UK
AL-BAHITH AL-ARABI. VFOAT Arab Researcher. No. 1 (Aug. 1984)-. Periodical. Arabic (English). qt. $6.00 single issue. 5 Belgrave Square, London SW1X 8PH England. **LC** DS36; .B34.

SU
AL-DARAH. Vol. 1 (March 1975)-. Periodical. Arabic (summaries and/or abstracts in English). qt. 20 riyals; $6.00 US. Darat Al-Malik Abd Al-Aziz, PO Box 2945, Riyadh 11461 Saudi Arabia. **Tel** 4412316 / 4412317, FAX 00966/1/4417020. **ED** Mohammad H. Zaidan and Abdullah H. Al-Hoqail. **LC** DS201; .D37. Index available. cum. index. **Bk Rev. Ad Acc. Circ:** 13,000 (ctrl).
Ind/Abst Middle East J.

QA
AL-DAWHAH. Added/Corp Qatar. Wizarat al-Ilam. **VFOAT** Aldoha. (19??)-. Periodical. Arabic. mo. Wizarat Al-Ilam, PO Box 2324 Qatar, Al-Dawhah Qatar. **LC** DS247Q3; D38.

LE
AL-DIYAR. Periodical. Arabic. 1.50 single issue. Sharikat Al-Diyar Al-Sihafiyah, PO Box 959, Beirut Lebanon. **LC** DS80.A2; D58. **UDC** 956.93.

US/8750-4952
AL-MUBTAATH. [Mubtaath]. **VFOAT** Mubtaath Magazine. Periodical. Arabic. mo. Free to Saudi Arabian Students. Al-Mubtaath Magazine, c/o Saudi Arabian Ed Mission, 601 New Hampshire Avenue NW, Washington DC 20037. **DD** 956. **UDC** 953.

KU
AL-MUJTAMA. V. 1- March 17, 1970-. Periodical. Arabic. wk. Jamiyat Al-Islah Al-Ijtimai, PO Box 4850, Al-Kuwayt Kuwait. **LC** DS41; .M84. **UDC** 953.68.

LE
AL-MUSAWWAR AL-JADID. (19??)-. Periodical. Arabic. wk. +L150.00. Adnan Hammudah, Nasif Al-Yaziji Street, Senaf Building/5th Floor, PO Box 5510 & 9503, Beirut Lebanon. **LC** DS36; .M697.

LE
AL-MUSTAQBAL AL-ARABI. Added/Corp Markaz Dirasat al-Wahdah al-Arabiyah (Beirut, Lebanon). **VFOAT** Arab Future. Vol. 1 (August 1978)-. Periodical. Arabic. mo. $60.00 (Arab countries), $80.00 (Europe, Cyprus, Iran, & Turkey), $90.00 (other) individual; $100.00 (Arab countries), $120.00 (other) institution. Centre for Arab Unity Studies, PO Box 113, 6001 Beirut, Lebanon. **LC** DS36; .M75.

LE
AL-NIDA. Periodical. Arabic. £L150.00. Shari Al-Mazraah, Milk Al-Ghandur, Raqm 35, PO Box 4744, Beirut Lebanon. **LC** DS80.A2; N54.

LE
AL-QAWMI AL-ARABI. Periodical. Arabic. wk. Kurnish Al-Mazraah, S B 13520 Shuran, Beirut Lebanon. **LC** DS63.1; .Q38.

LE
AL-QUDS. Periodical. Arabic. £L200.00. Binayat Al-Nasr Shari Sulayman Al-Bustani, PO Box 11/6071, Beirut Lebanon. **LC** DS41; .Q37.

QA
AL-RAYYAN / YUSDIRUHA MATHAF QATAR AL-WATANI BI-AL-DAWHAH. VFOAT Arrayan. Periodical. Arabic (summaries and/or abstracts in English). Rais Tahrir Al-Sahifah Al-Ilmiyah Mathaf Qatar Al-Watani, PO Box 879, Al-Dawhah Qatar. **LC** DS247.O63; R39.

SU
AL-SHARQ. V. 1- May 1978-. Periodical. Arabic. wk. 200 riyals 00 qursh. Al-Sharikah Al-Sharqiyah Lil-Sihafah Wa-Al-Tibaah Wa-Al-Ilam Shari Al-Amir Muhammad Imarat Al-Zamil, PO Box 2662-2663, Al-Damman 31461 Saudi Arabia. **Tel** (03)8571011, FAX (03)8578055. **ED** Ahmed Bin Abdulrahman Al Ghamdi and Abdul Wahab Al Aswani. **LC** DS247.S62; A27. **Bk Rev. Ad Acc. Circ:** 25,000. available on microfiche; available on microfilm; available on CD-ROM; available on diskette; available in microform.

IQ
AL-TAHRIR. VFOAT Tahreer. No. 1- May 1972-. Periodical. Arabic. mo. Al-Jabhah Al-Muttahidah Li-Tahrir Al-Sumal Al-Gharbi, PO Box 3067, Baghdad Iraq. **LC** DT411; .T34.

SU
AL-YAMAMAH. Periodical. Arabic. wk. 120 riyals. PO Box 4057, Al-Riyad Saudi Arabia. **LC** DS36; .Y35. **UDC** 953.2.

KU
AL-YAQZAH. VFOAT Yaqza. (1967)-. Periodical. Arabic. wk. Al-Yaqza, PO Box 6000, Safat Kuwait. **Tel** 011 965 614808. **LC** DS36; .Y36.

IR/0378-4215
ACTA IRANICA. DEUXIEME SERIE. HOMMAGES ET OPERA MINORA. (197?)-. Monographic series. Multiple languages. ir. Price varies per volume. E. J. Brill, Postbus 9000, 2300 PA Leiden Netherlands. **Tel** 011 31 71 312624, FAX 011 31 71 317532, telex 39296 BRILL NL. **UDC** 8. **Pr Rev.**

US/0732-6505
AIDS AND RESEARCH TOOLS IN ANCIENT NEAR EASTERN STUDIES. (AIDS AND RRESEARCH TOOLS IN ANCIENT NEAR EASTERN STUDIES : ARTANES.). [Aids res. tools anc. Near East. stud.]. **Added/Corp** International Institute for Mesopotamian Area Studies. **VFOAT** ARTANES; ARTANES, Aids and Research Tools in Ancient Near Eastern Studies. No. 1 (1977)-. Monographic series. English. ir. Price varies per volume. Undena Publications, PO Box 97, Malibu CA 90265. **Tel** (310)649-2612. **(Subscription address:** Crescent Academic Services, 29528 Madera Avenue, Shafter, CA 93263) **ED** G. Buccellati. **DD** 915. **Circ:** 300.
Desc: Practical volumes for teaching and research in ancient Near Eastern studies.

CN
AL-HILAL. VFOAT Hilal. (September 1892)-. Arabic (English). Twelve times a year. 24.00Can$. Al Hilal, 338 Hollyberry Trail, Willowdale Ontario M2H 2P6 Canada. **Tel** (416)493-4374, FAX (416)493-4374. **ED** Umme Ali. **LC** AP95.A6; H5. Index available in last issue of volume--attached. **Bk Rev. Ad Acc, Adv Mgr:** L. Owaisi. **Circ:** 5,000.
Desc: Covers all aspects of cultural life in the Arab world.

MR
AL-ISLAM AL-YAWM. Added/Corp ISESCO (Organization). **VFOAT** Islam Aujourd'Hui; Islam Today. Vol. 1, No. 1 (April 1983)-. Periodical. Arabic (English and French). sa. $12.00. Al Islam al Yawm / Islam Today, PO Box 755, 16 Mukarrar Sharia, Agdal al Rabat Morocco. **Tel** 011 212 7 72433, telex 326.45 M. **LC** DS35.3; .I83. **Circ:** 7,000.
Desc: Contains surveys about Islamic and education sciences and culture. Publishes two periodical reviews of the activities and programs of the Islamic educational, scientific and cultural organization.
Ind/Abst Middle East J.

IS
APRIL 17. Newsletter. English (Hebrew and Arabic). Alternative Information Center, PO Box 31417, Jerusalem Israel. **Tel** 011 00972 2 241159, 011 00972 2 253151, FAX 011 00972 2 253151.
Desc: Concerned with the urgent problems facing Palestinian political prisoners and reporting on local and international support campaigns.

US/0271-3519
ARAB STUDIES QUARTERLY. [Arab stud. q.]. Vol. 1 (Winter 1979)-. Academic Scholarly Publication. English. qt. $40.00 (institutions) US and Canada. Association of Arab-American University Graduates, PO Box 408, Normal IL 61761. **Tel** (309)452-6588. **ED** S K Farsoun Said. **LC** DS36; .A715. **DD** 909/0974927. **UDC** 950-011; 953; 930.85(=927). **Bk Rev. Ad Acc. Circ:** 2,000 (ctrl). Documents available from UMI Article Clearinghouse.
Desc: Scholarly journal which deals with Middle East history, economics, politics and culture.
Ind/Abst Acad. Search (July 1993-); Am. Hist. Life (1979-); Expand. Acad. Index (1992-); Hum. Rights Intern. Rep.; Humanit. Source (Jul. 1993-); Index Islam. Lit.; INFO-SOUTH Abstr.; Int. Bibliogr. Sociol.; Int. Polit. Sci. Abstr.; Mag. Search; Middle East Abstr. Index; Newsp. Period. Abstr. (1989-); PAIS Int. Print (1991-); Middle East J.

KE
ARAB WORLD, THE. Periodical. Multiple languages (English and Swahili). bm. Kenya League of Arab States, PO Box 30770, Nairobi Kenya. **LC** DS36; .A742. **DD** 909/.09/74927. **UDC** 930.9(53); 930.85(=927).

IT
ARABIA SAUDITA OGGI. ***Ceased.*** **Added/Corp** Saudi Arabia. Safarah (Italy). (19??)-?. Periodical. Italian. mo. Ambasciata Dell'Arabia Saudita, Rome 00198 Italy. **LC** DS201; .A69.

NE/0570-5398
ARABICA. [Arabica]. Vol. 1 (Jan. 1954)-. Academic Scholarly Publication. French (English, German and Arabic). Three times a year. Fl180.00 (institutions) Netherlands; $103.00 (institutions) other. E. J. Brill, Postbus 9000, 2300 PA Leiden Netherlands. **Tel** 011 31 71 312624, FAX 011 31 71 317532, telex 39296 BRILL NL. **ED** M. Arkoan. **LC** PJ6001; .A7. **DD** 492/.7/05. **[CCC]. Bk Rev. Ad Acc. Circ:** 575 (ctrl).
Desc: Focuses on multidisciplinary studies of ancient and contemporary problems concerning Arabic societies. Each issue contains a critical bulletin providing comprehensive information on the scholarly production and news of the world of Arabists.
Ind/Abst Am. Hist. Life (1966-1984); Index Islam. Lit.; Index Book Rev. Relig.; MLA Int. Bibl. Books Artic. Mod. Lang. Lit.; Numis. Lit.; Relig. Index One Period.; Middle East J.

UK/0959-4213
ARAM PERIODICAL. [ARAM Period.]. **Added/Corp** AM Society for Syro-Mesopotamian Studies. (1989)-. English. sa. £27.00. ARAM Periodical, Oriental Institute, Pusey Lane, Oxford OX1 2LE England. **Tel** 011 44 865 514041, FAX 011 44 865 516824. **ED** Dr. Shafiq Abouzayd. **DD** 956. **Pr Rev.**
Desc: Newsletter concerned with all aspects of

Syro-Mesopotamian cultures. Does not confine itself soley to Aramaic culture, but attempts to deal with all cultures of the geographical area influenced by Aramaic culture.

US/1044-1891
ARAMCO WORLD (1987). (ARAMCO WORLD.). [Aramco world]. **Added/Corp** Arabian American Oil Company. **VFOAT** ARAMCO World Magazine. **VAT** Arabian American Oil Company World. Vol. 38, No. 5 (Sept./Oct. 1987)-. Periodical. English. Six times a year. Free. ARAMCO Services Company, PO Box 2106, Public Affairs Department, Houston TX 77252. **Tel** (713)432-4147. **ED** Robert Arndt, (phone: (713)432-4425). **DD** 953. Index available. cum. index. **Circ:** 180,000 (ctrl). ***Continues*** *ARAMCO World Magazine, 0146-4132.*
Desc: Covers the history, culture, geography, natural history, and economic of the Arab and Muslim worlds, with special emphasis on the Middle East. It is nonpolitical, beautifully illustrated and widely used as supplementary material for students at junior-high to university levels.
Ind/Abst Energy Inf. Abstr.; Index Free Period.

IS
ARTICLE 17. Newsletter. English (Hebrew). Alternative Information Center, PO Box 31417, Jerusalem Israel. **Tel** 011 00972 2 241159, 011 00972 2 253151, FAX 011 00972 2 253151.
Desc: Deals with problems regarding Palestinians' resident status and family reunification in the occupied territories.

US/1058-644X
BIBLIOGRAPHIC GUIDE TO MIDDLE EASTERN STUDIES. [Bibliogr. guide Middle East. stud.]. **VFOAT** Middle Eastern Studies; Bibliographic Guide Middle East Studies; A.Bibliographic guide. P.Middle Eastern studies. (1990)-. English. $190.00. GK Hall & Co, 100 Front Street, Riverside NJ 08075. **Tel** (800)257-5755 ext. 2223. **DD** 956.

UK
BRITISH JOURNAL OF MIDDLE EASTERN STUDIES. **Added/Corp** British Society for Middle Eastern Studies. Vol. 18, No. 1 (1991)-. Periodical. English. sa. £20.00 UK; $40.00 US; £20.00 other. British Society for Middle Eastern Studies, Department of Politics, University of Exeter, Exeter EX4 4RJ England. **Tel** 011 44 392 263186. **ED** Paul Starkey. **LC** DS61.9.G7; B75a. **DD** 956/.005. Index available. **Bk Rev.** **Ad Acc.** **Pr Rev.** **Circ:** 1,000. ***Continues*** *British Society for Middle Eastern Studies. Bulletin - British Society for Middle Eastern Studies.*
Desc: Middle East oriented studies.
Ind/Abst Middle East J.

JA
CHUTO KENKYU. **Added/Corp** Chuto Chosakai. **VFOAT** Journal of Middle Eastern Studies. (1957)-. Periodical. Japanese. mo. $278.00. **(Subscription address:** Japan Publications Trading Company, Ltd., PO Box 5030, Tokyo International, Tokyo 100-31 Japan.**)** **LC** DS41; .C47.

NE
COPTIC STUDIES. **VFOAT** CS; C.S. Vol. 1 (1978)-. Monographic series. English (French and German). ir. Price varies per volume. E. J. Brill, Postbus 9000, 2300 PA Leiden Netherlands. **Tel** 011 31 71 312624, FAX 011 31 71 317532, telex 39296 BRILL NL.
Desc: Series covering Coptic philology.

NE/0929-0761
DEAD SEA DISCOVERIES. **See** Religion and Theology.

FR/0765-1074
DIRASAT KURDIYAH. **VFOAT** Mutalaat Kurdi; Studia Kurdica. 1 (Jan. 1984)-. Periodical. Arabic. 30.00F single issue. Studia Kurdica, Institut Kurde de Paris, 106 rue Lafayette, 75010 Paris France. **Tel** (01)48246464. **ED** Siyamend Othman. **LC** DS51.K7; D57. **Bk Rev.** **Circ:** 2,000.
Ind/Abst Middle East J.

●US/1060-4367
DOMES (MILWAUKEE, WIS.). (DOMES.). [Domes]. **Added/Corp** University of Wisconsin-Milwaukee. School of Library and Information Science. **VFOAT** Digest of Middle East Studies. (1992)-. Periodical. English. Four times a year (Winter, Spring, Summer, Fall). $50.00 one year; $90.00 two years. University of Wisconsin - Milwaukee / School of Library and Information Science, Box 413, Milwaukee WI 53201. **Tel** (414)229-4707, FAX (414)229-4848, telex 4909991372. **ED** Mohammed M. Aman. **LC** DS41; .D66. **DD** 956. **Bk Rev**, (Qty: 60/year). **Ad Acc.** **Pr Rev.** ctrl circ.
Desc: A review in English of all subjects relating to Islam and the Middle East, including Israel and all Arab and other Islamic countries.

US
EDEBIYAT: JOURNAL OF MIDDLE EASTERN LITERATURES. **See** Literature.

US/0736-945X
EGYPT THEN AND NOW. [Egypt then now]. **Added/Corp** Egypt. Safarah (U.S.). Cultural and Educational Bureau. (19??)-. Periodical. English. qt. Free. Cultural and Educational Bureau of the Embassy of Egypt in the USA, 2200 Kalorama Road NW, Washington DC 20008. **Tel** (202)265-6400. **ED** Abdessalam Diab. **LC** DT70; .E395. **DD** 962/.005. **Circ:** 2,000 (ctrl).
Desc: Strives to inform and educate the public about the interesting, unique facets of Egyptian culture and history along with the general educational system of Egypt.

AT
FAIROUZ. (19??)-. Arabic. mo. 102.00Aus$. Mid East Link Pty Ltd., 6 61 63 Haldon Street, Lakemba NSW 2195, Australia. **Tel** 11 61 2 7582444, FAX 11 61 2 7582799.

NE/0169-9423
HANDBUCH DER ORIENTALISTIK, 1. ABT. DER NAHE UND DER MITTLERE OSTEN. (HANDBUCH DER ORIENTALISTIK. ERSTE ABTEILUNG, NAHE UND DER MITTLERE OSTEN.). [Handb. Orient., 1. Abt. Nahe Mittl. Osten]. (1952)-. Monographic series. German. ir. Price varies per volume. E. J. Brill, Postbus 9000, 2300 PA Leiden Netherlands. **Tel** 011 31 71 312624, FAX 011 31 71 317532, telex 39296 BRILL NL.

US
HARVARD MIDDLE EASTERN STUDIES. **Added/Corp** Harvard University. Center for Middle Eastern Studies. (1958)-. Monographic series. English. ir. Price varies per volume. Harvard University Press, 79 Garden Street, Cambridge MA 02138. **Tel** (617)496-1344, (800)448-2242.

US/0887-9044
IDOC MIDDLE EAST QUARTERLY. [IDOC Middle East q.]. **Added/Corp** Arab-Israeli Research and Relations Project. No. 1 (Jan. 1974)-. Periodical. English. qt. **DD** 956.
Ind/Abst Am. Hist. Life (1974).

FR/0761-1285
INFORMATION AND LIAISON BULLETIN / INSTITUT KURDE DE PARIS. July 1983-. Bulletin. English (French, German and Italian). bm. Studia Kurdica, Institut Kurde de Paris, 106 rue Lafayette, 75010 Paris France. **Tel** (01)48246464. **LC** DS59.K86; I53.

US/0740-5375
INTERNATIONAL JOURNAL OF ISLAMIC AND ARABIC STUDIES. [Int. j. Islam. Arab. Stud.]. **Added/Corp** International Institute of Islamic and Arabic Studies. **VFOAT** Majallat Mahad Al-Dirasat Al-Islamiyah Wa-Al-Arabiyah Al-Alami. (1984)-. Periodical. English (Arabic, French and German). Twice a year. $30.00. International Institute of Islamic and Arabic Studies, PO Box 5482, Bloomington IN 47402. **Tel** (812)339-6180. **ED** Salman H. Al-Ani. **DD** 909. Index available. cum. index. **Ad Acc.** **Pr Rev.** **Circ:** 2,400 (ctrl).
Ind/Abst Geogr. Abstr. Human Geogr. (?-?); Index Islam. Lit.; Middle East J.

●US/1073-6697
INTERNATIONAL JOURNAL OF KURDISH STUDIES, THE. [Int. j. Kurd. stud.]. **Added/Corp** Kurdish Library (Brooklyn, New York, N.Y.). Vol. 6, No. 1 & 2 (1993)-. Periodical. English. Twice a year. $50.00. The Kurdish Library, 345 Park Place, Brooklyn NY 11238. **Tel** (718)783-7930. **LC** DS51.K7; K885. **DD** 956.1/0049159. ***Continues*** *Kurdish Studies, 1070-0870.*

UK/0020-7438
INTERNATIONAL JOURNAL OF MIDDLE EAST STUDIES. [Int. j. Middle East stud.]. Vol. 1, No. 1 (Jan. 1970)-. Academic Scholarly Publication. English. ir (6 issues). $131.00 US, Canada & Mexico; £86.00 other. Cambridge University Press, The Edinburgh Building, Shaftesbury Road, Cambridge CB2 2RU United Kingdom. **Tel** 011 44 223 312393, FAX 011 44 223 325959. **(Subscription address:** Cambridge University Press / North America, 110 Midland Avenue, Port Chester NY 10573.**)** **ED** Leila Fawaz. **LC** DS41; .I55. **DD** 915.6/03/305. **[CCC].** **Bk Rev.** **Pr Rev.** available on microfilm and microfiche from University Microfilms International (UMI). Documents available from The Genuine Article, UMI Article Clearinghouse.
Desc: Publishes original research on the political, social and cultural history of the Middle East from the seventh century to the present day. Also covers Spain, south-east Europe and the Soviet Union for the periods in which their territories were under the influence of Middle Eastern civilization. Particular attention is paid to the history, politics, economics, anthropology, sociology, literature and folklore of the area and to comparative religion, theology, law and philosophy.
Ind/Abst ABC POL SCI; Abstr. Anthropol.; Acad. Ind. [Computer File] (1992-); Acad. Search (Jan. 1994-); Am. Hist. Life (1970-); Arts Humanit. Citation Index [Select. Cov.]; Curr. Contents Soc. Behav. Sci.; Expand. Acad. Index (1989-); Geogr. Abstr. Human Geogr.; Index Islam. Lit.; INFO-SOUTH Abstr.; Int. Dev. Abstr.; Int. Polit. Sci. Abstr.; Leis. Recreat. Tour. Abstr.; Middle East Abstr. Index; MLA Int. Bibl. Books Artic. Mod. Lang. Lit.; Newsp. Period. Abstr. (1991-); Res. Alert [Full Cov.]; Rural Dev. Abstr.; Soc. Sci. Source (Jul. 1993-); Soc. Sci. Cit. Index [Full Cov.]; Soc. Sci. Index; Soc. Sci. Index Fulltext (Nov. 1988-) [Full Txt.]; Middle East J.; U.S. Polit. Sci. Doc.; World Agric. Econ.

US/0971-5223
INTERNATIONAL JOURNAL OF PUNJAB STUDIES. English. sa (Apr. and Oct.). $67.00. SAGE Periodical Press, 2455 Teller Road, Thousand Oaks CA 91320. **Tel** (805)499-0721, FAX (805)499-0871, telex 100799.

US/0892-4147
IRAN NAMEH. BUNYAD-I MUTALAAT-I IRAN. [Iran namah]. **Added/Corp** Foundation for Iranian Studies (Washington, D.C.). **VFOAT** Iran Nameh. Vol. 1 No. 1 (Autumn 1982)-. Periodical. English (Persian). Four times a year (Jan., Apr., July, Oct.). $35.00 (individual); $65.00 (institution). Foundation for Iranian Studies, 4343 Montgomery Avenue, Suite 200, Bethesda MD 20814. **Tel** (301)657-1990, FAX (310)657-4381. **ED** Hormoz Hekmat. **LC** DS251; .I72. cum. index. **Bk Rev**, (Qty: 8-10). **Ad Acc.** **Circ:** 1,000 (ctrl).
Ind/Abst Middle East J.

IR
IRAN YEARBOOK. English. Kayhan Research Association, Tehran Iran. **LC** DS251; .I755. **DD** 955/.05. **UDC** 955.

US/0021-0862
IRANIAN STUDIES. (IRANIAN STUDIES : BULLETIN OF THE SOCIETY FOR IRANIAN CULTURAL AND SOCIAL STUDIES.). [Iran. stud.]. **Added/Corp** Society for Iranian Studies. Society for Iranian Cultural and Social Studies. Vol. 1, No. 1 (Winter 1967)-. Periodical. English (French and German). Four times a year (Jan., Apr., July, Oct.). $40.00 (one year); $75.00 (two years). Society for Iranian Studies / Columbia University, 420 West 118th Street, Room 112 S1A, New York NY 10027. **Tel** (212)854-2584. **ED** Abbas Amanat (editor's address: PO Box 1504, Yale Station, Yale University, Department of History, Haven, CT 06520, phone: (203)432-1354). **DD** 915.5/003. **CODEN** IRSTEK. Index available. cum. index. **Bk Rev.** **Ad Acc.** **Pr Rev.** **Circ:** 500.
Ind/Abst Am. Hist. Life (1987-); Anthropol. Lit.; Middle East Abstr. Index; MLA Int. Bibl. Books Artic. Mod. Lang. Lit.; Middle East J.

US/0270-840X
IRANIAN STUDIES SEMINAR, ANNUAL PROCEEDINGS. [Iran. stud. semin., annu. proc.]. **Main/Corp** Iranian Studies Seminar (University of Pennsylvania). **Added/Corp** Iranian Studies Seminar (University of Pennsylvania) Annual Proceedings. (19??)-. English. an. Free. Iranian Studies Seminar, 325 University Museum/F1, University of Pennsylvania, Philadelphia PA 19174. **LC** DS251.5; .I58a. **DD** 955.

UK/0021-0889
IRAQ. [Iraq]. **Added/Corp** British School of Archaeology in Iraq. Vol. 1, Pt. 1 (April 1934)-. Periodical. English. an. $55.00. British School of Archaeology, 31-34 Gordon Square, London WC1 England. **Tel** 011 44 81 675 8343. **ED** J D Hawkins. **LC** DS78.A2; I7. **DD** 913.35. Index available. cum. index. **Circ:** 700.
Desc: Devoted to studies of history, art, archaeology, religion, economic and social life of Iraq and neighboring countries from earliest times to about 1700 AD.
Ind/Abst Anthropol. Index; Anthropol. Lit.; Art Archaeol. Tech. Abstr.; Avery Index Archit. Period. Suppl. Colum. Univ. (19??-199?); Index Book Rev. Relig.; Middle East Abstr. Index; Relig. Index One Period.

IQ
IRAQ (BAGHDAD, IRAQ). (IRAQ.). No. 137 (June 1, 1981)-. Periodical. English. bw. Translation and Foreign Languages Publishing House, Calliphs Street, PO Box 4074, Baghdad Republic of Iraq. **LC** DS67; .I67. **DD** 956.7/043/05. **UDC** 956.7. ***Continues*** *Iraq Today.*

US/0748-2639
IRAQ VIEWS & NEWS. [Iraq views news]. **VFOAT** Iraq Views and News. Periodical. English. bw. The Iraqi Press Office, 1801 P Street NW, Washington DC 20036. **LC** DS67; .I675. **DD** 956.7/005. **UDC** 956.7.

UK/0075-093X
ISLAMIC SURVEYS. (1962)-. Monographic series. English. ir. Columbia University Press, 136 South Broadway, Irvington NY 10533. **Tel** (914)591-9111. **LC** D199.3; .I8. **DD** 915.6.

UK
ISRAEL AFFAIRS. Vol. 1 (199?)-. English. qt. $115.00. Frank Cass & Company Ltd, Newbury House, 890-900 Eastern Avenue, Newbury Park, Ilford, Essex IG2 7HH United Kingdom. **Tel** 011 44 81 599 8866, FAX 011 44 81 599 0984, telex 897719.

●US/1065-7711
ISRAEL STUDIES BULLETIN. (ISRAEL STUDIES BULLETIN : A PUBLICATION OF THE ASSOCIATION FOR ISRAEL STUDIES / PUBLISHED UNDER THE AUSPICES OF THE MIDDLE EAST

CENTER, UNIVERSITY OF PENNSYLVANNIA.). [Israel stud. bull.]. **Added/Corp** Association for Israel Studies. University of Pennsylvania. Middle East Center. Vol. 7, No. 2 (Spring 1992)-. Bulletin. English. sa. $25.00. Israel Studies Bulletin, c/o Dr. Russell Stone, College of Liberal Arts, American University, Washington DC 20016. **DD** 956. ***Continues** Newsletter (Association for Israel Studies), 1050-5083.*

IS
ISRAEL STUDIES : THE REVIEW OF THE JERUSALEM INSTITUTE FOR ISRAEL STUDIES. No. 1 (Spring 1988)-. Periodical. English. Jerusalem Institute for Israel Studies, 20A Radak Street, Jerusalem 92186 Israel. **LC** DS101; .I647. **DD** 956.9405/05.

IS
ISRAELI DEMOCRACY. ***Ceased.*** **See** Political Science.

IS/0334-4118
JERUSALEM STUDIES IN ARABIC AND ISLAM. **Added/Corp** Universitah Ha-Ivrit Bi-Yerushalayim. Makhon Le-Limude Asyah Ve-Afrikah. Keren Maks Shlesinger. Vol. 1 (1979)-. English (Arabic and English). Twice a year. $50.00. Magnes Press, Hebrew University of Jerusalem, PO Box 7695, Jerusalem 91076 Israel. **Tel** 011 972 2 660341, 011 972 2 635291, FAX 011 972 2 633370, telex 25391. **LC** DS36; .J47. **DD** 909/.0974927.

IR
JIHAD (QOM, IRAN). (AL-JIHAD.). **VFOAT** Majallat Al-Jihad. (19??)-. Periodical. Arabic. mo. SB 201, Qum Iran. **LC** DS318.8; .J54.

IR
JIHAD (TEHRAN, IRAN : MONTHLY). (AL-JIHAD.). V. 1, No. 1, (Dec. 1982)-. Periodical. Arabic. mo. Al-Jumhuriyah Al-Islamiyah Fi, S B 235, Tehran Iran. **LC** DS318.8; .J542.

JO
JORDAN. Periodical. English. Ministry of Tourism and Antiquities, PO Box 224, Amman Jordan. **LC** DS153.A2; J67. **DD** 915.695/04/405. **UDC** 915.695.

UK
JOURNAL OF ISRAELI HISTORY, THE. (19??)-. English. Three times a year. $125.00. Frank Cass & Company Ltd, Newbury House, 890-900 Eastern Avenue, Newbury Park, Ilford, Essex IG2 7HH United Kingdom. **Tel** 011 44 81 599 8866, FAX 011 44 81 599 0984, telex 897719. ***Continues** Studies in Zionism, 0334-1771.*

US/0377-919X
JOURNAL OF PALESTINE STUDIES. [J. Palest. stud.]. **Added/Corp** Jamiat al-Kuwayt. Institute for Palestine Studies (Washington, D.C.) Muassasat al-Dirasat al-Filastiniyah. Vol. 1 (Autumn 1971)-. Periodical. English (French). qt (Jan., Apr., July, Oct.). $32.00 (individuals), $50.00 (institutions), $19.00 (students). University of California Press, 2120 Berkeley Way, Berkeley CA 94720. **Tel** (510)642-4191, (510)642-3907, FAX (510)642-9917. **ED** Hisham Sharabi. **LC** DS119.7; .J63. **DD** 327.5694/017/4927. **[CCC].** Index available. **Bk Rev. Ad Acc. Pr Rev. Circ:** 3,500. available on microfilm and microfiche from University Microfilms International (UMI). Documents available from The Genuine Article, UMI Article Clearinghouse.
Desc: A journal focusing on Palestinian affairs and the Arab-Israeli conflict.
Ind/Abst ABC POL SCI; Acad. Search (July 1993-); Altern. Press Index; Am. Hist. Life (1971-); Curr. Contents Soc. Behav. Sci.; Expand. Acad. Index (1992-); Hist. Source (July 1993-); Hum. Rights Intern. Rep.; Humanit. Source (Jul. 1993-); Index Islam. Lit.; INFO-SOUTH Abstr.; Int. Bibliogr. Sociol.; Int. Labour Doc.; Int. Polit. Sci. Abstr.; Mag. Search; Middle East Abstr. Index; Newsp. Period. Abstr. (1992-); PAIS Int. Print (1991-); Peace Res. Abstr. J. (1972-1973); Res. Alert [Full Cov.]; Soc. Plann. Policy Dev. Abstr.; Soc. Sci. Cit. Index [Full Cov.]; Sociol. Abstr.; Middle East J.

PK/0030-9796
JOURNAL OF THE PAKISTAN HISTORICAL SOCIETY. [J. Pak. Hist. Soc.]. **Main/Corp** Pakistan Historical Society. Vol. 1 (Jan. 1953)-. Academic Scholarly Publication. English (Arabic, Persian and Urdu). Four times a year (Jan., Apr., July, Oct.). $40.00. Pakistan Historical Society, 30 New Karachi Housing Society, Karachi 75400 Pakistan. **Tel** 011 92 21 4557847. **LC** DS376; .P296. **DD** 954.9/1/005. Index available. cum. index. **Bk Rev. Ad Acc. Circ:** 2,000. available with illustrations.
Ind/Abst Am. Hist. Life (1982-); Middle East Abstr. Index.

IR/0377-063X
JOURNAL OF THE REGIONAL CULTURAL INSTITUTE (IRAN, PAKISTAN, TURKEY). (JOURNAL OF THE REGIONAL CULTURAL INSTITUTE.). [J. Reg. Cult. Inst. (Iran, Pak., Turk.)]. **Main/Corp** Muassasah-i Farhangi-i Mintaqagahi. (Spring 1967)-. Periodical. English. qt. Regional Culture Institute, 15 Vasal E Shirazi, No of Eliz 11 Boulevard, Tehran Iran. **LC** DS266; .M82a. **DD** 950.
Ind/Abst Am. Hist. Life (1971-).

US/0149-1784
JOURNAL OF SOUTH ASIAN AND MIDDLE EASTERN STUDIES. [J. South Asian Middle East. stud.]. **Added/Corp** Pakistan American Foundation. Vol. 1, (Fall 1977)-. Periodical. English. Four times a year (Jan., Apr., July, Oct.). $25.00 (institutions), $20.00 (individual) US; $30.00 (other). Villanova University, 421 Lac Hall, Villanova PA 19085. **Tel** (215)519-4738 (215)519-4791, FAX (215)645-6913. **ED** Hafeez Malik. **LC** DS41; .J63. **DD** 950/.05. **Bk Rev. Ad Acc, Adv Mgr:** Havsman, **Tel** 215-645-4738. **Pr Rev. Circ:** 7,500.
Desc: In-depth analysis of political, economic and social developments in the modern Islamic and non-Islamic societies in South Asia, the Middle East and North Africa.
Ind/Abst Am. Hist. Life (1989-); Am. Bibliogr. Slavic East Europ. Stud.; Index Islam. Lit.; Int. Polit. Sci. Abstr.; Middle East Abstr. Index; PAIS Int. Print (1991-); Middle East J.

US/0888-9007
JUSER (LOS ANGELES, CALIF.). (JUSUR.). [Jusur]. **Added/Corp** Gustave E. von Grunebaum Center for Near Eastern Studies. University of California, Los Angeles. Graduate Students Association. Vol. 1, (1985)-. Periodical. English. an. $16.00 (institutions); $8.00 (individuals and faculty); $4.00 (students). Von Grunebaum for Near Eastern Studies, 10286 Bunche Hall, University of California, Los Angeles CA 90024. **Tel** (310)825-1181. **ED** Catherine E. Sweet. **LC** DS41; .J85. **DD** 956/.005. **Bk Rev. Ad Acc, Adv Mgr:** Robert Bond. **Circ:** 300.
Desc: Original research in all fields dealing with the Middle East. We give special attention to graduate students and junior scholars.
Ind/Abst Am. Hist. Life (1985-); PAIS Int. Print (1991-?); Middle East J.

US/1061-8457
KURDISH LIFE. [Kurd. life]. **Added/Corp** Kurdish Library (Brooklyn, New York, N.Y.). No. 1 (Fall 1991)-. Periodical. English. Four times a year (Seasonally). $20.00. The Kurdish Library, 345 Park Place, Brooklyn NY 11238. **Tel** (718)783-7930. **LC** DS51.K7; K883. **DD** 305.

US/1070-0870
KURDISH STUDIES. ***Title Change.*** [Kurd. stud.]. **Added/Corp** Kurdish Library (Brooklyn, New York, N.Y.). Vol. 5, No. 1 & 2 (Spring)-(Fall 1992). Periodical. English. sa. The Kurdish Library, 345 Park Place, Brooklyn NY 11238. **Tel** (718)783-7930. **LC** DS51.K7; K885. **DD** 956.1/0049159. ***Continues** Kurdish Times, 0885-386X.* ***Continued by** International Journal of Kurdish Studies, 1073-6697.*

US/1059-4698
LEBANON FILE / COUNCIL OF LEBANESE AMERICAN ORGANIZATIONS. [Leban. file]. **Added/Corp** Council of Lebanese American Organizations. (Jan. 1991)-. Periodical. English. $24.00. Clao-Lebanon File, PO Box 811165, Cleveland OH 44118-7116. **DD** 956.

IR
LUQMAN. **See** Religion and Theology-Islam, Bahaism, Theosophy.

UA
MAJALLAT AL-DIRASAT AL-SHARQIYAH. **Added/Corp** Jamiyat Khirriji Aqsam Al-Lughat Al-Sharqiyah Bi-al-Jamiat Al-Misriyah. No. 1 (Dec./Jan. 1983)-. Periodical. Arabic. sa. Dr Dhakiyah Muhammad Rushdi Qsim Al-Lughat Al-Sharqiyah, Kulliyat Al-Adab, Jamiat Al-Qahirah Egypt. **LC** DS41; .M33.

UA
MAJALLAT AL-SHARQ AL-AWSAT. **VFOAT** Journal of the Middle East. No. 1- Jan. 1974-. Arabic (English). an. Ain-Shams University, Abbasseyah, Cairo Egypt. **LC** DS41; .M34. **DD** 956/.005. **UDC** 956.

KU
MAJALLAT DIRASAT AL-KHALIJ WA-AL-JAZIRAH AL-ARABIYAH. **VFOAT** Journal of the Gulf and Arabian Peninsula Studies. Began in Jan. 1975. Arabic (English). qt. $40.00. Journal of the Gulf & Arabian Peninsula Studies, PO Box 17073, Khaldiah Kuwait. **Tel** 816824-816807. **ED** Bader J Al-Yocoub. **LC** DS201; .M34. **UDC** 953. **Bk Rev. Ad Acc.** available in microform.
Desc: Deals with political, economical, and sociological topics related to Gulf and Arabian Peninsula region.
Ind/Abst Soc. Plann. Policy Dev. Abstr.; Sociol. Abstr. (?-?); Middle East J.

IR/1015-2830
MAJOLLAH-'I BASTANSHINASI VA-TARIKH. **See** Archaeology.

LE
MAWQIF (BEIRUT, LEBANON). (AL-MAWQIF.). No. 1 (June 1, 1983)-. Periodical. Arabic. mo. £L300.00. Al-Mawqif, SB 11/7927 Beirut Lebanon. **LC** DS80.A2; M39.

US/0162-766X
MIDDLE EAST, ABSTRACTS AND INDEX. **See** History(General)-Abstracting, Bibliographies and Statistics.

US/0084-2311
MIDDLE EAST AND SOUTH ASIA, THE. [Middle East South Asia]. **VFOAT** Middle East & South Asia. (1967)-. English. an. $9.50. Stryker-Post Publications, PO Drawer 1200, Harpers Ferry WV 25425. **Tel** (800)995-1400. **ED** Ray L. Cleveland. **LC** DS44; .C55. **DD** 915. ctrl circ.
Desc: Addresses social, economic, political and controversial issues.

US
MIDDLE EAST CLIPBOARD, THE. **Added/Corp** American Educational Trust. (19??)-. Periodical. English. Fifty-two times a year. $600.00. American Educational Trust, PO Box 53062, Washington DC 20009. **Tel** (202)939-6052, FAX (202)265-4574, (202)232-6754. ctrl circ.
Desc: Clipping service of the top articles in major US, British, and other countries newspapers on the Middle East.
Ind/Abst Hum. Rights Intern. Rep.

US/0163-5476
MIDDLE EAST CONTEMPORARY SURVEY. (MIDDLE EAST CONTEMPORARY SURVEY / THE SHILOAH CENTER FOR MIDDLE EASTERN AND AFRICAN STUDIES, TEL AVIV UNIVERSITY.). [Middle East contemp. surv.]. **Added/Corp** Mekhon Shiloah Le-Heker Ha-Mizrah Ha-Tikhon Ve-Afrikah. Merkaz Dayan Le-Heker Ha-Mizrah Ha-Tikhon Ve-Afrikah (Universitat Tel-Aviv). **VFOAT** MECS; M.E.C.S. Vol. 1 (1977)-. English. an. Westview Press Inc, 5500 Central Avenue, Boulder CO 80301. **Tel** (303)444-3541, FAX (303)449-3356. **LC** DS62.8; .M53. **DD** 320.9/56/046.

US/0026-3141
MIDDLE EAST JOURNAL, THE. **See** History(General)-Abstracting, Bibliographies and Statistics.

US/0271-3160
MIDDLE EAST (NEW YORK, N.Y.), THE. (THE MIDDLE EAST : ISSUES AND EVENTS OF ... FROM THE NEW YORK TIMES INFORMATION BANK.). [Middle East]. **Added/Corp** New York Times Information Bank (Firm). (1978)-. English. an. Arno Press, 3 Park Avenue, New York NY 10016. **Tel** (212)725-2050. **LC** DS63.1; .M4843. **DD** 956/.005.

●US/1061-1924
MIDDLE EAST POLICY. **See** Political Science-International Relations.

LE
MIDDLE EAST SKETCH. Periodical. English. BAK Publications, Hashem A 1 Babon Building, Mneimne Street, PO Box 7367, Beirut Lebanon. **LC** DS41; .M525. **DD** 915.6/03/405. **UDC** 915.6.

US/0026-3184
MIDDLE EAST STUDIES ASSOCIATION BULLETIN. [Middle East Stud. Assoc. bull.]. **Added/Corp** Middle East Studies Association of North America. Middle East Studies Association of North America. Bulletin. **VFOAT** MESA Bulletin. Vol. 1 (May 1967)-. Periodical. English. sa. Free to subscribers of the International Journal of Middle East Studies. Middle East Studies Association / New York, New York University, Washington Square, New York NY 10003. **Tel** (212)598-2400. **ED** Jere Bacharach. **LC** DS41; .M533. **DD** 956/.0072. **CODEN** MESBEL. Index available. cum. index. **Bk Rev. Ad Acc. Circ:** 2,500 (ctrl).
Desc: Reviews of recently published books, and audio-visual materials. Short articles and notices.
Ind/Abst Am. Hist. Life (1980-); Geogr. Abstr. Human Geogr.; Index Islam. Lit.; Index Book Rev. Relig.; Int. Polit. Sci. Abstr.; Middle East Abstr. Index; Middle East J.

UK/0026-3206
MIDDLE EASTERN STUDIES. [Middle East. stud.]. Vol. 1 (Oct. 1964)-. Periodical. English. qt. $195.00. Frank Cass & Company Ltd, Newbury House, 890-900 Eastern Avenue, Newbury Park, Ilford, Essex IG2 7HH United Kingdom. **Tel** 011 44 81 599 8866, FAX 011 44 81 599 0984, telex 897719. **ED** Elie Kedourie and Sylvia Haim. **LC** DS41; .M535. **DD** 956/.005. **Bk Rev. Ad Acc, Adv Mgr:** Anne Kidson. **Pr Rev. Circ:** 700. available on microfilm and microfiche from University Microfilms International (UMI). Documents available from The Genuine Article, UMI Article Clearinghouse.
Desc: History and politics of Middle East, North Africa, Turkey, Iran and Israel in 19th and 20th centuries. Of special interest to scholars concerned with understanding the modern Middle East.
Ind/Abst ABC POL SCI; Abstr. Anthropol. (19??-); Acad. Abstr. Full Text Elite (Jan. 1992-); Acad. Abstr. (Jan.

History(General) —History of the Middle East

1992-); Acad. Search (Jan. 1992-); Am. Hist. Life (1970-); Br. Humanit. Index; Curr. Contents Soc. Behav. Sci.; Expand. Acad. Index (1989-); Geogr. Abstr. Human Geogr.; Index Islam. Lit.; INFO-SOUTH Abstr.; Int. Bibliogr. Sociol.; Int. Dev. Abstr.; Int. Polit. Sci. Abstr.; Mag. Search; Middle East Abstr. Index; Newsp. Period. Abstr. (1991-); Res. Alert [Full Cov.]; Rural Dev. Abstr.; Soc. Plann. Policy Dev. Abstr.; Soc. Sci. Source (Jan. 1992-); Soc. Sci. Index [Full Cov.]; Soc. Sci. Index; Soc. Sci. Index Fulltext (Oct. 1988-) [Full Txt.]; Sociol. Abstr.; Middle East J.; World Agric. Econ.

US/0731-8944
MIDEAST DIRECTIONS. [Mideast dir.]. MED 82-1 (June 1982)-. English. ir. Free. Library of Congress / Middle Eastern Division, Near-East Section, Washington DC 20540. **UDC** 956.

US/0888-2460
MIDEAST MONITOR. Ceased. (MIDEAST MONITOR / ASSOCIATION OF ARAB-AMERICAN UNIVERSITY GRADUATES, INC.). [Mideast monit.]. **VFOAT** AAUG Mideast Monitor. Vol. 1, No. 2 (Oct. 1984)-Ceased 1990. Periodical. English. bm. Association of Arab-American University Graduates, PO Box 408, Normal IL 61761. **Tel** (309)452-6588. **DD** 956. **UDC** 956. *Continues Middle East Focus (Belmont, Mass.).*

KU
MILAFF AL-ALAQAT AL-ARABIYAH AL-YABANIYAH / IDAD QISM AL-ALAQAT AL-DUWALIYAH. VFOAT Anba; Arabu Nihon Kankei Tsuzurikomi. No. 1, (May 1981)-. Periodical. Arabic. Al-Anba Newspaper, Airport Road/Press Area, Shuweikh, PO Box 23915, Safat 13100 Kuwait. **LC** DS63.2.J3; M54.

IS/0017-7083
MIZAH HE-HADASH. Added/Corp Hevrah ha-Mizrahit ha-Yisreelit. **VFOAT** New East; Modern East. Vol. 1, No. 1 No. 710, (October 1949)-. Periodical. Hebrew (summaries and/or abstracts in English). qt. $25.00 (individuals), $30.00 (institutions). Hebrew University of Jerusalem / Israel Oriental Society, Jerusalem Israel. **Tel** 011 972 2 883633. **LC** DS41; .M56. **DD** 956/.005.
Ind/Abst ABC POL SCI (19??-19??); Am. Hist. Life (1954-); Old Testam. Abstr.

US/0077-0027
MODERN MIDDLE EAST SERIES (NEW YORK). (MODERN MIDDLE EAST SERIES.). **Added/Corp** Columbia University. Middle East Institute. No. 1, (1970)-. Monographic series. English. ir. Price varies per volume. University of Texas Press, PO Box 7819, Austin TX 78713. **Tel** (512)471-4531, FAX (512)320-0668, telex 776453 UTEXPRES AUS.

US/0888-191X
NA'AMAT WOMAN. (NAAMAT WOMAN : MAGAZINE OF NAAMAT USA, THE WOMEN'S LABOR ZIONIST ORGANIZATION OF AMERICA.). **Added/Corp** Naamat USA (Organization). **VFOAT** Naamat Froy. Vol. 1, No. 1 (March-April 1986)-. Periodical. English (Yiddish). Five times a year. $20.00. Naamat USA, 200 Madison Avenue, Suite 2120, New York NY 10011. **Tel** (212)725-8010. **LC** DS150.L3; P5. **DD** 956.94/001. *Continues Pioneer Woman, 0032-0021.*
Ind/Abst Index Jew. Period. (199?-).

IS
NEWS FROM WITHIN. (19??)-. English. Twelve times a year. $60.00. Alternative Information Center, PO Box 31417, Jerusalem Israel. **Tel** 011 00972 2 241159, 011 00972 2 253151, FAX 011 00972 2 253151. **ED** Dr. Tikua Honig Parnass. Index available ($10.00). **Bk Rev** (Qty: 8-10). **Ad Acc**, **Adv Mgr:** Ingrid. **Circ:** 1,000 (ctrl). available on an online database.
Desc: A bulletin providing analysis, background information, and eye-witness reports of events and developments in both Palestinian and Israeli societies.

IS
OTHER FRONT, THE. English (Arabic). Fifty-two times a year. $65.00. Alternative Information Center, PO Box 31417, Jerusalem Israel. **Tel** 011 00972 2 241159, 011 00972 2 253151, FAX 011 00972 2 253151. **ED** Sergio Yahmi and N. Worshowski. Index available ($2.00 upon request). **Circ:** 500 (ctrl). available on an online database.
Desc: A review of the Israeli press, focusing on the peace camp, the Right and the center of the political spectrum - their statements and activities relating to the Israeli-Palestinian conflict.

US/0030-963X
PAKISTAN AFFAIRS. Added/Corp Pakistan. Embassy (U.S.) Information Division. Pakistan. Safarah (U.S.). Vol. 1, (Oct. 31, 1947)-. Periodical. English. Twenty-six times a year. Free. Embassy of Pakistan, 2315 Massachusetts Avenue Northwest, Washington DC 20008. **Tel** (202)939-6225 or 6226. **LC** DS376; .P27.

PK/0030-980X
PAKISTAN HORIZON. [Pak. horiz.]. **Added/Corp** Pakistan Institute of International Affairs. Vol. 1 (Mar. 1948)-. Periodical. English. qt (Jan., Apr., July, Oct.). $44.00. Friends Book House, Government Printing Office, Box 803, Karachi 1 Pakistan. **LC** DS376;

.P32. **DD** 954.7. Index Available, published separately, free-automatically sent.
Ind/Abst ABC POL SCI; Am. Hist. Life (1954-1956, 1969-); Index Islam. Lit.; Int. Bibliogr. Sociol.; Middle East Abstr. Index; Middle East J.

PK
PAKISTAN JOURNAL OF HISTORY AND CULTURE. V. 1, No. 1 (Jan./June 1980)-. Periodical. English. sa. $7.00. Pakistan Journal of History & Culture, PO Box 1230, Islamabad Pakistan. **LC** DS376; .P323. **DD** 954.9/005. **UDC** 954.9.
Ind/Abst Am. Hist. Life (1989-); Int. Bibliogr. Sociol.

PK/0377-2586
PAKISTAN PICTORIAL. No. 1 (Jan./Feb. 1973)-. Periodical. English. bm (6 issues). Pakistan Publications, Box 183, Shahrah Iraq, Karachi 1 Pakistan. **LC** DS376; .P3425. **DD** 954.9/105/05.

RU/0131-2642
PALESTINSKII SBORNIK. [Palest. sb.]. **Added/Corp** Rossiiskoe Palestinskoe Obshchestvo. (1954)-. Multiple languages. Izdatelstvo Nauka St. Petersburg, Mendeleevskaia Liniia 1, 199034 St. Petersburg, B-34 Russia. **Tel** 218-26-12. **(Subscription address:** Victor Kamkin, 4956 Boiling Brook Parkway, Rockville MD 20852.**) Continues** *Pravoslavnyi Palestinskii Sbornik.*
Ind/Abst BHA : Biblio. Hist. Art.

DK
PAYK-I NAJAT / JABHAH-I NAJAT-I IRAN. Added/Corp Jabhah-i Najat-i Iran. (19??)-. Periodical. Persian. da. Jabhah-i Najat-i Iran, PB 102, 2670 Greve Str., Copenhagen Denmark. **LC** DS318.72; .P394.

US/0069-3324
PUBLICATIONS - UNIVERSITY OF CHICAGO. CENTER FOR MIDDLE EASTERN STUDIES. Main/Corp University of Chicago. Center for Middle Eastern Studies. Vol. 1 1968-. Monographic series. English. ir. Price varies per volume. University of Chicago Press / Book Department, 11030 South Langley Avenue, Chicago IL 60628. **Tel** (800)621-2736, (312)568-1550, FAX (312)753-0811, telex 23933. **UDC** 956.

YE
QADAYA AL-ASR. VFOAT Kadaya Al-Asr. Periodical. Arabic. mo. Qadaya Al-Asr, Rais Al-Tahrir SB 5392, Al-Maalla Adan Yemen. **LC** DS247.A2; A278.

LE
QADAYA ARABIYAH. No. 1.- ; 1974-. Periodical. Arabic. £L4.00. Al-Muassasah Al-Arbiyah Lil-Dirasat Wa-Al-Nashr, SB 5460, Beirut Lebanon. **LC** DS36; .Q2.

SU
QAFILAT AL-ZAYT. Began in 1953. Periodical. Arabic. mo. Sharikat Aramku, Idarat Al-Alaqat Al-Ammah Al-Zahran Al-Mamlakah Al-Arabiyah Al-Saudiyah, PO Box 1389, Al-Zahran Saudi Arabia. **LC** DS36; .Q23.

IT
QUADERNI DI STUDI ARABI. Added/Corp Universita degli Studi di Venezia. Seminario di Letteratura Araba. Universita Degli Studi di Venezia. Dipartimento di Scienze Storico-Archeologiche e Orientalistiche. Universita Degli Studi di Venezia. Dipartimento di Scienze Storico-Archeologiche e Orientalistiche. Sezione Orientalistica. **VFOAT** QSA. Vol. 1 (1983)-. Italian (English, French and Spanish). an. L70000 Italy; L80000 other. Herder Editrice e Libreria SRL, Piazza Montecitorio 117-120, 00186 Rome Italy. **Tel** 011 39 6 679 4628, FAX 011 39 6 678 4751. **LC** DS36.8; .Q33. **DD** 909/.04927.

NR/0536-2288
RESEARCH BULLETIN (CENTRE OF ARABIC DOCUMENTATION). (RESEARCH BULLETIN / CENTRE OF ARABIC DOCUMENTATION, UNIVERSITY OF IBADAN.). **Added/Corp** Centre of Arabic Documentation. Vol. 1 (July 1964)-. Periodical. English. ir. Center of Arabic Documentation, Institute of African Studies, University of Ibadan Nigeria.

LE
SHUUN FILASTINIYAH. Added/Corp Munazzamat al-Tahrir al-Filastiniyah. Markaz al-Abhath. **VFOAT** Palestine Affairs. (1971)-. Periodical. Arabic. Twelve times a year. Palestine Research Center, PO Box 1691, Beirut Lebanon. **Tel** 011 351260. **LC** DS119.7; .S496.
Ind/Abst Middle East J.

NE
SOCIAL, ECONOMIC AND POLITICAL STUDIES OF THE MIDDLE EAST. VFOAT Etudes Sociales, Economiques et Politiques du Moyen Orient. Vol. 1 (1971)-. Monographic series. English (French). ir. Price varies per volume. E. J. Brill, Postbus 9000, 2300 PA Leiden Netherlands. **Tel** 011 31 71 312624, FAX 011 31 71 317532, telex 39296 BRILL NL.

NE
STUDIES IN THE HISTORY OF THE ANCIENT NEAR EAST. Vol. 1 (1982)-. Monographic series. English. ir. Price varies per volume. E. J. Brill, Postbus 9000, 2300 PA Leiden Netherlands. **Tel** 011 31 71 312624, FAX 011 31 71 317532, telex 39296 BRILL NL.

SJ/0378-8059
SUDANOW. [Sudanow]. **Added/Corp** Sudan. Wizarat al-Ilam wa-al-Thaqafah. Vol. 1, (June 1976)-. Periodical. English. mo. $50.00. Sudanow, PO Box 2561, Khartoum Sudan. **Tel** 77915/77913. **(Subscription address:** Subscription Office, Sudanow, PO Box 2651, Khartoum, Sudan**) ED** Fath El Rahman Mahgoub. **LC** DT154.1; .S92. **DD** 962.4/005. **Bk Rev**. **Ad Acc**. **Circ:** 4,000.
Ind/Abst Rural Dev. Abstr.

IR
TARIQ AL-THAWRAH. VFOAT Tariq Al-Thawra. Periodical. Arabic. Mintaqat, 13 SB 13/361, Tehran Iran. **LC** DS79.65; .T37.

IS
YERUSHILTON. Periodical. Hebrew. Pirum Zamir, Rehov Koresh 14, POB 1343, Yerushalayim Israel. **LC** DS109; .Y48.

US/0279-182X
YISRAEL SELLANU. (YISRAEL SHELANU.). **VFOAT** Israel Shelanu. (19??)-. Periodical. Hebrew. Fifty-two times a year. $50.00. Israel Shelanu BBSI Ltd., 5307 New Utrecht Avenue, Brooklyn NY 11219. **Tel** (718)972-1066. **(Subscription address:** PO Box 190432, Brooklyn, NY 11219; telephone: (718)338-8025**)** **LC** DS101; .Y48.

HOBBIES

US
8-TRACK MIND MAGAZINE. English. qt. $8.00 US, Canada & Mexico. 8-Track Mind Magazine, PO Box 90, East Detroit MI 48021. **Tel** (313)776-5427. **ED** F.R. Forster. **Circ:** 500.
Desc: Features the joys of collecting 8-track tapes and players as extolled by readers' letters and mostly unsolicited submissions.

US/0148-6691
AEROPHILE EXTRA. See Aeronautics, Astronautics.

US/0147-7668
AEROPHILE (SAN ANTONIO). Ceased. See Aeronautics, Astronautics.

US/0899-9171
AFAS QUARTERLY OF THE AUTOMOTIVE FINE ARTS SOCIETY. See Transportation-Automobiles.

US/1046-0470
AMERICAN AMATEUR JOURNALIST, THE. [Am. amat. journal.]. **VFOAT** AAJ. Periodical. English. bm. Free to members. American Amateur Press Association, Editor, 1923 20th Street, Portsmouth OH 45662. **Tel** (717)573-4526. **ED** Linda Donaldson. **DD** 071. **Bk Rev**. **Ad Acc**. **Circ:** 350 (ctrl).
Desc: Newsletter for writing, printing, and graphic arts as a hobby.

US/0196-5654
AMERICAN BOOK COLLECTOR (1980). (AMERICAN BOOK COLLECTOR.). [Am. book collect.]. New Series, Vol. 1 (Jan./Feb. 1980)-. Periodical. English. Eleven times a year (July/Aug. issues combined). $47.00 (one year), $127.00 (three year). Moretus Press Inc, PO Box 1080, Ossining NY 10562-1080. **Tel** (914)941-0409. **ED** Bernard McTigue. **LC** Z990; .A52. **DD** 002/.075/05. [CCC]. Index available. cum. index. **Bk Rev**. **Ad Acc**. **Circ:** 3,500. *Continues Book Collector's Market, 0162-2498.*
Desc: The American magazine for all collectors of books and literature. Features childrens' and illustrated books, press books/fine printing, American auctions, and more.
Ind/Abst Abstr. Engl. Stud.; Am. Hist. Life (1963-1976,1987-); Annu. Bibliogr. Engl. Lang. Lit.; ARTbibliogr. Mod. (1984-); Book Rev. Index; MLA Int. Bibl. Books Artic. Mod. Lang. Lit.

US/0164-7008
AMERICAN COLLECTOR'S JOURNAL, THE. See Antiques.

US
AMERICAN COUNTRY COLLECTIBLES. VFOAT Country Collectibles. Vol. I, No. I (Dec. 1991)-. Periodical. English. qt. $15.97. GCR Publishing Group, 1700 Broadway, 34th Floor, New York NY 10019. **Tel** (212)541-7100, (800)435-0715, FAX (212)245-1241.

(**Subscription address:** Kable Publishers Aide, 308 East Hitt Street, Subscription Department, Mt. Morris IL 61054-1473.) **ED** Florina McCain. **LC** NK805; .A665. **DD** 745.1/05. **Ad Acc.**
Desc: Magazine for everyone who enjoys collecting - as a pastime, as an investment and as a way to add color and character to a country style home.

●US/1061-9399
AMERICAN MODELER (RALEIGH, N.C.). (AMERICAN MODELER.). [Am. model.]. Vol. 1, No. 1 (Aug./Sept. 1992)-. Periodical. English. Six times a year. $14.95 US; $17.95 Canada and Mexico and Europe; and $19.95 other. Agency Photo Service, PO Box 1446, Raleigh NC 27602. **Tel** (919)779-3232. **ED** Robert Thomason. **DD** 745. **Bk Rev. Ad Acc. Circ:** 5000.
Desc: The newspaper of scale modeling reports on news and features of interest to hobbyist that build scale representations from plastic kits or scratch. Articles include "How-to", model collecting, museum collections of miniatures, industry news on companies and their products, competition events, trade shows, convention coverage, and reports on actual items and events of interest to enthusiast.

US/0883-0991
AMERICAN SPACEMODELLING. ***Title Change.*** [Am. spacemodel.]. **Added/Corp** National Association of Rocketry (U.S.). **VFOAT** American Space Modeling. Vol. 26, No. 7 (July 1984)-(199?)-. Periodical. English. bm. National Association of Rocketry, 1311 Edgewood Drive, Altoona WI 54720. **Tel** (713)499-5925. **ED** John Pursley. **LC** TL844; .M62. **DD** 629.47/5/0228. **Bk Rev. Ad Acc. Circ:** 7,500. ***Continues*** *Model Rocketeer, 0190-1060.* ***Continued by*** *Sport Rocketry, 1076-2701.*
Desc: Includes photographs, plans, and technical articles on the hobby of model rocketry.

US
AMERICAN TAXIDERMIST MAGAZINE. (19??)-. Trade Publication. English. Six times a year. $16.00 (one year), $30.00 (two year), $44.00 (three year). American Taxidermist Magazine, PO Box 549, Bernalillo NM 87004-0549. **Tel** (505)867-6226. **ED** T. E. Kelly. **Ad Acc. Circ:** 2,700 (ctrl).
Desc: Trade journal devoted to the technical and commercial aspects of taxidermy.

IT
ANNUARIO SEAT. VOL. G, P.TURISMO E TEMPO LIBERO. **See** Travel and Tourism.

●US/1065-3694
ANTIQUE & COLLECTORS REPRODUCTION NEWS. **See** Antiques.

US/0164-7237
ANTIQUE CAR TIMES. **See** Antiques.

●US/1069-5141
ANTIQUE DOLL WORLD. **See** Antiques.

US/0882-6897
ANTIQUE TRADER ANTIQUES & COLLECTIBLES PRICE GUIDE, THE. **See** Antiques.

US/0161-8342
ANTIQUE TRADER WEEKLY, THE. **See** Antiques.

US/0884-6294
ANTIQUES & COLLECTING HOBBIES. ***Title Change.*** **See** Antiques.

US
ANTIQUES & COLLECTING MAGAZINE. **See** Antiques.

FR/0151-6981
AQUARAMA. (1967)-. Periodical. French. bm. 210.00F France; 246.00F other. Aquarama, 24 rue de Verdun, 67000 Strasbourg France. **Tel** 011 33 88 619608, FAX 011 33 88 411074. **UDC** 639.93.

CN/0380-982X
ARMS COLLECTING. **Added/Corp** Museum Restoration Service (Ottawa, Ont.). Vol. 11 (Feb. 1973)-. Periodical. English. qt. $21.75 all, except Canada. Museums Restoration Service, Box 390, Bloomfield Ontario K0K 1G0 Canada. **Tel** (613)393-2980. **ED** S James Gooding. **DD** 623.4/4/075. Index available. **Bk Rev. Ad Acc. Circ:** 1,500 (ctrl). ***Continues*** *Canadian Journal of Arms Collecting, 0008-3992.*
Desc: History of arms technology. To include firearms, armor.

FR/0980-9465
ATELIER PARIS, L'. ***Ceased.*** **See** Interior Design.

AT
AUSTRALIAN ANTIQUE BOTTLES & COLLECTABLES. **See** Antiques.

AT/0816-3294
AUSTRALIAN DOLL DIRECTORY. [Aust. doll. dir.]. (1986)-. English. bm. 33.00Aus$ Australia; 63.00Aus$ New Zealand; 77.00Aus$ US. M.A. Brooks, PO Box 503, Mossvale New South Wales, 2577 Australia. **Tel** 11 61 4 8681338, FAX 11 61 4 4 8691438. **ED** Jack Brooks. **DD** 745.592202594. **Bk Rev. Ad Acc. Circ:** 20,000.
Desc: Teddy bear and doll collectors' and makers' magazine.

AT/0004-9875
AUSTRALIAN NUMISMATIC JOURNAL. **Added/Corp** Numismatic Society of South Australia. Vol. 1 (1950)-. English. Four times a year. 25.00Aus$ Australia; 35.00Aus$ others Comes with Australian Numismatic Society membership. Australian Numismatic Society, Box R4 Royal Exchange, Sydney NSW 2000 Australia. **ED** F. S. Dobbin. **Circ:** 250.

US/0898-2155
AUTOMOTIVE INVESTOR. **See** Transportation-Automobiles.

US/0148-5393
AZACA. V. 1- Aug. 1975-. Periodical. English (English). mo. $10.00. Christopher De L'Estrang, 36 South Main Street, New Hope PA 18938. **LC** Z41.A2; A98. **DD** 929.8.

US/0743-975X
BASEBALL & FOOTBALL CARDS. (BASEBALL & FOOTBALL CARDS / BY THE HOUSE OF COLLECTIBLES, INC.). [Baseb. footb. cards]. **Added/Corp** House of Collectibles. **VFOAT** Baseball and Football Cards. (19??)-. English. an. $3.50. Random House Inc., 400 Hahn Road, Westminster MD 21157. **Tel** (800)726-0600, (800)733-3000, FAX (800)659-2436. **LC** GV875.3; .B368. **DD** 769/.49796357029/473.

US/0746-7966
BASEBALL CARD NEWS. ***Title Change.*** [Baseb. card news]. (19??)-(19??). Periodical. English. bw. Krause Publications, 700 East State Street, Iola WI 54990-0001. **Tel** (715)445-2214, FAX (715)445-4087, telex 55 6461. **ED** Allan Kaye. **DD** 796. **Bk Rev. Ad Acc. Circ:** 27,428. ***Absorbed by*** *Sports Collectors Digest.*
Desc: Contains updates on new collectibles for baseball, football, hockey, basketball and other sports as well as non-sports card sets. Spotlights on baseball players and card sets.

US
BASEBALL CARD POCKET PRICE GUIDE / BY THE EDITORS OF SPORTS COLLECTORS DIGEST. **See** Recreation, Leisure-Sports.

US/0896-7563
BASEBALL CARD PRICE GUIDE MONTHLY. ***Title Change.*** (BASEBALL CARD PRICE GUIDE.). [Baseb. card price guide mon.]. **VFOAT** Price Guide Monthly. No. 1 (April 1988)-(1992). Periodical. English. mo. Krause Publications, 700 East State Street, Iola WI 54990-0001. **Tel** (715)445-2214, FAX (715)445-4087, telex 55 6461. **ED** Dan Albaugh. **DD** 769. **Circ:** 200,000. ***Continued by*** *Sports Card Price Guide Monthly, 1061-5512.*
Desc: The hobby's most complete price guide listing current values in two grades for more than 45,000 cards produced by Topps, Fleer, Donruss, Bowman, Goudey, Sportflics, Score and turn-of-the-century tobacco and candy cards. Also has handy guides for grading and pricing for novice and advanced collectors. Contains advertising for baseball cards and related items.

US/1058-0433
BASEBALL CARD UPDATE. [Baseb. card update]. (1991)-. Periodical. English. mo. $17.95. Jetpac Publishing, PO Box 120467, East Haven CT 06512. **DD** 796.

US/8750-5851
BASEBALL CARDS. ***Title Change.*** [Baseb. cards]. **VFOAT** Baseball Cards Magazine. Vol. 1, No. 1 (Spring 1981)-(19??). Periodical. English. mo. Krause Publications, 700 East State Street, Iola WI 54990-0001. **Tel** (715)445-2214, FAX (715)445-4087, telex 55 6461. **ED** Kit Kiefer. **LC** Discard. **DD** 741. **Bk Rev. Ad Acc. Circ:** 184,860 (ctrl). ***Continued by*** *Sports Cards, 1069-2282.*
Desc: Featuring baseball cards from all eras. Monthly guide to card collecting for beginners and advance collectors. Includes updated baseball card price guide in each issue, Q & A column, articles, and ads offering baseball cards and related items.

US/0199-946X
BASEBALL HOBBY NEWS. ***Ceased.*** (19??)-(Aug. 1993). Periodical. English. mo. Baseball Hobby News, 4540 Kearny Villa Road/Suite 215, San Diego CA 92123. **Tel** (619)565-2848, FAX (619)565-6608. **ED** Frank Barning. **Bk Rev. Ad Acc. Circ:** 16,500 (ctrl).
Desc: Complete coverage of baseball memorabilia, particularly baseball cards. Stories about new and old items, nostalgia, and numerous advertisements selling collectibles.

US/1044-775X
BASICALLY BUCKLES. Vol. 9, No. 6 (June 1989)-. Periodical. English. mo. Toy Farmer Limited, HC 2 Box 5, Lamoure ND 58458. **Tel** (800)533-8293, (701)883-5206. **LC** NK4890.B4; B37. **DD** 739. ***Continues*** *Buckle Buddies, 1043-2442.*
Desc: Magazine for collectors of belt buckles, watch fobs, key rings and related collectibles.

US/0886-0599
BECKETT BASEBALL CARD MONTHLY. [Beckett baseb. card mon.]. **VFOAT** Baseball Card Monthly; Beckett Monthly. (198?)-. Periodical. English. mo (12 issues). $19.95 (one year), $35.95 (two year), $47.95 (three year). Beckett Publications, 15850 Dallas Parkway, Dallas TX 75248. **Tel** (214)991-6657, FAX (214)991-8930. **ED** Fred Reed and Pepper Hastings. **DD** 796. **Ad Acc. Circ:** 465,000.
Desc: A non-investment, positive treatment of baseball card and baseball autograph collecting. Updated baseball card price guide and informational hobby articles and columns run monthly.

US/1055-8179
BECKETT BASKETBALL MAGAZINE. [Beckett basketb. mag.]. Issue #4 (Sept./Oct. 1990)-. Periodical. English. mo. $19.95 US; $29.86 Canada; $31.95 other. Beckett Publications, 15850 Dallas Parkway, Dallas TX 75248. **Tel** (214)991-6657, FAX (214)991-8930. (**Subscription address:** PO Box 1915, Marion, OH 43305, Telephone: (614)383-5772) **ED** Dr James Beckett. **LC** WMLC 90/0529. **DD** 796. Index available. **Ad Acc.** ***Continues*** *Beckett Basketball Card Magazine, 1055-8187.*
Desc: Contains interviews with star players, basketball card price guide, reader question and answer section, tips on the hobby and articles on collecting.

US/0744-723X
BIG REEL, THE. **See** Motion Picture.

US/0744-6179
BLADE MAGAZINE, THE. ***Title Change.*** [Blade mag.]. Vol. 9, No. 4 (June 1982)-(19??). Periodical. English. mo. American Blade Inc, PO Box 22007, Chattanooga TN 37422. **Tel** (615)894-0339, FAX (615)892-5007. **ED** Steve Shackleford. **LC** TS380; .A43. **DD** 621.9/32. **Ad Acc, Adv Mgr:** Luci Stone, **Tel** (615)894-0339. **Circ:** 60,000. ***Continues*** *American Blade, 0097-8949.* ***Continued by*** *Blade (Chattanooga, Tenn.), 1064-5853.*
Desc: The magazine of all aspects of the cutlery industry: sporting use, collecting, history, new products and innovations, legislation, knife making, art knives, official publication of the Knifemakers Guild.

UK
BOOK AND MAGAZINE COLLECTOR. Periodical. English. mo. Diamond Publishing Group Ltd., 45 St Marys Road, London W5 5RQ England.

US/0045-2521
BOOKPLATES IN THE NEWS. [Bookpl. news]. **Added/Corp** American Society of Bookplate Collectors and Designers. No. 1 (July 1970)-. Periodical. English. qt. $25.00. American Society of Bookplate Collectors and Designers, 605 North Stoneman Avenue, Suite F, Alhambra CA 91801. **Tel** (213)283-1936. **ED** Audrey Spencer Arellanes. **DD** 097; 769. Index available. cum. index. **Bk Rev. Ad Acc. Circ:** 200. available on microfilm from University Microfilms International (UMI).
Desc: Material relating to any aspect of bookplate art - contemporary and historical. Bookplate artists, collectors, exhibitions, competitions, literature (books and periodicals).
Ind/Abst Am. Bibliogr. Slavic East Europ. Stud.

US/1056-2346
BRASS MODELER & COLLECTOR. [Brass model. collect.]. **VFOAT** Brass Modeler and Collector. Vol. 1, No. 1 (Jan./Mar. 1991)-. Periodical. English. qt. $37.50. N J International Inc, 77 West Nicholai Street, Hicksville NY 11801. **Tel** (516)433-8720, FAX (516)938-5109. **DD** 790.

US/0885-8578
BREAKTHROUGH (ATLANTA, GA.). (BREAKTHROUGH.). [Breakthrough]. **Added/Corp** International Wildlife Artist Foundation. **VFOAT** Breakthrough Magazine. (19??)-. Periodical. English. Four times a year (Feb., May, Aug., Nov.). $21.00 (one year); $38.00 (two years). Breakthrough Magazine, PO Box 2945, Hammond LA 70404. **Tel** (504)345-7266, FAX (504)542-1831. **ED** Kathy Blomquist. **DD** 704. **Bk Rev**, (Qty: 1-2/yr). **Ad Acc. Circ:** 9,000.
Desc: An educational and how-to publication devoted to the serious wildlife artist. Filled with clearly illustrated step-by-step demonstrations, the main focus of the editorial material is related to taxidermy. However, due to the similarities of technique and reference materials needed, we also incorporate related wildlife art such as wood carving, sculpture, painting and photography.

US/1056-0130
BREAKTHROUGH (HAMMOND, LA.). (BREAKTHROUGH.). (19??)-. Periodical. English. Four times a year (Feb., May, Aug., Nov.). $25.00 (one year); $46.00 (two years). Breakthrough Magazine, PO Box 2945, Hammond LA 70404. **Tel** (504)345-7266, FAX

(504)542-1831. **ED** Larry and Kathy Blomquist. **DD** 700. Index available. cum. index. **Bk Rev. Ad Acc. Circ:** 8,500 (ctrl).
Desc: Devoted to the serious wildlife artist.

US/1056-8468
BRITISH MARQUE CAR CLUB NEWS. **See** Transportation-Automobiles.

UK/0308-6712
BRITISH TOYS & HOBBIES. [Br. toys hobbies]. (1976)-. Periodical. English. Twelve times a year. £121.00. British Toys & Hobbies Briefing, 80 Camberwell Road, London SE5 OEG England. **Tel** 011 44 71 7017271, FAX 011 44 71 7082437, telex 261507. ***Continues*** *British Toys, 0007-1897.*

CN/1182-5561
BULLETIN - ONTARIO HANDWEAVERS AND SPINNERS. **See** The Arts-Crafts and Decorative Arts.

US
BULLETIN (PEWTER COLLECTORS' CLUB OF AMERICA). (BULLETIN / THE PEWTER COLLECTORS CLUB OF AMERICA.). **Added/Corp** Pewter Collectors' Club of America. **VFOAT** PCCA Bulletin. (19??)-. Periodical. English. Twice a year. $30.00. Pewter Collectors Club of America, 740 Highview Drive, Wyckoff NJ 07481. **Tel** (201)891-0146. **LC** NK8400; .P47. **DD** 739.533.

US
BULLETIN (TOY TRAIN OPERATING SOCIETY : 1973). (BULLETIN / TOY TRAIN OPERATING SOCIETY INC.). **VFOAT** News Bulletin. Vol. 8, No. 1 (Jan. 1973)-. Bulletin. English. mo. $35.00. Toy Train Operating Society Inc, 25 West Walnut Street/Suite 305, Pasadena CA 91103. **Tel** (818)578-0673. **ED** Al Bailey, David Otth. **LC** TF197; .T59A. **DD** 625.1/9/05. Index available. cum. index. **Bk Rev. Ad Acc.** ctrl circ. ***Continues*** *News Bulletin (Toy Train Operating Society).*
Desc: A newsletter of classified toy train advertisements, history and operation of toy trains.

●US/1062-7383
CAGED BIRD HOBBYIST. **See** Zoology-Ornithology.

CN/1185-1856
CANADIAN SPORTSCARD COLLECTOR. [Can. sportscard coll.]. Vol. 1, No. 1 (Sept. 1990)-. Periodical. English. mo. 24.49Can$ Canada; $26.95 US; 38.95Can$ other. Canadian Sportscard Collector, 103 Lakeshore Road, Suite 202, St. Catherine's L2N 2T6 Canada. **Tel** (416)646-7744, FAX (416)646-0995. **DD** 769/.49796/0971.

CN/0703-895X
CANADIAN TOKEN, THE. **Added/Corp** Canadian Association of Token Collectors. Vol. 1, Issue No. 1 (July 1972)-. Periodical. English. bm (Jan., Mar., May, July, Sept., Nov.). 15.00Can$ Canada; 20.00Can$ other. Canadian Association of Token Collectors, 10 Wesanford Place, Hamilton Ontario L8P 1N6 Canada. **Tel** (905)528-3649. **ED** K. A. Palmer. **DD** 737/.3/0971. **Bk Rev. Circ:** 300 (ctrl).
Desc: Articles on the subject of Canadian tokens.
Ind/Abst Numis. Lit.

US/1048-6194
CAR MODELER. [Car model.]. Vol. 1, No. 1 (May 1990)-. Periodical. English. bm (Jan., Mar., May, July, Sept., Nov.). $16.00 (one year), $30.00 (two year) US; $19.00 (one year), $36.00 (two year) Canada & Mexico ; $22.00 (one year), $ $42.00 (two year) other. Highland Productions Inc., N50 West 13605 Overview Drive, Menomonee Falls WI 53051. **Tel** (414)783-7740, FAX (414)783-7710. **ED** Gary Schmidt. **DD** 629. **Bk Rev**, (Qty: 6-8). **Ad Acc, Adv Mgr:** Brain Taylor. **Circ:** 29,000.
Desc: By modelers, for modelers. Contains how-to articles covering all areas of the modeling hobby, from kit and resin reviews, contest coverage, model truck coverage, hobby happenings and more.

US/1059-9142
CARD COLLECTOR'S PRICE GUIDE. ***Title Change.*** [Card collect. price guide]. Vol. 1, No. 1 May (1992)-(Jan. 1995). Periodical. English. mo. Century Publishing Company, 990 Grove Street, Evanston IL 60201-4370. **Tel** (708)491-6440, (800)321-3333, FAX (708)491-0459. **LC** WMLC 91/4465. **DD** 790. ***Merged into*** *Combo, 1078-389X.*
Desc: Buy/sell price guide for non-sports trading cards.

US/0008-6916
CARRIAGE JOURNAL, THE. [Carriage J.]. **Added/Corp** Carriage Association of America. Carriage Association. Vol. 1 (June 1963)-. Periodical. English. qt. $25.00 library, $45.00 other. The Carriage Journal, RD #1 Box 115, Salem NJ 08079. **Tel** (609)935-1616, FAX (609)358-6138. **ED** Jill Ryder. **DD** 600; 973. Index available. cum. index. **Bk Rev**, (Qty: 10-12). **Ad Acc, Adv Mgr:** Diane Garrison. **Circ:** 4,500.
Desc: To foster the knowledge and research of collecting, restoring and driving horse-drawn vehicles.
Ind/Abst Art Archaeol. Tech. Abstr.

AT
CERAMIC STUDY GROUP NEWSLETTER. (19??)-. Newsletter. English. Ten times a year (Published monthly except Dec. and Jan.). 35.00Aus$. Ceramic Study Group Newsletter, PO Box 1528, Macquarie Center, Sydney, New South Wales, 2113 Australia. **Tel** 02 869 2195. **Bk Rev**, (Qty: 20). **Ad Acc. Circ:** 600 (ctrl).
Desc: Articles and information of interest to potters and those interested in pottery.

CN/1183-3033
CHARLTON HOCKEY CARD PRICE GUIDE, THE. ***Title Change.*** [Charlt. hockey card price guide]. **Added/Corp** Charlton International Inc. 1st Ed. (1991)-(1992). Periodical. English. sa. Charlton Press, 2010 Yonge Street, Toronto Ontario M4S 1Z9. **Tel** (416)488-4653. **DD** 769/.497962/0294. ***Continued by*** *Charlton Standard Catalogue of Hockey Cards, 1188-7737.*

US/0228-6947
CHARLTON STANDARD CATALOGUE OF ROYAL DOULTON FIGURINES, THE. [Charlton stand. cat. R. Doulton fig.]. **VFOAT** Royal Doulton Figurines. 2nd Ed. (1991)-. English. be. $14.95 per vol. Charlton Press, 2010 Yonge Street, Toronto Ontario M4S 1Z9. **Tel** (416)488-4653. **DD** 738.8/2/0294.

FR
CHASSE REVUE NATIONALE CHASSE. French. mo. Dawson France SA, BP 40, 91121 Palaiseau Cedex France. **Tel** 011 33 1 69104700, telex 220064F.

US/0094-1182
CIVIL WAR COLLECTORS' DEALER DIRECTORY, THE. **See** Antiques.

●US/1066-6281
CLASSIC AMUSEMENTS. [Class. amus.]. Issue 8 (Nov./Dec. 1992)-. Periodical. English. bm. Classic Amusements, PO Box 315, Clifton VA 22024. **DD** 688. ***Continues*** *Slot Machine-Juke Box Collector, 1058-8256.*

US/0009-8310
CLASSIC CAR. **See** Transportation-Automobiles.

US
CLASSIC CAR DIGEST. **See** Transportation-Automobiles.

US/0895-0997
CLASSIC TOY TRAINS. [Class. toy trains]. **VFOAT** CTT. (Fall 1987)-. Periodical. English. Eight times a year. $26.50 US; $35.00 other. Kalmbach Publishing Company, PO Box 1612, Waukesha WI 53187. **Tel** (414)796-8776 ext.411, FAX (414)796-0126. **ED** Dick Christianson. **DD** 625. **Bk Rev. Ad Acc. Circ:** 45,206.
Desc: A magazine for toy train collectors and operators. Each issue recalls and reports on the trains built by Lionel, American Flyer, Ives, LGB, and a variety of other manufacturers. Readers discover information on collecting, operating, repairing, and restoring toy trains.

UK/0961-5032
CLOCKMAKER (HINCKLEY). (THE CLOCKMAKER.). [Clockmaker Hinckley]. (Feb. 1990)-. Trade Publication. English. bm (6 issues). £15.50 UK; £18.50 US, Canada and Europe; £19.50 other. TEE Publishing, Fosse Way, Radford Semele, Leamington Spa CV31 1XN England. **Tel** 011 44 926 614101, FAX 011 44 926 614293. **ED** Charles Aked. **DD** 681.113. Index available. **Bk Rev. Ad Acc, Adv Mgr:** Susi Bolzicco, **Tel** same as publisher. **Pr Rev. Circ:** 3,000.
Desc: Designed for the amateur and professional clockmakers and restorers.

US/1056-4527
COLLECT, I. [I collect]. (1991)-. Periodical. English. mo. $5.00. Amazing Sports Publications, 655 Broadway, Suite 1055, Denver CO 80203. **DD** 790.

CN/0822-4927
COLLECTABLES AUCTION. [Collect. auction - Torex]. **Main/Corp** Torex. Periodical. English. $3.50 per no. Charlton Press, 2010 Yonge Street, Toronto Ontario M4S 1Z9. **Tel** (416)488-4653. **DD** 738.8/2/0294713541.

CN/0822-4889
COLLECTABLES AUCTION / CHARLTON AUCTIONS. [Collect. auction - Charlton Auctions]. **Main/Corp** Charlton Auctions. Periodical. English. $2.50 per no. Charlton Press, 2010 Yonge Street, Toronto Ontario M4S 1Z9. **Tel** (416)488-4653. **DD** 738.8/2/0294713541. ***Absorbed in part*** *Unreserved Public Mini Auction, 0822-7713.*

US/1076-4356
COLLECTIBLE NEWSPAPERS. [Collect. newsp.]. **Added/Corp** Newspaper Collectors' Society of America. Vol. 1, No. 1 (Feb./March 1984)-. English. qt. $18.00. Newspaper Collector Society of America, Box 19134, Lansing MI 48901. **Tel** (517)887-1255, FAX (517)887-2194. **ED** Rick Brown. **LC** PN4888.C57; C65. **DD** 070/.075. Index available. cum. index. **Bk Rev**, (Qty: 3). **Photos. Ad Acc.** Full Page (B&W) $45.00. Half Page (B&W) $25.00. **Circ:** 400.
Desc: Journalism and printing history for researchers, libraries, and collectors of antique newspapers.

US
COLLECTIBLE TRUCKS. **See** Transportation-Automobiles.

●US/1073-8142
COLLECTIBLES, COUNTRY & AMERICANA. **VFOAT** Collectibles, Country and Americana; Country Accents Collectibles. (1993)-. Periodical. English. Four times a year. $15.97. GCR Publishing Group, 1700 Broadway, 34th Floor, New York NY 10019. **Tel** (212)541-7100, (800)435-0715, FAX (212)245-1241. **(Subscription address:** Kable Publishers Aide, 308 East Hitt Street, Subscription Department, Mt. Morris IL 61054-1473.**)**
Desc: Magazine about vintage collectibles from the 1920's through the 1950's. Informative and fun to read with plenty on flea markets and garage sale finds.

●US/1068-347X
COLLECTING TOYS. **See** Gifts, Toys.

US/0888-1944
COLLECTOR CAR NEWS. [Collect. car news]. Vol. 25, No. 3 (March 1986)-. Periodical. English. mo. $18.75. Collector Car News, PO Box 2210, Palm Springs CA 92263. **Tel** (619)778-1370. **ED** W.L. Finefrock (editor's address: PO Box 2300, Santa Maria, CA 93455; editor's telephone number: (805)937-8575). **LC** TL7.A1; C62. **DD** 629.2/222/0750973. **Bk Rev. Ad Acc. Circ:** 10,000. ***Formed by the union of*** *Coast Car Collector, 0191-4758* ***and*** *Collectors Motor News, 0746-8687.*
Desc: News, features, calendar of car events.

US/0733-2130
COLLECTOR EDITIONS. [Collect. ed.]. (198?)-. Periodical. English. bm (6 issues). $19.97. Acquire Publishing Company, 170 Fifth Avenue, New York NY 10010. **Tel** (212)989-8700, (800)347-6969, FAX (212)645-8976. **ED** Joan M. Pursley. **LC** AM201; .C68. **DD** 069.5/05. **Circ:** 70,000. available on microfilm from University Microfilms International (UMI). ***Continues*** *Collector Editions Quarterly, 0199-929X.*
Desc: Reports on ceramics and glass, tabletop and collector art. Emphasis is placed on antiques and limited-edition contemporary products that are collectible.

US/1071-4162
COLLECTOR (HUNTER, N.Y.), THE. (THE COLLECTOR.). [Collector]. Vol. 1 (Sept. 1887)-. Periodical. English. mo (10-11 eacy year). $15.00 North America; $25.00 other. Walter R Benjamin Autographs, PO Box 255 Hunter, New York NY 12442. **Tel** (212)834-3902. **ED** W R Benjamin. **LC** Z41; .A2C6. **DD** 929.
Desc: For autograph and historical collectors.

UK
COLLECTOR'S CAR. (Sept. 1979)-. Periodical. English. mo. Reed Business Publishing / West Sussex, England, Perrymount Road, Haywards Heath, West Sussex RH16 3DH England. **Tel** 011 44 81 6523500. **LC** TL7.A1; C64. **DD** 629.2/222/075. ***Supersedes*** *V & V, Veteran & Vintage Magazine.*

CN/1183-2185
COLLECTORS' CHRONICLE, THE. [Collect. chron.]. Vol. 1 (Feb. 1991)-. Periodical. English. mo. $23.50 Canada; $37.75 other. Rainforest Publications Inc., #209-2010 Barclay Street, Vancouver British Columbia V6G 1L5 Canada. **DD** 769/.49796/05.

UK
COLLECTORS CLASSICS. Monographic series. English. Price varies per volume. Blues Unlimited Department CC, 38A Sackville Road, Bexhill-On-Sea Sussex England.

●US/1068-4808
COLLECTORS' INFORMATION BUREAU'S COLLECTIBLES MARKET GUIDE & PRICE INDEX. [Collect. Inf. Bur. collect. mark. guide price index]. **Added/Corp** Collectors' Information Bureau (U.S.). **VFOAT** Collectibles Market Guide & Price Index; Collectibles Market Guide and Price Index. 9th Ed. (1992)-. English. $13.95. Collector's Information Bureau, 2420 Burton SE, Grand Rapids MI 49546. **LC** NK1125; .A353. **DD** 745/.075. ***Continues*** *Collectibles Market Guide & Price Index to Limited Edition Plates, Figurines, Bells, Graphics, Steins, and Dolls, 1068-4794.*

US/0735-9357
COLLECTORS' MARKETPLACE DIRECTORY. NEW YORK CITY DESIGN. (COLLECTORS' MARKETPLACE DIRECTORY.). [Collect. marketpl. dir., N.Y. City ed.]. 1981-1982-. Directory. English. Artrepreneur/Boritz M A F, 945 Fifth Avenue, New York NY 10021. **LC** AM311.N5; C64. **DD** 300/.025/7471.

US/0744-5989
COLLECTORS' SHOWCASE (SAN DIEGO, CALIF.). **See** Antiques.

Hobbies

●US/1066-3649
COLLECTOR'S SOURCE. [Collect. source]. Vol. 1, No. 1 (Mar. 1993)-. Periodical. English. mo. $24.95. USA Weekend, 535 Madison Avenue, New York NY 10022. **Tel** (212)715-2011. **(Subscription address:** Small Publishing Fulfillment Service, 202 Twin Oaks Drive, Syracuse NY 13206.**) DD** 790.

UK
COLLECTORS WORLD (STAFFORD, STAFFORDSHIRE). (COLLECTORS WORLD.). Vol. 1, No. 1 (March/April 1983)-. Periodical. English. bm. Frank Allen Publishers Ltd, 14 Arcade Chambers High Street, Brentwood Essex England. **Absorbed** Antique Bottle Collecting.

●US/1078-389X
COMBO (EVANSTON, ILL.). See Recreation, Leisure-Games and Amusements.

US/1063-7982
COMIC BOOK COLLECTOR. *Title Change.* **See** Recreation, Leisure-Games and Amusements.

●US/1059-9401
COMICS RETAILER. [Comics retail.]. Vol. 1, No. 1 (Apr. 1992)-. Periodical. English. mo. $25.00 US; $30.00 Canada. Krause Publications, 700 East State Street, Iola WI 54990-0001. **Tel** (715)445-2214, FAX (715)445-4087, telex 55 6461. **LC** IN PROCESS. **DD** 658.
Desc: Covers the comics industry, including licensed comics products, videos, role playing games, trading cards, and apparel.

●US/1062-4503
COMICS VALUES ANNUAL. See Recreation, Leisure.

US/1052-486X
CONTEMPORARY DOLL MAGAZINE. [Contemp. doll mag.]. Vol. 1, No. 1 (Fall 1990)-. Periodical. English. bm. $19.90. Scott Publications, 30595 West Eight Mile Road, Livonia MI 48152. **Tel** (313)477-6650, (800)458-8237, FAX (810)477-6795. **ED** Lewis Goldstein. **LC** NK4894.U6; C66. **DD** 745.592/21/05.
Desc: A doll enthusiast magazine that exclusively covers contemporary dolls of all types. Included is advice for collectors and profiles of artists and manufacturers.

UK/0955-1298
CONTINENTAL MODELLER. [Cont. model.]. (1979)-. Periodical. English. Twelve times a year. £21.00 UK; £31.20 other. Pritchard Publications, Bear Seaton, Devon EX12 3NA England. **Tel** 011 44 0297 21542, telex 42603.

US
CRAFT DIGEST. English. Twelve times a year. $24.00. Craft Digest, PO Box 155, New Britain CT 06050. **Tel** (203)225-8875. **ED** Joseph Mehan. **Bk Rev**, (Qty: 30-40). **Ad Acc, Adv Mgr:** Harry Langenheim, **Tel** (203)489-4723. **Circ:** 3,500 (ctrl).

AT/1037-339X
CROSS STITCH. See Sewing and Needlework.

US/0732-5495
CRYPTOGRAPHY MAGAZINE. (198?)-. Periodical. English. bm (6 issues). $10.00. Cryptography Magazine, PO Box 641, Davis CA 95617. **Tel** (916)756-3720. **ED** William Estabrook. **Ad Acc. Circ:** 1,000.
Desc: Cryptograms and other puzzles, occasional stories, articles and contests. Suitable for beginners and experienced solvers.

GW/0941-8393
DATZ : AQUARIEN TERRARIEN. **Added/Corp** Verband Deutscher Vereine fuer Aquarien- und Terrarienkunde. Verband der Osterreichischen Aquarien- und Terrarienvereine. **VFOAT** DATZ-Aquarien Terrarier; DATZ-AT. (1991)-. Periodical. German. mo. Verlag Eugen Ulmer, Postfach 700561, D 70574 Stuttgart Germany. **Tel** 011 49 711 4507108, FAX 011 49 711 4507120, telex 7-23634. **Bk Rev. Ad Acc. Circ:** 16,500. **Continues** Aquarien- und Terrarien Zeitschrift, 0723-4066.
Ind/Abst Aquat. Sci. Fish. Abstr. (Computer File).

GW/0931-4393
DBZ. DEUTSCHE BRIEFMARKEN-ZEITUNG. [DBZ, Dtsch. Briefmarken-Ztg.]. **VFOAT** Deutsche Briefmarken-Zeitung. (1985)-. Periodical. German. bw (26 issues per year). DM146.00. DBZ Verlag Deutsche Briefmarkenzeitung, Postfach 1363, D-56377 Nassau Germany. **Tel** 011 49 2604 70148, FAX 011 49 2604 70151, telex 260 494 DBZ. **ED** Ludwig Trondle Lampertheim. **UDC** 656.833.91. **Bk Rev. Ad Acc. Circ:** 48,000 (ctrl). **Continues** DBZ. Deutsche Zeitung fuer Briefmarkenkunde, 0011-4790 **and** Phila-Report (Bendorf), 0720-2245.

US/1055-0364
DECOY MAGAZINE. [Decoy mag.]. (19??)-. Periodical. English. bm (Jan., Mar., May, Jul., Sep., Nov.). $30.00 (one year); $55.00 (two years). Decoy Magazine, PO Box 277, Burtonsville MD 20866. **Tel** (301)890-0262. **ED** Joe Engers. **LC** SK335; .D42. **DD** 745.593/6. **Bk Rev**, (Qty: 6). **Ad Acc. Circ:** 3,000.
Desc: Articles on decoy collecting and decoy makers, updated auction coverage, articles on collectible duck calls, fishing tackle and classic sporting art. Calendar of events, classifieds, book reviews, and museum news.

US/0896-7970
DIEHARD (BOSTON, MASS.). (DIEHARD.). [Diehard]. (1987)-. Periodical. English. mo. $21.95 (US); $29.95 (Canada). Coman Publishing Company, PO Box 2331, Durham NC 27702. **Tel** (919) 688-0218. **ED** Steve Almasey. **DD** 796. **Ad Acc, Adv Mgr:** Jan Cheves. **Circ:** 9,000 (ctrl). **Continues** Fan (Boston, Mass.), 0891-9151.

US/0742-373X
DIRECTORY OF MEMBERS / THE MANUSCRIPT SOCIETY. Main/Corp Manuscript Society (U.S.). Directory. English. ir (every 3 years). $5.00. David R Smith/Executive Director, 350 North Niagara Street, Burbank CA 91505. **LC** Z991; .M3614. **DD** 091/.025/73. **Circ:** 1,500. **Continues** Manuscript Society (U.S.). MS Directory.

US/0896-8322
DISCOVERIES (PORT TOWNSEND, WASH.). (DISCOVERIES.). Vol. 1, No. 1 (Jan./Feb. 1988)-. Periodical. English. Twelve times a year. $19.00 (one year); $30.00 (two years). Arena Publications, 17230 13 Mile Road, Roseville MI 48066. **Tel** (313)774-4311. **DD** 781.
Desc: Targeted toward the record collector.

CN/0706-5132
DIVER MAGAZINE. See Recreation, Leisure-Sports.

NE
DOEHETZELF. (19??)-. Dutch. mo (12 issues). Fl65.40 (latest issue). Medianet BV, Postbus 6298, 2001 LN Haarlem Netherlands. **Tel** 011 31 23 173311.

UK
DOLL & TOY. See Gifts, Toys.

CN/0840-3813
DOLL & TOY COLLECTOR (LONDON). *Ceased.* (DOLL & TOY COLLECTOR.). [Doll toy collect.]. **VFOAT** Doll and Toy Collector. (1988)-(199?). Periodical. English. bm. Box 454, Station B, London Ontario N6A 4W8 Canada. **DD** 688.7/221/0750971. **Continues** Canadian Doll Post, 0820-5140.

US/1052-0805
DOLL ARTISTRY. *Ceased.* (1990)-Ceased (May 1992). Periodical. English. bm. Hobby House Press, 900 Frederick Street, Cumberland MD 21502. **Tel** (301)759-3770. **ED** Carolyn Cook. **Separated from** Doll Reader, 0744-0901.
Desc: Editorial covers how to make dolls and create doll fashions.

US/0191-460X
DOLL NEWS. Added/Corp United Federation of Doll Clubs. (1???)-. Periodical. English. qt. Doll News, 8 B East Street, Parkville MO 64152.

US/0744-0901
DOLL READER. See Gifts, Toys.

US/0012-5229
DOLL TALK FOR COLLECTORS. *Ceased.* (1938)-?. Periodical. English. bm. Kimport Dolls, Box 495, Independence MO 64051. **Tel** (816)461-0757. **ED** Kim McKim. **Bk Rev. Circ:** 10,000.
Desc: Stories and features of interest to the doll collector.

US/1066-4726
DOLL WORLD (BERNE, IND.). See The Arts-Crafts and Decorative Arts.

US/1058-157X
DOLLS IN MINIATURE : THE MAGAZINE. [Dolls miniat.]. **VFOAT** DIM. (1991)-. Periodical. English. qt. $12.00. Dolls in Miniature, 3177 Bel Air Court, Camarillo CA 93010. **DD** 745.

US/0197-2626
DON CLEARY'S RECORD COLLECTORS DIRECTORY. See Sound Recordings and Systems.

●US/1065-7789
DOROTHY KAMM'S PORCELAIN COLLECTOR'S COMPANION. [Dorothy Kamm's porcelain collect. companion]. **VFOAT** Porcelain Collector's Companion. Vol. 1, No. 1 (Oct. 1992)-. Periodical. English. bm. $24.00. Dorothy Kamm's Porcelain Collector's Companion, PO Box 7460, Port St. Lucie FL 34985-7460. **DD** 738.

GW
DWJ, DEUTSCHES WAFFEN-JOURNAL. See Recreation, Leisure-Sports.

US/0737-1659
DX NEWS. (DX NEWS : THE MAGAZINE OF THE NATIONAL RADIO CLUB SINCE 1933 / NATIONAL RADIO CLUB.). **Added/Corp** National Radio Club (U.S.). (19??)-. Periodical. English. ir. $24.00 US; $25.00 Canada and Mexico; $36.00 other. National Radio Club, PO Box 118, Poquonock CT 06064. **Tel** (608)423-4159. **ED** Mike Knitter. Index available. cum. index. **Bk Rev. Circ:** 750 (ctrl). available on audiocassette.
Desc: The AM Broadcast Band Hobby magazine of the National Radio Club since 1933.

US/0199-5804
EJAG NEWS MAGAZINE, THE. See Transportation-Automobiles.

UK/0955-7644
ENGINEERING IN MINIATURE. [Eng. miniat.]. (1979)-. Periodical. English. mo. £19.20 UK; £25.40 other. TEE Publishing, Fosse Way, Radford Semele, Leamington Spa CV31 1XN England. **Tel** 011 44 926 614101, FAX 011 44 926 614293. **ED** N. Smedley and W. Tranter. **DD** 620.0028. Index available. **Bk Rev. Ad Acc, Adv Mgr:** Susi Bolzicco, **Tel** same as publisher. **Pr Rev. Circ:** 15,000.
Desc: Covers all types of model engineering.

UK
ESSEX SUCCULENT REVIEW. See Gardening and Horticulture.

US/1067-3202
EXPLORER KNIFE JOURNAL. See Recreation, Leisure-Sports.

AT/1035-0977
FACET TALK. [Facet talk]. **Added/Corp** Australian Facetors' Guild. (1981)-. Periodical. English. bm. 25.00Aus$ Australia; 35.00Aus$ other. Facetor's Guild, POB 399, Warwick Qld 4370 Australia. **Tel** (076)613-076. **(Subscription address:** 5 Altona Court, East Doncaster Victoria 3109 Australia**) DD** 736.2028. **Bk Rev. Ad Acc. Circ:** 1,200 (ctrl).
Desc: The official organ of the Australian Facetors Guild devoted to the interests of amateur and professional gem cutters.

IT
FARE ELETTRONICA. See Engineering-Electricity, Electrical Engineering, Electronics.

US/0277-979X
FINESCALE MODELER. [FineScale model.]. **VFOAT** Fine Scale Modeler. Vol. 1, No. 1 (Fall 1982)-. Periodical. Nine times a year. $26.95 US; $38.00 other. Kalmbach Publishing Company, PO Box 1612, Waukesha WI 53187. **Tel** (414)796-8776 ext.411, FAX (414)796-0126. **ED** Bob Hayden. **LC** TT154; .F54. **DD** 745.592/8/05. Index available. **Bk Rev. Ad Acc. Circ:** 77,144.
Desc: Information on constructing realistic and accurate models; includes new project ideas and tips and techniques.
Ind/Abst Index Inf.

US
FINGER LAKES TRAVEL GUIDE, THE. **Added/Corp** Finger Lakes Association. **VFOAT** I Love New York. (1978)-. English. an. $0.75. Finger Lakes Travel Guide, 309 Lake Street, Route 54, Penn Yan NY 14527. **Tel** (913)722-5050. **ED** H. F. Montague. **Ad Acc. Circ:** 15,000. **Continues** Finger Lakes Regional Travel Guide.

US/0015-4849
FLYING MODELS. (19??)-. Periodical. English. mo. $23.00 US; $29.00 Canada; $31.00 other. Carstens Publications Inc, PO Box 700, Newton NJ 07860. **Tel** (201)383-3355, FAX (201)383-4064. **ED** Robin Hunt. **Bk Rev. Ad Acc. Circ:** 32,000.
Desc: Covers model aviation for beginners and advanced modelers: radio control, control line, free flight. Also RC boats and cars.

US/1051-1997
FOOTBALL, BASKETBALL & HOCKEY COLLECTOR. *Ceased.* **VFOAT** Football Basketball Hockey Collector. (1990)-(July 1992). Periodical. English. mo. Krause Publications, 700 East State Street, Iola WI 54990-0001. **Tel** (715)445-2214, FAX (715)445-4087, telex 55 6461. **ED** Don Butler. **Ad Acc**.
Desc: Targets collectors of football, basketball and hockey cards and related memorabilia. Editorial covers news about cards, and collectibles, investment tips and comprehensive price guides.

GW
FREIZEIT REVUE. German. wk. $120.00 US. Burda GmbH, Postfach 1230, D-7602 Offenburg Germany. **Tel** 011 49 781-8401. **(Subscription address:** US: German Language Publications, Inc., 153 South Deanstreet, Englewood, NJ 07631**)**

US/1062-1482
GAUGE RAIL-ROADING, O. [O gauge rail-r.]. (19??)-. Periodical. English. bm (Feb., April, June, Aug., Oct., Dec.). $21.00 (1 year); $40.00 (2 year) US; $27.00 (1 year); $52.00 (2 year) other. Myron J Biggar Group Inc., PO Box 239, 692 Brandywine Road, Nazareth PA 18064. **Tel** (215)759-5367, FAX (215)759-0406. **ED**

Hobbies

Myron J. Biggar. **DD** 625. cum. index. **Bk Rev. Ad Acc. Circ:** 23,500. **Continues** O Scale Railroading, 0889-4167.

JA
GINKA. Japanese. qt. $83.00 California; $85.00 other US. **(Subscription address:** Kinokuniya Company Ltd., 38-1 Sakuragaoka 5, chome Setagaya-ku, Tokyo 156 Japan.**) ED** Bunka Shuppan-Kyoku.

US/0017-114X
GLEANINGS IN BEE CULTURE. *Title Change.* **See** Zoology.

US/1055-2685
GOLDMINE (1985). (GOLDMINE.). [Goldmine]. Vol. 11, No. 18 (Aug. 1985)-. Periodical. English. bw. $35.00 US; $71.95 other. Krause Publications, 700 East State Street, Iola WI 54990-0001. **Tel** (715)445-2214, FAX (715)445-4087, telex 55 6461. **LC** IN PROCESS. **DD** 780. **Continues** Record Collector's Goldmine, 8750-2577.
Desc: Music collector's marketplace Contains articles and columns on recording artists of the past and present, as well as complete discographies of those featured artists. Includes record show calendar for upcoming record shows nationwide.

CN/0017-5625
GUN TALK. **VFOAT** S.G.C.A. Gun Talk. Began publication in 1961. Periodical. English. qt. Saskatchewan Gun Collectors Association, Box 1334, Regina Saskatchewan S4P 0A0 Canada.

US/0883-4431
GUN TRADER'S GUIDE, THE. [Gun trader's guide]. 1st Ed.-. English. ir. $14.95 single issue. Stoeger Publishing Company, 55 Ruta Court, Ste 100 Hackensack NJ 07606. **Tel** (201)440-2700, telex 134511. **LC** TS532.4; .G87. **DD** 683.4/0075. Index available.
Desc: Up-to-date retail values of firearms manufactured since the turn of the century.

US/0897-5345
H.A.N.D.S. ON GUIDE. **See** The Arts-Crafts and Decorative Arts.

US/0145-6016
HOBBY ARTIST NEWS. Periodical. English. bm. $4.00. R Gillem, Route 2, Fort Atkinson IA 52144.

NE
HOBBY BULLETIN. (19??)-. Bulletin. mo (Jul./Aug. issue combined). Fl69.00. Uitgeverij De Muiderkring BV, POB 313, 1380 AH Weesp Netherlands. **Tel** 011 31 2940 15210.

UK/0142-6192
HOBBY ELECTRONICS. **See** Engineering-Electricity, Electrical Engineering, Electronics.

NE
HOBBY HANDIG. Dutch. bm. PVO Abonnementen Administratie Netherlands, Postbus 77, 5126 ZH Gilze Netherlands. **Tel** 011 31 1615 7450.

US/1053-8011
HOBBY INDEX. [Hobby index]. English. an. Index House, Box 716, Stevens Point WI 54481. **LC** Z6153.M63; H62; TT154. **DD** 016.688/1/05.

US
HOBBY MERCHANDISER ANNUAL TRADE DIRECTORY. Directory. English. an. $35.00. Hobby Publishing Inc, Box 420, Englishtown NJ 07726. **Tel** (201)446-4900, FAX (201)446-5488.

US/0744-1738
HOBBY MERCHANDISER (NEW YORK, N.Y.). (HOBBY MERCHANDISER.). Vol. 1, No. 1 (Jan. 1982)-. Trade Publication. English. Thirteen times a year. $20.00 US; $37.00 other. Hobby Publishing Inc, Box 420, Englishtown NJ 07726. **Tel** (201)446-4900, FAX (201)446-5488. **ED** Andrew Hecht. **LC** TT159; .H55. **DD** 382/.456887/0973. **Bk Rev. Ad Acc. Circ:** 8,500 (ctrl). **Continues in part** Craft, Model & Hobby Industry, 0011-0752.
Desc: Trade magazine serving model and hobby industry and radio control. Annual directory published in August.

US/1045-0602
HOBBYISTS' SOURCEBOOK. [Hobbyist sourceb.]. (1990)-. English. be. $49.95. Gale Research Inc., 835 Penobscot Building, Detroit MI 48226. **Tel** (800)877-GALE, (313)961-2242, FAX (313)961-6083, telex TWX 810-221-7086. **LC** GV1201.5; .H63. **DD** 790.1/3.
Desc: A one-stop reference listing of live, print, and electronic sources for information on more than 50 of the world's most popular hobbies, pursuits, and pastimes.

FI/0355-4317
HYMY. [Hymy]. **VFOAT** Hymylehti. (1972)-. Periodical. Finnish. sm. Fmk428.00. Laila Lehtinen, Kaukolantie 29, 02140 Espoo Finland. **UDC** 79. **Continues** Hymylehti, 0018-8298.

US/0098-9487
IAJRC JOURNAL. **See** Music.

US/0073-5930
INDEX TO HOW TO DO IT INFORMATION. **See** Hobbies-Abstracting, Bibliographies and Statistics.

US/1050-3994
INTERNATIONAL DOLL WORLD. *Title Change.* [Int. doll world]. Vol. 14, No. 2 (Apr. 1990)-(199?). Periodical. English. bm. House of White Birches, 306 East Parr Road, Berne IN 46711. **Tel** (219)589-8741, FAX (219)589-8093. **LC** TS2301.T7; N38. **DD** 688.7/221/05. **Continues** National Doll World, 0147-4685. **Continued by** Doll World (Berne, Ind.), 1066-4726.
Ind/Abst Index Inf.

US/0010-7646
JAYBEES. **Ceased.** (19??)-(19??). Periodical. English. mo. Claudine Moffatt, PO Box 36, Valley Park MO 63088.

FR
JOGGING INTERNATIONAL. English. 300.00F France; 380.00F other. Jogging International, 24 rue du Surmelin, 75020 Paris France. **Tel** 011 33 1 40300046.
Ind/Abst SPORT Discus.

US/0736-7724
JOURNAL OF THE AMERICAN SPORTING BOOK COLLECTOR, THE. Periodical. English. an. The American Sporting Book Holding Company, PO Box 504, Arlington VT 05250.

UK/0305-2133
JOURNAL OF THE PLAYING-CARD SOCIETY. **See** Recreation, Leisure-Games and Amusements.

SP
JUGUETECNICA. Spanish. mo. 6800ptas Spain; $68.00 US. Novofer SA, C/San German 5 1, 08004 Barcelona Spain. **Tel** 93-325 32 87, FAX 93-424 44 60. **Circ:** 10,000.

JA
KADO: ART OF FLOWER ARRANGEMENT. **See** Gardening and Horticulture-Florist Trade.

US/1062-9610
KIT CAR ILLUSTRATED. (1985)-. Periodical. English. Six times a year. $12.98 (one year); $19.98 (two year). McMullen Publishing Inc, 2145 West La Palma Avenue, PO Box 70015, Anaheim CA 92801-1785. **Tel** (714)572-2255, FAX (714)572-1864. **DD** 629. **Continues** Kit Car Quarterly.

US/0882-7362
KIT GUNS & HOBBY GUNSMITHING. **VFOAT** Kit Guns and Hobby Gunsmithing. 1st Ed.-. English. an. $11.95. Balund Inc, 2409 Westlawn Drive, Kettering OH 45440. **LC** TS535; .K5. **DD** 683.4/05.

US/0276-9042
KNIFE WORLD. [Knife world]. (1977)-. Periodical. English. mo. $15.00 (one year), $25.00 (two year), $35.00 (three year). Knife World, Box 3395, Knoxville TN 37917. **Tel** (615)397-1955, FAX (615)397-1969. **ED** C. Houston Price. Index available. **Bk Rev**, (Qty: 8). **Ad Acc. Circ:** 13,000 (ctrl).
Desc: Articles on knives and knife collecting.

US
KNITKING MAGAZINE. **See** Sewing and Needlework.

US/0898-8943
KNIVES ILLUSTRATED. [Knives illus.]. (1987)-. Periodical. English. Four times a year. $14.95 (one year); $26.95 (two year). McMullen Publishing Inc, 2145 West La Palma Avenue, PO Box 70015, Anaheim CA 92801-1785. **Tel** (714)572-2255, FAX (714)572-1864. **LC** TS380; .K579. **DD** 621.9/32/05.

US/0741-6091
KOVELS ON ANTIQUES AND COLLECTIBLES. **See** Antiques.

US
LINEUP. **See** Transportation.

GW/0175-7601
LOGBUCH, DAS. (LOGBUCH : JOURNAL OF MARITIME HISTORY AND MODEL SHIP BUILDING.). [Logbuch]. **VFOAT** Logbuch (Brilon). (1965)-. Periodical. German. qt. DM80.00. Arbeitskreis Historischer Schiffbau e. V., Hirschberger Weg 7, 59929 BRILON Germany. **Tel** 011 49 2961 8386. **ED** Hurst Menzel. **UDC** 689:629.12(091). Index available. **Bk Rev. Ad Acc.**
Desc: Strives to go beyond the scope of activities of usual interest to modelmakers. Primary topics range from background material on historic shipbuilding to types of vessels and individual vessels, as well as special problems in nautical technology.

US/0278-4114
LOOSE CHANGE. [Loose change]. (Fall 1977)-. Periodical. English. mo (10 issues). $39.00 US; $44.00 other. Mead Publishing Corporation, 1515 South Commerce Street, Las Vegas NV 89102-2703. **Tel** (702)387-8750. **ED** Daniel R. Mead. **LC** TJ1557; .L66. **DD** 629.8/2. cum. index. **Bk Rev. Ad Acc, Adv Mgr:** Nora Mead. **Circ:** 2,200.
Desc: Explores all aspects of coin-op gaming machines: equipment, history, collectors and collectibles, slot machines, jukeboxes, pinballs, vendors.

CN/0225-0721
MAGAZINE - CANADIAN ORNAMENTAL PHEASANT AND GAME BIRD ASSOCIATION. [Mag. - Can. Ornam. Pheasant Game Bird Assoc.]. **Main/Corp** Canadian Ornamental Pheasant and Game Bird Association. May 1979-. Periodical. English (French). mo. 18.00Can$ membership. Johanne Coppes, R R #3, Rockwood Ontario N0B 2K0 Canada. **Tel** (519)843-2049. **ED** William Brown. **DD** 636.5/9. **Ad Acc. Circ:** 900 (ctrl). **Continues** Canadian Ornamental Pheasant and Game Bird Association. Bulletin, 0225-0713.
Desc: Information regarding raising birds as a hobby; adds to acquire or dispose of birds and bird related items.

US/0195-7813
MANUSCRIPT SOCIETY NEWS, THE. [Manuscr. Soc. news]. **Added/Corp** Manuscript Society (U.S.). Vol. 1, No. 1 (Spring 1980)-. Periodical. English. Four times a year. $30.00 (insitutions), $25.00 (individuals), $50.00 (contributing), $75.00 (sustaining) Comes with Manuscript Society membership. The Manuscript Society, 350 North Niagara Street, Burbank CA 91505. **Tel** (818)845-3011. **ED** S. L. Carson. **LC** Z108; .M36. **DD** 091/.06/073. **Ad Acc. Circ:** 1,500 (ctrl).
Desc: A newsletter for members of the manuscript society, an organization of interest to autograph collectors, dealers, scholars, authors, archivists, institutions and many others.

US/0025-262X
MANUSCRIPTS (NEW YORK, N.Y.). (MANUSCRIPTS / MANUSCRIPT SOCIETY.). [Manuscripts]. **Added/Corp** Manuscript Society (U.S.). Vol. 5, No. 4 (Summer 1953)-. Periodical. English. qt. Free to members of the Manuscript Society. The Manuscript Society, 350 North Niagara Street, Burbank CA 91505. **Tel** (818)845-3011. **ED** David R. Chesnutt. **LC** Z41.A2; A925. **DD** 091. Index available. cum. index. **Ad Acc. Circ:** 1,450. **Continues** Autograph Collectors Journal.
Desc: Journal of the Manuscript Society, an international organization of persons and institutions devoted to the collection, preservation, use and enjoyment of autographs and manuscripts.
Ind/Abst Am. Hist. Life (1963-); Annu. Bibliogr. Engl. Lang. Lit.; MLA Int. Bibl. Books Artic. Mod. Lang. Lit.

PL/0137-883X
MAY MODELARZ. [May Model.]. (1958)-. Periodical. Polish. mo $36.00. **(Subscription address:** ARS Polona, PO Box 1001, 00068 Warsaw Poland.**) UDC** 689.

US/0025-6633
MEDAL COLLECTOR, THE. *Title Change.* (THE MEDAL COLLECTOR : OFFICIAL PUBLICATION OF THE ORDERS AND MEDALS SOCIETY OF AMERICA.). [Medal collect.]. **Added/Corp** Orders and Medals Society of America. (19??)-(19??). Periodical. English. mo. Medals Society of America, c/o John E. Lelle, PO Box 484, Glassboro NJ 08028. **Tel** (609)863-0148. **DD** 737. **Continues** Medal Collector Bulletin. **Continued by** Journal of the Orders and Medals Society of America.

UK/0026-4083
MILITARY MODELLING. (19??)-. Periodical. English. Twelve times a year. £21.00 UK; $53.00 other. Argus Specialist Publications, Queensway House, 2 Queensway Redhill, Surrey RH1 1QS England. **Tel** 0737 768611, FAX 0737 773993, telex 948669 TOPJNL G. **ED** Ken Jones. Index available. cum. index. **Bk Rev. Ad Acc.** ctrl circ.
Desc: Journal for modellers, wargamers, and military enthusiasts; includes full-color illustrations.

US/0199-9184
MINIATURE COLLECTOR. [Miniat. collect.]. (19??)-. Periodical. English. bm. $17.95 (one year), $33.95 (two year). Scott Publications, 30595 West Eight Mile Road, Livonia MI 48152. **Tel** (313)477-6650, (800)458-8237, FAX (810)477-6795. **DD** 745.

UK
MINIATURE WARGAMES. English. mo. £25.00 UK; £29.00 other. Pireme Publishing Limited, 34 Chatsworth Road, Charminster, Bournemouth Dorset BH8 8SW England. **Tel** 011 44 202 512355, FAX 011 44 202 499404. **ED** Iain Dickie. Index available. **Bk Rev**, (Qty: 70). **Ad Acc. Circ:** 14,000.

US/0826-9187
MINIATURES DEALER (CLIFTON, VA. : 1985). **Ceased.** (MINIATURES DEALER.). [Miniat. dealer]. Vol. 9, No. 3 (Mar. 1985)-Vol. 16 (May 1992).

Hobbies

Periodical. English. mo. Kalmbach Publishing Company, PO Box 1612, Waukesha WI 53187. **Tel** (414)796-8776 ext.411, FAX (414)796-0126. **ED** Geri Willems. **LC** NK4894.U6; M5. **DD** 688/.1. **Bk Rev. Ad Acc. Circ:** 2,000 (ctrl). ***Continues*** *Miniatures and Doll Dealer, 0747-0517.*
Desc: Services the doll house miniatures dealer, wholesaler, distributor, and manufacturer. Includes new products information, business articles, etc.

US/0896-7288
MINIATURES SHOWCASE. ***Ceased.*** [Miniat. showc.]. Vol. 1, No. 1 (Fall 1986)-(Nov. 1993). Periodical. English. bm. Kalmbach Publishing Company, PO Box 1612, Waukesha WI 53187. **Tel** (414)796-8776 ext.411, FAX (414)796-0126. **ED** Geraldine Willems. **DD** 688. **Bk Rev. Ad Acc. Circ:** 41,488.
Desc: A decorating magazine with tips, techniques and expert advice to inspire hobbyists of all skill levels.

US/0026-7295
MODEL AIRPLANE NEWS. See Aeronautics, Astronautics.

UK/0267-2715
MODEL AUTO REVIEW. [Model auto rev.]. (19??)-. Periodical. English. Ten times a year. £36.00 US & Hong Kong; £24.00 UK; £30.00 Europe; £39.50 Australia, New Zealand, & Japan; £32.50 Middle East. R & V Ward, Malvern House Publications, 120 Gledhow Valley Road, Leeds LS17 6LX United Kingdom. **Tel** 011 44 532 686685, FAX 011 44 532 686993. **ED** Roderick C. Ward. **Bk Rev. Ad Acc. Circ:** 6,000.
Desc: Leading publication worldwide for collectors of model and toy road vehicles. All scales, materials, kits and handbuilt. Mostly male adult readership.

US/0744-5059
MODEL AVIATION. [Model aviat.]. **Added/Corp** Academy of Model Aeronautics. (1937)-. Periodical. English. Twelve times a year. $18.00. Academy of Model Aeronautics, 5151 East Memorial Drive, Muncie IN 47302. **Tel** (317)287-1256. **ED** Jim Haught. **LC** TL770.A1; M62. **DD** 629.133. **Ad Acc. Circ:** 110,000. ***Absorbed*** *Air Youth Horizons.*
Desc: Deals with all categories of flying model aircraft with how-to and construction information.
Ind/Abst Index Inf.

CN/0317-7831
MODEL AVIATION CANADA. See Aeronautics, Astronautics.

US/0731-4795
MODEL BUILDER (1981). (MODEL BUILDER.). [Model build.]. (1981)-. Periodical. English. mo. $25.00 US; $35.00 Canada; $33.00 other. Gallant Models Inc, PO Box 669, 34249 Camino Capistrano, Capistrano Beach CA 92624. **Tel** (714) 496-5411, FAX (714) 496-5427. **ED** William C. Northrop, Jr. **LC** TL770.A1; M624. **DD** 629.133/1/305. **Ad Acc. Circ:** 60,000 (ctrl). ***Continues*** *R/C Model Builder, 0194-7079.*
Desc: Model Builder is about model airplanes, boats, product reviews and construction articles.

UK/0026-7325
MODEL ENGINEER, THE. [Model eng.]. Vol. 76, No. 1861 (Jan. 7, 1937)-. Periodical. English. Twenty-four times a year. £36.00 (24 issues), £18.00 (12 issues) UK; $96.00 (24 issues), $48.00 (12 issues) US. Argus Specialist Publications, Queensway House, 2 Queensway Redhill, Surrey RH1 1QS England. **Tel** 0737 768611, FAX 0737 773993, telex 948669 TOPJNL G. ***Continues*** *Model Engineer and Practical Electrician;* ***Absorbed*** *Home Mechanics; Ships and Ship Models.*
Desc: Caters to the practical model engineer as well as the theorist, with the objective of covering all aspects of the hobby in detail.

UK/0959-6909
MODEL ENGINEERS' WORKSHOP. [Model eng. workshop]. (1990)-. Periodical. English. bm. £15.00 UK; $38.00 other. Argus Specialist Publications, Queensway House, 2 Queensway Redhill, Surrey RH1 1QS England. **Tel** 0737 768611, FAX 0737 773993, telex 948669 TOPJNL G. **DD** 620.00228. ***Continues*** *World of Model Engineering, 0958-8078.*
Desc: A practical magazine designed to help the amateur machinist have an understanding of tools and equipment in the home engineering workshop. Contains drawings and instructions on how to make tools and perfect metal finishing techniques.

US/0026-7341
MODEL RAILROADER. [Model railr.]. Vol. 1, No. 1 (Jan. 1934)-. Periodical. English. mo. $34.95 US; $45.00 other. Kalmbach Publishing Company, PO Box 1612, Waukesha WI 53187. **Tel** (414)796-8776 ext.411, FAX (414)796-0126. **ED** Russ Larson. **LC** TF197; .M6. **DD** 625. **Bk Rev. Ad Acc. Circ:** 197,000. Documents available from UMI Article Clearinghouse.
Desc: Tips, projects, and photographs. Helps readers improve layouts and keep in touch with the hobby.
Ind/Abst Consum. Index Prod. Eval. Inf. Source; Gen. Period. Index (1985-); Mag. Index Plus (1989-); Newsp. Period. Abstr. (1988-); Mag. Index (1977-)(1959-).

US/0199-1914
MODEL RAILROADING. [Model railr.]. (19??)-. Periodical. English. Twelve times a year. $30.00 US; $38.50 other. Wiesner Publishing, 7009 South Potomac Street, Englewood CO 80112. **Tel** (303)397-7600, (800)945-0973, FAX (303)397-7619. **ED** Randall Lee. **LC** WMLC L 83/7271. **DD** 625. **Ad Acc, Adv Mgr:** Chris Lane. **Circ:** 15,000 (ctrl).
Desc: A how-to publication for model railroad construction, including layouts, track plans and prototype information.

UK/0953-0584
MODEL RAILWAYS (1987). (MODEL RAILWAYS.). [Model railw. 1987]. (1987)-. Periodical. English. Twelve times a year. £20.40 UK; $51.00 other. Argus Specialist Publications, Queensway House, 2 Queensway Redhill, Surrey RH1 1QS England. **Tel** 0737 768611, FAX 0737 773993, telex 948669 TOPJNL G. ***Continues*** *Your Model Railway, 0267-7016.*
Desc: Provides the general railway modelling enthusiast with the latest news, reviews and developments in the hobby, including competitions, quizzes, etc.

US/0191-6904
MODEL RETAILER (CLIFTON, VA.). (MODEL RETAILER.). [Model retail.]. (1975)-. Periodical. English. mo. $24.00. Kalmbach Publishing Company, PO Box 1612, Waukesha WI 53187. **Tel** (414)796-8776 ext.411, FAX (414)796-0126. **ED** Geoffrey Wheeler. **LC** WMLC L 83/7270. **DD** 381. **Bk Rev. Ad Acc.** ctrl circ.
Desc: Serves hobby retailers, distributors, and manufacturers. Includes: new product information, what's selling, business articles, etc.

UK
MODEL SHIPWRIGHT. (1971)-. Periodical. English. Four times a year (Mar., June, Sept., Dec.). £19.00 UK, $36.00 US, $43.00Can$ Canada, £21.00 other, (one year); £51.00 UK, $97.00 US, 116.00Can$ Canada, £56.00 other. Conway Maritime Press, 101 Fleet Street, London EC4Y 1DE England. **Tel** 011/44/71/583/2412, FAX 011/44/71/583/2412, telex 8814206. **(Subscription address:** Brasseys UK Ltd., Distribution Center, Blackhorse Road, Letchworth SG6 1HN England.**) ED** John Bowen. Index available (Bound in June issue.). **Bk Rev**, (Qty: varies). **Ad Acc, Adv Mgr:** J. Mannering, **Tel** 071 583 2412. **Circ:** 4,000.
Desc: These mix articles, reviews, and comment are from modelmakers from all over the world. Provides detailed information with authentic plans, clear diagrams, and photographs.

US/0892-2780
MODEL SHOPPER. [Model shopp.]. Periodical. English. mo. $11.95 US; $19.97 Canada and Mexico. Antic Publishing, 544 2nd Street, San Francisco CA 94170. **Tel** (415)957-1911. **ED** Dewitt Robboleth. **DD** 745. **Circ:** 48,000.
Desc: Edited for hobbyists who build gas and battery powered models. Offers how-to information and coverage of the latest model cars, airplanes and other items.

IT/0392-4076
MODELLISTICA. [Modellistica]. (1956)-. Periodical. Italian. mo. L80000 Italy; L105000 other. Vittorugo Chiodo, Borgo Pinti 95, 50121 Florence, Italy. **Tel** 011 39 55 2478487. **UDC** 793.7.

AT/0159-7191
MOROCCO BOUND. See Publishing-Books and Bookmaking.

US
MOUTHPIECE. See Zoology-Ornithology.

US/8750-5401
MOVIE COLLECTOR'S WORLD. [Movie collect. world]. Issue No. 200 (Nov. 30, 1984)-. Periodical. English. bw. $35.00 (one year), $50.00 (two year). Movie Collectors World, PO Box 309, Fraser MI 48026. **Tel** (313)774-4311, FAX (313)774-5450. **ED** Brian A. Bukantis. **DD** 791. **Bk Rev**, (Qty: 100). **Ad Acc. Circ:** 5,000. ***Continues*** *Movie & Film Collector's World, 0746-0325.*
Desc: Video and film hobbyist publication for trading, buying and selling tapes, posters and other movie memorabilia.

US/0731-8197
MRQ. VFOAT Miniature Railroad Quarterly. No. 1-. Periodical. English. qt. Tarjany Publications, PO Box 46, Calabasas CA 91302. **LC** WMLC L 83/107.

US/0898-5820
MUSCLE CARS OF THE .... See Transportation-Automobiles.

US/0739-327X
NATIONAL AUCTION BULLETIN. (19??)-. Periodical. English. sm. $49.00. National Auction Bulletin, 230 Basin Drive, Ft Lauderdale FL 33308. **Tel** (305)491-1799.

US/0027-884X
NATIONAL BUTTON BULLETIN, THE. [Natl. button bull.]. **Added/Corp** National Button Society. (19??)-. Bulletin. English. Five times a year (Feb., May, July, Oct., Dec.). $15.00 US & Canada; $20.00 (airmail) other. National Button Society, 2733 Juno Place, c/o Lois Pool, Akron OH 44333. **Tel** (216)864-3296. **DD** 687. Index available. **Bk Rev. Ad Acc. Circ:** 3,800. ***Continues*** *Button Bulletin.*
Desc: A non-profit organization devoted to the promotion of the hobby of button collecting. An organization of collectors, libraries, museums and members of the button trade in the United States and foreign countries.

US/0744-3889
NATIONAL JOURNAL (ALLENTOWN, PA.). See Glass and Ceramics.

US/1051-4600
NATIONAL KNIFE MAGAZINE, THE. [Natl. knife mag.]. **Added/Corp** National Knife Collectors Association. Vol. 7, No. 2 (July 1983)-. Periodical. English. mo. $32.00 US; $64.00 other. National Knife Collector Association, PO Box 21070, Chattanooga TN 37421. **Tel** (615)899-9456. **ED** Lisa Broyles. **DD** 623. **Bk Rev. Ad Acc. Circ:** 15,000 (ctrl). ***Continues*** *National Knife Collector, 0164-7547.*
Desc: Articles/reviews of knives, both old and new.

US/0747-5527
NATIONAL STAMPAGRAPHIC. See The Arts-Graphic Arts.

US
NAWCC BULLETIN. See Antiques.

US/0363-3284
NEW COLLECTOR'S DIRECTORY, THE. (1976)-. Directory. English. Padre Productions Inc, Box 1275, San Luis Obispo CA 93406. **Tel** (805)543-5404.

US/1061-7175
NON-SPORT MARKETPLACE. (NON-SPORT MARKETPLACE : THE NON-SPORT CARD HOBBY'S MOST OBJECTIVE, COMPREHENSIVE, AND REALISTIC PRICE REPORT.). [Non-sport marketpl.]. (1991)-. Periodical. English. Three times a year. $10.00, US; $15.00 Canada. Non-Sport Marketplace, PO Box 128, Plover WI 54467. **DD** 790.

US/0164-3290
NUTSHELL NEWS. See The Arts-Crafts and Decorative Arts.

US
OFFICIAL COLLECTORS JOURNAL, THE. VFOAT Collectors Journal; Journal. 1st Ed.-. English. an. $4.95. Random House Inc., 400 Hahn Road, Westminster MD 21157. **Tel** (800)726-0600, (800)733-3000, FAX (800)659-2436. **LC** AM201; .O34. **DD** 790.1/32/05.

US/0743-8702
OFFICIAL GUIDE TO BUYING & SELLING ANTIQUES AND COLLECTIBLES, THE. See Antiques.

US/1059-0056
OFFICIAL IDENTIFICATION AND PRICE GUIDE TO POSTCARDS, THE. [Off. identif. price guide postc.]. **VFOAT** Postcards. 1st Ed. (1991)-. English. House of Collectibles, 201 East 50th Street, New York NY 10022. **DD** 741.

US
OFFICIAL IDENTIFICATION GUIDE TO GUNMARKS. VFOAT ID Gunmarks. 2nd Ed. English. an. $9.95. Random House Inc., 400 Hahn Road, Westminster MD 21157. **Tel** (800)726-0600, (800)733-3000, FAX (800)659-2436. **LC** TS532.4; .O36. ***Continues*** *Official Guide to Gunmarks, 0747-6671.*

US/0748-3317
OFFICIAL PRICE GUIDE TO BASEBALL CARDS (1984), THE. (THE OFFICIAL PRICE GUIDE TO BASEBALL CARDS / BY THE HOUSE OF COLLECTIBLES, INC.). **Added/Corp** House of Collectibles. **VFOAT** Baseball. 3rd Ed. (1984)-. English. an. $8.89 (includes shipping/handling). Random House Inc., 400 Hahn Road, Westminster MD 21157. **Tel** (800)726-0600, (800)733-3000, FAX (800)659-2436. **LC** GV875.3; .O37. **DD** 769/.49796357/0973. ***Continues*** *Official Pete Rose ... Price Guide to Baseball Cards, 0749-3304.*

●US/1062-6980
OFFICIAL ... PRICE GUIDE TO BASKETBALL CARDS, THE. [Off. price guide basketb. cards]. **VFOAT** Basketball Cards; Official Price Guide Basketball Cards; Official Price Guide Basketball. 1st ed. (1992)-. English. $5.99. House of Collectibles, 201 East 50th Street, New York NY 10022. **DD** 769. ***Continues in part*** *Official Price Guide to Hockey and Basketball Cards, 1062-7227.*

●US/1069-8426
OFFICIAL PRICE GUIDE TO BEER CANS (1993), THE. (THE OFFICIAL PRICE GUIDE TO BEER CANS.). [Off. price guide beer cans]. **VFOAT** Beer Cans. 5th Ed. (Dec. 1993)-. Periodical. English. ir. Random House Inc., 400 Hahn Road, Westminster MD 21157. **Tel** (800)726-0600, (800)733-3000, FAX (800)659-2436. **DD** 739. ***Continues*** *Official Price Guide to Beer Cans and Collectibles, 0884-0237.*

Hobbies

US/0884-0237
OFFICIAL PRICE GUIDE TO BEER CANS & COLLECTIBLES, THE. ***Title Change.*** (THE OFFICIAL PRICE GUIDE TO BEER CANS & COLLECTIBLES / BY THE HOUSE OF COLLECTIBLES, INC.). [Official price guide beer cans collect.]. **Added/Corp** House of Collectibles. **VFOAT** Beer Cans. **VAT** Official Price Guide to Beer Cans and Collectibles. (198?)-(199?). English. an. Random House Inc., 400 Hahn Road, Westminster MD 21157. **Tel** (800)726-0600, (800)733-3000, FAX (800)659-2436. **LC** NK8459.B36; O36. **DD** 663. ***Continues*** *Official Price Guide to Beer Cans, 0748-1144.* ***Continued by*** *Official Price Guide to Beer Cans (New York, N.Y. : 1993), 1069-8426.*

US/0747-8747
OFFICIAL PRICE GUIDE TO BOTTLES, OLD & NEW, THE. [Off. price guide bottles old new]. **Added/Corp** House of Collectibles. **VFOAT** Bottles; Official Price Guide to Bottles, Old and New. (19??)-. English. an. $15.50 (includes shipping/handling). Random House Inc., 400 Hahn Road, Westminster MD 21157. **Tel** (800)726-0600, (800)733-3000, FAX (800)659-2436. **LC** NK5440.B6; O4. **DD** 748.8/2/075.

US/0882-2999
OFFICIAL ... PRICE GUIDE TO COLLECTIBLE CAMERAS, THE. [Off. price guide collect. cameras]. **VFOAT** Cameras. 2nd Ed. (1985)-. English. an. $9.95. Random House Inc., 400 Hahn Road, Westminster MD 21157. **Tel** (800)726-0600, (800)733-3000, FAX (800)659-2436. **LC** TR6.5; .O36. **DD** 771.3/075. ***Continues*** *Official Price Guide to Cameras, 0743-8664.*

US/8756-1654
OFFICIAL PRICE GUIDE TO COLLECTOR CARS, THE. [Off. price guide collect. cars]. **VFOAT** Cars. 1981-. English. an. Random House Inc., 400 Hahn Road, Westminster MD 21157. **Tel** (800)726-0600, (800)733-3000, FAX (800)659-2436. **ED** T Hudgeons. **LC** TL7.A1; K783. **DD** 629.2/222/075. ***Continues*** *Kruse Professional Price Guide to Collector Cars, 8756-1662.*

US/0747-7589
OFFICIAL PRICE GUIDE TO COLLECTOR GUNS, THE. (THE OFFICIAL PRICE GUIDE TO COLLECTOR GUNS / BY THE HOUSE OF COLLECTIBLES.). [Off. price guide collect. guns]. **Added/Corp** House of Collectibles. **VFOAT** Collector Guns; Guns. 1st Ed. (1984)-. English. an. Random House Inc., 400 Hahn Road, Westminster MD 21157. **Tel** (800)726-0600, (800)733-3000, FAX (800)659-2436. **LC** TS532.4; .O373. **DD** 683.4/075.

US/0747-7570
OFFICIAL PRICE GUIDE TO COLLECTOR HANDGUNS, THE. **Added/Corp** House of Collectibles. **VFOAT** Collector Handguns; Handguns. 1st Ed. (1983)-. English. an. $17.85 (latest edition). Random House Inc., 400 Hahn Road, Westminster MD 21157. **Tel** (800)726-0600, (800)733-3000, FAX (800)659-2436. **LC** TS532.4; .O374. **DD** 683.4/3/075.

US/0747-5357
OFFICIAL PRICE GUIDE TO COLLECTOR KNIVES, THE. [Off. price guide collect. knives]. **Added/Corp** House of Collectibles. **VFOAT** Collector Knives; Knives. (19??)-. English. an. $17.85. Random House Inc., 400 Hahn Road, Westminster MD 21157. **Tel** (800)726-0600, (800)733-3000, FAX (800)659-2436. **LC** TS380; .O34. **DD** 621.9/32/075.

US/0743-8710
OFFICIAL PRICE GUIDE TO COLLECTOR PLATES, THE. [Off. price guide collect. plates]. **VFOAT** Collector Plates; Plates. 1st Ed. (1983)-. English. an. $13.45 (includes shipping/handling). Random House Inc., 400 Hahn Road, Westminster MD 21157. **Tel** (800)726-0600, (800)733-3000, FAX (800)659-2436. **LC** NK4695.P55; O36. **DD** 738.2/4.

US/0747-8178
OFFICIAL PRICE GUIDE TO COLLECTOR PRINTS, THE. [Off. price guide collect. prints]. **Added/Corp** House of Collectibles. **VFOAT** Prints. 2nd Ed. (1979)-. English. an. $15.85 (includes shipping/handling). Random House Inc., 400 Hahn Road, Westminster MD 21157. **Tel** (800)726-0600, (800)733-3000, FAX (800)659-2436. **LC** NE885; .O36. **DD** 769/.12. ***Continues*** *Official Guide to Collector Prints, 0747-8348.*

US/0748-5840
OFFICIAL PRICE GUIDE TO COMIC BOOKS & COLLECTIBLES, THE. **Added/Corp** House of Collectibles. **VFOAT** Comic Books & Collectibles; Comic Books and Collectibles; Comics. (19??)-. English. ir. $9.95. Random House Inc., 400 Hahn Road, Westminster MD 21157. **Tel** (800)726-0600, (800)733-3000, FAX (800)659-2436. **ED** T. E. Hudgeons III. **LC** Z5956.C6; O38; PN6725. **DD** 741.5/0973/075.

US/0748-1365
OFFICIAL PRICE GUIDE TO FOOTBALL CARDS (1984), THE. (THE OFFICIAL PRICE GUIDE TO FOOTBALL CARDS / BY THE HOUSE OF COLLECTIBLES, INC.). [Off. price guide footb. cards]. **Added/Corp** House of Collectibles. **VFOAT** Football Cards; Football. 3rd Ed. (1984)-. English. an. $8.85 (includes shipping/handling). Random House Inc., 400 Hahn Road, Westminster MD 21157. **Tel** (800)726-0600, (800)733-3000, FAX (800)659-2436. **LC** GV959; .O36. **DD** 769/.49796357/0973. ***Continues*** *Official O.J. Simpson ... Price Guide to Football Cards, 0749-3290.*

US/1062-7227
OFFICIAL PRICE GUIDE TO HOCKEY AND BASKETBALL CARDS. ***Title Change.*** [Official price guide hockey basketb. cards]. **VFOAT** Hockey and Basketball Cards; Hockey & Basketball. 1st Ed. (1989)-(199?). English. an. House of Collectibles, 201 East 50th Street, New York NY 10022. **ED** James Beckett. **LC** GV568.5; .O34. **DD** 769/.49796/0973. ***Continues in part*** *Sport Americana Football, Hockey, Basketball, and Boxing Card Price Guide, 0732-1775.* ***Split into*** *Official ... Price Guide to Basketball Cards, 1062-6980* ***and*** *Official Price Guide to Hockey Cards, 1062-7138.*

US
OFFICIAL PRICE GUIDE TO HOCKEY CARDS. **VFOAT** Hockey Cards. 1st Ed. (1991)-. English (French). $5.99. House of Collectibles, 201 East 50th Street, New York NY 10022. ***Continues*** *Official Price Guide to Hockey and Basketball Cards.*

US/0748-5522
OFFICIAL PRICE GUIDE TO HUMMEL FIGURINES & PLATES, THE. (THE OFFICIAL PRICE GUIDE TO HUMMEL FIGURINES & PLATES / BY THE HOUSE OF COLLECTIBLES, INC.). **Added/Corp** House of Collectibles. **VFOAT** Hummel Figurines & Plates; Hummel Figurines and Plates; Hummels. (1981)-. English. an. $13.45 (includes shipping/handling). Random House Inc., 400 Hahn Road, Westminster MD 21157. **Tel** (800)726-0600, (800)733-3000, FAX (800)659-2436. **ED** E. Hudgeons III. **LC** NK4660; .O35. **DD** 738.8/2/094331.

US/0743-8672
OFFICIAL PRICE GUIDE TO KITCHEN COLLECTIBLES, THE. [Off. price guide kitchen collect.]. **VFOAT** Kitchen Collectibles; Kitchen. 1st Ed. (1984)-. English. an. $9.95. Random House Inc., 400 Hahn Road, Westminster MD 21157. **Tel** (800)726-0600, (800)733-3000, FAX (800)659-2436. **LC** TX656; .O36. **DD** 683/.82/075.

US/0747-5691
OFFICIAL PRICE GUIDE TO MILITARY COLLECTIBLES, THE. **VFOAT** Military Collectibles; Military. Began with vol. for 1982. English. an. Random House Inc., 400 Hahn Road, Westminster MD 21157. **Tel** (800)726-0600, (800)733-3000, FAX (800)659-2436. **LC** UC460; .O36. **DD** 355.1/4/075.

US/0747-5047
OFFICIAL PRICE GUIDE TO OLD BOOKS & AUTOGRAPHS, THE. **VFOAT** Old Books & Autographs; Old Books and Autographs; Books. (19??)-. English. ir. Price varies. Random House Inc., 400 Hahn Road, Westminster MD 21157. **Tel** (800)726-0600, (800)733-3000, FAX (800)659-2436. **LC** Z1000.5; .O35. **DD** 017/.8.

US/0747-5365
OFFICIAL PRICE GUIDE TO ORIENTAL COLLECTIBLES, THE. (THE OFFICIAL PRICE GUIDE TO ORIENTAL COLLECTIBLES / BY THE HOUSE OF COLLECTIBLES, INC.). [Off. price guide orient. collect.]. **Added/Corp** House of Collectibles. **VFOAT** Oriental Collectibles; Oriental. 1st Ed. (1984)-. English. ir. $9.95. Random House Inc., 400 Hahn Road, Westminster MD 21157. **Tel** (800)726-0600, (800)733-3000, FAX (800)659-2436. **LC** NK1068; .O37. **DD** 745.1/0951/075.

US/0747-5373
OFFICIAL PRICE GUIDE TO PAPER COLLECTIBLES, THE. ***Suspended.*** (THE OFFICIAL PRICE GUIDE TO PAPER COLLECTIBLES / BY THE HOUSE OF COLLECTIBLES, INC.). [Off. price guide pap. collect.]. **Added/Corp** House of Collectibles. **VFOAT** Paper Collectibles; Paper. (1980)-(19??). English. ir. **(Subscription address:** Random House Special Sales, Order Entry, 400 Hahn Road, Westminster MD 21157.**) LC** AM303.5; .O37. **DD** 790.1/32/0973.

US/0743-9792
OFFICIAL PRICE GUIDE TO PAPERBACKS & MAGAZINES, THE. **Added/Corp** House of Collectibles. **VFOAT** Paperbacks & Magazines; Paperbacks and Magazines; Books. 1st Ed. (1983)-. English. an. $13.85 (includes shipping/handling). Random House Inc., 400 Hahn Road, Westminster MD 21157. **Tel** (800)726-0600, (800)733-3000, FAX (800)659-2436. **LC** Z1033.P3; O35. **DD** 070.5/73/029.

US/8755-2787
OFFICIAL PRICE GUIDE TO SCIENCE FICTION & FANTASY COLLECTIBLES, THE. (THE OFFICIAL PRICE GUIDE TO SCIENCE FICTION & FANTASY COLLECTIBLES / BY THE HOUSE OF COLLECTIBLES, INC.). [Off. price guide sci. fict. fantasy collect.]. **Added/Corp** House of Collectibles. **VFOAT** Official Price Guide to Science Fiction and Fantasy Collectibles; S Fiction. 1st Edition (1985)-. Periodical. English. an. Price varies. Random House Inc., 400 Hahn Road, Westminster MD 21157. **Tel** (800)726-0600, (800)733-3000, FAX (800)659-2436. **ED** T. E. Hudgeons III. **LC** Z5917.S36; O37; PN3433.5. **DD** 016.80883/876.

US/0747-5055
OFFICIAL PRICE GUIDE TO SCOUTING COLLECTIBLES, THE. **See** Societies and Clubs.

US/0748-1128
OFFICIAL PRICE GUIDE TO STAR TREK AND STAR WARS COLLECTIBLES, THE. **Added/Corp** House of Collectibles. **VFOAT** Star Trek and Star Wars Collectibles; Star Trek and Star Wars Price Guide. 1st. Ed. (1983)-. English. an. $10.95 (includes shipping/handling). Random House Inc., 400 Hahn Road, Westminster MD 21157. **Tel** (800)726-0600, (800)733-3000, FAX (800)659-2436. **LC** PN1995.9.S694; O54. **DD** 791.45/72/075.

US/0475-1876
OLD CAR VALUE GUIDE. ***Ceased.*** **See** Transportation-Automobiles.

US/0048-1637
OLD CARS. **See** Transportation-Automobiles.

US/0895-9730
ORNAMENT COLLECTOR, THE. [Ornam. coll.]. Vol. 1, No. 1 (Dec. 1986)-. Periodical. English. Four times a year (Mar., June, Sept., Dec.). $21.95 (one year), $38.95 (two years). Rosie Wells Enterprises Inc., Route 1 Box 255, Canton IL 61520. **Tel** (309)668-2211, (309)668-2565, FAX (309)668-2795. **ED** Rosie Wells. **Ad Acc. Circ:** 6,500.

UK
PATCHWORK. English. £13.50 UK; $34.00 other. Argus Specialist Publications, Queensway House, 2 Queensway Redhill, Surrey RH1 1QS England. **Tel** 0737 768611, FAX 0737 773993, telex 948669 TOPJNL G.

US/1046-7963
PATTON'S ... FANTASY BASEBALL PRICE GUIDE. [Patton's fantasy baseb. price guide]. **VFOAT** Fantasy Baseball Price Guide. (1989)-. English. $8.95. Simon & Schuster, 1230 Avenue of the Americas, New York NY 10020. **Tel** (212)698-7000. **ED** Alex Patton. **LC** GV1202.F33; P38. **DD** 793.93.

US/1045-1188
PEN WORLD. [Pen world]. (19??)-. Periodical. English. Six times a year. $42.00 (one year), $107.00 (three year). World Publications / Texas, Box 6666, Kingwood TX 77325-6666. **Tel** (713)359-4363, FAX (713)359-4468. **ED** Nancy Olson. **LC** TS1262; .P46. **DD** 681/.6. **Ad Acc. Circ:** 10,000 (ctrl).
Desc: Covers vintage and contemporary fountain pens and related writing instruments.

GW/0031-7969
PHILOBIBLON. **See** The Arts-Art.

US/1052-9977
PICTURE FRAMING MAGAZINE. [Pict. fram. mag.]. (1990)-. Periodical. English. mo. $20.00. Hobby Publishing Inc, Box 420, Englishtown NJ 07726. **Tel** (201)446-4900, FAX (201)446-5488. **LC** WMLC 91/738. **DD** 749.

US
PLASTIC FIGURE AND PLAYSET COLLECTOR. **See** Gifts, Toys.

UK/0966-4033
PLAYING-CARD WORLD. **See** Recreation, Leisure-Games and Amusements.

US/1050-0790
POCKET PAGES. (POCKET PAGES : CALIFORNIA'S CARD SHOW DIGEST.). [Pocket pages]. **VFOAT** California's Card Show Digest. Vol. 1, No. 1 (Oct. 1991)-. Periodical. English. mo. $26.75. Pocket Pages, 19528 Ventura Boulevard, Suite 390, Tarzana CA 91356. **DD** 796.

US/0748-6510
POMONA : NORTH AMERICAN FRUIT EXPLORERS' QUARTERLY. **See** Gardening and Horticulture.

US/0740-1728
POST CARD COLLECTORS' BULLETIN. ***Ceased.*** [Post card collect. bull.]. (19??)-(1992). Bulletin.

English. bm. Krause Publications, 700 East State Street, Iola WI 54990-0001. **Tel** (715)445-2214, FAX (715)445-4087, telex 55 6461. **LC** NC1870; .P73. **DD** 741.68/3/05.

US/0746-6102
POSTCARD COLLECTOR. [Postc. collect.]. (1983)-. Periodical. English. mo. $23.95 (one year), $43.00 (two year); $59.00 (three year) US; $58.90 (one year), $109.50 (two year); $153.50 (three year) other. Joe Jones Publishing, PO Box 337, Iola WI 54945. **Tel** (800)331-0038, (715)445-5000, FAX (715)445-4053, . **ED** Deb Lengkeek. cum. index (yearly in the Annual). **Bk Rev. Ad Acc. Circ:** 7,867.
Desc: The leading magazine for postcard collectors contains the largest marketplace for antique as well as modern postcards. Informative articles and helpful columns aid the beginning and advanced postcard collector become knowledge about their collection. Includes postcard show calendar and auction results.

UK/0953-0592
PRACTICAL WARGAMER. [Pract. warg.]. (1987)-. Periodical. English. Six times a year. £11.70 UK; $30.00 other. Argus Specialist Publications, Queensway House, 2 Queensway Redhill, Surrey RH1 1QS England. **Tel** 0737 768611, FAX 0737 773993, telex 948669 TOPJNL G. **DD** 793.9.
Desc: Directed at wargamers of all levels - covers all aspects of wargaming and its peripheral interests; features factual, historical, fantasy, board games, role-playing, computing and modelling.

US/1058-1081
PROFESSIONAL MODEL NEWSLETTER. [Prof. model newsl.]. (1990)-. Newsletter. English. mo. $25.00. Professional Model Publications, Subscriptions, 201 North Wells, Suite 410, Chicago IL 60606. **DD** 746.

US/0734-1482
PROTOTYPE MODELER. ***Ceased.*** ?. Periodical. English. bm. Interurban Press, PO Box 6444, Glendale CA 91225. **Tel** (818)240-9130. **DD** 745. **Bk Rev. Ad Acc. Circ:** 8,200.
Desc: Model railroad hobbist magazine with emphasis on modeling from prototypes.

FR/0993-0701
PUCK (CHARLEVILLE-MEZIERES). (PUCK.). **Added/Corp** Institut International de la Marionnette. (1988)-. Periodical. French. an (Oct.). Price varies. Institut International de la Marionnette, 7 Place Winston Churchill, 08000 Charlevl Mezieres France. **Tel** 011 33 24 564455. available on microfilm from University Microfilms International (UMI).

IT/1121-5550
QUATTRORUOTINE ROZZANO. (QUATTRORUOTINE.). [Quattroruotine Rozzano]. (1965)-. Periodical. Italian. qt. L30000.00 Italy; L64000.00 other. Editoriale Domus, Via Achille Grandi 5-7, 20089 Rozzano Milan Italy. **Tel** 011 39 2 82472276, FAX 011 39 2 8255033. **UDC** 794.5. ***Continues*** *Notiziario del Club delle Quattroruotine, 1121-5569.*

US/1054-2256
RADIO CONTROL ACTION SERIES. (19??)-. English. qt. $16.00 (one year), $28.00 (two years), $39.00 (three years). Air Age Publishing, 251 Danbury Road, Wilton CT 06897. **Tel** (203)834-2900, FAX (203)762-9803. **(Subscription address:** PO Box 578, Mount Morris, IL 61054; Tel: 1-800-827-0598**)**

US/1043-8009
RADIO CONTROL BOAT MODELER. **See** The Arts-Crafts and Decorative Arts.

UK/0268-5248
RADIO CONTROL BOAT MODELLER. [Radio control boat model.]. (1985)-. Periodical. English. Six times a year. £9.60 UK; £12.60 Europe and Eire; £13.60 other. Argus Specialist Publications, Queensway House, 2 Queensway Redhill, Surrey RH1 1QS England. **Tel** 0737 768611, FAX 0737 773993, telex 948669 TOPJNL G. **DD** 623.8201.
Desc: Covers scale sailing and power models for the model boat builder.

US/0098-9215
RADIO CONTROL BUYERS GUIDE. **VFOAT** RC Buyers Guide. (1975)-. English. ir. $10.95. Boynton & Associates, 14101 G. Parke Long Court, Chantilly VA 22021. **Tel** (703)263-0900. **ED** George Zombakis. **LC** TT154.5; .R3. **DD** 629.04/022/8. **Ad Acc. Circ:** 20,000.
Desc: Descriptions and photos on thousands of products available for radio control modeling.

US/0886-1609
RADIO CONTROL CAR ACTION. [Radio control car action]. **VFOAT** Car Action; R/C Car Action. Vol. 1, No. 1 (Winter 1986)-. Periodical. English. mo. $30.00 (one year); $55.00 (two year); $75.00 (three year). Air Age Publishing, 251 Danbury Road, Wilton CT 06897. **Tel** (203)834-2900, FAX (203)762-9803. **(Subscription address:** Radio Control Car Action, PO Box 427, Mount Morris IL 61054.**)** **ED** Louis DeFrancesco Jr. **DD** 629. **Bk Rev. Ad Acc. Circ:** 125,000.
Desc: Covering the hobby of radio control cars. Reviews of new kits and major racing events, how-to articles and in-depth technical features. Columns address troubleshooting, off-road cars, monster trucks, on-road and electronics.

UK/0953-0576
RADIO CONTROL MODEL CARS. (1986)-. English. Twelve times a year. £19.20 UK; $56.00 other. Argus Specialist Publications, Queensway House, 2 Queensway Redhill, Surrey RH1 1QS England. **Tel** 0737 768611, FAX 0737 773993, telex 948669 TOPJNL G. ***Continues*** *Model Cars Monthly.*
Desc: Covers all aspects of the hobby of radio control model cars. Regular features include latest product releases and full-color up-to-date kit reviews, national and international race reports, and oncoming kit releases.

●US/1061-7213
RADIO CONTROL MODEL CARS (1992). (RADIO CONTROL MODEL CARS.). [Radio control model cars]. **VFOAT** RC Model Cars; R/C Model Cars. (1992)-. Periodical. English. mo. $25.00 US; $35.00 Canada; $33.00 other. Gallant Models Inc, PO Box 669, 34249 Camino Capistrano, Capistrano Beach CA 92624. **Tel** (714) 496-5411, FAX (714) 496-5427. **DD** 629. ***Continues*** *Radio Control Model Cars and Trucks, 1061-7205.*

US/1061-7205
RADIO CONTROL MODEL CARS AND TRUCKS. ***Title Change.*** [Radio control model cars trucks]. **VFOAT** R/C Model Cars Magazine; R/C Model Cars. (July 1990)-(1992). Periodical. English. mo. Gallant Models Inc, PO Box 669, 34249 Camino Capistrano, Capistrano Beach CA 92624. **Tel** (714) 496-5411, FAX (714) 496-5427. **DD** 629. ***Continues*** *Radio Control Model Cars, 0887-4689.* ***Continued by*** *Radio Control Model Cars.*

UK/0033-7838
RADIO CONTROL MODELS & ELECTRONICS. **VAT** Radio Control Models and Electronics. (19??)-. Periodical. English. Twelve times a year. $57.00. Argus Specialist Publications, Queensway House, 2 Queensway Redhill, Surrey RH1 1QS England. **Tel** 0737 768611, FAX 0737 773993, telex 948669 TOPJNL G. **ED** David Boddington. **Bk Rev. Ad Acc. Circ:** 33,000.
Desc: Specialist magazine on radio control model aircraft. Feature plans, practical articles, reviews, reports, consumer tests on all aspects of radio control flying disciplines.
Ind/Abst Index Inf.

UK/0269-8307
RADIO CONTROL MODELS & ELECTRONICS : RCM AND E. [RCM E]. (19??)-. Periodical. English. mo. £20.40 UK; $57.00 other. Argus Specialist Publications, Queensway House, 2 Queensway Redhill, Surrey RH1 1QS England. **Tel** 0737 768611, FAX 0737 773993, telex 948669 TOPJNL G. **DD** 621.

UK
RADIO CONTROL SCALE AIRCRAFT. **VFOAT** R/C Control Scale Aircraft. (19??)-. Periodical. English. Six times a year. £15.00 UK; $38.00 other. Argus Specialist Publications, Queensway House, 2 Queensway Redhill, Surrey RH1 1QS England. **Tel** 0737 768611, FAX 0737 773993, telex 948669 TOPJNL G. **LC** WMLC 93/894.
Desc: Combines scale radio control model know-how with full-size aircraft information; includes scale construction, international designs, engine tests, and a super scale plan feature.

UK/0144-0713
RADIO MODELLER. (19??)-. Periodical. English. Twelve times a year. £19.20 UK; $51.00 other. Argus Specialist Publications, Queensway House, 2 Queensway Redhill, Surrey RH1 1QS England. **Tel** 0737 768611, FAX 0737 773993, telex 948669 TOPJNL G. **ED** Alec Gee. Index available. **Bk Rev. Ad Acc. Circ:** 20,000.
Desc: Covers all aspects of radio-controlled model flight - power model and glider; slope soarer and thermal; and helicopter.

US/0033-877X
RAILROAD MODEL CRAFTSMAN. (19??)-. Periodical. English. mo. $25.00 US; $28.97 Canada; $33.00 other. Carstens Publications Inc, PO Box 700, Newton NJ 07860. **Tel** (201)383-3355, FAX (201)383-4064. **ED** William Schaumburg. **Bk Rev. Ad Acc. Circ:** 72,000. ***Continues*** *Model Railroad Craftsman.*
Desc: RMC reaches the model railroad enthusiast, beginner and advanced collectors. Contains information on scale and toy trains, how-to, plans, layouts, new products, books, meets and photos.

US/0199-3445
RAILROADIANA EXPRESS, THE. Periodical. English. qt. Railroadiana Collectors Association Inc, 330 Sophia Street, West Chicago IL 60185.

UK/0033-8931
RAILWAY MODELLER. [Railw. model.]. (1949)-. Periodical. English. Twelve times a year. £21.00 UK; £31.20 other. Pritchard Publications, Bear Seaton, Devon EX12 3NA England. **Tel** 011 44 0297 21542, telex 42603. **DD** 625.19.
Desc: Railroads models.

US
RARE BOOKS : TRENDS, COLLECTIONS, SOURCES. ***Ceased.*** (1983/84)-?. Periodical. English. an. R R Bowker, A Reed Reference Publishing Company, Part of Reed International PLC, PO Box 31, 121 Chanlon Drive, New Providence NJ 07974. **Tel** (908)464-6800, (800)521-8110, FAX (908)665-6688, telex 138-755. **ED** Alice D Schreyer. **NLM** Z 1029; R221.

US/0033-6866
RC MODELER (1969). (RC MODELER.). **Added/Corp** International Model Power Boat Association. National Association of Radio Control Clubs. National Miniature Pylon Racing Association. **VAT** Radio Control Modeler. (19??)-. Periodical. English. mo. $24.00. RC Modeler Corporation, PO Box 487, Sierra Madre CA 91024. **Tel** (818)355-1476. **ED** D. Dewey. **LC** TL770.A1; R14. **DD** 629.133/1. **Bk Rev. Ad Acc. Circ:** 150,000 (ctrl).
Desc: Devoted to hobby of the model building airplanes, boats, helicopters, and cars that are radio controlled.

US/8755-6154
RECORD COLLECTOR'S MONTHLY. [Rec. collect. mon.]. **VFOAT** RCM. (198?)-. Periodical. English. ir (2-3 issues). $15.00. Record Collector's Monthly Inc., PO Box 75, Mendham NJ 07945. **Tel** (201)543-9520, FAX (201)543-6033. **ED** Don Mennie. **LC** PAR. **DD** 789. **Bk Rev**, (Qty: 8-20/yr). **Ad Acc. Circ:** 2,500.
Desc: Covers collectible disc recordings from 1950 to 1970 - rock and roll, rhythm and blues, doo-wop, and rockabilly. Includes feature articles on recording artists, record labels, and up-to-date convention listings.

FR
REEF MISES A JOUR. (19??)-. French. qt. 1658.77F. Centre Sci Technique Baitment, 84 Avenue Jean Jaures, BP 2, 77421 Marne Vallee 2 France. **Tel** 011 33 1 64688282.

US/0742-9088
REPRODUCER, THE. (THE REPRODUCER : JOURNAL OF THE VINTAGE RADIO AND PHONOGRAPH SOCIETY, INC.). [Reproducer]. Periodical. English. qt. Free to major libraries. VRPS Inc, POB 165345, Irving TX 75016. **ED** George J Potter and Ken Deibel. **LC** TK6563; .R428. **DD** 621.3841/36/075. **Bk Rev. Ad Acc. Circ:** 450.
Desc: Covers antique radio and phonograph collecting, restoration methods, historical documentation, collectors, ads, and articles on radio equipment.

●US/1059-5759
RIFLE & SHOTGUN ANNUAL. **See** Recreation, Leisure-Sports.

US/0746-7672
RUBBERSTAMPMADNESS. **VFOAT** Rubber Stamp Madness. (19??)-. Periodical. English. bm. $20.00 (one year); $36.00 (two years). Rubberstampmadness, 408 SW Monroe, Corvallis OR 97330. **Tel** (503)752-0075. **ED** Roberta Sperling and Michael Malan (Managing Editor). **Ad Acc, Adv Mgr:** Susan Shumway. Full Page (B&W) $980.00. Half Page (B&W) $600.00. Full Page (Color) $1,265.00. Half Page (Color) $825.00. **Circ:** 13,000 (ctrl).

NE
RUNNERS. mo. Sportcom, Postbus 30, 1440 AA Purmerend Netherlands. **Tel** 011 31 02990 279950.

US/0193-7014
S9 HOBBY RADIO. **See** Communication-Broadcasting.

UK
SCALE AIRCRAFT MODELLING. English. mo. $56.60 US; £19.20 UK; £25.44 other. Hall Park Publications Ltd., 32 34 Simpson Road, Bletchley, Milton Keynes MK1 1BA England. **Tel** 011 44 908 377559, FAX 011 44 908 366744. **ED** Alan Hall. **Bk Rev**, (Qty: 12). **Ad Acc, Adv Mgr:** Andy Hale.

US
SCALE AUTO ENTHUSIAST. (1979)-. English. Six times a year (Feb., Apr., June, Aug., Oct., Dec.). $15.00 (one year) $ 28.00 (two year) US; $18.00 (one year), $34.00 (two year) Canada and Mexico; $21.00 (one year), $40.00 (two year) other. Highland Productions Inc., N50 West 13605 Overview Drive, Menomonee Falls WI 53051. **Tel** (414)783-7740, FAX (414)783-7710. **ED** Gary Schmidt. **Ad Acc, Adv Mgr:** Brian Taylor, **Tel** (414)783-7740. **Circ:** 64,000 (ctrl).
Desc: Covers all areas of hobby from cars to emergency vehicles, plastic to metal, out-of-the-box to scratchbuuilt. Contains how-to articles, kit and promo reviews, new items of interest, model car contest coverage, coming events listing and classifieds.

Hobbies

US/0145-8213
SCALE CABINETMAKER, THE. Vol. 1, (Oct. 1976)-. Periodical. English. Four times a year (Jan., Apr., July, Oct.). $22.00 (one year); $43.00 (two years). Dorsett Publication, PO Box 2038, Christiansburg VA 24073. **Tel** (703)382-4651. **ED** James H. Dorsett. **LC** TT178; .S32. **DD** 745.59/23/05. **Bk Rev. Ad Acc. Circ:** 2,400.
Desc: The how-to magazine in the miniatures hobby.

UK/0269-834X
SCALE MODELS INTERNATIONAL. [Scale models int.]. (198?)-. Periodical. English. Twelve times a year. £20.40 UK; $51.00 other. Argus Specialist Publications, Queensway House, 2 Queensway Redhill, Surrey RH1 1QS England. **Tel** 0737 768611, FAX 0737 773993, telex 948669 TOPJNL G. **Continues** Scale Models.
Desc: Covers news, reviews and conversion projects, plus full-size references and plans on all aspects of kit building - information on static scale models of aircraft, cars, trucks, and motorcycles.

US/0199-7327
SCALE R/C MODELER. **VFOAT** Scale RC Modeler. (19??)-. Periodical. English. mo. $35.50. Challenge Publications Inc., 7950 Deering Avenue, Canoga Park CA 91304. **Tel** (818)887-0550. **LC** TL770.A1; S29. **DD** 629.133/1343.

US
SDA NEWS / SURFACE DESIGN ASSOCIATION. **Main/Corp** Surface Design Association (U.S.). **VFOAT** Surface Design Association News. (19??)-. Periodical. English. Four times a year (Feb., May, Aug., Nov.). $45.00 (one year); $85.00 (two years); $125.00 (three years) Comes with Surface Design Association membership. Surface Design Association, PO Box 20799, Oakland CA 94620. **Tel FAX** (707)829-3285. **ED** Patricia Malarcher (editor's address: 93 Ivy Lane, Englewood, NJ 07631, phone: (201)568-1084). **LC** NK1160; .S96a. **Continues** Surface Design Association (U.S.) Newsletter.

UK
SEARCHER. English. mo $48.00. Searcher Publications, PO Box 43, Hindhead Sur GU26 6XG England. **Tel** 011 44 428 606109.

●**US/1064-3257**
SECRET OF THE PROS, THE. (THE SECRET OF THE PROS : THE NEWSLETTER FOR COLLECTORS, INVESTORS AND DEALERS OF TRADING CARDS.). (1992)-. Newsletter. English. mo. $29.97. The Secret of the Pros, 131 Langford Place, Suite 200, Charlottesville VA 22903.

UK
SILENT FLIGHT. English. Six times a year. £15.00 UK; $35.00 other. Argus Specialist Publications, Queensway House, 2 Queensway Redhill, Surrey RH1 1QS England. **Tel** 0737 768611, FAX 0737 773993, telex 948669 TOPJNL G.
Desc: Concentrates exclusively on model gliding and electric powered soarers. Offers advice on kits, assembly, motors, and radios.

US/0164-3509
SKINNED KNUCKLES. See Transportation-Automobiles.

US/1058-8256
SLOT MACHINE-JUKE BOX COLLECTOR. *Title Change.* [Slot mach.-juke box collect.]. **VFOAT** Slot Machine Juke Box Collector; Slot-Box Collector. **VAT** Slot Box Collector. Issue 1 (2nd Quarter of 1991)-(1992). Periodical. English. qt. Slot-Box Collector, 6560 Backlick Road, Suite 217, Springfield VA 22150. **LC** TJ1570; .S58. **DD** 688.7/52. **Continued by** Classic Amusements, 1066-6281.

US/0049-1845
SPECIAL-INTEREST AUTOS. See Transportation-Automobiles.

US/0190-1389
SPORT AMERICANA BASEBALL CARD PRICE GUIDE, THE. (1979)-. English. an (March). $16.95 Maryland residents; $17.69 other. Edgewater Book Co, PO Box 40238, Cleveland OH 44140. **Tel** (216)835-3108. **ED** Dr. James Beckett (editor's address: 15850 Dallas Parkway, Dallas, TX 75248; (214)991-6657. **LC** GV875.3; .B42. **DD** 769/.4/97963570973. **Circ:** 110,000.
Desc: Comprehensive listing of virtually all baseball cards produced from 1887 through 1993-94 and prices as determined through collector's input.

US
SPORT AMERICANA HOCKEY CARD PRICE GUIDE, THE. **VFOAT** Hockey Card Price Guide. (1991)-. English (French). Edgewater Book Co, PO Box 40238, Cleveland OH 44140. **Tel** (216)835-3108. **LC** GV847.6; .S66. **DD** 769/.49796962/0931.

US/1076-2701
SPORT ROCKETRY. [Sport rocket.]. **Added/Corp** National Association of Rocketry (U.S.). (199?)-. Periodical. English. bm. National Association of Rocketry, 1311 Edgewood Drive, Altoona WI 54720. **Tel** (713)499-5925. **ED** John Pursley. **LC** TL844; .M62. **DD** 629.47/5/0228. **Bk Rev. Ad Acc. Circ:** 7,500.
Continues American Spacemodeling, 0883-0991.
Desc: Includes photographs, plans, and technical articles on the hobby of model rocketry.

US/1050-365X
SPORTS CARD TRADER. [Sports card trader]. Vol. 1, No. 1 (May 1990)-. Periodical. English. mo. $29.95. Century Publishing Company, 990 Grove Street, Evanston IL 60201-4370. **Tel** (708)491-6440, (800)321-3333, FAX (708)491-0459. **LC** GV568.5; .S65. **DD** 769/.49796/0973.
Desc: Buy/sell price guide for baseball, football and hockey trading cards.

US/1069-2282
SPORTS CARDS. [Sports cards]. (19??)-. Periodical. English. mo. $18.95 US; $24.95 other. Krause Publications, 700 East State Street, Iola WI 54990-0001. **Tel** (715)445-2214, FAX (715)445-4087, telex 55 6461. **DD** 741. **Continues** Baseball Cards, 8750-5851.

US
SPORTS COLLECTORS DIGEST FOOTBALL, BASKETBALL & HOCKEY PRICE GUIDE / BY THE STAFF OF SPORTS COLLECTORS DIGEST. **VFOAT** Football, Basketball & Hockey Price Guide; Football, Basketball, and Hockey Price Guide. (1991)-. English. $14.95. Krause Publications, 700 East State Street, Iola WI 54990-0001. **Tel** (715)445-2214, FAX (715)445-4087, telex 55 6461. **LC** GV568.5; .S675. **DD** 769/.49796/0973.

UK/0144-249X
STANLEY GIBBONS POSTCARD CATALOGUE. **Added/Corp** Stanley Gibbons Publications Ltd. **VFOAT** Postcard Catalogue. 1st Ed. (1981)-. Publication. an. £5.95. Stanley Gibbons Limited, Parkside, Christchurch Road, Ringwood, Hants, BH24 3SH England. **Tel** 011 44 425 472363, FAX 011 44 425 470247. **LC** HE6184.P65; S7. **DD** 741.68/3/0750941. Each issue contains an index to its own contents (no volume index)--loose.

UK
STORY PAPERS COLLECTORS DIGEST. English. Story Papers Collectors Digest, 46 Overbury Avenue, Beckenham, Kent BR3 2PY United Kingdom.
Ind/Abst Child. Lit. Abstr. (19??-).

US/8750-3298
STREET RODDING ILLUSTRATED.
Ceased. See Transportation-Automobiles.

●**US/1068-5812**
TACKLE TESTER. [Tack. tester]. **Added/Corp** Tackle Tester Club. Vol. 4, No. 1 (Apr. 1993)-. Periodical. English. mo. Belvoir Publications Inc., 75 Holly Hill Lane, Greenwich CT 06836. **Tel** (203)661-6111, FAX (203)661-4802. **DD** 799. **Continues** Tackle Test, 1048-9215.

JA/0912-9715
TAMIYA MODEL MAGAZINE INTERNATIONAL. [Tamiya model mag. int.]. **VFOAT** Model Magazine International. (1985)-. Periodical. English. Six times a year. Argus Specialist Publications, Queensway House, 2 Queensway Redhill, Surrey RH1 1QS England. **Tel** 0737 768611, FAX 0737 773993, telex 948669 TOPJNL G. **DD** 745.592.
Desc: Covers a variety of modelling subjects, including radio control models and fine scale modelling. Also reviews, tips, and full-color how-to-build articles.

UK/1161-8566
TAMIYA MODEL MAGAZINE INTERNATIONAL FALQUEMONT. (TAMIYA MODEL MAGAZINE INTERNATIONAL.). (1991)-. Periodical. French. qt. £10.50 UK; $29.00 other. Argus Specialist Publications, Queensway House, 2 Queensway Redhill, Surrey RH1 1QS England. **Tel** 0737 768611, FAX 0737 773993, telex 948669 TOPJNL G. **UDC** 379.823(086.5).

●**US/1072-5121**
TAUNTON'S FINE COOKING. See Food and Food Industry.

US/0199-2988
TAXIDERMY REVIEW. (19??)-. Periodical. English. Taxidermy Review, PO Box 668, Sheridan MT 59749. **LC** QL63; .T35. **DD** 579/.4/05. **Continues** Wide World of Taxidermy.

US/0279-9731
TAXIDERMY TODAY. (19??)-. Trade Publication. English. qt (Jan., Apr., Jul., Oct). $22.00 US; $30.00 Canada and Mexico; $37.00 other. Taxidermy Today, 119 Gadsden Street, Chester SC 29706. **Tel** (803)377-7211, FAX (803)581-2557. **ED** Fredrick T. Ehrlich. **LC** QL63; .T37. **DD** 579/.4/05. **Bk Rev**, (Qty: varies). **Ad Acc. Circ:** 3,000.
Desc: Trade journal for taxidermists and related artists, both professional and hobbyist. Contains how-to articles, product and services reviews, introductions and sources of supplies.

US/0745-7189
TEDDY BEAR AND FRIENDS, THE. [Teddy Bear friends]. **VFOAT** Teddy Bear and Friends Magazine. Vol. 1, No. 1 (Spring 1983)-. Periodical. English. Six times a year. $17.95. Cowles Magazines, PO Box 8200, Harrisburg PA 17105. **Tel** (717)657-9555, (800)435-9610. (**Subscription address:** Kable Publishers Aide, 308 East Hitt Street, Subscription Department, Mt. Morris IL 61054-1473.) **ED** Carolyn Cook. **LC** NK8740; .T43. **DD** 745. Index available. cum. index. **Ad Acc. Circ:** 60,000 (ctrl).
Desc: Teddy bear making and dressing patterns, information for collectors, bear and animal values and fun paper dolls.

CN/0714-3788
TIPPS. (TIPPS, THE COLLECTOR'S JOURNAL.). [Tipps]. **VAT** Tipps Magazine. Vol. 1, No. 1 (Mar. 1982)-. Periodical. English. qt. $2.50 each number. Tipps The Collector's Journal, PO Box 5, Regina Saskatchewan S4P 2Z5 Canada. **DD** 790.1/32/097124.

●**US/1066-7423**
TODAY'S COLLECTOR (IOLA, WIS.). (TODAY'S COLLECTOR.). [Today's collect.]. (1993)-. Periodical. English. mo. $17.95 US; $31.75 other. Krause Publications, 700 East State Street, Iola WI 54990-0001. **Tel** (715)445-2214, FAX (715)445-4087, telex 55 6461. **DD** 790.

US/1056-8697
TOMART'S ACTION FIGURE DIGEST. [Tomart's action fig. dig.]. **VFOAT** Action Figure Digest. Vol. 1, No. 1 (1991)-. Periodical. English. qt. $16.00. Tomart Publications, PO Box 292150, Dayton OH 45429. **DD** 688.

AT/1035-9176
TOY & HOBBY RETAILER. See Gifts, Toys.

●**US**
TOY & HOBBY WORLD (1993). See Gifts, Toys.

US/1069-3254
TOY & HOBBY WORLD INTERNATIONAL. *Title Change.* See Gifts, Toys.

US
TOY & HOBBY WORLD. WEEKLY MARKET REPORT. *Ceased.* See Business-Retail.

US
TOY COLLECTORS DIRECTORY. Directory. English. an. Free to paid advertisers; $3.00 other. C Mack, Rural Route 3 Box 216, Saw Mill Road, Durham CT 06422. **LC** NK9509.15; .T69. **DD** 688.7/2/0750973.

US/0894-5055
TOY FARMER, THE. [Toy farmer]. (19??)-. Periodical. English. mo. $17.95 (one year), $29.95 (two years) US; $27.95 (one year), $49.95 (two years) other. Toy Farmer Limited, HC 2 Box 5, Lamoure ND 58458. **Tel** (800)533-8293, (701)883-5206. **ED** Claire Scheibe. **LC** IN PROCESS. cum. index. **Ad Acc, Adv Mgr:** Gwen Chappell. **Circ:** 27,000.

US/1051-2187
TOY TRUCKER & CONTRACTOR. [Toy truck. contract.]. **VFOAT** Toy Trucker and Contractor. Vol. 8, No. 3 (Mar. 1990)-. Periodical. English. mo. $17.95 (one year), $29.95 (two years) US; $27.95 (one year), $49.95 (two years) Canada; $27.95 other. Toy Farmer Limited, HC 2 Box 5, Lamoure ND 58458. **Tel** (800)533-8293, (701)883-5206. **LC** WMLC 91/1270. **DD** 629. **Continues** American Toy Trucker.

US/1060-9970
TRADING CARDS. [Trading cards]. Vol. 1, No. 1 (July 1991)-. English. mo. $17.95. LPF Inc., 9171 Wilshire Blvd/Suite 300, Beverly Hills CA 90210. (**Subscription address:** Kable Publishers Aide, 308 East Hitt Street, Subscription Department, Mt. Morris IL 61054-1473.) **LC** WMLC 91/729. **DD** 790.

US/0041-0829
TRAIN COLLECTORS QUARTERLY, THE. (TRAIN COLLECTORS QUARTERLY.). **Added/Corp** Train Collectors Association. Vol. 1 (Jan. 1955)-. Periodical. English. qt. $12.00 individuals; Free to School & Libraries. Train Collectors Association, PO Box 248, Strasburg PA 17579. **Tel** (717)687-8623. **ED** Bruce D Manson, Jr. **LC** TF197; .T68. **Bk Rev. Circ:** 26,000 (ctrl).
Desc: Historical writings and documentation relating to toy trains. Biographical information on toy train manufacturers, operating help for the toy train operator, and general news of the toy train industry.

US/1040-0001
TRAVEL COLLECTOR. *Ceased.* [Travel collect.]. Vol. 1, No. 1 (Oct. 1988)-(Sept. 1992). Periodical. English. mo. Travel Collector, PO Box 40,

Hobbies —Numismatics

Manawa WI 54949. **Tel** (414)596-1944. **ED** Dick Sherry. **DD** 910.
 Desc: Contains features and news for collectors of virtually anything.

US/0049-4593
TREASURE. (19??)-. Periodical. English. mo. $35.40 US; $45.40 other. Double Eagle Publishing / California, 31970 Yucaipa Blvd., Yucaipa CA 92399. **Tel** (714)794-4612, FAX (714)794-9452.

UK/0140-4539
TREASURE HUNTING. (1977)-. English. mo. £30.60 UK; £36.90 other. Greenlight Publishing House, Hatfield Peverel Chelmsford, Essex CM3 2HF England. **Tel** 011 44 245 381011. *Continues Metal Detecting.*

US/1041-4258
TUFF STUFF. [Tuff stuff]. (198?)-. Periodical. English. mo. $24.95 (one year), $44.95 (two years), $62.95 (three year) US; $32.95 (one year), $58.95 (two year), $79.95 (three year) other (includes postage). Tuff Stuff, PO Box 1637, Glen Allen VA 23060. **Tel** (804)264-0539, FAX (804)266-6874. **DD** 796.
 Desc: Includes complete price guides for baseball, basketball, football and hockey cards, ect. Informative articles and a wide variety of advertised products.

US/0899-496X
U.S. BOAT & SHIP MODELER. [U. S. boat ship model.]. **VFOAT** United States Boat and Ship Modeler; U.S. Boat and Ship Modeler. **VAT** United States Boat & Ship Modeler. (Summer 1987)-. Periodical. English. qt. $14.00 US; $20.00 Canada; $19.00 other. Gallant Models Inc, PO Box 669, 34249 Camino Capistrano, Capistrano Beach CA 92624. **Tel** (714) 496-5411, FAX (714) 496-5427. **LC** WMLC 93/773. **DD** 745.

US/1044-1344
U.S. TOY COLLECTOR MAGAZINE. See Gifts, Toys.

CN/0315-2383
UNITT'S CANADIAN PRICE GUIDE TO ANTIQUES & COLLECTABLES. See Antiques.

IT
VICINO ORIENTE. Added/Corp Universita di Roma. Istituto di Studi del Vicino Oriente. Vol. 1 (1978)-. Italian. ir. L100000. Herder Editrice e Libreria SRL, Piazza Montecitorio 117-120, 00186 Rome Italy. **Tel** 011 39 6 679 4628, FAX 011 39 6 678 4751.

US/1055-6060
VIDEO PROPHILES. *Ceased.* See Communication-Broadcasting.

US/1047-4420
VINTAGE FASHIONS. *Ceased.* See Clothing Industry and Fashion.

US/0736-198X
W.W. 1 AERO. See Aeronautics, Astronautics.

US
WANT ADVERTISER. Periodical. English. wk (51 per year). $175.00. WANT AD Publications, Inc., 740 Boston Post Road, Sudbury MA 01776-3397. **Tel** (508)443-4778, FAX (508)443-5253. **ED** Kim Grellier. **Ad Acc, Adv Mgr:** Mrs. Halter, **Tel** (508)443-4100. **Circ:** 65,000.
 Desc: Classified ads of miscellaneous items for sale by individuals rather than businesses.

US/0739-6457
WARMAN'S AMERICANA & COLLECTIBLES. [Warman's Am. collect.]. **VFOAT** Warman's Americana and Collectibles; Americana & Collectibles; Americana and Collectibles. 1st Ed. (1984)-. Periodical. English. be. $15.95. Warman Publishing Company, PO Box 1112, Willow Grove PA 19090-0703. **Tel** (215)657-1812. **LC** AM303.5; .W37. **DD** 790.1/32/0973.

US/0884-3791
WARREN'S MOVIE POSTER PRICE GUIDE. See Motion Picture.

US/1042-6094
WEEKEND WOODWORKING PROJECTS. [Weekend woodwork. prog.]. Vol. 1, Issue 1 (Jan. 1988)-. Periodical. English. Six times a year. $27.97 (one year); $48.00 (two years). Meredith Corporation, Locust at 17th, Des Moines IA 50309. **Tel** (515)284-3000. **(Subscription address:** Neodata / Colorado, PO Box 2606, Boulder Boulder CO 80322.) **DD** 684.
 Desc: Each issue includes 6-7 project plans for all skill levels such as clocks, pull toys, spice racks, laminated napkin rings and much more.

US/8750-295X
WESTERN WORLD AVON COLLECTORS NEWSLETTER. *Ceased.* (WESTERN WORLD AVON COLLECTORS NEWSLETTER / WESTERN WORLD AVON COLLECTORS NEWSLETTER).

Added/Corp Western World Avon Club. (19??)-Vol. 21, No. 6 (Dec. 1993). Newsletter. English. bm. Western World Avon Club, Box 23785, Pleasant Hill CA 94523. **ED** Floyd P Busby. **Circ:** 2,500.

UK/0265-8712
WHITE DWARF. [White dwarf]. (1977)-. Periodical. English (French). mo. $35.00 US; $45.00 Canada & Mexico; £27.50 UK; £35.00 Europe; 72.00Aus$ Australia and New Zealand; £45.00 other. Games Workshop Ltd., Chewton Street Hill Top Eastwood, Nottingham NG16 3HY England. **Tel** 011 44 773 769731, 760462. **(Subscription address:** Games Workshop Ltd / US, 3431 C, Benson Avenue, Balitiore MD 21227.) **ED** Robin Dews. **DD** 793.9.

US/0886-3407
WILDFOWL CARVING AND COLLECTING. See The Arts-Crafts and Decorative Arts.

CN/0826-2098
WILLOW TRANSFER QUARTERLY. See Glass and Ceramics.

US/0738-0143
WINNING SWEEPSTAKES NEWSLETTER. VFOAT WSN. Vol. 1, No. 1 (June 1983)-. Newsletter. English. mo. $24.00. Sebell Publishing Co., PO Box 1468, 965 Concord St., Framingham MA 01701. **Tel** (508)820-1800. **ED** Robin & Jeffrey Sklar. **Circ:** 100,000.
 Desc: Covers and analyzes chance of winning different sweepstakes.

US
WIZARD: THE GUIDE TO COMICS. (19??)-. English. mo. $37.95 (1 year), $59.50 (2 year), $3.95 (single issue) US; $45.95 (1 year), $4.95 (single issue) Canada; $69.95 other. Wizard Press Inc, 100 Red Schoolhouse Road, Building B-1, Chestnutridge NY 10977. **Tel** (914)426-1900, FAX (914)426-6071. **(Subscription address:** Wizard Press, PO Box 656, Yorktown Heights NY 10598.) **ED** Alan Binenstock. **Bk Rev,** (Qty: varies). **Ad Acc, Adv Mgr:** Colin Campbell, **Tel** (212)265-0986. **Pr Rev. Circ:** 300M (ctrl).
 Desc: Contains price guide, interviews with artists and writers, non-sport card section, toy section, hot comics, readers section, and show section. Overall the comic book industry for the collector and investor. General interest and lifestyle editorial.

US/0275-1569
YEAR BOOK (AMERICAN SOCIETY OF BOOKPLATE COLLECTORS AND DESIGNERS). (YEAR BOOK / AS OF BC & D.). [Year book - Am. Soc. Bookpl. Collect. Des.].
Added/Corp American Society of Bookplate Collectors and Designers. **VFOAT** Yearbook. Vol. 34 (1967/1968)-. English. an. $30.00 Comes with American Society of Bookplate Collectors & Designers membership. American Society of Bookplate Collectors and Designers, 605 North Stoneman Avenue, Suite F, Alhambra CA 91801. **Tel** (213)283-1936. **ED** Audrey Spencer Arellanes. **DD** 769. Index available. **Circ:** 200. *Continues Year Book ... of the American Society of Bookplate Collectors and Designers, Washington, D.C.*
 Desc: Contains artists who design them, individuals and institutions who use them, collectors who use and collect them; history of the bookplate throughout the centuries and around the world.

US
YELLOWBACK LIBRARY. See Literature.

ABSTRACTING, BIBLIOGRAPHIES AND STATISTICS

US/0073-5930
INDEX TO HOW TO DO IT INFORMATION. Added/Corp Norman Lathrop Enterprises. Abstracting, Indexing, and Dissemination Service. Norman Lathrop Enterprises. Information Abstracting, Indexing, and Dissemination Service Division. (1964)-. Abstracting/Indexing Service. English. an. Norman Lathrop Enterprises, PO Box 198, Wooster OH 44691. **Tel** (216)262-5587. **ED** Norman Lathrop. **LC** Z7913; .I64. Index available. cum. index.
 Desc: A subject guide to "how-to" articles appearing in craft, hobby, how-to, and special interest magazines. Includes information, instructions, plans, suggestions, and tips on how to solve and prevent problems, build and construct objects and to pursue a craft or hobby

US/0029-6031
NUMISMATIC LITERATURE. Added/Corp American Numismatic Society. No. 1 (Oct. 1947)-. Abstracting/Indexing Service. English. Twice a year (Mar. & Sept.). $11.00 US; $12.00 others. American Numismatic Society, Broadway at 155th Street, New York NY 10032. **Tel** (212)234-3130, FAX (212)234-3381, telex NUMISMA. **ED** M. H. Martin. **LC** Z6866; .A53. **DD** 016.737. Index available. **Circ:** 900.

 Desc: Survey of current publications in or related to numismatics with abstracts of their contents.
 Ind/Abst Am. Bibliogr. Slavic East Europ. Stud.

NUMISMATICS

SP
ACTA NUMISMATICA. (1971)-. Spanish. an. 7282ptas. Institut d'Estudis Catlanes, Carme 47, 08001 Barcelona Spain. **Tel** 011 34 3 3185407. **LC** CJ9; .A32.
 Ind/Abst BHA : Biblio. Hist. Art; Numis. Lit.

IQ
AL-MASKUKAT. Journal 1- July 1969-. Periodical. Arabic (summaries and/or abstracts in English). be. Directorate of Antiquities, Ministry Culture & Information, Baghdad Iraq. **Tel** 5376121. **LC** CJ3770; .M38. **Bk Rev.**

US/0884-5670
AMERICAN GUIDE TO U.S. COINS. *Suspended.* [Am. guide U. S. coins]. Began with 1964 Ed.-Suspended in (1992). English. an. Macmillan Publishing Co. / Indiana, 201 West 103rd Street, Indianapolis IN 46290. **Tel** (800)428-5331, (800)858-7674. **LC** CJ1830; .F7. **DD** 737.49/73.

US/1053-8356
AMERICAN JOURNAL OF NUMISMATICS (1989). (AMERICAN JOURNAL OF NUMISMATICS.). [Am. j. numis.]. **Added/Corp** American Numismatic Society. **VFOAT** AJN. 2nd Series (1989)-. English. an. $31.50 Comes with American Numismatic Society Regular and Publications membership. American Journal of Numismatics, Broadway at 155th Street, New York NY 10032. **Tel** (212)234-3130, telex NUMISMA. **LC** CJ1; .A63. **DD** 737/.05. available on microfilm from University Microfilms International (UMI). *Continues Museum Notes, 0145-1413.*

FR/0997-055X
ANNALES DU GROUPE NUMISMATIQUE DU COMTAT ET DE PROVENCE. (1970)-. Periodical. French. an. UDC 737 (449).
 Ind/Abst BHA : Biblio. Hist. Art.

IT/0578-9923
ANNALI / ISTITUTO ITALIANO DI NUMISMATICA. Added/Corp Istituto Italiano di Numismatica. **VFOAT** AIIN; Annali dell'Istituto Italiano di Numismatica. (1954)-. Periodical. Italian. ir. L80000. Istituto Italiano Numismatica, Via Quattro Fontane 11, 00184 Rome Italy. **Tel** 011 39 6 4743603. cum. index.
 Ind/Abst BHA : Biblio. Hist. Art; Numis. Lit.

CN/0318-4951
ANNUAL CONVENTION - CANADIAN NUMISMATIC ASSOCIATION. Main/Corp Canadian Numismatic Association. Began with 1970? issue. Periodical. English. Charlton Press, 2010 Yonge Street, Toronto Ontario M4S 1Z9. **Tel** (416)488-4653. **DD** 737.4/9/71. *Continues Canadian Numismatic Association. Convention Sale Catalogue, 0318-496X.*

US/0420-025X
ANTIKE MUNZEN UND GESCHNITTENE STEINE. Added/Corp Deutsches Archaologisches Institut. Vol. 1 (1969)-. Monographic series. German. ir. Price varies per volume. Walter de Gruyter Inc. / Hawthorne, 200 Saw Mill River Road, Hawthorne NY 10532. **Tel** (914)747-0110, GERMANY: 011/49/30/260050, FAX (914)747-1326, telex 646677. **(Subscription address:** Germany/ PO Box 110240, 1 Berlin 11 Germany)
 Ind/Abst Numis. Lit.

CN/0708-3181
ATLANTIC NUMISMATIST, THE. V. 15, No. 6- June 1979-. Periodical. English. mo. Atlantic Provinces Numismatic Association, PO Box 243, Armdale Post Office, Halifax NS B3L 4K1. **DD** 737/.06/2715. *Continues A. P. N. A. Newsletter, 0044-9903.*

US/0737-6634
AUCTION PRICES REALIZED. U.S. COINS. [Auction prices realiz., U. S. coins]. **VFOAT** Auction Prices Realized. US Coins; U.S. Coins; US Coins. (1982)-. English. an. $60.00. Krause Publications, 700 East State Street, Iola WI 54990-0001. **Tel** (715)445-2214, FAX (715)445-4087, telex 55 6461. **ED** Bob Wilhite. **LC** CJ1826; .R66. **DD** 737.4973. *Continues Rome's Prices Realized for U.S. Coins, 0277-6510.*
 Desc: Provides information on what buyers have paid for similar coins in a highly competitive market arena. Includes recent auction results, and covers the top sixty-five public numismatic auctions and more than 100,000 lots, with purchase prices.

AT/0004-8887
AUSTRALIAN COIN REVIEW. [Aust. coin rev.]. (1964)-. Periodical. English. mo. 32.00Aus$ Australia; 42.00Aus$ Asia and Oceania; 50.00Aus$ other. Jesat Pty Ltd., PO Box 5, Wombarra NSW, 2515

Australia. **Tel** 61 42 681434, FAX 61 42 681435. **DD** 737.494.
Ind/Abst Numis. Lit.

AT/1030-7915
AUSTRALIAN NUGGET JOURNAL. See Metals and Metallurgy.

AT/0004-9875
AUSTRALIAN NUMISMATIC JOURNAL. **Added/Corp** Numismatic Society of South Australia. (19??)-. Periodical. English. an. 15.00Aus$. Numismatic Society of South Australia, GPO Box 80, Adelaide 5001 South Australia. **ED** David Rampling. **LC** CJ1; .A92. **DD** 737/.099423. **Circ:** 250. ***Continues*** *South Australian Numismatic Journal.*
Desc: Articles on numismatics and kindred subjects, especially coins, tokens, paper money and medals; particularly those of Australia.
Ind/Abst Numis. Lit.

US/0164-0828
BANK NOTE REPORTER. (19??)-. Periodical. English. mo. $29.95 US; $40.25 other. Krause Publications, 700 East State Street, Iola WI 54990-0001. **Tel** (715)445-2214, FAX (715)445-4087, telex 55 6461. **ED** Dave Harper. **Bk Rev. Ad Acc. Circ:** 4,361 (ctrl).
Desc: Provides current prices for banknotes of the US and world. Active buy/sell marketplace for paper money collectors.
Ind/Abst Numis. Lit.

NE
BEELDENAAR, DE. **Added/Corp** Nederlands Genootschap voor Munt- en Penningkunde. Vereniging voor Penningkunst. (1977)-. Periodical. Dutch. bm (6 issues). Fl33.96 Netherlands & Belgium; Fl58.00 other. Stichting Beeldenaar, Postbus 11028, 2301 EA Leiden Netherlands. **Tel** 011 31 71 120748. **ED** M. Lagerwey. **LC** CJ9; .B4. Index available. **Bk Rev. Ad Acc. Circ:** 4,000 (ctrl). ***Formed by the union of*** *Geuzenpenning* ***and*** *De Florijn.*
Ind/Abst BHA : Biblio. Hist. Art.

GW/0300-4627
BLATT FUER SORTENWESEN. Periodical. German. mo. DM56.80. Deutscher Fachverlag GmbH, Verlagsgruppe, D 60264 Frankfurt Germany. **Tel** 011 49 69 75951001, telex 411 862.
Ind/Abst Vitis Vitic. Enol. Abstr.

UK/0143-8956
BRITISH NUMISMATIC JOURNAL. (THE BRITISH NUMISMATIC JOURNAL, INCLUDING THE PROCEEDINGS OF THE BRITISH NUMISMATIC SOCIETY.). [Br. numis. j.]. **Added/Corp** British Numismatic Society. Vol. 1 (1903)-. Periodical. English. an. £18.00 membership. British Numismatic Society, Royal Mint Pontyclum, Midgemorgan CF7 8YT England. **Tel** 011 44 81 958 8753. **LC** CJ2470; .B7. cum. index.
Ind/Abst Am. Hist. Life (1989-); Art Archaeol. Tech. Abstr.; BHA : Biblio. Hist. Art; Numis. Lit.

FR/0037-9344
BULLETIN DE LA SOCIETE FRANCAISE DE NUMISMATIQUE. [Bull. Soc. fr. numis.]. **Main/Corp** Societe Francaise de Numismatique. Vol. 3 (1948)-. Periodical. French. Ten times a year. Bibliotheque Nationale, 58 rue de Richelieu, 75084 Paris Cedex 02 France. **Tel** 011 33 1 47038385. **ED** M. Dhenin. cum. index. **Circ:** 800 (ctrl). ***Continues*** *Proces-Verbal de la Seance du ... .*
Desc: Ancient medieval and modern numismatics.
Ind/Abst BHA : Biblio. Hist. Art; Numis. Lit.

BE/0009-0344
BULLETIN TRIMESTRIEL - CERCLE D'ETUDES NUMISMATIQUES. [Bull. trimest. - Cercle etud. numis.]. (1964)-. Periodical. French. qt. **UDC** 737.
Ind/Abst BHA : Biblio. Hist. Art.

SP/0007-9502
CAESARAUGUSTA. See Archaeology.

CN/0702-3162
CANADIAN COIN NEWS. Vol 14, No. 2 (June 21/July 5, 1976)-. Periodical. English. Twenty-six times a year. 24.56Can$ Canada; 25.95Can$ US; 38.95Can$ others. Canadian Coin News, 103 Lakeshore Road,, Suite 202, St Catharines Ontario L2N 2T6 Canada. **Tel** (416)646-7744, FAX (416)646-0995. **ED** Bret Evans. **DD** 737/.05. **Bk Rev. Ad Acc. Circ:** 16000. ***Supersedes in part*** *Coin, Stamp, Antique News, 0010-0439.*
Desc: Brings the world of Canadian and world numismatics to the collectors and dealers. It offers regular, informed columns, feature articles and a very useful trends section.
Ind/Abst Can. Index; Numis. Lit.

CN/0008-4573
CANADIAN NUMISMATIC JOURNAL, THE. **Added/Corp** Canadian Numismatic Association. Vol. 1 (Jan. 1956)-. Periodical. English (French). Ten times a year (July/Aug. and Jan./Feb. combined). 30.00Can$. Canadian Numismatic Association, PO Box 226, Barrie Ontario L4M 4T2 Canada. **Tel** (705)737-0845, FAX (705)737-0293. **ED** Robert C. Willey. Index available. cum. index. **Bk Rev. Ad Acc. Circ:** 2,300 (ctrl). available on microfiche. ***Supersedes*** *Canadian Numismatic Association. The C.N.A. Bulletin., 0315-4882.*
Desc: To encourage and promote the science of numismatics by acquirement and study of coins, paper money, medals, tokens and all other numismatic items, with special emphasis on material pertaining to Canada.
Ind/Abst Can. Index; Numis. Lit.

RM/0256-0844
CERCETARI NUMISMATICE. [Cercet. numis.]. (1978)-. Periodical. Romanian. an. Muzeul de Istorie al Republicii Socialiste Romania, Calea Victoriei Nr. 12, Bucharest Romania. **UDC** 93.
Ind/Abst BHA : Biblio. Hist. Art.

CN/0228-152X
CHARLTON CANADIAN TRADE DOLLAR GUIDE, THE. [Charlton Can. trade dollar guide]. 1st- Ed.; 1980-. English. an. $7.95 per no. Charlton Press, 2010 Yonge Street, Toronto Ontario M4S 1Z9. **Tel** (416)488-4653. **DD** 737.4971.

CN/0703-5837
CHARLTON NUMISMATIC BULLETIN, THE. V. 1, No. 5- Fall 1976-. Bulletin. English. Charlton Press, 2010 Yonge Street, Toronto Ontario M4S 1Z9. **Tel** (416)488-4653. **DD** 737.4/9/71. ***Continues*** *Charlton Bulletin, 0381-677X.*

CN/1183-7101
CHARLTON STANDARD CATALOGUE OF THE CANADIAN NUMISMATIC ASSOCIATION'S MEDALS AND AWARDS, THE. [Charlton stand. cat. Can. Numis. Assoc. medals awards]. **Added/Corp** Canadian Numismatic Association. 1st Ed. (1991)-. English. be. $9.95. Charlton Press, 2010 Yonge Street, Toronto Ontario M4S 1Z9. **Tel** (416)488-4653. **DD** 737/.222.

CN/0706-0424
CHARLTON'S STANDARD CATALOGUE OF CANADIAN COINS. [Charlton's stand. cat. Can. coins]. **VFOAT** Charlton Standard Catalogue of Canadian Coins. 31st Ed. (Winter 1981)-. Periodical. English. an. 9.35Can$. Charlton Press, 2010 Yonge Street, Toronto Ontario M4S 1Z9. **Tel** (416)488-4653. **LC** CJ1860; .C47. **DD** 737.4971. ***Continues*** *Standard Catalogue of Canadian Coins., 0845-5708.*

US
CIVIL WAR TOKEN JOURNAL, THE. **Added/Corp** Civil War Token Society. (1987)-. Periodical. English. qt. $5.00. Civil War Token Society, 670 Korina Street, Vandenberg AFB CA 93437. **ED** Will Mumford. **Bk Rev. Ad Acc. Circ:** 850. ***Continues*** *Copperhead Courier.*
Desc: Published to promote the study of Civil War tokens along with historic, educational, and scientific lines.
Ind/Abst Numis. Lit.

US
CLASSICAL NUMISMATIC REVIEW. **Added/Corp** Classical Numismatic Group. (19??)-. Periodical. English. qt. Subscription: $40.00 US, £22 UK; addresses outside US and UK, $50.00 (£28) per year. B A Seaby Ltd, Numismatists, 7 Davies Street, London W1Y 1LL United Kingdom. **Tel** 071 495 2590, FAX 071 491 1595. **LC** CJ1; .C614. ***Absorbed*** *Seaby Coin & Medal Bulletin.*

US/1062-8169
COIN DEALER NEWSLETTER, THE. [Coin deal. newsl.]. **VFOAT** CDN; Greysheet. (19??)-. Newsletter. English. wk. $89.00 (1 year), $147.00 (2 year). The Coin Dealer Newsletter, Department CDN, PO Box 11099, Torrance CA 90510. **Tel** (213)515-7369, FAX (213)515-7534. **DD** 737.

UK
COIN HOARDS. **Main/Corp** Royal Numismatic Society (Great Britain). **Added/Corp** International Numismatic Commission. Vol. 1 (1975)-. Monographic series. English. ir. Price varies per volume. Spink & Son Ltd, 5-7 King Street St James, London SW1Y 6QS England. **Tel** 011 44 71 9307888, FAX 011 44 71 8394853, telex SPINK 916711. **LC** CJ153.A2; R68a. **DD** 737.4. **Circ:** 1,200.
Desc: Occasional journal to publish preliminary reports of coin hoards and summary descriptions of hoards published elsewhere. This journal also contains longer articles on hoard related topics.
Ind/Abst Br. Archaeol. Bibliogr.; Numis. Lit.

US
COIN MAGAZINE. mo. $15.00. Error Trends, PO Box 158, Oceanside NY 11572-0158. **Bk Rev. Ad Acc.** ctrl circ.

UK
COIN MONTHLY. English. mo. £20.60 UK; £22.10 other. Numismatic Publishing Company, Sovereign House, Brentwood Essex CM14 4SE England. **Tel** 0277 219876.

UK/0955-4386
COIN NEWS (HINDHEAD, ENGLAND). (COIN NEWS.). (198?)-. Periodical. English. Twelve times a year. £22.00 UK; £30.00 Europe and (surface mail) other; £40.00 (airmail) other. Token Publishing Ltd., 105 High Street, Honiton, Devon EX14 8PE England. **Tel** 11 44 0404 45414, FAX 11 44 0404 45313, telex 28883. **ED** J.W. Mussell. **LC** CJ1; .C49. **DD** 737/.05. **Ad Acc, Adv Mgr:** C. Hartman. **Circ:** 8,000. ***Continues*** *Coin & Medal News.*

US/0010-0412
COIN PRICES. (19??)-. Periodical. English. bm. $16.95 US; $22.00 other. Krause Publications, 700 East State Street, Iola WI 54990-0001. **Tel** (715)445-2214, FAX (715)445-4087, telex 55 6461. **ED** Bob Wilhite. **Circ:** 83,175.
Desc: Provides complete current market prices for all US coins. Values are listed in up to 12 grades of preservation. Provides pricing to keep collectors informed of fluctuations in the hobby.

US/0010-0447
COIN WORLD. (1960)-. Periodical. English. wk. $28.00 (one year), $49.00 (two year). Coin World, PO Box 150, Sidney OH 45367. **Tel** (513)498-0800, (800)253-4555. **(Subscription address:** Neodata, PO Box 2606, Boulder, CO 80322) **ED** Beth Deisher. **Bk Rev. Ad Acc. Circ:** 80,000. available on microfilm and microfiche from University Microfilms International (UMI).
Desc: The leading weekly publication for coin collectors, investors and hobbyists. The most comprehensive news coverage and price trends available hobbywide.
Ind/Abst Numis. Lit.

US/0361-0845
COIN WORLD ALMANAC. (1976)-. English. ir. $29.95 (hardbound), $15.95 (paper). Amos Press, PO Box 29, Sidney OH 45365. **Tel** (513)498-0802, (800)448-7293, FAX (513)498-0812. **LC** CJ1; .C576. **DD** 737.4/05.

US/1047-8000
... COIN WORLD GUIDE TO U.S. COINS, PRICES, AND VALUE TRENDS, THE. [Coin world guide U.S. coins, prices, value trends]. **VFOAT** Guide to U.S. Coins, Prices, and Value Trends. (1989)-. English. an. $4.50. New American Library, 120 Woodbine Street, Bergenfield NJ 07621. **Tel** (201)387-0600. **LC** PAR. **DD** 737.
Desc: Provides updated price information, a current market analysis, a brief history of U.S. coinage, and other relevant information.

UK/0307-6571
COIN YEARBOOK. [Coin year book]. (1970)-. English. an. Numismatic Publishing Company, Sovereign House, Brentwood Essex CM14 4SE England. **Tel** 0277 219876. **ED** Marion Hornett. **LC** CJ2471; .C6. **DD** 737.4/9/42. **Ad Acc. Circ:** 15,000. ***Continues*** *Coin Monthly Year Book.*
Desc: Presents features, reference articles, and more than 180 pages of illustrated coin prices, compiled from dealer's and auctioneer's selling prices.

US/0010-0455
COINAGE. [Coinage]. Vol. 1 (Winter 1964)-. Periodical. English. mo. $23.00. Miller Magazines Inc, 4880 Market Street, Ventura CA 93003. **Tel** (805)664-3824, FAX (805)664-3875. **ED** Karen Miller. **DD** 737.4/05. Index available. **Bk Rev. Ad Acc. Circ:** 74,020. available on microfilm and microfiche from University Microfilms International (UMI).
Desc: Covers coin collecting, and investing in gold and silver.
Ind/Abst Numis. Lit.

US/0270-4625
COINAGE MAGAZINE'S GOLD & SILVER. [Coin. mag. gold silver]. **VFOAT** Gold & Silver. **VAT** Coinage Magazine's Gold and Silver. Periodical. English. Miller Magazines Inc, 4880 Market Street, Ventura CA 93003. **Tel** (805)664-3824, FAX (805)664-3875. **LC** CJ113; .C63. **DD** 737.4.

US/0010-0471
COINS (IOLA, WIS.). (COINS.). Vol. 9 (1962)-. Periodical. English. mo. $22.95 US; $32.35 other. Krause Publications, 700 East State Street, Iola WI 54990-0001. **Tel** (715)445-2214, FAX (715)445-4087, telex 55 6461. **ED** Arlyn G. Seiber. **Bk Rev. Ad Acc. Circ:** 70,079. available on microfilm and microfiche from University Microfilms International (UMI). ***Continues*** *Coin Press Magazine.*
Desc: Features US coins accompanied by full-color photographs, collector columns, US world coin hobby news, US coin price guide covering most popular US coins. Hobby guide for novice or casual advanced collectors.
Ind/Abst Numis. Lit.

UK
COINS MARKET VALUES. English. an. Link House Magazines Ltd., Link House, Dingwall Avenue, Croydon Surrey CR9 2TA England. **Tel** 011 44 81 686 2599, FAX 011 44 81 760 5154, telex 947709. **ED** Richard West. **LC** CJ2476; .C64. **DD** 737.4941. **Ad Acc.**
Desc: A market price guide of British coins.

US/1048-0951
COLLECTORS BULLETIN (CANTON, ILL.). (COLLECTORS BULLETIN.). [Collect. bull.]. Vol. 6, No. 8 (Dec. 1989)-. Periodical. English. Six times a year. $21.95 (one year); $38.95 (two years). Rosie Wells

Hobbies — Numismatics

Enterprises Inc., Route 1 Box 255, Canton IL 61520. **Tel** (309)668-2211, (309)668-2565, FAX (309)668-2795. **ED** Rosie Wells. **DD** 790. **Ad Acc**, **Adv Mgr:** T. Behymer, **Tel** (309)668-2211. **Circ:** 6,500. *Continues Buy Sell Trade.*

US/0885-2995
COLLECTORS' JOURNAL OF ANCIENT ART. See The Arts-Art.

US/0010-1443
COLONIAL NEWSLETTER (HUNTSVILLE), THE. (THE COLONIAL NEWSLETTER.). V. 1- Oct. 1960-. Newsletter. English. qt. cum. index.
Ind/Abst Numis. Lit.

CN/0713-813X
CTD POCKET GUIDE, THE. [CTD pocket guide]. **VAT** Canadian Trade Dollars Pocket Guide. 1st Ed. (1982 i.e. 1981)-. English. an. $2.50 per volume. J G Cote, 12 Lyon Heights Road, Scarborough Ontario M1P 3V7 Canada. **DD** 737.4971.

US/0070-1882
CURRENT COINS OF THE WORLD. 1st Ed, (1966)-. Catalog. English. ir. Coin and Currency Institute, PO Box 1057, Clifton NJ 07014. **Tel** (201)471-1062, FAX (201)471-1062. **ED** A. Friedberg and I. Friedberg. **LC** CJ1755; .Y46. **DD** 737.4. Index available. **Bk Rev**. **Ad Acc.**
Desc: Comprehensive listing with photos and prices of all coins made in the world as of 1955 to date.

GW
DEUTSCHES MUNZPREIS-JAHRBUCH. German. 90.00. Battenberg, Ernst Battenberg Verlag, Munchen Germany. **LC** CJ2706; .D48. **DD** 737.4/9/43.

US/0270-8949
EDMUND'S UNITED STATES COIN PRICES. [Edmund's U.S. coin prices]. **Main/Corp** Edmund Publications Corporation (West Hempstead, N.Y.). **VFOAT** United States Coin Prices. Vol. 1 (Oct. 1980)-. English. qt. $20.00. Edmund's Publications Corporation / California, 300 North Sepulveda Boulevard, Suite 2050, El Segundo CA 90245. **Tel** (310)640-7840, (914)962-6297. **(Subscription address:** Edmund Publications, PO Box 338, Shrub Oak, NY 10588**) LC** CJ1826; .E35a. **DD** 737.4973.

US
ERROR TRENDS. English. mo. $15.00 (one year), $28.00 (two year), $40.00 (three year). Error Trends Coin Magazine, PO Box 158, Oceanside NY 11572-0158. **ED** Arnold Margolis. **Bk Rev**. **Ad Acc**. **Pr Rev**. **Circ:** 1500.
Desc: Devoted to error coin collecting in all of its phases.

US/0430-2958
FELL'S INTERNATIONAL COIN BOOK. (FELL'S INTERNATIONAL COIN BOOK / BY JACQUES DEL MONTE.). [Fell's int. coin book]. (19??)-. English. ir (Publishes every five or six years). $9.95 (paper edition); $14.95 (cloth edition). Frederick Fell Publishers Inc, 2131 Hollywood Boulevard, Suite 204, Hollywood FL 33020. **Tel** (305)925-5242, FAX (302)925-5244. **ED** Charles T. Mangrum, Stephen S. Strichart and Peggy Loewy-Wellisch. **LC** CJ1; .F44. **DD** 737.4. Index available. **Bk Rev**. **Ad Acc.**
Desc: The definitive guide to the identification and value of coins minted throughout the world. It also includes the latest international prices for old and rare coins, as well as for those which are in use today.

US/1041-6951
FELL'S UNITED STATES COIN BOOK. [Fell's U. S. coin book]. **VFOAT** United States Coin Book. 1st Ed. (1949)-. English. $9.95 (paperback), $14.95 (cloth). Frederick Fell Publishers Inc, 2131 Hollywood Boulevard, Suite 204, Hollywood FL 33020. **Tel** (305)925-5242, FAX (302)925-5244. **ED** Rod Hughes. **LC** CJ1826; .A67. **DD** 737. **Ad Acc**, **Adv Mgr:** Don Lessane.
Desc: Provides collectors with current information vital to wise and profitable numismatic investment.

US/0896-4432
FIRST STRIKE. [First strike]. Vol. 1, No. 1 (Spring 1987)-. Periodical. English. Four times a year. $28.00 North America; $33.00 other. American Numismatic Association, 818 North Cascade Avenue, Colorado Springs CO 80903. **Tel** (719)632-2646, FAX (719)634-4085. **ED** Barbara J Gregory and Marilyn A Reback. **DD** 737. cum. index. **Ad Acc**. **Circ:** 31,000 (ctrl).
Desc: A supplement to The Numismatist for emerging collectors.

XR/0862-1195
FOLIA NUMISMATICA. **Added/Corp** Moravske Muzeum v Brne. (198?)-. Czech. *Continues Moravske Numismaticke Zpravy.*

AU
FUNDMUNZEN DER ROMISCHEN ZEIT IN OSTERREICH. ABTEILUNG I, BURGENLAND, DIE. **Added/Corp** Osterreichische Akademie der Wissenschaften. Philosophisch-Historische Klasse. (1970)-. Monographic series. German. ir. Price varies per volume.

SP/0210-2137
GACETA NUMISMATICA. [Gac. numis.]. (1966)-. Periodical. Spanish. qt. **UDC** 737.
Ind/Abst BHA : Biblio. Hist. Art.

US/1052-8741
GARY NORTH'S RARE COIN INVESTMENT REVIEW. [Gary North's rare coin investm. rev.]. **Added/Corp** American Bureau of Economic Research. **VFOAT** Rare Coin Investment Review. Vol. 7, No. 7 (Aug. 10, 1990)-. Periodical. English. mo. $67.00. Rare Coin Investment Review, PO Box 8204, Fort Worth TX 76124. **DD** 332. *Continues Gary North's Investment Coin Review,* 8750-4502.

US/0072-8829
GUIDE BOOK OF UNITED STATES COINS, A. **VFOAT** Red Book of United States Coins. 1st Edition (1947)-. English. an (Summer). $11.45 (softcover); $14.45 (hardcover). Western Publishing Company, PO Box 700, Department M Sales, Racine WI 53401. **Tel** (201)471-1441, (800)236-7123. **(Subscription address:** Donovan Music, 732 Clinton Street, Waukwsha WI 53186.**) ED** R. S. Yeoman. **LC** CJ1826; .G785. **DD** 737.4.

GW/0072-9523
HAMBURGER BEITRAEGE ZUR NUMISMATIK. **Added/Corp** Hamburg. Museum fur Hamburgische Geschichte. Verein der Munzenfreunde in Hamburg. (1947)-. Periodical. German.
Ind/Abst BHA : Biblio. Hist. Art.

UK
HAMILTON'S COIN AND MEDAL DESPATCH. *Ceased.* **VFOAT** Coin and Medal Despatch. Vol. 1-( )-(?). English. A D Hamilton & Company Ltd, 7 St Vincent Place, Glasgow GL 2DW Scotland. **LC** CJ1; .H35. **DD** 737/.05.

KO
HANGUK HWAPYE KAGYOK TOROK / KIM IN-SIK CHO. Korean. an. W3,500. Kumhwa Chulpansa, 18 Kwanhundong Chongno-ku, Seoul Korea. **LC** CJ3730; .K55.

US/0884-0180
HAY DRAMAGITAKAN HANDES. (HAY DRAMAGITAKAN HANDES / HAY DRAMAGITAKAN ENKERAKTSUTIWN.). **Added/Corp** Armenian Numismatic Society (Los Angeles, Calif.). **VFOAT** Armenian Numismatic Journal. Vol. 1, No. 1 (Mar. 1975)-. Periodical. Armenian (English). qt. $6.00. 8511 Beverly Park Place, Pico Rivera CA 90660. **Tel** (310)695-0380. **ED** Y T Nercessian. **LC** CJ3481; .H39. **DD** 737/.09566/2. Index available. cum. index. **Bk Rev**. **Circ:** 175 (ctrl).
Desc: Covers unpublished Armenian coins, banknotes, and medals. The latest Armenian numismatic literature is abstracted (in English) in every issue.
Ind/Abst Numis. Lit.

CN/0316-9138
INSTANT (TORONTO). (THE INSTANT.). **Main/Corp** Israel Numismatic Society of Toronto. **VFOAT** Instant. Vol. 1; Jan. 1973-. Periodical. English. Israel Numismatic Society of Toronto, PO Box 395, Willowdale Ontario M2N 5T1 Canada. **DD** 737/.095694.

UK
INTERNATIONAL NUMISMATIC DIRECTORY. 1st- Ed.; 1973-. Directory. English. J J Krasnodebshi, 9 St Lawrence Road, SW9 GPW London England. **LC** CJ63; .I57. **DD** 737/.025.

IS/0021-2288
ISRAEL NUMISMATIC JOURNAL. [Isr. numis. j.]. **Added/Corp** Israel Numismatic Society. (1963)-. Periodical. English. ir. $30.00. Israel Exploration Society, 5 Avida Street, 91070 Jerusalem Israel. **Tel** 011 972 2 227991. **ED** Dan Barag. cum. index. **Bk Rev**. **Circ:** 400.
Desc: The sole periodical of the Israel Numismatic Society, publishing research about the coins of the Eastern Mediterranean.
Ind/Abst New Testam. Abstr.

GW/0323-6919
JAHRBUCH DES ARBEITSKREISES THURINGER MUNZ- UND GELDGESCHICHTE. 1986-. German. an. **LC** CJ2800; .J33. **DD** 737/.09431. *Continues Jahrbuch des Arbeitskreises Munz- und Geldgeschichte Thuringens.*
Ind/Abst Numis. Lit. (?-?).

GW/0075-2711
JAHRBUCH FUER NUMISMATIK UND GELDGESCHICHTE. **Added/Corp** Bayerische Numismatische Gesellschaft. (1949)-. German. an. DM42.00. Bayerische Numis Gesellschaft, Residenzstrasse 1, D 80333 Munich Germany. **Tel** 011 49 89 227221. **LC** CJ31; .J3. *Continues Deutsches Jahrbuch fur Numismatik.*
Ind/Abst BHA : Biblio. Hist. Art.

CN/0848-9610
JEFFREY HOARE NUMISMATIC AUCTION IN CONJUNCTION WITH TOREX. [Jeffrey Hoare numis. auction conjunction Torex]. **Main/Corp** Jeffrey Hoare Auctions. **Added/Corp** Torex. **VFOAT** Jeffrey Hoare Auctions; Numismatic Auction. English. sa. Charlton Press, 2010 Yonge Street, Toronto Ontario M4S 1Z9. **Tel** (416)488-4653. **DD** 737.4971/029/4713541. *Continues Numismatic Auction,* 0822-4951.

US/1050-3986
JOURNAL OF ECONOMIC ARCHAEOLOGY, THE. **VFOAT** CNVR. (1991)-. Periodical. English. mo. $149.00. Classical Investments Ltd, 67 Wall Street/Suite 2411, New York NY 10005.

AT
JOURNAL OF THE NUMISMATIC ASSOCIATION OF AUSTRALIA. **Added/Corp** Numismatic Association of Australia. (198?)-. Periodical. English.
Ind/Abst APAIS, Aust. Public Aff. Inf. Ser. (1985-).

II/0029-6066
JOURNAL OF THE NUMISMATIC SOCIETY OF INDIA, THE. **Main/Corp** Numismatic Society of India. Vol. 1 (1939)-. Periodical. English. sa. $25.00. Numismatic Society of India, PO Hindu University, Varanasi 5 India. **(Subscription address:** Prints India, 11 Darya Ganj, New Delhi 110002 India.**) LC** CJ3530; .N8. **DD** 737.06254. cum. index.
Ind/Abst Numis. Lit.

US
JOURNAL OF THE ORDERS AND MEDALS SOCIETY OF AMERICA, THE. **Added/Corp** Orders and Medals Society of America. **VFOAT** JOMSA. (19??)-. Periodical. English. Ten times a year (Jan./Feb. and Aug./Sep. issues combined). $20.00. Medals Society of America, c/o John E. Lelle, PO Box 484, Glassboro NJ 08028. **Tel** (609)863-0148. **ED** Michael A. Sundock. **LC** CJ5501; .O7. Index available. cum. index. **Bk Rev**. **Ad Acc**. **Circ:** 1,600 (ctrl). *Continues Medal Collector,* 0025-6633.

HU/0230-788X
MAGYAR EREMGYUJTOK EGYESULETE CSONGRAD MEGYEI SZERVEZETENEK KIADVANYAI, A. (1982)-. Hungarian. ir. **UDC** 061.2.
Ind/Abst Numis. Lit.

UK/0263-7707
MEDAL LONDON. (THE MEDAL.). [Medal]. **Added/Corp** British Art Medal Society. (1982)-. Periodical. English (French). Twice a year (Spring & Fall). £20.00 UK and Europe; £25.00 other. British Art Medal Trust, Department of Coins & Medals, British Museum, London WE1B 3DG England. **Tel** 011 44 71 636 1555 Ext. 8260. **ED** Phillip Artwood. **LC** CJ5501; .M43. **DD** 737/.22/05. (Every five years). cum. index. **Bk Rev**. **Ad Acc**. **Circ:** 1,100 (ctrl).
Desc: News and information on commemorative arts medals.
Ind/Abst BHA : Biblio. Hist. Art; Numis. Lit.

UK/0958-4986
MEDAL NEWS HINDHEAD. 1989. (MEDAL NEWS.). [Medal news Hindhead, 1989]. (1989)-. Periodical. English. Ten times a year. £24.00 UK; £28.50 other. Token Publishing Ltd., 105 High Street, Honiton, Devon EX14 8PE England. **Tel** 11 44 0404 45414, FAX 11 44 0404 45313, telex 28883. **ED** J.W. Mussell. **DD** 737.22. **Bk Rev**. **Ad Acc**, **Adv Mgr:** Mrs. C. Hartman. *Continues in part Coin & Medal News* (198?), 0955-4386.
Desc: Devoted to all aspects of orders, medals and decorations, campaign and military history, lifesaving and bravery awards.

IT
MEMORIE DELL'ACCADEMIA ITALIANA DI STUDI FILATELICI E NUMISMATICI. See Communication-Postal Communications.

CN/0822-4943
MILITARIA AUCTION - TOREX. (MILITARIA AUCTION.). [Mil. auction - Torex]. **Main/Corp** Torex. Periodical. English. ir. $2.50 each number. Charlton Press, 2010 Yonge Street, Toronto Ontario M4S 1Z9. **Tel** (416)488-4653. **DD** 737.223/0294713541.

AU/0029-9359
MITTEILUNGEN DER OSTERREICHICHEN NUMISMATISCHEN GESELLSCHAFT. [Mitt. Osterr. Numis. Ges.]. (1947)-. Periodical. German. bm. **UDC** 737.
Ind/Abst BHA : Biblio. Hist. Art.

US/0149-4279
MODERN GOLD COINAGE. [Mod. gold coin.]. **Added/Corp** Gold Institute. (1976)-. English. an. $50.00. Gold Institute, 1112 16th Street Northwest, Suite 240, Washington DC 20036. **Tel** (202)835-0185, FAX

Hobbies —Numismatics

(202)835-0155, telex 904233 DAV INC WSH. **LC** CJ113; .M6. **DD** 737.4/05. **Circ:** 600.
Desc: Contains complete data on all gold coins issued in the world each year prepared with the cooperation of the monetary authorities, central banks and mints of each country.

US/0149-7707
MODERN SILVER COINAGE. Added/Corp Silver Institute. (1972)-. Periodical. English. an. $40.00. Silver Institute, 1112 16th Street NW, Suite 240, Washington DC 20036. **Tel** (202)835-0155, **FAX** (202)783-2127, telex 904233 DAV INC WSH. **ED** John H. Lutley. **LC** CJ1546; .M6. **DD** 737.4.

MX
MONEDAS. Began with Jan. 1959 issue. Periodical. Spanish. Apartado Sociedad Numismatica de Puebla, Postal 329, Puebla Pue Mexico. **LC** CJ9; .M65.
Ind/Abst Numis. Lit.

SZ
MUNZEN REVUE. (19??)-. Periodical. English (German). mo. 72.00F. Verlag Munzen Revue AG, Blotzheimerstrasse 40, 4055 Basel Switzerland. **Tel** 011 44 61 445504. **ED** Albert Beck. **LC** CJ3240; .M86. **DD** 737.4943. **Bk Rev. Ad Acc. Circ:** 25,000 (ctrl).
Desc: Reporting over the numismatic market from the ancient till today - prize trends, events calendar-coins, medallions, banknotes, tokens, etc.
Ind/Abst Numis. Lit.

GW
MUNZENSAMMLER MIT DEM MUNZENMARKT, DER. Began with issue for Dec. 1973. Periodical. German. ir. 60.00 DM. DMV Verlag fur Munzliteratur GmbH, Eimermacherweg 30, W-4400 Munster Germany. **LC** CJ5; .M814. **DD** 737/.075.

GR
NOMISMATIKA KHRONIKA. Added/Corp Hellenike Nomismatike Hetaireia. (1972)-. Greek, Modern (Multiple languages; summaries and/or abstracts in English and Greek, Modern). $20.00. The Hellenic Numismatic Society, Didotou 45, 106 80 Athens Greece. **Tel** FAX 011 30 1 3634296. **ED** Anastasios P. Tzamalis. **LC** CJ9; .N65. Index available. cum. index. **Bk Rev**, (Qty: 2-3 per year). **Circ:** 500.
Desc: The journal of the Hellenic Numismatic Society containing articles covering the spectrum of Greek numismatics and related subjects by Greek and foreign authors. Articles are published in the original language and accompanied by a full or summarized translation in Greek or English.

SW/0078-107X
NORDISK NUMISMATISK ARSSKRIFT. SCANDINAVIAN NUMISMATIC JOURNAL. VFOAT Scandinavian Numismatic Journal. (19??)-. Periodical. Multiple languages. an. Scandinavian University Press, PO Box 2959 Toeyen, N 0608 Oslo 6 Norway. **Tel** 011 47 2 2575400, FAX 011 47 2 2575353, telex 71896 UROR N. **(Subscription address:** Scandinavian University Press, 200 Meacham Ave., Elmont NY 11003.**)**
Ind/Abst Numis. Lit.

SP/0029-6015
NUMISMA (MADRID). (NUMISMA). [Numisma]. **Added/Corp** Sociedad Iberoamericana de Estudios Numismaticos. (Oct./Dec. 1951)-. Periodical. English. qt. **LC** CJ9; .N75.
Ind/Abst Am. Hist. Life (1957-1963); BHA : Biblio. Hist. Art.

CN/0822-4900
NUMISMATIC AUCTION / CHARLTON AUCTIONS. [Numis. auction - Charlton Auctions].
Main/Corp Charlton Auctions. Periodical. English. $2.50 per no. Charlton Press, 2010 Yonge Street, Toronto Ontario M4S 1Z9. **Tel** (416)488-4653. **DD** 737.4971/029/4713541. **Absorbed in part** Unreserved Public Mini Auction, 0822-7713.

UK/0078-2696
NUMISMATIC CHRONICLE. Added/Corp Royal Numismatic Society. Vol. 126 (1966)-. Proceedings. English. an. £24.00. Spink & Son Ltd, 5-7 King Street St James, London SW1Y 6QS England. **Tel** 011 44 71 9307888, FAX 011 44 71 8394853, telex SPINK 916711. cum. index. **Continues** Numismatic Chronicle and Journal of the Royal Numismatic Society.
Desc: Proceedings of the Royal Numismatic Society form a separately paged section of each volume.
Ind/Abst BHA : Biblio. Hist. Art.

UK
NUMISMATIC CIRCULAR, THE. Main/Corp Spink & Son, Ltd., London. V. 1- Dec. 1892-. Periodical. English. Ten times a year. £10.00 UK; $40.00 US. Spink & Son Ltd, 5-7 King Street St James, London SW1Y 6QS England. **Tel** 011 44 71 9307888, FAX 011 44 71 8394853, telex SPINK 916711. **ED** D H Saville. Index available. **Bk Rev. Circ:** 3,000 (ctrl).
Ind/Abst Br. Archaeol. Bibliogr.; Numis. Lit.

US/0029-6031
NUMISMATIC LITERATURE. See Hobbies-Abstracting, Bibliographies and Statistics.

US/0029-604X
NUMISMATIC NEWS (KRAUSE PUBLICATIONS : 1977). (NUMISMATIC NEWS.). [Numis. news]. (19??)-. Periodical. English. wk. $27.95. Krause Publications, 700 East State Street, Iola WI 54990-0001. **Tel** (715)445-2214, FAX (715)445-4087, telex 55 6461. **ED** Bob Wilhite. **LC** CJ1; .N64. **DD** 737/.0973. **Bk Rev. Ad Acc. Circ:** 35,739 (ctrl).
Continues Numismatic News Weekly.
Desc: Each issue features a retail/wholesale value guide. Contains a current events and dates calendar noting coin shows and hobby happenings. Includes an advertising marketplace where coin collectors can buy and sell through the mail.
Ind/Abst Numis. Lit.

US/0078-2718
NUMISMATIC NOTES AND MONOGRAPHS (NEW YORK). (NUMISMATIC NOTES AND MONOGRAPHS.). **Added/Corp** American Numismatic Society. J. Paul Getty Museum. VFOAT Numismatic Notes and Monographs. No. 1 (1920)-. Monographic series. English. ir. Price varies per volume. American Numismatic Society, Broadway at 155th Street, New York NY 10032. **Tel** (212)234-3130, FAX (212)234-3381, telex NUMISMA. **ED** Marie H. Martin and Leslie A. Elam. **LC** UNC. **Circ:** 1,000.
Desc: This series consists of monographs which rely heavily on numismatic evidence.
Ind/Abst Numis. Lit.

US/0517-404X
NUMISMATIC STUDIES. Added/Corp American Numismatic Society. No. 1 (1938)-. Monographic series. English. ir. Price varies per volume. American Numismatic Society, Broadway at 155th Street, New York NY 10032. **Tel** (212)234-3130, FAX (212)234-3381, telex NUMISMA. **ED** Marie H. Martin and Leslie A. Elam. **LC** UNC. **Circ:** 1,000.
Desc: Publication in which numismatic evidence is a primary part of the analysis.
Ind/Abst Numis. Lit.

IT
NUMISMATICA, LA. (19??)-. Periodical. Italian. Eleven times a year. L60000 Italy; L75000 other. La Numismatica, Via Ferramola 14, 25121 Brescia Italy. **Tel** 011 39 30 3756211, FAX 011 39 30 3756211. Index available. cum. index. **Bk Rev**, (Qty: 20). **Ad Acc.** ctrl circ.
Desc: News and information for the numismatic collector.

SZ
NUMISMATICA E ANTICHITA. Vol. 1 (1972)-. Italian (English, French, German and Spanish). an. L130.000. Istituto Editoriale Cisalpino, La Goliardica-Via-Rezia 4, 20135 Milan Italy.
Desc: The history of coins and archaeological discoveries.

XR
NUMISMATICKE LISTY. Added/Corp Narodni Muzeum v Praze. Numismaticka Spolecnost Ceskoslovenska v Praze. (1963)-. Periodical. Czech. qt. **Continues** Numismaticke Listy Numismaticke Spolecnosti Ceskoslovenske v Praze.
Ind/Abst BHA : Biblio. Hist. Art.

XR/0546-9414
NUMISMATICKY SBORNIK. 1- 1953-. Czech (summaries and/or abstracts in Russian and French). **ED** Jiri Sejbal. **LC** CJ9; .N83. **DD** 737.4/05. **Circ:** 1,000.
Desc: Contains scientific studies on numismatics and reports on founds of coins in Czechoslovakia.
Ind/Abst BHA : Biblio. Hist. Art; Numis. Lit.

FR/0335-1971
NUMISMATIQUE ET CHANGE REVIGNY-SUR-ORNAIN. (1974)-. Periodical. French. mo (except Aug.). 205.68F France; 260.00F other. FSEPS, 12 rue Poincare, 55800 Revigny France. **Tel** 011 33 29 70 56 33. **UDC** 05.

AU/0250-7838
NUMISMATISCHE ZEITSCHRIFT. Added/Corp Osterreichische Numismatische Gesellschaft. (1869)-. Periodical. German. be. S580.00. Osterreich Numismatische Gesellschaft, Burgring 5, A-1010 Vienna Austria. **Tel** 011 43 1 52177381.
Ind/Abst BHA : Biblio. Hist. Art.

GW
NUMISMATISCHES NACHRICHTENBLATT. Added/Corp Numismatische Kommission der Lander in der Bundesrepublik Deutschland. Verband der Deutschen Munzvereine. (19??)-. Periodical. German. **LC** CJ5; .N84.
Ind/Abst BHA : Biblio. Hist. Art; Numis. Lit.

US/0029-6090
NUMISMATIST, THE. (1888)-. Periodical. English. mo. $28.00 US; $33.00 other. American Numismatic Association, 818 North Cascade Avenue, Colorado Springs CO 80903. **Tel** (719)632-2646, FAX (719)634-4085. **ED** Barbara G Gregory. **LC** CJ1; .N8. **DD** 737/.05. Index available. cum. index. **Bk Rev. Ad Acc. Circ:** 31,000 (ctrl). available on microfiche.
Desc: For collectors of coins, medals, tokens and paper money. Devoted to the science of numismatics, the journal publishes carefully documented, illustrated articles on US and world numismatics.
Ind/Abst Am. Bibliogr. Slavic East Europ. Stud.; Numis. Lit.

US/0029-6090
NUMISMATIST: FOR COLLECTORS OF COINS, MEDALS, TOKENS AND PAPER MONEY, THE. [Numismatist]. **Added/Corp** American Numismatic Association. American Numismatic Association. Proceedings. (Oct. 1893)-. Periodical. English. mo. $28.00 US; $33.00 other. American Numismatic Association, 818 North Cascade Avenue, Colorado Springs CO 80903. **Tel** (719)632-2646, FAX (719)634-4085. **DD** 737. Index available. **Continues** Numismatist and Year Book.

CI/0546-9422
NUMIZMATICKE VIJESTI / HRVATSKO NUMIZMATICKO DRUSTVO. Added/Corp Hrvatsko Numizmaticko Drustvo. (19??)-. Serbo-Croatian (Roman) (summaries and/or abstracts in English and German). an.
Ind/Abst BHA : Biblio. Hist. Art.

RU/0130-7754
NUMIZMATIKA I EPIGRAFIKA / AKADEMIIA NAUK SSSR, INSTITUT ARKHEOLOGII. Added/Corp Institut Arkheologii (Akademiia Nauk SSSR). (1960)-. Russian. Izdatelstvo Nauka / Akademiia Nauk, Publishing House of the Russian Academy of Sciences, Leninskii Porspekt 14, 117901 Moscow Russia. **Tel** 011 95 954-21-53, FAX 011 95 938-21-44, telex 411964.
Ind/Abst BHA : Biblio. Hist. Art.

UN/0550-371X
NUMIZMATIKA I SFRAGISTIKA / AKADEMIIA NAUK UKRAINSKOI SSR, INSTITUT ARKHEOLOGII. 1- 1963-. Russian. **LC** CJ23.
Ind/Abst Numis. Lit.

HU
NUMIZMATIKAI KOZLONY. Began in 1902. Hungarian (summaries and/or abstracts in English and German). Akademiai Road, 1085 Budapest Csepreghy U 4, Budapest Hungary. **LC** CJ2640; .N8.
Ind/Abst Numis. Lit.

PO
NUMMUS. 2. SERIE. VFOAT Nvmmvs. Vol. I-. Portuguese. Each issue contains an index to its own contents (no volume index)--loose. **Continues** Nummus, 0085-364X.
Ind/Abst BHA : Biblio. Hist. Art.

US/0193-9610
OFFICIAL BLACKBOOK PRICE GUIDE OF UNITED STATES COINS, THE. (THE OFFICIAL ... BLACKBOOK PRICE GUIDE OF UNITED STATES COINS / BY MARC HUDGEONS.). 16th Ed. (1979)-. English. an. $8.90. Random House Inc., 400 Hahn Road, Westminster MD 21157. **Tel** (800)726-0600, (800)733-3000, FAX (800)659-2436. **ED** T. Hudgeons. **LC** CJ1830; .O3. **DD** 737.4/9/73. **Continues** Official Black Book of United States Coins.

US/0195-3540
OFFICIAL BLACKBOOK PRICE GUIDE OF UNITED STATES PAPER MONEY, THE. (19??)-. English. an (current year edition published in previous year). $6.00. Random House Inc., 400 Hahn Road, Westminster MD 21157. **Tel** (800)726-0600, (800)733-3000, FAX (800)659-2436. **LC** HG591; .H83. **DD** 769.5/5973. **Continues** Official Blackbook Price Guide of United States Paper Money, 0195-3540.

US/0747-5683
OFFICIAL GUIDE TO COIN COLLECTING, THE. [Off. guide coin collect.]. VFOAT Coin Collecting. English. an. Random House Inc., 400 Hahn Road, Westminster MD 21157. **Tel** (800)726-0600, (800)733-3000, FAX (800)659-2436. **LC** CJ81; .O35. **DD** 737.4973/075.

US/8756-1646
OFFICIAL HEWITT-DONLON PRICE GUIDE TO UNITED STATES PAPER MONEY, THE. [Off. Hewitt-Donlon price guide U.S. pap. money]. VFOAT Official Hewitt Donlon Price Guide to United States Paper Money; Price Guide to United States Paper Money. English. an. $4.95. Random House Inc., 400 Hahn Road, Westminster MD 21157. **Tel** (800)726-0600, (800)733-3000, FAX (800)659-2436. **ED** M Hudgeons. **LC** HG591; .O38. **DD** 769.5/5973/0750973.

US/0747-8682
OFFICIAL INVESTORS GUIDE, BUYING, SELLING GOLD COINS, THE. See Business-Investments.

US/0747-8526
OFFICIAL INVESTORS GUIDE, BUYING, SELLING SILVER COINS, THE. See Business-Investments.

US/0747-8674
OFFICIAL INVESTORS GUIDE, BUYING, SELLING SILVER DOLLARS, THE. See Business-Investments.

US/0748-2108
OFFICIAL PRICE GUIDE TO MINT ERRORS AND VARIETIES, THE.
Added/Corp House of Collectibles. **VFOAT** Mint Errors and Varieties. 2nd Ed. (1978)-. English. Random House Inc., 400 Hahn Road, Westminster MD 21157. **Tel** (800)726-0600, (800)733-3000, FAX (800)659-2436. **LC** CJ125; .O35. **DD** 737.4973. ***Continues*** *Official Guide to Mint Errors, 0748-2094.*

CN/0048-1815
ONTARIO NUMISMATIST, THE. V. 1- Nov. 1961-. Periodical. English. mo. Ontario Numismatic Association, PO Box 33, Waterloo Ontario Canada.

US/0031-1162
PAPER MONEY. Vol. 1 (1962)-. Periodical. English. bm. $20.00 US; $25.00 Canada & Mexico; $30.00 other. Society of Paper Money Collectors, PO Box 186, Florissant MO 63031. **Tel** (314)542-1621. **LC** HG353; .P34. Index available (inserted in Jan. issue). cum. index. **Bk Rev**. **Ad Acc**. **Circ:** 1,800 (ctrl).
Ind/Abst Numis. Lit.

US/8756-6265
PROCEEDINGS / COINAGE OF THE AMERICAS CONFERENCE. [Proc. - Coin. Am. Conf.]. **Main/Corp** Coinage of the Americas Conference. Began in 1985?. Proceedings. English. an. Price varies per volume. American Numismatic Society, Broadway at 155th Street, New York NY 10032. **Tel** (212)234-3130, FAX (212)234-3381, telex NUMISMA. **DD** 737. **Circ:** 600.
Desc: Contains annual conference proceedings.

US/0197-5013
PROCEEDINGS OF GOLD AND MONEY SESSION AND GOLD TECHNICAL SESSION. [Proc. Gold Money Sess. Gold Tech. Sess.]. **Added/Corp** American Institute of Mining, Metallurgical and Petroleum Engineers. Oregon Section. Oregon. Dept. of Geology and Mineral Industries. **VFOAT** Gold and Money Session and Gold Technical Session. Proceedings. English. ir. $6.50. State Department of Geology and Mineral Industries, 800 Northeast Oregon Street, Suite 28, Portland OR 97232. **Tel** (503)731-4100, FAX (503)731-4066.
Ind/Abst GeoRef.

US/0095-263X
RARE COIN REVIEW. **Added/Corp** Bowers and Ruddy Galleries. (19??)-. English. ir. $69.00. Bowers and Merena Inc, Box 1224, Wolfeboro NH 03894. **Tel** (800)222-5993. **LC** CJ1; .R37. **DD** 737.4/05.

US
RARE COINS & MEDALS. **Main/Corp** Galerie des Monnaies of Geneva, Ltd. **VAT** Rare Coins and Medals. Vol. 1- Winter/Spring 1978-. Periodical. English. Galerie des Monnaies of Geneva Ltd, 970 Madison Avenue, New York NY 10021.

BE/0774-5885
REVUE BELGE DE NUMISMATIQUE ET DE SIGILLOGRAPHIE. **VFOAT** Belgisch Tijdschrift voor Numismatiek en Zegelkunde. (1908)-. Periodical. French. an. Societe Royale de Numismatique, 28A AV Roi Leopold, B 1330 Rixensart Belgium. **UDC** 737.
Ind/Abst BHA : Biblio. Hist. Art.

FR/0484-8942
REVUE NUMISMATIQUE. **Added/Corp** Societe Francaise de Numismatique, Paris. Vol. 1-20, (1836)-. French. ir. 342.80F France; 370.00F other. Societe Edition Belles Lettres, 95 Boulevard Raspail, 75006 Paris France. **Tel** 011 33 1 45487055, FAX 011 33 1 45449288, telex 200577.
Ind/Abst BHA : Biblio. Hist. Art; Numis. Lit.

SZ
REVUE SUISSE DE NUMISMATIQUE.
Added/Corp Schweizerische Numismatische Gesellschaft. **VFOAT** Schweizerische Numismatische Rundschau. (1891)-. Periodical. French (German). an. comes with membership. Schweizer Numismatische Gesell, Niederdorfstrasse 43 Italo Vecchi, CH 8001 Zurich Switzerland. cum. index.
Ind/Abst BHA : Biblio. Hist. Art.

IT
RIVISTA ITALIANA DI NUMISMATICA E SCIENZE AFFINI. **Added/Corp** Societa Numismatica Italiana, Milan. Vol. 1 (1888)-. Periodical. Italian. qt. **LC** CJ9; .R6. cum. index.
Ind/Abst BHA : Biblio. Hist. Art.

MM
SAID MALTA COIN, BANKNOTE, AND MEDAL CATALOGUE. **VFOAT** Malta Coin, Banknote, and Medal Catalogue. 1st Ed. (1982)-. English. Emmanuel Said Publishers, 32 Melita Street, PO Box 345, Valletta Malta. **LC** CJ3199.5; .S26. **DD** 737/.0945/85.

US/0049-1152
SAN. **Main/Corp** Society for Ancient Numismatics. Vol. 1 (July 1969)-. Periodical. English. qt. $7.00. Society of Ancient Numismatics, PO Box 730, Karin Cozzolino, Lomita CA 90717. **LC** CJ201; .S63a. **DD** 737/.05.
Ind/Abst Numis. Lit. (199?-).

SZ/0487-8019
SCHWEIZER MUNZBLATTER. (SCHWEIZER MUNZBLATTER. GAZETTE NUMISMATIQUE SUISSE.). **Added/Corp** Schweizerische Numismatische Gesellschaft. **VFOAT** Gazette Numismatique Suisse. (1949)-. Periodical. German (French). Four times a year. 100.00F. Schweizer Numismatische Gesell, Niederdorfstrasse 43 Italo Vecchi, CH 8001 Zurich Switzerland.
Ind/Abst BHA : Biblio. Hist. Art.

US/0090-404X
SCULPTORS. (INDEX OF SCULPTORS.). **Main/Corp** Franklin Mint. 1965/71-. English. Franklin Mint, Franklin Mint Center, Philadelphia PA 19091. **LC** CJ5813; .F7. **DD** 737/.092/2.

UK
SEABY COINS SUBSCRIPTION. English. ir. £25 US and United Kingdom; £35 other. Seaby/CNG, 14 Old Bond Street, London W1X 4JL UK. **Tel** 11 44 71 495 1888, FAX 11 44 71 499 5916, telex 27859, 261068.

CN/0380-8866
SHORE LINE, THE. V. 1- Jan. 1976-. Periodical. English. mo. North Shore Numismatic Society, PO Box 86241, North Vancouver BC V7L 4J8. **DD** 737/.062/71133. ***Supersedes*** *North Shore Numismatic Society.*

UK/0263-7677
SPINK NUMISMATIC CIRCULAR. [Spink numis. circ.]. **Added/Corp** Spink & Son. **VFOAT** Numismatic Circular. Vol. 90, No. 1 (Feb. 1982)-. Periodical. English. Ten times a year. £12.00 (UK & Europe) surface mail; £30.00 (other) airmail. Spink & Son Ltd, 5-7 King Street St James, London SW1Y 6QS England. **Tel** 011 44 71 9307888, FAX 011 44 71 8394853, telex SPINK 916711. ***Continues*** *Numismatic Circular.*
Ind/Abst BHA : Biblio. Hist. Art.

US
STANDARD CATALOG OF WORLD GOLD COINS / BY CHESTER L. KRAUSE AND CLIFFORD MISHLER. **VFOAT** World Gold Coins. (1986)-. Catalog. English. be. Krause Publications, 700 East State Street, Iola WI 54990-0001. **Tel** (715)445-2214, FAX (715)445-4087, telex 55 6461. **ED** C.R. Bruce II. **LC** CJ113; .S73. **DD** 737.4/3. ***Continues in part*** *Krause, Chester L. Standard Catalog of World Coins.*

UK
STANDARD CATALOGUE OF BRITISH COINS. **VFOAT** Coins of England and the United Kingdom; Coins of Scotland, Ireland and the Islands. (19??)-. English. an (Published in Sept.). £12.95. Seaby/CNG, 14 Old Bond Street, London W1X 4JL UK. **Tel** 11 44 71 495 1888, FAX 11 44 71 499 5916, telex 27859, 261068. **LC** CJ2476; .S82. **DD** 737.4/9/41. ***Continues*** *Seaby's Standard Catalogue of British Coins.*

MY/0126-9682
STANDARD CATALOGUE OF MALAYSIA-SINGAPORE-BRUNEI COINS AND PAPER MONEY. 3rd Ed. (1981)-. English. an. 25.00Mal$. International Stamp & Coin Company Ltd, 2.4 & 2.5 Pertama Shopping Complex/2nd Floor, Jalan Tuanku Abdul Rahman, 50100 Kuala Lumpur Malaysia. **Tel** 03-2926373. **ED** Steven Tan. **LC** CJ3624; .S75. **DD** 737/.09595. Index available. **Bk Rev**. **Circ:** 3,000 (ctrl). ***Continues*** *Coin & Paper Money Catalogue of Malaysia, Singapore & Brunei.*
Desc: Complete listing of Malaysia, Singapore and Brunei coins and paper money including JIM tokens, etc.

US/0741-9236
STANDARD ... U.S. COIN CATALOGUE. [Stand. U.S. coin cat.]. **Main/Corp** Scott Publishing Co. **VFOAT** Standard ... US Coin Catalogue. English. $2.95. Colin Smythe Limited, PO Box 6, Gerrards Cross, Buckinghamshire SL9 8XA England. **Tel** 0753 886000, FAX 0753 886469. **LC** CJ1826; .S32A. **DD** 737.4973.

II
STUDIES IN SOUTH INDIAN COINS. **Added/Corp** South Indian Numismatic Society. Vol. 1 (1991)-. English. **LC** CJ3549.I49; S78. **DD** 737.4954/8.

RM
STUDII SI CERCETARI DE NUMISMATICA. **Main/Corp** Institutul de Arheologie (Academia de Stiinte Sociale si Politice a Republicii Socialiste Romania). Vol. 5 (1971)-. Romanian (English, French, German, Romanian and Russian). ir. Editura Academia Republicii Socialiste Romania, Calea Victoriei Nr 125, R-79717 Bucuresti Romania. **Tel** telex 10376 PRSFI R. **LC** CJ3330; .A3. ***Continues*** *Academia Republicii Socialiste Romania. Institutul de Arheologie. Studii si Cercetari de Numismatica.*
Ind/Abst BHA : Biblio. Hist. Art; Numis. Lit.

US/0271-3993
SYLLOGE NUMMORUM GRAECORUM (NEW YORK). [Sylloge nummorum Graecorum]. **Added/Corp** American Numismatic Society. (1969)-. English. ir. Price varies per volume. American Numismatic Society, Broadway at 155th Street, New York NY 10032. **Tel** (212)234-3130, FAX (212)234-3381, telex NUMISMA. **ED** Marie H. Martin and Leslie A. Elam. **Circ:** 500.
Desc: This series is a systematic publishing of ancient Greek coins held in the collections of the American Numismatic Society.

US/0039-8233
TAMS JOURNAL. [TAMS j.]. **Main/Corp** Token and Medal Society. **VFOAT** Journal. **VAT** Token and Medal Society Journal. (1961)-. Periodical. English. Six times a year (Feb., Apr., Jun., Aug., Oct., Dec.). $20.00 Comes with Token and Medal Society membership. Token & Medal Society, PO Box 951988, Lake Mary FL 32795. **Tel** (407)321-8747. **ED** David Schenkman; (editor's address: PO Box 366, Bryantown, MD 20617 phone: (301)274-3441). Index available (bound in issue). cum. index (1960-1985 only). **Ad Acc**. **Circ:** 1,700 (ctrl).
Desc: Articles and news items on collecting of tokens and medals; some advertising by members, including free classified ads.

FR/0223-4300
TRESORS MONETAIRES. **Added/Corp** Bibliotheque Nationale (France). Centre d'Etude et de Publication des Trouvailles Monetaires. (1979)-. French. an. 325.00F France; 340.00F others. Bibliotheque Nationale, 58 rue de Richelieu, 75084 Paris Cedex 02 France. **Tel** 011 33 1 47038385. **LC** CJ3; .T74. **DD** 737.4944. Index available. cum. index.
Ind/Abst Numis. Lit.

US/0882-1674
TRIDENT (WASHINGTON, D.C.). See Hobbies-Philately.

US/0743-9350
U.S. COINS, CURRENCY & STAMPS. [U.S. coins, curr. stamps]. **VFOAT** US Coins, Currency & Stamps; U.S. Coins, Currency and Stamps. **VAT** United States Coins, Currency & Stamps. 1st Ed.-. English. an. $3.50. Random House Inc., 400 Hahn Road, Westminster MD 21157. **Tel** (800)726-0600, (800)733-3000, FAX (800)659-2436. **LC** CJ1826; .U22. **DD** 737.4973.

US/0271-3969
U.S. COINS OF VALUE. [U.S. coins value]. **VAT** United States Coins of Value. (1965)-. English. an. $2.25. Dell Publishing Company Inc., 1540 Broadway, 9th Floor, New York NY 10036-4021. **Tel** (212)782-8532, FAX (212)782-8338. **LC** CJ1826; .S782. **DD** 737.4973.

US/0198-6252
UKRAINSKYI FILATELIST / SOIUZ UKRAINSKYKH FILATELISTIV I NUMIZMATYKIV. See Hobbies-Philately.

US
VIRGINIA NUMISMATIST, THE. **Added/Corp** Virginia Numismatic Association. (1959)-. Periodical. English. Six times a year. $7.00. The Virginia Numismatist, 712 Westover Road, Richmond VA 23220. **Tel** (804)358-0525. **ED** James C. Ruehrmund. **Bk Rev**, (Qty: 3-4 per year). **Ad Acc**. **Circ:** 400.
Desc: Contains articles on coins, tokens, paper money, etc.; reviews of numismatic books and information on the activities of the Virginia Numismatic Association and its member clubs.
Ind/Abst Numis. Lit. (?-?).

PL
WIADOMOSCI NUMIZMATYCZNE.
Added/Corp Polskie Towarzystwo Archeologiczne. International Numismatic Congress. 6th, Rome, 1961. No. 1 (1957)-. Periodical. Polish (summaries and/or abstracts in English). qt. Price on Request. **(Subscription address:** ARS Polona, PO Box 1001, 00068 Warsaw Poland.) ***Supersedes*** *Biuletyn Numizmatyczny.*
Ind/Abst BHA : Biblio. Hist. Art; Numis. Lit. (199?-).

US/0145-9090
WORLD COIN NEWS. [World coin news]. (19??)-. Periodical. English. bw. $25.95 US; $48.25 other. Krause Publications, 700 East State Street, Iola WI 54990-0001. **Tel** (715)445-2214, FAX (715)445-4087, telex 55 6461. **ED** Colin R. Bruce. **DD** 737. **Ad Acc**. **Circ:** 6,863 (ctrl).
Desc: Includes hobby news, historical features on coins minted around the world, and an advertising marketplace offering collectors coins to buy or sell. Includes current world coin market prices and coin show calendar.
Ind/Abst Numis. Lit.

Hobbies —Philately

PHILATELY

CN/0316-5051
1+1. Monographic series. French (English). Price varies per volume. Editions Gilles Gheerbrant, 2130 Rue Crescent, Montreal Quebec H3G 2B8 Canada. **DD** 769/.9/04.

US/0363-6542
1869 TIMES. Added/Corp United States 1869 Pictorial Research Associates. **VAT** Eighteen Hundred and Sixty Nine Times. Vol. 1 (Nov. 1975)-. Periodical. English. qt. $15.00. 1869 Pictorial Research Associates Inc., c/o Jonathon Rose, 30 Golf Road, Pleasanton CA 94566. **LC** HE6185.U5; E37. **DD** 769.56973/05.

DK
AFA OSTEUROPA FRIMARKEHANDEL. Main/Corp Aarhus Frimrkehandel. **VFOAT** Osteuropa Frimrkekatalog. **VAT** Aarhus Frimrkehandel Osteuropa Frimrkekatalog. Danish. be. kr400.00. Aarhus Frimrkehandel, Bruunsgade 42, 8000 C Aarhus Denmark. **Tel** 06 125288, FAX 06 199281. **ED** Lars Boes. **LC** HE6185.E85; A27A. **Circ:** 10,000.
Desc: Stamp catalogue covering the Eastern Europe countries.

DK
AFA VESTEUROPA FRIMRKEKATALOG. Main/Corp Aarhus Frimrkehandel. **VFOAT** Vesteuropa Frimrkekatalog. **VAT** Aarhus Frimrkehandel Vesteuropa Frimrkekatalog. Began with Vol. for 1974. Danish. an. kr500.00. Aarhus Frimrkehandel, Bruunsgade 42, 8000 C Aarhus Denmark. **Tel** 06 125288, FAX 06 199281. **ED** Lars Boes. **LC** HE6185.E842; A16A. **Circ:** 7,500. **Supersedes in part** AFA Europa Frimrkekatalog.
Desc: Illustrated stamp catalogue covering Western Europe.

UK
AIR MAIL MAGAZINE. No. 1- Mar. 1939-. Periodical. English. mo. **LC** HE6187.

UK
AMATEUR COLLECTOR'S STAMP CATALOGUE OF SWITZERLAND, THE. VFOAT Stamp Catalogue of Switzerland. Began with 1951 issue. English. **ED** E H Spiro. **LC** HE6185.S9; A7.

US/0003-0473
AMERICAN PHILATELIST, THE. [Am. philat.]. **Added/Corp** American Philatelic Association. American Philatelic Society. **VFOAT** American Philatelist and Year Book of the American Philatelic Association; American Philatelist Year Book. Vol. 1, No. 1 (Jan. 10, 1887)-. Academic Scholarly Publication. English. Twelve times a year. $30.00 US; $33.00 Canada and Mexico; $36.00 other. American Philatelist, Box 8000, State College PA 16803. **Tel** (814)237-3803. **ED** Bill Welch. **LC** HE6187; .A6. **DD** 769.56/075/0973. **Bk Rev. Ad Acc. Circ:** 50,000 (ctrl).
Desc: Articles from humorous to scholarly on philately and the hobby of stamp collecting, and current events of the society.
Ind/Abst Art Archaeol. Tech. Abstr.

US/0163-1608
AMERICAN REVENUER, THE. (THE AMERICAN REVENUER : OFFICIAL ORGAN OF THE AMERICAN REVENUE ASSOCIATION.). Periodical. English. mo (combined issues in July-Aug. and Nov.-Dec.). $18.00. American Revenue Association, PO Box 56, Rockford IA 50468. **Tel** (515)756-3542, FAX (515)756-3542. **ED** Kenneth Trettin. **LC** HJ5321.Z7; A76. **DD** 769.5/7. Index available. cum. index. **Bk Rev. Ad Acc. Circ:** 1,500.
Desc: Dedicated to the study of revenue (tax) stamps of the world. Publishes original research articles and catalogue listings about these stamps.

CN/0384-6679
AMERICAN STAMP NEWS. English. bm. Gray Stamp Company, Station F, Toronto Ontario Canada.

VB
ANNUAL PHILATELIC EXHIBITION / BRITISH VIRGIN ISLANDS PHILATELIC SOCIETY. Added/Corp British Virgin Islands Philatelic Society. (May 26/27, 1990)-. English. **LC** HE6191; .P47.

SA
ARCADE STAMP CATALOGUE / AS. Main/Corp Arcade Stamp Shop. English. Shop No 5, Old Arcade, 100 Market Street, Johannesburg 2000 South Africa. **LC** HE6185.S622; A72A. **DD** 769.56968/075/0968.

US/0360-5205
ATA HANDBOOK. VFOAT A.T.A. Handbook; ATA Topical Handbook; A.T.A. Topical Handbook; Topical Handbook; Handbook. English. $4.00. American Topical Association, PO Box 630, Johnstown PA 15907. **Tel** (814)539-6301. **LC** HE6185; .A635. **DD** 769/.564/075.

Circ: 2,000. **Continues** Topical Handbook.
Desc: Listings of postage stamps by collector, topical interest.

AT
AUSTRALASIAN STAMP CATALOGUE. (19??)-. English. an. 24.95Aus$ (25th edition). Lighthouse Philatelics Pty Ltd., 10 Bartley Street, Chippendale NSW 2005 Australia. **Tel** 011 61 2 6985041. **ED** Brian Moore. **LC** HE6185.A82; A84. **DD** 769.56994. Index available. **Bk Rev. Circ:** 35,000.
Desc: An illustrated and priced catalogue of stamps from the Australian commonwealth (including Australian states issues) and Australian territories.

AT
AUSTRALIAN COMMONWEALTH SPECIALISTS' CATALOGUE, THE.
Ceased. (1926)-(19??). English. ir. Seven Seas Stamps, 62 Wingewarra Street, Dubbo New South Wales 2830 Australia. **Tel** (068)82 3955. **LC** HE6185.A82; A89. **DD** 769.56994/075/0994.

CN/0045-3129
B N A TOPICS. Added/Corp British North America Philatelic Society. Vol. 1 (1944)-. Periodical. English. bm. 20.00Can$ Comes with British North America Philatelic Society membership. British North America Philatelic Society, 6312 Carnarvon Street, Vancouver British Columbia, V6N 1K3 Canada. **Tel** (604)266-0112. **ED** Mike Street. **LC** HE6187; .B18. **DD** 769/.56/074. **Ad Acc. Circ:** 1,500.
Desc: Articles on various aspects of the philately of British North America, including the postage and revenue stamps and postal history of Canada and the provinces.

UK
BALE CATALOGUE OF ISRAEL POSTAGE STAMPS / COMPILED AND PUBLISHED BY MICHAEL H. BALE.
VFOAT Catalogue of Israel Postage Stamps. 10th Ed. (1979)-. English. be. £42.50 Canada. Negev Stamps Ltd, PO Box 1, Ilfracombe EX34 9BR England. **Tel** 11 44 271 862857. **ED** Michael H Bale. **LC** HE6185.P14; B3. **DD** 769.5695694/075. **Bk Rev. Circ:** 2,000. **Continues** Bale, Michael H. Bale Catalogue of Palestine & Israel Postage Stamps.
Desc: Comprehensive priced catalogue Israel postage.

CN
BALTIC PHILATELIST NUMISMATIST, THE. Periodical. English. $3.00. Baltic Philatelic Club, A Greblis, PO Box 5, Roxboro H8Y 3E8 Canada. **LC** HE6187; .B35. **DD** 769/.56948.

US/8756-5153
BAY PHIL, THE. (THE BAY PHIL : A MONTHLY PUBLICATION OF THE FRIENDS OF THE WESTERN PHILATELIC LIBRARY, INC.). **Added/Corp** Western Philatelic Library. Friends. (19??)-. Periodical. English. Six times a year (Feb., Apr., June, Aug., Oct., Dec.). $8.00. Friends Western Philatelic Lib, PO Box 2219, Sunnyvale CA 94087. **Tel** (408)733-0336.

IT
BOLAFFI'S ROMAN STATES AND VATICAN CITY SPECIALIZED STAMP CATALOGUE. VFOAT Bolaffi Specialized Stamp Catalogue, Roman States and Vatican City. English. John Raith, PO Box 144, Flushing NY 11365. **LC** HE6185.V32; B58. **DD** 769.56945/634.

IT
BOLLETTINO PREFILATELICO E STORICO-POSTALE. N. 6- Dec. 1978-. Italian. L10000. CCP 9/23511 Intestato Alleditrice del Corrier Maggiore, Via Dellarco 31, 35100 Padova Italy. **LC** HE6187; .B57. **Continues** Bollettino Prefilatelico Storico-Postale.

LH
BRIEFMARKENAUSGABE VOM ... / L'EMISSION DE TIMBRES-POSTE DU ... / THE STAMP ISSUE OF ... / FUERSTENTUM LIECHTENSTEIN, DIE.
Added/Corp Liechtenstein. Amt fuer Briefmarkengestaltung. Postmuseum des Fuerstentums Liechtenstein. **VFOAT** Emission de Timbres-Poste du ...; Stamp Issue of ... . (19??)-. English (French and German). Amt fuer Briefmarkengestaltung, GL-9490 Vaduz Liechtenstein. **LC** HE6185.L5; L53a. **DD** 769.569436/48. **Continues** Ausgabe (Liechtenstein. Amt fuer Briefmarkengestaltung).

US/0477-4612
BULLETIN OF THE POLONUS PHILATELIC SOCIETY. Main/Corp Polonus Philatelic Society. **VFOAT** Polonus Bulletin. Began with Aug. 1942 issue. Bulletin. English. bm. Polonus Philatelic Society, Po Box 82, River Grove IL 60171. **ED** M E Stexzynaki. **LC** HE6187; .P649A. **DD** 769.569438. cum. index.

CN/0384-7632
C P S NEWS LETTER (TORONTO). (C P S NEWS LETTER.). **Main/Corp** Canadian Philatelic

Society. Vol. 1 (June 1950)-. Periodical. English (French; summaries and/or abstracts in French). mo. Canadian Philatelic Society, 73 Adelaide Street West, Toronto Ontario M5H 1P5. **DD** 769/.56/0971.

CN/0824-6602
CAHIERS DE L'ACADEMIE (MONTREAL). (LES CAHIERS DE L'ACADEMIE.). Opus 1 (15 Nov. 1983)-. French. an. 20.00Can$ Canada; 25.00Can$ other. Academie Quebecoise d'Etudes Philateliques, CP 24 Succursale Beaubien, Montreal Quebec H2G 3C8 Canada. **DD** 769.56/05. **Circ:** 200 (ctrl).
Desc: Researches about philately and postal history by our members. Many subjects from many countries.

CN/0702-9268
CANADA SPECIALIZED POSTAGE STAMP CATALOGUE. Began with 1974. English. an. $15.00. Canada Specialized Ltd, Editorial Office, 330 Bay Street/Suite 703, Toronto Ontario M5H 2T8 Canada. **LC** HE6185.C22; C36. **DD** 769.56971/075/0971.

CN/0045-5253
CANADIAN PHILATELIST. [Can. philat.]. **Added/Corp** Canadian Philatelic Society. Royal Philatelic Society of Canada. **VFOAT** Philateliste Canedien. Vol. 1 (March 1950)-. Periodical. English (French; summaries and/or abstracts in French). bm. $30.00. Royal Philatelic Society of Canada, PO Box 5320 Station F, Ottawa Ontario K2C 3J1 Canada. **Tel** (613)224-4189, FAX (613)737-7704. **ED** Jim Haskett. Index available. **Bk Rev. Ad Acc. Circ:** 6,000 (ctrl).
Desc: Philatelic and postal history articles, worldwide with majority related to Canada. Letters to editor, new Canada issues, advertising, new members and interests.
Ind/Abst Can. Index.

CN/0702-3154
CANADIAN STAMP NEWS. Vol. 1 (June 28/July 12, 1976)-. Periodical. English. Twenty-six times a year. 24.95Can$ Canada; $25.94 US; 38.95Can$ other. Canadian Stamp News, 103 Lakeshore Road, Suite 202, St. Catherines L2N 2T6 Canada. **Tel** (416)646-7744, FAX (416)646-0995. **ED** Don Atanasuff. **DD** 769/.56/05. **Bk Rev. Ad Acc. Circ:** 20,000. **Supersedes in part** Coin, Stamp, Antique News, 0010-0439.
Ind/Abst Can. Index.

US/0746-004X
CANAL ZONE STUDY GROUP. (THE CANAL ZONE PHILATELIST / CANAL ZONE STUDY GROUP.). **VFOAT** C.Z.S.G. Philatelic Notes; CZSG Philatelic Notes; Canal Zone Philatelic Notes. Periodical. English. qt. $5.00 membership. A R Bew Secretary, Canal Zone Study Group, 20 South Carolina Avenue South, Atlantic City NJ 08401. **LC** HE6185.C24; C36. **DD** 769.5697287/5/05.

XR
CESKOSLOVENSKO. VFOAT Katalog Ceskoslovenskych Znamek. Czech. kcs40.00 single issue. Postovni Filatelisticka Sluzba V Nakl Dopravy A Spoju, Prague 1 NA Prikope 13, Prague Czech Republic. **LC** HE6185.C952; A3.

UK/0142-5625
CHANNEL ISLANDS SPECIALISED CATALOGUE OF STAMPS AND POSTAL HISTORY. [Channel Isl. spec. cat. stamps post. hist.]. **VFOAT** Stanley Gibbons Channel Islands Specialised Catalogue of Stamps and Postal History. (1979)-. English. be (every 2 years). £12.95 UK; £17.95 other. Stanley Gibbons Limited, Parkside, Christchurch Road, Ringwood, Hants, BH24 3SH England. **Tel** 011 44 425 472363, FAX 011 44 425 470247. **DD** 769.5694234.

CN/0822-482X
CHARLTON CANADA STAMP ALBUM & STORYBOOK, THE. VFOAT Canada Stamp Album & Storybook. 4th Ed. (1983)-. English. an. $6.00 per vol. Charlton Press, 2010 Yonge Street, Toronto Ontario M4S 1Z9. **Tel** (416)488-4653. **DD** 769.56971. **Continues** Charlton ... Canada Stamp & Storybook, 0709-4108.

US
CHINA PHILATELY. VFOAT Chung-Kuo Jen Min Yu Cheng; Chi Yu. No. 1 (Spring 1982)-. Periodical. English. Six times a year. $21.00. All China Philatelic Federation. **(Subscription address:** China International Book Trading Corporation, PO Box 399, Library Service Department, Beijing 100044 People's Republic of China.**)**
Desc: An informative, academic and commercial magazine. Keeps the reader informed of new issues in China; provides information and background material on rare Chinese stamps; and publishes the results of philatelic studies and findings.

US/0009-6008
CHRONICLE OF THE U.S. CLASSIC POSTAL ISSUES, THE. Added/Corp U.S. Philatelic Classics Society. **VFOAT** Chronicle. **VAT** Chronicle of the United States Classic Postal Issues. Vol. 17, No. 48 (Oct. 1964)-. Academic Scholarly Publication. English. qt. $16.00 members of the US Philatelic Classics Society, $24.00 non-members. US Philatelic Classics

Society, Briarwood, c/o Patricia S. Walker, Lisbon MD 21765. **LC** HE6187; .C5342. **DD** 769/.56973. Index available. **Bk Rev. Ad Acc. Circ:** 1,200. ***Continues*** *Chronicle of the U.S. Philatelic Classics Society.*
Desc: Journal of scholarly research on US and related stamps and postal history before 1900.

CH
CHUNG-KUO YU KAN. VFOAT China Philatelic Magazine. Periodical. Chinese. $80.00 nonmember. Chung-Kuo Chi Yu Hsieh Hui, PO Box 18, Taipei Taiwan. **LC** HE6204.T28; C49. **DD** 769.56/075.

US/0010-0838
COLLECTORS CLUB PHILATELIST, THE. [Collect. Club philat.]. **Main/Corp** Collectors Club (New York, N.Y.). **Added/Corp** Collectors Club (New York, N.Y.) Philatelist. Vol. 1 (Jan. 1922)-. Periodical. English. bm (six issues). The Collectors Club, 22 East 35th Street, New York NY 10016. **Tel** (212)683-0559. **ED** E. E. Fricks. **LC** HE6187; .C6. cum. index. **Circ:** 1,000.

US/0146-4728
DATZ PHILATELIC INDEX OF UNITED STATES POSTAGE STAMPS. VFOAT Philatelic Index of United States Postage Stamps. English. Numisphil Publications, PO Box 2743, Denver CO 80201. **LC** HE6185.U5; D35. **DD** 769/.56973/075.

UK/0308-549X
DAVID FIELD ALL-WORLD MINIATURE SHEET CATALOGUE. VFOAT All-World Miniature Sheet Catalogue. 1973-. English. £2.00. David Fields Holdings Ltd, 42 Berkeley Street, W1X 5FP London England. **LC** HE6230.M48; D37. **DD** 769/.56.

GW
DEUTSCHE BRIEFMARKEN REVUE / SD SAMMLER DIENST. German. mo. DM47.00 Germany; DM57.00 other. PSBN Verlagsgesellschaft GmbH, Konkordiastrasse 13, W-4000 Duesseldorf 1 Germany. **Tel** 011 49 211 394032.

CN/0827-2034
DIRECTORY - CANADIAN STAMP DEALERS' ASSOCIATION. (DIRECTORY.). [Dir. - Can. Stamp Deal. assoc.]. **Main/Corp** Canadian Stamp Dealers' Association. **VFOAT** Canadian Stamp Dealers' Association Directory; C.S.D.A. Directory. 1984-. Directory. English. an. Free. Canadian Stamp Dealers' Association, PO Box 1123, Adelaide Street, Toronto Ontario M5C 2K5 Canada. **DD** 769.56/025/71. **Ad Acc. Circ:** 10,000.
Desc: Members of Canadian Stamp Dealers' Association, listed by name and philatelic specialty.

US
DIRECTORY OF ATA MEMBERS. **Main/Corp** American Topical Association. **VAT** Directory of American Topical Association Members. 1989-. Directory. English. ir (issued every four years). $25.00. American Topical Association, PO Box 630, Johnstown PA 15907. **Tel** (814)539-6301. **LC** HE6188; .A7215. **DD** 769.56/4/06073. **Ad Acc.** ctrl circ. ***Continues*** *Membership Directory - American Topical Association.*

CN/0707-7203
ECHOS PHILATELIQUES. (ECHOS PHILATELIQUES : BULLETIN MENSUEL D'INFORMATION.). Bulletin. French. mo. $1.00 per number. Echos Philateliques, CP 398 Succursale A, Montreal Quebec H3C 2T1 Canada. **DD** 769.56/06/0714281. ***Continues*** *Philatelic Echos, 0707-7203.*

CU
FILATELIA CUBANA. Periodical. Spanish. Three times a year. $10.00. Ediciones Cubanas, Obispo 527, Altos ESQ Bernaza, CP 10100 Havana Cuba. **Tel** 011 632980, 631942, FAX 011 631011, telex 512337, 6540. **LC** HE6187; .F463. **DD** 769/.56/05. **Circ:** 10,000 (ctrl).
Desc: Specialized publication for collectors of stamps and first-day issues. Articles or stamp history, critical studies of Cuban Stamps. Extensive information on activities of the Federation.

PL
FILATELISTA : DWUTYGODNIK POLSKIEGO ZWIAZKU FILATELISTOW. (195?)-. Periodical. Polish. mo. $33.00. **(Subscription address:** ARS Polona, PO Box 1001, 00068 Warsaw Poland.**)**

US/0015-2714
FIRESIDE CHATS. Periodical. English. qt. $15.00. Franklin D Roosevelt Philatelic Society, 154 Laguna Court, St Augustine Shores FL 32086-7031. **Tel** (904)797-3513. **ED** Gustav Detjen Jr. **LC** HE6183.R67; F57. **DD** 769.56/49973917/0924. **Bk Rev. Ad Acc. Circ:** 440 (ctrl).
Desc: Information on Roosevelt stamps and related philatelic material, new issues, book reviews, historic data on Roosevelt administration, trading page and FD Roosevelt membership facts.

US/0428-4836
FIRST DAYS. Added/Corp American First Day Cover Society. (19??)-. Periodical. English. Eight times a year. $15.00. American First Day Cover Society, PO Box 5295, Fairlawn OH 44333. **Tel** (602)321-9206. **ED** Barry Newton. Index available. **Bk Rev. Ad Acc. Circ:** 4,000.
Desc: Covers a branch of philately concerned with the issue of stamps.

US/0190-7433
FLEETWOOD'S STANDARD FIRST DAY COVER CATALOG. Catalog. English. Fleetwood Publications, 1 Unicover Center, Cheyenne WY 82008. **LC** HE6184.C65; F533. **DD** 769.56/5/0294.

US/0196-5034
FOUNDATION BULLETIN (NEW YORK). (FOUNDATION BULLETIN.). Bulletin. English. qt. Free (foundation contributors). Philatelic Foundation, 270 Madison Avenue, New York NY 10016. **ED** John F Dunn.
Desc: Discussion of factors related to examination of stamps and covers for genuiness and faults, plus news on foundation activities.

US/0197-7202
FRANCE ... SPECIALIZED CATALOGUE OF ARTIST PROOFS, DE LUXE SHEETS, IMPERFORATES, COLOR ESSAYS, FIRST DAY COVERS, COLLECTIVE PROOFS, PRINTERS INSPECTION PROOFS, ILLUSTRATIONS. 1980-. English. an. $12.00. Orzano Publishing Company, PO Box 394, Islip New York 11751. **Tel** (516)968-8996. **ED** J Orzano. **LC** HE6185.F82; F67. **DD** 769.56944/075/0973. **Bk Rev. Ad Acc.**
Desc: Covers pricing of French artist proofs, deluxe sheets, imperforates, color essays, first day covers, collective proofs, printers inspection proofs including illustrations of each.

US/0732-5517
FROM THE DRAGON'S DEN. (FROM THE DRAGON'S DEN : OFFICIAL PUBLICATION OF THE RYUKYU PHILATELIC SPECIALIST SOCIETY.). Periodical. English. qt. $10.00 (membership) US; $15.00 (membership) other. Arthur L Askins, PO Box 4092, Berkeley CA 94704.

US/0275-4967
GERSHON'S ... SPECIALIZED CATALOGUE OF ISRAEL AND THE HOLY LAND. VFOAT Specialized Catalogue of Israel and the Holy Land. (19??)-. Catalog. English. $12.00. Gershon Litzman, 147 West 42nd Street, New York NY 10036. **LC** HE6185.I65; G47. **DD** 769.5695694.

UK
GIBBONS STAMP MONTHLY. (June 1977)-. Consumer Publication. English. Twelve times a year. £19.20. Stanley Gibbons Limited, Parkside, Christchurch Road, Ringwood, Hants, BH24 3SH England. **Tel** 011 44 425 472363, FAX 011 44 425 470247. **ED** Hugh Jefferies. **LC** HE6187; .S7352. **DD** 769.56/075/0941. Index available. cum. index. **Bk Rev**, (Qty: 50-100 per year). **Ad Acc, Adv Mgr:** Carol Flynn. **Circ:** 24,000. ***Continues*** *Stamp Monthly.*
Desc: Britain's leading philatelic magazine with news, specialized studies, and market information. Includes competitions, new collectors column and the exclusive Stanley Gibbons Catalogue Supplement.

CN/0316-7739
GRAND NEWS. Added/Corp Grand River Valley Philatelic Association. (Sept. 1969)-. English. Five times a year. 7.50Can$. Grand River Valley Philatelic Association, 116 Gilkison Street, Brantford Ontario N3T 2A3 Canada. **Tel** (519)759-4925, FAX (519)753-6190. **DD** 769/.56/0627134.

US/0098-2326
HEBERT'S CATALOGUE OF USED PLATE NUMBER SINGLES. English. $4.00. George G Shapiro, Trans Pacific Stamp Company, PO Box 48715, Los Angeles CA 90048. **LC** HE6185.U6; C28. **DD** 769/.56973. ***Continues*** *Catalogue of Used Plate Number Singles.*

GW
HESSISCHE POSTGESCHICHTE. **Added/Corp** Gesellschaft fuer Deutsche Postgeschichte. Bezirksgruppe Hessen. (19??)-. German. ir. Am Main Gesellschaft fur Deutsche, Postgeschichte Bezirksgruppe Hessen, Friedrich-Ebert-Anlage 58-72, Frankfurt Germany. **LC** HE6996.H4; H47a.

US/0146-0994
JAPANESE PHILATELY. Added/Corp International Society for Japanese Philately. (19??)-. Periodical. English. Six times a year. International Society of Japanese Philately, 530 East Indian Spring Drive, Silver Spring MD 20901. **Tel** (301)589-3686. **ED** Robert M. Spalding. **LC** HE6187; .J3. **DD** 769/.56952. Index available. cum. index. **Bk Rev. Ad Acc. Circ:** 1,500 (ctrl).
Desc: Relates Japanese philately to the history, culture and customs of Japan.

US/0278-436X
JAPOS BULLETIN. VFOAT J.A.P.O.S. Bulletin. **VAT** Journalists, Authors and Poets on Stamps Bulletin. (19??)-. Bulletin. English. qt. $9.00. J A P O S Study Group, c/o Gustav Detjen Jr, 154 Laguna Court, Augustine Shores FL 32086-7031. **Tel** (904)797-3513. **ED** Gustav Detjen Jr. **LC** HE6183.L59; J36. **DD** 769.56/3. **Bk Rev. Ad Acc. Circ:** 400.
Desc: Data on journalists, authors and poets featured on world-wide postage stamps, new issues, book reviews, market place pages, anecdotes, and stories, promotion of additional stamps honoring writers.

US/0447-953X
JOURNAL OF SPORTS PHILATELY. [J. sports philatel.]. **Added/Corp** Sports Philatelists International. Vol. 1, No. 1 (Sept. 1962)-. Periodical. English. Six times a year. $12.00 US and Canada. Sports Philatelists International, Box 2286, c/o John la Porta, La Grange IL 60525. **ED** Mark C. Maestrone. **LC** HE6187; .J62. **DD** 769.56/49796/05. Index available (published separately). **Bk Rev. Ad Acc. Circ:** 500 (ctrl).
Desc: Periodical for stamp collectors with interests in sports or Olympics. Includes articles on many topics, information on auctions, check lists, ads and membership information.
Ind/Abst SPORT Discus; SportSearch (May 1987-).

SW
KATALOG (SWEDEN. POSTENS FRIMARKSAVDELNING). (KATALOG / PFA.). English (French, German and Swedish). PFA Postens Frimarksavdelning, S-105 02 Stockholm Sweden. **LC** HE6185.S82.

KO
KOREAN STAMPS. Began in 1964. Periodical. English. bm. Korea Publications Export, Pyongyang DPRK Korea. **LC** HE6185.K7; K63. **DD** 769.569519/3.

US/0161-6234
LINN'S STAMP NEWS. Vol. 42, No. 28 (No. 2130) (Sept. 1, 1969)-. Periodical. English. wk. $33.00 (one year), $73.00 (two years) US; $59.00 (one year), $139.00 (two years) other. Amos Press, PO Box 29, Sidney OH 45365. **Tel** (513)498-0802, (800)448-7293, FAX (513)498-0812. **ED** Michael Laurence. **LC** HE6187; .L5. **DD** 769/.56/075. **Bk Rev. Ad Acc. Circ:** 77,000. available on microfilm from University Microfilms International (UMI). ***Continues*** *Linn's Weekly Stamp News.*
Desc: The world's largest weekly stamp newspaper combining comprehensive philatelic journalism, educational features and revealing market coverage.

US/0748-996X
LINN'S U.S. STAMP YEARBOOK. (LINN'S U.S. STAMP YEARBOOK : A COMPREHENSIVE RECORD OF TECHNICAL DATA, BACKGROUND AND STORIES BEHIND ALL OF THE STAMPS ...). [Linn's U. S. stamp yearb.]. **VFOAT** Linn's US Stamp Yearbook; U.S. Stamp Yearbook; US Stamp Yearbook. 1983-. English. an. $19.95 softcover, $30.00 hardcover. Linn's Stamp News, PO Box 29, Sidney OH 45365-0029. **Tel** (513)498-0801. **ED** George Amick. **LC** HE6185.U6; L54. **DD** 769.56973. Index available. **Circ:** 15,000.
Desc: A collection of photos, facts, stories and technical data on every U.S. stamp and postal product issued in 1988.

US/0146-6887
LINN'S WORLD STAMP ALMANAC. [Linn's world stamp alm.]. (1977)-. Consumer Publication. English. ir. $19.95. Amos Press, 911 Vandermark Road, Box 29, Sidney OH 45365. **Tel** (513)498-0801, FAX (513)498-0814. **LC** HE6194; .L56. **DD** 769/.56/075.

UK
LONDON PHILATELIST, THE. Added/Corp Philatelic Society (Great Britain) Royal Philatelic Society (Great Britain). Vol. 1, No. 1 (Jan. 1892)-. Periodical. English. Ten times a year (Jan/Feb. & July/Aug. combined). £36.00. Royal Philatelic Society of London, 41 Devonshire Place, London W1N 1PE, England. **Tel** 11 44 71 486 1044, FAX 11 41 71 486 0803. **ED** George E. Barker. **LC** HE6187; .L6. **Bk Rev. Ad Acc. Circ:** 1,600.
Desc: Presents articles on the stamps and postal history of all territories worldwide, plus news of the society and other philatelic bodies and their activities.

SP
MADRID FILATELICO. Periodical. Spanish. **ED** M Galvez Rodriguez. **LC** HE6187; .M3.

US
MEKEEL'S WEEKLY STAMP NEWS. **Added/Corp** State Historical Society of Wisconsin. **VFOAT** MeKeel's Weekly. Vol. 1 (Jan. 7, 1981)-. English. wk. $15.00 US; $25.00 other. Severn Wylie Jewett Company, Box 1660, Portland ME 04104. **Tel** (207)797-3221. **ED** George F Stilphen. **LC** Microfilm 01921 HE; HE6187. **Bk Rev. Ad Acc. Circ:** 5,000 (ctrl). ***Absorbed*** *Weekly Philatetic Era.*
Desc: News items and articles pertaining to stamp collecting.

UK/0305-3245
MEMBERSHIP DIRECTORY - PHILATELIC TRADERS' SOCIETY. [Membsh. dir. - Philat. Traders Soc.]. (19??)-. Monographic series. English. an (May). £5.00 UK; £8.00 others. Philatelic Traders Society Ltd., 107 Charterhouse

Hobbies — Philately

Street, London EC1M 6PT England. **Tel** 011 44 71 490 1005, FAX 011 44 71 253 0414. **ED** Derek Yardley. **Ad Acc. Circ:** 1,000 (ctrl).

GW
MICHEL BENELUX-KATALOG ... BELGIEN, NIEDERLANDE, LUXEMBURG. German. Schwaneberger Verlag GmbH, Muthmannstrasse 4, W-8000 Munchen 45 Germany. **LC** HE6185.B462; M53. **DD** 769.569492/075.

GW
MICHEL BRIEFE-KATALOG DEUTSCHLAND. German. Schwaneberger Verlag GmbH, Muthmannstrasse 4, W-8000 Munchen 45 Germany. **LC** HE6185.G3; M53. **DD** 769.56943/075/0943.

GW
MICHEL DEUTSCHLAND-SPEZIAL-KATALOG. **VFOAT** Deutschland-Spezial-Katalog. German. ir. Schwaneberger Verlag GmbH, Muthmannstrasse 4, W-8000 Munchen 45 Germany. **LC** HE6185.G3; M5.

GW/0301-6692
MICHEL EUROPA-KATALOG. [Michel Eur.-Kat.]. **VFOAT** Michel Europa, Katalog. German. Schwaneberger Verlag GmbH, Muthmannstrasse 4, W-8000 Munchen 45 Germany. **LC** HE6226; .M6. **Continues** Michel Briefmarkenkatalog: Europa, 0301-8857.

GW
MICHEL GANZSACHEN-KATALOG DEUTSCHLAND. **VFOAT** Ganzsachen-Katalog Deutschland. German. ir. Schwaneberger Verlag GmbH, Muthmannstrasse 4, W-8000 Munchen 45 Germany. **LC** HE6184.S73; M5. **DD** 769.56/6/0750943.

GW
MICHEL GROSSBRITANNIEN-SPEZIAL-KATALOG. German. Schwaneberger Verlag GmbH, Muthmannstrasse 4, W-8000 Munchen 45 Germany. **LC** HE6185.G62; M47. **DD** 769.56941/0750943.

GW
MICHEL ITALIEN-KATALOG ... MIT MALTA, SAN MARINO UND VATIKANSTAAT. German. Schwaneberger Verlag GmbH, Muthmannstrasse 4, W-8000 Munchen 45 Germany. **LC** HE6185.I7; M47. **DD** 769.56945/075/0943.

GW
MICHEL OSTERREICH-SPEZIAL-KATALOG. **VFOAT** Osterreich-Spezial-Katalog. German. ir. Schwaneberger Verlag GmbH, Muthmannstrasse 4, W-8000 Munchen 45 Germany. **LC** HE6185.A92; M48.

GW
MICHEL PRIVATGANZSACHEN-KATALOG BUNDESREPUBLIK DEUTSCHLAND, BERLIN, DEUTSCHE DEMOKRATISCHE REPUBLIK. **VFOAT** Privatganzsachen-Katalog Bundesrepublik Deutschland, Berlin, Deutsche Demokratische Republik. German. ir. Schwaneberger Verlag GmbH, Muthmannstrasse 4, W-8000 Munchen 45 Germany. **LC** HE6184.S73; M53. **DD** 769.55/6/0750943.

GW
MICHEL SKANDINAVIEN-KATALOG. German. Schwaneberger Verlag GmbH, Muthmannstrasse 4, W-8000 Munchen 45 Germany. **LC** HE6185.S382; M48. **DD** 769.56948/075/0943.

NE
MIJN STOKPAARDJE. (19??)-. Dutch. ir. Price varies per volume. Uitgeverij De Postiljon, Post Box 15041, 3501 BA Utrecht Netherlands. **Tel** 011 31 30 717988.

CN/0707-2937
MONTHLY COLLECTOR (SUDBURY). (THE MONTHLY COLLECTOR.). V. 1- Apr. 1978-. Periodical. English. mo. $4.00 The Monthly Collector, 269-50 Shelley Drive, Sudbury Ontario P3A 4S6 Canada. **DD** 769/.56/05.

US
NOBLE OFFICIAL CATALOG OF BUREAU PRECANCELS, THE. **VFOAT** Noble Official Catalog of United States Bureau Precancels. (19??)-. Catalog. English. an. **LC** HE6185.U6; M5. **Continues** Mitchell-Noble Official Catalog of Bureau Precancels.

IT
NUOVO CORRIERE FILATELICO, IL. Vol. 1- Oct. 1975-. Periodical. Multiple languages (English, French, German and Italian). 10.000. Societe di Studi Filatelici E Storico Postali, Via Cavour 38, 50129 Firenze Italy. **LC** HE6187; .N85.

US/0195-3559
OFFICIAL BLACKBOOK PRICE GUIDE OF UNITED STATES POSTAGE STAMPS, THE. [Off. blackbook price guide U.S. post. stamps]. (197?)-. English. an. $8.90 (includes shipping/handling). Random House Inc., 400 Hahn Road, Westminster MD 21157. **Tel** (800)726-0600, (800)733-3000, FAX (800)659-2436. **LC** HE6185.U6; H82. **DD** 769.56973/075.

US/0882-9071
ONCE UPON A TIME (ARLINGTON, TEX.). (ONCE UPON A TIME : NEWSLETTER OF THE ATA FOLKLORE-FAIRY TALE STUDY UNIT.). [Once time]. **Added/Corp** American Topical Association. Fairy-Tale/Folklore Study Unit. American Topical Association. Folktale-Fairy Tale Study Unit. American Topical Association. Folklore-Fairy Tale Study Unit. (Aug./Sept. 1975)-. Periodical. English. bm. $10.00 US; $15.00 other. ATA Fairy-Tale, Folklore Study Unit, 2509/Buffalo Drive, Arlington TX 76013. **Tel** (817)275-2801. **ED** Karen J. Cartier. **LC** HE6183.F35; O53. **DD** 769.56/493982. Index available. cum. index. **Circ:** 85.
Desc: Newsletter devoted to fairytales, folklore, legends and mythology which are portrayed on postage stamps of the world. Stories, authors, postmarks and new issues are presented.

US/8755-3562
OPINIONS (PHILATELIC FOUNDATION (NEW YORK, N.Y.)). (OPINIONS.). [Opinions - Philat. Found. (N.Y. N.Y.)]. **Added/Corp** Philatelic Foundation (New York, N.Y.). (1983)-. Periodical. English. Philatelic Foundation, 270 Madison Avenue, New York NY 10016. **LC** HE6187; .O65. **DD** 769.56/05.

US/0893-9055
PANTOGRAPH OF POSTAL STATIONERY, THE. Vol. 1 (July 15, 1972)-. Periodical. English. bm. $12.00 US; $16.00 other. United Postal Stationery Society, Central Office, PO Box 48, Redlands CA 92373. **DD** 790. **Ad Acc. Circ:** 1,500 (ctrl).

CN/0319-4094
PHILA-PRESSE. Vol. 1, March (1975)-. Periodical. French. mo. Federation Des Societes Philateliques Du Quebec, 502 H.V., Quebec G1R 4R8. **DD** 769/.56/062714.

CN/0822-4919
PHILATELIC AUCTION / CHARLTON AUCTIONS. [Philat. auction - Charlton Auctions]. **Main/Corp** Charlton Auctions. Periodical. English. $2.50 per no. Charlton Press, 2010 Yonge Street, Toronto Ontario M4S 1Z9. **Tel** (416)488-4653. **DD** 769.56971/029/4713541. **Absorbed in part** Unreserved Public Mini Auction, 0822-7713.

CN/0822-496X
PHILATELIC AUCTION - TOREX. (PHILATELIC AUCTION.). [Philat. auction - Torex]. **Main/Corp** Torex. Periodical. English. ir. $2.50 per no. Charlton Press, 2010 Yonge Street, Toronto Ontario M4S 1Z9. **Tel** (416)488-4653. **DD** 769.56/029/4713541.

AT
PHILATELIC BULLETIN. Title Change. Began with (Aug. 1953)-(1979). Bulletin. English. Australia Postal Commission, Box 357E GPO 3001, Melbourne Australia. **LC** HE6187; .P2438. **DD** 769/.56/075. cum. index. **Continued by** Australian Stamp Bulletin.

US
PHILATELIC CHIT CHAT FROM CHARLIE. Wonderlin, POB 3645, Peoria IL 61614.

US/0048-3710
PHILATELIC JOURNALIST, THE. Ceased. (1971)-(July 1988). Periodical. English. qt. The Philatelic Journalist, 154 Laguna Court, St Augustine Shores FL 32086-7031. **Tel** (904)797-3513. **ED** Gustav Detjen Jr. **LC** HE6187; .P353. **DD** 769.56/05. **Bk Rev. Ad Acc. Circ:** 900 (ctrl).
Desc: Information helpful to philatelic writers and publicists. Articles promote and publicize philately and philatelic literature. Also activities of members of the Society of Philaticians, a group of philatelic journalists. Reviews of philatelic books.

US/0270-1707
PHILATELIC LITERATURE REVIEW. [Philat. lit. rev.]. **Added/Corp** American Philatelic Research Library. (1942)-. Periodical. English. qt (4 issues). $30.00. American Philatelic Research Library, PO Box 8338, State College PA 16803. **Tel** (814)237-3803. **ED** William L. Welch Jr. **Bk Rev. Ad Acc. Circ:** 2,560 (ctrl).
Desc: Book reviews of current philatelic literature and articles concerning philatelic research, authors and literature.

US/0273-5598
PHILATELIC OBSERVER. (PHILATELIC OBSERVER : OFFICIAL ORGAN OF THE JUNIOR PHILATELISTS OF AMERICA.). [Philat. obs.]. **Added/Corp** Junior Philatelists of America. (19??)-. Periodical. English. bm. Philatelic Observer, 16 Lancaster Avenue, Maplewood NJ 07040. **DD** 769.

UK
PHILATELIC REVIEW. Periodical. English. qt. £2.00 UK; £3.00 (surface mail), £4.00 (airmail) other. **LC** HE6185.G6; P48. **DD** 769.56941/075/0941.

●US
PHILATELIC SHOPPER, THE. Vol. 1, No. 1 (June 1992)-. Periodical. English. mo. **LC** WMLC 91/5881.

CN/0381-7547
PHILATELIE AU QUEBEC. (PHILATELIE QUEBEC.). [Philat. Que.]. **Added/Corp** Federation Quebecoise de Philatelie. **VFOAT** Philatelie au Quebec. Vol 10 No 5 (Jan. 1984)-. Periodical. French. mo (10 issues). 40.00Can$ (institutions), 28.04Can$ (individuals). Philatelie Quebec, 4545 Pierre Coubertin CP 1000, Montreal QUE H1V 3R2 Canada. **Tel** (514)252-3035, FAX (514)251-8038. **ED** Francois Brisse. **DD** 769.56/05. **Bk Rev.** (Qty: 8 to 10). **Ad Acc, Adv Mgr:** Ivan Latulippe.
Desc: General philatelic interest including a section for young philatelists.
Ind/Abst Point Repere (1984-).

UK/0260-6739
PHILATELIST AND PJGB, THE. VAT Philatelist and Philatelic Journal of Great Britain. Periodical. English. bm. £12.00 UK; $18.38 US. Robson Lowe Ltd, 39 Poole Hill Auction House, Bournemouth England BH2 5PX. **Tel** (0202)295711, telex 41146. **ED** Robson Lowe, Peter Collins and Derryck Milne. **LC** HE6187; .P62. **DD** 769.56/075/0941. Index available. cum. index. **Bk Rev. Ad Acc.** rec'd circ. available on microfilm from University Microfilms International (UMI). **Formed by the union of** Philatelist and Philatelic Journal of Great Britain.

AT
PHILATELY FROM AUSTRALIA. **Added/Corp** Royal Philatelic Society of Victoria. Vol. 1 (Mar. 1949)-. Periodical. English. Four times a year. 15.00Aus$. Royal Philatelic Society of Victoria, 6 Avoca Street, South Yarra Victoria 3141 Australia. **Tel** (03)866 4706. **ED** G. Kellow. **LC** HE6187; .P642. **DD** 383.22. Index available. cum. index. **Circ:** 500.
Desc: Specialized Australian philately.

US/0885-7385
POSTA (LAKE OSWEGO, OR.), LA. (LA POSTA.). [Posta]. (19??)-. Periodical. English. Six times a year (Jan., Mar., May, July, Sept., Nov.). $15.00. La Posta, PO Box 135, Lake Oswego OR 97034. **Tel** (503)657-5685. **ED** Richard W. Helbock. **LC** HE6371; .P66. **DD** 383/.4973. **Bk Rev. Ad Acc. Circ:** 1,100.
Desc: Journal of American postal history covering all aspects of transport and handling of the mails.
Ind/Abst West. Hist. Q.

US/0272-5363
POSTAGE STAMP PRICES OF THE UNITED STATES, UNITED NATIONS, AND CANADA AND PROVINCES. [Post. stamp prices U.S., U.N., Can. prov.]. **VFOAT** Harris Reference Catalog of Postage Stamp Prices for United States, United Nations, Canada & Provinces; Harris Postage Stamp Catalogue. English. sa. $2.25. HE Harris, 645 Summer Street, Boston MA. **LC** HE6226; .H32A. **DD** 769.56973/029/4.

US/0554-8373
POSTAL STATIONERY. Began with July/Aug. 1948. Periodical. English. bm. $6.00. United Postal Stationery Society, Central Office, PO Box 48, Redlands CA 92373. **LC** HE6187; .P69. **DD** 769/.56. **Bk Rev. Ad Acc.** ctrl circ. **Continues** Postal Stationery Journal, 0278-6362.

SZ
POSTGESCHICHTE. **VFOAT** Histoire Postale; Postal History. Periodical. German (French). qt. 25.00F Switzerland; $25.00 US. Postgeschichte, Verlag, 8025 Zurich Switzerland. **Tel** 01 251 46 12. **ED** Hans R Schwarzenbach. **LC** HE6007; .P57. Index available. **Bk Rev. Ad Acc. Circ:** 2,000.
Desc: The only postal history journal in Central Europe.

US/0551-6897
POSTHORN, THE. [Posthorn]. **Added/Corp** Scandinavian Collectors Club. **VFOAT** Post Horn. (19??)-. Periodical. English. Four times a year. $14.00. Journal of Scandinavian Collectors Club, Box 302, Lawrenceville GA 30246-0302. **ED** Eugene C. Lesney. **DD** 769. **Circ:** 2,000.
Desc: Collection of Scandinavian philatelic items, philatelic history and related subjects.

US
PRICED CATALOGUE OF STAMPS OF FOREIGN COUNTRIES. **Main/Corp** Stanley Gibbons, Inc. **VFOAT** Stanley Gibbons Priced Catalogue of Stamps of Foreign Countries. English. be. Stanley Gibbons Limited, Parkside, Christchurch Road, Ringwood, Hants, BH24 3SH England. **Tel** 011 44 425 472363, FAX 011 44 425 470247. **ED** David Aggersberg.

Desc: A relatively detailed listing of the world's stamps. Fully priced in 21 volumes. Under constant editorial revision.

UK
PRIVATE POST, THE.
Added/Corp Cinderella Stamp Club. Cinderella Stamp Club. British Private Post Study Group. (1977)-. Periodical. English. ir. £4.00 UK; $6.40 US. Cinderella Stamp Club, 44 The Ridgeway, London NW11 8QS England. **Tel** (01)455-8438. **ED** L. N. Williams. **LC** HE6187; .P77. **DD** 769/.56941. Index available. cum. index. **Bk Rev. Pr Rev. Circ:** 500.
Desc: Studies of private mail carriage in Britain 1660-to date.

CN/0714-8941
PUBLIC STAMP AUCTION.
(L.C.D. STAMP AUCTION.). [Public stamp auction]. **Main/Corp** L.C.D. Stamp Co. English. Public Stamp Auction Catalog, 104, Mezzanine, 100 Richmond Street West, Toronto Ontario M5H 3K6 Canada. **DD** 769.56/029/4. ***Continues*** *Public Auction (L.C.D. Stamp Co.), 0714-8933.*

SA
R.S.A. POSTAGE STAMP CATALOGUE.
English. Arcade Stamp Shop, 97 Commissioner Street, Johannesburg South Africa. **LC** HE6185.S622; R18. **DD** 769/.56968.

CN/0383-1132
REFLETS DE LA PHILATELIE AU QUEBEC.
V. 1- March 1976-. Periodical. French. ir. $1.50 each number. Y Legris, 5817 rue Madore, Montreal Quebec H1M 1H3 Canada. **DD** 769/.569/71.

US/0748-2930
ROMANIAN PHILATELIC STUDIES.
Added/Corp Romanian Philatelic Club. (197?)-. Periodical. English. qt. Romanian Philatelic Club, 84-47 Kendrick Place, Jamaica Estates NY 11432. **LC** HE6185.R8; R65. **DD** 769.569498.

US/0036-181X
S.P.A. JOURNAL.
[S.P.A. j.]. **Main/Corp** Society of Philatelic Americans. **VAT** Society of Philatelic Americans Journal. V. 1- 1939-. Periodical. English. mo. Society Philatelic Americans, PO Box 9041, Wilmington DC 19809. **LC** HE6188 .B .S575. **DD** 383.2206273.
Desc: Includes the society's Year book.

US
SCOTT SPECIALIZED CATALOGUE OF UNITED STATES STAMPS.
Added/Corp Scott Publishing Co. **VFOAT** Scott United States Stamp Catalogue; Specialized Catalogue of United States Stamps. 51st Ed. (1973)-. English. an. $37.00 US; $38.00 other. Bloomsbury Books, 1123 Hull Terrace, Evanston IL 60202. **Tel** (708)869-3234. **ED** Richard Sine. ***Continues*** *Scott's Specialized Catalogue of United States Stamps.*
Desc: Comprehensive listing of US stamps using the exclusive Scott numbering system. Lists booklet panes, postal stationery, plate blocks, first day covers and plate number coils.

US/0737-0741
SCOTT STAMP MONTHLY.
[Scott stamp mon.]. **Added/Corp** Scott Publishing Co. Vol. 1, No. 1 (Nov. 1982)-. Periodical. English. mo. $16.95 (one year), $28.95 (two years). Amos Press, PO Box 29, Sidney OH 45365. **Tel** (513)498-0802, (800)448-7293, FAX (513)498-0812. **LC** HE6187; .S388. **DD** 769.56/075/00973. Index available (bound in last issue). ***Continues*** *Scott's Monthly Stamp Journal;* ***Absorbed*** *Scott Chronicle of New Issues, 0737-2809.*
Desc: A stamp collector's magazine that contains feature articles about new stamp issues as well as philatelic rarities. Magazine is of interest to both beginner and advanced collector.

US/0161-5084
SCOTT STANDARD POSTAGE STAMP CATALOGUE.
[Scott stand. post. stamp cat.]. **Main/Corp** Scott Publishing Co. **Added/Corp** Scott Publishing Co. **VFOAT** Standard Postage Stamp Catalogue. 129th Ed. (1973)-. English. Five times a year. $185.00 US; $190.00 others. Bloomsbury Books, 1123 Hull Terrace, Evanston IL 60202. **Tel** (708)869-3234. **LC** HE6226; .S48. **DD** 769.56/075. ***Continues*** *Scott's Standard Postage Stamp Catalogue, 0161-5084.*
Desc: Updated price list of stamps as well as other important information for the collector.

UK
SCOTTISH STAMP NEWS (EDINBURGH, SCOTLAND : 1987).
(SCOTTISH STAMP NEWS : THE JOURNAL OF THE ALBA STAMP GROUP.). Vol. 17, No. 2 (April 1987)-. Periodical. English. Alba Stamp Group, 40 Braedale Avenue, Motherwell ML1 3DX Scotland. **LC** HE6187; .S39. **DD** 769.56/075/09411. ***Continues*** *Newsletter (Alba Stamp Group).*

US
SEAPOSTER.
Periodical. English. bm. $10.00. Maritime Postmark Society, PO Box 10411, c/o Fred McGary, Midland TX 79702. **Tel** (915)699-6457. **ED** Martin W Longseth. **LC** HE6187; .S436. **Bk Rev. Ad Acc. Circ:** 300 (ctrl).
Desc: Articles of interest to collectors of maritime mail markings and the history and use of these marks.

MY/0127-1563
SINGAPORE STAMP CATALOGUE IN FULL COLOUR.
1st ed.-. English. an. 9.00Mal$ Malaysia; $4.00 US. International Stamp & Coin Company Ltd, 2.4 & 2.5 Pertama Shopping Complex/2nd Floor, Jalan Tuanku Abdul Rahman, 50100 Kuala Lumpur Malaysia. **Tel** 03-2926373. **ED** Steven Tan. **LC** HE6185.S532; S55. **DD** 769.569595/7/07509595. **Bk Rev. Circ:** 3,000 (ctrl).
Desc: Complete listing of Singapore stamps, miniature sheets, postal stationery, and first day covers.

CN/0583-4465
SISSONS STAMP AUCTION.
Main/Corp Sissions (J. N.) Limited. Monographic series. English. Price varies per volume. J N Sissons Ltd, 37 King Street East, Toronto Ontario M5C 1E9 Canada. **DD** 769/.569/71.

US
SOUTH AFRICAN STAMP COLOUR CATALOGUE, THE.
Began with 1977. English. an. $11.80. Harry Edelman, 111-137 Lefferts Boulevard, 50 Ozone Park, New York NY 11420. **LC** HE6185.S622; S68. **DD** 769.56968/075/0968.

SZ
SPEZIALKATALOG UBER DIE BRIEFMARKEN DER SCHWEIZ UND VON LIECHTENSTEIN.
German. Zumstein & Cie, Postfach 2585, CH-3001 Bern Switzerland. **LC** HE6185.S92; S67. **DD** 769.569494/075/09494.

US/0273-7078
STAMP AUCTION NEWS.
[Stamp auction news]. Periodical. English. mo. H L Lindquist Publications, 85 Canisteo Street, Hornell NY 12843-1544. **Tel** (607)324-2212, FAX (607)324-1753. **DD** 769.

AT
STAMP BULLETIN (SOUTH MELBOURNE, VIC.).
(STAMP BULLETIN.). Bulletin. English. Australian Stamp Bulletin, Locked Bag 8, South Melbourne Victoria 3205 Australia. **LC** HE6187; .A848. **DD** 769.56/075/0994. ***Continues*** *Australian Stamp Bulletin.*

US/0277-3899
STAMP COLLECTOR.
[Stamp collect.]. Vol. 50 (1976)-. Newspaper. English. wk. $20.00 (library), $29.90 (1 year), $49.90 (2 year) US; $40.00 (library), $49.90 (1 year), $89.90 (2 year) other. Van Dahl Publications Incorporated, PO Box 10, Albany OR 97321. **Tel** (503)928-3569, FAX (503)967-7262. **Bk Rev. Ad Acc. Circ:** 18,000. available on microfilm. ***Continues*** *Western Stamp Collector, 0043-4213.*
Desc: Dedicated to promoting the growth and enjoyment of philately for beginning and advanced collectors through the exchange of information and ideas.

US/8755-3139
STAMP DEALER FORUM.
[Stamp deal. forum]. No. 1 (Oct.1984)-. Periodical. English. bm. $12.00. Stamp Dealer Forum, PO Box 1013, Suisun CA 94585. **Tel** (707)429-5603. **ED** Ken Lerner. **DD** 769. **Bk Rev. Ad Acc. Circ:** 500.
Desc: Award winning, with substance for success oriented stamp (philatelic) dealers. Information you can use. Including computer use in the collectibles trade.

UK/0038-9277
STAMP LOVER, THE.
Main/Corp Junior Philatelic Society, London. Vol. 1 (June 1980)-. Bulletin. English. bm. $30.00 (non-members). National Philatelic Society, 107 Charterhouse Street, London EC1M 6PT England. **Tel** 011 44 71 251 5040. **ED** Michael Furnell. Index available. cum. index (Every 10 years). **Bk Rev. Ad Acc. Circ:** 3,000 (ctrl). available with illustrations.

UK/0307-6679
STAMP MAGAZINE.
[Stamp mag.]. Vol. 1 (1934)-. English. Twelve times a year (published last Friday of each month). £21.60 UK; £33.60 Europe; £32.00 other (postage included in all prices). **(Subscription address:** UK/ United Magazine Subscriptions, 1st Floor, Stephenson House, Brunel C, Milton Keynes, MK2 2EW England; telephone: 11 44 908 371981**)** ***Absorbed*** *Stamp Weekly* ***and*** *World Stamp Digest.*

US/0038-9315
STAMP WHOLESALER, THE.
(19??)-. Periodical. English. Twenty-eight times a year (published bi-weekly with special issues and April and October). $20.00 (one year), $40.00 (two year). Van Dahl Publications Incorporated, PO Box 10, Albany OR 97321. **Tel** (503)928-3569, FAX (503)967-7262. **ED** L. Jackson. **LC** HE6187; .S76. **DD** 383.2205. **Bk Rev. Ad Acc. Circ:** 5,000.
Desc: Stamp trade newspaper.

US/0038-9358
STAMPS (NEW YORK, N.Y. 1932).
(STAMPS.). [Stamps]. Vol. 1 No. 1 (Sept. 17, 1932)-. Periodical. English. wk. $18.80 US, Mexico and Canada; $45.40 other. H L Lindquist Publications, 85 Canisteo Street, Hornell NY 12843-1544. **Tel** (607)324-2212, FAX (607)324-1753. **ED** Denise Axtelo. **LC** HE6187; .S77. **DD** 769.56/05. Index available. **Bk Rev. Ad Acc. Circ:** 19,000 (ctrl). available on microfilm and microfiche from University Microfilms International (UMI). Documents available from UMI Article Clearinghouse, Magazine Collection.
Desc: Magazine for stamp collectors. News, current events, useful information on US and foreign stamps, market reports, postal history, and advertising to buy and sell.
Ind/Abst Gen. Period. Index (1985-); Mag. Index Plus (1989-); Newsp. Period. Abstr. (1989-); Mag. Index (1977-).

CN/0700-5555
STANDARD CANADIAN PLATE BLOCK CATALOGUE, THE.
VFOAT Canada Plate Block Catalogue. 1st- Ed. Periodical. English. $2.00 each number. K Bileski, Station B, Winnipeg Manitoba Canada. **DD** 769/.569/71.
Desc: Including the imprints and marginal inscriptions of British North America as originally compiled by Maj. K. Hamilton White.

UK
STANLEY GIBBONS SIMPLIFIED CATALOGUE STAMPS OF THE WORLD / STANLEY GIBBONS PUBLICATIONS.
VFOAT Stanley Gibbons Simplified Catalogue of Stamps of the World; Stamps of the World. (1983)-. English. an. 1994 edition not yet priced. Stanley Gibbons Limited, Parkside, Christchurch Road, Ringwood, Hants, BH24 3SH England. **Tel** 011 44 425 472363, FAX 011 44 425 470247. ***Continues*** *Stanley Gibbons Stamps of the World.*

UK/0142-9752
STANLEY GIBBONS STAMP CATALOGUE. PART 1: BRITISH COMMONWEALTH.
Main/Corp Stanley Gibbons Publications Ltd. (19??)-. English. an. 19.95Can$. Stanley Gibbons Limited, Parkside, Christchurch Road, Ringwood, Hants, BH24 3SH England. **Tel** 011 44 425 472363, FAX 011 44 425 470247. **LC** HE6226; .S83a. **DD** 769.56/075.

UK
STANLEY GIBBONS STAMP CATALOGUE. PART 16, CENTRAL ASIA.
1st Ed. (1981)-. Periodical. English. an. £8.50. Stanley Gibbons Limited, Parkside, Christchurch Road, Ringwood, Hants, BH24 3SH England. **Tel** 011 44 425 472363, FAX 011 44 425 470247. **LC** HE6185.T92; S7. **DD** 769.56958/075/0941.

US/0883-6760
STATE REVENUE NEWSLETTER, THE.
[State revenue newsl.]. Newsletter. English. bm. $4.00 US; $12.00 other. Harold A Effner Jr, 425 Sylvania Avenue, Avon By The Sea NJ 07717-1133. **Tel** (201)775-7737. **(Subscription address:** Box 629, Chappaqua, NY 10514-0629**)** **ED** Terence Hines. **DD** 769. Index available. cum. index. **Bk Rev. Ad Acc. Circ:** 250 (ctrl). available on microfilm from The State Historical Society of Wisconsin.
Desc: Publishes information on the revenue stamps issued by the states and municipalities of the United States.

UK/0142-615X
STONEHAM CATALOGUE OF BRITISH STAMPS, THE.
(1978)-. English. sa. Sarum Publications Ltd, 92-94 Fisherton Street, Salisbury United Kingdom. **Tel** 0722 412100, FAX 0722 412875. **LC** HE6185.G62; S79. **DD** 769.56941/075/0941. **Bk Rev. Ad Acc.**

US/0095-5418
STRICTLY U.S.
V. 1- Oct. 1974-. Periodical. English. qt. $3.00 US; $5.00 Canada and Mexico. Vancorp, 1961 Saddle HIll North, Dunedin FL 33528. **Tel** (813)784-1330. **ED** Donna von Stein. **LC** HE6187; .S83. **DD** 769/.56973.

SW/0347-1152
SVERIGES FRIMARKEN OCH HELSAKER / SVERIGES FILATELIST-FORBUND.
VFOAT S.F.F. Specialkatalog; Sverige-Katalogen; SFF Specialkatalog. Swedish (summaries and/or abstracts in English and German). an. £20.00. FACIT, Katalogintressenter AB, Box 302 32, Stockholm 104 25 Sweden. **Tel** 08/50 18 72. **LC** HE6185.S82; S92. **DD** 769.569485/075/09485. **Bk Rev. Ad Acc. Circ:** 20,000 (ctrl).

US/0198-7992
THAI PHILATELY.
[Thai philat.]. Began with Jan. 1978 issue. Periodical. English. qt. Free to members. Society for Thai Philately, PO Box 454, Plattsburgh NY 12901. **LC** HE6185.T45; T49. **DD** 769.569593.

IS
TOLDOT HA-DOAR SHEL ERETS YISRAEL.
VFOAT Holy Land Postal History. 1- Summer 1979-. Periodical. English. qt. $15.00 Israel;

$15.00, $21.00 (airmail) US; $19.00 (airmail) Europe. Ha-Agudah Le-Toldat Ha-Doar Shel Erets-Yisrael, POB 10175, Jerusalem 91101 Israel. **ED** Z Shimony and E Glassman. **LC** HE7186; .T64. **DD** 383/.495694. Index available. cum. index. **Bk Rev. Ad Acc. Circ:** 300 (ctrl).
Desc: Bulletin of news and research articles of postal history and philately of the Holy Land in all periods. Illustrated.

US/0090-7286
TOPICAL NEW ISSUES. English. an. $7.00. American Topical Association, PO Box 630, Johnstown PA 15907. **Tel** (814)539-6301. **ED** Allan Cunningham Sr. **LC** HE6187; .A635 subser. **DD** 769/.56/075. **Circ:** 2,000.
Desc: Listing of each year's worldwide postage stamps by topic pictured on stamp.

US/0040-9332
TOPICAL TIME. [Top. time]. **Added/Corp** American Topical Association. Vol. 1 No. 1 (1949/51)-. Periodical. English. Six times a year (Jan., Mar., May, July, Sept., Nov.). $15.00 US, $18.00 other Comes with American Topical Association membership. American Topical Association, PO Box 630, Johnstown PA 15907. **Tel** (814)539-6301. **ED** George Griffenhagen. **LC** HE6187; .T65. **DD** 769. Index available (Bound in January issue). cum. index. **Bk Rev**, (Qty: 20-50). **Ad Acc, Adv Mgr:** Don Smith, **Tel** (814)539-6301. **Circ:** 6,700 (ctrl).
Desc: Information on stamp collecting by topics shown on stamps, birds, trains, boy scouts and masonry, etc.

US/0882-1674
TRIDENT (WASHINGTON, D.C.). (TRIDENT / UKRAINIAN PHILATELIC AND NUMISMATIC SOCIETY.). **VFOAT** Visnik; UPNS Trident; Visnik Sufn. Periodical. English (Ukrainian). ir (6 times a year). $12.00. Ukrainian Philatelic and Numismatic Society, PO Box 14163, Washington DC 20044. **Tel** (703)360-2559. **ED** Wes Capar. **DD** 769. **Bk Rev. Ad Acc. Circ:** 300 (ctrl).
Desc: A newsletter of the society dealing with Ukrainian philately and numismatics, conventions, membership information, articles, and society events. Also includes three auctions every year.

CN/0148-673X
TRUMPETER (LONDON). (THE TRUMPETER.). **Added/Corp** Croatian Philatelic Society. (19??)-. Periodical. English (Serbo-Croatian (Roman)). Four times a year. $20.00. Croatian Philatelic Society, 2596 East 8th Avenue, Borger TX 79007. **Tel** (806)273-7225. **ED** Eck Spahich. **Bk Rev**, (Qty: 5-10). **Ad Acc. Circ:** 700 (ctrl).
Desc: Devoted to the study and exchange of information regarding Croatian, central European and Balkan postal issues, postal history, numismatism and other collectibles.

US/0743-9350
U.S. COINS, CURRENCY & STAMPS. See Hobbies-Numismatics.

US/0198-6252
UKRAINSKYI FILATELIST / SOIUZ UKRAINSKYKH FILATELISTIV I NUMIZMATYKIV. Added/Corp Soiuz Ukrainskykh Filatelistiv i Numizmatykiv. **VFOAT** Ukrainian Philatelist. Vol. 22, Ch. 37/38 (1975)-. Periodical. English (Ukrainian). sa. Ukrainian Philatelic and Numismatic Society, PO Box 14163, Washington DC 20044. **Tel** (703)360-2559. **ED** Ingert Kuzych. **LC** HE6185.U45; F54. **DD** 769.56947/71/075. Index available. cum. index. **Bk Rev. Ad Acc. Circ:** 300 (ctrl). ***Continues*** *Ukrainskyi Filatelist (Soiuz Ukrainskykh Filatelistiv).*
Desc: Society journal presenting articles and comprehensive studies of all aspects of Ukrainian philately (including Cinderella issues) and numismatics.

•CN/1193-8838
UNITRADE CATALOGUE SPECIALISE DES TIMBRES CANADIENS. [Unitrade cat. spec. timbres can.]. **Added/Corp** Unitrade Press. **VFOAT** Catalogue Specialise des Timbres Canadiens. (1992)-. French. ir (published in October or November). 13.95Can$. Unitrade Press, 91 Tycos Drive, Toronto Ontario M6B 1W3 Canada. **DD** 769.56971/029/4. ***Continues*** *Scott Catalogue Specialise des Timbres Canadiens., 1193-882X.*

•CN/1193-8811
UNITRADE SPECIALIZED CATALOGUE OF CANADIAN STAMPS. [Unitrade spec. cat. Can. stamps]. **Added/Corp** Unitrade Press. **VFOAT** Specialized Catalogue of Canadian Stamps. (1992)-. English. an. 13.95Can$. Unitrade Press, 91 Tycos Drive, Toronto Ontario M6B 1W3 Canada. **DD** 769.56971/029/4. ***Continues*** *Scott Specialized Catalogue of Canadian Stamps., 0840-3503.*

US/0732-3670
UTD PHILATELIC BULLETIN, THE. VFOAT U.T.D. Philatelic Bulletin. **VAT** University of Texas at Dallas Philatelic Bulletin. Vol. 1, No. 1 (Apr. 1982)-. Bulletin. English. ir. Free. University of Texas at Dallas, Department of Special Collections, Box 830643, Richardson TX 75083-0643. **Tel** (214)690-2570. **Circ:** 250.
Desc: This is a newsletter for Friends of the UTD Philatelic Library.

US/0510-2332
WESTERN EXPRESS. [West. express]. **Added/Corp** Western Cover Society. Vol. 1, (Jan. 1951)-. Periodical. English. qt (Jan., Apr., July,Oct.). $15.00. Western Cover Society, 27 Bridgewater Way, Pleasant Hill CA 94523. **ED** Alan H. Patera (Editor's phone: (503)635-1379). **LC** HE6185.U7; W5. **DD** 383.2. cum. index. **Bk Rev. Ad Acc. Circ:** 400.
Desc: Exchange of information and ideas on collecting philatelic memorabilia of the Far West including diaries, letters, photos and express covers.

UK/0260-1265
YEARBOOK AND PHILATELIC SOCIETIES' DIRECTORY. Added/Corp British Philatelic Federation. (19??)-. English. an. £7.50. The British Philatelic Centre, 107 Charterhouse Street, London EC1M 6PT England. **Tel** 01 251 5040, FAX 01 490 4253. **ED** A. Herbert and R. Grimsey. **LC** HE6188; .B713. **DD** 769.56/06/041. **Bk Rev. Ad Acc. Circ:** 4,000 (ctrl). ***Continues*** *B. P. F. Yearbook and Philatelic Societies' Directory.*
Desc: Concise information on all aspects of organised philately in Great Britain with some details on local and specialised societies worldwide.

JA
YUSHU NENKAN. VFOAT Stamp Collectors' Annual. 1971-. Japanese (Japanese). Kanai Stamp Company, c/o Osaka Kanai Building/4th Floor, 22 Doshima Funadaikumachi Kita-ku, Osaka Japan. **LC** HE6194; .Y87.

HOME ECONOMICS

US
100'S OF BAKING AND DESSERT IDEAS. VFOAT Hundreds of Baking and Dessert Ideas; 100's of Baking Ideas. (19??)-. English. an. Meredith Corporation, Locust at 17th, Des Moines IA 50309. **Tel** (515)284-3000.

US/0194-7176
A.H.E.A. ACTION. ***Title Change.*** (AHEA ACTION.). **Main/Corp** American Home Economics Association. **VAT** American Home Economics Association Action. Vol. 1 (Aug. 1974)-(1993). Periodical. English. Five times a year. American Home Economics Association, 1555 King Street, Alexandria VA 22314. **Tel** (703)706-4600, (800)424-8080, FAX (703)706-4663. **ED** Anne Swearingen. **LC** TX1; .A5375. **Ad Acc. Circ:** 30,000. available on microfilm and microfiche from University Microfilms International (UMI). ***Continued by*** *American Home Economics Association. Action.*
Desc: Informs members and the public of association, professional and national activities that affect families.

CN/0710-1694
ABOYEUR, L'. [Aboyeur]. No. 1 (Sept. 1975)-. Periodical. French. Free to members, $10.00 others. Association Des Cuisiniers De Quebec, 311 Sud, Rue Dorchester, Quebec G1K 5Z9 Canada. **DD** 641.5/06/0714.

LE
AL-MALAYIN. VFOAT Al Malayeen; Malayeen. V. 1, No. 1, (April 1983)-. Periodical. Arabic. mo. 15.00 single issue. Al-Muassasah Al-Ammah Lil-Ilam. **LC** TX335; .M246.

JO
AL-MUSTAHLIK. See Consumer Interests.

US/0736-170X
ALMOST FREE RECIPES AND COOKBOOKS UPDATES. VFOAT Almost Free Recipes & Cookbooks Updates; Almost Free Cookbooks & Recipes Updates; Almost Free Cookbooks and Recipes Updates. English. sa. $4.00 US; $4.00 (back issues). Prosperity and Profits, Unlimited Distribution Services, Box 570213, Houston TX 77257. **ED** A Doyle. **Bk Rev. Ad Acc. Circ:** 1,200 (ctrl). available on microfiche.
Desc: Excerpts from recipes and cookbooks, recipe and cookbook offerings, actual recipes, where to find or locate almost free recipes and cookbooks.

US/0892-6492
AMERICAN COUNTRY. [Am. ctry.]. **VFOAT** Mother Earth News American Country. Vol. 1, No. 1 (March 1987)-. Periodical. English. bm. $18.00 US; $24.00 Canada. American Country, PO Box 3132, Harlan IA 51593-2198. **DD** 640.

•US/0194-7176
AMERICAN HOME ECONOMICS ASSOCIATION ACTION. Main/Corp American Home Economics Association. (1993)-. Periodical. English. Five times a year. American Home Economics Association, 1555 King Street, Alexandria VA 22314. **Tel** (703)706-4600, (800)424-8080, FAX (703)706-4663. **ED** Anne Swearingen. **LC** TX1; .A5375. **Ad Acc. Circ:** 30,000. available on microfilm and microfiche from University Microfilms International (UMI). ***Continues*** *AHEA. Action.*
Desc: Informs members and the public of association, professional and national activities that affect families.

US/0892-1024
ART CULINAIRE (ATLANTA, GA.). (ART CULINAIRE.). [Art culin.]. (1986)-. Periodical. English. Four times a year. $59.00 (one year); $108.00 (two year); $147.00 (three year) US; $75.00 (one year), $140.00 (two year), $195.00 (three year) other. Culinaire Inc., PO Box 9268, Morristown NJ 07963-9268. **Tel** (201)993-5500, FAX (201)993-8779. **ED** Karen Hadley. **CODEN** ACULEH. Index Bound in First Issue. cum. index. **Bk Rev**, (Qty: 3-4). **Ad Acc. Circ:** 8,000.
Desc: Dedicated to the quality and beauty of professional food preparation. Contains recipes, including color photography of the presentation of the dish.
Ind/Abst Foods Adlibra.

GW/0045-0049
AUSBILDUNG UND BERATUNG IN LAND- UND HAUSWIRTSCHAFT / LAND- UND HAUSWIRTSCHAFTLICHER AUSWERTUNGS- UND INFORMATIONSDIENST. V. 8, No. 10 (Oct. 1955)-. Periodical. German. mo. BLV Verlagsgesellschaft MBH, Lothstrasse 29, D80797 Munich Germany. **Tel** 011 49 89 12705214. ***Continues*** *Nutzen Und Ordnung; Ausbilding Und Beratung in der Landwirtschaft.*

CN/0822-5168
AUTONOMOUS LIVING. [Auton. living]. Periodical. English. qt. $2.00 per no. Hipper Industries Ltd, PO Box 238 Station D, Scarborough Ontario M1R 5B7 Canada. **DD** 640/.5.

US/0278-7245
BAKING IDEAS. ***Ceased.*** (19??)-(19??). Periodical. English. an. Meredith Publications / Special Interest Section, 1716 Locust Street, Des Moines IA 50309. **Tel** (515)284-3000. **LC** TX761; .B19. **DD** 641.7/1.

CN/0826-5240
BARBIZON. [Barbizon]. No. 1-. Periodical. English. mo. $15.00. Barbizon Collective, PO Box 923, Kelowna BC V1Y 7P5 Canada. **DD** 640.

US/0737-1373
BARGAIN BOOK, THE. [Bargain book]. Vol. 1 No. 1 (Fall 1982)-. Periodical. English. qt. Free to Multi-Housing Rental Properties. Jacoby and Company, 2418A South Victor, Aurora CO 80014. **LC** TX955; .B37. **DD** 647/.92/068.

US/0897-0386
BEST RECIPES. See Food and Food Industry.

US/0006-0151
BETTER HOMES AND GARDENS. [Better homes gard.]. Vol. 2, No. 12 (Aug. 1924)-. Periodical. English. mo. $17.00 (one year), $34.00 (two year), $60.00 (three year). Meredith Corporation, Locust at 17th, Des Moines IA 50309. **Tel** (515)284-3000. **(Subscription address:** Neodata / Colorado, PO Box 2606, Boulder Boulder CO 80322.) **ED** David Jordon. **LC** NA7100; .B45. **DD** 747/.05. **Ad Acc. Circ:** 8,000,000. available on microfilm and microfiche from University Microfilms International (UMI); available on an online database (file 647/Full-Text) from DIALOG. Documents available from UMI Article Clearinghouse. ***Continues*** *Fruit, Garden and Home.*
Desc: Brings readers how-to features on food, recipes, decorating, remodeling, building, crafts, gardening, family health, travel money management, education and more. It's America's complete home and family service magazine.
Ind/Abst Abr. Read. Guide Period. Lit.; Acad. Abstr. Full Text Elite (Jan. 1984-); Acad. Abstr. (Jan. 1984-); Consum. Index Prod. Eval. Inf. Source; Foods Adlibra; Gen. Period. Index (1985-); Index Inf. (1971-); Mag. Artic. Summar. Elite (Jan. 1984-); Mag. Artic. Summar. Select (Jan. 1984-); Mag. Artic. Summar. CD-ROM (Jan. 1984-); Mag. Index Plus (1989-); Mag. Index Sel. Microfiche (1990-) [Full Txt.]; Mag. Index. Sel. (1986-); Mag. Search; Newsp. Period. Abstr. (1988-); Read. Guide Abstr. Select Ed.; Read. Guide Period. Lit.; Resource/One Ondisc (1988-); Mag. Index (1977-); TOM Gen. Index (1985-) [Full Txt.]; Vocat. Search (Jan. 1984-).

US/0006-6990
BON APPETIT. [Bon appet.]. Vol. 1 (Nov./Dec. 1956)-. Periodical. English. mo. $18.00. Conde Nast Publications / New York, 350 Madison Avenue, New York NY 10017. **Tel** (212)880-8800, (800)777-0700. **(Subscription address:** Neodata / Colorado, PO Box 2606, Boulder Boulder CO 80322.) **LC** TX633; .B65. **DD** 641/.013. **Ad Acc. Circ:** 1,300,000. available on microfilm and microfiche from University Microfilms International (UMI). Documents available from UMI Article Clearinghouse.
Desc: America's food and entertaining magazine about wining, dining and the good life - both at home and abroad. Features its popular columns 'Too Busy To Cook' and 'Cooking For Two'. Includes recommendations and reviews, travel notes, recipe exchange, comment and inquiry, famous chefs, cookery books, new products, and

100 kitchen-tested recipes.
Ind/Abst Abr. Read. Guide Period. Lit.; Acad. Abstr. Full Text Elite (Jan. 1984-); Acad. Abstr. (Jan. 1984-); Acad. Search (Jan. 1984-); Access (1978-?); Can. Index (?-?); Consum. Index Prod. Eval. Inf. Source; Foods Adlibra; Gen. Period. Index (1992-); Mag. Artic. Summar. Elite (Jan. 1984-); Mag. Artic. Summar. Select (Jan. 1984-); Mag. Artic. Summar. CD-ROM (Jan. 1984-); Mag. Index Plus (1992-); Mag. Search; Newsp. Period. Abstr. (1988-); Read. Guide Period. Lit.; Vocat. Search (Jan. 1984-).

US/1042-7139
BREAD PUDDING UPDATE. Vol. 1 Mar. (1989)-. Periodical. English. an. $17.95 US; $19.95 Canada; $21.95 other. Continnuus / Houston, PO Box 570213, Houston TX 77257. **Tel** (713)867-3438. **ED** A C Doyle. **Circ:** 1,500.
Desc: Recipes and possibilities for making bread pudding.

CN/0822-7918
BUDGETING FOR BASIC NEEDS AND BUDGETING FOR MINIMUM ADEQUATE STANDARD OF LIVING. [Budg. basic needs budg. minim. adequate stand. living]. 1983-. English (French). an. $8.00 U.S. per number. Montreal Diet Dispensary, 2182 Lincoln Avenue, Montreal Quebec H3H 1J3 Canada. **Tel** (514)937-5375. **DD** 640/.42/09714281. **Circ:** 300 (ctrl). ***Continues** Budgeting for Basic Needs, 0225-9729.*
Desc: These budgets establish the minimum adequate expenditure for the maintenance of health. It sets standards for each item according to age and sex. Individual allowances, as well as individual variances in cost per family size, age and sex, are calculated yearly.

US
BUENHOGAR (HEARST CORPORATION). (BUENHOGAR.). **Added/Corp** Hearst Corporation. (19??)-. Periodical. Spanish. bw. $59.90. Editorial America SA, 6355 Northwest 36th Street, Miami FL 33166. **Tel** (305)871-6400. **(Subscription address:** CDS, SIFD Agency Control, 1901 Bell Avenue, Demoine, IA 50315 (Phone: (515)246-6812))
Desc: The Spanish-language version of Good Housekeeping. Includes topics such as cooking, home decoration, health, education and child-care. Geared to the Hispanic woman.

CN/0008-3763
CANADIAN HOME ECONOMICS JOURNAL. [Can. home econ. j.]. **Added/Corp** Canadian Home Economics Association. **VFOAT** Revue Canadienne d'Economie Familiale. Vol. 1 (Nov. 1950)-. Periodical. English (French). qt (Jan., Apr., Jun., Oct.). 35.00Can$ (individuals), 50.00Can$ (institutions) Canada; 40.00Can$ (individuals), 55.00Can$ (institutions) US; 44.00Can$ (individuals), 59.00Can$ (institutions) other. Canadian Home Economics Association, 901-151 Slater Street, Ottawa Ontario K1P 5H3 Canada. **Tel** (613)238-8817, FAX (613)238-1677. **ED** Glenda Everett, Lethbridge Community College, (403)320-3343. **[CCC]**. Index available. cum. index. **Bk Rev**, (Qty: 4 per year). **Ad Acc**, **Adv Mgr:** M Martin, **Tel** (613)238-8817. **Circ:** 3,300 (ctrl). available in microform from Micromedia Limited; available on microfilm and microfiche from University Microfilms International (UMI).
Desc: Professional journal for those educated and/or working in the field of consumer and family studies, foods/nutrition, and home economics/human ecology.
Ind/Abst AGRICOLA [Select. Cov.]; Can. Index; Can. Period. Index; Curr. Index J. Educ.; Nutr. Abstr. Rev., Ser. B, Live Feeds and Feed.; Nutr. Abstr. Rev., Ser. A, Hum. Exp.; PAIS Int. Print (1991-); Potato Abstr.; Soyabean Abstr.; World Text. Abstr.

UK
CARE HOME MANAGEMENT. (19??)-. Periodical. English. qt. £130.50. Croner Publ Ltd, Croner House, London Road, Kingston upon Thames, Surrey KT2 6SR England. **Tel** 011 44 81 5473333, FAX 081 547-2637.

UK
CARE HOME MANAGEMENT RECORDS AND PROCEDURES. (19??)-. Periodical. English. £98.40. Croner Publ Ltd, Croner House, London Road, Kingston upon Thames, Surrey KT2 6SR England. **Tel** 011 44 81 5473333, FAX 081 547-2637.

US
CHEF INSTITUTIONAL. ***Title Change.*** Vol. 17, No. 6 (Oct. 1971)-(19??). English. bm. Talcott Publishing, 206 West Huron, Chicago IL 60610. **Tel** (312)664-4040, FAX (312)664-8947. ***Continues** Chef Mgazine.*
***Continued by** Chef.*
Ind/Abst Foods Adlibra.

FR/0980-8396
CHEF PARIS, LE. (1986)-. Periodical. French. Nine times a year. 352.60F France; 530.00F other. Editions Max Brezol Sarl, 9 rue Labie, 75838 Paris Cedex 17 France. **Tel** 011 33 1 45742162, FAX 011 33 1 45740103. **UDC** 641.

US/0883-9077
CHRISTMAS IS COMING! (HARDCOVER). **See** The Arts-Crafts and Decorative Arts.

CC
CHUNG-KUO SHIH PIN. **VFOAT** China Food. Periodical. Chinese. RMBY0.20. Chung-Kuo Kuo Chi Tu Shu Mao I Tsung Kung SSU, PO Box 2820, Beijing, People's Republic of China. **Tel** 23724. **LC** TX724.5.C5; C5788. **DD** 641.5951.

US
CONSUMER BUYING GUIDE (SKOKIE, ILL.). **See** Consumer Interests.

US/0010-826X
COOKBOOK DIGEST. **VAT** Cook Book Digest. No. 1 (Spring 1968)-. Periodical. English. bm (6 issues). $24.00. Hochman Associates, 950 Third Avenue, 16th Floor, New York NY 10022. **Tel** (212)371-4932. **(Subscription address:** CDS Agency Hard Copy, PO Box 4966, Des Moines IA 50340.**)** **ED** Rosalind Cole. **Ad Acc. Circ:** 250,000.
Desc: Digest of recipes and selections of material relating to cooking, entertaining, travel, domestic and international from cookbooks, photos, drawings.

●US/1060-7765
COOKBOOK REVIEW, THE. (1992)-. Periodical. English. bm. $19.95 (individual), $37.00 (institution). Cookbook Review, 60 Kinnaird Street, Cambridge MA 02139.

US
COOKING CONNECTION. (19??)-. English. Six times a year. $11.95. Recipes Unlimited, Box 1271, Burnsville MN 55337. **Tel** (612)890-6655, (800)328-2846. ***Continues** Microwave Times.*

US/1061-4729
COOKING CONTEST NEWSLETTER, THE. **See** Food and Food Industry.

●US/1068-2821
COOK'S ILLUSTRATED. [Cook's illus.]. Vol. 1, No. 1 (1992)-. Periodical. English. bm (Jan., Mar., May, July, Sept., Nov.). $24.95 US; $27.95 Canada; $36.95 other. Natural Health Ltd Partners, PO Box 569, Brookline Village MA 02147. **Tel** (617)232-1000. **ED** Maura Lyons. **DD** 641. Index available. **Bk Rev**, (Qty: 12). **Circ:** 150,000.
Desc: This magazine is about recipes, cookwares and cookbooks reviews, illustrations, professional shortcuts and blind taste-tests.

US/0731-8634
COOK'S INDEX. [Cook's index]. Vol. 1 (1989)-. English. te. $55.00. John Gordon Burke Publisher Inc., PO Box 1492, Evanston IL 60204. **Tel** (708)866-8625, FAX (708)866-8625. **LC** Z5776.G2; C59; TX651. **DD** 016.641.
Desc: An index of cookery periodicals and cookbooks from 1975-1987. All periodicals indexed contain recipes, and users are able to find regional dishes as well as plans and recipes for general entertaining.

US
CORPORATE CONSUMER FORUM TRENDLETTER. English. Four times a year. $40.00. Home Economists in Business, 5008-16 Pine Creek Drive, Westerville OH 43081. **Tel** (614)890-4342. **ED** Shawna Hooser. **Bk Rev**, (Qty: 4). **Ad Acc. Circ:** 2,200.
Desc: Covers HEIB (Home Economists in Business Association) news and professional development information, and consumer trends.

US/0195-7953
COSMOPOLITAN LIVING. Spring/Summer 1980-. Periodical. English. sa. $2.50 single issue. The Hearst Corporation, 250 West 55th Street, New York NY 10019. **Tel** (212)649-4014. **LC** TX303; .C67. **DD** 640.

US
COUNTRY COOKING. ***Ceased.*** (19??)-(19??). Periodical. English. an. Meredith Publications / Special Interest Section, 1716 Locust Street, Des Moines IA 50309. **Tel** (515)284-3000. **LC** TX715; .C86124. **DD** 641.59/173/4.

US/0732-2569
COUNTRY LIVING (NEW YORK, N.Y.). (COUNTRY LIVING.). [Ctry. living]. (198?)-. Periodical. English. mo. $17.97. The Hearst Corporation, 250 West 55th Street, New York NY 10019. **Tel** (212)649-4014. **(Subscription address:** CDS Agency Hard Copy, PO Box 4966, Des Moines IA 50340.**)** **LC** TX1; .G727. **DD** 640/.5. **Ad Acc.** available on microfilm and microfiche from University Microfilms International (UMI). Documents available from UMI Article Clearinghouse. ***Continues** Good Housekeeping's Country Living, 0274-4791.*
Desc: Responds to the renewed interest in country life.
Ind/Abst Acad. Abstr. Full Text Elite (March 1984-); Acad. Abstr. (Mar. 1984-); Acad. Search (Mar. 1984-); Garden Lit. (1992-); Gen. Period. Index (1989-); Mag. Artic. Summar. Elite (March 1984-); Mag. Artic. Summar. Select (March 1984-); Mag. Artic. Summar. CD-ROM (March 1984-); Mag. Index Plus (1989-); Mag. Search; Newsp. Period. Abstr. (1988-); Mag. Index (1989-).

CN/0849-0635
COUNTRY SIDE MAGAZINE. ***Ceased.*** [Ctry. side mag.]. **VFOAT** Country Side. Vol. 1, No. 1 (Spring 1989)-Vol.4, No.4 (1992). Periodical. English. qt. Country Estate, 7 LaBatt Avenue, Toronto Ontario M5A 3P2 Canada. **DD** 640/.5. ***Continues** Country Estate, 0822-8485.*

US/0279-9847
CREATIVE COOK'S DIGEST, THE. Periodical. English. bm. $11.95. M B Friedman, 8500 Andes, Austin TX 78759.

US/0145-7012
CREPE COOKBOOK FOR DINNERS & DESSERTS. (WOMAN'S DAY CREPE COOKBOOK FOR DINNERS & DESSERTS.). **VAT** Crepe Cookbook for Dinners and Desserts. No. 1-. English. $1.25 each issue. Fawcett Publications, 1 Fawcett Place, Greenwich CT 06830. **LC** TX770; .W65. **DD** 641.8.

FR/0989-3091
CUISINE ACTUELLE. (1987)-. Periodical. French. Twelve times a year. $90.11 France; $142.00 other. Prisma Presse, 6 rue Daru, 75379 Paris Cedex 08, France. **Tel** 011 33 1 44153000, FAX 011 33 1 47641042. **(Subscription address:** Ca M Interesse, Service Abbonements B 110, 60732 Ste Geneva Cedex 9 France.**)** **UDC** 641.55.

NZ/0113-1206
CUISINE AUCKLAND. (CUISINE.). [Cuisine Auckl.]. (1987)-. Periodical. English. Six times a year (Mar., May, July, Sept., Nov., Jan.). 40.00NZ$ New Zealand; 70.00NZ$ Australia; 100.00NZ$ other. Cuisine Publications Ltd., PO Box 37-349, Parnell Auckland New Zealand. **Tel** 011 64 9 3070702, FAX 011 64 9 3079044. **ED** Julie Dalzell (phone: 649 3070702). **DD** 641.509931. Index available. cum. index. **Bk Rev**, (Qty: 30). **Ad Acc**, **Adv Mgr:** M. Thomson, **Tel** 307 0702. **Circ:** 25,000.
Desc: Food, wine, and good living magazine of international appeal. Covers recipes, wine tastings, and reviews, travel.

US/0161-8741
DALLAS-FORT WORTH HOME GARDEN. ***Ceased.*** (DALLAS-FORT WORTH HOME & GARDEN.). **VFOAT** Dallas-Fort Worth Home and Garden. Periodical. English. mo. DFW Home and Garden, PO Box 25386, Houston TX 77265-5386. **Tel** (800)525-0643. **LC** TX311; .D32. **DD** 640/.5. ***Continues** Dallas-Ft. Worth Home Garden, 0161-8741.*

BL
DESFILE. Portuguese. ir. $65.00. Bloch Editores S A, rua do Russel 766/804, 22 210 Rio de Janeiro Brazil.

US/0569-5058
DIRECTORY - HOME ECONOMISTS IN BUSINESS, SECTION OF THE AMERICAN HOME ECONOMICS ASSOCIATION. **Main/Corp** American Home Economics Association. Home Economists in Business Section. **VFOAT** Home Economists in Business Membership Directory. (1992)-. Directory. English. an. $50.00 (individuals and non-members); $25.00 (college and university libraries, students). Home Economists in Business, 5008-16 Pine Creek Drive, Westerville OH 43081. **Tel** (614)890-4342. **ED** Shawna Hooser. **Ad Acc. Circ:** 2,200 (ctrl).
Desc: Membership Directory of Home Economists in Business professional organizations.

US/0889-8804
DOUBLE TALK. [Double talk]. (19??)-. Periodical. English. Four times a year (Jan., Mar., July, Oct.). $8.00 US; $10.00 Canada; $12.00 others. Double Talk, PO Box 412, Amelia OH 45102. **Tel** (513)231-8946. **DD** 649.

FR
ECONOMIE FAMILIALE, L'. **Added/Corp** International Federation of Home Economics. **VFOAT** Home Economics. (19??)-. Periodical. Multiple languages (English, French, German and Spanish). qt. 80.00F. Federation International l'Economie Familiale, 5 Av de la Porte Brancion, Paris 75015 France. **Tel** 011 33 1 48423474, FAX 011 33 1 42500989. **ED** Odette Goncet. **LC** TX1; .E65. **DD** 640/.5. **Bk Rev. Circ:** 5,500. ***Continues** Bulletin de la Federation Internationale pour l'Economie Familiale.*

FR
ECONOMIE FAMILIALE HOME ECONOMICS, L'. **VFOAT** Home Economics. (197?)-. Periodical. French (English, Spanish and German). qt. 80.00F. Federacion Internacional l'Economie Familiale, 5 Avenue de la Porte Brancion, 75015 Paris France. **Tel** 011 33 1 48423474. ***Continues** International Federation of Home Economics Bulletin.*

US
EDUCATORS GUIDE TO FREE HOME ECONOMICS AND CONSUMER EDUCATION MATERIALS. **Added/Corp** Educators Progress Service. 8th Ed. (1991)-. English. an.

$27.95. Educators Progress Service Inc, 214 Center Street, Randolph WI 53956. **Tel** (414)326-3126. **ED** Kathleen Suttles Nehmer. **LC** TX1; .E662. **Bk Rev**. ctrl circ. ***Continues*** *Educators Guide to Free Home Economics Materials, 0883-2811.*
Desc: Guide contains videotapes, films, filmstrips, and audiotapes available on a free-loan basis. Also provides printed materials available free of cost concerning consumer education and home economics.

US/0889-8421
EVERYTHING NATURAL. [Everything nat.]. Sept./Oct. 1986-. Periodical. English. bm. $18.00. Everything Natural, c/o Debra Dadd, PO Box 1506, Mill Valley CA 94942. **Tel** (415)663-1685. **ED** Debra Lynn Dadd. **DD** 640. Index available. cum. index. **Bk Rev. Ad Acc. Circ:** 2,000. ***Continues*** *Nontoxic & Natural Newsletter, 0882-2867.*
Desc: Natural alternatives to toxic chemicals found in everyday household products.

US/0738-6583
EXECUTIVE HOUSEKEEPING TODAY. [Exec. housekeep. today]. **Added/Corp** National Executive Housekeepers Association (U.S.). **VFOAT** EHT. Vol. 1, No. 1 (July 1980)-. Periodical. English. mo (12 issues). $22.00 US; $28.00 other. National Executive Housekeepers Assn, 1001 Eastwind Drive, Suite 301, Westerville OH 43081. **Tel** (614)895-7166, FAX (614)895-1248. **ED** Linda Gambaiani. **DD** 647. **NLM** W1; EX204FE. **Bk Rev**, (Qty: 4). **Ad Acc, Adv Mgr:** Dan Cufford. **Circ:** 7,000 (ctrl). available on an online database.
Desc: Geared toward professionals in the housekeeping field to cover; management, floor care, personnel staffing, design and much more.
Ind/Abst Hospit. Health Admin. Index (Feb. 1989-).

CN/0710-5878
FACS SHEET. (FACS SHEET / FACS, UNIVERSITY OF GUELPH.). [FACS sheet]. **Added/Corp** University of Guelph. College of Family and Consumer Studies. Vol. 1, No. 1 (Jan. 1978)-. Periodical. English. Free. College of Family & Consumer Studies, University of Guelph, Guelph Ontario N1G 2W1 Canada. **DD** 640.73/0971. ctrl circ.

US/0014-7206
FAMILY CIRCLE. VFOAT Everywoman's Family Circle. Vol. 1 (1932)-. Periodical. English. Seventeen times a year. $15.98. Family Circle Inc, 110 5th Avenue, New York NY 10011-5601. **Tel** (212)463-1000. **(Subscription address:** CDS Agency Hard Copy, PO Box 4966, Des Moines IA 50340.**) ED** Gay Bryant. **LC** AP2; .F174. **Ad Acc. Circ:** 7,000,000. Documents available from UMI Article Clearinghouse. ***Continues*** *Everywoman's.*
Desc: Women's service magazine covering food, home decorating, beauty, health, childcare, money management, family, crafts and travel.
Ind/Abst Acad. Abstr. Full Text Elite (July 1989-); Acad. Abstr. (July 1989-); Access (1975-); Consum. Health Nutr. Index (?-?); Index Inf. (1978-1984); Mag. Artic. Summar. Elite (July 1989-); Mag. Artic. Summar. Select (July 1989-); Mag. Artic. Summar. CD-ROM (July 1989-); Mag. Index Plus (1992-); Mag. Search; Newsp. Period. Abstr. (1988-); Vocat. Search (July 1989-).

US/0890-1481
FAMILY CIRCLE COOKBOOK. [Fam. circ. cookb.]. (1986)-. English. an. Family Circle Inc, 110 5th Avenue, New York NY 10011-5601. **Tel** (212)463-1000. **(Subscription address:** Communication Data Services, 112 Tenth Street, Des Moines IA 50309.**) LC** TX1; .F33. **DD** 641.5/05.

US/0425-676X
FAMILY ECONOMICS REVIEW. [Fam. econ. rev.]. **Added/Corp** Institute of Home Economics (U.S.) United States. Agricultural Research Service. Consumer and Food Economics Research Division. Consumer and Food Economics Institute (U.S.) United States. Science and Education Administration. United States. Agricultural Research Service. United States. Agricultural Research Service. Family Economics Research Group. (June 1957)-. Government Publication. English. qt. $7.50 domestic; $9.40 other. Superintendent of Documents, US Government Printing Office, Washington DC 20402. **Tel** (202)275-3328, FAX (202)786-2377. **LC** TX326.A1; F35. **DD** 640. available on microfilm and microfiche from University Microfilms International (UMI). Documents available from UMI Article Clearinghouse, Documents on Demand. ***Continues*** *Rural Family Living.*
Desc: Contains articles on a variety of topics concerning family economics. Topics covered include costs in areas, such as food, housing, clothing, energy, and raising children; family budgeting, economic well being of various groups; and other areas.
Ind/Abst AGRICOLA [Full Cov.]; Am. Stat. Index; Econ. Lit. Index; Expand. Acad. Index (1992-); Foods Adlibra; Newsp. Period. Abstr. (1992-); PAIS Int. Print; Soc. Plann. Policy Dev. Abstr.

US/0014-7230
FAMILY HANDYMAN, THE. [Fam. handyman]. (Jan./March 1951)-. Periodical. English. Ten times a year. $19.97. R D Publications, 28 West 23rd Street, New York NY 10010. **Tel** (800)365-5005, (212)366-8630. **(Subscription address:** CDS / SIFD Agency Control, 1901 Bell Avenue, Des Moines IA 50315.**) ED** Gary Havens. **LC** TX323; .F35. **DD** 643/.7/05. Index available. cum. index. **Ad Acc. Circ:** 1,300,000. available on microfilm and microfiche from University Microfilms International (UMI); available on an online database (file 647/Full-Text) from DIALOG. Documents available from UMI Article Clearinghouse, Magazine Collection. ***Absorbed*** *Home Garden's Natural Gardening Magazine, 0090-7650.*
Desc: Guide to home improvement and repair. Foolproof, step-by-step photo instructions help amateur do-it-yourselfers turn out professional results on a wide variety of home projects. Also in every issue: reviews of new products; using tools safely; auto and appliance repair; and hints shared by readers.
Ind/Abst Acad. Abstr. Full Text Elite (Jan. 1989-); Acad. Abstr. (Jan. 1989-); Consum. Index Prod. Eval. Inf. Source; Gen. Period. Index (1985-); Index Inf. (1964-); Mag. Artic. Summar. Elite (Jan. 1989-); Mag. Artic. Summar. Select (Jan. 1989-); Mag. Artic. Summar. CD-ROM (Jan. 1989-); Mag. Index Plus (1989-); Mag. Index. Sel. (1986-); Mag. Search; Newsp. Period. Abstr. (1986-); Read. Guide Abstr. Select Ed.; Read. Guide Period. Lit.; Mag. Index (1977-); Vocat. Search (Jan. 1989-).

CN/0709-3225
FINE CUISINE D'HENRI BERNARD, LA. [Fine cuisine Henri Bernard]. No. 1- Sept. 1979-. Periodical. French. mo. $1.50 per number. Editions Internationales Alain Stanke, 2100 rue Guy, Montreal Quebec H3H 2N4 Canada. **DD** 841.5/05.

US/0741-9015
FOOD & WINE (NEW YORK, N.Y.). (FOOD & WINE : THE GUIDE TO GOOD TASTE.). [Food wine]. **Added/Corp** International Review of Food and Wine Associates. **VFOAT** Food and Wine. Vol. 6, No. 6 (June 1983)-. Periodical. English. Twelve times a year. $26.00. American Express Publishing Company, 1120 Avenue of the Americas, New York NY 10036. **Tel** (212)382-5642. **(Subscription address:** CDS Agency Hard Copy, PO Box 4966, Des Moines IA 50340.**) LC** TX341; .I656. **DD** 641/.05. available on microfilm and microfiche from University Microfilms International (UMI). ***Continues*** *Monthly Magazine of Food and Wine, 0279-6740.*
Desc: Covers the art of preparing, presenting and enjoying fine food, wine and spirits. It features articles on dining out, entertaining and traveling and includes recommendations for recipes, wine, travel, equipment and appliances, trends, menu planning, and diet and nutrition.
Ind/Abst Access (1985-); Foods Adlibra.

GW/0016-1187
FREUNDIN MUNCHEN. [FreundinMunch.]. (1967)-. Periodical. German. bw (26 issues per year). $120.00 US. Burda GmbH, Postfach 1230, D-7602 Offenburg Germany. **Tel** 011 49 781-8401. **(Subscription address:** US: German Language Publications, Inc., 153 South Deanstreet, Englewood, NJ 07631 (telephone 201-871-1010 Elizabeth Koch)**) UDC** 088.

UK/0017-2081
GOOD HOUSEKEEPING (BRITISH EDITION). (GOOD HOUSEKEEPING.). [Good housekeep.]. **VFOAT** GH. Vol. 1 (March 1922)-. Periodical. English. mo. $57.00 US; $66.00 Canada. National Magazine Company Ltd., 72 Broadwick Street, London W1V 2BP England. **Tel** 011 44 71 5395214. **(Subscription address:** Tower Publishing, Tower House, Sovereign Park Market Harborough, Leicester LE16 9EF England.**)** ***Absorbed*** *Nash's Pall Mall Magazine.*

US/0017-209X
GOOD HOUSEKEEPING (U.S. ED.). (GOOD HOUSEKEEPING.). [Good housekeep.]. Vol. 62, No. 5 (May 1916)-. Periodical. English. mo. $17.97. The Hearst Corporation, 250 West 55th Street, New York NY 10019. **Tel** (212)649-4014. **(Subscription address:** CDS Agency Hard Copy, PO Box 4966, Des Moines IA 50340.**) LC** TX1; .G7. **DD** 640/.5. **Ad Acc.** available on microfilm and microfiche from University Microfilms International (UMI); available on an online database (file 647/Full-Text) from DIALOG. Documents available from UMI Article Clearinghouse. ***Continues*** *Good Housekeeping Magazine, 0731-1893.*
Desc: Contains a variety of articles and notes on topics of current health concern such as detecting breast cancer, infectious diseases, first aid, and parenting. Features regular department entitled "The Family Doctor".
Ind/Abst Abr. Read. Guide Period. Lit.; Acad. Abstr. Full Text Elite (Jan. 1984-); Acad. Abstr. (Jan. 1984-); Biogr. Index; Consum. Health Nutr. Index; Consum. Index Prod. Eval. Inf. Source; Energy Res. Abstr. (June 1980-); Foods Adlibra; Gen. Period. Index (1985-); Health Ref. Cent. (1987-) [Full Txt.] [Select. Cov.]; Index Inf.; Mag. Artic. Summar. Elite (Jan. 1984-); Mag. Artic. Summar. Select (Jan. 1984-); Mag. Artic. Summar. CD-ROM (Jan. 1984-); Mag. ASAP Plus [Full Txt.]; Mag. Index Plus (1989-); Mag. Index Sel. Microfiche (1990-) [Full Txt.]; Mag. Index. Sel. (1986-); Mag. Search; Newsp. Period. Abstr. (1988-); Read. Guide Abstr. Select Ed.; Read. Guide Period. Lit.; Mag. Index (1977-); TOM Gen. Index (1985-) [Full Txt.]; Vocat. Search (Jan. 1984-).

US/0017-2553
GOURMET. [Gourmet]. Vol. 1 (Jan. 1941)-. Periodical. English. mo. $20.00. Conde Nast Publications / New York, 350 Madison Avenue, New York NY 10017. **Tel** (212)880-8800, (800)777-0700. **(Subscription address:** Neodata / Colorado, PO Box 2606, Boulder Boulder CO 80322.**) LC** TX1; .G75. **DD** 641.505. **Ad Acc.** available on microfilm and microfiche from University Microfilms International (UMI). Documents available from UMI Article Clearinghouse, Magazine Collection.
Desc: The epicurean magazine that sets the standard of excellence for a new generation of knowledgeable and discriminating readers. Authentic menus and recipes that encourage the preparation of the great dishes of the world.
Ind/Abst Acad. Abstr. Full Text Elite (Jan. 1984-); Acad. Abstr. (Jan. 1984-); Acad. Search (Jan. 1984-); Consum. Index Prod. Eval. Inf. Source; Foods Adlibra; Garden Lit. (1992-); Gen. Period. Index (1985-); INFO-SOUTH Abstr.; Mag. Artic. Summar. Elite (Jan. 1984-); Mag. Artic. Summar. Select (Jan. 1984-); Mag. Artic. Summar. CD-ROM (Jan. 1984-); Mag. Index Plus (1989-); Mag. Index. Sel. (1986-); Mag. Search; Newsp. Period. Abstr. (1986-); Read. Guide Abstr. Select Ed.; Read. Guide Period. Lit.; Mag. Index (1977-); TOM Gen. Index (1992-) [Full Txt.]; Vocat. Search (Jan. 1984-).

NE/0926-6976
GROOTCONSUMENT AMSTERDAM. (GROOTCONSUMENT.). [Grootconsument Amst.]. **VFOAT** Gids Grootconsument. (1973)-. Periodical. Dutch. Ten times a year. Fl92.45. Hermes Media BV, Postbus 9940, 1006 AP Amsterdam Netherlands. **Tel** 011 31 20 669 1769. **UDC** 640.5.

FR/0767-8177
GUIDE CUISINE PARIS. [Guide cuis.Paris]. (1983)-. Periodical. French. Twelve times a year. 92.00F France; 142.00F others. Prisma Presse, 6 rue Daru, 75379 Paris Cedex 08, France. **Tel** 011 33 1 44153000, FAX 011 33 1 47641042. **(Subscription address:** Ca M Interesse, Service Abbonements B 110, 60732 Ste Geneva Cedex 9 France.**) UDC** 641.

CN/0823-6860
GUIDES FOR FAMILY BUDGETING. [Guides fam. budg.]. **Added/Corp** Social Planning Council of Metropolitan Toronto. (1964)-. English. an. $15.00. Social Planning Council of Metropolitan Toronto, 2 Carlton Street Suite 1001, Toronto Ontario M5B 1J3 Canada. **Tel** (416)351-0095. **DD** 640/.42/05.

GW/0017-8454
HAUSWIRTSCHAFT UND WISSENSCHAFT. Added/Corp Deutsche Gesellschaft fuer Hauswirtschaft. Institut fuer Hauswirtschaft. Gesellschaft fuer Hauswirtschaft, Munich. Bundesforschungsanstalt fuer Hauswirtschaft, Stuttgart. Vol. 1 (1952/1953)-. Periodical. German. Six times a year. DM80.00 Germany; DM91.00 other. Schneider Verlag GmbH SVH, Wilhelmstrasse 13, D 73666 Baltmannsweiler Germany. **Tel** 011 49 7153 41206, FAX 011 49 7153 48761. **Bk Rev.**

US/0194-2522
HOLLY HOBBIE'S HOME TIMES. Winter 1979-. Periodical. English. qt. Charter Concepts, Inc., 641 Lexington Avenue, New York NY 10022. **LC** TX1; .H56. **DD** 640/.5.

UK
HOME AND COUNTRY : THE MAGAZINE OF THE NATIONAL FEDERATION OF WOMEN'S INSTITUTES. **See** Women's Interests.

US/0073-3075
HOME AND GARDEN BULLETIN. No. 1- 1950-. Bulletin. English. ir. Price varies per volume. US Department of Agriculture, 14th Street and Independence Avenue SW, Washington DC 20250. **Tel** (202)720-5457. **LC** TX7; .U6. **DD** 640/.5. **CODEN** XAHGA2. cum. index.
Ind/Abst AGRICOLA [Full Cov.]; Nutr. Abstr. Rev., Ser. B, Live Feeds and Feed.; Nutr. Abstr. Rev., Ser. A, Hum. Exp.

US/1071-4782
HOME COOKING. [Home cook.]. (19??)-. Periodical. English. mo. $12.97. House of White Birches, 306 East Parr Road, Berne IN 46711. **Tel** (219)589-8741, FAX (219)589-8093. **(Subscription address:** Palm Coast Data, PO Box 420235, Agency Department, Palm Coast FL 32142.**) ED** Judi K. Merkel. **DD** 641. **Circ:** 60,000. ***Continues*** *Women's Circle Home Cooking, 0195-2439.*
Desc: Quick and easy methods for old-fashioned goodness, approximately 100 recipes in each issue.

●UK/0965-366X
HOME COOKING. [Home cook.]. (1992)-. Periodical. English. Twelve times a year. Argus Specialist Publications, Queensway House, 2 Queensway Redhill, Surrey RH1 1QS England. **Tel** 0737 768611, FAX 0737 773993, telex 948669 TOPJNL G. **DD** 641.5. ***Continues*** *Home & Freezer Digest, 0305-8751.*
Desc: Includes coverage of all matters of food and drink - diet, seasonal buys and kitchen product reviews.

CN/0018-4004
HOME EC NEWS. **Added/Corp** Alberta Teachers' Association. Home Economics Council. **VFOAT** Home Economics News. (Dec. 1970)-. Periodical. English. 30.00Can$ membership. Alberta Teachers Association, 11010-142 Street, Barnett House, Edmonton Alberta T5N 2R1 Canada. **Tel** (403)453-2411. ctrl circ. ***Supersedes*** *Newsletter of the Home Economics Council, A. T. A., 0382-537X.*

UK
HOME ECONOMICS. Vol. 1 (1955)-. Periodical. English. mo (except January, August). £19.95, £15.00 (students) UK; $45.00 North America; £24.00 other. Forbes Publications Ltd, 120 Bayswater Road, London W2 3JH England. **Tel** (71)229 9322. **ED** Dilys Wells. Index available. **Bk Rev. Ad Acc. Circ:** 4,500.
Desc: Home economics, health education, food and nutrition, consumer affairs, social education and lifeskills.

US/0046-7774
HOME ECONOMICS RESEARCH JOURNAL. [Home econ. res. j.]. **Added/Corp** American Home Economics Association. Vol. 1 (Sept. 1972)-. Periodical. English. qt (Mar., June, Sept., Dec.). $92.00. SAGE Periodical Press, 2455 Teller Road, Thousand Oaks CA 91320. **Tel** (805)499-0721, FAX (805)499-0871, telex 100799. **ED** Rodney Cate (University of Arizona). **LC** TX1; .H625. **DD** 640/.05. **CODEN** HERSA. **Acid Free.** available on microfilm and microfiche from University Microfilms International (UMI). Documents available from UMI Article Clearinghouse.
Desc: Publishes original research concerned with the general well-being of families and individuals. A major vehicle for the dissemination of new knowledge generated by home economics researchers, focusing on current issues in child development, clothing and textiles, family economics, consumer studies, family relationships, food and nutrition, housing technology and interior design.
Ind/Abst AGRICOLA [Full Cov.]; Curr. Index J. Educ.; Ergon. Abstr.; Expand. Acad. Index (1992-); Middle East Abstr. Index; Newsp. Period. Abstr. (1992-); Nutr. Abstr. Rev., Ser. A, Hum. Exp.; Rev. Med. Vet. Entomol.; Soc. Work Abstr. (Summer 1987-?) [Select. Cov.]; Text. Technol. Dig.

UK
HOME ECONOMIST, THE. Vol. 1, No. 1 (July 1981)-. English. bm. £40.00. Institute of Home Economics, Hobart House 40 Grosvenor Place, London SW1X 7AE England. **Tel** 011 44 71 8231109. **ED** Heather Higgins and Kurt Paulus. **Bk Rev. Ad Acc.**
Desc: Professional information resource on food, clothing, home management and design, household services and research related to the home and community.

CN/0225-5871
HOME OWNERS'. [Home own.]. No. 8- Winter 1979-. Periodical. English. qt. Free. Ontario Ltd., Suite 208, 1430 King Street West, Toronto Ontario M6K 1H8. **DD** 643. ctrl circ. ***Continues*** *Homeowners' Guide, 0225-588X.*

US/0146-9487
HOMEMAKER OF THE NATIONAL EXTENSION HOMEMAKERS COUNCIL, THE. **Main/Corp** National Extension Homemakers Council. V. 1- Spring 1977-. Periodical. English. bm. $9.97. DC Hipschmann, PO Box 8283, Rapid City SD 57709. **LC** TX1; .N28A. **DD** 640/.5. **Bk Rev. Ad Acc. Circ:** 275,000.
Desc: For women, including those working outside the home, practical approaches to making home a pleasant and comfortable place.

●US/1063-1747
HOW TO BE A PERFECT COOK. [How perfect cook]. (1992)-. Periodical. English. mo. $29.95. P.R.E. Services, 17095 Hopewell Road, Alpharetta GA 30201. **DD** 641.

US/1054-4747
IDEAS UNLIMITED (WASHINGTON, D.C.). (IDEAS UNLIMITED.). [Ideas unltd. (Wash. D. C.)]. (19??)-. English. Twelve times a year. $195.00. Newsletter Services Inc, 9700 Philadelphia Court, Lanham MD 20706. **Tel** (800)345-2611. **DD** 081.

CN/0836-0650
INNOVATIONS. [Innovations]. Vol. 17, No. 2 (Jan. 1988)-. Periodical. English. New Brunswick Teachers' Association, PO Box 752, Fredericton New Brunswick E3B 5R6 Canada. **Tel** (506)452-8921. **DD** 640/.7/0715. ***Continues*** *Winds of Change (Fredericton, N.B.), 0710-7781.*

US
INTERCHANGE. 1977-. English. **LC** TX165.A1; I57. **DD** 640/.7/1173.
Ind/Abst Work Relat. Abstr.

US/1055-3657
INTERNATIONAL FRIENDSHIP MAGAZINE. [Int. friendsh. mag.]. No. 911 (1991)-. Periodical. English. sa. $20.00. Heart to Heart Publications, PO Box 1898, MT. Pleasant SC 29465-1898. **DD** 646.

US/0162-8380
JEEPERS KREEPERS REFUND PEEPERS. Periodical. English. $6.75. Jeepers Kreepers Refund Peepers, Kitty Houghtaling/Jill Schumacher, Rion Road, Chichester NY 12416.

UK/0309-3891
JOURNAL OF CONSUMER STUDIES AND HOME ECONOMICS. See Consumer Interests.

CN/0705-7830
JOURNAL OF HOME ECONOMICS EDUCATION. [J. home econ. educ.]. **Added/Corp** Alberta Teachers' Association. Alberta Teachers' Association. Home Economics Council. Vol. 17, No. 1 (May 1978)-. Periodical. English. tq (2 or 3 times a year). 30.00Can$. Alberta Teachers Association, 11010-142 Street, Barnett House, Edmonton Alberta T5N 2R1 Canada. **Tel** (403)453-2411. **DD** 640.7. ***Continues*** *Home Echoes, 0018-4012.*

AT
JOURNAL OF HOME ECONOMICS. INSTITUTE OF AUSTRALIA. (19??)-. English. Four times a year. 35.00Aus$. Home Economics Association of Australia, PO Box 303, Broadway 2007 NSW Australia. **Tel** 011 61 2 358 2513. ***Continues*** *Home Economics Association of Australia Journal.*

US/0022-1570
JOURNAL OF HOME ECONOMICS (WASHINGTON). (THE JOURNAL OF HOME ECONOMICS.). [J. home econ.]. **Added/Corp** American Home Economics Association. Vol. 1 (Feb. 1909)-. Periodical. English. qt (4 issues). $75.00 (includes AHEA Action). American Home Economics Association, 1555 King Street, Alexandria VA 22314. **Tel** (703)706-4600, (800)424-8080, FAX (703)706-4663. **LC** TX1; .J7. Index available (free). **Bk Rev. Ad Acc. Pr Rev. Circ:** 30,000. available on microfilm and microfiche from University Microfilms International (UMI). Documents available from UMI Article Clearinghouse. ***Absorbed*** *Bulletin / American Home Economics Association.*
Desc: Professional journal of the American Home Economics Association.
Ind/Abst Acad. Abstr. Full Text Elite (July 1990-); Acad. Abstr. (July 1990-); Acad. Ind. [Computer File] (1992-); Acad. Search (July 1990-); AGRICOLA [Full Cov.]; Book Rev. Index; Curr. Index J. Educ.; Dairy Sci. Abstr.; Educ. Index; Expand. Acad. Index (1992-); INFO-SOUTH Abstr.; Mag. Artic. Summar. Elite (July 1990-); Mag. Artic. Summar. Select (July 1990-); Mag. Artic. Summar. CD-ROM (July 1990-); Mag. Search; Med. Rev. Dig.; Newsp. Period. Abstr. (1992-); Nutr. Abstr. Rev., Ser. B, Live Feeds and Feed.; Nutr. Abstr. Rev., Ser. A, Hum. Exp.; Soc. Work Abstr. (Summer 1987-) [Select. Cov.]; Text. Technol. Dig.; Vocat. Search (July 1990-).

AT/0158-6912
JOURNAL OF THE HOME ECONOMICS ASSOCIATION OF AUSTRALIA. ***Title Change.*** [J. Home Econ. Assoc. Aust.]. (1969)-(19??). Periodical. English. qt. Home Economics Association of Australia, PO Box 303, Broadway 2007 NSW Australia. **Tel** 011 61 2 358 2513. **DD** 640. Index available in last issue of volume--attached. ***Continued by*** *Journal of Home Economics Institute of Australia.*
Ind/Abst Aust. Educ. Index.

US
JOURNAL OF VOCATIONAL HOME ECONOMICS EDUCATION. **Added/Corp** American Vocational Association. Division of Home Economics Education. Vol. 1, No. 1 (Winter 1983)-. Periodical. English. Twice a year (May and Nov.). $25.00 (individual), $40.00 (institution). J Madison University, Gerontology Center, Dept Social Work- D Pomraning, Harrisonburg VA 22807. **Tel** (703)568-6169. **ED** Dr. Sue Couch and Dr. Ginny Felstehausen. **Pr Rev. Circ:** 35,000.

JA
KATEI GAHO. (19??)-. Periodical. Japanese. Twelve times a year. $207.00 California; $213.00 elsewhere US; $240.00 Europe; $264.00 Asia; $216.00 other. **(Subscription address:** Kinokuniya Book Stores of America, 1581 Webster Street, San Francisco CA 94115.**) ED** Sekai Bunka-Sha.

US/0889-843X
KIDS COOKING NEWSLETTER. [Kids cook. newsl.]. Oct. 1986-. Newsletter. English. mo. $24.00. GK Publications, 7479 Ohio Street, Mentor OH 44060. **DD** 642.

JA/0286-8237
KINJO GAKUIN DAIGAKU RONSHU, KASEIGAKU HEN. **VFOAT** Annual Report of Natural Science and Home Economics, Kinjo Gakuin College. Began in 1962. Periodical. Japanese (English). an. Kinjo Gakuin Daigaku Omori Moriyama-ku, Nagoya-shi Japan. **Tel** (052)798-0180. **LC** TX1; .K56. **Circ:** 700.

HU
KONZERV- ES PAPRIKAIPAR. **Added/Corp** Konzervipari Vallalatok Troesztje. Magyar Elelmiszeripari Tudomiamyos Egyesuelet. Konzervipari Szakosztaly. No. 1 (Jan./Feb. 1976)-. Academic Scholarly Publication. Hungarian (summaries and/or abstracts in Russian and German). qt. Lapkiado Vallalat, Lenin Korut 9-11, 1073 Budapest 7, Hungary. **Tel** 222-408. Documents available from CASDDS.
Ind/Abst Chem. Abstr.; Food Sci. Technol. Abstr.

US/0888-4811
KOSHER GOURMET MAGAZINE, THE. ***Title Change.*** [Kosher gourmet mag.]. (1986)-?. Periodical. English. bm. KGM Publications, PO Box 387A, Planetarium Station, New York NY 10024. **Tel** (212)595-1714. **ED** Gil Marks. **DD** 641. **Bk Rev. Ad Acc. Circ:** 5,000. ***Continued by*** *Kosher Gourmet and Jewish Perspective, 1053-2056.*
Desc: A manual for the modern Kosher consumer. Each issue offers Kosher recipes, consumer news, food ideas, and feature articles.

JA/0388-3612
KYORITSU JOSHI DAIGAKU KASEI GAKUBU KIYO. [Kyoritsu Joshi Daigaku Kasei Gakubu kiyo]. **VFOAT** Bulletin of the Faculty of Home Economics, Kyoritsu Women's University. (1973)-. Periodical. Multiple languages. an. Kyoritsu Women's University / Department of Home Economics, Tokyo Japan. **DD** 640. Documents available from CASDDS. ***Continues in part*** *Kyoritsu Joshi Daigaku Kiyo, 0388-3604.*
Ind/Abst Chem. Abstr.

US/0023-7124
LADIES' HOME JOURNAL. See Women's Interests.

SZ/0024-0028
LEBENSMITTEL-INDUSTRIE, DIE. ***Suspended.*** [Lebensm.-Ind.]. Jan. 1954-Suspended with No. 4, 1991. Academic Scholarly Publication. German. mo. $16.92. Deutscher Judo Verband, Redaktion Ippon Segewaldweg 40, D 12557 Berlin Germany. **Tel** 011 49 711 210770, telex 051 678. **LC** TX341; .L43. **CODEN** LEINAQ. **Pr Rev.** Documents available from CASDDS. ***Supersedes in part*** *Deutsche Genussmittel-Zeitschrift;* ***Continues*** *Deutsche Obst- und Gemuse-, Zucker und Susswarenzeitschrift.*
Ind/Abst Chem. Abstr.; Curr. Biotechnol.; Curr. Ref. Fish Res.; EMBASE; Food Sci. Technol. Abstr.; Int. Packag. Abstr.; SCISEARCH.

FR/0988-4343
LETTRE DES CUISINISTES, DES BAINISTES ET DES ELECTROMENAGISTES, LA. (1988)-. Periodical. French. wk. 1071.00F France and French overseas departments & territories; 1480.00F other. L'Officiel SA, Boite Postale 9037, 34041 Montpellier Cedex France. **Tel** 011 33 67 588228. **UDC** 67.

US/0882-4452
LIFE SKILLS NEWS. (LIFE SKILLS NEWS / DEPARTMENT OF HOME ECONOMICS, MONTCLAIR STATE COLLEGE, SCHOOL OF PROFESSIONAL STUDIES.). [Life skills news]. **Added/Corp** Montclair State College. Life Skills Center. (19??)-. Periodical. English. Three times a year. $6.00 US; $7.00 other. Life Skills Center, Montclair State College, Upper Montclair NJ 07043. **Tel** (201)893-4172. **ED** Joan Bernstein and Mary Ellen Fecanin. **DD** 640. **Circ:** 2,000 (ctrl). ***Continues*** *Life Skills Center News.*
Desc: Highlights current topics regarding education, family issues, consumer issues, and food and nutrition topics.

US/1059-2539
LIVING BETTER. [Living better]. **Added/Corp** Cooperative Extension Association of Nassau County. Home Economics Division. Cornell Cooperative Extension. Nassau County. Home Economics Program. (198?)-. Periodical. English. mo. **DD** 640.
Ind/Abst AGRICOLA [Select. Cov.].

CN/0315-9329
M.H.E.T.A. JOURNAL. [MHETA j.]. **Main/Corp** Manitoba Home Economics Teachers' Association. **Added/Corp** Manitoba Teachers' Society. Vol. 6, No. 1 (Nov. 1973)-. Periodical. English. Three times a year (Jan., May, Sept.). 30.00Can$. Manitoba Teachers Society, 191 Harcourt Street, Winnipeg Manitoba R3J 3H2 Canada. **Tel** (204)888-7961 ext.254, FAX (204)831-0877. **DD** 640.7. ***Continues*** *M.H.E.T.A. Bulletin, 0315-9310.*

US/1048-8383
MAGAZINE OF AMERICA'S BEST RECIPES, THE. See Nutrition and Dietetics.

IS
MAH KEDAI. No. 1- February 1975-. Periodical. Hebrew. bm. 5.00 single issue. Ha-Moatsah Ha-Yisreelit Le-Tsarkhanut, Rehov Hauniversitah 42, Tel-Aviv Israel. **LC** TX335; .M2215.

US/0889-4884
MAILBOX NEWS. (MAILBOX NEWS : MAID OF SCANDINAVIA'S MONTHLY PUBLICATION FOR FOOD ENTHUSIASTS.). [Mailb. news]. (19??)-. Periodical. English. Twelve times a year. $12.00. Maid of Scandinavia Company, 3244 Raleigh Avenue, Minneapolis MN 55416. **Tel** (612)927-7996, FAX (612)927-6215. **ED** Char Brown and Dee Dalquist. **DD** 641. Index available. cum. index. **Bk Rev. Circ:** 45,000 (ctrl). available on diskette.
Desc: For cake decorating and candymaking enthusiasts or those who like to be creative with food. Readers submit pictures of work and exchange ideas.

FR
MAISON ET TRAVAUX. French. Maison et Travaux, 16/18 rue de l Amiral Mouchez, F-75686 Paris Cedex 14 France.

FR/0025-0953
MAISON FRANCAISE, LA. [Maison fr.]. Vol. 1 No. 1 (Oct. 1946)-. Periodical. French. ir. 853.00F (airmail); 340.00F France; 568.00F other. La Maison Francaise, 17 rue D Uzes, 75002 Paris France. **ED** F Ollive. **LC** TX1; .M26. **DD** 747. cum. index.
Ind/Abst Avery Index Archit. Period. Suppl. Colum. Univ. (Jan. 1990-).

US/1057-5251
MARTHA STEWART LIVING. [Martha Stewart living]. **VFOAT** Living. (Winter 1990)-. Periodical. English. Ten times a year. $24.00. Time Inc. / New York, Time & Life Building, Rockefeller Center, New York NY 10020. **(Subscription address:** Neodata / Colorado, PO Box 2606, Boulder Boulder CO 80322.**)** **DD** 646. **Ad Acc.**

US/0024-8908
MCCALL'S. **See** Women's Interests.

CN/0317-9303
MEMOIRE AUX GOUVERNEMENTS CANADIEN ET QUEBECOIS. **Main/Corp** Federation des Associations Cooperatives d'Economie Familiale du Quebec. First issue in 1968. Periodical. French. Free to minister and members of the Federation. Federation des Associations Cooperatives d'Economie Familiale du Quebec, 3510 Est Boulevard St-Joseph, Montreal Quebec H1X 1W6 Canada. **DD** 640.73.

US/0197-372X
MICROWAVE TIMES, THE. ***Title Change.*** [Microw. times]. Vol. 1 (1975)-(19??). Periodical. English. bm. Recipes Unlimited, Box 1271, Burnsville MN 55337. **Tel** (612)890-6655, (800)328-2846. **ED** Janet Sadlack. **DD** 641. Index available. **Circ:** 300,000. available in braille (by CL Productions). ***Continued by*** *Cooking Connection.*
Desc: Recipes and information for microwave oven owners. Questions and answers, adapting recipes, idea exchange, new product information plus lots of recipes.
Ind/Abst Foods Adlibra.

UK/0264-9683
MODUS. **Added/Corp** National Association of Teachers of Home Economics. Vol. 1, No. 1 (Jan. 1983)-. Periodical. English. Eight times a year (Jan., March, April, May, June, Sept., Oct., and Nov.). £25.00 UK and Eire; £32.00 (surface mail) other. National Association of Teachers of Home Economics & Technology, Hamilton House, Mabledon Place, London WC1H 9BJ England. **Tel** 11 44 1 387-1441, FAX 11 44 1 383-7230. ***Continues*** *Housecraft.*
Ind/Abst Br. Educ. Index.

SI
MPH LIVING. Periodical. English. MPH Distributors Son BHD, 71177 Stamford Road, Singapore 6 Singapore. **LC** TX1; .F45. **DD** 640/.5. ***Continues*** *Female Living.*

US/8755-1713
NAHC WILD GAME COOKBOOK. [NAHC wild game cookb.]. **VFOAT** N.A.H.C. Wild Game Cookbook; Wild Game Cookbook. **VAT** North American Hunting Club Wild Game Cookbook. English. an. $15.95. National Association of Housing Cooperatives, 1614 King Street, Alexandria VA 22314. **Tel** (703)549-5201, FAX (703)684-8648. **LC** TX751; .N34. **DD** 641.6/91/05. **Circ:** 20,000.

US/0896-193X
NAILS. [Nails]. **VFOAT** Nails Magazine. (198?)-. Trade Publication. English. mo. $36.00. Nails Magazine, 2512 Artesia Boulevard, Redondo Beach CA 90278. **Tel** (310)376-8788, (800)334-8152. **DD** 646.

US/0192-6772
NATIONAL HOME CENTER NEWS. [Natl. home cent. news]. (19??)-. Periodical. English. Twenty-three times a year. $99.00 North America; $119.00 Canada; $279.00 other. Lebhar Friedman Inc., 3922 Coconut Palm Drive, Tampa FL 33619. **Tel** (800)927-9292, (813)664-6707. **ED** Ken Schept. **DD** 380. **[CCC]. Ad Acc. Circ:** 52,000 (ctrl). available on microfilm and microfiche from University Microfilms International (UMI); available on an online database (files 16,570/Full-Text) from DIALOG.
Desc: Newspaper to retailers, manufacturers and wholesalers in cumber, building material, hardware industry.
Ind/Abst F&S Index Plus Text, Int. [Full Txt.] [Select. Cov.]; Mark. Advert. Ref. Serv. [Full Txt.]; PROMT [Full Txt.]; Stat. Ref. Index.

AT/0028-249X
NEW IDEA MELBOURNE. (1929)-. Periodical. English. wk. 119.60Aus$ Australia; 156.00Aus$ other. Pacific Publications Pty Ltd, 32 Walsh Street, Melbourne VIC 3000 Australia. **Tel** 011 61 3 3207000.

JA/0913-5227
NIHON KASEI GAKKAISHI. (NIHON KASEI GAKKAI SHI.). [Nihon Kasei Gakkaishi]. **Added/Corp** Nihon Kasei Gakkai. **VFOAT** Journal of Home Economics of Japan. (1987)-. Periodical. Japanese (summaries and/or abstracts in English; table of contents in English). mo. $230.00. **(Subscription address:** Kyowa Book Company Inc., 1-38 Kanda Jinbo-Cho, Chiyoda-Ku Tokyo 101, Japan**)** **LC** TX1; .K37. **[CCC].** ***Continues*** *Kaseigaku Zasshi, 0449-9069.*

CN/0225-1272
NUTRIPLAN. [Nutriplan]. No. 1 (March 22, 1980)-. Periodical. French. wk. Nutriplan, 1115 Ouest rue Sherbrooke 2302, Montreal Quebec H3A AH3 Canada. **DD** 641.5/05.

US/1044-4637
ORIGINAL RECIPES. (1990)-. Periodical. English. mo. $18.00. Paul J Belanger, 1229 Broadway/Suite 376, Bangor ME 04401.

CN
PEOPLE AND PRACTICE. English. Four times a year. $14.00. SCH Family & Nutritional Science, 2205 East Mall, University of British Columbia, Vancouver BC V6T 1W5 Canada. **Tel** (604)822-6195, FAX (604)822-5143. **ED** Eleanore Vaines Ph.D. cum. index.
Desc: This series presents issues central to the profession practice of home economic.

GW/0031-630X
PETRA. **See** Women's Interests.

US/0270-9341
PHOENIX HOME/GARDEN. **See** Interior Design.

●US/1064-7503
PREVENTION'S QUICK AND HEALTHY LOW-FAT COOKING. **See** Food and Food Industry.

US/0893-2247
QUICK 'N EASY COOKIN'. ***Title Change.*** **VFOAT** Quick and Easy Cooking. Vol. 1, No. 1 (Sept./Oct. 1986)-(19??). Periodical. English. Six times a year. Parkside Publishing, PO Box 66, Davis SD 57021-0066. **Tel** (605)238-5704. **ED** Nancy A. Krome and Zeta Ovengard. **DD** 641. **Ad Acc. Circ:** 12,000. ***Continued by*** *Quick n Easy Country Cookin.*
Desc: Covers recipes, food preparation, crafts, sewing, gardening and inspirational articles.

●US/1075-7384
QUICK N EASY COUNTRY COOKIN. **VFOAT** Quick and Easy Country Cooking. (1994)-. English. Six times a year. $12.95. Parkside Publishing, PO Box 66, Davis SD 57021-0066. **Tel** (605)238-5704. ***Continues*** *Quick n Easy Cookin, 0893-2247.*

US
RECIPE SOURCES NEWSLETTER. Newsletter. English. an. $4.00 North America; $6.00 other. Restaurant Publishing / Houston, Box 570213, Houston TX 77257. **ED** A C Doyle. **Circ:** 2,000.
Desc: Sources of free, or inexpensive recipes.

CN/0709-9045
RESEARCH NEWSLETTER - FACULTY OF HOME ECONOMICS, UNIVERSITY OF ALBERTA. [Res. newsl. - Fac. Home Econ., Univ. Alta.]. **Main/Corp** University of Alberta. Faculty of Home Economics. No. 1 (1978)-. Newsletter. English. an. Limited free distribution. Faculty of Home Economics, University of Alberta, Edmonton Alberta T6G 2M8 Canada. **DD** 640/.7/2071233. ctrl circ.

FR
REVUE CULINAIRE, LA. (19??)-. French. Ten times a year. 244.86F France; 350.00F other. Mutuelle Cuisiniers de France, 45 rue Saint Roch, 75001 Paris France. **Tel** 011 33 1 42615275.

US
SAN DIEGO HOME / GARDEN. ***Title Change.*** [S. Diego home/gard.]. **VAT** San Diego Home Garden. (Sept. 1979)-(1993). Periodical. English. mo. San Diego Home Garden, 4577 Viewridge Avenue, San Diego CA 92123. **Tel** (619)571-1818, FAX (619)571-1889. **ED** Peter Jensen. **LC** TX1; .S245. **DD** 640/.5. **Ad Acc. Circ:** 34,104 (ctrl). available in microform. ***Continued by*** *San Diego Home/Garden Lifestyles, 1073-6891.*

●US/1073-6891
SAN DIEGO HOME/GARDEN LIFESTYLES. [S. Diego home/gard. lifestyles]. **VFOAT** San Diego Home Garden Lifestyles; San Diego Home/Garden. Vol. 15, No. 2 (Oct. 1993)-. Periodical. English. Twelve times a year. $18.00 US; $26.00 others. San Diego Home Garden, 4577 Viewridge Avenue, San Diego CA 92123. **Tel** (619)571-1818, FAX (619)571-1889. **DD** 051. **Ad Acc. Circ:** 45,000. ***Continues*** *San Diego Home/Garden, 0274-483X.*
Desc: A creative guide to San Diego lifestyles.

FR/0769-6094
SAVOIRS ET FORMATION. (1985)-. Periodical. French. Five times a year. 97.94F. Association de l'Enseignement et la Formation des Travailleurs Immigres / AEFTI, 16 rue de Valmy, F-93100 Montreuil France. **Tel** 011 33 1 42870220. **UDC** 362 : 325.14.

US/0883-475X
SCHOLASTIC CHOICES. [Scholast. choices]. **VFOAT** Choices. Vol. 1, No. 1 (Sept. 1985)-. Periodical. English. Eight times a year. $25.00. Scholastic Inc., 2931 East McCarty Street, PO Box 3710, Jefferson City MO 65102-9957. **Tel** (314)636-5271, (800)631-1586. **ED** Karen Glenn, Mark Bregman, Pearl Gaskins. **LC** TX1; .P7. **DD** 640/.5. Index available. **Bk Rev. Ad Acc. Circ:** 750,000 (ctrl). available on microfilm from Xerox; available on microfilm and microfiche from University Microfilms International (UMI). ***Continues*** *Co-Ed (Dayton, Ohio), 0009-9724.*
Ind/Abst Gen. Period. Index (Jan. 1985-Dec. 1985); Mag. Artic. Summar. Elite (July 1993-); Mag. Artic. Summar. CD-ROM (July 1993-); Mag. Index (Sept. 1985-Dec. 1985).

CN/0848-8258
SELECT HOMES & FOOD. ***Title Change.*** [Sel. homes food]. **VFOAT** Select Homes and Food. Vol. 16, No. 7 (Oct. 1989)-(19??). Periodical. English. Eight times a year. Telemedia Publishing Inc., 555 West 12th Avenue, Suite 300, North York Ontario V5Z 4L4 Canada. **Tel** (604)877-7732. **(Subscription address:** Indas, 35 Riviera Drive, Building 17, Markham Ontario L3R 8N4 Canada.**)** **LC** TX714; .S45. **DD** 640/.5. ***Formed by the union of*** *Select Homes (Vancouver, B.C.)., 0713-8075* ***and*** *Canadian Living's Food Magazine., 0831-5663.* ***Continued by*** *Canadian Select Homes.*
Ind/Abst Can. Index.

CH
SHIH PIN KO CHI. **VFOAT** Food Science and Technology. Periodical. Chinese. NT$0.20. Science Press, 16 Donghuangchenggen North Street, Beijing 100707, People's Republic of China. **Tel** 011 86 1 4019821, 011 86 1 4010642, FAX 011 86 1 4012180, 011 86 1 4019810, telex 210147. **LC** TX341; .S4. **DD** 641/.05.

KO
SIK SAENGHWAL. **VFOAT** Wolgan Sik Saenghwal. V. 1- (1984, 9)-. Periodical. Korean. mo. W10,000. Sik Saenghwal Kaeson Pom Kungmin Undong Ponbu, 731 Socho-dong Kangnam-ku, Seoul Korea. **LC** TX724.5.K65; S55.

US/0272-2003
SOUTHERN LIVING ... ANNUAL RECIPES. (19??)-. English. an. $29.95. Oxmoor House, PO Box 2463, Birmingham AL 35201. **Tel** (205)877-6000. **LC** TX715; .S6795. **DD** 641.5975/05.
Desc: Contains every recipe considered delectable enough to be published during the past year in Southern Living. Indexed three ways, and includes full-color photography.

US/1048-8413
SPECIALTY COOKING. **See** Nutrition and Dietetics.

US/1066-2898
SUPER SNACK NEWS. **See** Children and Youth Interests.

CN/0702-7133
T H E S A NEWSLETTER. [T.H.E.S.A. newsl.]. **Main/Corp** Teachers of Home Economics Specialists Association. Vol. 17 (Oct. 1976)-. Periodical. English. Five times a year. $45.00. British Columbia Teachers Federation, 100-550 West 6th Avenue, Vancouver British Columbia V5Z 4P2 Canada. **Tel** (604)871-2283, (800)663-9163, FAX (604)871-2294, (604)871-2290. **DD** 640.7. ***Continues*** *Teachers of the Home Economics Specialist Association. Newsletter, 0381-940X.*
Ind/Abst Can. Educ. Index (1965-1985).

KO
TAEHAN KAJONG HAHOE CHI. **Main/Corp** Taehan Kajong Hakhoe. **VFOAT** Journal of Korean Home Economics Association. Periodical. English (Korean). Yonse University, c/o College of Home Economics, Seoul Korea. **LC** TX1; .T33A. **DD** 640/.5.

US/0364-3824
TASTE. **Added/Corp** Culinary Institute of America. Fellows. (19??)-. Periodical. English. Twice a year. Free on request. Culinary Institute of America, Public Relations Department, Hyde Park NY 12538. **Tel** (914)452-9600. **LC** TX1; .T36. **DD** 641.5/05.

US/0735-6986
TEEN TIMES (WASHINGTON, D.C.). (TEEN TIMES; MAGAZINE OF THE FUTURE HOMEMAKERS OF AMERICA.). **Added/Corp** Future

Homemakers of America. (19??)-. Periodical. English. Four times a year (Jan., Mar., Sept., Nov.). $6.00. Future Homemakers of America, 1910 Association Drive, Reston VA 22091. **Tel** (703)476-4900.

FI/0355-0567
TEHO / TYOTEHOSEURA. **See** Agriculture.

FR/0989-6333
THURIES MAGAZINE. (1988)-. Periodical. French. Ten times a year. 509.30F France; 650.00F Europe; 750.00 French overseas departments and territories; 800.00F other. Thuries Magazine, La Bride, 81170 Cordes, France. **Tel** 011 33 1 63561606, FAX 011 33 1 63561699. **ED** Beatrice Balaye. **UDC** 641. Index available. cum. index. **Ad Acc**, **Adv Mgr Tel** 011 33 1 63561601. **Circ:** 45,000 (ctrl).

US/1065-366X
TIGHTWAD GAZETTE. [Tightwad gaz.]. (1990)-. Periodical. English. mo. $12.00 US; $14.50 Canada & Mexico; $21.00 other. Tightwad Gazette, R.R. Box 3570, Leeds ME 04263-9710. **Tel** (207)524-7962. **ED** Amy Dacyczyn. **DD** 640. Index available (Published seperately). cum. index. **Bk Rev**, (Qty: 2). **Circ:** 60,000.
Desc: Promotes thrift as a viable alternative lifestyle. Contains information on getting more out of every dollar.

US
TIPS & TOPICS (LUBBOCK, TEX.). ***Ceased.*** (TIPS & TOPICS.). **VFOAT** Tips and Topics. Vol. 22, No. 2, Winter (1981)-Ceased April (1988). Periodical. English. qt. Tips and Topics, College of Home Economics, PO Box 4170, Texas Tech University, Lubbock TX 79409. ***Continues*** *Tips and Topics in Home Economics, 0040-8042.*

JA/0371-831X
TOKYO KASEI DAIGAKU KENKYU KIYO. **Main/Corp** Tokyo Kasei Daigaku. **Added/Corp** Tokyo Kasei Daigaku. Reports of Studies of the Tokyo College of Domestic Science. Tokyo Kasei Daigaku. Bulletin of the Tokyo College of Domestic Science. **VFOAT** Reports of Studies of the Tokyo College of Domestic Science; Bulletin of the Tokyo College of Domestic Science. (1960)-. Academic Scholarly Publication. Japanese (English). an. Tokyo Kasei University, 18-1 Kaga 1-chome Itabashi-ku, Tokyo Japan. **LC** TX1; .T63a. **CODEN** TKDKBL. Documents available from CASDDS.
Ind/Abst Chem. Abstr.

US
TOMPKINS COUNTY HOME & GARDEN. **Added/Corp** Cooperative Extension Association of Tompkins County. **VFOAT** Home & Garden. (Jan. 1983)-. Periodical. English. mo. $6.00. Cornell Cooperative Extension of Tompkins County, 615 Willow Avenue, Ithaca NY 14850. **Tel** 272-2292. cum. index. **Circ:** 2,000 (ctrl). ***Continues*** *Dimension (Ithaca, N.Y.).*
Desc: Magazine of Cornell Cooperative Extension of Tompkins County. Articles on gardening, energy conservation, consumer affairs and family life.

FR
TOUTE LA BRODERIE LE JOURNAL DES BRODEUSES. French. Three times a year. $14.00 (one year), $27.00 (two year). Snege Editions, BP 7085, 23 rue Chalopin, 69341 Lyon Cedex 07 France. **Tel** 011 33 78 720688.

US/0191-3549
UNDERGROUND SHOPPER. NEW YORK CITY, THE. 1st- Ed. English. $4.95. Susann Publications Inc, Route 2 PO Box 176 H, Roanoke TX 76262. **LC** TX335; .U46. **DD** 380.1/45/00097471.

PN/0505-0146
VANIDADES CONTINENTAL. (1961)-. Periodical. Spanish. sm. $57.50. Editorial America SA, 6355 Northwest 36th Street, Miami FL 33166. **Tel** (305)871-6400. **(Subscription address:** CDS, SIFD Agency Control, 1901 Bell Avenue, Demoine, IA 50315 (Phone: (515)246-6812)) **ED** F. Calderon. available on microfilm and microfiche from University Microfilms International (UMI).
Desc: Covers topics such as home decoration, food, bar recipes, travel and arts, music, movies, books and features on international and local personalities.

●US/1065-6340
VEGETARIAN GOURMET. **See** Food and Food Industry.

CN/0702-7338
WHAT'S COOKING. V. 1- July/Aug. 1976-. Periodical. English. mo. Original Microwave oven Kitchens, 24 Ronson Drive, Rexdale Ontario M9W 1B4. **DD** 641.5/88.

US/0043-4590
WHAT'S NEW IN HOME ECONOMICS. [What's new home econ.]. (Sept. 1936)-. Periodical. English. Five times a year. $29.00 US; $47.00 other. University Publishing Co., 1429 Walnut Street, 4th Floor, Philadelphia PA 19102. **Tel** (215)563-3501. **ED** Jane Leichner. **LC** TX1; .W45. **DD** 640.5. **Bk Rev.** **Ad Acc.** **Circ:** 15,000. available on microfilm and microfiche from University Microfilms International (UMI).
Desc: Publication for professional home economists with lesson plan ideas, resources, curriculum and development in all areas of home economics. An easy to use guide for all family educators.
Ind/Abst AGRICOLA.

US/0198-0297
WOMAN'S DAY COOKING FOR TWO. No. 1- Sept. 1979-. Periodical. English. mo. $1.50 each issue. Diamandis Communications Inc, 1499 Monrovia Avenue, New Port Beach CA 92663. **Tel** (714)720-5300. **LC** TX1; .W65. **DD** 641.5/05.

US/0278-1026
WOMAN'S DAY DESSERT LOVER'S COOKBOOK. **VFOAT** Woman's Day Super Special Series Dessert Lover's Cookbook; Dessert Lover's Cookbook. No. 1 (Feb.-Mar. 1981)-. Periodical. English. bm. $1.69 each issue. Diamandis Communications Inc, 1499 Monrovia Avenue, New Port Beach CA 92663. **Tel** (714)720-5300. **LC** TX773; .W776. **DD** 641.8/6/05.

US/0195-6299
WOMAN'S DAY GREAT HOLIDAY BAKING IDEAS. **VFOAT** Great Holiday Baking Ideas. (19??)-. Periodical. English. mo. $2.95 each issue. Hachette Magazines Inc., 1633 Broadway, New York NY 10019. **Tel** (212)767-6000. **LC** TX769; .W73. **DD** 641.8/65.

US/1056-7836
WOMAN'S DAY HELPFUL HINTS LETTER. [Woman's day help. hints lett.]. **VFOAT** Helpful Hints Letter. Vol. 1, No. 1 (July/Aug. 1991)-. Periodical. English. Six times a year. $19.95. Opportunity Associates, 73 Spring Street, New York NY 10012. **Tel** (212)925-3180. **(Subscription address:** Palm Coast Data, PO Box 420235, Agency Department, Palm Coast FL 32142.) **DD** 640.

US
WORLD CONVENTION DATES. EVENT PLANNER'S GUIDE. **VFOAT** Event Planner's Guide. English. an. World Convent Dates, 500 Summer Street, Stamford CT 06901-1384. **LC** TX907; .W69. **DD** 647/.969.

JA
ZENKOKU TANKI DAIGAKU KIYO RONBUN SAKUIN. KASEIGAKU HEN. **VFOAT** Bulletin of Junior Colleges SIC Cumulative Index in Japan. 1950-1979-. Japanese. 35000. Saitama Fukushikai, 7-31 Horinouchi 3 Niiza-shi, Saitama-ken 352 Japan. **LC** Z5775; .Z46; TX1. available on microfiche.

HOMOSEXUALITY

US/0001-8996
ADVOCATE (LOS ANGELES, CALIF.), THE. (THE ADVOCATE.). [Advocate]. No. 33 (May 13-26, 1970)-. Periodical. English. bw (26 issues). $39.97 (one year), $75.95 (two year). Liberation Publications, 6922 Holywood Boulevard, 10th Floor, Los Angeles CA 90028. **Tel** (213)871-1225. **ED** Richard Rovilard. **DD** 301.41/57/05. Index available. **Bk Rev.** **Ad Acc.** **Circ:** 350,000 (ctrl). available on microfiche. Documents available from UMI Article Clearinghouse. ***Continues*** *Los Angeles Advocate.*
Desc: Information on the gay liberation movement and homosexuality.
Ind/Abst Acad. Ind. [Computer File] (1992-); Altern. Press Index; Expand. Acad. Index (1992-); Gen. Period. Index (1991-); LegalTrac (1980-); Mag. Index Plus (1991-); Newsp. Period. Abstr. (1988-); Mag. Index.

US/0893-7958
AMETHYST (ATLANTA, GA.). (AMETHYST : A JOURNAL FOR LESBIANS AND GAY MEN.). [Amethyst]. **Added/Corp** Southeastern Arts, Media & Education Project (Atlanta, Ga.). (Spring 1987)-. Periodical. English. sa (2 issues). $24.00 institution, $12.00 individual. SAME - Southeastern Arts, Media & Education Project, 75 Bennett Street Northwest, Suite N-1, Atlanta GA 30309. **Tel** (404)609-9590. **LC** WMLC 91/2975. **DD** 810.

CN/0824-2100
ANGLES (VANCOUVER). (ANGLES.). [Angles]. **Added/Corp** Vancouver Gay Community Centre Society. Vancouver Gay Community Centre. Newspaper Committee. 1st Issue (Dec. 1983)-. Periodical. English. mo. 30.00Can$ Canada; 35.00Can$ US; 45.00Can$ other. Lavender Publishing Ltd,, 1170 Bute Street, Vancouver British Columbia, V6E 1Z6 Canada. **Tel** (604)688-0265. **ED** Dan Guinan, Harry Hill, and John Doyle, Harry Hill and Dan Guinan. **DD** 306.7/66/09711. **Bk Rev.** **Ad Acc.** **Circ:** 15,000. ***Continues*** *Vancouver Gay Community Centre News.*
Desc: News, reviews, and commentary for lesbian/gay community in Western Canada.
Ind/Abst Film Lit. Index (19??-).

CN/0712-1954
ATTITUDE (MONTREAL). (ATTITUDE.). [Attitude]. Periodical. French. mo. $2.75 per no. Attitude, CP 115 Succursale H, Montreal Quebec H3G 2K5 Canada. **DD** 306.7/662/09714281.

US/0896-9531
BAD ATTITUDE. [Bad attitude]. Vol. 1, No. 1 (Spring 1984)-. Periodical. English. Six times a year. $30.00 US; $50.00 others. Bad Attitude, PO Box 110, Cambridge MA 02139. **Tel** (617)426-4469. **ED** Jasmine Sterling, (editor's address: PO Box 390110, Comb, MA 02139 phone: (508)372-6247). **Bk Rev**, (Qty: 10-12). **Ad Acc**, **Adv Mgr:** J. Sterling. **Circ:** 5,000.
Desc: Erotic fiction, articles, poetry, black and white photos and cartoons all concerning lesbian sexuality.

US
BAY AREA REPORTER : B.A.A. **See** Newspapers.

US/0883-4334
BAY WINDOWS. [Bay windows]. Vol. 1, No. 1 (Mar. 1983)-. Periodical. English. Fifty-one times per year. $40.00. Bay Windows, 1523 Washington Street, Boston MA 02118. **Tel** (617)266-6670 Ext. 214. **DD** 363.

NE
BEST GUIDE TO AMSTERDAM & BENELUX VENUES (FOR GAY MEN AND LESBIANS). **See** Travel and Tourism.

NE
BEST GUIDE TO GREAT BRITAIN (FOR GAY MEN). **See** Travel and Tourism.

●US
BETTER HOMOS AND GARDENS. Issue #1 (Spring 1992)-. Periodical. English. qt. **LC** HQ75; .B488.

US/1055-0976
BLACK AND GAY. **See** Ethnic Interests.

US/1049-3298
BLACK LACE. [Black lace]. No. 1 (Spring 1991)-. Periodical. English. qt. $5.95. BLK Publishing Company, PO Box 83912, Los Angeles CA 90083-0912. **Tel** (310)410-0808, FAX (310)410-9250. **ED** Alycee J. Lane. **DD** 305.
Desc: Erotic magazine for African-American lesbians. It features a collection of poetry, short stores, fantasy letters to the editor, and advice column, artwork, and erotic photography.

US/1043-0075
BLK (LOS ANGELES, CALIF.). (BLK.). [BLK]. (1988)-. Periodical. English. Twelve times a year. $18.00 one year; $30.00 two years. BLK Publishing Company, PO Box 83912, Los Angeles CA 90083-0912. **Tel** (310)410-0808, FAX (310)410-9250. **ED** Don Thomas. **LC** HQ75; .B54. **DD** 305. **Bk Rev**, (Qty: 36). **Ad Acc**, **Adv Mgr:** Cedric Whitfield, **Tel** (310)410-0808. **Circ:** 13,000. available on microfilm from University Microfilms International (UMI). Documents available from UMI Article Clearinghouse.
Desc: This magazine is for the lesbians and gays around the world.
Ind/Abst Altern. Press Index (199?-); Newsp. Period. Abstr. (1991-).

CN/0826-0508
BODY POLITIC XTRA. [Body polit. Xtra]. No. 1 (March 3, 1984)-. Periodical. English. sm. 42.95Can$. Pink Triangle Press, PO Box 7289, Station A, Toronto Ontario M5W 1X9 Canada. **Tel** (416)364-6320. **ED** Ken Popert. **DD** 306.7/66/09713541. **Ad Acc.** **Circ:** 10,000.
Desc: A guide to entertainment and local events in the city of Toronto.

US/1043-383X
CABIRION AND GAY BOOKS BULLETIN, THE. [Cabirion Gay books bull.]. **Added/Corp** Gay Academic Union. New York Chapter. Scholarship Committee. **VFOAT** Gay Books Bulletin; Cabirion/Gay Books Bulletin. No. 10 (Winter/Spring 1984)-. Bulletin. English. qt. Gay Academic Union, Box 480, Lenox Hill, New York NY 10021. **Tel** (212)242-7276. **LC** PN56.H57; G38. **DD** 810.9/353. ***Continues*** *Gay Books Bulletin, 1058-1480.*
Ind/Abst MLA Int. Bibl. Books Artic. Mod. Lang. Lit.

AT
CAMPAIGN AUSTRALIA. **VFOAT** Campaign. No. 75 (March 1982)-. Periodical. English. Twelve times a year. 55.00Aus$. Campaign Australia, PO Box A 228, Sydney S NSW 2000 Australia. **Tel** 011 61 2 3575722. **ED** Greg Gallaghan (phone: (02)332-3620). **Bk Rev**, (Qty: 12). **Ad Acc**, **Adv Mgr:** Dario Burgel, **Tel** (02)332 3666. **Circ:** 16,000 (ctrl). ***Continues*** *Campaign (Potts Point, N.S.W.).*

US/0146-7921
CHRISTOPHER STREET. [Christopher Str.]. Vol. 1 (July 1976)-. Periodical. English. mo. $27.00 US; $37.00 other. That New Magazine Inc., 28 West 25th Street, 4th Floor, New York NY 10159. **Tel** (212)627-2120, FAX (212)727-9321. **(Subscription address:** Christopher Street Magazine, PO Box 1475,

Church Street Station, New York NY 10008.) **ED** Thomas E. Steele. **LC** HQ75; .C48. **DD** 301.41/57/05. **Bk Rev. Ad Acc. Circ:** 8,000. available on microfilm and microfiche from University Microfilms International (UMI). Documents available from UMI Article Clearinghouse.
Desc: A literary magazine of interest to gay people.
Ind/Abst Acad. Ind. [Computer File] (1992-); Expand. Acad. Index (1989-); Mag. Index Plus (1991-); Newsp. Period. Abstr. (1989-); Mag. Index (Jan. 1991-).

●US/1064-8070
COLOR LIFE. (COLOR LIFE : THE LESBIAN, GAY, TWOSPIRIT & BISEXUAL, PEOPLE OF COLOR MAGAZINE.). **Added/Corp** Cairos Project. (1992)-. Periodical. English. mo. $25.00 (institutions). The Cairos Project, PO Box 1518, Ansonia Station, New York NY 10022-4689.

US/0891-6969
COMMON LIVES, LESBIAN LIVES. [Common Lives Lesbian Lives]. **VFOAT** Lesbian Lives; Common Lives/Lesbian Lives. No. 1 (Fall 1981)-. Periodical. English. qt (Jan., April, July, Oct.). $25.00 (institutions), $15.00 (individuals). Common Lives/Lesbian Lives, PO Box 1553, Iowa City IA 52244. **Tel** (319)335-1488. **ED** Lee Hageneier, Lorna Campbell, Joan Benson and Carla Randall. **DD** 306. **Bk Rev. Ad Acc. Circ:** 2,000.
Desc: Written and visual work by lesbians containing poetry, fiction, history, memoirs, correspondence, journal, photographs, drawings, drama, artwork, and essay.

US/1054-0296
COUPLES (BOSTON, MASS.). (COUPLES : A GAY & LESBIAN NEWSLETTER ON COUPLING.). [Couples]. Vol. 1, No. 1 (Mar. 1991)-. Newsletter. English. mo. $30.00. TWT Press, PO Box 155, Boston MA 02124-0002. **DD** 306.

US/1062-6247
DENEUVE (SAN FRANCISCO, CALIF.). (DENEUVE.). [Deneuve]. Vol. 1, No. 1 (May/June 1991)-. Periodical. English. bm. $24.00. FRS Enterprises, 4663 18th Street, San Francisco CA 94114. **DD** 305.

US/1055-7415
DRUMMER (SAN FRANCISCO, CALIF.). (DRUMMER.). [Drummer]. (1971)-. Periodical. English. mo. $70.00 North America; $110.00 other. Desmodus Inc, PO Box 410390, San Francisco CA 94141-0390. **Tel** (415)252-1195, FAX (415)252-9574. **ED** A F DeBlase and Joseph W Bean. **DD** 305. **Bk Rev. Ad Acc. Circ:** 30,000 (ctrl).
Desc: Leather lifestyles for gay men. Includes fiction, non-fiction, photos, and art.

US
DUNGEON MASTER. English. bm. $24.00 North America; $33.00 other. Desmodus Inc, PO Box 410390, San Francisco CA 94141-0390. **Tel** (415)252-1195, FAX (415)252-9574. **ED** A F DeBlase and T A Feldwebel. **Bk Rev. Ad Acc. Circ:** 7,000.
Desc: SM sexuality for gay men. Includes non-fiction: How to, safety, psychology, etc.

US/1043-3333
EVERGREEN CHRONICLES, THE. (1985)-Vol. 10 (1993)-. Periodical. English. Twice a year (June and December). $15.00 (individual), $20.00 (institution), US; $18.00 (individual), other; $12.00 Low income. Evergreen Chronicles, PO Box 8939, Minneapolis MN 55408. **Tel** (612)371-0382, FAX (612)371-0382. **ED** Jim Berg (612)649-4982. **DD** 810. Index available (Pulblished in June, $7.95). **Bk Rev**, (Qty: 5). **Ad Acc. Circ:** 2,000 (ctrl).

US/0046-3167
FAG RAG. [Fag rag]. (197?)-. Periodical. English. an. $10.00. Fag Rag, PO Box 331, Boston MA 02215. **Tel** (617)661-7534. **LC** HQ76.5; .F35. **DD** 306.
Ind/Abst Altern. Press Index.

●US/1078-0068
FERRARI'S PLACES OF INTEREST. [Ferrari's places interest]. **Added/Corp** Ferrari Publications (Firm). **VFOAT** Places of Interest. 13th Year (1992)-. English. an. $14.95. Ferrari Publications, PO Box 37887, Phoenix AZ 85069. **Tel** (602)863-2408. **LC** G1201.E63; P5. **DD** 910. ***Continues*** *Places of Interest, 0731-096x.*
Desc: Local experts tells about gay and lesbian life in cities around the world and what you, as a tourist, will encounter when you get there.

US/0744-6349
FIRST HAND. [First hand]. **VFOAT** Firsthand; First Hand Experiences for Loving Men. (19??)-. Periodical. English. Twelve times a year. $48.00. Jackie Lewis, PO Box 1314, Teaneck NJ 07666. **Tel** (201)836-9177. **ED** Jerry Douglas and Bob Harris. **Bk Rev. Ad Acc. Circ:** 70,000 (ctrl).
Desc: Gay men's first hand sexual experiences. Includes letters from readers and erotic fiction.

GW/0931-4091
FORUM HOMOSEXUALITAT UND LITERATURE. See Literature.

US
GALA REALIST. **VAT** Gay and Lesbian Atheists Realist. (Oct. 1989)-. Periodical. English. mo. Gay and Lesbian Atheists, PO Box 14142, San Francisco CA 94114. ***Continues*** *GALA Review.*

US
GAY AIRLINES & TRAVEL CLUB NEWSLETTER, THE. (19??)-. Newsletter. English. Four times a year. $20.00. Fan Club Publishing, PO Box 69A04, West Hollywood CA 90069. **Tel** (213)650-5112. **Bk Rev. Ad Acc. Circ:** 5,000.
Desc: Newsletter of the Gay Airline & Travel Club - a social organization for gay people seeking others interested in travel, collecting airline memorabilia, or who work in the airline or travel industries. Provides personal ads, articles, pictures, tours & excursions, parties, dinners & other social events.

CN/0226-0441
GAY CHRISTIAN WITNESS. (GAY CHRISTIAN WITNESS : AN OCCASIONAL PUBLICATION OF THE COUNCIL ON HOMOSEXUALITY AND RELIGION.). [Gay Christ. witness]. No. 1 (Mar. 1980)-. Periodical. English. Gay Christian Witness, PO Box 1912, Winnipeg Manitoba R3C 3R2 Canada. **DD** 261.8/3576.

US/0147-0728
GAY COMMUNITY NEWS (BOSTON, MASS.). ***Ceased.*** (GAY COMMUNITY NEWS.). [Gay community news]. **VFOAT** GCN. Vol. 1, No. 2 (June 28, 1973)-Vol. 19, No. 47/48, (1992). Periodical. English. wk. Gay Community News, 62 Berkeley Street, Boston MA 02116. **Tel** (617)426-4469. **LC** HQ75; .G37. **DD** 305. Documents available from UMI Article Clearinghouse. ***Continues*** *Gay Community Newsletter.*
Desc: This premier newsweekly is on the cutting edge of the gay/lesbian sexual liberation movement.
Ind/Abst Altern. Press Index; Expand. Acad. Index (1992-); Newsp. Period. Abstr. (1992-).

US/0730-3297
GAY/LESBIAN MEDIA DIRECTORY WORLDWIDE. [Gay/lesbian media dir. worldw.]. **VFOAT** Lesbian Media Directory Worldwide. **VAT** Gay Lesbian Media Directory Worldwide. (1981/82)-. Directory. English. Vox Populi Publications, PO Box 59154, Chicago IL 60659. **LC** HQ76.25; .G39. **DD** 016.3067/66/05.

US/0360-571X
GAY LUTHERAN, THE. **Added/Corp** Lutherans Concerned for Gay People. (July/Aug. 1974)-. Periodical. English. Ten times a year. Free on request. Lutherans Concerned, PO Box 19114A, Los Angeles CA 90019. **Tel** (213)663-7816.

CN/0381-6931
GAY MONTREAL. (1976)-. Periodical. French. wk. 0.50Can$ per number. Le Journal Gay Montreal, CP 568 Station Youville, Montreal Quebec H2P 2W1 Canada. **DD** 301.41/57/09714281.

UK
GAY NEWS. No. 1- 1972-. Periodical. English. bw. Gay News, 254 South 11th Street, Philadelphia PA 19107. **Tel** (215)625-8501, FAX (215)625-8501.

CN/0700-3536
GAY RISING. V. 1- Mar. 1975-. Periodical. English. ir. Gay Alliance Toward Equality, 193 Carlton Street, Toronto Ontario M5A 2K7 Canada. **DD** 301.41/57/0971.

UK
GAY TIMES. (19??)-. English. mo. £21.00 (UK); £48.00 (other). Millivres Ltd, 116-134 Bayham Street, London NW1 0BA England. **Tel** 11 44 71 2670021, FAX 01 44 71 2840329. ***Continues*** *Him Monthly; Gay News.*

UK/0950-6101
GAY TIMES LONDON. 1984. [Gay times Lond., 1984]. (19??)-. Periodical. English. mo. £21.00 (UK); £48.00 (other). Millivres Ltd, 116-134 Bayham Street, London NW1 0BA England. **Tel** 11 44 71 2670021, FAX 01 44 71 2840329. ***Continues*** *Him Monthly; Gay News.*

US
GAYELLOW PAGES. NORTHEAST ED. **VFOAT** Gay Yellow Pages. **VAT** Gay Yellow Pages. (1979)-. English. an. $10.00 US and Canada; $13.00 other. Renaissance House, Box 533 Village Station, New York NY 10014. **Tel** (212)674-0120. **ED** Frances Green. **Ad Acc. Circ:** 50,000.
Desc: Directory of services and businesses for the gay and lesbian community in USA and Canada.

CN/0712-3221
GENOS (WINNIPEG, MAN.). (GENOS : A GENDER-GENOCIDE.). [Genos]. Periodical. English. mo. Project Lambda, 299 Kennedy Street, Winnipeg Manitoba, R3B 2M7 Canada. **DD** 051.

US
GENRE. Vol. 1, No. 1 (Spring 1991)-. Periodical. English. mo (Dec./Jan. and Jul./Aug. issues combined). $19.95. Genre, 8033 Sunset Boulevard, #261, Los Angeles CA 90046. **Tel** (213)645-2115. **LC** WMLC 93/1073.

US/1059-065X
GLBAMES NEWSLETTER. [GLBAmes newsl.]. **Main/Corp** Gays, Lesbians, and Bisexuals of Ames. **VFOAT** GLBAmes; GLB Ames Newsletter. **VAT** Gays Lesbians and Bisexuals of Ames Newsletter. (April 1991)-. Newsletter. English. mo. $7.00. GLB Ames, PO Box 2283, Ames IA 50010-2283. ***Continues*** *GLA Newsletter, 1041-7729.*

●US/1068-0586
GLOBAL CITY REVIEW. See Literary and Political Reviews.

●US/1064-2684
GLQ (NEW YORK, N.Y.). (GLQ : A JOURNAL OF LESBIAN AND GAY STUDIES.). **VAT** Gay Lesbian Quarterly. (1992)-. Periodical. English. qt. $79.00 (academic institutions), $122.00 (corporate institutions). Gordon & Breach Science Publishers, Inc., PO Box 786, Cooper Station, New York NY 10276. **Tel** (212)206-8900, FAX (212)645-2459. **(Subscription address:** International Publishers Distributor at one of the following addresses: 820 Town Center Drive, Langhorne, PA 19047; or PO Box 90, Reading Berkshire RG1 8JL UK; or Kent Ridge PO Box 1180, Singapore 9111, Republic of Singapore) **[CCC].**
Desc: Publishes scholarship, criticism and commentary in the rapidly expanding interdisciplinary field of gay and lesbian studies.

CN/0315-0151
GO INFO. **Main/Corp** Gays of Ottawa. (July 1972)-. Periodical. English (French). mo (July/Aug. and Dec./Jan. issues combined). 17.50Can$ Canada; 18.00Can$ other. Association of Lesbians & Gays of Ottawa, PO Box 2919 Station D, Ottawa Ontario K1P 5W9 Canada. **Tel** (613)233-0152.

US/0145-5400
GPU NEWS. **Main/Corp** Gay Peoples Union. **VAT** Gap Peoples Union News. (1971)-. Periodical. English. mo. $10.00. Liberations Publicatons Inc, PO Box 92203, Milwaukee WI 53202.

●US
GSBA GUIDE/DIRECTORY. **Main/Corp** Greater Seattle Business Association. **VFOAT** GSBA Guide Directory; Greater Seattle Business Association Guide Directory. (1992)-. English. GSBA, PO Box 20263, Seattle WA 98102. **LC** HF296.S6; G73. ***Continues*** *GSBA Directory.*

US/1069-5281
HOTHEAD PAISAN. (HOTHEAD PAISAN, HOMICIDAL LESBIAN TERRORIST.). **VFOAT** Giant Ass Publishing Presentz Hothead Paisan, Homicidal Lesbian Terrorist. (1991)-. Periodical. English. qt. $14.00. Giant Ass Publishing, Box 214, New Haven CT 06502. **DD** 305. **Circ:** 5,000.

NE
ILGA PINK BOOK. **VFOAT** I.L.G.A. Pink Book. (1988)-. English. Homostudies RUU, Postbus 80140, 3508 TC, Utrecht The Netherlands. **Tel** 030-534779. **LC** HQ76.5; .I43. **DD** 306.7/66/05. **Bk Rev. Ad Acc.** ***Continues*** *Pink Book.*

US/0891-7140
JOURNAL OF GAY & LESBIAN PSYCHOTHERAPY. [J. gay lesbian psychother.]. **VFOAT** Journal of Gay and Lesbian Psychotherapy. Vol. 1, No. 1 (1989)-. Periodical. English. qt. $75.00 US; $105.00 other. The Haworth Press Inc, 10 Alice Street, Binghamton NY 13904-1580. **Tel** (607)722-5857, (800)3-HAWORTH, FAX (607)722-1424. **ED** David Scasta (editor's address: 1439 Pineville Road, New Hope, PA 18938). **LC** RC558; .J68. **DD** 616.85/83406. **NLM** W1; JO663M. **CODEN** JGLPE9. **Bk Rev. Ad Acc. Pr Rev. Acid Free. Circ:** 1,018. available on microfilm and microfiche from University Microfilms International (UMI). Documents available from UMI Article Clearinghouse, Haworth Document Delivery Service.
Desc: A practical, multidisciplinary forum for the exposition and discussion of issues relating to the use of psychotherapy with gay, lesbian, and bisexual clients. The journal is divided into two sections: a clinical section and an experimental section with emphasis on the clinical applications.
Ind/Abst Abstr. Anthropol. (19??-); Abstr. Res. Pastor. Care Couns. (19??-); Expand. Acad. Index (1992-); Newsp. Period. Abstr. (1989-); Psychol. Abstr. (1989-); PsycLit; Sage Fam. Stud. Abstr.; Soc. Plann. Policy Dev. Abstr.; Soc. Work Abstr. [Select. Cov.]; Stud. Women Abstr.

●US/1053-8720
JOURNAL OF GAY & LESBIAN SOCIAL SERVICES. **VFOAT** Journal of Gay and Lesbian Social Services. (1992)-. Periodical. English. qt. $60.00 US: $84.00 other. The Haworth Press Inc, 10 Alice Street, Binghamton NY 13904-1580. **Tel** (607)722-5857, (800)3-HAWORTH, FAX (607)722-1424. **ED** James J. Kelley (editor's address: Department of Social Work, California State University, 1250 Bellflower Boulevard,

Long Beach, CA 90840), and Raymond M. Berger. **Bk Rev. Ad Acc. Pr Rev. Acid Free.** available on microfiche. Documents available from Haworth Document Delivery Service.
Desc: In the field of social welfare. Focuses on a wide variety of policy, program, and practice issues aims to promote the well-being of homosexuals and bisexuals in contemporary society.
Ind/Abst Index Period. Artic. Relat. Law; Soc. Work Abstr.; Stud. Women Abstr.

US/0091-8369
JOURNAL OF HOMOSEXUALITY. [J. homosex.]. Vol. 1 (Fall 1974)-. Academic Scholarly Publication. English. qt (Published during the academic year). $200.00 US; $280.00 other. The Haworth Press Inc, 10 Alice Street, Binghamton NY 13904-1580. **Tel** (607)722-5857, (800)3-HAWORTH, FAX (607)722-1424. **ED** John Dececco (editor's address: San Francisco State University, Psychology Building, Room 502, San Francisco, CA 94132). **LC** HQ75; .J68. **DD** 301.41/57/05. **NLM** W1 JO672H. **CODEN** JOHOD7. **Bk Rev. Ad Acc. Pr Rev. Acid Free. Circ:** 822. available on microfilm and microfiche from University Microfilms International (UMI). Documents available from The Genuine Article, BIOSIS Document Express, UMI Article Clearinghouse, Haworth Document Delivery Service.
Desc: Devoted to theoretical, empirical, and historical research on homosexuality, heterosexuality, sexual identity, social sex roles, and the sexual relationships of both men and women.
Ind/Abst Abstr. Anthropol.; Abstr. Soc. Gerontol.; Abstr. Res. Pastor. Care Couns. (19??-); Acad. Ind. [Computer File] (1992-); Acad. Search (Jan. 1993-); Appl. Soc. Sci. Index Abstr.; Arts Humanit. Citation Index [Select. Cov.]; Biol. Abstr.; Crim. Justice Abstr.; Crim. Penol. Police Sci. Abstr.; Curr. Contents Soc. Behav. Sci.; EMBASE; Expand. Acad. Index (1989-); High. Educ. Abstr. (1977-); Hum. Resour. Abstr. (?-?); Index Med.; Index Book Rev. Relig.; Index Period. Artic. Relat. Law; INFO-SOUTH Abstr.; Mag. Search; Middle East Abstr. Index; Newsp. Period. Abstr. (1991-); PAIS Int. Print (1991-); Psychol. Abstr. (1974-); PsycINFO; PsycLit; Relig. Index One Period.; Res. Alert [Full Cov.]; Sage Fam. Stud. Abstr.; Soc. Plann. Policy Dev. Abstr.; Soc. Sci. Source (Jul. 1993-); Soc. Sci. Cit. Index [Full Cov.]; Soc. Sci. Index Fulltext (1988-) [Full Txt.]; Soc. Work Abstr. [Select. Cov.]; Sociol. Abstr.; Stud. Women Abstr.

US/0145-2398
KALOS. (KALOS: ON GREEK LOVE.). Vol. 1 (Spring 1976)-. Periodical. English. Three times a year. $8.50. Comita, PO Box 7071, Arlington VA 22207. **LC** HQ75; .K34. **DD** 301.41/57/05.

GW
KATALOG DER BIBLIOTHEK FUER INTERNATIONALE SCHULE ZEITSCHRIFTEN. (1987)-. German.

US/1048-9487
LAMBDA BOOK REPORT. [Lambda book rep.]. **Added/Corp** Lambda Rising, Inc. **VFOAT** Book Report. Vol. 2, No. 3 (Feb./Mar. 1990)-. Periodical. English. bm. $19.95 (one year), $34.95 (two year). Lambda Rising Inc, 1625 Connecticut Avenue Northwest, Washington DC 20009. **Tel** (202)462-7924, FAX (202)462-7257. **ED** Jim Marks. **LC** PN56.H57; L36. **DD** 809/.93353. **Bk Rev**, (Qty: 420). **Ad Acc, Adv Mgr:** L. Smith. **Circ:** 9,000. Documents available from UMI Article Clearinghouse. ***Continues** Lambda Rising Book Report, 0894-1416.*
Desc: Reviews all new gay and lesbian books published. Also includes information on books, trends, authors, and serious literary criticisms. Every new gay or lesbian book appears in each issue.
Ind/Abst Book Rev. Index; Newsp. Period. Abstr. (1989-).

US/1062-0680
LAW & SEXUALITY. (LAW & SEXUALITY : A REVIEW OF LESBIAN AND GAY LEGAL ISSUES.). [Law sex.]. **Added/Corp** Tulane Law School. **VFOAT** Law and Sexuality. Vol. 1 (Summer 1991)-. Periodical. English. an. $20.00 (institutions), $12.00 (individuals). Tulane University School of Law, 6801 Freret Street, New Orleans LA 70118. **Tel** (504)865-5990. **LC** K12; .A863. **DD** 346.7301/3/05; 347.3061305.
Ind/Abst Index Leg. Period. (1992-).

CN/1064-5950
LESBIAN AND GAY STUDIES NEWSLETTER : LGSN. [Lesbian gay stud. newsl.]. **Added/Corp** Gay and Lesbian Caucus for the Modern Languages. **VFOAT** LGSN. Vol. 16, No. 2 (July 1989)-. Newsletter. English. Three times a year (Mar., July, Nov.). $12.00 (individual); $20.00 (institution). Duke University Department of English, PO Box 90021, Durham NC 27709-0021. **Tel** (919)684-6508, FAX (919)684-4871. **ED** Shelton Waldrep. **DD** 305. **[CCC]. Bk Rev. Ad Acc. Circ:** 600 (ctrl). ***Continues** Gay Studies Newsletter, 1184-4752.*
Desc: The LGSN is one of the oldest continuously publishing gay or lesbian publications in the world. It is arguably the most important academic publication in the field of gay/lesbian /bisexual studies coming out of North America.

US/1064-4776
LESBIAN CONTRADICTION. [Lesbian contradict.]. **VFOAT** LESCON. (198?)-. Periodical. English. qt. $8.00 (individuals), $15.00 (institutions) US; $12.00 (individuals), $19.00 (institutions) Canada; $16.00 (individuals), $23.00 (institutions) other. Lesbian Contradiction, 584 Castro Street, Suite 356, San Francisco CA 94114. **ED** Jan Adams, Rebecca Gordon, and Angie Fa. **DD** 305. **Bk Rev**, (Qty: 8). **Circ:** 2,500. available on audiocassette.
Desc: A journal of irreverent feminism, by and for women who agree to disagree. Contains humor, commentary, analysis, and cartoons.
Ind/Abst Altern. Press Index.

US/8755-5352
LESBIAN ETHICS. **See** Ethics.

US/8755-9021
LESBIAN-GAY LAW NOTES. **See** Law.

US/1064-0819
LESBIAN HERSTORY ARCHIVES NEWSLETTER. [Lesbian Herstory Arch. newsl.]. **Added/Corp** Lesbian Herstory Educational Foundation. **VFOAT** Lesbian Herstory Archives News. (Mar. 1976)-. Newsletter. English. Twice a year. $10.00. Lesbian Herstory Education Foundation Inc, PO Box 1258, New York NY 10116. **Tel** (718)768-3953. **ED** Beth Haskell. **DD** 305. **Circ:** 8,000-10,000. ***Continues** Lesbian Herstory Archives.*
Desc: Newsletter about the work and holdings of the Lesbian Herstory Archives. Each issue includes a bibliography.

US/0739-1803
LESBIAN NEWS (CANOGA PARK, CALIF.), THE. (LESBIAN NEWS.). No. 1 Aug. (1975)-. Periodical. English. mo. $45.00. Lesbian News, PO Box 1430, Palm CA 92277. **Tel** (213)656-0258 ext. 113. **ED** Deborah Bergman. **Bk Rev. Ad Acc. Circ:** 90,000 (ctrl).
Desc: The nation's leading monthly magazine with news and features of interest to lesbians.

US/0361-5928
LESBIAN READER, THE. 1st- Ed.; Dec. 1975-. Periodical. English. qt. $4.50. Amazon Press, 395 60th Street, Oakland CA 94618. **LC** HQ75; .L45. **DD** 301.41/57.

●US/1077-5684
LESBIAN REVIEW OF BOOKS, THE. (1994)-. Periodical. English. Four times a year. $10.00. Lesbian Review of Books, PO Box 6369, Altadena CA 91003. **Tel** (818)398-4200.

CN/0712-8398
LESBO (MONTREAL). ***Ceased.*** (LESBO.). [Lesbo]. (1979)-(199?). Periodical. French. Editions De L'Oree, 3600 Boul Du Trichentenaire, Montreal Quebec H1B 5M8 Canada. **DD** 306.7/663/05.

US
MACH. (19??)-. English. qt. $26.00 North America; $40.00 other. Desmodus Inc, PO Box 410390, San Francisco CA 94141-0390. **Tel** (415)252-1195, FAX (415)252-9574. **ED** A. F. DeBlase and Joseph W. Bean. **Ad Acc. Circ:** 10,000 (ctrl).
Desc: Leather S&M fiction, art and photos for gay men.

US
MALCHUS : THE NATION'S LESBIAN & GAY CHRISTIAN MONTHLY. English. mo. $18.00. MALCHUS Lesbian & Gay Christian Monthly Journal, 6036 Richmond Highway, Suite 301, Alexandria VA 22303. **Tel** (703)329-7896. **Circ:** 1,100.

US
MEN OF ALL COLORS TOGETHER CHICAGO : [NEWSLETTER]. Main/Corp MACT Chicago. (May 1991)-. Periodical. English. mo. ***Continues** BWMT-Chicago.*

US/1072-8112
MILITARY & POLICE UNIFORM ASSOCIATION NEWSLETTER, THE. (1988)-. Newsletter. English. Four times a year. $20.00. Fan Club Publishing, PO Box 69A04, West Hollywood CA 90069. **Tel** (213)650-5112. **ED** Louis Wendruck. **Bk Rev. Ad Acc. Circ:** 1,000.
Desc: Newsletter of the Military & Police Uniform Association - a social organization for gay men seeking others interested in uniforms and the uniform lifestyle. Offers personal ads, articles, photos, stories and trading/for sale ads and social events.

US
MOM ... GUESS WHAT ... !. No. 1- Nov. 1978-. Periodical. English. mo. $15.00. Mom...Guess What!, 1725 L Street NW, Sacramento CA 95814-4023. **Tel** (916)441-6397. **Bk Rev. Ad Acc. Circ:** 21,000 (ctrl).
Desc: Gay news, reviews and political news.

US/0164-8381
NEW DAWN (NEW YORK). (NEW DAWN.). (197?)-. Periodical. English. bm. $7.50. New Dawn, PO Box 1849, Alexandria VA 22313-1849.

US/0744-060X
NEW YORK NATIVE. (1980)-. Periodical. English. wk. $49.00 US; $74.00 other. That New Magazine Inc., 28 West 25th Street, 4th Floor, New York NY 10159. **Tel** (212)627-2120, FAX (212)727-9321. **(Subscription address:** Christopher Street Magazine, PO Box 1475, Church Street Station, New York NY 10008.) **ED** John Hammond. **Bk Rev. Ad Acc. Circ:** 12,000 (ctrl).
Desc: Covering arts and news of interest to the gay and lesbian community. Investigative reporting on AIDS. Source of non-establishment information on epidemic.

US/0890-2224
ON OUR BACKS. [On our backs]. Vol. 1 (1984)-. Periodical. English. bm (6 issues). $34.95 US; $42.95 Canada; $59.95 other. On Our Backs, 526 Castro, San Francisco CA 94114. **Tel** (415)861-4723. **ED** Debi Sundahl. **LC** HQ75; .O5. **DD** 305.48/9664. Index available. cum. index. **Bk Rev**, (Qty: 20-40). **Ad Acc, Adv Mgr:** Marnie De Bois. **Circ:** 12,000(print), 36,000(readership).
Desc: Entertainment for the adventurous lesbian. Articles are authentic, intelligent, humorous and lusty.

US/0888-8833
OPEN HANDS. (OPEN HANDS : JOURNAL OF THE RECONCILING CONGREGATION PROGRAM.). [Open hands]. **Added/Corp** Affirmation: United Methodists for Lesbian/Gay Concerns. Vol. 2, No. 1 (Summer 1986)-. Periodical. English. Four times a year. $16.00 US; $20.00 other. Open Hands, 3801 North Keeler Avenue, Chicago IL 60641. **Tel** (312)736-5475, FAX (312)736-5526. **ED** Mary Jo Ostermen (editor's address: PO Box 2374 Boulder CO 80306; editor's phone: (303)666-8322). **DD** 287. Index available. **Bk Rev**, (Qty: 3-4). **Ad Acc. Circ:** 1,500. ***Continues** Manna for the Journey, 0884-8327.*

US
OUR OWN. English. mo (12 issues per year). $14.00 3rd Class Postage; $20.00 1st Class Postage. Our Own Inc, 739 Yarmouth Street, Norfolk VA 23510. **Tel** (804)625-0700, FAX (804)625-6024. **ED** Patrick Evans. **Bk Rev**, (Qty: 30). **Ad Acc, Adv Mgr:** Michelle Romano. **Circ:** 10,000 (ctrl).
Desc: Directed to the lesbian, gay and bisexual community.

US/1044-6699
OUR WORLD (DAYTONA BEACH, FLA.). **See** Travel and Tourism.

●US/1066-7776
OUT & ABOUT (NEW HAVEN, CONN.). (OUT & ABOUT.). [Out about]. **VFOAT** Out and About. (1992)-. Newsletter. English. Ten times a year. $49.00 US; $59.00 Canada and Mexico; $69.00 other. Out & About, 542 Chapel Street, New Haven CT 06511. **Tel** (203)789-8518, FAX (203)789-8759. **ED** Billy Kolber. **DD** 306. Index available (published separately). cum. index. **Bk Rev**, (Qty: 6/year). **Circ:** 3,500 (ctrl).
Desc: A travel newsletter for the gay and lesbian community.

NZ/0110-4454
OUT AUCKLAND. [OutAuckl.]. (1977)-. Periodical. English. Six times a year. 30.00NZ$ New Zealand; 40.00NZ$ other. Lawrence Publishing Company Ltd., Private Bag 92126, Auckland 1 New Zealand. **Tel** 011 64 9 3779031, FAX 011 64 9 3777767. **ED** Brett Sheppard. **Bk Rev. Ad Acc.** ctrl circ. ***Continues** New Zealand Gay News, 0110-0238.*
Desc: Gay community publication for New Zealand.

US/0896-7733
OUT/LOOK (SAN FRANCISCO, CALIF.). ***Ceased.*** (OUT/LOOK.). [Outlook]. **VFOAT** Outlook; Out Look. (1988)-(19??). Periodical. English. qt. Out/Look National Lesbian and Gay Quarterly, PO Box 146430, San Francisco CA 94114. **ED** Jan Zita Grover. **Bk Rev. Ad Acc. Circ:** 15,000. Documents available from UMI Article Clearinghouse.
Desc: Forum of political and cultural discussion of issues for the lesbian and gay community.
Ind/Abst Access (19??-1992); Altern. Press Index (-1992); Book Rev. Index; Gen. Period. Index (1985-?); Mag. Index Plus (1991-); Newsp. Period. Abstr. (1990-).

●US/1062-7928
OUT (NEW YORK, N.Y.). (OUT.). [Out]. (1992)-. English. Ten times a year. $24.95 (one year), $39.95 (two years) US; $31.00 (per year) Canada; $37.00 (per year) other. Out Magazine, PO Box 1935, Marion OH 43306-2035. **Tel** (212)334-9119, FAX (212)334-9227. **ED**

Homosexuality

Sara Petit. **Bk Rev**, (Qty: 3). **Ad Acc**, **Adv Mgr:** Harry Taylor, **Tel** (212)334-9119. **Circ:** 85,000.
Desc: Each issue opens with short personality pieces and pop culture blurbs, followed by journalistic features and interviews from three to six pages each, and closes with a piece on fashion and sundry food, advice, and horoscope columns. Looks at the world from a gay point of view rather than just covering the gay and lesbian community.

NE/0167-5907
PAIDIKA. Vol. 1, No. 1 (Summer 1987)-. Periodical. English. sa. $65.00. Paidika, Postbus 22630, 1100 DC Amsterdam Netherlands.

US/0731-096X
PLACES OF INTEREST. Title Change. [Places interest]. **Added/Corp** Ferrari Publications (Firm). **VFOAT** Map Guide USA and Canada. (1980)-(199?). English (French, German and Spanish). an. Ferrari Publications, PO Box 37887, Phoenix AZ 85069. **Tel** (602)863-2408. **LC** G1201.E63; P5. **DD** 910. **Continued by** Ferrari's Places of Interest, 1078-0068.
Desc: Local experts tells about gay and lesbian life in cities around the world and what you, as a tourist, will encounter when you get there.

US/1054-6804
PUTTING OUT : A PUBLISHING RESOURCE GUIDE FOR LESBIAN & GAY WRITERS. See Literature.

CN/0824-0965
QUEBEC G. [Que. G]. **VAT** Quebec Gai (1984). Summer 1984-. Periodical. French. mo. $2.50 per no. Productions Visuelles TYM, CP 941, Succursale Desjardins Montreal, Quebec H5B 1C1 Canada. **DD** 306.7/662/09714. **Continues** QG : Quebec Gai, 0824-0957.

US/1064-4059
QUEST : FOR A POSITIVE LIFESTYLE. **VFOAT** Quest Magazine. (May 1988)-. English. Twelve times a year. $24.00. DPBBB Enterprises Inc. / Quest, 432 South Broadway, Denver CO 80209. **Tel** (303)722-5965. **ED** Steve Cruz. **Bk Rev**, (Qty: 12/year). **Ad Acc. Circ:** 10,000.
Desc: Arts and entertainment news directed to the Colorado gay community.

CN/0712-838X
RENCONTRES GAIES. [Rencontres gaies]. Vol. 1, No. 1 Jan. 1982-. Periodical. French. $1.50 per number. Rencontres Gaies, CP 245, Succursale N, Montreal Quebec H2X 3M4 Canada. **DD** 306.7/662/09714.

US/0149-709X
RFD (WOLF CREEK). (RFD.). [RFD]. **VAT** Recruiting Feminist Drakes. (1974)-. Periodical. English. qt (Mar., June, Sept., Dec.). $18.00 (1 year), $34.00 (2 years). RFD, PO Box 68, Liberty TN 37095. **Tel** (615)536-5176. **ED** Ron Lambe. **DD** 810. **Bk Rev. Ad Acc. Circ:** 2,800 (ctrl). available on microfiche.
Desc: Country journal for gay men everywhere. Focuses on country living and alternative lifestyles exploring environmental concerns and gay men's experiences.
Ind/Abst Altern. Press Index.

CN/0831-375X
RG. (RG : REVUE GAIE.). [RG]. **VFOAT** Revue Gaie; Mensuel RG. Periodical. French. mo. $40.00, $3.00 (single issues). RG, Box 5245 Station C, Montreal Quebec H2X 3M4 Canada. **Tel** (514)523-9463. **DD** 306.7/662/09714. **Bk Rev. Ad Acc. Circ:** 25,000. available on diskette.
Desc: Includes topics on cinema, culture, music, novel, erotica, news, editorial, travel, and correspondence club.

UK/0958-188X
ROUGE. Issue 1 (Winter 1989/1990)-. Periodical. English. qt.

US
SAN FRANCISCO SENTINEL. See Newspapers.

US/1047-3971
SECOND STONE, THE. (THE SECOND STONE : THE NATIONAL NEWSPAPER FOR GAY AND LESBIAN CHRISTIANS.). [Second stone]. **VFOAT** Second Stone Newspaper. No. 1 (Nov. 1988)-. Periodical. English. Six times a year (Jan., Mar., May, July, Sept., Nov.). $15.00. Bailey Communications, PO Box 8340, New Orleans LA 70182. **Tel** (504)899-4014, **FAX** (504)891-7555. **ED** Jim Bailey. **DD** 051. **Bk Rev**, (Qty: 6). **Ad Acc, Adv Mgr:** J. Bailey, **Tel** (504)891-7555. ctrl circ.
Desc: The christian newsletter for the gays and lesbians.

CN
SHARE. (19??)-. English (French). qt. 10.00Can$. Share, Box 3357, Courtenay British Columbia V9N 5N5 Canada. **Tel** (604)335-2362. **ED** Arthur Corry. **Bk Rev. Ad Acc. Circ:** 300 (ctrl). available with illustrations.
Desc: Articles on the senior gay culture.

US/0196-1853
SINISTER WISDOM. [Sinister wisdom]. (July 1976)-. Periodical. English. Three times a year (Apr., Aug., Dec.). $30.00. Sinister Wisdom, PO Box 3252, Berkeley CA 94703. **Tel** (510)534-2335. **ED** Elana Dykewomon (editor's telephone: (510)562-2605). **LC** PS508.W7; S54. **DD** 810/.8/09287. **Bk Rev**, (Qty: 1-6). **Ad Acc, Adv Mgr:** Jamie Lee Evans. **Circ:** 3,500. available on audiocassette.
Desc: A journal for the lesbian imagination in the arts and politics.
Ind/Abst Altern. Press Index (?-199?); Index Am. Period. Verse; Romant. Move.

CN/0714-7376
SORTIE (MONTREAL). (SORTIE.). [Sortie]. No. 1 (Oct. 1982)-. Periodical. French. Six times a year. Studio Bograf Inc, 180 Ste-Catherine est, Bureau 624, Montreal Quebec H2X 1K3 Canada. **Tel** (514)871-1424. **DD** 306.7/66/05. Index available. **Bk Rev. Ad Acc. Circ:** 5,000 (ctrl). available on diskette.

CN/0708-109X
STANDOUT MAGAZINE. **VFOAT** Standout. Sept. 1978-. Periodical. English. mo. $10.00 Canada; $12.00 other. Outstanding Productions, PO Box 5071 Station A, Toronto Ontario M5W 1N4 Canada. **DD** 301.41/57/05.

●US/1070-0161
(THE) BRAVE NEW TICK. [Brave new tick]. Vol. 1, Issue 1 (Mar. 1993)-. Periodical. English. mo. Free. Graftographic Press, Box 24, S, Grafton MA 01560-0024. **Tel** (508)799-3769. **ED** Paul N. Dion. **DD** 051. **Ad Acc. Circ:** 85. **Continues** Bloated Tick.
Desc: Includes articles on gay rights, gay issues, art, poetry, and commentary.

US/1046-9613
TRIBE (BALTIMORE, MD.). (TRIBE : AN AMERICAN GAY JOURNAL.). [Tribe]. Vol. 1, No. 1 (Winter 1990)-. Periodical. English. Four times a year. $28.00. Columbia Publishing Company / Maryland, 234 East 25th Street, Baltimore MD 21218. **Tel** (301)366-7070. **DD** 810.
Desc: Gay literary journal, that offers about 100 carefully edited and printed essays, poems, and stories.

US/1063-2697
VANGUARD (EDUCATION INFORMATION NETWORK (LOS ANGELES, CALIF.)). Ceased. (VANGUARD : NEWS & VIEWS.). [Vanguard]. **Added/Corp** Education Information Network (Los Angeles, Calif.). (1990)-(19??). Periodical. English. bw. Education Information Network, PO Box 931898, Los Angeles CA 90028. **Tel** (213)466-1363. **DD** 305.

SA/0256-7008
VECTOR KLOOF. [VectorKloof]. (1975)-. Periodical. English. mo. R54.54 South Africa; $90.54 other. Pulse Publications Pty Ltd, Box 1884, Johannesburg 2000 South Africa. **Tel** 27 21 8352221, **FAX** 27 21 8351943. **ED** Johann Barnard. **UDC** 621.3. **Ad Acc.**
Ind/Abst Ei Page One.

US/0892-7375
VISIBILITIES. Ceased. [Visibilities]. Periodical. English. bm. Visibility Press Ltd, PO Box 1258 Peter Stuyvesant Station, New York NY 10009-1258. **Tel** (212)473-4635. **ED** Susan T Chasin. **DD** 051. **Bk Rev. Ad Acc. Circ:** 5,000 (ctrl).
Desc: A magazine by, for and about lesbians.

●US/1065-2914
VOICES (RENO, NEV.). (VOICES.). [Voices]. **VFOAT** Lesbian Voices. (Aug. 1992)-. Periodical. English. mo. $18.00. Triangle Impact Enterprises, PO Box 6923, Reno NV 89513-6923. **DD** 305.

US/0199-4395
WEEKLY NEWS (MIAMI, FLA.), THE. (THE WEEKLY NEWS : TWN.). [Wkly. news]. **Added/Corp** Dade County Coalition for Human Rights. **VFOAT** TWN. (197?)-. Newspaper. English. Fifty-two times a year (Wednesdays). $78.00. Weekly News, Inc., 901 NE 79th Street, Miami FL 33138. **Tel** (305)757-6333, **FAX** (305)756-6488. **ED** George Ferencz. **DD** 071. **Bk Rev. Ad Acc. Circ:** 32,000.
Desc: A weekly gay newspaper.

CN/0712-4279
WILDE TIMES. (WILDE TIMES / OSCAR WILDE MEMORIAL SOCIETY.). [Wilde times]. Oct. 1980-. Periodical. English. mo. Free. The Society / Wilde Times, Box 221, Winnipeg Manitoba R3C 3R5 Canada. **DD** 306.7/66/05.

US
WOMEN'S TRAVELLER. See Travel and Tourism.

●US/1064-489X
WORKING IT OUT. See Economics-Labor.

ABSTRACTING, BIBLIOGRAPHIES AND STATISTICS

US/1043-3333
EVERGREEN CHRONICLES, THE. See Homosexuality.

US/1047-3971
SECOND STONE, THE. See Homosexuality.

HORSES AND HORSEMANSHIP

US
ALABAMA THOROUGHBRED JOURNAL. **VFOAT** Alabama Thoroughbred Journal and Standardbred News. 1984-. English. mo. Alabama Thoroughbred, 1000 Financial Center, Birmingham AL 35203.

CN/1184-163X
ALBERTA STABLE DIRECTORY. [Alta. stable dir.]. **Added/Corp** Alberta. Alberta Agriculture. Alberta. Horse Industry Branch. (1990)-. Directory. English. **DD** 636.1/083/0257123.

CN/0227-0579
ALBERTA WILD ROSE QUARTER HORSE JOURNAL. (ALBERTA WILD ROSE QUARTER HORSE JOURNAL : OFFICIAL PUBLICATION OF THE ALBERTA QUARTER HORSE ASSOCIATION.). [Alta. wild rose quart. horse j.]. **Added/Corp** Quarter Horse Association of Alberta. **VFOAT** Quarter Horse Journal. **VAT** Quarter Horse Journal (Nanton). (Feb. 1981)-. Periodical. English. mo. 13.00Can$. Quarter Horse Association of Alberta, PO Box 9, Highway 800, Hill Spring Alberta T0K 1E0 Canada. **Tel** (403)626-3613, **FAX** (403)626-3600. **ED** Jacki French. **DD** 636.1/33/097123. **Bk Rev. Ad Acc. Circ:** 10,000 (ctrl). **Continues** Wild Rose Quarter Horse Country, 0228-0760.
Desc: Show and sale results, coming events listings, veterinary updates, profiles of youth, amateur and regular owners and trainers.

US/0274-6565
AMERICAN FARRIERS' JOURNAL. **Added/Corp** American Farrier's Association. American Farrier's Association. Newsletter. (197?)-. English. Six times a year (Nov.). $42.95. American Farriers Journal, PO Box 624, Brookfield WI 53008. **Tel** (414)782-4480, **FAX** (414)782-1252. **ED** Frank Lessiter. **DD** 682. [CCC]. **Ad Acc, Adv Mgr:** Alice Musser. **Circ:** 4,000 (ctrl).
Desc: Devoted to the farrier and his craft of horseshoeing.

US/0897-1498
AMERICAN HORSES IN SPORT. [Am. horses sport]. (1987)-. English. an. $5.00. Chronicle of the Horse Inc, PO Box 46, Middleburg VA 22117. **Tel** (703)687-6341, **FAX** (703)687-3937. **ED** John Strassburger. **LC** SF294.25; .A46. **DD** 798.2/0973. **Ad Acc. Circ:** 24,000. available on microfilm.
Desc: A review of the year for Grand Prix Jumping, combined training, show hunters, dressage and driving, plus profiles of the horse and horseman of the year in each discipline.

US
AMERICAN RACING MANUAL, THE. (1906)-. Periodical. English. an. $70.00. Daily Racing Form Inc, 10 Lake Drive, Hightstown NJ 08520. **Tel** (609)448-9100. **LC** SF325; .A5. **Continues** American Sporting Manual.

US/0162-0568
AMERICAN STEEPLECHASING. 1st- Ed.; 1977-. English. National Steeplechase & Hunt Association, Box 308, Elmont NY 11003. **LC** SF359.3.U6; A44. **Supersedes** Steeplechasing in America.

US/0730-2975
AMERICAN TRAKEHNER, THE. **Added/Corp** American Trakehner Association. (19??)-. Periodical. English. qt. $15.00 US; $25.00 other. American Trakehner Association, 1520 West Church Street, Newark OH 43055. **LC** Discard.

US/0003-1445
AMERICAN TURF MONTHLY. [Am. turf mon.]. (1946)-. Periodical. English. mo. 29.00 (one year), $50.00 (two year). American Turf Monthly, 306 Broadway, Lynbrook NY 11563. **Tel** (800)645-2240, **FAX** (516)569-0451. **ED** Ian Blair (editor's phone: (800)666-9488). **DD** 798. **Bk Rev. Ad Acc.** ctrl circ.

Desc: Nations largest thorougbred handicapping magazine includes systems, angles, features handicapping hints.

US
ANNUAL REPORT, HORSE RACING, HARNESS RACING. **Main/Corp** Pennsylvania. State Horse Racing Commission. **VFOAT** Horse Racing, Harness Racing, Annual Report; Annual Report, Harness Racing; Annual Report, Horse Racing. (1988)-. English. State Horse Racing Commission, Commonwealth of Pennsylvania, No. 2 Riverside Office Center, 2101 North Front Street, Harrisburg PA 17110. ***Formed by the union of*** *Pennsylvania. State Harness Racing Commission. Annual Report* ***and*** *Pennsylvania. State Horse Racing Commission. Annual Report of the Pennsylvania State Horse Racing Commission to Governor ... .*

US
ANNUAL REPORT OF THE CALIFORNIA HORSE RACING BOARD FOR THE PERIOD JULY 1 ... TO JUNE 30 ... . **Main/Corp** California Horse Racing Board. **VFOAT** Horse Racing in California. 6th (1975-1976)-. English. an. **LC** SF335.U6; C18. **DD** 353.97940085/8. ***Continues*** *Annual Report to the Governor and to the Legislature of the State of California.*

US
ANNUAL REPORT OF THE DELAWARE RACING COMMISSION TO THE GOVERNOR OF THE STATE OF DELAWARE. **Main/Corp** Delaware Racing Commission. English. an. Delaware Racing Commission, Delaware State Office Building, 820 French Street/3rd Level, Wilmington DE 19801. **Tel** (302)571-3288. **LC** SF335.U6; D44. **DD** 353.97510085/8. ctrl circ.

US
ANNUAL REPORT OF THE DELAWARE THOROUGHBRED RACING COMMISSION TO THE GOVERNOR OF THE STATE OF DELAWARE. **Main/Corp** Delaware Thoroughbred Racing Commission. English. an. Delaware Racing Commission, Delaware State Office Building, 820 French Street/3rd Level, Wilmington DE 19801. **Tel** (302)571-3288. **LC** SF335.U6; D45A. **DD** 353.97510085/8.

US/0083-3517
ANNUAL YEAR BOOK - UNITED STATES TROTTING ASSOCIATION, INC. (ANNUAL YEAR BOOK - UNITED STATES TROTTING ASSOCIATION.). **Main/Corp** United States Trotting Association. (19??)-. English. an. $15.00. US Trotting Association, 750 Michigan Avenue, Columbus OH 43215. **Tel** (614)224-2291, FAX (614)228-1385. **LC** SF325; .W2. **DD** 798/.46/0973. ***Continues*** *United States Trotting Association Year Book, Trotting and Pacing.*
Desc: Review of racing records of all Harness Horses racing in the United States and Canada.

US/1059-2997
ANVIL MAGAZINE. [Anvil mag.]. (Jan. 1991)-. Periodical. English. Twelve times a year. $49.50 (one year); $84.50 (two years); $118.50 (three years). The Anvil, PO Box 1810, Georgetown CA 95634. **Tel** (916)333-2142, FAX (916)333-2906. **ED** Rob Edwards. **DD** 682. ***Continues*** *Anvil (Georgetown, Calif.), 0890-2534.*

US/0892-385X
APPALOOSA JOURNAL. [Appaloosa j.]. **Added/Corp** Appaloosa Horse Club. Vol. 42, No. 1 (Jan. 1987)-. Periodical. English. Twelve times a year. $20.00 (one year), $38.00 (two years) US; $35.00 (one year), $68.00 (two years) other. Appaloosa Horse Club Inc, PO Box 8403, Moscow ID 83843. **Tel** (208)882-5578. **ED** Debbie Moors. **DD** 636. Index available (bound in Dec. issue). **Bk Rev**, (Qty: 2-3). **Ad Acc**, **Adv Mgr:** Gretchen Naccarato. **Circ:** 14,000. ***Continues*** *Appaloosa News, 0003-665X.*
Desc: News and features dedicated to the enjoyment of the Appaloosa breed and their owners.

UK/0402-7493
ARAB HORSE SOCIETY NEWS, THE. **Main/Corp** Arab Horse Society. **VFOAT** Arab Horse. (Autumn 1955)-. English. sa. Mossbrook Limited, Blackmore Road, Ebblake Estate, Verwd Dorset BH21 6BR England.

US/0194-6803
ARABIAN HORSE EXPRESS. Vol. 1 (1978)-. Periodical. English. mo. $25.00 (one year), $40.00 (two year) US; $33.00*(one year), $56.00 (two year) other. Arabian Horse Express, PO Box 845, Coffeyville KS 67337. **Tel** (316)251-7340. **ED** Kathleen Gallagher. (y). **Bk Rev**, (Qty: 12). **Ad Acc**, **Adv Mgr:** Tammy Gomez, **Tel** 1-800-533-9734. **Circ:** 10,500 (ctrl).
Desc: Arabian horse oriented equine publication. Includes regular information on training, regional news, vet forums, IAHA, AHSA, race news, and product news.

US/0191-2577
ARABIAN HORSE JOURNAL, THE. **VFOAT** Arabian Horse. (19??)-. Periodical. English. wk. $12.00. Titi Ferguson, 1850 Long Corner Road, Mt Airy MD 21771. **Tel** (301)831-5828. **LC** SF293.A8; A43. **DD** 636.1/1. ***Continues*** *Arabian Horse, 0097-9503.*

US/0279-8425
ARABIAN HORSE TIMES, THE. (19??)-. Trade Publication. English. Twelve times a year. $25.00 one year; $45.00 two year; $65.00 three year. Adams Corporation, PO Box 2464, New York NY 10163. **Tel** (507)835-3204. Index available. **Ad Acc. Circ:** 25,000 (ctrl).
Desc: Trade journal covering the Arabian horse industry around the world. Lots of color advertisements and articles.

US/0003-7494
ARABIAN HORSE WORLD. Vol. 1 (1960)-. Periodical. English. Twelve times a year. $36.00 US; $60.00 Canada; $75.00 other. Arabian Horse World, 824 San Antonio Avenue, Palo Alto CA 94303-4617. **Tel** (415)856-0500, FAX (415)326-5209, telex 263047. **Bk Rev. Ad Acc. Circ:** 18,000.
Desc: Equine magazine devoted to all aspects of the Arabian breed including care, health, breeding, horsemanship, showmanship and the Arabian horse industry in general.

US/0091-4401
ARIZONA THOROUGHBRED, THE. [Ariz. throughbred]. Periodical. English. bm. $15.00. Arizona Thoroughbred Association Inc, PO Box 41774, Phoenix AZ 85080-1774. **Tel** (602)942-1310. **ED** Jill A Smart. **Bk Rev. Ad Acc. Circ:** 4,000 (ctrl).
Desc: Thoroughbred breeders magazine with human interest stories regarding race horses and people with the racing industry.

CN/0226-627X
ATLANTIC POST CALLS. [Atl. post calls]. V. 1-Feb. 16, 1979-. Periodical. English. wk. $15.00. Cumberland Publishers, PO Box 280, Amherst Nova Scotia B4H 3Z2 Canada. **DD** 798.4/6/09715.

AT/0729-9397
ATRI TURF NOTES. **Added/Corp** stralian Turfgrass Research Institute. **VFOAT** Australian Turf Research Institute Turf Notes. (1982)-. Periodical. English. qt. 28.00Aus$. Australian Turf Grass Research Institute, 68 Victoria Avenue, Concord West NSW 2138 Australia. **ED** David S Drane (editor's address: PO Box 190, Concord West NSW 2138 Australia; editor's phone: 61 2 7361233. **DD** 635.96420288. Index available. cum. index. **Ad Acc**, **Adv Mgr:** same as editor. ctrl circ.

AT
AUSTRALIAN BLOODHORSE REVIEW. (19??)-. English. Twelve times a year. 79.00Aus$ Australia; 110.00Aus$ New Zealand; 120.00Aus$ other. Australian Bloodhorse Review, PO Box 286, Richmond 2753 Australia. **Tel** 011 61 45 885355, FAX 011 61 45 885478. **ED** M. Davis (editor's address: PO Box 561, Liverpool New South Wales 2170 Australia). **Circ:** 9,000.
Desc: A magazine devoted to thoroughbred.

AT/1032-6626
AUSTRALIAN EQUINE VETERINARIAN. English. Four times a year (Feb., May, Aug., Nov.). 135.00Aus$. Australian Equine Veterinary, PO Box 371, Artarmon NSW 2064 Australia. **Tel** 61 2 4115342, FAX 61 2 4133765. **ED** Cate Plummber. **Bk Rev. Ad Acc. Pr Rev. Circ:** 1,000 (ctrl).
Ind/Abst Index Vet.; Vet. Bull.

AT/0728-1226
AUSTRALIAN HORSE AND RIDER. [Aust. horse rider]. (1973)-. Periodical. English. mo. 36.00Aus$ Australia, 66.00Aus$ other. Prestige Publications, PO Box 687, Woolloonga QLD 4102 Australia. **Tel** 011 61 27 8911299. **DD** 798.20994.
Ind/Abst SPORT Discus.

AT
AUSTRALIAN QUARTER HORSE MAGAZINE. English. mo. 27.50Aus$. Australian Quarter Horse Association, PO Box 979, Tamworth NSW 2340 Australia. **Tel** 011 61 67 668333. **Ad Acc**, **Adv Mgr:** Michael Vink.

AT/0817-8550
AUSTRALIAN STOCK HORSE JOURNAL. [Aust. stock horse j.]. **Added/Corp** Australian Stock Horse Society. (1985)-. Periodical. English. Six times a year. 20.00Aus$ (Australia); 30.00Aus$ (other). Australian Stock Horse, 92 Kelly Street, Scone New South Wales, 2337 Australia. **Tel** 011 44 65 451122, FAX 011 44 65 452165. **ED** Joan Starr. **DD** 636.130994. **Ad Acc. Circ:** 6,250 (ctrl). ***Continues*** *Australian Stock Horse, 0314-9056.*
Desc: Offers a unique opportunity for advertisers to reach people who are interested in, own, use and show horses.

US/0005-366X
BACKSTRETCH, THE. **Added/Corp** United Thoroughbred Trainers of America. (1962)-. Periodical. English. Six times a year. $14.00 US; $17.00 Canada; $20.00 other. United Thoroughbred Trainers of America, 19899 West Nine Mile Road, Southfield MI 48075. **Tel** (313)354-3232, FAX (313)354-3157. **ED** Harriet Dalley. **LC** SF335.U6; B33. **DD** 798.4/00973. Index available. **Bk Rev**, (Qty: 60/year). **Ad Acc**, **Adv Mgr:** Shelia Eck, **Tel** (800)325-3487. **Circ:** 25,403.
Desc: Intended for those interested in thoroughbred horses and racing.

US/0006-4998
BLOOD-HORSE, THE. **VAT** Blood Horse. (1928)-. Periodical. English. wk (52 issues). $95.00 (US except Kentucky). The Thoroughbred Owners and Breeder Association, PO Box 4038, Lexington KY 40544. **Tel** (606)278-2361, (800)866-2361, FAX (606)276-4450, telex 21-8473. **(Subscription address:** Blood Horse, PO Box 7718, Riverton, NJ 08077) **ED** Edward L Bowen. **LC** SF277; .B55. **DD** 636.1/32/05. Index available. **Bk Rev. Ad Acc. Circ:** 22,000. available on microfilm and microfiche from University Microfilms International (UMI). ***Continues*** *Thoroughbred.*
Desc: Publication dedicated to the improvement of thoroughbred breeding and racing.

US
BLUE RIBBON, THE. (1939)-. Periodical. English. an (Aug.). $10.00. Celebration Inc, PO Box 1010, Shelbyville TN 37160. **Tel** (615)684-5915. **ED** Ron Thomas. **Bk Rev. Ad Acc. Circ:** 8,000.

CN/0838-1690
BULLETIN / CANADIAN EQUESTRIAN FEDERATION. [Bull. - Can. Equest. Fed.]. **Added/Corp** Canadian Equestrian Federation. No. 30 (Feb. 1988)-. Bulletin. English. qt. Free on request. Canadian Equestrian Federation, 333 River Road, Ottawa Ontario K1L 8H9 Canada. **Tel** (613)748-5632. **DD** 798.2/0971. ***Continues*** *Canadian Equestrian Federation Official Bulletin, 0710-9156.*
Ind/Abst SPORT Discus.

US/1057-9907
BUYER'S GUIDE / THOROUGHBRED TIMES, BLOODSTOCK RESEARCH, THE. **Added/Corp** Bloodstock Research Information Services. (July 15-18, 1991)-. Periodical. English. qt. Thoroughbred Publications Inc, PO Box 8237, Lexington KY 40533-9985. **Tel** (800)648-4637, (606-223-9800. **DD** 636.

US/0091-441X
CALIFORNIA HORSE REVIEW. [Calif. horse rev.]. (19??)-. Periodical. English. mo. $19.95. California Horse Review, PO Box 1238, Rancho Cordova CA 95741. **Tel** (916)638-1519. **ED** Jennifer Meyer. **Bk Rev. Ad Acc. Circ:** 6,500.
Desc: Focus is on California's all-breeds horse industry interests and activities. Horse trainers, breeders, show people, care, nutrition, equipment and how-to methods are featured.

US/0273-8287
CALIFORNIA HORSEMAN'S NEWS. **VFOAT** Horseman's News. Periodical. English. mo. $15.00. California Horseman's News, PO Box 474, San Marcos CA 92069. **Tel** (619)471-0130. **ED** Tracy Cahill. **Bk Rev. Ad Acc. Circ:** 14,000.
Desc: All breed equine tabloid full of horse news, stories, coming events and trends of the horse industry. Also includes a monthly veterinary and new products column.

●US/1061-1754
CALIFORNIA/NEVADA HORSEMAN'S DIRECTORY. [Calif./Nev. horseman's dir.]. **VFOAT** California Nevada Horseman's Directory; Horseman's Directory. (1992)-. Directory. English. $7.95. Kannberg and Associates, 439 Kirland Way, Kirland WA 98033. **DD** 636. ***Continues*** *Northern California Horseman's Directory.*

US
CALIFORNIA STALLION REGISTER. **Added/Corp** California Thoroughbred Breeders Association. (1975)-. Periodical. English. an. $13.00. California Thoroughbred Breeders Association, 201 Colorado Place, PO Box 750, Arcadia CA 91006. **Tel** (818)445-7800, FAX (8181)574-0852, telex 247505 CTB UR. ***Continues*** *The Thoroughbred of California.*

CN
CANADIAN ARABIAN HORSE STUD BOOK. **Main/Corp** Canadian National Live Stock Records. Vol. 1-. Periodical. English. ir. Canadian Arabian Horse Registry, #300 Terrace Plaza, 4445 Calgary Trail South, Edmonton Alberta T6H 5R7 Canada. **Tel** (403)436-4244. **Circ:** 1,700 (ctrl).
Desc: Record of purebred Arabian horses registered in the Canadian Arabian Horse Registry.

CN/0824-1414
CANADIAN ARABIAN RACING REFERENCE. [Can. Arab. racing ref.]. 1981/1982/1983-. English. an. $5.00 per no. Alberta Arabian Racing Association, 54 Bell Street, Red Deer Alta. T4R 1M8. **DD** 636.1/12.

CN/0840-6200
CANADIAN HORSEMAN (GUELPH). (CANADIAN HORSEMAN.). [Can. horseman]. Vol. 8, No. 1 (Jan/Feb. 1989)-. Periodical. English. Six times a year (Jan., Mar., May, July, Sept., Nov.). 18.95Can$ Canada;

29.95Can$ other. The Corinthian Publishing Company Ltd, Box 670, Aurora Ontario L4G 4J9 Canada. **Tel** (416)727-0107, FAX (416)841-1530. **ED** Lee Benson. **DD** 636.1/005. **Bk Rev**, (Qty: varies). **Ad Acc**, **Adv Mgr:** V. Evans. ***Continues*** *Horse Sense (Guelph, Ont.)., 0829-3244.*
Desc: Just general knowledge for the western and recreational rider and various disciplines addressed also.
Ind/Abst SPORT Discus.

CN/0820-6813
CANADIAN REINER, THE. [Can. reiner]. **VFOAT** Le Reiner Canadien; Reiner Canadien. V. 1, No. 1 (Jan./Feb. 1983)-. Periodical. English (French). bm. Free to Members. National Reining Horse Association of Canada, c/o Claude Payette, 1576 Bellevue, Carignan Quebec J3L 3P9 Canada. **DD** 636.1/0888.

CN/0008-5073
CANADIAN SPORTSMAN, THE. (1870)-. Periodical. English. Twice a week. $55.00 (one year), $95.00 (two year) US; 43.00Can$ (one year), 75.00Can$ (two year) Canada. Canadian Sportsman Ltd, Box 129, Staffordville NoJ 1Y0 Canada. **Tel** (519)866-5558, FAX (519)866-5596. **ED** Gary Foerster. Index available. **Ad Acc. Circ:** 6,000 (ctrl).
Desc: Contains information dealing with standard breeding and racing of horses.

CN/0830-0593
CANADIAN THOROUGHBRED. [Can. thoroughbred]. **VFOAT** Thoroughbred. Vol. 1, No. 1 (April 1986)-. Periodical. English. mo. 39.95Can$ Canada; 55.00Can$ other. Canadian Thoroughbred, 225 Industrial Parkway South, Box 820, Aurora Ontario L4G 4J9 Canada. **Tel** (416)727-0107, FAX (416)841-1530. **ED** Jennifer Monison. **DD** 798.4/3/0971. **Circ:** 3,500. ***Continues*** *Canadian Horse, 0008-378X;* ***Absorbed*** *British Columbia Thoroughbred.*

UK/0958-1820
CARRIAGE DRIVING. [Carriage driv.]. (1986)-. Periodical. English. Six times a year. £21.00 Europe & Eire; £25.00 US & Canada & Australia; £27.00 New Zealand; £15.00 UK; £28.00 others. TG Scott Subscriber Services, 6 Bourne Enterprise Center, Wrotham Road, Borough Green, Kent TN15 8DG England. **Tel** 011 44 01 732 884023, FAX 011 44 01 732 884034. **DD** 798.6.
Desc: Each issue contains many color illustrations and articles, reports on private driving, showing, driving trials, coaching, long distance driving and harness racing.

CN/0384-6156
CAVALIER (SAINT-GERMAIN-DE-GRANTHAM). (LE CAVALIER.). **Added/Corp** Association Cutting Horse du Quebec. Association des Cavaliers du Quebec. Association Quebecoise Quarter Horse. Club Quebecois Paint horse. Vol. 1 (April 1976)-. Periodical. French (English; summaries and/or abstracts in English). ir. $1.00 per no. Le Cavalier ENR, CP 233, Saint-Germain-de-Grantham Quebec J0C 1K0 Canada. **DD** 798/.2/05.

II
CENTAUR : HOUSE JOURNAL OF THE INDIAN ASSOCIATION OF EQUINE INTERESTS. **Added/Corp** Indian Association of Equine Interests. Vol. 1, No. 1 (July 1984)-. Periodical. English. qt. $21.00. Indian Association of Equine Interests, Mylapore, Madras, India. **(Subscription address:** Prints India, 11 Darya Ganj, New Delhi 110002 India.**)**
Ind/Abst Agrofor. Abstr.; For. Abstr.; Index Vet.; Nutr. Abstr. Rev., Ser. B, Live Feeds and Feed.; Protozoolog. Abstr.; Rev. Med. Vet. Entomol.

PL/0867-6704
CHAMPION KATOWICE. (CHAMPION.). [Champion Katow.]. (1991)-. Periodical. Polish. bm (6 issues). Price on Request. **(Subscription address:** ARS Polona, PO Box 1001, 00068 Warsaw Poland.**) UDC** 798.

CN/0829-4828
CHEVAL CANADIEN. (LE CHEVAL CANADIEN / LA SOCIETE DES ELEVEURS DE CHEVAUX CANADIENS.). [Cheval can.]. Began publishing between Nov. 1984 and May 1985. Periodical. French. mo. Free to members. Societe Eleveurs Chevaux Canadiens, 1745 St Hubert Street, Montreal Quebec H2L 3Z1 Canada. **DD** 636.1/009714.

FR
CHEVAL MAGAZINE. French. mo. 280.00F France; 380.00F other. Optipress, BP 60, 78490 Montfort L'Amaury France. **Tel** 011 33 1 34862922. **Ad Acc. Circ:** 130,000 (ctrl).

AU/1010-3422
CHEVAL (WIEN). (CHEVAL.). [Cheval]. No. 9 (Feb. 1978)-. Periodical. German. mo.
Ind/Abst Bibliogr. Agric.

FR
CHEVAUX DE PENNY. **See** Children and Youth Interests.

US/0009-5990
CHRONICLE OF THE HORSE, THE. [Chron. horse]. **Added/Corp** Masters of Foxhounds Association of America. Vol. 24 No. 19 (Jan. 6 1961)-. Periodical. English. wk. $38.50 (one year), $115.50 (three year). Chronicle of the Horse, PO Box 46, Middleburg VA 22117. **Tel** (703)687-6341. **ED** John Strassberger. **LC** SF321; .C45. **DD** 798.405. Index available. **Bk Rev. Ad Acc. Circ:** 20,959 (ctrl). available on microfilm and microfiche from University Microfilms International (UMI). ***Continues*** *Chronicle (Middleburg, Va.).*
Desc: English-type horse sports news.

JA
CHUO KEIBA NENKAN. **Added/Corp** Nihon Chuo Keibakai. (19??)-. Periodical. Japanese. Nihon Chuo Keibakai Kyosoba Sogo Kenkyujo, (Equine Research Institute, Japan Racing Association), 27-7 Tsurumaki 5-chome, Setagayaku Tokyoto 154 Japan. **LC** SF335.J3; C47.

AT/0814-2513
CLASS RACEHORSES OF AUSTRALIA AND NEW ZEALAND. [Cl. raceh. Aust. N. Z.]. (1984)-. English. an. 95.00Aus$ (Australia); 105.00Aus$ (other). AAP Racing Services, PO Box 54, Glebe 2037 Australia. **Tel** 011 61 02 236 8800. **ED** Peter Brown, Ken Boman. **DD** 798.400994. **Bk Rev.** ctrl circ.

US
CLASSIC. V. 1- Dec. 1975-. Periodical. English. bm. $12.00. Classic, 551 5th Avenue, New York NY 10017. **LC** SF277. **DD** 636.1/005.

●CN/1187-9327
CONTACT - ONTARIO EQUESTRIAN FEDERATION. (CONTACT.). [Contact - Ont. Equest. Fed.]. **Added/Corp** Ontario Equestrian Federation. (Winter 1992)-. Periodical. English. Three times a year. Free to members. Ontario Eqestrian Federation, 1220 Sheppard Avenue East, Willowdale Ontario M2K 2X1 Canada. **DD** 798.2. ***Continues*** *OEF News., 1187-9319.*

CN/0829-2930
CORINTHIAN HORSE SPORT. [Corinthian horse sport]. **VFOAT** Horse-Sport. Vol. 20, No. 2, (Feb. 1987)-. Periodical. English. Twelve times a year. 26.95Can$ Canada; 42.95Can$ other. The Corinthian Publishing Company Ltd, Box 670, Aurora Ontario L4G 4J9 Canada. **Tel** (416)727-0107, FAX (416)841-1530. **ED** Colette Hawkins. **DD** 798.2/0971/05. **Bk Rev**, (Qty: varies). **Ad Acc**, **Adv Mgr:** V. Mosher, **Tel** 727-0107. ***Continues*** *Corinthian Horse Sport in Canada, 1184-2318.*
Desc: In-depth information for the competitive English rider and including shows results, interviews and experts advice.
Ind/Abst Can. Index.

US/1061-3986
CUTTING HORSE. ***Title Change.*** [Cutting horse]. **Added/Corp** National Cutting Horse Association (U.S.). Vol. 45, No.1 Jan. (1992)-(199?). Periodical. English. mo. National Cutting Horse Association, 4704 Highway 377 South, Fort Worth TX 76116. **Tel** (817)244-6188. **LC** WMLC 91/5705. **DD** 798. ***Continues*** *Cuttin' Hoss Chatter, 0090-8711.* ***Continued by*** *Cutting Horse Chatter.*

US
CUTTING HORSE CHATTER. (19??)-. English. mo. $50.00. National Cutting Horse Association, 4704 Highway 377 South, Fort Worth TX 76116. **Tel** (817)244-6188. ***Continues*** *Cutting Horse.*

US
DAILY RACING FORM. (19??)-. Periodical. English. da (312 per year). $636.00. Daily Racing Form, 1301 North Elston Avenue, Chicago IL 60622. **Tel** (312)227-3000. **ED** Don Fleming. **LC** Microfilm 03003 SF; SF321. **Circ:** 35,147.

US/0199-5928
DERBY (NORMAN, OKLA.). ***Ceased.*** (DERBY.). [Derby]. Vol. 1, (Feb. 1980)-?. Periodical. English. bm (except Jan., Feb., March, and April). Derby, PO Box 5418, Norman OK 73070. **Tel** (405)364-9444. **ED** G Del Hollingsworth. **DD** 798. **Ad Acc. Circ:** 3,500 (ctrl).
Desc: Covering the thoroughbred racing and breeding industry in the central and southwestern United States. Includes award winning by nationally-known turf writers, stakes results, etc.

US/0012-5865
DRAFT HORSE JOURNAL, THE. Vol. 1 (1964)-. Periodical. English. qt (Mar., June, Sept., Dec.). $20.00 US; $25.00 other. Maurice & Jeanne Telleen, 201 1st SE, Box 670, Waverly IA 50677. **Tel** (319)352-4046. **ED** Maurice Telleen and Jeannine Telleen. **Bk Rev**, (Qty: 2). **Ad Acc. Circ:** 23,000.
Desc: A magazine serving the interests of all draft horse breeds and support industries.

US/0147-796X
DRESSAGE & CT. **VFOAT** Dressage and CT. **VAT** Dressage and combined training. (1971). Periodical. English. mo. $25.00 (one year), $44.00 (two year), $64.00 (three year) US; $35.00 (one year), $64.00 (two year), $94.00 (three year) other. Dressage & CT, PO Box 2460, 211 West Main St., New London OH 44851. **Tel** (419)929-6781, FAX (419)929-3800. **(Subscription address:** 211 W Main Street, New London, OH 44851**)** **ED** Ivan I Bezugloff Jr. **LC** SF309.5; .D7. **DD** 798.2/05. **Bk Rev. Ad Acc. Circ:** 10,000 (ctrl). ***Continues*** *Dressage and Combined Training, 0147-7951.*
Desc: Educational publication for two of the Olympic equestrian sports: dressage and combined training. Also reports on important national and international competitions.
Ind/Abst SPORT Discus; SportSearch (May 1987-).

US/0191-7714
EASTERN/WESTERN QUARTER HORSE JOURNAL. ***Ceased.*** [East./west. quart. horse j.]. **VFOAT** Eastern/Western; EWQHJ. **VAT** Eastern Western Quarter Horse Journal. (197?)-(June 1992). Periodical. English. mo. Eastern/Western Quarter Horse, Drawer 690, Middleboro MA 02346. **Tel** (617)947-6831. **ED** Christine Brune. **LC** WMLC L 83/9998. **DD** 636. **Ad Acc. Circ:** 9,000 (ctrl). ***Continues*** *Eastern Quarter Horse Journal, 0090-872X.*
Desc: Features interviews, national quarter horse standings, bloodline articles, etc. The official voice of the National Snaffle Bit Association.

CN/1182-9958
ENGLISH RIDER. [Engl. rider]. Vol. 1, No. 1 (June 1990)-. Periodical. English. qt. Golden Arc Publishing and Typesetting, 491 Book Road West, Ancaster, Ontario L9G 3L1 Canada. **Tel** (416)648-2035. **DD** 798.2/3/09713.

FR
EPERON, L'. **Added/Corp** Union Nationale Interprofessionnelle du Cheval. (?)-. Periodical. French. bm. L'Eperon, 51 rue Dumont d'Urville, 75116 Paris France.

US/0013-9831
EQUESTRIAN TRAILS. [Equest. trail.]. **Added/Corp** Equestrian Trails. (19??)-. Periodical. English. Twelve times a year. Free. Equestrian Trails, 13741 Foothill Boulevard, Suite 220, Sylmar CA 91342. **Tel** (818)362-6819. **ED** Tina Graboyes. **Bk Rev. Ad Acc. Circ:** 6,000 (ctrl).
Desc: Contains general equine information including owning, showing, and trail riding.

UK
EQUI. Periodical. English. bm. Equi, 9 Rostherne Avenue, Lowton St Lukes Warrington, Cheshire WA3 2QD England.
Ind/Abst SportSearch (May 1987-).

US/1047-8620
EQUINE ATHLETE, THE. [Equine athl.]. **Added/Corp** Association for Horse Medicine. Vol. 1, No. 1 (Dec. 1988)-. Periodical. English. bm (6 issues). $44.50 US; $50.00 Canada and Mexico; $65.00 other. Veterinary Practice Publishing Company, PO Box 4457, Santa Barbara CA 93140-4457. **Tel** (805)965-1028, FAX (805)965-0722. **DD** 636.
Desc: Equine sports medicine news journal for trainers and veterinarians.

US/0162-8941
EQUINE PRACTICE. [Equine pract.]. Vol. 1 (Jan./Feb. 1979)-. Periodical. English. Ten times a year. $36.00 US; $42.00 Canada and Mexico; $50.00 other. Veterinary Practice Publishing Company, PO Box 4457, Santa Barbara CA 93140-4457. **Tel** (805)965-1028, FAX (805)965-0722. **ED** Charles D. Vail. **LC** SF951; .E58. **DD** 636.1/08/905. **CODEN** EQPRDF. Index available. cum. index. **Bk Rev. Ad Acc. Circ:** 5,000. available on microfilm and microfiche from University Microfilms International (UMI). Documents available from The Genuine Article, BIOSIS Document Express.
Desc: Journal of equine medicine and surgery for the practitioner.
Ind/Abst AgBiotech News Inf.; AGRICOLA [Full Cov.]; Anim. Breed. Abstr.; Biol. Abstr.; Curr. Contents, Agric. Biol. Environ. Sci.; Grasslands For. Abstr.; Helminthol. Abstr. (1991-); Index Vet.; Nutr. Abstr. Rev., Ser. B, Live Feeds and Feed.; Protozoolog. Abstr.; Res. Alert [Select. Cov.]; Rev. Med. Vet. Entomol.; Rev. Med. Vet. Mycology; Sorghum Mill. Abstr.; Soyabean Abstr.; Vet. Bull.

US/0739-9065
EQUINE VETERINARY DATA. [Equine vet. data]. Vol. 1 (Jan. 1, 1980)-. Periodical. English. mo. $70.00 US; $80.00 Canada and Mexico; $95.00 other. Equine Veterinary Data, Box 1209, Wildomar CA 92595. **Tel** (714)678-1889, FAX (714)678-1885. **ED** William E Jones Yes. Index available. cum. index. **Circ:** 1,500 (ctrl).
Desc: Professional newsletter for equine practitioners. Latest information on veterinary care of horses.
Ind/Abst Index Vet.; Nutr. Abstr. Rev., Ser. B, Live Feeds and Feed.; Rev. Med. Vet. Entomol.

UK/0957-7734
EQUINE VETERINARY EDUCATION. [Equine vet. educ.]. **Added/Corp** British Equine Veterinary Association. **VFOAT** EVE. Vol. 1, No. 1 (Sept. 1989)-. Periodical. English. bm. £72.00 UK; £84.00 others; $126.00 US. TG Scott Subscriber Services, 6 Bourne Enterprise Center, Wrotham Road, Borough Green, Kent TN15 8DG England. **Tel** 011 44 01 732

884023, FAX 011 44 01 732 884034. **LC** SF955; .E68. **Desc:** The aim of this journal is to provide information about practical topics relating to situations encountered on daily basis by those involved in equine practice. **Ind/Abst** AGRICOLA [Full Cov.]; Anim. Breed. Abstr.; Helminthol. Abstr. (1991-); Index Vet.; Nutr. Abstr. Rev., Ser. B, Live Feeds and Feed.; Vet. Bull.

CN/0828-864X
EQUINEWS. Vol. 1, No. 2 (June 1984)-. Periodical. English. mo. 15.00Can$ Canada; 22.00Can$ others. Westview Publications, Site 15 Comp 5, Vernon BC V1T 6Y5 Canada. **Tel** 604 545-3560, FAX 604 545-7099. **ED** John Whittle. **DD** 798.2/09712. **Bk Rev. Ad Acc. Circ:** 15,000 (ctrl).
Desc: General interest, all-breed, all-discipline equine magazine, the official voice of the Horse Council of British Columbia, Arabian Associations and British Columbian competitive trail riders.

US/0149-0672
EQUUS. [Equus]. V. 1- Nov. 1977-. Periodical. English. mo. $24.00 (one year), $36.00 (two year) (surface mail). Fleet Street Corporation, 656 Quince Orchard Road, Gaithersburg MD 20878. **Tel** (301)977-3900. **LC** SF277; .E67. **DD** 636.1/08/905. Index available. **Ad Acc. Circ:** 110,000. available on microfilm and microfiche from University Microfilms International (UMI).
Desc: A horse health publication for laymen, featuring authoritative, well- illustrated articles on health care, behavior, training veterinary trends, exercise physiology. **Ind/Abst** AGRICOLA; SPORT Discus; SportSearch.

UK/0260-7468
EUROPEAN RACEHORSE, THE. [Eur. raceh.]. **VFOAT** European Race Horse. Began with Vol. 1, No. 1 (Mar. 1981)-. Periodical. English. Four times a year. £24.00. **DD** 636. ***Continues*** *British Racehorse, 0007-1706.*

CN/0822-7330
EXPRESS EQUESTRE. [Express equest.]. **VFOAT** Magazine Equestre. Vol. 1, No. 1-. Periodical. French. ir. $18.00. Express Equestre, CP 416 Succursale Bourassa, Montreal Quebec H2C 3G7 Canada. **DD** 798.2/09714.

US/0090-967X
FLORIDA HORSE, THE. Added/Corp Florida Thoroughbred Breeders' Association. Vol. 1, (1958)-. Periodical. English. Ten times a year. $45.00. Florida Horse, PO Box 2106, Ocala FL 32678. **Tel** (904)732-6700. **DD** 796.

US/1049-9032
FLORIDA THOROUGHBRED TIMES. [Fla. thoroughbred times]. **VFOAT** Florida Times. Vol. 2, No. 2 (Feb. 1990)-. Periodical. English. Twelve times a year. $18.00. Thoroughbred Publications Inc, PO Box 8237, Lexington KY 40533-9985. **Tel** (800)648-4637, (606-223-9800. **DD** 798. ***Separated from*** *Thoroughbred Times, 0887-2244.*

US/0884-1322
FOAL REGISTRATIONS, ILLINOIS CONCEIVED & FOALED STANDARDBREDS. VFOAT Foal Registrations, Illinois Conceived and Foaled Standardbreds; Illinois Conceived & Foaled Standardbreds; Illinois Conceived and Foaled Standardbreds. English. an. free. Illinois Department of Agriculture, PO Box 19281, Springfield IL 62794. **Tel** (217)782-2172, FAX (217)785-4505. **ED** Jered Hooker. **LC** SF293.S72; F62. **DD** 636.1/7. Index available. cum. index. **Circ:** 3,000 (ctrl).

US/0884-0105
FOAL REGISTRATIONS OF ILLINOIS CONCEIVED AND FOALED, AND ILLINOIS FOALED THOROUGHBREDS. VFOAT Illinois Foaled Thoroughbreds. English. an. Illinois Department of Agriculture, PO Box 19281, Springfield IL 62794. **Tel** (217)782-2172, FAX (217)785-4505. **LC** SF293.T5; F6. **DD** 636.1/32/09773.

IT
GUIDA DEL CAVALIERE. Italian. L3.500. L L Edizioni Equestri, Via Pastrengo 14, 20159 Milan Italy. **LC** SF310.I8; G84. **DD** 798/.23/0945.

US/1045-2648
HARNESS HANDBOOK, THE. (THE HARNESS HANDBOOK : THE LEADING HORSEMEN OF.). [Harness handb.]. 1989 Ed.-. Periodical. English. an. $8.00. US Trotting Association, 750 Michigan Avenue, Columbus OH 43215. **Tel** (614)224-2291, FAX (614)228-1385. **LC** SF339.5.U6; H37. **DD** 798.4/6/097305. ***Formed by the union of*** *Leading Horsemen* ***and*** *Leading Horses.*

US/0164-3703
HARNESS HORSEMEN INTERNATIONAL. Periodical. English. mo. $12.00 US; $18.00 other. Harness Horsemen International, Rocky Hill CT 06067. ***Continues*** *International Trotter and Pacer.*

CN/0381-7695
HARNESS WORLD. VFOAT Monde du Harnais. V. 1- Aug. 20, 1973-. Periodical. English (French). bm. $10.00. Harness World, PO Box 100, Cote Des Neiges, Montreal Quebec H3S 2S4 Canada. **DD** 798/.46/05.

UK/0951-2640
HEAVY HORSE WORLD. (HEAVY HORSE.). [Heavy horse world]. (1987)-. Periodical. English. Four times a year (Mar., June, Sept., Dec.). £10.00 UK; £14.50 other. Heavy Horse World, Park Cottage West Dean, Chichester WS PO18 0RX England. **Tel** 011 44 243 63364. **ED** Diane Zeunes. **DD** 636.15. **Bk Rev**, (Qty: 8). **Ad Acc. Circ:** 3,000.
Desc: Special magazine covering all aspects of horses. British breeds especially , and some overseas coverage.

US/0018-4683
HOOF BEATS (COLUMBUS, OHIO). (HOOF BEATS.). [Hoof beats]. **Added/Corp** United States Trotting Association. Vol. 1 (1933)-. Periodical. English. Twelve times a year. $18.00 US; $29.50 Canada; $45.00 other. US Trotting Association, 750 Michigan Avenue, Columbus OH 43215. **Tel** (614)224-2291, FAX (614)228-1385. **ED** Dean A. Hoffman. **DD** 798. **Bk Rev. Ad Acc. Circ:** 27,000 (ctrl).
Desc: News and feature stories about raising and racing harness horses. Extensive color photography. Freelance article accepted.

AT/0811-8698
HOOFBEATS. (1979)-. Periodical. English. bm. 20.00Aus$ Australia; 30.00Aus$ other. Hoofbeats, Lot 46 Leslie Road, Wandi Perth 6167 Australia. **Tel** 61 9 3970506, FAX 61 9 3970200. **ED** Sandra Hannan. **Bk Rev**, (Qty: Varies). **Ad Acc, Adv Mgr:** same as editor. **Circ:** 13,000.
Desc: Equestrian; informative and educational equestrian magazine which has training and veterinary articles profiles, "how to" articles and stories of general interest to horse owners.
Ind/Abst SPORT Discus.

●US
HOOFCARE & LAMENESS. VFOAT Hoofcare and Lameness. Issue No. 92-1 (Spring 1992)-. Periodical. English. qt. ***Continues*** *Hoofcare and Lameness Quarterly Report, 1062-3221.*

US
HOOFPRINTS. Added/Corp Hooved Animal Humane Society. Vol. 1, No. 1 (1973)-. Periodical. English. qt. $35.00. Hooved Animal Humane Society, PO Box 400, Woodstock IL 60098. **Tel** (815)337-5563.

AT
HOOFS AND HORNS. (1944)-. Periodical. English. mo. 43.00Aus$ (Australia); 59.00Aus$ (New Zealand, Papua, New Guinea, Fiji, Indonesia, Malaysia, India, China, & Japan); 66.00Aus$ (other). Rural Press / Victoria, PO Box 160, Port Melbourne Victoria 3207 Australia. **Tel** 11 61 3 2870900, telex 35668.

US/0199-6266
HOOSIER EQUESTRIAN. 1934-. Periodical. English. bm. Indiana Saddle Horse Association, 120 Garden Drive, PO Box 552, Westfield IN 46074.

CN/1183-3173
HORSE ACTION (WINFIELD). (HORSE ACTION.). [Horse act.]. Vol. 1, No. 1 (Oct. 1990)-. Periodical. English. mo. $12.00 per year. Horse Action, Rural Route 1, Suite 8, Comp. 8, Winfield, British Columbia V0H 2C0 Canada. **DD** 636.1.

US/0094-3355
HORSE AND HORSEMAN. (19??)-. Periodical. English. mo. $18.00 (US); $26.00 (others). Gallant Charger Publishing Inc., Box HH, 34249 Camino Capistrano, Capistrano Beach CA 92624. **Tel** (714)493-2101, FAX (714)240-8680. **ED** Jack Lewis. **Ad Acc. Circ:** 97,149.
Desc: Informative and entertaining stories on all facets of the horse world.
Ind/Abst AGRICOLA.

UK
HORSE AND HOUND HUNTER CHASERS AND POINT-TO-POINTERS. (19??)-. English. wk. $159.00. IPC Magazines Ltd., Perrymount Road, Haywards Heath, West Sussex RH16 3DH England. **Tel** 011 44 444 440421. **LC** SF359.3.G7; H67. **DD** 798/.45/0942.

UK/0262-5814
HORSE & PONY. (19??)-. English. Twenty-six times a year. £25.00 UK, £30.00 others (surface mail); £38.00 Europe, £42.00 Middle East & North Africa, £53.00 Pacific Island, Australasia & Far East, £50.00 others (airmail). EMAP National Publications Ltd, Farndon Road, Market Harborough, Leicestershire, LE16 9NR England. **Tel** 011 44 733 555161. **ED** Sarah Haw. available on microfilm from University Microfilms International (UMI).

US/0018-5159
HORSE & RIDER. [Horse rider]. **VFOAT** H & R. **VAT** Horse and Rider. (1968)-. Periodical. English. mo. $27.00. Cowles Magazines, PO Box 8200, Harrisburg PA 17105. **Tel** (717)657-9555, (800)435-9610. **LC** SF277; .H73. **DD** 798; 798/.2/05. **Bk Rev. Ad Acc. Circ:** 100,000. Documents available from UMI Article Clearinghouse. ***Continues*** *Western Life.*
Desc: Covers Western riding; articles on training theories and the latest information on health care, feeding and grooming.
Ind/Abst AGRICOLA; Mag. Artic. Summar. Elite (July 1989-); Mag. Artic. Summar. Select (July 1989-); Mag. Artic. Summar. CD-ROM (July 1989-); Mag. Search; Mid. Search (Jul. 1989-); Newsp. Period. Abstr. (1990-); Prim. Search (Jul. 1989-); SportSearch.

US/0193-2950
HORSE & RIDER ALL-WESTERN YEARBOOK. VFOAT All-Western Yearbook. **VAT** Horse and Rider All-Western Yearbook. No. 5 1975-. English. an. $2.95. Rich Publications Inc, 941 Calle Negocio, San Clemente CA 92672-6202. **Tel** (714)361-1955, FAX (714)361-0333. **DD** 798.

UK
HORSE AND RIDER (LONDON, ENGLAND). (HORSE AND RIDER.). Vol. 30, No. 347 (Jan. 1981)-. Periodical. English. mo (12 issues). £20.40 UK; £26.20 other. D J Murphy Publishing Ltd., 296 Ewell Road Surbiton, Surrey KT6 7AQ England. **Tel** 011 44 81 390 8547, FAX 011 44 81 390 8696. **ED** Kate O'Sullivan. **Bk Rev. Ad Acc. Circ:** 35,000. ***Continues*** *Light Horse.*
Desc: High quality equestrian magazine covering all topics relating to horses, including equitation, stable management and veterinary matters.

US/0145-9791
HORSE ILLUSTRATED. [Horse illus.]. Vol. 1, (1976)-. Periodical. English. Twelve times a year. $23.97. Fancy Publications, PO Box 6050, Mission Viejo CA 92690. **Tel** (714)855-8822, (800)426-2516, FAX (714)855-3045. **(Subscription address:** Neodata / Colorado, PO Box 2606, Boulder Boulder CO 80322.**) ED** Linda Lewis. **LC** SF277; .H74. **DD** 789/.2/05. **Circ:** 88,000.

US/0890-233X
HORSE INDUSTRY DIRECTORY. [Horse ind. dir.]. 1976-. Directory. English. an. $12.00. American Horse Council, 1700 K Street NW/#300, Washington DC 20001. **Tel** (202)296-4031. **ED** Mary D Midkiff and Virginia Reagan. **LC** SF278.5; .H65. **DD** 636. **CODEN** AESSE8. Index available. **Circ:** 10,000 (ctrl). Documents available from Ask*IEEE. ***Continues*** *Horse Industry Trade Press Directory.*
Desc: Comprehensive listing of major breed groups, health and humane organizations, racetracks and related groups, sporting organizations, and government information sources. Also listings for horse publications.
Ind/Abst INSPEC (1987-).

CN/0828-4679
HORSE INDUSTRY DIRECTORY OF CANADA. [Horse ind. dir. Can.]. 1984-. Directory. English. an. $10.00 per no. Whitehouse Publishing, 10205 Venables Drive, Vernon BC V1B 2K4. **DD** 636.1/0025/71.

AT/0817-7686
HORSE MAGAZINE. [Horse mag.]. (1984)-. Periodical. English. Twelve times a year. 37.50Aus$ Australia; 62.50Aus$ New Zealand & Papua New Guinea; 72.50Aus$ other. The Horse Magazine, Old Gembrook Road, Upper Pakenham VIC Australia. **Tel** 011 61 59 427447, FAX 011 61 59 427556. **ED** Christopher Hector. **DD** 636.100994. cum. index. **Ad Acc.**

US/0092-6353
HORSE PLAY. Added/Corp Maryland Horse Breeders Association. **VFOAT** Horseplay. (19??)-. Periodical. English. mo. $17.97 (one year), $33.94 (two years). Horseplay, 11 Park Avenue, PO Box 130, Gaithersburg MD 20884. **Tel** (301)840-1866, FAX (301)840-5722. **ED** Cordelia Doucet. Index available. **Bk Rev. Ad Acc. Circ:** 41,000.
Desc: America's number one English riding magazine. English riding sports coverage, horse care, and instruction.

CN/0380-2779
HORSE RACING MAGAZINE. (Aug./Sept. 1975)-. Periodical. English. mo. $10.00. Canadian Mass Publications, Suite 204/920 Alness Street, Downsview Ontario M3J 2H7 Canada. **DD** 798/.4/00971.

US
HORSE SHEETS. (19??)-. English. Twelve times a year. $15.00. Horse Sheets, PO Box 219, Fort Atkinson WI 53538. **Tel** (800)462-4837. ***Continues*** *Record Horseman.*

US
HORSE SHOW MAGAZINE. Added/Corp American Horse Shows Association. (1937)-. Periodical. English. ir. $35.00 (junior); $50.00 (adult) Comes with American Horse Shows Association membership. American Horse Shows Association, 220 East 42nd Street, New York NY 10017. **Tel** (212)759-3070. **LC** SF277; .A524.

US/0744-4257
HORSE TIMES. [Horse times]. (198?)-. Periodical. English. mo. $12.00. Horse Times, PO Box 351, Star ID 83669. **Tel** (208)467-4077. **ED** Jo Woodbury. Index available. **Bk Rev. Ad Acc. Circ:** 11,000.
Desc: Information about coming events, a seven-state calendar of events, features about all breeds of horses. The standings and results of horse activities in the intermountain west and pacific northwest.

US/0018-5191
HORSE WORLD. Vol. 1- Feb. 1949-. Periodical. English. Eleven times a year. $35.00 (one year), $60.00 (two years), $87.50 (three years). Dabora Inc, 730 Madison Street, Shelbyville TN 37160. **Tel** (615)684-8123. **ED** David L Howard. **Bk Rev. Ad Acc. Circ:** 2,500 (ctrl). ***Continues*** *United States Horseman.*
Desc: Brings you all the excitement and glamour of the saddle horse and morgan horse industry. Stories, results, winners, events and much more included.

UK/0018-5183
HORSE WORLD : PONY EXPRESS. Periodical. English. mo. Alan Exley Alan Exley, 181 Queen Victoria Street, London EC4 UK, 181 Queen Victoria Street, London EC4 UK,. **Tel** , , FAX , , telex , .

US/0897-4497
HORSE WORLD USA. ***Title Change.*** [Horse world USA]. **VAT** Horse World United States of America. Vol. 10, No. 6 (Jan. 1988)-(19??). Periodical. English. mo. Garri Publication Associates Inc, 114 West Hills Road, Huntington NY 11746. **Tel** (516)423-0620, FAX (516)423-0567. **ED** Diana De Rosa. **DD** 798. ***Continues*** *Eastern Horse World, 0745-9416.* ***Continued by*** *America's Equestrian, 1060-5975.*
Desc: An independent magazine available for all horsepeople and edited for the horse enthusiast, professional, amateur and horselover.

US/0162-8127
HORSECARE. ***Ceased.*** **VFOAT** Horse Care Magazine. **VAT** Horse Care. Vol. 1-Ceased (1991). English. an. Rich Publications Inc, 941 Calle Negocio, San Clemente CA 92672-6202. **Tel** (714)361-1955, FAX (714)361-0333. **LC** SF285.3; .H69. **DD** 636.1/083.

US/0018-5221
HORSEMAN (HOUSTON, TEX.). (HORSEMAN.). [Horseman]. (19??)-. Periodical. English. mo. $11.97. Horseman, 25025 I-45 North/Suite 390, Spring TX 77380. **Tel** (713)688-6611. available on microfilm and microfiche from University Microfilms International (UMI). Documents available from UMI Article Clearinghouse.
Ind/Abst AGRICOLA; Mag. Search; Newsp. Period. Abstr. (1988-1990); SportSearch.

US/1045-6066
HORSEMAN'S CONNECTION OF OREGON. [Horseman's connect. Or.]. 1st Ed. (1989)-. English. an. Equine Connection Inc, PO Box 20848, Portland OR 97220. **LC** SF278.54.O7; H67. **DD** 636.1/0025/795.

US/0018-5256
HORSEMEN'S JOURNAL, THE. ***Ceased.*** **Added/Corp** Horsemen's Benevolent and Protective Association. (19??)-(Dec. 1992). Periodical. English. mo. Horsemens Journal, PO Box 8237, Lexington KY 40533. **Tel** (606)223-9800. **ED** Kay Coyte. **DD** 798. **Bk Rev. Ad Acc. Circ:** 43,456 (ctrl). available on microfilm and microfiche from University Microfilms International (UMI). Documents available from UMI Article Clearinghouse.
Desc: Thoroughbred horse racing, owning, and training of race horses; also racing industry information including sales previews and legislative concerns.
Ind/Abst Newsp. Period. Abstr. (1988-).

US/0199-6436
HORSEMEN'S YANKEE PEDLAR. **VFOAT** Pedlar. (19??)-. Periodical. English. mo. $18.00 (one year); $29.00 (two years). Horsemens Yankee Pedlar, 785 South Bridge Street, Auburn MA 01501. **Tel** (508)832-9638, FAX (508)832-6744. **ED** Jane Sullivan. **Bk Rev. Ad Acc, Adv Mgr:** Kelley Small. **Circ:** 15,000.
Desc: All-breed, all-activity horse newspaper with up-to-date information.

CN/0840-6715
HORSEPOWER (AURORA). (HORSEPOWER: MAGAZINE FOR YOUNG HORSE LOVERS.). [Horsepower]. **VFOAT** Horse Power. (Oct./Nov. 1988)-. Periodical. English. Six times a year (Feb., Apr., June, Aug., Oct., Dec.). 15.95Can$ Canada; 29.95Can$ other. Corinthian Publishing Company Ltd, 225 Industrial Parkway South, PO Box 670, Aurora Ontario L4G 4J9 Canada. **Tel** (416)727-0107, FAX (416)841-1530. **ED** Susan Stafford. **DD** J798.2. **Bk Rev**, (Qty: varies). **Ad Acc, Adv Mgr:** V. Mosher.
Desc: General information for young riders. It listed puzzles, contests, cartoons, and a pen pal section.

CN/0225-4913
HORSES ALL. [Horses all]. Vol.1 (Oct. 1977)-. Periodical. English. mo. 14.02Can$ Canada; 15.00Can$ US; 39.00Can$ other. North Hill News Inc., 4000-19 Street Northeast, Calgary Alberta T2E 6P8, Canada. **Tel** (403)520-6633, FAX (403)291-0502. **ED** Mickey Dumont. **DD** 636.1/0097123. **Ad Acc. Circ:** 10,540 (ctrl).
Desc: Horse industry and horse association news. Official newspaper of western Canadian horse club and associations.

US/0046-7936
HORSES (CARLSBAD, CALIF.). (HORSES.). **VFOAT** Horses Magazine. (19??)-. Periodical. English. bm (Mar., June, Sept., Dec.). $19.95. Horses Magazine, 21 Greenview, Carlsbad CA 92008. **Tel** (919)931-9958, FAX (919)931-0650. **ED** John Quirk. **DD** 798. **Ad Acc. Circ:** 5,000 (ctrl).
Desc: The national and international magazine of the sport covering show jumping, dressage and eventing. Table-top quality. "Perfect bound." The leading Equestrian photographers of the world. Extensive use of color. Expertise and a lively sense of humor. The majority of readers save every issue.

US/0742-7999
HORSETRADER, THE. [Horsetrader]. **VFOAT** Horse Trader. (19??)-. Periodical. English. Twelve times a year. $15.00 US; $20.00 others. Horsetrader Inc., PO Box 728, Middlefield OH 44062. **Tel** (216)632-5266. **ED** Jerome Goldberg. **Ad Acc. Circ:** 36,000.
Desc: Strictly all advertising, display and classified: horse shows, clinics, sales, and horses for sale.

US/1057-8501
HUNTER & SPORT HORSE. [Hunt. sport horse]. **VFOAT** Hunter and Sport Horse. Vol. 1, Issue 2 (July/Aug. 1991)-. Periodical. English. bm. $15.99 (one year); $28.99 (two year). Midwest Hunter Inc, 12204 Covington Road, Ft Wayne IN 46804. **Tel** (219)625-4030, FAX (219)625-3480. **LC** WMLC 91/4668. **DD** 798. ***Continues*** *Midwest Hunter & Sport Horse, 1056-8182.*

FR
INFORMATION HIPPIQUE. **Added/Corp** Union Nationale Interprofessionnelle du Cheval. Periodical. French. bm. L Eperon, 174 Ave Charles de Gaulle, 92200 Neuilly Sur Seine France.

●US/1062-7146
INTERNATIONAL SADDLERY AND APPAREL JOURNAL. [Int. saddlery appar. j.]. **VFOAT** SAJ. Vol. 12, No. 1 (Jan. 1992)-. Periodical. English. mo. EEMG, Inc., PO Box 3039, Berea KY 40403-3039. **DD** 636. ***Continues*** *International Horse Digest, 1062-4201.*
Ind/Abst AGRICOLA.

CN/0712-497X
INTERNATIONAL THOROUGHBRED DIGEST. [Int. thoroughbred dig.]. No. 1 (Aug. 1981)-. Periodical. English. mo. 24.00Can$. International Thoroughbred Digest, 572 Cummer Avenue, Willowdale Ontario M2K 2M4 Canada. **DD** 636.1/32/0971.

US/0147-0833
JOURNAL OF EQUINE MEDICINE AND SURGERY, THE. [J. equine med. surg.]. V. 1 (Jan. 1977)-. Academic Scholarly Publication. English. mo (combined Nov./Dec.). $30.00 (licensed veterinarians) U.S. and Canada; $20.00 (students of veterinary medicine), $40.00 (libraries), $45.00 other. Veterinary Publications, Business and Editorial Offices, 44 Nassau Street, Princeton NJ 08540. **LC** SF951. **DD** 636.089/6/005. **NLM** W1 JO644C. **CODEN** JESUDA. Documents available from CASDDS.
Ind/Abst AGRICOLA; Chem. Abstr. (1977-1979); Index Vet.; Nutr. Abstr. Rev., Ser. B, Live Feeds and Feed.; Nutr. Abstr. Rev., Ser. A, Hum. Exp.; Life Sci. Collect.; Protozoolog. Abstr.; Vet. Bull.

US/0737-0806
JOURNAL OF EQUINE VETERINARY SCIENCE. [J. equine vet. sci.]. Vol. 1, No. 1 (Jan./Feb. 1981)-. Periodical. English. mo. $60.00 US; $70.00 Canada and Mexico; $85.00 other. Equine Veterinary Data, Box 1209, Wildomar CA 92595. **Tel** (714)678-1889, FAX (714)678-1885. **ED** William E Jones. **DD** 636. **NLM** W1 JO644CD. Index available. cum. index. **Bk Rev. Ad Acc. Pr Rev. Circ:** 3,500.
Desc: Scientific papers on equine veterinary matters and equine science update.
Ind/Abst AgBiotech News Inf.; AGRICOLA [Full Cov.]; Anim. Breed. Abstr.; Biodeter. Abstr. (1991-); Dairy Sci. Abstr.; Grasslands For. Abstr.; Helminthol. Abstr. (19??-19??); Index Vet.; Nutr. Abstr. Rev., Ser. B, Live Feeds and Feed.; Protozoolog. Abstr.; Rev. Med. Vet. Entomol.; Rev. Med. Vet. Mycology; SCISEARCH; Vet. Bull.; Wheat Barley Trit. Abstr.; World Agric. Econ.

●US
JOURNAL OF THE AMERICAN SHETLAND PONY CLUB. (1994)-. Periodical. English. bm. Pony Journal, Box 3415, Peoria IL 61614. Index available. **Ad Acc. Circ:** 1,400. ***Continues*** *Pony Journal, 0199-5537.*

CN/0381-1050
JR. RIDER, THE. **VAT** The Junior Rider. V. 1- Feb. 1977-. Periodical. English. qt. $3.00 Canada, $3.25 US. The Jr Rider, Rural Route 1, Kemptville Ontario K0G 1J0 Canada. **DD** 798/.2/05.

US/1041-2786
JUST HORSIN' AROUND. 1988-. Periodical. English. mo. $25.00. Jordan Hill Enterprises, Rt 10, Jordan Road, Franklin TN 37064. **Tel** (615)791-5656. **ED** Jane G Bradley. **DD** 798. **Circ:** 10,000.
Desc: A news and advice magazine for the Tennessee horseman. It covers a wide variety of topics including horse showing, horse jumping, polo, fox hunting, breed reports, and club news. Advice on care is also given.

US
KEENELAND. English. sa (Apr., Oct.). $5.50 (one year); $10.50 (two year). Paddock Publishing Inc, 904 North Broadway, Lexington KY 40505. **Tel** (606) 255-8860, FAX (606) 231-9223. **ED** Barbara Sutton. **Ad Acc.**
Desc: Dedicated to the Thoroughbred and Keeneland Race Course in particular.

PL
KON POLSKI. **Added/Corp** Panstwowe Wydawnictwo Rolnicze i Lesne. Vol. 11, No. 1 (1976)-. Periodical. Polish. Six times a year. Price on Request. **(Subscription address:** ARS Polona, PO Box 1001, 00068 Warsaw Poland.**)**

JA/0386-4634
KYOSHOBA SOGO KENKYUJO HOKOKU. (BULLETIN OF EQUINE RESEARCH INSTITUTE.). [Kyosoba Sogo Kenkyujo hokoku]. **VFOAT** Nihon Chuo Keibakai Kyosoba Sogo Kenkyujo Hokoku. No. 17 (1980)-. Academic Scholarly Publication. Japanese (English). Kyosoba Sogo Kenkyujo, 27-7 Tsurumaki 5-chome Setagaya-ku, Tokyo 154 Japan. **LC** SF951. **CODEN** BEQIDC. Documents available from BIOSIS Document Express, CASDDS. ***Continues*** *Experimental Reports of Equine Health Laboratory.*
Ind/Abst Biol. Abstr.; Chem. Abstr.; Dairy Sci. Abstr.; Helminthol. Abstr.; Index Vet.; Nutr. Abstr. Rev., Ser. B, Live Feeds and Feed.; Life Sci. Collect.; Protozoolog. Abstr.; SEA Abstr.; Vet. Bull.

US
LECTURES GIVEN AT THE STUD MANAGERS COURSE. **Main/Conf** Stud Managers Course, Lexington, Kentucky. 1st.- 1951-. Periodical. English. an. The Stud Managers Course, PO Box 4218, Lexington KY 40504.

US/0884-1284
LIST OF TATTOOED REGISTERED HARNESS HORSES. English. United States Trotting Association, 750 Michigan Avenue, Columbus OH 43215. **LC** SF339.5.U6; L57. **DD** 798.4/6/0973.

US/0892-6271
LONE STAR HORSE REPORT. [Lone horse rep.]. (198?)-. Periodical. English. mo. $10.00 (1 year), $15.00 (2 year). Lone Star Horse Report, PO Box 14767, Fort Worth TX 76117. **Tel** (817)838-8642, (800)852-0920, FAX (817)838-6410. **ED** Henry King. **DD** 636. **Bk Rev. Ad Acc. Circ:** 8,000.
Desc: Covers all horse uses from pleasure riding to pari-mutuel racing and all equine breeds from Miniatures to draft horses. Particularly edited for the chosen market of the North Central Texas counties surrounding the Dallas/Fort Worth metroplex, the largest concentration of horses in the United States.

US/0747-1912
LOUISIANA HORSE. [La. horse]. (Jan. 1969)-. Periodical. English. Six times a year. $12.00. The Louisiana Horse, PO Box 2098, Hammond LA 70404. **Tel** (504)345-6599. **DD** 632.

CN/0826-5682
MAGAZINE EQUESTRE (1984). (MAGAZINE EQUESTRE.). [Mag. equest.]. No. 11 (Spring 1984)-. Periodical. French. ir. $10.00. Magazine Equestre, CP 416 Succursale Bourassa, Montreal Quebec H2C 3G7 Canada. **DD** 636.1/005. ***Continues*** *Equestre, 0821-7904.*

US/0025-4274
MARYLAND HORSE, THE. Vol. 1, (1934)-. Periodical. English. mo (July/August issue combined). $30.00 US; $34.00 other. Maryland Horsebreeders Association, PO Box 427, Lutherville Timonium MD 21093. **Tel** (410)252-2100, FAX (301)560-0503. **ED** Richard W Wilcke. **LC** SF277; .M3. **DD** 636.12805. **Bk Rev. Ad Acc. Circ:** 4,400 (ctrl).
Desc: Thoroughbred racing and breeding in the Mid-Atlantic region serving owners, breeders, trainers and horse enthusiasts. Covers secondary throughbred markets as well.

US/1068-0810
MEMBERSHIP DIRECTORY - AMERICAN ASSOCIATION OF EQUINE PRACTITIONERS. **See** Veterinary Sciences.

US/1056-3245
MID-ATLANTIC THOROUGHBRED. [Mid-Atl. thoroughbred]. **Added/Corp** Maryland Horse Breeders Association. **VFOAT** Mid Atlantic Thoroughbred; Mid Atlantic Stallion Directory; Mid-Atlantic Sallion Directory. Vol. 1, No. 1 (1991)-. Periodical. English. bm. $20.00 US; $29.00 other. Maryland Horse Breeders Association, Box 427,

Timonium MD 21094. **Tel** (410)252-2100, FAX (410)560-0503. **ED** Richard Wilke. **LC** SF293.T5; M54. **DD** 636.1/32/02574. **Bk Rev. Ad Acc, Adv Mgr:** Kristen Mowery. **Circ:** 7,500.
Desc: Covers thoroughbred racing and breeding in the mid-atlantic region of the United States.

US/0279-4985
MINIATURE HORSE JOURNAL, THE.
Periodical. English. qt. International Miniature Horse Register, PO Box 907, Palos Verdes Estates CA 90274. **Tel** (310)375-1898.

US/0894-5632
MINNESOTA THOROUGHBRED JOURNAL. [Minn. thoroughbred j.]. **Added/Corp** Minnesota Thoroughbred Association. **VFOAT** Thoroughbred Journal. Vol. 1, No. 1 (Sept. 1987)-. Periodical. English. ir (9 issues). $25.00. Minnesota Thoroughbred Association, 1600 West Lake Street, Suite 130, Minneapolis MN 55408. **Tel** (612)827-2311. **DD** 798.

US/0747-1424
MODERN HORSE BREEDING : MHB. [Mod. horse breed.]. **VFOAT** M.H.B. Vol. 1, No. 1 (Jan. 1984)-. Periodical. English. ir (9 issues per year). $36.00 (one year), $65.00 (two year), $90.00 (three year). Modern Horse Breeding, 13017 Wisteria Drive 324, Germantown MD 20874. **Tel** (301)972-9279. **DD** 636.

CN/0228-0663
MON MEILLEUR. [Mon meilleur]. **VAT** Journal du Six/Trente-Six. V. 1- 27 Nov. 1977-. Periodical. French. wk. 0.50Can$ each number. Presse d'Action Economique, MTML Bureau 1903, 1650 Av Lincoln, Montreal Quebec H3H 1H1 Canada. **DD** 798.4/01/09714.

US/0027-1098
MORGAN HORSE, THE. Added/Corp American Morgan Horse Association. Morgan Horse Club. (1951)-. Periodical. English. Twelve times a year. $27.50 US; $49.50 Canada & Mexico; $57.50 others. American Morgan Horse Association, PO Box 960, Shelburne VT 05482-0960. **Tel** (802)985-4944, FAX (802)985-8897. **ED** Suzy Lucine. **LC** SF293.M8; M6. **DD** 636.1281. Index available. cum. index. **Ad Acc. Circ:** 7.300. ***Continues*** *Morgan Horse Magazine.*
Desc: Publishes profiles of famous horses from the past and present, biographical articles on trainers, breeders and other Morgan enthusiasts, interviews, coverage of events, articles on new developments in health, nutrition, medicine, or other sciences applicable to the Morgan.

US/1043-2590
MUSTANG!. (MUSTANG! : THE MAGAZINE FOR ADOPTERS OF WILD HORSES AND BURROS.). No. 1 (May 1989)-. Periodical. English. qt. $15.00 (one year), $28.00 (two year). Mustang Creek Inc., Rural Route 1, Box 112AA, Rollingstone MN 55969. **ED** Bev Sandlin and Josh Warburton. **DD** 636. **Bk Rev. Ad Acc.** ctrl circ.
Desc: Contains articles on wild horses and burros; also western heritage.

US/0027-9455
NATIONAL HORSEMAN, THE. [Natl. horseman]. (1???)-. Periodical. English. mo. $38.00. National Horseman, PO Box 43397, Middleton KY 40243. **Tel** (502)245-1125.

US/0886-5647
NATIONWIDE OVERNIGHT STABLING DIRECTORY. Directory. English. an. $19.95. Equine Travelers of America Inc, PO Box SD-322, Arkansas City KS 67005. **Tel** (316)442-8131 OR (515)637-4151, FAX (515)637-4155. **ED** James L McDaniel and Janice J Nelson. **LC** SF285.35; .N37. **DD** 636.1/08/3102573. **Circ:** 5,000.
Desc: Listings of overnight stabling available for traveling horsemen. Reservation service also available.

JA
NEGISHI KEIBA KINEN KOEN NENPO.
Main/Corp Negishi Keiba Kinen Koen. Began with issue for 1979. Periodical. Japanese. an. Baji Bunka Zaidan, 3 Negishidai 1 Naka-ku, Yokohama-shi 231 Japan. **LC** SF278.73.J32; N436A.

US/0886-4241
NEW MEXICO QUARTER HORSE, THE. [N.M. quart. horse]. **Added/Corp** New Mexico Quarter Horse Association. (19??)-. Periodical. English. an. $8.00. New Mexico Quarter Horse, Box 69, Pine Hill NM 87357. **Tel** (505)783-4347. **DD** 636.

CN/0835-5509
NEWSLETTER / EQUINE RESEARCH CENTRE AT GUELPH. [Newsl. - Equine Res. Cent. Guelph]. **Added/Corp** University of Guelph. Equine Research Centre. **VFOAT** Activities & Annual Report. Vol. 1, No. 4 (May 1987)-. Newsletter. English. Free. Equine Research Centre, University of Guelph, Guelph, Ontario N1G 2W1 Canada. **DD** 636.1/089/072. ***Continues*** *Newsletter (University of Guelph. Centre for Equine Research), 0837-1156.*
Ind/Abst SPORT Discus.

US
NEWSLETTER / TRI-STATE HORSEMEN'S ASSOCIATION. Main/Corp Tri-State Horsemen's Association. Newsletter. English. mo. 50 - 91st Lane NE, Minneapolis MN 55434.

US
NORTHEAST EQUINE JOURNAL. English. mo. $14.00. Equine Publication Inc, 312 Marlboro Street, Keene NH 03431. **Tel** (603)357-4271. **Bk Rev. Ad Acc. Circ:** 10,000.
Desc: Feature oriented horse publication.

US
OHIO THOROUGHBRED, THE. Added/Corp Ohio Thoroughbred Breeders and Owners. Vol. 4, No. 2 (April 1974)-. Trade Publication. English. bm. $18.00. Ohio Thoroughbred Breeders, 920 Rage Street/Suite 201, Cincinnati OH 45202. **Tel** (513)241-4589. **ED** Gayle Miller. **Ad Acc. Circ:** 1,500.
Desc: Intended to help develop and inform horsemen as to events in the breeding and thoroughbred-racing industry in the state of Ohio.

UK
PACEMAKER UPDATE INTERNATIONAL. ***Title Change.*** (19??)-(19??). English. Haymarket Publishing Ltd., 12 14 Ansdell Street, London W8 5TR England. **Tel** 011 44 483 733800, FAX 011 44 483 776573. **(Subscription address:** Haymarket Publishing Ltd, PO Box 219, Subscriptions Department, Woking Surrey GU21 1ZW, United Kingdom.**)** ***Merged with*** *Thoroughbred Breeder* ***to form*** *Pacemaker and Thoroughbred Breeder, 0967-4829.*

US/0894-4458
PACIFIC COAST JOURNAL. [Pac. Coast j.]. Vol. 22, No. 1 (Jan. 1985)-. Periodical. English. mo. $20.00 US; $25.00 other. Pacific Coast Quarter Horse Association, PO Box 255847, Sacramento CA 95865. **Tel** (916)924-7265. **ED** Jill L Scopinich. **DD** 636. **Circ:** 6,926. ***Continues*** *Quarter Horse of the Pacific Coast, 0093-8238.*

US/0164-5706
PAINT HORSE JOURNAL (1979). (PAINT HORSE JOURNAL.). **Added/Corp** American Paint Horse Association. (1979)-. Periodical. English. Twelve times a year. $23.00 (one year); $41.00 (two years). American Paint Horse Association, PO Box 961023, Fort Worth TX 76161. **Tel** (817)439-3400, FAX (817)439-3484. **ED** Darrell Dodds (phone: (817)439-3400 ext. 217). Index available. **Bk Rev**, (Qty: 10-12 per year). **Ad Acc, Adv Mgr:** Jackie McGinnis, **Tel** (817)439-3400 ext. 219. **Circ:** 16,200. ***Continues*** *Paint Horse.*
Desc: Published for horsemen who are interested in the American paint horse. Feature articles are varied but are all related to the paint horse industry.

US/0031-045X
PALOMINO HORSES. Added/Corp Palomino Horse Breeders of America. (19??)-. Periodical. English. mo. $17.50. Palomino Horse Breeders, 15253 East Skelly Drive, Tulsa OK 74116-2637. **Tel** (918)438-1234. **ED** Tracy Thompson. **Bk Rev. Ad Acc. Circ:** 5,800 (ctrl).
Desc: Information on equine-related human interest stories and breed association activities; reports on equine-related legislative activities; horse show results; activity calendar; and national equine events.

US/0882-9624
POA (1985). (POA : THE OFFICIAL PUBLICATION OF THE PONY OF THE AMERICAS CLUB, INC.). [POA]. **Added/Corp** Pony of the Americas Club. **VFOAT** POA Magazine. **VAT** Pony of America. Vol. 30, No. 3 (Apr. 1985)-. Periodical. English. mo. $20.00 (nonmembers), $25.00 (members). Pony of the Americas Club Inc, 5240 Elmwood Avenue, Indianapolis IN 46203. **Tel** (317)788-0107. **ED** Becky Lohman. **DD** 798. **Bk Rev. Ad Acc. Circ:** 1,700 (ctrl). ***Continues*** *Pony of America.*
Desc: Feature a Richard Shrake training column, spotlights on the POA breed and its owners, and articles on all topics in the equine industry.

US/0146-4574
POLO (GAITHERSBURG, MD.). See Recreation, Leisure-Sports.

UK
PONY. Vol. 25 i.e. 24, No. 12-. Periodical. English. mo. £12.60 UK; £18.60 other. D J Murphy Publishing Ltd., 296 Ewell Road Surbiton, Surrey KT6 7AQ England. **Tel** 011 44 81 390 8547, FAX 011 44 81 390 8696.

US/0199-5537
PONY JOURNAL, THE. ***Title Change.*** **Added/Corp** American Shetland Pony Club. American Miniature Horse Registry. Midwest Welsh Breeders. Northeastern Welsh Association. (1977)-(1993). Periodical. English. bm. Pony Journal, Box 3415, Peoria IL 61614. **ED** T. R. Huston. Index available. **Ad Acc. Circ:** 1,400. ***Continues*** *American Shetland Pony and American Miniature Horse Journal.* ***Continued by*** *Journal of the American Shetland Pony Club, American Miniature Horse Registry.*

US/0090-8762
PRACTICAL HORSEMAN. [Pract. horseman]. Vol. 1 (Jan. 1973)-. Periodical. English. mo. $33.00. Cowles Magazines, PO Box 8200, Harrisburg PA 17105. **Tel** (717)657-9555, (800)435-9610. **Ad Acc. Circ:** 55,000. ***Absorbed*** *Pennsylvania Horse.*
Desc: How-to-do-it publication for the serious English-style rider interested in breeding, training and conditioning horses for hunting, jumping, and training.
Ind/Abst SPORT Discus; SportSearch (May 1987-).

US/0741-4595
PRACTICAL TAX GUIDE FOR THE HORSE OWNER, A. [Pract. tax guide horse own.]. Began with 1983 Ed. English. an. Publishing Horizons, 623 High Street, Worthington OH 43085. **LC** KF6289.8.H6; T35. **DD** 343.7305/2/024636.

FR/0395-8639
PRATIQUE VETERINAIRE EQUINE. See Veterinary Sciences.

US/0195-6272
PREAKNESS, THE. Main/Corp Maryland Jockey Club. **VFOAT** Preakness Stakes. English. an. Maryland Jockey Club, Baltimore MD 21215. **ED** S Siciliano. **LC** SF357.P73; M37A. **DD** 799.4/3/097526. ***Continues*** *Pimlico Proudly Presents ... Running, Preakness.*

US
PROCEEDINGS - NATIONAL ADVISORY BOARD FOR WILD FREE-ROAMING HORSES & BURROS. Main/Corp National Advisory Board for Wild Free-Roaming Horses and Burros. Government Publication. English. an. US Department of the Interior Bureau of Land Management, 1849 C Street NW, Room 5660, Washington DC 20240. **Tel** (202)208-3801, FAX (202)208-5902.

US/0065-7182
PROCEEDINGS OF THE ANNUAL CONVENTION OF THE AMERICAN ASSOCIATION OF EQUINE PRACTITIONERS. [Proc. annu. conv. Am. Assoc. Equine Pract.]. **Main/Corp** American Association of Equine Practitioners. (1956)-. Proceedings. English. an (July). $35.00 (members); $73.00 (non-members) Comes with American Association of Equine Practitioners membership. American Association of Equine Practitioners, 4075 Iron Works Pike, Lexington KY 40511. **Tel** (606)233-0147, FAX (606)233-1968. **ED** Frank J. Milne. **DD** 636. **NLM** W1 PR584NN. Index available. cum. index. **Circ:** 5,200 (ctrl). available on microfilm from University Microfilms International (UMI).
Desc: Scientific papers given at the annual convention of equine medicine.
Ind/Abst AGRICOLA [Full Cov.]; Anim. Breed. Abstr.; Dairy Sci. Abstr.; Helminthol. Abstr. (1991-); Index Vet.; Nutr. Abstr. Rev., Ser. B, Live Feeds and Feed.; Life Sci. Collect.; Rev. Med. Vet. Mycology; Vet. Bull.

CN/0708-4978
PROCEEDINGS OF THE SUBCOMMITTEE ON OFF-TRACK BETTING. Main/Corp Canada. Parliament. Senate. Subcommittee on Off-Track Betting. **VFOAT** Deliberations du Sous-Comite sur les Paris Hors-Piste. **VAT** Off-Track Betting; Paris Hors-Piste. No. 1- Mar. 6, 1979-. Proceedings. English (French). Receiver General for Canada / Ottawa, Canada Comm Group Publishing, Ottawa Ontario K1A 0S9 Canada. **Tel** (819)956-4802, (800)661-2868. **LC** SF333.C2; C36A. **DD** 798.4/01/0971.

NE/0167-7926
PRZEWALSKI HORSE. No. 1- May 1978-. Periodical. English (Dutch). sa (June and December). DM22.00, $12.00. Foundation for Preservation & Protection of Przewalski Horse, Mathenesserstraat 101A, 3027 PD Rotterdam Netherlands. **Tel** 010-4370447. **Bk Rev. Ad Acc.** ctrl circ.
Desc: Information on projects reserves for the Przewalski horse research, behaviour, genetics, breeding, policy in captivity, in zoos and reserves, biology of the horse, etc.

CN/0228-0612
QUARTER CIRCLE. (THE QUARTER CIRCLE.). [Quart. circle]. **Added/Corp** B. C. Quarter Horse Association. (1978)-. Periodical. English. ir. Free. Quarter Horse Association, PO Box 3216, Langley British Columbia V3A 4R6 Canada. **Tel** (604)530-8667. **DD** 636.1/33/09711. **Bk Rev. Ad Acc. Circ:** 1,000 (ctrl).
Desc: Contains veterinary articles, training articles and quarter horse breed articles.

US/0164-6656
QUARTER HORSE JOURNAL (1953), THE. (THE QUARTER HORSE JOURNAL.). [Quart. horse j.]. (1953)-. Periodical. English. Twelve times a year. $17.00 one year; 42.50 three years. American Quarter Horse Association, PO Box 32470, Amarillo TX 79120. **Tel** (806)376-4811, FAX (806)372-6806. **ED** Audie Rackley, (806)376-4888. **LC** SF293.Q3; Q3. **Ad Acc, Adv Mgr:** Doug Hayes, **Tel** (806)372-1163. **Pr Rev.** ctrl circ. available on microfilm from University Microfilms International (UMI). ***Continues*** *Quarter Horse and the Quarter Horse Journal.*
Desc: New stories and pictures designed to improve the breeding and performance of the American Quarter Horse.

US/0093-8238
QUARTER HORSE OF THE PACIFIC COAST, THE. ***Title Change.*** [Quart. horse Pac. Coast]. **Main/Corp** Pacific Quarter Horse Association. (19??)-(19??). Periodical. English. mo. Pacific Coast Quarter Horse, PO Box 254822-Cal Expo GT 12, Sacramento CA 95825. **Tel** (916)922-9857. **DD** 636. ***Continued by*** *Pacific Coast Journal, 0894-4458.*

US/0899-3130
QUARTER RACING JOURNAL, THE. [Quart. racing j.]. **Added/Corp** American Quarter Horse Association. Vol. 1, No. 1 (Jan. 1988)-. Periodical. English. Twelve times a year. $17.00 (one year), $42.50 (three year) US; $34.00 (1 year) other. American Quarter Horse Association, PO Box 32470, Amarillo TX 79120. **Tel** (806)376-4811, FAX (806)372-6806. **ED** Audie Rackley, (806)376-4888. **LC** WMLC 93/1737. **DD** 798. Index available. **Ad Acc. Pr Rev. Circ:** 12,000 (ctrl).
Desc: The official racing voice of the American Quarter Horse Association. Dedicated to the advancement and improvement of the breeding and performance of the racing quarter horse.

US/0091-7516
QUARTER RACING RECORD, THE. ***Suspended.*** [Quart. racing rec.]. (1961)-Suspended. Periodical. English. mo. $20.00. Quarter Racing Record, 2033 Heritage Park Drive, Oklahoma City OK 73120-7502. **Tel** (817)656-9221. **ED** H David Smith. **LC** SF357.3; .Q37. **DD** 798.4/3. **Ad Acc. Circ:** 9,000.
Desc: Provides the most complete and in-depth coverage of the racing industry available today.

US/0888-0859
QUARTER RUNNING HORSE CHART BOOK, THE. [Quart. runn. horse chart book]. **Added/Corp** American Quarter Horse Association. Racing Dept. American Quarter Horse Association. Racing Division. American Quarter Racing Association. (Jan./Mar. 1949)-. Periodical. English. mo. $115.00. American Quarter Horse Association, PO Box 32470, Amarillo TX 79120. **Tel** (806)376-4811, FAX (806)372-6806. **ED** Dan Fick. **LC** SF321; .Q8. **Circ:** 500 (ctrl).
Desc: Race charts and statistical information concerning quarter horse racing.

UK
RACEFORM UP-TO-DATE FORM BOOK. English. an. £5.00. Sporting Chronicle Publications Ltd, PO Box 290 Thomson House, Manchester M60 4BJ England. **LC** SF335.G7; R29. **DD** 798.4/3/0941.

UK
RACEFORM UP-TO-DATE FORM BOOK. NATIONAL HUNT EDITION. English. an. £11.00. Sporting Chronicle Publications Ltd, PO Box 290 Thomson House, Manchester M60 4BJ England. **LC** SF359.3.G7; R32. **DD** 798.4/5/0941.

US/0733-6500
RACING, FARM, CORPORATE, AND STABLE NAMES. [Racing farm corp. stable names]. **Main/Corp** United States Trotting Association. (1960)-. English. an. United States Trotting Association, 750 Michigan Avenue, Columbus OH 43215. **LC** SF321; .U52. **DD** 798.4/6/02573. ***Continues*** *United States Trotting Association. Racing Farm and Stable Names.*

US/0033-7439
RACING STAR WEEKLY. (19??)-. Periodical. English. wk. $45.00. Star Publishing Company / New York, 438 West 37th Street, New York NY 10018. **Tel** (212)279-4619. **ED** Bob Smith. **Bk Rev. Ad Acc. Circ:** 12,000.

US/0744-6829
RACKING REVIEW, THE. (19??)-. Periodical. English. Twenty times a year. $20.00. The Racking Review, PO Box 777, Waynesboro TN 38485. **Tel** (615)722-3688. **DD** 798.

US/0736-0134
REGISTER OF THE AMERICAN SADDLEBRED HORSE ASSOCIATION (INCORPORATED), THE. **Added/Corp** American Saddlebred Horse Association. **VFOAT** American Saddlebred Horse Register; American Saddle Horse Register. Vol. No. 61 (1980)-. English. an. $70.00 (per issue). American Saddlebred Horse Association, c/o Kentucky Horse, 4093 Iron Works Pike, Lexington KY 40511-8433. **Tel** (606)259-2742. **LC** SF293.S12; A5. **DD** 636.1/3/0973. ***Continues*** *Register of the American Saddle-Horse Breeders' Association (Incorporated).*
Desc: Lists pedigrees of all American saddlebred horses registered during a given year. Also includes indexes by original owners, sires and registration numbers.

US
REPORT OF THE ... RACING SEASON / MAINE STATE HARNESS RACING COMMISSION. **See** Recreation, Leisure-Sports.

CN/1184-2059
REVUE DU CHEVAL ARABE DU QUEBEC, LA. [Rev. cheval arabe Que.]. **Added/Corp** Association du Cheval Arabe du Quebec. (Winter 1990)-. Periodical. French (summaries and/or abstracts in English). qt. Free for members. Association du Cheval Arabe du Quebec, 3280 Rue Belair, Sherbrooke, Quebec J1L 1B1 Canada. **DD** 636.1/12. ***Continues*** *Revue du Cheval Arabe., 1184-2040.*

CN/0380-2736
REVUE HIPPIQUE, LA. V. 1- Dec. 1970-. Periodical. French. Mijean, CP 66, Ste.Rose Quebec H7L 1K7.

UK
RIDING. English. wk. $86.00. Scott Publishing Ltd, Perrymound Road, Hayward Heath, West Sussex RH1 63BR England.

CN/0824-4812
RIGHT TRACK (TORONTO). (THE RIGHT TRACK.). [Right track]. Mar. 1, 1983-. Periodical. English. mo. $2.00 per no. Right Track, Suite 100-185, 2 Bloor Street West, Toronto Ontario M4W 3E2. **DD** 798.4/01/09713.

US/0738-8381
ROCKY MOUNTAIN QUARTER HORSE. **Added/Corp** Rocky Mountain Quarter Horse Association. (1963)-. Periodical. English. mo. $20.00. Rocky Mountain Quarterhorse Association, 318 Livestock Exchange Building, Denver CO 80216. **Tel** (303)296-1143, (303)478-2162.

CN/0708-5125
RULES OF STANDARDBRED RACING. (RULES OF STANDARDBRED RACING / ONTARIO RACING COMMISSION.). [Rules standardbred racing]. **Main/Corp** Ontario Racing Commission. **VFOAT** Standardbred Racing. (19??)-. English (French). an. Ontario Racing Commission, 10 Wellesley Street East, Toronto Ontario M7A 2K1 Canada. **Tel** (416)963-0520. **LC** KEO766.5.H65; A323. **Circ:** 12,000 (ctrl).

CN/0707-8919
RULES OF THOROUGHBRED RACING. (RULES OF THOROUGHBRED RACING, WITH QUARTERHORSE APPENDAGE / ONTARIO RACING COMMISSION.). **Main/Corp** Ontario Racing Commission. **VFOAT** Rules of Thoroughbred Racing. (19??)-. English. Ontario Racing Commission, 10 Wellesley Street East, Toronto Ontario M7A 2K1 Canada. **Tel** (416)963-0520. **LC** KEO766.5.H65; A324.

US/0036-2271
SADDLE AND BRIDLE. (1928)-. Periodical. English. mo. $38.00 US; $58.00 other. Saddle & Bridle, 375 North Jackson Avenue, St. Louis MO 63130. **Tel** (314)725-9115, FAX (314) 725-6440. **ED** Jeffrey A. Thompson. **LC** SF277; .S25. **DD** 798.05. Index available. **Bk Rev. Ad Acc, Adv Mgr:** Chris Thompson. **Circ:** 6,000 (ctrl).
Desc: Covers show horse breeds of Saddlebred, Morgan, Hackney, Arabian and the leading national horse shows.

US/0161-7842
SADDLE HORSE REPORT. (19??)-. Periodical. English. Fifty times a year. $50.00 (one year), $87.50 (two years), $125.00 (three years). Dabora Inc, 730 Madison Street, Shelbyville TN 37160. **Tel** (615)684-8123. **ED** David Howard. **DD** 798. **Ad Acc. Circ:** 4,500 (ctrl).
Desc: Contains all the latest news and information about the shows, horses, sales, and horsepeople in the Saddle Horse and Morgan Horse industry.

US/8755-3929
SHOW HORSE (BANGOR, ME.). (SHOW HORSE.). [Show horse]. Vol. 1, No. 1 (Dec. 1984)-. Periodical. English. mo. $24.00. Show Horse, PO Box 1270, Bangor ME 04401. **Tel** (207)947-0126. **ED** Stephen Kinney. **LC** SF295.185; .S56. **DD** 798.2/05. **Bk Rev. Ad Acc. Circ:** 5,000. ***Continues*** *Northeast Horseman, 0029-2990.*
Desc: A four-color, glossy magazine for the American Saddleseat; show ring traditions of horsemanship, Saddlebreds, Arabians and Morgans.

US/0744-3056
SIDE-SADDLE NEWS. (SIDE-SADDLE NEWS : OFFICIAL PUBLICATION OF THE INTERNATIONAL SIDE-SADDLE ORGANIZATION.). [Side-saddle news]. **VFOAT** Side Saddle News. Periodical. English. bm. $18.00. Side-Saddle News, Road 2/Box 2055, Mount Holly NJ 08060. **Tel** (609)261-1777. **ED** C B Kneeland. **Bk Rev. Ad Acc. Circ:** 800.
Desc: A magazine about side-saddles and side-saddle riding. Affluent circulation nation wide. Lists shows, clinics, runs, how-to articles and pictures. Its the largest of its type magazine in the world.

US/0093-3929
SOUTHERN HORSEMAN. (19??)-. Periodical. English. Twelve times a year. Southern Horseman, PO Box 71, Meridian MS 39302. **Tel** (601)693-6607.

US/0364-9237
SPEEDHORSE (MONTHLY), THE. (THE SPEEDHORSE.). [Speedhorse]. **VFOAT** Speed Horse. (1967)-. Periodical. English. mo (except Nov.). $20.00. Speedhorse Publications Inc, PO Box 1000, Norman OK 73070. **Tel** (405)364-0831. **ED** Diane C. Simmons. **LC** SF321; .Q3. **DD** 798/.43. **Bk Rev. Ad Acc. Circ:** 8,200 (ctrl). ***Continues*** *Quarter Racing World.*
Desc: Trade publications devoted to breeding and training for the quarter horse racing industry. Subject matter geared toward owners, trainers and breeders.

US/0098-5422
SPUR (DELAPLANE). (SPUR.). **Added/Corp** National Steeplechase and Hunt Association. Virginia Thoroughbred Association. (19??)-. Periodical. English. bm (6 issues). $24.00. Spur Publications Inc., 725 Broadstreet, Augusta GA 30901. **Tel** (706)722-6060, FAX (706)724-3873. **ED** Cathy C. Laws. **LC** SF277; .S63. **DD** 636.1/2/05. **Ad Acc. Circ:** 52,000. ***Continues*** *Spur of Virginia.*
Desc: Edited for owners, breeders, trainers, jockeys, and fans of the thoroughbred horse and sports of flat racing, steeplechasing, and polo. Feature oriented, in-depth profiles and color photo essays.

US/0163-7649
STABLE & KENNEL NEWS OF THE SOUTH. **VAT** Stable and Kennel News of the South. Periodical. English. mo. $6.00. Florida Horseman, PO Box 146, Altamonte Springs FL 32701. ***Formed by the union of*** *News of Georgia's Horses* ***and*** *Southern Dog Advertiser.*

US/1055-2979
STALLION DIRECTORY. [Stallion dir.]. **VFOAT** Stallion Directory for ...; Thoroughbred Times Stallion Directory. Directory. English. Record Publishing Company / Kentucky, 904 North Broadway, Lexington KY 40505. **LC** SF293.T5; S75. **DD** 636.1/32. ***Absorbed*** *Sire Book, 0272-3786.*

US
STALLION REGISTER FOR ... . **Added/Corp** Thoroughbred Owners and Breeders Association. (19??)-. English. an (Nov.). $27.75 Kentucky residents; $26.50 US; $31.50 others. Thoroughbred Owner Breeder Association, PO Box 4038, Lexington KY 40544. **Tel** (606)278-2361, (606)278-2361, FAX (606)276-4450, telex 21-8473. **ED** Ed Bowen. **LC** SF277; .B55 Suppl. **DD** 636.1/32/05. Index available. **Bk Rev. Ad Acc. Circ:** 22,500.
Desc: Concerns owning, breeding, selling and racing thoroughbred horses; reports important stakes races and various aspects of breeding, racing, training and care.

CN/0705-2553
STANDARDBRED, THE. [Standardbred]. Vol. 8, No. 20 (Sept. 27, 1978)-. Periodical. English. Twenty-six times a year. 30.00Can$ Canada; $35.00 US. The Standardbred News, PO Box 150, Circulation Department, Acton ONT L7J 2M3 Canada. **Tel** (519)853-5100, FAX (519)853-5040. **ED** Paul Nolan. **DD** 798.4/6/0971. **Ad Acc. Circ:** 6,000. ***Continues*** *Standardbred Magazine, 0827-8067.*
Ind/Abst SportSearch (May 1987-).

US/0083-3495
STANDARDBRED SIRES AND DAMS. **VFOAT** U.S.T.A. Sires and Dams. The Register. English. an. $60.00. United States Trotting Association, 750 Michigan Avenue, Columbus OH 43215. **ED** David Carr. **LC** SF293.S72; S74. **DD** 636.1/7.
Desc: Records are performance data on standard bred stallions and mares and their offspring.

UK
STATISTICAL RECORD, THE. **See** Horses and Horsemanship-Abstracting, Bibliographies and Statistics.

US/0149-3442
TACK 'N TOGS MERCHANDISING. (19??)-. Periodical. English. Thirteen times a year. $25.00. Miller Publishing Company, 12400 Whitewater Drive, Suite 160, Minnetonka MN 55343. **Tel** (612)931-0211. **(Subscription address:** CDS / SIFD Agency Control, 1901 Bell Avenue, Des Moines IA 50315.) **[CCC].** available on microfilm from University Microfilms International (UMI).

US/0149-9920
TEXAS HORSE-TRADER, THE. V. 1- Aug. 1977-. Periodical. English. mo. $10.00. E.W. Forbes and Associates, 1218 Autrey, Houston TX 77006.

US/0164-6168
TEXAS THOROUGHBRED (WICHITA FALLS, KAN.). (TEXAS THOROUGHBRED.). [Tex. thoroughbred]. **Added/Corp** Texas Thoroughbred Breeders Association. (19??)-. Periodical. English. Eleven times a year (June/July issues combined). $18.00. Texas Throughbred Breeders Association, PO Box 14967, Austin TX 78761. **Tel** (512)458-6133, FAX (512)453-5919. **ED** Anne Lang. **DD** 636. **Bk Rev. Ad Acc. Circ:** 2,500 (ctrl).
Desc: Feature photos pertinent to thoroughbred

breeding, horse health and racing in Texas and the Southwest. Official publication of the Texas Thoroughbred Breeder's Association.

US/0883-8038
THOROUGHBRED BUSINESS. [Thoroughbred bus.]. Vol. 1, No. 1 (Nov./Dec. 1985)-. Periodical. English. bm. $18.00 US; $32.00 Canada, free to qualified persons. Lexington Publishers, PO Box 21973, Lexington KY 40522-1973. **DD** 798.

US/0049-3821
THOROUGHBRED OF CALIFORNIA, THE. **Added/Corp** California Thoroughbred Breeders Association. (19??)-. Periodical. English. mo (12 issues). $42.00 (one year), $80.00 (two year), $116.00 (three year) US; $60.00 (one year), $115.00 (two year), $165.00 (three year) other. California Thoroughbred Breeders Association, 201 Colorado Place, PO Box 750, Arcadia CA 91006. **Tel** (818)445-7800, FAX (8181)574-0852, telex 247505 CTB UR. **ED** Nat Wess and Tracy Gantz. Index available. **Bk Rev**. **Ad Acc. Circ:** 3400 (ctrl). available on microfilm and microfiche from University Microfilms International (UMI).
Desc: Devoted to the improvement of racehorses in California; designed as an educational tool for horsemen.

US/0162-3117
THOROUGHBRED RECORD (1967). ***Title Change.*** (THOROUGHBRED RECORD.). [Thoroughbred rec.]. Vol. 186, No. 19 (Nov. 1967)-(1992). Periodical. English. mo. Thoroughbred Publications Inc., PO Box 8237, Lexington KY 40533. **Tel** (606)223-9800, (800)648-4637. **LC** SF293.T5; T3974. **DD** 798.4/.00973. available on microfilm and microfiche from University Microfilms International (UMI). ***Continues*** *Thoroughbred Record and the Racing Calendar, 0040-6414.* ***Merged into*** *Thoroughbred Times, 0887-2244.*
Ind/Abst SportSearch (May 1987-?).

US
THOROUGHBRED RECORD. FOREIGN STATISTICAL REVIEW, THE. **See** Horses and Horsemanship-Abstracting, Bibliographies and Statistics.

US/0739-5809
THOROUGHBRED STALLION RECORDS OF ... . [Thoroughbred stallion rec.]. **VFOAT** Blood Horse Thoroughbred Stallion Records of ...; Blood-Horse Thoroughbred Stallion Records of ... . 1981-. English. an. $60.00. **LC** SF293.T5; T43. **DD** 636.1/32. **Circ:** 1,000.
Desc: Contains statistics on every sire with a runner in the previous year, and every broodmare sire of a runner in that year. Includes an average earnings index, plus new indexes for evaluating 500 leading sires and broodmare sires.

US/0887-2244
THOROUGHBRED TIMES. [Thoroughbred times]. Vol. 1, Issue 1 (Sept. 20, 1985)-. Periodical. English. wk (Tues.). $52.95 Kentucky residents; $49.95 others in US; $110.00 Canada; $120.00 other. Thoroughbred Publications Inc., PO Box 8237, Lexington KY 40533. **Tel** (606)223-9800, (800)648-4637. **ED** Mark Simon. **LC** SF293.T5; T44. **DD** 636.1/32/05. **Bk Rev**. **Ad Acc. Circ:** 25,000 (ctrl). ***Absorbed*** *Thoroughbred Record.* ***Continued in part by*** *Florida Thoroughbred Times, 1049-9032.*
Desc: A newspaper for thoroughbred owners and breeders covering racing, public auctions, farm management, veterinary care, law, taxes, and statistics.

US/1046-9974
TIMES, IN HARNESS. [Times harness]. Vol. 1 No. 1 (Sept. 9 1989)-. Periodical. English. Fifty-two times a year. $68.00 US; $78.00 Canada; $245.00 other. Times Standard Inc, 8125 Jonestown Road, Harrisburg PA 17112. **Tel** (717)469-2000, FAX (717)469-2005. **ED** Frank Cotolo. **LC** WMLC L 83/8004. **DD** 798. **Ad Acc. Circ:** 6,800.
Desc: Edited for owners of harness race horses.

US/0274-8274
TRAIL BLAZER (PASO ROBLES). (TRAIL BLAZER.). **VFOAT** Trail Blazer for the Distance Rider. (197?)-. Periodical. English. Twelve times a year. $15.00. Trail Blazer, 5000 Carrizo Road, Atascadero CA 93422. **Tel** (805)544-4913. **ED** Susan Brannon. **DD** 798. **Ad Acc. Circ:** 12,300 (ctrl).
Desc: The voice of the sports of distance horse racing for 9 years. Technical training articles, schedule of events and human interest.

CN/0704-0733
TROT. **VFOAT** Maple Leaf Trot. **VAT** Trot Magazine. V. 1- Dec. 1974-. Periodical. English (French). mo. $13.93. Canadian Trotting Association, 233 Evans Avenue, Toronto Ontario M8Z 1J6 Canada. **Tel** (416)252-3565. **DD** 798/.46/0971.
Ind/Abst SportSearch (May 1987-).

US/0744-0103
USCTA NEWS. **VFOAT** U.S.C.T.A. News. **VAT** United States Combined Training Association News. 1971. Periodical. English. bm. $15.00 US; $20.00 Canada; $15.00 (surface mail), $33.00 (airmail) other. United States Combined Training, 292 Bridge Street, South Hamilton MA 01982. **Tel** (617)468-7133. **ED** Fifi Coles. **Bk Rev**. **Ad Acc. Circ:** 7,500 (ctrl).
Desc: Educational articles on all aspects of combined training, plus the latest rule changes, calendar of events, and profiles on horses and riders.
Ind/Abst SPORT Discus.

US/0882-5130
USDF BULLETIN. [USDF bull.]. Bulletin. English. qt. USDF, PO Box 80668, Lincoln NE 68501. **Tel** (402)474-7632. **DD** 798. **Circ:** 19,000.
Ind/Abst SPORT Discus.

US/0882-5009
USDF CALENDAR OF COMPETITIONS. **Added/Corp** United States Dressage Federation. **VFOAT** Calendar of Competitions. (19??)-. English. an. USDF, PO Box 80668, Lincoln NE 68501. **Tel** (402)474-7632. **Bk Rev**. **Ad Acc. Circ:** 4,000 (ctrl).
Desc: Recognized dressage competitions for year listed chronologically and by region, plus current dressage tests.

US/0882-4991
USDF DRESSAGE INSTRUCTORS, CLINICIANS, TRAINERS, JUDGES, TECHNICAL DELEGATES DIRECTORY. **VFOAT** USDF Dressage Directory; Dressage Directory. Directory. English. be. $5.00. USDF, PO Box 80668, Lincoln NE 68501. **Tel** (402)474-7632. **LC** SF309.5; .U77. **DD** 798.2/3/02573.

●US/1059-8456
VETERINARY UPDATE (LARGE ANIMALS). **See** Veterinary Sciences.

US/0505-8813
VOICE OF THE TENNESSEE WALKING HORSE. **Added/Corp** Tennessee Walking Horse Breeders and Exhibitors Association. **VFOAT** Voice. (1962)-. Periodical. English. mo (Sept./Oct. issues combined). $18.00 (one year), $34.00 (two year), $50.00 (three year). Tennessee Walking Horse, Exhibition Association, Box 286, Lewisburg TN 37091. **Tel** (615)359-1567, FAX (615)359-2539. **ED** P. J. Wamble. **Ad Acc, Adv Mgr:** David Kranich, **Tel** (615)359-1567. **Circ:** 4,000 (ctrl).
Desc: The official breed journal of the Tennessee Walking Horse.

US/0093-6928
WALKING HORSE REPORT. (19??)-. Periodical. English. Fifty times a year (weekly except Christmas and New Year's). $50.00 (one year), $87.50 (two years), $125.00 (three years). Dabora Inc, 730 Madison Street, Shelbyville TN 37160. **Tel** (615)684-8123. **ED** David Howard. **LC** SF293.T4; W35. **DD** 636.1/3. **Ad Acc. Circ:** 6,000 (ctrl).
Desc: Contains all the latest news and information about the shows, horses, sales, and horsepeople in the Walking Horse Industry.

US/8750-8109
WALKING HORSE WORLD. Vol. 3, No. 1 (Jan. 1985)-. Periodical. English. mo. $9.00. Walking Horse World, PO Box 1297, Lebanon TN 37087. **DD** 636. ***Continues*** *Bits 'n Shoes, 0746-1631.*

US/0043-3837
WESTERN HORSEMAN, THE. [West. horseman]. Vol. 1, No. 1 (Jan. 1936)-. Periodical. English. mo. $18.00 (1 year), $30.00 (2 year). Western Horseman Magazine, 3850 North Avenue, PO Box 7980, Colorado Springs CO 80933-7980. **Tel** (719)633-5524, (800)874-6774, FAX (719)633-1392. **(Subscription address:** Kable Publishers Aide, 308 East Hitt Street, Subscription Department, Mt. Morris IL 61054-1473.**)** **ED** Pat Close. **LC** SF277; .W52. **DD** 636.105. Index available (bound in issue). **Bk Rev**. **Ad Acc. Circ:** 180,598. available on microfilm and microfiche from University Microfilms International (UMI). Documents available from UMI Article Clearinghouse.
Desc: Magazine devoted to the western stock horse, including quarter horse and other breeds. Articles on training, breeding, showing, veterinary, rodeo, ranching, and general interest.
Ind/Abst Acad. Search (May 1984-June 1989); Biol. Agric. Index; INFO-SOUTH Abstr.; Mag. Artic. Summar. Elite (May 1984-June 1989); Mag. Artic. Summar. Select (May 1984-June 1989); Mag. Artic. Summar. CD-ROM (May 1984-June 1989); Mag. Search; Newsp. Period. Abstr. (1992-).

CN/0820-571X
WESTERN RIDER (1987). (THE WESTERN RIDER.). [West. rid.]. **VFOAT** Canadian Quarter Horse Journal. Vol. 17, No. 6 (Mar. 1987)-. Periodical. English. Twelve times a year. 25.00Can$ (one year); 40.00 (two years). Golden Arc Publishing and Typesetting, 491 Book Road West, Ancaster, Ontario L9G 3L1 Canada. **Tel** (416)648-2035. **DD** 798.2/05. Index available. **Bk Rev**. **Ad Acc.** ***Continues*** *The Canadian Rider, 0702-9071.*

US/0192-5210
YANKEE HORSETRADER. ***Ceased.*** **VAT** Yankee Horse Trader. (1978)-Vol. 9, No. 6 ?. Periodical. English. mo. Yankee Horse Trader, PO Box 226, Shaftsbury VT 05262-0226. **Tel** (802)442-8092. **ED** David Scribner. **Bk Rev**. **Ad Acc. Circ:** 5,000 (ctrl).
Desc: Offers in-depth columns and features on all aspects of the horse industry in the Eastern US, including veterinary news and profiles of horsemen.

ABSTRACTING, BIBLIOGRAPHIES AND STATISTICS

UK
STATISTICAL RECORD, THE. . Statistical Publication. English. qt. £99.00. Weatherbys, Sanders Road, Wellingborough NN8 4BX England. **Tel** (0933)76241, telex 311582. **ED** S Cheney. **Ad Acc.** ctrl circ.
Desc: Statistical analysis of racing performances during the calendar year in Great Britain and Ireland and of British bred winners overseas.

US
THOROUGHBRED RECORD. FOREIGN STATISTICAL REVIEW, THE. **VFOAT** Foreign Statistical Review; Foreign Stakes Supplement. 1984-. Statistical Publication. English. an. $39.95, $54.95 (with Statistical review). Thoroughbred Publications Inc., PO Box 8237, Lexington KY 40533. **Tel** (606)223-9800, (800)648-4637. **ED** David Heckerman. **LC** SF293.T5; T396. **DD** 636.1/32/021. **Bk Rev**. **Ad Acc. Circ:** 17,000. ***Continues in part*** *Thoroughbred Record Breeders Book.*
Desc: A thoroughbred breeding and racing publication over 113 years old.

HOTELS/MOTELS

UK
ABC WORLDWIDE HOTEL GUIDE. ***Title Change.*** **VFOAT** Worldwide Hotel Guide; ABC World Wide Hotel Guide. (Apr. 1986)-?. English. sa. ABC International / Boston, 131 Clarendon Street, Boston MA 02116. **LC** TX907; .A143. **DD** 647/.94/05. ***Continues in part*** *ABC Hotel Guide.* ***Continued by*** *Hotel & Trave Index (ABC International Ed.), 1056-4713.*

UK
AGENT'S HOTEL GAZETTEER : TOURIST CITIES OF EUROPE, THE. English. £5.00. **LC** TX910.A1; A35. **DD** 647/.954. ***Absorbed*** *Touropindex.*

US/0731-3152
ALA WHERE TO STAY BOOK, EAST. **VFOAT** A.L.A. Where to Stay Book, East. **VAT** Automobile Legal Association Where to Stay Book, East. 1981-. English. an. Free (members). ALA Auto and Travel Club, National Headquarters, 888 Worcester Street, Wellesley MA 02181. **Tel** (617)237-5200. **ED** Gerard J Gagnon. **LC** TX907; .A37. **DD** 647/.9474. ctrl circ. ***Continues in part*** *ALA Where to Stay Book, 0098-6518.*
Desc: A selected listing of hotels and motels in the Eastern United States and Canada.

US/8755-9242
ALA WHERE TO STAY BOOK, WEST. [ALA where stay book west]. **VFOAT** A.L.A. Where to Stay Book, West. **VAT** Automobile Legal Association Where to Stay Book, West. Periodical. English. an. Free (members). ALA Auto and Travel Club, National Headquarters, 888 Worcester Street, Wellesley MA 02181. **Tel** (617)237-5200. **ED** Gerard J Gagnon. **LC** TX907; .A373. **DD** 647/.9748. ctrl circ. ***Continues in part*** *ALA Auto & Travel Club. ALA Where to Stay Book, 0098-6518.*
Desc: A selected listing of hotels and motels in the Western United States, Canada and Mexico.

GW/0002-5895
ALLGEMEINE HOTEL- UND GASTSTATTEN-ZEITUNG. **VFOAT** Deutsche Hotel-Nachrichten mit Kuche und Keller. (1947)-. Periodical. German. wk. DM283.20 Germany; DM300.00 other. Hugo Matthaes Druckerei Verlag, Postfach 103144, W-7000 Stuttgart 10 Germany. **Tel** 011 49 711 21331. **UDC** 64.024.

●US/1063-0007
AMERICA'S WONDERFUL LITTLE HOTELS & INNS. THE MIDWEST. [Am. wonderful little hotels inns, Midwest]. **VFOAT** America's Wonderful Little Hotels and Inns. The Midwest. 1st ed. (1992)-. English. $12.95. St. Martin's Press, 175 Fifth Avenue, New York NY 10010. **Tel** (800)221-7945, (212)982-3900, FAX (212)777-6359. **DD** 917. ***Continues in part*** *America's Wonderful Little Hotels & Inns. Midwest, the Rocky Mountains, and the Southwest, 1057-6436.*

US
AMERICA'S WONDERFUL LITTLE HOTELS & INNS : THE MIDWEST, THE ROCKY MOUNTAINS, AND THE SOUTHWEST. **VFOAT** America's Wonderful Little Hotels and Inns; The Midwest, The Rocky Mountains, and

The Southwest. 1st Ed. (1991)-. Periodical. English. $11.95. St. Martin's Press, 175 Fifth Avenue, New York NY 10010. **Tel** (800)221-7945, (212)982-3900, FAX (212)777-6359.

●US/1062-9998
AMERICA'S WONDERFUL LITTLE HOTELS & INNS. THE ROCKY MOUNTAINS AND THE SOUTHWEST. [Am. wonderful little hotels inns, Rocky Mt. Southwest]. **VFOAT** America's Wonderful Little Hotels and Inns. The Rocky Mountains and the Southwest. 1st ed. (1992)-. English. $13.95. St. Martin's Press, 175 Fifth Avenue, New York NY 10010. **Tel** (800)221-7945, (212)982-3900, FAX (212)777-6359. **LC** TX907.3.M55; A45. **DD** 647.947301/05. ***Continues in part** America's Wonderful Little Hotels & Inns. Midwest, the Rocky Mountains and the Southwest, 1057-6436.*

SP
ANUARIO ESPANOL DE HOSTELERIA Y COLECTIVIDADES. Spanish. 4.500ptas Spain; 9.000ptas North America; 6.500ptas other. Puntex SA, c/ Mare de Deu del Coll 14, 08023 Barcelona Spain. **Tel** (93)237 71 24, FAX (93)217 55 73, telex 97131 GPMM E. **Circ:** 10,000.
Desc: Hotel firms, distributors, trademarks and products by sector.

HK
ASIAN HOTEL AND CATERING TIMES. English. mo. HK$430.00. Thomson Press Hong Kong Ltd, Tai Sang Commercial Building/19th Floor, 24-34 Hennessy Road, Room 1903, Hong Kong Hong Kong. **Tel** 11 852 5 283351, FAX 11 852 5 8650825, telex 61504 THOMS HX. **ED** Glenn Rogers. **Bk Rev**. **Ad Acc, Adv Mgr:** Teresa Chan. ctrl circ.

●UK/1054-4089
BEST BED & BREAKFAST IN ENGLAND, SCOTLAND & WALES, THE. [Best bed breakf. Engl. Scotl. Wales]. **VFOAT** Best Bed and Breakfast in England, Scotland and Wales; Best Bed and Breakfast; Best Bed & Breakfast. (1992)-. English. Globe Pequot Press, 6 Business Park Road, Old Saybrook CT 06475. **Tel** (800)243-0495, . **LC** TX907.5.G7; B47. **DD** 647.944103/05. ***Continues** Best Bed & Breakfast in the World, 1057-5472.*

●US/1061-7353
BEST PLACES TO STAY IN THE MID-ATLANTIC STATES. (1992)-. English. te. Houghton Mifflin Company, Wayside Road, Burlington MA 01803. **Tel** (800)225-3362, (617)272-1500.

●US/1060-7730
BEST PLACES TO STAY IN THE ROCKY MOUNTAIN STATES. (1992)-. English. be. $13.95. Houghton Mifflin Company, Wayside Road, Burlington MA 01803. **Tel** (800)225-3362, (617)272-1500.

US/1054-9773
BEST VACATION RENTALS. UNITED STATES AND CANADA. [Best vacat. rent. U. S. Can.]. **VFOAT** United States and Canada. 1st ed. (1991)-. English. be. $17.95. Prentice-Hall Press Legal & Financial Services, 15 Columbus Circle, Third Floor, New York NY 10023. **Tel** (212)373-7500. **LC** HD7289.3.U6; B47. **DD** 643/.2.

UK
BHRCA OFFICIAL GUIDE TO HOTELS AND RESTAURANTS IN GREAT BRITAIN, IRELAND AND OVERSEAS. **VFOAT** B.H.R.C.A. Official Guide to Hotels and Restaurants in Great Britain, Ireland and Overseas; Hotels and Restaurants in Britain; Hotels and Restaurants in Great Britain, Ireland and Overseas; British Hotels and Restaurants; Hotels & Restaurants in Great Britain, Ireland and Overseas; Hotels & Restaurants in Britain; British Hotels & Restaurants. English. an. $9.95. **LC** TX910.G7; B47. **DD** 647/.944101.

US
BLUE HOTEL, THE. No. 1 (1980)-. Periodical. English. Windflower Press, PO Box 82213, Lincoln NE 68501. **ED** T Kooser.

BL
BRASIL, MEETING FACILITIES. **VFOAT** Meeting Facilities in Brazil; Meeting Facilities. English. Embratur, Brazilian Tourism Authority, Praca Maua 7-11 And, Rio de Janeiro RJ Brazil. **LC** TX910.B8; B68. **DD** 647/.9.

UK
BRITISH HOTELIER & RESTAURATEUR : OFFICIAL MAGAZINE OF THE BRITISH HOTELS, RESTAURANTS & CATERERS ASSOCIATION. ***Title Change.*** **Added/Corp** British Hotels, Restaurants, and Caterers Association. **VFOAT** British Hotelier and Restaurateur. (19??)-(19??). Periodical. English. Ten times a year. British Hotels Restaurants and Caterers Association, 40 Duke Street, London W1M 6HR England. **Tel** 011 44 71 4996641. **ED** Ann Satchell. **Bk Rev**. **Ad Acc**. **Pr Rev**. **Circ:** 10,500 (ctrl). ***Continued by** Voice of the Hospitality Association.*
Desc: Reports on tourism, industry news, legislation, product news and articles of business. Help to top level management directors and proprietors.

US/0274-6093
CALIFORNIA INNTOUCH. **Added/Corp** California Hotel & Motel Association. Vol. 1 (June 1980)-. Periodical. English. Six times a year (Feb., Apr., June, Aug., Oct., Dec.). Free, (members); $35.00 (non-members). California Hotel/Motel Association, 414 29th Street, Sacramento CA 95815. **Tel** (916)444-5843, FAX (916)483-1210. **ED** Bill Howe. **Ad Acc. Circ:** 7,300 (ctrl).

CN/0229-4427
CANADIAN HOSPITALITY. (CANADIAN HOSPITALITY : THE VOICE OF THE HOSPITALITY INDUSTRY IN CANADA.). [Can. hosp.]. Vol. 1, No. 1 (Nov. 1980)-. Periodical. English. mo. Canadian Hospitality Publications, 124 West 8th Street North, Vancouver British Columbia V7M 3H2 Canada. **DD** 647/.9471. ***Continues** Hospitality Canada, 0318-7721.*

CN/1182-9923
CANADIAN HOTEL AND RESTAURANT (1990). ***Title Change.*** (CANADIAN HOTEL AND RESTAURANT : CH & R.). [Can. hotel restaur.]. **VFOAT** CH & R; Hotel and Restaurant; Hotel & Restaurant; Canadian Hotel & Restaurant. Vol. 68, No. 8 (Aug. 1990)-(19??). Periodical. English. mo. MacLean Hunter Publ. Limited / Toronto, 777 Bay Street, 8th Floor Agency Control, Toronto Ontario M5W 1A7 Canada. **Tel** (416)596-5000, (800)268-6811, FAX (416)596-5526. **DD** 647.9471/005. available on microfilm and microfiche from University Microfilms International (UMI). ***Continues** Hotel & Restaurant., 0846-5282. **Continued by** CH & R Product News & Menu Planner.*

CN
CANADIAN HOTEL & RESTAURANT. SOURCES DIRECTORY. **VFOAT** Foodservice & Lodging Directory. 1974-. Directory. English. an. 11.00Can$. Maclean Hunter Canada / Montreal, 1001 bvd. de Maisonneuve W., Montreal, Quebec H3A 3E1 Canada. **Tel** 514-845-5141, FAX 514-845-4302, telex 055-60604. **DD** 338.4/7/647941028. ***Supersedes** Canadian Hotel & Restaurant. Annual Directory Issue.*
Desc: Provides the operator with an accurate, alphabetically presented, and easy to read 'who's who' of foodservice and lodging suppliers in Canada.

CN/1185-5738
CANADIAN LODGING OUTLOOK. (CANADIAN LODGING OUTLOOK / PRICE WATERHOUSE; SMITH TRAVEL RESEARCH.). [Can. lodg. outlook]. **Added/Corp** Price Waterhouse (Firm) Smith Travel Research. Hotel Association of Canada. (Jan. 1991)-. Periodical. English. Twelve times a year. Free on request. Price Waterhouse Company, PO Box 190, Toronto Ontario M5X 1H7 Canada. **Tel** (416)863-1133. **DD** 338.4. ***Continues** Hotel Market Trends (Toronto, Ont.)., 1185-572X.*

US/0889-9797
CASINO CHRONICLE. [Casino chron.]. Vol. 1, No. 1 (June 6, 1983)-. Periodical. English. Forty-eight times a year. $155.00 US; $165.00 Canada; $170.00 Mexico; $205.00 other. Casino Chronicle, 1412 Chanticleer, Cherry Hill NJ 08003. **Tel** (609)751-8620. **ED** Ben A Borowsky. **DD** 795. **Bk Rev**, (Qty: (12-20)). **Ad Acc. Circ:** 1500.
Desc: Weekly newsletter which focuses on the casino gaming industry in Atlantic City, reporting monthly revenue and quarterly profit and loss statements, plus information relating to personnel, entertainment, marketing, transportation and other related issues to the casino/hotel industry.

UK/0008-7777
CATERER & HOTELKEEPER. **See** Food and Food Industry.

UK
CATERING. **See** Food and Food Industry.

AT
CENSUS OF TOURIST ACCOMMODATION ESTABLISHMENTS, WESTERN AUSTRALIA. **Main/Corp** Australian Bureau of Statistics. Western Australian Office. (1973/74)-. Government Publication. English. Four times a year. 20.00Aus$. Australian Bureau of Statistics / Western Australian Office, 30 Terrace Road, East Perth WA 6004 Australia. **LC** TX910.A7; A9a. **DD** 647/.94941/0212.

US/1042-5918
CHRIE COMMUNIQUE. [CHRIE comm.]. **Added/Corp** International CHRIE. **VAT** Council on Hotel, Restaurant, and Institutional Educational Communique. (198?)-. Periodical. English. sm (24 issues). $50.00. CHRIE Council on Hotel Restaurant and Institutional Education, 1200 17th Street Northwest, Department A Adair, Washington DC 20036. **Tel** (202)331-5990. **DD** 647. ***Continues** Hospitality Educator, 8750-7129.*

UK
CONFERENCE BLUE BOOK. (19??)-. English. an. £65.00. Benn Business Information Service Ltd, Riverbank House, Angel Lane, Tonbridge Kent TN9 1SE England. **Tel** 011 44 732 362666, FAX 011 44 732 770483, telex 95454 BBIS.

UK
CONFERENCE GREEN BOOK. [Conf. green book]. (1981)-. English. an. £65.00. Benn Business Information Service Ltd, Riverbank House, Angel Lane, Tonbridge Kent TN9 1SE England. **Tel** 011 44 732 362666, FAX 011 44 732 770483, telex 95454 BBIS. Index available. **Ad Acc, Adv Mgr:** Julia Allen. **Circ:** 7,000 (ctrl).
Desc: Fully regionalised listing of over 4,000 UK venues indexed alphabetically detailing telephone numbers, meeting room capacity in theatre style and number of bedrooms. Hundreds of individual full page entries give contact names and numbers; address details; delegate rates; details on meeting room dimension; lighting, sound, power and telephone facilities. Bars, restaurants, sports and conference facilities are also listed. Concentrates on special interest and leisure facilities.

UK
CONTINENTAL HOTEL GUIDE. **VFOAT** RAC Continental Hotel Guide. 1988-. English. an. RAC Motoring Services Ltd, RAC House, PO Box 100, South Croydon Surrey CR2 6XW England.

CN/0226-8922
CONVENTIONS & MEETINGS CANADA (1981). (CONVENTIONS & MEETINGS CANADA : OFFICIAL GUIDE TO MEETING LOCATIONS AND FACILITIES.). (1980)-. English. an (July). 39.00Can$. Effective Communications Ltd, 5762 Highway 7, Suite 207, Markham ONT L3P 1A8 Canada. **Tel** (905)471-1550. **DD** 647/.9471. ***Continues** Conventions & Meetings; Facilities and Services in Canada, 0315-100X.*

US/0010-8804
CORNELL HOTEL AND RESTAURANT ADMINISTRATION QUARTERLY, THE. [Cornell hotel restaur. adm. q.]. **Added/Corp** Cornell University. School of Hotel Administration. Vol. 1 (May 1960)-. Academic Scholarly Publication. English. Six times a year (1 volume). $150.00 US; $190.00 other. Elsevier Science Publishing Company Inc, Madison Square Station, PO Box 882, New York NY 10159-0882. **Tel** (212)633-3950, FAX (212)633-3990. **ED** Joan Livingston. **LC** TX901; .C67. **DD** 647.9505. **CODEN** CHRQA2. **[CCC].** available on microfilm and microfiche from University Microfilms International (UMI); available on an online database (file 648/Full-Text) from DIALOG. Documents available from UMI Article Clearinghouse.
Desc: Hotel and restaurant industry and related subjects.
Ind/Abst ABI/INFORM Glob. Ed.; ABI Inform Ondisc (May 1983-); Acad. Search (July 1993-); AGRICOLA [Select. Cov.]; Bus. ASAP (1992-) [Full Txt.]; Bus. Index (1985-); Bus. Period. Index; Bus. Source (Jul. 1993-); Foods Adlibra; Gen. BusinessFile (1985-); Gen. Period. Index (1985-); Health Plan. Adminis.; Hospit. Health Admin. Index (v21n4,1981-v29n4,1989); INFO-SOUTH Abstr.; Leis. Recreat. Tour. Abstr.; Mag. Search; Rural Dev. Abstr.; Trade Ind. ASAP [Full Txt.]; Trade Ind. Index (1981-) [Full Txt.]; UMI ABI/Inform--Bus. Period. Ondisc [Full Txt.]; Wilson Bus. Abstr.; World Agric. Econ.

US/0893-1291
COUNTRY INNS AND BACK ROADS (CONTINENTAL EUROPE ED.). ***Ceased.*** (COUNTRY INNS AND BACK ROADS : BY NORMAN T. SIMPSON.). [Ctry. inns back roads]. **VFOAT** Continental Europe. (1985)-(1991/1992 Edition). Periodical. English. be. Harper & Row Publishers Inc, 10 East 53rd Street, New York NY 10022. **Tel** (717)343-4761. **(Subscription address:** Keystone Industrial Park, Scranton, PA 18512) **DD** 647. ***Continues** Country Inns and Back Roads (European Ed.).*

US/1042-6248
COUNTRY INNS AND BACK ROADS. NORTH AMERICA. (COUNTRY INNS AND BACK ROADS. NORTH AMERICA : NEW ENGLAND, WEST COAST, CANADA, MIDDLE ATLANTIC, SOUTH, MIDWEST, ROCKY MOUNTAINS.). [Ctry. inns back roads, North A.]. **VFOAT** North America Country Inns and Back Roads. (1985)-. English. an. $12.95. Harper Collins Publishers, Keystone Industrial Park, Scranton PA 18512. **Tel** (800)242-7737, (800)233-4727, FAX (800)822-4090. **ED** Norman T. Simpson. **LC** E169.02; .C657. **DD** 647.947301. ***Continues** Country Inns and Back Roads.*

US/0893-1186
COUNTRY INNS AND BACKROADS. BRITAIN AND IRELAND. [Ctry. inns back roads]. **VFOAT** Britain and Ireland. (1980)-. English. be. $10.95. Harper & Row Publishers Inc, 10 East 53rd Street, New York NY 10022. **Tel** (717)343-4761. **(Subscription address:** Keystone Industrial Park, Scranton, PA 18512) **ED** Norman T Simpson. **LC** TX907.5.G7; C68. **DD** 647.

US/0898-560X
COUNTRY INNS, BED & BREAKFAST. [Ctry. inns, bed breakf.]. **VFOAT** Country Inns, Bed and

Breakfast; Country Inns; Country Inns/Bed & Breakfast. (Spring 1987)-. Periodical. English. qt. $17.95 (one year), $32.95 (two year). Country Inns Publications Inc, PO Box 182, South Orange NJ 07079. **Tel** (201)762-7090. **(Subscription address:** Kable Publishers Aide, 308 East Hitt Street, Subscriptions Department, Mt. Morris, IL 61054) **LC** TX901; .C68. **DD** 647.94.

US/0892-4481
COUNTRY INNS GAZETTE. [Ctry. inns gaz.]. (April 1987)-. Periodical. English. mo. $60.00. PO Box 6976, FDR Station, New York NY 10150. **LC** TX907.3.N35; C68. **DD** 647.9474.

SA
CVR HOTEL GUIDE TO SOUTHERN AFRICA, THE. VFOAT C.V.R. Hotel Guide to Southern Africa; Die CVR Hotelgids vir Suider-Afrika; C.V.R. Hotelgids vir Suider-Afrika; CVR Hotelgids vir Suider-Afrika. 1st Ed. (1981)-. Afrikaans (English). Chris van Rensburg Publications Pty Ltd, PO Box 25272, Ferreirasdorp, Johannesburg Republic of South Africa. **LC** DT752; .C49A. **DD** 647/.96801/05. ***Continues*** *CVR Travel & Hotel Guide to Southern Africa.*

US/1014-9600
DAILY SUBSISTANCE ALLOWANCE RATES. See Economics-International Economics.

UK
DEREK JOHANSEN'S RECOMMENDED HOTELS IN GREAT BRITAIN. English. an. £12.95 UK; £17.28 other. Johansens Publications Ltd, Great Western Mailing, Brunel House, Forde Road, Newtown Abbott, South Daxon TQ12 4PU England. **Tel** 0626-61121, FAX 0626-331402.

IO
DIRECTORY AKOMODASI JAWA, BALI DAN SUMATERA UTARA. Directory. Indonesian. Biro Pusat Statistik, JLN Dr Sutomo 8 Kotak, Pos 1003, Jakarta 10710 Indonesia. **Tel** 3728007, 374908. **LC** TX910.I6; D56.

IO
DIRECTORY HOTEL, LOSMEN DAN PENGINAPAN. Added/Corp Indonesia. Biro Pusat Statistik. (1973)-. Directory. Indonesian. Biro Pusat Statistik, JLN Dr Sutomo 8 Kotak, Pos 1003, Jakarta 10710 Indonesia. **Tel** 3728007, 374908. **LC** TX910.I6; D57.

IO/0304-1484
DIRECTORY HOTEL PARIWISATA & TRAVEL BUREAU. 1973-. Directory. Indonesian. Biro Pusat Statistik, JLN Dr Sutomo 8 Kotak, Pos 1003, Jakarta 10710 Indonesia. **Tel** 3728007, 374908. **LC** G155.I6; D56.

US/0742-3306
DIRECTORY OF HOSPITALITY EDUCATORS. [Dir. hosp. educ.]. **Added/Corp** American Hotel & Motel Association. Educational Institute. **VFOAT** Directory. (19??)-. English. sa. $35.00. Educational Institute of the American Hotel and Motel Association, PO Box 1240, East Lansing MI 48826. **Tel** (517)353-5500, FAX (517)353-5527, telex 810-251-0701. **ED** Karen Grannemann. **LC** TX911.3.M27; D57. **DD** 647/.94/071073. **Circ:** 5,000.
Desc: Geographic listing of academic institutions offering programs in hospitality management; alphabetic listing of educators teaching in the programs listed.

●US
DIRECTORY OF HOTEL & MOTEL COMPANIES. Added/Corp American Hotel Association Directory Corporation. American Hotel & Motel Association. **VFOAT** Directory of Hotel and Motel Companies. 61st Ed. (1992)-. Directory. English. an (March). $83.00 (includes 6% tax) Washington DC residents; $78.50 other. American Hotel and Motel Association, 1201 New York Avenue Northwest, Washington DC 20005. **Tel** (202)289-3100, (202)289-3165, FAX (202)289-3199. **LC** TX907; .D5. **DD** 647.947301/05. ***Continues*** *Directory of Hotel & Motel Systems.*

US
DIRECTORY OF HOTEL & MOTEL SYSTEMS. *Title Change.* Added/Corp American Hotel Association Directory Corporation. **VFOAT** Directory of Hotel and Motel Systems. (196?)-(199?). Directory. English. an. American Hotel and Motel Association, 1201 New York Avenue Northwest, Washington DC 20005. **Tel** (202)289-3100, (202)289-3165, FAX (202)289-3199. **ED** Richard Turner. **LC** TX907; .D5. **Ad Acc. Circ:** 9,000. ***Continues*** *Directory of Hotel Systems.* ***Continued by*** *Directory of Hotel & Motel Companies.*
Desc: Lists companies that own, operate or manage two or more properties. Gives address, phone number, officers, property names, total number of rooms and properties.

KE
DIRECTORY OF HOTELS IN KENYA. VFOAT Kenya Directory of Hotels. Directory. English. Kenya Marketing & Publications Company, Biashara Street, Raja Building, PO Box 10304, Nairobi Kenya. **LC** TX910.K4; D57. **DD** 647/.94676/2.

US/0277-8416
DISCOVERAMERICARD DIRECTORY OF CITIES & HOTELS, THE. VFOAT Directory of Cities & Hotels; Discoveramericard Directory of Cities and Hotels. 1980-1981-. Directory. English. $29.95. Discovericard International, PO Box 1984, New England Station, Hartford CT 06101. **LC** TX907; .D48. **DD** 647/.947301.

UK
EGON RONAY'S GUIDE TO HOTELS, RESTAURANTS, PUBS, INNS IN GREAT BRITAIN AND IRELAND AND LONDON PENSIONS. Added/Corp Egon Ronay Organisation. **VFOAT** Guide to Hotels, Restaurants, Pubs, Inns in Great Britain and Ireland and London Pensions. (19??)-. English. an. £8.60. Egon Ronay Organisation, Greencoat House, Francis Street, London SWIP 1 England. **LC** TX910.G7; E35. **DD** 647/.9442. **Ad Acc. Circ:** 100,000. ***Continues*** *Egon-Ronay-BMC Guide to Hotels, Restaurants, Pubs and Inns.*

UA
EGYPTIAN HOTEL GUIDE. English (Arabic). an. Egyptian Hotel Association, 8 El Sad El Ali Street, Dokki Guiza Egypt. **Tel** 712 134-34 88 468, telex 92355 ANIS UN. **ED** Tamy Daoud. **LC** TX910.E3; E37. **DD** 647/.9462/05. Index available. **Ad Acc. Circ:** 20,000 (ctrl).

US/0146-5171
EUROPEAN ACCOMMODATIONS DIRECTORY. Directory. English. American Automobile Association, 1000 AAA Drive, Heathrow FL 32746. **Tel** (407)444-7000. **LC** TX910.A1; E92. **DD** 647/.944.

US
EUROPE'S WONDERFUL LITTLE HOTELS AND INNS. 1st. Ed. (1978)-. English. ir. $17.95. St. Martin's Press, 175 Fifth Avenue, New York NY 10010. **Tel** (800)221-7945, (212)982-3900, FAX (212)777-6359.

US/0270-8434
EXXON TRAVEL CLUB MEXICO VACATION TRAVEL GUIDE. [Exxon Travel Club Mex. vacat. travel guide]. **Main/Corp** Travelvision. **Added/Corp** Exxon Travel Club. **VFOAT** Mexico Vacation Travel Guide; Exxon Travel Club Vacation Travel Guide, Mexico. (1977)-. English. an. $3.95. Simon & Schuster, 1230 Avenue of the Americas, New York NY 10020. **Tel** (212)698-7000. **LC** F1209; .T72a. **DD** 917.2/04833. ***Continues*** *Exxon Travel Club Mexico Illustrated Vacation Travel Guide, 0270-8442.*

US/0192-1347
FASTFACTS EUROPEAN HOTEL LOCATOR. Main/Corp Denhamwood, Inc. **Added/Corp** Denhamwood, Inc. European hotel locator. Vol 1 (1978)-. English. be. $75.00. Denhamwood Inc, 4069 Hayvenhurst Avenue, Encino CA 91436. **Tel** (818)992-3423. **LC** G1797.21.E635; D4. **DD** 912/.164794401. **Circ:** 5,000.
Desc: Instant reference to location and facilities of hotels in 45 major European cities.

US/0742-0722
FASTFACTS HOTEL MOTEL LOCATOR, UNITED STATES & CANADA. VFOAT Fastfacts U.S.A. and Canada; Hotel Motel Locator, United States and Canada; Hotel Motel Locator, United States & Canada; Hotel Motel Locator Fastfacts USA & Canada. English. ir. $85.00. Denhamwood Inc, 4069 Hayvenhurst Avenue, Encino CA 91436. **Tel** (818)992-3423. **LC** TX907; .F387. **DD** 647/.94701. **Circ:** 5,000. ***Continues*** *Fastfacts U.S.A. Hotel Motel Locator, 0197-9477.*
Desc: Instant reference to location and facilities of hotels and motels in over 180 cities.

US/0739-0807
FIELDING'S HAVENS AND HIDEAWAYS USA. VFOAT Fielding's Havens and Hideaways U.S.A.; Havens and Hideaways USA; Havens and Hideaways U.S.A. 1984-. English. an. $7.95. William Morrow & Company Inc, 1350 Avenue of the Americas, New York NY 10019. **LC** TX907; .F46. **DD** 647/.9473. ***Continues*** *Morrow Book of Havens and Hideaways.*

UK/0308-8464
FINANCIAL TIMES WORLD HOTEL DIRECTORY, THE. Main/Corp Financial Times Limited. **Added/Corp** Financial Times Limited. FT World Hotel Directory. **VFOAT** FT World Hotel Directory. (1975/1976)-. Directory. English. an. $162.00. Longman Group Ltd., Fourth Avenue, Longman House, Harlow Essex CM19 5SR England. **Tel** 011 44 279 429655, FAX 011 44 279 431059, telex 81259. **(Subscription address:** US & Canada: Gale Research Co., 835 Penobscot Building, Detroit, MI 48226) **LC** TX907; .F47a. **DD** 647/.94. **[CCC]. Ad Acc. Circ:** 3,000.
Desc: Directs users to 3,200 hotels in 140 countries around the world. Entries include hotel address, reservation system, style, location, and manager's name.

GW/0939-8414
FIRST CLASS ALFELD. [First classAlf.]. (198?)-. Periodical. German. mo (10 issues per year). DM70.00 Germany; DM80.00 other. Gilde Fachverlag GmbH & Co KG, Postfach 1351, Foehrster Strasse 8, 31043 Alfeld Germany. **Tel** 011 49 5181 80040, FAX 011 49 5181 800490. **ED** Susanne Staub. **UDC** 64. Index available. cum. index. **Ad Acc, Adv Mgr:** Uwe Krist. ctrl circ.
Desc: Information magazine for hotels and restaurants that specialize in first class treatment.

US/8750-6807
FLORIDA HOTEL & MOTEL JOURNAL. (FLORIDA HOTEL & MOTEL JOURNAL : THE OFFICIAL PUBLICATION OF THE FLORIDA HOTEL & MOTEL ASSOCIATION.). **Added/Corp** Florida Hotel & Motel Association. **VFOAT** Hotel & Motel. **VAT** Florida Hotel and Motel Journal. Vol. 8, No. 1 (Jan. 1985)-. Periodical. English. Twelve times a year. $25.68 Florida; $24.00 others. Accomodations, Inc., PO Box 1529, Tallahassee FL 32302. **Tel** (904)224-2888, FAX (904)222-3462. **ED** Jayleen Woods. **Bk Rev. Ad Acc, Adv Mgr:** Helen Sanders. **Circ:** 7,000 (ctrl). ***Continues*** *Florida Hotel & Motel News, 0192-3498.*
Desc: A management magazine, directed toward helping hoteliers achieve the results in their businesses. Authoritative and or generic articles provide advice, strategies, educational ideas and information concerning laws, taxes and current trends in the industry.

US/0015-4156
FLORIDA MOTEL JOURNAL. Vol. 1 (1951)-. English. ir. Florida Motel Journal, PO Box 705, Orlando FL 32802.

US
FODOR'S SELECTED RESORTS AND HOTELS OF THE U.S. Added/Corp Fodor's Travel Publications, Inc. **VFOAT** Selected Resorts and Hotels of the U.S. (1988)-. Periodical. English. ir. $15.85. Random House Inc., 400 Hahn Road, Westminster MD 21157. **Tel** (800)726-0600, (800)733-3000, FAX (800)659-2436. **LC** TX907.2; .F63. **DD** 647/.9473.

CN/0007-8972
FOODSERVICE & HOSPITALITY. See Restaurants.

US
FOREIGN LODGING LIST. Main/Corp Traveler's Information Exchange. 1976/78-. English. sa. $25.00 US; $30.00 other. Travelers Information Exchange MA 02116. **Tel** (617)536-5651. **ED** Jan Stankus. **LC** D910; .W82. **DD** 647/.94/05. **Bk Rev. Circ:** 600 (ctrl). ***Continues*** *Foreign Lodging List Issued by the Women's Rest Tour Association.*
Desc: Contains information sent in by members from personal travel experiences.

US/1064-3435
FROMMER'S COMPREHENSIVE TRAVEL GUIDE. BED & BREAKFAST, NORTH AMERICA. [Frommer's compre. travel guide, Bed breakf. N. Am.]. **VFOAT** Comprehensive Travel Guide. Bed & Breakfast, North America; Bed & Breakfast, North America; Bed and Breakfast, North America; Frommer's B and B North America; Frommer's Bed and Breakfast, North America; Frommer's Bed & Breakfast, North America; Frommer's B&B North America. 4th Ed.(1991)-. English. be. $14.95. Macmillan Publishing Co. / Indiana, 201 West 103rd Street, Indianapolis IN 46290. **Tel** (800)428-5331, (800)858-7674. **LC** TX907.2; .B44. **DD** 647.947303. ***Continues*** *Frommer's Bed & Breakfast, North America, 1051-6824.*

CN/0705-7520
GITE (ST-JOSEPH). (LE GITE.). **Added/Corp** Corporation des Proprietaires des Gites du Quebec. (1978)-. Periodical. French. Six times a year. Corp des Propietaires les Publications le Gite des Gites du Quebec, CP 67 St-Joseph, Cte Beauce Quebec G0S 2V0 Canada. **DD** 647/.94714. ***Continues*** *Tout sur le Gite, 0703-475X.*

CN/1187-421X
GITES DU PASSANT AU QUEBEC. [Gites passant Que.]. **Added/Corp** Federation des Agricotours du Quebec. **VFOAT** Bed and Breakfasts, Gites a la Ferme, Maisons de Campagne au Quebec; Bed and Breakfasts; Gites a la Ferme; Maisons de Campagne au Quebec. (1991)-. French (English). **DD** 647.94714/03. ***Continues*** *Le Reseau Quebecois des Gites du Passant, Gites a la Ferme et Maisons de Campagne., 1184-7425.*

CN/1187-421X
GITES DU PASSANT AU QUEBEC. [Gites passant Que.]. **Added/Corp** Federation des Agricotours du Quebec. **VFOAT** Bed and Breakfasts, Gites a la Ferme, Maisons de Campagne au Quebec; Bed and Breakfasts; Gites a la Ferme; Maisons de Campagne au Quebec. (1991)-. English (French). **DD** 647.94714/03. ***Continues*** *Le Reseau Quebecois des Gites du Passant, Gites a la Fferme et Maisons de Campagne.*

US
GUEST SECURITY BULLETIN. (19??)-. Bulletin. English. an. $15.00. Magna Publications Inc, 2718 Dryden Drive, Madison WI 53704. **Tel** (800)433-0499, (608)246-3591, FAX (608)246-3597.

SP
GUIA DE HOTELES : ESPANA. Spanish (Italian, Portuguese, German, French, English and Swedish). Direccion General de Empresas Actividades Turisticas, Alcala Num 44, Madrid 14 Spain. **LC** TX910.S7; G77. **DD** 647/.9446. ***Continues*** *Spain. Direccion General del Turismo. Hoteles de Espana.*

VE
GUIA TURISTICA Y HOTELES DE VENEZUELA. Multiple languages (English and Spanish). **LC** F2314; .G83.

SA/0376-5210
GUIDE TO THE HOTELS IN SOUTH AFRICA. **VFOAT** South Africa Hotel Guide; Suid-Afrika Hotel-Gids. English. $0.75. Rensburg Publications, PO Box 25272, Marshalltown South Africa. **LC** TX910.S55; G8. **DD** 647/.9468.

US
HAMPTONS : THE MAGAZINE OF THE WORLD'S MOST SOPHISTICATED RESORT, THE. **See** Travel and Tourism.

US
HISTORIC HOTELS OF AMERICA. **Added/Corp** National Trust for Historic Preservation in the United States. (1991)-. Periodical. English. $55.00. National Trust for Historic Preservation, 1785 Massachusetts Avenue Northwest, Washington DC 20036. **Tel** (202)673-4035.
Desc: Facts about prominent hotels, including architectural details and human interest stories.

UK
HORECA ENTRE. English. bw. F76.00. Standex Periodieken BV, Postbus 956, 3900 AZ Veenendaal Netherlands. **Tel** 011 31 8385 28008.

SP
HORECO. **See** Restaurants.

CN/0838-6854
HOSPITALITE, HOTELLERIE, RESTAURATION, L'. [Hosp. hotel. restaur.]. Vol. 9 No 5 (Sept./Oct. 1985)-. Periodical. French. bm. 4,75 $ le no. 26,00 $ par ann,ee. Hotellerie, Restauration, 10E Etage, 1001 Quest Boul., De Maisonneuve Montreal Quebec, H3A 3E1. **DD** 647/.94714. available on microfilm and microfiche from University Microfilms International (UMI). ***Formed by the union of*** *L'Hospitalite., 0704-6359* ***and*** *Hotellerie Restauration., 0225-6185.*

●NZ
HOSPITALITY. (1993)-. Periodical. English. Trade Publications Ltd., 300 Great South Road Greenlane, Newmarket Auckland New Zealand. **Tel** 011 64 9 9293000. ***Continues in part*** *Hospitality & Catering.*

US
HOSPITALITY & TOURISM EDUCATOR. **VFOAT** Hospitality and Tourism Educator. (Spring 1988)-. Periodical. English. Three times a year. $35.00. CHRIE Council on Hotel Restaurant and Institutional Education, 1200 17th Street Northwest, Department A Adair, Washington DC 20036. **Tel** (202)331-5990. **ED** Robert H Basselman and Jeffery A Fernsten. **Bk Rev. Ad Acc. Pr Rev. Circ:** 2,000.
Desc: A refereed periodical addressing issues key to education in this field.
Ind/Abst Leis. Recreat. Tour. Abstr.

US/1060-9350
HOSPITALITY RESEARCH JOURNAL. (HOSPITALITY RESEARCH JOURNAL : THE PROFESSIONAL JOURNAL OF THE COUNCIL ON HOTEL, RESTAURANT, AND INSTITUTIONAL EDUCATION.). [Hospitality res. j.]. **Added/Corp** Council on Hotel, Restaurant, and Institutional Education (U.S.). Vol. 14, No. 1 (1990)-. Periodical. English. Three times a year. $50.00. CHRIE Council on Hotel Restaurant and Institutional Education, 1200 17th Street Northwest, Department A Adair, Washington DC 20036. **Tel** (202)331-5990. **LC** TX911.3.M27; H66. **DD** 647/.94/711. ***Continues*** *Hospitality Education and Research Journal, 0741-5095.*
Ind/Abst Leis. Recreat. Tour. Abstr.

US/0363-1427
HOSPITALITY SERIES. No. 1- 1975-. Periodical. English. University of Minnesota / Arboretum Boulevard, 3675 Arboretum Boulevard, Chasha MN 55318. **LC** S77; .E228 subser. **DD** 630/.8 S.

US
HOSTELER (MINNEAPOLIS, MINN.). (MINNESOTA HOSTELER.). Periodical. English. ir. $2.00. American Youth Hostels / Minnesota, 475 Cedar, St Paul MN 55106. **Tel** (612)292-4126.

UK
HOSTELLING INTERNATIONAL, BUDGET ACCOMMODATION. **Added/Corp** International Youth Hostel Federation. **VFOAT** Budget Accommodation. (19??)-. Periodical. English (French, German and Spanish). an (Feb.). £10.95. American Youth Hostels, 733 15th Street Northwest, Suite 840, Washington DC 20005. **Tel** (202)783-6161, FAX (202)783-6171. **LC** TX931; .H67.

US/0332-4400
HOTEL & CATERING REVIEW (BLACKROCK, DUBLIN). (HOTEL & CATERING REVIEW.). **VFOAT** Hotel and Catering Review. (19??)-. Trade Publication. English. mo. 21p (Eire); 27p (other). Jemma Publishers, PO Box 1973, Rathmines Dublin, 6 Ireland. **Tel** 11 353 1 975500. **ED** Frank Corr. **Bk Rev. Ad Acc. Circ:** 4,000 (ctrl).
Desc: Trade magazine for the Irish catering industry.

UK
HOTEL AND CATERING TECHNOLOGY. English. mo. £25.00 UK and Northern Ireland; £55.00 US and Canada; £40.00 other. ASL Publishing Ltd, 38 Westgate Street, Ipswich Suffolk 1P1 3ED England. **Tel** 011 44 0473 230132.

US/0018-6082
HOTEL & MOTEL MANAGEMENT. [Hotel motel manage.]. **VFOAT** Hotel and Motel Management; H&MM. **VAT** Hotel and Motel Management. Vol. 182, No. 5 (May 1967)-. Periodical. English. Twenty-one times a year. $38.00 US and possessions; $63.00 Canada; $110.00 other. Advanstar Communications Inc., 131 West First Street, Duluth MN 55802. **Tel** (218)723-9477, (800)346-0085. **ED** Michael DeLuca. **DD** 647. **[CCC]. Ad Acc. Circ:** 42,596 (ctrl). available on microfilm and microfiche from University Microfilms International (UMI); available on an online database (file 16/Full-Text) from DIALOG. ***Continues*** *Hotel Management & Innkeeping.* ***Absorbed in part by*** *Motor Inn Journal.*
Desc: News and features on all aspects concerning the lodging industry.
Ind/Abst Acad. Search (Jan. 1993-); Bus. Index (1985-); Bus. Period. Index; Bus. Source (Jan. 1993-); F&S Index Plus Text, Int. [Full Txt.] [Select. Cov.]; Foods Adlibra; Gen. BusinessFile (1985-); Gen. Period. Index (1985-); INFO-SOUTH Abstr.; Mag. Search; PROMT [Full Txt.]; Trade Ind. Index (1981-); Vocat. Search (Jan. 1993-); Wilson Bus. Abstr.

US/0149-3639
HOTEL & RESORT INDUSTRY. **VAT** Hotel and Resort Industry. (1978)-. Periodical. English. Twelve times a year. Coastal Communications Corporation, 488 Madison Avenue, New York NY 10022. **Tel** (212)888-1500. **ED** Harvey Grotsky. **Ad Acc. Circ:** 42,000 (ctrl).
Desc: Articles on management, marketing, technology, furnishing, design, equipment, decor, security, supplies and varied products and services required to operate and maintain a lodging establishment.

II
HOTEL AND RESTAURANT GUIDE INDIA. **VFOAT** India Hotel and Restaurant Guide; India Hotel & Restaurant Guide. '81-. English. an. 25.00. Federation of Hotel and Restaurant Associations of India, 406 75-76 Nehru Place, New Delhi 110019 India. **LC** TX910.I5; A6. **DD** 647/.945401. ***Continues*** *Hotel Guide India (New Delhi, India : 1980).*

US/0162-9972
HOTEL & TRAVEL INDEX. [Hotel travel index]. **VAT** Hotel and Travel Index. (Nov. 1951)-. English. Four times a year. $89.00. Reed Travel Group / New Jersey, 500 Plaza Drive, Secaucus NJ 07096. **Tel** (201)902-2000, (800)360-0015, FAX (201)319-1628. **(Subscription address:** Hotel & Travel Index, PO Box 7654, Riverton NJ 08077.**) DD** 910. **CODEN** HTINDM. Index available (free). ***Continues*** *Travel Index.*

US/1056-4713
HOTEL & TRAVEL INDEX (ABC INTERNATIONAL ED.). **See** Aeronautics, Astronautics.

US
HOTEL BUSINESS. May (1992)-. English. mo. $25.00. ICD Publications, 1393 Veterans Highway, PO Box 420, Hauppauge NY 11788. **Tel** (516)979-7878. **Ad Acc. Circ:** 45,000 (ctrl).
Desc: Focuses on industry-related issues, such as legislation, analyses of statistics and finances.

NE
HOTEL- EN RESTAURANTGIDS NEDERLAND. **Added/Corp** Koninklijke Nederlandse Toeristen Bond ANWB. **VFOAT** Hotel/Restaurants Nederland. (19??)-. Dutch. an. **LC** TX910.N4; H67.

AT/1032-0954
HOTEL EXECUTIVE, THE. [Hotel exec.]. (1988)-. Periodical. English. mo. 48.00Aus$ Australia; 107.80Aus$ other. Rapid Run Distribution, PO Box 274, St. Kilda VIC 3182 Australia. **Tel** 011 61 03 5298211, FAX 011 61 3 5104869. **DD** 647.9494.

UK
HOTEL MANAGEMENT TODAY. English. mo. £25.00 UK; £55.00 other. ASL Publishing Ltd, 38 Westgate Street, Ipswich Suffolk 1P1 3ED England. **Tel** 011 44 0473 230132. ***Continues*** *Food Today.*

US/8750-5126
HOTEL/MOTEL SECURITY AND SAFETY MANAGEMENT. [Hotel/motel secur. saf. manage.]. **VFOAT** Hotel, Motel Security and Safety Management. (198?)-. Periodical. English. mo. $169.00 (one year), $298.00 (two year). Rusting Publications, PO Box 190, Port Washington NY 11050. **Tel** (516)883-1440. **ED** Robert Rusting. Index available. cum. index. **Bk Rev,** (Qty: 12 per year). **Circ:** 700.

GW
HOTEL RESTAURANT. **See** Restaurants.

SZ
HOTEL- UND GASTGEWERBE RUNDSCHAU. Periodical. German. 60.00. Forster Verlag Ag, Ottikerstrasse 59, CH-8033 Zurich Switzerland. **Tel** 1-9108022. **ED** Eva Frieden. **Ad Acc.**
Desc: Articles on food control and menus, dish washing in commercial kitchens, interior design of restaurants and hotels, product information, and recipes.

US
HOTEL UPDATE NEWSLETTER. Newsletter. English. Twelve times a year. Free. Entertainment Pubications, Inc., Hospitality Division, 2125 Butterfield Road, Troy MI 48084. **Tel** (313)637-8432, FAX (313)637-9777. **ED** Robert McHenry. **Bk Rev. Circ:** 10,000 (ctrl).
Desc: Information and updates on hotels.

●US/1065-8432
HOTELBUSINESS (HAUPPAUGE, N.Y.). (HOTELBUSINESS.). [HotelBus.]. **VFOAT** Hotel Business; HB. (1992)-. Periodical. English. mo. $35.00. ICD Publications, 1393 Veterans Highway, PO Box 420, Hauppauge NY 11788. **Tel** (516)979-7878. **ED** Peter Rameo. **DD** 647. Full Page (B&W) $6900.00. **Pub. Size:** Tabloid. **Circ:** 45,000.

IT
HOTELDOMANI. (19??)-. Italian. Nine times a year. L70000 Italy; L135000 Europe; L180000 other. Tecniche Nuove SPA, Via Ciro Menotti 14, 20129 Milan Italy. **Tel** 011 39 2 75701, FAX 011 39 2 7610351, telex 334647 TECHS I. **Ad Acc. Pr Rev.** ctrl circ.
Desc: The first and most established magazine in the hotel field. Deals with this world as a whole. The magazine is about all the various topics of the hotel culture: from the structural and technological aspects to the management problems and marketing strategies.

SA
HOTELIER & CATERER (NAIROBI). Ramsay Son & Parker Pty Ltd., PO Box 180, Howard Place, Pinelands 7450 South Africa. **Tel** 011 27 21 531 1391, FAX 011 27 21 531 3333, telex 526933.

SA
HOTELIER & CATERER : OFFICIAL MAGAZINE OF FEDHASA. **Added/Corp** Federated Hotel, Liquor and Catering Association of South Africa. **VFOAT** Hotelier and Caterer. (19??)-. English. mo. R99.00. Ramsay Son & Parker Pty Ltd., PO Box 180, Howard Place, Pinelands 7450 South Africa. **Tel** 011 27 21 531 1391, FAX 011 27 21 531 3333, telex 526933.

SI/0217-9695
HOTELIER SINGAPORE. [Hotelier Singap.]. (1985)-. Periodical. English. mo. Singapore Hotel Assn, 11 Dhoby Ghaut #15-04 Cathay B, Singapore 0922 Singapore. **Tel** 336 2955. **DD** 647.945957. ***Continues*** *Lu Guan, 0129-9565.*

SW/0283-748X
HOTELL & PENSIONAT. **Added/Corp** Svenska Turistforeningen. **VFOAT** Hotell Och Pensionat. Swedish. Svenska Turistforeningen, Box 25, Vasagatan 48, 10120 Stockholm Sweden. **LC** TX910.S8; H67. ***Continues*** *Hotell & Pensionat i Sverige, 0349-1579.*

FI
HOTELLILUOKITTELUTYORYHMA : MUISTIO. **Main/Corp** Matkailun Edistamiskeskus. Hotelliluokitteluty Oryhma. 1988-. Finnish. Matkailun Edistamiskeskus Asemapaallikonkatu 12B, PL 53, 00521 Helsinki Finland. **LC** TX910.F5; M38A.

FR
HOTELS, CAFES, RESTAURANTS EN ... . French. an. Institut National de la Statistique et des Etudes Economiques, 18 Bd Adolphe Pinard, 75675 Paris 14 France. **LC** TX910.F8; H57. **DD** 647.9444/021.

FR
HOTELS DE FRANCE, LES. **VFOAT** Guide National Officiel de l'Hotellerie Francaise. Began with 1979 Vol. French. an. 195.00F France; 205.00F other. Ecran Publicite, 190 Boulevard Haussmann, 75008 Paris France. **Tel** (1)45-63-10-54, FAX 42-89-08-72, telex 290131F. **LC** TX910.F8; H63. **DD** 647/.944401. **Circ:**

25,000. ***Continues*** *Hotels de la France et d'Outre-Mer.*
Desc: Provides in clear and exact form, not only all the necessary general touristic information, but also all the items concerning the category, the rates, the location and the amenities of all the approved Hotels, Motels and 'Relais de Tourisme'.

US/1047-2975
HOTELS (NEWTON, MASS.). (HOTELS : THE INTERNATIONAL MAGAZINE OF THE HOTEL AND HOTEL RESTAURANT INDUSTRY.). [Hotels]. Vol. 23, No. 10 (Oct. 1989)-. Periodical. English. mo. $75.00 US; $112.00 Canada; $105.00 Mexico; $135.00 (surface mail) other. Cahners Publishing Company, 249 West 17th Street, New York NY 10011. **Tel** (212)645-0067, FAX (212)242-6987. **(Subscription address:** Cahners Publishing Company / Colorado, Paid Subscription Service Center, PO Box 7610, Highlands Ranch CO 80126-7610.**) LC** TX901; .S19. **DD** 647.94/05. **[CCC]. Bk Rev. Ad Acc. Circ:** 60,000 (ctrl). ***Continues*** *Hotels & Restaurants International, 0744-3897.*
Desc: A business publication for the worldwide hotel industry. Each issue contains information on hotel development, investment, foodservice, design, sales and marketing, and business practices.
Ind/Abst Acad. Search (July 1993-); Bus. Index (1989-); Bus. Source (Jan. 1993-); Gen. BusinessFile (1989-); Gen. Period. Index (1989-); INFO-SOUTH Abstr.; Mag. Search; Trade Ind. Index (Oct. 1989-); Vocat. Search (July 1993-).

US/0746-9985
HSMAI MARKETING REVIEW. (HSMAI MARKETING REVIEW / HOTEL SALES & MARKETING ASSOCIATION INTERNATIONAL.). [HSMAI mark. rev.]. **Added/Corp** Hotel Sales & Marketing Association International. **VFOAT** H.S.M.A.I. Marketing Review; Marketing Review. **VAT** Hotel Sales and Marketing Association International Marketing Review. (198?)-. Periodical. English. qt. $20.00. Hotel Sales & Marketing Association International, 1300 L Street Northwest, Suite 800, Washington DC 20005. **Tel** (202)789-0089. ***Continues*** *HSMA Marketing Review, 0744-9011.*

UK
IBRM. English. ir. £17.00 UK; £21.00 Europe; £37.50 US; £41.00 other. Institute of Baths & Recreation Management, Giffard House, 36-38 Sherrard Street, Leicestershire LE13 1XJ England. **Tel** 011 44 664 65531, FAX 0664 501155. ***Continues*** *Baths Service and Recreation Management.*

II
INDIAN HOTELKEEPER AND TRAVELLER. Periodical. English. Twelve times a year. $8.45 India; $35.00 others. Indian Hotelkeeper and Traveller, 90-91 Maiden Hotel, 7 Alpier Road, Delhi 110054 India.

IO
INDONESIA HOTEL DIRECTORY.
Added/Corp Indonesia. Direktorat Jenderal Pariwisata. (1976)-. Directory. English. ir. Jakarta Directorate General of Tourism, Jalan Kramat Raya 81, Jakarta Indonesia. **LC** TX910.I6; I54.

SP
INDUSTRIA HOTELERA EN ESPANA.
Periodical. Spanish (English). an. Gasso-Horwath SA, Ronda Gral Mitre 126, 08021 Barcelona Spain. **Tel** 34-3-211 1900, FAX 34-3-211 1166, telex 50422 SEGA E. **ED** Jose Maria. **Bk Rev. Circ:** 2,000 (ctrl).

CN/0821-7610
INN BUSINESS (ESSEX, ONT.). (INN BUSINESS.). [Inn buss.]. (1983)-. Periodical. English. bm (6 issues). Zanny Limited, 11966 Woodbine Avenue, Gormley ONT L0H 1G0 Canada. **Tel** (905)887-4813. **ED** Kerry Turner. **DD** 338.4/76479471. **Bk Rev. Ad Acc. Circ:** 9,750 (ctrl). ***Continues*** *Canadian Inn Business, 0709-7077.*
Desc: Contains hotel and motel management and purchasing subjects such as how to run the business more profitably.

US/0895-2965
INN GUIDE, THE. [Inn guide]. 1st Ed. (1986)-. English. be. $39.00. The Inn Guide, California Inns, POB 3383, Santa Rosa CA 95402. **LC** TX907; .I573. **DD** 647/.9479401.

CN/0710-6386
INN MAGAZINE. [Inn mag.]. Periodical. English. ir. $23.21. Bosch Publishing Ltd, 10105 109th Street, Edmonton Alberta T5J 1M8 Canada. **Tel** (403)428-6455. **DD** 647/.9471.

CN/1193-1922
INNFOCUS (NORTH VANCOUVER). (INNFOCUS.). [Innfocus]. **VFOAT** Inn Focus; British Columbia and Yukon Innfocus; B.C. & Yukon Innfocus. Vol. 55, No. 5 (Aug./Sept. 1991)-. Periodical. English. bm. 20.95Can$. Naylor Communications Ltd, 100 Sutherland Avenue, Winnipeg Manitoba R2W 3C7 Canada. **Tel** (204)947-0222, FAX (604)985-7399. **DD** 647.9471101. ***Continues*** *British Columbia & Yukon Hotelier., 1182-0195.*

CN/0847-9356
INNKEEPER. [Innkeeper]. (Aug./Sept. 1989)-. Periodical. English. bm. $15.00 Canada; $20.00 other. Naylor Communications Ltd, 100 Sutherland Avenue, Winnipeg Manitoba R2W 3C7 Canada. **Tel** (204)947-0222, FAX (604)985-7399. **DD** 338.4/76479471. ***Continues*** *Ontario Innkeeper, 0705-2561.*

US/0746-6498
INNKEEPING WORLD. (19??)-. Periodical. English. Ten times a year (Monthly except Aug. and Dec.). $112.00 US and Canada; $144.00 other. Innkeeping World, PO Box 84108, c/o Charles Nolte, Seattle WA 98124. **Tel** (206)362-7125, FAX (206)362-7847. available on microfilm from University Microfilms International (UMI).
Desc: Focuses on hospitality trends worldwide and on all facets of hotel operation.

CN/0710-992X
INNSIDE NEWS. (INNSIDE NEWS / COMMONWEALTH HOLIDAY INNS OF CANADA.). [Innside news]. Periodical. English. ir. Free. Commonwealth Holiday Inns of Canada, 31 Fasken Drive, Rexdale Ontario M9W 1K8 Canada. **DD** 338.4/76479471. ctrl circ.

US/0361-4220
INTERNATIONAL GUILD GUIDE, THE.
See Restaurants.

FR
INTERNATIONAL HOTEL GUIDE. VFOAT Guide International des Hotels. 1951-. English. an. International Hotel Assn, 80 rue de la Roquette, 75011 Paris France.

GW/0340-0948
INTERNATIONAL HOTEL TELEX. English. Unitex-Verlag, Bavariaring 8-9, Munchen Germany. **LC** TX907; .I584. **DD** 647.94.

●US
INTERNATIONAL HOTEL TRENDS.
Added/Corp PKF Consulting (Firm). **VFOAT** Trends. (1993)-. English. PKF Publishing, 1728 Banks, Houston TX 77098. **Tel** (713)942-0414. ***Continues*** *Trends in the Hotel Industry. International Edition, 0278-3983.*

HK/0959-6119
INTERNATIONAL JOURNAL OF CONTEMPORARY HOSPITALITY MANAGEMENT. VFOAT Journal of Contemporary Hospitality Management. (April 1989)-. Periodical. English. Six times a year. $939.00. MCB University Press, 60 62 Toller Lane, Bradford West Yorkshire BD8 9BX England. **Tel** 011 44 274 499821, FAX 011 44 274 547143, telex 51317 MCBUNI G. **(Subscription address:** MCB University Press / US and Canada Subscriptions, PO Box 10812, Birmingham AL 35201-0812.**) ED** Richard E Teare and David Littlejohn. **LC** IN PROCESS. **Ad Acc.** Documents available from UMI Article Clearinghouse.
Desc: Communicates the latest developments and thinking in the management of hospitality operations worldwide. For hotel, catering and leisure industries.
Ind/Abst ABI/INFORM Glob. Ed.; Leis. Recreat. Tour. Abstr.

UK/0278-4319
INTERNATIONAL JOURNAL OF HOSPITALITY MANAGEMENT.
Added/Corp International Association of Hotel Management Schools. Vol. 1, No. 1 (1982)-. Periodical. English. qt. $261.00 The Americas; £175.00 other. Pergamon Press, An Imprint of Elsevier Science Ltd., The Boulevard, Langford Lane, Kidlington, Oxford OX5 1GB United Kingdom. **Tel** 011 44 865 843000, 011 44 865 843699, FAX 011 44 865 843010. **(Subscription address:** Elsevier Science Ltd. Oxford Fulfillment Centre, PO Box 800, Kidlington, Oxford OX5 1DX United Kingdom.**) ED** John O'Connor. **LC** TX911.3.M27; I56. **DD** 647/.94/05. **CODEN** IJHMDN. **[CCC].** available on microfilm and microfiche from University Microfilms International (UMI).
Ind/Abst Leis. Recreat. Tour. Abstr.; Women Manage. Rev. [Full Txt.].

AT
INTERSTATE ACCOMODATION DIRECTORY. Added/Corp Royal Automobile Club of Queensland. (19??)-. Directory. English. an. 2.00Aus$ (members), 8.00Aus$ (non-members). Royal Automobile Club of Queensland, 2649 Logan road, Eight Mile Plains, Queensland 4113 Australia. **Tel** 361-2435, FAX 849-0610. **LC** TX907; .I64. **DD** 647/.9494. Index available. **Ad Acc, Adv Mgr:** Karen Shields. Full Page (B&W) 2800Aus$. Half Page (B&W) 1800Aus$. Full Page (Color) 3770Aus$. Half Page (Color) 2430Aus$. **Circ:** 70,000 (ctrl).
Desc: Accommodation listing including facilities and tariffs for all Australian states except Queensland.

IO
INVENTARISASI AKOMODASI PROPINSI MALUKU. **See** Restaurants.

US/1056-5043
JAPAN HOTEL AND RESORT INVESTMENT REPORT. (July 1991)-. English. $295.00. Mead Ventures Inc, PO Box 44952, Phoenix AZ 85064. **Tel** (602)234-0044, FAX (602)234-0076.
Desc: Lists more than 200 Japanese-owned hotels in the United States along with purchase price.

UK
LET'S HALT AWHILE IN GREAT BRITAIN. English. an. Ashley Courtenay Ltd, 16 Little London, Chichester Sussex England. **Tel** (0243)775521, FAX 0243 531331, telex 86402 (CHITYP). **LC** TX910.G7; A67. **DD** 647/.9442. Index available. **Bk Rev. Circ:** 25,000. ***Continues*** *Ashley Courtenay's Let's Halt Awhile: England, Wales, Scotland, Ireland.*
Desc: Recommends approximately 1,500 hotels and inns throughout England, Scotland, Wales and major islands of Britain.

US/0894-5128
LODGING AND RESTAURANT INDEX.
See Travel and Tourism.

US/0148-0766
LODGING HOSPITALITY. [Lodg. hosp.]. Vol. 30, No. 6 (June 1974)-. Periodical. English. Twelve times a year. $60.00 US; $85.00 Canada; $90.00 Mexico; $100.00 other. Penton Publishing, 1100 Superior Avenue, Cleveland OH 44114-2543. **Tel** (216)696-7000, FAX (216)696-0836. **(Subscription address:** Penton Publishing, PO Box 96732, Chicago IL 60693.**) LC** TX901; .L6. **DD** 647/.94/05. **[CCC].** available on microfilm and microfiche from University Microfilms International (UMI); available on an online database (files 15,648/Full-Text) from DIALOG. ***Continues*** *Hospitality, Lodging, 0098-3306.*
Ind/Abst Acad. Search (July 1993-); Bus. ASAP (1990-) [Full Txt.]; Bus. Index (1985-); Bus. Period. Index; Bus. Source (Jan. 1993-); Gen. BusinessFile (1985-); Gen. Period. Index (1985-); INFO-SOUTH Abstr.; Mag. Search; Stat. Ref. Index; Trade Ind. ASAP [Full Txt.]; Trade Ind. Index (1981-) [Full Txt.]; UMI ABI/Inform--Bus. Period. Ondisc (Jan. 1991-) [Full Txt.]; Vocat. Search (July 1993-); Wilson Bus. Abstr.

US/1078-6503
LODGING MAGAZINE. ***Title Change.*** [Lodg. mag.]. **Added/Corp** American Hotel Association Directory Corporation. **VFOAT** Lodging. Vol. 16, No. 2 (Oct. 1990)-(199?). Periodical. English. Twelve times a year (Except July/Aug. issues combined). American Hotel and Motel Association, 1201 New York Avenue Northwest, Washington DC 20005. **Tel** (202)289-3100, (202)289-3165, FAX (202)289-3199. **ED** Phillip Hayward (phone: (202)289-3169). **DD** 647. **Ad Acc, Adv Mgr:** Janet Dodson, **Tel** (202)289-3160. **Circ:** 36,000 (ctrl). ***Continues*** *Lodging, 0360-9235.* ***Continued by*** *Lodging (Washington, D.C. : 1993), 1078-5795.*
Desc: Information on the management of the American Hotel & Motel Association. Geared toward professionals & executives in the hotel and motel industry.

FI
MAJOITUSLIIKKEIDEN KAPASITEETTI.
See Restaurants.

FI
MAJOITUSTILASTO, MAJOITUSLIIKKEIDEN KAPASITEETIN KAYTTO. VFOAT Accommodation Statistics, Utilization of Lodging Services' Capacity. Multiple languages (English, Finnish and Swedish). Valtion Painatuskeskus, PO Box 516, SF 00101 Helsinki Finland. **Tel** 011 358 0 5660266. **LC** TX901; .M34.

CN/0849-3685
MEMBERSHIP DIRECTORY & BUYERS' GUIDE / ONTARIO HOTEL AND MOTEL ASSOCIATION. [Membsh. dir. buy. guide - Ont. Hotel Motel Assoc.]. **Main/Corp** Ontario Hotel and Motel Association. (1990)-. Consumer Publication. English. Free to members. Ontario Hotel and Motel Association Roster, 6725 Airport Road, Suite 102, Mississauga, Ontario L4V 1V2 Canada. **DD** 647.94713. ***Continues*** *Ontario Hotel and Motel Association. Membership and Allied Members Directory., 0836-7760.*

UK
MICHELIN GREAT BRITAIN AND IRELAND. Main/Corp Michelin Tyre Company, Ltd. **VFOAT** Great Britain and Ireland. (19??)-. Periodical. Multiple languages (English, French, German and Italian). $5.25. Manufacture Francaise des Pneumatiques Michelin, 46 avenue de Breteuil, 75431 Paris Cedex 07 France. **(Subscription address:** Michelin Travel Publications, PO Box 19008, Greenville SC 29602.**) LC** TX910.G7; M45b. **DD** 647/.9441.
Desc: Selection of hotels and restaurants in Great Britain and Ireland.

UK
MICHELIN GREATER LONDON. Main/Corp Michelin Tyre Company, Ltd. (19??)-. Multiple languages (English, French, German and Spanish). ir. Manufacture Francaise des Pneumatiques Michelin, 46 avenue de Breteuil, 75431 Paris Cedex 07 France. **(Subscription**

address: Michelin Travel Publications, PO Box 19008, Greenville SC 29602.) **LC** TX910.G7; M45a. **DD** 914.21/04/857.
Desc: Selected hotels and restaurants in greater London. Extract from Michelin / Great Britain and Ireland.

US/1075-5926
MOBIL TRAVEL GUIDE. FREQUENT TRAVELERS' GUIDE TO MAJOR CITIES. **See** Travel and Tourism.

US/1040-1075
MOBIL TRAVEL GUIDE. NORTHEAST. **See** Travel and Tourism.

US/0161-1925
MOTEL ECONOMY GUIDE : FLORIDA & I-95. **VAT** Motel Economy Guide. Florida and Interstate Ninety-Five. 1978-. English. $2.95. Seaholm Interstate Directories 12561. **LC** TX907; .M87. **DD** 647/.94759.

US
MOTEL OCCUPANCY IN VERMONT. **Added/Corp** Vermont. Agency of Development and Community Affairs. (19??)-. English. an. Vermont Agency of Development and Community Affairs, Montpelier VT 05602. **Tel** (802)828-3211. **ED** George A Donovan. **LC** TX909; .M58. **DD** 647/.94743020212. **Circ:** 200.

US/0272-8699
NATIONAL DIRECTORY AND ATLAS OF BUDGET MOTELS. 1981-. Directory. English. an. $4.95. Michael West Inc, PO Box 520, East Setauket NY 11733. **LC** TX907; .N257. **DD** 647/.947302.

US/0146-3950
NATIONAL DIRECTORY OF BUDGET MOTELS. (1975)-. Directory. English. an. $6.95. Pilot Books, 103 Cooper Street, Babylon NY 11702-2319. **Tel** (516)422-2225, FAX (516)422-2227. **ED** Raymond Carlson. **LC** TX907; .N26. **DD** 647/.9473.
Desc: Nationwide guide to over 2,200 low-cost chain motel accommodations in the US and Canada. It also includes headquarter listings, toll-free phones and additional information.

NZ
NEW ZEALAND HOTEL/MOTEL INVENTORY AND ROOM OCCUPANCY RATES (LICENSED). **See** Hotels/Motels-Abstracting, Bibliographies and Statistics.

CN
NEWFOUNDLAND AND LABRADOR. ACCOMMODATIONS. English. an. Department of Development and Tourism, Tourism Branch, PO Box 2016, St John's Newfoundland A1C 5R8 Canada. **LC** TX910.N43; N48. **DD** 647/.947180/05. ***Continues*** *Newfoundland and Labrador (Accommodation Guide).*

US/1059-0730
NORTH AMERICAN BED & BREAKFAST REGISTRY, THE. [N. Am. bed breakf. regist.]. **VFOAT** North American Bed and Breakfast Registry. Fall (1991)-. English. qt. $38.50. Wakeman & Costine Publications, 3526 South Florida Avenue, PO Box 6958, Lakeland FL 33807-9917. **LC** TX907.2; .N673. **DD** 647.947503.

UK
NORTHERN IRELAND. English. **LC** TX910.G7; N67. **DD** 647/.94416/05.

CN/0707-087X
NOVA SCOTIA HOSTELLER. **Added/Corp** Canadian Hostelling Association. Nova Scotia. Vol. 20, No. 5 (Oct. 1977)-. Periodical. English. Canadian Hostelling Association / South Halifax, Nova Scotia Region, PO Box 3010, South Halifax Nova Scotia B3J 3G6 Canada. **Tel** (902)425-5450. **DD** 647/.94/062716. **Circ:** 1,000. ***Continues*** *Atlantic Hosteller, 0318-5818.*
Desc: International hostel news, local trip information, and Nova Scotia hostels and activities.

CN/1184-0390
NOVA SCOTIA PICTORIAL COUNTRY INNS, BED & BREAKFAST AND MUCH MORE. [N.S. pict. ctry. inns bed breakf. much more]. 4th Ed. (1990)-. English. Stone House Publishing, PO Box 9301, Station A, Halifax Nova Scotia B3K 5N5 Canada. **DD** 647.94716/005. ***Continues*** *Hines, Sherman, 1941- Nova Scotia Pictorial Bed & Breakfast and Unique Inns., 0848-080X.*

US/1053-0002
OAG BUSINESS TRAVEL PLANNER (NORTH AMERICAN ED.). (OAG BUSINESS TRAVEL PLANNER : THE OFFICIAL GUIDE TO LODGING AND TRAVEL RELATED SERVICES.). **Added/Corp** Official Airline Guides, Inc. American Hotel & Motel Association. **VFOAT** Business Travel Planner; Hotel & Motel Redbook : The Official Lodging Directory of the American Hotel & Motel Association; Hotel and Motel Redbook. **VAT** Official Airline Guides Business Travel Planner. Vol. 32, No. 3 (Sept./Nov. 1990)-. Periodical. English. Four times a year. $142.00. Official Airline Guides, 2000 Clearwater Drive, Oak Brook IL 60521. **Tel** (800)323-3537. **(Subscription address:** Neodata / Colorado, PO Box 2606, Boulder Boulder CO 80322.) **LC** TX907; .O34. **DD** 647/.94701. **CODEN** OBTEE2. ***Continues*** *OAG Travel Planner, Hotel & Motel Redbook (North American Ed.), 0894-1726.*

●US/1073-0338
OAG OFFICIAL TRAVELER. TRAVEL GUIDE. (OAG OFFICIAL TRAVELER. TRAVEL GUIDE : THE GOVERNMENT, MILITARY, AND CRC'S GUIDE TO LODGING AND TRAVEL RELATED SERVICES / OFFICIAL AIRLINE GUIDES.). [OAG off. travel., Travel guide]. **Added/Corp** Official Airline Guides, Inc. **VFOAT** Official Traveler; Travel Guide; OAG, The Official Traveler's Travel Guide. **VAT** Official Airline Guides Official Traveler. Travel Guide. Vol. 1, No. 1 (Apr.-June 1992)-. Periodical. English. Twelve times a year. $39.95. Official Airline Guides, 2000 Clearwater Drive, Oak Brook IL 60521. **Tel** (800)323-3537. **LC** TX907.2; .O24. **DD** 647.947301.

●US/1075-1548
OAG TRAVEL PLANNER (EUROPEAN ED.). (OAG TRAVEL PLANNER.). **Added/Corp** Official Airline Guides, Inc. American Hotel & Motel Association. **VFOAT** Travel Planner. **VAT** Official Airline Guides Travel Planner. Vol. 14, No. 3 (Jan.-Mar. 1992)-. Directory. English. qt. Official Airline Guides / Illinois, 2000 Clearwater Drive, Oak Brook IL 60521. **Tel** (800)323-3537, FAX (312)574-6091, telex 210144 OAGO UR. **(Subscription address:** Neodata / Colorado, PO Box 2606, Boulder Boulder CO 80322.) **ED** Richard A. Nelson and Margaret E. Pritt. **LC** TX907.5.E85; O24. **DD** 647/.94401. **CODEN** OTRPEF. **Ad Acc. Circ:** 22,000. available on an online database from OAG Electronic Edition Travel Service. ***Continues*** *OAG Travel Planner, Hotel & Motel Redbook (European Ed.), 0894-1718.*
Desc: Provides travel facts, complete lodging information, airport diagrams, maps and reservation telephone numbers for over 14,000 destinations throughout the United States, Canada, Mexico and the Caribbean. Includes data and visuals on travel to and through European cities.

US
OFFICERS' REPORT & DAILY CONVENTION PROCEEDINGS - HOTEL AND RESTAURANT EMPLOYEES AND BARTENDERS INTERNATIONAL UNION. **Main/Corp** Hotel and Restaurant Employees and Bartenders International Union. **VAT** Officers' Report and Daily Convention Proceedings. 34th- 1957-. Proceedings. English. ir. Hotel and Restaurant Employees and International Union, 1219 28th Street Northwest, Washington DC 20007-3316. **Tel** (202)393-4373. ***Continues*** *Hotel and Restaurant Employees and Bartenders International Union. Officers Report and Proceedings.*

UK
OFFICIAL GUIDE, HOTELS AND RESTAURANTS IN GREAT BRITAIN AND IRELAND, THE. **VFOAT** BHRA Guide to Hotels and Restaurants; Hotels and Restaurants in Great Britain and Ireland. English. an. British Hotels & Restaurants, 13 Cork Street, London W1Y 2BH England.

US/1043-1195
OFFICIAL GUIDE TO AMERICAN HISTORIC INNS, THE. [Off. guide Am. hist. inns]. **Added/Corp** Association of American Historic Inns. **VFOAT** American Historic Inns. (1989)-. English. Association of American Historic Inns, Box 336, Dana Point CA 92629. **Tel** (714)499-4022, FAX (714)496-7050. **ED** Deborah Sabach. **LC** TX907.2; .O38. **DD** 647.947303. Index available. **Bk Rev. Circ:** 67,000.
Desc: Most comprehensive guide to bed and breakfast and historic country inns available. Describes 195 inns in detail, over 700 illustrations, an appendix listing 5,000 inns. Covers the oldest inns in America starting from 1637 include 100 inns built prior to 1776.

FR
OFFICIAL GUIDE TO THE HOTELS-RESTAURANTS, COUNTRY HOTELS & INNS OF FRANCE, THE. **VFOAT** Country Hotels & Inns of France; Country Hotels and Inns of France. English (French). $10.95. Federation Nationale des Logis et Auberges de France, 25 rue Jean-Mermoz, 75008 Paris France. **LC** TX910.F8; O36. **DD** 647.944401. ***Continues*** *Official Guide to the Country Hotels & Inns of France.*

US
OFFICIAL HOTEL AND RESORT GUIDE. ***Title Change.*** **VFOAT** OHRG. (196?)-(19??). English. ir. Reed Travel Group / New Jersey, 500 Plaza Drive, Secaucus NJ 07096. **Tel** (201)902-2000, (800)360-0015, FAX (201)319-1628. **Bk Rev. Ad Acc.** ctrl circ. ***Continued by*** *Official Hotel Guide.*

US/1056-1862
OFFICIAL HOTEL GUIDE. [Offic. hotel guide]. (1991)-. English. an (published in April as 3 bound volumes). $225.57. Reed Travel Group / New Jersey, 500 Plaza Drive, Secaucus NJ 07096. **Tel** (201)902-2000, (800)360-0015, FAX (201)319-1628. **LC** TX907; .O43. **DD** 647.94/025.
Desc: Detailed descriptions of 30,000 hotels and resorts worldwide.

US/0094-5242
OFFICIAL MEETING FACILITIES GUIDE. ***Title Change.*** [Offic. meet. facil. guide]. (Spring 1974)-Vol. 18 (1992). English. sa. Reed Travel Group / New Jersey, 500 Plaza Drive, Secaucus NJ 07096. **Tel** (201)902-2000, (800)360-0015, FAX (201)319-1628. **LC** TX907; .O46. **DD** 647/.94. **CODEN** OMFGDE. ***Continued by*** *Official Meeting Facilities Guide, North America, 1070-4515.*
Desc: Current, complete information on over 1400 premier meeting sites worldwide.
Ind/Abst Curr. Lit. Fam. Plan. (19??-199?).

US/1054-3309
OFFICIAL MEETING FACILITIES GUIDE, EUROPE. [Off. meet. facil. guide Eur.]. **VFOAT** Europe; OMFGE; Official Meeting Facilities Guide-Europe. Vol. 1, No. 1 (Autumn/Winter 1991)-. English. Twice a year. £100.00. Reed Travel Group / New Jersey, 500 Plaza Drive, Secaucus NJ 07096. **Tel** (201)902-2000, (800)360-0015, FAX (201)319-1628. **LC** TX907.5.E85; O44. **DD** 657.944.

●US/1070-4515
OFFICIAL MEETING FACILITIES GUIDE, NORTH AMERICA. [Offic. meet. facil. guide N. Am.]. **VFOAT** OMFG; Official Meeting Facilities Guide. Vol. 19, No. 1 (Spring/Summer 1992)-. English. sa (published in March and September). $61.80. Reed Travel Group / New Jersey, 500 Plaza Drive, Secaucus NJ 07096. **Tel** (201)902-2000, (800)360-0015, FAX (201)319-1628. **LC** TX907; .O46. **DD** 647/.94. ***Continues*** *Official Meeting Facilities Guide, 0094-5242.*

US/0030-1183
OHIO TAVERN NEWS. **See** Restaurants.

CN/0707-8102
ONTARIO/CANADA ACCOMMODATIONS. [Ont./Can. accommod.]. **VFOAT** Ontario Canada Accommodations. 1982-. English. Ontario Ministry of Tourism and Recreation, Province of Ontario, Queen's Park, Toronto Ontario M7A 2E5 Canada. **LC** TX910.C2; O59. **DD** 647/.94713. ***Continues*** *Ontario. Ministry of Industry and Tourism. Ontario-Canada Accommodation, 0707-8102.*

PK/0250-4359
PAKISTAN HOTEL & RESTAURANT GUIDE. **VFOAT** Pakistan Hotel and Restaurant Guide. English. an. Rs50.00 Pakistan; $5.00 US. Maulai Enterprise, J-6/2 Al-Naseer Sharifabad, F B Area/Block 1, Karachi 75900 Pakistan. **Tel** 682764, 684293, 687425. **ED** Syed Wali Ahmad Maulai. **LC** TX910.P35; P312. **DD** 647/.94549/1. Index available. **Ad Acc. Circ:** 5,000.
Desc: Hotels, motels, restaurants, youth hostels, business and shopping chapter, exchange rates, hotel telegraph code for ordering rooms, a must for every traveller visiting Pakistan. Approved and recognised by Pakistan Hotels Association and Ministry of tourism, government of Pakistan.

PK
PAKISTAN HOTEL AND TRAVEL REVIEW. V. 1- June 1978-. Periodical. English. mo. Rs300.00 Pakistan; $30.00 US. Maulai Enterprise, J-6/2 Al-Naseer Sharifabad, F B Area/Block 1, Karachi 75900 Pakistan. **Tel** 682764, 684293, 687425. **ED** Syed Wali Ahmad Maulai. **LC** TX910.P35; P315. **DD** 338.4/647945491. Index available. **Bk Rev. Ad Acc. Circ:** 5,000.
Desc: Airlines, hotels, eating houses, calendar of events, feature articles, travel news and views, interviews of important personalities in hotel and travel field. Approved by Pakistan Hotels Association and Ministry of Tourism, Government of Pakistan.

PK/0552-8968
PAKISTAN HOTEL GUIDE. English. an. Rs50.00 Pakistan; $5.00 other. Publishers Correspondents and Advertising, 118/1 Sharifabad 19, Karachi Pakistan. **Tel** 682764. **ED** S W A Maulai. **LC** TX910.P35; P32. **DD** 647/.94549/1. Index available. **Ad Acc. Circ:** 5,000.
Desc: Hotels, motels, restaurants, youth hotels, business and shopping chapter, exchange rates, hotel telegraph code for ordering rooms, approved and recognised by Ministry of Tourism, Government of Pakistan and Pakistan Hotels Association.

PK
PAKISTAN HOTELS & TOURISM. **VAT** Pakistan Hotels and Tourism. (1975)-. English. an. Rs5.00. Bhatti Publications, 103-B Gulberg, Lahore Pakistan. **ED** Mukhtar Bhatti. **LC** DS376.8; .B47. **DD** 915.49/1/045. ***Supersedes*** *Hotels and Restaurants of Pakistan.*

FR
PARIS AND ENVIRONS : HOTELS AND RESTAURANTS. **Main/Corp** Pneu Michelin (Firm). English. an. $3.95. Michelin Guides and Maps, PO Box 3305, Spartanburg SC 29304. **Tel** (803)599-0850. **LC** TX910.F8; M35B. **DD** 647/.9444/3601.

Hotels/Motels

PE
PERU, GUIA DE HOTELES Y TURISMO.
Added/Corp International Hotel & Tourism Consultants (Firm). **VFOAT** Guia de Hoteles y Turismo; Peru, Guia de Hoteles. Spanish (English). **Continues** Peru, Guia de Hoteles.

CN/1180-999X
PRAIRIE-HOTELIER. Ceased. [Prairie-hotel.].
Added/Corp Manitoba Hotel Association. Alberta Hotel Association. Hotels Association of Saskatchewan. Vol. 15, No. 1 (Jan./Feb. 1990)-(Fall 1993). Periodical. English. bm. Naylor Communications Ltd, 100 Sutherland Avenue, Winnipeg Manitoba R2W 3C7 Canada. **Tel** (204)947-0222, FAX (604)985-7399. **DD** 338.4/76479471201. **Continues** Prairie Hotelman., 0705-2189.

UK
PREMIER HOTELS OF GREAT BRITAIN.
46th Ed. (1985)-. English. an. $15.95. Pelican Publishing Company, PO Box 3110, Gretna LA 70054. **Tel** (504)368-1175, (800)843-1724, FAX (504)368-1195. Index available.
Desc: Lists with information on hotels located throughout the country.

UK/0959-2687
PROFESSIONAL HOTEL & RESTAURANT INTERIORS. See Interior Design.

UK/0952-5424
PROGRESS IN TOURISM, RECREATION, AND HOSPITALITY MANAGEMENT. See Travel and Tourism.

US/1047-4668
RECOMMENDED COUNTY INNS. [Recomm. ctry. inns, N. Engl.]. **VFOAT** Country Inns. New England; New England. 11th Ed. (1989)-. English. Globe Pequot Press, 6 Business Park Road, Old Saybrook CT 06475. **Tel** (800)243-0495, . **ED** Editor: E. Squier. **LC** TX907; .G93. **DD** 647.947401. **Continues** Guide to the Recommended Country Inns of New England, 0093-4585.

CN/1183-6008
REPERTOIRE DES TARIFS PREFERENTIELS HOTELIERS. Title Change. (REPERTOIRE DES TARIFS PREFERENTIELS HOTELIERS / MINISTERE DES APPROVISIONNEMENTS ET SERVICES.). [Repert. tarifs prefer. hotel.]. **Added/Corp** Quebec (Province). Ministere des Approvisionnements et Services. **VAT** Repertoire des Tarifs Preferentiels Hoteliers Accordes aux Employes du Gouvernement. (1992)-(1993). Periodical. French. **DD** 647.94714. **Continued by** Tarifs Preferentiels Hoteliers ... Accordes aux Employes du Gouvernement du Quebec, 1196-2755.

US/0886-9863
RESORT & HOTEL MANAGEMENT. Ceased. See Business-General Management.

US/8750-1252
RESORT DEVELOPMENT & OPERATION. VFOAT Resort Development and Operation; Resort Development & Operations. (May 1990)-. Periodical. English. Eight times a year. $40.00 US; $55.00 Canada and Mexico; $70.00 other. CHB Co. Inc, PO Box 5627, Bellingham WA 98227. **Tel** (206)676-4146, FAX (206)647-1311. **ED** Carl Burlingame. **Bk Rev**, (Qty: 2-5). **Ad Acc. Circ:** 3,600. **Continues** Resort Development.
Desc: Trade news and trends in resort development.

US/0897-5833
RESORTS & GREAT HOTELS. [Resorts great hotels]. **VFOAT** Resorts and Great Hotels. (1987)-. Periodical. English. an (June). $15.00 US; $20.00 Canada & Mexico; $25.00 Europe, South America & Caribbean; $30.00 others. Resorts and Great Hotels, 123 West Padre, Santa Barbara CA 93105. **Tel** (805)687-1422. **ED** Annette Burden. **DD** 647. **Ad Acc. Adv Mgr:** Don Fritzen, **Tel** (805)687-1422.

GW/0344-4422
RESTAURANT- & HOTEL-MANAGEMENT. VFOAT Restaurant- und Hotel-Management; Restaurants- & Hotels-Management; Restaurants und Hotels-Management. (1971)-. Periodical. German. mo. DM72.00 Germany; DM82.80 other. Rhenania Fachverlag GmbH, Postfach 601220, Possmoorweg 5, W-2000 Hamburg 60 Germany. **Tel** 011 49 40 27170, FAX 011 49 40 27172056, telex 2173465 or 213214. **UDC** 64.024.1 :65.012.4.

AT/0725-9379
RETAIL ESTABLISHMENTS AND SELECTED SERVICE ESTABLISHMENTS, HOTELS AND ACCOMMODATION, TASMANIA / AUSTRALIAN BUREAU OF STATISTICS.
Added/Corp Australian Bureau of Statistics. Tasmanian Office. (19??)-. English. ir. Australian Bureau Statistics / Tasmanian Office, Commonwealth Government Centre, 188 Collins Street, Hobart GPO Box 66A, Hobart Tasmania 7001 Australia. **Tel** (002)205889. **LC** TX910.A7; R47. **DD** 647/.994601/05.
Desc: Covers details of numbers of establishments, persons employed, wages and salaries, turnover, stocks, purchases, tranfers-in and selected expenses, value added, fixed capital expenditure less disposals and accommodation capacity.

FR
REVUE TECHNIQUE EQUIP HOTEL.
French. mo. 239.96F France; 450.00F other. Revue Equip Hotel, 10 rue de Beffroi, 92200 Neuilly sur Seine France. **Tel** 011 33 1 46400101, FAX 011 33 1 46401949.

US/0098-4507
SAV-ON-HOTELS. VFOAT Sav-on-Hotels Across Europe. English. an. Traveltips, PO Box 11061, Oakland CA 94611. **LC** TX910.A1; S27. **LC** 647/.944.
Desc: Guide to selected European budget hotels and other economy lodgings.

UK
SCOTLAND, HOTELS & GUEST HOUSES. Added/Corp Scottish Tourist Board. **VAT** Scotland, Hotels and Guest Houses. (19??)-. English.
Continues Scotland, Where to Stay, Hotels and Guest Houses.
Desc: Provides a guide to Scottish bed and breakfast residences, hotels, and taverns.

UK
SCOTLAND, WHERE TO STAY, HOTELS AND GUEST HOUSES. Title Change.
Added/Corp Scottish Tourist Board. **VFOAT** Hotels and Guest Houses; Ou Se Loger en Ecosse. (1980)-(19??). English. an. Scottish Tourist Board, 23 Ravelston Terrace, Edinburgh EH4 3EU England. **Tel** 031-332-2433. **LC** TX910.S3; S28. **DD** 647/.941101/05. **Continues** Where to Stay in Scotland ... Hotels, Guesthouses, and University Accommodation. **Continued by** Scotland, Hotels & Guest Houses.

UK
SIGNPOST. (1935)-. English. £8.95. Fountain Court, Steelhouse Lane, Birmingham B4 6DT England. **Tel** (021)236-5979, FAX (021)200-1159. **ED** C. F. Carney-Smith. **LC** TX910.G7; S55. **DD** 647/.9442. **Bk Rev. Ad Acc. Circ:** 10,000.
Desc: Guide to hotels in the UK, illustrated in color.

GW
SILENCIUM. (19??)-. German. Sisu Steinschulte Verlag, Bismarckstr 10, W-5300 Bonn 2 Germany. **Tel** 0228/361063, FAX 0228/351130, telex 885 540. Index available. **Ad Acc.**
Desc: A hotel magazine for the Silence-hotel group.

US/0890-281X
SPECIAL EVENTS. [Spec. events]. Periodical. English. bm. Miramar Publishing Company / California, 6133 Bristol Parkway, PO Box 3640, Culver City CA 90231. **Tel** (310)337-9717, (800)543-4116. **DD** 338.

US/1040-600X
SUCCESSFUL HOTEL MARKETER, THE. Title Change. [Success. hotel mark.]. Vol. 1, No. 1 (1988)-(Jan. 1994). Periodical. English. Twelve times a year. Magna Publications Inc, 2718 Dryden Drive, Madison WI 53704. **Tel** (800)433-0499, (608)246-3591, FAX (608)246-3597. **ED** William Merrick. **DD** 658. [CCC]. Index available. cum. index. **Bk Rev. Ad Acc. Pr Rev. Circ:** 1,500. **Absorbed by** Total Quality in Hospitality, 1069-5591.
Desc: Reports on hotel/motel marketing promotions and ideas.

CK
TARIFAS HOTELERAS. VFOAT Colombia, Tarifas Hoteleras. Spanish. Ministerio de Desarollo Economico, Calle 19 No 6-68 Piso 7, Bogota Colombia. **LC** TX910; .C7137. **DD** 647/.94861/05.

US
TEXAS HOTEL REVIEW (SAN ANTONIO, TEX. : 1988). Ceased. (TEXAS HOTEL REVIEW.). Jan. (1988)-Ceased with Dec. (1988). Periodical. English. mo. Hotel Review Company, 900 Congress Avenue/Suite 310, Austin TX 78701. **Tel** (512)828-3566. **ED** Spencer Derden. **Ad Acc.** ctrl circ. **Continues** Southwest Hotel-Motel Review.

IO
TINGKAT PENGHUNIAN KAMAR HOTEL. Began in 1976. Indonesian. an. Rp1,500 Indonesian; $1.00 US. Central Bureau of Statistics / Indonesia, c/o Dr. Sutomo, 8 Jalan, PO Box 3, Jakarta Indonesia. **Tel** 372808 374908 Ext.342. **LC** TX910.I6; T56. ctrl circ.

●US/1069-5591
TOTAL QUALITY IN HOSPITALITY. [Total qual. hosp.]. Vol. 1, No. 1 (June 1993)-. Periodical. English. mo. $127.00 US and Canada; $147.00 other. Magna Publications Inc, 2718 Dryden Drive, Madison WI 53704. **Tel** (800)433-0499, (608)246-3591, FAX (608)246-3597. **DD** 338. **Absorbed** Successful Hotel Marketer.

SZ
TOURISM & HOTEL SECURITY WORLDWIDE MAGAZINE. Added/Corp International Hotel Security Association. World Tourism Organization. **VFOAT** Tourism and Hotel Security Worldwide Magazine; Hotel Security Worldwide; Tourism Hotel Security Worldwide Magazine. (19??)-. Periodical. English (French). sa.
Ind/Abst Leis. Recreat. Tour. Abstr.

IS
TOURISM AND HOTEL SERVICES STATISTICS QUARTERLY. See Travel and Tourism-Abstracting, Bibliographies and Statistics.

SZ
TOURISMUS IN DER SCHWEIZ IN DER HOTELLERIE UND DEN UBRIGEN BEHERBERGUNGSFORMEN. VFOAT Tourisme en Suisse dans l'Hotellerie et les Autres Formes d'Hebergement. French (German). an. 6.00 each issue. Bundesamt fuer Statistik, Schwarztorstrasse 96, CH 3003 Bern Switzerland. **Tel** 031 3236011, FAX 031 3236061. **LC** TX910.S9; T65. **DD** 338.4/76479449401/0212.

LE
TOURIST & HOTEL GUIDE FOR LEBANON. See Travel and Tourism.

FR/0150-7540
TOUTES LES NOUVELLES DE L'HOTELLERIE ET DU TOURISME. [Toute nouv. Hotel. tour.]. (1971)-. Periodical. French. mo (July/Aug. issue combined). 132.22F France; 160.00F other. Toutes les Nouvelles de l'Hotl. and du Tourisme, 4 rue Barye, 75017 Paris France. **Tel** 011 33 1 47660548. **UDC** 64.024 + 380.8.

US/0145-7810
TRAVEL MASTER. Periodical. English. sa. $20.00. 645 Stewart Avenue, Garden City NY 11530. **LC** TX907; .T815. **DD** 647/.94.

US/0278-3983
TRENDS IN THE HOTEL INDUSTRY. INTERNATIONAL EDITION. Title Change. (TRENDS IN THE HOTEL INDUSTRY.). [Trends hotel industr. Int. ed.]. **Added/Corp** Pannell, Kerr, Forster (Firm). **VFOAT** Trends. (1980)-(1992). English. an. PKF Publishing, 1728 Banks, Houston TX 77098. **Tel** (713)942-0414. **LC** TX901; .T73. **DD** 338.4/7647/9401. **Continues** Trends in the Hotel Business. International Ed. **Continued by** International Hotel Trends (San Francisco, Calif. : 1993).

US/0276-5357
TRENDS IN THE HOTEL INDUSTRY. USA EDITION. (TRENDS IN THE HOTEL INDUSTRY.). [Trends hotel ind., USA ed.]. **Added/Corp** Pannell, Kerr, Forster (Firm). **VAT** Trends in the Hotel Industry. United States of America Edition. (1980)-. English. an. $195.00. PKF Publishing, 1728 Banks, Houston TX 77098. **Tel** (713)942-0414. **(Subscription address:** Trends in the Hotel Industry, Subscription Office, PO Box 11318, Birmingham AL 35202-1318. **) LC** TX909.A1; H3. **DD** 338.4/7647947301. **Continues** Trends in the Hotel-Motel Business, 0741-7985.

IT
TURISMO D'ITALIA. (19??)-. Periodical. Italian. Ten times a year. L95000 (members of FAIAT); L130000 (non-member) Italy; L140000 (non-member) other. Ediman SRL, C SO San Gottardo 39, 20136 Milan, Italy. **Tel** 011 39 2 58103791. **ED** Maria Paola Cavallazzi and Giovann Coldmbo. cum. index. **Bk Rev. Ad Acc. Pr Rev. Circ:** 15,000 (ctrl).
Desc: Motel and restaurant management, tourism and hotel products.

GW
UNTERNEHMAN UND ARBEITSSTATTEN. REIHE 1.4, KOSTENSTRUKTUR IM GASTGEWERBE / HERAUSGEBER STATISTISCHES BUNDESAMT. VFOAT Kostenstruktur im Gastgewerbe; Fachserie 2. Periodical. German. ir (quadrennial). DM7.00. W Kohlhammer Verlag GmbH, Postfach 800430, D 70549 Stuttgart Germany. **Tel** 011 49 711 78631, FAX 011 49 711 7863263, telex 7-255820. **LC** HC290.5.C7; A3. **Continues** Fachserie C, Unternehmen und Arbeitsstatten. Reihe 1, die Kostenstruktur in der Wirtschaft, VI, Gastgewerbe.

SP
VACACIONES EN CASAS DE LABRANZAS. Main/Corp Spain. Direccion General de Empresas y Actividades Turisticas. Spanish. Ministerio de Comercio y Secretaria de Estado de Turismo, Alcala Num 44, Madrid-14 Spain. **LC** TX910.S7; S63A.

NE
VERGADERACCOMMODATIEGIDS. Dutch. an. Intermedia BV, Postbus 4, 2400 M Alphen Rijn Netherlands. **Tel** 011 31 1720 66855.

FI/0357-749X
VITRIINI. Trade Publication. Finnish (summaries and/or abstracts in Swedish). mo. 260. ISO Roobertink 6A, 00120 Helsinki 12 Finland. **Tel** (90)648022. **ED** Lena Heikkila. **LC** TX901; .H86. **Bk Rev. Ad Acc. Circ:** 3,500 (ctrl). ***Continues*** *Hotelli- Ja Ravintolalehti.*
Desc: Trade magazine for restaurants, hotels, cafes, and cafeterias.

UK
VOICE OF THE HOSPITALITY ASSOCIATION. (19??)-. English. Ten times a year. £33.00. British Hotels Restaurants and Caterers Association, 40 Duke Street, London W1M 6HR England. **Tel** 011 44 71 4996641. ***Continues*** *British Hotelier and Restauranteur.*

UK
WHERE TO STAY IN SCOTLAND, BED AND BREAKFAST. ***Title Change.*** **VFOAT** Ou se Loger en Ecosse. English. an. Scottish Tourist Board, 23 Ravelston Terrace, Edinburgh EH4 3EU England. **Tel** 031-332-2433. **LC** TX907; .S365. **DD** 647/.94411/05. **Ad Acc. Circ:** 38,000. ***Continues*** *National Register of Accommodation.* ***Continued by*** *Scotland, Where to Stay, Bed and Breakfast.*
Desc: More than 2,000 bed and breakfast establishments throughout Scotland offering inexpensive accommodations.

US/0894-6027
WORLDWIDE HOTEL INDUSTRY. [Worldw. hotel ind.]. **VFOAT** Annual Report on International Hotel Operations. 1986 Ed.-. English. an. $65.00. Horwath & Horwath International, 919 3rd Avenue, New York NY 10022. **Tel** (212)980-3100, FAX (212)751-5161, telex 236501. **LC** TX901; .H5. **DD** 338.4/7647/9401021.
Ind/Abst Stat. Ref. Index.

US
WORLDWIDE LODGING INDUSTRY. DIGEST / HORWATH & HORWATH INTERNATIONAL. **Added/Corp** Horwath & Horwath International. (1982)-. English. an. $250.00. Horwath International, 415 Madison Avenue, New York NY 10017. **Tel** (212)838-5566.
Desc: Deals with hotels and taverns.

CN/0316-8298
WRIGLEY'S HOTEL DIRECTORY. 18th-1928-. Directory. English. an. Wrigley Directories Ltd, 7385 Laburnum Street, Vancouver British Columbia V6P 5N2 Canada. **DD** 647/.947. ***Continues*** *Wrigley's Hotel Red Book, 0316-8301.*

YU
YUGOSLAVIA; HOTEL AND TOURIST DIRECTORY. **VFOAT** Hotelsko-Turisticki Adresar. Directory. Multiple languages (English, French, German and Serbo-Croatian (Roman)). Privredni Pregled, Marsala Birjuzova 3-5, Belgrad Yugoslavia. **LC** TX910.Y8; Y83.

YU
YUGOSLAVIA. HOTELSKE CENE. **VFOAT** Hotelske Cene; Hotel Rates. English (French, German, Italian and Serbo-Croatian (Roman)). Opste Udruzenje Turisticke Privrede Jugoslavije, Terazije 15-23, Belgrad Yugoslavia. **LC** TX910.Y8; Y82.

US/1060-720X
ZAGAT UNITED STATES TRAVEL SURVEY. CENTRAL STATES. [Zagat U. S. travel surv., Cent. states]. **Added/Corp** Zagat Survey (Firm). **VFOAT** United States Travel Survey. Central States; Zagat U.S. Travel Survey; Central U.S. Travel, Zagat Survey. (1991)-. English. $9.95. Zagat Survey, 4 Columbus Circle, New York NY 10019. **LC** TX907.3.M55; Z33. **DD** 647.947701. ***Continues in part*** *Zagat United States Hotel Survey, 1054-3627.*

US/1060-7196
ZAGAT UNITED STATES TRAVEL SURVEY. WESTERN STATES. [Zagat U. S. travel surv., West. states]. **Added/Corp** Zagat Survey (Firm). **VFOAT** United States Travel Survey. Western States; Zagat U.S. Travel Survey; Western U.S. Travel, Zagat Survey. (1991)-. English. $9.95. Zagat Survey, 4 Columbus Circle, New York NY 10019. **LC** TX907.3.W47; Z33. **DD** 647.947801. ***Continues in part*** *Zagat United States Hotel Survey, 1054-3627.*

ABSTRACTING, BIBLIOGRAPHIES AND STATISTICS

UK
HCIMA QUARTERLY BIBLIOGRAPHY OF HOTEL AND CATERING MANAGEMENT. **Main/Corp** Hotel Catering and Institutional Management Association. **Added/Corp** Hotel, Catering and Institutional Management Association. Vol. 1 (April 1980)-. Bibliography. English. qt. £58 UK; £70 other. Hotel Catering and Institutional Management Association, 191 Trinity Road, London SW17 7HN England. **Tel** 11 44 81 6724251, FAX 11 44 81 6821707.

NZ
NEW ZEALAND HOTEL/MOTEL INVENTORY AND ROOM OCCUPANCY RATES (LICENSED). English. an. 25.00NZ$. Tourist and Publicity Department, Private Bag, Wellington New Zealand. **Tel** 04728-860. **LC** TX910.N45; N44A. **DD** 647/.9493101. ***Continues*** *New Zealand Accommodation Inventory and Room Occupancy Rates.*

HOUSEHOLD HARDWARE AND APPLIANCES

IT
ANNUARIO SEAT. VOL. E, ARREDAMENTO. **VFOAT** Annuario S.E.A.T. Vol. E, Arredamento; Arredamento. Italian. an. Free. Via Aurelio Saffi 18, 10138 Turin Italy. **Tel** 011-33301, FAX 4472953, telex 212248 I. **LC** HD9773.I79; A56. **DD** 338.4/76841/002545. Index available. cum. index. **Ad Acc. Circ:** 27,100.
Desc: Yearbook of Italian companies in domestic furnitures, household appliances, commodities for the house classified in categories. Additional information on specific market situation in Italy available.

US/0003-6781
APPLIANCE. [Appliance]. Vol. 26, No. 7 (July 1969)-. Periodical. English. mo. $68.00 US; $78.00 (surface mail), $198.00 (air mail) other. Dana Chase Publications Inc, 1110 Jorie Boulevard CS 9019, Suite 203, Oak Brook IL 60522-9019. **Tel** (708)990-3484, FAX (708)990-0078. **ED** Scot Stevens. **LC** TP812.A1; F5. **[CCC]. Ad Acc. Circ:** 29,000 (ctrl). available on microfilm and microfiche from University Microfilms International (UMI). ***Continues*** *MPM. Metal Products Manufacturing, 0160-6328;* ***Absorbed*** *Appliance Engineer.*
Desc: Reaches the production, engineering, purchasing and marketing functions among the producers of consumer, commercial and business appliances worldwide. Includes news, statistical data and production highlights.
Ind/Abst Ceram. Abstr.; F&S Index Plus Text, Int. [Select. Cov.]; Gas Abstr.; PROMT; Stat. Ref. Index; Trade Ind. ASAP [Full Txt.]; Trade Ind. Index [Full Txt.].

US/0003-679X
APPLIANCE MANUFACTURER. [Appl. manuf.]. Vol. 1 (Jan. 1953)-. Trade Publication. English. mo. $55.00 US; $65.00 Canada and Mexico; $125.00 other (includes Appliance Manufacturer Directory). Business News Publishing Company, 755 West Big Beaver Road, Suite 1000, Troy MI 48084. **Tel** (810)362-3700, FAX (810)362-0317, telex 230295. **ED** Norman Remich. **LC** HD9697.U4; A65. **DD** 680. **[CCC]. Ad Acc. Circ:** 35,000 (ctrl). available on microfilm and microfiche from University Microfilms International (UMI). Documents available from Ask*IEEE.
Desc: Serves design engineers, production engineers and management worldwide in the manufacture of consumer, commercial or business appliances and equipment.
Ind/Abst Bus. ASAP (1990-) [Full Txt.]; Bus. Index (1985-); Bus. Period. Index; Bus. Source (Jan. 1993-); F&S Index Plus Text, Int. [Select. Cov.]; Gas Abstr. (?-?); Gen. BusinessFile (1985-); Gen. Period. Index (1985-); INSPEC (June 1984-Dec. 1985); Mag. Search; Predicasts; PROMT; Trade Ind. ASAP [Full Txt.]; Trade Ind. Index (1981-) [Full Txt.]; Vocat. Search (Jan. 1993-); Wilson Bus. Abstr.

US
APPLIANCE MANUFACTURER. DIRECTORY. **VFOAT** Annual Directory Issue. (19??)-. Directory. English. an. $25.00 US; $35.00 Canada and Mexico; $40.00 other. Business News Publishing Company, 755 West Big Beaver Road, Suite 1000, Troy MI 48084. **Tel** (810)362-3700, FAX (810)362-0317, telex 230295. **(Subscription address:** 5900 Harper Road, Suite 105, Solon, OH 44139; telephone: (216)349-3060**)**

US/0003-6803
APPLIANCE SERVICE NEWS. (1950)-. Periodical. English. mo. $15.25 US; $23.00 other. Gamit Enterprises Inc, 110 West Saint Charles Road, PO Box 789, Lombard IL 60148. **Tel** (312)932-9550. **ED** William Wingstedt. **LC** TK1; .A675. **Bk Rev. Ad Acc. Circ:** 52,000 (ctrl).
Desc: Business and technical news for appliance service dealers and do-it-yourselfers.

US
APPLIANCES AND RECREATION. (19??)-. English. mo. $225.00. Predicasts Inc., A Ziff Communications Company, 11001 Cedar Avenue, Cleveland OH 44106. **Tel** (800)321-6388, (216)795-3000, FAX (216)229-9944, telex 985 604. **(Subscription address:** Information Access Company, PO Box 61000, Department 1851, San Francisco, CA 94161; Phone: (800)321-6388**)**

US/1041-388X
AQUA (DULUTH, MINN.). (AQUA.). Vol. 13, No. 9 (Sept. 1988)-. Periodical. English. mo. $25.00 US; $60.00 Canada; $90.00 other. Athletic Business Publications, 1842 Hoffman Street, Suite 201, Madison WI 53704. **Tel** (800)722-8764, (608)249-0186. **LC** TH6485; .S67. **DD** 728/.9. ***Continues*** *Spa and Sauna, 0886-9472.*
Ind/Abst Geogr. Abstr. Human Geogr.; Int. Dev. Abstr.

HK
ASIAN SOURCES HARDWARES FOR WORLD MARKETS. **See** Economics-Industry and Production.

US/0094-4955
BLUE BOOK OFFICIAL LAWN EQUIPMENT TRADE-IN GUIDE. ***Ceased.*** **VFOAT** Official Lawn Equipment Trade-In Guide. (19??)-(19??). English. Intertec Publishing Corporation, 9800 Metcalf, Overland Park KS 66212. **Tel** (913)341-1300. **LC** HD9486.6.L373; U64. **DD** 681/.7631.

UK/0966-4890
BRUSHES INTERNATIONAL DIRECTORY. [Brushes int. dir.]. (1990)-. Directory. English. an. £23.00 UK; £27.00 Europe; £30.00. Turret Group, 177 Hagden Lane, Watford Herts WD1 8LN United Kingdom. **Tel** 011 44 923 228577, FAX 011 44 923 221346. **DD** 338.76796025. ***Continues*** *Directory of the Brush and Allied Trades, 0305-4861.*

US/0007-2710
BRUSHWARE (WASHINGTON, D.C.). (BRUSHWARE.). [Brushware]. (1948)-. Periodical. English. Six times a year (Jan., Mar., May, July, Sept., Nov.). $35.00 US; $50.00 Canada and Mexico; $70.00 other. Centaur & Company, 5 Willowbrook Court, Potomac MD 20854. **Tel** (301)983-1152, FAX (301)982-4006. **ED** Tom Goldberg. **LC** TS2301.B8; A4. **DD** 679. **Bk Rev. Ad Acc, Adv Mgr:** C. Wurzer, **Tel** (301)983-1152. **Circ:** 1,800. ***Continues*** *Brooms, Brushes & Mops.*
Desc: A key personnel in the brush, roller, broom, mop and applicator industry.

US/0890-9008
BUILDING SUPPLY & HOME CENTERS. ***Title Change.*** **See** Building and Construction.

CN/0045-4915
CANADIAN HANDGUN. 1965-. Periodical. English. qt. Ontario Handgun Association, 135 Centre Street East, Richmond Hill Ontario L4C 1A5 Canada.
Ind/Abst SportSearch (May 1987-).

US/8755-254X
CHILTON'S HARDWARE AGE (1984). (CHILTON'S HARDWARE AGE.). [Chilton's hardw. age]. **VFOAT** Hardware Age. Vol. 221, No. 1 (Jan. 1984)-. Periodical. English. mo. $75.00. Chilton Company, 201 King of Prussia Road, Radnor PA 19089. **Tel** (610)964-4122, (800)695-1214, FAX (610)964-4978, telex 6851035 CHILTON UW. **DD** 683. **[CCC].** available on microfilm and microfiche from University Microfilms International (UMI). ***Continues*** *Hardware Age (1981), 8755-2558.*
Desc: Hardware publication for do-it-yourselfers, home center retailers and wholesalers.
Ind/Abst Bus. ASAP (1990-) [Full Txt.]; Bus. Index (1985-); F&S Index Plus Text, Int. [Select. Cov.]; Gen. BusinessFile (1985-); Gen. Period. Index (1985-); Mag. Search; PROMT; Trade Ind. ASAP [Full Txt.]; Trade Ind. Index (1984-) [Full Txt.]; Vocat. Search (Jan. 1993-).

CH/1012-3520
CHINA SOURCES. HARDWARE. **VFOAT** Hardware. Vol. 9, No. 6 (July 1988)-. Periodical. English. mo. $50.00 (surface mail), $80.00 (air mail). Sino Communication Company Ltd, Block B 5-Fl Vita Tower, 29 Wong Chuk Hang Road, Hong Kong Hong Kong. **Tel** 5-557355, telex 65932 SINOC HX. **LC** HD9745.C54; C56. **DD** 382/.45683/029451. ***Continues*** *China Sources;* ***Absorbed*** *China Trader.*

US/1052-9179
CONSUMER GUIDE TO HOME ENERGY SAVINGS. [Consum. guide home energy sav.]. **Added/Corp** American Council for an Energy-Efficient Economy. **VFOAT** Home Energy Savings. (1991)-. English. an. ACEE / American Council for an Energy-Efficient Economy, 2140 Shattuck Avenue, Suite 202, Berkeley CA 94704. **Tel** (510)549-9914. **LC** TJ163.5.D86; C66. **DD** 644.

AT
COUNTERPOINT. English. mo. $48.00Aus Australia; $110.00Aus$ other. Reed Business Publishing Pty Ltd. / Australia, 1 5 Railway Street, Level 12 North Tower, Chatswood W 2067 NSW Australia. **Tel** 011 61 2 3725222, FAX 011 61 2 4197533. **ED** Sarah Hawthorn. **Ad Acc, Adv Mgr:** Hugh Salmon, **Tel** 61-2-372-5222.

Circ: 5050 (ctrl).
Desc: Industry news, trends, product information, marketing and regular opinions on electrical appliance industry.

US
CURRENT INDUSTRIAL REPORTS. MA-36E, ELECTRIC HOUSEWARES AND FANS. ***Ceased.*** **Added/Corp** United States. Bureau of the Census. **VFOAT** Electric Housewares and Fans. (1965)-(19??). English. an. Superintendent of Documents, US Government Printing Office, Washington DC 20402. **Tel** (202)275-3328, FAX (202)786-2377. **LC** HD9971.5.E543; U543. **DD** 338.4/768383/0973. ***Continues*** *Current Industrial Reports. M36E, Electric Housewares and Fans.*
Desc: Presents timely data on the production, inventories, and orders of approximately 5,000 products, which represents 40 percent of all US manufacturing.

US/0888-4501
DEALERSCOPE MERCHANDISING. **See** Business-Retail.

●US/1064-6280
DEALERSCOPE MERCHANDISING GOLDBOOK. [Dealerscope merch. goldb.]. (1993)-. English. an. $385.00 US; $391.00 Canada; $410.00 other. North American Publishing Company, 401 North Broad Street, Philadelphia PA 19108. **Tel** (215)238-5300, (800)777-8074, FAX (215)238-5283. **DD** 338.
Desc: Gives immediate access to essential inside facts on hundreds of top consumer electronics retailers, manufacturers, distributors and manufacturer's representatives.

NE
DHZ MARKT. Dutch. Eleven times a year. Fl68.10 Netherlands; Fl85.00 (libraries). Verenigde Periodieken BV, Postbus 433, 2040 AK Zandvoort Netherlands. **Tel** 02507 19334, FAX 02507-17516. **Bk Rev. Ad Acc.** ctrl circ.
Desc: Do-It-Yourself tool magazine.

US/0732-1252
DIRECTORY, CERTIFIED APPLIANCES AND ACCESSORIES. [Dir., certif. appl. accessories]. **Added/Corp** American Gas Association. Laboratories. **VFOAT** Directory of Certified Appliances and Accessories. (Jan. 1967)-. Directory. English. mo. $76.00. American Gas Association / Cleveland, 8501 East Pleasant Valley Road, Cleveland OH 44131. **Tel** (216)524-4990, FAX (216)642-3463, telex 263574 AGA. **LC** TP714; .A63. **DD** 683/.8. **Circ:** 4,500 (ctrl). ***Continues*** *Directory, Approved Appliances, Listed Accessories.*
Desc: Lists appliances and controls, the designs of which have been found by the American Gas Association Laboratories to comply with applicable national standards.

US/0882-536X
DIRECTORY OF HARDLINES DISTRIBUTORS. **VFOAT** Chain Store Guide ... Directory of Hardlines Distributors. (1988)-. Directory. English. be. $225.00 continental US; $235.00 other US; $250.00 other. Lebhar Friedman Inc., 3922 Coconut Palm Drive, Tampa FL 33619. **Tel** (800)927-9292, (813)664-6707. **LC** HD9745.U4; D52. **DD** 381/.4568/02573. Index available. available on magnetic tape. ***Continues*** *Directory of Hardware & Housewares Distributors, 0882-536X.*
Desc: Provides company profiles of houseware, paint and paint sundries, electrical, heating, cooling, plumbing, lumber, building supplies and lawn and garden distributors serving 6.5 million retailer, contractor and commercial accounts.

US/0272-0167
DIRECTORY OF HOME CENTER OPERATORS & HARDWARE CHAINS. [Dir. home cent. oper. hardw. chains]. **VFOAT** Home Center Operators & Hardware Chains. **VAT** Directory of Home Center Operators and Hardware Chains. (19??)-. Directory. English. an. $255.00 continental US; $265.00 other US; $280.00 other. Lebhar Friedman Inc., 3922 Coconut Palm Drive, Tampa FL 33619. **Tel** (800)927-9292, (813)664-6707. **ED** Christopher Warne. **LC** HD9745.U4; D485. **DD** 381/.45683/02573. Index available. ***Continues*** *Directory: Home Centers & Hardware Chains, Auto Supply Chains, 0094-8667.*
Desc: Profiles on 6,300 home centers, lumber/building material companies and hardware chains, 200 specialty paint/home decorating chains serving 22,700 units, Also covers 23 buying groups serving 85,000 stores.

US/0093-8718
DIRECTORY OF HOME CENTERS. (19??)-. English. an. $90.00. Lebhar Friedman Inc., 3922 Coconut Palm Drive, Tampa FL 33619. **Tel** (800)927-9292, (813)664-6707. **LC** HD9745.U4; D53. **DD** 381/.45/68302573.

UK
DIY WEEK. **VAT** Do It Yourself Week. Vol. 327, No. 4951 (Sept. 2, 1988)-. Periodical. English. wk. £58.00. Benn Business Information Service Ltd, Riverbank House, Angel Lane, Tonbridge Kent TN9 1SE England. **Tel** 011 44 732 362666, FAX 011 44 732 770483, telex 95454 BBIS. **LC** HD9745.G7; H3. **DD** 381/.45683/0941. ctrl circ. available on an online database (file 16/Full-Text) from DIALOG. ***Continues*** *Hardware Trade Journal.*
Desc: Covers markets and product news in DIY, decor, garden and housewares knowledgeably and comprehensively every week, backing this with in-depth reports on individual market sectors, and current trends.
Ind/Abst PROMT [Full Txt.].

US/0889-2989
DO-IT-YOURSELF RETAILING. [Do-it-yours. retail.]. **Added/Corp** National Retail Hardware Association (U.S.). **VFOAT** Do It Yourself Retailing. Vol. 150, No. 7 (June 1986)-. Periodical. English. mo. $5.00 (U.S., personal), $5.50 (Canada, personal), $15.00 (schools and libraries). National Retailing Hardware Association, 5822 West 74th Street, Indianapolis IN 46278. **Tel** (317)297-1190. **LC** TS200; .N3. **DD** 338.4/7683/0973. available on an online database (files 570,648/Full-Text) from DIALOG. ***Continues*** *DIY Retailing, 8750-2569.*
Ind/Abst Bus. ASAP (1990-) [Full Txt.]; Bus. Index (1986-); F&S Index Plus Text, Int. [Select. Cov.]; Gen. BusinessFile (1986-); Mark. Advert. Ref. Serv.; PROMT; Trade Ind. ASAP [Full Txt.]; Trade Ind. Index [Full Txt.].

UK/0262-8279
ELECTRIC LIVING JOURNAL : ELECTRICAL ASSOCIATION FOR WOMEN. (Spring 1982)-. Periodical. English. qt. Electric Living Journal, 25 Foubert's Place, London W1V 2AL England. ***Continues*** *Electric Living.*

US
ELECTRICAL APPLIANCE AND UTILIZATION EQUIPMENT DIRECTORY. **Added/Corp** Underwriters' Laboratories. (197?)-. Directory. English. an (June). $22.00. Underwriters Laboratories Inc., 333 Pfingsten Road, Northbrook IL 60062. **Tel** (708)272-8800 Ext.3542, FAX (708)272-8129, telex 6502543343. ***Continues*** *Electrical Appliance and Utilization Equipment List.*

US/1065-6677
EXPORT EN ESPANOL. [Export esp.]. (19??)-. Periodical. Spanish. Six times a year. $50.00. Hunter Publishing Company Inc., 25 Northwest Point Boulevard, Suite 800, Elk Grove Village IL 60007-1036. **Tel** (708)427-9512, FAX (708)427-2097. **DD** 382. ***Continues*** *Exportador, 0279-456X.*
Desc: Directed to importers, distributors, and dealers interested in consumer hardgoods, including heating, ventilation, air conditioning, refrigeration, etc.

US/0014-519X
EXPORT (NEW YORK, N.Y.). (EXPORT.). [Export]. (19??)-. Periodical. English. Six times a year. $50.00. Hunter Publishing Company Inc., 25 Northwest Point Boulevard, Suite 800, Elk Grove Village IL 60007-1036. **Tel** (708)427-9512, FAX (708)427-2097. **ED** Robert Weingarten. **DD** 382. **Bk Rev. Ad Acc. Circ:** 28,056 (ctrl).
Desc: Directed to importers, distributors, and dealers interested in consumer hardgoods, including heating, ventilation, air conditioning, refrigeration, etc.

CH
GIFTS AND HOUSEWARES ACCESSORIES. English. mo. $120.00. Gifts and Housewares Association, PO Box 34-23, Taipei Taiwan. **Tel** 011 86 2 7210454, 011 86 2 7411325.

CN/0711-7973
GOURMET BOUTIQUE. Vol. 1, No. 1 (March/April 1982)-. Periodical. English (French). ir. $17.00. Packard Communications, 801 York Mills Road, Don Mills Ontario M3B 1X7 Canada. **DD** 643/.3/05.

FR/0767-1830
GUIDE DES CONVENTIONS INTERNATIONALES DE SECURITE SOCIALE. (GUIDE DES CONVENTIONS INTERNATIONALES.). [Guide conv. int. secur. soc.]. (196?)-. French. Four times a year (basic volume and three updates per year). 331.75F France; 498.00F other. UCANSS, 33 Avenue du Maine, BP 45 & 46, 75755 Paris Cedex 15 France. **Tel** 011 33 1 45388149, 011 33 1 45388148. **UDC** 368.4 (094.2).

US/1059-1672
GUNS & AMMO ... HANDGUN ANNUAL. **VFOAT** Guns and Ammo ... Handgun Annual; Handgun Annual; G and A Handgun Annual; G & A Handgun Annual. (1984)-. English. an. $4.95 US; $6.00 Canada. Petersen Publishing Company, 6420 Wilshire Bouldevard, Los Angeles CA 90048. **Tel** (213)782-2485. **LC** TS537; .G865. **DD** 683.4/32/05.

CN/0847-9968
HARDWARE & HOME CENTRE MAGAZINE. [Hardw. home cent. mag.]. **VFOAT** Hardware and Home Centre Magazine; Centre. Vol. 12, No. 7 (Oct. 1988)-. Periodical. English. Eight times a year. 18.00Can$ Canada; 38.50Can$ other. Southam Information and Technology Group Inc., 1450 Don Mills Road, Don Mills Ontario M3B 2X7 Canada. **Tel** (416)445-6641, (800)668-2374, FAX (416)442-2261. **DD** 338.4/7684/00971. ***Continues*** *Hardware, Home, Building Supply Centre., 0847-995X.*

US/0017-7709
HARDWARE MERCHANDISER (CHICAGO). ***Ceased.*** (HARDWARE MERCHANDISER.). (1949)-Ceased Vol. 40 (Jan. 1989). Periodical. English. mo. Irving-Cloud Publishing Company, 417 North Hough Street, Barrington IL 60010. **Tel** (708)382-3405, FAX (708)674-7015. **ED** Pam Taylor. **Ad Acc. Circ:** 70,200 (ctrl).
Desc: Edited for retail and wholesale hardware markets.

CN/1199-2786
HARDWARE MERCHANDISING (1993). (HARDWARE MERCHANDISING.). (199?)-. Periodical. English. Ten times a year. 37.00Can$ Canada; 74.00Can$ other. MacLean Hunter Ltd. Business Publishers / Canada, Box 9100, Station A, Toronto ONT M5W 1A5 Canada. **Tel** (416)946-8420, (800)567-0444. **(Subscription address:** Indas, 35 Riviera Drive, Building 17, Markham Ontario L3R 8N4 Canada.**)** ***Continues*** *Hardware Merchandising, Building Supply Dealer, 0831-0807.*

CN/0831-0807
HARDWARE MERCHANDISING, BUILDING SUPPLY DEALER. ***Title Change.*** [Hardw. merch. build. supply deal.]. **VFOAT** Hardware Merchandising. **VAT** Hardware Merchandising (1985). (August 1985)-(199?). Periodical. English. Nine times a year. Maclean Hunter Canada / Montreal, 1001 bvd. de Maisonneuve W., Montreal, Quebec H3A 3E1 Canada. **Tel** 514-845-5141, FAX 514-845-4302, telex 055-60604. **ED** Sally Praskey. **DD** 338.4/7683/0971. **Ad Acc. Circ:** 17,000 (ctrl). available on microfilm from University Microfilms International (UMI). ***Continues*** *Hardware & Housewares Merchandising, 0827-1429.* ***Continued by*** *Hardware Merchandising (1993), 1199-2786.*
Desc: Hardware and building supplies; including everything from lumber and insulation to upscale kitchen and bath furnishings.

CN/0384-3394
HARDWARE, TOOL AND CUTLERY MANUFACTURERS (PRELIMINARY ED.). ***Ceased.*** (HARDWARE, TOOL AND CUTLERY MANUFACTURERS.). [Hardw. tool cutlery manuf.]. **Main/Corp** Statistics Canada. Manufacturing and Primary Industries Division. **VFOAT** Fabricants de Quincaillerie, d'Outillage et de Coutellerie. English (French). an. Statistics Canada, Publications Sales & Services, Main Building Room 1710, Ottawa Ontario K1A 0T6 Canada. **Tel** (613)951-5078, (800)267-6677, FAX (613)951-1584, telex 053-3585.

US/1053-7260
HOME HOW-TO NEWS. [Home how-to news]. **VFOAT** Home How To News. Vol. 1, No. 1 (Jan./Feb. 1991)-. Periodical. English. bm. $34.96. CY Decosse, Inc., 5900 Green Oak Drive, Minnetonka MN 55343. **DD** 643.

CN/0714-8151
HOME RENOVATIONS. [Home renov.]. **VFOAT** Renovations. Vol. 1, No. 9 (Feb./March 1982)-. Periodical. English. mo. $1.00 per no. Brant Publications, 605-402 West Pender Street, Vancouver BC V6B 1T6. **DD** 643/.7/05. ***Continues*** *Renovation West, 0710-4790.*

CN/0318-5273
HOUSEHOLD FACILITIES AND EQUIPMENT. (HOUSEHOLD FACILITIES AND EQUIPMENT / PREPARED IN THE SPECIAL SURVEYS DIVISION, DOMINION BUREAU OF STATISTICS, ...). [Househ. facil. equip.]. **Added/Corp** Canada. Dominion Bureau of Statistics. Special Surveys Division. Canada. Dominion Bureau of Statistics. Consumer Finance Research Staff. Statistics Canada. Consumer Finance Research Staff. Statistics Canada. Consumer Income and Expenditure Division. Statistics Canada. Housing Surveys and Data Dissemination Section. Statistics Canada. Household Surveys Division. **VFOAT** Equipement Menager. Vol. 1 (Sept. 1953)-. Periodical. English (French). an. 30.00Can$ Canada; $36.00 US; $42.00 other. Statistics Canada, Publications Sales & Services, Main Building Room 1710, Ottawa Ontario K1A 0T6 Canada. **Tel** (613)951-5078, (800)267-6677, FAX (613)951-1584, telex 053-3585. **LC** HD7305.A3; A35. **DD** 301.5/4/0971.
Desc: Estimates of household and dwelling size, tenure, type of dwelling, heating facilities, water supply, cooking facilities, bathroom facilities and household appliances such as refrigerators, microwave ovens, washing machines and clothes dryers in Canadian homes. Includes items such as telephones, radios, TVs and cars.

CN/0226-4560
HOUSEHOLD FACILITIES BY INCOME AND OTHER CHARACTERISTICS. **See** Economics.

CN/0848-502X
HOUSEHOLD FACILITIES BY INCOME AND OTHER CHARACTERISTICS, REVISED ESTIMATES. **See** Household Hardware and Appliances-Abstracting, Bibliographies and Statistics.

Household Hardware and Appliances

CN/0829-9889
HOUSEWARES CANADA. *Ceased.*
[Housewares Can.]. Vol. 1, No. 1 (Jan./Feb. 1985)- Ceased with Vol. 8, No. 2 (199?). Periodical. English. qt. Centre Publications, Suite 3, 2000 Ellesmere Road, Scarborough Ontario M1H 2W4. **DD** 381/.456838/0971.

UK
HOUSEWARES EUROPE. (19??)-. Periodical. English. Four times a year. £20.00. Benn Publications Ltd., Sovereign Way, Tonbridge TNQ 1RW England. **Tel** 011 44 732 364422, FAX 011 44 732 361534, telex 0732 95132 BENTON G.

US/0747-3885
HOUSEWARES MERCHANDISING. Vol. 1, No. 1 (Jan./Feb. 1984)-. Periodical. English. qt. $10.00. Dinan Communications, INC., 134 Main Street, New Canaan CT 06840.

UK/0264-8563
HOUSEWARES TONBRIDGE. [Housewares Tonbridge]. (1983)-. Periodical. English. Eleven times a year. £42.00 UK; £60.00 other. Benn Publications Ltd., Sovereign Way, Tonbridge TNQ 1RW England. **Tel** 011 44 732 364422, FAX 011 44 732 361534, telex 0732 95132 BENTON G. **DD** 338.76838.

US/0883-7155
INTERNATIONAL DESIGN YEARBOOK, THE. See Interior Design-Home Furnishings.

US/0277-0792
KEYNOTES (DALLAS, TEX.). (KEYNOTES.). English. mo (except combined June and July). Associated Locksmiths of America, 3003 Live Oak Street, Dallas TX 75204. **LC** TS519; .K49A. **DD** 638/.3/05.

FI
KOTITALOUSESINEIDEN KORJAUS. **Main/Corp** Finland. Tilastokeskus. **VFOAT** Reparation Av Hushallsvaror. 1972-. Multiple languages (Finnish and Swedish). Tilastokeskus, PL 504, Annankatu 44, 00101 Helsinki Finland. **Tel** 358-0-17341, FAX 358-0-17342474, telex 1002111 TILASTO SF. **LC** HD9999.H83; F53A.

US/1050-2254
LOCKSMITH LEDGER INTERNATIONAL. [Locksmith ledger int.]. **VFOAT** Locksmith Ledger. Vol. 48, No. 6 (May 1988)-. Periodical. English. mo (with additional issue in Jan.). $36.00 US; $50.00 Canada; $95.00 other. Locksmith Publishing Corporation, 850 Busse Highway, Park Ridge IL 60068. **Tel** (708)692-5940, FAX (708)692-4604. **LC** IN PROCESS. **DD** 683. *Continues* Locksmith Ledger, 0273-625X.

US
MAJOR HOME APPLIANCE INDUSTRY FACT BOOK. Added/Corp Association of Home Appliance Manufacturers (Chicago, Ill.). **VFOAT** Major Home Appliance Industry Factbook. (1991)-. English. *Continues* Major Appliance Industry Facts Book.

US/0744-2130
MAJOR HOUSEHOLD APPLIANCES. (CURRENT INDUSTRIAL REPORTS. MA-36F, MAJOR HOUSEHOLD APPLIANCES / U.S. DEPARTMENT OF COMMERCE, BUREAU OF THE CENSUS.). Government Publication. English. an. $1.25. US Department of Commerce / Bureau of the Census, Data User Services Division, Customer Services, Washington DC 20233-0800. **Tel** (301)763-4100. **(Subscription address:** Superintendent of Documents, US Government Printing Office, Washington DC 20402.**)** **LC** HD9971.5.E543; U545. **DD** 380.1/4568388/0973.
Desc: Presents timely data on the production, inventories, and orders of approximately 5,000 products, which represents 40 percent of all US manufacturing.

US/0047-8717
NARDA NEWS. Main/Corp National Appliance and Radio-TV Dealers Association. **Added/Corp** National Appliance & Radio-TV Dealers Association. News. **VAT** National Appliance and Radio-TV Dealers Association News. (1961)-. Periodical. English. mo. $48.00 (US); $72.00 (other). National Appliance and Radio-TV Dealers Association, 10 East 22nd Street, Lombard IL 60148. **Tel** (312)454-0944. **LC** HD9697.U4; N22.

US/0364-3719
NATIONAL LOCKSMITH, THE. VFOAT Locksmith News. Began with issue for Vol. 2, No. 2 (Feb. 1976). Periodical. English. mo. $22.00 US; $25.00 Canada; $30.00 other. National Publishing Company, 698 Bonded Parkway, Streamwood IL 60103. **LC** TS519.N3; A33. **DD** 683/.3/05. *Continues* National Locksmith.
Desc: Issues for Feb. 1976-Apr. 1976 include sections: "The Locksmith News."

US/0272-7854
NAVY ARMS MUZZLELOADERS' JOURNAL. English. $2.25 US; $2.75 Canada. Aqua Field Publications Inc, 66 West Gilbert Street, Shrewsbury NJ 07702. **Tel** (201)842-8300. **LC** TS536.6.M8; N38. **DD** 683.4.

US/0743-8672
OFFICIAL PRICE GUIDE TO KITCHEN COLLECTIBLES, THE. See Hobbies.

US
PATENT DIGEST. See Copyright, Intellectual Property.

FR
PLASIR DE LA MAISON. French. ir. 115.00F France, Belgium and Luxembourg; 218.00F other. Bureau Ingenierie Informatique, BP 41 Service Abonnements, 60700 Sacy Le Grand France. **Tel** 011 33 44 727755, 011 33 44 692626.

US/0742-4442
POCKET PRICE GUIDE. Added/Corp Sargent, Jim Schleyer, Jim W. R. Case & Sons Company. **VFOAT** Case Pocket Price Guide. (19??)-. English. $9.50. Knife Nook, Box 243, Burke VA 22015. **ED** Jim Sargent and Jim Schleyer. **LC** TS380; .P6. **DD** 621.9/32/0750973.

US
POWER TOOLS. English. an. $79.00. Orion Research Corporation, 14555 North Scottsdale Road, Suite 330, Scottsdale AZ 85260. **Tel** (800)844-0759, (602)951-1114, FAX (602)951-1117.
Desc: Gives used pricing information on 8,970 products.

CN/0825-1339
PRODUCTION, SALES, AND STOCKS OF MAJOR APPLIANCES. (PRODUCTION, SALES AND STOCKS OF MAJOR APPLIANCES / STATISTICS CANADA, INDUSTRY). [Prod. sales stocks major appliances]. **Added/Corp** Statistics Canada. Manufacturing and Primary Industries Division. Statistics Canada. Industry Division. **VFOAT** Production, Ventes, et Stocks d'Appareils Menagers. Vol. 1, No. 1 (April 1984)-. Periodical. English (French). mo. 60.00Can$ Canada; $72.00 US; $84.00 other. Statistics Canada, Publications Sales & Services, Main Building Room 1710, Ottawa Ontario K1A 0T6 Canada. **Tel** (613)951-5078, (800)267-6677, FAX (613)951-1584, telex 053-3585. **ED** Laurie Vincent. **LC** HD9971.5.E543; C226. **DD** 338.4/768388/0971. *Circ:* 270. *Formed by the union of Domestic Refrigerators and Freezers, 0380-6081 and Domestic Washing Machines and Clothes Dryers, 0380-609X.*
Desc: Sales by province, production and stocks for Canada for washing machines, clothes dryers, refrigerators, freezers, ranges and dishwashers.

●US/1064-2668
PROFESSIONAL VCR REPAIR TRAINING MANUAL AND BUSINESS PLAN, THE. VFOAT Training Manual and Business Plan. (1992)-. English. $55.00. Hido's Success Guides, 33227 Bainbridge Road, Cleveland OH 44139.

SZ
SCHUSS UND WAFFE. (1984)-. Periodical. German. sa. Verlag Stocker-Schmid, Hasenbergstrasse 7, Postfach 66, CH-8953 Dietikon Switzerland. **LC** TS532; .S38. **DD** 683.4/005.

CN/0410-5907
SPECIFIED DOMESTIC ELECTRICAL APPLIANCES. (SPECIFIED DOMESTIC ELECTRICAL APPLIANCES / PREPARED IN THE METAL AND CHEMICAL PRODUCTS SECTION, INDUSTRY AND MERCHANDISING DIVISION.). [Specif. domest. electr. appl.]. **Added/Corp** Canada. Dominion Bureau of Statistics. Metal and Chemical Products Section. Canada. Dominion Bureau of Statistics. Industry and Merchandising Division. Canada. Dominion Bureau of Statistics. Industry Division. Canada. Dominion Bureau of Statistics. Manufacturing and Primary Industries Division. Statistics Canada. Manufacturing and Primary Industries Division. Statistics Canada. Industry Division. **VFOAT** Certains Appareils Electriques Menagers. Vol. 1, No. 1 (Jan. 1958)-. Periodical. English (French). mo. 60.00Can$ Canada; $72.00 US; $84.00 other. Statistics Canada, Publications Sales & Services, Main Building Room 1710, Ottawa Ontario K1A 0T6 Canada. **Tel** (613)951-5078, (800)267-6677, FAX (613)951-1584, telex 053-3585. **ED** L. Vincent. **DD** 338.4/768383/0971. *Circ:* 500. available on microfiche.
Desc: Statistics on manufacturing of small electrical appliances, kitchen appliances, vacuum cleaners, and home comfort products.

US
STOVE, FURNACE & ALLIED APPLIANCE WORKERS' JOURNAL. VFOAT Stove, Furnace & Allied Appliance Workers International Union of N.A. Journal. Periodical. English. qt. Stove, Furnace and Allied Appliance Workers International Union, 2929 South Jefferson Avenue, St Louis MO 63118.

US
SUPPLEMENTAL DIRECTORY OF CERTIFIED APPLIANCES AND ACCESSORIES / AMERICAN GAS ASSOCIATION LABORATORIES. Added/Corp American Gas Association. Laboratories. (1967)-. Periodical. English. Twelve times a year. $76.00. American Gas Association / Cleveland, 8501 East Pleasant Valley Road, Cleveland OH 44131. **Tel** (216)524-4990, FAX (216)642-3463, telex 263574 AGA.

UK
TELEVISION; SERVICING, CONSTRUCTION, COLOUR, DEVELOPMENTS. See Engineering-Electricity, Electrical Engineering, Electronics.

GW
WESTEUROPA : QUELLEN ZUM MARKT FUR ELEKTROHAUSGERATE. Main/Corp Bundesstelle fur Aussenhandelsinformation (Germany). German. DM10.00. Bundesstelle fuer Aussenhandelsinformation, Agrippastr 87 93, D 50676 Cologne Germany. **Tel** 011 49 221 2057316, FAX 011 49 221 2057212. **LC** HD9971.5.E543; E84A.

US/0160-3299
WOODSTOVE FIREPLACE AND EQUIPMENT DIRECTORY. Directory. English. an. $2.00. Mitchell Associates, Inc., 106 Market Street, PO Box 4474, Manchester NH 03108. **LC** TH7438; .W66. **DD** 338.4/7/69722.

ABSTRACTING, BIBLIOGRAPHIES AND STATISTICS

CN/0848-502X
HOUSEHOLD FACILITIES BY INCOME AND OTHER CHARACTERISTICS, REVISED ESTIMATES. (HOUSEHOLD FACILITIES BY INCOME AND OTHER CHARACTERISTICS, REVISED ESTIMATES / STATISTICS CANADA, HOUSEHOLD SURVEYS DIVISION / EQUIPEMENT MENAGER SELON LE REVENU ET D'AUTRES CARACTERISTIQUES, ESTIMATIONS REVISEES / STATISTIQUE CANADA, DIVISION DES ENQUETES-MENAGES.). [Househ. facil. income other charact. revis. estim.]. **Added/Corp** Statistics Canada. Household Surveys Division. **VFOAT** Equipement Menager Selon le Revenu et d'Autres Caracteristiques, Estimations Revisees. (1986)-. Statistical Publication. English (French). an. 35.00Can$. Statistics Canada, Publications Sales & Services, Main Building Room 1710, Ottawa Ontario K1A 0T6 Canada. **Tel** (613)951-5078, (800)267-6677, FAX (613)951-1584, telex 053-3585. **DD** 339.4/1/0971. *Continues* Household Income, Facilities and Equipment, Revised Estimates., 0848-4988.

HOUSING AND URBAN DEVELOPMENT

US
1990 CENSUS PROFILE. Added/Corp United States. Bureau of the Census. **VFOAT** Census Profile. No. 1 (Mar. 1991)-. Government Publication. English. US Department of Commerce / Bureau of the Census, Data User Services Division, Customer Services, Washington DC 20233-0800. **Tel** (301)763-4100. **(Subscription address:** Superintendent of Documents, US Government Printing Office, Washington DC 20402.**)**

US/0148-2289
A-95 CLEARINGHOUSE REPORT. Main/Corp Vermont. State Planning Office. **VAT** A-Ninety-Five Clearinghouse Report. English. an. State Planning Office / Vermont, Montpelier VT 05602. **LC** HT393.V6; V47A. **DD** 309.2/5/09743.

JA/0389-9160
A + U. See Architecture.

NE
AANWINSTENLIJST : LIJST VAN AANWINSTEN DER BIBLIOTHEKEN VAN DE RPD EN HET HIROV. Main/Corp Netherlands. Rijksplanologische Dienst. No. 5 (1987)-. Periodical. Dutch. mo. Rijksplanologische Dienst Nirov Bibliotheek, Willem Witsenplein 6, 2596 BK S-Gravenhage Netherlands. *Continues* Lijst van Aanwisten der Bibliotheken.

US/1061-4354
ABA JOURNAL OF AFFORDABLE HOUSING & COMMUNITY DEVELOPMENT LAW. [ABA j. afford. hous. community dev. law]. **Added/Corp** American Bar Association. Forum Committee on Affordable Housing and Community Development Law. **VFOAT** Journal of Affordable Housing & Community Development Law; Journal of Affordable Housing and Community Development Law. **VAT** American Bar Association Journal of Affordable Housing and Community Development Law. Vol. 1, No. 1 (Fall/Winter 1991)-. Periodical. English. qt. $40.00. American Bar Association, 750 North Lake Shore Drive, Chicago IL 60611. **Tel**

(312)988-5522, (312)988-5241, FAX (312)988-5528, telex 270593. **ED** Jeffrey Kuta. **DD** 344. **Circ:** 1,200.
Desc: Covers the developments in current housing situations and community development law.

US/0272-7978
ABSTRACTS. STATE APPALACHIAN DEVELOPMENT PLANS AND INVESTMENT PROGRAMS. (ABSTRACTS - APPALACHIAN REGIONAL COMMISSION.). **Main/Corp** Appalachian Regional Commission. **VFOAT** State Appalachian Development Plans and Investment Programs. English. an. Appalachian Regional Commission, 1666 Connecticut Avenue Northwest, Washington DC 20235. **Tel** (202)673-7968, FAX (202)673-7930. **LC** HT392.5.A7; A66A. **DD** 361.6/0974.

IE/0306-9907
ACCOUNTS OF THE NORTHERN IRELAND HOUSING EXECUTIVE. (ACCOUNTS OF THE NORTHERN IRELAND HOUSING EXECUTIVE, TOGETHER WITH THE REPORT OF THE COMPTROLLER AND AUDITOR-GENERAL THEREON.). [Acc. North. Irel. Hous. Exec.]. **Main/Corp** Northern Ireland Housing Executive. (1972)-. English. an. 8.50p. HMSO, IDB House, 64 Chichester Street, Belfast BT1 4PS Northern Ireland. **Tel** 0232 238451, FAX 0232 230782. **LC** HD7336.A3; N59a. **DD** 354/.416/.00865. ***Continues*** *Accounts, Together with the Report of the Comptroller and Auditor-General Thereon.*

CN/0711-9674
ACQUISITIONS - CANADIAN HOUSING INFORMATION CENTRE. ***Title Change.*** (ACQUISITIONS / INFORMATION RESOURCE SERVICE [I.E. CANADIAN HOUSING INFORMATION CENTRE].). [Acquis. - Can. Hous. Inf. Cent.]. **Main/Corp** Canadian Housing Information Centre. **VFOAT** Nouvelles Publications. **VAT** Nouvelles Publications - Centre Canadien de Documentation sur l'Habitation; Acquisitions - Central Mortgage and Housing Corporation, National Office, Information Resource Service; Nouvelles Publications - Societe Centrale d'Hypotheques et de Logement, Bureau National, Services des Sources d'Information. (Mar. 1979)-No. 3 (Mar. 1993). Periodical. English (French). mo. Canada Mortgage and Housing Corporation, 700 Montreal Road, Ottawa, Ontario K1A 0P7 Canada. **Tel** (613)748-2550, FAX (613)748-7855. **DD** 016.3635. **Circ:** 450. ***Continues*** *Canada. Urban Affairs Canada. Information Resource Service. Acquisitions., 0711-9364;* ***Absorbed*** *Societe Centrale d'Hypotheques et de Logement. Bibliotheque. Library Bulletin.* ***Continued by*** *Canadian Housing Information Centre. Acquisitions List, 1197-7485.*
Desc: Material added to the library of the Canadian Housing Information Centre.

●CN/1197-7485
ACQUISITIONS LIST - CANADIAN HOUSING INFORMATION CENTRE. (ACQUISITIONS LIST / LISTE DES ACQUISITIONS.). [Acquis. list - Can. Hous. Inf. Cent.]. **Main/Corp** Canadian Housing Information Centre. **VFOAT** Liste des Acquisitions. **VAT** Liste des Acquisitions - Centre Canadien de Documentation sur l'Habitation. No. 4 (Apr. 1993)-. Periodical. English (French). mo. Canada Mortgage and Housing Corporation, 700 Montreal Road, Ottawa, Ontario K1A 0P7 Canada. **Tel** (613)748-2550, FAX (613)748-7855. **DD** 016.3635. ***Continues*** *Canadian Housing Information Centre. Acquisitions., 0711-9674.*

FR
ACTIVITES - ASSOCIATION POUR LES ETUDES D'AMENAGEMENT ET D'URBANISME DE LA REUNION. **Main/Corp** Association pour les Etudes d'Amenagement et d'Urbanisme de la Reunion. French. 21,50 Single Issue. BP 1168, 97483 Saint-Denis France. **LC** HT395.R4; A87A. **DD** 307.7/6/0606981.

FR
ACTIVITES - COMITE D'EXPANSION DE LA METROPOLE NORD. **Main/Corp** Comite d'Expansion de la Metropole Nord. French. E S C - Batiment C, Avenue Gaston Berger, Lille France. **LC** HT395.F73; L53A. **DD** 309.2/62/094428.

US/0361-9753
ACTIVITIES - THE TENNESSEE STATE PLANNING OFFICE. **Main/Corp** Tennessee State Planning Office. English. Tennessee State Planning Office, 208 Central Service Building, Nashville TN 37219. **LC** HT393.T4; T46A. **DD** 309.2/5/09768.

SP
ACTUACIONS RESIDENCIALS / INSTITUT CATALA DEL SOL, GENERALITAT DE CATALUNYA, DEPARTAMENT DE POLITICA TERRITORIAL I OBRES PUBLIQUES. **Main/Corp** Institut Catala del Sol (Spain). **VFOAT** Sol Residencial. Catalan. an. Institut Catala del Sol, Generalitat de Catalunya, Department de Politica Territorial i Obres Publiques, Corsega 289 6E, 08008 Barcelona Spain. **LC** HD1390.5; .I57A.

US
ADVANCES FOR PUBLIC WORKS PLANNING PROGRAM. **Main/Corp** United States. Dept. of Housing and Urban Development. Office of Housing. Government Publication. English. US Department of Housing and Urban Development, 451 Seventh Street SW, Washington DC 20401. **Tel** (202)708-0980, FAX (202)708-0299.

●US/1073-4600
AFRICAN RURAL AND URBAN STUDIES. (1994)-. Periodical. English. Three times a year. $40.00 (institutions), $30.00 (individuals) US; $60.00 (institutions), $50.00 (individuals) other. Michigan State University Press, 1405 South Harrison Road, Manly Miles 25, East Lansing MI 48823-5202. **Tel** (517)355-9543, FAX (800)678-2120, (517)336-2611. ***Formed by the union of*** *Rural Africana, 0085-5839* ***and*** *African Urban Studies, 0736-6760.*

US/0747-6108
AFRICAN URBAN QUARTERLY. [Afr. urban q.]. **Added/Corp** State University of New York at Albany. African and Afro-American Studies Dept. **VFOAT** AUQ. Vol. 1, No. 1 (Jan. 1986)-. Periodical. English. Four times a year. $50.00 (individuals), $100.00 (institutions) Kenya, $80.00 (individuals), $150.00 (institutions) others (surface mail) $70.00 (individuals), $120.00 (institutions) Kenya, $100.00 (individuals), $170.00 (institutions) others (airmail). African Urban Quarterly Limited, PO Box 51336, Nairobi Kenya. **Tel** 11 254 2 216574, FAX 11 254 2 336885, telex 22095. **ED** Robert A. Obudho (phone: 011 254 2 444911). **LC** HT148.A2; A36. **DD** 307.7/6/096. Index available. cum. index. **Bk Rev**. **Ad Acc**. **Pr Rev**. **Circ:** 3,000.
Desc: Covers all aspects of urbanization and regional planning in Africa. Topics covered include agriculture, demography, transportation, environmental studies, as they affect the quality of human life in urban areas. Serves as a forum for exchange of views between researchers, international organizations and research institutes throughout the world.
Ind/Abst Abstr. Anthropol.; Geogr. Abstr. Human Geogr.; Int. Dev. Abstr.; Int. Polit. Sci. Abstr.; Linguist. Lang. Behav. Abstr.; Popul. Index (?-?); Soc. Plann. Policy Dev. Abstr.; Sociol. Abstr.

US/0736-6760
AFRICAN URBAN STUDIES (EAST LANSING, MICH.). ***Ceased.*** (AFRICAN URBAN STUDIES.). [Afr. urban stud.]. No. 1, (Spring 1978)-No. 21. Academic Scholarly Publication. English. Three times a year. Michigan State University African Studies Center, East Lansing MI 48824. **Tel** (517)353-1700, FAX (517)353-7254, telex 650 277 3148. **ED** Harold Marcus. **LC** HT148.A2; A37. **DD** 307.7/6/096. **Bk Rev**. **Circ:** 205. ***Continues*** *African Urban Notes.*
Desc: The only scholarly journal concerning urban society, urbanization and cities in the world's fastest growing continent.
Ind/Abst Am. Hist. Life (1980-); Int. Dev. Abstr. (?-?); Middle East Abstr. Index.

US
AGENDA SYNOPSIS. English. bw. $25.00. Agenda Synopsis, 1231 I Street RM 200, Sacramento CA 95814. **Tel** (916)449-5604.

IV/1018-8568
AGRIPROMO ABIDJAN. (1973)-. Periodical. French. Four times a year (Jan., Apr., July, Oct.). 92.00F (surface mail); 116.00F (airmail). Inst Afri Pour Dev Eco Soc, Inades, 08 BP 8, Abidjan 08 Ivory Coast. **Tel** 011 225 441594. **UDC** 63. cum. index. **Ad Acc. Circ:** 8,000 (ctrl).
Desc: Information and interest in rural development.

US/0147-8419
ALABAMA PLANNING RESOURCE CHECKLIST : COUNTY/REGIONAL SERIES. English. State Capitol, Santa Fe NM 87503. **LC** Z7164.R33; A58; HT393.A2. **DD** 016.3092/5/09761.

US/0191-8125
ALI-ABA COURSE OF STUDY. LAND PLANNING AND REGULATION OF DEVELOPMENT : MATERIALS. **See** Law.

US/0191-2240
ALI-ABA COURSE OF STUDY : SECTION 8 HUD-SUBSIDIZED HOUSING, NEW TAX-EXEMPT FINANCING TECHNIQUES : MATERIALS. **See** Law.

US/0091-2352
ALL LOW-RENT PUBLIC HOUSING PROGRAMS, REGION 1: BOSTON. **Main/Corp** United States. Department of Housing and Urban Development. Financial Management Branch. (19??)-. Government Publication. English. qt. US Department of Housing and Urban Development, 451 Seventh Street SW, Washington DC 20401. **Tel** (202)708-0980, FAX (202)708-0299. **LC** HD7294.A3; U55a. **DD** 301.5/4.

US/0091-2433
ALL LOW-RENT PUBLIC HOUSING PROGRAMS, REGION 2: NEW YORK. **Main/Corp** United States. Department of Housing and Urban Development. Financial Management Branch. (19??)-. Government Publication. English. qt. US Department of Housing and Urban Development, 451 Seventh Street SW, Washington DC 20401. **Tel** (202)708-0980, FAX (202)708-0299. **LC** HD7295.A3; U55a. **DD** 301.5/4.

US/0091-2514
ALL LOW-RENT PUBLIC HOUSING PROGRAMS, REGION 3: PHILADELPHIA. **Main/Corp** United States. Department of Housing and Urban Development. Financial Management Branch. (19??)-. Government Publication. English. qt. US Department of Housing and Urban Development, 451 Seventh Street SW, Washington DC 20401. **Tel** (202)708-0980, FAX (202)708-0299. **LC** HD7295.A3; U55b. **DD** 301.5/4.

US/0091-2522
ALL LOW-RENT PUBLIC HOUSING PROGRAMS, REGION 4: ATLANTA. **Main/Corp** United States. Department of Housing and Urban Development. Financial Management Branch. (19??)-. Government Publication. English. qt. US Department of Housing and Urban Development, 451 Seventh Street SW, Washington DC 20401. **Tel** (202)708-0980, FAX (202)708-0299. **LC** HD7296.A3; U55a. **DD** 301.5/4.

US/0091-4770
ALL LOW-RENT PUBLIC HOUSING PROGRAMS, REGION 5: CHICAGO. **Main/Corp** United States. Department of Housing and Urban Development. Financial Management Branch. (19??)-. Government Publication. English. qt. US Department of Housing and Urban Development, 451 Seventh Street SW, Washington DC 20401. **Tel** (202)708-0980, FAX (202)708-0299. **LC** HD7297.A3; U55a. **DD** 301.5/4.

US/0091-245X
ALL LOW-RENT PUBLIC HOUSING PROGRAMS, REGION 6: FORT WORTH. **Main/Corp** United States. Department of Housing and Urban Development. Financial Management Branch. (19??)-. Government Publication. English. qt. US Department of Housing and Urban Development, 451 Seventh Street SW, Washington DC 20401. **Tel** (202)708-0980, FAX (202)708-0299. **LC** HD7303.T4; U5a. **DD** 301.5/4.

US/0091-2530
ALL LOW-RENT PUBLIC HOUSING PROGRAMS, REGION 7: KANSAS CITY. **Main/Corp** United States. Dept. of Housing and Urban Development. Financial Management Branch. (19??)-. Government Publication. English. qt. US Department of Housing and Urban Development, 451 Seventh Street SW, Washington DC 20401. **Tel** (202)708-0980, FAX (202)708-0299. **LC** HD7303.K3; U5a. **DD** 301.5/4.

US
ALL LOW-RENT PUBLIC HOUSING PROGRAMS, REGION 8: DENVER. **Main/Corp** United States. Dept. of Housing and Urban Development. Financial Management Branch. (19??)-. Government Publication. English. qt. US Department of Housing and Urban Development, 451 Seventh Street SW, Washington DC 20401. **Tel** (202)708-0980, FAX (202)708-0299. **LC** HD7301; .U55a. **DD** 301.5/4.

US/0091-2441
ALL LOW-RENT PUBLIC HOUSING PROGRAMS, REGION 9: SAN FRANCISCO. **Main/Corp** United States. Department of Housing and Urban Development. Financial Management Branch. (19??)-. Government Publication. English. qt. US Department of Housing and Urban Development, 451 Seventh Street SW, Washington DC 20401. **Tel** (202)708-0980, FAX (202)708-0299. **LC** HD7303.C2; U5a. **DD** 301.5/4.

US/0091-2344
ALL LOW-RENT PUBLIC HOUSING PROGRAMS, REGION 10: SEATTLE. **Main/Corp** United States. Dept. of Housing and Urban Development. Financial Management Branch. (19??)-. Government Publication. English. qt. US Department of Housing and Urban Development, 451 Seventh Street SW, Washington DC 20401. **Tel** (202)708-0980, FAX (202)708-0299. **LC** HD7302.A3; U56a. **DD** 301.5/4.

US
ANNALI DEL DIPARTIMENTO DI STUDI DELLEUROPA ORIENTALE. **Added/Corp** United States. Bureau of the Census. United States. Dept. of Housing and Urban Development. Office of Policy Development and Research. **VFOAT** American Housing Survey for the Phoenix Metropolitan Area in ... . (1985)-. English. ir. Herder Editrice e Libreria SRL, Piazza Montecitorio 117-120, 00186 Rome Italy. **Tel** 011 39 6 679 4628, FAX 011 39 6 678 4751. ***Continues*** *Current*

Housing and Urban Development

Housing Reports. H-170, Annual Housing Survey, Phoenix, Ariz., Standard Metropolitan Statistical Area. Housing Characteristics for Selected Metropolitan Areas.

GW/0570-1864
ANNALS OF REGIONAL SCIENCE, THE. [Ann. reg. sci.]. **Added/Corp** Western Regional Science Association. Western Washington State College. Western Washington University. (1967)-. Periodical. English. Four times a year. DM298.00. Springer-Verlag GmbH & Company KG, Heidelberger Platz 3, D 14197 Berlin Germany. **Tel** 011 49 30 8207223, FAX 011 49 30 8214091, telex 183 319 SPBLN D. **(Subscription address:** Springer Verlag New York Inc. / for North America, 44 Hartz Way, Secaucus NJ 07096.**) ED** D T Batten and T R Lakshmanan. **LC** HT390; .A55. **DD** 309.2/5/05. **[CCC]**. cum. index. **Bk Rev**. **Pr Rev**. **Circ:** 1,100 (ctrl). available on microfilm and microfiche from University Microfilms International (UMI). Documents available from The Genuine Article. **Supersedes** *Papers and Proceedings of the Western Section Regional Science Association.*
Desc: A periodical in the emerging interdisciplinary field of regional and urban studies, location of economic activity, planning, transportation, etc.
Ind/Abst ABC POL SCI; Avery Index Archit. Period. Suppl. Colum. Univ.; Contents Recent Econ. J.; Curr. Contents Soc. Behav. Sci.; Econ. Lit. Index; Geogr. Abstr. Human Geogr. (?-?); GeoRef; Int. Bibliogr. Sociol.; Int. Dev. Abstr. (?-?); J. Econ. Lit. (1985-); J. Plan. Lit.; PAIS Int. Print; Popul. Index; Res. Alert [Full Cov.]; Sage Urban Stud. Abstr. Soc. Sci. Cit. Index [Full Cov.]; SportSearch; World Agric. Econ.

CN/0824-1430
ANNUAIRE / CORPORATION PROFESSIONNELLE DES URBANISTES DU QUEBEC. [Annu. - Corp. prof. urban. Que.]. **Main/Corp** Corporation Professionelle des Urbanistes du Quebec. French. an. Corporation Professionelle des Urbanistes du Quebec, 85 St. Paul Street West, 4th Floor / Room B5, Montreal Quebec H2Y 3V4 Canada. **Tel** (514)849-1177. **DD** 711/.4/025714.

II/0533-5752
ANNUAL ADMINISTRATION REPORT ON SCHEDULED AREAS IN GUJARAT STATE. **Main/Corp** Gujarat, India (State). Periodical. English. Editions Masson, 120 BD Street Germain, 75280 Paris Cedex 06 France. **Tel** (1)46342760, FAX (1)45872999. **LC** HN690.G8.

US
ANNUAL AUDIT PLAN. **Main/Corp** United States. Dept. of Housing and Urban Development. Office of Inspector General. **VFOAT** Audit Plan. Government Publication. English. an. US Department of Housing and Urban Development, 451 Seventh Street SW, Washington DC 20401. **Tel** (202)708-0980, FAX (202)708-0299.

US
ANNUAL AWARDS CEREMONY / U.S. DEPARTMENT OF HOUSING AND URBAN DEVELOPMENT. **Main/Corp** United States. Dept. of Housing and Urban Development. Government Publication. English. an. US Department of Housing and Urban Development, 451 Seventh Street SW, Washington DC 20401. **Tel** (202)708-0980, FAX (202)708-0299.

US
ANNUAL DEMOGRAPHIC DATA FOR MIGRANT FAMILY HOUSING CENTERS. See Population Studies.

US
ANNUAL HOUSE MARKET REPORT : THE STATE OF THE HOUSING MARKET. 1981-. English. an. Free. Connecticut Department of Housing, 1179 Main Street, PO Box 2910, Hartford CT 06101. **Tel** (203)566-5264. **LC** HD7303.C8; C635A. **DD** 363.5/09746. Index available. cum. index. ctrl circ. **Continues** *Connecticut Housing Market.*

US
ANNUAL HOUSING SURVEY. (ANNUAL HOUSING SURVEY, UNITED STATES AND REGIONS.). 1973-. Government Publication. English. an. US Department of Commerce / Bureau of the Census, Data User Services Division, Customer Services, Washington DC 20233-0800. **Tel** (301)763-4100. **(Subscription address:** Superintendent of Documents, US Government Printing Office, Washington DC 20402.**)**
Desc: Pt. A-General housing characteristics. Pt. B-Indicators of housing and neighborhood quality. Pt. C-Financial characteristics of the housing inventory. Pt. D-Housing characteristics of ... .

US
ANNUAL PLAN REVIEW: AREA I. **Main/Corp** Fairfax County (Va.). Office of Comprehensive Planning. **Added/Corp** Fairfax County (Va.). Planning Commission. (19??)-. English. an. Office of Comprehensive Planning, 4100 Chain Bridge Road, Fairfax VA 22030. **LC** HT393.V62; F3417a.

US
ANNUAL PLAN REVIEW: AREA II. **Main/Corp** Fairfax County (Va.). Office of Comprehensive Planning. **Added/Corp** Fairfax County (Va.). Planning Commission. (19??)-. English. an. County of Fairfax, 4100 Chain Bridge Road, Fairfax VA 22030. **LC** HT393.V62; F3417c. **DD** 361.6/1/09755291.

US
ANNUAL PLAN REVIEW: AREA III. **Main/Corp** Fairfax County (Va.). Office of Comprehensive Planning. **Added/Corp** Fairfax County (Va.). Planning Commission. (19??)-. English. an. County of Fairfax, 4100 Chain Bridge Road, Fairfax VA 22030. **LC** HT393.V62; F3417b. **DD** 711/.3/09755291.

US
ANNUAL PLAN REVIEW: AREA IV. **Main/Corp** Fairfax County (Va.). Office of Comprehensive Planning. **Added/Corp** Fairfax County (Va.). Planning Commission. (19??)-. English. an. County of Fairfax, 4100 Chain Bridge Road, Fairfax VA 22030. **LC** HT393.V62; F3417d. **DD** 711/.3/09755291.

US
ANNUAL PLAN REVIEW - OFFICE OF COMPREHENSIVE PLANNING (VIRGINIA). **Main/Corp** Fairfax County (Va.). Office of Comprehensive Planning. English. an. Office of Comprehensive Planning, 4100 Chain Bridge Road, Fairfax VA 22030. **LC** HT167.5.V8; F34A. **DD** 711/.4/09755291.

●US
ANNUAL PLAN UPDATING THE NEW YORK STATE COMPREHENSIVE HOUSING AFFORDABILITY HOUSING ACT. **Added/Corp** New York (State). Task Force on the National Affordable Housing Act. (1993)-. English.

US
ANNUAL REPORT. **Main/Corp** Hawaii Community Development Authority. English. Hawaii Community Development Authority, 680 Ala Moana Boulevard, Honolulu HI 96813. **LC** HN79.H33; C64a. **Continues** *Review of the Year - Hawaii Community Development Authority.*

CN/0822-4382
ANNUAL REPORT - ALBERTA DEPARTMENT OF HOUSING. (ANNUAL REPORT.). [Annu. rep. - Alta. Dep. Hous.]. **Main/Corp** Alberta. Dept. of Housing. 1982/1983-. English. an. Alberta Housing and Public Works, 207 Legislative Bldg., Edmonton T5K 2B6. **LC** HD4010.A4; A4A. **DD** 354.71230086/5/05. **Continues in part** *Alberta. Alberta Housing and Public Works. Annual Report, 0702-3111.*

CN/0837-6816
ANNUAL REPORT / AMHC, ALBERTA MORTGAGE AND HOUSING CORPORATION. [Annu. rep. - Alta. Mortg. Hous. Corp.]. **Main/Corp** Alberta Mortgage and Housing Corporation. 1984/85-. English. an. Alberta Mortgage and Housing Corporation, 9405-50 Street, Edmonton Alberta T6B 2T4 Canada. **Tel** (403)468-3535, FAX (403)468-3555. **LC** HD7305.A3; A63A. **DD** 332.3/2/097123. ctrl circ. **Continues** *Annual Report / Alberta Housing Corporation, 0706-411X.*

AT/0310-4559
ANNUAL REPORT AND STATEMENT OF ACCOUNTS - RURAL RECONSTRUCTION BOARD (HOBART). (ANNUAL REPORT AND STATEMENT OF ACCOUNTS.). **Main/Corp** Rural Reconstruction Board. 1971/72-. English. an. Government Printing Tasmania, 188 Collins Street, Hobart Tasmania Australia. **LC** HD2182; .R85A. **DD** 354/.946/008233.

US/0091-3510
ANNUAL REPORT - CAPITAL AREA PLANNING COUNCIL. (ANNUAL REPORT.). **Main/Corp** Capital Area Planning Council. (19??)-. English. an. **LC** HT393.T48; C33a. **DD** 309.2/5/09764.

US/0091-1577
ANNUAL REPORT - CINCINNATI CITY PLANNING COMMISSION. (ANNUAL REPORT.). **Main/Corp** Cincinnati. (Ohio). City Planning Commission. English. an. City of Cincinnati, Planning Commission, Cincinnati OH 45236. **LC** HT168.C52. **DD** 352/.96/0977178.

US
ANNUAL REPORT - CITY OF NEW YORK, MAYOR'S OFFICE OF MODEL CITIES. **Main/Corp** New York (City). Mayor's Office of Model Cities. **VFOAT** Model Cities Re-Structured, Annual Report of the Mayors Office of Model Cities. English. an. Mayor's Office of Model Cities, 280 Broadway, New York NY 10007. **LC** HT177.N5; N465A. **DD** 352.0747/1.

US/0363-4183
ANNUAL REPORT - DEPARTMENT OF HOUSING & COMMUNITY DEVELOPMENT. **Main/Corp** California Dept. of Housing and Community Development. **VAT** Annual Report - Department of Housing and Community Development. (19??)-. English. California Department of Housing & Community Development, PO Box 951050, Sacramento CA 94252. **Tel** (916)445-4775, FAX (916)323-2815. **LC** KFC820; .A83. **DD** 353.9/794/00865.

AT/1037-5171
ANNUAL REPORT / DEPARTMENT OF PLANNING AND HOUSING. **Main/Corp** Victoria. Dept. of Planning and Housing. (1990/1991)-. English. **Formed by the union of** *Victoria. Dept. of Planning and Urban Growth Annual Report* **and** *Victoria. Ministry of Housing and Construction. Report of the Director General of Housing and Construction for the Period from... .*

US/0743-1767
ANNUAL REPORT / HAWAII COASTAL ZONE MANAGEMENT PROGRAM. [Annu. rep. - Hawaii Coast. Zone Manage. Program]. **Main/Corp** Hawaii Coastal Zone Management Program. English. an. Hawaii Coastal Zone Management Program, Department of Planning and Economic Development, Honolulu HI. **LC** HT393.H3; H377A. **DD** 353.99690082/326.

PH
ANNUAL REPORT / HOME DEVELOPMENT MUTUAL FUND (PHILIPPINES). **Main/Corp** Home Development Mutual Fund (Philippines). English. an. PAG-IBIG Fund Building, 317 Buendia Avenue Est Makati, Metro Manila Philippines. **LC** HD7366.A4; H64A. **DD** 354.5990086/5045.

CN/0835-0213
ANNUAL REPORT - MINISTRY OF HOUSING (TORONTO. 1986). (ANNUAL REPORT.). [Annu. rep. - Minist. Hous.]. **Main/Corp** Ontario. Ministry of Housing. **Added/Corp** Ontario Housing Corporation. Ontario Land Corporation. **VFOAT** Rapport Annuel. **VAT** Rapport Annuel - Ministere du Logement (Toronto. 1988). (1985/1986)-. English. an. $2.50. **LC** HD7305.A3; O57a. **DD** 354.7130086/5/06. **Absorbed** *Ontario. Ministry of Housing. Rapport Annuel (1986), 0835-0221;* **Continues in part** *Ontario. Ministry of Municipal Affairs and Housing. Annual Report, 0821-9079.*

II
ANNUAL REPORT / NATIONAL INSTITUTE OF RURAL DEVELOPMENT. **Main/Corp** National Institute of Rural Development (India). (19??)-. English (Hindi). an. National Institute of Rural Development, Rajendranagar, Hyderabad 500 030 India. **Tel** 48001-4, telex 425-6510. **ED** R. P. Kapoor. **LC** HN690.Z9; C666. **DD** 307.7/2/0954. **Circ:** 1,000 (ctrl). **Continues** *National Institute of Rural Development (India). Annual Report for ... of the National Institute of Rural Development.*
Desc: Publication giving details of NIRD's activities during the financial year.

US/0545-6533
ANNUAL REPORT - NEW YORK STATE HOUSING FINANCE AGENCY. **Main/Corp** New York State Housing Finance Agency. English. an. New York State Housing Finance Agency, 1250 Broadway, New York NY 10001. **LC** HD7303.N7; N45. **DD** 353.9/747/00865.

ZA
ANNUAL REPORT OF THE DEPARTMENT OF TOWN AND COUNTRY PLANNING. **Main/Corp** Zambia. Dept. of Town and Country Planning. (1978)-. English. Department of Town and Country Planning, Lusaka Zambia. **LC** HT169.Z35; Z34a. **Continues** *Zambia. Dept. of Town and Country Planning. Report of the Department of Town and Country Planning.*

KE
ANNUAL REPORT OF THE DIRECTOR, HOUSING DEVELOPMENT AND MANAGEMENT DEPARTMENT FOR THE YEAR.../CITY COUNCIL OF NAIROBI. **Main/Corp** Nairobi (Kenya). City Council. Housing Development Dept. English. an. $35.00 US. Housing Development Department. **Tel** 791231. **LC** HN800.K43; C65. **DD** 352.94/4/0967625. **Bk Rev**. **Ad Acc**. **Circ:** 200. **Continues** *Nairobi (Kenya). Dandora Community Development Project Dept. Annual Report.*
Desc: Annual report of the Nairobi City Commission's Director of Housing Development Department.

Housing and Urban Development

KE
ANNUAL REPORT OF THE DIRECTOR OF SOCIAL SERVICES & HOUSING FOR THE YEAR - MOMBASA KENYA. See Sociology-Social Services and Welfare.

CN
ANNUAL REPORT / PRINCE EDWARD ISLAND HOUSING CORPORATION.
Main/Corp Prince Edward Island Housing Corporation. 1975-76-. English. an. Free upon request. Prince Edward Island Housing Corporation, PO Box 2000, Charlottetown Prince Edward Island C1A 7N8 Canada. **ED** Don Pridmore. **LC** HD7305.P76; P74A. **DD** 354.7170086/5/06. **Circ:** 250 (ctrl). **Continues** Annual Report - Prince Edward Island Housing Authority, 0701-5283.

US/0098-941X
ANNUAL REPORT - SOUTH DAKOTA HOUSING DEVELOPMENT AUTHORITY. **Main/Corp** South Dakota Housing Development Authority. 1973/74-. English. an. South Dakota Housing Development Authority, 120 East Capitol, Pierre SD 57501. **LC** HD7303.S8; S68A. **DD** 353.9/783/00865.

US/0091-0678
ANNUAL REPORT - STATE PLANNING OFFICE. EXECUTIVE DEPARTMENT. STATE OF MAINE. (ANNUAL REPORT.). **Main/Corp** Maine. State Planning Office. 1972-. English. an. State Planning Office / Maine, 189 State Street, Augusta ME 04333. **LC** HC107.M2; M35A. **DD** 353.9/741/008.

US/0277-0563
ANNUAL REPORT / TEXAS COASTAL AND MARINE COUNCIL. **Main/Corp** Texas Coastal and Marine Council. English. an. Texas Coastal and Marine Council, Box 13407, Austin TX 78711. **LC** HT393.T48; T495A. **DD** 353.97640082/326.

UK
ANNUAL REPORT / THE SCOTTISH CIVIC TRUST. **Main/Corp** Scottish Civic Trust. (1980/81)-. English. an. Scottish Civic Trust, 24 George Square, Glasgow G2 1EF Scotland. **Tel** 041-221-1466. **Continues** Scottish Civic Trust Year Book.

UK/0308-082X
ANNUAL REPORT - TOWN AND COUNTRY PLANNING ASSOCIATION.
Main/Corp Town and Country Planning Association (Great Britain). (1900)-. English. an (Mar., or Apr.) £2.00 UK; £2.50 others. Town and Country Planning Association, 17 Carlton House Terrace, London SW1Y 5AS England. **Tel** 011 44 71 930 8903. **ED** David Boke. **LC** HT169.G7; T68a. **DD** 309.2/12/062421. **Ad Acc**. **Circ:** 1,300 (ctrl).
Desc: Review of the activities of the Town and Country Planning Association.

US
ANNUAL REPORT / U.S. NATIONAL HOUSING AGENCY. **Main/Corp** United States. National Housing Agency. 1st (1942)-. English. US National Housing Agency, Washington DC 20410.

CN
ANNUAL REPORT - URBAN AFFAIRS (OTTAWA). See Public Administration.

RH
ANNUAL REVIEW / DEPARTMENT OF PHYSICAL PLANNING, MINISTRY OF LOCAL GOVERNMENT, RURAL AND URBAN DEVELOPMENT. **Main/Corp** Zimbabwe. Dept. of Physical Planning. (198?)-. English. an. **LC** HD992.A1; Z56a. **DD** 354.68910081/8/06.

II
ANNUAL STATEMENT OF ACCOUNTS - HOUSING BOARD. RAJASTHAN, INDIA.
Main/Corp Rajasthan, India. Housing Board. English. 3.00. India Housing Board, C-38 Bhagwantdass Road, Jaipur-1 India. **LC** HD7361.R28; R32A. **DD** 354/.54/400865.

US
ANNUAL SUMMARY OF DWELLING UNITS AUTHORIZED BY BUILDING PERMITS (NEW JERSEY). **Main/Corp** New Jersey. Office of Business Economics. English. an. Labor Market and Demographic Research, Policy and Planning, New Jersey Department of Labor, CN 388, Trenton NJ 08625-0388. **Tel** (609)984-2593. **LC** HD7303.N5; N6A. **DD** 338.4/7/690809749.

US/0095-4810
ANNUAL WORK PROGRAM - SOUTHWEST NEW MEXICO COUNCIL OF GOVERNMENTS. (ANNUAL WORK PROGRAM.). **Main/Corp** Southwest New Mexico Council of Governments. English. an. Southwest New Mexico Council of Governments, PO Box 1211, 211 1/2 North Bullard, Silver City NM 88061. **LC** HT393.N55; S68A. **DD** 711/.3/09789.

II
ANUDANOM KI MANGEM (INDIA. MINISTRY OF WORKS AND HOUSING).
Title Change. **Main/Corp** India (Republic). Ministry of Works and Housing. **VFOAT** Demands for Grants. (19??)-(19??). Multiple languages (Hindi and English). an. Government of India Press Ministry of Housing and Works, Minto Road, New Delhi India. **LC** HD4291; .M55a. **DD** 354/.54/00865. **Continued by** Anudanom ki Mangem, Nagara Vikasa Mantralaya.

II
ANUDANOM KI MANGEM, NAGARA VIKASA MANTRALAYA. **Main/Corp** India. Ministry of Urban Development. **VFOAT** Demands for Grants of Ministry of Urban Development. (19??)-. English (Hindi). Government of India Press Ministry of Housing and Works, Minto Road, New Delhi India. **LC** HD4291; .M55a. **DD** 354/.54/00865. **Continues** India. Ministry of Works and Housing. Anudanom ki Mangem.

US/0192-0030
APARTMENT AGE. **Added/Corp** Apartment Association Los Angeles-Western Cities. Apartment Association of Greater Los Angeles. California Apartment Association. (1967)-. Periodical. English. mo. $41.00 (one year). Apartment Age Magazine, 621 South Westmoreland Avenue, Los Angeles CA 90020. **Tel** (213)384-4131, FAX (213) 382-3970. **ED** Kevin B Postema. **LC** HD1361; .A63. Index available. **Bk Rev**. **Ad Acc**. **Circ:** 38,300 (ctrl).
Desc: Legal, political, informational news for rental housing owners, primarily in Los Angeles County.

CN/0318-9651
APARTMENT & BUILDING. Feb. 1975-. English. bm. $6.00. Apartment & Building, PO Box 69465 Station K, Vancouver British Columbia V5L 4W2 Canada. **DD** 647/.92/05. **Supersedes** Apartment & Building Owners Journal, 0316-5574.

CN/0225-9532
APARTMENT WORLD IN WINNIPEG. [Apt. world Winn.]. V. 1- Nov./Dec. 1979-. Periodical. English. ir. $1.50 per number. Cougar Communications, Po Box 791, Winnipeg Man. R3C 2N4. **DD** 363.5.

US
APPLICATION THROUGH INSURANCE, SINGLE FAMILY, SECTION 203(N). **Main/Corp** United States. Dept. of Housing and Urban Development. Office of Housing. 1979-. Government Publication. English. US Department of Housing and Urban Development, 451 Seventh Street SW, Washington DC 20401. **Tel** (202)708-0980, FAX (202)708-0299.

●**IT**
AQUAPOLIS. **Suspended**. Vol. 1, No. 1 (Jan./Feb. 1992)-(199?). Periodical. English (Italian). bm. Grafiche Veneziane Srl., Castello 5653, 30122 Venezia, Italy.

IT/0392-615X
ARCHIVIO DELLE LOCAZIONI E DEL CONDOMINIO. [Arch. locaz. condomin.]. (1979)-. Periodical. Italian. qt. L100000 Italy; L150000 Europe; L200000 other. Casa Editrice La Tribuna, Via Don Minzoni 51, 29100 Piacenza Italy. **Tel** 011 39 523 759015, 011 39 523 759020. **UDC** 347.453.3.

IT/0004-0177
ARCHIVIO DI STUDI URBANI E REGIONALI. (May 1968)-. Periodical. Italian. Three times a year. L87000.00 Italy; L130000.00 other. Franco Angeli Riviste SRL, Viale Monza 106, 20127 Milan Italy. **Tel** 011 39 2 2827651, 011 39 2 289562. **LC** HT101; .A72.
Ind/Abst Int. Bibliogr. Sociol.

CN/0820-5523
ARDOISE (QUEBEC). **Ceased**. (L'ARDOISE.). [Ardoise]. **Added/Corp** Mouvement d'Education Populaire et d'Action Communautaire du Quebec. (1983)-(19??). Periodical. French. ir. **DD** 361.8/09714.
Desc: Contains information on community organization and development, adult education, and social participation.

JA
AREA DEVELOPMENT IN JAPAN.
Added/Corp Nihon Chiiki Kaihatsu SentÂa. (Sept. 1968)-. Periodical. English. sa. Japan Center for Area Development Research, Iino Building 2-1-1 Uchisawaicho Chiyoda-ku, Chiyoda Ku Tokyo Japan. **LC** HT395.J3; A8. **DD** 309.2/62/0952.

US
AREAWIDE ACTION PLAN OF THE UPPER CUMBERLAND DEVELOPMENT DISTRICT. **Main/Corp** Upper Cumberland Development District. 1978-. English. an. Upper Cumberland Development District, Burgess Falls Road, Cookeville TN 38501. **LC** HT393.T4; U66A. **DD** 361.6/09768/5.

US/0004-1564
ARIZONA MOBILE CITIZEN. **Ceased**. (19??)-(June 1993). Periodical. English. wk. Arizona Mobile Citizen, PO Box 5397, Phoenix AZ 85010. **Tel** (602)275-1776. **ED** Ruth C Kaseman. **Bk Rev**. **Ad Acc**. **Circ:** 18,000-20,000.

US/1061-7035
ASHI TECHNICAL JOURNAL OF HOME INSPECTION AND IN-SERVICE BUILDING COMPONENT FAILURES.
[ASHI tech. j. home insp. in-serv. build. compon. fail.]. **Added/Corp** American Society of Home Inspectors. **VFOAT** ASHI Technical Journal. **VAT** American Society of Home Inspectors Technical Journal of Home Inspection and In-Service Building Component Failures. (1991)-. Periodical. English. sa. $49.00. American Society of Home Inspectors, 1735 North Lynn Street, Suite 950, Arlington VA 22209-2022. **DD** 643.

US
AUDIT GUIDE AND STANDARDS FOR COMMUNITY DEVELOPMENT BLOCK GRANT RECIPIENTS. See Sociology-Social Services and Welfare.

US
AUDIT GUIDE FOR AUDITS OF HUD APPROVED NONSUPERVISED MORTGAGES FOR USE BY INDEPENDENT PUBLIC ACCOUNTANTS. See Business-Accounting.

AT/0811-3130
AURISA NEWS. [AURISA news]. **Added/Corp** Australian Urban and Regional Information Systems Association. **VFOAT** Australian Urban and Regional Information Systems Association News. (1983)-. Periodical. English. Six times a year (Feb., Apr., June, Aug., Oct., Dec.). 30.00Aus$. Aurisa, PO Box E307, Queen Victoria Terrace 2600 Australia. **Tel** 011 61 6 2734054, FAX 011 61 6 2734057. **DD** 025.067110994. **Ad Acc**. **Circ:** 900 (ctrl). Documents available from the publisher. **Continues** AURISA Newsletter.

AT/0729-3682
AUSTRALIAN PLANNER : JOURNAL OF THE ROYAL AUSTRALIAN PLANNING INSTITUTE. [Aust. plann.]. **Added/Corp** Royal Australian Planning Institute. **VFOAT** Journal of the Royal Australian Planning Institute. Vol. 20, No. 1 (Feb. 1982)-. Periodical. English. qt. 55.00Aus$ Australia; 70.00Aus$ other. Royal Australian Planning Institute Inc, 615 Burwood Road Rapi House, Hawthorn Victoria 3122 Australia. **Tel** 011 61 3 8190728, FAX 011 61 3 8190676. **ED** Rcihard Cardew. **Bk Rev**. **Ad Acc**. **Circ:** 3,500. **Continues** Royal Australian Planning Institute Journal.
Desc: Articles and reviews on urban and regional planning and environmental topics current in Australia and Southeast Asia. Official organ of the Royal Australian Planning Institute.
Ind/Abst APAIS, Aust. Public Aff. Inf. Ser. (1982-); Archit. Period. Index (1982-); Avery Index Archit. Period. Suppl. Colum. Univ. (1990-); PAIS Int. Print (1991-).

AT/0728-6309
AUSTRALIAN PLANNING APPEAL DECISIONS. **Ceased**. See Law.

US/8750-8788
AUTHORITY (WASHINGTON, D.C.), THE. (THE AUTHORITY.). [Authority]. Periodical. English. qt. $50.00. Housing and Development Law Institute, PO Box 2847, Washington DC 20013. **Tel** (202)265-8102. **ED** Jane Lang McGrew. **Circ:** 200.
Desc: Compilation of cases, summarized and indexed, decided in federal and state courts involving public agencies which administer assisted housing and development programs. Includes a legal comment on a significant current legal issue.

US/0899-5540
AUTOMATED BUILDER. [Autom. build.]. Vol. 25, No. 8 (Aug. 1988)-. Periodical. English. mo. Free to qualified subscribers; $40.00 US; $80.00 (surface mail), $150.00 (airmail) other. CMN Associates Incorporated, PO Box 120, Carpinteria CA 93013. **Tel** (805)684-7659, FAX (805)684-1765. **ED** Don Carlson. **LC** TH4819.P7; A92. **DD** 693/.97/05. Index available. **Bk Rev**. **Ad Acc**. **Circ:** 26,000 (ctrl). available on microfilm and microfiche from University Microfilms International (UMI). **Continues** Automation in Housing & Manufactured Home Dealer, 0740-3534.
Desc: Covers technology and marketing of housing.
Ind/Abst Avery Index Archit. Period. Suppl. Colum. Univ. (Aug. 1988-199?); Bibliogr. Mission. (Aug. 1988)-.

SI
BANDAR. V. 1- 1969-. Periodical. English. **LC** HT169.S56; S53. **DD** 309.2/62/095952.

Housing and Urban Development

GW
BAUTATIGKEIT UND WOHNUNGEN. REIHE 3: BESTAND AN WOHNUNGEN, FORTGESCHRIEBENE ERGEBNISSE. **Main/Corp** Germany (West). Statistisches Bundesamt. **Added/Corp** Germany (West). Statistisches Bundesamt. Bestand an Wohnungen. **VFOAT** Bautatigkeit und Wohnungen. Reihe 3; Bestand an Wohnungen; Fachserie 5. **VAT** Bautatigkeit und Wohnungen. Reihe Drei: Bestand an Wohnungen. (1976)-. German. **LC** HD9715.G3; A356. **Continues** Germany (West). Statistisches Bundesamt. Bauwirtschaft, Bautatigkeit, Wohnungen. Reihe 6: Bestand an Wohnungen. (Fortgeschriebene Ergebnisse).

AU/0005-9102
BERICHTE ZUR RAUMFORSCHUNG UND RAUMPLANUNG. Main/Corp Osterreichische Gesellschaft Fur Raumforschung und Raumplanung. 1957-. Periodical. German. bm. DM94.20. Springer-Verlag New York Inc., 175 5th Avenue, New York NY 10010. **Tel** (212)460-1500, telex 232 235 SPB UR. **(Subscription address:** Springer Verlag New York Inc. / for North America, 44 Hartz Way, Secaucus NJ 07096.**) Supersedes** Berichte / Osterreichische Gesellschaft fur Raumforschung und Raumplanung. **Ind/Abst** Bibliogr. Carto.; Geogr. Abstr. Phys. Geogr.; Geogr. Abstr. Human Geogr.; GeoRef; Leis. Recreat. Tour. Abstr.; Rural Dev. Abstr.; World Agric. Econ.

US/1047-5192
BERKELEY PLANNING JOURNAL. [Berkeley plan. j.]. **Added/Corp** University of California, Berkeley. Dept. of City and Regional Planning. Vol. 1, No. 1 (Spring 1984)-. Periodical. English. an (Fall). $25.00 (institutions), $10.00 (individuals). Berkeley Planning Journal, UC Department City Regional Planning, Berkeley CA 94720. **Tel** (510)642-3256, FAX (510)643-9576. **ED** Rolf Pendall and Elizabeth Smith. **LC** HT390; .B44. **DD** 307.1/216/05. **Bk Rev**. (Qty: varies). **Pr Rev. Circ:** 300. **Ind/Abst** Avery Index Archit. Period. Suppl. Colum. Univ. (1990); Environ. Period. Bibliogr.

US
BI-ANNUAL REPORT / DETROIT CITY PLANNING COMMISSION. Main/Corp Detroit (Mich.). City Planning Commission. **VFOAT** Biannual Report; Biennial Report. (198?)-. English. be. City of Detroit City Planning Commission, City Planning Commission, 202 City-County Building, Detroit MI 48226. **Tel** (313)224-6225. **LC** NA9127.D6; A15. **DD** 352.9/6/097743405. **Continues** Detroit (Mich.). City Planning Commission. Two-year Report ... .

SZ
BIBLIOGRAPHIE DER ORTS-, REGIONAL- UND LANDESPLANUNG. 1972-. German. an. Verlag der Fachvereine Austieferung, Postfach 566, CH-6314 Unteraegeri Switzerland. **LC** Z7165.S9; B5.

US
BIENNIAL REPORT AND OVERVIEW, AREA REDEVELOPMENT ADMINISTRATION. 1975/77-. English. be. 480 Cedar Street, St Paul MN 55101. **LC** HC107.M63; P6325. **DD** 353.9/776/0082.

US
BIENNIAL REPORT / IRCD, IOWA RURAL COMMUNITY DEVELOPMENT PROGRAM. Main/Corp Iowa Rural Community Development Program. 1979-1980-. English. be. Office for Planning and Programming, 523 East 12th Street, Des Moines IA 50319. **LC** HN79.I83; C64. **DD** 307.7/2/09777.

BL
BNH EM RESUMO. Main/Corp Banco Nacional da Habitacao. Yearly V. 1- (No. 1-); May/June 1976-. Portuguese. Banco Nacional da Habitacao, Av Rio Branco 37-Conj 704, Rio de Janeiro Brazil. **LC** HD7323.A3; B3C.

DK/0006-5285
BO BEDRE. [Bo bedre]. **VFOAT** Manedsmagasinet Bo Bedre. (1961)-. Periodical. Danish. mo (12 issues per year). kr978.00. Munksgaard International Publishers Ltd, PO Box 2148, DK-1016 Copenhagen K Denmark. **Tel** 011 45 33 12 70 30, FAX 011 45 33 12 93 87, telex 19431 MUNKS DK. **DD** 640. **CODEN** 64.

US/1055-6192
BOCA NATIONAL PROPERTY MAINTENANCE CODE. [BOCA natl. prop. maint. code]. **Main/Corp** Building Officials and Code Administrators International. **VFOAT** National Property Maintenance Code. **VAT** Building Officials and Code Administrators National Property Maintenance Code. 3rd Edition (1990)-. English. ir (Every three years). $18.00 (members), $27.00 (non-members). BOCA International, 4051 West Flossmoore Road, Country Club Hills IL 60478. **Tel** (708)799-2300, FAX (708)799-4981. **LC** KF5701.Z95; B85. **DD** 343.73/078624; 347.30378624. **Continues** Building Officials and Code Administrators International. BOCA National Existing Structures Code, 0897-0076.

SP
BOLETIN DE JURISPRUDENCIA Y RESOLUCIONES ADMINISTRATIVAS SOBRE URBANISMO Y VIVIENDA. See Law.

NE/0166-9370
BOS, BERICHTEN OVER STADSVERNIEUWING. [B.O.S. Ber. stadsvernieuwing]. **VFOAT** Berichten Over Stadsvernieuwing; B.O.S. 1.- Vol., Winter 1975/76-. Academic Scholarly Publication. Dutch. Centrale Afdeling Voorlichting. **LC** HT178.N4; B67. **Ind/Abst** EMBASE.

BL
BRAZIL DEVELOPMENT SERIES. VFOAT Serie Desenvolvimento Brasileiro; Desenvolvimento Brasileiro. Multiple languages (English and Portuguese). Telepress Servico de Imprensa Ltda, rua Sete de Abril 264 40 Andar, Sao Paulo Brazil. **LC** HC187; .B866. **DD** 338.981.

US/0273-1169
BUDGET GUIDELINES : CONDOMINIUMS, PLANNED DEVELOPMENTS, STOCK COOPERATIVES, COMMUNITY ASSOCIATIONS. VFOAT Condominiums, Planned Developments, Stock Cooperatives, Community Associations. 1st- Ed.; 1980-. English. an. Wyndham Company Inc, 25283 Cabot Road/Suite 101, Laguna Hills CA 92653. **LC** HD7287.65; .W95. **DD** 643/.2.

UK/0263-7960
BUILT ENVIRONMENT (LONDON, 1978). (BUILT ENVIRONMENT.). [Built environ.]. **Added/Corp** Regional Studies Association (London, England). Vol. 4 (June 1978)-. Academic Scholarly Publication. English. Four times a year (Mar., June, Sept., Dec.). £55.00 UK & Republic of Ireland; £60.00 others. Alexandrine Press, PO Box 15, 51 Cornmarket Street, Oxford OX1 3EB England. **Tel** 011 44 865 724627, FAX 011 44 865 792309, telex 22914 CCC G. **ED** Peter Hall and David Banister. **LC** HD7333.A3; B797. **DD** 301.5/4/0941. **[CCC].** **Bk Rev** (Qty: 10). **Circ:** 600. **Continues** Built Environment Quarterly, 0308-1508. **Desc:** Relevant to all involved with urban and regional planning and related disciplines. Enables practitioners to keep abreast of developments in the planning world, and provides excellent source material for academics and their students. **Ind/Abst** Archit. Period. Index (1977-); Avery Index Archit. Period. Suppl. Colum. Univ. (1988-); Coal Abstr.; EMBASE; Ergon. Abstr. (?-?); Geogr. Abstr. Human Geogr.; Highw. Res. Abstr.; J. Plan. Lit.; Middle East Abstr. Index; Soft. Abstr. Eng.; Trop. Dis. Bull.

CN/0380-1977
BULLETIN DU C. R. I. U. Main/Corp Universite de Montreal. Centre de Recherche et d'Innovation Urbaines. No. 1- 1973-. Bulletin. French. Price varies per volume. Centre de Recherches et d'Innovation Urbaine, Universite de Montreal, CP 6128, Montreal Quebec H3C 3J7 Canada. **DD** 711/.07/20714281.

US
BULLETIN OF NICCA / NICARAGUAN CENTER FOR COMMUNITY ACTION. Added/Corp Nicaraguan Center for Community Action. **VFOAT** NICCA Bulletin. (19??)-. Bulletin. English. Twelve times a year. $10.00. Nicaraguan Perspectives, PO Box 1004, Nicaraguan Information Ct, Berkeley CA 94701. **Tel** (415)549-1387.

FR
BULLETIN OFFICIEL DU MINISTERE DE L'EQUIPEMENT ET DE L'AMENAGEMENT DU TERRITOIRE. Main/Corp France. Ministere de l'Equipement et de l'Amenagement du Territoire. (19??)-. French. Four times a year. 338.00F France; 625.00F other. Direction des Journaux Officiels, 26 rue Desaix, 75727 Paris Cedex 15 France. **Tel** 011 33 1 40587500. **LC** LAW. **DD** 344/.44/06. **Continues** Bulletin Officiel du Ministere de l'Equipement.

JA
BULLETIN / UNITED NATIONS CENTRE FOR REGIONAL DEVELOPMENT. Main/Corp United Nations Centre for Regional Development. Bulletin. English. United Nations Centre for Regional Development, Nagono 1-47-1 Nakamura-ku, Nagoya 450 Japan. **Tel** 011 81 52 561-9377, FAX 011 81 52 561-9375, telex J59620 UNCENTRE. **LC** HT390; .U5313. **DD** 341.7/59.

GW/0007-5884
BUNDESBAUBLATT. [Bundesbaublatt]. **Added/Corp** Germany (West). Bundesministerium fuer Staedtebau und Wohnungswesen. (1952)-. Trade Publication. German. mo. DM275.00 Germany; DM318.00 other. Bauverlag GmbH, Postfach 1460, D 65173 Wiesbaden Germany. **Tel** 011 49 6123 7000, FAX 011 49 6123 700122. **Bk Rev. Ad Acc. Circ:** 4,400.

Desc: Publication covering all aspects of the housing industry. **Ind/Abst** EMBASE; Energy Res. Abstr. (Nov. 1978-).

DK/0007-7658
BYPLAN. [Byplan]. **Added/Corp** Norsk Byplanforening. Dansk Byplanlaboratorium. Vol. 1 (1948)-. Periodical. Danish. Six times a year. kr356.00 Scandinavia; kr440.00 others. Arkitektens Forlag / The Danish Architectural Press, Nyhavn 43, DK-1051 Copenhagen K Denmark. **Tel** 011 45 33 136200, FAX 011 45 33 912770. **ED** Arne Jaardniand. Index available. cum. index. **Bk Rev. Ad Acc. Desc:** Journal on town, regional, and national planning. **Ind/Abst** Int. Civil Eng. Abstr.; Soft. Abstr. Eng.

US/0526-6459
C H P C PROGRESS. (19??)-. Periodical. English. 20 West 40th Street, New York NY 10018. **DD** 711.

CN/0315-4920
C P A C REVIEW. Main/Corp Community Planning Association of Canada. **VFOAT** A C U Revue. V. 23, No. 6- July 1973-. Periodical. Multiple languages. mo. Community Planning Association of Canada / Ottawa, 425 Gloucester Street, Ottawa K1R 5E9, Canada. **DD** 711/.4/0971. **Continues** Community Planning Review, 0010-387X.

CN/0711-2475
CAHIER DE RECHERCHE - FACULTE DE L'AMENAGEMENT, UNIVERSITE DE MONTREAL. (CAHIER DE RECHERCHE.). [Cah. rech. - Fac. amenage., Univ. Montr.]. 01-. Monographic series. French. Price varies per volume. Faculte de l'Amenagement, Universite de Montreal, 5620 Av Darlington, Montreal Quebec H3T 1T2 Canada. **Tel** (514)343-6835. **DD** 710.

CN/0712-0370
CAHIER TECHNIQUE - DIRECTION GENERALE DE LA PLANIFICATION. OFFICE OF PLANIFICATION ET DE DEVELOPPEMENT DU QUEBEC. (CAHIER TECHNIQUE.). [Cah. tech. - Dir. gen. planif. dev. Que.]. **VFOAT** Cahiers Techniques. No. 1-. Periodical. French. Gouvernement du Quebec, 600 St Amable 4E Etage, Quebec Quebec G1R 4Z1 Canada. **DD** 711/.09714.

AE
CAHIERS DE L'AMENAGEMENT : PUBLICATION DE L'UNITE DE RECHERCHE EN AMENAGEMENT TERRITORIAL / MINISTERE DE L'AMENAGEMENT DU TERRITOIRE, DE L'URBANISME ET DE LA CONSTRUCTION, AGENCE NATIONALE POUR L'AMENAGEMENT DU TERRITOIRE. Added/Corp Algeria. Wihdat al-Bahth fi al-Tahyiah al-Umraniyah. **VFOAT** Manashir al-Tahyiah al-Umraniyah. (Sept. 1986)-. French. qt. **LC** HT395.A39; C33.

FR/0014-4711
CAHIERS DE L'EXPANSION REGIONALE, LES. Title Change. [Cah. expans. reg.]. **Added/Corp** Conseil National des Economies Regionales. Conseil National des Economies Regionales de la Productivite (France) Conseil International des Economies Regionales. **VFOAT** Expansion Regionale. (1959)-19??). Periodical. French. **LC** HT395.F7; C34. **DD** 361.6/0944. **Continued by** Inter Regions, 0240-9925.

FR/0153-6184
CAHIERS DE L'INSTITUT D'AMENAGEMENT ET D'URBANISME DE LA REGION D'ILE-DE-FRANCE. [Cah. Inst. amenage. urban. reg. Ile-de-Fr.]. **Main/Corp** Institut d'Amenagement et d'Urbanisme de la Region d'Ile-de-France. Vol. 42 (July 1976)-. Periodical. French. qt. 580.00F. Institut d'Amenagement et d'Urbanisme, 251 rue de Vaugirard, 75740 Paris Cedex 15 France. **Tel** 011 33 1 40437937. **LC** HT166; .F72A. **DD** 301.36/1/05. **Continues** Cahiers de l'Institut d'Amenagement et d'Urbanisme de la Region Parisienne. **Ind/Abst** Avery Index Archit. Period. Suppl. Colum. Univ. (1989-); PAIS Int. Print (1991-).

CN/0823-7980
CALGARY INDUSTRIAL LAND SURVEY. (CALGARY INDUSTRIAL LAND SURVEY AS OF ....). [Calg. ind. land surv.]. **Added/Corp** Calgary (Alta.). Long Range Planning and Research Division. Calgary (Alta.). Planning Dept. (1980)-. English. an. City of Calgary Planning Information Centre, PO Box 2100, Calgary Alberta T2P 2M5 Canada. **DD** 333.77/097123/3.

US/1056-2486
CALIFORNIA APARTMENT INVESTMENT SURVEY (SACRAMENTO COUNTY ED.), THE. (THE CALIFORNIA APARTMENT INVESTMENT SURVEY.). (1991)-. English. qt. $269.00. Realvest Research Associates, Inc., PO Box 10888, Oakland CA 94610.

US/0194-2913
CALIFORNIA COMMUNITIES. ***Title Change.*** **Added/Corp** California. Dept. of Housing and Community Development. No. 5 (Sept. 1977)-(19??). Periodical. English. qt. California Department of Housing & Community Development, PO Box 951050, Sacramento CA 94252. **Tel** (916)445-4775, FAX (916)323-2815. ***Continues*** *Communities.* ***Continued by*** *California Neighborhoods.*
Ind/Abst Calif. Period. Index; Calif. Period. Microfi.

US/0741-6083
CALIFORNIA HOUSING PLAN, THE. (THE CALIFORNIA HOUSING PLAN : STRATEGY FOR STATE ACTION.). **Main/Corp** California. Dept. of Housing and Community Development. **VFOAT** 101 Steps to Better Housing. (19??)-. English. be. California Department of Housing & Community Development, PO Box 951050, Sacramento CA 94252. **Tel** (916)445-4775, FAX (916)323-2815. **LC** HD7303.C2; C24a. **DD** 363.5/56/09794. ***Continues*** *California Statewide Housing Plan ... Update.*

US/1052-8946
CALIFORNIA LAND USE AND PLANNING LAW. (CALIFORNIA LAND-USE AND PLANNING LAW / DANIEL J. CURTIN, JR.). [Calif. land use plan. law]. **VFOAT** California Land Use and Planning Law. (198?)-. English. an. $42.00. Solano Press, PO Box 773A, Point Arena CA 95468. **Tel** (707)884-4508. **LC** KFC811; .C87. **DD** 346.79404/5; 347.940645. ***Continues*** *California Planning Law and Land Use Regulations;* ***Absorbed*** *Subdivision Map Act Manual, 1042-3796.*

US
CALIFORNIA NEIGHBORHOODS. (19??)-. Periodical. English. Twice a year. Free on request. California Department of Housing & Community Development, PO Box 951050, Sacramento CA 94252. **Tel** (916)445-4775, FAX (916)323-2815. **ED** Paul Kranhold. **Circ:** 5,000. ***Continues*** *California Communities.*

US/0891-382X
CALIFORNIA PLANNING & DEVELOPMENT REPORT. [Calif. plan. dev. rep.]. **VFOAT** California Planning and Development Report; CP 6 DR. Vol. 1, No. 1 (Nov. 1986)-. Periodical. English. mo. $189.00 new; $199.00 renew. California Planning & Development Report, 1275 Sunnycrest Avenue, Ventura CA 93003. **LC** HT169.C2; C34. **DD** 338.

US/1053-4164
CALIFORNIA REAL ESTATE TRENDS. FORECAST FOR HOUSING AND THE ECONOMY. See Real Estate.

CN/1185-653X
CANADA'S CAPITAL, OURS IN COMMON. ANNUAL REPORT. [Can. cap. ours common, annu. rep.]. **Main/Corp** Canada. National Capital Commission. **VFOAT** Capitale nationale, on s'y Retrouve. Rapport Annuel. (1991)-. English (French). **DD** 354.710071/3.

CN/0824-3727
CANADA'S HOUSING CRISIS. [New Democratic Party]. Periodical. English. Free. Canada's Housing Crisis, c/o New Democratic Party, House of Commons, Ottawa Ontario K1A 0A6 Canada. **DD** 363.5/0971.

CN/0826-7278
CANADIAN HOUSING. [Can. hous.]. **Added/Corp** Canadian Association of Housing and Renewal Officials. **VFOAT** Habitation Canadienne. Vol. 1, No. 1 (Fall 1984)-. Periodical. English (French). qt. 40.00Can$ (one year), 65.00Can$ (two year) Canada; 50.00Can$ (one year), 75.00Can$ (two year) other. Canadian Housing Renewal Association, 304 251 Laurier Avenue West, Ottawa Ontario K10 5J6 Canada. **Tel** (613)594-3007. **ED** Heather Lang-Rurtz. **DD** 363.5/0971. **Bk Rev. Ad Acc. Circ:** 1,000. ***Continues*** *Impact, 0707-7599.*
Desc: Professional journal geared to organizations (municipal, provincial, federal, and grass-roots) involved in affordable housing, shelter, urban, renewal, and rehabilitation of homes and neighborhoods.
Ind/Abst Can. Index.

CN/0823-020X
CANADIAN HOUSING. MONTHLY ANALYSIS. [Can. hous. mon. anal.]. Vol. 2, No. 9 (June 1977)-. Periodical. English. mo. 330.00Can$ Canada. Clayton Research Associates Ltd, 1580 Kingston Road, Scarborough Ontario M1N 1S2 Canada. **Tel** (905)699-5645, FAX (416)699-2252. **ED** 3050435455. **DD** 333.33/8. **Circ:** 300 (ctrl). ***Continues*** *Canadian Housing Forecast and Analysis. Monthly Canadian Housing Commentary, 0700-3080.*
Desc: Free trade with Canada will present new market opportunities for US firms. Authoritative commentary on Canadian housing trends and forecasts.

CN/0705-4580
CANADIAN JOURNAL OF REGIONAL SCIENCE, THE. **Added/Corp** Dalhousie University. Regional and Urban Studies Centre. INRS-Urbanisation. **VFOAT** Revue Canadienne des Sciences Regionales. Vol. 1, No. 1 (Spring 1978)-. Periodical. English (French). Three times a year (Spring, Summer, Autumn). 50.00Can$. University of New Brunswick Department of Economics, PO Box 4400, Fredericton New Brunswick E3B 5A3 Canada. **Tel** (506)453-4828. **ED** William Coffey, Jacques Ledent. **LC** HT395.C3; C354. **DD** 361.6/0971. **Bk Rev**, (Qty: approx. 6/year; English and French). **Ad Acc. Circ:** 450.
Desc: Canadian regional development policy, policy and methods of regional analysis.

●CN/1188-3774
CANADIAN JOURNAL OF URBAN RESEARCH. [Can. j. urban res.]. **Added/Corp** University of Winnipeg. Institute of Urban Studies. Vol. 1, Issue 1 (June 1992)-. English. sa. 42.06Can$ institutions; 28.04Can$ (individuals) Canada; 40.00Can$ (individuals) other. Institute of Urban Studies, University of Winnipeg, 515 Portage Avenue, Winnipeg Manitoba R3B 2E9 Canada. **Tel** (204)786-9409. **ED** Mary Ann Dennis. **DD** 307.76/05. Index available. cum. index. **Bk Rev. Ad Acc. Pr Rev. Circ:** 170. available on microfilm from Micromedia Limited.
Desc: Contribution to the field of urban studies from ideological, disciplinary, and methodological perspectives.

US
CAPSULES / SOUTHERN RURAL DEVELOPMENT CENTER. **Added/Corp** Southern Rural Development Center. (1981)-. Periodical. English. Ten times a year. Free. Southern Rural Development Center, Box 5446, Mississippi State MS 39762. **Tel** (601)325-3207.

US/0164-0070
CAROLINA PLANNING. [Carol. plann.]. **Added/Corp** University of North Carolina at Chapel Hill. Dept. of City and Regional Planning. Vol. 1 (Summer 1975)-. Periodical. English. Twice a year (Jan. & Sept.). $12.00 (one year), $20.00 (two year). University of North Carolina, Department of City and Regional Planning, Campus Box 3140, Chapel Hill NC 27599-3140. **Tel** (919)962-3983. **ED** John Anton and Steven Stichter. **LC** HT393.N8; C37. **DD** 309.2/12/09756. cum. index. **Circ:** 1,000.
Desc: A forum for discussion of planning problems and related public policy issues facing planning professionals in both the Southeast and the rest of the nation.
Ind/Abst Avery Index Archit. Period. Suppl. Colum. Univ. (Fall 1989, Fall 1990); Energy Res. Abstr. (May 1980-); PAIS Int. Print.

US/1050-3811
CD-HOUSING REGISTER, THE. [CD-hous. reg.]. **VAT** Community Development Housing Register. (19??)-. Periodical. English. sm. $387.00. CD Publications, 8204 Fenton Street, Silver Spring MD 20910. **Tel** (800)666-6380, (301)588-6380, FAX (301)588-6385. **DD** 643.

US/0891-1029
CENTER CITY REPORT. (CENTER CITY REPORT / INTERNATIONAL DOWNTOWN EXECUTIVES ASSOCIATION.). [Cent. city rep.]. **Added/Corp** International Downtown Executives Association. (19??)-. Periodical. English. Four times a year. $50.00. International Downtown Association, 915 Fifteenth Street Northwest, Suite 900, Washington DC 20005. **Tel** (202)783-4963, FAX (202)347-2161. **ED** Dale Doyle. **DD** 711. **Circ:** 1,000 (ctrl).
Ind/Abst Urban Aff. Abstr.

CN/0710-5851
CENTREFOLD (BRANDON). (CENTREFOLD / COMMUNITY RESOURCE CENTRE.). [Centrefold]. **Main/Corp** Brandon University. Rural Community Resource Centre. Spring 1978-. Periodical. English. qt. Community Resource Centre, Brandon University, Brandon Manitoba R7A 6A9 Canada. **DD** 307.7/2/0607127.

II
CHANGING VILLAGES / CONSORTIUM ON RURAL TECHNOLOGY. Periodical. English. bm. Foundation for Rural Recovery and Development, 10 Panchshila Park Shopping Centre, New Delhi 110017 India.
Ind/Abst Agrofor. Abstr. (1991-); Field Crop Abstr.; Hortic. Abstr.; Rice Abstr.

UK/0306-3178
CHARTERED SURVEYOR : URBAN QUARTERLY. **VFOAT** Urban Quarterly. V. 1- Aug. 1973-. Periodical. English. qt. £0.50. Royal Institution of Chartered Surveyors, PO Box 87, London EC4P 4HL England. **Tel** 01 353 2300, telex 25212 BUILDA-G. **LC** HD591.A1; C47. **DD** 526.9/05. available on microfilm from University Microfilms International (UMI).
Ind/Abst Archit. Period. Index.

US/1046-8196
CHF NEWSBRIEFS. [CHF newsb.]. **VAT** Cooperative Housing Foundation Newsbriefs. Vol. 20, No. 3 (Aug. 1988)-. Periodical. English. qt. Free. Cooperative Housing Foundation, 20090-1280. **Tel** (301)587-4700, FAX (301)587-2626, telex 440271 CHR UL. **ED** Alicia J George. **DD** 361. **Circ:** 3,000. ***Continues*** *Newsbriefs (Cooperative Housing Foundation (U.S.)), 0895-5735.*
Desc: Describes Cooperative Housing Foundation activities around the world as well as developments in the shelter sector.

JA
CHIIKIGAKU KENKYU. **Added/Corp** Nihon Chiiki Gakkai. (19??)-. Japanese (English). an. ¥6000. Nihon Chiiki Gakkai, c/o Kohno Office, Institute of Socio-Economic Planning, University of Tsukuba, Tsukuba Ibaraki 305 Japan. **Tel** (0298)53-5071. **ED** Hirotada Kohno et al. **LC** HT395.J3; C483. Index available. **Circ:** 700 (ctrl).

CC
CHINA CITY PLANNING REVIEW. **Added/Corp** Chung-kuo Chien Chu Hsueh Hui. Cheng Shih Kuei Hua Hsueh Shu Wei Yuan Hui. Chung-kuo Cheng Shih Kuei Hua She Chi Yen Chiu Yuan. China Urban Planning Society. Vol. 1, No. 1 (Nov. 1985)-. Periodical. English (translations available in Chinese). sa. **LC** HT169.C6; C442. **DD** 711/.4/095105.
Ind/Abst Avery Index Archit. Period. Suppl. Colum. Univ. (1988).

UK
CHINA URBAN STATISTICS. ***Ceased.*** **See** Housing and Urban Development-Abstracting, Bibliographies and Statistics.

KO
CHIYOK SAHOE KAEBAL YONGU. **Added/Corp** Hanguk Chiyok Sahoe Kaebal Hakhoe. **VFOAT** Community Development Review. (19??)-. Periodical. Korean (summaries and/or abstracts in English). **LC** HN730.5.Z9; C6153.
Ind/Abst Soc. Work Abstr.

JA
CHUBUKEN NO MIRAIZO. **Added/Corp** Chunichi Shimbun, Nagoya, Japan. Chunichi Shimbun Sha. Nagoya Honsha. Kaihatsukyoku. (1972)-. Periodical. Japanese. ¥1300. Chunichi Shimbun Honsha, 6-1 Sannomatu 1-chome, Naka-ku 460, Nagoya Japan. **LC** HT395.J32; C533.

CC
CHUNG-KUO CHENG SHIH CHIEN SHE NIEN CHIEN = ZHONG GUO CHENG SHI JIAN SHE NIAN JIAN / "CHUNG-KUO CHENG SHIH CHIEN SHE NIEN CHIEN" PIEN WEI HUI. **Added/Corp** "Chung-Kuo Cheng Shih Chien She Nien Cien" Pien Wei Hui. **VFOAT** Zhong Guo Cheng Shi Jian She Nian Jian. (1986/1987)-. Chinese. an. $42.00. China National Publishing Import & Export Corporation, 16 Gongti E Rd., Chaoyang Dist., Beijing 100704, People's Republic of China. **Tel** 011 8601 50630169, 5066688, FAX 011 8601 5063101, 5063010, telex 22313. **LC** IN PROCESS; HT169.C6; C48.

KO
CHUTAEK KUMYUNG. **VFOAT** Housing Finance Quarterly Review. Periodical. Korean (English). bm. W1400. The Korea Housing Bank, 36-3 Yoido-dong Youngdeungpo-ku Seoul Korea. **Tel** 784-7711, 32933, telex KOHOBA K27879. **ED** Soo-Kon Rhee. **LC** HD7367.5.A3; C47. Index available. cum. index. **Circ:** 3,000 (ctrl).

BG
CIRDAP STUDY SERIES. **Added/Corp** Center on Integrated Rural Development for Asia and the Pacific. **VAT** Center on Integrated Rural Development for Asia and the Pacific Study Series. No. 1 (1982)-. Monographic series. English. CIRDAP, Documentation Officer, Bard Campus, Kotbari, Comilla, Bangladesh. **LC** UNC.
Ind/Abst Int. Dev. Abstr.; Soils Fert.; World Agric. Econ.

UK/0264-2751
CITIES (LONDON, ENGLAND). (CITIES.). [Cities]. Vol. 1, No. 1 (Aug. 1983)-. Periodical. English. Six times a year. $395.00 The Americas; £265.00 other. Butterworth Heinemann Publishers, Linacre House, Jordan Hill, Oxford OX2 8DP England. **Tel** 011 44 865 310366. **(Subscription address:** Elsevier Science Ltd. Oxford Fulfillment Centre, PO Box 800, Kidlington, Oxford OX5 1DX United Kingdom.) **ED** Jennifer Nicholson. **LC** HT119; .C563. **DD** 307.7/6/05. **[CCC].** Index available. **Bk Rev. Ad Acc.** available on microfilm and microfiche from University Microfilms International (UMI). Documents available from Documents on Demand.
Desc: Provides a comprehensive range of articles for policy and decision makers at local, national and international levels, and for all analysts of urban policies. Papers, commentaries, book reviews, conference reviews, a bibliography of recently published articles and books, research reports, an international conference calendar and a selection of special features are presented in each issue.
Ind/Abst Avery Index Archit. Period. Suppl. Colum. Univ. (Feb. 1990-); Environ. Abstr.; Geogr. Abstr. Phys. Geogr.; Geogr. Abstr. Human Geogr.; Int. Bibliogr. Sociol.; Int. Dev. Abstr.; J. Ferrocement; J. Plan. Lit.; Linguist. Lang. Behav. Abstr.; PAIS Int. Print (1991-); Sage Urban Stud. Abstr (?-?); Soc. Plann. Policy Dev. Abstr.; Sociol. Abstr.; Urban Aff. Abstr.

IT/0009-7640
CITTA E SOCIETA. ***Title Change.*** Vol. 1 (Jan./Feb. 1966)-(19??). Periodical. Italian. qt. Citta e Societa, Piazza S Ambrogio 21, 20123 Milan Italy. **DD** 301.3. ***Continued by*** *Solidarieta Lombardia.*
Ind/Abst Archit. Period. Index (1979-19??).

US/0893-0465
CITY & SOCIETY. (CITY & SOCIETY : JOURNAL OF THE SOCIETY FOR URBAN ANTHROPOLOGY.). [City soc.]. **VFOAT** City and Society. Vol. 1, No. 1 (June 1987)-. Periodical. English. an. $30.00. American Anthropological Association, 4350 North Fairfax Dr, Suite 640, Arlington VA 22203. **Tel** (703)528-1902 ext. 3031, FAX (703)528-3546. **ED** Alvin Wolfe. **LC** HT101; .C544. **DD** 307.7/6/05. **CODEN** CISOEC. **Ad Acc. Pr Rev. Circ:** 500 (ctrl). available on microfilm from University Microfilms International (UMI). Documents available.
Desc: Cross-disciplinary studies of urban communities and complex societies, from the perspective of urban anthropology and related disciplines.
Ind/Abst Am. Hist. Life (1987-); Anthropol. Lit.; Linguist. Lang. Behav. Abstr.; Sage Urban Stud. Abstr; Soc. Plann. Policy Dev. Abstr.; Sociol. Abstr.

US/0199-0330
CITY LIMITS. [City limits]. **Added/Corp** Association of Neighborhood Housing Developers. (19??)-. Periodical. English. Ten times a year (June/July and Aug./Sept. issues combined). $20.00 (individuals and community groups), $35.00 (others) US. City Limits Community Information Service, Inc., 40 Prince Street, New York NY 10012. **Tel** (212)925-9820, FAX (212)966-3407. **ED** Andrew White. **LC** HN79.N43; C63. **DD** 307.7/6/09747. **Bk Rev. Ad Acc, Adv Mgr:** Faith Wiggins, **Tel** (917)253-3887. **Circ:** 4,500. available on microfilm from University Microfilms International (UMI).
Desc: An urban affairs monthly news magazine; news/analysis of critical urban issues - housing, homelessness, neighborhood revitalization, economic development, land use, etc.
Ind/Abst Altern. Press Index; Avery Index Archit. Period. Suppl. Colum. Univ. (1990-);(1984-).

US
CITY OF LOS ANGELES PLANNING AND ZONING CODE : CHAPTER 1 OF THE LOS ANGELES MUNICIPAL CODE. **Main/Corp** Los Angeles (Calif.). **VFOAT** Los Angeles City Planning and Zoning Code. (19??)-. Periodical. English. ir. Building News Inc., 3055 Overland Avenue, Los Angeles CA 90034. **Tel** (310)202-7775, (800)873-6397. Index available. **Bk Rev. Ad Acc.**

SP
CIUDAD Y TERRITORIO. ***Title Change.*** **See** Public Administration.

●SP
CIUDAD Y TERRITORIO--ESTUDIOS TERRITORIALES. **Added/Corp** Spain. Ministerio de Obras Publicas, Transportes y Medio Ambiente. **VFOAT** Ciudad y Territorio Estudios Territoriales; Ciudad y Territorio; Estudios Territoriales; Ciudad y Territorio y Estudios Territoriales; CyTET. Vol. 1, No. 97 (Oct. 1993)-. Periodical. Spanish. qt. 5000ptas Spain; 7000ptas others. Ministerio de Obras Publicas y Transportes y Medio Ambiente, Paseo de la Castellana, 67, 28071 Madrid Spain. **Tel** 011 34 1 5977263, 5977266, FAX 011 34 1 5546351. **LC** HT395.S7; C58. **DD** 307.76/0946/05. ***Formed by the union of*** *Ciudad y Territorio* ***and*** *Estudios Territoriales.*

US
CLAIMS COLLECTION HANDBOOK. **Main/Corp** United States. Dept. of Housing and Urban Development. Office of Administration. 1979-. Government Publication. English. US Department of Housing and Urban Development, 451 Seventh Street SW, Washington DC 20401. **Tel** (202)708-0980, FAX (202)708-0299. ***Continues*** *Procedures for Claims Collection Officers to Follow to Implement Claims Collection Act of 1966.*

US
CLASSIFICATION NUMBERS AND INDEXES. **Added/Corp** United States. Dept. of Housing and Urban Development. Office of Administration. (19??)-. Government Publication. English. US Department of Housing and Urban Development, 451 Seventh Street SW, Washington DC 20401. **Tel** (202)708-0980, FAX (202)708-0299.

●CN/1193-6517
CLAYTON COMPLETIONS REPORT. [Clayton complet. rep.]. **Added/Corp** Clayton Research Associates. (Feb. 1992)-. Periodical. English. qt. Clayton Research Associates Ltd, 1580 Kingston Road, Scarborough Ontario M1N 1S2 Canada. **Tel** (905)699-5645, FAX (416)699-2252. **DD** 333.33/8. ***Continues*** *Clayton Completions Forecast., 1183-8450.*

CN/1183-8442
CLAYTON HOUSING FORECAST. [Clayton hous. forecast]. **Added/Corp** Clayton Research Associates. Vol. 1, No. 1 (July 1991)-. Periodical. English. qt. Clayton Research Associates Ltd, 1580 Kingston Road, Scarborough Ontario M1N 1S2 Canada. **Tel** (905)699-5645, FAX (416)699-2252. **DD** 338.4/76908/0971. ***Continues*** *Canadian Housing. Quarterly Forecast., 0824-2429.*

CN/1183-8434
CLAYTON HOUSING REPORT. [Clayton hous. rep.]. **Added/Corp** Clayton Research Associates. Vol. 1, No. 1 (July 1991)-. Periodical. English. mo. 353.74Can$. Clayton Research Associates Ltd, 1580 Kingston Road, Scarborough Ontario M1N 1S2 Canada. **Tel** (905)699-5645, FAX (416)699-2252. **DD** 333.33/8. ***Continues*** *Canadian Housing. Monthly Analysis., 0823-020X.*

US/1054-8998
CLEARING (ELIZABETHTOWN, N. Y.), THE. (THE CLEARING.). **Added/Corp** Housing Assistance Program of Essex County (Essex County, N.Y.). Vol. 1, No. 1 (Summer 1991)-. Periodical. English. qt. Free. Housing Assistance Program of Essex County, Inc., PO Box 157, Elizabethtown NY 12932. **DD** 363.

FR
CODE DE L'URBANISME. **Main/Corp** France. 1.- Ed.; 1977-. French. Dalloz, 35 rue Tournefort, 75240 Paris Cedex 05 France. **Tel** 011 33 1 40515434 or 40515454, FAX 45 87 37 48, telex 206 446 F.

FR
CODE DES LOYERS ET DE LA COPROPRIETE. **Main/Corp** France. (197?)-. French. Dalloz, 35 rue Tournefort, 75240 Paris Cedex 05 France. **Tel** 011 33 1 40515434 or 40515454, FAX 45 87 37 48, telex 206 446 F. **LC** IN PROCESS.
Desc: Contains information necessary to everyday use in the fields of civil codes and procedure, including ordinances and decrees. Arranged in alphabetical order.

US
CODE OF FEDERAL REGULATIONS. 24, HOUSING AND URBAN DEVELOPMENT. **See** Law.

IT
CODICE DELLE LOCAZIONE. (19??)-. Periodical. Italian. qt. IPSOA Editore SRL, Casella Postale 12055, Mastrangelo, 20120 Milan Italy. **Tel** 011 39 2 82476248. Index available (Included).

VE/0505-1762
COLECCION ESPACIO Y FORMA. **Main/Corp** Venezuela. Universidad Central, Caracas. Facultad de Arquitectura y Urbanismo. Vol. 1 1958-. Periodical. Spanish. Universidad Central de Venezuela / Facultad de Arquitectura y Urbanismo, Caracas Venezuela.

CM
COMMUNAUTES AFRICAINES : REVUE TRIMESTRIELLE. (19??)-. Periodical. French. Four times a year. 500.00CFAF (two years). APICA, BP 5946, Douala-Akwa Cameroon. **Tel** 42-12-28, telex s/c 5744.

CN/0711-480X
COMMUNIQUE - CANADIAN ASSOCIATION OF HOUSING AND RENEWAL OFFICIALS. (COMMUNIQUE : INFORMATION ON HOUSING.). [Commun. - Can. Assoc. Hous. Renew. Off.]. Periodical. English. Free to Members. Association of Colleges of Applied Arts and Technology of Ontario, Suite 703, 2 Sheppard Avenue East, Willowdale Ontario M2N 2Y7. **DD** 363.5/0971.

US/0199-9346
COMMUNITIES (LOUISA). (COMMUNITIES.). [Communities]. **Added/Corp** Community Publications Cooperative. **VFOAT** Best of Communities. No. 1 (Dec. 1972)-. Periodical. English. qt (Spring, Summer, Fall, Winter). $25.00 (institutions), $18.00 (individuals) US; $45.00 (institutions), $33.00 (individuals) other. Communities, Rt 1 Box 155, Sandhill Farm, Rutledge MO 63563. **Tel** (816) 883-5545, FAX (816)883-5545. **ED** Diana Christian. **DD** 301.4. **Bk Rev**, (Qty: 6). **Ad Acc. Circ:** 3,000. available on microfilm from Bell & Howell's Underground Newspaper Collection. ***Formed by the union of*** *Communitarian; Communitas, 0278-3606* ***and*** *Alternatives.*
Desc: Reporting on all aspects of intentional communities movements.
Ind/Abst Altern. Press Index (?-199?); Linguist. Lang. Behav. Abstr.; Soc. Plann. Policy Dev. Abstr.; Sociol. Abstr. (?-?).

US/0743-1864
COMMUNITY AFFAIRS QUARTERLY. Vol. 1, No. 1 (Fall 1983)-. Periodical. English. qt. Texas Department of Community Affairs, PO Box 13166 Capitol Station, Austin TX 78711. **LC** HN79.T4; C59. **DD** 307/.14/09764. ***Continues*** *TDCA Bulletin, 0738-0291.*

US/0896-9159
COMMUNITY CHANGE. (COMMUNITY CHANGE / CENTER FOR COMMUNITY CHANGE.). [Community change]. **Added/Corp** Center for Community Change. (1987)-. Periodical. English. qt. $20.00 (one year), $30.00 (two year). Center for Community Change, 1000 Wisconsin Avenue, Washington DC 20007. **Tel** (202)342-0567, FAX (202)342-0567. **ED** Timothy Saasta. **DD** 362. **Bk Rev**, (Qty: 4). **Circ:** 3,000 (ctrl). ***Continues*** *Federal Programs Monitor.*
Desc: Commentary about issues affecting the poor, reports about important developments and profiles of successful community organizations.

US/0363-1613
COMMUNITY DEVELOPMENT BLOCK GRANT PROGRAM. DIRECTORY OF ALLOCATIONS FOR FISCAL YEARS ... . Government Publication. English. US Department of Housing and Urban Development, 451 Seventh Street SW, Washington DC 20401. **Tel** (202)708-0980, FAX (202)708-0299. **LC** HN90.C6; U6A. **DD** 309.2/62/0973. available on microfiche (Vols. for (1976 - 1981-) destributed to depository libraries).

US/0094-2324
COMMUNITY DEVELOPMENT DIGEST (WASHINGTON). (COMMUNITY DEVELOPMENT DIGEST.). [Community dev. dig.]. (197?)-. Periodical. English. sm. $387.00. CD Publications, 8204 Fenton Street, Silver Spring MD 20910. **Tel** (800)666-6380, (301)588-6380, FAX (301)588-6385. **ED** Byron Fielding. **DD** 333. Index available. ***Continues*** *Housing and Renewal Index;* ***Absorbed*** *Infrastructure, 0742-1990.*
Desc: Reports on community development block grants and other community development programs with state and local case studies, local news and citations of federal actions. Features documentation of HUD memoranda.

US
COMMUNITY DEVELOPMENT EVALUATION SERIES. No. 1- 1971-. Government Publication. English. US Department of Housing and Urban Development, 451 Seventh Street SW, Washington DC 20401. **Tel** (202)708-0980, FAX (202)708-0299. **LC** HN90.C6; C66. **DD** 309.2/6/0973.

CN/0823-6062
COMMUNITY DEVELOPMENT (GUELPH). (COMMUNITY DEVELOPMENT : THE NEWSLETTER OF THE ONTARIO COMMUNITY DEVELOPMENT SOCIETY.). [Community dev.]. V. 1, Issue 1 (April 1982)-. Newsletter. English. qt. Free to members. Ontario Community Development Society, Room 011, Johnston Hall, Guelph Ontario N1G 2W1. **DD** 307/.14/09713.

US
COMMUNITY DEVELOPMENT REPORTER. English. mo (12 issues per year). $495.00. Community Development Reporter, PO Box 17616, Philadelphia PA 19135. **Tel** (215)333-1717. **ED** James P. Walton. cum. index.
Desc: Compendium of federal regulations, statutes, executive orders and circulars relating to community development block program.

US/1045-4322
COMMUNITY ECONOMICS (GREENFIELD, MASS.). (COMMUNITY ECONOMICS.). **Added/Corp** Institute for Community Economics (Greenfield, Mass.). (1983)-. Periodical. English. qt. $30.00 (institutions), $15.00 (individuals) US; $20.00 other. Institute for Community Economics, 57 School Street, Springfield MA 01105. **Tel** (413)746-8660, FAX (413)746-8862. **ED** Kirby White, Lisa Berger. **DD** 330. cum. index. **Bk Rev**, (Qty: 3-5). **Circ:** 7,000.
Desc: Reports on the activities and issues facing the community investment for those interested in affordable housing and land reform.

US
COMMUNITY MATRIX FOR DEVELOPMENT PROJECTS. **Main/Corp** Alaska. Division of Economic Enterprise. **VFOAT** Community Project Matrix. English. an. Alaska Department of Commerce and Economic Development, 333 Willoughby Avenue, 9th Floor, Juneau AK 99801. **Tel** (907)465-2500, FAX (907)463-3841. **LC** HN79.A583; C63A. **DD** 307.7/09798.

AT/0814-401X
COMMUNITY QUARTERLY. [Community q.]. (1984)-. Periodical. English. qt (Mar., June, Sept., Dec.). 36.00Aus$ Australia; 42.00Aus$ Asia and Oceania; 44.00Aus$ other. Employ Working Effectively Inc, PO Box 275, St. Kilda 3182 Australia. **Tel** 011 61 3 5253384. **ED** Fae Dent and Chris Morris. **DD** 307.1409945. Index available. **Bk Rev**, (Qty: 6). **Ad Acc. Circ:** 1,000.
Desc: Practical examples of community development in action.

US/0277-6189
COMMUNITY SERVICE NEWSLETTER. **Added/Corp** Community Service, Inc. **VFOAT** Community Comments. Vol. 24 (Jan./Feb. 1976)-. Periodical. English. bm (6 issues). $25.00. Community Service Inc, Box 243, Yellow Springs OH 45387. **Tel** (513)767-2161. **ED** Jane Morgan. **Bk Rev. Circ:** 400 (ctrl). ***Continues*** *Community Comments Newsletter.*
Desc: Articles on how to improve your community and on understanding the importance of the small community to our democratic way of life.

US/0277-464X
COMMUNITY UPO. Main/Corp United Planning Organization. **VAT** Community United Planning Organization. (19??)-. Periodical. English. Community Planning Organization, 1021 14th Street NW, Washington DC 20005.

US
COMPENDIUM OF HUMAN SETTLEMENTS STATISTICS / DEPARTMENT OF INTERNATIONAL ECONOMICS AND SOCIAL AFFAIRS, STATISTICAL OFFICE / RECUEIL DES STATISTIQUES DES ETABLISSEMENTS HUMAINS / DEPARTEMENT DES AFFAIRES ECONOMIQUES ET SOCIALES INTERNATIONALES, BUREAU DE STATISTIQUE. See Housing and Urban Development-Abstracting, Bibliographies and Statistics.

US/0097-7810
COMPENDIUM OF RESEARCH CONTRACTS AND REPORTS - (DEPT. OF HOUSING AND URBAN DEVELOPMENT). Main/Corp United States. Dept. of Housing and Urban Development. Office of Policy Development and Research. 1973-. Government Publication. English. an. US Department of Housing and Urban Development, 451 Seventh Street SW, Washington DC 20401. **Tel** (202)708-0980, FAX (202)708-0299. **LC** HD7293.A49; H673B. **DD** 301.5/4/072073.

US/0272-5800
COMPENDIUM OF RESEARCH REPORTS. [Compend. res. rep.]. Began with Aug. 1979. Government Publication. English. sa. US Department of Housing and Urban Development, 451 Seventh Street SW, Washington DC 20401. **Tel** (202)708-0980, FAX (202)708-0299. **LC** HD7293.A1; U532A. **DD** 361.6/0973.

US
COMPETITIONHOTLINE. See Architecture.

US/0198-9715
COMPUTERS, ENVIRONMENT AND URBAN SYSTEMS. [Comput., environ. urban syst.]. Vol. 5, No. 1/2 (1980)-. Academic Scholarly Publication. English. Six times a year. $552.00 The Americas; £370.00 other. Pergamon Press, An Imprint of Elsevier Science Ltd., The Boulevard, Langford Lane, Kidlington, Oxford OX5 1GB United Kingdom. **Tel** 011 44 865 843000, 011 44 865 843699, FAX 011 44 865 843010. **(Subscription address:** Elsevier Science Ltd. Oxford Fulfillment Centre, PO Box 800, Kidlington, Oxford OX5 1DX United Kingdom.) **ED** Gordon A. Gobert. **LC** HT166; .C6212. **DD** 307.7/6/02854. **CODEN** CEUSD5. **[CCC]. Pr Rev.** available on microfilm and microfiche from University Microfilms International (UMI). Documents available from Article Express International, The Genuine Article, Ask*IEEE, Documents on Demand. ***Continues*** *Urban Systems, 0147-8001.*
Ind/Abst Avery Index Archit. Period. Suppl. Colum. Univ. (1989-); Bioeng. Abstr.; Civ. Struct. Eng. Abstr.; Compumath Citation Index [Full Cov.]; Comput. Abstr.; Comput. Inf. Syst. Abstr. J. [Full Cov.]; Curr. Contents Eng. Tech. Appl. Sci.; Curr. Geogr. Publ. (199?-); Educ. Adm. Abstr.; Ei Page One; Elect. Comm. Abstr.; EMBASE; Energy Inf. Abstr.; Energy Res. Abstr. (Jan. 1981-); Eng. Index Annu.; Environ. Abstr.; Environ. Eng. Abstr.; Environ. Period. Bibliogr.; Geogr. Abstr. Phys. Geogr.; Geogr. Abstr. Human Geogr.; Health Saf. Sci. Abstr.; INSPEC (1981-); Int. Dev. Abstr.; Mater. Sci. Eng. Abstr.; Pollut. Abstr. Indexes; Psychol. Abstr. (1980-); PsycINFO; PsycLit; Res. Alert [Full Cov.]; Sage Urban Stud. Abstr; SCISEARCH; Soc. Sci. Cit. Index [Select. Cov.]; Urban Aff. Abstr.

US/0742-9320
CONDOMINIUM, HOMEOWNER & COOPERATIVE COMMUNITY ASSOCIATIONS INFORMATION RESOURCE. VFOAT Condominium, Homeowner and Cooperative Community Associations Information Resource. (1984)-. English. an. $13.95. Condo Management Maintenance Corporation, 65 Highway 22, PO Box 4908, Clinton NJ 08809. **Tel** (201)735-4438. **ED** Lester J. Giese. **LC** Z7164.H8; C696; HD7287.67.U5. **DD** 016.643/2. **Bk Rev. Ad Acc. Circ:** 1,000 (ctrl).
Desc: Resource of organizations, magazines, newsletters, state agencies, software and books that support and provide information on the management of condominiums.

US/0095-487X
CONDOMINIUM WORLD. *Title Change.* Vol. 1 (Autumn 1974)-(19??). Periodical. English. qt. Warren Gorham & Lamont Inc., Park Square Building, 31 St. James Avenue, Boston MA 02116-4112. **Tel** (617)423-2020, (800)950-1207, FAX (617)423-2026. **LC** HD7287.67.U5; C65. **DD** 333.3/3. ***Merged into*** *Real Estate Review, 0034-0790.*

US/0362-7586
CONSOLIDATED DEVELOPMENT DIRECTORY. Directory. English. an. US Department of Housing and Urban Development Federal Housing Commissioner, 451 Seventh Street SW, Room 9100, Washington DC 20410. **Tel** (202)708-3600, FAX (202)755-2580. **LC** HD7293.A49; P83A. **DD** 301.5/4/02573.

US
CONSTRUCTION REPORTS. C45, HOUSING UNITES AUTHORIZED FOR DEMOLITION IN PERMIT-ISSUING PLACES. VFOAT Housing Units Authorized for Demolition in Permit-Issuing Places. 1969-. Government Publication. English. an. US Department of Commerce / Bureau of the Census, Data User Services Division, Customer Services, Washington DC 20233-0800. **Tel** (301)763-4100. **(Subscription address:** Superintendent of Documents, US Government Printing Office, Washington DC 20402.) ***Continues*** *Construction Reports. C45, Permits Issued for Demolition of Residential Structures in Selected Cities.*

US/0363-8537
CONSTRUCTION REPORTS: NEW ONE-FAMILY HOMES SOLD AND FOR SALE. Main/Corp United States. Bureau of the Census. **Added/Corp** United States. Dept. of Housing and Urban Development. (1962)-. Government Publication. English. ir. $25.00 domestic; $31.25 other. Superintendent of Documents, US Government Printing Office, Washington DC 20402. **Tel** (202)275-3328, FAX (202)786-2377.
Desc: Provides preliminary information regarding new privately owned, one-family houses sold during the month and for sale at the end of the month.

UV
CONSTRUIRE ENSEMBLE / CESAO. Periodical. French. bm. CESAO, BP 305, Bobo-Dioulasso Burkina Faso. **LC** HN821.Z9; C63. **DD** 307.7/2/0966.

IT/0010-7050
CONSULENTE IMMOBILIARE. [Consul. immob.]. (1957)-. Periodical. Italian. sm (24 issues per year). L210000. Pirola Editore, CP 10444, Via Parabiago 19, 20151 Milan Italy. **Tel** 011 39 2 3022888. **UDC** 333.33. **Ad Acc, Adv Mgr Tel** 3022.1. **Circ:** 14,000.

US/0097-9759
COOPERATIVE HOUSING BULLETIN. [Coop. hous. bull.]. **Added/Corp** National Association of Housing Cooperatives. **VFOAT** CHB. (19??)-. Periodical. English. bm. $50.00. National Association of Housing Cooperatives, 1614 King Street, Alexandria VA 22314. **Tel** (703)549-5201, FAX (703)684-8648. **ED** Roger Wilcox and Kate Lau. **DD** 334. **Bk Rev. Ad Acc. Circ:** 2,700 (ctrl). ***Continues*** *What's Happening in Housing Cooperatives.*
Desc: News affecting housing cooperatives, laws, regulations, court cases, training opportunities, technical assistance articles and news about existing cooperatives.

US/0589-6355
COOPERATIVE HOUSING JOURNAL. [Coop. hous. j.]. **Added/Corp** National Association of Housing Cooperatives. (1969)-. Periodical. English. an. $50.00 (Comes with Cooperative Housing Bulletin.). National Association of Housing Cooperatives, 1614 King Street, Alexandria VA 22314. **Tel** (703)549-5201, FAX (703)684-8648. **ED** Roger Willcox, Herbert J. Levy, Katharine Jones Law. **DD** 334. **Ad Acc. *Continues*** *Cooperative Housing Quarterly.*
Desc: Articles of lasting value for leaders of housing cooperatives. Published by the NAHC, it is the only national housing cooperative organization.

US
COOPERATIVE HOUSING LAW AND PRACTICE, FORMS. (19??)-. English. ir. Matthew Bender & Company Inc., 1275 Broadway, Albany NY 12204. **Tel** (800)833-9844, (518)487-3000.

CN/0226-0344
COTTAGER MAGAZINE, THE. [Cottager mag.]. **VAT** Cottager. V. 1- March 1980-. Periodical. English. ir. $5.50. MLC Publications, Cottager Magazine, 130 Lewis Street, Ottawa Ontario K2P 0S7 Canada. **DD** 643/.2.

US
COUNCIL NOTES. Main/Corp Illinois. University at Urbana-Champaign. Small Homes Council-Building Research Council. (1975)-. Periodical. English. ir. $4.00 (two year). University of Illinois / Small Homes Council, Small Homes Council Building, Research Council, Urbana IL 61801. **Tel** (217)333-1802. **ED** Henry R Spies. **Circ:** 2,500.
Desc: Consumer-oriented brochures on residential planning, construction and maintenance.

US/0082-9455
COUNTY AND CITY DATA BOOK. See Housing and Urban Development-Abstracting, Bibliographies and Statistics.

US
COUNTY AND CITY STATISTICS CD-ROM. See Housing and Urban Development-Abstracting, Bibliographies and Statistics.

US/0149-5208
COUNTYWIDE ANNUAL PLAN REVIEW / FAIRFAX COUNTY, VA. OFFICE OF COMPREHENSIVE PLANNING. Main/Corp Fairfax County, Va. Office of Comprehensive Planning. **VFOAT** Annual Plan Review for Countywide Items. English. Office of Comprehensive Planning, 4100 Chain Bridge Road, Fairfax VA 22030. **LC** HT393.V62; F34177. **DD** 711/.3/09755291.

CN/0317-0780
CPAC BOOKSHOPPE. (CPAC BOOKSHOPPE. LA LIBRAIRIE DE L'ACU.). **Main/Corp** Community Planning Association of Canada. **VFOAT** La Librairie de l'ACU. (1974)-. Periodical. English. Community Planning Association of Canada / Ottawa, 425 Gloucester Street, Ottawa K1R 5E9, Canada. **DD** 016.711/4/0971.

US
CPD NOTES / HEADQUARTERS, COMMUNITY PLANNING AND DEVELOPMENT. Main/Corp United States. Office of Community Planning and Development. **VFOAT** Community Planning and Development Notes. (1991)-. Periodical. English. mo. Office of Community Planning and Development, 451 7th Street SW, Washington DC 20410.

US/0743-1635
CPL BIBLIOGRAPHY. See Housing and Urban Development-Abstracting, Bibliographies and Statistics.

US
CRITICAL PATH PROCESSING TERMINAL OPERATING PROCEDURES. Government Publication. English. US Department of Housing and Urban Development, 451 Seventh Street SW, Washington DC 20401. **Tel** (202)708-0980, FAX (202)708-0299.

US
CURA REPORTER. Main/Corp University of Minnesota. Center for Urban and Regional Affairs. **VFOAT** CURA. Began publication with: 1970. Periodical. English. Five times a year. Free. Center for Urban and Regional Affairs, University of Minnesota, 330 Humphrey Center, 301 19th Avenue South, Minneapolis MN 55455. **Tel** (612)625-1551. **ED** Judith H Weir. Index available. cum. index. **Pr Rev. Circ:** 5,000.
Desc: Research reports on projects related to urban and regional development in Minnesota.

US/0896-6761
CURRENT CONSTRUCTION REPORTS. C20, HOUSING STARTS. (CURRENT CONSTRUCTION REPORTS. C20, HOUSING STARTS / U.S. DEPT. OF COMMERCE, BUREAU OF THE CENSUS.). [Curr. constr. rep., C20 Hous. starts]. **Added/Corp** United States. Bureau of the Census. **VFOAT** Housing Starts. (Aug. 1987)-. Government Publication. English. mo. $20.00 US; $25.00 other. US Department of Commerce / Bureau of the Census, Data User Services Division, Customer Services, Washington DC 20233-0800. **Tel** (301)763-4100. **(Subscription address:** Superintendent of Documents, US Government Printing Office, Washington DC 20402.) **LC** HD9715.U5; A275. **DD** 338.4/76908/0973021. Documents available from Documents on Demand. ***Continues*** *Construction Reports. C20, Housing Starts, 0498-8442.*
Ind/Abst Am. Stat. Index.

US/0896-6737
CURRENT CONSTRUCTION REPORTS. C21, NEW RESIDENTIAL CONSTRUCTION IN SELECTED METROPOLITAN STATISTICAL AREAS. [Curr. constr. rep., C21 New resid. constr. sel. metrop. stat. areas]. **Added/Corp** United States. Bureau of the Census. United States. Dept. of Housing and Urban Development. **VFOAT** New Residential Construction in Selected Metropolitan Statistical Areas. C21-87-Q2 (2nd Quarter 1987)-. Government Publication. English. qt. $9.00 US; $11.25 other. US Department of Housing and Urban Development, 451 Seventh Street SW, Washington DC 20401. **Tel** (202)708-0980, FAX (202)708-0299. **LC** HD9715.U5; A275. **DD** 338.4/76908/0973021. ***Continues*** *Construction Reports. C21, New Residential Construction in Selected Standard Metropolitan Statistical Areas, 0145-0212.*

US
CURRENT CONSTRUCTION REPORTS. C25, NEW ONE-FAMILY HOUSES SOLD /U.S. DEPT. OF COMMERCE, BUREAU OF THE CENSUS [AND] U.S. DEPT. OF HOUSING AND URBAN DEVELOPMENT. Added/Corp United States. Bureau of the Census. United States. Dept. of Housing and Urban Development. **VFOAT** New One-Family Houses Sold; New One Family Houses Sold. (Jan. 1991)-. Government Publication.

Housing and Urban Development

English. mo. $25.00 US; $31.25 other. Superintendent of Documents, US Government Printing Office, Washington DC 20402. **Tel** (202)275-3328, FAX (202)786-2377. **LC** HD7293.A1; C65. **DD** 381/.45690837/0973021. *Formed by the union of Current Construction Reports. C25, New One-Family Houses Sold and for Sale, 0896-9256 and Current Construction Reports. C27, Price Index of New One-Family Houses Sold, 0896-6710.*

US
CURRENT HOUSING REPORTS. H-111, HOUSING VACANCIES AND HOMEOWNERSHIP. **Added/Corp** United States. Bureau of the Census. **VFOAT** Housing Vacancies and Homeownership. (1988)-. Government Publication. English. qt. $12.00 US; $15.00 other. Superintendent of Documents, US Government Printing Office, Washington DC 20402. **Tel** (202)275-3328, FAX (202)786-2377. Documents available from Documents on Demand. *Continues Current Housing Reports. H-111, Housing Vacancies, 0498-8469.*
Ind/Abst Am. Stat. Index.

US
CURRENT HOUSING REPORTS. H-111, HOUSING VACANCIES AND HOMEOWNERSHIP, ANNUAL STATISTICS. **Added/Corp** United States. Bureau of the Census. **VFOAT** Housing Vacancies and Homeownership, Annual Statistics. (1987)-. Government Publication. English. qt. $12.00 US; $15.00 other. Superintendent of Documents, US Government Printing Office, Washington DC 20402. **Tel** (202)275-3328, FAX (202)786-2377. **LC** HD7293.A1; C865. **DD** 363.5/1/0973021. *Continues Current Housing Reports. Series H-111, Housing Vacancies. Vacancy Rates and Characteristics of Housing in the United States, Annual Statistics.*
Ind/Abst Predicasts Forecasts.

US
CURRENT HOUSING REPORTS. H-131, CHARACTERISTICS OF APARTMENTS COMPLETED. **Added/Corp** United States. Bureau of the Census. United States. Dept. of Housing and Urban Development. **VFOAT** Characteristics of Apartments Completed. Government Publication. English. an. US Department of Commerce / Bureau of the Census, Data User Services Division, Customer Services, Washington DC 20233-0800. **Tel** (301)763-4100. **(Subscription address:** Superintendent of Documents, US Government Printing Office, Washington DC 20402.**)** **LC** HD7287.6.U5; U54a. **DD** 338.4/7/690831.

US/1048-7565
CURRENT HOUSING REPORTS. H-150, AMERICAN HOUSING SURVEY FOR THE UNITED STATES IN ... . [Curr. hous. rep., H-150 Am. hous. surv. U. S.]. **Added/Corp** United States. Bureau of the Census. United States. Dept. of Housing and Urban Development. Office of Policy Development and Research. **VFOAT** American Housing Survey for the United States in ... . (1985)-. Government Publication. English. be. US Department of Commerce, 14th Street & Constitution Avenue NW, Washington DC 20230. **Tel** (202)482-2000, FAX (202)482-3772. **LC** HD7293.A1; C862. **DD** 363.5/1/0973021. *Formed by the union of Current Housing Reports. Series H-150, Annual Housing Survey, United States and Regions. Part A, General Housing Characteristics, 0195-3699; Current Housing Reports. Series H-150, Annual Housing Survey, United States and Regions. Part B, Indicators of Housing and Neighborhood Quality by Financial Characteristics, 0882-0600; Current Housing Reports. Series H-150, Annual Housing Survey, United States and Regions. Part C, Financial Characteristics of the Housing Inventory, 0192-1894; Current Housing Reports. Series H-150, Annual Housing Survey, United States and Regions. Part D, Housing Characteristics of Recent Movers, 0192-1908; Current Housing Reports. Series H-150, Annual Housing Survey, United States and Regions. Part E, Urban and Rural Housing Characteristics, 0195-3575 and Current Housing Reports. Series H-150, Annual Housing Survey, United States and Regions. Part F, Energy-Related Housing Characteristics, 0736-9697.*

US
CURRENT HOUSING REPORTS. H-170, AMERICAN HOUSING SURVEY FOR THE CHICAGO METROPOLITAN AREA IN ... . **Added/Corp** United States. Bureau of the Census. United States. Dept. of Housing and Urban Development. Office of Policy Development and Research. **VFOAT** American Housing Survey for the Chicago Metropolitan Area in ... . (1987)-. Government Publication. English. ir. US Department of Commerce / Bureau of the Census, Data User Services Division, Customer Services, Washington DC 20233-0800. **Tel** (301)763-4100. **(Subscription address:** Superintendent of Documents, US Government Printing Office, Washington DC 20402.**)**

US
CURRENT HOUSING REPORTS. H-170, AMERICAN HOUSING SURVEY FOR THE PORTLAND METROPOLITAN AREA IN ... . **Added/Corp** United States. Bureau of the Census. United States. Dept. of Housing and Urban Development. Office of Policy Development and Research. **VFOAT** American Housing Survey for the Portland Metropolitan Area in ... . **VAT** Portland Metropolitan Area in ... . (1986)-. Government Publication. English. ir. US Department of Commerce / Bureau of the Census, Data User Services Division, Customer Services, Washington DC 20233-0800. **Tel** (301)763-4100. **(Subscription address:** Superintendent of Documents, US Government Printing Office, Washington DC 20402.**)** *Continues Current Housing Reports. H-170, Annual Housing Survey, Portland, Oreg.-Wash., Standard Metropolitan Statistical Area. Housing Characteristics for Selected Metropolitan Areas.*

US
CURRENT HOUSING REPORTS. H-170, ANNUAL HOUSING SURVEY, HONOLULU, HAWAII, STANDARD METROPOLITAN STATISTICAL AREA. HOUSING CHARACTERISTICS FOR SELECTED METROPOLITAN AREAS. See Housing and Urban Development-Abstracting, Bibliographies and Statistics.

US
CURRENT HOUSING REPORTS. H-170, ANNUAL HOUSING SURVEY, HOUSTON, TEX., STANDARD METROPOLITAN STATISTICAL AREA. HOUSING CHARACTERISTICS FOR SELECTED METROPOLITAN AREAS. See Housing and Urban Development-Abstracting, Bibliographies and Statistics.

US
CURRENT HOUSING REPORTS. H-170, ANNUAL HOUSING SURVEY, LOUISVILLE, KY.-IND. STANDARD METROPOLITAN STATISTICAL AREA. HOUSING CHARACTERISTICS FOR SELECTED METROPOLITAN AREAS. See Housing and Urban Development-Abstracting, Bibliographies and Statistics.

US
CURRENT HOUSING REPORTS. H-170, ANNUAL HOUSING SURVEY, NEW YORK, NY., STANDARD METROPOLITAN STATISTICAL AREA. HOUSING CHARACTERISTICS FOR SELECTED METROPOLITAN AREAS. See Housing and Urban Development-Abstracting, Bibliographies and Statistics.

US
CURRENT HOUSING REPORTS. H-170, ANNUAL HOUSING SURVEY, ORLANDO, FLA., STANDARD METROPOLITAN STATISTICAL AREA. HOUSING CHARACTERISTICS FOR SELECTED METROPOLITAN AREAS. **VFOAT** Annual Housing Survey, Orlando, Fla., Standard Metropolitan Statistical Area. Housing Characteristics for Selected Metropolitan Areas. Began with 1974. Government Publication. English. ir. US Department of Commerce / Bureau of the Census, Data User Services Division, Customer Services, Washington DC 20233-0800. **Tel** (301)763-4100. **(Subscription address:** Superintendent of Documents, US Government Printing Office, Washington DC 20402.**)**

US
CURRENT HOUSING REPORTS. H-170, ANNUAL HOUSING SURVEY, RALEIGH, N.C., STANDARD METROPOLITAN STATISTICAL AREA. HOUSING CHARACTERISTICS FOR SELECTED METROPOLITAN AREAS. **VFOAT** Annual Housing Survey, Raleigh, N.C., Standard Metropolitan Statistical Area. Housing Characteristics for Selected Metropolitan Areas. Began with 1976. Government Publication. English. te. US Department of Commerce / Bureau of the Census, Data User Services Division, Customer Services, Washington DC 20233-0800. **Tel** (301)763-4100. **(Subscription address:** Superintendent of Documents, US Government Printing Office, Washington DC 20402.**)**

US
CURRENT HOUSING REPORTS. H-170, ANNUAL HOUSING SURVEY, SACRAMENTO, CALIF., STANDARD METROPOLITAN STATISTICAL AREA. HOUSING CHARACTERISTICS FOR SELECTED METROPOLITAN AREA. See Housing and Urban Development-Abstracting, Bibliographies and Statistics.

US
CURRENT HOUSING REPORTS. H-170, ANNUAL HOUSING SURVEY, SEATTLE-EVERETT, WASH., STANDARD METROPOLITAN STATISTICAL AREA. HOUSING CHARACTERISTICS FOR SELECTED METROPOLITAN AREAS. **VFOAT** Annual Housing Survey, Seattle-Everett, Wash., Standard Metropolitan Statistical Area. Housing Characteristics for Selected Metropolitan Areas. Began with 1976. Government Publication. English. te. $9.00. US Department of Commerce / Bureau of the Census, Data User Services Division, Customer Services, Washington DC 20233-0800. **Tel** (301)763-4100. **(Subscription address:** Superintendent of Documents, US Government Printing Office, Washington DC 20402.**)** available on microfiche (Vols. for (1979)- distributed to depository libraries).
Desc: A sample survey of housing units in the United States.

US
CURRENT HOUSING REPORTS. H-170, ANNUAL HOUSING SURVEY, ST. LOUIS, MO-ILL., STANDARD METROPOLITAN STATISTICAL AREA. HOUSING CHARACTERISTICS FOR SELECTED METROPOLITAN AREAS. See Housing and Urban Development-Abstracting, Bibliographies and Statistics.

US
CURRENT HOUSING REPORTS. H171, SUPPLEMENT TO THE AMERICAN HOUSING SURVEY FOR SELECTED METROPOLITAN AREAS IN ... . **Added/Corp** United States. Bureau of the Census. United States. Dept. of Housing and Urban Development. Office of Policy Development and Research. **VFOAT** Supplement to the American Housing Survey for Selected Metropolitan Areas in ... . (1984)-. Government Publication. English. US Department of Commerce / Bureau of the Census, Data User Services Division, Customer Services, Washington DC 20233-0800. **Tel** (301)763-4100. **(Subscription address:** Superintendent of Documents, US Government Printing Office, Washington DC 20402.**)** **LC** HD7293.A1; A53. *Continues Current Housing Reports. Series H-171, Annual Housing Survey, Supplementary Reports. No. 1, Summary of Housing Characteristics for Selected Metropolitan Areas, 0194-0643.*

US/1056-7739
D.C. ZONING NEWS, THE. [D. C. zoning news]. **VFOAT** Zoning News; DC Zoning News. **VAT** District of Columbia Zoning News. Vol. 1, No. 1 (July 9, 1990)-. English. McGrath Publishing Company, PO Box 9001, Wilmington NC 28402. **LC** IN PROCESS. **DD** 333.

JA
DAITOSHIKEN YORAN: SHUTOKEN KINKI-KEN CHUBU-KEN. **Added/Corp** Japan. Kokudocho. Daitoshien Seibikyoku. (19??)-. Periodical. Japanese. Kokudocho Daitoshiken Seibikyoku, 6-19 Azabudai 1-chome Minato-ku, Tokyo Japan. **LC** HT395.J32; K364.

SW/0348-2863
DALARNAS MUSEUMS SERIE AV RAPPORTER. **Added/Corp** Dalarnas Museum. **VFOAT** Serie AV Rapporter. (197?)-. Monographic series. Swedish. ir. Price varies per volume. **LC** UNC.

FI/0359-7105
DATUTOP, DEPARTMENT OF ARCHITECTURE, TAMPERE UNIVERSITY OF TECHNOLOGY OCCASIONAL PAPERS. See Architecture.

US/0271-1753
DEPARTMENT OF HOUSING AND URBAN DEVELOPMENT ANNUAL REPORT TO CONGRESS ON INDIAN AND ALASKA NATIVE HOUSING AND COMMUNITY DEVELOPMENT PROGRAMS. [Dep. Hous. Urban Dev. annu. rep. Congr. Indian Alsk. native hous. co

mmunity dev. programs]. **Main/Corp** United States. Dept. of Housing and Urban Development. Office of the Special Assistant to the Secretary for Indian and Alaska Native Programs. 1978/79-. Government Publication. English. an. US Department of Housing and Urban Development, 451 Seventh Street SW, Washington DC 20401. **Tel** (202)708-0980, FAX (202)708-0299. **LC** E98.H58; U55A. **DD** 363.5/9. available on microfiche (Vols. for (1983-) distributed to depository libraries). ***Continues*** *Annual Report to Congress. Indian and Alaska Native Housing and Commodity Development Programs.*

NO/0800-2045
DERAP WORKING PAPERS. [DERAP work. pap.]. **VFOAT** Development Research and Action Programme Working Papers; DERAP Arbeidsnotater. (1963)-. Monographic series. Multiple languages. ir. **DD** 300.
Ind/Abst Geogr. Abstr. Human Geogr.; Int. Dev. Abstr.

II/0376-8260
DETAILED DEMAND FOR GRANTS OF HOUSING AND URBAN DEVELOPMENT DEPARTMENT. **Main/Corp** Jammu and Kashmir. Housing and Urban Development Dept. (19??)-. English. Ranbir Government Press / Housing and Urban Development, Jammu and Kashmir, Housing and Urban Development Department, Jammu India. **LC** HD7361.K3; J33a. **DD** 354/.54/600722.

●US/1062-5348
DEVELOPERS AND BUILDERS NEWS. [Dev. build. news]. Began in 1992. English. wk. $500.00. Durga Publications, 1409 North Cedar Crest Blvd., Box 105, Allentown PA 18104. **DD** 690. ***Continues*** *Residential Construction News.*

US
DEVELOPMENT SERIES. V. 1- Spring 1975-. English. $10.00. University of Washington College of Architecture and Urban Planning, Seattle WA 98195. **LC** HT166; .D42. **DD** 309.2/62/05.

FR
DIAGONAL. **Added/Corp** France. Direction de l'Amenagement Foncier et de l'Urbanisme. Groupe d'Etudes et de Recherches. France. Direction de l'Amenagement Foncier et de l'Urbanisme. (19??)-. Periodical. French. ir. 8.50F single issue. 64 rue de la Federation, 75015 Paris France. **LC** HT169.F7; D5. **DD** 309.2.

US/0363-0013
DIRECTORY : AREAWIDE PLANNING ORGANIZATIONS, STATE OF IOWA. **VFOAT** Areawide Planning Organizations, State of Iowa. Directory. English. Office for Planning and Programming, 523 East 12th Street, Des Moines IA 50319. **LC** HT393.I8; D56. **DD** 309.2/12/025777.

CN/0714-0541
DIRECTORY: NORTHERN ONTARIO. [North. Ont. dir.]. **Added/Corp** Ontario. Ministry of Northern Affairs. (1978)-. English. be. 4.50Can$. Ministry of Northern Development and Mines, Communications Services, 159 Cedar Street/6th Floor, Sudbury Ontario P3E 6A5 Canada. **Tel** FAX (705)670-7108. **LC** HT127; .D57. **DD** 361./0025/7131. **Circ:** 3,000.
Desc: Provides information on communities and Indian reserves located north of the French River, with a minimum population of twenty-five.

CN/0226-8558
DIRECTORY OF HOUSING CO-OPERATIVES. **See** Economics-Cooperatives.

US
DIRECTORY OF INDIANA LOCAL AND REGIONAL PLANNING AND DEVELOPMENT COMMISSIONS, A. **Added/Corp** Indiana. State Planning Services Agency. (19??)-. English. State Planning Services Agency, 143 West Market Street, Suite 300/Harrison Building, Indianapolis IN 46204. **LC** HT393.I6; D57. **DD** 352.9/6/025772.

US/0098-1095
DIRECTORY OF LOCAL HOUSING AUTHORITIES. **Added/Corp** United States. Dept. of Housing and Urban Development. Office of Housing Management. (19??)-. Directory. English. Housing Management, US Department of Housing and Urban Development, Washington DC 20410. **LC** HD7293.A49; H673c. **DD** 352/.75/0973.

US/0090-7812
DIRECTORY OF MISSOURI'S REGIONAL PLANNING SYSTEM, A. **Added/Corp** Missouri. Dept. of Community Affairs. Missouri. Dept. of Community Affairs. Office of Planning. (19??)-. Directory. English. Missouri Department of Community Affairs, 505 Missouri Boulevard, Jefferson City MO 65101. **LC** HT393.M8; D57. **DD** 309.2/5/025778.

US/0160-4856
DIRECTORY OF PUBLIC HOUSING AGENCIES. (DIRECTORY OF PUBLIC HOUSING AGENCIES / U.S. DEPARTMENT OF HOUSING AND URBAN DEVELOPMENT.). [Dir. public hous. agencies]. Government Publication. English. US Department of Housing and Urban Development, 451 Seventh Street SW, Washington DC 20401. **Tel** (202)708-0980, FAX (202)708-0299. **LC** HD7293.A1; D57. **DD** 352/.75/02573.

US/0094-5994
DIRECTORY: SUB-STATE PLANNING DISTRICTS IN OKLAHOMA. **Added/Corp** Oklahoma. Office of Community Affairs and Planning. **VFOAT** Sub-State Planning Districts in Oklahoma. (19??)-. Directory. English. Office of Community Affairs and Planning, 4901 North Lincoln, Oklahoma City OK 73105. **LC** HT393.O45; D56. **DD** 309.2/5/025766.

US/0196-8203
DISCLOSURE (CHICAGO). **See** Consumer Interests.

SW/0347-0962
DOCUMENT - SWEDISH COUNCIL FOR BUILDING RESEARCH. (DOCUMENT.). [Doc. - Swed. Counc. Build. Res.]. **Added/Corp** Statens rad for Byggnadsforskning (Sweden). (1975)-. Academic Scholarly Publication. English. Price varies per volume. Swedish Council for Building Research, Sankt Goransgatan 66, International Section, S-112 33 Stockholm Sweden. **Tel** 08/54 0640, FAX +46-8-6537462. **CODEN** DSCRDL. Documents available from Article Express International.
Ind/Abst Avery Index Archit. Period. Suppl. Colum. Univ. (1990-); Bioeng. Abstr.; Ei Page One; EMBASE; Eng. Index Annu.

CL
DONDEVIVIR : REVISTA DE PROPIEDADES. **VFOAT** Donde Vivir. (1980)-. Periodical. Spanish. mo. Edif Centro Nuevo, 2214 Of 145, Santiago Chile.

US/0145-1715
DOWNTOWN PLANNING & DEVELOPMENT ANNUAL. **VAT** Downtown Planning and Development Annual. 1977-. English. an. Downtown Research and Development, 270 Madison Avenue, New York NY 10016. **LC** HT175; .D68. **DD** 309.2/62/0973.

GW
DV MITTEILUNGEN. **Main/Corp** Deutscher Verband fur Wohnungswesen, Stadtebau und Raumplanung. Periodical. German. qt. Duncker und Humblot Verlag, Postfach 410329, D-12113 Berlin Germany. **Tel** 011 49 30 79000612, 011 49 30 79000613. ***Continues*** *Deutscher Verband fur Wohnungswesen, Stadtebau und Raumplanung. Mitteilungen.*

US/1054-0903
ECONOMIC DEVELOPMENT ABROAD. [Econ. dev. abroad]. (March 1986)-. Periodical. English. bm. CUED, 1730 K Street NW, Washington DC 20006. **DD** 338.

●US/1055-8284
ECONOMIC HOME OWNER, THE. (1993)-. Periodical. English. qt. $29.99. Publishing & Business Consultants, PO Box 75392, Los Angeles CA 90075. **Tel** (213)732-3477, FAX (213)732-9123. **ED** Andeson Napoleon Atia. **Ad Acc.** Full Page (B&W) $5750.00. Half Page (B&W) $3575.00. Full Page (Color) $8750.00 (2 color). Half Page (Color) $5500.00 (2 color). **Circ:** 168,000 total.
Desc: Of interest to those who live in houses, condos or apartments. Features articles on general health, finance and investments, home repair and maintenance.

IT/0422-5619
EDILIZIA POPOLARE. No. 1- 1954-. Periodical. Italian. Edilizia Popolare SRL, Quadrato della Concordia 9, 00144 Rome Italy. **Tel** 011 39 6 5925693, 94 OR 95. cum. index.
Ind/Abst Archit. Period. Index.

IT
EDILIZIA RESIDENZIALE PUBBLICA NOTIZ ANIACAP. Italian. L25000. Aniacap Palazzo della Civilta, Del Laboro, 00144 Rome Italy.

IT
EDILIZIA SCOLASTICA E CULTURALE. (Jan.-Apr. 1986)-. Periodical. Italian. Three times a year. L79500 Italy; L100000 other. Editoriale Finanz Le Monnier, PB 202, Via Meucci 2, 50015 Grassina Florence Italy. **Tel** 011 39 55 64910. **LC** WMLC 93/1744. ***Continues*** *Edilizia Scolastica.*

GR
EKISTIC INDEX OF PERIODICALS. **Added/Corp** Athens Center of Ekistics. **VFOAT** Ekistic Index. Vol. 18, No. 104 (Jan./June 1985)-. English. sa. $150.00. Athens Center of Ekistics, 24 Strat Syndesmou Street, Box 3471, Athens 102 10 Greece. **Tel** 011 30 1 3623216, FAX 011 30 1 3633395, telex 215227. **ED** M Connou. **LC** Z5942; .E38; HT151. **DD** 016.307. Index available. **Circ:** 200. ***Continues*** *Ekistic Index.*

GR/0013-2942
EKISTICS. [Ekistics]. **Added/Corp** Athenaiko Kentro Oikistikes. Doxiadis Associates. **VFOAT** Oikistikee. (1957)-. Periodical. English. bm. $80.00. Athens Center of Ekistics, 24 Strat Syndesmou Street, Box 3471, Athens 102 10 Greece. **Tel** 011 30 1 3623216, FAX 011 30 1 3633395, telex 215227. **ED** P. Psomopoulos. **LC** HN1; .E45. **NLM** W1 EK22. Index available. cum. index. **Circ:** 2,500. available on microfilm and microfiche from University Microfilms International (UMI). Documents available from The Genuine Article, UMI Article Clearinghouse, Documents on Demand. ***Continues*** *Tropical Housing and Planning Monthly Bulletin.*
Desc: Deals with all aspects of the problems in science of human settlements.
Ind/Abst Acad. Search (July 1993-); Appl. Soc. Sci. Index Abstr.; Archit. Period. Index; Curr. Contents Soc. Behav. Sci.; Curr. Geogr. Publ. (199?-); EMBASE (May-Aug. 1986, Jan.-June 1988, Jan. 1989-); Environ. Abstr.; Expand. Acad. Index (1989-); Geogr. Abstr. Phys. Geogr.; Geogr. Abstr. Human Geogr.; Highw. Res. Abstr.; INFO-SOUTH Abstr.; Int. Bibliogr. Sociol.; Int. Dev. Abstr.; Leis. Recreat. Tour. Abstr.; Middle East Abstr. Index; Newsp. Period. Abstr. (1991-); PAIS Int. Print; Res. Alert [Full Cov.]; Rural Dev. Abstr.; Soc. Sci. Source (Jul. 1993-); Soc. Sci. Index Fulltext (May 1986-) [Full Txt.]; World Agric. Econ.

UK
ENCYCLOPEDIA OF PLANNING LAW AND PRACTICE. **See** Law.

UK/0308-518X
ENVIRONMENT & PLANNING A. (ENVIRONMENT & PLANNING: A.). [Environ. plan. A]. **VAT** Environment and Planning A. Vol. 6 (Jan./Feb. 1974)-. Periodical. English. mo. £390.00 UK; $645.00 US. Pion Ltd., 207 Brondesbury Park, London NW2 5JN England. **Tel** 011 44 81 459 0066, FAX 011 44 81 451 6454, telex 94016265 PION G. **ED** A. Wilson. **LC** HT166; .E55. **DD** 309.2/5/05. Index available. **Bk Rev. Ad Acc. Pr Rev.** Documents available from The Genuine Article, UMI Article Clearinghouse, Documents on Demand. ***Continues in part*** *Environment & Planning, 0013-9173.*
Desc: Covers urban and regional problems and planning, ranging from human geography and planning through economics, sociology and politics, to civil engineering (for transport), mathematics and statistics.
Ind/Abst Acad. Search (Jan. 1993-); AGRICOLA; Arts Humanit. Citation Index [Select. Cov.]; Avery Index Archit. Period. Suppl. Colum. Univ.; Bibliogr. Carto.; Commun. Abstr.; Curr. Contents Soc. Behav. Sci.; Curr. Geogr. Publ. (199?-); Econ. Lit. Index; EMBASE (1990-); Energy Inf. Abstr.; Environ. Abstr.; Environ. Period. Bibliogr.; Expand. Acad. Index (1989-); Fish Rev.; Geogr. Abstr. Human Geogr.; Highw. Res. Abstr.; Int. Abstr. Oper. Res. [Select. Cov.]; Int. Bibliogr. Sociol.; Int. Civil Eng. Abstr.; Int. Dev. Abstr.; J. Econ. Lit. (1986); J. Plan. Lit.; Leis. Recreat. Tour. Abstr.; Mag. Search; Newsp. Period. Abstr. (1989-); Life Sci. Collect.; Popul. Index; Res. Alert [Full Cov.]; Sage Public Adm. Abstr.; Sage Urban Stud. Abstr; Soc. Sci. Cit. Index [Full Cov.]; Soc. Sci. Index; Soc. Sci. Index Fulltext (Nov. 1988-) [Full Txt.]; Soft. Abstr. Eng.; Transp. Res. Abstr.

UK/0265-8135
ENVIRONMENT AND PLANNING. B, PLANNING & DESIGN. **VFOAT** Planning & Design; Planning and Design. Vol. 10, No. 1 (March 1983)-. Periodical. English. bm. £137.00 UK; $235.00 US. Pion Ltd., 207 Brondesbury Park, London NW2 5JN England. **Tel** 011 44 81 459 0066, FAX 011 44 81 451 6454, telex 94016265 PION G. **LC** NA2005; .E58. **DD** 720/.5. **CODEN** EPBDEX. Index available. **Bk Rev. Ad Acc. Pr Rev.** Documents available from The Genuine Article. ***Continues*** *Environment & Planning. B, 0308-2164.*
Desc: Publishes research in urban systems and design science in the field of urban and regional planning, especially research on urban form and morphology, planning theories and processes, decisionmaking, and spatial analysis.
Ind/Abst Acad. Search (Jan. 1993-); Archit. Period. Index; Arts Humanit. Citation Index [Select. Cov.]; Avery Index Archit. Period. Suppl. Colum. Univ. (1989-); Bibliogr. Carto.; Curr. Contents Soc. Behav. Sci.; Geogr. Abstr. Phys. Geogr.; Geogr. Abstr. Human Geogr.; Highw. Res. Abstr.; Int. Abstr. Oper. Res. [Select. Cov.]; Int. Bibliogr. Sociol.; Int. Dev. Abstr.; J. Plan. Lit.; Res. Alert [Full Cov.]; Sage Urban Stud. Abstr; Soc. Sci. Cit. Index [Full Cov.].

US/1044-033X
ENVIRONMENTAL AND URBAN ISSUES. [Environ. urban issues]. **Added/Corp** Joint Center for Environmental and Urban Problems. **VFOAT** Environmental and Urban Issues ... Florida, the Nation, the World. Vol. 15, No. 2 (Jan. 1988)-. Periodical. English. qt (Jan., Apr., July, Oct.). Free to US & Canada. Environmental & Urban Issues, Florida Atlantic University, Florida International University, FAU/FIU Joint Center, 220 SE 2nd Ave. #709, Ft. Lauderdale FL 33301. **Tel** (305)355-5255. **ED** M. J. Matthews. **LC** HC107.F63; E543. **DD** 333.7/09759/05. Index Bound in First Issue.

Bk Rev. Circ: 3,000 (ctrl). ***Continues*** *Florida Environmental and Urban Issues, 0145-5885.*
Desc: Presents articles that contribute to the understanding and solution of problems relating to growth, the environment and urbanization.
Ind/Abst J. Plan. Lit.; PAIS Int. Print (1991-).

UK/0013-9270
ENVIRONMENTAL HEALTH (LONDON). (ENVIRONMENTAL HEALTH / INSTITUTION OF ENVIRONMENTAL HEALTH.). [Environ. health]. Vol. 89, No. 6 (June 1981)-. Academic Scholarly Publication. English. mo. £58.00. Institution of Environmental Health Officers, Chadwick House, Rushworth Street, London SE1 0RB England. **Tel** (01)928-6006. **ED** H J King. **Bk Rev. Ad Acc. Circ:** 7,500 (ctrl). available on microfilm from University Microfilms International (UMI). ***Continues*** *Environmental Health (Environmental Health Officers Association (London, England)).*
Desc: Covers all aspects of environmental health, housing, food hygiene, water and air pollution, health and safety, legal reports, and new products.
Ind/Abst EMBASE; Environ. Period. Bibliogr. (?-?); Food Sci. Technol. Abstr.; Life Sci. Collect.; Protozoolog. Abstr.; Saf. Health Work.

CN/0711-6780
ENVIRONMENTS. [Environments]. **Added/Corp** University of Waterloo. Faculty of Environmental Studies. Vol. 14, No. 1 (1982)-. Periodical. English (French). ir (3 issues per volume). 35.00Can$ (institutions), 27.00Can$ (individuals) Canada; 45.00Can$ (institutions), 35.00Can$ (individuals) other. Environments, Faculty of Environmental Studies, ES1/Room 325, University of Waterloo, Waterloo Ontario N2L 3G1 Canada. **Tel** (519)885-1211 ext. 3586, FAX (519)-746-2031, telex 069-55259. **ED** H. S. Coblentz. **DD** 711/.05. **CODEN** ENVREP. Index available (Bound in 20th issue.). cum. index. **Bk Rev. Circ:** 450. ***Continues*** *Contact, 0317-8625.*
Desc: Aims to present the outside readers to areas of knowledge in which university personnel and practitioners at Waterloo and elsewhere, and public officials, are currently engaged. Contains the knowledge and addresses of the people in the fields of environment, development and design.
Ind/Abst AQUAREF; Can. Index; Can. Period. Index; Ecol. Abstr.; Environ. Period. Bibliogr.; Geogr. Abstr. Phys. Geogr. (?-?); Geogr. Abstr. Human Geogr.; Int. Dev. Abstr.; Leis. Recreat. Tour. Abstr.; Middle East Abstr. Index; Rural Dev. Abstr.; World Agric. Econ.

US/0745-4821
EQUAL OPPORTUNITY IN HOUSING. **Added/Corp** United States Department of Housing and Urban Development. Prentice-Hall, Inc. (1971)-. Periodical. English. bw. $345.00. Prentice-Hall Law and Business, 270 Sylvan Avenue, Englewood Cliffs NJ 07632. **Tel** (800)223-0231, (201)894-8538, FAX (201)894-8666.

FR
EQUIPEMENT ENERGETIQUE DES LOGEMENTS NEUFS, L'. **VFOAT** Marche du Logement Neuf: Agglomerations et Zones Touristiques. French. an. Documentation Francaise, 29 Quai Voltaire, 75344 Paris Cedex 7 France. **Tel** 011 33 1 40157000, FAX 011 33 1 40157230, telex 204 826 DOCFRAN. **LC** TH4809.F8; E68. **DD** 696/.0944/021.

JA
ESP, ECONOMY SOCIETY POLICY. **Added/Corp** Keizai Kikaku Kyokai. Japan. Keizai Kikakucho. **VFOAT** Economy Society Policy. (19??)-. Periodical. Japanese (Japanese). mo. ¥250. Keizai Kikaku Kyokai, c/o Sanyo Building, 19-1 Shinbashi 1, Minato-ku 105, Tokyo Japan. **LC** HT395.J3; E18.

FR/0014-0481
ESPACES ET SOCIETES. **See** Architecture.

PE
ESPACIO. No. 1-. Periodical. Spanish. S/2,800. Editorial Val Carcel, Diez Canseco 146 Of 604, Lima 18 Peru. **LC** HT166; .E784.

BL
ESPACO & DEBATES. **VFOAT** Espaco e Debates; E&D. Vol. 1, No. 1 (Jan. 1981)-. Periodical. Portuguese. Three times a year. $50.00 (individuals), $60.00 (institutions). Nucleo Estudos Reg Urganosner, Rua Cajaiba 144, CEP 05025 Sao Paulo Spa Brazil. **LC** HT390; .E85.

UV
ESSOR RURAL. No. 1- July. 1973-. Periodical. French. 1,200. Secretariat Permanent, B P 7007, Ouagadougou Burkina Faso. **LC** HN810.U64; C63. **DD** 309.2/63/096625.

SP/0211-6871
ESTUDIOS TERRITORIALES. ***Title Change.*** **Added/Corp** Centro de Estudios de Ordenacion del Territorio y Medio Ambiente (Spain) Instituto del Territorio y Urbanismo (Spain). Vol. 1 (Jan./March 1981)-(19??). Periodical. Spanish. Three times a year. Ministerio de Obras Publicas y Transportes y Medio Ambiente, Paseo de la Castellana, 67, 28071 Madrid Spain. **Tel** 011 34 1 5977263, 5977266, FAX 011 34 1 5546351. **LC** HT395.S7; E85. cum. index. **Bk Rev. Pr Rev. Circ:** 1,250. ***Split into*** *Ciudad y Territorio* ***and*** *Ciudad y Territorio--Estudios Territoriales.*
Desc: Regional science, regional planning, land use planning, urbanism, urban planning and town planning.

CL/0250-7161
EURE. (EURE. REVISTA LATINOAMERICANA DE ESTUDIOS URBANO REGIONALES.). [EURE]. **Added/Corp** Universidad Catolica de Chile. Centro de Desarrollo Urbano y Regional. Consejo Latinoamericano de Ciencias Sociales. Comision de Desarrollo Urbano y Regional. **VFOAT** Revista Latinoamericana de Estudios Urbano Regionales. Vol. 1 (Oct. 1970)-. Periodical. Spanish. Three times a year. $37.00 The Americas; $30.00 others. Pontificia Universidad Catolica Chile, Casilla 114 D Alameda 340 213, Santiago Chile. **Tel** 011 56 2 2224516 ext 2417. **ED** Fernando Riveros. **LC** HT127.5; .E18. ***Continues*** *Cuadernos de Desarrollo Urbano Regional.*
Ind/Abst Avery Index Archit. Period. Suppl. Colum. Univ. (June 1990); HAPI Hisp. Am. Period. Index; Int. Bibliogr. Sociol.; PAIS Int. Print.

BE
EUROPA DES CAPITALES. **Main/Corp** Union of the Capitals of the European Community. **VFOAT** Europa of the Capitals. V. 1- 1973-. Multiple languages (English, French, Italian, Dutch and German). Unity of the Capitals of European Community, 10 rue du Chene, Bruxelles Belgium. **LC** HT131; .U54A.

●UK/0965-4313
EUROPEAN PLANNING STUDIES. **Added/Corp** Association of European Schools of Planning. Vol. 1, No. 1 (1993)-. Periodical. English. qt (Mar., Jun., Sep., Dec.). £120.00. Carfax Publishing Company, PO Box 25 Abingdon, Oxfordshire OX14 3UE England. **Tel** 011 44 235 555335, FAX (0279)31067, telex 817484. **(Subscription address:** US and Canada/ PO Box 2025, Dunnellon, FL 34430-2025; telephone:(904)489-6996) **LC** HT395.E85; E855. **[CCC].** available on microfiche.
Desc: Provides a forum for ideas and information about spatial development processes and policies in Europe. Published articles of a theoretical, empirical and policy-relevant nature and is particularly concerned with integrating knowledge of processes with practical policy proposals, implementation and evaluation.

UK/0969-7764
EUROPEAN URBAN AND REGIONAL STUDIES. (19??)-. Periodical. English. Four times a year. £99.00 Europe; £107.00 Other (Institutions). Longman Group Ltd., Fourth Avenue, Longman House, Harlow Essex CM19 5SR England. **Tel** 011 44 279 429655, FAX 011 44 279 431059, telex 81259.

US/0161-9535
EVALUATION OF THE URBAN HOMESTEADING DEMONSTRATION PROGRAM, ANNUAL REPORT. **Main/Corp** United States. Dept. of Housing and Urban Development. Office of Policy Development and Research. 1st- 1977-. English. an. Iowa Department of Corrections, 523 East 12th Street, Capitol Annex, Des Moines IA 50319. **Tel** (515)281-4811, FAX (515)281-7345. **LC** HD7293.A49; H673D. **DD** 353.008/65.

US/0098-6798
EXAMINATION OF FINANCIAL STATEMENTS OF THE PENNSYLVANIA AVENUE DEVELOPMENT CORPORATION. **See** Public Administration.

CN/0318-5125
EXPANSION DES CITES ET VILLES. V. 2- 1972-. Periodical. French. Societe D'Edition Montrealaise, Bureau 202, 8602 Est, Rue Sherbrooke, Montreal Quebec H1L 1B7 Canada. **DD** 971.4/04.

US/0191-2208
EXPENSE ANALYSIS, CONDOMINIUMS, COOPERATIVES, & PLANNED UNIT DEVELOPMENTS. **See** Real Estate.

US/0091-4932
F.H.A. HOMES. (FHA HOMES.). **Added/Corp** United States. Federal Housing Administration. United States. Dept. of Housing and Urban Development. United States. Dept. of Housing and Urban Development. Housing Information & Statistics Division. United States. Dept. of Housing and Urban Development. Information Systems Division. **VFOAT** Data for States and Selected Areas on Characteristics of FHA Operations Under Section 203. **VAT** Federal Home Administration Homes. (19??)-. English. an. US Department of Housing and Urban Development Federal Housing Commissioner, 451 Seventh Street SW, Room 9100, Washington DC 20410. **Tel** (202)708-3600, FAX (202)755-2580. **LC** HD7293.A49; H69a. **DD** 363.5/8. available on microfiche (Vols. for (1983-) distributed to depository libraries).

US
F H A TRENDS OF HOME MORTGAGE CHARACTERISTICS. **Main/Corp** United States. Federal Housing Administration. Government Publication. English. qt. US Department of Housing and Urban Development, 451 Seventh Street SW, Washington DC 20401. **Tel** (202)708-0980, FAX (202)708-0299. Documents available from Documents on Demand.
Ind/Abst Am. Stat. Index.

HU/0237-4323
FALU, A. [Falu]. (1985)-. Newsletter. Hungarian. qt. $20.00. Agroinform Kiado es Nyomda Kft., Kitaibel pal u. 4, 1024 Budapest II, Hungary. **Tel** 0135-1927, FAX 135-0344. **ED** Tibor Ferenczi. **UDC** 71.
Ind/Abst Agric. Eng. Abstr.

CN/0229-3110
FEEDBACK (CALGARY). (FEEDBACK : THE CALGARY REGIONAL PLANNING COMMISSION NEWSLETTER.). [Feedback]. **Added/Corp** Calgary Regional Planning Commission. Vol. 1, No. 1 (May 1980)-. Periodical. English. qt. Calgary Regional Planning Commission, 4303 11th Street South East, Calgary Alberta T2G 4X1 Canada. **DD** 711/.3/0971233. ***Continues*** *Calgary Regional Planning Commission News, 0229-3102.*

US/0275-1267
FHA HOMES. DATA FOR STATES AND SELECTED AREAS ON CHARACTERISTICS OF FHA OPERATIONS UNDER SECTION 245, GRADUATED PAYMENT MORTGAGE PROGRAM. (FHA HOMES. DATA FOR STATES AND SELECTED AREAS ON CHARACTERISTICS OF FHA OPERATIONS UNDER SECTION 245, GRADUATED PAYMENT MORTGAGE PROGRAM / U.S. DEPARTMENT OF HOUSING AND URBAN DEVELOPMENT.). **VFOAT** Data for States and Selected Areas on Characteristics of FHA Operations Under Section 245, Graduated Payment Mortgage Program. **VAT** Federal Housing Administration Homes. Data for States and Selected Areas on Characteristics of Federal Housing Administration Operations Under Section Two Hundred Forty-Five, Graduated Payment Mortgage Program. Government Publication. English. US Department of Housing and Urban Development, 451 Seventh Street SW, Washington DC 20401. **Tel** (202)708-0980, FAX (202)708-0299. **LC** HD7293.A1; U533A. **DD** 363.5/0973. available on microfiche (Vols. for (1983-) distributed to depository libraries).

US/0145-5648
FHA MONTHLY REPORT OF OPERATIONS. HOME MORTGAGE PROGRAMS. **VFOAT** Home Mortgage Programs. Oct. 1976-. Government Publication. English. qt. US Department of Housing and Urban Development, 451 Seventh Street SW, Washington DC 20401. **Tel** (202)708-0980, FAX (202)708-0299. ***Continues*** *FHA Monthly Report of Operations. Home Mortgage Programs, 0145-5648.*

US/0145-5656
FHA MONTHLY REPORT OF OPERATIONS. PROJECT MORTGAGE INSURANCE PROGRAMS. **VFOAT** Project Mortgage Insurance Programs. Government Publication. English. mo. US Department of Housing and Urban Development, 451 Seventh Street SW, Washington DC 20401. **Tel** (202)708-0980, FAX (202)708-0299. ***Continues*** *FHA Monthly Report of Operations. Project Mortgage Insurance Programs, 0145-5656.*

US
FIELD PROCEDURES FOR MONITORING RELOCATION AND REAL PROPERTY ACQUISITION ACTIVITIES. Government Publication. English. ir. US Department of Housing and Urban Development, 451 Seventh Street SW, Washington DC 20401. **Tel** (202)708-0980, FAX (202)708-0299.

US
FINANCIAL OPERATIONS AND ACCOUNTING PROCEDURES FOR INSURED MULTIFAMILY PROJECTS. Government Publication. English. US Department of Housing and Urban Development, 451 Seventh Street SW, Washington DC 20401. **Tel** (202)708-0980, FAX (202)708-0299. ***Continues*** *Handbook of FHA Requirements Governing Fiscal Operations, Accounting, and Financial Reports for Multifamily Housing Projects.*

US/0145-1081
FINANCIAL STATEMENTS - DEPARTMENT OF HOUSING AND URBAN DEVELOPMENT, OFFICE OF FINANCE AND ACCOUNTING. (FINANCIAL STATEMENTS AS OF ...). **Main/Corp** United States. Dept. of Housing and Urban Development. Office of Finance and Accounting. Government Publication.

English. sa. US Department of Housing and Urban Development, 451 Seventh Street SW, Washington DC 20401. **Tel** (202)708-0980, FAX (202)708-0299.

US
FLORIDA HOUSING LAND ACQUISITION AND SITE DEVELOPMENT AND TRUST FUND... ANNUAL REPORT TO GOVERNOR ... . **Main/Corp** Florida. Dept. of Veteran and Community Affairs. English. an. Florida Department of Veteran and Community Affairs, 2571 Executive Circle East, Tallahassee FL 32301. **LC** HD7288.78 .U52; F573A. **DD** 353.97590086/5045.

US/0279-0297
FLORIDA PLANNING (TALLAHASSEE, FLA. : 1981). (FLORIDA PLANNING.). V. 1, No. 1 (April 1981)-. Periodical. English. mo. $15.00. Florida Planning, c/o Oliver Kerr, Metro Dade County Planning/Suite 1220, Miami FL 33128.

CN/0712-2691
FOCUS (RED DEER). (FOCUS : RED DEER REGIONAL PLANNING COMMISSION NEWSLETTER.). [Focus]. **Added/Corp** Red Deer Regional Planning Commission. Vol. 1, No. 1 (Mar. 1981)-. Newsletter. English. Four times a year. Free. Red Deer Advocate, 2950 Bremner Avenue, Red Deer Alberta T4N JG3 Canada. **Tel** (403)343-2400. **ED** Charles Dack. **DD** 711/.3/0971233. **Circ:** 900.
Desc: Describe and publicize land use planning work of the Red Deer Regional Planning Commission.

US/1056-5159
FORECAST OF HOUSING ACTIVITY. (FORECAST OF HOUSING ACTIVITY / NAHB.). [Forecast hous. act.]. **Added/Corp** National Association of Home Builders (U.S.) Economics, Mortgage Finance, and Housing Policy Division. (19??)-. Periodical. English. mo. $690.00 (NAHB members), $750.00 (nonmembers). National Association of Home Builders, 15th and M Street NW, Washington DC 20005. **Tel** (202)822-0203. **LC** HD7293.A1; F67. **DD** 333.33/0973/05.

GW/0341-244X
FORSCHUNGEN ZUR RAUMENTWICKLUNG. German. Bundesforschungsanstalt fur Landeskunde und Raumordnung, Informationszentrum Raum und Bau der Fraunhofer-Gesellschaft, Nobelstrasse 12, 7000 Stuttgart 80 Germany. **Tel** (0711)68 68-500. ***Supersedes*** *Institut fur Raumordnung Mitteilungen, 0537-8060.*
Desc: Monographs on regional and urban planning, collected reports on the work of the Federal Research Institute for regional geography and regional planning.

GW/0515-9083
FORSCHUNGS- UND SITZUNGSBERICHTE. **Main/Corp** Akademie fur Raumforschung und Landesplanung (Hannover, Germany). Vol. 1 (1950)-. Periodical. German. Akademie fur Raumforschung und Landesplanung, Hohenzollernstrasse 11, W-3000 Hannover 1 Germany. **Tel** (0577)34842, FAX (0577)348247. **Bk Rev. Ad Acc. Circ:** 500.

GW
FORSCHUNGSDOKUMENTATION RAUMORDNUNG, STADEBAU, WOHNUNGSWESEN. ***Ceased.*** **Added/Corp** Bundesforschungsanstalt fur Landeskunde und Raumordnung. Fraunhofer-Gesellschaft. Informationsverbundzentrum Raum und Bau. (1978)-(19??). German. mo. Bundesforschungsanstalt fur Landeskunde und Raumordnung, Informationszentrum Raum und Bau der Fraunhofer-Gesellschaft, Nobelstrasse 12, 7000 Stuttgart 80 Germany. **Tel** (0711)68 68-500. **LC** Z7164.R33; F68; HT395.G4. **Bk Rev. Circ:** 200 (ctrl). available on an online database. ***Supersedes*** *Dokumentation Laufender Forschungsarbeiten zur Raumentwicklung.*
Desc: Research documentation on regional planning, town planning and housing. Documents cover some 1,000 current and completed research projects.

US/0741-3483
FROM THE STATE CAPITALS. URBAN DEVELOPMENT. ***Title Change.*** [From state cap., Urban dev.]. **VFOAT** Urban Development. (Jan. 1984)-?. Periodical. English. mo. Wakeman Walworth Inc., 300 North Washington Street #204, Alexandria VA 22314. **Tel** (703)549-8606. **ED** Emily Novick. **[CCC].** ***Continues*** *From the State Capitals. Housing and Redevelopment (New Haven, Conn.), 0734-1075.* ***Continued by*** *From the State Capitals Economic Development.*
Desc: Grants, renewal and development incentives, bonding and loan programs, mortgage laws, housing codes, condominium conversion regulations, rent control guidelines.

NE
GEMEENTESTEM, DE. (19??)-. Dutch. sm (24 issues). Fl214.00. Samson Bedrijfsinformatie, Postbus 4, 2400 HA Alphen Rij Netherlands. **Tel** 011 31 1 72066633. **(Subscription address:** Intermedia BV, Postbus 4, 2400 MA Alphen Rijn Netherlands.**)** **LC** WMLC L 83/8482.

GW
GEMEINDEVERZEICHNIS FUER NIEDERSACHSEN. **Added/Corp** Niedersachsisches Landesverwaltungsamt. (19??)-. German. Nieders. Landeramt fuer Statisik, Postfach 44 60, 30044 Hanover Germany. **Tel** 0511 98 98 321, FAX 0511 98 98 400. **LC** HT137; .G43. **DD** 309.2/62/094359. **Bk Rev. Circ:** 2,000. ***Continues*** *Amtliches Gemeindeverzeichnis fuer Niedersachsen.*
Desc: Names of all towns and villages in lower saxony.

US/0069-9047
GENERAL SERIES - CENTER FOR REAL ESTATE AND URBAN ECONOMIC STUDIES, SCHOOL OF BUSINESS ADMINISTRATION, UNIVERSITY OF CONNECTICUT. **See** Real Estate.

NO/0435-3684
GEOGRAFISKA ANNALER. SERIES B, HUMAN GEOGRAPHY. [Geogr. ann., Ser. B]. (1965)-. Periodical. English. Three times a year. Kr490.00, $85.00. Scandinavian University Press, PO Box 2959 Toeyen, N 0608 Oslo 6 Norway. **Tel** 011 47 2 2575400, FAX 011 47 2 2575353, telex 71896 UROR N. **(Subscription address:** Scandinavian University Press, 200 Meacham Ave., Elmont NY 11003.**)** **ED** Goeran Hoppe. **CODEN** GAHGAJ. Index available. **Bk Rev. Ad Acc. Pr Rev. Circ:** 900 (ctrl). Documents available from BIOSIS Document Express. ***Continues in part*** *Geografiska Annaler.*
Desc: Presenting research within the field of human geography.
Ind/Abst Anthropol. Lit.; Bibliogr. Carto.; Biol. Abstr.; Curr. Geogr. Publ. (199?-); Geogr. Abstr. Human Geogr.; Int. Dev. Abstr.; Leis. Recreat. Tour. Abstr.; Rural Dev. Abstr.; World Agric. Econ.

US/0146-5295
GEORGIA MUNICIPAL YEARBOOK, THE. English. an. Georgia Municipal Association, 201 Pryor Street Southwest, Atlanta GA 30303. **Tel** (404)688-0472. **LC** HD4606.G4; G46. **DD** 363.5.

UK/0264-6315
GREATER LONDON INTELLIGENCE JOURNAL. [Greater Lond. intell. j.]. Began with June 1977. Periodical. English. ir. £2.50. GLC South Bank Bookshop, County Hall, London SE1 7PB England. **LC** HT169.G72; L645. **DD** 307/.12/09421. ***Continues*** *Greater London Intelligence Quarterly, 0305-7747.*
Ind/Abst Br. Humanit. Index.

US
GROUP PRACTICE FACILITIES. Government Publication. English. US Department of Housing and Urban Development, 451 Seventh Street SW, Washington DC 20401. **Tel** (202)708-0980, FAX (202)708-0299.

US/0017-4815
GROWTH AND CHANGE. (GROWTH AND CHANGE : A JOURNAL OF URBAN AND REGIONAL POLICY.). [Growth change]. **Added/Corp** University of Kentucky. College of Business and Economics. Vol. 1 (Jan. 1970)-. Periodical. English. qt. $32.00 (individual), $67.00 US(institutions); $47.00 (individual), $82.00 (institution)other. Growth and Change, 301 Mathews Building, University of Kentucky, Lexington KY 40506-0047. **Tel** (606)257-3827, (606)257-7675. **ED** Richard E. Gift & Thomas R. Leinbach. **LC** HT390; .G74. **DD** 301.3/72/05. **CODEN** GRCHDH. **[CCC].** Index available. cum. index. **Bk Rev. Ad Acc. Pr Rev. Circ:** 1,000. available on microfilm and microfiche from University Microfilms International (UMI). Documents available from The Genuine Article, UMI Article Clearinghouse.
Desc: Refereed journal of urban and regional issues. Research from economists, policy analysts, geographers, etc., on issues in regional economics.
Ind/Abst ABC POL SCI; ABI/INFORM Glob. Ed.; ABI Inform Ondisc (July 1976-); ABI/INFORM Ondisc: Expr. Ed.; Acad. Search (July 1993-); AGRICOLA [Select. Cov.]; Bus. Index (1985-); Coal Abstr.; Curr. Contents Soc. Behav. Sci.; Econ. Lit. Index; Energy Res. Abstr. (Aug. 1977-); Expand. Acad. Index (1992-); Gen. BusinessFile (1985-); Gen. Period. Index (1985-); Geogr. Abstr. Human Geogr.; Health Saf. Sci. Abstr.; INFO-SOUTH Abstr.; Int. Dev. Abstr.; Int. Polit. Sci. Abstr.; J. Econ. Lit.; J. Plan. Lit.; Leis. Recreat. Tour. Abstr.; Mag. Search; Middle East Abstr. Index; Newsp. Period. Abstr. (1992-); PAIS Int. Print (1991); Pollut. Abstr. Indexes; Popul. Index (?-?); Res. Alert [Full Cov.]; Rural Dev. Abstr.; Sage Urban Stud. Abstr; Soc. Sci. Cit. Index [Full Cov.]; Soils Fert.; Trade Ind. Index; UMI ABI/Inform--Bus. Period. Ondisc (Spring 1988-) [Full Txt.]; U.S. Polit. Sci. Doc.; Urban Aff. Abstr.; World Agric. Econ.

CN
GUIDE DES RESSOURCES PROFESSIONNELLES EN URBANISME. (GUIDE ES RESSOURCES PROFESSIONNELLES EN URBANISME / CORPORATION PROFESSIONNELLE DES URBANISTES DU QUEBEC.). [Guide ressour. prof. urban.]. **Main/Corp** Corporation Professionnelle des Urbanistes du Quebec. (1988)-. French. an. 16.00Can$. Corporation Professionnelle des Urbanistes du Quebec, 85 St. Paul Street West, 4th Floor / Room B5, Montreal Quebec H2Y 3V4 Canada. **Tel** (514)849-1177. **DD** 711/.4/025714.

US/0889-051X
GUIDE TO FLORIDA RETIREMENT LIVING. **See** Senior Citizens.

CN/0700-5040
HABITABEC. V. 1- April 23, 1976-. Periodical. French (English). wk. $54.17. Habitabec, 8620 rue Berri, Montreal Quebec H2P 2G4 Canada. **Tel** (514)389-5944. **DD** 338.4/7/69009714.

UK/0197-3975
HABITAT INTERNATIONAL. [Habitat int.]. **Added/Corp** World Environment and Resources Council. Vol. 2, No. 5/6 (1977)-. Academic Scholarly Publication. English. qt. $574.00 The Americas; £385.00 other. Pergamon Press, An Imprint of Elsevier Science Ltd., The Boulevard, Langford Lane, Kidlington, Oxford OX5 1GB United Kingdom. **Tel** 011 44 865 843000, 011 44 865 843699, FAX 011 44 865 843010. **(Subscription address:** Elsevier Science Ltd. Oxford Fulfillment Centre, PO Box 800, Kidlington, Oxford OX5 1DX United Kingdom.**)** **ED** O. H. Koenigsberger, S. Groak, and B. Bernstein. **LC** GF101; .H28. **DD** 307.76. **[CCC]. Pr Rev.** available on microfilm and microfiche from University Microfilms International (UMI). Documents available from Documents on Demand. ***Continues*** *Habitat, 0361-3690.*
Ind/Abst Curr. Aware. Biol. Sci., CABS; Curr. Contents Soc. Behav. Sci.; EMBASE; Energy Inf. Abstr.; Energy Res. Abstr. (June 1980-); Environ. Abstr.; Environ. Period. Bibliogr.; Geogr. Abstr. Human Geogr.; GeoRef; Int. Dev. Abstr.; Int. Labour Doc.; J. Ferrocement; Life Sci. Collect.; Sage Fam. Stud. Abstr. (?-?); Sage Race Relat. Abstr.; Sage Urban Stud. Abstr; Soc. Plann. Policy Dev. Abstr.; Sociol. Abstr.

KE/0251-7205
HABITAT NEWS. [Habitat news]. **Added/Corp** United Nations Centre for Human Settlements. Vol. 1, No. 1 (March 1979)-. Periodical. English (French and Spanish). Three times a year (includes NGO News as insert). Free on request. UNCHS / United Nations Centre for Human Settlements (Habitat), Chief, Information, Audio-Visual and Documentation Division, PO Box 30030, Nairobi Kenya. **Tel** 011 254 2 621234, FAX 011 254 2 520724, telex 22996. **ED** Ellen Kitonga. **LC** HD7285; .H28. **DD** 307/.05. Index available. cum. index. **Bk Rev. Circ:** 9,500. ***Continues*** *Human Settlements, 0046-8231;* ***Absorbed*** *Habitat Foundation News; Vision Habitat News.*
Desc: Research and development, technical co-operation, training and public information in the human settlements field.
Ind/Abst Avery Index Archit. Period. Suppl. Colum. Univ. (1984-); Int. Dev. Abstr. (?-?); Middle East Abstr. Index.

●FR
HABITAT : SUPPLEMENT ... AUX CAHIERS DE L'IAURIF. **Added/Corp** Institut d'Amenagement et d'Urbanisme de la Region d'Ile-de-France. **VFOAT** Cahiers de l'Institut d'Amenagement et d'Urbanisme de la Region d'Ile-de-France; Supplement ... au Cahiers de l'IAURIF; Cahiers de l'IAURIF. No 1 (April 1992)-. Periodical. French. qt.

SZ
HABITATION. ***Suspended.*** **Added/Corp** Union Suisse pour l'Amelioration du Logement. Vol. 1 (1929)-(Oct. 1991). Periodical. English. mo. L'Habitation, Clos de Bulle 8, 1004 Lausanne Switzerland. **Tel** 011 41 21 234582.

UK/0952-8156
HABS. HOUSING ABSTRACTS. [HABS, Hous. abstr.]. **VFOAT** Housing Abstracts. (1987)-. English. sm. £80.00. London Research Centre, 81 Black Prince Road, London SE1 7SZ England. **Tel** 011 44 71 627 9666, FAX 011 44 71 627 9674. **ED** Judith Barton. **DD** 016.3635. Index available. cum. index. **Circ:** 500. available on an online database.
Desc: Provides abstracts of press comment, reports and journal articles on housing issues.

US
HANDBOOK AND REPORT TO THE COMMISSIONERS - BUFFALO MUNICIPAL HOUSING AUTHORITY. (HANDBOOK & REPORT TO THE COMMISSIONERS.). **Main/Corp** Buffalo Municipal Housing Authority. **VFOAT** BMHA Handbook & Report to the Commissioners. 1st-1976-. Periodical. English. Buffalo Municipal Housing Authority, 901 City Hall, Buffalo NY 14202.

US
HARVARD CITY PLANNING STUDIES. Vol. 1 (1930)-. Monographic series. English. ir. Price varies per volume. Harvard University Press, 79 Garden Street, Cambridge MA 02138. **Tel** (617)496-1344, (800)448-2242.

US
HARVARD STUDIES IN URBAN HISTORY. (19??)-. Monographic series. English. ir. Price varies per volume. Harvard University Press, 79 Garden Street, Cambridge MA 02138. **Tel** (617)496-1344, (800)448-2242.

CN/0848-8622
HEMSON PLANNING & DEVELOPMENT REPORT. [Hemson plan. dev. rep.]. **VFOAT** Hemson Planning and Development Report. Vol. 7, No. 16 (Sept. 13, 1989)-. Periodical. English. Two issues per month (except July and August). 400.00Can$. Hemson Consulting Ltd, 30 St Patrick Street, Suite 1000, Toronto Ontario, M5T 3A3 Canada. **Tel** 9416)593-5090, FAX (416)595-7144. **DD** 307.1/2/09713541. ***Continues*** *Planning and Development Hotline, 0828-1203.*

JA
HIKAKU TOSHISHI KENKYU. VFOAT Comparative Urban History Review. V. 1, No. 1 (June 1982)-. Periodical. Japanese (English, German and French). sa. ¥5000 Japan; $35.00 US. Hikaku Toshishi Kenkyukai, c/o Rikkyo Daigaku, Keizaigakubu Kenkyushitsu Nishi, Ikebukuro 3-chome Toshima-ku, Tokyo 171 Japan. **Tel** 03-985-2342. **ED** T Kato, Y Morita, K Ogura, T Sakata, K Takahashi, K Ugawa, M Uozumi, and A Yoshie. **LC** HT151; .H48. **Bk Rev. Circ:** 250 (ctrl).

US/1051-5852
HISTORIC NEIGHBORHOODS NEWSLETTER. [Hist. neighb. newsl.]. **Added/Corp** Historic Neighborhoods Foundation (Boston, Mass.). (Fall 1989)-. Newsletter. English. qt (4 issues). Comes with Historic Neighborhoods Foundation membership. Historic Neighborhoods Foundation, 2 Boylston Street, Boston MA 02116. **Tel** (617)426-1885. **DD** 720. ***Continues*** *Newsletter (Historic Neighborhoods Foundation (Boston, Mass.) : 1989).*

JA
HITO TO KOKUDO. Added/Corp Japan. Kokudocho. **VFOAT** People and National Land Policy. Vol. 1 (1952)-. Periodical. Japanese. bm. ¥450. Kokudo Keikaku Kyokai, 21 Kotohiracho, Minato-ku 105 Tokyo Japan. **LC** HT395.J3; H56.

US/1053-0762
HOME GROUND. (HOME GROUND : THE JOURNAL OF THE HOME HABITAT SOCIETY.). [Home ground]. **Added/Corp** Home Habitat Society. Vol. 1, No. 1 (Winter 1991)-. Periodical. English. qt. $20.00 (includes membership). Home Habitat Society, 11824 Taneytown Pike, Taneytown MD 21787. **DD** 333.

US
HOMEOWNERSHIP FOR LOWER-INCOME FAMILIES, SECTION 235 (I), BASIC INSTRUCTIONS. Government Publication. English. ir. US Department of Housing and Urban Development, 451 Seventh Street SW, Washington DC 20401. **Tel** (202)708-0980, FAX (202)708-0299.

UK/0018-4233
HOMES AND GARDENS INCORPORATING HOME. (1919)-. Periodical. English. mo. £25.00 (one year), £42.50 (two year), £56.25 (three year) UK; $53.60 (one year), $89.60 (two year), $118.60 (three year) US and Canada; £76.00 (one year), £129.20 (two year), £171.00 (three year) Middle East, Africa, South America, South Asia; £34.00 (one year), £57.80 (two year), £76.50 (three year) other. Reed Business Publishing / West Sussex, England, Perrymount Road, Haywards Heath, West Sussex RH16 3DH England. **Tel** 011 44 81 6523500. **[CCC].**

US/0740-7211
HOMES INTERNATIONAL. *Suspended.* [Homes int.]. Periodical. English. bm. $26.75. Holiday Home International Corporation, 51 Weaver Street, Greenwich CT 06830. ***Continues*** *Holiday Homes International, 0149-0257.*

US
HOMEWORKS. English. Twenty-six times a year. $200.00. National Community Development Association, 522 21st Street NW Suite 120, Washington DC 20006. **Tel** (202)293-7587, FAX (202)887-5546.

UK
HOUSE BUILDER. Added/Corp House Builders' Federation (Great Britain). **VFOAT** House Builder and Estate Developer; House Builder & Estate Developer. Vol. 39, No. 3 (Mar. 1980)-. Periodical. English. Ten times a year. £60.00 UK; £90.00 other. House Builder Publication Ltd., 82 New Cavendish Street, London W1M 8AD England. **Tel** 011 44 71 580-5588. **ED** Phillip Cooke. **LC** HD9715.A1; F423. **DD** 338.4/76908/0941. **Ad Acc. Circ:** 23,000 (ctrl). ***Continues*** *Housebuilder.*
Desc: Politics and economics of private sector house building market. Marketing of new homes. Methods and materials, land supply problem and urban renewal.
Ind/Abst Archit. Period. Index.

US/0018-6554
HOUSING AFFAIRS LETTER. [Hous. aff. lett.]. **VFOAT** Housing Affairs. (19??)-. Periodical. English. wk (50 issues). $373.00. CD Publications, 8204 Fenton Street, Silver Spring MD 20910. **Tel** (800)666-6380, (301)588-6380, FAX (301)588-6385. **ED** Bryon Fielding. **LC** HD7293.A1; H688. **DD** 333. Index available.
Desc: Complete coverage of housing news, legislation, regulations and the mortgage and construction markets.

AT
HOUSING AND CONSTRUCTION QUARTERLY. Mar. 1975-. Periodical. English. Australian Government Publishing Service, GPO Box 84, Canberra ACT 2601 Australia. **Tel** 011 61 6 2954411, FAX 011 61 6 2954455. **LC** HD7379.A3; H58. **DD** 301.5/4/0994. ***Continues*** *Housing Quarterly.*

US/0091-5939
HOUSING & DEVELOPMENT REPORTER. [Hous. dev. report.]. **Added/Corp** Bureau of National Affairs (Washington, D.C.). **VFOAT** Housing and Development Reporter. No. 1 (May 16, 1973)-. English. wk. $919.95 US and Canada; $1,186.45 other. Warren Gorham & Lamont Inc., Park Square Building, 31 St. James Avenue, Boston MA 02116-4112. **Tel** (617)423-2020, (800)950-1207, FAX (617)423-2026. **ED** Bruce Lane, Chuck Edson and Barry Jacobs. **LC** KF5729.A1; H68. **DD** 344/.73/063635. **[CCC].**
Desc: Covers current legislative developments, administrative actions and judicial opinions affecting housing, urban affairs and community development.

UK/0018-6589
HOUSING & PLANNING REVIEW. (HOUSING AND PLANNING REVIEW : THE JOURNAL OF THE NATIONAL HOUSING AND TOWN PLANNING COUNCIL.). [Hous. plann. rev.]. **VAT** Housing and Planning Review. Vol. 20, No. 1 (Sept./Oct. 1964)-. Periodical. English. bm. £15.50. National Housing & Town Planning Council, 14-18 Old Street, London EC1V 9AB England. **Tel** 01-251-2363. **ED** John Buchanan. cum. index. **Bk Rev. Ad Acc. Circ:** 2,400. ***Continues*** *British Housing and Planning Review;* ***Absorbed*** *Housing and Planning News-Bulletin.*
Desc: Current housing and planning.
Ind/Abst Appl. Soc. Sci. Index Abstr.; Avery Index Archit. Period. Suppl. Colum. Univ. (Dec. 1989-); J. Ferrocement; Sage Race Relat. Abstr.

MY
HOUSING & PROPERTY DIGEST. VFOAT Housing and Property Digest. Periodical. English. $10.00. Annual Magazine Arcade, 198-200 2nd Floor Bangunan Teck Jln Pudu, Kuala Lumpur Malaysia. **LC** HD7363.6.A3; H66. **DD** 333.33/09595.

US/0888-2746
HOUSING AND SOCIETY. [Hous. soc.]. **Added/Corp** American Association of Housing Educators. American Association of Housing Educators. Proceedings. Vol. 5 (1978)-. Periodical. English. Three times a year (Jan., May, Sept.). $50.00 Comes with American Association of Housing Educators membership. American Association of Housing Educators, Texas A&M, College of Architecture, College Station TX 77843. **Tel** (409)845-0986, FAX (409)845-4491, telex (510)892-7689. **DD** 363. ***Continues*** *Housing Educators Journal.*
Ind/Abst AGRICOLA [Full Cov.]; Avery Index Archit. Period. Suppl. Colum. Univ. (1988-); PAIS Int. Print.

US
HOUSING ASSISTANCE PAYMENTS PROGRAM. SUBSTANTIAL REHABILITATION PROCESSING HANDBOOK. VFOAT Substantial Rehabilitation Processing Handbook. Government Publication. English. US Department of Housing and Urban Development, 451 Seventh Street SW, Washington DC 20401. **Tel** (202)708-0980, FAX (202)708-0299.

US
HOUSING CHARACTERISTICS FOR SELECTED METROPOLITAN AREAS. 1974-. Government Publication. English. US Department of Commerce / Bureau of the Census, Data User Services Division, Customer Services, Washington DC 20233-0800. **Tel** (301)763-4100. **(Subscription address:** Superintendent of Documents, US Government Printing Office, Washington DC 20402.**)**

US
HOUSING CHEAP OR ON A BUDGET NEWSLETTER. Newsletter. English. be. $7.50 North America; $11.50 other. Center for Self Sufficiency / Distribution Services, c/o Prosperity & Profits Unlimited, PO Box 570213, Houston TX 77257-0213. **ED** A C Doyle. **Circ:** 1,500. available on audiocassette.
Desc: Ideas for housing cheap, or on a budget.

US
HOUSING COUNSELING HANDBOOK. Government Publication. English. US Department of Housing and Urban Development, 451 Seventh Street SW, Washington DC 20401. **Tel** (202)708-0980, FAX (202)708-0299.

US/1056-5140
HOUSING ECONOMICS. [Hous. econ.]. **Added/Corp** National Association of Home Builders (U.S.). Economics, Mortage Finance, and Housing Policy Division. Vol. 33, No. 6 (June 1987)-. Periodical. English. mo. $125.00 (NAHB members), $150.00 (nonmembers) regular subscription; $175.00 (NAHB member), $205.00 (nonmembers) combined subscription with Housing Market Statistics. National Association of Home Builders, 15th and M Street NW, Washington DC 20005. **Tel** (202)822-0203. **LC** HD7293.A1; H614. **DD** 338.4/769/08097305. ***Continues*** *Economic News Notes for the Building Industry. Monthly Report and Housing Starts Bulletin.*

US
HOUSING FINANCE AND DEVELOPMENT AGENCIES PROCESSING HANDBOOK. Government Publication. English. US Department of Housing and Urban Development, 451 Seventh Street SW, Washington DC 20401. **Tel** (202)708-0980, FAX (202)708-0299.

AT/1031-0320
HOUSING FINANCE FOR OWNER OCCUPATION, AUSTRALIA. **See** Housing and Urban Development-Abstracting, Bibliographies and Statistics.

US
HOUSING IN FLORIDA. Main/Corp Florida Governor. 2nd (1974)-. English. an. Free. Florida Department of Community Affairs, Division of Technical Assistance, 2571 Executive Center Circle East, Tallahassee FL 32301. **LC** HD7303.F6; F518A. **DD** 363.5/09759. ***Continues*** *Annual Report on State Housing Goals (Tallahassee), 0091-9942.*

SA
HOUSING IN SOUTHERN AFRICA. Target Communications, PO Box 3445, 2125 Randburg Transvaal, South Africa. **Tel** 011 27 11 886-4583, 886-4584, 886-4585.

US/0277-8491
HOUSING LAW BULLETIN. **See** Law.

UK
HOUSING LAW REPORTS. **See** Law.

UK/0261-0280
HOUSING (LONDON. 1978). (HOUSING.). [Housing]. **Added/Corp** Institute of Housing (Great Britain). Vol. 14, No. 4 (April 1978)-. Periodical. English. mo (ten issues a year). £40.00 UK; £45.00 other. Inside Communications Ltd., Octavia House, Westwood Business Park, Westwood Way, Coventry CV4 8JP, England. **Tel** 44 203 694393, FAX 44 203 695001. **ED** Rosalind Bayley. Index available. **Ad Acc, Adv Mgr:** H Cox, **Tel** 44 71 8374280. **Circ:** 12,000. ***Continues*** *Housing Monthly, 0950-1924.*
Desc: Provides detailed information on new initiations and keeps housing professionals aware of developments in their fast moving world.
Ind/Abst Appl. Soc. Sci. Index Abstr.; Avery Index Archit. Period. Suppl. Colum. Univ. (Feb., April, Dec. 1989, 1990-); Bus. Index (1981-?).

US/0363-4744
HOUSING MARKET REPORT. [Hous. mark. rep.]. **Added/Corp** Community Development Services. (197?)-. Periodical. English. sm. $314.00. CD Publications, 8204 Fenton Street, Silver Spring MD 20910. **Tel** (800)666-6380, (301)588-6380, FAX (301)588-6385. **ED** James Kelder. **LC** HD7293.A1; H687. **DD** 332.
Desc: Focuses on national and regional housing markets and marketing; unique housing outlook panel provides monthly forecasts of starts, interest rates and other indicators.

US/1056-5132
HOUSING MARKET STATISTICS. (HOUSING MARKET STATISTICS / NATIONAL ASSOCIATION OF HOME BUILDERS.). [Hous. mark. stat.]. **Added/Corp** National Association of Home Buildiers (U.S.) Economics, Mortgage Finance, and Housing Policy Division. (1991)-. Periodical. English. mo. $90.00 (members of the National Association of Home Builders), $105.00 (nonmembers) regular subscription; $175.00 (members), $205.00 (nonmembers) combined subscription with Housing Economics. National Association of Home Builders, 15th and M Street NW, Washington DC 20005. **Tel** (202)822-0203. **DD** 333. ***Continues*** *Current Housing Situation.*

US/1071-2585
HOUSING NEW JERSEY. [Hous. N.J.]. **Added/Corp** New Jersey Institute of Technology. Housing New Jersey, Inc. Vol. 1, Issue 1 (June 1991)-. Periodical. English. mo. $45.00 (non profit); $90.00 (profit) organizations. Housing New Jersey, 303 George Street, Suite 400, New Brunswick NJ 08901. **Tel** (908) 545-6166, FAX (908) 545-5653. **ED** Joni Scanlon. **DD** 363. **Bk Rev**, (Qty: 3-4). **Circ:** 2,500 (ctrl).

US
HOUSING NEW JERSEY. English. $45.00 (non profit); $90.00 (profit) organizations. Housing New Jersey, 303 George Street, Suite 400, New Brunswick NJ 08901. **Tel** (908) 545-6166, FAX (908) 545-5653.

CN/0710-7323
HOUSING NEWSLETTER (OTTAWA). (HOUSING NEWSLETTER.). [Hous. newsl.]. No. 1 (Oct. 1980)-. Newsletter. English. Free. Social Planning Council of Ottawa-Carelton, 256 King Edward Avenue, Ottawa Ontario K1N 7M1 Canada. **Tel** (613)236-9585. **DD** 363.5/09713/83. ctrl circ.

US/0145-1359
HOUSING PERFORMANCE INDICATORS. [Hous. perform. indic.]. 1975-. Government Publication. English. mo. US Department of Housing and Urban Development, 451 Seventh Street SW, Washington DC 20401. **Tel** (202)708-0980, FAX (202)708-0299. ***Continues*** *HPMC Performance Indicators.*

US/1051-1482
HOUSING POLICY DEBATE. [Hous. policy debate]. **Added/Corp** Federal National Mortgage Association. Office of Housing Policy Research. Vol. 1, Issue 1, (1990)-. Periodical. English. Four times a year. Free. Federal National Mortgage Association, 3900 Wisconsin Avenue Northwest, Washington DC 20016. **Tel** (202)752-7000. **LC** HD7293.A1; H65. **DD** 363.5/8/097305. available on microfilm and microfiche from University Microfilms International (UMI).
Ind/Abst Econ. Lit. Index; Int. Bibliogr. Sociol.; PAIS Int. Print.

US/0742-6178
HOUSING PRODUCTION (BALTIMORE, MD.). (HOUSING PRODUCTION.). Began with 1971. English. an. $25.00. Baltimore Regional Council of Governments, 601 N Howard Street, Baltimore MD 21201-4585. **Tel** (301)333-3333, FAX (301)659-1260. **ED** Gail Owen. **LC** HD7304.B2; H63. **DD** 338.4/769083/097526. **Circ:** 150.
Desc: Summary and analysis of residential construction information in the Baltimore metropolitan area; includes data on number of housing units authorized by type.

AT/0813-7978
HOUSING QUEENSLAND. [Hous. Qld.]. (1983)-. Periodical. English. Four times a year. $20.00. Housing Industry Association, PO Box 3573, South Brisbane QLD 4101 Australia. **Tel** 011 61 8461298, FAX 011 61 846 3794. **DD** 690.809943. ***Continues*** *Queensland Housing Industry Costing Guide.*

US/0732-9342
HOUSING REPORT FOR KENTUCKY. 1979-. English. an. $15.00. Urban Studies Center, University of Louisville, Louisville KY 40292. **Tel** (502)588-6626. **ED** C Theodore Koebel. **LC** HD7303.K4; H68. **DD** 363.5/09769. **Circ:** 1,000 (ctrl).
Desc: Comprehensive source of facts, figures, and analyses of supply and demand factors affecting housing markets throughout Kentucky. Data by county, state and selected metropolitan areas.

UK/0018-6651
HOUSING REVIEW (LONDON). (HOUSING REVIEW.). [Hous. rev.]. **Added/Corp** Housing Centre (Great Britain). Vol. 6, No. 1 (Jan./Feb. 1957)-. Periodical. English. Six times a year. £35.00. Housing Centre Trust, 20 Vestry Street, London N1 7RE England. **Tel** 011 44 71 253 6103. **ED** Joan Ash. Index available. **Bk Rev. Ad Acc. Circ:** 2,500 (ctrl). available on microfilm and microfiche from University Microfilms International (UMI). ***Continues*** *Housing Centre Review.*
Desc: Leader articles, reports of meetings, notes on current topics, reviews and letters.
Ind/Abst Appl. Soc. Sci. Index Abstr.; Archit. Period. Index; Avery Index Archit. Period. Suppl. Colum. Univ.; Geogr. Abstr. Human Geogr.; J. Plan. Lit.; Sage Race Relat. Abstr.

UK/0267-3037
HOUSING STUDIES. [Hous. stud.]. Vol. 1, No. 1 (Jan. 1986)-. Periodical. English. qt. £68.00. Carfax Publishing Company, PO Box 25 Abingdon, Oxfordshire OX14 3UE England. **Tel** 011 44 235 555335, FAX (0279)31067, telex 817484. **(Subscription address:** US and Canada/ PO Box 2025, Dunnellon, FL 34430-2025; telephone:(904)489-6996) **[CCC].** Index available. **Bk Rev. Ad Acc. Circ:** 750. available on microfilm and microfiche from University Microfilms International (UMI).
Desc: Explores the changing nature of housing problems and policies and examines the wider economic, political, financial, social, and legal issues associated with housing internationally.
Ind/Abst Appl. Soc. Sci. Index Abstr.; Geogr. Abstr. Human Geogr.; Int. Dev. Abstr.; Soc. Plann. Policy Dev. Abstr.; Stud. Women Abstr.

US
HUD INTERNATIONAL INFORMATION SERIES. **Main/Corp** United States. Dept. of Housing and Urban Development. Office of International Affairs. (April 30, 1970)-. Government Publication. English. US Department of Housing and Urban Development, 451 Seventh Street SW, Washington DC 20401. **Tel** (202)708-0980, FAX (202)708-0299.
Ind/Abst Archit. Period. Index (Dec. 1977-).

US
HUD SALES CONNECTION, THE. **Added/Corp** United States. Dept. of Housing and Urban Development. Vol. 1, No. 1 (1991)-. Government Publication. English. qt. US Department of Housing and Urban Development, 451 Seventh Street SW, Washington DC 20401. **Tel** (202)708-0980, FAX (202)708-0299.

IT
ICIE INNOVAZIONE. ***Suspended.*** (19??)-29/30 (1992). Italian. Four times a year. ICIE Soc Coop RL, Via Nomentana 133, 00161 Rome Italy. **Tel** 011 39 6 8845848.

US/0361-6932
ILLINOIS REGIONAL PLANNING AGENCY DIRECTORY. Directory. English. Department of Local Government Affairs, Office of Research and Planning, 303 East Monroe, Springfield IL. **LC** HT393.I4; I43. **DD** 309.2/5/025773.

IT
IMPERMEABILIZZARE. BE MA Editrice, Via Teocrito 50, 20128 Milan, Italy. **Tel** 011 39 2 2552451.

US
INCOME/EXPENSE ANALYSIS : FEDERALLY-ASSISTED APARTMENTS. **Added/Corp** Institute of Real Estate Management. **VFOAT** Federally Assisted Apartments. (1986)-. English. an. ***Continues in part*** *Income/Expense Analysis: Apartments, 0194-1941.*

US
INDEX TO CPL EXCHANGE BIBLIOGRAPHIES. **Added/Corp** Council of Planning Librarians. (1975)-. Monographic series. English. Sixteen times a year. $285.00. American Planning Association, 1313 East 60th Street, Chicago IL 60637. **Tel** (312)955-9100, FAX (312)955-8312.

II/0046-9017
INDIAN JOURNAL OF REGIONAL SCIENCE. [Indian j. reg. sci.]. **Added/Corp** Regional Science Association (India). Indian Institute of Technology (Kharagpur, India). (1968)-. Periodical. English. sa. $20.00. Indian Institute of Technology and Planning, Kharagpur West Bengal 721302 India. **Tel** 2221-2224, telex 6401-201 ITKG IN. **(Subscription address:** Prints India, 11 Darya Ganj, New Delhi 110002 India.**) ED** A N Bose and C R Pathak. **LC** HT395.I5; .I6. **DD** 309.2/5/0954. Index available. **Bk Rev. Ad Acc. Circ:** 525 (ctrl).
Desc: Regional science, regional city planning, regional development, theory concept, and case studies.
Ind/Abst AGRICOLA; Appl. Soc. Sci. Index Abstr.; Curr. Lit. Sci. Sci.; Int. Bibliogr. Sociol.; Int. Dev. Abstr. (?-?); Rice Abstr.; Rural Dev. Abstr.; World Agric. Econ.

CN/0709-6836
INDUSTRIE DE L'HABITATION MANUFACTUREE, L'. [Ind. habitat. manuf.]. **VFOAT** Manufactured Housing Industry. V. 1- Jan. 1977-. Periodical. English (French). bm. Clay Publishing Company Ltd, Bewdley Ontario K0L 1E0 Canada. **Tel** (416)797-2281. **DD** 338.4/7/6292260971. ***Continues in part*** *Mobile Home & Recreational Vehicle Industry, 0380-4917.*

FR
INFORMATION BULLETIN, MUNICIPAL AND REGIONAL MATTERS. Began with No. 1, Mar. 1969. Bulletin. English. sa. Manhattan Publishing Company, PO Box 650, Croton-on-Hudson NY 10520. **Tel** (914)271-5194. **LC** HT390; .I45. **DD** 361.6/094.

GW/0340-1774
INFORMATIONEN ZUR MODERNEN STADTGESCHICHTE : IMS. **VFOAT** IMS. (Oct. 1970)-. Periodical. German. sa. **LC** DD91; .I54.
Ind/Abst Am. Hist. Life (1989-).

GW/0303-2493
INFORMATIONEN ZUR RAUMENTWICKLUNG. [Inf. Raumentwickl.]. **Added/Corp** Bundesforschungsanstalt fuer Landeskunde und Raumordnung. (Jan. 1974)-. Periodical. German. ir. DM66.00. Selbstverlag der Bundesforschungsanstalt fuer Landeskunde und Raumordnung AM, Michaelshof 8, Postfach 200130, D 53131 Bonn 2 Germany. **Tel** 011 49 228 826209. **LC** HT395.G4; I664. ***Formed by the union of*** *Rundbrief - Institut fuer Landeskunde* ***and*** *Informationen - Institut fuer Raumordnung.*
Ind/Abst EMBASE; Energy Res. Abstr. (March 1979-); Geogr. Abstr. Human Geogr.; GeoRef; PAIS Int. Print (1991-); World Agric. Econ.

UK/0260-7239
INSTITUTE OF HOUSING YEAR BOOK, THE. **Added/Corp** Institute of Housing (Great Britain). (19??)-. Periodical. English. an. The Institute of Housing, 12 Upper Belgrave Street, London SW1X 8BA England. **LC** HD7333.A3; I465a. **DD** 363.5/06/041. ***Continues*** *Year Book and List of Members (Institute of Housing (Great Britain)).*

CN/0712-788X
INSTITUTE OF URBAN STUDIES PUBLICATION. (REPORT.). [Inst. Urban Stud. publ.]. Monographic series. English. Price varies per volume. Institute of Urban Studies, University of Winnipeg, 515 Portage Avenue, Winnipeg Manitoba R3B 2E9 Canada. **Tel** (204)786-9409. **DD** 307.7/6/0971274.

FR/0240-9925
INTER REGIONS. [Inter reg.]. **Added/Corp** Conseil National des Economies Regionales et de la Productivite (France). (19??)-. Periodical. French. Eleven times a year (July & August issue combined). 372.18F France; 380.00F Europe; 472.18F others. Conseil National Economies Region, 219 Boulevard Street Germain, 75007 Paris France. **Tel** 011 33 1 42223529, FAX 011 33 1 45499446. ***Continues*** *Cahiers de l'Expansion Regionale, 0014-4711.*

US
INTERIM GUIDE FOR ENVIRONMENTAL ASSESSMENT. **Main/Corp** Planning Environment International. Government Publication. English. an. US Department of Housing and Urban Development, 451 Seventh Street SW, Washington DC 20401. **Tel** (202)708-0980, FAX (202)708-0299.

US/0146-6518
INTERNATIONAL JOURNAL FOR HOUSING SCIENCE AND ITS APPLICATIONS. [Int. j. hous. sci. appl.]. **Added/Corp** International Association for Housing Science. Vol. 1 (Aug. 1977)-. Periodical. English. Four times a year. $200.00 (one year); $360.00 (two years). International Journal for Housing Science, PO Box 340525, Coral Gables FL 33134. **Tel** (305)446-9462, FAX (305) 348-3797, telex 441582 TLX SVC ATTENTION URAL. **ED** Oktay Ural. **LC** HD7285; .I533. **DD** 301.5/4/05. **CODEN** IJHADL. **[CCC].** Index available. **Bk Rev. Ad Acc. Circ:** 1,000 (ctrl). available on microfilm and microfiche from University Microfilms International (UMI); Microfilms International Marketing Corp.; and Pergamon Press. Documents available from Article Express International.
Ind/Abst Archit. Period. Index; Avery Index Archit. Period. Suppl. Colum. Univ. (1989-); Bioeng. Abstr.; Concr. Abstr.; Ei Page One; Energy Res. Abstr. (March 1979-); Eng. Index Annu.; Int. Civil Eng. Abstr.; J. Ferrocement; Soft. Abstr. Eng.

UK/0309-1317
INTERNATIONAL JOURNAL OF URBAN AND REGIONAL RESEARCH. [Int. j. urban reg. res.]. **VFOAT** Revue Internationale de Recherche Urbaine et Regionale; Urban Regional Research. Vol. 1 (Mar. 1977)-. Academic Scholarly Publication. English (French). Four times a year. £83.00 UK and Europe; $142.00 North America; £91.50 other. Basil Blackwell Publishers Ltd, 108 Cowley Road, Oxford 0X4 1JF England. **Tel** 011 44 865 791100, FAX 011 44 865 791347, telex 837022 OXBOOK G. **(Subscription address:** Blackwell Publishers / UK, Marston Book Services, PO Box 87, Oxford OX2 0DT England.**) ED** Michael Harlowe. **LC** HT101; .I57. **DD** 361.6/05. **[CCC]. Bk Rev. Pr Rev.** available on microfilm and microfiche from University Microfilms International (UMI). Documents available from The Genuine Article, UMI Article Clearinghouse.
Desc: Publishes the studies of conflicting interests in urban and regional development related to fundamental, economic, social and political processes at local, national and international levels.
Ind/Abst ABC POL SCI; Am. Hist. Life (1983-); Appl. Soc. Sci. Index Abstr.; Avery Index Archit. Period. Suppl. Colum. Univ. (1989/1990-); Curr. Contents Soc. Behav. Sci.; Curr. Geogr. Publ. (199?-); Expand. Acad. Index (1992-); Geogr. Abstr. Human Geogr.; Int. Bibliogr. Sociol.; Int. Dev. Abstr.; J. Plan. Lit.; Leis. Recreat. Tour. Abstr.; Middle East Abstr. Index; Newsp. Period. Abstr. (1992-); PAIS Int. Print (1991-?); Res. Alert [Full Cov.]; Rural Dev. Abstr.; Sage Urban Stud. Abstr (?-?); Soc. Plann. Policy Dev. Abstr.; Soc. Sci. Cit. Index [Full Cov.]; Sociol. Abstr. [Full Cov.]; World Agric. Econ.

VE
INTERNATIONAL RURAL HOUSING JOURNAL, THE. English. ir. International Rural Housing Journal, Apartado de Curreo 16-224, Caracas Venezuela. **LC** HD7289.A3; I63. **DD** 363.5/9.

II
ITPI JOURNAL. **Added/Corp** Institute of Town Planners, India. **VFOAT** Journal. Vol. 4, No. 1 & 2 (June/Sept. 1985)-. Periodical. English. Four times a year (Mar., June, Sept., Dec.). $45.00. Institute of Town Planners, 4-A Ring Road, Indraprastha Estate, New Delhi 110002 India. **Tel** 3318571, 3327812. **LC** HT169.I5; I5. **Bk Rev. Ad Acc. Circ:** 1,500 (ctrl). ***Continues*** *Journal of Institute of Town Planners, India.*

GW/0515-9091
JAHRESBERICHT (AKADEMIE FUR RAUMFORSCHUNG UND LANDESPLANUNG (GERMANY)). (JAHRESBERICHT / AKADEMIE FUER RAUMFORSCHUNG UND LANDESPLANUNG.). **Added/Corp** Akademie Fur Raumforschung und Landesplanung (Germany). German. an. Akademie fur Raumforschung und Landesplanung, Hohenzollernstrasse 11, W-3000 Hannover 1 Germany. **Tel** (0577)34842, FAX (0577)348247. **LC** HT395.G4; J34. **DD** 361.6/0943. **Bk Rev. Ad Acc. Circ:** 500. ***Continues*** *Arbeitsbericht (Akademie Fur Raumforschung und Landesplanung (Germany)).*
Desc: Covers regional analysis, spatial structure, spatial planning, regional planning, urban planning, regional policy, environmental research, land use planning, forecasting, and regionalization.

●US/1070-5422
JOURNAL OF COMMUNITY PRACTICE. (1994)-. Periodical. English. qt (4 issues). $60.00 US; $84.00 other. The Haworth Press Inc, 10 Alice Street, Binghamton NY 13904-1580. **Tel** (607)722-5857, (800)3-HAWORTH, FAX (607)722-1424. **ED** Marie Weil, DSW. **Acid Free.** Documents available from Haworth Document Delivery Service.
Desc: Forum for the development, debate and exchange of ideas on community practice in research, theory development, intervention models, curriculum development and teaching.
Ind/Abst Guide Soc. Sci. Relig. (1994-); Index Period. Artic. Relat. Law (1994-); Oper. Res./Manag. Sci. (1994-); Sociol. Abstr. (1994-); Transp. Res. Abstr. (1994-).

●UK/0964-0568
JOURNAL OF ENVIRONMENTAL PLANNING AND MANAGEMENT. **Added/Corp** University of Newcastle Upon Tyne. Dept. of Town and Country Planning. **VFOAT** Environmental Planning and Management. Vol. 35, No. 1 (1993)-. Periodical. English. qt. £168.00. Carfax Publishing Company, PO Box 25 Abingdon, Oxfordshire OX14 3UE England. **Tel** 011 44 235 555335, FAX (0279)31067, telex 817484. **(Subscription address:** US and Canada/ PO Box 2025, Dunnellon, FL 34430-2025; telephone:(904)489-6996) **LC** NA9000; .P58. **DD** 711. **[CCC].** available on microfiche. Documents available from Documents on Demand. ***Continues*** *Planning Outlook, 0032-0714.*
Desc: Focus is on the integrated planning and management of environmental resources. Topics covered encompass applied research, the application of new approaches and techniques, and the evaluation of policy and practice.
Ind/Abst Ecol. Abstr.; Environ. Abstr.; Geogr. Abstr. Human Geogr.; Int. Bibliogr. Sociol.

US/0272-7374
JOURNAL OF HOUSING (1979). (JOURNAL OF HOUSING.). [J. hous.]. **Added/Corp** National Association of Housing and Redevelopment Officials. Vol. 36 No. 9 (Oct. 1979)-. Periodical. English. bm (6 issues). $24.00 (one year), $42.00 (two year). National Association of Housing Redevelopment, 1320 18th Street Northwest, 4th Floor, Washington DC 20036. **Tel** (202)429-2960. **ED** Terence K. Cooper. **LC** HD7285; .J68. **DD** 363.5/0973. **CODEN** JOHOA4. **Ad Acc. Circ:** 12,500 (ctrl). available on microfilm and microfiche from University Microfilms International (UMI). Documents available from UMI Article Clearinghouse, Documents on Demand. ***Continues*** *JOH. Journal of Housing, 0272-7374.*
Desc: Covers new achievements in public housing and community development.
Ind/Abst ABI/INFORM Glob. Ed.; ABI Inform Ondisc (Oct. 1979-); Acad. Search (July 1993-); AGRICOLA; Avery Index Archit. Period. Suppl. Colum. Univ. (1989/1990-); Bus. Index (1985-); Environ. Abstr.; Expand. Acad. Index (1984-); Gen. BusinessFile (1985-); Gen. Period. Index (1985-); Index Period. Artic. Relat. Law; INFO-SOUTH Abstr.; J. Plan. Lit.; Mag. Search; Manage. Contents; Newsp. Period. Abstr. (1991-); PAIS Int. Print (1991-); Soc. Sci. Source (Jul. 1993-); Soc. Sci. Index; Soc. Sci. Index Fulltext (Nov. 1988-) [Full Txt.]; Soc. Work Abstr. (?-?); Urban Aff. Abstr.

US/1051-1377
JOURNAL OF HOUSING ECONOMICS. [J. hous. econ.]. **VFOAT** Housing Economics. Vol. 1, No. 1 (Mar. 1991)-. Academic Scholarly Publication. English. qt (4 issues). $127.00 US and Canada; $155.00 other. Academic Press, Inc., 6277 Sea Harbor Drive, Orlando FL 32887. **Tel** (800)543-9534, (407)345-4100, FAX (407)363-9661. **ED** Henry O. Pollakowski. **LC** IN PROCESS; HD7293.Z9; J68. **DD** 333. **[CCC].**
Desc: Provides a focal point for the publication of economic research related to housing. Provides broad coverage of topics, including international comparisons, impacts on the public sector, and construction industry studies.

US/0276-3893
JOURNAL OF HOUSING FOR THE ELDERLY. [J. hous. elderly]. Vol. 1, No. 1 (Spring/Summer 1983)-. Periodical. English. sa. $160.00 US; $224.00 other. The Haworth Press Inc, 10 Alice Street, Binghamton NY 13904-1580. **Tel** (607)722-5857, (800)3-HAWORTH, FAX (607)722-1424. **ED** Leon Pastalan (editor's address: 2226 Art and Architecture Building, The University of Michigan, Ann Arbor, MI 48109-2069). **LC** HD7287.9; .J68. **DD** 363.5/9. **Bk Rev. Ad Acc. Pr Rev. Acid Free. Circ:** 206. available on microfilm and microfiche from University Microfilms International (UMI). Documents available from Haworth Document Delivery Service.
Desc: Directed towards gerontological professionals and the design, planning, and management professionals in the architecture and housing/urban planning/public policy fields who are responsible for the residential environments of the elderly in their communities.
Ind/Abst Abstr. Soc. Gerontol.; AGRICOLA [Select. Cov.]; Archit. Period. Index; Index Period. Lit. Aging; J. Plan. Lit.; PAIS Int. Print (1991-); Psychol. Abstr. (1983-); PsycINFO; PsycLit; Sage Fam. Stud. Abstr. (?-?); Sage Urban Stud. Abstr; Soc. Plann. Policy Dev. Abstr.; Soc. Work Abstr. [Select. Cov.]; Urban Aff. Abstr.

US/1052-7001
JOURNAL OF HOUSING RESEARCH. [J. hous. res.]. **Added/Corp** Federal National Mortgage Association. Office of Housing Policy Research. Vol. 1, Issue 1 (1990)-. Periodical. English. Fannie Mae, 3900 Wisconsin Avenue NW, Washington DC 20016. **LC** HD7293.A1; J68. **DD** 363.5/0973/05. available on microfilm and microfiche from University Microfilms International (UMI).
Ind/Abst Econ. Lit. Index; Int. Bibliogr. Sociol.; PAIS Int. Print.

US/0739-456X
JOURNAL OF PLANNING EDUCATION AND RESEARCH. (JOURNAL OF PLANNING EDUCATION AND RESEARCH / ASSOCIATION OF COLLEGIATE SCHOOLS OF PLANNING.). [J. plann. educ. res.]. **Added/Corp** Association of Collegiate Schools of Planning (U.S.). Vol. 1, No. 1 (Summer 1981)-. Periodical. English. Four times a year (Mar., June, Sept., Dec.). $30.00 (individual), $60.00 (institutions), US; $35.00 (individual), $65.00 (institutions), other. Association of Collegiate Schools of Planning, Department of Urban & Regional Planning, Florida State University, Tallahassee FL 32306-2030. **Tel** (904)644-9653, FAX (904)644-6041. **ED** Ms. Cavell Kyser. **LC** HT392; .J68. **DD** 361.6/07/1073. Index available. **Bk Rev**, (Qty: 25). **Ad Acc, Adv Mgr:** C. Kyser. **Pr Rev. Circ:** 1,200 (ctrl). Documents available from Documents on Demand.
Desc: Covers theory and research in urban planning and applied in the educational or professional settings. Topics includes economic development, housing, land use, transportation, mediation and environment.
Ind/Abst Avery Index Archit. Period. Suppl. Colum. Univ. (Fall 1988-); Environ. Abstr.; Environ. Period. Bibliogr.; Geogr. Abstr. Human Geogr.; Int. Dev. Abstr.; J. Plan. Lit.; PAIS Int. Print (1991-); Sage Public Adm. Abstr. (?-?); Sage Urban Stud. Abstr.

US/0885-4122
JOURNAL OF PLANNING LITERATURE. **See** Housing and Urban Development-Abstracting, Bibliographies and Statistics.

II
JOURNAL OF RURAL RECONSTRUCTION. **Added/Corp** Afro-Asian Rural Reconstruction Organization. (199?)-. Periodical. English. sa. ***Continues*** *Rural Reconstruction, 0557-6644.*
Ind/Abst Appl. Soc. Sci. Index Abstr.; Int. Dev. Abstr.

US/0194-4363
JOURNAL OF THE AMERICAN PLANNING ASSOCIATION. [J. Am. Plan. Assoc.]. **Main/Corp** American Planning Association. **VFOAT** JAPA. Vol. 45, No. 1 (Jan. 1979)-. Academic Scholarly Publication. English. Four times a year. $36.00 US; $50.00 other. American Planning Association, 1313 East 60th Street, Chicago IL 60637. **Tel** (312)955-9100, FAX (312)955-8312. **ED** Raymond J. Burby and Edward Kaiser. **LC** HD87.5; .A46a. **DD** 361.6/0973. **CODEN** JAPAD9. **Bk Rev. Ad Acc. Pr Rev. Circ:** 12,000. available on microfilm and microfiche from University Microfilms International (UMI). Documents available from Article Express International, The Genuine Article, UMI Article Clearinghouse, Documents on Demand. ***Continues*** *Journal of the American Institute of Planners, 0002-8991.*
Desc: Articles for and by academics and practitioners in urban and regional planning: community development, economics, housing, policymaking, urban design, real estate, land use, environment, and transportation.
Ind/Abst ABC POL SCI; ABI/INFORM Glob. Ed.; ABI Inform Ondisc (Jan. 1979-); Acad. Search (July 1993-); AGRICOLA; Am. Hist. Life (1979-); Appl. Soc. Sci. Index Abstr.; Archit. Period. Index (Jan. 1979-); Art Index; Arts Humanit. Citation Index [Select. Cov.]; Avery Index Archit. Period. Suppl. Colum. Univ. (Spring 1986-Summer 1987, Winter 1990-); BHA : Biblio. Hist. Art; Bioeng. Abstr.; Bus. ASAP (1992-) [Full Txt.]; Bus. Index (1985-); Curr. Contents Soc. Behav. Sci.; Curr. Index J. Educ.; Ei Page One; EMBASE; Energy Inf. Abstr.; Energy Res. Abstr. (1979-); Eng. Index Annu.; Environ. Abstr.; Environ. Period. Bibliogr.; Expand. Acad. Index (1984-); Gen. BusinessFile (1985-); Gen. Period. Index (1985-); Geogr. Abstr. Phys. Geogr.; Geogr. Abstr. Human Geogr.; Highw. Res. Abstr.; Index Period. Artic. Relat. Law (19??-19??); INIS Atomindex [Micro.]; Int. Bibliogr. Sociol.; Int. Civil Eng. Abstr.; J. Plan. Lit.; Mag. Search; Manage. Contents; Middle East Abstr. Index; Newsp. Period. Abstr. (1991-); PAIS Int. Print (1991-); Res. Alert [Full Cov.]; Risk Abstr.; Sage Urban Stud. Abstr; Soc. Sci. Source (Jul. 1993-); Soc. Sci. Cit. Index [Full Cov.]; Soc. Sci. Index; Soc. Sci. Index Fulltext (Autumn 1988-) [Full Txt.]; Soc. Work Abstr. (?-?); Soft. Abstr. Eng.; UMI ABI/Inform--Bus. Period. Ondisc (Spring 1988-) [Full Txt.]; U.S. Polit. Sci. Doc.; Urban Aff. Abstr.

US/1045-8077
JOURNAL OF THE URBAN AND REGIONAL INFORMATION SYSTEMS ASSOCIATION. (JOURNAL OF THE URBAN AND REGIONAL INFORMATION SYSTEMS ASSOCIATION / URISA.). [J. Urban Reg. Inf. Syst. Assoc.]. **Added/Corp** Urban and Regional Information Systems Association. **VFOAT** Journal; URISA Journal. Vol. 1, No. 1 (Fall 1989)-. Periodical. English. sa. $68.00 (one year), $134.00 (two year), $199.00 (three year), institutions; $30.00 (one year), $60.00 (two year), $90.00 (three year), individuals. University of Wisconsin Press, Journal Division, 114 North Murray Street, Madison WI 53715. **Tel** (608)262-4952, FAX (608)262-8909. **LC** HT390; .J67. **DD** 361.6/0285. **CODEN** URJOEO.

US/0735-2166
JOURNAL OF URBAN AFFAIRS. [J. urban aff.]. **Added/Corp** Virginia Polytechnic Institute and State University. Division of Environment and Urban Systems. Urban Affairs Association (U.S.). Vol. 3, No. 4 (Fall 1981)-. Periodical. English. qt. $160.00 (institutions), $60.00 (individuals) US; $180.00 (institutions), $70.00 (individuals) (surface mail), $200.00 (institutions), $80.00 (individuals) (air mail) other. JAI Press Inc., 55 Old Post Road, Suite 2, PO Box 1678, Greenwich CT 06836-1678. **Tel** (203)661-7602, FAX (203)661-0792. **ED** Scott Cummings and Theodore Koebel. **LC** HT101; .J65. **DD** 307.7/6/0973. **CODEN** JUAFEM. **[CCC]. Bk Rev. Ad Acc. Circ:** 450. ***Formed by the union of*** *Urban Interests, 0192-4974* ***and*** *Urban Affairs Papers, 0735-2158.*
Desc: Addresses contemporary urban issues of interest to scholars, practitioners, policy makers, and students.
Ind/Abst Avery Index Archit. Period. Suppl. Colum. Univ. (1988-1989); Geogr. Abstr. Human Geogr.; Int. Polit. Sci. Abstr.; J. Plan. Lit.; Middle East Abstr. Index; PAIS Int. Print; Sage Public Adm. Abstr.; Sage Urban Stud. Abstr; Soc. Plann. Policy Dev. Abstr.; Soc. Sci. Cit. Index [Full Cov.].

US/0096-1442
JOURNAL OF URBAN HISTORY. **See** History(General).

US/0733-9488
JOURNAL OF URBAN PLANNING AND DEVELOPMENT. **See** Engineering-Civil Engineering.

●US/1063-0732
JOURNAL OF URBAN TECHNOLOGY, THE. [J. urban technol.]. Vol. 1, No. 1 (Fall 1992)-. Periodical. English. Three times a year. $54.00 (institutions), $45.00 (individuals). Journal of Urban Technology, 300 Jay Street, Brooklyn NY 11201. **Tel** (718)260-5392. **LC** IN PROCESS; HT101; .J687. **DD** 307.

JA
KAIHATSU KOHO. **Added/Corp** Hokkaido Kaihatsu Kyokai. (19??)-. Periodical. Japanese. mo. ¥18000. Hokkaido Kaihatsu Kyokai, (Hokkaido Development Association), Sapporo Kahihatsu Sogo Chosa, Nishi 19-chome Kita-2 jo, Chuoko Sapporoshi Hokkaido 60 Japan. **LC** HT395.J32; H636.

JA
KAIHATSU RONSHU. **Main/Corp** Hokkai Gakuen Daigaku Kaihatsu Kenkyujo. Issue No. 1 (1965)-. Periodical. Japanese. sa. Hokkai Gakuen University / Institute of Development Policy Studies, Asahi-machi-4, Sapporo Toyohira 062 Japan. **Tel** 011 841 1161. **LC** HT395.J32; H634a.

SZ
KANTON BERN (N.G.) LEERWOHNUNGSBESTAND ... / AMT FUR STATITISK DES KANTONS BERN. **VFOAT** Canton de Berne (N.F.), Logements Vacants au Service de Statistique du Canton de Berne. French (German). an. **LC** HD7353.B42; K37. **DD** 363.5/1/094945.

JA/0387-2513
KEIKAKU GYOSEI / NIHON KEIKAKU GYOSEI GAKKAI. **VFOAT** Planning Administration. Periodical. Japanese. ¥1500. Gakuyo Shobo, 7-5 Fujimi 1 Chiyoda-ku, Tokyo 102 Japan. **LC** HT395.J3; K413.

US/1063-0074
KELLEY BLUE BOOK MANUFACTURED HOUSING USED VALUE GUIDE. [Kelley blue book manuf. hous. used value guide]. **Added/Corp** Kelley Blue Book Co. **VFOAT** Manufactured Housing

Used Value Guide; Manufactured Homes and Park Locations; Official Manufactured Housing Guide Used Values; Manufactured Homes & Park Locations; Manufactured Home Used Values Park Location Guide; Manufactured Housing Guide. (198?)-. English. Twice a year. $45.00 US; $55.00 other. Kelley Blue Book, PO Box 19691, Irvine CA 92713. **Tel** (714)770-7704. **LC** HD9715.7.A1; K44a. **DD** 690/.879/02973. ***Continues*** *Manufactured Housing and Mobile Home Guide, 0748-8734.*

US
KNOX COUNTY CAPITAL IMPROVEMENTS PROGRAM. **Main/Corp** Metropolitan Planning Commission of Knoxville and Knox County, Tennessee. English. an. City Hall Park, Knoxville TN 37902.
Desc: Each annual report covers a five year planning period, e.g., 1977/82, 1978/83.

NO
KOMMUNALTEKNIKK. Norwegian. an. Norsk Kommunalteknikk, Haakon Viis Gate 9, Oslo 1 Norway.

FI
KR-TIEDOTE / SISAASIAINMINISTERIO, KAAVOITUS- JA RAKENNUSOSASTO. **Main/Corp** Finland Sisaasiainministerio Kaavoitus- Ja Rakennusosasto. **Added/Corp** Finland. Sisaasiainministerio. Kaavoitus- Ja Rakennusosasto. Finland. Ymparistoministerio. Kaavoitus- Ja Rakennusosasto. **VAT** Kaavoitus Ja Rakentaminen Tiedote. (19??)-. Finnish. ir. Valtion Painatuskeskus, PO Box 516, SF 00101 Helsinki Finland. **Tel** 011 358 0 5660266. **LC** HT169.F5; F56a.

IT
LABIRINTI. (19??)-. Italian. qt. L40000.00. Associazione Orestiadi di Gibellina, PZA XV Gennaio 1968 1, 91024 Gibellina Italy. **Tel** 011 39 924 67639.

US/0023-768X
LAND USE DIGEST. **See** Real Estate.

US/0271-5228
LANDLORD TENANT LAW BULLETIN. **See** Law.

US/1050-3196
LANDLORD-TENANT RELATIONS REPORT. [Landlord-tenant relat. rep.]. **VFOAT** Landlord Tenant Relations Report. No. 84-1 (Jan. 1984)-. Periodical. English. mo. $134.00 US and Mexico; $144.00 Canada; $174.00 other. CD Publications, 8204 Fenton Street, Silver Spring MD 20910. **Tel** (800)666-6380, (301)588-6380, FAX (301)588-6385. **DD** 333. Index available (free).
Desc: Coverage of developments affecting rental topics. Emphasis on court actions, state and local news, L-T commission proceedings, and HUD. Provides helpful advice and communication tips.

US/0883-0746
LANDLORD VS. TENANT/NYC. **See** Law.

NE/0169-2046
LANDSCAPE AND URBAN PLANNING. [Landsc. urban plan.]. Vol. 13, No. 1 (Feb. 1986)-. Academic Scholarly Publication. English. Nine times a year (3 volumes). Fl1137.00. Elsevier Science Publishers BV, PO Box 211, 1000 AE Amsterdam Netherlands. **Tel** 011 31 20 5803642, FAX 011 31 20 5862696, telex 15682. **ED** A E Weddle. **LC** HT166; .L33. **DD** 307.1/216/05. **CODEN** LUPLEZ. **[CCC]**. **Pr Rev.** available on microfilm and microfiche from University Microfilms International (UMI). Documents available from The Genuine Article, BIOSIS Document Express, Documents on Demand. ***Formed by the union of*** *Landscape Planning, 0304-3924* ***and*** *Urban Ecology, 0304-4009;* ***Absorbed*** *Reclamation & Revegetation Research, 0167-644X.*
Desc: Concerned with conceptual, scientific and design approaches to land use.
Ind/Abst Agrofor. Abstr.; Arts Humanit. Citation Index [Select. Cov.]; Avery Index Archit. Period. Suppl. Colum. Univ. (1989-); Biol. Abstr. (1986-); Coal Abstr.; Curr. Contents, Agric. Biol. Environ. Sci.; Curr. Contents Arts Humanit.; Curr. Geogr. Publ. (199?-); Dairy Sci. Abstr.; Ecol. Abstr.; Ecology Abstr.; Ei Page One; Environ. Abstr.; Environ. Period. Bibliogr.; Fish Rev.; Geogr. Abstr. Phys. Geogr. (?-?); Geogr. Abstr. Human Geogr.; GeoRef; Health Saf. Sci. Abstr.; Int. Dev. Abstr.; Irr. Drain. Abstr.; J. Plan. Lit.; Leis. Recreat. Tour. Abstr.; Pollut. Abstr. Indexes; Res. Alert [Full Cov.]; Rice Abstr.; Rural Dev. Abstr.; Sage Urban Stud. Abstr; Soc. Sci. Cit. Index [Full Cov.]; Soils Fert.; Wildl. Rev.; World Agric. Econ.

US/0075-8167
LATIN AMERICAN UURBAN RESEARCH. **Added/Corp** University of Florida. Center for Latin American Studies. Massachusetts Institute of Technology. Center for International Studies. (1970)-. English. an. SAGE Periodical Press, 2455 Teller Road, Thousand Oaks CA 91320. **Tel** (805)499-0721, FAX (805)499-0871, telex 100799. **ED** F. F. Rabinovitz and F. M. Trueblood. **LC** HT127.5; .L38. **DD** 301.3/6/098. **Acid Free.**

US/0193-8290
LAW & HOUSING JOURNAL. **See** Law.

CN/0703-9581
LEBRETON. V. 1- July/Aug. 1977-. Periodical. English (French). Lebreton, 540 Wellington Street, Ottawa Ontario K1R 6K5 Canada. **DD** 711/.4/0971384.

CN/0843-5278
LIAISON - INTERGOVERNMENTAL COMMITTEE ON URBAN AND REGIONAL RESEARCH. (LIAISON.). [Liaison - Intergov. Comm. Urban Reg. Res.]. **Added/Corp** Intergovernmental Committee on Urban and Regional Research (Canada). **VFOAT** Liaison, Newsletter of the Intergovernmental Committee on Urban and Regional Research. **VAT** Liaison - Comite Intergouvernemental de Recherches Urbaines et Regionales. Vol. 1, No. 1 (May/June 1989)-. Periodical. English (French). bm (6 issues). 60.00Can$. ICURR / Intergovernmental Committee on Urban and Regional Research, 150 Eglinton Avenue East, Suite 301, Toronto Ontario M4P 1E8 Canada. **Tel** (416)973-5629, FAX (416)973-1375. **ED** Wayne Berry. **DD** 352.071/05. **Bk Rev**, (Qty: 30). **Ad Acc. Circ:** 1,000. ***Continues*** *Interaction, 0226-2878.*

US
LIHC MONTHLY REPORT. (19??)-. Periodical. English. mo. $179.00 (one year), $250.00 (two year). Novogradac Fortenbach and Company, 110 Sutter Street, Suite 100, San Francisco CA 94104. **Tel** (415)616-2058, FAX (415)616-2049. **ED** Carol L. Hough. Index available. cum. index (Available as of 10/94). **Ad Acc. Circ:** 1,500.
Desc: News, opinion, features, and commentary on the field of low-income housing tax credits.

NE
LIST OF MEMBERS - INTERNATIONAL FEDERATION FOR HOUSING AND PLANNING. **Main/Corp** International Federation for Housing and Planning. Multiple languages (English, French and German). ir. International Federation for Housing and Planning, 43 Wassenaarseweg, 2596 The Hague Netherlands. **Tel** (31)(070) 24 45 57, telex 31578. **LC** HD7285; .I515. **DD** 301.5/4. **Circ:** 600 (ctrl).
Desc: List of members, governing bodies, rules, standing cites and working groups.

US/0147-8974
LOCAL AUTHORITIES PARTICIPATING IN LOW-RENT HOUSING PROGRAMS. **Main/Corp** United States. Dept. of Housing and Urban Development. Assisted Housing Branch. June 30, 1971-. Government Publication. English. US Department of Housing and Urban Development, 451 Seventh Street SW, Washington DC 20401. **Tel** (202)708-0980, FAX (202)708-0299. **LC** HD7293.A49; P84A. **DD** 301.5/4. ***Continues*** *Local Authorities Participating in PHA Low-Rent Housing Programs.*

IT
LOCAZIONI E CONDOMINIO : CASI E QUESTIONI. (19??)-. Italian. Three times a year. Iposa Srl, Cas Postale 12055, Delendati, 20120 Milan Italy. **Tel** 011 39 2 77971. Index available.

US/0148-6160
LOUISIANA PLANNING DIRECTORY. 1976-. Directory. English. be. Louisiana State Planning Office, 4528 Bennington Avenue, Baton Rouge LA 70808. **LC** JK4730; .L58. **DD** 353.9/763/002.

US
LOW-RENT HOUSING HOMEOWNERSHIP OPPORTUNITES. **Added/Corp** United States. Dept. of Housing and Urban Development. Office of Administration. **VFOAT** Low-Rent Housing Homeownership Opportunities Handbook. (19??)-. Government Publication. English. US Department of Housing and Urban Development, 451 Seventh Street SW, Washington DC 20401. **Tel** (202)708-0980, FAX (202)708-0299.

CN/0228-684X
LUTTES URBAINES. Vol. 1, No. 1-. Periodical. French. $8.00. Luttes Urbaines, CP 263, Drummondville Quebec J2B 6V7 Canada. **DD** 307.7/6/09714.

FR/1164-4079
MACADAM NICE. **See** Transportation-Roads and Traffic.

JA/0287-0150
MACHI & SUMAI. **VFOAT** Machi to Sumai. Periodical. Japanese. qt. Jutaku Toshi Seibi Kodan, 14-ban 6-go Kudan Kita 1-chome Chiyoda-ku, Tokyo Japan. **LC** HD7285; .M32.

II/0589-090X
MAIN RECOMMENDATIONS, PROCEEDINGS AND AGENDA NOTES. ***Title Change.*** **Main/Conf** Conference on Community Development and Panchayati Raj. Proceedings. English. Department of Community Development and Panchayati Raj Parliament House, New Delhi 110 001 India. ***Continued by*** *Conference of Chief Ministers and State Ministers for Community Development and Panchayati Raj. Proceedings and Agenda Notes.*
Desc: Vols. for include Main recommendations, proceedings, and agenda notes of the conference of State Ministers of community Development and Panchayati Raj. ... .

US/0897-2559
MAIN STREET NEWS. [Main str. news]. **Added/Corp** National Main Street Center (U.S.). **VFOAT** Main Street. (April 1985)-. Periodical. English. mo. comes with membership. National Trust for Historic Preservation, 1785 Massachusetts Avenue Northwest, Washington DC 20036. **Tel** (202)673-4035. **DD** 307. cum. index.
Ind/Abst Urban Aff. Abstr.

CN/0226-6857
MAISONS D'ICI. [Maisons ici]. Vol. 1 (April 1980)-. Periodical. French. mo. $20.00 Canada; $23.00 other. Mediadix, 859 rue St-Jacques, St-Jean-Sur-Richelieu Quebec J3B 6Z8 Canada. **DD** 690/.8/09714.

US
MAJOR DEVELOPMENT ANNOUNCEMENTS ANNUAL REPORT / ATLANTA REGIONAL COMMISSION. **Main/Corp** Atlanta Regional Commission. **VFOAT** Major Development Trends in the Atlanta Region. English. Atlanta Regional Comm., Northside Parkway, 200 Northcreek, Atlanta GA 30327. **Tel** (404)364-2502, FAX (404)364-2599. ***Continues*** *Major Development Trends in the Atlanta Region.*

CN/0319-4620
MAJOR REPORT - CENTRE FOR URBAN AND COMMUNITY STUDIES, UNIVERSITY OF TORONTO. **Main/Corp** University of Toronto. Centre for Urban and Community Studies. **Added/Corp** University of Toronto. Centre for Urban and Community Studies. (1???)-. Monographic series. English. ir. Price varies per volume. Centre for Urban and Community Studies, 455 Spadina Avenue, Room 426, Toronto Ontario M5S 2G8 Canada. **Tel** (416)978-2072. **DD** 301.36. cum. index. **Circ:** 200.
Desc: Urban studies, planning, social structure, housing and public policy.

US/0891-8821
MAKING CITIES LIVABLE NEWSLETTER. [Mak. cities livable newsl.]. **VFOAT** MCL Newsletter; M.C.L. Newsletter. Vol. 1, No. 1 (Feb. 1987)-. Newsletter. English. qt. $85.00. Center for Urban Well-Being, PO Box 7586, Carmel CA 93921. **DD** 307.

US/0147-3433
MANAGEMENT OF HOUSING. Government Publication. English. US Department of Housing and Urban Development, 451 Seventh Street SW, Washington DC 20401. **Tel** (202)708-0980, FAX (202)708-0299. **LC** TX960; .M35. **DD** 353.008/65.

US/0193-6808
MANAGING HOUSING LETTER. [Manag. hous. lett.]. (197?)-. Periodical. English. mo. $141.00. CD Publications, 8204 Fenton Street, Silver Spring MD 20910. **Tel** (800)666-6380, (301)588-6380, FAX (301)588-6385. **ED** Jim Kelder. **DD** 643. Index available.
Desc: News and advice for owners and managers of public, private and subsidized rental housing; includes news from Washington, plus practical management tips.

CN
MANITOBA COMMUNITY REPORTS. ***Title Change.*** English. Manitoba Department of Industry & Commerce, 505 Norway Building, Winnipeg Manitoba Canada. **LC** HT127; .M35. **DD** 330.97127/005. ***Continued by*** *Report on Manitoba Communities.*

US
MANUAL OF ACCEPTABLE PRACTICES. **Main/Corp** United States. Dept. of Housing and Urban Development. **VFOAT** Manual of Acceptable Practices to the HUD Minimum Property Standards. English. ir. Council of American Building Officials, 5202 Leesburg Pike, Falls Church VA 22041. **Tel** (202)783-3238.

US/1047-2967
MANUFACTURED HOME MERCHANDISER. [Manuf. home merch.]. Vol. 37, No. 10 (Oct. 1989)-. Periodical. English. mo. Free (trade), $36.00 (nontrade) US; $48.00 other. Mobile Manufactured Home, 203 North Wabash Avenue, Suite 800, Chicago IL 60601. **Tel** (312)236-3528. **LC** HD7395.M6; M62. **DD** 338.4/7690879/05. **Ad Acc. Circ:** 17,000 (ctrl). available on microfilm and microfiche from University Microfilms International (UMI). ***Continues*** *Mobile/Manufactured Home Merchandiser, 0191-9768.*
Ind/Abst Bus. Index (1989-); Gen. BusinessFile (1989-); Trade Ind. Index (Oct. 1989-).

US/0276-1645
MANUFACTURED HOMES APPRAISAL GUIDE, OFFICIAL VALUATION GUIDE. **VFOAT** Dealers Confidential Manufactured Homes Appraisal Guide. English. sa. $32.00. PO Box 2197, Everett WA 98203. **LC** HD7289.62.U6; M36. **DD** 338.4/3629226/0973.

Housing and Urban Development

US/0277-7924
MANUFACTURED HOUSING DEALER. ANNUAL DIRECTORY & BUYER'S GUIDE. **VFOAT** Manufactured Housing Dealer. Annual Directory and Buyers Guide; Manufactured Housing Industry Directory; Manufactured Housing Dealer Magazine. Annual Directory. Began with Vol. for 1979. Directory. **an.** $9.00. TL Enterprises, 29901 Agoura Road, Agoura CA 91301. **Tel** (800)234-3450, (805)389-0300. **LC** HD9715.7.U6; M643. **DD** 381/.45690879/02573. **Continues** Mobile-Modular Housing Dealer. Annual Directory and Buyer's Guide, 0097-7233.

US/0733-2351
MANUFACTURED HOUSING INDUSTRY ... BUYER'S MANUAL. **VFOAT** Buyer's Manual. 1981-. English. **an.** $20.00. JCL Corporation, 1308 Northwood Drive, Nappannee IN 46550. **LC** HD9715.5.U6; M36. **DD** 690/.879/029473.

US/0197-1816
MANUFACTURED HOUSING NEWSLETTER. (19??)-. Periodical. English. mo. $96.00 (one year), $168.00 (two year), $216.00 (three year) US; $116.00 (one year) other (includes postage). Manufactured Housing Newsletter, PO Box 6300, Battlement Mesa CO 81636. **Tel** (206)746-6272. **ED** Hal Carlson.
Desc: Covers news and detects trends in component, pre-cut, panelized, modular, and mobile home industries. Contains interviews with newsmakers. Follows regulatory, marketing, and financial events.

US
MANUFACTURED HOUSING QUARTERLY. Ceased. **VFOAT** Manufactured Housing. Ceased (1986). Periodical. English. qt. Manufactured Housing Institute, 1745 Jefferson Davis Highway, Arlington VA 22202. **Tel** (703)979-6620.

PO
MAPUTO ANTES DE INDEPENDENCIA: GEOGRAFIA DE UMA CIDADE COLONIAL. Portuguese. Instituto de Investigacao Cientifica Tropical, Centro de Documentacao e Informacao, rua Jau 47, 1 300 Lisbon Portugal. **Tel** 645321. **LC** HT169.M852.

CN
MARCHE (OTTAWA-CARLETON (ONTARIO). DEPARTEMENT DE L'URBANISME. GROUPE DE PARTICIPATION PUBLIQUE), EN. (EN MARCHE : UN BULLETIN D'INFORMATION / PAR LE GROUPE DE PARTICIPATION PUBLIQUE, DIRECTION DE POLITIQUES ET PROGRAMMES, SERVICE DE PLANIFICATION.). **VFOAT** In Process. Vol. 1, No. 3 (June 1979)-. Bulletin. French (English). Free. Groupe de Participation Publique, Service de Planification Municipalite Regionale d'Ottawa-Carleton, 8E Etage/222 rue Queen, Ottawa Ontario K1P 5Z3 Canada. **DD** 352.9/6/0971383. ctrl circ. **Continues** In Process (Ottawa-Carleton (Ontario). Departement de l'Urbanisme. Groupe de Participation Publique), 0711-2971.

US/0363-8286
MARKET ABSORPTION OF APARTMENTS. (CURRENT HOUSING REPORTS. H-130, MARKET ABSORPTION OF APARTMENTS.). [Mark. absorpt. apartm.]. **Added/Corp** United States. Bureau of the Census. United States. Dept. of Housing and Urban Development. **VFOAT** Market Absorption of Apartments. (1???)-. Government Publication. English. qt (annual index). $8.50 domestic; $10.65 other. Superintendent of Documents, US Government Printing Office, Washington DC 20402. **Tel** (202)275-3328, FAX (202)786-2377. **LC** HD7287.6.U5; A3. **DD** 333.33/8. Documents available from Documents on Demand.
Ind/Abst Am. Stat. Index.

CN/0576-2944
MDRP. **Main/Corp** MacKenzie Delta Research Project. **Added/Corp** Canada. Northern Science Research Group. Northern Co-Ordination and Research Centre. (1967)-. Monographic series. English. Price varies per volume. Northern Science Research Group, Department of Indian & Northern Affairs, Ottawa Ontario K1A 0H4 Canada. **Tel** (613)951-7276, (800)267-6677, telex 053-3585. **LC** HT395.C32; M35. **DD** 917.1; 309.2/5/0971221S.

AG
MEDIO AMBIENTE Y URBANIZACION. **Added/Corp** Consejo Latinoamericano de Ciencias Sociales. Comision de Desarrollo Urbano y Regional. Vol. 6, No. 21 (Dec. 1987)-. Periodical. Spanish. qt. $30.00 Argentina, Chile, Bolivia, Paraguay, Uruguay and Brazil; $35.00 elsewhere Latin America; $50.00 other. Centro de Estudios Urbanos y Regionales, Corrientes 2835, 1193 Buenos Aires, Argentina. **Tel** 011 54 1 9613050. **LC** HT127.5; .B65. **Continues** Boletin de Medio Ambiente y Urbanizacion, 0326-7857.
Ind/Abst PAIS Int. Print.

CN/0829-9153
METRO PLANNING REVIEW. (METRO PLANNING REVIEW / EDMONTON METROPOLITAN REGIONAL PLANNING COMMISSION.). [Metro plan. rev.]. **Added/Corp** Edmonton Metropolitan Regional Planning Commission. Vol. 1, Issue No. 1 (Winter 1986)-. Periodical. English. ir. Free. Edmonton Metropolitan Regional Planning Commission, 10303 Jasper Avenue, 9th Floor, Edmonton Alberta T5J 3N6 Canada. **Tel** (403)423-5701. **ED** Philippa Fairbairn. **DD** 307/.12/0971233. Circ: 1,000. **Continues** Regional Update, 0822-8981.
Desc: Contains planning matters in the Edmonton Region and general planning-related issues.

FR/0223-5633
METROPOLIS (PARIS). (METROPOLIS.). [Metropolis]. **VFOAT** International Metropolis. (1974)-. Periodical. French (English). mo. 47.50F, 70.00F (airmail). Coept, 27 rue du Chateau-d'eau, 75010 Paris France. **Tel** (1)42-40-61-87, FAX (1)42 40 06 20. **Bk Rev. Ad Acc.**
Desc: Urbanism, environmental planning, architecture transports, and telecommunications.

US/0893-8490
METROPOLITAN REVIEW (CHICAGO, ILL.). (METROPOLITAN REVIEW.). [Metrop. rev.]. **VFOAT** Metropolitan Review of Architecture, Art, Design, Urban Planning, Interiors, Culture, Theory, History, The City & The House. Vol. 1, No. 1 (Jan./Feb. 1988)-. Periodical. English. an (Summer). $25.00 (one year); $45.00 (two years). Metropolitan Press Publications Inc., 1165 North Clark Street, 2nd Floor, Chicago IL 60610. **Tel** (312)280-0131. **DD** 725. Index available ($6.00). **Ad Acc.**
Desc: Regular issues feature such new building types as the skyscraper, corporate facilities, institutions, public spaces, residential design, town planning and landscape architecture - everything from the city to the house.

US/1061-981X
METROPOLITAN RICHMOND APARTMENTS FOR RENT. [Metrop. Richmond apartm. rent]. **VFOAT** Apartments for Rent. (Aug. 27, 1991)-. Periodical. English. bw. Free. Adler Group Inc., 8601 Georgia Avenue, Silver Spring MD 20910. **Tel** (609)988-0092, FAX (609)988-0093. **DD** 333.

US/1061-9607
MHFA UPDATE. (MHFA UPDATE : QUARTERLY NEWSLETTER OF THE MASSACHUSETTS HOUSING FINANCE AGENCY.). **Added/Corp** Massachusetts Housing Finance Agency. **VAT** Massachusetts Housing Finance Agency Update. Vol. 10, No. 4 Summer (1991)-. Newsletter. English. qt. Massachusetts Housing Finance Agency, 50 Milk Street, Boston MA 02109. **Continues** MHFA Newsletter, 0741-1014.

US
MICHIGAN HOUSING MARKET INFORMATION SYSTEM MONOGRAPH SERIES, THE. No. 1- 1975-. English. Michigan State Housing Development Authority, 300 South Capitol Avenue, Lansing MI 48926. **Tel** (517)373-8370. **LC** HV86; .M536 subser. **DD** 361/.9774.

US/1047-1359
MIN FAX. [Min fax]. **Added/Corp** Marketing Information Network. **VFOAT** Minfax. (19??)-. Periodical. English. Twelve times a year. $125.00. Marketing Information Network, 475 Fifth Avenue, Suite 503, New York NY 10017. **Tel** (212)670-0711. **ED** Edward C. Birkner, Mary Weber, and Elizabeth Birkner. **DD** 333. Index available. cum. index. **Bk Rev. Circ:** 500. **Absorbed** Span.
Desc: A newsletter of real estate development and investment. News and housing plus house plans and designs.

US
MINIMUM PROPERTY STANDARDS FOR CARE-TYPE HOUSING. **Main/Corp** United States. Dept. of Housing and Urban Development. Government Publication. English. qt. US Department of Housing and Urban Development, 451 Seventh Street SW, Washington DC 20401. **Tel** (202)708-0980, FAX (202)708-0299.

US
MINIMUM PROPERTY STANDARDS FOR MULTIFAMILY HOUSING. **Main/Corp** United States. Dept. of Housing and Urban Development. (19??)-. Government Publication. English. ir. $88.75. Superintendent of Documents, US Government Printing Office, Washington DC 20402. **Tel** (202)275-3328, FAX (202)786-2377. **Continues** United States. Federal Housing Administration. Minimum Property Standards for Multifamily Housing.

US
MINIMUM PROPERTY STANDARDS FOR ONE-AND TWO-FAMILY DWELLINGS. **Main/Corp** United States. Dept. of Housing and Urban Development. (19??)-. Government Publication. English. ir. Superintendent of Documents, US Government Printing Office, Washington DC 20402. **Tel** (202)275-3328, FAX (202)786-2377. **Continues** Minimum Property Standards for One- and Two-Family Dwellings.

US/0149-9610
MISSOURI OVERALL PROGRAM DESIGN AND ANNUAL WORK PROGRAM. **Main/Corp** Missouri. Division of Budget and Planning. **VFOAT** Missouri Overall Program Design and Annual Work Program Fiscal Year. 1977-. English. an. Division of Budget and Planning, B-9 Capitol Building, Jefferson City MO 65101. **LC** HT393.M8; M56A. **DD** 309.2/5/09778. **Continues** Missouri Overall Program Design, 0360-9634.

GW/0011-9822
MITTEILUNGEN - DEUTSCHE AKADEMIE FUER STADTEBAU UND LANDESPLANUNG. **Main/Corp** Deutsche Akademie fur Stadtebau und Landesplanung. Periodical. German.
Ind/Abst PAIS Int. Print (1991-).

UK
MOBILE & HOLIDAY HOMES. **VFOAT** Mobile and Holiday Homes. English. mo. £13.20 UK; £19.20 other. Link House Magazines Ltd., Link House, Dingwall Avenue, Croydon Surrey CR9 2TA England. **Tel** 011 44 81 686 2599, FAX 011 44 81 760 5154, telex 947709. **ED** Anne Webb. **LC** TL297; .M6. **DD** 643/.2. Index available. cum. index. **Bk Rev. Ad Acc.** **Continues** Mobile Home and Holiday Caravan, 0306-5839.
Desc: The only UK magazine covering the static carvan market for both residential and leisure use.

US/8750-0655
MOBILE HOME LIVING. (MOBILE HOME LIVING : THE OFFICIAL VOICE OF THE MOBILE HOME OWNERS OF AMERICA.). Periodical. English. bm. $7.50. MHOA, PO Box 753, Bothwell WA 98041. **Tel** (206)485-4343. **ED** Cher Griffin. **Ad Acc. Circ:** 3,500.

US/0270-4005
MONETARY POLICY REPORT FROM THE COMMITTEE ON BANKING, HOUSING, AND URBAN AFFAIRS, UNITED STATES SENATE. See Business-Banking and Finance.

US
MORTGAGE INSURANCE FOR THE PURCHASE OR REFINANCING OF EXISTING MULTIFAMILY HOUSING PROJECTS. See Insurance.

US/0742-8073
MOTOR HOME TRADE-IN GUIDE. Title Change. [Motor home trade-in guide]. 15th Ed. (1983)-?. English. an. Intertec Publishing Corporation, 9800 Metcalf, Overland Park KS 66212. **Tel** (913)341-1300. **LC** HD9715.7.U6; O36. **DD** 381/.45690879/0973. **Continues** Official Motor Home Trade-In Guide, 0093-1195. **Continued by** Motor Home & Truck Camper Trade-In Guide.

IT
MPTOZOAROP / EDILIZIA RESIDENZA PUBBLICA. (19??)-. Italian. Edilizia Populare Srl, Quadrato della Concordia 9, 00144 Rome Eur Italy.

US/0744-169X
MULTI-HOUSING MAINSTREAM. (MULTI-HOUSING MAINSTREAM / NATIONAL APARTMENT ASSOCIATION). **Added/Corp** National Apartment Association (U.S.). (198?)-. Periodical. English. mo. National Apartment Association, 1111 14th Street NW/Suite 900, Washington DC 20005.

US/0146-0919
MULTI-HOUSING NEWS. **VFOAT** MHN; MHN Multi-Housing News. (19??)-. Periodical. English. Six times a year. $30.00 US; $46.00 Canada & Mexico; $90.00 other. Miller Freeman Inc., 600 Harrison Street, San Francisco CA 94107. **Tel** (415)905-2337, FAX (415)905-2240, telex 278273. **(Subscription address:** JCI, PO Box 1766, Riverton NJ 08077.**) [CCC].** **Continues** Apartment Construction News.

US
MULTI-HOUSING NEWSLETTER. **VFOAT** Multi Housing Newsletter; MHN. Vol. 1, No. 8 (Dec. 18, 1991)-. Newsletter. English. sm. $345.00 US and Canada; $385.00 other. Miller Freeman Inc., 600 Harrison Street, San Francisco CA 94107. **Tel** (415)905-2337, FAX (415)905-2240, telex 278273.

CN/0702-7206
MUNICIPAL AND PLANNING LAW REPORTS. See Law.

US
NADA MANUFACTURED HOUSING APPRAISAL GUIDE. (19??)-. English. Three times a year. $95.00. NADA Appraisal Guides, PO Box

7800, Costa Mesa CA 92628. **Tel** (714)556-8511, (800)966-6232, FAX (714)556-8715. ***Continues*** *NADA Mobile Home Manufactured Housing Appraisal Guide.*

US/0363-6453
NAHRO ROSTER. **Main/Corp** National Association of Housing and Redevelopment Officials. **VAT** National Association of Housing and Redevelopment Officials Roster. English. an. $24.00. National Association of Housing and Redevelopment Officials, 2600 Virginia Avenue NW, Washington DC 20037. **Tel** (202)333-2020. **ED** Terence Cooper. **LC** HD7293.A1; N238A. **DD** 350/.865/02573. **Bk Rev. Ad Acc. Circ:** 12,500 (ctrl).
Desc: The journals' content consists of public housing developments, community revitalization and legislation in the industry.

IT/0027-7835
NAPOLI NOBILISSIMA. **See** The Arts.

US/1059-3071
NATIONAL HOUSING REGISTER. [Natl. hous. regist.]. (1991)-. Periodical. English. National Housing Register, 27239 Meadowbrook Drive, Davis CA 95616-5049. **DD** 363.

XR
NAVRH A BYDLENI. Periodical. Czech (summaries and/or abstracts in English, German and Russian). an. Ustav Bytove A Odevni, Kultury Prague 1, Na Prikope 27 Czech Republic. **LC** TH4809.C95; N39.

US/0743-4529
NCPC QUARTERLY. (NCPC QUARTERLY / NATIONAL CAPITAL PLANNING COMMISSION.). **Added/Corp** United States. National Capital Planning Commission. **VFOAT** N.C.P.C. Quarterly. **VAT** National Capital Planning Commission Quarterly. (Winter 1981)-. Periodical. English. qt. Free on request. National Capital Planning Commission, 1325 G Street Northwest, Washington DC 20576. **Tel** (202)724-0176. **LC** HT394.W3; U5a. **DD** 361.6/09753. ctrl circ. ***Continues*** *Quarterly Review of Commission Proceedings, 0098-308X.*
Desc: Narrative photos of federal projects in the Washington DC area.

US/0160-211X
NEBRASKA ANNUAL HOUSING REPORT. **Main/Corp** Nebraska. Dept. of Economic Development. Division of Research. **Added/Corp** Nebraska. Division of Community Affairs. (19??)-. English. an. Nebraska Department of Economic Development, Box 94666, 301 Centinnial Mall, Lincoln NE 68509. **Tel** (402)471-3111. **LC** HD7303.N2; N42a. **DD** 301.5/4/09782.

US/0740-526X
NEIGHBORHOOD IDEAS. [Neighb. ideas]. V. 1- Sept. 1976-. Periodical. English. mo. $20.00. Neighborhood Ideas, PO Box 39208, Washington DC 20016.

US/0193-791X
NEIGHBORHOOD WORKS, THE. [Neighb. works]. **Added/Corp** Center for Neighborhood Technology (Chicago, Ill.). (Jan. 1978)-. Periodical. English. Six times a year. $40.00 (one year), $60.00 (two year) institutions, $30.00 (one year), $45.00 (two year) individuals. Neighborhood Works, 2125 West North Avenue, Chicago IL 60647. **Tel** (312)278-4800. **ED** Patti Wolter (editor's phone: (312)278-4800 ext. 113). cum. index. **Bk Rev. Ad Acc, Adv Mgr:** Bridget, **Tel** (312)278-4800 ext. 113. **Circ:** 2,000.
Desc: Resources for urban communities involving community development issues focused around energy, housing, food and environmental quality.
Ind/Abst Altern. Press Index; Urban Aff. Abstr.

NE/0920-1580
NETHERLANDS JOURNAL OF HOUSING AND ENVIRONMENTAL RESEARCH. ***Title Change.*** **Added/Corp** Gestructureerde Samenwerking (Organization : Netherlands) Nederlands Instituut voor Ruimtelijke Ordeningen Volkshuisvesting. **VFOAT** Housing and Environmental Research; H & E. Vol. 1, No. 1 (1986)-(19??). Periodical. English. qt. Delft University Press, Stevinweg 1, 2628 CN Delft The Netherlands. **Tel** 011 31 15 783254. ***Continued by*** *Netherlands Journal of Housing and the Built Environment.*
Desc: Publishes results of research in the environmental field and contributes to the enhancement of the quality of this research and to the exchange of scientific contacts between researchers beyond.

NE
NETHERLANDS JOURNAL OF HOUSING AND THE BUILT ENVIRONMENT. **Added/Corp** Gestructureerde Samenwerking (Organization : Netherlands) Nederlands Instituut voor Ruimtelijke Ordeningen Volkshuisvesting. **VFOAT** H E; Housing and the Built Environment. Vol. 6, No. 1 (1991)-. Periodical. English. qt. Fl145.00. Delft University Press, Stevinweg 1, 2628 CN Delft The Netherlands. **Tel** 011 31 15 783254. ***Continues*** *Netherlands Journal of Housing and Environmental Research.*

US
NEW JERSEY BUILDING PERMITS, ANNUAL SUMMARY. an. Free. Labor Market & Demographics, New Jersey Department of Labor, CN 388, Trenton NJ 08625. **Tel** (609)292-2323.
Desc: Annual data on residential and non-residential building and demolition permits.

US/0277-9218
NEW JERSEY MUNICIPAL DATA BOOK, THE. (THE NEW JERSEY MUNICIPAL DATA BOOK / COMPILED BY NEW JERSEY ASSOCIATES.). **Added/Corp** New Jersey Associates. (19??)-. English. an (Oct.). $80.00. Information Publications, 3790 El Camino Real/Suite 162, Palo Alto CA 94306. **Tel** (415)965-4449. **LC** HT123.5.N5; N53. **DD** 307.7/6/09749.

US/0097-8213
NEW SETTLER'S GUIDE FOR WASHINGTON, D.C. AND COMMUNITIES IN NEARBY MARYLAND AND VIRGINIA, THE. (19??)-. English. an. $7.00. New Settlers Guide, 8824 Tuckerman Lane, Potomac MD 20854. **Tel** (301)299-7507. **ED** Robert B. Minogue. **LC** F192.3; .N445. **DD** 917.53. **Ad Acc. Circ:** 15,000.
Desc: Vital facts for Washington, Maryland, Virginia and eleven surrounding counties, 80 individual communities, type of community, public, private schools, recreation, taxes, services, etc.

CN/0705-1034
NEWSLETTER. **Main/Corp** Housing and Urban Development Association of Canada. Economic Research Committee. (1971/72)-. Newsletter. English. ir. Canadian Home Builders' Association, 200 Elgin Street/5th Floor, Ottawa Ontario K2P 1L5 Canada. **Tel** (613)230-3060, FAX (613)232-4635. **DD** 301.5/4/0971.

US
NEWSLETTER - AMERICAN PLANNING ASSOCIATION, TEXAS CHAPTER. **Main/Corp** American Planning Association. Texas Chapter. **Added/Corp** Texas. University at Austin. Graduate Program in Community and Regional Planning. Vol. 6, No. 4 (Nov. 1978)-. Newsletter. English. ***Continues*** *Newsletter - American Institute of Planners, Texas Chapter.*

IT
NEWSLETTER IMMOBILIARE. Newsletter. Italian. mo. L70000. Pirola Editore, CP 10444, Via Parabiago 19, 20151 Milan Italy. **Tel** 011 39 2 3022888.

CN/1188-1429
NEWSLETTER - LONDON (ONT.). PLANNING DIVISION. (NEWSLETTER / CITY OF LONDON, PLANNING DIVISION.). [Newsl. - Lond. (Ont.), Plan. Div.]. **Added/Corp** London (Ont.). Planning Division. Vol. 1, No. 1 (June 1991)-. Newsletter. English. qt. Limited free distribution. City of London, Planning Division, 300 Dufferin Avenue, PO Box 5035, London Ontario N6A 4L9 Canada. **DD** 711.

US/0147-9334
NEWSLETTER - MARYLAND DEPARTMENT OF STATE PLANNING. **Main/Corp** Maryland. Dept. of State Planning. Vol. 13, No. 3 (Mar. 1960)-. Newsletter. English. bm. 301 West Preston Street, Baltimore MD 21201. **LC** HC107.M3; M266a. **DD** 338.9752. ***Continues*** *News Letter - Maryland State Planning Commission, 0147-9431.*

SW
NEWSLETTER OF SWEDISH BUILDING RESEARCH. **See** Building and Construction.

US/0584-4266
NEWSLETTER - SOUTHEASTERN WISCONSIN REGIONAL PLANNING COMMISSION. **Main/Corp** Southeastern Wisconsin Regional Planning Commission. Vol. 1 (1961)-. Newsletter. English. bm. Free, Wisconsin; $12.00 other. Southeastern Wisconsin Regional Planning Commission, PO Box 1607, Waukesha WI 53187. **Tel** (414)547-6721. **ED** Kurt W. Bauer. **LC** HT393.W6; S68c. **Circ:** 2,000 (ctrl).
Desc: Summary of the commission's work in a more popular vein. Summarizes and digests larger major publications and informs the constituency of items of general interest.

NO/0802-8818
NORD REVY : TIDSSKRIFT FOR REGIONAL UDVIKLING, NAERINGSLIV, MILJOE. **Added/Corp** Nordiska Arbetsgruppen for Regionalpolitisk Forskning. **VFOAT** Nord Revy. Vol. 1 (1990)-. Periodical. Norwegian (Swedish and Danish; summaries and/or abstracts in English). bm. Kr550.00, $98.00. Scandinavian University Press, PO Box 2959 Toeyen, N 0608 Oslo 6 Norway. **Tel** 011 47 2 2575400, FAX 011 47 2 2575353, telex 71896 UROR N. **(Subscription address:** Scandinavian University Press, 200 Meacham Ave., Elmont NY 11003.) **ED** Lars Hedegaard. **LC** DL55; .N63. **Pr Rev.**
Desc: Scandinavian journal of regional development, business and the environment.
Ind/Abst Geogr. Abstr. Human Geogr.

JA/0912-9731
NOSON KEIKAKU GAKKAISHI. [Noson Keikaku Gakkaishi]. **VFOAT** Journal of Rural Planning Association. (1982)-. Periodical. Multiple languages. qt. Noson Keikaku Gakkai, (Rural Planning Assoc.), c/o Nihon Daigaku Nojuigakubu, Nogyo Kogakuka Nogyo Kenchikugaku, Kenkyushitsu, 1866, Kameino, Fuzisawashi, Kanagawaken 252, Japan. **DD** 338.1.
Ind/Abst For. Abstr.; Leis. Recreat. Tour. Abstr.

CN/0226-9988
NOTES DE RECHERCHE (UNIVERSITE DE MONTREAL. FACULTE DE L'AMENAGEMENT). (NOTES DE RECHERCHE / FACULTE DE L'AMENAGEMENT, UNIVERSITE DE MONTREAL.). [Notes rech. - Fac. amenage., Univ. Montr.]. French. Faculte de l'Amenagement, Universite de Montreal, 5620 Av Darlington, Montreal Quebec H3T 1T2 Canada. **Tel** (514)343-6835. **ED** Denys Marchand. **DD** 711/.4/05. **Circ:** 500.
Desc: Research reports or preliminary writings on subject related to architecture, landscape architecture, urban and regional planning, industrial design. Theoretical or practical approaches from faculty staff and Ph.D. students.

●US/1071-9466
NTIS ALERT. REGIONAL & URBAN PLANNING & TECHNOLOGY. [NTIS alert, Reg. urban plan. technol.]. **Added/Corp** United States. National Technical Information Service. **VFOAT** Regional & Urban Planning & Technology; Regional and Urban Planning and Technology; National Technical Information Service Alert. Regional & Urban Planning & Technology. Vol. 92, No. 14 (Apr. 15, 1992)-. Periodical. English. Twenty-four times a year. $160.00 US; $225.00 other. National Technical Information Service - NTIS, Room 2027S, 5285 Port Royal Road, Springfield VA 22161. **Tel** (703)487-4630, (703)487-4660, (703)487-4650, FAX (703)321-8547, telex 89-9405. **DD** 307. Index Available Received separately--bound from publisher. ***Formed by the union of*** *NTIS Alert. Urban & Regional Technology & Development, 1071-9482* ***and*** *NTIS Alert. Problem-Solving Information for State & Local Governments, 1071-9474.*
Desc: Provides information on economic and community development, emergency services and planning, housing, recreation, etc.

US
NTIS ALERT. URBAN & REGIONAL TECHNOLOGY & DEVELOPMENT. ***Title Change.*** **Added/Corp** United States. National Technical Information Service. **VFOAT** Urban and Regional Technology and Development; Urban & Regional Technology & Development; National Technical Information Service Alert. Urban and Regional Technology and Development. Vol. 92, No. 1 (Jan. 7, 1992)-(Mar. 24, 1992). Periodical. English. wk. National Technical Information Service - NTIS, Room 2027S, 5285 Port Royal Road, Springfield VA 22161. **Tel** (703)487-4630, (703)487-4660, (703)487-4650, FAX (703)321-8547, telex 89-9405. ***Continues*** *Urban & Regional Technology & Development, 0163-1535.* ***Merged with*** *NTIS Alert. Problem-Solving Information for State & Local Government* ***to form*** *NTIS Alert. Regional & Urban Planning & Technology.*

US/0888-5303
NUC URBAN EXCHANGE. (NUC URBAN EXCHANGE : THE NATIONAL URBAN COALITION NEWSLETTER.). [NUC urban exch.]. **VFOAT** Urban Exchange. **VAT** National Urban Coalition Urban Exchange. Began in 1986. Newsletter. English. bm. National Urban Coalition, 8601 Georgia Avenue/Suite 500, Silver Spring MD 20910. **DD** 352.

US
OCCASIONAL PAPER - PROGRAM IN URBAN AND REGIONAL STUDIES. **Main/Corp** Cornell University. Program in Urban and Regional Studies. No. 7-. Monographic series. English. ir. Price varies per volume. Cornell University Purs Publs, 209 West Sibley Hall, Ithaca NY 14853. **Tel** (607)256-6262. ***Continues*** *Occasional Paper - Center for Urban Development Research.*

TZ
OCCASIONAL PAPERS ON COMMUNITY DEVELOPMENT - EAST AFRICAN LITERATURE BUREAU. **Main/Corp** East African Literature Bureau. 1- 1962-. English. East African Literature Bureau. **LC** HN800.E13; A3. **DD** 309.2/6/0967.

BE
OCMW FOCUS. (19??)-. Dutch. mo (June/July and Aug./Sept. issues combined). 566.04F Belgium; $18.97 US. Vereniging Van Belg Sted Gemen, Aarlenstraat 53 Bus 4, 1040 Brussels Belgium. **Tel** 011 32 2 233 21 11, 011 32 2 2332011, FAX 011 32 2 231 15 23. **Bk Rev.**
Desc: Covers social work by public service.

US/0191-6335
OFFICIAL CALIFORNIA APARTMENT JOURNAL. **Added/Corp** Apartment Association California Southern Cities. **VFOAT** Apartment Journal. (19??)-. Periodical. English. mo. Official California Apartment Journal Inc, PO Box 17038, Long Beach CA 90807. **Tel** (310)426-8341. **Bk Rev. Ad Acc. Circ:** 6,000 (ctrl).
Desc: Rental housing management; professionalism is fostered thru educational materials and reports on new products, techniques; reports on legislative activity affecting rental housing business.

US/0360-1463
OFFICIAL COMPREHENSIVE DEVELOPMENT PLAN. **Main/Corp** Atlanta (Ga.). Bureau of Planning. English. an. 700 City Hall, 68 Mitchell Street SW, Atlanta GA 30303. **LC** HT168.A7; A74A. **DD** 711/.4/0975823.

US
OHIOSCAPES NEWSLETTER. Newsletter. English. qt. free. Ohio Department of Economic and Community Development, PO Box 1001, Columbus OH 43266. **Tel** (614)466-2285. **ED** Mary Dupler. **Bk Rev. Circ:** 1600 (ctrl).
Desc: Designed to provide Community Development Block Grant Program recipients with up-to-date information regarding all aspects of the program.

JA
OKINAWA NO SHINKO KAIHATSU. **Main/Corp** Japan. Okinawa Kaihatsucho. (19??)-. Periodical. Japanese. Okinawa Kaihatsucho, 6-1 Nagatacho 1-chome Chiyoda-ku, Tokyo 100 Japan. **LC** HT395.J32; O383.

CN/0228-8494
OMH. OFFICES MUNICIPAUX D'HABITATION. (OMH ... : BULLETIN D'INFORMATION DE L'ASSOCIATION DES OFFICES MUNICIPAUX D'HABITATION DU QUEBEC.). [OMH, Off. munic. habitat.]. **Added/Corp** Association des Offices Municipaux d'Habitation du Quebec. **VAT** Offices Municipaux d'Habitation. (1975)-. Bulletin. French. ir. Free to members. Association des Offices Municipaux d'Habitation du Quebec, Bureau 222/2095 Ouest Boul Charest, Sainte-Foy Quebec G1N 4L8 Canada. **Tel** (418)683-9010. **DD** 363.5/09714. Index available. **Ad Acc. Circ:** 3,500.

CN/0702-5459
ON-SITE (EDMONTON). (ON-SITE.). V. 1- Feb. 1977-. Periodical. English. mo. Free. Hudac Alberta Council, 201-11230-119 Street, Edmonton Alta. T5G 2X3. **DD** 363.5/097123.

US/0747-3435
ORANGE COUNTY APARTMENT NEWS. (ORANGE COUNTY APARTMENT NEWS / APARTMENT ASSOCIATION OF ORANGE COUNTY.). **Added/Corp** Apartment Association of Orange County. **VFOAT** Apartment News. (19??)-. Periodical. English. Twelve times a year. $36.00. Apartment Association of Orange County, PO Box 4809, Garden Grove CA 92642. **Tel** (714)638-5550. **ED** William H. Kraus. Index available. **Ad Acc. Circ:** 5,800 (ctrl).

US
ORGANIZATION: OFFICE OF THE ASSISTANT SECRETARY FOR POLICY DEVELOPMENT AND RESEARCH. **Added/Corp** United States. Dept. of Housing and Urban Development. (19??)-. Government Publication. English. US Department of Housing and Urban Development, 451 Seventh Street SW, Washington DC 20401. **Tel** (202)708-0980, FAX (202)708-0299.

US/0892-192X
OUR REGION. ***Ceased.*** (OUR REGION : A PUBLICATION OF THE ERIE AND NIAGARA COUNTIES REGIONAL PLANNING BOARD.). **VFOAT** Our Erie & Niagara Region. (Spring/Summer Issue 1986)-(19??). Periodical. English. qt. Erie and Niagara Counties Regional Planning Board, 3103 Sheridan Drive, Amherst NY 14226. **Tel** (716)837-2035. **ED** David J Evans. **Circ:** 1,000.

US
OUR ... YEAR / REGIONAL PLANNING COUNCIL. **Main/Corp** Regional Planning Council (MD.). **VFOAT** Annual Report of the Regional Planning Council. English. an. Regional Planning Council Government, 601 North Howard Street, Baltimore MD 21201-4585. **Tel** (301)333-3333, FAX (301)659-1260. **LC** HT394.B3; R42A. **DD** 352.9/6/0975271.

US
OVERALL PROGRAM DESIGN FOR COMPREHENSIVE METROPOLITAN PLANNING AND DECISION MAKING. **Main/Corp** Metroplan. English. Continental Building, 100 Main Street, Little Rock AR 72201. **LC** HT393.A8; M45A. **DD** 309.2/5/09767.

CN/0048-4326
P I B C NEWS. **Main/Corp** Planning Institute of British Columbia. Vol. 13, No. 2 (July 1970)-. Periodical. English. Six times a year. 35.00Can$ North & South America; 40.00Can$ other. Planning Institute of British Columbia, #20 10551 Shellbridge Columbia, Richmond British Columbia V6X 2W9 Canada. **Tel** (604)270-2061, FAX (604)660-2271. **ED** Bob Burgess & Graham Stallard. **Ad Acc. Circ:** 500. ***Continues*** *P I B C Newsletter, 0380-6650.*

US/0738-1867
PACIFIC MOUNTAIN QUARTERLY. Vol. 1, No. 1 (Spring 1983)-. Periodical. English. qt. Free to those involved in rural development services. Rural Community Assistance Corporation, 1900 K Street, Suite 202, Sacramento CA 95814.

IT/1120-3544
PAESAGGIO URBANO. Italian. bm. L72000 (individuals), L130000 (institutions). Maggioli Editore, Casella Postale 290, 47037 Rimini, Italy. **Tel** 011 39 541 628666, FAX 011 39 541 742217.

CN/0833-1871
PAPERS IN CANADIAN ECONOMIC DEVELOPMENT. [Pap. Can. econ. dev.]. **Added/Corp** University of Waterloo. Faculty of Environmental Studies. Economic Development Program. Industrial Developers Association of Canada. Vol. 1 (1987)-. Periodical. English. Economic Development Program, University of Waterloo, Waterloo, Ontario N2L 3G1 Canada. **LC** HC111; .P36. **DD** 338.971/005.
Ind/Abst Geogr. Abstr. Human Geogr.

US/1056-8190
PAPERS IN REGIONAL SCIENCE : THE JOURNAL OF THE REGIONAL SCIENCE ASSOCIATION INTERNATIONAL. [Pap. reg. sci.]. **Added/Corp** Regional Science Association International. Regional Science Association International. Meeting. Regional Science Association International. European Congress. Regional Science Association International. Pacific Conference. **VFOAT** Journal of the Regional Science Association International; Journal of the RSAI. Vol. 70, No. 1 (Jan. 1991)-. Periodical. English. qt (Mar, June, Sept, Dec). $120.00. Regional Science Association, University of Illinois, 901 S Mathews Street, Urbana IL 61801-3682. **Tel** (217)333-9895, FAX (217)244-1785. **LC** HT390; .R44. **DD** 307. ***Continues*** *Papers, 0486-2902.*
Ind/Abst World Agric. Econ.

CN/0225-2724
PAPERS ON PLANNING AND DESIGN. (PAPERS ON PLANNING AND DESIGN / DEPT. OF URBAN AND REGIONAL PLANNNING, UNIVERSITY OF TORONTO,). [Pap. plann. des.]. **Added/Corp** University of Toronto. Dept. of Urban and Regional Planning. **VFOAT** Papers on Planning & Design. (197?)-. Monographic series. English. ir. price varies per volume. University of Toronto / Department Geography, 230 College Street, Toronto Ontario M5S 1A1 Canada. **Tel** (416)978-3376. **LC** UNC.

IT/0031-1731
PARAMETRO. [Parametro]. (1970)-. Periodical. Italian (English; summaries and/or abstracts in French and German). Six times a year. L98000 Italy; L140000 others. Faenza Editrice, Via P de Crescenzi 44, 48018 Faenza Italy. **Tel** 011 39 546 663488, FAX 011 39 546 660440, telex 550387.
Ind/Abst Archit. Period. Index (1970-19??); Avery Index Archit. Period. Suppl. Colum. Univ. (Sept. 1989-).

FR
PARIS PROJET. **Added/Corp** Atelier Parisien d'Urbanisme. (19??)-. Periodical. French. Three times a year. 350.00F (France); 400.00F (other). Atelier Parisien d'Urbanisme, 17 Boulevard Morland, 75181 Paris Cedex 04 France. **Tel** 11 33 1 42712814. **LC** HT178.F72; P37. **DD** 307/.12/0944361.
Desc: Publishes articles concerning the city's statistical data, demographic and economic studies, transportation, and Urban development.
Ind/Abst Avery Index Archit. Period. Suppl. Colum. Univ. (1990-); Geogr. Abstr. Human Geogr.

US/1040-7340
PAS MEMO. (PAS MEMO / AMERICAN SOCIETY OF PLANNING OFFICIALS, PLANNING ADVISORY SERVICE.). [PAS memo]. **Added/Corp** American Society of Planning Officials. Planning Advisory Service. American Planning Association. Planning Advisory Service. **VFOAT** Planning Advisory Service Memos. **VAT** Planning Advisory Service Memo. (1971)-. Periodical. English. Twelve times a year. Price varies. American Planning Association, 1313 East 60th Street, Chicago IL 60637. **Tel** (312)955-9100, FAX (312)955-8312. **DD** 350.
Ind/Abst Avery Index Archit. Period. Suppl. Colum. Univ. (Apr. 1989, Mar. 1990); Ecol. Abstr.; Geogr. Abstr. Human Geogr.

CN/1187-2713
PATRIMOINE TRIFLUVIEN. [Patrim. trifluvien]. **Added/Corp** Societe de Conservation et d'Animation du Patrimoine de Trois-Rivieres. No. 1 (Apr 1991)-. French. Free for members. Societe de Conservation et D'Animation du Patrimoine de Trois-Rivieres, CP 1391, Trois-Rivieres, Quebec G9A 5L2 Canada. **DD** 971.4/45/05. ***Continues*** *Patrimoine (Trois-Rivieres, Quebec)., 1187-2721.*

●US/1059-2016
PBC HOUSING BRIEFS. **VFOAT** Housing Briefs. **VAT** Publishing and Business Consultants Housing Briefs. (1993)-. Newsletter. English. qt. Publishing & Business Consultants, PO Box 75392, Los Angeles CA 90075. **Tel** (213)732-3477, FAX (213)732-9123.

US
PDR, RESEARCH AND TECHNOLOGY PROGRAM. **Main/Corp** United States. Dept. of Housing and Urban Development. Office of Policy Development and Research. **VFOAT** Research and Technology. **VAT** Policy Development Research, Research and Technology Program. Government Publication. English. US Department of Housing and Urban Development, 451 Seventh Street SW, Washington DC 20401. **Tel** (202)708-0980, FAX (202)708-0299. **LC** HT167.2; .U53E. **DD** 301.36/0973.

US/0197-2545
PERSPECTIVE (LUBBOCK). (PERSPECTIVE.). **Main/Corp** South Plains Association of Governments. English. an. South Plains Association of Governments, 1323 58th Street, Lubbock TX 79412. **LC** HT393.T48; S66B. **DD** 361.6/09764/84.

BL/0101-8612
PESQUISA MUNICIPAL / FUNDACAO SISTEMA ESTADUAL DE ANALISE DE DADOS, SEADE. Began with V. for 1979/1980. Portuguese. be. SEADE, Av Casper Libero 464, 01033 Sao Paulo SP Brazil. **Tel** 011 55 11 2279788. **LC** HT129.B7; P47. **DD** 307.7/6/098161.

IT
PIANO. ***Ceased.*** Vol. 1 (Oct. 1976/Jan. 1977)-?. Periodical. Multiple languages (English and Italian). Three times a year. Medicea, Porta S Maria 8, 50122 Firenze Italy. **LC** HT166.

NQ
PIEDRA BOCONA, LA. **Added/Corp** Italy. Direzione Generale per la Cooperazione Allo Sviluppo. Vol. 1, No. 1 (July 1991)-. Periodical. Spanish. mo. Cooperacion Italian para el Desarollo, Apdo. 93, Granada Nicaragua. **Tel** 2839. **ED** Ronaldo Puerto Lazo.

LV
PILSETU VESTURES PROBLEMAS. **Main/Corp** Petera Stuckas Latvijas Valsts Valsts Universitate. Visparejas Vestures Katedra. (1974)-. Multiple languages (Latvian and Russian). **LC** DK511.L17; R5a.

US/0279-9278
PLACE IN THE COUNTRY, A. **Added/Corp** New England Farm and Home Association. (19??)-. Periodical. English. Twelve times a year. $8.00. New England Farm Bulletin, Box 67, Cohasset MA 02025. **Tel** (617)383-0158.

CN/0032-0544
PLAN CANADA. [Plan Can.]. **Added/Corp** Town Planning Institute of Canada. Canadian Institute of Planners. Vol. 1 (1959)-. Periodical. English (French). Six times a year. 61.60Can$ (institutions), 55.00Can$ (individuals) Canada; 77.00Can$ (institutions), 61.60Can$ other. Canadian Institute of Planners, 541 Sussex Drive, Second Floor, Ottawa Ontario K1N 6Z6 Canada. **Tel** (613)562-4646. **ED** John Curry, Norma Reveler and Ron Keeble. **LC** NA9000; .T582. **[CCC].** Index available. **Bk Rev. Ad Acc. Circ:** 3,300. available on microfiche from University Microfilms International (UMI). ***Supersedes in part*** *Town Planning.*
Desc: Land use planning, housing, community economic development, urban design, environmental planning and strategic planning.
Ind/Abst Archit. Period. Index; Avery Index Archit. Period. Suppl. Colum. Univ. (Jan., July, Sept. 1989); Can. Index; Can. Period. Index; J. Plan. Lit.; PAIS Int. Print (1991-).

KE
PLAN EAST AFRICA. English. East Africa Publishing House, Dundee Close off London Road, PO Box 30571, Nairobi Kenya. **LC** HT169.A3; P57. **DD** 309.2/62/0967.

SW/1100-0678
PLANERA BYGGA BO. **Added/Corp** Sweden. Plan- och Bostadsverket. **VFOAT** Boverkets Tidskrift. (1988)-. Periodical. Swedish. bm. Svensk Byggtjanst, Box 7853, 103 99 Stockholm Sweden. **LC** HT395.S8; A58. ***Continues*** *Plan o Bygg, 0280-4131.*

SI/0129-2838
PLANEWS. **VFOAT** Tse Hua Chi Kan. Periodical. English. Singapore Institute of Planners, General PO Box 3600, Singapore. **LC** HT169.S55; S5. **DD** 307/.12/095957. ***Continues*** *SIP Journal.*

UK/0309-1384
PLANNER (LONDON). ***Ceased.*** (THE PLANNER.). [Plann.]. Vol. 59, No. 7 (July/Aug. 1973)-(Sept. 1993). Periodical. English. Fifty times a year. Royal Town Planning Association, 26 Portland Place, London W1N 4BE England. **Tel** 011 44 71 6369107. **ED** Anthony Fyson. Index available. **Bk Rev. Ad Acc. Circ:** 16,873. Documents available from Article Express International. ***Continues*** *Royal Town Planning Institute. Journal;* ***Absorbed*** *Planner News, 0953-1106.*
Desc: Professional journal of town and country planning.
Ind/Abst Account. Tax Datab. (1986-) [Full Txt.]; Appl. Soc. Sci. Index Abstr.; Archit. Period. Index (1973-19??); Bioeng. Abstr.; Br. Humanit. Index; Ei Page One; EMBASE (Feb., July 1989, 1990-); Eng. Index Annu.; Int. Civil Eng. Abstr.; Int. Dev. Abstr.; J. Plan. Lit.; Leis. Recreat. Tour. Abstr.; Middle East Abstr. Index.

US
PLANNING & DEVELOPMENT. Macomb County Department of Planning & Economic Development, 115 South Groesbeck Highway, Mount Clemens MI 48043.

US
PLANNING & DEVELOPMENT NEWS. **Added/Corp** Macomb County (Mich.). Dept. of Planning, Community and Economic Development. **VFOAT** Planning & Development; Planning and Development News; News. Vol. 1, No. 1 (Sept. 1988)-. Periodical. English. bm. Macomb County Department of Planning and Economic Development, 115 South Groesbeck Highway, Mount Clemens MI 48043. ***Continues*** *Planning.*

UK
PLANNING AND DEVELOPMENT STATISTICS. ESTIMATES. **See** Housing and Urban Development-Abstracting, Bibliographies and Statistics.

US
PLANNING AND ZONING : A LAW BULLETIN PUBLISHED BY THE INSTITUTE OF GOVERNMENT, THE UNIVERSITY OF NORTH CAROLINA AT CHAPEL HILL. **Added/Corp** University of North Carolina at Chapel Hill. Institute of Government. No. 1 (Jan. 1991)-. Bulletin. English. Institute of Government, University of North Carolina at Chapel Hill, CB #3300 Knapp Building, Chapel Hill NC 27599-3330. **Tel** (919)966-4119, FAX (919)962-2707. **LC** IN PROCESS.

US/0738-114X
PLANNING & ZONING NEWS. (PLANNING & ZONING NEWS : A PUBLICATION OF THE PLANNING & ZONING CENTER, INC.). **Added/Corp** Planning & Zoning Center (Lansing, Mich.). **VFOAT** Planning and Zoning News. (19??)-. English. mo (12 issues). $150.00. Planning and Zoning Center Inc., 302 South Waverly Road, Lansing MI 48917. **Tel** (517)886-0555, FAX (517)886-0564. **ED** Mark A. Wyckoff. **LC** HD211.M5; P57. **DD** 346.77404/5; 347.740645. Index available. cum. index. **Bk Rev. Ad Acc. Circ:** 2,650 (ctrl).
Desc: Focuses on current court, legislative, and municipal initiatives in the preparation and implementation of local plans and land use regulations. Its primary focus is on Michigan.
Ind/Abst PAIS Int. Print (1991-).

UK/0268-3644
PLANNING APPEAL DECISIONS (ANDOVER, ENGLAND). (PLANNING APPEAL DECISIONS.). **Added/Corp** Great Britain. Dept. of the Environment. **VFOAT** PAD; Planning Appeals. 1 PAD 1-101 (Autumn 1985)-. English. Six times a year. £240.00 Europe; £252.00 other. Sweet & Maxwell Ltd., South Quay Plaza, 183 Marsh Wall, London E14 9FT England. **Tel** 011 44 264 342899, FAX 011 44 264 342723, telex 929089 ITPINF G. **LC** KD1125; .A556. **DD** 346.4204/5; 344.20645.

UK/0495-9728
PLANNING BULLETIN. **Main/Corp** Town and Country Planning Association. Bulletin. English. wk. £49.00 UK; £61.00 other. Town & Country Planning Association, 17 Carlton House Terrace, London SW1Y 5AS England. **Tel** 011 44 1 930 8903.

US/0001-2610
PLANNING (CHICAGO, ILL. 1969). (PLANNING.). [Planning]. **Added/Corp** American Planning Association. American Society of Planning Officials. Vol. 35 (Jan. 1969)-. Academic Scholarly Publication. English. Twelve times a year. $40.00. American Planning Association, 1313 East 60th Street, Chicago IL 60637. **Tel** (312)955-9100, FAX (312)955-8312. **ED** Sylvia Lewis, Ruth Knack and Dennis McClendon. **LC** HC101; .A57. **DD** 330.9/73/092. **CODEN** PLNNDB. Index available. cum. index. **Bk Rev. Ad Acc. Circ:** 24,000 (ctrl). available on microfilm and microfiche from University Microfilms International (UMI). Documents available from UMI Article Clearinghouse, Documents on Demand. ***Continues*** *ASPO Newsletter. American Society of Planning Officials;* ***Absorbed*** *Practicing Planner, 0161-6994.*
Desc: Magazine devoted to city planning. Covers trends, techniques and news of US communities. Has won national editorial and design awards.
Ind/Abst ABI/INFORM Glob. Ed.; ABI Inform Ondisc (Sept. 1983-); Acad. Search (July 1993-); Avery Index Archit. Period. Suppl. Colum. Univ. (1989-); Bus. ASAP (1992-) [Full Txt.]; Bus. Index (1985-); EMBASE; Environ. Abstr.; Environ. Period. Bibliogr.; Gen. BusinessFile (1985-); Gen. Period. Index (1985-); Geogr. Abstr. Phys. Geogr.; Geogr. Abstr. Human Geogr.; J. Plan. Lit.; PAIS Int. Print (1991-); Sage Urban Stud. Abstr; Trade Ind. ASAP [Full Txt.]; Trade Ind. Index [Full Txt.]; UMI ABI/Inform--Bus. Period. Ondisc (Dec. 1987-) [Full Txt.]; Urban Aff. Abstr.

US/1058-5605
PLANNING COMMISSIONERS JOURNAL. [Plan. comm. j.]. Vol. 1, No. 1 (Nov./Dec. 1991)-. Periodical. English. Six times a year (Jan., Apr., July, Oct.). $32.00 municipalities with a population of 25,000 to 75,000 US; $51.20 other. Champlain Planning Press, PO Box 4295, Burlington VT 05406. **Tel** (802)864-9083, FAX (802)862-1882. **ED** Wayne Seville. **DD** 307. Index Bound in First Issue (Bound in Fall issue). **Circ:** 3,600.
Desc: Covers a wide range of planning issues: zoning, land use law, transportation, housing, ethics and more. Regular columnists and features.

CN/0228-2410
PLANNING GUIDELINE SERIES. [Plann. guidel. ser.]. **Main/Corp** Nova Scotia. Community Planning Division. V. 1- 1976-. Monographic series. English. Price varies per volume. Department of Municipal Affairs / Nova Scotia, Community Planning, Provincial Building, PO Box 216, Halifax Nova Scotia B3J 2M4 Canada. **DD** 711/.4.

US/1071-1953
PLANNING HISTORY PRESENT. (PLANNING HISTORY PRESENT / SOCIETY FOR AMERICAN CITY AND REGIONAL PLANNING HISTORY.). [Plan. hist. present]. **Added/Corp** Society for American City and Regional Planning History. Vol. 1, No. 1 (1987)-. Periodical. English. Twice a year (Mar., & Sept.). $35.00 Comes with for American City and Regional Planning History membership. Society for American City and Regional Planning History, 3655 Darbyshire Drive, Hilliard OH 43026-2534. **Tel** (614)876-2319. **ED** Laurence C. Gerckehs (phone: 614)876-2170). **DD** 307. **Bk Rev**, (Qty: varies). **Ad Acc. Circ:** 360 (ctrl).

US/0048-4318
PLANNING IN NORTHEASTERN ILLINOIS. **Added/Corp** Northeastern Illinois Metropolitan Area Planning Commission. Northeastern Illinois Planning Commission. Vol. 5, No. 3 (May/June 1963)-. Periodical. English. Four times a year. Free on request. Northeastern Illinois Planning Commission, 400 West Madison Street, Chicago IL 60606. **Tel** (312)454-0400. ***Continues*** *Metropolitan Area Planning.*

US/0091-4053
PLANNING LEGISLATION IN NEW YORK STATE. **See** Law.

US/0885-6737
PLANNING NEWS (ALBANY, N.Y.). (PLANNING NEWS.). [Plan. news]. **VFOAT** NYPF Planning News. (1975)-. Periodical. English. qt. $60.00 (individual); $25.00 (library). New York Planning Federation, 488 Broadway, Suite 313, Albany NY 12207-2911. **Tel** (518)489-8116. **ED** Sheila A Clifford. **LC** HT393.N7; N495. **DD** 361.6/09747. Index available. **Bk Rev. Ad Acc. Circ:** 9,700 (ctrl). ***Continues*** *New York State Planning News.*
Desc: Serves as a resource for information on the purposes and techniques of planning, zoning and land use control.
Ind/Abst Avery Index Archit. Period. Suppl. Colum. Univ. (1989/1990-).

AT/0313-3796
PLANNING NEWS SOUTH MELBOURNE. (1975)-. Periodical. English. Eleven times a year (Except Jan.). 70.00Aus$. Royal Australian Planning Institute, 615 Burwood Road, Hawthorn 3122 Australia. **Tel** 011 61 3 8190930, FAX 011 61 3 8190676. **ED** Gary Arnold. **Bk Rev**, (Qty: few). **Ad Acc, Adv Mgr:** J. Jenkins, **Tel** 05 819 0930. **Circ:** 750 (ctrl).

UK/0266-5433
PLANNING PERSPECTIVES : PP. [Plan. perspect.]. **VFOAT** PP. Vol. 1, No. 1 (Jan. 1986)-. English. qt. $255.00 US and Canada; £150.00 Europe; £160.00 other. E & FN Spon Ltd, 2 6 Boundary Row, London SE1 8HN England. **Tel** 011 44 71 865 0066. **(Subscription address:** Chapman & Hall, Cheriton House, North Way, Andover, Hampshire, SP10 5BE England.) **ED** Gordon Cherry, Anthony Sutcliffe. **[CCC]. Bk Rev. Ad Acc. Pr Rev. Circ:** 250. available on microfilm from University Microfilms International (UMI).
Desc: Reflects the interests of those concerned with the planning of the environment who seek to provide explanations for the origins and consequences of planning ideas, methods and activities. Subject areas include historical studies of all aspects of planning, with the emphasis on the industrial era.
Ind/Abst Am. Hist. Life (1989-); Archit. Period. Index; Avery Index Archit. Period. Suppl. Colum. Univ. (Jan. 1989, Jan. 1990-); Geogr. Abstr. Human Geogr.; Int. Dev. Abstr.

UK/0269-7459
PLANNING PRACTICE + RESEARCH. [Plan. pract. res.]. **VFOAT** Planning Practice and Research. (1986)-. Periodical. English. qt. $114.00. Carfax Publishing Company, PO Box 25 Abingdon, Oxfordshire OX14 3UE England. **Tel** 011 44 235 555335, FAX (0279)31067, telex 817484. **ED** Joe Doak. **DD** 711.40941. Index available. **Bk Rev. Ad Acc. Pr Rev.**
Desc: Critical evaluation of planning in practice. Aims to strengthen the links between planners in practice and those in planning education and research.
Ind/Abst Geogr. Abstr. Human Geogr.; Int. Bibliogr. Sociol.; J. Plan. Lit.; PAIS Int. Print (1991-); World Agric. Econ.

NZ
PLANNING QUARTERLY (NEW ZEALAND PLANNING INSTITUTE). (PLANNING QUARTERLY.). **Added/Corp** New Zealand Planning Institute. (June 1982)-. Periodical. English. Four times a year (Mar., June, Sept., Dec.). 40.00NZ$ New Zealand; 65.00NZ$ other. Associated Group Media Ltd, Private Bag 99915, Newmarket, Auckland 1031 New Zealand. **Tel** 11 64 9 3795393, FAX 11 64 9 3089523, telex 79121057. **ED** Cathy Sheehan. **Ad Acc, Adv Mgr:** Chris Joel. **Circ:** 1,200. ***Continues*** *Town Planning Quarterly.*
Desc: Town and country planning and related subjects including sociology, geography, social and environmental matters and economics.
Ind/Abst Avery Index Archit. Period. Suppl. Colum. Univ. (1989); Ecol. Abstr.; Geogr. Abstr. Human Geogr.; Int. Civil Eng. Abstr.; Int. Dev. Abstr. (?-?).

US
PLANNING, ZONING, AND DEVELOPMENT LAWS. **See** Law.

CN/0380-6723
PLANS. 1- 1968-. Periodical. English. bm. Free to members of the Association, $2.00 others. Community Planning Association of Canada / Nova Scotia Division, PO Box 211, 1815 Hollis Street, Halifax Nova Scotia B3L 4K1 Canada. **DD** 309.2'5'09715.

PE
PLAZA MAYOR. No. 1 (Mar./April, 1982)-. Periodical. Spanish. Four times a year (Mar., June, Sept., Dec.). $60.00. Editora Tecnica, Avenue of Alvarez Calderon 180 of 8, San Isidro Lima 27 Peru. **Tel** 403285 LUIS DORICH. **ED** Luis Dorich Torres. Index available. cum. index. **Bk Rev. Ad Acc. Circ:** 5,000.
Desc: Urban and regional planning, architecture, housing, ecology, local government and other subjects concerning the development of communities mainly in developing countries.

US
POPULATION AND LAND USE BULLETIN. ***Ceased.*** **Added/Corp** San Diego (Calif.). Planning Dept. **VFOAT** Population and Land Use. (19??)-(19??). Bulletin. English. an. City of San Diego, Planning Department, 202 C Street, San Diego CA 92101. **Tel** (714)236-6480.

US
POPULATION ESTIMATE AND HOUSING INVENTORY FOR THE CITY OF LOS ANGELES AS OF OCTOBER 1 ... (LOS ANGELES (CALIF.)). (POPULATION ESTIMATE AND HOUSING INVENTORY FOR THE CITY OF LOS ANGELES AS OF OCTOBER 1 ...). English. Department of City Planning, Data Support Unit, Room 507/Los Angeles City Hall, Los Angeles CA 90012. **LC** HD7304.L7; P66. **DD** 312/.09794/94. ***Continues*** *Estimated Housing Inventory by Geographic Areas, 0733-4117.*

BL
POVOADOS DO ESTADO DA BAHIA. Portuguese. Departamento de Geografia E Estatistica, Avenida Luiz Viana Filho S/N - Paralela, Salvador Brazil. **LC** HT129.B7; P68.

US/0163-8602
PRESIDENT'S NATIONAL URBAN POLICY REPORT, THE. (THE PRESIDENT'S NATIONAL URBAN POLICY REPORT / PREPARED BY THE U.S. DEPARTMENT OF HOUSING AND URBAN DEVELOPMENT.). **Main/Corp** United States. Dept. of Housing and Urban Development. **Added/Corp** United States. President. **VFOAT** National Urban Policy Report. 1st (1978)-. English. ir. $4.00 (latest edition). HUD User, PO Box 6091, Rockville MD 20850. **Tel** 800 245-2691 or, (301)251-5154. **LC** HT123; .U43a. **DD** 301.36/1/0973.

Housing and Urban Development

FR
PRIX DE REVIENT DES LOGEMENTS NEUFS EN ... / MINISTERE DE L'URBANISME ET DU LOGEMENT, DIRECTION DES AFFAIRES ECONOMIQUES ET INTERNATIONALES, LE. French. 31.50F single issue. Documentation Francaise, 29 Quai Voltaire, 75344 Paris Cedex 7 France. **Tel** 011 33 1 40157000, FAX 011 33 1 40157230, telex 204 826 DOCFRAN. **LC** HD7338.A3; P74. **DD** 338.4/369083/0944021.

IT
PROBLEMI DEL TERRITORIO. (1979)-. Monographic series. Italian. Price varies per volume. Edizioni Scientifiche Italiane, Via Chiatamone 7, 80121 Naples Italy. **Tel** 011 39 81 7645768, 011 39 81 7645443, FAX 011 39 81 7646477.

US/0092-8445
PROCEEDINGS OF THE ANNUAL GOVERNOR'S WORKSHOP ON INTERGOVERNMENTAL RELATIONS AND REGIONAL PLANNING (SAN ANTONIO). (PROCEEDINGS.). **Main/Conf** Governor's Workshop on Intergovernmental Relations and Regional Planning. Proceedings. English. an. Office of the Governor / Austin, PO Box 12428, Austin TX 78711. **Tel** (512)463-1919. **LC** HT393.T48; G67A. **DD** 309.2/5/09764.

US/0730-3009
PROCEEDINGS OF THE INSTITUTE ON PLANNING, ZONING, AND EMINENT DOMAIN. See Law.

US
PROCUREMENT POLICIES AND PROCEDURES. Main/Corp United States. Dept. of Housing and Urban Development. Office of Administration. Government Publication. English. US Department of Housing and Urban Development, 451 Seventh Street SW, Washington DC 20401. **Tel** (202)708-0980, FAX (202)708-0299.

UK/0305-9006
PROGRESS IN PLANNING. [Prog. plann.]. (1973)-. Monographic series. English. Six times a year. $298.00 The Americas; £200.00 other. Pergamon Press, An Imprint of Elsevier Science Ltd., The Boulevard, Langford Lane, Kidlington, Oxford OX5 1GB United Kingdom. **Tel** 011 44 865 843000, 011 44 865 843699, FAX 011 44 865 843010. **(Subscription address:** Elsevier Science Ltd. Oxford Fulfillment Centre, PO Box 800, Kidlington, Oxford OX5 1DX United Kingdom.) **ED** Derek R. Diamond, J. B. McLoughlin, and B. Massam. **LC** HT166; .P744. **DD** 307/.12/05. **[CCC]. Pr Rev.** available on microfilm and microfiche from University Microfilms International (UMI). Documents available from The Genuine Article, Documents on Demand.
Ind/Abst Appl. Soc. Sci. Index Abstr.; Curr. Contents Soc. Behav. Sci.; Energy Inf. Abstr.; Environ. Abstr.; Geogr. Abstr. Human Geogr.; Highw. Res. Abstr.; Int. Bibliogr. Sociol.; Int. Dev. Abstr.; J. Plan. Lit.; Res. Alert [Full Cov.]; Sage Urban Stud. Abstr (?-?); Soc. Sci. Cit. Index [Full Cov.].

UK/0956-4187
PROGRESS IN RURAL POLICY AND PLANNING. VFOAT PIRPAP. Vol. 1 (1991)-. Periodical. English. Belhaven Press, 25 Floral Street, London WC2E 9DS England. **LC** HT401; .P76.
Continues International Yearbook of Rural Planning, 0952-3847.

KE
PROJECT INFORMATION REPORT. *Title Change.* **Main/Corp** United Nations Centre for Human Settlements. (19??)-(19??). English (French, Spanish and Arabic). an. UNCHS / United Nations Centre for Human Settlements (Habitat), Chief, Information, Audio-Visual and Documentation Division, PO Box 30030, Nairobi Kenya. **Tel** 011 254 2 621234, FAX 011 254 2 520724, telex 22996. **LC** HT51; .U55a. **DD** 307/.06/01. **Ad Acc. Circ:** 10,000. *Continued by* United Nations Centre for Human Settlements. Operational Activities Report.
Desc: Covers current technical cooperation projects (159 projects in 77 countries).

US
PROJECT MONOGRAPH (INSTITUTE FOR URBAN DESIGN (U.S.)). (PROJECT MONOGRAPH / INSTITUTE FOR URBAN DESIGN.). No. 1 (Sept. 1984)-. Monographic series. English. qt. Price varies per volume. Institute for Urban Design, 47 Barrow Street, New York NY 10014. **Tel** (212)741-2041.
Desc: Non-profit education and research organization for architects, landscape architects, city planners, public administrators and developers concerned with the design of cities.

US
PROPERTY DISPOSITION HANDBOOK. Government Publication. English. an. $26.50. US Department of Housing and Urban Development, 451 Seventh Street SW, Washington DC 20401. **Tel** (202)708-0980, FAX (202)708-0299. **ED** Kiley and Moselle. Index available. cum. index. **Bk Rev. Ad Acc. Pr Rev.** ctrl circ.
Desc: Labor and material cost for residential, commercial, and industrial construction.

US
PROPERTY DISPOSITION HANDBOOK; ONE TO FOUR FAMILY PROPERTIES. English. US Department of Housing and Urban Development Federal Housing Commissioner, 451 Seventh Street SW, Room 9100, Washington DC 20410. **Tel** (202)708-3600, FAX (202)755-2580.

UK
PROPERTY, PLANNING, AND COMPENSATION REPORTS. See Law.

NE
PROSPECT. Added/Corp International Federation for Housing and Planning. (1988)-. Periodical. English. International Federation for Housing and Planning, 43 Wassenaarseweg, 2596 The Hague Netherlands. **Tel** (31)(070) 24 45 57, telex 31578. *Continues* IFHP News Sheet.
Ind/Abst Avery Index Archit. Period. Suppl. Colum. Univ. (1988-); Geogr. Abstr. Phys. Geogr.; Geogr. Abstr. Human Geogr.; Int. Dev. Abstr.

US
PUBLIC HOUSING DEVELOPMENT HANDBOOK. Government Publication. English. ir. US Department of Housing and Urban Development, 451 Seventh Street SW, Washington DC 20401. **Tel** (202)708-0980, FAX (202)708-0299.

US/0887-4468
PUBLIC INNOVATION ABROAD. [Public innov. abroad]. **Added/Corp** Academy for State and Local Government. International Center. Vol. 10, No. 2 (Feb. 1986)-. Periodical. English. qt. $48.00 (one year), $80.00 (two years), $116.00 (three years) North America; $60.00 (one year), $104.00 (two years), $152.00 (three years) other; Transportation quarterly issues only: $20.00 US, Canada and Mexico; $24.00 overseas. International Center, Academy for State and Local Government, 444 N Capitol St, Suite 345, Washington DC 20001. **Tel** (202)434-4850, FAX (202)434-4851. **ED** George G Wynne. **DD** 352. **Bk Rev. Circ:** 1,500. *Continues* Urban Innovation Abroad, 0163-6499.
Desc: Covers public transportation technology, innovation and trends from around the world relevant to US concerns.

US
PUBLICATION - MIDDLE TENNESSEE SECTION, TENNESSEE STATE PLANNING OFFICE. Main/Corp Tennessee. State Planning Office. Middle Tennessee Section. English. HCA, PO Box 24350, Nashville TN 37202-4350. **LC** HT167.5.T2; A3. **DD** 309.2/5/09768. *Continues* MTO Publication.

CN/0826-0273
PUBLICATION (UNIVERSITY OF GUELPH. UNIVERSITY SCHOOL OF RURAL PLANNING AND DEVELOPMENT). (PUBLICATION / UNIVERSITY SCHOOL OF RURAL PLANNING AND DEVELOPMENT.). [Publ. - Univ. Sch. Rur. Plann. Dev.]. Monographic series. English. Price varies per volume. University School of Rural Planning and Development, University of Guelph, Guelph Ontario N1G 2W1 Canada. **DD** 333.7. *Continues* Publication (University of Guelph. Centre for Resources Development), 0318-3505.

US/0072-1298
PUBLICATIONS - GEORGIA. UNIVERSITY. INSTITUTE OF COMMUNITY AND AREA DEVELOPMENT. Main/Corp University of Georgia. Institute of Community and Area Development. Vol. 1 (1962)-. English. University of Georgia Institute of Community and Area Development, Athens GA 30602. **DD** 353.9; 711.

MY
PURNAMA RAYA. V. 1- Jan./Mar. 1974-. Periodical. Multiple languages (English). $3.50 single issue. Perbadanan Pembangunan Bandar, 44 Jalan Sultan Ismail, Kuala Lumpur Malaysia. **LC** HT178.M34; P87. **DD** 309.2/62/09595.

IT
QUADERNI DI DIRITTO URBANISTICO. (19??)-. Italian. ir. Price varies per volume. Cel Srl, Via G Pascoli 6, 24020 Gorle BG Italy. **Tel** 011 39 35 299033.

IT/0394-0926
QUADERNI DI URBANISTICA E INFORMAZIONI. Added/Corp Istituto Nazionale di Urbanistica. (1986)-. Monographic series. Italian. ir. Price varies per volume. Ist Nazionale di Urbanistica, Via S Caterina Da Siena 46, 00186 Rome Italy. **Tel** 011 39 6 6793559.

IT/1120-9232
QUADERNI EMILIANI. [Quad. emiliani]. **VFOAT** Q/E. Vol. 1, Oct. (1978)-. Periodical. Italian. Three times a year. L18000. c/c Postale N 21716402, Intestato Alla Cooperativa Libraria Universitaria, Editrice Bologna Italy. **LC** HT145.I8; Q34.

SP
QUADERNS D'ARQUITECTURA I URBANISME. See Architecture.

SP
QUADERNS D'ARQUITECTURA I URBANISME. EXTRA. See Architecture.

US/0363-5775
QUARTERLY BULLETIN - DEPARTMENT OF REGIONAL PLANNING, COUNTY OF LOS ANGELES, CALIFORNIA. Main/Corp Los Angeles Co., Calif. Dept. of Regional Planning. No. 125 (July 1974)-. Bulletin. English. qt. Department of Regional Planning, 320 West Temple Street, Los Angeles CA 90012. **LC** HT393.C32; L655. **DD** 352/.96/0979493. *Continues* Los Angeles Co., Calif. Regional Planning Commission. Quarterly Bulletin - Regional Planning Commission, County of Los Angeles, California.

CN/0845-4078
QUINQUENNIAL REVIEW. [Quinquenn. rev. - City Tor. Plan. Dev. Dep.]. **Added/Corp** Toronto (Ont.). Planning and Development Dept. (1981)-. English. ir. Planning and Development Department, Economic Development Division, 18th Floor/East Tower City Hall, Toronto Ontario M5H 2N2 Canada. **Tel** (416)362-7185. **DD** 711/.4/09713541. *Absorbed* Condominium Monitor, 0836-2491; Office Monitor, 0823-9967; Housing monitor., 0823-9959.

US/0147-9059
RAM DIGEST, THE. [RAM dig.]. **VAT** Registered Apartment Manager Digest. Periodical. English. qt. Free to members. National Association of Home Builders, 15th and M Street NW, Washington DC 20005. **Tel** (202)822-0203. **ED** Michele McCarthy. **LC** TX957; .R35. **DD** 658. **Ad Acc. Circ:** 5,000.
Desc: Serves the concerns of multihousing (particularly rental) builders, developers, owners, and managers: marketing, maintenance, resident relations, personnel management, design, legislation, etc.

YU
RASPODELA STANOVA I KREDITA ZA STANOVE U ... GODINI / SOCIJALISTICKA REPUBLIKA SRBIJA, REPUBLICK ZAVOD ZA STATISTIKU. Serbo-Croatian (Roman). **LC** HD7355.5.S4; R37.

SZ
RAUMPLANUNG, INFORMATIONSHEFTE / EJPD, BUNDESAMT FUR RAUMPLANUNG. VFOAT Amenagement du Territoire, Bulletin d'Information. Periodical. German (French). ir. 22.00F. Bundesamt fur Raumplanung, Eigerstr 65, 3003 Bern Switzerland. **Tel** 031/61 40 60. **LC** HT395.S9; R36. **DD** 361.6/09494. Index available. **Bk Rev. Circ:** 3,000 (ctrl).
Desc: Specific land use and spatial planning problems in Switzerland.

CN/0845-5341
RE-NEW (PORT HOPE). *Title Change.* (RE-NEW.). [Re-New]. Vol. 3, No. 1 (March/April 1989)-(19??). Periodical. English. ir. Bluestone House Inc., 12 Mill Street South, Port Hope Ontario L1A 2S5 Canada. **Tel** (905)885-2449, FAX (905)885-5355. **ED** Susan Jane Anstey. **DD** 643/.7/05. **Bk Rev.** (Qty: 8-10/yr). **Ad Acc. Adv Mgr:** Vicki Mosher. **Circ:** 8,500. *Separated from* Century Home, 0838-9330. *Merged into* Century Home, 0838-9330.

US
RECENT RESEARCH RESULTS / U.S. DEPARTMENT OF HOUSING AND URBAN DEVELOPMENT, OFFICE OF POLICY DEVELOPMENT AND RESEARCH. Added/Corp United States. Dept. of Housing and Urban Development. Office of Policy Development and Research. HUD USER (U.S.). **VFOAT** RRR. (Sept. 1979)-. English. mo. Free. Department of Housing and Urban Development / Maryland, PO Box 6091, Rockville MD 20850-0691. **Tel** (202)708-1600. **ED** Michael Siewert. **Circ:** 9,000 (ctrl).
Desc: Provides news and information on the activities of the Office of Policy Development and Research and other offices at the US Department of Housing and Urban Development.

US/0731-0153
REDBOOK / TAA, TEXAS APARTMENT ASSOCIATION. **Main/Corp** Texas Apartment Association. English. Texas Apartment Association Inc., 6225 Highway 290 East #204, Austin TX 78723. **LC** KFT1317; .T48. **DD** 346.76404/34; 3476406434.

CN/0710-1821
REGINA. ROSS INDUSTRIAL PARK. [Regina, Ross Ind. Park]. 1980-. English. an. Properties Department, City of Regina, PO Box 1790, Regina Saskatchewan S4P 3C8 Canada. **DD** 711/.5524/0971244. ***Continues*** *Ross Industrial Park, Regina, 0710-1813.*
Desc: Fully serviced industrial land available at competitive prices. Development controls in place to protect investment.

US
REGION TOMORROW, THE. **Added/Corp** Regional Plan Association (New York, N.Y.). Issue No. 1 (Apr. 1991)-. Periodical. English. Regional Plan Association, 570 Lexington Avenue, New York NY 10022. **Tel** (212)398-1140, FAX (212)768-9136.

US/0732-586X
REGION (WASHINGTON, D.C.), THE. (THE REGION.). **Added/Corp** Metropolitan Washington Council of Governments. Vol. 21, No. 3 (Summer 1980)-. Periodical. English. Twice a year. Free. Metropolitan Washington Council of Governments, 777 North Capitol Street Northeast, Washington DC 20002-4239. **Tel** (202)962-3256. **ED** Sherry Conway Appel. **LC** HT394.W3; R44. **DD** 361.6/09753. **Circ:** 6,000 (ctrl). ***Continues*** *Regional Report (Metropolitan Washington Council of Governments), 0539-5429.*
Desc: A review and analysis of issues concerning the residents of the metropolitan Washington region including economic development, transportation, environmental, human services and public safety issues.
Ind/Abst Urban Aff. Abstr.

AT
REGIONAL DEVELOPER. Mar./Apr. 1979-. Periodical. English. Department of Decentralisation, New South Wales 2000 Australia. **LC** HC620.I53; N48. **DD** 338/.09944. ***Continues*** *New South Wales Horizons.*

JA/0250-6505
REGIONAL DEVELOPMENT DIALOGUE. [Reg. dev. dialogue]. **Added/Corp** United Nations Centre for Regional Development. Vol. 1 (Spring 1980)-. Periodical. English. Twice a year. United Nations Centre for Regional Development, Nagono 1-47-1 Nakamura-ku, Nagoya 450 Japan. **Tel** 011 81 52 561-9377, FAX 011 81 52 561-9375, telex J59620 UNCENTRE. **(Subscription address:** UNIPUB, 4611 F Assembly Drive, Lanham MD 20706.**)** **ED** Hidehiko Sazanami and Chakrit Noranitipadungkarn. **LC** HT390; .R38. **DD** 338.9/009172/4. Index available. cum. index. **Ad Acc. Circ:** 1,000 (ctrl). available on microfiche (from Congressional Information Service Inc.). ***Continues*** *Asian Development Dialogue.*
Desc: Provides a forum for critical discussion of urban and regional development problems, policies, and perspectives among academicians and practitioners. Bridges the gap between concept and reality, policy and practice in regional development.
Ind/Abst Geogr. Abstr. Phys. Geogr.; Geogr. Abstr. Human Geogr.; Int. Dev. Abstr.; Int. Labour Doc.; PAIS Int. Print; Rural Dev. Abstr.; Sage Urban Stud. Abstr (?-?); Soc. Plann. Policy Dev. Abstr.

AT
REGIONAL DEVELOPMENT JOURNAL, THE. **Added/Corp** Australia. Dept. of Post-War Reconstruction. Regional Planning Division. Vol. 1, No. 1 (May 1949)-. English. ir. Department of Post-War Planning, Regional Planning, Canberra, Australia. **LC** WMLC L 83/2812.

NZ
REGIONAL DEVELOPMENT NEWS. English. qt. Editor Regional Development News, Department of Trade and Industry, Private Bag, Wellington New Zealand. **LC** HT395.N45; R43. **DD** 338.9931/005.

US/0034-3374
REGIONAL PLAN NEWS. ***Title Change.*** **See** Public Administration.

CN/0824-6556
REGIONAL REVIEW NEWSLETTER. [Reg. rev. newsl.]. Feb. 1983-. Newsletter. English. qt. South Peace Regional Planning Commission, 200 Windsor Court, 9835-101 Aveneu, Brande Prairie, Alta T8V 5V4 Canada. **DD** 711/.3/0971231.

NE/0166-0462
REGIONAL SCIENCE AND URBAN ECONOMICS. [Reg. sci. urban econ.]. Vol. 5 (Feb. 1975)-. Academic Scholarly Publication. English. Six times a year (1 volume). Fl785.00. Elsevier Science Publishers BV, PO Box 211, 1000 AE Amsterdam Netherlands. **Tel** 011 31 20 5803642, FAX 011 31 20 5862696, telex 15682. **ED** Urs Schweizer, Ake E Andersson, and Walter Isard. **LC** HB9; .R33. **DD** 330/.01/51. **CODEN** RGUEA3. **[CCC]. Bk Rev. Ad Acc. Pr Rev.** available on microfilm and microfiche from University Microfilms International (UMI). Documents available from The Genuine Article, UMI Article Clearinghouse. ***Continues*** *Regional and Urban Economics, 0034-3331.*
Desc: The editors desire to have the interdisciplinary character of regional science as well as the development of the more specialized field of urban economics.
Ind/Abst ABC POL SCI (1991-present); ABI/INFORM Glob. Ed.; ABI Inform Ondisc (Feb. 1981-); Abstr. AIT Rep. Publ. Energy; Acad. Search (July 1993-); Bus. Index (1985-1990); Coal Abstr.; Contents Recent Econ. J.; Curr. Contents Soc. Behav. Sci.; Econ. Lit. Index (Feb. 1981-); Energy Res. Abstr. (Mar. 1981-); Environ. Period. Bibliogr. (?-?); Gen. BusinessFile (1985-1990); Gen. Period. Index (1985-); Geogr. Abstr. Phys. Geogr.; Geogr. Abstr. Human Geogr. (1991-); Highw. Res. Abstr.; Int. Bibliogr. Sociol.; Int. Dev. Abstr.; J. Econ. Lit.; J. Plan. Lit.; Mag. Search; Res. Alert [Full Cov.]; Sage Urban Stud. Abstr (1975-); Soc. Plann. Policy Dev. Abstr.; Soc. Sci. Cit. Index [Full Cov.]; Sociol. Abstr.; Trade Ind. Index.

US/0166-0462
REGIONAL SCIENCE AND URBAN ECONOMICS [MICROFORM]. Vol. 5 (Feb. 1975)-. Academic Scholarly Publication. English. Elsevier Science Publishers BV, PO Box 211, 1000 AE Amsterdam Netherlands. **Tel** 011 31 20 5803642, FAX 011 31 20 5862696, telex 15682. **LC** Microfilm (o) 91/6001. **[CCC].** ***Continues*** *Regional and Urban Economics, 0034-3331.*
Ind/Abst PAIS Int. Print (?-?).

PK/0254-7988
REGIONAL STUDIES (INSTITUTE OF REGIONAL STUDIES (ISLAMABAD, PAKISTAN)). (REGIONAL STUDIES.). **Added/Corp** Institute of Regional Studies (Islamabad, Pakistan). Vol. 1 No. 1 (Winter 1982)-. Periodical. English. Four times a year. $38.00. Institute of Regional Studies, NAFDEC Complex 56 F Blue Area, Islamabad Pakistan. **LC** DS331; .R43. **DD** 954/.005.
Ind/Abst Middle East J.

US/0361-0691
REGIONAL TOPICS. V. 1- Mar. 1969-. Periodical. English. qt. Tri-County Regional Planning Commission, 19 North High Street, Akron OH 44308.

US/0034-3420
REGION'S AGENDA, THE. **Added/Corp** Regional Plan Association (New York, N.Y.). Vol. 1 (Sept. 1970)-. Periodical. English. ir. $50.00 (Individuals); $500.00 (corporate); Comes with Regional Plans Association Membership. Regional Plan Association, 570 Lexington Avenue, New York NY 10022. **Tel** (212)398-1140, FAX (212)768-9136. **ED** Mary C. Rivers. **Circ:** 4,000 (ctrl).
Desc: Research and analysis of economic development, transportation, open space, social conditions, and land use decisions that affect the New York Metropolitan Region.

BL
RELATORIO DAS ATIVIDADES DA COMPANHIA DE HABITACAO DO ESTADO DE SANTA CATARINA. **Main/Corp** Companhia de Habitacao do Estado de Santa Catarina. Portuguese. Rua Almirante Lamego, 2 C P 858, Florianopolis 88000 Brazil. **LC** HD9715.B84; H33A.

UK/0263-7499
RENT REVIEW & LEASE RENEWAL. **See** Real Estate.

US
RENT SUPPLEMENT HANDBOOK. Government Publication. English. US Department of Housing and Urban Development, 451 Seventh Street SW, Washington DC 20401. **Tel** (202)708-0980, FAX (202)708-0299.

CN/0382-3547
REPERTOIRE DES TAUX DE LOCATION. **Main/Corp** Quebec (Province) Section des Taux de Location. (1975)-. French. an. $3.50. Ministere des Travaux Publico et de l'Approvisement, Section des Taux de Location, Quebec Canada. ***Supersedes*** *Quebec (Province) Service des Taux de Location. Repertoire des Taux de Location., 0382-3547.*

US/0529-8172
REPORT. **Main/Corp** Citizens' Housing and Planning Council of New York. (19??)-. Periodical. English (Spanish). an. Citizens Housing & Planning Council, 218 West 40th Street/12th Floor, New York NY 10018-1509. **Tel** (212)391-9030. **DD** 331.83. **Bk Rev.**

TZ
REPORT & ACCOUNTS - CAPITAL DEVELOPMENT AUTHORITY. **Main/Corp** Tanzania. Capital Development Authority. **VFOAT** Report and Accounts. 1st- 1973/74-. English. Capital Development Authority, PO Box 913, Dodoma Tanzania. **LC** HT169.T332; D627A. **DD** 354/.678/0086.

UK
REPORT - GREAT BRITAIN. SCOTTISH DEVELOPMENT DEPT. **Main/Corp** Great Britain. Scottish Development Dept. English. an. **LC** HT169.G7; A38.

US
REPORT - MICHIGAN STATE HOUSING DEVELOPMENT AUTHORITY. ***Title Change.*** **Main/Corp** Michigan State Housing Development Authority. English. an. Michigan State Housing Development Authority, 401 South Washington, Lansing MI 48909. **Tel** (517)335-2006. **LC** HD7303.M5; M5A. **DD** 353.9/774/00865. ***Continues*** *MSHDA Review.* ***Continued by*** *MSHDA Review, Newsletter.*

UK
REPORT OF PROCEEDINGS - TOWN AND COUNTRY PLANNING SUMMER SCHOOL. **Main/Corp** Town and Country Planning Summer School. Proceedings. English. an. **LC** NA9185; .T6. **DD** 711.082.

AT
REPORT OF THE DIRECTOR GENERAL OF HOUSING AND CONSTRUCTION FOR THE PERIOD FROM ... . ***Title Change.*** **Main/Corp** Victoria. Ministry of Housing and Construction. **VFOAT** Annual Report of the Director General of Housing and Construction. (July 1987/June 1988)-(19??). English. an. Ministry of Housing and Construction, 250 Elizabeth Street, Melbourne NSW 3000 Australia. **LC** HD7379.V5; V535a. **DD** 354.9450086/06. ***Formed by the union of*** *Annual Report of the Director of Housing, Victoria, 0810-4972* ***and*** *Annual Report / Victoria Public Works Dept.* ***Merged with*** *Victoria. Dept. of Planning and Urban Growth. Annual Report* ***to form*** *Victoria. Dept. of Planning and Housing. Annual Report.*

US
REPORT OF THE VIRGINIA HOUSING STUDY COMMISSION. **Main/Corp** Virginia. Housing Study Commission. English. Department of Purchases and Supply, 6 North 6th Street/Suite 202, Richmond VA 23210. **LC** J87; .V9 DATE C, subser; HD7303; D7303. **DD** 328.755/07/208 S; 301.5/4/09755.

US/0160-8266
REPORT - PLANNING ADVISORY SERVICE. (REPORT / AMERICAN PLANNING ASSOCIATION, PLANNING ADVISORY SERVICE.). [Rep. - Plan. Advis. Serv.]. **Added/Corp** American Planning Association. Planning Advisory Service. **VFOAT** APA/PAS Report; PAS Report; P.A.S. Report. **VAT** American Planning Association/Planning Advisory Service Report; APA PAS Report. No. 336 (Oct. 1978)-. Monographic series. English. Twelve times a year. Price varies per volume. American Planning Association, 1313 East 60th Street, Chicago IL 60637. **Tel** (312)955-9100, FAX (312)955-8312. **ED** J. Hecimovich. **LC** NA9108; .A545. **DD** 309.2/2. cum. index. ***Continues*** *Report (American Society of Planning Officials. Planning Advisory Service), 0160-8266.*
Desc: Eight annual reports directed to land use planners and related professionals, each on an individual topic.
Ind/Abst Geogr. Abstr. Human Geogr.

US/0740-9443
RESEARCH AND TECHNOLOGY PROGRAM. (FISCAL YEAR ... RESEARCH AND TECHNOLOGY PROGRAM.). [Res. technol. program]. **VFOAT** Research and Technology. Government Publication. English. an. US Department of Housing and Urban Development, 451 Seventh Street SW, Washington DC 20401. **Tel** (202)708-0980, FAX (202)708-0299. **LC** HD7293.A1; F57. **DD** 353.0086/5/06.

CN/0828-4121
RESEARCH BULLETIN - CITY OF TORONTO PLANNING AND DEVELOPMENT. RESEARCH AND INFORMATION SECTION. (RESEARCH BULLETIN / CITY OF TORONTO PLANNING AND DEVELOPMENT DEPT., RESEARCH AND INFORMATION SECTION.). [Res. bull. - City Tor. Plann. Dev. Dept., Res. Inf. Sect.]. (Dec. 1981)-. Bulletin. English. 3.00Can$. Planning and Development Department, Economic Development Division, 18th Floor/East Tower City Hall, Toronto Ontario M5H 2N2 Canada. **Tel** (416)362-7185. **ED** Steve Dyns. **DD** 307/.12/09713541. **Circ:** 1,000 (ctrl). ***Continues*** *Research Bulletin (Toronto (Ont.). Planning and Development Dept. Policy and Research Division), 0828-4113.*
Desc: An ongoing series of planning research studies dealing with demographic/economic and social issues in Toronto.

US
RESEARCH IN URBAN POLICY. **VFOAT** RUP. Vol. 1 (1985)-. Monographic series. English. ir. $73.25. JAI Press Inc., 55 Old Post Road, Suite 2, PO Box 1678, Greenwich CT 06836-1678. **Tel** (203)661-7602, FAX (203)661-0792. **ED** Terry Nichols Clark. **LC** HT101; .R38. **DD** 307.7/6/0973.
Ind/Abst Soc. Plann. Policy Dev. Abstr.

Housing and Urban Development

CN/0316-0068
RESEARCH PAPER - CENTRE FOR URBAN AND COMMUNITY STUDIES. UNIVERSITY OF TORONTO. (RESEARCH PAPER - UNIVERSITY OF TORONTO, CENTRE FOR URBAN AND COMMUNITY STUDIES.). **Main/Corp** University of Toronto. Centre for Urban and Community Studies. No. 21-. Periodical. English. ir. Centre for Urban and Community Studies, 455 Spadina Avenue, Room 426, Toronto Ontario M5S 2G8 Canada. **Tel** (416)978-2072. **DD** 301.3/6. cum. index. **Bk Rev. Ad Acc. Circ:** 250 (ctrl). *Continues* University of Toronto. Centre for Urban and Community Studies. Research Report, 0316-005X.
 Desc: Urban studies, planning, social structure, housing and public policy.

US/0741-725X
RESIDENTIAL ENERGY CONSUMPTION SURVEY. HOUSING CHARACTERISTICS. (RESIDENTIAL ENERGY CONSUMPTION SURVEY. HOUSING CHARACTERISTICS / ENERGY INFORMATION ADMINISTRATION, OFFICE OF ENERGY MARKETS AND END USE, END USE ENERGY DIVISION, U.S. DEPARTMENT OF ENERGY.). [Resid. energy consum. surv., Hous. charact.]. **VFOAT** Housing Characteristics; R.E.C.S., Housing Characteristics; RECS, Housing Characteristics. 1980-. Government Publication. English. an. US Department of Energy, 1000 Independence Avenue SW, Washington DC 20585. **Tel** (202)586-5000, FAX (202)586-4073. **LC** HD7293.A1; R47. **DD** 333.79/13/0973.

US
RESIDENTIAL ENERGY CONSUMPTION SURVEY [COMPUTER FILE] / ENERGY INFORMATION ADMINISTRATION, OFFICE OF ENERGY MARKETS AND END USE, ENERGY END USE DIVISION. See Energy.

CN/0835-1074
RESIDENTIAL GENERAL CONTRACTORS AND DEVELOPERS. See Building and Construction.

CN/0712-6468
RESIDENTIAL LAND AND HOUSING SURVEY / THE CITY OF CALGARY, PLANNING DEPARTMENT. [Resid. land hous. surv.]. English. an. 5.00Can$. City of Calgary Planning Information Centre, PO Box 2100, Calgary Alberta T2P 2M5 Canada. **DD** 711/.4/0971233.

US/1062-7316
RETIREMENT HOUSING BUSINESS REPORT. *Title Change.* [Retire. hous. bus. rep.]. (1992)-(1993). Periodical. English. mo. CD Publications, 8204 Fenton Street, Silver Spring MD 20910. **Tel** (800)666-6380, (301)588-6380, FAX (301)588-6385. **DD** 362. *Continues* Retirement Housing Report, 0890-7757. *Merged into* Housing the Elderly Report, 1050-3234.

US/0048-749X
REVIEW OF REGIONAL STUDIES, THE. [Rev. reg. stud.]. Vol. 1 (Fall 1970)-. Academic Scholarly Publication. English. Three times a year. $30.00. University of Tennessee Dept. of Economics, Stolely Management Center, Knoxville TN 37996. **Tel** (615)974-3303. **ED** Henry W Herzog, Jr., Alan M Schlottmann. **LC** HT390; .R45. **DD** 309.2/5/05. **Circ:** 1,000 (ctrl). available on microfilm.
 Desc: Scholarly analysis of regional aspects of social systems.
 Ind/Abst Econ. Lit. Index; Geogr. Abstr. Phys. Geogr.; Geogr. Abstr. Human Geogr.; Int. Dev. Abstr.; J. Econ. Lit.; J. Plan. Lit.; Popul. Index.

RH/1016-2240
REVIEW OF RURAL AND URBAN PLANNING IN SOUTHERN AND EASTERN AFRICA : JOURNAL OF THE ASSOCIATION OF RURAL & URBAN PLANNERS IN SOUTHERN & EASTERN AFRICA. **Added/Corp** Association of Rural & Urban Planners in Southern & Eastern Africa. **VFOAT** Review of Rural & Urban Planning in S & E Africa. (198?)-. Periodical. English. tq. $72.00 (institutions); $48.00 (individuals). University of Zimbabwe / Department of Law, PO Box MP 167, Mount Pleasant, Harare Zimbabwe. **Tel** 011 263 0 303211 ext. 1813, FAX 011 263 4 303273. **LC** HT395.A356; R48. **DD** 307.1/2/0967605.
 Ind/Abst Int. Bibliogr. Sociol.; Rural Dev. Abstr.

JA
REVIEW OF URBAN AND REGIONAL DEVELOPMENT STUDIES: RURDS. **Added/Corp** Applied Regional Science Conference. Tokyo Kokusai Daigaku. Urban Development Institute. **VFOAT** RURDS. Vol. 1, No. 1 (January 1989)-.

Periodical. English. sa. $40.00. Urban Dvlp Inst, Nakanishi 6F, 8 4 Takanadobaba 4 Chome, Shijuku-ku Tokyo 169 Japan. **Tel** 011 81 3 3672659. **LC** HT390; .R48.
 Ind/Abst Int. Bibliogr. Sociol.; Int. Dev. Abstr.

US
REVIEWING AND PROCESSING COMMUNITY DEVELOPMENT BLOCK GRANT ENTITLEMENT APPLICATIONS. Government Publication. English. US Department of Housing and Urban Development, 451 Seventh Street SW, Washington DC 20401. **Tel** (202)708-0980, FAX (202)708-0299.

BL
REVISTA BRASILEIRA DE PLANEJAMENTO. 1- April 1976-. Periodical. Portuguese. Three times a year. Instituto Brasileivo de Planejamento, Av Ipiranga 1555, 5O Andar 90.000, Porto Alegre Brazil. **LC** HC186; .R375.

BL
REVISTA DA FUNDACAO JONES DOS SANTOS NEVES. **Main/Corp** Fundacao Jones dos Santos Neves. Yearly V. 1, Jan./March 1978-. Portuguese. Cr$80.00. Fundacao Jones dos Santos Neves, Avenida Cesar Hilal, 437-1 Andar, Vitoria Brazil. **LC** HF395.B72; E763.

US/0185-1861
REVISTA INTERAMERICANA DE PLANIFICACION. [Rev. interam. planif.]. **Added/Corp** Interamerican Planning Society. Vol. 6, No. 21 (Mar. 1972)-. Periodical. Spanish. qt (Mar., June, Sept., Dec.). $30.00 Latin America; $40.00 Europe; $42.00 Asia, Africa, & Oceania. Sociedad Interamericana de Planificacion, PO Box 1566, San Antonio TX 78296. **Tel** (210)227-8760, FAX (210)227-0918. **ED** Luis E. Camacho. **LC** HC95.A1; R47. **DD** 309.2/5/098. cum. index. **Ad Acc. Circ:** 2,000 (ctrl). *Continues* Interamerican Planning Society. Revista.
 Desc: Covers the relation of economic and social planning for development in Latin America.
 Ind/Abst HAPI Hisp. Am. Period. Index; Int. Bibliogr. Sociol.; Int. Labour Doc.; LABORDOC.

FR
REVUE D'ECONOMIE REGIONAL ET URBAINE. Vol.1, No.1 (1978)-. Periodical. French. ir. 410.00F France; 550.00F other. A D I C U E E R, 93 Avenue du Recteur Pineau, 86022 Poiters Cedex France. **Tel** 16 49 462743. **Bk Rev. Circ:** 500 (ctrl).
 Desc: Covers inter-regional, micro-regional and urban development. Also contains policy research and studies.

FR/0242-5629
REVUE DES LOYERS ET DES FERMAGES, DE LA PROPRIETE COMMERCIALE, DES FONDS DE COMMERCE, DE LA CONSTRUCTION ET DE LA COPROPRIETE IMMOBILIERES. See Real Estate.

CN/0707-9699
REVUE INTERNATIONALE D'ACTION COMMUNAUTAIRE (MONTREAL). (REVUE INTERNATIONALE D'ACTION COMMUNAUTAIRE.). [Rev. int. action communaut.]. **VFOAT** International Review of Community Development. (Spring 1979)-. Periodical. French (summaries and/or abstracts in English and Spanish). sa. 36.00Can$ (institutions); 24.00Can$ (individuals) Canada; 30.00Can$ (individuals) other. Ecole de Service Social, CP 6128 Universite de Montreal, Montreal Quebec H3C 3J7 Canada. **Tel** (514)343-7222. **(Subscription address:** Periodica Inc., PO Box 444, 1155 Ducharme, Outremont Quebec H2V 4R6 Canada.**)** **DD** 309.2/6/05. *Supersedes* Community Development, 0020-854X.
 Ind/Abst Int. Polit. Sci. Abstr.; Point Repere (1983-); Soc. Plann. Policy Dev. Abstr.; Sociol. Abstr.

CN/0842-957X
REVUE QUEBECOISE DURBANISME. [Rev. que. urban.]. **Added/Corp** Association Quebecoise d'Urbanisme. Vol. 8, No 1 (October 1987)-. Periodical. French. Association Qeubecoise d'Urbanisme, CP 1315, Place Bonaventure, Montreal Quebec H5A 1H1. **DD** 711/.4/09714. *Continues* Contact (Association Quebecoise d'Urbanisme)., 0824-6084.

●US
RIVERSIDE SOUTH FORUM. **Added/Corp** Riverside South Planning Corporation (New York, N.Y.). Issue No. 1 (1992)-. Periodical. English.

US
ROBERT-Z'BERG URBAN OPEN SPACE AND RECREATION PROGRAM ANNUAL REPORT. English. an. Department of Parks and Recreation, PO Box 2390, Sacramento CA 95811. **Tel** (916)322-7000.

UK
ROOF. **Added/Corp** Shelter (Organization). (19??)-. Periodical. English. bm. $85.05 US and Canada; $65.24 UK; $81.55 other. Shelter / London, 88 Old Street, London EC1V 9HU, England. **Tel** 011 44 71 253-0202. **ED** Tim Mars. **LC** HD7333.A3; R63. Index available. cum. index. **Bk Rev. Ad Acc. Circ:** 4,000 (ctrl).
 Desc: Concerned with housing policy, practice, law, special notes for advisors, parliament, with an investigative and campaigning emphasis.
 Ind/Abst Appl. Soc. Sci. Index Abstr.; Sage Race Relat. Abstr.

US
ROUNDUP / LOW INCOME HOUSING INFORMATION SERVICE. **Added/Corp** Low Income Housing Information Service (Washington, D.C.). (198?)-. Periodical. English. mo (10 issues). Free to members; Membership: $15.00 (individuals), $25.00 (private or community based organizations), $150.00 (governmental & national organizations). Low Income Housing Information Service, 1012 14th Street NW, Suite 1200, Washington DC 20005. **Tel** (202)662-1530, FAX (202)393-1973. **ED** Rich West. **Bk Rev. Circ:** 1,300. *Continues* Low Income Housing Round-Up.
 Desc: Source of information on federal low income housing programs and activities in Congress.

CN/0831-148X
ROYAL LEPAGE SURVEY OF CANADIAN HOUSE PRICES. [R. LePage surv. Can. house prices.]. (Winter 1985)-. Periodical. English. Three times a year. Free. Royal Lepage, 39 Wynford Drive/4th Floor, Don Mills Ontario M3C 9Z9 Canada. **DD** 338.4/3/6908640971. *Continues* Royal Trust Survey of Canadian House Prices, 0706-8506.

US
RSRI ABSTRACTS. **Main/Corp** Regional Science Research Institute. **VAT** Regional Science Research Institute Abstracts. Vol. 1 (June 1976)-. Periodical. English. ir. Free on request. Regional Science Research Institute, PO Box 329, Hightstown NJ 08520. **Tel** (609)448-6966. **ED** Benjamin H. Stevens and Michael L. Lahr. **Circ:** 900.
 Desc: Abstracts activities of the Regional Science Research Institute.

NE
RUIMTELIJKE VERKENNINGEN. **Added/Corp** Netherlands. Rijksplanologische Dienst. (1985/1986)-. Dutch. **LC** HC321; .A3572. *Continues* Jaarverslag Rijksplanologische Dienst.

US
RURAL ADVOCATE, THE. **Main/Corp** Michigan. Rural Development Program. **Added/Corp** Michigan. Dept. of Commerce. Vol. 1, No. 1, (1990)-. Periodical. English.

UK/0140-4768
RURAL DEVELOPMENT ABSTRACTS / [PREPARED BY THE COMMONWEALTH BUREAU OF AGRICULTURAL ECONOMICS]. See Housing and Urban Development-Abstracting, Bibliographies and Statistics.

US/0197-4904
RURAL DEVELOPMENT COUNCIL PUBLICATION (FAIRBANKS). (PUBLICATION / ALASKA RURAL DEVELOPMENT CORPORATION.). No. 1-. Monographic series. English. Price varies per volume. University of Alaska Cooperative Extension Service, Fairbanks AK 99701.

SW/0346-7287
RURAL DEVELOPMENT STUDIES. [Rural dev. stud.]. **Added/Corp** Sveriges Lantbruksuniversitet. U-Landsavdelningen. Sveriges Lantbruksuniversitet. International Rural Development Centre. No. 1 (1972)-. Monographic series. English. **LC** UNC.
 Ind/Abst For. Abstr.

BG
RURAL DEVELOPMENT STUDIES (UNIVERSITY OF RAJSHAHI. DEPT. OF ECONOMICS). (RURAL DEVELOPMENT STUDIES.). **Added/Corp** Rajasahi Bisvabidyalaya. Dept. of Economics. International Bank for Reconstruction and Development. (19??)-. Monographic series. English. Price varies per volume. Bangladesh Institute of Development Studies, E-17 Agargaon, PO Box 3854, Dhaka 7 Bangladesh. **Tel FAX** 880-2-813023.
 Ind/Abst Agrofor. Abstr. (1991-).

ET
RURAL PROGRESS. V. 1- Oct. 1977-. Periodical. English. The Editor Rural Progress, PO Box 3001, Addis Ababa Ethiopia. **LC** HN771; .R87. **DD** 309.2/63/096.

Housing and Urban Development

Formed by the union of Rural Development Newsletter and African Women.
Ind/Abst Int. Labour Doc.; Rural Dev. Abstr.; World Agric. Econ.

II/0557-6644
RURAL RECONSTRUCTION (NEW DELHI). Title Change. (RURAL RECONSTRUCTION.). [Rural reconstr.]. **Added/Corp** Afro-Asian Rural Reconstruction Organization. Vol. 1 (1966)-(199?). Periodical. English. qt. **LC** HN1; .R85. **DD** 307.7/2/05. *Continued by Journal of Rural Reconstruction.*
Ind/Abst Appl. Soc. Sci. Index Abstr. (?-?); Int. Dev. Abstr. (?-?).

II
RURAL SYSTEMS. **Added/Corp** National Council of Rural Development (India). Vol. 1, No. 1 (Mar. 1983)-. Periodical. English. qt. $40.00. National Council of Rural Development, Varanasi, India. (**Subscription address:** Prints India, 11 Darya Ganj, New Delhi, 110002 India, (Phone: 011 91 11 3268645)) **LC** HN49.C6; R89. **DD** 307.1/4/05.

PE
RURALTER : REVISTA DE DESARROLLO RURAL ALTERNATIVO / CENTRO INTERNACIONAL DE COOPERACION PARA EL DESARROLLO AGRICOLA, CICDA. **Added/Corp** Centro Internacional de Cooperacion para el Desarrollo Agricola. No. 1 (1986)-. Periodical. Spanish. sa. Centro Internacional de Cooperacion para el Desarrollo Agricola - CICDA, Coordinacion America Latina, Aptdo. 3720, Lima 100, Peru.
Ind/Abst PAIS Int. Print.

JA/0917-0553
RURDS. REVIEW OF URBAN AND REGIONAL DEVELOPMENT STUDIES. [RURDS, Rev. urb. reg. dev. stud.]. **VFOAT** Review of Urban and Regional Development Studies; Journal of the Applied Regional Science Conference. (1989)-. Periodical. English. Twice a year. $40.00 (surface mail), $48.00 (airmail). Urban Development Institute, Nakanishi 6F, 8 4 Takanadobaba 4 Chome, Shijuku ku Tokyo 169 Japan. **Tel** 11 81 3 3672659, FAX 11 81 3 3678451. **ED** Koichi Mera. **DD** 333.38. **Pr Rev. Circ:** 1,000.

RU
RUSSKII GOROD. No. 1 (1976)-. Periodical. Russian. an. 1.30rub. Izdatelstvo Moskovskogo Universiteta, K-9 Ulitsa Gertsena 5/7, Moscow Russia. **Tel** (301)881-5973. **LC** HT145.S58; R87.

KO
SAE MAUL UNDONG YONGU (HANSA TAEHAK. SAE MAUL UNDONG YONGUSO). (SAE MAUL UNDONG YONGU.). Periodical. Korean (summaries and/or abstracts in English). Hansa Taehak Sae Maul Undong Yonguso, 2288 Taemyong-dong Nam-ku, Taegu Korea. **LC** HN730.5.Z9; C665824.

KO
SAE MAUM NONMUNJIP. **Added/Corp** Chungnam Taehakkyo. Pusol Sae Maul Yonguso. **VFOAT** Journal of Saemaum. (1988)-. Periodical. Korean (summaries and/or abstracts in English). **LC** HN730.5.Z9; C66588. *Continues Sae maum nonchong.*

US/0090-5747
SAGE URBAN STUDIES ABSTRACTS. See Housing and Urban Development-Abstracting, Bibliographies and Statistics.

PH
SAMBAHAYAN. National Housing Authority, Quezon Memorial Circle, Elliptical Road, Diliman, Quezon City Philippines.

US/0192-1738
SAN FERNANDO VALLEY APARTMENT OWNER BUILDER. **VFOAT** Apartment Owner Builder; San Fernando Valley Apartment Owner/Builder. (19??)-. Periodical. English. mo. $9.00 (one year), $15.00 (two year) zip codes beginning 900-935; $24.00 (one year), $43.00 (two year) other. Apartment News Publications, 3220 East Willow, Long Beach CA 90806. **Tel** (213)636-8351. **Circ:** 60,000.

NR/0331-0523
SAVANNA. See Economics.

US
SCAG: A RECORD OF ACCOMPLISHMENT. See Public Administration.

SW/0281-5737
SCANDINAVIAN HOUSING AND PLANNING RESEARCH. [Scand. hous. plan. res.]. **VFOAT** Scandinavian Housing & Planning Research; SHPR. Vol. 1, No. 1 (Feb. 1984)-. Periodical. English. qt. Kr760.00, $120.00. Scandinavian University Press, PO Box 2959 Toeyen, N 0608 Oslo 6 Norway. **Tel** 011 47 2 2575400, FAX 011 47 2 2575353, telex 71896 UROR N. (**Subscription address:** Scandinavian University Press, 200 Meacham Ave., Elmont NY 11003.)
Ind/Abst Geogr. Abstr. Human Geogr.; Int. Bibliogr. Sociol.; J. Plan. Lit.; Sage Urban Stud. Abstr.

GW/0417-1500
SCHRIFTENREIHE. **Main/Corp** Deutsche Akademie fur Stadtebau und Landesplanung. 1- 1950-. Periodical. German. Deutsche Akademie fur Stadtebau und Landesplanung, Dusseldorf Germany.

CN
SCOOP. (19??)-. Periodical. English. Ten times a year. 13.37Can$. Co-operative Housing Federation of British Columbia, 4676 Main Street, Vancouver BC V5V 3R7 Canada. **Tel** (604)879-5111, FAX (604)879-4611. **ED** Coie Dudley. **Ad Acc.** ctrl circ.

UK
SCOTTISH HOUSING STATISTICS / SCOTTISH DEVELOPMENT DEPARTMENT. See Housing and Urban Development-Abstracting, Bibliographies and Statistics.

●UK/0144-8196
SCOTTISH PLANNING & ENVIRONMENTAL LAW. **Added/Corp** Law Society of Scotland. Planning Exchange. **VFOAT** Scottish Planning and Environmental Law. No. 39 (June 1993)-. Periodical. English. tq. £27.00 UK; £35.00 other. Planning Exchange, 186 Bath Street, Glasgow G2 4HG Scotland. **Tel** 011 44 41 3328541. **LC** KDC446.A13; S25. **DD** 346.41104/5; 344.110645. *Continues Scottish Planning Law & Practice.*

US/0740-4271
SECONDARY MORTGAGE MARKETS. See Business-Banking and Finance.

US
SECTION 802(C)(2) : INTEREST SUBSIDY GRANTS PROCESSING HANDBOOK. **VFOAT** Interest Subsidy Grants Processing Handbook. Government Publication. English. ir. US Department of Housing and Urban Development, 451 Seventh Street SW, Washington DC 20401. **Tel** (202)708-0980, FAX (202)708-0299.

US
SELECTED PAPERS PRESENTED AT THE ANNUAL MEETING - SOUTHERN REGIONAL SCIENCE ASSOCIATION. **Main/Corp** Southern Regional Science Association. **VFOAT** Papers. 1968-. English. an. University of Tennessee College of Business Administration, Knoxville TN 37916. **LC** HT390. **DD** 338.973.

CN/0705-1506
SEMINAR PAPERS - ASSOCIATION OF ONTARIO HOUSING AUTHORITIES. **Main/Corp** Association of Ontario Housing Authorities. (1977)-. Periodical. English. an. Limited free distribution. Ontario Housing Authorities, 405-111 Avenue Road, Toronto Ontario M5R 3J8. **DD** 301.5/4.

AT
SHELTER. **Added/Corp** Australia. Dept. of Housing. Vol. 1 (Aug. 1973)-. Periodical. English. Australian Department of Housing, PO Box 690, Canberra Australian Capital Territory 2601 Australia. **LC** HD7379.A3; S5. **DD** 301.5/4/0994.

US/0885-9612
SHELTERFORCE. [Shelterforce]. **Added/Corp** Shelterforce Collective. National Lawyers Guild. National Housing Institute (U.S.) Shelterforce Inc. **VFOAT** Shelter Force. Vol. 1, (1975)-. Periodical. English. Six times a year (Jan., Mar., May, July, Sept., Nov.). $16.20 (individual), $25.50 (insitutions) US; $34.20 Canada; $38.70 other. Shelterforce, 439 Main Street, Orange NJ 07050. **Tel** (201)678-3110, FAX (201)678-0014. **ED** Patrick Morrissy. **LC** HD7293.A1; S53. **DD** 363.5/0973/05. cum. index. **Bk Rev. Ad Acc. Adv Mgr:** Dale Coleman, **Tel** (201)678-3110. **Circ:** 2,400 (ctrl). available on microfilm.
 Desc: National housing publication reporting on news from around the country, analysis and policies relating to tenants and low and moderate income people.
 Ind/Abst Altern. Press Index; Soc. Plann. Policy Dev. Abstr.; Sociol. Abstr.

JA
SHIN TOSHI. **Added/Corp** Toshi Keikaku Kyokai. Japan. Kensetsusho. Toshikyoku. (19??)-. Periodical. Japanese. Twelve times a year. $144.00. (**Subscription address:** Kyowa Book Company Inc., 1 38 Kanda Jinbocho Chiyoda-ku, Tokyo 101 Japan.) **LC** HT169.J3; S5.

US/0417-1225
SHOPPING CENTERS IN THE DETROIT REGION. **Main/Corp** Detroit Metropolitan Area Regional Planning Commission. (19??)-. Periodical. English. an. Metro Regional Planning Commission, 800 Cadillac Square Building, Detroit MI 48201. **DD** 658.8.

SI
SIP JOURNAL. **Main/Corp** Singapore Institute of Planners. (Sept. 1971)-. English. an. Singapore Institute of Planners, GPO Box 3600, 23 Outram Park, Singapore 0316 Singapore. **LC** HT169.S55; S5.

IT
SISTEMI URBANI. Vol. 1, No. 1 (April 1979)-. Periodical. Italian (English and French). Three times a year. L190000 Italy; L300000 other. Guida Editori Spa, Via D Morelli 16/B, 80121 Naples Italy. **Tel** 011 39 81 7644288. **LC** HT166; .S572. **DD** 307/.12/05.

US
SITE SELECTION. (19??)-. English. Four times a year. $75.00. Conway Data Inc., 40 Technology Park Suite 200, Norcross GA 30092. **Tel** (404)446-6996, (800)554-5686, FAX (404)263-8825. *Absorbed Site Selection Europe; Site Selection & Industrial Development, 1041-3073.*

US/0194-2735
SMALL CITY AND REGIONAL COMMUNITY, THE. V. 1- 1978-. English. be. $19.00 US; $25.00 other. Foundation Press, University of Wisconsin-Stevens Point, Stevens Point WI 54481. **Tel** (715)346-2708. **ED** Robert Wolensky and Edward J Miller. **LC** HT123; .S57. **DD** 307.7/6/0973. **Circ:** 500 (ctrl). available on microfiche.
 Desc: Proceedings on the conferences of the small city and regional community.

US/0196-1683
SMALL TOWN. [Small town]. **Added/Corp** Small Towns Institute (U.S.). Vol. 1 (July 1969)-. Periodical. English. Six times a year (Jan., Mar., May, July, Sept., Nov.). $45.00 (institutions), $40.00 (individuals). Small Towns Institute, PO Box 517, Ellensburg WA 98926. **Tel** (509)925-1830. **ED** Kenneth Munsell. **LC** HT101; .S63. cum. index. **Bk Rev. Circ:** 1,600.
 Desc: Publishes case studies of innovative programs dealing with the issues and problems facing small communities in the United States and Canada.
 Ind/Abst AGRICOLA [Full Cov.]; Sage Urban Stud. Abstr (?-?); Urban Aff. Abstr.

●US/1061-9933
SMALL TOWN OBSERVER, THE. [Small town obs.]. (1992)-. Periodical. English. Four times a year. $24.00. The Small Town Observer, PO Box 324, Bend OR 97709. **Tel** (503)382-0316. **ED** Thomas H. Evons. **DD** 917. **Bk Rev. Ad Acc, Adv Mgr:** Thom Evons, **Tel** (503)383-3746. **Circ:** 5,000. *Continues Northwest Relocation News.*
 Desc: Documents the move from large urban areas to small rural towns. Profiles of towns, interviews with people making the move. Focuses on the problems as well as the opportunities for the people and towns.

CN/0711-3102
SMC NATIONAL REPORT. [SMC natl. rep.]. **Main/Corp** Housing and Urban Development Association of Canada. Sales and Marketing Council. Vol. 5, No. 1-. Periodical. English. mo. Housing and Urban Development Association of Canada, 10th Floor, 15 Toronto Street, Toronto Ontario M5C 2E3 Canada. **DD** 333.33/06/071. *Continues Sales and Marketing Council Newsletter, 0225-073X.*

PO
SOCIEDADE E TERRITORIO. (198?)-. Periodical. Portuguese. Three times a year. 6800$0 Spain; 7900$0 Europe; 9600$0 other. Edicoes Afrontamento, Apartado 1309, 4201 Porto Portugal. **Tel** 011 351 2 489271, FAX 011 351 2 491777. **LC** WMLC 93/3506; HD481.A1; S62.

JA
SOGO TOSHI KENKYU. **VFOAT** Comprehensive Urban Studies. (Nov. 1977)-. Periodical. Japanese (summaries and/or abstracts in English). an. Tokyo Toritsu Daigaku Toshi Kenkyu Senta, (Center for Urban Studies, Metropolitan University), 1-1 Yakumo 1, Meguro-ku Tokyo 152 Japan. **LC** HT101; .S63. **DD** 301.36/05.

IT
SOLIDARIETA LOMBARDIA. (19??)-. Italian. Four times a year. L20000. Citta e Societa, Piazza S Ambrogio 21, 20123 Milan Italy. *Continues Citta e Societa.*

CN/0828-6574
SOLPLAN REVIEW. [Solplan rev.]. **Added/Corp** Drawing-Room Graphic Services. (Feb. 1985)-. Periodical. English. Six times a year (Feb., Apr., June, Aug., Oct., Dec.). 38.00Can$ Canada, 46.00Can$ other, (one year); 72.00Can$ Canada, 88.00Can$ other (two years). Drawing Room Graphic Services, PO Box 86627, North Vancouver BC V7L 4L2 Canada. **Tel** (604)689-1841, FAX (604)689-1401. **ED** Richard Kadulsky, (phone: (604)689-1841). **DD** 693.8/32/05. **CODEN** SREVEW. cum. index. **Bk Rev. Ad Acc. Circ:** 5,000.

RU
SOTSIALNO-EKONOMICHESKOE RAZVITIE MOSKVY I KRUPNEISHIKH GORODOV SSSR. **Added/Corp** Gosudarstvennaia Biblioteka SSSR Imeni V.I. Lenina.

Nauchno-Issledovatelskii Otdel Bibliografovedeniia i Nauchno-Vspomogatelnoi Bibliografii. (1987)-. Russian. ir. ***Continues*** *Sotsialno-Ekonomicheskoe* ***and*** *Razvitie Moskvy.*

US
SOUNDINGS FROM AROUND THE WORLD. English. Twice a year. $5.00 Northern Hemisphere/industrial nations; Free to addresses in Southern Hemisphere/developing nations. World Neighbours, 4127 Northwest 122nd Street, Oklahoma City OK 73120-8869. **Tel** (800)242-6387, (405)752-9700, FAX (405)752-9393, telex 5106002674.
Desc: Reviews and/or describes materials (including price and ordering information) for use in the development field. An excellent reference for rural development workers. Available in English only.

US/0147-8559
SOUTH ATLANTIC URBAN STUDIES. ***Ceased.*** [South Atl. urban stud.]. V. 1- (1977)-?. English. an. University of South Carolina Press, 205 Pickens Street, Columbia SC 29208. **Tel** (803)778-2500, (800)777-5243. **LC** HT108; .S68. **DD** 301.36/3/0975.

US
SOUTHERN COMMUNITIES. English. bm. $15.00 (1 year), $27.00 (2 year), $39.00 (3 year). Southern Neighborhoods Network, PO Box 121133, Nashville TN 37212. **Tel** (615)292-1798, . ***Absorbed*** *Community Economic Reporter, 0882-8636; Southern Neighborhoods, 0735-8644.*

US
SPOTLIGHT. English. qt (with one special issue). $95.00. Waterfront Center, 1536 44th Street NW, Washington DC 20007. **Tel** (202)337-0356. ***Continues*** *Waterfront World, 0733-0677.*

US/0361-6444
SPUR REPORT. [SPUR rep.]. **Main/Corp** San Francisco Planning and Urban Renewal Association. **Added/Corp** San Francisco Planning and Urban Renewal Association. **VFOAT** SPUR News. **VAT** San Francisco Planning and Urban Renewal Association Report; San Francisco Planning and Urban Research Association Report. No. 1 (May 1963)-. Periodical. English. Twelve times a year. $35.00. San Francisco Planning and Urban Research Association, 312 Sutter Street, San Francisco CA 94108. **Tel** (415)781-8726. **ED** Michael S. McGill. **DD** 322. **Circ:** 1,500 (ctrl).
Desc: Public policy analyses of issues facing the San Francisco Bay area.

RU
SREDNEVEKOVYI GOROD. Vol. 1 (1968)-. Russian. 0.78rub each issue. Saratov N.G. Chernyshevskii State University, Astrakhanskaya Ulitsa 83, 410071 Saratov Russia. **Tel** 24-16-96, FAX 24-04-46, telex 241125. **LC** HT131; .S7.

SW/0280-4549
STAD OCH LAND. **See** Gardening and Horticulture.

GW
STADT, REGION, LAND. Periodical. German. ir. Institut fur Stadtbauwesen, Rwth Aachen, W-5100 Aachen Mies-van-der-Rohe-Strasse Germany. **LC** HT169.G3; S73. **DD** 307.7/6/0943.

GW/0585-0096
STADTBAUWELT. (1964)-. Periodical. German. qt (4 issues). DM100.00. Bertelsmann Fachzeitschriften GmbH, Carl-Bertelsmann Strasse 270, D-33311 Frankfurt Germany. **Tel** 011 49 5241 802199. **(Subscription address:** Translibris GmbH, PO Box 301373, D 50783 Cologne Germany.**)**

GW
STADTEBAUBERICHT. **Main/Corp** Germany (West). Bundesministerium fur Raumordnung, Bauwesen und Stadtebau. German. Deishmanns Aue, W-53 Bonn-Bad Godesberg Germany. **LC** HT169.G3; G38A. **DD** 309.2/62/0943.

US/0196-1098
STATE INVESTMENT PLAN. **Main/Corp** Georgia. Office of Planning and Budget. English. an. Georgia Office of Planning and Budget, 270 Washington Street Southwest, Room 611, Atlanta GA 30334. **Tel** (404)656-3820. **LC** HT393.G4; G46A. **DD** 361.6/09758.

US
STATISTICAL SUMMARY OF DEPARTMENTAL ACTIONS. **See** Housing and Urban Development-Abstracting, Bibliographies and Statistics.

US
STATISTICAL SUMMARY OF PROGRAMS / NEW YORK STATE DIVISION OF HOUSING AND COMMUNITY RENEWAL. **See** Housing and Urban Development-Abstracting, Bibliographies and Statistics.

IO
STATISTIK PERUMAHAN DAN LINGKUNGANNYA. **See** Housing and Urban Development-Abstracting, Bibliographies and Statistics.

AU
STEINE SPRECHEN. **Added/Corp** Verein fur Denkmal- und Stadtbildpflege. (19??)-. Periodical. German.
Ind/Abst BHA : Biblio. Hist. Art.

IT/0391-3929
STORIA DELLA CITTA. ***Ceased.*** [Stor. citta]. No. 1 (Sept. 1976)-Issue 56 (Dec. 1993). Periodical. Italian (English and French). qt. **(Subscription address:** Agenzia Italiana Esportazione, Via Manzoni 12, 20089 Rozzano Milan, Italy.**)** **LC** HT111; .S73. **DD** 307.7/6/09.
Ind/Abst Art Archaeol. Tech. Abstr.; Avery Index Archit. Period. Suppl. Colum. Univ. (1988-1990); BHA : Biblio. Hist. Art (?-?).

IT
STORIA URBANA. Volume 1, No. 1 (Jan. 1977)-. Periodical. Italian (summaries and/or abstracts in English). Three times a year. L116000 Italy; L150000 other. Franco Angeli Riviste SRL, Viale Monza 106, 20127 Milan Italy. **Tel** 011 39 2 2827651, 011 39 2 289562. **ED** L. Bortolotti. **LC** HT145.I8; .S75.
Ind/Abst Am. Hist. Life (1990-); Avery Index Archit. Period. Suppl. Colum. Univ. (Jan. 1989-); BHA : Biblio. Hist. Art.

US
STREET TALK. **Added/Corp** Regional Rehabilitation Institute. (June 1977)-. Periodical. English. Regional Housing Rehabilitation Institute, 157 Church Street, New Haven CT 06510. **Tel** (203)787-8372.

UK/0957-6517
STREETWISE : THE MAGAZINE OF URBAN STUDIES. [Streetwise Brighton]. **Added/Corp** National Association for Urban Studies (Great Britain). **VFOAT** Magazine of Urban Studies. Issue No. 1 (Autumn 1989)-. Periodical. English. qt. £22.50 (institutions and libraries), £15.50 (individuals, schools, and voluntary organizations), £10.00 NAUS members, UK; £26.50 (institutions and libraries), £19.50 (individuals, schools, and voluntary organizations), £14.00 NAUS members, other. Lewis Cohen Urban Studies Center, 68 Grand Parade, Brighton Poly East Sussex BN2 2JY England. **Tel** 011 44 273 673416, FAX 011 44 273 679179. ***Continues*** *BEE. Bulletin of Environmental Education, 0045-1266.*
Desc: Information on cities and towns and urban policy.
Ind/Abst Br. Educ. Index; Geogr. Abstr. Phys. Geogr.; Geogr. Abstr. Human Geogr.

CN/0822-5044
SUBVENTIONS. [Subventions]. Periodical. French. Salon National De L'Habitation, 2197 Est, Rue Sherbrooke, Montreal Quebec H2K 1C9. **DD** 363.5/8/09714.

US
SUPPLEMENTAL MANAGEMENT FUND FOR SUBSIDIZED MULTIFAMILY PROJECTS. Government Publication. English. ir. US Department of Housing and Urban Development, 451 Seventh Street SW, Washington DC 20401. **Tel** (202)708-0980, FAX (202)708-0299.

US/0363-7514
SURVEY OF MUNICIPAL PLANNING AND REGULATORY ACTIVITY, A. **Main/Corp** Maine. State Planning Office. English. Maine State Planning Office, 184 State Street, Augusta ME 04333. **LC** HT167; .M34A. **DD** 309.2/62/09741.

US
SURVEY OF REGIONAL LITERATURE, THE. **Added/Corp** Bryant College. Center for Regional Analysis. **VFOAT** SRL. (19??)-. Periodical. English. qt. $60.00 (institutions), $45.00 (individuals) North America; $60.00 other. Bryant College, 450 Douglas Pike, Smithfield RI 02917. **Tel** (401)232-6470, FAX (401)232-6319. **ED** R. D. Norton. Index available (Index by arthor and geographic reference). **Circ:** 300.
Desc: Lists current book annotations and journal abstracts concerning cities and regions worldwide. Each issue also profiles a region, topic, or issue of special interest.

SW/0032-0560
SWEDISH TOWN AND COUNTRY PLANNING REVIEW, THE. (PLAN.). **Added/Corp** Foreningen for Samhallsplanering (Sweden). Vol. 1, (1947)-. Periodical. Swedish (English; summaries and/or abstracts in English). Six times a year. Kr500.00 Europe; Kr570.00 others. Swedish Society Town Country Planning, PO Box 15013, S-800 15 Gavle Sweden. **Tel** 011 46 26 687500, FAX 011 46 26 611536. **ED** Goran Cars (phone: (046) 8 7907938). **LC** HT169.S8; P5. Index available (6th iss.). **Bk Rev**, (Qty: 6). **Ad Acc. Circ:** 2,500.
Desc: Issues relating to the general planning of urban and rural areas. Seeks to provide a forum for a colloquy on these problems between technical, economic and social experts and representatives of central and local government, the business community and the general public.
Ind/Abst Int. Civil Eng. Abstr.; Soft. Abstr. Eng.

FR
TABLEAU DE BORD CONJONCTUREL DU LOGEMENT. **Main/Corp** France. Direction du Batiment et des Travaux Publics et de la Conjoncture. Periodical. French. qt. 340.00F, add 25.00F for (airmail) postage. Documentation Francaise, 29 Quai Voltaire, 75344 Paris Cedex 7 France. **Tel** 011 33 1 40157000, FAX 011 33 1 40157230, telex 204 826 DOCFRAN. **LC** HD7338.A3; F723A. **DD** 338.4/7/69080944.
Desc: This publication summarizes in graph format, economic trends in building, housing, and public works.

UA
TANMIYAT AL-MUJTAMA. **VFOAT** Tanmiat El-Mogtama; Community Development. Periodical. Arabic (English). qt. $5.00. 31 Shari Lubnan, Al-Muhandisin. **LC** HN786.Z9; C67.

GW
TATIGKEITSBERICHT DES ILS. **Main/Corp** Institut fur Landes- und Stadtentwicklungsforschung des Landes Nordrhein-Westfalen. **VAT** Tatigkeitsbericht des Institut fur Landes- und Stadtentwicklungsforschung des Landes Nordrhein-Westfalen. 1971/74-. German. Institut fur Landes und Stadtentwicklungsforschung des Landes Nordrhein-Westfalen, Dortmund Germany. **LC** HT395.G42; N687B.

US/0083-4718
TECHNICAL BULLETIN - URBAN LAND INSTITUTE. (TECHNICAL BULLETIN.). [Tech. bull. - Urb. Land Inst.]. Began with: No. 1 (Mar. 1945). Bulletin. English. ir. Price varies per volume. Urban Land Institute, 625 Indiana Ave Northwest, Washington DC 20004. **Tel** (202)624-7000, (800)321-5011. **LC** NA9000; .U67. **DD** 333.77/0973.

US/0584-4290
TECHNICAL REPORT - SOUTHEASTERN WISCONSIN REGIONAL PLANNING COMMISSION. **Main/Corp** Southeastern Wisconsin Regional Planning Commission. No. 1 (1965)-. Monographic series. English. ir. Price varies per volume. Southeastern Wisconsin Regional Planning Commission, PO Box 1607, Waukesha WI 53187. **Tel** (414)547-6721. **LC** HT390; .S685. ctrl circ.
Desc: Documents the findings of basic inventories such as detailed soil surveys, potential park and open space sites, and horizontal and vertical control surveys to various public and private agencies within the region.

HU/0230-4805
TELEPULESFEJLESZTES. **Added/Corp** Varosepitesi Tudomanyos es Tervezo Intezet. Hungary. Epitesugyi es Varosfejlesztesi Miniszterium. (19??)-. Periodical. Hungarian (translations available in English, French, German and Russian).
Ind/Abst Leis. Recreat. Tour. Abstr.; World Agric. Econ.

UK
TELLING AND DUXBURY : PLANNING LAW AND PROCEDURE. **See** Law.

US/0040-3083
TENANT. **Added/Corp** Metropolitan Council on Housing. **VFOAT** Inquilino. (197?)-. Periodical. English (Spanish). Eleven times a year (monthly except Aug.). $5.00 institution; $2.50 individual. Metropolitan Council on Housing, 102 Fulton Street, Suite 302, New York NY 10038. **Tel** (212)693-0550, FAX (212)693-0555. **ED** Judith Mahoney Pasternak. **Circ:** 4,000 (ctrl).

CN/1195-423X
TENANTS BULLETIN. Bulletin. English. qt (Mar., June, Sept., Dec.). 25.00Can$. Federation Metro Tenants Association, 344 Bloor Street, Suite 403, Toronto ONT M5S 3A7 Canad. **Tel** (416)921-8583, FAX (416)921-4177. **ED** Peter Bruer (416)921-9494. **Ad Acc. Circ:** 20,000.
Desc: Covering issues of concerns, interest and information of use to residential tenants in the greater Toronto area.

UK/0142-7849
THIRD WORLD PLANNING REVIEW. [Third world plann. rev.]. Vol. 1 (Spring 1979)-. Periodical. English. qt (4 issues). $170.00 (institution) US. Liverpool University Press, PO Box 147, Liverpool L69 3BX England. **Tel** (051)794 2233, FAX (051)708 6502, telex 627095. **(Subscription address:** Turpin Distribution Services Limited, Blackhorse Road, Letchworth, Hertfordshire SG6 1HN, United Kingdom.**)** **ED** Richard J. Kirkby. **LC** HT169.5; .T5. **DD** 361.6/09172/4. **[CCC].** Index available. cum. index. **Bk Rev. Ad Acc. Pr Rev. Circ:** 600. available on microfilm and microfiche from University Microfilms International (UMI). Documents available from The Genuine Article.
Desc: Intended as a forum for communication between planning practitioners, teachers, research workers and students. Concerned with housing, the use and development of resources and energy, transport and communications, rural development, demographic

change, surveying and planning techniques, the problems of very large metropolitan areas, and the relationship between economic and physical planning.
Ind/Abst Archit. Period. Index (1979-1983); Avery Index Archit. Period. Suppl. Colum. Univ. (1990-); Br. Humanit. Index (19??-); Curr. Contents Soc. Behav. Sci. (19??-); Geogr. Abstr. Human Geogr. (19??-); Int. Bibliogr. Sociol. (19??-); Int. Civil Eng. Abstr. (19??-); Int. Dev. Abstr. (19??-); Int. Labour Doc. (19??-); Res. Alert (19??-) [Full Cov.]; Rural Dev. Abstr. (19??-); Sage Fam. Stud. Abstr. (?-?); Sage Urban Stud. Abstr (19??-); Soc. Plann. Policy Dev. Abstr. (19??-); Soc. Sci. Cit. Index (19??-) [Full Cov.]; Sociol. Abstr. (19??-); Soft. Abstr. Eng. (19??-).

NE/0040-747X
TIJDSCHRIFT VOOR ECONOMISCHE EN SOCIALE GEOGRAFIE : TESG. **See** Economics.

US
TIMEKEEPER'S HANDBOOK. Government Publication. English. US Department of Housing and Urban Development, 451 Seventh Street SW, Washington DC 20401. **Tel** (202)708-0980, FAX (202)708-0299.

CN/1187-5887
TODAY'S SENIORS HOUSING CHOICES GUIDE. [Today's sr. hous. choices guide]. **VFOAT** Housing Choices Guide. (1991)-. English. Metroland Printing Publishing & Distributing, 3145 Wolfedale Road, Mississauga, Ontario L5C 3A9 Canada. **Tel** (416)273-5680, FAX (416)273-4991. **DD** 362.5/946.

JA
TOSHI KENKYU HOKOKU. **Added/Corp** Tokyo Toritsu Daigaku. Toshi Kenkyu Iinkai. No. 46/49 (Oct. 1974)-. Periodical. Japanese. ir. Free on request. Tokyo Metropolitan University / Center for Urban Studies, 1-1 Minami Ohsawa Hachioji, Tokyo 192-03 Japan. **Tel** 0426-77-2351, FAX 0426-77-2352. **LC** HT151; .T69.

AT/0040-9995
TOWN-PLANNING AND LOCAL GOVERNMENT GUIDE, THE. Vol. 1 (July 1956)-. Periodical. English. mo. $160.00. The Law Book Company Limited, 44-50 Waterloo Road, North Ryde New South Wales, 2113 Australia. **Tel** 011 61 2 8870177, FAX 011 61 2 8887240, telex ASBOOK 27445. **ED** Kenneth Gifford. **LC** LAW. **DD** 340. cum. index.
Desc: Arranged alphabetically under subject matter headings, this publication covers spectrum of legal matters of relevance at local government level.
Ind/Abst Aust. Leg. Mon. Dig.

NR/0331-0485
TOWN PLANNING MANUAL. Monographic series. English. Price varies per volume. Town Planning Division, Western State of Nigeria, Ibadan Nigeria. **LC** HT169.N62; W467. **DD** 309.2/62/096692.

UK/0041-0020
TOWN PLANNING REVIEW. (THE TOWN PLANNING REVIEW.). [Town plan. rev.]. **Added/Corp** University of Liverpool. Dept. of Civic Design. Liverpool School of Architecture. Dept. of Civic Design. Vol. 1 (April 1910)-. Periodical. English. qt (4 issues). $170.00 (institution) US and Canada. Liverpool University Press, PO Box 147, Liverpool L69 3BX England. **Tel** (051)794 2233, FAX (051)708 6502, telex 627095. **(Subscription address:** Turpin Distribution Services Limited, Blackhorse Road, Letchworth, Hertfordshire SG6 1HN, United Kingdom.) **ED** David W. Massey. **LC** NA9000; .T6. **[CCC].** Index available. cum. index. **Bk Rev. Ad Acc.** available in microform from Kraus Microform. Documents available from Documents on Demand.
Desc: A forum for communication between planning practitioners, teachers, research workers and students, and for a widely-interested but non-specialist readership. The review's field of interest covers all aspects of Urban and Regional planning, including rural planning, transport planning, landscape design, housing and new towns.
Ind/Abst Appl. Soc. Sci. Index Abstr.; Archit. Period. Index (1910,1977-); Art Index; Avery Index Archit. Period. Suppl. Colum. Univ. (1989-); Br. Archaeol. Bibliogr.; Br. Humanit. Index; Contents Pages Manage.; Curr. Technol. Index; Environ. Abstr.; Environ. Period. Bibliogr.; Geogr. Abstr. Human Geogr.; Int. Bibliogr. Sociol.; Int. Civil Eng. Abstr. (-1985); Int. Dev. Abstr. (?-?); J. Plan. Lit.; Middle East Abstr. Index (1986-); PAIS Int. Print; Life Sci. Collect.; Sage Urban Stud. Abstr (1910-); Soft. Abstr. Eng.

CN/0847-9119
TRAMES (MONTREAL). (TRAMES.). [Trames]. **Added/Corp** Universite de Montreal. Faculte de l'Amenagement. **VFOAT** Revue de l'Amenagement. Vol. 1, No 1 (Autumn 1988)-. Periodical. French. ir (2 to 3 issues per year). 30.00Can$ (institutions), 20.00Can$ (individuals). Faculte d Amenagement Univesite Montreal, C.P. 6128 Succ A, Montreal Quebec H3C 3J7, Canada. **Tel** (514)343-6003, FAX (514)343-2183. **DD** 711/.4/09714. **Ad Acc, Adv Mgr:** C Nadeau. **Circ:** 250 (ctrl).
Ind/Abst Point Repere (1990-).

UK
TRANSACTIONS OF THE MARTIN CENTRE FOR ARCHITECTURAL & URBAN STUDIES. **See** Architecture.

US/0300-6026
TRENDS IN HOUSING. [Trends hous.]. **Added/Corp** National Committee Against Discrimination in Housing. Vol. 1 (Aug. 1956)-. Periodical. English. bm (Feb., Apr., Jun., Aug., Oct., Dec.). $20.00 (1 year), $30.00 (2 year). Trends in Housing, 1629 K Street NW/Suite 802, Washington DC 20006. **Tel** (202)833-4456, FAX (202)775-7465. **ED** Natalie P Shear. **LC** HD7293.A1; T74. **DD** 363. **Bk Rev. Ad Acc. Circ:** 15,000.
Desc: The only newsletter focusing on housing discrimination issues nationwide.

US
TWO YEAR BUDGET / SIGNAL HILL REDEVELOPMENT AGENCY. **Main/Corp** Signal Hill (Calif.). Redevelopment Agency. (1991)-. English. be. ***Continues** Annual Budget.*

CN/0828-2390
U.B.C. PLANNING PAPERS. CANADIAN PLANNING ISSUES. [U.B.C. plan. pap., Can. plan. issues]. **Added/Corp** University of British Columbia. School of Community and Regional Planning. **VFOAT** Canadian Planning Issues. (198?)-. Monographic series. English. Price varies per volume. **DD** 361.6/0971.
Ind/Abst Geogr. Abstr. Human Geogr.

US/0502-9716
U.S. HOUSING MARKETS. (U.S. HOUSING MARKETS / PREPARED BY ADVANCE MORTGAGE CORPORATION.). [U.S. hous. mark.]. **Added/Corp** Advance Mortgage Corporation. Lomas & Nettleton Company. Lomas Mortgage USA. **VFOAT** United States Housing Markets; US Housing Markets. **VAT** United States Housing Markets. (19??)-. English. Twelve times a year. $180.00 US & Canada; $205.00 others. US Housing Markets, 33300 5 Mile Road, Suite 202, Livonia MI 48154. **Tel** (313)422-6100. **ED** Brian H. Bragg. **LC** HD7293.A1; U17. **DD** 381/.456908/0973. Index available. **Circ:** 1,200 (ctrl).
Desc: List surveys plus special reports and pre-publication releases on housing activity in US, 53 markets and nine regions. Analyses of US market and of market sectors, influences.

US/0364-443X
ULRF REPORTS. **Main/Corp** Urban Land Research Foundation. **VAT** Urban Land Research Foundation Reports. 1- Apr. 1974-. English. Urban Land Research Foundation, 1200 18th Street NW, Washington DC 20036.

JA
UNCRD WORKING PAPERS. **Added/Corp** United Nations Centre for Regional Development. **VFOAT** Working Papers; UNCRD Working Paper. No. 82/1 (1982)-. Monographic series. English. Price varies per volume. United Nations University Press, 53-70, Jingumae 5 Chome, Shibuya-ku Tokyo 150, Japan. **Tel** 81 3 34992811, FAX 81 3 34992828, telex J25442.
Ind/Abst Geogr. Abstr. Human Geogr.; Int. Dev. Abstr.

US
UNIFIED ISSUANCES SYSTEM. Government Publication. English. US Department of Housing and Urban Development, 451 Seventh Street SW, Washington DC 20401. **Tel** (202)708-0980, FAX (202)708-0299.

US/0501-1213
UNIFORM HOUSING CODE. **See** Building and Construction.

UK/0305-103X
URBAN ABSTRACTS. **Added/Corp** Greater London Council. No. 1 (April 1974)-. English. mo. £98.00 UK; £113.00 other. London Research Centre, 81 Black Prince Road, London SE1 7SZ England. **Tel** 011 44 71 627 9666, FAX 011 44 71 627 9674. **ED** Richard Golland. **Ad Acc. Circ:** 1,000. ***Continues** Planning and Transportation Abstracts.*
Desc: Journal of abstracts of recent acquisitions by the Research Library (formerly GLC Research Library), covering social and technical aspects of urban affairs.

US/0042-0816
URBAN AFFAIRS QUARTERLY. [Urban aff. q.]. Vol. 1 (Sept. 1965)-. Academic Scholarly Publication. English. qt (Mar., June, Sept., Dec.). $169.00. SAGE Periodical Press, 2455 Teller Road, Thousand Oaks CA 91320. **Tel** (805)499-0721, FAX (805)499-0871, telex 100799. **ED** Dennis R. Judd (University of Missouri, St. Louis). **LC** HT101; .U67. **DD** 309.2/62. **[CCC]. Pr Rev. Acid Free.** available on microfilm and microfiche from University Microfilms International (UMI). Documents available from The Genuine Article, UMI Article Clearinghouse, Documents on Demand.
Desc: Emphasizes state-of-the-art research and scholarly analysis on urban themes: urban life, metropolitan systems, urban economic development and urban policy.
Ind/Abst ABC POL SCI; Acad. Abstr. Full Text Elite (Jan. 1992-); Acad. Abstr. (Jan. 1992-); Acad. Search (Jan. 1992-); Am. Hist. Life (1971-); Appl. Soc. Sci. Index Abstr.; Avery Index Archit. Period. Suppl. Colum. Univ. (Mar., Dec. 1990); Crim. Justice Abstr.; Curr. Contents Soc. Behav. Sci.; Curr. Geogr. Publ. (199?-); Curr. Index J. Educ.; EMBASE; Environ. Abstr.; Expand. Acad. Index (1989-); Geogr. Abstr. Human Geogr.; INFO-SOUTH Abstr.; Int. Bibliogr. Sociol.; Int. Dev. Abstr.; Int. Polit. Sci. Abstr.; J. Plan. Lit.; Mag. Search; Middle East Abstr. Index; Multicult. Educ. Abstr.; Newsp. Period. Abstr. (1991-); PAIS Int. Print; Res. Alert [Full Cov.]; Sage Race Relat. Abstr.; Sage Urban Stud. Abstr; Soc. Plann. Policy Dev. Abstr.; Soc. Sci. Source (Jan. 1992-); Soc. Sci. Cit. Index [Full Cov.]; Soc. Sci. Index; Soc. Sci. Index Fulltext (Sept. 1988-) [Full Txt.]; Soc. Work Abstr. [Select. Cov.]; Sociol. Abstr.; Sociol. Educ. Abstr.; Stud. Women Abstr.; U.S. Polit. Sci. Doc.; Urban Aff. Abstr.

●US
URBAN AGE, THE. Vol. 1, No. 1 (Sept. 1992)-. Periodical. English (French and Spanish). Four times a year. Free to developing countries; $40.00 other. World Bank Publications, 1818 H Street Northwest, Washington DC 20433. **Tel** (202)473-1155, (202)473-1155, FAX (202)522-3224, telex WUI 64145 WORLDBANK. **(Subscription address:** World Bank Publications, PO Box 7247 8619, Philadelphia, PA 19170) **ED** Mary McNeil & Bonnie Bradford. **Bk Rev**, (Qty: 20). ***Continues** Urban Edge (English Edition), 0163-6510.*

US/0146-0544
URBAN AMERICA. English. $24.00. Institute for the Study of the City, 419 Park Avenue South, New York NY 10016. **LC** HT123; .U716. **DD** 301.36/0973.

CN/0708-3823
URBAN AND REGIONAL RESEARCH IN CANADA. **VFOAT** Recherches Urbaines et Regionales au Canada. 1975/76-. French (English). Service des Sources d'Information, Departement d'Etat Charge des Affaires Urbaines, Ottawa Ontario K1A 0P6 Canada. **DD** 016.30136/07/2071.

UK/0067-8961
URBAN AND REGIONAL STUDIES. **Main/Corp** Birmingham, England. University. Centre for Urban and Regional Studies. **Added/Corp** Birmingham, England. University. Centre for Urban and Regional Studies. (1970)-. English. Unwin Hyman Ltd., 15 17 Broadwick Street, London W1V 1FP England. **Tel** 011 44 71 439 3126. **DD** 309.1; 711.

CN/0709-4140
URBAN CANADA (SELECTED PUBLICATIONS). (URBAN CANADA. CANADA URBAIN.). **VFOAT** Canada Urbain. **VAT** Canada Urbain (Publications Choisies). (1977)-. Periodical. English (French). Micromedia Limited, 20 Victoria Street, Toronto Ontario M5C 2N8 Canada. **Tel** (416)362-5211, (800)387-2689, FAX (416)362-6161, telex 06524668. **DD** 301.36/0971. ***Continues** Canadian Urban Sources, 0317-2775.*

US/0898-5049
URBAN DESIGN & PRESERVATION QUARTERLY. [Urban des. preserv. q.]. **Added/Corp** American Planning Association. Urban Design and Preservation Division. **VFOAT** Urban Design and Preservation Quarterly. Vol. 10, No. 3 & 4 (Summer & Fall 1987)-. Periodical. English. qt. $20.00 (member), $40.00 (nonmember). American Planning Association, 1313 East 60th Street, Chicago IL 60637. **Tel** (312)955-9100, FAX (312)955-8312. **DD** 711. ***Continues** UD Review, 0749-7547.*

UK/0141-6979
URBAN DESIGN FORUM. [Urban des. forum]. **Added/Corp** Oxford Polytechnic. Dept. of Town Planning. No. 1 (Feb. 1978)-. Periodical. English.
Ind/Abst Archit. Period. Index (Feb. 1978-1983).

US/0895-8076
URBAN DESIGN UPDATE: NEWSLETTER OF THE INSTITUTE FOR URBAN DESIGN. [Urban des. update]. **Added/Corp** Institute for Urban Design (U.S.). **VFOAT** Update. Vol. 1, No. 1 (July/Aug. 1985)-. Periodical. English. bm. $90.00. Institute for Urban Design, 47 Barrow Street, New York NY 10014. **Tel** (212)741-2041. **ED** Ann Ferebee. **LC** NA9000; .U7334. **DD** 352. **Bk Rev. Ad Acc.**

US/0253-3324
URBAN DEVELOPMENT DEPARTMENT TECHNICAL PAPER. [Urban Dev. Dep. tech. paper]. **VFOAT** Urban Development Department Technical Notes. Monographic series. English. ir. Price varies per volume. World Bank Publications, 1818 H Street Northwest, Washington DC 20433. **Tel** (202)473-1155, (202)473-1155, FAX (202)522-3224, telex WUI 64145 WORLDBANK.

US/0163-6510
URBAN EDGE (ENGLISH ED.), THE. ***Title Change.*** (THE URBAN EDGE.). [Urban edge]. **Added/Corp** International Bank for Reconstruction and Development. Council for International Urban Liaison. (1977)-(199?). Periodical. English. Ten times a year.

Council for International Urban Liaison, 818 18th Street NW, Washington DC 20006. **Tel** (202)334-8065. **ED** John Dinges. **LC** CURRENT ISSUES ONLY. **Bk Rev. Circ:** 7,000. ***Continued by*** *Urban Age (English Edition).*
Desc: Provides worldwide coverage of urban development activities in developing countries.
Ind/Abst J. Ferrocement; Urban Aff. Abstr.

●UK/0963-9268
URBAN HISTORY. Vol. 19, Pt. 1 (Apr. 1992)-. Academic Scholarly Publication. English. Three times a year. $81.00 (individuals), $53.00 (institutions). Cambridge University Press, The Edinburgh Building, Shaftesbury Road, Cambridge CB2 2RU United Kingdom. **Tel** 011 44 223 312393, FAX 011 44 223 325959. **(Subscription address:** Cambridge University Press / North America, 110 Midland Avenue, Port Chester NY 10573.**) ED** Richard Rodger. **LC** HT101; .U675. **DD** 301.36/09. ***Continues*** *Urban History Yearbook, 0306-0845.*
Desc: Contents include research based articles, historiographical and methodological surveys, appraisals of source materials and surveys of urban development in individual countries.

II/0970-9045
URBAN INDIA. (URBAN INDIA : JOURNAL OF THE N.I.U.A.). [Urban India]. **Added/Corp** N.I.U.A. (Organization : India). Vol. 1, No. 1 (Sept. 1981)-. Periodical. English. qt. $19.00. National Institute of Urban Affairs, 11 Nyaya Marg Chanakyapuri, New Delhi 110021 India. **Tel** 3014580. **(Subscription address:** Prints India, 11 Darya Ganj, New Delhi, 110002 India, (Phone: 011 91 11 3268645)**) ED** Savita Pande. **LC** HT147.I5; U68. **DD** 307.7/6/0954. **Bk Rev. Circ:** 500.
Desc: Focuses on urban issues mainly in India. Each number generally deals with a topical theme related to housing and urban development. Contributors are worldwide.

US/0042-0891
URBAN LAND. **Added/Corp** Urban Land Institute. Urban Land Institute. Bulletin Urban Land Institute. News Bulletin. Vol. 1 (July 1941)-. Periodical. English. mo. $220.00 US; $290.00 other. Urban Land Institute, 625 Indiana Ave Northwest, Washington DC 20004. **Tel** (202)624-7000, (800)321-5011. **ED** Libby Howland. **LC** NA9000; .U7. **DD** 711.05. **Bk Rev. Circ:** 16,500. available on microfilm and microfiche from University Microfilms International (UMI). Documents available from Documents on Demand.
Desc: Covers trends and issues in land use and development.
Ind/Abst Archit. Period. Index; Avery Index Archit. Period. Suppl. Colum. Univ. (Apr., June, July 1989, Feb. 1990-); Environ. Abstr.; Highw. Res. Abstr.; Index Period. Artic. Relat. Law; J. Plan. Lit.; Middle East Abstr. Index; Sage Urban Stud. Abstr; Urban Aff. Abstr.

US/0042-0905
URBAN LAWYER, THE. **See** Law.

●US
URBAN MANAGEMENT PROGRAM. **Added/Corp** World Bank. **VFOAT** Urban Management Program Policy Paper. (1992)-. Monographic series. English. Price varies per volume. World Bank Publications, 1818 H Street Northwest, Washington DC 20433. **Tel** (202)473-1155, (202)473-1155, FAX (202)522-3224, telex WUI 64145 WORLDBANK.

US/0732-8265
URBAN OUTLOOK. ***Title Change.*** [Urban outl.]. **Added/Corp** Business Publishers. Vol. 4, No. 10 (May 4, 1982)-Vol. 14, No. 22 (Nov. 30, 1992). Periodical. English. mo. Alexander Research & Communications, Inc, 215 Park Avenue South, Suite 1301, New York NY 10003. **Tel** (212)228-0246, FAX (212)228-0376. **ED** Laurence A Alexander. **LC** NA9000; .D457. **Bk Rev.** ***Continues*** *Urban Planning Reports, 0735-3839;* ***Absorbed*** *Urban Futures Idea Exchange, 0147-7137.* ***Absorbed by*** *Financial Local Government.*
Desc: Newsletter for professionals concerned with meeting the unique challenges of today's urban areas. Focuses on planning and land use, energy and environment, urban technology, infrastructure, health, economic development, demographics and lifestyles, education, housing, grants, and funding, crime and security.

US/0095-1528
URBAN PLANNING QUARTERLY. V. 1-Autumn 1974-. Periodical. English. qt. $10.00. University of Washington Department of Urban Planning, 410 Gould Hall, Seattle WA 98195. **LC** HT166; .U743. **DD** 309.2/62/05.

AT/0811-1146
URBAN POLICY AND RESEARCH. Vol. 1, No. 1 (Dec. 1982)-. Periodical. English. qt. $48.21 (institution), $36.15 (individual) US; 60.00Aus$ (institution), 45.00Aus$ (individual). Urban Policy and Research, GPO Box 2476V, Attn: V. Eckersley, Melbourne Victoria 3001 Australia. **Tel** 011 61 3 6602226. Index available (Bound in issue).
Ind/Abst APAIS, Aust. Public Aff. Inf. Ser. (19??-).

US/0529-0740
URBAN RENEWAL PROGRESS REPORT. **Main/Corp** Chicago (Ill.). Dept. of City Planning. Periodical. English. Department of Urban Renewal, 318 S Michigan, Chicago IL 60604.

US/0417-1152
URBAN RENEWAL SERIES - DETROIT. CITY PLAN COMMISSION. **Main/Corp** Detroit. City Plan Commission. 1- 1962-. Periodical. English. City Planning Commission, Detroit MI 48226.

●US/1062-2292
URBAN REPORT (WASHINGTON, D.C.), THE. (THE URBAN REPORT / OFFICE OF HOUSING AND URBAN PROGRAMS, U.S. AGENCY FOR INTERNATIONAL DEVELOPMENT.). [Urban rep.]. **Added/Corp** United States. Agency for International Development. Office of Housing and Urban Programs. Vol. 1, No. 1 (Jan. 1992)-. Periodical. English. qt. Free. Usaid's Office of Housing and Urban Programs, Room 401 SA-2, Washington DC 20523-0214. **DD** 307.

US/0732-7277
URBAN RESEARCH REVIEW. (URBAN RESEARCH REVIEW : HOWARD UNIVERSITY INSTITUTE FOR URBAN AFFAIRS AND RESEARCH PUBLICATION.). Began in 1976. Periodical. English. qt. IUAR, 2900 Van Ness Street NW, Washington DC 20008.

UK/0042-0980
URBAN STUDIES (HARLOW). (URBAN STUDIES.). [Urban stud.]. Vol. 1, No. 1 (May 1964)-. Periodical. English. Ten times a year. £174.00 (includes special double issue Urban Studies Review). Carfax Publishing Company, PO Box 25 Abingdon, Oxfordshire OX14 3UE England. **Tel** 011 44 235 555335, FAX (0279)31067, telex 817484. **(Subscription address:** US and Canada/ PO Box 2025, Dunnellon, FL 34430-2025; telephone:(904)489-6996**) ED** W. Lever, U. Money and G. Wood. **LC** HT103; .U7. **DD** 307/.12. **[CCC].** cum. index. **Bk Rev. Ad Acc. Pr Rev.** available on microfiche. Documents available from The Genuine Article, UMI Article Clearinghouse.
Desc: International forum for discussion on urban affairs and regional planning.
Ind/Abst Acad. Search (July 1993-); Am. Hist. Life (1967-); Appl. Soc. Sci. Index Abstr.; Archit. Period. Index (1964,1978-); Avery Index Archit. Period. Suppl. Colum. Univ. (1989-); BHA : Biblio. Hist. Art; Br. Humanit. Index; Contents Recent Econ. J.; Curr. Contents Soc. Behav. Sci.; Curr. Geogr. Publ. (199?-); Curr. Technol. Index; Econ. Lit. Index; Educ. Adm. Abstr. (?-?); EMBASE; Expand. Acad. Index (1989-); Geogr. Abstr. Human Geogr.; Highw. Res. Abstr.; Hist. Abstr., Part B, Twent. Century Abstr.; INFO-SOUTH Abstr.; Int. Bibliogr. Sociol.; Int. Dev. Abstr.; Int. Polit. Sci. Abstr.; J. Econ. Lit.; J. Plan. Lit.; Linguist. Lang. Behav. Abstr.; Mag. Search; Middle East Abstr. Index; Newsp. Period. Abstr. (1991-); PAIS Int. Print; Life Sci. Collect.; Res. Alert [Full Cov.]; Rural Dev. Abstr.; Sage Fam. Stud. Abstr.; Sage Public Adm. Abstr.; Sage Urban Stud. Abstr; SCISEARCH; Soc. Plann. Policy Dev. Abstr.; Soc. Sci. Source (Jul. 1993-); Soc. Sci. Cit. Index [Full Cov.]; Soc. Sci. Index; Soc. Sci. Index Fulltext (Aug. 1988-) [Full Txt.]; Sociol. Abstr.; Stud. Women Abstr.

●FR/1240-0874
URBANISME. No. 256 (Sept. 1992)-. Periodical. French. mo. 880.00F France; $226.46 other. Publs Architecture & Urbanisme, 57 Rue de Seine, 75006 Paris France. **Tel** 33 1 40510404. **(Subscription address:** Urbanismes, Svc. Abbonnement, 36 rue de Picpus, 75012 Paris France.**)** ***Continues*** *Urbanismes & Architecture, 1145-5187.*
Ind/Abst BHA : Biblio. Hist. Art (19??-).

FR/1145-5187
URBANISMES & ARCHITECTURE. ***Title Change.*** **VFOAT** Urbanismes et Architecture; Urbanismes. No. 231-232 (Oct.-Nov. 1989)-No. 255 (Mar. 1992). Periodical. French. mo. Publications du Moniteur, 17 rue d'Uzes, 75108 Paris Cedex 02 France. **Tel** 011 33 1 40133030, FAX 011 33 1 40419495 customer service, 40133037 advertising, telex UPRESSE 680876 F. available on microfilm and microfiche from University Microfilms International (UMI). ***Continues*** *Urbanisme, 0042-1014.* ***Continued by*** *Urbanisme (Paris, France : 1992), 1240-0874.*

SP/0213-9391
URBANISMO / COAM. **Added/Corp** Colegio Oficial de Arquitectos de Madrid. No. 1 (May 1987)-. Periodical. Spanish (summaries and/or abstracts in English). Three times a year. Colegio Oficial Arquitectos de Madrid, Barquillo 12 5A Pla, 28004 Madrid Spain. **Tel** 011 34 1 5218200.
Ind/Abst Archit. Period. Index (May 1988-); Avery Index Archit. Period. Suppl. Colum. Univ. (Sept. 1987, Jan. and May 1988, Jan. and Sept. 1989, Jan, May and Sept. 1990).

SP/0213-1110
URBANISMO REVISTA. ***Suspended.*** **Added/Corp** Laboratorio de Urbanismo de Barcelona. **VFOAT** UR; UR Revista. No. 1 (Jan. 1985)-(19??). Periodical. Spanish. Three times a year. Laboratorio de Urbanismo Ur Re, Diagonal 649, 08028 Barcelona Spain. **Tel** 011 34 3 4016402.
Ind/Abst Avery Index Archit. Period. Suppl. Colum. Univ. (1988-1989).

XR
URBANISMUS A UZEMNI PLANOVANI. **Added/Corp** Brunn. Vyzkumny Ustav Vystavby a Architektury. Urbanisticke Pracoviste. (19??-). Periodical. Multiple languages (Russian, English and German). bm. $15.30. Artia Pegas Press Ltd., Palac Metro Narodni TR 25, 11000 Prague 1 Czech Republic. **Tel** 011 42 2 24196265 or 24196266, 24196266. **(Subscription address:** Artia Pegas Press Ltd., Palac Metro Narodni Trida 25, 11210 Prague 1 Czech Republic.**)**

IT/0042-1022
URBANISTICA. ***Suspended.*** [Urbanistica]. (1949)-(19??). Periodical. Italian (summaries and/or abstracts in French and English). Three times a year. Free. Franco Angeli Riviste SRL, Viale Monza 106, 20127 Milan Italy. **Tel** 011 39 2 2827651, 011 39 2 289562. **LC** NA9000; .U74. cum. index. ***Continues in part*** *Urbanistica.*
Ind/Abst Avery Index Archit. Period. Suppl. Colum. Univ. (1988/89-).

IT/0392-5005
URBANISTICA INFORMAZIONI. (URBANISTICA INFORMATIONI : RIVISTA BIMESTRALE DELL'INU ISTITUTO NAZIONALE DI URBANISTICA.). [Urban inf.]. **Added/Corp** Istituto Nazionale di Urbanistica. (1972)-. Periodical. Italian. bm. L70000, $48.56 Italy; L140000, $97.12 other. Istituto Nazionale di Urbanistica, Via S Caterina da Siena 46, 00186 Rome Italy. **Tel** (06)6793559. Index available (Free). **Ad Acc. Circ:** 6,000 (ctrl).
Desc: Urban and regional planning; national or international politics related to city and territory (laws, plans, experiences, etc.).

IT
URBANISTICAIPOTESI. Periodical. Italian. Libreria Editrice Fiorentina, Via Ricasole 105-107, R 50122 C C P 5/11965, Firenze Italy. **LC** HT101; .U75. **DD** 309.2/6/094551.

US/0898-7661
URISA MEMBERSHIP DIRECTORY. [URISA membsh. dir.]. **Main/Corp** Urban and Regional Information Systems Association. **VFOAT** Membership Directory. **VAT** Urban and Regional Information Systems Association Membership Directory. Directory. English. Council for Liberal Learning, Association of American Colleges, 1818 R Street NW, Washington DC 20009. **Tel** (202)387-3760. **DD** 351. ***Continues*** *URISA Directory of Members, 0733-0634.*

CN/0833-966X
VACANT URBAN RESIDENTIAL LAND SURVEY, ... UPDATE. [Vacant urban resid. land surv. update]. 1984-. English. an. Free. Regional Municipality of Ottawa-Carleton, Planning Department, 222 Queen Street, Ottawa Ontario K1P 5V9 Canada. **Tel** (613)560-2053. **DD** 333.77/11/0971383. ctrl circ. available on microfiche (from Micromedia, Toronto). ***Continues*** *Vacant Urban Residential Land Update, 0833-9678.*
Desc: Maps and status of every parcel of vacant land zoned for residential uses. Includes analysis of land consumption on availability of land.

SZ
VADEMECUM (HERGISWIL (NIEDWALDEN, SWITZERLAND)). (VADEMECUM / IHA, GFM.). **VFOAT** I.H.A. Vademecum; IHA Vademecum. Periodical. German (summaries and/or abstracts in French). an. IHA Institute fur Marktanalysen AG, 6052 Hergiswil/NW Switzerland. **LC** HA1593; .V33. **DD** 314.94.

US/0892-6433
VANGUARD. (VANGUARD / THE COMMUNITY DEVELOPMENT SOCIETY.). [Vanguard]. **Added/Corp** Community Development Society. (19??)-. Periodical. English. ir. $55.00. Community Development Society / Wisconsin, 1123 North Water Street, c/o Mikki Soltis, Milwaukee WI 53202. **Tel** (414) 276-8788, FAX (414) 276-7704. **ED** L. R. Hughes (editor's address: Lincoln University, Jefferson City, Mo). **DD** 301. Index available. **Ad Acc.** ctrl circ. available on microfilm from University Microfilms International (UMI); available on microfiche from University Microfilms International (UMI).
Desc: Newsletter of the community development society.

CN/0823-0153
VANIEROIS, LE. [Vanierois]. 1st Year, No 1 (Feb. 1983)-. Periodical. French. mo. 217 Belanger, Ville de Vanier Quebec G1M 1V6 Canada. **Tel** 683-3941. **DD** 971.4/47/005. **Ad Acc. Circ:** 6,000 (ctrl).
Desc: Local information on the specific problems of the city; in particular, problems concerning housing and unemployment.

NE
VERNIEUWDESTAD. 1973/74-. Dutch. Ministerie van Volkshuisvesting en Ruimtelijke Ordening, Staatsuitgeverij, Gravenhage Netherlands. **LC** HT178.N4; V47.

Housing and Urban Development —Abstracting, Bibliographies and Statistics

BE
VERSLAG VAN DE RAAD VAN BEHEER OVER DE VERRICHTINGEN. **Main/Corp** Societe Nationale du Logement. Dutch. an. Free. Nationale Maatschappij Voor de Huisvesting, Breydelstraat 12, 1040 Brussels Belgium. **Tel** (02)2305125. **LC** HD7343.A3. **Circ:** 3,000 (ctrl).
Desc: Activity report.

SA
VERSLAG VAN DIE DIREKTEUR-GENERAAL, GEMEENSKAPSONTWIKKELING VIR DIE TYDPERK ... . **Main/Corp** South Africa. Dept. of Community Development. **VFOAT** Report of the Director-General, Community Development for the Period ... . (197?)-. Afrikaans (English). an. R11.10. The Government Printer, Bosman Street, Private Bag X85, Pretoria 0001 South Africa. **Tel** 012-323-9731, FAX 012-323-0009. **LC** HN801.Z9; C672B. **DD** 307/.336/0968. *Continues* Verslag van die Sekretaris Van Gemeenskapsbou.

CN/0382-9227
VIBRATIONS (OTTAWA. 1975). (VIBRATIONS.). Apr. 1975-. Periodical. English. ir. Vibrations, 2061 Prescott Highway, Ottawa Ontario K2E 7A4 Canada. **DD** 711/.4/0971384. *Supersedes Vibes, 0382-9219.*

BG
VILLAGE REPORT SERIES. **Added/Corp** Bangladesh Institute of Development Studies. (1982)-. Monographic series. English. Price varies per volume. Bangladesh Institute of Development Studies, E-17 Agargaon, PO Box 3854, Dhaka 7 Bangladesh. **Tel** FAX 880-2-813023.

MX
VIVIENDA. Periodical. Spanish. sa. $3,000 Mexico; $4,000 US. Instituto del Fondo Nacional de la Vivienda Para los Trabajadores, Revista Vivienda Barranca del Muerto No 280, Mexico 20 DF Mexico. **Tel** 651-94-00 (1141 Y 1142). **LC** HD7285; .V49. **Circ:** 1,300.

NE
VOICE OF THE PEDESTRIAN, THE. *Suspended.* **VFOAT** La Voix du Pieton; Die Stimme des Fussgangers. Periodical. English (French and German). Four times a year. Fl110.00 Netherlands; Fl125.00 other. International Federation of Pedestrians, 43 Wassenaarseweg, 2596 CG The Hague Netherlands. **Tel** +31 70 24 45 57, FAX +31 70 24 69 16, telex 21578 INTER NL REF I 999. **ED** Jon H Leons. **LC** HE5601; .V64. **DD** 388.4/1. **Ad Acc.**

UK
VOLUNTARY HOUSING. **Added/Corp** National Federation of Housing Societies. (19??)-. Periodical. English. mo. £56.00 (institutions), £41.50 (individuals). National Federation of Housing Association, 175 Grays Inn Road, London WC1X 8UP England. **Tel** 011 44 71 278 6571. **LC** HD7333.A3; V64.
Ind/Abst Avery Index Archit. Period. Suppl. Colum. Univ. (Jan. 1990-).

US/8756-0801
WASHINGTON UNIVERSITY JOURNAL OF URBAN AND CONTEMPORARY LAW. See Law.

US/0733-0677
WATERFRONT WORLD. *Title Change.* [Waterfr. world]. **Added/Corp** Waterfront Center (U.S.). Vol. 1, No. 1 (Jan./Feb. 1982)-(19??). Periodical. English. bm. Waterfront Center, 1536 44th Street NW, Washington DC 20007. **Tel** (202)337-0356. **ED** Ann Breen and Dick Rigby. **Bk Rev** **Ad Acc. Circ:** 1,500 (ctrl). *Continued by Spotlight.*
Desc: News, features, literature review, editorials, calendar, resource listings on all aspects of urban waterfront development/restoration preservation, emphasis on North America.

US/1056-9545
WEEKLY READER OF HOUSING AND COMMUNITY NEWS, THE. (THE WEEKLY READER OF HOUSING AND COMMUNITY NEWS / ANHD.). **Added/Corp** Association for Neighborhood and Housing Development (New York, N.Y.). **VFOAT** Weekly Reader; ANHD Weekly Reader. (19??)-. Periodical. English. Forty-eight times a year (Mondays, except twice in summer & twice in winter). $60.00 (institutions), $30.00 (individuals). Association for Neighborhood & Housing Development Inc, 305 Seventh Avenue, 20th Floor, New York NY 10001-6008. **Tel** (212)463-9600, FAX (212)463-9606.
Desc: Provides information on tenants rights, community development, organizational and program fundraising, and legal and legislative developments. Also includes a calendar of events, job notices, and updates on group activities.

NE
WEGWIJS. Dutch. bm. Veilig Verkeer Nederland, Postbus 287, 1200 AG Hilversum Netherlands. **Tel** 035 211411.

UK/0262-8333
WELSH HOUSING STATISTICS / WELSH OFFICE / YSTADEGAU TAI CYMRU / Y SWYDDFA GYMREIG. **Added/Corp** Great Britain. Welsh Office. **VFOAT** Ystadegau tai Cymru. No. 1 (1981)-. Statistical Publication. English. an. Welsh Office Publications Unit, Crown Building, Cathay's Park, Cardiff CF1 3NQ Wales. **Tel** 011 44 222 825111. **LC** HD7334.A3; W43. **DD** 338.4/769083/09429.

CN/0836-4397
WEST VANCOUVER REPORT. (WEST VANCOUVER REPORT / THE CORPORATION OF THE DISTRICT OF WEST VANCOUVER.). [West Vanc. rep.]. **Main/Corp** West Vancouver (B.C.). (198?)-. Periodical. English. Free. Corporation of the District of West Vancouver, 750-17th Street, West Vancouver British Columbia V7V 3T3 Canada. **DD** 711/.4/0971133. *Continues West Vancouver (B.C.) West Vancouver Municipal News., 0227-5309.*

US/0192-1576
WESTERN LOS ANGELES COUNTY APARTMENT OWNER/BUILDER. **VFOAT** Apartment Owner Builder. V. 1- 1967-. Periodical. English. mo. $10.00. Apartment News Publications, 3220 East Willow, Long Beach CA 90806. **Tel** (213)636-8351.

IO
WIDYAPURA. Periodical. Indonesian. bm. Pusat Penelitian Masalah Pekotaan dan Linkungan Dki Jakarta, Jl Medan Merdeka Selatan 8-9 Blok G Lantai 22, Jakarta Pusat Indonesia. **LC** HT110; .W48.

US/0190-1109
WILEY SERIES IN URBAN RESEARCH, THE. (19??)-. Monographic series. English. ir. Price varies per volume. John Wiley & Sons Inc / New Jersey, 1 Wiley Drive, Somerset NJ 08875. **Tel** (800)225-5945, (908)469-4400. **(Subscription address:** John Wiley & Sons / England, Baffins Lane, Chichester, West Sussex PO19 1UD England.**)**

AU
WOHNBAU. **Added/Corp** Austria. Bundesministerium fuer Bauten und Technik. Wohnbauforschung. (1974)-. Periodical. German. mo. S250.00. Grimmelshausengasse 1, Vienna Austria. **LC** TH4805; .W58. **DD** 690/.8/05.

AU
WOHNBAUFORSCHUNG IN OSTERREICH. **Added/Corp** Forschungsgesellschaft fur Wohnen, Hauen und Planen. (19??). Consumer Publication. German. bm. 570.00. Forschungsgellschaft fur Wohnen, Lowengasse 47, 1030 Vienna III Austria. **Tel** 0222 712 62510, FAX 0222 712 625121. **LC** HD7337.A3; W58. Index available. **Bk Rev**, (Qty: 20). **Ad Acc. Circ:** 350.
Desc: All scientific problems of housing of the sectors planning, technology, financing, law and documentation.

GW
WOHNGELD IN NORDRHEIN-WESTFALEN. See Housing and Urban Development-Abstracting, Bibliographies and Statistics.

AU/0933-2766
WOHNRECHTLICHE BLAETTER. See Law.

AU
WOHNUNGEN, DIE. **Main/Corp** Osterreichisches Statistisches Zentralamt. German. **LC** HA1173; .A27 subser.

US/0094-1891
WOODALL'S DIRECTORY OF MOBILE HOME COMMUNITIES. 24th- Ed.; 1971-. Directory. English. an. $5.95. Woodall Publishing Company, 28167 North Keith Drive, Lake Forest IL 60015. **Tel** (708)362-6700. **LC** TX907; .W66. **DD** 647/.9473. *Continues Woodall's Mobile Home Park Directory.*

US/0091-5505
WOODALL'S MOBILE HOME LIFESTYLE. Periodical. English. Three times a year. Woodall Publishing Company, 28167 North Keith Drive, Lake Forest IL 60015. **Tel** (708)362-6700. **LC** TX1100; .W66. **DD** 643. *Continues Woodall's Mobile Modular Housing Today.*

US/0093-7274
WOODALL'S MOBILE/MODULAR LIVING. **VFOAT** Mobile/Modular Living. English. an. $1.25. Woodall Publishing Company, 28167 North Keith Drive, Lake Forest IL 60015. **Tel** (708)362-6700. **LC** TX1100; .W67. **DD** 643.

US/0883-9689
WORKING PAPER - JOINT CENTER FOR HOUSING STUDIES OF MIT AND HARVARD UNIVERSITY. (WORKING PAPER.). [Work. pap. - Jt. Cent. Hous. Stud. MIT Harv. Univ.]. **Added/Corp** Joint Center for Housing Studies of MIT and Harvard University. Began in 1985. Monographic series. English. Price varies per volume. Joint Center for Urban Studies of MIT and Harvard University, 53 Church Street, Cambridge MA 02138. **DD** 363. *Continues Working Paper (Joint Center for Urban Studies), 0275-2964.*

CN/0713-8466
WORKING PAPER - SCHOOL OF URBAN & REGIONAL PLANNING. UNIVERSITY OF WATERLOO. (WORKING PAPER.). [Work. pap. - Sch. Urban Reg. Plann., Univ. Waterloo]. **VAT** Working Paper Series - School of Urban & Regional Planning. University of Waterloo. Monographic series. English. ir (four to six issues per year). Price varies per volume. School of Urban and Regional Planning, Faculty of Environmental Studies, University of Waterloo, Waterloo Ontario N2L 3G1 Canada. **Tel** (519)885-1211. **ED** Norman Pressman. **DD** 333.73/0971.

HK
WU YU NIEN CHIEN. **VFOAT** Housing Directory. 1983-. Periodical. Chinese. an. $50.00. Wu Yu Kuan Li Yu Hsien Kung SSU, 23/F Wu Sang House, 655 Nathan Road, Kowloon Hong Kong. **LC** HD7371.A3; W8. **DD** 363.5/0951/25.

US/0160-0869
YEAR END REPORT - KANSAS ECONOMIC OPPORTUNITY OFFICE. See Economics.

US
ZONING AND LAND USE CONTROLS / BY PATRICK J. ROHAN ; CONTRIBUTORS, GARY I. COHEN ... [ET AL.]. (19??)-. English. ir. Matthew Bender & Company Inc., 1275 Broadway, Albany NY 12204. **Tel** (800)833-9844, (518)487-3000. cum. index.

US/0731-5791
ZONING AND PLANNING LAW HANDBOOK. See Law.

US/0161-8113
ZONING AND PLANNING LAW REPORT. See Law.

US/0514-7905
ZONING BULL. (BOSTON, MASS.). (ZONING BULLETIN.). [Zoning bull.]. Vol. 1, Ch. 1 (July 1953)-. Bulletin. English. Twenty-four times a year. $79.81. Quilan Publishing Company, 23 Drydock Avenue, Boston MA 02110. **Tel** (617)542-0048. **LC** LAW. **DD** 346. **[CCC].** available on microfilm and microfiche from University Microfilms International (UMI).

US/8755-3856
ZONING NEWS. (ZONING NEWS / AMERICAN PLANNING ASSOCIATION.). [Zoning news]. **Added/Corp** American Planning Association. American Planning Association. Planning Advisory Service. PAS memo. (1984)-. Periodical. English. mo. $45.00 US; $54.00 other. American Planning Association, 1313 East 60th Street, Chicago IL 60637. **Tel** (312)955-9100, FAX (312)955-8312. **DD** 307.
Ind/Abst Urban Aff. Abstr.

US/0748-0083
ZONING REPORT (MARGATE, FL.), THE. (THE ZONING REPORT.). (July 30, 1983)-. Periodical. English. ir (14 issues per year). $58.00. The Zoning Report, Box 6529, 1404 North State Road 7#269, Margate FL 33063. **ED** Charles Reed. **DD** 346. Index available. cum. index. **Bk Rev**, (Qty: 2-4). **Circ:** 500.
Desc: Practical guide for writing improved regulations for solving local government zoning and subdivision problems.

ABSTRACTING, BIBLIOGRAPHIES AND STATISTICS

US/0066-3840
ANNUAL BULLETIN OF HOUSING AND BUILDING STATISTICS FOR EUROPE. [Annu. bull. hous. build. stat. Eur.]. **Main/Corp** United Nations. Economic Commission for Europe. **Added/Corp** United Nations. Economic Commission for Europe. Bulletin Annuel de Statistiques du Logement et de la Construction pour l'Europe. United Nations. Economic Commission for Europe. Ezhegodnyi Biulleten Evropeiskoi Zhilishchnoi i Stroitelioi Statistiki. **VFOAT** Bulletin Annuel de Statistiques du Logement et de la Construction pour l'Europe; Ezhegodnyi Biulleten Evropeiskoi Zhilishchnoi i Stroitelioi Statistiki. 1st (1957)-. Government Publication. English (French and Russian). an. $25.00. United Nations Publications, 2 United Nations Plaza, Room DC2 0853, Department 007C, New York NY 10017. **Tel** (212)963-8303, (800)253-9646. **LC** HD9715.A1; U48. **DD** 338.4769.
Desc: Information on dwelling construction, materials

used and employment in the construction industry. Also includes wholesale price indices of building materials in Europe, Canada and the United States.

CN/0316-4691
BIBLIOGRAPHIC SERIES - CENTRE FOR URBAN AND COMMUNITY STUDIES. UNIVERSITY OF TORONTO. (BIBLIOGRAPHIC SERIES - UNIVERSITY OF TORONTO, CENTRE FOR URBAN AND COMMUNITY STUDIES.). Began publication in 1970?. Monographic series. English. ir. Price varies per volume. Centre for Urban and Community Studies, 455 Spadina Avenue, Room 426, Toronto Ontario M5S 2G8 Canada. **Tel** (416)978-2072. **DD** 016.30136. **Circ:** 200.
Desc: Urban studies, planning, social structure, housing and public policy.

BL/0102-9290
BOLETIM BIBLIOGRAFICO. [Bol. bibliogr. - Assessor. tec. doc. Banco Nac. Habitac.]. **Main/Corp** Banco Nacional da Habitacao. Assessoria Tecnica de Documentaca. V. 1- Jan. 1976-. Bulletin. Portuguese. Banco Nacional de Habitacao, Av Rio Branco 37-Conj 704, Rio de Janeiro Brazil. **LC** Z5942; .B3A; HT169.B7. **DD** 016.3092/62/0981.

AT
BUILDING ACTIVITY, WESTERN AUSTRALIA. **Added/Corp** Australian Bureau of Statistics. Western Australian Office. (198?)-. English. qt. 10.70Aus$. Australian Bureau of Statistics, PO Box 10, Belconnen Australian Capital Territory, 2616 Australia. **Tel** 011 61 6 2527911, FAX 011 61 6 2516009. ***Continues*** *Building and Housing, Western Australia.*
Desc: Number of dwelling units and value of residential buildings, value of alterations and additions to residential buildings and value of non-residential building by class of building, and more.

UK
CHINA URBAN STATISTICS. ***Ceased.*** (1985)-(1986). English. an. Gale Research Inc., 835 Penobscot Building, Detroit MI 48226. **Tel** (800)877-GALE, (313)961-2242, FAX (313)961-6083, telex TWX 810-221-7086. **LC** HT147.C48; C4. **DD** 315.1.

US
COMPENDIUM OF HUMAN SETTLEMENTS STATISTICS / DEPARTMENT OF INTERNATIONAL ECONOMICS AND SOCIAL AFFAIRS, STATISTICAL OFFICE = RECUEIL DES STATISTIQUES DES ETABLISSEMENTS HUMAINS / DEPARTEMENT DES AFFAIRES ECONOMIQUES ET SOCIALES INTERNATIONALES, BUREAU DE STATISTIQUE. **Added/Corp** United Nations. Statistical Office. **VFOAT** Recueil des Statistiques des Etablissements Humains. 4th Ed. (1983)-. Statistical Publication. English (French). ir. United Nations Publications, 2 United Nations Plaza, Room DC2 0853, Department 007C, New York NY 10017. **Tel** (212)963-8303, (800)253-9646. **LC** HD7287; .C585. **DD** 363.5/021. ***Continues*** *Compendium of Housing Statistics.*

US/0082-9455
COUNTY AND CITY DATA BOOK. [Cty. city data book]. **Added/Corp** United States. Bureau of the Census. 1st Ed. (1949)-. English. ir. Superintendent of Documents, US Government Printing Office, Washington DC 20402. **Tel** (202)275-3328, FAX (202)786-2377. **LC** HA202; .A36. **DD** 317.3. **NLM** W2 A B9CO. available on CD-ROM (As: County & City Data Book [Computer File]); available on microfiche. ***Continues in part*** *Cities Supplement* ***and*** *County Databook.*
Desc: Brings together a variety of social and economic data from the Census Bureau and other sources for the United States, regions, divisions, states, counties, incorporated cities of 25,000 or more, and places of 2,500 or more.

US
COUNTY AND CITY STATISTICS CD-ROM. (19??)-. English. mo. $990.00 Educational institutions and non-profit organizations; $1200.00 other. Slater Hall Information Products, 1301 Pennsylvania Avenue Northwest, Washington DC 20004. **Tel** (202)393-2666.

US/0743-1635
CPL BIBLIOGRAPHY. [CPL bibliogr.]. **Added/Corp** Council of Planning Librarians. **VAT** Council of Planning Librarians Bibliography. No. 4 (1979)-. Bibliography. English. mo. $285.00. American Planning Association, 1313 East 60th Street, Chicago IL 60637. **Tel** (312)955-9100, FAX (312)955-8312. **ED** Patricia Coatsworth. **LC** UNC. **DD** 020. Index available. **Pr Rev. Circ:** 300 (ctrl). ***Supersedes*** *Council of Planning Librarians. Exchange Bibliography.*
Desc: Bibliographies in the fields of planning urban development, zoning, transportation and housing.

US
CURRENT HOUSING REPORTS. H-170, ANNUAL HOUSING SURVEY, HONOLULU, HAWAII, STANDARD METROPOLITAN STATISTICAL AREA. HOUSING CHARACTERISTICS FOR SELECTED METROPOLITAN AREAS. **Added/Corp** United States. Bureau of the Census. United States. Dept. of Housing and Urban Development. Office of Policy Development and Research. **VFOAT** Annual Housing Survey, Honolulu, Hawaii, Standard Metropolitan Statistical Area. (19??)-. Government Publication. English. US Department of Commerce / Bureau of the Census, Data User Services Division, Customer Services, Washington DC 20233-0800. **Tel** (301)763-4100. **(Subscription address:** Superintendent of Documents, US Government Printing Office, Washington DC 20402.**)**

US
CURRENT HOUSING REPORTS. H-170, ANNUAL HOUSING SURVEY, HOUSTON, TEX., STANDARD METROPOLITAN STATISTICAL AREA. HOUSING CHARACTERISTICS FOR SELECTED METROPOLITAN AREAS. **VFOAT** Annual Housing Survey, Houston, Tex., Standard Metropolitan Statistical Area. Government Publication. English. US Department of Commerce / Bureau of the Census, Data User Services Division, Customer Services, Washington DC 20233-0800. **Tel** (301)763-4100. **(Subscription address:** Superintendent of Documents, US Government Printing Office, Washington DC 20402.**)**

US
CURRENT HOUSING REPORTS. H-170, ANNUAL HOUSING SURVEY, LOUISVILLE, KY.-IND. STANDARD METROPOLITAN STATISTICAL AREA. HOUSING CHARACTERISTICS FOR SELECTED METROPOLITAN AREAS. **Added/Corp** United States. Bureau of the Census. United States. Dept. of Housing and Urban Development. Office of Policy Development and Research. **VFOAT** Annual Housing Survey, Louisville, Ky.-Ind. Standard Metropolitan Statistical Area. (1976)-. Government Publication. English. ir. US Department of Commerce / Bureau of the Census, Data User Services Division, Customer Services, Washington DC 20233-0800. **Tel** (301)763-4100. **(Subscription address:** Superintendent of Documents, US Government Printing Office, Washington DC 20402.**)**

US
CURRENT HOUSING REPORTS. H-170, ANNUAL HOUSING SURVEY, NEW YORK, NY., STANDARD METROPOLITAN STATISTICAL AREA. HOUSING CHARACTERISTICS FOR SELECTED METROPOLITAN AREAS. **VFOAT** Annual Housing Survey, New York, N.Y., Standard Metropolitan Statistical Area. Began with 1976. Government Publication. English. ir. US Department of Commerce / Bureau of the Census, Data User Services Division, Customer Services, Washington DC 20233-0800. **Tel** (301)763-4100. **(Subscription address:** Superintendent of Documents, US Government Printing Office, Washington DC 20402.**)**

US
CURRENT HOUSING REPORTS. H-170, ANNUAL HOUSING SURVEY, SACRAMENTO, CALIF., STANDARD METROPOLITAN STATISTICAL AREA. HOUSING CHARACTERISTICS FOR SELECTED METROPOLITAN AREA. **VFOAT** Annual Housing Survey, Sacramento, Calif., Standard Metropolitan Statistical Area. Began with 1976. Government Publication. English. ir. US Department of Commerce / Bureau of the Census, Data User Services Division, Customer Services, Washington DC 20233-0800. **Tel** (301)763-4100. **(Subscription address:** Superintendent of Documents, US Government Printing Office, Washington DC 20402.**)**

US
CURRENT HOUSING REPORTS. H-170, ANNUAL HOUSING SURVEY, ST. LOUIS, MO-ILL., STANDARD METROPOLITAN STATISTICAL AREA. HOUSING CHARACTERISTICS FOR SELECTED METROPOLITAN AREAS. **Added/Corp** United States. Bureau of the Census. United States. Dept. of Housing and Urban Development. Office of Policy Development and Research. **VFOAT** Annual Housing Survey, St. Louis, Mo.-Ill., Standard Metropolitan Statistical Area. (1976)-. Government Publication. English. ir. US Department of Commerce / Bureau of the Census, Data User Services Division, Customer Services, Washington DC 20233-0800. **Tel** (301)763-4100. **(Subscription address:** Superintendent of Documents, US Government Printing Office, Washington DC 20402.**)**

AT/1032-0865
DIRECTORY OF HOUSING RELATED STATISTICS. [Dir. hous. relat. stat.]. **Added/Corp** Australian Bureau of Statistics. (1988)-. English. be. 30.00Aus$. Australian Bureau of Statistics, PO Box 10, Belconnen Australian Capital Territory, 2616 Australia. **Tel** 011 61 6 2527911, FAX 011 61 6 2516009. **DD** 363.50994021.
Desc: Presents details of housing related statistics produced by both government and non-government sources. Intended to acquaint users with the wide range of housing related data currently available.

US
HOUSING AND URBAN AFFAIRS ... : A BIBLIOGRAPHIC GUIDE TO THE MICROFORM COLLECTION. **VFOAT** Housing Update; Housing and Urban Affairs : A Bibliographic Guide to the ... Documents Update. 1965/76-. English. an.
Desc: The documents in each collection were chosen from the holdings of the library of the Department of Housing and Urban Development.

AT/1031-0320
HOUSING FINANCE FOR OWNER OCCUPATION, AUSTRALIA. [Hous. finance own. occup. Aust.]. **Added/Corp** Australian Bureau of Statistics. (1978)-. Periodical. English. mo. 10.70Aus$. Australian Bureau of Statistics, PO Box 10, Belconnen Australian Capital Territory, 2616 Australia. **Tel** 011 61 6 2527911, FAX 011 61 6 2516009. **DD** 332.7220994. ***Continues*** *Housing Finance for Owner Occupation, 0313-1092.*
Desc: Secured finance commitments to individuals for construction of dwellings, purchase of new and established dwellings by banks, permanent building societies and other lenders.

US/0885-4122
JOURNAL OF PLANNING LITERATURE. [J. plan. lit.]. **Added/Corp** Ohio State University. City and Regional Planning Dept. Vol. 1, No. 1 (Winter 1985-86)-. Abstracting/Indexing Service. English. qt (Feb., May, Aug., Nov.). $127.00. SAGE Periodical Press, 2455 Teller Road, Thousand Oaks CA 91320. **Tel** (805)499-0721, FAX (805)499-0871, telex 100799. **ED** Kenneth Pearlman (Ohio State University). **LC** Z5942; .J68; HT166. **DD** 016.3071/2. **[CCC]. Acid Free. Circ:** 900. available on microfilm.
Desc: Publishes review articles providing a comprehensive and critical evaluation of a particular subject, abstracts of recent literature in the field of city and regional planning and bibliographical listings.
Ind/Abst Geogr. Abstr. Human Geogr.; Int. Bibliogr. Sociol.; Int. Dev. Abstr. (?-?); PAIS Int. Print (1991-); Sage Urban Stud. Abstr.

UK
PLANNING AND DEVELOPMENT STATISTICS. ESTIMATES. **Main/Corp** Chartered Institute of Public Finance and Accountancy. Statistical Information Service. (19??)-. English. an. Chartered Institute of Public Finance and Accountancy, 2 3 Robert Street, London WC2N 6BH England. **Tel** 011 44 1 895 8823. **LC** HT169.G72; E583. **DD** 309.2/12/0941.

UK/0140-4768
RURAL DEVELOPMENT ABSTRACTS / [PREPARED BY THE COMMONWEALTH BUREAU OF AGRICULTURAL ECONOMICS]. **Added/Corp** Commonwealth Bureau of Agricultural Economics. Commonwealth Agricultural Bureaux. (Mar. 1978)-. Abstracting/Indexing Service. English. bm. $247.00 US. CAB International Centre, Wallingford, Oxon OX10 8DE United Kingdom. **Tel** 44 491 832111, FAX 44 491 833508, telex 847964 (COMAGG G). **LC** HN49.C6; R874. **DD** 016.307/14. **Ad Acc.** available on magnetic tape and CD-ROM; available on an online database from Tsukuba Daigaku; CAN/OLE; STN International; JICST; DATA-STAR; DIMDI; ESA-IRS; BRS; and DIALOG.

US/0090-5747
SAGE URBAN STUDIES ABSTRACTS. [Sage urban stud. abstr.]. **VFOAT** Urban Studies Abstracts. Vol. 1 (Feb. 1973)-. Abstracting/Indexing Service. English. qt (Feb., May, Aug., Nov.). $292.00. SAGE Periodical Press, 2455 Teller Road, Thousand Oaks CA 91320. **Tel** (805)499-0721, FAX (805)499-0871, telex 100799. **LC** HT51; .S24. **DD** 301.36. **Bk Rev. Acid Free. Circ:** 750. available on microfilm and microfiche from University Microfilms International (UMI).
Desc: Publishes cross-indexed abstracts of important recent literature (plus related citations) on all aspects of urban studies.

UK
SCOTTISH HOUSING STATISTICS / SCOTTISH DEVELOPMENT DEPARTMENT. No. 1 (1st Quarter 1978)-. English. qt. **LC** HD7335.A3; S39. **DD** 338.4/769083/09411. ***Continues*** *Housing Return for Scotland.*

Humanities

US
STATISTICAL SUMMARY OF DEPARTMENTAL ACTIONS. Main/Corp Los Angeles, Calif. Dept. of City Planning. **Added/Corp** Los Angeles (Calif.) Dept. of City Planning. Annual Report Summary of the Department of City Planning. **VFOAT** Annual Report Summary of the Department of City Planning. (19??)-. Statistical Publication. English. an. Department of City Planning, Data Support Unit, Room 507/Los Angeles City Hall, Los Angeles CA 90012. **LC** HT168.L6; L68A. **DD** 352/.96/0979494.

US
STATISTICAL SUMMARY OF PROGRAMS / NEW YORK STATE DIVISION OF HOUSING AND COMMUNITY RENEWAL. Main/Corp New York (State). Division of Housing and Community Renewal. (Mar. 31, 1981)-. Statistical Publication. English. an. New York State Division of Housing and Community Renewal, 2 World Trade Center, New York NY 10047. **LC** HD7303.N7; N393a. **DD** 363.5/8/09747021. *Continues* New York (State). Division of Housing and Community Renewal. Management Information and Research Bureau. Statistical Summary of Programs.

IO
STATISTIK PERUMAHAN DAN LINGKUNGANNYA. 1981-. Indonesian. Biro Pusat Statistik, JLN Dr Sutomo 8 Kotak, Pos 1003, Jakarta 10710 Indonesia. **Tel** 3728007, 374908. **ED** Desa Lingkungan Hidup. **LC** HD7365.A3; S7. Index available. **Bk Rev**.

GW
WOHNGELD IN NORDRHEIN-WESTFALEN. Main/Corp North Rhine-Westphalia (Germany). Landesamt fur Datenverarbeitung und Statistik. 1974/76-. German. an. DM4.00. Landesamt fuer Datenverarbeitung und Statistik Nordrhein-Westfalen, Postfach 101105, 40002 Duesseldorf Germany. **Tel** (0211)944901, FAX (0211)442006, telex 8586654 LDST D. **LC** HA1320.N6; A32 subser; HD7339.N6 N6. **Circ:** 200.
 Desc: Statistical returns on public housing allowances.

HUMANITIES

US/1041-536X
ACLS OCCASIONAL PAPER. (ACLS OCCASIONAL PAPER / AMERICAN COUNCIL OF LEARNED SOCIETIES.). [ACLS occas. paper]. **Added/Corp** American Council of Learned Societies. **VFOAT** American Council of Learned Societies Occasional Paper. (1987)-. Monographic series. English. ir. Free on request. American Council of Learned Societies, 228 East 45th Street, 16th Floor/ACLS, New York NY 10017. **Tel** (212)697-1505. **LC** AS36.N5; A82. **DD** 001.
 Desc: Seeks to familiarize teachers with current developments in the humanities, support their development of curricular materials based on their studies, and disseminate those materials.

IT/0001-494X
ACME. (ACME; ANNALI DELLA FACOLTA DI LETTERE E FILOSOFIA DELL'UNIVERSITA DEGLI STUDI DI MILANO.). [Acme]. **Added/Corp** Universita di Milano. Facolt-a di Lettere e Filosofia. Vol. 1 (Jan./June 1948)-. Periodical. Italian. Three times a year. L60000 Italy; L75000 other. Cisalpino IST Edit Universitar, via Ferrarese 119 2, 40128 Bologna Italy. **Tel** 011 39 51 370337. cum. index.
 Ind/Abst Am. Human. Life (1965-); MLA Int. Bibl. Books Artic. Mod. Lang. Lit.; Numis. Lit.

FI/0355-578X
ACTA ACADEMIAE ABOENSIS. SER. A. HUMANIORA. [Acta Acad. Aboensis, Ser. A]. **Main/Corp** Abo Akademi. Vol. 29 (1965)-. Monographic series. Multiple languages (Swedish, English and German). ABO Akademis Forlag, Kaskisgatan 2 C 14, SF-20700 ABO Finland. *Continues* Abo Akademi. Acta Academiae Aboensis. Humaniora.
 Ind/Abst Annu. Bibliogr. Engl. Lang. Lit.; MLA Int. Bibl. Books Artic. Mod. Lang. Lit.

DK
ACTA JUTLANDICA; AARSKRIFT ... HUMANISTISK SERIE. Main/Corp Aarhus Universitet. 1-. Periodical. Danish. Aarhus University Press, Aarhus University, Building 170, DK-8000 Aarhus C Denmark. **Tel** 011 45 86 197033, FAX 011 45 86 198433, telex 16600.

SP
ACTA SALMANTICENSIA, FILOSOFIA Y LETRAS. (1945)-. Monographic series. Spanish. Price varies per volume. Ediciones Universidad de Salamanca, Apartado Postal 325, 37080 Salamanca Spain. **Tel** 011 34 23 294598, FAX 011 34 23 263046.

SW/0345-0147
ACTA UNIVERSITATIS UMENSIS. (ACTA UNIVERSITATIS UMENSIS. UMEA STUDIES IN THE HUMANITIES.). [Acta Univ. Umensis]. **Added/Corp** Umea Universitet. **VFOAT** Umea Studies in the Humanities. (1975)-. Monographic series. Swedish. Price varies per volume. **LC** UNC.
 Ind/Abst MLA Int. Bibl. Books Artic. Mod. Lang. Lit.

PL/0239-6661
ACTA UNIVERSITATIS WRATISLAVIENSIS. Added/Corp Uniwersytet Wrocawski im. Bolesawa Bieruta. Vol. 1 No. 1 (1962)-. Monographic series. Polish (summaries and/or abstracts in English, French, German and Russian; table of contents in English). ir. Price varies per volume. **(Subscription address:** ARS Polona, PO Box 1001, 00068 Warsaw Poland.**) LC** AS262.B84; A18. **DD** 060. **CODEN** AWMFAR. *Formed by the union of* Uniwersytet Wrocawski. Zeszyty Naukowe, Ser. A **and** Uniwersytet Wrocawski. Zeszyty Naukowe, Ser. B.
 Ind/Abst Geogr. Abstr. Phys. Geogr.; Geogr. Abstr. Human Geogr.; Leis. Recreat. Tour. Abstr.; Math. Rev.; Rural Dev. Abstr.; Soc. Plann. Policy Dev. Abstr.; Sociol. Abstr. (?-?); World Agric. Econ.; Zentralbl. Math. Ihre Grenzgeb.

FR/1140-6011
ACTIVITE PHILOSOPHIQUE ET SOCIALE, SCIENTIFIQUE, MEDICALE ET LITTERAIRE, L'. VFOAT Activite Philosophique, Sociale, Scientifique, Medicale, Esthetique et Litteraire. (1956)-. Periodical. French. tq. L30000.00. Centrum Ignatianum Spiritual, Borgo S Spirito CP 6139, 00195 Rome Italy. **Tel** 11 39 6 6569841. **UDC** 61. *Continues* CIS (Paris), 1140-6003.

IQ
AFAQ ARABIYAH. See The Arts.

UK
AFGHANICA : THE AFGHANISTAN STUDIES NEWSLETTER. Vol. 1, No. 1 (Sept. 1987)-. Newsletter. English. sa (2 issues). £12.00 UK, £15.00 other (institution). Afghanica, Jagellonian University, Al Mickiewicza 9/11, 31 120 Krakow Poland. **ED** Ms. Kinga Maciuszak. **LC** IN PROCESS. **Bk Rev** (Qty: 2-3).
 Desc: Information on conferences, seminars and lectures on Afghanistan and the area. Covers humanistic studies, literature, linguistics, anthropology, sociology, history and religion.

SA/0256-2804
AFRICA INSIGHT. See Social Sciences.

●UK/1352-2175
AFRICAN STUDIES ABSTRACTS : THE ABSTRACTS JOURNAL OF THE AFRICAN STUDIES CENTRE, LEIDEN. See Social Sciences-Abstracting, Bibliographies and Statistics.

US/0002-1016
AGORA (POTSDAM). Suspended. (AGORA.). [Agora]. **Added/Corp** State University College at Potsdam, N.Y. Vol. 1 (Fall 1969)-(1991). English. Twice a year. State University of New York / Potsdam, College at Potsdam, C/O Dr. M. Bergman, Potsdam NY 13676. **Tel** (315)267-2005. **LC** AS30; .A35. **DD** 001.3/05.
 Ind/Abst Annu. Bibliogr. Engl. Lang. Lit.; MLA Int. Bibl. Books Artic. Mod. Lang. Lit.; Philos. Index.

AT
AICCM BULLETIN. (19??)-. English. ir. 50.00Aus$ (individuals); 50.00Aus$ (institutions) Comes with Australian Institute for the Conservation of Cultural Material membership. Institute for the Conservation of Cultural Material Inc, GPO Box 1638, Canberra Australian Capital Territory 2601 Australia. **Tel** 011 61 6 2434531. *Continues* ICCM Bulletin.

CL/0568-3939
AISTHESIS. VFOAT Aisethesis. No. 1-. Spanish. an. **LC** BH25; .A57.
 Ind/Abst HAPI Hisp. Am. Period. Index.

US/0731-5880
AITIA. See Philosophy.

LE/0002-3973
AL-ABHATH. Added/Corp American University of Beirut. **VFOAT** Abhath. Vol. 1 (March 1948)-. Periodical. Arabic (English, French and German). an. $15.00. Al Abhath, c/o American University of Beirut, Beirut Lebanon. **Tel** 011 340740. **LC** AS595.A6; A36. cum. index.
 Ind/Abst Am. Hist. Life (1956-); Int. Bibliogr. Sociol.; Numis. Lit.; Middle East J. (?-?).

SP
ALBUM. Spanish. bm. 3.300ptas Spain; $125.00 other. Letras y Artes Sa, Juan Alvarez Mendizabal 58, 28008 Madrid Spain. **Tel** 011 34 1 248 9027. **Pr Rev. Circ:** 25,000 (ctrl).

US/0361-0144
AMERICAN HUMANITIES INDEX, THE. See Humanities-Abstracting, Bibliographies and Statistics.

GW
AMTSBLATT DES HESSISCHEN KULTUSMINISTERS. Main/Corp Hesse (Germany). Kultusministerium. Periodical. German. mo. 30.00. Der Hessische Kultusminister, Luisenplatz 10, W-6200 Wiesbaden Germany. cum. index. *Continues* Hesse (Germany). Ministerium fur Erziehung und Volksbildung. Amtsblatt.

CC
AN-HUI SHIH TA HSUEH PAO. Added/Corp An-Hui Shih Fan Ta Hsueh. **VFOAT** An-Hui Shih Ta Hsueh Pao, Che Hsueh She Hui Ko Hsueh Pan; Anhui Shida Xuebao. (19??)-. Periodical. Chinese. qt. RMBY20.00. China National Publishing Company, 380 Bei Su Zhou Lu, Shanghai, People's Republic of China. **LC** AS452.A5; A3. **Bk Rev. Ad Acc.** ctrl circ. *Continues* An-Hui Shih Fan Ta Hsueh Hsueh Pao.
 Desc: Introducing Chinese philosophy, political science, and famous thinking.

GW
ANALECTA SLAVICA. Vol. 1 (1972)-. Monographic series. Multiple languages (Czech, Polish and Russian). ir. Price varies per volume. Physica-Verlag GmBh & Company, Postfach 105280, D-69042 Heidelberg Germany. **Tel** 06221 487-492, FAX 06221 487177 und 487366, telex 461723 sphdb-d.

CU/1017-8937
ANALES DEL CARIBE. (1981)-. Periodical. Spanish (English and French). an. $14.00 US; $18.00 other. Casa de Las Americas, Calle 3 Y G, El Vedado, La Habana Cuba. **Tel** 32 3587, 32 1590, telex CAMER CU 51-1019. **(Subscription address:** Subdireccion de Exportacion, Ediciones Cubanas, Apartado 605, La Habana Cuba**) ED** Emilio Jorge Rodriguez. **UDC** 300(729). Index available. cum. index. **Bk Rev. Ad Acc.**
 Desc: Publication specialized on Caribbean culture and society, includes research studies and original articles.

MX/0185-1276
ANALES DEL INSTITUTO DE INVESTIGACIONES ESTETICAS. See The Arts-Art.

UK
ANGLO NORMAN DICTIONARY. Ceased. Ceased with Vol. 8, 1992. English. ir. Modern Humanities Research Association, Kings College Strand, London WC2R 2LS England. **Tel** 44 71 836 5454.

FI/0355-113X
ANNALES ACADEMIAE SCIENTIARUM FENNICAE. DISSERTATIONES HUMANARUM LITTERARUM. [Ann. Acad. Sci. Fenn., Diss. hum. litt.]. **Added/Corp** Suomalainen Tiedeakatemia. **VFOAT** Dissertationes Humanarum Litterarum. (1973)-. Monographic series. English (German and French). ir. Price varies per volume. Academia Scientarum Fennica, Mariankatu 5, 00170 Helsinki 17 Finland. **ED** Heikki Palva. **LC** UNC. Index available. **Circ:** 500-800 (ctrl).
 Ind/Abst Linguist. Lang. Behav. Abstr.; MLA Int. Bibl. Books Artic. Mod. Lang. Lit.; Soc. Plann. Policy Dev. Abstr.; Sociol. Abstr.

CM
ANNALES DE LA FACULTE DES LETTRES ET SCIENCES HUMAINES SERIE SCIENCES HUMAINES / UNIVERSITE DE YAOUNDE. Vol. 1, No. 1 (Jan. 1985)-. Periodical. French. sa. Universite de Yaounde, Faculte des Lettres et Sciences Humaines, Prof. Sondengam BP 812, Yaounde Cameroon. *Continues in part* Annales de la Faculte des Lettres et Sciences Humaines de Yaounde.
 Ind/Abst MLA Int. Bibl. Books Artic. Mod. Lang. Lit.

FR
ANNALES DE L'ACADEMIE DE MACON / SOCIETE DES ARTS, SCIENCES, BELLES-LETTRES, ET AGRICULTURE DE SAONE-ET-LOIRE. Main/Corp Academie de Macon. Societe des Arts, Sciences, Belles-Lettres, et Agriculture de Saone-et-Loire. (1851)-(1876); 2nd. Ser. (1877)-(1895); 3rd. Ser. (1896)-(1988); 4th Ser. (1989)-. French. *Continues* Academie de Macon. Societe des Arts, Sciences, Belles-Lettres, et Agriculture de Saone-et-Loire. Compte-Rendu des Travaux.
 Ind/Abst BHA : Biblio. Hist. Art.

FR/0182-855X
ANNALES PUBLIEES PAR L'UNIVERSITE DE TOULOUSE - LE MIRAIL. See Education-Higher Education.

Humanities

HU/0524-8981
ANNALES UNIVERSITATIS SCIENTIARUM BUDAPESTINENSIS DE ROLANDO EOTVOS NOMINATAE. SECTIO HISTORICA. [Ann. Univ. Sci. Budap. Rolando Eotvos nom. Sect. hist.] **Main/Corp** Eotvos Lorand Tudomanyegyetem. V. 1- 1957-. Periodical. Hungarian (English, French, German and Russian). an. Eotvos Lorand Tudomanyegyetem, Bolcseszettudomanyi Kar, Pesti BUL, H-1052 Budapest Hungary. **Tel** 36 11 180 966. **(Subscription address:** ELTE Boleseszettudomanyi Kar, Torteneti Konyvtar, Pesti BUL, H-1052 Budapest Hungary) **ED** Istvan Dioszegi. **LC** AS142.B9; A2. **Bk Rev**. ctrl circ.
Ind/Abst Am. Hist. Life (1960-1971, 1974-).

IT
ANNALI DELLA FACOLTA DI LETTERE E FILOSOFIA. Main/Corp Universita degli Studi di Perugia. Facolta di Lettere e Filosofia. (1964)-. Periodical. Italian. an.
Ind/Abst MLA Int. Bibl. Books Artic. Mod. Lang. Lit.

US/0192-2858
ANNALS OF SCHOLARSHIP. [Ann. scholarsh.]. Vol. 1 (Winter 1980)-. Periodical. English. qt (published within the seasons). $60.00 (one year) $120.00 (two year) $180.00 (three year) institution; $32.00 (one year) $64.00 (two yera) $96.00 (three year) individual. Wayne State University Press, 4809 Woodward Avenue, The Leonard N. Simons Building, Detroit MI 48201-1309. **Tel** (313)577-6119, (313)577-6120, FAX (313)577-6131. **LC** AS30; .A56. **DD** 081.
Desc: Promotes inquiries into the history and current development of disciplinary criteria and the ways in which scholars and their research influence and are influenced by institutional, political, or social factors.
Ind/Abst BHA : Biblio. Hist. Art; MLA Int. Bibl. Books Artic. Mod. Lang. Lit.

US/0503-1001
ANNALS OF THE UKRAINIAN ACADEMY OF ARTS AND SCIENCES IN THE UNITED STATES. [Ann. Ukr. Acad. Arts Sci. U.S.]. **Main/Corp** Ukrainian Academy of Arts and Sciences in the United States. Vol. 1, No. 1 (Winter 1951)-. English. ir. $35.00. Annnals of the Ukrainian Academy of Arts & Science, 206 West 100th Street, New York NY 10025. **Tel** (212)222-1866. **LC** AS36.U4; A35. **DD** 061.3. cum. index. **Bk Rev**. **Pr Rev. Circ:** 500-1,000.
Ind/Abst Am. Hist. Life (1955-).

FR
ANNUAIRE DE LA RECHERCHE / UNIVERSITE DE PARIS 1 PANTHEON-SORBONNE. French. an. 12 Place du Pantheon, Paris France. **LC** AS158; .A66. **DD** 001.4/025/44.

UK
ANNUAL BULLETIN OF THE MODERN HUMANITIES RESEARCH ASSOCIATION. Main/Corp Modern Humanities Research Association. Bulletin. English. ir. George Washington University / 2127 G Street Northwest, Washington DC 20015. **Tel** (202)994-1000.

ZA
ANNUAL REPORT - UNIVERSITY OF ZAMBIA. SCHOOL OF HUMANITIES & SOCIAL SCIENCES. Main/Corp University of Zambia. School of Humanities and Social Sciences. (19??)-. English. University of Zambia School of Humanities and Social Services, Lusaka Zambia. **LC** LG469.L8; A33. **DD** 378.689/4.

SP/0211-5611
ANTHROPOS (BARCELONA, SPAIN). (ANTHROPOS). No. 1 (April 1981)-. Periodical. Spanish (Spanish, Romanian and English). mo. $80.39 Spain; $93.07 other. Anthropos Editorial, Apartado 387, 08190 Sant Cugat del Valles Barcelona Spain. **Tel** 011 34 3 5894884. **LC** Z2685; .A58. **DD** 015.46. Index available. cum. index. **Bk Rev**. **Ad Acc**. **Circ:** 10,000 (ctrl).
Desc: A basic reference in the Hispanic cultural production. Aims to investigate the leading and creative cultural agents and document the Culture scientifically.

SP/1130-2089
ANTHROPOS. SUPLEMENTOS. [Anthropos, Supl.]. (1987)-. Periodical. Spanish (Catalan, French, English and Portuguese). Six times a year. 7.388ptas Italy; 9.450ptas Europe; 10.750ptas US; 11.050ptas Africa; 12.350ptas Asia; 12.450ptas Australia. Anthropos Editorial, Apartado 387, 08190 Sant Cugat del Valles Barcelona Spain. **Tel** 011 34 3 5894884. **ED** Ramon Gabarros. **UDC** 001. Index available. cum. index. **Pr Rev. Circ:** 5,000 (ctrl).
Desc: Periodical thematically related to "Anthropos".

AT/1030-3839
ANTITHESIS. Added/Corp University of Melbourne. English Dept. Vol. 1, No. 1 (1987)-. Periodical. English. sa (May & Oct.). $35.00 (institutions), $25.00 (individuals). Antithesis, English Department, University of Melbourne, Parkville VIC 3052 Australia. **Tel** 011 61 3 344 5506. **ED** Richard Harling, Eleanor Hogan, Barbara Hogarth.
Ind/Abst APAIS, Aust. Public Aff. Inf. Ser. (1989-).

RM/0066-4987
ANUAR DE LINGVISTICA SI ISTORIE LITERARA. See Linguistics.

CE
AQUINAS JOURNAL. See Social Sciences.

GW/0003-9233
ARCHIV FUER KULTURGESCHICHTE. See History(General).

GW
ARCHIV FUER VERGLEICHENDE KULTURWISSENSCHAFT. Vol. 1 (196?)-. Periodical. German. ir. Price varies. Verlag Anton Hain Athenaeum, Wormer Strasse 99, D 55294 Bodenheim Germany. **Tel** 011 49 6135 3057.

CK/0570-7293
ARCO. (Mar./Apr. 1959)-. Periodical. Spanish. mo. $50.00. Promotora de Medios de Comunicacion Social, Carrera 6 No. 35-39, Apartado Aereo 8624, Bogota DE Colombia. **Tel** 011 57 1 2851500. **LC** AP63; .A662. **Bk Rev. Circ:** 10,000. available with illustrations.
Ind/Abst HAPI Hisp. Am. Period. Index (19??-).

US
ARION / BOSTON UNIVERSITY. See Literature.

US
ARIS FUNDING REPORTS. CREATIVE ARTS AND HUMANITIES REPORT. See The Arts.

SW/0349-0416
ARSBOK / KUNGL. HUMANISTISKA VETENSKAPS-SAMFUNDET I UPPSALA. [Arsb. - K. Hum. vetensk.-samf. Upps.]. **Main/Corp** K. Humanistiska Vetenskapssamfundet i Uppsala. **VFOAT** Annales Societatis Litterarum Humaniorum Regiae Upsaliensis. (1943)-. Swedish. **LC** WMLC 91/1019.
Ind/Abst Am. Hist. Life (1963-); BHA : Biblio. Hist. Art.

AT/0812-7158
ARTISAN MELBOURNE. See Education-Teaching and Curriculum.

US
ARTS & HUMANITES SEARCH. See The Arts.

US
ARTS & HUMANITIES CITATION INDEX. CITATION INDEX, PERMUTERM SUBJECT INDEX. Added/Corp Institute for Scientific Information. (1978)-. Academic Scholarly Publication. English. ir. Institute for Scientific Information, 3501 Market Street, Philadelphia PA 19104. **Tel** (215)386-0100, (800)523-1850, FAX (215)386-6362, telex 84-5305. **(Subscription address:** Institute for Scientific Information, PO Box 71416, Chicago, IL 60694)

US/1060-9202
ARTS & HUMANITIES CITATION INDEX (COMPACT DISC ED.). See The Arts.

US/0162-8445
ARTS & HUMANITIES CITATION INDEX. PERMUTERM SUBJECT INDEX. Added/Corp Institute for Scientific Information. (1978)-. Academic Scholarly Publication. English. ir. Institute for Scientific Information, 3501 Market Street, Philadelphia PA 19104. **Tel** (215)386-0100, (800)523-1850, FAX (215)386-6362, telex 84-5305. **(Subscription address:** Institute for Scientific Information, PO Box 71416, Chicago, IL 60694)

US/0162-8445
ARTS & HUMANITIES CITATION INDEX (PRINT ED.). See Humanities-Abstracting, Bibliographies and Statistics.

US
ASIA FOUNDATION QUARTERLY, THE. *Title Change*. **Added/Corp** Asia Foundation. (Autumn 1986)-(19??). Periodical. English. qt. Asia Foundation, 465 California Street, 14th Floor, San Francisco CA 94104. **Tel** (415)982-4640, FAX (415)392-8863. **ED** Gay Morris. **LC** DS1; .A5753. ctrl circ. *Continues* Asia Foundation News, 0735-0740. *Continued by* Asia Foundation News (San Francisco, Calif. : 1991).
Desc: Contains articles and information about the Foundation's programs.

KO/0251-3110
ASIAN & PACIFIC QUARTERLY OF CULTURAL AND SOCIAL AFFAIRS. *Title Change*. [Asian Pac. q. cult. soc. aff.]. **Added/Corp** Cultural and Social Centre for the Asian and Pacific Region. **VFOAT** Asian and Pacific Quarterly of Cultural and Social Affairs. Vol. 6, No. 2 (Autumn 1974)-Vol. 24, No. 1 (Autumn 1992). Periodical. English. Three times a year. Asian & Pacific Quarterly, CPO Box 3129, Seoul Korea. **Tel** 02 679-5651. available on microfilm from University Microfilms International (UMI). *Continues* Asian Pacific Quarterly of Cultural and Social Affairs, 0251-3110. *Continued by* Asian Pacific Quarterly.
Ind/Abst Am. Hist. Life (1972-).

●KO
ASIAN PACIFIC QUARTERLY. Added/Corp Cultural and Social Centre for the Asian and Pacific Region. **VFOAT** APQ; A.P.Q. Vol. 25, No. 1 (Autumn 1993)-. Periodical. English. Four times a year. Free. Asian & Pacific Quarterly, CPO Box 3129, Seoul Korea. **Tel** 02 679-5651. *Continues* Asian & Pacific Quarterly of Cultural and Social Affairs.

IT/0391-8149
ATTI DELLA ACCADEMIA NAZIONALE DEI LINCEI. MEMORIE CLASSE DI SCIENZE MORALI STORICHE E FILOLOGICHE. [Atti Accad. Naz. Lincei, Mem. Cl. Sci. morali stor.]. (1948)-. Monographic series. Multiple languages. tw. **UDC** 1. *Continues* Atti della Accademia d'Italia - Memorie della Classe di Scienze Morali Storiche e Filologiche.
Ind/Abst BHA : Biblio. Hist. Art.

IT
ATTI E MEMORIE (ACCADEMIA NAZIONALE DI SCIENZE, LETTERE E ARTI (MODERA, ITALY) : 1984). (ATTI E MEMORIE / ACCADEMIA NAZIONALE DI SCIENZE, LETTERE E ARTI, MODENA.). **Added/Corp** Accademia Nazionale di Scienze, Lettere e Arti (Modena, Italy). Ser. 7, Vol. 1 (1984)-. Italian. an. *Continues* Memorie (Accademia Nazionale di Scienze, Lettere e Arti (Modera, Italy)).
Ind/Abst BHA : Biblio. Hist. Art; Numis. Lit.

IT/0365-4710
ATTI E MEMORIE / ACCADEMIA VIRGILIANA DI MANTOVA. Added/Corp Accademia Nazionale Virgiliana. Vol. 27 (1949)-. Periodical. Italian. *Continues* Atti e Memorie (Reale Accademia Virgiliana di Scienze, Lettere ed Arte).
Ind/Abst BHA : Biblio. Hist. Art.

IT/0393-2397
ATTI E MEMORIE DELLA ACCADEMIA PETRARCA DI LETTERE, ARTI E SCIENZE. (1930)-. Periodical. Italian. an. **UDC** 5. **CODEN** 8.
Ind/Abst BHA : Biblio. Hist. Art.

IT/0394-1663
ATTI E MEMORIE DELLA SOCIETA TIBURTINA DI STORIA E D'ARTE GIA ACCADEMIA DEGLI AGEVOLI E COLONIA DEGLI ARCADI SIBILLINI. (1929)-. Periodical. Italian. an. **UDC** 908. **CODEN** 061.12.
Ind/Abst BHA : Biblio. Hist. Art.

IT/0392-0836
ATTI E MEMORIE DELL'ACCADEMIA TOSCANA DI SCIENZE E LETTERE LA COLOMBARIA. [Atti mem. Accad. toscana sci. lett., La Colombaria]. **Added/Corp** Accademia Toscana di Scienze e Lettere La Colombaria. Vol. 17 (1952)-. Italian. an. Casa Editrice Leo S. Olschki, Viuzzo del Pozzetto, Casella Postale 66, 50126 Florence Italy. **Tel** 011 39 55 6530684, FAX 011 39 55 6530214. *Continues* Atti e Memorie dell'Accademia Fiorentina di Scienze Morali la Colombaria.
Ind/Abst BHA : Biblio. Hist. Art.

IT
ATTI / ISTITUTO VENETO DI SCIENZE, LETTERE ED ARTI. Added/Corp Istituto Veneto di Scienze, Lettere ed Arti. (1943)-. Italian. **LC** AS222; .V31. *Continues* Atti (Reale Istituto Veneto di Scienze, Lettere ed Arti (Venice, Italy).
Ind/Abst Numis. Lit.

IT/0004-8062
AUREA PARMA. (AVREA PARMA : RIVISTA QUADRIMESTRALE DI STORIA, LETTERATURA E ARTE.). [Aurea Parma]. **VFOAT** Aurea Parma. (1912)-. Periodical. Italian. tq. L60000.00 Italy; L120000.00 other. GDP Editrice SRL, Via Emilio Casa 5 A, 43100 Parma Italy. **Tel** 011 39 521 2159. cum. index.
Ind/Abst BHA : Biblio. Hist. Art (19??-); MLA Int. Bibl. Books Artic. Mod. Lang. Lit. (19??-).

AT/0004-9328
AUSTRALIAN HUMANIST, THE. Added/Corp Council of Australian Humanist Societies. No. 1 (Dec. 1966)-. Periodical. English. Three times a year (Feb., June, & Oct.). 5.00Aus$. Australian Humanist,

Humanities

138 B Princess Street, Kew 3101 Australia. **Tel** 11 61 3 8536443. **ED** James Gerrand. **Bk Rev**, (Qty: 3). **Ad Acc, Adv Mgr:** Jamey, **Tel** 03 853 6662. **Circ:** 600.

FR/0067-4222
BAROQUE (MONTAUBAN). See Literature.

SP/0210-0088
BASILISCO (OVIEDO, SPAIN). See Philosophy.

GW/0067-4729
BAYERISCHES JAHRBUCH FUER VOLKSKUNDE. Added/Corp Bayerische Landesstelle fur Volkskunde. Bayerische Akademie der Wissenschaften. Institut fur Volkskunde. **VFOAT** Beitrage zur Munchener Volkskunde. (1950)-. German. an. *Supersedes Bayerische Hefte fur Volkskunde.*
Ind/Abst BHA : Biblio. Hist. Art.

AT/0811-3653
BEAGLE : OCCASIONAL PAPERS OF THE TERRITORY MUSEUM OF ARTS AND SCIENCES, THE. [Beagle]. Vol. 1, No. 1 (Feb. 10, 1983)-. Monographic series. English (summaries and/or abstracts in French). an. Price varies per volume. Museums & Art Galleries of the Northern Territory, GPO Box 4646, Darwin Northern Territory 0801 Australia. **Tel** (089)824211, **FAX** (089)411258. **ED** J N A Hooper. **CODEN** BEAGET. **Bk Rev**. **Pr Rev. Circ:** 300 (ctrl). Documents available from BIOSIS Document Express.
Ind/Abst AESIS Q.; Biol. Abstr. (1987-).

JA
BEPPU DAIGAKU KIYO. Main/Corp Beppu Daigaku. **VFOAT** Memoirs of Beppu University. Japanese. Free. Deppu Daigaku, 82 Ishigaki, Beppu Japan. **Tel** 0977-67-0101. **ED** Shigemi Goto. **LC** AS552.B46; A2. **Circ:** 500 (ctrl).
Desc: Collection of papers by professors and lecturers chiefly on the arts, history (Japanese, Asian, and Western), literature (Japanese and English) and linguistics.

UK/0966-8772
BHI PLUS [COMPUTER FILE]. See Humanities-Abstracting, Bibliographies and Statistics.

●US/1064-301X
BIBLION (NEW YORK, N.Y.). (BIBLION : THE BULLETIN OF THE NEW YORK PUBLIC LIBRARY.). [Biblion]. **Added/Corp** New York Public Library. Vol. 1, No. 1 (Fall 1992)-. Bulletin. English. Twice a year. $60.00 US; $80.00 other. Greenwood Press Inc., PO Box 5007, Westport CT 06881-5007. **Tel** (203)226-3571, FAX (203)222-1502. **DD** 027. *Continues Bulletin of Research in the Humanities, 0160-0168.*
Ind/Abst Am. Hist. Life (1966-1971).

BL/0102-6968
BOLETIM - CENTRO DE LETRAS E CIENCIAS HUMANAS. (BOLETIM.). [Bol. - Cent. Let. Cienc. Hum.]. (1980)-. Bulletin. Portuguese. sa. Universidade Estadual de Londrina, Centro de Letras e Ciencias Humanas, Campus Universitario, Caixa Postal 6001, CEP 86051-970 Londrina-Parana Brazil. **ED** J. Carlos Thomson. **UDC** 3.

BL
BOLETIM / UNIVERSIDADE ESTADUAL DE LONDRINA, CCH, CENTRO DE LETRAS E CIENCIAS HUMANAS. See Social Sciences.

SP/0210-7481
BOLETIN DE LA REAL ACADEMIA DE BUENAS LETRAS DE BARCELONA. [Bol. R. Acad. Buenas Let. Barcelona]. **Main/Corp** Academia de Buenas Letras de Barcelona. (1902)-. Spanish. an. 2500ptas. Real Academia de Buenas Letras, C Obispo Casador 3, 08002 Barcelona Spain. **Tel** 011 34 3 3150010.
Ind/Abst Am. Hist. Life (1967-1970); BHA : Biblio. Hist. Art.

SP/0034-060X
BOLETIN DE LA REAL ACADEMIA DE CORDOBA, DE CIENCIAS, BELLAS LETRAS Y NOBLES ARTES. Added/Corp Real Academia de Cordoba, de Ciencias, Bellas Letras y Nobles Artes. **VFOAT** Boletin de la Real Academia de Cordoba. (19??)-. Periodical. Spanish. an. **LC** AS302; .C6. **DD** 056/.1. *Continues Academia de Ciencias, Bellas Letras y Nobles Artes de Cordoba. Boletin de la Academia de Ciencias, Bellas Letras y Nobles Artes de Cordoba.*
Ind/Abst Am. Hist. Life (1955-1963); BHA : Biblio. Hist. Art.

SP/0210-1475
BOLETIN DE LA SOCIEDAD CASTELLONENSE DE CULTURA. [Bol. Soc. Castellon. Cult.]. **Main/Corp** Sociedad Castellonense de Cultura. Vol. 1 (Jan./March 1920)-. Periodical. Spanish. qt. 1500ptas Spain; 2500ptas other. Sociedad Castellonense de Cultura, Hierba Casa Abadia/Aptdo 16, 12001 Castellon Spain. **Tel** 011 34 64 232024. **LC** DP302.C55; A17. Index available in last issue of volume--attached. cum. index.
Ind/Abst Am. Hist. Life (1968-1969); BHA : Biblio. Hist. Art.

IT
BOLLETTINO DELL'ANNO ... / SOCIETA TARQUINIENSE DI ARTE E STORIA. Added/Corp Societa Tarquiniense di Arte e Storia. No. 7 (1978)-. Periodical. Italian. an. *Continues Bollettino delle Attivita.*
Ind/Abst BHA : Biblio. Hist. Art.

IT
BOLLETTINO D'INFORMAZIONI / CENTRO DI RICERCHE INFORMATICHE PER I BENI CULTURALI. See The Arts.

IT/1121-6425
BOLLETTINO STORICO DELLA CITTA DI FOLIGNO / ACCADEMIA FULGINIA DI LETTERE, SCIENZE E ARTI. See History(General)-History of Europe.

UK/0007-0815
BRITISH HUMANITIES INDEX. See Humanities-Abstracting, Bibliographies and Statistics.

PO/0870-7618
BROTERIA 1925. [Broter. 1925]. **VFOAT** Fe Ciencias Letras; Revista Contemporanea de Cultura; Cultura e Informacao. (1925)-. Periodical. Portuguese. mo (10 issues). $30.00 Spain and Portugal; $40.00 other. Broteria Revista de Cultura, R Maestro Antonio Taborda 14, 1293 Lisbon Codex Portugal. **Tel** 011 351 1 3961660. **UDC** 008(05). *Continues Broteria. Serie de Vulgarizacfao Cientifica, 0871-0465.*

CN/0707-8048
BULLETIN - CANADIAN FEDERATION FOR THE HUMANITIES. Main/Corp Canadian Federation for the Humanities. V. 4, No. 3- Fall 1978-. Bulletin. English (French). Three times a year. Canadian Federation for the Humanities, 151 Slater Street, Ottawa Ontario K1P 5H3 Canada. **Tel** (613)236-4686. **DD** 061/.1. *Continues Humanities Research Council of Canada. Bulletin, 0315-9566.*

FR
BULLETIN DE CORRESPONDANCE HELLENIQUE. SUPPLEMENT. Added/Corp Ecole Francaise d'Athenes. Vol. 1 (1973)-. Bulletin. French. ir. Price varies per volume. Diffusion de Boccard, 11 rue de Medicis, 75006 Paris France. **Tel** 011 33 1 43260037.
Ind/Abst Numis. Lit.

JA/0495-7725
BULLETIN DE LA MAISON FRANCO-JAPONAISE. Main/Corp Tokyo. Maison Franco-Japonaise. Vol. 1-14 (1927-47); New Series, Vol. 1 (1951)-. Bulletin. French. ir (every 2 or 3 years). price varies. Maison Franco Japonaise, 3 Nichome Surugadai Kanda, Chiyoda-ku Tokyo 101 Japan. **Tel** 03-291-1144, FAX 03-291-8360, telex 2223454 MAIFRA J. **LC** AS552; .T715. **Circ:** 1,000 (ctrl).
Desc: Publishes works of French post-graduate level researchers on social and cultural aspects of Japan.
Ind/Abst MLA Int. Bibl. Books Artic. Mod. Lang. Lit.

BE/0776-1295
BULLETIN DE LA SOCIETE D'ART ET D'HISTOIRE DU DIOCESE DE LIEGE. Main/Corp Societe d'Art et d'Histoire du Diocese de Liege. (1881)-. Bulletin. French. an. cum. index.
Ind/Abst BHA : Biblio. Hist. Art.

FR/0755-2483
BULLETIN DE LA SOCIETE DES ETUDES LITTERAIRES, SCIENTIFIQUES ET ARTISTIQUES DU LOT. [Bull. Soc. etud. lit. sci. artist. Lot]. (1873)-. Periodical. French. qt. **UDC** 908 (447.3).
Ind/Abst BHA : Biblio. Hist. Art.

FR/1148-8557
BULLETIN DE LA SOCIETE DES LETTRES, SCIENCES ET ARTS DE LA CORREZE. Main/Corp Societe des Lettres, Sciences et Arts de la Correze. (1879)-. Bulletin. French. qt. **LC** DC611.C77; S7. cum. index.
Ind/Abst BHA : Biblio. Hist. Art.

FR
BULLETIN DE L'ACADEMIE DES SCIENCES ET LETTRES DE MONTPELLIER. Main/Corp Academie des Sciences et Lettres de Montpellier. V. 1- 1909- ; New Series V. 1- 1970-. Bulletin. French. an. Academie des Sciences et Lettres de Montpellier, Service des Publications et echanges, Bibliotheque Interuniversitaire, 4 rue Ecole Mage-34000 Montpellier. **Tel** 67 52 70 82. **LC** AS162. ctrl circ.
Desc: Letters on medicine and science by academicians.

SG/0018-9642
BULLETIN DE L'INSTITUT FONDAMENTAL D'AFRIQUE NOIRE. SERIE B: SCIENCES HUMAINES. [Bull. Inst. fond. Afr. noire, Ser. B]. **Added/Corp** Institut Fondamental d'Afrique Noire. **Added/Corp** Institut Fondamental d'Afrique Noire. **VFOAT** Sciences Humaines. Vol. 28 (Jan./April 1966)-. Bulletin. French (English). qt (4 issues). Institut Fondamental d'Afrique Noire, Boite Postale 206, Cheikh Anta Diop, Dakar Senegal. **Tel** 011 221 250090. **LC** DT1; .I5123. available on diskette. *Continues Bulletin de l'Institut Francais d'Afrique Noire. Serie B : Sciences Humaines, 0378-3871.*
Ind/Abst Am. Hist. Life (1964-); Anthropol. Lit.; Int. Labour Doc.; MLA Int. Bibl. Books Artic. Mod. Lang. Lit.

FR/1153-2599
BULLETIN HISTORIQUE ET SCIENTIFIQUE DE L'AUVERGNE 1933. (1933)-. Periodical. French. qt. **UDC** 908(445.9).
Ind/Abst BHA : Biblio. Hist. Art.

UK/0301-102X
BULLETIN OF THE JOHN RYLANDS UNIVERSITY LIBRARY OF MANCHESTER. [Bull. J. Rylands Univ. Libr. Manchester]. **Added/Corp** John Rylands University Library of Manchester. Vol. 55, (Autumn 1972)-. Bulletin. English. Three times a year (Spring, Summer, Autumn). £60.00 US & Canada; £40.00 other. The John Rylands University Library of Manchester, Oxford Road, Manchester M13 9PP England. **Tel** 011 44 61 275 3757 9, FAX 011 44 61 273 7488, telex 666517. **ED** Dr. Dorothy Clayton. Index Bound in First Issue. cum. index. **Circ:** 1,000 (ctrl). available on microfilm and microfiche from University Microfilms International (UMI). Documents available from The Genuine Article. *Continues Bulletin of the John Rylands Library, 0021-7239.*
Desc: Examines material about the humanities, social sciences, and on the history and the philosophy of the natural and physical sciences.
Ind/Abst Abstr. Engl. Stud.; Am. Hist. Life (1957-);; Annu. Bibliogr. Engl. Lang. Lit.; Arts Humanit. Citation Index [Full Cov.]; BHA : Biblio. Hist. Art; Br. Archaeol. Bibliogr. (?-?); Br. Humanit. Index; Curr. Contents Arts Humanit.; Index Book Rev. Relig.; Libr. Inf. Sci. Abstr.; MLA Int. Bibl. Books Artic. Mod. Lang. Lit.; New Testam. Abstr.; Old Testam. Abstr.; Recent. Publ. Artic.; Relig. Index One Period. (1980-); Relig. Theol. Abstr.; Res. Alert [Full Cov.]; RILA, Int. Rep. Lit. Art; Romant. Move.; Soc. Sci. Cit. Index [Select. Cov.].

II/0033-9156
BULLETIN OF THE RAMAKRISHNA MISSION INSTITUTE OF CULTURE. Main/Corp Ramakrishna Mission, India. Institute of Culture. Vol. 1 (Jan. 1960)-. Bulletin. English. mo. $25.00. Ramakrishna Mission, Institute of Culture, Calcutta, India. **(Subscription address:** Prints India, 11 Darya Ganj, New Delhi, 110002 India, (Phone: 011 91 11 3268645)) **LC** B133.R34; R3.

CI/0350-1604
BULLETIN SCIENTIFIQUE. SECTION B, SCIENCES HUMAINES. [Bull. sci., B, Sci. hum.]. **Added/Corp** Savjet Akademija Nauka SFRJ. Savjet Akademija Nauka i Umjetnosti SFRJ. **VFOAT** Sciences Humaines. No 1-3, (Jan. 1965)-. Bulletin. English. sa. $50.00. Hrvatska Akademija Znanosti i Umjetnosti / Croatian Academy of Sciences & Arts, Zrinski TRG 11, 41000 Zagreb Croatia. **Tel** 011 38 41 433 661, FAX 011 38 41 433 383. **LC** AS346; .S313. *Continues in part Bulletin Scientifique.*

FR/1160-5634
BULLETIN - SOCIETE ACADEMIQUE DU BAS-RHIN POUR LE PROGRES DES SCIENCES, DES LETTRES, DES ARTS ET DE LA VIE ECONOMIQUE. See The Arts.

JA
BUNKAGAKU NENPO (KOBE DAIGAKU. BUNKAGAKU KENKYUKA). (BUNKAGAKU NENPO.). **Added/Corp** Kobe Daigaku. Bunkagaku Kenkyuka. **VFOAT** Annual Reports of Humanities and Social Sciences. No. 1 (March 1982)-. Japanese. an. Kobe Daigaku Daigakuin Bunkagaku Kenkyuka, 1 Rokkodai-cho 1, Nada-ku 657, Kobe-shi Japan. **Tel** 078-881-1212, FAX 078-881-8238. **LC** AS552.K47; A23. **Circ:** 700 (ctrl).

BU/0204-9864
BYZANTINO BULGARICA. See History(General)-History of Europe.

FR/0395-8418
CAHIERS DE FONTENAY, LES. (1975)-. Periodical. French. Three times a year. 150.00F (45.00F postage) France; 146.00F (35.00F postage) other. Cahiers de Fontenay, 31 Avenue Lombard, F-92260 Fontenay Roses France. **(Subscription address:** Les Cahiers de Fontenay, 31, A5. Lombart B.P.81, 92266 Fontenay Aux Roses Cedex) **ED** Michael Coquery. **Pr Rev.**
Desc: Articles in all fields of the humanities.

CN/0839-4555
CAHIERS DU CENTRE D'ETUDES DE L'ASIE DE L'EST. [Cah. Cent. etud. Asie Est]. **Added/Corp** Universite de Montreal. Centre d'Etudes de l'Asie de l'Est. **VFOAT** Cahiers du Centre d'Etude de l'Asie de l'Est. No. 1 (April 1980)-. Monographic series. French. ir (2 issues). 8.00Can$. EBSI Universite de Montreal, CP 6128 Succursale A, Montreal Quebec H3C 3J7 Canada. **Tel** (514)343-7422, (514)343-6444, FAX (514)343-2283, telex 05267389. **ED** Charles Le Blanc (editor's telephone: (514)343-5800). **LC** UNC. cum. index. **Bk Rev**, (Qty: 2). **Ad Acc. Pr Rev. Circ:** 500.
Desc: Research refereed journal having for objective the publication of original manuscripts, notes, essays, documents, bibliographical studies and book reviews in the field of humanities by specialists of East and Southeast Asia. The journal is used as reference by students, professors, researcheres, specialists and professionals.

FR
CAHIERS RATIONALISTES, LES. See Science and Technology.

CN
CALGARY INSTITUTE FOR THE HUMANITIES SERIES. English. an. Humanities Press, 165 1st Avenue, Atlantic Highlands NJ 07716. **Tel** (908)872-1441, (800)221-3845, FAX (908)872-0717, telex 752233. Index available.
Desc: Monographs on broad range of current and historical, cultural issues in the humanities.

TR
CARINDEX, SOCIAL SCIENCES AND HUMANITIES. See Social Sciences.

US/1041-4959
CARING PEOPLE (WASHINGTON, D.C.). (CARING PEOPLE.). [Caring people]. Vol. 1, No. 1 (Dec. 1988)-. Periodical. English. qt. $18.00. National Association for Home Care, 519 C Street Northeast, Stanton Park, Washington DC 20002. **Tel** (202)547-7424, FAX (202)547-3540.

US/0008-6681
CARNEGIE MAGAZINE. [Carnegie mag.]. **Added/Corp** Carnegie Institute. Carnegie Institute of Technology. Carnegie Library of Pittsburgh. Vol. 2, No. 1 (April 1928)-. Periodical. English. bm. $12.00. Carnegie Museum of Natural History, 4400 Forbes Avenue, Pittsburgh PA 15213. **Tel** (412)622-3315, FAX (412)622-8837. **LC** AS36; .P765. **DD** 607.11/74886. available on microfilm and microfiche from University Microfilms International (UMI). ***Continues** Bulletin of the Carnegie Institute.*
Ind/Abst Annu. Bibliogr. Engl. Lang. Lit.; ARTbibliogr. Mod.; Avery Index Archit. Period. Suppl. Colum. Univ. (19??-199?).

US/0147-2127
CAS FORUM. See Education-Higher Education.

US/1059-8308
CAUDA PAVONIS. (CAUDA PAVONIS : THE HERMETIC TEXT SOCIETY NEWSLETTER.). [Cauda pavonis]. **Added/Corp** Hermetic Text Society. **VFOAT** Hermetic Text Society Newsletter. (19??)-. Newsletter. English. Twice a year. $10.00 (individuals) US; $12.00 other. Washington State University / Department of English, Pullman WA 99164-5020. **Tel** (509)335-3023, 335-5020. **ED** Stanton J. Linden. **DD** 540. **Pr Rev. Circ:** 500.
Desc: Publishes scholarly material on all aspects of alchemy and Hermeticism and their influence on literature, philosophy, art, religion and the history of science and medicine.
Ind/Abst MLA Int. Bibl. Books Artic. Mod. Lang. Lit.

FR/0240-4656
CELEBRER PARIS. [Celebrer Paris]. (1979)-. Periodical. French. Ten times a year. 210.58F France; 215.00F other EEC; 250.00F other. Editions du CERF, BP 65, 77932 Perthes Cedex France. **Tel** 011 33 1 44181212. **UDC** 282. ***Continues** Notes de Pastorale Liturgique, 0546-6849.*

US/0162-0177
CENTENNIAL REVIEW, THE. (CR. THE CENTENNIAL REVIEW.). [Centen. rev.]. **Added/Corp** Michigan State University. College of Arts and Letters. **VFOAT** Centennial Review. Vol. 19 (1975)-. Periodical. English. Three times a year (Jan., April, Oct.). $12.00 (one year), $18.00 (two year). Michigan State University / 312 Linton Hall, East Lansing MI 48824-1044. **Tel** (517)355-1905, FAX (517)353-5368. **ED** R.K. Meiners and Cheryllee Finney. **DD** 051. Index available. **Ad Acc, Adv Mgr:** C. Finney. **Circ:** 1,000. available on microfilm and microfiche from University Microfilms International (UMI). Documents available from The Genuine Article. ***Continues** Centennial Review, 0162-0177.*
Desc: Committed to reflection on intellectual work, particularly as set in the university and its environment.
Ind/Abst Abstr. Engl. Stud.; Am. Hist. Life (1963-); Am. Humanit. Index; Annu. Bibliogr. Engl. Lang. Lit.; Arts Humanit. Citation Index [Full Cov.]; BHA : Biblio. Hist. Art; Curr. Contents Arts Humanit.; Index Am. Period. Verse; Linguist. Lang. Behav. Abstr.; Lit. Crit. Regist. (1975-); MLA Int. Bibl. Books Artic. Mod. Lang. Lit.; Res. Alert [Full Cov.]; Romant. Move. (1975-); Soc. Plann. Policy Dev. Abstr.; Sociol. Abstr. (1975-).

US/0273-3323
CENTRAL PARK. Vol. 1, No. 1 (Spring 1981)-. Periodical. English. Twice a year. $5.00. Central Park Magazine, PO Box 1446, New York NY 10023. **Tel** (718)596-1967.
Ind/Abst Am. Humanit. Index; Index Am. Period. Verse.

CH
CHENG-KUNG TA HSUEH HSUEH PAO. JEN WEN, SHE HUI, KO CHI, I HSUEH PIEN. Added/Corp Kuo li Cheng-Kung ta Hsueh. **VFOAT** Journal of Cheng Kung University. Humanities, and Social Science, Science, Engineering, and Medicine Section. (Nov. 1991)-. Periodical. Chinese (English). **LC** AS452; .T33. ***Formed by the union of** Cheng-Kung ta Hsueh Hsueh pao. Jen wen, she hui Pien **and** Cheng-Kung ta Hsueh Hsueh pao. Ko chi, i Hsueh Pien, 1013-0829.*

US/0590-983X
CHICOREL INDEX SERIES. Vol. 1 (1970)-. Monographic series. English. ir. Price varies per volume. American Library Publishing Company, PO Box 4272, Sedona AZ 86340-4272. **Tel** (602)284-1162. **ED** Marietta S. Chicorel. **DD** 016; 800. **Bk Rev.**
Desc: A series of locator guides for the social services, education and humanities. Suitable for high school through university and research libraries.

US/0149-7006
CHICOREL INDEX TO ABSTRACTING AND INDEXING SERVICES : PERIODICALS IN HUMANITIES AND THE SOCIAL SCIENCES. VFOAT Index to Abstracting and Indexing Services. 1st- Ed.; 1974-. Periodical. English. American Library Publishing Corporation, PO Box 2014, Sedona AZ 86336. **Tel** (602)284-1162. **LC** Z6293; .C54. **DD** 016.05. **NLM** Z 6293 C533.

US/0887-5731
CHRONICLES (ROCKFORD, ILL.). (CHRONICLES : A MAGAZINE OF AMERICAN CULTURE.). **Added/Corp** Rockford Institute. Vol. 10, No. 3 (March 1986)-. Periodical. English. mo. $24.00 (one year), $38.00 (two year), $64.00 (three year). The Rockford Institute, 934 North Main Street, Rockford IL 61103. **Tel** (815)964-5053, FAX (815)965-1826. **ED** Thomas J. Fleming. **LC** E169.12; .C483. **DD** 973/.05. cum. index. **Bk Rev. Ad Acc. Circ:** 14,500. ***Continues** Chronicles of Culture, 0163-1187.*
Desc: Features coverage of contemporary literature and the arts.
Ind/Abst Annu. Bibliogr. Engl. Lang. Lit.

PO/0871-1992
CIDADE DE EVORA, A. Added/Corp Evora, Portugal Commissao Municipal de Turismo. No. 1 (1943)-. Periodical. Portuguese. an.
Ind/Abst BHA : Biblio. Hist. Art.

BL/0101-8515
CIENCIA HOJE : REVISAT DE DIVULGACAO CIENTIFICA DA SOCIEDADE BRASILEIRA PARA O PROGRESSO DA CIENCIA. See Science and Technology.

MX/0185-0903
CITAS LATINOAMERICANAS EN CIENCIAS SOCIALES Y HUMANIDADES : CLASE. See Social Sciences.

CN/0315-906X
CLASSMATE. See Education.

DR/0009-9376
CLIO (SANTO DOMINGO). (CLIO : ORGANO DE LA ACADEMIA DOMINICANA DE LA HISTORIA.). [Clio]. **Added/Corp** Academia Dominicana de la Historia. Vol. 1 (Jan./Feb. 1933)-. Periodical. Spanish. bm. $30.00. Academia Dominicana de la Historia, Calle de las Mercedes 50, Santo Domingo, Dominican Republic. **LC** F1931; .C54. cum. index. **Bk Rev. Ad Acc. Circ:** 500. available on microfilm and microfiche from University Microfilms International (UMI).
Desc: Articles and reviews dealing with interplay of literature, history, and philosophy of history. Other interests in this context: religion, myth, philosophy.
Ind/Abst Am. Hist. Life (1955-).

FR/0588-1757
COLLECTION D'ESTHETIQUE. 1- 1967-. Periodical. French. ir. Klincksieck, 11 rue de Lille, 75007 Paris France. **Tel** 1-42-60-38-25. **(Subscription address:** CDU-Sedes, 88 Boulevard St Germain, 75005 Paris France) **ED** Marc Jimenez.

US/0010-1966
COLUMBIA LIBRARY COLUMNS. [Columbia libr. columns]. **Added/Corp** Friends of the Columbia Libraries. Vol. 1 (Fall 1951)-. Periodical. English. Three times a year. $12.00 US; $15.00 other. Friends of Columbia Libraries, 535 West 114th Street, New York NY 10027. **Tel** (212)854-2231. **ED** Rudolph Ellenbogen, Rare Book and Manuscript Library, Butler Library, 535 West 114th Street, New York, NY 10027 USA; Telephone: (212)854-8480. **LC** Z671; .C63. **DD** 020.5. **Circ:** 750.
Desc: Articles in the social sciences and humanities, primarily English and American literature broadly based on the collections in the Columbia University libraries.
Ind/Abst Abstr. Engl. Stud.; Annu. Bibliogr. Engl. Lang. Lit.; Child. Lit. Abstr. (19??-); Libr. Lit.; MLA Int. Bibl. Books Artic. Mod. Lang. Lit.

IT/0375-6181
COMMENTARI DELL'ATENEO DI BRESCIA. [Comment. Ateneo Brescia]. (1813)-. Periodical. Italian. an. **CODEN** CMABCCMABC. ***Continues** Commentari dell' Accademia di Scienze, Lettere, Agricoltura ed Arti del Dipartimento del Mela.*
Ind/Abst BHA : Biblio. Hist. Art.

●US/0961-754X
COMMON KNOWLEDGE. Added/Corp University of Texas at Dallas. Vol. 1, No. 1 (Spring 1992)-. Periodical. English. tq (3 issues). $52.00 institutions, $28.00 individuals US; $65.00 institutions, $41.00 individuals other. Oxford University Press / New York, 200 Madison Avenue, New York NY 10016. **Tel** (212)679-7300, (919)677-0977, (800)451-7556, (800)445-9714, FAX (919)677-1303. **(Subscription address:** Oxford University Press / USA, Journals Marketing Department, Oxford University Press, 2001 Evans Road, Cary NC 27513.) **LC** AP2; .C66. **[CCC].** available on microfilm and microfiche from University Microfilms International (UMI).
Desc: Explores the world on a broader scale through the eyes and experiences of its contributors, many of whom are international intellectuals. Strives to create a common community of professors and the public in both the West and East.

US/0739-473X
COMMUNITY COLLEGE HUMANIST, THE. (THE COMMUNITY COLLEGE HUMANIST : CCH : A TRI-ANNUAL PUBLICATION OF THE COMMUNITY COLLEGE HUMANITIES ASSOCIATION.). **Added/Corp** Community College Humanities Association (U.S.). **VFOAT** CCH; C.C.H. (19??)-. Periodical. English. Three times a year. $40.00. Community College Humanities Association, 1700 Spring Garden Street, Philadelphia PA 19130. **Tel** (215)751-8860.

US/0748-0741
COMMUNITY COLLEGE HUMANITIES REVIEW, THE. (THE COMMUNITY COLLEGE HUMANITIES REVIEW : CCHR.). [Community coll. humanit. rev.]. **VFOAT** CCHR; C.C.H.R.; Humanities Review. No. 5 (Winter 1983-1984)-. Periodical. English. an. $7.50. Community College Humanities Review, Union County College, 1033 Springfield Avenue, Cranford NJ 07016. **DD** 001. ***Continues in part** Community College Humanities Association. Review and Proceedings of the Community College Humanities Association, 0739-4721.*

US/0733-4540
COMPARATIVE CIVILIZATIONS REVIEW. See Social Sciences.

FR/0065-0536
COMPTES RENDUS DES SEANCES - ACADEMIE DES INSCRIPTIONS & BELLES-LETTRES. [C. r. seances annee - Acad. inscr. b.-lett.]. **Main/Corp** Academie des Inscriptions & Belles-Lettres (France). (1857)-. Periodical. French. qt. 675.00F. Diffusion de Boccard, 11 rue de Medicis, 75006 Paris France. **Tel** 011 33 1 43260037. **LC** AS162; .P315. **DD** 054/.1. cum. index. Documents available from The Genuine Article.
Ind/Abst Arts Humanit. Citation Index [Full Cov.]; BHA : Biblio. Hist. Art; Curr. Contents Arts Humanit.; Numis. Lit.; Res. Alert [Full Cov.].

NE/0010-4817
COMPUTERS AND THE HUMANITIES. [Comput. humanit.]. Vol. 1 (Sept. 1966)-. Periodical. English. bm. $470.00. Kluwer Academic Publishers, Postbus 322, 3300 AH Dordrecht, The Netherlands. **Tel** 011 (31) 78 524400, FAX 011 31 78 183273, telex 20083. **ED** Glyn Holmes, Terrence Erdt, Joel Goldfield, and Christian Delcourt (European editor). **LC** Z699.5.H8; C65. **NLM** Z 699.A1 C7363. **CODEN** COHUAD. **[CCC]. Pr Rev. Acid Free.** available on microfilm and microfiche from University Microfilms International (UMI). Documents available from The Genuine Article, UMI

Article Clearinghouse, Ask*IEEE.
Desc: Consistently published work at the forefront of computer applications in the humanities, including work on literature of all periods and genres, languages and linguistics, musicology, history, art history, and humanistically oriented social science. Publishes reports on the latest research in these areas, as well as pedagogical applications. Occasionally special issues are published, allowing a thorough coverage of particulary vital topics, such as natural language processing, computer-assisted instruction, artificial intelligence, and surveys of computing activities in such countries as Canada, France and Italy.
Ind/Abst Abstr. Engl. Stud.; Acad. Search (July 1993-); Am. Hist. Life (1967-); Am. Humanit. Index; Annu. Bibliogr. Engl. Lang. Lit.; ARTbibliogr. Mod.; ARTbibliogr. Curr. Titles; Arts Humanit. Citation Index [Full Cov.]; BHA : Biblio. Hist. Art; Book Rev. Index (1984-); Compumath Citation Index [Full Cov.]; Comput. Lit. Index; Comput. Rev.; Curr. Contents Arts Humanit.; Curr. Index J. Educ. (March 1990); Data Process. Dig.; Educ. Technol. Abstr.; Expand. Acad. Index (1989-); Humanit. Index; Humanit. Source (Jul. 1993-); INFO-SOUTH Abstr.; Inf. Instruc. Technol. (1984-); INSPEC (May 1969-); Linguist. Lang. Behav. Abstr.; Mag. Search; MLA Int. Bibl. Books Artic. Mod. Lang. Lit.; Music Index (?-19??); Newsp. Period. Abstr. (1991-); Res. Alert [Full Cov.]; RILM Abstr.; Romant. Move.; SCISEARCH; Soc. Plann. Policy Dev. Abstr.; Soc. Sci. Cit. Index [Select. Cov.]; Sociol. Abstr.

●IT/1121-6875
CONCERTINO MILANO. (CONCERTINO). [ConcertinoMilano]. (1992)-. Periodical. Italian. bm. L32000. Concertino Giancarlo Buzzi, Via Mose Bianchi 59, 20149 Milan Italy. **Tel** 011 39 2 435679. **ED** Giancarlo Buzzi. **UDC** 37.031. **Ad Acc.**

FR/1142-5067
CONNAISSANCE DE L'EURE. (1971)-. Periodical. French. **UDC** 061.22(442.4). ***Continues*** *Recueil des Travaux de la Societe d'Agriculture, Sciences, Arts et Belles-Lettres, 1142-5075.*
Ind/Abst BHA : Biblio. Hist. Art.

US/0196-9099
CONTRIBUTIONS IN BLACK STUDIES. [Contrib. black stud.]. **Added/Corp** Five College Black Studies Executive Committee. No. 2 (1979)-. English. ir. $4.00 (individuals), $6.00 (institutions). Five College Black Studies, 310 New Africa House, University of Massachusetts, Amherst MA 01003. **Tel** (413)545-0980. **ED** Ernest Allen Jr. **LC** E185.5; .C874. **DD** 973/.00496073. Index available. cum. index. **Bk Rev. Ad Acc. Circ:** 1,000. ***Continues*** *Contributions in Black Studies, 0196-9099.*
Desc: An interdisciplinary journal encompassing the humanities and social sciences, societies, cultures, histories, and politics of the black world.
Ind/Abst Am. Hist. Life (1986-); Linguist. Lang. Behav. Abstr.; Soc. Plann. Policy Dev. Abstr.; Sociol. Abstr.

US/0147-1031
CONTRIBUTIONS IN INTERCULTURAL AND COMPARATIVE STUDIES. **Added/Corp** Council on Intercultural and Comparative Studies. No. 1 (1976)-. Monographic series. English. ir. Price varies per volume. Greenwood Press Inc., PO Box 5007, Westport CT 06881-5007. **Tel** (203)226-3571, FAX (203)222-1502. **LC** UNC.

FR/0304-310X
CORREO, EL. **Main/Corp** Unesco. (1948)-. Periodical. Spanish (English and French). mo. $55.00. UNESCO / France, 31 rue Francois Bonvin, 75732 Paris Cedex 15 France. **Tel** 011 33 1 45684564, 011 33 1 45684565, FAX 011 33 1 42733007, telex 204461 Paris. **(Subscription address:** UNIPUB, 4611 F Assembly Drive, Lanham MD 20706.**)**

IT
CORRISPONDENZE. No. 1 (Spring 1987)-. Periodical. Italian. Three times a year.

US/0740-3399
CREATION SOCIAL SCIENCE AND HUMANITIES QUARTERLY. ***Ceased.*** **See** Social Sciences.

US/0011-1589
CRITICISM (DETROIT). (CRITICISM.). [Criticism]. Vol. 1 (Winter 1959)-. Periodical. English. qt (Jan., Apr., Jul., Oct.). $50.00 (one year), $90.00 (two year), $142.00 (three year) institutions; $28.00 (one year), $52.00 (two year), $78.00 (three year) individuals. Wayne State University Press, 4809 Woodward Avenue, The Leonard N. Simons Building, Detroit MI 48201-1309. **Tel** (313)577-6119, (313)577-6120, FAX (313)577-6131. **ED** Ross Pudaloff. **LC** AS30.W3; A2. **DD** 051. Index available (bound in issue). **Bk Rev. Ad Acc. Circ:** 1,200 (ctrl). available on microfilm and microfiche from University Microfilms International (UMI). Documents available from The Genuine Article, UMI Article Clearinghouse.
Desc: Examines literature and arts of all periods and nations either individually or in their inter-relationships and also the critical theory regarding them.
Ind/Abst Abstr. Engl. Stud.; Acad. Search (July 1993-); Arts Humanit. Citation Index [Full Cov.]; BHA : Biblio. Hist. Art; Book Rev. Index; Curr. Contents Arts Humanit.; Expand. Acad. Index (1989-); Film Lit. Index (1986-1991); Humanit. Index; Humanit. Source (Jul. 1993-); INFO-SOUTH Abstr.; Lit. Crit. Regist.; Mag. Search; Middle East Abstr. Index; MLA Int. Bibl. Books Artic. Mod. Lang. Lit.; Newsp. Period. Abstr. (1991-); Res. Alert [Full Cov.]; Romant. Move.; Soc. Sci. Cit. Index [Select. Cov.].

US/0890-8885
CROSS TIMBERS REVIEW. ***Ceased.*** [Cross timbers rev.]. Vol. 1, No. 1 (May 1984)-(19??). Periodical. English. sa. Cisco Junior College, Cisco TX 76437. **Tel** (817)442-3282. **ED** Monte Lewis. **DD** 808. **Circ:** 250.
Desc: History and biography; poetry and fiction; articles and essays on the literature and culture of the southwest.

PR
CUADERNOS DE LA FACULTAD DE HUMANIDADES. **Main/Corp** Puerto Rico. University. Faculty of Humanities. No. 1-. Periodical. English (Spanish). Universidad de Puerto Rico / Recinto, Recinto de Rio Piedras, Rio Piedras 00931 Puerto Rico. **LC** AS74.P8; A25. **DD** 056/.1.

IT
CULTURA, LA. Vol. 1 (Jan. 1963)-. Periodical. Italian. Three times a year. L64000 Italy; L120000 other. Societa Editrice il Mulino, Strada Maggiore 37, 40125 Bologna Italy. **Tel** 011 39 51 256011, FAX 011 39 51 256034. **Bk Rev. Ad Acc. Circ:** 1,300. ***Supersedes*** *Cultura.*
Desc: A journal of humanistic studies founded in 1881 by Ruggero Bonghi. It publishes important contributions in the fields of philosophy, history and literature.
Ind/Abst MLA Int. Bibl. Books Artic. Mod. Lang. Lit.

●UK
CULTURAL STUDIES FROM BIRMINGHAM. **Added/Corp** University of Birmingham. Dept. of Cultural Studies. No. 1 (1992)-. Periodical. English. an. £6.00 (individuals), £12.00 (institutions) UK; £8.00 (individuals), £15.00 (institutions) others. Crees, University of Birmingham, PO Box 363, Birmingham B15 2TT England. **Tel** 011 44 0214146349 Ext. 2247, FAX 011 44 0214146707.

US/1048-8650
CULTURAL VISTAS. (CULTURAL VISTAS / LOUISIANA ENDOWMENT FOR THE HUMANITIES.). [Cult. vistas]. **Added/Corp** Louisiana Endowment for the Humanities. Vol. 1, No. 1 (Spring 1990)-. Periodical. English. qt. $12.00. Louisiana Endowment for the Humanities, 1001 Howard Avenue, Suite 3110, New Orleans LA 70113. **Tel** (504)523-4352, FAX (504)529-2358. **ED** Michael Sartisky. **DD** 976. Index available. cum. index. **Bk Rev**, (Qty: 12). **Ad Acc. Circ:** 11,000.
Desc: Developed to provide a place for discussion, revelation, and exchange to enhance knowledge and appreciation of the history and culture of Louisiana.

AT/1033-8713
CULTURE AND POLICY / ICPS. **Added/Corp** Griffith University. Institute for Cultural Policy Studies. Vol. 1, No. 1 (Aug. 1989)-. Periodical. English. an. 100.00 Australia, 135.00 other (institutions); 350.00 Australia, 400.00 other (corporate subscriptions); 20.00 Australia, $35.00 other (individuals). Institute of Cultural Policy Studies, Division of Humanities, Griffith University, Nathan Queensland 4111 Australia. **Tel** 011 61 7 2757111, FAX 07 875 7730. **LC** IN PROCESS.

●US/1063-634X
CULTUREFRONT (NEW YORK, N.Y.). (CULTUREFRONT.). [Culturefront]. **Added/Corp** New York Council for the Humanities. **VFOAT** Culture Front. Vol. 1, No. 1 (May 1992)-. Periodical. English. Three times a year. $15.00 individuals, $25.00 institutions US; add $8.40 postage Canada. New York Council for the Humanities, 198 Broadway, 10th Floor, New York NY 10038. **Tel** (212)233-1131, FAX (212)233-4607. **LC** CB3; .C85.
Desc: A journal of humanities, presenting news and a variety of views on the production, interpretation and politics of culture.

US/0163-3155
CURRENT CONTENTS. ARTS & HUMANITIES. **See** The Arts-Abstracting, Bibliographies and Statistics.

JA/0386-7293
CURRENT CONTENTS OF ACADEMIC JOURNALS IN JAPAN. THE HUMANITIES AND SOCIAL SCIENCES. [Curr. contents acad. j. Jpn., Humanit. soc. sci.]. **Added/Corp** Center for Academic Publications Japan. **VFOAT** Humanities and Social Sciences. (1974/1975)-. English. an. $122.00. **(Subscription address:** Kyowa Book Company Inc., 1 38 Kanda Jinbocho Chiyoda-ku, Tokyo 101 Japan.**)** **LC** AI19.J3; C85. **DD** 059/.956. ***Continues*** *Current Contents of Academic Journals in Japan.*

UK/0267-1972
CURRENT RESEARCH IN BRITAIN. THE HUMANITIES. (CURRENT RESEARCH IN BRITAIN. THE HUMANITIES : CRB.). [Curr. res. Br., Humanit.]. **Added/Corp** British Library. Lending Division. **VFOAT** CRB. Humanities. 1st Ed. (1985)-. English. an. £40.00 UK; £44.00 other. British Library / Lending Division, Boston Spa, Wetherby West Yorkshire LS 237BQ England. **Tel** 0937 546060, FAX 0937 546333, telex 557381. **LC** AZ188.G7; C87. **DD** 001.3/072041. ***Continues in part*** *Research in British Universities, Polytechnics and Colleges.*

BG/1013-543X
DACCA UNIVERSITY STUDIES. PART A, THE. **See** The Arts.

JA/0386-1082
DAITO BUNKA DAIGAKU KIYO. JINBUN KAGAKU. [Daito Bunka Daigaku kiyo. Jinbun kagaku]. **VFOAT** Bulletin of Daito Bunka University. Humanities. (1975)-. Periodical. Multiple languages. an. **DD** _a060. ***Continues in part*** *Daito Bunka Daigaku Kiyo (1972), 0386-1066.*
Ind/Abst MLA Int. Bibl. Books Artic. Mod. Lang. Lit.

CN/0418-4297
DAUGAVAS VANAGU MENESRAKSTS. **Added/Corp** Daugavas Vanagi (Organization). Centrala Valde. **VFOAT** D V Menesraksts. (Jan./Feb. 1965)-. Periodical. Latvian. bm. Daugavas Vanago Publishing Co, 125 Broadview Avenue, Toronto Ontario M4M 2E9 Canada. **LC** AP95.L4; D35. ***Continues*** *Daugavas Vanagi, 0416-7805.*
Ind/Abst Am. Bibliogr. Slavic East Europ. Stud.

FR/0246-2346
DEBAT, LE. No. 1 (May 1980)-. Periodical. French. ir (5 issues per year). 348.68F France and French overseas departments and territories; 374.00F other. Editions Gallimard, 5 rue Sebastien Bottin, 75328 Paris Cedex 7 France. **Tel** 011 33 1 49544200. **(Subscription address:** Editions Gallimard Services Abonnements, 49 rue de la Vanne, 92126 Montrouge France.**)** **LC** AP20; .D36. **DD** 054/.1. Index available. **Circ:** 5,200.
Ind/Abst Int. Polit. Sci. Abstr.; PAIS Int. Print (1991-).

UK/0965-156X
DEBATTE OXFORD. (DEBATTE.). (1992)-. Periodical. English. sa (spring and fall). $84.00. Carfax Publishing Company, PO Box 25 Abingdon, Oxfordshire OX14 3UE England. **Tel** 011 44 235 555335, FAX (0279)31067, telex 817484.
Desc: Studies in the humanities for modern Germany.

GW
DELPHIN. **See** The Arts.

FR/0419-1633
DIOGENE (EDITION FRANCAISE). (DIOGENE.). [Diogene]. **Added/Corp** International Council for Philosophy and Humanistic Studies. Unesco. (Nov. 1952)-. Periodical. French (English). Four times a year. 166.50F France; 170.00F French Territories and Possessions; 187.00F other. Editions Gallimard, 5 rue Sebastien Bottin, 75328 Paris Cedex 7 France. **Tel** 011 33 1 49544200. **(Subscription address:** Sodis, 128 Avenue Mal Lattre Tass, BP 149, 77043 Lagny France.**)** **DD** 100.
Ind/Abst Int. Polit. Sci. Abstr.; Philos. Index.

IT/0392-1921
DIOGENES (ENGLISH ED.). **See** Philosophy.

US/0887-0551
DIRECTORY OF GRANTS IN THE HUMANITIES. [Dir. grants humanit.]. (1986)-. Directory. English. an (Apr.). $84.50 North America; $101.40 others. Oryx Press, 4041 North Central Avenue, #700, Phoenix AZ 85012-3397. **Tel** (800)279-ORYX, (602)265-2651, FAX (602)265-6250, (800)279-4663, (800)279-6799. **(Subscription address:** Eurospan Ltd., Journals and Serials Division, 3 Henrietta Street, Covent Garden, London WC2E 8LU England.**)** **LC** AZ188.U5; D56. **DD** 001.
Desc: Contains over 2,500 funding programs that support research or performance in literature, language, ethics and fine arts. Each entry includes a program describing functions, goals, restrictions and deadlines.

SP
DIRIGIDO POR ... . Spanish. Dirigido Por SA, RBLA de Catalunya 108/3, 08008 Barcelona Spain.

US/0419-4209
DISSERTATION ABSTRACTS INTERNATIONAL. A, THE HUMANITIES AND SOCIAL SCIENCES. [Diss. abstr. int., A, Humanit. soc. sci.]. **Added/Corp** University Microfilms. Xerox University Microfilms. University Microfilms International. Vol. 30, No. 1 (July 1969)-. English. mo. $1,700 US and Canada; $2,025 other. University Microfilms International, 300 North Zeeb Road, Ann Arbor MI 48106-1346. **Tel** (313)761-4700, (800)521-0600 Exts. 2490, 2491, FAX (313)973-1540. **LC** Z5053; .D57. **DD** 011/.7. **NLM** Z 5055.U5 D615. Index available (free). available on microfiche from University Microfilms International (UMI). ***Continues*** *Dissertation Abstracts. A, Humanities and Social Sciences, 0095-9154.*
Ind/Abst AgBiotech News Inf.; Agric. Eng. Abstr. (1991-); Agrofor. Abstr. (19??-19??); Dairy Sci. Abstr.; Field Crop Abstr.; For. Prod. Abstr. (1991-); For. Abstr.; Hortic. Abstr.; Index Vet.; Irr. Drain. Abstr.; Leis. Recreat. Tour.

Abstr.; Linguist. Lang. Behav. Abstr.; Maize Abstr.; MLA Int. Bibl. Books Artic. Mod. Lang. Lit.; Music Index; Nematol. Abstr.; Nutr. Abstr. Rev., Ser. B, Live Feeds and Feed.; Nutr. Abstr. Rev., Ser. A, Hum. Exp.; Ornamental Hort. (1991-); Pig News Inf.; Popul. Index; Postharvest News Inf.; Potato Abstr.; Poult. Abstr.; Protozoolog. Abstr.; Recent. Publ. Artic.; Rev. Agric. Entomol.; Rev. Med. Vet. Entomol.; Rice Abstr.; Rural Dev. Abstr.; Seed Abstr.; Soc. Plann. Policy Dev. Abstr.; Sociol. Abstr.; Soils Fert.; Sorghum Mill. Abstr.; Soyabean Abstr.; Sug. Indus. Abstr.; Wheat Barley Trit. Abstr.; World Agric. Econ.

AU/0419-4225
DISSERTATIONEN DER UNIVERSITAT WIEN. **See** Science and Technology.

NE
DOCUMENTATIEBLAD / LEIDEN AFRIKA-STUDIECENTRUM. ***Title Change.*** **See** Social Sciences-Abstracting, Bibliographies and Statistics.

BE/0774-6318
DODONAEUS. [Dodonaeus]. (1962)-. Periodical. French. bm. Dodonaeus, 21 Plaslaar, Lier Belgium. **UDC** 582.852.

GW/0012-6063
DREI (STUTTGART, GERMANY : 1948). (DIE DREI : ZEITSCHRIFT FUER WISSENSCHAFT, KUNST, UND SOZIALES LEBEN.). **Added/Corp** Anthroposophische Gesellschaft in Deutschland. (1948)-. Periodical. German. Twelve times a year. DM55.00. Verlag Freies Geistesleben, Haussmanstrasse 76, D 70188 Stuttgart Germany. **[CCC].** ***Continues*** *Anthroposophie.*

US/0094-3037
EAST CENTRAL EUROPE. [East cent. eur.]. **VFOAT** Europe du Centre-Est. V. 1- 1974-. Periodical. English (French, Italian, German and Russian). sa. $20.00 (one year), $63.00 (three year). CMTS USC / Charles Schlacks Jr. Publisher, 734 West Adams Boulevard, Kerckhoff Hall, Los Angeles CA 90089. **Tel** (203)743-6510. **ED** Charles Schlacks Jr. **LC** DR2; .E16. **DD** 914.3/03/05. **Bk Rev. Ad Acc. Circ:** 300 (ctrl). available on microfilm and microfiche from University Microfilms International (UMI).
Desc: Studies on East Germany, Poland, Czechoslovakia and Hungary in the humanities and social sciences.
Ind/Abst Am. Hist. Life (1974-); Am. Bibliogr. Slavic East Europ. Stud.

JA
EIGO SEINEN. THE RISING GENERATION. **VFOAT** The Rising Generation. Periodical. Japanese (English). mo. $150.00. **(Subscription address:** Kyowa Book Company, Inc., 1-38 Kanda Jinbo-Cho, Chiyoda-Ku Tokyo 101, Japan**)**
Ind/Abst MLA Int. Bibl. Books Artic. Mod. Lang. Lit.

CK
ESCRITOS. **Added/Corp** Medelln, Colombia. Universidad Pontificia Bolivariana. Facultad de Filosofia y Letras. No. 1 (July 1974)-. Periodical. Spanish. ir. Free. University Pontificia Bolivariana, Facultad de Filosofia y Letras, Medellin-Colombia. **Tel** 011 57 4 497116. **ED** Carlos Enrique Londono. **LC** AS82.M4; A2. **Bk Rev. Circ:** 600.
Desc: Theory and application on Columbian and Latinamerican texts, concerning science, philosophy, and literature. Feature education perspectives, projections and special concerns. Information on linguistics and language teaching.

US/0361-5634
ESSAYS IN ARTS AND SCIENCES. [Essays arts sci.]. **Added/Corp** University of New Haven. Vol. 1, (1971)-. English. an (Fall). $10.00 (individual), $.00 (institutions) standing order; $15.00 with institutions & individual standing order. New Haven University, 300 Orange Avenue, West Haven CT 06516. **Tel** (203)932-7000. **ED** E. E. David Sloane Jewell. **LC** AS36; .N34515. **DD** 081. **Bk Rev. Pr Rev. Circ:** 500 (ctrl).
Desc: Interdisciplinary journal devoted to a broad range of subjects.
Ind/Abst Abstr. Engl. Stud.; Lit. Crit. Regist.; Middle East Abstr. Index; MLA Int. Bibl. Books Artic. Mod. Lang. Lit.; Romant. Move.

SP
ESTUDIOS HUMANISTICOS. GEOGRAFIA, HISTORIA, ARTE. **VFOAT** Geografia, Historia, Arte. Vol. 6 (1984)-. Spanish. an. Universidad de Leon / Filosofia, Facultad de Filosofia y Letras, Leon Spain. ***Continues in part*** *Estudios Humanisticos.*

BL
ESTUDOS UNIVERSITARIOS. Vol. 1- 1970-. Portuguese. Universidade Federal de Pernambuco, Cidade Universitaria, Recife Brazil. **LC** AS80.A1; E857.

FR/0338-361X
ETUDES CORSES. **Added/Corp** Association des Chercheurs en Sciences Humaines, Domaine Corse. Centre National de la Recherche Scientifique (France). No. 1 (1973)-. Periodical. French. sa.
Ind/Abst BHA : Biblio. Hist. Art.

FR/0014-1941
ETUDES (PARIS. 1897). (ETUDES.). [Etudes]. **Added/Corp** Jesuits. (1897)-. Periodical. French. Eleven times a year. 440.74F France; 550.00F other. Assas Editions, 14 rue d'Assas, 75006 Paris France. **Tel** 011 33 1 44394848, FAX 011 33 1 40490192. ***Continues*** *Etudes Religieuses, Philosophiques, Historiques et Litteraires.*
Ind/Abst Am. Hist. Life (1955, 1964-); Int. Labour Doc.; MLA Int. Bibl. Books Artic. Mod. Lang. Lit.; New Testam. Abstr.; Philos. Index; Point Repere (1983-); Abr. Cathol. Period. Lit. Index; Cathol. Period. Lit. Index.

FR/0153-9221
ETUDES VAUCLUSIENNES. **Added/Corp** Faculte des Lettres et Sciences Humaines d'Avignon. Departement d'Histoire. Faculte des Lettres et Sciences Humaines d'Avignon. Departement de Geographie. (19??)-. Periodical. French. sa. 80F. Etudes Vauclusiennes, Facutle des Lettres et des Sciences Humanies, 5 rue Violette, 84000 Avignon France. **LC** DC611.V356; E83. **Circ:** 1,000.
Ind/Abst BHA : Biblio. Hist. Art.

US/0098-2474
EXPLORATIONS IN RENAISSANCE CULTURE. [Explor. Renaiss. cult.]. Vol. 1 (1974)-. English. an (Winter). Free (members); $10.00 (non-members). Explorations Renaissance Culture, A. W. Fields, PO Box 44612, USL Station, Lafayette LA 70503. **Tel** (318)231-6857. **ED** Albert W. Fields. **LC** CB361; .E9. **DD** 940/.21. **Ad Acc. Pr Rev. Circ:** 400 (ctrl).
Desc: Interdisciplinary journal of Renaissance studies and an academic journal.
Ind/Abst Annu. Bibliogr. Engl. Lang. Lit.; MLA Int. Bibl. Books Artic. Mod. Lang. Lit.

US/1043-2493
EXPLORATIONS. SPECIAL SERIES. [Explor., Spec. ser.]. **Added/Corp** Levy Humanities Series (Organization). **VFOAT** Special Series. Vol. 1 (1987)-. English. an (publlished in winter). $10.00. Explorations Renaissance Culture, A. W. Fields, PO Box 44612, USL Station, Lafayette LA 70503. **Tel** (318)231-6857. **ED** Albert W. Fields. **DD** 909. **Pr Rev. Circ:** 500.
Desc: Academic articles on literature, history and art of the Rennaissance.
Ind/Abst MLA Int. Bibl. Books Artic. Mod. Lang. Lit.

GW/0179-8367
FEMINIST, DER. **See** Women's Interests.

US/0897-1323
FLORA LEVY LECTURE IN THE HUMANITIES, THE. (U.S. DISTRIBUTION JOURNAL.). [Flora Levy lect. humanit.]. **Added/Corp** University of Southwestern Louisiana. Vol. 1 (1980)-. English. BMT Publications Inc, Seven Penn Plaza, New York NY 10001. **Tel** (800)223-9638, (212)594-4120. **DD** 001.
Ind/Abst Bus. Index (1988-); Gen. BusinessFile (1988-); Gen. Period. Index (1988-).

SP/0015-5594
FOLIA HUMANISTICA. [Folia humanist.]. Vol. 1 (Jan. 1963)-. Periodical. Spanish. bm. $70.00. Editorial Glarma S A, Londres 17, Madrid 28 Spain. **(Subscription address:** International Subscription Inc., 30 Montgomery Street, 7th Floor, Jersey City, NJ 07302; Phone: (800)544-6748 or (201)451-9420**)** **LC** AS301; .F64. Documents available from The Genuine Article.
Ind/Abst Am. Hist. Life (1967-1985); ARTbibliogr. Mod.; Arts Humanit. Citation Index [Full Cov.]; Curr. Contents Arts Humanit.; Res. Alert [Full Cov.]; Soc. Sci. Cit. Index [Select. Cov.].

DK/0105-712X
FOLK OG FORSKNING / UDG. AF UNIVERSTETSFORENINGEN FOR DET SYDLIGE OG VESTLIGE JYLLAND. **Added/Corp** Universtetsforeningen for det Sydlige og Vestlige Jylland. No. 1 (1977)-. Periodical. Danish. Four times a year. kr100.00 Denmark; $20.00 US. Universitetsforeningen for det Sydlige, 09 Vestlige Jylland, Sekretariat: Irisvej 14, DK 6700 Esbjerg Denmark. **Tel** 05142745. **ED** Ann Bilde MacLaurin. **LC** AS281.A1; F64. Index available. cum. index. **Bk Rev. Circ:** 2,000 (ctrl).
Desc: Disseminating results within maritime medicine, fishery economics, east and west studies. Regional development, agriculture, farming, thrombosis research and migration information is also included.

US/0015-6000
FOLLIA DI NEW YORK. (1893)-. Periodical. Italian (English). mo. $33.00 US; $63.00 other. Italian National Magazine Company, Incorporated, 111 Patterson Street, Hoboken NJ 07030. **Tel** (212)966-5420. **Bk Rev. Ad Acc.** ctrl circ.
Desc: Contains original poems, cultural articles and book reviews concentrating on the Italian experience and the cultural facets of the immigrant to USA and Canada.

IT
FONDAMENTI. (1985)-. Periodical. Italian (summaries and/or abstracts in English). Three times a year. Giardini Editori Stampatori, Via Santa Bibbiana 28, 56127 Pisa Italy. **Tel** 011 39 50 934242.

US/0743-2259
FOOTWORK. **Added/Corp** Passaic County Community College (N.J.). (198?)-. Periodical. English. an. $5.00. Passaic County College, College Boulevard, Cultural Affairs, Paterson NJ 07509. **Tel** (201)684-6555, (201)684-5904. **Bk Rev. Ad Acc. *Continues*** *Footwork Magazine.*
Desc: Literary publication containing poetry and fiction.
Ind/Abst Am. Humanit. Index; Index Am. Period. Verse.

SA/0015-8054
FORT HARE PAPERS. **See** Science and Technology.

US/0533-0130
FRANKLIN LECTURES IN THE SCIENCES AND HUMANITIES, THE. **See** Social Sciences.

UK/0957-1558
FRENCH CULTURAL STUDIES. **VFOAT** FCS. Vol. 1, No. 1 (Feb. 1990)-. Periodical. English. Three times a year. £44.00 (institutions), £23.00 (individuals) UK; $95.00 (institutions), $49.00 (individuals) North & South America & Japan; £47.00 (institutions), £25.00 (individuals) other. Alpha Academic, Mill Lane, Chalfont St Giles, Buckingham HP8 4NR England. **Tel** 44 494 872509. **LC** DC415; .F74. **CODEN** FCUSEP.
Desc: A unique journal devoted to publishing original research across the broad spectrum of of modern and contemporary French culture. Its prime concern is to foster serious academic work on French culture in literature, cinema, the media, visual arts, and cultural policy.
Ind/Abst Acad. Search (July 1993-); Humanit. Source (Jul. 1993-).

JA
FUKUOKA DAIGAKU JINBUN RONSO. **Main/Corp** Fukuoka Daigaku. Kenkyujo. **VFOAT** Fukuoka University Review of Literature and Humanities. Japanese (English). qt. Fukuoka Daigaku Kenkyusho, 8-19-1 Nanakuma Jonan-ku, Fukuoka 814-01 Japan. **LC** AS552.F95; A25. **Circ:** 920.

US/1064-0037
FURMAN HUMANITIES REVIEW. [Furman humanit. rev.]. **Added/Corp** Furman University. Vol. 1 (May 1988)-. Periodical. English. an (published in April or May). Free. Furman Department of Classical and Modern Languages, Furman University, Greenville SC 29613. **Tel** (803)294-2000. **ED** David Bost (803)294-3177. **LC** AS30; .F86. **DD** 001.3/05. **Pr Rev. Circ:** 1,250.
Desc: Publishes undergraduate papers in the humanities.

US/0190-4701
FURMAN STUDIES. [Furman stud.]. **Added/Corp** Furman University. Vol. 31, No. 5 (Winter 1949)-. Periodical. English. an. Free. Furman University, Greenville SC 29613. **Tel** (803)294-3152. **ED** Gilbert Allen. **LC** AS36; .F86. **DD** 051. **Bk Rev. Ad Acc. Circ:** 500. ***Continues*** *Furman University Studies.*
Desc: Contains essays relating to the liberal arts. Most authors are members of the Furman community.
Ind/Abst Annu. Bibliogr. Engl. Lang. Lit.; MLA Int. Bibl. Books Artic. Mod. Lang. Lit.; Romant. Move.

US/1059-3454
GARLAND REFERENCE LIBRARY OF THE HUMANITIES. [Garland ref. libr. humanit.]. **VFOAT** Reference Library of the Humanities. (19??)-. Monographic series. English. ir. Garland Publishing, 1000A Sherman Avenue, Hamden CT 06514. **Tel** (800)627-6273, (203)281-4487, FAX (203)230-1186. **LC** UNC. **DD** 001.
Ind/Abst Math. Rev.; MLA Int. Bibl. Books Artic. Mod. Lang. Lit.

US/0894-9832
GENDERS (AUSTIN, TEX.). (GENDERS.). [Genders]. (Spring 1988)-. Periodical. English. Three times a year. $40.00 (institution), $24.00 (individual). New York University Press, 70 Washington Square South, New York NY 10012. **Tel** (212)998-2575. **(Subscription address:** New York University Press, Order Department, 70 Washington Square South, New York NY 10012.**)** **ED** Ann Kibbey. **LC** NX1; .G6. **DD** 700/.5. **[CCC]. Bk Rev. Ad Acc. Circ:** 700 (ctrl). available on microfilm and microfiche from University Microfilms International (UMI). Documents available from UMI Article Clearinghouse.
Desc: Art and humanity journal with a primary interest in gender studies, exploring the definitions of gender as expressed in art, literature, history and films.
Ind/Abst Am. Hist. Life (1988-); Am. Humanit. Index; Annu. Bibliogr. Engl. Lang. Lit.; Arts Humanit. Citation Index [Full Cov.]; BHA : Biblio. Hist. Art; Curr. Contents Arts Humanit.; Expand. Acad. Index (1992-); Film Lit. Index (19??-); MLA Int. Bibl. Books Artic. Mod. Lang. Lit.; Newsp. Period. Abstr. (1992-); Soc. Plann. Policy Dev. Abstr.; Soc. Sci. Cit. Index [Select. Cov.]; Women Stud. Abstr.

●US
GERMANIC NOTES AND REVIEWS. **VFOAT** GNR. Vol. 23, No. 1 (Spring 1992)-. Periodical. English (German). Twice a year (Mar. & Sept.). $10.00 US; $11.00 other. Bemidji State University, c/o R. Krummel, Department of Modern Classical Language, Bemidji MN 56601. **Tel** (218)751-6265. **ED** Richard F. Krummel. **LC** PD1; .G38. **Bk Rev. Ad Acc. Pr Rev. Circ:** 500 (ctrl). Documents available from The Genuine Article. ***Continues*** *Germanic Notes, 0016-8882.*
Desc: All aspects of literature, history, and folklore of German-speaking countries, Low Countries, and Scandinavia.
Ind/Abst Arts Humanit. Citation Index [Full Cov.]; Curr. Contents Arts Humanit.; Res. Alert [Full Cov.]; Soc. Sci. Cit. Index [Select. Cov.].

BN/0350-0020
GODISNJAK - AKADEMIJA NAUKA I UMJETNOSTI BOSNE I HERCEGOVINE. CENTAR ZA BALKANOLOSKA ISPITIVANJA. (GODISNJAK / ANNUAIRE / ACADEMIE DES SCIENCES ET DES ARTS DE BOSNIE-HERZEGOVINE.). [God. - Akad. nauka umjet. Bosne Herceg., Cent. balk. ispit.]. **Added/Corp** Akademija Nauka i Umjetnosti Bosne i Hercegovine. Centar za Balkanoloska Ispitivanja (Akademija Nauka i Umjetnosti Bosne i Hercegovine). **VFOAT** Annuaire. (1966)-. Serbo-Croatian (Roman). an. ***Continues*** *Godisnjak (Naucno Drustvo Bosne i Hercegovine).*
Ind/Abst MLA Int. Bibl. Books Artic. Mod. Lang. Lit.

GW
GOTTINGER MISZELLEN. No. 1-. Periodical. Multiple languages (English and French). bm. DM65.00 US. Redaktion Seminar fur Agyptologie der Universitat, 34 Gottingen, Prinzenstrasse 21, Gottingen Germany. **Tel** 0551-394400. **LC** DT56.8; .G63. Index available.
Desc: Ancient Egypt (Pharyonic to Coptic) including art, history, religion, language, literature and method.
Ind/Abst Art Archaeol. Tech. Abstr.

GW/0017-1549
GOTTINGISCHE GELEHRTE ANZEIGEN. (GOTTINGISCHE GELEHRTE ANZEIGEN / UNTER DER AUFSICHT DER GESELLSCHAFT DER WISSENSCHAFTEN.). [Gott. gel. Anz.]. **Added/Corp** Akademie der Wissenschaften in Gottingen. Gesellschaft der Wissenschaften zu Gottingen. (1802)-. Periodical. German. ir (2 double issues per year). DM84.00. Vandenhoeck & Ruprecht, Robert Bosch Breite 6, D-37079 Goettingen Germany. **Tel** 011 49 551 695911, FAX 011 49 551 695917, telex 965226 VAN d. **[CCC].** Index available (free). cum. index. **Bk Rev**. ctrl circ. ***Continues*** *Gottingische Anzeigen von Gelehrten Sachen.*
Ind/Abst Annu. Bibliogr. Engl. Lang. Lit.; BHA : Biblio. Hist. Art; Romant. Move.

US/0436-306X
GRANDS DOCUMENTS. LES EDITIONS DE MINUIT. **VFOAT** Les Editions de Minuit. French. 7 rue Bernard Palissy, Paris 75006 France. **DD** 080.

GW/0017-3185
GRANI. **See** General Interest-General Interest-Europe.

PO/0434-9415
GULBENKIANA. Vol. 1 (1960)-. Portuguese. Centro de Estudos Historicos Ultramarinos, Calcada da Boa Hora, 30 Palacio de Ega, 14406393 Portugal. **DD** 946.9.

JA/0367-4061
GUNMA DAIGAKU KYOYOBU KIYO. [Gunma Daigaku Kyoyobu kiyo]. **Added/Corp** Gunma Daigaku. Kyoyobu. **VFOAT** Gunma Journal of Liberal Arts and Science. (1967)-. Japanese (English; summaries and/or abstracts in English). an. **CODEN** GDKKAX. Documents available from CASDDS.
Ind/Abst Chem. Abstr.

TU
HACETTEPE UNIVERSITY BULLETIN OF HUMANITITES. Bulletin. an. $4.00. Hacettepe University Turkish, Middle East Soc & Econ Research, Institute Beytepe Ankara Turkey. **Acid Free.**
Ind/Abst Am. Hist. Life (1969-1977).

US/0198-6449
HALCYON (RENO). (HALCYON.). [Halcyon]. 1979-. Periodical. English. an. $10.00. Nevada Humanities Committee Inc, PO Box 8029, Reno NV 89507. **Tel** (702)784-6587. **ED** Wilbur Shepperson. **LC** AP2; .H14. **DD** 051. cum. index. **Circ:** 3,000.
Desc: Includes guest articles and essays of general humanistic interest.
Ind/Abst Am. Hist. Life (1981-); West. Hist. Q.

UA
HAWLIYAT KULLIYAT AL-INSANIYAT WA-AL-ULUM AL-IJTIMAIYAH. **VFOAT** Bulletin of the Faculty of Humanities and Social Sciences. Periodical. Arabic (English). an. University of Qatar, PO Box 2713, Doha Qatar. **LC** AS587.D38; A2. **DD** 059/.927.

GR
HELLENIKA VIVLIA. GREEK BOOKS. **VFOAT** Greek Books. (1975)-. Monographic series. Greek, Modern (English). ir. Price varies per volume. Society of Macedonia Studies, Ethnikis Amynis 4, GR 546 21 Thessaloniki Greece. **Tel** 011 30 31 271195. Index available in last issue of volume--attached.

FI/0439-5530
HORISONT. (KULTURTIDSKRIFTEN HORISONT.). [Horisont]. (1954)-. Periodical. Swedish. Six times a year. $25.00 Europe; $36.00 other. Sven Erik Klinkmann, Henrikagatan 7 9 4 N, 65320 Vasa Finland. **UDC** 82.

PR/0018-5027
HORIZONTES (PONCE, P.R.). (HORIZONTES.). [Horizontes]. **Added/Corp** Catholic University of Puerto Rico. Vol. 1, No. 1 (Oct. 1957)-. Periodical. Spanish. Twice a year (Apr. & Oct.). $7.50 Puerto Rico; $8.50 others. Universidad Catolica Puerto Rico, Avendia Las Americas, Ponce PR 00731. **Tel** (809)841-2000.
Ind/Abst Am. Hist. Life (1967-1976, 1979-); ARTbibliogr. Mod. (1984-); MLA Int. Bibl. Books Artic. Mod. Lang. Lit.

US/1055-1182
HRD DIGEST AND ABSTRACTS. ***Ceased.*** (1991)-(1992). Periodical. English. mo. Inventure Publications / College Park, 4431 Lehigh Road, Suite 162, College Park MD 20740.

HK
HSIN YA HSUEH SHU CHI KAN. NEW ASIA ACADEMIC BULLETIN. **Main/Corp** Chinese University of Hong Kong. New Asia College. **Added/Corp** Chinese University of Hong Kong. New Asia College. New Asia Academic Bulletin. **VFOAT** New Asia Academic Bulletin. (1978)-. Academic Scholarly Publication. English (Chinese). ir. Chinese University of Hong Kong, New Asia College, Shatin New Territories Hong Kong. **Tel** 0-633111. **LC** PL2274; .H65a. **DD** 809. **Circ:** 1,000.
Desc: Carries academic articles on a specific topic such as East-West comparative literature, Confucianism, China's management reforms, anthropology, etc.

US/0742-2075
HUDSON VALLEY REGIONAL REVIEW, THE. (THE HUDSON VALLEY REGIONAL REVIEW : HVRR.). [Hudson Val. reg. rev.]. **Added/Corp** Bard College. Center. **VFOAT** HVRR. Vol. 1, No. 1 (Mar. 1984)-. Periodical. English. sa (Mar. and Sept.). $10.00 institutions; $8.00 individuals. Hudson Valley Studies / Bard College, Room 200 Box 180, Tewksbury, Ammandale-on-the-Hudson NY 12504. **Tel** (914)758-6971. **ED** Richard Wiles & William Wilson. **LC** F127.H8; H87. **DD** 974.7/3. Index available in last issue of volume--attached. cum. index. **Bk Rev**, (Qty: 8). **Circ:** 700 (ctrl).
Desc: A journal of regional studies, both historical and contemporary, encompassing the arts, humanities, etc., with special emphasis on the Hudson Valley region.
Ind/Abst Am. Hist. Life.

US/1045-6767
HUMAN NATURE (HAWTHORNE, N.Y.). (HUMAN NATURE : AN INTERDISCIPLINARY BIOSOCIAL PERSPECTIVE.). [Hum. nat.]. Vol. 1, No. 1 (1990)-. Periodical. English. qt (Jan., Apr., July, Oct.). $145.00. Walter de Gruyter Inc. / Hawthorne, 200 Saw Mill River Road, Hawthorne NY 10532. **Tel** (914)747-0110, GERMANY: 011/49/30/260050, FAX (914)747-1326, telex 646677. **ED** Jane B. Lancaster (University of Mexico). **LC** GN365.9; .H86. **DD** 304.5/05. **NLM** W1; HU448ML. **CODEN** HNATER. **[CCC].**
Desc: Dedicated to advancing the interdisciplinary investigation of the biological, social and environmental factors that underlie human behavior.
Ind/Abst Int. Bibliogr. Sociol.; Psychol. Abstr.; Soc. Plann. Policy Dev. Abstr.; Sociol. Abstr.; Mag. Index.

US/0742-115X
HUMANA CIVILITAS. V. 1-. Monographic series. English. ir. Price varies per volume. Undena Publications, PO Box 97, Malibu CA 90265. **Tel** (310)649-2612. **Circ:** 500.
Desc: History, philosophy, religion, and science under the auspices of the Center for Medical and Renaissance studies, UCLA.

DK/0903-2401
HUMANIORA (COPENHAGEN, DENMARK : 1988). (HUMANIORA.). 1988-. Periodical. Danish. sa. Kr75.00 Denmark; Kr128.00 North America; Kr104.00 other. Forskningsdirektoratet, H C Andersens Boulevard 40, 1553 Copenhagen V Denmark. **Tel** +45 33 11 43 99, FAX +45 33 32 35 01, telex 15652 FS. **ED** Peter Schoening. **Circ:** 2,500 (ctrl).
Desc: A presentation of results from selected research projects financed by the Danish Research Council for the Humanities. In addition all new projects are listed.

GW/0439-884X
HUMANISMUS UND TECHNIK. **See** History(General).

GW
HUMANISTISCHE BIBLIOTHEK. REIHE III: SKRIPTEN. **Added/Corp** Munich. Universitat. Seminar fur Philosophie und Geistesgeschichte des Humanismus. Centro Italiano di Studi Umanistici e Filosofici. Vol. 1, (1972)-. Monographic series. German. ir. Price varies per volume. Wilhelm Fink Verlag, Ohmstrasse 5, D 80802 Munich Germany. **Tel** 011 49 89 348017, 348018.

GW/0018-7445
HUMANITAS BERLIN, DDR. ***Ceased.*** (1961)-(19??). Newspaper. German. bw (26 issues per year). VEB Verlag und Gesundheit GMBH, Neue Grunestrasse 18, D-10179 Berlin, Germany. **Tel** 011 49 30 2700516. **UDC** 61. **CODEN** 614.

FR/0242-6870
HUMANITE PARIS, L'. (L'HUMANITE.). [Humanite Paris]. (1904)-. Periodical. French. da. 2460.00F. L'Humanite, 5 Bis rue Jean Juares, F-93528 Saint Denis France. **Tel** 011 33 1 49227323. **UDC** 07.

CN/0229-4699
HUMANITIES ASSOCIATION OF CANADA NEWSLETTER. [Humanit. Assoc. Can. newsl.]. **VFOAT** Bulletin de l'Association Canadienne des Humanites; HAC Newsletter; Bulletin de l'ACH; Humanities Newsletter; Bulletin des Humanites. Newsletter. English (French). Three times a year. Free to members. Humanities Association of Canada, Canterbury College, 172 Patricia Road, Windsor Ontario N9B 3B9 Canada. **ED** J Gordon Haggert. **DD** 001.3/06/071.

US/0882-5475
HUMANITIES EDUCATION. ***Title Change.*** [Humanit. educ.]. **Added/Corp** National Association for Humanities Education. Vol. 1, No. 1 (Jan. 1984)-(19??). Periodical. English. qt. National Association for Humanities Education, University of Minnesota, Department of Philosophy, and Humanities, Duluth MN 55812. **Tel** (218)726-8237. **ED** Fred E H Schroeder. **DD** 001. **Bk Rev. Ad Acc. Circ:** 500. ***Continues*** *Humanews.* ***Continued by*** *Interdisciplinary Humanities, 1056-6139.*
Desc: Dedicated to the teaching of integrated studies among the humanities arts and related fields in schools, colleges, and museums.

US/0018-7577
HUMANITIES IN THE SOUTH. (HUMANITIES IN THE SOUTH : NEWS-LETTER OF THE SOUTHERN HUMANITIES CONFERENCE.). [Humanit. South]. **Added/Corp** Southern Humanities Conference. No. 1 (April 1951)-. Periodical. English. Twice a year. $25.00 institutions; $20.00 individuals. Southern Humanities Council, University of Tennessee at Chattanooga, Chattanooga TN 37403. **Tel** (615)755-4153. **LC** WMLC L 83/4657.
Ind/Abst Abstr. Engl. Stud. (Fall 1985-); Am. Humanit. Index; Lit. Crit. Regist.; MLA Int. Bibl. Books Artic. Mod. Lang. Lit.

US/0095-5981
HUMANITIES INDEX. **See** Humanities-Abstracting, Bibliographies and Statistics.

US/0095-5981
HUMANITIES INDEX. CD-ROM. (1985)-. English. qt ((annual cumulations)). $1,295.00. H W Wilson Company, 950 University Avenue, Bronx NY 10452. **Tel** (800)367-6770, (718)588-8400, FAX (718)590-1617, telex 4990003 HWILSON. **ED** Joanna Greenspan. Index available. cum. index. ctrl circ. available on diskette from WILSONSEARCH; available on an online database from WILSONLINE; available on magnetic tape from WILSONTAPE; available in print.
Desc: Author and subject index to periodicals in the fields of archaeology and classical studies, area studies, folklore, history, language and literature, literary and political criticism, performing arts, philosophy, religion and theology and related subjects.

●US/1073-1962
HUMANITIES SOURCE. **See** Humanities-Abstracting, Bibliographies and Statistics.

US/0018-7526
HUMANITIES (WASHINGTON). (HUMANITIES / NATIONAL ENDOWMENT FOR THE HUMANITIES.). [Humanities]. **Added/Corp** National Endowment for the Humanities. Vol. 1, No. 1 (Jan./Feb. 1980)-. Government Publication. English. bm. $15.00 domestic; $18.75 other. Superintendent of Documents, US Government Printing Office, Washington DC 20402. **Tel** (202)275-3328, FAX (202)786-2377. **ED** Mary Lou Beatty. **LC** LB2301; .H83. Index available. cum. index. **Circ:** 4,000 (ctrl). available on microfilm and microfiche from University Microfilms International (UMI). ***Continues*** *National Endowment for the Humanities. Humanities, 0018-7526.*
Desc: Review of current work and thought in the humanities. Informs potential applicants, grantees, and the public about the current programs and activities of the agency.
Ind/Abst Can. Period. Index (19??-); Curr. Index J. Educ.; Leis. Recreat. Tour. Abstr.

GW/0018-7615
HUMBOLDT SPANISCHE AUSGABE. (1960)-. Periodical. Spanish. tq. Free on request. Inter Nationes EV, Postfach 200749, D 53137 Bonn Germany. **Tel** 11 49 2288801, FAX 11 49 228 880355, telex 228308. **ED** Margaret Kraft. **UDC** 009(7-8) = 60 = 690. **Bk Rev. Circ:** 12,000 (ctrl).
Desc: Covers German / Latin American cultural relations.

JA
IBARAKI DAIGAKU JIMBUNGAKUBU KIYO : JIMBUNGAKUKA RONSHU. **Main/Corp** Ibaraki Daigaku. Jimbungakuka. **VFOAT** Studies in Humanities. French (Japanese). Ibaraki Daigaku Jimbungakubu, 1-1 Bunkyo 2-chome, Mito Japan. **Tel** 0292-26-1621. **LC** AS552.I2; A25. **Circ:** 250 (ctrl). ***Continues*** *Ibaraki Daigaku Jimbungakubu Kiyo: Bungakuka Ronshu.*
Desc: A university bulletin that treats theses of history, literature, philosophy, and psychology.

NE/0923-7135
INCOGNITA (LEIDEN, NETHERLANDS). ***Ceased.*** (INCOGNITA.). Vol. 1, (1990)-(199?). Periodical. English. Twice a year. E. J. Brill, Postbus 9000, 2300 PA Leiden Netherlands. **Tel** 011 31 71 312624, FAX 011 31 71 317532, telex 39296 BRILL NL. **ED** I P Couliano. **[CCC].**

US/0191-0574
INDEX TO SOCIAL SCIENCES & HUMANITIES PROCEEDINGS. See Social Sciences.

II/0378-2964
INDIAN HORIZONS. [Indian horiz.]. **Added/Corp** Indian Council for Cultural Relations. Vol. 21 (Jan. 1972)-. Periodical. English (Spanish, French and Arabic). Four times a year (Jan., Apr., July, Oct.). Indian Country Cultural Relations, Azad Bhavan Indraprastha Estate, New Delhi 110002 India. **Tel** 3319310. **(Subscription address:** Prints India, 11 Darya Ganj, New Delhi 110002 India.**) ED** Ashok Srinivasan. **LC** DS501; .I36. **DD** 915.4/005. **Bk Rev. Circ:** 1,400 (ctrl). available on microfilm and microfiche from University Microfilms International (UMI). Documents available from The Genuine Article. ***Continues*** *Indo-Asian Culture, 0019-7203.*
Desc: Journal of Indian culture and the arts, of cultural relations, past and present, between India and the world. Contents include articles, fiction, reviews, and brief notices of new books.
Ind/Abst Am. Hist. Life (1955-1964, 1968-); Arts Humanit. Citation Index (19??-19??) [Full Cov.]; Curr. Contents Arts Humanit.; MLA Int. Bibl. Books Artic. Mod. Lang. Lit.; Res. Alert [Full Cov.].

XR/0231-5386
INFORMACNI PRIRUCKA / CESKOSLOVENSKA AKADEMIE VED. See Societies and Clubs.

BL/0100-0365
INFORME CIENCIA E ARTE : BOLETIM. V. 1- Sept./Oct. 1973-. Bulletin. Portuguese. Universidade Federal de Sao Carlos, KM 235 Caica Postal 384, Sao Carlos Brazil. **LC** AS80.U55; A26.

KO
INMUN KWAHAK. Added/Corp Songgyungwan Taehakkyo (Seoul, Korea). Pusol Inmun Kwahak Yonguso. **VFOAT** Journal of the Humanities. (1971)-. Periodical. Korean (summaries and/or abstracts in English and French). **LC** AS559.S49; A15.
Ind/Abst MLA Int. Bibl. Books Artic. Mod. Lang. Lit.

FR
INRIATHEQUE. French. Institut National de Recherche et Informatique en Automatique Sedis Diffusion, Dom Voluceau Rocqnct, BP 105, 78153 Le Chesnay Cedex France. **Tel** 011 33 1 39635627, telex 697033 F.

FR
INTELLECTICA / REVUE DE L'ARC. (19??)-. French. sa. 189.57F France; 250.00F other. Lish CNRS, 54 BD de Raspail, 75270 Paris France. **Tel** 011 33 1 49542000. **(Subscription address:** EC2, 269 rue de la Garenne, 92024 Nanterre Cedex France.**)**

US/1055-0542
INTELLIGENT SYSTEMS : THE NEWSLETTER OF THE FOUNDATION FOR INTELLIGENT SYSTEMS IN THE SOCIAL SCIENCES, ARTS & HUMANITIES. See Social Sciences.

●US/1056-6139
INTERDISCIPLINARY HUMANITIES. (INTERDISCIPLINARY HUMANITIES: DEDICATED TO THE TEACHING OF INTEGRATED STUDIES AMONG THE HUMANITIES, ARTS AND RELATED FIELDS IN SCHOOLS, COLLEGES AND CULTURAL INSTITUTIONS.). [Interdiscip. humanit.]. **Added/Corp** National Association for Humanities Education (U.S.). Vol. 9, No. 1 (Winter 1992)-. Periodical. English. Four times a year. $20.00. National Association for Humanities Education, University of Minnesota, Department of Philosophy, and Humanities, Duluth MN 55812. **Tel** (218)726-8237. **LC** AZ183.U5; I585. **DD** 001.3. ***Continues*** *Humanities Education, 0882-5475.*

US/1042-4032
INTERNATIONAL JOURNAL OF HUMANITIES AND PEACE, THE. [Int. j. humanit. peace]. **VFOAT** IJHP. Vol. 6, No. 7 (Spring 1989)-. English. an (occasionally 2 volumes). $18.00 one year; $25.00 other. International Journal Humanities Peace, 1436 North Evergreen Drive, Flagstaff AZ 86001. **Tel** (602)774-4793. **ED** Dr. Vasant V. Merchant. **LC** AS9; .I58. **DD** 001.3/05. **CODEN** IJHAEM. **Bk Rev**, (Qty: 5-6). ctrl circ. ***Continues*** *Arizona Humanities Association Journal.*
Desc: This annual is a non-profit, educational, voluntary, and tax deductible organization. It is dedicated to the pursuit of excellent in Humanities-Education-Peace and a global vision and universal understanding among ethnic and culturally diverse groups nationally and internationally.

US/0896-2294
INTERNATIONAL JOURNAL ON THE UNITY OF THE SCIENCES. *Suspended.* See Science and Technology.

CN/0825-0456
INTERNATIONAL SEMIOTIC SPECTRUM. [Int. semiot. spectr.]. **VFOAT** Semiotic Spectrum. **VAT** ISS. International Semiotic Spectrum. No. 1 (Jan. 1984)-. Periodical. English. sa. $20.00 U.S. Toronto Semiotic Circle, c/o Victoria College, NAB 305, 73 Queen's Park Crescent East, Toronto Ontario M5S 1K7 Canada. **Tel** (416)585-4456. **ED** Paul Bouissac. **DD** 001.51. Index available. cum. index. **Bk Rev. Ad Acc. Circ:** 7,000 (ctrl).
Desc: Publishes concise articles (state-of-the-art in AI, Cognitive Science, Communication, Semiotics) with illustrations, bibliographies and short book reviews. Also reports on semiotic activities worldwide (associations, conferences, and publications).

GW
INTERNATIONALE BIBLIOGRAPHIE DER ZEITSCHRIFTENLITERATUR AUS ALLEN GEBIETEN DES WISSENS. See Literary and Political Reviews-Abstracting, Bibliographies and Statistics.

IT
INTERSEZIONI. Vol. 1, No. 1 (April 1981)-. Periodical. Italian. tq. L68000.00 Italy; L120000.00 (surface mail), L140000.00 (airmail) other. Societa Editrice il Mulino, Strada Maggiore 37, 40125 Bologna Italy. **Tel** 011 39 51 256011, FAX 011 39 51 256034. **ED** Andrea Battistini. **LC** CB3; .I5. **Bk Rev. Circ:** 1,500.
Desc: Deals with history of ideas, which can serve as a crossroad for research in various sectors: philosophy, history of science, criticism, sociology and psychology.

PH
IPC PAPERS: INSTITUTE OF PHILIPPINE CULTURE. Monographic series. English. ir. Price varies per volume. Institute of Philippine Culture, PO Box 154, Ateneo Manila Univ, Manila Philippines.

IT/0392-7601
ITALICA ROMA. (1982)-. Spanish. an. **UDC** 902.
Ind/Abst BHA : Biblio. Hist. Art.

BE/0774-2851
JAARBOEK - ARCA LOVANIENSIS ARTES ATQUE HISTORIAE RESERANS DOCUMENTA. See The Arts.

GW/0373-9767
JAHRBUCH DER AKADEMIE DER WISSENSCHAFTEN IN GOTTINGEN. See The Arts.

CN/0448-9179
JAUNA GAITA. [Jauna gaita]. **Added/Corp** American Latvian Youth Association. Jauna Gaita. Celinieks. Jauna Gaita. No. 1 (1955)-. Periodical. Latvian. qt. 28.00Can$ Canada; $28.00 other. Jauna Gaita, 23 Markland Drive, Etobicoke ONT M9C 1M8 Canada. **Tel** (905)621-0898. **ED** L. Zandbergs. Index available. cum. index. **Bk Rev.** ctrl circ.
Ind/Abst Am. Bibliogr. Slavic East Europ. Stud.; MLA Int. Bibl. Books Artic. Mod. Lang. Lit.

JA/0386-8729
JIMBUN GAKUHO TOKYO. 1950. [Jimbun gakuho Tokyo. 1950]. **VFOAT** Journal of Social Sciences and Humanities (Tokyo. 1950). (1950)-. Periodical. Multiple languages. **DD** _a060.
Ind/Abst Am. Hist. Life (1954-1972).

UK/0449-0789
JOHN COFFIN MEMORIAL LECTURE, THE. Added/Corp University of London. (19??)-. Monographic series. English. ir. Price varies per volume. Humanities Press, 165 1st Avenue, Atlantic Highlands NJ 07716. **Tel** (908)872-1441, (800)221-3845, FAX (908)872-0717, telex 752233.

US/0021-8510
JOURNAL OF AESTHETIC EDUCATION, THE. [J. aesthet. educ.]. **Added/Corp** Illinois. Office of the Superintendent of Public Instruction. University of Illinois (Urbana-Champaign Campus). **VFOAT** Aesthetic Education. (Spring 1966)-. Periodical. English. qt. $42.00 (one year), $75.60 (two year), institutions; $28.00 (one year), $50.40 (two year), individuals. University of Illinois Press, 1325 South Oak Street, Champaign IL 61820. **Tel** (217)333-0950, FAX (217)244-8082. **ED** Ralph A. Smith. **LC** N1; .J58. **DD** 701.1707. **CODEN** JAEDBT. **[CCC].** Index available (bound in Oct. issue). **Bk Rev. Ad Acc. Circ:** 1,200. available on microfilm and microfiche from University Microfilms International (UMI). Documents available from The Genuine Article.
Desc: Articles on arts and humanities, aesthetics, administration and policy.
Ind/Abst Abstr. Engl. Stud.; Annu. Bibliogr. Engl. Lang. Lit.; Art Index; ARTbibliogr. Mod.; Arts Humanit. Citation Index [Full Cov.]; BHA : Biblio. Hist. Art; Book Rev. Index; Contents Pages Educ.; Curr. Contents Arts Humanit.; Curr. Index J. Educ.; Educ. Index; Educ. Technol. Abstr.; Film Lit. Index; Music Artic. Guide; Philos. Index; Psychol. Abstr. (1968-); PsycINFO (?-?); PsycLit; Res. Alert [Full Cov.]; Soc. Sci. Cit. Index [Select. Cov.]; Sociol. Educ. Abstr.

SA/0258-9001
JOURNAL OF CONTEMPORARY AFRICAN STUDIES : JCAS. VFOAT JCAS; J.C.A.S. Vol. 1 Oct. (1981)-. Academic Scholarly Publication. English. Twice a year (June and December). $30.00. Institute Society & Economic Research, Rhodes University, PO Box 94, Grahamstown 6140, South Africa. **Tel** 11 27 461 22023 ext 550. **ED** Denis Ventes. **LC** DT1; .J67. **DD** 960/.05. Index available. **Bk Rev. Ad Acc. Circ:** 1,000 (ctrl).
Desc: An interdisciplinary journal of writing in the human sciences promoting scholarly understanding of developments and change in Africa.
Ind/Abst Int. Bibliogr. Sociol.; Int. Labour Doc.; Rice Abstr.

US/1048-597X
JOURNAL OF ERITREAN STUDIES. ***Ceased.*** (JOURNAL OF ERITREAN STUDIES : JES.). [J. Eritrean stud.]. **Added/Corp** Research and Information Centre on Eritrea (Rome, Italy). **VFOAT** JES. Vol. 1, No. 1 (Summer 1986)-(19??). Periodical. English. sa. Research and Information Centre on Eritrea, PO Box 894, Grambling LA 71245. **LC** DT391; .J68. **DD** 963/.5/005.

MW
JOURNAL OF HUMANITIES (ZOMBA, MALAWI). (JOURNAL OF HUMANITIES : JH). **VFOAT** JH. No. 1 (April 1987)-. English. an. K5.00 Malawi; $4.00 US. University of Malawi / Humanities, Chancellor College, Faculty of Humanities, PO Box 280, Zomba Malawi. **Tel** 522222. **ED** Didier N Kaphagawani. **LC** AS621.A1; J68. **DD** 001.3/096897. **Bk Rev. Ad Acc.**

US/1041-3545
JOURNAL OF MEDICAL HUMANITIES, THE. See Medical Science and Technology.

UK
JOURNAL OF MEDITERRANEAN STUDIES. *Title Change.* (19??)-(19??). English. sa. Frank Cass & Company Ltd, Newbury House, 890-900 Eastern Avenue, Newbury Park, Ilford, Essex IG2 7HH United Kingdom. **Tel** 011 44 81 599 8866, FAX 011 44 81 599 0984, telex 897719. ***Continued by*** *Mediterranean Historical Review.*

MM/1016-3476
JOURNAL OF MEDITERRANEAN STUDIES. Added/Corp University of Malta. Mediterranean Institute. **VFOAT** JMS. Vol. 1, No. 1 (1991)-. Periodical. English (French and Italian). sa (Jan., July). $55.00 (individual), $100.00 (institution) US; $25.00 (individual), $50.00 (institution) other. Mediterranean Institute, University of Malta, Msida Malta. **Tel** 011 356 333903-6 331734, FAX 011 356 336450. **(Subscription address:** Turpin Distribution Services Limited, Blackhorse Road, Letchworth, Hertfordshire SG6 1HN, United Kingdom.**) ED** Dr. Paul Sant Cassia (phone: 44 91 374 2870). **LC** DE1; .J695. **DD** 909/.09822. **CODEN** JMESEP. **Bk Rev**, (Qty: 15-20). **Ad Acc, Adv Mgr:** Tita Bonnica, **Tel** 356 343572. **Circ:** 200. available on CD-ROM and an online database.
Desc: Deals with Mediterranean societies and cultures in History, Art, Literature, Classics, and Anthropology and Archaeology.
Ind/Abst Anthropol. Lit.; Int. Bibliogr. Sociol.

●US/1060-149X
JOURNAL OF PRE-RAPHAELITE STUDIES (1992), THE. (JOURNAL OF PRE-RAPHAELITE STUDIES.). [J. pre-Raphael. stud.]. **VFOAT** JPRS. (1992)-. Periodical. English. Twice a year. $40.00 (institutions), $25.00 (individuals). Kutztown University / Art Department, Professor Lisa Norris,

Kutztown PA 19530. **Tel** (215)683-4000. **ED** Lisa Norris. **DD** 700. **Bk Rev. Pr Rev. Circ:** 450. *Continues Journal of Pre-Raphaelite and Aesthetic Studies, 0835-7099.*
Desc: Covers art, literature, aesthetic theory, and cultural history, mainly in Great Britain, from the Victorian period to the end of the 19th century.
Ind/Abst Annu. Bibliogr. Engl. Lang. Lit.; BHA : Biblio. Hist. Art; MLA Int. Bibl. Books Artic. Mod. Lang. Lit.; RILA, Int. Rep. Lit. Art; Soc. Sci. Cit. Index [Select. Cov.].

PK
JOURNAL OF SOCIAL SCIENCES & HUMANITIES. See Social Sciences.

KO/0023-4044
JOURNAL OF SOCIAL SCIENCES AND HUMANITIES (SEOUL). (JOURNAL OF SOCIAL SCIENCES AND HUMANITIES.). [J. soc. sci. hum.]. **Added/Corp** Hanguk Yonguwon (Seoul, Korea). (19??)-. Periodical. English. sa. **LC** DS901; .H322. **DD** 951.9/005. *Continues Bulletin of the Korean Research Center.*
Ind/Abst Am. Hist. Life (1975-); Int. Bibliogr. Sociol.

II/0022-4855
JOURNAL OF TAMIL STUDIES. [J. Tamil stud.]. **Added/Corp** International Association of Tamil Research. International Institute of Tamil Studies. Vol. 1 & 2, (Apr. 1969)-. Periodical. English (Tamil). Twice a year (June, Dec.). $12.00. International Institute of Tamil Studies, CPT Campus Adyar, Madras 600113 India. **Tel** 011 91 44 412992. **ED** S. Chellappau and K. Subbiah Pillai. **LC** PL4758.A2; J65. **Bk Rev**. **Circ:** 1,000 (ctrl). *Supersedes Tamil Culture.*
Desc: Areas of language and literature, linguistics, drama, folk arts, music, dance, costumes, grammar comparative literature and palm leaf manuscripts.
Ind/Abst MLA Int. Bibl. Books Artic. Mod. Lang. Lit.

US/0361-5154
JOURNAL OF THE HUMANITIES AND SOCIAL SCIENCES. 1975-. English. an. $4.00. Virginia State College, Box 57, Petersburg VA 23803. **LC** E185.5; .J82. **DD** 973/.04/96073.

II
JOURNAL OF THE MADRAS UNIVERSITY. SECTION A, HUMANITIES. **Added/Corp** University of Madras. Vol. 15, No. 1 (July 1943)-. English. Twice a year. Rs33.00. University of Madras Registrar, University Building Chepauk, Madras 600 005 India. **LC** AS472; .M152. **DD** 001.3/05. *Continues in part Journal of the Madras University.*

PK/0034-5431
JOURNAL OF THE RESEARCH SOCIETY OF PAKISTAN. See Social Sciences.

CN/0228-1635
JOURNAL OF UKRAINIAN STUDIES. [J. Ukr. stud.]. **Added/Corp** Canadian Institute of Ukrainian Studies. **VFOAT** Journal; Zhurnal. **VAT** Zurnal Ukrajinoznaucyh Studij. Vol. 5 No. 1 (Spring 1980)-. Periodical. English (Ukrainian). Twice a year (Summer and Winter). $15.00 (individual); $20.00 (institution). Canadian Institute of Ukrainian Studies, University of Alberta, 352 Athabasca Hall, Edmonton Alberta T6G 2E8 Canada. **Tel** (403)492-2972, FAX (403)492-4967, telex 037-2023. **ED** Dr. Zenon Kohut. **LC** DK508.A2; J68. **DD** 947/.71/005. cum. index. **Bk Rev**. **Circ:** 800 (ctrl). *Continues Journal of Ukrainian Graduate Studies, 0701-1792.*
Desc: Articles, surveys, and reviews about subjects and books dealing with Ukraine and Ukrainians in the past and present in the areas of the humanities and the social sciences.
Ind/Abst Am. Hist. Life (1988-); Am. Bibliogr. Slavic East Europ. Stud. (19??-19??); MLA Int. Bibl. Books Artic. Mod. Lang. Lit.

JA/0911-0682
JUNSHIN GAKUHO. [Junshin gakuho]. **VFOAT** Annual Report of Modern Humanities Institute. (1982)-. Periodical. Multiple languages. an. **DD** 200.
Ind/Abst Am. Hist. Life (1954-1962).

JA
KANAZAWA DAIGAKU KYOYOBU RON SHU: JIMBUN KAGAKU HEN. Main/Corp Kanazawa Daigaku. Kyoyobu. **VFOAT** Studies in Humanities. Began in 1964. Multiple languages (Japanese and German). 1-1 Marunouchi, Kanazawa Japan. **LC** AS552.K26; A27.

US/0022-8745
KANSAS QUARTERLY. See General Interest-General Interest-North America.

US/0191-1031
KENTUCKY REVIEW (LEXINGTON. 1979), THE. (THE KENTUCKY REVIEW.). [Ky. rev.]. **Added/Corp** University of Kentucky Library Associates. Vol. 1, (Autumn 1979)-. Periodical. English. Three times a year (Jan., May, Sept.). $10.00. The Kentucky Review, C/O K. Ellenberg, University of Kentucky Libraries, Lexington KY 40506-0039. **Tel** (606)257-8408, FAX (606)257-1563. **ED** Bradley Carrington and Gordon Hogg. **LC** AS30; .K46. **DD** 051. Index available. cum. index. **Ad Acc. Circ:** 1,200-1,400 (ctrl).
Desc: Articles and interviews relating to American, English, and world literature, history, philosophy, art, architecture, music, folklore, typography, cinema, or other topics in the humanities.
Ind/Abst Am. Humanit. Index; BHA : Biblio. Hist. Art; Lit. Crit. Regist.; MLA Int. Bibl. Books Artic. Mod. Lang. Lit.

GW/0170-0391
KHIPU. See The Arts.

NR/0331-8168
KIABARA. (KIABARA : JOURNAL OF THE HUMANITIES, UNIVERSITY OF PORT HARCOURT.). [Kiabara]. **Added/Corp** University of Port Harcourt. School of Humanities. (June 1978)-. Periodical. English (Niger-Kordofanian). Twice a year (June & Dec.). N7.00 (institutions), N5.00 (individuals). University of Port Harcourt, PMB 5323 School of Humanities, Port Harcourt Nigeria. **LC** AS633.A1; K52. **DD** 070.5/94/096694.
Ind/Abst MLA Int. Bibl. Books Artic. Mod. Lang. Lit.

PH
KINAADMAN. WISDOM. See History(General)-History of Asia.

JA
KOCHI DAIGAKU KYOIKU GAKUBU KENKYU HOKOKU. DAI 2-BU. VFOAT Bulletin of the Faculty of Education, Kochi University. Series 2. Began with No. 19- published in 1967. Japanese (Japanese). Kochi Daigaku Kyoiku Gakubu, 5-ban 1-go Akebono-cho 2-chome, Kochi-shi-Japan. **LC** AS552.K5245; A24. *Continues in part Kochi Daigaku Kyoiku Gakubu Kenkyu Hokoku.*

KO
KOREA OBSERVER. Added/Corp Hanguk Haksul Yonguwon (Korea). **VFOAT** Hanguk Haksul Yongu. Vol. 1, No. 1 (Oct. 1968)-. Periodical. English. qt. $40.00 (one year), $68.00 (two year). Institute of Korean Studies, CPO Box 3410, Seoul 100-634 Korea. **Tel** 82 2 569 5574, FAX 82 2 564 1190. **ED** In June Kim, Myungsoon Shin and Joon Koo Lee. **LC** DS901; .K717. **DD** 915.19/03/05. Index available. cum. index. **Bk Rev** (Qty: 4). **Ad Acc, Adv Mgr:** B.Y. Kim. **Circ:** 3,000 (ctrl).
Desc: For the purpose of encouraging Korean studies, especially within the humanities and social sciences, and for promoting cultural exchanges with other nations.
Ind/Abst Int. Bibliogr. Sociol.; PAIS Int. Print (1991-).

KO
KOREANA. See The Arts-Art.

RM
KORUNK. (1926)-. Periodical. Hungarian. mo. $54.00. **(Subscription address:** Orion Press SRL, SPL Independentei 202-A, Bucharest 6 Romania.) **LC** AP82; .K65.
Desc: Socio-cultural and political review.
Ind/Abst MLA Int. Bibl. Books Artic. Mod. Lang. Lit.

IT
KOS : RIVISTA DI CULTURA E STORIA DELLE SCIENZE MEDICHE, NATURALI E UMANE DIRETTA DA MASSIMO PIATTELLI PALMARINI. See Science and Technology.

GW/0724-343X
KULTUR CHRONIK. See The Arts.

RU
KULTURA I KULTURNOE STROITELSTVO. Added/Corp Informtsentr po Problemam Kultury I Iskusstva (Soviet Union) Soviet Union. Ministerstvo Kultury. (19??)-. Russian. 0.36rub (single issue). Gosudarstvennaia Biblioteka, Informatsionnyi Tsentr, Imeni V. I. Lenina, Prospekt Kalinina 3, 121019 Moscow Russia. **LC** Z5579; .K84; CB428.

PL/0023-5172
KULTURA I SPOECZENSTWO. [Kult. spoecz.]. **Added/Corp** Polska Akademia Nauk. Zakad Socjologii i Historii Kultury. (1957)-. Periodical. Polish. qt. **LC** AS261; .P624.
Ind/Abst Am. Hist. Life (1957-1970,1975-); Soc. Plann. Policy Dev. Abstr.

SW/0083-6796
KUNGL. VITTERHETS-, HISTORIE- OCH ANTIKVITETSAKADEMIENS ARSBOK. [K. Vitterh.- hist.- antikvitetsakad. arsb.]. (1926)-. Periodical. Swedish. an. **UDC** 061.1:930.85.
Ind/Abst BHA : Biblio. Hist. Art.

JA
KYODO KENKYU KATSUDO HOKOKUSHO. See Social Sciences.

JA
KYOYO RONSO. Added/Corp Hogaku Kenkyu. Keio Gijuku Daigaku. Hogaku Kenkyukai. (19??)-. Periodical. Multiple languages (Japanese, English and German). qt. ¥500 Japan; ¥300 US. Keio Gijuku Daigaku Hogaku Keknyukai, 15-45 Mita 2-chome Minato-ku 108, Tokyo Japan. **Tel** 03-453-4511. **ED** S Taguchi. **LC** AS552.K36; A3. Index available. cum. index. **Circ:** 1,300.
Desc: The articles included are mostly the theses on English, French and German languages and literatures by the scholars attached to the law department of Keio University.

US/0275-410X
LAMAR JOURNAL OF THE HUMANITIES. [Lamar. J. Humanit.]. **Added/Corp** Lamar University. College of Liberal Arts. Lamar University. **VFOAT** Journal of the Humanities. (1975)-. Periodical. English. sa (May and Nov.). $6.00. Lamar University / College of Arts, PO Box 10023, Beaumont TX 77710. **Tel** (409)880-8596. **ED** Ronald H. Fritze. **LC** AS30; .L35. **DD** 051. **Bk Rev. Pr Rev. Circ:** 300.
Desc: Publishes articles of inter-disciplinary or general interest in the fields of literature, history, contemporary culture, and in the fine arts.
Ind/Abst Am. Hist. Life (1986-); MLA Int. Bibl. Books Artic. Mod. Lang. Lit.

IT/0393-6813
LATIUM. (LATIUM / ISTITUTO DI STORIA E DI ARTE DEL LAZIO MERIDIONALE, CENTRO DI ANAGNI.). [Latium]. **Added/Corp** Istituto di Storia e di Arte del Lazio Meridionale (Italy). Centro di Anagni. (1984)-. Italian. an.
Ind/Abst BHA : Biblio. Hist. Art.

GH
LEGON JOURNAL OF THE HUMANITIES. V. 1 (1974)-. Periodical. English. Ghana Publishing Corporation, Private Post Bag, Tema Ghana. **LC** AS631.A1; L43. **DD** 052.
Ind/Abst MLA Int. Bibl. Books Artic. Mod. Lang. Lit.

XV/0374-0315
LETOPIS SLOVENSKE AKADEMIJE ZNANOSTI IN UMETNOSTI. Added/Corp Akademija Znanosti in Umetnosti v Ljubljani. Slovenska Akademija Znanosti in Umetnosti. **VFOAT** Rapport sur l'Activite de la Bibliotheque de l'Academie Slovene des Sciences et des Arts; Yearbook of the Slovene Academy of Sciences and Arts; Yearbook of the Slovenian Academy of Sciences and Arts. (1942)-. Periodical. Slovenian. qt. **LC** AS346; L58. **NLM** W1 SL635.
Ind/Abst BHA : Biblio. Hist. Art.

SP/0210-3516
LETRAS DE DEUSTO. [Let. Deusto]. **Added/Corp** Universidad de Deusto. Facultad de Filosofia y Letras. Vol. 1 No. 1 (Jan./June 1971)-. Periodical. Spanish. Five times a year. $60.00. Ediciones Mensajero, Apartado 73, 48080 Bilbao Spain. **Tel** 011 34 94 4470358. **ED** Ignacio Elizalde.
Desc: Studies on literature, arts, history.
Ind/Abst Am. Hist. Life (1972-); Annu. Bibliogr. Engl. Lang. Lit.; MLA Int. Bibl. Books Artic. Mod. Lang. Lit.; Romant. Move.

FR/0335-1793
LIBERATION PARIS. 1973. (LIBERATION.). [Liberation Paris, 1973]. (1973)-. Newspaper. French. da. 2350.00F Switzerland; 1720.00F Belgium; 1655.24F France; 3180.00F other. Liberation, 11 rue Beranger, 75154 Paris Cedex 03 France. **Tel** 011 33 1 42761712. **UDC** 070.2(1-4)(44).

US/0024-2241
LIBRARY CHRONICLE OF THE UNIVERSITY OF TEXAS AT AUSTIN, THE. [Libr. chron. Univ. Tex. Austin]. **Added/Corp** University of Texas at Austin. General Libraries. University of Texas at Austin. Humanities Research Center. **VFOAT** Library Chronicle. New Ser., No. 1 (March 1970)-. English. Four times a year. $30.00 domestic; $50.00 overseas. Harry Ransom Humanities Research Center, The University of Texas Austin, PO Drawer 7219, Austin TX 78713-7219. **Tel** (512)471-8944, FAX (512)471-9646. **ED** Dave Oliphant. **LC** Z881; .T383. **DD** 027. Index available in last issue of volume--attached. **Ad Acc. Circ:** 300. available on microfilm from University Microfilms International (UMI). Documents available from The Genuine Article. *Continues Library Chronicle of the University of Texas, 0885-4351.*
Desc: Literary and art criticism, correspondence of authors and artists, theatre and film history, research in bibliography and book arts, reproduction of photographs and artworks.
Ind/Abst Abstr. Engl. Stud.; Am. Hist. Life (1970-); Annu. Bibliogr. Engl. Lang. Lit.; ARTbibliogr. Mod.; Arts Humanit. Citation Index [Full Cov.]; BHA : Biblio. Hist. Art; Curr. Contents Arts Humanit.; MLA Int. Bibl. Books Artic. Mod. Lang. Lit.; Res. Alert [Full Cov.]; Romant. Move.

US/0278-9671
LITERATURE AND MEDICINE. See Medical Science and Technology.

UK
M.H.R.A. Added/Corp Modern Humanities Research Association. No. 1 (April 1927)-. Bulletin. English. ir. Modern Humanities Research Association, Kings College Strand, London WC2R 2LS England. **Tel** 44 71 836 5454. **LC** PB1; .M15. *Supersedes Modern Humanities Research Association. Bulletin - Modern Humanities Research Association.*
Ind/Abst MLA Int. Bibl. Books Artic. Mod. Lang. Lit.

XN/0350-3089
MACEDONIAN REVIEW. [Maced. rev.]. **Added/Corp** Kulturen Zivot. Vol. 1 (1971)-. Periodical. English. Three times a year. $20.00. Macedonian Review, PO Box 85, Skopje Macedonia. **Tel** 011 38 91 239134, 011 38 91 226105. **ED** Boris Vishinski. Index available (bound in last issue). **Bk Rev. Ad Acc. Circ:** 5,000 (ctrl). available on microfilm from University Microfilms International (UMI).
Desc: Articles on Macedonian history, culture, literature and arts, as well as Macedonian short stories, poetry and book reviews.
Ind/Abst Am. Hist. Life (1971-); ARTbibliogr. Mod.; MLA Int. Bibl. Books Artic. Mod. Lang. Lit.

JA
MACHIKANEYAMA RONSO: SHIGAKUHEN. VFOAT Machikaneyama Ronso: History. No. 5- 1972-. Japanese (summaries and/or abstracts in English). Osaka Daigaku Bungakubu, 1-1 Machikaneyamacho, Toyonaka Osaka Japan. **Tel** (06)844-1151. **LC** D1; .M26. **Circ:** 400 (ctrl). ***Continues in part*** *Machikaneyama Ronso.*
Desc: Articles in human sciences containing philosophy, history, literature, arts, and Japanology.

JA/0387-4818
MACHIKANEYAMA RONSO : TETSUGAKUHEN. VFOAT Machikaneyama Ronso Philosophy. No. 5- 1972-. Japanese (summaries and/or abstracts in English). an. Osaka Daigaku Bungakubu, 1-1 Machikaneyamacho, Toyonaka Osaka Japan. **Tel** (06)844-1151. **LC** B8.J3; M28. **Circ:** 500 (ctrl). ***Continues in part*** *Machikaneyama Ronso.*

SZ
MACOLIN. German, French and Italian. mo. 33.00F. SIGWERB AG, PF 173 Dorfmattenstr 26, CH 5612 Villmergen Switzerland. **Tel** 011 41 57 230505, FAX 011 41 57 231550.

US/1052-018X
MAINE SCHOLAR, THE. [Me. sch.]. **Added/Corp** University of Maine System. Vol. 1, No. 1 (Autumn 1988)-. English. an (Nov.). $12.00 (individuals); $15.00 (institutions). The Maine Scholar, 96 Falmouth Street, Portland ME 04103. **Tel** (207)780-4330. **ED** Wanda P. Whitten (editor's address: 102 Bedford Street, Portland ME 04103, phone: (207)780-4749). **LC** WMLC L 83/7645. **DD** 001. **Pr Rev.**

SU
MAJALLAT KULLIYAT AL-ADAB WA-AL-ULUM AL-INSANIYAH. VFOAT Journal of the Faculty of Arts and Humanities. Periodical. Arabic (English). an. Faculty of Arts and Humanities, King Abdul Azia University Jeddah, PO Box 9032, Jeddah Saudi Arabia. **LC** AS599.4.A1; M34. **DD** 059/.927.

GR/0076-289X
MAKEDONIKA (THESSALONIKA). (MAKEDONIKA.). [Makedonika]. **Added/Corp** Hetaireia Makedonikp-son Spoudp-son. (1940)-. Periodical. Greek, Modern. an. $30.00. Society for Macedonian Studies, 4 Ethnikis Amynis Avenue, GR 546 21 Thessaloniki Greece. **Tel** 011 30 31 271195. cum. index. **Bk Rev**, (Qty: 4-5). **Circ:** 600 (ctrl).
Desc: History, archaeology, folklore and linguistics of north Greece.
Ind/Abst Am. Hist. Life (1955-); MLA Int. Bibl. Books Artic. Mod. Lang. Lit.

US/0025-2603
MANUSCRIPTA (ST. LOUIS, MO.). (MANUSCRIPTA.). [Manuscripta]. **Added/Corp** St. Louis University. Library. Pius XII Memorial Library. Vol. 1 (Feb. 1957)-. Academic Scholarly Publication. English. Three times a year. $20.00 US; $22.00 other. St Louis University / Library, Piux XII Memorial Library, 3650 Lindell Boulevard, St Louis MO 63108. **Tel** (314)658-3090, FAX (314)658-3108. **ED** Charles J Ermatinger. **LC** Z6602; .M36; Z810.V369. **DD** 091. cum. index. **Bk Rev**, (Qty: 15). **Circ:** 900. Documents available from The Genuine Article. ***Supersedes*** *Manuscripta, 0025-2603;* ***Continues in part*** *Historical Bulletin / St. Louis, 0361-5456.*
Desc: Scholarly articles directed at teaching or research in the humanities and history; also studies of the manuscripts in the collections of the Vatican Film Library.
Ind/Abst Abstr. Engl. Stud.; Am. Hist. Life (1953-); Am. Humanit. Index; Annu. Bibliogr. Engl. Lang. Lit.; Arts Humanit. Citation Index [Full Cov.]; BHA : Biblio. Hist. Art; Curr. Contents Arts Humanit.; Index Book Rev. Humanit.; Middle East Abstr. Index; MLA Int. Bibl. Books Artic. Mod. Lang. Lit.; Old Testam. Abstr.; Recent. Publ. Artic.; Res. Alert [Full Cov.]; RILA, Int. Rep. Lit. Art; Abr. Cathol. Period. Lit. Index; Cathol. Period. Lit. Index.

US/0025-4878
MASSACHUSETTS REVIEW, THE. [Mass. rev.]. **Added/Corp** University of Massachusetts (Amherst campus). Vol. 1 (Oct. 1959)-. Periodical. English. qt. $20.00 (one year), $35.00 (two year), $53.00 (three year) institutions, $15.00 (one year), $27.00 (two year), $40.00 (three year) individuals US; $25.00 (one year), $45.00 (two year), $68.00 (three year) institutions, $20.00 (one year), $37.00 (two year), $55.00 (three year) individuals other. Massachusetts Review, University of Massachusetts, Memorial Hall, Amherst MA 01003. **Tel** (413)545-2689. **ED** Mary Heath, Jules Chametzky and Paul Jenkins. **LC** AS30.M3; A22. **DD** 051. Index available. **Bk Rev. Ad Acc. Circ:** 2,000. available on microfilm and microfiche from University Microfilms International (UMI). Documents available from The Genuine Article, UMI Article Clearinghouse.
Desc: A beautifully printed magazine of literature, the arts and public affairs. Two outstanding features are its art reproductions and special issues. 172 pages of fiction poetry, literary criticism, and current events.
Ind/Abst Abstr. Engl. Stud.; Acad. Abstr. Full Text Elite (July 1990-); Acad. Abstr. (July 1990-); Acad. Ind. [Computer File] (1987-); Acad. Search (July 1990-); Am. Hist. Life (1968-); Am. Bibliogr. Slavic East Europ. Stud.; Am. Humanit. Index; Annu. Bibliogr. Engl. Lang. Lit.; ARTbibliogr. Mod.; Arts Humanit. Citation Index [Full Cov.]; BHA : Biblio. Hist. Art; Curr. Contents Arts Humanit.; Expand. Acad. Index (1987-); Film Lit. Index; Humanit. Index; Humanit. Source (Jul. 1990-); Index Am. Period. Verse; INFO-SOUTH Abstr.; Lit. Crit. Regist.; Mag. Search; MLA Int. Bibl. Books Artic. Mod. Lang. Lit.; Newsp. Period. Abstr. (1991-); Res. Alert [Full Cov.]; Romant. Move.; Soc. Plann. Policy Dev. Abstr.; Sociol. Abstr.

BE
MEDEDELINGEN VAN DE KONINKLIJKE ACADEMIE VOOR WETENSCHAPPEN, LETTEREN EN SCHONE KUNSTEN VAN BELGIE, KLASSE DER LETTEREN. **Main/Corp** Vlaanse Academie voor Wetenschappen, Letteren en Schone Kusten van Belgie. Klasse der Letteren. Vol. 1- 1939-. Dutch (English, German and French). ir. Koninklijke Academie voor Wetenschappen, Letteren en Schone Kunsten Van Belgie, Hertogsstraat 1, B-1000 Brussels Belgium. **Tel** 011 32 2 5112623, FAX 011 32 2 5110143. **ED** G Verbeke. Index available. cum. index. **Circ:** 800. Documents available from Ask*IEEE.
Desc: Proceedings of the humanities section of the Academy, containing articles related to history, philosophy, legal sciences, psychology, linguistics, theology, etc.
Ind/Abst BHA : Biblio. Hist. Art; INSPEC (1968-); Nematol. Abstr.

BE
MEDEDELINGEN VAN DE KONINKLIJKE ACADEMIE VOOR WETENSCHAPPEN, LETTEREN EN SCHONE KUNSTEN VAN BELGIE, KLASSE DER SCHONE KUNSTEN. **Added/Corp** Koninklijke Academie voor Wetenschappen, Letteren en Schone Kunsten van Belgiee. Klasse der Schone Kunsten. Vol. 34 (1972)-. Monographic series. Dutch (English). ir. Price varies per volume. Koninklijke Academie voor Wetenschappen, Letteren en Schone Kunsten Van Belgie, Hertogsstraat 1, B-1000 Brussels Belgium. **Tel** 011 32 2 5112623, FAX 011 32 2 5110143. **ED** G. Verbeke. **LC** NX5; .V58. Index available. **Circ:** 800. ***Continues*** *Mededelingen van de Koninklijke Vlaamse Academie voor Wetenschappen, Letteren en Schone Kunsten van Belgie, Klasse der Schone Kunsten.*
Desc: Proceedings of the fine arts section of the Academy, containing articles on fine arts and music.

US/0892-2772
MEDICAL HUMANITIES REVIEW. See Medical Science and Technology.

MM
MEDITERRANEAN STUDIES. VFOAT Journal of Mediterranean Studies. V. 1- Winter/Spring 1978-. Periodical. English (summaries and/or abstracts in French and Arabic). sa. $8.00 individual, $12.00 libraries, and institutions. Midsea Books Ltd, 3A Strait Street, Valletta Malta. **LC** DE1; .M43. **DD** 909/.09822. **UDC** 908.4-015. ***Formed by the union of*** *Journal of the Faculty of Arts (Royal University of Malta)* ***and*** *Economic and Social Studies (Valletta, Malta).*

FR/1157-075X
MEMOIRES. Main/Corp Academie des Sciences, Belles-Lettres et Arts de Savoie. 2nd Ser., Vol. 12 (1872); 3rd Ser., Vol. 1 (1873)- Vol. 12, (1887); 4th Ser., 4 Vol. 1 (1887)- Vol. 12 (1910); 5th Ser. Vol. 1 (1911)- Vol.12, (1951); 6th Ser. Vol. 1 -. Periodical. French. ***Continues*** *Academie Imperiale des Sciences, Belles-Lettres et Arts de Savoie. Memoires.*
Ind/Abst BHA : Biblio. Hist. Art.

FR/0182-628X
MEMOIRES - ACADEMIE DES SCIENCES, BELLES LETTRES ET ARTS D'ANGERS. [Mem. - Acad. sci., belles lett. Angers]. (1972)-. Periodical. French. **UDC** 908. ***Continues*** *Memoires - Academie des Sciences, Belles Lettres et Arts, 0182-6298.*
Ind/Abst BHA : Biblio. Hist. Art.

FR/0249-6747
MEMOIRES DE LA COMMISSION DES ANTIQUITES DU DEPARTEMENT DE LA COTE-D'OR. Main/Corp Commission des Antiquites du Departement de la Cote-d'Or. **Added/Corp** Academie des Sciences, Arts et Belles-Lettres de Dijon. (1832)-. French.
Ind/Abst BHA : Biblio. Hist. Art.

FR/0369-1896
MEMOIRES DE L'ACADEMIE DES SCIENCES, INSCRIPTIONS ET BELLES-LETTRES DE TOULOUSE. [Mem. Acad. sci., inscr. b.-lett. Toulouse]. **Main/Corp** Academie des Sciences, Inscriptions et Belles-Lettres de Toulouse. (1870)-. French. **CODEN** MSBTAG. ***Continues*** *Academie des Sciences, Inscriptions et Belles-Lettres de Toulouse. Memoires de l'Academie Imperiale des Sciences, Inscriptions et Belles-Lettres de Toulouse.*
Ind/Abst BHA : Biblio. Hist. Art.

BE/0373-7667
MEMOIRES ET PUBLICATIONS DE LA SOCIETE DES SCIENCES, DES ARTS ET DES LETTRES DU HAINAUT. See The Arts.

US/0069-8970
MEMOIRS OF THE CONNECTICUT ACADEMY OF ARTS AND SCIENCES. [Mem. Conn. Acad. Arts Sci.]. **Main/Corp** Connecticut Academy of Arts and Sciences. Vol. 1, Part 1 (1810)-. Monographic series. English. ir. Price varies per volume. Connecticut Academy of Arts and Sciences, PO Drawer 93A, Yale Station, New Haven CT 06520. **ED** James Thorpe III. **LC** Q11. Index available. **Bk Rev. Ad Acc.** ctrl circ. available on microfilm from University Microfilms International (UMI).

US/0026-2005
MICHIGAN ACADEMICIAN. [Mich. acad.]. **Added/Corp** Michigan Academy of Science, Arts, and Letters. Vol. 1 (Winter 1969)-. Periodical. English. qt (Feb., May, Aug., Nov.). $45.00 US; $50.00 other. Michigan Academy of Science Art & Letters, The University of Michigian, Argus Building II, 400 Fourth Street, Ann Arbor MI 48109-4816. **Tel** (313)936-2938, FAX (313)763-2447. **ED** Kathleen F. Duke. **LC** AS30; .M478. **DD** 051. **CODEN** MACDAH. Index available. cum. index. **Bk Rev**, (Qty: 8-12). **Pr Rev. Circ:** 1,100 (ctrl). Documents available from BIOSIS Document Express, CASDDS. ***Continues*** *Michigan Academy of Science, Arts, and Letters. Papers of the Michigan Academy of Science, Arts, and Letters, 0096-2694.*
Desc: Outstanding papers from those presented at annual meetings of Michigan Academy of Science, Arts and Letters. Subjects cover 35 different disciplines.
Ind/Abst Abstr. Anthropol.; Abstr. Engl. Stud.; AGRICOLA [Select. Cov.]; Am. Hist. Life (1969-); Annu. Bibliogr. Engl. Lang. Lit.; ARTbibliogr. Mod.; Biol. Abstr.; Chem. Abstr.; Curr. Geogr. Publ. (199?-); Film Lit. Index (19??-); GeoRef; Int. Aerosp. Abstr.; J. Econ. Lit.; MLA Int. Bibl. Books Artic. Mod. Lang. Lit.; Life Sci. Collect.; Psychol. Abstr.; Romant. Move.; Soc. Plann. Policy Dev. Abstr.; Sociol. Abstr.

US
MICHIGAN STUDIES IN THE HUMANITIES. Added/Corp Horace H. Rackham School of Graduate Studies. (1980)-. Monographic series. English. ir. University of Michigan / Michigan Slavic Publications, 3040 Modern Language Building, Ann Arbor MI 48108. **Tel** (313)763-4496.
Ind/Abst MLA Int. Bibl. Books Artic. Mod. Lang. Lit.

US/0026-637X
MISSISSIPPI QUARTERLY, THE. [Miss. q.]. **Added/Corp** Mississippi State University. College of Arts and Sciences. Mississippi State College. Social Science Research Center. Mississippi State University. Social Science Research Center. Vol. 7 (Oct. 1953)-. Periodical. English. qt (March/April, June/July, Oct./Nov., Jan./Feb.). $12.00 US; $16.00 other. Mississippi State University / The Mississippi Quarterly, Box 5272, Mississippi State MS 39762. **Tel** (601)325-3069, FAX (601)325-3299, telex 785045. **ED** Robert L. Phillips, Jr. **LC** AS30.M58; A2. **DD** 051. Index available ((published in fall)). **Bk Rev. Ad Acc. Pr Rev. Circ:** 900. available on an online database from University Microfilms International (UMI); available on microfilm. Documents available from The Genuine Article, UMI Article Clearinghouse. ***Continues*** *Social Science Bulletin.*
Desc: Publishes articles, notes, queries, and book reviews on materials in the humanities and the social sciences dealing with the South, past and present.
Ind/Abst Abstr. Engl. Stud.; Acad. Search (July 1993-); Am. Hist. Life (1963-); Am. Humanit. Index; Annu. Bibliogr. Engl. Lang. Lit.; Arts Humanit. Citation Index [Full Cov.]; Curr. Contents Arts Humanit.; Expand. Acad. Index (1989-); Humanit. Index; Humanit. Source (Jul. 1993-); INFO-SOUTH Abstr.; Lit. Crit. Regist.; Mag. Search; MLA Int. Bibl. Books Artic. Mod. Lang. Lit.; Newsp. Period. Abstr. (1991-); Res. Alert [Full Cov.]; Romant. Move.; Soc. Plann. Policy Dev. Abstr.; Soc. Sci. Cit. Index [Select. Cov.]; Sociol. Abstr.; West. Hist. Q.

US/0026-7503
MODERN AUSTRIAN LITERATURE. See Literature.

US/0093-5778
MONTCLAIR JOURNAL OF SOCIAL SCIENCES AND HUMANITIES, THE. ***Suspended.*** See Social Sciences.

JA/0027-0741
MONUMENTA NIPPONICA. See History(General)-History of Asia.

JA
MUGENDAI. Periodical. Japanese. qt. Free. Nihon Ai Bi Emu Kabushiki Kaisha, 2-12 Roppongi 3 Minato-ku, Tokyo-to 106 Japan. **Tel** 03-586-111, 03-589-0644. **ED** Shokichi Maeno. **LC** ML5; .M625. Index available. cum. index. **Bk Rev. Circ:** 45,000 (ctrl).
Desc: Main themes are: the relationship between science, technology and man, exchanges between different cultures, and Japanese studies.

TU
NASHRAH AL-IKHBARIYAH (RESEARCH CENTRE FOR ISLAMIC HISTORY, ART, AND CULTURE). See The Arts.

US/0077-2879
NASSAU REVIEW, THE. [Nassau rev.]. **Added/Corp** Nassau Community College. Vol. 1 (Spring 1964)-. English. an. Nassau Community College, Garden City NY 11530. **DD** 810.
Ind/Abst MLA Int. Bibl. Books Artic. Mod. Lang. Lit.

SA/1015-0935
NATAL MUSEUM JOURNAL OF HUMANITIES. Added/Corp Natal Museum (Pietermaritzburg, South Africa). **VFOAT** Journal of Humanities; Tydskrif vir Geesteswetenskappe; Natal Museum Tydskrif vir Geesteswetenskappe. Vol. 1 (July 1989)-. English (German and French). an. R70.00. Natal Museum, 237 Loop Street, Pietermaritzburg, 3201 South Africa. **Tel** 0331-51404. **ED** J Londt. **LC** AZ188.S6; N38. Index available. cum. index. **Pr Rev. Circ:** 200 (ctrl).

US/8755-5492
NATIONAL ENDOWMENT FOR THE HUMANITIES ... ANNUAL REPORT. [Annu. rep. - Natl. Endow. Humanit.]. **Main/Corp** National Endowment for the Humanities. **Added/Corp** National Endowment for the Humanities. Annual Report. **VFOAT** Annual report. (1979)-. English. an. Free. National Endowment for the Humanities, 1100 Pennsylvania Avenue NW, Washington DC 20506. **Tel** (202)786-0438. **DD** 001. ***Continues*** *National Endowment for the Humanities. Report, 8755-5514.*

US/8755-514X
NEBRASKA REVIEW (OMAHA, NEB.), THE. (THE NEBRASKA REVIEW.). [Neb. rev.]. **Added/Corp** University of Nebraska at Omaha. Creative Writing Program. Vol. 13, No. 1 (Winter 1984)-. Periodical. English. sa. $9.00. Nebraska Review, University of Nebraska Omaha, Writers Workshop, Omaha NE 68182-0324. **Tel** (402)554-2771. **ED** Art Homer. **LC** IN PROCESS. **DD** 810. **Ad Acc. Circ:** 650. ***Continues*** *Smackwarm, 0732-1198.*
Desc: Original poetry and fiction by contemporary writers. Dedicated to creative rather than critical writing.

SP/1130-0426
NEUVA REVISTA DE POLITICA, CULTURA Y ARTE. See Social Sciences.

US/0738-9671
NEW MEXICO HUMANITIES REVIEW. ***Ceased.*** [N.M. humanit. rev.]. Vol. 1, No. 1 (Jan. 1978)-No. 37 (1993). Periodical. English. tq. New Mexico Tech, Humanities Department, Box A, Socorro NM 87801. **Tel** (505)835-5445. **ED** Jerry Bradley and John Rothfork. **LC** PS501; .N474. **DD** 810/.8. Index available (first issue). cum. index. **Bk Rev**, (Qty: 20/yr). **Ad Acc. Circ:** 650 (ctrl).
Desc: Literature for general academic readership - poetry, fiction, essays, reviews, and art. Southwestern themes and interdisciplinary approaches.
Ind/Abst MLA Int. Bibl. Books Artic. Mod. Lang. Lit.

US/0028-6583
NEW REPUBLIC (NEW YORK, N.Y.). (THE NEW REPUBLIC.). [New repub.]. Vol. 1 (Nov. 7, 1914)-. Periodical. English. Forty-eight times a year. $69.97 (one year), $120.00 (two year). New Republic, 1220 19th Street Northwest, Washington DC 20036. **Tel** (202)331-7494. **(Subscription address:** Kable Publishers Aide, 308 East Hitt Street, Subscriptions Department, Mt. Morris, IL 61054) **ED** Michael Kinsley. **LC** AP2; .N624. **DD** 051. **Bk Rev. Ad Acc. Pr Rev. Circ:** 90,000. available on microfilm and microfiche from University Microfilms International (UMI); available on an online database (files 647,648/Full-Text) from DIALOG. Documents available from The Genuine Article, UMI Article Clearinghouse, Documents on Demand.
Desc: A journal of analysis and opinion. Facts and forecasts of current events. Reviews and essays on books, films, television, music and theatre.
Ind/Abst ABI/INFORM Glob. Ed.; ABI Inform Ondisc (March 1975-Oct. 1977); Abr. Read. Guide Period. Lit.; Acad. Abstr. Full Text Elite (Jan. 1984-Dec. 1986, July 1989-) [Full Txt.]; Acad. Abstr. (July 1989-); Acad. Ind. [Computer File] (1984-); Acad. Search (July 1989-); Am. Hist. Life (1955-1958); Am. Bibliogr. Slavic East Europ. Stud.; Annu. Bibliogr. Engl. Lang. Lit.; Arts Humanit. Citation Index [Select. Cov.]; Book Rev. Digest; Book Rev. Index; Crim. Justice Abstr.; Energy Inf. Abstr.; Environ. Abstr.; Expand. Acad. Index (1984-); Film Lit. Index; Gen. Period. Index (1985-); Hum. Rights Intern. Rep.; Index Am. Period. Verse; Index Period. Artic. Relat. Law (1977-); INFO-SOUTH Abstr.; Infobank (Jan. 1969-); Mag. Artic. Summar. Elite (Jan. 1984-Dec. 1986, July 1989-) [Full Txt.]; Mag. Artic. Summar. Select (Jan. 1984-Dec. 1986, July 1989-); Mag. Artic. Summar. CD-ROM (Jan. 1984-Dec. 1986, July 1989-); Mag. ASAP Plus [Full Txt.]; Mag. ASAP Sel. [Full Txt.]; Mag. Express (1986-) [Full Txt.]; Mag. Index Plus (1989-); Mag. Index Sel. Microfiche (1986-) [Full Txt.]; Mag. Index. Sel. (1986-); Mag. Search; Med. Rev. Dig.; Middle East Abstr. Index (March 1975-Oct. 1977); Newsp. Period. Abstr. (1986-); Peace Res. Abstr. J. (1964-1966, 1973-1979, 1981, 1985-1986); Read. Guide Abstr. Select Ed.; Read. Guide Period. Lit.; Res. Alert [Full Cov.]; Resource/One Ondisc; Romant. Move.; Soc. Plann. Policy Dev. Abstr.; Soc. Sci. Source (Jan. 1984-Dec. 1986, Jul. 1989-) [Full Txt.]; Soc. Sci. Cit. Index [Full Cov.]; Sociol. Abstr. (?-?); SportSearch (1955-1958); Mag. Index (1977-); TOM Gen. Index (1985-) [Full Txt.]; Vocat. Search (Jan. 1984-) [Full Txt.].

NZ
NEW ZEALAND SLAVONIC JOURNAL. [N. Z. Slav. j.]. **Added/Corp** Victoria University of Wellington. Dept. of Russian. (1974)-. Periodical. English (Russian). an (Aug.). 50.00NZ$. Victoria University of Wellington / Department of Russian, PO Box 600, Wellington New Zealand. **Tel** 011 64 4 4715322, FAX 011 64 4 4965419, telex 30882. **ED** I. Zohrab and C. Dowsett. **LC** PG1; .N47. Index available. cum. index. **Bk Rev. Circ:** 150 (ctrl).
Desc: Publishes articles and book reviews on Russian and other Slavonic literature, languages, history and general culture, including those of the Soviet Union and its Slavonic neighbors.
Ind/Abst Am. Hist. Life (1971-); Annu. Bibliogr. Engl. Lang. Lit.; MLA Int. Bibl. Books Artic. Mod. Lang. Lit.

TU
NEWSLETTER (RESEARCH CENTRE FOR ISLAMIC HISTORY, ART, AND CULTURE). See The Arts.

CN/0715-433X
NEWSLETTER / THE CALGARY INSTITUTE FOR THE HUMANITIES. [Newsl. - Calg. Inst. Humanit.]. **Main/Corp** Calgary Institute for the Humanities. Sept. 1980-. Newsletter. English. an. Free. Calgary Institute for the Humanities, University Library University of Calgary, 2500 University Drive NW, Calgary Alberta T2N 1N4 Canada. **Tel** (403)220-7238. **ED** H G Coward. **DD** 001.3/06/071233. ctrl circ.

NE/0028-9930
NIEUWE WEST-INDISCHE GIDS. See Social Sciences.

US/0890-5495
NINETEENTH CENTURY CONTEXTS. See Literature.

US
NORTH CAROLINA HUMANITIES. English. sa (May and Nov.). $15.00. NC Humanitites Review-UNCW, 601 South College Road, Wilmington NC 28403. **ED** Philip Gerard (919)395-3329 Department of English, UNC Wilmington, Wilmington, NC 28403. **Circ:** 300.

CK/0020-370X
NOTICIAS CULTURALES. No. 1- July 15, 1961-. Periodical. Spanish. bm. Instituto Caro y Cuervo, Apartado 51502, Bogota Colombia. **Tel** 011 57 1 2557753, FAX 011 57 1 2170243. **LC** WMLC L 83/8499. **Circ:** 3,000 (ctrl).

FR
NOTRE-DAME DU LIBAN. (19??)-. Periodical. French. sm. Notre-Dame du Liban, 15 rue d'Ulm, 75005 Paris France. **LC** DC718.L43; N67. **DD** 305.8/9275692044/05.

FR/0029-456X
NOTRE TEMPS PARIS. 1968. [Notre temps Paris, 1968]. (1968)-. Periodical. French. mo. 241.92F France; 321.00F other. Bayard Presse, Svc Client, 3 rue Bayard/Dept 2, 75393 Paris Cedex 08 France. **Tel** 011 33 1 44356060, 011 33 1 44356262. **UDC** 36.

IT
NOUVA UMANITA. (197?)-. Periodical. Italian. Six times a year. L33000 Italy: L40000 others. Citta Nuova Editrice, Via Degli Scipioni 265, 00192 Rome Italy. **Tel** 011 39 6 3216212.

PO
NOVA RENASCENCA. Added/Corp Associacao Cultural "Nova Renascenca.". Vol. 1, No. 1 (Fall 1980)-. Periodical. Portuguese. ir. $53.00. Fundacao Antonio Almeida, R Tenente Valadim 231 331, 4100 Porto Portugal. **Tel** 011 352 2 667418692607. **LC** AP65; .N68. **DD** 056/.9.

US/0029-5337
NOVYJ ZURNAL. (NOVYI ZHURNAL.). [Novyj z.]. **VFOAT** New Review. Vol. 1 (1942)-. Periodical. Russian. Four times a year. $90.70 US; $95.70 other. New Review, 611 Broadway / Room 842, New York NY 10012. **Tel** (212)353-1478, FAX (212)353-1478. **ED** Turi Kashkarov. **LC** AP50; .N685. **DD** 947. Index available. cum. index. **Bk Rev. Circ:** 1,300 (ctrl).
Desc: Includes Russian literary and political pieces, poetry, memoirs and historical documents.
Ind/Abst Abstr. Bull. Inst. Pap. Sci. Tech.; Am. Hist. Life; MLA Int. Bibl. Books Artic. Mod. Lang. Lit.; Recent. Publ. Artic.

SP/0029-5795
NUESTRO TIEMPO. Added/Corp Universidad de Navarra. Instituto de Periodismo. Vol. 1, No. 1 (July 1954)-. Periodical. Spanish. mo (monthly with Jan./Feb. issues combined). $80.00. Servicio de Publicaciones de la Universidad de Navarra SA, Edificio Muga, Campus Universitario, 31008 Pamplona Spain. **Tel** 011 34 48 282700 ext. 2887. **LC** AS301; .N8. **[CCC].**

IT
NUOVA COLLEZIONE DI TESTI UMANISTICI INEDITI ORARI. Italian. ir. Casa Editrice Leo S. Olschki, Viuzzo del Pozzetto, Casella Postale 66, 50126 Florence Italy. **Tel** 011 39 55 6530684, FAX 011 39 55 6530214.

●IT
NUOVI STUDI LIVORNESI / ASSOCIAZIONE DI STORIA, LETTERE E ARTI LIVORNESI. Added/Corp Associazione di Storia, Lettere e Arti Livornesi. **VFOAT** NSL. Vol. 1 (1993)-. Periodical. Italian. an. **LC** DG975.L4; S78. ***Continues*** *Studi Livornesi.*
Ind/Abst BHA : Biblio. Hist. Art.

JA
OBIRIN RON SHU : IPPAN KYOIKU HEN. Main/Corp Obirin Daigaku. Tanki Daigaku. **VFOAT** Journal of Social Sciences and Humanities. Japanese (Japanese). Obirin Tanki Daigaku, 3758 Tokiwa-Machi, Machida Tokyo 194-02 Japan. **LC** AS552.O2; A36.

SA/0065-387X
OCCASIONAL PAPERS. Main/Corp Africa Institute. (1968)-. Monographic series. English. ir. Price varies. Africa Institute of South Africa, PO Box 630, Pretoria 0001 South Africa. **Tel** 011 27 12 328-6970, FAX 011 27 12 323-8153. **Pr Rev. Circ:** 200.
Desc: Papers on African affairs.

GW/0474-1242
OLYMPISCHE FORSCHUNGEN. Vol. 1 (1944)-. Monographic series. German. Price varies per volume. Walter de Gruyter Inc., PO Box 303421, D 10728 Berlin Germany. **Tel** 011 49 30 260050, FAX 011 49 30 26005251. **(Subscription address:** US and Canada/ 200 Saw Mill River Road, Hawthorne, NY 10532**)**

MX/0185-5727
PALABRA Y EL HOMBRE, LA. [Palabra hombre]. **Added/Corp** Universidad Veracruzana. (Jan./March 1957)-(Oct./Dec. 1968)-. Periodical. Spanish. qt. $75.00 (US); $90.00 (Canada & Latin America) $120.00 (others except Mexico). Universidad Veracruz, Apartado Postal 97, Xalapa Vera Cruz Mexico. **Tel** (281)7 18 16. **ED** Raul Hernandez Viveros. **LC** AS63; .J353. **DD** 056/.1. Index available. **Bk Rev. Ad Acc. Circ:** 2,000 (ctrl).
Desc: Covers literature, history, and sociology. A multidisciplinary journal of the humanities.
Ind/Abst Am. Hist. Life (1966, 1970-); Arts Humanit. Citation Index (19??-19??) [Full Cov.]; HAPI Hisp. Am. Period. Index; MLA Int. Bibl. Books Artic. Mod. Lang. Lit.

US/0736-9123
PAPERS IN COMPARATIVE STUDIES. [Pap. comp. stud.]. **Added/Corp** Ohio State University. Division of Comparative Studies in the Humanities. Ohio State University. Center for Comparative Studies in the Humanities. Vol. 1 (1981)-. English. an. $10.00. Ohio State University / Papers in Comparative Studies, 306 Dulles Hall, 230 West 17th Avenue, Columbus OH 43210. **Tel** (614)292-2559. **LC** AS30; .P36. **DD** 001.3.
Ind/Abst MLA Int. Bibl. Books Artic. Mod. Lang. Lit.

UK/0953-8577
PARAGRAPH POOLE. (PARAGRAPH.). [PARagraph Poole]. (1987)-. Periodical. English. Three times a year. £19.75 UK; $38.50 US. Edinburgh University Press, 22 George Square, Edinburgh EH8 9LF Scotland. **Tel** 011 44 31 650 6207, FAX 011 44 31 662 0053. **DD** 646.79. **Bk Rev. Ad Acc, Adv Mgr:** Kathryn MacLean. **Circ:** 1,000.
Desc: Devoted to furthering the understanding of French critical thought in English-speaking countries. Publishes essays and review articles in English which explore critical theory in general and its application to literature, other arts, and society.
Ind/Abst Film Lit. Index (19??-).

Humanities

US/1056-6783
PASSAGES (EVANSTON, ILL.).
(PASSAGES : A CHRONICLE OF THE HUMANITIES.).
[Passages]. **Added/Corp** Northwestern University (Evanston, Ill.) Program of African Studies. Issue 1 (1991)-. Periodical. English. sa. Free. Northwestern University African Studies, Program of African Studies, 620 Library Place, Evanston IL 60201. **Tel** (708)491-7684. **DD** 305.

CN/0702-7125
PAST & PRESENT (WATERLOO). (PAST & PRESENT.). Oct. 1976-. Periodical. English. ir. Free in Canada. Past & Present, University of Waterloo, Waterloo Ontario N2L 3G1 Canada. **Tel** (519)885-1211. **ED** Brian Hendley. **DD** 300/.5. Index available. cum. index. **Bk Rev. Circ:** 1,800 (ctrl).
Desc: An arts faculty publication that publishes articles of current research and of the humanities.

●UY
PATRIOMONIO CULTURAL. (1992)-.
Spanish. sa. Ministerio de Educacion y Cultura, Comision del Patrimonio Historico,, Artistico y Cultural de la Nacion, Ituziango 1255, Montevideo Uruguay. **Tel** 95-79-42.

PH
PCSS POLICY MONOGRAPH SERIES.
(1984)-. Monographic series. English. Price varies per volume. President's Center for Special Studies, 14 Ilang-Ilang Street.

US/0885-3886
PHENOMENOLOGICAL INQUIRY. See Philosophy.

US/0734-3140
PITTSBURGH UNDERGRADUATE REVIEW, THE. [Pittsburgh undergrad. rev.].
Added/Corp University of Pittsburgh. University Honors Program. Vol. 1, No. 1 (Spring 1981)-. Academic Scholarly Publication. English. sa (May and Dec.). $7.00. Pittsburgh Undergraduate, 3500 Cathedral of Learning, Pittsburgh PA 15260. **Tel** (412)624-00121. **ED** Michael Kwadrat. **LC** AS30; .P57. **DD** 051. **Circ:** 1,000.
Desc: A nationally recognized scholarly journal dedicated to publishing undergraduate analytical essays in the humanities, natural and social sciences.

●US/1061-6012
PLATTSBURGH STUDIES IN THE HUMANITIES. (1992)-. Monographic series.
English. Price varies per volume. Peter Lang Publishing, 62 West 45th Street, 4th Floor, New York NY 10036. **Tel** (212)764-1471, (800)770-5264, telex 6973364 PLNY.

US/0032-2970
POLISH REVIEW (NEW YORK. 1956), THE. See Social Sciences.

US
POLISH STUDIES PROGRAM MONOGRAPHS. (1982)-. Monographic series.
English. Price varies per volume. Central Connecticut State University, New Britain CT 06050.

FR/0182-6220
POMME D'API. [Pomme api]. (1965)-. Periodical. French. mo (10 issues). 34.1Can$. Bayard Presse, Svc Client, 3 rue Bayard/Dept 2, 75393 Paris Cedex 08 France. **Tel** 011 33 1 44356060, 011 33 1 44356262. **UDC** 08.

US/1053-1920
POSTMODERN CULTURE. (POSTMODERN CULTURE : [COMPUTER FILE]. AN ELECTRONIC JOURNAL OF INTERDISCIPLINARY CRITICISM.). [Postmod. cult.]. **VFOAT** PMC. Vol. 1, No. 1 (Fall 1990)-. Periodical. English. tq (3 issues). Free through electronic mail; Diskette or microfiche: $30.00 institutions, $15.00 individuals US; $35.00 institutions, $20.00 individuals other. Oxford University Press / New York, 200 Madison Avenue, New York NY 10016. **Tel** (212)679-7300, (919)677-0977, (800)451-7556, (800)445-9714, FAX (919)677-1303. **(Subscription address:** Oxford University Press / USA, Journals Marketing Department, Oxford University Press, 2001 Evans Road, Cary NC 27513.**) DD** 909. available on microfiche from Internet; and BITNET; available on diskette.
Desc: Examines the culture, literature, and social issues of the postmodern era.

PL/0521-9310
PRACE. SERIA A. Main/Corp Bydgoskie Towarzystwo Naukowe. Wydzial Nauk Humanistycznych. Vol. 1 (1963)-. Periodical. Polish.
(Subscription address: ARS Polona, PO Box 1001, 00068 Warsaw Poland.**) DD** 060.

NE/0165-4373
PRANA. [Prana]. (1975)-. Periodical. Dutch. Six times a year. Fl1367.92. Ankh-Hermes BV, Smyrnastraat 5, 7413 BA Deventer Netherlands. **Tel** 011 31 3 2312900. **UDC** 1.

FR/1154-7707
PRECIS ANALYTIQUE DES TRAVAUX DE L'ACADEMIE DES SCIENCES, BELLES-LETTRES ET ARTS DE ROUEN. Main/Corp Academie des Sciences, Belles-Lettres et Arts de Rouen. (1744)-. French. an. cum. index.
Ind/Abst BHA : Biblio. Hist. Art.

US/0032-8456
PRINCETON UNIVERSITY LIBRARY CHRONICLE, THE. [Princeton Univ. Libr. chron.].
Added/Corp Princeton University. Library. Friends. Vol. 1 (Nov. 1939)-. Academic Scholarly Publication. English. Three times a year (Spring, Fall, Winter). $30.00. Princeton University Library, Rare Books Department, 1 Washington Road, Princeton NJ 08544. **Tel** (609)258-3155, FAX (609)258-4105. **(Subscription address:** Marieta Lazanski, (609)258-3155**) ED** Patricia H. Marks. **LC** Z733.P93; C5. **DD** 027.774967. Index available. **Pr Rev. Circ:** 1,300. available on microfilm and microfiche from University Microfilms International (UMI). *Absorbed* Biblia.
Desc: Publishes articles of scholarly importance in the humanities, the social and natural sciences, and about books and book collecting. Written for the general reader.
Ind/Abst Abstr. Engl. Stud.; Am. Hist. Life (1963-); Annu. Bibliogr. Engl. Lang. Lit.; MLA Int. Bibl. Books Artic. Mod. Lang. Lit.; Recent. Publ. Artic.; Romant. Move.; Writ. Am. Hist.

SW/0546-8175
PRIX NOBEL, LES. Main/Corp Nobelstiftelsen. (1901)-. Academic Scholarly Publication. French (English). an. Kr366.00 (1992 ed.). Almqvist & Wiksell International, PO Box 4627, S-11691 Stockholm Sweden. **Tel** 011-46-8-6408800. **LC** AS911; .N72. **NLM** AS 911 N744P. **CODEN** PRIXAL. Documents available from CASDDS.
Ind/Abst Chem. Abstr.

IS/0578-9230
PROCEEDINGS (AKADEMYAH HA-LEUMIT HA-YISREELIT LE-MADAIM). (PROCEEDINGS / ISRAEL ACADEMY OF SCIENCES AND HUMANITIES.).
Added/Corp Akademyah ha-Leumit ha-Yisreelit le-Madaim. Vol. 1, No. 1 (1963)-. Monographic series. English. ir. Price varies per volume. Academy of Sciences and Humanities, PO Box 4040, Jerusalem 91040 Israel. **Tel** 011 972 2 636211, FAX 011 972 2 666059. **ED** S. Reem. **Circ:** 450.
Desc: Printing of lectures delivered under the auspices of the Israel Academy of Sciences and Humanities.

UK/0024-0281
PROCEEDINGS OF THE LEEDS PHILOSOPHICAL AND LITERARY SOCIETY, LITERARY AND HISTORICAL SECTION. See Societies and Clubs.

UK/0369-9986
PROCEEDINGS OF THE LEEDS PHILOSOPHICAL AND LITERARY SOCIETY. SCIENTIFIC SECTION. [Proc. Leeds Philos. Lit. Soc. Sci. sect.]. **Main/Corp** Leeds Philosophical and Literary Society. Vol. 1, (Oct. 1925)-. Proceedings. English. ir. Price varies per volume. Central Museum, Calverley Pt, Leeds LS1 3AA England. **Tel** 011 44 532 452894. **ED** P. T. Speakman. **LC** AS122; .L263. **DD** 062. **CODEN** PIOAAL. Index available. cum. index. **Pr Rev. Circ:** 600. Documents available from BIOSIS Document Express, Ask*IEEE, CASDDS.
Desc: Short to medium length original reports in any area of science.
Ind/Abst Biol. Abstr.; Chem. Abstr.; GeoRef; INSPEC (1968-); Life Sci. Collect.

AT/0067-1592
PROCEEDINGS - THE AUSTRALIAN ACADEMY OF THE HUMANITIES.
Main/Corp Australian Academy of the Humanities. Vol. 1 (1970)-. Proceedings. English. an. 16.00Aus$. The Australian Aademy of the Humanities, GPO Box 93, Canberra Australian Capital Territory 2601 Australia. **Tel** (062)487744, FAX (062)486827. **Acid Free. Circ:** 300 (ctrl). Documents available from FAXON Xpress. *Supersedes* Report / Australian Humanities Research Council.
Desc: Annual proceedings and lecture.

US/1064-7961
PROFESSIONAL SCHOLAR. *Ceased.*
(PROFESSIONAL SCHOLAR : THE NEWSLETTER FOR SCHOLARSHIP OF DISCOVERY, INTEGRATION, APPLICATION, AND DISSEMINATION.). [Prof. sch.]. (1992)-(Feb. 1994). Newsletter. English. Ten times a year. Magna Publications Inc, 2718 Dryden Drive, Madison WI 53704. **Tel** (800)433-0499, (608)246-3591, FAX (608)246-3597. **DD** 370.

US/0033-1058
PROMENY (CZECHOSLOVAK SOCIETY OF ARTS AND SCIENCES IN AMERICA).
(PROMENY.). [Promeny]. **VFOAT** Metamorphoses; Premeny. Vol. 1 (1964)-. Periodical. Czech (Slovak). qt. $22.00 (members), $30.00 (nonmembers). Karel Hruby, Theirsteinerrain 90, CH-4059 Basel Switzerland. **Tel** (718)479-0870. **(Subscription address:** Ruzena Bunza, 75-70 199th Street, Flushing, NY 11366**) ED** K Hruby, L Durovic, J Krejci, J Lochman, Z Skvorecka, J Spetko, J Vladislav, R Welleck and Z Brodska. **LC** AP53; .P7. **Bk Rev. Circ:** 1,200.
Desc: Features Czech and Slovak letters and theoretical essays on the humanities, literature and art of Central Europe. Each issue is illustrated.
Ind/Abst Am. Bibliogr. Slavic East Europ. Stud. (19??-19??); MLA Int. Bibl. Books Artic. Mod. Lang. Lit.

US/0098-0900
PROTOCOL OF THE COLLOQUY OF THE CENTER FOR HERMENEUTICAL STUDIES IN HELLENISTIC AND MODERN CULTURE. See Classical Studies.

PL/0033-2194
PRZEGLAD HUMANISTYCZNY. [Prz. humanist.]. (1957)-. Periodical. Polish. bm. $99.00. **(Subscription address:** ARS Polona, PO Box 1001, 00068 Warsaw Poland.**) LC** AS261; .P7.
Ind/Abst Annu. Bibliogr. Engl. Lang. Lit.; BHA : Biblio. Hist. Art; MLA Int. Bibl. Books Artic. Mod. Lang. Lit.; Soc. Plann. Policy Dev. Abstr.; Sociol. Abstr. (?-?).

CN/0845-4450
PUBLIC (TORONTO). See The Arts.

VE/0506-6034
PUBLICACION - VENEZUELA. UNIVERSIDAD CENTRAL. CONSEJO DE DESARROLLO CIENTIFICO Y HUMANISTICO. Main/Corp Venezuela. Universidad Central, Caracas. Consejo de Desarrollo Cientifico y Humanistico. Vol. 1 (1961)-. Spanish. Universidad Central de Venezuela / Consejo de Desarrollo Cientifico Humanistico, Caracas Venezuela. **DD** 060.

UK/0581-0280
PUBLICATIONS. Main/Corp Modern Humanities Research Association. Vol. 1 (1969)-. Monographic series. English. ir. Price varies per volume. W. S. Maney and Son Ltd., Hudson Road, Leeds LS9 7DL England. **Tel** 011 44 532 497481, FAX 011 44 532 486983. **(Subscription address:** W.S. Maney & Son Limited, PO Box YR7, Leeds, LS9 7UU England.**)**

FR/1163-2283
QUALITA PARIS. (QUALITA.). (19??)-. Periodical. French. qt. Free on request. EDF DDSC, 2 rue Louis Murat, F-75008 Paris France. **Tel** 011 33 1 40422870. **UDC** 621.3(44).

FR/0767-9432
QUALITIQUE PARIS. (QUALITIQUE.). [Qualitique Paris]. (1988)-. Periodical. French (summaries and/or abstracts in English, German and Spanish). Ten times a year. 582.74F France; 695.00F Europe; 795.00F other. Editions Labeau, Qualitique, 9 rue Albert Einstein, 77420 Champs sur Marne France. **Tel** 011 33 1 64682193. **(Subscription address:** Editions Labeau, 23 25 rue Fernand Combette, F 93100 Montreuil France.**) UDC** 658.56.

CN/0033-6041
QUEEN'S QUARTERLY. See Social Sciences.

US/1041-8385
QUI PARLE. [Qui parle]. **Added/Corp** University of California, Berkeley. (1987)-. Periodical. English (French). Twice a year (Fall & Spring). $10.00 (individuals), $20.00 (institutions). Qui Parle, Townsend Center Humanities, 460 Stephens Hall, University of California, Berkeley CA 94720. **Tel** (510)643-9670, FAX (510)643-5284. **ED** Sarah Pelmas. **LC** PN1; .Q5. **DD** 809/.005. **Bk Rev, (Qty:** 4). **Ad Acc. Circ:** 500. *Continues* Ca Parle.
Ind/Abst MLA Int. Bibl. Books Artic. Mod. Lang. Lit.

SP
QUINTESSENCE. (19??)-. Spanish. Ediciones Doyma SA, Travesera de Gracia 17 21, 08021 Barcelona Spain. **Tel** 011 34 3 2000711, 011 34 3 4145706, FAX 011 34 3 2091136, telex 51964 INK E.

US/0731-4817
RACKHAM JOURNAL OF THE ARTS AND HUMANITIES, THE. [Rackham j. arts humanit.]. **Added/Corp** University of Michigan. **VFOAT** RAJAH. Vol. 2, No. 1 (Fall 1980)-. Periodical. English (French, Spanish and German). an. $4.00. Rajah / University of Michigan, 411 Mason Hall, Ann Arbor MI 48109. **Tel** (313)763-2351. **ED** Catharine Krieps, Thomas Mussio, Mary Lacey, John Cantu, Raymond Lee, Gina Hauskneckt and Julie Burch Mussio. **LC** PN2; .R25. **DD** 700/.5. Index available. cum. index. **Ad Acc.** *Continues Rackham Literary Studies*, 0360-7887.
Desc: An interdisciplinary journal that publishes nearly exclusively the work of graduate students at the University of Michigan.
Ind/Abst Abstr. Engl. Stud.; MLA Int. Bibl. Books Artic. Mod. Lang. Lit.

Humanities

FR/0033-9075
RAISON PRESENTE. See Philosophy.

US/1071-0043
RAVEN (TRENTON, N.J.). See Social Sciences.

SP/0034-0235
RAZON Y FE. (RAZON Y FE; REVISTA HISPANO-AMERICANA DE CULTURA.). [Razon fe]. Year 1, Vol. 1 (Sept. 1901)-. Periodical. Spanish. ir (10 issues). $58.00 US (surface mail). Centro Loyola, Pablo Aranda 3, 28006 Madrid Spain. **Tel** 011 34 1 565-4930, 562-6604, FAX 011 34 1 563-4073. **ED** Juan Garcia-Perez. **LC** AP60; .R2. Index available. cum. index. **Bk Rev. Ad Acc. Circ:** 7,000 (ctrl).
Desc: Relation between religion and culture in wide sense: politics, economy, social and cultural questions.
Ind/Abst Am. Hist. Life (1955-1974); Bibliogr. Mission.; MLA Int. Bibl. Books Artic. Mod. Lang. Lit.; New Testam. Abstr.

FR/0399-1989
RECHERCHES GERMANIQUES. [Rech. ger.]. **Added/Corp** Universite des Sciences Humaines de Strasbourg. No. 1 (1971)-. French. an. 90.00F France. Universite des Sciences Humaines, 22 rue Descartes, 67084 Strasbourg Cedex France. **Tel** 011 33 88 417317. **ED** Gonthier-Louis Fink. **LC** DD61; .R28. **Ad Acc.**
Desc: German studies.
Ind/Abst MLA Int. Bibl. Books Artic. Mod. Lang. Lit.; Romant. Move.

CN/0700-9283
RECORDS OF EARLY ENGLISH DRAMA. See Theater.

UK/0486-3720
RENAISSANCE AND MODERN STUDIES. [Renaiss. mod. stud.]. Vol. 1 (1957)-. English. an. Price varies per volume. Renaissance & Modern Studies, University of Nottingham, Hispanic Studies, Nottingham NG7 2RD England. **Tel** 011 44 602 515800. **LC** AS121; .R4. **DD** 042. available on microfilm and microfiche from University Microfilms International (UMI).
Ind/Abst Abstr. Engl. Stud.; Am. Hist. Life (1961-); Annu. Bibliogr. Engl. Lang. Lit.; Br. Humanit. Index; MLA Int. Bibl. Books Artic. Mod. Lang. Lit.

IT/0393-2931
RENDICONTI DELLA ACCADEMIA DI ARCHEOLOGIA LETTERE E BELLE ARTI NAPOLI. See The Arts.

IT
RENDICONTI / INSTITUTO LOMBARDO ACCADEMIA DI SCIENZE E LETTERE, CLASSE DI LETTERE E SCIENZE MORALI E STORICHE. Added/Corp Istituto Lombardo-Accademia di Scienze e Lettere. Classe di Lettere, Scienze Morali e Storiche. Vol. 92, No. 1 (1958)-. Italian (English and French). ir (1-2 issues per volume). Price varies per volume. Instituto Lombardo Accademia di Scienze e Lettere, Via Borgonuovo 25, 20121 Milan Italy. **Tel** 011 39 2 86461388. **LC** AS222.I85; A3. **DD** 055/.1. **NLM** W1 IS82. **Continues** Rendiconti (Istituto Lombardo di Scienze e Lettere. Classe di Lettere e Science Morali e Storiche).
Ind/Abst MLA Int. Bibl. Books Artic. Mod. Lang. Lit.

UK/0309-7994
REPORT AND TRANSACTIONS - THE DEVONSHIRE ASSOCIATION FOR THE ADVANCEMENT OF SCIENCE, LITERATURE AND ART. See The Arts.

US/0147-569X
REPORT FROM ASPEN INSTITUTE BERLIN. Main/Corp Aspen Institute Berlin. Vol. 1 (1976)-. Multiple languages (English and German). $3.00. Aspen Institute for Humanistic Studies, 360 Bryant Street, Palo Alto CA 94302. **LC** AS1; .A86a. **DD** 060.

US/0095-2230
REPORT OF ACTIVITIES FOR THE STATE DEPARTMENT OF ART, HISTORICAL AND CULTURAL PRESERVATION. Main/Corp Louisiana. Dept. of Art, Historical and Cultural Preservation. 1973-. English. an. Old State Capitol, Corner North Boulevard and St Phillip Streets, Baton Rouge LA 70801. **LC** N8849; .L68A. **DD** 353.9/763/0085.

US/0734-6018
REPRESENTATIONS (BERKELEY, CALIF.). (REPRESENTATIONS.). [Representations]. Vol. 1, No. 1 (Feb. 1983)-. Periodical. English. qt (Feb., May, Aug., Nov.). $36.00 (individuals), $67.00 (institutions), $24.00 (students). University of California Press, 2120 Berkeley Way, Berkeley CA 94720. **Tel** (510)642-4191, (510)642-3907, FAX (510)642-9917. **ED** Stephen Greenblatt and Carla Hesse 322 Wheeler Hall, University of California, Berkeley, CA 94720. **LC** NX1; .R46. **DD** 700/.5. **[CCC]. Bk Rev. Ad Acc. Pr Rev.**

Circ: 2,600. available on microfilm and microfiche from University Microfilms International (UMI). Documents available from The Genuine Article.
Desc: Interdisciplinary research on and theory of history, literature and art.
Ind/Abst Am. Hist. Life (1983-); Am. Humanit. Index (-199?); Annu. Bibliogr. Engl. Lang. Lit.; ARTbibliogr. Mod.; Arts Humanit. Citation Index [Full Cov.]; BHA : Biblio. Hist. Art; Child. Lit. Abstr. (19??-); Curr. Contents Arts Humanit.; Film Lit. Index (19??-); Lit. Crit. Regist.; MLA Int. Bibl. Books Artic. Mod. Lang. Lit.; Res. Alert [Full Cov.]; Soc. Sci. Cit. Index [Select. Cov.].

US/8755-3864
RESEARCH CENTER FOR THE ARTS AND HUMANITIES REVIEW. Suspended. See The Arts.

UK
RESEARCH IN HUMANITIES COMPUTING : SELECTED PAPERS FROM THE AALC/ACH CONFERENCE. Added/Corp Association for Literary and Linguistic Computing. Association for Computers and the Humanities. (1991)-. Monographic series. English. ir. Price varies per volume. Oxford University Press, Walton Street, Oxford OX2 6DP England. **Tel** 011 44 865 56767, FAX 011 44 865 267773, telex 837330 OXPRES G. **(Subscription address:** Oxford University Press / USA, Journals Marketing Department, Oxford University Press, 2001 Evans Road, Cary NC 27513.) **ED** Susan Hockey and Nancy Ide. **LC** AZ105; .R47. **DD** 001.3/0285. available with illustrations.

II
RESEARCH JOURNAL : HUMANITIES & SOCIAL SCIENCE. Main/Corp Indore, India (City). University. V. 1- Aug. 1972-. Multiple languages (English and Hindi). sa. RS5.00. University of Indore, University House, Indore 452-001 India. **LC** AS472.I53; A36. **DD** 378.54/3.

UK/0956-9014
RESEARCH ON LATIN AMERICA IN THE HUMANITIES AND SOCIAL SCIENCES IN THE UNIVERSITIES AND POLYTECHNICS OF THE UNITED KINGDOM. Added/Corp University of London. Institute of Latin American Studies. (1988)-. Bibliography. English. ir (every 3-4 years). £4.50. Institute of Latin American Studies, 31 Tavistock Square, London WC1H 9HA England. **Tel** 071 3871 5671, FAX 071 385 5024. **ED** A. Bell. **LC** Z1601; .R47. **Formed by the union of** Theses in Latin American Studies at British Universities in Progress and Recently Completed, 0307-109X **and** Latin American Studies in the Universities of the United Kingdom. Staff Research in Progress or Recently Completed in the Humanities and Social Sciences.

US
RESEARCH PROGRAMS GUIDELINES. See The Arts.

US/0147-0922
RESEARCH PROGRAMS - NATIONAL ENDOWMENT FOR THE HUMANITIES. Main/Corp National Endowment for the Humanities. English. National Endowment for the Humanities, 1100 Pennsylvania Avenue NW, Washington DC 20506. **Tel** (202)786-0438. **LC** LB2336; .N36B. **DD** 001.4/4.

BL/0001-3846
REVISTA DA ACADEMIA PAULISTA DE LETRAS. Main/Corp Academia Paulista de Letras (Sao Paulo, Brazil). (1937)-. Periodical. Portuguese. qt. **LC** AS80; .S313. **DD** 056/.9. cum. index.
Ind/Abst HAPI Hisp. Am. Period. Index.

●BL/0104-0111
REVISTA DE CIENCIAS HUMANAS : REVISTA DA UFPR. Added/Corp Universidade Federal do Parana. Setor de Ciencias Humanas, Letras e Artes. **VFOAT** Ciencias Humanas. Vol. 1, No. 1 (1992)-. Periodical. Portuguese (summaries and/or abstracts in English, French, Italian and Spanish). sa. 40.00Arg$. Universidade Federal de Parana, Sector de Ciencias Humanas, Letras e Artes, Travessa Alfredo Bufren 140, 80020-240 Curitaba, Parana Brazil. **Tel** 011 41 224-6623. **ED** Roberto Gomes. **LC** IN PROCESS.

MX
REVISTA DE LA UNIVERSIDAD AUTONOMA DE YUCATAN. Added/Corp Universidad Autonoma de Yucatan. Vol. 26, No. 151 (July/Sept. 1984)-. Periodical. Spanish. ir. Free. Universidad de Yucatan, Calles 57 Por 60, Merida Yucatan Mexico. **LC** AS63.M5; A3. **Continues** Universidad de Yucatan. Revista de la Universidad de Yucatan, 0185-1381.
Ind/Abst MLA Int. Bibl. Books Artic. Mod. Lang. Lit.

FR/0080-2484
REVUE BIBLIOGRAPHIQUE DE SINOLOGIE. See Humanities-Abstracting, Bibliographies and Statistics.

FR/1141-1325
REVUE DE LA HAUTE-AUVERGNE. Added/Corp Societe des Lettres, Sciences et Arts "la Haute-Auvergne". (1???)-. Periodical. French. qt. **LC** DC611.A94; R5. **DD** 944/.59005. cum. index.
Ind/Abst BHA : Biblio. Hist. Art.

CN/0316-6368
REVUE DE L'UNIVERSITE DE MONCTON (1976). See Education-Higher Education.

FR/0035-2748
REVUE DU VIVARAIS. See The Arts.

IT/0080-3073
RINASCIMENTO. [Rinascimento]. **Added/Corp** Istituto Nazionale di Studi sul Rinascimento. **VFOAT** Rinascita. 2. Serie. (1950)-. Italian. an. L97000 Italy; L130000 other. Casa Editrice Leo S. Olschki, Viuzzo del Pozzetto, Casella Postale 66, 50126 Florence Italy. **Tel** 011 39 55 6530684, FAX 011 39 55 6530214. **LC** DG533.A1; R57. Documents available from The Genuine Article. **Supersedes** Rinascita (Florence, Italy).
Desc: Covers humanities and the Renaissance.
Ind/Abst Am. Hist. Life (1976-); Arts Humanit. Citation Index [Full Cov.]; BHA : Biblio. Hist. Art; Curr. Contents Arts Humanit.; MLA Int. Bibl. Books Artic. Mod. Lang. Lit.; Res. Alert [Full Cov.]; Romant. Move.

JA/0389-9535
RISSHO DAIGAKU JINBUN KAGAKU KENKYUJO NENPO. BESSATSU. VFOAT Annual Bulletin of the Institute of Humanistic Sciences, Rissho University. Periodical. Japanese. Rissho Daigaku Jinbun Kagaku Kenkyujo, 2-banchi Osaki 4-chome, Shinagawa-ku Tokyo Japan. **LC** AS552.R56; A242.

IT/0035-5739
RIVISTA ABRUZZESE. [Riv. abruzz.]. Vol. 1, No. 1 (1947)-. Periodical. Italian. Four times a year. L40000. Rivisat Abruzzese, via C Fagiani 37, 66034 Lanciano CH Italy. **Tel** 011 39 872 49445.
Ind/Abst BHA : Biblio. Hist. Art; MLA Int. Bibl. Books Artic. Mod. Lang. Lit.

PL/0035-7707
ROCZNIKI HUMANISTYCZNE. [Rocz. humanist.]. **Added/Corp** Katolicki Uniwersytet Lubelski. Towarzystwo Naukowe. Wydzia Historyczno-Filologiczny. Katolicki Uniwersytet Lubelski. Towarzystwo Naukowe. **VFOAT** Annales de Lettres et Sciences Humaines; Annals of Arts. (1949)-. Monographic series. Polish. qt (4 issues). **(Subscription address:** ARS Polona, PO Box 1001, 00068 Warsaw Poland.) **LC** AS261; .R6.
Ind/Abst Am. Hist. Life (1979-); BHA : Biblio. Hist. Art; MLA Int. Bibl. Books Artic. Mod. Lang. Lit.

FR
ROMANIA. French. Dawson France SA, BP 40, 91121 Palaiseau Cedex France. **Tel** 011 33 1 69104700, telex 220064F.

RM/0048-8550
ROMANIA LITERARA. See Literature.

FR
ROUGE. (19??)-. French. ir. 392.00F France; 500.00F other. Presse Edition Communication, 2 rue Richard Lenoir, 93108 Montreuil France. **Tel** 011 33 1 48590080.

BE
RUIMTE VOOR CULTUUR. Ceased. (19??)-(1992). Dutch. qt. FEVECC, Bondgenotenlaan 52, B-1190 Brussels Belgium. **Tel** 02 347 27 59, FAX 02 346 14 32. Index available. **Bk Rev. Ad Acc.** ctrl circ.
Desc: Articles on culture.

JA/0289-0917
RYUKOKU KIYO. Added/Corp Ryukoku Daigaku. (197?)-. Periodical. Japanese (English). sa. **CODEN** RYKIER. Documents available from CASDDS.
Ind/Abst Chem. Abstr.

US
SALARY STUDY. See Sociology-Social Services and Welfare.

US/0036-3529
SALMAGUNDI (SARATOGA SPRINGS). (SALMAGUNDI.). [Salmagundi]. **Added/Corp** Skidmore College. No. 1 (Fall 1965)-. Periodical. English. qt. $20.00 US; $25.00 other. Skidmore College, Saratoga Springs NY 12866. **Tel** (518)584-5000. **ED** Peggy and Robert Boyers. cum. index. **Bk Rev. Ad Acc.** Documents available from The Genuine Article, UMI Article Clearinghouse.
Desc: Publishes debates, travel pieces, new fiction, interviews with Sontag, Kundera, and Gordimer; symposia, and regular columns. Published by Skidmore College.
Ind/Abst Abstr. Engl. Stud.; Acad. Search (Jan. 1993-); Am. Hist. Life (1987-); Am. Bibliogr. Slavic East Europ. Stud.; Am. Humanit. Index; Arts Humanit. Citation Index [Full Cov.]; Curr. Contents Arts Humanit.; Expand. Acad. Index (1989-); Film Lit. Index; Humanit. Index; Humanit. Source (Jul. 1993-); Index Am. Period. Verse; INFO-SOUTH Abstr.; Mag. Search; MLA Int. Bibl. Books

Artic. Mod. Lang. Lit.; Newsp. Period. Abstr. (1990-); Res. Alert [Full Cov.]; Soc. Plann. Policy Dev. Abstr.; Soc. Sci. Cit. Index [Select. Cov.].

US/0097-8051
SAN JOSE STUDIES. [San Jose stud.]. Vol.1 (Feb. 1975)-. Academic Scholarly Publication. English. Three times a year. $18.00 US; $21.00 other (institutions); $12.00 US; $15.00 other individuals. San Jose Studies, San Jose State University, c/o O C Williams, San Jose CA 95192. **Tel** (408)924-4476. **ED** Fauneil J Rinn. **LC** AS36.C17; A3. **DD** 051. Index available. **Circ:** 500. available on microfilm from University Microfilms International (UMI).
Desc: Journal of general and scholarly interest featuring critical, creative, and informative writing in the arts, businesses, humanities, social sciences, and sciences; also includes poetry and fiction.
Ind/Abst Am. Hist. Life (1975-); Am. Humanit. Index; Annu. Bibliogr. Engl. Lang. Lit.; ARTbibliogr. Mod. (1984-); Child. Lit. Abstr. (19??-); MLA Int. Bibl. Books Artic. Mod. Lang. Lit.; Romant. Move.; Soc. Plann. Policy Dev. Abstr.; Sociol. Abstr.; Women Stud. Abstr.

US/0161-7729
SCHOLARS' FACSIMILES AND REPRINTS (SERIES). See Linguistics.

GW
SCHRIFTEN ZUR LITERATUR- UND GEISTESGESCHICHTE. 1984-. Monographic series. German. Price varies per volume. Dr. Ernst Hauswedell & Co. Verlag, Rosenbergstrasse 113, D 70193 Stuttgart Germany. **Tel** 011 49 711 638265.

IS
SCOPUS. **See** College and School Publications.

UK/1350-7508
SCOTLANDS. (1994)-. Periodical. English. Twice a year. £35.00 UK & Europe; $65.00 US; £38.00 other. Edinburgh University Press, 22 George Square, Edinburgh EH8 9LF Scotland. **Tel** 011 44 31 650 6207, FAX 011 44 31 662 0053. **ED** Christopher MacLachlan. **Ad Acc, Adv Mgr:** Kathryn MacLean. **Circ:** 500.
Desc: Contains articles and essays celebrating the richness of Scottish literature, history, music, art, film and television.

US/0190-731X
SCRIBLERIAN AND THE KIT-CATS, THE. [Scriblerian Kit-Cats]. **Added/Corp** Goldsmiths' College. Dept. of English. Temple University. Dept. of English. Northeastern University (Boston, Mass.). Dept. of English. **VFOAT** Scriblerian. Vol. 4, No. 2 (Spring 1972)-. Periodical. English. Twice a year (May & Dec.). $15.00 (individuals); $20.00 (institutions). Temple University / English Department, College of Liberal Arts, Anderson Hall 939, Philadelphia PA 19122. **Tel** (215)204-7539, (215)204-7000. **ED** Peter A. Tasch, Roy S. Wolper, and Arthur J. Weitzman. **DD** 824. Index available. **Bk Rev. Ad Acc. Circ:** 1,200 (ctrl). Documents available from The Genuine Article. ***Continues*** *Scriblerian, 0036-9640.*
Desc: Reviews, notes, queries, illustrations, and ephemera on the Scriblerians and Kit-Cats and the acquaintances.
Ind/Abst Abstr. Engl. Stud.; Am. Humanit. Index; Annu. Bibliogr. Engl. Lang. Lit.; Arts Humanit. Citation Index [Full Cov.]; Curr. Contents Arts Humanit.; MLA Int. Bibl. Books Artic. Mod. Lang. Lit.; Res. Alert [Full Cov.]; Soc. Sci. Cit. Index [Select. Cov.].

CN/0226-8418
SCRIPTA MEDITERRANEA. (SCRIPTA MEDITERRANEA : BULLETIN OF THE SOCIETY FOR MEDITERRANEAN STUDIES ...). [Scr. Mediterr.]. **Added/Corp** Society for Mediterranean Studies (Toronto, Ont.). **VFOAT** SM. Vol. 1 (1980)-. English (French and Italian). an. $25.00. University of Toronto / New College, Box 308, Department of French, Toronto Ontario M5S 1A1 Canada. **ED** Anthony Percival. **LC** DE1; .S375. **DD** 909/.0982/2. Index available. **Bk Rev. Circ:** 100.
Desc: The journal of the Society for Mediterranean Studies, an international learned society based in Canada and devoted to the study of all aspects of Mediterranean culture and civilization, past and present, with a special interest in interdisciplinary and cross-cultural investigation.
Ind/Abst Recent. Publ. Artic.

AT/0158-1953
SEARMG NEWSLETTER. (1979)-. Newsletter. Three times a year. £15.00 (members). Anutech Pty Limited, GPO Box 4, Canberra Act, 2601 Australia. **Tel** 011 61 6 2492479, FAX 011 61 6 2575088. **ED** I. Soegito. **Bk Rev. Ad Acc. Circ:** 350. ***Continues*** *Southeast Asian Research Materials Group Newsletter, 0311-290X.*

●IT
SECONDO RINASCIMENTO, IL. No. 1 (Mar./Apr. 1992)-. Periodical. Italian. Five times a year. L80000. Editore Spirali-Vel SRL / Spirali Edizione SRL, Via Fratelli Gabba 3, 20121 Milan Italy. **Tel** 02-805-4417, FAX 02-869-2631. **(Subscription address:** Via Bellezza 11, 20136 Milan, Italy (telephone 02-5831-5871)) **ED** Armando Verdiglione. ***Formed by the union of*** *Spirali del Secondo Rinascimento* ***and*** *Spirales (Milan, Italy).*

KO/0377-5240
SEOUL NATIONAL UNIVERSITY FACULTY PAPERS : HUMANITIES AND SOCIAL SCIENCE SERIES, A & B. **See** Education-Higher Education.

CN/0316-8379
SERIAL TITLES IN THE HUMANITIES AND SOCIAL SCIENCES (WINDSOR). (SERIAL TITLES IN THE HUMANITIES AND SOCIAL SCIENCES; A HOLDINGS LIST.). **Main/Corp** University of Windsor. Library. 1st Ed. (1966)-. Periodical. English. an. Free. Library / Winsdor, University of Windsor, Windsor Ontario N9B 3P4 Canada. **DD** 016.3/005.

IT
SFERA ROMA. ***Ceased.*** (SFERA.). [Sfera Roma]. (1988)-(Dec. 1994). Periodical. Italian. bm. Editrice Sigma Tau, Via Sudafrica 20, 00144 Rome Italy. **Tel** 011 39 6 91391. **ED** Giulio Macchi. **Circ:** 7,000.
Desc: Each issue concerned with two contrasting subjects, taking into account the differences between them; also focusing on those elements tending to render them complementary.

JA/0285-0427
SHIZUOKA DAIGAKU KYOYOBU KENKYU HOKOKU. JINBUN SHAKAI KAGAKU HEN. **VFOAT** Reports of Faculty of Liberal Arts, Shizuoka University. Humanities and Social Sciences. V. 17, No. 1-. Periodical. English (Japanese). Shizuoka Daigaku Kyoyobu, 836 Oya, Shizuoka-shi 422 Japan. **LC** AS552.S477; A3. ***Continues*** *Shizuoka Daigaku Kyoyobu Kenkyu Hokoku. Dai 1-Bu.*

JA
SHIZUOKA DAIGAKU KYOYOBU KENKYU HOKOKU. SHIZEN KAGAKU HEN. **VFOAT** Reports of the Department for Liberal Arts. Sciences; Reports of the Faculty of Liberal Arts, Shizuoka University. Sciences. Periodical. English (Japanese). an. Shizuoka Daigaku Kyoyobu, 836 Oya, Shizuoka-shi 422 Japan. **LC** Q4; .S5225. ***Continues in part*** *Shizuoka Daigaku Kyoyobu Kenkyu Hokoku.*

CH/0258-8412
SI YU YAN. (SSU YU YEN.). [Si yu yan]. **VFOAT** Thought and Word. (Feb. 1963)-. Periodical. Chinese. bm. $20.00. The Thought and Word Association 6F, 24 Ai Kuo East Road, Taipei Taiwan. **LC** AS455.A1; .S77. **DD** 059/.951. **Bk Rev. Ad Acc. Circ:** 1,000.
Desc: Includes humanities and social sciences articles.
Ind/Abst Am. Hist. Life (1970-).

IT/0037-458X
SICULORUM GYMNASIUM. [Siculorum gymnasium]. **Added/Corp** Universita di Catania. Facolta di Lettere e Filosofia. Universita di Catania. Facolta di Lettere e Filosofia. Biblioteca. (Jan./June 1948)-. Periodical. Italian. sa. L75000.00. Siculorum Gymnasium Universita Facolta Lettere, PZA Dante 32, 95124 Catania Italy. **Tel** 011 39 95 7102722. **LC** AS221; .S55.
Ind/Abst Annu. Bibliogr. Engl. Lang. Lit.; MLA Int. Bibl. Books Artic. Mod. Lang. Lit.

PH/0037-5284
SILLIMAN JOURNAL. [Silliman j.]. **Added/Corp** Silliman University. James W. Chapman Research Foundation. Vol. 1 (Jan. 1954)-. Periodical. English. qt (4 issues). $24.00. Silliman University, PO Box 606, Dumaguete 6200 Philippines. **LC** AS540; .S5. **DD** 068.9914. **Bk Rev. Circ:** 400 (ctrl). available on microfilm and microfiche from University Microfilms International (UMI).
Ind/Abst Index Philip. Period.; MLA Int. Bibl. Books Artic. Mod. Lang. Lit.; Philip. Sci. Technol. Abstr.

KO
SIN INGAN. **VFOAT** The New Humanity; New Humanity. Periodical. Korean (Korean). mo. W500 each issue. **LC** BL2240.C5; S55.

GW/0342-5991
SITZUNGSBERICHTE DER BAYERISCHEN AKADEMIE DER WISSENSCHAFTEN. PHILOSOPHISCH-HISTORISCHE KLASSE. **See** Classical Studies.

US/0037-6779
SLAVIC REVIEW. **See** Literary and Political Reviews.

US/0093-8335
SMITHSONIAN OPPORTUNITIES FOR RESEARCH AND STUDY IN HISTORY, ART, SCIENCE. Began with 1972. English. Office of Fellowships and Grants, Room 3300/l'Enfant Plaza, Smithsonian Institution, Washington DC 20560. **LC** Q11.S8; S86. **DD** 001.4/3/09753. ***Continues*** *Opportunities for Research and Advanced Study, 0191-3158.*

SZ
SNB QUARTALSHEFT. (19??)-. German. ir. 30.00F Europe; 55.00F other. Zuerichsee Zeitschriftenverlag, Seestrasse 86, CH 8712 Staefa Switzerland. **Tel** 011 41 1 9285611.

NE/0303-8300
SOCIAL INDICATORS RESEARCH. **See** Social Sciences.

CN
SOCIALIST STUDIES/ETUDES SOCIALIST: A CANADIAN ANNUAL. **See** Social Sciences.

FR/0153-9353
SOCIETE DES AMIS DES ARTS ET SCIENCES DE TOURNUS. [Soc. amis arts sci. Tournus]. **VFOAT** Societe des Amis des Arts et des Sciences de Tournus. (1879)-. Periodical. French. an. **UDC** 008.
Ind/Abst BHA : Biblio. Hist. Art.

UK/0262-7280
SOUTH ASIA RESEARCH. **Added/Corp** University of London. Centre of South Asian Studies. No. 1 (May 1981)-. Periodical. English. sa (2 issues). £23.00 UK and Europe; $40.00 other. Oxford University Press, Walton Street, Oxford OX2 6DP England. **Tel** 011 44 865 56767, FAX 011 44 865 267773, telex 837330 OXPRES G. **(Subscription address:** Oxford University Press / USA, Journals Marketing Department, Oxford University Press, 2001 Evans Road, Cary NC 27513.**) ED** D. Engels, D. Moodley, J. Rogers, S. Malik, I. Chowdhur Sengupta, C Pinney, J. Whelpton, D. Arnold, M. Anderson, M. Hutt Arnold, M. Anderson and M. Hutt. **LC** DS331; .S656. **DD** 954/.005. **[CCC].** cum. index. **Bk Rev. Ad Acc. Circ:** 300. available on microfiche.
Desc: Covers the humanities and social science fields of South Asian studies with emphasis on research in progress and contributions by younger scholars.
Ind/Abst Am. Hist. Life; Geogr. Abstr. Human Geogr. (?-?); Int. Bibliogr. Sociol.; Int. Dev. Abstr.

US/0038-2876
SOUTH ATLANTIC QUARTERLY, THE. [South Atl. q.]. **Added/Corp** Duke University. Vol. 1 (Jan. 1902)-. Academic Scholarly Publication. English. qt (4 issues). $60.00 (institutions), $24.00 (individuals) US; $72.00 (institutions), $36.00 (individuals) other. Duke University Press, PO Box 90660, Durham NC 27708-0660. **Tel** (919)687-3600, (919)688-5134 (orders), FAX (919)688-4574, telex 802829. **ED** Fredric Jameson. **LC** AP2; .S75. **DD** 051. **[CCC]. Bk Rev. Ad Acc. Circ:** 1,100 (ctrl). available on microfilm and microfiche from University Microfilms International (UMI). Documents available from The Genuine Article, UMI Article Clearinghouse.
Desc: Scholarly periodical in general humanities, publishing essays and reviews of current interest in literature, politics, history, and the arts.
Ind/Abst Abstr. Engl. Stud.; Acad. Abstr. Full Text Elite (July 1990-); Acad. Abstr. (July 1990-); Acad. Ind. [Computer File] (1987-); Acad. Search (July 1990-); Am. Hist. Life (1954-); Am. Humanit. Index; Annu. Bibliogr. Engl. Lang. Lit.; Arts Humanit. Citation Index [Full Cov.]; Book Rev. Index; Curr. Contents Arts Humanit.; Expand. Acad. Index (1987-); Film Lit. Index (19??-); Humanit. Index; INFO-SOUTH Abstr.; Lit. Crit. Regist.; Middle East Abstr. Index (1954-); MLA Int. Bibl. Books Artic. Mod. Lang. Lit.; Newsp. Period. Abstr. (1991-); Res. Alert [Full Cov.]; Romant. Move.; Sage Race Relat. Abstr. (1954-); Soc. Sci. Source (Jul. 1990-); Soc. Sci. Cit. Index [Select. Cov.]; SportSearch; West. Hist. Q. (1954-); Women Stud. Abstr.

US/0038-4186
SOUTHERN HUMANITIES REVIEW. [South. humanit. rev.]. **Added/Corp** Auburn University. Vol. 1 (Spring 1967)-. Periodical. English. qt (4 issues). $15.00 one year; $20.00 two years. Southern Humanities Review, 9088 Haley Center, Auburn University, Auburn University AL 36849. **Tel** (205)844-9088. **ED** Dan R. Latimer and R.T. Smith. **LC** AS36.A86; A35. Index available (Dec. iss.). **Bk Rev,** (Qty: 50-70). **Ad Acc. Pr Rev. Circ:** 700. available on microfilm and microfiche from University Microfilms International (UMI). Documents available from The Genuine Article, UMI Article Clearinghouse.
Desc: Publishes fiction, critical essays, and poetry on the arts, literature, philosophy, religion and history.
Ind/Abst Abstr. Engl. Stud.; Acad. Search (July 1993-); Am. Hist. Life (1969-); Am. Humanit. Index; Annu. Bibliogr. Engl. Lang. Lit.; Arts Humanit. Citation Index [Full Cov.]; Book Rev. Index (1984-); Curr. Contents Arts Humanit.; Expand. Acad. Index (1989-); Film Lit. Index; Humanit. Index; Humanit. Source (Jul. 1993-); Index Am. Period. Verse; Index Book Rev. Humanit.; INFO-SOUTH Abstr.; Lit. Crit. Regist.; Mag. Search; MLA Int. Bibl. Books Artic. Mod. Lang. Lit.; Newsp. Period. Abstr. (1991-); Ref. Sources; Res. Alert [Full Cov.]; Romant. Move.

UK
SPANISH STUDIES. **See** History(General)-History of Europe.

CE/0378-486X
SRI LANKA JOURNAL OF THE HUMANITIES, THE. [Sri Lanka j. humanit.]. **Added/Corp** University of Sri Lanka, Peradeniya Campus. University of Peradeniya. Vol. 1 (June 1975)-. Periodical. English. an. Price varies. University of Ceylon, Department of English, Peradeniya Sri Lanka. **ED** Merlin Peris. **LC** AS475.A1; S74. **DD** 052. **Bk Rev. Circ:** 600. ***Continues** Ceylon Journal of the Humanities.*
Desc: Articles on art and culture, philosophy, history, and sociology, more especially on Sri Lanka.
Ind/Abst Abstr. Engl. Stud.; Int. Bibliogr. Sociol.

CN/0839-4377
SSHRC NEWS. **See** Social Sciences.

US/0277-4720
ST. JOHNS REVIEW (1981), THE. **See** Education-Higher Education.

PH/0036-3014
ST. LOUIS UNIVERSITY RESEARCH JOURNAL. [St. Louis Univ. res. j.]. **Main/Corp** St. Louis University (Philippines). Graduate School of Arts and Sciences. **Added/Corp** Saint Louis University (Philippines). Graduate School of Arts and Sciences. Research Journal. **VAT** Saint Louis University Research Journal. Vol. 1 (March 1970)-. Periodical. English. sa. $44.95. Research Journal Editorial Office / St. Louis University, PO Box 71, Baguio City 0216 Philippines. **Tel** 011 63 442 3043. **ED** Felino L. Lorente. **LC** AS540.S34; A25. **DD** 051. Index available. cum. index. **Bk Rev. Circ:** 1,000 (ctrl). ***Supersedes** Saint Louis Quarterly.*
Desc: An interdisciplinary journal in the sciences and the humanities.
Ind/Abst Abstr. Engl. Stud.; Middle East Abstr. Index; MLA Int. Bibl. Books Artic. Mod. Lang. Lit.; Philip. Sci. Technol. Abstr.

US/1048-3721
STANFORD HUMANITIES REVIEW. [Stanford humanit. rev.]. Vol. 1, No. 1 (Spring 1989)-. Periodical. English. Twice a year (Spring & Fall). $40.00. Stanford Humanities Review, Mariposa House, Stanford CA 94305. **Tel** (415)725-6747. **ED** Stefano Franchi. **LC** AS30; .S72. **DD** 028.1. **Bk Rev**, (Qty: 10). **Ad Acc. Circ:** 250.
Ind/Abst BHA : Biblio. Hist. Art.

IT
STUDI GORIZIANI. (STUDI GORIZIANI / RIVISTA A CURA DELLA BIBLIOTECA GOVERNATIVA DI GORIZIA.). **Added/Corp** Biblioteca Governativa di Gorizia (Italy). Vol. 1 (1923)-. Periodical. Italian. sa. L24000. Biblioteca Statale Isontina, Via Mameli 12, 34170 Gorizia Italy. **Tel** 011 39 481 531802. **ED** Silvestri Otello. **LC** DG975.G673; S78. **DD** 945/.392/005. **Bk Rev. Circ:** 600 (ctrl).
Desc: Regional studies of the history and arts of Gorizia, Italy, also studies on linguistics, literature and social sciences of that region.
Ind/Abst BHA : Biblio. Hist. Art.

IT
STUDI LIVORNESI / ASSOCIAZIONE DI STORIA, LETTERE E ARTI LIVORNESI. ***Title Change.*** **Added/Corp** Associazione di Storia, Lettere e Arti Livornesi. Vol. 1 (1986)-(1992). Periodical. Italian. an. **LC** DG975.L4; S78. **DD** 945/.56/005. ***Continued by** Nuovi Studi Livornesi.*
Ind/Abst BHA : Biblio. Hist. Art (?-?).

IT
STUDI SCIACCHIANI. **Added/Corp** Societa Degli Amici di Michele Federico Sciacca. Vol. 1, No. 1 (Jan./June 1985)-. Periodical. Italian. sa. $50.00. Arcipelago Sociedad Internationale Unita. Scienze, Casella Postale 997, 16100 Genova Italy.

IT/0392-0690
STUDI TRENTINI DI SCIENZE STORICHE. [Studi trent. sci. stor.]. **Added/Corp** Societa di Studi Trentini di Scienze Storiche. Vol. 7 (1926)-. Periodical. Italian. qt. L25000. Istituto Studi Trentini, Via Petrarca 36, 38100 Trento Italy. **Tel** 011 39 461 983388. ***Supersedes in part** Studi Trentini.*
Ind/Abst Am. Hist. Life (1991-); BHA : Biblio. Hist. Art; MLA Int. Bibl. Books Artic. Mod. Lang. Lit.

IT
STUDI URBINATI. B, SCIENZE UMANE E SOCIALI. **Added/Corp** Universita di Urbino. **VFOAT** Scienze Umane e Sociali; Stvdi Vrbinati. (1988)-. Italian. Edizioni Quattroventi di Anna Veronesi, Via Dini 16/Casella Postale 156, 60129 Urbino Italy. **LC** AS221; .S78. ***Continues** Studi Urbinati. B1, Storia, Geografia; Studi Urbinati. B2, Filosofia, Pedagogia, Psicologia; Studi Urbinati. B3, Linguistica, Letteratura, Arte; Studi Urbinati. B4, Economia, Sociologia.*

PL/0081-637X
STUDIA ESTETYCZNE. **Added/Corp** Polska Akademia Nauk. Instytut Filozofli i Socjologii. Vol. 1 (1964)-. Polish (summaries and/or abstracts in English and Russian). ir. **(Subscription address:** ARS Polona, PO Box 1001, 00068 Warsaw Poland.**)** **LC** BH6; .S78.
Ind/Abst BHA : Biblio. Hist. Art.

US
STUDIES IN ENGLISH AND AMERICAN LITERATURE, LINGUISTICS, AND CULTURE. **See** Literature.

US/0888-5753
STUDIES IN POPULAR CULTURE. [Stud. pop. cult.]. **Added/Corp** Popular Culture Association in the South. Vol. 1, No. 1 (Winter 1977)-. Periodical. English. Twice a year (April and Oct.). $20.00. Studies in Popular Culture, c/o .D Calhoun, French / Jefferson Community College SW, Louisville KY 40272. **Tel** (502)935-9840, FAX (502)935-9840. **ED** Dennis R. Hall, (502)852-4182). **LC** E169.1; .S935. **DD** 306/.4/0973. **Bk Rev**, (Qty: varies). **Circ:** 300.
Desc: Academic journal on all aspects of popular culture.
Ind/Abst Child. Lit. Abstr. (19??-); Film Lit. Index (19??-); MLA Int. Bibl. Books Artic. Mod. Lang. Lit.

US
STUDIES IN THE HUMANITIES. Vol. 1 (March 1969)-. Academic Scholarly Publication. English. Twice a year (June & Dec.). $12.00 (institutions); $5.00 (individuals). Indiana University of Pennsylvania / English Department, 110 Leonard Hall, Indiana PA 15705. **Tel** (412)357-6486, FAX (412)357-3056. **ED** Malcolm Hayward. **Bk Rev. Ad Acc. Pr Rev. Circ:** 300 (ctrl).
Desc: Multidisciplinary studies in literature, film, and aesthetics. A scholarly, refereed journal of articles in the humanities.
Ind/Abst Am. Bibliogr. Slavic East Europ. Stud.; Am. Humanit. Index; Annu. Bibliogr. Engl. Lang. Lit.; Film Lit. Index; Lit. Crit. Regist.; MLA Int. Bibl. Books Artic. Mod. Lang. Lit.; Romant. Move.

UK/0083-7199
STUDIES OF THE WARBURG INSTITUTE. **Main/Corp** London. University. Warburg Institute. **Added/Corp** Warburg Institute. Vol. 1 (1936)-. Monographic series. English (German and Latin). ir. Price varies per volume. Warburg Institute, University of London, Woburn Square, London WC1H OAB England. **Tel** 011 44 71 5809663, FAX (01)580-9663. **ED** J. B. Trapp. **Circ:** 165 (ctrl).
Desc: Series concerns the strands that link medieval and modern civilization with its origins in the ancient cultures of the Near East and the Mediterranean.

US
SUBSTANCE. English. University of California Department of French and Italian, Santa Barbara CA 93106.
Ind/Abst Am. Humanit. Index; Lit. Crit. Regist.

SJ/0375-2984
SUDAN NOTES AND RECORDS. [Sudan notes rec.]. **VFOAT** Sudan fi Dafatir wa-Mudawwanat. (1918)-. English. Sudan Notes and Records, PO Box 555, Khartoum Sudan. **ED** Yusuf Fadl Hasan. **CODEN** SUNRAE. Index available. cum. index. **Bk Rev. Ad Acc. Circ:** 2,000.
Desc: Publication presenting the results of academic research in Sudan in both the natural and social sciences, and the humanities.
Ind/Abst Ethnoarts Index; GeoRef.

GW/0082-0660
SYMBOLON. ***Ceased.*** **See** Religion and Theology.

MG
TALOHA. **Added/Corp** Universite de Madagascar. Vol. 1 (June 1965)-. French (English and Malagasy). an. 3600FMG. Universite de Madagascar / History, Departement d'Histoire, PB 566, Antananarivo Madagascar.
Ind/Abst Anthropol. Index; Anthropol. Lit.

FR
TECHNIQUES NOUVELLES EN SCIENCES DE L'HOMME. 1984-. French. Les Belles Lettres, 95 Boulevard Raspail, 75006 Paris France. **Tel** (1)45.48.70.55, FAX (1)45.44.92.88, telex 200577 F. **LC** AS161; .B39 subser; AS162.B44.

US/0894-3354
TEXAS JOURNAL OF IDEAS, HISTORY, AND CULTURE. [Tex. j. ideas hist. cult.]. **Added/Corp** Texas Committee for the Humanities. **VFOAT** Texas Journal. Vol. 8, No. 1 (Fall/Winter 1985)-. Periodical. English. sa. $25.00. Texas Committee for the Humanities, Banister Place A, 3809 South 2nd Street, Austin TX 78704. **Tel** (512)440-1991. **ED** Catherine Williams. **LC** F386; .T39. **DD** 976.4/005. **Bk Rev**, (Qty: 10-12). **Ad Acc, Adv Mgr:** Judith H. Diaz. **Circ:** 10,000 (ctrl). ***Continues** Texas Humanist.*

UK/0957-0322
TEXTS AND DISSERTATIONS. [Texts diss.]. **Added/Corp** Modern Humanities Research Association. **VFOAT** MHRA Texts and Dissertations. No. 10 (1979)-. Monographic series. English. ir. W. S. Maney and Son Ltd., Hudson Road, Leeds LS9 7DL England. **Tel** 011 44 532 497481, FAX 011 44 532 486983. ***Continues** Modern Humanities Research Association. Dissertation Series.*
Ind/Abst MLA Int. Bibl. Books Artic. Mod. Lang. Lit.

JA
TEZUKAYAMA DAIGAKU RONSHU. **Main/Corp** Tezukayama Daigaku. **VFOAT** Tezukayama University Review. English (Japanese). Tezukayama Daigaku Kyoyo Gakkai, Tezukayama 4-chome, Nara Japan. **LC** AS552.T4; A29. **DD** 759.951.

US/0196-0121
THANATOLOGY ABSTRACTS. **See** Psychology.

SA/0040-5817
THEORIA (PIETERMARITZBURG). (THEORIA.). [Theoria]. **Added/Corp** University of Natal. Faculty of Arts. Natal University College. Faculty of Arts. (1947)-. Academic Scholarly Publication. English (Afrikaans). Twice a year. R25.00 (individual); R35.00 (institution). University of Natal Press, PO Box 375, 3200 Pietermaritzbrg, South Africa. **Tel** 11 27 0331 63320, FAX 011 27 0331 63497. **ED** Raphael De Kadt, (editor's address: Department of Politics, University of Natal, King George V Avenue, Durban South Africa). **LC** AS615; .N315. **DD** 082. **Bk Rev. Circ:** 120.
Desc: Scholarly, non-disciplinary journal in the humanities, arts and social sciences.
Ind/Abst Annu. Bibliogr. Engl. Lang. Lit.; MLA Int. Bibl. Books Artic. Mod. Lang. Lit.

MY/0128-357X
THIRD WORLD RESURGENCE. **Added/Corp** Third World Network (George Town, Penang). No. 1, (Sept. 1990)-. Periodical. English (Spanish). Twelve times a year. £11.00 (individuals), £16.00 (institutions), Europe & UK; $20.00 (individuals), $30.00 (institutions), US & Canada. Third World Network, 87 Cantonment Road, 10250 Penang Malaysia. **Tel** 011-60-4-373511, 60-4-373713, FAX 011-60-4-368106, telex MA40989. **(Subscription address:** Third World Network, 336 Pinner Road, Middlesex HA1 4LB, UK; Michelle Syverson and Associates, 1442-A Walnut Street, Suite 81, Berkeley, CA 49709, USA.**)** **ED** Martin Khor. **Bk Rev.**
Desc: An international network of groups and individuals involved in efforts to bring about a greater articulation of the needs and rights of peoples in the Third World.

SP/0210-6310
TOLETUM. **VFOAT** Boletin de la Real Academia de Bellas Artes y Ciencias Historicas de Toledo. (1918)-. Periodical. Spanish. tq. **UDC** 7.
Ind/Abst BHA : Biblio. Hist. Art.

US/0049-4127
TOPIC (WASHINGTON). ***Suspended.*** (TOPIC.). [Topic]. **Added/Corp** Washington and Jefferson College (Washington, Pa.). No. 1 (1960/61)-Suspended. Periodical. English. an. $1.00. Topic Journal of the Liberal Arts, Washington and Jefferson College, Washington PA 15301. **LC** AS30; .T6. **DD** 881/.01/09.
Ind/Abst Abstr. Engl. Stud.; MLA Int. Bibl. Books Artic. Mod. Lang. Lit.

JA/0386-5975
TOYAMA DAIGAKU JINBUN GAKUBU KIYO. [Toyama Daigaku Jinbun Gakubu kiyo]. **VFOAT** Journal of the Faculty of Humanities, Toyama University. Periodical. Japanese. Toyama Daigaku Jinbun Gakubu, 3190 Gofuku, Toyama-shi Japan. **LC** AS552.T719; A34.
Ind/Abst Soc. Plann. Policy Dev. Abstr.; Sociol. Abstr. (?-?).

CN/0035-9122
TRANSACTIONS OF THE ROYAL SOCIETY OF CANADA. (TRANSACTIONS OF THE ROYAL SOCIETY OF CANADA. MEMOIRES DE LA SOCIETE ROYALE DU CANADA.). [Trans. R. Soc. Can.]. **Main/Corp** Royal Society of Canada. **VFOAT** Memoires de la Societe Royale du Canada. Vol. 1 (1882)-Vol. 12 (1894); Series 2, Vol. 1 (1895)-Vol. 12 (1906); Series 3, Vol. 1 (1907)-Vol. 56 (1961); Series 4, Vol. 1 (1962)-. English (French). an (July). 20.00Can$. Royal Society of Canada, PO Box 9734, Ottawa Ontario K1G 5J4 Canada. **Tel** (613)991-6990. **ED** John M. Robson. **DD** 081. **CODEN** TRSCAI. Index available. **Circ:** 1,500. Documents available from Ask*IEEE.
Desc: This publication, consisting of selected papers given at the annual meeting of the Society, is distributed to all fellows and (by exchange) to some other learned societies, and is available by subscription to libraries, institutions, and individuals.
Ind/Abst AGRICOLA [Select. Cov.]; Am. Hist. Life (1954-); Can. Period. Index (19??-); GeoRef; INSPEC (1970-).

JA/0287-7805
TSUDA-JUKU DAIGAKU KIYO. [Tsuda-juku Daigaku kiyo]. **Main/Corp** Tsuda-Juku Daigaku. **VFOAT** Journal of Tsuda College. Began with 1969 issue. Japanese (English). an. Free. Tsuda-Juku Daigaku Kiyo, 2-1-1 Tsuda-machi, Kodaira-shi Tokyo 187 Japan. **Tel** 0423-42-5136, FAX 0423-41-2444. **LC** AS552.T76; A35. **Pr Rev. Circ:** 1,000.
Desc: Tsuda College journal.
Ind/Abst Math. Rev.

JA/0389-8032
TSURUMI DAIGAKU KIYO. DAI 4-BU, JINBUN SHAKAI HEN. **VFOAT** Bulletin of Tsurumi College. Part 4, Studies in Humanities and Social Science. Japanese (Japanese). Tsurumi Daigaku, 1-3 Tsurumi 2 Tsurumi-ku, Yokohama-shi 230 Japan. **LC** AS552.Y647; A3.

PL/0860-7222
TURBULENCE / [INITIATED BY THERMAL MACHINERY INSTITUTE, TECHNICAL UNIVERSITY OF CZESTOCHOWA, POLAND]. **Added/Corp** Politechnika Czestocowska. Thermal Machinery Institute. Vol. 1 (1989)-. Periodical. English. an. Price on Request. **(Subscription address:** ARS Polona, PO Box 1001, 00068 Warsaw Poland.) **LC** IN PROCESS.

TK
TURKMENISTAN YLYMLAR AKADEMIIASYNYNG KHABARLARY. GUMANITAR YLYMLARY. **See** Social Sciences.

FI/0082-6987
TURUN YLIOPISTON JULKAISUJA SARJA B: HUMANIORA. (TURUN YLIOPISTON JULKAISUJA. ANNALES UNIVERSITATIS TURKUENSIS. SERIES B: HUMANIORA.). [Turun Yliop. julk., Sar. B]. **Main/Corp** Turun Yliopisto. **Added/Corp** Turun Yliopisto Annales Universitatis Turkuensis. Series B: Humaniora. **VFOAT** Annales Universitatis Turkuensis. Series B: Humaniora. (1923)-. Monographic series. Multiple languages (English, Finnish, French, German and Latin). **LC** AS262.T84; A3. **CODEN** AUTBD5.
Ind/Abst Annu. Bibliogr. Engl. Lang. Lit.; Psychol. Abstr. (1927-).

SW/0348-7997
TVARSNITT. **Added/Corp** Humanistisk-Samhallsvetenskapliga Forskningsradet (Sweden). No. 1 (1979)-. Periodical. Swedish. qt. Kr96.00. Swedish Science Press, PO Box 118, S 751 04 Uppsala Sweden. **Tel** 011 46 18 365566, FAX 011 48 18 365277.

SA/0041-4751
TYDSKRIF VIR GEESTESWETENSKAPPE. [Tydskr. geesteswet.]. **Added/Corp** Suid-Afrikaanse Akademie vir Wetenskap en Kuns. (March 1961)-. Periodical. Afrikaans (summaries and/or abstracts in English and German). Four times a year. R38.00. Suid Afrik Akad Wetenskap Kuns, Box 538, Pretoria 0001 South Africa. **Tel** 011 27 12 3285082. **LC** AS611; .S817. ***Supersedes in part*** *Tydskrif vir Wetenskap en Kuns.*
Ind/Abst MLA Int. Bibl. Books Artic. Mod. Lang. Lit.

FR/0041-5278
UNESCO COURIER, THE. [Unesco cour.]. **Added/Corp** Unesco. (June 1989)-. Periodical. English. mo. $55.00. UNESCO / France, 31 rue Francois Bonvin, 75732 Paris Cedex 15 France. **Tel** 011 33 1 45684564, 011 33 1 45684565, FAX 011 33 1 42733007, telex 204461 Paris. **(Subscription address:** UNIPUB, 4611 F Assembly Drive, Lanham MD 20706.) **LC** AS4.U8; A14. **NLM** W1; UN103WK. available in braille; available on microfilm and microfiche from University Microfilms International (UMI); available on an online database (file 647/Full-Text) from DIALOG. Documents available from UMI Article Clearinghouse. ***Continues*** *Courier (Paris, France : 1984), 0041-5278.*
Desc: Each issue is devoted to a main theme of universal interest, viewed from a variety of cultural standpoints by authors from different countries.
Ind/Abst Acad. Abstr. Full Text Elite (Jan. 1989-) [Full Txt.]; Acad. Abstr. (Jan. 1989-); Acad. Ind. [Computer File] (1984-); Acad. Search (Jan. 1989-); Expand. Acad. Index (1984-); Gen. Period. Index (1985-); INFO-SOUTH Abstr.; Mag. Artic. Summar. Elite (Jan. 1989-) [Full Txt.]; Mag. Artic. Summar. Select (Jan. 1989-); Mag. Artic. Summar. CD-ROM (Jan. 1989-); Mag. ASAP Plus [Full Txt.]; Mag. Express (1989-) [Full Txt.]; Mag. Index Plus (1989-); Mag. Search; Middle East Abstr. Index; Newsp. Period. Abstr. (1988-); Peace Res. Abstr. J.; Read. Guide Abstr. Select Ed.; Read. Guide Period. Lit.; Resource/One Ondisc; Soc. Sci. Source (Jan. 1989-); Mag. Index (1977-); TOM Gen. Index (1993-) [Full Txt.]; Vocat. Search (Jan. 1989-) [Full Txt.].

MX
UNIVERSIDAD. **Added/Corp** Universidad Autonoma de Queretaro. (1978)-. Periodical. Spanish (summaries and/or abstracts in English). $100.00. Edificio de Rectoria, Centro Universitario, Cerro de las Campanas, Queretaro Qro Mexico. **LC** AS63.A1; U54.

GW/0341-0129
UNIVERSITAS. ENGLISH LANGUAGE EDITION (STUTTGART). ***Ceased.*** (UNIVERSITAS.). [Universitas. Engl. lang. ed.]. Vol. 1 (1956)-Vol. 36. Periodical. English. qt. Wissenschaftliche Verlagsgesellschaft mbH, Postfach 101061, D 70009 Stuttgart Germany. **Tel** 011 49 711 258200, FAX 011 49 711 2582290, telex 723636 DAZ D. **ED** Christian Rotta. **LC** AP4; .U57. Index available in last issue of volume--attached. **Bk Rev. Ad Acc. Circ:** 6,800 (ctrl).
Desc: Journal for science, arts and literature.
Ind/Abst Am. Hist. Life (1956-1957); Annu. Bibliogr. Engl. Lang. Lit.; GeoRef; MLA Int. Bibl. Books Artic. Mod. Lang. Lit.; Philos. Index.

GW/0041-9079
UNIVERSITAS (STUTTGART). (UNIVERSITAS.). [Universitas]. Vol. 1 (April 1946)-. Periodical. German. mo. DM108.00. Wissenschaftliche Verlagsgesellschaft mbH, Postfach 101061, D 70009 Stuttgart Germany. **Tel** 011 49 711 258200, FAX 011 49 711 2582290, telex 723636 DAZ D. **ED** Christian Rotta. **LC** AP30; .U567. **DD** 053/.1; 053. **CODEN** UNIVA8. **[CCC].**
Desc: An interdisciplinary journal for the sciences and humanities.
Ind/Abst Am. Hist. Life (1954-1957); Annu. Bibliogr. Engl. Lang. Lit.; Art Archaeol. Tech. Abstr.; Energy Res. Abstr. (June 1978-); GeoRef; MLA Int. Bibl. Books Artic. Mod. Lang. Lit.; Philos. Index.

US/0887-204X
UNIVERSITY OF FLORIDA HUMANITIES MONOGRAPHS. (UNIVERSITY OF FLORIDA HUMANITIES MONOGRAPH / UNIVERSITY OF FLORIDA.). [Univ. Fla. humanit. monogr.]. **Added/Corp** University of Florida. No. 31 (1970)-. Monographic series. English. ir. Price varies per volume. University of Florida Press, 15 Northwest 15th Street, Gainesville FL 32611. **Tel** (904)392-5717, (800)226-3822. **DD** 051. ***Continues*** *University of Florida Monographs. Humanities, 0071-6189.*
Ind/Abst MLA Int. Bibl. Books Artic. Mod. Lang. Lit.

US/0085-2473
UNIVERSITY OF KANSAS PUBLICATIONS. HUMANISTIC STUDIES. **Added/Corp** University of Kansas. **VFOAT** Humanistic Studies; University of Kansas Humanistic Studies. Vol. 6, No. 4 (1940)-. Monographic series. English. ir. Peter Lang Publishing, 62 West 45th Street, 4th Floor, New York NY 10036. **Tel** (212)764-1471, (800)770-5264, telex 6973364 PLNY. ***Continues*** *Humanistic Studies (Lawrence, Kan.), 0085-2473.*
Ind/Abst MLA Int. Bibl. Books Artic. Mod. Lang. Lit. (19??-).

US/0077-6386
UNIVERSITY OF NEBRASKA STUDIES. [Univ. Neb. stud.]. Vol. 1 (1941). New Series No. 1 (Nov. 1945)-. English. ir. University of Nebraska / Love Memorial Library, Lincoln NE 68588. **DD** 051. available on microfilm and microfiche from University Microfilms International (UMI). ***Continues*** *University Studies (University of Nebraska (Lincoln Campus)).*
Ind/Abst MLA Int. Bibl. Books Artic. Mod. Lang. Lit. (19??-).

UK
UNIVERSITY OF NOTTINGHAM MONOGRAPHS IN THE HUMANITIES. **VFOAT** Monographs in the Humanities. Vol. 1; 1980-. Monographic series. English. Price varies per volume. Secretary, Department of Philosophy, University of Nottingham, Nottingham NG7 2RD England. **Tel** (0602) 484848, FAX (0602)420825, telex 37346 (UNINOT G). **ED** R A Cardwell. **Bk Rev. Circ:** 400.

CN/0042-0247
UNIVERSITY OF TORONTO QUARTERLY. [Univ. Tor. q.]. **Main/Corp** University of Toronto. **VFOAT** Letters in Canada. Vol. 1-3, No. 2, (Mar. 1895)-. Periodical. English. qt (Jan., Apr., July, Oct.). $55.00. University of Toronto Press, 5201 Dufferin Street, Downsview Ontario M3H 5T8 Canada. **Tel** (416)667-7781, (416)667-7782, FAX (416)667-7803. **ED** A. Bewell. **[CCC]. Ad Acc. Circ:** 1,000 (ctrl). available on microfilm and microfiche from University Microfilms International (UMI). Documents available from The Genuine Article, UMI Article Clearinghouse.
Desc: This journal publishes interdisciplinary articles and reviews of international repute. The Letters in Canada issue reviews fiction, poetry, and drama in Canada. General readers and specialists in fields related to the humanities appreciate the journal's breadth of view.
Ind/Abst Abstr. Engl. Stud.; Acad. Search (July 1993-); Am. Hist. Life (1959-); Annu. Bibliogr. Engl. Lang. Lit.; Arts Humanit. Citation Index [Full Cov.]; BHA : Biblio. Hist. Art; Can. Index; Can. Period. Index; Curr. Contents Arts Humanit.; Expand. Acad. Index (1989-); Humanit. Index; Humanit. Source (Jul. 1993-); INFO-SOUTH Abstr.; Lit. Crit. Regist.; Mag. Search; MLA Int. Bibl. Books Artic. Mod. Lang. Lit.; Newsp. Period. Abstr. (1990-); Res. Alert [Full Cov.]; Romant. Move.

CN
UP TO DATE (HUMAN RESOURCE). English. mo. 64.00Can$. Up to Date Publications, 7270 Woodbine Avenue, Suite 204, Markham Ontario L3R 4B9 Canada. **Tel** (416)479-7895, FAX (905)479-2990. **ED** Alan Roadburg. Index available. cum. index.

NE/0925-3440
VERZEKERINGS MAGAZINE. [Verzek. mag.]. (1991)-. Periodical. Dutch. wk (Wed.). 147.50F Belgium; 200.00F Europe. Nijgh Periodicken BV, Postbus 122, 3100 AC Schiedam Netherlands. **Tel** 011 31 10 4274174. **UDC** 368. ***Continues*** *VVP Magazine, 0922-7415.*

US/0709-4698
VICTORIAN PERIODICALS REVIEW. **See** Literary and Political Reviews.

AG
VIGENCIA. **Added/Corp** Universidad de Belgrano. Fundacion Editorial de Belgrano para la Educacion, la Ciencia y la Tecnologia. Vol. 1 Sept./Oct. (1968)-. Periodical. Spanish. mo. $30.00. Editorial Belgrano, Teodoro Garcia 2090, Buenos Aires, Argentina. **ED** Enrique Pugliese. **LC** AS78; .B414. **DD** 056/.1. **Bk Rev. Ad Acc. Circ:** 15,000.

SP
VINIYOGA. (19??)-. Periodical. Spanish (French). Four times a year. 2800ptas Spain; 4300ptas other. Asociacion Viniyoga Espana, Barcelona 30, 08400 Granollers Spain. **Tel** 011 34 3 8709504.

BE
VLAAMSE GIDS, DE. (19??)-. Periodical. Dutch. bm. 700F. Uitgeverij J Hoste / Abo Dienst, Emile Jacqmainlaan 105, 1000 Brussels Belgium. **Tel** (02)2193290. **ED** Uitg J. Hoste. **Bk Rev. Ad Acc. Circ:** 13,000.
Desc: A cultural periodical; apart from giving cultural information, it defends the principles of liberty and tolerance.
Ind/Abst Annu. Bibliogr. Engl. Lang. Lit.; MLA Int. Bibl. Books Artic. Mod. Lang. Lit.

FR/0763-9686
VOCABLE (ENGLISH ED.). (1984)-. French (German and Spanish). bw (except Aug.). 242.90F France; 400.94F French Possessions & Europe; 695.06F others (paper edition); 834.74F France; 1150.00F French Overseas Dept. & Territories & Europe; 1510.00F others (cassette edition). Vocable, Service Abonnements, BP 1, 59440 Avesnes Sur Helpe France. **Tel** 011 33 27614040. available on audiocassette.

US/0043-0609
WASHINGTON INTERNATIONAL ARTS LETTER. Vol. 1 (June 1962)-. Periodical. English. qt. $124.00. Washington International Arts Letter, PO Box 12010, Des Moines IA 50312. **Tel** (515)243-8691. **ED** James Duncan. **LC** NX1; .W3. **Bk Rev. Circ:** 15,000. available on microfilm and microfiche from University Microfilms International (UMI).
Desc: A newsletter and digest concerning patronage and developments in the arts, humanities and education. Includes 10 issues per year comprised of the quarterly grants and support report and a bi-monthly resources and trends report. Both the quarterly and the bi-monthly reports are also available separately.

US/0891-8899
WEBER STUDIES. [Weber stud.]. **Added/Corp** Weber State College. School of Arts and Humanities. Vol. 1 (Spring 1984)-. Periodical. English. Three times a year (Jan., May, Sept.). $20.00 (institutions), $10.00 (individuals). Weber Studies, Weber State University, School of Arts and Humanities, Ogden UT 84408. **Tel** (801)626-6657, (801)626-6473. **ED** Neila C. Seshachari. **LC** AS30; .W38. **DD** 051. cum. index. **Bk Rev**, (Qty: 12-18). **Ad Acc. Acid Free. Circ:** 1,100.
Desc: Original fiction, critical essays, biographies, and poetry. Topics include art, literature, history, political science, sociology, philosophy, and the sciences.
Ind/Abst Abstr. Engl. Stud. (Spring 1987-)(spring 1987-); Am. Humanit. Index; Index Am. Period. Verse; MLA Int. Bibl. Books Artic. Mod. Lang. Lit.; Soc. Plann. Policy Dev. Abstr.; Sociol. Abstr. (Spring 1987-).

CH/0508-3052
WEN SHIH CHE HSUEH PAO / KUO LI TAIWAN TA HSUEH. **Added/Corp** Kuo li Tai-wan ta Hsueh. Wen Hsueh Yuan. **VFOAT** Bulletin of the College of Liberal Arts, National Taiwan University; Kuo li Tai-wan ta Hsueh wen Shih che Hsueh pao. (1950)-. Periodical. Chinese. sa. National Taiwan University, College of Liberal Arts, Taipei, Taiwan. **LC** AS455.T263; A38.
Ind/Abst Am. Hist. Life (1966-).

US/0083-9167
WHERE AMERICA'S LARGE FOUNDATIONS MAKE THEIR GRANTS. ***Ceased.*** [Where Am. large found. make their grants]. (1971/72)-?. English. be. Public Service Materials Center, 5130 Macarthur Boulevard Northwest, 2nd Floor, Washington DC 20016. **Tel** (202)966-6838. **DD** 001.

UK/0083-9248
WHIDDEN LECTURES. **Added/Corp** McMaster University, Hamilton, Ont. (1956)-. Monographic series. English. ir. Price varies per volume. Oxford University Press, Walton Street, Oxford OX2 6DP England. **Tel** 011 44 865 56767, FAX 011 44 865 267773, telex 837330 OXPRES G. **(Subscription address:** Oxford University Press / USA, Journals Marketing Department, Oxford University Press, 2001 Evans Road, Cary NC 27513.)

US/0740-6789
WILLAMETTE JOURNAL OF THE LIBERAL ARTS, THE. **See** The Arts.

US/0512-1175
WISCONSIN ACADEMY REVIEW.
Added/Corp Wisconsin Academy of Sciences, Arts and Letters. Vol. 1 (Winter 1954)-. Academic Scholarly Publication. English. Four times a year (Mar., June, Sept., Dec.). $30.00. Wisconsin ACA Science Art & Letters, 1922 University Avenue, Madison WI 53705. **Tel** (608)263-1693, FAX (608)262-2639. **ED** Faith Miracle, Bill Urbrock. **Circ:** 1,800.
Desc: Relating to the Wisconsin people. Scholarly journal dealing with various subjects of concern and interest.

GW/0512-1426
WISSENSCHAFT UND GESELLSCHAFT. (19??)-. Monographic series. German. ir. Price varies per volume. Akademie-Verlag GmbH, Muehlenstrasse 33 34, D 13162 Berlin Germany. **Tel** 011 49 30 47889300, FAX 011 49 30 47889357. **DD** 600; 300; 500.
Desc: The institute of theory, history and organization of science of the academy of sciences publishes results of research into philosophical, historic, social and economic aspects of science trends.

US/0884-2930
WYOMING, THE HUB OF THE WHEEL.
[Wyo. hub wheel]. **VFOAT** Wyoming. No. 1 (Spring 1986)-. Periodical. English. sa. $9.00 (U.S.), $12.00 (foreign), $15.00 (cassette). **DD** 810. available on audiocassette.
Ind/Abst Am. Humanit. Index (199?-).

US/1041-6374
YALE JOURNAL OF LAW & THE HUMANITIES. See Law.

JA
ZASSHI KIJI SAKUIN, JINBUN SHAKAI HEN. Added/Corp Kokuritsu Kokkai Toshokan (Japan). Ukeire Seiribu. Kokuritsu Kokkai Toshokan (Japan). Etsuranbu. Kokuritsu Kokkai Toshokan (Japan). Sanko Shoshibu. **VFOAT** Japanese Periodicals Index Humanities and Social Science; Japanese Periodicals Index. Vol. 1, No. 1 (Sept. 1948)-. Periodical. Japanese. qt. ¥21200. Kokuritsu Kokkai Toshokan, (National Diet Library), 1-10-1 Nagatacho Chiyoda-ku, Tokyo 100 Japan. **Tel** 03 3581-2331, FAX 03 3597-9104. **LC** AI19.J3; Z38. cum. index. **Bk Rev. Circ:** 1,120 (ctrl).
Desc: A classified index to articles and essays contained in 1,850 titles of domestic periodicals.

PL
ZESZYTY NAUKOWE. Main/Corp Wyzsza Szkoa Pedagogiczna W Gdansku. Wydzia Humanistyczny. 1-. Polish. **(Subscription address:** ARS Polona, PO Box 1001, 00068 Warsaw Poland.) **LC** AS248.W9; A45. **DD** 001.3.
Ind/Abst SportSearch (May 1987-).

US/0036-2050
ZPRAVY - SVU. Main/Corp Czechoslovak Society of Arts and Sciences in America. **VFOAT** SVU News. **VAT** Zpravy - Spolecnost pro Vedy a Umeni; Zpravy - Czechoslovak Society of Arts and Sciences in America. V. 1- Sept. 1959-. Periodical. Czech. bm. Czechoslovak Society of Arts and Science, 2 Fordham Hill Oval-9G, New York NY 10468. **Tel** (212)365-5094. **LC** E184.B67; C988. **Bk Rev. Circ:** 1,000.
Desc: Czechoslovak Society of Arts and Sciences activities, members' achievements in arts and sciences. Czech and Slovak exile literature reviews.

ABSTRACTING, BIBLIOGRAPHIES AND STATISTICS

US/0361-0144
AMERICAN HUMANITIES INDEX, THE.
(AMERICAN HUMANITIES INDEX.). Vol. 1 (Spring/Summer 1975)-. Abstracting/Indexing Service. English. an. $250.00. Whitston Publishing Company Inc, PO Box 958, Troy NY 12181. **Tel** (518)283-4363. **LC** AI3; .A278. **DD** 016.051. **Circ:** 250.
Desc: An index to creative, critical, and scholarly serials in the arts and humanities. It currently indexes over 480 journals many of which are not indexed at all elsewhere or that are available only in indexing services not universally nor easily available.

FR/0248-3912
ARCHIVES ET DOCUMENTS, MICRO-EDITION. SCIENCES HUMAINES. (ARCHIVES ET DOCUMENTS, MICRO-EDITION. SCIENCES HUMAINES / INSTITUT D'ETHNOLOGIE.). [Arch. doc. micro-ed. Sci. hum.]. **Added/Corp** Institut d'Ethnologie (Musee de l'Homme). **VFOAT** Archives et Doeuments, Micro-Edition. Sciences Humaines, Sciences Naturelles. (1979)-. French (summaries and/or abstracts in English). an. Institut d'Ethnologie Musee de l'Homme, Palais de Chaillot, Place du Trocadero 75116 Paris France. **Tel** 45 53 82 15. **LC** Z5111; .A73; GN316. **DD** 016.306. *Continues in part* Archives et Documents, Micro-Edition, 0338-8905; *Absorbed* Archives et Documents, Micro-Edition. Sciences Naturelles.

US/0162-8445
ARTS & HUMANITIES CITATION INDEX (PRINT ED.). (ARTS & HUMANITIES CITATION INDEX.). [Arts humanit. cit. index]. **VAT** Arts and Humanities Citation Index. (1976)-. Abstracting/Indexing Service. English. sa. $5330.00 (print); $5665.00 (CD-ROM); $7275.00 (combination print and CD-ROM). Institute for Scientific Information, 3501 Market Street, Philadelphia PA 19104. **Tel** (215)386-0100, (800)523-1850, FAX (215)386-6362, telex 84-5305. **(Subscription address:** Institute for Scientific Information, PO Box 71416, Chicago IL 60694.) **LC** AI3; .A63. **DD** 016.05. available on magnetic tape and an online database (as Arts & Humanities Search); available on CD-ROM from Institute for Scientific Information.
Desc: Contains specialized bibliographies in the arts and humanities. Covers leading journals from the full range of arts and humanities disciplines.

UK/0966-8772
BHI PLUS [COMPUTER FILE].
Abstracting/Indexing Service. English. qt. £795.00. Bowker Saur Ltd., A Reed Reference Publishing Company, Part of Reed International PLC, 59-60 Grosvenor Street, London WIX 9DA England. **Tel** 011 44 71 4935841, FAX 011 44 71 4991590. **ED** Lyn Duffus. available in print (British Humanities Index).
Desc: Provides access to a wide range of information - covering the arts, history, economics, philosophy, politics and society.

UK/0007-0815
BRITISH HUMANITIES INDEX. [Br. humanit. index]. **Added/Corp** Library Association. (1962)-. Abstracting/Indexing Service. English. qt. £415.00 EEC; £455.00 other. Bowker Saur Ltd., A Reed Reference Publishing Company, Part of Reed International PLC, 59-60 Grosvenor Street, London WIX 9DA England. **Tel** 011 44 71 4935841, FAX 011 44 71 4991590. **(Subscription address:** World-Wide Subscription Services, Unit 4, Gibbs Reed Farm Pashley Road, Ticehurst TN5 7HE England.) **LC** AI3; .B7. **DD** 011/.34. available on CD-ROM (BHI Plus). *Supersedes in part* Subject Index to Periodicals.
Desc: A current, easy-to-use guide to important British journals covering all areas of the humanities. Reference tool for librarians, academics, information specialists, researchers and everyone who needs to locate, recall or monitor current information.

US/0095-5981
HUMANITIES INDEX. [Humanit. index]. Vol. 1 (1975)-. Abstracting/Indexing Service. English. qt. Print edition sold on the service basis. H W Wilson Company, 950 University Avenue, Bronx NY 10452. **Tel** (800)367-6770, (718)588-8400, FAX (718)590-1617, telex 4990003 HWILSON. **ED** Joanna Greenspon. **LC** AI3; .H85. **DD** 016.0013. Index available. cum. index. ctrl circ. available on CD-ROM from WILSONDISC; available on diskette from WILSONSEARCH; available on magnetic tape from WILSONTAPE; available on an online database from WILSONLINE. *Supersedes in part* Social Sciences & Humanities Index, 0037-7899.
Desc: Author and subject index to periodicals in the fields of archaeology and classical studies, area studies, folklore, history, language and literature, literary and political criticism, performing arts, philosophy, religion and theology and related subjects.

US/1063-3294
HUMANITIES INDEX (CD-ROM ED.).
(HUMANITIES INDEX [COMPUTER FILE].). [Humanit. index]. **Added/Corp** H.W. Wilson Company. (198?)-. English. qt. $1295.00. H W Wilson Company, 950 University Avenue, Bronx NY 10452. **Tel** (800)367-6770, (718)588-8400, FAX (718)590-1617, telex 4990003 HWILSON. **LC** AI3. **DD** 001. available on magnetic tape from WILSONTAPE; available on diskette from WILSONSEARCH; available on an online database from WILSONLINE.
Desc: Provides information on art, archaeology and classical studies, area studies, dance, drama, film, folklore, history, journalism and communications, language and literature, music, performing arts, philosophy, and religion and theology.

●US/1073-1962
HUMANITIES SOURCE. (HUMANITIES SOURCE [COMPUTER FILE] EBSCO CD-ROM.). [Humanit. sources]. **Added/Corp** EBSCO Publishing (Firm). **VFOAT** EBSCO CD-ROM. (1993)-. Abstracting/Indexing Service. English. mo. $1495.00. EBSCO Publishing / Boston, 83 Pine Street, Peabody MA 01960. **Tel** (800)653-2726 North America, (508)535-8500, FAX (508)535-8545. **ED** Melissa Kummerer. **DD** 001. *Absorbed* History Source CD-ROM, 1063-9799.
Desc: Provides access to abstracts and indexing coverage of over 400 journals in the disciplines of philosophy, literature, religion and the arts. The product also includes ASCII full text for several journals, including The Writer, Germanic Review, Journal of Popular Film & Television and more.

US/1042-4032
INTERNATIONAL JOURNAL OF HUMANITIES AND PEACE, THE. See Humanities.

FR/0080-2484
REVUE BIBLIOGRAPHIQUE DE SINOLOGIE. (1955)-. Bibliography. French (English). an. 250.00F. Editions EHESS, 131 Boulevard Saint Michel, 75005 Paris France. **Tel** 011 33 43 544715. **ED** Danielle Elisseeff and Michel Cartier. **Circ:** 400.
Desc: Surveys of numerous articles appearing in the field of Chinese human sciences.

JA
ZASSHI KIJI SAKUIN. JINBUN SHAKAI HEN (CUMULATIVE EDITION). (ZASSHI KIJI SAKUIN. JINBUN SHAKAI HEN / KANSHU, KOKURITSU KOKKAI TOSHOKAN SANKO SHOSHIBU.). **VFOAT** Japanese Periodicals Index. Humanities and Social Science. 1948-1954-. Japanese (Japanese). ¥35000 each volume of 11 vol. set. **(Subscription address:** Kinokuniya Company Ltd., 38-1 Sakuragaoka 5, chome Setagaya-ku, Tokyo 156 Japan.) **LC** AI19.J3; Z3814.

HYPNOSIS

US/0002-9157
AMERICAN JOURNAL OF CLINICAL HYPNOSIS, THE. (AMERICAN JOURNAL OF CLINICAL HYPNOSIS : OFFICIAL JOURNAL [OF] THE AMERICAN SOCIETY OF CLINICAL HYPNOSIS AND THE ACADEMY OF APPLIED PSYCHOLOGY IN DENTISTRY.). [Am. j. clin. hypn.]. **Added/Corp** Academy of Applied Psychology in Dentistry (U.S.) American Society of Clinical Hypnosis. Vol. 1, No. 1 (July 1958)-. Academic Scholarly Publication. English. Four times a year. $30.00 (individuals), $45.00 (institutions) Canada & Mexico; $37.60 (individuals), $52.60 (institutions) others. American Society of Clinical Hypnosis, 2250 East Devon Avenue, Suite 291, Des Plaines IL 60018. **Tel** (312)297-3317. **ED** Thurman Mott Jr. **LC** RC490; .A4. **NLM** W1 AM45. **CODEN** AJHNA3. **Bk Rev. Ad Acc. Pr Rev. Circ:** 5,200. available on microfilm and microfiche from University Microfilms International (UMI). Documents available from The Genuine Article, BIOSIS Document Express.
Ind/Abst Annals Behav. Med.; Biol. Abstr.; Curr. Contents Soc. Behav. Sci.; EMBASE; Index Med.; Index Period. Artic. Relat. Law (19??-19??); Middle East Abstr. Index; Life Sci. Collect.; Psychol. Abstr. (1966-); PsycINFO; PsycLit; Res. Alert [Full Cov.]; Soc. Sci. Cit. Index [Full Cov.].

AT/0156-0417
AUSTRALIAN JOURNAL OF CLINICAL AND EXPERIMENTAL HYPNOSIS. [Aust. j. clin. exp. hypn.]. **Added/Corp** Australian Society for Clinical and Experimental Hypnosis. Vol. 6 (Nov. 1978)-. Periodical. English. sa. 20.00Aus$ (individuals), 35.00Aus$ (institutions) Australia; 25.00Aus$ (individuals), 40.00Aus$ (institutions) other. Australian Journal of Clinical and Experimental Hypnosis, Edward Wilson Building, Austin Hospital, Heidelberg VIC 3084 Australia. **Tel** 011 61 3 4596499. **ED** Wendy-Louise Walker. **NLM** W1 AU558D. **CODEN** AJCHDV. **Bk Rev. Pr Rev. Circ:** 1,400 (ctrl). Documents available from BIOSIS Document Express. *Continues* Australian Journal of Clinical Hypnosis.
Desc: Academic journal with papers, case notes, and letters regarding clinical and experimental use of hypnosis. Australian and international contributors.
Ind/Abst Biol. Abstr.; EMBASE; Psychol. Abstr. (1978-); PsycINFO; PsycLit.

AT/0810-0713
AUSTRALIAN JOURNAL OF CLINICAL HYPNOTHERAPY AND HYPNOSIS, THE.
Added/Corp Australian Society of Clinical Hypnotherapists. (198?)-. Periodical. English. Twice a year (Mar. & Sept). 25.00Aus$ (individuals), 31.00Aus$ (institutions) Australia and New Zealand; 30.00Aus$ (individuals), 38.00Aus$ (institutions) other. Australian Academic Press Pty. Ltd., 32 Jeays Street, Bowen Hills Queensland 4006 Australia. **Tel** 011 61 7 2571176, FAX 011 61 7 2525908. **ED** Zoltan Keleman. **NLM** W1; AU558DK. **Bk Rev. Ad Acc. Adv Mgr:** Stephen May. **Circ:** 500. *Continues* Australian Journal of Clinical Hypnotherapy, 0159-7175.
Desc: Publishes original clinical, research, theoretical, historical and related reports dealing with the professional application of hypnosis and hypnotherapy.
Ind/Abst EMBASE; Psychol. Abstr. (1980-); PsycLit.

UK/0960-5290
CONTEMPORARY HYPNOSIS : THE JOURNAL OF THE BRITISH SOCIETY OF EXPERIMENTAL AND CLINICAL HYPNOSIS. Added/Corp British Society of Experimental and Clinical Hypnosis. Vol. 8, No. 1 (Feb. 1991)-. Periodical. English. Three times a year. £30.00

(individuals), £45.00 (institutions). Whurr Publishers Ltd, 19B Compton Terrace, London N1 2UN England. **Tel** 011 44 71 359 5979, FAX 011 44 71 226 5290. **(Subscription address:** Turpin Distribution Services Limited, Blackhorse Road, Letchworth, Hertfordshire SG6 1HN, United Kingdom.**) ED** Dr. Brian Fellows. **NLM** W1; CO769MQA. **CODEN** COHYET. Index available. **Bk Rev. Ad Acc.** Full Page (B&W) ú150.00. **Pr Rev. Acid Free. Circ:** 450. available on microfilm and microfiche from University Microfilms International (UMI). ***Continues*** *British Journal of Experimental and Clinical Hypnosis, 0265-1033.*
Desc: The journal has two main objectives: to provide a forum for the critical discussion of ideas, theories, findings, prodedures and social policies associated with the topic of hypnosis; and to disseminate information on all aspects of theory, research and practice.
Ind/Abst Annals Behav. Med.; Psychol. Abstr. (1982-); PsycINFO.

GW/0933-1093
EXPERIMENTELLE UND KLINISCHE HYPNOSE : ZEITSCHRIFT DER DEUTSCHEN GESELLSCHAFT FUER HYPNOSE. Added/Corp Deutsche Gesellschaft fuer Hypnose. Vol. 1, No. (1983)-. Periodical. German (English). sa. Verlag Dr. Winkler, Postfach 10 26 65, 4630 Bochum 1 Germany. **NLM** W1; EX519E.
Ind/Abst PsycINFO (1987-); PsycLit.

US/0882-6072
HYPNOSIS REPORTS. ***Ceased.*** [Hypn. rep.]. Vol. 1, No. 1 (April 1985)-(1988). Periodical. English. mo. Harte Center for Hypnosis Inc, 37 East 28th Street, New York NY 10016. **Tel** (212)481-7240. **ED** Richard Harte. **DD** 154. **Bk Rev.**

US/0882-8652
HYPNOTHERAPY TODAY. (HYPNOTHERAPY TODAY : JOURNAL OF THE AMERICAN ASSOCIATION OF PROFESSIONAL HYPNOTHERAPISTS.). Periodical. English. qt. Hypnotherapy Today, PO Box 731, McLean VA 22101. **Tel** (703)448-9623. **ED** William S Brink. **DD** 615. **Bk Rev. Circ:** 1,800 (ctrl).
Desc: Publishes articles and reports on theory, techniques, professional practice, and other topics related to therapeutic hypnosis. Reviews books which would be of interest to hypnotherapists.

US/0020-7144
INTERNATIONAL JOURNAL OF CLINICAL AND EXPERIMENTAL HYPNOSIS, THE. [Int. j. clin. exp. hypn.]. **Added/Corp** Society for Clinical and Experimental Hypnosis (U.S.). Vol. 7, No. 1 (Jan. 1959)-. Academic Scholarly Publication. English. qt (Jan., Apr., July, Oct.). $123.00. SAGE Periodical Press, 2455 Teller Road, Thousand Oaks CA 91320. **Tel** (805)499-0721, FAX (805)499-0871, telex 100799. **ED** Fred H. Frankel. **LC** RC490; .S623. **DD** 615.8512. **NLM** W1 IN766DI. **CODEN** IJEHAO. **Bk Rev. Ad Acc. Pr Rev. Acid Free. Circ:** 2,700 (ctrl). available on microfilm and microfiche from University Microfilms International (UMI). Documents available from The Genuine Article, BIOSIS Document Express. ***Continues*** *Journal of Clinical and Experimental Hypnosis, 0095-988X.*
Desc: Publishes research and clinical papers dealing with hypnosis in psychology, psychiatry, the medical and dental specialties and allied areas of science.
Ind/Abst Annals Behav. Med.; Biol. Abstr.; Curr. Contents Soc. Behav. Sci.; EMBASE; Index Med.; Middle East Abstr. Index; Life Sci. Collect.; Psychol. Abstr. (1959-); PsycINFO; PsycLit; Res. Alert [Full Cov.]; Soc. Sci. Cit. Index [Full Cov.]; Soc. Work Abstr. [Select. Cov.].

JA/0581-3131
JAPANESE JOURNAL OF HYPNOSIS. Twice a year. Japanese Society of Hypnosis, Otsuka, Bunkyo-ku, Tokyo 112 Japan.
Ind/Abst PsycINFO (1985-).

US
JOURNAL OF CLINICAL HYPNOTHERAPY AND HYPNOANALYSIS. (19??)-. English. qt. $70.00 (institutions), $42.50 (individuals) US; $104.00 (institutions), $86.50 (individuals) other. International Universities Press Inc., 59 Boston Post Road, PO Box 1524, Madison CT 06443-1524. **Tel** (203)245-4000, FAX (203)245-0775, telex 282986 IUP BK.

IT
RASSEGNA DI PSICOTERAPIE, IPNOSI : ORGANO UFFICIALE QUADRIMESTRALE DELLA F.I.S.P.I.R. (FEDERAZIONE ITALIANA STUDIO PSICOTERAPIE, IPNOSI E STATI DI RILASSAMENTO). VFOAT Rassegna di Psicoterapie. Vol. 13, N. 1 (Jan.-April 1986)-. Periodical. Italian. Three times a year. Edizioni Minerva Medica, Corso Bramante 83-85, 10126 Turin Italy. **Tel** 011 39 11 678282, FAX 011 39 11 674502. **NLM** W1; RA689G. ***Continues*** *Rassegna di Ipnosi e Psicoterapie.*

INDUSTRIAL HEALTH AND SAFETY

NZ
ACC INJURY STATISTICS. WORK. Added/Corp Accident Compensation Corporation (New Zealand). **VFOAT** Injury Statistics. Work; Work. **VAT** Accident Compensation Corporation Injury Statistics. Work. Vol. 1 (1991)-. English.

CN/0044-5878
ACCIDENT PREVENTION. [Accid. prev.]. **Added/Corp** Industrial Accident Prevention Association (Ont.) Industrial Accident Prevention Associations. No. 1 (Apr. 1953)-. Periodical. English. Six times a year. 18.00Can$ Canada; 24.00Can$ US; 33.00Can$ other. Industrial Accident Prevention Association, 250 Yonge Street, 28th Floor, Toronto Ontario M5B 2N4 Canada. **Tel** (416)506-8888, FAX (416)506-8880. **ED** Susan Stanton. Index Bound in First Issue. **Bk Rev**, (Qty: 4). **Ad Acc. Pr Rev. Circ:** 18,000 (ctrl). ***Supersedes*** *Memorandum for Industrial Executives.*
Desc: Information concerning, and promotion of, safety and health both on and off the job, for workers in the province of Ontario.
Ind/Abst Saf. Health Work.

CN
ACCIDENT PREVENTION MAGAZINE. English. Ten times a year. 32.10Can$ Canada; $40.00 US; $55.00 other. Industrial Accident Prevention Association, 250 Yonge Street, 28th Floor, Toronto Ontario M5B 2N4 Canada. **Tel** (416)506-8888, FAX (416)506-8880. **ED** Susan Stanton. **Bk Rev. Circ:** 37,000 (ctrl). ***Continues*** *Guide to Safety.*
Desc: Health and safety articles, news, products and features for the manufacturing and retail firms in Ontario.

US
ACCIDENT PREVENTION MANUAL FOR BUSINESS & INDUSTRY. Main/Corp National Safety Council. 1st. Ed. (1946)-. English. ir. $79.95. National Safety Council, 1121 Spring Lake Drive, Itasca IL 60143. **Tel** (800)621-7615, (708)775-2294, FAX (708)285-0797. **LC** T55; .N3. **DD** 614.85.
Desc: Three-volume set with information on occupational safety and health.

US/0882-4274
ACGIH TRANSACTIONS. [ACGIH trans.]. **Main/Corp** American Conference of Governmental Industrial Hygienists. **VAT** American Conference of Government Industrial Hygienists Transactions. 1982-. English. an. ACGIH, Building D5, 6500 Glenway Avenue, Cincinnati OH 45211. **LC** HD7260; .A45. **DD** 363.1/1/0973. **NLM** W1; AN626KH v.4 etc. ***Continues*** *American Conference of Governmental Industrial Hygienists. Transactions of the Annual Meeting.*

US/1070-9274
ACTS FACTS. (ACTS FACTS / ACTS.). [ACTS facts]. **Added/Corp** ACTS (Association). **VFOAT** Acts Facts Newsletter. (19??)-. Periodical. English. mo (12 issues per year). $10.00 US; $12.00 Canada; $16.00 other. Arts Crafts and Theater Safety, 181 Thompson Street #23, New York NY 10012. **Tel** (212)777-0062, FAX Call ahead for connection. **ED** Monona Rossol. **DD** 346. Index available (Bound in Dec. issue - $1.00). cum. index. **Bk Rev**, (Qty: 2-3). **Circ:** 500.
Desc: Occupational health, safety and regulatory information for people in the arts and theatre.

US/0276-5063
ADVANCES IN MODERN ENVIRONMENTAL TOXICOLOGY. [Adv. mod. environ. toxicol.]. (1980)-. Academic Scholarly Publication. English. ir. Price varies per volume. Princeton Scientific Publishing Company Inc., PO Box 2155, Princeton NJ 08543. **Tel** (609)683-4750, FAX (609)683-0838. **ED** M A Mehlman. **LC** UNC. **NLM** W1; AD682D. **CODEN** AETODY. **[CCC].** Index available. **Ad Acc. Circ:** 1,500. Documents available from CASDDS.
Desc: This is a series of volumes dealing with topics of interest to professional biological chemists, toxicologists, pharmacologists, occupational physicians, industrial hygienists, and scientists working in related disciplines.
Ind/Abst AGRICOLA [Select. Cov.]; Chem. Abstr.; EMBASE.

FR/0290-0106
ALARMES, PROTECTION, SECURITE. (1981)-. Periodical. French. bm. 295.11F France; 480.00F other. Editions Sedep, 8 rue de la Michodiere, 75002 Paris France. **Tel** 011 33 1 47424100. **UDC** 620.1. **Ad Acc.** ***Continues*** *Alarmes Protection Vols, 0240-8155.*
Desc: Industrial security, electronic security, physical security, and information on theft and fire.

IT/0393-7054
AMBIENTE E SICUREZZA SUL LAVORO. [Ambiente sicur. lav.]. (1985)-. Periodical. Italian. Nine times a year (includes supplements). L170000.00 Italy; L185000.00 Europe; L215000.00 other. Edizioni Protezione Civile SPA, Via dell Acqua Traversa 187/189, 00135 Rome Italy. **Tel** 011 39 6 3313000, FAX 011 39 6 3313212, telex 626462 EPCINFI. **UDC** 331.823. Index available in last issue of volume--attached. **Bk Rev. Ad Acc, Adv Mgr:** Davide Carissimi. **Circ:** 10,000.

US/0002-8894
AMERICAN INDUSTRIAL HYGIENE ASSOCIATION JOURNAL. [Am. Ind. Hyg. Assoc. j.]. **Added/Corp** American Industrial Hygiene Association. **VFOAT** Industrial Hygiene Journal; Journal. Vol. 19, No. 1 (Feb. 1958)-. Academic Scholarly Publication. English. mo. $110.00 US; $135.00 Canada and Mexico; $175.00 (includes airmail charge) other. American Industrial Hygiene Association, 2700 Prosperity Avenue, Suite 250, Fairfax VA 22031. **Tel** (703)849-8888, FAX (703)207-3561. **(Subscription address:** American Industrial Hygiene Association, PO Box 27632, Richmond, VA 23261**) ED** Paul D. Halley. **LC** RC963; .A135. **DD** 613. **NLM** W1 AM4365. **CODEN** AIHAAP. **[CCC].** Index available (bound in all issues). cum. index. **Bk Rev. Ad Acc. Pr Rev. Acid Free. Circ:** 10,000. available on microfilm and microfiche from University Microfilms International (UMI). Documents available from The Genuine Article, BIOSIS Document Express, UMI Article Clearinghouse, CASDDS, Documents on Demand. ***Continues*** *American Industrial Hygiene Association Quarterly, 0096-820X.*
Desc: The primary vehicle of communication among members of the industrial hygiene profession throughout the world publishing the most peer reviewed articles in its field. Printed on acid-free paper.
Ind/Abst ABI/INFORM Glob. Ed.; ABI Inform Ondisc (March 1975-Oct. 1975); Acoust. Abstr.; Agric. Eng. Abstr. (1991-); Air Pollut. Titles; Anal. Abstr.; Appl. Sci. Technol. Index; Art Archaeol. Tech. Abstr.; BioBusiness; Biol. Abstr.; Chem. Abstr.; Chem. Hazards Ind.; Coal Abstr.; Cumul. Index Nurs. Allied Health Lit.; Curr. Contents, Agric. Biol. Environ. Sci.; EMBASE; Energy Res. Abstr.; Eng. Mater. Abstr.; Environ. Abstr.; For. Prod. Abstr. (1991-); For. Abstr.; Health Saf. Sci. Abstr.; Index Med.; Index Vet.; Ind. Hyg. Dig.; INIS Atomindex [Micro.]; Int. Aerosp. Abstr.; Lab. Hazards Bull.; Lit. Pat. Abstr., Oilfield Chem. (1972-); Lit. Abstr., Catal. Catal.; Lit. Abstr., Health Environ.; Lit. Abstr., Pet. Refin. Petrochem.; Lit. Abstr., Pet. Substit.; Lit. Abstr., Transp. Storage; MINPROC; Mintec, Min. Technol. Abstr.; Pig News Inf.; Pollut. Abstr. Indexes; Res. Alert [Full Cov.]; Rev. Med. Vet. Mycology; Risk Abstr.; Saf. Health Work; Sci. Cit. Index; SCISEARCH; Soc. Sci. Cit. Index [Select. Cov.]; Sug. Indus. Abstr.; Vet. Bull.; Toxicol. Abstr.; Trop. Dis. Bull.; World Ceram. Abstr.; World Surf. Coat. Abstr.

GW/0177-3062
AMTLICHE MITTEILUNGEN DER BUNDESANSTALT FUER ARBEITSSCHUTZ. Added/Corp Bundesanstalt fuer Arbeitsschutz (Germany). (19??)-. German. Four times a year. Free. Bundesanstalt fuer Arbeitsschutz, Postfach 170202, D44061 Dortmund Germany. **Tel** 011 49 231 9071 306, FAX 011 49 0231 9071 454, telex 822 153 BAU D.
Ind/Abst Trop. Dis. Bull.

BL
ANAIS DO CONPAT. Main/Corp Congresso Nacional de Prevencao de Acidentes do Trabalho. (19??)-. Portuguese. Free on request. Fundacentro, rua Capote Valente 710, CEP 05409 Sao Paulo SP Brazil. **Tel** 011 55 11 8536588. **LC** HD7683; .C66a.

UK/0003-4878
ANNALS OF OCCUPATIONAL HYGIENE, THE. [Ann. occup. hyg.]. **Added/Corp** British Occupational Hygiene Society. Vol. 1 (Dec. 1958)-. Academic Scholarly Publication. English (French). bm. $455.00 The Americas; £305.00 other. Pergamon Press, An Imprint of Elsevier Science Ltd., The Boulevard, Langford Lane, Kidlington, Oxford OX5 1GB United Kingdom. **Tel** 011 44 865 843000, 011 44 865 843699, FAX 011 44 865 843010. **(Subscription address:** Elsevier Science Ltd. Oxford Fulfillment Centre, PO Box 800, Kidlington, Oxford OX5 1DX United Kingdom.**) ED** John McK Ellison (editor's address: c/o TUC Centenary Institute of Occupational Health, London School of Hygiene and Tropical Medicine, Keppel Street, London WC1E 7HT United Kingdom). **LC** RC963; .A213. **DD** 613.6/2/05. **NLM** W1 AN617. **CODEN** AOHYA3. **[CCC]. Pr Rev.** available on microfilm and microfiche from University Microfilms International (UMI). Documents available from Article Express International, The Genuine Article, BIOSIS Document Express, CASDDS, Documents on Demand.
Desc: Covers the emission, measurement and control of gases, fumes, dusts, radiation and noise, ventilation, personal protection, sampling and analytical techniques, dose-response relationships and hygiene standards. Features include refereed original research reports and short communications, and state-of-the-art reviews. Also includes letters to the editor and reports of meetings.
Ind/Abst Acoust. Abstr.; AGRICOLA [Select. Cov.]; Agric. Eng. Abstr.; Air Pollut. Titles; Anal. Abstr.; BioBusiness; Biol. Abstr.; Biol. Dig.; Chem. Abstr.; Chem. Hazards Ind.; Coal Abstr.; Curr. Aware. Biol. Sci., CABS; Curr. Biotechnol.; Curr. Contents Life Sci.; EMBASE; Energy Inf. Abstr.; Energy Res. Abstr.; Eng. Index Annu.; Environ. Abstr.; Ergon. Abstr.; Health Saf. Sci. Abstr.;

Health Plan. Adminis.; Index Med.; Ind. Hyg. Dig.; Int. Aerosp. Abstr.; Lab. Hazards Bull.; Life Sci. Collect.; Pollut. Abstr. Indexes; Protozoolog. Abstr.; Res. Alert [Full Cov.]; Rev. Med. Vet. Entomol.; Risk Abstr.; Saf. Health Work; Sci. Cit. Index; SCISEARCH; Soc. Sci. Cit. Index [Select. Cov.]; Toxicol. Abstr.; Trop. Dis. Bull.; World Ceram. Abstr.

US
ANNUAL REPORT - ALABAMA. DEPT. OF INDUSTRIAL RELATIONS. DIVISION OF SAFETY AND INSPECTION. Main/Corp Alabama. Dept. of Industrial Relations. Division of Safety and Inspection. **VFOAT** Statistical Annual Report. 1959/60-. English. an. Alabama Department of Industrial Relations, Industrial Relations Building, 649 Monroe Street, Montgomery AL 36131. **Tel** (205)261-5465. **LC** HD3663.A2; A33. **DD** 363.1/19622/09761. **Circ:** 1,500 (ctrl). ***Continues*** *Annual Statistical Report - Alabama Department of Industrial Relations, Division of Safety and Inspection.*

AT
ANNUAL REPORT / DEPARTMENT OF OCCUPATIONAL HEALTH, SAFETY & WELFARE. Main/Corp Western Australia. Dept. of Occupational Health, Safety & Welfare. **Added/Corp** Western Australia. Occupational Health, Safety, and Welfare Commission. (1986)-. English. an. Department of Occupational Health, Safety & Welfare, Perth WA Australia. **LC** RC967; .W49a. **DD** 354.941001/61.

FI
ANNUAL REPORT / INSTITUTE OF OCCUPATIONAL HEALTH. Main/Corp Tyoterveyslaitos. (19??)-. Periodical. English (Finnish). an. Free. Institute of Occupational Health, Topeliuksenkatu 41 a A, SF-00250 Helsinki Finland. **Tel** 358 0 47471, FAX 358 0 4747548, telex 121 394. **ED** Suvi Lehtinen. **LC** RC968; .T96a. **DD** 354.4897/0084/1. **Circ:** 4,000 (ctrl).
Desc: A report which describes the development of occupational health and safety in Finland and the activities of the Institute of Occupational Health.

US
ANNUAL REPORT / THE DIVISION OF SAFETY AND HYGIENE, BUREAU OF WORKERS' COMPENSATION. Main/Corp Ohio. Division of Safety and Hygiene. (1989)-. English. 30 West Spring Street, Columbus OH 43266-0581. **DD** 353.9/771/00783. ***Continues*** *Annual Report of the Division of Safety and Hygiene.*

US/1047-322X
APPLIED OCCUPATIONAL AND ENVIRONMENTAL HYGIENE. [Appl. occup. environ. hyg.]. **Added/Corp** American Conference of Governmental Industrial Hygienists. Vol. 5, No. 1 (Jan. 1990)-. Academic Scholarly Publication. English. mo (1 volume). $178.00 US; $263.00 (air mail), $220.00 (surface mail) other. Elsevier Science Publishing Company Inc, Madison Square Station, PO Box 882, New York NY 10159-0882. **Tel** (212)633-3950, FAX (212)633-3990. **LC** RC963.A1; A67. **DD** 613.6/2/05. **NLM** W1; AP516M. **CODEN** AOEHE9. **[CCC]. Ad Acc. Pr Rev.** Documents available from CASDDS, Documents on Demand. ***Continues*** *Applied Industrial Hygiene, 0882-8032.*
Ind/Abst Chem. Abstr. (1990-); EMBASE; Environ. Abstr.; Ergon. Abstr.; Health Saf. Sci. Abstr.; Ind. Hyg. Dig. (199?-); Pollut. Abstr. Indexes; Risk Abstr.

NO/0332-7124
ARBEIDERVERN. [Arbeidervern]. 1.- Vol.; Apr. 1973-. Periodical. Norwegian. bm. Kr90.00. Direktoratet for Arbeidstilsynet, Fr Nansens Vie 14 Boks 8103, DEP 0032 Oslo 1 Norway. **Tel** (02)957000, FAX (02)466214. **ED** Tor Skjervagen. **LC** HD7200; .A32A. **Bk Rev. Ad Acc. Circ:** 41,000 (ctrl).
Desc: Covers worker protection and working environment.
Ind/Abst Energy Res. Abstr. (Sept. 1980-); Saf. Health Work.

●NE/0920-119X
ARBEIDSOMSTANDIGHEDEN. Added/Corp Nederlands Instituut Voor Arbeidsomstandigheden. (1992)-. Periodical. Dutch. mo. Fl 185.00. Libresso BV, Postbus 878, 7400 GA Deventer Netherlands. **Tel** 011 31 5700 47421. ***Continues*** *Maandblad Voor Arbeidsomstandigheden, 0920-119X.*

●NE
ARBEIDSOMSTANDIGHEDEN ACTUEEL. Added/Corp Nederlands Instituut Voor Arbeidsomstandigheden. (1992)-. Periodical. Dutch. mo. Nederlands Instituut voor Arbeidsomstandigheden, Postbus 5665, 1007 AR Amsterdam Netherlands. **Tel** 020-5498611.

GW/0300-581X
ARBEITSMEDIZIN, SOZIALMEDIZIN, PRAVENTIVMEDIZIN. [Arbeitsmed., Sozialmed., Praventivmed.]. 8.- Yearly Volume; Jan. 1973-. Academic Scholarly Publication. German. mo. $103.00. AW Gentner Verlag, Postfach 101742, D-70015 Stuttgart Germany. **Tel** 011 49 711 636720, FAX 011 49 711 6367247, telex 841 722244. **LC** RC963; .A2142. **NLM** W1 AR125QP. **CODEN** ASPVAS. Index available. **Bk Rev. Ad Acc. Pr Rev. Circ:** 4,500. Documents available from BIOSIS Document Express. ***Continues*** *Arbeitsmedizin, Sozialmedizin, Arbeitshygiene, 0003-7753.*
Ind/Abst Biol. Abstr.; Chem. Hazards Ind.; Coal Abstr.; EMBASE; Energy Res. Abstr. (Sept. 1976-); Lab. Hazards Bull.; Life Sci. Collect.; Rev. Agric. Entomol.; Rev. Med. Vet. Mycology; Saf. Health Work; SCISEARCH; SportSearch; Trop. Dis. Bull.

GW/0138-1555
ARBEITSSCHUTZ, ARBEITSHYGIENE. [Arb.schutz, Arb.hyg.]. 16. Yearly (1/80)-. Periodical. German. qt. 13.00M. Zentralinstitut fuer Arbeitschutz, Gerhart-Hauptmann Str. 1, 8020 Dresden, Germany. **Tel** telex ZVA 26221. **NLM** W1 AR128P. **Bk Rev. Ad Acc. Circ:** 8,000 (ctrl). ***Continues*** *Informationen Arbeitsschutz, Arbeitshygiene, 0138-1458.*
Desc: Occupational safety research, accidents, diseases, noise and vibration control, analysis, statistics, management and planning, training and education, safety techniques, safetylaw, publications, etc.

GW
ARBEITSSICHERHEIT. Added/Corp Germany (West). Bundesministerium fuer Arbeit und Sozialordnung. (1986)-. German. ir. DM120.00 (5 volume set). Rudolf Haufe Verlag, Hindenburgstrasse 64, D 79102 Freiburg I BR Germany. **Tel** 011 49 761 36830, FAX 011 49 761 3683236, telex 841 772442. **LC** HD7707; .A7.

SW/0347-7193
ARBETSMILJO. VFOAT Working Environment. Swedish (Swedish). Arbetsmiljo, Kungsholms Hamnplan 3, Stockholm 112 20 Sweden. **LC** HD7731; .A72.

SW
ARBETSMILJON I SIFFROR. MILFOSTATISTISK ARSBOK. VFOAT Miljostatistisk Arsbok; Yearbook of Environmental Statistics; Working Environment in Figures. (1985)-. Swedish. SCB Statistiska Centralbyran, 11581 Stockholm Sweden. **LC** HD7731; .A73.

IT
ARCHIVIO DI SCIENZE DEL LAVORO. Vol. 1 (1985)-. Periodical. Italian (summaries and/or abstracts in English). qt. Istituto Poligrafico Zecca Stato, Piazza Verdi 10, 00198 Rome Italy. **Tel** 011 39 6 85082307, 011 39 6 85082221. **NLM** W1; AR554F. ***Continues*** *Lavoro Umano.*
Ind/Abst Trop. Dis. Bull.

CR/0004-1254
ARHIV ZA HIGIJENU RADA I TOKSIKOLOGIJU. [Arh. hig. rada toksikol.]. **Added/Corp** Institut za Medicinska Istrazivanja (Jugoslavenska Akademija Znanosti i Umjetnosti) Institut za Medicinska Istrazivanja i Medicinu Rada (Jugoslavenska Akademija Znanosti i Umjetnosti) Udruzenje za Medicinu Rada SFRJ. Udruzenje Toksikologa Jugoslavije. **VFOAT** Archives of Industrial Hygiene & Toxicology. Vol. 7, No. 1 (1956)-. Academic Scholarly Publication. English (summaries and/or abstracts in English, German and Russian). Four times a year. $48.00. Institute Medical Research & Occupational Health, Ksaverska Cesta 2, 41001 Zabreb Croatia. **Tel** 38 41 434537. **LC** RA1211; .A73. **NLM** W1 AR786. **CODEN** AHRTAN. Index available (bound in Dec. issue). **Bk Rev** (Qty: 25-30). **Ad Acc, Adv Mgr Tel** 38 41 434188 Ext. 56. **Pr Rev. Circ:** 1,000 (ctrl). Documents available from BIOSIS Document Express, CASDDS. ***Continues*** *Arhiv Za Higijenu Rada.*
Desc: Fields of interest: occupational and environmental health, toxicology. Official journal of the Croatian Association on Occupational Health and the Croatian Toxicological Society.
Ind/Abst Biol. Abstr.; Chem. Abstr.; EMBASE; Ergon. Abstr.; Health Saf. Sci. Abstr.; Health Plan. Adminis.; Index Med.; Ind. Hyg. Dig.; Nutr. Abstr. Rev., Ser. A, Hum. Exp.; Life Sci. Collect. (1985-); Pollut. Abstr. Indexes; Rev. Med. Vet. Entomol.; Saf. Health Work; Toxicol. Abstr.; Wheat Barley Trit. Abstr.

US/1057-9419
ASA NEWSLETTER - APPLIED SCIENCE AND ANALYSIS, INC, THE. **See** Military and Defense.

US/1046-0438
ASBESTOS MANAGEMENT SOURCEBOOK. **See** Building and Construction.

CN/0226-9422
AT THE CENTRE (HAMILTON). ***Ceased.*** (AT THE CENTRE.). [At Cent.]. **Main/Corp** Canadian Centre for Occupational Health and Safety. **VFOAT** Au Centre. Vol. 2, No. 1 (June 1979)-No. 15 (Apr. 1992). Periodical. English (French). bm. **DD** 354.710083/028/9. ***Continues*** *Canadian Centre for Occupational Health and Safety. Planning Secretariat. At the Centre., 0226-9422.* ***Continued in part by*** *Canadian Centre for Occupational Health and Safety. Au Centre.*
Ind/Abst Chem. Hazards Ind.; Ergon. Abstr.; Lab. Hazards Bull.; Trop. Dis. Bull.

AT/0005-0180
AUSTRALIAN SAFETY NEWS. (19??)-. English. 45.00Aus$ Australia; 100.00Aus$ other. National Safety Council of Australia, 322 Glenferrie Road, Malvern VIC 3144 Australia. **Tel** 011 61 3 824 8822.
Ind/Abst Ergon. Abstr.

CN/0821-2937
B.C. WORKER'S HEALTH NEWSLETTER. [B.C. work. health newsl.]. **VAT** British Columbia Workers' Health Newsletter. No. 1 (May/June 1982)-. Newsletter. English. qt. 15.00Can$ (individuals), 21.00Can$ (union/community), 30.00Can$ (institutions) Canada; $16.25 (individuals), $20.75 (union/community), $22.50 (institutions) US; 25.00Can$ (individuals), 35.00Can$ (union/community), 45.00Can$ (institutions) other. Labour Studies Program, 2055 Purcell Way, North Vancouver British Columbia V7J 3H5 Canada. **Tel** (684)984-4954. **ED** Ken Hansen and Ed Lavalle. **DD** 363.1/1/09711. **Circ:** 300.
Desc: Concerned about the health and and safety of all Canadian workers.

GW/0170-5911
BASF-STUDIE. Added/Corp Badische Anilin- und Soda-Fabrik. Aerztliche Abteilung. (1971)-. Monographic series. German. Price varies per volume. F K Schattauer Verlagsgesellschaft mbH, Postfach 10 45 45, D 70040 Stuttgart Germany. **Tel** 011 49 711 2298726. **NLM** W1 B422K.

GW/0171-2144
BERICHT UBER DAS ... INTERNATIONALE KOLLOQUIUM UBER DIE VERHUTUNG VON ARBEITSUNFALLEN UND BERUFSKRANKHEITEN IN DER CHEMISCHEN INDUSTRIE. [Ber. Int. Kolloqu. Verhut. Arb.unf. Berufskrankh. Chem. Ind.]. **Added/Corp** International Social Security Association. International Section for the Prevention of Occupational Accidents and Diseases in the Chemical Industry. **VFOAT** Report of the ... International Symposium on the Prevention of Occupational Accidents and Diseases in the Chemical Industry. (1970)-. English (French and German). **CODEN** BIKIDA. Documents available from CASDDS.
Ind/Abst Chem. Abstr.

US/0090-7480
BEST'S SAFETY DIRECTORY. (BEST'S SAFETY DIRECTORY; SAFETY-SECURITY-POLLUTION CONTROL PRODUCTS.). [Best's saf. dir.]. **Added/Corp** A.M. Best Company. (19??)-. English. an. $43.75. AM Best Company, Ambest Road, Oldwick NJ 08858. **Tel** (908)439-2200 ext. 5653, telex 837744. **LC** T55.A1; B4. **DD** 338.4/7/620860257. **NLM** W 26 B561. **[CCC]. Ad Acc.** ***Continues*** *Best's Environmental Control and Safety Directory, 0067-6322.*
Desc: The most complete sourcebook for occupational safety-health needs. Contains information on regulatory standards, safety techniques, product descriptions, applications and purchase sources.

GW/0173-0487
BIA REPORT. [BIA Rep.]. **VFOAT** B.I.A. Report. Began in 1981?. Academic Scholarly Publication. German. ir. Price varies per volume. Berufsgenossenschaftliches Institut fur Arbeitssicherheit Augustin 2 Bundesrepublik, Deutschland Germany. **Tel** 02241-231-02, FAX 02241-231-234, telex 889 460 BIA D. **CODEN** BRPODE. **Circ:** 400-800 (ctrl). Documents available from CASDDS.
Ind/Abst Chem. Abstr. (1981-1982).

US/0149-0923
BIORESEARCH TODAY. INDUSTRIAL HEALTH & TOXICOLOGY. ***Ceased.*** **VFOAT** Industrial Health & Toxicology. **VAT** Bioresearch Today. Industrial Health and Toxicology. Ceased (Dec. 1991). English. mo. BioSciences Information Service, Biological Abstracts / BIOSIS, 2100 Arch Street, Philadelphia PA 19103-1399. **Tel** (800)523-4806 US, (215)587-4800 Pennsylvania and worldwide, FAX (215)587-2016, telex 831739.
Desc: Current awareness journal including abstracts and content summaries of studies involving industrial health and toxicology.

BL
BOLETIM ESTATISTICO. Main/Corp Fundacao Jorge Duprat Figueiredo de Seguranca e Medicina do Trabalho. (19??)-. Bulletin. Portuguese. Fundacentro, rua Capote Valente 710, CEP 05409 Sao Paulo SP Brazil. **Tel** 011 55 11 8536588. **LC** HD7262.5.B7; F86a. **DD** 363.1/12/0981.

SP/0210-2439
BOLETIN BIBLIOGRAFICO DE LA PREVENCION. **See** Economics-Labor.

UK/0007-1072
BRITISH JOURNAL OF INDUSTRIAL MEDICINE. ***Title Change.*** [Br. j. ind. med.]. **Added/Corp** British Medical Association. Vol. 1, No. 1 (Jan. 1944)-Vol. 50, No. 12 (Dec. 1993). Academic Scholarly Publication. English. qt. BMJ / British Medical Journal Publishing Group, British Medical Association House, Tavistock Square, London WC1H 9JR England. **Tel** 011 44 71 3874499, FAX 011 44 71 383 6402, telex 290034 HBJ MN. **ED** H.A. Waldron. **LC** RC963; .A23. **DD** 331.82205. **NLM** W1; BR539. **CODEN** BJIMAG. **[CCC].** cum. index. **Pr Rev.** available on microfilm and microfiche from University Microfilms International (UMI). Documents available from The Genuine Article, BIOSIS Document Express, CASDDS, Documents on Demand. ***Continued by*** *Occupational and Environmental Medicine, 1351-0711.*
Desc: Authoritative papers on aspects of occupational medicine. Covers the pneumoconioses, occupational cancers, industrial toxicology and psychology.
Ind/Abst Acoust. Abstr.; Air Pollut. Titles; Art Archaeol. Tech. Abstr.; BioBusiness; Biol. Abstr.; Chem. Abstr.; Chem. Hazards Ind.; Coal Abstr.; Curr. Aware. Biol. Sci., CABS; Curr. Contents Clin. Med.; Curr. Contents Life Sci.; EMBASE; Environ. Abstr.; Environ. Period. Bibliogr.; Ergon. Abstr.; For. Prod. Abstr. (19??-19??); For. Abstr.; Health Saf. Sci. Abstr.; Health Plan. Adminis.; Hospit. Health Admin. Index; Index Med.; Ind. Hyg. Dig.; Lab. Hazards Bull.; Leadscan; Lit. Pat. Abstr., Oilfield Chem. (1972-); Lit. Abstr., Catal. Catal.; Lit. Abstr., Health Environ.; Lit. Abstr., Pet. Refin. Petrochem.; Lit. Abstr., Pet. Substit.; Lit. Abstr., Transp. Storage; Maize Abstr.; Nutr. Abstr. Rev., Ser. B, Live Feeds and Feed.; Nutr. Abstr. Rev., Ser. A, Hum. Exp.; Life Sci. Collect.; Pollut. Abstr. Indexes; Postharvest News Inf.; Potato Abstr.; Protozoolog. Abstr.; Res. Alert [Full Cov.]; Rev. Agric. Entomol.; Rev. Med. Vet. Entomol.; Rev. Med. Vet. Mycology; Rev. Plant Pathol.; Risk Abstr.; Saf. Health Work; Sci. Cit. Index; SCISEARCH; Soc. Sci. Cit. Index [Select. Cov.]; Soils Fert.; Surf. Treat. Technol. Abstr.; Text. Technol. Dig. (19??-199?); Toxicol. Abstr.; Trop. Dis. Bull.; Weed Abstr.; World Ceram. Abstr.; World Surf. Coat. Abstr.; World Text. Abstr.

FR
BULLETIN DE DOCUMENTATION. No. 1 (Jan. 1981)-. Bulletin. French. ir. 180.00F. Institut National de Recherche & Securite, 4 rue Andre Boulle, 94942 Creteil Cedex 09 France. **Tel** 011 33 1 42070606. **LC** TA145; .B85. Index available. cum. index. **Circ:** 3,000. ***Continues*** *Documentation Technique (Electricite de France).*

FR/0376-6187
BULLETIN DE DOCUMENTATION INRS. **Added/Corp** Institut National de Recherche et de Securite. International Occupational Safety and Health Information Centre. **VAT** Bulletin de Documentation - Institut National de Recherche et de Securite. Vol. 1, (1974)-. Bulletin. French. Seven times a year. 210.00F France; 260.00 other. Institut National de Recherche & Securite, 4 rue Andre Boulle, 94942 Creteil Cedex 09 France. **Tel** 011 33 1 42070606. **NLM** ZWA 400 B938. ***Supersedes*** *Bulletin Bibliographique de la Prevention, 0045-3498 .*
Desc: Bibliographic bulletin related to health and safety at the workplace.

US/0271-3888
BULLETIN / HOLMES SAFETY ASSOCIATION. Jan. 1979-. Bulletin. English. mo. MSHA Holmes Safety Association, PO Box 25367, Denver CO 80225. **LC** TN295; .B76. **DD** 622/.9/05. ***Continues*** *Holmes Safety Association Monthly Safety Topic, 0272-3190.*

●US
BWC NEWS. See Economics-Labor.

BE/0376-7639
CAHIERS DE MEDECINE DU TRAVAIL. See Medical Science and Technology.

FR/0010-244X
CAHIERS DES COMITES DE PREVENTION DU BATIMENT ET DES TRAVAUX PUBLICS. [Cah. com. prev. batim. trav. publics]. **Added/Corp** Organisme de Prevention du Batiment et des Travaux Publics. Organisme de Prevention du Batiment et des Travaux Publics. L'Activite de l'O.P.P.B.T.P. (1947)-. Periodical. French. bm. 138.00F (one year), 256.00F (two years) France; 256.00F (one year), 468.00F (two years) other. Organisme Professionnel de Prevention du Batiment et des Travaux Publics, 204 Rond Point du Pont Sevres, 92516 Boulgne Blnct CDX France. **Tel** 33 1 46092000, FAX 33 1 46092740. **ED** Pierre Verges. **LC** TA192; .C32. **Ad Acc. Circ:** 18,000 (ctrl). ***Continues*** *Cahiers des Comites de Securite du Batiment et des Travaux Publics.*
Ind/Abst CIS Abstr.; Coal Abstr.; Saf. Health Work.

FR/0153-5552
CAHIERS - S.E.M.A. (CAHIERS SEMA.). [Cah. - S.E.M.A.]. **Added/Corp** Societe d'Economie et de Mathematique Appliquees. (1977)-. French. an. ***Continues*** *Metra.*
Ind/Abst Int. Abstr. Oper. Res. (?-?); Saf. Health Work.

US/1054-1209
CAL-OSHA REPORTER. [Cal-OSHA report.]. **VFOAT** Cal OSHA Reporter; California OSHA Rreport. (1973)-. Periodical. English. Fifty times a year (Except last 2 weeks of Dec.). $227.00. Cal-OSHA Reporter, PO Box 36, San Pablo CA 94806. **Tel** (510)233-1880 or 837-7100, FAX (510)233-1249 or 837-3900. **ED** Anne Bell. **DD** 344. Index available (Jan. iss.). **Circ:** 1,080 (ctrl).
Desc: Update on news, law, meetings and legal decisions regarding California and FED-OSHA for safety and health specialists, lawyers, regulators, unions, insurers. Includes research compendium.

CN/0709-5252
CANADIAN OCCUPATIONAL HEALTH & SAFETY NEWS. Vol. 1, No. 7 (June 12, 1978)-. Periodical. English. wk. 373.00Can$ Canada; 419.00Can$ other. Southam Information and Technology Group Inc., 1450 Don Mills Road, Don Mills Ontario M3B 2X7 Canada. **Tel** (416)445-6641, (800)668-2374, FAX (416)442-2261. **ED** Scott Williams. **DD** 614.8/52/0971. Index available. **Bk Rev. Circ:** 1,200. available on an online database (file 636/Full-Text) from DIALOG. ***Continues*** *Canadian Industrial Health & Safety News, 0701-8983.*
Desc: Canada's only national, independent OH&S newsletter, reports the latest information on management techniques, legislation, hazards and issues. Examines successful corporate strategies, new training and education resources, career opportunities.
Ind/Abst PTS Newsl. Database [Full Txt.].

CN/0008-4611
CANADIAN OCCUPATIONAL SAFETY. [Can. occup. saf.]. Vol. 1, No. 3, (July 1963)-. Periodical. English. bm. 16.00Can$ Canada; 48.00Can$ US; 72.00Can$ other. Clifford Elliot & Associates Ltd, PO Box 358, Oakville Ontario L6J 5A2 Canada. **Tel** (905)842-2884, FAX (905)842-8226. **ED** Ms Jackie Roth. **Ad Acc, Adv Mgr:** Ralph Elliot. **Circ:** 10,500 (ctrl). ***Continues*** *Canadian Occupational Safety Magazine, 0315-1611.*
Desc: Feature articles, technical papers and product news relating to the industrial health and safety field in Canada.
Ind/Abst Chem. Hazards Ind.; Lab. Hazards Bull.; Saf. Health Work.

CN/0825-608X
CANADIAN OCCUPATIONAL SAFETY AND HEALTH LAW MONTHLY REPORT. See Law.

CN/0710-0973
CASE HISTORY OF AN ACCIDENT OR INCIDENT. [Case hist. accid. incid.]. Periodical. English. mo. Industrial Accident Prevention Association, 250 Yonge Street, 28th Floor, Toronto Ontario M5B 2N4 Canada. **Tel** (416)506-8888, FAX (416)506-8880. **DD** 363.1/1/079.

US/1057-1981
CCPS/AICHE DIRECTORY OF CHEMICAL PROCESS SAFETY SERVICES. See Chemistry.

UK
CERAMICS, HEALTH AND SAFETY. **Main/Corp** Great Britain. Health and Safety Executive. 1971/77-. English. Health & Safety Executive, Room 414 St Hughs House Stanley, Btle Merseyside L20 3QY England. **Tel** 011 44 51 951 4000, FAX 011 44 51 922 5394, telex 628235. **LC** RC965.C43; G73A. **DD** 363.1/19666/0941.

US
CHARACTERISTICS OF OCCUPATIONAL INJURIES AND ILLNESSES IN ARKANSAS. English. Arkansas Department of Labor, PO Box 2981, Little Rock AR 72203.

US/0733-8384
CHARACTERISTICS OF WORK-RELATED INJURIES AND ILLNESSES IN MAINE. **Main/Corp** Maine. Bureau of Labor. Research and Statistics Division. English. an. Free. Research & Statistics Division, Bureau of Labor Standards, State House Station 45, Augusta ME 04333-0045. **Tel** (207)289-6400, FAX (207)289-6449. **ED** John L Rioux, Janet Callahan, and Terry Hathaway. **LC** HD7262.5.U62; M23A. **DD** 363.1/19/09741. **Circ:** 1,000 (ctrl).
Desc: Statistical compiliation of injury and illness characteristics for State of Maine.

US/0145-3599
CHARTBOOK ON OCCUPATIONAL INJURIES AND ILLNESSES. **Main/Corp** United States. Bureau of Labor Statistics. Government Publication. English. US Department of Labor / Bureau of Labor Statistics, 441 G Street NW, Washington DC 20212. **Tel** (202)606-7800, FAX (202)606-7797. **LC** HD8051.A7876 subser; HD7262.5. **DD** 331.1/08 S; 614.8/52/0973.

UK/0265-5721
CHEMICAL HAZARDS IN INDUSTRY. See Industrial Health and Safety-Abstracting, Bibliographies and Statistics.

●US/1074-9098
CHEMICAL HEALTH & SAFETY. **Added/Corp** American Chemical Society. **VFOAT** Chemical Health and Safety. (1994)-. Periodical. English. bm. $250.00 (institution) US. American Chemical Society, 1155 Sixteenth Street Northwest, Washington DC 20036. **Tel** (800)333-9511, (800)227-5558, (614)447-3776, FAX (202)833-7736. **(Subscription address:** American Chemical Society / Ohio, Department L 0011, Columbus OH 43268-0011.**)**

US/8755-2566
CHILTON'S INDUSTRIAL SAFETY & HYGIENE NEWS. [Chilton's ind. saf. hyg. news]. **VFOAT** Industrial Safety & Hygiene News; Chilton's Industrial Safety and Hygiene News. (198?)-. Periodical. English. mo. $50.00 US & Canada; $65.00 other. Chilton Company, 201 King of Prussia Road, Radnor PA 19089. **Tel** (610)964-4122, (800)695-1214, FAX (610)964-4978, telex 6851035 CHILTON UW. **ED** David Johnson. **DD** 658. **CODEN** CIHNEM. **[CCC]. Ad Acc. Circ:** 57,000 (ctrl). available on microfilm and microfiche from University Microfilms International (UMI). ***Continues*** *Industrial Safety & Hygiene News, 0278-8217.*
Desc: Product reports and feature articles in ISHN assist industrial safety-hygiene personnel in selective equipment and services that improve on-the-job employee safety and health.
Ind/Abst BioBusiness (1989-).

US/0271-2873
CITATOR OF THE DECISIONS OF THE OCCUPATIONAL SAFETY AND HEALTH REVIEW COMMISSION. [Cit. decis. Occup. Saf. Health Rev. Comm.]. **Main/Corp** United States. Occupational Safety and Health Review Commission. (1979)-. English. Occupational Safety and Health Review Commission, 1825 K Street NW, Washington DC 20006. **Tel** (202)634-7943. **LC** KF3568.34; .O242. **DD** 344.73/0465/02648. ***Continues*** *Citator to Decisions of the Occupational Safety and Health Review Commission, 0271-2873.*

US/1043-8017
CLEANROOMS (FLEMINGTON, N.J.). (CLEANROOMS.). [CleanRooms]. **VFOAT** Clean Rooms; Clear Rooms Magazine; Cleanrooms Magazine. (198?)-. Periodical. English. Twelve times a year. $33.00 US and Canada; $89.00 other. PennWell Publishing Company, 1421 South Sheridan, PO Box 1260, Tulsa OK 74101. **Tel** (918)835-3161, (800)331-4463, FAX (918)831-9497. **(Subscription address:** CleanRooms Magazine, Publishing Services, PO Box 1260, Tulsa OK 74101.**) ED** Tom Brotzman. **LC** TH7692; .C54. **DD** 620.8/6. **Ad Acc. Circ:** 45,000 (ctrl).
Desc: Contamination control technology; feature articles, news items and product information on cleanroom-related products and services.

FR/0248-742X
COLLECTION DE MONOGRAPHIES DE MEDECINE DU TRAVAIL. [Collect. monogr. med. trav.]. (1981)-. Monographic series. French. ir. Price varies per volume. Masson 120, Boulevard Saint-Germain, Paris VI France. **NLM** W1; CO17QK.

CN/0712-936X
COMMUNIQUE / HUMAN FACTORS ASSOCIATION OF CANADA. [Commun. - Hum. Factors Assoc. Can.]. **Added/Corp** Human Factors Association of Canada. (1971)-. Periodical. English (French). Six times a year (Feb., Apr., June, Aug., Oct., Dec.). 100.00Can$ (associate); 130.00Can$ (full) Comes with Human Factors Association of Canada membership. Human Factors Association of Canada, 6519B Mississauga Road, Mississauga Ontario L5N 1A5 Canada. **Tel** (905)567-7193. **ED** Sharon McFadden and Luc Desnoyers. **DD** 613.6/2/05. **Bk Rev. Ad Acc. Circ:** 400 (ctrl).

●UK/1351-5802
COMPETENCY. (1993)-. Periodical. English. qt. £160.00 UK; £170.00 other. Eclipse Publications Ltd, 18 20 Highbury Place, London N5 1QP England. **Tel** 011 44 71 354 5858.

US
CONNECTICUT OCCUPATIONAL INJURY AND ILLNESS SURVEY. **Added/Corp** Connecticut. Labor Dept. Connecticut. Occupational Safety and Health Division. Connecticut. Occupational Safety and Health Statistics Unit. **VFOAT** Connecticut Occupational Injuries and Illnesses; Occupational Injuries and Illnesses in Connecticut. (1990)-. English. ***Continues*** *Connecticut. Labor Dept. Occupational Injuries and Illnesses in Connecticut.*
Desc: Looks at industrial accidents and hygiene.

CN/0704-6766
CONSTRUCTION SAFETY JOURNAL. See Building and Construction.

US/0744-7167
CONSTRUCTION SUPERVISION & SAFETY LETTER. ***Ceased.*** **See** Building and Construction.

US/0093-5093
COURSE ANNOUNCEMENT - DIVISION OF TRAINING. NATIONAL INSTITUTE FOR OCCUPATIONAL SAFETY AND HEALTH. (COURSE ANNOUNCEMENT.). **Main/Corp** National Institute for Occupational Safety and Health. Division of Training. English. National Institute for Occupational Safety and Health, 4676 Columbia Parkway, Cincinnati OH 45226. **Tel** (513)533-8236. **LC** HD7654; .N33A. **DD** 614.8/52.

UK/0967-8344
CRONER'S HEALTH & SAFETY AT WORK. (19??)-. Periodical. English. bm. £216.00. Croner Publ Ltd, Croner House, London Road, Kingston upon Thames, Surrey KT2 6SR England. **Tel** 011 44 81 5473333, FAX 081 547-2637.

CN/0713-3421
CSSE CONTACT. [CSSE contact]. **VAT** Canadian Society of Safety Engineering Contact. Periodical. English (French). bm. 35.00Can$. Canadian Society of Safety Engineering, 6519B Mississauga Road, Mississauga Ontario L5N 1A6 Canada. **Tel** (416)567-7192, FAX (416)567-7191. **ED** Peter Fletcher. **DD** 363.1/1/06071. **Ad Acc. Circ:** 2,000 (ctrl). ***Continues*** *Membership Newsletter / Canadian Society of Safety Engineering.*

US
CURRENT HOUSING REPORTS. H-170, AMERICAN HOUSING SURVEY FOR THE HARTFORD METROPOLITAN AREA IN ... . **Added/Corp** United States. Bureau of the Census. United States. Dept. of Housing and Urban Development. Office of Policy Development and Research. **VFOAT** American Housing Survey for the Hartford Metropolitan Area in ... . (1987)-. Government Publication. English. ir. US Department of Commerce / Bureau of the Census, Data User Services Division, Customer Services, Washington DC 20233-0800. **Tel** (301)763-4100. **(Subscription address:** Superintendent of Documents, US Government Printing Office, Washington DC 20402.**)** ***Continues*** *Current Housing Reports. H-170, Annual Housing Survey, Hartford, Conn., Standard Metropolitan Statistical Area. Housing Characteristics for Selected Metropolitan Areas.*

US
CURRENT HOUSING REPORTS. H-170, AMERICAN HOUSING SURVEY FOR THE MIAMI-FT. LAUDERDALE METROPOLITAN AREA IN ... . **Added/Corp** United States. Bureau of the Census. United States. Dept. of Housing and Urban Development. Office of Policy Development and Research. **VFOAT** American Housing Survey for the Miami-Ft.Lauderdale Metropolitan Area in ... . (1986)-. Government Publication. English. ir. US Department of Commerce / Bureau of the Census, Data User Services Division, Customer Services, Washington DC 20233-0800. **Tel** (301)763-4100. **(Subscription address:** Superintendent of Documents, US Government Printing Office, Washington DC 20402.**)** ***Continues*** *Current Housing Reports. H-170, Annual Housing Survey, Miami, Fla., Standard Metropolitan Statistical Area. Housing Characteristics for Selected Metropolitan Areas.*

US
CURRENT HOUSING REPORTS H-170, AMERICAN HOUSING SURVEY FOR THE NEW ORLEANS METROPOLITAN AREA IN ... . **Added/Corp** United States. Bureau of the Census. United States. Dept. of Housing and Urban Development. Office of Policy Development and Research. **VFOAT** American Housing Survey for the New Orleans Metropolitan Area in ... . **VAT** New Orleans Metropolitan Area in ... . (1986)-. Government Publication. English. ir. US Department of Commerce / Bureau of the Census, Data User Services Division, Customer Services, Washington DC 20233-0800. **Tel** (301)763-4100. **(Subscription address:** Superintendent of Documents, US Government Printing Office, Washington DC 20402.**)** ***Continues*** *Current Housing Reports. H-170, Annual Housing Survey, New Orleans, La., Standard Metropolitan Statistical Area. Housing Characteristics for Selected Metropolitan Areas.*

CN/0225-9990
DANGEROUS AND/OR UNUSUAL OCCURRENCES. **Main/Corp** British Columbia. Ministry of Energy, Mines and Petroleum Resources. July/Sept. 1978-. Periodical. English. Ministry of Energy, Parliament Buildings, Victoria British Columbia V8V 1X4 Canada. **DD** 622/.8/09711. ***Continues*** *Dangerous and/or Unusual Occurences, 0225-9990.*

US/0270-3777
DANGEROUS PROPERTIES OF INDUSTRIAL MATERIALS REPORT. [Danger. prop. ind. mater. rep.]. Vol. 1, No. 1 (Sept./Oct. 1980)-. Academic Scholarly Publication. English. Four times a year. $220.00 US; $262.00 other. Van Nostrand Reinhold Company Inc., 115 5th Avenue, New York NY 10003. **Tel** (212)254-3232, FAX (212)673-1239, telex 272562. **(Subscription address:** Dangerous Properties of Industrial Materials, PO Box 1897, Lawrence KS 66044-8897.**)** **ED** N. Irving Say. **LC** T55.3.H3; D36. **DD** 604.7/05. **CODEN** DPIRDU. **[CCC]. Ad Acc. Circ:** 2,000. available on microfilm and microfiche from University Microfilms International (UMI). Documents available from CASDDS, Documents on Demand.
Desc: Answers to health and safety questions, data on the chemical properties of substances in the workplace, and professional guidance on the laws of OSHA, EPA, and other regulatory agencies.
Ind/Abst Abstr. Bull. Inst. Paper Chem.; Abstr. Bull. Inst. Pap. Sci. Tech.; Art Archaeol. Tech. Abstr.; BioBusiness (1989-1990); Chem. Abstr.; Chem. Hazards Ind.; Electron. Commun. Abstr. J.; Environ. Abstr.; Health Saf. Sci. Abstr.; ISMEC Bull.; Lab. Hazards Bull.; Life Sci. Collect.; Pollut. Abstr. Indexes; Saf. Sci. Abstr. J.; Text. Technol. Dig.; Toxicol. Abstr.

US/0193-7987
DECISIONS - FEDERAL MINE SAFETY AND HEALTH REVIEW COMMISSION. (DECISIONS / FEDERAL MINE SAFETY AND HEALTH REVIEW COMMISSION.). **Main/Corp** United States. Federal Mine Safety and Health Review Commission. (March 1979)-. Government Publication. English. mo. $99.00. Superintendent of Documents, US Government Printing Office, Washington DC 20402. **Tel** (202)275-3328, FAX (202)786-2377. **LC** KF3574.M5; A4914. **DD** 344/.73/0465. **NLM** WA 33; AA1 U685d.

US
DECISIONS OF THE OCCUPATIONAL SAFETY AND HEALTH REVIEW BOARD. **See** Law.

RU
DEISTVIE PROIZVODSTVENNYKH FAKTOROV NA ORGANIZM I MERY ZASHCHITY. **Added/Corp** Gosudarstvennaia Publichnaia Nauchno-Tekhnicheskaia Biblioteka (Akademiia Nauk SSSR). (1976)-. Multiple languages (Russian and Multiple languages). bm. 0.28rub (single issue). Izdatelstvo Nauka / Akademiia Nauk, Publishing House of the Russian Academy of Sciences, Leninskii Porspekt 14, 117901 Moscow Russia. **Tel** 011 95 954-21-53, FAX 011 95 938-21-44, telex 411964. **LC** Z6675.I5; D44; RC963.A1.

CN/0703-6426
DIRECTORY, OCCUPATIONAL SAFETY AND HEALTH LEGISLATION IN CANADA. **See** Law.

FR/0339-6517
DOCUMENTS POUR LE MEDECIN DU TRAVAIL. [Doc. pour med. trav.]. (1973)-. Periodical. French. qt. Institut National de Recherche & Securite, 4 rue Andre Boulle, 94942 Creteil Cedex 09 France. **Tel** 011 33 1 42070606. **UDC** 61.
Desc: Technical, medical and legal information for the occupational practitioners.

BE/0773-6231
DOE HET VEILIG. [Doe veilig]. (1948)-. Periodical. Dutch. bm. 300.00F. Provinciaal Veiligheids Instituut, Jezusstraat 28 30, 2000 Antwerpen Belgium. **Tel** 03 231 28 04. **ED** A. Voet. **UDC** 658.382.3. **Bk Rev. Ad Acc. Circ:** 2,000 (ctrl).
Desc: Information on occupational health and safety.

AT/1035-3046
ECONOMIC AND LABOUR RELATIONS REVIEW : ELRR, THE. **Added/Corp** University of New South Wales. Industrial Relations Research Centre. University of New South Wales. Centre for Applied Economic Research. **VFOAT** ELRR. Vol. 1, No. 1 (June 1990)-. Periodical. English. Twice a year (June and December). 30.00Aus$ (individuals), 55.00Aus$ (institutions) Australia; 50.00Aus$ (individuals), 75.00Aus$ (institutions) other. Center Applied Economic Research, PO Box 1, Faculty of Commerce and Economics, Kensington New South Wales 2033 Australia. **Tel** 011 02 697-3343, FAX 011 61 02 3138591. **ED** John Nevile. **Ad Acc. Pr Rev. Circ:** 300.
Desc: Produced jointly by the Centre for Applied Economic Research as the Industrial Relations Research Centre at the University of New South Wales. Focus is contemporary issues and developments in the fields of economics and labor relations.

US/0732-5665
ELECTRICAL ACCIDENT INVESTIGATION HANDBOOK. ***Suspended.*** [Electr. accid. invest. handb.]. Periodical. English. ir. $130.00. Electrodata Inc, PO Box 206, Glen Echo MD 20812.

US
EMERGENCY MANAGEMENT OF HAZARDOUS MATERIALS INCIDENTS. (19??)-. English. ir. $64.75 nonmembers; $58.25 members. National Fire Protection Association, 1 Batterymarch Park, PO Box 9101, Quincy MA 02269-9101. **Tel** (617)770-3000, (800)344-3555.
Desc: Information about hazardous chemicals, incident mitigation, and personal safety.

US/0747-9085
EMERGENCY MANAGEMENT TODAY : AN INFORMATION SERVICE OF EMERGENCY MANAGEMENT INFORMATION SERVICES. **See** Civil Defense.

US/0747-816X
EMERGENCY RESPONSE GUIDEBOOK. (EMERGENCY RESPONSE GUIDEBOOK : GUIDEBOOK FOR HAZARDOUS MATERIALS INCIDENTS.). **Added/Corp** United States. Materials Transportation Bureau. United States. Dept. of Transportation. Office of Hazardous Materials Transportation. (1984)-. English. te (every three years). $7.95. Labelmaster, PO Box 46402, Chicago IL 60646. **Tel** (800)358-6200, (312)478-0900. **LC** T55.3.H3; E45. **DD** 604.7/028/9. **NLM** WA 39; E39. ***Continues*** *Hazardous Materials ... Emergency Response Guidebook.*

US/0749-0003
EMPLOYEE ASSISTANCE QUARTERLY. [Empl. assist. q.]. Vol. 1, No. 1 (Fall 1985)-. Academic Scholarly Publication. English. qt (Published the academic year). $185.00 US; $259.00 other. The Haworth Press Inc, 10 Alice Street, Binghamton NY 13904-1580. **Tel** (607)722-5857, (800)3-HAWORTH, FAX (607)722-1424. **ED** Keith McClellan (editor's address: Multi-Resource Centers, 24725 West 12 Mile Road, Suite 310, Southfield, MI 48034). **LC** HF5549.5.A4; L32. **DD** 362.2/9286. **NLM** W1; EM696N. **Bk Rev. Ad Acc. Pr Rev. Acid Free. Circ:** 207. available on microfilm and microfiche from University Microfilms International (UMI). Documents available from Haworth Document Delivery Service. ***Continues*** *Labor-Management Alcoholism Journal, 0361-1205.*
Desc: Takes as its mission the development of scholarly and research literature regarding work-based alcoholism programs and the employee assistance movement.
Ind/Abst Anbar Account. Finan. Abstr. [Full Txt.]; Anbar Mark. Distr. Abstr. [Full Txt.]; Anbar Top Manage. Abstr. [Full Txt.]; EMBASE; Hum. Resour. Abstr.; Int. Labour Doc.; Manage. Bibliogr. Rev.; Oper. Prod. Manage. Abstr. [Full Txt.]; PAIS Int. Print (1991-); Person. Train. Abstr. [Full Txt.]; Person. Manage. Abstr.; Psychol. Abstr. (1985-); PsycINFO; PsycLit; Sage Fam. Stud. Abstr.; Soc. Plann. Policy Dev. Abstr.; Soc. Work Abstr. [Select. Cov.]; Urban Aff. Abstr.; Women Manage. Rev. [Full Txt.]; Work Relat. Abstr.

AT
EMPLOYMENT INJURIES QUEENSLAND. **See** Industrial Health and Safety-Abstracting, Bibliographies and Statistics.

AT/1033-6133
EMPLOYMENT INJURIES, TASMANIA. **See** Industrial Health and Safety-Abstracting, Bibliographies and Statistics.

UK
ENCYCLOPEDIA OF HEALTH & SAFETY AT WORK. (1962)-. English. ir. £170.00 Europe; £179.00 other. Sweet & Maxwell Ltd., South Quay Plaza, 183 Marsh Wall, London E14 9FT England. **Tel** 011 44 264 342899, FAX 011 44 264 342723, telex 929089 ITPINF G.

US/0738-3746
ENVIRONMENT, SAFETY, HEALTH AT DOE FACILITIES. **Main/Corp** United States. Dept. of Energy. Assistant Secretary for Environmental Protection Safety, and Emergency Preparedness. **VFOAT** Environment, Safety, Health at D.O.E. Facilities. **VAT** Environment, Safety, Health at Department of Energy Facilities. Fiscal Year 1980-. English. an. National Technical Information Service - NTIS, Room 2027S, 5285 Port Royal Road, Springfield VA 22161. **Tel** (703)487-4630, (703)487-4660, (703)487-4650, FAX (703)321-8547, telex 89-9405. **LC** HD7262.5.U6; O63. **DD** 363.1/19621042/0973. ***Continues*** *Operational Accidents & Radiation Exposures at DOE Facilities, 0276-7880.*

US
EOHSI INFOLETTER. **See** Environmental Issues.

SP
ERGA; PUBLICACION BIBLIOGRAFICA SOBRE CONDICIONES DEL TRABAJO. Spanish. ir. 3180.00ptas European Economic Communities. Inst Nac Seguridad Higiene Trabajo, Calle Dulcet 2 10, 08034 Barcelona Spain. **Tel** 011 34 3 2800102. **UDC** 61.

NE
EURO COURSES. HEALTH PHYSICS AND RADIATION PROTECTION. **Added/Corp** Commission of the European Communities. Directorate-General Telecommunications. Information Industries and Innovation. Scientific and Technical Communications Service. **VFOAT** Health Physics and

Radiation Protection. Vol. 1 (1991)-. Monographic series. English. ir. Price varies. Kluwer Academic Publishers, Postbus 322, 3300 AH Dordrecht, The Netherlands. **Tel** 011 (31) 78 524400, FAX 011 31 78 183273, telex 20083. **NLM** W1; EU576H.

US
EXCEL. (19??)-. Newsletter. English. qt. $24.00. Center for Excellence in Construction Safety / CECS, West Virginia University, PO Box 6031, Morgantown WV 26506. **Tel** (304)293-4152, FAX (304)293-3395. **ED** Janet Della-Ginstina. **Circ:** 500 (ctrl). ***Continues** CECS Newsletter.*

NE/0014-4398
EXCERPTA MEDICA. SECTION 35. OCCUPATIONAL HEALTH AND INDUSTRIAL MEDICINE. See Industrial Health and Safety-Abstracting, Bibliographies and Statistics.

GW
EXPLOSIONSSCHUTZ-RICHTLINIEN. (19??)-. German. ir. Universitatsverlag Carl Winter, POB 106140, D 69051 Heidelberg Germany. **Tel** 011 49 6221 770260.

UK
FACILITIES MANAGEMENT. See Economics-Industry and Production.

CN/0226-0484
FATAL ACCIDENT SUMMARY (VICTORIA). (FATAL ACCIDENT SUMMARY.). [Fatal accid. summ. (Victoria)]. **Main/Corp** British Columbia. Ministry of Energy, Mines and Petroleum Resources. Periodical. English. Ministry of Energy, Parliament Buildings, Victoria British Columbia V8V 1X4 Canada. **DD** 622/.8/09711. ***Continues** Fatal Accident Summary, 0226-0484.*

CN/1181-6988
FITNESS WORKS!. See Health and Personal Fitness.

US
FLAMMABLE AND COMBUSTIBLE LIQUIDS CODE. (19??)-. English. ir. $21.50 nonmembers; $19.50 members. National Fire Protection Association, 1 Batterymarch Park, PO Box 9101, Quincy MA 02269-9101. **Tel** (617)770-3000, (800)344-3555.

US
FLAMMABLE AND COMBUSTIBLE LIQUIDS CODE HANDBOOK. (19??)-. English. ir. $64.75 nonmembers; $58.25 members. National Fire Protection Association, 1 Batterymarch Park, PO Box 9101, Quincy MA 02269-9101. **Tel** (617)770-3000, (800)344-3555.

●CN/1183-9856
FLEET SAFETY & HEALTH. (FLEET SAFETY & HEALTH / ONTARIO SAFETY LEAGUE.). [Fleet saf. health]. **Added/Corp** Ontario Safety League. **VFOAT** Fleet Safety and Health. Vol. 1, No. 1 (Jan. 1992)-. Periodical. English. mo. Ontario Safety League, 21 Four Seasons Place, Suite 100, Etobiocoke Ontario M9B 6J8 Canada. **DD** 629.2. ***Continues** The Fleet Supervisor., 0702-5777.*

GW
FORTSCHRITTE DER SICHERHEITSTECHNIK : BERICHTE AUS DER DECHEMA-FACHAUSSCHUSSE. 1986-. Periodical. German (German). VCH Publishers Inc, 220 East 23rd Street, New York NY 10010. **Tel** (212)683-8333, , FAX (212)481-0897. **(Subscription address:** VCH Publishers Inc., 303 Northwest 12th Avenue, Journals Department, Deerfield FL 33442.**)** **LC** QD53; .D45 subser; T55.A1. **DD** 363.11/05.

GW
GEFAHRGUT - DANGEROUS GOODS CD-ROM. German (German, English and French). Springer-Verlag GmbH & Company KG, Heidelberger Platz 3, D 14197 Berlin Germany. **Tel** 011 49 30 8207223, FAX 011 49 30 8214091, telex 183 319 SPBLN D. **(Subscription address:** Springer Verlag New York Inc. / for North America, 44 Hartz Way, Secaucus NJ 07096.**)**
Desc: Covering up to 7 databases, this products offers a whole variety of information on environmentally risky substances. Especially important for fire brigades, police, rescue services, hospitals, transportation companies, airports, seaports, railroads, documentation and information centers, etc.

RU/0016-9919
GIGIENA TRUDA I PROFESSIONALNYE ZABOLEVANIJA. (GIGIENA TRUDA I PROFESSIONALNYE ZABOLEVANIIA.). [Gig. tr. prof. zabol.]. **Added/Corp** Soviet Union. Ministerstvo Zdravookhraneniia. Vsesoiuznoe Nauchnoe Obshchestvo Gigienistov (Soviet Union). (1957)-. Academic Scholarly Publication. Russian (summaries and/or abstracts in English; table of contents in English). mo. $99.95. **(Subscription address:** East View Publications Inc., 3020 Harbor Lane North, Suite 110, Minneapolis MN 55447.**)** **NLM** W1 GI135. **CODEN** GTPZAB. **[CCC].** Documents available from Article Express International, BIOSIS Document Express, CASDDS.
Ind/Abst Bioeng. Abstr.; Biol. Abstr.; Chem. Abstr.; Coal Abstr.; Ei Page One; Eng. Index Annu.; Index Med.; Ind. Hyg. Dig.; Int. Aerosp. Abstr.; Int. Labour Doc.; Saf. Health Work; Trop. Dis. Bull.

IT
GIORNALE DEGLI IGIENISTI INDUSTRIALI. Assn Italiana Igienisti Indust, Via Clefi 9, 20146 Milan Italy. **Tel** 011 39 2 48006079.

CC/1000-7164
GONGYE WEISHENG YU ZHIYEBING. (KUNG YEH WEI SHENG YU CHIH YEH PING.). [Gongye weisheng yu zhiyebing]. **Added/Corp** An Kang Lao Tung Wei Sheng Yen Chiu So. **VFOAT** Gongyeweisheng yu Zhiyebing; Industrial Health and Occupational Diseases. (1973)-. Periodical. Chinese (summaries and/or abstracts in English; table of contents in English). bm. **NLM** W1; KU701JP. **CODEN** GWZHEW. Documents available from CASDDS.
Ind/Abst Chem. Abstr.

NE
HANDBOEK ARBEIDS - EN MILIEUVEILIGHEID. Dutch. qt. Kluwer BV, Postbus 23, 7400 GA Deventer Netherlands. **Tel** 011 31 5700 33155, 011 31 5700 48999, FAX 011 31 5700 11504, telex 42829. **ED** H Hekman. Index available. cum. index. **Pr Rev. Circ:** 1,500. ***Continues** Handboek Voor Bedrijfsveilligheid.*
Desc: Articles about industrial health and safety, security and environmental problems.

UK
HANDBOOK OF OCCUPATIONAL HYGIENE. (1980)-. English. qt. £376.60. Croner Publ Ltd, Croner House, London Road, Kingston upon Thames, Surrey KT2 6SR England. **Tel** 011 44 81 5473333, FAX 081 547-2637. **ED** Bryan Harvey.

GW
HANDBUCH PERSONLICHE SCHUTZAUSRUSTUNGEN. (19??)-. German. ir (plus 2 updates). DM128.00. Ecomed Verlagsgesellschaft GmbH, Postfach 1752, D 86895 Landsberg Germany. **Tel** 011 49 8191 125544, FAX 011 49 8191 125513.

US/0743-8826
HAZARD PREVENTION. (HAZARD PREVENTION : JOURNAL OF THE SYSTEM SAFETY SOCIETY.). [Hazard prev.]. **Added/Corp** System Safety Society (U.S.). (19??)-. Periodical. English. qt (4 issues). $45.00 US; $50.00 Canada and Mexico; $60.00 other. System Safety Society, 5 Export Drive/Suite A, Sterling VA 22170-4421. **Tel** (703)450-0310. **ED** Sonya Kaiser. **LC** TA169.7; .H39. **DD** 620.8/6/05. **Bk Rev. Ad Acc. Circ:** 1,500 (ctrl).
Desc: Application of management and engineering techniques for limiting hazards in systems and products, reducing product liability risk and promoting the system safety concept in high tech projects.
Ind/Abst Health Saf. Sci. Abstr.; Int. Aerosp. Abstr.; Pollut. Abstr. Indexes.

UK
HAZARDOUS INFORMATION AND PACKAGING. (19??)-. Periodical. English. £141.10. Croner Publ Ltd, Croner House, London Road, Kingston upon Thames, Surrey KT2 6SR England. **Tel** 011 44 81 5473333, FAX 081 547-2637.

US
HAZARDOUS MATERIALS RESPONSE HANDBOOK. (19??)-. English. ir. $64.75 nonmembers; $58.25 members. National Fire Protection Association, 1 Batterymarch Park, PO Box 9101, Quincy MA 02269-9101. **Tel** (617)770-3000, (800)344-3555.
Desc: Covers hazardous materials preparedness, from recognizing risks to decontamination.

UK/0267-7296
HAZARDS. [Hazards]. (1984)-. Periodical. English. Five times a year. £8.00 (individuals), £18.00 (institutions) UK & Europe; £10.00 (individuals), £25.00 (institutions) other. Hazards, PO Box 199, Sheffield S1 1FQ England. **DD** 363.110941. Index available. cum. index. **Bk Rev. Pr Rev. Circ:** 3,000. ***Continues** Hazards Bulletin, 0140-0525.*
Desc: Information for trade union safety representatives on health and safety at work.
Ind/Abst Chem. Hazards Ind.; Curr. Technol. Index; Lab. Hazards Bull.

AT
HAZARDS AUSTRALIA. English. Four times a year (Mar., July, Sept., Dec.). 45.00Aus$. Qualified Workers Health Centre, 2nd Floor, Trades Hall, 16 Peel Street, South Brisbane, Queensland, 4101 Australia. **Tel** 011 61 7 8462719. **ED** P. Grassick and T. Smith. **Pr Rev. Circ:** 500.

●UK/0966-906X
HAZARDS IN THE OFFICE. (Jan. 1993)-. Newsletter. English. bm. £52.00 EC; $98.00 US; £57.00 other. Royal Society of Chemistry, Thomas Graham House, Science Park, Cambridge CB4 4WF England. **Tel** 011 44 223 420066, FAX 011 44 223 423429, telex 818293 ROYAL. **(Subscription address:** Turpin Distribution Services Limited, Blackhorse Road, Letchworth, Hertfordshire SG6 1HN, United Kingdom.**)**
Desc: Concerned exclusively with office hazards. Provides up-to-date information on the hidden hazards in the office environment and the vital safety procedures to be adopted to prevent injury.

UK/0269-8188
HEALTH & SAFETY AT WORK. [Health saf. work]. **VFOAT** Health and Safety at Work. No. 1- 1972-. Academic Scholarly Publication. English. Price varies per volume. Her Majesty's Stationery Office, 51 Nine Elms Lane, London SW8 5DR England. **Tel** 011 44 71 873 8459, 011 44 71 873 8499, FAX 011 44 71 873 8499, 011 44 71 873 8456, telex 297138. **(Subscription address:** PO Box 276, Public Centre, London SW8 5DT England**)** **NLM** W1 HE264G. ***Continues** Safety, Health and Welfare New Series.*
Ind/Abst Coal Abstr.; EMBASE; Ergon. Abstr.; World Text. Abstr.

UK/0141-8246
HEALTH & SAFETY AT WORK (CROYDON). (HEALTH & SAFETY AT WORK.). [Health Saf. Work]. Vol. 1 (1978)-. Periodical. English. mo. £44.00 UK; £76.00 other. Tolley Publishing Company Ltd, Tolley House, 2 Addiscombe Road, Croydon, Surrey CR9 5AF United Kingdom. **Tel** 011 44 81 6869141, FAX 011 44 81 6863155, 011 44 81 7600588. **ED** Craig McLellan, Circulation Manager. **[CCC]. Bk Rev. Ad Acc. Circ:** 11,500. available on microfilm and microfiche from University Microfilms International (UMI).
Desc: An independent, authoritative voice on health, safety and environmental matters in the factory, office or on site. Provides a forum for expert comment and informed discussion. Contains news of legal decisions and the implications of legislation, guidance on expert services, equipment and training. Also contains reviews of training material.
Ind/Abst Alum. Ind. Abstr.; Anbar Account. Finan. Abstr. [Full Txt.]; Anbar Mark. Distr. Abstr. [Full Txt.]; Anbar Top Manage. Abstr. [Full Txt.]; Art Archaeol. Tech. Abstr.; Chem. Bus. Bull.; Chem. Bus. NewsBase (1989-); Chem. Bus. Update; Chem. Hazards Ind.; Curr. Technol. Index; Energy Res. Abstr. (Nov. 1979-); Lab. Hazards Bull.; Leadscan; Manage. Market. Abstr.; Manage. Bibliogr. Rev.; Met. Abstr.; Oper. Prod. Manage. Abstr. [Full Txt.]; Person. Train. Abstr. [Full Txt.]; Women Manage. Rev. [Full Txt.]; World Surf. Coat. Abstr.

●UK
HEALTH AND SAFETY AT WORK DIRECTORY, THE. (1994)-. Directory. English. Kluwer Publishing Ltd, Croner House, London Road, Kingston Upun, Thames Surrey KT2 6SY England. **Tel** 081-547-3333, FAX 081-547-2037. **NLM** WA 22; FA1 H4. ***Continues** Health and Safety Directory.*

AT/0727-3304
HEALTH AND SAFETY BULLETIN. [Health saf. bull.]. (1981)-. English. 80.00Aus$ non-profit organizations, 160.00Aus$ income-generating organizations Australia; 140.00Aus$ non-profit organizations, 220.00Aus$ income-generating organizations other. Victorian Trades Hall Council, Safety Unit, Box 93 Trades Hall, Carlton S VIC 3053 Australia. **Tel** 011 61 03 662 3511, FAX 011 61 03 663 2127. **DD** 363.110994.

UK
HEALTH AND SAFETY IN INDUSTRY AND COMMERCE. VFOAT Health and Safety. Vol. 2, No. 11 (July 1979)-. Periodical. English. mo. £82.50 UK; £87.50 other. Springfield Information Services / Petersborough, PO Box 31, Cross Street Court, Peterborough PE1 1SD England. **Tel** 011 44 733 267272. Documents available from UMI Article Clearinghouse. ***Continues** Health and Safety in Industry.*
Ind/Abst ABI/INFORM Glob. Ed.; Chem. Hazards Ind.; Int. Packag. Abstr.; Lab. Hazards Bull.; Manage. Market. Abstr.; Print. Abstr.

UK/0140-8534
HEALTH & SAFETY MONITOR. [Health saf. monit.]. Periodical. English. mo. £90.00 UK; £105.00 other. Monitor Press, Rectory Road, Great Waldingfield, Sudbury Suffolk CO10 0TL United Kingdom. **Tel** 011 44 787 378607. **LC** KD3168.A13; H4. **DD** 344.41/0465/05. Index available. **Bk Rev.** ctrl circ.
Desc: Read by senior executives and safety officers, company secretaries and legal representatives as well as union officials; outlines in plain language the new codes of practice, guidance notes and fresh regulations.
Ind/Abst Manage. Market. Abstr.

UK
HEALTH AND SAFETY RESEARCH AND TECHNOLOGICAL SERVICES. ***Ceased.***
Main/Corp Great Britain. Health and Safety Executive. Research and Laboratory Services Division. (1984)-(19??). English. an. Health & Safety Executive,

Room 414 St Hughs House Stanley, Btle Merseyside L20 3QY England. **Tel** 011 44 51 951 4000, FAX 011 44 51 922 5394, telex 628235. **LC** T55.A1; G74a. **DD** 363.1/1/072041. ***Continues*** *Health and Safety Research.*

US/0892-9351
HEALTH AND SAFETY SCIENCE ABSTRACTS. See Public Health and Safety-Abstracting, Bibliographies and Statistics.

AT/1033-1425
HEALTH AT WORK NEWSLETTER. ***Suspended.*** [Health work newsl.]. (1989)-(1994). Newsletter. English. Four times a year. 30.00Aus$ institutions; 12.00Aus$ individuals. Health Promotion in Workplace, PO Box 2, Woden ACT 2606 Australia. **Tel** 011 61 062 822 144, FAX 011 61 062 825 147. **DD** 613.0994.

UK
HEALTH CARE RISK REPORT. (19??)-. Periodical. English. £185.00 UK; £200.00 other. Eclipse Publications Ltd, 18 20 Highbury Place, London N5 1QP England. **Tel** 011 44 71 354 5858.

US/0277-8521
HEALTH HAZARD EVALUATION SUMMARIES. [Health hazard eval. summ.]. **Added/Corp** National Institute for Occupational Safety and Health. (April 1980)-. English. US Department of Health and Human Services, 200 Independence Avenue Southwest, Washington DC 20201. **NLM** W1 HE344D.

CN/0824-5681
HEALTH, LABOR & SAFETY REPORT. [Health labor saf. rep.]. **VAT** Health, Labor and Safety Report. Vol. 1, No. 1 (May 1983)-. Periodical. English. bm. $27.00. Health Labor & Safety Report, PO Box 3355 Station D, Edmonton Alberta T5L 2J2 Canada. **DD** 363.1/1/097123.

UK
HEALTH SERVICE REPORT. (19??)-. Periodical. English. £135.00 UK; £140.00 other. Eclipse Publications Ltd, 18 20 Highbury Place, London N5 1QP England. **Tel** 011 44 71 354 5858.

US/1050-575X
HEALTHCARE HAZARDOUS MATERIALS MANAGEMENT. See Public Health and Safety.

US
HEALTHCARE PLANNING AND MARKETING. SOCIETY FOR HEALTHCARE PLANNING AND MARKETING OF THE AMERICAN HOSPITAL ASSOCIATION. Added/Corp American Hospital Association. Society for Healthcare Planning and Marketing. **VFOAT** Health Care Planning and Marketing. Vol. 10, No. 6 (Nov./Dec. 1987)-. Periodical. English. ir. $110.00 (members); $150.00 (non-members) Comes with Society for Healthcare Planning Marketing membership. Society for Healthcare Planning and Marketing, 840 North Lake Shore Drive, Chicago IL 60611. **Tel** (312)280-6086. **NLM** W1; HE608T. ***Continues*** *Hospital Planning and Marketing, 0891-3269.*

US/1057-199X
HEALTHY OFFICE REPORT, THE. (THE HEALTHY OFFICE REPORT : PUBLICATION OF THE NATIONAL SAFE WORKPLACE INSTITUTE.). [Heal. off. rep.]. **Added/Corp** National Safe Workplace Institute. Vol. 1, No. 1 (June 15, 1991)-. Periodical. English. mo. $59.00. National Safe Workplace Institute, 122 South Michigan Avenue, Suite 1450, Chicago IL 60603. **DD** 363.

GW/0085-1469
HEFTE ZUR UNFALLHEILKUNDE. [Hefte Unfallheilkd.]. Issue 1 (1929)-. Periodical. German. ir (four-six issues per year). DM70.00 to DM160.00. Springer-Verlag GmbH & Company KG, Heidelberger Platz 3, D 14197 Berlin Germany. **Tel** 011 49 30 8207223, FAX 011 49 30 8214091, telex 183 319 SPBLN D. **(Subscription address:** Springer Verlag New York Inc. / for North America, 44 Hartz Way, Secaucus NJ 07096.) **ED** J Rehn, L Schweiberer, H Tocherine. **NLM** W1 HE683. **CODEN** HUFHAR. Index available. **Circ:** 800. Documents available from BIOSIS Document Express.
Desc: Monographs on topics of trauma surgery.
Ind/Abst Biol. Abstr.; EMBASE; Health Plan. Adminis.; Index Med.

FR/0181-9739
HISTOIRE DES ACCIDENTS DU TRAVAIL. [Hist. accid. trav.]. **Added/Corp** Universite de Nantes. Centre de Recherches d'Histoire Economique et Sociale. (1975)-. Periodical. French.
Ind/Abst Am. Hist. Life (1963-1971,1984-1985).

US/0145-1561
IAIABC JOURNAL. Main/Corp International Association of Industrial Accident Boards and Commissions. **VAT** International Association of Industrial Accident Boards and Commissions Journal. (Spring 1976)-. Periodical. English. ir. International Association of Industrial Accident Boards and Commissions, PO Box 13449, One LeFleurs Square, Jackson MS 39236. **Tel** (601)366-4582. **LC** HD7090; .I43a. **DD** 368.4/1/005.

FR/1017-1606
IARC MONOGRAPHS ON THE EVALUATION OF CARCINOGENIC RISKS TO HUMANS. See Medical Science and Technology-Neoplasma, Neoplastic.

IT
IGIENE DEL LAVORO. (19??)-. Italian. EPC Spa, Via dell'Acqua Traversa 187/189, 00135 Rome Italy. **Tel** 011 39 6 3313000, FAX 011 39 6 3313212.

US/1062-2799
IIR REVIEW, THE. [IIR rev.]. **Added/Corp** Institute for Injury Reduction. **VAT** Institute for Injury Reduction Review. Vol. 1, No. 1 (Winter 1991)-. Periodical. English. sa. $50.00. Institute for Injury Reducation, 375 Prince George's Boulevard, Suite 200, Upper Marlboro MD 20772. **DD** 363.

US/0270-4242
INDEX TO DECISIONS OF THE OCCUPATIONAL SAFETY AND HEALTH REVIEW COMMISSION. English. qt. Occupation Safety and Health Commission, Washington DC 20006. **LC** KF3568.3.A2; O252. **DD** 344.73/0465/02646.

II/0019-5278
INDIAN JOURNAL OF INDUSTRIAL MEDICINE. [Indian j. ind. med.]. **Added/Corp** Indian Association of Occupational Health. (19??)-. Periodical. English. qt. $50.00. Indian Association of Occupational Health, 82-B Shakespeare Sarani, Calcutta 700017 India. **(Subscription address:** Prints India, 11 Darya Ganj, New Delhi 110002 India.) **NLM** W1 IN211. **CODEN** IJIDAW. Documents available from BIOSIS Document Express.
Ind/Abst BioBusiness; Biol. Abstr.; Saf. Health Work.

II/0019-5391
INDIAN JOURNAL OF OCCUPATIONAL HEALTH. [Indian j. occup. health]. **Added/Corp** Society for the Study of Industrial Medicine. Bombay Branch. Indian Association of Occupational Health. Bombay Branch. (Aug. 1958)-. Periodical. English. qt. $20.00. Society for the Study of Industrial Medicine, 243 Kerwadi Main Road, Bombay 4 Maharashtra India. **(Subscription address:** Prints India, 11 Darya Ganj, New Delhi 110002 India.) **LC** RC963; .A367. **NLM** W1 IN2225.
Ind/Abst Acoust. Abstr.; Saf. Health Work.

US
INDUSTRIAL FIRE SAFETY. ***Ceased.*** **See** Fire Prevention.

JA/0019-8366
INDUSTRIAL HEALTH. [Ind. health]. **Added/Corp** Rodo Eisel Kenkyujo, Kawasaki, Japan. Vol. 1 (Oct. 1963)-. Academic Scholarly Publication. English. qt. Free on request. National Institute of Industrial Health, 211 Nagao 6 Chome Tamaku, Kawasaki 214 Japan. **Tel** 011 81 44 865 6111. **LC** RC963; .A368. **DD** 613.6/2/05. **NLM** W1 IN3738. **CODEN** INHEAO. **Pr Rev.** Documents available from The Genuine Article, BIOSIS Document Express, CASDDS. ***Supersedes*** *Bulletin of the National Institute of Industrial Health.*
Ind/Abst Acoust. Abstr.; Anal. Abstr.; BioBusiness; Biol. Abstr.; Chem. Abstr.; Chem. Hazards Ind.; CSA Neuro. Abstr. (?-?); Curr. Contents Life Sci.; EMBASE; Energy Res. Abstr.; For. Prod. Abstr. (1991-); Health Saf. Sci. Abstr.; Health Plan. Adminis.; Index Med.; Ind. Hyg. Dig.; Lab. Hazards Bull.; Life Sci. Collect.; Pollut. Abstr. Indexes; Res. Alert [Full Cov.]; Saf. Health Work; Sci. Cit. Index; SCISEARCH; Soc. Sci. Cit. Index [Select. Cov.]; SportSearch; Trop. Dis. Bull.

US/0890-3018
INDUSTRIAL HEALTH & HAZARDS UPDATE. [Ind. health hazards update]. **VFOAT** Industrial Health and Hazards Update. (19??)-. Periodical. English. mo. $249.00 US; $269.00 Canada; $309.00 (surface), $349.00 (air) other. Merton Allen Associates, PO Box 15640, Plantation FL 33318-5640. **DD** 363. available on an online database (file 16,636/Full-Text) from DIALOG.
Ind/Abst PROMT [Full Txt.]; PTS Newsl. Database [Full Txt.].

UK
INDUSTRIAL HEALTH AND SAFETY. (19??)-. Periodical. English. qt. £164.20. Croner Publ Ltd, Croner House, London Road, Kingston upon Thames, Surrey KT2 6SR England. **Tel** 011 44 81 5473333, FAX 081 547-2637.

US/0019-8382
INDUSTRIAL HYGIENE DIGEST. See Industrial Health and Safety-Abstracting, Bibliographies and Statistics.

US
INDUSTRIAL HYGIENE FIELD OPERATIONS MANUAL. Main/Corp United States. Occupational Safety and Health Administration. **VFOAT** Occupational Safety and Health, Industrial Safety FOM. (1???)-. English. $32.00. US Department of Labor Occupational Safety & Health Administration, 200 Constitution Avenue NW, Room S315, Washington DC 20210. **Tel** (202)219-8151, FAX (202)219-5986.

US/0147-5401
INDUSTRIAL HYGIENE NEWS (PITTSBURGH). (INDUSTRIAL HYGIENE NEWS.). Vol. 1, (Mar. 1978)-. Periodical. English. Seven times a year. $25.00 (US & Canada): $30.00 (other). Rimbach Publishing Company, 8650 Babcock Boulevard, Pittsburgh PA 15237. **Tel** (412)364-5366. **ED** Richard Rimbach and David Lavender. **Bk Rev. Ad Acc. Circ:** 60,500 (ctrl).
Desc: Edited for the person responsible for monitoring, evaluating, controlling health hazards in the work environment.

US/0734-0346
INDUSTRIAL SAFETY AND APPLIED HEALTH PHYSICS ANNUAL REPORT FOR ... . [Ind. saf. appl. health phys. annu. rep.]. **Main/Corp** Oak Ridge National Laboratory. Industrial Safety and Applied Health Physics Division. Began with: 1977. English. an. National Technical Information Service - NTIS, Room 2027S, 5285 Port Royal Road, Springfield VA 22161. **Tel** (703)487-4630, (703)487-4660, (703)487-4650, FAX (703)321-8547, telex 89-9405. **NLM** W2 A O12A. ***Continues*** *Applied Health Physics and Safety Annual Report, 0146-6712.*

II/0019-8765
INDUSTRIAL SAFETY & HEALTH BULLETIN. ***Ceased.*** **VAT** Industrial Safety and Health Bulletin. Ceased Feb. 1985. Bulletin. English. Directorate General of Factory, Central Labour Institute Building, Sion, Bombay 22 India.

II/0301-4746
INDUSTRIAL SAFETY CHRONICLE. [Ind. saf. chron.]. Periodical. English. qt. $3.00. National Safety Council / India, Central Labour Institute Building, Sion Bombay-22 DD India. **LC** T55.A1; I593. **DD** 614.8/52/05. **NLM** W1 IN393S.
Ind/Abst Saf. Health Work.

UK/0262-3226
INDUSTRIAL SAFETY DATA FILE. [Ind. saf. data file]. (1982)-. Periodical. English. Twelve times a year. $257.00 US and Canada. Wilmington Publishing Ltd., PO Box 200, Field End Road, Ruislip Middx HA4 OSY England. **Tel** 011 44 81 841 3970, FAX 011 44 81 841 9676. **DD** 363.110941. ***Continues*** *Industrial Safety, 0019-8757.*

FR/0378-9993
INDUSTRY AND ENVIRONMENT (ENGLISH EDITION). (INDUSTRY AND ENVIRONMENT.). [Ind. environ.]. **Added/Corp** United Nations Environment Programme. **VFOAT** Industry and Environment Quarterly Newslatter. Vol. 1, No. 1 (Oct./Nov./Dec. 1978)-. Academic Scholarly Publication. English. qt. $45.00 (add $10.00 for airmail postage). United Nations Publications, 2 United Nations Plaza, Room DC2 0853, Department 007C, New York NY 10017. **Tel** (212)963-8303, (800)253-9646. **(Subscription address:** United Nations Publications, Subscription Office, PO Box 361, Birmingham AL 35201-0361.) **ED** Jacqueline Aloisi de Larderel. **LC** TD169; .I5. **CODEN** IENVDB. Index available. cum. index. **Bk Rev. Pr Rev. Circ:** 5,500 (ctrl). Documents available from Documents on Demand.
Desc: Worldwide policy papers and technical articles on industry and environment issues.
Ind/Abst Abstr. Bull. Inst. Pap. Sci. Tech.; BioBusiness (1988); Chem. Bus. Bull.; Chem. Bus. NewsBase (1985-); Chem. Bus. Update; Chem. Hazards Ind.; Ei Page One; EMBASE; Environ. Abstr.; Food Sci. Technol. Abstr.; Lab. Hazards Bull.; Leadscan; PAIS Int. Print (1991-); Pollut. Abstr. Indexes.

US/0887-1086
INDUSTRY AND HEALTH CARE (CAMBRIDGE, MASS.). ***Ceased.*** (INDUSTRY AND HEALTH CARE.). [Ind. health care]. Vol. 1-Ceased ?. Monographic series. English. qt. Boston University / School of Medicine, 80 East Concord Street, Boston MA 02118. **Tel** (617)247-5000. **DD** 658. ***Continues*** *Industry and Health Care, 0887-1086.*
Ind/Abst Hospit. Health Admin. Index.

US/8756-2405
INJURIES IN OIL AND GAS DRILLING AND SERVICES. [Inj. oil gas drill. serv.]. Government Publication. English. US Department of Labor / Bureau of Labor Statistics, 441 G Street NW, Washington DC 20212. **Tel** (202)606-7800, FAX (202)606-7797. **LC** HD7269.P4; I53. **DD** 363.1/19622338/021.

US/0095-0432
INJURY EXPERIENCE IN COAL MINING. (INJURY EXPERIENCE IN COAL MINING / U.S. DEPARTMENT OF LABOR, MINE SAFETY AND HEALTH ADMINISTRATION.). Began with 1948. English. an. US Department of Labor Mine Safety & Health Administration, 4015 Wilson Boulevard, Arlington VA 22203. **Tel** (703)235-1452, FAX (703)235-1563. **LC** TN23; .U4 subser. **DD** 622 S; 312/.43. **NLM** W2 A B8701EI. available on microfiche (Vols. for (1981-) distributed to depository libraries).

US/0270-0042
INJURY EXPERIENCE IN METALLIC MINERAL MINING. (INJURY EXPERIENCE IN METALLIC MINERAL MINING / U.S. DEPARTMENT OF LABOR, MINE SAFETY AND HEALTH ADMINISTRATION.). [Inj. exp. met. miner min.]. **Added/Corp** United States. Mine Safety and Health Administration. (1978)-. English. an. US Department of Labor Mine Safety & Health Administration, 4015 Wilson Boulevard, Arlington VA 22203. **Tel** (703)235-1452, FAX (703)235-1563. **LC** TN295; .I536. **DD** 312/.43. **NLM** W2; A M601ia. available on microfiche (Vols. For (1982)- distributed to depository libraries). ***Continues*** *Injury Experience in the Metallic Mineral Industries, 0160-8452.*

US/0270-2053
INJURY EXPERIENCE IN SAND AND GRAVEL MINING. (INJURY EXPERIENCE IN SAND AND GRAVEL MINING / U.S. DEPARTMENT OF LABOR, MINE SAFETY AND HEALTH ADMINISTRATION.). [Inj. exp. sand gravel min.]. Began with 1978. English. an. US Department of Labor Mine Safety & Health Administration, 4015 Wilson Boulevard, Arlington VA 22203. **Tel** (703)235-1452, FAX (703)235-1563. **LC** TN295; .U57A. **DD** 363.1/19622/3620973. **NLM** W2; A M601ib. available on microfiche (Vols. for (1982-) distributed to depository libraries). ***Continues*** *Injury Experience in the Sand and Gravel Industry, 0191-6645.*

US
INJURY EXPERIENCE IN STONE MINING / U.S. DEPARTMENT OF LABOR, MINE SAFETY AND HEALTH ADMINISTRATION. **Added/Corp** United States. Mine Safety and Health Administration. Health and Safety Analysis Center (U.S.). Division of Mining Information Systems. (1978)-. English. an. US Department of Labor Mine Safety & Health Administration, 4015 Wilson Boulevard, Arlington VA 22203. **Tel** (703)235-1452, FAX (703)235-1563. **LC** TN295; .U58a subser.; TN951.A5. **DD** 363.1/19622/0973. **NLM** W2; A M601ic. available on microfiche (Vols. for (1984-) distributed to depository libraries). ***Continues*** *United States. Mine Safety and Health Administration. Injury Experience in Quarrying, 0098-4906.*

GW/0340-0131
INTERNATIONAL ARCHIVES OF OCCUPATIONAL AND ENVIRONMENTAL HEALTH. [Int. arch. occup. environ. health]. **VFOAT** Occupational and Environmental Health; Internationales Archiv fur Arbeits- und Umweltmedizin. Vol. 35, No. 1 (1975)-. Academic Scholarly Publication. English (French and German). Six times a year. DM1196.00. Springer-Verlag GmbH & Company KG, Heidelberger Platz 3, D 14197 Berlin Germany. **Tel** 011 49 30 8207223, FAX 011 49 30 8214091, telex 183 319 SPBLN D. **(Subscription address:** Springer Verlag New York Inc. / for North America, 44 Hartz Way, Secaucus NJ 07096.**) ED** G Lehnert. **LC** RC963.A1; I58. **DD** 614.8/52/05. **NLM** W1 IN7043. **CODEN** IAEHDWIAOHDE. **[CCC].** available on microfilm and microfiche from University Microfilms International (UMI). Documents available from The Genuine Article, BIOSIS Document Express, CASDDS, Documents on Demand. ***Continues*** *Internationales Archiv fur Arbeitsmedizin, 0020-5923.*
Desc: Permits measures to be introduced which greatly advance the possibilities of providing health protection for workers and the general public.
Ind/Abst Acoust. Abstr.; Agric. Eng. Abstr. (1991-); Anal. Abstr.; BioBusiness; Biol. Abstr.; Chem. Abstr.; Chem. Hazards Ind.; CIS Abstr.; Coal Abstr.; Cumul. Index Nurs. Allied Health Lit.; Curr. Contents Clin. Med.; Curr. Contents Life Sci.; Dairy Sci. Abstr.; EMBASE; Energy Inf. Abstr.; Energy Res. Abstr. (April 1978-); Environ. Abstr.; Ergon. Abstr.; For. Prod. Abstr. (1991-); For. Abstr.; Health Saf. Sci. Abstr.; Index Med.; Lab. Hazards Bull.; Leadscan; Med. Abstr. Newsl.; Nutr. Abstr. Rev., Ser. B, Live Feeds and Feed.; Nutr. Abstr. Rev., Ser. A, Hum. Exp.; Nutr. Res. Newsl.; Life Sci. Collect.; Pollut. Abstr. Indexes; Poult. Abstr.; Res. Alert [Full Cov.]; Rev. Agric. Entomol.; Saf. Health Work; Sci. Cit. Index; SCISEARCH; Soc. Sci. Cit. Index [Select. Cov.]; SportSearch; Toxicol. Abstr.; Trop. Dis. Bull.; Weed Abstr.

●US/1077-3525
INTERNATIONAL JOURNAL OF OCCUPATIONAL AND ENVIRONMENT HEALTH. **See** Environmental Issues.

US/1053-9557
INTERNATIONAL JOURNAL OF OCCUPATIONAL HEALTH AND TOXICOLOGY. (1991)-. Periodical. English. qt. $200.00. Princeton Scientific Publishing Company Inc., PO Box 2155, Princeton NJ 08543. **Tel** (609)683-4750, FAX (609)683-0838.

●PL
INTERNATIONAL JOURNAL OF OCCUPATIONAL MEDICINE AND ENVIRONMENTAL HEALTH. **Added/Corp** Instytut Medycyny Pracy Im. Prof. Dr. Med. Jerzego Nofera. Polskie Towarzystwo Medycyny Pracy. (1994)-. Periodical. English. Four times a year. $200.00. Nofer Inst of Occupational Medicine, PO Box 199, 8 Southwest Tersey Street, 90-950 Lodz Poland. **Tel** 011 48 42 314745, 011 48 42 314625, 011 48 42 314911, e mail:GeoNet Mull:imp-dyrekcja, FAX 011 48 42 348331, 011 48 42 556102, telex 885360 IMP PL, 885130 CITOZ PL, 885130 IMP PL. **ED** Janusz Indulski. Index available (annual authors index). **Bk Rev**, (Qty: 4). **Ad Acc. Pr Rev.** ctrl circ. ***Continues*** *Polish Journal of Occupational Medicine and Environmental Health, 0867-8383.*

US
INTERNATIONAL LOSS CONTROL REVIEW. (19??)-. English. Four times a year. International Loss Control Institute, PO Box 1898, Atlanta Highway, Longanville GA 30249. **Tel** (404)466-2208, FAX (404)466-4318. **Circ:** 1,200. ***Continues*** *International Risk Control Review, 0739-389X.*

US/0739-389X
INTERNATIONAL RISK CONTROL REVIEW. ***Title Change.*** **See** Industrial Health and Safety-Abstracting, Bibliographies and Statistics.

CN/0822-2754
IRSST / IRSST, INSTITUT DE RECHERCHE EN SANTE ET EN SECURITE DU TRAVAIL DU QUEBEC, L'. **Added/Corp** IRSST (Quebec). **VAT** Institut de Recherche en Sante et en Securite du Travail du Quebec. Vol. 1, No. 1 (Winter 1984)-. Periodical. French. qt. Free. Institut de Recherche en Sante et en Securite du Travail du Quebec, 505 Boulevard Maisonneuve Ouest, Montreal Quebec H3A 3C2 Canada. **Tel** (514)288-1551 ext. 240. **DD** 363.1/1/09714. **Bk Rev. Circ:** 5,000.

GW
JAHRESBERICHT DER GEWERBEAUFSICHT. **Main/Corp** Baden-Wuerttemberg (Germany). Ministerium fuer Arbeit, Gesundheit und Sozialordnung. (19??)-. Trade Publication. German. Umweltministerium Baden-Wurttemberg, Kernerplatz 9, 70182 Stuttgart Germany. **Tel** (0711)126-0, FAX (0711)126-2881, telex 7111-643 UMIN BW. **LC** LAW. **DD** 344/.4347/0465. **Bk Rev. Acid Free. Circ:** 5,000 (ctrl).

US/0149-7510
JOB SAFETY & HEALTH; AN ADVISORY BULLETIN ON GOVERNMENT AND INDUSTRY SAFETY POLICIES, PROCEDURES AND PRACTICES. **Added/Corp** Bureau of National Affairs. **VAT** Job Safety and Health, and Advisory Bulletin on Government and Industry Safety Policies, Procedures and Practices. (19??)-. Periodical. English. ir. $660.00. Bureau of National Affairs Inc., 9435 Key West Avenue, Rockville MD 20850. **Tel** (800)372-1033, (301)258-1033, FAX (301)948-5823. **ED** Eileen Z. Joseph. **[CCC].**

US/1057-5820
JOB SAFETY & HEALTH QUARTERLY. (JOB SAFETY & HEALTH QUARTERLY : JS & HQ / U.S. DEPARTMENT OF LABOR, OCCUPATIONAL SAFETY AND HEALTH ADMINISTRATION.). [Job saf. health q.]. **Added/Corp** United States. Occupational Safety and Health Administration. **VFOAT** Job Safety and Health Qquarterly; JS & HQ; JS and HQ. Vol. 1, No. 1 (Fall 1989)-. Government Publication. English. qt. $8.50 domestic; $10.65 other. Superintendent of Documents, US Government Printing Office, Washington DC 20402. **Tel** (202)275-3328, FAX (202)786-2377. **LC** IN PROCESS. **DD** 363.
Desc: Features articles on job safety and health topics and current information on OSHA.

US/0148-4079
JOB SAFETY & HEALTH REPORT. ***Title Change.*** **VAT** Job Safety and Health Report. (1971)-(19??). Periodical. English. bw. Business Publishers Inc., 951 Pershing Drive, Silver Spring MD 20910-4464. **Tel** (301)587-6300, (800)274-0122, FAX (301)585-9075. **[CCC].** ***Continued by*** *Occupational Health and Safety Letter.*
Desc: Report on occupational safety and health nationwide. Covers OSHA, NIOSH, OSHRC, and MSHA as well as the courts, industry initiatives, and the labor movement.

US/0149-7510
JOB SAFETY & HEALTH (WASHINGTON. 1977). (JOB SAFETY & HEALTH.). **Added/Corp** Bureau of National Affairs (Washington, D.C.). **VAT** Job Safety and Health (Washington. 1977). No. 1 (Dec. 13, 1977)-. Periodical. English. bw. $660.00. Bureau of National Affairs Inc., 9435 Key West Avenue, Rockville MD 20850. **Tel** (800)372-1033, (301)258-1033, FAX (301)948-5823. **[CCC].**

US/1040-4198
JOB SAFETY CONSULTANT. ***Title Change.*** [Job saf. consult.]. (Sept. 1982)-(1993). Periodical. English. mo. Business Research Publications, 1333 H Street Northwest, 2nd Floor West, Washington DC 20005. **Tel** (202)842-3022, (800)822-6338, FAX (202)842-3023. **DD** 363. ***Continues*** *OSHA Reports.* ***Merged into*** *OSHA Compliance Advisor.*
Desc: Shows you how to maintain worker health and safety in compliance with OSHA and other statutory regulations.

US
JOINT NIOSH/OSHA CURRENT INTELLIGENCE BULLETIN. **Main/Corp** National Institute for Occupational Safety and Health. **VFOAT** Current Intelligence Bulletin. Bulletin. English. Price varies per volume. Publications Dissemination Dts, 4676 Columbia Parkway, Cincinnati OH 45226.

AT/0815-6409
JOURNAL OF OCCUPATIONAL HEALTH AND SAFETY, AUSTRALIA AND NEW ZEALAND, THE. Vol. 1, No. 1 (Aug. 1985)-. Periodical. English. Six times a year. 308.00Aus$ Australia & New Zealand; 317.00Aus$ others. CCH Australia Ltd, PO Box 230, North Ryde New South Wales, 2113 Australia. **Tel** 011 61 02 888 2555, FAX 011 61 02 888 7324. **NLM** W1; JO801PS.
Desc: A comprehensive and developing range of topics are covered, including work stress, chemicals at work, impact of technological change, manual handling, noise, risk management, rehabilitation, and more.
Ind/Abst EMBASE.

US/0096-1736
JOURNAL OF OCCUPATIONAL MEDICINE. ***Title Change.*** (JOM. JOURNAL OF OCCUPATIONAL MEDICINE.). [J. occup. med.]. **Added/Corp** American Occupational Medical Association. American Academy of Occupational Medicine. Industrial Medical Association (U.S.). **VFOAT** Journal of Occupational Medicine; JOM. Vol. 10 (Jan. 1968)-(199?). Academic Scholarly Publication. English. mo. Williams & Wilkins Company, 428 East Preston Street, Baltimore MD 21202-3993. **Tel** (410)528-4000, (800)638-6423, FAX (410)528-8596, telex 87669. **(Subscription address:** Williams & Wilkins, PO Box 64380, Baltimore, MD 21264-4380**) ED** Lloyd Tepper. **DD** 331. **NLM** W1 JO802. **CODEN** JJOMDZJOCMA7. **[CCC]. Pr Rev.** available on microfilm from University Microfilms International (UMI). Documents available from , The Genuine Article, BIOSIS Document Express, CASDDS, , Documents on Demand, Quick Copies. ***Continues*** *Journal of Occupational Medicine, 0096-1736.* ***Continued by*** *Journal of Occupational and Environmental Medicine, 1076-2752.*
Desc: Original articles on occupational medical practice, including: epidemiology, toxicology, health screening, ergonomics, assessment, rehabilitation, health education, and administration.
Ind/Abst BioBusiness; Biol. Abstr.; Bus. Index (1981-Dec. 1984); Chem. Abstr.; Chem. Hazards Ind.; CIS Abstr.; Coal Abstr.; Cumul. Index Nurs. Allied Health Lit.; Curr. Contents Clin. Med.; EMBASE; Energy Inf. Abstr.; Energy Res. Abstr. (Jan. 1981-); Environ. Abstr.; Environ. Period. Bibliogr.; Ergon. Abstr.; For. Prod. Abstr.; Health Saf. Sci. Abstr.; Health Devices Alerts; Health Index (1989-); Health Period. Database; Health Ref. Cent. (Jan. 1989-) [Full Cov.]; Hospit. Health Admin. Index; Index Med.; Index Vet.; Ind. Hyg. Dig.; Int. Aerosp. Abstr.; Int. Nurs. Index; Iowa Drug Inf. Serv. (1971-); Lab. Hazards Bull.; Nucl. Sci. Abstr.; Nutr. Res. Newsl.; Life Sci. Collect.; Physic. Medline Plus; Pollut. Abstr. Indexes; Protozoolog. Abstr.; Res. Alert [Full Cov.]; Rev. Agric. Entomol.; Rev. Med. Vet. Entomol.; Risk Abstr.; Saf. Health Work; Sci. Cit. Index; SCISEARCH; Soc. Sci. Cit. Index [Select. Cov.]; Toxicol. Abstr.; Trade Ind. Index (1981-?);; Trop. Dis. Bull.; Work Relat. Abstr.; World Surf. Coat. Abstr.

US/1053-0487
JOURNAL OF OCCUPATIONAL REHABILITATION. [J. occup. rehabil.]. Vol. 1, No. 1 (Mar. 1991)-. Periodical. English. Four times a year. $195.00 institutions, $50.00 individuals US; $230.00 institutions, $59.00 individuals other. Plenum Press, 233 Spring Street, New York NY 10013-1578. **Tel** (212)620-8000, (800)221-9369, FAX (212)463-0742, (212)807-1047, telex 23/421139. **ED** Michael Feuerstein. **LC** RC964; .J68. **DD** 616.9/803. **NLM** W1; JO802PCL. **CODEN** JOCTEW. **[CCC].**
Desc: Provides a multidisciplinary forum for the publication of original research, theoretical papers, review articles, and case studies related to the mechanisms and management of work-related disability.

Industrial Health and Safety

US/0022-4375
JOURNAL OF SAFETY RESEARCH. [J. saf. res.]. **Added/Corp** National Safety Council. Vol. 1 (1969)-. Periodical. English. qt. $328.00 The Americas; £220.00 other. Pergamon Press, An Imprint of Elsevier Science Ltd., The Boulevard, Langford Lane, Kidlington, Oxford OX5 1GB United Kingdom. **Tel** 011 44 865 843000, 011 44 865 843699, FAX 011 44 865 843010. **(Subscription address:** Elsevier Science Ltd. Oxford Fulfillment Centre, PO Box 800, Kidlington, Oxford OX5 1DX United Kingdom.**)** **ED** Thomas Planek. **LC** HV675.A1; J68. **DD** 614.85/05. **NLM** W1 JO872H. **CODEN** JSFRAV. **[CCC]**. **Pr Rev.** available on microfilm and microfiche from University Microfilms International (UMI). Documents available from Article Express International, The Genuine Article, BIOSIS Document Express, UMI Article Clearinghouse.
Ind/Abst Bioeng. Abstr.; Biol. Abstr.; Coal Abstr.; Curr. Contents Soc. Behav. Sci.; Ei Page One; EMBASE; Eng. Index Annu.; Ergon. Abstr.; Expand. Acad. Index (1992-); Health Saf. Sci. Abstr.; Newsp. Period. Abstr. (1992-); Pollut. Abstr. Indexes; Psychol. Abstr. (1969-); PsycINFO; PsycLit; PsycScan: Appl. Psych.; Res. Alert [Full Cov.]; Risk Abstr.; Saf. Health Work; Soc. Sci. Cit. Index [Full Cov.].

US/0098-4108
JOURNAL OF TOXICOLOGY AND ENVIRONMENTAL HEALTH. See Medical Science and Technology-Toxicology.

JA/0387-821X
JOURNAL OF UOEH. See Public Health and Safety.

US/1053-3826
KELLER'S INDUSTRIAL SAFETY REPORT. [Keller's ind. saf. rep.]. **VFOAT** Industrial Safety Report. Vol. 1, No. 1 (Jan. 1991)-. Periodical. English. Twelve times a year. $98.85. J. J. Keller & Associates, PO Box 548, Neenah WI 54957-0368. **Tel** (800)558-5011, (414)722-2848. **DD** 344.

UK/0261-2917
LABORATORY HAZARDS BULLETIN. See Industrial Health and Safety-Abstracting, Bibliographies and Statistics.

IE
LABOUR INSPECTION : REPORT FOR ... OF THE INDUSTRIAL INSPECTORATE AND GENERAL INSPECTORATE, DEPARTMENT OF LABOUR. **VFOAT** Labour Inspection Report for ... . English. ir. Government Publications, 4 5 Harcourt Road, Dublin 2 Ireland. **Tel** 011 353 1 6613111 Ext.4005. **LC** HD7262.5.I73; L33. **DD** 363.1/1/09417. **Circ:** 1,000.

CH
LAO TUNG PAO HU. **VFOAT** Lao Dong Bao Hu. Periodical. Chinese. NT$0.18. Science Press, 16 Donghuangchenggen North Street, Beijing 100707, People's Republic of China. **Tel** 011 86 1 4019821, 011 86 1 4010642, FAX 011 86 1 4012180, 011 86 1 4019810, telex 210147. **LC** T55.A1; L34. **DD** 363.1/1/0951.

CH
LAO TUNG WEI SHENG YU HUAN CHING I HSUEH. **VFOAT** Labour Health and Environmental Medicine. Began in 1978. Periodical. Chinese. bm. NT$0.40. Post Office, Tien-Chin Shih, People's Republic of China. **LC** RC963.A1; L36. **DD** 613.6/2/05.

IT/0390-2528
LAVORO SICURO. [Lav. sicuro]. (1974)-. Periodical. Italian. mo (9 issues). L115000 Italy. Masson S.P.A, Via Statuto 2/4, 20121 Milan Italy. **Tel** 011 39 2 63671, FAX 011 39 2 6367211. **ED** Vittorio Vedovato. **UDC** 331. **Circ:** 5,100.
Desc: Provides news on the latest achievements in different sectors of prevention: accident prevention, fire-fighting, industrial hygiene and medicine, and product safety. A useful tool for small and medium-sized companies, manufacturers, traders and end-users.

US/1051-533X
LEGAL QUARTERLY DIGEST OF MINE SAFETY AND HEALTH DECISIONS. See Law.

CN/0833-899X
LIST OF CERTIFIED OCCUPATIONAL HEALTH AND SAFETY PRODUCTS. [List certif. occup. health saf. prod.]. (1982)-. English. Free. Canadian Standards Association, 178 Rexdale Boulevard, Rexdale Ontario M9W 1R3 Canada. **Tel** (416)747-4000, (416)747-4044, telex 06-989344. **DD** 687.16.

SZ
LIST OF PERIODICALS ABSTRACTED. **Main/Corp** International Labor Office. International Occupational Safety and Health Information Centre. **VFOAT** Liste des Periodiques Depoutilles; Zerzeichnis der Erfassten Zeitschriften. 1965-. Multiple languages. ir. International Occupational Safety and Health Information Centre, CH1211 Geneve 22 Switzerland. **Tel** 41/22/996740, FAX (41)22 798-8685, telex 22 271. **LC** Z7164.A17; I52A; HD7260. **DD** 016.6148/5/05. **NLM** ZWA 400 L773.
Desc: Lists names and publishers of all periodicals abstracted at least once by Information Centre since 1960.

UK/0097-2312
LOSS PREVENTION. *Title Change.* See Engineering-Chemical Engineering.

UK/0260-9576
LOSS PREVENTION BULLETIN. [Loss prev. bull.]. (1974)-. Periodical. English. bm (6 issues). £180.00 (institutions), £45.00 (universities) UK; £220.00 (institutions), £55.00 (universities) other. Institution of Chemical Engineers, Davis Building, 165-189 Railway Terrace, Rugby Warwickshire CV21 3HQ England. **Tel** 011 44 1788 578214, FAX 011 44 1788 560833, telex 311780. **ED** Simon Jones. Index available (ú70.00 on computer disk).

IO
MAJALAH HYGIENE PERUSAHAAN, KESEHATAN-KESELAMATAN KERJA, DAN JAMINAN SOSIAL. **VFOAT** Indonesian Journal of Industrial Hygiene, Occupational Health-Safety, and Social Security; Hygiene Perusahaan, Kesehatan-Keselamatan Kerja, Dan Jaminan Sosial. Multiple languages (English and Indonesian). **LC** RC967; .M336. **NLM** W1 MA492JE. **Continues** Madjalah Hygiene Perusahaan, Kesehatan-Keselamatan Kerja, Dan Djaminan Sosial.

US
MATERIAL SAFETY DATA SHEETS SERVICE. **Added/Corp** Information Handling Services. **VFOAT** VSMF, Material Safety Data Sheets Service; Material Safety Data Sheets. Issue 82-11 (Nov. 1982)-. English. bm. Genium Publishing Corporation, One Genium Plaza, Schenectady NY 12304. **Tel** (518)377-8854, FAX (518)377-1891.

US/0742-4647
MEALEY'S LITIGATION REPORTS. ASBESTOS. See Law.

SP/0465-546X
MEDICINA Y SEGURIDAD DEL TRABAJO. [Med. segur. trab.]. (Oct./Dec. 1952)-. Periodical. Spanish. qt. $5.77 Spain; $12.00 other. Facultad de Medicina Pabellon 8, Ciudad Universitaria, 28040 Madrid Spain. **LC** RC963; .A44. **DD** 616.9/803/05. **NLM** W1 ME6397. **CODEN** MSTRAW. Documents available from BIOSIS Document Express, CASDDS.
Ind/Abst Biol. Abstr.; Chem. Abstr.; Ergon. Abstr.; Indice Med. Esp.; Ind. Hyg. Dig.; Saf. Health Work; Trop. Dis. Bull.

CN/1186-8058
MEMBERSHIP DIRECTORY / CANADIAN SOCIETY FOR INDUSTRIAL SECURITY. [Membsh. dir. - Can. Soc. Ind. Secur.]. **Main/Corp** Societe Canadienne de la Surete Industrielle. **VFOAT** Repertoire de nos Membres. (1991)-. Directory. French (English). Free for Members. Societe Canadienne de la Surete Industrielle, 23 Rue Princess, Carleton Place, Ontario K7C 2M6 Canada. **DD** 651.

CN/1186-8058
MEMBERSHIP DIRECTORY / CANADIAN SOCIETY FOR INDUSTRIAL SECURITY. [Membsh. dir. - Can. Soc. Ind. Secur.]. **Main/Corp** Canadian Society for Industrial Security. **VFOAT** Repertoire de nos Membres - Societe Canadienne de la Surete Idustriele. (1991)-. Directory. English (French). Free to members. Canadian Society for Industrial Security, 3 Unity Road, Toronto Ontario M4J 5A3 Canada. **Tel** (416)461-4109. **DD** 651.

US/0097-9368
MESA SAFETY REVIEWS. **Main/Corp** United States. Mining Enforcement and Safety Administration. Health and Safety Analysis Center. Periodical. English. mo. Mining Enforcement & Safety Administration Information Office, 4015 Wilson/Room 516, Arlington VA 22203. **Tel** (202)235-1456.

US
MINE INJURIES AND WORKTIME. **Added/Corp** United States. Mine Safety and Health Administration. United States. Mine Safety and Health Administration. Division of Mining Information Systems. **VFOAT** Mine Injuries and Worktime. (1978)-. Periodical. English. qt. Free on request. US Department of Labor Mine Safety and Health Administration / Colorado, PO Box 25367, Denver CO 80225. **Circ:** 3,000 (ctrl). *Formed by the union of* Coal-Mine Injuries and Worktime, 0275-1976 *and* Metal and Nonmetal Mine Injuries.
Desc: Tabular detail of injuries, employment and hours worked in the coal, metal, non-metal, stone, sand, and gravel mining industries in the US.
Ind/Abst AESIS Q.; Coal Abstr.; Energy Res. Abstr. (Oct. 1978-).

US
MINERALS HEALTH AND SAFETY CONTRACT RESEARCH, DEVELOPMENT, AND DEMONSTRATION IN FISCAL YEAR ... / BY STAFF, DIVISION OF MINERALS HEALTH AND SAFETY TECHNOLOGY. **Added/Corp** United States. Bureau of Mines. Division of Minerals Health and Safety Technology. (1980)-. Government Publication. English. an. US Department of the Interior / Bureau of Mines, 810 7th Street NW, Room 604, Washington DC 20241. **Tel** (202)501-9300. *Continues* Mine Health and Safety Contract Research, Development and Demonstration.

US
MONITOR. **Added/Corp** University of California. Center for Labor Research and Education. Labor Occupational Health Program. **VFOAT** Labor Occupational Health Program Monitor. (1974)-. Periodical. English. sa. $10.00. Labor Occupational Health Program, 2521 Channing Way, Berkeley CA 94720. **Tel** (510)642-5507, FAX (510)643-5698. **ED** Eugene S. Darling. **Bk Rev**, (Qty: 3-4). **Circ:** 2,000.
Desc: Newsletter on occupational safety and health. News, original articles on hazards and regulatory issues. Book and film reviews. For union leaders and members, professionals, etc.
Ind/Abst Urban Aff. Abstr.

HU/0230-2896
MUSZAKI INFORMACIO. KORSZERU MUNKAFELTETELEK, MUNKAVEDELEM. **VFOAT** Korszeru Munkafeltetelek, Munkavedelem. Began with issue for Jan. 1981. Periodical. Hungarian. bw. 1,200ft. Orszagos Muszaki Informacios Kozpont es Konyvtar, Reviczky U 6 Budapest III Hungary. **Tel** BUDAPEST 338 728. **ED** Istran Klauz and Gyula Pasti. **LC** RC963; .A444. **Ad Acc. Circ:** 1,000. *Continues* Muszaki Informacio. Korszeru Munkafeltetelek.

US
NATIONAL BOARD INSPECTION CODE; A MANUAL FOR BOILER AND PRESSURE VESSEL INSPECTORS. **Main/Corp** National Board of Boiler and Pressure Vessel Inspectors. **VFOAT** Manual for Pressure Vessel Inspectors. (19??)-. Periodical. English. be. $50.00. National Board of Boiler and Pressure Vessel Inspectors, 1055 Crupper, Columbus OH 43229. **Tel** (614)888-8320.

US
NATIONAL COAL LEADER. (199?)-. Periodical. English. mo. $12.00. National Independent Coal Leader, PO Box 354, Richlands VA 24641. **Tel** (703)963-2779, FAX (703)964-6342. **ED** Barbara Altizer and Emily Fisher (editor's address: PO Box 250, Richlands VA 24641; editor's phone: (703)963-2779). **LC** HD9541; .N37. **Ad Acc. Circ:** 8,500. *Continues National Independent Coal Leader.*
Desc: Coal trade paper promoting the use by Coal Nationwide.

US
NEW JERSEY SENSOR NEWS / DIVISION OF OCCUPATIONAL AND ENVIRONMENTAL HEALTH. **Added/Corp** New Jersey. Division of Occupational & Environmental Health. **VFOAT** SENSOR News. (Sept. 1991)-. English. **LC** RC964; .N45. **DD** 616.9/803/09749.

NZ/1171-0462
NEW ZEALAND JOURNAL OF OCCUPATIONAL THERAPY. **Added/Corp** New Zealand Association of Occupational Therapists. **VFOAT** NZJOT. Vol. 41, No. 1 (Winter 1990)-. Periodical. English. Twice a year. 40.00NZ$ New Zealand; 50.00NZ$ other. New Zealand Occupational Therapist, PO Box 68 / 291 Newton, Auckland New Zealand. **Tel** 011 64 9 602720. **ED** Ms. C. Hocking. **NLM** W1; NE973P. cum. index. **Bk Rev**, (Qty: 8/year). **Ad Acc. Continues** *Journal of the New Zealand Association of Occupational Therapists Inc.*

CN/0822-028X
NEWSLETTER / TORONTO OCCUPATIONAL HEALTH RESOURCE COMMITTEE. [Newsl. - Tor. Occup. Health Resour. Comm.]. **Added/Corp** Toronto Occupational Health Resource Committee. **VAT** Toronto Occupational Health Resource Committee Newsletter. Vol. 1, No. 1 (May 1982)-. Newsletter. English. qt. Subscription by Donation. Toronto Occupational Health Resource Committee, Suite 300, 717 Pape Avenue, Toronto Ontario M4K 3S9. **DD** 363.1/1/09713.

US
NFPA INSPECTION MANUAL. (19??)-. English. ir. $58.50 nonmembers; $52.75 members. National Fire Protection Association, 1 Batterymarch Park, PO Box 9101, Quincy MA 02269-9101. **Tel** (617)770-3000, (800)344-3555.

Desc: Facts about interior finish, electrical and heating systems, building construction, combustible dusts, metals, plastics, etc.

US/0883-7457
NIOSH CERTIFIED EQUIPMENT LIST AS OF ... . [NIOSH certif. equip. list]. **VFOAT** Certified Equipment List as of ... . **VAT** National Institute for Occupational Safety and Health Certified Equipment List. English. ir. US Department of Health and Human Services, 200 Independence Avenue Southwest, Washington DC 20201. **LC** HD7653; .N66. **DD** 620.8/6/0973. available on microfiche (Vols. for (1984-) distributed to depository libraries). ***Continues*** *NIOSH Certified Equipment.*

US/0893-4940
NIOSH CURRENT INTELLIGENCE BULLETIN. [NIOSH curr. intell. bull.]. **Main/Corp** National Institute for Occupational Safety and Health. **Added/Corp** National Institute for Occupational Safety and Health. Office of Extramural Coordination and Special Projects. **VFOAT** Current Intelligence Bulletin. **VAT** National Institute for Occupational Safety and Health Current Intelligence Bulletin. (1975)-. Monographic series. English. ir. Price varies per volume. National Technical Information Service - NTIS, Room 2027S, 5285 Port Royal Road, Springfield VA 22161. **Tel** (703)487-4630, (703)487-4660, (703)487-4650, FAX (703)321-8547, telex 89-9405. **DD** 363. **NLM** W1 CU788JC.

US/0742-7603
NIOSH REPORT ON OCCUPATIONAL SAFETY AND HEALTH. (NIOSH REPORT ON OCCUPATIONAL SAFETY AND HEALTH FOR FISCAL YEAR ... UNDER PUBLIC LAW 91-596.). [NIOSH rep. occup. saf. health]. **Added/Corp** National Institute for Occupational Safety and Health. **VFOAT** N.I.O.S.H. Report on Occupational Safety and Health for Fiscal Year ... Under Public Law 91-596; Report on Occupational Safety and Health for FY ... Under Public Law 91-596. **VAT** National Institute for Occupational Safety and Health report on occupational safety and health for fiscal year ... under public law 91-596. (19??)-. Periodical. English. an. Free on request. National Institute for Occupational Safety and Health, 4676 Columbia Parkway, Cincinnati OH 45226. **Tel** (513)533-8236. **LC** RC967; .N55. **DD** 616.9/803/072073. **NLM** W2; A N1655n. available on microfiche (Vols. for (1981-) distributed to depository libraries).

CN/0710-0922
NOUVELLES (CANADA. DIVISION DU TRANSPORT DES MARCHANDISES DANGEREUSES). (NOUVELLES : MARCHANDISES DANGEREUSES.). [Nouv. marchandises dangereuses]. **VFOAT** Bulletin sur les Marchandises Dangereuses. Vol. 1, No. 1 (Sept. 1980)-. Periodical. French. ir. Free. Transports Canada / Division du Transport des Marchandises Dangereuses, Ottawa Ontario K1A 0N5 Canada. **DD** 363.1/756/0971.

US/0892-2055
NUCLEAR PLANT JOURNAL. **See** Energy.

●UK/1351-0711
OCCUPATIONAL AND ENVIRONMENTAL MEDICINE. Vol. 51, No. 1 (Jan. 1994)-. Periodical. English. mo. £139.00 (surface mail). BMJ / British Medical Journal Publishing Group, British Medical Association House, Tavistock Square, London WC1H 9JR England. **Tel** 011 44 71 3874499, FAX 011 44 71 383 6402, telex 290034 HBJ MN. **NLM** W1; OC563. **CODEN** OEMEEM. ***Continues*** *British Journal of Industrial Medicine, 0007-1072.*
Desc: Deals with industrial and occupational medicine and environmental health.

US/0029-7909
OCCUPATIONAL HAZARDS. [Occup. hazards]. Vol. 2 (Oct. 1939)-. Periodical. English. Twelve times a year. $45.00 US; $65.00 Canada; $90.00 Mexico; $95.00 other. Penton Publishing, 1100 Superior Avenue, Cleveland OH 44114-2543. **Tel** (216)696-7000, FAX (216)696-0836. **(Subscription address:** Penton Publishing, PO Box 96732, Chicago IL 60693.**) ED** Gregg LaBar, Peter Sheridan, Stephen Minter, Sandy Moretz, and John Bruening. **DD** 363. **NLM** W1 OC546L. **CODEN** OCHAAZ. **[CCC].** Index available. cum. index. **Bk Rev. Ad Acc. Circ:** 60,000 (ctrl). available on microfilm and microfiche from University Microfilms International (UMI); available on an online database (files 15,149,648/Full-Text) from DIALOG. Documents available from UMI Article Clearinghouse. ***Continues*** *Occupational Hazards & Safety.*
Desc: Serves industrial officials responsible for safety management and plant protection. Articles regularly cover industrial safety and hygiene, occupational health, insurance, first aid, medical care, training and handling of hazardous materials. Staff-written material is based on personal interviews and frequent plant visits.
Ind/Abst ABI/INFORM Glob. Ed.; ABI Inform Ondisc (Aug. 1979-); Acad. Search (July 1993-); Acoust. Abstr. (Aug. 1979-); Bus. ASAP (1990-) [Full Txt.]; Bus. Index (1985-); Bus. Period. Index (1990-); Bus. Source (Jan. 1993-); Chem. Hazards Ind.; Gen. BusinessFile (1985-); Gen. Period. Index (1985-); Health Index (1992-); Health Ref. Cent. (1987-) [Full Txt.] [Select. Cov.]; INFO-SOUTH Abstr.; Lab. Hazards Bull.; Mag. Search; Person. Manage. Abstr.; Saf. Health Work; Trade Ind. ASAP [Full Txt.]; Trade Ind. Index [Full Txt.]; UMI ABI/Inform--Bus. Period. Ondisc (Dec. 1987-) [Full Txt.]; Vocat. Search (July 1993-); Wilson Bus. Abstr.; Work Relat. Abstr. (1974-).

UK/0029-7917
OCCUPATIONAL HEALTH. [Occup. health]. **Added/Corp** Royal College of Nursing Society of Occupational Health Nursing. Vol. 1 (1949)-. Periodical. English. Twelve times a year. £39.00 (individuals), £55.00 (institutions) UK, £59.00 others (surface mail); £110.00 (airmail) others. Aldwych Publishing, A. Clark, 230-234 Long Lane, London SE1 4QE England. **Tel** 11 44 71 4034353, 011 44 71 4077541, FAX 11 44 71 4030233. **ED** Helen Kogan. **[CCC].** Index available (bound in March issue). cum. index. **Bk Rev. Ad Acc, Adv Mgr:** Peter Collis. **Circ:** 4,700. available on microfilm and microfiche from University Microfilms International (UMI).
Desc: Provides members of the occupational health team with articles and news, features covering all aspects of safety and health in the workplace.
Ind/Abst Acoust. Abstr.; Appl. Soc. Sci. Index Abstr.; Chem. Hazards Ind.; Coal Abstr.; Cumul. Index Nurs. Allied Health Lit.; EMBASE; Eng. Mater. Abstr.; Ind. Hyg. Dig. (19??-19??); Int. Nurs. Index; Lab. Hazards Bull.; Saf. Health Work; SportSearch.

US/0362-4064
OCCUPATIONAL HEALTH & SAFETY. [Occup. health saf.]. **VFOAT** Occupational Health and Safety; International Journal of Occupational Health & Safety. (Jan./Feb. 1976)-. Periodical. English. mo (12 issues, plus Sourcebook). $73.50 US; $99.50 Canada; $91.50 Mexico; $103.50 other. Stevens Publishing Corporation, 225 North New Road, Waco TX 76702-2604. **Tel** (800)727-7573, (817)776-9000. **(Subscription address:** Stevens Publishing Corp., PO Box 2573, Waco TX 76702.**) LC** RC963; .A37. **DD** 363.11/0973. **NLM** W1 OC565DH. **CODEN** OHSADQ. **[CCC].** Index available (bound in Dec. issue). available on microfilm and microfiche from University Microfilms International (UMI). Documents available from Ask*IEEE, CASDDS. ***Continues*** *International Journal of Occupational Health & Safety, 0093-2205.*
Ind/Abst Acad. Search (Jan. 1993-); Art Archaeol. Tech. Abstr.; BioBusiness; Bus. Period. Index; Bus. Source (Jan. 1993-); Chem. Abstr.; Chem. Hazards Ind.; Cumul. Index Nurs. Allied Health Lit.; EMBASE; Energy Res. Abstr. (1980-); Foods Adlibra; Health Saf. Sci. Abstr.; Health Source (Jan. 1993-); Index Med.; Ind. Hyg. Dig.; INFO-SOUTH Abstr.; INSPEC (May/June 1976-); Lab. Hazards Bull.; Mag. Search; PAIS Int. Print (1991-); Life Sci. Collect.; Saf. Health Work; Vocat. Search (Jan. 1993-); Wilson Bus. Abstr.; Work Relat. Abstr.

CN
OCCUPATIONAL HEALTH & SAFETY CANADA. English. Six times a year. Corpus Information Service Ltd, 1450 Don Mills Road, Don Mills Ontario M3B 2X7 Canada. **Tel** (416)445-7101, telex 06-966612.
Ind/Abst Can. Period. Index (19??-).

AT
OCCUPATIONAL HEALTH AND SAFETY DIRECTORY. (19??)-. English. an. 130.00Aus$. Newsletter Information Service, PO Box 693, Manly New South Wales 2095 Australia. **Tel** 011 61 2 9777500.

US
OCCUPATIONAL HEALTH AND SAFETY HEALTH FACILITIES REPORT. (19??)-. Periodical. English. mo. $298.50 US; $322.50 Canada; $305.50 Mexico; $315.50 other. Stevens Publishing Corporation, 225 North New Road, Waco TX 76702-2604. **Tel** (800)727-7573, (817)776-9000. **(Subscription address:** Stevens Publishing Corp., PO Box 2573, Waco TX 76702.**)** ***Absorbed*** *Medical Waste Management.*

CN/0706-5019
OCCUPATIONAL HEALTH AND SAFETY LAW. **See** Law.

US/0196-058X
OCCUPATIONAL HEALTH AND SAFETY LETTER. (1971)-. Periodical. English. bw. $286.00. Business Publishers Inc., 951 Pershing Drive, Silver Spring MD 20910-4464. **Tel** (301)587-6300, (800)274-0122, FAX (301)585-9075. **ED** Gershon W. Fishbein. **NLM** W1 OC565BK. **[CCC].** available on an online database (files 15,636/Full-Text) from DIALOG. ***Continues*** *Job Safety and Health Report.*
Desc: Regulatory and political aspects of occupational health and safety.
Ind/Abst PTS Newsl. Database [Full Txt.].

CN/0846-9229
OCCUPATIONAL HEALTH & SAFETY MAGAZINE. [Occup. health saf. mag.]. **Added/Corp** Alberta Workers' Health, Safety and Compensation. Occupational Health and Safety Division. Alberta. Occupational Health and Safety Division. Alberta. Alberta Community and Occupational Health. Alberta. Alberta Occupational Health and Safety. **VFOAT** Occupational Health and Safety Magazine; OH&S Magazine. Vol. 8, No. 3 (Dec. 1985)-. Periodical. English. Three times a year. Free on request. Alberta Labour Communications, 10808-99th Avenue Room 506, Edmonton Alberta T5K 0G5 Canada. **DD** 363.1/1/097123. ***Continues*** *Occupational Health & Safety, 0705-6052.*

US/0896-3835
OCCUPATIONAL HEALTH & SAFETY NEWS DIGEST. (OCCUPATIONAL HEALTH & SAFETY NEWS.). [Occup. health saf. news dig.]. **VFOAT** OH & S News; OH & S News Digest; Occupational Health and Safety News; Occupational Health & Safety News Digest; Occupational Health&Safety News Digest; Occupational Health and Safety News Digest; OH and S News; O.H. and S News Digest; OH&S News Digest. Vol. 1, No. 1 (Feb. 1985)-. Periodical. English. sm (24 issues). $358.50 US; $382.50 Mexico; $402.50 other. Stevens Publishing Corporation, 225 North New Road, Waco TX 76702-2604. **Tel** (800)727-7573, (817)776-9000. **(Subscription address:** Stevens Publishing Corp., PO Box 2573, Waco TX 76702.**) DD** 613. **CODEN** OHSDE2.
Ind/Abst BioBusiness (1989-).

FI/0250-6602
OCCUPATIONAL HEALTH FOUNDATION, INSTITUTE OF OCCUPATIONAL HEALTH. Main/Corp Tyoterveyssaatio. 1973-. Periodical. English. Institute of Occupational Health Finland, Topeliuksenkatu 41AA, SF-00250 Helsinki Finland. **Tel** 011 358 0 47471, FAX 011 358 0 4747548, telex 121 394 TLTX ST. **NLM** W1 TY344AC. ***Continues*** *Occupational Health Foundation and the Institute of Occupational Health, Helsinki, Finland, Annual Report, 0358-3449.*

AT/1032-0989
OCCUPATIONAL HEALTH MAGAZINE. [Occup. health mag.]. (1988)-. Periodical. English. mo. Free to subscribers of Occupational Health Newsletter. Newsletter Information Service, PO Box 693, Manly New South Wales 2095 Australia. **Tel** 011 61 2 9777500. **DD** 363.110994. ***Continues*** *Occupational Health and Safety Products and Services, 1032-0970.*

US
OCCUPATIONAL HEALTH MANAGEMENT. ***Ceased.*** (19??)-(Dec. 1994). English. American Health Consultants, 3525 Piedmont Road, Suite 400, Atlanta GA 30305. **Tel** (800)688-2421, (404)262-7436.
Desc: Devoted to helping you achieve success with your hospital's occupational health management program.

AT
OCCUPATIONAL HEALTH NEWSLETTER. (19??)-. English. sm. 345.00Aus$. Newsletter Information Service, PO Box 693, Manly New South Wales 2095 Australia. **Tel** 011 61 2 9777500.

UK/0951-4600
OCCUPATIONAL HEALTH REVIEW (LONDON). (OCCUPATIONAL HEALTH REVIEW.). [Occup. health rev.]. **Added/Corp** Industrial Relations Services. (198?)-. Periodical. English. bm. £155.00 UK; £171.00 other. Eclipse Publications Ltd, 18 20 Highbury Place, London N5 1QP England. **Tel** 011 44 71 354 5858. **(Subscription address:** Industrial Relations Services, 18 20 Highbury Place, London N5 1QP England.**) ED** John Manos and John Green. **NLM** W1; OC574D. Index available. cum. index. **Circ:** 1,500.
Desc: A publication for both managers with an interest, but not professional involvement, in occupational health and for all those with a special interest in the subject - nurses, doctors, occupational hygienists, toxicologists, safety officers and chemists.
Ind/Abst Chem. Hazards Ind.; Lab. Hazards Bull.; Manage. Market. Abstr.; World Surf. Coat. Abstr.

●US/1061-0251
OCCUPATIONAL HYGIENE. (1992)-. English. Four times a year. Gordon & Breach Science Publishers, Inc., PO Box 786, Cooper Station, New York NY 10276. **Tel** (212)206-8900, FAX (212)645-2459. **(Subscription address:** International Publishers Distributor at one of the following addresses: 820 Town Center Drive, Langhorne, PA 19047; or PO Box 90, Reading Berkshire RG1 8JL UK; or Kent Ridge PO Box 1180, Singapore 9111, Republic of Singapore**) NLM** W1; OC576P. **[CCC].**
Desc: Presents the most recent developments in the science of anticipation, recognition, evaluation and control of occupational hazards.

US
OCCUPATIONAL INJURIES AND ILLNESSES IN CONNECTICUT. ***Title Change.*** **Main/Corp** Connecticut. Labor Dept. (19??)-(19??). English. an. Connecticut Labor Department, 200 Folly Brook Boulevard, Wethersfield CT 06109. **Tel** (203)566-4380. **ED** P Joseph Peraro. **LC** HD7262.5.U62; C83. **DD** 312/.4/309746. ***Continued by*** *Connecticut Occupational Injury and Illness Survey.*

US/0198-7771
OCCUPATIONAL INJURIES AND ILLNESSES IN MAINE. English. an. Research & Statistics Division, Bureau of Labor Standards, State House Station 45, Augusta ME 04333-0045. **Tel** (207)289-6400, FAX (207)289-6449. **ED** John L Rioux, Bradford Brown and Terry Hathaway. **LC** HD7262.5.U62; M25. **DD** 312/.43/09741. **Circ:** 1,000.
Desc: Statistical compilation of injury and illness rate for the state of Maine.

US
OCCUPATIONAL INJURIES AND ILLNESSES IN ... SUMMARY. Government Publication. English. an. $2.00. US Department of Labor / Bureau of Labor Statistics, 441 G Street NW, Washington DC 20212. **Tel** (202)606-7800, FAX (202)606-7797.

US/0162-010X
OCCUPATIONAL INJURIES AND ILLNESSES IN THE UNITED STATES BY INDUSTRY. (OCCUPATIONAL INJURIES AND ILLNESSES IN THE UNITED STATES BY INDUSTRY / C.U.S. DEPARTMENT OF LABOR, BUREAU OF LABOR STATISTICS.). **Added/Corp** United States. Bureau of Labor Statistics. (1973)-. English. Four times a year. $14.50. Superintendent of Documents, US Government Printing Office, Washington DC 20402. **Tel** (202)275-3328, FAX (202)786-2377. **LC** HD7262.5.U6; U54a. **DD** 614.8/52/0973. **NLM** W2; A B88o. ***Continues*** *Occupational Injuries and Illnesses by Industry.*

US
OCCUPATIONAL INJURIES AND ILLNESSES. IOWA. 1972-. English. an. Iowa Division of Labor, Inspections and Reporting Bureau, 1000 East Grand Avenue, Des Moines IA 50319. **Tel** (515)281-3606. **Circ:** 300 (ctrl). ***Continues*** *1971 Occupational Injuries and Illnesses Survey (Des Moines, Iowa).*
Desc: Results of annual occupational injuries and illnesses survey.

US/0272-0957
OCCUPATIONAL INJURIES AND ILLNESSES. SUMMARY (WASHINGTON). (OCCUPATIONAL INJURIES AND ILLNESSES, SUMMARY.). [Occup. inj. illn., Summ.]. **Main/Corp** United States. Bureau of Labor Statistics. Government Publication. English. US Department of Labor / Bureau of Labor Statistics, 441 G Street NW, Washington DC 20212. **Tel** (202)606-7800, FAX (202)606-7797. **LC** HD805L; .A7876 subser; HD7262.5. 5.U6. **DD** 331.1/0973 S; 312/.43/0973.

US/0885-114X
OCCUPATIONAL MEDICINE (PHILADELPHIA, PA.). (STATE OF THE ART REVIEWS. OCCUPATIONAL MEDICINE.). [Occup. med.]. **VFOAT** Occupational Medicine; State of the Art Reviews in Occupational Medicine. Vol. 1, No. 1 (Jan./March 1985 I.E. 1986)-. Academic Scholarly Publication. English. Four times a year. $86.00 US and Possessions; $96.00 other. Hanley & Belfus Inc., 210 South 13th Street, Philadelphia PA 19107. **Tel** (215)546-7293, FAX (215)790-9330. **ED** John J Hanley. **LC** RC963.A1; S83. **DD** 616.9/803/05. **NLM** W1; OC583F. **CODEN** SAOME4. **[CCC].** Index available. **Pr Rev. Circ:** 2,500. Documents available from The Genuine Article, BIOSIS Document Express, CASDDS.
Desc: Covers medical problems of the work place. Each issue reviews a focal problem, such as pulmonary disease, back pain, etc.
Ind/Abst Biol. Abstr. (1986-); Chem. Abstr. (1986-); Chem. Hazards Ind.; Index Med. (1986-); Lab. Hazards Bull.; Res. Alert [Select. Cov.]; SCISEARCH; Soc. Sci. Cit. Index [Select. Cov.].

SZ/0029-7984
OCCUPATIONAL SAFETY AND HEALTH ABSTRACTS. ***Title Change.*** Periodical. English. International Occupational Safety and Health Information Centre, CH1211 Geneve 22 Switzerland. **Tel** 41/22/996740, FAX (41)22 798-8685, telex 22 271. ***Continued by*** *CIS Abstracts, 0302-7651.*

UK/0143-5353
OCCUPATIONAL SAFETY & HEALTH (BIRMINGHAM). (OCCUPATIONAL SAFETY & HEALTH.). [Occup. saf. health]. **Added/Corp** Royal Society for the Prevention of Accidents. Vol. 1, (March 1971)-. Periodical. English. Twelve times a year. £43.00 UK; £68.65 other. Royal Society for the Prevention of Accidents, Cannon House, Priory Queensway, Birmingham B4 6BS England. **Tel** 011 44 21 200 2461, FAX 021 200 1254. **ED** Jacky Steemson. **LC** T55.A1; B72. **DD** 614.85/2/05. **NLM** W1 OC597N. Index available. **Bk Rev. Ad Acc. Circ:** 10,400. ***Continues*** *British Journal of Occupational Safety.*
Ind/Abst Anal. Abstr.; Chem. Hazards Ind.; Coal Abstr.; Curr. Technol. Index; Lab. Hazards Bull.; Manage. Market. Abstr.; Saf. Health Work; World Text. Abstr.

US/0737-1268
OCCUPATIONAL SAFETY AND HEALTH LAW. **See** Law.

US/0146-3632
OCCUPATIONAL SAFETY AND HEALTH (NEW YORK). (1976)-. Monographic series. English. Price varies per volume. Marcel Dekker Inc., 270 Madison Avenue, New York NY 10016. **Tel** (212)696-9000, (800)228-1160, FAX (212)685-4540, telex 421419. **(Subscription address:** Marcel Dekker Inc, PO Box 5017, Monticello NY 12701.**) LC** UNC. **NLM** W1 OC597M.
Desc: Each volume presents a different aspect of occupational safety and health. Topics include fire loss control, practical electrical safety, cancer risk assessment and more.

US/0095-3237
OCCUPATIONAL SAFETY & HEALTH REPORTER. **Added/Corp** Bureau of National Affairs (Washington, D.C.). **VAT** Occupational Safety and Health Reporter. Vol. 1 (May 6, 1971)-. Periodical. English. wk. $1030.00 (includes binder). Bureau of National Affairs Inc., 9435 Key West Avenue, Rockville MD 20850. **Tel** (800)372-1033, (301)258-1033, FAX (301)948-5823. **ED** Mary R. Worobec. **LC** KF3570.A1; O25. **DD** 344/.73/046505. **[CCC].**
Desc: Notification and reference service which provides information on federal and state regulation of occupational safety and health, standards, legislation, enforcement activities, research, and legal decisions.
Ind/Abst Ind. Hyg. Dig. (19??-).

SZ/0078-3129
OCCUPATIONAL SAFETY AND HEALTH SERIES. (OCCUPATIONAL SAFETY AND HEALTH SERIES / INTERNATIONAL LABOUR ORGANISATION.). [Occup. saf. health ser.]. **Added/Corp** International Labour Office. International Labour Organisation. No. 1 (196?)-. Academic Scholarly Publication. English. ir. Price varies per volume. International Labour Office - ILO, Publications Sales Service, CH-1211 Geneva 22 Switzerland. **Tel** 011 41 22 7996111. **(Subscription address:** International Labor Office / Albany, NY, 49 Sheridan Avenue, Albany NY 12210.**) NLM** W1 OC598. **CODEN** OSHSDY. Documents available from BIOSIS Document Express, CASDDS.
Desc: Occasional technical monographs and reports on occupational health and safety protection against sickness, disease and injury.
Ind/Abst Biol. Abstr.; Chem. Abstr.

US/0161-9446
OCCUPATIONAL SAFETY AND HEALTH TRAINING GRANTS. 1976/77-. Periodical. English. US Department of Health and Human Services, 200 Independence Avenue Southwest, Washington DC 20201. **NLM** WA 22 AA1 O15.
Desc: Listing of grants available to colleges, universities, and other instructional institutions in the United States. Geographical arrangement under broad topics, e.g., Industrial hygiene.

US
OCCUPATIONAL SAFETY AND HEALTH. VOLUME 1. GENERAL INDUSTRY STANDARDS. **Main/Corp** United States. Occupational Safety and Health Administration. (19??)-. Periodical. English. ir. US Department of Labor Occupational Safety & Health Administration, 200 Constitution Avenue NW, Room S315, Washington DC 20210. **Tel** (202)219-8151, FAX (202)219-5986.

US
OCCUPATIONAL SAFETY AND HEALTH. VOLUME 3. CONSTRUCTION STANDARDS. **Main/Corp** United States. Occupational Safety and Health Administration. (19??)-. Periodical. English. ir. Construction Standards, US Department of Labor, Occupational Safety and Health Administration, Washington DC 20402.

US
OCCUPATIONAL SAFETY AND HEALTH. VOLUME 4. OTHER REGULATIONS AND PROCEDURES. **Main/Corp** United States. Occupational Safety and Health Administration. Periodical. English. ir. Other Regulations and Procedures, US Department of Labor, Occupational Safety and Health Administration, Washington DC 20402.

US
OCCUPATIONAL SAFETY AND HEALTH. VOLUME 5. FIELD OPERATIONS MANUAL. **Main/Corp** United States. Occupational Safety and Health Administration. (19??)-. Periodical. English. ir. Field Operations Manual, US Department of Labor, Occupational Safety and Health Administration, Washington DC 20402.

US/0164-212X
OCCUPATIONAL THERAPY IN MENTAL HEALTH. [Occup. ther. ment. health]. Vol. 1 (Spring 1980)-. Periodical. English. qt. $175.00 US; $245.00 other. The Haworth Press Inc, 10 Alice Street, Binghamton NY 13904-1580. **Tel** (607)722-5857, (800)3-HAWORTH, FAX (607)722-1424. **ED** Diane Gibson (editor's address: Activity Therapy Department, The Sheppard and Enoch Pratt Hospital, POB 6815, Towson, MD 21204). **LC** RC487; .O26. **DD** 616.89/1652/05. **NLM** W1 OC601N. **CODEN** OTMHDX. **Bk Rev. Ad Acc. Pr Rev. Acid Free. Circ:** 725. available on microfilm and microfiche from University Microfilms International (UMI). Documents available from BIOSIS Document Express, Haworth Document Delivery Service.
Desc: Presents timely material specifically for occupational therapists in mental health clinics, hospitals, schools, human service agencies and transitional living programs.
Ind/Abst Abstr. Soc. Gerontol.; Abstr. Res. Pastor. Care Couns. (19??-); Biol. Abstr.; Cumul. Index Nurs. Allied Health Lit.; EMBASE; Except. Child Educ. Resour.; Psychol. Abstr. (1980-); PsycINFO; PsycLit; Soc. Work Abstr. [Select. Cov.].

PL/0029-8220
OCHRONA PRACY. [Ochr. pr.]. (July 1952)-. Periodical. Polish (table of contents in English and Russian). mo. $57.00. **(Subscription address:** ARS Polona, PO Box 1001, 00068 Warsaw Poland.**)** ***Continues*** *Bezpieczenstwo I Higiena Pracy.*
Ind/Abst Coal Abstr.; Saf. Health Work.

CN/0827-4576
OH&S CANADA. [OH S Can.]. **Added/Corp** Corpus Information Services. **VFOAT** OHS Canada; Occupational Health & Safety Canada. Vol. 1, No. 1 (July/Aug. 1985)-. Periodical. English. bm. 83.00Can$ (one year), 139.00Can$ (two year), 197.00Can$ (three year) Canada; 114.00Can$ (one year), 191.00Can$ (two year), 271.00Can$ (three year) US; 124.00Can$ (one year), 208.00Can$ (two year), 294.00Can$ (three year) other. Southam Information and Technology Group Inc., 1450 Don Mills Road, Don Mills Ontario M3B 2X7 Canada. **Tel** (416)445-6641, (800)668-2374, FAX (416)442-2261. **ED** Cindy Moser. **DD** 363.1/1/05. Index available. **Bk Rev. Ad Acc. Circ:** 7,000 (ctrl). available on microfilm and microfiche from University Microfilms International (UMI).
Desc: A practical guide that covers OH&S law, medicine, hazardous substances, industrial hygiene, workers' compensation, wellness and controversial issues.

CN
OH&S SURVIVAL KIT. an. 137.00Can$. Southam Information and Technology Group Inc., 1450 Don Mills Road, Don Mills Ontario M3B 2X7 Canada. **Tel** (416)445-6641, (800)668-2374, FAX (416)442-2261.

RU/0131-2618
OKHRANA TRUDA I SOTSIALNOE STRAKHOVANIE. [Ohr. tr. so. strahovanie]. **Added/Corp** Vsesoiuznyi Tsentralnyi Sovet Professionalnykh Soiuzov. (1958)-. Periodical. Russian. mo. $99.95. **(Subscription address:** East View Publications Inc., 3020 Harbor Lane North, Suite 110, Minneapolis MN 55447.**)**
Ind/Abst LABORDOC; Saf. Health Work.

SP
ORDENANZAS LABORALES PARA LA INDUSTRIA Y COMERCIO : SEGURIDAD E HIGIENE EN EL TRABAJO, PLAN NACIONAL Y ORDENANZA GENERAL. **Main/Corp** Spain. Ministerio de Trabajo. **VFOAT** Seguridad e Higiene en El Trabajo. Spanish. 250. Ediciones Salvatierra, c/o Fernando No 30, Barcelona Spain. **LC** LAW.

US/0094-7776
OSAHRC REPORTS. **See** Law.

US
OSHA 1910 COMPLIANCE MANUAL. (19??)-. English. Thirty times a year. $424.79 (comes with OSHANews). Merritt Company, 1661 Ninth Street, PO Box 955, Santa Monica CA 90406. **Tel** (310)450-7234, (800)638-7597, FAX (310)396-4563.

US
OSHA 1926 COMPLIANCE MANUAL. (19??)-. English. an. $424.79 (includes OSHANews). Merritt Company, 1661 Ninth Street, PO Box 955, Santa Monica CA 90406. **Tel** (310)450-7234, (800)638-7597, FAX (310)396-4563.

US/1065-9277
OSHA CD-ROM. (OSHA CD-ROM [COMPUTER FILE].). [OSHA CD-ROM]. **Main/Corp** United States. Occupational Safety and Health Administration. **VFOAT** Occupational Safety and Health Administration CD-ROM. OSHA A92-1 (Oct. 1991)-. Government Publication. English. qt. $88.00 US; $110.00 other. Superintendent of Documents, US Government Printing Office, Washington DC 20402. **Tel** (202)275-3328, FAX (202)786-2377. **LC** HD7654. **DD** 363.
Desc: System requirements: IBM XT, AT, PS/2 or compatible, 640K, DOS 3.3 or higher, MS-DOS CD-ROM extensions 2.0 or higher, VGA/EGA adapter and color monitor, CD-ROM drive, and hard disk.

US/0896-9949
OSHA COMPLIANCE ADVISOR. [OSHA compliance advis.]. **VAT** Occupational Safety and Health

Administration Compliance Advisor. Issue No. 101 (Feb. 1, 1988)-. Periodical. English. Twenty-four times a year. $269.95. Business & Legal Reports, 39 Academy Street, Madison CT 06443. **Tel** (203)245-7448, (800)727-5257, FAX (203)245-2559. **ED** John Brady. **DD** 344. **[CCC]**. Index available. ***Absorbed*** *Job Safety Consultant, 1040-4198.*
Desc: Reports on OSHA related activities.

US
OSHA PUBLICATIONS & TRAINING MATERIAL. **Main/Corp** United States. Occupational Safety and Health Administration. **VAT** Occupational Safety and Health Administration Publications and Training Material. English. US Department of Labor Occupational Safety & Health Administration, 200 Constitution Avenue NW, Room S315, Washington DC 20210. **Tel** (202)219-8151, FAX (202)219-5986.

US/0896-9957
OSHA TRAINING BULLETIN FOR SUPERVISORS. [OSHA train. bull. superv.]. **Added/Corp** United States. Occupational Safety and Health Administration. **VAT** Occupational Safety and Health Administration Training Bulletin for Supervisors. Issue No. 174 (Feb. 1988)-. Bulletin. English. mo. $89.88. Business & Legal Reports, 39 Academy Street, Madison CT 06443. **Tel** (203)245-7448, (800)727-5257, FAX (203)245-2559. **DD** 363. **[CCC]**. ***Continues*** *Hazardous Materials Training Bulletin for Supervisors, 0887-9125.*

US/1057-1485
OSHA WEEK. [OSHA week]. **Added/Corp** National Institute for Occupational Safety and Health. **VFOAT** OSHAweek. **VAT** National Institute for Occupational Safety and Health Week. (19??)-. Periodical. English. wk. $372.00 US; $417.00 Canada; $382.00 Mexico; $408.00 other. Stevens Publishing Corporation, 225 North New Road, Waco TX 76702-2604. **Tel** (800)727-7573, (817)776-9000. **(Subscription address:** Stevens Publishing Corp., PO Box 2573, Waco TX 76702.**) DD** 362.

US/0740-1418
OSHANEWS. (OSHA NEWS : BIMONTHLY BULLETIN OF OCCUPATIONAL SAFETY AND HEALTH LEGISLATION AND ACTIVITIES FOR SUBSCRIBERS TO THE OSHA REFERENCE MANUAL.). [OSHAnews]. **VAT** Occupational Safety and Health Administration News. (197?)-. English. bm. comes with OSHA Compliance Manual. Merritt Company, 1661 Ninth Street, PO Box 955, Santa Monica CA 90406. **Tel** (310)450-7234, (800)638-7597, FAX (310)396-4563.

US/0148-821X
PENNSYLVANIA WORK INJURIES. **Main/Corp** Pennsylvania. Bureau of Occupational Injury and Disease Compensation. Data Input Section. English. Bureau of Occupational Injury and Disease Compensation, Data Imput Section, Harrisburg PA. **LC** HD7262.5.U62; P4. **DD** 312/.4/309748.

US
PIPELINE ACCIDENT REPORTS. BRIEF FORMAT / NATIONAL TRANSPORTATION SAFETY BOARD. **Added/Corp** United States. National Transportation Safety Board. Issue No. 1 (1977)-. English. ir. National Technical Information Service - NTIS, Room 2027S, 5285 Port Royal Road, Springfield VA 22161. **Tel** (703)487-4630, (703)487-4660, (703)487-4650, FAX (703)321-8547, telex 89-9405.

US
PLANT, TECHNOLOGY & SAFETY MANAGEMENT SERIES. **Added/Corp** Joint Commission on Accreditation of Healthcare Organizations. **VFOAT** Plant, Technology, and Safety Management Series; PTSM Series. (1985)-. Monographic series. English. qt. Joint Commission on Accreditation of Hospitals, 1 Renaissance Boulevard, Headquarters Center, Oakbrook Terrace IL 60181. **Tel** (708)916-5800. **NLM** W1; PL105T.

FR
PREVENIR LES RISQUES DU METIER. French. qt. 23.00F. Institut National de Recherche & Securite, 4 rue Andre Boulle, 94942 Creteil Cedex 09 France. **Tel** 011 33 1 42070606. ***Continues*** *Risques du Metier.*

●US/1056-9588
PREVENTING INJURY. [Prev. inj.]. Vol. 1, No. 1 (Winter 1992)-. Periodical. English. qt. $100.00. TBI Press, 6210 Campbell Road, Dallas TX 75248. **DD** 658.

FR/0766-5687
PREVENTIQUE. ***Title Change.*** **Added/Corp** Association des Industriels de France Contre les Accidents du Travail. (1985)-(199?). Periodical. French. bm. AIF Services SA, 10 rue de Calais, 75009 Paris France. **LC** T55.A1; R45. **DD** 363.1/1/0944. **CODEN** PRVNEQ. ***Continues*** *Revue de la Securite, 0035-1261.* ***Merged with*** *Revue Generale de Securite* ***to form*** *Securite.*
Ind/Abst Int. Labour Doc. (?-?); LABORDOC (?-?).

HT
PREVOYANCE : PUBLICATION DE L'OFFICE D'ASSURANCE ACCIDENTS DU TRAVAIL, MALADIE, ET MATERNITE. No. 1 (Feb. 1981)-. Periodical. French. Office d'Assurance Accidents du Travail Maladie et Maternite, BP No 1324, Port-au-Prince Haiti. **LC** HD7672; .A35. **DD** 363.1/17/097294. ***Continues*** *Prevention (Port-au-Prince, Haiti).*

US
PROCEEDINGS OF THE ... ANNUAL INSTITUTE ON COAL MINING HEALTH, SAFETY AND RESEARCH. **Main/Conf** Institute on Coal Mining Health, Safety, and Research. Proceedings. English. an. Department of Mining and Minerals Engineering, Virginia Polytechnic Institute and State University, Blacksburg VA 24061. **Tel** (703)961-6671, telex 910 333-1. **ED** J R Lucas, D R Forshey and W H Sutherland. **Circ:** 150 (ctrl).
Desc: Articles by representatives of industry, government, academia and UMWA on small mines, health and safety, ground control, substance abuse, etc.

US/0148-4176
PROCEEDINGS OF THE ANNUAL MEETING - NATIONAL ACADEMY OF ARBITRATORS. MEETING. (PROCEEDINGS OF THE ... ANNUAL MEETING, NATIONAL ACADEMY OF ARBITRATORS.). [Proc. annu. meet. - Natl. Acad. Arbitr., Meet.]. **Main/Corp** National Academy of Arbitrators. Meeting. **Added/Corp** BNA Incorporated. 8th (1955)-. Proceedings. English. an. $40.00. Bureau of National Affairs Inc., 9435 Key West Avenue, Rockville MD 20850. **Tel** (800)372-1033, (301)258-1033, FAX (301)948-5823. **LC** HD5481; .N32. **DD** 331. cum. index. ***Continues*** *National Academy of Arbitrators. Meeting. Selected Papers From the First Seven Annual Meetings of the National Academy of Arbitrators.*
Ind/Abst Index Leg. Period.; Leg. Resour. Index; LegalTrac (1990-).

US
PRODUCT SAFETY NEWS. English. mo. $120.00. Institute for Product Safety, PO Box 1931, Durham NC 27702. **Tel** (919)489-2357, FAX (919)490-4954. **ED** Sherie Harless (919)489-2357. Index available. cum. index. **Ad Acc.**

US/0099-0027
PROFESSIONAL SAFETY. [Prof. saf.]. **Added/Corp** American Society of Safety Engineers. Vol. 19, No. 10 (Oct. 1974)-. Periodical. English. mo. $60.00 US, Canada & Mexico; $70.00 other. American Society of Safety Engineers, 1800 East Oakton Street, Des Plaines IL 60018. **Tel** (312)692-4121. **ED** Ellen Zielinski. **LC** T55.A1; A418a. **DD** 620.8/6/05. **CODEN** PRSAD5. Index available. cum. index. **Bk Rev. Ad Acc. Circ:** 20,000. available on microfilm and microfiche from University Microfilms International (UMI); available on an online database (file 15/Full-Text) from DIALOG. Documents available from Article Express International, UMI Article Clearinghouse. ***Continues*** *American Society of Safety Engineers. ASSE Journal.*
Desc: Keeps the professional safety specialists informed on developments in the research and technology of accident prevention.
Ind/Abst ABI/INFORM Glob. Ed.; ABI Inform Ondisc (Jan. 1985-); Acoust. Abstr.; Alum. Ind. Abstr.; Appl. Sci. Technol. Index; Bioeng. Abstr.; Chem. Hazards Ind.; Coal Abstr.; Ei Page One; Eng. Mater. Abstr.; Eng. Index Annu.; Ergon. Abstr.; Health Saf. Sci. Abstr.; Hospit. Health Admin. Index; Lab. Hazards Bull.; Manage. Market. Abstr.; Met. Abstr.; Saf. Health Work; UMI ABI/Inform--Bus. Period. Ondisc (Dec. 1987-) [Full Txt.].

BE/0771-2839
PROMOSAFE (NEDERLANDSE ED.). (PROMOSAFE.). [Promosafe]. **Added/Corp** Association Nationale pour la Prevention des Accidents du Travail. (19??)-. Periodical. Dutch. bm. 500.00F. Anpat, rue Gachard 88 Boite 4, 1050 Brussels Belgium. **Tel** 011 32 2 6480337. **LC** T55.A1; P73.
Ind/Abst Chem. Hazards Ind.; Int. Labour Doc.; Lab. Hazards Bull.; LABORDOC; Saf. Health Work.

PL
PRZYJACIEL PRZY PRACY. **Added/Corp** Centralna Rady Zwiazkow Zawodowych w Polsce. (Oct. 1949)-. Periodical. Polish. mo. $33.00. **(Subscription address:** ARS Polona, PO Box 1001, 00068 Warsaw Poland.**) LC** T55.A1; P77.
Ind/Abst Saf. Health Work.

IT
PULIZIA INDUSTRIALE E SANIFICAZIONE. Italian. mo. Mo Ed Co Srl, Via Paolo Da Cannobio 9, 20122 Milan Italy. **Tel** 02-878724, 02-878577, FAX 02-89010728. **Ad Acc, Adv Mgr:** Dr Pellizzari. **Circ:** 6000 (ctrl).

US/0195-9344
QUARTERLY INJURY & ILLNESS INCIDENCE REPORT. **Main/Corp** Western Wood Products Association. **VAT** Quarterly Injury and Illness Incidence Report. (19??)-. English. qt. $18.00. Western Wood Products Association, Yeon Building, 522 Southwest Fifth Avenue, Portland OR 97204-2122. **Tel** (503)224-3930, FAX (503)224-3934.
Desc: Year to date injury control index and annual summary of injury experience of the Western Woods Region, includes injury rates for lumber manufacturing only.

SZ/0258-0748
QUARTERLY NEWSLETTER - INTERNATIONAL COMMISSION ON OCCUPATIONAL HEALTH. [Q. newsl. - Int. Comm. Occup. Health]. **VFOAT** Bulletin Trimestriel - Commission Internationale de la Medecine du travail; Quarterly Newsletter - ICOH; Bulletin Trimestriel - CIMT. (1982)-. Periodical. English (French). qt. International Association on Occupational Health, Av J Crosnier 10, 1206 Geneva Switzerland. **UDC** 61.

FR/0242-6277
R.G.S. REVUE GENERALE DE SECURITE. ***Title Change.*** **VFOAT** Revue Generale de Securite. (1981)-(1992). Periodical. French. mo. AIF Services SA, 10 rue de Calais, 75009 Paris France. **UDC** 614.8. ***Merged with*** *Preventique, 0766-5687* ***to form*** *Securite (General), 1244-5053.*

US/0740-0640
RADIATION PROTECTION MANAGEMENT. [Radiat. prot. manage.]. Vol. 1, No. 1 (Oct. 1983)-. Academic Scholarly Publication. English. bm. $156.00 (1 year), $291.00 (2 year) (individuals); $390.00 (1 year), $726.00 (2 year) (libraries and institutions); $45.00 (1 year), $90.00 (2 year) (qualified individual). Radiation Safety Assn Inc, 10 Pendleton Drive, Hebron CT 06248. **Tel** (203)228-0824, FAX (203)228-4402. **ED** K Paul Steinmeyer. **NLM** W1; RA164T. **CODEN** RPMAEI. Index available. **Bk Rev. Ad Acc. Pr Rev. Circ:** 1,000. Documents available from CASDDS.
Desc: A technical journal presenting practical, work-related information for applied radiation protection programs at nuclear power plants and industrial facilities. Also covers respiratory protection and waste management.
Ind/Abst Chem. Abstr. (1983-).

NO
RAPPORT OM VIRKSOMHETEN. **Main/Corp** Norway. Direktoratet for Arbeidstilsynet. Norwegian. **LC** HD3740; .A23a. ***Continues*** *Arsmelding for Arbeidstilsynet.*

UK
REGISTER OF VALVES. **See** Petroleum and Natural Gas.

US/0361-2546
REGISTRY OF TOXIC EFFECTS OF CHEMICAL SUBSTANCES [MICROFORM]. **See** Medical Science and Technology-Toxicology.

US
REGULATORY GUIDE / U.S. NUCLEAR REGULATORY COMMISSION, OFFICE OF STANDARDS DEVELOPMENT. **Main/Corp** U.S. Nuclear Regulatory Commission. Office of Standards Development. (19??)-. English. ir. Price varies. National Technical Information Service - NTIS, Room 2027S, 5285 Port Royal Road, Springfield VA 22161. **Tel** (703)487-4630, (703)487-4660, (703)487-4650, FAX (703)321-8547, telex 89-9405.
Desc: Contains information on power reactors, test reactors, fuels and material, environmental siting, plant protection, occupational health, and anti-trust reviews.

UK/0951-8320
RELIABILITY ENGINEERING & SYSTEM SAFETY. **See** Engineering.

CN/0826-3116
REPERTOIRE DES ACTIVITES DE FORMATION ET D'INFORMATION. [Repert. act. form. inf.]. **Main/Corp** Association pour la Sante et la Securite du Travail, Secteur Affaires Sociales. Fall 1983-. Periodical. French. qt. Free. Association Sante Securite du Travail, 801 Sherbrooke East 12th Floor, Montreal Quebec H2L 1K7 Canada. **Tel** (514)524-6871, (800)361-4528. **DD** 363.1/1/070714. ctrl circ.

SA/0377-970X
REPORT OF THE COMPENSATION COMMISSIONER FOR OCCUPATIONAL DISEASES. **Main/Corp** South Africa. Compensation Commissioner for Occupational Diseases. **VFOAT** Verslag van die Vergoedingskommissaris vir Bedryfsiektes. Apr. 1973/Mar. 1974-. Periodical. Afrikaans (English). Pretoria Government Printer, Department of Water Affairs, Private Bag X85, Pretoria 0001 South Africa. **NLM** W2 HU5 C73R.

SA
REPORT OF THE MEDICAL BUREAU FOR OCCUPATIONAL DISEASES. **Main/Corp** South Africa. Medical Bureau for Occupational Diseases. **VFOAT** Verslag van die Mediese

Buro vir Bedryfsicktes; Verslag van die Mediese Buro Vir Bedryfsiektes. 1973/74-. Afrikaans (English). R2.05. Medical Bureau for Occupational Diseases, The Government Printer, Private Bag X85, Pretoria South Africa. **LC** RC963.A1. **DD** 354/.68/0077. **NLM** W2; HU5 S51r. ***Continues*** *Verslag van die Mediese Buro Vir Mynwerkers.*

US
REPORT TO THE ALASKA LEGISLATURE - DIVISION OF OCCUPATIONAL SAFETY AND HEALTH. **Main/Corp** Alaska. Division of Occupational Safety and Health. English. Alaska Department of Labor, Administrative Services, Research & Analysis Section, PO Box 25501, Juneau AK 99802-5501. **Tel** (907)465-4500. **LC** HD7655.A4; A43A. **DD** 353.97980078/3.

US
REPORTED OCCUPATIONAL INJURIES AND ILLNESSES, SOUTH DAKOTA. **Main/Corp** South Dakota. State Center for Health Statistics. **VFOAT** South Dakota Employers' First Reports of Injuries & Illnesses. English. **LC** RC964; .S667A. **DD** 312/.3980309783. ***Continues*** *Reported Occupational Injuries and Illnesses, South Dakota, 0148-3226.*

UK/0265-9581
RESEARCH PAPER (GREAT BRITAIN. HEALTH AND SAFETY EXECUTIVE). (RESEARCH PAPER / HEALTH AND SAFETY EXECUTIVE.). [Res. pap. - Health Saf. Exec.]. **VFOAT** H.S.E. Research Paper. 9-. Academic Scholarly Publication. English. Price varies per volume. Her Majesty's Stationery Office, 51 Nine Elms Lane, London SW8 5DR England. **Tel** 011 44 71 873 8459, 011 44 71 873 8499, FAX 011 44 71 873 8499, 011 44 71 873 8456, telex 297138. **NLM** W1 RE232U. Documents available from CASDDS. ***Continues*** *Technical Paper (Great Britain. Health and Safety Laboratories), 0142-1719.*
Ind/Abst Chem. Abstr.; Coal Abstr.

US/0882-0953
RESPIRATORY PROTECTION NEWSLETTER. ***Ceased.*** [Radiol. respir. prot. newsl.]. Vol. 1, No. 1 (Jan. 1985)-Vol. 9, No. 6 (Dec. 1993). Newsletter. English. bm. Radiation Safety Associates Inc, PO Box 107, Hebron CT 06248. **Tel** (203)228-0487. **ED** Paul Steinmeyer. **DD** 363. Index available. cum. index. **Bk Rev.** **Circ:** 200 (ctrl).
Desc: Respiratory protection and related subjects as they apply to the nuclear industry.

FI/0357-5993
REVIEWS - INSTITUTE OF OCCUPATIONAL HEALTH. (REVIEWS.). [Rev. - Inst. Occup. Health]. Began in 1976?. Monographic series. English. Price varies per volume. Institute of Occupational Health Finland, Topeliuksenkatu 41AA, SF-00250 Helsinki Finland. **Tel** 011 358 0 47471, FAX 011 358 0 4747548, telex 121 394 TLTX ST. **NLM** W1 RE257CEB.

BL/0303-7657
REVISTA BRASILEIRA DE SAUDE OCUPACIONAL. (REVISTA BRASILEIRA DE SAUDE OCUPACIONAL / MINISTERIO DO TRABALHO E PREVIDENCIA SOCIAL, FUNDACENTRO, FUNDACAO JORGE DUPRAT FIGUEIREDO DE SEGURANCA E MEDICINA DO TRABALHO.). **Added/Corp** Fundacao Jorge Duprat Figueiredo de Seguranca e Medicina do Trabalho. Fundacao Centro Nacional de Seguranca, Higiene e Medicina do Trabalho (Brazil). (Jan./Mar. 1973)-. Periodical. Portuguese. Four times a year. Fundacentro, rua Capote Valente 710, CEP 05409 Sao Paulo SP Brazil. **Tel** 011 55 11 8536588. **LC** IN PROCESS. **NLM** W1 RE346B. **CODEN** RBSOEQ.
Ind/Abst Chem. Hazards Ind.; Int. Labour Doc.; Lab. Hazards Bull.; LABORDOC.

BL
REVISTA DE SEGURANCA & I.E. E PREVENCAO. Portuguese. 300.00. Instituto Nacional de Prevencao de Acidentes, Caixas Postais 6.441 E 6.321, Sao Paulo CEP 01037 Brazil. **LC** HD7262.5.B7; R48.

FR
REVUE GENERALE DE SECURITE. ***Title Change.*** (19??)-(19??). French. Ten times a year. Societe Alpine de Publications, 7 Chemin de Gordes, 38100 Grenoble France. **Tel** 011 33 76 432864. ***Merged with*** *Preventique, 0766-5687* ***to form*** *Securite.*
Ind/Abst Infomat Int. Bus.

BE
REVUE INTERNATIONALE DE DROIT ECONOMIQUE. **Added/Corp** Association Internationale de Droit Economique. **VFOAT** R.I.D.E.; RIDE. (1986)-. Periodical. French. Three times a year. 3000.00F Belgium; 3350.00F other Europe; 3400.00F other. De Boeck Wesmael SA, Fond Jean Paques 4, 1348 Louvain La Neuve Belgium. **Tel** 011 32 10 482509, FAX 32 (0) 2 6273650. **LC** K21; .I556. **DD** 345/.0264; 342.5264.

US/0888-8582
RIGHT TO KNOW COMPLIANCE ADVISOR. ***Ceased.*** [Right to know compliance advis.]. **Added/Corp** Business & Legal Reports (Firm). **VFOAT** Right to Know. (19??)-(19??). Periodical. English. bm. Business & Legal Reports, 39 Academy Street, Madison CT 06443. **Tel** (203)245-7448, (800)727-5257, FAX (203)245-2559. **ED** John Brady. **LC** KF3566.A3; R54. **DD** 344.73/0465; 347.304465. Index available.
Desc: Report on OSHA related activities. Summaries of federal register entries.

US
RIGHT-TO-KNOW PLANNING REPORT : CHEMICAL HAZARD COMMUNICATION AND EMERGENCY PLANNING. **VFOAT** Chemical Hazard Communication and Emergency Planning. (1987)-. Monographic series. English. bw. Comes with Right to Know Planning Guide. Bureau of National Affairs Inc., 9435 Key West Avenue, Rockville MD 20850. **Tel** (800)372-1033, (301)258-1033, FAX (301)948-5823. **(Subscription telephone:** FAX (301)948-5823**)** **ED** Eileen Z Joseph.
Desc: A newsletter providing information on new community right-to-know and community emergency response programs.

IT/0391-2825
RIVISTA DI MEDICINA DEL LAVORO ED IGIENE INDUSTRIALE. [Riv. med. lav. ig. ind.]. (Jan.-Mar. 1977)-. Academic Scholarly Publication. Italian (summaries and/or abstracts in English and French). qt (4 issues). L50000 Italy. Casa Editrice Libraria Idelson Gnocchi, via Alcide De Gasperi 55, 80133 Naples Italy. **Tel** 011 39 81 5524733. **ED** Luigi Ambrosi. **NLM** W1 RI53F. **CODEN** RMLIDF. **Bk Rev.** Documents available from CASDDS. ***Continues*** *Folia Medica (Naples, Italy).*
Desc: Covers occupational medicine.
Ind/Abst Chem. Abstr.; EMBASE.

SZ
RIVISTA SVIZZERA SICUREZZA LAVORO. **VFOAT** Schweizerische Blatter fur Arbeitssicherheit; Cahiers Suisse de la Securite du Travail. Italian (German and French). Free. Ist Naz Svizzero Assn Con Inf, 6002 Luzern Postfach, Fluhmattstrasse 1 Switzerland. **Tel** 011 41 215378. Index available. **Ad Acc.** ctrl circ.
Desc: Aim is to promote safety in work by describing certain situations in each issue.

US/1054-5050
ROY ANDERSON'S ROAD WORK SAFETY REPORT. **See** Transportation-Roads and Traffic.

US
SAFE FOREMAN. English. Twelve times a year. $10.00. The United Safety Service, PO Box 645, Wheaton IL 60187. **Tel** (708)665-1303.

US/0896-9051
SAFE WORKER. [Safe work.]. **Added/Corp** National Safety Council. Vol. 1 (May 1928)-. Periodical. English. mo. $19.00 (one year), $33.00 (two year). National Safety Council, 1121 Spring Lake Drive, Itasca IL 60143. **Tel** (800)621-7615, (708)775-2294, FAX (708)285-0797. **(Subscription address:** National Safety Council, PO Box 429, Itasca IL 60143.**)** **LC** HD7262; .S25. **DD** 331.82305.

US/0748-1403
SAFETY ALERT. (SAFETY ALERT / AMERICAN PULPWOOD ASSOCIATION.). [Saf. alert]. **Added/Corp** American Pulpwood Association. (19??)-. Periodical. English. American Pulpwood Association, 1025 Vermont Avenue Northwest, Suite 1020, Washington DC 20005. **Tel** (202)347-2900. **DD** 634.

US/0891-1797
SAFETY & HEALTH. (SAFETY & HEALTH : SH / NATIONAL SAFETY COUNCIL.). [Saf. health]. **Added/Corp** National Safety Council. **VFOAT** Safety and Health; SH. Vol. 135, No. 1 (Jan. 1987)-. Periodical. English. Twelve times a year. $56.00. National Safety Council, 1121 Spring Lake Drive, Itasca IL 60143. **Tel** (800)621-7615, (708)775-2294, FAX (708)285-0797. **(Subscription address:** National Safety Council, PO Box 429, Itasca IL 60143.**)** **ED** Austin Weber. **DD** 614. **NLM** W1; SA124M. Index available. **Bk Rev.** **Ad Acc.** **Circ:** 35,000. available on microfilm and microfiche from University Microfilms International (UMI). Documents available from UMI Article Clearinghouse. ***Continues*** *National Safety and Health News, 8756-5366.*
Desc: Official occupational safety and health publication of the National Safety Council. Provides practical information to help employers manage their safety, health and environmental concerns.
Ind/Abst Abstr. Bull. Inst. Pap. Sci. Tech.; Acad. Search (Jan. 1994-); Bus. Index (1987-); Bus. Period. Index; Chem. Hazards Ind.; Ei Page One; Expand. Acad. Index (1992-); Gen. BusinessFile (1987-); Gen. Period. Index (1987-); Health Ref. Cent. (1987-) [Select. Cov.]; Health Source (Jul. 1993-); Ind. Hyg. Dig. (1987-19??); INFO-SOUTH Abstr.; Lab. Hazards Bull.; Mag. Search; Newsp. Period. Abstr. (1992-); Trade Ind. Index; Wilson Bus. Abstr.; Work Relat. Abstr.

SZ/1010-7053
SAFETY AND HEALTH AT WORK : ILO-CIS BULLETIN. **See** Industrial Health and Safety-Abstracting, Bibliographies and Statistics.

AT/1032-0024
SAFETY AND TRAINING NEWS. (SAFETY & TRAINING NEWS.). [Saf. train. news]. (1988)-. English. ir. New South Wales Coal Association, PO Box A244, Sydney NSW 2000 Australia. **Tel** 02 2676488. **DD** 622.805. ***Continues*** *Training and Safety News, 1032-0016.*
Ind/Abst AESIS Q.

CN/0835-8184
SAFETY INFOGRAM. (INFOGRAM SECURITE.). [Saf. infogram]. **Added/Corp** Centre Canadien d'Hygiene et de Securite au Travail. **VFOAT** Safety Infogram. (1987)-. Periodical. French (English). ir. 4.50Can$ Canada; 5.50Can$ other. Canadian Centre for Occupational Health and Safety (CCOHS), 250 Main Street East, Hamilton ONT L8N 1H6 Canada. **Tel** (416)572-2981, (416)572-4493, FAX (416)572-2206, telex 0618532. **DD** 363.1/175/0971. ***Continues*** *CCINFOGRAM., 0837-5879.*

SA/0377-8592
SAFETY MANAGEMENT. [Saf. manage.]. **Added/Corp** National Occupational Safety Association. **VFOAT** Veiligheidsbestuur. Vol 1 (Dec. 1974)-. Periodical. English (Afrikaans). mo. R34.00 local; $34.00 overseas. National Occupational Safety Association / NOSA, PO Box 26434, Arcadia 0007 South Africa. **Tel** (012)21-7736, FAX (012)324 2393, telex 322262 SA. **ED** Steven Naude. **LC** T55.A1 .; S23. **Ad Acc.** **Circ:** 26,000 (ctrl). ***Supersedes*** *Safety Digest* ***and*** *Safety in Industry.*
Desc: Aimed at the industrial spectrum, with emphasis on safety, occupational health and environmental protection matters, products, and developments.
Ind/Abst Curr. Technol. Index; Saf. Health Work.

US/1069-2118
SAFETY MANAGEMENT (WATERFORD, CONN.). (SAFETY MANAGEMENT.). [Saf. manag.]. **Added/Corp** National Foremen's Institute. (19??)-. Periodical. English. mo. $97.92 (US); $118.44 (Canada). Bureau of Business Practice, 24 Rope Ferry Road, Waterford CT 06386. **Tel** (800)243-0876, (203)442-4365, (800)876-9105, FAX (203)443-1123. **DD** 363.

US/0270-4447
SAFETY NEWS (DENVER). (SAFETY NEWS / WATER & POWER RESOURCES SERVICE.). [Saf. news]. **Added/Corp** United States. Dept. of the Interior. Water and Power Resources Service. United States. Bureau of Reclamation. 4th Quarter (1979)-. Periodical. English. Four times a year. Free. Engineering and Research Center, PO Box 25007, Attention D 160, Denver CO 80225. **Tel** (303)236-8098. **LC** T55.A1; R4. **DD** 363.1/1933391/00973. ***Continues*** *Reclamation Safety News, 0034-1436.*
Ind/Abst Health Saf. Sci. Abstr.; Saf. Health Work.

UK
SAFETY PRACTITIONERS' YEAR BOOK, THE. **VFOAT** Safety Practitioners' Yearbook. 1st Ed. (1986)-. English. an. Paramount Publishing Ltd, 17 21 Shenley Road, Borehamwood, Herts WD6 IRT England. **Tel** 011 44 81 207-5599, FAX 011 44 81 207-2598. **LC** T55.A1; S235.

US
SAFETY PRODUCTION PLAN PROGRAM. English. $61.32 US; $77.28 Canada; (includes Supervisor's Safety Clinic & Supervisor's Memory Jogger). Bureau of Business Practice, 24 Rope Ferry Road, Waterford CT 06386. **Tel** (800)243-0876, (203)442-4365, (800)876-9105, FAX (203)443-1123.

FR/0765-913X
SAFETY RESEARCH NEWS. [Saf. res. news]. (1982)-(198?). Periodical. English (French). Four times a year. Institut National de Recherche & Securite, 4 rue Andre Boulle, 94942 Creteil Cedex 09 France. **Tel** 011 33 1 42070606. **UDC** 331.823.
Desc: Information on new trends in occupational health and safety. Description of organizations engaged in research works and of their activities.

NE/0925-7535
SAFETY SCIENCE. [Saf. sci.]. Vol. 14, No. 1 (May 1991)-. Academic Scholarly Publication. English (French and German). Nine times a year (3 volumes). Fl855.00. Elsevier Science Publishers BV, PO Box 211, 1000 AE Amsterdam Netherlands. **Tel** 011 31 20 5803642, FAX 011 31 20 5862696, telex 15682. **LC** HD7262; .J68. **DD** 614.8/52/05. **NLM** W1; SA125L. **CODEN** SSCIEO. **[CCC].** available on microfilm and microfiche from University Microfilms International (UMI). Documents available from Article Express International, The Genuine Article, BIOSIS Document Express. ***Continues*** *Journal of Occupational Accidents, 0376-6349.*
Ind/Abst Biol. Abstr.; Coal Abstr.; Curr. Contents Eng. Tech. Appl. Sci.; Ei Page One; EMBASE; Eng. Index Annu.; Ergon. Abstr.; Highw. Res. Abstr.; Pollut. Abstr. Indexes; Res. Alert [Select. Cov.]; Soc. Sci. Cit. Index [Select. Cov.].

CN/0842-5477
SAFETY SMARTS. [Saf. smarts]. Vol. 1, Issue 1 (Apr./May 1987)-. Periodical. English. bm (6 issues). $14.19. Bongarde Communications, 2315 Government Street, Pentiction BC V2A 4W5 Canada. **Tel** (604)493-2200, (800)668-9300, FAX (604)493-1970. **(Subscription address:** Bongarde Communications, PO Box 428, Oroville WA 98844.**)** **DD** 363.1/1/05.

CN
SAFETY TALKS. (19??)-. Periodical. English. bm (6 issues). $291.88. Bongarde Communications, 2315 Government Street, Pentiction BC V2A 4W5 Canada. **Tel** (604)493-2200, (800)668-9300, FAX (604)493-1970. **(Subscription address:** Bongarde Communications, PO Box 428, Oroville WA 98844.**)**

US/1069-2037
SAFETY (WATERFORD, CONN.). (SAFETY.). [Safety]. **Added/Corp** Bureau of Business Practice. **VFOAT** Safety Compliance Letter. No. 1405 (March 1986)-. Periodical. English. Twelve times a year. $108.36 (US); $131.52 (other). Bureau of Business Practice, 24 Rope Ferry Road, Waterford CT 06386. **Tel** (800)243-0876, (203)442-4365, (800)876-9105, FAX (203)443-1123. **ED** Laurie-Beth Roberts. **LC** HD7653; .O18. **DD** 363.1/1/0973. ***Continues*** *OSHA Compliance Letter, 0092-5799.*

US
SAFEWORKER. (19??)-. Periodical. English. Twelve times a year. $19.00. National Safety Council, 1121 Spring Lake Drive, Itasca IL 60143. **Tel** (800)621-7615, (708)775-2294, FAX (708)285-0797.

JA/0370-8217
SAIKO TO HOAN. ***Ceased.*** [Saiko to hoan]. **Added/Corp** Kogyo Gijutsuin Kogai Shigen Kenkyujo (Japan). **VFOAT** Mining and Safety. (1953)-(1992). Academic Scholarly Publication. Japanese (summaries and/or abstracts in English). mo. Kogyo Gijutsuin Kogai Shigen kenkyujo, (National Research Inst. for Pollution & Resources, Agency of Industrial Science & Technology), 16-3, Onogawa, Tsukubashi, Ibarakiken 305 Japan. **(Subscription address:** Maruzen Company Ltd., PO Box 5050, Import & Export Department, Tokyo 100 31 Japan.**)** **CODEN** SAHOA5. **Ad Acc. Circ:** 1,500 (ctrl). Documents available from CASDDS.
Desc: Introduces technical improvement concerning the production of the mining industry.
Ind/Abst Chem. Abstr.; Coal Abstr.

SP/0210-6612
SALUD Y TRABAJO (MADRID). (SALUD Y TRABAJO : REVISTA DEL SERVICIO SOCIAL DE HIGIENE Y SEGURIDAD DEL TRABAJO.). [Salud trab.]. **Added/Corp** Spain. Servicio Social de Higiene y Seguridad del Trabajo. Instituto Nacional de Seguridad e Higiene en el Trabajo (Spain). (1976)-. Periodical. Spanish. bm. 1500ptas Spain; $11.77 US; 2200ptas other. Inst Nac Seguridad Higiene Tra, Torrelaguna 73, 28027 Madrid Spain. **Tel** 011 34 1 4037000. **LC** HD7735; .S24. **DD** 363.1/1/0946. **NLM** W1 SA389. Index available. **Circ:** 4,500 (ctrl).
Desc: Goal of this journal is to spread information on programs and projects concerning accident prevention on the job and job-related illnesses. Also contains news and research studies on job safety and security.
Ind/Abst Ergon. Abstr.; Indice Med. Esp.; Saf. Health Work.

JA
SANGYO ANZEN KENKYUJO TOKUBETSU KENKYU HOKOKU. VFOAT Special Research Report. Japanese (summaries and/or abstracts in English). Rodosho Sangyo Anzen Kenkyujo, (Research Inst. of Industrial Safety, Ministry of Labour), 35-1, Shiba 5 Chome, Minatoku, Tokyoto 108, Japan. **LC** T55.A1; S24.

JA/0047-1879
SANGYO IGAKU. (SANGYO IGAKU. JAPANESE JOURNAL OF INDUSTRIAL HEALTH.). [Sangyo igaku]. **Added/Corp** Nippon Sangyo Eisei Kyokai. **VFOAT** Japanese Journal of Industrial Health. Vol. 1 (Feb. 1959)-. Academic Scholarly Publication. English (summaries and/or abstracts in English). bm. $176.00. Japanese Association of Industrial Health, c/o Public Health Building, 78 Hanazono-cho, Shinuuku, Tokyo 160 Japan. **(Subscription address:** Kyowa Book Company Inc., 1-38 Kanda Jinbo-Cho, Chiyoda-Ku Tokyo 101, Japan**)** **NLM** W1 SA649A. **CODEN** SAIGBL. Documents available from BIOSIS Document Express, CASDDS.
Ind/Abst BioBusiness; Biol. Abstr.; Chem. Abstr.; CSA Neuro. Abstr. (?-?); EMBASE; Index Med.; Ind. Hyg. Dig. (19??-); Life Sci. Collect.; Pollut. Abstr. Indexes; Rev. Med. Vet. Entomol.; Saf. Health Work; SportSearch; Trop. Dis. Bull.

JA/0388-337X
SANGYO IGAKU JANARU. [Sangyo igaku janaru]. **VFOAT** Occupational Health Journal. Began in 1978. Academic Scholarly Publication. Japanese. $100.00. Sangyo Igaku Shinko Zaidan, (Occupational Health Promotion Foundation), Toho Biru, 5-1, Akasaka 2 Chome, Minatoku, Tokyoto 107 Japan. **(Subscription address:** Kyowa Book Company Inc., 1-38 Kanda Jinbo-Cho, Chiyoda-Ku, Tokyo 101, Japan (Phone: 03-3293-0727)**)** **NLM** W1; SA648J. **CODEN** SIJADW. Documents available from CASDDS.
Ind/Abst Chem. Abstr.

JA
SANGYO IGAKU SOGO KENKYUJO NEMPO. Main/Corp Rodosho Sangyo Igaku Sogo Kenkyujo. (1976)-. Periodical. Japanese (English). an. Free. Rodosho Sangyo Igaku Sogo Kenkyujo, 21-1 Nagao 6-chome, Tama-ku 213, Kawasaki Japan. **Tel** 044-865-6111, FAX 044-865-6116. **ED** Shigeji Koshi. **LC** RC963.A1; R62a. **Circ:** 400 (ctrl). ***Continues*** *Rodo Eisei Kenkyujo Nempo.*

FI/0355-3140
SCANDINAVIAN JOURNAL OF WORK, ENVIRONMENT & HEALTH. [Scand. j. work, environ. & health]. **VAT** Scandinavian Journal of Work, Environment and Health. Vol. 1- (March 1975)-. Academic Scholarly Publication. English. bm. Fmk800.00 (Scandinavia); Fmk900.00 (other). Scandinavian Journal of Work Environment, Topeliuksenkatu 41 AA, SF-00250 Helsinki Finland. **Tel** 358 0 479 968. **ED** Sven Hernberg. **LC** RC963.A1; S29. **DD** 616.9/803/05. **NLM** W1 SC154K. **CODEN** SWEHDO. **[CCC].** Index available. **Bk Rev. Pr Rev. Circ:** 1,500 (ctrl). available on microfilm and microfiche from University Microfilms International (UMI). Documents available from The Genuine Article, BIOSIS Document Express, CASDDS. ***Formed by the union of*** *Nordisk Hygienisk Tidskrift, 0029-1374* ***and*** *Work, Environment, Health, 0300-3221.*
Desc: Original scientific articles and reviews concerning occupational health and the work environment in the fields of medicine, toxicology, epidemiology, hygiene, safety, ergonomics, sociology, psychology, and physiology.
Ind/Abst Acoust. Abstr.; Anal. Abstr.; Appl. Soc. Sci. Index Abstr.; Biol. Abstr.; Chem. Abstr.; Chem. Hazards Ind.; Coal Abstr.; CSA Neuro. Abstr. (?-?); Cumul. Index Nurs. Allied Health Lit.; Curr. Contents Clin. Med.; Ei Page One; EMBASE; Energy Res. Abstr. (June 1978-); Ergon. Abstr.; For. Prod. Abstr.; For. Abstr.; Geogr. Abstr. Human Geogr.; Health Saf. Sci. Abstr.; Index Med.; Ind. Hyg. Dig.; Lab. Hazards Bull.; Nutr. Res. Newsl.; Life Sci. Collect.; Pollut. Abstr. Indexes; Psychol. Abstr. (1984-); PsycINFO; PsycLit; Res. Alert [Full Cov.]; Rev. Agric. Entomol.; Rev. Med. Vet. Mycology; Risk Abstr.; Saf. Health Work; Sci. Cit. Index; SCISEARCH; Soc. Sci. Cit. Index [Select. Cov.]; Toxicol. Abstr.; Trop. Dis. Bull.; Weed Abstr.; World Surf. Coat. Abstr.

GW/0932-4712
SCHRIFTENREIHE DER BUNDESANSTALT FUER ARBEITSSCHUTZ. GEFAHRLICHE ARBEITSSTOFFE. ***Title Change.*** [Schr.reihe Bundesanst. Arb.schutz, Gefahrl. Arb.stoffe]. **Added/Corp** Bundesanstalt fuer Arbeitsschutz (Germany). (1984)-?. Academic Scholarly Publication. German. Wirtschaftsverlag NW, Verlag fur Neue Wissenschaft GmbH, Postfach 101110, D-27511 Bremerhaven Germany. **Tel** 011 49 471 46093, 011 49 471 46094, 011 49 471 46095, FAX 011 49 471 42765. **CODEN** SBAAE7. Documents available from CASDDS. ***Continued by*** *Forschungsanwendung, 0932-4836; Gefahrliche Arbeitsstoffe, 0932-4712; Regelwerke, 0932-478X; Sonderschriften, 0932-481X* ***and*** *Tagungsberichte, 0932-4828.*
Ind/Abst Chem. Abstr. (1986-).

●FR
SECURITE. Vol. 1, No. 1 (Jan./Feb. 1993)-. Periodical. French. ir (10 issues). $124.38 US. Societe Alpine de Publications, 7 Chemin de Gordes, 38100 Grenoble France. **Tel** 011 33 76 432864. **LC** T55.A1; S43. **DD** 363.11/05. **CODEN** SURIEB. ***Formed by the union of*** *Preventique, 0766-5687* ***and*** *Revue Generale de Securite.*

SZ/1015-6356
SECURITE, ENVIRONEMENT. [Secur. environ.]. **VFOAT** Sicherheit, Umweltschutz; Revue Suisse de la Securite. Vol. 1 (Jan./March 1988)-. Periodical. French. qt. 50.00F Switzerland; 150.00F other. Editions Marcel Meichtry, 26 Chemin de la Caroline, CH1213 Petit Lancy Switzerland. **Tel** 011 41 22 7911027, FAX 011 41 22 7928834. **ED** Jean-Louis Noverraz. **LC** PAR. cum. index. **Bk Rev. Ad Acc. Circ:** 10,000 (ctrl). ***Continues*** *Revue Suisse de la Securite et de l'Environnement.*

FR/0755-2386
SECURITE ET MEDECINE DU TRAVAIL. (1969)-. Periodical. French. qt. 550.00F (nonmember) France; 360.00F EEC; 560.00F other. AFTIM, 1 Place Uranie, 94340 Joinville Le Pont France. **Tel** 011 33 1 48857059, FAX 011 33 1 48850299. **ED** M. Bellaguet. **UDC** 616. **Bk Rev**, (Qty: 4). **Ad Acc.**

UK/0262-9836
SELECTED ABSTRACTS ON OCCUPATIONAL DISEASES. **See** Industrial Health and Safety-Abstracting, Bibliographies and Statistics.

US/0732-7722
SHEPARD'S FEDERAL OCCUPATIONAL SAFETY AND HEALTH CITATIONS. **See** Law.

JA
SHOKUBA NO ANZEN KANRI OYOBI EISEI KANRI NI KANSURU SOGO JITTAI CHOSA KEKKA HOKOKUSHO. Main/Corp Japan. Rodosho. Tokei Johobu. (19??)-. Periodical. Japanese. Daijin Kanbo, 8-9, Ginza 2-chome, Chuo-ku Tokyo 104 Japan. **LC** HD7757; .A15a.

GW/0037-4504
SICHER IST SICHER. (1961)-. Periodical. German. mo. DM108.20. Verlag Wilhelm Kluge, PTFCH 510322, Saalmannstrasse 9, W 1000 Berlin 51 F R Germany. **Tel** 011 49 30 4135025, FAX 011 49 30 4139417. **UDC** 331.82. **CODEN** 614.8.01-027.

GW/0300-3329
SICHERHEITSINGENIEUR. [Sicherheitsingenieur]. (1970)-. Trade Publication. German. Twelve times a year. DM131.40 Germany; DM160.20 other. Dr. Curt Haefner Verlag GmbH, Bachstrasse 14, Postfach 106060, D 69050 Heidelberg Germany. **Tel** 011 49 6221 49063. **ED** Curt Haefner. **[CCC].** Index available. cum. index. **Bk Rev. Ad Acc. Circ:** 4,000 (ctrl).
Desc: Independent trade journal for job safety and safety technology for the job safety professional, planner and builder; also for managers in industry and public service.
Ind/Abst Coal Abstr.; Energy Res. Abstr. (Sept. 1973-); Ergon. Abstr.; Saf. Health Work.

US
SOUTH CAROLINA OCCUPATIONAL INJURIES AND ILLNESSES SURVEY. **Added/Corp** South Carolina. Dept. of Labor. Division of Data Management and Statistics. **VFOAT** Occupational Injuries and Illnesses Survey. (19??)-. Periodical. English. an. Free on request. South Carolina Division of Labor, PO Box 11329, Columbia SC 29211. **Tel** (803)734-9594.

US/0270-5273
STATE DATA ON OCCUPATIONAL INJURIES AND ILLNESSES. Main/Corp United States. Bureau of Labor Statistics. Government Publication. English. US Department of Labor / Bureau of Labor Statistics, 441 G Street NW, Washington DC 20212. **Tel** (202)606-7800, FAX (202)606-7797. **LC** HD8051; .A7876 subser; HD7262.5. 5.U6. **DD** 331.1/0973 S; 312/.43/0973.

US
STATE OF WYOMING CHARACTERISTICS OF RECORDABLE OCCUPATIONAL INJURIES AND ILLNESSES. **See** Industrial Health and Safety-Abstracting, Bibliographies and Statistics.

IT
STATISTICHE PER LA PREVENZIONE. Main/Corp Istituto Nazionale per l'Assicurazione Contro Gli Infortuni Sul Lavoro. Centro di Informazione E di Documentazione Infortunistica. May/Dec. 1974-. Italian. sa. L16320. Inail Direz Generale, Serv Rel Int Est, Via IV Noviembre 144, 00187 Rome Italy. **Tel** 011 39 6 672041. **ED** Carla Maciocci. **LC** HD7102.I8; I83A. **DD** 321/.4/30945. **Circ:** 2,700.
Desc: Detailed information on the occupational accidents reported and settled with compensation in the first six months and entire year. Information includes: type of accidents, location of injury, agent of injury, action of or to injured person, specific ages of workers, and hour in which the accident occurred.

CN/1181-781X
STATISTICS INFOGRAM. (INFOGRAM STATISTIQUE.). [Stat. infogram]. **Added/Corp** Centre Canadien d'Hygiene et de Securite au Travail. **VFOAT** Statistiques sur les Accidents du Travail au Canada. (1990)-. Periodical. French (English). **DD** 363.11/0971/021.

JA/0081-928X
SUMITOMO SANGYO EISEI. [Sumitomo sangyo eisei]. **Added/Corp** Sumitomo Byoin. Sangyo Eisei Kenkyushitsu. **VFOAT** Sumitomo Bulletin of Industrial Health. (1965)-. Academic Scholarly Publication. Japanese (summaries and/or abstracts in English). Sumitomo Byoin, Naka-no-Shima 5-2-2, Kita-ku, Osaka-shi 530 Japan. **CODEN** SSEIBV. Documents available from CASDDS.
Ind/Abst Chem. Abstr.; EMBASE.

US
SUMMARY OF OCCUPATIONAL INJURIES AND ILLNESSES. Added/Corp Indiana. Dept. of Labor. Research and Statistics Division. United States. Bureau of Labor Statistics. Vol. 9 (1988)-. English. Indiana Division of Labor, 1013 State Office Building, Indianapolis IN 46204. **LC** HD7262.5.U62; I68. **DD** 363.1/12/09772021. ***Formed by the union of***

Industrial Health and Safety

Characteristics of Occupational Injuries and Illnesses in Indiana **and** *Numbers and Rates of Occupational Injuries and Illnesses in Indiana.*

FI
SUOMALAISTA TYOTERVEYS- JA TYOTURVALLISUUSALAN KIRJALLISUUTTA. (1977)-. Periodical. Finnish. an. Tyoterveyslaitos, Julkaisutoimisto, Laajaniityntie 1, 01620 Vantaa 62 Finland. **LC** Z6675.I5; S86; RC963.

FI
SUOMEN TYSUOJELUKIRJALLISUUS. **Added/Corp** Tyoterveyslaitos. (1977)-. English. sa. Institute of Occupational Health of Finland, Topeliuksenkatu 41 a A, SF-00250 Helsinki Finland. **Tel** 0358-0-47471. **LC** Z6675.I5; S864; HD7727.3.

US/1043-2191
SUPERVISOR (ENGLEWOOD, N.J.), EL. (EL SUPERVISOR.). [Supervisor]. **Added/Corp** Inter American Safety Council. (19??)-. Periodical. Spanish. mo. $12.40 (members International American Safety Council); $15.50 (non-members). International American Safety Council, 33 Park Place, Englewood NJ 07631. **Tel** (201)871-0004. **ED** Santiago Egana. **LC** HD7262; .S82. **DD** 363. **Ad Acc. Circ:** 20,000 (ctrl).
 Desc: Accident prevention loss control for supervisors.

US/1061-7736
SUPERVISORS REPORT. [Superv. rep.]. **VFOAT** Occupational Health and Safety Supervisors Report; Occupational Health & Safety Supervisors Report; OHS Supervisors Report. (1991)-. Periodical. English. mo. $129.00. Washington News, Inc., 225 North New Road, Waco TX 76702. **DD** 331.

US/0145-0263
TECHNICAL NOTES - OCCUPATIONAL SAFETY AND HEALTH ADMINISTRATION. (TECHNICAL NOTES / OCCUPATIONAL SAFETY AND HEALTH ADMINISTRATION, U.S. DEPARTMENT OF LABOR.). **Added/Corp** United States. Occupational Safety and Health Administration. (19??)-. Periodical. English. ir. US Department of Labor Occupational Safety & Health Administration, 200 Constitution Avenue NW, Room S315, Washington DC 20210. **Tel** (202)219-8151, FAX (202)219-5986.

US
THRESHOLD LIMIT VALUES AND BIOLOGICAL EXPOSURE INDICES FOR .... **Added/Corp** American Conference of Governmental Industrial Hygienists. (198?)-. English. an (July). $11.20 (all except taxable Ohio residents); $10.08 (Canadian); $8.96 (others). American Conference of Governmental Industrial Hygienists, 6500 Glenway Avenue, Building D-7, Cincinnati OH 45211. **Tel** (513)661-7881, FAX (513)661-7195. **LC** RA1229.5; .T57. **DD** 615.9/02.
 Continues *TLVs, Threshold Limit Values for Chemical Substances in the Work Environment Adopted by ACGIH for ...* .

US/0734-3302
TODAY'S SUPERVISOR. [Today's superv.]. **Added/Corp** National Safety Council. Vol. 46, No. 11 (Nov. 1982)-. Periodical. English. Twelve times a year. $19.00. National Safety Council, 1121 Spring Lake Drive, Itasca IL 60143. **Tel** (800)621-7615, (708)775-2294, FAX (708)285-0797. **(Subscription address:** National Safety Council, PO Box 429, Itasca IL 60143.) **ED** Kathy Henderson. **LC** HD7260; .N345. **DD** 658.3/02/05. available on microfilm and microfiche from University Microfilms International (UMI). **Continues** *Industrial Supervisor, 0019-879X.*

JA
TOXIC AND HAZARDOUS INDUSTRIAL CHEMICALS SAFETY MANUAL. English. an. $115.00. Intl Tech Info Inst, 1-6-5 Nishishibashi Minatoku, Tokyo Japan.

US/0199-3178
TOXIC SUBSTANCES JOURNAL. *Title Change.* **See** Medical Science and Technology-Toxicology.

US/0748-2337
TOXICOLOGY AND INDUSTRIAL HEALTH. **See** Medical Science and Technology-Toxicology.

US
TRANSACTIONS BULLETIN - INDUSTRIAL HYGIENE FOUNDATION OF AMERICA. **Main/Corp** Industrial Hygiene Foundation of America. **VFOAT** Industrial Hygiene Foundation Annual Meeting; Transactions Bulletin - Industrial Hygiene Foundation; Transactions Bulletin - Industrial Hygiene Foundation of America, Inc. No. 8 (19??)-. Bulletin. English. 5231 Centre Street, Pittsburgh PA 15232. **LC** HD7260; .I377. **DD** 613.62. **Continues** *Transactions Series, Bulletin - Industrial Hygiene Foundation of America.*

FR/0373-1944
TRAVAIL & SECURITE. (TRAVAIL & I.E. ET SECURITE.). [Trav. & secur.]. **Main/Corp** Institut National de Recherche et de Securite. (1949)-. Periodical. French. Eleven times a year (July / Aug. issue combined). 280.00F France; 260.00F other. Institut National de Recherche & Securite, 4 rue Andre Boulle, 94942 Creteil Cedex 09 France. **Tel** 011 33 1 42070606. **LC** HD7262; .I62a. **DD** 614.8/52.
 Ind/Abst Coal Abstr.; Int. Labour Doc.; Saf. Health Work; SportSearch.

CN/0829-0369
TRAVAIL ET SANTE. [Trav. sante.]. Vol. 1, No. 1 (Spring 1985)-. Periodical. French (summaries and/or abstracts in English). qt. 25.00Can$ Canada; 40.00Can$ other. Groupe Communication Sansectra, Case Postale 1089, Napierville Quebec J0J 1L0 Canada. **Tel** (514)245-7285. **DD** 363.1/1/05. **Bk Rev. Ad Acc. Circ:** 2,500.
 Ind/Abst Ergon. Abstr.; Point Repere.

AI
TRUDY KLINICHESKOGO OTDELA INSTITUTA. **Added/Corp** Nauchno-Issledovatelskii Institut Gigieny Truda i Profzabolevanii, Erivan. Klinicheskii Otdel. (1970)-. Russian. **NLM** W1 TR956G.

FI/0041-4816
TYO TERVEYS TURVALLISUUS. **Added/Corp** Tyoterveyssaatio. No. 1, (1975)-. Periodical. Finnish. Sixteen times a year. Fmk345.00. Tyo Terveys Turvallisus, Topeliuksenkatu 41 AA, SF-00250 Helsinki Finland. **Tel** 358-0-47471, FAX 358 0 47 47 478, telex 358-0-414634. **ED** Matti Tapiainen. **Bk Rev**, (Qty: 10). **Ad Acc; Adv Mgr:** Mr. Ingmar Quist, **Tel** 358 0 213246. **Circ:** 80,000 (ctrl).
 Desc: It aims to provide specialists throughout the world with current information on occupational health and safety.
 Ind/Abst Ergon. Abstr.; Saf. Health Work.

FI/0359-1255
TYOTERVEISET. (1981)-. Periodical. Finnish. qt. Free on request. Institute of Occupational Health Finland, Topeliuksenkatu 41AA, SF-00250 Helsinki Finland. **Tel** 011 358 0 47471, FAX 011 358 0 4747548, telex 121 394 TLTX ST. **ED** Suvi Lehtinen. **UDC** 658.3. Index available. **Circ:** 10,000.
 Desc: Scientific articles on occupational health and safety.

BE
VEILIG BOUWEN. (19??)-. French (Dutch). Six times a year. 1500F. Natl Actiecom Veiligheid Hygie, Bouwbedrijf Poincarelaan 70, 1070 Brussels Belgium. **Tel** 02 523 40 93, FAX 02 522 74 50.

GW
VERWALTUNGSBERICHT DES BEZIRKS BONN DER BERGBAU-BERUFSGENOSSENSCHAFT / HERAUSGEGEBEN VON DER BEZIRKSVERWALTUNG BONN DER BERGBAU-BERUFSGENOSSENSCHAFT. **Main/Corp** Bergbau-Berufsgenosenschaft (Germany). Bezirksverwaltung Bonn. (19??)-. Corporate Report. German. an. Bergbau-Berufsgenosenschaft, Hybscgeudtstrasse 23, W-44789 Bochum Germany. **Tel** 02 34 3160. **LC** HD7269.M61; G32a. **DD** 363.1/19622/0943021. **Acid Free.**

CN
W H M I S COMPLIANCE MANUAL. English. Carswell / Canada, 2075 Kennedy Road, Scarborough Ontario M1T 3V4 Canada. **Tel** (416)609-3800, (800)387-5164.

US
WALL SAFETY POSTER. English. Twelve times a year. $107.76 US; $131.16 Canada. Bureau of Business Practice, 24 Rope Ferry Road, Waterford CT 06386. **Tel** (800)243-0876, (203)442-4365, (800)876-9105, FAX (203)443-1123.

US
WASHINGTON STATE WORK INJURY AND ILLNESS SUMMARY. 1980-. English. an. Free. Department of Labor and Industries, Data Analysis Section, 905 Plum Street Mail Stop HC-217-1, Olympia WA 98504-0631. **Tel** (206)586-1816. **ED** Pamela Hill. **LC** HD7262.5.U62; W33. **DD** 312/.43/09797. **NLM** W2; AW2 D52w. **Circ:** 1,250. **Continues** *Washington State Work Injuries and Illnesses.*
 Desc: Summary of work related injuries and illnesses. Includes charts and tables for nature, source, type, body part, occupation and industries.

CN
WHMIS HANDBOOK, THE. (19??)-. English. an. 143.00Can$. Southam Information and Technology Group Inc., 1450 Don Mills Road, Don Mills Ontario M3B 2X7 Canada. **Tel** (416)445-6641, (800)668-2374, FAX (416)442-2261.

CN/0705-7814
WISE OWL NEWS (TORONTO). (WISE OWL NEWS.). **VFOAT** Canadian Wise Owl News. 1967-. Periodical. English. sa. Free. Editor of Wise Owl News CNIB, 1929 Bayview Avenue, Toronto Ontario M4G 3E8 Canada. **DD** 614.8/52.

FI/0783-6899
WORK HEALTH SAFETY. [Work health saf.]. (1982)-. English. an. **UDC** 613.6.
 Ind/Abst Ergon. Abstr.

CN/0835-233X
WORK INJURIES. (WORK INJURIES / STATISTICS CANADA, LABOUR DIVISION, UNEMPLOYMENT INSURANCE STATISTICS SECTION.). [Work inj.]. **Added/Corp** Statistics Canada. Unemployment Insurance Statistics Section. **VFOAT** Accidents du Travail. (1985)-. English (French). an. 33.00Can$ Canada; $40.00 US; $47.00 other. Statistics Canada, Publications Sales & Services, Main Building Room 1710, Ottawa Ontario K1A 0T6 Canada. **Tel** (613)951-5078, (800)267-6677, FAX (613)951-1584, telex 053-3585. **LC** HD7262.5.C3; W65. **DD** 363.1/1/0971021. **Continues** *Work Injuries Statistics, 0837-4325.*

UK
WORKERS HEALTH INTERNATIONAL NEWSLETTER. Newsletter. English. qt. $24.00. Workers Health International Newsletter, PO Box 199, Sheffield S1 1FQ England. **Tel** 011 44 742 24411.

US
WORKPLACE HEALTH. *Title Change.* No. 1 (May 1992)-(19??). English. Twelve times a year. Vitality Magazine, 8080 North Central, Suite 1510, Dallas TX 75206. **Tel** (214)691-1480, FAX (214)891-8202. **Continued by** *Workplace Vitality, 1074-4452.*

AU
WORKPLACE HEALTH & SAFETY MANUAL. English. 440.00Aus$. CCH Australia Ltd, PO Box 230, North Ryde New South Wales, 2113 Australia. **Tel** 011 61 02 888 2555, FAX 011 61 02 888 7324.
 Desc: Takes a structured, procedural approach to workplace health and safety practice - from a full explanation of the basic concepts and issues through to successful program implementation.

●US/1059-1044
WORKPLACE SAFETY AWARENESS PROGRAM. (1992)-. Periodical. English. mo. $156.84. J. J. Keller & Associates, PO Box 548, Neenah WI 54957-0368. **Tel** (800)558-5011, (414)722-2848.

●US/1074-4452
WORKPLACE VITALITY. (1994)-. Periodical. English. mo $59.00 (non-members); $49.00 (members of National Wellness Association). Vitality Magazine, 8080 North Central, Suite 1510, Dallas TX 75206. **Tel** (214)691-1480, FAX (214)891-8202. **Continues** *Workplace Health.*

US
WORLD AUTOMOTIVE ENVIRONMENT & SAFETY BULLETIN. **See** Transportation-Automobiles.

US/0899-8035
YEAR BOOK OF OCCUPATIONAL AND ENVIRONMENTAL HEALTH. [Year b. occup. environ. med.]. **VFOAT** Yearbook of Occupational and Environmental Health. (1990)-. English. an. $59.95. Mosby Year Book Inc., 11830 Westline Industrial Drive, St Louis MO 63146. **Tel** (800)325-4177, (314)872-8370, FAX (314)432-1380, telex 44-2402. **LC** RC963.A1; Y43. **NLM** ZWA 30; Y39.

GW/0340-2444
ZEITSCHRIFT FUER ARBEITSWISSENSCHAFT. **See** Economics-Labor.

CC/1001-9391
ZHONGHUA LAODONG WEISHENG ZHIYEBING ZAZHI. (CHUNG-HUA LAO TUNG WEI SHENG CHIH YEH PING TSA CHIH.). [Zhonghua laodong weisheng zhiyebing zazhi]. **Added/Corp** Tien-Chin Shih lao Tung wei Sheng yen Chiu so. Tien-Chin Shih lao Tung wei Sheng Huan Ching i Hsueh Hsueh hui. **VFOAT** Zhonghua Laodong Weisheng Zhiyebing Zazhi; Chinese Journal of Industrial Hygiene and Occupational Diseases. (1983)-. Periodical. Chinese (table of contents in English). bm. Tianjin Industrial Hygiene and Occupational Diseases Institute, 265 Ma Chang Dao Street, Hexi District, Tianjin, People's Republic of China. **NLM** W1; CH982KF. **CODEN** ZLWZEX. Documents available from CASDDS.
 Ind/Abst Chem. Abstr. (1986-); Ind. Hyg. Dig. (19??-).

ABSTRACTING, BIBLIOGRAPHIES AND STATISTICS

UK/0265-5721
CHEMICAL HAZARDS IN INDUSTRY. [Chem. hazards ind.]. **Added/Corp** Royal Society of Chemistry (Great Britain). **VFOAT** CHI. No. 1 (Jan. 1984)-. Abstracting/Indexing Service. English. mo (12 issues). £309.00 EC; $620.00 US; £325.00 other. Royal Society of Chemistry, Thomas Graham House, Science Park, Cambridge CB4 4WF England. **Tel** 011 44 223 420066, FAX 011 44 223 423429, telex 818293 ROYAL. **(Subscription address:** Turpin Distribution Services Limited, Blackhorse Road, Letchworth, Hertfordshire SG6 1HN, United Kingdom.**)** **NLM** ZWA 400; C517. **CODEN** CHINEK. **[CCC].** Index available. **Ad Acc. Circ:** 1,000. available on an online database from STN International; ESA-IRS; ORBIT; DIALOG; and DATA-STAR.
Desc: A current awareness periodical dealing with health and safety, chemical and biological hazards, plant safety, legislation, protective equipment and storage relating to the chemical and allied industries. Contains approximately 200 items drawn from the world's primary literature. The references include document titles, bibliographic details and abstracts. Each issue contains a subject and a chemical index.
Ind/Abst World Surf. Coat. Abstr.

XR/0302-4288
CZECHOSLOVAK BIBLIOGRAPHY ON INDUSTRIAL HYGIENE AND OCCUPATIONAL DISEASES. [Czech. bibliogr. ind. hyg. occup. dis.]. **Added/Corp** Institut Hygieny a Epidemiologie. Vyskumny Ustav Priemyslenej Hygieny a Chorob z Povolania. Vol. 16 (1971)-. Bibliography. English. **LC** RC963; .A453. **NLM** ZWA 400 C998. ***Continues** Prague. Ustav Hygieny Prace a Chorub z Povolani. Scientific Reports on Industrial Hygiene and Occupational Diseases in Czechoslovakia, 0322-8142.*
Desc: Information on industrial hygiene and occupational diseases.
Ind/Abst World Text. Abstr.

AT
EMPLOYMENT INJURIES QUEENSLAND. **Added/Corp** Australian Bureau of Statistics. Queensland Office. **VFOAT** Employment Injuries. (1986/1987)-. Periodical. English. an. Price varies. Australian Bureau of Statistics, PO Box 10, Belconnen Australian Capital Territory, 2616 Australia. **Tel** 011 61 6 2527911, FAX 011 61 6 2516009. ***Continues** Industrial Accidents (Brisbane, Qld.).*
Desc: Employment injuries by industry group, occupation group, type of employment injury, extent of disability, sex, duration of disability, and more.

AT/1033-6133
EMPLOYMENT INJURIES, TASMANIA. **Added/Corp** Australian Bureau of Statistics. Tasmanian Office. (1987/1988)-. English. an. 10.70Aus$. Australian Bureau of Statistics, PO Box 10, Belconnen Australian Capital Territory, 2616 Australia. **Tel** 011 61 6 2527911, FAX 011 61 6 2516009. ***Continues** Industrial Accidents, Tasmania, 0314-1721.*
Desc: Fatal and non-fatal accidents -- time lost, cost of claims, type of accident, accident factor, nature of injury, site of injury, month of occurrence, industry group, occupational group, age group and duration of time lost.

NE/0014-4398
EXCERPTA MEDICA. SECTION 35. OCCUPATIONAL HEALTH AND INDUSTRIAL MEDICINE. (OCCUPATIONAL HEALTH AND INDUSTRIAL MEDICINE.). [Excerpta medica. Section thirty five. Occupational health and industrial medicine]. **Added/Corp** Excerpta Medica Foundation. Vol. 1 (Jan. 1971)-. Abstracting/Indexing Service. English. Sixteen times a year (2 vols.). Fl2004.00. Excerpta Medica Publishing Group, PO Box 548, 1000 AM Amsterdam Netherlands. **Tel** 011 31 20 5803243. **(Subscription address:** Excerpta Medica Journals, PO Box 85, Limerick Ireland.**)** **LC** RC963; .A446. **DD** 613.6/2/08. **NLM** ZW 1 E978P. **CODEN** EMOHAH. **[CCC].** available on microfilm from University Microfilms International (UMI); available on CD-ROM.
Desc: This journal is subdivided into a large number of specific chapters on the basis of either the type of problem being considered, the anatomical area or organ system being affected or the nature of the injurious agent.
Ind/Abst Anal. Abstr.

US/0019-8382
INDUSTRIAL HYGIENE DIGEST. [Ind. hyg. dig.]. **Added/Corp** Industrial Hygiene Foundation of America. Industrial Health Foundation. Vol. 1 (1937)-. Abstracting/Indexing Service. English. mo. $150.00 (one year), $270.00 (two year) US; $162.00 (one year), $294.00 (two year) other. Industrial Health Foundation, 34 Penn Circle West, Pittsburgh PA 15206. **Tel** (412)363-6600, FAX (412)363-6605. **ED** Marianne C. Kaschak. **NLM** ZWA 400 I416. **CODEN** IHYDA. Index available. cum. index. **Bk Rev. Circ:** 2,000 (ctrl). Documents available from Documents on Demand.
Desc: Compilation of abstracts of environmental and occupational health literature.
Ind/Abst CIS Abstr.; Energy Inf. Abstr.; Environ. Abstr.; Saf. Health Work.

US/0739-389X
INTERNATIONAL RISK CONTROL REVIEW. ***Title Change.*** [Int. risk control rev.]. **Added/Corp** International Loss Control Institute. **VFOAT** Risk Control Review. (1981)- Vol. 13, No. 2, (19??). Abstracting/Indexing Service. English. qt. International Loss Control Institute, PO Box 1898, Atlanta Highway, Longanville GA 30249. **Tel** (404)466-2208, FAX (404)466-4318. **ED** Robert M Arnold Jr and James R Callison Jr. **LC** HD61; .I57. **DD** 363.1/06. Index available. **Circ:** 1,500. ***Continued by** International Loss Control Review.*
Desc: Contains abstracts of safety/loss control related articles from over 150 magazines. Excellent resource for keeping professionals current with their reading.

UK/0261-2917
LABORATORY HAZARDS BULLETIN. [Lab. hazards bull.]. **Added/Corp** Royal Society of Chemistry (Great Britain). (April 1981)-. Abstracting/Indexing Service. English. mo (12 issues). £154.00 EC; $310.00 US; £164.00 other. Royal Society of Chemistry, Thomas Graham House, Science Park, Cambridge CB4 4WF England. **Tel** 011 44 223 420066, FAX 011 44 223 423429, telex 818293 ROYAL. **(Subscription address:** Turpin Distribution Services Limited, Blackhorse Road, Letchworth, Hertfordshire SG6 1HN, United Kingdom.**)** **CODEN** LHBUD2. **[CCC].** Index available. **Ad Acc. Circ:** 1,000. available on an online database from STN International; ESA-IRS; ORBIT; DIALOG; and DATA-STAR.
Desc: A current awareness periodical which reports on safety measures, potential hazards and new legislation affecting the well-being of employees working in laboratories. Contains approximately 60-70 references drawn from current scientific and technical literature. The references include document titles, bibliographic citations and abstracts. Each issue contains a chemical and a subject index. In addition, each issue includes a Hazards Data Sheet relating to a specific chemical compound.

SZ/1010-7053
SAFETY AND HEALTH AT WORK : ILO-CIS BULLETIN. **Added/Corp** International Occupational Safety and Health Information Centre. International Labour Office. **VFOAT** ILO-CIS Bulletin. Vol. 1, No. 1-2 (1987)-. Abstracting/Indexing Service. English (French). bm. $230.00. International Labour Office - ILO, Publications Sales Service, CH-1211 Geneva 22 Switzerland. **Tel** 011 41 22 7996111. **ED** Jukka Takala and Michele Nahmias. **LC** T55.A1; I62a. **NLM** ZWA 400; C14. **CODEN** SHWOEV. Index available. cum. index (annual and five year). **Bk Rev. Ad Acc. Circ:** 1,500 (ctrl). available on CD-ROM; available on an online database. ***Continues** International Occupational Safety and Health Information Centre. CIS Abstracts, 0302-7651.*
Desc: Abstracts of recent publications in OCC safety and health. List of courses and conferences. "News and Activities" column.
Ind/Abst Ergon. Abstr.

UK/0262-9836
SELECTED ABSTRACTS ON OCCUPATIONAL DISEASES. [Sel. abstr. occup. dis.]. (1982)-. Periodical. English. qt. £8.00 UK; £9.44 other Europe and EIRE; £11.24 other. Department of Health and Social Security Library, PO Box 21, Stanmore, Middlesex HA7 1AY England. **Tel** 011 44 71 9722000, 9728161. **DD** 016.6169803.

US
STATE OF WYOMING CHARACTERISTICS OF RECORDABLE OCCUPATIONAL INJURIES AND ILLNESSES. (1986)-. English. an. Free. Wyoming Department of Labor & Statistics, Herschler Building, Cheyenne WY 82002. **Tel** (307)777-7340. **ED** Albert J Wolff. **LC** RC964; .W95A. **DD** 363.1/1/09787021. **Circ:** 250 (ctrl). ***Continues** State of Wyoming Characteristics of Occupational Injuries and Illnesses.*
Desc: Occupational injury and illness characteristic statistics for recordable industrial accidents.

INSURANCE

AT/0314-8580
A.I.I. JOURNAL. [A.I.I. j.]. **VFOAT** Australian Insurance Institute Journal. (1977)-. Periodical. English. Five times a year. 35.00Aus$. Australian Insurance Institute, 31 Queen Street, 15th Floor, Melbourne Victoria, 3000 Australia. **Tel** 011 61 3 6294021, FAX 011 61 3 6294204, telex 139668. **ED** Mark Sheeman. **DD** _a368.994. **Bk Rev. Ad Acc.**

US
ACCIDENT AND HEALTH BUSINESS.
See Public Health and Safety.

AT
ACCIDENT COMPENSATION. VICTORIA. (19??)-. English. ir. 455.00Aus$ (includes 1 looseleaf volume, 6 updates, plus bulletins). Butterworths Pty Ltd, 271-273 Lane Cove Road, PO Box 345, North Ryde NSW 2113 Australia. **Tel** 011 61 2 3354444, FAX 011 61 2 3354655. ***Continues** Workers Compensation. Victoria.*
Desc: Source of the legislation relating to accident compensation and workers compensation in Victoria, with detailed commentary on its application and consequences.

US
ACTUARIAL DIGEST, THE. English. bm. Free US; $18.00 Canada. Actuarial Digest Publishing Company, 5600 Roswell Road NE/Suite 276N, Atlanta GA 30342. **Tel** (404)256-5871.

US/0732-5428
ACTUARIAL RESEARCH CLEARING HOUSE. (ACTUARIAL RESEARCH CLEARING HOUSE : ARCH.). **Added/Corp** Society of Actuaries. **VFOAT** ARCH; A.R.C.H. (19??)-. English. ir (2-3 times a year). $35.00. Society of Actuaries, PO Box 95668, Chicago IL 60694. **Tel** (708)706-3526. **ED** Charles S. Fuhrer and Arnold F. Shapiro. **LC** HG8779; .A28. **DD** 368.3/2/00151. **Circ:** 320 (ctrl).
Desc: Items of actuarial research and proceedings of the annual Actuarial Research Conference.

US/1046-5081
ACTUARIAL REVIEW, THE. [Actuar. rev.]. **Added/Corp** Casualty Actuarial Society. (1974)-. Periodical. English. qt. $10.00 US; 16.00Can$ Canada. Casualty Acturial Society, 1100 North Glede #600, Arlington VA 22201. **Tel** (703)276-3100. **DD** 368.

US/0148-3145
ACTUARIAL TABLES EFFECTIVE FOR TERMINATIONS. **Main/Corp** Pension Benefit Guaranty Corporation. (19??)-. Government Publication. English. ir. Superintendent of Documents, US Government Printing Office, Washington DC 20402. **Tel** (202)275-3328, FAX (202)786-2377. **LC** HD7106.U5; P394b. **DD** 331.2/52/0973.
Desc: Information on old age pensions.

US/0363-9274
ACTUARIAL VALUATION, NEBRASKA STATE PATROLMEN'S RETIREMENT SYSTEM. **Main/Corp** Milliman & Robertson, Inc. English. William & Robertson Inc, Suite 308/8990 West Didge Road, Omaha NE 68114. **LC** HV8145.N37; M55A. **DD** 331.2/52. ***Continues** Actuarial Report, Nebraska State Patrolmen's Retirement System.*

US/0001-7825
ACTUARY. **Added/Corp** Society of Actuaries. Vol. 1, (1967)-. Periodical. English. Ten times a year (Except July/Aug.). $15.00. Society of Actuaries, PO Box 95668, Chicago IL 60694. **Tel** (708)706-3526. **ED** Diana Montgomery. **Bk Rev. Circ:** 13,000 (ctrl).
Desc: Newsletter of the Society of Actuaries.

IT
ADS : NOTIZIARIO SETTIMANALE ASSICURATIVO ECONOMICO FINANZIARIO. Italian. wk. L370000 Italy; L400000 Europe; L450000 other. Agenzia Di Stampa, Vicolo Sciarra 61, 00187 Rome Italy. **Tel** 011 39 6 6841811.

US/0163-8939
ADVANCED SALES REFERENCE SERVICE. **Added/Corp** National Underwriter Company. (19??)-. English. ir (includes monthly updates). $410.00 US; $421.00 Canada; $421.50 other. National Underwriter Company, 505 Gest Street, Cincinnati OH 45203-0874. **Tel** (513)721-2140, (800)543-0874. ***Continues** Diamond Life Bulletins.*
Desc: Eight-volume series covering insurance and tax planning for proprietorships, partnerships and corporations.

US
ADVANCED UNDERWRITING SERVICE.
See Public Administration-Public Finance and Taxation.

SP
AL VOCANTE. Spanish. Three times a year. free. Asociacion Hispana de Servicio al Automovilista SA, Rios Rosas 32 - P 3, 28003 Madrid Spain. **ED** Francisco Rebollo Delnoto. **Ad Acc. Circ:** 25,000.

US
ALABAMA MEDICAID. ***Title Change.*** **Added/Corp** Alabama. Medical Services Administration. (19??)-(19??). English. an. **LC** HD7102.U5; A25. **DD** 362.1/04252/09761. ***Continues** Medicaid Trends in Alabama.* ***Continued by** Alabama Medicaid Agency. Annual Report.*

Insurance

US
ALASKA PERSONAL LINES STATISTICAL ANALYSIS, PRIVATE PASSENGER AUTOMOBILE INSURANCE, HOMEOWNERS INSURANCE / DIVISION OF INSURANCE, DEPARTMENT OF COMMERCE AND ECONOMIC DEVELOPMENT, STATE OF ALASKA. See Insurance-Abstracting, Bibliographies and Statistics.

CN/0712-9343
ALBERTA INSURANCE DIRECTORY. [Alta. insur. dir.]. 1st Ed. (1982)-. Directory. English. an. $17.00 per volume. Arbutus Publications, PO Box 35070 Station E, Vancouver British Columbia V6M 4G1 Canada. **DD** 368/.0025/7123.

US/0271-3578
ALI-ABA COURSE OF STUDY : ABA SECTION OF TAXATION, ANNUAL ADVANCED STUDY SESSIONS, BUSINESS AND ESTATE PLANNING WITH LIFE AND DISABILITY INSURANCE : MATERIALS. See Law-Estate Planning.

US/0735-2883
ALL ABOUT MEDICAID. Ceased. Vol. 1, No. 1 (Nov. 18, 1982)-(Jan. 1987). Periodical. English. bw. Carson Communications, 6130 Franconia Station Lane, Alexandria VA 22310. **Tel** (703)922-9475.

US/0735-2891
ALL ABOUT MEDICARE. Ceased. [All about med.]. Vol. 1, No. 1 (Jan. 17, 1983)-(Jan. 1987). Periodical. English. bw. Carson Communications, 6130 Franconia Station Lane, Alexandria VA 22310. **Tel** (703)922-9475.

US/0002-7200
AMERICAN AGENT & BROKER. VAT American Agent and Broker. (Oct. 1969)-. Periodical. English. mo. $12.00 US; $20.00 other. American Agent & Broker, 408 Olive Street, St. Louis MO 63102. **Tel** (314)421-5445. **ED** David A. Baetz, George F. Williams. **LC** HG9651; .L6. **DD** 368/.9/73. **Bk Rev. Ad Acc. Circ:** 39,000 (ctrl). available on microfilm and microfiche from University Microfilms International (UMI); available on an online database (file 15/Full-Text) from DIALOG. Documents available from UMI Article Clearinghouse. **Continues** Local Agent.
 Desc: Magazine of sales and management information exclusively for independent property-casualty agents and brokers.
 Ind/Abst ABI/INFORM Glob. Ed.; ABI Inform Ondisc (Oct. 1987-); UMI ABI/Inform--Bus. Period. Ondisc (Oct. 1987-) [Full Txt.].

US/0095-3520
AMORTIZATION, INSURANCE PREMIUM AND OUTSTANDING PRINCIPAL BALANCE TABLES FOR HOME MORTGAGES AND LOANS INSURED UNDER THE NATIONAL HOUSING ACT. See Business-Banking and Finance.

CG
ANNUAIRE OFFICIEL DES ASSURANCES AFRICAINES. 1.- Ed.; 1978-. English (French). B P 5287, Kinshasa Congo. **LC** HG8720.A6; A53. **DD** 368/.96.

US/0192-8643
ANNUAL CONFERENCE OF STATE MEDICAID DIRECTORS. CONFERENCE REPORT. Added/Corp Institute for Medicaid Management. United States. Medicaid Bureau. (19??)-. English. an. US Department of Health and Human Services, 200 Independence Avenue Southwest, Washington DC 20201. **LC** HD7102.U4; C584a. **DD** 368.4/2/00973.

US/0736-9026
ANNUAL CONTRACTOR EVALUATION REPORT FOR BLUE CROSS/BLUE SHIELD OF MICHIGAN. PART B CARRIER. See Economics-Labor.

US/0093-8017
ANNUAL EVALUATION OF THE NEW YORK STATE UNEMPLOYMENT INSURANCE FUND. See Economics-Labor.

CN/0319-3535
ANNUAL REPORT - ALBERTA HAIL AND CROP INSURANCE CORPORATION. Main/Corp Alberta Hail and Crop Insurance Corporation. English. an. Hail and Crop Insurance Corporation, 1110 First Street SW, Calgary Alta T2R 0V2. **LC** HG9968.H35; C253. **DD** 368.1/22.

US
ANNUAL REPORT - AMERICAN COLLEGE. Main/Corp American College (Bryn Mawr, Pa.). (1974)-. English. American College of Life Underwriters, 270 Bryn Mawr Avenue, Bryn Mawr PA 19010. **Continues** Annual Report - American College of Life Underwriters.

US
ANNUAL REPORT AND STATISTICAL DATA - DIVISION OF INSURANCE (MISSOURI). See Insurance-Abstracting, Bibliographies and Statistics.

US
ANNUAL REPORT AND SUMMARY OF ANNUAL STATEMENTS BY THE DIRECTOR OF INSURANCE TO ... GOVERNOR, FOR YEAR ENDING DECEMBER 31 ... INCLUDING FISCAL REPORT FOR YEAR ENDING JUNE 30 ... . **Main/Corp** Illinois. Dept. of Insurance. 48th (1982)-. English. Illinois Department of Insurance, 320 West Washington Street, Springfield IL 62767. **Tel** (217)782-4515, FAX (217)782-5020. **LC** HG8511.I3; A452. **DD** 353.9773082/55/05. **Continues** Annual Report Including Summary of Annual Statements by the Director of the Department of Insurance to ... Governor, State of Illinois for the Year Ending December 31 ... Including Fiscal Report for Year Ending June 30 ... .

US
ANNUAL REPORT, CAL-VET INSURANCE PLANS. July 1, 1980-. English. an. California Department of Veterans Affairs, 1227 O Street, Sacramento CA 95814. **Tel** (916)445-2688. **LC** UB358.C2; C24. **DD** 355.1/15. **Continues** Cal-Vet Insurance Plans.

II/0304-6966
ANNUAL REPORT: DIRECTORS' REPORT, BALANCE SHEET AND ACCOUNTS. Main/Corp Deposit Insurance Corporation. (19??)-. English. an. Deposit Insurance Corporation, Vidyut Bhavan, Pathakwadi, Post Bag No. 2810, India. **(Subscription address:** Prints India, 11 Darya Ganj, New Delhi 110002 India.**) LC** HG1662.I4; D44a. **DD** 368.8/54/00954.

AT/0311-953X
ANNUAL REPORT - EXPORT PAYMENTS INSURANCE CORPORATION. Main/Corp Export Payments Insurance Corporation. English. 0.40Aus$. Government Printer / Australia, PO Box 84, Canberra, Australian Capital Territory, 2600 Australia. **LC** J905; .L3 subser; HG9970.C69. **DD** 328.94/01 S; 368.8/7/006594. **Continues** Annual Report and Financial Statement - Export Payments Insurance Corporation, 0311-9521.

●CN/1192-0254
ANNUAL REPORT / FINANCIAL INSTITUTIONS COMMISSION. See Business-Banking and Finance.

US
ANNUAL REPORT FOR THE YEAR ... / STATE OF ARKANSAS, EMPLOYMENT SECURITY DIVISION, DEPARTMENT OF LABOR. See Economics-Labor.

CN/0317-7947
ANNUAL REPORT - INSURANCE CORPORATION OF BRITISH COLUMBIA. Main/Corp Insurance Corporation of British Columbia. **VAT** Insurance Corporation of British Columbia. Annual Report. 1st- 1973/74-. Periodical. English. an. Insurance Corporation of Canada, 1055 West Georgia Street, Vancouver British Columbia V6E 3R4 Canada. **LC** HG9970.A68; C35A. **DD** 368/.006/2711.

CN/0542-5395
ANNUAL REPORT - MANITOBA CROP INSURANCE CORPORATION. Main/Corp Manitoba Crop Insurance Corporation. 1962-. Periodical. English. an. Free. Manitoba Crop Insurance Corporation, 886 St. James Street, Winnipeg Manitoba R3G 3J7 Canada. **LC** HG9968.C75. **DD** 368.1. **Supersedes** Crop Insurance Agency (Man.). Annual Report, 0317-476X.

US
ANNUAL REPORT / MARYLAND HOUSING FUND. Main/Corp Maryland Housing Fund. English. an. Maryland Housing Fund, 45 Calvert Street, Annapolis MD 21401. **LC** HG9992.35.M3; M37A. **DD** 353.97520086/5045.

US
ANNUAL REPORT - NEW JERSEY. STATE AGENCY FOR SOCIAL SECURITY. See Sociology-Social Services and Welfare.

US
ANNUAL REPORT OF THE DEPARTMENT OF COMMERCE AND INSURANCE. See Business-Commerce.

US
ANNUAL REPORT OF THE DEPARTMENT OF INSURANCE OF THE STATE OF INDIANA FOR THE FISCAL YEAR ENDING SEPTEMBER 30 ... . **Added/Corp** Indiana. Dept. of Insurance. 1st (1920/1921)-. Periodical. English. an. Auditor of the State of Indiana, 240 State House, Indianapolis IN 46204. **Continues** Annual Report of the Auditor of the State of Indiana, Year ... Insurance Department; **Continues in part** Indiana. Auditor's Office. Annual Report of the Auditor of State, 0362-3041.

US
ANNUAL REPORT OF THE KANSAS INSURANCE DEPARTMENT. Main/Corp Kansas. Insurance Dept. **VFOAT** Century One; Annual Report. 101st (1970)-. English. Kansas Insurance Department, 420 SW 9th Street, Topeka KS 66612. **Tel** (913)296-7805, FAX (913)296-2283. **Continues** Kansas. Insurance Dept. Annual Report of the Commissioner of Insurance of the State of Kansas.

US
ANNUAL REPORT OF THE NEW YORK STATE SENATE STANDING COMMITTEE ON INSURANCE. Main/Corp New York (State). Legislature. Senate. Standing Committee on Insurance. (1985)-. English. New York Legislature, Albany NY 12236. **Continues** Chairman's Report.

CN/0225-8579
ANNUAL REPORT OF THE SUPERINTENDENT OF INSURANCE (QUEBEC. 1977). (ANNUAL REPORT OF THE SUPERINTENDENT OF INSURANCE (QUEBEC).). [Annu. rep. Supt. Insur.]. **Main/Corp** Quebec (Province). Service des Assurances. **VAT** Annual Report of the Quebec Superintendent of Insurance. English. an. Editeur Officiel du Quebec, 1283 Boul Charest Ouest, Quebec Quebec G1N 2C9 Canada. **LC** HG8550.Z8; Q429A. **DD** 354.7140082/55/06.

US
ANNUAL REPORT / OFFICE OF THE GOVERNOR, DIVISION OF MEDICAID. Main/Corp Mississippi. Division of Medicaid. 16th (July 1, 1984-June 30, 1985)-. English. an. PO Box 16786, Jackson MS 39236-0786. **LC** HD7102.U4; M55A. **DD** 353.97620084/1045/06. **Continues** Annual Report - Mississippi Medicaid Commission.

CN/1183-9309
ANNUAL REPORT - ONTARIO INSURANCE COMMISSION. (ANNUAL REPORT.). [Annu. rep. - Ont. Insur. Comm.]. **Main/Corp** Ontario Insurance Commission. **VFOAT** Rapport Annuel. **VAT** Rapport Annuel - Commission des Assurances de l'Ontario. (1991)-. English (French). **DD** 368.

CN/1183-9309
ANNUAL REPORT - ONTARIO INSURANCE COMMISSION. (RAPPORT ANNUEL.). [Annu. rep. - Ont. Insur. Comm.]. **Main/Corp** Commission des Assurances de l'Ontario. **VFOAT** Annual Report. **VAT** Rapport Annuel - Commission des Assurances de l'Ontario. (1991)-. French (English). **DD** 368.

CN/0227-5864
ANNUAL REPORT / ONTARIO SHARE AND DEPOSIT INSURANCE CORPORATION. See Business-Banking and Finance.

US/0362-4218
ANNUAL REPORT - STATE OF NEW JERSEY, DEPARTMENT OF INSTITUTIONS AND AGENCIES, DIVISION OF MEDICAL ASSISTANCE AND HEALTH SERVICES-MEDICAID. (MEDICAID ANNUAL REPORT.). **Main/Corp** New Jersey. Division of Medical Assistance and Health Services. English. an. Department of Institutions & Agencies, 324 East State Street, Trenton NJ 08608. **LC** HD7102.U5; N52A. **DD** 368.4/2/009749. **Continues** New Jersey. Division of Medical Assistance and Health Services. Annual Report.

CN/0229-7108
ANNUAL REPORT / SUPERINTENDENT OF INSURANCE. Main/Corp Alberta. Superintendent of Insurance. English. Office of the Superintendent of Insurance and Real Estate, 10065 Jasper Avenue, Edmonton Alberta T5J 3B1 Canada. **LC** HG8550; .A15a. **DD** 368/.97123/05. **Continues in part**

Insurance

Annual Report, Superintendent of Insurance - Alberta. Office of the Superintendent of Insurance and Real Estate.

CN/0715-2647
ANNUAL REPORT - TERRITORIAL HOSPITAL INSURANCE SERVICES AND MEDICARE. (ANNUAL REPORT FOR THE PERIOD ENDING MARCH 31 ... / TERRITORIAL HOSPITAL INSURANCE SERVICES AND MEDICARE.). [Annu. rep. - Territ. Hosp. Insur. Serv. Med.]. **Main/Corp** Northwest Territories. Territorial Hospital Insurance Services. English. an. Culture and Communications, Government of the Northwest Territories, PO Box 1320, Yellowknife Northwest Territories X1A 2L9 Canada. **LC** HD7102.C22; N576A. **DD** 354.719/2008256.

US/0145-9171
ANNUAL REPORT TO THE GOVERNOR AND LEGISLATURE ON PREPAID HEALTH PLANS, PHPS. (ANNUAL REPORT TO THE GOVERNOR AND LEGISLATURE ON PREPAID HEALTH PLANS, PHPS (CALIFORNIA).). **Main/Corp** California. Dept. of Health. English. an. California Health and Welfare Agency Department of Social Services, 744 P Street, Sacramento CA 95814. **LC** RA413.5.U6; C33. **DD** 353.9/794/00841.

US
ANNUAL STATISTICAL BULLETIN / NATIONAL COUNCIL ON COMPENSATION INSURANCE. See Economics-Abstracting, Bibliographies and Statistics.

●US
ANNUAL STATISTICAL SUPPLEMENT, ... TO THE SOCIAL SECURITY BULLETIN. See Sociology-Social Services and Welfare.

US/1058-6504
ANNUAL WORKERS' COMPENSATION CONFERENCE, THE. See Economics-Labor.

US
ANNUITIES FROM THE BUYER'S POINT OF VIEW. Main/Corp American Institute for Economic Research. (19??)-. English. an. $10.00. American Institute for Economic Research, Division Street, Great Barrington MA 01230. **Tel** (413)528-1216, **FAX** (413)528-0103. **ED** Robert A. Gilmour. **Circ:** 1,000,000 (ctrl). *Supersedes in part* American Institute for Economic Research. Life Insurance and Annuities from the Buyer's Point of View.

US/1071-4510
ANNUITY & LIFE INSURANCE SHOPPER. See Business-Investments.

SP/0303-4763
ANUARIO ESTADISTICO DE SEGUROS. See Insurance-Abstracting, Bibliographies and Statistics.

US/1041-1585
APPRAISAL REVIEW & MORTGAGE UNDERWRITING JOURNAL. See Real Estate.

IT/0392-5145
ARCHIVIO DI MEDICINA LEGALE E DELLE ASSICURAZIONI. See Medical Science and Technology-Forensic Medicine, Medical Jurisprudence.

FR/0150-6854
ARGUS ET LA SEMAINE, L'. [Argus Sem.]. **VFOAT** Argus, la Semaine. (1940)-. Periodical. French. wk. 969.64F France; 1320.00F other. Argus des Assurances, 2 rue de Chateaudun, 75441 Paris Cedex 09 France. **Tel** 011 33 1 45961300. **UDC** 368. *Continues* L'Argus (Paris, 1877), 0004-1173; La Semaine, 0150-6846.

SI/0218-2696
ASIA INSURANCE REVIEW. [Asia insur. rev.]. (1991)-. Periodical. English. Six times a year (Jan., Mar., May., Jul., Sep., Nov.). 90.00Sing$ Singapore, Malaysia & Brunei; 115.00Sing$ Asia/Oceania; 130.00Sing$ Africa, Middle East, Europe & America. Ins Communications Pte Ltd, 47 Ann Siang Road #06-00, Singapore 0106 Singapore. **Tel** 65 2245583, **FAX** 65 2241091. **ED** Sivam Susramanian. **DD** 368.005. **Ad Acc**, **Adv Mgr:** Joanna Org. **Circ:** 5,000 (ctrl).
Desc: A professional insurance magazine covering issues relating to insurance, reinsurance, broking, loss adjusting, IT in insurance interviews with regulators, etc.

AU
ASSECURANZ-COMPASS. (1893)-. German (English and French). an. 12995.00F. Assecuranz Compass, 256 Moliere Avenue, 1060 Brussels Belgium. **Tel** 011 32 2 6470975, FAX 011 32 2 3473340, telex 62903. **LC** HG8015; .A8. **DD** 368/.005. Index available. **Ad Acc**, **Adv Mgr:** G Vermeirsch, **Tel** 02-345-9070.

Circ: 2,500.
Desc: Two volumes of facts and figures covering insurance, insurance-related companies worldwide. Information: address, management, board, branches, working field, group membership, subsidiaries, foreign representatives, share capital, foundation year, and annual report summary.

IT/0004-5098
ASSICURAZIONE; QUINDICINALE DI TECHNICA, CRONACA E GIURISPRUDENZA ASSICURATIVA. (1884)-. Periodical. Italian. Eleven times a year. L50000.00 Italy; L8000.00 others. L Assicurazioni SRL, Piazza Della Vittoria 6/16, 16121 Genoa Italy. **Tel** 011 39 10 540887, telex 610336 INA RM. **Bk Rev**. **Ad Acc**. **Circ:** 2,000.
Desc: Law, economy, and finance of private insurance with particular regards to literature and sentences.

IT
ASSICURAZIONI. Vol. 1 (Jan./Feb. 1934)-. Periodical. Italian (summaries and/or abstracts in English, French and German). an. Casa Editrice Felice, Va Meucci 2, 50015 Grassina FI Italy. cum. index.

IT
ASSICURAZIONI SOCIALI OBBLIGATORIE. IPSOA Editore SRL, Casella Postale 12055, Mastrangelo, 20120 Milan Italy. **Tel** 011 39 2 82476248.

IT
ASSINEWS. (19??)-. Italian. qt. L250000 (insurance companies & banks), L150000 (all except insurance companies & banks) Italy; L250000 other. Assinform, Viale Trento 4, 33170 Pordenone Italy. **Tel** 011 39 434 26136, FAX 011 39 434 521578. Index available. **Bk Rev**. **Ad Acc**.
Desc: Publication deals with insurance law, news, and techniques of insurance.

IE
ASSURANCE COMPANIES / DEPARTMENT OF INDUSTRY, COMMERCE, AND ENERGY. English. an. Government Publications, 4 5 Harcourt Road, Dublin 2 Ireland. **Tel** 011 353 1 6613111 Ext.4005. **LC** HG8604; .A52. **DD** 368/.9417.

FR/0004-6019
ASSURANCE FRANCAISE. No. 1 (1947)-. Periodical. French. Twenty-two times a year. 1060.00F Americas, South Africa, and Near East; 773.75F France; 790.00F other EEC; 1100.00F other. Societe d'Editions et Publications Assurance Francaise, 55 rue de Chateaudun, 75009 Paris France. **Tel** 011 33 1 48742836, 011 33 1 45268900.

CN/0714-430X
ASSURANCE I.A.R.D. AU CANADA. (LES ASSURANCES I.A.R.D. AU CANADA / BUREAU D'ASSURANCE DU CANADA.). [Assur. I.A.R.D. Can.]. **VAT** Assurances Incendie, Accidents, Risques Divers au Canada. French. an. $0.50 per volume. Bureau d'Assurance du Canada, Bureau 920/1080 Cote du Beaver Hall, Montreal Quebec H2Z 1S8 Canada. **DD** 368/.971.

CN/0004-6027
ASSURANCES. [Assurances]. Vol. 1, (Jan. 1933)-. Periodical. French (English). Four times a year (Jan., Apr., July, Oct.). 50.00Can$ Canada; 54.00Can$ other. Assurances, 1140 Ouest Boulevard de Maisonneuve, Montreal Quebec H3A 3H1 Canada. **Tel** (514)282-9841, FAX (514)282-1364, telex 055 60657. **ED** Remi Moreau. **LC** HG8015; .A86. **DD** 368.05. Index available. **Ad Acc**. **Circ:** 1,000.
Desc: In-depth articles in French and English on insurance, reinsurance, and insurance law. Special sections: case laws, documentation and book reviews.
Ind/Abst Can. Period. Index; Index Can. Leg. Period. Lit.; Ins. Period. Index (-199?); Point Repere (1983-).

CN/1186-835X
ASSUREUR DES COMMERCES, L'. [Assur. commer.]. **Added/Corp** Corporation Bernard Pelletier & Associes. Vol. 1, No 1 (Spring 1991)-. Periodical. French. sa. Free Limited Distribution. Corporation Bernard Pelletier & Associates, Bureau B-103, 131 Rue Richer, Hull Quebec J8Y 4T8 Canada. **DD** 368.8.

CN/0715-8564
ASSUREUR VIE A L'ECOUTE. (L'ASSUREUR VIE A L'ECOUTE : MENSUEL DE L'ASSOCIATION DES ASSUREURS-VIE DE QUEBEC.). [Assur.-vie ecoute]. **Main/Corp** Association des Assureurs-Vie de Quebec. Dec. 1977-. Periodical. French. mo. Limited free distribution to members. A.A.V.Q., 1135 Chemin St-Louis Canada. **DD** 368.3/006071447. *Continues* Association des Assureurs-Vie de Quebec. L'Assureur a l'Ecoute, 0824-9733.

CN/0706-635X
ASSURVIE. V. 1, No. 2- Nov. 1978-. Periodical. French. qt. $10.00. Assurvie Inc., CP 61, 2020 Rue University, Montreal Quebec. **DD** 368.3/2/009714. *Continues* Assure-Vie, 0705-5773.

UK/0515-0361
ASTIN BULLETIN. Added/Corp International Actuarial Association. ASTIN Section. Permanent Committee for International Actuarial Congresses. ASTIN Section. **VAT** Actuarial Studies in Non-Life Insurance Bulletin. (1958)-. Bulletin. English (French). Twice a year. £2500.00. NV Druk Ceuterick, Brusselsestraat 153, B3000 Louvain Belguim. **Tel** 011 32 16 228181. **ED** Hans Buhlmann and D. Harry Reid. Index available. **Bk Rev**. **Ad Acc**. **Circ:** 2,000.
Desc: Publishes papers written from any quantitative point of view attacking theoretical and applied problems in any field faced with elements of insurance and risk.

US/0277-643X
ATSIS JOURNAL. (ATSIS JOURNAL : THE JOURNAL OF THE ASA T. SPAULDING INSURANCE SOCIETY.). **VFOAT** A.T.S.I.S. Journal. **VAT** Asa T. Spaulding Insurance Society Journal. 1981-82-. Periodical. English. an. Free. Asa T Spaulding Insurance Society, 2345 Sherman Avenue, Washington DC 20059. **LC** HG8011; .A87. **DD** 368/.005.

IT/0021-2520
ATTI UFFICIALI / ISTITUTO NAZIONALE DELLA PREVIDENZA SOCIALE. Main/Corp Istituto Nazionale Delle Previdenza Sociale. **Added/Corp** Istituto Nazionale della Previdenza Sociale (Italy). Servizio Affari Generali e Relazione Pubbliche. (1944)-. Italian. mo. L70000. Istituto Nazionale della Previdenza Sociale, Via Ciro il Grande 21, CP 10024, 00144 Rome Italy. **Tel** 011 39 6 59054090. **LC** HD7182; .I86a. *Continues* Istituto Nazionale Fascista della Previdenza Sociale (Italy). Atti Ufficiali.

US/0193-2918
AUDIT OF THE FINANCIAL STATEMENTS OF FEDERAL CROP INSURANCE CORPORATION. Main/Corp United States. General Accounting Office. (19??)-. English. an. Free. US General Accounting Office / Maryland, Document Handling and Information Services Facility, PO Box 6015, Gaithersburg MD 20877. **Tel** (202)275-6241. **LC** HG9968.C7; U53. **DD** 353.008/233. *Continues* Audit of Federal Crop Insurance Corporation, 0092-7791.

US/0148-0464
AUDIT REPORT, DEPARTMENT OF INSURANCE, TENNESSEE BOARD OF BARBER EXAMINERS. See Public Administration-Public Finance and Taxation.

GW/0933-8357
AUSSENDIENST-INFORMATIONEN. TRAININGSKURS FUR SYSTEMATISCHES VERKAUFEN. [Aussend.-Inf., Train.kurs syst. Verkauf.]. **VFOAT** Al. Aussendienst-Informationen. Trainingskurs fur Systematisches Verkaufen. (19??)-. Periodical. German (Italian, French, Dutch, Finnish, English, Swedish, Spanish and Norwegian). sm. DM173.04 Germany; DM161.70 other. Verlag Norbert Mueller GMBH, Postfach 810605, W-8000 Munich 81 Germany. **Tel** 011 44 89 998900, FAX 89 913256. **ED** Renate vom Hofe. **UDC** 658.8.011.1. Index available. cum. index. **Bk Rev**. **Circ:** 18,000 (ctrl).

US/0279-9006
AUSTIN INSURANCE REPORT. ADMINISTRATIVE EDITION. (AUSTIN INSURANCE REPORT.). (19??)-. English. Fifty-one times per year. $75.60 Texas; $70.00 others. Austin Insurance Report, PO Box 12368, Austin TX 78711. **Tel** (512)478-5663. **ED** Homer Olsen and Bill Kidd.

AT/0728-5736
AUSTRALIAN & NEW ZEALAND INSURANCE CASES. [Aust. N. Z. insur. cases]. (1982)-. English. be. **DD** 346.9310860264 346.940860264.
Ind/Abst Aust. Leg. Mon. Dig.

CN/0317-7815
AUTOMOBILE INSURANCE EXPERIENCE. (AUTOMOBILE INSURANCE EXPERIENCE. RAPPORT STATISTIQUE SUR L'ASSURANCE AUTOMOBILE.). [Automob. insur. exp.]. **Added/Corp** Insurance Bureau of Canada. **VFOAT** Rapport Statistique sur l'Assurance Automobile. (1971)-. Periodical. English (French). an. Insurance Bureau of Canada, 181 University Avenue, 13th Floor, Toronto Ontario M5H 3M7 Canada. **Tel** (416)362-2031, FAX (416)361-5952. **DD** 368.2/32/00971. *Supersedes* Automobile Experience by Province & Statistical Territory and by Type of Automobile, Coverage, Classification, 0317-7807.
Desc: Report covers the five previous policy years.

Insurance

US/0093-0466
AUTOMOBILE INSURANCE LOSSES COLLISION COVERAGES VARIATIONS BY MAKE AND SERIES. (AUTOMOBILE INSURANCE LOSSES, COLLISION COVERAGES, VARIATIONS BY MAKE AND SERIES : MODELS.). **Main/Corp** Highway Loss Data Institute. (1972)-. English. Highway Loss Data Institute, 10005 North Globe Road, Arlington VA 22201. **Tel** (703)247-1600. **LC** HG9970.A5; H5A. **DD** 368.3/84/0140973.
Ind/Abst Stat. Ref. Index.

US/0734-547X
AUTOMOBILE INSURANCE LOSSES, INJURY COVERAGES. CLAIM FREQUENCY RESULTS FOR ... MODELS. [Automob. insur. losses inj. cover., Claim freq. results models]. English. an. Highway Loss Data Institute, 10005 North Globe Road, Arlington VA 22201. **Tel** (703)247-1600. **LC** HG9970.3; .A85. **DD** 368.5/72/00973.
Desc: Vols. for 1974/75-1974/76 include results of more than one year.

CN/0319-5767
AVENANT. (L'AVENANT.). **Added/Corp** Bureau d'Assurance du Canada. Service des Realtions Publiques. (1974)-. Periodical. French. ir. L'Avenant, Bureau 902/135 Est rue Sherbrooke, Montreal Quebec H2X 1C6 Canada. **DD** 368/.006/271.

US/0149-4120
AVERAGE MONTHLY WORKERS COVERED BY KENTUCKY UNEMPLOYMENT INSURANCE LAW BY INDUSTRIAL DIVISION AND COUNTY. (AVERAGE MONTHLY WORKERS COVERED BY KENTUCKY UNEMPLOYMENT INSURANCE LAW BY INDUSTRIAL DIVISION AND COUNTY / COMMONWEALTH OF KENTUCKY, DEPARTMENT FOR HUMAN RESOURCES, DIVISION FOR RESEARCH & SPECIAL PROJECTS.). **Added/Corp** Kentucky. Dept. for Human Resources. Division for Research & Special Projects. Kentucky. Division for Unemployment Insurance. (19??)-. English. an. Kentucky Department of Human Resources, Division for Unemployment Insurance, Frankfort KY 40601. **LC** HD7096.U6; K469. **DD** 368.4/4/009769.

IS/0005-2299
AVODAH U-VITUAH LEUMI. See Economics-Labor.

US/8756-5374
BAD FAITH LAW REPORT, THE. See Law.

US/0278-7644
BANK INSURANCE SURVEY. *Title Change.* **Added/Corp** American Bankers Association. American Bankers Association. Insurance and Protection Division. (19??)-(19??). English. an. American Bankers Association, 1120 Connecticut Avenue Northwest, Washington DC 20036. **Tel** (202)663-5221, **FAX** (202)828-4544. **(Subscription telephone:** (202)663-7667) **LC** HG9974.3; .B36. **DD** 368.8. *Continued by* Bank Insurance Survey Report, 1068-025X.

US/1068-025X
BANK INSURANCE SURVEY REPORT. [Bank insur. surv. rep.]. **Added/Corp** American Bankers Association. (19??)-. English. an. American Bankers Association, 1120 Connecticut Avenue Northwest, Washington DC 20036. **Tel** (202)663-5221, , FAX (202)828-4544. **LC** HG9974.3; .B36. **DD** 368.8. *Continues* Bank Insurance Survey, 0278-7644.

US
BARCLAYS INSURANCE LAW REPORT (CALIFORNIA EDITION). See Law.

LE
BAYAN (BEIRUT, LEBANON : 1970). (AL-BAYAN.). Began in 1970. Periodical. Arabic. mo. $50.00 individuals, $75.00 associations. Sahat Al-Tabaris Jadat F Shihab Binayat Kamil Al-Qubi Al-Tabiq Al-Sadis, S B 11-1510, Beirut Lebanon. **LC** HG187.3; .B39.

GW/0522-6457
BEITRAGE ZUR GANZHEITLICHEN WIRTSCHAFTS- UND GESELLSCHAFTSLEHRE. (1966)-. Monographic series. German. ir. Price varies per volume. Duncker und Humblot Verlag, Postfach 410329, D-12113 Berlin Germany. **Tel** 011 49 30 79000612, 011 49 30 79000613. **DD** 330.

UK/0268-764X
BENEFITS & COMPENSATION INTERNATIONAL. [Benefits compens. int.]. **VFOAT** Benefits and Compensation International. (19??)-. Periodical. English. mo (10 issues). $400.00. Pension Publications Ltd, Hope House, 45 Great Peter Street, London SW1P 3LT England. **Tel** 011 41 71 2220288, FAX (71)799 2163, telex 261401. **ED** Irena St John-Brooks. Index available. **Bk Rev. Ad Acc. Pr Rev.**

Circ: 1,184. available on microfilm. Documents available from UMI Article Clearinghouse. *Continues* Benefits International.
Desc: For international companies, containing articles by local practitioners on employee benefits, pensions, investments and remuneration.
Ind/Abst ABI/INFORM Glob. Ed.; Gen. BusinessFile (1992-); Ins. Period. Index.

US/8756-1263
BENEFITS QUARTERLY. See Economics-Labor.

DK/0905-0965
BERETNING FRA FINANSTILSYNET. (1988)-. Danish. an. Danske Boghandlers Kommission, Stilgan Street 228, 2800 Copenhagen Denmark. **LC** HG8655; .D45A. *Continues* Forsikringsselskaber og Pensionskasser M.V.

AU
BERICHT - PENSIONSVERSICHERUNGSANSTALT DER ANGESTELLTEN. See Economics-Labor.

US/1064-8038
BEST'S AGENTS GUIDE. LIFE-HEALTH. [Best's agents guide. Life health]. **Added/Corp** A.M. Best Company. (1991)-. English. ir. AM Best Company, Ambest Road, Oldwick NJ 08858. **Tel** (908)439-2200 ext. 5653, telex 837744. **LC** HG8943; .B27. **DD** 368.3/2/002573. *Continues* Best's Agents Guide to Life Insurance Companies, 0094-9973.
Desc: Uniformly presented facts, figures and other valuable information on over 1,600 life insurance companies.

US
BEST'S AGGREGATES & AVERAGES. LIFE-HEALTH. **Added/Corp** A.M. Best Company. **VFOAT** Best's Aggregates and Averages. Life-Health. 5th Annual Ed. (1986)-. English. an. $95.00. AM Best Company, Ambest Road, Oldwick NJ 08858. **Tel** (908)439-2200 ext. 5653, telex 837744. **LC** HG8941; .B48. **DD** 368.3/2/00973. *Continues* Best's Industry Composite of Life-Health Companies, 0737-1063.
Desc: Examines the consolidated financial and operating legal reserve life/health insurers from three viewpoints: graphical, narrative and statistical.

US/0270-5974
BEST'S AGGREGATES & AVERAGES. PROPERTY-CASUALTY. **Added/Corp** A.M. Best Company. **VFOAT** Best's Aggregates and Averages. Property-Casualty. 37th Annual Ed. (1976)-. English. an. $265.00. AM Best Company, Ambest Road, Oldwick NJ 08858. **Tel** (908)439-2200 ext. 5653, telex 837744. **[CCC].** *Continues* A.M. Best Company. Best's Aggregates & Averages. Property-Liability, 0271-3853.

US/0271-0927
BEST'S DIRECTORY OF RECOMMENDED INSURANCE ADJUSTERS. [Best's dir. recomm. insur. adjust.]. **Added/Corp** A.M. Best Company. **VFOAT** Best's Directory of Recommended Insurance Adjusters. 50th Ed. (1980)-. Directory. English. an. $55.00. AM Best Company, Ambest Road, Oldwick NJ 08858. **Tel** (908)439-2200 ext. 5653, telex 837744. **LC** HG8525; .B35. **DD** 368/.014. *Continues* Best's Recommended Independent Insurance Adjusters, 0091-830X.
Desc: Includes nearly 1,000 pages with listings for more than 3,500 insurance adjusting firms throughout the world. Listings are arranged alphabetically by city within each state, Canadian province, and foreign country.

US/0277-1551
BEST'S DIRECTORY OF RECOMMENDED INSURANCE ATTORNEYS. See Law.

US/0145-4420
BEST'S EXECUTIVE DATA SERVICE: LIFE-HEALTH INDUSTRY MARKETING RESULTS. **Main/Corp** A.M. Best Company. **VFOAT** Life-Health Industry Marketing Results. (1976)-. English. AM Best Company, Ambest Road, Oldwick NJ 08858. **Tel** (908)439-2200 ext. 5653, telex 837744. **LC** HG8941; .A22a. **DD** 368/.9/73.

US/0743-5320
BEST'S EXECUTIVE DATA SERVICE. LIFE-HEALTH INDUSTRY MARKETING RESULTS. ACCIDENT & HEALTH LINES-EXPERIENCE BY STATE. **Added/Corp** A.M. Best Company. **VFOAT** Life-Health Industry Marketing Results. Accident & Health Lines-Experience by State. (19??)-. English. an. $2361.00 (full package). AM Best Company, Ambest Road, Oldwick NJ 08858. **Tel** (908)439-2200 ext. 5653, telex 837744. **LC** HG9331; .B44. **DD** 368/.8/006.
Desc: Provides accident and health insurance reports for six types of business plus a total summary report for each state ordered.

US/8755-9730
BEST'S EXECUTIVE DATA SERVICE. LIFE-HEALTH INDUSTRY MARKETING RESULTS. EXPERIENCE OF PUERTO RICO. **Added/Corp** A.M. Best Company. **VFOAT** Life-Health Industry Marketing Results. Experience of Puerto Rico. (19??)-. English. an. $330.00. AM Best Company, Ambest Road, Oldwick NJ 08858. **Tel** (908)439-2200 ext. 5653, telex 837744. **LC** HG8556.7; .A137. **DD** 368.3/8/006.
Desc: Provides six life insurance and six accident and health reports, plus total summary reports for all business written in Puerto Rico.

US/0743-5312
BEST'S EXECUTIVE DATA SERVICE. LIFE-HEALTH INDUSTRY MARKETING RESULTS. LIFE LINES-EXPERIENCE BY STATE. **Added/Corp** A.M. Best Company. **VFOAT** Life-Health Industry Marketing Results. Life Lines-Experience by State. (19??)-. English. an. $2361.00 (full package). AM Best Company, Ambest Road, Oldwick NJ 08858. **Tel** (908)439-2200 ext. 5653, telex 837744. **LC** HG8941; B477. **DD** 368.3/2/006.
Desc: Provides life insurance reports for six lines of business plus a total summary report for each state ordered.

US
BEST'S EXECUTIVE DATA SERVICE. REPORT A 4 - HIGH RISK AUTO STUDY. **Main/Corp** A.M. Best Company. (19??)-. English. $845.00 per set. AM Best Company, Ambest Road, Oldwick NJ 08858. **Tel** (908)439-2200 ext. 5653, telex 837744. **LC** HG9970.A5; B46. **DD** 368.2/32/00973.
Desc: Offers a thorough analysis of the underwriting results of companies writing predominantly nonstandard auto businesses.

US/0275-4975
BEST'S EXECUTIVE DATA SERVICE. REPORT A2, EXPERIENCE OF PUERTO RICO. PROPERTY AND CASUALTY INSURANCE. **Added/Corp** A.M. Best Company. **VFOAT** Best's Executive Data Service, Experience of Puerto Rico; Property and Casualty Insurance. Report A2, Experience of Puerto Rico. (19??)-. English. $68.00 per line plus $125.00 per state. AM Best Company, Ambest Road, Oldwick NJ 08858. **Tel** (908)439-2200 ext. 5653, telex 837744. **LC** HG8556.7; .A14. **DD** 368/.97295.
Desc: Basic resource for insurance company management seeking to evaluate underwriting, sales and loss experience, or in comparing their results with those of other companies, by state and by line.

US/0094-3150
BEST'S EXECUTIVE DATA SERVICE. REPORT A6- COMPARATIVE EXPERIENCE BY STATE (STATE LEADERS). **Main/Corp** A.M. Best Company. (19??)-. English. an. $68.00 per line + $125.00 per state. AM Best Company, Ambest Road, Oldwick NJ 08858. **Tel** (908)439-2200 ext. 5653, telex 837744. **LC** HG8501; .A35c. **DD** 368.1/00973.
Desc: Comprehensive analysis of regional carriers, their market shares, loss experience, and relative rankings.

US/0198-9553
BEST'S EXECUTIVE DATA SERVICE. REPORT A7-, FIVE YEAR EXPERIENCE BY STATE. [Best's exec. data serv., Rep. A7-Five year exp. State]. **Main/Corp** A.M. Best Company. (19??)-. English. $68.00 per line plus $125.00 per state. AM Best Company, Ambest Road, Oldwick NJ 08858. **Tel** (908)439-2200 ext. 5653, telex 837744. **LC** HG8501; .A35a. **DD** 368/.973.
Desc: Examines the state, by line premium-loss record of the 50 largest property-casualty companies, ranked by premium volume, over the past five years.

US
BEST'S FLITCRAFT COMPEND. *Ceased.* **Added/Corp** A.M. Best Company. No. 81 (1968)-(1994). English. an. AM Best Company, Ambest Road, Oldwick NJ 08858. **Tel** (908)439-2200 ext. 5653, telex 837744. **LC** HG8881; .F68. **DD** 368.3'2'002573. *Continues* Flitcraft Compend, 0733-9631.
Desc: A world of data on premiums, cash and paid-up values, dividends, options and other categories on 275 life companies writing over 91% of the life insurance sold in the United States.

US
BEST'S INSURANCE MANAGEMENT REPORTS. **Added/Corp** A.M. Best Company. **VFOAT** Insurance Management Reports. (Nov. 5, 1979)-. Periodical. English. wk. $325.00 (must specify edition: Life-Health or Property-Casual). AM Best Company, Ambest Road, Oldwick NJ 08858. **Tel** (908)439-2200 ext. 5653, telex 837744.
Desc: Regular coverage on four key areas: the financial scene; the outlook in Washington; statistics covering various aspects of the business; and comment or analysis dealing with current events or developments.

Insurance

US

BEST'S INSURANCE REPORTS. LIFE-HEALTH. Added/Corp A.M. Best Company. 63rd Ed. (1968/1969)-. English. ir. $850.00 (Full Service). AM Best Company, Ambest Road, Oldwick NJ 08858. **Tel** (908)439-2200 ext. 5653, telex 837744. **Continues** Best's Life Insurance Reports.

US/0148-3218
BEST'S INSURANCE REPORTS, PROPERTY-CASUALTY. Added/Corp A.M. Best Company. 77th- Ed.(1976)-. English. an. $850.00 (Full Service). AM Best Company, Ambest Road, Oldwick NJ 08858. **Tel** (908)439-2200 ext. 5653, telex 837744. **LC** HG9655; .B5. **DD** 368.1/006/573. **[CCC]. Continues** Best's Insurance Reports, Property-Liability.
Desc: Provides coverage of more than 3,200 property casualty companies operating in the United States.

US/0362-8701
BEST'S INSURANCE SECURITIES RESEARCH SERVICE. Ceased. Main/Corp A.M. Best Company. (1968)-?. English. ir. AM Best Company, Ambest Road, Oldwick NJ 08858. **Tel** (908)439-2200 ext. 5653, telex 837744. **LC** HG5123.I6; B37A. **DD** 332.6/7.

US/0148-3064
BEST'S KEY RATING GUIDE : PROPERTY-CASUALTY. Added/Corp A.M. Best Company. 70th Ed.(1976)-. English. an. $90.00. AM Best Company, Ambest Road, Oldwick NJ 08858. **Tel** (908)439-2200 ext. 5653, telex 837744. **LC** HG9765; .B4. **DD** 368/.9/73. **[CCC]. Continues** Best's Key Rating Guide. Property-Liability, 0731-5546.
Desc: Examines up to five years of performance for some 1,700 major property-casualty firms operating in the United States. Also contains summary exhibits for up to 2,000 smaller mutual companies.

US/0572-6301
BEST'S MARKET GUIDE. Added/Corp United Statistical Associates. 1st Ed.(1970)-. English. ir. $1425.00. AM Best Company, Ambest Road, Oldwick NJ 08858. **Tel** (908)439-2200 ext. 5653, telex 837744. **LC** HG4926.A3; B4. **DD** 332.67.
Desc: The most comprehensive source of data on corporate stock, bonds, and municipal bond holdings of insurance companies or groups.

US

BEST'S RATING MONITOR. Added/Corp A.M. Best Company. (198?)-. Periodical. English. bw. AM Best Company, Ambest Road, Oldwick NJ 08858. **Tel** (908)439-2200 ext. 5653, telex 837744. **LC** HG8501; B47. **Continues** Best's Insurance Management Reports. Advance Rating Release (Property/Casualty Edition).

US/0197-2405
BEST'S RETIREMENT INCOME GUIDE. Ceased. Main/Corp A.M. Best Company. **Added/Corp** A.M. Best Company. Retirement Income Guide. (19??)-(1994). English. sa. AM Best Company, Ambest Road, Oldwick NJ 08858. **Tel** (908)439-2200 ext. 5653, telex 837744. **LC** HD7106.U5; B45a. **DD** 368.3/7/00973.
Desc: Reference source for the annuities of the companies. than 350 annuity plans now being sold. Covers 90 percent of all offerings marketing in the United States.

US/0005-9706
BEST'S REVIEW. (LIFE-HEALTH INSURANCE EDITION). (BEST'S REVIEW.). [Best's rev.]. Vol. 69, No. 9 (1969)-. Periodical. English. mo. $16.00 US and Canada; $17.00 other. AM Best Company, Ambest Road, Oldwick NJ 08858. **Tel** (908)439-2200 ext. 5653, telex 837744. **LC** HG8751; .B4. **NLM** W1 BE9548. **CODEN** BRLHB5. **[CCC].** available on microfilm and microfiche from University Microfilms International (UMI); available on an online database from DIALOG. Documents available from UMI Article Clearinghouse, Ask*IEEE. **Formed by the union of** Best's Insurance News (Life Ed.), 0275-0988 **and** Flitcraft Courant.
Desc: Coverage of marketing, legislative and financial trends, comments on developments of industry-wide significance, new product developments, company reports, and details regarding management changes and market share studies.
Ind/Abst ABI/INFORM Glob. Ed.; ABI Inform Ondisc (Aug. 1971-); ABI/INFORM Ondisc; Expr. Ed. (Jan. 1987-); Acad. Search (July 1993-); Account. Art.; Bus. ASAP (1990-) [Full Txt.]; Bus. Index (1985-); Bus. Period. Index; Bus. Source (Jul. 1993-); Comput. Lit. Index; F&S Index Plus Text, Int. [Select. Cov.]; Fed. Tax Artic.; Gen. BusinessFile (1985-); Gen. Period. Index (1985-); Hospit. Health Admin. Index; Ins. Period. Artic. Relat. Law (19??-19??); INFO-SOUTH Abstr.; INSPEC (April 1982-); Ins. Period. Index; Mag. Search; PROMT; Stat. Ref. Index; Trade Ind. ASAP [Full Txt.]; Trade Ind. Index (1981-) [Full Txt.]; UMI ABI/Inform--Bus. Period. Ondisc (Jan. 1987-) [Full Txt.]; Wilson Bus. Abstr.; Work Relat. Abstr.

US/0161-7745
BEST'S REVIEW (PROPERTY/CASUALTY INSURANCE ED.). (BEST'S REVIEW.). [Best's rev.]. Vol. 77, No. 1 (May 1976)-. Periodical. English. mo. $16.00 US, Canada and Mexico; $17.00 other. AM Best Company, Ambest Road, Oldwick NJ 08858. **Tel** (908)439-2200 ext. 5653, telex 837744. **LC** HG8011; .B35. **DD** 368/.973. **CODEN** BRPIDU. **[CCC].** available on microfilm from University Microfilms International (UMI); available on an online database from DIALOG. Documents available from Ask*IEEE, UMI Article Clearinghouse. **Continues** Best's Review. (Property/Liability Insurance Edition), 0005-9714.
Desc: In-depth coverage of marketing, legislative and financial trends, comments on developments of industrywide significance, new product developments, company reports, and details regarding management changes, market share studies and more.
Ind/Abst ABI/INFORM Glob. Ed.; ABI Inform Ondisc (May 1976-); ABI/INFORM Ondisc: Expr. Ed. (Jan. 1987-); Acad. Search (July 1993-); Bus. ASAP (1990-) [Full Txt.]; Bus. Index (1985-); Bus. Period. Index; Bus. Source (Jul. 1993-); Comput. Lit. Index; F&S Index Plus Text, Int. [Select. Cov.]; Fed. Tax Artic.; Gen. BusinessFile (1985-); Gen. Period. Index (1985-); INFO-SOUTH Abstr.; INSPEC (April 1982-); Ins. Period. Index; Mag. Search; PROMT; Stat. Ref. Index; Trade Ind. ASAP [Full Txt.]; Trade Ind. Index (1981-) [Full Txt.]; UMI ABI/Inform--Bus. Period. Ondisc (Jan. 1987-) [Full Txt.]; Wilson Bus. Abstr.

US

BEST'S SETTLEMENT OPTIONS MANUAL. Ceased. 27th Ed. (1968)-(April 1988). English. an. AM Best Company, Ambest Road, Oldwick NJ 08858. **Tel** (908)439-2200 ext. 5653, telex 837744. **Continues** Settlement Options.
Desc: Provides current settlement option provisions on 95 percent of all policies issued in North America since 1900.

US/0191-4510
BEST'S UNDERWRITING GUIDE FOR COMMERCIAL LINES. Main/Corp A.M. Best Company. (1976?)-. English. qt. $275.00 (Includes main volume, one year's supplements and newsletter). AM Best Company, Ambest Road, Oldwick NJ 08858. **Tel** (908)439-2200 ext. 5653, telex 837744. **LC** HG8011; .B36A. **DD** 368/.012/05.
Desc: Created to assist company underwriters and agents in the decision-making process by providing the tools necessary to evaluate a risk. Treats commercial business on the basis of risk classification.

GW

BETRIEBSKRANKENKASSEN. Main/Corp Bundesverband der Betriebskrankenkassen (Germany). (19??)-. German. bm. Bundesverband der Bertriebskrankenkasse, Kronprinzenstrasse 6, 45128 Essen Germany. **LC** HD7102.G3; B813a. **NLM** W1 BE9573. **Ad Acc.**

GW

BEVOLKERUNG UND ERWERBSTATIGKEIT. REIHE 4.2.2, ENTGELTE UND BESCHAFTIGUNGSDAUER DER ARBEITNEHMER. See Law.

GW/0723-7561
BG, DIE. (BERUFSGENOSSENSCHAFT.). **VFOAT** Berufsgenossenschaft (1979). (1979)-. Periodical. German. mo. DM112.80. Erich Schmidt Verlag GmbH, Postfach 304240, D 10724 Berlin Germany. **Tel** 011 49 30 25008525. **UDC** 331.82:331.041.2. **[CCC].**

US

BIENNIAL REPORT / TENNESSEE DEPARTMENT OF EMPLOYMENT SECURITY. See Economics-Labor.

US

BLUE BOOK OF ADJUSTERS. 1937-. English. an. National Association of Independent Insurance Adjusters, PO Box 4027, Bellvue WA 98009. **LC** HG8525. **DD** 368/.014/02573.

US/0272-2445
BLUE BOOK OF PENSION FUNDS, THE. See Economics-Labor.

CN/0831-6503
BLUE CHART REPORT, THE. [Blue chart rep.]. **Added/Corp** Stone & Cox Limited. (1985)-. English. 22.50Can$ Canada; 25.50Can$ other. Stone & Cox Ltd Publishers, 111 Peter Street, Suite 202, Toronto Ontario M5V 2H1 Canada. **Tel** (416)599-0772. **DD** 368/.971. **Continues** The Blue Chart Supplement With Selected Performance Indicators., 0831-649X.

US/0095-7100
BNA PENSION REPORTER. Title Change. See Economics-Labor.

US/1051-4775
BNA'S WORKERS' COMPENSATION REPORT. See Economics-Labor.

MX

BOLETIN INFORMATIVO (INTER-AMERICANA CONFERENCE ON SOCIAL SECURITY). See Sociology-Social Services and Welfare.

UK/0965-450X
BOOTH'S NIC BRIEF. [Booth's NIC brief]. (1988)-. English. mo. £132.00. Booth and Company Limited, 1 Amherst Neville Street, Leeds LS1 4DW England. **Tel** 011 44 532 31300, FAX 011 44 532 313200. **ED** Neil D. Booth. Index available. cum. index. **Circ:** 1,000. available on diskette.
Desc: Journal covers all aspects of national insurance. Social Security contribution law and practice, including changes in legislation and planning opportunities for tax minimization for employees in the UK scheme.

IT

BORSA DEI NOLI. (19??)-. Italian. wk. L60000 Italy; L120000 other. Pubblicrea S di F, Corso Gastaldi 11/33, 16100 Genoa Italy. **Tel** 011 39 10 308848.

US/0273-0995
BRIEF (CHICAGO. 1980), THE. See Law.

UK

BRITISH INSURANCE INDUSTRY, THE. 1982 Ed.-. English. Chiltern Publishing, 18 Burgess Wood Road, Beaconsfield Bucks HP9 1EQ England. **Tel** 011 44 494 673062, FAX 011 44 494 678914.

UK/0961-2114
BROKER (LONDON). (THE BROKER.). [Broker Lond.]. (1987)-. Periodical. English. qt. £55.00. Lloyd's of London Press Ltd, Sheepen Place, Colchester, Essex, CO3 3LP England. **Tel** 011 44 206 772113, US: (212)529-9500, US: (800)955-6937, FAX 011 44 206 772680, US: (212)529-9826, telex 987321 LLOYDS G. **(Subscription address:** Lloyd's of London Press Inc. / North America, 611 Broadway, Suite 308, New York NY 10012.) **DD** 381.45368. **Continues** British Insurance Broker, 0141-6197.

US/0273-6551
BROKER WORLD. [Brok. world]. Vol. 1 (Sept./Oct. 1980)-. Periodical. English. mo. $6.00 (one year), $11.00 (two year), $16.00 (three year). Insurance Publications Inc., PO Box 11310, Overland Park KS 66207. **Tel** (913)383-9191, (800)762-3387, FAX (913)381-1247. **ED** Sharon A Chace. **LC** WMLC 93/789. **DD** 368. **Ad Acc, Adv Mgr:** Robb Edwards. Documents available from UMI Article Clearinghouse.
Desc: Published to advance the practice of professionalism in the life and health insurance industry.
Ind/Abst ABI/INFORM Glob. Ed.; ABI Inform Ondisc (Jan. 1988-).

CN/0227-437X
"BROWN CHART" FOR ALL LINES OF GENERAL INSURANCE, PROVINCIAL RESULTS: ... REPORT, THE. Title Change. [Brown chart all lines gen. insur., Prov. results, Rep.]. **VFOAT** Provincial Results; Stone & Cox Brown Chart: Provincial Results in Canada; Donnees Provinciales, l'Annuaire Brun: Rapport ... . 1977-. Periodical. English (French). an. Stone & Cox Ltd Publishers, 111 Peter Street, Suite 202, Toronto Ontario M5V 2H1 Canada. **Tel** (416)599-0772. **LC** HG8550.A4; S8A. **DD** 368/.971. **Continues** Brown Chart of Provincial Results. Report, 0316-1927. **Continued by** Brown Chart of Provincial Results, 0316-1927.

FR

BULLETIN ADMINISTRATIF DES ASSURANCES. See Law.

CN/1180-3681
BULLETIN / CANADIAN INSTITUTE OF ACTUARIES. [Bull. - Can. Inst. Actuar.]. **Added/Corp** Canadian Institute of Actuaries. **VFOAT** Bulletin. **VAT** Bulletin - Institut Canadien des Actuaires. Vol. 1, No. 1 (May 1990)-. Periodical. English (French). Ten times a year. 25.00Can$ Canada; 30.00Can$ others. Canadian Institute of Actuaries, 360 Albert Street, Suite 1040, Ottawa, Ontario K1R 7X7 Canada. **Tel** (613)236-8196. **DD** 368/.01/06071.

US/0588-7127
BULLETIN. COMMISSION ON INSURANCE TERMINOLOGY. Main/Corp Commission on Insurance Terminology. (1965)-. Periodical. English. American College of Life Underwriters, 270 Bryn Mawr Avenue, Bryn Mawr PA 19010. **DD** 368.

FR

BULLETIN DU SERVICE SOCIAL DES CAISSES D'ASSURANCE MALADIE. (1970)-. Bulletin. French. ir. **NLM** W1 BU649S. **Supersedes** Bulletin du Service Social des Organismes de Securite Sociale.

FR
BULLETIN OFFICIEL DES ASSURANCES / REPUBLIQUE FRANCAISE, MINISTERE DE L'ECONOMIE. See Law.

●US/1075-9018
BUSINESS CLAIMS CASUALTY BULLETIN. (1994)-. English. Twelve times a year. $59.85. Quinlan Publishing Company, 23 Drydock Avenue, Boston MA 02210-2387. **Tel** (617)542-0048, (800)229-2084, FAX (617)345-9646. ***Continues*** *Risk Manager Law Bulletin.*

US/0007-6864
BUSINESS INSURANCE. [Bus. insur.]. **Added/Corp** Crain Communications Inc. Advertising Publications, Inc. Vol. 1, (Oct. 30, 1967)-. Periodical. English. Fifty-two times a year. $80.00 US & Possessions, $118.00 Canada, $200.00 others (regular delivery); $175.00 US & Possessions, $185.00 Canada, $200.00 others (airmail). Crain Communications Inc., 1400 Woodbridge, Detroit MI 48207. **Tel** (313)446-6000, (800)992-9970. **(Subscription address:** Crain Communciations Inc., 965 East Jefferson Avenue, Detroit, MI 48207**) ED** Kathryn J. McIntyre. **LC** HG8011; .B87. **DD** 368.8/1/005. **CODEN** BUINEW. **[CCC]. Bk Rev. Ad Acc. Circ:** 45,000. available on microfilm and microfiche from University Microfilms International (UMI); available on an online database (file 16/Full-Text) from DIALOG. Documents available from UMI Article Clearinghouse.
Desc: News on risk management, employee benefit issues, commercial insurance and reinsurance market developments.
Ind/Abst ABI/INFORM Glob. Ed. (Jan. 1975-); ABI Inform Ondisc (Jan. 1975-); ABI/INFORM Ondisc: Expr. Ed. (Jan. 1987-); Acad. Search (July 1993-); BioBusiness; Bus. Index (1985-); Bus. Period. Index; Bus. Source (Jul. 1993-); Cumul. Index Nurs. Allied Health Lit.; Curr. Lit. Fam. Plan.; F&S Index Plus Text, Int. [Full Txt.] [Select. Cov.]; Gen. BusinessFile (1985-); Gen. Period. Index (1985-); Health Plan. Adminis.; Hospit. Health Admin. Index (1978-1986); INFO-SOUTH Abstr.; Ins. Period. Index; Mag. Search; PROMT [Full Txt.]; Trade Ind. Index (1981-); UMI ABI/Inform--Bus. Period. Ondisc (Nov. 1987-) [Full Txt.]; Wilson Bus. Abstr.

US/0275-0317
BUSINESS INSURANCE. EDITORIAL INDEX. ***Ceased.*** (BUSINESS INSURANCE. ... EDITORIAL INDEX / COMPILED BY THE INDEXING CENTER, MICRO PHOTO DIVISION, BELL & HOWELL COMPANY, WOOSTER, OHIO.). [Bus. insur., Ed. index]. **Added/Corp** Bell & Howell Co. Indexing Center. **VFOAT** Annual Index to Business Insurance; Business Insurance. 1st Quarter (Jan./Feb./Mar. 1981)-(Jan. 1994). English. qt. Crain Communications Inc., 1400 Woodbridge, Detroit MI 48207. **Tel** (313)446-6000, (800)992-9970. **LC** HG8011; .B87 Suppl. **DD** 368.8/1/005.

US/0091-3545
CALIFORNIA EMPLOYER CONTRIBUTIONS TO THE UNEMPLOYMENT FUND. See Economics-Labor.

US/0890-4871
CALIFORNIA INSURANCE LAW REPORT. See Law.

US
CALIFORNIA INSURANCE NEWS / CALIFORNIA, DEPARTMENT OF INSURANCE. **Added/Corp** California. Dept. of Insurance. Vol. 1, No. 1 (Summer 1991)-. English. qt. California Department of Insurance, 100 Van Ness Avenue, 17th Floor, San Francisco CA 94102. **Tel** (415)557-9624, FAX (213)736-4891. **LC** KFC290.A15; P762. ***Continues*** *Producer's Newsletter (Sacramento, Calif. : 1986).*

US/0883-9867
CALIFORNIA WORKERS' COMPENSATION ENQUIRER. VFOAT CWCE. (198?)-. Periodical. English. mo. $55.00. California Workers' Compensation Enquirer, PO Box 5460, Los Alamitos CA 90721. **Tel** (213)430-8707.

US/0199-2414
CALUNDERWRITER. Added/Corp California Association of Life Underwriters. (19??)-. Periodical. English. Twelve times a year. $12.00. CALUnderwriter, PO Box 6459, Oakland CA 94603. **Tel** (510)638-2450. **ED** Dan Crouch. **Circ:** 11,477.

CN/0713-1755
CANADA PENSION PLAN CONTRIBUTION AND UNEMPLOYMENT INSURANCE PREMIUM TABLES. See Economics-Labor.

CN/0824-2585
CANADIAN CASES ON THE LAW OF INSURANCE. See Law.

CN/0008-3828
CANADIAN INDEPENDENT ADJUSTER, THE. Added/Corp Canadian Independent Adjusters' Conference. Vol. 1, (Spring 1958)-. Periodical. English. Four times a year (Mar., June, Sept., Dec.). $38.00 (three years). Journal Management, 216 Market Square, Newmarket Ontario L3Y 4A8 Canada. **Tel** (905)895-1518. **Bk Rev. Ad Acc. Circ:** 5,000 (ctrl).
Desc: Educational articles on general insurance claims work, insurance coverages, engineering articles, case law reports, recent trends in casualty insurance, and claims.

CN/0008-3879
CANADIAN INSURANCE. [Can. insur.]. 1905-. Trade Publication. English. mo (13 issues per year-twice in May). 20.00Can$ (one year), 38.00Can$ (two year) Canada; $17.02 US. Stone & Cox Ltd Publishers, 111 Peter Street, Suite 202, Toronto Ontario M5V 2H1 Canada. **Tel** (416)599-0772. **ED** M F Steeler. **Bk Rev. Ad Acc. Circ:** 11,000 (ctrl). Documents available from UMI Article Clearinghouse. ***Absorbed*** *Insurance Agent & Broker in Canada, 0020-4595; Corporate Insurance in Canada, 0315-8098.*
Desc: A journal of the Canadian insurance trade covering both property/casualty and life insurance.
Ind/Abst ABI/INFORM Glob. Ed.; ABI Inform Ondisc (July 1979-); Ins. Period. Index.

CN/0318-0352
CANADIAN INSURANCE CLAIMS DIRECTORY. (1933)-. Directory. English. an. $37.50. University of Toronto Press Book Department, 5201 Dufferin Street, Downsview Ontario M3H 5T8 Canada. **Tel** (416)667-7791, FAX (416)667-7832. **ED** Gwen Peron. **DD** 368/.014/02571. Index available. **Ad Acc, Adv Mgr:** J. Young. **Circ:** 2,200.

CN/0588-6562
CANADIAN INSURANCE LAW REPORTER. See Law.

CN/0836-0456
CANADIAN INSURANCE LAW REVIEW. See Law.

CN/0822-109X
CANADIAN JOURNAL OF INSURANCE LAW. See Law.

CN/0706-5582
CANADIAN JOURNAL OF LIFE INSURANCE. [Can. j. life insur.]. Vol. 1 (Sept. 1978)-. Periodical. English. ir. Price varies. Canadian Journal of Life, PO Box 365, Elmira Ontario N3B 2Z7 Canada. **Tel** (519)669-2693. **ED** R. Alastair Rickard. **DD** 368.3/2/00971. **Bk Rev.** available in microform. Documents available from UMI Article Clearinghouse.
Desc: A magazine for those with a thoughtful interest in the life insurance business.
Ind/Abst ABI/INFORM Glob. Ed.

CN/0836-4001
CANADIAN LIFE AND HEALTH INSURANCE FACTS. [Can. life health insur. facts]. **Added/Corp** Canadian Life and Health Insurance Association. (1986)-. English. an. 5.00Can$. Canadian Life and Health Insurance Association, 1 Queen Street East, Suite 1700, Toronto Ontario M5C 2X9 Canada. **Tel** (416)777-2221. **DD** 368.3/00971. ***Formed by the union of*** *Canadian Health Insurance Facts, 0829-2086* ***and*** *Canadian Life Insurance Facts, 0068-9157.*

CN
CANADIAN PROPERTY AND CASUALTY INSURANCE SERVICE : QUARTERLY REPORT. Main/Corp Data Resources of Canada. **VFOAT** Insurance Service: Quarterly. V. 1- April 1979-. Periodical. English. qt. Data Resources of Canada, 80 Bloor Street West/Suite 505, Toronto Ontario M5S 2V1 Canada. **LC** HG8550; .A33A. **DD** 368.5/00971.

CN/0008-5251
CANADIAN UNDERWRITER. [Can. underwrit.]. (1934)-. Periodical. English. mo. 24.95Can$ (one year), 39.00Can$ (two year), 54.00Can$ (three year) Canada; 40.00Can$ (one year), 64.00Can$ (two year), 90.00Can$ (three year) other. Southam Information and Technology Group Inc., 1450 Don Mills Road, Don Mills Ontario M3B 2X7 Canada. **Tel** (416)445-6641, (800)668-2374, FAX (416)442-2261. available on microfilm and microfiche from University Microfilms International (UMI). Documents available from UMI Article Clearinghouse.
Ind/Abst ABI/INFORM Glob. Ed.; Ins. Period. Index.

CN/0317-1264
CANADIAN UNDERWRITER. ANNUAL STATISTICAL REVIEW. See Insurance-Abstracting, Bibliographies and Statistics.

US
CAPITOL REPORTER. See Business-Banking and Finance.

US/1056-814X
CAPTIVE INSURANCE COMPANY DIRECTORY. (CAPTIVE INSURANCE COMPANY DIRECTORY / COMPILED AND EDITED BY THE STAFF OF RISK PLANNING GROUP, INC.). [Capt. insur. co. dir.]. **Added/Corp** Risk Planning Group. Tillinghast, Nelson & Warren. Tillinghast (Firm). (1982)-. Directory. English. an. $150.00 North America; £80.00 other. Tillinghast Publications, 695 East Main Street, Suite 600, Stamford CT 06901. **Tel** (203)326-5400, FAX (203)326-5498. **ED** Corinne Rammming. **DD** 368. ***Continues in part*** *Risk Management Reports, 0199-6827.*
Desc: Contains the most current information on captive insurance companies, parent/sponsors, and managers in various domiciles. An invaluable tool for risk managers, investment advisors, bankers, insurance agents and brokers, captive managers, and others who need to keep informed of the captive movement.

US/1056-8158
CAPTIVE INSURANCE COMPANY REPORTS. (CAPTIVE INSURANCE COMPANY REPORTS : CICR.). [Capt. insur. co. rep.]. **Added/Corp** Risk Planning Group. Tillinghast (Firm). **VFOAT** CICR. (Oct. 1977)-. Periodical. English. Twelve times a year. $120.00 (universities); $185.00 other. Tillinghast Publications, 695 East Main Street, Suite 600, Stamford CT 06901. **Tel** (203)326-5400, FAX (203)326-5498. **ED** Hugh Rosenbaum. **DD** 368. cum. index. **Circ:** 1,500. available on microfilm from University Microfilms International (UMI).
Desc: A newsletter covering worldwide reinsurance, tax, and regulatory developments in the captive movement, edited by Hugh Rosembaum. Included are comprehensive reports and comparisons of new and existing captive domiciles, with frequent updates; reports on reinsurance and fronting conditions and their effects on captives; and the latest impact of tax legislation and court cases.

UK/0262-7701
CAPTIVE INSURANCE COMPANY REVIEW. [Captive insur. co. rev.]. (1981)-. English. Twelve times a year. £275.00 UK; $450.00 other. Risk & Insurance Research Group, 4 Henrietta Street, Covent Gard, London WC2E 8PS England. **Tel** 011 44 71 836 0614, FAX 011 44 71 379 6355, telex 23446. **DD** 368.

US/1065-1292
CAROLINA AGENT, THE. [Carol. agent]. **Added/Corp** Carolinas Association of Professional Insurance Agents. (19??)-. Periodical. English. qt. $18.00 (non-members), $14.00 (members). Carolinas Association of Professional Insurance Agents, 3109 Charles B Root Wynd, Raleigh NC 27612. **Tel** (919)782-5807. **ED** Sally Sherman. **DD** 368. **Ad Acc. Circ:** 800 (ctrl).

US/1061-9259
CASE MANAGER. [Case manag.]. **Added/Corp** Individual Case Management Association. (19??)-. Periodical. English. Four times a year (Feb., May, July, Oct.). $30.00. Systemedic Corporation, 10809 Executive Center Drive, Suite 105, Little Rock AR 72211. **Tel** (501)227-5553, FAX (501)227-8362. **ED** Nathania Sawyer. **DD** 650. **Ad Acc, Adv Mgr:** Pam Adelstein, **Tel** (501)227-5553. **Pr Rev. Circ:** 18,000.
Desc: This is publication of the Individual Case Management Association, a national organization providing educational, marketing and networking support to medical case managers and other related professionals who coordinate and manage services involving large or serious claims in both the health and workers' compensation claims industry. Articles, columns and departments address the need for shared experiences, practical information and treatment/care resources in the broad medical case management and managed care professions.

US/1046-6487
CASUALTY ACTUARIAL SOCIETY FORUM. (CASUALTY ACTUARIAL SOCIETY FORUM / CASUALTY ACTUARIAL SOCIETY.). [Casualty Actuar. Soc. forum]. **Added/Corp** Casualty Actuarial Society. **VFOAT** CAS Forum. (1987)-. Periodical. English. sa. $30.00 US; 40.00Can$ Canada. Casualty Acturial Society, 1100 North Glede #600, Arlington VA 22201. **Tel** (703)276-3100. **DD** 368.

UK/0268-0815
CASUALTY RETURN / LLOYD'S REGISTER OF SHIPPING. Added/Corp Lloyd's Register of Shipping (Firm : 1914-). (1984)-. English. an. $110.00. Lloyd's Register of Shipping / London, 71 Senchurch Street, London EC3 M4BS England. **Tel** 011 44 71 7099166. **(Subscription address:** Lloyd's Register of Shipping, 17 Battery Place, New York NY 10004.**) LC** HE565.A3; C37. ***Continues*** *Lloyd's Register of Shipping (Firm : 1914-) Casualty Return; Statistical Summary of Merchant Ships Totally Lost, Broken Up, etc., 0261-2712.*
Desc: An annual statistical summary, including all merchant ships totally lost or reported broken up during the year. Individual ships are also listed with brief details of casualty or disposal. Returns include information such as analysis of casualties and disposals by ship-type and registration and total losses categorized by type of loss.

Insurance

US/0748-951X
CGL REPORTER. [CGL report.]. **VFOAT** C.G.L. Reporter. **VAT** Comprehensive General Liability Reporter. Vol. 1, No. 1 (1983)-. Periodical. English. Twice a year. $180.00. International Risk Management Institute, 12222 Merit Drive, Suite 1660, Dallas TX 75251. **Tel** (214)960-7693, (800)827-4242, FAX (214)960-6037. **ED** Jill B. Berkeley. **DD** 368. Index available. cum. index. **Circ:** 600.
 Desc: A research tool indexing and summarizing major cases involving insurance coverage problems arising under the comprehensive general liability policy for use in insurance law litigation.

KO
CHABOTAP. **Added/Corp** Hanguk Chadongcha Pohom Chusik Hoesa. (19??)-. Periodical. Korean. mo. Hanguk Chandongcha Pohom Chusik Hoesa, 21-9 Cho-dong Chung-ku, Seoul Korea. **LC** HG9970.4.K6; C48.

US/0740-3925
CHECKBOOK'S GUIDE TO HEALTH INSURANCE PLANS FOR FEDERAL EMPLOYEES. **VFOAT** Guide to Health Insurance Plans for Federal Employees; Health Insurance Plans for Federal Employees. English. an. $3.95. Checkbook Insurance Guide, 806 15th Street NW/Suite 925, Washington DC 20005. **Tel** (202)347-9612. **ED** W Francis and others. **LC** JK794.H38; C47. **DD** 353.001/234.

US
CHILD HEALTH PLUS, HEALTH PLAN FOR KIDS : ANNUAL REPORT TO THE GOVERNOR & LEGISLATURE, CHILD HEALTH INSURANCE PLAN. **Added/Corp** New York (State). Dept. of Health. **VFOAT** Annual Report to the Governor & Legislature, Child Health Insurance Plan. (1991)-. English. New York State Health Department, Empire State Plaza Tower Building, Room 1408, Albany NY 12237. **Tel** (518)474-2011, FAX (518)474-4471.

US
CHRONOLOGICAL SUMMARY OF OREGON'S UNEMPLOYMENT INSURANCE PROGRAM FROM THE BEGINNING OF THE OPERATION TO DATE / PREPARED BY RESEARCH & STATISTICS SECTION. **Added/Corp** Oregon. Employment Division. Research and Statistics Section. (1980)-. English. an. Oregon Department of Human Resources Development, 155 Cottage Street NE, Salem OR 97310. **LC** HD7096.U6; O694. **DD** 353.97950082/56. **Continues** Chronological Summary of Oregon's Unemployment Insurance Program.

US/0743-3840
CLAIMS ADMINISTRATION, INSURANCE, TORT COURT DECISIONS DIGEST. (CLAIMS ADMINISTRATION - INSURANCE - TORT COURT DECISIONS DIGEST / AMERICAN INSURANCE ASSOCIATION.). English. wk. American Insurance Association Serv Group, PO Box 2095, Rahway NJ 07065. **Tel** (201)388-0332. **LC** KF1247.8; .C55. **DD** 346.7303; 347.3063. **Continues** Claims Administration Digest Court Decisions, 0743-3875.

US/0743-3859
CLAIMS ADMINISTRATION, WORKERS' COMPENSATION COURT DECISIONS DIGEST. (CLAIMS ADMINISTRATION - WORKERS' COMPENSATION COURT DECISIONS DIGEST / AMERICAN INSURANCE ASSOCIATION.). Began in 1982. English. wk. American Insurance Association Serv Group, PO Box 2095, Rahway NJ 07065. **Tel** (201)388-0332. **LC** KF3613.36; .C55. **Continues** Claims Administration Workers' Compensation Digest Court Decisions, 0743-3867.

US/0895-7991
CLAIMS (SEATTLE, WASH.). (CLAIMS.). [Claims]. Vol. 35, No. 10 (Oct. 1987)-. Periodical. English. mo. $38.00 US; $53.00 Canada; $93.00 other. Insurance Week Inc., 1001 Fourth Avenue Plaza, Suite 3029, Seattle WA 98154. **Tel** (206)624-6965, FAX (206)624-5021. **ED** Merle D. Gors. **DD** 368. **Bk Rev**. **Ad Acc**. **Circ:** 6,300. **Continues** Insurance Adjuster, 0020-4579.
 Desc: Contains news and features regarding property-casualty claims field.

US/0277-9595
COLORADO INSURANCE INDUSTRY STATISTICAL REPORT. See Insurance-Abstracting, Bibliographies and Statistics.

US/0743-5037
COLORADO MEDICINE. DIRECTORY OF PHYSICIANS. *Title Change.* **Main/Corp** Colorado Medical Society. **Added/Corp** Copic Trust. **VFOAT** Colorado Medicine Directory of Physicians; Directory of Physicians, Colorado. (1980)-(19??). English. an. Colorado Medical Society, PO Box 17550, Denver CO 80217. **Tel** (303)779-5455. **NLM** W 22 AC6 C718c. **Continues** Directory of Physicians, 0420-0640. **Continued by** Colorado Medical Society Physician's Resource Book.

CN/0382-7038
COMMENT (DON MILLS). (COMMENT.). [Comment]. **VFOAT** C L U Comment. No. 1- Jan. 1967-. Periodical. English (French). bm. Institute of Chartered Life Underwriters of Canada, 41 Lesmill Road, Don Mills Ontario M3B 2T3 Canada. **Tel** (416)444-5251. Index available. **Circ:** 25,000 (ctrl).

US
COMMUNITIES PARTICIPATING IN THE NATIONAL FLOOD INSURANCE PROGRAM. Government Publication. English. US Department of Housing and Urban Development, 451 Seventh Street SW, Washington DC 20401. **Tel** (202)708-0980, FAX (202)708-0299.

US
COMPARISON OF STATE UNEMPLOYMENT INSURANCE LAWS. **Added/Corp** United States. Unemployment Insurance Service. (19??)-. Government Publication. English. ir. $45.00 US; $56.25 other. Superintendent of Documents, US Government Printing Office, Washington DC 20402. **Tel** (202)275-3328, FAX (202)786-2377.

ZA
COMPENSATION MIRROR. See Economics-Labor.

US/0732-5282
COMPENSATION (WASHINGTON, D.C. : 1982). See Economics-Labor.

US/0742-924X
CONNECTICUT INSURANCE LAW REVIEW, THE. See Law.

US/1048-9851
CONTINGENCIES (WASHINGTON, D.C.). (CONTINGENCIES.). [Contingencies]. **Added/Corp** American Academy of Actuaries. (1989)-. Periodical. English. bm (6 issues). $24.00. American Academy of Actuaries, 1720 I Street Northwest, 7th Floor, Washington DC 20006. **Tel** (202)223-8196, FAX (202)872-1948. **ED** Dana Murphy. **DD** 368. Index available. **Bk Rev**, (Qty: 10-12/yr). **Ad Acc**, **Adv Mgr:** J. Solomon. **Pr Rev**. **Circ:** 20,000 (ctrl).
 Desc: In-depth insight into the world of actuarial analysis and logic. Timely features on how the actuarial profession impacts daily financial and business decisions.

US/0361-9400
CONTINUOUS WAGE AND BENEFIT HISTORY. See Economics-Labor.

UK
CORPORATE COVER. Corporate Report. English. Eleven times a year. £60.00 UK; £70.00 Europe; £75.00 other. Euromoney Publications PLC, Nestor House, Playhouse Yard, London EC4Z 5EX England. **Tel** 011 44 71 779 8888, FAX 011 44 71 779 8617, telex 290700 EUROMON G.
 Desc: Only specialist commercial insurance and risk management magazine produced for the information needs of the European insurance buyer and commercial broker. Contains the latest news and analysis from the marketplace with specialist articles on insurance and risk management practices.

CN/1182-610X
CORPUS WORKERS' COMPENSATION HANDBOOK. [Corpus work. compens. handb.]. **Added/Corp** Corpus Information Services. **VFOAT** Worker's Compensation Handbook. No. 1 (1990)-. English. te. 197.00Can$. Southam Information and Technology Group Inc., 1450 Don Mills Road, Don Mills Ontario M3B 2X7 Canada. **Tel** (416)445-6641, (800)668-2374, FAX (416)442-2261. **DD** 368.4/1/00971.

AT/0312-6757
COVER NOTE SYDNEY. [Cover note Syd.]. (1975)-. Periodical. English. wk. 415.00Aus$. Newsletter Information Service, PO Box 693, Manly New South Wales 2095 Australia. **Tel** 011 61 2 9777500. **DD** 368.994.

US/8755-7444
COVERAGE (CHAMPAIGN, ILL.), THE. (THE COVERAGE.). Vol. 1 (Fall 1984)-. Periodical. English. qt. Eisner-Endsley, 1004 Harrington, Champaign IL 61821. **DD** 368.

US/0162-2706
CPCU JOURNAL. [CPCU j.]. **Main/Corp** Society of Chartered Property and Casualty Underwriters. **VFOAT** Journal. **VAT** Chartered Property and Casualty Underwriters Journal. Vol. 31 Mar. (1978)-. Periodical. English. qt (4 issues). $20.00. Society of Chartered Property and Casual Underwriters, Kahler Hall, Providence Road CB#9, Malvern PA 19355. **Tel** (215)251-2743. **ED** Michael L. Murray. **LC** HG8011; .S63. **DD** 368/.005. Index available. cum. index. **Bk Rev**. **Ad Acc**. **Circ:** 20,000 (ctrl). available on microfilm and microfiche from University Microfilms International (UMI); available on an online database (file 15/Full-Text) from DIALOG. Documents available from UMI Article Clearinghouse, UMI Article Clearinghouse. **Continues** CPCU Annals, 0037-9824.
 Desc: Features articles and commentary by leading insurance and business practitioners about property/casualty insurance topics and general business practices.
 Ind/Abst ABI/INFORM Glob. Ed.; ABI Inform Ondisc (March 1978-); Gen. BusinessFile (1992-); Ins. Period. Index; UMI ABI/Inform--Bus. Period. Ondisc [Full Txt.].

US/0007-8883
CPCU NEWS. **Main/Corp** Society of Chartered Property and Casualty Underwriters. **VAT** Society of Chartered Property & Casualty Underwriters News. (19??)-. Periodical. English. mo (10 issues). $9.00. Society of Chartered Property and Casual Underwriters, Kahler Hall, Providence Road CB#9, Malvern PA 19355. **Tel** (215)251-2743.

US/1054-1063
CREDIT INSURANCE NEWSLETTER, THE. [Credit insur. newsl.]. Vol. 1, No. 1 (Feb. 1991)-. Newsletter. English. Four times a year (Apr., June, Sept., Dec.). $75.00. Creditre Corporation, 4107 Greenway Court, Colleyville TX 76034. **Tel** (817)788-8121. **DD** 332.

US/0899-6350
CRITTENDEN INSURANCE MARKETS, COMMERCIAL LINES. [Crittenden insur. mark. commer. lines]. **Added/Corp** Crittenden Newsletters, Inc. **VFOAT** Crittenden Insurance Markets; Insurance Markets, Commercial Lines. (1986)-. Periodical. English. ir (49 issues per year). $387.00. Crittenden Research Inc., PO Box 1150, Novato CA 94948. **Tel** (415)382-2400, FAX (415)382-2476. **DD** 368.

US/1044-9884
CSR ADVISOR, THE. [CSR advis.]. **VAT** Customer Service Representative Advisor. Vol. 1, No. 1 (July 1989)-. Periodical. English. mo. $136.00 US; $163.00 other. Standard Publishing Company, 155 Federal Street, Boston MA 02110. **Tel** (617)457-0604, (617)457-0600, FAX (617)457-0608. **ED** Diana Montgomery. **DD** 368. Index available.

US
CYCLOPEDIA OF INSURANCE IN THE UNITED STATES. 1st Ed; 1890-. Periodical. English. Index Publishing, 123 Will Street, New York NY 10007. **LC** HG8523. **DD** 368.973.
 Desc: Issuess for 1916-include section: Biographical sketches.

GW/0012-0618
DEUTSCHE RENTENVERSICHERUNG. (DEUTSCHE RENTENVERSICHERUNG / HERAUSGEGEBEN VOM VERBAND DEUTSCHER RENTENVERSICHERUNGSTRAGER.). [Dtsch. Rentenversicher.]. **Added/Corp** Verband Deutscher Rentenversicherungstrager. (1962)-. Periodical. German. ir (published every 5th week). DM160.00. Wirtschaftsdienst Verlag UND, Druckerei GmbH Lange Str 13, W 6000 Frankfurt 1 Germany.

IT/0012-2653
DIFESA SOCIALE. See Public Health and Safety.

CN
DIGEST OF BENEFIT ENTITLEMENT PRINCIPLES. See Economics-Labor.

CN/0710-2429
DIRECTORY - CANADIAN LIFE AND HEALTH INSURANCE ASSOCIATION. (DIRECTORY.). [Dir. - Can. Life Health Ins. Assoc.]. **Main/Corp** Canadian Life and Health Insurance Association. **VFOAT** Repertoire. **VAT** Repertoire - Association Canadienne des Compagnies d'Assurances de Personnes. 1981/82-. Directory. English (French). Canadian Life and Health Insurance Association, 1 Queen Street East, Suite 1700, Toronto Ontario M5C 2X9 Canada. **Tel** (416)777-2221. **DD** 368.3/0025/71. **Continues** Canadian Life Insurance Association. Directory, 0707-6150.

UK
DIRECTORY OF INSURANCE BROKERS, LOSS ADJUSTORS AND CLAIMS ASSESSORS, THE. Directory. English. an. £0.80. A P Crawley, 13/14 Charterhouse Square, London EC1M 6AY England. **LC** HG8596; .D5. **DD** 368/.0025/42. **Continues** Directory of Insurance Brokers and Claims Assessors.

US
DIRECTORY OF INSURANCE COMPANIES LICENSED IN NEW YORK STATE. Directory. English. New York Insurance Department, 160 West Broadway, New York NY 10013. **Tel** (212)602-0434, FAX (212)602-0437. **LC** HG8526.N7; A33. **DD** 368/.0025/747. **Continues** Names and Addresses of Insurance Companies Listed in New York State Issued by the New York Insurance Dept.

Insurance

US/0732-1767
DIRECTORY OF INSURANCE COMPANIES (SANTA FE, N.M.). (DIRECTORY OF INSURANCE COMPANIES.). Directory. English. an. **LC** HG8526.N6; D57. **DD** 368/.0025/789.

US/0732-9857
DIRECTORY / SECTION OF TORT AND INSURANCE PRACTICE. See Law.

IT
DIRITTO E TECNICA DELLA CIRCOLAZIONE STRADALE E ASSICURAZIONE OBBLIGATORIA DI RCA. See Law.

●IT
DIRITTO ED ECONOMIA DELL'ASSICURAZIONE. See Law.

US/0195-4482
DISABILITY NEWSLETTER. (19??)-. Newsletter. English. Three times a year (Mar., June, Nov.). $85.00. Milliman & Robertson Inc., 8500 Normdale Lake Boulevard, Suite 1850, Minneapolis MN 55437. **Tel** (612)897-5300, FAX (612)897-5301. **Circ:** 800.
Desc: Covers issues and current developments in both individual and group disability income insurance, long term care insurance, and continuing care retirement communities. Addresses all aspects of the disability income insurance field, including claim administration, underwriting, financial analysis, rehabilitation, and marketing.

US/1046-6444
DISCUSSION PAPER PROGRAM / CASUALTY ACTUARIAL SOCIETY. [Discuss. pap. program - Casualty Actuar. Soc.]. **Added/Corp** Casualty Actuarial Society. (1979)-. Monographic series. English. Price varies per volume. Casualty Acturial Society, 1100 North Glede #600, Arlington VA 22201. **Tel** (703)276-3100. **DD** 368.

CN
DISPOSITIONS DES REGIMES ET LES COTISANTS EN ..., LES. See Economics-Labor.

US
DISTRICT PAID INSURANCE PROGRAMS IN CALIFORNIA SCHOOL DISTRICTS. Main/Corp California. Bureau of School Apportionments and Reports. English. $2.50. California State Department of Education, PO Box 944272, 721 Capitol Mall, Sacramento CA 94244. **Tel** (916)657-2451, (916)445-7608, FAX (916)657-3000. **LC** LB2842.2; .C19C. **DD** 331.2/55.

US
DUN'S GUIDE TO GROUP INSURANCE PLANS. Added/Corp Dun's Marketing Services. (1987/1988)-. Directory. English. an. Dun & Bradstreet Information Services, 3 Sylvan Way, Parsippany NJ 07054. **Tel** (201)605-6000, (800)526-0651. **LC** HG8058; .G76. **DD** 368.3/0025/73. **Continues** Group Insurance Standard Directory.

UK/0965-9676
EAST EUROPEAN INSURANCE REPORT. [East Eur. insur. rep.]. Periodical. English. mo. £375.00 UK; £388.00 other. Financial Times Business Information Ltd., Tower House, Southampton Street, London WC2E 7HA England. **Tel** 011 44 71 353 1040.
Ind/Abst PROMT [Full Txt.]; PTS Newsl. Database [Full Txt.].

NE
EISS YEARBOOK / ANNUAIRE EISS. See Sociology-Social Services and Welfare.

US/0013-6808
EMPLOYEE BENEFIT PLAN REVIEW. [Empl. benefit plan rev.]. **Added/Corp** Charles D. Spencer & Associates. (1946)-. Periodical. English. mo (12 issues). $56.00 North America; $98.00 other. Charles D. Spencer & Associates, 250 South Wacker Drive, Suite 600, Chicago IL 60606-5834. **Tel** (312)993-7900, FAX (312)993-7910. **ED** Bruce F. Spencer. **LC** HD7106.U5; E55. **DD** 331.252. **NLM** W1 EM696P. **CODEN** EBPVAL. **Bk Rev. Ad Acc. Circ:** 15,200 (ctrl) available on microfilm and microfiche from University Microfilms International (UMI). Documents available from UMI Article Clearinghouse.
Desc: Current developments in corporate retirement plans and health care programs including pensions, profit-sharing, flexible benefits, ESOPS, medical, life, disability, dental, PPO, HMO, and VEBA's.
Ind/Abst ABI/INFORM Glob. Ed.; ABI Inform Ondisc (Sept. 1975-); Acad. Search (July 1993-); Account. Art.; Bus. Index (1985-); Bus. Period. Index; Bus. Source (Jan. 1993-); Cumul. Index Nurs. Allied Health Lit.; Fed. Tax Artic.; Gen. BusinessFile (1985-); Gen. Period. Index (1985-); Health Plan. Adminis.; Hospit. Health Admin. Index (1980-1987); INFO-SOUTH Abstr.; Ins. Period. Index; Mag. Search; Manage. Contents (1974-); PROMT; UMI ABI/Inform--Bus. Period. Ondisc [Full Txt.]; Vocat. Search (July 1993-); Wilson Bus. Abstr.

US/0740-9087
EMPLOYERS' HEALTH COSTS SAVINGS LETTER. See Medical Science and Technology.

US/0735-3286
EMPLOYMENT SECURITY STATISTICAL BULLETIN. See Economics-Abstracting, Bibliographies and Statistics.

SW
ENSKILDA FORSAKRINGSFORETAG. See Insurance-Abstracting, Bibliographies and Statistics.

VE
ESTADISTICA Y ACTUARIADO. See Insurance-Abstracting, Bibliographies and Statistics.

CL/0577-8174
ESTADISTICAS (CHILE. SERVICIO DE SEGURO SOCIAL). See Insurance-Abstracting, Bibliographies and Statistics.

UK
EUROPEAN INSURANCE MARKET. English. Twenty-six times a year. £305.00 UK; $505.00 US & Canada. DYP Insurance Reinsurance Res. Grp. Ltd., 181 Queen Victoria St. Bridge House, London EC4V 4DD England. **Tel** 011 44 71 236 2175, FAX 011 44 71 489 1487.

UK/0960-0981
EUROPEAN INSURANCE MARKET. [Eur. insur. market]. (1990)-. Periodical. English. ir. $470.00. DYP Insurance Reinsurance Res. Grp. Ltd., 181 Queen Victoria St. Bridge House, London EC4V 4DD England. **Tel** 011 44 71 236 2175, FAX 011 44 71 489 1487. **DD** 368.94.

UK
EUROPEAN INSURANCE STRATEGIES. English. ir. $595.00. Evandale Publishing Ltd, 3840 East Castle Street, London W1N 7PE England. **Tel** 011 44 71 436 7028.

US/0273-026X
EXAMINATION OF THE FINANCIAL STATEMENTS OF FHA INSURANCE OPERATIONS. [Exam. financ. statements FHA insur. oper.]. **Main/Corp** United States. General Accounting Office. **VAT** Examination of the Financial Statements of Federal Housing Administration Insurance Operations. English. an. US General Accounting Office / District of Columbia, 441 G Street NW, Room 4528, Washington DC 20548. **Tel** (202)275-2812. **LC** HG9992.3; .U54B. **DD** 353.0072/31.

US/0740-1388
EXCESS EXPRESS. (19??)-. Periodical. English. mo. Comes with Strategies for Insurance Coverages. Merritt Company, 1661 Ninth Street, PO Box 955, Santa Monica CA 90406. **Tel** (310)450-7234, (800)638-7597, FAX (310)396-4563. **ED** Heinz J. Pulverman. **Bk Rev. Circ:** 2,000.
Desc: Information on new and innovative insurance techniques; how to use both conventional and specialty markets.

US
EXPERIENCE BY STATE (BY LINE). LIFE/HEALTH. REPORT FORMAT, ACCIDENT & HEALTH LINES, FIVE YEAR STUDY. VFOAT Life/Health. (1990)-. English. an. AM Best Company, Ambest Road, Oldwick NJ 08858. **Tel** (908)439-2200 ext. 5653, telex 837744. **LC** HG8941; .B476. **DD** 368.3/8/006573. **Continues** Best's Executive Data Service. Life-Health Industry Marketing Results. Five Year Experience by State Accident & Health Lines, 0743-5835.

US
EXPERIENCE BY STATE (BY LINE). LIFE/HEALTH. REPORT FORMAT, ACCIDENT & HEALTH LINES, ONE YEAR STUDY. VFOAT Best's Life-Health Industry Marketing Results. (1990)-. English. AM Best Company, Ambest Road, Oldwick NJ 08858. **Tel** (908)439-2200 ext. 5653, telex 837744. **LC** IN PROCESS.

US
EXPERIENCE BY STATE (BY LINE). LIFE/HEALTH. REPORT FORMAT, LIFE LINE, FIVE YEAR STUDY. VFOAT Life/Health; Life Health; Best's Executive Data Service, Five Year by Line/By State Marketing History. (1990)-. English. an. AM Best Company, Ambest Road, Oldwick NJ 08858. **Tel** (908)439-2200 ext. 5653, telex 837744. **LC** .B4765. **DD** 368.3/006/573. **Continues** Best's Executive Data Service. Life-Health Industry Marketing Results. Five Year Experience by State Life Lines, 0743-5304.

US
EXPERIENCE BY STATE (BY LINE). LIFE/HEALTH. REPORT FORMAT, LIFE LINES ONE YEAR STUDY. (1990)-. English. AM Best Company, Ambest Road, Oldwick NJ 08858. **Tel** (908)439-2200 ext. 5653, telex 837744.

US
EXPERIENCE BY STATE (BY LINE). PROPERTY/CASUALTY. REPORT FORMAT A8, FIVE YEAR STUDY. Added/Corp A.M. Best Company. **VFOAT** Property/Casualty; Property Casualty. Best Database Services, P/C Experience by State (by Line). (1990)-. English. an. $68.00 per line plus $125.00 per state. AM Best Company, Ambest Road, Oldwick NJ 08858. **Tel** (908)439-2200 ext. 5653, telex 837744. **Continues** Best's Executive Data Service. Property and Casualty Insurance. Report A 8, Five Year Experience by State, 0275-6242.
Desc: Summarizes the experience of the next 50 largest carriers.

US
EXPERIENCE BY STATE (BY LINE). REPORT FORMAT, A5, TWO YEAR STUDY. PROPERTY/CASUALTY. VFOAT Property/Casualty. Report Format, A5, Two Year Study.; Best Datbase Services, P/C Experience by State (By Line). (1990)-. English. $68.00 per line plus $125.00 per state. AM Best Company, Ambest Road, Oldwick NJ 08858. **Tel** (908)439-2200 ext. 5653, telex 837744.
Desc: Tool for making marketing and underwriting comparisons that go beyond the previous year's data. Provides a two-year study of critical trends in premiums written.

US
EXPERIENCE BY STATE (BY LINE). REPORT FORMAT, A6, TWO YEAR STUDY. PROPERTY/CASUALTY. VFOAT Property/Casualty. Report Format, A6, Two Year Study; Property Casualty. Report Format, A6, Two Year Study. (1990)-. English. $68.00 per line plus $125.00 per state. AM Best Company, Ambest Road, Oldwick NJ 08858. **Tel** (908)439-2200 ext. 5653, telex 837744.
Desc: Details up to 50 state leaders and direct writers with by-line results given for each state in which a carrier is a significant writer.

US
EXPERIENCE BY STATE (BY LINE). REPORT FORMAT, A7, FIVE YEAR STUDY. PROPERTY/CASUALTY. Added/Corp A.M. Best Company. **VFOAT** Property/Casualty. Report Format, A7, Five Year Study; Property Casualty. Report Format, A7, Five Year Study. (1990)-. English. $68.00 per line plus $125.00 per state. AM Best Company, Ambest Road, Oldwick NJ 08858. **Tel** (908)439-2200 ext. 5653, telex 837744.
Desc: Examines the by-state, by-line premium-loss record of the 50 largest property/casualty companies.

US/0098-6402
EXPERIENCE OF FEDERAL AGENCIES UNDER THE PROGRAM OF SELF-INSURING FIDELITY LOSSES PURSUANT TO PUBLIC LAW 92-310. Main/Corp United States. Dept. of the Treasury. **VAT** Experience of Federal Agencies Under the Program of Self-Insuring Fidelity Losses Pursuant to Public Law Ninety-Two-Three Hundred and Ten. English. Department of Treasury, 15th Street and Pennsylvania Avenue NW, Washington DC 20220. **Tel** (202)566-2000. **LC** HG9970.S5; U56A. **DD** 353.001/324.

UK
EXPORT FINANCE. (1982)-. Periodical. English. $125.00. Euromoney Publications PLC, Nestor House, Playhouse Yard, London EC4Z 5EX England. **Tel** 011 44 71 779 8888, FAX 011 44 71 779 8617, telex 290700 EUROMON G. **ED** James Ball and Martin Knight.
Desc: Provides analysis of the techniques and practices of export finance and export finance agencies. Examines in detail the export finance, insurance and guarantee systems of 36 countries worldwide, including lists of all the schemes available, eligibility for finance and performance figures for the agencies described.

JA
FACT BOOK, NON-LIFE INSURANCE IN JAPAN. Main/Corp Nihon Songai Hoken Kyokai. English (Japanese). an. ¥65000. The Marine and Fire Insurance Association of Japan Inc, Non-Life Insurance Building, 9 Kanda Awajicho 2-chome, Chiyoda-ku, Tokyo Japan. **Tel** 255-1211, FAX 255-5376, telex 2224829. **ED** Takashi Kumakiri. **LC** HG8705; .A34A. **DD** 368/.952. **Circ:** 900.

US
FACTBOOK AND MEMBERSHIP DIRECTORY / MORTGAGE INSURANCE COMPANIES OF AMERICA. Main/Corp Mortgage Insurance Companies of America. (19??)-.

Insurance

Directory. English. an. Free on request. Mortgage Insurance Company of America, 805 15th Street NW, Suite 1110, Washington DC 20005. **Tel** (202)371-2899. **ED** Patty Kosciuszko. **LC** HG9992; .M67. *Continues Mortgage Insurance Companies of America. Factbook and Directory.*
Desc: Purpose is to explain the mortgage insurance industry and introduce its participants.

CN/0319-1826
FACTS OF THE GENERAL INSURANCE INDUSTRY IN CANADA. Added/Corp
Insurance Bureau of Canada. (1972)-. English (French). an. price varies per volume. Insurance Bureau of Canada, 181 University Avenue, 13th Floor, Toronto Ontario M5H 3M7 Canada. **Tel** (416)362-2031, FAX (416)361-5952. **DD** 368/.971.
Desc: Compendium of statistics and general information on property/automobile insurance industry in Canada.

CN/0836-3374
FAITS SUR LES ASSURANCES DE PERSONNES AU CANADA.
[Faits assur. pers. Can.]. (1986 Ed.)-. French. an. Free. Association Canadienne des Compagnies d'Assurances de Personnes, 666 Ouest, Rue Sherbrooke, Montreal Quebec H3A 1E7. **DD** 368.3/00971. *Formed by the union of Faits sur l'Assurance-Vie au Canada, 0317-5359 and Faits sur l'Assurance-Maladie au Canada, 0831-9596.*

US
FEDERAL & STATE INSURANCE WEEK.
VFOAT Federal and State Insurance Week; Insurance Week. (1987)-. Periodical. English. wk. $347.00. JR Publishing Inc., PO Box 6654, McLean VA 22106. **Tel** (703)532-2235. **LC** HG8501; .F43. wk.available on an online database (file 636/Full-Text) from DIALOG.
Ind/Abst PTS Newsl. Database [Full Txt.].

US
FEDERAL DISASTER ASSISTANCE PROGRAM, INSURANCE HANDBOOK FOR PUBLIC ASSISTANCE. VFOAT
Insurance Handbook for Public Assistance. Government Publication. English. US Department of Housing and Urban Development, 451 Seventh Street SW, Washington DC 20401. **Tel** (202)708-0980, FAX (202)708-0299.

US
FEDERAL PERSONNEL MANUAL SYSTEM. FPM SUPPLEMENT 870-1. LIFE INSURANCE. See Public Administration-Civil Service.

US
FEDERAL TAXATION OF LIFE INSURANCE COMPANIES.
English. an. Matthew Bender & Company Inc., 1275 Broadway, Albany NY 12204. **Tel** (800)833-9844, (518)487-3000.

US/0887-0942
FEDERATION OF INSURANCE & CORPORATE COUNSEL QUARTERLY.
[Fed. Insur. Corp. Couns. q.]. **Added/Corp** Federation of Insurance & Corporate Counsel (U.S.). **VFOAT** Federation of Insurance and Corporate Counsel Quarterly; FICC Quarterly. Vol. 36, No. 1 (Fall 1985)-. Periodical. English. qt. $26.00; $20.00 (law college), $26.00 (all other) libraries. Federation of Insurance & Corporate Counsel, 302 Centre Lane, Walpole MA 02081. **Tel** (508)668-6859, FAX (508)668-6892. **ED** John J Kircher Marquette University Law School, 1103 West Wisconsin Avenue, Milwaukee, WI 53233 (editors telephone (414) 288-7095); Curr. Law Index (1985-); Gen. BusinessFile (1992-); Index Leg. Period.; Ins. Period. Index (199?-); Leg. Resour. Index (1985-); LegalTrac (1985-). **LC** K6; .E3. **DD** 346.73/086/05; 347.3068605. ctrl circ. available on microfilm and microfiche from University Microfilms International (UMI). Documents available from UMI Article Clearinghouse. *Continues Federation of Insurance Counsel Quarterly, 0430-2583.*
Ind/Abst ABI/INFORM Glob. Ed.; ABI Inform Ondisc (Fall 1987-); Curr. Law Index (1985-); Gen. BusinessFile (1992-); Index Leg. Period.; Ins. Period. Index (199?-); Leg. Resour. Index (1985-); LegalTrac (1985-).

●US
FEHB GUIDE FOR CSRS/FERS ANNUITANTS. Added/Corp
Federal Employees Health Benefits Program (U.S.) United States. Office of Personnel Management. Retirement and Insurance Group. **VFOAT** CSRS/FERS Annuitants. (1994)-. English. US Office of Personnel Management, 1900 E Street Northwest, Washington DC 20415. **Tel** (202)632-6256. *Continues Enrollment Information & Plan Comparison Chart for CSRS/FERS Annuitants.*

●US
FEHB GUIDE. OPEN SEASON FOR FEDERAL CIVILIAN EMPLOYEES / FEDERAL EMPLOYEES HEALTH BENEFITS PROGRAM. Added/Corp
Federal Employees Health Benefits Program (U.S.) United States. Office of Personnel Management. Retirement and Insurance Group. **VFOAT** Open Season for Federal Civilian Employees. (1994)-. English. US Office of Personnel Management, 1900 E Street Northwest, Washington DC 20415. **Tel** (202)632-6256. *Continues Enrollment Information & Plan Comparison Chart. Open Season for Federal Civilian Employees.*

●US
FEHB GUIDE. OPEN SEASON FOR FEDERAL CIVILIAN EMPLOYEES / FEDERAL EMPLOYEES HEALTH BENEFITS PROGRAM (LARGE PRINT EDITION). Added/Corp
Federal Employees Health Benefits Program (U.S.) United States. Office of Personnel Management. Retirement and Insurance Group. **VFOAT** Open Season for Federal Civilian Employees. (1994)-. English. US Office of Personnel Management, 1900 E Street Northwest, Washington DC 20415. **Tel** (202)632-6256. *Continues Enrollment Information & Plan Comparison Chart. Open Season for Federal Civilian Employees.*

●US
FEHB GUIDE. OPEN SEASON FOR FEDERAL CIVILIAN EMPLOYEES IN POSITIONS OUTSIDE THE CONTINENTAL UNITED STATES / FEDERAL EMPLOYEES HEALTH BENEFITS PROGRAM. Added/Corp
Federal Employees Health Benefits Program (U.S.) United States. Office of Personnel Management. Retirement and Insurance Group. **VFOAT** Open Season for Federal Civilian Employees in Positions Outside the Continental United States. (1994)-. English. US Office of Personnel Management, 1900 E Street Northwest, Washington DC 20415. **Tel** (202)632-6256. *Continues Enrollment Information & Plan Comparison Chart. Open Season for Federal Civilian Employees in Positions Outside the Continental United States.*

●US
FEHB GUIDE. OPEN SEASON FOR INDIVIDUALS ELIGIBLE TO ENROLL FOR TEMPORARY CONTINUATION OF COVERAGE, COVERAGE UNDER THE SPOUSE EQUITY LAW OR SIMILAR STATUTES PROVIDING COVERAGE TO FORMER SPOUSES / FEDERAL EMPLOYEES HEALTH BENEFITS PROGRAM. Added/Corp
Federal Employees Health Benefits Program (U.S.) United States. Office of Personnel Management. Retirement and Insurance Group. **VFOAT** Open Season for Individuals Eligible to Enroll for Temporary Continuation of Coverage, Coverage Under the Spouse Equity Law or Similar Statutes Provding Coverage to Former Spouses. (1994)-. English. US Office of Personnel Management, 1900 E Street Northwest, Washington DC 20415. **Tel** (202)632-6256. *Continues Enrollment Information & Plan Comparison Chart. Open Season for Individuals Eligible to Enroll for Temporary Continuation of Coverage, Coverage Under the Spouse Equity Law or Similar Statutes Provding Coverage to Former Spouses.*

●US
FEHB GUIDE. OPEN SEASON FOR INDIVIDUALS RECEIVING COMPENSATION FROM THE OFFICE OF WORKERS' COMPENSATION PROGRAMS (OWCP). Added/Corp
Federal Employees Health Benefits Program (U.S.) United States. Office of Personnel Management. Retirement and Insurance Group. **VFOAT** Open Season for Individuals Receiving Compensation from the Office of Workers' Compensation Programs (OWCP). (1994)-. English. US Office of Personnel Management, 1900 E Street Northwest, Washington DC 20415. **Tel** (202)632-6256. *Continues Enrollment Information & Plan Comparison Chart. Open Season for Individuals Receiving Compensation from the Office of Workers' Compensation Programs (OWCP).*

●US
FEHB GUIDE. OPEN SEASON FOR RETIREMENT SYSTEMS PARTICIPATING IN THE FEDERAL EMPLOYEES HEALTH BENEFITS PROGRAM. Added/Corp
Federal Employees Health Benefits Program (U.S.) United States. Office of Personnel Management. Retirement and Insurance Group. **VFOAT** Open Season for Retirement Systems Participating in the Federal Employees Health Benefits Program; Retirement Systems Participating in the Federal Employees Health Benefits Program. (1994)-. English. US Office of Personnel Management, 1900 E Street Northwest, Washington DC 20415. **Tel** (202)632-6256. *Continues Enrollment Information & Plan Comparison Chart. Open Season for Retirement Systems Participating in the Federal Employees Health Benefits Program.*

●US
FEHB GUIDE. OPEN SEASON FOR UNITED STATES POSTAL SERVICE EMPLOYEES / FEDERAL EMPLOYEES HEALTH BENEFITS PROGRAM. Added/Corp
Federal Employees Health Benefits Program (U.S.) United States. Office of Personnel Management. Retirement and Insurance Group. **VFOAT** Open Season for United States Postal Service Employees. (1994)-. English. US Office of Personnel Management, 1900 E Street Northwest, Washington DC 20415. **Tel** (202)632-6256. *Continues Enrollment Information & Plan Comparison Chart. Open Season for United States Postal Service Employees.*

CN/0225-2449
FELLOWSHIP PROGRAM - INSURANCE INSTITUTE OF CANADA. Title Change.
(FELLOWSHIP PROGRAM.). [Fellowsh. program - Insur. Inst. Can.]. **Main/Corp** Insurance Institute of Canada. **VFOAT** Programme F.I.A.C. **VAT** Programme Fellow Institute d'Assurance du Canada. 1979/80-. English (French). an. Insurance Institute of Canada, 55 University Avenue, Toronto Ontario M5J 2H7. **DD** 368/.007/1071. ctrl circ. *Formed by the union of Institut d'Assurance du Canada. Annuaire, 0225-2414 and Insurance Institute of Canada. Education Programs, 0702-7397. Continued by Programme F.I.A.C.*

US/0145-5656
FHA MONTHLY REPORT OF OPERATIONS. PROJECT MORTGAGE INSURANCE PROGRAMS. See Housing and Urban Development.

US/0747-6582
FIDELITY & SURETY NEWS : FSN. See Law.

●US/1066-7350
FINANCE, INSURANCE & REAL ESTATE USA. See Business-Banking and Finance.

US
FINANCIAL OPERATIONS AND ACCOUNTING PROCEDURES FOR INSURED MULTIFAMILY PROJECTS. See Housing and Urban Development.

US/0889-0552
FINANCIAL PLANNING FOCUS [SOUND RECORDING].
[Financ. plan. focus]. **Added/Corp** American Society of Chartered Life Underwriters. **VFOAT** Focus. (198?)-. Periodical. English. qt. $99.00 members; $129.00 nonmembers (print). American Society of CLU & ChFC, PO Box 59, Bryn Mawr PA 19010. **Tel** (215)526-2500, FAX (215)527-4010. **ED** Vince Mallon. **DD** 332. Index available. **Circ:** 2,500 (ctrl).

US/0270-5656
FINANCIAL REVIEW OF ALIEN INSURERS.
[Financ. rev. alien insur.]. **Main/Corp** National Association of Insurance Commissioners. **VFOAT** NAIC Financial Review of Alien Insurers. English. qt. $275.00. National Association of Insurance Commissioners, PO Box 263, Department 42, Kansas City MO 64193. **Tel** (816)842-3600, (816)374-7259, FAX (816)471-7004. **ED** Maxi Moody. **LC** HG8021; .N37A. **DD** 368/.0068/1. **Circ:** 250 (ctrl).
Desc: Contains financial data on foreign insurance companies doing business in the United States.

US/0149-0109
FINANCING THE OREGON UNEMPLOYMENT INSURANCE PROGRAM. See Economics-Abstracting, Bibliographies and Statistics.

US/0738-8187
FIRE AND CASUALTY, LIFE AND DISABILITY INSURANCE MANUAL.
Added/Corp California. Dept. of Insurance. (1982)-. English. an. **LC** HG9751.C2; A3. **DD** 368/.9794. *Continues Fire and Casualty Insurance Manual.*

US/0163-8882
FIRE CASUALTY & SURETY BULLETINS 301. STANDARD LINES SET. VAT
Fire Casualty and Surety Bulletins Three Hundred and One. (19??)-. English. an (three-volume set with monthly supplements). $297.00. National Underwriter Company, 505 Gest Street, Cincinnati OH 45203-0874. **Tel** (513)721-2140, (800)543-0874. Index available (free - on disk). available on diskette.

US
FIRE CASUALTY & SURETY BULLETINS 304. GUIDE TO POLICIES.
(19??)-. English. mo (two-volume set with monthly updates). $133.00. National Underwriter Company, 505 Gest Street, Cincinnati OH 45203-0874. **Tel** (513)721-2140, (800)543-0874. Index available (free - on disk). available on diskette.

Insurance

US
FIRE CASUALTY & SURETY BULLETINS 308. COMPANIES & COVERAGES. (19??)-. English. an (with monthly supplements). $108.00. National Underwriter Company, 505 Gest Street, Cincinnati OH 45203-0874. **Tel** (513)721-2140, (800)543-0874. Index available (free - on disk). available on diskette.

US/0163-8874
FIRE CASUALTY & SURETY BULLETINS 325. COMPLETE SERVICE. VAT Fire Casualty and Surety Bulletins Three Hundred and Twenty-Five. (19??)-. English. mo (six-volume set with monthly updates). $520.00. National Underwriter Company, 505 Gest Street, Cincinnati OH 45203-0874. **Tel** (513)721-2140, (800)543-0874. Index available (free - on disk). available on diskette.

●**US/1073-7111**
FLEXIBLE BENEFITS. (1993)-. English. mo. $202.00. Panel Publishers, A Division of Aspen Publishers, Inc., 7201 McKinney Circle, PO Box 990, Frederick MD 21705-9727. **Tel** (800)638-8437. **(Subscription address:** Aspen Publishers Inc., PO Box 990, Frederick MD 21701.**) ED** Gregory E. Mathews, CPA and Bruce G. Carveth.
Desc: Provides advice from experts, excerpts from current literature, regulatory and legal updates and how-to articles on the design, administration, communication, cost factors, and advantages of flexible benefit plans.

US/0743-3441
FLORIDA UNDERWRITER. [Fla. underwrit.]. **Added/Corp** National Underwriter Company. Vol. 1, No. 1 (May 1984)-. Periodical. English. Twelve times a year. $16.50 one year; $27.50 two years. National Underwriter Company, 505 Gest Street, Cincinnati OH 45203-0874. **Tel** (513)721-2140, (800)543-0874. **DD** 368.
Desc: Special issues on meeting planning, auto insurance, conventions, automation, etc. Also includes excess and surplus lines directory, life/health broker directory, and a statistical review.

US
FLORIDA WORKERS COMPENSATION INSTITUTE REPORTER. English. Sixteen times a year (Published semi-monthly during the regular legislative session, and monthly during the balance of the year.). $177.00. Healthtrac Inc, PO Box 13552, Tallahassee FL 32317. **Tel** (904)222-8180, (800)533-5259, FAX (904)222-4893. **ED** Creston Nelson-Morrill. **Circ:** 290 (ctrl).
Desc: Information and news on workers compensation in Florida.

CN/0384-5958
FORESIGHT (MONTREAL). (FORESIGHT.). V. 1- July 1976-. Periodical. English. bm. $15.00. Insurance Brokers' Association of the Province of Quebec, Room 1570, 550 Sherbrooke Street West, Montreal Quebec H3A 1C8. **DD** 368/.9/714.

SW/0015-7880
FORSAKRINGSTIDNINGEN (STOCKHOLM, SWEDEN). (FORSAKRINGSTIDNINGEN : FT.). **Added/Corp** Svenska Forsakringsbolags Riksforbund. **VFOAT** FT; F.T. (1964)-. Periodical. Swedish. ir. 70.00. Forsakringsbolagens Serviceaktiebolag, Strandvagen 5 B, 114 51 Stockholm Sweden. **LC** HG8015; .F62. **NLM** W1 FO113.

NO/0801-0056
FORSIKRINGSSELSKAPER. Main/Corp Norway. Forsikringsradet. **VFOAT** Societes d'Assurances. 1912-. Norwegian. I Kommisjon Hos H Aschehoug Og Universitetsforlaget, Sehesteds Plass, Oslo 1 Norway. **LC** HA1501; subser. **DD** 368/.9481.

US
FORUM (CHICAGO), THE. See Law.

CN/0380-3147
FORUM (DON MILLS). (FORUM.). **Added/Corp** Life Underwriters Association of Canada. (May 1971)-. Periodical. English (French). Ten times a year. 30.00Can$. Life Underwriters Association of Canada, 41 Lesmill Road, Don Mills Ontario M3B 2T3 Canada. **Tel** (416)444-5251, (800)563-5822, FAX (416)444-8031. **ED** Valarie Osborne. Index available. **Bk Rev. Ad Acc. Circ:** 18,500 (ctrl). **Supersedes** Life Underwriters' News, 0024-323X.
Desc: Provides industry news along with information on provincial and federal government activities affecting the industry and sales ideas to life insurance agents.

US/0016-0105
FRATERNAL MONITOR, THE. VFOAT FM. Vol. 1, No. 1 (Aug. 1, 1890)-. Periodical. English. mo. $25.00. Fraternal Monitor, 7233 North Olney Street, Indianapolis IN 46240. **Tel** (317)842-3636. **(Subscription address:** Dearborn Financial Publishing, Inc., Subscription Office, PO Box 830350, Birmingham AL 35283-0350.**)**

US
FRAUD BUREAU NEWSLETTER. Added/Corp California. Dept. of Insurance. Fraud Bureau. Vol. 5, No. 1 (April 1990)-. Newsletter. English. **LC** KFC290.A15; F7. **Continues** Fraud Bureau : [Newsletter].

US/0016-1748
FROM THE STATE CAPITALS. INSURANCE REGULATION. [From state cap., Insur. regul.]. **VFOAT** Insurance Regulation. (19??)-. Periodical. English. wk. $211.50 (one year) $378.00 (two year) public and institutional libraries; $235.00 (one year), $420.00 (two year) other. Wakeman Walworth Inc., 300 North Washington Street #204, Alexandria VA 22314. **Tel** (703)549-8606. **ED** Emily Novick. **DD** 346. **[CCC].**
Desc: Reports on various states' regulation of policies, rates and benefits for all types of insurance including life, health, automobile and malpractice. Also details actions concerning insurance related issues.

US/1058-0808
GAMA NEWS JOURNAL. [GAMA news j.]. **Added/Corp** General Agents and Managers Association. **VAT** General Agents and Managers Association journal. (199?)-. Periodical. English. bm. $20.00 (non-members); free (members of General Agents Manager's Conference). General Agents Manager's Conference, 1922 F Street Northwest, Washington DC 20006. **Tel** (202)331-6088, FAX (202)785-5712. **ED** Connie Creswell & Renee Pietrangelo. **DD** 658. Index available. cum. index. **Bk Rev. Ad Acc. Pr Rev. Circ:** 10,000. **Continues** GAMC News Journal, 1052-424X.
Desc: A practitioner's guide to agency management.

CN/0380-223X
GENERAL INSURANCE REGISTER. Added/Corp Stone & Cox Limited. **VFOAT** Register. (1976)-. English. an (Jan.). 36.00Can$ Canada; 41.00Can$ other. Stone & Cox Ltd Publishers, 111 Peter Street, Suite 202, Toronto Ontario M5V 2H1 Canada. **Tel** (416)599-0772. **ED** John D. Wyndham. **LC** HG9783; .S8. **DD** 368/.971. **Ad Acc. Circ:** 2,500. **Continues** Stone & Cox General Insurance Year Book, Canada, 0081-5772.
Desc: Directory of property and casualty services in Canada. Including adjusters, appraisers, legal, brokers, and company listings.

SZ
GENEVA PAPERS ON RISK AND INSURANCE : ISSUES AND PRACTICE. English. qt. 170.00F (one year), 480.00F (three years) Switzerland; 195.00F (one year), 555.00F (three years) other. Assn Intl Etudes Economie de l'Assurance, 18 Chemin Rieu, 1208 Geneva Switzerland. **Tel** 011 41 22 470938, FAX 011 41 22 472078. **Continues** Geneva Papers on Risk and Insurance.

US/0926-4957
GENEVA PAPERS ON RISK AND INSURANCE THEORY. [Geneva pap. risk insur., Theory]. (1991)-. Periodical. English. sa. $199.00. Kluwer Academic Publishers / Massachusetts, PO Box 358, Accord Station, Hingham MA 02018. **Tel** (617)871-6600. **ED** Henri Louberge and Harris Schlesinger. **UDC** 368.1. **[CCC]. Pr Rev. Acid Free.** Documents available from The Genuine Article. **Continues** The Geneva Papers on Risk and Insurance, 0252-1148.
Desc: The papers have included articles from Nobel-prize winning economists as well as from chief executive officers of some of the world's top insurance companies. The main criteria for the journal is that papers advance our understanding of risk and insurance theory.
Ind/Abst Curr. Contents Soc. Behav. Sci.; Int. Bibliogr. Sociol.; J. Econ. Lit.; Res. Alert [Full Cov.]; Soc. Sci. Cit. Index [Full Cov.].

IT
GIORNALE DELLE ASSICURAZIONI. (19??)-. Italian. mo. L84000 Italy; L96400 other. Arnoldo Mondadori Editore, UFF Cont Abbonamenti, 20090 Segrate MI Italy. **Tel** 011 39 2 75422015, telex 320457 MONDMI I.

US/1057-8714
GLOBAL GUARANTY'S CREDIT ENHANCEMENT AND FINANCIAL GUARANTY DIRECTORY. [Glob. Guarant. credit enhanc. financ. guarant. dir.]. **Added/Corp** Global Guaranty Group. **VFOAT** Credit Enhancement and Financial Guaranty Directory; Directory of Ccredit Enhancements and Financial Guarantors; Global Guaranty Directory. (1991)-. Directory. English. Global Guaranty Group, 1 State Street Plaza, New York NY 10004. **LC** HG9997; .G56. **DD** 368.8/3/0065.

US/1056-8123
GOVERNMENTAL RISK MANAGEMENT REPORTS. [Gov. risk manage. rep.]. **Added/Corp** Risk Planning Group. Tillinghast (Firm). Vol. 1 (Apr. 1979)-. Periodical. English. mo. $75.00 universities; $125.00 other. Tillinghast Publications, 695 East Main Street, Suite 600, Stamford CT 06901. **Tel** (203)326-5400, FAX (203)326-5498. **ED** Jenny Emery. **DD** 368. **Pr Rev. Circ:** 1,000. available on microfilm from University Microfilms International (UMI).
Desc: Newsletter for public entities, focusing on risk financing and control, legislative changes, recent court decisions, and alternative risk financing mechanisms.

US/0743-6904
GREATER NEW YORK DIRECTORY, THE. (THE GREATER NEW YORK DIRECTORY / DENTAL INSURANCE SERVICES INCORPORATED.). **VFOAT** Directory; Insurance Directory. Directory. English. an. Dental Insurance Services, PO Box 485, Belmont MA 02178. **LC** HD7104.5.U52; N484. **DD** 368.3/823/00257471.

US/0730-2460
GROUP INSURANCE PLANS. HEALTH, DENTAL, PRESCRIPTION, OPTICAL. Added/Corp New Jersey Education Association. **VFOAT** NJEA Research. (19??)-. English. ir. $1.00. New Jersey Education Association, PO Box 1211, 180 West State Street, Trenton NJ 08607. **Tel** (609)599-4561 ext. 208, FAX (609)599-1266. **LC** HG9397.5.N4; G76. **DD** 368.3/82/009749.

CN/0821-1493
GROUP INSURANCE SURVEY. (GROUP INSURANCE SURVEY, NON-UNION SALARIED EMPLOYEES OF THE PRIVATE SECTOR IN CANADA.). [Group insur. surv.]. English. te. $165.00 per vol. Wyatt Company / Canada, 141 Adelaide Street West, Toronto Ontario M5H 3L5 Canada. **DD** 368.3/00971.

CN/0710-4588
GUIDES OF UNDERWRITERS' LABORATORIES OF CANADA. (GUIDES OF UNDERWRITERS' LABORATORIES OF CANADA / UNDERWRITERS' LABORATORIES OF CANADA.). [Guides Underwrit. Lab. Can.]. **Main/Corp** Underwriters' Laboratories of Canada. English. an. Free. Underwriters Laboratories of Canada, 7 Crouse Road, Scarborough Ontario M1R 3A9 Canada. **DD** 690/.02/18. ctrl circ.

US/0889-4183
HALES REPORT, INSURANCE BROKERAGE, THE. Added/Corp Hales & Associates, Inc. (Oak Brook, Ill.). **VFOAT** Hales Report. (19??)-. Periodical. English. mo. $150.00. Hales and Associates Inc., Two Westbrook Corporation Center, Suite 840, Westchester IL 60154. **Tel** (708)409-0080, FAX (708)409-1211. **ED** Laura Mazzyca-Toops. **DD** 332. Index available. cum. index. **Circ:** 1,300.

US/0361-2902
HANDBOOK OF EMPLOYMENT SECURITY PROGRAM STATISTICS. See Economics-Abstracting, Bibliographies and Statistics.

UK
HANDBOOK OF INSURANCE. (19??)-. Periodical. English. £234.10. Croner Publ Ltd, Croner House, London Road, Kingston upon Thames, Surrey KT2 6SR England. **Tel** 011 44 81 5473333, FAX 081 547-2637.

UK
HANDBOOK OF MOTOR INSURANCE. (19??)-. Periodical. English. £228.00. Croner Publ Ltd, Croner House, London Road, Kingston upon Thames, Surrey KT2 6SR England. **Tel** 011 44 81 5473333, FAX 081 547-2637.

UK
HANDBOOK OF PENSIONS. (19??)-. Periodical. English. tq. £277.75. Croner Publ Ltd, Croner House, London Road, Kingston upon Thames, Surrey KT2 6SR England. **Tel** 011 44 81 5473333, FAX 081 547-2637.

US
HANSON'S MANUAL OF EXAMINATION AND INSURANCE LAW HANDBOOK. See Law.

US/0017-7962
HARTFORD AGENT. A JOURNAL OF FIRE INSURANCE, THE. Added/Corp Hartford Fire Insurance Company, Hartford. (1909)-. Periodical. English. Four times a year. Free on request. ITT Hartford Insurance Group, Corporate Relations T 1 56 Hartford Plaza, Hartford CT 06115. **Tel** (203)547-5000.

●**US/1075-024X**
HEALTH ALLIANCE ALERT. [Health alliance alert]. **Added/Corp** Faulkner & Gray's Healthcare Information Center. Vol. 9, No. 1 (Jan. 14, 1994)-. Periodical. English. bw. $450.00. Faulkner & Gray Inc., 11 Penn Plaza, 17th Floor, New York NY 10001. **Tel**

Insurance

(212)967-7000, (800)535-8403. **DD** 362. **NLM** W1; HE233. *Formed by the union of* Health Business, 1062-6107 *and* Managed Care Alert.

US
HEALTH AND HEALTH INSURANCE : THE PUBLIC'S VIEW. Added/Corp Health Insurance Institute (New York, N.Y.) Health Insurance Association of America. (1978)-. Periodical. English. Health Insurance Association of America, 1025 Connecticut Avenue Northwest, Washington DC 20036. **Tel** (202)223-7780. **LC** HG9395; .H36.

US/0197-4246
HEALTH CARE FINANCING ADMINISTRATION RULINGS ON MEDICARE, MEDICAID, PROFESSIONAL STANDARDS REVIEW, AND RELATED MATTERS. [Health Care Financ. Admin. Rulings Medicare, Medicaid, Prof. Stand. Rev. Related Matters]. **Main/Corp** United States. Health Care Financing Administration. **Added/Corp** United States. Health Care Financing Administration. Rulings on Medicare, Medicaid, Professional Standards Review, and Related Matters. **VFOAT** Rulings on Medicare, Medicaid, Professional Standards Review, and Related Matters. (Nov. 1978)-. Government Publication. English. qt. Superintendent of Documents, US Government Printing Office, Washington DC 20402. **Tel** (202)275-3328, FAX (202)786-2377. **LC** KF3608.A4; A494. **DD** 344.73/03210425. **NLM** W 32.5 AA1 H36.

AT/0727-1611
HEALTH INSURANCE SURVEY, AUSTRALIA. See Insurance-Abstracting, Bibliographies and Statistics.

US/0017-9019
HEALTH INSURANCE UNDERWRITER, THE. [Health insur. underwrit.]. **Added/Corp** National Association of Health Underwriters. International Association of Health Underwriters. (19??)-. Periodical. English. Eleven times a year (July/Aug. issues combined). $40.00 (one year); $180.00 Comes with National Association of Health Underwriters membership. National Association Health Underwriters, 1000 Connecticut Avenue Northwest, Suite 1111, Washington DC 20036. **Tel** (202)223-5533. **LC** HG9371; .H32. **DD** 368.3/82/01205. **NLM** W1 HE365.

US/0899-8965
HEALTH LEGISLATION AND REGULATION. See Law.

CN/0823-6348
HERMINE. [Hermine +]. V. 1, No 1 (Feb. 1, 1983)-. Periodical. French. mo. Free. Hermine, 14 Place de Belvedere Canada. **DD** 368/.9714/05.

US
HINE'S DIRECTORY OF INSURANCE ADJUSTERS. VFOAT Directory of Insurance Adjusters. Directory. English. an. $20.00. Hine's Legal Directory Inc., PO Box 280, Glen Ellyn IL 60138. **Tel** (708)462-9670. **ED** J R Collins. **LC** HG8021; .H5. **Ad Acc. Circ:** 7,000 (ctrl). *Continues* Hine's Insurance Adjusters.
Desc: Directory of independent insurance claim adjusters.

US
HINE'S INSURANCE COUNSEL. See Law.

JA/0286-5890
HIROSAKI DAIGAKU HOKEN KANRI GAIYO. Japanese. Hirosaki Daihgaku Hoken Kanri Senta, 1 Bunkyo-cho, Hirosaki-shi Japan. **LC** LB3499.J32; H574 .

US/1050-9038
HMO MAGAZINE. [HMO mag.]. **Added/Corp** Group Health Association of America. **VAT** Health Maintenance Organizations Magazine. Vol. 31, No. 3 (May/June 1990)-. Periodical. English. bm. $75.00 (one year), $120.00 (two year), $155.00 (three year). Group Health Association of America, Department 0612, Washington DC 20073. **Tel** (202)778-3247, FAX (202)331-7487. **DD** 362. *Continues* GHAA News, 0887-9087.
Desc: Coverage of topics affecting the managed care industry.

JA
HOKEN ROPPO / HOKEN SEIDO KENKYUKAI HEN. See Law.

JA
HOKENGAKU ZASSHI. See Law.

US
HOMEOWNERS ANALYSIS. English. $39.00. Rough Notes Company Inc, 1200 North Meridian Street, Indianapolis IN 46206. **Tel** (317)634-1541, (800)428-4384, FAX (317)634-1041.

US
HOMEOWNERS GUIDE. English. $39.00. Rough Notes Company Inc, 1200 North Meridian Street, Indianapolis IN 46206. **Tel** (317)634-1541, (800)428-4384, FAX (317)634-1041.

US
HOMEOWNERS PROGRAM GUIDE. English. $27.00. Rough Notes Company Inc, 1200 North Meridian Street, Indianapolis IN 46206. **Tel** (317)634-1541, (800)428-4384, FAX (317)634-1041.

US/1074-8334
HOSPITAL PAYMENT & INFORMATION MANAGEMENT. Ceased. See Medical Science and Technology-Hospital Administration and Medical Centers.

US/1060-7838
HOSPITAL'S MEDICARE POLICY & PAYMENT REPORT, THE. Title Change. See Medical Science and Technology-Hospital Administration and Medical Centers.

UK/0265-5934
HULL CLAIMS ANALYSIS. 1984-. Periodical. English. mo. **LC** K1226.A13; H85. **DD** 346.41/08622. available on microfilm and microfiche from University Microfilms International (UMI).

CN/0712-5887
IBAO NEWS. (IBAO NEWS : A NEWSLETTER FOR THE MEMBERS OF THE INSURANCE BROKERS ASSOCIATION OF ONTARIO.). [IBAO news]. **VAT** Insurance Brokers Association of Ontario News. Vol. 17, No. 1 (Sept. 1981)-. Newsletter. English. mo. Free to members. Insurance Brokers Association of Ontario, Suite 633, 67 Yonge Street, Toronto Ontario M5E 1J8. **DD** 368/.971. *Continues* Independent Insurance Agents & Brokers of Ontario. IIABO News, 0706-6376.

US
IBIS REVIEW. Added/Corp Charles D. Spencer & Associates. **VFOAT** Review. No. 1 (July 1986)-. Periodical. English. mo (12 issues). $100.00. Charles D. Spencer & Associates, 250 South Wacker Drive, Suite 600, Chicago IL 60606-5834. **Tel** (312)993-7900, FAX (312)993-7910. **ED** Bruce F. Spencer and Laurie W. Letts. Index available. **Ad Acc. Circ:** 2,300.
Desc: Provides descriptions and commentary on topics of importance to international benefits specialists, such as pensions, death benefits and health care.
Ind/Abst F&S Index Plus Text, Int. [Select. Cov.]; PROMT.

UK/1353-1573
IDS PENSIONS SERVICE BULLETIN. See Law-Labor Law.

US/0094-7660
ILLINOIS INSURANCE. V. 1- Sept. 1969-. Periodical. English. bm. Illinois Department of Insurance, 320 West Washington Street, Springfield IL 62767. **Tel** (217)782-4515, FAX (217)782-5020. **ED** Nan Nases. **LC** HG8538.I3; I6. **DD** 368/.9/773. **Circ:** 4,700 (ctrl). available on microfilm from University Microfilms International (UMI).
Desc: Regulatory newsletter of Illinois Department of Insurance provides information on insurance law regulations, department policies, and activities.

●US/1067-2338
ILLINOIS WORKERS' COMPENSATION LAW BULLETIN. See Law.

US/0736-8399
INA PROFESSIONAL LIABILITY BULLETIN, ATTORNEYS. See Law.

US/0270-2061
INCL JOURNAL. See Law.

US
INDEPENDENT ADJUSTER, THE. Added/Corp National Association of Independent Insurance Adjusters. (19??)-. Periodical. English. qt. $6.00. Insurance Week Inc., 1001 Fourth Avenue Plaza, Suite 3029, Seattle WA 98154. **Tel** (206)624-6965, FAX (206)624-5021.

US/0002-7197
INDEPENDENT AGENT. [Indep. agent]. **Added/Corp** National Association of Insurance Agents. Independent Insurance Agents of America. Vol. 66, No. 5 (Jan. 1969)-. Periodical. English. Twelve times a year. $24.00. National Association of Insurance Agents, 127 South Peyton Street, Alexandria VA 22314. **Tel** (703)683-4422. **LC** HG9651; .A5. **DD** 368/.9/73. available on microfilm and microfiche from University Microfilms International (UMI). *Continues* American Agency Bulletin.

US
INDEX-DIGEST OF PRECEDENT DECISIONS. Main/Corp California. Unemployment Insurance Appeals Board. (19??)-. English. Twelve times a year. $30.00. California Unemployment Insurance Appeals, PO Box 944275, Sacramento CA 95814. **Tel** (916)445-5678. **Circ:** 250 (ctrl).
Desc: Summaries of issued precedent decisions.

US/0195-7805
INDIANA UNDERWRITER, THE. Ceased. Added/Corp National Underwriter Company. Vol. 1, No. 1 (Nov. 20, 1979)-(April 1994). Periodical. English. mo. National Underwriter Company, 505 Gest Street, Cincinnati OH 45203-0874. **Tel** (513)721-2140, (800)543-0874. **LC** HG8538.I6; I5.

FR
INDICATEUR STATISTIQUE (CAISSE NATIONALE DE L'ASSURANCE MALADIE DES TRAVAILLEURS SALARIES (FRANCE)). See Economics-Labor.

CR
INFORME ESTADISTICO (INSTITUTO NACIONAL DE SEGUROS (SAN JOSE, COSTA RICA)). See Insurance-Abstracting, Bibliographies and Statistics.

US
INITIAL CLOSING COMMITMENT FOR PROJECT MORTGAGE INSURANCE. Government Publication. English. ir. US Department of Housing and Urban Development, 451 Seventh Street SW, Washington DC 20401. **Tel** (202)708-0980, FAX (202)708-0299.

●US/1065-2736
INSIDE WORKERS' COMPENSATION. See Economics-Labor.

US
INSOURCE CUSTOM SERVICE (CD-ROM). (1992)-. English. NILS Publishing Company, PO Box 2507, Chatsworth CA 91313-2507. **Tel** (818)998-8830, (800)423-5910, FAX (818)718-8482.
Desc: Offers subscribers comprehensive law information for the states they do business in.

UK
INSTITUTE OF ACTUARIES (GREAT BRITAIN). (LIST OF MEMBERS.). **Main/Corp** Institute of Actuaries (Great Britain). (19??)-. English. an (Jan.). £25.00. Institute of Actuaries / England, 4 Worcester Street, Napier House, Oxford OX1 2AW England. **Tel** 011 44 865 794144, FAX 011 44 865 794094. **LC** WMLC 91/674.

UK
INSTITUTE OF ACTUARIES YEAR BOOK, THE. Ceased. Ceased (1986). English. an. Alden Press Ltd, Osney Mead, Oxford OX2 0EF England.

NE/0167-8558
INSURANCE ABSTRACTS AND REVIEWS. Title Change. Vol. 1, No. 1 (June 1982)-(1992). Periodical. English. Nationale Nederladen, Copr Affairs, Box 29701, 2502 LS Hague The Netherlands. **[CCC].** *Merged into* Insurance Mathematics and Economics, 0167-6687.

AT
INSURANCE ACT OF 1960 : ANNUAL REPORT FOR THE YEAR ENDED ON THE 30TH OF JUNE ..., THE. English. an. **LC** WMLC L 83/7938.

US/0020-4587
INSURANCE ADVOCATE. [Insur. advocate]. 1889. Periodical. English. wk (except 1st week in July and last week in Dec.). $30.00. Roberts Publishing Corporation, 45 John Street, New York NY 10038. **Tel** (212)233-3768, FAX (212)964-9885. **ED** Emanuel Levy. **DD** 368. **Bk Rev. Ad Acc. Circ:** 7,400. available on microfilm and microfiche from University Microfilms International (UMI). *Continues* Echo.
Desc: Editorial material of interest to all segments of insurance business including attorneys, legislators, regulators, gathered from countrywide sources, news, articles, opinions are featured.

UK/0142-6265
INSURANCE AGE. [Insur. age]. (1979)-. Periodical. English. mo. £50.00 UK; £76.00 Europe; £76.00 other. EMAP Business & Computer Publishing Ltd., 1 Lincoln Court 1 Lincoln Road, Peterborough PE1 2RP England. **Tel** 011/44/733/68900, FAX 011/44/733/349290. **(Subscription address:** EMAP Business Publishing, Ferrari House Audit House, Field End, Ruislip Middlesex HA4 9UY England.**)** **(Subscription address:** EMAP Business Publishing, Ferrari House, Audit Hs Field End, Ruislip Middlesex HA4 9UY England**)**
Ind/Abst Infomat Int. Bus.

Insurance

US/0074-0675
INSURANCE ALMANAC (ENGLEWOOD. 1933), THE. (THE INSURANCE ALMANAC.). (193?)-. English. an (July). $122.25. Underwriter Printing & Publishing Company, 50 East Palisade Avenue, Englewood NJ 07631. **Tel** (201)569-8808, (800) 526-4700. **ED** Donald Wolff. **Bk Rev**. **Ad Acc**. **Circ**: 10,000 (ctrl). *Continues Insurance Almanac and Who's Who in Insurance, 0363-4108.*
Desc: The who, what, when and where of insurance. Listings of agencies, companies, adjusters, appraisers, auditors, insurance officials and organizations.

AT/0311-0192
INSURANCE & BANKING RECORD, THE. See Business-Banking and Finance.

US/0735-3944
INSURANCE AND EMPLOYEE BENEFITS LITERATURE. Added/Corp Special Libraries Association. Insurance and Employee Benefits Division. No. 374 (July/Aug. 1981)-. Periodical. English. bm. $15.00 U.S. and Canada, $20.00 other. Equifax Inc, c/o Michael McDavid, PO Box 4081, Atlanta GA 30302. **Tel** (404)885-8320. **ED** Kathleen Kelleher. **Bk Rev**. **Circ**: 300 (ctrl). *Continues Insurance Literature, 0734-6689.*
Desc: Annotated bibliography for books, documents, and other publications from all aspects of the insurance and employee benefits industries.

US/0736-0126
INSURANCE AND FINANCIAL REVIEW, THE. [Insur. financ. rev.]. Vol. 16, No. 1 (Jan. 1983)-. Periodical. English. Twelve times a year. Philo Smith and Company Inc., 2950 Summer Street, Stamford CT 06905. **Tel** (203)348-7365. **ED** Philo Smith. **LC** HG8011; .I58. **DD** 332.6/722. **Circ**: 1,000. *Continues Insurance Stock Review.*
Desc: Insurance and financial services industry review by company; also a topic of current interest.

US/1055-4556
INSURANCE & LIABILITY REPORTER. [Insur. liabil. report.]. **Added/Corp** American Insurance Attorneys. Insurance and Liability Reporter. Vol. 1, No. 1 (Feb. 15, 1991)-. Periodical. English. sm. $525.00. NILS Publishing Company, PO Box 2507, Chatsworth CA 91313-2507. **Tel** (818)998-8830, (800)423-5910, FAX (818)718-8482. **DD** 368.

UK/0950-5377
INSURANCE & REINSURANCE SOLVENCY REPORT. [Insur. reinsur. solv. rep.]. **VFOAT** Insurance and Reinsurance Solvency Report. (1986)-. Periodical. English. Fifty times a year. £355.00 UK; $585.00 US & Canada. DYP Insurance Reinsurance Res. Grp. Ltd., 181 Queen Victoria St. Bridge House, London EC4V 4DD England. **Tel** 011 44 71 236 2175, FAX 011 44 71 489 1487. **DD** 368.

US/0892-5887
INSURANCE AND RISK MANAGEMENT--FOR BUSINESS AND GOVERNMENT. [Insur. risk manage.-- bus. gov.]. **Added/Corp** Bureau of National Affairs (Washington, D.C.). **VFOAT** Insurance and Risk Management. Vol. 1, No. 1 (March 31, 1987). Periodical. English. sm. $398.00 US, Canada and Mexico; $420.00 other. Buraff Publications Inc., 714 Church Street, Alexandria VA 22314. **Tel** (800)333-1291, (703)739-8500. **ED** Corby Anderson. **DD** 368. **[CCC]**. *Continues in part Loss Prevention and Control, 0191-2763.*
Desc: Newsletter on risk management and loss prevention and control, including news briefs, tax tips, state developments, liability issues, regulatory developments, and coverage of specific insurance and risk management topics.

US/1054-0733
INSURANCE & TECHNOLOGY. [Ins. technol.]. **VFOAT** Insurance and Technology. Vol. 15, No. 5 (Oct/Nov 1990)-. Periodical. English. Twelve times a year. $48.00 US; $60.00 Canada & Mexico; $105.00 other. Miller Freeman Inc., 600 Harrison Street, San Francisco CA 94107. **Tel** (415)905-2337, FAX (415)905-2240, telex 278273. **LC** HG8075; .I56. **DD** 368/.00285/53. **[CCC]**. Documents available from Ask*IEEE. *Continues Insurance Software Review, 0892-8533.*
Ind/Abst Comput. Bus. (19??-); Comput. Lit. Index (19??-); Gen. BusinessFile (1992-); INSPEC (1987-).

US/0898-5170
INSURANCE ANTITRUST & TORT REFORM REPORT. *Title Change.* See Law-Corporate Law.

US/0736-5969
INSURANCE BENEFITS SURVEY. TWIN CITY AREA. English. be. Personnel Surveys, Inc., 1608 Northstar Center, Minneapolis MN 55402. **LC** HG8539.M56; I57. **DD** 331.25/5.

UK/0260-2385
INSURANCE BROKERS' MONTHLY AND INSURANCE ADVISER. [Insur. brok. mon. insur. advis.]. **VFOAT** Brokers' Monthly and Insurance Adviser. (1978)-. Periodical. English. Twelve times a year. £32.00 UK; £59.00 (airmail), £40.00 (surface mail) other. Insurance Publishing & Printing Co., 7 Stourbridge Road Lye, Stourbridge, West Midlands DY9 7DG England. **Tel** 011 44 384 895228, FAX 011 44 384 893666. **ED** Brian Susman. **DD** 368. **Bk Rev**, (Qty: 10). **Ad Acc**, **Adv Mgr**: Jane Sones, **Tel** 0689 785156. **Circ**: 8,000 (ctrl). available on an online database from DIALOG; available in print. *Continues Insurance Brokers' Monthly, 0020-4633.*
Ind/Abst Infomat Int. Bus.

UK
INSURANCE BUSINESS: ANNUAL REPORT. Main/Corp Great Britain. Dept. of Trade and Industry. (197?)-. English. an. £10.00. Her Majesty's Stationery Office, 51 Nine Elms Lane, London SW8 5DR England. **Tel** 011 44 71 873 8459, 011 44 71 873 8499, FAX 011 44 71 873 8499, 011 44 71 873 8456, telex 297138. **(Subscription address:** Her Majesty's Stationery Office, PO Box 276; Publications Centre, London SW8 5DT England.) **LC** HG8594; .A37b. **DD** 368/.942. *Continues Great Britain. Board of Trade. Insurance Business.*

US
INSURANCE COMPANY MARKET RANK. English. an. $150.00 (includes updates). Harkey and Associates Inc., PO Box 159025, 2000 Richard Jones Road, Suite 170, Nashville TN 37215. **Tel** (615)385-4131, FAX (615)385-4979.

US/0749-2847
INSURANCE COMPANY RATINGS REPORTER. Added/Corp Prime Management, Inc. (Sept. 1984)-. Periodical. English. mo. $495.00. Prime Management Inc, 155 Montgomery Street/Suite 301, San Francisco CA 94101. **DD** 368.

US/8755-6162
INSURANCE COMPUTING NEWSLETTER. [Insur. comput. newsl.]. **VFOAT** ICN. Began in 1984?. Newsletter. English. mo. $65.00. Insurance Computing Newsletter, Overland Park KS 66212-4221. **DD** 368.

US/0193-0516
INSURANCE CONFERENCE PLANNER. [Insur. conf. plann.]. Vol. 12 No. 2 (July 1976)-. Periodical. English. bm. $42.00 US; $64.00 other; $96.00 (airmail). Laux Company Inc, 63 Great Road, Maynard MA 01754. **Tel** (508)897-5552, FAX (508)897-6824. **ED** Susan Hatch. **DD** 658. **Ad Acc**, **Adv Mgr**: B Ventre. **Circ**: 7,500 (ctrl). Documents available from UMI Article Clearinghouse. *Continues in part Insurance Magazine, 0275-2611.*
Desc: The executives guide to incentive travel and meeting/conference planning in the insurance field.
Ind/Abst ABI/INFORM Glob. Ed.; ABI Inform Ondisc (Dec. 1976-Oct. 1977).

UK
INSURANCE CONTRACT LAW. (19??)-. Periodical. English. £323.80. Croner Publ Ltd, Croner House, London Road, Kingston upon Thames, Surrey KT2 6SR England. **Tel** 011 44 81 5473333, FAX 081 547-2637.

US
INSURANCE DEPARTMENT SERVICE / ALL STATE SERVICE. English. ir. $2,500.00. Underwriter Printing & Publishing Company, 50 East Palisade Avenue, Englewood NJ 07631. **Tel** (201)569-8808, (800) 526-4700.

US
INSURANCE DIRECTORY. *Title Change.* **Added/Corp** Alabama. Dept. of Insurance. Alabama. Bureau of Insurance. (19??)-(196?). Directory. English. an. **LC** HG8511.A2; A4. **DD** 368.9761. *Continued by Insurance Agents Directory.*

UK
INSURANCE DIRECTORY AND YEAR BOOK : POST MAGAZINE ALMANACK, THE. Directory. English. an. £120.00. Buckley Press Ltd, 58 Fleet Street, London EC4Y 1JU England. **Tel** 011 44 71 5833030.
Desc: Contains issues relating to statistics and facts of ordinary life, industrial life, motor, property, liability, personal accident, pecuniary loss and marine, etc.

US/0020-4668
INSURANCE ECONOMICS SURVEYS. V. 1- July 1944-. Periodical. English. bm. $7.50. Insurance Economics Society, 303 Atlantic Avenue/#206, Virginia Beach VA 23451. **Tel** (202)393-2541. **ED** John B O'Day. **Bk Rev**. **Circ**: 15,000 (ctrl).
Desc: Dedicated to the progress of America's private enterprise and reviews issues such as national health insurance, social security, medicare, taxing, fringe benefits and unisex insurance rates.

US/0095-2923
INSURANCE FORUM, THE. [Insur. forum]. Vol. 1, No. 1 (Jan. 1, 1974)-. Periodical. English. mo. $60.00. Insurance Forum, PO Box 245, Ellettsville IN 47429. **Tel** (812)876-6502. **ED** Joseph M. Belth. **LC** HG8501; .I55. **DD** 368/.973/05. Index available. cum. index. **Bk Rev** available on microfilm and microfiche from University Microfilms International (UMI).
Desc: Discussion of important public policy issues in insurance.
Ind/Abst Ins. Period. Index.

FI/0356-9993
INSURANCE IN FINLAND. [Insur. Finl.]. (1960)-. Periodical. English. sa. UDC 368.
Ind/Abst Selec. Coop. Index Manage. Period.

IE/0791-7201
INSURANCE INDUSTRY INTERNATIONAL. English. mo (10 issues). $749.00. Lafferty Publications Ltd. / Dublin, Tower Ida Centre Pearse St., Dublin 2 Ireland. **Tel** 011 353 1 6718022, FAX 01-718520.

US/0887-7858
INSURANCE INDUSTRY LITIGATION REPORTER : THE NATIONAL JOURNAL OF RECORD OF INSURANCE LITIGATION. See Law.

US
INSURANCE INDUSTRY NEWSLETTER. Newsletter. English. wk. $117.00. Insurance Field Company, PO Box 948, Northbrook IL 60065. **Tel** (708)498-0100. **ED** George V R Smith. *Supersedes The Insurance Field.*
Desc: Gives current information on insurance activities in the ever-changing, fast breaking insurance world every Monday morning.

US/0020-4714
INSURANCE JOURNAL. (19??)-. Periodical. English. bw (26 issues per year). $156.00. Insurance Journal, 9191 Towne Centre Drive, Suite 550, San Diego CA 92122. **Tel** (619)455-7717, FAX (619)546-1462. **ED** Karen St.George. **Ad Acc**, **Adv Mgr**: Dena Kaplan. **Circ**: 10,000 (ctrl). available on microfilm and microfiche from University Microfilms International (UMI).
Desc: California's property casualty magazine.

US/0148-2688
INSURANCE LAW. See Law.

UK
INSURANCE LAW & PRACTICE. English. qt. £100.00. Tolley Publishing Company Ltd, Tolley House, 2 Addiscombe Road, Croydon, Surrey CR9 5AF United Kingdom. **Tel** 011 44 81 6869141, FAX 011 44 81 6863155, 011 44 81 7600588.

US/0892-4422
INSURANCE LAW ANTHOLOGY. See Law.

AT/1030-2379
INSURANCE LAW JOURNAL (SYDNEY, N.S.W.). (INSURANCE LAW JOURNAL.). Vol. 1, No. 1 (Jan. 1988)-. English. Three times a year (Feb., July, Nov.). 125.00Aus$. Butterworths Pty Ltd, 271-273 Lane Cove Road, PO Box 345, North Ryde NSW 2113 Australia. **Tel** 011 61 2 3354444, FAX 011 61 2 3354655. **ED** A. A. Tarr. **LC** K9; .N7473. **DD** 346.94/086/05; 349.4068605. Index available. **Bk Rev**.
Desc: Contains articles on current developments in insurance law.
Ind/Abst Index Leg. Period.; Leg. Resour. Index; LegalTrac (1988-).

UK
INSURANCE LAW MONTHLY. (19??)-. English. mo. £134.00 UK; £156.00 other. Monitor Press, Rectory Road, Great Waldingfield, Sudbury Suffolk CO10 0TL United Kingdom. **Tel** 011 44 787 378607. **ED** R. M. Merkin. Index available. **Bk Rev**.
Desc: Newsletter for specialists in the insurance and reinsurance industry.

UK
INSURANCE LAW REPORTS (HARLOW, ESSEX). See Law.

US/0744-1045
INSURANCE LITIGATION REPORTER. See Law.

US/0097-6245
INSURANCE MAGAZINE'S GOLD BOOK OF INSURANCE MARKETING. VFOAT Gold Book of Insurance Marketing. English. an. $10.00. Insurance Magazine, 1100 High Ridge Road, Stamford CT 06905. **LC** HG8943; .G63. **DD** 368/.9/73. *Continues Gold Book of Life Insurance Selling and Marketing.*

US/0538-2629
INSURANCE MARKET PLACE, THE. **VFOAT** Rough Notes' Market Place. English. an. Rough Notes Company Inc, 1200 North Meridian Street, Indianapolis IN 46206. **Tel** (317)634-1541,

(800)428-4384, FAX (317)634-1041. **LC** HG8523; .I614. **DD** 368/.00973. available on microfilm from University Microfilms International (UMI).

CN/0317-1272
INSURANCE MARKETER, THE. Vol. 1 (1973)-. English. an. 54.00Can$ Canada; 90.00Can$ others Comes with Canadian Underwriter. Southam Information and Technology Group Inc., 1450 Don Mills Road, Don Mills Ontario M3B 2X7 Canada. **Tel** (416)445-6641, (800)668-2374, FAX (416)442-2261. **LC** HG8550.A6; I57. **DD** 368/.971.

US/1040-6867
INSURANCE MARKETING INSIDER. [Insur. mark. insid.]. Periodical. English. mo. $118.00 North America; $153.40 other. Shelby Publishing Corporation, 210 Lincoln Street, Suite 700, Boston MA 02111-2491. **Tel** (617)423-0978, FAX (617)482-7820. **DD** 368. **Bk Rev. Ad Acc. Circ:** 2,000 (ctrl). ***Continues*** *Liner's Insurance Marketing Insider, 0892-1458.*
Desc: Insurance sales newsletter.

NE/0167-6687
INSURANCE MATHEMATICS & ECONOMICS. [Insur., math. econ.]. **VFOAT** Insurance, Mathematics and Economics. Vol. 1, No. 1 (Jan. 1982)-. Academic Scholarly Publication. English. Six times a year (2 volumes). Fl930.00. Elsevier Science Publishers BV, PO Box 211, 1000 AE Amsterdam Netherlands. **Tel** 011 31 20 5803642, FAX 011 31 20 5862696, telex 15682. **ED** F De Vylder, H Gerber, M J Goovaerts, J Haezendonck, S Klugman, and G C Taylor. **CODEN** IMECDX. **[CCC]. Pr Rev.** available on microfilm and microfiche from University Microfilms International (UMI). Documents available from The Genuine Article, UMI Article Clearinghouse, Ask*IEEE.
Desc: An international journal which intends to strengthen communication between individuals and groups who produce and apply research results in insurance mathematics, thus helping to correct the current fragmentation of research in the field.
Ind/Abst ABI/INFORM Glob. Ed.; ABI Inform Ondisc (July 1983-); Compumath Citation Index [Full Cov.]; Curr. Contents Soc. Behav. Sci.; Curr. Index Stat.; INSPEC (Jan. 1984-); Math. Rev.; Res. Alert [Full Cov.]; Risk Abstr.; Soc. Sci. Cit. Index [Full Cov.]; Zentralbl. Math. Ihre Grenzgeb.

US/0074-073X
INSURANCE PERIODICALS INDEX. See Insurance-Abstracting, Bibliographies and Statistics.

US/1055-5749
INSURANCE PHONE BOOK & DIRECTORY. [Insur. phone book dir.]. **Added/Corp** U.S. Directory Service. **VFOAT** Insurance Phone Book and Directory. (19??)-. Directory. English. an. $95.30. Reed Reference Publishing, 121 Chanlon Road, New Providence NJ 07974. **Tel** (908)464-6800, (800)521-8110 Ext. 3387, (800)223-1797, FAX (908)665-3560. **LC** HG8525; .I62. **DD** 368/.0025/73.

US/0020-4803
INSURANCE RECORD (DALLAS, TEX.), THE. (THE INSURANCE RECORD.). (19??)-. Periodical. English. Twenty-six times a year (Published every other Thursday). $15.00 (one year); $30.00 (three year). The Record Publishing Company, PO Box 225770, Dallas TX 75265. **Tel** (214)630-0687, FAX (214)631-2476. **ED** Glen E. Hargis. **Ad Acc, Adv Mgr:** C. J. Hargis. **Circ:** 2,300.
Desc: News articles written for the insurance agent in Texas, Louisiana, Oklahoma and Arkansas. Primary emphasis on new lines, current legislation and management changes.

AT
INSURANCE RECORD OF AUSTRALIA & NEW ZEALAND, THE. VAT Insurance Record of Australia and New Zealand. V. 1- (Nov. 1976-). Periodical. English. ir. 55.00Aus$, Australia; 110.00Aus$ other. Craftsman Publications, Private Bag 260, Burwood Victoria 3125 Australia. **Tel** (03)288-9622. **ED** George Wilson. **LC** HG8732; .I56. **DD** 368/.9/94. **Bk Rev. Ad Acc. Circ:** 1,800. ***Supersedes*** *Insurance & Banking Record.*
Desc: Personnel movements, company news, articles and notes on the Australian insurance industry.

FJ
INSURANCE REPORT AND STATISTICS OF FIJI. See Insurance-Abstracting, Bibliographies and Statistics.

JA/0910-5719
INSURANCE. SEIMEI HOKEN TOKEI-GO. See Insurance-Abstracting, Bibliographies and Statistics.

US/0749-1840
INSURANCE SERVICE. COMMERCIAL INSURANCE MARKET STUDY / DATA RESOURCES, INC. [Insur. serv., Commer. insur. mark. study]. **Added/Corp** Data Resources, Inc. **VFOAT** Commercial Insurance Market Study. (19??)-. English. DRI McGraw Hill, 24 Hartwell Avenue, Lexington MA 02173. **Tel** (617)863-5100. **LC** HG8059; .I58. **DD** 368.8/1/00973.

US
INSURANCE SERVICE ECONOMIC INDICATORS / DRI, DATA RESOURCES, INC. Added/Corp Data Resources, Inc. (19??)-. Periodical. English. DRI McGraw Hill, 24 Hartwell Avenue, Lexington MA 02173. **Tel** (617)863-5100. **LC** HG8501; .I57. **DD** 368/.973.

US/0276-6361
INSURANCE SERVICE QUARTERLY REVIEW. (INSURANCE SERVICE QUARTERLY REVIEW / DATA RESOURCES, INC.). **Added/Corp** Data Resources, Inc. (19??)-. English. qt. DRI McGraw Hill, 24 Hartwell Avenue, Lexington MA 02173. **Tel** (617)863-5100. **LC** HG8011; .D37a. **DD** 368/.973. ***Continues*** *DRI Insurance Service Quarterly Review, 0364-3298.*

US/0271-2628
INSURANCE SERVICE: REGIONAL REVIEW. [Insur. serv., Reg. rev.]. **Main/Corp** Data Resources, Inc. (19??)-. English. DRI McGraw Hill, 24 Hartwell Avenue, Lexington MA 02173. **Tel** (617)863-5100. **LC** HG8501; .D37a. **DD** 368/.973.

US/0892-8533
INSURANCE SOFTWARE REVIEW. ***Title Change.*** [Ins. softw. rev.]. Periodical. English. qt. International Computer Programs Inc / Barbara Lahiff, 823 East Westfield Boulevard, Indianapolis IN 46220. **Tel** 800-428-6179, (317)251-7727. **LC** HG8075; .I56. **DD** 368. **CODEN** INSREK. **[CCC].** available on microfilm and microfiche from University Microfilms International (UMI). Documents available from UMI Article Clearinghouse. ***Continues*** *ICP Insurance Software, 0747-1297.* ***Continued by*** *Insurance & Technology, 1054-0733.*
Ind/Abst ABI/INFORM Glob. Ed.; ABI Inform Ondisc; Data Process. Dig.

JA/0910-5727
INSURANCE. SONGAI HOKEN TOKUBETSU TOKEI-GO. See Insurance-Abstracting, Bibliographies and Statistics.

US/1057-0349
INSURANCE SOUTH MAGAZINE. [Insur. south mag.]. **VFOAT** Insurance South. (July 1991)-. Periodical. English. bm. $18.00. Insurance South, Inc., PO Box 331, Mount Vernon VA 22121-0331. **DD** 368.

UK/0268-1935
INSURANCE SYSTEMS BULLETIN. [Insur. syst. bull.]. (1985)-. Bulletin. English. mo (10 issues). £269.00. IBC Publishing, 57-61 Mortimer St., London W1N 7TD England. **Tel** 011 44 71 637 4383, FAX 011 44 71 636 6314. **DD** 368.00285. **Bk Rev**, (Qty: 10-20). **Circ:** 1,000 (ctrl). available on an online database. Documents available from BLDSC. ***Absorbed*** *Insurance Systems International.*

UK/0954-5514
INSURANCE SYSTEMS INTERNATIONAL. ***Title Change.*** [Insur. syst. int.]. (1988)-(19??). Periodical. English. qt. IBC Publishing, 57-61 Mortimer St., London W1N 7TD England. **Tel** 011 44 71 637 4383, FAX 011 44 71 636 6314. **DD** 368.00285. ***Merged into*** *Insurance Systems Bulletin.*

CN/0714-8402
INSURANCE T.R.A.C. REPORT, CANADA. (INSURANCE T.R.A.C. REPORT (CANADA) / RAPPORT D'ASSURANCE 'T.R.A.C.'.). [Insur. T.R.A.C. rep., Can.]. **Added/Corp** Canada. Dept. of Insurance. I.P. Sharp Associates. T.R.A.C. Insurance Services. Office of the Superintendent of Financial Institutions Canada. **VFOAT** Rapport d'Assurance 'T.R.A.C.'; T.R.A.C. Report; Tests Ratios Analyses Charts Report; Rapport d'Assurance 'T.R.A.C.' (Canada). **VAT** Insurance Tests Ratios Analyses Charts Report, Canada; Rapport d'Assurance 'Tests Ratios Analyses Charts'; T.R.A.C. (Toronto); Tests Ratios Analyses Charts. (1982)-. English (French). an. 94.00Can$ Canada; 109.00Can$ other. TRAC Insurance Services, 600 133 Richmond Street, Toronto Ontario M5H 2L3 Canada. **Tel** (416)363-8266. **ED** Patricia Collins. **DD** 368/.971. **Circ:** 1,100.
Desc: A publication analyzing the solvency, profitability and underwriting practices of more than 300 property/casualty insurance companies in Canada.

US/0890-9164
INSURANCE TAX REVIEW, THE. (THE INSURANCE TAX REVIEW / TAX ANALYSTS.). [Insur. tax rev.]. **Added/Corp** Tax Analysts (Firm : U.S.). (Oct. 1986)-. Periodical. English. mo. $499.00. Tax Analysts, 6830 North Fairfax Drive, Arlington VA 22213. **Tel** (703)533-4400, (800)955-3444. **LC** KF6495.I5; I57. **DD** 343.7305/267; 347.3035267. **[CCC].**

US/0276-6280
INSURANCE THEFT LOSSES. VANS, PICKUPS AND UTILITY VEHICLES, ... MODELS. Added/Corp Highway Loss Data Institute. (1979)-. English. an. Highway Loss Data Institute, 10005 North Globe Road, Arlington VA 22201. **Tel** (703)247-1600. **LC** HG9970.3; .I55. **DD** 368.5/72.

US/1042-7333
INSURANCE TIMES (NEWTON, MASS.). (INSURANCE TIMES.). [Insur. times]. (198?)-. Periodical. English. Twenty-six times a year. $39.95 (one year), $69.00 (two years), $89.00 (three years). Insurance Times, 20 Park Plaza, Suite 1101, Boston MA 02116. **Tel** (617)292-7117. **ED** Andrew Simpson. **DD** 368. **Ad Acc. Circ:** 7,600 (ctrl). available on microfiche. ***Continues*** *New England Insurance Times, 0888-4935.*
Desc: Carries current news and original feature reports on the entire insurance industry: property, casualty, life, health, and related financial services.

US
INSURANCE TRENDS. English. mo. $390.00. Conning & Company, 185 Asylum Street, City Place II, Hartford CT 06103. **Tel** (203) 520-1521, FAX (203) 520-1504.

US/0020-4846
INSURANCEWEEK. VAT Insurance Week. (19??)-. Periodical. English. Fifty-two times a year. $30.00 US; $32.46 Washington; $45.00 Canada; $85.00 others. Insurance Week, 1001 4th Avenue Plaza, Suite 3029, Seattle WA 98154. **Tel** (206)624-6965, FAX (206)624-5021. **ED** Douglas Canfield. **Ad Acc. Circ:** 5,800 (ctrl).

US
INSURED PROJECT SERVICING HANDBOOK. Added/Corp United States. Dept. of Housing and Urban Development. Office of Housing Management. (19??)-. Government Publication. English. ir. US Department of Housing and Urban Development, 451 Seventh Street SW, Washington DC 20401. **Tel** (202)708-0980, FAX (202)708-0299.

UK
INSURING FOREIGN RISKS. (19??)-. Periodical. English. ir. £269.45. Croner Publ Ltd, Croner House, London Road, Kingston upon Thames, Surrey KT2 6SR England. **Tel** 011 44 81 5473333, FAX 081 547-2637.

US/0192-9046
INTERFACE. INSURANCE INDUSTRY. ***Title Change.*** **Added/Corp** International Computer Programs, Inc. **VFOAT** Insurance Industry; ICP Interface. Insurance Industry. (Jan. 1976)-. Periodical. English. qt. International Computer Programs Inc / Barbara Lahiff, 823 East Westfield Boulevard, Indianapolis IN 46220. **Tel** 800-428-6179, (317)251-7727. **LC** HG8075; .I53. **DD** 368/.0028/54. available on microfilm from University Microfilms International (UMI). ***Continued by*** *ICP Interface. Insurance Industry, 0745-0419.*

US/0018-8611
INTERNATIONAL BENEFITS INFORMATION SERVICE. (IBIS. INTERNATIONAL BENEFITS INFORMATION SERVICE.). [Int. benefits inf. serv.]. **Added/Corp** Charles D. Spencer & Associates. **VFOAT** IBIS. (Sept. 1969)-. Periodical. English. mo. $810.00 Chicago; $802.50 Illiinois; $750.00 other. Charles D. Spencer & Associates, 250 South Wacker Drive, Suite 600, Chicago IL 60606-5834. **Tel** (312)993-7900, FAX (312)993-7910. Index available (free).
Ind/Abst Grasslands For. Abstr.; Ins. Period. Index (1986-).

UK/0966-7733
INTERNATIONAL BROKER, THE. [Int. brok.]. (1992)-. Newspaper. English. Twelve times a year. £275.00 UK; $450.00 others. Risk & Insurance Research Group, 4 Henrietta Street, Covent Gard, London WC2E 8PS England. **Tel** 011 44 71 836 0614, FAX 011 44 71 379 6355, telex 23446.

●UK/0968-2090
INTERNATIONAL INSURANCE LAW REVIEW. See Law.

US/0020-6997
INTERNATIONAL INSURANCE MONITOR. [Int. insur. monit.]. **VFOAT** IIM. Vol. 14 (Jan. 1960)-. Periodical. English. Four times a year. $25.00. Chase Communications Group, 2535 Beechwood Avenue, PO Box 9001, Mt Vernon NY 10552. **Tel** (914)699-2020. **LC** HG8011; .W47. **DD** 368. Index available. **Bk Rev. Ad Acc. Circ:** 3,200. available on microfilm and microfiche from University Microfilms International (UMI); available on an online database (file 771/Full-Text) from DIALOG. Documents available from UMI Article Clearinghouse. ***Continues*** *West East Insurance Monitor.*
Desc: Reporting developments in insurance, legislation for same and changes in personnel and organizations worldwide.

Ind/Abst ABI/INFORM Glob. Ed.; ABI Inform Ondisc (Sept. 1979-); Ins. Period. Index (1974-199?); UMI ABI/Inform--Bus. Period. Ondisc (Sep. 1987-) [Full Txt.].

UK
INTERNATIONAL INSURANCE REPORT. **Added/Corp** Risk Research Group. Risk & Insurance Research Group. (19??)-. Periodical. English. Twelve times a year. £245.00 UK; $400.00 other. Risk & Insurance Research Group, 4 Henrietta Street, Covent Gard, London WC2E 8PS England. **Tel** 011 44 71 836 0614, FAX 011 44 71 379 6355, telex 23446.
Desc: News and articles on the international insurances.

US/0020-9651
INTERPRETER (DURHAM, N.C.), THE. (THE INTERPRETER / INSURANCE ACCOUNTING AND STATISTICAL ASSOCIATION.). [Interpreter]. **Added/Corp** Insurance Accounting and Systems Association. Insurance Accounting and Statistical Association. (Aug. 1940)-. Statistical Publication. English. bm. $12.00. Insurance Accounting and Systems Association, PO Box 51340, Durham NC 27717. **Tel** (919)489-0991. available on microfilm and microfiche from University Microfilms International (UMI).
Ind/Abst Account. Tax Datab. (1976-) [Full Txt.].

NE/0166-3658
INZET. [Inzet]. (1977)-. Periodical. Dutch. mo (11 issues). Fl66.04. VNZ, Redaktie Inzet, Postbus 520, 3700 AM Zeist, Netherlands. **Tel** 011 31 3404 88361. **UDC** 368.4. ***Formed by the union of** Unie, 0165-7364 **and** Ziekenfondsgids, 0304-470X.*

NE
JAARBOEK/VADEMECUM VOOR HET VERZEKERINGSWEZEN. 64 Ed. (1973)-. Dutch. Marnixstraat 16, Den Haag The Netherlands. **LC** HG8642; .J148. ***Formed by the union of** Vademecum Voor het Nederlandsche Verzekeringswezen **and** Jaarboek Voor het Assurantie-en Hypotheekwezen.*

NE
JAARVERSLAG / ALGEMEEN WERKLOOSHEIDSFONDS. **Main/Corp** Algemeen Werkloosheidsfonds. Dutch. Algemeen Werkloosheidsfonds, Postbus 100, 2700 AC Zoetermeer Netherlands. **LC** HD7096.N3; A58.

NE
JAARVERSLAG - SOCIALE VERZEKERINGSRAAAD. **See** Sociology-Social Services and Welfare.

AU/0379-2595
JAHRBUCH - STEIERMARKISCHE GEBIETSKRANKENKASSE FUR ARBEITER UND ANGESTELLTE. **See** Medical Science and Technology.

AU/0457-1231
JAHRESBERICHT. **See** Economics-Labor.

AU
JAHRESBERICHT DER TIROLER GEBIETSKRANKENKASSE. **Main/Corp** Tiroler Gebietskrankenkasse. **VFOAT** T.G.K.K. Bericht; TGKK Bericht. German. an. Tiroler Gebietskrankenkasse, Klara-Polt-Weg 2, 6020 Innsbruck Austria. **LC** HD7102.A92; T53. **DD** 368.3/82/00943642. ***Continues** Tiroler Gebietskrankenkasse fur Arbieter und Angestellte. Jahresbericht.*

JA/0910-4534
JAPAN INSURANCE NEWS. [Jpn. insur. news]. (1974)-. Periodical. English. bm (Jan., Mar., May, July, Sept., Nov.). $77.00 Asia; $82.00 US, Canada, Central America, Australia, and New and Middle East; $86.00 other. Hoken Kenkyu-Jo, 17-3-1 Chome Honmachi, Shibuya-Ku Tokyo Japan. **Tel** 011 81 3 3376 3331, FAX 011 81 3 3376 7125. **DD** 368. Index available (available and Jan. issue). **Ad Acc. Circ:** 3,000.

CH
JEN SHOU PAO HSIEN YEH WU TUNG CHI NIEN PAO. **Main/Corp** Tai-Pei Shih Jen Shou Pao Hsien Shang Yeh Tung Yeh Kung Hui. **VFOAT** Annual Report of Life Insurance, Republic of China. Chinese (English). Life Insurance Operation, Development Committee of Taipei, Life Insurance Association, 4-6 Alley 4 Lane 217/Sec 3 Chung Hsiao East Road, Taipei Taiwan. **LC** HG9171; .T34.

US/1040-1008
JOHN BURTON'S WORKERS' COMPENSATION MONITOR. [John Burton's work. compens. monit.]. **VFOAT** Workers' Compensation Monitor. Vol. 1, No. 1 (Jan. 1988)-. Periodical. English. bm. $180.00. LRP Publications, 747 Dresher Road, PO Box 980, Horsham PA 19044-0980. **Tel** (800)341-7874, (215)784-0860, FAX (215)784-9639, (215)784-0870. **ED** John Burton. **LC** KF3611.A3; J64. **DD** 368.
Desc: Provides analytical articles, digests of important publications, summaries of significant decisions, summaries of important laws, administrative rules, and regulations; and highlights of recent personnel changes and forthcoming conferences in the field.

US/0739-7186
JOHN HANCOCK COMPANIES ... ANNUAL REPORT. [John Hancock co. annu. rep.]. **Main/Corp** John Hancock Mutual Life Insurance Company. 1982-. English. an. John Hancock Mutual Life Insurance Company, John Hancock Place, PO Box 111, Boston MA 02117. **LC** HG8963.J6; A3. **DD** 368.3/2/006073. ***Continues** John Hancock Mutual Life Life Insurance Company. Annual Report.*

US/0021-7204
JOHN LINER LETTER, THE. [John Liner lett.]. Vol. 1 (Dec. 1963)-. Periodical. English. mo. $166.95 Massachusetts; $159.00 other US; $206.70 other. Standard Publishing Company, 155 Federal Street, Boston MA 02110. **Tel** (617)457-0604, (617)457-0600, FAX (617)457-0608. **DD** 368. Index available. cum. index.

US/0894-1807
JOHN LINER REVIEW : THE QUARTERLY REVIEW OF BUSINESS INSURANCE, THE. [John Liner rev.]. Vol. 1, No. 1 (Spring 1987)-. Periodical. English. qt. $106.00 US; $137.40 other. Standard Publishing Company, 155 Federal Street, Boston MA 02110. **Tel** (617)457-0604, (617)457-0600, FAX (617)457-0608. **ED** Roger Pierce. **LC** WMLC 93/1542. **DD** 368. Index available. cum. index. **Ad Acc. Circ:** 6,000 (ctrl). available on microfilm from University Microfilms International (UMI).
Desc: Targeted to corporate insurance buyers, risk managers, and agents and brokers specializing in property, casualty, health and benefit insurance. Covers market conditions and current legislative and regulatory issues, and reports on software and books in the field.

BG
JOURNAL - BANGLADESH INSURANCE ACADEMY. **Main/Corp** Bangladesh Insurance Academy. Vol. 1- Mar. 1975-. Periodical. English. mo. TK4.00 per copy. Bangladesh Insurance Academy, Corner Court, 29 Toyenbee Circular Road, Motijheel Bangladesh. **LC** HG8013; .B34A. **DD** 368/.9/5492.

UK
JOURNAL / CHARTERED INSURANCE INSTITUTE, THE. **Main/Corp** Chartered Insurance Institute. **VFOAT** Chartered Insurance Institute Journal. (March 1989)-. Periodical. English. bm. £18.00. Chartered Insurance Institute, 20 Aldermanbury, London EC2V 7HY England. **Tel** 011 44 071 6063835, FAX 011 44 071 7260131. **ED** Susan Sheen. **Bk Rev**, (Qty: 3-6 per year). **Ad Acc, Adv Mgr:** David Hughes, **Tel** 011 44 071 5833030. **Circ:** 62,000. ***Continues** CII Journal.*
Desc: News of CII professional training and education activities, and technical articles on insurance and financial services; also book listings and legal reviews.

●US/1064-6647
JOURNAL OF ACTUARIAL PRACTICE. [J. actuar. pract.]. **VFOAT** JAP. Vol. 1, No. 1 (1993)-. Periodical. English. Twice a year (May & Nov.). $70.00 (individuals), $140.00 (institutions) US, Canada, & Mexico; $75.00 (individuals), $150.00 (institutions) others. Absalom Press, PO Box 22098, Lincoln NE 68542. **Tel** (402)421-8149, FAX (402)421-8149. **ED** Colin M. Ramsay. **LC** HG8779; .J68. **DD** 368/.01/05. **Pr Rev.**

US/0278-5420
JOURNAL OF AGENT AND MANAGEMENT SELECTION AND DEVELOPMENT, THE. ***Suspended.*** (THE JOURNAL OF AGENT AND MANAGEMENT SELECTION AND DEVELOPMENT / BEHAVIORAL SCIENCE RESEARCH PRESS.). [J. agent manage.sel. dev.]. Vol. 1 No. 1 (Mar. 1981)-Vol. 1 No. 4 (1983). Periodical. English. ir. Behavioral Science Res Press, 2695 Villa Creek 180, Dallas TX 75234. **Tel** (214)243-8543. **LC** HG8091; .J68.

US/0021-874X
JOURNAL OF AMERICAN INSURANCE. [J. Am. insur.]. Vol. 1 (July 1924)-. Periodical. English. qt. Alliance of American Insurers, 1501 Woodfield Road, Schaumburg IL 60173-4980. **Tel** (312)490-8543. **ED** Robert S Mendenhall and Joseph Franz. **LC** HG8011; .J6. **DD** 368.05. **NLM** W1 JO535J. cum. index. **Circ:** 20,500 (ctrl). available on microfilm and microfiche from University Microfilms International (UMI). Documents available from Ask*IEEE, UMI Article Clearinghouse.
Desc: Deals with economic, personal, legal issues affecting property and casualty insurance and the American economy.
Ind/Abst ABI/INFORM Glob. Ed.; ABI Inform Ondisc (Sept. 1971-); Bus. ASAP (1992-) [Full Txt.]; Bus. Index (1985-); Bus. Source (Jul. 1993-); Gen. BusinessFile (1985-); Gen. Period. Index (1985-); Highw. Res. Abstr.; Index Period. Artic. Relat. Law; Ind. Hyg. Dig. (19??-19??); INFO-SOUTH Abstr.; INSPEC (Winter 1982/1983-1990); Ins. Period. Index; Mag. Search; PAIS Int. Print (1991-?); Trade Ind. ASAP [Full Txt.]; Trade Ind. Index [Full Txt.]; UMI ABI/Inform--Bus. Period. Ondisc (Spring 1988-1990) [Full Txt.]; Urban Aff. Abstr.

US/1057-5073
JOURNAL OF HEALTH CARE BENEFITS. [J. health care benefits]. **VFOAT** Health Care Benefits. Vol. 1, No. 1 (Sept./Oct. 1991)-. Periodical. English. bm. $132.75 US; $207.75 other. Warren Gorham & Lamont Inc., Park Square Building, 31 St. James Avenue, Boston MA 02116-4112. **Tel** (617)423-2020, (800)950-1207, FAX (617)423-2026. **LC** HG9395; .J68. **DD** 368.3/82/0097305. **NLM** W1; JO67BGE. **[CCC].**

US/0198-9839
JOURNAL OF INFORMATION MANAGEMENT. ***Suspended.*** [J. inf. manage.]. **VFOAT** Journal, Information Management. Vol. 1 (Fall 1979)-. English. Three times a year. $7.00 single issue. Life Office Management Association, 5770 Powers Ferry Road, Atlanta GA 30327. **Tel** (404)951-1770. **LC** HG8835; .J68. **DD** 368.3/2/002854. available on microfilm from University Microfilms International (UMI). Documents available from Ask*IEEE, UMI Article Clearinghouse.
Ind/Abst ABI/INFORM Glob. Ed.; ABI Inform Ondisc (Fall 1982-); INSPEC (Fall 1983-Spring 1988); UMI ABI/Inform--Bus. Period. Ondisc (Spring 1988-Spring 1988) [Full Txt.].

US
JOURNAL OF INSURANCE ISSUES. **Added/Corp** Western Risk and Insurance Association. Vol. 14, No. 1 (Jan. 1991)-. Periodical. English. sa. $20.00 US; $30.00 other. Western Risk and Insurance Association, PO Drawer DF, c/o R. Hershburger, Mississippi State MS 39762. **Tel** (601)325-2341, FAX (601)325-2410. **LC** HG8011; .J578. ***Continues** Journal of Insurance Issues and Practices, 0738-8934.*

US/0743-6661
JOURNAL OF INSURANCE MEDICINE (NEW YORK, N.Y.). (JOURNAL OF INSURANCE MEDICINE / ALIMDA.). [J. insur. med.]. **Added/Corp** Association of Life Insurance Medical Directors of America. Vol. 10, No. 4 (Oct./Dec. 1979)-. Periodical. English. qt. $45.00. Creative Concept Publishing, PO Box 8446, Kenmore WA 98028. **Tel** (206)368-8331, FAX (206)368-8331. **DD** 368. **NLM** W1 JO715D. Index available. cum. index. **Bk Rev. Ad Acc. Pr Rev. Circ:** 900. ***Continues** Insurance Medicine.*

US/0736-248X
JOURNAL OF INSURANCE REGULATION. [J. insur. regul.]. **Added/Corp** National Association of Insurance Commissioners. **VFOAT** J.I.R; JIR. Vol. 1, No. 1 (Sept. 1982)-. Periodical. English. Four times a year. $58.00 Missouri; $50.00 others. National Association of Insurance Commissioners, PO Box 263, Department 42, Kansas City MO 64193. **Tel** (816)842-3600, (816)374-7259, FAX (816)471-7004. **ED** Barbara Heaney. **LC** K10; .O867. **DD** 346.73/086/05; 347.3068605. **Circ:** 1,500 (ctrl). available on an online database (files 15,485/Full-Text) from DIALOG.
Desc: Contains articles on current insurance regulatory issues and offers point/counterpoint views.
Ind/Abst Ins. Period. Index; PAIS Int. Print.

●US/1069-4064
JOURNAL OF PENSION BENEFITS. (1993)-. Periodical. English. qt. $126.00. Panel Publishers, A Division of Aspen Publishers, Inc., 7201 McKinney Circle, PO Box 990, Frederick MD 21705-9727. **Tel** (800)638-8437. **(Subscription address:** Aspen Publishers Inc., PO Box 990, Frederick MD 21701.) **ED** Joan Gucciardi, MSPA, MAAA, EA.
Desc: Provides pension professionals with new ideas, insights, and views on trends, cost management and liability. Topics included are 401(k) plans, flexible benefits, legal developments, small business plans and much more.

US/0022-4367
JOURNAL OF RISK AND INSURANCE, THE. [J. risk insur.]. **Added/Corp** American Risk and Insurance Association. Vol. 31 (March 1964)-. Periodical. English. Four times a year. $90.00 US; $95.00 (surface mail), $100.00 (airmail) other. American Risk Insurance Association, California State University, School of Business Administration, Sacramento CA 95819-6088. **Tel** (916)278-6609, (916)278-7386, FAX (916)278-5437. **ED** J. David Cummins, Wharton School, Universtiy of Pennsylvania, 3641 Locust Walk, Philadelphia PA 19104; (215)898-5644. **LC** HG8011; .J64. **DD** 368/.973. **Ad Acc. Pr Rev.** ctrl circ. available on microfilm and microfiche from University Microfilms International (UMI); available on an online database (file 648/Full-Text) from DIALOG. Documents available from The Genuine Article, UMI Article Clearinghouse. ***Continues** Journal of Insurance (Bloomington, Ill.), 1047-3483.*
Desc: Both theoretical and empirical studies focus on the economic, financial, legal, managerial, marketing, and social aspects of risk and uncertainty.
Ind/Abst ABI/INFORM Glob. Ed.; ABI Inform Ondisc (Sept. 1971-); Acad. Search (July 1993-); Bus. ASAP (1990-) [Full Txt.]; Bus. Index (1985-); Bus. Period. Index; Bus. Source (Jul. 1993-); Contents Pages Manage.; Curr. Contents Soc. Behav. Sci.; Econ. Lit. Index; Gen. BusinessFile (1985-); Gen. Period. Index (1985-); INFO-SOUTH Abstr.; Ins. Period. Index; J. Econ. Lit.;

Insurance

Mag. Search; Manage. Contents (1974-); PAIS Int. Print (1991-); Public Aff. Inf. Serv. Bull.; Res. Alert [Full Cov.]; Soc. Sci. Cit. Index [Full Cov.]; Wilson Bus. Abstr.

US/1052-2875
JOURNAL OF THE AMERICAN SOCIETY OF CLU & CHFC. [J. Am. Soc. CLU ChFC]. **VAT** Journal of the American Society of Chartered Life Underwriters and Chartered Financial Consultants. Vol. 40, No. 6 (Nov. 1986)-. Periodical. English. bm. $32.00 (one year), $58.00 (two year), $82.00 (three year). American Society of CLU & CHFC, PO Box 59, Bryn Mawr PA 19010. **Tel** (215)526-2500, FAX (215)527-4010. **ED** Betty Thomson. **LC** HG8751; .A53. **DD** 368.3/2/00973. Index available. cum. index. **Ad Acc. Circ:** 38,000 (ctrl). available on microfilm and microfiche from University Microfilms International (UMI). Documents available from UMI Article Clearinghouse. **Continues** Journal of the American Society of CLU, 0742-9517.
Desc: To advance the philosophy and practice of professionalism in insurance specifically, and the broad field of financial services generally.
Ind/Abst ABI/INFORM Glob. Ed.; ABI Inform Ondisc (Oct. 1971-); Acad. Search (July 1993-); Account. Art.; Bus. Source (Jul. 1993-); Fed. Tax Artic.; Gen. Period. Index (1985-); INFO-SOUTH Abstr.; LegalTrac (1982-); UMI ABI/Inform--Bus. Period. Ondisc (Nov. 1987-) [Full Txt.].

UK/0020-2681
JOURNAL OF THE INSTITUTE OF ACTUARIES. [J. Inst. Actuar.]. Vol. 25, Pt. 5 (Jan. 1886)-. English. Three times a year. $60.00. Alden Press Ltd, Osney Mead, Oxford OX2 0EF England. **NLM** W1 JO931M. cum. index. **Continues** Assurance Magazine and Journal of the Institute of Actuaries.
Desc: List of members issued with Vol. 35 with separate paging.
Ind/Abst Popul. Index.

US/1059-4167
JOURNAL OF WORKERS COMPENSATION, THE. [J. work. compens.]. Vol. 1, No. 1 (Fall 1991)-. Periodical. English. qt. $115.00 US; $149.60 other. Standard Publishing Company, 155 Federal Street, Boston MA 02110. **Tel** (617)457-0604, (617)457-0600, FAX (617)457-0608. **LC** HD7103.65.U6; J68. **DD** 368.4/1/0097305. **Ad Acc.**

JA
KANI SEIMEI HOKEN NO SHIBORITSU SHOGAI HASSEIRITSU NI KANSURU CHOSA. Main/Corp Japan. Kani Hokenkyoku. (19??)-. Periodical. Japanese. Kani Hokenkyoku, 3-2 Kasumigaseki 1-chome Chiyoda-ku, Tokyo 100 Japan. **LC** HG9165; .A45d.

FI/0355-4821
KANSANELAKELAITOKSEN JULKAISUJA. M. Added/Corp Kansanelakelaitos (Finland). **VFOAT** Publications of the Social Insurance Institution, Finland. M. (1967)-. Monographic series. Finnish (English). Price varies per volume. **NLM** W1; PU736J.
Ind/Abst Int. Bibliogr. Sociol.

US
KANSAS FINAL COMPREHENSIVE SOCIAL SERVICE PLAN, TITLE XX SOCIAL SECURITY ACT. See Sociology-Social Services and Welfare.

●US/1069-1847
KANSAS INSURANCE AGENT & BROKER. [Kansas insur. agent brok.]. **Added/Corp** Professional Independent Insurance Agents of Kansas. **VFOAT** Kansas Insurance Agent and Broker. (1992)-. Periodical. English. Six times a year (Jan., Mar., May, July, Sept., Nov.). $30.00. Professional Independent Insurance Agent Kansas, 815 Topeka Avenue, Topeka KS 66612. **Tel** (913)232-0561, FAX (913)232-6817. **ED** Sue Schulte. **DD** 368. **Ad Acc. Circ:** 1,000.
Desc: This features articles and news on insurance trading.

US/0889-0560
KEEPING CURRENT. Added/Corp American Society of Chartered Life Underwriters. Continuing Education Division. (19??)-. Periodical. English. Four times a year (Mar., June, Sept., Dec.). $129.00 (non members); $99.00 (members). American Society of Chartered Life Underwriters, PO Box 59, Bryn Mawr PA 19010. **Tel** (215)526-2500, FAX (215)527-1499. **ED** Vince Mallom, (phone: (215)526-2514). cum. index. **Circ:** 5000.
Desc: Life insurance practical applications.

●US
KELLY INSURANCE DIRECTORY: NATIONWIDE HOSPITAL INSURANCE BILLING DIRECTORY. Added/Corp Francis B. Kelly and Associates. **VFOAT** Nationwide Hospital Insurance Billing Directory. (1991/1992)-. Directory. English. Francis Kelly and Associates, 123 Veteran Avenue, Los Angles CA 90024.

LC HG9395; .N37. **DD** 368.3/82/002573. **Continues** Nationwide Hospital Insurance Billing Directory, 1052-9659.

JA
KENKO HOKEN KUMIAI JIGYO NEMPO. Added/Corp Kenko Hoken Kumiai Rengokai. Japan. Koseisho. Hokenkyoku. (1957)-. Periodical. Japanese. Kenko Hoken Kumiai Rengokai, (National Federation of Health Insurance Society), 24-4 Minamiaoyama 1 chome, Minatoku Tokyo 107 Japan. **LC** HG9399.J3; K45.

US/1071-8230
KIRSCHNER'S INSURANCE DIRECTORIES. NORTHERN CALIFORNIA. [Kirschner's insur. dir., North. Calif.]. **VFOAT** Kirschner's Insurance Directory. Northern California. (1981)-. English. sa. $29.90. Kirschner's Insurance Directories, P.O.Box 1087, Folsom CA 95763. **Tel** (916)983-7170, FAX (916)983-1704. **DD** 368. Index available. **Ad Acc. Circ:** 5,500.

US/1071-8222
KIRSCHNER'S INSURANCE DIRECTORIES. PACIFIC NORTHWEST. [Kirschner's insur. dir., Pac. Northwest]. **VFOAT** Kirschner's Insurance Directory. Pacific Northwest. (19??)-. English. sa. $29.90. Kirschner's Insurance Directories, P.O.Box 1087, Folsom CA 95763. **Tel** (916)983-7170, FAX (916)983-1704. **DD** 368.

US/1071-8249
KIRSCHNER'S INSURANCE DIRECTORY. SOUTHERN CALIFORNIA. [Kirschner's insur. dir., South. Calif.]. **VFOAT** Kirschner's Insurance Directory. Southern California. (19??)-. Directory. English. sa. $29.90. Kirschner's Insurance Directories, P.O.Box 1087, Folsom CA 95763. **Tel** (916)983-7170, FAX (916)983-1704. **DD** 368. Index available. **Ad Acc. Circ:** 6,500.

GW/0342-0809
KOMPASS (BOCHUM), DER. (DER KOMPASS; ZEITSCHRIFT FUER SOZIALVERSICHERUNG IM BERGBAN.). [Kompass]. (1886)-. German. mo. DM85.70. Verlag Glueckauf GmbH, Postfach 185619, D-45206 Essen Germany. **Tel** 011 49 2054 924200, 011 49 2054 924201, 011 49 2054 924202, telex 08579545. Index Available, published separately, free-automatically sent. Documents available from BLDSC.
Desc: Covers all aspects of insurance for the mining industry.
Ind/Abst Coal Abstr.; Saf. Health Work.

KO
KOREA NON-LIFE INSURANCE INDUSTRY. Title Change. Main/Corp Taehan Sonhae Pohom Hyophoe. (Jan. 1979)-(19??). English. sa. Korea Non-Life Insurance Association, 80 Susong-dong Chongro-gu, KPO Box 1379, Seoul Korea. **Tel** (02)739-4163, telex SONBO K27947. **ED** Hong Jo. **LC** HG8707; .A28a. **DD** 338.4/736895195. **Circ:** 1,500. **Continued by** Korea Non-Life Insurance.

GW/0301-4835
KRANKENVERSICHERUNG (BERLIN), DIE. (DIE KRANKENVERSICHERUNG.). (Oct. 1949)-. Periodical. German. Twelve times a year. DM143.40. Erich Schmidt Verlag GmbH, Postfach 304240, D 10724 Berlin Germany. **Tel** 011 49 30 25008525. **LC** HD7102.G3; K63. **NLM** W1 KR274H. **[CCC].** **Bk Rev. Ad Acc.** available on microfilm.
Desc: Social insurance.

SW
LAGEN OM ALLMAN FORSAKRING OCH ANDRA FORFATTNINGAR OM SOCIALFORSAKRING M.M. See Sociology-Social Services and Welfare.

MY/0126-8252
LAPORAN TAHUNAN ... KETUA PENGARAH INSURANS. Main/Corp Malaysia. Bahagian Insuran. **VFOAT** Annual Report of the Director General of Insurance. English (Malay). an. $15.00. Ketua Pengarah Percetakan Negara Semenanjung Malaysia, Jl Chan Sow Lin, Kuala Lumpur 07-03 Malaysia. **LC** HG8704.66; .A24. **DD** 368/.9595.

US
LAW OF LIABILITY INSURANCE. See Law.

US/0023-9631
LEADERS MAGAZINE (LEXINGTON). (LEADERS MAGAZINE.). [Leaders magazine]. Periodical. English. bm. $11.95 (one year), $22.00 (two year), $29.00 (three year) US; $15.95 (one year), $26.00 (two years) Canada; $18.50 (one year), $29.00 (two years) other. Insurance Publications, 100 Dennis Drive, Lexington KY 40503. **Tel** (606)277-6221, (800)356-5936, FAX (606)277-8059. **ED** Fred R Kissling Jr. **Bk Rev. Ad Acc. Circ:** 10,000. available on microfilm and microfiche from University Microfilms International (UMI). **Continues** Leader's Digest.
Desc: Ideas on selling all types of insurance, disability, life, etc. The life insurance sales digest.

US
LECTURES - DALLAS. SOUTHERN METHODIST UNIVERSITY. CASUALTY AND PROPERTY INSURANCE INSTITUTE. Main/Corp Dallas. Southern Methodist University. Casualty and Property Insurance Institute. 1st (1951?)-. English. be.

US/0148-2750
LEGAL MALPRACTICE REVIEW. See Law.

US/0094-0623
LEGAL NOTES FOR INSURANCE. See Law.

US
LEGAL SECTION PROCEEDINGS / THE ... ANNUAL MEETING OF THE LEGAL SECTION OF THE AMERICAN COUNCIL OF LIFE INSURANCE. Main/Corp American Council of Life Insurance. Legal Section. Meeting. **VFOAT** ACLI Legal Section Proceedings. (1984)-. Proceedings. English. an. American Council of Life Insurance, 1001 Pennsylvania Avenue Northwest, Washington DC 20004. **Tel** (202)624-2372. **Continues** Proceedings of the Annual Meeting of the Legal Section of the American Council of Life Insurance, 0196-805X.

UK
LIABILITY RISK AND INSURANCE. English. Twelve times a year. £290.00 UK; $480.00 US & Canada. DYP Insurance Reinsurance Res. Grp. Ltd., 181 Queen Victoria St. Bridge House, London EC4V 4DD England. **Tel** 011 44 71 236 2175, FAX 011 44 71 489 1487.

US/0742-5120
LICENSING, COUNTERSIGNING, AND SURPLUS LINE LAWS FOR THE 50 STATES, DISTRICT OF COLUMBIA, PUERTO RICO, AND THE VIRGIN ISLANDS. See Law.

US/1053-2838
LIFE & HEALTH INSURANCE SALES. [Life health insur. sales]. **VFOAT** Life and Health Insurance Sales; Insurance Sales. Vol. 133, No. 4 (April 1990)-. Periodical. English. mo. $25.00 (one year), $40.25 (two year), $55.50 (three year) US; $35.00 (one year), $60.25 (two year), $85.50 (three year) other. Rough Notes Company Inc, 1200 North Meridian Street, Indianapolis IN 46206. **Tel** (317)634-1541, (800)428-4384, FAX (317)634-1041. **LC** HG8751; .I6. **DD** 368.3/8/00688. **Continues** IS, Insurance Sales, 0199-4581.

US/0024-3078
LIFE ASSOCIATION NEWS. [Life assoc. news]. **Added/Corp** National Association of Life Underwriters. **VFOAT** LAN. Vol. 1 (Sept. 1906)-. Periodical. English. mo. $6.00 US; $28.00 other. National Association of Life Underwriters, 1922 F Street NW, Washington DC 20006. **Tel** (202)331-6070, FAX (202)835-9608. **ED** Ian MacKenzie. **LC** HG8751; .L47. **DD** 368.305. Index available. cum. index. **Bk Rev. Ad Acc. Circ:** 145,000 (ctrl). available on microfilm and microfiche from University Microfilms International (UMI); available on an online database (file 15/Full-Text) from DIALOG. Documents available from UMI Article Clearinghouse.
Desc: Directed to the individual life and health insurance agents who make up the National Association of Life Underwriters. Its purpose is to enhance the professionalism of its readers. More than half of each issue is devoted to articles from successful life insurance agents demonstrating the use of life and health insurance products in solving problems for their clients.
Ind/Abst ABI/INFORM Glob. Ed.; ABI Inform Ondisc (Feb. 1972-); Account. Art. (1974-); Fed. Tax Artic.; Ins. Period. Index (-19??); Manage. Contents (1974-); Ref. Sources; UMI ABI/Inform--Bus. Period. Ondisc (Dec. 1987-) [Full Txt.].

US/0047-4606
LIFE COMPANY TAX NEWSLETTER. See Law.

CH
LIFE INSURANCE BUSINESS IN TAIWAN. English. an. Taipei Life Insurance Association, 5th Floor/152 Sung Chiang Road, Taipei Taiwan. **LC** HG9171; .A25. **DD** 338.4/736832/00951249.

US
LIFE INSURANCE BUYING. Main/Corp American Council of Life Insurance. Statistical Services. English. Free. Statistical Services of the American Council of Life Insurance, 1850 K Street NW, Washington DC 20006-2284. **Tel** (202)862-4000.

US/0075-9406
LIFE INSURANCE FACT BOOK. Added/Corp American Council of Life Insurance. Institute of Life Insurance (New York, N.Y.). (1946)-. English. an. American Council of Life Insurance, 1001 Pennsylvania Avenue Northwest, Washington DC 20004. **Tel**

Insurance

(202)624-2372. **ED** Suzanne K. Stemnock. **LC** HG8943; .L5. **DD** 368.3058. **NLM** W1 LI404K. ctrl circ.
Ind/Abst Predicasts Forecasts; Stat. Ref. Index.

US/0024-3116
LIFE INSURANCE IDEAS. (LIFE INSURANCE IDEAS : IBP, LIFE INSURANCE PLANNING.). **Main/Corp** Institute for Business Planning, Inc. Periodical. English. sm. $204.00. Institute for Business Planning Inc, Subscription Service Center, IBP Plaza, Englewood Cliffs NJ 07632.

IE/0956-327X
LIFE INSURANCE INTERNATIONAL. (LIFE INSURANCE INTERNATIONAL : LII.). [Life insur. int.]. **VFOAT** LII. (1989)-. Periodical. English. mo (10 issues). $749.00. Lafferty Publications Ltd. / Dublin, Tower Ida Centre Pearse St., Dublin 2 Ireland. **Tel** 011 353 1 6718022, FAX 01-718520.
Desc: Bulletin for senior executives in financial institutions that provide life insurance and other forms of contractual savings.

US/0024-3132
LIFE INSURANCE PLANNING. Main/Corp Institute for Business Planning, Inc. (19??)-. English. Thirty-seven times a year (includes one volume, monthly supplements, and semi-monthly newsletters). $279.00. Prentice-Hall Law and Business, 270 Sylvan Avenue, Englewood Cliffs NJ 07632. **Tel** (800)223-0231, (201)894-8538, FAX (201)894-8666.

US/0024-3140
LIFE INSURANCE SELLING. [Life insur. sell.]. (19??)-. Periodical. English. ir. $8.00. Commerce Publishing Company, 408 Olive Street, St Louis MO 63102. **Tel** (314)421-5445. **ED** Larry Albright. **LC** HG8751; .L65. **Bk Rev. Ad Acc**. **Circ:** 43,125. available on microfilm and microfiche from University Microfilms International (UMI). **Absorbed** Selling Insurance.
Desc: A magazine of tested sales ideas for life insurance salespeople and financial planners. Includes sales techniques, insurance trends, new policies, and office aids.
Ind/Abst Ins. Period. Index (-199?).

CN/0835-2933
LIFE INSURANCE TABLES. [Life insur. tables]. **Added/Corp** Stone & Cox Limited. **VFOAT** Tables d'Assurance-Vie. (1987)-. English (French). $21.00 per Vol. Stone & Cox Ltd Publishers, 111 Peter Street, Suite 202, Toronto Ontario M5V 2H1 Canada. **Tel** (416)599-0772. **DD** 368.3/2011/0971. **Continues** Stone & Cox Life Insurance Tables, 0081-5780.

US/0889-0986
LIMRA'S MARKETFACTS. [LIMRA's mark.Facts]. **Added/Corp** Life Insurance Marketing and Research Association. **VFOAT** LIMRA's Market Facts; Market Facts; Marketfacts. **VAT** Life Insurance Marketing and Research Association's Marketfacts. (198?)-. Periodical. English. Six times a year (Jan., Mar., May, July, Sept., Nov.). £36.00 Europe / $45.00 nonmembers, $90.00 LIMRA members. Life Insurance Market and Research Association Inc, PO Box 208, Hartford CT 01641. **Tel** (203)677-0033 (800)235-4672, FAX (203)678-0187. **DD** 368. **Continues** Marketfacts.
Ind/Abst Ins. Period. Index (1987-199?).

US/0892-1458
LINER'S INSURANCE MARKETING INSIDER. Title Change. [Liner's insur. mark. insid.]. **Added/Corp** John Liner Insurance and Risk Management Advisors Inc. **VFOAT** Insurance Marketing Insider. Vol. 1, No. 1 (Jan. 1987)-(198?). Periodical. English. mo. Standard Publishing Company, 155 Federal Street, Boston MA 02110. **Tel** (617)457-0604, (617)457-0600, FAX (617)457-0608. **ED** Diana Montgomery. **DD** 368. Index available. cum. index. **Continued by** Insurance Marketing Insider, 1040-6867.

US/0428-1365
LIST OF MEMBER INSTITUTIONS - FEDERAL SAVINGS AND LOAN INSURANCE CORPORATION. (LIST OF MEMBER INSTITUTIONS.). **Main/Corp** Federal Savings and Loan Insurance Corporation. (19??)-. English. Federal Savings and Loan Insurance Corporation, 320 1st Street NW, Washington DC 20552. **LC** HG1662.U5; F42b. **DD** 368.8/54/01673.

US/0537-9350
LIST OF WORTHWHILE LIFE AND HEALTH INSURANCE BOOKS, A.
Added/Corp American Council of Life Insurance. Institute of Life Insurance (New York, N.Y.) Health Insurance Institute (New York, N.Y.). (1968)-. English. an. Free. American Council of Life Insurance, 1001 Pennsylvania Avenue Northwest, Washington DC 20004. **Tel** (202)624-2372. **LC** Z7164.I7; L58; HG8771. **DD** 016.3683/2. **NLM** ZW 275 AA1 L72. **Formed by the union of** List of Current Health Insurance Books, 0360-2214 **and** List of Worthwhile Life Insurance Books, 0537-9369.

US
LLOYD'S INSURANCE INTERNATIONAL. English. mo. $249.00. Lloyd's of London Press Inc., 611 Broadway/Suite 308, New York NY 10012. **Tel** (212)529-9500, FAX (212)529-9826, telex 7105812659. **ED** Jeff Myhre. cum. index. **Circ:** 600.
Continues Lloyd's Marine Insurance International, 0268-1927; Lloyd's Non-Marine Insurance International.
Desc: Covers developments in the world-wide insurance markets: property, casualty, aviation, marine, fire, motor, accidents and natural disasters. Provides news of policy innovations, mergers and acquisitions, legal cases, regulations, political developments affecting insurance and corporate results. Provides commentary and analysis for the entire insurance world.

UK/0265-8356
LONDON MARKET NEWSLETTER. [Lond. mark. newsl.]. (1982)-. Periodical. English. Fifty times a year. £355.00 UK; $585.00 US & Canada. DYP Insurance Reinsurance Res. Grp. Ltd., 181 Queen Victoria St. Bridge House, London EC4V 4DD England. **Tel** 011 44 71 236 2175, FAX 011 44 71 489 1487. **ED** Graham Village. **DD** 368.2009421. **Bk Rev**. available on microfiche.
Desc: News, features and statistical surveys on international insurance and reinsurance centered on the london market.

US/0024-6832
LOUISIANA INSUROR. Added/Corp Louisiana Association of Insurance Agents, inc. (194?)-. Periodical. English. Six times a year. Independent Insurance Agent of Louisiana, 1 American Place/Suite 2020, Baton Rouge LA 70825. **Tel** (504)387-5149.

US/0090-6506
MAJOR MEDICAL PLANS : SELECTED COLLECTIVE BARGAINING AGREEMENTS, CALIFORNIA. Main/Corp California. Dept. of Industrial Relations. Division of Labor Statistics and Research. English. California Department of Industrial Relations, 395 Oyster Pt. Boulevard, San Francisco CA 94101. **Tel** (415)982-4773, FAX (415)557-8964. **LC** HD7102.U5; C23. **DD** 331.89.

US/1059-6186
MALECKI ON INSURANCE. [Malecki insur.]. Vol. 1, No. 1 (Nov. 1991)-. Periodical. English. mo. $122.00. Malecki Communications, 4959 Delhi Road, Cincinnati OH 45238. **Tel** (513)451-6046, FAX (513)451-0023. **DD** 368.

US/1042-4091
MANAGED CARE LAW OUTLOOK. See Law.

US/8756-6001
MANAGEMENT COMPENSATION SURVEY OF THE INSURANCE INDUSTRY. See Economics-Labor.

US/0748-6316
MANAGEMENT SUMMARY. (MANAGEMENT SUMMARY / NATIONAL COUNCIL ON COMPENSATION INSURANCE.). **Added/Corp** National Council on Compensation Insurance. (19??)-. English. an. National Council on Compensation Insurance, 1 Penn Plaza, New York NY 10001. **LC** HD7103.65.U6; M35. **DD** 368.4/1012.

US/0025-1968
MANAGER'S MAGAZINE. [Manager's mag.]. **Added/Corp** Life Insurance Marketing and Research Association. Life Insurance Sales Research Bureau. Vol. 1, (Jan. 1926)-. Periodical. English. Twelve times a year. $65.00 (nonmembers), $45.00 (members) surface mail; £48.00 Europe. Life Insurance Market and Research Association Inc, PO Box 208, Hartford CT 01641. **Tel** (203)677-0033 (800)235-4672, FAX (203)678-0187. **ED** Valerie E. C. Barker. **LC** HG8751; .M3. **DD** 368.305. Index available. cum. index. **Bk Rev**. **Circ:** 13,000 (ctrl). available on microfilm and microfiche from University Microfilms International (UMI). Documents available from UMI Article Clearinghouse. **Supersedes** Quarterly Review of Life Insurance and Business Conditions.
Desc: Articles for insurance field management.
Ind/Abst ABI/INFORM Glob. Ed.; ABI Inform Ondisc (Summer 1976-); Acad. Search (July 1993-); Bus. ASAP (1992-) [Full Txt.]; Bus. Index (1985-); Bus. Source (Jul. 1993-); Gen. BusinessFile (1985-); Law Office Inf. Serv.; Mag. Search; UMI ABI/Inform--Bus. Period. Ondisc (Feb. 1987-) [Full Txt.].

●US/1065-3937
MANAGING EMPLOYEE HEALTH BENEFITS. See Business-General Management.

US/0161-2174
MAP, MONITORING ATTITUDES OF THE PUBLIC. Main/Corp American Council of Life Insurance. **VFOAT** MAP Survey. English. an. Free. American Council of Life Insurance, 1001 Pennsylvania Avenue Northwest, Washington DC 20004. **Tel** (202)624-2372. **LC** HG8943; .A47A. **DD** 301.15/43/3683200973. **Continues** MAP Report: Monitoring Attitudes of the Public.

UK/0265-8410
MARINE & AVIATION INSURANCE REPORT. [Mar. aviat. insur. rep.]. **VFOAT** Marine and Aviation Insurance Report. (1984)-. Periodical. English. Twelve times a year. £305.00 UK; $505.00 US & Canada. DYP Insurance Reinsurance Res. Grp. Ltd., 181 Queen Victoria St. Bridge House, London EC4V 4DD England. **Tel** 011 44 71 236 2175, FAX 011 44 71 489 1487. **DD** 368.2400941.

CN/0228-8923
MARINE AND INSURANCE NEWS. [Mar. insur. news]. July 1980-. Periodical. English. mo. Knops Consultants, 1256 Lake Sundance Crescent Southeast, Calgary Alberta T2J 2S8 Canada. **DD** 368.2/2/00971.

UK/0268-1927
MARINE INSURANCE INTERNATIONAL. Title Change. Vol. 1, No. 1 (Aug. 1985)-?. Periodical. English. bw. Lloyd's of London Press Ltd, Sheepen Place, Colchester, Essex, CO3 3LP England. **Tel** 011 44 206 772113, US: (212)529-9500, US: (800)955-6937, FAX 011 44 206 772880, US: (212)529-9826, telex 987321 LLOYDS G. **(Subscription address:** US/ 611 Broadway, Suite 523, New York, NY 10012**)** **Bk Rev**. **Circ:** 200. **Continued by** Absorbed into Lloyd's Insurance International.

US
MARKET INTEREST RATE FOR PROJECT MORTGAGE INSURANCE. Government Publication. English. ir. US Department of Housing and Urban Development, 451 Seventh Street SW, Washington DC 20401. **Tel** (202)708-0980, FAX (202)708-0299.

CN/0822-3998
MARKETING OPTIONS. See Business-Marketing.

US/0893-1011
MEALEY'S LITIGATION REPORTS. BAD FAITH. See Law.

US/8755-9005
MEALEY'S LITIGATION REPORTS. INSURANCE. See Law.

●US/1075-380X
MEALEY'S LITIGATION REPORTS. INSURANCE FRAUD. [Mealey's litig. rep., Insur. fraud]. **Added/Corp** Mealey Publications. **VFOAT** Insurance Fraud. Vol. 1, Issue #1 (Feb. 1994)-. Periodical. English. mo. $390.00. Mealey Publications, PO Box 446, Wayne PA 19087-0446. **Tel** (215)688-6566, FAX (215)688-7552. **LC** IN PROCESS. **DD** 346.

US/1043-8416
MEALEY'S LITIGATION REPORTS. INSURANCE INSOLVENCY. See Law.

US/1055-307X
MEALEY'S LITIGATION REPORTS. PUNITIVE DAMAGES & TORT REFORM.
Added/Corp Mealey Publications. **VFOAT** Punitive Damages & Tort Reform; Punitive Damages and Tort Reform. Vol. 5, Issue #15 (Feb. 8, 1991)-. Periodical. English. Twenty-four times a year. $695.00. Mealey Publications, PO Box 446, Wayne PA 19087-0446. **Tel** (215)688-6566, FAX (215)688-7552. **ED** Scott Jacobs. **LC** KF1246.A3; M43. **DD** 346.7303/05; 347.306305. **[CCC].** Index available ((published separately)). cum. index. **Continues** Insurance Antitrust & Tort Reform Report, 0898-5170.
Desc: Covers precedent-setting civil litigation in product liability and personal injury cases, punitive damages, legislative initiatives to revise tort laws and subsequent legal challenges, and antitrust litigation against insurance companies.

US/0193-9483
MEDICAL ASSISTANCE, MEDICAID (LANSING). See Sociology-Social Services and Welfare.

US/0743-8079
MEDICAL BENEFITS. [Med. benefits]. (Jan. 1984)-. Periodical. English. Twenty-four times a year. $178.00. Panel Publishers, A Division of Aspen Publishers, Inc., 7201 McKinney Circle, PO Box 990, Frederick MD 21705-9727. **Tel** (800)638-8437. **(Subscription address:** Aspen Publishers Inc., PO Box 990, Frederick MD 21701.**)** **ED** Margaret Mucklo and Bruce G. Carveth. **DD** 368. **NLM** W1; ME228M. Index available (free).
Desc: Digest of current research and news related to health care costs for American business.
Ind/Abst Work Relat. Abstr. (?-19??).

Insurance

US
MEDICAL MALPRACTICE. (19??)-. English. ir. Price varies. Matthew Bender & Company Inc., 1275 Broadway, Albany NY 12204. **Tel** (800)833-9844, (518)487-3000.

US
MEDICAL SECTION PROCEEDINGS : THE ... ANNUAL MEETING OF THE MEDICAL SECTION OF THE AMERICAN COUNCIL OF LIFE INSURANCE. Main/Corp American Council of Life Insurance. Medical Section. Meeting. 8th (June 25-29, 1983)-. Proceedings. English. an. American Council of Life Insurance, 1001 Pennsylvania Avenue Northwest, Washington DC 20004. **Tel** (202)624-2372. **LC** HG8886.A3; .A44A. *Continues Proceedings / American Council of Life Insurance. Medical Section.*

US/0743-5959
MEDICARE AND MEDICAID DATA BOOK, THE. See Sociology-Social Services and Welfare.

●US/1068-1019
MEDICARE AND MEDICAID LAW BULLETIN. [Medicare Medicaid law bul.]. (Sept. 1992)-. Periodical. English. wk. $250.00. LRP Publications, 747 Dresher Road, PO Box 980, Horsham PA 19044-0980. **Tel** (800)341-7874, (215)784-0860, FAX (215)784-9639, (215)784-0870. **DD** 346.
Desc: Provides summaries of decisions relating to Medicare and Medicaid.

US/1047-1863
MEDICARE COMPLIANCE ALERT. [Medicare compliance alert]. Vol. 1, No. 1 (Oct. 2, 1989)-. Periodical. English. Twenty-four times a year. $370.00. United Communications Group, 11300 Rockville Pike, Suite 1100, Rockville MD 20852. **Tel** (301)816-8950 ext. 223, FAX (301)816-8945. **DD** 368. **NLM** W1; ME5509B.

US/0733-4672
MEDICARE EXPLAINED. Added/Corp Commerce Clearing House. (1979)-. English. an (March). $17.50. Commerce Clearing House Inc., 4025 West Peterson Avenue, Chicago IL 60646-6085. **Tel** (312)583-8500, FAX (708)940-4600. **LC** KF3608.A4; M42. **DD** 344.73/0226; 347.304226. **NLM** W 32.5; AA1 M42. *Continues in part Social Security and Medicare Explained.*
Desc: Guidance on every important aspect of Medicare. Reflects new Medicare cost-sharing obligation for beneficiaries and discusses the Physician's Medicare Fee Schedule.

US/0730-143X
MEDICARE, HEALTH INSURANCE FOR THE AGED AND DISABLED. SUMMARY-UTILIZATION AND REIMBURSEMENT BY PERSON. Title Change. See Sociology-Social Services and Welfare.

US
MEDICARE HOSPITAL MANUAL. Added/Corp United States. Health Care Financing Administration. **VFOAT** Hospital Manual; Health Insurance for the Aged Hospital Manual. (1977)-. Government Publication. English. ir. $380.00 US; $475.00 other. Superintendent of Documents, US Government Printing Office, Washington DC 20402. **Tel** (202)275-3328, FAX (202)786-2377.
Desc: Procedures for filing prompt and accurate claims for services rendered to aged patients under the provisions of the Health Insurance for the Aged Act.

US/1068-2465
MEDICARE MANAGER. [Medicare manag.]. (Jan. 1991)-. Periodical. English. Twelve times a year. $117.00. Shannon Publications, 9441 LBJ Freeway, Box 2, Suite 510, Dallas TX 75243. **Tel** (214)644-0159, FAX (214)644-1538. **ED** Ellen Bradley. **DD** 368. ctrl circ.
Desc: Written for the doctors or their office managers. Offer tips, solutions and applications for incorporating medicare rules & regulations into the office procedures. Covers Part B reimbursement and management issues.

US/0896-4815
MEDICARE-MEMORANDUM (OUTPATIENT CLINIC ED.). See Sociology-Social Services and Welfare.

US/0730-7942
MEDICARE, USE OF SKILLED NURSING FACILITIES. 1976-1977-. English. Health Care Financing Administration, 6325 Security Boulevard, Room 700, Baltimore MD 21207. **Tel** (410)966-3000, FAX (410)966-5267. **NLM** W2 A H23M.

AG
MERCADO ASEGURADOR. Spanish (translations available in English). mo (11 issues per year - Jan./Feb. issues combined). $190.00. EDISEG SRL, Tucuman 1516 3A, 1050 Buenos Aires, Argentina. **Tel** 011 54 1 476-0356, FAX 011 54 1 393-7245. Index Available in first issue of next volume--attached.

●US
MERCER GUIDE TO SOCIAL SECURITY AND MEDICARE. Added/Corp William M. Mercer, Inc. **VFOAT** Guide to Social Security and Medicare; Mercer Guide to Social Security & Medicare. (1992)-. English. an. $10.00. William Mercer Inc., 1500 Meidinger Tower, Louisville KY 40202. **Tel** (502)561-4541. **LC** HD7123.U5; M47. *Continues Guide to Social Security and Medicare.*

CN
MERCER PENSION MANUAL, THE. Carswell Publications, 2330 Midland Avenue, Agincourt Ontario M1S 1P7 Canada. **Tel** (416)291-8421.

●US/1061-2610
MICHIGAN INSURANCE HANDBOOK. (MICHIGAN INSURANCE HANDBOOK / PREPARED BY PUBLIC SECTOR CONSULTANTS, INC.). [Mich. insur. handb.]. **Added/Corp** Public Sector Consultants, Inc. (1991-92)-. English. be. Public Sector Consultants, Inc., Knapp's Centre, 300 South Washington Square, Suite 401, Lansing MI 48933. **DD** 368. *Continues Michigan Insurance Issues Handbook, 1061-2602.*

US/0026-2935
MID AMERICA INSURANCE. (19??)-. Periodical. English. Twelve times a year. $10.00. Insurance Publications Inc., PO Box 11310, Overland Park KS 66207. **Tel** (913)383-9191, (800)762-3387, FAX (913)383-1247. **ED** Jim Willman. **Ad Acc. Circ:** 25,000 (ctrl). Documents available from UMI Article Clearinghouse.
Desc: Ideas on the application and sale of life and health insurance products.
Ind/Abst ABI/INFORM Glob. Ed.; ABI Inform Ondisc (Jan. 1988-).

US/0740-8366
MINNESOTA INSURANCE. VFOAT Insurance Minnesota. Vol. 1, No. 1 (Dec. 1982)-. Periodical. English. mo (12 issues). $17.00 (1 year), $30.00 (2 year). Minnesota Insurance, 1107 Hazeltine Boulevard, Suite 539, Chaska MN 55318. **Tel** (612)448-8816. **ED** Jack Meusey. **Ad Acc. Circ:** 4,500 (ctrl).

CN/0825-0138
MINUTES OF PROCEEDINGS AND EVIDENCE OF THE SPECIAL COMMITTEE ON PENSION REFORM. See Economics-Labor.

CN/0315-7253
MINUTES OF PROCEEDINGS OF THE ANNUAL CONFERENCE - ASSOCIATION OF SUPERINTENDENTS OF INSURANCE OF THE PROVINCES OF CANADA. See Law.

US/1052-7869
MISSISSIPPI WORKERS' COMPENSATION REPORTER. [Miss. work. compens. rep.]. **VFOAT** MWCR. Vol. 1, No. 1 (May 15, 1989)-. Periodical. English. Twenty-four times a year. $100.00 (one year), $150.00 (two year). Jackson Legal Publication, Post Office Box 12528, Jackson MS 39236. **Tel** (601)856-2326, FAX (601)957-9309. **ED** J.A. Fortenberry. **LC** KFM6942; .A516. **DD** 344.762/021; 347.620421. Index available. cum. index. **Circ:** 500.
Desc: A briefing service on all workers' compensation decisions handed down by the Mississippi Workers' Compensation Commission and the Mississippi Supreme Court. Subscriptions include a complimentary subscription to the Workers' Compensation Watch, a legislative tracking service covering workers' compensation.

SZ/0042-3815
MITTEILUNGEN DES VEREINIGUNG SCHWEIZERISCHER VERSICHERUNGSMATHEMATIKER. (MITTEILUNGEN / VEREINIGUNG SCHWEIZERISCHER VERSICHERUNGSMATHEMATIKER.). [Mitt. Ver. schweiz. Versicherungsmath.]. **Added/Corp** Vereinigung Schweizerischer Versicherungsmathematiker. (1980)-. Periodical. German (English, French and Italian). sa. 150.00F Switzerland; 160.00F other. Staempfli & Cie SA, Postfach 8326, CH-3001 Bern Switzerland. **Tel** 011 41 31 3006666, telex 031 911 515 EDMZ CH. [CCC].
Continues Mitteilungen der Vereinigung Schweizerischer Versicherungsmathematiker.
Ind/Abst Math. Rev.

US
MONTHLY JOB SERVICE STATISTICS. Added/Corp Washington (State). Employment Security Dept. Vol. 43, No. 1 (Jan. 1986)-. Periodical. English. mo. Research and Analysis Branch, Washington State Employment Security Department, Box 9046, Olympia WA 98507. **Tel** (206)438-4800, FAX (206)438-4846. *Continues Statistical Summary of Activities for the Month.*

US/1047-9961
MONTHLY SURVEY OF LIFE INSURANCE SALES IN THE UNITED STATES (1986). (MONTHLY SURVEY OF LIFE INSURANCE SALES IN THE UNITED STATES.). [Mon. surv. life insur. sales U. S.]. **Added/Corp** LIMRA International (Organization). **VFOAT** Life Insurance Sales in the United States. (Jan. 1986)-. Periodical. English. mo. $625.00. Life Insurance Market and Research Association Inc, PO Box 208, Hartford CT 01641. **Tel** (203)677-0033 (800)235-4672, FAX (203)678-0187. **DD** 368. *Continues Monthly Survey of Life Insurance Sales in the United States and Canada.*

US
MORNINGSTAR VARIABLE ANNUITIES / LIFE. (19??)-. English. bw. $295.00 US; $355.00 Canada and Mexico; $495.00 other. Morningstar Inc, 225 West Wacker Drive, Chicago IL 60606. **Tel** (312)696-6000, (800)876-5005.

US/1076-2167
MORNINGSTAR VARIABLE ANNUITY/LIFE SOURCEBOOK. Ceased. [Morningstar var. annuity/life sourceb.]. **Added/Corp** Morningstar, Inc. **VFOAT** Variable Annuity/Life Sourcebook; Variable Annuity Life Source Book. (1993)-(1994). English. an. Morningstar Inc, 225 West Wacker Drive, Chicago IL 60606. **Tel** (312)696-6000, (800)876-5005. **DD** 368. *Continues Variable Annuity Sourcebook, 1062-3361.*

US
MORTGAGE CREDIT ANALYSIS FOR MORTGAGE INSURANCE ON ONE TO FOUR FAMILY PROPERTIES. Government Publication. English. US Department of Housing and Urban Development, 451 Seventh Street SW, Washington DC 20401. **Tel** (202)708-0980, FAX (202)708-0299.

US
MORTGAGE CREDIT ANALYSIS FOR PROJECT MORTGAGE INSURANCE. Government Publication. English. US Department of Housing and Urban Development, 451 Seventh Street SW, Washington DC 20401. **Tel** (202)708-0980, FAX (202)708-0299.

US
MORTGAGE GUARANTY. VFOAT Mortgage Guaranty Insurance. 1980-. English. an. Department of Consumer Affairs Regulation and Licensing / Missouri, Division of Insurance, PO Box 690, Jefferson City MO 65120. **LC** HG9992.35.M8; M67. **DD** 368.8/52/009778.

US
MORTGAGE INSURANCE FOR THE PURCHASE OR REFINANCING OF EXISTING MULTIFAMILY HOUSING PROJECTS. Government Publication. English. ir. US Department of Housing and Urban Development, 451 Seventh Street SW, Washington DC 20401. **Tel** (202)708-0980, FAX (202)708-0299.

●UK/0965-8629
MOTOR INSURANCE MARKET. [Mot. insur. mark.]. (1992)-. Periodical. English. Twelve times a year. £210.00 UK; $350.00 US & Canada. DYP Insurance Reinsurance Res. Grp. Ltd., 181 Queen Victoria St. Bridge House, London EC4V 4DD England. **Tel** 011 44 71 236 2175, FAX 011 44 71 489 1487. **DD** 368.0920941.

CN/0828-6159
MUTUALISTE, LE. [Mutualiste]. Vol. 1, No. 1 (Sept./Oct. 1983)-. Periodical. French. en. Free. Federation des Mutuelles d'Incendie, Bureau 300/2014 Ouest Boulevard Charest, Ste Foy Quebec G1N 4N6 Canada. **DD** 368.1/1/009714. ctrl circ. *Continues Revue d'Information de la Mutualite Quebecoise.*

US/1044-8799
NACORE'S ... COMPENSATION & BENEFITS SURVEY. [NACORE's compens. benefits surv.]. **VFOAT** NACORE's ... Compensation and Benefits Survey; Compensation & Benefits Survey; Compensation and Benefits Survey. **VAT** National Association of Corporate Real Estate Executives' ... Compensation and Benefits Survey. (1989)-. English. an. $40.00 (members), $150.00 (nonmembers). NACORE International, 471 Spender Drive South/Suite 8, West Palm Beach FL 33409. **DD** 331.

US/0146-5481
NAIC MALPRACTICE CLAIMS. Main/Corp National Association of Insurance Commissioners. **VAT** National Association of Insurance Commissioners Malpractice Claims. V. 1- Dec. 1975-. English. qt. $28.00. National Association of Insurance Commissioners, PO Box 263, Department 42, Kansas City MO 64193. **Tel** (816)842-3600, (816)374-7259, FAX (816)471-7004. **LC** HG8054.P5; N37A. **DD** 368.5.

US/0741-0727
NAIC NEWS, THE. (THE NAIC NEWS : OFFICIAL NEWSLETTER OF THE NATIONAL ASSOCIATION OF

INSURANCE COMMISSIONERS.). **Added/Corp** National Association of Insurance Commissioners. **VFOAT** N.A.I.C. News. Vol. 1. No. 1 (Dec. 1983)-. Periodical. English. Twelve times a year. $155.00. National Association of Insurance Commissioners, PO Box 263, Department 42, Kansas City MO 64193. **Tel** (816)842-3600, (816)374-7259, FAX (816)471-7004.

US/0147-3476
NATIONAL DIRECTORY OF MEDICARE HOME HEALTH AGENCIES. Directory. English. 6401 Security Boulevard, Baltimore MD 21235. **LC** RA445; .N275. **DD** 362.6/11/402573.

US/1040-2926
NATIONAL ESTIMATOR. (NATIONAL ESTIMATOR : JOURNAL OF THE NATIONAL ESTIMATING SOCIETY.). [Natl. estim.]. **Added/Corp** National Estimating Society (U.S.) Society of Cost Estimating and Analysis. **VFOAT** Estimator. (19??)-. Periodical. English. Twice a year. $30.00 US; $40.00 others. Society Cost Estimating and Analysis, 101 South Whiting Street, Suite 201, Alexandria VA 22304. **Tel** (703)751-8069, FAX (703)461-7328. **ED** Lee Baseman. **DD** 368. **Ad Acc. Pr Rev. Circ:** 2,000. ***Continues*** *Estimator (Huntsville, Ala.).*

US/0743-7927
NATIONAL INSURANCE LAW REVIEW. **See** Law.

JM
NATIONAL INSURANCE SCHEME : ANNUAL REPORT YEAR ENDING ... / MINISTRY OF LABOUR AND NATIONAL INSURANCE. **Added/Corp** Jamaica. Ministry of Labour and National Insurance. Jamaica Information Service (Jamaica). **VFOAT** Annual Report on the National Insurance Scheme for the Year Ending .... English. **LC** WMLC 91/391.

US
NATIONAL UNDERWRITER CITY INSURANCE TELEPHONE DIRECTORY. (19??)-. Directory. English. an. $13.75. National Underwriter Company, 505 Gest Street, Cincinnati OH 45203-0874. **Tel** (513)721-2140, (800)543-0874.
Desc: Alphabetical listings of information on agencies, adjusters, company claims personnel, agents and brokers, companies, GA's and organizations (covers life, health, and property and casualty). Published for eight areas.

US/0893-8202
NATIONAL UNDERWRITER (LIFE, HEALTH / FINANCIAL SERVICES ED.). (NATIONAL UNDERWRITER.). [Natl. underwrit.]. **Added/Corp** National Underwriter Company. **VFOAT** National Underwriter. Life & Health / Financial Services; Life & Health / Financial Services; Life and Health Financial Services. 90th Year, No. 52 (Dec. 29, 1986)-. Periodical. English. wk. $75.00 (1 year), $130.00 (2 year); $167.00 (one year), $313.00 (two year) other. National Underwriter Company, 505 Gest Street, Cincinnati OH 45203-0874. **Tel** (513)721-2140, (800)543-0874. **LC** IN PROCESS. **DD** 368. available on microfilm and microfiche from University Microfilms International (UMI). Documents available from UMI Article Clearinghouse. ***Continues*** *National Underwriter. Life & Health Insurance Ed., 0028-033X.*
Ind/Abst ABI/INFORM Glob. Ed.; ABI Inform Ondisc (1986-); Bus. ASAP (1990-) [Full Txt.]; Bus. Index (1987-); Bus. Period. Index (1986-); Fed. Tax Artic.; Gen. BusinessFile (1987-); Gen. Period. Index (1987-); Hospit. Health Admin. Index (1986-); PROMT [Full Txt.]; Trade Ind. ASAP [Full Txt.]; Trade Ind. Index (1986-) [Full Txt.]; Wilson Bus. Abstr.

US/1050-6357
NATIONAL UNDERWRITER PROFILES. HEALTH INSURERS. [Natl. underwrit. profiles. Health insur.]. **Added/Corp** National Underwriter Company. **VFOAT** Health Insurers. (1990)-. Directory. English. an. $41.50. National Underwriter Company, 505 Gest Street, Cincinnati OH 45203-0874. **Tel** (513)721-2140, (800)543-0874. **LC** HG9956; .A6. **DD** 368.3/82/006573. **NLM** W1; NA779W. ***Continues*** *Argus Chart of Health Insurance, 0897-6732.*
Desc: Analysis and figures to determine companies' financial and underwriting performance results.

US/1050-5857
NATIONAL UNDERWRITER PROFILES. LIFE INSURERS. [Natl. Underwrit. profiles, Life insur.]. **Added/Corp** National Underwriter Company. **VFOAT** Life Insurers. (1990)-. Periodical. English. an. $41.50. National Underwriter Company, 505 Gest Street, Cincinnati OH 45203-0874. **Tel** (513)721-2140, (800)543-0874. **LC** HG8955; .U5. **DD** 368.3/2/006573. ***Continues*** *Life Financial Reports, 0271-1559.*

US/1050-6365
NATIONAL UNDERWRITER PROFILES. PROPERTY / CASUALTY INSURERS. [Natl. underwrit. profiles, Prop./casualty insur.]. **Added/Corp** National Underwriter Company. **VFOAT** Property / Casualty Insurers; Property, Casualty Insurers. (1990)-. Periodical. English. an. $41.40. National Underwriter Company, 505 Gest Street, Cincinnati OH 45203-0874. **Tel** (513)721-2140, (800)543-0874. **LC** HG9765; .A68; HG8501; .N37. **DD** 368/.006/573. ***Continues*** *Argus F.C. & S. Chart, 0360-8921.*
Desc: Financial amounts and ratios to determine companies' performance and operating characteristics.

US/1042-6841
NATIONAL UNDERWRITER (PROPERTY & CASUALTY / RISK & BENEFITS MANAGEMENT EDITION). (NATIONAL UNDERWRITER.). [Natl. underwriter]. **Added/Corp** National Underwriter Company. **VFOAT** National Underwriter, Property and Casualty, Risk and Benefits Management; National Underwriter, Property & Casualty / Risk & Benefits Management. 93rd Year, No. 2 (Jan. 9, 1989)-. Periodical. English. wk. $79.00 (1 year), $133.00 (2 year) US; $187.00 (one year), $332.00 (two year) other. National Underwriter Company, 505 Gest Street, Cincinnati OH 45203-0874. **Tel** (513)721-2140, (800)543-0874. **DD** 368. **CODEN** NUCEE5. available on microfilm and microfiche from University Microfilms International (UMI). ***Continues*** *National Underwriter (Property & Casualty/Employee Benefits Edition), 0898-8897.*
Ind/Abst Acad. Search (July 1993-); BioBusiness (1989)(1989-); Bus. ASAP (1990-) [Full Txt.]; Bus. Index (1989-); Bus. Source (Jul. 1993-); Fed. Tax Artic.; Gen. BusinessFile (1987-); Gen. Period. Index (1989-); INFO-SOUTH Abstr.; Mag. Search; PROMT [Full Txt.]; Trade Ind. ASAP [Full Txt.]; Trade Ind. Index [Full Txt.].

US
NCSL STATE LEGISLATIVE SUMMARY : LIABILITY INSURANCE. ***Ceased.*** **Added/Corp** National Conference of State Legislatures. **VFOAT** Liability Insurance; N.C.S.L. State Legislative Summary.; Summary, Liability Insurance; National Conference of State Legislatures State Legislative Summary. (19??)-(19??). English.

US/0162-3974
NEIGHBORS. V. 1- Fall 1975-. Periodical. English. mo. Alabama Farm Bureau Federation AL 36116. **Tel** (205)288-3900. **ED** Jay Burnett.

US/0747-8038
NEWSLETTER - ASSOCIATION OF FAMILY AND CONCILIATION COURTS. CALIFORNIA CHAPTER, THE. (THE NEWSLETTER / CALIFORNIA CHAPTER OF FAMILY AND CONCILIATION COURTS.). Newsletter. English. qt. $75.00 members. SAGE Periodical Press, 2455 Teller Road, Thousand Oaks CA 91320. **Tel** (805)499-0721, FAX (805)499-0871, telex 100799. **LC** KFC116.A15; N49. **DD** 346.79401/5/0269 347.4906150269. **Acid Free.**

TZ
NGAO. Periodical. Multiple languages (English and Swahili). National Insurance Corporation of Tanzania, Insurance House, PO Box 9264, Dar es Salaam Tanzania. **LC** HG8015; .N47. **DD** 368/.9/678.

US
NON-CASH BENEFITS SIC SURVEY. **See** Economics-Labor.

SW/0029-1358
NORDISK FORSAKRINGSTIDSKRIFT. **Added/Corp** Forsikringsforeningen i Kbenhavn. Suomen Vakuutusyhdistys.Norske Forsikringsforening. Svenska Forsakringsforeningen. Forsakringssallskapet i Goteborg. (1921)-. Periodical. Swedish. **LC** HG8015; .N6. **DD** 368.058. cum. index. ***Supersedes*** *Forsakringsforeningens Tidskrift.*
Ind/Abst Selec. Coop. Index Manage. Period.

IT
NOTIZIARIO ASSICURATIVO. Italian (English). mo. L60.000. Publiass Srl, Via Dei Gracchi 30, 20146 Milan Italy. **Tel** 02-8357642, FAX 89401513. **Ad Acc. Circ:** 3,000.
Desc: Articles, interviews, tests and news.

IT
NOTIZIARIO ASSINDUSTRIA GENOVA. Italian. sm. Ausind Srl, Via Gropallo 10/2, 16122 Genoa Italy. **Tel** 011 39 10 5367587.

UK/0952-231X
OCCUPATIONAL PENSIONS. [Occup. pensions]. (1987)-. Periodical. English. mo. £140.00 UK; £155.00 other. Eclipse Publications Ltd, 18 20 Highbury Place, London N5 1QP England. **Tel** 011 44 71 354 5858. **DD** 331.2520941.

US
OHIO UNDERWRITER. **Added/Corp** National Underwriter Company. Vol. 21, No. 1 (Jan. 1988)-. Periodical. English. Twelve times a year. $16.50 one year; $27.50 two years. National Underwriter Company, 505 Gest Street, Cincinnati OH 45203-0874. **Tel** (513)721-2140, (800)543-0874. ***Continues*** *Ohio Underwriter Insurance News.*
Desc: Information on the broker market, life brokerage, statistical review life/health, statistical review property/casualty, excess and surplus lines, etc.

CN/0712-3388
OLD AGE SECURITY, GUARANTEED INCOME SUPPLEMENT, SPOUSE'S ALLOWANCE. [Old age secur., guaranteed income suppl., spouse's allow.]. **VFOAT** Securite de la Vieilleuse, Supplement de Revenu Garanti, Allocation au Conjoint. English (French). Health and Welfare of Canada Information Directorate, Ottawa Ontario K1A 0K9 Canada. **Tel** (613)954-8576. **DD** 368.4/3011/0971.

US/0885-4416
ON THE RISK. (ON THE RISK : JOURNAL OF THE ACADEMY OF LIFE UNDERWRITING.). [On the risk]. **Added/Corp** Academy of Life Underwriting. (1985)-. Periodical. English. qt (Mar., June, Sept., Dec.). $30.00 (nonmembers), $20.00 (members) North America; $45.00 other. On the Risk, PO Box 267, Claymont DE 19703-0267. **Tel** (302) 421-8956, FAX (302) 421-8964. **(Subscription address:** Paul McDaniel, Underwriting VP, General American Life Insurance Company, 13045 Tesson Ferry Road, St. Louis, MO 63128**) ED** Hank George (phone: (414)423-0967). **DD** 368. Index available. **Bk Rev**, (Qty: 4). **Ad Acc. Circ:** 3,600 (ctrl).
Desc: Journal of the Academy of Life Underwriting, publishing articles on home office life and health underwriting.

US/1046-8013
OPEN SEASON GUIDE. [Open seas. guide]. **Added/Corp** Employee Benefits Review, Inc. **VFOAT** Employee Benefits Review's Open Season Guide. (1990)-. Periodical. English. an. $11.90 (nonmembers), $9.90 (members). National Association Retired Federal Employees, 1533 New Hampshire Northwest, Washington DC 20036. **Tel** (202)234-0832. **LC** JK794.H4; O64. **DD** 353.001/234. ***Continues*** *Selecting the Right Federal Health Plan ... Open Season, 1041-1518.*

US
ORGANIZATION : FEDERAL INSURANCE ADMINISTRATION. **VFOAT** Federal Insurance Administration. Government Publication. English. US Department of Housing and Urban Development, 451 Seventh Street SW, Washington DC 20401. **Tel** (202)708-0980, FAX (202)708-0299.

AU
OSTERREICHISCHE SOZIALVERSICHERUNG, DIE. **See** Sociology-Social Services and Welfare.

US
OUR VOICE. **See** Economics-Labor.

PK
PAKISTAN INSURANCE YEAR BOOK, THE. Began with 1948 issue. English. NGM Communication, PO Box 2627, Karachi 75900 Pakistan. **Tel** 011 92 21 428625. **LC** HG8704.5; .A3. **DD** 368/.95491.

US/0893-8121
PART B NEWS. [Part B news]. Vol. 1, No. 1 (May 1987)-. Periodical. English. Twenty-four times a year. $446.00 (one year), $882.00 (two year). United Communications Group, 11300 Rockville Pike, Suite 1100, Rockville MD 20852. **Tel** (301)816-8950 ext. 223, FAX (301)816-8945. **DD** 368.
Desc: Guides hospital executives, group practice administrators and other health care managers through the complex rules of the Medicare Part B reimbursement program to ensure they get every Part B dollar they are entitled to. Features advance warnings on Part B law, regulation and funding changes coming from Washington plus practical, nuts-and-bolts advice on Part B claims.
Ind/Abst Health Plan. Adminis.; Hospit. Health Admin. Index (1989-1991).

UK
PAY AND BENEFITS SOURCEBOOK. **See** Business-Accounting.

AT/1035-3615
PENSIONERS VOICE (SYDNEY). (1958)-. Periodical. English. mo (11 issues). 9.00Aus$. Combined Pensioners Association, Level 5 / 405 Sussex Street, Haymarket New South Wales 2000 Australia. **Tel** 011 61 2 2811811.

UK
PENSIONS MANAGEMENT. English. Financial Times Business Information Ltd, Central House, 27 Park Street, Croydon CR0 1YD England. **Tel** 011 44 81 680 3786.

UK
PENSIONS TODAY. English. Monitor Press, Rectory Road, Great Waldingfield, Sudbury Suffolk CO10 0TL United Kingdom. **Tel** 011 44 787 378607.

UK/0307-191X
PENSIONS WORLD. [Pensions World]. (1972)-. Periodical. English. Twelve times a year. £89.00 Europe; £42.00 other. Tolley Publishing Company Ltd, Tolley

Insurance

House, 2 Addiscombe Road, Croydon, Surrey CR9 5AF United Kingdom. **Tel** 011 44 81 6869141, FAX 011 44 81 6863155, 011 44 81 7600588.

CN/0228-3212
PERFORMANCE COMPARISON, CANADIAN POOLED PENSION FUNDS. See Economics-Labor.

UK
PERMANENT HEALTH INSURANCE : THE CITY FINANCIAL REVIEW. (19??)-. Periodical. English. an. £112.85. Croner Publ Ltd, Croner House, London Road, Kingston upon Thames, Surrey KT2 6SR England. **Tel** 011 44 81 5473333, FAX 081 547-2637.

US
PERSONAL INJURY LAW DEFENSE BULLETIN : A NEWSLETTER FOR DEFENSE COUNSEL, INSURANCE AND CORPORATE CLAIMS MANAGEMENT, THE. See Law-Corporate Law.

US/0730-7950
PERSONS ENROLLED FOR MEDICARE. [Pers. enroll. Medicare]. 1979-. English. an. Health Care Financing Administration, 6325 Security Boulevard, Room 700, Baltimore MD 21207. **Tel** (410)966-3000, FAX (410)966-5267. **NLM** W2 A S63MF. *Continues* Medicare, Persons Enrolled, 0730-7969.

CN/0843-0985
PERSPECTIVES - INSTITUT D'ASSURANCE DU CANADA. (PERSPECTIVES.). [Perspect. - Inst. assur. Can.]. Vol. 3, No. 1 (Dec. 1987)-. Periodical. French. Insurance Institute of Canada, 55 University Avenue, Toronto Ontario M5J 2H7. **DD** 368/.006/071. *Continues* Volume 2, 0225-1655.

CN/0843-0977
PERSPECTIVES - INSURANCE INSTITUTE OF CANADA. (PERSPECTIVES.). [Perspect. - Insur. Inst. Can.]. Vol. 3, No. 1 (Dec. 1987)-. Periodical. English. Insurance Institute of Canada, 55 University Avenue, Toronto Ontario M5J 2H7. **DD** 368/.006/071. *Continues* Volume 2, 0225-168X.

CN/0712-8223
PERSPECTIVES STATISTIQUES (QUEBEC). See Sociology-Social Services and Welfare.

US
PF&M ANALYSES. English. Twelve times a year. %300.00 US; $320.00 other. Rough Notes Company Inc, 1200 North Meridian Street, Indianapolis IN 46206. **Tel** (317)634-1541, (800)428-4384, FAX (317)634-1041.

UK/0032-2679
PH, POLICY HOLDER INSURANCE JOURNAL. **VFOAT** Policy Holder Insurance Journal. **VAT** Policy Holder, Policy Holder Insurance Journal. (19??)-. Periodical. English. wk. $68.96. Buckley Press Ltd, 58 Fleet Street, London EC4Y 1JU England. **Tel** 011 44 71 5833030. **LC** HG8013; .P6. **DD** 368/.005. *Continues* Policy-Holder.
Desc: Policy holder law supplement.

GW/0176-3261
PKV PUBLIK. [PKV publik]. **VFOAT** Private Krankenversicherung Publik. (1984)-. Periodical. German. ir (6 issues). DM6.30. Verlag Versicherungswirtschaft, Klosestrasse 20 24, D-76137 Karlsruhe Germany. **Tel** 011 49 721 35090, FAX 011 49 721 31833. **UDC** 368.382. *Continues* PKV-Information, 0723-8959.

KO
POHOM HAKHOE CHI. **VFOAT** Korean insurance Journal. Periodical. Korean (Korean). Hanguk Pohom Hakhoe, 35 Tongui-dong, Chongno-ku, Seoul South Korea. **LC** HG8015; .P58.

KO
POHOM TONGGYE YONBO. See Insurance-Abstracting, Bibliographies and Statistics.

KO
POHOM TONGGYE YON'GAM. See Insurance-Abstracting, Bibliographies and Statistics.

CN/0710-1538
POINT DE VUE SUR LES ASSURANCES. [Point vue assur.]. **Added/Corp** Bureau d'Assurance du Canada. (19??)-. Periodical. French. Bureau d'Assurance du Canada, Bureau 920/1080 Cote du Beaver Hall, Montreal Quebec H2Z 1S8 Canada. **DD** 368/.971.

XR
POJISTNY OBZOR. Czech (table of contents in Russian and English). mo. (**Subscription address:** Artia Pegas Press Ltd., Palac Metro Narodni Trida 25, 11210 Prague 1 Czech Republic.) **LC** HG8015; .P6.

KO
POJUNG SABO. **Added/Corp** Taehan Pojung Pohom Chusik Hoesa. **VFOAT** Korea Fidelity & Surety Quarterly Review; Korea Fidelity and Surety Quarterly Review. (19??)-. Periodical. Korean (Korean). qt. Not for sale. Taehan Pojung Pohom Chusik Hosea, 136-74 Yonji-Dong Chongno-ku, Seoul Korea. **LC** HG9997.4.K6; P64.

US/1045-9936
POLICIES IN REVIEW. [Policies rev.]. Ed. 1 (Aug. 1988)-. Periodical. English. mo. $227.50 US; $295.25 other. Standard Publishing Company, 155 Federal Street, Boston MA 02110. **Tel** (617)457-0604, (617)457-0600, FAX (617)457-0608. **ED** Roger Pierce. **LC** HG8501; .P64. **DD** 368/.973/05. **Circ:** 1,000.
Desc: Detailed analysis of major non-standard insurance policies.

US/0163-8920
POLICY STATISTICS SERVICE. *Ceased.* See Insurance-Abstracting, Bibliographies and Statistics.

UK
POST MAGAZINE. Vol. 147 No. 36 (Sept. 4, 1986)-. Periodical. English. wk. £75.00 UK; £85.00 other. Buckley Press Ltd, 58 Fleet Street, London EC4Y 1JU England. **Tel** 011 44 71 5833030. **LC** HG8013; .P64. **DD** 368/.005. available on an online database (files 771,772,799/Full-Text) from DIALOG. *Continues* Post Magazine and Insurance Monitor.
Ind/Abst Infomat Int. Bus.

US/1054-2396
PPO LETTER, THE. (THE PPO LETTER : THE INDEPENDENT NEWSLETTER FOR THE PPO INDUSTRY.). [PPO lett.]. **VAT** Preferred Provider Organization Letter. Vol. 1, No. 1 (Jan. 28, 1991)-. Newsletter. English. Twenty-five times a year. $397.00. Business Information Services Inc., 12811 North Point Lane, Laurel MD 20708. **Tel** (301)604-4001, FAX (301)604-5126. **ED** James Gutman. **DD** 368. [**CCC**]. **Circ:** 500. available on an online database from NEWSNET.
Desc: Focuses on news developments and trends in such aspects as terms of PPO contracts, state and federal regulation affecting PPO's new contract provisions sought by employers and insurers, PPO marketing strategies, and how to choose providers.

US
PRACTICAL RISK MANAGEMENT. **Added/Corp** Warren, McVeigh & Griffin. (Jan. 1974)-. Periodical. English. bm (6 issues). $335.00 US; $345.00 Canada; $360.00 other. Practical Risk Management, PO Box 1439, Alameda CA 94501. **Tel** (510)865-3628, FAX (510)253-9645. Index available. cum. index.
Desc: Each issue includes risk management notes.

YU
PRAVNE SVESKE. **Added/Corp** Udruzenje Pravnika Socijalno Zravstvene Delatnosti SR Srbije. (1969)-. Periodical. Serbo-Croatian (Cyrillic). qt. **LC** LAW.

US
PRECEDENT DECISIONS : BENEFIT, RULING, TAX AND DISABILITY. **Main/Corp** California. Unemployment Insurance Appeals Board. No. 1/49 (1968/1969)-. English. $15.00. Employment Development Department, 800 Capitol Mall, MIC 85, Sacramento CA 95814. **Tel** (916)445-1952. **LC** KFC596; .A556. **Circ:** 400.
Desc: Unemployment insurance precedent decisions.

BL
PREVIDENCIA, A. Periodical. Portuguese. bm. 150. Sindicato dos Corretores de Seguros e de Capitalizac, rua do Rosario 99 - 5 O Andar, Rio de Janeiro Brazil. **Tel** 021 22102031. **ED** Sergio dos Santos Netto. **LC** HG8015; .P65. **DD** 368/005. **Ad Acc**. **Circ:** 6,000.
Desc: Prints news of the investment scene, articles on business opportunities, and sales techniques. Includes international news and excerpts from foreign newspapers.

US/0277-7967
PRINCIPLES AND PRESENTATION. INSURANCE. **VFOAT** Principles & Presentation. Insurance. 1979-. English. an. $20.00. Peat Marwick Mitchell & Company / New York, 345 Park Avenue, New York NY 10154. **Tel** (212)758-9700. **LC** HG8501; .P74. **DD** 657/.83603/0973.

US
PRISM. (19??)-. Newsletter. English. qt. Public Risk Insurance Services & Management Inc. / PRISM, 411 East Third Avenue, Eugene OR 97401. **Tel** (503)686-0168, (800)447-7476. **ED** Loretta Gale.
Desc: Publication for public entities and insurance brokers.

US
PRIVATE PASSENGER AUTOMOBILE INSURANCE. 1980-. English. an. Missouri Division of Insurance Statistical Section, PO Box 690, Jefferson City MO 65102. **LC** HG9970.35.M8; P74. **DD** 368/.092/09778.

US
PROCEEDINGS - AMERICAN BAR ASSOCIATION. SECTION OF INSURANCE, NEGLIGENCE AND COMPENSATION LAW. See Law.

CN/0229-0995
PROCEEDINGS / CANADIAN INSTITUTE OF ACTUARIES. **Main/Corp** Canadian Institute of Actuaries. General Meeting. **VFOAT** Deliberations. Proceedings. English (French). Three times a year. Canadian Institute of Actuaries, 360 Albert Street Suite 1040, Ottawa Ontario K1R 7X7 Canada. **Tel** (613)236-8196. **LC** HG8779; .C36a. **DD** 368.3/2/0097105. *Continues* Canadian Institute of Actuaries. General Meeting. Deliberations, 0229-0995.

US
PROCEEDINGS / CONFERENCE OF CONSULTING ACTUARIES, THE. **Main/Corp** Conference of Consulting Actuaries. Meeting. Vol. 41 (1991)-. Proceedings. English. **LC** HG8754; .C6. **DD** 368.301. *Continues* Conference of Actuaries in Public Practice. Meeting. Proceedings, 0589-039X.
Desc: Information concernig life insurance and actuaries.

US/0740-1485
PROCEEDINGS OF THE ANNUAL MEETING - MILLION DOLLAR ROUND TABLE (DES PLAINES, ILL.). (PROCEEDINGS OF THE ... ANNUAL MEETING, MILLION DOLLAR ROUND TABLE.). [Proc. annu. meet. - Million Dollar Round Table (Des Plaines, Ill.)]. **Main/Corp** Million Dollar Round Table (Des Plaines, Ill.). 1973-. Proceedings. English. an. Million Dollar Round Table, 325 West Touhy, Park Ridge IL 60060. **Tel** (708)692-6378. **LC** HG8944; .M55A. **DD** 368.3/2/00973. *Continues* Proceedings of the Million Dollar Round Table ... Annual Meeting.

US/0075-9414
PROCEEDINGS OF THE ... ANNUAL MEETING OF THE LIFE INSURERS CONFERENCE. **Main/Conf** Life Insurers Conference. Meeting. 51st (Apr. 13-15, 1961)-. Proceedings. English. an. **LC** HG8754; .L48. **DD** 368.3/2/00973. *Continues* Proceedings of the ... Convention of the Life Insurers Conference.

US/0893-2980
PROCEEDINGS OF THE CASUALTY ACTUARIAL SOCIETY. [Proc. Casualty Actuar. Soc.]. **Main/Corp** Casualty Actuarial Society. Vol. 7, No. 16 (1921)-. Proceedings. English. an. $50.00 US; 64.00Can$ Canada. Casualty Acturial Society, 1100 North Glede #600, Arlington VA 22201. **Tel** (703)276-3100. **DD** 368. *Continues* Casualty Actuarial and Statistical Society of America. Proceedings of the Casualty Actuarial and Statistical Society of America.

US/0363-0358
PROCEEDINGS OF THE NATIONAL ASSOCIATION OF INSURANCE COMMISSIONERS. **Main/Corp** National Association of Insurance Commissioners. Meeting. 84th, Vol. 1 (1953)-. Proceedings. English. sa. National Association of Insurance Commissioners, PO Box 263, Department 42, Kansas City MO 64193. **Tel** (816)842-3600, (816)374-7259, FAX (816)471-7004. **LC** HG8016; .N2. **DD** 368/.973. *Continues* National Convention of Insurance Commissioners. Meeting. Proceedings of the ... Annual Session of the National Association of Insurance Comissioners.

US/0160-4163
PROCEEDINGS OF THE SEMINAR OF THE CONFERENCE OF INSURANCE LEGISLATORS. **Main/Conf** Conference of Insurance Legislators. **VFOAT** Proceedings of the Seminar on the Health Care System. Proceedings. English. National Insurance Law Service, 21625 Prairie Street, PO Box 2507, Chatsworth CA 91311. **Tel** (818)998-8830, (800)423-5910. **LC** HG8522; .C66. **DD** 368/.9/73.

US/0148-8899
PROFESSIONAL AGENT, THE. **Added/Corp** Professional Insurance Agents. V. 45, No. 12 (Dec. 1976)-. Periodical. English. mo. $20.00 (nonmembers); $12.00 (members). Professional Agent, 400 North Washington Street, Alexandria VA 22314. **Tel** (703)836-9340, FAX (703)836-1279. **ED** Alan Prochoroff. **LC** HG8011; .M85. **DD** 368/.9/73. **Ad Acc**. **Circ:** 30,000 (ctrl). available on microfilm from University Microfilms International (UMI). *Continues* Mutual Review.
Desc: Property, casualty insurance, small business management for independent insurance agents.

US/0883-8240
PROFESSIONAL INSURANCE AGENTS OF NEW YORK. [Prof. insur. agents N. Y.]. **VFOAT** Professional Insurance Agents. Periodical. English. mo. $25.00. Professional Insurance Agents of New York State Inc, Old Route 9W, PO Box 98, Glenmont NY 12077. **DD** 368. *Continues* Triangle, 0744-9801.

Insurance

US/0555-3385
PROFESSIONAL LIABILITY NEWSLETTER. (1968)-. Newsletter. English. mo (except Aug.) $45.00 US; $55.00 other. Professional Liability, PO Box 834, Berkeley CA 94701. **Tel** (415)741-8723. **ED** D S Rubsamen.

US/0194-3871
PROGRAM ADMINISTRATION REVIEW OF THE SOCIAL SECURITY DISABILITY INSURANCE AND THE SUPPLEMENTAL SECURITY INCOME VOCATIONAL REHABILITATION PROGRAMS. See Economics-Labor.

CN/0820-0777
PROGRAMME D'ASSOCIE / INSTITUT D'ASSURANCE DU CANADA. [Programme assoc. - Inst. assur. Can.]. **Main/Corp** Institut d'Assurance du Canada. **VFOAT** Programme d'Introduction aux Assurances I.A.R.D. (1982/83)-?. French. an. Free. Institut D'Assurance Du Canada, 3 E Etage, 122 Rue St. Patrick, Toronto Ontario Canada M5T 2X8. **DD** 368/.007/1071. ctrl circ. **Continues** Programme A.I.A.C., Programme d'Introduction aux Assurances I.A.R.D., 0225-2422. **Continued in part by** Programme d'Introduction aux Assurances I.A.R.D., 1187-9238.

CN/0820-6120
PROGRAMME F.I.A.C. (PROGRAMME F.I.A.C. / INSTITUT D'ASSURANCE DU CANADA.). [Programme F.I.A.C.]. **Main/Corp** Insurance Institute of Canada. **VAT** Programme Fellow de l'Institute d'Assurance du Canada. 1982/1985-. Periodical. English (French). ir. Free. Insurance Institute of Canada, 55 University Avenue, Toronto Ontario M5J 2H7. **DD** 368/.007/1171. ctrl circ. **Separated from** Insurance Institute of Canada. Fellowship Program, 0225-2449.

CN/1187-645X
PROPERTY AND CASUALTY INSURANCE. [Prop. casualty insur.]. **Added/Corp** Canada. Industry, Science and Technology Canada. **VFOAT** Assurance de Biens et Risques Divers. (1990/1991)-. English (French). **DD** 368.

CN/1187-645X
PROPERTY AND CASUALTY INSURANCE. (ASSURANCE DE BIENS ET RISQUES DIVERS.). [Prop. casualty insur.]. **Added/Corp** Canada. Industrie, Sciences et Technologie Canada. **VFOAT** Property and Casualty Insurance. (1991)-. French (English). **DD** 368.

US/1050-4710
PROPERTY/CASUALTY INSURANCE FACTS. [Prop./casualty insur. facts]. **Added/Corp** Insurance Information Institute. **VFOAT** Property Casualty Insurance Facts; Property/Casualty Fact Book; Insurance Facts. (1990)-. English. Insurance Information Institute, 110 William Street, New York NY 10038. **Tel** (212)669-9226, FAX (212)732-1916. **DD** 368. **Continues** Insurance Facts.
Ind/Abst Predicasts Forecasts; Stat. Ref. Index.

CN/0823-8138
PROSPECTIVE (MONTREAL. 1984). (PROSPECTIVE.). [Prospective]. V. 1, No. 1, (April/May 1984)-. Periodical. French (English). bm. 30.00Can$. Association Provinciale des Assureurs-Vie du Quebec, Suite 701/511 Place d'Armes, Montreal Quebec H2Y 2W7 Canada. **Tel** (514)288-4454. **ED** Claude Perrier. **DD** 368.3/2/0060714. **Ad Acc**. **Circ**: 6,500. **Continues** Asseureurs-Vie Quebec, 0383-2376.
Desc: Information on matters of interest for members who are life insurance underwriters.

US
PROSPECTS FOR AUTOMOBILE INSURANCE UNDERWRITING RESULTS. English. Conning & Company, 185 Asylum Street, City Place II, Hartford CT 06103. **Tel** (203) 520-1521, FAX (203) 520-1504. **LC** HG9970.3; .P76. **DD** 368.5/72/00973.

US
PROSVETA ENLIGHTENMENT.
Added/Corp Slovenska Narodna Podporna Jednota. **VFOAT** Enlightenment. (July 1916)-. Newspaper. Slovenian (English). Fifty-two times a year (Published on Wed.). $16.00. Slovene National Benefit Society, 166 Shore Drive, Burr Ridge IL 60521. **Tel** (312)887-7660. **ED** Jay Sedmak (editor's address: 166 Shore Drive, Burr Ridge, IL 60521). **Ad Acc, Adv Mgr**: Jean. **Circ**: 22,000. available on microfilm. **Continues** Glasilo SNPJ.
Desc: Fraternal newspaper that contains items of interest based on members, lodges, and various cultural events, along with items of fraternal insurance.

NE/0165-0734
PS. PERIODIEK VOOR SOCIALE VERZEKERNIG, SOCIALE VOORZIENINGEN EN ARBEIDSRECHT.
[PS, Period. soc. verzek. soc. voorzien. arbeidsr.]. **VFOAT** Periodiek Voor Sociale Verzekernig. Sociale Voorzieningen en Arbeids- Recht. (1976)-. Periodical. Dutch. bw. Fl173.03. Kluwer BV, Postbus 23, 7400 GA Deventer Netherlands. **Tel** 011 31 5700 33155, 011 31 5700 48999, FAX 011 31 5700 11504, telex 42829. **UDC** 331.

US
PUBLIC EMPLOYEE BENEFIT PLANS. See Public Administration-Civil Service.

CN
QUARTERLY REPORT / INSURERS ADVISORY ORGANIZATION OF CANADA / IAO. (19??)-. English. Four times a year (Mar., June., Sept., Dec.). 120.00 Can$ Canada; 150.00Can$ other. Insurers Advisory Organization, 18 King Street East, Suite 700, Toronto, Ontario, M5C 1C4 Canada. **Tel** (416)368-1801, FAX (416)348-9559. **ED** James K. Christie. **Circ**: 250.

●US
RAILROAD RETIREMENT AND UNEMPLOYMENT INSURANCE SYSTEMS HANDBOOK. **Added/Corp** United States. Railroad Retirement Board. **VFOAT** Railroad Retirement Handbook. (1992)-. English. US Railroad Retirement Board, 844 Rush, Chicago IL 60611. **Continues** Handbook of Railroad Retirement and Unemployment Insurance Systems.

CN/0225-3208
RAPPORT ANNUEL DU SURINTENDANT DES ASSURANCES (QUEBEC. 1977).
Ceased. (RAPPORT DU SURINTENDANT DES ASSURANCES.). **Main/Corp** Quebec (Province). Direction Generale des Assurances. **VAT** Rapport Annuel du Surintendant des Assurances du Quebec. 98E (1980)-?. French. an. Editeur Officiel du Quebec, 1283 Boul Charest Ouest, Quebec Quebec G1N 2C9 Canada. **LC** HG8550.Z8; Q427. **DD** 354.7140082/55/06. **Continues** Rapport Annuel du Surintendant des Assurances, 0225-3208.

CN/0715-7770
RAPPORT ANNUEL / OFFICE DE LA SECURITE DU REVENU DES CHASSEURS ET PIEGEURS CRIS. See Sociology-Social Services and Welfare.

CN/0380-4585
RAPPORT ANNUEL - REGIE DES RENTES DU QUEBEC. **Main/Corp** Regie des Rentes du Quebec. (1966)-. French. an. Regie des Rentes du Quebec, Case Postale 5200, Quebec Quebec G1K 7S9 Canada. **Tel** (418)643-8309. **LC** HD7130.Q4; A3. **DD** 354.7140082/56. Index available.

CN
RAPPORT ANNUEL - SERVICE DES ASSURANCES. **Main/Corp** Quebec (Province). Service des Assurances. French. an. Editeur Officiel du Quebec, 1283 Boul Charest Ouest, Quebec Quebec G1N 2C9 Canada. **LC** HG8550.Z8; Q427. **DD** 354.714/0082/55/06.

FR
RAPPORT D'ACTIVITIE - CAISSE NATIONALE DE L'ASSURANCE MALADIE DES TRAVAILLEURS SALARIES. See Economics-Labor.

US
RBRVS STEP BY STEP. (19??)-. English. an. $200.00. St. Anthony's Publishing Co., 500 Montgomery Street /Suite 700, Alexandria VA 22314. **Tel** (800)632-0123 ext. 5746. **(Subscription address:** St. Anthony Publishing Inc., PO Box 14212, Washington DC 20044.**)**
Desc: Explains Medicare's final decisions on physician payment; includes coding guidelines for global surgery, modifiers, visit codes, etc., with clip-and-save reference sheets.

UK
REACTIONS. English. Twelve times a year. $320.00 US and Canada; £145.00 UK; £165.00 Europe; $360.00 other. Euromoney Publications PLC, Nestor House, Playhouse Yard, London EC4Z 5EX England. **Tel** 011 44 71 779 8888, FAX 011 44 71 779 8617, telex 290700 EUROMON G.
Desc: Reports, reviews and analyses the latest developments in the insurance world to keep you abreast of your market.

UK/0953-5640
REACTIONS (LONDON). (RE ACTIONS.). [ReActions]. **VFOAT** ReActions. (19??)-. Periodical. English. mo. Reactions Ltd, 39-41 North Road, London N7 9DP England. Documents available from UMI Article Clearinghouse.
Ind/Abst ABI/INFORM Glob. Ed.; ABI Inform Ondisc (Dec. 1985-); Ins. Period. Index (199?-).

GW/0343-9771
RECHT UND SCHADEN. See Law.

US/0730-2983
RECORD - SOCIETY OF ACTUARIES. MEETING. (RECORD / SOCIETY OF ACTUARIES.). **Main/Corp** Society of Actuaries. Meeting. Vol. 1, No. 1 (May 1975)-. Periodical. English. Four times a year. $30.00 schools & universities; $60.00 others. Society of Actuaries, PO Box 95668, Chicago IL 60694. **Tel** (708)706-3526. **ED** Linda M. Delgadito. **LC** HG8754; .S6. **DD** 368.3/005. **Circ**: 13,000 (ctrl).
Desc: Papers presented at regional and annual meetings of the Society of Actuaries.

UK
REFERENCE BOOK OF MARINE INSURANCE CLAUSES. **Main/Corp** Witherby and Company, London. English. an. Witherby and Company Ltd, 5 Plaintain Place, Crosby Row, London SE1 1YN England. **LC** KD1845.A65; W57. **DD** 344.41/0862.

US/0091-357X
REGISTER OF RETIREMENT BENEFIT PLANS REPORTED UNDER THE WELFARE AND PENSION PLANS DISCLOSURE ACT. See Economics-Labor.

UK
REGULATION OF INSURANCE. (19??)-. Periodical. English. £297.60. Croner Publ Ltd, Croner House, London Road, Kingston upon Thames, Surrey KT2 6SR England. **Tel** 011 44 81 5473333, FAX 081 547-2637.

UK/0048-7171
REINSURANCE. [Reinsurance]. (May 1969)-. Periodical. English. mo. £55.00 UK and airmail Europe; £75.00 airmail Far East and Pacific Rim; £65.00 airmail other. Buckley Press Ltd, 58 Fleet Street, London EC4Y 1JU England. **Tel** 011 44 71 5833030. **LC** HG8059.R4; R43. **DD** 368/.012. available on an online database (files 771,772,799/Full-Text) from DIALOG.
Ind/Abst Ins. Period. Index (1989-); PAIS Int. Print.

US
REINSURANCE DIGEST. Vol. 4, No. 6 (Nov./Dec. 1988)-. Periodical. English. Four times a year. $45.00 US; $49.00 Canada. Reinsurance Communications Company, 82 Wall Street/Suite 1105, New York NY 10005. **Tel** (212)797-7377. **Continues** United States Reinsurance Report, 0890-846X.

US/0747-5276
REINSURANCE DIRECTORY. [Reinsur. dir.]. Directory. English. an. $29.50. College of Insurance, 123 William Street, New York NY 10038. **LC** HG8083; .R38. **DD** 368/.012.

UK
REINSURANCE LAW. See Law.

UK/0961-7264
REINSURANCE LAW REPORTS. See Law.

UK/0266-8653
REINSURANCE MARKET REPORT.
[Reinsur. mark. rep.]. (1984)-. Periodical. English. Fifty times a year. £385.00 UK; $630.00 US & Canada. DYP Insurance Reinsurance Res. Grp. Ltd., 181 Queen Victoria St. Bridge House, London EC4V 4DD England. **Tel** 011 44 71 236 2175, FAX 011 44 71 489 1487. **DD** 368.012.

US/0034-3641
REINSURANCE REPORTER. [Reinsur. report.]. Periodical. English. qt. Reinsurance Reporter, Life/Health Reinsurance Division, Lincoln National Corporation, 1300 South Clinton, Box 1110, Fort Wayne IN 46801. **DD** 368.

BL
RELATORIO ANUAL / IRB. **Main/Corp** Instituto de Resseguros do Brasil. **Added/Corp** Instituto de Resseguros do Brasil. Annual Report. **VFOAT** Annual Report. (1970)-. Portuguese. **LC** HG8571; .I65. **DD** 368.86. **Continues** Instituto de Resseguros do Brasil. Relatorio.

IT
RELAZIONI E BILANCIO / INA, ISTITUTO NAZIONALE DELLE ASSICURAZIONI.
Main/Corp Istituto Nazionale Delle Assicurazioni. (19??)-. Italian. an. Istituto Nazionale delle Assicurazioni, Via Sallustiana 51, Rome Italy. **Tel** 06/67221, FAX 06/47224523, telex 610336. **LC** HG9086; .I7. **DD** 368//.945. **Circ**: 1,000. **Continues** Istituto Nazionale Delle Assicurazioni. Consiglio di Amministrazione. Relazioni e Bilancio del Consiglio di Amministrazione e del Collegio dei Sindaci.

BB
REPORT AND ACCOUNTS AT ... / INSURANCE CORPORATION OF BARBADOS. **Main/Corp** Insurance Corporation of Barbados. **VFOAT** Annual Report and Statement of Accounts. English. an. Insurance Corporation of

Barbados, Corner James and Roebuck Streets, Bridgetown Barbados. **LC** HG8556.9.Z9; I574. **DD** 354.7298/1008255/06.

II
REPORT - COMMITTEE ON GOVERNMENT ASSURANCES. **Main/Corp** Tamil Nadu. Legislature. Legislative Council. Committee on Government Assurances. 664h- 1968/69-. English. India Legislative Council, Committee on Government Assurances, Fort St George, Madras 600009 India. **LC** JQ533; .A3. **DD** 328.54/82/0765. ***Continues*** *Madras (State). Legislature. Legislative Council. Committee on Assurances. Report.*

UK
REPORT OF THE CHIEF REGISTRAR / REGISTRY OF FRIENDLY SOCIETIES. **Main/Corp** Great Britain. Registry of Friendly Societies. 1979-. English. an. **LC** HG9245.G7; G74A. **DD** 334/.7/0941. ***Absorbed*** *Report of the Industrial Assurance Commissioner.*

RH
REPORT OF THE COMMISSIONER OF INSURANCE FOR THE YEAR ENDED ... / ZIMBABWE. **Added/Corp** Zimbabwe. Commissioner of Insurance. Dec. 31, (1987)-. English. **LC** HG8724.4; .A33a. **DD** 368/.96891. ***Continues*** *Zimbabwe. Registrar of Insurance. Report of the Registrar of Insurance for the Year Ended December 31 ... .*

US
REPORT OF THE COMMISSIONER OF INSURANCE - KANSAS. **Main/Corp** Kansas. Insurance Dept. 1st- 1871-. English. an. Kansas Insurance Department, 420 SW 9th Street, Topeka KS 66612. **Tel** (913)296-7805, FAX (913)296-2283. **DD** 368.9781; 368.93.
Desc: Vol. for 1880 includes Compilation of the insurance lasw of the States of kansas in force April 15, 1881.

SA
REPORT OF THE COMPULSORY MOTOR VEHICLE INSURANCE SECTION AND OF THE MOTOR VEHICLE ASSURANCE FUND. **Main/Corp** South Africa. Dept. of Transport. **VFOAT** Verslag van die Afdeling Verpligte Motorvoertuigassuransie en van die Motorvoertuigassuransiefonds. Multiple languages (Afrikaans and English). **LC** HG9970.A68; S68A. **DD** 368.5/72/00968.

US
REPORT OF THE INSURANCE DIVISION OF IOWA. **Main/Corp** Iowa. Insurance Division. English. Full Depository, 707 Savings and Loan Building, Des Moines IA 50309. ***Continues*** *Report / Iowa. Insurance Dept. Report.*

US
REPORT OF THE SELECT COMMITTEE ON INSURANCE RATES, REGULATION AND RECODIFICATION OF THE INSURANCE LAW. **See** Law.

SA
REPORT OF THE UNEMPLOYMENT INSURANCE FUND FOR THE YEAR ENDED ... / DEPARTMENT OF MANPOWER UTILISATION. ***Title Change.*** **Added/Corp** South Africa. Dept. of Manpower Utilisation. South Africa. Dept. of Manpower. **VFOAT** Verslag van die Werkloosheidversekeringsfonds vir dir Jaar Geeindig ... . (19??)-(19??). Afrikaans (English). an. Unemployment Insurance Fund, PO Box 1851, Pretoria 0001 Republic of South Africa. **LC** HD7096.S5; S683a. **DD** 354.680082/56. ***Continued by*** *Unemployment Insurance Fund ... Annual Report.*
Desc: Contains information on the administration of insurance, benefits and payments to dependants of deceased, unemployed, maternity, and illness benefits.

CN/1191-3398
REPORT ON THE BUDGET FOR THE DEVELOPMENT USES OF UNEMPLOYMENT INSURANCE. ***Title Change.*** **See** Sociology-Social Services and Welfare.

II
REPORTS AND SUMMARIES OF DISCUSSIONS / INTERNATIONAL SOCIAL SECURITY ASSOCIATION, COMMITTEE ON PROVIDENT FUNDS. **Main/Corp** International Social Security Association. Committee on Provident Funds. Meeting. English. Regional Office for Asia and the Pacific, International Social Security Association, B-66 Defence Colony, New Delhi 110024 India. **Tel** 62-5001. **LC** HD7252; .I57A. **DD** 368.4/009172/4. cum. index. ***Continues*** *International Social Security Association. Committee on Provident Funds. Meeting. Reports and Summary of Discussions.*

UK/0143-9669
REREPORT, THE. **Added/Corp** Institute for International Research. **VAT** Reinsurance Report. Issue 80 (April 14, 1980)-. Periodical. English. bw (25 issues per year). $870.00. Evandale Publishing Ltd, 3840 East Castle Street, London W1N 7PE England. **Tel** 011 44 71 436 7028.

US
RESEARCH IN UNEMPLOYMENT INSURANCE. CHARACTERISTICS OF THE INSURED UNEMPLOYED. **See** Economics-Labor.

US/0887-1752
RESOURCE (ATLANTA, GA.). (RESOURCE: THE MAGAZINE OF THE LIFE OFFICE MANAGEMENT ASSOCIATION.). [Resource]. **Added/Corp** Life Office Management Association. **VFOAT** LOMA Resource. Vol. 4, No. 3 (June/July/Aug. 1979)-. Periodical. English. mo. Free (members); $36.00 (nonmembers). LOMA / Life Office Management Association, 5770 Powers Ferry Road, Atlanta GA 30327. **Tel** (404)951-1770, FAX (404)984-0441. **ED** Ron Clark. **DD** 368. **Ad Acc.** ***Continues*** *LOMA Resource (Life Office Management Association).*

IT
RESPONSABILITA CIVILE E PREVIDENZA. **See** Law.

UK/0034-6349
REVIEW, THE. (1869)-. Periodical. English. Twelve times a year. £95.00 UK, £115.00 others; $145.00 US. EMAP Business & Computer Publishing Ltd., 1 Lincoln Court 1 Lincoln Road, Peterborough PE1 2RP England. **Tel** 011/44/733/68900, FAX 011/44/733/349290. **(Subscription address:** EMAP Business Publishing, Ferrari House Audit House, Field End, Ruislip Middlesex HA4 9UY England.) **ED** Anne Myers. **LC** HG8013; .R4. **DD** 368.05. **Bk Rev. Ad Acc. Circ:** 4,995 (ctrl).
Desc: Reinsurance and international insurance and all subjects relating to these industries, such as economics, accounting, investment, financial analyses and world business trends.

BL/0019-0446
REVISTA DO IRB / INSTITUTO DE RESSEGUROS DO BRASIL. **VFOAT** IRB; I.R.B. Periodical. Portuguese. ir. Free. Inst do Resseguros do Brazil, Marechal Camera 171, Rio de Janeiro Brazil ZC-00. **Tel** (640)297-1212. **ED** Romilds Oliveira Motta. **Bk Rev. Ad Acc. Circ:** 6,200 (ctrl). ***Continues*** *Instituto de Resseguros do Brasil. Revista.*
Desc: Brazilian insurance market and reinsurance are the main subjects.

BE/0771-1530
REVUE BELGE DE SECURITE SOCIALE. **See** Sociology-Social Services and Welfare.

FR/0337-730X
REVUE FRANCAISE DU DOMMAGE CORPOREL. [Rev. fr. dommage corpor.]. **Added/Corp** Federation Francaise des Associations de Medecins-Conseils de Societes d'Assurances. (1975)-. Periodical. French. qt. 521.33F France; 650.00F other. JB Bailliere, 37 Avenue des Champs Elysees, 75008 Paris France. **Tel** 011 33 1 49536900. **NLM** W1; RE854G. ***Continues*** *Bulletin des Medecins-Conseils de Societes d'Assurances.*

BE
REVUE GENERAL DES ASSURANCES ET DE RESPONSABILITIES. Dutch. ir. 2300.00F. Revue Generale des Assurances Responsabilites, Groeselenberg 128, B-1180 Bruxelles Belgium. **Tel** 02 3431181.

US/1053-556X
RISK & BENEFITS JOURNAL, THE. [Risk benefits j.]. **VFOAT** Risk and Benefits Journal. Vol. 1, No. 1 (Nov./Dec. 1991)-. Periodical. English. bm. Free. Allied Health Care Publications, 4676 Admiralty Way, Suite 202, Marina Del Rey CA 90292. **LC** HG9395; .R57. **DD** 658.3/254.

US/0893-2654
RISK & BENEFITS MANAGEMENT. ***Ceased.*** [Risk benefits manage.]. **VFOAT** Risk and Benefits Management. Vol. 1, No. 1 (Dec. 1986)-Ceased (May 1988). Periodical. English. mo. Brentwood Publishing, 1640 5th Street, Santa Monica CA 90401. **Tel** (310)826-8388, telex 71-371-7714. **ED** Kwok-Sze Wong. **DD** 368. Index available. **Bk Rev. Ad Acc. Circ:** 15,000 (ctrl).
Desc: For risk, insurance and benefits managers; covers insurance, employee benefits, loss control, risk analysis and planning.

US/1050-9232
RISK & INSURANCE. (RISK & INSURANCE : THE MAGAZINE FOR RISK AND REINSURANCE EXECUTIVES.). [Risk insur.]. **VFOAT** Risk and Insurance. Vol. 1, No. 1 (June/July 1990)-. Periodical. English. Twelve times a year. $59.95 (postage included). Axon Magazine Group, 747 Dresher Road, Department AA, PO Box 980, Horsham PA 19044. **Tel** (215)784-0860. **ED** Richard Jaccoma. **LC** HG8054.5; .R52. **DD** 368/.973/05. **[CCC].**
Desc: Targets insurance industry executives and risk and insurance managers at corporations, nonprofit institutions and government agencies.

US/0743-9458
RISK LINE. [Risk line]. Periodical. English. bm. Risk Management Publishing Company, 2030 East Broadway/Suite 110, Tucson AZ 85719.

US/0035-5593
RISK MANAGEMENT. [Risk manage.]. **Added/Corp** American Society of Insurance Management. Risk and Insurance Management Society. Vol. 16, No. 4 (July/Aug. 1969)-. Periodical. English. mo. $54.00. Risk and Insurance Management Society, 205 East 42nd Street, New York NY 10164. **Tel** (212)286-9364. **ED** Mark Schussel. **LC** HG8059.C7; N312. **DD** 658. **CODEN** RMGTDN. Index available. **Ad Acc. Circ:** 12,000 (ctrl). available on microfilm and microfiche from University Microfilms International (UMI); available on an online database (files 15,16,485,648,771,772/Full-Text) from DIALOG. Documents available from Ask*IEEE, UMI Article Clearinghouse. ***Continues*** *National Insurance Buyer.*
Desc: News and feature articles of interest to risk and employee benefit managers.
Ind/Abst ABI/INFORM Glob. Ed.; ABI Inform Ondisc (Aug. 1989-); ABI/INFORM Ondisc: Expr. Ed.; Acad. Search (July 1993-); Account. Tax Datab. (1974-) [Full Txt.]; Bus. ASAP (1990-) [Full Txt.]; Bus. Index (1985-); Bus. Period. Index; F&S Index Plus Text, Int.; Gen. BusinessFile (1985-); Gen. Period. Index (1985-); Health Plan. Adminis.; Hospit. Health Admin. Index; INFO-SOUTH Abstr.; INSPEC (1982-); Ins. Period. Index; Mag. Search; PROMT; Risk Abstr.; Trade Ind. ASAP; Trade Ind. Index; UMI ABI/Inform--Bus. Period. Ondisc (Oct. 1987-) [Full Txt.]; Wilson Bus. Abstr.

US
RISK MANAGEMENT AND INSURANCE AUDIT TECHNIQUES. (19??)-. English. Twice a year. $157.00 US; $204.10 other. Standard Publishing Company, 155 Federal Street, Boston MA 02110. **Tel** (617)457-0604, (617)457-0600, FAX (617)457-0608.

●US/0732-2666
RISK MANAGEMENT FOR EXECUTIVE WOMEN. [Risk manage. exec. women]. (1992)-. Periodical. English. qt. $125.00 (institutions), $85.00 (individuals) US; $151.00 Canada; $185.00 other. Cox Publications, PO Box 20316, Billings MT 59104-0316. **Tel** (406)256-8822. **ED** Meridith B. Cox. **Bk Rev. Circ:** 155. ***Continues*** *California Risk Management Report for the Female Executive.*
Desc: Information on insurance, business risks and legislation to help female executives make effective risk management decisions.

US/1070-0102
RISK MANAGEMENT LETTER, THE. [Risk manage. lett.]. **Added/Corp** Warren, McVeigh & Griffin. (19??)-. Periodical. English. Five times a year. $28.00. Warren McVeigh & Griffin Inc, 1420 Bristol Street, Suite 220, Newport Beach CA 92660. **Tel** (714)752-1058, FAX (714)955-1929. **ED** Ron Rakich. **LC** HG8011; .R57. **DD** 368. **Pr Rev.**

US/0740-1396
RISK MANAGEMENT NEWSLETTER. ***Ceased.*** [Risk manage. newsl.]. Ceased (Dec. 1990). Periodical. English. mo. James Mooney and Company, PO Box 50, 262 Mountain Avenue, Springfield NJ 07081. **Tel** (201)376-3500. **ED** Heinz J. Pulverman. **Circ:** 2,000.

US/0199-6827
RISK MANAGEMENT REPORTS. [Risk manage. rep.]. **Added/Corp** Risk Planning Group. Tillinghast (Firm). Vol. 1 (1974)-. Periodical. English. an. $200.00 US; $225.00 (airmail) other. Tillinghast Publications, 695 East Main Street, Suite 600, Stamford CT 06901. **Tel** (203)326-5400, FAX (203)326-5498. **ED** H Felix Kloman. **DD** 368. Index available. cum. index. **Bk Rev. Circ:** 1,000 (ctrl). available on microfilm from University Microfilms International (UMI). ***Continued in part by*** *Captive Insurance Company Directory, 1056-814X.*
Desc: A journal on all aspects of risk management and insurance. Contains "Current Comment" which provides a view of current topics and trends affecting risk management and "Good Reading" a review of literature in terms of accuracy, interest and application.

US
RISK MANAGER LAW BULLETIN. ***Title Change.*** [Risk manage. law bull.]. **VFOAT** RMLB; R.M.L.B. Vol. 13, No. 1 (Jan. 1992)-(19??). Periodical. English. Twelve times a year. Quinlan Publishing Company, 23 Drydock Avenue, Boston MA 02210-2387. **Tel** (617)542-0048, (800)229-2084, FAX (617)345-9646. **LC** KF1215.A59; B87. **DD** 346.73/08681; 347.3068681. ***Continues*** *Corporate Insurance Law Bulletin, 1040-3132.* ***Continued by*** *Business Claims Casualty Bulletin.*

US/0197-7539
RISK REPORT, THE. **Added/Corp** International Risk Management Institute. Vol. 5, No. 1 (Sept. 1982)-.

Insurance

Periodical. English. mo. International Risk Management Institute, 12222 Merit Drive, Suite 1660, Dallas TX 75251. **Tel** (214)960-7693, (800)827-4242, FAX (214)960-6037. Index available (Free). **Continues** RIMCO Risk Report.

UK
RISK UPDATE. English. Twelve times a year. £225.00 UK; $375.00 US & Canada. DYP Insurance Reinsurance Res. Grp. Ltd., 181 Queen Victoria St. Bridge House, London EC4V 4DD England. **Tel** 011 44 71 236 2175, FAX 011 44 71 489 1487.

US/0035-8525
ROUGH NOTES (INDIANAPOLIS). (ROUGH NOTES.). [Rough notes]. (18??)-. Trade Publication. English. mo. $25.00 (one year), $40.25 (two years), $55.50 (three years) US; $35.00 (one year), $60.25 (two year), $85.50 (three year). Rough Notes Company Inc, 1200 North Meridian Street, Indianapolis IN 46206. **Tel** (317)634-1541, (800)428-4384, FAX (317)634-1041. **ED** Thomas McCoy. **LC** HG8011; .R7. **Ad Acc.** ctrl circ. available on microfilm and microfiche from University Microfilms International (UMI). Documents available from UMI Article Clearinghouse.
Desc: Property casualty insurance trade magazine. Articles by agency experts or insurance journalists.
Ind/Abst ABI/INFORM Glob. Ed.; ABI Inform Ondisc (May 1972-); Ins. Period. Index.

US/0161-7125
ROUND THE TABLE. (ROUND THE TABLE / MILLION DOLLAR ROUND TABLE.). **Added/Corp** Million Dollar Round Table (Des Plaines, Ill.). (19??)-. Periodical. English. bm (6 issues). $10.00. Million Dollar Round Table, 325 West Touhy, Park Ridge IL 60060. **Tel** (708)692-6378. **ED** Mary Kay Ams. **LC** HG8876; .R695. **DD** 368.3/2/00688. **Circ:** 20,000.

US/1059-0447
S & P'S INSURER SOLVENCY REVIEW (LIFE-HEALTH ED.). (S & P'S INSURER SOLVENCY REVIEW / STANDARD AND POOR'S INSURANCE RATING SERVICES.). [S & P's insur. solv. rev.] **Added/Corp** Standard and Poor's Insurance Rating Services. **VFOAT** S&P's Insurer Solvency Review; S and P's Insurer Solvency Review; Insurer Solvency Review; Insurer Solvency Review. Life-Health. **VAT** Standard and Poor's Insurer Solvency Review. Spring (1991)-. English. an. $115.00. Standard & Poor's Corporation, 25 Broadway, New York NY 10004. **Tel** (212)208-8775. **LC** HG8941; .S2. **DD** 368.3/006/573.

US/1059-0455
S & P'S INSURER SOLVENCY REVIEW (PROPERTY-CASUALTY ED.). (S & P'S INSURER SOLVENCY REVIEW / STANDARD AND POOR'S INSURANCE RATING SERVICES.). [S & P's insur. solv. rev.]. **Added/Corp** Standard and Poor's Insurance Rating Services. **VFOAT** S&P's Insurer Solvency Review; S and P's Insurer Solvency Review; Insurer Solvency Review; Insurer Solvency Review. Property-Casualty. **VAT** Standard and Poor's Insurer Solvency Review. Spring (1991)-. English. an. $115.00. Standard & Poor's Corporation, 25 Broadway, New York NY 10004. **Tel** (212)208-8775. **LC** HG8501; .S15. **DD** 368/.006/573.

US/0146-292X
S.S. HUEBNER FOUNDATION MONOGRAPH SERIES. **Added/Corp** S.S. Huebner Foundation for Insurance Education. **VFOAT** Huebner Foundation Monograph. **VAT** Solomon Stephen Huebner Foundation Monograph Series. No. 1 (1972)-. Monographic series. English. ir. Price varies per volume. University of Pennsylvania / Huebner, 430 Vance Hall, 3733 Spruce Street, Philadelphia PA 19104. **Tel** (215)898-2515. **ED** J. David Cummins. **LC** UNC. **Circ:** 1,000.
Desc: Research monographs on risk and insurance topics including economics of insurance markets, financial management of insurance companies, and public policy issues.

KO
SAENGMYONG POHOM SEMU. 1982-. Korean. Saengmyong Pohom Hyophoe, 60-1 3-ka Chungmuro Chung-ku, Seoul Korea. **LC** HG8848; .S3.

SW/0346-1238
SCANDINAVIAN ACTUARIAL JOURNAL. [Scand. actuar. j.]. **Added/Corp** Danske Aktuarforening. Finlands Aktuarieforeningen. Norske Aktuarforening. Svenska Aktuarieforeningen. (1974)-. Periodical. English. sa. Kr410.00, $66.00. Scandinavian University Press, PO Box 2959 Toeyen, N 0608 Oslo 6 Norway. **Tel** 011 47 2 2575400, FAX 011 47 2 2575353, telex 71896 UROR N. **(Subscription address:** Scandinavian University Press, 200 Meacham Ave., Elmont NY 11003.) **ED** Von Bahr, Norber, Ramlau-Hansen, and Ruohonen. **LC** HG8751; .S55. **DD** 368.3/6/01105. **CODEN** SAJODI. **Bk Rev. Ad Acc. Circ:** 500. **Supersedes** Skandinavisk Aktuarietidskrift.
Desc: Mathematical methods for insurance: probability theory, statistics, operations research, numerical analysis, computer science, demography, mathematical economics, practical actuarial method.

Ind/Abst Curr. Index Stat.; Math. Rev.; Stat. Theory Method Abstr. (1976-1981, 1983-1984, 1986); Zentralbl. Math. Ihre Grenzgeb.

SZ
SCHWEIZERISCHE VERSICHERUNGS ZEITSCHRIFT. REVUE SUISSE D'ASSURANCES. **VFOAT** Revue Suisse d'Assurances. (193?)-. Periodical. German (French). bm. 84.00F Switzerland; 92.00F other. Verlag Peter Lang AG, Jupiterstrasse 15, CH-3000 Bern 15 Switzerland. **Tel** 011 41 31 9411122, FAX 011 41 31 321131.

SZ
SCHWEIZERISCHE VERSICHERUNGSZEITSCHRIFT. REVUE SUISSE D'ASSURANCES. **VFOAT** Revue Suisse d'Assurances. (19??)-. Periodical. German. mo. **LC** HG8015; .S35. cum. index.

SZ/0255-9072
SCHWEIZERISCHE ZEITSCHRIFT FUER SOZIALVERSICHERUNG UND BERUFLICHE VORSORGE. [Schweiz. Z. Sozialversicher. berufl. Vorsorge]. **Added/Corp** Konferenz der Kantonalen Stiftungsaufsichtsbehorden (Switzerland) Konferenz der Kantonalen BVG-Aufsichtsbehorden (Switzerland). **VFOAT** Revue Suisse des Assurances Sociales et de la Prevoyance Professionnelle; SZS; S.Z.S. (1982)-. Periodical. German. bm (6 issues). 95.00F Switzerland; 108.00F other. Staempfli & Cie SA, Postfach 8326, CH-3001 Bern Switzerland. **Tel** 011 41 31 3006666, telex 031 911 515 EDMZ CH. Index Available in last issue of each volume--loose separately paged. **Continues** Schweizerische Zeitschrift fuer Sozialversicherung.

US/0363-4922
SECURITY LETTER. See Business-Personnel Management.

MX/0379-0304
SEGURIDAD SOCIAL. See Economics-Labor.

JA/0287-2641
SEIMEI HOKEN KEIEI. **Added/Corp** Seimei Hoken Keiei Gakkai. **VFOAT** Seimeihoken Keiei; Life Insurance Management. (19??)-. Periodical. Japanese. bm. ¥4000 membership. Seimei Hoken Keiei Gakkai, c/o Seimei Hoken Bunka, Kenkyujo Tokyo Jimusho 8-ban 8-go Yaesu 2-chome, Chuo-ku Tokyo 104 Japan. **LC** HG9245.J3; S45.

US
SELECTIVE DIGEST OF THE LAW OF INSURANCE AND RELATED TOPICS. (1985/86)-. English. an. $20.00. Bar List Publishing Company, 425 Huehl, Northbrook IL 60062. **Tel** (708)498-0100. **Separated from** Insurance Bar.

US
SENTINEL, THE. **Added/Corp** Factory Insurance Association. (19??)-. Periodical. English. Four times a year. Free on request. Industrial Risk Insurers, PO Box 5010, Hartford CT 06102-5010. **Tel** (203)520-7300, FAX (203)549-5780, 527-3160, telex 9-9349. **ED** Anson Smith (editor's address: 85 Woodland Street, PO Box 5010, Hartford, CT 06102-5010 USA; telephone: (203)520-7442). **Circ:** 65,000.
Desc: Information on company property loss prevention.

US/0732-104X
SERVICEMEN'S AND VETERAN'S GROUP LIFE INSURANCE PROGRAMS, ANNUAL REPORT. See Military and Defense.

JA
SHAKAI FUKUSHI NO DOKO. See Sociology-Social Services and Welfare.

US/1055-8667
SHEPARD'S NEW JERSEY INSURANCE LAW & REGULATION REPORTER. See Law.

CN/0705-1786
SHOPPERS' GUIDE TO CANADIAN LIFE INSURANCE PRICES (SUDBURY, ONT. : 1980). (SHOPPERS' GUIDE TO CANADIAN LIFE INSURANCE PRICES.). 1980 Ed.-. English. an. W E McLeod, 15 Eden Point Drive, Sudbury Ontario P3E 4V6 Canada. **ED** William E McLeod. **DD** 368.3/2/00971. **Continues** Consumer's Association of Canada. Shoppers' Guide to Canadian Life Insurance Prices, 0705-1786.

US
SHORTCUT2. (1987)-. English. Four times a year. $350.00 (includes installation package, updates, and newsletters). National Underwriter Company, 505 Gest Street, Cincinnati OH 45203-0874. **Tel** (513)721-2140, (800)543-0874. **Continues** Agents & Buyers Market Service.
Desc: A market-tracking system on software. Aids

insurance professionals in identifying offerings of both standard and specialty insurance companies and brokers in hundreds of industries and free-standing coverages.

US/0883-6825
SHOW-ME UNDERWRITER, THE. (THE SHOW-ME UNDERWRITER : THE OFFICIAL MAGAZINE OF THE MISSOURI ASSOCIATION OF LIFE UNDERWRITERS.). **VFOAT** Show Me Underwriter. Periodical. English. bm. $3.00. Missouri Association of Life Underwriters, PO Box 1729, Jefferson City MO 65101. **Tel** (314)634-5202. **ED** Annette Wankum. **Ad Acc. Circ:** 2,800.

US
SINGLE FAMILY COINSURANCE PROGRAM. **Added/Corp** United States. Federal Housing Administration. **VFOAT** Coinsurance Handbook. (1976)-. Government Publication. English. US Department of Housing and Urban Development, 451 Seventh Street SW, Washington DC 20401. **Tel** (202)708-0980, FAX (202)708-0299.

US/0736-8348
SMART'S INSURANCE BULLETIN. [Smart's Insur. bull.]. (19??)-. Newsletter. English. wk. $245.00. James Whitaker & Associates, 1 Waters Park Drive, Suite 104, San Mateo CA 94403. **Tel** (415)341-2432, FAX (415)341-3304. **ED** Frederick L. Pilot. [CCC]. Index available. **Circ:** 800.
Desc: Provides timely reporting & analysis of regulatory, political & legal developments affecting the California property and casualty industry.

US/0882-6234
SOCIAL SECURITY ALERT (1985). (SOCIAL SECURITY ALERT / THE RESEARCH INSTITUTE OF AMERICA.). Vol. 1, No. 1 (Mar. 1985)-. Periodical. English. mo. $72.00. Research Institute of America, 117 East Stevens Avenue, Valhalla NY 10595. **Tel** (800)431-9025. **DD** 368.

II/0250-4057
SOCIAL SECURITY DOCUMENTATION. ASIAN SERIES. **Main/Corp** International Social Security Association. Regional Office for Asia and Oceania. Monographic series. English. ir. Price varies per volume. International Social Security Association, Case Postale 1, CH-1211 Geneva 22 Switzerland. **Tel** 011 41 22 7996617, FAX 011 41 22 7986385.

SZ
SOCIAL SECURITY DOCUMENTATION. EUROPEAN SERIES. English (French and German). ir. (one or two volumes per year). 20.00F. International Social Security Association, Case Postale 1, CH-1211 Geneva 22 Switzerland. **Tel** 011 41 22 7996617, FAX 011 41 22 7986385.
Desc: Studies and reports of meetings concerning aspects of social security of special interest for industrialised countries.

AT/0726-1195
SOCIAL SECURITY JOURNAL. See Sociology-Social Services and Welfare.

NE
SOCIALE VERSEKERING, PENSIOENVERSEKERING, LEVENSVERZEKERING / CENTRAAL BUREAU VOOR DE STATISTIEK. See Sociology-Social Services and Welfare.

CN/0846-1961
SOCIETAIRE (MONTREAL). (LE SOCIETAIRE.). [Societaire]. **Added/Corp** Association des Courtiers d'Assurances de la Province de Quebec. **VFOAT** Bulletin; Bulletin le Societaire. Vol. 1, No 1 (Jan/Feb. 1991)-. Periodical. French. mo. Free for Members. Association des Courtiers d'Assurances de la Province de Quebec, 550 Ouest rue Sherbrooke/Bureau 1570, Montreal Quebec H3A 1C8 Canada. **DD** 368. **Continues** Info (Association des Courtiers d'Assurances de la Province de Quebec)., 0846-1953.

US/0038-0075
SOCIETY PAGE. Periodical. English. bm. American Society of CLU-CHFC, 270 Bryn Mawr Avenue, Bryn Mawr PA 19010. **Tel** (215)526-2500. **ED** Deanne L Sherman. **Circ:** 36,000 (ctrl).
Desc: A newsletter containing Society news, announcements of services, and articles on trends in insurance and financial services.

US/8756-1093
SOFTWHERE. INSURANCE. See Computers-Software.

JA
SONGAI HOKEN KENKYU. **Added/Corp** Songai Hoken Jigyo Kenkyujo (Japan). (19??)-. Japanese. Four times a year. $74.50. Songai Hoken Jigyo Kenkujo, 6-5 Kanda Surugadai 3, Chiyoda-ku 101, Tokyo Japan. **(Subscription address:** Japan Publications Trading Company, Ltd., PO Box 5030, Tokyo International, Tokyo 100-31 Japan.) **LC** HG9956; .S635.

Insurance

NO
SOSIAL TRYGD. See Sociology-Social Services and Welfare.

RU
SOTSIALNOE OBESPECHENIE. Vol. 1 (1926)-. Periodical. Russian. mo. $79.95. **(Subscription address:** East View Publications Inc., 3020 Harbor Lane North, Suite 110, Minneapolis MN 55447.**)** Index available. **Ad Acc.**
Ind/Abst Int. Labour Doc.

US/0073-148X
SOURCE BOOK OF HEALTH INSURANCE DATA. Added/Corp Health Insurance Institute (New York, N.Y.) Health Insurance Association of America. Public Relations Division. Health Insurance Association of America. Policy Development and Research Dept. **VFOAT** Sourcebook of Health Insurance Data. 1st Edition (1959)-. English. an. $26.92 (latest edition). Health Insurance Association of America, 1025 Connecticut Avenue Northwest, Washington DC 20036. **Tel** (202)223-7780. **(Subscription address:** Professional Books Distributors, 1650 Bluegrass Lakes Parkway, Alpheretta GA 30201.**) LC** HG9396; .S6. **DD** 368.380973. **NLM** W1 SO893.
Ind/Abst Predicasts Forecasts; Stat. Ref. Index.

US/0038-4216
SOUTHERN INSURANCE. (19??)-. Periodical. English. Twelve times a year. $12.00. Chase Communications Group, 2535 Beechwood Avenue, PO Box 9001, Mt Vernon NY 10552. **Tel** (914)699-2020. **ED** Alvin J. Davis. **Bk Rev. Ad Acc. Circ:** 3,400 (ctrl).
Supersedes Insurance Agent.
Desc: Carries trade literature, personnel news, coming events, financial news, book reviews, and staff articles, all concerning the insurance industry.

GW/0173-394X
SOZIALLEISTUNGEN. REIHE 1: VERSICHERTE IN DER KRANKEN- UND RENTENVERSICHERUNG. See Sociology-Social Services and Welfare.

UK/0957-0063
SPACE INSURANCE REPORT. [Space insur. rep.]. (1989)-. English. Twelve times a year. £315.00 UK; $520.00 US. DYP Insurance Reinsurance Res. Grp. Ltd., 181 Queen Victoria St. Bridge House, London EC4V 4DD England. **Tel** 011 44 71 236 2175, FAX 011 44 71 489 1487. **DD** 368.

US
SPECIAL REVIEW OF THE DEPARTMENT OF HEALTH AND SOCIAL SERVICES, DIVISION OF PUBLIC ASSISTANCE, MEDICAL ASSISTANCE PAYMENTS FOR ABORTIONS, A. See Sociology-Social Services and Welfare.

US
SPECIALTY COVERAGE MARKET REPORTS : SCMR. Added/Corp Rough Notes Co. **VFOAT** SCMR. (19??)-. Periodical. English. mo. $70.00 US; $80.00 other. Rough Notes Company Inc, 1200 North Meridian Street, Indianapolis IN 46206. **Tel** (317)634-1541, (800)428-4384, FAX (317)634-1041. **ED** Wally Clapp. **Circ:** 500.

US/0740-1329
SPENCER'S RETIREMENT PLAN SERVICE. (SPENCER'S RETIREMENT PLAN SERVICE : SRPS.). [Spencer's Retire. plan serv.]. **VFOAT** S.R.P.S.; SRPS. (19??)-. Periodical. English. mo. $340.00 Chicago; $337.00 Illinois; $315.00 other. Charles D. Spencer & Associates, 250 South Wacker Drive, Suite 600, Chicago IL 60606-5834. **Tel** (312)993-7900, FAX (312)993-7910. **ED** Ross D. Spencer. **Circ:** 800 (ctrl).
Desc: Covers small-plan benefits for consultants. Also covers pensions, not only from the legal angle, but with practical applications.

US
ST. ANTHONY'S ICD-9-CM CODING FOR PHYSICIAN REIMBURSEMENT.
Added/Corp St. Anthony Hospital Publications (Firm). **VFOAT** Saint Anthony's ICD-9-CM Coding for Physician Reimbursement. (198?)-. Periodical. English. mo. $159.00. St. Anthony's Publishing Co., 500 Montgomery Street /Suite 700, Alexandria VA 22314. **Tel** (800)632-0123 ext. 5746. **(Subscription address:** St. Anthony Publishing Inc., PO Box 14212, Washington DC 20044.**) NLM** W1; SA162.

NE
STAND ZIEKENGELDVERZEKERING VERSLAG OVER ... / SOCIALE VERZEKERINGSRAAD. VFOAT Stand Ziekengeldverzekering. Dutch. an. Sociale Verzekeringsraad, Postbus 100, 2700 AC Zoetemeer Netherlands. **LC** HD7102.N4; N46A. **DD** 368.3/8/009492.
Continues Verslag van de Stand der Ziekengeldverzekering.

US/0038-9390
STANDARD (BOSTON), THE. (THE STANDARD.). (1865)-. Periodical. English. wk (Weekly except every other week in July and Aug.). $40.00. Standard Publishing Company, 155 Federal Street, Boston MA 02110. **Tel** (617)457-0604, (617)457-0600, FAX (617)457-0608. **ED** Frank R. Pate. **LC** HG9651; .S8. **Ad Acc, Adv Mgr:** Barbara Crockett.

US
STATE OF MONTANA, DEPARTMENT OF LABOR AND INDUSTRY, WORKMEN'S COMPENSATION DIVISION, REPORT ON REVIEW OF CERTAIN INSURANCE AND DISABILITY COMPENSATION OPERATIONS. See Economics-Labor.

US/0097-8825
STATE OF NEVADA BOND TRUST FUND AUDITOR REPORT. Main/Corp Nevada. Legislative Auditor. English. Legislative Auditor, Legislative Building, Capitol Complex, Carson City NV 89710. **LC** HG9970.S6; N355A. **DD** 353.9/793/00825.

US/0095-1382
STATISTICAL TABLES - DEPARTMENT OF EMPLOYMENT SECURITY. See Insurance-Abstracting, Bibliographies and Statistics.

US
STATISTICAL TABLES FROM ANNUAL STATEMENTS. See Insurance-Abstracting, Bibliographies and Statistics.

GW
STATISTIK DER ORTSKRANKENKASSEN IN DER BUNDESREPUBLIK DEUTSCHLAND : ALTERSGLIEDERUNG DER MITGLIEDER. See Insurance-Abstracting, Bibliographies and Statistics.

CN/0846-8001
STATISTIQUES FINANCIERES EN ..., LES. See Economics-Abstracting, Bibliographies and Statistics.

US
SUPERGROWTH. Newsletter. English. Six times a year. $80.00. Russell Miller Inc., 300 Montgomery Street, San Francisco CA 94104. **Tel** (415)956-7474. **Circ:** 3,500.

CN/0713-1763
SUPPLEMENTARY CANADA PENSION PLAN CONTRIBUTION AND UNEMPLOYMENT INSURANCE PREMIUM TABLES. See Economics-Labor.

CN/0713-178X
SUPPLEMENTARY UNEMPLOYMENT INSURANCE PREMIUM TABLES ... PROVINCE OF QUEBEC. (SUPPLEMENTARY UNEMPLOYMENT INSURANCE PREMIUM TABLES FOR 10 - 13 - 22 PAY PERIODS.). [Suppl. Unemploy. Insur. prem. tables ... Prov. Que.]. **VFOAT** Tables Supplementaires de Primes d'Assurance-Chomage pour 10 - 13 - 22 Periodes de Paie. **VAT** Tables Supplementaires de Primes d'Assurance-Chomage ... Province de Quebec. Periodical. English (French). Revenue Canada Taxation, 875 Heron Road, Ottawa Ontario K1A 0L8 Canada. **Tel** (613)957-3508, FAX (613)941-0914. **DD** 354.710082/56.

SW
SVENSK FORSAKRINGS-ARSBOK. THE SWEDISH INSURANCE YEAR-BOOK. Added/Corp Svenska Forsakringsforeningen. **VFOAT** The Swedish Insurance Year-Book. (1916)-. Swedish (Swedish). Kr.50.00. **LC** HG5621; .S84.

●US/1061-401X
TAX FACTS. INSURANCE AND EMPLOYEE BENEFITS ED. (TAX FACTS.). (1992)-. English. an. $29.95. Tax Facts, 505 Gest Street, Cincinnati OH 45203.

US/0496-9685
TAX FACTS ON LIFE INSURANCE. [Tax facts life insur.]. **Added/Corp** National Underwriter Company. (19??)-. English. an. $19.25. National Underwriter Company, 505 Gest Street, Cincinnati OH 45203-0874. **Tel** (513)721-2140, (800)543-0874. **LC** KF6428.L5; T38. **DD** 343/.73/052.
Desc: Provides current income, estate, and gift tax information.

US/0093-3368
TEXAS INSURANCE FACT BOOK. 1973-. English. an. $2.00. Bureau of Business Research / Texas, University of Texas at Austin, Box 7459, Austin TX 78713. **Tel** (512)471-1616, FAX (512)471-1063. **LC** HG8018; .S8 subser; HG8538.T4. **DD** 368/.9764.

US/0264-6307
TEXAS INSURANCE LAW REPORTER. See Law.

US/0040-8190
TITLE NEWS. [Title news]. **Added/Corp** American Land Title Association. American Title Association. Vol. 3, No. 2 (Mar. 1924)-. Periodical. English. bm. $48.00 nonmember; $30.00 other. American Land Title Association, 1828 L Street Northwest, Suite 705, Washington DC 20036. **Tel** (800)787-2582, (202)296-3671. **ED** Adina Conn. **DD** 368. Index available. cum. index. **Ad Acc.** ctrl circ. *Continues Monthly Bulletin of the American Title Association.*
Ind/Abst Bus. Index (1985-); Curr. Law Index (1983-); Gen. BusinessFile (1985-); Ins. Period. Index (-19??); Leg. Resour. Index (1983-); LegalTrac (1983-); Trade Ind. Index.

US
TLTA NEWS. Added/Corp Texas Land Title Association. **VFOAT** Texas Land Title Association News. (19??)-. English. Four times a year (Jan., Apr., July, Oct.). $16.00. Texas Land Title Association / TLTA, 220 West Seventh Street, Suite 201, Austin TX 78701. **Tel** (512)472-6593, FAX (512)472-5931. **ED** Christine Turneabe. **Ad Acc.** Full Page (B&W) $625.00 (members). Half Page (B&W) $425.00 (members). **Circ:** 1,600 (ctrl).
Desc: The non-profit state trade association for title insurance companies, title insurance agents and abstracters involved in the conveyance of titles to real property in Texas. Designed to keep members informed about relevant industry issues and association activities, the magazine helps members improve their skills and increase their knowledge and also fosters pride in being part of the Texas title insurance industry.

UK
TOLLEY'S NATIONAL INSURANCE CONTRIBUTIONS. English. £27.95. Tolley Publishing Company Ltd, Tolley House, 2 Addiscombe Road, Croydon, Surrey CR9 5AF United Kingdom. **Tel** 011 44 81 6869141, FAX 011 44 81 6863155, 011 44 81 7600588. **ED** Neil Booth.
Desc: Contains details of the Social Security (Contributions) Act 1991 implementing the new NI charge for employers providing company cars. Also contains new DSS leaflets and changes in DSS interpretation and practice.

UK
TOLLEY'S SOCIAL SECURITY AND STATE BENEFITS. English. an (November). £29.95. Tolley Publishing Company Ltd, Tolley House, 2 Addiscombe Road, Croydon, Surrey CR9 5AF United Kingdom. **Tel** 011 44 81 6869141, FAX 011 44 81 6863155, 011 44 81 7600588. **ED** Jim Mathewman.
Desc: Contains all important developments in the law and includes the changes brought about by the most recent Social Security legislation and case law. Examines eighty types of benefit and assistance. List of key points precedes the explanation of all major benefits and references to relevant legislation are included throughout.

US/0885-856X
TORT & INSURANCE LAW JOURNAL. See Law.

●US/1064-4709
TRANSACTIONS OF THE ACADEMY OF INSURANCE MEDICINE: 1992, VOLUME LXXVI. (1992)-. English. an. Association of Life Insurance Medical Directors, 1 Monarch Place, c/o W J Baker MD, Springfield MA 01133. **Tel** (413)784-6637. **ED** Charles B Arnold, MD. Index available. *Continues Transactions of the Association of Life Insurance Medical Directors of America, Annual Meeting, 0066-9598.*
Ind/Abst Energy Res. Abstr.; Index Med.

US/0066-9598
TRANSACTIONS OF THE ASSOCIATION OF LIFE INSURANCE MEDICAL DIRECTORS OF AMERICA, ANNUAL MEETING. *Title Change.* [Trans. Assoc. Life Insur. Med. Dir. Am. annu. meet.]. **Main/Corp** Association of Life Insurance Medical Directors of America. (1941)-(1992). English. an. Association of Life Insurance Medical Directors, 1 Monarch Place, c/o W J Baker MD, Springfield MA 01133. **Tel** (413)784-6637. **DD** 368. **NLM** W1 TR225Q. cum. index. available on microfilm from University Microfilms International (UMI). *Continues Association of Life Insurance Medical Directors of America. Abstract of the Proceedings of the Annual Meeting of the Association of Life Insurance Medical Directors of America, 0734-6239. Continued by Transactions of the Academy of Insurance Medicine: 1992, Volume LXXVI.*
Ind/Abst Energy Res. Abstr. (Aug. 1982-); Index Med.

Insurance

UK/0071-3686
TRANSACTIONS OF THE FACULTY OF ACTUARIES. Main/Corp Faculty of Actuaries in Scotland. Vol. 1 (1901)-. Periodical. English. ir (3 or 4 per year). £9.00. Faculty of Actuaries, 40 44 Thistle Street, Edinburgh EH2 1EN Scotland. **Tel** 011 44 31 2204555. **ED** L.J.G. Purdie. **LC** HG8754; .F4. Index available. cum. index. **Bk Rev.** ctrl circ. **Continues** Transactions of the Actuarial Society of Edinburgh.
Desc: Official journal of the Faculty of Actuaries.
Ind/Abst Stat. Theory Method Abstr. (1959-1963).

US
TRANSACTIONS OF THE SOCIETY OF ACTUARIES COMMITTEE REPORTS. English. ir. Society of Actuaries, PO Box 95668, Chicago IL 60694. **Tel** (708)706-3526.

US/0037-9794
TRANSACTIONS - SOCIETY OF ACTUARIES. Main/Corp Society of Actuaries. Vol. 1, No. 1 (1949)-. Academic Scholarly Publication. English. an. $55.00. Society of Actuaries, PO Box 95668, Chicago IL 60694. **Tel** (708)706-3526. **ED** Jerry Enoch. **LC** HG8754; .S6. **DD** 368.3/005. Index available. cum. index. **Pr Rev. Circ:** 10,000. **Supersedes** Actuarial Society of America. Transactions; American Institute of Actuaries. Record.
Desc: Scholarly journal of papers in actuarial science and in the life and health insurance and employee benefits industry.
Ind/Abst Math. Rev.; Stat. Theory Method Abstr. (1982).

US/0094-422X
TRANSCRIBINGS, ANNUAL CONFERENCE - AMERICAN SOCIETY OF PENSION ACTUARIES. See Economics-Labor.

US
TRENDS IN EMPLOYMENT & WAGES COVERED BY UNEMPLOYMENT INSURANCE. Added/Corp New Jersey. Division of Labor Market and Demographic Research. **VFOAT** Trends in Employment and Wages Covered by Unemployment Insurance; New Jersey Covered Employment Trends. (1988)-. Periodical. English. an. Division of Labor Market and Demographic Research, New Jersey Department of Labor, CN 388, Trenton NJ 08625-0388. **Tel** (609)292-0076, FAX (609)984-6833. **LC** HD7096.U6; N59. **DD** 331.12/5/00749. **Continues** New Jersey Covered Employment Trends, 0737-1810.

●SZ/1019-4126
TRENDS IN SOCIAL SECURITY. See Economics-Labor.

US
U.S. DECENNIAL LIFE TABLES. ACTUARIAL TABLES BASED ON UNITED STATES LIFE TABLES. See Insurance-Abstracting, Bibliographies and Statistics.

US
U.S. DECENNIAL LIFE TABLES. METHODOLOGY OF THE NATIONAL AND STATE LIFE TABLES FOR THE UNITED STATES. See Insurance-Abstracting, Bibliographies and Statistics.

PL
UBEZPIECZENIA MAJATKOWE I OSOBOWE. Main/Corp Poland. Gowny Urzad Statystyczny. (1965/68)-. Polish. an. $4.50 Poland; $5.50 North America; $5.00 other. Zaklad Wydawnictw Statystycznych, Al Niepodleglosci 208, 00-925 Warszawa Poland. **Tel** 253241, telex 814581A GUS. **LC** HA1451; .S47 subser; HG8651. **Circ:** 900 (ctrl).
Desc: Statistical data of property and personal insurance.

KO
UIRYO POHOM TONGGYE YONBO. Added/Corp Uiryo Pohom Kwalli Kongdan (Korea). **VFOAT** Medical Insurance Statistical Year Book; Medical Insurance Statistical Yearbook. Korean (English). **LC** HG9399.K8; U5. **Continues** Uiryo Pohom Yonbo.

KO
UIRYO POHOM YONBO. Title Change. VFOAT Annual Report. Korean (Korean). an. **LC** HG9399.K83; U378. **Continued by** Uiryo Pohom tonggye yonbo (Seoul, Korea).

US
UL TRENDS. Added/Corp Underwriters' Laboratories. **VFOAT** Trends. **VAT** Underwriters Laboratories Trends. (19??)-. Periodical. English. Three times a year. Free on request. Underwriters Laboratories Inc., 333 Pfingsten Road, Northbrook IL 60062. **Tel** (708)272-8800 Ext.3542, FAX (708)272-8129, telex 6502543343.

US/1062-6441
UNDERWRITER ALERT. [Underwrit. alert]. (19??)-. Periodical. English. bm. $130.00 (7 issues). Underwriter Alert, PO Box 2990, Binghamton NY 13902. **Tel** (607)724-3992, FAX (607)724-3992. **ED** John J. Krinik (Editor's Address: 6 Hartley Road, Binghampton, NY 13901). **DD** 368. Index available (bound in 7th issue of each volume). cum. index. **Circ:** 400.
Desc: Survey of news, information, and trends - medical, financial, legal, sales - for the home office life and health underwriter.

US
UNDERWRITERS' HANDBOOK. (19??)-. Directory. English. an. $48.50. National Underwriter Company, 505 Gest Street, Cincinnati OH 45203-0874. **Tel** (513)721-2140, (800)543-0874.
Desc: Listings for 35 states of property, health, and casualty and life agencies segmented by city, including principals, address, phone number and companies represented.

US/0041-6622
UNDERWRITERS' REPORT. (19??)-. Periodical. English. Fifty-one times per year (except last week of the year). $45.00. Underwriters Report, 667 Mission Street, San Francisco CA 94105. **Tel** (415)981-3221, FAX (415)974-5041. **ED** Roy Pasini. **LC** WMLC L 83/3719. **Ad Acc. Circ:** 6,500. available on microfilm from University Microfilms International (UMI).
Desc: News events related primarily to property-casualty insurance industry; secondarily to life insurance industry.

US
UNDERWRITING : TECHNICAL DIRECTION FOR PROJECT MORTGAGE INSURANCE. Government Publication. English. ir. US Department of Housing and Urban Development, 451 Seventh Street SW, Washington DC 20401. **Tel** (202)708-0980, FAX (202)708-0299.

CN/0713-1771
UNEMPLOYMENT INSURANCE PREMIUM TABLES ... PROVINCE OF QUEBEC. (UNEMPLOYMENT INSURANCE PREMIUM TABLES / TABLES DE PRIMES D'ASSURANCE-CHOMAGE.). [Unemploy. Insur. prem. tables ... Prov. Que.]. **Added/Corp** Canada. Taxation. **VFOAT** Tables de Primes d'Assurance-Chomage. **VAT** Tables de Primes d'Assurance-Chomage ... Province de Quebec. (19??)-. Periodical. English (French). Revenue Canada Taxation, 875 Heron Road, Ottawa Ontario K1A 0L8 Canada. **Tel** (613)957-3508, FAX (613)941-0914. **DD** 354.710082/56.

US/8756-9892
UNEMPLOYMENT INSURANCE QUALITY APPRAISAL RESULTS. (UNEMPLOYMENT INSURANCE QUALITY APPRAISAL RESULTS FOR FY ... / PREPARED BY EMPLOYMENT AND TRAINING ADMINISTRATION, UNEMPLOYMENT INSURANCE SERVICE.). **Added/Corp** United States. Unemployment Insurance Service. (19??)-. English. an. US Department of Labor Employment & Training Administration, 200 Constitutions Avenue NW, Room S307, Washington DC 20210. **Tel** (202)219-6050, FAX (202)219-6827. **LC** HD7096.U5; U6375. **DD** 368.4/4/00973. available on microfiche (Vols. for (1983-) distributed to depository libraries).

CN/0828-3176
UNEMPLOYMENT INSURANCE STATISTICS. ANNUAL SUPPLEMENT (OTTAWA). (UNEMPLOYMENT INSURANCE STATISTICS, ANNUAL SUPPLEMENT ... / STATISTICS CANADA, LABOUR DIVISION, UNEMPLOYMENT INSURANCE STATISTICS SECTION.). [Unempl. insur. stat., Annu. suppl.]. **Added/Corp** Statistics Canada. Unemployment Insurance Statistics Section. Canada. Employment and Immigration Canada (Commission). **VFOAT** Statistiques sur l'Assurance-Chomage, Supplement Annuel ... . (1985)-. English (French). an. Free to subscribers to Unemployment Insurance Statistics. Statistics Canada, Publications Sales & Services, Main Building Room 1710, Ottawa Ontario K1A 0T6 Canada. **Tel** (613)951-5078, (800)267-6677, FAX (613)951-1584, telex 053-3585. **LC** HD7096.C2; U53. **DD** 368.4/1/00971021.

CN/0829-1098
UNEMPLOYMENT INSURANCE STATISTICS (OTTAWA). (UNEMPLOYMENT INSURANCE STATISTICS / STATISTICS CANADA, LABOUR DIVISION, UNEMPLOYMENT INSURANCE STATISTICS SECTION.). [Unemploy. insur. stat.]. **Added/Corp** Statistics Canada. Unemployment Insurance Statistics Section. **VFOAT** Statistiques sur l'Assurance Chomage; Statistiques sur l'Assurance-Chomage. Vol. 44, No. 4 (April 1985)-. English (French). mo. 160.00Can$ Canada; $192.00 US; $224.00 other. Statistics Canada, Publications Sales & Services, Main Building Room 1710, Ottawa Ontario K1A 0T6 Canada. **Tel** (613)951-5078, (800)267-6677, FAX (613)951-1584, telex 053-3585. **LC** HD7096.C2; A34. **DD** 368.4/1/00971021. **Continues** Statistical Report on the Operation of the Unemployment Insurance Act, 0382-4098.

CL
VALORES Y SEGUROS / SUPERINTENDENCIA DE VALORES Y SEGUROS. Periodical. Spanish. qt. $15.00 single issue. Superintendencia de Valores Y Seguros, Alameda 874, 6 Y 7 Pisos. **LC** HG5341; .V34. **DD** 332.63/2/0983.

US
VALUATION ANALYSIS FOR HOME MORTGAGE INSURANCE. Added/Corp United States. Dept. of Housing and Urban Development. Office of Housing Production and Mortgage Credit. (19??)-. Government Publication. English. US Department of Housing and Urban Development, 451 Seventh Street SW, Washington DC 20401. **Tel** (202)708-0980, FAX (202)708-0299.

US
VALUATION ANALYSIS FOR PROJECT MORTGAGE INSURANCE. Government Publication. English. US Department of Housing and Urban Development, 451 Seventh Street SW, Washington DC 20401. **Tel** (202)708-0980, FAX (202)708-0299.

●US/1065-3473
VANTAGE (WORCESTER, MASS.). (VANTAGE : A PUBLICATION OF STATE MUTUAL LIFE ASSURANCE COMPANY OF AMERICA FOR ITS MARKETING/SALES TEAMS.). [Vantage]. **Added/Corp** State Mutual Life Assurance Company of America. (1992)-. Periodical. English. qt. Free. Allmerica Financial, 440 Lincoln Street, Worcester MA 01653. **DD** 658.

US/1062-3361
VARIABLE ANNUITY SOURCEBOOK. Title Change. [Var. annuity sourceb.]. **Added/Corp** Morningstar, Inc. **VFOAT** Morningstar's Variable Annuity Sourcebook. (1992)-(1992). English. an. Morningstar Inc, 225 West Wacker Drive, Chicago IL 60606. **Tel** (312)696-6000, (800)876-5005. **LC** HG8790; .V37. **DD** 368.3/75/002573. **Continued by** Morningstar Variable Annuity/Life Sourcebook.

GW/0933-4548
VERSICHERUNGSMEDIZIN. See Medical Science and Technology.

GW
VERSICHERUNGSRECHT. (19??)-. Periodical. German. Thirty-six times a year. DM323.12. Verlag Versicherungswirtschaft, Klosestrasse 20 24, D-76137 Karlsruhe Germany. **Tel** 011 49 721 35090, FAX 011 49 721 31833.

GW/0042-4358
VERSICHERUNGSWIRTSCHAFT. [Versicherungswirtschaft]. (1946)-. Periodical. German. Twenty-four times a year. DM159.24. Verlag Versicherungswirtschaft, Klosestrasse 20 24, D-76137 Karlsruhe Germany. **Tel** 011 49 721 35090, FAX 011 49 721 31833.
Ind/Abst Energy Res. Abstr. (Feb. 1972-).

SA
VERSLAE VAN DIE GEKOSE KOMITEE VOOR PENSIOENE. See Economics-Labor.

NE
VERSLAG VAN DE VERZEKERINGSKAMER INGEVOLGE DE WET OP HET SCHADEVERZEKERINGSBEDRIJF OVER HET JAAR ... . 1980-. Dutch (summaries and/or abstracts in English and French). an. **LC** HG8641; .N47A. **Continues** Verslag van de Verzekeringskamer Ingevolge de Wet op Het Schadeverzekeringsbedrijf Betrefende de Financiele Gegevens van de Ondernemingen en de Werkzaamheden en Bevindingen van de Kamer.

GW
VERWALTUNGSBERICHT DES BEZIRKS BONN DER BERGBAU-BERUFSGENOSSENSCHAFT / HERAUSGEGEBEN VON DER BEZIRKSVERWALTUNG BONN DER BERGBAU-BERUFSGENOSSENSCHAFT. See Industrial Health and Safety.

NE
VERZEKERINGS ARCHIEF, HET. Verbond Van Verzekeraars Ned, Postbus 990, 2501 CZ Den Haag Netherlands.

NE
VERZEKERINGS MAGAZINE VVP. Dutch. wk. Nijg Periodieken BV, Postbus 122, 3100 AC Schiedam Netherlands. **Tel** 011 31 10 4274174.

Insurance

●CN/1191-1077
VIESAGE (MONTREAL). (VIESAGE.).
[ViEsage]. **Added/Corp** Association des Intermediaires en Assurance de Personnes du Quebec. Section Montreal. **VFOAT** Vie Sage. Vol. 1, No 1 (Febr. 1992)-. Periodical. French. bm. Free for Members. De Personnes Du Quebec, CP 126 Succursale Place D'Armes, Montreal (Quebec) H2Y 3H9. **DD** 368.3.

CN/0827-2654
VIEWPOINT - INSURANCE BUREAU OF CANADA. *Ceased.* (VIEWPOINT.). [Viewp. - Insur. Bur. Can.]. Feb. 1980-(19??). Periodical. English. Insurance Bureau of Canada, 181 University Avenue, 13th Floor, Toronto Ontario M5H 3M7 Canada. **Tel** (416)362-2031, FAX (416)361-5952. **DD** 368./971/05. *Continues* Viewpoint on Insurance, 0827-2662.

US/0190-3535
VIEWPOINT (NEW YORK. 1968).
(VIEWPOINT.). Periodical. English. HIAA Consumer & Professional Relations Division, 1025 Connecticut Avenue NW/1200, Washington DC 20036-5405. **NLM** W1 VI42F. *Supersedes* Health Insurance Viewpoints, 0017-9027.

US
WEEKLY INSURED UNEMPLOYMENT REPORT. (19??)-. Periodical. English. wk. Research and Analysis Branch, Washington State Employment Security Department, Box 9046, Olympia WA 98507. **Tel** (206)438-4800, FAX (206)438-4846.

●US/1074-2158
WEISS RESEARCH'S INSURANCE SAFETY DIRECTORY. **Added/Corp** Weiss Research, Inc. (West Palm Beach, Fla.). **VFOAT** Weiss Insurance Safety Directory; Insurance Safety Directory. (July 1992)-. Directory. English. Four times a year (Jan., Apr., July, Oct.). $438.00 one year; $699.00 two years. Weiss Research Inc., PO Box 2923, Attn: Jenifer Epler, West Palm Beach FL 33402. **Tel** (407)684-8100, FAX (407)684-9039. **ED** Martin D. Weiss (editor's address: 2200 N. Florida Mango Road, West Palm Beach, FL 33409). **LC** HG8098; .I56. *Continues* Insurance Safety Directory, 1061-7329.

US
WEST'S SOCIAL SECURITY REPORTING SERVICE. SOCIAL SECURITY CASES FROM U.S. SUPREME COURT, U.S. COURT OF APPEALS, U.S. DISTRICT COURTS, U.S. CLAIMS COURT, U.S. BANKRUPTCY COURTS, STATE APPELLATE COURTS. See Law.

US/0193-9718
WHAT IT COSTS. **Main/Corp** Rough Notes Co. (19??)-. English. be. $39.00. Rough Notes Company Inc, 1200 North Meridian Street, Indianapolis IN 46206. **Tel** (317)634-1541, (800)428-4384, FAX (317)634-1041. **LC** HG8076; .R68a. **DD** 338.4/3.

US/0363-1036
WHO WRITES WHAT IN LIFE AND HEALTH INSURANCE. (WHO WRITES WHAT IN LIFE AND HEALTH INSURANCE / COMPILED BY REFERENCE BOOK DEPARTMENT, THE NATIONAL UNDERWRITER COMPANY.). [Who writes what life health ins.]. **Added/Corp** National Underwriter Company. Reference Book Dept. National Underwriter Company. **VFOAT** Who Writes What. 32nd Annual Ed. (1974)-. English. an. $27.00. National Underwriter Company, 505 Gest Street, Cincinnati OH 45203-0874. **Tel** (513)721-2140, (800)543-0874. **LC** HG8861; .N3. **DD** 368.3/2/00973. *Continues* Who Writes What?, 0275-1518.
Desc: Guide to finding new, unusual and hard-to-place life, group health and disability insurance.

US
WHO'S WHO IN RISK MANAGEMENT. See Biographies.

GW/0932-4658
WISSENSCHAFTLICHE REIHE / ZENTRALINSTITUT FUER DIE KASSENARZTLICHE VERSORGUNG IN DER BUNDESREPUBLIK DEUTSCHLAND. [Wiss. Reihe Zent.inst. Kassenartl. Versorg. Bundesrepub. Dtschld.]. **Added/Corp** Zentralinstitut fur die Kassenarztliche Versorgung in der Bundesrepublik Deutschland. **VFOAT** Wissenschaftliche Reihe des Zentralinstituts fur die Kassenarztliche Versorgung in der Bundesrepublik Deutschland. (197?)-. Monographic series. German (summaries and/or abstracts in English). Deutscher Aerzte Verlag GmbH, Postfach 404265, D-50832 Cologne Germany. **Tel** 011 49 2234 7011219. **NLM** W1 WI96. *Continues* Schriftenreihe - Zentralinstitut fur die Kassenarztliche Versorgung in der Bundesrepublik Deutschland, 0341-5473.

CN/0706-5574
WITHOUT PREJUDICE (EDMONTON). (WITHOUT PREJUDICE.). **Added/Corp** University of Alberta. Faculty of Law. (Spring 1978)-. Periodical. English. mo. 60.00Can$ Canada; 75.00Can$ other. Ontario Insurance Adjust Association, Group Box 6 Site 2 RR # 1, Brechin Ontario L0K 1B0 Canada. **Tel** (705)484-5561. **ED** Jim Cameron. **DD** 340/.07/1171233. **Bk Rev**. **Ad Acc**. **Circ:** 2,000 (ctrl).
Desc: Official journal of Ontario Insurance Adjusters Association. Educational and industry news on all matters of insurance from a claims view point.
Ind/Abst Int. Bibliogr. Sociol.

KO
WOLGAN KYOBO. **VFOAT** Kyobo. Periodical. Korean. mo. Taehan Kyoyuk Pohom Chusik Hoesa, 1-1 Chongno 1-Ka Chongno-ku, Seoul Korea. **LC** HG9168.Z9; T338. ctrl circ.

US/0043-7751
WOODMEN OF THE WORLD MAGAZINE. *Title Change.* **Added/Corp** Woodmen of the World Life Insurance Society (U.S.). **VFOAT** Wood Men of the World Magazine; Wood Men Magazine; Woodmen Magazine. Vol. 47, No. 10 (Oct. 1937)-(19??). Periodical. English. mo. Woodmen of the World Magazine, 1700 Farnam Street, Omaha NE 68102. **Tel** (402)342-1890. **ED** Leland A Larson. **LC** HS1510.W78; A17. **Ad Acc**. **Circ:** 465,000 (ctrl). *Continues* Sovereign Visitor. *Continued by* Woodmen (Omaha, Neb.), 1069-1790.
Desc: Regular features include sections about the adult lodge units, ranger units for youngsters under 16, a joke page, and general interest material.

US
WORK INJURY MANAGEMENT. English. mo (published monthly with June/July and Dec./Jan. issues combined). $125.00. Managed Health Associates, 1430 Willamette Street, Suite 213, Eugene OR 97401-4049. **Tel** (503)484-5853, FAX (503)484-1476. **ED** Patrick Devlin. **Ad Acc**. ctrl circ.

US/1054-7819
WORKERS' COMP ADVISOR (CALIFORNIA ED.). See Economics-Labor.

US
WORKERS COMP INSURANCE AND LAW. (19??)-. English. $58.50. LRP Publications, 747 Dresher Road, PO Box 980, Horsham PA 19044-0980. **Tel** (800)341-7874, (215)784-0860, FAX (215)784-9639, (215)784-0870.

●US/1066-2669
WORKERS' COMP MANAGED CARE. [Work. comp manag. care]. **Added/Corp** Business Information Services. Vol. 1, No. 1 (Nov. 1992)-. Periodical. English. Twelve times a year. $238.00. Business Information Services Inc., 12811 North Point Lane, Laurel MD 20708. **Tel** (301)604-4001, FAX (301)604-5126. **ED** James H. Gutman. **DD** 331. **[CCC].**
Desc: News and information exclusively about the medical side of worker's compensation.

US
WORKERS' COMPENSATION DESK BOOK. English. an. $62.45. LRP Publications, 747 Dresher Road, PO Box 980, Horsham PA 19044-0980. **Tel** (800)341-7874, (215)784-0860, FAX (215)784-9639, (215)784-0870.
Desc: Reference source for the most precedential workers' compensation developments and decisions for the previous year.

CN/0847-5857
WORKERS' COMPENSATION MANAGING CLAIMS. [Work. compens. manag. claims]. **VFOAT** Managing Claims, Workers' Compensation. Vol. 1, No. 1 (Jan. 1990)-. Periodical. English. Twelve times a year. 395.00Can$ one year; 675.00Can$ two years. Concord Publishing Ltd, 14 Prince Arthur Avenue, Suite 209, Toronto, Ontario M5R 2A9 Canada. **Tel** (416)964-2758, FAX (416)964-0659. **DD** 658.3/254/09713. Index available ((Dec-Feb) iss.). cum. index.
Desc: Is designed to provide accurate and authoritative information.

US/1052-6358
WORKERS COMPENSATION OUTLOOK (BOSTON, MASS.). See Economics-Labor.

AT
WORKERS' COMPENSATION REPORTS. *Suspended.* See Law.

AT
WORKERS' COMPENSATION REPORTS, WESTERN AUSTRALIA. **Added/Corp** Workers' Compensation Board of W.A. **VFOAT** Western Australia. Vol. 1 (1982)-. English. **LC** LAW. **DD** 344.941/021; 349.410421.
Ind/Abst Aust. Leg. Mon. Dig.

US/0149-371X
WORKERS COVERED BY KENTUCKY UNEMPLOYMENT INSURANCE LAW BY COUNTY. **Main/Corp** Kentucky. Dept. for Human Resources. Division for Research and Special Projects. English. Kentucky Department of Human Resources, Division for Unemployment Insurance, Frankfort KY 40601. **LC** HD7096.U6; K47. **DD** 368.4/4/009769.

●US/1063-4363
WORKFORCE (WASHINGTON, D.C.). See Economics-Labor.

US
WORKMENS' COMP NEWSLETTER. (19??)-. English. bw. $93.09. Merritt Company, 1661 Ninth Street, PO Box 955, Santa Monica CA 90406. **Tel** (310)450-7234, (800)638-7597, FAX (310)396-4563.

US/0097-9163
WORKMEN'S COMPENSATION DATA. See Economics-Labor.

US
WORKMEN'S COMPENSATION FOR OCCUPATIONAL INJURIES AND DEATH. See Economics-Labor.

UK
WORLD INSURANCE REPORT.
Added/Corp Financial Times Business Information Ltd. **VFOAT** Financial Times World Insurance Report; WIR. (19??)-. English. Twenty-five times a year (Except the week of Christmas). £645.00 UK; £670.00 others. Financial Times England, 8 16 Great New Street, London EC4A 3BN England. **Tel** 011 44 71 353 0305, 353 1040, FAX 011 44 353 0846. **ED** Lynn MacRikhic. **LC** HG8013; .W67. **DD** 368/.005. Index available. **Bk Rev**. available on microfiche.
Desc: Covers all categories of risk and non risk-carrying organizations related to insurance and reinsurance worldwide. It systematically fills a significant informations gap between insurer security, solvency and credit-rating services. Also reports on likely future preformance including financial status and claims. Includes comparative tables of company results for speedy and revealing comparisons.
Ind/Abst PROMT [Full Txt.]; PTS Newsl. Database [Full Txt.].

UK/0955-4823
WORLD INSURANCE REPORT CORPORATE. [World insur. rep. corp.]. **VFOAT** World Corporate Insurance Report. (1988)-. Corporate Report. English. bw. £354.00 UK; £373.00 other. Financial Times Business Information Ltd., Tower House, Southampton Street, London WC2E 7HA England. **Tel** 011 44 71 353 1040. **DD** 368. available on an online database (files 16,636/Full-Text) from DIALOG.
Ind/Abst PROMT [Full Txt.]; PTS Newsl. Database [Full Txt.].

UK
WORLD POLICY GUIDE. Periodical. English. mo. £634.00 UK; $1,040.00 US; $650.00 other. Financial Times Business Information Ltd., Tower House, Southampton Street, London WC2E 7HA England. **Tel** 011 44 71 353 1040. **ED** Sue Copeman. **LC** HG8013; .W673. **DD** 368/.005. Index available. **Bk Rev**. available on microfiche.
Desc: A comprehensive source of information on new products and policy innovations in the commercial insurance market. It looks in depth at specific markets, analysing participants, availability of cover, rating systems, insurer requirements, losses and special considerations.

US/0569-2032
YEAR BOOK - AMERICAN ACADEMY OF ACTUARIES. **Main/Corp** American Academy of Actuaries. **VFOAT** Yearbook. (1967)-. English. an. $25.00. American Academy of Actuaries, 1720 I Street Northwest, 7th Floor, Washington DC 20006. **Tel** (202)223-8196, FAX (202)872-1948. **LC** HG8754; .A5515. **DD** 368/.0062/73. **Bk Rev**. **Circ:** 8,800 (ctrl).
Desc: Directory of the Board of directors, committees and members. It includes the organizations laws, qualification standards, and guide to professional conduct.

US/0534-4352
YEAR BOOK - INSURANCE ACCOUNTING AND STATISTICAL ASSOCIATION. **Main/Corp** Insurance Accounting and Statistical Association. (19??)-. Statistical Publication. English. an. Edwin C Carlson, Insurance Accounting and Statistical Association, 406 West 34th Street, Kansas City MO 64111. **LC** HG8019; .I48. **DD** 657/.836.

US
YEAR BOOK / SOCIETY OF ACTUARIES. **Main/Corp** Society of Actuaries. **VFOAT** Yearbook. (19??)-. English. an (Jan.). $25.00. Society of Actuaries, PO Box 95668, Chicago IL 60694.

Insurance —Abstracting, Bibliographies and Statistics

Tel (708)706-3526. ED Linda M. Delgadillo. LC HG8754; .S63. DD 368/.01/06073. Circ: 13,000. Formed by the union of Actuarial Society of America. Year Book and American Institute of Actuaries. Year Book.
Desc: Information listing of committees, SOA bylaws, rules, regulations, board of directors, and meetings dates.

UK
YEAR BOOK / THE FACULTY OF ACTUARIES. Main/Corp Faculty of Actuaries in Scotland. (1938/1939)-. English. an. £3.00. Faculty of Actuaries, 40 44 Thistle Street, Edinburgh EH2 1EN Scotland. Tel 011 44 31 2204555. LC HG8602; .A64. DD 368.9411.

US/0194-3979
YEARBOOK - AMERICAN SOCIETY OF PENSION ACTUARIES. See Economics-Labor.

CN/0068-8975
YEARBOOK - CANADIAN INSTITUTE OF ACTUARIES. (YEAR BOOK - CANADIAN INSTITUTE OF ACTUARIES / ANNUAIRE - INSTITUT CANADIEN DES ACTUAIRES.). Main/Corp Canadian Institute of Actuaries. VFOAT Annuaire - Institut Canadien des Actuaires. (1966)-. Periodical. Multiple languages (English and French). an. Free (members). 100.00Can$ (nonmembers). Canadian Institute of Actuaries, 306 Albert Street, Suite 1040, Ottawa Ontario K1R 7X7 Canada. Tel (613)236-8196. LC WMLC L 83/7000. DD 368/.01/06271.

US/0895-6022
YEARBOOK - CASUALTY ACTUARIAL SOCIETY. [Yearb. - Casualty Actuar. Soc.]. Main/Corp Casualty Actuarial Society. No. 1 (1922)-. English. an. $40.00 US; 52.00Can$ Canada. Casualty Acturial Society, 1100 North Glede #600, Arlington VA 22201. Tel (703)276-3100. LC HG9956; .C35. DD 368.

US/0276-7325
YEAR'S WORK - INSURANCE INSTITUTE FOR HIGHWAY SAFETY, THE. See Transportation-Roads and Traffic.

● US/1065-495X
YOUR CHICAGO EXPRESS. (YOUR CHICAGO EXPRESS : THE VOICE OF C.A.L.U.). Main/Corp Chicago Association Life Underwriters. VFOAT Chicago Express. Vol. 50, No. 3 (May/June 1992)-. Periodical. English. bm. Chicago Association of Life Underwriters, 65 West Wackler Place, Suite 1107, Chicago IL 60601. Continues Chicago Association Life Underwriters.; Activities, 0744-8503.

US
YOUR MEDICARE HANDBOOK FOR RAILROAD RETIREMENT BENEFICIARIES. Added/Corp United States. Railroad Retirement Board. VFOAT Your Medicare Handbook. (19??)-. English.

GW/0044-2585
ZEITSCHRIFT FUER DIE GESAMTE VERSICHERUNGS-WISSENSCHAFT. [Z. gesamte Versicherungs-Wiss.]. Added/Corp Deutscher Verein fuer Versicherungs-Wissenschaft. (1???)-. Periodical. German. Four times a year. DM118.69. Verlag Versicherungswirtschaft, Klosestrasse 20 24, D-76137 Karlsruhe Germany. Tel 011 49 721 35090, FAX 011 49 721 31833. LC HG8015; .Z5. DD 368/.005. [CCC].
Ind/Abst Energy Res. Abstr. (Aug. 1978-).

ABSTRACTING, BIBLIOGRAPHIES AND STATISTICS

US
ALASKA PERSONAL LINES STATISTICAL ANALYSIS, PRIVATE PASSENGER AUTOMOBILE INSURANCE, HOMEOWNERS INSURANCE / DIVISION OF INSURANCE, DEPARTMENT OF COMMERCE AND ECONOMIC DEVELOPMENT, STATE OF ALASKA. VFOAT Alaska ... Private Passenger Auto Insurance and Homeowners Insurance. Statistical Publication. English. an. Alaska Department of Commerce, Department of Commerce & Economic Development, PO Box D, Juneau AK 99811. Tel (907)465-2521. ED Bob Sims. LC HG9970.A55; A434. DD 368/.096/0979805. Circ: 3,000.
Desc: Analysis and comparison of homeowners and auto results in Alaska.

US
ANNUAL REPORT AND STATISTICAL DATA - DIVISION OF INSURANCE (MISSOURI). Main/Corp Missouri. Division of Insurance. Statistical Publication. English. an. Missouri Division of Insurance, 11th Floor, Jefferson Building, Jefferson City MO 65101. LC HG8511.M8; D58A. DD 368/.9/778.

SP/0303-4763
ANUARIO ESTADISTICO DE SEGUROS. Added/Corp Mexico. Comision Nacional Bancaria y de Seguros. (19??)-. Spanish. Comision Nacional Bancaria y de Seguros, Republica de el Salvador Num 47, Mexico City DF Mexico. LC HG8552; .A85.

CN/0317-1264
CANADIAN UNDERWRITER. ANNUAL STATISTICAL REVIEW. (1934)-. Statistical Publication. English. an. 30.00Can$. Southam Information and Technology Group Inc., 1450 Don Mills Road, Don Mills Ontario M3B 2X7 Canada. Tel (416)445-6641, (800)668-2374, FAX (416)442-2261. DD 368/.971.

US/0277-9595
COLORADO INSURANCE INDUSTRY STATISTICAL REPORT. Statistical Publication. English. an. $5.00. Department of Regulatory Agencies, Division of Insurance, 303 West Colfax/Suite 500, Denver CO 80204. Tel (303)620-4300. LC HG8101.C6; C64. Circ: 250 (ctrl). Continues Insurance Industry in Colorado, Statistical Report, 0361-6568.
Desc: Insurance operations in Colorado for calendar year and division operations for fiscal year.

SW
ENSKILDA FORSAKRINGSFORETAG. VFOAT Private Insurance Companies. Swedish (summaries and/or abstracts in English). an. Box 5053, Stockholm S10242 5 Sweden. LC HA1521; .F65. Continues Enskilda Forsakringsanstalter.

VE
ESTADISTICA Y ACTUARIADO. Statistical Publication. Spanish. Edificio Stolmar, Mezzanina 1 - Altagracia a Salas, Caracas Venezuela. LC HA1; .E85.

CL/0577-8174
ESTADISTICAS (CHILE. SERVICIO DE SEGURO SOCIAL). Main/Corp Chile. Servicio de Seguro Social. 1952/56?-. Statistical Publication. Spanish. an. Servicio de Seguro Social, Av Bulnes 418, Santiago 31133384 Chile. LC WMLC L 83/1933. DD 368.4. NLM W2 DC5 D15E. Continues in part Chile. Caja de Seguro Obligatorio. Annuario Estadistico.

UK
FINANCIAL TIMES WORLD INSURANCE YEARBOOK, THE. Added/Corp Financial Times (London, England). VFOAT FT, World Insurance Yearbook; World Insurance. (1976/77)-. English. an. $215.00. Gale Research Inc., 835 Penobscot Building, Detroit MI 48226. Tel (800)877-GALE, (313)961-2242, FAX (313)961-6083, telex TWX 810-221-7086. (Subscription address: PO Box 1584, Birmingham, AL 35201) LC HG8019; .F48. DD 368/.005. Each issue contains an index to its own contents (no volume index)--loose. Ad Acc. Circ: 1,200.
Desc: Presents detailed corporate and financial information on over 1,200 insurance companies worldwide.

US/0195-8631
HEALTH CARE FINANCING REVIEW. [Health care financ. rev.]. Added/Corp United States. Health Care Financing Administration. Office of Research and Demonstrations. United States. Health Care Financing Administration. Office of Research, Demonstrations, and Statistics. Vol. 1, Issue 1 (Summer 1979)-. Government Publication. English. qt (annual issue). $19.00 US; $23.75 other. Superintendent of Documents, US Government Printing Office, Washington DC 20402. Tel (202)275-3328, FAX (202)786-2377. ED Gerri Michael-Dyer. LC RA410.53; .H415. DD 338.4/33621/0973. NLM W1 HE299KF. Index available. cum. index. Bk Rev. Pr Rev. Circ: 5,000 (ctrl). available on microfilm and microfiche from University Microfilms International (UMI); available at an online database (files 15,149,485/Full-Text) from DIALOG. Documents available from UMI Article Clearinghouse, Documents on Demand.
Desc: Health care financing issues and innovative delivery systems as related to the Medicare and Medicaid programs.
Ind/Abst ABI/INFORM Glob. Ed.; ABI Inform Ondisc (Summer 1985-); Abstr. Soc. Gerontol.; Acad. Abstr. Full Text Elite (Jan. 1992-); Acad. Abstr. (Jan. 1992-); Acad. Search (Jan. 1992-); Account. Tax Datab. (Summer 1985-) [Full Txt.]; Am. Stat. Index; Bus. Source (Jan. 1992-); EMBASE; Expand. Acad. Index (1989-); Health Period. Database [Full Txt.]; Health Plan. Adminis.; Health Ref. Cent. (Jan. 1989-) [Full Txt.] [Full Cov.]; Health Source (Jan. 1992-); Hospit. Health Admin. Index; Hospit. Manage. Rev.; INFO-SOUTH Abstr.; Mag. Search; Newsp. Period. Abstr. (1991-); PAIS Int. Print; Soc. Sci. Source (Jan. 1992-); Soc. Sci. Index; Soc. Sci. Index Fulltext (Fall 1988-) [Full Txt.]; Soc. Work Abstr. (Spring 1987-) [Select. Cov.]; UMI ABI/Inform--Bus. Period. Ondisc (Fall 1987-) [Full Txt.].

AT/0727-1611
HEALTH INSURANCE SURVEY, AUSTRALIA. [Health insur. surv., Aust.]. (1979)-. English. ir. 15.30Aus$. Australian Bureau of Statistics, PO Box 10, Belconnen Australian Capital Territory, 2616 Australia. Tel 011 61 6 2527911, FAX 011 61 6 2516009. DD 368.38200994.
Desc: Contains statistics showing the level of private health insurance of contributor units and persons, cross-classified by: type of insurance cover, contribution rate, recent changes to cover, composition and income of contributor unit, reasons for insuring, and more.

CR
INFORME ESTADISTICO (INSTITUTO NACIONAL DE SEGUROS (SAN JOSE, COSTA RICA)). (INFORME ESTADISTICO.). Spanish. Apartado Postal 10061, San Jose Costa Rica.

US/0074-073X
INSURANCE PERIODICALS INDEX. Added/Corp Special Libraries Association. Insurance Division. (1963)-. Abstracting/Indexing Service. English. an. $100.00. NILS Publishing Company, PO Box 2507, Chatsworth CA 91313-2507. Tel (818)998-8830, (800)423-5910, FAX (818)718-8482. ED Orivle Anderson. LC HG8011; .I545. DD 368/.005. Circ: 500. available on an online database from WESTLAW; NEXIS; LEXIS; and DIALOG.
Desc: The only periodicals index that covers all lines of insurance--indexing over 40 journals and magazines (over 15,000 articles every year).

FJ
INSURANCE REPORT AND STATISTICS OF FIJI. Main/Corp Fiji. Bureau of Statistics. (1977)-. English. an. Commissioner of Insurance, Government Buildings, Seva Fiji. LC J961; .H835 subser; HG8738. DD 300 S; 368/.99611. Continues Fiji. Bureau of Statistics. Insurance Statistics of Fiji.

JA/0910-5719
INSURANCE. SEIMEI HOKEN TOKEI-GO. [Insurance. Seimei hoken tokei-go]. VFOAT Statistics of Life Insurance Business in Japan; Inshuaransu. Seimei Hoken Tokei-Go. (19??)-. Periodical. Japanese. an (Sept.). ¥2300.00 Japan; ¥3420.00 US, Canada, Mexico and Latin America (life); ¥9180.00 US, Canada, Mexico and Latin America (life and non-life combined). Hoken Kenkyu-Jo, 17-3-1 Chome Honmachi, Shibuya-Ku Tokyo Japan. Tel 011 81 3 3376 3331, FAX 011 81 3 3376 7125. ED Toshiaki Shirai (Chief Editor). DD 368.

JA/0910-5727
INSURANCE. SONGAI HOKEN TOKUBETSU TOKEI-GO. [Insurance. Songai hoken tokubetsu tokei-go]. VFOAT Insurance. Annual Special Issue; Statistics of Japanese Non-Life Insurance Business; Inshuaransu. Songai Hoken Tokubetsu Tokei-Go; Inshuaransu. Songai Hoken Tokei-Go. (19??)-. Periodical. Japanese. an (Oct.). ¥9180.00 US, Canada, Mexico and Latin America (life and non-life combined). Hoken Kenkyu-Jo, 17-3-1 Chome Honmachi, Shibuya-Ku Tokyo Japan. Tel 011 81 3 3376 3331, FAX 011 81 3 3376 7125. ED Toshiaki Shirai (Chief Editor). DD 368.

NZ
INSURANCE STATISTICS (NEW ZEALAND). (INSURANCE STATISTICS.). Added/Corp New Zealand. Dept. of statistics. (19??)-. English. an. 7.15NZ$. Government Printing Office / New Zealand, 10 Mulgrave Street, Wellington New Zealand. Tel 011 64 4 4737211, FAX 011 64 4 734943, telex GOVPRINT NZ 31320. LC WMLC L 83/4324.
Desc: The New Zealand insurance industry.

KO
POHOM TONGGYE YONBO. Added/Corp Taehan Sonhae Pohom Hyophoe. VFOAT Insurance Statistics Yearbook. (19??)-. English (Korean). an. LC HG8707; .A27. DD 368/.95195.

KO
POHOM TONGGYE YON'GAM. VFOAT Insurance Statistics Yearbook. Year 1977-. Korean (Korean). LC HG8707.A4; P63.

US/0163-8920
POLICY STATISTICS SERVICE. Ceased. Ceased (Dec. 1990). English. ir. National Underwriter Company, 505 Gest Street, Cincinnati OH 45203-0874. Tel (513)721-2140, (800)543-0874.

FR
SOLIDARITE, SANTE. ETUDES STATISTIQUES / MINISTERE DES AFFAIRES SOCIALES ET DE LA SOLIDARITE NATIONALE. See Public Health and Safety-Abstracting, Bibliographies and Statistics.

US/0741-9767
STATISTICAL BULLETIN - METROPOLITAN LIFE INSURANCE COMPANY (1984). (STATISTICAL BULLETIN : SB.). [Stat. bull. - Metrop Life Insur. Co.]. Added/Corp

Metropolitan Life Insurance Company. **VFOAT** SB. Vol. 65, No. 1 (Jan./March 1984)-. Statistical Publication. English. qt (Jan., Apr., Jul., Oct.). $40.00 library and non-profit organization; $50.00 other. Sheridan Press, PO Box 465, Hanover PA 17331. **Tel** (800)352-2210, (717)632-3535, FAX (717)633-8900. **(Subscription address:** Fulco, 30 Broad Street, Denville NJ 07834.) **ED** Charles B. Arnold and Joan W. Parks. **LC** HG8963.M5; A3. **DD** 304.6/0973. **NLM** W1; ST316EAB. Index available (bound in last issue). cum. index. **Circ:** 4,500. available on microfilm and microfiche from University Microfilms International (UMI). ***Continues*** *Statistical Bulletin (Metropolitan Life Foundation), 0736-4822.*
Desc: National and geographic analyses of major demographic/ demiologic subjects and medical data for health and business professionals.
Ind/Abst Bus. ASAP (1990-) [Full Txt.]; Bus. Index (Jan. 1985-Dec. 1985); Bus. Period. Index; Energy Res. Abstr. (1984-); Gen. BusinessFile (1985-); Index Med.; PAIS Int. Print (1991-); Popul. Index; Stat. Ref. Index.

US/0095-1382
STATISTICAL TABLES - DEPARTMENT OF EMPLOYMENT SECURITY. (STATISTICAL TABLES - STATE OF VERMONT, DEPARTMENT OF EMPLOYMENT SECURITY.). **Main/Corp** Vermont. Dept. of Employment Security. Statistical Publication. English. Vermont Department of Employment Security, PO Box 488, Montpelier VT 05602. **LC** HD7096.U6; V519B. **DD** 331.1/09743.

US
STATISTICAL TABLES FROM ANNUAL STATEMENTS. **Main/Corp** New York (State). Insurance Dept. **Added/Corp** New York (State). Insurance Dept. **VFOAT** NY Statistical Tables. (19??)-. Statistical Publication. English. an. $6.50. Superintendent of Insurance Agency B-1, Empire State Plaza, Albany NY 12257. **Tel** (518)474-4557. **LC** HG8511.N7; A34.
Desc: Includes statistical tables from annual statements and an annual report of the superintendent of insurance to the legislature.

US/0532-6109
STATISTICS OF FRATERNAL BENEFIT SOCIETIES. **Added/Corp** National Fraternal Congress of America. (1966)-. English. an (July). $11.00. National Fraternal Congress of America, 1300 Iroquois Drive, Room 260, Naperville IL 60540. **Tel** (708)355-6633. **LC** HG9226; .F72. **DD** 368.3/63/00973. ***Continues*** *Combined Statistics and Consolidated Chart of Fraternal Societies.*

GW
STATISTIK DER ORTSKRANKENKASSEN IN DER BUNDESREPUBLIK DEUTSCHLAND : ALTERSGLIEDERUNG DER MITGLIEDER. **Main/Corp** Bundesverband der Ortskrankenkassen. German. Postfach 844, 53 1 Bonn-Bad Germany. **LC** HD7102.G73; B834C.

US/0739-4691
TEXAS BLUE BOOK OF LIFE INSURANCE STATISTICS (1982), THE. (THE TEXAS BLUE BOOK OF LIFE INSURANCE STATISTICS.). [Tex. blue book life insur. stat.]. **VFOAT** Texas Blue Book. (196?)-. English. an (Sept.). $34.00. The Record Publishing Company, PO Box 225770, Dallas TX 75265. **Tel** (214)630-0687, FAX (214)631-2476. **ED** John H. Leslie. **LC** HG8961.T4; T4. **DD** 368.3/2/0068. Index available. **Ad Acc**, **Adv Mgr:** C. J. Hargis. **Circ:** 1,000. available on diskette. ***Continues*** *Texas Life Record.*
Desc: A three year comparison of financial and sales statistics of life insurance companies annual reports to Texas State Board of Insurance. Includes addresses, phone numbers, and key personnel.

US
U.S. DECENNIAL LIFE TABLES. ACTUARIAL TABLES BASED ON UNITED STATES LIFE TABLES. **VFOAT** Actuarial Tables Based on United States Life Tables. English. ir. US Department of Health & Human Services National Center for Health Statistics, 6525 Belcrest Road, Room 1140, Hyattsville MD 20782. **Tel** (301)436-7016, FAX (301)436-4258.

US
U.S. DECENNIAL LIFE TABLES. METHODOLOGY OF THE NATIONAL AND STATE LIFE TABLES FOR THE UNITED STATES. **VFOAT** Methodology of the National and State Life Tables for the United States. Periodical. English. ir. US Department of Health & Human Services / Public Health Service, 200 Independence Avenue SW, Room 716G, Washington DC 20201. **Tel** (202)690-6867, FAX (202)690-6274.

INTERIOR DESIGN

●US/1064-9948
100 DESIGNERS' FAVORITE ROOMS. **VFOAT** One Hundred Designers' Favorite Rooms; Barons Who's Who Presents 100 Designers' Favorite Rooms. (1993)-. English. $30.00. Barons Who's Who, 412 North Coast Highway, Suite B-110, Laguna Beach CA 92651. **Tel** (714)497-8615.

US/0278-0844
1001 HOME IDEAS. ***Suspended.*** [1001 home ideas]. **VFOAT** One Thousand One Home Ideas; One Thousand and One Home Odeas. (1981)-(19??). Periodical. English. mo. $22.00 (one year), $44.00 (two year) non-trade, $15.97 (one year), $32.97 (two year) trade. Family Media Inc, 3 Park Avenue, New York NY 10016. **(Subscription address:** 1,001 Home Ideas, PO Box 6023, Palm Coast, FL 32037-6023) **ED** Ellen Frankel. **LC** NK1700; .O5. available on microfilm and microfiche from University Microfilms International (UMI); available on an online database from OCLC EPIC; and DIALOG. Documents available from UMI Article Clearinghouse. ***Continues*** *1001 Home/Decorating Ideas, 0731-8782.*
Desc: Adds new color and life to a home.
Ind/Abst Newsp. Period. Abstr. (1988-1991).

FR
ABC. **VFOAT** ABC Decor; ABC Document. **VAT** Antiquites, Beaux-Arts, Curiosites. (1964)-. Periodical. French. mo. ABC Decor, 8 rue St Marc, 75 Paris 2 France.

IT/0001-3218
ABITARE. **See** Architecture.

IT/1120-6772
ABITARE CON ARTE. [Abitare arte]. (1990)-. Periodical. Italian (English). tq. L50000 (one year) L90000 (two year) Italy; L90000 (one year) L160000 (two year) other. Azzurra Editrice SRL, Via Della Moscova 49, 20121 Milan Italy. **Tel** 011 39 2 29010364, FAX 011 39 2 29002192. **UDC** 64. **Bk Rev**. **Ad Acc**, **Adv Mgr:** Brivio Givsi. ctrl circ.
Desc: Covers classic and contemporary furniture.

US
ACCESSORIES TODAY. **Added/Corp** Decorative Accessories Industry. (19??)-. English. **LC** WMLC 93/779.
Ind/Abst F&S Index Plus Text, Int. [Select. Cov.]; PROMT.

SP
AD : REVISTA INTERNACIONAL DE DECORATION, DISENO Y ARQUITECTURA. (19??)-. Spanish. Eleven times a year. 5.5000ptas. Ediciones VIP SA, Gran Via Carlos 111 124 - P5, 08034 Barcelona Spain. **Tel** (343)2050261, FAX (343)2050261, telex 97834 PUER E. **ED** Maria Victoria Aroca. **Bk Rev**. **Ad Acc**. **Pr Rev. Circ:** 30.
Desc: Journal on architecture, interior decoration and design characterized by features on houses accompanied by exclusive photos of very high quality.

GW/0173-8046
AIT. ARCHITEKTUR, INNENARCHITEKTUR, TECHNISCHER AUSBAU. **See** Architecture.

IT/0392-5730
AMBIENTE CUCINA, L'. [Amb. cucina]. **VFOAT** Decors Cuisine; Kitchen; Kuche. (1977)-. Periodical. Multiple languages (English). bm (6 issues). L44000 Italy. Masson S.P.A, Via Statuto 2/4, 20121 Milan Italy. **Tel** 011 39 2 63671, FAX 011 39 2 6367211. **ED** Fabrizio Gomarasca. **UDC** 645.63. **Bk Rev**. **Ad Acc. Circ:** 22,100 (ctrl).
Desc: Covers kitchen interior design, up-dated production, existing furnishing solutions, reportages from the main sectorial exhibitions in Italy and abroad, technical and cultural themes, studies and market researches.

GW
AMBIENTE (OFFENBURG, GERMANY). (AMBIENTE.). (1980)-. Periodical. German. Ten times a year. $120.00. Burda GmbH, Postfach 1230, D-7602 Offenburg Germany. **Tel** 011 49 781-8401. **(Subscription address:** US: German Language Publications, Inc., 153 South Deanstreet, Englewood, NJ 07631)

●CN/1195-227X
ARCHITECTURE AND DESIGN INSITE. [Archit. des. insite]. **VFOAT** Insite. Vol. 3, No. 1 (Sept. 1993)-. Periodical. English (summaries and/or abstracts in French). Six times a year. 32.00Can$ (one year); 74.00Can$ (three years). Manor Communications Co., 312 Dolmite Drive, Suite 217, Downsview Ontario M3J 2N2 Canada. **Tel** (905)667-9609. **DD** 729/.05. ***Continues*** *International Contract (Downsview, Ont.), 1183-9708.*

FR/0980-9465
ATELIER PARIS, L'. ***Ceased.*** (1986)-(1992). Periodical. English (French). Ten times a year. SNEC, 41 rue Barrault, 75013 Paris France. **Tel** 011 33 1 45676721. **UDC** 76. **CODEN** 74.

US/0199-1531
AUSTIN HOMES & GARDENS. ***Suspended.*** **VAT** Austin Homes and Gardens. V. 1- July 1979-Suspended. Periodical. English. mo. $12.00. Austin Homes & Gardens, PO Box 1684, Austin TX 78767. **Tel** (512)443-8936. **ED** Hazel W Gully and June W Hayes. Index available. **Bk Rev**. **Ad Acc. Circ:** 10,000.
Desc: Features architecture, design, gardening, dining, fitness, and travel. Departments include events, reviews, society, gardening, dining, and travel.
Ind/Abst Index Period. Artic. Relat. Law.

AT
AUSTRALASIAN FURNISHING TRADE JOURNAL. (19??)-. English. Five times a year. 46.00Aus$ Australia; 86.00Aus$ other. Furnishing Publications Pty, 5 Faigh Street, Mulgrave Victoria 3170 Australia. **Tel** 011 61 3 5625844, FAX 011 61 3 5625412. **ED** Keith Dunn. **Bk Rev**. **Ad Acc**, **Adv Mgr:** Joanne Royal. **Circ:** 3,500.

AT
AUSTRALIAN COUNTRY LOOKS. (19??)-. Periodical. English. mo. 54.00Aus$ Australia; 42.00Aus$ New Zealand & Papua New Guinea; 113.00Aus$ US & Canada; 95.00Aus$ Singapore, Malaysia, Taiwan; 104.00Aus$ Hong Kong, China, Japan, India; 120.00Aus$ other. Federal Publishing Co Pty Ltd, PO Box 199, 180 Bourke Road, Alexandria New South Wales, 2015 Australia. **Tel** 011 61 2 693 6666, FAX 011 61 2 693 9935. **(Subscription address:** Federal Publishing Co. Pty Ltd., PO Box 199, Alexandria NSW 2015 Australia.)

AT
AUSTRALIAN DESIGN SERIES. English. mo. 57.00Aus$ Australia; 92.00Aus$ New Zealand; 96.50Aus$ other. Australian Consolidated Press, GPO Box 5252, Sydney New South Wales 2001 Australia. **Tel** 02 282 8000, FAX 02 282 8254.

AT/0007-928X
AUSTRALIAN HOME BEAUTIFUL. (1925)-. Periodical. English. mo. 48.00Aus$ Australia; 66.00Aus$ other. Pacific Publications Pty Ltd, 32 Walsh Street, Melbourne VIC 3000 Australia. **Tel** 011 61 3 3207000. ***Continues*** *Australian Home Builder.*

AT
AUSTRALIAN HOUSE AND GARDEN. (19??)-. Periodical. English. mo. 50.40Aus$ Australia; 77.00Aus$ New Zealand; 139.00Aus$ other. Australian Consolidated Press Ltd, GPO Box 5252, Sydney New South Wales 2001 Australia. **Tel** 011 61 2 2600000.

JA
AXIS. **VFOAT** Akushisu. (1981)-. Periodical. Japanese (table of contents in English). qt. ¥12000.00. Axis Incorporated, 5 17 1 Roppongi Minato Ku, Tokyo Japan. **Tel** 011 81 3 3587 2781.
Desc: Covers interior design.

CN/0829-982X
AZURE (TORONTO). (AZURE.). [Azure]. Vol. 2, No. 15/16 (May/June 1985)-. Periodical. English. Six times a year. 19.95Can$ Canada; 35.95Can$ other. Azure Publishing Inc, 2 Silver Avenue, Toronto Ontario M6R 3AZ Canada. **Tel** (416)588-2588, FAX (416)588-2357. **ED** Nelda Roger. **DD** 971.3/541. **Ad Acc**, **Adv Mgr:** Sergio Sgaramella. **Circ:** 12,000 (ctrl). ***Continues*** *Village Gazette (Toronto, Ont.), 0829-3406.*
Desc: Concerned with all features of design; examines the various sources that have an impact on design--culture, new aesthetics, technological advances and social issues.

IT
BAGNO OGGI E DOMANI, IL. Italian (French, English and German). Nine times a year. $112.00. Editoriale PEG Spa, Via Fratelli Bressan 2, 20126 Milan Italy. **Tel** 011 39 2 2579841, FAX 011 39 2 255-2779, telex 323088 PEGMOS I. **ED** Grazia Gamberoni. **Bk Rev**. **Ad Acc. Circ:** 31,700 (ctrl).
Desc: Bathroom interior design, up-dated production, existing furnishing solutions, reportages from the main sectorial exhibitions in Italy and abroad, technical and cultural themes, studies and market researches.

CN/0225-9206
BATH & KITCHEN MARKETER. ***Ceased.*** [Bath & kitchen mark.]. Vol. 1 (Nov. 1979)-(Aug. 1992). Trade Publication. English. Five times a year. Southam Information and Technology Group Inc., 1450 Don Mills Road, Don Mills Ontario M3B 2X7 Canada. **Tel** (416)445-6641, (800)668-2374, FAX (416)442-2261. **ED** Ronald H. Shuker. **DD** 747.7/8/05. **Bk Rev**. **Ad Acc**. ctrl circ.
Desc: Serves contractors and retailers who design, sell or install plumbing fixtures, kitchen cabinets and related accessories for new and renovated residential bathrooms and kitchens in Canada.

AT/0310-1452
BELLE (SYDNEY, N.S.W.). See Architecture.

US/0743-2461
BEST-SELLING HOME PLANS FROM HOME MAGAZINE. [Best-sell. home plans from Home mag.]. **VFOAT** Best Selling Home Plans from Home Magazine; Best Selling Home Plans; Home Plans; Best-Selling Home Plans. (198?)-. Periodical. English. Six times a year. $20.00. Hachette Magazines Inc., 1633 Broadway, New York NY 10019. **Tel** (212)767-6000. **(Subscription address:** Neodata / Colorado, PO Box 2606, Boulder Boulder CO 80322.**) LC** NA7205; .H74. **DD** 728/.37/0223. **Ad Acc. Circ:** 800,000. ***Continues*** *Hudson Home Plans, 0194-3316.*

US
BETTER HOMES AND GARDENS DECORATING IDEAS. (February, 1980)-. Periodical. English. Four times a year. Meredith Corporation, Locust at 17th, Des Moines IA 50309. **Tel** (515)284-3000. **ED** Bill Yates. **Bk Rev. Ad Acc.** ctrl circ.

US/0277-836X
BETTER HOMES AND GARDENS DECORATING IDEAS. WINDOW & WALL IDEAS. (WINDOW & WALL IDEAS.). **VFOAT** Window and Wall Ideas; Window and Wall Decorating Ideas. (19??)-. Periodical. English. ir. Available on newsstand only. Meredith Corporation, Locust at 17th, Des Moines IA 50309. **Tel** (515)284-3000. **LC** NK2121; .B47. ***Continues*** *Window & Wall Decorating Ideas, 0363-5406.*

US
BETTER HOMES AND GARDENS KITCHEN & BATH IDEAS. **VFOAT** Kitchen & Bath Ideas. (19??)-. English. Available on newsstand only. Meredith Corporation, Locust at 17th, Des Moines IA 50309. **Tel** (515)284-3000. **LC** TX653; .B47. **DD** 643/.3/05.

US/0899-4382
BLUE RIBBON HOME PLANS. **VFOAT** Home Plans. English. qt. $7.10. The Garlinghouse Company, PO Box 1717, Middletown CT 06457. **Tel** (203)632-0500, FAX (203)632-0712. **ED** Ed Rothwell. **LC** NA7205; .B55. **DD** 728.3/7/0223. **Bk Rev. Ad Acc.** ctrl circ.
Desc: Features over 130 home plan designs with hundreds of illustrations. The designs cover a broad range of styles and tastes.

US/1060-3190
CALIFORNIA HOMES AND LIFESTYLES. [Calif. homes lifestyles]. (198?)-. Periodical. English. mo. $24.00. McFadden Publishing, 17911 Skypark Circle/Suite D, Irvine CA 92714. **Tel** (714)241-9221. **DD** 747. ***Continues*** *California Homes, 0734-5453.*

CN/0008-3887
CANADIAN INTERIORS. [Can. inter.]. **VFOAT** CI. Vol. 1 (April 1964)-. Periodical. English. bm. 40.00Can$ Canada; 89.00Can$ other. Crailer Communications, 113 Davenport Road, Toronto Ontario M5R 1H8 Canada. **Tel** (416)966-9944. available on microfilm and microfiche from University Microfilms International (UMI).
Ind/Abst Can. Index.

CN
CANADIAN SELECT HOMES. (19??)-. Periodical. English. Eight times a year. 17.95Can$ Canada; 26.00Can$ US; 34.00Can$ other. Telemedia Publishing Inc., 555 West 12th Avenue, Suite 300, North York Ontario V5Z 4L4 Canada. **Tel** (604)877-7732. **(Subscription address:** Indas, 35 Riviera Drive, Building 17, Markham Ontario L3R 8N4 Canada.**) *Continues*** *Select Homes.*

US/0192-4486
CARPET & RUG INDUSTRY. [Carpet rug ind.]. **VFOAT** Carpet and Rug Industry. **VAT** Carpet and Rug Industry. (1973)-. Periodical. English. Twelve times a year. $48.00 US; $53.00 Canada & Mexico; $64.00 others. Rodman Publications Corporation, 17 S Franklin Turnpike, PO Box 555, Ramsey NJ 07446. **Tel** (201)825-2552, FAX (201)825-0553. **ED** Frank O'Neill. **LC** HD9937.U6; C32. **[CCC]. Ad Acc. Circ:** 5,500 (ctrl).
Ind/Abst F&S Index Plus Text, Int. [Select. Cov.]; Mark. Advert. Ref. Serv.; PROMT; Text. Technol. Dig.; World Text. Abstr.

BL
CASA & I.E. E DECORACAO. Periodical. Portuguese. $40.00 single issue. Editoria Vecchi, rua do Resende 144, Rio de Janeiro Brazil. **LC** NK1700; .C37. **DD** 747/.8/83.

IT/0008-7173
CASA VOGUE. Periodical. Italian (summaries and/or abstracts in English). Eleven times a year. L42350 Italy; L77800 other. Edizioni Conde Nast Spa, Piazza Castello 27, 20121 Milan Italy. **Tel** 011 39 2 85611. **Bk Rev. Ad Acc. Circ:** 50,000 (ctrl).
Desc: The leader magazine on Italian and international design in the more beautiful and up-to-date houses, signed by top architects, designers or decorators.
Ind/Abst ARTbibliogr. Mod.

US
CHINA DECORATOR, THE. Periodical. English. mo. $25.00 (one year), $48.00 (two year). China Decorator, PO Box 575, Shingle Springs CA 95682. **Tel** (916)677-1455, FAX (916)677-1408.

US/0195-1416
COLONIAL HOMES. See Architecture.

AT
COMFORTABLE LIVING AND QUEENSLAND HOMES./FOR AUSTRALIA. English. qt. 21.80Aus$. Graphic Publishing, PO Box 348, Springwood QLD 4127 Australia. **Tel** 011 61 7 8081614, FAX 011 61 7 2089329.

US/0894-4083
COUNTRY ACCENTS. [Ctry. accents]. (198?)-. Periodical. English. bm (6 issues). $17.97. GCR Publishing Group, 1700 Broadway, 34th Floor, New York NY 10019. **Tel** (212)541-7100, (800)435-0715, FAX (212)245-1241. **(Subscription address:** Kable Publishers Aide, 308 East Hitt Street, Subscription Department, Mt. Morris IL 61054-1473.**) LC** TX1; .C854. **DD** 640/.5.
Desc: Guide for ideas and information on country home decorating, antiques and craft projects.

US/0731-2164
COUNTRY DECORATING IDEAS. (1980)-. Periodical. English. qt. $14.97 (two year). Harris Publications, 1115 Broadway/8th Floor, New York NY 10010. **Tel** (212)807-7100. **ED** Jack C Davis. **Ad Acc.**

US/0737-3740
COUNTRY HOME. [Ctry. home]. **VFOAT** Country Home and Kitchen Ideas. (Spring 1983)-. Periodical. English. bm (6 issues). $18.00. Meredith Corporation, Locust at 17th, Des Moines IA 50309. **Tel** (515)284-3000. **(Subscription address:** Neodata / Colorado, PO Box 2606, Boulder Boulder CO 80322.**) ED** Jean LemMon. **LC** TH4850; .C68. **DD** 643/.1/0973. **Ad Acc. Circ:** 880,000. ***Continues*** *Country Home & Kitchen Ideas, 0731-5597.*
Desc: A lifestyle publication for those who enjoy living the country life in or out of the country. In-depth articles on decorating, building, renovation, food, gardening, etc.
Ind/Abst Access (1984-); Garden Lit. (1992-).

UK/0951-3019
COUNTRY HOMES AND INTERIORS. (COUNTRY HOMES & INTERIORS.). [Ctry. homes inter.]. (19??)-. Periodical. English. mo. $55.25 US and Canada; £23.40 UK; £32.50 other. IPC Magazines Ltd., Perrymount Road, Haywards Heath, West Sussex RH16 3DH England. **Tel** 011 44 444 440421.

US
COUNTRY LIVING COUNTRY KITCHENS. $2.95 (single copy). The Hearst Corporation, 250 West 55th Street, New York NY 10019. **Tel** (212)649-4014. **ED** Rachel Newman.
Desc: Offers advice on everything from planning and budgeting to new products on the market. Articles include a variety of recipe and entertaining suggestions.

UK
COUNTRY LIVING. (ENGLAND EDITION). English. mo. $72.00. National Magazine Company Ltd., Perrymount Road, Haywards Heath, West Sussex RH16 3DH England. **Tel** 011 44 444 440421.

US/1047-3955
COUNTRY SAMPLER. (COUNTRY SAMPLER : COUNTRY DECORATING IDEAS & WHERE TO BUY COUNTRY ACCESSORIES.). (198?)-. Periodical. English. Six times a year (Jan., Mar., May, July, Sept., Nov.). $26.61. Sampler Publications Inc, 707 Kautz Road, St Charles IL 60174. **Tel** (708)377-8000 ext.270. **(Subscription address:** Kable News, PO Box 352, Mt. Morris, IL 61054**) DD** 747. **Ad Acc.**
Desc: Showcases varieties of country decorating styles. Features catalog sections offering handcrafted products and accessories.

●US/1066-7245
COUNTRY SAMPLER'S WEST. [Ctry. sampl. west]. **VFOAT** West. Vol. 4, No. 1 (Apr. 1993)-. Periodical. English. bm (6 issues). $19.96. Sampler Publications Inc, 707 Kautz Road, St Charles IL 60174. **Tel** (708)377-8000 ext.270. **(Subscription address:** Kable Publishers Aide, 308 East Hitt Street, Subscription Department, Mt. Morris IL 61054-1473.**) DD** 747. **Ad Acc. *Continues*** *Southwest Sampler, 1047-4242.*

US/1053-9980
COUNTRY VICTORIAN ACCENTS. ***Title Change.*** [Ctry. Vic. accents]. Vol. 2, No. 4 (Winter 1991)-(199?). Periodical. English. qt. GCR Publishing Group Inc, 1700 Broadway/34th Floor, New York NY 10019. **Tel** (212)541-7100, FAX (212)245-1241. **LC** WMLC 91/1137. **DD** 747. ***Continues*** *Country Victorian Decorating, 1052-1224.* ***Continued by*** *Country Victorian Decorating & Lifestyle, 1071-0256.*

US/1071-0256
COUNTRY VICTORIAN DECORATING & LIFESTYLE. [Ctry. Vic. decor. lifestyle]. **VFOAT** Country Victorian Decorating and Lifestyle. (199?)-. Periodical. English. bm (6 issues). $19.97. GCR Publishing Group, 1700 Broadway, 34th Floor, New York NY 10019. **Tel** (212)541-7100, (800)435-0715, FAX (212)245-1241. **(Subscription address:** Kable Publishers Aide, 308 East Hitt Street, Subscription Department, Mt. Morris IL 61054-1473.**) DD** 747. ***Continues*** *Country Victorian Accents, 1053-9980.*
Desc: Magazine for those who love all things Victorian, a way of decorating and a lifestyle of a gracious bygone age.

UK
DECORATING CONTRACTOR ANNUAL DIRECTORY. Directory. English. an. £16.20 UK; £18.30 other. Kingslea Press Limited, 137 Newhall Street, Birmingham B3 1SF. **Tel** 021 236 8112, FAX 021-200 1480, telex 338024 Bircom-G Kingslea.
Desc: Comprehensive listings of manufacturers, merchants, and product buyers' guide for the decorating contractor.

US/0011-7404
DECORATING RETAILER. **Added/Corp** National Decorating Products Association. (19??)-. Periodical. English. Twelve times a year. $9.00 (one year), Decorating Registry; $20.00 (one year) Decorating Retailer; $25.00 (one year), Wallcovering Directory. National Decorating Products, 1050 North Lindbergh Boulevard, St. Louis MO 63132. **Tel** (314)991-3470, FAX (314)991-5039.
Ind/Abst Mag. Search; Vocat. Search (Jan. 1993-).

US
DECORATING WITH ART & ANTIQUES. ***Ceased.*** **VFOAT** Decorating with Art and Antiques. (Oct. 1990)-(19??). English.

CN/0705-1093
DECORATION CHEZ-SOI. **VFOAT** Chez-Soi. Vol. 1 (Mar. 1978)-. Periodical. French. Ten times a year. 44.00Can$ Canada; 88.00Can$ other. Publications Quebecor le Nordais, 5800 rue St. Denis, Bar 605, Montreal Quebec H2S 3L5 Canada. **Tel** (514)272-6330. **DD** 747/.05. **Bk Rev. Ad Acc. Circ:** 100,000 (ctrl).
Desc: Interior home decorating magazine. Aiming at people participating in their home decoration. New products, and new ideas.

CN/0828-4946
DECORATION JET SET AMBIANCE. [Decor. jet set ambiance]. **VFOAT** Decoration Ambiance; Decoration Ambiance Jet Set. **VAT** Decoration Jet Set (1983). V. 4, No. 3, (Fall 1983)-. Periodical. French. ir. $9.00. Jet Set Ambiance, Suite 23, 4246 Est, Jean Talon, Montreal Quebec H1S 1J7. **DD** 747.211/4/05. ***Continues*** *Decoration, 0714-458X.*

CN/0315-047X
DECORMAG. [Decormag]. **VFOAT** Maisons et Jardins. Vol. 1 (Aug 1972)-. Periodical. French. Ten times a year. 19.94Can$ Canada; 38.20Can$ other. Publications Transcontinental Inc, 1100 Rene-Levesque, 24Fl Boulevard West, Montreal Quebec H3B 4X9 Canada. **Tel** (514)392-9000, FAX (514)392-4724. **ED** Francine Tremblay, Claude Gervais, and Dominique Lamarche. **DD** 747.211. **Circ:** 75,000 (ctrl).
Desc: This publication features art and antiques, fashion, cuisine, plants, architecture, travel and leisure.
Ind/Abst Point Repere (1983-).

US/0891-5997
DESIGN FIRM DIRECTORY (ENVIRONMENTAL AND INTERIOR DESIGN ED.). (THE DESIGN FIRM DIRECTORY.). [Des. firm dir.]. (1987)-. Directory. English. an. $44.00. Wefler and Associates, PO Box 1167, Evanston IL 60204. **Tel** (312)454-1940. **LC** NK1167; .D47. **DD** 745.4/025/73. ***Continues in part*** *Design Directory, 0195-4326.*
Desc: National listing of firms and consultants in graphic and industrial design.

FI/0418-7717
DESIGN IN FINLAND. **Added/Corp** Suomen Ulkomaankauppaliitto. (1981)-. English (German and Japanese). an. $25.00. Finnish Foreign Trade Association, PO Box 908, Arkadiankatu 4-6 BSF, 00101 Helsinki 10 Finland. **Tel** 011 358 0 69591, FAX 011 358 0 694-0028, telex 121696. **ED** Jussi Sipila, Cynthia Dale, Elina Joensuu, and Danuta Manninen. **Ad Acc. Circ:** 30,000. ***Continues*** *Designed in Finland, 0418-7717.*
Desc: Publication on Finnish design industry. Includes articles on furniture, architecture, and designers.

US/0277-3538
DESIGN SOLUTIONS. See Architecture.

US/1041-0422
DESIGN TIMES. [Des. times]. (Oct./Nov. 1988)-. Periodical. English. bm. $19.95 one year; $35.95 two year; $47.95 three year. Design Times, 715 Boylston Street, Boston MA 02116. **Tel** (617)859-9690. **DD** 747. **Ad Acc. Circ:** 15,000 (ctrl).

UK/0950-3676
DESIGN WEEK. **VFOAT** DesignWeek. (1986)-. English. Fifty times a year. £50.00 UK; £85.00 Europe; £95.00 other. Centaur Communications Ltd., St Giles House, 50 Poland Street, London W1V 4AX England. **Tel**

011 44 71 439 4222, FAX 011 44 71 734 6748, telex 261352. available on an online database (files 771,772,799/Full-Text) from DIALOG.

AT/0810-6029
DESIGN WORLD. See Architecture.

US/0192-1487
DESIGNERS WEST. ***Ceased.*** [Des. West]. (1953)-(1992). Periodical. English. mo. Designers World Corporation, 8914 Santa Monica Boulevard, Los Angeles CA 90069. **LC** NK2004; .D45. **DD** 729. Index available. **Bk Rev. Ad Acc. Circ:** 34,000 (ctrl).
Desc: Covers the field of western interior design, including contract and residential work.

US
DESIGNERS WEST RESOURCE DIRECTORY. 1970-. Directory. English. an. $30.00 (twelve issues and directory) US; $35.00 (twelve issues and directory) other; $10.00 (directory only). Designers West, 8914 Santa Monica Boulevard, PO Box 69660, Los Angeles CA 90069-0660. **Tel** (310)657-8231, FAX (310)657-3673. **ED** Barbara L Shepherd. **LC** NK2004; .D46. **DD** 747/.025/78. **Ad Acc. Circ:** 40,000.
Desc: Western sources for products and services offered to the interior design trade by both national and regional manufacturers.

US/1057-8277
DESIGNERS WORLD. ***Ceased.*** [Des. world]. **VFOAT** DW. Vol. 1 No. 1 (Sept. 1991)-(April 1993). Periodical. English. mo. Designers World Corporation, 8914 Santa Monica Boulevard, Los Angeles CA 90069. **LC** NK1700; .D47. **DD** 729.

UK
DESIGNING. ***Ceased.*** **Added/Corp** Council of Industrial Design (Great Britain). (19??)-(19??). Periodical. English. Three times a year. Design Council, 28 Haymarket, London SW1Y 4SU England. **Tel** 011 44 71 839 8000, FAX 011 44 71 925 2130, telex 8812963.

AU/1035-0500
DESIGNINK. ***Ceased.*** **See** Architecture.

NE
DHZ VAKHANDEL. Bureau Van Vliet BV, PO Box 20, 2040 AA Zandvoort Netherlands.

NE
DOEHETZELF. **See** Hobbies.

PL/0867-2105
DOM I WNETRZE. **VFOAT** Dom & Wnetrze. (1992)-. Periodical. Polish. bm (6 issues). Price on Request. **(Subscription address:** ARS Polona, PO Box 1001, 00068 Warsaw Poland.**)** **UDC** 643. **CODEN** 645.

IT/0012-5377
DOMUS. (DOMUS : ARTE E STILE NELLA CASA, ARTE E STILE NELL'INDUSTRIA (INDUSTRIAL DESIGN).). [Domus]. No. 1 (Jan. 1928)-. Periodical. Italian (English). Eleven times a year. $150.00; $180.00 combined subscription with Dossier. Editoriale Domus, Via Achille Grandi 5-7, 20089 Rozzano Milan Italy. **Tel** 011 39 2 82472276, FAX 011 39 2 8255033. **ED** Mario Bellini. **LC** N4; .D6. **DD** 709. **Bk Rev. Ad Acc. Circ:** 62,000. Documents available from The Genuine Article.
Desc: Review for architecture interiors design art. Features are eclecticism and sensibility for new trends.
Ind/Abst Archit. Period. Index (1977-); Art Index; ARTbibliogr. Mod.; Arts Humanit. Citation Index (19??-19??) [Full Cov.]; Avery Index Archit. Period. Suppl. Colum. Univ. (1990-); Curr. Contents Arts Humanit.; Res. Alert [Full Cov.].

US/1046-1957
ELLE DECOR. [Elle decor]. Vol. 1, No. 1 (Winter 1990)-. Periodical. English. bm (6 issues). $20.00. Hachette Magazines Inc., 1633 Broadway, New York NY 10019. **Tel** (212)767-6000. **(Subscription address:** Neodata / Colorado, PO Box 2606, Boulder Boulder CO 80322.**)** **LC** NK1700; .E43. **DD** 747/.05.
Desc: Brings the flavor and spirit of Elle Magazine to the world of home design and decoration...the American home style magazine with a French accent and an international outlook.
Ind/Abst Access (1991-); Avery Index Archit. Period. Suppl. Colum. Univ. (Mar. 1990-).

UK
ELLE DECORATION. English. bm. £13.20 UK; £23.00 other. World Wide Subscription Services, Unit 4, Gibbs Reed Farm, East Sussex TN5 7HE England. **Tel** (0580)200657, FAX (0580)200616.

UK/0957-8943
ELLE DECORATION BRITISH ED. (ELLE DECORATION.). [Elle Decor. Br. Ed.]. (1989)-. Periodical. English. Ten times a year. £46.00 Europe. World Wide Subscription Services, Unit 4, Gibbs Reed Farm, East Sussex TN5 7HE England. **Tel** (0580)200657, FAX (0580)200616. **DD** 747.

FR/0988-1476
ELLE DECORATION NEUILLY-SUR-SEINE. (1987)-. Periodical. French. Eight times a year. 194.91F France; 307.00F others. EDI 7, 6 rue Ancelle, 92525 Neuilly Sur Seine, Cedex France. **Tel** 011 33 1 40886000. **UDC** 08 : 654.

US/0279-4438
FACILITIES DESIGN & MANAGEMENT. [Facil. des. manage.]. **VFOAT** Facilities Design and Management. Vol. 1, No. 1 (Jan. 1982)-. English. mo. $65.00 US; $67.00 Canada & Mexico; $125.00 other. Miller Freeman Inc., 600 Harrison Street, San Francisco CA 94107. **Tel** (415)905-2337, FAX (415)905-2240, telex 278273. **ED** Anne Fallucchi. **LC** HF5547.2; .F33. **DD** 747/.8523/05. **[CCC]. Bk Rev. Ad Acc. Circ:** 30,500 (ctrl). available on microfilm and microfiche from University Microfilms International (UMI); available on an online database (file 15/Full-Text) from DIALOG. Documents available from UMI Article Clearinghouse.
Desc: Office design, planning, and management. Focus on interior spaces. Also including telecommunications and real estate.
Ind/Abst ABI/INFORM Glob. Ed. (19??-); ABI Inform Ondisc (Jan. 1988-); Avery Index Archit. Period. Suppl. Colum. Univ. (Aug. 1989); Constr. Index (199?-); UMI ABI/Inform--Bus. Period. Ondisc [Full Txt.].

US/0898-9494
FLORIDA HOME & GARDEN. [Fla. home gard.]. **VFOAT** Florida Home and Garden. Vol. 4, No.7 (April 1988)-. Periodical. English. mo. Florida Media Affiliates Inc, PO Box 019068, Miami FL 33101. **Tel** (305)445-4500, FAX (305)445-4600. **(Subscription address:** Fulfillment Corporation of America, PO Box 1962, Marion OH 43305.**)** **LC** WMLC L 83/7467. **DD** 747. ***Continues*** *South Florida Home & Garden, 0743-863X.*

SW/0015-766X
FORM. **Added/Corp** Svenska Slojdforeningen. Foreningen Svensk Form. (1905)-. Periodical. Swedish (summaries and/or abstracts in English). Six times a year. Kr725.00 Includes membership in Swedish Society Industrial Design. Foreningen Svensk Form, Renstiernas Gata 12, S 11628 Stockholm Sweden. **Tel** 011 46 8 6443303. **ED** Kerstin Wickman. **Bk Rev. Ad Acc. Circ:** 7,000 (ctrl).
Desc: Sweden's only magazine specializing in design and environment matters.

US/1044-3576
GARDEN STATE HOME & GARDEN. [Gard. State home gard.]. **VFOAT** Home & Garden; Garden State Home and Garden; Home and Garden; Garden State Home & Garden Magazine. Periodical. English. mo. $15.00. Micromedia Limited, 20 Victoria Street, Toronto Ontario M5C 2N8 Canada. **Tel** (416)362-5211, (800)387-2689, FAX (416)362-6161, telex 06524668. **DD** 747. ***Continues*** *New Jersey Home & Garden, 0890-3921.*

IT/1120-236X
HABITAT UFFICIO. [Habitat uff.]. (1981)-. Periodical. Multiple languages. Seven times a year. L6000.00 Italy (surface mail); L150000.00 Europe, L200000.00 Africa & Asia & America, L250000.00 other (airmail). Alberto Greco Editore, Via Del Fusaro 8, 20146 Milan Italy. **Tel** 011 39 2 4819086 or 4691895, FAX 011 39 2 4819091, telex 315367. **UDC** 651.2.

US/0897-022X
HARDWOOD FLOORS. **See** Forestry-Lumber and Wood.

GW
HAUS, DAS. (19??)-. Periodical. German. Ten times a year. $40.00 US. Burda GmbH, Postfach 1230, D-7602 Offenburg Germany. **Tel** 011 49 781-8401. **(Subscription address:** US: German Language Publications, Inc., 153 South Deanstreet, Englewood, NJ 07631**)**

GW/0017-9876
HEIMTEX. (19??)-. Periodical. German. Twelve times a year. DM144.00. Westdeutsche Verlagsanstalt GmbH, Ahmser Strasse 190, 32052 Herford Germany. **Tel** 011 49 05221 7750, FAX 011 49 05221 775 215. **(Subscription address:** Westdeutsche Verlagsanstalt GmbH, Postfach 3054, D 32046 Herford Germany.**)** **UDC** 645.1. **[CCC].**

CN/0823-6348
HERMINE. **See** Insurance.

US
HOME ACCENTS TODAY. (19??)-. English. mo (8 issues). $29.95 US; $50.00 Canada and Mexico; $50.00 (surface mail), $100.00 (airmail) other. Cahners Publishing Company, 249 West 17th Street, New York NY 10011. **Tel** (212)645-0067, FAX (212)242-6987. **(Subscription address:** Cahners Publishing Company / North Carolina, Circulation Department, PO Box 2754, High Point NC 27261-2754.**)** ***Continues*** *Accessories/Today.*
Desc: Edited for retailing and manufacturing executives of residential/household home accents. Reports on the changes in the economy, government and society that are having an impact on the profitability of home accent retailing and manufacturing.

US
HOME AND CONDO. **See** Gardening and Horticulture.

US/1078-0289
HOME FASHIONS. [Home fash.]. **VFOAT** Home Fashions Magazine. (199?)-. Periodical. English. mo. $30.00 US; $60.00 other. Fairchild Publications Inc, 7 West 34th Street, 4th Floor, New York NY 10001. **Tel** (212)630-4230. **DD** 746. ***Continues*** *Home Fashions Magazine, 0896-7962.*

US/0896-7962
HOME FASHIONS MAGAZINE. ***Title Change.*** [Home fash. mag.]. **VFOAT** Home Fashions. Vol. 8, No. 12 (Nov. 1987)-(199?). Periodical. English. mo. Fairchild Publications Inc, 7 West 34th Street, 4th Floor, New York NY 10001. **Tel** (212)630-4230. **LC** TS1760; .H65. **DD** 746.9/05. available on an online database (files 16,570/Full-Text) from DIALOG. ***Continues*** *Home Fashions Textiles, 0195-654X.* ***Continued by*** *Home Fashions, 1078-0289.*
Ind/Abst F&S Index Plus Text, Int. [Full Txt.] [Select. Cov.]; Mark. Advert. Ref. Serv. [Full Txt.]; PROMT [Full Txt.]; Text. Technol. Dig.

US/1050-494X
HOME MAGAZINE'S BEST IDEAS KITCHEN AND BATH. [Home mag. best ideas kitchen bath]. **VFOAT** Kitchen and Bath; Kitchen & Bath; Home Magazine's Best Kitchen & Bath Ideas; Home Magazine's Best Kitchen and Bath Ideas. (1990)-. Periodical. English. Four times a year (Feb., May, Aug., Nov.). $7.90. Hachette Magazines Inc., 1633 Broadway, New York NY 10019. **Tel** (212)767-6000. **LC** TH4816.3.K58; H64. **DD** 643/.3/05. ***Continues*** *Home Magazine's Best Kitchen & Bath Ideas, 1049-9105.*

US/0278-2839
HOME (ORADELL, N.J.). (HOME.). [Home]. (June 1981)-. Periodical. English. Ten times a year. $22.00. Hachette Magazines Inc., 1633 Broadway, New York NY 10019. **Tel** (212)767-6000. **(Subscription address:** Neodata / Colorado, PO Box 2606, Boulder Boulder CO 80322.**)** **ED** Olivia Beuhl. **LC** TX311; .H77. **DD** 643/.05. **Ad Acc. Circ:** 540,769. Documents available from UMI Article Clearinghouse. ***Continues*** *Hudson Home Magazine, 0194-1089.*
Desc: A comprehensive idea resource for everything from building decisions and financing to remodeling, decorating, gardening and home entertaining.
Ind/Abst AGRICOLA; Mag. Artic. Summar. Elite (July 1994-); Newsp. Period. Abstr. (1988-).

US/0363-8758
HOME PLANNING AND DECORATING. Began with March 1972 issue. Periodical. English. qt. $9.95. Hudson Home Publications, 175 S San Antonio Rd., Los Altos CA 94022. **Tel** (310)937-5486. **LC** TX311; .H66. **DD** 643/.05. ***Continues*** *Interior Planning and Design.*

US/0364-653X
HOME PLANS & PROJECTS. **See** Architecture.

US/1043-8831
HOME-TECH REMODELING AND RENOVATION COST ESTIMATOR. [HomeTech remodel. renov. cost estim.]. **VFOAT** Remodeling and Renovation Cost Estimator. 18th Annual Ed. (1983)-. English. an. $49.50. Home Tech Publications, 5161 River Road, Bethesda MD 20816. **Tel** (800)678-8392. **ED** Henry Reynolds. **LC** TH4816; .H654. **DD** 643/.7/0299. **Circ:** 20,000. ***Formed by the union of*** *Home-Tech Restoration and Renovation Cost Estimator* ***and*** *Home-Tech Remodeling and Home Improvement Cost Estimator.*
Desc: Annual estimating manuals to compute labor and materials costs for home improvement, remodeling and repairs. Cost of books includes quarterly regional indexes listing price changes.

US/0364-6548
HOMES FOR LEISURE LIVING. **See** Architecture.

●US/1062-9254
HOSPITALITY DESIGN. (HOSPITALITY DESIGN: HD.). [Hosp. des.]. **VFOAT** HD. Vol. 14, No. 5 (May 1992)-. Periodical. English. ir (10 issues). $45.00 US. Bill Communications Inc., 355 Park Avenue South, New York NY 10010-1789. **Tel** (800)821-6897, (212)592-6262, FAX (212)592-6209. **(Subscription address:** Bill Communications, 200 South Route 130, Cinnamin, NJ 08077**)** **LC** NA7800; .R47. **DD** 729. ***Continues*** *Restaurant/Hotel Design International, 0898-9079.*
Desc: Features comprehensive 4-6 page stories, illustrated with architectural-quality photographs, on new (and newly-renovated) hotels, resorts, restaurants, senior living, and medical facilities. It also offers coverage of news, trends, people, and products in the hospitality design industry.

Ind/Abst Acad. Search (July 1993-); INFO-SOUTH Abstr.; Trade Ind. Index (May 1992-); Vocat. Search (July 1993-).

UK/0043-5759
HOUSE & GARDEN (BRITISH EDITION, 1948). (HOUSE & GARDEN.). [House gard.]. **VAT** House and Garden. (19??)-. Periodical. English. mo. $80.00. Conde Nast Publications Ltd, Perrymount Road, Haywards Heath, West Sussex RH16 3DH England. **Tel** 011 44 444 440421, FAX 011 44 444 440619. **(Subscription address:** International Subscriptions, 30 Montgomery Street, 7th Floor, Jersey City NJ 07302.**)** ***Absorbed*** *Wine and Food Magazine.*
Ind/Abst Archit. Period. Index (1947-); Gen. Period. Index (1985-); Mag. Index Plus (1989-); Mag. Index Sel. Microfiche (1990-) [Full Txt.]; TOM Gen. Index (1985-) [Full Txt.].

US/0018-6406
HOUSE & GARDEN (NEW YORK). ***Ceased.*** (HOUSE & GARDEN.). [House gard.]. **VFOAT** House and Garden; HG. Vol. 1, (June 1901)-(1993). Periodical. English. mo. Conde Nast Publications / New York, 350 Madison Avenue, New York NY 10017. **Tel** (212)880-8800, (800)777-0700. **ED** Louis Oliver Gropp. **LC** NA7100; .H6. **DD** 640/.5. **Bk Rev. Ad Acc. Circ:** 500,000. available on microfilm and microfiche from University Microfilms International (UMI). Documents available from UMI Article Clearinghouse, Magazine Collection. ***Absorbed*** *American Homes and Gardens, 1049-1104; Living for Young Homemakers.*
Desc: Has a commitment to the best in design, art and interiors. Features outstanding photography and commentary. Also illustrates the use of creativity in homes throughout the world.
Ind/Abst Acad. Abstr. Full Text Elite (Jan. 1984-June 1993); Acad. Abstr. (Jan. 1984-June 1993); Acad. Search (Jan. 1984-June 1993); ARTbibliogr. Mod.; Biogr. Index; Consum. Index Prod. Eval. Inf. Source; Garden Lit. (1992-); INFO-SOUTH Abstr.; Mag. Artic. Summar. Elite (Jan. 1984-June 1993); Mag. Artic. Summar. Select (Jan. 1984-); Mag. Artic. Summar. CD-ROM (Jan. 1984-June 1993); Mag. Search; Newsp. Period. Abstr. (1988-); Read. Guide Abstr. Select Ed.; Read. Guide Period. Lit.; Resource/One Ondisc (1988-); Mag. Index (1977-); Vocat. Search (Jan. 1984-June 1993).

US/0018-6422
HOUSE BEAUTIFUL. See Architecture.

US
HOUSE BEAUTIFUL'S HOME BUILDING. See Building and Construction.

US
HOUSE BEAUTIFUL'S HOME REMODELING AND DECORATING. **VFOAT** Home Remodeling and Decorating. Spring (1987)-. English. Three times a year. $2.95 (single copy) US; $3.95 (single copy) Canada. The Hearst Corporation, 250 West 55th Street, New York NY 10019. **Tel** (212)649-4014. **ED** Jim Kemp. **Ad Acc.**
Desc: Creative ideas and information on home design, furnishings, lighting, wall and floor covering and window treatments are featured regularly. Remodeling articles include advice on additions and restoration along with practical information for adapting the featured design and remodeling ideas to the readers own homes.

US
HOUSE BEAUTIFUL'S KITCHENS, BATHS. English. Three times a year. $2.95 (single copy) US; $3.95 (single copy) Canada. The Hearst Corporation, 250 West 55th Street, New York NY 10019. **Tel** (212)649-4014. **ED** Jim Kemp. **Ad Acc.**
Desc: Designs and uses for cabinets, appliances, fixtures, flooring and building materials are emphasized. Regular features include storage ideas and hints for using space more efficiently. Design and product information is geared to match various tastes and budgets.

US/1074-4274
HOUSE (WESTHAMPTON BEACH, N.Y.). (HOUSE. LIFESTYLE OF THE ISLAND.). [House]. (19??)-. Periodical. English. Six times a year (Jan., Mar., May, July, Sept., Nov.). $12.00. Sheahan Publications, Suffolk County Airport, Westhampton Beach NY 11978. **Tel** (516)288-5400, FAX (516)288-5420. **DD** 051. **Ad Acc, Adv Mgr Tel** (516)288-5400. **Circ:** 26,000 (ctrl). ***Continues*** *House in the Hamptons.*
Desc: General news and information on interior design, decoration, kitchen and bath design, architecture, landscaping, and lighting and many more ideas.

US/0161-1895
I.D.E.A.S. INTERIORS, DESIGN, ENVIRONMENT, ARTS, STRUCTURES. (A.I.D.E.A.S. INTERIORS, DESIGN, ENVIRONMENT, ARTS, STRUCTURES.). **VFOAT** Interiors, Design, Environment, Arts, Structures; IDEAS. (19??)-. Periodical. English. Four times a year. $21.30 Florida; $20.00 (one year), $34.00 (two years) US; $22.00 (one year), $36.00 (two years) US Possessions & Canada; $32.00 (one year), $59.00 (two years) other. Dodi Publications, PO Box 343392, Coral Gables FL 33114. **Tel** (305)238-0557. **ED** Al Alschuler. **Ad Acc, Adv Mgr:** R. Rachlin.

CN/0822-4269
IDEES DE MA MAISON, LES. [Idees maison]. No. 1 (Sept. 1983)-. Periodical. French. Ten times a year. 44.00Can$ Canada; 88.00Can$ other. Publications Quebecor le Nordais, 5800 rue St. Denis, Bar 605, Montreal Quebec H2S 3L5 Canada. **Tel** (514)272-6330. **DD** 747/.05.

US/1055-5013
IHD, THE HANDBOOK. ***Title Change.*** [IDH, handb.]. **VFOAT** IDH. **VAT** Interior Decorators' Handbook, The Handbook. (Spring/Summer 1990)-(1992). English. sa. Columbia Communications Inc., 370 Lexington Avenue, New York NY 10017. **Tel** (212)532-9290. **LC** NK1705; .I34. **DD** 747/.029/473. ***Continues*** *Interior Decorators' Handbook, 0733-8511.* ***Continued by*** *Interior Decorators' Handbook (New York, N.Y. : 1993).*

US/0446-0138
INDOOR COMFORT NEWS. (19??)-. Periodical. English. mo (12 issues). $12.00. Institute of Heating & Air Conditioning Industry, 606 North Larchmont Boulevard, Suite 4A, Los Angeles CA 90004. **Tel** (310)467-1158. **ED** Charlene Klink. **Circ:** 15,500.

II/0970-1761
INSIDE OUTSIDE. [Inside outs.]. Vol. 1 (Nov./Dec. 1977)-. Periodical. English. bm. $36.00. Debonair Publications Pvt Ltd, 289 Shahid Bhagat Singh Road, Bombay 400 001 India. **(Subscription address:** Prints India, 11 Darya Ganj, New Delhi 110002 India.**) LC** NK2076.A1; I57. **DD** 745.4/49/54.
Ind/Abst Archit. Period. Index (1981-).

US/0192-1657
INSTALLATION & CLEANING SPECIALIST. **VAT** Installation and Cleaning Specialist. (19??)-. Periodical. English. Twelve times a year. $38.00 US & Canada; $60.00 others. Specialist Publications Inc, 17835 Ventura Boulevard, Suite 312, Encino CA 91316. **Tel** (818)345-3550, FAX (818)344-9647. **ED** Howard Olansky. **LC** TS1779.5; .I53. **DD** 698.9/05. **Ad Acc. Circ:** 16,500. ***Continues*** *Installation Specialist.*
Desc: Lets you zero in on firms that provide professional floor care and service... that clean, repair, install, maintain and service carpet, hard surface floors and related indoor/outdoor surfaces.

DK
INTERIEUR. (19??)-. Periodical. Danish.

US/0733-8511
INTERIOR DECORATORS' HANDBOOK. ***Title Change.*** [Inter. decor. hand book]. **VFOAT** Interior Decorators' Hand Book. Periodical. English. sa. Columbia Communications Inc., 370 Lexington Avenue, New York NY 10017. **Tel** (212)532-9290. **ED** Laura Blank. **DD** 747. **Bk Rev. Ad Acc. Circ:** 20,000 (ctrl). ***Continued by*** *Ihd, The Handbook, 1055-5013.*
Desc: Purchasing guide of furniture, furnishings, and services for the interior designer.

●US
INTERIOR DECORATORS' HANDBOOK : IDH. **VFOAT** IDH, Interior Decorators' Handbook; IDH. (1993)-. English. sa. Columbia Communications Inc., 370 Lexington Avenue, New York NY 10017. **Tel** (212)532-9290. **LC** NK1705; .I34. ***Continues*** *IDH, the Handbook, 1055-5013.*

US/0020-5508
INTERIOR DESIGN (NEW YORK, N.Y.). (INTERIOR DESIGN.). [Inter. des.]. (1950)-. Periodical. English. mo. $47.97 US; $63.97 (includes GST) Canada; $149.97 other. Cahners Publishing Company, 249 West 17th Street, New York NY 10011. **Tel** (212)645-0067, FAX (212)242-6987. **(Subscription address:** Interior Design, PO Box 2606, Boulder CO 80322-2606.**) DD** 729. **[CCC].** available on microfilm and microfiche from University Microfilms International (UMI). Documents available from UMI Article Clearinghouse. ***Continues*** *Interior Design and Decoration.*
Desc: Residential and commercial interiors are featured every month. Covers the business as well as the beauty, of interior design. Each issue contains valuable insights and inspiration on managing the business, legal issues and trade practices. Delivers the information design professionals need to keep ahead of the game.
Ind/Abst Acad. Search (July 1993-); Art Index; ARTbibliogr. Mod.; Avery Index Archit. Period. Suppl. Colum. Univ. (1990-); Bus. Index (1985-); Gen. BusinessFile (1985-); Gen. Period. Index (1985-); Health Plan. Adminis.; Hospit. Health Admin. Index; INFO-SOUTH Abstr.; Mag. Search; Newsp. Period. Abstr. (1992-); Stat. Ref. Index; Trade Ind. ASAP [Full Txt.]; Trade Ind. Index (1981-) [Full Txt.]; Vocat. Search (July 1993-).

CN/1188-0635
INTERIOR MOTIVES. [Inter. motiv.]. No. 1 (1991)-. Periodical. English. qt. Limited free distribution. Classic House Interiors Inc., 50 Lockridge Avenue, Unit 10, Unionville Ontario L3R 8X5. **DD** 729.

US/1059-5287
INTERIORS & SOURCES. [Inter. sources]. **VFOAT** Interiors and Sources; IS. (198?)-. Periodical. English. Nine times a year. $27.00 US; $50.00 other. L C Clark Publishing Company Inc, PO Box 13079, North Palm Beach FL 33408. **Tel** (407)627-3393, FAX (407)627-3447, telex 350839. **DD** 747. **Ad Acc, Adv Mgr Tel** (708)498-9880. **Circ:** 27,000 (ctrl).

US/0164-8470 #y 0148-012x
INTERIORS (NEW YORK, N.Y. : 1978). (INTERIORS.). [Interiors]. **Added/Corp** Interior Designers Group. Vol. 138, No. 3 (Oct. 1978)-. Periodical. English. mo. $35.00 US; $53.00 Canada; $70.00 other (surface mail). Billboard Publications Inc., 1515 Broadway Billboard, New York NY 10036. **Tel** (212)764-7300, FAX (305)755-7048, telex WU TWX 710-581-6279. **(Subscription address:** Fulfillment Corp of America, 205 West Center Street, Marion, OH 43302**) LC** TS1300; .I67. **DD** 747/.05. **[CCC].** available on microfilm from University Microfilms International (UMI). Documents available from UMI Article Clearinghouse. ***Continues*** *Contract Interiors, 0148-012X.*
Desc: Complete coverage of the commercial design industry for the design professional and student of design.
Ind/Abst Acad. Ind. [Computer File] (1992-); Archit. Period. Index (1978-); Art Index; ARTbibliogr. Mod. (1978-); Avery Index Archit. Period. Suppl. Colum. Univ. (1989/1990-); Constr. Index (199?-); Expand. Acad. Index (1992-); Health Plan. Adminis.; Hospit. Health Admin. Index; Newsp. Period. Abstr. (1992-).

UK
INTERIORS QUARTERLY. ***Title Change.*** (19??)-(19??). English. qt. Cheerman Limited, Halpern House 301, 305 Euston Road, London NW1 3SS England. **Tel** 011 44 71 2783000. ***Absorbed by*** *World Architecture.*

CN/1183-9708
INTERNATIONAL CONTRACT (DOWNSVIEW). ***Title Change.*** (INTERNATIONAL CONTRACT.). [Int. contract des.]. **VFOAT** International Contract Magazine. Vol. 1, No. 1 (Aug./Sept. 1991)-Vol. 2, No. 6 (July 1993). Periodical. English. bm. Manor Communications Co., 312 Dolmite Drive, Suite 217, Downsview Ontario M3J 2N2 Canada. **Tel** (905)667-9609. **DD** 729/.05. ***Continues*** *Contract (Concord, Ont.), 1184-2512.* ***Continued by*** *Architecture and Design Insite, 1195-227X.*

IT/0020-9538
INTERNI. [Interni]. (1967)-. Periodical. Italian (summaries and/or abstracts in English). Sixteen times a year. $240.00. Agenzia Italiana di Esportazione, Via Manzoni 12, 20089 Rozzano Milan, Italy. **Tel** 011 39 2 57512575. **LC** NK1700; .I65. **DD** 747/.05. ***Continues*** *Rivista dell'Arredamento, 0392-8462.*

HU/0231-195X
IPARI FORMATERVEZESI SZAKIRODALMI TAJEKOZTATO. (1983)-. Periodical. Hungarian. qt. 2.300. Orszagos Muszaki Informacios Kozpont es Konyvtar (O.M.I.K.K.), National Technical Information Centre and Library Museum, u 17, PO Box 12, 1428 Budapest, Hungary. **Tel** (361)118-1994, FAX (361)138-2414, telex 22-4944 OMIKK H. **(Subscription address:** OMIKK Budapest, POB 12, H-1428, Hungary**) ED** Eva Szentpali. **UDC** 016. **Circ:** 85.
Desc: Articles on design in industry.

●US/1071-7641
JOURNAL OF INTERIOR DESIGN. [J. inter. design]. **Added/Corp** Interior Design Educators Council. Vol. 19, No. 1 (1993)-. Periodical. English. sa (May and Nov). $50.00 (institutions), $35.00 (individuals). Journal of Interior Design, 633 South Shore Drive, Dr. P. Flanagan, Madison WI 53715. **Tel** (608)246-6310. **ED** Paul Eshelman. **LC** NK1700; .J68. **DD** 729. **CODEN** JOIDEE. ***Continues*** *Journal of Interior Design Education and Research, 0147-0418.*

US/0147-0418
JOURNAL OF INTERIOR DESIGN EDUCATION AND RESEARCH. ***Title Change.*** [J. inter. des. educ. res.]. **Added/Corp** Interior Design Educators Council. (19??)-Vol. 18, No. 1 & 2 (1993). English. sa. Jeanne S Rymer, University of Delaware, Alison Hall, Newark DE 19716. **Tel** (509)335-6845. **ED** Paul Esaelman (editor's address: Cornell University, MVR Hall, Ithaca, NY 14853). **LC** NK1700; .J68. **DD** 729. cum. index. **Bk Rev. Pr Rev. Circ:** 500 (ctrl). ***Continued by*** *Journal of Interior Design.*
Desc: Current interior design research, educational trends, critical reviews of current work, book reviews.
Ind/Abst AGRICOLA; Ergon. Abstr.

NE
KARWEI. Uitgeverij De Schouw, Waterlandlaan 37, 1441 RS Purmerend Netherlands.

US/0730-2487
KITCHEN & BATH BUSINESS. [Kitchen bath bus.]. **VFOAT** Kitchen and Bath Business; KBB. Vol. 27, No. 10 (Oct. 1981)-. Periodical. English. mo. $45.00 US; $54.00 Canada; $90.00 other. Miller Freeman Inc., 600 Harrison Street, San Francisco CA 94107. **Tel** (415)905-2337, FAX (415)905-2240, telex 278273.

(Subscription address: JCI, PO Box 1766, Riverton NJ 08077.**)** **LC** TT197; .K427. **DD** 683/.88/05. **[CCC].** ***Continues*** *Kitchen Business, 0023-1932;* ***Absorbed*** *Plastic Laminating.*

US/8750-9504
KITCHEN & BATH CONCEPTS. ***Title Change.*** [Kitchen bath concepts]. **VFOAT** Kitchen and Bath Concepts. Vol. 1, No. 1 (Feb./March 1985)-(19??). Periodical. English. bm. QR Publishing, 20 E Jackson, Chicago IL 60604. **Tel** (312)922-5402. **LC** TH4816.3.K58; B37. ***Absorbed by*** *Qualified Remodeler, 0098-9207.*

US/8750-345X
KITCHEN & BATH DESIGN NEWS. [Kitchen bath des. news]. **VFOAT** Kitchen and Bath Design News. (198?)-. Periodical. English. Twelve times a year. $50.00 US; $65.00 Canada; $120.00 other. PTN Publishing Company, 445 Broad Hollow Road, Melville NY 11747. **Tel** (516)845-2700, FAX (516)845-7109. **DD** 683.

US/0731-5600
KITCHEN AND BATH IDEAS. (19??)-. Periodical. English. qt. $3.99. Meredith Publications / Special Interest Section, 1716 Locust Street, Des Moines IA 50309. **Tel** (515)284-3000. **LC** TH4816; .K58. **DD** 643/.3/05.

US
KITCHEN & BATH SOURCE BOOK. **VFOAT** Kitchen and Bath Source Book. Vol. 2 (1990)-. English. $24.95. MBC Data Distributor Publications Inc, Indianapolis IN. ***Continues*** *Hutton's Kitchen & Bath Source Book.*

US
KITCHEN AND FAMILY ROOM IDEAS. (19??)-. English. an. Available on newsstand only. Meredith Corporation, Locust at 17th, Des Moines IA 50309. **Tel** (515)284-3000. **LC** TX653; .K53. **DD** 643.3/05.

HU
LAKASKULTURA. (19??)-. Periodical. Polish. Six times a year. $20.00. **(Subscription address:** Kultura, PO Box 149, H 1389 Budapest 62 Hungary**)** **LC** NK1700; .L35.

US
LIVING NOW. V. 1- Spring 1970-. Periodical. English. qt. Holt Rinehart & Winston, 1st Anne's Road Eastbourne, East Sussex BN21 3UN England. **Tel** (212)688-9100. **LC** NA7100; .L515. **DD** 728/.05. ***Formed by the union of*** *Home Modernizing Guide* ***and*** *New Homes Guide.*

FR/0025-0945
MAISON & JARDIN. **VAT** Maison et Jardin. Vol. 1, No. 1 (1950)-. Periodical. French. Ten times a year. $75.00. Les Editions Conde Nast, Service Abonnements B620, 60732 S Genevieve Cedex 9 France. **Tel** 011 33 45 673505, 44 034400. **(Subscription address:** International Subscriptions, 30 Montgomery Street 7th Floor, Jersey City, NJ 07302**)**

GW/0025-2697
MAPPE, DIE. [Mappe]. Apr. (1880)-. Periodical. German. mo (12 issues). DM153.60 Germany, DM166.20 other. Verlag Georg DW Callwey GmbH, Postfach 800409, D 81604 Munich Germany. **Tel** 011 49 89 43600533. **ED** Klaus Halmburger. **LC** NK1700; .M3. **[CCC].** Index available. **Bk Rev. Ad Acc. Circ:** 30,300 (ctrl).
Desc: Information on interior decorating, decorative arts and colors in interior decoration.
Ind/Abst Art Archaeol. Tech. Abstr.; Biodeter. Abstr.; Surf. Treat. Technol. Abstr.; World Surf. Coat. Abstr.

US
MCCALL'S EARLY AMERICAN DECORATING & CRAFTS. **VFOAT** Early American Decorating & Crafts. V. 1-. English. $1.75 single issue. ABC Leisure Magazine Inc, 825 7th Avenue, New York NY 10019. **Tel** (212)265-8360. **LC** TT23; .M3. **DD** 747.214.

US/0162-8151
MCGRAW-HILL HOMEBOOK, THE. **VFOAT** Homebook. **VAT** McGraw-Hill Home Book. 1979-. Periodical. English. an. McGraw Hill Publishing Company, Inc., 1221 Avenue of the Americas, New York NY 10020. **Tel** (212)512-6410, (800)525-5003, FAX (212)512-6111. **LC** TH4817; .M38. **DD** 643/.7.

GW/0343-0642
MD LEINFELDEN. (1974)-. Periodical. Multiple languages. mo. DM220.80 Germany; DM232.80 other. Konradin Verlags Gruppe, Robert Kohlhammer GmbH, D-70765 Leinfelden Germany. **Tel** 011 49 711 7594370, 011 49 711 7594229. **UDC** 645.4. **CODEN** 728. **[CCC].** ***Continues*** *MD : Moebel Interior Design, 0024-8029.*

US/1058-7233
METRO (WINTER PARK, FLA.). (METRO : SHOWCASING THE ORLANDO COMMUNITY, ITS PEOPLE, AND THEIR HOMES.). [Metro]. Vol. 3, No. 1 (Sep. 1991)-. Periodical. English. mo. $18.00 US; $42.00 Canada. Newtech Solutions, Inc., 1330 Palmetto Avenue, Winter Park FL 32789. **DD** 747. ***Continues*** *Metro Orlando Home, 1047-9856.*

US/0273-2858
METROPOLITAN HOME. [Metrop. home]. Vol. 13, No. 4 (Apr. 1981)-. Periodical. English. bm (6 issues). $16.00. Hachette Magazines Inc., 1633 Broadway, New York NY 10019. **Tel** (212)767-6000. **(Subscription address:** Neodata / Colorado, PO Box 2606, Boulder Boulder CO 80322.**)** **LC** NK1700; .A57. **DD** 051. **Bk Rev. Ad Acc. Circ:** 700,000. available on microfilm and microfiche from University Microfilms International (UMI); available on an online database (file 647/Full-Text) from DIALOG. Documents available from UMI Article Clearinghouse. ***Continues*** *Apartment Life, 0092-0444.*
Desc: A trend conscious, life-style magazine with emphasis on the stylish home, creative living, wondrous collections, fragrant gardens and much more.
Ind/Abst Acad. Abstr. Full Text Elite (July 1989-); Acad. Abstr. (July 1989-); Access (1984-); Avery Index Archit. Period. Suppl. Colum. Univ. (1990-); Consum. Index Prod. Eval. Inf. Source; Index Inf. (1978-1980); Mag. Artic. Summar. Elite (July 1989-); Mag. Artic. Summar. Select (July 1989-); Mag. Artic. Summar. CD-ROM (July 1989-); Mag. Search; Newsp. Period. Abstr. (1988-); Mag. Index (1981-); Vocat. Search (July 1989-).

UK
METROPOLITAN HOME. (UK EDITION). English. ir. £24.00 UK; £46.00 other. IPC Business Press, Oakfield HS, Perrymount Road, Hayward Heath, West Sussex RH16 3DH England. **Tel** 011 44 444 440421, FAX 011 44 444 440619, telex 892084 REEDBP G.

NE
MEUBEL. Dutch. wk. Lakerveld BV, PB 43250, 2504 AG Den Haag Netherlands. **Tel** 070 643930.

HK
MO TENG CHIA TING. MODERN HOME. **VFOAT** Modern Home. (March 1977)-. Periodical. Chinese. Twelve times a year. $73.00 US; $90.00 Canada. Evergreen Publishing and Stationery, 136 South Atlantic Boulevard, Monterey Park CA 91754. **Tel** (818)284-9066, FAX (818)284-1571. **LC** NK1700; .M6.

IT/0391-3635
MODO DESIGN MAGAZINE. [Modo]. (1977)-. Periodical. Italian (summaries and/or abstracts in English). mo. L70000 Italy; L140000 other. Ricerche Design Editrice SRL, Via Room 21, 20094 Corsico MI Italy. **Tel** 011 39 2 4491149 or, 4405544. **Bk Rev. Ad Acc. Circ:** 35,000.
Desc: Covers design in both theoretical and actual applications, from computer image to urban design.
Ind/Abst Archit. Period. Index (1977-); ARTbibliogr. Mod.; Avery Index Archit. Period. Suppl. Colum. Univ. (1984,1990-).

BU/0204-5060
NASH DOM : [IZDANIE NA KOMITETA ZA KULTURA]. **Added/Corp** Bulgaria. Komitet za Kultura. (19??)-. Periodical. Bulgarian. bm. DM95.00. Pavlovich No 6 Ul Nikolai, Sofia 1142 Bulgaria. **(Subscription address:** Kubon & Sagner, ABT Zeitschriftenimport, D 80328 Munich Germany.**)** **LC** NK2067.A1; N37. **DD** 747.2/94977/05.

US/1059-3500
NC HOME. ***Ceased.*** [NC home]. **VAT** North Carolina Home. Vol. 1, No. 1 (Feb. 1992)-Vol. 3, No. 1. Periodical. English. bm. The News & Observer Publishing Company, 5435 77 Center Drive, Suite 50, Charlotte NC 28217. **Tel** (704)523-6987, FAX (704)523-4211. **ED** Lee Childs. **DD** 729. **Ad Acc, Adv Mgr:** Glenn Benton.
Desc: Stories about elegant homes & gardens in North Carolina.

NZ/0110-098X
NEW ZEALAND HOME AND BUILDING. [N.Z. home & build.]. **VFOAT** Home and Building. (1976)-. Periodical. English. Six times a year (Feb., Apr., June, Aug., Oct., Dec.). 30.80NZ$ New Zealand; 78.80NZ$ Australia and Pacific Islands; 132.80NZ$ other. Associated Group Media Ltd, Private Bag 99915, Newmarket, Auckland 1031 New Zealand. **Tel** 11 64 9 3795393, FAX 11 64 9 3089523, telex 79121057. **ED** Vicki Holder. **DD** 720. **Bk Rev**, (Qty: 3-5). **Ad Acc, Adv Mgr:** Gaye Billings. ctrl circ. ***Continues*** *Home and Building, 0018-392X.*
Desc: Covers interior design and renovation in New Zealand homes, restaurants, etc.
Ind/Abst Archit. Period. Index (Vol. 38 No. 6, 1976-).

BE
NIEUW NEUF. ***Title Change.*** **See** Architecture.

JA
NOBU. **VFOAT** NOB. Fall Edition 1974-. Periodical. Japanese (Japanese). Intra America Beauty Network, PO Box 629, 14 Commerce Drive, North Branford CT 06471. **Tel** (800)634-8500, (203)484-2665. **LC** NK1700; .N6.

US/0898-1191
NORTHERN CALIFORNIA HOME & GARDEN. ***Ceased.*** [North Calif. home gard.]. **VFOAT** Northern California Home and Garden; NCH+G. Vol. 1, No. 1 (Nov. 1987)-(19??). Periodical. English. mo. Westar Media Inc., PO Box 51823, Palo Alto CA 94303. **Tel** (415)368-8800, FAX (415)368-6251. **ED** Ann Bertelsen. **DD** 747. **Bk Rev. Ad Acc. Circ:** 65,000.

SP
ON DISENO. Spanish (English). Ten times a year (Except Jan. and Aug.). 12500.00ptas Spain; 15500.00 ptas Europe; 36000.00 ptas other. Aram Ediciones SA, Travesera de Dalt 82, 08024 Barcelona Spain. **Tel** 93-2192156, FAX 2192902. **ED** Carmen Ferrer. Index available. **Bk Rev. Ad Acc.** ctrl circ.
Desc: Contemporary spanish furniture, interior design and graphic design.
Ind/Abst Avery Index Archit. Period. Suppl. Colum. Univ. (No. 104, 1989-).

NE
ONDERHOUD INTERIEUR. (19??)-. Periodical. Dutch. Seven times a year (1 manual plus 6 updates). Fl450.00. Misset Uitgeverij BV, Postbus 4, 7000 BA Doetinchem, Netherlands. **Tel** 011 31 8340 49911. Index available (free).

US
OPEN HOUSE. Periodical. English. sa (published spring and fall). $18.00 US; $38.00 other. Open House Magazine Inc, PO Box 371610, Miami FL 33137. **Tel** (305)576-6011. **ED** Patricia G. Ernst. **Circ:** 20,000.
Desc: Luxury publication of interior design and architecture.

US/1044-4807
ORIENTAL RUG REVIEW. [Orien. rug rev.]. Vol. 1, No. 9 (Dec. 1981)-. Periodical. English. Six times a year. $48.00 (one year), $80.00 (two years). Oriental Rug Auction Review Inc, PO Box 709, Meredith NH 03253-0709. **Tel** (603)744-9191, FAX (603)744-6933. **LC** NK2808; .O734. **DD** 746.7/5/09505. ***Continues*** *Oriental Rug Auction Review, 0740-7017.*

IT/0391-7487
OTTAGONO. ***Title Change.*** **See** Architecture.

IT/0391-7487
OTTAGONO. ***Title Change.*** [Ottagono]. **Added/Corp** Consorzio Pubblicita Industria Arredamento. (April 1966)-(19??). Periodical. Italian (English; summaries and/or abstracts in English). qt. Consorzio Gestione Biblioteche, Vle Trento Palazzo Garbini, 01100 Viterbo Italy. **Tel** 39 761 2226623. **ED** Giuliana Gramigna. Index available. **Circ:** 25,000 (ctrl). ***Merged with*** *Ottagono. English. Ottagono* ***to form*** *Ottagono (Milan, Italy : 1991).*
Desc: Magazine of architecture, furniture and industrial design.
Ind/Abst Archit. Period. Index (1977-1986)(1977-); ARTbibliogr. Mod. (1981-); Avery Index Archit. Period. Suppl. Colum. Univ. (1989-); BHA : Biblio. Hist. Art.

CN/0822-8256
OUR LITTLE YELLOW BOOK. [Our little yellow book]. V. 1, No. 1 July 1983-. Periodical. English. bm. Free. Shir-Cel Publishing & Marketing, #350, 500 Kingsway Plaza, Burnaby BC V5H 2E4. **DD** 643/.7/05.

US/0735-9713
PAINTING & WALLCOVERING CONTRACTOR. **See** Paints and Painting.

UK/0966-1530
PERIOD HOUSE & ITS GARDEN. [Period House Gard.]. **VFOAT** Period House and Its Garden. (1992)-. Periodical. English. mo. Orpheus Publications, 7 St. Johns Road, Harrow Middlesex HA1 2EE England. **Tel** 011 44 81 863-4040, FAX 011 44 81 424-9945. **(Subscription address:** Orpheus Subscriptions Departmenmt, PO Box 648, Harrow, Middlesex, HA1 2NW; England.**)** **DD** 728.0941. ***Continues*** *Old-house Journal, 0961-5962.*

UK/0958-1987
PERIOD LIVING. [Period living]. (1990)-. Periodical. English. mo. £24.00 UK; £32.00 other. EMAP Consumer Magazine, 1st Floor, Stephenson House Brunel C, Milton Keynes MK2 2EW England. **Tel** 011 44 71 437 9011, FAX 011 44 71 434 0656, telex 266400. ***Absorbed*** *Traditional Homes.*

US/0270-9341
PHOENIX HOME/GARDEN. **VFOAT** Phoenix Home, Garden; Phoenix Home and Garden; Phoenix Home & Garden. Vol. 1, No 1 (Nov. 1980)-. Periodical. English. mo. $15.00 (one year), $26.00 (two year). Phoenix Home and Garden, 4041 North Central Avenue, Suite A-100, Phoenix AZ 85012. **Tel** (602)234-0840, FAX (602)277-7857. **(Subscription address:** Phoenix Home & Garden, PO Box 34308, Phoenix, AZ 85067**)** **ED** Manya Winsted. **LC** TX311; .P48. **DD** 640/.5. **Ad Acc. Circ:** 35,000.
Desc: For families concerned with achieving a rewarding lifestyle in their home environments.

UK/0959-2687
PROFESSIONAL HOTEL & RESTAURANT INTERIORS. [Prof. hotel restaur. inter.]. **VFOAT** Professional Hotel and Restaurant Interiors. (1989)-. Periodical. English. bm. £24.00 UK; £40.00 other. Albatross Publications, PO Box 193, Dorking Surrey RH5 5YF England. **Tel** 0306 712712. **ED** Carol Andrews. **DD** 747. **Bk Rev. Ad Acc. Circ:** 4,000 (ctrl). ***Continues*** *Professional Interiors, 0955-4793.*
Desc: Covers all aspects of interior decor for hotels and restaurants.

Interior Design

US/0882-6781
PROFESSIONAL OFFICE DESIGN. *Title Change.* [Prof. off. des.]. Vol. 1, No. 1 (Spring 1985)-(19??). Periodical. English. qt. New York Law Publishing Company, 345 Park Avenue South, New York NY 10010. **Tel** (212)741-8300, (800)888-8300. **DD** 725. *Continued by* Designer Specifier, 1047-5362.
Ind/Abst Law Office Inf. Serv.

UK
PROFESSIONAL PAINTER & DECORATOR. See Paints and Painting.

CN/1182-0470
PROFESSIONAL RENOVATION. [Prof. renov.]. **VFOAT** Professional Renovation Magazine. (Spring 1990)-. Periodical. English. sa. $10.00. Homes Publishing Group, 40 Ridgetop Road, Scarborough Ontario M1R 4G3 Canada. **Tel** (416)754-1660, FAX (416)754-4554. **ED** Robin Robinson. **DD** 643/.7/05. Index available. **Bk Rev. Ad Acc. Circ:** 50,000 (ctrl).
Desc: Consumer guide to complete renovations done by professionals.

US/0882-1518
PROFESSIONAL UPHOLSTERER, THE. *Ceased.* (THE PROFESSIONAL UPHOLSTERER : OFFICIAL PUBLICATION OF THE NATIONAL ASSOCIATION OF PROFESSIONAL UPHOLSTERERS.). **Added/Corp** National Association of Professional Upholsterers (U.S.). Vol. 1, No. 1 (April 1984)-(July 1989). Periodical. English. bm. Cahners Publishing Company, 249 West 17th Street, New York NY 10011. **Tel** (212)645-0067, FAX (212)242-6987. **(Subscription address:** PO Box 173306, Denver, CO 80217-3306) **ED** Karl Kunkel and Gary Evans. **DD** 338. **Bk Rev. Ad Acc. Circ:** 11,000. available on microfilm and microfiche from University Microfilms International (UMI).
Desc: Official publication of the National Association of Professional Upholsterers is dedicated to serving the information needs of today's professional reupholsterer.
Ind/Abst Text. Technol. Dig.

US
RECORD HOUSES AND APARTMENTS OF THE YEAR. Main/Corp Architectural Record. **VFOAT** Record Houses; Record Houses and Apartments; Architectural Record Houses. (1976)-. Periodical. English. an. $12.00 US; $14.00 other. McGraw Hill Publishing Company, Inc., 1221 Avenue of the Americas, New York NY 10020. **Tel** (212)512-6410, (800)525-5003, FAX (212)512-6111. *Continues* Record Houses.

US/0277-6219
RECORD INTERIORS. [Rec. inter.]. (1981)-. English. an. $6.00. McGraw Hill Publishing Company, Inc., 1221 Avenue of the Americas, New York NY 10020. **Tel** (212)512-6410, (800)525-5003, FAX (212)512-6111. **LC** NK1700; .R4. **DD** 747.213.

●**US/1060-3735**
REMODEL NOW. [Remodel now]. Winter (1992)-. Periodical. English. qt. $25.00. Social Issues Resources Series Inc, PO Box 2348, Boca Raton FL 33427. **Tel** (800)327-0513, (407)994-0079. **DD** 643.

CN/0822-2479
RESOURCE DIRECTORY (TORONTO). (RESOURCE DIRECTORY.). [Resour. dir.]. 1984-. Directory. English (French). an. Source Handbook Publications, Suite 1200, 1 St. Clair Avenue West, Toronto Ontario M4K 1V4 Canada. **ED** Joanna Maxwell. **DD** 338.4/7747/02571. **Bk Rev. Ad Acc. Circ:** 10,000 (ctrl).
Desc: Provides a comprehensive list of sources available to the design trade.

US/1047-8841
RETAIL STORE IMAGE. [Retail store image]. Vol. 1, No. 1 (Jan./Feb. 1990)-. Periodical. English. Six times a year (Jan., Mar., May, July, Sept., Nov.). $35.00. Argus Business, 6151 Powers Ferry Road, Atlanta GA 30339. **Tel** (404)995-2500, (800)233-3359. **ED** Katherine Field. **DD** 658. **[CCC]. Circ:** 25,000 (ctrl). available on microfilm and microfiche from University Microfilms International (UMI).
Desc: Aimed at an audience including interior design consulting firms, interior designers, architects, CEOs and owners of retail establishments, visual merchandising executives, store planners and retail headquarters executives.

US
S & B REPORT. English. mo (11 issues - July/Aug. issue combined). $49.00 (one year), $79.00 (two year). Lazar Media Group, 112 East 36th Street, Fourth Floor, New York NY 10016. **Tel** (212)679-5400, FAX (212)679-5400. **ED** Eve Miceli & Elysa Lazar. **Ad Acc.** ctrl circ.

JA/0563-0991
S D; SPACE DESIGN. See Architecture.

GW/0036-6277
SCHOENER WOHNEN. (1960)-. Periodical. German (English). mo. $70.00. Gruner und Jahr Ag & Co, Abonnenten Service, D 20080 Hamburg Germany. **Tel** 011 49 40 37030. **LC** NK1700; .S36. **DD** 747/.05. available on microfilm from University Microfilms International (UMI).

UK
SCOTTISH HOME AND COUNTRY. Periodical. English. mo.
Ind/Abst Museum Abstr.

US/1043-0946
SEARCH (DEVON, PA.). (SEARCH.). [Search]. (Jan., Feb., Mar. 1988)-. Periodical. English. qt. $99.00 (1 year), $180.00 (2 year), $250.00 (3 year) (hard copy) $215.00 (computerized library ed.) US; $109.00 (1 year), $200.00 (2 year), $280.00 (3 year) (hard copy) $235.00 (computerized library ed.) Canada; $121.00 (1 year), $224.00 (2 year), $316.00 (3 year) (hard copy), $259.00 (computerized library ed.) other;. Search Publishing Inc, 102 Brighton Circle, Devon PA 19333. **Tel** (215)889-0535, FAX (215)889-9497. **ED** Don Colangelo. **LC** NA1; .S53. **DD** 016.72/05. cum. index. **Circ:** 800.
Desc: Comprehensive index to leading periodicals read by architects and interior designers. Special features include extensive keyword list, reference to quality illustrations and listing of full design team.

CN/0848-8258
SELECT HOMES & FOOD. *Title Change.* See Home Economics.

FR/0990-6029
SEMAINE AMEUBLEMENT INFORMATION, LA. (1987)-. Periodical. French. Forty-eight times a year. 685.60F France; 1500.00F other (combined with Le Nouvel de l'Ameublement). Editions GM Perrin, 88 Boulevard de Charonne, 75980 Paris Cedex 20 France. **Tel** 011 33 1 43489951. **UDC** 645.4. *Continues* Ameublement Information, 0295-4206.

US/0149-516X
SOUTHERN ACCENTS. [South. accents]. Vol. 1, (Fall 1977)-. Periodical. English. bm (6 issues). $24.95. Southern Progress Corporation, PO Box 1748, Birmingham AL 35201. **Tel** (205)877-6000. **(Subscription address:** Southern Accents, 500 Office Park Drive, Birmingham AL 35223.) **LC** NK2002; .S68. **DD** 747/.8/8. **Bk Rev. Ad Acc. Circ:** 258,330 (ctrl). available on microfilm and microfiche from University Microfilms International (UMI).
Desc: Edited for those who recognize and appreciate the gracious lifestyle of the South. Features the interiors and gardens of fine Southern residences.
Ind/Abst Avery Index Archit. Period. Suppl. Colum. Univ. (1989/90-); Garden Lit. (1992-).

US/0199-896X
SOUTHERN CALIFORNIA HOME & GARDEN. See Architecture.

US/1047-4242
SOUTHWEST SAMPLER. *Title Change.* [Southwest sampl.]. Vol. 1, No. 1 (Spring 1990)-(199?). Periodical. English. Six times a year. Sampler Publications Inc, 707 Kautz Road, St Charles IL 60174. **Tel** (708)377-8000 ext.270. **DD** 747. **Ad Acc.** *Continued by* Country Sampler's West, 1066-7245.

US/0190-4205
ST. LOUIS HOME/GARDEN. Periodical. English. mo. St Louis Home & Garden Magazine, 10300 Watson Road, St Louis MO 63127.

US/0192-8732
STORES OF THE YEAR. Added/Corp Retail Reporting Bureau (New York, N.Y.). Vol. 1 (1980)-. English. ir. $49.95 (per copy). Retail Reporting Bureau, c/o John Burr, 302 5th Avenue, New York NY 10001. **Tel** (212)279-7000, (800)251-4545, FAX (212)279-7014. **ED** Martin M. Pegler. **LC** NK2195.S89; S76. **DD** 747/.8521. **Ad Acc.**
Desc: Covers visual merchandising and design ideas; considered a standard reference work for the retail industry. Hardcover book features more than 300 color photos.

FR/0982-8354
STUDIO MAGAZINE. French. mo. 349.00F France; 469.00F other. Editions Mondiales, 9 11 13 Rue du Col Pierre Avia, 75754 Paris Cedex 15 France. **Tel** 011 33 1 46622162. **(Subscription address:** Studio Magazine Serv Abonnements, BP 502, F 60732 Ste Genevieve France)

US/0146-8243
SWEET'S INTERIORS MARKET. 1977-. English. McGraw Hill Publishing Company, Inc., 1221 Avenue of the Americas, New York NY 10020. **Tel** (212)512-6410, (800)525-5003, FAX (212)512-6111. **LC** NK1705; .S94. **DD** 338.4/7/74702573.

SP
TET : THE EAST TRADE. mo. $40.00. Editorial Ofice, Apartado 14 013, 28027 Madrid Spain. **Tel** 011 34 1 2672403.

US/1059-0307
TODAY'S FACILITY MANAGER. [Today's facil. manager]. **VFOAT** Facility Manager. Vol. 3, No. 5 (Sept. 1991)-. Periodical. English. Eight times a year. $30.00. Business Facilities, PO Box 2060, Red Bank NJ 07701. **Tel** (908)842-7433. **ED** Heidi Schwartz. **LC** NA4170; .C67; MF5547.2; .B87. **DD** 729. **Ad Acc. Circ:** 30000 (ctrl). *Continues* Business Interiors, 1044-3584.

US/0883-4660
TRADITIONAL HOME. [Tradit. home]. **VFOAT** Better Homes and Gardens Traditional Home. (198?)-. Periodical. English. Six times a year. $18.00. Meredith Corporation, Locust at 17th, Des Moines IA 50309. **Tel** (515)284-3000. **(Subscription address:** Neodata / Colorado, PO Box 2606, Boulder Boulder CO 80322.) **LC** NK2002; .T73. **DD** 747.213/05.
Desc: Helps readers create the traditional lifestyle with ideas for decorating, renovating, entertaining and collecting.

UK/0950-2181
TRADITIONAL HOMES. *Title Change.* **VFOAT** Traditional Garden. (Oct. 1984)-(19??). Periodical. English. mo. EMAP Consumer Magazine, 1st Floor, Stephenson House Brunel C, Milton Keynes MK2 2EW England. **Tel** 011 44 71 437 9011, FAX 011 44 71 434 0656, telex 266400. *Absorbed* Period Homes. *Absorbed by* Period Living and Traditional Homes, 0958-1987.
Ind/Abst Archit. Period. Index (Oct. 1984-); Avery Index Archit. Period. Suppl. Colum. Univ. (Jan. 1990-); Child. Lit. Abstr. (19??-).

UK/0950-219X
TRADITIONAL INTERIOR DECORATION. (1986)-. English. qt.
Ind/Abst Archit. Period. Index (Oct./Nov. 1987-Mar./Apr. 1989).

IT/0503-0455
UFFICIOSTILE. [Ufficiostile]. (1968)-. Periodical. Italian. bm. L63000 Italy. Masson S.P.A, Via Statuto 2/4, 20121 Milan Italy. **Tel** 011 39 2 63671, FAX 011 39 2 6367211. **ED** Mara Solari. **UDC** 651. **Circ:** 13,000.
Desc: Covers the problems relevant to space office organization. Reports in brief on the most interesting and topical issues related to planning and interior design. It presents articles and special reports on the main world exhibitions, and interviews with famous designers.

US/1040-8150
VERANDA (ATLANTA, GA.). (VERANDA.). [Veranda]. Vol. 1, No. 1 (Spring 1987)-. Periodical. English. qt. $12.00. Veranda, PO Box 550426, c/o Lisa Newsom, Atlanta GA 30355. **Tel** (404)261-3603. **LC** NK2002; .V47. **DD** 747.215/05. **Bk Rev. Ad Acc. Circ:** 80,000.
Desc: Publishes fine interiors, gardens, table settings, floral displays, recipes, travel, southern prose and social calendar.

AT
VICTORIAN HOMES. English. qt. 21.80Aus$. Graphic Publishing, PO Box 348, Springwood QLD 4127 Australia. **Tel** 011 61 7 8081614, FAX 011 61 7 2089329.

US/0744-415X
VICTORIAN HOMES. See Architecture.

US/1047-3947
VICTORIAN SAMPLER. (VICTORIAN SAMPLER : VICTORIAN DECORATING IDEAS & WHERE TO BUY VICTORIAN ACCESSORIES.). [Vic. sampler]. (1989)-. Periodical. English. Six times a year (Jan., Mar., May, July, Sept., Nov.). $19.96 one year; $33.98 two years. Sampler Publications Inc, 707 Kautz Road, St Charles IL 60174. **Tel** (708)377-8000 ext.270. **(Subscription address:** Kable News, 308 East Hill Street, Mt. Morris, IL 61054) **DD** 747. **Ad Acc.**
Desc: Covers Victorian-style home decor. Presents homes, accessories, table settings, gardens, and traditional decorating.

FR/0767-0508
VOGUE DECORATION. *Title Change.* (1985)-(1993). Periodical. French. bm. Les Editions Conde Nast, Service Abonnements B620, 60732 S Genevieve Cedex 9 France. **Tel** 011 33 45 673505, 44 034400. **UDC** 747. *Continues* M.J. Maison & Jardin International, 0762-3127. *Merged into* Maison & Jardin, 0025-0945.

IT
VOTRE MAISON. (19??)-. Periodical. Italian. bm. L40000 Italy; L160000 other. A Pieroni SRL, Viale Vittorio Veneto 28, 20124 Milan Italy. **Tel** 39 2 29000282, 29002876.

US/0273-6837
WALL PAPER (NEW YORK, N.Y.), THE. (THE WALL PAPER.). (1980)-. Periodical. English. Twelve times a year. $18.00 (one year), $28.00 (two year). Wall Publications Inc. / Maurice S. Murray, 570 7th Avenue, New York NY 10018. **Tel** (212)869-4960. **Bk Rev. Ad Acc. Circ:** 16,000 (ctrl).
Ind/Abst Constr. Index (-199?).

US/1055-4394
WALLCOVERINGS, WINDOWS & INTERIOR FASHION. [Wallcover. wind. inter. fash.]. **VFOAT** Wallcoverings, Windows, and Interior Fashion; Wallcoverings. (1991)-. Periodical. English. mo. $18.00 (1 year), $33.00 (2 year). Publishing Dynamics

Inc, 15 Bank Street/Suite 101, Stamford CT 06901. **Tel** (203)357-0028, FAX (203)357-0075. **ED** G. Lisa Sullivan. **LC** HD9843.U6; W3. **DD** 338. **Ad Acc. Circ:** 16,900 (ctrl). ***Continues*** *Wallcoverings Magazine, 8750-8184.* **Ind/Abst** Vocat. Search (July 1993-).

US/0049-7398
WESTERN FLOORS. **Added/Corp** Western Floor Covering Association. WFCA news. (19??)-. Periodical. English. mo. $40.00 (1 year), $66.00 (2 year), $88.00 (3 year) US; $52.00 (1 year) Canada; $72.00 (1 year) other. Specialist Publications Inc, 17835 Ventura Boulevard, Suite 312, Encino CA 91316. **Tel** (818)345-3550, FAX (818)344-9647. **ED** Howard Olansky. **LC** HD9937.U5; W46. **Ad Acc. Circ:** 15,400.

CN/0824-0604
WESTERN LIVING (VANCOUVER ED.). (WESTERN LIVING.). [West. living]. Vol. 14, No. 3 (March 1984)-. Periodical. English. mo (10 issues). 18.00Can$ Canada; 32.00Can$ US; 34.00Can$ other. Telemedia Publishing, Suite 300 E, Tower 555 West 12th Avenue, Vancouver, British Columbia V5Z 4G4, Canada. **Tel** (604)877-7732, FAX (604)877-4848, (604)877-4849. **ED** Paula Brook. **LC** AP5; .W47. **DD** 051. **Ad Acc, Adv Mgr:** Janet MacDonald. **Circ:** 252,500 (ctrl). ***Continues in part*** *Western Living (British Columbia Ed.), 0821-7017.*

UK
WHAT'S NEW IN INTERIORS. English. qt. £24.00 UK and Northern Ireland; $48.00 other. Morgan Grampian, 40 Beresford Street Woolwich, London SE18 6BQ England. **Tel** 011 44 81 855 7777, FAX 011 44 81 855 5548, telex 896238.

US/0897-5914
WHO'S WHO IN INTERIOR DESIGN. (WHO'S WHO IN INTERIOR DESIGN / BARONS WHO'S WHO.). [Who's who inter. des.]. **Added/Corp** Barons Who's Who (Firm). (1988/89)-. English. an. $175.00. Barons Who's Who, 412 North Coast Highway, Suite B-110, Laguna Beach CA 92651. **Tel** (714)497-8615. **LC** NK2004.2; .W48. **DD** 729/.092/273; B.
Desc: Contains entries for over 2,300 persons involved in both contract and residential interior design in the U.S.

US/0886-9669
WINDOW FASHIONS. [Window fash.]. **Added/Corp** Industrial Fabrics Association International. **VFOAT** Window Fashions Magazine; WF. Vol. 6, No. 1, Jan. (1986)-. Periodical. English. Twelve times a year. $30.00 US; $40.00 Canada; $65.00 Central America; $70.00 South America Europe; $85.00 other. Window Fashions, 4225 White Bear Parkway, Suite 400, St. Paul MN 55102. **Tel** (612)293-1544, telex 290282. **ED** Susan Schultz. **DD** 747. **Bk Rev. Ad Acc, Adv Mgr:** Dori Michard. **Circ:** 25,000 (ctrl). ***Continues*** *WES, 0746-7400.*
Desc: Design and merchandising trade publication serving retailers, dealers, specialty stores, designers, department stores, homestores and decorating centers involved with window treatments. Includes news, new products, trends, design ideas, how-to articles, and company and personality profiles.

FR
WINDOWS MAGAZINE. (19??)-(1992). French. mo. 240.00F France; 480.00F other. Bosquet Edition, Informat, BP 710, 92053 Paris La Defense France. **Tel** 46 92 27 60, FAX 46 92 27 73. **Ad Acc. Pr Rev. Circ:** 35,000.
Desc: Publication dedicated to windows and other graphic interfaces and their use in films.

US/0888-6822
WISCONSIN HOME GALLERY MAGAZINE. [Wisc. home gallery mag.]. **VFOAT** Home Gallery; Wisconsin Home Gallery; Home Gallery Magazine. (198?)-. Periodical. English. Ten times a year. $12.00 US; $17.00 other. Wisconsin Home Gallery, West 51 North 185 Fillmore Avenue, Cedarburg WI 53012. **Tel** (414)377-7398, FAX (414)377-1583. **ED** Stephen T. Bothe. **DD** 728. **Ad Acc, Adv Mgr:** Dick Strauss. **Circ:** 48,000.
Desc: Showcases area remodeling, building, landscaping, decorating and unique homes.

UK/0264-083X
WORLD OF INTERIORS, THE. [World inter.]. (1982)-. Periodical. English. Eleven times a year. $77.00. Quadrant Subscription Services Ltd, Oakfield House, Perrymount Road, Haywards Heath, West Sussex RH16 3DH England. **Tel** (01)828-5571. **LC** NK1700; .W64. **DD** 729. ***Continues*** *Interiors (London), 0263-1520.*
Ind/Abst ARTbibliogr. Mod.; Avery Index Archit. Period. Suppl. Colum. Univ. (1990-).

HOME FURNISHINGS

●US/1069-4188
AMERICAN FURNITURE. [Am. furnit.]. **Added/Corp** Chipstone Foundation. (1993)-. English. an. $45.00 US; $50.00 other. University Press of New England, 23 South Main Street, Hanover NH 03755. **Tel** (800)421-1561, (603)643-7110, FAX (603)643-1540. **DD** 645.

GW
ANNUAL REVIEW OF EUROPEAN EXPORT INDUSTRIES : FURNITURE. **VFOAT** Revue Annuelle des Industries Europeennes d'Exportation : Meubles; Jahresschau der Europaischen Export-Industrie : Mobel. 1978-. English (French and German). an. $53.00. Industrieschau Verlagsgesellschaft MBH, PO Box 4034, Berliner Allee 8, W-6000 Darmstadt Germany. **Tel** (06151)33411, FAX (06151)33164, telex 419257. **(Subscription address:** US/ Western Hemisphere Publishing Corporation, PO Box 710, Newcastle, CA 95658**) LC** TS803; .A64. **DD** 382/.45/684100254. **Ad Acc. Circ:** 8,000. available on CD-ROM from ABC Database.
Desc: Comprises the entire furniture manufacturing industry of 28 European countries.

IT
ANNUARIO SEAT. VOL. E, ARREDAMENTO. **See** Household Hardware and Appliances.

US/0893-5556
BED TIMES. [Bed times]. **Added/Corp** National Association of Bedding Manufacturers. International Sleep Products Association. **VFOAT** Bedtimes. Vol. 115, No. 3 (Mar. 1987)-. Periodical. English. mo. $25.00 (ISPA members), $35.00 (nonmembers) US; $30.00 (ISPA members), $40.00 (nonmembers) other. International Sleep Products Association, 333 Commerce Street, Alexandria VA 22314-2801. **Tel** (703)683-8371, FAX (703)683-4503. **ED** Tracy Savidge. **LC** TX315; .B4. **DD** 684.1/5/05. **CODEN** BEDTEF. Index available. **Ad Acc. Circ:** 2,600. ***Continues*** *Bedding Magazine, 0277-9129.*

US
BETTER HOMES AND GARDENS DECORATING. (19??)-. Periodical. English. qt. $3.50. Meredith Publications / Special Interest Section, 1716 Locust Street, Des Moines IA 50309. **Tel** (515)284-3000. ***Continues*** *Better Homes and Gardens Furnishings and Decorating Ideas, 0092-7961.*

US/0743-894X
BETTER HOMES AND GARDENS WOOD. [Better homes gard. wood.]. **VFOAT** Wood; Wood Magazine. No. 1 (Sept./Oct. 1984)-. Periodical. English. Nine times a year. $22.00 (one year); $39.00 (two year); $58.50 (three year). Meredith Corporation, Locust at 17th, Des Moines IA 50309. **Tel** (515)284-3000. **(Subscription address:** Neodata / Colorado, PO Box 2606, Boulder Boulder CO 80322.**) ED** Larry Clayton. **LC** TT180; .B44. **DD** 684/.08/05. **Ad Acc. Circ:** 500,000.
Desc: Provides project plans, updates on tools and techniques, shop tips, and articles on master craftsmen.
Ind/Abst Index Inf. (1984-).

UK/0305-733X
BLINDS AND SHUTTERS. [Blinds and shutters]. (195?)-. Periodical. English. qt. £30.00 UK; £38.00 (surface), £46.00 (air mail) other. Turret Group, 177 Hagden Lane, Watford Herts WD1 8LN United Kingdom. **Tel** 011 44 923 228577, FAX 011 44 923 221346.

GW/0341-3659
BM. BAU- + MOBELSCHREINER. **VFOAT** Bau- und Mobelschreiner; BM. Bau- und Mobelschreiner; Bau- + Mobelschreiner. (1957)-. Periodical. German. mo. DM174.00 Germany; DM188.40 other. Konradin Verlags Gruppe, Robert Kohlhammer GmbH, D-70765 Leinfelden Germany. **Tel** 011 49 711 7594370, 011 49 711 7594229. **UDC** 684.

IT
CAMINO. (19??)-. Italian. Four times a year. L36000.00 Italy; L55000.00 other. Serv Int Abbon Periodici, Via Baldissera 4, 20129 Milan Italy. **Tel** 011 39 2 2043828.

CN/0319-0803
CANADA'S FURNITURE MARKET. 1975-. English. 60.00Can$. Maclean Hunter Canada / Montreal, 1001 bvd. de Maisonneuve W., Montreal, Quebec H3A 3E1 Canada. **Tel** 514-845-5141, FAX 514-845-4302, telex 055-60604. **DD** 381/.45/684100971.
Desc: Reports Canadian production, imports of furniture with a report on the specific industries manufacturing furniture items.

CN/0826-6204
CANADIAN FURNITURE AND FURNISHINGS DIRECTORY. [Can. furnit. furnish. dir.]. (198?)-. Directory. English. an. 27.00Can$ Canada; $45.00 other. Sentinel Business Publications, 7575 Trans Canada Highway, Suite 500, St. Laurent Quebec H4T 1V6 Canada. **Tel** (514)333-1116, FAX (514)631-8858. **ED** Carol Clifford. **DD** 338.4/76841/02571. **Ad Acc. Circ:** 7,412 (ctrl). ***Continues*** *Lloyd's Canadian Furniture and Furnishings Directory, 0068-8789.*
Desc: Comprehensive listings by product category of suppliers to the furniture and home furnishings industries.

CN/0826-7642
CANADIAN HOUSE AND HOME. [Can. house home]. V. 6, Issue No. 1 (Feb./March 1984)-. Periodical. English. ir (Feb/Mar, Apr, May/June, July/Aug, Sept, Oct, Nov, Dec/Jan). 23.00Can$ Canada; 33.50Can$ other. Canadian House and Home, 511 King St West/Suite 120, Toronto Ontario M5V 2Z4 Canada. **Tel** (416)593-0666, FAX (416)591-1630. **ED** Katherine Vansittart, Suite 120, 511 King St W, Toronto, Ontario. **DD** 747/.05. **Bk Rev,** (Qty: 24-40 approx.). **Ad Acc, Adv Mgr:** Kathryn O'Hara, **Tel** (416)593-0666. **Circ:** 104,000. ***Continues*** *House and Home (Toronto, Ont.), 0822-7764.*

US/0092-0495
CARPET AND RUG INSTITUTE REVIEW. (REVIEW : STATE OF THE INDUSTRY.). **Main/Corp** Carpet and Rug Institute. English. an. **LC** HD9937.U5; C37. **DD** 338.4/7/7467973. ***Continues*** *Carpet Industry Review; Industry Review.*

IT
CASA OGGI. Ten times a year. L100000 Italy; L150000 other. Serv Int Abbon Periodici, Via Baldissera 4, 20129 Milan Italy. **Tel** 011 39 2 2043828.

IT/1120-6381
CASA SUI CAMPI, LA. [Casa campi]. (1990)-. Periodical. Italian. mo. L60000. Edagricole, PO Box 2157, 40100 Bologna Italy. **Tel** 011 39 51 492211 Ext. 22, FAX 011 39 51 493660, telex 510336 EDAGRI. **UDC** 631.1.

IT/0394-882X
CASA TESSIL REPORTER. **See** Textiles.

IT
CASAVIVA. (19??)-. Periodical. Italian. mo. L36000 Italy; L79800 other. Arnoldo Mondadori Editore, UFF Cont Abbonamenti, 20090 Segrate MI Italy. **Tel** 011 39 2 75422015, telex 320457 MONDMI I.

US/0740-8285
CASUAL LIVING. (CASUAL LIVING : THE MAGAZINE OF LEISURE & LIFESTYLE PRODUCTS.). (19??)-. Periodical. English. Eleven times a year (10 issues plus annual directory). $20.00 US; $50.00 others; $125.00 (airmail). Bolger, 3301 Como Avenue Southeast, Minneapolis MN 55414. **ED** Tammy Galvin, (phone: 800)999-6311). **LC** HD9773.U4; C37. **DD** 381/.4568418/0973. **Ad Acc.** ctrl circ. ***Continues*** *Casual Living & Summer and Casual Furniture.*
Desc: The magazine is for the casual furnishing industry.

●US/1064-3648
CFX (HIGHLAND PARK, ILL.). (CFX : THE CONTRACT FURNITURE EXCHANGE.). [CFX]. **Added/Corp** DesignNetwork International. **VFOAT** Contract Furniture Exchange. (July 1, 1992)-. Periodical. English. wk. $99.00. Design Network International, Ltd., 417 Central Avenue, Highland Park IL 60035. **Tel** (708)831-0300. **DD** 648.

CN/0715-5689
CITY & COUNTRY HOME. ***Ceased.*** [City ctry. home]. **VAT** Home (Toronto). Vol. 1, No. 1 (Fall 1982)-(Winter 1994). Periodical. English. Six times a year. MacLean Hunter Ltd. Business Publishers / Canada, Box 9100, Station A, Toronto ONT M5W 1A5 Canada. **Tel** (416)946-8420, (800)567-0444. **DD** 747/.05. available on microfilm and microfiche from University Microfilms International (UMI); and Micromedia Limited. ***Continues*** *Home Decor/Canada, 0227-6496.*
Ind/Abst Can. Index.

US/0272-6904
COLORADO HOMES & LIFESTYLES. **VFOAT** Colorado Homes and Lifestyles. Vol. 1, No. 1 (Dec./Jan. 1981)-. Periodical. English. bm. $11.99 (1 year), $16.99 (2 year), $23.00 (3 year) US; $19.99 (1 year), $32.99 (2 year), $47.00 (3 year) Canada; $23.99 (1 year), $39.99 (2 year), $59.00 (3 year) other. Wiesner Publishing, 7009 South Potomac Street, Englewood CO 80112. **Tel** (303)397-7600, (800)945-0973, FAX (303)397-7619. **ED** Laurel Lund. **LC** TX301; .C56. **DD** 640/.5. **Ad Acc. Circ:** 26,000.
Desc: A home and lifestyle magazine that will inform and entertain with features on Colorado's most beautiful homes, as well as how-to information on redecorating and remodeling.

GW
CONTINENTAL HOMEWARES. ***Ceased.*** **See** Glass and Ceramics.

US/1053-5632
CONTRACT DESIGN. [Contract des.]. Vol. 32, Issue 10 (Oct. 1990)-. Periodical. English. mo. $65.00 US; $67.00 Canada & Mexico; $90.00 other. Miller Freeman Inc., 600 Harrison Street, San Francisco CA 94107. **Tel** (415)905-2337, FAX (415)905-2240, telex 278273. **(Subscription address:** JCI, PO Box 1766, Riverton NJ 08077.**) LC** TS840; .C65. **DD** 747/.05. **[CCC].** cum. index. available on microfilm and microfiche from University Microfilms International (UMI). ***Continues*** *Contract (New York, N.Y. : 1960), 0010-7832.*
Ind/Abst Constr. Index (199?-); Hospit. Health Admin. Index (Oct. 1990-Dec. 1992).

FR/0751-6320
COURRIER DU MEUBLE PARIS, LE. [Courr. meuble Paris]. (1958)-. Periodical. French. Forty-seven times a year. 636.63F France; 1030.00F other. Editions du Tigre, 23 rue Joubert, 75009 Paris France. **Tel** 011 33 1 48745250, 011 33 1 48788758, FAX (1)40 16 43 65, telex 283769 F. **UDC** 684.

US/1045-8816
DECORATIVE RUG, THE. [Decor. rug]. **VFOAT** Decorative Rug Magazine. (198?)-. Periodical. English. mo. $65.00 (one year), $120.00 (two years). Oriental Rug Auction Review Inc, PO Box 709, Meredith NH 03253-0709. **Tel** (603)744-9191, FAX (603)744-6933. **DD** 746. **Bk Rev. Ad Acc, Adv Mgr:** Peter Woodman, **Tel** (603)744-9191. **Circ:** 6500. ***Continues*** *Decorative Rug Market.*
Desc: Monthly journal for the area rug professional.

US/1053-4571
DIGEST FOR HOME FURNISHERS. [Dig. home furnish.]. (1974)-. Periodical. English. Four times a year. $3.50. Minnesota 300, 6700 Penn Avenue South, Minneapolis MN 55423. **Tel** (612)861-3403. **ED** Richard English. **DD** 684. **Ad Acc. Circ:** 3,000 (ctrl). ***Continues*** *Home Furnishings Market Digest.*
Desc: Edited for owners, managers, buyers and sales personnel of retail home furnishings establishments. Articles regarding retail stores, management merchandising, display and personnel.

US/0749-4556
DIRECTOIRE. NEW YORK METROPOLITAN ED., INCLUDING SUBURBAN DESIGNER RESOURCES, LE. (LE DIRECTOIRE.). **VFOAT** New York le Directoire. English (English). an. Western Pacific Publishing, 10 East 39th Street, Suite 1000, New York NY 10016. **LC** HD9773.U6; N494. **DD** 684/.0029/47471.

US/0888-0158
DIRECTORY OF HOME FURNISHINGS RETAILERS. [Dir. home furnish. retail.]. **VFOAT** Home Furnishings Retailers; Chain Store Guide. (1987)-. Directory. English. an. $239.00. Chain Store Guide Information Services, 425 Park Avenue, New York NY 10022. **Tel** (212)371-9400, FAX (212)826-6390. **ED** Kevin Edison. **LC** HD9773.U4; D57. **DD** 381/45684/002573. Index available. available on diskette (and telemarketing cards, galley reports); available on magnetic tape; available on labels.
Desc: Profiles on 5,297 furniture and horizontal home furnishings, retail companies operating 13,509 stores and over 56 major wholesale/distributors each with $1,000,000 minimum annual sales. Listings identify sales volume, price lines, distribution centers, trading areas, the names/titles of 14,285 key executives, etc.

UK/0070-6604
DIRECTORY TO THE FURNISHING TRADE. [Dir. furnish. trade]. (1966)-. English. an. £95.00 UK; £105.00 other. Benn Publications Ltd., Sovereign Way, Tonbridge TNQ 1RW England. **Tel** 011 44 732 364422, FAX 011 44 732 361534, telex 0732 95132 BENTON G. **(Subscription address:** Benn Business Information Services, Riverbank House Angel Lane, Tonbridge Kent TN9 1SE England.**) ED** Andrea Vizard. **DD** 338.7684002541. **Circ:** 2,500. ***Continues*** *Cabinet Maker & Retail Furnisher Directory to the Furnishing Trade.*
Desc: Up-to-date information on 14,000 British manufacturers, agents, distributors wholesalers and retailers of bedding, upholstery, carpets, fabrics and accessories. Trademarks and trade names, trade association and business information. Alphabetical and Geographical listing of 7,000 UK retailers.

IT
DOSSIER CASA. (19??)-. Italian. Eleven times a year. L30000. Sedim Srl, Via Pomba 1, 10123 Turin Italy. **Tel** 011 39 11 8124098.

US/0279-4918
DRAPERIES & WINDOW COVERINGS. **VFOAT** Draperies and Window Coverings. (198?)-. Periodical. English. Thirteen times a year. $33.00. L C Clark Publishing Company Inc, PO Box 13079, North Palm Beach FL 33408. **Tel** (407)627-3393, FAX (407)627-3447, telex 350839. **DD** 338.

NE
EIGEN HUIS & INTERIEUR. (19??)-. Dutch. mo (12 issues). Medianet BV, Postbus 6298, 2001 LN Haarlem Netherlands. **Tel** 011 31 23 173311.

CN/0319-616X
F C N, FLOOR COVERING NEWS. **VFOAT** Floor Covering News. V. 1- Jan. 1976-. Periodical. English. ir. $30.18. Maclean Hunter Canada / Montreal, 1001 bvd. de Maisonneuve W., Montreal, Quebec H3A 3E1 Canada. **Tel** 514-845-5141, FAX 514-845-4302, telex 055-60604. **DD** 338.4/7/69890971. available on microfilm and microfiche from University Microfilms International (UMI). ***Supersedes in part*** *H G R, Home Goods Retailing, 0319-0919.*

DK
FAIR FACTS (GLOSTRUP, DENMARK). (FAIR FACTS.). Vol. 1, No. 1 (March 1989)-. Danish (English, French and German). Four times a year. $33.00. Arnold Busck International AS, Kobmagergade 49, PO Box 2180, 1150 Copenhagen K Denmark. **Tel** 011 45 33 122453.

UK/0014-5904
FIRA BULLETIN. [FIRA bull.]. **Added/Corp** Furniture Industry Research Association (Great Britain). **VFOAT** F.I.R.A. Bulletin. **VAT** Furniture Industry Research Association Bulletin. (196?)-. Bulletin. English. qt. £55.00 UK; £68.00 other. Furniture Industry Research Association, Maxwell Road Stevenage, Hertfordshire SG1 2EW England. **Tel** 011 44 438 313433, FAX (0438)727607, telex 827653 FIRA G. **ED** A.D. Spillard. **LC** TS840; .F672. **DD** 338.4/76841/005. Index available. **Ad Acc. Circ:** 1,300 (ctrl). ***Continues*** *FIRA Technical Bulletin.*
Desc: Technical articles relevant to the furniture industry: techniques, processes, materials, components etc.
Ind/Abst AGRICOLA; Art Archaeol. Tech. Abstr.; Fluid Abstr., Civil Eng.; Fluid Abstr. Proc. Eng.; FLUIDEX (1973-1989); For. Prod. Abstr.; For. Abstr.; Pap. Board Abstr.; Saf. Health Work; World Ceram. Abstr.; World Surf. Coat. Abstr.; World Text. Abstr.

US/0163-2930
FIRA NAFM. (NAFM/FIRA BULLETIN.). **Main/Corp** National Association of Furniture Manufacturers. **VFOAT** FIRA/NAFM Magazine. **VAT** Furniture Industry Research Association, National Association of Furniture Manufacturers. Vol. 1 (Dec. 1977)-. Bulletin. English. qt. National Association of Furniture Manufacturers, 8401 Connecticut Avenue NW, Washington DC 20015. **LC** TS840; .N25A. **DD** 684.1/05.
Desc: Contains a summary of FIRA bulletins 57-59. Future issues will also reprint information contained in FIRA bulletins as well as technical articles from U. S. trade and technology.

US/1041-2506
FLOOR COVERING BUSINESS. [Floor cover. bus.]. Vol. 60, No. 2 (Oct. 1988)-. Periodical. English. mo. $60.00 US; $150.00 other. International Thomson Retail Press Inc, 345 Park Avenue South, New York NY 10010. **Tel** (212)887-8400. **LC** HD9937.A1; F5. **DD** 645/.1/068. available on an online database (file 648/Full-Text) from DIALOG. ***Continues*** *Modern Floor Covering Business, 1041-1089.*
Ind/Abst Bus. Index (1988-1989); Gen. BusinessFile (1988-1989); Gen. Period. Index (1988-1989); Mag. Search.

US/1045-5116
FLOOR COVERING NEWS / U.S.A. [Floor cover. news/U. S. A.]. **VFOAT** Floor Covering News, U.S.A. **VAT** Floor Covering News / United States of America. (1989)-. Periodical. English. wk. $25.00 US and Canada; $100.00 other. Altron Communications, 29-10 Thomson Avenue, Long Island NY 11101. **Tel** (718)706-7830. **DD** 338. ***Continues*** *Floor Covering News, 0899-9961.*

●CN/1193-8781
FLOOR COVERING PLUS. See Building and Construction.

US/0015-3761
FLOOR COVERING WEEKLY. (1952)-. Periodical. English. wk. $48.00 US; $60.00 Canada; $104.00 other. Hearst Business Communications, 1790 Broadway, New York NY 10019. **Tel** (212)969-7500, FAX (212)969-7564. **ED** Janet Mogan Daly. **Ad Acc. Circ:** 21,250.
Desc: Includes new products, personnel, business activities, market and convention reports, merchandising techniques, style trends, dealer promotions, financial reports, government actions, interviews, investigative reports, and much, much more.
Ind/Abst Text. Technol. Dig.

●US/1064-7627
FLOOR FOCUS. See Building and Construction.

US/0164-5749
FLOTATION SLEEP INDUSTRY. [Flotat. sleep ind.]. (1972)-. Periodical. English. mo. $17.50 US and possessions; $25.00 Canada; $70.00 other. Advanstar Communications Inc., 131 West First Street, Duluth MN 55802. **Tel** (218)723-9477, (800)346-0085. **ED** Leslie Baer-Frohoff. **DD** 338. **Ad Acc. Circ:** 9,040.
Desc: Directed to waterbed specialty and conventional retail stores that sell flotation sleep systems.

US/0734-1571
FLOTATION SLEEP INDUSTRY. BUYERS GUIDE. **VFOAT** Buyers Guide. Consumer Publication. English. an. $17.50 US, includes magazine subscription; $40.00 Canada, includes magazine subscription. Hester Communications, 1700 East Dryer Road/Suite 250, Santa Ana CA 92705. **Tel** (714)250-8060. **LC** HD9971.5.W383; U544. **DD** 684.1/5.

RM
FORESTA: ROMANIAN WOOD AND FURNITURE REVIEW. See Forestry-Lumber and Wood.

AT/0816-5947
FURNISHING FLOORS. DOMESTIC AND CONTRACT. [Furnish. floors, domest. contract]. (1984)-. Periodical. English. bm (5 issues). 40.00Aus$ Australia; 76.00Aus$ other. Furnishing Publications Pty, 5 Faigh Street, Mulgrave Victoria 3170 Australia. **Tel** 011 61 3 5625844, FAX 011 61 3 5625412. **ED** Keith Dunn. **DD** 747.405. **Bk Rev. Ad Acc, Adv Mgr:** Joanne Royal. **Circ:** 3,500. ***Continues*** *Furnishing Floors, 0314-0156.*

US/0894-8348
FURNITURE & CABINET MANUFACTURING. ***Title Change.*** [Furnit. cabinet manuf.]. **VFOAT** Furniture and Cabinet Manufacturing. Vol. 33, No. 5 (June 1987)-?. Periodical. English. mo. Furniture & Cabinet Manufacturing, PO Box 38281, Germantown TN 38138. **DD** 684. ***Continues*** *Furniture Manufacturing Management, 0192-799X.* ***Continued by*** *Modern Woodworking.*

CN/0828-9891
FURNITURE AND FIXTURE INDUSTRIES. (FURNITURE AND FIXTURE INDUSTRIES / STATISTICS CANADA, INDUSTRY DIVISION, CENSUS OF MANUFACTURES SECTION.). [Furnit. fixt. ind.]. **Added/Corp** Statistics Canada. Census of Manufactures Section. Statistics Canada. Industry Division. Statistics Canada. Annual Survey of Manufactures Section. **VFOAT** Industries du Meuble et des Articles d'Ameublement. (1983)-. English (French). an. 38.00Can$ Canada; $46.00 US; $54.00 other. Statistics Canada, Publications Sales & Services, Main Building Room 1710, Ottawa Ontario K1A 0T6 Canada. **Tel** (613)951-5078, (800)267-6677, FAX (613)951-1584, telex 053-3585. **LC** HD9773.C2; F87. **DD** 338.4/76841/00971. ***Continues*** *Furniture Manufacturers, 0319-8928.*
Desc: Annual census of manufacturers.

UK/0016-3058
FURNITURE HISTORY. (FURNITURE HISTORY : THE JOURNAL OF THE FURNITURE HISTORY SOCIETY.). [Furnit. hist.]. **Added/Corp** Furniture History Society (London, England). Vol. 1 (1965)-. Academic Scholarly Publication. English. Five times a year (1 journal and 4 newsletters). £16.00 UK; £18.00 Europe; £20.00 other. Furniture History, c/o Brian Austen, 1 Mercedes Cottages, St John's Road, Haywards Heath, West Sussex RH16 4EH England. **Tel** 011 44 444 413845. **ED** Sarah Medlam (editor's address: Collection of Furniture & Woodwork, Victoria & Albert Museum, South Kensington,London SW7 2RL, England; 011 44 71 938 8406. **LC** NK2528; .F8. **DD** 749.2205. Index available. cum. index. **Bk Rev. Circ:** 1,350 (ctrl).
Desc: Dedicated to the publication of scholarly articles on the history and development of furniture and furnishings. World-wide in scope though concentrating on Europe and North America.
Ind/Abst Art Archaeol. Tech. Abstr.; Art Index; ARTbibliogr. Mod. (1983-); BHA : Biblio. Hist. Art; Br. Archaeol. Bibliogr.; Br. Humanit. Index.

UK
FURNITURE LITERATURE : A SELECT BIBLIOGRAPHY ON FURNITURE AND ALLIED SUBJECTS. Bibliography. English. £15.00 members, £35.00 nonmembers. Furniture Industry Research Association, Maxwell Road Stevenage, Hertfordshire SG1 2EW England. **Tel** 011 44 438 313433, FAX (0438)727607, telex 827653 FIRA G. **LC** Z5995 .F87 1975 TS880. **DD** 016.6841.

UK
FURNITURE LITERATURE. SUPPLEMENT. **Main/Corp** Furniture Industry Research Association. English. £15.00 members, £35.00 nonmembers. Furniture Industry Research Association, Maxwell Road Stevenage, Hertfordshire SG1 2EW England. **Tel** 011 44 438 313433, FAX (0438)727607, telex 827653 FIRA G. **LC** Z5995; .F87 1975 SUPPL; TS880. **DD** 016.6841.
Desc: Includes all relevant literature added to the stock of FIRA Library.

CN/0849-6692
FURNITURE MAGAZINE. ***Suspended.*** [Furnit. mag.]. **VFOAT** Canada's Furniture Magazine. Vol. 9, No. 2 (May/June 1989)-(May 1992). Periodical. English (summaries and/or abstracts in French). bm. $22.00 Canada; $36.00 other. Victor Publishing Company Ltd, 312 Dolomite Drive, Suite 217, Downsview Ontario M3J 2N2 Canada. **Tel** (905)667-9609. **DD** 381/.456841/00971. ***Continues*** *Canada's Furniture Magazine, 0711-0030.*

UK/0306-0519
FURNITURE MANUFACTURER. See Manufacturing.

US/1047-4676
FURNITURE RETAILER (GREENSBORO, N.C.). ***Title Change.*** (FURNITURE RETAILER : OFFICIAL JOURNAL OF THE NATIONAL HOME FURNISHINGS ASSOCIATION.). [Furnit. retail.]. **Added/Corp** National Home Furnishings Association (U.S.). Vol. 1, No. 1 (Apr. 1989)-Vol. 5, No. 12 (Dec. 1993). Periodical. English. mo. National Home Furnishings Association, 1301 Carolina Street, Greensboro NC 27401. **Tel** (919)378-6065. **LC** TS840; .N28. **DD** 338.4/7684/0097305. ***Continues*** *NHFA's CompetitivEdge, 0745-189X.* ***Continued by*** *Home Furnishings Executive (Greensboro, N.C.), 1073-5585.*

US/0194-360X
FURNITURE/TODAY. [Furnit./today]. **VFOAT** Furniture Today. (197?)-. Periodical. English. wk (49 issues). $89.97 US, Canada & Mexico; $250.00 (surface mail), $550.00 (airmail) other. Cahners Publishing Company, 249 West 17th Street, New York NY 10011. **Tel** (212)645-0067, FAX (212)242-6987. **(Subscription address:** Cahners Publishing Company / North Carolina, Circulation Department, PO Box 2754, High Point NC 27261-2754.**)** **ED** Bill Peterson. **DD** 338. **[CCC]. Ad Acc. Circ:** 20,000. available on microfilm and microfiche from University Microfilms International (UMI).
Desc: Edited for retail executives in the nation's furniture and department stores and for manufacturing executives at all levels of the furniture industry.
Ind/Abst PROMT [Full Txt.]; Trade Ind. Index.

US/0738-890X
FURNITURE WORLD (NEW YORK, N.Y.). (FURNITURE WORLD.). [Furnit. world]. **VFOAT** Furniture World South/West. Vol. 62, No. 4 (April 1983)-. Periodical. English. Thirteen times a year. $16.00 (one year), $36.00 (three years) US; $39.00 Canada; $85.00 other. Towse Publishing Company, 530 5th Avenue, Pelham NY 10803. **Tel** (914)738-6744, FAX (914)738-6820. **LC** TS840; .T5. **DD** 381/456841/00973. **Ad Acc. Circ:** 20,000 (ctrl). ***Continues*** *Furniture World and Furniture Buyer and Decorator, 0016-3104;* ***Absorbed*** *Furniture South, 0016-3074.*

HK
GIFTS & HOME PRODUCTS. VFOAT Gifts and Home Products. (199?)-. Periodical. English. mo. $85.00 (1 year), $130.00 (2 year) surface mail; $170.00 (air mail) Far East and India; $225.00 (air mail) other. Trade Media Ltd / Hong Kong, GPO Box 11411, Hong Kong Hong Kong. **Tel** 011 852 555-4777, FAX 011 852 870-0637. **LC** HD9999.G493; E183. **DD** 380.1/4567/095. ***Continues*** *Asian Sources Gifts & Home Products, 1010-9579.*

US/0273-5695
HEARTH AND HOME (GILFORD, N.H. : 1989). See Energy.

US/0746-7885
HFD. [HFD]. **VFOAT** H.F.D. **VAT** Home Furnishings Daily. (19??)-. Periodical. English. wk. $38.00 (trade), $44.95 (nontrade) US; $100.00 Canada; $200.00 other. Fairchild Publications Inc, 7 West 34th Street, 4th Floor, New York NY 10001. **Tel** (212)630-4230. **(Subscription address:** Home Furnishings Daily, PO Box 3088, Southeastern, PA 19393**)** **LC** HF5001; .R45. **DD** 381/.45683/0973. available on an online database (files 16,570,648/Full-Text) from DIALOG. ***Continues*** *HFD/Retailing Home Furnishings, 0162-9158.*
Ind/Abst Bus. ASAP (1990-) [Full Txt.]; Bus. Index (1985-); F&S Index Plus Text, Int. [Full Txt.] [Select. Cov.]; Gen. BusinessFile (1985-); Infobank; Mark. Advert. Ref. Serv. [Full Txt.]; PROMT [Full Txt.]; Trade Ind. ASAP [Full Txt.]; Trade Ind. Index [Full Txt.].

AU/0018-3776
HOLZ IM HANDWERK. (1958)-. Periodical. German. Twelve times a year. S500.00. Internationaler Holzmarkt, Anton Frank Gasse 17, 1180 Vienna Austria. **Tel** 011 43 222 4706756, FAX 011 43 222 4706723. **ED** Ing H. Kraus. **Ad Acc. Circ:** 5,000.
Desc: Informs furniture makers on up-to-date themes from the whole reach of the furniture-making industry, the outfittings-industry and commerce. Includes new methods, new machinery, tools, and pictured reports of furniture design, plans and illustrations.

IT
HOME. See Textiles.

●US/1073-5585
HOME FURNISHINGS EXECUTIVE (GREENSBORO, N.C.). (HOME FURNISHINGS EXECUTIVE.). [Home furnish. exec.]. Vol. 1, No. 1 (Jan. 1994)-. Periodical. English. mo. $48.00. Pace Communication, 1301 Carolina Street, Greensboro NC 27401. **Tel** (910)378-6065, FAX (910)275-286. **ED** Patricia N. Bowling. **DD** 338. Index available (bound in December issue). **Bk Rev. Ad Acc. Circ:** 14,000 (ctrl). ***Continues*** *Furniture Retailer (Greensboro, N.C.), 1047-4676.*

US/8750-4979
HOME FURNISHINGS REPRESENTATIVES CONTACT. [Home furnish. represent. contact]. **VFOAT** Contact; Home Furnishings Contact. Periodical. English. Eight times a year. International Home Furnishings Representatives Association, 209 South Main Street, Space M-1215, PO Box 670, High Point NC 27261-0670. **Tel** (919)889-3920, FAX (919)883-8245. **ED** Lynn Fick. **DD** 684. **Ad Acc. Circ:** 5,000 (ctrl).
Desc: Provides news of the home furnishings industry and listings of lines available to sales representatives who are members of the association.

UK/0954-1071
HOME FURNISHINGS TONBRIDGE. (HOME FURNISHINGS). [Home furnish. Tonbr.]. (1988)-. English. Six times a year. £30.00 UK; £45.00 other. Benn Publications Ltd., Sovereign Way, Tonbridge TNQ 1RW England. **Tel** 011 44 732 364422, FAX 011 44 732 361534, telex 0732 95132 BENTON G. **DD** 338.476840941.

CN/0848-8312
HOME GOODS RETAILING. [Home goods retail.]. Vol. 35, No. 2 (Feb./March 1989)-. Periodical. English. mo. $30.00 Canada; $55.00 other. Maclean Hunter Canada / Montreal, 1001 bvd. de Maisonneuve W., Montreal, Quebec H3A 3E1 Canada. **Tel** 514-845-5141, FAX 514-845-4302, telex 055-60604. **DD** 338.4/7684/00971. ***Continues*** *H G R, Home Goods Retailing, 0319-0919.*

US/1045-9367
HOME IMPROVEMENT CENTER. ***Ceased.*** **See** Building and Construction.

US/0162-9077
HOME LIGHTING & ACCESSORIES. VAT Home Lighting and Accessories. (1923)-. Periodical. English. mo. $30.00 (one year), $60.00 (three years) US and Mexico; $40.00 other. Doctorow Communications Inc., 1033 Clifton Avenue, PO Box 2147, Clifton NJ 07013. **Tel** (201)779-1600, FAX (201)779-3242. **ED** Peter Wulff. **[CCC]. Ad Acc. Circ:** 10,300 (ctrl).
Desc: Feature stories on lighting stores. Columns on all aspects of retailing.

NE/0168-4663
HOUT- EN MEUBELINDUSTRIE, EXCL. METALEN MEUBELEN / CENTRAAL BUREAU VOOR DE STATISTIEK, HOOFDAFDELING STATOSTOELEM VAN INDUSTRIE EN BOUWNIJVERHEID. **VFOAT** Hout- en Meubelindustrie, Exclusief Metalen Meubelen; Manufacture of Wood, Woodproducts, Including Furniture. 1981-. Dutch (summaries and/or abstracts in English). an. Fl8.00. Centraal Bureau voor de Statistiek, AFD ALG Zaken, Postbus 959, 2270 AZ Voorburg Netherlands. **Tel** 011 31 70 3373800, FAX 011 31 038 7429, telex 32692 CBS NL. **LC** HD9765.N4; N48A. ***Continues*** *Netherlands. Centraal Bureau voor de Statistiek. Hout- en Meubelindustrie, Excl. Metalen Meubelen Produktiestatistieken.*

FI/0786-003X
HUONEKALU- JA MUU TEOLLISUUS. **VFOAT** Mobel- Och Annan Industri. Finnish (Swedish). an. Tilastokeskus, PL 504, Annankatu 44, 00101 Helsinki Finland. **Tel** 358-0-17341, FAX 358-0-17342474, telex 1002111 TILASTO SF. **LC** HD9773.F5; H86.

FR/0750-0181
I.N. REVUE DES TECHNIQUES NOUVELLES EN SERRURERIE MENUISERIE MIROITERIE. See Building and Construction-Carpentry and Woodwork.

US/0192-1657
INSTALLATION & CLEANING SPECIALIST. See Interior Design.

US/0883-7155
INTERNATIONAL DESIGN YEARBOOK, THE. [Int. des. yearb.]. **VFOAT** International Design Year Book. Vol. 1 (1985/86)-. English. an. $100.00 (yearbook 7), $85.00 (yearbooks 2-5), $80.00 (yearbooks 6-7). Abbeville Press Inc, 80 Northfield Avenue, Building 424, Edison NJ 08837. **Tel** (212)888-1969, FAX (212)644-5085, telex 428141. **LC** NK1160; .I57. **DD** 745.4/442.
Desc: A yearbook on the design in furniture, appliances, and domestic products.

IT
INTERNI ANNUAL. See Economics-Industry and Production.

FR/0750-3288
JOURNAL DE LA MAISON, LE. [J. maison]. (1968)-. Periodical. French. Ten times a year. 274.24F France; 365.00F other. Editions Bonnier, 20 rue de Billancourt, BP 406, 92103 Boulogne Cedex France. **Tel** 011 33 1 48250505. **UDC** 64.

CN/0712-9262
JOURNAL / Q.F.M.A. [J. - Q.F.M.A.]. **Main/Corp** Quebec Furniture Manufacturers' Association. **VAT** Journal - Quebec Furniture Manufacturers' Association Journal. Anglais. Vol. 1, No. 1 (Apr. 1981)-. Periodical. English. mo. Free. Journal Q F M A, PO Box 1002 Place Bonaventure, Montreal Quebec H5A 1E9 Canada. **DD** 338.4/76841/0060714. ***Continues in part*** *Quebec Furniture Manufacturers Association. Bulletin, 0382-7135.*

NE/1380-7676
KEUKEN & INTERIEUR MAGAZINE. **VFOAT** Keuken en Interieur Magazine; KIM International. (1987)-. Periodical. Dutch. Six times a year. Fl72.00. Bruil Tijdschriften, Postbus 100, Keppelseweg 44, 7000 AC Doetinchem Netherlands. **Tel** 011 31 834024033. ***Continues*** *Keuken & Afbouw Magazine, 1380-3379.*

US/0892-743X
LDB INTERIOR TEXTILES. See Textiles.

GW
MARKT INTERN MOEBELHANDEL. German. wk. DM489.11 Germany; DM459.84 Europe; DM470.24 other. Markt Intern Verlag GmbH, Grafenberger Allee 30, 4000 Duesseldorf Germany. **Tel** 011 49 2 11 66980.

US/0272-1562
MCCALL'S DECORATING BOOK. VFOAT Mccall's Do-It-Yourself Decorating Book. V. 1- 1980-. English. $1.95 per copy. ABC Leisure Magazine Inc, 825 7th Avenue, New York NY 10019. **Tel** (212)265-8360. **LC** TT387; .M32. **DD** 746/.05.

BE/0772-6287
MEUBELECHO. French (Dutch). bm. 1300F Belgium; 2000F other. Echo du Meuble, Rue Fin Finstraat 4, 1080 Brussels Belgium. **Tel** 02 4240064, FAX 02 424 1215. **ED** Geert Degrande. Index available. **Ad Acc. Circ:** 5,000 (ctrl).
Desc: Information to help retailers in the furniture business raise their sales.

IT
MIA CASA. Alberto Peruzzo Editore Srl, V Le Marelli 165, 20099 Sesto San Giovanni Italy.

GW/0047-7796
MK. MOBEL-KULTUR. [MK, Mobel-Kult.]. **VFOAT** Mobel-Kultur. (1949)-. Periodical. German. mo. DM310.00. Ferdinand Holzmann Verlag, Postfach 601049, D 22210 Hamburg Germany. **Tel** 011 49 40 6320180. **UDC** 684. **Ad Acc. Circ:** 8,500 (ctrl).

IT/0026-7112
MOBILE MILANO, IL. [MobileMilano]. (1957)-. Periodical. Italian. bw. L50000 Italy; L100000 other. Il Mobile, Via R Serra 14, 20148 Milan Italy. **Tel** 011 39 2 3270337. **UDC** 684.

NE/0165-5302
MOBILIA (AMSTERDAM). [Mobilia Amst.]. (1959)-. Trade Publication. Dutch. Eleven times a year. Fl88.21 Netherlands; Fl123.00 other. Uitgeverij Mobilia BV, Postbus 15341, 1001 MH Amsterdam, Netherlands. **Tel** 011 31 20 6206934, 011 31 20 6206954. **ED** Olga Smalhout-Holst. **UDC** 749. **Bk Rev**, (Qty: 5-10/yr). **Ad Acc, Adv Mgr:** Paul Pekelharing. **Pr Rev. Circ:** 6,300.
Desc: A trade magazine for home decorators, institutional decorators, architects, and interior architects.

GW
MODERNE KUECHE, DIE. Added/Corp Arbeitsgemeinschaft die Moderne Kueche. (19??)-. Periodical. German. Six times a year. DM57.30 Germany; DM66.60 other. Die Planung Verlagsgesellschaft GmbH, Holzhofallee 25-31, 6100 Darmstadt Germany. **Tel** 011 49 6151 314104, FAX 011 49 6151 387307. **LC** TX653; .M63. **Circ:** 7,000.

SP/0027-2930
MUEBLE, EL. [Mueble]. **VFOAT** Mueble Actual. (1962)-. Periodical. Spanish. mo. 3300ptas Spain; 10485ptas Europe; 13200ptas other. Editorial Origen, Perez Galdos 36, 08012 Barcelona, Spain. **Tel** 011 34 3 4157374. **UDC** 645.

FR
NOUVEL OFFICIEL DE L'AMEUBLEMENT. (19??)-. French. Ten times a year. 430.00F. Editions G.M. Perrin, 88 Boulevard de Charonne, 75020 Paris France. **Tel** 011 33 1 43489951, telex 216 219 F. **ED** Nell Boix. **Bk Rev. Ad Acc. Circ:** 8,000.

UK
NURSERY TRADER. English. Turrent Group, Circulation Dept, PO Box 64, Rickmansworth Herts WD3 1SN England.

US/8755-609X
OFFICIAL IDENTIFICATION GUIDE TO EARLY AMERICAN FURNITURE, THE. [Off. identif. guide early Am. furnit.]. **VFOAT** Early American Furniture; Identification Furniture; ID Furniture. 1st Ed.-. English. an. $9.95. Random House Inc., 400 Hahn Road, Westminster MD 21157. **Tel** (800)726-0600, (800)733-3000, FAX (800)659-2436. **LC** NK2406; .O35. **DD** 749.214.

US/8755-5522
OFFICIAL IDENTIFICATION GUIDE TO VICTORIAN FURNITURE, THE. [Off. identif. guide vic. furnit.]. **VFOAT** Victorian Furniture; Identification Furniture; ID Furniture. 1st Ed.-. English. an. $9.95. Random House Inc., 400 Hahn Road, Westminster MD 21157. **Tel** (800)726-0600, (800)733-3000, FAX (800)659-2436. **LC** NK2407; .O34. **DD** 749.213/075/0973.

US/0743-8737
OFFICIAL PRICE GUIDE TO WICKER, THE. [Off. price guide wicker]. **VFOAT** Wicker. 1st Ed. (1983)-. English. ir. Random House Inc., 400 Hahn Road, Westminster MD 21157. **Tel** (800)726-0600, (800)733-3000, FAX (800)659-2436. **LC** NK2712.7; .O36. **DD** 749.213/075.

International Assistance and Development

US/1057-5731
PATHFINDER (DALLAS, TEX.).
(PATHFINDER : STRATEGIES FOR INTELLIGENT PRODUCTS & SERVICES FOR THE HOME.). [Pathfinder]. **Added/Corp** Parks Associates. (1990)-. Periodical. English. bm. $395.00 US; $430.00 Canada; $420.00 other. Parks Associates, 5310 Harvest Hill Road, Suite 235, Dallas TX 75230. **Tel** (214)490-1113, FAX (214)490-1133. **ED** Myra Moore. **DD** 645. **Circ:** 200.
Desc: Contains information on intelligent products and services for the home. Covers consumer industries such as home systems, cable television, telecommunications, consumer electronics, and emerging technologies.

AT/1036-3181
PERIOD HOME RENOVATOR BUYER'S GUIDE. (19??)-. English. Four times a year (During the seasons). 31.95Aus$ (one year); 61.90Aus$ (two years); 91.00Aus$ (three years). Publicity Press Pty Ltd, 252 Bay Street, Port Melbourne 3207 Australia. **Tel** 011 61 03 6466788. **ED** Fiona Whittle (phone: 03 6466788). **Bk Rev. Ad Acc. Adv Mgr:** Liz Webster, **Tel** 6466788. ctrl circ. **Continues** Period Home Renovators Guide, 0818-710X.

GW
PORZELLAN + GLAS : P + G / ORGAN DES BUNDESVERBANDES DES GLAS-, PORZELLAN- UND KERAMIK-EINZELHANDELS. *Ceased.* **See** Glass and Ceramics.

IT
PRODURRE PER ABITARE. 1978-. Italian. an. Editrice Segesta, Corso Monforte 15, 20122 Milan Italy.

CN/1180-5897
QUARTERLY SHIPMENTS OF HOUSEHOLD FURNITURE PRODUCTS. [Q. shipm. househ. furnit. prod.]. **Added/Corp** Statistics Canada. Industry Division. **VFOAT** Livraisons Trimestrielles des Produits de Meubles de Maison. Vol. 1, No. 1 (Mar. 1990)-. Periodical. English (French). qt. Statistics Canada, Publications Sales & Services, Main Building Room 1710, Ottawa Ontario K1A 0T6 Canada. **Tel** (613)951-5078, (800)267-6677, FAX (613)951-1584, telex 053-3585. **DD** 338.4/76841/00971021.
Desc: Annual census of manufacturers.

AG
REVISTA - CAMERA DE COMERCIANTES EN ARTEFACTOS PARA EL HOGAR. Main/Corp Camera de Comerciantes en Artefactos Para el Hogar. Spanish. Bartolome Mitre 2162, Buenos Aires Argentina. **LC** HD9773.A73; C35A.

FR/0242-8903
REVUE DE L'AMEUBLEMENT, LA. [Rev. ameubl.]. (1913)-. Periodical. French. mo. 489.72F France; 950.00F other. Editions du Tigre, 23 rue Joubert, 75009 Paris France. **Tel** 011 33 1 48745250, 011 33 1 48788758, FAX (1)40 16 43 65, telex 283769 F. **UDC** 64.

US/0037-7260
SMALL WORLD (GUILFORD). (SMALL WORLD.). [Small world]. (19??)-. Periodical. English. Twelve times a year. $18.00 US; $25.00 Canada and Mexico; $56.00 other. Earnshaw Publications Inc., 475 Fire Island Avenue, Babylon NY 11702. **Tel** (516)661-4637. **ED** Tom Hudson. **Bk Rev. Ad Acc. Circ:** 10,000 (ctrl).
Desc: Nursery furniture and accessories and toys.

IT
SPAZIO CASA. Italian. mo. L52800 Italy; L80000 other. Rusconi Editore Spa, Servicio Abbonements, V Le Sarca 235, 20126 Milan Italy. **Tel** 011 39 2 66192634.

CN/1181-9464
STATISTIQUES SUR L'INDUSTRIE DU MEUBLE. See Building and Construction-Carpentry and Woodwork.

DK
STC NEWS. Main/Corp Scandinavian Trade Center for Home Furnishings. (19??)-. Periodical. Multiple languages (Danish, English and German). Scandinavian Trade Center for Home Furnishings, Bella Centret, DK-2400 NV Copenhagen Denmark. **LC** TS840; .S315. **DD** 338.4/7/68400948.

US/0895-934X
SUN BELT FLOOR COVERING. [Sun belt floor cover.]. **VFOAT** Sunbelt Floor Covering. Vol. 1, No 1 (Sept. 1987)-. Periodical. English. Target Publications, PO Box 810195, Dallas TX 75381. **Tel** (214)484-4474. **DD** 338. **Ad Acc. Circ:** 22,242 (ctrl).
Formed by the union of Southwest Floor Covering, 0279-6902 *and* Southeast Floor Covering, 0894-5047.
Desc: Floor covering information for floor covering retailers.

FR/0039-8780
TABLE ET CADEAU, L'OBJET POUR LA MAISON. VFOAT Table et Cadeau. (1961)-. Periodical. French. Ten times a year. 350.00F, 52.00F (single issue) France; 485F other. Group Cepp Editions Ampere, 25 rue Dagorno, 75012 Paris France. **Tel** 011 33 1 43473020, FAX 011 33 1 43473080.

US/0192-9550
TILE & DECORATIVE SURFACES. [Tile decor. surf.]. **VFOAT** Tile and Decorative Surfaces. **VAT** Tile and Decorative Surfaces. (1???)-. Periodical. English. Twelve times a year. $50.00 US; $55.00 Canada & Mexico; $60.00 others. Tile & Decorative Surfaces, 6300 Variel Avenue, Suite I, Woodland Hills CA 91367. **Tel** (818)704-5555, FAX (818)704-6500, telex 181545 TELE MAG CD. **ED** John Maynard. **DD** 693. Index available.
Bk Rev. Ad Acc. Pr Rev. Circ: 15,295 (ctrl).
Desc: Covers the manufacture, sale, distribution and proper installation of ceramic, marble and granite tiles.
Ind/Abst Constr. Index.

US/1056-2052
UPHOLSTERY DESIGN & MANUFACTURING. See Manufacturing.

US/0896-5935
UPHOLSTERY MANUFACTURING. [Upholstery manuf.]. (198?)-. Periodical. English. mo (except Nov.). Delta Communications Inc, Subsidiary of Cahners Publishing Company, 455 North Cityfront Plaza Drive, Chicago IL 60611. **Tel** (312)222-2000, FAX (312)222-2026. **LC** WMLC 93/4764. **DD** 684. **Continues** Upholstery Manufacturing Management, 0746-5017.

NE
VT WONEN. Medianet BV, Postbus 6298, 2001 LN Haarlem Netherlands. **Tel** 011 31 23 173311.

●US/1058-9821
WEEKEND WOODCRAFTS. (WEEKEND WOODCRAFTS : EASY PROJECTS TO BUILD & FINISH.). [Weekend woodcrafts]. **VFOAT** Weekend Wood Crafts; Woodcrafts. Issue #1 (Feb. 1992)-. Periodical. English. bm. $17.00. EGW Publishing Company, 1041 Shary Circle, Concord CA 94518. **Tel** (510)671-9852, (800)777-1164, FAX (510)671-0692.
(**Subscription address:** Neodata / Colorado, PO Box 2606, Boulder Boulder CO 80322.) **LC** WMLC 91/2932. **DD** 684.

US/1064-3575
ZIGZAG'S MONDAY MORNING QUARTERBACK. (ZIGZAG'S MONDAY MORNING QUARTERBACK : THE NEWSLETTER OF THE CONTRACT FURNITURE INDUSTRY.). **VFOAT** Zig Zag's Monday Morning Quarterback; Monday Morning Quarterback. (Apr. 19, 1990)-. Periodical. English. wk. $199.00 US; $204.00 Canada and Mexico; $229.00 other. Zig Zag Corporation, PO Box 638, Highland Park IL 60035. **Tel** (708)831-0300. **DD** 338. **Circ:** 25,000.

GW
ZUHAUSEWOHNEN. VFOAT Zuhause Wohnen. No. 10 (Oct. 1991)-. Periodical. German. Twelve times a year. DM80.40. Jahreszeiten Verlag GmbH, Postfach 60 12 20, D 22212 Hamburg Germany. **Tel** 011 49 40 27173529. **Continues** Zuhause.

INTERNATIONAL ASSISTANCE AND DEVELOPMENT

US/0503-4922
A.I.D. ECONOMIC DATA BOOK, NEAR EAST AND SOUTH ASIA. See International Assistance and Development-Abstracting, Bibliographies and Statistics.

US/0096-1507
A.I.D. RESEARCH AND DEVELOPMENT ABSTRACTS. See International Assistance and Development-Abstracting, Bibliographies and Statistics.

US
ADVANCES IN DEVELOPMENTAL POLICY STUDIES. (19??)-. English. an. $73.25. JAI Press Inc., 55 Old Post Road, Suite 2, PO Box 1678, Greenwich CT 06836-1678. **Tel** (203)661-7602, FAX (203)661-0792. **ED** Stuart Nagel.

GW
AFRICAN DEVELOPMENT PERSPECTIVES YEARBOOK. Added/Corp Research Group on African Development Perspectives Bremen. Vol. 1 (1989)-. English.
Ind/Abst LABORDOC.

NR/0044-667X
AFRISCOPE. [Afriscope]. V. 1 (June 1971)-. Periodical. English. mo. Pan Afriscope Publications, PMB 1119, Yaba Lagos Nigeria. **LC** HC501; .A63. **DD** 309.1/6/03. available on microfilm and microfiche from University Microfilms International (UMI).
Ind/Abst Am. Hist. Life (1972-1975); MLA Int. Bibl. Books Artic. Mod. Lang. Lit.

CN/0713-0465
AGRICULTURAL AID TO DEVELOPING COUNTRIES. [Agric. aid dev. ctries.]. **Main/Corp** British Columbia. Ministry of Agriculture and Food. **VFOAT** British Columbia Agricultural Aid to Developing Countries and World Disaster Areas. 1980/81-. English. an. British Columbia Ministry of Agriculture & Fisheries, Parliament Building, Room 028, Victoria British Columbia V9A 1M9 Canada. **Tel** (604)387-1978. **LC** HD1417; .B74A. **DD** 338.1/8/091724. **Continues** Agricultural Aid to Developing Countries, 0713-0465.

US
AID RESEARCH AND DEVELOPMENT ABSTRACTS ARDA. (19??)-. English. Four times a year. $10.00 US; $25.00 other. Agency for International Development, 1500 Wilson Boulevard, Suite 1010, Arlington WV 22209.
Desc: Each issue presents abstracts of 100 development related reports, studies and books presenting findings in areas such as agriculture, education, economics and health.

FR
ANNUAL REPORT - CAISSE CENTRALE DE COOPERATION ECONOMIQUE. Main/Corp Caisse Centrale de Cooperation Economique (France). (197?)-. French (English). Caisse Centrale de Cooperation Economique, Cite Du Retigo, 35-37 rue Boissy D'Anglas, 75379 Paris Cedex 08 France. **Tel** 1 42 66 93 66, telex 21632 F. **LC** HC60; .C25b. **DD** 354/.44/00825.

AU
ANNUAL REPORT / THE OPEC FUND. Main/Corp OPEC Fund for International Development. (1979)-. English (French, Spanish and Arabic). an. Free. OPEC Fund for International Development, PO Box 995 Parkring 8, 1011 Vienna Austria. **Tel** 011 43 1 515640, FAX 011 43 1 214 98 27. **LC** HC60; .O58a. **DD** 338.91/09172/4. **Pr Rev. Circ:** 5,000. **Continues** OPEC Special Fund.

US/0252-2942
ANNUAL REPORT - WORLD BANK. (THE WORLD BANK ANNUAL REPORT.). [Annu. rep. - World Bank]. **Main/Corp** International Bank for Reconstruction and Development. **Added/Corp** International Development Association. International Finance Corporation. Multilateral Investment Guarantee Agency. (1982)-. English. an. 4.00Can$. World Bank Publications, 1818 H Street Northwest, Washington DC 20433. **Tel** (202)473-1155, (202)473-1155, FAX (202)522-3224, telex WUI 64145 WORLDBANK. **LC** HG3881; .I5. **DD** 332.1/532/05. **Continues** World Bank. World Bank Annual Report, 0252-2942.
Desc: Information on economic assistance and international banking.

CN/0715-240X
ANNUAL REVIEW / ALBERTA AGENCY FOR INTERNATIONAL DEVELOPMENT. [Annu. rev. - Alta. Agency Int. Dev.]. **Main/Corp** Alberta Agency for International Development. **VFOAT** Fiscal Year, Summaries of Projects by Non-Governmental Organizations by countries; Summaries of Projects by Non-Governmental Organizations and by Countries. **VAT** Alberta Agency for International Development Summary Review. (1982)-. English. an. Alberta Agency for International Development, 14th Floor/CN Tower, 10004-104 Avenue, Edmonton Alberta T5J 0K5 Canada. **LC** HC60; .A459a. **DD** 338.91/7123/005. **Continues** Alberta International Assistance Program. Alberta International Assistance Program Summary Review, 0711-0650.

NE
ASPECTEN VAN INTERNATIONALE SAMENWERKING : MAANDBLAD VAN HET DIRECTORAAT-GENERAAL INTERNATIONALE SAMENWERKING VAN HET MINISTERIE VAN BUITENLANDSE ZAKEN. Periodical. Dutch. ir. Voorlichtingsdienst Ontwikkelingssamenwerking, Plein 17, 2511 CS Den Haag Netherlands. **LC** HC60; .N4578. **Continues** Internationale Samenwerking.

CN/1181-604X
AU COURANT - CANADIAN COUNCIL FOR INTERNATIONAL CO-OPERATION. (AU COURANT.). [Au courant - Can. Counc. Int. Co-op.]. **Added/Corp** Canadian Council for International Co-operation. **VFOAT** Au Courant. **VAT** Au Courant - Conseil Canadien pour la Cooperation Internationale. Vol. 1, No. 1 (July/Aug. 1990)-. Periodical. English (French). mo (10 issues). 27.00Can$. Canadian Council for International Cooperation, 1 Nicholas Street, Suite 300,

Ottawa, Ontario K1N 7B7 Canada. **Tel** (613)241-7007, FAX (613)241-5302, telex 0636700492. **DD** 338.9/17101724.
Ind/Abst Bus. ASAP (1992-) [Full Txt.]; Gen. Period. Index (1985-); Manage. Contents.

AT
AUSTRALIAN CAMBODIAN QUARTERLY. **Added/Corp** Australian Cambodian Support Committee. (198?)-. Periodical. English. qt. Australian Cambodian Support Committee, Trades Hall Box 3, 4 Goulburn Street, Sydney NSW 2000 Australia. ***Continues** Australian Kampuchean Quarterly.*

AT
AUSTRALIA'S OVERSEAS AID PROGRAM. **Added/Corp** Australia. (1987/88)-. Government Publication. English. an. Australian Government Publishing Service, GPO Box 84, Canberra ACT 2601 Australia. **Tel** 011 61 6 2954411, FAX 011 61 6 2954455. ***Continues** Australia's Overseas Development Assistance Program.*

●CN/1199-1844
BAOBAB INTERNATIONAL. [Baobab int.]. **Added/Corp** Canadian Crossroads International. Vol. 1, No. 1 (Spring 1993)-. Periodical. English (summaries and/or abstracts in French). qt. Free. Canadian Crossroads International, 31 Madison Avenue, Toronto Ontario M5R 2S2 Canada. **Tel** (416)967-0801, FAX (416)967-9078. **DD** 361.7. ***Continues** Crossworld., 0225-3992.*

CN/0715-4267
BULLETIN (INTER PARES (ORGANIZATION)). (BULLETIN / INTER PARES.). [Bull. - Inter Pares]. **VAT** Inter Pares Bulletin. Bulletin. English. Free. Inter Pares Bulletin, 205 Pretoria Avenue, Ottawa Ontario K1S 1X1 Canada. **DD** 338.91/71/01724.

CN/0849-1259
C-FAR NEWSLETTER. [C-FAR newsl.]. **Added/Corp** Citizens for Foreign Aid Reform. **VAT** Citizens for Foreign Aid Reform Newsletter (1989). (1989)-. Newsletter. English. mo. $15.00 per year, single copies. (Extra copies: 10 for $2.00; 100 for $10.00; 500 for $40.00). Citizens for Foreign Aid Reform, PO Box 332, Rexdale Ontario M9W 5L3 Canada. **DD** 338.9/171/005. ***Continues** Newsletter (Citizens for Foreign Aid Reform), 0826-4228.*

US
CATALOG OF STATE ASSISTANCE PROGRAMS. (THE RED BOOK : CATALOG OF STATE ASSISTANCE PROGRAMS.). **Added/Corp** Maryland. Office of Planning. **VFOAT** Catalog of State Assistance Programs. (19??)-. Catalog. English. Department of State Planning, State Office Building, Baltimore MD 21201. **Tel** (410)225-4490. **LC** HJ485; .M25a. **DD** 336.1/85. ***Continues** Maryland. Dept. of State Planning. Catalog of State Assistance Programs, 0097-9309.*

FR
CCIC INFORMATION. English (French). Four times a year. 200.00F France; 220.00F other. SEPIC, 9 rue Cler, 75007 Paris France. **Tel** 11 33 1 47051759, FAX 11 33 1 45569092.

●US/1061-6691
CD-DIS (ARLINGTON, VA.). (CD-DIS [COMPUTER FILE]: A.I.D.'S DEVELOPMENT INFORMATION SYSTEM/ U.S. AGENCY FOR INTERNATIONAL DEVELOPMENT, CENTER FOR DEVELOPMENT INFORMATION & EVALUATION.). [CD-DIS]. **Added/Corp** United States. Agency for International Development. Center for Development Information and Evaluation (U.S.). **VAT** Compact Disc Development Information System. No. 1 (Mar. 1992)-. English. qt. $123.00 US; $140.00 other; $53.00 single copies. LTS Corporation, 1500 Wilson Blvd., Suite 1010, Arlington VA 22209-2404. **DD** 362. **Circ:** 250.
Desc: The CD-DIS, a CD-ROM (compact) disk containing the complete A.I.D. Document and Project Databases, and the full text of selected A.I.D. reports and publications, including the Agency's Congressional Presentation and over 100 project evaluations. The databases currently identify over 8,000 projects initiated since 1974 and 70,000 associated project and technical reports.

DK/0106-0805
CDR PROJECT PAPERS. ***Title Change.*** **Added/Corp** Centret for Udviklingsforskning (Denmark) Bangladesh Institute of Development Studies. **VFOAT** C.D.R. project papers. N.A. **VAT** Centre for Development Research project papers. (19??-1992). Monographic series. English. Centre for Development Research, NY Kongensgade 9, DK-1472 Copenhagen K Denmark. **Tel** 45 114 5700, FAX 45 33 140125. **LC** HC59.69; .C37. **DD** 330.9172/4. **Circ:** 400 (ctrl). ***Continued by** CDR Project Paper, 0904-4698.*
Desc: Presents the results of the centre's social science research projects on development issues in Third World countries.
Ind/Abst Rural Dev. Abstr.

●US
CHOICES : THE HUMAN DEVELOPMENT MAGAZINE / UNDP. **Added/Corp** United Nations Development Programme. Division of Public Affairs. Vol. 1, No. 1 (Apr. 1992)-. Periodical. English. qt. $16.00 (one year), $30.00 (two year). United Nations Development Program, Room DC1-1900, One UN Plaza, New York NY 10017. **Tel** (212)906-5328, FAX (212)906-5364. **LC** HC59.8; .W672. ***Continues** World Development (New York, N.Y.).*
Desc: Highlights international development. Topics include health, education, agriculture, politics, women's issues and more.
Ind/Abst Read. Guide Period. Lit.

UK/0141-8513
COMMONWEALTH CURRENTS. **Added/Corp** Commonwealth Secretariat. (April 1978)-. Periodical. English. bm. Free. Commonwealth Secretariat / London, Marlborough House, Pall Mall, London SW1Y 5HX England. **Tel** 44 71 8393411, telex 27678. **ED** Dale Gunthorp. **LC** DA10; .C62. **DD** 909/.09/71241. **Bk Rev. Circ:** 30,000 (ctrl). ***Formed by the union of** Commonwealth Record of Recent Events **and** Commonwealth Diary of Coming Events.*
Desc: Reports on the work of the Commonwealth Secretariat in effecting international cooperation for development among commonwealth member countries.

AT
COMMONWEALTH PAYMENTS TO OR FOR VICTORIA. **Added/Corp** Victoria. Treasury Dept. English. Government Printer / Treasury Department, PO Box 203, North Melbourne Victoria, 3051 Australia. **LC** HJ1753; .V52a. **DD** 336.1/85. ***Continues** Payments to or for Victoria by the Commonwealth.*

US/0273-2181
COMMUNIQUE (OVERSEAS DEVELOPMENT COUNCIL). (COMMUNIQUE.). [Communique]. Periodical. English. mo. Overseas Development Council, 1717 Massachusetts Avenue NW, Washington DC 20036. **Tel** (202)234-8701. ***Supersedes** Communique on Development Issues.*

IT
COMPASS (ROME, ITALY). (COMPASS : NEWSLETTER OF THE SOCIETY FOR INTERNATIONAL DEVELOPMENT.). **Added/Corp** Society for International Development. (19??)-. Newsletter. English. qt. Society of International Development, Palazzo Civilta del Lavoro, 00144 Rome Italy. **Tel** 011 39 6 5917897, FAX 011 39 6 5919836, telex 612339. **LC** HD72; .C65. **DD** 338.9/005.

IT/0393-3059
COOPERAZIONE. **Added/Corp** Italy. Ministero Degli Affari Esteri. Dipartimento per la Cooperazione allo Sviluppo. (19??)-. Periodical. English (Italian and French; translations available in Italian). ir. L75000.00 Italy; L150000.00 other. Editalia Edizioni D Italia, Via di Palla Corda 7, 00186 Rome Italy. **Tel** 011 39 6 6541592, FAX 011 39 6 6869561. **LC** HC59.8; .C66. **DD** 338.91/45/005.

IT/0391-674X
COOPERAZIONE. ***Ceased.*** [Cooperazione]. (1972)-(1994). Periodical. Italian (French and English). Eleven times a year. Editalia Edizioni D Italia, Via di Palla Corda 7, 00186 Rome Italy. **Tel** 011 39 6 6541592, FAX 011 39 6 6869561. **UDC** 334.

INT/0304-3118
COURRIER DE L'UNESCO, LE. (COURRIER DE L'UNESCO.). [Courr. Unesco]. **VFOAT** Courrier - Unesco. (1947)-. Periodical. French. mo. 132.00F Third World Countries, 211.00F others (surface mail);. UNESCO / France, 31 rue Francois Bonvin, 75732 Paris Cedex 15 France. **Tel** 011 33 1 45684564, 011 33 1 45684565, FAX 011 33 1 42733007, telex 204461 Paris. **UDC** 341.16:001. **CODEN** NU053.
Ind/Abst Point Repere (1979-).

CN/0380-1438
CRDI EXPLORE, LE. [CRDI explore]. **Main/Corp** Centre de Recherches pour le Developpement International (Canada). **VAT** Cenrre de Recherches pour le Developpement International Informe. Vol. 4 (Mar. 1975)-. Periodical. French. qt. 16.00Can$. International Development Research Center, PO Box 117, Richmond Hill Ontario L4C 4X9 Canada. **Tel** (905)475-4145, FAX (416)940-3606. **ED** Eileen Conway. ***Separated from** IDRC Reports, 0315-9981.*
Ind/Abst Can. Period. Index (1987-).

CN/0225-3992
CROSSWORLD (LONDON, ONT.). ***Title Change.*** (CROSSWORLD.). [Crossworld]. **Added/Corp** Canadian Crossroads International. Vol. 5, No. 2 (Apr. 1979)-(1992). Periodical. English (French; summaries and/or abstracts in French). qt. Canadian Crossroads International, 31 Madison Avenue, Toronto Ontario M5R 2S2 Canada. **Tel** (416)967-0801, FAX (416)967-9078. **ED** Caroline Connell. **DD** 361.2/6. **Bk Rev. Circ:** 2,500 (ctrl). ***Continues** Canadian Crosswords International. Newsletter, 0225-3984. **Continued by** Baobab International, 1199-1844.*
Desc: A news magazine on national (Canadian) and international development.

GW
DED BRIEF. **Main/Corp** Deutscher Entwicklungsdienst. **VAT** Deutscher Entwidklungsdienst Brief. (1964)-. Periodical. German. qt. Free. Deutscher Entwicklungsdienst, Kladower Damm 299, 14089 Berlin Germany. **Tel** 049 030 36509-0, FAX 049 30 365271, telex 182900 DED. **LC** HC60; .D4649a. **Bk Rev**, (Qty: 6-8). **Acid Free. Circ:** 20,000.
Desc: The work of volunteers and their experiences in personnel development cooperation. Each issue concentrates on a special subject, such as nutrition, water, self-help, women in third world countries and other related topics.

PE
DEUDA EXTERNA LATINOAMERICANA : CUADERNOS. **Added/Corp** Instituto para la Deuda Externa Latinoamericana. **VFOAT** Cuadernos; Revista "Cuadernos"; Cuadernos de la Deuda Externa Latinoamericana. (Jan-Mar 1991)-. Periodical. Spanish. qt. Instituto para la Deuda Externa Latinoamericana, Avenue Del Pinar Number 302, Chacarilla del Estanque San Borja, Lima 41 Peru. **LC** HJ8514.5; .D483.

US/0066-1090
DEVELOPING WORLD : A U F S READINGS. **VAT** Developing World: American Universities Field Staff Readings. Began with V. 1, 1966. English. American Universities Field Staff, 620 Union Drive, Indianapolis IN 46202-2897.

NZ
DEVELOPMENT. **Added/Corp** New Zealand. External Aid Division. Vol. 1 (Apr. 1978)-. Periodical. English. qt. **LC** HC411; .D48. **DD** 338.9/931/0505.
Ind/Abst CSA Neuro. Abstr.; Int. Polit. Sci. Abstr.; J. Ferrocement; Microbiol. Abstr. Sect. C; Middle East Abstr. Index.

XV
DEVELOPMENT & INTERNATIONAL COOPERATION. **Added/Corp** Center za Proucevanje Sodelovanja z Dezelami v Razvoju-- Ljubljana. **VFOAT** Development and International Cooperation. Vol. 7, No. 12 (June 1991)-. Periodical. English. sa. ***Continues** Development & South-South Cooperation, 0352-7670.*
Ind/Abst Middle East J.

US/8756-0488
DEVELOPMENT ANTHROPOLOGY NETWORK. (DEVELOPMENT ANTHROPOLOGY NETWORK : BULLETIN OF THE INSTITUTE FOR DEVELOPMENT ANTHROPOLOGY.). [Dev. anthropol. netw.]. **Added/Corp** Institute for Development Anthropology (Binghamton, N.Y.). **VFOAT** Network. Vol. 1, No. 1 (Dec. 1981)-. Periodical. English. Twice a year (July & Dec.). $15.00. Institute for Development Anthropology, PO Box 2207, Binghamton NY 13902. **Tel** (607)772-6244. **ED** Michael Horowitz, Peter Little, Muneera Salem Murdock and Michael Painter. **DD** 306. Index available. cum. index. **Circ:** 1,900.
Desc: Includes substantive articles on third world development issues by specialists in varied geographic and subject areas.
Ind/Abst Agrofor. Abstr. (1991-); For. Abstr.; Nutr. Abstr. Rev., Ser. A, Hum. Exp.; Rural Dev. Abstr.

US/0146-0617
DEVELOPMENT ASSISTANCE PROGRAMS OF U. S. NON-PROFIT ORGANIZATIONS IN EL SALVADOR. **Main/Corp** Technical Assistance Information Clearing House. **VAT** Development Assistance Programs of United States Non-Profit Organizations in El Salvador. (19??)-. English. 200 Park Avenue South, New York NY 10003. **LC** HC148.A1; T4. **DD** 361.7/025/73.

FR
DEVELOPMENT CO-OPERATION EFFORTS AND POLICIES OF THE MEMBERS OF THE DEVELOPMENT ASSISTANCE COMMITTEE; REVIEW. **Main/Corp** Organisation for Economic Co-Operation and Development. Development Assistance Committee. **VFOAT** Twenty-Five Years of Development Co-Operation; Development Co-Operation in the 1990's; Development Co-Operation. (Dec. 1972)-. English. an. OECD Publications and Information Center, 2 rue Andre-Pascal, 75775 Paris Cedex 16 France. **Tel** 011 33 1 45248167, US:(202)785-6323, FAX 011 33 1 45248500 OR 45248176, telex 620 160 OCDE. **(Subscription address:** US/2001 L Street NW, Suite 700, Washington, DC 20036; telephone: (202)785-6323**) LC** HC60; .O688. **DD** 338.91/172/4. ***Continues** Organisation for Economic Co-Operation and Development. Development Assistance Committee. Development Assistance Efforts and Policies in ... of the Members of the Development Assistance Committee.*
Desc: Includes analysis of the current situation, detailed statistics on financial flows to developing countries, and information on the policies of OECD/DAC members and other donors, including OPEC countries.

US/0192-1312
DEVELOPMENT COMMUNICATION REPORT. See Communication.

FR
DEVELOPMENT COOPERATION. English (French). an. OECD Publications and Information Center, 2 rue Andre-Pascal, 75775 Paris Cedex 16 France. **Tel** 011 33 1 45248167, US:(202)785-6323, FAX 011 33 1 45248500 OR 45248176, telex 620 160 OCDE. **Ad Acc.**
Desc: Contains information on aid and programs for developing countries.

AT
DEVELOPMENT DOSSIER / ACFOA. **Added/Corp** Australian Council for Overseas Aid. Vol. 1 (1980)-. Periodical. English. Four times a year. 32.00Aus$ Australia; 34.00Aus$ other. Australian Council for Overseas Aid, Private Bag 3, Deakin ACT 2600 Australia. **Tel** 011 61 62851816, FAX 011 61 1 62851720, telex 61643. **LC** HC59.69; .D48. **DD** 330.9172/4. **Ad Acc. Circ:** 1,000. ***Continues*** *Development News Digest.*

IT
DEVELOPMENT HOTLINE. English. Twenty-two times a year. $65.00 (institutions), $50.00 (individuals) developed countries; $30.00 (institutions), $15.00 (individuals) developing countries. Society of International Development, Palazzo Civilta del Lavoro, 00144 Rome Italy. **Tel** 011 39 6 5917897, FAX 011 39 6 5919836, telex 612339.

UK/0961-4524
DEVELOPMENT IN PRACTICE. **Added/Corp** Oxfam. Vol. 1, No. 1 (Spring 1991)-. Periodical. English. Three times a year. £30.00 Europe; £40.50 Far East and Australasia; £37.50 other. Oxfam Publications, 274 Banbury Road, Oxford OX2 7DZ England. **Tel** 011 41 865 313196, FAX 011 41 865 313117. **ED** Deborah Eade. Index available (bound in third issue). **Bk Rev**, (Qty: approx. 60 per year). **Ad Acc, Adv Mgr:** T. Milner, **Tel** (0805)313196. **Circ:** 500.
Ind/Abst Rural Dev. Abstr.

UK/0950-6764
DEVELOPMENT POLICY REVIEW. (DEVELOPMENT POLICY REVIEW : THE JOURNAL OF THE OVERSEAS DEVELOPMENT INSTITUTE.). [Dev. policy rev.]. **Added/Corp** Overseas Development Institute (London, England). Vol. 1, No. 1 (May 1983)-. Academic Scholarly Publication. English. Four times a year (Jan., Apr., July, Oct.). $151.00 North America; £97.50 others. Basil Blackwell Publishers Ltd, 108 Cowley Road, Oxford 0X4 1JF England. **Tel** 011 44 865 791100, FAX 011 44 865 791347, telex 837022 OXBOOK G. **(Subscription address:** Blackwell Publishers / UK, Marston Book Services, PO Box 87, Oxford OX2 0DT England.**) ED** Sheila Page. **LC** HC59.7; .D48. **DD** 338.91/09171/4. **CODEN** DPORER. **Bk Rev. Ad Acc.** ***Continues*** *ODI Review, 0078-7116.*
Desc: Provides a forum for new research and for the exchange of views and information between people directly concerned with development in business, government, and other organizations.
Ind/Abst Agrofor. Abstr. (1991-); Cot. Trop. Fibr. Abstr. Bibliogr.; For. Abstr.; Geogr. Abstr. Human Geogr.; Int. Dev. Abstr.; Int. Labour Doc.; Linguist. Lang. Behav. Abstr.; Middle East Abstr. Index; PAIS Int. Print (1991-); Rural Dev. Abstr.; Soc. Plann. Policy Dev. Abstr.; Sociol. Abstr.; World Agric. Econ.

IT/1011-6370
DEVELOPMENT (ROME). (DEVELOPMENT.). [Development]. **Added/Corp** Society for International Development. **VFOAT** Developpement; Desarrollo; International Development Review; Revue du Developpement. (1978)-. Academic Scholarly Publication. English (French and Spanish). qt. £40.00 UK & Europe; $60.00 North America; £40.00 other. Basil Blackwell Publishers Ltd, 108 Cowley Road, Oxford 0X4 1JF England. **Tel** 011 44 865 791100, FAX 011 44 865 791347, telex 837022 OXBOOK G. **(Subscription address:** Blackwell Publishers / UK, Marston Book Services, PO Box 87, Oxford OX2 0DT England.**) ED** Maurice Williams. **LC** HC60; .I546. **DD** 338.91/05. **Circ:** 10,000. available on microfilm and microfiche from University Microfilms International (UMI). Documents available. ***Continues*** *Revista del Desarrollo Internacional, 0095-7062;* ***Absorbed*** *Focus, Technical Cooperation, 0146-8502.*
Desc: Aims beyond the confines of the strictly professional community and intends to catalyse the debate among a broader public.
Ind/Abst ABC POL SCI; AgBiotech News Inf.; Calcium Calcif. Tissue Abstr.; Genet. Abstr.; Hum. Rights Intern. Rep.; Int. Bibliogr. Sociol.; Int. Labour Doc.; LABORDOC; Linguist. Lang. Behav. Abstr.; PAIS Int. Print (1991-); Soc. Plann. Policy Dev. Abstr.; Sociol. Abstr.; U.S. Polit. Sci. Doc. (199?-).

SA
DEVELOPMENT SOUTHERN AFRICA (SANDTON, SOUTH AFRICA). (DEVELOPMENT SOUTHERN AFRICA.). **Added/Corp** Development Bank of Southern Africa. Vol. 1, No. 1 (May 1984)-. Periodical. English. Four times a year. $30.00. Development Bank of Southern Africa, PO Box 1234, Half Way House, 1685 South Africa. **Tel** 011 313 3911, FAX 011 313 3086, 011 313 3072, telex 4-25546 SA. **ED** R. J. W. van der Kooy. **LC** HC900.A1; D48. Index available. cum. index. **Bk Rev. Ad Acc. Circ:** 1,800-2,000 (ctrl).
Desc: Promotes research and discussion as well as publishes papers, reviews, notes, on development issues relating to underdeveloped regions and communities in Southern Africa.
Ind/Abst For. Prod. Abstr. (1991-); For. Abstr.; Int. Bibliogr. Sociol.; Irr. Drain. Abstr.; Maize Abstr.; Nutr. Abstr. Rev., Ser. A, Hum. Exp.; Potato Abstr.; Rev. Agric. Entomol.; Rice Abstr.; Rural Dev. Abstr.; Soils Fert.; World Agric. Econ.

US
DISAM JOURNAL OF INTERNATIONAL SECURITY ASSISTANCE MANAGEMENT, THE. **Added/Corp** Defense Institute of Security Assistance Management (U.S.). **VFOAT** DISAM Journal. **VAT** Defense Institute of Security Assistance Management Journal of International Security Assistance Management. (19??)-. Periodical. English. Four times a year. $12.00. Treasurer of the United States, DISAM, DRP Building 125, 2335 7th Street, Wright-Patterson AFB OH 45433-5000. **Tel** (513)255-2994, (513)255-3669, FAX (513)255-4319. **LC** UA12; .D57. **DD** 355/.032. ***Continues*** *DISAM Newsletter.*
Ind/Abst Air Univ. Libr. Index Mil. Period.

US/1012-8069
DISCUSSION PAPER - IFC. (DISCUSSION PAPER / INTERNATIONAL FINANCE CORPORATION.). [Discuss. paper - IFC]. **Added/Corp** International Finance Corporation. No. 1 (1988)-. Monographic series. English. Price varies per volume. World Bank Publications, 1818 H Street Northwest, Washington DC 20433. **Tel** (202)473-1155, (202)473-1155, FAX (202)522-3224, telex WUI 64145 WORLDBANK.
Ind/Abst Geogr. Abstr. Human Geogr.; Int. Dev. Abstr.

FI/0780-9212
DOCUMENT OF MINISTRY FOR FOREIGN AFFAIRS, FINNISH INTERNATIONAL DEVELOPMENT AGENCY. [Doc. Minist. Foreign Aff., Fin. Int. Dev. Agency]. 1983-. Monographic series. English. ir. Price varies per volume. ***Continues*** *Document of Ministry for Foreign Affairs, Department for International Development Co-Operation, 0359-291X.*

CN
EARTHBEAT. English. Ten times a year. 15.00Can$ Canada; 25.00Can$ US. Saskatchewan Council for International Cooperation, 2138 McIntyre Street, Regina Saskatchewan, S4P 2R7 Canada. **Tel** (306)757-4669, FAX (306)757-3226. **ED** Lori Latta. **Circ:** 1,000.

SZ/0012-9143
ECHO. ***Title Change.*** **See** Education-Teaching and Curriculum.

CL
ESTUDIOS E INFORMES DE LA CEPAL. **Added/Corp** United Nations. Economic Commission for Latin America. (1981)-. Monographic series. Spanish. ir. Price varies per volume. CEPAL / United Nations Economic Commission for Latin America / Chile, Publications Sales Section, CEPAL Casilla 179-D, Santiago Chile. **LC** UNC.
Ind/Abst World Agric. Econ.

UK/0957-8811
EUROPEAN JOURNAL OF DEVELOPMENT RESEARCH, THE. **Added/Corp** European Association of Development Research and Training Institutes. Vol. 1, No. 1 (June 1989)-. Periodical. English. Twice a year. $95.00. Frank Cass & Company Ltd, Newbury House, 890-900 Eastern Avenue, Newbury Park, Ilford, Essex IG2 7HH United Kingdom. **Tel** 011 44 81 599 8866, FAX 011 44 81 599 0984, telex 897719. **ED** Helen O'Neill and David Lehmann. **LC** HC59.69; .E976. Index available. **Bk Rev. Ad Acc, Adv Mgr:** Anne Kidson. **Pr Rev.**
Desc: Covers policy, theory and practice in all aspects of development studies for social scientists, governments and non-government organizations at national regional and international levels.
Ind/Abst Int. Dev. Abstr.; Int. Labour Doc.; LABORDOC.

TG
FAMILLE ET DEVELOPPEMENT. **See** Public Health and Safety.

IT
FAO INVESTMENT CENTRE TECHNICAL PAPER. **VFOAT** F.A.O. Investment Centre Technical Paper; FAO Document Technique du Centre d'Investissement; FAO Documento Tecnico del Centro de Inversiones; Liang Nung Tsu Chih Tou Tzu Chung Hsin Chi Shu Wen Chi. **VAT** Food and Agriculture Organization of the United Nations Investment Centre Technical Paper. Monographic series. English (Arabic, Spanish, Chinese and French). Price varies per volume.

US/0015-1947
FINANCE & DEVELOPMENT. **See** Economics-International Economics.

US/0430-473X
FINANCES & DEVELOPPEMENT. (FINANCES ET DEVELOPPEMENT.). [Financ. dev.]. **Added/Corp** International Monetary Fund. World Bank Group. World Bank. International Bank for Reconstruction and Development. (Mar. 1968)-. Periodical. French. qt. World Bank Publications, 1818 H Street Northwest, Washington DC 20433. **Tel** (202)473-1155, (202)473-1155, FAX (202)522-3224, telex WUI 64145 WORLDBANK. available on microfilm from University Microfilms International (UMI).
Ind/Abst LABORDOC.

NZ/0110-0424
FLOW OF RESOURCES FROM NEW ZEALAND TO DEVELOPING COUNTRIES, THE. **Main/Corp** New Zealand. Ministry of Foreign Affairs. English. New Zealand Ministry of Foreign Affairs, Private Bag, Wellington 1 New Zealand. **Tel** 64 4 728877, FAX 64 4 729596, telex NZ 3441. **LC** HC60; .N4755A. **DD** 338.91/172/40931.

IT/0259-4064
FOOD AID IN FIGURES. **Added/Corp** Food and Agriculture Organization of the United Nations. **VFOAT** Aide Alimentaire en Chiffres. Vol. 1 (1983)-. English (French and Spanish). ir. Food and Agriculture Organization (FAO) / Italy, GIPC166 via Terme di Caracalla, 00100 Rome Italy. **Tel** 011 39 6 522 52925, FAX 011 39 6 522 55784. **(Subscription address:** Unipub, 4611 F Assembly Drive, Lanham MD 20706.**) LC** HV696.F6; F625. **DD** 363.8/83/021.

ET
FOOD AND AGRICULTURE IN AFRICA / UNITED NATIONS ECONOMIC COMMISSION FOR AFRICA, FOOD AND AGRICULTURE ORGANIZATION OF THE UNITED NATIONS. **Added/Corp** Joint ECA/FAO Agriculture Division. United Nations. Economic Commission for Africa. Food and Agriculture Organization of the United Nations. **VFOAT** ECA/FAO Agriculture Division Staff Papers. No. 1 (1991)-. Periodical. English. United Nations Economic Commission for Africa, PO Box 3001, Addis Ababa Ethiopia. **Tel** (212)754-8302, telex 21029 VNECA ET.

JA/0379-5721
FOOD AND NUTRITION BULLETIN. **See** Nutrition and Dietetics.

US/0360-4594
FOOD AND NUTRITION PROGRAMS. **Main/Corp** United States. Food and Nutrition Service. English. an. United States Department of Agriculture Food & Nutrition Service, 3101 Park Center Drive, Room 803, Alexandria VA 22302. **Tel** (703)305-2062, FAX (703)305-2908. **LC** HV696.F6; U617A. **DD** 362.5/0973.

US
FOOD FOR PEACE PROGRAM ANNUAL REPORT. **Added/Corp** United States. President. (19??)-. English. an.

US/0362-4153
FOREIGN ASSISTANCE PROGRAM. **Main/Corp** United States. Agency for International Development. **VFOAT** Foreign Assistance Programs. (1963)-. English. an. US Department of State Agency for International Development, Office of Public Affairs, Washington DC 20523. **LC** HC60; .U472. **DD** 338.91/172/4073. ***Continues*** *United States. Agency for International Development. Report to the Congress on the Foreign Assistance Program.*

●NO
FORUM FOR DEVELOPMENT STUDIES. **Added/Corp** Norsk Utenrikspolitisk Institutt. Norsk Forening for Utviklingsforskning. **VFOAT** FORUM. No. 1 (1992)-. Periodical. English. sa. ***Continues*** *Forum for Utviklingsstudier, 0332-8244.*

FR
GEOGRAPHICAL DISTRIBUTION OF FINANCIAL FLOWS TO DEVELOPING COUNTRIES. **Added/Corp** Organisation for Economic Co-Operation and Development. **VFOAT** Repartition Geographique des Ressources Financieres Mises A la Disposition des Pays en Developpement. (1974)-. English (French). an. $66.00. OECD Publications and Information Center, 2 rue Andre-Pascal, 75775 Paris Cedex 16 France. **Tel** 011 33 1 45248167, US:(202)785-6323, FAX 011 33 1 45248500 OR 45248176, telex 620 160 OCDE. **(Subscription address:** OECD Publications Center, 2001 L Street, Suite 700, Washington DC 20036.**) LC** HC60; .O73d. **DD** 338.91/091724/00212. ***Continues*** *Geographical Distribution of Financial Flows to Less Developed Countries.*
Desc: The unique source of data on the origin, volume, purpose and terms of the aid and other resource flows channelled to over 130 developing countries.

US
GEOGRAPHICAL DISTRIBUTION OF FINANCIAL FLOWS TO LESS DEVELOPED COUNTRIES (COMMITMENTS). **Main/Corp** Organisation for Economic Co-Operation and Development. Development Assistance Committee. **Added/Corp** Organisation for Economic Co-operation and Development. Development Assistance Committee. Repartition Geographique des Ressources Financieres Mises a la Disposition des Pays Moins Developpes (Engagements). **VFOAT** Repartition Geographique des Ressources Financieres Mises a la Disposition des Pays Moins Developpes (Engagements). (19??)-. Multiple languages (English and French). tq. $32.00. OECD Publications and Information Center, 2 rue Andre-Pascal, 75775 Paris Cedex 16 France. **Tel** 011 33 1 45248167, US:(202)785-6323, FAX 011 33 1 45248500 OR 45248176, telex 620 160 OCDE. **(Subscription address:** OECD Publications Center, 2001 L Street, Suite 700, Washington DC 20036.) **LC** HC60; .O73a. **DD** 338.91. available on microfiche; available on magnetic tape.
Desc: Presents data on aid and other resource flows to developing countries and territories from individual, bilateral, and multilateral sources.

GW
GERMAN TRIBUNE. THIRD WORLD REVIEW, THE. **VFOAT** Third World Review. No. 1 (May 11, 1980)-. Periodical. English. Friedrich Reinecke Verlag GmbH, Hartwicusstrasse 3 4, W-2000 Hamburg 76 F R Germany. **Tel** 011 49 40 2285279, FAX 040/2285260, telex 2-14-733.

US/0882-3251
GLOBAL DEVELOPMENT REPORT. [Glob. dev. rep.]. **Added/Corp** World Academy of Development and Cooperation. (1984)-. Newsletter. English. qt. World Academy of Development and Cooperation, 4500 College Avenue, College Park MD 20740. **DD** 338.

US/1056-649X
GRANTS FOR FOREIGN AND INTERNATIONAL PROGRAMS. **See** Philanthropy.

US/0733-6608
GRASSROOTS DEVELOPMENT. (GRASSROOTS DEVELOPMENT : JOURNAL OF THE INTER-AMERICAN FOUNDATION.). [Grassroots dev.]. Vol. 6, No. 1-. Periodical. English (Spanish and Portuguese). qt. Free. Inter-American Foundation / Arlington, 1515 Wilson Boulevard, Arlington VA 22209. **Tel** (703)841-3821, FAX (703)841-0973, telex 247008 IAF. **ED** Kathryn Shaw. **LC** HC121; .J68. **DD** 338.91/7308/0601. Index available. cum. index. **Bk Rev. Circ:** 14,000. available on microfilm from University Microfilms International (UMI). ***Continues** Journal of the Inter-American Foundation, 0733-6640.*
Desc: Reports how the poor in Latin America and the Caribbean organize and work to improve their lives. Its purpose is to explore how development assistance can contribute more effectively to self-help efforts.
Ind/Abst AGRICOLA [Select. Cov.]; Cot. Trop. Fibr. Abstr. Bibliogr.; Dairy Sci. Abstr.; Geogr. Abstr. Human Geogr.; HAPI Hisp. Am. Period. Index; Index Free Period.; Int. Dev. Abstr.; Int. Labour Doc.; J. Ferrocement; J. Plan. Lit.; LABORDOC; PAIS Int. Print (1991-); Rural Dev. Abstr.

US
GUIDE TO SOURCES OF INTERNATIONAL POPULATION ASSISTANCE. SUPPLEMENT. (Oct. 1977)-. English. UN Fund for Population Activities, 220 East 42nd Street/17th Floor, New York NY 10017. **LC** HB848; .G83 SUPPL. **DD** 309.22/3.

AU
GUIDE TO TRAINING OPPORTUNITIES FOR INDUSTRIAL DEVELOPMENT. **Added/Corp** United Nations Industrial Development Organization. **VFOAT** Apercu des Moyens de Formation pour le Developpement Industriel; Repertorio de Oportunidades de Capacitacion para el Desarrollo Industrial. 1st Ed. (1972)-. English (French and Spanish). an. Industrial Human Resources Development Branch, Department of Industrial Operations, UNIDO, POB 300, A-1400 Vienna Austria. **Tel** (0222)211310, FAX (0222)237280, telex 135612. **LC** HD5715.5.D44; G85. **DD** 331.25/92/0251724. **Circ:** 3,000 (ctrl).

FR/0990-915X
HISTOIRES DE DEVELOPPEMENT LYON. (HISTOIRES DE DEVELOPPEMENT.). (1988)-. Periodical. French. qt. 220.00F France; 240.00F other. CIEDEL, 30 Rue Sainte Helene, 69002 Lyon France. **Tel** 011 33 1 78378324. **UDC** 327:338.
Ind/Abst LABORDOC.

US/0740-1116
HUNGER NOTES. [Hunger notes]. **Added/Corp** World Hunger Education Service. Vol. 2, No. 8 (Jan. 1977)-. Periodical. English. mo. $18.00 individuals; $45.00 institutions. World Hunger Education Service, PO Box 29056, Washington DC 20017. **Tel** (202)269-1075. **ED** Patricia L Kutzner. **Bk Rev. Ad Acc. Circ:** 1,000 (ctrl). ***Continues** Hunger Workshop Notes.*
Desc: Focuses on the underlying causes of hunger and poverty in developing countries and in the United States. Seeks inter-disciplinary solutions, with guide to further information.
Ind/Abst AGRICOLA; Hum. Rights Intern. Rep.

CN/0315-9981
I D R C REPORTS. (THE IDRC REPORTS / INTERNATIONAL DEVELOPMENT RESEARCH CENTRE.). [IDRC rep.]. **Added/Corp** International Development Research Centre (Canada). **VFOAT** I.D.R.C. Reports; C.R.D.I. Informe; CRDI Informe. **VAT** International Development Research Centre Reports. Vol. 1, No. 1 (March 1972)-. Academic Scholarly Publication. English (French). qt. 20.00Can$. International Development Research Center, PO Box 117, Richmond Hill Ontario L4C 4X9 Canada. **Tel** (905)475-4145, FAX (416)940-3606. **ED** Eileen Conway. **LC** HC59.69; .I37. **DD** 909/.09724. **CODEN** IDRIDJ. Index available. **Bk Rev. Circ:** 25,000 (ctrl). Documents available from CASDDS, Documents on Demand. ***Continued in part by** International Development Research Centre (Canada). CRDI, 0380-1438.*
Desc: Covers third world development issues and particular scientific research made in third world countries.
Ind/Abst Agric. Eng. Abstr.; Biocont. News Inf. (1991-); Can. Index (?-?); Can. Period. Index (19??-);; Chem. Abstr. (1972-1983); Energy Res. Abstr. (1979-); Environ. Abstr.; Environ. Period. Bibliogr.; Food Sci. Technol. Abstr.; For. Abstr.; J. Ferrocement; Nutr. Abstr. Rev., Ser. B, Live Feeds and Feed.; Nutr. Abstr. Rev., Ser. A, Hum. Exp.; Rev. Agric. Entomol.; Rev. Med. Vet. Entomol.; SEA Abstr.; Trop. Dis. Bull.; Weed Abstr.

SZ
ICARA REPORT / INTERNATIONAL CONFERENCE ON ASSISTANCE TO REFUGEES IN AFRICA. **Added/Corp** International Conference on Assistance to Refugees in Africa. **VFOAT** I.C.A.R.A. Report. No. 1 (Jan. 28, 1981)-. Periodical. English (Arabic, Chinese, French, Spanish and Russian). ir. ICARA Secretariat, External Affairs Division, UNHCR Palais des Nations, CH-1211 Geneva 10 Switzerland. **Tel** 39 84 58, telex 415740 HCR CH. ctrl circ.

US
IN REVIEW / INTER-AMERICAN FOUNDATION. **Main/Corp** Inter-American Foundation. (1991)-. English. Inter-American Foundation, Ballston Metro Center, 901 North Stuart Street, 10th Floor, Arlington VA 22203. **LC** HC121; .I63a. ***Continues** Annual Report.*

US/1047-4803
INTERNATIONAL BULLETIN FOR THE RECONSTRUCTION & DEVELOPMENT OF ARMENIA. [Int. bull. reconstr. dev. Armen.]. **VFOAT** International Bulletin for the Reconstruction and Development of Armenia; International Bulletin. Vol. 1, No. 1 (Dec. 1989)-. Bulletin. English. ir. Zoryan Institute, 19 Day Street, Cambridge MA 02140-1203. **Tel** (617)497-6713. **LC** HV600 1988; .A754. **DD** 363.3/495/09566205.

UK/0262-0855
INTERNATIONAL DEVELOPMENT ABSTRACTS. **See** International Assistance and Development-Abstracting, Bibliographies and Statistics.

US/0738-1425
INTERNATIONAL DEVELOPMENT RESOURCE BOOKS. (INTERNATIONAL DEVELOPMENT RESOURCE BOOKS / PREPARED UNDER THE AUSPICES OF THE CENTER FOR ADVANCED STUDY OF INTERNATIONAL DEVELOPMENT, MICHIGAN STATE UNIVERSITY.). [Int. dev. resour. books]. **Added/Corp** Michigan State University. Center for Advanced Study of International Development. No. 1, (1984)-. Monographic series. English. ir. Price varies per volume. Greenwood Press Inc., PO Box 5007, Westport CT 06881-5007. **Tel** (203)226-3571, FAX (203)222-1502. **ED** Pradip Ghosh. **LC** UNC.

US/1060-815X
INTERNATIONAL DRUG PREVENTION QUARTERLY OF THE NAE PROJECT, THE. (THE INTERNATIONAL DRUG PREVENTION QUARTERLY OF THE NAE PROJECT : A PUBLICATION OF DEVELOPMENT ASSOCIATES, INC., FOR THE U.S. AGENCY FOR INTERNATIONAL DEVELOPMENT (A.I.D.).). [Int. drug prev. q. NAE Proj.]. **VFOAT** International Drug Prevention Quarterly. Vol. 1, no. 1 (Fall 1991)-. Periodical. English. qt. International Drug Prevention Quarterly, Development Associates Inc., 1730 North Lynn Street, Arlington VA 22209. **DD** 363. ***Continues** Asian Drug Prevention Quarterly, 1047-7764.*

II
INTERNATIONAL JOURNAL OF DEVELOPMENT PLANNING LITERATURE. **Added/Corp** Jan Tinbergen Institute of Development Planning. Vol. 1, No. 1 (Jan./March 1986)-. Periodical. English. qt. $50.00. Jan Tinbergen Institute of Development Planning, PO Box 91, Rohtak 124001 India. **(Subscription address:** Prints India, 11 Darya Ganj, New Delhi, 110002 India, (Phone: 011 91 11 3268645)) **LC** HD72; .I58. **DD** 338.9/005.
Ind/Abst Rural Dev. Abstr.

CN/0703-8976
INTERNATIONAL PROJECT BOOKLET. No. 1 (Feb. 1977)-. Monographic series. English. Price varies per volume. Institute of Environmental Studies, Douglas College, PO Box 2503, New Westminster British Columbia V3L 5B2 Canada. **DD** 309.2/232/54.

NE/0927-5770
INZET AMSTERDAM. (INZET.). [Inzet Amst.]. (1992)-. Periodical. Dutch. bm. Secretariaat Veldwerk, Keizersgracht 181, 1016 DR Amsterdam Netherlands. **Tel** 011 31 20 257212. **UDC** 339.96 + 341.232. ***Formed by the union of** CON-Tekst (Wageningen), 0168-8421 **and** Veldwerk (Amsterdam), 0922-2782 KNV-Kortom (Amsterdam), 0922-355X NIO-Kroniek (Amsterdam), 0927-5657 Stand Van Zaken, 0927-5894.*

AT/0816-5165
ISLANDS/AUSTRALIA WORKING PAPERS. [Isl./Aust. work. pap.]. **Added/Corp** Australian National University. National Centre for Development Studies. (1985)-. Monographic series. English. ir. Price varies per volume. **DD** 330.99.
Ind/Abst Geogr. Abstr. Human Geogr.; Int. Dev. Abstr.

GW
JAHRBUCH - DEUTSCHES ROTES KREUZ. **See** Sociology-Social Services and Welfare.

US
JOINT FORUM FOR PHILIPPINE PROGRESS NEWS. English. an. Free. Carnegie Council on Ethics and International Affairs, 170 East 64th Street, New York NY 10021. **Tel** (212)838-4120, FAX (212)752-2432, telex CRIAPAX NEW YORK. **ED** Christopher J Sigur. **Circ:** 3,000 (ctrl).
Desc: Reports on private sector investments of the US and Japan in the Philippines; progress of the Philippine Assistance Program and the efforts of the US and Japan to work cooperatively to promote growth and development in the Philippines.

US/0022-037X
JOURNAL OF DEVELOPING AREAS, THE. [J. dev. areas]. **Added/Corp** Western Illinois University. Vol. 1 (Oct. 1966)-. Periodical. English. Four times a year. $35.00 (institutions), $25.00 (individuals) North America; $35.00 other. Journal of Developing Areas, West Illinois University, 232 Morgan Hall, Macomb IL 61455. **Tel** (309)298-1108, FAX (309)298-2585. **ED** Nicholas C. Pano. **LC** HC59.7; .J65. **DD** 338.91/172/4. **CODEN** JDARB4. Index available (Bound in the 4th issue, published in July). **Bk Rev**, (Qty: 80). **Ad Acc, Adv Mgr:** Joan Pano. **Circ:** 1,400 (ctrl). Documents available from The Genuine Article, UMI Article Clearinghouse, Documents on Demand.
Desc: Main interest focuses on political, economic, social, cultural, historical, and comparative studies of the third world and the development process.
Ind/Abst ABC POL SCI; ABI/INFORM Glob. Ed.; ABI Inform Ondisc (July 1979-); Abstr. Anthropol.; Acad. Search (July 1993-); AgBiotech News Inf.; AGRICOLA [Select. Cov.]; Am. Hist. Life (1966-); Appl. Soc. Sci. Index Abstr.; Arts Humanit. Citation Index [Select. Cov.]; Asia.-Pac. Econ. Lit.; Bus. Index (1985-); Bus. Period. Index; Curr. Contents Soc. Behav. Sci.; Econ. Lit. Index (19??-); Energy Inf. Abstr.; Environ. Abstr.; Expand. Acad. Index (1992-); Gen. BusinessFile (1985-); Gen. Period. Index (1985-); Geogr. Abstr. Human Geogr.; HAPI Hisp. Am. Period. Index; Health Saf. Sci. Abstr.; Hum. Resour. Abstr.; INFO-SOUTH Abstr.; Int. Bibliogr. Sociol.; Int. Dev. Abstr.; Int. Exec.; Int. Labour Doc.; Int. Polit. Sci. Abstr.; J. Econ. Lit.; J. Plan. Lit.; LABORDOC; Leis. Recreat. Tour. Abstr.; Mag. Search; Middle East Abstr. Index; Newsp. Period. Abstr. (1992-); Nutr. Abstr. Rev., Ser. A, Hum. Exp.; PAIS Int. Print (1991-); Pollut. Abstr. Indexes; Res. Alert [Full Cov.]; Rice Abstr.; Rural Dev. Abstr.; Sage Public Adm. Abstr.; Soc. Plann. Policy Dev. Abstr.; Soc. Sci. Cit. Index [Full Cov.]; Sociol. Abstr.; Soils Fert.; Middle East J.; Trade Ind. Index (1981-); U.S. Polit. Sci. Doc. (July 1979-); Wilson Bus. Abstr.; Women Stud. Abstr.; World Agric. Econ.

II
KRISHI SAMEEKSHA. (19??)-. Government Publication. Hindi. mo. Rs100.00. Ministry of Agriculture / Directorate of Economics and Statistics, A 2E 3 Kasturba Gandhi Marg Barracks, New Delhi 110 001 India.

CN/0715-3023
LAND AND HUMAN SETTLEMENTS. (LAND AND HUMAN SETTLEMENTS. OCCASIONAL PAPERS.). [Land hum. settl.]. **Added/Corp** University of British Columbia. Centre for Human Settlements. Vol. 1 (1982)-. Monographic series. English. ir. Price varies per volume. Centre for Human Settlements, University of British Columbia V6T 1W5 Canada. **Tel** (604)228-5254. **ED** H. Peter Oberlander. **DD** 333. **Bk Rev. Circ:** 1,000.
Desc: Impact of urbanization upon developing countries

International Assistance and Development

and their systematic response within national policies and those recommended by UN Centre for Human Settlements.

US
LATIN AMERICA AND THE CARIBBEAN : SELECTED ECONOMIC AND SOCIAL DATA. Added/Corp United States. Agency for International Development. (July 1991)-. English. sa. US International Development Cooperation Agency, Agency for International Development, Washington DC 20523.

BE
LIBERTE (BRUSSELS, BELGIUM). (LIBERTE.). Added/Corp Centre d'Aide au Developpement dans la Liberte et le Progres (Brussels, Belgium). (19??)-. Periodical. French. (every three months). Centre d'Aide au Developpement dans la Liberte et le Progress, rue de Naples 39, 1050 Bruxelles Belgium. ED Charles Petitjean. LC HC60; .L466. DD 330.9172/4. Bk Rev, (Qty: 4). ctrl circ.

CN/0823-1729
LISTE DES PERIODIQUES / CENTRE D'INFORMATION SUR LE DEVELOPPEMENT. [Liste period. - Cent. inf. dev.]. Main/Corp Canadian International Development Agency. Development Information Centre. VFOAT Periodicals List. 1982-. English (French, Spanish, Portuguese, German and Chinese). an. DD 016.33891/05.

MY
MALAYSIAN JOURNAL OF ECONOMIC STUDIES : JOURNAL OF THE MALAYSIAN ECONOMIC ASSOCIATION AND THE FACULTY OF ECONOMICS AND ADMINISTRATION, UNIVERSITY OF MALAYA. Added/Corp Persatuan Ekonomi Malaysia. Universiti Malaya. Fakulti Ekonomi dan Pentadbiran. Vol. 25, No. 1 (June 1988)-. Periodical. English. sa. $20.00. Malaysian Economic Association, PO Box 1127, Jalan Pantai Baru, Kuala Lumpur Malaysia. LC HC445.5.A1; K33. DD 330.9595/005. Continues Kajian Ekonomi Malaysia, 0126-5350.

CN/0226-1995
MARCHE INTERNATIONAL (PIERREFONDS). (MARCHE INTERNATIONAL.). [Marche int.]. V. 1- Dec. 1979. Periodical. English (French). mo. $48.00. Entreprises AMAF, Marche International, 6084 Clark Street, Pierrefonds Quebec H8Z 2G4 Canada. DD 330.9172/4.

RU
MEZHDUNARODNOE EKONOMICHESKOE SOTRUDNICHESTVO. Added/Corp Council for Mutual Economic Assistance. Secretariat. (1991)-. Periodical. Russian. mo. Sovet Ekonomicheskoi Vzaimopomoshchi Sekretariat, Prospekt Kalinina 56, Moscow Russia. LC HC244; .S59582d. CODEN MEKSEW. Continues Ekonomicheskoe Sotrudnichestvo Stran-chlenov SEV.

CN
MINUTES OF PROCEEDINGS AND EVIDENCE OF THE SUB-COMMITTEE ON INTERNATIONAL DEVELOPMENT OF THE STANDING COMMITTEE ON EXTERNAL AFFAIRS AND NATIONAL DEFENSE. Main/Corp Canada. Parliament. House of Commons. Sub-Committee on International Development. VFOAT Proces-Verbaux et Temoignages du Sous-Comite sur le Developpement International du Comite Permanent des Affaires Exterieures et de la Permanent des Affaires Exterieures et de la Defense Nationale. July 22, 1975-. Proceedings. English (French). Parliament Building, Queen's Park, Toronto Ontario M7A 1B6 Canada. LC HC60; .C2876A. DD 338.91/172/4071.

●TC
NATIONAL DEVELOPMENT PROGRAMME / GOVERNMENT OF THE TURKS AND CAICOS ISLANDS, BRITISH WEST INDIES. Main/Corp Turks and Caicos Islands. Added/Corp Turks and Caicos Islands. Financial Secretary's Office. (1988/89 to 1992/93)-. English.

NE
NETHERLANDS DEVELOPMENT COOPERATION POLICY. Main/Corp Netherlands (Kingdom, 1815-). Departement Van Buitenlandse Zaken. Voorlichtingsdienst Ontwikkelingssamenwerking. 1978-. English. Development Cooperation, Information Department of the Ministry of Foreign Affairs, Plein 17, The Hague Netherlands. LC HC60; .N4575B. DD 338.91/492. Continues Netherlands Development Policy.

US/0196-9420
NEWSLETTER - NATIONAL COUNCIL FOR INTERNATIONAL VISITORS. [Newsl. - Natl. Counc. Int. Visit.]. Main/Corp National Council for International Visitors. Vol. 23, No. 4 (Oct. 1979)-. Newsletter. English. qt. Free. National Council for International Visitors, 1420 K St. N.W., Suite 800, Washington DC 20005-2401. Tel (202)842-1414, FAX (202)289-4625. ED Claire P. Burke. LC HV1; .N36a. DD 362.8. Bk Rev. Circ: 8,500. Continues Coserv Across the U.S.A.

UK
NEWSLETTER / PASTORAL DEVELOPMENT NETWORK. Main/Corp Pastoral Development Network (Overseas Development Institute). Newsletter. English.
Ind/Abst Anim. Breed. Abstr.; Dairy Sci. Abstr.; Plant Genet. Resour. Abstr.

TU/1010-9935
ODTU GELISME DERGISI. (ODTU GELISME DERGISI / METU STUDIES IN DEVELOPMENT.). [ODTU gelis. derg.]. Added/Corp Orta Dogu Teknik Universitesi (Ankara, Turkey). Iktisadi ve Idari Bilimler Fakultesi. Orta Dogu Teknik Universitesi (Ankara, Turkey). Idari Ilimler Fakultesi. VFOAT METU Studies in Development; Gelisme Dergisi. (1980)-. Periodical. English (Turkish). Four times a year. $40.00. Middle East Technical University, Faculty of Economic and Administrative Sciences, Ankara 06531 Turkey. Tel 011 91 41 2101000 ext. 2006. LC HD72; .O37. DD 338.9/005. Continues Gelisme Dergisi, 1010-9927.
Ind/Abst Math. Rev.; Zentralbl. Math. Ihre Grenzgeb.

FR
OECD DEVELOPMENT COOPERATION REVIEW. English. an. $32.00. OECD Publications and Information Center, 2 rue Andre-Pascal, 75775 Paris Cedex 16 France. Tel 011 33 1 45248167, US:(202)785-6323, FAX 011 33 1 45248500 OR 45248176, telex 620 160 OCDE. (Subscription address: OECD Publications Center, 2001 L Street, Suite 700, Washington DC 20036.)
Desc: Annual review of member countries foreign aid programs. Includes statistical information.

US
OFDA ANNUAL REPORT / OFFICE OF U.S. FOREIGN DISASTER ASSISTANCE, AGENCY FOR INTERNATIONAL DEVELOPMENT. Main/Corp United States. Agency for International Development. Office of U.S. Foreign Disaster Assistance. VFOAT Annual Report. (1986)-. English. LC HV553; .U45a. DD 363.3/48/05. Continues Annual Report / United States. Agency for International Development. Office of US Foreign Disaster Assistance.

US/0472-3724
ONU CRONICA MENSUAL. See Political Science-International Relations.

UK
OVERSEAS DEVELOPMENT. Added/Corp Great Britain. Overseas Development Administration. Great Britain. Ministry of Overseas Development. No. 1 (Nov. 1966)-. Periodical. English. ir. Free on request. Overseas Development Administration / London, Eland House, Stag Place, London SW1 England. ED David Harris. Bk Rev. Circ: 20,000.
Desc: News and illustrated features on Britain's aid program to the Third World, including articles of scientific interest, book reviews and news about voluntary agencies.

AT/1031-5969
PACIFECON SURVEY OF DEVELOPMENT ACTIVITY IN NEW ZEALAND. (1984)-. English. Seventeen times a year (Every three weeks). 1050.00Aus$. Pacific Economics Pty. Ltd., PO Box A1450, Sydney New South Wales 2000 Australia. Tel 011 61 2 2679882, FAX 011 61 2 2641760.

US
PADF IN ACTION. Main/Corp Pan American Development Foundation. VFOAT Action. English (Spanish). an. Pan American Development Foundation, 1889 F Street Northwest, Washington DC 20006. Tel (202)789-3000, telex 64128. ED Camille Grosdidier.
Desc: Combats poverty in Latin America/Caribbean through vocational training, loans for small businesses, health care, forestry, agricultural projects. Provides emergency disaster relief and reconstruction assistance.

US/0884-9196
PEACE CORPS TIMES. [Peace Corps times]. Began with Vol. 1, No. 1, March 1978. Periodical. English. qt. Peace Corps, Washington DC 20525. Tel (202)606-3010, FAX (202)606-3110. (Subscription address: 1990 K Street NW, Washington, DC 20024) LC HC60.5; .P43. DD 361.2/6/05. Circ: 17,500 (ctrl).
Desc: General and technical material published for Peace Corps volunteers serving worldwide.

FR
PERSPECTIVES. French (English and Spanish). qt. 100.00F. UNESCO / France, 31 rue Francois Bonvin, 75732 Paris Cedex 15 France. Tel 011 33 1 45684564, 011 33 1 45684565, FAX 011 33 1 42733007, telex 204461 Paris.

NE/0926-1524
POVERTY AND DEVELOPMENT. [Poverty dev.]. (1991)-. Monographic series. English. ir. Price varies per volume. The Hague Development Cooperation Information Department, Ministry of Foreign Affairs, PO Box 20061, 2500 EB Den Haag, The Netherlands. ED Laetitia van Drunen and Fred van der Kraaij. UDC 330.5 :339.3.

CE/0588-4241
PROGRESS OF THE COLOMBO PLAN. Main/Corp Colombo Plan Bureau. Periodical. English. Columbo Plan Bureau, 12 Melbourne Avenue, Colombo 4 Sri Lanka Ceylon.

US/0749-3789
PROJECT CONCERN INTERNATIONAL ... ANNUAL REPORT. [Proj. Concern Int. annu. rep.]. Main/Corp Project Concern International (Organization). English. an. Project Concern International, 3550 Afton Road, PO Box 85323, San Diego CA 92138. LC R722; .A24. DD 362.1/0425. Continues Project Concern's Annual Report, 0749-3770.

YU/0351-3564
PUBLIC ENTERPRISE / INTERNATIONAL CENTER FOR PUBLIC ENTERPRISES IN DEVELOPING COUNTRIES. Added/Corp International Center for Public Enterprises in Developing Countries. Vol. 1, No. 1 (1980)-. Periodical. English. qt. $60.00 (one year), $100.00 (two years). Kumarian Press Inc, 630 Oakwood Avenue, Suite 119, West Hartford CT 06110. Tel (203)953-0214, FAX (203)953-8579. ED Edo Pirkmajer, Titova 104, 61109 Ljubljana, PO Box 92, Yugoslavia, (phone) 38-61 182-331. LC HD4420.8; .P82. DD 351.009/2/05. Index available. cum. index. Bk Rev. Pr Rev. ctrl circ.
Desc: Designed to stimulate awareness of the crucial role of the public sector in developing countries.
Ind/Abst Soc. Plann. Policy Dev. Abstr.

SP
PUEBLOS DEL TERCER MUNDO. Periodical. Spanish. ir. 1.500ptas. Fray Juan Gil 5, Madrid-2 Spain. LC D880; .P83. DD 909/.09734.
Ind/Abst Bibliogr. Mission.

CN/0706-6937
RAFIKI. Began publication in Mar. 1978?. Periodical. English. ir. $5.00. Toronto Miles For Millions, PO Box One Million, Station A, Toronto Ontario M5W 1S1. DD 909/.09/724082.

FR
RAPPORT ANNUEL - CAISSE CENTRALE DE COOPERATION ECONOMIQUE. Main/Corp Caisse Centrale de Cooperation Economique (France). French. an. Caisse Centrale de Cooperation Economique, Cite Du Retigo, 35-37 rue Boissy D'Anglas, 75379 Paris Cedex 08 France. Tel 1 42 66 93 66, telex 21632 F. LC HC60; .C24. DD 338.944. Continues Caisse Centrale de Cooperation Economique. Rapport d'Activite.

CI/0352-4728
RAZVOJ. Added/Corp Institut za Zemlje u Razvoju (Zagreb, Croatia) Institut za Razvoj i Meunarodne Odnose (Zagreb, Croatia). VFOAT Development. (1984)-. Periodical. Serbo-Croatian (Roman) (summaries and/or abstracts in English). qt. LC HD72.; R39.
Ind/Abst LABORDOC.

FI/0782-7881
REGERINGENS BERATTELSE TILL RIKSDAGEN OM UTVECKLINGSSAMARBETET. See Economics.

US/0503-485X
REPORT ON THE HEALTH, POPULATION AND NUTRITION ACTIVITIES OF THE AGENCY FOR INTERNATIONAL DEVELOPMENT, DEPARTMENT OF STATE. (REPORT ON THE HEALTH, POPULATION AND NUTRITION ACTIVITIES.). Main/Corp United States. Agency for International Development. (19??)-. English. LC RA390.U5; A65a. DD 353.008/4. NLM W2 A A25R.

SZ
REVUE INTERNATIONALE DE LA CROIX-ROUGE. (Jan. 15, 1919)-. Periodical. French. Six times a year. $20.00. Intl Comm of Red Cross, Com Edoc, 17 Avenue de la Paix, Geneva Switzerland. Tel (022)730 2077 78, FAX (022)733 2057, telex 414226. Index available. Bk Rev, (Qty: 12/yr). Pr Rev. Circ: 8000 (ctrl).

Desc: Red Cross principles, humanitarian law in today's world, ICRC activities and subjects of interest to the Red Cross such as environment.

NE
SAMSAM. Periodical. Dutch. Ten times a year. Free. Samsam, Mauritskade 63, 1092 AD Amsterdam Netherlands. **Tel** 020-5688440. **LC** HC59.7; .S268. **Circ:** 510,000 (ctrl).

US/1014-739X
SDA WORKING PAPER SERIES. (SOCIAL DIMENSIONS OF ADJUSTMENT IN SUB-SAHARAN AFRICA.). [SDA working pap. ser.]. **Added/Corp** International Bank for Reconstruction and Development. (1990)-. Monographic series. English. Price varies per volume. World Bank Publications, 1818 H Street Northwest, Washington DC 20433. **Tel** (202)473-1155, (202)473-1155, FAX (202)522-3224, telex WUI 64145 WORLDBANK. **DD** 960.
Ind/Abst Int. Dev. Abstr.

US/0194-4495
SEEDS (DECATUR, GA.). (SEEDS / A NEW GENERATION.). [Seeds]. **Added/Corp** Oakhurst Baptist Church (Decatur, Ga.). (1977)-. Periodical. English. qt. $40.00 (institutions), $20.00 (individuals) US; $54.00 (institutions), $34.00 (individuals) other. Seeds, PO Box 6170, Waco TX 76706. **Tel** (817)775-7745. **ED** Katherine Cook. **Bk Rev**, (Qty: 15-20). **Ad Acc**, **Adv Mgr:** Susan Hansen, **Tel** (817)755-7745. **Pr Rev. Circ:** 3,000.
Desc: Informs Christian people about the realities of hunger and poverty, and offers a variety of positive ways to respond to the needs of the poor.

SZ
SERIE DE INFORMES TECNICOS DE LA OMS. (19??)-. Spanish (French, Spanish, Arabic, Chinese and Russian). ir (approximately 15 per year). 132.00F. World Health Organization, Distribution and Sales, 20 Avenue Appia, CH-1211 Geneva 27 Switzerland. **Tel** 011 41 22 7912111, FAX 011 41 22 7880401.
Desc: Reports by leading experts commissioned to advise the world's scientific and medical communities on a way to tackle a selected health or medical problem.

SW/0282-6011
SIDA RAPPORT. **Added/Corp** Sweden. Styrelsen for Internationell Utveckling. Vol. 1 (1985)-. Periodical. Swedish. Eight times a year. Kr238.00. Ord and Bild, Box 2390, 403 16 Goteborg Sweden. **Tel** 46 31 7741740, FAX 46 31 7742018. **ED** Johan Oberg. **LC** HC60; .S84. Index available. cum. index. **Bk Rev**. **Ad Acc. Circ:** 2,500 (ctrl). ***Continues*** *Rapport Fran SIDA.*
Desc: Published by the Swedish International Development Authority as an independent journal for analysis and debate on aid and development. It also contains feature writing on the Third World.

SZ
SOINS. French. sm. 130.00F (individuals), 190.00F (institutions). OPISA, 33 Chemin des Hutins, 1247 Anieres Geneva Switzerland. **Tel** 011 41 22 7512347. **Bk Rev.**

NE
STUDIES IN DEVELOPMENT AND PLANNING (ROTTERDAM). V. 1- 1973-. Monographic series. English. ir. Price varies per volume. Rotterdam University Press, Badhuisweg 232, 2597 JS The Hague Netherlands.

US
SUMMARY OF ONGOING RESEARCH AND TECHNICAL ASSISTANCE PROJECTS IN AGRICULTURE. **Main/Corp** United States. Agency for International Development. English. an. US Department of State, 2201 C Street NW, Room 5819, Washington DC 20520. **Tel** (202)647-9859.

US/0273-2599
THIRD WORLD (BOCA RATON). (THIRD WORLD.). [Third world]. V. 1, Article 1-. English. an. Social Issues Resources Series Inc, PO Box 2348, Boca Raton FL 33427. **Tel** (800)327-0513, (407)994-0079. **ED** E C Goldstein. **LC** HC57.7; .T45. **DD** 909/.09724.
Desc: Interdisciplinary resource material consisting of reprinted articles from popular and professional journals, newspapers, magazines and government documents.

UK
THIRD WORLD REPORTS. **VFOAT** Third World Reports. (19??)-. Periodical. English. wk. $220.00. CSI Syndication Service, Wild Acre Plaw Hatch, West Sussex RH19 4JL England. **Tel** 011 44 342 810875, FAX 011 44 342 3905400, telex 305 892822. **ED** Colin Legum. **LC** D880; .C64. **DD** 909/.09724. cum. index. **Bk Rev**. **Ad Acc.** ctrl circ.
Desc: Reports dealing with political, social and economic matters in the Third World and their relations with the West, Soviet Bloc and China.

US/8755-8831
THIRD WORLD RESOURCES. [Third world resour.]. Vol. 1, No. 1 (Spring 1985)-. Periodical. English. qt. $35.00. Third World Resources, 464 19th Street, Oakland CA 94612. **Tel** (510)835-4692, FAX (510)835-3017. **ED** Thomas P. Fenton and Mary J. Heffron. **DD** 330. Index available. **Bk Rev. Ad Acc. Circ:** 2,000 (ctrl). available on microfiche.
Desc: Concise descriptive and evaluative listings of third world-related resources (organizations, books, periodicals, pamphlets, and audiovisuals). Contains unique 4-page pullout of resources on one region.
Ind/Abst Book Rev. Index; Hum. Rights Intern. Rep.

US/0894-1319
THIRD WORLD WEEK. ***Ceased.*** [Third world week]. **VFOAT** Third-World Week. Vol. 1, No. 13, Feb.(1987)-Ceased June (1991). Periodical. English. wk. South North News Service Inc., 4 West Wheelock, Department CS, Hanover NH 03755. **Tel** (603)643-5071, FAX (603)643-9599. **DD** 990. ***Continues*** *Third World Report, 0891-933X.*
Desc: A compilation of news articles from developing countries that the South-North News Service transmit daily to subscribing newspapers.

PK
THIRDWORLD. **VFOAT** Third World. Vol. 12, No. 11 (Nov. 1988)-. Periodical. English. mo. ThirdWorld, 47-A/2 Block G Pechs, Karachi-29 Pakistan. **LC** HC59.7; .T454. **DD** 909/.09724/05. ***Continues*** *Third World International.*

US/0742-1524
TOGETHER (MONROVIA, CALIF.). (TOGETHER : A JOURNAL OF WORLD VISION INTERNATIONAL.). [Together]. **Added/Corp** World Vision International. No. 1 (Oct./Dec. 1983)-. Periodical. English. qt. $15.00. World Vision, 919 West Huntington Drive, Monrovia CA 91016. **Tel** (818)303-8811, FAX (818)303-7651, telex 275335. **LC** WMLC 93/1069.

US/0738-6311
TOUCHING. (TOUCHING / WORLD RELIEF.). [Touching]. Began in 1980?. Periodical. English. qt. World Relief, PO Box WRC, Wheaton IL 60189.

TU
TURKIYE'YE AMERIKAN IKTISAD YARDMLAR. **Added/Corp** Turkey. Maliye Bakanlg. Turkey. Hazine Genel Mudurlugu. Milletleraras Iktisadi Isbirligi Teskilat (Turkey). Genel Sekreterlik. Vol. 42 (1960)-. Turkish. sa. **LC** HC491; .T86. ***Continues*** *Turkiye'de Marshall Plan.*

CN/0705-3452
TWO THIRDS. [Two thirds]. Vol. 1 (1st Quarter 1978)-. Periodical. English (French). Three times a year. 25.00Can$. Two Thirds, Simon Fraser University, Centre for Canadian Studies, Burnaby British Columbia V5A 1S6 Canada. **Tel** 936-8848. **ED** Jorge Gilbert. **LC** HC59.69; .T86. **DD** 909/.09/724. Index available. **Bk Rev. Ad Acc. Circ:** 1,000 (ctrl).
Desc: Covers information on Third World Countries.
Ind/Abst Hum. Rights Intern. Rep.

SZ/0250-9377
UNDRO NEWS. ***Title Change.*** (UNDRO NEWS / OFFICE OF THE UNITED NATIONS DISASTER RELIEF CO-ORDINATOR.). [UNDRO news]. **Added/Corp** Office of the United Nations Disaster Relief Co-ordinator. **VAT** Office of the United Nations Disaster Relief Co-Ordinator News. (Mar. 1980)-(1992). Periodical. English (French). bm. Office of the United Nations Disaster Relief Co-Ordinator, Palais des Nations, CH-1211 Geneva 10 Switzerland. **Tel** 022734 60 11, FAX (22)733-5623, telex 28148 UNDR. **ED** Odette Mengin. **LC** HV553; .U16. **DD** 363.3/4526/05. **Bk Rev. Ad Acc. Circ:** 6,000 (ctrl). ***Continues*** *UNDRO Newsletter.* ***Continued by*** *DHA UNDRO News.*
Desc: Provides factual information on UNDRO activities in disaster relief, preparedness and prevention; current disaster situations; and technical developments in disaster-related fields.
Ind/Abst GeoRef.

SZ
UNVNEWS / THE UNITED NATIONS VOLUNTEERS PROGRAMME. **Main/Corp** United Nations Volunteers. **VFOAT** UNV News; News. No. 45 (June 1988)-. Periodical. English (French and Spanish). qt. United Nations Publishers Geneva, Palais des Nations, C115 Services Ventes, CH-1211 Geneva 10 Switzerland. **Tel** 011 41 227988400, 7985850. **LC** HC60; U468a. **DD** 361.2/6. ***Continues*** *UNV Newsletter.*

CN/1184-0692
USC COUNTRY PROFILE. INDONESIA. (USC COUNTRY PROFILE. INDONESIA / USC CANADA.). [USC ctry. profile, Indones.]. **Main/Corp** Unitarian Service Committee of Canada. **VAT** Unitarian Service Committee of Canada Country Profile. Indonesia. (1990)-. English. USC Canada, 56 Sparks Street, Ottawa, Ontario K1P 5B1 Canada. **DD** 307.1/4/09598. ***Formed by the union of*** *Unitarian Service Committee of Canada. USC Project Summaries. Indonesia., 0834-1001* ***and*** *Indonesia Fact Sheet., 0826-0060.*

CN/1184-0757
USC COUNTRY PROFILE. LESOTHO. (USC COUNTRY PROFILE. LESOTHO / USC CANADA.). [USC ctry. profile, Lesotho]. **Main/Corp** Unitarian Service Committee of Canada. **VAT** Unitarian Service Committee of Canada Country Profile. Lesotho. (1990)-. English. USC Canada, 56 Sparks Street, Ottawa, Ontario K1P 5B1 Canada. **DD** 307.1/4/096885. ***Formed by the union of*** *Unitarian Service Committee of Canada. USC Project Summaries. Lesotho., 0834-0986* ***and*** *Lesotho Fact Sheet., 0826-0079.*

CN/1184-0730
USC COUNTRY PROFILE. MALI. (USC COUNTRY PROFILE. MALI / USC CANADA.). [USC ctry. profile, Mali]. **Main/Corp** Unitarian Service Committee of Canada. **VAT** Unitarian Service Committee of Canada Country Profile. Mali. (1990)-. English. USC Canada, 56 Sparks Street, Ottawa, Ontario K1P 5B1 Canada. **DD** 307.1/4/096623. ***Formed by the union of*** *Unitarian Service Committee of Canada. USC Project Summaries. Mali., 0843-3550.*

CN/1184-0722
USC COUNTRY PROFILE. NEPAL. (USC COUNTRY PROFILE. NEPAL / USC CANADA.). [USC ctry. profile, Nepal]. **Main/Corp** Unitarian Service Committee of Canada. **VAT** Unitarian Service Committee of Canada Country Profile. Nepal. (1990)-. English. USC Canada, 56 Sparks Street, Ottawa, Ontario K1P 5B1 Canada. **DD** 307.1/4/095496. ***Formed by the union of*** *Unitarian Service Committee of Canada. USC Project Summaries. Nepal., 0834-096X* ***and*** *Nepal Fact Sheet., 0826-0052.*

CN/1184-0714
USC COUNTRY PROFILE. SWAZILAND. (USC COUNTRY PROFILE. SWAZILAND / USC CANADA.). [USC ctry. profile, Swazil.]. **Main/Corp** Unitarian Service Committee of Canada. **VAT** Unitarian Service Committee of Canada Country Profile. Swaziland. (1990)-. English. USC Canada, 56 Sparks Street, Ottawa, Ontario K1P 5B1 Canada. **DD** 307.1/4/096887. ***Formed by the union of*** *Unitarian Service Committee of Canada. USC Project Summaries. Swaziland., 0834-0978* ***and*** *Swaziland Fact Sheet., 0826-0036.*

NE/0922-2782
VELDWERK AMSTERDAM. ***Title Change.*** (VELDWERK.). (1988)-(1992). Periodical. Dutch. qt. Secretariaat Veldwerk, Keizersgracht 181, 1016 DR Amsterdam Netherlands. **Tel** 011 31 20 257212. **UDC** 331.5. **Bk Rev. Ad Acc. Pr Rev. Circ:** 1,600 (ctrl). ***Merged with*** *CON-Tekst (Wageningen), 0168-8421* ***and*** *KNV-Kortom (Amsterdam), 0922-355X NIO-Kroniek (Amsterdam), 0927-5657 Stand Van Zaken, 0927-5894* ***to form*** *Inzet (Amsterdam), 0927-5770.*
Desc: A magazine of development workers. Most editions have a theme such as health, disaster, or solidarity; links field experience with policy and awareness in the First World.

CG/0506-8894
VIE DU TIERS-MONDE. **Added/Corp** Congo (Democratic Republic) Institut National d'Etudes Politiques. (1967)-. Periodical. French. mo. Institut National d'Etudes Politiques, Kinshasa Congo. **DD** 967.5.

CN/0382-0327
VOICE OF RADOM. V. 1- Jan. 1957-. Periodical. English (Yiddish). mo. United Radomer Relief for US and Canada, c/o A Glass, 4415 Bathurst Street/Room 201, Downsview Ontario Canada. **LC** DS101; .V59.

US/0275-5599
WASHINGTON REPORT ON THE HEMISPHERE. [Wash. rep. hemisph.]. **Added/Corp** Council on Hemispheric Affairs (U.S.). **VFOAT** C.O.H.A.'s Washington Report on the Hemisphere. Vol. 1, No. 4 (Nov. 11, 1980)-. Periodical. English. bw (24 issues per year). $185.00 individuals; $235.00 religious and media organizations; $298.50 institutions. Council on Hemisphere Affairs, 724 9th Street Northwest, Suite 401, Washington DC 20001. **Tel** (202)393-3322, FAX (202)393-3423. **ED** Larry Birns. Index available. **Bk Rev**, (Qty: 24). **Circ:** 2,000 (ctrl). ***Continues*** *COHA's Washington Report on the Hemisphere.*
Desc: Monitors the full spectrum of U. S.- Latin American as well as U. S.- Canadian-Latin American relations from a Washington perspective. Analysis includes political, economic, trade union, diplomatic, developmental, human rights, and legislative issues through a descriptive and analytical approach.
Ind/Abst Hum. Rights Intern. Rep.

US/1059-4175
WHO'S DOING WHAT?. (WHO'S DOING WHAT? : A DIRECTORY OF US ORGANIZATIONS & INSTITUTIONS EDUCATING ABOUT DEVELOPMENT & OTHER GLOBAL ISSUES.). [Who's doing what?]. **Added/Corp** National Clearinghouse on Development Education. American Forum for Global Education. 2nd Ed. (1991)-. Directory. English. be. $12.00. National Clearinghouse on Development Education, 45 John Street, Suite 908, New York NY 10038. **DD** 327. ***Continues*** *Who's Doing What in Development Education?.*

US/1046-7548
WHY - WORLD HUNGER YEAR. (WHY.). [Why - World Hung. Year]. **Added/Corp** World Hunger Year. **VFOAT** Why Magazine. No. 1 (Spring 1989)-. Periodical. English. Four times a year. $18.00 (1 year), $30.00 (2 year) US; $25.00 (1 year), $50.00 (2 year)

other. World Hunger Year Inc., 505 Eighth Avenue, 21st Floor, New York NY 10018. **Tel** (212)629-8850, FAX (212)465-9274. **LC** HC79.P6; W48. **DD** 363.8/05. available on microfilm and microfiche from University Microfilms International (UMI). ***Continues** Food Monitor, 0162-0045.*
Desc: Covers articles on how to teach about hunger, food collections, displays and programs to raise public awareness of worldwide hunger and poverty.
Ind/Abst Altern. Press Index (199?-); PAIS Int. Print.

US
WORKING PAPER / HELEN KELLOGG INSTITUTE FOR INTERNATIONAL STUDIES, UNIVERSITY OF NOTRE DAME. **Added/Corp** Helen Kellogg Institute for International Studies. (Dec. 1983)-. Monographic series. English (Spanish). ir. $50.00. Helen Kellogg Institute for International Studies, University of Notre Dame, Notre Dame IN 46556. **Tel** (219)239-6580, FAX (219)631-6717. **ED** Caroline Domingo. **LC** UNC.
Ind/Abst Geogr. Abstr. Human Geogr.; Int. Dev. Abstr.

AT/0816-5181
WORKING PAPERS IN TRADE AND DEVELOPMENT. [Work. pap. trade dev.]. **Added/Corp** Australian National University. Research School of Pacific Studies. Dept. of Economics. Australian National University. National Centre for Development Studies. No. 86/1 (1986)-. Monographic series. English. Price varies per volume. Anutech Pty Limited, GPO Box 4, Canberra Act, 2601 Australia. **Tel** 011 61 6 2492479, FAX 011 61 6 2575088. **ED** Peter G. Warr. **LC** HC59.69; .W65. **DD** 330.9172/4. Index available. cum. index. **Acid Free. Circ:** 350 (ctrl).
Ind/Abst Geogr. Abstr. Human Geogr.; Int. Dev. Abstr.; Irr. Drain. Abstr.

IT/1010-9099
WORLD FOOD PROGRAMME JOURNAL. [J. - World Food Programme]. **Added/Corp** World Food Programme. World Food Programme. Public Affairs & Information Branch. **VFOAT** Journal; WFP Journal. No. 1 (Jan./March 1987)-. Periodical. English (French and Spanish). Four times a year. Free on request. World Food Programme, Via Cristoforo Colombo, 426, 00145 Rome, Italy. **Tel** 011 39 6 626675, FAX 52282840, telex 626675 WFP I. **ED** Paul Mitchell. **LC** HV696.F6; W7. Documents available from Documents on Demand. ***Continues** World Food Programme News, 0049-8084.*
Desc: Description of work of World Food Programme (WFP) and various WFP projects that are being undertaken worldwide with help of food aid projects for agricultural development, vulnerable groups, etc.
Ind/Abst Environ. Abstr.; Int. Dev. Abstr.

UK/0161-2352
WORLD GOODWILL NEWSLETTER. [World Goodwill newsl.]. **Main/Corp** World Goodwill. Newsletter. English (French, German, Spanish, Italian, Danish, Dutch, Greek, Modern and Icelandic, Portuguese). qt. World Goodwill Newsletter, 113 University Place/11th Floor, New York NY 10003. **Tel** (212)982-8770. **ED** Jan Nation. **Circ:** 18,000.

US
WORLD NEIGHBORS IN ACTION. English (French and Spanish). Twice a year. $10.00 for 4 issues (two year subscription to a single address or one year subscription to two addresses) sent to addresses in Northern Hemisphere/industrial nations; Free when sent to addresses in the Southern Hemisphere/developing nations. World Neighbours, 4127 Northwest 122nd Street, Oklahoma City OK 73120-8869. **Tel** (800)242-6387, (405)752-9700, FAX (405)752-9393, telex 5106002674.
Desc: A how-to-do-it newsletter treating a different topic of interest to development workers in each issue. Previous topics have included: caring for the elderly, nutrition, composting, and neighborhood development.

US
WORLD VISION. **Added/Corp** World Vision International. Vol. 16 (Jan. 1972)-. Periodical. English. bm. Free on request. World Vision, 919 West Huntington Drive, Monrovia CA 91016. **Tel** (818)303-8811, FAX (818)303-7651, telex 275335. **ED** Terry Madison. Index available. cum. index. **Bk Rev. Circ:** 200,000 (ctrl).
***Formed by the union of** World Vision Magazine **and** World Vision Heartline.*
Desc: Articles on third world issues (refugees, hunger, famine relief, water, rights of women and children, etc.) that inform, educate, promote action among Christians and the church worldwide to meet these dire human needs.

ABSTRACTING, BIBLIOGRAPHIES AND STATISTICS

US/0503-4922
A.I.D. ECONOMIC DATA BOOK, NEAR EAST AND SOUTH ASIA. **Main/Corp** United States. Agency for International Development. Statistics and Reports Division. No. 243, Apr. (1967)-. Periodical. English. ir. National Technical Information Service - NTIS, Room 2027S, 5285 Port Royal Road, Springfield VA 22161. **Tel** (703)487-4630, (703)487-4660, (703)487-4650, FAX (703)321-8547, telex 89-9405. **Circ:** 18,500 (ctrl).
Desc: Bulletin listing a sampling of reports contained in the NTIS database in five categories: manufacturing processing industry, agriculture and food, construction, and management and economic development.

US/0096-1507
A.I.D. RESEARCH AND DEVELOPMENT ABSTRACTS. **Added/Corp** United States. Agency for International Development. Division of Documentation and Information. United States. Agency for International Development. Bureau for Technical Assistance. LTS Corporation. **VFOAT** AID Research and Development Abstracts; ARDA; A.R.D.A. **VAT** Agency for International Development Research and Development Abstracts. Vol. 1, No. 4 (1974)-. Abstracting/Indexing Service. English. Four times a year. $10.00. ARDA / Agency for International Development US, 1500 Wilson Boulevard, Suite 1010, Arlington VA 22209-2404. **Tel** (703)351-4006, FAX (703)351-4039, telex 3730100 LTSCORP. **ED** Roger A. Reynolds. **LC** HD82; .U535a. **DD** 016.33891/172/4073. Index available. **Circ:** 4,000 (ctrl). ***Continues** A.I.D. Reference Center. A.I.D. Research Abstracts, 0094-4599.*
Desc: Provides annotative abstracts of AID-produced reports on a wide variety of topics related to international development - agriculture, health, private enterprise, housing, environment, and economics.

US
AID RESEARCH AND DEVELOPMENT ABSTRACTS ARDA. **See** International Assistance and Development.

UK/0262-0855
INTERNATIONAL DEVELOPMENT ABSTRACTS. [Int. dev. abstr.]. **Added/Corp** University College of Swansea. Centre for Development Studies. Vol. 1 (1982)-. Abstracting/Indexing Service. English. Six times a year. $477.00 The Americas; £320.00 other. Elsevier Geo Abstracts, An Imprint of Elsevier Science Ltd., The Boulevard, Langford Lane, Kidlington, Oxford OX5 1GB United Kingdom. **Tel** 011 44 865 843000, 011 44 865 843699, FAX 011 44 865 843010. **(Subscription address:** Elsevier Science Ltd. Oxford Fulfillment Centre, PO Box 800, Kidlington, Oxford OX5 1DX United Kingdom.**) ED** Marion Amos. **LC** HC59.69; .I57. **DD** 909/09724. **[CCC].** Index available. **Bk Rev. Ad Acc. Circ:** 350. available on microfilm and microfiche from University Microfilms International (UMI). ***Absorbed** International Development Index, 0262-0862.*
Desc: Provides an information service designed to assist researchers, fieldworkers, teachers and students in identifying recent material.

JEWELRY

US/0192-7507
ACCENT. Periodical. English. mo. $26.00 US; $38.00 Canada; $52.00 (surface mail), $120.00 (airmail) other. Sonja Gilbert / Chestnut Street, 60 Chestnut Street, Suite 201, Devon PA 19333. **Tel** (215)293-1112. **ED** Mitch Plotnick. **Ad Acc.** ctrl circ. available on microfilm and microfiche from University Microfilms International (UMI).
Desc: Fashion jewelry and watch forecasts for upcoming season. Editorial includes jewelry packaging and display, and changes and innovations in the fashion jewelry and watch industry.

US/0193-0931
AMERICAN JEWELRY MANUFACTURER. [Am. jewel. manuf.]. **Added/Corp** Manufacturing Jewelers and Silversmiths of America. **VFOAT** AJM. (1956)-. Periodical. English. Twelve times a year. $36.00 US & US Possessions, $46.00 Canada & Central America, $74.00 others (surface mail); $119.00 (airmail). Manufacturing Jewelers & Silversmiths of America, Inc., 100 India Street, Providence RI 02903. **Tel** (401)274-3840, FAX (401)274-0265. **ED** Clark Heidger. **LC** TS720; .A53. **[CCC]. Bk Rev. Ad Acc. Circ:** 4,500.
Desc: Technical aspects of jewelry manufacturing and crafting with news of the manufacturing jewelry industry.
Ind/Abst Eng. Mater. Abstr.

BE/0777-0626
ANTWERP FACETS. [Antwerp Facets]. (1989)-. Trade Publication. English (Dutch). qt. 800.00F. Diamond High Council, Hovenierstraat 22, B 2018 Antwerp Belgium. **Tel** 011 32 3 2220511, FAX 011 32 3 2220724. **ED** M. Van Den Abeelen. **UDC** 621.921.34. **Bk Rev. Ad Acc. Circ:** 7,000. ***Continues** Informatieblad Hoge Raad voor Diamant (Antwerpen), 0770-4305.*
Desc: Information for the international diamond trade and industry.

SP
ANUARIO ESPANOL DE JOYERIA Y RELOJERIA. Spanish. 4.500ptas; Spain; 9.00ptas North America; 6.500ptas other. PUNTEX SA, c/o Mare de Deu del Coll 14, 08023 Barcelona Spain. **Tel** (93)237 71 24, FAX (93)217 57 83, telex 97131 GPMM E. **Bk Rev. Ad Acc. Circ:** 10,000.
Desc: Jewelry business with their representatives. Distributors for foreign firms, trademarks, products by sector and workshops.

GW
ART AUREA. **See** The Arts-Art.

SP
ARTE Y JOYA INTERNATIONAL. Spanish. Five times a year. $160.00 (two year) US. Publicaciones Joyeras SA, Calle via Layetana 71, 08003 Barcelona, Spain. **Tel** 011 34 3 3180710.

HK
ASIAN JEWELRY. English. ir. Bliss Press Ltd, 1/F Flat B, Blue Pool Mansion 1, Blue Pool, Happy Valley Hong Kong. **Tel** 852 5 8910155.

AT/0004-9174
AUSTRALIAN GEMMOLOGIST, THE. [Aust. gemmol.]. **Added/Corp** Gemmological Association of Australia. (19??)-. Academic Scholarly Publication. English. Four times a year (Feb., May, Aug., Nov.). 26.00Aus$ Australia; 31.00Aus$ New Zealand; 34.00Aus$ Malaysia & Singapore & China & Hong Kong & India & Japan & Sri-Lanks & Taiwan; 38.00Aus$ Europe & South America & Africa; 36.00 US & Asia & others. Gemmological Association of Australia, PO Box 35, South Yarra 3141 Victoria Australia. **Tel** 011 61 3 5104154. **ED** W. H. Hicks (phone: (03)826 9003). **CODEN** AGMLB2. Index available (May iss.). cum. index. **Bk Rev. Ad Acc. Circ:** 2,500. Documents available from CASDDS.
Desc: Original articles of gemmological interest, abstracts from journals, book reviews and evaluation of instruments.
Ind/Abst AESIS Q.; Chem. Abstr.; GeoRef.

NE
BEDRIJFSGEGEVENS VOOR DE DETAILHANDEL IN UURWERKEN EN GGOUDEN EN ZILVEREN WWERKEN. **Main/Corp** Economisch Instituut Voor Het Midden- en Kleinbedrijf. (19??)-. Dutch. **LC** HD9747.N4; E25a.

SP/0210-7228
BOLETIN DEL INSTITUTO GEMOLOGICO ESPANOL. (1972)-. Periodical. Spanish. tq. Free upon request. Instituto Gemologico Espanol, Victor Hugo 1-3, Madrid 4 Spain. **Tel** 971-5326267. **UDC** 549.091. **Bk Rev. Ad Acc. Pr Rev. Circ:** 5,000 (ctrl).
Desc: Information on professional gemology.

UK/0266-2558
BRITISH JEWELLER 1983. [Br. jeweller1983]. (1983)-. Periodical. English. mo. £50.00 UK; £85.00 Europe & Eire; £100.00 other. British Jewellery, Wentworth House, Peterborough PE1 1DS England. **Tel** 011 44 7 3363100. **(Subscription address:** EMAP Business Publishing, Ferrari House Audit House, Field End, Ruislip Middlesex HA4 9UY England.**) DD** 338.47739270941. ***Continues** British Jeweller and Watch Buyer, 0007-0866.*

CN/0226-7446
CANADIAN GEMMOLOGIST. (THE CANADIAN GEMMOLOGIST.). [Can. gemmol.]. **Added/Corp** Canadian Gemmological Association. No. 1 (April 1976)-. Periodical. English. Four times a year (Mar., Jun., Sep., Dec.). $25.00. The Canadian Gemmologist, 21 Dundas Square Suite 1209, Toronto Ontario M5B 1B7 Canada. **Tel** (416)603-0451. **ED** Willow Wight. **DD** 736/.2/05. **Bk Rev**, (Qty: 4). **Ad Acc. Pr Rev. Circ:** 1,000 (ctrl). ***Continues** Canadian Gemmological Association. News Letter.*
Desc: Includes articles of interest to gemmologists plus information about relevant happenings such as international meetings and about association activities.

CN/0008-3917
CANADIAN JEWELLER. [Can. jewel.]. (1960)-. Periodical. English. Six times a year. 28.04Can$ Canada; 72.00Can$ others. Style Communications, 1448 Lawrence Avenue East, Suite 302, Toronto Ontario M4A 2V6 Canada. **Tel** (416)755-5199, FAX (416)755-9123. **ED** Simon Hally. **Ad Acc, Adv Mgr:** A. Thomas, **Tel** (416)755-5799. **Circ:** 7,000 (ctrl). available on microfilm from University Microfilms International (UMI). ***Continues** Trader and Canadian Jeweller, 0315-8802.*
Desc: Business and product information for jewelers in Canada, primarily aimed at the retail sector.

US/0363-5767
CASTING & JEWELRY CRAFT. **VAT** Casting and Jewelry Craft. V. 1- May/June 1976-. Periodical.

English. bm. $7.50. Alian Publications Inc, 66 James Drive, Ringwood NJ 07456. **LC** TT212; .C35. **DD** 739.27/05.

BE
DIAMANT. English, Dutch and French. mo (with July and Aug. issue combined). $85.00. Diamant, Consciencestr 7, 2018 Antwerp Belgium. **Tel** 011 32 3 2392250, FAX 011 32 3 2394354.

NE/0920-5578
DIAMANT-, GOUD- EN ZILVERVERWERKENDE INDUSTRIE, SIERADENINDUSTRIE. VFOAT Diamond Cutting and Polishing and Manufacture of Goldsmith's and Silversmith's Ware and Jewellery. 1983-1984-. Dutch (summaries and/or abstracts in English). Fl15.00. Central Bureau voor de Statistiek, Prinses Beatrixlaan 428, Postbus 959, 2270 AZ Voorburg Netherlands. **LC** HD9677.N4; D53. ctrl circ.

UK
DIAMANTAIRE. English. Ten times a year. £150.00 UK; £270.00 others. British Sulphur Corporation Ltd, 31 Mount Pleasant, London WC1X 0AD England. **Tel** 011 44 71 8375600, FAX 011 44 71 8370292, telex 918918 SULFEX G. **ED** Mark Cockle.
Desc: Provides up-to-the-minute reporting on the movement of rough and polished diamonds through the major trade centres.

US/0954-5581
DIAMOND INSIGHT. [Diam. insight]. (1988)-. Periodical. English. Eleven times a year (Except Aug.). $325.00. Tryon Merchantile Incorporated, 790 Madison Avenue, Suite 602, New York NY 10021. **Tel** (212)570-4180, FAX (212)772-1286. **ED** Guido Giovannini-Torelli. **DD** 338. Bound Index published separately, free upon request (In Oct.). cum. index. **Bk Rev**, (Qty: 2-3).
Desc: Vital intelligence on the world's important stones, future price indicators and key behind the trends.

UK/0957-0446
DIAMOND INTERNATIONAL. (19??)-. Periodical. English. bm. $150.00 US and Canada; £75.00 other. CRU Publishing Limited, 31 Mount Pleasant, London WC1X 0AD England. **Tel** 011 44 71 8375600, FAX 011 44 71 8370292, telex 918918 SULFEX G. **ED** Mark Cockle. **Bk Rev**, (Qty: 1 or 2). **Ad Acc, Adv Mgr:** Diane Taylor.
Desc: Reporting on all aspects of the world diamond industry, from mining through to cutting and polishing and on to retail.

SA
DIAMOND NEWS & S.A. JEWELLER. Periodical. English. mo. R18.00 South Africa; R78.00 (airmail), R25.00 (surface mail) US. Jewelery Council of South Africa, PO Box 9478, Johannesburg 2000 South Africa. **Tel** 011 296441, telex 488353. **ED** Jon Beverley. **LC** HD9677.S6; D52. **DD** 338.2/7/820968. Index available. cum. index. **Bk Rev. Ad Acc. Circ:** 1,500. ***Continues*** *Diamond News and South African Jeweller.*
Desc: Articles of interest to the jewelry, diamond industry, matchmaking and gold.

US/0199-9753
DIAMOND REGISTRY BULLETIN, THE. [Diamond regist. bull.]. **Main/Corp** Diamond Registry. (19??)-. Bulletin. English. Eleven times a year (monthly with June/July issue combined). $97.00 (one year), $250.00 (three years) US and Canada; $125.00 (one year), $350.00 (three years) other. Diamond Registry, 580 5th Avenue, Suite 806, New York NY 10036. **Tel** (212)575-0444, FAX (212)575-0722. **ED** Joseph Schlussel. **Bk Rev. Ad Acc.**
Desc: Important independent insiders information on present and future outlook of the diamond market and a special confidential wholesale price list for all shapes and sizes.

II
DIAMOND WORLD. (1973)-. English. bm. $30.00. Gem & Jewelry Information Center India, A 95 Journal House Janta Colony, Jaipur 302 004 India. **Tel** 011 91 141 44398, FAX 011 91 141 42973, telex 365-2410 KALA IN. **ED** Vidya Vinod Kala. **Bk Rev**, (Qty: 3-4). **Ad Acc, Adv Mgr:** Alok Kala. **Circ:** 12,000 (ctrl).
Desc: Covers diamonds trade and industry. Includes market report, technical notes, new equipment, news and notes, etc.

IS
DIAMOND WORLD REVIEW. Added/Corp World Federation of Diamond Bourses. Vol. 1 (May 1975)-. Periodical. English (Japanese). bm. $78.00. International Diamond Publishing Limited, PO Box 3237, 52131 Ramat Gan Israel. **Tel** 011 972 3 7512165, telex 35770 COIN IL (ATTN: INTERNATIONAL DIAMOND PUBLIC). **ED** Michael Segal. **LC** TS753; .D48. **DD** 338.4/7/7362305. **Bk Rev. Ad Acc. Circ:** 5,000 (ctrl).
Desc: Information from diamond mining, manufacturing and consumer countries for diamantaires, precious stone dealers and jewelers.

SP
DUPLEX BIJOUX. (19??)-. Spanish. Three times a year. $48.00. Duplex Creativos SA, Via Layetana 71 Principal 1, 08003 Barcelona Spain. **Tel** 011 34 3 318 3738, FAX 011 34 3 318 5984. **ED** Pedro Perez. **Circ:** 6,000.

SZ/0014-2603
EUROPA STAR. See Jewelry-Clocks and Watches.

GW
EUROPEAN JEWELER SPECIAL. English (German). sa. Free Free. Ruhle-Diebener-Verlag GmbH + Co KG, Wolfschlugener Strasse 5 A, Post Box 70 04 50, W-7000 Stuttgart 70 Germany. **Tel** 0711/76 50 75-76, FAX 0711/76 65 51. **ED** Senta Bergmaier and Peter Henselder. **LC** HD9747.E85; E94. **DD** 338.4/76882/09405. **Ad Acc. Circ:** 12,300.
Desc: Market oriented export magazine for jewelry, watches clocks, stones and pearls. Branch news from all over the world, highlighting fairs and exhibitions; providing statistics.

US/0273-5423
EXECUTIVE JEWELER. *Ceased.* Vol. 1 (Dec./Jan. 1981)-?. Periodical. English. bm. Executive Jeweler, 222 Wisconsin Avenue, Lake Forest IL 60045. **Tel** (312)295-2483.

US
FASHION INTERNATIONAL. See Clothing Industry and Fashion.

US/1056-2559
FASHION JEWELRY PLUS. [Fash. jewel. plus]. (198?)-. Periodical. English. bm. $20.00 (one year), $30.00 (two year). Larkin Group, 100 Wells Avenue, Newton MA 02159. **Tel** (617)964-5100, 800-869-7469, FAX (617)964-2752. **DD** 391.

●US/1044-3622
GEM & LAPIDARY QUARTERLY. Added/Corp Gem & Lapidary Wholesalers. **VFOAT** Gem and Lapidary Quarterly. (1992)-. Periodical. English. qt. Free. Gem & Lapidary Wholesalers, Inc., PO Box 98, Flora MS 39071.

BE
GEMSTONE PRICE REPORT. English. Eleven times a year. $290.00. Intero SA, 124 Dieweg, 1180 Brussels Belgium. **Tel** 011 32 2 3748239. **Bk Rev.** ctrl circ. ***Continues*** *Precioustone Newsletter.*
Desc: Gemological publication price lists for diamonds and colored stones.

US/0882-6269
GEMSTONE REGISTRY BULLETIN, THE. VFOAT Gemstone Registry; Bulletin. (19??)-. Bulletin. English. Eleven times a year. $97.00 (Comes with Diamond Registry Bulletin). The Diamond Registry, 580 5th Avenue, Suite 806, New York NY 10036. **Tel** (212)575-0444. **ED** Joseph Schlussel. **Bk Rev. Ad Acc.**
Desc: Important independent insiders information on present and future outlook of the gem market. Other information on the jewelry market, special confidential price list for all gem stones.

GW/0017-1573
GOLD + SILBER, UHREN + SCHMUCK. Periodical. German (summaries and/or abstracts in English and French). mo. DM180.00. Konradin Verlagsgruppe, Postfach 100252, Ernst Mey Str 8, W-7022 Leinfelden Echterdingen 1 Germany. **Tel** (0711)75940, telex 7 255 421. **ED** Konrad Kohlhammer. **[CCC]. Bk Rev. Ad Acc. Circ:** 10,208 (ctrl).
Desc: A trade oriented business publication for clocks and watches, gold and silverware, precious stones and costume jewelry.

UK/0953-0355
GOLDSMITHS REVIEW. [Goldsmiths rev.]. (1987)-. English. an. £5.00. Worshipful Company of Goldsmiths, Goldsmith Hall, Foster Lane, London EC2 6BN England. **Tel** 011 44 71 606-7010, FAX 011 44 71 606-1511. **ED** David Beasley. **Pr Rev. Circ:** 6,000 (ctrl). ***Continues*** *Review - Worshipful Company of Goldsmiths* ***and*** *Goldsmiths Gazette, 0951-5887.*
Desc: Includes articles on silver and jewellery, antique and modern.

GW
GZ : GOLDSCHMIEDE UND UHRMACHER ZEITUNG. VFOAT Goldschmiede und Uhrmacher Zeitung. (April 1987)-. Periodical. German (summaries and/or abstracts in English). mo. DM195.96. Ruehle Diebener Verlag, Postfach 700450, West 7000 Stuttgard 70 Germay. **Tel** 011 49 711 976670. **ED** S. Bergmaier and P. Henselder. **Bk Rev. Ad Acc. Circ:** 15,100 (ctrl). ***Continues*** *Goldschmiede Zeitung, European Jeweler, Uhrmacher Zeitschrift.*
Desc: Information on jewelry, goldsmithing, silverware, gemstones, and a presentation of artists and technical novelties.

HK
HONG KONG JEWELLERY. English (Chinese). qt. $38.00 South East Asia; $50.00 other. Ridgeville Ltd., 21 Man Lok Street, Unit 7, 3 Floor, Hunghom Kowloon Hong Kong. **Tel** 011 852 3 344311.

JA/0385-5090
HOSEKI GAKKAI SHI. [Hoseki Gakkaishi]. **Added/Corp** Hoseki Gakkai Nihon. **VFOAT** Journal of the Gemmological Society of Japan. Vol. 1, No. 1 (1974/10)-. Academic Scholarly Publication. Japanese (summaries and/or abstracts in English). qt. Hoseki Gakkai Nihon, (Gemmological Society of Japan), 9-2-601 Tsukiji 2 chome, Chuoku Tokyoto 104 Japan. **(Subscription address:** Japan Publications Trading Company, Ltd., PO Box 5030, Tokyo International, Tokyo 100-31 Japan.**) LC** TS750; .H54. **CODEN** HOGAD6. Documents available from CASDDS.
Ind/Abst Chem. Abstr.; GeoRef.

UK
INTERNATIONAL JEWELLERY & GIFTS. VFOAT International Jewellery and Gifts. Began with Vol. 3, No. 1, (Jan. 1960)-. English. mo. Heywood & Company Ltd, Carlton House, 66 69 G Queen Street, London WC2 England. **LC** WMLC L 83/2152. ***Continues*** *International Jewellers' Digest.*

US/1070-0242
JEWELERS' CIRCULAR-KEYSTONE (1990). (JEWELERS' CIRCULAR-KEYSTONE : JCK.). [Jewel. circ.-keyst.]. **VFOAT** JCK; Jewelers' Circular Keystone. Vol. 161, No. 1 (Jan. 1990)-. Periodical. English. Thirteen times a year. $95.00. Chilton Company, 201 King of Prussia Road, Radnor PA 19089. **Tel** (610)964-4122, (800)695-1214, FAX (610)964-4978, telex 6851035 CHILTON UW. **LC** TS720; .C46. **DD** 671. ***Continues*** *Chilton's Jewelers' Circular/Keystone, 0194-2905.*
Ind/Abst Bus. ASAP (1990-) [Full Txt.]; Bus. Index (1985-); Gen. BusinessFile (1985-); Gen. Period. Index (1985-); Mag. Search.

CN/0822-4897
JEWELLERY AUCTION / CHARLTON AUCTIONS. [Jewel. auction - Charlton Auctions]. **Main/Corp** Charlton Auctions. Periodical. English. $2.50 per no. Charlton Press, 2010 Yonge Street, Toronto Ontario M4S 1Z9. **Tel** (416)488-4653. **DD** 739.27/029/471354. ***Absorbed in part*** *Unreserved Public Mini Auction, 0822-7713.*

CN/0822-4935
JEWELLERY AUCTION - TOREX. (JEWELLERY AUCTION.). [Jewel. auction - Torex]. **Main/Corp** Torex. Periodical. English. ir. $3.50 per no. Charlton Press, 2010 Yonge Street, Toronto Ontario M4S 1Z9. **Tel** (416)488-4653. **DD** 739.27/029/4713541.

●UK/0961-4559
JEWELLERY INTERNATIONAL. [Jewel. int.]. (1991)-. Periodical. English. Six times a year. £35.00 UK; $70.00 others. British Sulphur Corporation Ltd, 31 Mount Pleasant, London WC1X 0AD England. **Tel** 011 44 71 8375600, FAX 011 44 71 8370292, telex 918918 SULFEX G. **ED** Mark Cockle. **DD** 739.27. **Bk Rev**, (Qty: 1 or 2). **Ad Acc, Adv Mgr:** Diane Taylor. **Circ:** 10,000.
Desc: The magazine to report jewellery news from a truly global perspective.

CN/0710-4820
JEWELLERY JOURNAL. (JEWELLERY JOURNAL / CANADIAN JEWELLERS ASSOCIATION.). [Jewel. j.]. Vol. 4, No. 1 (Spring 1981)-. Periodical. English. qt. Free to members. Canadian Jewellers Association, 100 Front Street West, Toronto Ontario M5J 1E3. **DD** 338.4/773927/0971. ***Continues*** *Canadian Jewellery News, 0710-4812.*

HK
JEWELLERY NEWS ASIA. English. mo. $77.00. Jewellery News Asia / Guardian, Sixth Floor #601-#603, 32 Oi Kwan Road, Wanchai Hong Kong. **Tel** 011 852 832 2011, FAX 011 852 832 9208. **ED** Peter Brindisi. **Ad Acc, Adv Mgr:** Karen Chow.

HK
JEWELLERY REVIEW. (19??)-. English. Six times a year. $65.00 US & Asia; $90.00 others. Brilliant - Art Publishing Ltd, GPO Box 985, 1101 Tung Wai Commercial Building, 111 Gloucester Road, Wanchai Hong Kong. **Tel** 011 852 511 6077, FAX 011 852 507 5855. **ED** Raymond Lam & Anthony Moore. Index available (Advertisers index & product index). **Ad Acc.**
Desc: Keep you ahead of non-reading competitors because it an excellent, exclusive source of trade information on the jewellery industry in Hong Kong. Features the activities of leading jewellery manufacturers and pays special attention to developments in China.

UK/0268-2087
JEWELLERY STUDIES. [Jewel. stud.]. (1985)-. Periodical. English. an.
Ind/Abst BHA : Biblio. Hist. Art.

CN/0383-9818
JEWELLERY WORLD. **Added/Corp** Canadian Jewellers Association. Vol. 1 (June/July 1976)-. Periodical. English. bm. 100.00Can$. Jewellery World, 20 Eglinton Avenue West, Suite 1203, Toronto Ontario M4R 1K8 Canada. **Tel** (416)480-1450, FAX (416)480-2342. **ED** Jonathon Reid (editor's address: 1108-20 Eglinton Avenue West, Toronto Ontario M4R 1K8 Canada). **DD** 338.4/7/739270971. **Ad Acc**, **Adv Mgr:** G Staines. **Circ:** 6,700 (ctrl).

SP
JEWELRY DUPLEX. (19??)-. Spanish. sa. $150.00. Duplex Creativos SA, Via Layetana 71 Principal 1, 08003 Barcelona Spain. **Tel** 011 34 3 318 3738, FAX 011 34 3 318 5984. **Circ:** 15,000.

US/1075-8143
JEWELRY MARKETING REVIEW. **See** Business-Marketing.

II/0022-1244
JOURNAL OF GEM INDUSTRY. **VFOAT** Jarnala Apha Jaima Indastri. (1963)-. Periodical. English (Hindi). mo. $25.00 (one year), $70.00 (three year). Gem & Jewelry Information Center India, A 95 Journal House Janta Colony, Jaipur 302 004 India. **Tel** 011 91 141 44398, FAX 011 91 141 42973, telex 365-2410 KALA IN. **ED** Alok Kala. **LC** TS720; .J75. **DD** 338.4/7/739270954. **Bk Rev**, (Qty: 3-4). **Ad Acc**. **Circ:** 14,000 (ctrl).

SZ/0368-4172
JOURNAL SUISSE DE HORLOGERIE ET DE BIJOUTERIE. (1921)-. Periodical. French. Six times a year (Feb., Apr., June, Aug., Oct. Dec.). 80.00F. Editions Scriptar SA, Chemin du Creux de Corsy 25, 1093 Conv Lausanne Switzerland. **Tel** 011 41 21 791065, FAX 011 41 21 174084. **UDC** 681.11.

SP/0213-120X
JOYAS & JOYEROS. **VFOAT** Joyas y Joyeros; Magazine de Joyas & Joyeros. (1985)-. Periodical. Spanish. Eight times a year. $66.38 Spain; $99.19 other. Tecnipublicaciones SA, C Fernando VI No 27, 28004 Madrid Spain. **Tel** 011 34 1 3197889, FAX 341 4101069, telex 43905 YEBE E. **UDC** 671.1. Index available. **Bk Rev**. **Ad Acc**. **Circ:** 8,000.

CN/0823-1346
JW PLUS. [JW plus]. **VAT** Jewellery World Plus. Vol. 1, No. 1 (Jan. 1982)-. Periodical. English. bm. Canadian Jewellers Institute, 20 Eglinton Avenue West, Canada Trust Tower, Suite 1203/Box 2021, Toronto Ontario M4R 1K8 Canada. **DD** 338.4/773927/0971.

US/0023-8457
LAPIDARY JOURNAL, THE. [Lapid. j.]. Vol. 1 (April 1947)-. Periodical. English. mo. $24.00 (includes Buyer's Guide). Lapidary Journal Inc., 60 Chestnut Avenue, Suite 201, Devon PA 19333. **Tel** (215)293-1112, FAX (215)293-1717. **ED** Merle Berk. **LC** NK7300; .L36. **DD** 739.27/05. **CODEN** LAJOA6. Index available. **Bk Rev**. **Ad Acc**. **Circ:** 35,500. Documents available from UMI Article Clearinghouse.
Desc: Famous authors help readers discover the gemstones and minerals that go into jewelry making, and then provide information and workshops for projects readers can create, or simply marvel.
Ind/Abst AESIS Q.; Gen. Period. Index (1985-); GeoRef; Index Inf. (1978-); Int. Aerosp. Abstr.; Mag. Index Plus (1989-); Newsp. Period. Abstr. (1988-); Mag. Index (1959-)(1977-).

AT/0729-5898
LEMEL. [LEMEL]. (1982)-. Periodical. English. Four times a year. 35.00Aus$. Jewellers & Metalsmiths GP Aus, PO Box 396, Scarborough WA 6019 Australia. **Tel** 011 61 9 3418238, FAX 011 61 9 2452053. **ED** David Walker (editor's phone: 011 61 9 3847468). **DD** 739.2706094. **Bk Rev**. **Ad Acc**, **Adv Mgr:** Felicity Peters. **Circ:** 400 (ctrl).
Desc: Technical and related information regarding jewelry and metalsmithing.

FR/0987-3872
LETTRE D'ORION MAGAZINE, LA. (LA LETTRE D'ORION.). (1983)-. Periodical. French. bw. 205.70F France; 500.00F other. Publicat Sarl, 17 Boulevard Poissonniere, 75002 Paris France. **Tel** 011 33 1 40265126. **UDC** 681.11.

CN/0068-9041
LLOYD'S CANADIAN JEWELLERY AND GIFTWARE DIRECTORY. 41st Ed. (1965)-. Directory. English. an. 30.00Can$ Canada; $37.50 US. Sentinel Business Publications, 7575 Trans Canada Highway, Suite 500, St. Laurent Quebec H4T 1V6 Canada. **Tel** (514)333-1116, FAX (514)631-8858. **ED** Carol Clifford. **DD** 338.4/7/688. **Ad Acc**. **Circ:** 5,500 (ctrl). ***Continues*** *Willson's Canadian Jewellery and Giftware Directory.*
Desc: A directory of product listings and suppliers of jewelry and giftware for retailers.

●US/1062-8460
LOUPE (SANTA MONICA, CALIF.). (LOUPE : GIA WORLD NEWS.). **Added/Corp** Gemological Institute of America. (1992)-. Periodical. English. qt. Free. Gemological Institute of America, 1660 Stewart Street, PO Box 2110, Santa Monica CA 90406. **Tel** (310)829-2991 Ext. 301, FAX (310)829-2269. ***Formed by the union of*** *Through the Loupe; Scope* ***and*** *GIA Net News.*

US/0892-1989
MARGARETOLOGIST, THE. [Margaretologist]. **Added/Corp** Center for Bead Research (Lake Placid, N.Y.). Vol. 1, No. 1 (1985)-. Periodical. English. Twice a year. $25.00 (two years) regular, $75.00 (two years) patron Comes with Centre for Bead Research membership. Center for Bead Research, 4 Essex Street, Lake Placid NY 12946. **Tel** (581)523-1794. **ED** Peter Francis Jr. **DD** 745. **Bk Rev**. **Circ:** 120.
Desc: Reports studies on the history, technology and use of beads from prehistoric to modern times conducted by the Center for Bead Research.

IT
MODA E BIJOUX. ***Suspended.*** (19??)-No. 15 (1992). Italian (English). qt. L20.000 Italy; $45.00 other. Nihon Yakugakkai, (Pharmaceutical Soc. of Japan), 12-15, Shibuya 2 Chome, Shibuyaku, Tokyoto 150, Japan. **ED** Florinda Gaudio. **Ad Acc**. **Circ:** 25,000.
Desc: Covers costume jewellery, fashion and fashion accessories. Audience is jewellery shops, perfumery, manufacturers, businessmen, and buyers in the sector.

US/0744-2513
MODERN JEWELER (1981). (MODERN JEWELER.). (19??)-. Periodical. English. mo. $25.00 US, Canada, and Mexico; $100.00 other. Vance Publishing Corporation, 400 Knightsbridge Parkway, Lincolnshire IL 60069. **Tel** (800)255-5113, (708)634-2600. **LC** HD9747.U5; M63. **DD** 381/.456882/0973. available on microfilm and microfiche from University Microfilms International (UMI). ***Continues*** *Modern Jeweler (National Executive Edition).*

US/0027-9544
NATIONAL JEWELER. (19??)-. Periodical. English. Twenty-four times a year. $100.00 US; $122.00 Canada & Mexico; $190.00 (surface mail), $480.00 (airmail) other. Miller Freeman Inc., 600 Harrison Street, San Francisco CA 94107. **Tel** (415)905-2337, FAX (415)905-2240, telex 278273. **(Subscription address:** JCI, PO Box 1766, Riverton NJ 08077.**)** **LC** HD9747.U54; N3. **[CCC].**

CN/0824-2194
NEWSVIEWS / CANADIAN JEWELLERS INSTITUTE. **Added/Corp** Canadian Jewellers Institute. (1980)-. Periodical. English. qt. Free to members. Canadian Jewellers Institute, 20 Eglinton Avenue West, Canada Trust Tower, Suite 1203/Box 2021, Toronto Ontario M4R 1K8 Canada. **DD** 338.4/773927/0971. ***Continues*** *CJI Newsletter.*

US/0029-3490
NORTHWESTERN JEWELER, THE. ***Title Change.*** **Added/Corp** Iowa Jewelers and Watchmakers Association. (19??)-(19??). Periodical. English. mo. Northwestern Jeweler, 142 West Main Street, Albert Lea MN 56007. **Tel** (507)373-2316. **ED** Paiit Reick. Index available. **Ad Acc**. **Circ:** 3,500 (ctrl). ***Continued by*** *Jewelers Inc., 1060-2151.*
Desc: Business magazine for the jewelry industry.

US/0742-5805
OFFICIAL PRICE GUIDE TO ANTIQUE JEWELRY, THE. [Off. price guide antique jewelry]. **VFOAT** Jewelry. 1st Edition (1982)-. Trade Publication. English. an. Price varies. Random House Inc., 400 Hahn Road, Westminster MD 21157. **Tel** (800)726-0600, (800)733-3000, FAX (800)659-2436. **ED** A. G. Kaplan. **LC** NK7312; .O35. **DD** 739.27/075.

CN/0833-2282
OPERATING RESULTS. RETAIL JEWELLERY STORES. (OPERATING RESULTS, RETAIL JEWELLERY STORES / STATISTICS CANADA, MERCHANDISING AND SERVICES DIVISION, RETAIL TRADE SECTION.). [Oper. results, Retail jewel. stores]. **Added/Corp** Statistics Canada. Retail Trade Section. **VFOAT** Resultats de l'Exploitation, Bijouteries au Detail; Operating Results, Independent Retail Jewellery Stores; Resultats de l'Exploitation, Magasins Independants de Vente au Detail de Bijouterie. (1981)-. English (French). an. 15.00Can$ Canada; $16.00 other. Statistics Canada, Publications Sales & Services, Main Building Room 1710, Ottawa Ontario K1A 0T6 Canada. **Tel** (613)951-5078, (800)267-6677, FAX (613)951-1584, telex 053-3585. **LC** HD9747.C3; O63. **DD** 381/.4573927/0971021. ***Continues*** *Operating Results. Independent Retail Jewellery Stores, 0834-4418.*
Desc: Presents data on independent retail jewelry stores: operating results, gross profit, detailed expense items and net profit as a percentage of net sales for incorporated and unincorporated firms. These ratios are stratified by sales size and by province or region wherever possible. Includes data analysis, methodology and a bibliography.

IT/0471-7376
ORAFO ITALIANO. [Orafo ital.]. (1947)-. Periodical. Italian. Eleven times a year. L130000.00 Italy; L200000.00 other. L'Orafo Italiana Srl, Via Nervesa 2, 20139 Milan Italy. **Tel** 011 39 2 5392288. **ED** Gianni Roggini. **UDC** 739.27. **Bk Rev**. **Ad Acc**. **Pr Rev**. **Circ:** 9,000.
Desc: Presents a panorama of what's happening in the goldware and jewelry sector.

US/0148-3897
ORNAMENT (LOS ANGELES, CALIF.). (ORNAMENT.). [Ornament]. Vol. 4, No. 1 (Apr. 1979)-. Periodical. English. qt. $25.00 US; $29.00 other. Ornament, PO Box 2349, San Marcos CA 92079. **Tel** (619)599-0222, (800)888-8950. **ED** Robert K Liu. **LC** NK7300; .B42. **DD** 739.27/05. **Ad Acc**. **Circ:** 35,000. ***Continues*** *Bead Journal, 0094-2448.*
Desc: Ancient, ethnic and contemporary jewelry, personal adornment, costumes and clothing.
Ind/Abst Anthropol. Index; Art Archaeol. Tech. Abstr.; Art Index; ARTbibliogr. Mod. (1983-); Br. Archaeol. Bibliogr. -?; Ethnoarts Index.

UK/0034-6063
RETAIL JEWELLER. (19??)-. Periodical. English. bw. £40.00 UK; £52.50 Europe; £70.00 other. EMAP Readerlink, Audit House, 260 Field End Road, Ruislip Middlesex HA4 9LT England. **Tel** 011 44 081 868 4499, FAX 011 44 081 429 3117. **(Subscription address:** EMAP Business Publishing, Ferrari House Audit House, Field End, Ruislip Middlesex HA4 9UY England.**)**

FR/0398-9011
REVUE DE GEMMOLOGIE A.F.G. [Rev. gemmol. afg.]. **Main/Corp** Association Francaise de Gemmologie. No. 49 (Dec. 1976)-. Periodical. French. Four times a year. 195.89F France; 200.00F EEC countries; 300.00F other. Association Francaise de Gemmologie, 163 rue Saint-Honore, F 75001 Paris France. **Tel** 011 33 1 48749193. ***Continues*** *Revue de Gemmologie.*
Desc: Information on precious stones and gem cutting.
Ind/Abst Geol. Abstr.; GeoRef.

BE/0040-0866
TECHNICA (BASEL). (TECHNICA.). [Technica]. (1952)-. Academic Scholarly Publication. French (Dutch). Eleven times a year. 1500F Belgium; 2500F Europe; 3500F other. Technica, Bd de Smet De Naeyer 290A, 1090 Brussels Belgium. **Tel** 24282245, FAX 24283078. **ED** National Jewellers Association. **LC** T4; .T177. **CODEN** TCHNAR. **[CCC]. Bk Rev**. **Ad Acc**. **Circ:** 3,000. Documents available from Ask*IEEE. ***Absorbed*** *Schweisstechnik, 0376-2181.*
Desc: Contains information on jewelry, watches, precious metals and stones.
Ind/Abst Alum. Ind. Abstr.; EMBASE; Energy Res. Abstr.; INSPEC (1968-); Met. Abstr. (1968-); Saf. Health Work.

IT
VALENZA GIOIELLI. (19??)-. Italian. Four times a year. $65.00. Agenzia Italiana di Esportazione, Via Manzoni 12, 20089 Rozzano Milan, Italy. **Tel** 011 39 2 57512575. ***Continues*** *L'Orafo Valenzano.*

IT
VOGUE GIOIELLO. Three times a year. $40.00. Edizioni Conde Nast Spa, Piazza Castello 27, 20121 Milan Italy. **Tel** 011 39 2 85611.

UK/0043-1079
WATCHMAKER, JEWELLER & SILVERSMITH (1941). ***Ceased.*** (WATCHMAKER JEWELLER AND SILVERSMITH.). [Watch. jewel. silversmith 1941]. **VFOAT** Watchmaker, Jeweller and Silversmith (1941); WJS. Watchmaker Jeweller and Silversmith. (1941)-(19??). Periodical. English. mo. Nexus Business Communications, Warwick House, Azalea Drive, c/o Dr. Swanle, Kent BR8 8HY England. **Tel** 011 44 322 660070. **DD** 681.11. ***Continues*** *Watchmaker and Jeweller, Silversmith and Optician.*

GW
ZEITSCHRIFT DER DEUTSCHEN GEMMOLOGISCHEN GESELLSCHAFT. **Main/Corp** Deutsche Gemmologische Gesellschaft. (1951)-. Periodical. German. an. $57.00. E. Schweizerbartsche Verlagsbuchhandlung, Johannesstrasse 3A, D-70176 Stuttgart Germany. **Tel** 011 49 711 625001, FAX 011 49 711 625005, telex 723363 SCHB D. **ED** H Bank and G Lenzen. **CODEN** ZDGGB7. **Bk Rev**. **Ad Acc**. ctrl circ. Documents available from Petroleum Abstracts Document Delivery Service.
Ind/Abst Geol. Abstr.; GeoRef; Life Sci. Collect.; Pet. Abstr.

CLOCKS AND WATCHES

US/0192-7507
ACCENT. See Jewelry.

UK/0003-5785
ANTIQUARIAN HOROLOGY AND THE PROCEEDINGS OF THE ANTIQUARIAN HOROLOGICAL SOCIETY. **Added/Corp** Antiquarian Horological Society. Antiquarian Horological Society. Proceedings of the Antiquarian Horological Society. **VFOAT** Antiquarian Horology. Vol. 1 (Dec. 1953)-. Periodical. English. Four times a year. £35.00 UK; £60.00 others Comes with Antiquarian Horological Society membership. Antiquarian Horological Society, New House High Street, Ticehurst, Wadhurst SSX TN5 7AL England. **Tel** 011 44 580 200155. **ED** David Penney. **Bk Rev**. **Ad Acc. Circ:** 3,000 (ctrl).
Desc: Its aims are to serve all those interested in antique clocks, watches and other time-measuring instruments.
Ind/Abst ARTbibliogr. Mod.; BHA : Biblio. Hist. Art.

UK/0954-593X
ANTIQUE CLOCKS. ***Title Change.*** Vol. 11, No. 1 (June 1988)-(19??). Periodical. English. mo. Model & Allied Publications Ltd, PO Box 35, Wolsey House, Wolsey Road, Hemel Hempstead Herts HP2 4SS England. ***Continues** Clocks, 0141-5107.* ***Continued by** Clocks (Hemel Hempstead, England).*

SP
ANUARIO DE LA RELOJERIA PARA ESPANA E HISPANOAMERICA. Spanish (French and English). an. 6000ptas Spain; $60.00 other. Ediciones Cedel, Mallorca 257, 1#, 08008 Barcelona Spain. **ED** Jose O. Avila. **LC** HD9999.C6; S62. **DD** 380.1/45/6811102546. Index available. **Bk Rev. Ad Acc. Circ:** 4,000.
Desc: Provides complete addresses of industrials and traders of jewelry, watchmaking, silversmith's craft, imitation jewelry, metal art, gemmology and religious art.

HK/0254-1173
ASIAN SOURCES TIMEPIECES. [Asian sources timepieces]. **VFOAT** Timepieces. (1980)-. Periodical. English. mo. $75.00 (1 year), $120.00 (2 year) surface mail. Trade Media Ltd / Hong Kong, GPO Box 11411, Hong Kong Hong Kong. **Tel** 011 852 555-4777, FAX 011 852 870-0637. Index available. **Ad Acc. Circ:** 19,500 (ctrl).
Desc: Import-export, business to business four-color magazine covering watches, clock, and cronometers from Asia.

FR/0766-6934
BIJOUTIER : REVUE FRANCAISE DES BIJOUTIERS HORLOGERS, LE. **VFOAT** Revue Francaise des Bijoutiers Horlogers. French. Twelve times a year. 300.00F France; 480.00F other. Pierre Johanet & Fils Editeurs SA, 7 Avenue Fd Roosevelt, 75008 Paris France. **Tel** 33 1 43590887, FAX 33 1 42255947, telex 649712 F. ***Continues** RFBH.*

CN/0712-2799
BYTOWN TIMES. [Bytown times]. **Added/Corp** National Association of Watch and Clock Collectors. Ottawa Valley Chapter, No. 111. (1979)-. Periodical. English. ir (five issues per year). $16.00. National Association of Watch and Clock Collectors, Ottawa Valley Chapter # 111, 14 Kinnear Street, Ottawa Ontario K1Y 3R4 Canada. **Tel** (613)728-1242. **ED** Peter Bomford. **DD** 681.1/1/0607138. **Bk Rev. Circ:** 500 (ctrl).
Desc: Provides information on forthcoming events and meetings; previous meetings; National Association news; articles on morology; and auction news. First published in 1979.

UK
CLOCKS. ***Title Change.*** (19??)-(19??). Periodical. English. mo. Model & Allied Publications Ltd, PO Box 35, Wolsey House, Wolsey Road, Hemel Hempstead Herts HP2 4SS England. ***Continued by** Antique Clocks, 0954-593X.*
Desc: Articles range from the clocks in Oxfordshire churches to Tavern clocks. Recommended for museums and libraries serving clock collectors.

UK
CLOCKS. (19??)-. Periodical. English. Twelve times a year. £28.80 UK; $70.00 other. Argus Specialist Publications, Queensway House, 2 Queensway Redhill, Surrey RH1 1QS England. **Tel** 0737 768611, FAX 0737 773993, telex 948669 TOPJNL G. ***Continues** Antique Clocks, 0954-593X.*
Desc: A journal for horological collectors and restorers. Includes features by horological authors with information on restorations, historical data, construction, auction news, sundials, watches and barometers.

US/0730-2924
COMPLETE GUIDE TO AMERICAN POCKET WATCHES, THE. **VFOAT** Official Guide Book to American Pocket Watches. 1st. Ed. (1981)-. English. $9.95 (U.S.), $11.20 (foreign). Overstreet Publications Inc, 780 Hunt Cliff Drive NW, Cleveland TN 37311. **Tel** (615)472-4135. **ED** Walter Presswood. **LC** NK7492; .C65. **DD** 681.1/14. **Ad Acc. Circ:** 15,000.
Desc: Includes over 10,000 current market prices, rare watch list, over 110 famous watch manufacturers, over 770 illustrations with color, wrist watches and European pocket watches.

SZ/0014-2603
EUROPA STAR. [Eur. star]. (1959)-. Periodical. Multiple languages. Six times a year. $50.00 (one year); $90.00 (two years); $130.00 (three years). Hugo Buchser SA, Route des Acacias 25, PO Box 30, CH-1211 Geneva 24, Switzerland. **Tel** 011 41 22 3003737, FAX 011 41 22 3003748. **ED** Pierre Morgan (Watch Editor), Anne Chabanel (Fashion Editor) and Anthony Morland (Jewelry Editor). **UDC** 681.11. **Ad Acc**.
Desc: An international watch and jewelry magazine with 7 regional editions.

FR/0015-9573
FRANCE HORLOGERE, LA. [Fr. horlog.]. (1901)-. Periodical. French. mo (with June-July and Aug.-Sept. combined). 323.21F France; 570.00F other. La France Horlogere, BP 169, 25014 Besancon Cedex France. **Tel** 011 33 81 821490. **UDC** 681.11.

HK
HONG KONG WATCHES & CLOCKS. Periodical. English. sa. $40.00. Hong Kong Trade Development Council, 38th Floor/Office Tower, Convention Plaza, 1 Harbour Road, Hong Kong. **Tel** 852 5844333, FAX 852 8240249, telex 7395 CONHK HX. **ED** Saul Lockhart. **Ad Acc. Circ:** 20,000 (ctrl).
Desc: Features Hong Kong's watch and clock industry.

US/0273-3374
HOROLOGICAL DIALOGUES. [Horol. dialogues]. V. 1- 1979-. Periodical. English. R Stenard, 60 First Street, Garden City NY 11530. **LC** TS540; .H74. **DD** 681.1/13/075.

UK/0018-5108
HOROLOGICAL JOURNAL. (THE HOROLOGICAL JOURNAL : THE SPECIAL ORGAN OF THE BRITISH HOROLOGICAL INSTITUTE.). [Horol. j.]. **Added/Corp** British Horological Federation. British Horological Institute. Vol. 1 (Sept. 1858)-. Periodical. English. Twelve times a year. £43.00 UK; £48.00 Europe; £52.48 other. British Horological Institute, Upton Hall, Upton Newark, Notts NG23 5TE England. **Tel** 011 44 636 813795, 011 44 636 813796, FAX 011 44 636 812258. **ED** Timothy Treffry. **LC** TS540; .H8. Index available. **Bk Rev. Ad Acc, Adv Mgr:** Helen Bartlett. **Circ:** 3,500 (ctrl). Documents available from Ask*IEEE. ***Continues** Watch & Clockmaker.*
Desc: Covers all aspects of technical horology, i.e. modern mechanical, electrical, eletronic, and antorian mechanical, together with constructional articles and international horological news.
Ind/Abst INSPEC (Apr. 1989-).

US/0145-9546
HOROLOGICAL TIMES. **Added/Corp** American Watchmakers Institute. Vol. 1 (Jan 1977)-. Periodical. English. mo. $40.00. AWI Central, PO Box 11011, 3700 Harrison Avenue, Cincinnati OH 45214. **Tel** (513)661-3838. **LC** TS540; .H82. **DD** 681/.11/05. Index available. cum. index. **Bk Rev. Ad Acc. Circ:** 10,000. ***Supersedes** News of and for the Watchmakers Industry, 0160-2012.*

SZ
INDICATEUR SUISSE. French (German, English, Italian and Spanish). an. 50.00F France; 60.00F Europe; 80.00F US. Indicateur Suisse/Swiss Directory, Route de la Glane 31, 1700 Fribourg Switzerland. **Tel** 037-24 47 25, telex 942 273. **ED** Marie Dunand. **LC** TS540; .I53. **DD** 681.1/14/025494. **Ad Acc. Circ:** 4,000.
Desc: Provides an address and reference guide to the Swiss watch industry; lists watch manufacturers and retailers, periphery industries and jewelers. Covers electronics and components, micro-technology, machines and tools.

SZ
JAHRBUCH DER UHRENINDUSTRIE UND IHRER VERWANDTEN ZWEIGE. **VFOAT** Annuaire de l'Industrie de la Montre et de Ses Branches Annexes; Uhren Rundschau Jahrbuch. Multiple languages (French and German). 11.00. Vogt Schild AG, Druck Verlag, Postfach 748 Zuchwilserstr 21, CH 4501 Solothurn Switzerland. **Tel** 011 41 65 247247. **LC** HD9999.C6; S944.

JA
JOURNAL OF HOROLOGICAL INSTITUTE OF JAPAN. (19??)-. Periodical. Japanese. qt. $140.00. **(Subscription address:** Maruzen Company Ltd., PO Box 5050, Import & Export Department, Tokyo 100 31 Japan.**)**

UK/0518-0333
MONOGRAPH / ANTIQUARIAN HOROLOGICAL SOCIETY. **Main/Corp** Antiquarian Horological Society. No. 1- 1960-. Monographic series. English. Price varies per volume. Cambridge University Press, The Edinburgh Building, Shaftesbury Road, Cambridge CB2 2RU United Kingdom. **Tel** 011 44 223 312393, FAX 011 44 223 325959. **(Subscription address:** US/ 110 Midland Avenue, Port Chester, NY 10573**)**

US/0743-9571
OFFICIAL PRICE GUIDE TO ANTIQUE CLOCKS, THE. **VFOAT** Antique Clocks; Clocks. 1st. Ed. (1983)-. English. an. $13.85 (latest edition). Random House Inc., 400 Hahn Road, Westminster MD 21157. **Tel** (800)726-0600, (800)733-3000, FAX (800)659-2436. **LC** NK7492; .O37. **DD** 681.1/13/09730750973.

NE/0925-0182
OPTISCHE IN FOTOTECHNISCHE INDUSTRIE, KLOKKEN- EN UURWERKINDUSTRIE / CENTRAAL BUREAU VOOR DE STATISTIEK, HOOFDAFDELING STATISTIEKEN VAN INDUSTRIE EN BOUWNIJVERHEID. **VFOAT** Manufacture of Optical and Photo-Technical Products, Manufacture of Clocks and Clockwork. 1980-1981-. Dutch (summaries and/or abstracts in English). an. Fl8.00. Centraal Bureau voor de Statistiek, AFD ALG Zaken, Postbus 959, 2270 AZ Voorburg Netherlands. **Tel** 011 31 70 3373800, FAX 011 31 038 7429, telex 32692 CBS NL. **LC** HD9707.N42; O67. available on audiocassette.

IT
OROLOGI. (19??)-. Italian. mo. L64000.00 Italy; L165000.00 Europe; L230000.00 America, Africa & Asia; L285000.00 other. Technimedia Srl, Via Carlo Perrier 9, 00157 Rome Italy. **Tel** 011 39 6 418921.

SZ/0039-7520
SWISS WATCH AND JEWELRY JOURNAL. **VFOAT** Journal Suisse d'Horlogerie et le Bijoutier. English. Six times a year (Feb., Apr., June, Aug., Oct., Dec.). 80.00F. Editions Scriptar SA, Chemin du Creux de Corsy 25, 1093 Conv Lausanne Switzerland. **Tel** 011 41 21 791065, FAX 011 41 21 174084.

UK
TIMEPIECE. 1981-. English. mo. $38.75 one year, $92.75 two years. Watch and Clock Book Society, PO Box 22, Ashford England. **Tel** (0233)21262. **ED** Norman Stuckey and Linda Palmer. **LC** NK7500.L65; T54. **DD** 681.1/13/075. Index available. cum. index. **Bk Rev. Ad Acc. Circ:** 2,500.
Desc: Specialist publication devoted to clocks and watches throughout the world.

GW
UHREN, JUWELEN, SCHMUCK. **Added/Corp** Zentralverband der Uhrmacher fuer das Bundesgebiet. Bundesverband der Juweliere und Uhrmacher. Forderungswerk Konigstein. (Jan. 1973)-. Trade Publication. German. mo. DM196.00. Bielefelder Verlagsanstalt KG, Niederwall 53, D 33602 Bielefeld Germany. **Tel** 011 49 521 595520. **LC** TS540; .U43. Index available. **Bk Rev. Ad Acc. Circ:** 9,700 (ctrl). ***Continues** Uhr.*
Desc: A practice-oriented trade magazine for the whole market of watches, horology, jewels, gold and silver items, precious stones and pearls-for management, product information, purchasing, selling and special technology.

SZ
UHREN RUNDSCHAU. REVUE DE LA MONTRE. **VFOAT** Revue de la Montre. Periodical. Multiple languages (French and German). 50.00. Vogt Schild AG, Druck Verlag, Postfach 748 Zuchwilserstr 21, CH 4501 Solothurn Switzerland. **Tel** 011 41 65 247247. **LC** HD9999.C6; S982. ***Formed by the union of** Schweizer Uhr **and** Swiss Watch.*

US/0279-6198
WATCH & CLOCK REVIEW. [Watch clock rev.]. **VAT** Watch and Clock Review. Vol. 48, No. 1 (Jan. 1981)-. Trade Publication. English. mo (11 issues per year). $19.50 (one year), $35.00 (two year), $50.00 (three year). Golden Bell Press, 2403 Champa Street, Denver CO 80205. **Tel** (303)296-1600. **ED** Jayne Barrick. **LC** TS540; .A6. **DD** 681.1/1/05. **Bk Rev. Ad Acc. Circ:** 15,000 (ctrl). available on microfilm and microfiche from University Microfilms International (UMI). ***Continues** American Horologist and Jeweler, 0002-8797.*
Desc: Trade journal for the watch and clock industry.

HK
WATCH REVIEW. (19??)-. Periodical. English. Six times a year (Feb., Apr., June, Aug., Oct. Dec.). $100.00 Asia; $120.00 other. Brillian Art Publishing Inc., GPO Box 985, Hong Kong. **Tel** 011 852 5116077, FAX 011 852 5075855. **Ad Acc.**
Desc: The professional trade source for the watch and clock industries and for very well-defined reasons: it brings you in-depth feature the latest market trends; offers from makers featuring exclusive salable items; new design concept; trade news covering both Hong Kong and China.

JOURNALISM

CN/0384-9325
"30". (LE 30.). **Added/Corp** Federation Professionnelle Des Journalistes du Quebec. **VAT** "Trente". Vol. 1, (Dec. 1976)-. Periodical. French. Ten times a year (Except January and December). 35.00Can$ Canada; 46.00Can$ other. Les Editions Le 30 Incorporees, 2083 Beaudry # 302, Montreal Quebec H2L 3G4 Canada. **Tel** (514)522-8033, FAX 514)522-6071. **DD** 070/.06/2714.

US/0747-8909
AEJMC NEWS. (AEJMC NEWS : THE NEWSLETTER OF THE ASSOCIATION FOR EDUCATION IN JOURNALISM AND MASS COMMUNICATION.). [AEJMC news]. **Added/Corp** Association for Education in Journalism and Mass Communication. **VFOAT** A.E.J.M.C. News. **VAT** Association for Education in Journalism and Mass Communication News. Vol. 17, No. 1 (Oct. 1983)-. Newsletter. English. bm (6 issues). $10.00. Association for Education in Journalism and Mass Communication, University of South Carolina, 1621 College Street, Columbia SC 29208-0251. **Tel** (803)777-2005, FAX (803)777-4728. **ED** Lillian Coleman. **DD** 070. **Ad Acc**. **Circ:** 5,000 (ctrl). *Continues AEJMC Newsletter*.
 Desc: Contains news and general information on education in journalism and mass communication. Publication is distributed to members of the Association (AEJMC).

US
AGENDA. (19??)-. English. Ten times a year. $20.00. National Federation of Press Women, c/o L. L. Wolfe, PO Box 99, Blue Springs MO 64015. **Tel** (816)229-1666. *Continues The Press Woman*.

US/0738-7792
AIM REPORT. [AIM rep.]. **Main/Corp** Accuracy in Media, Inc. **VAT** Accuracy in Media Report. Vol. 1, (1972)-. Periodical. English. Twenty-four times a year. $27.95 US, $36.95 Canada, $40.00 others (regular mail); $36.95 first class mail. Accuracy in Media, 4455 Connecticut Avenue, Suite 330, Washington DC 20008. **Tel** (202)364-4401, FAX (202)364-4098. **ED** Reed Irvine and Joe Goulden. **DD** 070. Index available (Next iss. ($20.00)). **Circ:** 17,000.
 Desc: Exposes media abuse and inaccuracies in print and electronic media.

US/0191-328X
ALASKA TODAY. *Ceased.* ( )-(Sept. 1987). English. an. Alaska Today, Department of Journalism & Broadcasting, University of Alaska, Fairbanks AK 99701. **LC** F901; .A377. **DD** 979.8/.005.

US/0149-5186
ALPHABETIZED DIRECTORY OF AMERICAN JOURNALISTS. (ALPHABETIZED DIRECTORY OF AMERICAN JOURNALISTS: ASSOCIATED PRESS, UNITED PRESS INTERNATIONAL, AMERICA'S DAILY NEWSPAPERS.). (19??)-. Directory. English. $7.95. PO Box 231, Kokomo IN 46901. **LC** PN4871; .A45. **DD** 071/.3/025.

US/0730-1766
ALTERNATIVE MEDIA. *Ceased.* See Political Science.

US/0882-1127
AMERICAN JOURNALISM. (AMERICAN JOURNALISM : THE PUBLICATION OF THE AMERICAN JOURNALISM HISTORIANS ASSOCIATION.). [Am. j.]. **Added/Corp** American Journalism Historians Association. Vol. 1, No. 1 (Summer 1983)-. Periodical. English. Four times a year. $25.00. College of Journalism / University of Georgia, PO Box 281, Athens GA 30602. **Tel** (706)542-5033. **ED** John Pauly. **LC** PN4700; .A39. **DD** 071/.3/09. Index available. **Bk Rev**, (Qty: 60-80 per year). **Ad Acc**, **Adv Mgr:** Alf Pratte, **Tel** (801)378-2077. **Pr Rev**. **Circ:** 400.
 Desc: It focuses on all aspects of journalism and mass media history. Prints articles, review essays and research notes on mass communication history.
 Ind/Abst Commun. Abstr.

●US/1067-8654
AMERICAN JOURNALISM REVIEW. (AMERICAN JOURNALISM REVIEW : AJR.). [Am. j. rev.]. **Added/Corp** University of Maryland at College Park. College of Journalism. **VFOAT** AJR. Vol. 15, No. 2 (Mar. 1993)-. Periodical. English. Ten times a year (published monthly with Jan./Feb. and Jul./Aug. issues combined). $24.00 (one year), $44.00 (two year) surface mail. Washington Journalism Review, 4716 Pontiac Street, Suite 310, College Park MD 20740. **Tel** (301)431-4771, (800)827-0771. **ED** Rem Reider. **LC** AP2; .W18; PN4700; .W38. **DD** 071. *Continues Washington Journalism Review (1983), 0741-8876*.
 Desc: National media magazine.
 Ind/Abst Acad. Search (July 1993-).

US
AMERICAN MEDICAL WRITERS ASSOCIATION AMWA JOURNAL. See Medical Science and Technology.

US/1061-4230
AMERICA'S CENSORED NEWSLETTER. *Ceased.* [Am. censored newsl.]. **VFOAT** Censored Newsletter. (1992)-Vol. 2 No. 5 (May 1993). Periodical. English. mo. Censored Publications, PO Box 310, Cotati CA 94931. **DD** 071.

US/0194-004X
AMWA FREELANCE DIRECTORY, THE. *Title Change.* **Main/Corp** American Medical Writers Association. **Added/Corp** American Medical Writers Association. **VFOAT** Freelance Directory. **VAT** American Medical Writers Association Freelance Directory. 1st Ed. (1975)-?. Directory. English. an. American Medical Writers Association, 9650 Rockville Pike, Bethesda MD 20814-3928. **Tel** (301)986-9119. **ED** Norman Grossblatt. **NLM** WZ 22 AA1 A16. Index available. **Circ:** 3,500. *Continued by Freelance Directory*.
 Desc: Freelance directory of medical communication services.

CN/0849-3928
ANNUAIRE - UNION DES ECRIVAINES ET ECRIVAINS QUEBECOIS. (ANNUAIRE.). [Annu. - Union ecrivaines ecrivains que.]. **Main/Corp** Union des Ecrivaines et Ecrivains Quebecois. (1990)-. French. 6.00Can$ per volume. Union des Ecrivaines et Ecrivains Quebecois, Bureau 510, 1030 Rue Cherrier, Montreal, Quebec H2L 1H9 Canada. **DD** 331.88/1184/025714. *Continues Union des Ecrivains Quebecois. Annuaire., 0848-0621*.

US/0193-4562
APF REPORTER. **Main/Corp** Alicia Patterson Foundation. **Added/Corp** Alicia Patterson Foundation. Reporter. **VAT** Alicia Patterson Foundation Reporter. Vol. 1 (June 1978)-. Periodical. English. Four times a year (Seasonally). Free. Alicia Patterson Foundation, 1001 Pennsylvania Avenue, Suite 1250, Washington DC 20004. **Tel** (202)393-5995. **ED** Margaret Engel (phone: (301)951-8512). **LC** AP2; .A3067a. **DD** 051. [CCC]. Index available. cum. index. **Circ:** 4,000 (ctrl). available on an online database from Internet; and America Online.
 Ind/Abst Index Free Period.

IO
ASEAN PRESS YEARBOOK ... . 1979-. English. **LC** PN4699; .A73. **DD** 079/.59.

KO/0304-8667
ASIAN PRESS, THE. English. $3.00. Institute for Communication Research, Seoul National University, Readership Research Center, Dong Song Dong, Seoul Korea. **LC** PN4709; .A85. **DD** 079/.5.

US
ASNE : PROCEEDINGS OF THE ... CONVENTION OF THE AMERICAN SOCIETY OF NEWSPAPER EDITORS. **Main/Corp** American Society of Newspaper Editors. Convention. **VFOAT** A.S.N.E.; Proceedings of the ... Convention of the American Society of Newspaper Editors. (1982)-. Proceedings. English. an. $25.00. American Society of Newspaper Editors, PO Box 4090, Reston VA 22090-1700. **Tel** (703)648-1148. **ED** Elise Burroughs. Index available (bound in all issues). **Circ:** 1,200. *Continues American Society of Newspaper Editors. Convention. Problems of Journalism (1948)*.
 Desc: Proceedings of the annual convention.

●US/1062-0036
AT RANDOM. See Publishing.

AT/0810-2686
AUSTRALIAN JOURNALISM REVIEW : AJR. **Added/Corp** Journalism Education Association (Australia). **VFOAT** AJR; A.J.R. (19??)-. Periodical. English. Twice a year (June, Dec.). 20.00Aus$ (individual); 40.00Aus$ (institution). Queensland University of Technology, Business Comm Drive, Granato Box 2434, Brisbane QLD 4001 Australia. **Tel** 011 61 7 8641729. **ED** LA Granato (editor's address: School of Media & Journalism, QUT GPO Box 2334, Brisbane 4001 Australia). **LC** PN4701; .A9. **DD** 079/.94/05. cum. index. **Bk Rev**. **Ad Acc**. **Pr Rev**. **Circ:** 300.
 Desc: Articles about various aspects of news media in Australia and overseas.
 Ind/Abst APAIS, Aust. Public Aff. Inf. Ser.; Commun. Abstr.

US
AWP CHRONICLE. **Added/Corp** Associated Writing Programs. **VFOAT** Associated Writing Programs Chronicle. Vol. 21, No. 4 (May 1989)-. Periodical. English. bm. $18.00. Associated Writing Programs, Old Dominion University, Norfolk VA 23529. **Tel** (804)683-3839. **LC** PN101; .A88. *Continues Associated Writing Programs. AWP Newsletter*.

GW/0409-1949
BERLINER ABHANDLUNGEN ZUM PRESSERECHT. German. ir. Duncker und Humblot Verlag, Postfach 410329, D-12113 Berlin Germany. **Tel** 011 49 30 79000612, 011 49 30 79000613.

US/1056-8034
BEST AMERICAN SPORTS WRITING, THE. [Best Am. sports writ.]. (1991)-. English. $21.95, $9.95. **DD** 813.

US/0195-895X
BEST NEWSPAPER WRITING. 1979-. English. an. $3.95. Poynter Inst Media Studies, 801 Third Street South, St Petersburg FL 33701. **Tel** (813)821-9494. **ED** Roy Peter Clark. **LC** PN4726; .B38. **DD** 081.

US/0737-2612
BEST OF NEWSPAPER DESIGN (MEMBER ED.), THE. (THE BEST OF NEWSPAPER DESIGN.). [Best newsp. des.]. **Added/Corp** Society of Newspaper Designers. Society of Newspaper Design. **VFOAT** Best in Newspaper Design. (1980)-. English. an. Society of Newspaper Designers, PO Box 17279, Baltimore MD 21203. **LC** Z253.5; .B48. **DD** 686.2/252. Documents available from UMI Article Clearinghouse.
 Ind/Abst Newsp. Period. Abstr. (1991-).

US/0093-5697
BLACK PRESS PERIODICAL DIRECTORY, THE. 1973-. Directory. English. $45.00. Systems Catalog Inc, 78 Merchant Street, Newark NJ 07105. **LC** Z6944.N39; B45. **DD** 070/.025/73.

UY
BRECHA (MONTEVIDEO, URUGUAY). (BRECHA). Vol. 1, No. 1 (Oct. 11, 1985)-. Periodical. Spanish. wk. $60.00 US. Brecha, Avda Uruguay 844, Montevideo Uruguay. **Tel** 91-67-23. **ED** Hugo Alfaro and Ruben Svirsky. **LC** AP63; .B78. **DD** 079/.895/13. **Bk Rev**. **Ad Acc**. **Circ:** 16,000. available on microfilm.
 Desc: News - political and cultural commentaries and reviews.
 Ind/Abst Hum. Rights Intern. Rep.

CN/0701-1229
BULLETIN - AGENCE DE PRESSE LIBRE DU QUEBEC. **Main/Corp** Agence de Presse Libre du Quebec. No 1- 18/25 Mar. 1971-. Bulletin. French. wk. 5.00Can$. Agence De Presse Libre Du Quebec Inc., 3459 Rue St.Hubert, Montreal Quebec H2L 3Z8. **DD** 070.4/35/09714.

CN/1184-0641
BULLETIN - CANADIAN ASSOCIATION OF JOURNALISTS. *Ceased.* (BULLETIN / THE CANADIAN ASSOCIATION OF JOURNALISTS.). [Bull. - Can. Assoc. Journal.]. **Added/Corp** Canadian Association of Journalists. No. 41 (Fall 1990)-(199?). Bulletin. English (summaries and/or abstracts in French). qt. Centre for Investigative Journalism, Carleton University, 324 St Patrick's Building, Ottawa Ontario K1S 5B6 Canada. **Tel** (613)788-7424, FAX (613)788-5604. **DD** 071/.1. *Continues Bulletin (Centre for Investigative Journalism)., 0822-207X*.
 Ind/Abst Can. Period. Index (19??-).

US/0003-1178
BULLETIN OF THE AMERICAN SOCIETY OF NEWSPAPER EDITORS, THE. [Bull. Am. Soc. Newspr. Ed.]. **Main/Corp** American Society of Newspaper Editors. **VFOAT** ASNE Bulletin. (19??)-. Bulletin. English. Nine times a year. $20.00 (one year), $35.00 (two years), $45.00 (three years) US & Canada; $25.00 (one year), $45.00 (two years), $60.00 (three years) other. American Society of Newspaper Editors, PO Box 4090, Reston VA 22090-1700. **Tel** (703)648-1148. **ED** Beverly Kees. **LC** PN4700; .A58. **Bk Rev**. **Circ:** 2,500. Documents available from UMI Article Clearinghouse.
 Desc: The nation's oldest journalism review explores major press controversies and offers practical advice on the nuts-and-bolts of daily newspaper editing.
 Ind/Abst Expand. Acad. Index (1992-); Newsp. Period. Abstr. (1989-).

US/1041-3669
BULL'S EYE (LYNBROOK, N.Y.). (BULL'S EYE.). Vol. 1, No. 1 (June 1988)-. Periodical. English. mo. $20.00. Bull's Eye Publications Inc, PO Box 36, Lynbrook NY 11563. **Tel** (516)593-1061. **DD** 070.
 Desc: Compiles editorial cartoons and arranges them by subject matter. Presents cartoons about major issues done by international cartoonist, with a showcase of his work.

US/0731-5449
BYLINE (EVANSTON, ILL.). (BYLINE : NORTHWESTERN'S JOURNALISM QUARTERLY.). (197?)-. Periodical. English. Three times a year. $10.00. Byline, PO Box 130596, Edmond OK 73013. **Tel** (405)348-5591, FAX (405)348-5591. **ED** Hope Edelman and Bob Brent. **Ad Acc**. **Circ:** 2,000 (ctrl).

Desc: Focuses on all aspects of the media. We review and analyze current issues in print and broadcast journalism, advertising and education.

US/0744-4249
BYLINE (OKLAHOMA CITY, OKLA.). (BYLINE : A MCCARVILLE PUBLICATION.). (198?)-. Periodical. English. Eleven times a year (July/Aug. issues combined). $20.00. Byline, PO Box 130596, Edmond OK 73013. **Tel** (405)348-5591, FAX (405)348-5591. **ED** Marcia Preston and Kathryn Fanning. **DD** 808. Index available. cum. index. **Ad Acc. Circ:** 3,000.
Desc: A magazine for writers and poets which aims toward helping them establish successful careers as writers. There are short fictions and poetry and hosts writing contests.

US/1049-1767
CAPITOL WEEKLY. [Capitol wkly.]. (1989)-. Periodical. English. wk. $59.00. Capitol Weekly Corporation, 1930 9th Street, Suite 200, Sacramento CA 95814. **Tel** (916)444-7665, FAX (916)444-6326. **DD** 071.

US/0008-8129
CATHOLIC JOURNALIST. (1945)-. Periodical. English. mo. $12.00. Catholic Journalist, 119 North Park Avenue, Rockville Centre NY 11570. **Tel** (516)766-3400. **ED** James A Doyle. **Bk Rev. Ad Acc. Circ:** 2,600 (ctrl). available on microfilm from University Microfilms International (UMI).
Desc: News and information about and for Catholic newspapers, magazines and book publishers and others interested in this field.

CN/1184-6569
CATTW BULLETIN. See Education-Teaching and Curriculum.

US/1056-9227
CHAPTER ONE FOR THE UNPUBLISHED WRITER IN ALL OF US. [Chapter one unpubl. writ. all us]. **VFOAT** Chapter One. Vol. 1, Issue 1 (1991)-. Periodical. English. bm. $10.95. J. A. B. Publishing, PO Box 4086, Cary NC 27519-4086. **DD** 810.

US/1058-6326
CHIPS OFF THE WRITER'S BLOCK CATHARSIS. VFOAT Catharsis. Premier Issue (Summer 1991)-. Periodical. English. $5.00 (single issue). Chips off the Writer's Block, PO Box 83371, Los Angeles CA 90083. **DD** 811.

CC
CHUNG-KUO HSIN WEN NIEN CHIEN. VFOAT Zhongguo Xinwen Nianjian. 1982-. Chinese. an. China Social Sciences Publishing House, Jia 158 Gulou Xiadajie, Beijing 100720, People's Republic of China. **LC** PN4705; .C49 . **DD** 079/.51. **Ad Acc.**

US/0888-8191
CIRCULATION MANAGEMENT (SPRINGFIELD, OR.). (CIRCULATION MANAGEMENT.). [Circ. manage.]. **VFOAT** CM. (198?)-. Periodical. English. Eleven times a year. $32.00 US; $49.00 other. Ganesa Corporation, 611 Broadway Room 401, New York NY 10012. **Tel** (212)979-0730, FAX (212)979-0961. **ED** Karlene Lukovitz. **LC** PN4784.C6; C47. **DD** 050/.688. **CODEN** CIRMEZ. **[CCC]. Ad Acc, Adv Mgr:** G. Bartmen, **Tel** (212)979-0730. **Circ:** 10,000 (ctrl). Documents available from Ask*IEEE.
Ind/Abst INSPEC (Jan. 1988-).

US/0192-5040
CITY AND REGIONAL MAGAZINE DIRECTORY. Added/Corp Conference Management Corporation. (1977)-. Directory. English. an. $19.95. Conference Management Corporation, PO Box 4900, 17 Washington Street, Norwalk CT 06856. **Tel** (203)852-0500. **LC** Z6951; .C576; PN4877. **DD** 051.

US/0198-6554
C:JET. (C : JET, COMMUNICATION : JOURNALISM EDUCATION TODAY.). [C:JET]. **Added/Corp** Journalism Education Association (U.S.). **VFOAT** Communication: Journalism Education Today. Vol. 11 (Fall 1977)-. Periodical. English. Four times a year. $40.00 Comes with Journalism Education Association membership. Journalism Education Association, Kansas State Univestity, Hall 103, Manhattan KS 66506. **Tel** (913)532-5532. **LC** PN4788; .C65. **DD** 373.18/97. ***Continues*** *Communication, 0010-3535.*
Ind/Abst Curr. Index J. Educ. (March 1990).

US
COACHES' CORNER, THE. Vol. 1, No. 1 (Mar. 1986)-. Periodical. English. Four times a year (Mar., June, Sept., Dec.). $7.00 (one year); $12.00 (two years). Coaches Corner, 2230 East Bradford Avenue, Suite #6, Milwaukee WI 53211. **Tel** (414)224-2387. **ED** Paul Salsini and Lucille Deview (phone: (414)964-8819). **Bk Rev. Circ:** 130.
Desc: News and information on coaches writers.

US/1062-6727
COLE PAPERS, THE. [Cole pap.]. (1989)-. Periodical. English. mo. $117.00 US; $125.00 Canada; $135.00 other. Cole Group, 2590 Greenwich, Suite 9, San Francisco CA 94123. **Tel** (415)673-2424, FAX (415)673-2449. **ED** David M. Cole. **DD** 070. **Bk Rev**, (Qty: 3-5). **Circ:** 1,000. available on an online database from NEWSNET.
Desc: Devoted to coverage of technology, journalism and publishing. Emphasis is on professional publishing systems for newspapers and magazines. Stories include coverage of the major industry meetings (NEXPO, Folio, Digital Photography and the Seybold Seminars) and reviews of suppliers and software.

US/0739-1056
COLLEGE MEDIA REVIEW. [Coll. media rev.]. **Added/Corp** College Media Advisers, Inc. (U.S.). Vol. 22, No. 4 (Summer 1983)-. Periodical. English. qt (Jan., Apr., July, Oct.). $15.00 (one year), $25.00 (two year). College Media Review, Journal Department, Memphis State University, Memphis TN 38152. **Tel** (901)678-2403, FAX (901)678-4798. **ED** David Nelson (phone: (512)245-2656). ***Continues*** *College Press Review, 0010-1117.*
Desc: Articles research pertaining to all aspects of college media advising.
Ind/Abst High. Educ. Abstr. (1973-).

US/0162-0010
COLORADO EDITOR. Added/Corp Colorado Press Association. (19??)-. Periodical. English. Twelve times a year. $5.00. Colorado Press Association, 1336 Glenarm Place, Denver CO 80204. **Tel** (303)571-5117. **ED** Marge Easton. **LC** PN4700; .C6. **DD** 070.5. **Circ:** 655.

US/0010-194X
COLUMBIA JOURNALISM REVIEW. [Columbia journal. rev.]. Vol. 1, (Spring 1962)-. Periodical. English. bm. $21.00. Columbia University / Columbia Journalism Review, 700A Journalism Building, New York NY 10027. **Tel** (212)854-2716, FAX (212)854-7837, telex 220094 COLUUR. **(Subscription address:** PO Box 1943, Marion, OH 43302-1943**) ED** Suzanne Braun Levine. **LC** PN4700; .C64. **DD** 070/.05. Index available. cum. index. **Bk Rev. Ad Acc. Circ:** 31,000. available on microfilm and microfiche from University Microfilms International (UMI); available on an online database (file 648/Full-Text) from DIALOG. Documents available from UMI Article Clearinghouse.
Desc: The Columbia Journalism Review monitors the nation's news media--press, radio, and TV. It seeks to assess the performance fo journalists and help define--or redefine--standards of honest, responsible service. Indispensable for the media professional and the concerned new consumer.
Ind/Abst ABI/INFORM Glob. Ed.; ABI Inform Ondisc (Jan. 1975-April 1975); Acad. Abstr. Full Text Elite (Sept. 1984-June 1989); Acad. Abstr. (Sept. 1984-June 1989); Acad. Ind. [Computer File] (1987-); Acad. Search (Sept. 1984-June 1989); Annu. Bibliogr. Engl. Lang. Lit.; Book Rev. Digest; Book Rev. Index; Expand. Acad. Index (1987-); Film Lit. Index; Hum. Rights Intern. Rep.; Humanit. Index; Index Period. Artic. Relat. Law (19??-19??); INFO-SOUTH Abstr.; Mag. Artic. Summar. Elite (Sept. 1984-June 1989); Mag. Artic. Summar. Select (Sept. 1984-June 1989); Mag. Artic. Summar. CD-ROM (Sept. 1984-June 1989); Mag. Express (1988-) [Full Txt.]; Mag. Search; Middle East Abstr. Index; Newsp. Period. Abstr. (1988-); Pop. Period. Index; Read. Guide Abstr. Select Ed.; Read. Guide Period. Lit.; Resource/One Ondisc; Topicator.

CN/0702-7990
COMMUNICATOR (VANCOUVER). (COMMUNICATOR.). Began with May 1976 issue. Periodical. English. Royal Navy Communications, B Branch Whitehall, London SW1 England. **DD** 071/.11.

US/1041-7117
COMMUNICATOR (WASHINGTON, D.C. 1988). (COMMUNICATOR : THE MAGAZINE OF THE RADIO-TELEVISION NEWS DIRECTORS ASSOCIATION.). [Communicator]. **Added/Corp** Radio-Television News Directors Association. **VFOAT** RTNDA Communicator. Vol. 42, No. 8 (Aug. 1988)-. Periodical. English. Twelve times a year. $75.00. Radio-Television News Directors Association, 1717 K Street Northwest, Suite 615, Washington DC 20006. **Tel** (202)659-6510, (800)807-8632, FAX (202)223-4007. **DD** 384. ***Continues*** *Radio-Television News Directors Association. RTNDA Communicator, 0033-7153.*

US
COMMUNIQUE / GANNETT CENTER FOR MEDIA STUDIES. Added/Corp Gannett Center for Media Studies. Vol. 1, No. 1 (Sept. 1986)-. Periodical. English. Eleven times a year (published monthly with July/Aug issue combined). free on request. Freedom Forum Media Studies Center, Columbia University, Financial Department, 2950 Broadway, New York NY 10027. **Tel** (212)678-6600, FAX (212)678-6663. **ED** Jeanne Sahadi.

US
COMMUNITY COLLEGE JOURNALIST : OFFICIAL PUBLICATION OF THE COMMUNITY COLLEGE JOURNALISM ASSOCIATION. Added/Corp Community College Journalism Association (U.S.). **VFOAT** Journalist; CCJA Journalist. Vol. 11, No. 3 (Fall 1983)-. Periodical. English. qt. $40.00. Community College Journalism Association, 3376 Hill Canyon Avenue, Thousand Oaks CA 91360-1119. **Tel** (805)492-4440, FAX (805)493-3479. **ED** Tom Pasqua (Editor's Address: 760 Monterey, Chula Vista, CA 92010; Editor's Phone: (619)422-6465). **Bk Rev. Ad Acc. Circ:** 400 (ctrl). available on microfiche from ERIC. ***Continues*** *Journalist (Community College Journalism Association (U.S.)).*

US/8756-7911
COMPUTERITER. See Computers-Microcomputers, Personal Computers.

AG
COMUNICACION Y CULTURA. ***Suspended.*** **See** Communication.

SP/0214-0039
COMUNICACION Y SOCIEDAD. See Communication.

US/0277-5956
CONNECTICUT NEWS HANDBOOK. (19??)-. English. an. $99.95. Connecticut Information Company, PO Box 2402, Short Beach CT 06405. **Tel** (203)397-4511. **ED** Thomas C. Clarie. **LC** AI21.H37; C66. **DD** 071/.46/3. **Circ:** 50.

CN/0045-835X
CONTENT FOR CANADIAN JOURNALISTS (1984). ***Title Change.*** (CONTENT FOR CANADIAN JOURNALISTS.). [Content Can. journal.]. **Added/Corp** Friends of Content. **VFOAT** Content. (May/June 1984)-(19??). Periodical. English. bm. Canadian Association of Journalists, 1125 Colonel by Dr. Carleton Un, Ottawa Ontario K1S 5B6 Canada. **Tel** (613)788-7424. **DD** 071/.1. ***Continues*** *Content (Montreal, Quebec), 0832-0950.* ***Continued by*** *Media.*
Desc: Canada's national periodical of news, comment and analysis about journalism. Primary purpose is to help raise professional standards and enhance the craft's sense of its social and cultural responsibilities, while helping the general public understand how the media behave. Book reviews, profiles and personal comment are regular features.
Ind/Abst Can. Period. Index.

FR
CORRESPONDANCE DE LA PRESSE. French. da. 19150.00F France; 20450.00F other. Societe Generale de Presse et d'Editions, 13 Avenue de l'Opera, 75001 Paris France. **Tel** 011 33 1 40151789.

UK
CPU NEWS : JOURNAL OF THE COMMONWEALTH PRESS UNION. Added/Corp Commonwealth Press Union. (Jan. 1989)-. Periodical. English. bm (6y). £12.00 UK; £20.00 other. Commonwealth Press Union, Studio House, 184 Fleet Street, London ED4A 2DU England. **Tel** 011 44 71 242 1056, FAX 011 44 71 831 4923, telex 9356565. **ED** Eric Blott. **Bk Rev**, (Qty: 4/5). **Ad Acc, Adv Mgr:** Ms. Wade. **Circ:** 2,000 (ctrl). ***Continues*** *CPU.*

UK
CPU : QUARTERLY OF THE COMMONWEALTH PRESS UNION. VFOAT CPU Quarterly; CPUQ; Commonwealth Press Union Quarterly. Periodical. English. qt. $15.33. Commonwealth Press Union, Studio House, 184 Fleet Street, London ED4A 2DU England. **Tel** 011 44 71 242 1056, FAX 011 44 71 831 4923, telex 9356565. **Bk Rev. Ad Acc.** ctrl circ.

US/0738-2901
DEADLINE (CHICAGO, ILL.). (DEADLINE.). [Deadline]. **Added/Corp** GEI Communications. (1983)-. Periodical. English. mo. GEI Communications, 4747 West Peterson Avenue, Chicago IL 60646.
Ind/Abst U.S. Polit. Sci. Doc. (199?-).

●FR/1165-8606
DECISIONS MEDIAS. See Communication.

XR/0011-8214
DEMOCRATIC JOURNALIST, THE. Added/Corp International Organization of Journalists. Vol. 1 (Nov. 1953)-. Periodical. English. mo. $12.50. IOJ Publishing, Rooseveltova 18, 160 00 Prague Czech Republic. **Tel** 011 42 2 2316412. **(Subscription address:** Artia Pegas Press Ltd., Palac Metro Narodni Trida 25, 11210 Prague 1 Czech Republic.**) ED** Rudolf Prevratil. **LC** PN4701; .D4. **DD** 070. **Bk Rev. Circ:** 8,000 (ctrl).
Desc: The leading publications of the International Organization of Journalists.

RU
DEMOKRATICHESKII ZHURNALIST. Added/Corp Mezhdunarodnaia Organiztsiia Zhurnalistov. (1961)-. Periodical. Russian. mo. $99.95. **(Subscription address:** East View Publications Inc., 3020 Harbor Lane North, Suite 110, Minneapolis MN 55447.)

US/1050-9224
DESIGN (WASHINGTON, D.C., 1980). (DESIGN : THE JOURNAL OF THE SOCIETY OF NEWSPAPER DESIGNERS.). [Design]. **Added/Corp** Society of Newspaper Designers. Society of Newspaper

Design. No. 1 (Mar. 1980)-. Periodical. English. qt. $55.00 (professional membership), $35.00 (student membership). Society of Newspaper Design, PO Box 4075, Reston VA 22090. **Tel** (703)620-1083. **ED** Ray Chattman, Executive Director. **DD** 070. **Ad Acc, Adv Mgr:** Ray Chattman, **Tel** (703)620-1083.
Desc: Information on newspaper layout and typography.
Ind/Abst Expand. Acad. Index (1992-).

●US/1061-6039
DEVELOPING YOUR CREATIVE WRITING STYLE AND LEARNING THE CRAFT OF WRITING. **See** Literature.

CK
DIRECTORIO DE PERIODISTAS PROFESIONALES DE COLOMBIA. 1-1979-. Spanish. Servicios de Comunicacion Social Ltda, Apartado Aereo 12003, Bogota DE Colombia. **LC** PN5053; .A18.

US/0278-8829
DIRECTORY / AMERICAN SOCIETY OF JOURNALISTS AND AUTHORS. **Main/Corp** American Society of Journalists and Authors. (19??)-. English. an. $78.75. Moonbeam Publications Inc, 18530 Mack Avenue, Grosse Pointe MI 48236. **Tel** (800)445-2391, (313)884-5255, FAX (313)884-5166. **LC** PN4841; .S62. **DD** 070/.025/73. ***Continues*** *American Society of Journalists and Authors. Directory of Professional Writers.*

CN/0833-9821
DIRECTORY OF MEMBERS - PERIODICAL WRITERS ASSOCIATION OF CANADA. (DIRECTORY OF MEMBERS / (P.W.A.C.) PERIODICAL WRITERS ASSOCIATION OF CANADA.). [Dir. memb. - Period. Writ. Assoc. Can.]. **Main/Corp** Periodical Writers Association of Canada. (1985/86)-. English. an (Feb.). $15.00. Periodical Writers Association of Canada, 24 Ryerson Avenue, Toronto Ontario M5T 2P3 Canada. **Tel** (416)868-6914, (416)504-1645, FAX (416)860-0826. **ED** Jane Widerman. **DD** 070.1/75/02571. **Ad Acc.** ***Continues*** *Directory of Professional Members, 0829-0857.*
Desc: Directory of professional free lance periodical writers.

●CN/1197-5148
DIRECTORY OF SOURCES FOR EDITORS, REPORTERS & RESEARCHERS, THE. [Dir. sources ed. report. res.]. **VFOAT** Directory of Sources; Sources. 30th Ed. (Summer 1992)-. Directory. English. sa. Sources, 4 Phipps Street, Suite 109, Toronto Ontario M4Y 1J5 Canada. **Tel** (416)964-7799, FAX (416)964-8763. **DD** 061/.1. Index available. **Bk Rev. Ad Acc. Circ:** 15,000 (ctrl). ***Continues*** *Sources (B. Zwicker : Publisher)., 0700-480X.*

US/0195-6124
DIRECTORY - OUTDOOR WRITERS ASSOCIATION OF AMERICA. **Main/Corp** Outdoor Writers Association of America. **VFOAT** OWAA Outdoor Writers Directory. 1979/80-. Directory. English. an. Outdoor Writers Association of America Inc, 2017 Cato Avenue, Suite 101, State College PA 16801. **Tel** (814)234-1011. **ED** Carol J Kersavage. **LC** PN4871; .O9. **DD** 070.4/497965. **Circ:** 2,500 (ctrl). ***Continues*** *OWAA National Outdoor Writers Directory.*

US/0196-7134
DOCUMENTARY EDITING. **Added/Corp** Association for Documentary Editing. Vol. 6, No. 1 (March 1984)-. Periodical. English. Four times a year. $25.00. Rhode Island Historical Society, 110 Benevolent Street, Providence RI 02906. **Tel** (401)331-8575, FAX (401)751-7930. **ED** C. James Taylor (editor's telephone: (803)777-6526). Index available (bound in Dec. issue). cum. index. **Bk Rev**, (Qty: 15). **Circ:** 500. ***Continues*** *Newsletter of the Association for Documentary Editing.*

GW/0417-9994
DORTMUNDER BEITRAGE ZUR ZEITUNGSFORSCHUNG. 1.- V. 1958-. Periodical. German. Verlag Dokumentation, Postfach 711009, W-8000 Muenchen 71 Germany. **Tel** 089/791040, telex 5212067. **LC** PN4703. ***Supersedes*** *Dortmund. Westfalisch-Niederrheinisches Institut fuer Zeitungsforschung. Mitteilungen; Dortmund. Westfalisch-Niederrheinisches Institut fuer Zeitungsforschung. Veroffentlichungen.*

FR
DROIT DE LA PRESSE. French. 550.00F. LITEC, Service Abonnements, 6 rue Victor Cousin, 75005 Paris France. **Tel** 011 33 1 46332237, FAX 011 33 1 46335032.

CN/0959-793X
DUMFRIES AND GALLOWAY COURIER. ***Ceased.*** (THE DUMFRIES AND GALLOWAY COURIER [MICROFORM].). Dec. 6, 1809 issue-Ceased with Mar. 25, 1884 issue. English. Preston Microfilming Services, 2215 Queen Street East, Toronto Ontario M4E 1E8 Canada. **Tel** (416)699-7154. **DD** 072/.9147.

FR
ECHO DE LA PRESSE (PARIS, FRANCE). (L'ECHO DE LA PRESSE.). No. 1 (Jan. 13, 1989)-. Periodical. French. Forty-Five times a year. 1,126.35F European Union; 1,560.00F other. Liaisons & Convergence, 1 Avenue East Belin, F-92856 Rueil Mal France. **Tel** 011 33 1 41299872, FAX 011 33 1 47575420, telex 613128. **LC** PN4702; .E22. **DD** 070.4/05. **Ad Acc.** ***Continues*** *Echo de la Presse et de la Publicite, 0755-0529.*

SA/0256-0054
ECQUID NOVI. **Added/Corp** Randse Afrikaanse Universiteit. Departement Kommunikasieleer. Vol. 1 No. 1 (1980)-. Periodical. Afrikaans (English). Twice a year. $25.00 (individuals), $50.00 (institutions). Science Africa, PO Box 40221, Arcadia 0007 South Africa. **Tel** 011 27 12 3486660.

US/0013-094X
EDITOR & PUBLISHER. **See** Publishing.

US/0424-4923
EDITOR & PUBLISHER INTERNATIONAL YEAR BOOK. **VFOAT** Editor and Publisher International Year Book; Editor and Publisher Year Book; Editor & Publisher Year Book. **VAT** Editor and Publisher International Year Book. (1959)-. English. an. $90.00 US & Canada; $113.00 other. Editor & Publisher Company, 11 West 19th Street, New York NY 10011. **Tel** (212)675-4380. **LC** PN4700; .E42. **DD** 070.5/025; 655; 070.172. available on microfilm and microfiche from University Microfilms International (UMI). ***Continues*** *Editor & Publisher. International Year Book Number.*

US
EDITOR & PUBLISHER. SYNDICATE DIRECTORY. **VFOAT** Syndicate Directory; Annual Syndicate Directory. (19??)-. Directory. English. an. $7.00. Editor & Publisher Company, 11 West 19th Street, New York NY 10011. **Tel** (212)675-4380. **ED** Robert U. Brown. **Ad Acc. Circ:** 30,000.
Desc: Complete listing of all newspaper syndicates and syndicated writers and services.

US/0736-1785
EDITORIAL EXCELLENCE. [Editor. excell.]. **Added/Corp** National Conference of Editorial Writers (U.S.). Vol. 1 (1982)-. Monographic series. English. ir. Price varies per volume. National Conference of Editorial Writers, 6223 Executive Boulevard, Rockville MD 20852. **Tel** (301)984-3015. **LC** PN4778; .E34. **DD** 070.4/12.

US
EDITOR'S DIGEST. **See** Publishing.

US/0746-3014
EDITOR'S FORUM (KANSAS CITY, MO.). (EDITOR'S FORUM.). [Ed. forum]. (198?)-. Periodical. English. mo. $104.00 one year, $192.40 two years. Editors Forum, PO Box 411806, Kansas City MO 64141. **Tel** (913)236-9235. **ED** William R. Brinton, (phone: (913)384-2555). **DD** 070. **Bk Rev**, (Qty: 4). **Circ:** 1,000. available on diskette. ***Continues*** *The Newsletter Forum, 0272-4642.*
Desc: Contains useful information and tips on writing editing, makeup, design and photography. Articles are on headlines, interviews, writing and editing. A look at what other editors are doing to improve their publications and tips on secrets of publishing newsletters.

US/0888-3173
EDITORS' NOTES. ***Ceased.*** (EDITORS' NOTES : BULLETIN OF THE CONFERENCE OF EDITORS' OF LEARNED JOURNALS.). [Ed. notes]. **Added/Corp** Conference of Editors of Learned Journals. **VFOAT** CELJ Bulletin. Vol. 1, No. 1 (Spring 1982)-(19??). Bulletin. English. Twice a year. Council Editors Learned Journals, Clarkson University, Box 5750, Potsdam NY 13699-5750. **Tel** (315)268-3987, FAX (315)268-3983. **ED** Edna Steeves (editor's address: University of Rhode Island Kingston RI 02881; editor's phone: (401)789-7131). **LC** PN4778; .E36. **DD** 070.4/1/05. **Ad Acc. Circ:** 600 (ctrl).
Desc: Articles on editing a scholarly journal.
Ind/Abst Abstr. Engl. Stud.; MLA Int. Bibl. Books Artic. Mod. Lang. Lit.

US/0735-8490
EDITORS ONLY. Vol. 1, No. 1 (Nov. 1982)-. Newsletter. English. Twelve times a year. $89.00 US; $95.00 Canada and Mexico; $105.00 other. Editors Only, PO Box 17108, Fountain AZ 85269. **Tel** (602)837-6492, FAX (602)837-6872. **ED** Bill Dunkerley (Editor's Telephone: (203)827-8896). **Bk Rev**, (Qty: 2). **Circ:** 500 (ctrl). available on an online database from NEWSNET.
Desc: A newsletter to promote editorial achievements and excellence.

US/0883-8569
EDITOR'S WORKSHOP NEWSLETTER. [Ed. workshop newsl.]. **VFOAT** EWN. (198?)-. Newsletter. English. mo. $119.00 US; $134.00. Ragan Communications Inc., 212 West Superior Street, Suite 200, Chicago IL 60610. **Tel** (312)335-0037, (800)878-5331, FAX (312)335-9583. **DD** 070. ***Continues in part*** *Ragan Report Workshops Notebook. Supplement.*

US
ENCYCLOMEDIA : MAGAZINE EDITION. **VFOAT** Magazine Edition, Encyclomedia; Magazine Encyclomedia. English. an. Decisions Publications, 342 Madison Avenue, New York NY 10017.

US/0895-2310
EXTRA! (NEW YORK, N.Y. 1987). (EXTRA! : THE NEWSLETTER OF FAIR (FAIRNESS & ACCURACY IN REPORTING).). [Extra!]. **Added/Corp** Fairness & Accuracy in Reporting (Organization). Vol. 1, No. 1 (June 1987)-. Newsletter. English. Six times a year. $40.00 institutions; $30.00 individuals. FAIR, 130 West 25th Street, New York NY 10001. **Tel** (212)633-6700. **ED** Jim Naureckas. **LC** PN4700; .E97. **DD** 070. **Circ:** 15,000.
Desc: Offers well-documented criticism in an effort to correct media bias and imbalance.
Ind/Abst Altern. Press Index (199?-); Hum. Rights Intern. Rep.

US/0739-0033
FILLERS FOR PUBLICATIONS. (19??)-. Periodical. English. mo. $117.00 (Fillers with 1 supplement), $84.00 (1 supplement only) (1 year); $124.00 (Fillers only), $208.00 (Fillers with 1 supplement), $308.00 (with all 3 supplements), $134.00 (1 supplement only) (2 year). Fillers for Publications, 7015 Prospect PL North East, Alburquerque NM 87110. **Tel** (505)884-7636, FAX (505)888-0477.
Desc: Copy for editors including health and safety, seasonal, general interest, business, features of various lengths; column stretchers; humorous pieces; editorials.

US/0196-8548
FINDER BINDER. ARIZONA'S UPDATED MEDIA DIRECTORY. (FINDERBINDER. STATE OF ARIZONA.). **Added/Corp** Rita Sanders Advertising & Public Relations Agency. **VFOAT** Arizona's Updated Media Directory; Finderbinder. **VAT** Finderbinder. Arizona's Updated Media Directory. (1980)-. English. Twelve times a year. $176.05. Arizona's Updated Media Directory, 432 East Southern Avenue, Tempe AZ 85282. **Tel** (602)967-8714, FAX (602)894-6216. **ED** Sandy Painter. **LC** P88.8; .F5615. **Circ:** 700 (ctrl).
Desc: Media Directory

US
FIRST DRAFT. (19??)-. Newsletter. English. mo. $139.00 US; $154.00 other. Ragan Communications Inc., 212 West Superior Street, Suite 200, Chicago IL 60610. **Tel** (312)335-0037, (800)878-5331, FAX (312)335-9583.

US/0426-5920
FLORIDA PRESS, THE. ***Ceased.*** [Fla. press]. **Added/Corp** Florida Press Association. Vol. 1, No. 1 (Jan. 1958)-(July 1990). English. qt. Florida Press Association, 336 E College Avenue/Suite 103, Tallahassee FL 32301-1554. **DD** 071.

US/1040-3205
FOCUSES (BOONE, N.C.). (FOCUSES.). Vol. 1, No. 1 (Spring 1988)-. Periodical. English. sa. $15.00 (institutions), $10.00 (individuals). Appalachian State University Department of English, Boone NC 28608. **Tel** (704)262-2000. **ED** William C. Wolff. **LC** WMLC 93/424. **DD** 808.
Desc: Journal devoted to the teaching of writing.

US/1056-9413
FOIA UPDATE. (FOIA UPDATE / U.S. DEPARTMENT OF JUSTICE, OFFICE OF INFORMATION LAW AND POLICY.). [FOIA updat.]. **Added/Corp** United States. Dept. of Justice. Office of Information Law and Policy. United States. Dept. of Justice. Office of Information and Privacy. **VAT** Freedom of Information Act Update. Vol. 1, No. 1 (Autumn 1979)-. Government Publication. English. qt. $5.00 domestic; $6.25 other. Superintendent of Documents, US Government Printing Office, Washington DC 20402. **Tel** (202)275-3328, FAX (202)786-2377.
Desc: Contains updated news articles pertaining to the Freedom of Information Act.
Ind/Abst Index U.S. Gov. Period.

US/0888-3955
FOLLOWUP FILE. Periodical. English. wk. $185.00. Stone Scott Company, 16 North Marengo Avenue, Suite 600, Pasadena CA 91101. **Tel** (818)585-0232. **ED** Roger D. Scott. ctrl circ.
Desc: Story information for journalists.

●US/1067-4926
FORBES MEDIACRITIC. [Forbes mediaCrit.]. **Added/Corp** Forbes Inc. **VFOAT** Forbes Media Critic; Media Critic; MediaCritic. Vol. 1, No. 1 (1993)-. Periodical. English. qt (4 issues). $29.95 US; $39.95 Canada; $44.95 other. American Heritage, Forbes Building, 60 Fifth Avenue, New York NY 10011. **Tel** (212)206-5512, (212)620-1804. **DD** 302. ***Continues in part*** *MediaGuide, 1042-2129.*

●US/1067-4918
FORBES MEDIAGUIDE 500. [Forbes mediaGuide 500]. **Added/Corp** Forbes Inc. **VFOAT** Forbes Media Guide 500; Forbes MediaGuide Five Hundred; MediaGuide 500; Media Guide; MediaGuide. (1993)-. Periodical. English. an. $22.45. Forbes Magazine, 60 Fifth Avenue, New York NY 10011. **Tel**

(212)620-2200, (800)825-0061. **(Subscription address:** Forbes Media Guide, PO Box 6615, Syracuse NY 13217.) **LC** PN4877; .F58. **DD** 302. ***Continues in part*** *MediaGuide, 1042-2129.*

●US/1063-1267
FREE PRESS (COLUMBUS, OHIO), THE. (THE FREE PRESS.). **Added/Corp** Columbus Institute for Contemporary Journalism. (April 1992)-. Periodical. English. mo. $12.00. Columbus Free Press, 1066 North High Street, Columbus OH 43201. **Tel** (614)294-9200. ***Continues*** *Columbus Freepress (Columbus, Ohio : 1976).*

US
FREELANCE DIRECTORY. Main/Corp American Medical Writers Association. (198?)-. Directory. English. American Medical Writers Association, 9650 Rockville Pike, Bethesda MD 20814-3928. **Tel** (301)986-9119. ***Continues*** *American Medical Writers Association.; AMWA Freelance Directory.*

●US/1064-9050
FREELANCE WRITER'S NEWSLETTER (KNOXVILLE, TENN.). (FREELANCE WRITER'S NEWSLETTER.). [Freel. writ. newsl.]. Issue 101 (1992)-. Newsletter. English. $36.00 (12 issues). Fine Arts Press, 1311-A Broadway, PO Box 3491, Knoxville TN 37927. **DD** 070.

US/0731-549X
FREELANCE WRITER'S REPORT. (FREELANCE WRITER'S REPORT / FFWA.). **Added/Corp** Cassell Communications. Florida Freelancae Writers Association. Vol. 1, No. 1 (March 1982)-. Periodical. English. mo. $39.00 (one year), $64.00 (two years) US; $51.00 (one year), $88.00 (two years) Canada; $54.00 (one year), $94.00 (two years) other. CNW Publishing, Editing & Promotion Inc., Maple Ridge Road, North Sandwich NH 03259. **Tel** (800)351-9278, (603)284-6367, FAX (603)284-6648. **ED** Dana K Cassell. **Bk Rev**, (Qty: 50). **Ad Acc. Circ:** 1,000.

US/0016-0636
FREELANCER'S NEWSLETTER. Vol. 1 (1970)-. Periodical. English. sm (except monthly in Sept. and July). $50.00. Circle Publication Inc, c/o Jo Ann Bardin, 307 Westlake Drive, Austin TX 78746. **Tel** (512)327-1208. **ED** Jo Ann Bardin. **Bk Rev. *Absorbed*** *In Black and White.* ***Absorbed in part by*** *Editorial Eye, 0193-7383.*
Desc: Articles and news of interest to freelancers, a marketing aid for writers and photographers. Computerized resume service for subscribers.

US/1059-5937
FRONT PAGE NEWS PLUS BUSINESS. (FRONT PAGE NEWS (PLUS BUSINESS) [COMPUTER FILE].). [Front page news plus bus.]. **VFOAT** Front Page News; Front-Page-News. (1989)-. Periodical. English. qt. $499.95. Buckmaster Publishing - Virginia, Route 4, Box 1630, Mineral VA 23117. **Tel** (703)894-5777. **LC** AN. **DD** 071.

JA
FURI JANARISUTO NENKAN. (1976)-. Periodical. Japanese. ¥3800. Masukomi Hyoronsha, 13-16 Roppongi 3 Minato-ku, Tokyo-to 106 Japan. **LC** PN4705; .F87.

AG
GACETA. Main/Corp Federacion Argentina de Periodistas. Vol. 1- 1970-. Spanish. Lavalle 1125, P 3O of 8, 1048 Buenos Aires Argentina. **LC** PN4705; .F4. ***Supersedes*** *Periodista Argentino.*

US/0433-163X
GANNETTEER. Added/Corp Gannett Company. (Jan 1955)-. Periodical. English. mo. Gannett Company / New York, Lincoln Tower, Rochester NY 14604. **Tel** (716)546-8600. **DD** 070.

NE
GAZETTE; INTERNATIONAL JOURNAL OF SCIENCE OF THE PRESS. Vol. 1 (Jan. 1955)-. Periodical. English. H E Stenfert Kroese, PO Box 33, Morssingel 9 13, 2312 AZ Leiden Netherlands. **LC** PN4699; .G3. **DD** 070.5. ***Continues*** *Revue International de Science de la Presse.*

US
GENERAL ASSSEMBLY - INTER AMERICAN PRESS ASSOCIATION. ASAMBLEA GENERAL - SOCIEDAD INTERNAMERICANA DE PRENSA. **Main/Corp** Inter-American Press Association. **Added/Corp** Inter-American Press Association. Asamblea General - Sociedad Interamericana de Prensa. **VFOAT** Asamblea General - Sociedad. (19??)-. English (Spanish). an. $25.00. Interamerican Press Association, 2911 Northwest 39th Street, Miami FL 33142. **Tel** (305)634-2465, telex 522873. **LC** PN4712; .I5. **DD** 070/.06/01. **Circ:** 1,700.
Desc: Transcript of annual general assembly in original languages (English and Spanish).

US/8750-6181
GPA BULLETIN, THE. ***Title Change.*** (THE GPA BULLETIN / GEORGIA PRESS ASSOCIATION.). **Added/Corp** Georgia Press Association. **VAT** Georgia Press Association Bulletin. Issue No. 1 (Dec. 12, 1984)-(19??). Bulletin. English. bw. GPA, Georgia Press Building, 1075 Spring Street NW, Atlanta GA 30309. ***Continued by*** *GA Press Bulletin, 1067-2931.*

US/0017-3541
GRASSROOTS EDITOR. [Grassroots ed.]. **Added/Corp** International Society of Weekly Newspaper Editors. International Conference of Weekly Newspaper Editors. Vol. 1, No. 1 (Jan. 1960)-. Periodical. English. qt (4 issues). $14.00 US and Canada; $16.00 other. South Dakota State University / Department of Journalism, Box 2235, Brookings SD 57007. **Tel** (605)688-4171. **ED** Richard W. Lee. **DD** 070. **Bk Rev. Circ:** 700. available on microfilm and microfiche from University Microfilms International (UMI).
Desc: Articles relate to the interests and problems of journalists involved with community newspapers.

US/0017-5021
GUARDIAN (NEW YORK, N.Y.), THE. (THE GUARDIAN.). [Guardian]. **Added/Corp** Institute for Independent Social Journalism, Inc. (New York, N.Y.). Vol. 20 No. 19 (Feb. 10, 1968)-. Periodical. English. wk. $50.00 (one year), $90.00 (two years), $120.00 (three years) institutions US; $33.50 (one year), $59.50 (two years) individuals US; $68.00 (one year), $126.00 (two years) institutions Canada; $51.50 (one year), $95.50 (two years) individuals Canada; $100.00 (one year), $180.00 (two years) institutions Asia, Africa, Mideast and Pacific airmail; $83.50 individuals Asia, Africa, Mideast and Pacific airmail; $80.00 (one year), $210.00 (two years) institutions other; $63.50 (one year), $119.50 (two years) individuals other. Institute for Independent Social Journalism Inc, 33 West 17th Street, New York NY 10011. **Tel** (212)691-0404. **ED** William A Ryan. **LC** AP2; .N244. **DD** 071/.3. Index available. **Bk Rev. Ad Acc. Circ:** 20,000 (ctrl). available on microfilm from University Microfilms International (UMI). ***Continues*** *National Guardian, 0362-5583.*
Desc: A U.S. left newsweekly, offering news and analysis of national and international events. Also film, music and book reviews. Reports from Central America, southern Africa and the Mideast.
Ind/Abst Altern. Press Index; Chicano Index; Child. Lit. Abstr.; Index Bus. Reports; Int. Packag. Abstr.; Print. Abstr.

US
GUIDE TO BUSINESS AND FINANCIAL NEWS MEDIA. Added/Corp Larriston Communications (Firm : U.S.). **VFOAT** Business and Financial News Media. (198?)-. English. an. $70.00 nonprofit organizations, $85.00 other. Larriston Communications, PO Box 20229, New York NY 10025. **Tel** (212)864-0150. **ED** Valerie Walls. **LC** PN4888.C59; G85. **DD** 071/.3/025. **Circ:** 1,000. ***Continues*** *Guide to U.S. Business, Financial and Economic News Correspondents and Contacts, 0747-7244.*
Desc: A publicity guide listing the national and local media outlets and the editors and correspondents who cover business, finance and economic news.

US
GUIDE TO MEDICAL AND SCIENCE NEWS MEDIA. VFOAT Medical and Science News Media. 1987-. English. an. $70.00 nonprofit organizations, $85.00 other. Larriston Communications, PO Box 20229, New York NY 10025. **Tel** (212)864-0150. **LC** PN4888.M43; G84. **DD** 070.4/4961. **Circ:** 1,000. ***Continues*** *Guide to U.S. Medical and Science News Correspondents and Contents, 0747-7252.*
Desc: A publicity guide listing the national and local media outlets and the editors and correspondents who cover medical, science and health news.

US/0017-5404
GUILD REPORTER, THE. See Economics-Labor.

US
HANDS ON (RABUN GAP, GA.). See Education.

KO/0897-697X
HAN'GUK KYONGJE SINMUN. [Han'guk kyongje sinmun]. **VFOAT** Korea Economic Daily. Periodical. Korean. da. $25.00. Korea Econom Daily America Inc, PO Box 8156, 42-15 Crescent Street, Long Island City NY 11101. **Tel** (718)706-8787. **DD** 071.
Ind/Abst PROMT [Full Txt.]; PTS Newsl. Database [Full Txt.].

KO
HANGUK SINMUN PANGSONG YONGAM. VFOAT Korean Press Annual. Began with 1976 Vol. Korean. W16,000. Hanguk Sinmun Yonguso, 31 1-ka Taepyong-no, Chung-ku, Seoul South Korea. **LC** P92.K6; H33.

US/0746-2425
HIGH SCHOOL NEWS AND GRAPHICS. VFOAT High School News & Graphics; High School News. (198?)-. Periodical. English. bw. $150.00. Tribune Media Services, 435 North Michigan Avenue, Chicago IL 60611. **Tel** (800)637-4082, FAX (312)222-2581. **LC** LA229; .H495. **DD** 373.18/05.
Desc: Provides news about what's happening in other schools around the country and articles about issues that affect today's high school students. Gives story ideas, news and feature stories, topics for journalism class assignments, reporting strategies, tips for faculty advisers, graphics, and more.

US/1048-3373
HIGH SCHOOL WRITER, THE. [High Sch. Writ.]. (19??)- Vol. 8 (Sept. 1992)-. Periodical. English. Nine times a year. $49.50. Writer Publications, PO Box 718, Grand Rapids MN 55744. **Tel** (218)326-8025. **ED** Roxanne Kain. **DD** 808. **Ad Acc.** ctrl circ. ***Continues*** *High School Writer of the Midwest, 1040-760X.*
Desc: Providing a real audience for student writers.

US/0742-5538
HISTORICAL GUIDES TO THE WORLD'S PERIODICALS AND NEWSPAPERS. [Hist. guide world's period. newsp.]. (1982)-. Monographic series. English. ir. Price varies per volume. Greenwood Press Inc., PO Box 5007, Westport CT 06881-5007. **Tel** (203)226-3571, FAX (203)222-1502.

US/0749-1255
HOTLINE - NEWSLETTER ASSOCIATION OF AMERICA. (HOTLINE.). [Hotline - Newsl. Assoc. Am.]. **Added/Corp** Newsletter Association of America. (19??)-. Periodical. English. ir. $250.00 Comes with Newsletter Association of American membership. Newsletter Association of America, 1341 G Street Northwest, Suite 603, Washington DC 20005. **ED** Frederick D. Goss. **DD** 070. Index available.

CH
HSIN WEN TA HSUEH. Added/Corp Fu Tan ta Hsueh (Shanghai, China). Hsin Wen Hsi. **VFOAT** Xin Wen da Xue. (19??)-. Periodical. Chinese. NT$0.65. Shang-Hai Hsin Hua Shu Tien, Shanghai, People's Republic of China. **LC** PN4722; .H8. **DD** 070/.05.

CC
HSIN WEN YEN CHIU TZU LIAO. **Added/Corp** Chung-kuo she hui ko Hseh Yuan. Hsin wen yen Chiu so. **VFOAT** Hsin Wen Yen Chiu Tzu Liao Tsung Kan. Vol. 1 (August 1979)-. Periodical. Chinese. RMBY0.80. Chung-Kuo She Hui Ko Hsueh Chu Pan She, Hsin Hua Shu Tien Pei-Ching Fa Hsing So, Beijing, People's Republic of China. **LC** PN4705; .H74. **DD** 079/.51.

US/0441-389X
HUDSON'S WASHINGTON NEWS MEDIA CONTACTS DIRECTORY. [Hudson's Wash. news media contacts dir.]. **VFOAT** Washington News Media Contacts Directory. (1968)-. Directory. English. an. $155.00. Newsletter Clearinghouse, PO Box 311, Rhinebeck NY 12572. **Tel** (914)876-2081, FAX (914)876-2561. **ED** Howard Penn Hudson. **LC** Z6953.W2; H8. **DD** 071/.53. **Bk Rev. Ad Acc.** ctrl circ.
Desc: Guide to the Washington DC press corps; contains information on more than 4,529 correspondents for wire services, news bureaus, newspapers, syndicates, radio, TV, magazines, newsletters, photo services, free-lance writers and others. Includes complete addresses, phone numbers, fields of interest, also a subject index covering 98 categories.

US/0018-8409
IAPA NEWS. Main/Corp Inter-American Press Association. No. 197 (Oct. 1970)-. Periodical. English. Twelve times a year. $25.00. Interamerican Press Association, 2911 Northwest 39th Street, Miami FL 33142. **Tel** (305)634-2465, telex 522873. **ED** Harry Caicedo. **LC** PN4712; .I52. **Ad Acc. *Continues*** *Press of the Americas.*
Ind/Abst Hum. Rights Intern. Rep.

GW/0946-4441
IBI DIENST. (1965)-. Newsletter. German. mo. DM398.00. Gesellschaft fuer Innerbetriebliche Kommunikation, Vor Dem Tor 16, D 31552 Rodenberg Germany. **Tel** 011 49 5723 4336, FAX 011 49 5723 3707. **Ad Acc.** Full Page (B&W) DM960.00. Half Page (B&W) DM480.00. **Acid Free. Circ:** 500.
Desc: Information for editors of house organs and specialists in internal communication.

US/0099-0876
INDEX TO PRAVDA. (PRAVDA. INDEX). **Added/Corp** American Association for the Advancement of Slavic Studies. (Jan. 1975)-. English. mo. $225.00. Ohio State University / Pravda, 2043 Millikin Road, Columbus OH 43210. **LC** AI21.P73; P7. **DD** 077/.31.

US/1058-4730
INFORMATION PUBLISHING. (INFORMATION PUBLISHING : BUSINESS/PROFESSIONAL MARKETS & MEDIA.). [Inf. pub.]. **Added/Corp** Simba Information, Inc. (1991)-. English. $1,495.00. Simba Information Inc., 213 Danbury Road, Wilton CT 06897-7430. **Tel** (203)834-0033 ext. 133, FAX (203)884-1771. **DD** 070.

CN
INTERNATIONAL PRESS JOURNAL.
Began with Jan./Feb. 1957 issue. Periodical. English. $50.00. Press Journal, PO Box 3285 Station F, Willowdale Ontario M2R 3G6 Canada. **Tel** (416)491-1201. **ED** Bali Sethi. **LC** PN4699; .I57. **DD** 071/.1/3. **Bk Rev**. **Circ:** 1,000.
Desc: International coverage on serials, who's who, yearbooks, trade directories on all subjects. Review of serial publications from all over the world.

US/0731-0978
INVESTIGATIVE REPORTER, THE. [Invest. rep.]. Vol. 1, No. 1 (Jan. 1982)-. Periodical. English. $18.00. The Investigative Reporter, 1401 16 NW, Washington DC 20036. **ED** Jack Anderson.

XR
IOJ NEWS LETTER / THE INTERNATIONAL ORGANIZATION OF JOURNALISTS. Periodical. English. sm. International Organization of Journalists / Czech Republic, Parizska 9, Prague 1 Czech Republic.

SZ/0019-0314
IPI REPORT. Vol. 1, (May 1952)-. Periodical. English. mo. 225.00F. International Press Institute, Wyderweg 10, CH 8047 Zurich Switzerland. **Tel** 011 41 1 4921419, FAX 011 41 1 4934080, telex 25950. **LC** PN4712. Documents available from UMI Article Clearinghouse.
Ind/Abst Expand. Acad. Index (1992-); Hum. Rights Intern. Rep.; Newsp. Period. Abstr. (1992-).

US/0164-7016
IRE JOURNAL, THE. [IRE j.]. **Main/Corp** Investigative Reporters and Editors, Inc. **VAT** Investigative Reporters and Editors Journal. Vol. 1, (Oct./Nov. 1978)-. Periodical. English. Six times a year (Jan., Mar., May, July, Sept., Nov.). $25.00 one year. University of Missouri School of Journalism, 213 Walter Williams Hall, Columbia MO 65211. **Tel** (314)882-3364, FAX (314)882-5431. **ED** Steve Weinberg (editor's address: 100 Neft Hall, Columbia, MO 65211, (314)882-2042). Index available. **Bk Rev**, (Qty: 8). **Circ:** 5,000. available on microfilm and microfiche from University Microfilms International (UMI). Documents available from UMI Article Clearinghouse.
Desc: Devoted to issues and techniques of information gathering in the journalism field.
Ind/Abst Expand. Acad. Index (1992-); Hum. Rights Intern. Rep.; Newsp. Period. Abstr. (1992-).

US/0897-0696
ISSUES IN WRITING. [Issues writ.]. **Added/Corp** University of Wisconsin--Stevens Point. Dept. of English. Vol. 1, No. 1 (Fall 1988)-. Periodical. English. Twice a year. $14.00. Issues in Writing, University of Wisconsin, English Department, Stevenspoint WI 54481. **Tel** (715)346-4342, FAX (715)346-4215. **ED** Roberta Stokes, W. John Coletta. **DD** 808. **CODEN** ISWRE7. Index available in last issue of volume--attached. cum. index. **Bk Rev**, (Qty: 10). **Ad Acc. Circ:** 500.
Ind/Abst Abstr. Anthropol. (19??-); Soc. Plann. Policy Dev. Abstr.

BU/0324-1238
IZKUSTVO. [Izkustvo]. (1951)-. Periodical. Bulgarian. Ten times a year. DM74.00. Komitet za Kultura, Sofia Bulgaria. **(Subscription address:** Kubon & Sagner, ABT Zeitschriftenimport, D 80328 Munich Germany.**)** **UDC** 7.
Ind/Abst BHA : Biblio. Hist. Art.

●US/0360-0939
JACA : JOURNAL OF THE ASSOCIATION FOR COMMUNICATION ADMINISTRATION. **See** Communication.

US/0146-4957
JOHN PETER ZENGER AWARD FOR FREEDOM OF THE PRESS AND THE PEOPLE'S RIGHT TO KNOW, THE. [John Peter Zenger award freedom press people's right know]. 1966-. Monographic series. English. an. Price varies per volume. University of Arizona Press, 1230 North Park Avenue, Suite 102, Tucson AZ 85719. **Tel** (602)882-3065, (800)426-3797. **LC** PN4738; .J57. **DD** 323.44/5. ***Continues*** *John Peter Zenger Award for Freedom of the Press.*

US/0893-5386
JOURNAL HOLDINGS IN THE NATIONAL CAPITAL AREA. [J. hold. natl. cap. area]. **Added/Corp** Interlibrary Users Association (Washington, D.C.). 7th Edition (1987)-. English. be. $30.00 (members); $190.00 (non-members) Comes with Interlibrary Users Association membership. Interlibrary Users Association, 3119 Miller Heights Road, Oakton VA 22124. **Tel** (703)902-5913. **(Subscription address:** Macron Systems Inc., 212 Elmhurst Circle, Evans City PA 16033.**)** **LC** Z6945; .J8; PN4801. **DD** 011/.34/09753. **NLM** Z 6945; J86. ***Continues*** *Journal Holdings in the Washington-Baltimore Area, 0362-4544.*

CN/0384-6784
JOURNAL L'ECLAIREUR ABITIBIEN.
VFOAT Eclaireur. V. 1 Jan. 1977-. Periodical. French. mo. 0.50Can$ per no. J. Albert, CP 248 Val D'Or, Abitibi Quebec Jp9 4P3 Canada. **DD** 071/.14/13.

●US/1065-755X
JOURNAL OF CREATIVE WRITING AND BIBLIOTHERAPY, THE. (1993)-. Periodical. English. qt. $20.00. Theraplan Inc., 3015 Woodsdale Boulevard, Lincoln NE 68502-5053. **Tel** (402)421-3172.

MY/0128-3863
JOURNAL OF DEVELOPMENT COMMUNICATION, THE. **See** Communication.

UK/0265-5942
JOURNAL OF NEWSPAPER AND PERIODICAL HISTORY. ***Ceased.*** Vol. 1, No. 1 (Winter 1984)-(1992). Periodical. English. an (2 issues per year). Greenwood Press Inc., PO Box 5007, Westport CT 06881-5007. **Tel** (203)226-3571, FAX (203)222-1502. **ED** Michael Harris. **LC** PN4699; .J65. **DD** 070/.09. Index available. cum. index. **Bk Rev. Ad Acc.** available on microfilm.
Desc: Provides a focus for all those with a professional or academic interest in press history within a chronological span extending from the seventeenth to the twentieth century.
Ind/Abst Am. Hist. Life (1984-); Annu. Bibliogr. Engl. Lang. Lit.; Commun. Abstr.; Libr. Inf. Sci. Abstr.; MLA Int. Bibl. Books Artic. Mod. Lang. Lit.

US/1077-694X
JOURNALISM & MASS COMMUNICATION ABSTRACTS. (199?)-. English. an. $20.00 US; $30.00 other (institution). Association for Education in Journalism and Mass Communication, University of South Carolina, 1621 College Street, Columbia SC 29208-0251. **Tel** (803)777-2005, FAX (803)777-4728. ***Continues*** *Journalism Abstracts, 0075-4412.*

US/0895-6545
JOURNALISM & MASS COMMUNICATION DIRECTORY. [Journal. mass commun. dir.]. **Added/Corp** Association for Education in Journalism and Mass Communication. **VFOAT** Journalism and Mass Communication Directory; Journalism Directory. Vol. 4 (1986)-. Directory. English. an (April). $20.00 US; $30.00 other. Association for Education in Journalism and Mass Communication, University of South Carolina, 1621 College Street, Columbia SC 29208-0251. **Tel** (803)777-2005, FAX (803)777-4728. **LC** PN4788; .J6. **DD** 070/.07/1173. ***Continues*** *Journalism Directory, 0735-3103.*

US/1077-6958
JOURNALISM & MASS COMMUNICATION EDUCATOR. (19??)-. English. qt (4 issues). $35.00 US; $40.00 other (institution). Association for Education in Journalism and Mass Communication, University of South Carolina, 1621 College Street, Columbia SC 29208-0251. **Tel** (803)777-2005, FAX (803)777-4728. ***Continues*** *Journalism Educator, 0022-5517.*
Desc: Teaching techniques, new courses and technology, statistical information on students, schools, and careers in journalism.

US/1077-6966
JOURNALISM & MASS COMMUNICATION MONOGRAPHS. (199?)-. English. ir (6-7 times per year). $35.00 (institution); $30.00 (individual) US; $40.00 (institution); $35.00 (individual) other. Association for Education in Journalism and Mass Communication, University of South Carolina, 1621 College Street, Columbia SC 29208-0251. **Tel** (803)777-2005, FAX (803)777-4728. **ED** Joe McKerns. ***Continues*** *Journalism Monographs, 0022-5525.*
Desc: In-depth research on a specific topic in the field of journalism.

US/1077-6990
JOURNALISM & MASS COMMUNICATION QUARTERLY. (199?)-. English. qt (4 issues). $50.00 US; $60.00 other (institution). Association for Education in Journalism and Mass Communication, University of South Carolina, 1621 College Street, Columbia SC 29208-0251. **Tel** (803)777-2005, FAX (803)777-4728. ***Continues*** *Journalism Quarterly, 0196-3031.*

US/0094-7679
JOURNALISM HISTORY. [Journal. hist.]. **Added/Corp** California State University Foundation. California State University, Northridge. Dept. of Journalism. Vol. 1 (Spring 1974)-. Periodical. English. qt. $15.00 (individuals), $35.00 (institutions) US, Canada, and Mexico; $25.00 (individuals), $45.00 (institutions) other. Greenspun School of Communication, University of Nevada, 4505 Maryland Parkway, Las Vegas NV 89154. **Tel** (702)895-3964, FAX (702)895-4805. **ED** Barbara Cloud. **LC** PN4700; .J65. **DD** 071/.3. Index available. **Bk Rev**, (Qty: 50). **Ad Acc. Pr Rev. Circ:** 600. available on microfilm and microfiche from University Microfilms International (UMI). Documents available from UMI Article Clearinghouse.
Desc: Publish articles on full scope of topics related to mass communications history. Emphasize contextual treatments and new approaches and understanding.
Ind/Abst Acad. Search (July 1993-); Am. Hist. Life (1974-); Commun. Abstr. (?-?); Expand. Acad. Index (1989-); Humanit. Index; Humanit. Source (Jul. 1993-); INFO-SOUTH Abstr.; Mag. Search; Middle East Abstr. Index; Newsp. Period. Abstr. (1991-); Ref. Sources; Writ. Am. Hist.

US/0449-3354
JOURNALISM SCHOLARSHIP GUIDE.
English. an. Dow Jones Newspaper Fund Inc., PO Box 300, Princeton NJ 08543-0300. **Tel** (609)452-2820, FAX (609)520-5804.

UK
JOURNALISM STUDIES REVIEW.
Added/Corp University College of South Wales and Monmouthshire. Vol. 1 June (1976)-. Periodical. English. an. £1.50. Wale University College, 34 Cathedral Road, Cardiff Wales United Kingdom. **LC** PN4701; .J67. **DD** 070/.05.

FR/0449-3370
JOURNALISME. **Added/Corp** Strasbourg. Universite. Centre International d'Enseignement Superieur du Journalisme. **VFOAT** Journalisme. No. 22 (1964)-. Periodical. French (English). qt. Lenseignemont du Journalisme, 10 rue Schiller, Strasbourg France. ***Continues*** *Enseignement du Journalisme.*

GW
JOURNALISMUS. V. 1- 1960-. German. ir (one to two issues per year). price varies. Universitatsverlag Konstanz, Postfach 1322, W-7750 Konstanz Germany. **Tel** 07531/23300, 07531/23598. **(Subscription address:** Ernst Pfister GmbH, Kommissionsbuchhandlung, Postfach 64 85, D-7750 Konstanz West Germany; Postfach 590, CH-8280 Kreuzlingen Schweiz West Germany**)** **ED** Franz Ronneberger, Paul Briguow and Karl Bringmann. **LC** PN4703; .J58. **Ad Acc. Circ:** 500 to 2,000.
Desc: Monographics in loose order, concerning Journalism. Ranging from "Ethics of Journalism" to "PC and Journalism".

UK/0022-5541
JOURNALIST. **Added/Corp** National Union of Journalists (Gt. Brit.). Vol. 1 (1908)-. Periodical. English. Six times a year. £9.50 UK & Ireland; £13.00 others. National Union of Journalists, 314-320 Grays Inn Road, London WC1X 8DP England. **Tel** 011 41 71 278-7916, FAX 011 41 71 837- 8143, telex 892384. **ED** Tim Gopsill. **Bk Rev. Ad Acc. Circ:** 34,000 (ctrl).
Desc: Journal of the British and Irish National Union of Journalists. Mailed to the vast majority of journalists in newspapers, broadcasting, magazines, book and public relations.

NE/0022-555X
JOURNALIST, DE. **Added/Corp** Federatie van Nederlandse Journalisten. Vol. 1 (1950)-. Periodical. Dutch. mo. Fl174.00. NVJ Administratie, Postbus 75997, 1070 AZ Amsterdam Netherlands. **Tel** 011 31 20 6766771. **LC** PN4705; .J6. ***Formed by the union of*** *Katholieke Journalist; Christen Journalist* ***and*** *Journalist.*

SI
JOURNALIST. PAO JEN. WARTAWAN, THE. **Added/Corp** Hsin-Chia-Po Chuan Kuo Hsin Wen Kung Tso Che Hsieh Hui. **VFOAT** Pao Jen; Wartawan. No. 1, (1978)-. Chinese (English and Malay). Singapore National Union of Journalists, 17-D Hilton Towers, Leonie Hill, Hsin-Chia-Po Singapore 9 Singapore. **LC** PN4699; .J67. **DD** 079/.5957.

GW
JOURNALISTEN-HANDBUCH. German. Wilhelmstrasse 42 62, Weisbaden Germany. **LC** PN4703; .W4. ***Continues*** *Wer Schreibt Woruber? Journalisten-Handbuch.*

XR
JOURNALISTS' AFFAIRS. **Added/Corp** International Organization of Journalists. (19??)-. Periodical. English. bw. International Organization of Journalists / Czech Republic, Parizska 9, Prague 1 Czech Republic. **LC** PN4712.I54; J67. **DD** 070/.05.

US/0022-8737
KANSAS PUBLISHER, THE. [Kans. publ.]. V. 16- Sept. 1949-. Periodical. English. mo. Kansas Press Association, PO Box 1773, Topeka KS 66601. **DD** 071. Documents available from UMI Article Clearinghouse. ***Continues*** *Jayhawker Press.*
Ind/Abst ABI/INFORM Glob. Ed.; ABI Inform Ondisc (March 1975-Aug. 1977).

JA
KIJI NO UCHIGAWA / ASAHI SHINBUNSHA HEN. 1-. Japanese. ¥250 single issue. Asahi Shinbunsha, 3-2 Tsukiji 5 Chuo-ku, Tokyo-to 104 Japan. **LC** PN5407.R5; K46.

JA
KIROKU. April 1979-. Periodical. Japanese. ¥4000. Kirokusha, 26-16 Nakano 5, Nakano-ku 164, Tokyo Japan. **LC** PN5401; .K57.

US/1057-0055
LAST WORD (FRIENDSWOOD, TEX.), THE. (THE LAST WORD : WRITING NEWS FOR WORKING WRITERS.). Vol. 1, No. 1 (Mar. 1991)-. Periodical. English. qt. $6.00. Word Wright International, PO Box 1426, Friendswood TX 77546. **DD** 810.

FR/1148-3164
LETTRE DE REPORTERS SANS FRONTIERES, LA. (198?)-. Periodical. French. mo. 250.00F. Reporters sans Frontieres, 17 rue Abbe 2 l'Epee, 34000 Montpellier France. **Tel** 33 67 798182. **ED** Chantal de Caoabianca. **UDC** 070-051. **Pr Rev. Circ:** 2,000 (ctrl). ***Continues*** *La Lettre de l'Observatoire de l'Information, 0997-3931.*

US/1046-7912
LIES OF OUR TIMES. See Political Science.

US/8756-2219
LITERARY AGENTS OF NORTH AMERICA MARKETPLACE. (LITERARY AGENTS OF NORTH AMERICA.). [Lit. agents North Am. marketpl.]. **Added/Corp** Author Aid/Research Associates International. **VFOAT** Literary agents of North America. (1983/84)-. English. an. $24.95 (per volume). Author Aid/Research Associates International, 340 East 52nd Street, New York NY 10022. **Tel** (212)758-4213, (212)980-9179. **ED** Arthur Orrmont and Leonie Rosenstier. **LC** PN163; .L57. **DD** 070.5/2/02573.

US/1043-9595
LITTLE PEOPLE'S PRESS, THE. [Little people's press]. (1989)-. Periodical. English. mo. $24.00. Premier Corporation, 421 Moor Park Avenue, Moorpark CA 93021. **DD** 051.

US/0882-049X
MAGAZINE DESIGN & PRODUCTION. ***Title Change.*** [Mag. des. prod.]. **VFOAT** Magazine Design and Production. Vol. 1, No. 1 (May 1985)-(1992). Periodical. English. mo. South Wind Publishing Company, 4551 West 107th Street/Suite 343, Overland Park KS 66207. **Tel** (913)642-6611, FAX (913)642-6676. **ED** Michael Scheibach. **LC** Z253.5; .M26. **DD** 686. **Bk Rev. Ad Acc. Circ:** 17,000 (ctrl). ***Continued by*** *Signature (Prairie Village, Kan.), 1068-1949.*
Desc: Articles on magazine design and production techniques and technologies, such as paper, printing, prepress, computers, and typesetters.
Ind/Abst Abstr. Bull. Inst. Pap. Sci. Tech.; Graph. Arts Bull. Inst. Pap. Sci. Technol. (Feb. 1989-March 1989., May 1989-June 1989, Aug. 1989-Nov. 1989).

UK
MAGAZINE WEEK. English. £25.00 UK; £46.00 other. Bouverie Publishing Company Ltd, 141 147 Temple Chambers, London EC4Y ODT England. **Tel** 011 44 825 765075, 011 44 71 5836463.

US/0193-7707
MASS COMM REVIEW. See Communication.

US/0025-5122
MASTHEAD, THE. [Masthead]. **Added/Corp** National Conference of Editorial Writers (U.S.). (Spring 1949)-. Periodical. English. qt. $25.00 (one year), $45.00 (two year), $63.75 (three year) US; $30.00 (one year), $50.00 (two year), $78.75 (three year) surface mail, $37.00 (one year), $57.00 (two year), $75.75 (three year) air mail, other. National Conference of Editorial Writers, 6223 Executive Boulevard, Rockville MD 20852. **Tel** (301)984-3015. **ED** David J. Fenech. **LC** PN4700; .M3. cum. index. **Bk Rev. Circ:** 1,000 (ctrl). Documents available from UMI Article Clearinghouse.
Desc: Journal devoted to all aspects of writing and producing editorials and determining editorial policy. Professional issues, timely editorial topics and journalism education are also covered.
Ind/Abst ABI/INFORM Glob. Ed.; ABI Inform Ondisc (Fall 1975-Fall 1977); Expand. Acad. Index (1992-); Index Free Period.; Newsp. Period. Abstr. (1992-).

HK
MEDIA. No. 1- Nov. 1977-. Periodical. English. sm. $60.00. Specialist Publications Ltd, 12 Fl Rhenish Ctr, 248 Hennessy Road, Hong Kong Hong Kong. **Tel** 5 8335022. ***Supersedes*** *Media.*

CN
MEDIA. (19??)-. English. Four times a year. 14.00Can$. Canadian Association of Journalists, 1125 Colonel by Dr. Carleton Un, Ottawa Ontario K1S 5B6 Canada. **Tel** (613)788-7424. ***Continues*** *Content.*

US
MEDIA CULTURE REVIEW. See Communication.

US/0195-6779
MEDIA HISTORY DIGEST. ***Ceased.*** [Media hist. dig.]. Vol. 1, No. 1 (Fall 1980)-(Fall 1994). Periodical. English. Twice a year. Editor & Publisher Company, 11 West 19th Street, New York NY 10011. **Tel** (212)675-4380. **ED** Hiley Ward. **LC** P87; .M36. **DD** 001.51/0973. **Ad Acc. Circ:** 1,000.
Desc: Digest type publication covering the history of news media in short story form.

US
MEDIA MONITOR. Added/Corp Center for Media and Public Affairs (Washington, D.C.). Vol. 1, No. 1 (Mar. 1987)-. Periodical. English. bm. $55.50. Center for Media & Public Affairs, 2100 L Street Northwest, Suite 300, Washington DC 20037. **Tel** (202)223-2942, FAX (202)872-4014. **ED** Dr. S. Robert Lichter and Dr. Linda Lichter. cum. index. **Circ:** 2,000 (ctrl).
Desc: Its purpose is to analyze scientifically how news and entertainment media treat social and political issues.

US/0885-4610
MEDIAFILE. [MediaFile]. **Added/Corp** Media Alliance. **VFOAT** Media File. (1980)-. Newsletter. English. bm (6 issues). $25.00. Media Alliance, 814 MIssion Street, Suite 205, San Francisco CA 94103. **Tel** (415)663-1911. **ED** Pam Pfiffner. **DD** 070. **Bk Rev. Ad Acc.** ctrl circ.
Desc: A membership newsletter that list media reviews.
Ind/Abst Altern. Press Index (-199?).

US/1042-2129
MEDIAGUIDE (MORRISTOWN, N.J.). ***Title Change.*** (MEDIAGUIDE.). [MediaGuide]. **VFOAT** Jude Wanniski's ... MediaGuide; Media Guide. (1986)-(1992). English. an. Polyconomics Inc, 86 Maple Avenue, Morristown NJ 07960. **ED** J. Wanniski. **LC** PN4888.P6; M37. **DD** 302.2/32/0973. ***Split into*** *Forbes Media Guide 500, 1067-4918* ***and*** *Forbes MediaCritic, 1067-4926.*
Desc: Covers short, objective, critical reviews of ten of America's leading daily newspapers and some 40 news-stand periodicals.

IT
MEDIAS. Italian. Three times a year. L1100000. Electas Milano, Via Coni Zugna 8, 20144 Milan Italy. **Tel** 011 39 2 48195581, FAX 011 39 2 48195850.
Desc: Contains articles on journalism, newspapers, journals and television.

US/0360-5752
MEMBERSHIP DIRECTORY AND AMERICAN CORRESPONDENTS OVERSEAS. Main/Corp Overseas Press Club of America. (19??)-. Directory. English. $10.00. Overseas Press Club of America, 35 East 39th Street, New York NY 10016. **LC** PN4871; .O882. **DD** 070.4/025/73. ***Continues*** *Directory of the Overseas Press Club of America and American Correspondents Overseas.*

IT/0392-5498
MILLIMETRO, IL. [Millimetro]. (1964)-. Periodical. Italian. Four times a year (Jan., Mar., July, Oct.). L62000.00 Italy; L80000.00 others. St. Pauls International SPA, Via Duccio di Boninsegna, 10, 20145 Milan Italy. **Tel** 011 39 2 48008838, FAX 011 39 2 48194565. **UDC** 087. **Bk Rev. Ad Acc. Circ:** 6,000.

US
MLA HANDBOOK FOR WRITERS OF RESEARCH PAPERS. (19??)-. Periodical. English. ir. $10.50. Modern Language Association of America, 10 Astor Place, New York NY 10003-6981. **Tel** (212)614-6382, FAX (212)477-9863. **ED** Joseph Gibaldi, Walter Achtert. **Acid Free.**
Desc: Guides writers through the stages of preparing a paper: research and drafting, mechanics, typing, and documentation.

US
MUCKRAKER : JOURNAL OF THE CENTER FOR INVESTIGATIVE REPORTING. Added/Corp Center for Investigative Reporting (U.S.). (Fall 1991)-. Periodical. English. qt. $40.00 (institutions), $20.00 (individuals). CIR Publications, 530 Howard Street, 2nd Floor, San Francisco CA 94105. **Tel** (800)733-0015. **ED** James Curtiss, Diana Hembree. **LC** PN4781; .M8. ***Continues*** *In House (Center for Investigative Reporting (U.S.).*
Desc: Includes reprints of Center stories first published in other outlets, as well as original investigative reports, commentary, methodology and other features.

US/0893-3472
N (MINNEAPOLIS, MINN.). ***Ceased.*** (N : A NEWSLETTER FOR NEWSLETTERS.). [N]. **Added/Corp** Poll & Erickson. **VFOAT** Newsletter for Newsletters. Vol. 1, No. 1 (July 1986)-(April 1993). Newsletter. English. bm. Poll Communications Group, 126 3 Street North, Suite 200, Minneapolis MN 55401. **Tel** (612)338-7664, FAX (612)338-5423. **ED** Scott Holter. **DD** 070. Index available. **Circ:** 7,000.
Desc: For people who produce newsletters or write for newsletters.

CN/0832-1329
NASA GAZETA. (NASHA GAZETA : BRUSSKII OBSHCHESTVENNO-POLITICHESKII EZHENEDELNIK.). [Nasa gaz.]. **VFOAT** Through Our Eyes. (Oct. 30, 1985)-. Periodical. English (Russian). ir. $1.50 per issue. Nasha Gazeta, PO Box 6118 Station J, Ottawa Ontario K2A 1T2 Canada. **DD** 071/.1.

IT
NASCERE. Nascere, Via General Govone 56, 20155 Milan Italy. ***Continues*** *Bollettino Aippo.*

AT/0310-365X
NEW JOURNALIST. [New journal.]. Began in 1972. Periodical. English. qt. $16.00. New Journalist, PO Box K750, Hay Market 2000 Australia. **LC** PN4701; .N35. **DD** 079/.94.
Ind/Abst APAIS, Aust. Public Aff. Inf. Ser. (1974-).

US/0732-0892
NEW YORK TIMES FILE, CRITICAL ISSUES. RESEARCH GUIDE AND INDEX, THE. [N. Y. times file crit. issues, Res. guide index]. **Added/Corp** University Microfilms International. Microfilming Corporation of America. (1982)-. English. an. University Microfilms International, 300 North Zeeb Road, Ann Arbor MI 48106-1346. **Tel** (313)761-4700, (800)521-0600 Exts. 2490, 2491, FAX (313)973-1540. **LC** AI21.N44; N47. **DD** 071/.47/1.

US/0741-9317
NEWARK PRESS. Began with issue for Oct. 1982?. Periodical. English. bm. $10.00. Newark Press, 8123 19th Place, Adelphi MD 20783.

US
NEWS NOTES & DEADLINES. English. bm. $65.00 (one year), $115.00 (two year). Association of College & University Offices, 1001 Connecticut Avenue #901, Washington DC 20036. **Tel** (202)659-2104, FAX (202)835-1159. **ED** Lisa Tomak, Tel. (202)659-2105. **Bk Rev**, (Qty: 6).

US/0199-2422
NEWS PHOTOGRAPHER. See Photography and Video.

CN/0703-217X
NEWSLETTER - CANADIAN SCIENCE WRITER'S ASSOCIATION. Main/Corp Canadian Science Writer's Association. (1971)-. Periodical. English. ir. Free. Ontario Research Foundation, Sheridan Park Research Committee, Mississauga Ontario L5K 1B3 Canada. **Tel** (416)822-4111, FAX (416)823-1446, telex 06-982311. **DD** 070.4/49/5. ctrl circ.

CN/0827-3146
NEWSLETTER - COACH HOUSE PRESS. (NEWSLETTER.). [Newsl. - Coach House Press]. Began with Feb. 1977 issue. Newsletter. English. Free. Coach House Press, 401 Huron Street, Toronto Ontario M5S 2G5 Canada. **DD** 070.5/09713/541. ctrl circ.

US/0885-6966
NEWSLETTER NEWSLETTER, THE. [Newsl. newsl.]. (19??)-. Newsletter. English. mo. $34.95 (one year), $64.90 (two year), $89.80 (three year). Communication Resources Inc, 4150 Belden Village Street NW, Suite 400, North Canton OH 44718. **Tel** (216)493-7880, FAX (216)493-7897. **ED** Robert W Fisher. **DD** 070. Index available. **Circ:** 25,000 (ctrl).
Desc: Material to help in producing church newsletters. Provides artwork, layout techniques, and new ideas.

US/0028-9507
NEWSLETTER ON NEWSLETTERS, THE. (1964)-. Newsletter. English. sm. $120.00 (one year), $226.00 (two years), $315.00 (three years) US & Canada; $140.00 (one year), $266.00 (two years), $375.00 (three years) other. Newsletter Clearinghouse, PO Box 311, Rhinebeck NY 12572. **Tel** (914)876-2081, FAX (914)876-2561. **ED** Howard Penn Hudson. Index available. **Ad Acc.** ctrl circ.
Desc: For the newsletter professional--covering world or newsletters-information on management editing graphics promotions-reviews of new NLS.

US/0889-4590
NEWSPAPER FINANCIAL EXECUTIVE JOURNAL. (NEWSPAPER FINANCIAL EXECUTIVE JOURNAL / INTERNATIONAL NEWSPAPER FINANCIAL EXECUTIVES.). [Newsp. financ. exec. j.]. **Added/Corp** International Newspaper Financial Executives. **VFOAT** Journal. Vol. 39, No. 3 (Dec. 1985)-. Periodical. English. Ten times a year. $100.00. International Newspaper Financial Executives, Box 16573, Dulles Airport, Washington DC 20041. **Tel** (703)648-1160, FAX (703)476-5961. **ED** Will Nash. **DD** 071. Index available. **Bk Rev. Ad Acc. Circ:** 1,500 (ctrl). ***Continues*** *Newspaper Controller, 0028-9558.*
Ind/Abst Account. Tax Datab. (1974-) [Full Txt.].

US/0889-8499
NEWSPAPERS CAREER DIRECTORY. [Newsp. career dir.]. **Added/Corp** Career Press Inc. Visible Ink Press. 1st Ed. (1987)-. Directory. English. be. $29.95 (hardcover), $17.95 (softcover). Gale Research Inc., 835 Penobscot Building, Detroit MI 48226. **Tel** (800)877-GALE, (313)961-2242, FAX (313)961-6083, telex TWX 810-221-7086. **LC** PN4797; .N45. **DD** 070/.023/73.
Desc: Covers internships, opportunities for minorities, starting out as a reporter, breaking into editorial at a large

paper, photojournalism, art and graphics, circulation, newspaper research, classified advertising sales and national account sales.

US/0270-9783
NEWSWIRE. **Added/Corp** Journalism Education Association (U.S.). **VFOAT** JEA Newswire. **VAT** Journalism Education Association Newswire; News Wire. Vol. 1 (1973)-. Periodical. English. qt. comes with membership. Journalism Education Association, KSU, Kedzie Hall 103, Manhattan KS 66506. **Tel** (913)532-5532. **LC** PN4788; .N4.

US/0028-9817
NIEMAN REPORTS. [Nieman rep.]. **Added/Corp** Nieman Alumni Council. Society of Nieman Fellows. Harvard University. Nieman Foundation. (Feb. 1947)-. Periodical. English. qt. $20.00 (one year), $35.00 (two year). Nieman Reports, PO Box 4951, Manchester NH 03108. **Tel** (617)495-2237. **ED** Fay Leviero. **LC** PN4700; .N57. **DD** 070. **Bk Rev. Circ:** 1,300. available on microfilm and microfiche from University Microfilms International (UMI). Documents available from UMI Article Clearinghouse.
Desc: Provides a forum for discussion of media-related issues by journalists, educators and public figures.
Ind/Abst ABI/INFORM Glob. Ed.; ABI Inform Ondisc (Fall 1974-Spring 1977); Annu. Bibliogr. Engl. Lang. Lit.; Expand. Acad. Index (1989-); Index Period. Artic. Relat. Law; Middle East Abstr. Index; Newsp. Period. Abstr. (1992-).

US/1062-6166
OCCASIONAL PAPER - FREEDOM FORUM MEDIA STUDIES CENTER. (OCCASIONAL PAPER.). [Occas. pap. - Freedom Forum Media Stud. Cent.]. **Added/Corp** Freedom Forum Media Studies Center. **VFOAT** Center Occasional Paper. No. 9 (Nov. 1991)-. Monographic series. English. **DD** 302. ***Continues*** *Occasional Paper (Gannett Foundation Media Center).*

US/0896-5730
OHIO WRITER. [Ohio writ.]. Began (Sept. 1987)-. Periodical. English. bm. $18.00. Ohio Writer, PO Box 528, Willoughby OH 44094. **Tel** (216)257-6410. **DD** 808. **Bk Rev. Ad Acc.**

US/0163-7010
OXBRIDGE DIRECTORY OF NEWSLETTERS. (1979)-. Directory. English. an. $345.00. Oxbridge Communications Inc., 150 5th Avenue, Room 302, New York NY 10011. **Tel** (212)741-0231, FAX (212)633-2938. **ED** Barry Lee. **LC** Z6944.N44; S82. **DD** 071/.3/025. **NLM** Z 6944.N44; O98. Index available. **Ad Acc.** available on labels; available on magnetic tape. ***Continues*** *Standard Directory of Newsletters.*
Desc: The largest directory of the North American newsletter business with 20,000 listings in 200 subject categories.

US/0883-6752
PAGES (CHICAGO, ILL.). (PAGES.). [Pages]. **VFOAT** Pages of Filler-Editorials- Cartoons-Art-Puzzles and other Useful Materials. (198?)-. Periodical. English. Twelve times a year. $185.00 (without disk service); $235.00 (including disk); $285.00 (with disk service). Berry Publishing Company, 300 North State Street, Suite 5821, Chicago IL 60610. **Tel** (312)222-9245, FAX (312)222-9637. **ED** Shirley Lambert and Daniel Berry. **DD** 070. **Bk Rev**, (Qty: 12). **Circ:** 5,000. ***Continues*** *Steam from the Boiler.*
Desc: Publication editorial and filler materials including management, health, quality, work habit, motivation articles, puzzles, cartoons, jokes, clipart, and one-liners for use by the editor.

MY
PANDUAN AKHBAR DAN MEDIA. PRESS AND MEDIA GUIDE. **Added/Corp** Malaysia. Jabatan Penerangan. **VFOAT** Press and Media Guide. (19??)-. Multiple languages (English and Malay). Jabatan Penerangan Malaysia, Kementerian Penerangan, Jalan Tun Perak, Kuala Lumpur Malaysia. **LC** Z6958.M3; P36; PN5449.M35.

CH
PAO HSUEH. **VFOAT** Journalism Magazine. Vol. 1- (1951)-. Periodical. Chinese (Chinese). sa. $2.00. Chung-Hua Min Kuo Hsin Wen Pien Chi Jen Hsieh Hui, 14-3 Hsi Ning South Road, Taipei Taiwan. **LC** PN4705; .P36. **DD** 070/.05.

IO
PERS INDONESIA. Dec. 1974-. Periodical. Indonesian. Ditjen PPG Departamen Penerangan, Jalan Veterna 7C Atas, Jakarta Indonesia. **LC** PN4705; .P45.

US/0895-4712
POLITICAL PIX. ***Ceased.*** [Polit. pix]. (1987)-?. Periodical. English. wk. Ambience Inc, PO Box 804Z, Norwich VT 05055-0804. **DD** 070.

●US/1062-824X
PONIECKI NEWSLETTER/INFORMATOR. **Added/Corp** Wadisaw Poniecki Charitable Foundation. **VFOAT** Poniecki Newsletter Informator; Poniecki. (1992)-. Periodical. English. Free. Wadisaw Poniecki Charitable Foundation, 8637 Arbor Drive, El Cerrito CA 94530-2728.

PL
PRASA POLSKA. **Added/Corp** Stowarzyszenie Dziennikarzy Polskich. (June 1947)-. Periodical. Polish. Twelve times a year. $48.00. **(Subscription address:** ARS Polona, PO Box 1001, 00068 Warsaw Poland.**) LC** PN5355.P6; P7.

UK/0435-2459
PRESS AND THE PEOPLE : THE ... ANNUAL REPORT OF THE GENERAL COUNCIL OF THE PRESS, THE. ***Ceased.*** **Main/Corp** Press Council. **Added/Corp** Press Council. Annual Report of the Press Council. **VFOAT** Annual Report of the Press Council. 1st (Oct. 1954)-37th (1990). English. an. The Press Council, No 1 Salisbury Square, London EC4Y 8AE England. **Tel** 01-353-1248, FAX 01-353-1248. **LC** PN5111.P73; A25. **DD** 070/.05. Index available. **Circ:** 2,000.
Desc: Adjudications of the Press Council on complaints received each year; includes a statistical analysis of the British press.

CN/0706-9286
PRESS REVIEW (TORONTO). (PRESS REVIEW.). [Press rev.]. Vol. 1 (Jan./Feb. 1977)-. Periodical. English. Four times a year. 17.00Can$ US & Canada; 20.00Can$ others. Press Review, PO Box 368 Station A, Toronto Ontario M5W 1C2 Canada. **Tel** (416)368-0512. **ED** Sheila Johnston. **DD** 071/.1. **Bk Rev. Ad Acc. Circ:** 16,000 (ctrl).
Desc: A communication national news media magazine covering newspaper, radio and television events, progress and controversy. Public relations and corporate and government relations are featured also.

US/0032-7824
PRESS WOMAN, THE. ***Title Change.*** **Added/Corp** National Federation of Press Women. **VFOAT** PW. (1937)-(19??). Periodical. English. Six times a year. National Federation of Press Women, c/o L. L. Wolfe, PO Box 99, Blue Springs MO 64015. **Tel** (816)229-1666. **ED** Lois Lauer Wolfe. **Ad Acc. Circ:** 5,000. ***Continued by*** *Agenda.*
Desc: Articles of interest to the journalism profession with major emphasis on women in media careers.

BE/0478-1546
PRESSE. (19??)-. French (English). an. 575F. Assn Belge des Editde Journaux, Paepsemlaan 22 Bus 7, 1070 Brussels Belgium. **Tel** 011 32 2 5229660.

SZ
PRESSE DER SOWJETUNION, DIE. German. wk. Deutscher Judo Verband, Redaktion Ippon Segewaldweg 40, D 12557 Berlin Germany. **Tel** 011 49 711 210770, telex 051 678. **LC** AP30; .P78.

GW
PRESSE-INFORMATION / DEUTSCHE VERKEHRSWACHT. Periodical. German. bm. Umschau Verlag, Postfach 110262, D-60037 Frankfurt Germany. **Tel** 011 49 69 2600692, FAX 011 49 69 2600223, telex 411964.

GW/0935-8064
PRESSE UND SPRACHE. (1988)-. Periodical. German. mo. DM36.60. Eilers & Schuenemann Verlag, Postfach 106067, D 2800 Bremen Germany. **Tel** 011 49 421 3690347, FAX 011 49 421 3690339, telex 841 244397. **UDC** 803. Index available. cum. index. **Bk Rev. Ad Acc.** ctrl circ. ***Continues*** *Unsere Zeitung.*
Desc: Articles from different German newspapers.

DK
PRESSENS ARBOG / UDGIVET AF DANSK PRESSEHISTORISK SELSKAB. **Added/Corp** Dansk Pressehistorisk Selskab. Began in 1974. Periodical. Danish. kr75.00. Dag Hammarskjold, Alle 33, 2100 Kbenhavn Denmark. **LC** PN4705; .P74. **DD** 078. ***Continues*** *Pressehistorisk Arbog.*

RU/0321-3501
PROBLEMY ZHURNALISTIKI. **Added/Corp** Moskovskii Gosudarstvennyi Universitet Im. M.V. Lomonosova. Fakultet Zhurnalistiki. Vol. 1 (1973)-. Russian. St Petersburg State University / Izdatelstvo Leningradskogo Universiteta, Universitetskaia Nab 7/9, 199034 St Petersburg Russia. **Tel** 011 95 218-97-88, FAX 011 95 218-51-52, telex 121481. **LC** PN5271; .P75.

●US/1064-5403
PROCEEDINGS OF THE ASSOCIATION FOR EDUCATION IN JOURNALISM AND MASS COMMUNICATION SOUTHEAST COLLOQUIUM. (PROCEEDINGS OF THE ASSOCIATION FOR EDUCATION IN JOURNALISM AND MASS COMMUNICATION SOUTHEAST COLLOQUIUM / HISTORY, LAW, AND NEWSPAPER DIVISIONS.). **Main/Conf** Association for Education in Journalism and Mass Communication Southeast Colloquium. **Added/Corp** Association for Education in Journalism and Mass Communication. **VFOAT** Southeast Colloquium; Proceedings of the AEJMC Southeast Colloquium. (1992)-. Proceedings. English. AEJMC / Georgia, Department of Communication, Georgia State University, Atlanta GA 30303.

US/0048-5942
PUBLISHERS' AUXILIARY. See Publishing.

GW/0033-4006
PUBLIZISTIK. [Publizistik]. **Added/Corp** Deutsche Gesellschaft fuer Publizistik. Deutsche Gesellschaft fuer Publizistik- und Zeitungswissenschaft. Deutsche Gesellschaft fuer Publizistik- und Kommunikationswissenschaft. (Jan./Feb. 1956)-. Periodical. German (English and French). qt. DM112.60. Westdeutscher Verlag GmbH, Postfach 5829, D 65048 Wiesbaden Germany. **Tel** 011 49 611 160220. **(Subscription address:** VVA Bertelsmann Distributors GmbH, Postfach 7777, D-33310 Guetersloh Germany.**) ED** Wilmont Haacke, Wolfgang R. Langenbucher, Franz Ronneberger, and Ulrich Saxer. **LC** PN4703; .P8. **DD** 070/.05. **[CCC].** Index available. cum. index. **Bk Rev. Ad Acc. Circ:** 1,200.
Desc: Magazine for sciences of printing, radio, film, public relations, advertising, communication and rhetoric.
Ind/Abst Int. Bibliogr. Sociol.; Int. Polit. Sci. Abstr.; Soc. Plann. Policy Dev. Abstr.; Sociol. Abstr.

US/1051-8126
PULSO DEL PERIODISMO. (PULSO). [Pulso periodismo]. **Added/Corp** Florida International University. Programa Centroamericano de Periodismo. **VFOAT** Pulso. Vol. 1, No. 1 (Mar. 1990)-. Periodical. Spanish. qt (Feb., May, Aug., Nov.). $15.00. Florida International University Central American Journal, North Miami Campus, North Miami FL 33181. **Tel** (305)348-2000 or, 940-5625. **ED** John Virtue (editor's address: 3000 Northeast 145th Street, ACII 135, North Miami, FL 33181; phone (305)940-5935. **LC** PN4988; .P85. **DD** 079/.728/05. cum. index. **Bk Rev**, (Qty: 4). **Ad Acc, Adv Mgr:** Mary Van Meter, **Tel** (303)964-8400. **Circ:** 4,500 (ctrl).
Desc: Covers in the areas of print, radio and TV activities in Latin America.

US/1054-6804
PUTTING OUT : A PUBLISHING RESOURCE GUIDE FOR LESBIAN & GAY WRITERS. See Literature.

KO
PYONJIBIN HYOPHOE PO. **Added/Corp** Hanguk Sinmun Pyonjibin Hyophoe. **VFOAT** Sinmun Pyonjibin Hyophoe Po. Vol. 1 (1981)-. Periodical. Korean. **LC** PN4705; .P96.

US/0033-6505
QUILL AND SCROLL (IOWA CITY). (QUILL AND SCROLL.). [Quill scroll]. **Added/Corp** Quill and Scroll Society. **VFOAT** Quill and Scroll. (19??)-. Periodical. English. Four times a year (Feb., Apr., Oct., Dec.). $12.00 (one year); $23.00 (two years); $34.00 (three years). Quill and Scroll Society, School of Journalism, University of Iowa, Iowa IA 52242. **Tel** (319)335-5795. **ED** Richard P. Johns. **Bk Rev. Ad Acc. Circ:** 15,000 (ctrl). available on microfilm and microfiche from University Microfilms International (UMI).
Desc: Publishes articles and information related to secondary schools. It also includes newspapers, yearbooks, and other publications.
Ind/Abst Curr. Index J. Educ.

US/0033-6475
QUILL (CHICAGO), THE. (THE QUILL.). [Quill]. **Added/Corp** Society of Professional Journalists, Sigma Delta Chi. Sigma Delta Chi. (1912)-. Periodical. English. Ten times a year. $27.00 US; $32.00 Canada; $37.00 others. Society of Professional Journalists, PO Box 77, c/o Greg Christopher, Greencastle IN 46135. **Tel** (317)653-3333, FAX (317)653-4631. **ED** Brian Steffens (editor's address: 16 South Jackson Street, Greencastle, IN 46135). **LC** PN4700; .Q5. **DD** 070.5. **Bk Rev**, (Qty: 10/yr). **Ad Acc, Adv Mgr:** Gregory Christopher. **Circ:** 18,000. available on microfilm and microfiche from University Microfilms International (UMI). Documents available from UMI Article Clearinghouse.
Desc: A magazine for journalists. It is seen as a resource for those in the media to develop and/or further their careers. It covers such topics as freedom of information, ethics, diversity, education, and resources.
Ind/Abst Acad. Search (July 1993-); Expand. Acad. Index (1989-); Humanit. Index; Humanit. Source (Jul. 1993-); INFO-SOUTH Abstr.; Mag. Search; Newsp. Period. Abstr. (1989-); Trade Ind. ASAP [Full Txt.]; Trade Ind. Index [Full Txt.].

US/0146-1222
R. I. BULLETIN. **Main/Corp** ANPA Research Institute. **VAT** Research Institute Bulletin. Bulletin. English. Newspaper Association of America, 11600 Sunrise Valley Drive, Reston VA 22091. **Tel** (703)648-1286. **LC** PN4734; .A43A. **DD** 338.7/61/07050973.

RU
RASPROSTRANENIE PECHATI.
Added/Corp Russia (1923-U.S.S.R.) Glavnoe Upravlenie po Rasprostraneniiu Pechati. (June 1948)-. Periodical. Russian. Six times a year. $99.95. **(Subscription address:** East View Publications Inc., 3020 Harbor Lane North, Suite 110, Minneapolis MN 55447.**)**

IT
RASSEGNA DELLA STAMPA. (19??)-. Periodical. Italian. mo. L80000 Italy; L100000 other. Assn Fra Le Soc Italiane Azioni, Piazza Venezia 11, 00187 Rome, Italy. **Tel** 011 39 6 6784413.

RU
REGISTR PERIODICHESKIKH IZDANII STRAN-CHLENOV MTSNTI. CHAST II: VSPOMOGATELNYE UKAZATELI.
Main/Corp Mezhdunarodnyi Tsentr Nauchnoi i Tekhnicheskoi Informatsii. (19??)-. Multiple languages (Russian and Multiple languages). qt. 2.50rub single issue. Avtomatizirovannaia Sluzhba Registratsi Periodicheskikh Izd, Smolenskaia-Sennaia Pl. 32/34, 121200 Moscow Russia. **LC** Z6945; .M557b; PN4699.

SZ
REPERTOIRE DE LA PRESSE SUISSE.
VFOAT Leitfaden der Schweizer Presse. Began with 1969/70 vol. Multiple languages (French, German and Italian). **LC** Z6956.S92; R46; PN5334.

CN/1183-4978
REPERTOIRE DES JOURNALISTES DU QUEBEC ET ANNUAIRE DES ENTREPRISES DE PRESSE. [Repert. journal. Que. annu. entrep. presse]. **Added/Corp** Federation Professionnelle des Journalistes du Quebec. Association des Journalistes Independants du Quebec. **VFOAT** Repertoire des Journalistes du Quebec. (1990)-. French. 15.00Can$. Association des Journalistes Independants du Quebec, CP 5728, Succursale C, Montreal, Quebec H2X 3N4 Canada. **DD** 070.4/025/714.

UK/1350-4010
REPORTAGE; THE INTERNATIONAL MAGAZINE OF PHOTOJOURNALISM.
(199?)-. English. Four times a year. $36.00 North America. Wordsearch Ltd., #26 Cramer Street, London W1M 3HE England. **Tel** 011 44 71 4867419, FAX 011 44 71 4861451. **(Subscription address:** Wordsearch Ltd. / North America Subscriptions, Subscrition Office, PO Box 1584, Birmingham AL 35201-1584.**)**
Desc: Contains information on photojournalism.

US/0739-3121
REPORTER (LOS ANGELES, CALIF.).
(REPORTER.). [Reporter]. **Added/Corp** George Dubow Agency. (19??)-. Periodical. English. mo (except July and Aug.). $36.00 (Reporter only), $54.00 (1 supplement), $88.00 (all 3 supplements) (1 year); $58.00 (Reporter only), $91.00 (1 supplement), $149.00 (all 3 supplements) (2 year). George Dubow Agency, 7015 Prospect Place Northeast, Albuquerque NM 87110. **Tel** (505)884-7636. **DD** 071.

CN/0712-7243
RESOURCE-MAG. ***Ceased.*** [Resour.-mag]. Vol. 1, No. 1 (Jan. 1982)-(Sept. 1993). Trade Publication. English. Ten times a year (Monthly except Jan./Feb. and July/Aug. combined). Resource Mag, 20 Tettenhall Road, Islington ONT M9A 2C3 Canada. **Tel** (416)231-7796. **ED** Lynn McFadgen. **DD** 070.5/72/0688. **Bk Rev. Circ:** 600.
Desc: A marketing newsletter for the magazine trade. Includes promotion tips, news and developments, with practical advice and newsletter for editors, publishers, circulation directors and advertising sales staff.

US/0892-581X
RIGHTING WORDS. [Righting words]. Vol. 1, No. 1 (Jan./Feb. 1987)-. Periodical. English. qt. $24.00 US and Possessions; $34.00 Canada; $40.00 other. Feredonna Communications, Drawer 23010, Knoxville TN 37933. **Tel** (615)584-1918. **ED** Michael Scott Ward. **DD** 808. Index available. cum. index. **Bk Rev. Ad Acc. Circ:** 1,200.

CN/0838-0651
RYERSON REVIEW OF JOURNALISM.
[Ryerson rev. j.]. **Added/Corp** Ryerson Polytechnical Institute. School of Journalism. (1984)-. English. sa. Limited free distribution. Ryerson Polytechnical Institute, School of Journalism, 350 Victoria Street, Toronto, Ontario M5B 2K3 Canada. **DD** 070/.05.
Ind/Abst Can. Period. Index (1990-).

US/0272-8079
S/N. SPEECHWRITER'S NEWSLETTER.
See Communication.

FI
SAL VUOSIKIRJA. **Main/Corp** Suomen Aikakauslehdentoimittajain Liitoo. **VFOAT** S.A.L. Vuosikirja. Finnish. an. Yrjonkatu 11 C 16, 00120 Helsinki 12 Finland. **Tel** 604 897. **ED** Kari Varmirkko. **LC** PN5355.F5; S86A. **Circ:** 1,500.

US/1054-6774
SAN DIEGO WRITERS MONTHLY. [S. Diego writ. mon.]. Vol. 1, No. 1 (Feb. 1991)-. Periodical. English. mo. $23.00 San Diego, California; $26.00 other. San Diego Writers Monthly, 3910 Chapman Street, San Diego CA 92110. **Tel** (619)226-0896. **ED** Michael T. MacCarthy. **DD** 808. Index available (bound in Feb. issue). cum. index. **Bk Rev**, (Qty: 24). **Ad Acc. Circ:** 2,000 (ctrl).
Desc: Literary magazine designed to highlight the writing and reading community of southern California. Publishes fiction, non-fiction, poetry, essays and interviews. Accepts unsolicited work.

CN/0821-7246
SCIENCE LINK. (SCIENCE LINK / CANADIAN SCIENCE WRITER'S ASSOCIATION.). [Sci. link]. Periodical. English. Six times a year. 50.00Can$. Canadian Science Writers Association, Science Information Sources, Ontario Science Centre, 770 Don Mills Road/Room A-104, Don Mills Ontario M3C 1T3 Canada. **Tel** (416)481-2532, FAX (416)968-6681. **ED** Geoff Foulds. **DD** 070.4/495/0971. **Bk Rev. Ad Acc. Circ:** 350 (ctrl).
Desc: Covers professional development of journalists and public relations people communicating science and technology in Canada. Covers media news and leads on science stories, plus CSWA activities.

US/1071-4103
SCIPHERS (COLLEGE STATION, TEX.).
(SCIPHERS : PUBLICATION OF THE SCIENCE WRITING EDUCATORS GROUP.). [Sciphers]. **Added/Corp** Association for Education in Journalism and Mass Communication. Science Communication Interest Group. Science Writing Educators Group. (Nov. 1979)-. Newsletter. English. qt. $10.00 (one year), $18.00 (two year) US; $30.00 (one year), $38.00 (two year) other. University of Missouri / Science Journalism, PO Box 838, Columbia MO 65205. **ED** Susanna Aosnig (editor's address: Department of Journalism, Texas A&M University, College Station, TX 77843-4111; phone: (409)845-5372). **LC** PN4784.T3; S9. **DD** 070. **Bk Rev. Circ:** 100. ***Continues*** *SWEG.*
Desc: Newsletter of the Science Communication Interest Group of the Association for Education in Journalism and Mass Communications.

JA
SENMON SHINBUN YORAN. Japanese. Nihon Senmon Shinbun Kyokai, 2-12 Toranomon 1 Minato-ku, Tokyo-to 105 Japan. **LC** Z6958.J3; S46; PN5404.

US
SIGNALS. **See** Agriculture.

US/0894-9239
SMALL STREET JOURNAL (COLORADO SPRINGS, COLO.). ***Ceased.*** (THE SMALL STREET JOURNAL.). [Small str. j.]. -Ceased March 1989. Periodical. English. mo. Innovative Learning Concepts, 888 Dublin Boulevard/Suite B, Colorado Springs CO 80918-7003. **Tel** (719)593-2448, (719)471-1008. **DD** 071. ***Continues*** *Fun Day Times, 0891-5938.*

CN/0700-480X
SOURCES (TORONTO). ***Title Change.*** (SOURCES.). [Source]. 8th Ed. (Fall 1981)- 29th Ed. (Winter 1991/92). Periodical. English (French). Twice a year. Sources, 4 Phipps Street, Suite 109, Toronto Ontario M4Y 1J5 Canada. **Tel** (416)964-7799, FAX (416)964-8763. **ED** Barrie Zwicker. **DD** 061/.1/05. Index available. **Bk Rev. Ad Acc. Circ:** 15,000 (ctrl). ***Separated from*** *Content (Montreal, Quebec), 0045-835X.* ***Continued by*** *Directory of Sources for Editors, Reporters & Researchers, 1197-5148.*
Desc: Articles of interest to the media. Contact persons in 1,200 organizations, 7,000 subjects.

US
SPR STUDENT PRESS REVIEW. (19??)-. English. qt. $22.00. Columbia Scholastic Press Association, Box 11, Columbia University, New York NY 10027-6969. **Tel** (212)280-3311. ***Continues*** *Student Press Review.*
Ind/Abst Curr. Index J. Educ.

US/0274-9777
SPS NEWSREPORT. ***Ceased.*** **Main/Corp** Student Press Service. **VFOAT** Student Press Service News Report. Periodical. English. bm. Student Press Service News Report, Cardinal Station, Washington DC 20064. **Tel** (202)635-6087. **ED** Stacey Grundman. **Circ:** 800. ***Continues*** *Newsreport - Student Press Service.*
Desc: A national news service for high schools and colleges which researches and reports on federal policy and activity affecting youth.

US/0036-2972
ST. LOUIS JOURNALISM REVIEW, THE.
[St. Louis journal. rev.]. **VFOAT** SJR. **VAT** Saint Louis Journalism Review. Vol. 1 No. 1 (Oct./Nov. 1970)-. Periodical. English. Ten times a year (monthly with July/Aug. and Dec./Jan. issues combined). $25.00 (one year), $42.00 (two years), $51.00 (three years), $66.00 (five years) US; $35.00 (one year), $62.00 (two years), $81.00 (three years), $116.00 (five years) other. St Louis Journalism Review, 8380 Olive Boulevard, St Louis MO 63132. **Tel** (314)991-1699, FAX (314)997-1898. **ED** Charles L Klotzer. **LC** PN4899.S25; S25. **DD** 071/.78/66. **[CCC]. Bk Rev. Ad Acc. Circ:** 10,000 (ctrl). Documents available from UMI Article Clearinghouse. ***Absorbed*** *Focus Midwest.*
Desc: A critique of media (press, broadcasting, tv, cable, public relations, advertising, etc.) primarily local but also nationally. Also covers issues ignored by the media.
Ind/Abst ABI/INFORM Glob. Ed.; ABI Inform Ondisc (Dec. 1974-Jan. 1976); Altern. Press Index; Expand. Acad. Index (1992-); Newsp. Period. Abstr. (1989-).

US/0739-9146
STATUS NEWS. **Main/Corp** Association for Education in Journalism. Committee on the Status of Women in Journalism Education. (Sept. 1977)-. Periodical. English. Three times a year. $3.00 members, $4.00 nonmembers. Southern Illinois University School of Journalism, Carbondale IL 62901. **Tel** (618)536-3361.

SZ
STREUDATEN DER SCHWEIZER PRESSE : ZEITUNGEN, ANZEIGER UND AMTSBLATTER. **VFOAT** Donnees de Diffusion de la Presse Suisse : Journaux, Feuilles d'Annonces et Feuilles Officielles. Multiple languages (French and German). Seestrasse 5, Postfach 623, 8027 Zurich Switzerland. **LC** PN5337.C5; S77.

US
STUDENT PRESS, THE. 1971-. English. an. R Rosen Press, 29 East 21st Street, New York NY 10010. **LC** LB3621. **DD** 378.1/98/97.

US/0160-3825
STUDENT PRESS LAW CENTER REPORT. **See** Law.

US
STUDENT PRESS REVIEW. ***Title Change.*** (19??)-(19??). English. qt. Columbia Scholastic Press Association, Box 11, Columbia University, New York NY 10027-6969. **Tel** (212)280-3311. ***Continues*** *School Press Review.* ***Continued by*** *SPR Student Press Review.*
Ind/Abst Curr. Index J. Educ.

US
STYLE (MINNEAPOLIS, MINN.). (STYLE.). **Added/Corp** American Association of Sunday and Feature Editors. (1984)-. English. an. Free. American Newspapers Publishing Association, PO Box 17407, Dulles International, Washington DC 20041. **Tel** (703)648-1104. **LC** PN4784.F37; S79.
Ind/Abst Expand. Acad. Index (1989-).

US/0197-9892
SUBSCRIBER AND PRIMARY AUDIENCE STUDY DIGEST, THE. [Subscr. prim. audience study dig.]. Fall 1979-. Periodical. English. sa. $25.00. The Media Book Inc, 75 East 5th Street, New York NY 10022. **LC** PN4888.R37; S82. **DD** 070.5/72/0688.

BU/0205-1656
SUVREMENNA ZHURNALISTIKA / [SBZH, NAUCHNO-INFORMATSIONEN TSENTUR]. **Added/Corp** Suiuz na Bulgarskite Zhurnalisti. Nauchno-Informatsionen Tsentur. (19??)-. Periodical. Bulgarian (summaries and/or abstracts in English and Russian). qt. 6.00lv. Bratia Miladinovi No 12, 1000 Sofia Bulgaria. **Tel** 871356, telex 022635. **ED** Todor Abazov. **LC** P87; .S87. Index available. **Bk Rev. Circ:** 1,000.
Desc: Devoted to mass media theory, criticism and history. Published by the research and information centre of journalism at the union of Bulgarian journalists.

US/1055-2723
SYNDICATED COLUMNIST CONTACTS.
[Synd. columnist contacts]. (1990)-. English. $130.00 (includes SOURCE BOOK MONTHLY CHANGE BULLETINS and DAILY UPDATING SERVICE). BPi Media Services, 1515 Broadway, New York NY 10036. **Tel** (800)753-6675, (518)753-6675, FAX (518)374-7889. **ED** Mitch Tebo. **LC** PN4888.S9; S93. **DD** 071/.3/02573. ***Continues*** *Syndicated Columnists (1987), 1046-6738.*
Desc: Designed to aid publicists in targeting print media. Contains information regarding over 1500 columns, 70+ syndicated packages and over 150 syndicating organizations. Focuses on comprehensive editorial details regarding each column.

CH
TAN-CHIANG WEN LI HSUEH YUAN CHUNG WAI CHI KAN PAO CHIH MU LU. TAMKANG LIST OF SERIALS. **Added/Corp** Chueh-Sheng Chi Nien Tu Shu Kuan. Tui Kuang Fu Wu Tsu. **VFOAT** Tamkang List of Serials; Chung Wai Chi Kan Pao Chih Mu Lu. (19??)-. Chinese (English). an. Department of Reader Services, Chueh Shen Memorial Library, Tamkang College of Arts and Sciences, Taipei Taiwan. **LC** Z6958.T34; T39; PN4832. **DD** 011/.34.

US/0162-0002
TEACHER WRITER. VAT Teacher-Writer. Vol. 1, (July/Aug. 1978)-. Periodical. English. bm. Ed Mart International, Department 60-F, 177 White Plains Road, Tarrytown NY 10591.

US/1049-2704
TITLES MAGAZINE. ***Suspended.*** [Titles mag.]. **VFOAT** Titles. (March/April 1990)-?. Periodical. English. bm. $15.00 US; $21.00 other. Larkspur Publishing, 200 Gate Five Road/Suite 214, Sausalito CA 94965. **Tel** (415)331-1211. **ED** Christine Nordbye. **DD** 071. **Ad Acc. Circ:** 60,000 (ctrl).
Desc: Targeted to retailers of mass market magazines and paperback books.

US
TJFR BUSINESS NEWS REPORTER. (19??)-. English. sm. $595.00 (one year), $998.00 (two year). TJFR Publishing Company, 545 North Maple Avenue, 2nd Floor, Ridgewood NJ 07450. **Tel** (201)444-6061, FAX (201)444-5919. **ED** Dean Rotbart. **Ad Acc.**
Desc: Gives the inside story on America's most influential journalists.

US/0193-4953
TOWERS CLUB USA NEWSLETTER. ***Title Change.*** **Main/Corp** Towers Club USA. **Added/Corp** Towers Club USA. Newsletter. **VAT** Towers Club United States of America Newsletter. Issue #1 (Jan. 1993)-(19??). Newsletter. English. mo (except May and Dec.). Towers Club USA Newsletter, PO Box 2038, Vancouver WA 98668-2038. **Tel** (206)574-3084. **ED** Jerry Buchanan. **Bk Rev. Ad Acc. Circ:** 7,000 (ctrl). ***Continued by*** *Jerry Buchanan's Info Marketing Report, 1066-5250.*
Desc: Covers all aspects of writing and marketing how-to-do-it books and reports. Neophytes or professional freelance writers gain tremendous advantage in profit-taking.

US/0738-9094
TRAVELWRITER MARKETLETTER. **VFOAT** Travel Writer Market Letter. (19??)-. Periodical. English. mo. $60.00 (one year), $115.00 (two years), $160.00 (three years). Travelwriter Marketletter, 301 Park Avenue, Suite 1850, New York NY 10022. **Tel** (212)759-6744, FAX (212)758-9209. **ED** Robert Milne. **[CCC]. Bk Rev. Circ:** 1,000. ***Formed by the union of*** *Update (Society of American Travel Writers)* ***and*** *Freelance Update.*
Desc: This journal is to help travel writers and photographers to sell their articles and photos.

US/1046-2163
TRENDS IN COLLEGE MEDIA. [Trends coll. media]. **Added/Corp** Associated Collegiate Press (U.S.). Vol. 69, No. 1 (September 1989)-. Periodical. English. ir. $12.00 US; $17.00 other; $20.00 combined with Trends in High School Media. National Scholastic Press Association, Associated Collegiate Press, University of Minnesota, 620 Rarig Center Minneapolis MN 55455. **Tel** (612)625-8335, FAX (612) 626-0720. **LC** LB3621.6; .T7. **DD** 378. available on microfilm from University Microfilms International (UMI). ***Continues in part*** *Scholastic Editor's Trends in Publications, 0745-2357.*

US
TRENDS IN COMMUNIST MEDIA. Periodical. English. wk. National Technical Information Service - NTIS, Room 2027S, 5285 Port Royal Road, Springfield VA 22161. **Tel** (703)487-4630, (703)487-4660, (703)487-4650, FAX (703)321-8547, telex 89-9405.

US/1046-2155
TRENDS IN HIGH SCHOOL MEDIA. (TRENDS IN HIGH SCHOOL MEDIA / NATIONAL SCHOLASTIC PRESS ASSOCIATION.). [Trends high school media]. **Added/Corp** National Scholastic Press Association. Vol. 69, No. 1 (October 1989)-. Periodical. English. qt. $12.00 US; $17.00 other; $20.00 combined with Trends in College Media. National Scholastic Press Association, Associated Collegiate Press, University of Minnesota, 620 Rarig Center Minneapolis MN 55455. **Tel** (612)625-8335, FAX (612) 626-0720. **LC** LB3621.5; .T7. **DD** 373. available on microfilm from University Microfilms International (UMI). ***Continues in part*** *Scholastic Editor's Trends in Publications, 0745-2357.*

US
TRINITY DIGEST. (19??)-. English. wk. Trinity Evangelical Divinity School, 2065 Half Day Road, Bannockburn, Deerfield IL 60015. **Tel** (708)945-8800. **Bk Rev. Ad Acc. Circ:** 1,500 (ctrl). ***Continues*** *Trinity Journal, 0360-3032.*

US/0360-3032
TRINITY JOURNAL. ***Title Change.*** [Trinity j.]. **Added/Corp** Trinity Evangelical Divinity School. (1974)-(19??). English. Twice a year. Trinity Evangelical Divinity School, 2065 Half Day Road, Bannockburn, Deerfield IL 60015. **Tel** (708)945-8800. **ED** Douglas Moo. **LC** BR1; .T72. **DD** 230/.05. available on microfilm and microfiche from University Microfilms International (UMI). ***Continues*** *Trinity Studies, 0360-2915.* ***Continued by*** *Trinity Digest.*
Ind/Abst Christ. Period. Index; Guide Soc. Sci. Relig.; Index Book Rev. Relig. (19??-19??); New Testam. Abstr.; Old Testam. Abstr.; Relig. Index One Period. (1980-19??); Relig. Theol. Abstr.

US/0196-5093
U.S. PUBLICITY DIRECTORY. BUSINESS & FINANCE. ***Ceased.*** [U. S. public. dir., Bus. finance]. **VAT** United States Publicity Directory. Business and Finance. Directory. English. sa. John Wiley & Sons, Inc., 605 Third Avenue, New York NY 10158-0012. **Tel** (212)850-6000, (212)850-6645, FAX (212)850-6088, telex 12-7063. **(Subscription address:** John Wiley & Sons / England, Baffins Lane, Chichester, West Sussex PO19 1UD England.**) LC** Z6951; .U14; PN4888.C59. **DD** 070.5/92/02573.

US/0196-5107
U.S. PUBLICITY DIRECTORY. COMMUNICATION SERVICES. [U. S. public. dir., Commun. serv.]. **VFOAT** USPD, U.S. Publicity Directory. Communications Services. **VAT** United States Publicity Directory. Communication Services. (1980)-. English. sa. John Wiley & Sons, Inc., 605 Third Avenue, New York NY 10158-0012. **Tel** (212)850-6000, (212)850-6645, FAX (212)850-6088, telex 12-7063. **(Subscription address:** John Wiley & Sons / England, Baffins Lane, Chichester, West Sussex PO19 1UD England.**) LC** P88.8; .U16. **DD** 071/.3.

US/0196-5085
U.S. PUBLICITY DIRECTORY. MAGAZINES. **VFOAT** USPD. U.S. Publicity Directory. Magazines. **VAT** United States Publicity Directory. Magazines. (Summer 1980)-. Directory. English. sa. John Wiley & Sons, Inc., 605 Third Avenue, New York NY 10158-0012. **Tel** (212)850-6000, (212)850-6645, FAX (212)850-6088, telex 12-7063. **(Subscription address:** John Wiley & Sons / England, Baffins Lane, Chichester, West Sussex PO19 1UD England.**) LC** Z6951; .U17; PN4877. **DD** 051.

US/0196-5077
U.S. PUBLICITY DIRECTORY. NEWSPAPERS. **VFOAT** USPD, U.S. Publicity Directory. Newspapers. **VAT** United States Publicity Directory. Newspapers. Summer 1980-. Directory. English. sa. John Wiley & Sons, Inc., 605 Third Avenue, New York NY 10158-0012. **Tel** (212)850-6000, (212)850-6645, FAX (212)850-6088, telex 12-7063. **(Subscription address:** John Wiley & Sons / England, Baffins Lane, Chichester, West Sussex PO19 1UD England.**) LC** Z6951; .U18; PN4867. **DD** 071/.3.

CN/0380-1403
UKRAJINSKYJ ZURNALIST. (UKRAINSKYI ZHURNALIST.). **VFOAT** Ukrainian Journalist. Began in 1968. Periodical. Ukrainian. The Ukrainian Journalist, 140 Bathurst Street, Toronto Ontario M5V 2R3 Canada. **DD** 070/.023.

UK
UNDERGROUND AND ALTERNATIVE PRESS IN BRITAIN, THE. **VFOAT** Underground Press. 1972-. English. an. Harvester Wheatsheaf, Campus 400, Maylands Avenue, Hemel Hempstead, Hertfordshire HP2 7EZ England. **Tel** 011 44 442 881900. **LC** Z6944.U5; U48; PN5124.U53. **DD** 015.41035.

CU
UPEC. **Main/Corp** UPEC. **VAT** Union de Periodistas de Cuba. Spanish. Buro Ejecutivo, Union de Periodistas de Cuba, Calle 23 No 452 Esquina A I, Habana Cuba. **LC** PN4705; .U6A. **DD** 079/.7291.

SZ
VERBREITUNGSDATEN DER SCHWEIZER PRESSE. Zollikerstrasse 27, Postfach 272, 8032 Zurich Switzerland.

RU
VESTNIK MOSKOVSKOGO UNIVERSITETA. SERIIA X : ZHURNALISTIKA. **Main/Corp** Moscow. Universitet. (1977)-. Academic Scholarly Publication. Russian. Six times a year. $119.95. Izdatelstvo Moskovskogo Universiteta, K-9 Ulitsa Gertsena 5/7, Moscow Russia. **Tel** (301)881-5973. **(Subscription address:** East View Publications Inc., 3020 Harbor Lane North, Suite 110, Minneapolis MN 55447.**) LC** PN4705; .M67a. Documents available from CASDDS. ***Supersedes*** *Vestnik. Seriia XI: Zhurnalistika.*
Ind/Abst Chem. Abstr.

US/0741-8876
WASHINGTON JOURNALISM REVIEW (1983). ***Title Change.*** (WASHINGTON JOURNALISM REVIEW : WJR.). [Washington journal. rev.]. **Added/Corp** University of Maryland at College Park. College of Journalism. **VFOAT** WJR; W.J.R. Vol. 5, No. 1 (Jan./Feb. 1983)-(1993). Periodical. English. mo (except bimonthly Jan./Feb., July/Aug.). Broadcast Interview Source, 2233 Wisconsin Avenue NW, #540, Washington DC 20007-4104. **Tel** (800)955-0311, (202)333-4904, FAX (202)342-5411. **ED** Bill Monroe and Jim Broadwater. **LC** PN4700; .W38. **Bk Rev. Ad Acc. Circ:** 30,000. available on microfilm and microfiche from University Microfilms International (UMI). Documents available from UMI Article Clearinghouse. ***Continues*** *WJR, 0743-9881.* ***Continued by*** *American Journalism Review, 1067-8654.*
Desc: Examines and reports on the press in all its forms in order to illuminate an institution that profoundly influences our lives.
Ind/Abst Access (?-?); ACM Guide Comput. Lit.; Am. Bibliogr. Slavic East Europ. Stud.; Book Rev. Index; Comput. Rev.; Dent. Abstr. (-199?); Expand. Acad. Index (1989-); Film Lit. Index (19??-); Humanit. Index; Humanit. Source (Jul. 1993-); Index Period. Artic. Relat. Law; INFO-SOUTH Abstr.; Mag. Search; Newsp. Period. Abstr. (1991-); Read. Guide Period. Lit.

●MW
WASI : [BULLETIN]. See Literature.

CN/1184-678X
WESTWORD (EDMONTON). (WESTWORD / WRITERS GUILD OF ALBERTA.). [WestWord]. **Added/Corp** Writers Guild of Alberta. **VFOAT** West Word; Writers Guild of Alberta WestWord. Vol. 10, No. 6 (Nov. 1990)-. Periodical. English. Six times a year. 30.00Can$ (institutions), 25.00Can$ (individuals). Writers Guild of Alberta, 10523-100 Avenue, Wordworks Building, Edmonton Alberta T5J 0A8 Canada. **Tel** (403)426-5892, FAX (403)424-7943. **ED** Dave Panchyk and Cath Jackel. **DD** 808/.02/05. **Ad Acc, Adv Mgr:** Darlene Diver. **Circ:** 1,000 (ctrl). ***Continues*** *Newsletter (Writers Guild of Alberta)., 0821-4204.*
Desc: A newsletter of the Writers Guild of Alberta. It contains articles and information of interest to writers in general and WGA members in particular.

CN/1186-8872
WINGS : WOMEN IN NEWS GATHERING. [Wings, Women news gathering]. **Added/Corp** Manitoba Media Women. Canadian Association of Journalists. **VFOAT** Women in News Gathering. (Summer 1991)-. Periodical. English. qt. Free to members of the Canadian Association of Journalists. $10.00 per year, others. Women in News Gathering (WINGs), c/o Shirley Muir, 605 Stradbrook, Winnipeg Manitoba R3L 0K3 Canada. **DD** 070.4.

CN/1180-5145
WORD (ST. JOHN'S). (WORD / THE WRITERS' ALLIANCE, WRITERS' ALLIANCE OF NEWFOUNDLAND AND LABRADOR.). [Word]. **Added/Corp** Writers' Alliance of Newfoundland and Labrador. **VFOAT** Writers' Alliance Word; WANL Newsletter. **VAT** Word - Writers' Alliance of Newfoundland and Labrador. (Dec. 1989/Jan. 1990)-. Periodical. English. mo. Free to members. Writers' Alliance of Newfoundland and Labrador, PO Box 2681, St. John's, Newfoundland A1C 5M5 Canada. **DD** 808/.02/060718.

US/0084-1323
WORKING PRESS OF THE NATION, THE. See Journalism-Abstracting, Bibliographies and Statistics.

CN/0225-5790
WORLD PRESS DIGEST. [World press dig.]. V. 1- Oct. 1979-. Periodical. English. mo. World Press Digest Canada Ltd, 258 Sheppard Avenue East/Suite 7, Willowdale Ontario M2N 3B1 Canada. **Tel** (416)225-5013. **DD** 051.

CN/1182-901X
WRITE ANGLES. [Write angles]. **Added/Corp** Calgary Writers Association. (1990)-. Periodical. English. mo. Limited free distribution. Calgary Writers Association, Box 3, 1325-44th Avenue North East, Calgary, Alberta T2E 6L5 Canada. **DD** C810/.6/09712338. ***Continues*** *Hints 'n' Prods., 0842-6406.*

UK/0084-2699
WRITERS DIRECTORY, THE. [Writ. dir.]. (1973)-. Directory. English. ir. $130.00. Gale Research Inc., 835 Penobscot Building, Detroit MI 48226. **Tel** (800)877-GALE, (313)961-2242, FAX (313)961-6083, telex TWX 810-221-7086. **LC** PS1; .W73. **DD** 808.
Desc: Provides biobibliographical entries for more than 17,000 living writers. Writers are from many countries and all writers listed have had at least one book published in English. Entries furnish personal and career data, a chronological list of publications, and present address. A separate section lists authors by writing category.

US/1053-1793
WRITER'S GUIDELINES (PITTSBURG, MO.). (WRITER'S GUIDELINES.). [Writ. guidel.]. **Added/Corp** Writer's Corporation of America. **VFOAT** WGM; Writer's Guidelines Magazine. Vol.4, No. 1 (Jan./Feb. 1991)-. Newsletter. English. bm. $25.00 US; $40.00 other. Writer's Corporation of America, PO Box 608, Pittsburgh MO 65724. **Tel** (417)993-5544, FAX (417)993-5544. **ED** Susan Salaki. **DD** 810. **Bk Rev. Ad Acc. Circ:** 750 (ctrl). ***Continues*** *Guidelines Magazine, 1046-9184.*
Desc: Grass roots approach to the world of writing and editing.

US/0196-5611
WRITERS GUILD DIRECTORY. **Added/Corp** Writers Guild of America, West. (19??)-. Directory. English. an. $17.50 US; $25.00 other. Writers Guild of

Journalism

America, 8955 Beverly Boulevard, Los Angeles CA 90048. **Tel** (310)550-1000, FAX (310)550-8185. **LC** PS5; .W7318. **DD** 810/.25/73.

US/0084-2710
WRITER'S HANDBOOK, THE. (1936)-. English. an. $32.70. Writer Inc, 120 Boylston Street, Boston MA 02116-4615. **Tel** (617)423-3157. **ED** Sylvia K. Burack. **LC** PN137; .W73. **DD** 029.6. Index available.
Desc: Includes practical advice and instruction by leading writers, with 100 chapters on how to write and sell non-fiction books, romances, poetry, short stories, novels, articles, plays and science fiction.

CN/0225-610X
WRITER'S LIFELINE. [Writ. lifeline]. No. 106 (Jan. 15, 1979)-. Periodical. English. mo. $18.00. Libra Press, 7650 Kimbel Street, Unit 35, Mississauga, Ontario, L5S 1L2 Canada. **Tel** (416)671-8376. **DD** 808/.02/05. **Bk Rev**. **Ad Acc**. **Circ:** 1,500. **Continues** Lifeline, 0316-0602.
Desc: A specialized magazine for freelance, professional, and beginning writers.

US/1054-2299
WRITER'S NETWORK, THE. [Writ. netw.]. (Jan. 1991)-. Periodical. English. bm. $18.00. Black Hawk Publishing Co., PO Box 24, Mt. Freedom NJ 07970-0024. **DD** 808.

US/1055-0224
WRITERS' WORKSHOP. [Writ. workshop]. **Added/Corp** Southwest Writers' Workshop (Albuquerque, N.M.). **VFOAT** Writers' Workshop Magazine. Vol. 91, No. 3 (1991)-. Periodical. English. mo. $25.00. Sandia Publishing Corporation, PO Box 35819, Albuquerque NM 87176. **DD** 808.

US/1057-0772
WRITER'S WORLD (BIG STONE GAP, VA.). (WRITER'S WORLD.). [Writ. world]. (1990)-. Periodical. English. bm. $15.00. Writer's World, 204 East 19th Street, Big Stone Gap VA 24219. **DD** 810.

US/0084-2737
WRITER'S YEARBOOK. (19??)-. English. an (published in Jan.). $3.95. Writer's Digest Books, 1507 Dana Avenue, Cincinnati OH 45207. **Tel** (513)531-2222, (800)289-0963, FAX (513)531-4744. **ED** A. M. Mathieu. **LC** PN111; .W7. available on microfilm and microfiche from University Microfilms International (UMI).
Desc: New articles and updated listings on how and where to sell your writings, including the top markets for nonfiction writers.

US/1050-4788
WRITING CONCEPTS. [Writ. concepts]. (1990)-. Periodical. English. mo. $77.00 US; $107.00 other. Communications Concepts Inc, 2100 National Press Building, Washington DC 20045. **Tel** (703)425-7751, FAX (703)425-8930. **(Subscription address:** PO Box 1608, Springfield, VA 22151-0608) **DD** 808.
Desc: Provides practical advice from peers for nonfiction writers and editors and addresses new problems they are facing. Focuses on the changing needs of writers, editors and publication managers.

US/0279-7208
WRITING (HIGHLAND PARK, ILL.). See Education.

●US/1065-6154
WRITING IT RIGHT. (1992)-. Periodical. English. qt. $48.00. RZ Communications, 528 NE 80th Street, Seattle WA 98115.

US/0741-7594
YOUNG AUTHOR'S MAGAZINE. **VFOAT** Young Author's. Vol. 1, No. 1 (Jan./Feb. 1984)-. Periodical. English. qt. $10.95. Theraplan Inc., 3015 Woodsdale Boulevard, Lincoln NE 68502. **Tel** (402)421-3172, FAX (402)421-8095.

RU/0130-3589
ZHURNALIST. **Added/Corp** Soiuz Zhurnalistov SSSR. Konferatsiia Zhurnalistskikh Soiuzov. (Jan. 1967)-. Periodical. Russian. mo. $109.95. **(Subscription address:** East View Publications Inc., 3020 Harbor Lane North, Suite 110, Minneapolis MN 55447.**) LC** PN5274; .Z646. **Bk Rev**. available on microfilm from University Microfilms International (UMI). **Continues** Sovetskaia Pechat.
Ind/Abst Curr. Dig. Post Sov. Press.

RU/0134-8442
ZHURNALIST, PRESSA, AUDITORIIA / LENINGRADSKII GOSUDARSTVENNYI UNIVERSITET IM. A.A. ZHDANOVA. **Added/Corp** Leningradskii Gosudarstvennyi Universitet Imeni A.A. Zhdanova. (1975)-. Periodical. Russian. 1.30rub. St Petersburg State University / Izdatelstvo Leningradskogo Universiteta, Universitetskaia Nab 7/9,

199034 St Petersburg Russia. **Tel** 011 95 218-97-88, FAX 011 95 218-51-52, telex 124181. **LC** PN4749; .Z58. **DD** 070/.05.

UN/0132-8425
ZHURNALIST UKRAINY. **Added/Corp** Spilka Zhurnalistiv URSR. Spilka Zhurnalistiv Ukrainy. (19??)-. Ukrainian. mo. 0.15rub (single issue). Spilka Zhurnalistiv URSR, Brest-Litovskii Prospekt 94, Kiev Ukraine. **LC** PN5278.U4; Z58.

ABSTRACTING, BIBLIOGRAPHIES AND STATISTICS

UK
UK PRESS GAZETTE. Vol. 1 (1965)-. English. wk. £53.75. Maclean Hunter Ltd. / UK, Chalk Lane Cockfosters Road, Barnet Herts EN4 0BU England. **Tel** 011 44 81 2423000, FAX 011 44 81 9759753, telex 299072. available on an online database (files 771,772,799/Full-Text) from DIALOG. **Absorbed** Media Reporter.

US/0084-1323
WORKING PRESS OF THE NATION, THE. [Work. press nation]. (1947)-. Directory. English. an. $385.00. National Register Publishing Company Inc., PO Box 31, 121 Chanlon Road, New Providence NJ 07974. **Tel** (800)521-8110, (800)323-6772, FAX (908)665-6688. **ED** Nancy Veatch. **LC** Z6951; .W6. **DD** 071.47. Index available. available on magnetic tape. **Continues** Working Press of New York City; **Absorbed** Gebbie House Magazine Directory, 0072-0526.
Desc: Provides the names of today's "newsmakers" - the writers, reporters, editors, and executives who decide whether or not to run a story. Includes phone numbers, material requirements, deadlines, etc., for newspapers, magazines, TV, and radio.

LAW

US/0744-6748
1ST READING (SACRAMENTO, CALIF.). (1ST READING / CHA.). **Added/Corp** California Hospital Association. **VFOAT** First Reading. (198?)-. Periodical. English. ir (21 issues). $30.00 members. California Association of Hospitals and Health Systems, PO Box 1100, Sacramento CA 95812. **Tel** (916)443-7401. **ED** Ted Fourhas. **Circ:** 1,380.
Desc: Covers legislation affecting the healthcare industry.

US/0892-7308
11TH CIRCUIT LAW LETTER. Ceased. [11th Circuit law lett.]. **Added/Corp** United States. Court of Appeals (11th Circuit). **VFOAT** Eleventh Circuit Law Letter. (198?)-(199?). Periodical. English. bw. Georgia Law Letter Publishers, 10 Park Place South, PO Box 1597, Atlanta GA 30301-1597. **LC** KF112 11th.1; .A14. **DD** 348.73/048; 347.30848.

US/1053-9549
AACD LEGAL SERIES, THE. Title Change. [AACD leg. ser.]. **Added/Corp** American Association for Counseling and Development. **VAT** American Association for Counseling and Development Legal Series. Vol. 1 (1991)-(199?). Monographic series. English. American Association for Counseling and Development, 5999 Stevenson Avenue, Alexandria VA 22304. **DD** 340.
Continued by ACA Legal Series, 1064-2226.

US
AALL PUBLICATION SERIES. Main/Corp American Association of Law Libraries. (1960)-. Monographic series. English. ir. Price varies. Fred B. Rothman & Company, 10368 West Centennial Road, Littleton CO 80127. **Tel** (800)457-1986, (303)979-5657, FAX (303)978-1457, telex 87669.

US/0740-4050
ABA/BNA LAWYERS' MANUAL ON PROFESSIONAL CONDUCT. CURRENT REPORTS. **Added/Corp** American Bar Association. Bureau of National Affairs (Washington, D.C.) American Bar Association. ABA/BNA Lawyers' Manual on Professional Conduct. **VFOAT** A.B.A./B.N.A. Lawyers' Manual on Professional Conduct. Current Reports. **VAT** American Bar Association, Bureau of National Affairs Lawyer's Manual on Professional Conduct. Vol. 1, No. 1 (Jan. 25, 1984)-. English. bw (26 issues). $659.00 (full service). Bureau of National Affairs Inc., 9435 Key West Avenue, Rockville MD 20850. **Tel** (800)372-1033, (301)258-1033, FAX (301)948-5823. **ED** Robert A. Robbins. **[CCC]**. cum. index. **Bk Rev**. **Circ:** 2,000 (ctrl).
Desc: Reports on developments affecting lawyers' professional lives, with accompanying loose-leaf manual that covers full range of ethical and professional topics.

US/0747-0088
ABA JOURNAL. [ABA j.]. **Added/Corp** American Bar Association. **VFOAT** A.B.A. Journal. (Jan. 1984)-. Periodical. English. mo. $66.00. American Bar Association, 750 North Lake Shore Drive, Chicago IL 60611. **Tel** (312)988-5522, (312)988-5241, FAX (312)988-5528, telex 270593. **ED** Laurence Bodine, George Gold, Robert Yates and Gary Hengstler. **LC** K1; .M385. **DD** 349.73/05; 347.3005. Index available. cum. index. **Bk Rev**. **Ad Acc**. **Circ:** 370,000 (ctrl). available on microfilm and microfiche from University Microfilms International (UMI). Documents available from The Genuine Article, UMI Article Clearinghouse. **Continues** American Bar Association Journal, 0002-7596.
Desc: Articles which provide insight into problems facing society that have legal implications.
Ind/Abst Acad. Ind. [Computer File] (1992-); Acad. Search (July 1993-); Account. Tax Datab. (1974-); Arts Humanit. Citation Index [Select. Cov.]; Book Rev. Index; Bus. Source (Jul. 1993-); Curr. Contents Soc. Behav. Sci.; Curr. Lit. Fam. Plan.; Expand. Acad. Index (1984-); INFO-SOUTH Abstr.; Law Office Inf. Serv.; Leg. Resour. Index (1984-); LegalTrac (1980-); Mag. Express (1988-) [Full Txt.]; Mag. Search; Newsp. Period. Abstr. (1988-); PAIS Int. Print; Res. Alert [Full Cov.]; Resource/One Ondisc; Soc. Sci. Cit. Index [Full Cov.]; Trade Ind. Index; Women Stud. Abstr.

US/1061-4354
ABA JOURNAL OF AFFORDABLE HOUSING & COMMUNITY DEVELOPMENT LAW. See Housing and Urban Development.

US/0883-4695
ABA SOFTWARE REVIEW. (ABA SOFTWARE REVIEW / LEGAL TECHNOLOGY ADVISORY COUNCIL, AMERICAN BAR ASSOCIATION.). **Added/Corp** Legal Technology Advisory Council (American Bar Association). **VFOAT** Software Review; LTAC Software Review. **VAT** American Bar Association Software Review; Legal Technology Advisory Council Software Review. Vol. 1, No. 2 (May 1985)-. Periodical. English. ir. American Bar Association, 750 North Lake Shore Drive, Chicago IL 60611. **Tel** (312)988-5522, (312)988-5241, FAX (312)988-5528, telex 270593. **LC** KF320.A9; A23. **DD** 340/.028/553.

●CN/1193-3100
ABORIGINAL JUSTICE BULLETIN. [Aborig. justice bull.]. **Added/Corp** Legal Services Society of British Columbia. Native Programs. Vol. 1, No. 1 (Spring 1992)-. Bulletin. English. qt. **DD** 347.71/0089/9705.

AT
ABORIGINAL LAW BULLETIN. Added/Corp University of New South Wales. Aboriginal Law Research Unit. No. 1 (Aug. 1981)-. Periodical. English. Six times a year (Feb., Apr., June, Aug., Oct., Dec.). 20.00Aus$ (individuals), 25.00Aus$ (institutions) Australia; 25.00Aus$ (individuals), 30.00Aus$ (institutions) others. Aboriginal Law Centre/UNSW, Faculty of Law, PO Box 1, Kensington New South Wales, 2033 Australia. **Tel** 011 61 2 385 2256, FAX 011 61 2 313 7209. **ED** Margie Cronin, and Jennifer Kremmer. Index available (published separately). cum. index. **Bk Rev**, (Qty: 6-12). **Ad Acc**. **Pr Rev**. **Circ:** 2,600 (ctrl).
Desc: This journal gives up-to-date information and articles on issues involving law and aboriginal and Torres Strait Islander peoples.
Ind/Abst Aust. Leg. Mon. Dig.

●US/1064-1289
ABOVEGROUND TANK STATE REGULATORY GUIDE. [Aboveground tank state regul. guide]. **VFOAT** Above Ground Tank State Regulatory Guide. 1st Ed. (1992)-. English. $195.00. CEEM Publications, 10521 Braddock Road, Fairfax VA 22032. **DD** 344.

US/0191-6688
ACCESS REPORTS, PRIVACY. (197?)-. Periodical. English. bw. $127.00. Plus Publications, Inc., 2626 Pennsylvania Avenue NW, Washington DC 20037. **LC** KF2.A15; A25. **DD** 342.73/0858.
Ind/Abst Hum. Rights Intern. Rep.

US/0191-6696
ACCESS REPORTS REFERENCE FILE. **Added/Corp** United States. Laws, Statutes, etc. **VFOAT** Reference File; Reference File: Federal. Vol. 1 (1975)-. Periodical. English. mo. $450.00. Access Reports Inc, 1624 Dogwood Lane, Lynchburg VA 24503. **Tel** (804)384-5334, FAX (804)846-6928. **ED** Harry A. Hammitt. **Circ:** 200 (ctrl).

US/8756-4262
ACCOUNTANTS' LIABILITY. See Business-Accounting.

US/0730-7721
ACCOUNTING FOR LAWYERS. See Business-Accounting.

Law

ZA
ACCOUNTS FOR THE YEAR ENDED 31ST DECEMBER ... : AUDITOR-GENERAL'S REPORT / REPUBLIC OF ZAMBIA, THE COUNCIL OF LEGAL EDUCATION. See Public Administration-Public Finance and Taxation.

NZ
A'COURT'S BUSINESS HANDBOOK NEW ZEALAND EDITION. (A'COURT'S BUSINESS HANDBOOK.). [A'Court's bus. handb.N.Z. ed.]. **VFOAT** Business Handbook. (1991)-. English. an. 95.00Aus$ Australia; 115.00Aus$ other. A Court Publications, 24 Ra Ora Drive, East Tamaki New Zealand. **Tel** 64 9 2741441. *Formed by the union of A' Court's Business Handbook (Wellington & Provinces Ed.), 0112-4684; A'Court's Business Handbook (South Island Edition), 0113-2067 and A'Court's Business Handbook (Auckland & Provinces Ed.), 0112-1804.*

US/1052-1674
ACQUISITION ISSUES. See Public Administration-Public Finance and Taxation.

AT/0813-6270
ACT NEWSLETTER - SOCIETY FOR COMPUTERS AND THE LAW, A.C.T. (1984)-. Newsletter. English. ir. **Ind/Abst** Aust. Leg. Mon. Dig.

VC/0001-5199
ACTA APOSTOLICA SEDIS, COMMENTARIUM OFFICIALE. See Religion and Theology-Catholicism.

SA/0065-1346
ACTA JURIDICA (CAPE TOWN). (ACTA JURIDICA.). [Acta jurid.]. **Added/Corp** University of Cape Town. Faculty of Law. (1958)-. English. an (Dec). R104.50 South Africa; R34.13 US. Juta Subscription Services, PO Box 14373, Kenwyn 7790 South Africa. **Tel** 011 27 21 7975101, FAX (021)761-5010, telex 523072 SA. **ED** I. Leeman. **LC** Law. **Circ:** 378 (ctrl). *Continues Butterworths South African Law Review.*
Desc: This magazine discusses articles and other information on current legal problems.
Ind/Abst Index Foreign Leg. Per.

XR/0567-8242
ACTA UNIVERSITATIS CAROLINAE. IURIDICA. MONOGRAPHIA. *Suspended.* **Added/Corp** Universita Karlova. (19??)-(19??). Monographic series. Czech. Price varies per volume. Charles University / Univerzita Karlova, Ovocnytrh 5, 116 36 Prague 1 Czech Republic. **Tel** 228441.
Ind/Abst Index Foreign Leg. Per.

PL/0208-6069
ACTA UNIVERSITATIS LODZIENSIS. FOLIA IURIDICA. **VFOAT** Folia Iuridica. 1-. Monographic series. Polish (French). Price varies per volume. **LC** K1; .C72. *Continues in part Acta Universitatis Lodziensis. Seria I, Nauki Humanistyczno--Spoeczne.*

VE/0254-072X
ACTAS PROCESALES DEL DERECHO VIVO. [Actas procesales derecho vivo]. V. 1- 1971-. Periodical. Spanish. mo. Grafiunic, 6593, Carmelitas, Caracas 101. **LC** K1; .C75.

FR
ACTION JURIDIQUE CFDT. (19??)-. French. Eight times a year. 250.73F France; 316.00F other. CFDT Presse, 4 Boulevard de la Villette, 75955 Paris Cedex 19 France. **Tel** 011 33 1 42038140. Index available. cum. index. **Ad Acc. Circ:** 5,600 (ctrl).

US
ACTION KIT FOR HOSPITAL LAW. Vol. 1 (March 1972)-. Periodical. English. mo. $495.00 (also comes with Action Kit for Hospital Law complete package). Action Kit for Hospital Law, 4614 5th Avenue, Pittsburgh PA 15213. **Tel** (800)245-1205, (412)687-8275. **LC** KF3825.A73; A25.

BE
ACTIVITE DES COURS ET TRIBUNAUX. STATISTIQUES DIVERSES. See Law-Abstracting, Bibliographies and Statistics.

CN/0846-3980
ACTIVITY REPORT - PUBLIC LEGAL EDUCATION AND INFORMATION SERVICE OF NEW BRUNSWICK. See Public Administration.

XM
ACTS FOR THE YEAR ... / ST. VINCENT & THE GRENADINES. Main/Corp Saint Vincent and the Grenadines. English. an. 32.00. Government Printing Office / Saint Vincent and the Grenadines, Kingstown St Vincent and The Grenadines. **LC** KGW5008; .A23. *Continues Saint Vincent. Laws, etc. Acts.*

SP/1130-9946
ACTUALIDAD ADMINISTRATIVA MADRID. [Actual. adm. Madr.]. (1985)-. Periodical. Spanish. Forty-eight times a year. 62000.00ptas. Actualidad Editorial SA, Calle Aragoneses 7, 28100 Alcobendas Madrid Spain. **Tel** 011 34 1 6616284. **UDC** 35.

SP/0213-6929
ACTUALIDAD FINANCIERA. [Actual. financ.]. (1986)-. Periodical. Spanish. Forty-eight times a year. 58000.00ptas. Actualidad Editorial SA, Calle Aragoneses 7, 28100 Alcobendas Madrid Spain. **Tel** 011 34 1 6616284. **UDC** 336. **Bk Rev.**

SP/0213-7097
ACTUALIDAD LABORAL. [Actual. labor.]. (1984)-. Periodical. Spanish. Forty-eight times a year. 64500.00ptas. Actualidad Editorial SA, Calle Aragoneses 7, 28100 Alcobendas Madrid Spain. **Tel** 011 34 1 6616284. **UDC** 349.2.
Ind/Abst Int. Labour Doc.

SP
ACTUALIDAD LABORAL LEGISLACION. Spanish. 40000ptas. Actualidad Editorial SA, Calle Aragoneses 7, 28100 Alcobendas Madrid Spain. **Tel** 011 34 1 6616284. **Bk Rev.**

SP/0213-6562
ACTUALIDAD PENAL. [Actual. penal]. (1986)-. Periodical. Spanish. wk. 40000ptas. Actualidad Editorial SA, Calle Aragoneses 7, 28100 Alcobendas Madrid Spain. **Tel** 011 34 1 6616284. **UDC** 343. **Bk Rev.**

SP
ACTUALIDAD TRIBUTARIA. Spanish. 40000ptas. Actualidad Editorial SA, Calle Aragoneses 7, 28100 Alcobendas Madrid Spain. **Tel** 011 34 1 6616284. **Bk Rev.**

SP
ACTUALIDAD TRIBUTARIA LEGISLACION. Spanish. 40000ptas. Actualidad Editorial SA, Calle Aragoneses 7, 28100 Alcobendas Madrid Spain. **Tel** 011 34 1 6616284. **Bk Rev.**

SP
ACTUALIDAD Y DERECHO. Spanish. 40000ptas. Actualidad Editorial SA, Calle Aragoneses 7, 28100 Alcobendas Madrid Spain. **Tel** 011 34 1 6616284. **Bk Rev.**

FR/0044-6157
ACTUALITE FIDUCIAIRE, L'. [Actual. fiduc.]. (1927)-. Periodical. French. mo (except Aug.). 286.97F France; 366.00F other. Nouvelles Editions Fiduciaires, 2 Bis rue de Villiers, 92300 Levallois Perret France. **Tel** 011 33 1 47581320. **UDC** 336.2. **[CCC].**

FR
ACTUALITE JURIDIQUE : DROIT ADMINISTRATIF, L'. **VFOAT** AJDA. (19??)-. Periodical. French. Eleven times a year. 670.00F. Publications du Moniteur, 17 rue d'Uzes, 75108 Paris Cedex 02 France. **Tel** 011 33 1 40133030, FAX 011 33 1 40419495 customer service, 40133037 advertising, telex UPRESSE 680876 F. **LC** K1; .C78. **DD** 342.44/06/05; 344.402605. Index available (free). *Continues Actualite Juridique.*
Ind/Abst Index Foreign Leg. Per.

FR/0001-7736
ACTUALITE JURIDIQUE. PROPRIETE IMMOBILIERE, L'. **VFOAT** Propriete Immobiliere; A.J.P.I.; AJPI. Periodical. French. mo. 335.00F. 17 rue d'Uzes, 75002 Paris France. **LC** LAW. **DD** 346.4404/3/05; 344.4064305.

FR/0753-874X
ACTUALITE LEGISLATIVE DALLOZ. [Actual. legis. Dalloz]. Vol.1, No. 1 (Jan. 20, 1983)-. Periodical. French. sm. 545.00F France; 690.00F other. Dalloz, 35 rue Tournefort, 75240 Paris Cedex 05 France. **Tel** 011 33 1 40515434 or 40515454, FAX 45 87 37 48, telex 206 446 F. **ED** Pierre Seydoux. **DD** 349.44; 344.4. *Continues Bulletin Legislative Dalloz (1962), 0755-2424.*
Desc: Looks at legislative evolution through texts and commentaries. Announces congresses, reviews, books and periodical articles touching on legislation, and prints ministerial responses with clarifications.
Ind/Abst Index Foreign Leg. Per.

BE
ACTUALITES DU DROIT : REVUE DE LA FACULTE DE DROIT DE LIEGE. **Added/Corp** Faculte de Droit de Liege. (1991)-. Periodical. French. qt. 5800.00F. E Story Scientia, 228 Boulevard E Brockstael, 1020 Brussels Belgium. **Tel** 011 32 2 4223911. **LC** K1; .N465. **DD** 349.493; 344.93. *Continues Annales de Droit de Liege, 0771-3029.*

US/1067-4713
ADA POLICY & LAW. *Ceased.* **VFOAT** Americans with Disabilities Act Policy & Law; ADA Policy and Law. Vol. 1, No. 1 (Jan. 18, 1993)-(19??). Periodical. English. mo. LRP Publications, 747 Dresher Road, PO Box 980, Horsham PA 19044-0980. **Tel** (800)341-7874, (215)784-0860, FAX (215)784-9639, (215)784-0870. **LC** IN PROCESS. **DD** 344. **[CCC].**

TU/1011-730X
ADALET DERGISI. [Adalet derg.]. (1943)-. Periodical. Turkish. bm (6 issues). $9.00 US, Canada and Pan America; $7.20 Europe; $1.80 Turkey; $7.80 other. Adalet Bakanligi Yayin, Mudurlugu Bakanliklar, Ankara Turkey. **UDC** 35.

AT/0065-1915
ADELAIDE LAW REVIEW, THE. [Adel. law rev.]. Vol. 1 (April 1960)-. Periodical. English. sa. 40.00Aus$. University of Adelaide / Law School, Helen Creeper, Adelaide SA 5005 Australia. **Tel** 011 61 8 3034440. **DD** 349.94/05; 349.4005. Index available. **Ad Acc. Circ:** 700 (ctrl). available on microfilm and microfiche from University Microfilms International (UMI).
Ind/Abst APAIS, Aust. Public Aff. Inf. Ser. (1963-); Aust. Leg. Mon. Dig.; Curr. Law Index (1980-); Index Leg. Period.; Leg. Resour. Index (1981-); LegalTrac (1984-).

US/8756-3630
ADELPHIA LAW JOURNAL. [Adelphia law j.]. **Added/Corp** Sigma Nu Phi Legal Fraternity. Vol. 1, No. 1 (Spring 1982)-. Periodical. English. an. $10.00. Adelphia Law Journal, 7135 West Higgins, Chicago IL 60656. **Tel** (312)631-3557, FAX (312)631-3508. **ED** Vito M. Evola. **LC** K1; .D43. **DD** 340/.05.
Desc: Covers current law topics.
Ind/Abst Curr. Law Index (1982-); Index Leg. Period.; Leg. Resour. Index (1982-); LegalTrac (1983-).

IO
ADIL (KUALA LUMPUR, MALAYSIA). (ADIL / PERSATUAN PEGAWAI-PEGAWAI PERKHIDMATAN KEHAKIMAN DAN PERUNDANGAN.). **Added/Corp** Persatuan Pegawai-Pegawai Perkhidmatan Kehakiman dan Perundangan (Malaysia). (19??)-. Periodical. English (Malay). qt. The Attorney General's Chamber, Tingkat 11, Bangunan Bank Rakyat, JL Tangsi, Kuala Lumpur Malaysia. **LC** K1; .D44. **DD** 349.595/05; 345.95005.

US/0147-3603
ADMINISTRATION OF JUSTICE MEMORANDA. English. ir. $2.00 per issue. University of North Carolina at Chapel Hill Institute of Government, CB 3330, Knapp Building, Chapel Hill NC 27599-3330. **Tel** (919)966-4119, FAX (919)962-0654. **ED** Robert L Farb. **LC** KFN7908.A15; U6. **DD** 347/.756. **Circ:** 1,000 (ctrl).
Desc: Discusses current issues of concern to North Carolina law enforcement and judicial officials.

US
ADMINISTRATIVE LAW BULLETIN. (19??)-. Bulletin. English. bw. $109.00. Pike & Fischer Inc., 4600 East-West Highway, Suite 200, Bethesda MD 20814-1438. **Tel** (301)654-6262, FAX (301)654-6297.

AT/0726-5816
ADMINISTRATIVE LAW DECISIONS. [Adm. law decis.]. (1978)-. English. an. **DD** 342.9406.
Ind/Abst Aust. Leg. Mon. Dig.

●US
ADMINISTRATIVE LAW JOURNAL OF THE AMERICAN UNIVERSITY, THE. **Added/Corp** Washington College of Law. Vol. 6, No. 1 (Spring 1992)-. Periodical. English. Four times a year. $15.00 (Alumni of Washington College of Law), $20.00 (other) US; $22.00 other. Administrative Law Journal / Washington College of Law, American University, 4410 Massachusetts Avenue Northwest, Washington DC 20016. **Tel** (202)885-3412. **ED** Michael Lawrence Kolis. Index available. *Continues Administrative Law Journal (Washington, D.C.), 1052-2913.*

UK/0957-9710
ADMINISTRATIVE LAW REPORTS. [Adm. law rep.]. (1989)-. English. sm (26 issues). £104.70 UK; £110.90 other. Barry Rose Law Periodicals Ltd., Little London, Chichester West Sussex PO19 1PG England. **Tel** 011 44 243 787841, 011 44 243 783637, FAX 011 44 243 779174, 011 44 243 779278. **ED** Ian McLeod. Index available. **Ad Acc, Adv Mgr:** Mrs. Curtis.
Desc: Reports reflect the growth in the importance of administrative law that has been one of the most notable developments in English law in the last few decades.
Ind/Abst Can. Legal Lit. (19??-).

US
ADMINISTRATIVE LAW, THIRD SERIES. **Added/Corp** Pike and Fischer, Inc. Vol. 1, No. 1 (May 9, 1989)-. English. ir. $630.00. Pike & Fischer Inc., 4600 East-West Highway, Suite 200, Bethesda MD 20814-1438. **Tel** (301)654-6262, FAX (301)654-6297.

US/0096-1493
ADMINISTRATIVE REGISTER OF KENTUCKY. **Added/Corp** Kentucky. General Assembly. Legislative Research Commission. (1974)-. English. mo. $48.00; $150.00 combined subscription with Kentucky Administrative Regulations Service. Kentucky State Treasurer / Room 64, State Capitol, Frankfort KY 40601. **Tel** (502)564-8100. **ED** Susan C. Harding. **LC** KFK1236; .A35. **DD** 348/.769/025. **Circ:** 800 (ctrl).
Desc: Proposed Kentucky regulations, amendments, emergency regulations, and public hearings scheduled.

US/0747-6612
ADVANCE ANNOTATION SERVICE TO THE CODE OF ALABAMA 1975. **Added/Corp** Alabama. Laws, etc. (Code : 1975) Michie Company. No. 1 (1980/1981)-. Periodical. English. Three times a year. $60.00. Michie Company, PO Box 7587, Charlottesville VA 22906-7587. **Tel** (804)972-7600, (800)542-0957, FAX (800)643-1280.

US/8756-873X
ADVANCED IMMIGRATION WORKSHOP. [Adv. immigr. workshop]. English. an. Practising Law Institute, 810 Seventh Avenue, New York NY 10019-5818. **Tel** (212)765-5700, FAX (212)581-4670 general correspondence, (212)265-4742 orders and billing inquiries. **LC** KF4819.3; .A34. **DD** 342.73/082; 347.30282. ***Continues*** *Advanced Immigration, 8756-4270.*

US/1043-755X
ADVANCED MUNICIPAL BONDS WORKSHOP. [Adv. munic. bonds workshop]. (1988)-. English. an. Practising Law Institute, 810 Seventh Avenue, New York NY 10019-5818. **Tel** (212)765-5700, FAX (212)581-4670 general correspondence, (212)265-4742 orders and billing inquiries. **LC** KF6775.Z9; A39. **DD** 346.73/0922. ***Continues*** *Advanced Municipal Bonds, 0883-0886.*

US/0198-9448
ADVANCED REAL ESTATE LAW COURSE. 1st- 1979-. English. an. State Bar of Texas, PO Box 12487, Capitol Station, Austin TX 78711. **Tel** (512)463-1411. **LC** KFT1326; .A93. **DD** 346.76404/37.

US
ADVANCED UNDERWRITING SERVICE. **See** Public Administration-Public Finance and Taxation.

UK/0267-0763
ADVERTISING LAW & PRACTICE. ***Title Change.*** [Advert. law pract.]. **VFOAT** Advertising Law and Practice. Vol. 1, No. 1 (Oct. 1984)-. Periodical. English. bm. Frank Cass & Company Ltd, Newbury House, 890-900 Eastern Avenue, Newbury Park, Ilford, Essex IG2 7HH United Kingdom. **Tel** 011 44 81 599 8866, FAX 011 44 81 599 0984, telex 897719. **LC** KD2206.A13; A38. **DD** 343.41/082; 344.10382. ***Continued by*** *Merged into Journal of Media Law and Practice, 0144-0373.*

US/0093-1985
ADVERTISING LAW ANTHOLOGY. Vol. 1 (1973)-. English. sa. $299.90. International Library Law Book Publishers, 101 Lakeforest Boulevard, Suite 270, Gaithersburg MD 20877. **Tel** (800)359-3349, (301)990-7755, FAX (301)990-7642. **ED** Donald J. Hoyes. **LC** KF1614.A73; A925. **DD** 343/.73/082. Index available. cum. index. **Bk Rev**, (Qty: 2).
Desc: Presents advertising law review articles by year, printed in their entirety, in the field of advertising from over 900 US law review journals. Introduction and overview by highly respected experts in advertising law.

BL
ADVOCACIA DINAMICA : ADV. **VFOAT** ADV; A.D.V. Periodical. Portuguese. ir. Coad Atualizadora Fiscal Ltda, Av Nove de Julho 3 766, Jardim Paulista, Sao Paulo Brazil. **LC** KHD72.2; .A38. **DD** 348.81/046; 348/10846.

SP
ADVOCACIA DINAMICA, SELECOES JURIDICAS : ADV. **VFOAT** Juridicas A.D.V.; Selecoes Juridicas ADV. Periodical. Portuguese. mo. Sistema Coad de Atualizacao Profissional, Avenida Nove de Julho 3 766, Jardim Paulista, CEP 01406, Sao Paulo SP Brazil. **LC** K1; .D85. **DD** 349.81/05; 348.1/005.

CN/0382-456X
ADVOCATE, THE. Vol. 1 (Sept. 1964)-. Periodical. English. University of Toronto Faculty of Law, Toronto Ontario M5S 1A1 Canada.
Ind/Abst Can. Legal Lit.

US/0515-4987
ADVOCATE (BOISE, IDAHO), THE. (THE ADVOCATE.). [Advocate]. **Added/Corp** Idaho State Bar. Idaho State Bar Foundation. Third District Bar Association (Idaho). Vol. 1, No. 1 (Oct. 1957)-. English. Twelve times a year. $30.00. Idaho State Bar, Box 895, Boise ID 83701. **Tel** (208)334-4500, FAX (208)334-4515. **ED** Jeannie M. Omel. **LC** KF200; .A35. **DD** 340.05. **Bk Rev**, (Qty: 6). **Ad Acc. Pr Rev. Circ:** 3,500. ***Absorbed*** *Idaho State Bar News Bulletin.*
Ind/Abst Curr. Law Index (1980-); Leg. Resour. Index (1980-); LegalTrac (1980-).

US/0568-0425
ADVOCATE (BOSTON, MASS.). (THE ADVOCATE : A PUBLICATION OF SUFFOLK UNIVERSITY LAW SCHOOL.). **Added/Corp** Suffolk University. Law School. Vol. 1, No. 1 (Fall 1968)-. Periodical. English. sa (Fall & Spring). $6.00. Suffolk University / Law, School of Law, 41 Temple Street, Boston MA 02114. **Tel** (617)573-8000, 573-8610. **LC** KF292.S8414; A423. **DD** 349.73; 347.3.

US
ADVOCATE / BRONX COUNTY BAR ASSOCIATION, THE. **Added/Corp** Bronx County Bar Association. (198?)-. Periodical. English. Bronx County Bar Association, 851 Grand Concourse, Bronx NY 10451. ***Continues*** *Bronx County Bar Journal.*
Ind/Abst Fed. Tax Artic.

US/0199-1876
ADVOCATE (LOS ANGELES TRIAL LAWYERS ASSOCIATION). (ADVOCATE.). **Added/Corp** Los Angeles Trial Lawyers Association. (Jan. 1973)-. Periodical. English. Eleven times a year. $50.00. Los Angeles Trial Lawyers Association, 3435 Wilshire Boulevard, Suite 1114, Los Angeles CA 90010. **Tel** (213)487-1212. **LC** KFC1025.A15; A38. **DD** 347.794/057.

CN/0044-6416
ADVOCATE (VANCOUVER). (THE ADVOCATE.). [Advocate]. **Added/Corp** Vancouver Bar Association. Vol. 1 (March 1943)-. Periodical. English. bm. 20.00Can$. Vancouver Bar Association, Business Office, 4765 Pilot House Road, Vancouver British Columbia V7W 1J2 Canada. **Tel** (604)925-2122, FAX (604)925-2065. **ED** David Roberts. Index available. cum. index. **Bk Rev. Ad Acc, Adv Mgr:** G. Roberts. **Circ:** 7,400. available on microfiche from Williams S Hein & Co.
Desc: Published by the Vancouver Bar Association and contains legal and educational matter, making particular reference to the practice of law in British Columbia.
Ind/Abst Can. Legal Lit.; Index Can. Leg. Period. Lit.

NE
ADVOCATENBLAD. **Added/Corp** Nederlandsche Advocaten-Vereeniging. (Jan. 15, 1918)-. Dutch. Twenty-three times a year. Fl197.50. W. E. J. Tjeenk Willink, Box 25, 8000 AA Zwolle Netherlands. **Tel** 011 31 38 228819, 011 31 38 211444. **(Subscription address:** PVO Abonnementenservices, PO Box 77, 5126 ZH Gilze Netherlands.**) LC** LAW.

US
ADVOCATE'S ADVOCATE. ***Ceased.*** (April 1988)-(199?). English. mo. Advocacy Institute, 1730 Rhode Island Avenue NW, Suite 600, Washington DC 20036. **Tel** (202)659-8475. **ED** Stan Cohen. **Bk Rev. Circ:** 500.
Desc: The guide to advocacy for public interest advocates.

CN/0824-3344
ADVOCATES' SOCIETY JOURNAL, THE. [Advocates' Soc. j.]. **Added/Corp** Advocates' Society. (June 1982)-. Periodical. English. ir. 50.00Can$. The Advocates Society, 160 Queen Street West, Toronto Ontario M5H 3H3 Canada. **Tel** (416)597-0243. **DD** 347.71/05/05.
Ind/Abst Can. Legal Lit.; Index Can. Leg. Period. Lit.

BL
ADVOGADO, O. Periodical. Portuguese. Rua Coelho Rodrigues, 1.202 1O Andar Salas 101/2, Teresina Brazil. **LC** LAW. **DD** 340/.06/281.

SW/0281-3505
ADVOKATEN (STOCKHOLM). (ADVOKATEN.). [Advokaten]. **Added/Corp** Sveriges Advokatsamfund. (1983)-. Swedish (English). ir. Kr225.00. Swedish Bar Association, PO Box 27321, S10254 Stockholm Sweden. **Tel** 011 46 8 245870. **ED** Curt Falkenstam. Index available. **Bk Rev. Ad Acc. Circ:** 5,000. ***Continues*** *Tidskrift (Sveriges Advokatsamfund), 0040-6902.*
Desc: Publishes news service interviews, reportage law, debates, and scientific law studies.

US/0360-5485
AFFILIATE, THE. [Affiliate]. **Added/Corp** American Bar Association. Young Lawyers Section. American Bar Association. Young Lawyers Division. Vol. 1 (July 1975)-. English. bm (6 issues). $18.00. American Bar Association, 750 North Lake Shore Drive, Chicago IL 60611. **Tel** (312)988-5522, (312)988-5241, FAX (312)988-5528, telex 270593. **LC** KF325.26; .A35. **DD** 340/.05.

BE
AFRICAN LAW BIBLIOGRAPHY. Bibliography. English (French). an. 2000F. Universite Libre de Bruxelles, 50 Avenue F D Roosevelt CP 188, 1050 Brussels Belgium. **Tel** 011 32 2 6423611. **ED** J Vanderlinden. cum. index. **Bk Rev. Circ:** 200.

BE
AFRICAN LAW BIBLIOGRAPHY. SUPPLEMENT. **Added/Corp** Nordic Law Consultants Geneve-Helsinki. **VFOAT** Bibliographie de Droit Africain. Supplement. 1st (1977/1980)-. Bibliography. English (Multiple languages). an. Universite Libre de Bruxelles, 50 Avenue F D Roosevelt CP 188, 1050 Brussels Belgium. **Tel** 011 32 2 6423611.

ET/0002-0052
AFRICAN LAW DIGEST. ***Suspended.*** Vol. 1, No. 1 (1965)-Vol. 10, No. 1 (1974). English. Three times a year. $40.00. Addis Ababa University Faculty of Law, PO Box 1176, Addis Ababa, Ethiopia. **Tel** 110844. **ED** Yeshak Teshome. **DD** 349.6/05; 346.005. Index available in last issue of volume--attached. **Circ:** 500.

●CN/1189-5136
AGENDA DES JURISTES, L'. [Agenda juristes]. (1992/1993)-. French. 39.95Can$. Editions Yvon Blais, Case Postale 180, Cowansville Quebec J2K 3H6 Canada. **Tel** (514)263-1086, (800)363-3047, FAX (514)263-9256. **DD** 340.

AT/0312-4592
AGIS : ATTORNEY-GENERAL'S INFORMATION SERVICE. **Added/Corp** Australia. Attorney-General's Dept. Library. **VFOAT** Attorney-General's Information Service. Vol. 1 (1975)-. Government Publication. English. sm (24 issues). 195.00Aus$. Australian Government Publishing Service, GPO Box 84, Canberra ACT 2601 Australia. **Tel** 011 61 6 2954411, FAX 011 61 6 2954455. **ED** Christine Hawke. **LC** K33; .A36. **DD** 016.34994/05; 016.3499405. **Pr Rev.** ctrl circ.
Desc: Comprehensively indexes and abstracts all Australian and New Zealand legal journal material.

NE/0167-4242
AGRARISCH RECHT. (AGRARISCH RECHT / STICHTING DE PACHT.). [Agrar. recht]. **Added/Corp** Stichting de Pacht. (198?)-. Academic Scholarly Publication. Dutch. Twelve times a year. Fl187.50. Libresso BV, Postbus 878, 7400 GA Deventer Netherlands. **Tel** 011 31 5700 47421. **LC** K16; .A25. Index available. **Ad Acc. Circ:** 1,600 (ctrl). ***Continues*** *Pacht.*
Ind/Abst EMBASE.

GW/0340-840X
AGRARRECHT. [Agrarrecht]. **Added/Corp** Deutsche Gesellschaft fuer Agrarrecht. (19??)-. German. mo. DM258.00 Germany; DM271.40 other. Landwirtschaftsverlag GmbH, Postfach 480249, D 48079 Muenster Hiltrup Germany. **Tel** 011 49 2501 8010, FAX 011 49 2501 801204, telex 892665 LANDV D. **ED** B. Bendel. **LC** K1; .G7. **DD** 343/.43/076. **[CCC].** Index available. **Bk Rev. Circ:** 1,200.
Ind/Abst Coal Abstr.; Dairy Sci. Abstr.; EMBASE; Index Vet.; Leis. Recreat. Tour. Abstr.; Rev. Agric. Entomol.; Rural Dev. Abstr.; Soils Fert.; World Agric. Econ.

US/1051-2780
AGRICULTURAL LAW DIGEST. **See** Agriculture.

US
AIDS LAW AND LITIGATION REPORTER. **See** Medical Science and Technology-Allergy and Immunology.

US/0896-6370
AIDS LAW REPORTER, THE. ***Ceased.*** [AIDS law report.]. **Added/Corp** National Legal Research Group. **VFOAT** Law Reporter. **VAT** Acquired Immune Deficiency Syndrome Law Reporter. (Oct. 1987)-Ceased (Nov. 1989). English. mo. National Legal Research Group Inc, PO Box 7187, Charlottesville VA 22906. **Tel** (800)727-6574, (804)977-5690, FAX (804)295-4667. **LC** KF3803.A54; A13. **DD** 344.73/04369792; 347.3044369792.

US/0887-1493
AIDS POLICY & LAW. [AIDS policy law]. **VFOAT** AIDS Policy and Law. **VAT** Acquired Immune Deficiency Syndrome Policy and Law. Vol. 1, No. 1 (Jan. 29, 1986)-. Periodical. English. sm. $487.00 US, Canada and Mexico; $509.00 other. Buraff Publications Inc., 714 Church Street, Alexandria VA 22314. **Tel** (800)333-1291, (703)739-8500. **(Subscription telephone:** FAX (301)948-5823**) ED** Richard Hagan. **LC** KF3803.A54; A133. **DD** 344.73/0465; 347.304465. **NLM** W1; AI696DE. **[CCC].**
Desc: Covers the practical and legal issues of AIDS: the

latest developments on the federal, state and local levels, fair employment practices, litigation, legislation, regulation, policy guidelines, case studies, interviews, and more.
Ind/Abst Curr. Lit. Fam. Plan.

US/1059-8871
AIDSMONTHLY (LEGAL ED.). ***Ceased.*** **See** Medical Science and Technology-Allergy and Immunology.

●NE
AIR AND SPACE LAW. **See** Aeronautics, Astronautics.

US/0747-7449
AIR AND SPACE LAWYER: FORUM COMMITTEE ON AIR AND SPACE LAW. AMERICAN BAR ASSOCIATION, THE. [Air space lawyer]. **Added/Corp** American Bar Association. Forum Committee on Air and Space Law. Vol. 1, No. 1 (Fall 1983)-. Periodical. English. qt (4 issues). $40.00. American Bar Association, 750 North Lake Shore Drive, Chicago IL 60611. **Tel** (312)988-5522, (312)988-5241, FAX (312)988-5528, telex 270593. **LC** KF2400.A15; A37. **DD** 343.73/097; 347.30397.

BL
AJURIS. **Added/Corp** Associacao dos Juizes do Rio Grande do Sul. Vol. 1 July (1974)-. Portuguese. ir. Livraria Sulina, Av Borges de Madeiros, Porto Alegre 1030 Brazil. **LC** K1; .J87.

US/0002-371X
AKRON LAW REVIEW. [Akron law rev.]. **Added/Corp** University of Akron. School of Law. University of Akron. College of Law. Vol. 1 (Fall 1967)-. English. Three times a year (Quarterly with issues 3 and 4 combined). $20.00. Akron Law Review, School of Law, University of Akron, Akron OH 44325. **Tel** (216)972-7335. **ED** James Spallino, Jr., (phone: (216)972-7335). **LC** K1; .K76. **DD** 340/.05. cum. index. **Circ:** 500.
Desc: Current information and development in law.
Ind/Abst Bowne Dig. Corp. Sec. Lawyers; Curr. Law Index (1980-); Fed. Tax Artic.; Index Leg. Period.; Leg. Resour. Index (1980-); LegalTrac (1980-).

GW/0568-7551
AKTUELLE BEITRAGE DER STAATS- UND RECHTSWISSENSCHAFT. **Added/Corp** Akademie fuer Staats- und Rechtswissenschaft der DDR. Informationszentrum Staat und Recht. (196?)-. Monographic series. German. ir. Price varies per volume. Akad Staats Rechtswissenschaft, August Bebel Str 89, D 14482 Postdam Germany. **LC** UNC. ***Continues*** *Aktuelle Beitrage zur Staats- und Rechtswissenschaft aus den Sozialistischen Landern.*
Desc: Comprises studies, monographs, minute-books, omnibus volumes concerning topics of political and legal sciences.

JO
AL-JARIDAH AL-RASMIYAH LIL-MAMLAKAH AL-URDUNIYAH AL-HASHIMIYAH. **Main/Corp** Jordan. No. 256- May 25, 1946-. Arabic. ***Continues*** *Jaridah Al-Rasmiyah Li-Imarat Sharq Al-Urdun.*

KU
AL-KUWAYT AL-YAWM. **Main/Corp** Kuwait. V. 1- ; 1954-. Arabic. wk. Ufilm Al-Kuwayt, SB 15, Al-Safah Kuwait. **LC** LAW.

US/0162-2986
ALA BRIEF. (BRIEF.). **VAT** American Lawyers Association Brief. Periodical. English. American Lawyers Association, 292 Madison Avenue, New York NY 10017. **LC** KF200; .B735. **DD** 340/.06/273.
Ind/Abst LegalTrac (1982-1989).

US/1045-1153
ALA NEWS (VERNON HILLS, ILL.). (ALA NEWS.). [ALA news]. **Added/Corp** Association of Legal Administrators. **VAT** Association of Legal Administrators News. (Aug. 1982)-. Periodical. English. bm. $36.00. Association of Legal Administrators, 175 East Hawthorn Parkway, Vernon Hills IL 60061. **Tel** (708)816-1212. **DD** 340. ***Continues*** *Legal Administrator.*

US
ALABAMA ADMINISTRATIVE MONTHLY. **Added/Corp** Alabama. Legislative Reference Service. Vol. 1, No. 1 (Oct. 1982)-. English. mo. $50.00. Legal Reference Service, Alabama House Division, Room 435, Montgomery AL 36130. **Tel** (205)261-7560, FAX (205)424-4358. **ED** Edna Brooks. **LC** KFA36; .A4. **DD** 348.761/025/05; 347.610825/05. **Circ:** 270.

US
ALABAMA LAW OF DAMAGES. English. ir. $94.95 One volume including latest pocket part supplement; $38.95 Separate pocket part supplement. Harrison Company Publishers, 3110 Crossing Park, PO Box 7500, Norcross GA 30091-7500. **Tel** (800)241-3561, (404)447-9150.

US/0002-4279
ALABAMA LAW REVIEW. [Ala. Law Rev.]. **Added/Corp** University of Alabama. (Fall 1948)-. Periodical. English. Three times a year. $30.00. University of Alabama / School of Law, PO Box 870380, Tuscaloosa AL 35487-0380. **Tel** (205)348-1175. **ED** Sarah W. Wiggins. **LC** K1; .L3. **DD** 340/.05. **Bk Rev**. **Circ:** 1,300. available on microfilm.
Desc: Covers the civil, economic, political, natural, literary, and ecclasiastical history of the state of Alabama and her people, reviews of books about Alabama and the South, and reports on the activities of the Alabama Historical Association.
Ind/Abst Bowne Dig. Corp. Sec. Lawyers; Curr. Law Index (1980-); Fed. Tax Artic.; Index Leg. Period.; Leg. Resour. Index (1980-); LegalTrac (1980-); PAIS Int. Print (1991-).

US/0002-4287
ALABAMA LAWYER, THE. (THE ALABAMA LAWYER : OFFICIAL ORGAN STATE BAR OF ALABAMA.). [Ala. lawyer]. **Added/Corp** Alabama State Bar. Vol. 1, No. 1 (Jan. 1940)-. Periodical. English. Six times a year. $20.00 US; $25.00 other. Alabama Lawyer, PO Box 4156, Montgomery AL 36101. **Tel** (205)269-1515, FAX (205)261-6310. **ED** Robert A. Huffaker. **LC** KF200; .A38. **DD** 340/.05. Index Available, published separately, free-automatically sent. cum. index. **Bk Rev**. **Ad Acc**. **Circ:** 9,000 (ctrl). available in microform. ***Continues*** *Alabama Bar Bulletin, 0741-2908.*
Desc: Official publication of the Alabama State Bar containing association news, court decisions, and other articles of interest to Alabama lawyers.
Ind/Abst Curr. Law Index (1980-); Fed. Tax Artic.; Index Leg. Period.; Leg. Resour. Index (1980-); LegalTrac (1980-).

US/0145-4390
ALABAMA LEGAL DIRECTORY, THE. **Added/Corp** Legal Directories Publishing Company. (1976)-. English. an (Feb.). $26.00. Legal Directories Publishing Company, 9111 Garland Road, PO Box 189000, Dallas TX 75218. **Tel** (214)321-3238, 800 447-5375. **LC** KF192.A5; A55. **DD** 340/.025/761. **Ad Acc**.
Desc: A digest of federal and state officials, law firms and individual lawyers, with pertinent information on county offices and jurisdiction of the courts at all levels.

US
ALABAMA-MESSENGER, THE. **VFOAT** Alabama Messenger. Vol. 51, No. 29 (July 17, 1971)-. Newspaper. English. wk. $10.00. Alabama Messenger, 706 Frank Nelson Building, Birmingham AL 35203. **Tel** (205)252-3672. ***Formed by the union of*** *Birmingham Messenger* ***and*** *Alabama Legal Advertiser.*

US/0747-6620
ALABAMA RULES ANNOTATED. (ALABAMA RULES ANNOTATED : INCLUDING THE RULES OF THE COURTS IN ALABAMA, THE RULES OF THE FEDERAL DISTRICT COURTS, AND THE RULES OF THE ELEVENTH CIRCUIT COURT OF APPEALS OF THE UNITED STATES.). [Ala. rules annot.]. **Added/Corp** Michie Company. (1983)-. English. an. $40.00. Michie Company, PO Box 7587, Charlottesville VA 22906-7587. **Tel** (804)972-7600, (800)542-0957, FAX (800)643-1280. **LC** KFA529; .A194. **DD** 347.761/051; 347.610751.

US/0276-1025
ALASKA BAR RAG, THE. **Added/Corp** Alaska Bar Association. **VFOAT** Bar Rag. Vol. 1, No. 1 (Sept. 1978)-. Periodical. English. Six times a year. $25.00. Alaska Bar Rag, PO Box 100279, Anchorage AK 99510. **Tel** (907)272-7469. **ED** Peter Maassu. **LC** KF200; .A414. **DD** 349.798/05; 347.98005. **Ad Acc**. **Circ:** 3,500.
Desc: A publication for and about members of the Alaska Bar Association.

US
ALASKA COURT RULES, STATE AND FEDERAL. **Added/Corp** West Publishing Company. (1990)-. Periodical. English. West Publishing Company, 610 Opperman Drive, PO Box 64526, Eagan MN 55123-1308. **Tel** (612)687-5618, (800)328-9352, FAX (612)687-5388, (800)562-2329. ***Continues*** *Alaska Rules of Court, State and Federal.*

US/0275-1895
ALASKA DIRECTORY OF ATTORNEYS. Directory. English. sa. $40.00. Todd Communications, 203 West 15th Street/Suite 102, Anchorage AK 99501. **Tel** (907)274-8633. **ED** Bonnie Ulrich. **LC** KF192.A55; A4. **DD** 349.798/025; 347.980025. **Ad Acc**. **Circ:** 2,600.
Desc: Alphabetical listing of all members of Alaska Bar Association - business address and phone; Alaska Judicial Court System, law enforcement agencies, process servers, court reporters, and title companies.

US/0883-0568
ALASKA LAW REVIEW. [Alsk. law rev.]. **Added/Corp** Duke University. School of Law. Alaska Bar Association. Vol. 1, No. 1 (Summer 1984)-. Periodical. English. sa (Published in June & Dec.). $20.00. Duke University School of Law, 006 Law Towerview & Science Drive, Durham NC 27706. **Tel** (919)684-5966, FAX (919)684-3417. **ED** John J. Hoffman. **LC** K1; .L325. **DD** 349.798/05; 347.98005. **Bk Rev**. **Ad Acc**. **Circ:** 2,500. ***Continues*** *UCLA-Alaska Law Review, 0886-263X.*
Desc: Book reviews and notes pertaining to legal issues of interest to Alaska.
Ind/Abst Bowne Dig. Corp. Sec. Lawyers; Curr. Law Index (1984-); Fed. Tax Artic.; Index Leg. Period.; Leg. Resour. Index (1984-); LegalTrac (1984-); PAIS Int. Print.

US/1059-4280
ALBANY LAW JOURNAL OF SCIENCE & TECHNOLOGY. [Albany law j. sci. technol.]. **Added/Corp** Albany Law School. **VFOAT** Alb. L.J. Sci. & Tech. Vol. 1 (1991)-. English. Twice a year. $20.00. Albany Law School of Union University, 80 New Scotland Avenue, Albany NY 12208. **Tel** (518)445-2311, (518)445-2372, FAX (518)445-2315. **LC** K1; .L323. **DD** 344/.09505; 342.409505. **Ad Acc**, **Adv Mgr:** J. Seymalak, **Tel** (518)472-5855. **Circ:** 750 (ctrl).

US/0002-4678
ALBANY LAW REVIEW. [Albany law rev.]. **Added/Corp** Albany Law School. Vol. 12 (June 1948)-. Periodical. English. Four times a year. $25.00. Albany Law Scholl / Union Unversity, 80 New Scotland Avenue, Albany NY 12208. **Tel** (518)445-2372, (518)445-2311. **LC** LAW. **[CCC]**. Index available. cum. index. **Bk Rev**. **Ad Acc**. **Circ:** 800 (ctrl). available on microfilm from University Microfilms International (UMI). ***Continues*** *Albany Law Review of Recent Decisions.*
Ind/Abst Bowne Dig. Corp. Sec. Lawyers; Crim. Justice Abstr.; Crim. Penol. Police Sci. Abstr.; Curr. Law Index (1980-); Fed. Tax Artic.; Index Leg. Period.; Leg. Resour. Index (1980-); LegalTrac (1980-).

CN/0319-7980
ALBERTA DECISIONS, CIVIL AND CRIMINAL CASES. (1974)-. English. Twelve times a year. 320.00Can$. Western Legal Publications Ltd., 301 One Alexander Street, Vancouver BC V6A 1B2 Canada. **Tel** (800)663-0422, (604)687-5671. **DD** 348/.7123/048. cum. index.
Desc: All available civil and criminal judgements from Alberta Court of Appeal, Court of Queen's Bench and District Courts of Alberta digested by subjects.

CN/0703-3117
ALBERTA LAW REPORTS. Vol. 1 (1908)-. English. mo. price varies per volume. Carswell / Canada, 2075 Kennedy Road, Scarborough Ontario M1T 3V4 Canada. **Tel** (416)609-3800, (800)387-5164. **ED** Margaret James. Index available. cum. index. **Ad Acc**.
Desc: Full text reports of all significant decisions of the courts of Alberta and of Federal Court and Supreme Court of Canada cases relevant to Alberta.
Ind/Abst Can. Legal Lit.

CN/0002-4821
ALBERTA LAW REVIEW. [Alta. Law Rev.]. **Added/Corp** University of Alberta. Faculty of Law. Canadian Petroleum Law Foundation. **VFOAT** Constitutional Studies; Etudes Constitutionnelles. (Fall 1955)-. Periodical. English. Four times a year (Jan., Mar., Aug., Oct.). 45.00Can$. Alberta Law Review, University of Alberta, Faculty of Law, Edmonton Alberta T6G 2H5 Canada. **Tel** (403)492-5681, FAX (403)492-4924. **ED** Scott Reeves and Janice Wright. Index available. cum. index. **Bk Rev**. **Ad Acc**. **Circ:** 3,000. available on microfilm and microfiche from University Microfilms International (UMI). ***Supersedes*** *Alberta Law Quarterly.*
Desc: Law articles, case comments, book reviews, and legislation updates; contains articles about all aspects of the law and the legal profession, addressing both academic and practical issues.
Ind/Abst Can. Legal Lit.; Curr. Law Index (1980-); Index Can. Leg. Period. Lit.; Index Leg. Period.; Leg. Resour. Index (1980-); LegalTrac (1980-).

CN/0830-9760
ALBERTA PARLIAMENTARY DIGEST. [Alta. parliam. dig.]. (Mar. 15, 1985)-. Periodical. English. ir (about 20 issues (one issue per week of session of Legislature)). 93.00Can$ Canada; 103.00Can$ Pan American countries; 113.00Can$ other. Alberta Parliamentary Digest, 335 21 10405 Jasper Avenue, Edmonton Alberta T5J 3S2 Canada. **Tel** (403)426-6960, FAX (403)426-7263. **ED** Michael Cregg. **DD** 328.7123/005. **Circ:** 500.
Desc: Summary of Government bills introduced; policy announcements main issues in question period; proclamations; bills progress of reading chart for Alberta Legislature.

CN
ALBERTA. PUBLIC AFFAIRS. TABLE OF ALBERTA LEGISLATION. (19??)-. English. ir. Alberta Statutes Province / Queens Printer, Province

Treasury, 11510 Kingsly Avenue, Edmonton Alberta T5G 2Y5 Canada. **Tel** (403)427-4952. ***Continues*** *List of Alberta Publications and Legislation, 0837-7375.*

CN/0713-892X
ALBERTA WEEKLY LAW DIGEST. [Alta. wkly. law dig.]. **Added/Corp** Carswell Legal Publications. Issue No. 1 (Jan. 7, 1982)-. Periodical. English. Fifty times a year. 385.00Can$. Carswell / Canada, 2075 Kennedy Road, Scarborough Ontario M1T 3V4 Canada. **Tel** (416)609-3800, (800)387-5164. **ED** Laura M. Wright. **DD** 348.7123/046. Index available. cum. index.
Desc: A pre-reporting service consisting of digests of all available judgements of the Supreme Court of Canada and the Federal Court in cases originating in the province.

US/0044-7560
ALI-ABA CLE REVIEW. **Main/Corp** American Law Institute-American Bar Association Committee on Continuing Professional Education. **VAT** American Law Institute, American Bar Association Continuing Legal Education Review. (1970)-. Periodical. English. mo. Free. American Law Institute, 4025 Chestnut Street, Philadelphia PA 19104-3099. **Tel** (215)243-1661, (800)253-6397, FAX (215)243-1664. **ED** Mark T. Carroll. Index available. **Bk Rev**, (Qty: 6 per year). **Circ:** 89,000 (ctrl). available on microfilm and microfiche from University Microfilms International (UMI). ***Continues*** *ALI-ABA CLE Review, 0044-7560.*
Desc: Ads on ALI-ABA CLE courses, books, audio and videocassettes, and periodicals.

US/0191-3689
ALI-ABA CONFERENCE. CONFERENCE ON FEDERAL INCOME TAX SIMPLIFICATION: PAPERS.
Main/Conf ALI-ABA Conference on Federal Income Tax Simplification. **Added/Corp** American Law Institute-American Bar Association Committee on Continuing Professional Education. American Law Institute. American Bar Association. Section of Taxation. **VAT** American Law Institute-American Bar Association Conference. Conference on Federal Income Tax Simplification: Papers. (19??)-. English. American Law Institute, 4025 Chestnut Street, Philadelphia PA 19104-3099. **Tel** (215)243-1661, (800)253-6397, FAX (215)243-1664. **LC** KF6369.3; .A12. **DD** 343/.73/052.

US/0145-6342
ALI-ABA COURSE MATERIALS JOURNAL. [ALI-ABA course mater. j.]. **Added/Corp** American Law Institute-American Bar Association Committee on Continuing Professional Education. **VAT** American Law Institute-American Bar Association Course Materials Journal. Vol. 1, (1976)-. Periodical. English. Six times a year (Feb., Apr., June, Aug., Oct., Dec.). $40.00. American Law Institute, 4025 Chestnut Street, Philadelphia PA 19104-3099. **Tel** (215)243-1661, (800)253-6397, FAX (215)243-1664. **ED** Mark T. Carroll (phone: (215)243-1604). **LC** K1; .L45. **DD** 340/.0973. Index available (June iss.). cum. index. **Ad Acc, Adv Mgr:** K. Lawner. **Circ:** 3,292. available on microfilm and microfiche from University Microfilms International (UMI).
Desc: Collection of outlines and written presentations on legal issues given at ALI-ABA courses.
Ind/Abst Bowne Dig. Corp. Sec. Lawyers; Curr. Law Index (1980-); Leg. Resour. Index (1980-); LegalTrac (1980-).

US/0277-3252
ALI-ABA COURSE OF STUDY. ABA SECTION OF TAXATION, ANNUAL OF TAXATION, ANNUAL ADVANCED STUDY SESSIONS, ADVANCED TAX PLANNING FOR REAL ESTATE TRANSACTIONS: MATERIALS.
(ADVANCED TAX PLANNING FOR REAL ESTATE TRANSACTIONS : ALI-ABA COURSE OF STUDY, MATERIALS.). **VFOAT** ALI-ABA Course of Study, Materials. **VAT** American Law Institute American Bar Association Course of Study. American Bar Association Section of Taxation, Annual Advanced Study Sessions, Advanced Tax Planning for Real Estate Transactions: Materials. English. an. American Law Institute, 4025 Chestnut Street, Philadelphia PA 19104-3099. **Tel** (215)243-1661, (800)253-6397, FAX (215)243-1664. **LC** KF6540.Z9; A37. **DD** 343.7305/46; 347.303546.

US/0192-821X
ALI-ABA COURSE OF STUDY. ALI-ABA CONFERENCE ON ERISA : MATERIALS.
Main/Conf I-ABA Conference on ERISA. **Added/Corp** American Law Institute-American Bar Association Committee on Continuing Professional Education. **VFOAT** ALI-ABA Conference on ERISA : Materials. **VAT** American Law Institute-American Bar Association Course of Study. American Law Institute-American Bar Association Conference on Employee Retirement Income Security Act : Materials. (19??)-. English. American Law Institute, 4025 Chestnut Street, Philadelphia PA 19104-3099. **Tel** (215)243-1661, (800)253-6397, FAX (215)243-1664. **LC** KF3512.Z9; A125. **DD** 344/.73/01252.

US/0190-9673
ALI-ABA COURSE OF STUDY. ATOMIC ENERGY LICENSING AND REGULATION : MATERIALS. **VAT** American Law Institute-American Bar Association Course of Study. Atomic Energy Licensing and Regulation: Materials. English. American Law Institute, 4025 Chestnut Street, Philadelphia PA 19104-3099. **Tel** (215)243-1661, (800)253-6397, FAX (215)243-1664. **LC** KF2138.Z9; A15. **DD** 343/.73/092.

US/0191-0272
ALI-ABA COURSE OF STUDY. BASIC LAW OF PENSIONS AND DEFERRED COMPENSATION: MATERIALS. **Main/Conf** I-ABA Course of Study: Basic Law of Pensions and Deferred Compensation. **Added/Corp** American Law Institute-American Bar Association Committee on Continuing Professional Education. University of Notre Dame. Law School. **VFOAT** Basic Law of Pensions and Deferred Compensation: Materials. **VAT** American Law Institute-American Bar Association Course of Study. Basic Law of Pensions and Deferred Compensation: Materials. (19??)-. English. an. $150.00 (two volumes). American Bar Association, 750 North Lake Shore Drive, Chicago IL 60611. **Tel** (312)988-5522, (312)988-5241, FAX (312)988-5528, telex 270593. **LC** KF3512.Z9; A133. **DD** 344/.73/01252.

US/0271-3535
ALI-ABA COURSE OF STUDY. BROKER-DEALER REGULATION: MATERIALS. **Main/Conf** I-ABA Course of Study: Broker-Dealer Regulation. **Added/Corp** American Law Institute-American Bar Association Committee on Continuing Professional Education. Federal Bar Association. Securities Law Committee. **VFOAT** Broker-Dealer Regulation: Materials. **VAT** American Law Institute, American Bar Association Course of Study. Broker Dealer Regulation: Materials. (19??)-. English. an (Published in January). $80.00. American Law Institute, 4025 Chestnut Street, Philadelphia PA 19104-3099. **Tel** (215)243-1661, (800)253-6397, FAX (215)243-1664. **LC** KF1071.Z9; A14. **DD** 346.73/0926.

US/0191-202X
ALI-ABA COURSE OF STUDY. CONDOMINIUM CONVERSIONS: MATERIALS. **Main/Conf** I-ABA Course of Study: Condominium Conversions. **Added/Corp** American Law Institute-American Bar Association Committee on Continuing Professional Education. **VFOAT** Condominium Conversions: Materials. **VAT** American Law Institute-American Bar Association Course of Study. Condominium Conversions: Materials. (19??)-. English. American Law Institute, 4025 Chestnut Street, Philadelphia PA 19104-3099. **Tel** (215)243-1661, (800)253-6397, FAX (215)243-1664. **LC** KF581.Z9; A115. **DD** 346/.73/0433.

US/0191-2623
ALI-ABA COURSE OF STUDY. DOMESTIC TAXATION OF HARD MINERALS : MATERIALS. **Main/Conf** ALI-ABA Course of Study: Domestic Taxation of Hard Minerals. **VFOAT** ALI-ABA Course of Study: Materials. **VAT** American Law Institute-American Bar Association Course of Study. Domestic Taxation of Hard Minerals: Materials. English. American Law Institute, 4025 Chestnut Street, Philadelphia PA 19104-3099. **Tel** (215)243-1661, (800)253-6397, FAX (215)243-1664. **LC** KF6495.M5. **DD** 343/.73/055.

US/0190-9339
ALI-ABA COURSE OF STUDY. EMINENT DOMAIN : MATERIALS. **VAT** American Law Institute-American Bar Association Course of Study. Eminent Domain: Materials. English. American Law Institute, 4025 Chestnut Street, Philadelphia PA 19104-3099. **Tel** (215)243-1661, (800)253-6397, FAX (215)243-1664. **LC** KF5599.Z9; A18. **DD** 343/.73/025.

US/0191-2585
ALI-ABA COURSE OF STUDY : ENERGY AND THE LAW, PROBLEMS AND CHALLENGES OF THE LATE 70'S : MATERIALS. **Main/Conf** ALI-ABA Course of Study: Energy and the Law, Problems and challenges of the Late 70's. **VAT** American Law Institute-American Bar Association Course of Study. Energy and the Law, Problems and Challenges of the Late Seventies: Materials. English. American Law Institute, 4025 Chestnut Street, Philadelphia PA 19104-3099. **Tel** (215)243-1661, (800)253-6397, FAX (215)243-1664. **LC** KF2120.Z9; A135. **DD** 343/.74/092.

US/0272-8990
ALI-ABA COURSE OF STUDY. ENERGY LAW : MATERIALS. **VFOAT** Energy Law: Materials. **VAT** American Law Institute-American Bar Association Course of Study. Energy Law. Materials. English. an. American Law Institute, 4025 Chestnut Street, Philadelphia PA 19104-3099. **Tel** (215)243-1661, (800)253-6397, FAX (215)243-1664. **LC** KF2120.Z9; A144. **DD** 346.7304/679; 347.3064679.

US/0191-2224
ALI-ABA COURSE OF STUDY. ERISA AND THE FEDERAL SECURITIES LAWS : MATERIALS. **Main/Conf** I-ABA Course of Study : ERISA and the Federal Securities Laws. **Added/Corp** American Law Institute-American Bar Association Committee on Continuing Professional Education. Federal Bar Association. Securities Law Committee. **VFOAT** ERISA and the Federal Securities Laws : Materials. **VAT** American Law Institute, American Bar Association Course of Study. Employee Retirement Income Security Act and the Federal Securities Laws : Materials. (19??)-. English. American Law Institute, 4025 Chestnut Street, Philadelphia PA 19104-3099. **Tel** (215)243-1661, (800)253-6397, FAX (215)243-1664. **LC** KF3512.Z9; A134. **DD** 344/.73/01252.

US/0191-4308
ALI-ABA COURSE OF STUDY. ERISA-PHASE II : MATERIALS. **Main/Conf** I-ABA Course of Study : ERISA-Phase II. **Added/Corp** American Law Institute-American Bar Association Committee on Continuing Professional Education. Joint Committee on Continuing Legal Education (Va.). **VFOAT** ERISA-Phase II : Materials. **VAT** American Law Institute, American Bar Association Course of Study. Employee Retirement Income Security Act, Phase Two : Materials. (19??)-. English. American Law Institute, 4025 Chestnut Street, Philadelphia PA 19104-3099. **Tel** (215)243-1661, (800)253-6397, FAX (215)243-1664. **LC** KF3512.Z9; A136. **DD** 344/.73/01252.

US/0191-2372
ALI-ABA COURSE OF STUDY. FEDERAL ELECTION LAW: MATERIALS. **Main/Conf** ALI-ABA Course of Study: Federal Election Law. **Added/Corp** American Law Institute-American Bar Association Committee on Continuing Professional Education. **VFOAT** Federal Election Law: Materials. **VAT** American Law Institute, American Bar Association Course of Study. Federal Election Law: Materials. (19??)-. English. American Law Institute, 4025 Chestnut Street, Philadelphia PA 19104-3099. **Tel** (215)243-1661, (800)253-6397, FAX (215)243-1664. **LC** KF4886.Z9; A15. **DD** 342/.73/07.

US/0191-3859
ALI-ABA COURSE OF STUDY. FEDERAL RULES OF EVIDENCE : MATERIALS. **VAT** American Law Institute-American Bar Association Course of Study. Federal Rules of Evidence: Materials. English. American Law Institute, 4025 Chestnut Street, Philadelphia PA 19104-3099. **Tel** (215)243-1661, (800)253-6397, FAX (215)243-1664. **LC** KF8935.Z9; A135. **DD** 347/.73/6.

US/0270-9686
ALI-ABA COURSE OF STUDY. INVESTMENT ADVISER REGULATION : MATERIALS. **VAT** American Law Institute-American Bar Association Course of Study. Investment Adviser Regulation. Materials. English. American Law Institute, 4025 Chestnut Street, Philadelphia PA 19104-3099. **Tel** (215)243-1661, (800)253-6397, FAX (215)243-1664. **LC** KF1072.Z9; A143. **DD** 346.73/092.

US/0191-8125
ALI-ABA COURSE OF STUDY. LAND PLANNING AND REGULATION OF DEVELOPMENT : MATERIALS. **VAT** American Law Institute-American Bar Association Course of Study. Land Planning and Regulation of Development: Materials. English. American Law Institute, 4025 Chestnut Street, Philadelphia PA 19104-3099. **Tel** (215)243-1661, (800)253-6397, FAX (215)243-1664. **LC** KF5698.Z9; A13. **DD** 346/.73/045.

US/0190-9592
ALI-ABA COURSE OF STUDY. LAND USE LITIGATION, CRITICAL ISSUES FOR ATTORNEYS, DEVELOPERS, AND PUBLIC OFFICIALS : MATERIALS.
Main/Conf I-ABA Course of Study: Land Use Litigation, Critical Issues for Attorneys, Developers, and Public Officials. **Added/Corp** American Law Institute-American Bar Association Committee on Continuing Professional Education. Urban Land Institute. **VFOAT** Land Use Litigation, Critical Issues for Attorneys, Developers, and Public Officials: Materials. **VAT** American Law Institute, American Bar Association Course of Study. Land Use Litigation, Critical Issues for Attorneys, Developers, and Public Officials. Materials. (19??)-. English. American Law Institute, 4025 Chestnut Street, Philadelphia PA 19104-3099. **Tel** (215)243-1661, (800)253-6397, FAX (215)243-1664. **LC** KF5698.Z9; A16. **DD** 346/.73/045.

Law

US/0191-1945
ALI-ABA COURSE OF STUDY : LEGAL ASPECTS OF MUSEUM OPERATIONS : MATERIALS. VAT American Law Institute-American Bar Association Course of Study. Legal Aspects of Museum Operations: Materials. English. American Law Institute, 4025 Chestnut Street, Philadelphia PA 19104-3099. **Tel** (215)243-1661, (800)253-6397, FAX (215)243-1664. **LC** KF4305.Z9; A136. **DD** 344/.73/093.

US/0191-1589
ALI-ABA COURSE OF STUDY. LEGAL ISSUES IN THE COAL INDUSTRY : MATERIALS. VAT American Law Institute-American Bar Association Course of Study. Legal Issues in the Coal Industry: Materials. English. American Law Institute, 4025 Chestnut Street, Philadelphia PA 19104-3099. **Tel** (215)243-1661, (800)253-6397, FAX (215)243-1664. **LC** KF1830.Z9; A17. **DD** 343/.73/077.

US/0191-3069
ALI-ABA COURSE OF STUDY : LEGAL PROBLEMS OF MUSEUM ADMINISTRATION : MATERIALS. VAT American Law Institute-American Bar Association Course of Study. Legal Problems of Museum Administration: Materials. English. American Law Institute, 4025 Chestnut Street, Philadelphia PA 19104-3099. **Tel** (215)243-1661, (800)253-6397, FAX (215)243-1664. **LC** KF4305.Z9; A139. **DD** 344/.73/093.

US/0191-2046
ALI-ABA COURSE OF STUDY. LITIGATION UNDER THE FEDERAL SECURITIES LAWS : MATERIALS. VAT American Law Institute-American Bar Association Course of Study. Litigation under the Federal Securities Laws. English. American Law Institute, 4025 Chestnut Street, Philadelphia PA 19104-3099. **Tel** (215)243-1661, (800)253-6397, FAX (215)243-1664. **LC** KF1440; .A178. **DD** 346/73/0920269.

US/0190-387X
ALI-ABA COURSE OF STUDY MATERIALS. CONSTRUCTION CONTRACTING IN THE MIDDLE EAST: PROBLEMS AND SOLUTIONS. (ALI-ABA COURSE OF STUDY : CONSTRUCTION CONTRACTING IN THE MIDDLE EAST, PROBLEMS AND SOLUTIONS : MATERIALS.). **Main/Conf** ALI-ABA Course of Study: Construction Contracting in the Middle East. **VFOAT** Construction Contracting in the Middle East: Problems and Solutions. **VAT** American Law Institute-American Bar Association Course of Study Materials. Construction Contracting in the Middle East: Problems and Solutions. English. American Law Institute, 4025 Chestnut Street, Philadelphia PA 19104-3099. **Tel** (215)243-1661, (800)253-6397, FAX (215)243-1664. **LC** LAW. **DD** 343/.56/078.

US/0190-3888
ALI-ABA COURSE OF STUDY MATERIALS. PRACTICE AND PROCEDURE IN FEDERAL TAX CONTROVERSIES: TAX COURT AND ELSEWHERE. (ALI-ABA COURSE OF STUDY : PRACTICE AND PROCEDURE IN FEDERAL TAX CONTROVERSIES, TAX COURT AND ELSEWHERE : MATERIALS.). **VFOAT** Practice and Procedure in Federal Tax Controversies: Tax Court and Elsewhere. **VAT** American Law Institute-American Bar Association Course of Study Materials. Practice and Procedure In Federal Tax Controversies: Tax Court and Elsewhere. English. an. American Law Institute, 4025 Chestnut Street, Philadelphia PA 19104-3099. **Tel** (215)243-1661, (800)253-6397, FAX (215)243-1664. **LC** KF6320; .A917. **DD** 343/.73/040269.

US/0191-2003
ALI-ABA COURSE OF STUDY : MODERN REAL ESTATE TRANSACTIONS : MATERIALS. Main/Corp ALI-ABA Course of Study: Modern Real Estate Transactions. **VAT** American Law Institute-American Bar Association Course of Study. Modern Real Estate Transactions: Materials. English. American Law Institute, 4025 Chestnut Street, Philadelphia PA 19104-3099. **Tel** (215)243-1661, (800)253-6397, FAX (215)243-1664. **LC** KF665.Z9; A14. **DD** 346/.73/0436.

US/0272-8982
ALI-ABA COURSE OF STUDY. PRODUCTS LIABILITY : PREVENTION, LITIGATION, AND LAW REFORM : MATERIALS. VAT American Law Institute-American Bar Association Course of Study. Products Liability. Prevention, Litigation, and Law Reform. Materials. English. an. American Law Institute, 4025 Chestnut Street, Philadelphia PA 19104-3099. **Tel** (215)243-1661, (800)253-6397, FAX (215)243-1664. **LC** KF1296.Z9; A16. **DD** 346.7303/82.

US/0190-9347
ALI-ABA COURSE OF STUDY. REAL ESTATE CONDOMINIUMS AND PUDS : MATERIALS. VAT American Law Institute, American Bar Association Course of Study. Real Estate Condominiums and Planned Unit Developments: Materials. English. American Law Institute, 4025 Chestnut Street, Philadelphia PA 19104-3099. **Tel** (215)243-1661, (800)253-6397, FAX (215)243-1664. **LC** KF581.Z9; A14. **DD** 346/.73/0433.

US/0730-4722
ALI-ABA COURSE OF STUDY. REAL ESTATE SYNDICATIONS. MATERIALS. (REAL ESTATE SYNDICATIONS : ALI-ABA COURSE OF STUDY, MATERIALS.). **VFOAT** ALI-ABA Course of Study, Materials. **VAT** American Law Institute-American Bar Association Course of Study. Real Estate Syndications. Materials. English. American Law Institute, 4025 Chestnut Street, Philadelphia PA 19104-3099. **Tel** (215)243-1661, (800)253-6397, FAX (215)243-1664. **LC** KF1079.Z9; R424. **DD** 346.7304/3; 347.30643.

US/0191-2240
ALI-ABA COURSE OF STUDY : SECTION 8 HUD-SUBSIDIZED HOUSING, NEW TAX-EXEMPT FINANCING TECHNIQUES : MATERIALS. VAT American Law Institute-American Bar Association Course of Study. Section Eight Housing and Urban Development-Subsidized Housing, New Tax-Exempt Financing Techniques: Materials. English. American Law Institute, 4025 Chestnut Street, Philadelphia PA 19104-3099. **Tel** (215)243-1661, (800)253-6397, FAX (215)243-1664. **LC** KF695.Z9; A18. **DD** 346/.73/0436.

US/0190-9657
ALI-ABA COURSE OF STUDY. SELECTED PROBLEMS IN TAX PLANNING FOR AGRICULTURE : MATERIALS. VAT American Law Institute-American Bar Association Course of Study. Selected Problems in Tax Planning for Agriculture: Materials. English. American Law Institute, 4025 Chestnut Street, Philadelphia PA 19104-3099. **Tel** (215)243-1661, (800)253-6397, FAX (215)243-1664. **LC** KF6369.8.F3; A14. **DD** 343/.73/053.

US/0191-2380
ALI-ABA COURSE OF STUDY : STATE AND LOCAL TAXATION AND FINANCE : MATERIALS. VAT American Law Institute-American Bar Association Course of Study. State and Local Taxation and Finance: Materials. English. an. American Law Institute, 4025 Chestnut Street, Philadelphia PA 19104-3099. **Tel** (215)243-1661, (800)253-6397, FAX (215)243-1664. **LC** KF6730.Z9; A17. **DD** 343/.73/043.

US/0272-8133
ALI-ABA COURSE OF STUDY. TAX PLANNING FOR AGRICULTURE : MATERIALS. VFOAT Tax Planning for Agriculture: Materials. **VAT** American Law Institute-American Bar Association Course of Study. Tax Planning for Agriculture: Materials. English. American Law Institute, 4025 Chestnut Street, Philadelphia PA 19104-3099. **Tel** (215)243-1661, (800)253-6397, FAX (215)243-1664. **LC** KF6369.8.F3; A16. **DD** 343.7305/581.

US/0190-9975
ALI-ABA COURSE OF STUDY. THE SUPREME COURT AND THE FEDERAL SECURITIES LAWS, IMPLICATIONS FOR LIABILITIES : MATERIALS. Main/Corp ALI-ABA Course of Study: The Supreme Court and the Federal Securities Laws: Implications for Liabilities. **VAT** American Law Institute-American Bar Association Course of Study. The Supreme Court and the Federal Securities Laws: Implications for Liabilities: Materials. English. American Law Institute, 4025 Chestnut Street, Philadelphia PA 19104-3099. **Tel** (215)243-1661, (800)253-6397, FAX (215)243-1664. **LC** KF1440; .A188. **DD** 346/.73/0666.

US/0271-2504
ALI-ABA COURSE OF STUDY. TRIAL EVIDENCE IN FEDERAL AND STATE COURTS, A CLINICAL STUDY OF RECENT DEVELOPMENTS: MATERIALS. Main/Conf ALI-ABA Course of Study: Trial Evidence in Federal and State Courts: A Clinical Study of Recent Developments. **Added/Corp** American Law Institute-American Bar Association Committee on Continuing Professional Education. South Carolina Bar. **VFOAT** Trial Evidence in Federal and State Courts, a Clinical Study of Recent Developments: Materials. **VAT** American Law Institute-American Bar Association Course of Study. Trial Evidence in Federal and State Courts, A Clinical Study of Recent Developments: Materials. (19??)-. English. an. American Law Institute, 4025 Chestnut Street, Philadelphia PA 19104-3099. **Tel** (215)243-1661, (800)253-6397, FAX (215)243-1664. **LC** KF8935.Z9; A16. **DD** 347.73/6.

US/0164-5757
ALI REPORTER, THE. Main/Corp American Law Institute. **VAT** American Law Institute Reporter. V. 1- Oct. 1978-. Periodical. English. qt. American Law Institute, 4025 Chestnut Street, Philadelphia PA 19104-3099. **Tel** (215)243-1661, (800)253-6397, FAX (215)243-1664. **ED** Michael Greenwald. **LC** KF200; .A455. **DD** 349.73/05. **Bk Rev. Circ:** 2,750 (ctrl).
Desc: Newsletter of the American Law Institute.

SP/0214-803X
ALIMENTALEX (MADRID). See Food and Food Industry.

UK
ALL ENGLAND LAW REPORTS, THE.
Added/Corp Great Britain. Parliament. House of Lords. Great Britain. Supreme Court of Judicature. Great Britain. Privy Council. Vol. 1 (1948)-. English. wk. Butterworth & Co. Ltd. / Kent, England, Borough Green, Sevenoaks Kent TN15 8PH England. **Tel** 011 44 732-884567, FAX 011 44 732-885996. **Absorbed** Law Times Reports; **Continues** All England Law Reports of Cases Decided in the House of Lords, The Privy Council, All Divisions of the Supreme Court, and Courts of Special Jurisdiction.
Desc: Widely used series of law reports. The coverage is comprehensive and includes all fields of law and all leading cases.

UK
ALL ENGLAND LAW REPORTS ANNUAL REVIEW, THE. (1982)-. English. an. £37.00. Butterworth & Co. Ltd. / Kent, England, Borough Green, Sevenoaks Kent TN15 8PH England. **Tel** 011 44 732-884567, FAX 011 44 732-885996. **LC** K1; .L527. **DD** 349.42; 344.2.

UK
ALL ENGLAND LAW REPORTS (INCORPORATING THE LAW TIMES REPORTS AND THE LAW JOURNAL REPORTS) OF CASES DECIDED IN THE HOUSE OF LORDS, THE PRIVY COUNCIL, ALL DIVISIONS OF THE SUPREME COURT, AND COURTS OF SPECIAL JURISDICTION, THE. Added/Corp Great Britain. Courts. Great Britain. Parliament. House of Lords. Great Britain. Privy Council. Judicial Committee. Great Britain. Supreme Court of Judicature. (1936)-. English. ir. Butterworth & Co. Ltd. / Kent, England, Borough Green, Sevenoaks Kent TN15 8PH England. **Tel** 011 44 732-884567, FAX 011 44 732-885996. **(Subscription address:** Butterworth Heinemann Publishers, 225 Wildwood Avenue, Unit B, Woburn MA 01801.) **ED** Peter Hutchesson. **Absorbed** Law Times Reports **and** Law Journal Reports.
Desc: Some 18,000 cases decided by the courts since 1936 are reported chronologically in a single series of volumes.
Ind/Abst Aust. Leg. Mon. Dig.

II
ALL INDIA PREVENTION OF FOOD ADULTERATION CASES. VFOAT Prevention of Food Adulteration Cases. (19??)-. English. mo. Rs30.00. International Law Book Company Gate, Delhi-6 India. **LC** LAW. **DD** 344/.54/04232; 345.4044232.

US
ALL NEWSLETTER / ACADEMIC LAW LIBRARIES SPECIAL INTEREST SECTION, AMERICAN ASSOCIATION OF LAW LIBRARIES. See Library and Information Sciences.

II
ALLAHABAD LAW JOURNAL. Added/Corp Great Britain. Privy Council. Judicial Committee. India. Courts. India (Dominion) Courts. India (Republic) Courts. Vol. 1 (1904)-. English. Twenty-six times a year. $60.00. **(Subscription address:** Prints India, 11 Darya Ganj, New Delhi 110002 India.)

HU/0002-564X
ALLAM- ES JOGTUDOMANY. Added/Corp Magyar Tudomanyos Akademia, Budapest. Allam- es Jogtudomanyi Intezet. Magyar Tudomanyos Akademia, Budapest. Allam- es Jogtudomanyi Intezet. Allam- es Jogtudomanyi Intezet Ertesitoje. Vol. 1 (1957)-. Academic Scholarly Publication. Hungarian. qt. $29.00. Akademiai Kiado, Publishing House of the Hungarian Academy of Sciences, Prielle Kornelia u. 19-35, H-1117 Budapest Hungary. **Tel** 011 36 1 1811991, FAX 011 36 1 1811991, telex 22-6228 AKNYO H. **(Subscription address:** Kultura, PO Box 149, H 1389 Budapest 62 Hungary.) **ED** I. Szabo. Index available. **Bk Rev. Ad Acc.**
Ind/Abst Index Foreign Leg. Per.; Int. Polit. Sci. Abstr.; Leis. Recreat. Tour. Abstr.; Rural Dev. Abstr.; World Agric. Econ.

US/0516-7094
ALLEGHENY LAWYER, THE. Began with Nov. 1958 issue. Periodical. English. mo. $90.00. Allegheny County Bar Association, 310 Grant Street, #420 Grant Building, Pittsburgh PA 15219-2203. **Tel** (412)261-6161. **ED** James I Smith. **LC** KF200; .A42. **DD** 340/.0974885. **Bk Rev. Circ:** 6,200 (ctrl).
Desc: Newsletter sent to all members of the Bar Association. It informs the lawyers of upcoming educational as well as social events; information of lawyers activities in organizations and communities.

US/0738-8152
ALPHABETICAL DIRECTORY OF ATTORNEYS IN NEW YORK STATE. **Added/Corp** New York Lawyers Diary and Manual (Firm). **VFOAT** Directory of Attorneys in New York State. (1982)-. Directory. English. an (Dec.). $40.00 (subscribers); $50.00 (non-subscribers). Skinder Strauss Associates, PO Box 50, Newark NJ 07101. **Tel** (800)444-4041, (201)642-1440, FAX (201)642-4280. **LC** KF192.N45; A43. **DD** 349.747/025; 347.470025. **Circ:** 1,000 (ctrl).
Desc: This is designed for locating an attorney or law firms when only their name is known.

PH/0117-1577
ALTERNATIVE LAW FORUM. [Altern. law forum]. (1985)-. Periodical. English. qt. **DD** 341.481.
Ind/Abst Hum. Rights Intern. Rep.

US/0191-863X
ALTMAN WEIL PENSA REPORT TO LEGAL MANAGEMENT, THE. [Altman Weil rep. leg. manage.]. **Main/Corp** Altman & Weil Publications, Inc. **Added/Corp** Altman & Weil Publications, Inc. Report to Legal Management. **VFOAT** Altman and Weil Report to Legal Management; Report to Legal Management. (1974)-. English. Twelve times a year. $195.00 one year; $350.00 two years. Altman Weil Pensa Publications Inc, PO Box 625, 2 Campus Boulevard, Newton Square PA 19073. **Tel** (215)359-9900, FAX (215)359-0467. **ED** James Wilber (phone: (414)886-1304). **LC** KF318.A1; A38. **DD** 651/.9/34. **[CCC].** Index Bound in First Issue (Oct. iss. (Free)). cum. index. **Circ:** 1,100.
Desc: Law office management and purchasing, including compensation, insurance, word processing and data processing, use of space, agencies; based on the experiences of Altman & Weil management consultants.
Ind/Abst Law Office Inf. Serv.

US/0738-6672
ALUMNAE/I DIRECTORY - RUTGERS LAW SCHOOL (NEWARK, N.J.). **See** College and School Publications-Alumni.

US
ALUMNI DIRECTORY / ALBANY LAW SCHOOL OF UNION UNIVERSITY. **See** College and School Publications-Alumni.

US/0162-0371
ALUMNI DIRECTORY - THE UNIVERSITY OF CHICAGO LAW SCHOOL. **See** College and School Publications-Alumni.

US/0572-4953
AMERICAN ASSOCIATION OF LAW LIBRARIES NEWSLETTER. **See** Library and Information Sciences.

US/1059-2474
AMERICAN BANK LAWYER, THE. [Am. bank lawyer]. **Added/Corp** Texas Association of Bank Counsel. Vol. 1, No. 1 (Nov. 1991)-. Periodical. English. Twelve times a year. $60.00. Texas Tech University / School of Law, PO Box 40004, Lubbock TX 79409-0004. **Tel** (806)742-3920. **DD** 346.

●US/1068-0861
AMERICAN BANKRUPTCY INSTITUTE LAW REVIEW, THE. [Am. Bankruptcy Inst. law rev.]. **Added/Corp** American Bankruptcy Institute. St. John's University (New York, N.Y.). School of Law. Vol. 1, No. 1 (Spring 1993)-. Periodical. English. sa. $52.00. LRP Publications, 747 Dresher Road, PO Box 980, Horsham PA 19044-0980. **Tel** (800)341-7874, (215)784-0860, FAX (215)784-9639, (215)784-0870. **DD** 346.
Desc: Analyzes specific topics in the bankruptcy field.

US/1046-5197
AMERICAN BAR, THE. [Am. bar]. **VFOAT** American Bar, The Canadian Bar, The International Bar. (1918)-. English. an (March). $275.00. Forster Long Inc, 3280 Ramos Circle, Sacramento CA 95827. **Tel** (916)362-3276, FAX 916362-5643. **ED** Marie T. Finn. **LC** KF190; .I5. **DD** 340.

US/0094-3584
AMERICAN BAR REFERENCE HANDBOOK, THE. (1974)-. English. an (Mar.). $50.00. Forster Long Inc, 3280 Ramos Circle, Sacramento CA 95827. **Tel** (916)362-3276, FAX 916362-5643. **DD** 340/.025/73. ***Continues*** *American Bar International Reference Handbook, 0090-2675.*

US/0197-8195
AMERICAN CIVIL LIBERTIES UNION RECORDS AND PUBLICATIONS UPDATE, THE. **Main/Corp** American Civil Liberties Union. English. be. Microfilming Corporation of America, 21 Harristown Road, Glen Rock NJ 07452. **LC** KF4742.3; .A53. **DD** 016.3234/0973.

US/8755-1675
AMERICAN COMPUTER LAW DIGEST. [Am. comput. law dig.]. Vol. 1, No. 1 (1984)-. Periodical. English. Four times a year. $50.00. American Computer Law Digest Inc, PO Box 39235, Friendship Station, Washington DC 20016. **Tel** (202)232-0800. **ED** C. R. Costa and A. E. Major Jr. **LC** KF390.5.C6; A492. **DD** 343.73/078004/02648; 347.3037800402648. **Bk Rev. Circ:** 2,000 (ctrl).
Desc: Recent briefs and discussions of court decisions and legislation affecting computer users and marketers.

US/0145-7993
AMERICAN INDIAN JOURNAL. [Am. Indian J.]. **Added/Corp** Institute for the Development of Indian Law. Vol. 1 (Oct. 1975)-. Periodical. English. Four times a year. $50.00. Institute Development of Indian Law, 2501 Blackwelder Street, School of Law, Oklahoma OK 73106. **Tel** (405-521-5361. **LC** KF8201.A3; A4. **DD** 346/.73/013. cum. index. available on microfilm and microfiche from University Microfilms International (UMI). ***Formed by the union of*** *Education Journal of the Institute for the Development of Indian Law, 0090-0958* ***and*** *Legislative Review.*
Ind/Abst Am. Hist. Life (1986-); Contents Pages Educ.; Curr. Index J. Educ.; Curr. Law Index (1980-); Leg. Resour. Index (1980-1982, 19??-); LegalTrac (1980-).

US/0002-8886
AMERICAN INDIAN LAW NEWSLETTER. ***Ceased.*** [Am. Indian law newsl.]. Vol. 1, No. 1 (May 3, 1968)-Vol. 23, No. 1 (?). Newsletter. English. bm. American Indian Law Center, PO Box 4456 Station A, Albuquerque NM 87196. **Tel** (505)277-5462. **ED** Marc Mannes. **LC** KF8201.A3; A44. **DD** 346.7301/3. **Circ:** 700 (ctrl).
Desc: Contains articles on issues of interest to those concerned with American Indian law.

US/0094-002X
AMERICAN INDIAN LAW REVIEW. [Am. Indian law rev.]. **Added/Corp** University of Oklahoma. College of Law. Vol. 1, (Winter 1973)-. English. Twice a year (June, Dec.). $15.00. University of Oklahoma College of Law, 300 Timberdell, Norman OK 73019. **Tel** (405)325-2840, FAX (405)325-6282. **ED** Michael Ridgeway. **LC** K1; .M437. **DD** 342/.73/087. cum. index. **Bk Rev**, (Qty: 1). **Ad Acc, Adv Mgr:** Waters, **Tel** (405)325-5191. **Circ:** 850 (ctrl).
Desc: Concentrates on American Indian law, Indian lands, Indian welfare, Indian rights, and the Bureau of Indian Affairs.
Ind/Abst Curr. Law Index (1980-); Index Leg. Period.; J. Plan. Lit.; Leg. Resour. Index (1980-); LegalTrac (1980-); Sel. Water Resour. Abstr.; West. Hist. Q.; Writ. Am. Hist.

US/0733-1290
AMERICAN JOURNAL OF FORENSIC PSYCHOLOGY, THE. **See** Medical Science and Technology-Forensic Medicine, Medical Jurisprudence.

US/0065-8995
AMERICAN JOURNAL OF JURISPRUDENCE (NOTRE DAME), THE. (THE AMERICAN JOURNAL OF JURISPRUDENCE.). [Am. j. jurisprud.]. **Added/Corp** University of Notre Dame. Law School. Vol. 14 (1969)-. English. an. $25.00. Notre Dame Law School, PO Box 486, Notre Dame IN 46556. **Tel** (219)239-5918, (219)255-2938. **ED** Charles E Rice. **LC** K14; .A867. **DD** 340.1. cum. index. **Bk Rev. Ad Acc. Pr Rev. Circ:** 1,100. available on microfilm and microfiche from University Microfilms International (UMI). ***Continues*** *Natural Law Forum, 0199-9702.*
Desc: Natural law theory and philosophy.
Ind/Abst ABC POL SCI; Crim. Penol. Police Sci. Abstr. (1980-); Curr. Law Index (1980-); Index Leg. Period.; Leg. Resour. Index (1980-); LegalTrac (1981-); Abr. Cathol. Period. Lit. Index; Cathol. Period. Lit. Index.

US/0098-8588
AMERICAN JOURNAL OF LAW & MEDICINE. [Am. j. law med.]. **Added/Corp** American Society of Law and Medicine. **VAT** American Journal of Law and Medicine. Vol. 1 (Mar. 1975)-. Academic Scholarly Publication. English. qt. $70.00. American Society of Law, Medicine and Ethics, 765 Commonwealth Avenue, 16th Floor, Boston MA 02215. **Tel** (617)262-4990, FAX (617)437-7596. **ED** Abby Wayne. **LC** K1; .M445. **DD** 344/.73/041. **NLM** W1 AM475. **CODEN** AJLMDN. **[CCC]. Bk Rev. Pr Rev. Circ:** 9,000. available on microfilm and microfiche from University Microfilms International (UMI). Documents available from The Genuine Article, BIOSIS Document Express, UMI Article Clearinghouse.
Desc: An interdisciplinary law review which contains professional articles, and analyses of legislature and judicial developments.
Ind/Abst Biol. Abstr.; Curr. Contents Soc. Behav. Sci.; Curr. Law Index (1980-); Curr. Lit. Fam. Plan. (19??-199?); EMBASE; Energy Res. Abstr. (March 1982-); Expand. Acad. Index (1984-); Health Devices Alerts; Health Plan. Adminis.; Hospit. Manage. Rev. (19??-19??); Index Med.; Index Leg. Period.; INIS Atomindex [Micro.]; Leg. Resour. Index (1980-); LegalTrac (1980-); Linguist. Lang. Behav. Abstr.; Newsp. Period. Abstr. (1990-); Res. Alert [Full Cov.]; Soc. Plann. Policy Dev. Abstr.; Soc. Sci. Cit. Index [Full Cov.]; Sociol. Abstr.

US/0002-9319
AMERICAN JOURNAL OF LEGAL HISTORY, THE. [Am. J. Leg. Hist.]. **Added/Corp** Temple University. School of Law. American Society for Legal History. Vol. 1, No. 1 (Jan. 1957)-. Periodical. English. qt (Jan., April, July, Oct.). $25.00 (individuals), $35.00 (institutions) US; $25.00 (individuals), $35.00 (institutions) Canada; $45.00 other. American Journal of Legal History, North Broad Street & Montgomery Avenue, Philadelphia PA 19122. **Tel** (215)787-1256, FAX (215)787-1785. **ED** John M Lindsey. Index available. **Bk Rev. Ad Acc. Pr Rev. Circ:** 1,200. Documents available from The Genuine Article.
Ind/Abst ABC POL SCI; Am. Hist. Life (1957-); Arts Humanit. Citation Index [Select. Cov.]; Bowne Dig. Corp. Sec. Lawyers (1957-); Crim. Justice Abstr.; Curr. Contents Soc. Behav. Sci.; Index Leg. Period.; Leg. Resour. Index (1980-); LegalTrac (1957,1980); Res. Alert [Full Cov.]; Soc. Sci. Cit. Index [Full Cov.]; Soc. Work Abstr. (?-?); West. Hist. Q. (1957-).

US/0160-0281
AMERICAN JOURNAL OF TRIAL ADVOCACY, THE. [Am. J. Trial Advocacy]. **Added/Corp** Samford University. Center for Advocacy and Clinical Education. Vol. 1 (Fall 1977)-. Periodical. English. Three times a year. $24.00 (one year), $45.00 (two year). Cumberland School of Law, 800 Lakeshore Drive, Room 305D, Birmingham AL 35229. **Tel** (205)870-2959. **ED** Jeffrey K. Hollis. **LC** K1; .M446. **DD** 347/.73/705. Index available. **Bk Rev. Ad Acc. Circ:** 2,000. available on microfilm and microfiche from University Microfilms International (UMI); available on an online database from WESTLAW.
Desc: Law review dedicated to the advancement of trial advocacy as a specialty within the law. Vehicle for the intellectual study of trial litigation.
Ind/Abst Crim. Justice Period. Index; Curr. Law Index (1980-); Index Leg. Period.; Leg. Resour. Index (1980-); LegalTrac (1980-).

US
AMERICAN LAW OF MINING. **Main/Corp** Rocky Mountain Mineral Law Foundation. (19??)-. English. an. $343.50. Matthew Bender & Company Inc., 1275 Broadway, Albany NY 12204. **Tel** (800)833-9844, (518)487-3000.

●US/1062-2446
AMERICAN LAW REPORTS. ALR 5TH, ANNOTATIONS AND CASES. [Am. law rep., ALR 5th, annot. cases]. **Added/Corp** Lawyers Co-Operative Publishing Company. **VFOAT** ALR 5th. Vol. 1 (1992)-. English. ir. Lawyers Cooperative Publishing Company, Aqueduct Building, Rochester NY 14694. **Tel** (800)527-0430, (716)546-5530. **LC** KF132; .A55. **DD** 348.73/46; 347.3084. ***Continues*** *American Law Reports. ALR 4th: Cases and Annotations, 0730-837X.*

US
AMERICAN LAW REPORTS. ALR FEDERAL: CASES AND ANNOTATIONS. **VFOAT** ALR Fed. Vol. 1 (1969)-. English. Five times a year. Lawyers Cooperative Publishing Company, Aqueduct Building, Rochester NY 14694. **Tel** (800)527-0430, (716)546-5530. **LC** KF132; .A47. **DD** 345/41.
Desc: Contains full reports of leading cases from the federal courts, followed by exhaustive annotations on points of federal law of particular current.

US/8750-8214
AMERICAN LAW REVIEW (DALLAS, TEX.), THE. (THE AMERICAN LAW REVIEW.). [Am. law rev.]. V. 16, No. 4 (Jan. 21, 1985)-. Periodical. English. wk. $24.00 US; $50.00 other. Financial Trend, Inc., 7616 LBJ Freeway, Dallas TX 75251. **LC** K1; .M4475. **DD** 349.73/05. available on microfilm from University Microfilms International (UMI). ***Continues*** *Financial Trend, 0040-4195.*

US/8755-4461
AMERICAN LAWYER GUIDE TO LEADING LAW FIRMS, THE. ***Suspended.*** [Am. lawyer guide lead. law firms]. **VFOAT** Guide to Leading Law Firms. Began 1983-84-Suspended. English. an. $1,495 Corporations; $859.00 other. Am-Law Publishing Corporation, 2 Park Avenue, New York NY 10016. **LC** KF190; .A5617. **DD** 340/.025/73. ***Continues*** *American Lawyer Guide to Law Firms, 0740-1507.*

US
AMERICAN LAWYER MANAGEMENT SERVICE, THE. English. Four times a year. $225.00 (firms with 100 or fewer attorneys), $295.00 (firms with 101 or more attorneys). American Lawyer Media, L.P., 600 3rd Avenue, New York NY 10016. **Tel** (212)973-2800.

US/0162-3397
AMERICAN LAWYER (NEW YORK. 1979), THE. (THE AMERICAN LAWYER.). [Am. law.]. Vol. 1, No. 1 (Feb. 1979)-. Periodical. English. Ten times a year (monthly with Jan./Feb. & July/Aug. issues combined). $375.00 (regular rate). American Lawyer Media, L.P., 600 3rd Avenue, New York NY 10016. **Tel** (212)973-2800. **ED** Steven Brill. **LC** K1; .M448. **DD** 349.73/05; 347.3005. **[CCC]. Bk Rev. Ad Acc. Circ:** 20,000. available on microfiche from University Microfilms International (UMI).
Desc: Serious well-written journalism regarding the business of lawyering. Unique view of people and events shaping the world of law and business highly regarded in those communities.
Ind/Abst Access (1981-); Curr. Law Index (1980-); Curr. Lit. Fam. Plan. (19??-199?); Law Office Inf. Serv.; Leg. Resour. Index (1980-); LegalTrac (1980-).

US/1050-4109
AMERICAN REVIEW OF INTERNATIONAL ARBITRATION, THE. (THE AMERICAN REVIEW OF INTERNATIONAL ARBITRATION / PARKER SCHOOL OF FOREIGN AND COMPARATIVE LAW, COLUMBIA UNIVERSITY.). [Am. rev. int. arbitr.]. **Added/Corp** Parker School of Foreign and Comparative Law. Vol. 1, No. 1 (Apr. 1990)-. Periodical. English. Four times a year. $120.00 US; $243.80 Netherlands; $230.00 other. Transnational Juris Publishers, 1 Bridge Street/ Candy Dubenski, Irvington NY 10533. **Tel** (914)591-4288, FAX (914)591-2688. **ED** Vratislav Pechota, 435 West 116 Street, New York, NY 10027; Telephone: (212)854-2691. **DD** 341. **Bk Rev. Ad Acc, Adv Mgr:** Elisa Varian, **Tel** (914)591-4288.
Desc: The first and only American quarterly publication with a focus on U.S. developments in international commercial arbitration. Contains articles and commentaries by authoritative contributors who analyze the significance, trends and developments in this growing area.

US/0003-1453
AMERICAN UNIVERSITY LAW REVIEW, THE. [Am. Univers. law rev.]. **Added/Corp** Washington College of Law. Vol. 6 (Jan. 1957)-. Periodical. English. Six times a year. $30.00 US; $35.00 other. Washington College of Law, 4410 Massachusetts Avenue NW, Washington DC 20016. **Tel** (202)885-2652, FAX (202)885-1039. Index available in last issue of volume--attached. **Bk Rev. Ad Acc, Adv Mgr:** Martine Tavakoli. **Pr Rev. Circ:** 1,600. available on microfilm and microfiche from University Microfilms International (UMI). ***Continues*** *American University Intramural Law Review, 0275-1674.*
Desc: Student and outside author notes and comments on various areas of the law.
Ind/Abst Bowne Dig. Corp. Sec. Lawyers; Crim. Justice Abstr.; Crim. Justice Period. Index; Curr. Law Index (1980-); Fed. Tax Artic.; Index Leg. Period.; Leg. Resour. Index (1980-); LegalTrac (1980-).

US/8756-3428
AMICUS CURIAE (CORAL GABLES, FLA.). (AMICUS CURIAE / UNIVERSITY OF MIAMI, SCHOOL OF LAW.). 1985-. English. an. University of Miami School of Law, 1311 Miller Drive, 460 Law Library, PO Box 248087, Coral Gables FL 33124. **Tel** (305)284-2464, FAX (305)284-2349. **LC** KF292.M44; A418. **DD** 340/.07/11759381.

US/0161-0783
AMICUS JURIS. 1st- issue. Periodical. English. sa. Memphis State University / Student Bar Association, Memphis TN 38152. **LC** KF200; .A46. **DD** 340/.09768.

SZ
AMTLICHE SAMMLUNG DES BUNDESRECHTS. **Main/Corp** Switzerland. (Jan. 12, 1988)-. Periodical. German. Fifty-two times a year (Wed.). F86.50 Switzerland; F109.50 others. Staempfli & Cie SA, Postfach 8326, CH-3001 Bern Switzerland. **Tel** 011 41 31 3006666, telex 031 911 515 EDMZ CH. ***Continues*** *Switzerland. Laws, etc. (Recueil des Lois Federales : 1920-1978). German.* ***and*** *Sammlung der Eidgenossischen Gesetze.*

BL
ANAIS FORENSES DO ESTADO DE MATO GROSSO. **Main/Corp** Mato Grosso, Brazil (State). Tribunal de Justica. Portuguese. $70.00. Tribunal de Justica / Ciuaba, Brazil, rua Joaquim Murtinho, 46-10 Andar Sala 3, Caixa Postal 258, Ciuaba Brazil. **DD** 348/.817/043.

RM
ANALELE UNIVERSITATII BUCURESTI. DREPT. **Main/Corp** Universitatea Din Bucuresti. Vol. 26 (1977)-. Periodical. Romanian (French and Romanian). an. DM164.00. **(Subscription address:** Kubon & Sagner, ABT Zeitschriftenimport, D 80328 Munich Germany.**)** **LC** K2; .U28.
Ind/Abst BHA : Biblio. Hist. Art.

SP
ANALES DE DERECHO. No. 1-. Periodical. Spanish. Secretariado de Publicaciones e Intercambio Cientifico, Universidad de Murcia, Murcia Spain. **LC** K1; .N42. **DD** 340/.0946.

MX
ANALES DE JURISPRUDENCIA. (19??)-. Spanish. qt. Direccion Anales Jurisprudencia, Conjunto Pino S Torre E 3 Piso, Mexico 1 DF Mexico.

SP/0008-7750
ANALES DE LA CATEDRA FRANCISCO SUAREZ. See Philosophy.

UY
ANALES DEL FORO. Periodical. Spanish. bw. Ituizaingo, 1495 Piso 2, Montevideo Uruguay. **LC** KHU72; .A23. **DD** 348.895/026; 348.950826.

US
ANALYSES OF PROPOSED CONSTITUTIONAL AMENDMENTS FOR ELECTION ... . **VFOAT** Analyses of Proposed Constitutional Amendments Appearing on ... Ballot. English. Texas Legislative Council, PO Box 12128 Capitol Station, Austin TX 78711. **LC** KFT1601 1876 .A7; T483. **DD** 342.764/035; 347.640235.

US
ANALYSIS OF FEDERAL AND STATE CAMPAIGN FINANCE LAW. English. sm. US Federal Election Commission, 999 E Street NW, Washington DC 20463. **Tel** (800)424-9530.

US/0896-9752
ANALYSIS OF REVISIONS OF THE UNIFORM BUILDING CODE, U.B.C. STANDARDS ... . [Anal. rev. unif. build. code]. **Main/Corp** International Conference of Building Officials. **VFOAT** U.B.C. Standards; Uniform Mechanical Code; Uniform Housing Code; Uniform Code for the Abatement of Dangerous Buildings; Uniform Sign Code; Uniform Fire Code. **VAT** Analysis of Revisions of the Uniform Building Code, Uniform Building Code Standards ...; Uniform Building Code Standards. English. an. ICBO Evaluation Service Inc., 5360 South Workman Mill Road, Whittier CA 90601. **Tel** (213)699-0541, FAX (213)692-3853. **DD** 343.

US/1059-518X
ANDERSON'S OHIO CASE LOCATOR. **VFOAT** Ohio Case Locator. (1991)-. English. qt. Anderson Publishing, 2035 Reading Road, Cincinnati OH 45202. **Tel** (513)421-4142, (800)582-7295, FAX (513)562-8116.

II
ANDHRA LAW TIMES. SUPPLEMENT. **VFOAT** ALT Acts, Rules, Cent. and AP; A.L.T. Acts, Rules, Cent. & A.P. English. an. Andhra Law Times, 16-11-418/3 Balaji Sadan Kilsukhnagar, Hyderabad 500-036 India. **DD** 348.54/84023; 345.4840823.

US/0887-7866
ANDREWS SCHOOL ASBESTOS ALERT. ***Ceased.*** [Andrews sch. absestos alert]. (August 1984)-(May 1989). Periodical. English. mo. Andrews Publications Inc., 1646 West Chester Pike, PO Box 1000, Westtown PA 19395. **Tel** (610)399-6600, (800)345-1101, FAX (610)399-6610. **DD** 344.

●US/1067-6996
ANDREWS' TOXIC TORTS ANNUAL. **Added/Corp** Andrews Publications (Firm). (1993)-. English. an. $95.00. Andrews Publications Inc., 1646 West Chester Pike, PO Box 1000, Westtown PA 19395. **Tel** (610)399-6600, (800)345-1101, FAX (610)399-6610.

US
ANGELINA COUNTY COURT DIGEST. v. 1- Nov. 8, 1977-. Periodical. English. bm. $15.00. 110-112 West Shepherd, PO Box 1487, Lufkin TX 74901. **LC** KFT1799.A53; A42. **DD** 340/.09764173.

FR/1156-4148
ANGLE DROIT PARIS. (ANGLE DROIT.). (1990)-. Periodical. French. Eleven times a year. 1950.00F France; 2100.00F other. Edicom, 21 rue Tournefort, 75005 Paris France. **Tel** 33 1 47072929, FAX 33 1 47073066, 33 1 4703129. **ED** T. P. Jovandet. **UDC** 354.32. Index available (Jan.). cum. index. **Bk Rev. Ad Acc. Circ:** 500.
Desc: Dedicated to the law of communication including TV, cable, radio and telecommunications.

UK/0308-6569
ANGLO-AMERICAN LAW REVIEW, THE. [Anglo-Am. law rev.]. Vol. 1 (Jan./March 1972)-. Periodical. English. qt. £78.00 UK; £80.00 other. Barry Rose Law Periodicals Ltd., Little London, Chichester West Sussex PO19 1PG England. **Tel** 011 44 243 787841, 011 44 243 783637, FAX 011 44 243 779174, 011 44 243 779278. **ED** Martin Partington. **LC** K1; .N45. **DD** 340/.05. **[CCC].** Index available. **Bk Rev. Ad Acc.**
Desc: The journal was founded in 1972 to act as a bridge between the law of those countries where the writ of common law still runs.
Ind/Abst Crim. Penol. Police Sci. Abstr. (19??-); Curr. Law Index (1980-); Index Leg. Period. (19??-); Leg. Resour. Index (1980-); LegalTrac (1981-).

US
ANIMAL LAW NEWSLETTER / ANIMAL PROTECTION COMMITTEE, YOUNG LAWYER'S DIVISION, AMERICAN BAR ASSOCIATION. (19??)-. English. sa (2 issues). $10.00. American Bar Association, 750 North Lake Shore Drive, Chicago IL 60611. **Tel** (312)988-5522, (312)988-5241, FAX (312)988-5528, telex 270593. ***Continues*** *Animal Law Report.*

US/0730-6792
ANIMAL RIGHTS LAW REPORTER. Jan. 1980-. Periodical. English. mo. $195.00. Perceptions Press Inc, 4200 Wisconson Avenue NW, Suite 106/345, Washington DC 20016. **LC** KF390.5.A5; A132. **DD** 346.73/046954; 347.30646954.
Desc: An objective analysis of the animal rights movement. Examines issues tactics, personalities, new regulations and literature.

FR/0066-202X
ANNALES AFRICAINES. [Ann. afr.]. (1954)-. French. an. 775.00F. Editions A Pedone, 13 rue Soufflot, 75005 Paris France. **Tel** 011 33 1 43540597. **DD** 349.66/05; 346.6005. cum. index.
Ind/Abst Am. Hist. Life (1956-1975).

BE/0770-6472
ANNALES DE DROIT DE LOUVAIN. **Added/Corp** Association des Diplomes en Droit de l'Universite de Louvain. (1981)-. French. qt. price varies per volume. Maison F Larcier SA, 39 rue des Minimes, B-1000 Bruxelles Belgium. **Tel** 011 32 2 512-4712, 512-9679. **(Subscription address:** Acces Plus, Fond Jean Paques 4, B1348 Louvain la Neuve Belgium.**)** **LC** K1; .N47. **DD** 340/.05. ***Continues*** *Annales de Droit.*
Ind/Abst Index Foreign Leg. Per.; Int. Polit. Sci. Abstr.

CG
ANNALES DE LA FACULTE DE DROIT. **Main/Corp** Universite Nationale du Zaire. Campus de Kinshasa. Faculte de Droit. Vol. 1 (1972)-. French. Presses Universitaries du E Zaire, Banque Commerciale Zairoise 923.957/26, Kinshasa Zaire. **LC** K25; .N567. **DD** 340/.096751.
Ind/Abst Index Foreign Leg. Per.

FR/1150-3637
ANNALES DE L'IRETIJ MONTPELLIER, LES. (LES ANNALES DE L'IRETIJ.). **VFOAT** Annales de l'Institut de Recherche et d'Etudes pour le Traitement de l'Information Juridique. (1989)-. Monographic series. French. an. Price varies per volume. IRETIJ / Faculte de Droit, 39 Rue de l'Universite, 34060 Montpellier Cedex France. **Tel** 011 33 67 604555. **UDC** 340.

GW
ANNALES. RECHTS- UND WIRTSCHAFTSWISSENSCHAFTLICHE ABTEILUNG. **Main/Corp** Universitat des Saarlandes. Vol. 1 (1963)-. Monographic series. German. ir. Price varies per volume. Carl Heymanns Verlag KG, Luxemburger Strasse 449, D 50939 Cologne Germany. **Tel** 011 49 221 460100, telex 8 881 888.

HU/0524-899X
ANNALES UNIVERSITATIS SCIENTIARUM BUDAPESTINENSIS DE ROLANDO EOTVOS NOMINATAE. SECTIO IURIDICA. [Ann. Univ. Sci. Budap. Rolando Eotvos nom. Sect. iurid.]. Vol. 1 (1959)-. English (French, German and Russian). an. $30.00. Eotvos Lorand Tudomanyegyetem, Bolcseszettudomanyi Kar, Pesti BUL, H-1052 Budapest Hungary. **Tel** 36 11 180 966.
Ind/Abst Am. Hist. Life (1979-); Index Foreign Leg. Per.

IT
ANNALI DEL SEMINARIO GIURIDICO. (19??)-. Italian. ir. L150000 (Volume 42). Palumbo G B & C Spa, Via Ricasoli N 59, 90139 Palermo Italy. **Tel** 011 39 91 588850, 011 39 91 334961.

IT
ANNALI DELLA FACOLTA DI GIURISPRUDENZA DI GENOVA. (19??)-. Italian. Twice a year. Giuffre Editore SPA, Via Busto Arsizio 40, 20151 Milan Italy. **Tel** 011 398 2 38089200. **ED** Enrico Zanelli.
Desc: Reports on the scientific work of lecturers and researchers in the various law institutes. Also provides an up-to-date overview of significant themes whose many sides receive scientific treatment.

FR/0570-1953
ANNEE CANONIQUE, L'. **Added/Corp** Societe Internationale de Droit Canonique et de Legislations Religieuses Comparees. Vol. 1 (1952)-. French (English, Italian and Spanish). an. 350.00F. Letouzey et Ane, 87

Law

Boulevard Raspail, 75006 Paris France. **Tel** 011 33 1 45488014.
Ind/Abst Bibliogr. Mission.

BE/0066-2461
ANNUAIRE ADMINISTRATIF ET JUDICIAIRE DE BELGIQUE. ADMINISTRATIEF EN GERECHTELIJK JAARBOEK VOOR BELGIE. See Public Administration.

CN/1180-9434
ANNUAIRE DE JURISPRUDENCE ET DE DOCTRINE DU QUEBEC. [Annu. jurisprud. doctrin. Que.]. **Added/Corp** Societe Quebecoise d'Information Juridique. (1989)-. French. Societe Quebecoise d'Information Juridique, 10 rue St Jacques Bureau 101, Montreal Quebec H2Y 1L3 Canada. **Tel** (514)842-8745, FAX (514)844-8984. **DD** 348.714/046. **Continues** Annuaire de Jurisprudence du Quebec., 0066-2496.

FR
ANNUAIRE LP. (19??)-. French. an (May). 1030.00F. Editions de Sante, 5 rue Las Cases, 75007 Paris, France. **Tel** 011 33 1 45519494. **LC** KJV5377.A15; A56. **DD** 344.44/0423; 344.404423.

FR
ANNUAIRE LP CEE. French. an. Editions de Sante, 5 rue Las Cases, 75007 Paris, France. **Tel** 011 33 1 45519494.

FR
ANNUAIRE STATISTIQUE DE LA JUSTICE. See Law-Abstracting, Bibliographies and Statistics.

CN/0316-6120
ANNUAIRE TELEPHONIQUE JUDICIAIRE DU QUEBEC. (ANNUAIRE TELEPHONIQUE JUDICIAIRE DU QUEBEC. THE QUEBEC LEGAL TELEPHONE DIRECTORY.). **VFOAT** Quebec Legal Telephone Directory.; Annuaire Telephonique Judiciaire.; Legal Telephone Directory. 23rd Edition (1967/68)-. Directory. French (English and French). Twice a year (Jan., Aug.). 35.00Can$. Wilson & Lafleur Ltd., 40 Rue Notre Dame East, Montreal, Quebec H2Y 1B9 Canada. **Tel** (514)875-6326, FAX (514)875-8356. **DD** 340/.025/714. **Ad Acc**. **Circ**: 10,000. **Continues** Annuaire Telephonique Judiciaire de la Province de Quebec, 0316-6139.
Desc: Complete legal telephone directory with business telephone number and full address in Quebec (lawyers, notaries, etc).

US/1052-8350
ANNUAL COMPUTER LAW INSTITUTE. (ANNUAL COMPUTER LAW INSTITUTE : [COURSE HANDBOOK].). [Annu. Comput. Law Inst.]. **Added/Corp** Practising Law Institute. **VFOAT** Computer Law Institute. 9th (1987)-. English. an (Nov.). $80.00. Practising Law Institute, 810 Seventh Avenue, New York NY 10019-5818. **Tel** (212)765-5700, FAX (212)581-4670 general correspondence, (212)265-4742 orders and billing inquiries. **LC** KF390.5.C6; C645. **DD** 346.
Continues Computer Law Institute, 0884-1578.
Desc: Current trends in computer law.

US/0747-8135
ANNUAL CONVENTION REFERENCE MATERIALS. (ANNUAL CONVENTION REFERENCE MATERIALS / THE ASSOCIATION OF TRIAL LAWYERS OF AMERICA.). [Annu. Conv. ref. mater.]. **Main/Corp** Association of Trial Lawyers of America. Convention. **VFOAT** Reference Materials. English. an. The Association of Trial Lawyers of America, 1050 31st Street NW, Washington DC 20007. **LC** KF8915.A2; A87. **DD** 349.73; 347.3.

US/0277-0520
ANNUAL DIRECTORY / HAWAII STATE BAR ASSOCIATION. Main/Corp Hawaii State Bar Association. Directory. English. an. Free to Hawaii members of State Bar Association; $15.00 North America; $18.00 other. Crossroads Press Inc., PO Box 833, Honolulu HI 96808. **Tel** (808)521-0021. **LC** KF192.H3; B37. **DD** 349.969/025; 349.690025. **Ad Acc**. **Circ**: 3,600. **Continues** Bar Association of Hawaii. Annual Directory.

US/0273-7000
ANNUAL ENERGY LITIGATION INSTITUTE : EFFECTIVE STRATEGIES & TECHNIQUES. [Annu. Energy Litig. Inst. Eff. Strategies & tech.]. **Main/Conf** Energy Litigation Institute. **VAT** Annual Energy Litigation Institute. Effective Strategies and Techniques. (19??)-. English. an. Prentice-Hall Law and Business, 270 Sylvan Avenue, Englewood Cliffs NJ 07632. **Tel** (800)223-0231, (201)894-8538, FAX (201)894-8666. **LC** KF1860.Z9; E54. **DD** 346.7304/679/0269.

US/0731-4493
ANNUAL FALL MEETING / SECTION OF LITIGATION, AMERICAN BAR ASSOCIATION. Main/Corp American Bar Association. Section of Litigation. Fall Meeting. (19??)-. English. an. $35.00. American Bar Association, 750 North Lake Shore Drive, Chicago IL 60611. **Tel** (312)988-5522, (312)988-5241, FAX (312)988-5528, telex 270593. **LC** KF8915.A2; A47. **DD** 347.74/7; 347.3077.

US/0147-1309
ANNUAL IMMIGRATION AND NATURALIZATION INSTITUTE. (ANNUAL IMMIGRATION AND NATURALIZATION INSTITUTE. PROGRAM.). **Main/Corp** Immigration and Naturalization Institute. English. an. Practising Law Institute, 810 Seventh Avenue, New York NY 10019-5818. **Tel** (212)765-5700, FAX (212)581-4670 general correspondence, (212)265-4742 orders and billing inquiries. **LC** KF4819.3; .I46. **DD** 342/.73/082.

US
ANNUAL IMMIGRATION AND NATURALIZATION INSTITUTE. PROCEEDINGS. Main/Corp Immigration and Naturalization Institute. **Added/Corp** Practising Law Institute. (19??)-. English. an. Practising Law Institute, 810 Seventh Avenue, New York NY 10019-5818. **Tel** (212)765-5700, FAX (212)581-4670 general correspondence, (212)265-4742 orders and billing inquiries. **LC** KF4819.A2; I426. **DD** 342/.73/082.

US/0273-5253
ANNUAL INSTITUTE ON MINERAL LAW. (ANNUAL INSTITUTE ON MINERAL LAW. [PROCEEDINGS].). [Annu. Inst. Miner. Law].
Added/Corp Louisiana State University and Agricultural and Mechanical College. Law School. Louisiana State University and Agricultural and Mechanical College. General Extension Division. Louisiana State University (Baton Rouge, La.). Law School. Louisiana State University (Baton Rouge, La.). General Extension Division. Louisiana State University (Baton Rouge, La.). Division of Continuing Education. Louisiana State University (Baton Rouge, La.). Institute of Continuing Legal Education. Louisiana State University System. Institute of Continuing Legal Education. Paul M. Hebert Law Center. Institute of Continuing Legal Education. (1956)-. English. ir. Louisiana State University / Continuing Legal Education, Room 275/Old Law Building, Baton Rouge LA 70803. **Tel** (504)388-5837. **LC** KF1849.A2; I57. **DD** 346.7304/6823; 347.30646823.
Continues Institute on Mineral Law. Proceedings of the Annual Institute on Mineral Law, 0076-1087.
Ind/Abst Index Leg. Period. (?-?); Leg. Resour. Index.

US
ANNUAL INSTITUTE ON SECURITIES REGULATION. Main/Corp Institute on Securities Regulation. 1st- 1970-. Periodical. English. an. Practising Law Institute, 810 Seventh Avenue, New York NY 10019-5818. **Tel** (212)765-5700, FAX (212)581-4670 general correspondence, (212)265-4742 orders and billing inquiries. **LC** KF1440; .I532. **DD** 346.73/0666.
Desc: Deals with all areas of securities regulation law.
Ind/Abst Bus. Index (1985-); Gen. BusinessFile (1985-); Index Leg. Period.; Leg. Resour. Index; LegalTrac; Trade Ind. Index.

US
ANNUAL LAW SCHOOL SUMMER SCHOOL PROGRAMS AT HOME AND ABROAD. English. an. $27.50. Graduate Group, 86 Norwood Road, West Hartford CT 06117-2236. **Tel** (203)232-3100. **ED** Mara Whitman. **Bk Rev**.
Desc: Information on summer programs offered at law schools around the world.

UK
ANNUAL OF INDUSTRIAL PROPERTY LAW. English. an. $40.00. **DD** 346.048.
Ind/Abst Leg. Resour. Index; LegalTrac.

AT/0155-025X
ANNUAL REPORT / ADMINISTRATIVE REVIEW COUNCIL. Main/Corp Administrative Review Council (Australia). **VFOAT** Administrative Review Council ... Annual Report. (1977)-. Government Publication. English. an. 18.00Aus$. Australian Government Publishing Service, GPO Box 84, Canberra ACT 2601 Australia. **Tel** 011 61 6 2954411, FAX 011 61 6 2954455. **DD** 342.94/066; 349.40266.

CN
ANNUAL REPORT / ALBERTA LAW REFORM INSTITUTE. Main/Corp Alberta Law Reform Institute. (1988/89)-. English. an. Alberta Law Reform Institute, 402 Law Centre, University of Alberta, Edmonton Alberta T6G 2H5 Canada. **Tel** (403)492-5291, (403)492-3374, FAX (403)492-1790. **LC** KEA149.I56; A163. **DD** 340/.3/097123. **Circ**: 2,000 (ctrl). **Continues** Annual Report / University of Alberta. Institute of Law Research and Reform.

US
ANNUAL REPORT / AMERICAN ARBITRATION ASSOCIATION. Main/Corp American Arbitration Association. (1973)-. English. ir. $200.00 Universities & Libraries; $250.00 Law Libraries; $100.00 individuals schools & other libraries (Comes with Arbitration Journal & Arbitration Times Membership). American Arbitration Association, 140 West 51st Street, New York NY 10020. **Tel** (212)484-4011, (212)484-4014, FAX (212)765-4874, telex 12463. **LC** KF9086; .A53. **DD** 347.73/9; 347.3079.

CN
ANNUAL REPORT - CANADIAN BAR ASSOCIATION. ALBERTA BRANCH. Main/Corp Canadian Bar Association. Alberta Branch. (1981/82)-. English. an. Canadian Bar Association / Alberta Branch, 1830 540 5th Avenue Southwest, Calgary Alberta T2P 0M2 Canada. **Tel** (403)263-3707. **LC** KE366.7.A4; A53. **DD** 340/.06/07123.

AT
ANNUAL REPORT / DEPARTMENT OF JUSTICE, QUEENSLAND GOVERNMENT. Main/Corp Queensland. Dept. of Justice. (19??)-. Government Publication. English. an. Queensland Department of Justice, Brisbane Queensland Australia. **DD** 354.943065/06.

US/0096-8854
ANNUAL REPORT / FEDERAL JUDICIAL CENTER. Main/Corp Federal Judicial Center. English. an. Federal Judicial Center, Dolly Madison House, 1520 H Street NW, Washington DC 20005. **Tel** (202)633-6347. **LC** KF8719; .A34. **DD** 347.73/2. available on microfiche (Vols. for (1982-) distributed to depository libraries).

US
ANNUAL REPORT / ILLINOIS GUARDIANSHIP AND ADVOCACY COMMISSION. Ceased. Main/Corp Illinois Guardianship and Advocacy Commission. (1980)-(19??). English. an. Office of Public Information / Chicago, 123 West Madison/Suite 1700, Chicago IL 60602. **LC** KFI1565; .A853. **DD** 344.773/044; 347.730444.

US/0093-2396
ANNUAL REPORT - INTERIM COMPLIANCE PANEL (WASHINGTON). (ANNUAL REPORT TO THE CONGRESS OF THE UNITED STATES.). **Main/Corp** United States. Interim Compliance Panel. 1970-. English. an. Interim Compliance Panel, Room 800, 1730 K Street NW, Washington DC 20006. **LC** KF3574.M53; A84. **DD** 614.8/52.

CN/0706-3806
ANNUAL REPORT - JUSTICE DEVELOPMENT COMMISSION (BRITISH COLUMBIA). Main/Corp British Columbia. Justice Development Commission. 1977/78-. English. an. Justice Development Commission, 1016 Langley Street, Victoria BC V8W 1V8 Canada. **LC** KEB532.A72; J77. **DD** 354/.711/088.

CN/0709-9983
ANNUAL REPORT - JUSTICE INSTITUTE OF BRITISH COLUMBIA. Main/Corp Justice Institute of British Columbia. 1978/79-. English. an. Justice Institute of British Columbia, 4180 West 4th Avenue, Vancouver British Columbia VcR 4J5 Canada. **DD** 874/.013.

UK
ANNUAL REPORT / JUSTICE SOCIETY. Main/Corp Justice (Society). 1st (1958)-. English. an. £2.00. Justice, British Sect Intl Com Jurists, 95A Chancery Lane, London WC2A 1DT England. **Tel** 011 44 71 4056018. **LC** KD456.J87; J87. **DD** 340/.1. **Pr Rev**.
Desc: Annual Report of the work of the society.

AT
ANNUAL REPORT / LAW LIBRARY, SUPREME COURT OF WESTERN AUSTRALIA. See Library and Information Sciences.

CN/0382-1463
ANNUAL REPORT - LAW REFORM COMMISSION OF CANADA. Main/Corp Law Reform Commission of Canada. **VFOAT** Rapport Annuel. 1st- 1971/72-. English (French). an. Law Reform Commission of Canada, 130 Albert Street/7th Floor, Ottawa Ontario K1A 0L6 Canada.

US/0882-9845
ANNUAL REPORT - LOUISIANA STATE BAR ASSOCIATION. (ANNUAL REPORT.). **Main/Corp** Louisiana State Bar Association. (19??)-. English. an. Louisiana State Bar Association, 210 Okeefe Avenue, Suite 600, New Orleans LA 70112. **Tel** (504)522-9172. **LC** KF332.L8; .L68135.

US/0362-1383
ANNUAL REPORT - MASSACHUSETTS ADVOCACY CENTER. Main/Corp Massachusetts Advocacy Center. 1st- 1974-. English. an. Massachusetts Advocacy Center, 2 Park Square, Boston MA. **LC** KFM2840; .M38. **DD** 353.9/744.

US/0360-4659
ANNUAL REPORT OF THE JUDICIAL COUNCIL OF NEW MEXICO. **Main/Corp** New Mexico. Judicial Council. (19??)-. English. an. University of New Mexico School of Law, 1117 Stanford NE, Albuquerque NM 87131. **Tel** (505)277-4820, 277-8659. **LC** KFN4108; .A834. **DD** 347/.789.

CN/0381-2510
ANNUAL REPORT OF THE LAW REFORM COMMISSION OF BRITISH COLUMBIA. **Main/Corp** Law Reform Commission of British Columbia. (1970)-. English. an. Free. Law Reform Commission of British Columbia, 865 Hornsby, Suite 3601, Vancouver British Columbia V6Z 2H4 Canada. **Tel** (604)660-2366. **DD** 340/.3/09711.

CN/0825-7361
ANNUAL REPORT OF THE PRIVACY COMMISSIONER. (ANNUAL REPORT / PRIVACY COMMISSIONER.). [Annu. rep. Priv. Comm.]. **Main/Corp** Canada. Privacy Commissioner of Canada. **VFOAT** Rapport Annuel du Commissaire a la Protection de la Vie Privee. (1983/1984)-. English (French). an. Free. Privacy Commissioner of Canada, 112 Kent Street/3rd Floor, Ottawa Ontario K1A 1H3 Canada. **Tel** (613)995-2410, FAX (613)995-1510. **ED** Sally Jackson. **LC** JC596.2.C2; C36a. **DD** 354.710081/1/06. **Circ:** 7,000. ***Continues** Canadian Human Rights Commissioner. Annual Report of the Privacy Commissioner, 0825-7361.*
Desc: Annual report of the Federal Privacy Ombudsman, containing commentary on data protection issues during the year. Highlights of the office's operations including selected case reports, data matching reviews, compliance audits, and statistics on the year's caseload and inquiries.

CN/0318-5044
ANNUAL REPORT - OFFICE OF THE FARMERS' ADVOCATE (ALBERTA). **Main/Corp** Alberta. Office of the Farmers' Advocate. (1???)-. English. an. Office of the Farmers Advocate, 1101 Agriculture Building, 9718-107 Street, Edmonton Alberta Canada. **DD** 343/.7123/0760269.

US
ANNUAL REPORT ON HAZARDOUS MATERIALS TRANSPORTATION : HAZARDOUS MATERIALS TRANSPORTATION ACT (TITLE I, PUBLIC LAW 93-633). **Main/Corp** United States. Materials Transportation Bureau. 10th (calendar year 1979)-. English. an. US Department of Transportation / Research and Special Programs Administration, Washington DC 20590. available on microfiche. ***Continues** United States. Dept. of Transportation. Annual Report on Hazardous Materials Transportation, 0277-3309.*

US/0739-8247
ANNUAL REPORT ON THE WORK OF THE GEORGIA COURTS. **Main/Corp** Georgia. Administrative Office of the Courts. July 1, 1981 to June 30, 1982-. English. an. Georgia Justice Center, Suite 500, 84 Peachtree Street, Atlanta GA 30303. **LC** KFG508 .A813. **DD** 353.9758008/8. ***Continues** Georgia. Administrative Office of the Courts. Annual Report, 0363-9320.*

CN/0709-4949
ANNUAL REPORT / PUBLIC AND PRIVATE RIGHTS BOARD. [Annu. rep. - Public Priv. Rights Board]. **Main/Corp** Saskatchewan. Public and Private Rights Board. English. an. Public and Private Rights Board, Room 501/Shell Building, 2240 Albert Street, Regina Saskatchewan S4P 3V7 Canada. **LC** KES495.A72; R543. **DD** 354.71240082/326.

IE
ANNUAL REPORT - RESTRICTIVE PRACTICES COMMISSION. (IRELAND). **Main/Corp** Ireland (Eire). Restrictive Practices Commission. (19??)-. English. **LC** KDK552; .A85. **DD** 354/.417/00827.

UK/0080-7915
ANNUAL REPORT / SCOTTISH LAW COMMISSION. **Main/Corp** Scottish Law Commission. 1st (1965/1966)-. English. an. £6.00. Her Majesty's Stationery Office, 51 Nine Elms Lane, London SW8 5DR England. **Tel** 011 44 71 873 8459, 011 44 71 873 8499, FAX 011 44 71 873 8499, 011 44 71 873 8456, telex 297138. **(Subscription address:** PO Box 276, Public Centre, London SW8 5DT England**)** **LC** KDC320; .A87. **DD** 349.411/06; 344.11006. **[CCC].**

CE
ANNUAL REPORT / THE LAW COMMISSION, SRI LANKA. **Main/Corp** Sri Lanka. Niti Komisan Departamentuva. English. an. 1.85. Government Publications Bureau, PO Box 500, Colombo Sri Lanka. **DD** 340/.3/095493.

UK
ANNUAL REPORT / THE MEDICAL AND DENTAL DEFENCE UNION OF SCOTLAND LIMITED. **See** Medical Science and Technology.

US/0561-1784
ANNUAL REPORT - THE SOUTHWESTERN LEGAL FOUNDATION. **Main/Corp** Southwestern Legal Foundation. (1958)-. English. an. Free. Southwestern Legal Foundation, PO Box 830707, University of Texas in Dallas, Richardson TX 75080. **Tel** (214)690-2370, telex 284522 SWLF UR. **ED** Janice R. Moss. **Circ:** 2,000 (ctrl).
Desc: Describes activities and programs sponsored by one of foundation's six centers.

UK
ANNUAL REPORT / UNIVERSITY OF LONDON, INSTITUTE OF ADVANCED LEGAL STUDIES. **Main/Corp** University of London. Institute of Advanced Legal Studies. (1947/1948)-. Corporate Report. English. an. Free. Institute of Advanced Legal Studies, University of London, Charles Clore House, 17 Russell Square, London WC1B 5DR United Kingdom. **Tel** 011 44 71 637 1731, FAX 011 44 71 436 8824, telex 269 400 SH UL. **LC** KD456.I6; U55. **DD** 340/.071/1421. **Circ:** 400 (ctrl).

US
ANNUAL REPORTS. **Main/Corp** American Law Institute-American Bar Association Committee on Continuing Professional Education. **VFOAT** ALI-ABA ... Annual Report. (1991)-. Periodical. English. ALI-ABA, 4025 Chestnut Street, Philadelphia PA 19104. ***Continues** Annual Report of the Executive Director.*

US/0739-6627
ANNUAL REPORTS - OREGON STATE BAR. (ANNUAL REPORTS / OREGON STATE BAR.). **Main/Corp** Oregon State Bar. **Added/Corp** Oregon State Bar. Annual Reports in Conjunction with the ... Meeting ... . **VFOAT** Oregon State Bar Annual Reports; Annual Reports for the Oregon State Bar in Conjunction with its ... Meeting ...; Annual Reports in Conjunction with the ... Meeting ... . (1979)-. English. an. Oregon State Bar, 5200 Southwest Meadows Road, Lake Oswego OR 97035. **Tel** (503)620-0222 ext 340, (800)452-8260, FAX (503)684-1366. **LC** KF332.O7; O7732. **DD** 340/.06/0795. ***Continues** Oregon State Bar. Committee Reports ... Annual Meeting.*

US/0738-0798
ANNUAL REVIEW, NORTH CAROLINA. **VFOAT** Annual Review, N.C. 3rd (1982)-. English. an. Wake Forest-Cle, PO Box 7206 Reynolds Station, Winston Salem NC 27109-7206. **LC** KFN7481; .A54. **DD** 349.756; 347.56. ***Continues** Annual Review Institute, North Carolina, 0277-2345.*

IE/0791-1084
ANNUAL REVIEW OF IRISH LAW. [Annu. rev. Ir. law]. (1987)-. English. an. $125.00; 85.00p. Round Hall Press, Kill Lane, Blackrock County, Dublin Ireland. **Tel** 011 353 1 2892922, FAX 011 353 1 2893072. **ED** R. Byrne and W. Binchy.

US/0364-3417
ANNUAL REVIEW OF POPULATION LAW. **Added/Corp** United Nations Fund for Population Activities. International Advisory Committee on Population and Law. United Nations Population Fund. Harvard Law School. Library. (1974)-. English. an. $45.00. Annual Review Population Law, Harvard University, ILS-458, Cambridge MA 02138. **Tel** (617) 495-9623, FAX (617) 495-4449. **LC** K2000.A53; A5. **DD** 344.04/8. **NLM** WA 33.1 A615. ctrl circ.

US/0160-1555
ANNUAL SECURITIES SEMINAR COURSE HANDBOOK. **Main/Corp** Institute of Continuing Legal Education, Ann Arbor, Mich. English. an. University of Michigan / Institute of Continuing Legal Education, 1020 Greene Street, Ann Arbor MI 48109-1444. **Tel** (313)764-0533, FAX (313)763-2412. **LC** KFM4414.A1; I5. **DD** 346/.774/0666.

US/0066-4413
ANNUAL SURVEY OF AMERICAN LAW. [Annu. surv. Am. law]. **Added/Corp** New York University. School of Law. (1942)-. English. Four times a year. New York University School of Law, 110 West Third Street, New York NY 10012. **Tel** (212)998-6540, (212)998-6560, FAX (212)995-4032. **ED** Joseph Profaci. **LC** KF178; .A5. **DD** 349/.73; 347.3. **Ad Acc. Circ:** 2,000. available on an online database. Documents available from UMI Article Clearinghouse.
Desc: Provides a perceptive analytic account of the year's legal development, covering legal trends and important recent decisions and legislation.
Ind/Abst Curr. Law Index (1980-); Expand. Acad. Index (1984-); Index Leg. Period.; Leg. Resour. Index (1980-); LegalTrac (1980-); Newsp. Period. Abstr. (1988-); Trade Ind. Index.

AT/0727-4076
ANNUAL SURVEY OF AUSTRALIAN LAW, AN. [Annu. surv. Aust. law]. (1981)-. English. an. 69.50Aus$ (renewals). University of Adelaide / Law School, Helen Creeper, Adelaide SA 5005 Australia. **Tel** 011 61 8 3034440. **LC** K1; .N4. **DD** 349.94; 349.4. ***Continues** Annual Survey of Law, 0314-5530.*
Desc: Presents a conspectus of important developments in all major areas of Australian law.
Ind/Abst Aust. Leg. Mon. Dig.; Index Leg. Period.; Leg. Resour. Index; LegalTrac (1988-).

US/0160-5658
ANNUAL SURVEY OF COLORADO LAW. [Annu. surv. Colo. law]. English. an. $48.00. Continuing Legal Education in Colorado, 600 17th Street/Suite 520, South Denver CO 80202. **Tel** (303)753-3351. **LC** KFC1870; .A55. **DD** 340/.09788. available on an online database.
Ind/Abst Curr. Law Index (1984-); Leg. Resour. Index (1984-); LegalTrac (1983-).

II/0570-2666
ANNUAL SURVEY OF INDIAN LAW. **Added/Corp** Indian Law Institute. (19??)-. English. an. Rs600.00. Indian Law Institute, Bhagwandass Road, New Delhi India. **Tel** 011 91 11 389429 or 389849. **ED** Alice Jacob. **Circ:** 1,000 (ctrl).
Desc: Contains a sufficient analysis of major developments and decisions of the Supreme Court and High Courts each year in the principal fields of Indian law.

SA/0376-4605
ANNUAL SURVEY OF SOUTH AFRICAN LAW. **Added/Corp** University of the Witwatersrand. Faculty of Law. **VFOAT** Annual Survey of S.A. Law; Annual Survey of SA Law. (1947)-. English. an. International Specialized Book Services, 5602 NE Hassalo Street, Portland OR 97213. **Tel** (800)547-7734.

IT
ANNUARIO ... DELLE AUTONOMIE LOCALI. Italian. an. Edizioni Autonomie Locali, Via Barnaba Oriani 16, 00197 Rome Italy. **Tel** 011 39 6 8078893. **LC** K1; .N55. **DD** 349.45.

UK/0262-3234
ANTHONY & BERRYMAN'S MAGISTRATES' COURT GUIDE. [Anthony Berryman's magistr. court guide]. **VFOAT** Magistrates Court Guide (1974). (1974)-. English. an. £18.95. Butterworth & Co. Ltd. / Kent, England, Borough Green, Sevenoaks Kent TN15 8PH England. **Tel** 011 44 732-884567, FAX 011 44 732-885996. **ED** Paul Carr. **DD** 344.205120519. ***Continues** Magistrates' Court Guide (1964).*
Desc: Provides a complete and up-to-date source of information in all aspects of the activities of magistrates' courts.

PN/0553-0814
ANUARIO DE DERECHO (PANAMA : 1981). (ANUARIO DE DERECHO / UNIVERSIDAD DE PANAMA, FACULTAD DE DERECHO Y CIENCIAS POLITICAS, CENTRO DE INVESTIGACION JURIDICA.). **Added/Corp** Universidad de Panama. Centro de Investigacion Juridica. Universidad de Panama. Facultad de Derecho y Ciencias Politicas. Vol. 11 (1981)-. Spanish. an. $15.00 US; $10.00 others. Universidad de Panama / Juridica, Centro Investigacion Juridica, Panama Republic of Panama. **Tel** 11 507 239279, 011 507 236888. **LC** K16; .A5. ***Continues** Revista Juridica Panamena.*
Ind/Abst Index Foreign Leg. Per.

SP/0304-4319
ANUARIO DE HISTORIA DEL DERECHO ESPANOL. [Anu. hist. derecho esp.]. **Added/Corp** Centro de Estudios Historicos (Spain) Instituto Francisco de Vitoria. Instituto Nacional de Estudios Juridicos (Spain). Vol. 1 (1924)-. Spanish. an. 6420ptas Spain; 6500ptas others. Ministerio de Justicia Centro, Publicaciones, Gran Via 76 8, 28013 Madrid Spain. **Tel** 011 34 1 5475422. **DD** 349.46/09; 344.6009. **Circ:** 500 (ctrl).
Ind/Abst Am. Hist. Life (1961-1974).

UY
ANUARIO DEL MINISTERIO DE JUSTICIA. Vol. 1 (1979)-. Spanish. an. Ministerio de Justicia, Centro de Publicaciones, Gran via 76-8, 28013 Madrid Spain. **Tel** 011 34 1 5475422. **LC** K1; .N9156. **DD** 348.895/025; 348.950825.

MX/0185-3295
ANUARIO JURIDICO. **Added/Corp** Universidad Nacional Autonoma de Mexico. Instituto de Investigaciones Juridicas. Vol. 1 (1974)-. Spanish. an. $25.00. UNAM - Institute of Investigaciones Juridicas, Universidad Nacional Autonoma de Mexico, Ciudad Universitaria, Mario de la Cueva, 04510 Mexico DF Mexico. **Tel** 011 52 5 622-7461, 616-1784, FAX 011 52 5 665-2193. **ED** Eugenio Hurtado Marquez. **LC** K1; .N92. **Bk Rev. Ad Acc. Pr Rev. Circ:** 1,000 (ctrl).
Desc: A reprint and commentary on essays of great relevance for legal studies and Mexican law. Represents a panorama of the judicial bibliography published throughout one year.

II
ANUDANOM KI MANGEM (INDIA. MINISTRY OF LAW AND JUSTICE).
Main/Corp India (Republic). Ministry of Law and Justice. **VFOAT** Demands for Grants. (19??)-. Multiple languages (Hindi and English). Government of India Press Ministry of Law and Justice, Minto Road, New Delhi India. **DD** 354/.54/065. ***Continues*** *India (Republic). Ministry of Law. Anuanom ki Mangem.*

GW
ANWALTSBLATT.
Periodical. German. Deutscher Anwaltverein, Adenauerallee 106, 5300 Bonn 1 Germany. **LC** K1; .N95. **DD** 340/.0943.

US
APLA NEWSLETTER.
Added/Corp Association for Political and Legal Anthropology. American Anthropological Association. **VAT** Association for Political and Legal Anthropology Newsletter. (198?)-. Newsletter. English. ir. $10.00. American Anthropological Association, 4350 North Fairfax Dr, Suite 640, Arlington VA 22203. **Tel** (703)528-1902 ext. 3031, FAX (703)528-3546. ***Continues*** *Newsletter (Association for Political and Legal Anthropology).*

IT
APOLLINARIS; COMMENTARIUS IURIDICO-CANONICUS.
Added/Corp Pontificia Universita Lateranense. Pontificium Institutum Utriusque Iuris. Vol. 1 (1928)-. Periodical. Latin (English, French, Italian and Spanish). Four times a year. L75000 Italy; L100000 others. Pontificia Universita Lateranense, Piazza S Giovanni Laterano 4, 00120 Citta del Vaticano. **Tel** 011 39 6 69886401, FAX 011 39 6 69886103. Index available. **Bk Rev**.
Ind/Abst Abr. Cathol. Period. Lit. Index; Cathol. Period. Lit. Index.

US/1056-9111
APPELBAUM/GRISSO REPORT ON LAW AND MENTAL HEALTH, THE.
Ceased. **VFOAT** Appelbaum Grisso Report on Law and Mental Health. (1992)-Ceased (1992). Periodical. English. bm. Williams & Wilkins Company, 428 East Preston Street, Baltimore MD 21202-3993. **Tel** (410)528-4000, (800)638-6423, FAX (410)528-8596, telex 87669. Documents available from Quick Copies.

IT
APPENDICE NUOVISSIMO DIGESTO.
Utet Ed Giuridica, Via Corte d'Appello 6, 10122 Turin Italy. **Tel** 011 39 11 530406.

US
APPLICANTS GUIDE, JUVENILE JUSTICE PROGRAMS ..., VICTIMS OF CRIME ACT-VICTIM ASSISTANCE PROGRAM.
Main/Corp New Jersey. State Law Enforcement Planning Agency. **VFOAT** Applicants Guide; Juvenile Justice Programs; Juvenile Justice Plan for New Jersey. (1990)-. English. State Law Enforcement Planning Agency / New Jersey, CN 083, Trenton NJ 08625. ***Continues*** *New Jersey. State Law Enforcement Planning Agency. Juvenile Justice Plan for New Jersey, Applicants Guide.*

UK/0267-6621
APPLIED COMPUTER AND COMMUNICATIONS LAW.
Title Change. **Added/Corp** Legal Studies and Services Limited. **VFOAT** Computer and Communications Law. (198?)-(1992). Periodical. English. mo. Monitor Press, Rectory Road, Great Waldingfield, Sudbury Suffolk CO10 0TL United Kingdom. **Tel** 011 44 787 378607. **LC** KD667.C65; A66. **DD** 343.41/078004; 344.10378004. ***Absorbed*** *Computer Law (Sudbury, Suffolk, England).* ***Continued by*** *IT Law Today.*

UK/0268-0556
ARAB LAW QUARTERLY.
[Arab law q.]. **Added/Corp** Society of Arab Comparative and International Law. Vol. 1, Pt. 1 (Nov. 1985)-. Periodical. English. qt. $606.00. Graham & Trotman Ltd, Sterling House, 66 Wilson Road, London SW1V 1DE England. **Tel** 44 71 8211123. **ED** W.M. Ballantyne and Mark Hoyle. **LC** K1; .R24. **DD** 340.5/9/05. **CODEN** ALQUEJ. **Pr Rev. Acid Free.**
Desc: Covers all aspects of Arab laws, both Shari's and secular. It provides an important forum of authoritative articles on the laws and legal developments throughout the twenty countries of the Arab world, and also includes notes on recent legislation and case law, guidelines on future changes, and reviews of the latest literature.
Ind/Abst Index Foreign Leg. Per.; Middle East J.

NE
ARBEIDSRECHT.
See Economics-Labor.

US/0733-6160
ARBITRATION & THE LAW.
(ARBITRATION & THE LAW : AAA GENERAL COUNSEL'S ANNUAL REPORT.). [Arbitrat. law]. **Main/Corp** American Arbitration Association. Office of the General Counsel. **Added/Corp** American Arbitration Association. Office of the General Counsel. Annual report. **VFOAT** Arbitration and the Law. (1981)-. English. an. $50.00. American Arbitration Association, 140 West 51st Street, New York NY 10020. **Tel** (212)484-4011, (212)484-4014, FAX (212)765-4874, telex 12463. **ED** Linda M Miller. **LC** KF9085.A15; A5. **DD** 347.73/9; 347.3079. Index available. **Circ:** 3,800.
Desc: Highlights the most significant legal developments in dispute resolution during the year.

US/0003-7893
ARBITRATION JOURNAL, THE.
Title Change. [Arbitrat. j.]. **Added/Corp** American Arbitration Association. New York Chamber of Commerce. Inter-American Commercial Arbitration Commission. (Jan. 1937)-(Sept. 1993). Periodical. English. qt. American Arbitration Association, 140 West 51st Street, New York NY 10020. **Tel** (212)484-4011, (212)484-4014, FAX (212)765-4874, telex 12463. **ED** Linda Miller. **LC** K1; .R25. **DD** 380.12605. Index available. **Bk Rev. Pr Rev. Circ:** 8,500 (ctrl). available on microfilm and microfiche from University Microfilms International (UMI). Documents available from The Genuine Article, UMI Article Clearinghouse. ***Continued by*** *Dispute Resolution Journal, 1074-8105.*
Desc: Its in-depth articles by practitioners and scholars analyze the latest trends in labor-management relations, commercial dispute settlement, construction, accident claims and international arbitration. Regular features include book reviews, digests of key court decisions, a listing of recent Eastman Arbitration Library acquisitions, and an opinion page.
Ind/Abst ABI/INFORM Glob. Ed. (Dec. 1974-); ABI Inform Ondisc (Dec. 1974-); Acad. Search (July 1993-Sept. 1994); Am. Hist. Life (1969-1974); Bowne Dig. Corp. Sec. Lawyers (1969-1974); Bus. Index (1985-); Bus. Period. Index; Bus. Source (Jul. 1993-); Curr. Contents Soc. Behav. Sci.; Curr. Law Index (1980-); Gen. BusinessFile (1985-); Gen. Period. Index (1985-); Index Leg. Period.; INFO-SOUTH Abstr.; Int. Labour Doc.; Leg. Resour. Index (1980-); LegalTrac (1969-1974, 1980-); Mag. Search; Person. Manage. Abstr.; Res. Alert [Full Cov.]; Soc. Sci. Cit. Index [Full Cov.]; SportSearch; Trade Ind. Index (1981-?); Wilson Bus. Abstr.; Work Relat. Abstr.

UK/0003-7877
ARBITRATION (LONDON, ENGLAND).
(ARBITRATION : THE JOURNAL OF THE INSTITUTE OF ARBITRATORS.). **Added/Corp** Chartered Institute of Arbitrators (Great Britain) Institute of Arbitrators (Great Britain). Vol. 20, No. 3 (Sept. 1954)-. Periodical. English. qt. £67.00. Institute of Arbitrators, 24 Angel Gate 326 City Road, London EC1V 2RS England. **Tel** 011 44 71 837 4483. ***Continues*** *Arbitration Journal (London, England).*
Desc: Covers arbitration and award.

SZ/1013-7432
ARBITRATION MATERIALS.
Title Change. Vol. 1, No. 1 (Mar. 1989)-(January 1994). Periodical. English. qt. Werner Publishing Company Ltd., PO Box 5134, CH 1211 Geneva 11 Switzerland. **Tel** 011 41 22 3103422. ***Merged with*** *World Trade Materials* ***to form*** *World Trade and Arbitration Materials.*

US
ARBITRATION NEWSLETTER.
No. 71 (May 1, 1955)-. Newsletter. English. ir. Cornelius Printing Company, USWA Circulation Department, 2457 East Washington Street, Indianapolis IN 46201.

AT
ARBITRATION REPORTS.
Main/Corp Australia. Public Service Board. English.
Ind/Abst Aust. Leg. Mon. Dig.

US/8756-5455
ARBITRATION TIMES.
(ARBITRATION TIMES : NEWS AND VIEWS FROM THE AMERICAN ARBITRATION ASSOCIATION.). [Arbitr. times]. (Spring 1982)-. Periodical. English. qt. Free. American Arbitration Association, 140 West 51st Street, New York NY 10020. **Tel** (212)484-4011, (212)484-4014, FAX (212)765-4874, telex 12463. **ED** Betty Blaisdell Berry and Linda M Miller. **LC** HD5503; .A8163. **DD** 331.89/143/0973. **Circ:** 70,000 (ctrl). ***Continues*** *American Arbitration Association. News and Views, 0093-6979.*
Desc: Reports on AAA activities and other matters of interest to the community of dispute resolution professionals. Readers are kept abreast of current developments in the area, from the passage of new arbitration laws to announcements of new publications and videotapes. Included are sections on labor news, international court decisions, legislation, education and training, and people in the news, etc.
Ind/Abst Work Relat. Abstr.

AT/0729-7904
ARBITRATOR BARTON.
(ARBITRATOR / AU.). [ArbitratorBarton]. (1982)-. Periodical. English. Four times a year (Feb., May, Aug., Nov.). 20.00Aus$. Institute of Arbitrators of Australia, 1022 Williams Street, Melbourne, Vic 3000, Australia. **Tel** 011 61 03 614 3891, FAX 011 61 03 629 3753. **ED** H. C. Amrose. **DD** 331.891430994. Index available (Bound in May issue.). cum. index. **Ad Acc. Circ:** 2,000. ***Continues*** *Commercial Arbitrator, 0729-5359.*

GW/0003-9160
ARCHIV FUER KATHOLISCHES KIRCHENRECHT.
Added/Corp Katholischer Juristenverein. (1857)-. Periodical. German (Latin). ir. Price varies per volume. Verlag Kirchheim & Company GmbH, Postfach 2524, D 55015 Mainz Germany. **Tel** 011 49 6131 960700, FAX 011 49 6131 638843. **ED** W. Aymans. **DD** 262.9/05. Index available. cum. index. **Bk Rev. Circ:** 600.
Ind/Abst Bibliogr. Mission.; Canon Law Abstr.

GW/0001-2343
ARCHIV FUER RECHTS- UND SOZIALPHILOSOPHIE.
Added/Corp Internationale Vereinigung fuer Rechts- und Sozialphilosophie. **VFOAT** Archives de Philosophie du Droit et de Philosophie Sociale; Archives for Philosophy of Law and Social Philosophy; ARSP. Vol. 1 (Oct. 1907)-. Periodical. German (English, French and Spanish). qt. DM198.00. Franz Steiner Verlag GmbH, Postfach 101061, D 70009 Stuttgart Germany. **Tel** 011 49 0711 2582372, FAX 011 49 0711 2582290, telex 723636 daz d. **ED** Werner Maihofer. **[CCC]. Bk Rev. Ad Acc. Circ:** 800.
Desc: Articles and reviews dedicated to philosophy of law and social philosophy.
Ind/Abst Index Foreign Leg. Per.; Int. Bibliogr. Sociol.; Int. Polit. Sci. Abstr.; Philos. Index; Soc. Plann. Policy Dev. Abstr.; Sociol. Abstr. (?-?).

FR/0066-6564
ARCHIVES DE PHILOSOPHIE DU DROIT.
(19??)-. Monographic series. French. ir. Price varies per volume. Dalloz, 35 rue Tournefort, 75240 Paris Cedex 05 France. **Tel** 011 33 1 40515434 or 40515454, FAX 45 87 37 48, telex 206 446 F. **[CCC].**
Ind/Abst Index Foreign Leg. Per.; Int. Polit. Sci. Abstr.

IT/1120-687X
ARCHIVIO DELLA NUOVA PROCEDURA PENALE.
VFOAT ANPP; A.N.P.P. (1990)-. Periodical. Italian. bm. L100000 Italy; L150000 other Europe; L200000 other. Casa Editrice La Tribuna, Via Don Minzoni 51, 29100 Piacenza Italy. **Tel** 011 39 523 759015, 011 39 523 759020. **LC** KKH4601.3; .A73. **DD** 345.45/05; 344.5055.

IT
ARCHIVIO GIURIDICO.
Vol. 1 (Apr. 1868)-. Periodical. Italian. bm. L100000 (Italy); L120000 (other). Enrico Mucchi Editore SRL, Via Emilia Est 1527, 41100 Modena Italy. **Tel** 011 39 59 374094, FAX 059/374096. cum. index.
Ind/Abst Index Foreign Leg. Per.

IT
ARCHIVIO GIURIDICO DELLA CIRCOLAZIONE E DEI SINISTRI STRADALI.
Casa Editrice La Tribuna, Via Don Minzoni 51, 29100 Piacenza Italy. **Tel** 011 39 523 759015, 011 39 523 759020.

IT/0393-1374
ARCHIVIO GIURIDICO DELLE OPERE PUBBLICHE.
[Arch. giurid. opere pubbliche]. (1975)-. Periodical. Italian. sa. Promedi SRL, Via Nicotera 29, 00195 Rome Italy. **Tel** 011 39 6 3230100. **UDC** 34.

IT/0004-0304
ARCHIVIO PENALE.
[Arch. Penale]. (1945)-. Periodical. Italian. qt. L160000.00 (institutions), L120000.00 (individuals) Italy; L200000.00 other. Edizioni Scientifiche Italiane, Via Chiatamone 7, 80121 Naples Italy. **Tel** 011 39 81 7645768, 011 39 81 7645443, FAX 011 39 81 7646477. **UDC** 34. **CODEN** ARPE-B.

PL/0066-6882
ARCHIVUM IURIDICUM CRACOVIENSE.
(1968)-. Polish. an. Price varies. Polska Akademia Nauk, Rynek 9,, 50-106 Wroclaw, Poland. **Tel** 48-71-386-25, FAX 48-71-448-103, telex 0712771. **(Subscription address:** ARS Polona, PO Box 1001, Krakowskie Przedmiescie 7, 00-068 Warsaw, Poland) **ED** Franciszek Studnicki. **Circ:** 600.
Desc: Information on various aspects of law including civil, labor, international and constitutional.

CN/0712-1873
ARCHTYPE (TORONTO).
See Physically Impaired.

US/0004-1386
ARIZONA ADVOCATE.
Periodical. English. ir. University of Arizona College of Law, Tucson AZ 85721. **Tel** (602)621-5593.

US/1040-4090
ARIZONA ATTORNEY.
[Ariz. atty.]. Vol. 25, No. 1 (Sept. 1988)-. Periodical. English. mo (August and September are combined). 30.00. State Bar of Arizona, 363 North First Avenue, Phoenix AZ 85004. **Tel** (602)252-4804, FAX (602)271-4930. **ED** Patricia Gannon. **LC** K1; .R47. **DD** 340. **Bk Rev. Ad Acc. Circ:** 11,200 (ctrl). available on microfilm. ***Formed by the union of*** *Arizona Bar Journal, 0004-1424* ***and*** *Arizona Bar Briefs, 0745-4384.*
Desc: Scholarly legal magazine designed for attorneys in Arizona.
Ind/Abst Leg. Resour. Index; LegalTrac (1988-).

US/1049-9342
ARIZONA ENVIRONMENTAL LAW LETTER. [Ariz. environ. law lett.]. Vol. 1, No. 1 (June 1990)-. Periodical. English. mo. $137.00. M. Lee Smith Publishers and Printers, 162 4th Avenue North, PO Box 198867, Nashville TN 37219. **Tel** (615)242-7395, (800)274-6774, FAX (615)256-6601. **ED** Steve Owens, Mike Patten, and Kim Williamson, (address) Brown and Bain, PO Box 400, Phoenix, AZ 85001, (phone)602-351-8000. **DD** 344.
Desc: Newsletter reporting the latest state specific environmental law developments that affect companies in that state.

US/0004-153X
ARIZONA LAW REVIEW. [Ariz. law rev.]. **Added/Corp** University of Arizona. College of Law. Vol. 1 (Spring 1959)-. Periodical. English. qt. $26.00 US; $28.00 other. Arizona Law Review, University of Arizona, College of Law, Tucson AZ 85721. **Tel** (602)621-1764. **ED** Russ Mancuso. **LC** K1; .R48. cum. index. **Circ:** 2,000. available on an online database from WESTLAW.
Desc: Contains legal articles written by law professors, justices, practitioners, and law students.
Ind/Abst Bowne Dig. Corp. Sec. Lawyers; Crim. Penol. Police Sci. Abstr.; Curr. Law Index (1980-); Energy Res. Abstr. (Nov. 1977-); Fed. Tax Artic.; Index Leg. Period.; INIS Atomindex [Micro.]; Leg. Resour. Index (1980-); LegalTrac (1980-); West. Hist. Q.

US/0094-4246
ARIZONA LEGISLATIVE SERVICE. VFOAT ARS Legislative Service. English. West Publishing Company, 610 Opperman Drive, PO Box 64526, Eagan MN 55123-1308. **Tel** (612)687-5618, (800)328-9352, FAX (612)687-5388, (800)562-2329. **(Subscription telephone:** FAX (612)688-3570) **LC** KFA2431. **DD** 348/.791/02.

US/0164-4297
ARIZONA STATE LAW JOURNAL. [Ariz. state law j.]. **Added/Corp** Arizona State University. College of Law. (1974)-. Periodical. English. Four times a year (Jan., Apr., July, Oct.). $20.00. Arizona State University College of Law, Tempe AZ 85287. **Tel** (602)965-7715, (602)965-6181, FAX (602)965-2427. **ED** John J Tuchi (editor's phone: (602)965-6287). **LC** K1; .R5. **DD** 340/.05. cum. index. **Bk Rev**, (Qty: 0-4). **Ad Acc. Circ:** 770 (ctrl). ***Continues*** *Law and the Social Order.*
Ind/Abst Bowne Dig. Corp. Sec. Lawyers; Curr. Law Index (1980-); Index Leg. Period.; Leg. Resour. Index (1980-); LegalTrac (1980-); PAIS Int. Print (1991-).

US/0742-0226
ARIZONA STATE UNIVERSITY LAW FORUM. [Ariz. State Univ. law forum]. **Added/Corp** Arizona State University. College of Law. **VFOAT** Law Forum; Arizona State Law Forum. Vol. 6, No. 1 (Spring 1983)-. Periodical. English. **LC** KF292.A744; A423. **DD** 340/.07/11791. ***Continues*** *Arizona State Law Forum, 0888-3157.*
Ind/Abst Fed. Tax Artic.; Leg. Resour. Index (1983-); LegalTrac (198?-).

US/1052-293X
ARKANSAS LAW NOTES. (ARKANSAS LAW NOTES : REPORTS TO THE ARKANSAS BAR / BY THE FACULTY OF THE UNIVERSITY OF ARKANSAS SCHOOL OF LAW.). [Ark. law notes]. **Added/Corp** University of Arkansas, Fayetteville. School of Law. (1983)-. Periodical. English. an. Free. Arkansas Law Notes, University of Arkansas, Waterman Hall, Fayetteville AR 72701. **Tel** (501)575-5601. **LC** K1; .R548. **DD** 349.767; 347.67.
Ind/Abst Fed. Tax Artic.; Index Leg. Period.

US/0004-1831
ARKANSAS LAW REVIEW. [Ark. law rev.]. **Added/Corp** Arkansas Bar Association. University of Arkansas (Fayetteville Campus). School of Law. University of Arkansas, Fayetteville. School of Law. Vol. 22 (Spring 1968)-. Periodical. English. Four times a year. $15.00. Arkansas Law Review, University of Arkansas, Waterman Hall, Fayetteville AR 72701. **Tel** (501)575-5601. **ED** Beth Myers. **LC** K1; .R552. **DD** 340/.05. Index available (volume 45 #4). cum. index. available on microfilm. ***Continues*** *Arkansas Law Review and Bar Association Journal.*
Ind/Abst Bowne Dig. Corp. Sec. Lawyers (1980-); Crim. Justice Abstr. (1980-); Curr. Law Index (1980-); Fed. Tax Artic.; Index Leg. Period.; Leg. Resour. Index (1980-); LegalTrac (1980-).

US/0571-0502
ARKANSAS LAWYER. [Ark. lawyer]. **Added/Corp** Arkansas Bar Association. Vol. 1 (June 1967)-. Periodical. English. Four times a year (Jan., Apr., July, Oct.). $15.00. Arkansas Bar Association, 400 West Markham, Little Rock AR 72201. **Tel** (501)375-4605. **ED** Ruth Williams. **LC** KF200; .A73. **DD** 340/.09767. **Bk Rev. Ad Acc. Circ:** 3,500.
Desc: The official publication of the Arkansas Bar Association. Presents a broad spectrum of bar issues, from an historical, innovative and informational perspective.
Ind/Abst Curr. Law Index (1980-); Law Office Inf. Serv.; Leg. Resour. Index (1980-); LegalTrac (1981-).

US
ARKANSAS LEGAL DIRECTORY, THE. VFOAT Legal Directory. Directory. English. an. $15.00. Legal Directories Publishing Company, 9111 Garland Road, PO Box 189000, Dallas TX 75218. **Tel** (214)321-3238, 800 447-5375. **LC** KF192.A75; A73. **DD** 349.767/025; 347.670025. ***Continues in part*** *Arkansas, Louisiana, and Mississippi Legal Directory.*

NO/0004-2072
ARKIV FOR LUFTRETT. (19??)-. Norwegian. ir. Scandinavian University Press, PO Box 2959 Toeyen, N 0608 Oslo 6 Norway. **Tel** 011 47 2 2575400, FAX 011 47 2 2575353, telex 71896 UROR N. **(Subscription address:** Scandinavian University Press, 200 Meacham Ave., Elmont NY 11003.)

BL
ARQIOVPS DPS TROBIMAOS DE ALCADA : ORGAO OFICIAL DOS TRIBUNAIS DE ALCADA DO ESTADO DO RIO DE JANEIRO. VFOAT A.T.A.; ATA. 1 (Jan./June 1983)-. Portuguese. sa. Jura Editora, Av Visconde de Guarapuava 2435 1O. Andar, CEP 80.000 Curitiba Parana Brazil. **LC** KHD8105; .A23. **DD** 348.81/53043; 348.1530843.

BL
ARQUIVOS DO INSTITUTO DE DIREITO SOCIAL. Main/Corp Instituto de Direito Social (Sao Paulo, Brazil). Portuguese. Instituto de Direito Social, Avenida Paulista No 726, Sao Paulo Brasil. **LC** K9; .I55. **DD** 344.81.

BL/0100-1213
ARQUIVOS DO MINISTERIO DA JUSTICA. [Arq. Minist. Justica]. **Main/Corp** Brazil. Ministerio da Justica. Portuguese. Rua Mexico 128 60 Andar, Rio de Janeiro Brazil. **LC** K2; .R25. **DD** 340/.0981. ***Continues*** *Arquivos / Brazil. Ministerio da Justica e Negocios Interiores.*

SZ
ARRETS DU TRIBUNAL FEDERAL SUISSE. RECUEIL OFFICIEL. Main/Corp Switzerland. Bundesgericht. **VFOAT** Arrets du Tribunal Federal Suisse. Recueil Officiel. Vol. 1 (1875)-. Monographic series. German. ir. Price varies per volume. Imprimeries Reunies Lausanne, 5 Chemin du Closel, CH 1020 Renens Switzerland. **Tel** 011 41 21 6350036. cum. index.

NE/0004-2870
ARS AEQUI. [Ars aequi]. **Added/Corp** Stichting Ars Aequi. (1951)-. Periodical. Dutch. Eleven times a year. F55.00. Stichting Ars Aequi, Postbus 1043GEL 70, 6501 BA Nijmegen Netherlands. **Tel** 031 80 224441.
Ind/Abst EMBASE; Index Foreign Leg. Per.

US/0886-1013
ART LAW AND ACCOUNTING REPORTER. [Art law account. report.]. **Added/Corp** Volunteer Lawyers and Accountants for the Arts. Texas Accountants and Lawyers for the Arts. Vol. 1, No. 1 (July 1982)-. Periodical. English. Four times a year. $25.00. Texas Accountants and Lawyers for the Arts, 1540 Sul Ross, Houston TX 77006. **Tel** (713)526-4876, FAX (713)526-1299. **ED** Annabel Levy. **LC** KF4288.A15; A78. **DD** 344.73/097; 347.30497. Index available. **Pr Rev.**

●NE/0924-8463
ARTIFICIAL INTELLIGENCE AND LAW. **See** Computers-Artificial Intelligence.

US
ARTS, ENTERTAINMENT & SPORTS LAW NEWS. VFOAT Arts, Entertainment and Sports Law News. (19??)-. English. American Bar Association, 750 North Lake Shore Drive, Chicago IL 60611. **Tel** (312)988-5522, (312)988-5241, FAX (312)988-5528, telex 270593. ***Continues*** *Lawyers and the Arts Committee Newsletter.*

US/0273-3048
ASBESTOS LITIGATION REPORTER. [Asbestos litig. report.]. (Feb. 1979)-. Periodical. English. sm. $950.00. Andrews Publications Inc., 1646 West Chester Pike, PO Box 1000, Westtown PA 19395. **Tel** (610)399-6600, (800)345-1101, FAX (610)399-6610. **ED** Leonard E. B. Andrews. **LC** KF1297.A73; A493. **DD** 346.7303/82; 347.306382. cum. index. ctrl circ.
Desc: Focuses on the most recent developments in suits alleging personal injuries from exposure to asbestos. Also reports selected developments in suits brought to recover the cost of removing or encapsulating asbestos building materials.

US/1059-6232
ASBESTOS MDL 875 UPDATE. [Asbestos MDL 875 update]. Vol. 1, No. 1 (Oct. 2, 1991)-. English. sm (24 issues). $650.00. Andrews Publications Inc., 1646 West Chester Pike, PO Box 1000, Westtown PA 19395. **Tel** (610)399-6600, (800)345-1101, FAX (610)399-6610. **LC** KF226; .A8. **DD** 346.7303/8; 347.30638.
Desc: A journal that provides a concise summary of the developments in the federal multi-district pretrial asbestos litigation proceedings now pending in Philadelphia.

US/1041-5130
ASBESTOS PROPERTY LITIGATION REPORTER. See Building and Construction.

PH
ASEAN LAW JOURNAL. Added/Corp ASEAN Law Association. Foundation. University of the Philippines. Vol. 1, No. 1 (Sept. 1982)-. English. an. $4.00 (single copy). **LC** K1; .S73. **DD** 349.5/05; 342.5005.
Ind/Abst Index Foreign Leg. Per.

HK/1022-0267
ASIA LAW. (19??)-. English. Ten times a year. $480.00. Asia Law & Practice Ltd, 2F 29 Hollywood Road, Central Hong Kong Hong Kong. **Tel** 011 852 5 5449918. ***Formed by the union of*** *Asian Law and Practice* ***and*** *Asian Corporate Law.*

HK
ASIA LAW AND PRACTICE. ***Title Change.*** **VFOAT** ALP. Vol. 1, No. 1 (January 30, 1989)-(19??). Periodical. English. Ten times a year. Asia Law & Practice Ltd, 2F 29 Hollywood Road, Central Hong Kong Hong Kong. **Tel** 011 852 5 5449918. ***Merged with*** *Asian Corporate Law* ***to form*** *Asia Law.*

US/0145-0220
ASIAN LAW FORUM. V. 1- 1976-. English. an. $1.25. Temple University / Sociology, Department of Sociology, Philadelphia PA 19122. **DD** 340/.095.

US/0090-6352
ASSESSMENT AND VALUATION LEGAL REPORTER. ***Title Change.*** **See** Public Administration-Public Finance and Taxation.

IS/0334-3871
ASSIA, JEWISH MEDICAL ETHICS. See Medical Science and Technology.

US
ASSOCIATION LAW AND POLICY. English. bw. $195.00. American Society of Association Executives, 1575 Eye Street NW, Washington DC 20005. **Tel** (202)626-2735, (202)626-2722, FAX (202)371-8825. **ED** Robert Spurrier Boege. Index available (two/yr). cum. index. **Bk Rev**, (Qty: 4-5/yr). **Ad Acc, Adv Mgr:** R.S. Boege, **Tel** (202)626-2703. **Circ:** 1800.
Desc: A comprehensive compilation of association and nonprofit-related legal topics. tracks development in nonprofit taxation antitrust, postal, copyright, employment law, and legislative developments.

PO
ASSUNTOS EUROPEUS. VFOAT Asseur. Vol. 1, No. 1 (Feb. 1982)-. Periodical. English (French and Portuguese). Three times a year. $35.00. Assuntos Europeus Secretario, C P 21302, 1100 Lisbon Portugal. **LC** K1; .S865. **DD** 349.4/05; 342/.05.

US/0746-4177
ATLA ADVOCATE. VFOAT A.T.L.A. Advocate. **VAT** Association of Trial Lawyers of America Advocate. Vol. 9, No. 6 (Oct. 1983)-. Periodical. English. mo. Association of Trial Lawyers of America, 1050 31st Street Northwest, Washington DC 20007. **Tel** (800)424-2725 ext. 307, FAX (202)298-6849. ***Continues*** *ATLA Bar News, 0164-8160.*

US/8755-9390
ATLA MASTERS AT WORK. [ATLA masters work]. **VAT** American Association of Trial Lawyers Masters at Work. 1-. English. an. Association of Trial Lawyers of America, 1050 31st Street Northwest, Washington DC 20007. **Tel** (800)424-2725 ext. 307, FAX (202)298-6849. **LC** KF8915; .A89. **DD** 347.73/7; 347.3077.

US
ATLANTA LAW LIBRARIES ASSOCIATION NEWSLETTER. Newsletter. English. Four times a year (Seasonally). $10.00. Atlanta Law Libraries Association, PO Box 57234 / Newsletter Ed, Atlanta GA 30343. **Tel** (404)656-3468. **ED** Pamela Deemer. **Bk Rev. Ad Acc, Adv Mgr:** Roger Glenn, **Tel** 800-633-4604 ext. 461. **Circ:** 200.
Desc: Articles and news concerning law libraianship, databases, Atlanta Law Libraries Association and American Association of Law libraries.

CN/0713-8970
ATLANTIC PROVINCES REPORTS. [Atl. prov. rep.]. Vol. 1 (1975)-. English. ir. Maritime Law Book Ltd, PO Box 302, Fredericton New Brunswick, E3B 4Y9 Canada. **Tel** (506)453-9921, (800)561-0220. **DD** 348/.715/042.
Desc: Contains all of the judgments of the New Brunswick Court of Appeals, the Nova Scotia Court of Appeals, the Prince Edward Island Court of Appeals, the NewFoundland Court of Appeals.

US
ATLANTIC REPORTER DIGEST. V. 1- 1930-. English. West Publishing Company, 610 Opperman Drive, PO Box 64526, Eagan MN 55123-1308. **Tel** (612)687-5618, (800)328-9352, FAX (612)687-5388, (800)562-2329. **(Subscription telephone:** FAX (612)688-3570) **DD** 345.415.

US/0004-7104
ATOMIC ENERGY LAW JOURNAL. [At. energy law j.]. Vol. 1, No. 1 (Winter 1959)-. Periodical. English. Four times a year. Invictus Publishing Corporation, 180 South Broadway, White Plains NY 10605. **DD** 346.7304/67924; 347.306467924.
Ind/Abst Curr. Law Index (1980-); INIS Atomindex [Micro.]; Leg. Resour. Index (1980-?); LegalTrac.

IT
ATTI PARLAMENTARI. RESOCONTI STENOGRAFICI DELLE SEDUTE. **Main/Corp** Italy. Parlamento. Senato. 4. Commissione Permanente Difesa. (1968/72)-. Periodical. Italian. L265.000. Libreria del Senato Repubblica, Via del Teatro Valle 37, 00186 Rome Italy. **Tel** 011 39 67062505. ***Continues*** *Atti Parlamentari. Resoconti delle Sedute in Sede Deliberante.*

IT
ATTI UFFICIALI. **Main/Conf** Congresso Internazionale per l'Elettronica. 7th (1960)-. Periodical. Italian. Twelve times a year. L45000. Istit Nazionale Previdenza Soc, Via Ciro Il Grande 21, CP 10024, 00144 Rome Italy. **Tel** 011 39 6 59054995. ***Supersedes*** *Rassegna Internazionale Elettronica e Nucleare, Rome. Atti del Congresso Scientifico.*

US/0571-8279
ATTORNEY-CPA, THE. (THE ATTORNEY-CPA : A PUBLICATION OF THE AMERICAN ASSOCIATION OF ATTORNEY-CERTIFIED PUBLIC ACCOUNTANTS, INC.). [Attorney-CPA]. **Added/Corp** American Association of Attorney-Certified Public Accountants. **VFOAT** Attorney-C.P.A.; Attorney CPA. (19??)-. Periodical. English. Five times a year (Jan., Mar., May, July, Oct.). $30.00. American Association of Attorney-Certified Public Accountants Inc., 24196 Alicia Parkway, Suite K, Mission Viejo CA 92691. **Tel** (714)768-0336, FAX (714)768-7062. **ED** Ronald M. DeVore. **LC** KF297.A1; A86. **DD** 349.73; 347.3. **Bk Rev**, (Qty: varies). **Ad Acc. Circ:** 2,000 (ctrl). available on an online database (file 485/Full-Text) from DIALOG.
Desc: Prints information on topics of interest to persons dually licensed as attorneys-at-law and certified public accountants. Provides technical professional information, updates on dual license regulations, member and association news.
Ind/Abst Account. Tax Datab. (1974-).

US/0732-7552
ATTORNEY FEE AWARDS REPORTER. ***Title Change.*** [Atty. fee awards rep.]. Vol. 5, No. 4 (June 1982)-(19??). Periodical. English. bm. Prentice-Hall Law and Business, 270 Sylvan Avenue, Englewood Cliffs NJ 07632. **Tel** (800)223-0231, (201)894-8538, FAX (201)894-8666. **ED** Harvey Miller and Andrea Grumfest. **LC** KF8995.A59; F42. **DD** 347.73/77; 347.30777. **Bk Rev. Ad Acc. Circ:** 500 (ctrl). ***Continues*** *Federal Attorney Fee Awards Reporter, 0193-3353.* ***Merged into*** *Inside Litigation.*
Desc: Information and analysis of current fee awards to attorneys by state and federal courts.

US
ATTORNEY GENERAL'S DIGEST, THE. **Added/Corp** Maryland. Dept. of Law. (19??)-. Periodical. English. qt. Free upon request. Maryland Office of Attorney, General 1, South Calvert St, Baltimore MD 21202. **Tel** (301)576-6300. **LC** KFM1761.A59; A85.

US/0361-3844
ATTORNEYS AND AGENTS REGISTERED TO PRACTICE BEFORE THE U.S. PATENT AND TRADEMARK OFFICE. **VAT** Attorneys and Agents Registered to Practice Before the United States Patent and Trademark Office. Government Publication. English. an. US Department of Commerce, 14th Street & Constitution Avenue NW, Washington DC 20230. **Tel** (202)482-2000, FAX (202)482-3772. **LC** KF3165.A3; A8. **DD** 346/.73/0486025. available on microfiche (Vols. for (1982-) distributed to depository libraries). ***Continues*** *Attorneys and Agents Registered to Practice Before the U.S. Patent Office.*

US/0745-421X
ATTORNEYS COMPUTER REPORT. [Atty. comput. rep.]. (198?)-. Periodical. English. mo. Professional Publications Inc, 1201 Peachtree Street Northeast, Atlanta GA 30309. **Tel** (404)455-7600. **LC** KF320.A9; A883. **DD** 340/.0085.

US/1057-5596
ATTORNEY'S GUIDE TO STATE BAR ADMISSION REQUIREMENTS. [Atty. guide state bar admiss. requir.]. **Added/Corp** Federal Reports, Inc. 1st Ed. (1991)-. English. $7.50. Federal Reports, Inc., 1010 Vermont Avenue NW, Suite 408, Washington DC 20005. **DD** 340.

US/0745-1369
ATTORNEYS MARKETING REPORT. ***Title Change.*** [Atty. mark. rep.]. Vol. 1, No. 1 (July 1982)-(19??). Periodical. English. Twelve times a year. James Publishing Group, Inc., PO Box 25202, Santa Ana CA 92799. **Tel** (714)755-5450, FAX (714)556-4133. **ED** Suzanne Verity and William J. Haines. **LC** KF316.5.A15; A88. **DD** 340/.068/8. **[CCC]. Bk Rev.** ***Merged into*** *Law Firm Marketing and Profit Report.*
Desc: How law firms can market their services. Practical advice on what some inventive firms are doing.
Ind/Abst Law Office Inf. Serv.

US/8750-2763
ATTORNEYS PERSONNEL REPORT. [Atty. pers. rep.]. (Aug. 1984)-. Periodical. English. mo. $197.00 (one year), $354.00 (two year). Attorneys Personnel Report, PO Box 80280, Atlanta GA 30366. **Tel** (404)455-7600. **ED** Susanne Verity. **LC** PAR. **DD** 338. **Ad Acc.** ctrl circ.
Desc: Directed to the particular personnel needs of the law office. Concerns with interviewing, recruiting, compensation and general management.

US
AUDIO LAWYER, THE. (THE AUDIO LAWYER. SOUND RECORDING.). **Added/Corp** American Law Institute-American Bar Association Committee on Continuing Professional Education. Vol. 1, No. 1 (1983)-. Periodical. English. Eight times a year. $99.00. American Law Institute, 4025 Chestnut Street, Philadelphia PA 19104-3099. **Tel** (215)243-1661, (800)253-6397, FAX (215)243-1664. **ED** William S. Stevens. **LC** RZA 0557. Index available. **Circ:** 125.
Desc: Audiocassettes containing spoken articles and recorded lectures of general interest to attorneys in the US.

GW
AUSLANDISCHES WIRTSCHAFTS- UND STEUERRECHT. **VFOAT** AWST; Schriftenreihe Auslandisches Wirtschafts- und Steuerrecht. Monographic series. German. Price varies per volume. Bundesstelle fuer Aussenhandelsinformation, Agrippastr 87 93, D 50676 Cologne Germany. **Tel** 011 49 221 2057316, FAX 011 49 221 2057212. ***Continues*** *Sonderveroffentlichung (Bundesstelle fur Aussenhandelsinformation (Germany). Legislativer Dienst).*
Ind/Abst Index Foreign Leg. Per.

●US/1065-7460
AUSTIN DAILY RECORD. [Austin Dly. Rec.]. **VFOAT** Daily Record. (1992)-. Periodical. English. da. Austin Daily Record, 503 West 1st Street, Austin TX 78701. **DD** 340. ***Continues*** *Austin Area Legal Record, 0896-730X.*

US/1063-1534
AUSTIN LAWYER'S MAGAZINE. ***Ceased.*** [Austin lawyer's mag.]. **Added/Corp** Austin Young Lawyers Association Foundation. Travis County Bar Association (Tex.). Vol. 1, No. 1 (1992)-(199?). Periodical. English. qt. Austin Lawyer's Magazine, 700 Lavace, Suite 602, Austin TX 78701-3102. **DD** 340. ***Continues*** *Austin Lawyer, 1071-0353.*

AT
AUSTRALASIAN GAY AND LESBIAN LAW JOURNAL. **See** Sexual Life.

AT/0816-3030
AUSTRALIAN ADMINISTRATIVE LAW BULLETIN, THE. [Aust. adm. law bull.]. **VFOAT** Australian Administrative Law Service Bulletin. (1985)-. Bulletin. English. mo. **DD** 342.94005.
Ind/Abst Aust. Leg. Mon. Dig.

AT/0814-8589
AUSTRALIAN BAR REVIEW. **Added/Corp** Australian Bar Association. Vol. 1, No. 1 (March 1985)-. Periodical. English. Three times a year. 145.00Aus$. Butterworths Pty Ltd, 271-273 Lane Cove Road, PO Box 345, North Ryde NSW 2113 Australia. **Tel** 011 61 2 3354444, FAX 011 61 2 3354655. **ED** J.D. Heydon. **LC** K1; .U768. **DD** 349.94/05; 349.4005. Index available. **Bk Rev.**
Desc: Articles that provide analysis for basic problems of legal doctrine and procedure.
Ind/Abst Aust. Leg. Mon. Dig.; Index Leg. Period.; Leg. Resour. Index; LegalTrac (1991-).

AT/1035-2295
AUSTRALIAN CAPITAL TERRITORY LEGISLATION CATALOGUE. [Aust. Cap. Territ. legis. cat.]. (1990)-. Government Publication. English. mo. 150.00Aus$. Australian Government Publishing Service, GPO Box 84, Canberra ACT 2601 Australia. **Tel** 011 61 6 2954411, FAX 011 61 6 2954455. **DD** 015.9470532.

AT/0726-5956
AUSTRALIAN CONSUMER SALES AND CREDIT LAW REPORTER. [Aust. consum. sales credit law report.]. (1978)-. English. an. 725.00Aus$. CCH Australia Ltd, PO Box 230, North Ryde New South Wales, 2113 Australia. **Tel** 011 61 02 888 2555, FAX 011 61 02 888 7324. **DD** 343.9407.
Desc: Provides information on the legislation and case law in commercial legal practice. Coverage includes all the key aspects, complete with detailed commentary, cases and legislation.
Ind/Abst Aust. Leg. Mon. Dig.

AT/1036-0425
AUSTRALIAN CURRENT LAW. LEGISLATION. Issue No. 1 (Jan. 1991)-. English. ir. $565.00 combination subscription with Reporter and Year Book sections of Australian Current Law. Butterworths Pty Ltd, 271-273 Lane Cove Road, PO Box 345, North Ryde NSW 2113 Australia. **Tel** 011 61 2 3354444, FAX 011 61 2 3354655. ***Continues in part*** *Australian Current Law, 0045-0405.*
Desc: Alert subscribers to the latest amendments to all Acts, Regulations and Rules of Federal , State and Territory parliaments.

AT/1036-0417
AUSTRALIAN CURRENT LAW. REPORTER. Issue No. 1 (Jan. 11, 1991)-. Periodical. English. ir. $565.00 combination subscription with Legislation and Year Book sections of Australian Current Law. Butterworths Pty Ltd, 271-273 Lane Cove Road, PO Box 345, North Ryde NSW 2113 Australia. **Tel** 011 61 2 3354444, FAX 011 61 2 3354655. ***Continues in part*** *Australian Current Law, 0045-0405.*
Desc: Provides digests of all available judgements from the High Court, the Federal Court, and the Supreme Courts.

AT/0067-1843
AUSTRALIAN DIGEST, THE. (19??)-. English. Six times a year. 300.00Aus$. The Law Book Company Limited, 44-50 Waterloo Road, North Ryde New South Wales, 2113 Australia. **Tel** 011 61 2 8870177, FAX 011 61 2 8887240, telex ASBOOK 27445. **(Subscription address:** Law Book Company, Australia Level 7 132 Arthur St., N Sydney NSW 2060 Australia.**) ED** J. M. Bennett. Index available. cum. index. **Circ:** 2,500.
Desc: The principal reference for the research of Australian case law. Covers cases from all Australian courts and Australian appeals to Privy Council.

AT/1034-3059
AUSTRALIAN DISPUTE RESOLUTION JOURNAL. Vol. 1, No. 1 (Feb. 1990)-. Periodical. English. qt. 132.00Aus$ Vol. 3, 1992). The Law Book Company Limited, 44-50 Waterloo Road, North Ryde New South Wales, 2113 Australia. **Tel** 011 61 2 8870177, FAX 011 61 2 8887240, telex ASBOOK 27445.
Ind/Abst Aust. Leg. Mon. Dig.; Leg. Resour. Index; LegalTrac (1990-).

AT
AUSTRALIAN HIGH COURT AND FEDERAL COURT PRACTICE. English. ir. 910.00Aus$. CCH Australia Ltd, PO Box 230, North Ryde New South Wales, 2113 Australia. **Tel** 011 61 02 888 2555, FAX 011 61 02 888 7324.
Desc: Provides accurate and complete coverage of the practice and procedures of the High Court and Federal Court as well as administrative law.
Ind/Abst Aust. Leg. Mon. Dig.

AT/0726-5883
AUSTRALIAN INDUSTRIAL LAW REVIEW. (1961)-. Periodical. English. wk.
Ind/Abst Aust. Leg. Mon. Dig.

AT/1033-9345
AUSTRALIAN INSOLVENCY BULLETIN. [Aust. insolv. bull.]. (1988)-. Bulletin. English. qt. 130.00Aus$. Insolvency Practitioners Association, GPO Box 3921, Sydney 2001 Australia. **Tel** 61 2 2464023, FAX 61 2 2621512. **ED** Dew Blackwell (editor's phone: 61 2 2846666). **DD** 346.94078. **Ad Acc. Circ:** 670. ***Continues*** *Australian Bankruptcy Bulletin, 0045-0286.*

AT/0814-9046
AUSTRALIAN INTELLECTUAL PROPERTY CASES. [Aust. intellect. prop. cases]. **Added/Corp** CCH Australia Limited. (1984)-. English. an. **DD** 346.9404802642.
Ind/Abst Aust. Leg. Mon. Dig.

AT/0729-3356
AUSTRALIAN JOURNAL OF LAW AND SOCIETY. [Aust. j. law soc.]. **Added/Corp** Macquarie University. School of Law. **VFOAT** Australian Journal of Law & Society. Vol. 1, No. 1 (1982)-. Periodical. English. an. $15.00 (individual), $30.00 (institutions). Australian Journal Law Society, School of Law, Macquarie University, Sydney NSW 2109 Australia. **Tel** 011 61 2 8057111. **ED** Gill H. Boehringer Stewart. **LC** K1; .U7824. **DD** 340/.115/05. **Bk Rev. Ad Acc. Pr Rev. Circ:** 300.
Desc: Seeks to provide a forum to reflect the growing awareness that law cannot be properly studied in isolation from society.
Ind/Abst APAIS, Aust. Public Aff. Inf. Ser.; Aust. Leg. Mon. Dig.; Curr. Law Index (1984-); Index Leg. Period.; Leg. Resour. Index (1984-); LegalTrac (1983-).

AT/0004-9611
AUSTRALIAN LAW JOURNAL, THE. [Aust. law j.]. Vol. 1 (May 5, 1927)-. Periodical. English. ir. $265.00. The Law Book Company Limited, 44-50 Waterloo Road, North Ryde New South Wales, 2113 Australia. **Tel** 011 61 2 8870177, FAX 011 61 2 8887240, telex ASBOOK 27445. **ED** J G Starke and J M Bennett. . **DD** 347.05. Index available. **Bk Rev. Ad Acc.** ctrl circ.
Desc: Australia's leading journal on legal matters.

Includes fast reports of the decisions of the high court.
Ind/Abst APAIS, Aust. Public Aff. Inf. Ser. (1963-); Aust. Leg. Mon. Dig.; Curr. Law Index (1980-); Energy Res. Abstr. (Sept. 1980-); Index Leg. Period.; Leg. Resour. Index (1980-); LegalTrac (1980-).

AT
AUSTRALIAN LAW JOURNAL REPORTS, THE. **Added/Corp** Australia. Courts. Vol. 32 (1958)-. English. mo. The Law Book Company Limited, 44-50 Waterloo Road, North Ryde New South Wales, 2113 Australia. **Tel** 011 61 2 8870177, FAX 011 61 2 8887240, telex ASBOOK 27445. ***Supersedes in part*** *Australian Law Journal, 0004-9611.*
Ind/Abst Aust. Leg. Mon. Dig.

●AT/1039-6616
AUSTRALIAN LAW LIBRARIAN. **Added/Corp** Australian Law Librarian's Group. Vol. 1, No. 1 (Feb. 1993)-. Periodical. English. Six times a year (Feb., Apr., June, Aug., Oct., Dec.). 48.00Aus$ Australia; 50.00Aus$ others (surface mail); 70.00Aus$ (airmail). Australian Law Librarian's Group, PO Box E40, Queen Victoria Terrace, Canberra ACT 2600 Australia. **Tel** 011 61 6 2506577, FAX 011 61 6 2505941. **ED** Julia Butler. **LC** Z675.L2; A97. **Bk Rev. Ad Acc. Circ:** 500. ***Continues*** *Newsletter (Australian Law Librarian's Group), 0311-5984.*
Ind/Abst Aust. Educ. Index; Aust. Libr. Inf. Sci. Abstr.; Leg. Inf. Manage. Index.

AT
AUSTRALIAN LAW NEWS. ***Title Change.*** **Added/Corp** Law Council of Australia. **VFOAT** Law News. Vol. 12, No. 2 (Sept. 1977)-(19??). Periodical. English. mo. Law Council of Australia, GPO Box 1989, Edinburgh Avenue, Canberra Act 2601 Australia. **Tel** 011 61 6 2473788, FAX 011 61 6 2480639, telex 62406. **ED** Barrie Virtue. **Bk Rev. Ad Acc, Adv Mgr Tel** 03-6631578. **Circ:** 28,000 (ctrl). ***Continues*** *Law Council Newsletter.* ***Continued by*** *Australian Lawyer.*
Ind/Abst Aust. Leg. Mon. Dig.

AT/0310-0014
AUSTRALIAN LAW REPORTS. **Added/Corp** Australia. High Court. Australian Capital Territory. Supreme Court. Vol. 1 (1973)-. English. 170.00Aus$. Butterworths Pty Ltd, 271-273 Lane Cove Road, PO Box 345, North Ryde NSW 2113 Australia. **Tel** 011 61 2 3354444, FAX 011 61 2 3354655. **ED** J.G. Starke and J.M. Bennett. **DD** 348/.94/04. ***Continues*** *Australian Argus Law Reports.*
Desc: Publication for lawyers in Australia who want to keep up to date. Contains major articles from Australia's leading legal writers.
Ind/Abst Aust. Leg. Mon. Dig.

AT
AUSTRALIAN LAWYER. (19??)-. English. Eleven times a year. 55.00Aus$. Law Council of Australia, GPO Box 1989, Edinburgh Avenue, Canberra Act 2601 Australia. **Tel** 011 61 6 2473788, FAX 011 61 6 2480639, telex 62406. ***Continues*** *Australian Law News.*
Desc: Articles and information about the Australia lawyers.

AT
AUSTRALIAN LEGAL DIRECTORY. **Added/Corp** Law Council of Australia. (1979)-. Directory. English. ir. 102.00Aus$. Butterworths Pty Ltd, 271-273 Lane Cove Road, PO Box 345, North Ryde NSW 2113 Australia. **Tel** 011 61 2 3354444, FAX 011 61 2 3354655. **DD** 349.94/025; 349.4025. Index available. **Circ:** 2,000 (ctrl).
Desc: Provides a comprehensive listing of barristers and solicitors practicing in Australia and legal institutions throughout Australia.

AT/0004-9646
AUSTRALIAN LEGAL MONTHLY DIGEST. **See** Law-Abstracting, Bibliographies and Statistics.

AT/0812-857X
AUSTRALIAN MINING AND PETROLEUM LAW ASSOCIATION YEARBOOK. **Added/Corp** Australian Mining and Petroleum Law Association. **VFOAT** AMPLA Yearbook. (1983)-. English. an. 195.00Aus$ Australia; 205.00Aus$ other. Australian Mining and Petroleum Law Association Ltd, 360 Little Bourke Street/4th Floor, Melbourne Vic 3000 Australia. **Tel** 011 61 3 6702544, FAX 011 61 3 6702616, telex 35307. **ED** A. G. Magree. **LC** K1; .U783. **DD** 343.94/0775; 349.403775. Index available. cum. index (In 1994 edition). **Circ:** 750. ***Continues*** *Australian Mining and Petroleum Law Journal, 0157-2083.*
Desc: Over 40 articles covering the complex field of the law relating to natural resources in Australia. Major articles and commentaries prepared by acknowledged experts. Provides a diversity of discussion on pertinent issues from government agreements, Australian and international views on sole risk, joint ventures, assignment clauses, oil and gas piplines, case studies on technology and the law and much more.
Ind/Abst AESIS Q.; Aust. Leg. Mon. Dig.; Curr. Law Index (1980-); Leg. Resour. Index (1980-?); LegalTrac (1983-1987).

AT/0728-6309
AUSTRALIAN PLANNING APPEAL DECISIONS. ***Ceased.*** Vol. 1, No. 1 (June 1982)-(19??). English. Sixteen times a year. The Law Book Company Limited, 44-50 Waterloo Road, North Ryde New South Wales, 2113 Australia. **Tel** 011 61 2 8870177, FAX 011 61 2 8887240, telex ASBOOK 27445. **ED** Kenneth Gifford Robert Michael Hayes. Index available. cum. index.
Desc: Contains decisions of the judges of the Local Government Court of Queensland, Assessors of the Land and Environment Court of New South Wales, and decisions of the South Australian Planning Tribunal, the Planning Appeals Boards of Tasmania and Victoria, and the Western Australian Town Planning Board.
Ind/Abst Aust. Leg. Mon. Dig.

AT/0311-094X
AUSTRALIAN TAX REVIEW. [Aust. tax rev.]. **Added/Corp** Law Book Company. Vol. 1 (Nov. 1971)-. English. qt. 185.00Aus$ (volume 21). The Law Book Company Limited, 44-50 Waterloo Road, North Ryde New South Wales, 2113 Australia. **Tel** 011 61 2 8870177, FAX 011 61 2 8887240, telex ASBOOK 27445. **ED** I C F Spry. **LC** K1; .U79. **DD** 343.9404/05. **Bk Rev. Ad Acc.** available on microfilm and microfiche from University Microfilms International (UMI); available on an online database (file 485/Full-Text) from DIALOG. Documents available from UMI Article Clearinghouse.
Desc: Analyses of taxation law and policy through articles and case notes.
Ind/Abst ABI/INFORM Glob. Ed.; Account. Tax Datab. (Mar. 1992-) [Full Txt.]; APAIS, Aust. Public Aff. Inf. Ser. (1973-); Aust. Leg. Mon. Dig.; Curr. Law Index (1980-); Index Leg. Period.; Leg. Resour. Index (1980-); LegalTrac (1980-).

AT/0814-9054
AUSTRALIAN TORTS REPORTS. [Aust. torts rep.]. **Added/Corp** CCH Australia Limited. (1984)-. English. an. CCH Australia Ltd, PO Box 230, North Ryde New South Wales, 2113 Australia. **Tel** 011 61 02 888 2555, FAX 011 61 02 888 7324.
Ind/Abst Aust. Leg. Mon. Dig.

US/0740-6819
AUTOMATED LAW OFFICE CONSULTANT, THE. Vol. 1, No. 1 (July 1982)-. Periodical. English. mo. $65.00. Roadrunner Publications, PO Box 13548, Austin TX 78711.

US/0278-4726
AUTOMOTIVE LITIGATION REPORTER. [Automot. litig. rep.]. (19??)-. Periodical. English. sm. $850.00. Andrews Publications Inc., 1646 West Chester Pike, PO Box 1000, Westtown PA 19395. **Tel** (610)399-6600, (800)345-1101, FAX (610)399-6610. **ED** Leonard E. B. Andrews. **LC** KF1297.A8; A492. **DD** 346.7303/82; 347.306382. cum. index. ctrl circ.
Desc: Provides comprehensive coverage of automotive product liability litigation. Focus is primarily on cases involving alleged automotive defects.

US
AVIATION CASES / CCH. ***Ceased.*** **Added/Corp** Commerce Clearing House. **VFOAT** CCH Aviation Cases. **VAT** Commerce Clearing House Aviation Cases. Vol. 1 (1945)-(Sept. 1992). English. Commerce Clearing House Inc., 4025 West Peterson Avenue, Chicago IL 60646-6085. **Tel** (312)583-8500, FAX (708)940-4600. **ED** A. E. Schechter. **LC** KF2400; .A513.
Desc: Bound volumes of cases on federal aviation regulation, insurance and liability problems.

US/0273-7310
AVIATION LAW REPORTS. **Added/Corp** Commerce Clearing House. (19??)-. English. sm. $1,740.00. Commerce Clearing House Inc., 4025 West Peterson Avenue, Chicago IL 60646-6085. **Tel** (312)583-8500, FAX (708)940-4600.

US/0737-7746
AVIATION LITIGATION REPORTER. [Aviat. litig. rep.]. (May 23, 1983)-. Periodical. English. sm. $825.00. Andrews Publications Inc., 1646 West Chester Pike, PO Box 1000, Westtown PA 19395. **Tel** (610)399-6600, (800)345-1101, FAX (610)399-6610. **ED** L. Andrews. **LC** KF2454.A59; A95. **DD** 346.7303/22; 347.306322. cum. index. ctrl circ.
Desc: Covers developments in lawsuits arising from commercial carrier, military, private plane and helicopter crashes. Typically, the suits involve product liability claims, the Warsaw Convention liability limits, the Federal Tort Claims Act and other issues.

US
AVISO, THE. 1979-. English (English). an. $7.95. **LC** KF193.D3; A9. **DD** 349.764/2811/025; 347. 62428110025.

B

CN/0849-6013
C LAWYERS' TELEPHONE, FAX AND SERVICES DIRECTORY. [B.C. lawyers' teleph. fax serv. dir.]. **Added/Corp** Canadian Bar Association. British Columbia Branch. **VAT** British Columbia Lawyers' Telephone, FAX and Services Directory. (1989/1990)-. Directory. English. an (Oct.). $35.00. Canadian Bar Association of British Columbia, 1148 Hornby Street, Suite 504, Vancouver British Columbia, V6Z 2C3 Canada. **Tel** (604)687-3404. **DD** 340/.025/711. ***Continues*** *Canadian Bar Association. British Columbia Branch. Membership and Services Directory., 0842-5183.*

CN/0382-5744
BACKGROUND PAPER - INSTITUTE OF LAW RESEARCH AND REFORM, UNIVERSITY OF ALBERTA. **Main/Corp** University of Alberta. Institute of Law Research and Reform. No. 1- 1975-. Monographic series. English. Price varies per volume. Institute of Law Research and Reform, 402 Law Centre, University of Alberta, Edmonton Alberta T6G 2H5 Canada. **DD** 346/.71/04342.

US/8756-5374
BAD FAITH LAW REPORT, THE. [Bad faith law rep.]. Vol. 1, No. 1 (Feb. 1985)-. Periodical. English. Ten times a year (monthly except Jan. & July). $240.00 (new subscription), $195.00 (renewal subscription). Stratton Press, PO Box 96, San Ramon CA 94583. **Tel** (415)735-1719. **ED** Stephen S Ashley (editor's address: PO Box 22391, San Francisco CA 94122; editor's phone: (415)759-5270). **LC** KF1301.5.I58; B33. **DD** 346.7303; 347.3063. cum. index. **Circ:** 850 (ctrl).
Desc: A compendium of all the latest developments in the field of bad faith. Summarizes all recent appellate decisions nationwide.

US/0092-0959
BALDWIN'S OHIO LEGISLATIVE SERVICE. **Added/Corp** Banks-Baldwin Law Publishing Company. **VFOAT** Ohio Legislative Service. (1971)-. English. Twelve times a year. Banks-Baldwin Law Publishing Company, PO Box 1974, University Center, Cleveland OH 44106. **Tel** (216)721-7373. **LC** KFO15; .B34. **DD** 348/.771/026.
Desc: Full text of all laws enacted by the General Assembly, complete with purpose clauses and effective dates.

US
BALDWIN'S OHIO REVISED CODE, WITH RULES OF PRACTICE, ANNOTATED. **Main/Corp** Ohio. English. Banks-Baldwin Law Publishing Company, PO Box 1974, University Center, Cleveland OH 44106. **Tel** (216)721-7373.

US
BALDWIN'S OHIO TAX LAW AND RULES. **Main/Corp** Ohio. **Added/Corp** Banks-Baldwin Law Publishing Company, Cleveland. **VFOAT** Ohio Tax Law and Rules. (1966)-. English. ir. $125.00. Banks-Baldwin Law Publishing Company, PO Box 1974, University Center, Cleveland OH 44106. **Tel** (216)721-7373. cum. index.
Desc: Published in cooperation with state tax agencies, this is the official guide to Ohio taxation.

US/0739-1234
BALDWIN'S OHIO TAX SERVICE. [Baldwin's Ohio tax serv.]. **Added/Corp** Banks-Baldwin Law Publishing Company. **VFOAT** Ohio Tax Service. (1978)-. English. qt. must order direct. Banks-Baldwin Law Publishing Company, PO Box 1974, University Center, Cleveland OH 44106. **Tel** (216)721-7373. **ED** Maryann B. Gall. **LC** KFO470.A6; B324. **DD** 343.77104; 347.71034.
Desc: Issues cover current developments by providing: status of bills, full text of official acts, tax agency rules, illustrative forms and decisions and opinions both reported and unreported.

US
BALTIMORE COUNTY GUIDE TO LAWS COVERING TENANT-LANDLORD RELATIONS IN THE CITY I.E. COUNTY AND THE STATE. **Main/Corp** Baltimore Neighborhoods, Inc. 1975-. English. an. Baltimore Neighborhoods Inc, 319 East 25th Street, Baltimore MD 21218. **LC** KFM1799.B32; L3523. **DD** 346.7527104/34.

●US
BANK AND CORPORATE GOVERNANCE LAW REPORTER. **See** Business-Banking and Finance.

UK/0961-7256
BANKING LAW REPORTS. [Bank. law reports]. (1991)-. Periodical. English. mo. £140.00 UK; £155.00 overseas. Business & Medical Publications Limited, Saxeway Business Centre, Chartridge Lane, Chesham, Bucks HP5 2SH England. **Tel** 011 44 494 792621, FAX 011 44 494 793098, telex 86402. **DD** 344.1068202642.
Desc: All about banking law reports.

US/0092-3877
BAR (AUSTIN). (BAR.). [Bar]. Periodical. English. mo. State Bar of Texas, PO Box 12487, Capitol Station, Austin TX 78711. **Tel** (512)463-1411. **LC** KF200; .B35. **DD** 340/.06/2764.

US/0749-0615
BAR BRIEF (BEVERLY HILLS, CALIF.). (BAR BRIEF : THE NEWSLETTER OF THE BEVERLY HILLS BAR ASSOCIATION.). [Bar brief]. **Main/Corp** Beverly Hills Bar Association. Newsletter. English. qt. $40.00. Beverly Hills Bar Association, 300 South Beverly Drive, Suite 201, Beverly Hills CA 90212. **Tel** (213)553-6644, FAX (213)284-8290. **ED** David M Shacter. **LC** KF200; .B48. **DD** 340/.06/0794. **Ad Acc. Circ:** 2,600 (ctrl).
Desc: Legal articles on all substantive law issues.

US
BAR BULLETIN. Bulletin. English. Seattle-King County Bar Association, 320 Central Building, Seattle WA 98104. **Tel** 624-9365.

US/0005-5824
BAR EXAMINER, THE. [Bar exam.]. V. 1- Nov. 1931-. English. qt. Free. National Conference of Bar Examiners, 333 North Michigan Avenue/Suite 1025, Chicago IL 60601-4090. **Tel** (312)641-0963, FAX (312)641-2052. **ED** Stuart Duhl, Ann Fisher. **DD** 347.069. cum. index. **Bk Rev. Circ:** 2,500 (ctrl). available on microfilm and microfiche from University Microfilms International (UMI).
Desc: Articles of interest to bar admitting authorities.
Ind/Abst Curr. Law Index (1980-); Leg. Resour. Index (1980-); LegalTrac (1981-).

US/0099-1031
BAR LEADER. [Bar lead.]. **Added/Corp** American Bar Association. (March/April 1975)-. Periodical. English. bm. $29.99. American Bar Association, 750 North Lake Shore Drive, Chicago IL 60611. **Tel** (312)988-5522, (312)988-5241, FAX (312)988-5528, telex 270593. **LC** KF200; .B355. **DD** 340/.06/273. ***Formed by the union of*** *Bar Activities* ***and*** *Bar Keys Communications Coordinator.*
Ind/Abst Curr. Law Index (1980-); Law Office Inf. Serv.; Leg. Resour. Index (1980-); LegalTrac (1980-).

US/1052-4541
BAR LETTER - STATE BAR OF NEVADA. ***Title Change.*** (BAR LETTER : NEWSLETTER OF THE STATE BAR OF NEVADA.). **Added/Corp** State Bar of Nevada. Vol. 1, No. 1 (Oct. 1989)-Vol. 4, No. 10 (Oct. 1992). Newsletter. English. mo. **LC** KF200; .B356. **DD** 349.793/05; 347.93005. ***Merged with*** *Inter Alia, 0092-6086* ***to form*** *Nevada Lawyer, 1068-882X.*
Desc: Concerned with the state bar of Nevada, bar associations, and the practice of law.

US/0546-4714
BAR NOTES. [Bar notes]. **Main/Corp** North Carolina Bar Association. **VFOAT** Barnotes. (1950)-. Periodical. English. bm. North Carolina Bar Association, 1312 Annapolis Drive, PO Box 12806, Raleigh NC 27605. **LC** KF200; .N655. **DD** 340/.06/0756. cum. index.
Ind/Abst Fed. Tax Artic.; Law Office Inf. Serv.

US/0271-2024
BAR REPORT. [Bar rep.]. **Main/Corp** District of Columbia Bar. (19??)-. Periodical. English. ir. comes with Washington Lawyer. District of Columbia Bar, 1250 H Street Northwest, Sixth Floor, Washington DC 20005. **Tel** (202)737-4700, FAX (202)626-3471. **LC** KF200; .D6. **DD** 349.753/06.

BB
BARBADOS LAW REPORTS. Main/Corp Barbados. **Added/Corp** Barbados. Ministry of the Attorney General. Vol. 1 (1948/1957)-. English. **LC** KGL1012; .A23. **DD** 348.7298/1043; 347.29810843.

US/0893-2506
BARCLAYS CALIFORNIA SUPREME COURT SERVICE. [Barclays Calif. Supreme Court serv.]. **Added/Corp** Barclays Law Publishers. Vol. 5, No. 25 (June 2, 1986)-. Periodical. English. wk. $465.00. Barclays Law Publishers, 400 Oyster Point Boulevard, South San Francisco CA 94080. **Tel** (800)888-3600, (415)244-6611, FAX (415)244-0408. **LC** KFC45.1; .B37. **DD** 347.794/046/05; 347.94074605. ***Continues*** *California Supreme Court Service (San Francisco, Calif.), 0741-5370.*

US
BARCLAYS INSURANCE LAW REPORT (CALIFORNIA EDITION). (19??)-. English. mo. $245.00. Barclays Law Publishers, 400 Oyster Point Boulevard, South San Francisco CA 94080. **Tel** (800)888-3600, (415)244-6611, FAX (415)244-0408. **(Subscription address:** PO Box 3066, South San Francisco CA 94080) **ED** R Michael James. **Circ:** 275 (ctrl).

US/1044-0194
BARCLAYS LAW LIBRARY. [Barclays law libr.]. **Added/Corp** Barclays Law Publishers. Vol. 11, No. 1 (Jan. 1989)-. English. mo. $395.00. Barclays Law Publishers, 400 Oyster Point Boulevard, South San Francisco CA 94080. **Tel** (800)888-3600, (415)244-6611, FAX (415)244-0408. **LC** K2; .A674. **DD** 348.73/046/0979405; 347.308460979405. ***Continues*** *Barclays California Law Monthly, 8755-772X.*

US
BARCLAYS UNITED STATES EIGHTH CIRCUIT SERVICE. Added/Corp United States. Court of Appeals (8th Circuit) Barclays Law Publishers. **VFOAT** United States Eighth Circuit Service; Eighth Circuit Service; Eighth Circuit Review; Rules of the United States Court of Appeals for the Eighth Circuit. Vol. 2, No. 1 (Sept. 18, 1987)-. Periodical. English. bw. $445.00. Barclays Law Publishers, 400 Oyster Point Boulevard, South San Francisco CA 94080. **Tel** (800)888-3600, (415)244-6611, FAX (415)244-0408. **LC** KF112 8th .1; .B37. ***Continues*** *Eighth Circuit Newsletter, 0891-0839.*

US/0893-2492
BARCLAYS UNITED STATES NINTH CIRCUIT SERVICE. [Barclays U. S. Ninth Circuit serv.]. **Added/Corp** United States. Court of Appeals (9th Circuit) Barclays Law Publishers. **VFOAT** Ninth Circuit Review; Rules of the United States Court of Appeals for the Ninth Circuit. Vol. 2, No. 16 (June 19, 1986)-. Periodical. English. wk. $435.00. Barclays Law Publishers, 400 Oyster Point Boulevard, South San Francisco CA 94080. **Tel** (800)888-3600, (415)244-6611, FAX (415)244-0408. **LC** KF112 9th .1; .B37. **DD** 347.73/24051/05; 347.3072405105. ***Continues*** *United States Ninth Circuit Service, 0883-864X.*

US/1046-1337
BARCLAYS UNITED STATES SECOND CIRCUIT SERVICE. [Barclays U. S. Second Circuit serv.]. **Added/Corp** United States. Court of Appeals (2nd Circuit) Barclays Law Publishers. **VFOAT** United States Second Circuit Service; Second Circuit Service; Second Circuit Review; Rules of the United States Court of Appeals for the Second Circuit. (1988)-. Periodical. English. bw. $435.00. Barclays Law Publishers, 400 Oyster Point Boulevard, South San Francisco CA 94080. **Tel** (800)888-3600, (415)244-6611, FAX (415)244-0408. **DD** 348. cum. index.

US/1045-9006
BARCLAYS UNITED STATES SEVENTH CIRCUIT SERVICE. [Barclays U. S. Seventh Circuit serv.]. **Added/Corp** United States. Court of Appeals (7th Circuit) Barclays Law Publishers. **VFOAT** United States Seventh Circuit Service; Seventh Circuit Service; Seventh Circuit Review; Rules of the United States Court of Appeals for the Seventh Circuit. Vol. 1, No. 1 (Oct. 25, 1988)-. Periodical. English. bw. $435.00. Barclays Law Publishers, 400 Oyster Point Boulevard, South San Francisco CA 94080. **Tel** (800)888-3600, (415)244-6611, FAX (415)244-0408. **LC** KF112 7th .1; .B37. **DD** 348.73/048; 347.30848. cum. index.

US/0899-3475
BARCLAYS UNITED STATES TENTH CIRCUIT SERVICE. [Barclays U. S. Tenth Circuit serv.]. **Added/Corp** Barclays Law Publishers. **VFOAT** Tenth Circuit Review; Rules of the United States Court of Appeals for the Tenth Circuit. Vol. 5, No. 1-2 (Oct. 28, 1987)-. Periodical. English. bm. $435.00. Barclays Law Publishers, 400 Oyster Point Boulevard, South San Francisco CA 94080. **Tel** (800)888-3600, (415)244-6611, FAX (415)244-0408. **LC** KF112 10th.1; .T46. **DD** 348.73/046/05; 347.3084605. ***Continues*** *Tenth Circuit Newsletter, 0887-1515.*

NR/0331-0086
BARRISTER, THE. Added/Corp Nigeria. University, Nsukka. Law Students' Association. (1967)-. Periodical. English. University of Nigeria, Nsukka Nigeria. **LC** K2; .A7. **DD** 3401.09669. ***Supersedes*** *Law Student.*
Ind/Abst Curr. Law Index (1980-); Law Office Inf. Serv.; Leg. Resour. Index (1980-); LegalTrac (1980-).

US/0094-5277
BARRISTER (CHICAGO). (BARRISTER.). [Barrister]. **Added/Corp** American Bar Association. Young Lawyers Section. Vol. 1 (Feb. 1974)-. English. qt (4 issues). $19.95. American Bar Association, 750 North Lake Shore Drive, Chicago IL 60611. **Tel** (312)988-5522, (312)988-5241, FAX (312)988-5528, telex 270593. **ED** Anthony Monahan. **LC** K2; .A68. **DD** 340/.05. **Ad Acc. Circ:** 150,000 (ctrl). ***Continues*** *Law Notes (American Bar Association. Young Lawyers Section), 0732-8370.*
Desc: The magazine for the young lawyer, reporting on law, the practice of law and law-firm management.
Ind/Abst Fed. Tax Artic.; Index Leg. Period.; Leg. Resour. Index (1980-).

US
BARRISTER LAW JOURNAL. English. mo. $25.00. Bar Association of San Francisco, 685 Market Street, Suite 700, San Francisco CA 94105. **Tel** (415)764-1600.

US/0739-2494
BARRISTER (PHILADELPHIA, PA.), THE. (THE BARRISTER / PENNSYLVANIA TRIAL LAWYERS ASSOCIATION.). [Barrister]. **Added/Corp** Pennsylvania Trial Lawyers Association. (19??)-. Periodical. English. Four times a year (Mar., July, Oct., Nov.). $32.00. Pennsylvania Trial Lawyers Association, 121 South Broad Street, Suite 800, Philadelphia PA 19107. **Tel** (215)546-6451, FAX (215)546-5430. **ED** Lee Swartz, (phone: (215)784-1941 Ext. 338). **LC** KF200; .B3565. **DD** 340. Index available. cum. index. **Bk Rev,** (Qty: 4). **Ad Acc, Adv Mgr:** Carla Davard. **Pr Rev. Circ:** 3,700.
Desc: A scholar legal journal with pratical and theorectical articles geared to the Pennsylvania trial lawyers.

US/0408-6007
BARRISTER (UNIVERSITY OF MIAMI. SCHOOL OF LAW). (THE BARRISTER.). **Added/Corp** Bar and Gavel Legal Society. University of Miami. School of Law. (19??)-. Periodical. English. an. Free. University of Miami School of Law, 1311 Miller Drive, 460 Law Library, PO Box 248087, Coral Gables FL 33124. **Tel** (305)284-2464, FAX (305)284-2349.

PH/0116-8657
BARRISTERS BULLETIN. Vol. 1, No. 1 (Apr. 1989)-. Bulletin. English. mo.

US/0883-8682
BARRISTERS NEWSLETTER. (BARRISTERS NEWSLETTER / LOS ANGELES COUNTY BAR ASSOCIATION.). **Main/Corp** Los Angeles County Bar Association. Vol. 1, No. 1 (Jan. 1985)-. Newsletter. English. qt. Los Angeles County Bar Association, PO Box 55020, Los Angeles CA 90055. **Tel** (213)896-6503, FAX (213)623-4328. **DD** 340.

US/1062-2489
BARRON'S GUIDE TO LAW SCHOOLS. **See** Education-Higher Education.

PH
BATAS AT KATARUNGAN. Vol. 1, No. 1 (Feb. 1982)-. Periodical. English (English). sa. $20.00. University of the Philippines Law Center, Diliman Quezon City Philippines. **LC** K2; .A73. **DD** 349.599/05; 345.99005.

SZ/1017-0588
BAURECHT. [Baurecht]. **VFOAT** Droit de la Construction; B.R./D.C.; BR/DC. Periodical. Multiple languages (French and German). qt. 41.00F Switzerland; $20.00 US. Seminar fur Schweizerisches Baurecht, Universitat, 1700 Freiburg Switzerland. **Tel** 37 21 92 04, FAX 37 219 702. **ED** Peter Gauch and Pierre Tercier. **LC** K2; .A74. **DD** 343.494/07869005; 344. 94037869005. Index available. cum. index. **Circ:** 4,500.
Desc: Information on specific problems of Swiss construction law. Appreciation and criticism of the jurisdiction in this area.
Ind/Abst Energy Res. Abstr. (Sept. 1980-).

US
BAY AREA GUILD NEWSLETTER. Newsletter. English. mo (except Jan., April, July, Oct.). $25.00. National Lawyers Guild / Bay Area, 558 Capp Street, San Francisco CA 94110. **Tel** (415)285-5067. **ED** Rob Petitpas. **Ad Acc. Circ:** 850.
Desc: Calendar of events, brief notes for the National Lawyers Guild / San Francisco Bay Area.

GW/0522-5337
BAYERISCHE VERWALTUNGSBLATTER. VFOAT BayVBl. Bayerische Verwaltungsblatter. (1870)-. Periodical. German. sm. Richard Boorberg Verlag GmbH, Levelingstrasse 6A, W-8000 Munich 80 Germany. **Tel** 011 49 89 4360000. **UDC** 342(430.1-43.6). **[CCC].**

US/0005-7274
BAYLOR LAW REVIEW. [Bayl. law rev.]. **Added/Corp** Baylor University. Law School. Vol. 1, No. 1 (Summer 1948)-. Periodical. English. qt. $28.00. Baylor University /Baylor Law Review, PO Box 97156, Waco TX 76798. **Tel** (817)755-3487. **LC** K2; .A78. **DD** 349.764; 347.64. **Bk Rev. Ad Acc. Circ:** 1,250.
Desc: Articles treat all areas of Texas and federal law, with articles by leading authorities and comments and case notes by student authors.
Ind/Abst Bowne Dig. Corp. Sec. Lawyers; Fed. Tax Artic.; Index Leg. Period.; Leg. Resour. Index (1980-); LegalTrac (1980-); PAIS Int. Print (1991-); Women Stud. Abstr.

US
BCBA NEWS / BUCKS COUNTY BAR ASSOCIATION. Added/Corp Bucks County Bar Association. **VFOAT** B.C.B.A. News; Bucks County Law Reporter. (19??)-. Periodical. English. Bucks County Bar Association, 135 East State Street, Doylestown PA 18901. **LC** KF200; .B38. **DD** 340/.060748.

SP/0213-6945
BCE. BOLETIN DE DERECHO DE LAS COMUNIDADES EUROPEAS. ***Ceased.*** **See** Political Science-International Relations.

US
BEAVER COUNTY LEGAL JOURNAL, THE. Vol. 1 (Mar. 25, 1939/Mar. 16, 1940)-. Periodical. English. wk. $40.00. Beaver County Legal Journal, 775 4th Street, Beaver PA 15009. **Tel** (412) 728-7622. **LC** Microfilm 0173 .
Desc: Comprising all the advanced reports of the opinions of the several courts of Beaver County, Pennsylvania.

UK/0735-3936
BEHAVIORAL SCIENCES & THE LAW. [Behav. sci. law]. **VFOAT** Behavioral Sciences and the Law. Vol. 1, No. 1 (1983)-. Periodical. English. qt. $255.00. John Wiley & Sons Ltd., Baffins Lane, Chichester West Sussex PO19 1UD England. **Tel** 0243 779777, FAX 0243 776128 BTG:JWP001, telex 86290 WIBOOKG. **(Subscription address:** John Wiley / Philadelphia, PO Box 7247, Philadelphia PA 19170.**) ED** Robert Wettstein. **LC** K2; .E3. **DD** 344.73/044/05; 347.3044405. **NLM** W1; BE132H. **CODEN** BSLADR. **[CCC]. Ad Acc. Circ:** 600. available on an online database; available on microfilm and microfiche from University Microfilms International (UMI). Documents available from The Genuine Article.
Desc: The journal explores the dynamic relationship between mental health and law. Each issue is devoted to specific topics, such as malpractice, terrorism, post-traumatic stress disorder, informed consent, insanity defense, personal defense, etc.
Ind/Abst Crim. Justice Abstr.; Curr. Contents Soc. Behav. Sci.; Curr. Law Index (1984-); EMBASE; Leg. Resour. Index (1984-); LegalTrac (1984-); Psychol. Abstr. (1983-); PsycINFO; PsycLit; Res. Alert [Full Cov.]; Soc. Sci. Cit. Index [Full Cov.].

GW/0172-4770
BEITRAEGE ZUM AUSLAENDISCHEN OEFFENTLICHEN RECHT UND VOELKERRECHT. Added/Corp Max-Planck-Institut fuer Auslaendisches Oeffentliches Recht und Voelkerrecht. No. 1 (1927)-. Monographic series. German. ir. Price varies per volume. Springer-Verlag GmbH & Company KG, Heidelberger Platz 3, D 14197 Berlin Germany. **Tel** 011 49 30 8207223, FAX 011 49 30 8214091, telex 183 319 SPBLN D. **(Subscription address:** Springer Verlag New York Inc. / for North America, 44 Hartz Way, Secaucus NJ 07096.**)**
Desc: Numbered series covering law.

US/0276-1505
BENCH AND BAR OF MINNESOTA, THE. [Bench bar Minn.]. **Added/Corp** Minnesota State Bar Association. Minnesota State Bar Association. Official Membership directory. **VFOAT** Bench & Bar of Minnesota. Vol. 1, No. 1 (Dec. 1943)-. Periodical. English. mo (11 issues). $25.00. Minnesota State Bar Association, 514 Nicollet Hall, Suite 300, Minneapolis MN 55402. **Tel** (612)333-1183, (800)882-6722, FAX (612)333-4927. **ED** Judson P. Haverkamp. **LC** KF200; .B46. **DD** 340/.05. Index available. cum. index. **Bk Rev**, (Qty: 60). **Ad Acc, Adv Mgr:** Julie A. Schaeffer, **Tel** (612)473-9677. **Circ:** 13,000 (ctrl). available on microfiche from Hein and Company. ***Continues*** *Bench and Bar of Minnesota (Saint Paul, Minn.).*
Desc: Focus on substantive law and the legal profession.
Ind/Abst Curr. Law Index (1980-); Fed. Tax Artic.; Law Office Inf. Serv.; Leg. Resour. Index (1980-); LegalTrac (1980-).

US/0270-5206
BENDER'S DICTIONARY OF 1040 DEDUCTIONS. Added/Corp Matthew Bender (Firm). **VFOAT** Dictionary of 1040 Deductions. **VAT** Bender's Dictionary of One Thousand and Forty Deductions. (1980)-. English. an. $32.00. Matthew Bender & Company Inc., 1275 Broadway, Albany NY 12204. **Tel** (800)833-9844, (518)487-3000. **ED** K Egan. **LC** KF6385; .B46. **DD** 343.7305/23/0321.

US
BENDER'S FORMS OF DISCOVERY. Main/Corp Bender (Matthew) and Company, Incorporated. (1???)-. English. ir. Matthew Bender & Company Inc., 1275 Broadway, Albany NY 12204. **Tel** (800)833-9844, (518)487-3000.

US/0732-6564
BENDER'S ... PAYROLL TAX GUIDE. [Bender's payr. tax guide]. **VFOAT** Payroll Tax Guide. English. Matthew Bender & Company Inc., 1275 Broadway, Albany NY 12204. **Tel** (800)833-9844, (518)487-3000. **LC** KF6436; .B46. **DD** 343.7305/242; 347.3035242.

US
BENDER'S UNIFORM COMMERCIAL CODE SERVICE. (19??)-. Periodical. English. ir. Matthew Bender & Company Inc., 1275 Broadway, Albany NY 12204. **Tel** (800)833-9844, (518)487-3000.

US/0747-9131
BENEFITS TODAY. *Ceased.* (BENEFITS TODAY / BNA.). [Benefits today]. Vol. 1, No. 1 (July 20, 1984)-(1993). Periodical. English. bw. Bureau of National Affairs Inc., 9435 Key West Avenue, Rockville MD 20850. **Tel** (800)372-1033, (301)258-1033, FAX (301)948-5823. **(Subscription address:** 9435 Key West Avenue, Rockville MD 20850; telephone: (301)948-5823**) ED** David A Sayre. **LC** KF3509.A15; B46. **DD** 343.7305/242. **[CCC].** Index available. cum. index.
Desc: Covers all major benefit trends including pensions, health and life insurance, dental care, Medicare, ESOPs, cafeteria plans and innovative company policies.

IO
BERITA BADAN PEMBINAAN HUKUM NASIONAL. Main/Corp Badan Pembinaan Hukum Nasional. V. 1.- Jan. 1975-. Indonesian. Pusat Dokumentasi Hukum Bphn, Jalan Medan Merdeka 9, Jakarta Indonesia.

GW/0409-1264
BERKELEY-KOELNER RECHTSSTUDIEN. (1961)-. Monographic series. German. ir. Price varies per volume. Verlag CF Mueller, Verlags GS, D-69018 Heidelberg Germany. **Tel** 011 49 6221 4890. **DD** 340.

US/0882-4312
BERKELEY WOMEN'S LAW JOURNAL. [Berkeley women's law j.]. **Added/Corp** University of California, Berkeley. School of Law. Vol. 1, No. 1 (Fall 1985)-. English. an. $17.00 (individuals), $38.00 (institutions), $9.00 (students/low income). University of California Press, 2120 Berkeley Way, Berkeley CA 94720. **Tel** (510)642-4191, (510)642-3907, FAX (510)642-9917. **LC** K2; .E75. **DD** 342.73/0878/05; 347.30287805. **[CCC]. Bk Rev. Ad Acc.** available on microfilm and microfiche from University Microfilms International (UMI).
Desc: A multidisciplinary law journal devoted to critical legal issues affecting women, especially poor women, women of color, disabled women and lesbians.
Ind/Abst Altern. Press Index; Index Leg. Period.; Leg. Resour. Index; LegalTrac (1980-).

US/8750-3379
BERKS COUNTY LAW JOURNAL. [Berks Cty. law j.]. **Added/Corp** Berks County, Pa. Courts. Berks County Bar Association. Vol. 1 (1908/09)-. English. wk (Thurs.). $30.00. Berks County Law Journal, 544 Court Street, PO Box 1058, Reading PA 19603-1058. **Tel** (610)375-4593, FAX (610)373-0256. **ED** George M. Lutz. **DD** 348. Index available. cum. index. **Ad Acc, Adv Mgr:** J. Gwinther, **Tel** (610)375-4591. **Circ:** 715 (ctrl).
Desc: Contains bar news, local opinions, legal notices, and commerical advertisements.

GW/0523-0209
BERLINER JURISTISCHE ABHANDLUNGEN. (1959)-. German. ir. Duncker und Humblot Verlag, Postfach 410329, D-12113 Berlin Germany. **Tel** 011 49 30 79000612, 011 49 30 79000613.

US/0277-1551
BEST'S DIRECTORY OF RECOMMENDED INSURANCE ATTORNEYS. Added/Corp A.M. Best Company. A.M. Best Company. Legal/Claims Division. **VFOAT** Directory of Recommended Insurance Attorneys. 52nd Ed. (1981)-. Directory. English. an. $65.00. AM Best Company, Ambest Road, Oldwick NJ 08858. **Tel** (908)439-2200 ext. 5653, telex 837744. **LC** KF195.I5; B47. **DD** 346.74/086/025; 347.30686025. ***Continues*** *Best's Recommended Insurance Attorneys.*
Desc: Contains more than 2,000 pages, listing over 4,000 top law firms. Listings are arranged alphabetically by city within each state, Canadian province and foreign country for ease of reference.

GW/0005-9935
BETRIEB, DER. (DER BETRIEB; WOCHENSCHRIFT FUER BETRIEBSWIRTSCHAFT, STEUERRECHT, WIRTSCHAFTSRECHT, ARBEITSRECHT.). [Betrieb]. (1948)-. Periodical. German. Fifty-two times a year. DM367.29 Germany; DM447.00 other. Handelsblatt GmbH, Postfach 102716, D-40018 Duesseldorf Germany. **Tel** 011 49 211 8871730. **[CCC].**
Ind/Abst Coal Abstr.; Energy Res. Abstr. (Dec. 1982-).

US/1051-628X
BEVERLY HILLS BAR ASSOCIATION JOURNAL. [Beverly Hills Bar Assoc. j.]. **Added/Corp** Beverly Hills Bar Association. **VFOAT** Beverly Hills Bar Journal. Vol. 11, No. 4 (July/Aug. 1977)-. Periodical. English. qt. $40.00. Beverly Hills Bar Association, 300 South Beverly Drive, Suite 201, Beverly Hills CA 90212. **Tel** (213)553-6644, FAX (213)284-8290. **ED** David Lich. **LC** K2; .E84. **DD** 340/.05. Index available. cum. index. **Ad Acc. Circ:** 3,300 (ctrl). available on microfiche. ***Continues*** *Journal of the Beverly Hills Bar Association.*
Desc: Deals with legal topics, both substantive and procedural.
Ind/Abst Curr. Law Index (1980-); Leg. Resour. Index (1980-); LegalTrac (1980-).

GW
BEVOLKERUNG UND ERWERBSTATIGKEIT. REIHE 4.2.2, ENTGELTE UND BESCHAFTIGUNGSDAUER DER ARBEITNEHMER. VFOAT Entgelte und Beschaftigungsdauer der Arbeitnehmer. (1983/84)-. German. an. DM9.70. W Kohlhammer Verlag GmbH, Postfach 800430, D 70549 Stuttgart Germany. **Tel** 011 49 711 78631, FAX 011 49 711 7863263, telex 7-255820. **LC** HD7103.5.G3; B48.

CK/0121-5183
BEYOND LAW / MAS ALLA DEL DERECHO. Added/Corp Instituto Latinoamericano de Servicios Legales Alternativos. **VFOAT** Mas Alla del Derecho. Issue No. 1 (Feb. 1991)-. Periodical. English. Three times a year. $20.00 Latin America and the Caribbean; $30.00 other. ILSA - Instituto Latinoamericano de Servicios Legales Alternativos, PO Box 077844, Bogota Colombia. **Tel** 011 57 1 2455995, 011 57 1 2884437, FAX 011 57 1 2884854. **LC** K2; .E86. **DD** 340/.115.

US/0360-2745
BIBLIOGRAPHIC GUIDE TO LAW. See Law-Abstracting, Bibliographies and Statistics.

NE
BIBLIOGRAPHIE DE LA COUR INTERNATIONALE DE JUSTICE / PREPAREE PAR LA BIBLIOTHEQUE DE LA COUR. See Law-Abstracting, Bibliographies and Statistics.

US
BIENNIAL REPORT / JOINT COMMITTEE FOR REVIEW OF ADMINISTRATIVE RULES. Main/Corp Wisconsin. Legislature. Joint Committee for Review of Administrative Rules. English. be. David G Berger Co-Chairman, Joint Committee for Review of Administrative Rules, Room 329/South State Capitol, Madison WI 53702. **LC** KFW2821.5.O85; A242. **DD** 328.775/07456.

US
BIENNIAL REPORT / THE JUDICIAL COUNCIL OF THE STATE OF MINNESOTA. Main/Corp Minnesota. Judicial Council. English. be. ***Continues*** *Report.*

US
BIENNIAL REPORT TO THE LEGISLATURE - MONTANA LEGISLATIVE ASSEMBLY. ADMINISTRATIVE CODE COMMITTEE. Main/Corp Montana. Legislative Assembly. Administrative Code Committee. English. be. Montana Legislative Council, State Capitol/Room 138, Helena MT 59620-1706. **Tel** (406)444-3064, FAX (406)444-3036. **LC** KFM9011.6; .A35. **DD** 342.786/06/05.

II
BIHAR BAR COUNCIL JOURNAL. Main/Corp Bihar State Bar Council. Periodical. English. mo. $.030. Bihar State Bar Council, High Court Building, Patna - 1 India. **DD** 348/.5412/046.

US/1062-4600
BILL BOARD : LEGISLATIVE NEWS FOR OHIO JUDGES / OHIO JUDICIAL CONFERENCE. [Bill board]. **Added/Corp** Ohio Judicial Conference. Vol. 1, Issue 1 (Dec. 1991)-. Periodical. English. mo. Free. Bill Board, Ohio Judicial Conference, 88 East Broad Street, Suite 1100, Columbus OH 43215. **DD** 340.

US/0006-2499
BILL OF RIGHTS JOURNAL, THE. [Bill Rights j.]. **Added/Corp** National Emergency Civil Liberties Committee (U.S.). Vol. 1, No. 1 (Dec. 1968)-. English. an. $15.00 Comes with Rights. National Emergency Civil Liberties Committee, 175 5th Avenue, New York NY 10010. **LC** K2; .I43. **DD** 323.4/0973. available on microfilm and microfiche from University Microfilms International (UMI).
Ind/Abst Altern. Press Index; Curr. Law Index (1980-); Hum. Rights Intern. Rep.; Leg. Resour. Index (1980-); LegalTrac (1980-).

US/1048-8936
BIMONTHLY REVIEW OF LAW BOOKS. [Bimon. rev. law books]. Vol. 1, No. 1 (Jan./Feb. 1990)-. Periodical. English. Six times a year (Jan., Mar., May, July, Sept., Nov.). $75.00. Fred B. Rothman & Company, 10368 West Centennial Road, Littleton CO 80127. **Tel** (800)457-1986, (303)979-5657, FAX (303)978-1457, telex 87669. **ED** Edward J. Bandes and Michael Rustad. **LC** KF1; .B58. **DD** 349.73; 347.3.
Desc: Provides law librarians, legal academics and lawyers with a professionally edited journal whose pages are devoted exclusively to the prompt reviewing of contemporary legal scholarship on diverse legal topics.

●US/1063-3596
BIOETHICS BULLETIN (WASHINGTON, D.C.). (BIOETHICS BULLETIN : BULLETIN OF THE COORDINATING GROUP ON BIOETHICS AND THE LAW, AMERICAN BAR ASSOCIATION.). [Bioeth. bull.]. **Added/Corp** American Bar Association. Coordinating Group on Bioethics and the Law. **VFOAT** ABA Bioethics Bulletin. Vol. 1, No. 1 (Spring 1992)-. Bulletin. English. Three times a year. Free on request. American Bar Association, 750 North Lake Shore Drive, Chicago IL 60611. **Tel** (312)988-5522, (312)988-5241, FAX (312)988-5528, telex 270593. **ED** Leanne Pfautz.

Law

US/1048-1788
BIORESEARCH TODAY. FOOD & DRUG LEGISLATION. *Ceased.* **VFOAT** BioResearch Today. Food & Drug Legislation; Food and Drug Legislation. Vol. 1, No. 1-2 (Jan./Feb. 1990)-Ceased (Dec. 1991). English. mo. BioSciences Information Service, Biological Abstracts / BIOSIS, 2100 Arch Street, Philadelphia PA 19103-1399. **Tel** (800)523-4806 US, (215)587-4800 Pennsylvania and worldwide, FAX (215)587-2016, telex 831739. **DD** 344.
Desc: Current awareness journal including abstracts and content summaries of studies involving food and drug legislation.

US/0091-4002
BIRK'S. VFOAT Birk's Register of Commercial Attorneys. English. 3539 Hennepin Avenue, Minneapolis MN 55408. **LC** KF195.C57; B5. **DD** 346/.73/07025.

US/0892-7227
BIRTH TRAUMA. [Birth trauma]. **Added/Corp** Medical Education, Inc. Kitch, Saurbier, Drutchas, Wagner & Kenney, P.C. **VFOAT** Birth Trauma Newsletter. (1985)-. Periodical. English. qt. $50.00. Medical Education Inc, 1 Michigan Avenue/Suite 720, Lansing MI 48933. **Tel** (517)372-3979, FAX (517)372-0441. **ED** Gary C Brown. **DD** 346. **Bk Rev. Circ:** 250 (ctrl).
Desc: Medical and legal information regarding risk management for obstetrics and guidelines of how to avoid malpractice.

RU/0557-5257
BIULLETEN VERKHOVNOGO SUDA SSSR. Main/Corp Russia (1923- U.S.S.R.). Verkhovnyi Sud. (1942)-. Periodical. Russian. bm. $119.95. **(Subscription address:** East View Publications Inc., 3020 Harbor Lane North, Suite 110, Minneapolis MN 55447.**)**

●US
BLAST : THE BULLETIN OF LAW/SCIENCE & TECHNOLOGY / AMERICAN BAR ASSOCIATION, SECTION OF SCIENCE AND TECHNOLOGY. Added/Corp American Bar Association. Section of Science and Technology. **VFOAT** Bulletin of Law, Science and Technology. No. 88 (Jan. 1994)-. Periodical. English. ir. American Bar Association, 750 North Lake Shore Drive, Chicago IL 60611. **Tel** (312)988-5522, (312)988-5241, FAX (312)988-5528, telex 270593. *Continues* Bulletin of Law, Science & Technology, 0362-3769.

SZ
BLATTER FUR EIN NEUES BODENRECHT. Periodical. French (German). qt. 2.50F each issue. Schweizerische Gesellschaft fur Ein Neues Bodenrecht, Postfach 2276, 3001 Bern Switzerland. **LC** K2; .L37. **DD** 346.49404/32; 344.9406432.

US
BLUE BOOK / ILLINOIS STATE BAR ASSOCIATION. Main/Corp Illinois State Bar Association. **VFOAT** Bluebook; ISBA Blue Book. (19??)-. English. Illinois State Bar Association, 424 South Second, Springfield IL 62701. **Tel** (217)525-1760, FAX (217)525-0712. **LC** KF332.I4; I432. **DD** 340/.06/0773. *Continues* Annual Reports of Officers, Committees, Sections, and Other Bar-related Groups.

US/0887-154X
BLUE SKY PRACTICE FOR PUBLIC AND PRIVATE OFFERINGS. [Blue sky pract. public priv. ltd. offer.]. (1984)-. English. an. Clark Boardman Callaghan, 155 Pfingsten Road, Deerfield IL 60015. **Tel** (800)323-8067. **ED** P. M. Fass and D. A. Wittner. **LC** KF1070.Z95; B56. **DD** 346.73/0666; 347.306666.

US/1062-9971
BLUEBOOK (CAMBRIDGE, MASS.), THE. (THE BLUEBOOK : A UNIFORM SYSTEM OF CITATION.). [Bluebook]. **Added/Corp** Harvard Law Review Association. **VFOAT** Uniform System of Citation. 15th Ed. (1991)-. English. ir. $7.50. Harvard Law Review Association, Gannett House, Cambridge MA 02138. **Tel** (617)495-4650. **LC** KF245; .B58. **DD** 348.73/47; 347.30847. *Continues* Uniform System of Citation.

US/0889-9312
BNA CRIMINAL PRACTICE MANUAL. CURRENT REPORTS. [BNA crim. pract. man. Curr. rep.]. **VFOAT** BNA Criminal Practice Manual. **VAT** Bureau of National Affairs Criminal Practice Manual. Current Reports. Vol. 1, No. 1 (Jan. 14, 1986)-. Periodical. English. bw. $389.00. Bureau of National Affairs Inc., 9435 Key West Avenue, Rockville MD 20850. **Tel** (800)372-1033, (301)258-1033, FAX (301)948-5823. **ED** Judith C. Mroczka. **DD** 345. **[CCC].**
Desc: A notification and reference service consisting of a desk reference binder covering the entire court process from arrest through sentencing, and a newsletter covering developments in clinical law, evidence and procedures, and practice techniques.

US/1058-7365
BNA'S EASTERN EUROPE REPORTER. See Business-Investments.

●US/1064-2137
BNA'S HEALTH LAW REPORTER. Added/Corp Bureau of National Affairs (Washington, D.C.). **VFOAT** Health Law Reporter. **VAT** Bureau of National Affair's Health Law Reporter. (1992)-. Periodical. English. wk. $985.00. Bureau of National Affairs Inc., 9435 Key West Avenue, Rockville MD 20850. **Tel** (800)372-1033, (301)258-1033, FAX (301)948-5823. **[CCC].**

US
BOCA BASIC HOUSING-PROPERTY MAINTENANCE CODE, THE. Main/Corp Building Officials and Code Administrators International. **VAT** Building Officials and Code Administrators Basic Housing-Property Maintenance Code. English. te. Building Officials & Code Administrators International Inc, 4051 West Flossmoor Road, Country Club Hills IL 60477. **Tel** (312)947-2580. **LC** KF5701; .B8. **DD** 343/.73/078.

US/1055-6192
BOCA NATIONAL PROPERTY MAINTENANCE CODE. See Housing and Urban Development.

US
BOILER AND PRESSURE VESSEL SAFETY ACT AND RULES AND REGULATIONS. Main/Corp Illinois. **Added/Corp** Illinois. Division of Boiler and Pressure Vessel Safety. (1978)-. English. Superintendent of Boiler and Pressure Vessel Safety, 302 Amory Building, Springfield IL 62706. **LC** KFI1580.5.S7; A293. **DD** 344.771/0472; 347.7104472. Index available in last issue of volume--attached. *Continues* Illinois. Laws, Statutes, Etc. Boiler Safety Act, and Boiler Rules and Regulations Formulated and Published by Authorization of the Board of Boiler Rules.

BL
BOLETIM - CENTRO DE ESTUDOS, PROCURADORIA GERAL DO ESTADO. Main/Corp Sao Paulo (Brazil : State). Procuradoria Geral do Estado. Centro de Estudos. V. 1- 1/15 Jan. 1977-. Bulletin. Portuguese. bm. Praca da Liberdade, 272-3 Andar, 01503 Sao Paulo Brazil.

BL
BOLETIM DA BIBLIOTECA. Main/Corp Petroleo Brasileiro, S.A. Servico Juridico. Biblioteca. Bulletin. Portuguese. Sejor, Av Republica do Chile 65 170, S/1751 Rio de Janeiro Brazil. **DD** 016.34981.

BL
BOLETIM DA PROCURADORIA GERAL. Main/Corp Rio de Janeiro (State). Departamento de Estradas de Rodagem. PRocuradoria Geral. Yearly V. 1- (No. 1-); 1973-. Bulletin. Portuguese. Praca Fonseca Ramos S/No, Edificio Sede do DER/RJ, 6 Pavimento, Porto Alegre Brazil. **DD** 343/.815/0944.

PO
BOLETIM DO MINISTERIO DA JUSTICA. Added/Corp Portugal. Ministerio da Justica. July (1947)-. Bulletin. Portuguese. mo. 10,500$00 Portugal; 17,500$00 other. Gabinete Gestao Financeiro, Praca do Comercio, 1194 Lisbon Codex Portugal. **Tel** 011 351 1 3474364. **DD** 348.469/046; 344.690846. Index available. cum. index. **Circ:** 5,000 (ctrl). *Continues* Portugal. Ministerio da Justica. Boletim Oficial do Ministerio da Justica.
Desc: Prints speeches, research articles, legislation, conference reports, judgements and bibliography.
Ind/Abst Index Foreign Leg. Per.

US
BOLETIM ELEITORAL. Main/Corp Brazil. Tribunal Regional Eleitoral de Sao Paulo. Bulletin. Portuguese. Tribunal Regional Editoral de Sao Paulo, rua Francisca Miquelina 123-9 PO S Andar, 01381 Sao Paulo Brazil. **DD** 342/.81/07.

BL
BOLETIM INFORMATIVO ADUANEIRAS. Bulletin. Portuguese. $2150. Edicoes Aduaneiras Ltda, Cx P 30.280, Sao Paulo Brazil. **DD** 343.8105/6/05; 348.1035605.

BL
BOLETIM INFORMATIVO MENSAL (PORTO ALEGRE, BRAZIL). (BOLETIM INFORMATIVO MENSAL : BIM / CORREGEDORIA-GERAL DA JUSTICA.). **VFOAT** BIM; B.I.M. Bulletin. Portuguese. mo. Corregedoria-Geral de Justica Palacio da Justica, 4O Andar, Porto Alegre Brazil. **LC** KHD8330.A15; B65. **DD** 347.81/65/005; 348.16507005.

BL
BOLETIM INFORMATIVO - PROCURADORIA GERAL DO ESTADO. Main/Corp Bahia, Brazil (State). Procuradoria Geral do Estado. Bulletin. Portuguese. Procuradoria Geral do Estado, Travessa da Ajuda No 2 - 20 Andar, Salvador Brazil. **LC** K2; .A43. **DD** 340/.09814.

US/0731-8111
BOLETIN ANGLOHISPANO. Vol. 1, No. 1 (Oct. 1980)-. Periodical. English (Spanish). bm. $15.00. Bola Publications, 8769 Devon Avenue, Hesperia CA 92345. **ED** Ricardo Nance. **LC** KFC81; .B64. **DD** 349.794/05; 347.94005. **Bk Rev. Circ:** 500.
Desc: English-Spanish-English glossary of Mexican Spanish.

PE
BOLETIN / COMISION ANDINA DE JURISTAS. Added/Corp Comision Andina de Juristas. (198?)-. Spanish. qt. **LC** KH54.C66; A23. **DD** 342.8/085/05; 348.028505.
Ind/Abst Hum. Rights Intern. Rep.

SP
BOLETIN DE JURISPRUDENCIA Y RESOLUCIONES ADMINISTRATIVAS SOBRE URBANISMO Y VIVIENDA. Main/Corp Spain. Ministerio de la Vivienda. (19??)-. Spanish. Servicio Central de Publicaciones, Ministerio de la Presidencia, Fuencarral, 45, 6, 28004 Madrid Spain. **Tel** 011 34 522 81 91.

SP/0212-4750
BOLETIN DE LEGISLACION DE LAS COMUNIDADES AUTONOMAS : BCA. See Public Administration.

SP
BOLETIN DE LEGISLACION INDUSTRIAL. Spanish. mo. 4200.00ptas. Ctro Publ Min Industria Energi, Doctor Fleming 7-2, 28036 Madrid Spain. **Tel** 011 34 1 3440362, 011 34 1 3440553.

SP
BOLETIN INFORMATIVO DEL DEPARTAMENTO DE DERECHO POLITICO. 3 (Spring 1979)-. Periodical. Spanish. qt. 900ptas. Secretario del Boletin, Departamento de Derecho Politico, Universidad Nacional de Educacion A, Education A Distancia Ciudad Universitaria, Madrid 3 Spain. **LC** K2; .O36. **DD** 349.46/05; 344.6005. *Continues* Boletin Informativo del Departamento de Derecho Politico e Internacional.

VE
BOLETIN INFORMATIVO - INSTITUTO DE FILOSOFIA DEL DERECHO. Main/Corp Universidad del Zulia. Instituto de Filosofia del Derecho. Yearly V. 4, No. 7-. Periodical. Spanish. Universidad del Zulia, Apartado 1490, Maracaibo Venezuela. **DD** 340/.1. *Continues* Boletin Informativo - Centro de Estudios de Filosofia del Derecho.

SP
BOLETIN OFICIAL DEL ESTADO : GACETA DE MADRID. Main/Corp Spain. **VFOAT** Gaceta de Madrid. Vol. 301, No. 50 (Feb. 1961)-. Spanish. da (Mon.-Sat.). 25410ptas Canary Islands, Ceuta & Melilla; 26172ptas Spain; 47250ptas others. Boletin Oficial Del Estado, Trafalgar 27, 28071 Madrid Spain. **Tel** 011 34 1 5382208. **ED** Jose Luis and Muera Villar. **DD** 349.46/05. Index available. cum. index. available on microfiche. *Formed by the union of* Boletin Oficial del Estado *and* Gaceta de Madrid.
Desc: Official journal of the Spanish government. Reports all legislative decisions and resolutions.

SP
BOLETIN OFICIAL, MINISTERIO DE EDUCACION Y CIENCIA. ACTOS ADMINISTRATIVOS. Main/Corp Spain. Ministerio de Educacion y Ciencia. Spanish. wk. Ministerio de Educacion, Alcoa 34, Madrid Spain. **LC** L511; .A44. **DD** 379.46. *Continues* Spain. Ministerio de Educacion. Boletin Oficial, Ministerio de Educacion. Actos Administrativos.

IT
BOLLETTINO DEI CHIMICI IGIENISTI. PARTE LEGISLATIVA. COMUNITA ECONOMICHE EUROPEE. Vol. 35, E1 (Feb. 1984)-. Periodical. Italian. Centro Scientifico Torinese, Via Borgone 57, 10139 Turin Italy. **Tel** 011 39 11 331493. **LC** KJE6172.A4; B65. **DD** 344.4/0423. *Continues in part* Bollettino dei Chimici dell'Unione Italiana dei Laboratori Provinciali, 0390-8585.

IT/0006-6893
BOLLETTINO TRIBUTARIO D'INFORMAZIONI. [Boll. Tribut. inf.]. (1933)-. Periodical. Italian. sm (23 issues per year). L155000 Italy; L310000 other. Bollettino Tributario d'Informazione, Via L Manara 1, 20122 Milan Italy. **Tel** 011 39 2 540-1010. **UDC** 336.2. Index available. cum. index. **Circ:** 20,000 (ctrl). available on CD-ROM.
Desc: Information on the Italian system of taxation and comments on sentences, laws, and state strategies.

IT/1120-544X
BOLLETTINO UFFICIALE DEGLI IDROCARBURI E DELLA GEOTERMIA / MINISTERO DELL'INDUSTRIA, DEL COMMERCIO E DELL'ARTIGIANATO, DIREZIONE GENERALE DELLE MINIERE, UFFICIO NAZIONALE MINERARIO PER GLI IDROCARBURI E LA GEOTERMIA. See Petroleum and Natural Gas.

IT
BOLLETTINO UFFICIALE MINISTERO LAVORI PUBLICI. Italian. mo. L90.000 (subscription), L10.000 (single copy). Istituto Poligrafico Zecca Stato, Piazza Verdi 10, 00198 Rome Italy. **Tel** 011 39 6 85082307, 011 39 6 85082221. **Pr Rev.**

AT/1033-4505
BOND LAW REVIEW. **Added/Corp** Bond University (Gold Coast, Qld.). School of Law. Vol. 1, No. 1 (May 1989)-. Periodical. English. Twice a year (June & Dec.). 40.00Aus$. Bond University, Gold Coast Law School, Queensland 4229 Australia. **Tel** 011 61 75 925011, FAX 011 61 75 952246. **ED** Professor Di Everett. **LC** K2; .O46. **DD** 349.94/05; 349.405. **Bk Rev. Ad Acc, Adv Mgr:** Everett, **Tel** 011 61 75 951060. **Circ:** 1,000 (ctrl).
Ind/Abst Aust. Leg. Mon. Dig.; Index Leg. Period.; Leg. Resour. Index; LegalTrac (1989-).

US/0749-5323
BOOKS ON TRIAL (NEW YORK, N.Y.). (BOOKS ON TRIAL : A REPORT FROM THE CLEARINGHOUSE ON SCHOOL BOOK-BANNING LITIGATION, NATIONAL COALITION AGAINST CENSORSHIP.). [Books trial]. **Added/Corp** Clearinghouse on School Book-Banning Litigation (U.S.). (Jan. 1985)-. English. an. $5.00. National Coalition Against Censorship, 275 7th Avenue, 20th Place, New York NY 10001. **Tel** (212)807-6222. **ED** Leanne Katz. **DD** 344. **Circ:** 5,000 (ctrl).
Desc: A comprehensive source of information on litigation concerning censorship in US public schools, with a listing of books, magazines and films involved.

US/0524-1111
BOSTON BAR JOURNAL. [Boston bar j.]. **Added/Corp** Boston Bar Association. Vol. 1, No. 1 (Jan. 1957)-. Periodical. English. Five times a year (Jan., Mar., May, Sept., Nov.). $40.00. Boston Bar Association, 16 Beacon Street, Boston MA 02108. **Tel** (617)742-0615, FAX (617)523-0127. **LC** KF200; .B66. **DD** 349.73/05; 347.3005. **Ad Acc. Pr Rev. Circ:** 8,000 (ctrl). available on an online database from WESTLAW. ***Continues** Bar Bulletin (Boston, Mass.).*
Desc: Contains information pertaining to law review
Ind/Abst Bowne Dig. Corp. Sec. Lawyers; Curr. Law Index (1980-); Fed. Tax Artic.; Law Office Inf. Serv.; Leg. Resour. Index (1980-); LegalTrac (1980-).

US/0161-6587
BOSTON COLLEGE LAW REVIEW. [Boston Coll. law rev.]. **Main/Corp** Boston College. Law School. Vol. 19 (Nov. 1977)-. Periodical. English. ir (five issues per year). $22.00 US; $25.00 other. Boston College Law School, 885 Centre Street, Newton Centre MA 02159. **Tel** (617)552-8550, FAX (617)552-2615. **LC** K2; .O8. **DD** 340/.05. Index available. **Ad Acc. Circ:** 1,000 (ctrl). ***Continues** Boston College Industrial and Commercial Law Review.*
Ind/Abst Bowne Dig. Corp. Sec. Lawyers; Curr. Law Index (1980-); Fed. Tax Artic.; Index Leg. Period.; Leg. Resour. Index (1980-); LegalTrac (1980-); PAIS Int. Print (1991-).

US/0741-8477
BOSTON UNIVERSITY JOURNAL OF TAX LAW. ***Ceased.*** [Boston Univ. j. tax law]. **VFOAT** Journal of Tax Law. Vol. 1 (March 1983)-Ceased with Vol. 9. Periodical. English. an. Boston University / Brookline, MA, 745 Commonwealth Avenue, Room 435, Boston MA 02215. **Tel** (617)353-6480. **LC** K2; .O86. **DD** 343.7304/05; 347.303405.
Ind/Abst Fed. Tax Artic.; Index Leg. Period.; Leg. Resour. Index; LegalTrac (1990-).

US/0006-8047
BOSTON UNIVERSITY LAW REVIEW. [Boston Univ. law rev.]. **Main/Corp** Boston University. School of Law. **Added/Corp** Boston University. School of Law. Law Review. Vol. 1 (Jan. 1921)-. Periodical. English. Five times a year. $25.00 US; $30.00 other. Boston University School of Law, 765 Commonwealth Avenue, Boston MA 02215. **Tel** (617)353-3157, (617)353-3115. Index available. **Bk Rev. Ad Acc. Pr Rev. Circ:** 4,000. Documents available from The Genuine Article.
Desc: A legal journal containing up-to-date articles by law professors and practicing attorneys, professional quality notes and case comments by student members.
Ind/Abst Bowne Dig. Corp. Sec. Lawyers; Crim. Justice Abstr.; Curr. Contents Soc. Behav. Sci.; Curr. Law Index (1980-); Fed. Tax Artic.; Index Leg. Period.; Leg. Resour. Index (1980-); LegalTrac (1980-); NEXIS; Res. Alert [Full Cov.]; Soc. Sci. Cit. Index [Full Cov.].

US
BOTTOM LINE, THE. **Added/Corp** State Bar of California. Economics of Law Practice Section. Vol. 1 (1979)-. Periodical. English. bm. $40.00. State Bar of California, 555 Franklin Street, San Francisco CA 94102. **Tel** (415)561-8200, FAX (415)561-8228.

NE/0165-1528
BOUWRECHT. [Bouwrecht]. (1964)-. Periodical. Dutch. mo (12 issues per year). Fl296.50. Kluwer BV, Postbus 23, 7400 GA Deventer Netherlands. **Tel** 011 31 5700 33155, 011 31 5700 48999, FAX 011 31 5700 11504, telex 42829. **(Subscription address:** Libresso BV, Postbus 23, 7400 GA Deventer Netherlands.**)**

US/0162-1726
BOYCOTT LAW BULLETIN. **VFOAT** Middle East Monthly. (1978)-. Periodical. English. Twenty-four times a year. $495.00. NU TEC Publishing Inc., PO Box 73326, Houston TX 77273. **Tel** (713)444-6562, FAX (713)444-6564. **ED** Joe Kamalick. **LC** KF1987.A15; A56. **DD** 343.73/087. Index available. cum. index. ***Continues** Anti-Boycott Bulletin, 0149-3310.*
Desc: Provides news and analysis on U.S. antiboycott laws and regulations and on others country boycott requirements.

UK/0308-4574
BRACTON LAW JOURNAL, THE. [Bracton law j.]. **Added/Corp** Bracton Law Society. Vol. 1 (1965)-. Periodical. English. an (Apr.). £7.50. University of Exeter Press, Reed Hall, Streatham Drive, Exeter EX4 4RJ United Kingdom. **Tel** 011 44 392 263202. **LC** K2; .R14. **DD** 349.41/05.
Ind/Abst Curr. Law Index (1982-); Index Leg. Period.; Leg. Resour. Index (1982-); LegalTrac (1983-).

●US/1062-1814
BREAST IMPLANT LITIGATION REPORTER. [Breast implant litig. report.]. **Added/Corp** Andrews Publications, Inc. (Mar. 1992)-. Periodical. English. sm (24 issues). $685.00. Andrews Publications Inc., 1646 West Chester Pike, PO Box 1000, Westtown PA 19395. **Tel** (610)399-6600, (800)345-1101, FAX (610)399-6610. **DD** 346.
Desc: The publication tracks and reports on the most recent and significant developments in lawsuits alleging personal injuries from breast implants. Covers pre-trial proceedings, trials, and appeals. Plus FDA actions, criminal investigations and company news.

US/1066-8411
BRIDGEPORT LAW REVIEW. ***Title Change.*** [Bridgeport law rev.]. **Added/Corp** Bridgeport School of Law at Quinnipiac College. **VFOAT** Bridgeport Law Review Quinnipiac College. Vol. 12, No. 2 (Winter 1992)-(199?). Periodical. English. qt. Quinnipiac College School of Law, 303 University Avenue, Bridgeport CT 06604. **Tel** (203)576-4068. **LC** K25; .N5678. **DD** 340/.05 2 19. ***Continues** University of Bridgeport Law Review, 0735-2832.* ***Continued by** Quinnipiac Law Review.*
Desc: Contains law reviews.
Ind/Abst Curr. Law Index; Index Leg. Period.

US/0520-9617
BRIEF (BOSTON), THE. ***Title Change.*** (THE BRIEF.). **Added/Corp** Boston University. School of Law. Vol. 1 (July 1958)-(19??). Periodical. English. ***Superseded by** Brief, 0520-9617.*

US/0273-0995
BRIEF (CHICAGO. 1980), THE. (THE BRIEF.). [Brief]. **Added/Corp** American Bar Association. Tort and Insurance Practice Section. Vol. 9, No. 3 (May 1980)-. Periodical. English. qt. $26.00. American Bar Association, 750 North Lake Shore Drive, Chicago IL 60611. **Tel** (312)988-5522, (312)988-5241, FAX (312)988-5528, telex 270593. **ED** Anne Mendelson and James Carr. **LC** KF1164.A1; A45. **Ad Acc. Circ:** 22,000 (ctrl). ***Continues** INCL Brief.*
Desc: Recent trends and how-to articles for tort and insurance lawyers.
Ind/Abst Curr. Law Index (1980-); Ins. Period. Index (1989-); Leg. Resour. Index (1980-?).

US/0164-789X #y 0164-789
BRIEF TIMES REPORTER, THE. (197?)-. Periodical. English. Fifty-two times a year. $254.00. The Public Record Corporation, PO Box 18186, 1666 Lafayette Street, Denver CO 80218. **Tel** (303)832-8262, (800)487-8262, FAX (303)861-5821. Index available (Publish 3 times a year).

CN/0715-3759
BRIEFLY SPEAKING. (BRIEFLY SPEAKING : A MONTHLY REPORT FOR MEMBERS OF THE CANADIAN BAR ASSOCIATION-ONTARIO.). Vol. 1, No. 1 (Sept. 1980 I.E. 1979)-. Periodical. English (French). mo. Free. Briefly Speaking, CBAO Centre, Suite 1000/120 Adelaide Street West, Toronto Ontario M5K 1T1 Canada. **Tel** (416)869-1047. **ED** Linda Adlam. **DD** 340/.06/0713. **Circ:** 15,000 (ctrl).
Desc: Newsletter informing members of the Association of activities within the profession.

US
BRIEFS / AMERICAN ASSOCIATION OF COLLEGES FOR TEACHER EDUCATION. **Added/Corp** American Association of Colleges for Teacher Education. **VFOAT** AACTE Briefs. Vol. 7, No. 6 (Aug. 1986)-. Periodical. English. bw. $25.00 US; $35.00 other. American Association of Colleges for Teacher Education, One Dupont Circle Northwest, Suite 610, Washington DC 20036-1186. **Tel** (202)293-2450, FAX (202)457-8095. ***Continues** AACTE Briefs, 0731-602X.*
Desc: Distributed to all AACTE representatives, reports on current events concerning teacher education in education, government and public policy communities.

●US
BRIGHAM YOUNG UNIVERSITY EDUCATION AND LAW JOURNAL. **Added/Corp** Brigham Young University. Dept. of Educational Leadership. J. Reuben Clark Law School. (Spring 1993)-. English. an. $8.00 (one year); $15.00 (two years). Brigham Young University / Law School Accounting, 358B JRCB, Provo UT 84602. **Tel** (801)378-6600, FAX (801)378-2188. **Ad Acc. Circ:** 200 (ctrl). ***Continues** Brigham Young University Journal of Law and Education.*

US/0360-151X
BRIGHAM YOUNG UNIVERSITY LAW REVIEW. [Brigh. Young Univ. law rev.]. (1975)-. English. ir (four issues). $20.00 (one year), $36.00 (two year), $50.00 (three year). Brigham Young University / Law School Accounting, 358B JRCB, Provo UT 84602. **Tel** (801)378-6600, FAX (801)378-2188. **LC** K2; .R48. **DD** 340/.05. Index available. cum. index. **Ad Acc, Adv Mgr:** Amy, **Tel** (801)378-5677. **Circ:** 600 (ctrl). available on CD-ROM; available on microfilm and microfiche from University Microfilms International (UMI). Documents available from UMI Article Clearinghouse.
Desc: Articles and student pieces reviewing laws and cases relating to the legal system.
Ind/Abst ABI/INFORM Glob. Ed.; ABI Inform Ondisc (1978-); Bowne Dig. Corp. Sec. Lawyers; Curr. Law Index (1980-); Fed. Tax Artic.; Index Leg. Period.; Leg. Resour. Index (1980-); LegalTrac (1980-).

CN/0715-4798
BRITISH COLUMBIA DECISIONS, STATUTE CITATOR. [B.C. decis., statut. cit.]. **Added/Corp** British Columbia. Court of Appeal. British Columbia. Supreme Court. British Columbia. County Courts. British Columbia. Provincial Court. Western Legal Publications Ltd. (1978)-. Periodical. English. Thirteen times a year. 110.00Can$. Western Legal Publications Ltd., 301 One Alexander Street, Vancouver BC V6A 1B2 Canada. **Tel** (800)663-0422, (604)687-5671. **DD** 348.
Desc: Digests of all available decisions pertaining to interpretation and application of British Columbia statutes decided by Supreme Court of Canada and British Columbia Courts filed by subject.

CN/0824-7986
BRITISH COLUMBIA GAZETTE. PART II, REGULATIONS, THE. [B.C. gaz., Part II, Regul.]. **Main/Corp** British Columbia. Vol. 1, No. 1 (Apr. 17, 1958)-. English. Twenty-six times a year. 90.00Can$. Crown Publications Inc., 521 Fort Street, Victoria, British Columbia, V8W 1E7 Canada. **Tel** (604)386-4636, FAX (604)386-0221. **DD** 348.711/025/05. **CODEN** BRCGES. Index available (free). available on microfilm; available on microfiche.

CN/0703-3060
BRITISH COLUMBIA LAW REPORTS (CALGARY). (BRITISH COLUMBIA LAW REPORTS.). (1977)-. Periodical. English. ir (two or three times a year). 115.00Can$. Carswell / Canada, 2075 Kennedy Road, Scarborough Ontario M1T 3V4 Canada. **Tel** (416)609-3800, (800)387-5164. **ED** Darrell E. Burns. **DD** 348/.711/043. Index available. cum. index. **Ad Acc.**
Desc: Includes all judgements of value from the courts of British Columbia and appeals therefrom to the Supreme Court of Canada.

CN/0713-8865
BRITISH COLUMBIA WEEKLY LAW DIGEST. [B.C. wkly. law dig.]. Issue No. 1 (Jan. 6, 1982)-. Periodical. English. wk. 410.00Can$ Canada; $356.75 other. British Columbia Weekly Law Digest, 2330 Maitland Avenue, Agincourt Ontario M1S 1P7 Canada. **Tel** (416)291-8421. **ED** David Gill. **DD** 348.711/046. Index available. cum. index.
Desc: Case summaries of all available judgements of the courts of British Columbia plus relevant Supreme Court of Canada decicions.

UK/0953-5705
BRITISH EQUAL OPPORTUNITIES CASES. 1986-. English. Tax, Business and Law Publisher, Telford Road, Bicester Oxfordshire OX6 0XD England. **LC** KD3102; .A513. **DD** 344.41/01133.

US/0161-5823
BROADCASTING AND THE LAW. Vol. 14, No. 24 (Dec. 15, 1984)-. Periodical. English. sm. $120.00. Broadcasting and the Law., One SE Third Avenue, Suite 1450, Miami FL 33131-1715. **Tel** (305)530-8322. **ED** John M Spencer. **LC** KF2801.A3; P47. **DD** 343.73/09945. Index available. **Circ:** 1,500 (ctrl). Documents available from UMI Article Clearinghouse. ***Continues** Perry's Broadcasting and the Law.*
Desc: Reports laws and regulations affecting radio and

TV stations. Answers questions about management, personnel, news, programming, promotions, advertising and technical requirements. Covers FCC, FTC, FEC, EEOC, OSHA, courts and more.
Ind/Abst Expand. Acad. Index (1992-); Newsp. Period. Abstr. (1992-).

US/0007-232X
BROOKLYN BARRISTER. **Added/Corp** Brooklyn Bar Association. Vol. 1 (Mar. 1950)-. Periodical. English. ir. Free. Brooklyn Law School, 250 Joralemon Street, Brooklyn NY 11201. **Tel** (718)780-7971. available on microfilm and microfiche from University Microfilms International (UMI).
Ind/Abst Fed. Tax Artic.

US/0007-2362
BROOKLYN LAW REVIEW. [Brooklyn law rev.]. **Added/Corp** Brooklyn Law School. Vol. 1 (April 1932)-. Periodical. English. qt. $16.00. Brooklyn Law School, 250 Joralemon Street, Brooklyn NY 11201. **Tel** (718)780-7971. **LC** K2; .R65. **DD** 340. **Bk Rev. Circ:** 1,000 (ctrl).
Desc: Legal periodical on topics of current interest to the legal community; annual review of important second circuit cases.
Ind/Abst Bowne Dig. Corp. Sec. Lawyers; Crim. Justice Abstr.; Curr. Law Index (1980-); Fed. Tax Artic.; Index Leg. Period.; Leg. Resour. Index (1980-); LegalTrac (1980-).

HU/0524-904X
BUDAPESTI EOETVOES LORAND TUDOMANYEGYETEM ALLAM ES JOGTUDOMANYI KARANAK ACTAI. (A BUDAPESTI EOTVOS LORAND TUDOMANYEGYETEM ALLAM ES JOGTUDOMANYI KARANAK ACTAI / SZERKESZTI A KAR TUDOMANYOS ES MODSZERTANI BIZOTTSAGA.). [Budap. Eoetvoes Lorand Tudomanyegy. Allam es Jogtud. Kar.]. **Main/Corp** Budapest. Tudomany-Egyetem. Allam- es Jogtodomanyi Kar. **Added/Corp** Eoetvoes Lorand Tudomanyegyetem. Allam- es Jogtudomanyi Kar. **VFOAT** Acta Facultatis Politico-Iuridicae Universitatis Scientiarum Budapestinensis de Rolando Eoetvoes Nominatae. Vol. 1 (1959)-. Hungarian (summaries and/or abstracts in French, German and Russian; table of contents in French, German and Russian). ir. Eotvos Lorand Tudomanyegyetem, Allam es Jogtudomanyi Kar, Pf 109, 1364 Budapest, Hungary. **Tel** 1-174-930, FAX 1-1174-114.
Ind/Abst Am. Hist. Life (1974-).

US/0197-4955
BUFFALO LAW JOURNAL. [Buffalo law j.]. (19??)-. Periodical. English. sw. $75.00. Buffalo Publishing Company, 472 Delaware Avenue, Buffalo NY 14202. **Tel** (716)822-6220, FAX (716)882-3020. **ED** Jennifer Lyons, (phone: (716)882-6220). **LC** K2; .U34. **DD** 349.747/05. **Ad Acc. Circ:** 1,100.
Desc: Legal, business, commercial news and public records information.

US/0023-9356
BUFFALO LAW REVIEW. [Buffalo law rev.]. V. 1- Spring 1951-. Periodical. English. Three times a year. $27.00. State University of New York / Buffalo, Amherst Campus, 605 John Lord O' Brien Hall, Buffalo NY 14260. **Tel** (716)645-2059. **ED** Bruce Brown. **LC** K2; .U35. **DD** 340/.05. **Bk Rev. Pr Rev. Circ:** 600 (ctrl). Documents available from The Genuine Article, Documents on Demand.
Desc: A compilation of legal research regarding every facet of the law, of interest to practicing attorneys and legal scholars.
Ind/Abst Arts Humanit. Citation Index [Select. Cov.]; Bowne Dig. Corp. Sec. Lawyers; Crim. Penol. Police Sci. Abstr.; Curr. Contents Soc. Behav. Sci.; Curr. Law Index (1980-); Environ. Abstr.; Fed. Tax Artic.; Index Leg. Period.; Leg. Resour. Index (1980-); LegalTrac (1980-); Linguist. Lang. Behav. Abstr.; Res. Alert [Full Cov.]; Soc. Plann. Policy Dev. Abstr.; Soc. Sci. Cit. Index [Full Cov.]; Sociol. Abstr.

AT/0815-6050
BUILDING AND CONSTRUCTION LAW. **See** Building and Construction.

UK/0266-0628
BUILDING LAW MONTHLY. [Build. law mon.]. (1983)-. Periodical. English. mo. £135.00 UK; £157.00 other. Monitor Press, Rectory Road, Great Waldingfield, Sudbury Suffolk CO10 0TL United Kingdom. **Tel** 011 44 787 378607. **DD** 344.2037862402648.

CN/0318-8809
BUILDING PERMITS. **See** Building and Construction.

US
BUILDING REGULATION. Vol. 1, No. 1 (Spring 1979)-. Periodical. English. qt. Virginia Department of Housing and Community Development, 4th Street Office Building, 205 North 4th Street, Richmond VA 23219. **LC** KFV2859.A1; A133. **DD** 343.755/07869/005; 347. 55037869005.

RM
BULETINUL OFICIAL AL REPUBLICII SOCIALISTE ROMANIA. PARTEA A III-A. SUPLIMENT. **Main/Corp** Romania. **Added/Corp** Romania. Consiliul de Stat. (1975)-. Romanian. $80.00. Buletinul Oficial Biroul de Publicitate Si Difuzare, Pentru Buletinul Oficial, Str Mendeleev Nr 7 Sectorul 1, Bucuresti Romania.

FR
BULLETIN ADMINISTRATIF DES ASSURANCES. **Main/Corp** France. Ministere de l'Economie. Bulletin. French. qt. 8077F. Imprimerie Nationale / France, BP 514, 59505 Douai Cedex France. **Tel** 011 33 27 937090. **DD** 346.44/086; 344.40686. **Bk Rev.** ***Continues** Bulletin Administratif des Assurances - France. Ministere de l'Economie et des Finances.*
Desc: Publication of laws, texts etc. regulating the insurance business.

CN/1183-9791
BULLETIN - COUNTY OF CARLETON LAW ASSOCIATION. (BULLETIN.). [Bull. - Cty. Carlet. Law Assoc.]. **Added/Corp** County of Carleton Law Association. Vol. 1, No. 1 (Sept. 1, 1991)-. Bulletin. English (summaries and/or abstracts in French). Free to members. County of Carleton Law Association, c/o Courthouse Law Library, 2004-161 Elgin Street, Ottawa Ontario K2P 2K1 Canada. **DD** 340.

CN/0829-1802
BULLETIN DE DROIT IMMOBILIER. [Bull. droit immob.]. Vol. 1, No. 1 (June 1985)-. Bulletin. French. mo. 125.00Can$. Editions Yvon Blais, Case Postale 180, Cowansville Quebec J2K 3H6 Canada. **Tel** (514)263-1086, (800)363-3047, FAX (514)263-9256. **ED** Lise Szmigielski. **DD** 346.71404/3/05. Index available. cum. index. **Bk Rev. Circ:** 500.
Desc: Review of changes in the law and jurisprudence of real Quebec.

FR/1019-0600
BULLETIN DE L'INSTITUT INTERNATIONAL DE DROIT D'EXPRESSION FRANCAISE. [Bull. Inst. int. droit expr. fr.]. (1991)-. Periodical. French. sa.
Ind/Abst Hum. Rights Intern. Rep.

FR
BULLETIN DES ARRETS DE LA COUR DE CASSATION. **Main/Corp** Belgium. Cour de Cassation. **VFOAT** Arrets de la Cour de Cassation de Belgique. Bulletin. French. mo. $99.78. Imprimerie Nationale / France, BP 514, 59505 Douai Cedex France. **Tel** 011 33 27 937090. **Bk Rev.** ***Continues** Belgium. Cour de Cassation. Bulletin.*
Desc: Deals mostly with the decisions rendered by the Civil Court of France (Commercial and Social Courts).

CN/0226-3033
BULLETIN D'INFORMATION. RETAIL SALES TAX ACT. LOI SUR LA TAXE DE VENTE AU DETAIL. (BULLETIN D'INFORMATION.). No. 1/77- April 1977-. Bulletin. French. Retail Sales Tax Act, Loi Vente Taxe Detail, Toronto Ontario Canada. **DD** 343.71305/52/05.

US/0363-8499
BULLETIN INDEX-DIGEST SYSTEM. SERVICE FOUR. EXCISE TAX. (BULLETIN INDEX-DIGEST SYSTEM. SERVICE 4, EXCISE TAXES / DEPARTMENT OF THE TREASURY, INTERNAL REVENUE SERVICE.). **Added/Corp** United States. Internal Revenue Service. **VFOAT** Service 4 Excise Tax. (1965/1968)-. Bulletin. English. an (cumulative supplements). $19.00. Claitors Law Books, 3165 South Acadian, Baton Rouge LA 70808. **Tel** (504)344-0476, (800)274-1403. **(Subscription address:** Claitors Law Books, PO Box 3333, Baton Rouge, LA 70821**)** **LC** KF6600.A57; I5. **DD** 343/.73/055.
Desc: Contains the Finding List and Digests for all permanent tax matters published in the Internal Revenue Bulletin-Excise Taxes.

US/0363-3594
BULLETIN INDEX-DIGEST SYSTEM, SERVICE ONE. INCOME TAX. (BULLETIN INDEX-DIGEST SYSTEM. SERVICE ONE, INCOME TAX / DEPARTMENT OF THE TREASURY, INTERNAL REVENUE SERVICE.). **Added/Corp** United States. Internal Revenue Service. United States. Internal Revenue Service. Internal Revenue Bulletin. Cumulative bulletin. **VFOAT** Bulletin Index-Digest System. Service 1, Income Taxes; Income Tax; Income Taxes; Service 1 Income Tax. **VAT** Bulletin Index Digest System. Service One, Income Tax. (1953)-. Bulletin. English. $42.00. Claitors Law Books, 3165 South Acadian, Baton Rouge LA 70808. **Tel** (504)344-0476, (800)274-1403. **(Subscription address:** Claitors Law Books, PO Box 3333, Baton Rouge, LA 70821**)** **LC** KF6362.3; .I5. **DD** 343/.73/05202648. ***Continues in part** Index-Digest Supplement.*
Desc: Finding list and digests for all permanent tax matters published in the Internal Revenue Bulletin, each consists of a basic manual and cumulative supplements for an indeterminate period.

UK/0963-9675
BULLETIN / INSTITUTE OF ADVANCED LEGAL STUDIES (UNIVERSITY OF LONDON). **Added/Corp** University of London. Institute of Advanced Legal Studies. **VFOAT** IALS Bulletin,. Issue 1 (Spring Term 1988/1989)-. Bulletin. English. tq (Oct., Jan., April). Institute of Advanced Legal Studies, University of London, Charles Clore House, 17 Russell Square, London WC1B 5DR United Kingdom. **Tel** 011 44 71 637 1731, FAX 011 44 71 436 8824, telex 269 400 SH UL. **Ad Acc, Adv Mgr:** B. Crothers. **Circ:** 750.

CN/0701-0303
BULLETIN JURIDIQUE. (BULLETIN JURIDIQUE - ASSOCIATION DE LA CONSTRUCTION DE MONTREAL ET DU QUEBEC.). **Main/Corp** Association de la Construction de Montreal et du Quebec. Vol. 1 (May 1975)-. Bulletin. French. mo. Association de la Construction de Montreal et du Quebec, 4970 Place de la Savane, Montreal Quebec H4P 1Z6 Canada. **DD** 352/.992/09714.

BE
BULLETIN LEGISLATIF BELGE. No. 1 (1931)-. Bulletin. French. wk. 9,550F (airmail), 8,850F (surface mail). Maison F Larcier SA, 39 rue des Minimes, B-1000 Bruxelles Belgium. **Tel** 011 32 2 512-4712, 512-9679. **ED** Paul Schetter and Blaude Lamberts. Index available.

XR
BULLETIN OF CZECHOSLOVAK LAW. ***Ceased.*** **Added/Corp** Jednota Ceskoslovenskych Pravniku. Bulletin of Czechoslovak Law. (1925)-(Dec. 1992). Periodical. Multiple languages (English and French). qt. **(Subscription address:** Artia Pegas Press Ltd., Palac Metro Narodni Trida 25, 11210 Prague 1 Czech Republic.**)**
Ind/Abst Index Foreign Leg. Per.; Index Vet.; Vet. Bull.

US/0362-3769
BULLETIN OF LAW, SCIENCE & TECHNOLOGY. ***Title Change.*** [Bull. law sci. technol.]. **Added/Corp** American Bar Association. Section of Science and Technology. **VAT** Bulletin of Law, Science and Technology. No. 1 (Jan. 1976)-No. 87 (Oct. 1993). Periodical. English. qt. American Bar Association, 750 North Lake Shore Drive, Chicago IL 60611. **Tel** (312)988-5522, (312)988-5241, FAX (312)988-5528, telex 270593. **ED** Bertram R. Cottine. **LC** KF325.188; .B8. **DD** 344/.73/095062. ctrl circ. ***Continued by** Blast (Chicago, Ill.).*
Desc: Provides information about current developments in law, science, and technology that it believes to be of professional interest to the Section's members and other readers.
Ind/Abst Curr. Law Index (1980-Dec. 1985); Leg. Resour. Index (1980-Dec. 1985); LegalTrac (1980-1985).

US/0146-2989
BULLETIN OF MEDIEVAL CANON LAW. [Bull. mediev. canon law]. **Added/Corp** Institute of Medieval Canon Law. Bulletin of Canon Law Institute of Research and Study in Medieval Canon Law. Bulletin of Medieval Canon Law. New Series, Vol. 1, (1971)-. Bulletin. English (French, German, Italian and Spanish). an. $20.00. Institute of Medieval Canon Law, PO Box 23651, Oakland CA 94623. **Tel** (510)642-5081. **ED** Stephan Kuttner Pennington. cum. index. **Ad Acc. Circ:** 600 (ctrl).
Desc: Articles concerning the history of Canon law and its impact on the law and institutions of medieval Europe with an emphasis on manuscript research, annotated bibliography.
Ind/Abst Bibliogr. Mission.; Canon Law Abstr.

CN/1193-8536
BULLETIN OF PROCEEDINGS - CANADA. SUPREME COURT. (BULLETIN OF PROCEEDINGS.). [Bull. proc. - Can., Supreme Court]. **VFOAT** Bulletin des Procedures. (1992)-. Proceedings. Multiple languages. wk (every week during court sessions). Free (Chief Justices & Law Faculties in Canada); 107.00Can$ (including tax) other. Supreme Court of Canada, Wellington Street, Ottawa Ontario K1A 0J1 Canada. **Tel** (613)995-4330, FAX (613)996-3063. **DD** 347.71035. cum. index. **Circ:** 250 (ctrl). ***Continues** Bulletin of Proceedings Taken in the Supreme Court of Canada, 0384-2487.*

CN/0384-2487
BULLETIN OF PROCEEDINGS TAKEN IN THE SUPREME COURT OF CANADA. ***Title Change.*** (BULLETIN OF PROCEEDINGS TAKEN IN THE SUPREME COURT OF CANADA. BULLETIN DES PROCEDURES DEVANT LA COUR SUPREME DU CANADA.). [Bull. proc. taken Supreme Court Can.]. **Main/Corp** Canada. Supreme Court. **VFOAT** Bulletin des Procedures Devant la Cour Supreme du Canada. (19??)-(1992). Bulletin. English (French). Supreme Court of Canada, Wellington Street, Ottawa Ontario K1A 0J1 Canada. **Tel** (613)995-4330, FAX (613)996-3063. ***Continued by** Canada. Supreme Court.; Bulletin of Proceedings, 1193-8536.*

US/0091-634X
BULLETIN OF THE AMERICAN ACADEMY OF PSYCHIATRY AND THE LAW. See Medical Science and Technology-Psychiatry.

AT/0726-5239
BULLETIN OF THE AUSTRALIAN SOCIETY OF LEGAL PHILOSOPHY. [Bull. Aust. Soc. Legal Philos.]. (1976)-. English. Twice a year. 30.00Aus$ Australia; 35.00Aus$ other. Australian Society for Legal Philosophy, 173-175 Phillip Street/ Jurispruden, Sydney 2000 Australia. **Tel** 011 61 02 232 5944, FAX 011 61 02 221 5635. **ED** Professor Alice Tay. **DD** 340.1. **Bk Rev. Pr Rev. Circ:** 260.
Desc: To promote study and discussion in the philosophy of law, including work on legal topics from the standpoints of the social and cultural sciences.

FR
BULLETIN OFFICIEL DES ANNONCES CIVILES ET COMMERCIALES. ***Title Change.*** **Main/Corp** France. **Added/Corp** France. Journal officiel. (19??-19??). Bulletin. French. da. Direction des Journaux Officiels, 26 rue Desaix, 75727 Paris Cedex 15 France. **Tel** 011 33 1 40587500. **DD** 346/.44/0705. ***Continues*** *France.; Bulletin Officiel des Annonces Commerciales.* ***Split into*** *Bulletin Officiel des Annonces Civiles et Commerciales. BODACC "A", 0298-296X; Bulletin Officiel des Annonces Civiles et Commerciales. BODACC "B", 0298-2978* ***and*** *Bulletin Officiel des Annonces Civiles et Commerciales. BODACC "C", 0298-2986.*

FR
BULLETIN OFFICIEL DES ASSURANCES / REPUBLIQUE FRANCAISE, MINISTERE DE L'ECONOMIE. **Main/Corp** France. Ministere de l'Economie. (19??)-. Bulletin. French. 22.00 Single Issue. Ministere de l'Economie, Direction des Assurances, 54 rue de Chateaudun, Paris 9E France. **DD** 346.44/086; 344.40686. ***Continues*** *France. Ministere de l'Economie. Bulletin Administratif des Assurances.*

FR/0750-0416
BULLETIN OFFICIEL DU MINISTERE DE LA JUSTICE (FRANCE). [Bull. off. Minist. justice]. **Main/Corp** France. Ministere de la Justice. Bulletin. French. qt. 105.00F. 27 rue de la Convention, 75732 Paris Cedex 15 France.

FR
BULLETIN OFFICIEL DU SECRETARIAT D'ETAT AUX DEPARTEMENTS ET TERRITOIRES D'OUTRE-MER (FRANCE). **Main/Corp** France. Secretariat d'Etat aux Departements et Territoires d'Outre-Mer. May/June 1974-. Bulletin. French. Secretariat d'Etat aux Departements et Territoires d'Outre-Mer, 27 rue Oudinot, Paris 7E France. **DD** 342/.44/06. ***Continues*** *Bulletin Officiel du Secretaire d'Etat Aupres du Premier Ministre Charge des Departements et Territoires d'Outre-Mer.*

CN/0822-5699
BULLETIN SSQ RESPECTING SOCIAL LAWS. [Bull. SSQ respect. soc. laws]. **VAT** Bulletin Services de Sante du Quebec Respecting Social Laws. Vol. 12 (Jan. 1983)-. Bulletin. English (French). an. Free. SSQ Mutuelle d'Assurance, 2525 Boulevard Laurier, CP 10500, Sainte-Foy Quebec G1V 4H6 Canada. **Tel** (418)651-7000. **DD** 344.714/02. **Circ:** 5,000 English, 85,000 French. ***Continues*** *Bulletin SSQ sur les Lois Sociales. English, 0713-8458.*
Desc: Resume of ten most important social laws - federal and province of Quebec. Reflects situation of January first of current year.

IT
BULLETTINO DELL'ISTITUTO DI DIRITTO ROMANO. **Main/Corp** Istituto di Diritto Romano, Rome. **Added/Corp** Rome. Universita. Instituto di Diritto Romano. Vol. 1 (1888); New Series Vol. 1 (1934/58); Vol. 1 (1959)-. Italian (English and German). an. L150000.00. Giuffre Editore SPA, Via Busto Arsizio 40, 20151 Milan Italy. **Tel** 011 398 2 38089200. **ED** Mario Talamanca.
Desc: Holds a unique position in the active promotion of studies on Roman Law in Italy and abroad.

GW
BUNDESGESETZBLATT. **Main/Corp** Germany (West). **Added/Corp** Germany (West). Bundesministerium der Justiz. (19??)-. Periodical. German (French and English). ir. price varies per volume. Bundesanzeiger Verlagsges GmbH, Postfach 1320, D 53003 Bonn Germany. **Tel** 011 49 228 3820812. ***Supersedes*** *Reichsgetzblatt; Verordnungsblatt fur die Britische Zone; Getetzblatt der Verwaltung des Vereinigten Wirtschaftgebietes.*
Desc: Contains treaties and other international agreements as well as agreements between the Bund and the Lander, and further statutory order.
Ind/Abst Coal Abstr.; Energy Res. Abstr. (April 1974-).

AU
BUNDESGESETZBLATT FUER DIE REPUBLIK OSTERREICH. **Main/Corp** Austria. (19??)-. Periodical. German. da. S1359.00. Verlag der Oesterreichischen, Staatsdruckerei Rennweg 12A, A-1037 Vienna Austria. **Tel** 011 43 1 797893766.
Ind/Abst Coal Abstr.

UK
BUSINESS LAW EUROPE. (19??)-. English. mo. £340.00 UK; £360.00 other. Financial Times England, 8 16 Great New Street, London EC4A 3BN England. **Tel** 011 44 71 353 0305, 353 1040, FAX 011 44 353 0846. ***Continues*** *Business Law Brief.*

US/1066-2596
BUSINESS LEGAL MATERIALS, RUSSIA. [Bus. leg. mater. Russ.]. (1992)-. Periodical. English. mo. $175.00 (libraries), $225.00 (other institutions and individuals)) US and Canada; $190.00 (libraries), $250.00 (other institutions and individuals) other. Russian Information Services, 89 Main Street, Box 2, Montpelier VT 05602. **Tel** (802)223-4955, FAX (802)223-6105. **ED** Paul Richardson. **DD** _a346. Index available.
Desc: Monthly compendium listing all laws of Russia relating to foreign trade and investment.

AN/1013-7777
BUTLLETI OFICIAL DEL PRINCIPAT D'ANDORRA. [Butll. of. Principat Andorra]. **Main/Corp** Andorra. (1989)-. Periodical. Catalan. bw.

UK/0959-3438
BUTTERWORTH LECTURES. [Butterworth lect.]. (1989)-. English. an. £19.95. Butterworth & Co. Ltd. / Kent, England, Borough Green, Sevenoaks Kent TN15 8PH England. **Tel** 011 44 732-884567, FAX 011 44 732-885996. **DD** 340.
Desc: Series given under the auspices of the Faculty of Laws of Queen Mary and Westfield College, University of London.

UK
BUTTERWORTH'S CONSTRUCTION LAW MANUAL. English. Butterworth & Co. Ltd. / Kent, England, Borough Green, Sevenoaks Kent TN15 8PH England. **Tel** 011 44 732-884567, FAX 011 44 732-885996. **(Subscription address:** Promotion Department, Butterworth & Co. Ltd., Freepost, 88 Kingsway, London WC2B 6BR England**)**
Desc: Addresses the common law issues such as formation of contract, privity, exclusion clauses and third parties. Also examines the aspects of the law peculiar to the construction industry, such as certification, retention moneys and variation of the contract, assignment, warranties and bonds, etc.

UK/0968-1418
BUTTERWORTHS EC CASE CITATOR AND SERVICE. [Butterworths EC case cit. serv.]. **VFOAT** Butterworths European Community Case Citator and Service. (1991)-. English. Twice a year (with a fortnightly updating service). £450.00. Butterworth & Co. Ltd. / Kent, England, Borough Green, Sevenoaks Kent TN15 8PH England. **Tel** 011 44 732-884567, FAX 011 44 732-885996. **ED** Stuart Isaacs. **DD** 341.0268.
Desc: Enables practitioners to find the main report references for all cases which are or have been before the Court.

●UK/0969-3912
BUTTERWORTH'S EC LEGISLATION IMPLEMENTATOR. **VFOAT** Butterworth's European Community Legislation Implementator. (1993)-. English. Twice a year. £145.00. Butterworth & Co. Ltd. / Kent, England, Borough Green, Sevenoaks Kent TN15 8PH England. **Tel** 011 44 732-884567, FAX 011 44 732-885996.
Desc: Lists all directives since UK accession and shows whether they have been implemented in the UK.

SA
BUTTERWORTHS INDEX AND NOTER-UP TO THE SOUTH AFRICAN LAW REPORTS. **Added/Corp** Butterworth & Co. (SA). (19??)-. English. an (Feb.). R80.00. Butterworth & Company / South Africa, PO Box 792, Durban 4000 South Africa. **Tel** 011 27 31 294247, FAX 011 27 31 283255. **ED** T. Coghlan. **DD** 346.80848. Index available. cum. index. ctrl circ.

SI/0951-5720
BUTTERWORTHS LAW DIGEST MALAYSIA, SINGAPORE AND BRUNEI. [Butterworths law dig. Malays. Singap. Brunei]. (May 1987)-. Periodical. English. mo. 275.00Sing$. Butterworths Asia, (A subsidiary of Reed International (Singapore) Pte. Ltd.), 3 Shenton Way, Number 1403, Singapore 0106 Republic of Singapore. **Tel** 011 65 2203684, FAX 011 65 2255026. **ED** Teo Keang Sood and Walter Woon. Index available. cum. index. **Bk Rev. Ad Acc. Circ:** 600.
Desc: The journal features digests of all significant recent cases in Malaysia, Singapore and Brunei. Notes on recent statues and subsidiary legislation from Singapore and Malaysia; digests of relevant cases and statues judicially considered.

UK
BUTTERWORTHS ORANGE TAX HANDBOOK. 1st Ed. (1976/1977)-. English. an. £20.00. Butterworth & Co. Ltd. / Kent, England, Borough Green, Sevenoaks Kent TN15 8PH England. **Tel** 011 44 732-884567, FAX 011 44 732-885996. **ED** Moiz Sadikali. **LC** KD5415; .B88. **DD** 343/.41/04.
Desc: Contains the up-to-date text of all the enactments relating to inheritance tax, national insurance contributions, stamp duty and value added tax. The material is chronologically arranged and fully indexed and cross-referenced.

UK
BUTTERWORTH'S UK TAX GUIDE. **Added/Corp** Butterworths (Firm). **VFOAT** Butterworth's U.K. Tax Guide; UK Tax Guide. (1982/1983)-. English. an. £16.95. Butterworth & Co. Ltd. / Kent, England, Borough Green, Sevenoaks Kent TN15 8PH England. **Tel** 011 44 732-884567, FAX 011 44 732-885996. **LC** KD5359; .B87. **DD** 343.4204; 344.2034. **Circ:** 24,000.
Desc: A major narrative dealing with all UK taxes, showing how they work and the policy behind them. Numerous cross-references, worked examples and tax tables are provided.

UK
BUTTERWORTHS YELLOW TAX HANDBOOK. 15th Ed. (1976/1977)-. English. an. £20.00. Butterworth & Co. Ltd. / Kent, England, Borough Green, Sevenoaks Kent TN15 8PH England. **Tel** 011 44 732-884567, FAX 011 44 732-885996. **ED** Moiz Sadikali. **LC** KD5423.99; .B87. **DD** 343/.42/04. ***Continues*** *Butterworths Tax Handbook.*
Desc: Provides the text of the legislation relating to income tax, capital gains tax and corporation tax in the amended and updated form needed for accurate assessments.

UK
BUYING AND SELLING LAW. (19??)-. Periodical. English. bm. £152.85. Croner Publ Ltd, Croner House, London Road, Kingston upon Thames, Surrey KT2 6SR England. **Tel** 011 44 81 5473333, FAX 081 547-2637.

US/0896-2383
BYU JOURNAL OF PUBLIC LAW, THE. [BYU j. public law]. **Added/Corp** J. Reuben Clark Law School. **VFOAT** Journal of Public Law; B.Y.U. Journal of Public Law. **VAT** Brigham Young University Journal of Public Law. Vol. 1, No. 1 (1986)-. Periodical. English. Twice a year (Apr., Nov.). $10.00 one year; $18.00 two years; $26.00 three years. Brigham Young University / Law School Accounting, 358B JRCB, Provo UT 84602. **Tel** (801)378-6600, FAX (801)378-2188. **LC** K2; .Y8. **DD** 342.73; 347.302. **Ad Acc. Circ:** 250 (ctrl).
Ind/Abst Index Leg. Period.; Leg. Resour. Index; LegalTrac (1990-).

CN/0704-0393
C L I C 'S LEGAL MATERIALS LETTER. ***Ceased.*** [CLIC leg. mater. lett.]. **Main/Corp** Canadian Law Information Council. **VFOAT** Bulletin d'Information Juridique. **VAT** Canadian Law Information Council's Legal Materials Letter. No. 1 (1977)-(1989). Periodical. English (French). bm. Canadian Law Information Council / Ottawa, 161 Laurier Avenue West, 5th Floor Ottawa, Ontario K1P 5J2 Canada. **Tel** (613)236-9766. **ED** John J Pyl. **DD** 340/.0971. Index available. **Bk Rev. Circ:** 500.
Desc: Provides features on new legal materials, reviews of recent books, annotations of recently released books, pamphlets, videos, etc., that deal with Canadian law.
Ind/Abst Can. Legal Lit.

US/1068-3631
CABLE T.V. AND NEW MEDIA LAW & FINANCE. See Communication-Broadcasting.

US/0161-6811
CABLE TELEVISION LAW : MUNICIPAL LAW OFFICERS EDITION. Periodical. English. mo. Communications Law Publishers, 1819 H Street North West, Washington DC 20036. **LC** KF2844.A15; C3. **DD** 343/.73/0994.

US/0749-7652
CABLE TV LAW REPORTER. [Cable TV law report.]. **Added/Corp** Paul Kagan Associates. **VFOAT** Cable Television Law Reporter. No. 1 (Sept. 6, 1984)-. English. sm. $550.00. Kagan World Media Inc., 126 Clock Tower Place, Carmel CA 93923-8734. **Tel** (408)624-1536, FAX (408)625-3225. **ED** Dwight Beach. **LC** KF2844.A59; C33. **DD** 343.73/09946; 347.3039946.
Desc: Newsletter on the latest and most important legal cases, including antitrust, first amendment, franchising, taxation, copyright, rate regulation, privacy and international law.

BL
CADERNO DE DIREITO ECONOMICO. No. 1-. Periodical. Portuguese. sa. Cr$45.00-Cr$65.00 Brazil; $15.00 US. Centro de Estudos de Extensao Universitaria, Avenida Professor Alfonso, Bovero 175,

01254 Sao Paulo Brazil. **Tel** (011)577, 2822, (011)872-1877. **LC** K3; .A29. **DD** 348.103805. **Circ:** 3,000.
Desc: Collection of articles by specialists, responding to topical questions on a specific theme of contributory and tax legislation.

BL
CADERNO DE PESQUISAS TRIBUTARIAS. No. 1-. Portuguese. an. $25.00. Centro de Estudos de Extensao Universitaria, Avenida Professor Alfonso, Bovero 175, 01254 Sao Paulo Brazil. **Tel** (011)577, 2822, (011)872-1877. **LC** K3; .A34. **DD** 343/.81/0405. **Bk Rev. Circ:** 10,000.
Desc: Collection of articles by specialists responding to topical questions on legislated or non-legislated issues in contributory and tax laws.

BE/0007-9758
CAHIERS DE DROIT EUROPEEN. [Cah. droit eur.]. (1965)-. Periodical. French. Six times a year. 5200.00F. Etablissements Emile Bruylant, 67 rue de la Regence, 1000 Brussels Belgium. **Tel** 011 32 2 5129845. **Ind/Abst** Index Foreign Leg. Per.; Int. Labour Doc.; Int. Polit. Sci. Abstr.

CN/0007-974X
CAHIERS DE DROIT (QUEBEC). (LES CAHIERS DE DROIT.). [Cah. droit]. Vol. 1, No. 1 (Dec. 1954)-. Periodical. French. qt. 45.00Can$. Wilson & Lafleur Ltd., 40 Rue Notre Dame East, Montreal, Quebec H2Y 1B9 Canada. **Tel** (514)875-6326, FAX (514)875-8356. **ED** Henri Brun. cum. index. **Bk Rev. Circ:** 1,600. available on microfilm and microfiche from University Microfilms International (UMI).
Desc: The review seeks to promote the juridical science and informs in a critical manner about the condition of law in the province of Quebec.
Ind/Abst Can. Legal Lit.; Index Foreign Leg. Per.; Index Leg. Period.; Leg. Resour. Index (1980-); LegalTrac (1980-); Point Repere (1983-).

FR/1148-4683
CAHIERS DE L'EUROPE PARIS. See Sociology-Social Services and Welfare.

FR/0982-3573
CAHIERS DU BARREAU DE PARIS, LES. Added/Corp Barreau de Paris. No. 1 (1987)-. Periodical. French. ir. 170.00F (latest edition). Aux Amateurs de Livres International, 62 Avenue de Suffren, 75015 Paris France. **Tel** 011 33 1 45671838.

II
CALCUTTA LAW JOURNAL. English. Twenty-four times a year. $32.00. Law Publishers and Booksellers, Sardar Patel Marg, PO Box 1077, Allahabad 211 001 India. **Tel** 011 91 532 604524, 602298. Index available. **Bk Rev. Ad Acc. Pr Rev.**

US/1044-9345
CALIFORNIA ARBITRATIONS. [Calif. arbitr.]. Vol. 10, No. 1 (Jan. 15, 1989)-. Periodical. English. Twelve times a year. California Arbitrations, PO Box 29, Monte Rio CA 95462. **LC** KFC310.A15; J87. **DD** 346.79403/05; 347.9406305. ***Continues** Jury Verdicts Weekly. Judicial Arbitrations Biweekly, 0888-0654.*

US
CALIFORNIA DURABLE POWER OF ATTORNEY HANDBOOK. Added/Corp California Continuing Education of the Bar. Continuing Education of the Bar--California. **VFOAT** Durable Power of Attorney Handbook; Durable Power of Attorney. (1988)-. English. an. $48.00. California Continuing Education of the Bar, 2300 Shattuck Avenue, Berkeley CA 94704. **Tel** (510)642-8000, (800)232-3444. **LC** KFC336; .C35. **DD** 346.794/029; 347.940629.
Desc: Presents a thorough treatment of technical requirements and highlights areas that have potential for abuse.

US/0271-2741
CALIFORNIA GOVERNMENT CONTRACTS. [Calif. gov. contracts]. V. 1- Aug. 1979-. Periodical. English. mo. $45.00. California Procurement Publications, 580 University Avenue/Suite 201, Sacramento CA 95825. **LC** KFC224.A15; C34. **DD** 346.794/023/05.

US
CALIFORNIA GOVERNMENT TORT LIABILITY PRACTICE / ARVO VAN ALSTYNE. (1980)-. English. $150.00. California Continuing Education of the Bar, 2300 Shattuck Avenue, Berkeley CA 94704. **Tel** (510)642-8000, (800)232-3444.
Desc: Includes a thorough discussion of the procedure to perfect claims and actions against public entities and public employees.

US
CALIFORNIA HEALTH LAW REPORT. ***Ceased.*** (19??)-(Dec. 1992). English. mo. Robert Anderson Publishing Company, 9323 Tech Center Drive, Suite 1700, Sacramento CA 95822. **Tel** (916)856-5050. **(Subscription address:** PO Box 22970, Sacramento CA 95822**) ED** Leigh Gruhn Nurre. **Bk Rev. Ad Acc. Pr Rev. Circ:** 350 (ctrl).
Desc: Provides concise information on healthcare and legal issues that affect healthcare professionals; including legislative action, agency regulation changes, court decisions and attorney general opinion.

US/1047-6466
CALIFORNIA INSURANCE LAW & REGULATION REPORTER. [Calif. insur. law regul. report.]. **Added/Corp** Litigation Research Group (San Francisco, Calif). **VFOAT** California Insurance Law and Regulation Reporter; California Insurance Law. Vol. 1, No. 1 (Nov. 1989)-. English. mo. $355.00. Shepards McGraw-Hill Inc, 555 Middle Creek Parkway, PO Box 35300, Colorado Springs CO 80935-3530. **Tel** (719)488-3000, FAX (800)525-0053. **ED** John DiMugno and Nadia Holober. **LC** KFC290.A15; C348. **DD** 346.794/086/05; 347.94068605.
Desc: Reviews every reported insurance and insurance related development in the state. Within days of an important decision, this timely newsletter gives you information you need to make fast, accurate decisions for yourself and your clients.

US/0890-4871
CALIFORNIA INSURANCE LAW REPORT. [Calif. insur. law rep.]. **Added/Corp** Data Research, Inc. (Rosemount, Minn.). Vol. 1, No. 1 (Oct. 1986)-. English. Twelve times a year. $217.00. Data Research Inc., PO Box 490, Rosemount MN 55068. **Tel** (612)452-8267, (800)365-4900. **LC** KFC290.A15; C35. **DD** 346.794/086/05; 347.94068605. Index available.
Desc: Information on the California insurance law.

US/1058-8205
CALIFORNIA LAND USE LAW & POLICY REPORTER. [Calif. land use law policy report.]. **Added/Corp** Shepard's/McGraw-Hill. **VFOAT** California Land Use Law and Policy Reporter; California Land Use. Vol. 1, No. 1 (Sept. 1991)-. Periodical. English. mo. $231.60. Shepards McGraw-Hill Inc, 555 Middle Creek Parkway, PO Box 35300, Colorado Springs CO 80935-3530. **Tel** (719)488-3000, FAX (800)525-0053. **ED** Robert Schuster. **LC** KFC811.A59; C35. **DD** 346.79404/5; 347.940645.

US/0008-1221
CALIFORNIA LAW REVIEW. [Calif. law rev.]. **Added/Corp** University of California, Berkeley. School of Law. University of California, Berkeley. School of Jurisprudence. Vol. 1, No. 1 (Nov. 1912)-. Periodical. English. bm (Jan., Mar., May, July, Oct., Dec.). $38.00 US; $47.00 (postage included) other. University of California Press, 2120 Berkeley Way, Berkeley CA 94720. **Tel** (510)642-4191, (510)642-3907, FAX (510)642-9917. **LC** K3; .A433. **DD** 340/.05. **CODEN** CLARDJ. **[CCC].** cum. index. **Pr Rev. Circ:** 1,900. available on microfilm and microfiche from University Microfilms International (UMI). Documents available from The Genuine Article, UMI Article Clearinghouse, UMI Article Clearinghouse, UMI Article Clearinghouse.
Desc: Published for the students of Boalt Hall School of Law at the University of California, Berkeley.
Ind/Abst ABC POL SCI; ABI/INFORM Glob. Ed.; ABI Inform Ondisc (Sept. 1976-); Bowne Dig. Corp. Sec. Lawyers; Commun. Abstr.; Crim. Justice Abstr.; Curr. Contents Soc. Behav. Sci.; Curr. Law Index (1980-); Expand. Acad. Index (1984-); Fed. Tax Artic.; Index Leg. Period.; Leg. Resour. Index (1980-); LegalTrac (1980-); Newsp. Period. Abstr. (1989-); PAIS Int. Print (1991); Res. Alert [Full Cov.]; Soc. Sci. Cit. Index [Full Cov.]; Urban Aff. Abstr.; Women Stud. Abstr.

US/0279-4063
CALIFORNIA LAWYER. [Calif. lawyer]. **Added/Corp** State Bar of California. (1981)-. Periodical. English. mo. $48.00. California Lawyer Magazine, 1390 Market Street, Suite 1210, San Francisco CA 94102. **Tel** (415)252-0500, FAX (415)252-0288. **ED** Ray Reynolds. **LC** KF200; .C34. **DD** 349.795/05; 347.95005. Index Bound in First Issue (Dec. issues). **Bk Rev**, (Qty: 30). **Ad Acc, Adv Mgr:** Steven Phillips, **Tel** (415)252-0500. **Circ:** 140,000 (ctrl). available on microfiche from LEXIS. ***Continues** California State Bar Journal, 0161-9241.*
Desc: The State Bar of California, containing articles and features pertaining to the personal and professional lives of the attorneys.
Ind/Abst Account. Art.; Bowne Dig. Corp. Sec. Lawyers (1981-); Curr. Law Index (1984-); Fed. Tax Artic.; Index Leg. Period.; Law Office Inf. Serv.; Leg. Resour. Index (1981-?, 1984-); LegalTrac (1981-).

US/1052-2379
CALIFORNIA LAWYERS. [Calif. lawyers]. **Added/Corp** Daily Journal (Firm) State Bar of California. **VFOAT** Directory of California Lawyers. Jan. (1990)-. Directory. English. sa. $20.00. Daily Journal Corporation, 915 East First Street, Los Angeles CA 90012. **Tel** (213)229-5300, FAX (213)680-3682. **LC** KF192.C3; C325. **DD** 349.794/025; 347.940025. ***Continues** California Attorneys, 1046-7777.*

US
CALIFORNIA LEGAL DIRECTORY, THE. (19??)-. Directory. English. an. $34.00. Legal Directories Publishing Company, 9111 Garland Road, PO Box 189000, Dallas TX 75218. **Tel** (214)321-3238, 800 447-5375. **LC** KF192.C3; C34. **DD** 340/.025/794. ***Continues** Pacific Coast Legal Directory.*

US/0097-9902
CALIFORNIA LIBRARY LAWS. Main/Corp California State Library. 1974-. English. an. California State Library, PO Box 942837, Sacramento CA 94237. **Tel** (916)445-4027. **LC** KFC675.A29; C34. **DD** 344/.794/092.

US/0883-6116
CALIFORNIA LOCAL PROBATE RULES. Added/Corp California Continuing Education of the Bar. (1971)-. English. $56.00. California Continuing Education of the Bar, 2300 Shattuck Avenue, Berkeley CA 94704. **Tel** (510)642-8000, (800)232-3444. **LC** KFC205.A39; C35. **DD** 346.79405/2; 347.940652.
Desc: Up-to-date compendium of the probate rules and procedures for each county in California.

US/1040-2640
CALIFORNIA PARALEGAL MAGAZINE. ***Ceased.*** [Calif. paralegal mag.]. (1989)-(Dec. 1992). Periodical. English. qt. California Paralegal Magazine, PO Box 6960, Los Osos CA 93412. **Tel** (805)772-8806. **(Subscription address:** PO Box 6960, Los Osos CA 93412**) ED** Valery E Goodman-Plater. **LC** KF320.L4; C35. **DD** 340/.08834. Index available. **Bk Rev. Ad Acc. Circ:** 2,000 (ctrl).
Desc: Information, education and inspiration for California paralegals.

US
CALIFORNIA PHARMACY LAWS, WITH RULES AND REGULATIONS. Main/Corp California. **Added/Corp** California. State Board of Pharmacy. California. Dept. of Consumer Affairs. (19??)-. English. Board of Pharmacy, 1021 O Street, Sacramento CA 95814. **LC** KFC546.5.P4; A296. **DD** 344/.794/042. ***Continues** California. Laws, Statutes, Etc. Pharmacy Laws of California and Administrative Rules of Board of Pharmacy.*

US/1052-2921
CALIFORNIA REAL PROPERTY JOURNAL. (CALIFORNIA REAL PROPERTY JOURNAL : OFFICIAL PUBLICATION OF THE REAL PROPERTY LAW SECTION, STATE BAR OF CALIFORNIA.). [Calif. real prop. j.]. **Added/Corp** State Bar of California. Real Property Law Section. Vol. 1, No. 1 (Winter 1982)-. Periodical. English. Four times a year. $40.00 (membership). State Bar of California, 555 Franklin Street, San Francisco CA 94102. **Tel** (415)561-8200, FAX (415)561-8228. **DD** 346. ***Continues** Real Property News.*
Ind/Abst Index Leg. Period.

●US/1072-7833
CALIFORNIA REGULATORY LAW BULLETIN. (1993)-. English. wk. $230.00. Barclays Law Publishers, 400 Oyster Point Boulevard, South San Francisco CA 94080. **Tel** (800)888-3600, (415)244-6611, FAX (415)244-0408.

US/0739-7860
CALIFORNIA REGULATORY LAW REPORTER, THE. [Calif. regul. law report.]. **Added/Corp** University of San Diego. Center for Public Interest Law. Vol. 1, No. 1 (Spring 1981)-. Periodical. English. Four times a year (Jan., Apr., July, Oct.). $58.00. Center for Public Interest Law, 5998 Alcala Park, University of San Diego, San Diego CA 92110. **Tel** (619)260-4806. **ED** Robert C. Fellmeth and Julianne D'Angelo. **LC** KFC430.A15; C35. **DD** 343.794/08; 347.94038. Index available (Bound in Winter iss. ($14.50)). cum. index. **Circ:** 1,500 (ctrl). ***Absorbed** Check-Up.*
Desc: Covers and analyzes policy decisions, rulemaking, and legislation affecting sixty California regulatory agencies. Also includes summaries of Litigation, the activities of public interest organizations, feature articles and commentaries.

US/1041-2654
CALIFORNIA REGULATORY NOTICE REGISTER. [Calif. regul. not. regist.]. **Added/Corp** California. Office of Administrative Law. **VFOAT** Regulatory Notice Register; Z Register. Register 88, No. 1-Z (Jan. 1, 1988)-. English. Fifty-two times a year. $162.00. California Administrative Law, Office of Administrative Law, 555 Capitol Mall, Suite 1290, Sacramento CA 95814. **Tel** (916)323-6225. **ED** Karen Morris (phone: (916)324-7954). **LC** KFC36; .C3. **DD** 343. Index available. cum. index. **Circ:** 950 (ctrl). ***Continues** California Administrative Notice Register.*
Desc: Contains notices of proposed regulatory actions by state regulatory agencies to adopt, amend or repeal regulations contained in the California Code of Regulations.

US/0094-2057
CALIFORNIA SCHOOL LAW DIGEST. [Calif. sch. law dig.]. (19??)-. English. mo. $130.00 (one year), $250.00 (two year). Whitaker Newsletter, PO Box 340, 313 South Avenue, Suite 202, Fanwood NJ 07023-0340. **Tel** (201)889-6336, FAX (201)889-6339. **(Subscription address:** Whitaker Newsletters, PO Box 192, Fanwood NJ 07923.**) ED** Fred Rossi. **LC** KFC648.A59; G73. **DD** 344/.794/0705. **[CCC]. Bk Rev. Circ:** 500.
Desc: Covers legal developments (appellate court

decisions) affecting California public schools (student rights, employment discrimination and teacher dismissals).

US/0744-6756
CALIFORNIA TORT REPORTER. **VFOAT** CTR. Vol. 1 (Jan. 1980)-. Periodical. English. mo (10 issues). $290.00. Shepards McGraw-Hill Inc, 555 Middle Creek Parkway, PO Box 35300, Colorado Springs CO 80935-3530. **Tel** (719)488-3000, FAX (800)525-0053. **ED** Leonard Sacks and Neil Levy. cum. index.
Desc: It's the only source for timely summaries and interpretations of every tort-related action by the California Supreme Court of Appeal, US Supreme Court, Ninth Circuit Court, Federal District Court, and the California legislature.

US/0008-1639
CALIFORNIA WESTERN LAW REVIEW. [Calif. west. law rev.]. **Added/Corp** California Western School of Law. Vol. 1, No. 1 (Spring 1965)-. Periodical. English. Twice a year. $20.00 US; $25.00 other. California Western School of Law, 225 Cedar Street, San Diego CA 92101. **Tel** (619)239-0391, (800)225-4252, FAX (619)696-9999. **ED** Michael P. Fitzgerald and Laura R. Hillock. cum. index. **Bk Rev**. **Ad Acc**. **Circ:** 1,400 (ctrl). available in microform; available on an online database.
Desc: Lead articles and student notes and comments as well as book reviews on general areas of law.
Ind/Abst Commun. Abstr.; Crim. Justice Abstr.; Crim. Penol. Police Sci. Abstr.; Curr. Law Index; Fed. Tax Artic.; Index Leg. Period.; Leg. Resour. Index (1980-); LegalTrac (1980-); PAIS Int. Print.

US/1048-5392
CALLAGHAN'S LAW REVIEW DIGEST. [Callaghan's law rev. dig.]. **VFOAT** Law Review Digest. Vol. 34, No. 2 (March/April 1985)-. English. bm. $90.00. Clark Boardman Callaghan, 155 Pfingsten Road, Deerfield IL 60015. **Tel** (800)323-8067. **ED** L A Bakken. **DD** 348. ***Continues*** *Law Review Digest.*

US
CAMBRIA COUNTY LEGAL JOURNAL. English. Fifty-two times a year. $60.00. Cambria County Bar Association, PO Box 338, Ebensburg PA 15931. **Tel** (814)472-9530. **ED** D. J. Damin. **Ad Acc**. ctrl circ.

UK/0084-8328
CAMBRIAN LAW REVIEW, THE. [Cambr. law rev.]. (1970)-. English. an (Mar.). $25.00. University College of Wales, H Owen Building, Aberystwyth SY23 3DD Wales UK. **Tel** 011 44 970 623111, FAX 0970622729, telex 35181 ABYUCW G. **LC** K3; .A44. **DD** 340/.05. **Bk Rev**, (Qty: 10). **Ad Acc**. **Circ:** 500.
Desc: A law review covering articles of a general academic interest both British and comparative and with British legal history bibliography and book reviews.
Ind/Abst Curr. Law Index (1980-); Index Leg. Period.; Leg. Resour. Index (1980-); LegalTrac (1980-).

UK/0008-1973
CAMBRIDGE LAW JOURNAL, THE. [Camb. law j.]. **Added/Corp** Cambridge University Law Society. Vol. 1, No. 1 (1921)-. Academic Scholarly Publication. English. Three times a year (March, July and November). $84.00 US, Canada & Mexico; £39.00 other. Cambridge University Press, The Edinburgh Building, Shaftesbury Road, Cambridge CB2 2RU United Kingdom. **Tel** 011 44 223 312393, FAX 011 44 223 325959. **(Subscription address:** Cambridge University Press / North America, 110 Midland Avenue, Port Chester NY 10573.**)** **ED** C. C. Turpin. **DD** 340/.05. Index Available, published separately, free-automatically sent. cum. index. **Bk Rev**. available on microfilm from University Microfilms International (UMI).
Desc: The journal's range includes jurisprudence and legal history, with a special emphasis placed on contemporary developments. A feature of the journal is the "Case and Comment" section in which members of the Cambridge Law Faculty and other contributors analyze recent judicial decisions, new legislation and current law reform proposals. The case notes and articles are designed to have the widest appeal to those interested in the law - whether as practitioners, students, teachers, judges, or administrators - and to provide an opportunity to keep them abreast of new ideas and the progress of legal reform.
Ind/Abst Br. Humanit. Index; Crim. Justice Abstr.; Curr. Law Index (1980-); Fed. Tax Artic.; Index Leg. Period.; Int. Bibliogr. Sociol.; Leg. Resour. Index (1980-); LegalTrac (1983-).

UK
CAMBRIDGE STUDIES IN ENGLISH LEGAL HISTORY. (1959)-. Monographic series. English. ir. Price varies per volume. Cambridge University Press, The Edinburgh Building, Shaftesbury Road, Cambridge CB2 2RU United Kingdom. **Tel** 011 44 223 312393, FAX 011 44 223 325959. **(Subscription address:** North America/ Cambridge University Press, 40 West 20th Street, New York, NY 10011-4211; telephone: (212)924-3900**)**

US/0748-2396
CAMP RESORT LAW REPORT. [Camp resort law rep.]. Vol. 1, No. 1 (May 1984)-. Periodical. English. bm. $75.00. Land Development Institute Ltd, 1401 16th Street Northwest, Washington DC 20036. **Tel** (202)232-2144, FAX (202)232-4757. **ED** Stuart Marshall, William Ingersoll and Lisa Marsh. Index available. cum. index. **Circ:** 200 (ctrl).
Desc: News on federal, state and local laws regarding campground development; court campground development and court and administrative decisions.

US/0884-8351
CAMPAIGN FINANCE LAW. (CAMPAIGN FINANCE LAW / AMERICAN LAW DIVISION, CONGRESSIONAL RESEARCH SERVICE, LIBRARY OF CONGRESS.). **Added/Corp** Library of Congress. Congressional Research Service. American Law Division. Clearinghouse on Election Administration (U.S.) D.T. Skelton Service Associates. Instructional Systems Corporation. Insight Group. (19??)-. English. an. $38.00. Superintendent of Documents, US Government Printing Office, Washington DC 20402. **Tel** (202)275-3328, FAX (202)786-2377. **(Subscription address:** US Government Bookstore, O'Neil Building, 2023 3rd Avenue North, Birmingham, AL 35203**)** **LC** KF4920.Z95; L5. **DD** 342.73/078; 347.30278. ***Continues*** *Analysis of Federal and State Campaign Finance Law, Summaries, and Quick-Reference Charts, 0190-0498.*
Desc: Contains legal memorandums summarizing state campaign finance regulations. Includes quick reference charts and opinions.

US/0094-1921
CAMPAIGN LAW REPORTER. **See** Political Science.

US/0361-056X
CAMPAIGN PRACTICES REPORTS. ***Ceased.*** **VFOAT** CP Reports. Vol. 1 (June 17, 1974)-Ceased Vol. 20 (1991). Periodical. English. bw (26 issues). Congressional Quarterly Inc., 1414 22nd Street Northwest, Washington DC 20037. **Tel** (202)887-8500, (800)432-2250 ext. 621, FAX (202)728-1863. **LC** KF4885.A15; C34. **DD** 342/.73/0705. **[CCC].**

US/0198-8174
CAMPBELL LAW REVIEW. [Campbell law rev.]. **Added/Corp** Campbell University (Buies Creek, N.C.). School of Law. Vol. 1 (1979)-. Periodical. English. Three times a year (Winter, Spring and Summer). $15.00. Campbell University School of Law, PO Box 1165, Buis Creek NC 27506. **Tel** (919)893-1799. **ED** Donald Higley. **LC** K3; .A452. **DD** 349.756/05; 347.56005. Index available (Bound in 3rd issue). **Ad Acc**, **Adv Mgr:** Don Hegley, **Tel** (919)893-4111. **Circ:** 520.
Ind/Abst Bowne Dig. Corp. Sec. Lawyers; Curr. Law Index (1981-); Fed. Tax Artic.; Index Leg. Period.; Leg. Resour. Index (1981-)(1980-); LegalTrac (1980-).

US/0742-8987
CAMPBELL'S LIST. (CAMPBELL'S LIST; A DIRECTORY OF SELECTED LAWYERS.). [Campbell's list]. **VFOAT** Campbell's List of Members of an Association for the Prompt Service of Papers ... . (19??)-. Directory. English. an. $10.00. Campbells List Inc., 100 East Ventris Avenue, PO Box 428, Maitland FL 32751. **Tel** (407)644-8298. **ED** John A. Campbell Jr. **Circ:** 6,500 (ctrl).
Desc: A directory of selected lawyers since 1879. We will accept referrals from out-of-town lawyers and clients. All are in general practice and most handle collections.

CN/0384-2568
CANADA FEDERAL COURT REPORTS. [Can. Fed. Court rep.]. **Main/Corp** Canada. Federal Court. **VFOAT** Recueil des Arrets de la Cour Federale du Canada. (1971)-. Periodical. Multiple languages (English and French). Twelve times a year. 78.00Can$. Canada Communication Group Publishers, Order Processing, Ottawa Ontario K1A 0S9 Canada. **Tel** (819)956-4800, (819)956-4802. **LC** KE142; .A23. **DD** 349.71; 347.1. ***Supersedes*** *Canada. Exchequer Court. Canada Exchequer Court Reports., 0384-255X.*

CN/0045-4192
CANADA GAZETTE. PART 1. (THE CANADA GAZETTE, PART I. LA GAZETTE DU CANADA, PARTIE I.). [Can. gaz., 1]. **Main/Corp** Canada. **VFOAT** Gazette du Canada, Partie I; Statement of the Assets and Liabilities of the Chartered Banks of Canada; Chartered Banks of Canada, Statement of Assets and Liabilities; Statement of Assets and Liabilities, Chartered Banks of Canada. Vol. 104 (Jan. 3, 1970)-. Periodical. English (French). wk. Canada Communication Group Publishers, Order Processing, Ottawa Ontario K1A 0S9 Canada. **Tel** (819)956-4800, (819)956-4802. available on microfilm from Micromedia Limited. ***Continues*** *Canada. The Canada Gazette.*

CN/0045-4206
CANADA GAZETTE. PART 2. (CANADA GAZETTE. PART II MICROFORM.). [Can. gaz., 2]. **Main/Corp** Canada. **VFOAT** La Gazette du Canada. Partie II; Gazette du Canada. Partie II; Canada Gazette. Part II, Statutory Orders and Regulations; Canada Gazette. Part II, Statutory Instruments; Gazette du Canada. Partie II, Decrets, Ordonnances et Reglements Statutaires; Gazette du Canada. Partie II, Textes Reglementaires. Periodical. English (French). Micromedia Limited, 20 Victoria Street, Toronto Ontario M5C 2N8 Canada. **Tel** (416)362-5211, (800)387-2689, FAX (416)362-6161, telex 06524668. **DD** 348.71/02/05.

CN/0045-4230
CANADA SUPREME COURT REPORTS. **Main/Corp** Canada. Supreme Court. **VFOAT** Recueil des Arrets de la Cour Supreme du Canada. (1970)-. Periodical. English (French). ir. 122.25Can$. Carswell / Canada, 2075 Kennedy Road, Scarborough Ontario M1T 3V4 Canada. **Tel** (416)609-3800, (800)387-5164.

CN/0317-2821
CANADA. TAX APPEAL BOARD CASES. INDEX. SUPPLEMENT. (TAX APPEAL BOARD CASES INDEX.). **Main/Corp** Canada. Tax Appeal Board. 1968-. Periodical. English. an. R De Boo, 81 Curlew Drive, Don Mills Ontario M3A 3P7 Canada. **DD** 343/.71/0402648.

CN/0008-3003
CANADIAN BAR REVIEW. REVUE DU BARREAU CANADIEN, THE. [Can. Bar rev.]. **Added/Corp** Canadian Bar Association. **VFOAT** Revue du Barreau Canadien. (Jan. 1923)-. Periodical. English (French). qt. $75.00 Canada; $95.00 other. Canadian Bar Association, Suite 902 50 O'Connor Street, Ottawa Ontario K1P 6L2 Canada. **Tel** (613)237-2925. **ED** Dr. A.J. McClean. **Bk Rev**. **Ad Acc**. **Circ:** 35,000 (ctrl). ***Formed by the union of*** *Canada Law Journal; Canadian Law Times.*
Ind/Abst Leg. Resour. Index (1980-).

•CN/1188-3081
CANADIAN CASE AND STATUTE CITATIONS. **Added/Corp** Carswell Legal Publications. **VFOAT** References Jurisprudentielles et Legislatives Canadiennes. No. 1 (Jan. 10, 1992)-. Periodical. English. mo. Thomson Professional Publishing Canada, 2075 Kennedy Road, Scarborough Ontario M1T 3V4.

CN/1188-3081
CANADIAN CASE AND STATUTE CITATIONS / REFERENCES JURISPRUDENTIELLES ET LEGISLATIVES CANADIENNES. ***Ceased.*** [Can. case statute cit.]. **Added/Corp** Thomson Professional Publishing Canada. Carswell Company. **VFOAT** References Jurisprudentielles et Legislatives Canadiennes. (Jan. 10, 1992)-(Dec. 1992). Periodical. English (French; summaries and/or abstracts in French). mo. Thomson Professional Publishing Canada, 2075 Kennedy Road, Scarborough Ontario M1T 3V4. **LC** KE173; .C357. **DD** 348.71/047. ***Continues*** *Canadian Citations, 0835-9776.*

CN/0824-2585
CANADIAN CASES ON THE LAW OF INSURANCE. [Can. cases law insur.]. **VFOAT** C.C.L.I. **VAT** C.C.L.I. Canadian Cases on the Law of Insurance. Vol. 1, Pt. 1 (Sept./Oct. 1983)-Vol. 49, Pt. 2 (Sept. 1991); Vol. 1, Pt. 1 (Nov. 1991)-. Periodical. English (French). ir. 130.00Can$. Carswell / Canada, 2075 Kennedy Road, Scarborough Ontario M1T 3V4 Canada. **Tel** (416)609-3800, (800)387-5164. **ED** Marvin G. Baer and James A. Rendall. **DD** 346.71/086/02642. Index available. cum. index. **Ad Acc**.
Desc: Features all important decisions in insurance law from all Canadian jurisdictions selected by experts in the field.
Ind/Abst Can. Legal Lit.; Index Can. Leg. Period. Lit.; LegalTrac.

CN/0317-0055
CANADIAN COMMUNICATIONS LAW REVIEW. (CANADIAN COMMUNICATIONS LAW REVIEW. LA REVUE CANADIENNE DE DROIT DES COMMUNICATIONS.). **Added/Corp** University of Toronto. Faculty of Law. **VFOAT** La Revue Canadienne de Droit des Communications. Vol. 1 (1969)-. Periodical. English. an (Dec.). $7.88. McCarthy & McCarthy, Box 48 T-D Centre, Toronto Ontario M5K 1E6 Canada. **Tel** (416)362-1812. **DD** 343/.71/099.
Desc: Contains in-depth articles in privacy, libel, freedom of speech, censorship, defamation, expanding technologies, and a host of other issues facing our information society.

CN/0822-6709
CANADIAN COMPUTER LAW REPORTER. ***Ceased.*** [Can. comput. law report.]. Vol. 1, Issue 1 (Nov. 1983)-(19??). Periodical. English. mo (10 issues). Insight Press, 55 University Avenue, Suite 1700, Toronto Ontario M5J 2V6, Canada. **Tel** (416)777-1363, (416)777-2020, FAX (416)777-1292. **DD** 346.71/07.
Ind/Abst Can. Legal Lit.

CN/0317-6495
CANADIAN CURRENT TAX. (CANADIAN CURRENT TAX : WEEKLY REPORT AND COMMENTARY / BY MARTIN L. O'BRIEN.). [Can curr. tax]. **Added/Corp** Butterworth & Co. (Canada). Issues 1/2 (Jan. 2 1981)-. English. Twelve times a year. 235.00Can$. Butterworth & Company Ltd. / Canada, 75 Clegg Road, Markham Ontario L6G 1A1 Canada. **Tel** (905)479-2665, (800)668-6481. **ED** Vern Krishna. **DD** 343.7105/2. ***Continues*** *CIT Canadian Current Tax, Weekly Report and Commentary, 0317-6495.*

Desc: Provides coverage of controversial tax issues written by naationally acclaimed experts from Canada's leading law and accounting firms.
Ind/Abst Can. Legal Lit.; Index Can. Leg. Period. Lit.

CN/0228-3409
CANADIAN CUSTOMS AND EXCISE REPORTS. ***Title Change.*** **Added/Corp** Butterworth & Co. (Canada). Vol. 1 (1980)-(19??). English. ir. Butterworth & Company Ltd. / Canada, 75 Clegg Road, Markham Ontario L6G 1A1 Canada. **Tel** (905)479-2665, (800)668-6481. **DD** 343.7105/6/02648. ***Continued by*** *National Trade & Tariff Service.*

CN/0068-8649
CANADIAN DEPRECIATION GUIDE. **Main/Corp** CCH Canadian Limited. 3rd- Ed.; 1951-. Periodical. English. CCH Canadian Ltd., 6 Garamond Court, Don Mills Ontario M3C 1Z5 Canada. **Tel** (416)441-2992, FAX (416)441-3418. **DD** 343/.71/052. ***Continues*** *The New Depreciation System, 0316-828X.*

CN/0588-6562
CANADIAN INSURANCE LAW REPORTER. **VFOAT** Canadian Insurance Law Reports. 1951/55-. Periodical. English. CCH Canadian Ltd., 6 Garamond Court, Don Mills Ontario M3C 1Z5 Canada. **Tel** (416)441-2992, FAX (416)441-3418. **LC** KE1145.8; .C36. **DD** 346/.71/086. ***Continues*** *Insurance Law Reporter.*
Desc: Prompt reporting of insurance decisions from all Canadian courts.

CN/0836-0456
CANADIAN INSURANCE LAW REVIEW. [Can. insur. law rev.]. **Added/Corp** Carswell Legal Publications. Vol. 1, No. 1 (March 1988)-. Periodical. English. Three times a year. 180.00Can$. Carswell / Canada, 2075 Kennedy Road, Scarborough Ontario M1T 3V4 Canada. **Tel** (416)609-3800, (800)387-5164. **ED** J. F. Graham. **DD** 346.71/086/05. **Bk Rev. Ad Acc.**
Desc: A national journal focusing on the most topical issues being faced by the Canadian insurance industry.
Ind/Abst Can. Legal Lit.; Index Can. Leg. Period. Lit.

CN/0822-109X
CANADIAN JOURNAL OF INSURANCE LAW. [Can. j. insur. law]. **VFOAT** Insurance Law. Vol. 1, No. 1 (Sept. 1983)-. Periodical. English (French). Six times a year. 180.00Can$. Butterworth & Company Ltd. / Canada, 75 Clegg Road, Markham Ontario L6G 1A1 Canada. **Tel** (905)479-2665, (800)668-6481. **ED** Lazar Sarna. **LC** KE1142; .C36. **DD** 346.71/086/05; 347.2068605. Index available. cum. index. **Bk Rev.**
Desc: Presents concise, cogent articles on recent developments affecting insurance, pensions and benefits.
Ind/Abst Can. Legal Lit.; Index Can. Leg. Period. Lit.

CN/0841-8209
CANADIAN JOURNAL OF LAW AND JURISPRUDENCE, THE. [Can. j. law jurisprud.]. **Added/Corp** University of Western Ontario. Faculty of Law. **VFOAT** CJLJ; C.J.L.J. Vol. 1, No. 1 (Jan. 1988)-. Periodical. English (French). sa (approximately January and June). 54.00Can$. University of Western Ontario / Faculty of Law, London Ontario N6A 3K7 Canada. **Tel** (519)679-2111 Ext. 8448, FAX (519)661-3790. **ED** Richard Bronaugh and Peter G. Barton (editors' phone: (519)679-2111 Ext. 8442). **LC** K27; .E855. **DD** 349.713/05; 347.13005; 340/.05. **Bk Rev. Ad Acc, Adv Mgr:** Nanette Love. **Circ:** 500. available on microfilm from WESTLAW. ***Continues*** *University of Western Ontario Law Review, 0703-900X.*
Desc: Forum for the publication of scholarly writing in general jurisprudence and legal philosophy. Articles address the nature of law, substantive and procedural law, constitutional law, legal and judicial reasoning, ethical aspects of legal practice, and concrete issues facing contemporary society.
Ind/Abst Can. Legal Lit.; Index Can. Leg. Period. Lit.; Index Leg. Period.; Leg. Resour. Index; LegalTrac (1987-).

CN/0829-3201
CANADIAN JOURNAL OF LAW AND SOCIETY. [Can. j. law soc.]. **Added/Corp** University of Calgary. Research Unit for Socio-Legal Studies. **VFOAT** Revue Canadienne de Droit et Societe; Law and Society; Droit et Societe; CJLS/RCDS. Vol. 1 (1986)-. English (French). sa (June and December). $50.00 (institutions), $30.00 (individuals). University of Calgary Press, 2500 University Drive Northwest, Calgary Alberta T2N 1N4 Canada. **Tel** (403)220-7578. **ED** Rainer Knopff and Ann Griffiths. **LC** K3; .A496. **DD** 340/.11505. **CODEN** CJLSEU. **Bk Rev. Ad Acc. Pr Rev. Circ:** 300 (ctrl).
Desc: A refereed journal dedicated to the promotion and publication of writing on law and the legal system.
Ind/Abst Can. Index (?-?); Can. Legal Lit.; Can. Period. Index (19??-); Crim. Justice Abstr.; Index Can. Leg. Period. Lit. (1992-).

CN/0832-8781
CANADIAN JOURNAL OF WOMEN AND THE LAW. [Can. j. women law]. **Added/Corp** National Association of Women and the Law. **VFOAT** Revue Juridique la Femme et le Droit. Vol. 1, No. 1 (1985)-. Periodical. English (French). sa. 69.55Can$ (institutions), 42.80Can$ (individuals) Canada; 70.00Can$ (institutions), 40.00Can$ (individuals) other. Canadian Journal of Women and the Law, 575 King Edward Avenue, Ottawa Ontario, K1N 6N5 Canada. **Tel** (613)564-5617, FAX (613)564-7190. **ED** Elizabeth A. Sheehy. **DD** 342.71/0878. **CODEN** CJWLEU. **Bk Rev. Ad Acc. Pr Rev. Circ:** 1,500. available on microfiche from Micromedia Limited.
Desc: Canada's legal periodical dedicated to providing in-depth analysis of legislation and legal issues of concern to women. Multi-disciplinary approach makes it a vital resource to academicians, lawyers, researchers and policymakers who require current information on arguments and decisions, along with activists interested in the social impact of current legal developments and strategies.
Ind/Abst Can. Index; Can. Legal Lit.; Can. Period. Index (19??-); Hum. Rights Intern. Rep.; Index Can. Leg. Period. Lit. (1992-); Index Leg. Period.; Leg. Resour. Index; LegalTrac (1980-); PAIS Int. Print (1991-); Women Stud. Abstr.

CN/1180-176X
CANADIAN LAW LIBRARIES. (CANADIAN LAW LIBRARIES / BIBLIOTHEQUES DE DROIT CANADIENNES.). [Can. law livr.]. **Added/Corp** Canadian Association of Law Libraries. **VFOAT** Bibliotheques de Droit Canadiennes. Vol. 15, No. 1 (Feb. 1990)-. Newsletter. English (French). Five times a year (Feb., Apr., Aug., Oct., Dec.). 60.00Can$. Canadian Association of Law Libraries, PO Box 1570, 190 Railway Station, Kingston Ontario, K7L 5C8 Canada. **Tel** (613)531-9338, FAX (613)531 0626, tolex 0527284. **DD** 340/.0971/05. Index available (Bound in April issue). **Bk Rev,** (Qty: 25-30). **Ad Acc. Pr Rev. Circ:** 600. ***Continues*** *Canadian Association of Law Libraries. Newsletter, 0319-5376.*
Ind/Abst Can. Period. Index (19??-); Index Can. Leg. Period. Lit. (1992-); Leg. Inf. Manage. Index (1990-).

CN/0703-2129
CANADIAN LAWYER. [Can. lawyer]. (Oct. 1977)-. Periodical. English. mo (except Jan., Aug., and special issue in April). 52.43Can$ Canada; 59.00Can$ other. Canadian Lawyer Magazine Ltd., 240 Edward Street, Aurora Ontario L4G 3S9 Canada. **Tel** (416)841-6480, FAX (416)841-5078. **ED** Catherine Kentridge. **LC** K3; .A497. **DD** 349.71/05; 347.1005. **Bk Rev. Ad Acc, Adv Mgr:** Jayne Townsend. **Circ:** 29,816 (ctrl). available on microfilm and microfiche from University Microfilms International (UMI).
Desc: For members of the legal professions, legal suppliers and consultants, and anyone interested in the contemporary practice of law. Covers trends and developments bringing change to the professions, mergers and expansions involving law firms, investigative articles on cases and events, social issues from a legal perspective and the legal technology market.
Ind/Abst Can. Index (?-?); Can. Legal Lit.; Can. Period. Index (19??-); Crim. Justice Period. Index; Curr. Law Index (1980-); Index Can. Leg. Period. Lit.; Law Office Inf. Serv.; Leg. Resour. Index (1980-); LegalTrac (1980-).

CN/0832-9257
CANADIAN LEGAL LITERATURE. **See** Law-Abstracting, Bibliographies and Statistics.

CN/1184-7190
CANADIAN LEGAL SERVICES DIRECTORY. [Can. leg. serv. dir.]. (1990)-. Directory. English. $20.00 per year. Lake Publishing, Box 1812, Kelowna, British Columbia V1Y 8P2 Canada. **DD** 340/.025/711. ***Continues*** *Canadian Legal Services., 1182-0381.*

CN/0225-2279
CANADIAN NATIVE LAW REPORTER. [Can. nativ. law rep.]. **Added/Corp** University of Saskatchewan. Native Law Centre. (1979)-. Periodical. English (French). qt (Mar., June, Sept., Dec.). 55.00Can$. University of Saskatchewan Native Law Centre, Saskatoon Saskatchewan S7N 0W0 Canada. **Tel** (306)966-6189, FAX (306)966-6207. **ED** Zandra Wilson. **LC** KE7705.8; .C36. **DD** 346.7101/3; 347.10613. Index available (bound in each issue). cum. index (in fourth issue). **Bk Rev,** (Qty: infrequent). **Circ:** 500. ***Continues*** *Canadian Native Law Bulletin, 0706-9790.*
Desc: Specialized law report series providing comprehensive coverage of native law judgments in Canada. Research features include subject index, states judicially considered, year-end cumulative indexes, articles and reviews.
Ind/Abst Can. Legal Lit.; Index Can. Leg. Period. Lit.; Leg. Resour. Index; LegalTrac (1980-).

CN/0825-608X
CANADIAN OCCUPATIONAL SAFETY AND HEALTH LAW MONTHLY REPORT. [Can. occup. saf. health law mon. rep.]. **Added/Corp** Corpus Information Services. **VFOAT** Monthly Report. Vol. 1 No. 1 (June 1984)-. Periodical. English. 959.00Can$ Canada; 1047.00Can$ other. Southam Information and Technology Group Inc., 1450 Don Mills Road, Don Mills Ontario M3B 2X7 Canada. **Tel** (416)445-6641, (800)668-2374, FAX (416)442-2261. **ED** Mark Sabourin. **DD** 344.71/0465/05. Index available. **Bk Rev.**
Desc: Loose-leaf encyclopedia of Canadian industrial health and safety legislation. Subscription includes bi-monthly updates.

CN/0319-2431
CANADIAN TAX NEWS. [Can. tax news]. Vol. 1 (May 1973)-. Periodical. English (French). mo. $139.00. Carswell / Canada, 2075 Kennedy Road, Scarborough Ontario M1T 3V4 Canada. **Tel** (416)609-3800, (800)387-5164. **ED** Donald R Huggett. **Circ:** 500.
Desc: Tax newsletter offering informative coverage on all major issues in Canadian tax law.
Ind/Abst Index Can. Leg. Period. Lit.

CN/0319-7085
CANNONS OF CONSTRUCTION, THE. **Added/Corp** University of Alberta. Faculty of Law. (1970). Periodical. English. Four times a year. Free. International Osbudsman Institute, University of Alberta, Law Faculty, Edmonton ALTA T6G 2H5 Canada. **Tel** (403)492-3196.

NZ/0112-0581
CANTERBURY LAW REVIEW, THE. [Canterb. law rev.]. Vol. 1, No. 1 (1980)-. Periodical. English. ir. $30.00. William W. Gaunt and Sons Inc, 3011 Gulf Drive, Gaunt Building, Holmes Beach FL 34217. **Tel** (800)942-8683, (813)778-5211. **LC** K3; .A5. **DD** 349.931/05; 349.31005.
Ind/Abst Curr. Law Index (1982-); Index Leg. Period.; Leg. Resour. Index (1982-); LegalTrac (1980-).

UK/0953-5586
CAP LEGISLATION. **See** Agriculture.

US/0090-8789
CARBON COUNTY LAW JOURNAL, THE. **Added/Corp** Carbon County Bar Association. (19??)-. English. wk. $36.00. Carbon County Bar Association, Box 6, Jim Thorpe PA 18229. **Tel** (717)325-3097, FAX (717) 325-9132. **ED** James A Wimmer, Roger N Nanovic, and Anthony Roberti. **LC** KFP52.C37; C33. **DD** 348/.74826/043. Index available. cum. index. **Ad Acc.**
Desc: Publishes the opinions of the Carbon County Court of Common Pleas, a list of recorded deeds and mortgages, a list of filed judgments and legal advertisements.

US/0741-515X
CARDIOLOGISTS' LEGAL LETTER. [Cardiol. leg. letter]. **Added/Corp** Merck Sharp & Dohme. Vol. 1, No. 1 (Feb. 1983)-. Periodical. English. mo. Free. Merck Sharp and Dohme / PA, Division of Merck Sharp and Company Inc, West Point PA 19486. **LC** KF2910.C37; A134. **DD** 346.7303/32/05; 347.306332/05.

US/0736-7694
CARDOZO ARTS & ENTERTAINMENT LAW JOURNAL. [Cardozo arts entertain. law j.]. **VFOAT** Cardozo Arts and Entertainment Law Journal. Vol. 1 (Spring 1982)-. Periodical. English. ir. $30.00. Benjamin N Cardozo School of Law, Yeshiva University, 55 5th Avenue, Room 121, New York NY 10003. **Tel** (212)790-0292. **ED** Elana Gershen. **LC** K3; .A687. **DD** 344.73/097/05; 347.3049705. **Bk Rev. Ad Acc. Circ:** 300 (ctrl).
Desc: Arts and entertainment law.
Ind/Abst Commun. Abstr.; Curr. Law Index (1984-); Film Lit. Index; Index Leg. Period.; Leg. Resour. Index (1984-); LegalTrac (1983-); PAIS Int. Print (1991-).

US/0270-5192
CARDOZO LAW REVIEW. [Cardozo law rev.]. **Added/Corp** Benjamin N. Cardozo School of Law. **VFOAT** Hegel and Legal Theory. Vol. 1 (Spring 1979)-. Periodical. English. Eight times a year. $30.00. Yeshiva University / Cardozo Law School, 55 5th Avenue, New York NY 10003. **Tel** (212)790-0355, FAX (212)790-0355. **ED** Douglas Epstein. **LC** K3; .A69. **DD** 349.747/05. Index available. **Bk Rev,** (Qty: 5). **Ad Acc. Circ:** 1,000.
Desc: Contains articles, essays, book reviews, and student authored notes on a wide variety of legal issues of interest to the legal and academic communities.
Ind/Abst Bowne Dig. Corp. Sec. Lawyers; Curr. Law Index (1981-); Index Leg. Period.; Leg. Resour. Index (1981-);; LegalTrac (1980-).

US/1043-1500
CARDOZO STUDIES IN LAW AND LITERATURE. [Cardozo stud. law lit.]. **Added/Corp** Jacob Burns Institute for Advanced Legal Studies. Vol. 1, No. 1 (Spring 1989)-. Periodical. English. sa. $50.00 (institutions), $20.00 (individual) US; $54.00 (institutions), $24.00 (individual) other. Benjamin N Cardozo Law School, 55 Fifth Avenue, Yeshiva U, New York NY 10003. **Tel** (212)790-0370, FAX (212)790-0345. **ED** Richard Weisberg. **LC** K3; .A694. **DD** 340/.05. **Bk Rev. Ad Acc, Adv Mgr:** Averlyn Archer, **Tel** (212)790-0370. **Pr Rev. Circ:** 750.
Desc: Created to address the growing interest among literary scholars, lawyers, and judges in the relationship between law and literature. This journal, among other topics, explores the legal themes in fiction, hermeneutics and legal rhetoric and style, and the relationship between ethics and aesthetics.
Ind/Abst Index Leg. Period.; Leg. Resour. Index; LegalTrac (1989-).

JM/0255-7118
CARIBBEAN JOURNAL OF LEGAL INFORMATION : BULLETIN OF THE CARIBBEAN ASSOCIATION OF LAW LIBRARIANS, THE. Vol. 4, No. 1 (March 1987)-. Bulletin. English. sa. $15.00. Caribbean Law Librarian, c/o Norman Manley Law School/Mona Campus, PO Box 231, Jamaica West Indies. **ED** Leslie P Fenty. **LC** Z673.C284; C37. ***Continues** Caribbean Law Librarian, 0255-7118.*
Ind/Abst Leg. Inf. Manage. Index.

UK
CARVER. English. ir. £215.00 (13th edition). Sweet & Maxwell Ltd., South Quay Plaza, 183 Marsh Wall, London E14 9FT England. **Tel** 011 44 264 342899, FAX 011 44 264 342723, telex 929089 ITPINF G.

●CN/1188-2948
CASE LAW DIGESTS. **VFOAT** Sommaires de la Jurisprudence; Canadian Current Law Case Law Digests; C.C.L. Case Law Digests. No. 1 (Jan. 17, 1992)-. Periodical. English (summaries and/or abstracts in French). mo. $555.00 (includes subscription to: Canadian case and statute citations; Legislation (Scarborough, Ont.); and, Canadian legal literature). Thomson Professional Publishing Canada, 2075 Kennedy Road, Scarborough Ontario M1T 3V4. ***Continues** Jurisprudence (Scarborough, Ont.), 1183-0611.*

UK/0955-9078
CASE SEARCH MONTHLY. [Case search mon.]. **Added/Corp** European Law Centre. **VFOAT** Gazetteer of European Law; Case Search Monthly. (1989)-(1993). English. mo. 200.00. Sweet & Maxwell Ltd., South Quay Plaza, 183 Marsh Wall, London E14 9FT England. **Tel** 011 44 264 342899, FAX 011 44 264 342723, telex 929089 ITPINF G. **LC** KJE923; .C37. **DD** 348.4/022; 344.080022.

US/0749-7709
CASE UPDATE. (CASE UPDATE / EASTERN MINERAL LAW FOUNDATION.). [Case update]. **Added/Corp** Eastern Mineral Law Foundation (U.S.). Vol. 1, No. 1 (Fall 1983)-. Periodical. English. Three times a year. $100.00. Eastern Mineral Law Foundation, West Virginia University Law Center, PO Box 6130, Morgantown WV 26506. **Tel** (304)293-2470. **ED** Sharon J. Daniels, Steven P. McGowan, William B. Ellis, William G Williams and Gary R. Weitkamp. **DD** 346. **Bk Rev**. **Ad Acc. Circ:** 700 (ctrl). available on diskette.
Desc: Concise summary of pertinent legal decisions related to mineral law in the Eastern United States.

US/0008-7262
CASE WESTERN RESERVE LAW REVIEW. [Case West. Reserve law rev.]. **Added/Corp** Franklin Thomas Backus School of Law. Vol. 19 (Nov. 1967)-. Periodical. English. qt. $25.00. Case Western Reserve University / School of Law, 11075 East Boulevard, Cleveland OH 44106. **Tel** (216)368-3304, FAX (216)368-6144. **ED** Eric Kinder. **LC** K3; .A786. **DD** 349.73/05. Index available. **Ad Acc, Adv Mgr:** Carolyn Speaker. **Circ:** 600. available on microfilm and microfiche from WESTLAW; available on CD-ROM and an online database. ***Continues** Western Reserve law review, 0270-2150.*
Ind/Abst Bowne Dig. Corp. Sec. Lawyers; Curr. Law Index (1980-); Fed. Tax Artic.; Index Leg. Period.; Leg. Resour. Index (1980-); LegalTrac (1980-).

US
CASES DECIDED IN THE SUPREME COURT OF VIRGINIA. **Main/Corp** Virginia. Supreme Court. **VFOAT** Virginia Reports. V. 212- ; 1971/1972-. English. Supreme Court of Virginia, Office of the Executive Secretary, 100 North 9th Street/3rd Floor, Richmond VA 23219. **Tel** (804)786-6455. **LC** KFV2445; .A2. **DD** 348.755/043. ***Continues** Cases Decided in the Supreme Court of Appeals of Virginia.*

US/1044-2987
CATALOG OF CURRENT LAW TITLES. [Cat. curr. law titles]. No. 1 (Jan./Feb. 1989)-. Catalog. English. bm. $248.00. Ward & Associates, 317 South Division, Suite 66, Ann Arbor MI 48104. **Tel** (313)665-3520, FAX (313)665-7880. **ED** Peter D Ward and Margaret A Goldblatt. **LC** KF4; .C395. **DD** 016.34/005. ***Continues** National Legal Bibliography. Recent Acquisitions of Major Legal Libraries, 0739-1951.*

●US/1049-796X
CATALOG OF CURRENT LAW TITLES, ANNUAL. [Cat. curr. law titles annu.]. (1991)-. Catalog. English. an. $295.00. William S. Hein & Company Inc., 1285 Main Street, Buffalo NY 14209. **Tel** (716)882-2600, (800)828-7571, FAX (716)883-8100, telex 91-209 WM S HEIN BUF. **DD** 016. ***Continues in part** National Legal Bibliography, Annual.*

US/0008-8137
CATHOLIC LAWYER, THE. [Cathol. lawyer]. **Added/Corp** St. Thomas More Institute for Legal Research. Vol. 1, No. 1 (Jan. 1955)-. Periodical. English. Four times a year. $5.00. St Johns University, Law Review Association, Grand Central & Utopia Parkways, Jamaica NY 11432. **Tel** (718)990-6654, FAX (718)990-6649. **ED** Professor Edward D. Cavanagh (editor's address: St John's University, School of Law, 8000 Utopia Parkway, Jamaica NY 11439; editor's phone: (718)990-6621). **LC** K3; .A788. **DD** 349.73/02422; 347.3002422. Index available (biennially in fourth issue). cum. index. **Circ:** 1,700.
Desc: Magazine devoted to timely legal problems having ethical, canonical, or theological implications.
Ind/Abst Canon Law Abstr.; Curr. Law Index (1980-); Fed. Tax Artic.; Index Leg. Period.; Leg. Resour. Index (1980-); LegalTrac (1980-); Abr. Cathol. Period. Lit. Index; Cathol. Period. Lit. Index.

US/0008-8390
CATHOLIC UNIVERSITY LAW REVIEW (1975). (CATHOLIC UNIVERSITY LAW REVIEW.). [Cathol. Univers. law rev.]. **Added/Corp** Columbus School of Law. Vol. 25 (Fall 1975)-. Periodical. English. Four times a year. $28.00 US; $33.00 other. Catholic University Law Review, Room 1 Leahy Hall, Washington DC 20064. **Tel** (202)319-5144. **ED** Edward McAndrew. **LC** K3; .A79. **DD** 340/.05. Index available. **Bk Rev**, (Qty: 1-4). **Circ:** 520. Documents available from The Genuine Article. ***Continues** Catholic University of America Law Review (1972).*
Desc: Legal publication featuring professional- and student-authored articles. Special issues include communications law and a District of Columbia survey.
Ind/Abst Bowne Dig. Corp. Sec. Lawyers (1980-); Commun. Abstr.; Curr. Contents Soc. Behav. Sci.; Curr. Law Index (1980-); Fed. Tax Artic.; Index Leg. Period.; Leg. Resour. Index (1980-); LegalTrac (1980-); Res. Alert [Full Cov.]; Risk Abstr. (19??-19??); Soc. Sci. Cit. Index [Full Cov.].

US/0411-3012
CAVEAT. 1- 1956?-. Periodical. English. ir. University of Illinois College of Law, Urbana IL 61801.

US/0197-193X
CAVEAT VENDOR. Periodical. English. Caveat Vendor, PO Box 12487 Capitol Station, Austin TX 78711. **LC** KFT1430.A59; C38. **DD** 343/.73/071/05.

CJ/0376-7779
CAYMAN GAZETTE. No. 1 (Jan. 6, 1975)-. English. sm. $269.52. Cayman Islands Government, Information Services, Tower Building, Government Administration Building, Grand Cayman British West Indies. **Tel** (809)94-98092, FAX 97544, telex 4260 CIGOVT. **DD** 340/.0972921. Index available. **Circ:** 500.
Desc: Official publication of the Cayman Islands Government.

UK/0269-977X
CAYMAN ISLANDS LAW REPORTS, THE. **Added/Corp** Cayman Islands. Grand Court. Cayman Islands. Court of Appeal. (1984)-. English. ir. price varies per volume. Law Reports International, Trinity College, Oxford OX1 3BH England. **Tel** 011 44 865 279883, FAX 011 44 865 279911. **ED** A. Milner. **LC** KGM13; .A24. **DD** 348.7292/1046; 347.29210846. **Circ:** 200 (ctrl).
Desc: Selected case reports from all superior courts of Cayman Islands.

US/0892-1822
CBA RECORD. [CBA rec.]. **Added/Corp** Chicago Bar Association. **VAT** Chicago Bar Association Record. Vol. 1, No. 1 (Jan. 1987)-. Periodical. English. Ten times a year (July/Aug. and Dec./Jan. issues combined). $25.00 (one year); Comes with Chicago Bar Association membership. Chicago Bar Association, 321 South Plymouth Court, Chicago IL 60604. **Tel** (312)554-2000. **ED** Michael B. Hyman and David A. Anderson. **LC** KF200; .C35. **DD** 340/.06/0773. **Bk Rev**. **Ad Acc. Circ:** 22,000 (ctrl). available on microfilm and microfiche from University Microfilms International (UMI). ***Continues** Chicage Bar Record.*
Ind/Abst Fed. Tax Artic.; Leg. Resour. Index; LegalTrac (1987-).

US/0162-4237
CEMETERY BUSINESS & LEGAL GUIDE. **See** Funeral Service.

US
CENTRAL DISTRICT ALMANAC. English. bw (published biweekly except in Aug., and Dec.). $350.00 US and Canada; $440.00 other. Central District Almanac., 500 South Madison Avenue, # 20, Pasedena CA 91101. **Tel** (213)626-2428, FAX (213)626-2503. **ED** Bill Girdner. Index available. cum. index. **Ad Acc. Circ:** 200. available on microfilm.
Desc: Provides information on oral and written rulings for the federal courts in the central district that, for the most part, go unpublished.

US/0363-7980
CENTRAL SCHOOL LAW DIGEST. V. 1- Feb. 1976-. English. mo. School Law Digest Corporation, PO Box 1752, Fresno CA 93717-1752. **LC** KF4114; .C4. **DD** 344/.77/0705.

US
CENTRE COUNTY LEGAL JOURNAL. V. 1- 1960-. Periodical. English. be. **LC** MICROFILM 0181 . Each issue contains an index to its own contents (no volume index)--loose.
Desc: Includes decisions of the courts of Centre County, PA.

UK
CHAMBERS & PARTNERS DIRECTORY OF THE LEGAL PROFESSION. Directory. English. be. £21.95. Chambers & Partners, 74 Long Lane, London EC1A 9ET England. **Tel** 011 44 71 6069371. **(Subscription address:** Biblios Distribution Service, Star Road Partridge Green, Sussex PH1 38LD England**)**

US
CHECKLISTS OF BASIC AMERICAN LEGAL PUBLICATIONS. **Added/Corp** American Association of Law Libraries. **VFOAT** Checklists Basic American Legal Publications. (1962)-. English. ir. Fred B. Rothman & Company, 10368 West Centennial Road, Littleton CO 80127. **Tel** (800)457-1986, (303)979-5657, FAX (303)978-1457, telex 87669. **ED** Marcia Zubrow.
Desc: A checklist of basic American legal publications i.e. state session laws, state reports, etc. Very useful for law libraries.

US/0148-7973
CHEMICAL REGULATION REPORTER. [Chem. regul. rep.]. **Main/Corp** Bureau of National Affairs (Washington, D.C.). Vol. 1 (Mar. 18, 1977)-. Periodical. English. wk. $680.00. Bureau of National Affairs Inc., 9435 Key West Avenue, Rockville MD 20850. **Tel** (800)372-1033, (301)258-1033, FAX (301)948-5823. **ED** Bernard S. Chabel. **LC** KF3958.A15; B87. **DD** 344/.73/042. **[CCC].**
Desc: A notification and reference service consisting of six binders that comprehensively cover federal chemical regulations.

CC
CHENG FA LUN TAN : CHUNG-KUO CHENG FA TA HSUEH HSUEH PAO. **Added/Corp** Chung-Kuo Cheng Fa Ta Hsueh. **VFOAT** Chung-Kuo Cheng Fa Ta Hsueh Hsueh Pao; Zhengfa Luntan; Tribune of Political Science and Law; Journal of China University of Political Science and Law. (1985)-. Periodical. Chinese (table of contents in English). bm. $11.10. **(Subscription address:** China International Book Trading Corporation, PO Box 399, Library Service Department, Beijing 100044 People's Republic of China.**)** **LC** K3; .H39. **DD** 340/.05. ***Continues** Chung-Kuo Cheng Fa Ta Hsueh Hsueh Pao.*
Desc: Tribune of political science and law.

US
CHESTER COUNTY LAW REPORTER. English. wk (52 issues per year). $40.00 members of Chester County Bar Association; $60.00 other. Chester County Law Reporter, 15 West Gay Street, West Chester PA 19380. **Tel** (215)692-1889. **ED** Richard Meanix Esquire. **Bk Rev**.
Desc: Contains opinions, legal notices, and sheriff sales.

US
CHESTER COUNTY REPORTS. **Added/Corp** Chester County Bar Association. Vol. 3 (1947)-. Periodical. English. ir. $50.00. Geo T. Bisel Company, 710 South Washington Square, Philadelphia PA 19106. **Tel** (800)247-3526. ***Continues** Chester County Reports, Containing Reports of Cases Decided by the Supreme Court of Pennsylvania and the Several County Courts of the Commonwealth.*

US/0009-3505
CHICAGO BAR RECORD. ***Ceased.*** [Chicago bar rec.]. **Added/Corp** Chicago Bar Association. Vol. 16 (Oct. 1934)-(19??). Periodical. English. bm. Chicago Bar Association, 321 South Plymouth Court, Chicago IL 60604. **Tel** (312)554-2000. available on microfilm and microfiche from University Microfilms International (UMI). ***Continues** Chicago Bar Association Record.*
Ind/Abst Index Leg. Period. (?-?); Leg. Resour. Index (1980-?); LegalTrac (1980-1986).

US/0362-6148
CHICAGO DAILY LAW BULLETIN. [Chic. dly. law bull.]. (1873)-. Bulletin. English. ir (254 per year). $150.00. Chicago Lawyer, 415 North State Street, Chicago IL 60610. **Tel** (312)644-7800, FAX (312)644-4255. ***Continues** Chicago Daily Law Record.*
Ind/Abst Chicano Index; Leg. Resour. Index (1984-); LegalTrac (1980-).

US/0009-3599
CHICAGO-KENT LAW REVIEW. [Chic.-Kent law rev.]. **Added/Corp** Chicago-Kent College of Law. **VFOAT** Chicago Kent Law Review. Vol. 17 (Dec. 1938)-. Periodical. English. tq (3 issues). $23.00 US and Canada; $26.00 other (latest volume). Chicago Kent College of Law, 565 West Adams Street, Chicago IL 60661. **Tel** (312)906-5190, FAX (312)906-5280. **LC** K3; .H45. **DD** 340. **Bk Rev**. available on CD-ROM. ***Continues** Chicago-Kent Review.*
Desc: Follows a symposium format -- the lead articles of each issue are devoted exclusively to a specific topic.
Ind/Abst Bowne Dig. Corp. Sec. Lawyers; Curr. Law Index (1980-); Fed. Tax Artic.; Index Leg. Period.; Leg. Resour. Index (1980-); LegalTrac (1980-).

US
CHICAGO LAW LIBRARY BULLETIN. **See** Library and Information Sciences.

US/0199-8374
CHICAGO LAWYER. [Chic. lawyer]. **VFOAT** Massachusetts Bay Transportation Authority Budget. (Nov. 1 1978)-. Periodical. English. mo. $40.00 (one year), $70.00 (two year), $90.00 (three year). Chicago Lawyer, 415 North State Street, Chicago IL 60610. **Tel** (312)644-7800, FAX (312)644-4255. **ED** Rob Warden. **LC** K3; .H463. **DD** 349.773/05; 347.73005. **Bk Rev. Ad Acc. Circ:** 6,000 (ctrl). available on microfilm and microfiche from University Microfilms International (UMI).
Desc: A newspaper geared toward the Cook county legal community.

US/1061-8899
CHICANO-LATINO LAW REVIEW. [Chicano-Lat. law rev.]. **Added/Corp** University of California, Los Angeles. School of Law. **VFOAT** Chicano Latino Law Review. Vol. 11, No. 1 (Spring 1991)-. Periodical. English. sa. $15.00 US; $19.00 other. Chicano Law Review, 405 Hilgard Avenue, UCLA Law School, Los Angeles CA 90024. **Tel** (310)825-2894, FAX (310)206-6489. **ED** Lillianna Gonzales. **LC** K3; .H47. **DD** 340/.05. **Bk Rev**, (Qty: 2-6). ctrl circ. ***Continues*** *Chicano Law Review, 0090-3620.*
Desc: Deals with the Hispanic community and its concerns, including the environment and education.
Ind/Abst Index Leg. Period.; Leg. Resour. Index.

US/1058-5516
CHILD ABUSE, NEGLECT, AND THE FOSTER CARE SYSTEM. [Child abuse negl. foster care syst.]. (1990)-. English. Practising Law Institute, 810 Seventh Avenue, New York NY 10019-5818. **Tel** (212)765-5700, FAX (212)581-4670 general correspondence, (212)265-4742 orders and billing inquiries. **DD** 344.

UK
CHILD LAW. English. qt. £75.00. Tolley Publishing Company Ltd, Tolley House, 2 Addiscombe Road, Croydon, Surrey CR9 5AF United Kingdom. **Tel** 011 44 81 6869141, FAX 011 44 81 6863155, 011 44 81 7600588.

US
CHILDREN AND THE LAW COMMITTEE NEWSLETTER. **See** Sociology-Social Services and Welfare.

HK/1011-2359
CHINA CURRENT LAWS. ***Ceased.*** (1987)-(19??). Periodical. English (Chinese). qt. Longman Group Ltd., Fourth Avenue, Longman House, Harlow Essex CM19 5SR England. **Tel** 011 44 279 429655, FAX 011 44 279 431059, telex 81259.
Desc: Designed for lawyers and companies involved in China trade and investment. It provides reliable information on selected developments in Chinese legislation, including materials not translated elsewhere.

HK
CHINA LAW AND PRACTICE. Vol. 1, No. 1 (January, 1987)-. English. ir (10 issues per year). $792.00. Asia Law & Practice Ltd, 2F 29 Hollywood Road, Central Hong Kong Hong Kong. **Tel** 011 852 5 5449918. **LC** K3; .H48. **DD** 349.51/05; 345.1005.

US/0891-6829
CHINA LAW REPORTER. [China law report.]. **Added/Corp** American Bar Association. Section of International Law. American Bar Association. Section of International Law and Practice. **VFOAT** Chung-Kuo Fa Lu Chi Kan. Vol. 1, No. 1 (Summer 1980)-. Periodical. English. qt (4 issues). $43.00. American Bar Association, 750 North Lake Shore Drive, Chicago IL 60611. **Tel** (312)988-5522, (312)988-5241, FAX (312)988-5528, telex 270593. **ED** Tao-Tai Hsia and Thomas J. Pasmussen. **LC** K3; .H49. **DD** 349.51/05; 345.1/005. ctrl circ.
Desc: Concerned mainly with practical issues facing lawyers and scholars.
Ind/Abst Curr. Law Index (1982-); Index Leg. Period.; Leg. Resour. Index (1982-); LegalTrac (1980-).

UK
CHINA LAW YEARBOOK. **Added/Corp** Fa Lu Chu Pan She. 1st Ed. (1987)-. English. an. $43.00. The Law Publishing House, Taipinglu/Haidian District, Beijing, People's Republic of China. **(Subscription address:** China Natl Publs Imp Exp Corp, PO Box 88, Beijing 100704 China**)** **DD** 349.51; 345.1.

US/0009-4609
CHINESE LAW AND GOVERNMENT. **Added/Corp** M.E. Sharpe, Inc. International Arts and Sciences Press. (1968)-. Academic Scholarly Publication. English (table of contents in Chinese; translations available in Chinese). bm. $520.00 US; $571.00 other. M. E. Sharpe Inc., 80 Business Park Drive, Armonk NY 10504. **Tel** (914)273-1800, (800)541-6563, FAX (914)273-2106. **ED** Michael Y. M. Kau. **LC** K3; .H5. **DD** 340/.0951. **Bk Rev. Ad Acc. Pr Rev. Circ:** 300 (ctrl). available on microfilm and microfiche from University Microfilms International (UMI). Documents available from The Genuine Article.
Desc: Significant scholarly works and policy documents in the fields of politics and government. Works of major significance from Japanese, Russian, and Taiwan sources sometimes included.
Ind/Abst Curr. Contents Soc. Behav. Sci.; Index Foreign Leg. Per.; Int. Polit. Sci. Abstr.; LABORDOC; PAIS Int. Print (1991-); Res. Alert [Full Cov.]; Soc. Sci. Cit. Index [Full Cov.].

US
CHIROPRACTIC LEGAL UPDATE. (19??)-. Periodical. English. bm. $99.00. Health Services Publications Ltd., PO Box 206, Fincastle VA 24090. **Tel** (703)473-3312, FAX (703)473-2744. **ED** C. Jacob Ladenheim, Louis Sportelli and Rob Sherman.
Desc: Articles on the legal aspects of chiropractics.

UK
CHITTY ON CONTRACTS. English. £225.00. Sweet & Maxwell Ltd., South Quay Plaza, 183 Marsh Wall, London E14 9FT England. **Tel** 011 44 264 342899, FAX 011 44 264 342723, telex 929089 ITPINF G.

UK
CHRONOLOGICAL TABLE OF THE STATUTES. **Added/Corp** Great Britain. Statute Law Committee. 59th Ed. (Dec. 1947)-. English. sa. Her Majesty's Stationery Office, 51 Nine Elms Lane, London SW8 5DR England. **Tel** 011 44 71 873 8459, 011 44 71 873 8499, FAX 011 44 71 873 8499, 011 44 71 873 8456, telex 297138. **(Subscription address:** Her Majesty's Stationery Office, PO Box 276, Publications Centre, London SW8 5DT England.**)** **LC** KD142.3; .G74. **DD** 348.41/022; 344.10822. ***Continues*** *Great Britain. Statute Law Committee. Chronological Table of and Index to the Statutes to the End of the Session of ... .*

US
CHROSTWAITE'S PENNSYLVANIA MUNICIPAL LAW REPORTER. Vol. 48 (19??)-. English. bm (6 issues). $99.00. Penns Valley Publishing, 4104 York Street, Harrisburg PA 17111. **Tel** (717)558-7700. ***Continues in part*** *Municipal Law Reporter.*

JA
CHUKAI JIDOSHA ROPPO. **Main/Corp** Japan. **Added/Corp** Japan. Unyusho. Jidoshakyoku. **VFOAT** Jidosha Roppo. (19??)-. Periodical. Japanese. ¥2200. Daiichi Hoki Shuppan Kabushiki Kaisha, 11-17 Minami Aoyama 2 Minato-ku, Tokyo-to 107 Japan.

TH
CHULALONGKORN LAW REVIEW. **Added/Corp** Chulalongkonmahawitthayalai. Khana Nitisat. Vol. 1 (1982)-. English. an. Chulalongkorn University Faculty of Law, 10330 Bangkok Thailand. **Tel** 011 66 2 2157436. **LC** K3; .H82. **DD** 349.593; 345.93.
Ind/Abst Index Foreign Leg. Per.

CC
CHUNG-HUA JEN MIN KUNG HO KUO CHUAN KUO JEN MIN TAI PIAO TA HUI CHANG WU WEI YUAN HUI KUNG PAO. **Main/Corp** China. Chuan Kuo Jen Min Tai Piao Ta Hui. Chang Wu Wei Yuan Hui. **VFOAT** Kung Pao. (1957)-. Periodical. Chinese. ir. $14.46. **(Subscription address:** China International Book Trading Corporation, PO Box 399, Library Service Department, Beijing 100044 People's Republic of China.**)**

CC/1002-4611
CHUNG-HUA JEN MIN KUNG HO KUO TSUI KAO JEN MIN FA YUAN KUNG PAO. **Main/Corp** China. Tsui Kao Jen Min Fa Yuan. **Added/Corp** China. Tsui Kao Jen Min Fa Yuan. Pan Kung Ting. **VFOAT** Zhonghua Renmin Gongheguo Zuigao Renmin Fayuan Gongbao. (1985)-. Periodical. Chinese. ir. $6.20. **(Subscription address:** China International Book Trading Corporation, PO Box 399, Library Service Department, Beijing 100044 People's Republic of China.**)** **LC** KNQ18; .C48.

CC
CHUNG-KUO FA LU NIEN CHIEN = LAW YEAR BOOK OF CHINA. **VFOAT** Law Year Book of China. (1987)-. Chinese. an (Dec.). $35.00. China National Publishing Import & Export Corporation, 16 Gongti E Rd., Chaoyang Dist., Beijing 100704, People's Republic of China. **Tel** 011 8601 50630169, 5066688, FAX 011 8601 5063101, 5063010, telex 22313. **LC** KNQ440.A13; C48.

CH
CHUNG WEN FA LU LUN WEN SO YIN / SHENG TSE-LIANG PIEN. **VFOAT** Index to Chinese Legal Periodicals. Chinese (Chinese). an. Soochow University Press, Wai Shuang Hsi Shih Lin, Taipei Taiwan. **Tel** 886-2-8819471. **ED** Tung Wu Ta Hsueh Tu Shu Kuan. **LC** K33; .C5. **DD** 349.51/016; 345.10016.

US
CHURCH LAW & TAX REPORT. **Added/Corp** Christian Ministry Resources (Firm). **VFOAT** Church Law and Tax Report. (198?)-. Periodical. English. Six times a year (Jan., Mar., May, July, Sept., Nov.). $78.00 (one year); $140.00 (two year). Christian Ministry Resources, PO Box 2301, Mathews NC 28106. **Tel** (800)222-1840, FAX (704)841-8039. **ED** James F. Cobble. **LC** KF4865.A15; C47. **Circ:** 13,000.
Desc: Covers ecclesiastical law for church and state church property.

IT
CIAO 2001. (19??)-. Italian. Twenty-four times a year. L50000 Italy; L70000 other. Editrice Europea Athena 2001, Lgo Tevere Dei Mellini 39, 00193 Rome Italy. **Tel** 011 39 6 3222529.

●SZ
CIJL YEARBOOK. **Added/Corp** Centre for the Independence of Judges and Lawyers. **VAT** Centre for the Independence of Judges and Lawyers Yearbook. Vol. 1 (1992)-. Periodical. English. an. 25.00F. International Commission of Jurists, 26 Chemin Joinville, PO Box 160, CH 1216 Geneva Switzerland. **Tel** 011 41 22 7884747. **LC** K115.A2; C54. **DD** 340/.05. ***Continues*** *CIJL Bulletin, 0252-0354.*

US
CIS LAW REPRINTS. SECURITIES REGULATION SERIES : THE SUPREME COURT OF THE UNITED STATES PETITIONS AND BRIEFS. **VFOAT** Securities Regulation Series; Supreme Court of the United States Petitions and Briefs; CIS Law Reprints. Securities Law Series; Securities Law Series. English. ir. Congressional Information Service Inc, 4520 East-West Highway, Suite 800, Bethesda MD 20814-3389. **Tel** (800)638-8380, (301)654-1550, FAX (301)654-4033, telex 292386 CIS UR. ***Continues*** *BNA's Law Reprints. Securities Regulation Series.*

US/0009-7446
CITATION (CHICAGO, ILL.). (THE CITATION.). [Citation]. **Added/Corp** American Medical Association. Law Dept. American Medical Association. Law Division. American Medical Association. Office of the Counsel. (May 9, 1958)-. Periodical. English. Twenty-four times a year (Published 1st & 15th of each month). $130.00 (one year), $230.00 (two year), $330.00 (three year) US; $150.00 (one year), $260.00 (two year), $380.00 (three year) Canada; $150.00 (one year), $290.00 (two year), $420.00 (three year) other. Citation Publishing Corporation, Box 3538 RFD, Long Grove IL 60047. **Tel** (708)438-2020, (800)626-5210, FAX (708)438-2299. **ED** Sheri A. Thomson. **LC** KF3821.A59; C57. **DD** 340. **NLM** W1 CI961. Index available. cum. index. **Ad Acc. Circ:** 2,400 (ctrl).
Desc: Summaries of the latest court decisions affecting physicians and other health professionals.
Ind/Abst Health Devices Alerts; Int. Pharm. Abstr.

II
CITIZEN ACTION. Vol. 1, No. 1 (1979)-. Periodical. English. qt.
Ind/Abst Hum. Rights Intern. Rep.

US/0270-8299
CITIZENS LAW ADVISOR. **Added/Corp** Citizens Law Library. (19??)-. Periodical. English. qt. $12.00. Citizen Law Library, 7 S Wirth Street, PO Box 1745, Leesburg VA 22075. **Tel** (703)777-2007. **LC** K3; .I85. **DD** 349.73/05; 347.3005.

US
CITY OF CHICAGO BUILDING CODE. **Main/Corp** Chicago (Ill.). **VFOAT** Chicago Building Code. (1977)-. English. an. $62.80. Chicago Building Code, 415 North State Street, Chicago IL 60610. **Tel** (312)644-7806, FAX (312)644-4255. **ED** D.D. Telshaw. **LC** KFX1242; .A1963. **DD** 343.773/1107869; 347.7311037869. Index available. **Ad Acc, Adv Mgr:** Tom Youpel, **Tel** (312)644-7800. **Circ:** 2,500. ***Continues*** *Chicago. Ordinances, etc. City of Chicago Building Code and Contractors Register.*
Desc: Ordinances regulating building construction in Chicago.

UK/0306-9788
CITY OF LONDON LAW REVIEW. ***Ceased.*** (CITY OF LONDON LAW REVIEW : JOURNAL OF THE MANSFIELD LAW CLUB, CITY OF LONDON POLYTECHNIC.). [City Lond. law rev.]. (1974)-?. Periodical. English. sa. City of London Polytechnic, Law Department, 84 Moorgate, London E1 7NT England. **Tel** (02)283-1030. **LC** K3; .I86. **DD** 349.42/05; 344.2005. **Bk Rev. Ad Acc. Circ:** 300.
Desc: The journal contains articles and case notes of topical interest. The contributors are predominantly academics, practitioners and members of the English judiciary.
Ind/Abst Curr. Law Index (1980-); Leg. Resour. Index (1980-?); LegalTrac (1980-1984).

US
CITY OF LOS ANGELES BUILDING CODE. **Main/Corp** Los Angeles (Calif.). **Added/Corp** Los Angeles (Calif.) Building Code. (19??)-. Periodical. English. ir. $109.00. Building News Inc., 3055 Overland Avenue, Los Angeles CA 90034. **Tel** (310)202-7775, (800)873-6397.

BS
CIVIL CAUSE. **Main/Corp** Botswana. High Court. (19??)-. English. Botswana Government High Court, PO Box 87, Government Printer, Gaborone Botswana. **DD** 348/.681/041.

SP/0212-6095
CIVITAS. REVISTA ESPANOLA DE DERECHO DEL TRABAJO. [Civitas, Rev. esp. derecho trab.]. **VFOAT** Revista Espanola de Derecho del Trabajo. (1980)-. Periodical. Spanish. bm. 12942ptas Spain; 14000ptas other. Editorial Civitas Sa, Egnacio Ellacuria 3, 28017 Madrid Spain. **Tel** 011 34 1 725-3156. **ED** Editorial Civitas, S A. **UDC** 349.2. cum. index. **Bk Rev. Circ:** 2,000.
Desc: Commentaries on labour legislation, court cases and bibliography.

US/0364-3603
CLAIMS FORUM. Vol. 1 (March/April 1976)-. Periodical. English. bm. $18.00. J R Hendee, PO Box 322, Medina NY 14103. **LC** KF2258.A15; C5. **DD** 343/.73/093.

US/0746-7168
CLASS ACTION REPORTS. [Class action rep.]. Vol. 1 (1972)-. Periodical. English. bm (Jan., Mar., May, July, Sept., Nov.). $320.00 US & Canada; $350.00 Europe & Asia. Class Action Reports, 4900 Massachusetts Avenue Northwest, Suite 230, Washington DC 20016. **Tel** (202)364-1031, FAX (202)363-6912. **ED** Beverly C. Moore, Jr. **LC** K3; .L36. **DD** 340. Index available (bound in all issues). cum. index. **Ad Acc.** ctrl circ.
Desc: Digests state and federal class action decisions in all areas of the law. Covers settlements and attorney fee awards in class actions. Offers useful up-to-date information for class action attorneys, corporate and government attorneys, judges, law students, and attorneys law libraries.

US
CLASSIFIED INDEX, TRULY AGREED TO AND FINALLY PASSED HOUSE AND SENATE BILLS. **Main/Corp** Missouri. General Assembly. Committee on Legislative Research. **Added/Corp** Missouri. General Assembly. House of Representatives. Missouri. General Assembly. Senate. (19??)-. English. **LC** KFM7815; .M57. **DD** 348.778/01; 347.78081.

US/0148-4346
CLE BULLETIN. **Main/Corp** West Virginia. University. College of Law. V. 1-. Bulletin. English. West Virginia University Law Center, Morgantown WV 26506. **LC** KFW1257; .C65. **DD** 340/.09754.

US
CLE JOURNAL AND REGISTER, THE. **Added/Corp** American Law Institute-American Bar Association Committee on Continuing Professional Education. Vol. 34, No. 1 (Jan. 1988)-. Periodical. English. Six times a year (Jan., Mar., May, July, Sept., Nov.). $75.00. American Law Institute, 4025 Chestnut Street, Philadelphia PA 19104-3099. **Tel** (215)243-1661, (800)253-6397, FAX (215)243-1664. **ED** Mark T. Carroll (phone: (215)243-1604). **LC** KF275; .J563. Index available (Nov. iss.). cum. index. **Bk Rev**, (Qty: unlimited). **Ad Acc**, **Adv Mgr:** Kathy Lawner, **Tel** (215)243-1659. **Pr Rev. Circ:** 465. ***Continues*** *CLE Register.*
Desc: Lists courses, publications, and audiovisual aids in continuing legal education. Provides and reports developments on specialization, mandatory continuing education, and recertification. Indexed by date, location and subject matter; plus articles on improving continuing legal education.

US
CLE TV: THE LAWYERS' VIDEO MAGAZINE. Periodical. English. sm. American Law Institute, 4025 Chestnut Street, Philadelphia PA 19104-3099. **Tel** (215)243-1661, (800)253-6397, FAX (215)243-1664. **LC** K3; .L4. **DD** 349.73/071/1.

US/1070-0099
CLEAN AIR PERMITS. (CLEAN AIR PERMITS : MANAGER'S GUIDE TO THE ... CLEAN AIR ACT.). [Clean air permits]. **Added/Corp** Thompson Publishing Group. (199?)-. Periodical. English. mo. $298.00. Thompson Publishing Group, 7711 Anderson Road, Tampa FL 33634. **Tel** (800)677-3789, (813)282-8607. **DD** 344.

CN
CLEF, LA. (19??)-. French. Four times a year. 30.00Can$. La CLEF, 327 Boulevard Saint Joseph, Hull Quebec J8Y 3Z1 Canada. **Tel** (819)776-6533, FAX (819)776-0726. **ED** Claude Savoie. Index available. cum. index. **Bk Rev**. **Ad Acc.** ctrl circ. ***Continues*** *Tele-CLEF.*

US/0893-3596
CLERGY MALPRACTICE ALERT. ***Suspended.*** [Clergy malpract. alert]. Vol. 1, No. 1 (Feb. 1987)-?. Periodical. English. mo. $36.00. Jomac Publishing Inc, 621 SW Morrison/1450, Portland OR 97205. **Tel** (503)224-5811. **DD** 346.

UK
CLERK & LINDSELL ON TORTS. English. ir. £186.00 (16th edition). Sweet & Maxwell Ltd., South Quay Plaza, 183 Marsh Wall, London E14 9FT England. **Tel** 011 44 264 342899, FAX 011 44 264 342723, telex 929089 ITPINF G.

US/0160-1598
CLEVELAND BAR JOURNAL (1968). (CLEVELAND BAR JOURNAL.). **Added/Corp** Bar Association of Greater Cleveland. (1968)-. Periodical. English. mo (11 issues with June/July combined). $12.00. Cleveland Bar Association, 113 St. Clair, Suite 225, Cleveland OH 44114-1253. **Tel** (216)696-3525, FAX (216)696-2413. **ED** Randy Orr. **LC** KF200; .C55. **DD** 340/.0977132. **Ad Acc**, **Adv Mgr:** John Moore, **Tel** (216)721-2455. **Circ:** 5,300. ***Continues*** *Cleveland Bar Association. Journal.*
Desc: Journal for lawyers who are members of the Cleveland Bar Association.
Ind/Abst Law Office Inf. Serv.

US/0145-1545
CLEVELAND-MARSHALL LAW NOTES. (19??)-. Periodical. English. Four times a year. Cleveland State University, 1801 Euclid, Cleveland OH 44115. **Tel** (216)687-2336, FAX (216)687-6881. **LC** KF292.C514; A414. **DD** 340/.07/1177132.

US/0009-8876
CLEVELAND STATE LAW REVIEW. [Clevel. State law rev.]. **Added/Corp** Cleveland-Marshall College of Law. Vol. 18, No. 3 (Sept. 1969)-. English. qt. $20.00. Cleveland State University, 1801 Euclid, Cleveland OH 44115. **Tel** (216)687-2336, FAX (216)687-6881. **ED** Shannon Place. **LC** K3; .L48. **DD** 340/.05. Index available. **Ad Acc**, **Adv Mgr:** John Dyer, **Tel** (216)687-2336. **Circ:** 900 (ctrl). ***Continues*** *Cleveland-Marshall Law Review, 1048-2792.*
Ind/Abst Bowne Dig. Corp. Sec. Lawyers; Crim. Penol. Police Sci. Abstr.; Curr. Law Index (1980-); Fed. Tax Artic.; Index Leg. Period.; Leg. Resour. Index (1980-); LegalTrac (1980-).

CN/1186-8694
CLIA LOSS PREVENTION BULLETIN / CANADIAN LAWYERS INSURANCE ASSOCIATION. [CLIA loss prev. bull.]. **Added/Corp** Canadian Lawyers Insurance Association. **VFOAT** Loss Prevention Bulletin. **VAT** Canadian Lawyers Insurance Association Loss Prevention Bulletin. Issue No. 1 (May 1991)-. Bulletin. English. Three times a year. Distribution limited to members. Canadian Lawyers Insurance Association, 600 919 11th Avenue SW, Calgary Alberta T2R 1P3 Canada. **DD** 346.7103.

US/0276-752X
CLIENT COUNSELING UPDATE : CCU. **Added/Corp** American Bar Association. Law Student Division. **VFOAT** CCU. Vol. 1, No. 1 (Oct. 1980)-. Periodical. English. ir. $6.00. American Bar Association, 750 North Lake Shore Drive, Chicago IL 60611. **Tel** (312)988-5522, (312)988-5241, FAX (312)988-5528, telex 270593. **ED** Sherry VanDonk-Gouwers. **LC** KF311.A15; C54. **DD** 340/.02373. **Bk Rev**. **Ad Acc.** ctrl circ.
Desc: Newsletter contains news articles concerning client counseling.

US
CLINICAL LAW REVIEW : A JOURNAL OF LAWYERING AND LEGAL EDUCATION. (19??)-. English. Twice a year. $20.00 US; $23.00 other. Clinical Law Review, 249 Sullivan Street, New York NY 10012-1079. **Tel** (212)998-6430, FAX (212)995-4031. **ED** Stephen Ellmann, Isabelle Gunning, Randy Hertz.

US/1058-8485
CLLI'S COMMERCIAL PROPERTY LAW DIGESTS. ***Ceased.*** [CLLI's commer. prop. law dig.]. **VFOAT** Commercial Property Law Digests; Commercial Property. (Sept 1991)-(199?). Periodical. English. mo. Brownstone Publishers, 149 Fifth Avenue, 16th Floor, New York NY 10010. **Tel** (212)473-8200, (800)643-8095, FAX (212)995-9205. **DD** 346.

US
CLM, CONSUMER LAW MONTHLY. **VFOAT** Consumer Law Monthly. Periodical. English. mo. PO Box 3496, Walnut Creek CA 94598. **LC** KFC375.A15; C2. **DD** 343/.794/0705.

US
COAL LAW & REGULATION / [PATRICK C. MCGINLEY, DONALD VISH, EDITORS]. ***Ceased.*** (19??)-(May 1992). English. Matthew Bender & Company Inc., 1275 Broadway, Albany NY 12204. **Tel** (800)833-9844, (518)487-3000.

CN/1184-7476
CODE CRIMINEL, L.R.C. (1985), CH. C-46, ET LOIS CONNEXES. [Code crim. L.R.C. (1985) ch. C-46 lois connexes]. **Main/Corp** Canada. **Added/Corp** Centre de Documentation Juridique du Quebec. **VFOAT** Code Criminel et Lois Connexes; Criminal Code and Related Statutes; Criminal Code, R.S.C., 1985, C. C-46, and Related Statutes. (1990)-. Periodical. English (French). sa. Wilson & Lafleur Ltd., 40 Rue Notre Dame East, Montreal, Quebec H2Y 1B9 Canada. **Tel** (514)875-6326, FAX (514)875-8356. **DD** 345.71/002632.

CN/1184-7514
CODE DE PROCEDURE CIVILE DU QUEBEC, L.R.Q. C-25, ET LOIS ET REGLEMENTS CONNEXES. [Code proced. civ. Que. L.R.Q. c.C-25 lois reglem. connexes]. **Main/Corp** Quebec (Province). **Added/Corp** Centre de Documentation Juridique du Quebec. **VFOAT** Code de Procedure Civile du Quebec; Code of Civil Procedure of Quebec; Code of Civil Procedure of Quebec, L.R.Q. C-25, and Related Statutes and Regulations. (1990)-. Periodical. English. sa. Wilson & Lafleur Ltd., 40 Rue Notre Dame East, Montreal, Quebec H2Y 1B9 Canada. **Tel** (514)875-6326, FAX (514)875-8356. **DD** 347.714/002632.

CN/1184-7506
CODE DE PROCEDURE CIVILE (EDITIONS THEMIS). (CODE DE PROCEDURE CIVILE). [Code proced. civ.]. **Main/Corp** Quebec (Province). **VFOAT** Code of Civil Procedure. (1990)-. French. Editions Themis, University of Montreal, Faculty of Law, PO Box 6128 SUCC-A Centre-Ville, Montreal Que H3C 3J7 Canada. **Tel** (514)739-9945, FAX (514)343-2199. **ED** Jean-Maurice Brisson. **DD** 347.714/002632.

US
CODE OF FEDERAL REGULATIONS. 7, AGRICULTURE. **Main/Corp** United States. Dept. of Agriculture. **Added/Corp** United States. Office of the Federal Register. **VFOAT** Agriculture; CFR. 7, Agriculture. (19??)-. English. an. Superintendent of Documents, US Government Printing Office, Washington DC 20402. **Tel** (202)275-3328, FAX (202)786-2377.

US
CODE OF FEDERAL REGULATIONS. 16, COMMERCIAL PRACTICES. **Added/Corp** United States. Office of the Federal Register. **VFOAT** Commercial Practices; CFR. 16, Commercial Practices. (19??)-. English. an. Superintendent of Documents, US Government Printing Office, Washington DC 20402. **Tel** (202)275-3328, FAX (202)786-2377. available on microfiche.
Desc: Special edition of the Federal Register, containing a codification of documents.

US
CODE OF FEDERAL REGULATIONS. 21, FOOD AND DRUGS. **Added/Corp** United States. Office of the Federal Register. **VFOAT** Food and Drugs; CFR. 21, Food and Drugs. (19??)-. English. an. Superintendent of Documents, US Government Printing Office, Washington DC 20402. **Tel** (202)275-3328, FAX (202)786-2377. **NLM** KF 70.A3 C66. available on microfiche.
Desc: Special edition of the Federal Register, containing a codification of documents.

US
CODE OF FEDERAL REGULATIONS. 23, HIGHWAYS. **Main/Corp** United States. Dept. of Transportation. **Added/Corp** United States. Office of the Federal Register. **VFOAT** Highways; CFR. 23, Highways. (19??)-. English. an. $28.00. Superintendent of Documents, US Government Printing Office, Washington DC 20402. **Tel** (202)275-3328, FAX (202)786-2377. available on microfiche.
Desc: Special edition of the Federal Register, containing a codification of documents.

US
CODE OF FEDERAL REGULATIONS. 24, HOUSING AND URBAN DEVELOPMENT. **Added/Corp** United States. Office of the Federal Register. **VFOAT** Housing and Urban Development; CFR. 24, Housing and Urban Development. (19??)-. English. an. Superintendent of Documents, US Government Printing Office, Washington DC 20402. **Tel** (202)275-3328, FAX (202)786-2377. available on microfiche.
Desc: Special edition of the Federal Register containing a codification of documents.

US
CODE OF FEDERAL REGULATIONS. 26, INTERNAL REVENUE. **Main/Corp** United States. Internal Revenue Service. **Added/Corp** United States. Office of the Federal Register. **VFOAT** Internal Revenue; CFR. 26, Internal Revenue. (19??)-. English. an. Superintendent of Documents, US Government Printing Office, Washington DC 20402. **Tel** (202)275-3328, FAX (202)786-2377. available on microfiche.
Desc: Special edition of the Federal Register, containing a codification of documents.

US
CODE OF FEDERAL REGULATIONS. 27, ALCOHOL, TOBACCO PRODUCTS AND FIREARMS. **Main/Corp** United States. Dept. of the Treasury. **Added/Corp** United States. Office of the Federal Register. **VFOAT** Alcohol, Tobacco Products and Firearms; CFR. 27, Alcohol, Tobacco Products and Firearms. (19??)-. English. an. Superintendent of Documents, US Government Printing Office, Washington DC 20402. **Tel** (202)275-3328, FAX (202)786-2377. available on microfiche.
Desc: Special edition of the Federal Register, containing a codification of documents.

US/0276-8445
CODE OF FEDERAL REGULATIONS. 30, MINERAL RESOURCES. [Code fed. regul., 30, Miner. resour.]. **Added/Corp** United States. Office of the Federal Register. **VFOAT** Mineral Resources; CFR. 30, Mineral Resources. **VAT** Code of Federal Regulations. Thirty, Mineral Resources. (19??)-. English. an. Superintendent of Documents, US Government Printing Office, Washington DC 20402. **Tel** (202)275-3328, FAX (202)786-2377. available on microfiche.
Desc: Special edition of the Federal Register, containing a codification of documents.

US
CODE OF FEDERAL REGULATIONS. 31, MONEY AND FINANCE, TREASURY. **Main/Corp** United States. Dept. of the Treasury. **Added/Corp** United States. Office of the Federal Register. **VFOAT** Money and Finance, Treasury; CFR. 31, Money and Finance, Treasury. (19??)-. English. an. Superintendent of Documents, US Government Printing Office, Washington DC 20402. **Tel** (202)275-3328, FAX (202)786-2377. available on microfiche.
Desc: Special edition of the Federal Register, containing a codification of documents.

US
CODE OF FEDERAL REGULATIONS. 42, PUBLIC HEALTH. **Main/Corp** United States. Dept. of Health and Human Services. **Added/Corp** United States. Office of the Federal Register. **VFOAT** Public Health; CFR. 42, Public Health. (19??)-. English. an. Superintendent of Documents, US Government Printing Office, Washington DC 20402. **Tel** (202)275-3328, FAX (202)786-2377. **NLM** KF 70.A3 C669. available on microfiche. ***Continues*** *Code of Federal Regulations. 42, Public Health.*
Desc: Special edition of the Federal Register, containing a codification of documents.

US
CODE OF FEDERAL REGULATIONS. 44, EMERGENCY MANAGEMENT AND ASSISTANCE. **Added/Corp** United States. Office of the Federal Register. **VFOAT** Emergency Management and Assistance; CFR. 30, Emergency Management and Assistance. (19??)-. English. an. $36.00. Superintendent of Documents, US Government Printing Office, Washington DC 20402. **Tel** (202)275-3328, FAX (202)786-2377. available on microfiche.
Desc: Special edition of the Federal Register, containing a codification of documents.

US
CODE OF FEDERAL REGULATIONS. 47, TELECOMMUNICATIONS. **Added/Corp** United States. Office of the Federal Register. **VFOAT** Telecommunications; CFR. 47, Telecommunications. (19??)-. English. an. $39.50. Superintendent of Documents, US Government Printing Office, Washington DC 20402. **Tel** (202)275-3328, FAX (202)786-2377. available on microfiche.
Desc: Special edition of the Federal Register, containing a codification of documents.

US
CODE OF FEDERAL REGULATIONS. 49, TRANSPORTATION. **Added/Corp** United States. Office of the Federal Register. **VFOAT** Transportation; CFR. 49, Transportation. (19??)-. English. an. $285.00 (parts 100-177), $94.00 (parts 350-399). Regulations Management Corporation, 1505 Arlington Road, Bloomington IN 47404. **Tel** (812)333-7347. **NLM** KF 70.A3 C669. available on microfiche.
Desc: Special edition of the Federal Register, containing a codification of documents.

US/0276-6906
CODE OF FEDERAL REGULATIONS. CFR INDEX AND FINDING AIDS. [Code Fed. regul., CFR index find. aids]. **Added/Corp** United States. Office of the Federal Register. **VFOAT** CFR Index and Finding Aids; Code of Federal Regulations. CFR Index; CFR Index. (1977)-. English. an. $31.00. Superintendent of Documents, US Government Printing Office, Washington DC 20402. **Tel** (202)275-3328, FAX (202)786-2377. **DD** 342. **NLM** KF 70.A3 C674. available on microfiche. ***Formed by the union of*** *Code of Federal Regulations. CFR Index* ***and*** *Code of Federal Regulations. Finding Aids.*
Desc: Special edition of the Federal Register.

US
CODE OF FEDERAL REGULATIONS. LSA, LIST OF CFR SECTIONS AFFECTED. **Added/Corp** United States. National Archives. United States. Office of the Federal Register. **VFOAT** L.S.A., List of C.F.R. Sections Affected; List of C.F.R. Sections Affected; List of CFR Sections Affected; LSA, List of CFR Sections Affected. (Aug 1977)-. Government Publication. English. mo (December, March, June and September issues are annuals). $24.00 US; $30.00 other. Superintendent of Documents, US Government Printing Office, Washington DC 20402. **Tel** (202)275-3328, FAX (202)786-2377. **NLM** KF 70.A3 C675. available on microfiche (Vols. for (1987)- distributed to depository libraries). ***Continues*** *Code of Federal Regulations. Cumulative List of CFR Sections Affected, 0363-8839.*
Desc: A listing of amendatory actions published in the Federal Register. Entries indicate type of change.

US
CODE OF FEDERAL REGULATIONS. N.1, GENERAL PROVISIONS. **Added/Corp** United States. Office of the Federal Register. **VFOAT** General Provisions; CFR. 1, General Provisions. (19??)-. Government Publication. English. an. $23.00. Superintendent of Documents, US Government Printing Office, Washington DC 20402. **Tel** (202)275-3328, FAX (202)786-2377. available on microfiche (Vols. for (1985-) distributed to some depository libraries).
Desc: Special edition of the Federal Register, containing a codification of documents.

US
CODE OF GEORGIA: ANNOTATED. English. ir. $798.00. Harrison Company Publishers, 3110 Crossing Park, PO Box 7500, Norcross GA 30091-7500. **Tel** (800)241-3561, (404)447-9150.

US
CODE OF GEORGIA, UNANNOTATED EDITION. ***Ceased.*** Ceased (1989). English. ir. Harrison Company Publishers, 3110 Crossing Park, PO Box 7500, Norcross GA 30091-7500. **Tel** (800)241-3561, (404)447-9150.

US
CODE OF LAWS OF SOUTH CAROLINA; ANNOTATED. **Main/Corp** South Carolina. (19??)-. English. ir. Lawyers Cooperative Publishing Company, Aqueduct Building, Rochester NY 14694. **Tel** (800)527-0430, (716)546-5530.
Desc: Official code of the state of South Carolina.

FR
CODE RURAL; CODE FORESTIER - (FRANCE). **Main/Corp** France. **Added/Corp** France. Laws, Statutes, etc. Code Forestier. French. Dalloz, 35 rue Tournefort, 75240 Paris Cedex 05 France. **Tel** 011 33 1 40515434 or 40515454, FAX 45 87 37 48, telex 206 446 F.
Desc: Covers agricultural laws and legislation, as well as forestry law and legislation.

IT
CODICE DELLA GIURISPRUDENZA. (19??)-. Periodical. Italian. tq. IPSOA Editore SRL, Casella Postale 12055, Mastrangelo, 20120 Milan Italy. **Tel** 011 39 2 82476248. Index available.

IT
CODICE DELLA GIURISPRUDENZA PREVIDENZIALE. (19??)-. Periodical. Italian. Three times a year. IPSOA Editore SRL, Casella Postale 12055, Mastrangelo, 20120 Milan Italy. **Tel** 011 39 2 82476248. Index available.

IT
CODICE D'ITALIA. TESTO VIGENTE. SCHEDE DI AGGIORNAMENTO. Italian. mo. Ist Geografico de Agostini, Via Giovanni da Verrazano 15, 28100 Novara Italy. **Tel** 011 39 321 4712015.

US/0191-4839
CODIFICATION OF PRESIDENTIAL PROCLAMATIONS AND EXECUTIVE ORDERS. **Main/Corp** United States. President. **VFOAT** Presidential Proclamations and Executive Orders. Began with 1961/77. English. National Archives and Records Administration, Eighth Street and Pennsylvania Avenue NW, Washington DC 20408. **Tel** (202)523-3220. **LC** KF70; .A473. **DD** 348/.73/1. **NLM** KF 70 .A473.

SP
COLECTANEA DE JURISPRUDENCIA CANONICA. **Main/Corp** Universidad Pontificia de Salamanca. Facultad de Derecho Canonico. (19??)-. Spanish. ir. 1950ptas. Universidad Pontificia de Salamanca, Apartado de Correos 541, 37080 Salamanca Spain. **Tel** 011 34 23 215140.

BL
COLETANEA DE RESOLUCOES DO CONSELHO DELIBERATIVO. COLETANEA DE ATOS DA PRESIDENCIA. **Main/Corp** Instituto do Acucar e do Alcool (Brazil). 1972-. Portuguese. Instituto do Acucar e do Alcool, Caixa Postal 420, Rio de Janeiro Brazil. ***Formed by the union of*** *Coletanea de Atos* ***and*** *Coletanea de Atos da Presidencia.*

US
COLLECTION AGENCY ACT WITH RULES AND REGULATIONS - (CALIFORNIA). **Main/Corp** California. English. Bureau of Collection and Investigative Services, 1920 20th Street, Sacramento CA 95814. **LC** KFC446.C6; A294. **DD** 346.794/077.
Desc: Including the California Robbins-Rosenthal fair debt collection practices act (with list of sections preempted by the Federal fair debt collection practices act), general provisions.

US/0192-1371
COLLEGE ADMINISTRATOR AND THE COURTS, THE. Vol. 1 (April 1978)-. English. qt. $59.50. College Administration Publications Inc, 830D Fairview Road, PO Box 15898, Asheville NC 28813. **Tel** (704)277-8777. **ED** Robert D. Bickel. **LC** KF4225.A59; B45 Suppl. **DD** 344/.73/074. Index available. cum. index. **Circ:** 2,000.
Desc: Briefs prepared for college administrators involving higher court decisions affecting administration of institutions of higher education.

US/0010-101X
COLLEGE LAW BULLETIN. Vol. 1, Nov. 1968-. Bulletin. English. mo. US National Student Association, 2115 South Street NW, Washington DC 20008.

US/0045-737X
COLLEGE LAW DIGEST. ***Title Change.*** Jan. 15, 1970-. Periodical. English. mo (13 issues yearly). National Association of College and University Attorneys, 1 Dupont Circle, Washington DC 20036. **Tel** (303)979-5657. **ED** Thomas E Blackwell. **LC** KF4225.A59; N383. **DD** 344/.73/074. ***Continues*** *West's Education Law Reporter. Special Pamphlet.* ***Absorbed by*** *West's Education Law Reporter. Special Pamphlet.*

US/0145-1472
COLLEGE STUDENT AND THE COURTS, THE. (19??)-. Periodical. English. qt. $59.50. College Administration Publications Inc, 830D Fairview Road, PO Box 15898, Asheville NC 28813. **Tel** (704)277-8777. **ED** D.Parker Young and Donald D. Gehring. **LC** KF4243.A59; Y68 1977 Suppl. **DD** 344.73/079; 347.30479. Index available. cum. index. **Circ:** 2,800 (ctrl).
Desc: Briefs of higher court decisions involving student institutional relationships in higher education.

US/1048-3683
COLORADO BANKRUPTCY COURT REPORTER, THE. [Colo. bankruptcy court report.]. **Added/Corp** Public Record Corporation. (198?)-. English. Four times a year. $131.00. The Public Record Corporation, PO Box 18186, 1666 Lafayette Street, Denver CO 80218. **Tel** (303)832-8262, (800)487-8262, FAX (303)861-5821. **ED** Jeffrey Cohen and C. Forrest Morgan III. **DD** 346. Index available ($20.00). **Bk Rev. Ad Acc.** ctrl circ. ***Continues*** *Bankruptcy Court Reporter, 0886-9774.*
Desc: Information on the Colorado bankruptcy courts.

US/0363-7867
COLORADO LAWYER. [Colo. lawyer]. **Added/Corp** Colorado Bar Association. Vol. 1, No. 1 (Jan. 1972)-. Periodical. English. mo. $35.00 (library), $85.00 (regular) US; $120.00 (library), $170.00 (regular) other. Colorado Bar Association, 1900 Grant Street, Suite 940, Denver CO 80203. **Tel** (303)860-1115, FAX (303)894-0821. **ED** Arlene Abady. **LC** K3; .O346. **DD** 340/.09788. Index available. cum. index (five-year). **Bk Rev**, (Qty: 2-4). **Ad Acc, Adv Mgr:** Suellen Palcanis, **Tel** (303)377-1673. **Circ:** 13,000 (ctrl). available on microfiche (from Hein and Company).
Desc: Articles on substantive law, Colorado appellate court opinions, court business and special legal features.
Ind/Abst Curr. Law Index (1980-); Fed. Tax Artic.; Index Leg. Period.; Law Office Inf. Serv.; Leg. Resour. Index (1980-); LegalTrac (1980-).

US
COLORADO LEGISLATIVE COUNCIL RECOMMENDATIONS. **Main/Corp** Colorado. General Assembly. Legislative Council. **VFOAT** Report to the Colorado General Assembly, Recommendations for .... English. an. State Capitol, Room 46, Denver CO 80203. **LC** KFC1820; .L4 subser; KFC1806. **DD** 300.9788 S; 348.788/01; 300. 9788 S; 347.88081.

US/0744-9828
COLORADO REPORTER COLORADO CASES REPORTED IN PACIFIC REPORTER, SECOND SERIES. [Colo. rep. Color. cases rep. Pac. rep.]. **VFOAT** Colorado Reporter;

West's Colorado Reporter. English. wk (except last week in Sept., and 1st week in Oct.). $60.00. West Publishing Company, 610 Opperman Drive, PO Box 64526, Eagan MN 55123-1308. **Tel** (612)687-5618, (800)328-9352, FAX (612)687-5388, (800)562-2329. **(Subscription telephone:** FAX (612)688-3570**)** **DD** 348.

US/0090-7944
COLUMBIA HUMAN RIGHTS LAW REVIEW. See Political Science-Civil Rights.

US/1062-6220
COLUMBIA JOURNAL OF GENDER AND LAW. [Columbia j. gend. law]. **Added/Corp** Columbia University. School of Law. Vol. 1, No. 1 (1991)-. Periodical. English. sa. $40.00 (institution); $15.00 (individual & public interest organizations); $10.00 (students). Columbia University School of Law, 435 West 116th Street, New York NY 10027. **Tel** (212)854-4398, (212)854-3742. **(Subscription address:** Columbia Journal of Gender and Law, Box E-10, 435 West 116th Street, New York NY 10027.**)** **LC** K3; .O348. **DD** 346.7301/34/05; 347.30613405.
Ind/Abst Index Leg. Period. (1992-).

US/0010-1923
COLUMBIA JOURNAL OF LAW AND SOCIAL PROBLEMS. [Columbia j. law soc. probl.]. **Added/Corp** Columbia University. School of Law. Vol. 1 (June 1965)-. Periodical. English. qt. $35.00 US; $40.00 other; $11.00 (single issue). Columbia University School of Law, 435 West 116th Street, New York NY 10027. **Tel** (212)854-4398, (212)854-3742. **(Subscription address:** Columbia Journal of Law and Social Problems, Box D-27, 435 West 116th Street, New York NY 10027.**)** **ED** Nicholas Lobenthal. (free on request). cum. index. **Bk Rev. Pr Rev. Circ:** 800. Documents available from The Genuine Article, UMI Article Clearinghouse.
Desc: A law journal focusing on general legal issues and their impact on pressing social concerns.
Ind/Abst ABC POL SCI; Bowne Dig. Corp. Sec. Lawyers; Crim. Justice Abstr.; Curr. Contents Soc. Behav. Sci.; Curr. Law Index (1980-); Educ. Adm. Abstr. (?-?); Expand. Acad. Index (1992-); Hum. Resour. Abstr.; Index Leg. Period.; J. Plan. Lit.; Leg. Resour. Index (1980-); LegalTrac (1980-); Newsp. Period. Abstr. (1992-); PAIS Int. Print (1991-); Res. Alert [Full Cov.]; Sage Fam. Stud. Abstr.; Sage Public Adm. Abstr. (?-?); Soc. Sci. Cit. Index [Full Cov.]; Urban Aff. Abstr.

US
COLUMBIA LAW ALUMNI BULLETIN (NEW YORK, N.Y. : 1980). See College and School Publications-Alumni.

US/0010-1958
COLUMBIA LAW REVIEW. [Columbia law rev.]. **Added/Corp** Columbia University. School of Law. Vol. 1 (Jan. 1901)-. Periodical. English. Eight times a year. $40.00. Columbia University School of Law, 435 West 116th Street, New York NY 10027. **Tel** (212)854-4398, (212)854-3742. **(Subscription address:** Columbia Law Review, Box A-26, 435 West 116th Street, New York NY 10027.**)** **LC** K3; .O355. **DD** 340/.05. **NLM** W1 CO285. **[CCC]. Bk Rev. Ad Acc. Pr Rev. Circ:** 3,200 (ctrl). Documents available from The Genuine Article, UMI Article Clearinghouse, UMI Article Clearinghouse.
Desc: Explores current legal issues; usually contains several pieces written by students and two to three written by judges, lawyers, practitioners or professors.
Ind/Abst ABC POL SCI; ABI/INFORM Glob. Ed.; ABI Inform Ondisc (Nov. 1972-Dec. 1974); Bowne Dig. Corp. Sec. Lawyers; Crim. Justice Abstr.; Crim. Penol. Police Sci. Abstr. (1974-); Curr. Contents Soc. Behav. Sci.; Curr. Law Index (1980-); Expand. Acad. Index (1989-); Fed. Tax Artic.; Health Plan. Adminis.; Index Leg. Period.; Int. Bibliogr. Sociol.; Int. Polit. Sci. Abstr. (1980-); Leg. Resour. Index (1980-); LegalTrac (Nov. 1972-Dec. 1974, 1980); Newsp. Period. Abstr. (1989-); PAIS Int. Print (1991-); Res. Alert [Full Cov.]; Soc. Sci. Cit. Index [Full Cov.]; West. Hist. Q.; Women Stud. Abstr.

US
COLUMBIA LAW SCHOOL NEWS. Vol. 1 (April 1947)-. Periodical. English. Columbia Law School, 435 West 116th Street, Box A-27, New York NY 10027.

US/0888-4226
COLUMBIA-VLA JOURNAL OF LAW & THE ARTS. [Columbia-VLA j. law arts]. **Added/Corp** Volunteer Lawyers for the Arts. Columbia University. School of Law. **VFOAT** Columbia VLA Journal of Law and the Arts; Journal of Law & the Arts; Journal of Law and the Arts; Law & the Arts; Law and the Arts. **VAT** Columbia-Volunteer Lawyers for the Arts Journal of Law & The Arts. Vol. 10, No. 1 (Autumn 1985)-. Periodical. English. qt. $35.00. Volunteer Lawyers for the Arts, 1 East 53rd Street 6th Floor, New York NY 10022. **Tel** (212)319-2787. **(Subscription address:** Columbia University School of Law, 453 West 116th Street, Box D 28, New York NY 10027.**)** **ED** Michael S. Simon. **LC** K1; .R56. **DD** 344/.097/05; 342.49705. **Circ:** 550. ***Continues*** *Art & The Law, 0743-5266.*
Desc: A journal of arts entertainment and communications law, published in conjunction with the Columbia University School of Law.

Ind/Abst ARTbibliogr. Mod.; Curr. Law Index (1985-); Index Leg. Period.; Leg. Resour. Index (1985-); LegalTrac (1985-).

US/0147-6696
COMMENTARIES. [Commentaries]. Began in 1968. English. qt. Boston University School of Law, 765 Commonwealth Avenue, Boston MA 02215. **Tel** (617)353-3157, (617)353-3115. **LC** KF1; .C65. **DD** 340.

US
COMMENTATOR. Added/Corp Los Angeles. Southwestern University. Student Bar Association. Periodical. English. mo. Southwestern University School of Law, 675 South Westmoreland, Los Angeles CA 90005. **Tel** (310)738-6762.
Ind/Abst Peace Res. Abstr. J. (1966-1968).

US/0098-4957
COMMERCIAL BAR, THE. (19??)-. English. an. Commercial Publishing Company, 740 South Fulton Avenue, Mt Vernon NY 10550. **LC** KF195.C57; C645. **DD** 346.07/025.

AT
COMMERCIAL DISPUTE RESOLUTION JOURNAL. (19??)-. English. Three times a year. 150.00Aus$. Butterworths Pty Ltd, 271-273 Lane Cove Road, PO Box 345, North Ryde NSW 2113 Australia. **Tel** 011 61 2 3354444, FAX 011 61 2 3354655.
Desc: Provides informed discussions and practical guidance on the mediation of commercial disputes.

US
COMMERCIAL LAW ANNUAL. Added/Corp Callaghan and Company. (1991)-. English. Clark Boardman Callaghan, 155 Pfingsten Road, Deerfield IL 60015. **Tel** (800)323-8067. **LC** KF872; .C65. **DD** 346.73/07/05; 347.306705.

AT/0819-4262
COMMERCIAL LAW QUARTERLY. [Commer. law q.]. **Added/Corp** Commercial Law Association of Australia. (1987)-. Periodical. English. qt. 205.00Aus$ (Public Companies & Educational Institutions), 175.00Aus$ (Law & Accounting Firms), 100.00Aus$ (individuals) Australia; 45.00Aus$ (other). Commercial Law Association, GPO Box 5186, Sydney NSW 2001 Australia. **Tel** 61 2 2313520. **DD** 346.940705. Index available. ***Continues*** *Bulletin - Commercial Law Association, 0819-6354.*
Ind/Abst Aust. Leg. Mon. Dig.

US/0736-0517
COMMERCIAL LEASE LAW INSIDER. (19??)-. Periodical. English. Twelve times a year. $227.00. Brownstone Publishers Inc, 149 Fifth Avenue, 16th Floor, New York NY 10010. **Tel** (212)473-8200, FAX (212)995-9205. **ED** Alan S. Parker. **LC** KF593.C6; A133. **DD** 346.7304/3462; 347.30643462. Index available.
Desc: Written primarily for owners, managers, attorneys and other real estate professionals. A practical, plain-english newsletter dealing with commercial leasing issues.

US/0898-5634
COMMERCIAL LEASING LAW & STRATEGY. [Commer. leas. law strategy]. **VFOAT** Commercial Leasing Law and Strategy; Commercial Leasing. (1988)-. Periodical. English. mo. $175.00. Leader Publications, 345 Park Avenue South, New York NY 10010. **Tel** (800)888-8300 ext. 6170, (212)545-6170, FAX (212)696-1848. **ED** Stephanie McEvily (editor's phone (516)766-7993). **LC** KF593.C6; A134. **DD** 346.7304/3462/05; 347.3064346205.
Desc: Covers issues of importance to people in commercial real estate, focusing on legal aspects.

US
COMMERICAL LAWS OF THE WORLD. BERMUDA. (19??)-. English. ir. $100.00. Foreign Tax Law Publishers Inc., PO Box 2189, Ormond Beach FL 32175-2189. **Tel** (904)253-5785, FAX (904)257-3003.

US/0587-2936
COMMITTEE REPORTS - LOCAL GOVERNMENT LAW SECTION OF THE AMERICAN BAR ASSOCIATION.
Main/Corp American Bar Association. Section of Local Government Law. (19??)-. English. an. American Bar Association, 750 North Lake Shore Drive, Chicago IL 60611. **Tel** (312)988-5522, (312)988-5241, FAX (312)988-5528, telex 270593. **LC** KF5300.A73; A4. **DD** 342/.73/09.

●US/1068-5871
COMMLAW CONSPECTUS. (COMMLAW CONSPECTUS : JOURNAL OF COMMUNICATIONS LAW.). **Added/Corp** Columbus School of Law. **VFOAT** Comm Law Conspectus; Journal of Communications Law. **VAT** Communications Law Conspectus. (1993)-. Periodical. English. Twice a year. $25.00. Columbus School of Law, Catholic University of America, Washington DC 20064. **Tel** (202)319-5144. **ED** Jennifer P. Brovan. cum. index. **Bk Rev. Ad Acc.** ctrl circ. available on an online database from WESTLAW; and LEXIS.

US/0277-2930
COMMODITIES LAW LETTER. ***Title Change.*** [Commod. law lett.]. (198?)-Vol. 11, No. 11 & 12 (Jan./Feb. 1992). Periodical. English. mo. Commodities Law Press Association, 40 Broad Street, Suite 2000, New York NY 10004. **Tel** (212)612-9545. **ED** Richard A Miller. **LC** KF1085.A15; C65. **DD** 343.73/08/05; 347.303805. cum. index. **Bk Rev. Circ:** 300 (ctrl). ***Continued by*** *Futures International Law Letter.*
Desc: Report and analysis of legal developments affecting commodities/futures and securities industry. For lawyers, accountants, and executives.
Ind/Abst Curr. Law Index (1984-); Leg. Resour. Index (1984-); LegalTrac (1981, 1984-).

US/0160-659X
COMMON LAW LAWYER, THE. Periodical. English. bm. International Common Law Exchange Society, PO Box 51, Palo Alto CA 94302. **Tel** (415)962-8073. **LC** K110.I53; A15. **DD** 340/.2/05.
Ind/Abst Curr. Law Index (1981-); Leg. Resour. Index (1981-?); LegalTrac (1980-1987).

UK/0588-7445
COMMON MARKET LAW REPORTS.
Added/Corp European Law Centre. **VFOAT** C.M.L.R.; CMLR. (Oct. 1962)-. Periodical. English. wk. £495.00 Europe; £520.00 other. Sweet & Maxwell Ltd., South Quay Plaza, 183 Marsh Wall, London E14 9FT England. **Tel** 011 44 264 342899, FAX 011 44 264 342723, telex 929089 ITPINF G. **ED** Neville March Hunnings. **DD** 341. Index available. cum. index. **Ad Acc. Circ:** 900.

NE/0165-0750
COMMON MARKET LAW REVIEW.
[Common mark. law rev.]. **Added/Corp** British Institute of International and Comparative Law. Rijksuniversiteit te Leiden. Europa Instituut. Vol. 1, No. 1 (June 1963)-. Periodical. English. bm. $844.00. Martinus Nijhoff Publishers, Subsidiary of Kluwer Academic Publishers, Koraalrood 50, 2718 SC Zoetermeer Netherlands. **Tel** 011 31 79 684400. **ED** Henry G Schermers, David O'Keefe, Wulf-Henning Roth, Piet Jan Slot, C.W.A. Timmermans and Jan A Winter. **DD** 349.4/05; 344.005. **CODEN** CMLRDD. **[CCC].** cum. index. **Bk Rev. Ad Acc. Pr Rev. Acid Free.** available on microfilm and microfiche from University Microfilms International (UMI). Documents available from The Genuine Article.
Desc: Designed to further the understanding and implementation of community law within the twelve Member States and to disseminate legal thinking on Community Law Matters.
Ind/Abst Arts Humanit. Citation Index [Select. Cov.]; Contents Recent Econ. J.; Curr. Contents Soc. Behav. Sci.; Curr. Law Index (1980-); Index Foreign Leg. Per.; Int. Labour Doc.; Int. Polit. Sci. Abstr. (1980-); LABORDOC; Leg. Resour. Index (1980-); LegalTrac (1980-); Leis. Recreat. Tour. Abstr.; PAIS Int. Print (1991-); Res. Alert [Full Cov.]; Rural Dev. Abstr.; Selec. Coop. Index Manage. Period; Soc. Sci. Cit. Index [Full Cov.]; World Agric. Econ.

AT/1036-9589
COMMONWEALTH BILLS TABLE AND ASSOCIATED MATERIAL. [Commonw. bills table assoc. mater.]. **Added/Corp** Australian Government Publishing Service. Legal Publishing Unit. **VFOAT** Commonwealth Bills and Associated Material. (1991)-. Government Publication. English. bw. 650.00Aus$. Australian Government Publishing Service, GPO Box 84, Canberra ACT 2601 Australia. **Tel** 011 61 6 2954411, FAX 011 61 6 2954455. **DD** 348.9405.

NW
COMMONWEALTH CODE OF THE NORTHERN MARIANA ISLANDS. English. Commonwealth Law Revision Commission, PO Box 307, Saipan Northern Mariana Islands 96950.

US
COMMONWEALTH COURT REPORTS.
Main/Corp Pennsylvania. Commonwealth Court. **Added/Corp** Pennsylvania. Commonwealth Court. Reports. **VFOAT** Pennsylvania Commonwealth Court Reports. Vol. 1 (1970/1971)-. Periodical. English. mo. Murrelle Printing Company Inc, Box 100, 201 West Lockhart Street, Sayre PA 18840. **Tel** (717)888-2244. **ED** William Wilks. **LC** KFP49; .A2. **DD** 348/.748/043. **Circ:** 1,000.
Desc: Opinions of the Commonwealth Court of Pennsylvania.

UK/0305-0718
COMMONWEALTH LAW BULLETIN.
Added/Corp Commonwealth Secretariat. No. 1 (July 1974)-. Bulletin. English. qt. £60.00. Commonwealth Secretariat / London, Marlborough House, Pall Mall, London SW1Y 5HX England. **Tel** 44 71 8393411, telex 27678. **ED** Jeremy Pope. **DD** 348/.009171241. Index available. cum. index. **Bk Rev**, (Qty: 4). **Ad Acc. Circ:** 1800.
Desc: Up-to-date notes on recent legislation, case law and law reform proposals, in the 49 commonwealth independent countries, and at the international level.
Ind/Abst Aust. Leg. Mon. Dig.; Leg. Resour. Index; LegalTrac (1980-).

AT/0069-7133
COMMONWEALTH LAW REPORTS, THE. **Main/Corp** Australia. High Court. Vol. 1 (1903/1904)-. English. ir. $172.00. The Law Book Company Limited, 44-50 Waterloo Road, North Ryde New South Wales, 2113 Australia. **Tel** 011 61 2 8870177, FAX 011 61 2 8887240, telex ASBOOK 27445. **ED** J D Merralls. **DD** 348.94/041; 349.40841.
Desc: Contains the authorised reports of the Court is regarded as being among the foremost authoritative series of national law reports.
Ind/Abst Aust. Leg. Mon. Dig.

AT
COMMONWEALTH OF AUSTRALIA GAZETTE. PERIODIC. **Main/Corp** Australia. English. **DD** 340/.0944. ***Supersedes in part*** *Australian Government Gazette.*

AT
COMMONWEALTH OF AUSTRALIA GAZETTE. PUBLIC SERVICE. **Main/Corp** Australia. (July 7, 1977)-. Government Publication. English. wk (50 issues). 395.00Aus$. Australian Government Publishing Service, GPO Box 84, Canberra ACT 2601 Australia. **Tel** 011 61 6 2954411, FAX 011 61 6 2954455. **DD** 340/.0994. ***Supersedes in part*** *Australian Government Gazette.*
Desc: Contains notices concerning administrative matters within the Australian Public Service. These include advertisements for vacancies and announcements of promotions and transfers.

AT
COMMONWEALTH TAXATION BOARD OF REVIEW DECISIONS. NEW SERIES. **Main/Corp** Australia. Taxation Board of Review. (19??)-. English. ir. Butterworths Pty Ltd, 271-273 Lane Cove Road, PO Box 345, North Ryde NSW 2113 Australia. **Tel** 011 61 2 3354444, FAX 011 61 2 3354655.

VC/0393-0327
COMMUNICATIONES - PONTIFICIA COMMISSIO CODICI IURIS CANONICI RECOGNOSCENDO. (COMMUNICATIONES.). [Commun. - Pontif. comm. codici iuris canon. recognoscendo]. **Added/Corp** Catholic Church. Pontificia Commissio Codici Iuris Canonici Recognoscendo. Vol. 1, (June 1969)-. Periodical. Italian. Twice a year. $24.81 Italy; $38.00others. Liberia Editrice Vaticana, Citta del Vaticano, 00120 Vatican City. **Tel** 011 39 6 69883529, telex 2024 DIRGENTEL VA.
Ind/Abst Bibliogr. Mission.; Canon Law Abstr.; Abr. Cathol. Period. Lit. Index; Cathol. Period. Lit. Index.

US/0162-9093
COMMUNICATIONS AND THE LAW. [Commun. law]. Vol. 1 (Winter 1979)-. Periodical. English. qt. $95.00 US; $105.00 other. Fred B. Rothman & Company, 10368 West Centennial Road, Littleton CO 80127. **Tel** (800)457-1986, (303)979-5657, FAX (303)978-1457, telex 87669. **ED** Theodore R Kupferman. **LC** K3; .O39. **DD** 343/.73/09905. **CODEN** COMLDE. **Ad Acc. Circ:** 800. available on microfilm and microfiche from University Microfilms International (UMI). Documents available from UMI Article Clearinghouse, UMI Article Clearinghouse, Ask*IEEE, UMI Article Clearinghouse.
Desc: Devoted to the study of expanding technology, aggressive use of the media by business, censorship, and judicial affairs.
Ind/Abst ABI/INFORM Glob. Ed. (Feb. 1987-); ABI Inform Ondisc (Feb. 1984-); Commun. Abstr.; Curr. Law Index (1980-); Expand. Acad. Index (1992-); Film Lit. Index (19??-); Index Leg. Period.; INSPEC (Feb. 1987-); J. Plan. Lit.; Leg. Resour. Index (1980-); LegalTrac (1980-); Newsp. Period. Abstr. (1992-); UMI ABI/Inform--Bus. Period. Ondisc [Full Txt.].

US/0898-2457
COMMUNICATIONS LAW (1982). (COMMUNICATIONS LAW.). [Commun. law]. **Added/Corp** Practising Law Institute. (1982)-. English. an (Nov.). $90.00. Practising Law Institute, 810 Seventh Avenue, New York NY 10019-5818. **Tel** (212)765-5700, FAX (212)581-4670 general correspondence, (212)265-4742 orders and billing inquiries. **LC** KF4774; .N48. **DD** 343.73/0998; 347.303998. ***Continues*** *Annual Communications Law Institute, 0898-2449.*

US/0737-7622
COMMUNICATIONS LAWYER : PUBLICATION OF THE FORUM COMMITTEE ON COMMUNICATIONS LAW, AMERICAN BAR ASSOCIATION. [Commun. lawyer]. **Added/Corp** American Bar Association. Forum Committee on Communications Law. Vol. 1, No. 1 (Winter 1983)-. Periodical. English. qt (4 issues). $35.00. American Bar Association, 750 North Lake Shore Drive, Chicago IL 60611. **Tel** (312)988-5522, (312)988-5241, FAX (312)988-5528, telex 270593. **LC** KF2750.A15; C65. **DD** 343.73/099; 347.30399.

CN/0824-2186
COMMUNIQUE (LAW SOCIETY OF MANITOBA). (COMMUNIQUE / THE LAW SOCIETY OF MANITOBA.). [Commun. - Law Soc. Manit.]. Sept. 1982-. Periodical. English. mo. Free to members. Law Society of Manitoba, 101-219 Kennedy Street, Suite 201, Winnepeg Manitoba R3C 1S8 Canada. **Tel** (204)942-5571. **ED** Graeme Garson. **DD** 340/.06/07127. **Circ:** 2,000 (ctrl).
Desc: Publication goes to law society membership to keep them current with operations of society, rule changes, new governing body to members and any matters of general interest to membership.

US/0730-6970
COMMUNIS SCRIPTURA. Periodical. English. The Missouri Bar, 326 Monroe, Jefferson City MO 65101. **Tel** (314)635-4128. **LC** KFM8195.7.L38; A133. **DD** 340/.07/12778.

US/0190-1192
COMMUNITY ASSOCIATION LAW REPORTER. [Community assoc. law report.]. **Added/Corp** Community Associations Institute. (January 1978)-. Periodical. English. mo. $125.00 members, $150.00 nonmembers. Community Associations Institute, 1630 Duke Street, Alexandria VA 22314. **Tel** (703)548-8600, FAX (703)684-1581. **ED** Wayne S.Hyatt (Editor's Address: Hyatt & Rhoads, P.C., 1200 Peachtree Center South Tower, 225 Peachtree St., NE, Atlanta GA 30303). **LC** KF581.A15; C65. **DD** 346/.73/043305. Index available. cum. index. **Ad Acc**, **Adv Mgr:** Jeff Sanderson. **Circ:** 3,400.
Desc: Reports on and analyzes court cases dealing with condominiums, co-operatives, and homeowner associations.

US
COMMUNITY DEVELOPMENT REPORTER. **See** Housing and Urban Development.

US/0069-7893
COMPARATIVE JURIDICAL REVIEW. [Comp. jurid. rev.]. **Added/Corp** Pan American Institute of Comparative Law. Rainforth Foundation. Vol. 1 (1964)-. English (Spanish). ir. Free on request. Rainforth Foundation, 3001 Ponce de Leon Boulevard, Coral Gables FL 33134. **Tel** (305)446-7856. **ED** Mario Diaz-Cruz. **DD** 340. cum. index. **Bk Rev. Circ:** 1,000.
Ind/Abst Curr. Law Index (1980-); Index Foreign Leg. Per.; Leg. Resour. Index (1980-); LegalTrac (1980-).

SY
COMPENDIUM OF LAWS AND JURISPRUDENCE OF THE REPUBLIC OF LEBANON. Multiple languages (English and French). PO Box 539, Damascus Syria. **DD** 340/.095692.

SY
COMPENDIUM OF LAWS OF THE FEDERATION OF ARAB REPUBLICS. English. PO Box 539, Damascus Syria. **DD** 340/.0962.

US/0362-5532
COMPILATION OF LAW RELATING TO THE PRACTICE OF VETERINARY MEDICINE AND SURGERY. ***Title Change.*** (COMPILATION OF LAWS RELATING TO THE PRACTICE OF VETERINARY MEDICINE AND SURGERY, WITH RULES AND REGULATIONS, GENERAL PROVISIONS OF THE BUSINESS AND PROFESSIONS CODE, INCLUDING THE CONSUMER AFFAIRS ACT, AND EXCERPTS FROM THE GOVERNMENT CODE - (CALIFORNIA).). [Compil. laws relat. pract. vet. med. surg.]. **Added/Corp** California. Board of Examiners in Veterinary Medicine. English. Consumer Affairs Building, 1020 N Street, Sacramento CA 95814. **LC** KFC547.V3; A294. **DD** 344/.794/049. ***Continued by*** *Compilation of Laws Relating to the Practice of Veterinary Medicine, Surgery and Animal Health Technology with Rules and Regulations, General Provisions of the Business and Professions Code, Including the Consumer Affairs Act (California).*

PH/0115-2203
COMPILATION OF PRESIDENTIAL DECREES - (PHILIPPINES). **Main/Corp** Philippines. V. 1- (No. 1/245-); Sept. 24, 1972/July 15, 1973-. English. Rural Bankers Legal Reference Center, 317 Samanillo Building, Manila Phillipines. **DD** 348/.599/01.

US/0882-9136
COMPILATION OF STATE AND FEDERAL PRIVACY LAWS. [Compil. state fed. priv. laws]. **VFOAT** Compilation of State & Federal Privacy Laws. (1978)-. English. an. $109.00 US and Canada; $135.00 other. Privacy Journal, PO Box 28577, Providence RI 02908. **Tel** (401)274-7861. **ED** Robert Ellis Smith. **LC** KF1262.A29; C66. **DD** 342.73/0858; 347.302858. Index available. cum. index. **Bk Rev. Pr Rev.** available on microfilm; available on an online database from NEWSNET.
Desc: Contains more than 600 laws protecting confidentiality of information, described and cited, by category and by state.

US/0741-9066
COMPLEAT LAWYER, THE. **Added/Corp** American Bar Association. Section of General Practice. Vol. 1, No. 1 (Winter 1984)-. Periodical. English. qt (4 issues). $23.00. American Bar Association, 750 North Lake Shore Drive, Chicago IL 60611. **Tel** (312)988-5522, (312)988-5241, FAX (312)988-5528, telex 270593. **LC** K3; .O46. **DD** 349.73/05; 347.3005. ***Formed by the union of*** *Docket Call* ***and*** *Law Notes for the General Practitioner.*
Ind/Abst Curr. Law Index (1984-); Law Office Inf. Serv.; Leg. Resour. Index (1984-); LegalTrac (1984-).

US
COMPLIANCE ALERT. **See** Business-Banking and Finance.

US/1044-1794
COMPUTER COUNSEL. **See** Business-General Management.

US/0361-7203
COMPUTER LAW AND TAX REPORT. Vol. 1 (Aug. 1974)-. Periodical. English. mo. $280.00. Roditti Reports Corporation, 954 Lexington Avenue, Suite 283, New York NY 10021. **Tel** (212)758-1464. **LC** KF1890.C6; A243. **DD** 343/.73/070285. **[CCC].**

US/0883-6019
COMPUTER LAW ANNUAL. ***Ceased.*** [Comput. law annu.]. 1985-Ceased (19??). English. an. Advanstar Communications Inc., 131 West First Street, Duluth MN 55802. **Tel** (218)723-9477, (800)346-0085. **LC** K3; .O47. **DD** 343.73/078004/05 347.307800405.

US/0894-1858
COMPUTER LAW FORMS HANDBOOK. [Comput. law forms handb.]. (1986)-. English. an. $90.00. Clark Boardman Callaghan, 155 Pfingsten Road, Deerfield IL 60015. **Tel** (800)323-8067. **LC** KF905.C6; C638. **DD** 343 73/078004/0269; 347.303780040269.

US/0164-8756
COMPUTER/LAW JOURNAL. ***Title Change.*** [Comput./law j.]. **Added/Corp** Center for Computer/Law. **VAT** Computer Law Journal. Vol. 1 (Spring 1978)-Vol. 12, No. 2 (Dec. 1993). Periodical. English. qt. Center for Computer Law, 4010 Palos Verdes Drive N, Suite 105, Rolling Hills Est. CA 90274. **Tel** (310)544-7372. **ED** Michael D Scott. **LC** K3; .O48. **DD** 340/.028/54. **CODEN** COLJD3. **[CCC].** Index available. cum. index (every five years). **Bk Rev. Circ:** 1,000. Documents available from Ask*IEEE. ***Merged with*** *Software Law Journal, 0886-3628* ***to form*** *John Marshall Journal of Computer & Information Law.*
Desc: An international journal on the legal problems of the computer, telecommunications, and information industries.
Ind/Abst Acad. Search (Jan. 1994-); ACM Guide Comput. Lit.; Bowne Dig. Corp. Sec. Lawyers; Commun. Abstr.; Comput. Lit. Index; Comput. Rev.; Curr. Law Index (1980-); Gen. Period. Index (1985-); Index Leg. Period.; INFO-SOUTH Abstr.; Inf. Sci. Abstr.; INSPEC (Spring 1980-); Leg. Resour. Index (1980-); LegalTrac (1980-); Mag. Search; Pollut. Abstr. Indexes.

US/0741-8809
COMPUTER LAW MONITOR, THE. [Comput. law monit.]. Vol. 1, No. 1 (Aug. 1983)-. Periodical. English. qt. $49.50 US; $57.50 other. Research Publishers Inc., PO Box 9267, Asheville NC 28815. **Tel** (704)298-8291. **ED** Patricia A Hollander. **LC** KF390.5.C6; A493. **DD** 343.73/078004; 347.30478004. **Circ:** 250 (ctrl).
Desc: Briefs of selected significant higher court decisions affecting the field of computer related systems.

US
COMPUTER LAW NEWSLETTER. ***Ceased.*** (1983)-(19??). Newsletter. English. bm. Warner and Stockpole, 28 State Street East Saltzberg, Boston MA 02109. **LC** KFM2484.5.C65.C65; A133. **DD** 343.744/07800164 44037800164.

US/0739-7771
COMPUTER LAW REPORTER. [Comput. law report.]. Vol. 1, No. 1 (July 1982)-. Periodical. English. mo. $1431.00 Washington DC; $1350.00 other. Law Reporters, 1519 Connecticut Avenue Northwest, Suite 200, Washington DC 20036. **Tel** (202)462-5755. **ED** Neil J. Cohen. **LC** KF390.5.C6; C649. **DD** 343.73/07800164; 347.3037800164. Index available. cum. index. **Bk Rev. Circ:** 300 (ctrl).
Desc: Articles, decisions and documents in various areas of computer-related law.

NE
COMPUTER LAW SERIES. English. ir. Kluwer Law and Taxation Publishers, Staverenstraat 32015, PO Box 23, 7400 GA Deventer Netherlands. **Tel** 011 31 5700 47261.

US/0747-8933
COMPUTER LAW STRATEGIST. [Comput. law strateg.]. Vol. 1, No. 1 (May 1984)-. Periodical. English. mo. $245.00. Leader Publications, 345 Park Avenue South, New York NY 10010. **Tel** (800)888-8300 ext. 6170, (212)545-6170, FAX (212)696-1848. **ED** Julian S. Millstein. **LC** KF390.5.C6; C653. **DD**

343.73/07800164; 347.3037800164. cum. index.
Desc: Reports on judicial, legislative and regulatory developments in computer law, including copyright, licensing, contracts, computer crime, warranties and financing.

CN/0824-4790
COMPUTER LAW (TORONTO). (COMPUTER LAW.). [Comput. law]. Vol. 1 No. 1 (Jan. 1984)-. Periodical. English. mo. $495.00. Computer Law Research Institute, 44 Albany Avenue, 2nd Floor, Toronto Ontario M5R 3C3 Canada. **DD** 346.71/07.
Ind/Abst Comput. Lit. Index; Index Can. Leg. Period. Lit.

US/0742-1192
COMPUTER LAWYER, THE. [Comput. lawyer]. **Added/Corp** Law & Business, Inc. Vol. 1, No. 1 (Feb. 1984)-. Periodical. English. Twelve times a year. $352.63. Prentice-Hall Law and Business, 270 Sylvan Avenue, Englewood Cliffs NJ 07632. **Tel** (800)223-0231, (201)894-8538, FAX (201)894-8666. **ED** Ronald Johnston, Allen Grogan, Miles R. Gilbourne. **LC** KF390.5.C6; A133. **DD** 343.73/07800164/05; 347.303780016405. **CODEN** COLAEB. **Bk Rev. Circ:** 1,500. ***Absorbed** Software Protection, 0733-1274.*
Desc: Provides action-oriented advice by nationally known computer lawyers to resolve the problems that face manufacturers, developers, distributors and users of computer and telecommunication products and services.
Ind/Abst Comput. Lit. Index; Index Leg. Period.

GW/0179-1990
COMPUTER UND RECHT (KOLN). (COMPUTER UND RECHT.). [Comput. Recht]. Vol. 1 (Oct. 1985)-. Periodical. German. mo. DM382.65 Germany; DM436.00 other. Verlag Dr. Otto Schmidt KG, Postfach 511026, D 50946 Cologne Germany. **Tel** 011 49 221 93738450. **LC** KK164.C66; C66. **DD** 343.43/07800164; 344.3037800164. **CODEN** CRECE3. **[CCC].** Documents available from Ask*IEEE. ***Absorbed** Informatik und Recht, 0179-0463.*
Ind/Abst Index Foreign Leg. Per. (Jan. 1989-); INSPEC (Jan. 1989-).

US/8756-2642
COMPUTER USER'S LEGAL REPORTER, THE. ***Suspended.*** [Comput. user's leg. report.]. Premier issue (No. 1) (July/Aug. 1984)-. Periodical. English. Four times a year. Computer Law Corporation, PO Box 375, Charlottesville VA 22902-0375. **Tel** (804)977-6343, FAX (804)977-8570. **ED** Charles Pritzker Lickson. **LC** KF390.5.C6; A134. **DD** 343.73/07800164; 347.3037800164.
Desc: A quick, easy to read source for legal news regarding computer use.

UK/0140-3249
COMPUTERS AND LAW. **See** Computers.

AT/0811-7225
COMPUTERS AND LAW SYDNEY. **See** Computers.

IT
COMUNICAZIONI E STUDI. ***Ceased.*** **Main/Corp** Milan. Universita. Istituto di Diritto Internazionale e Straniero. -Ceased with Vol. 17, No. 18, 1985. Italian. Giuffre Editore SPA, Via Busto Arsizio 40, 20151 Milan Italy. **Tel** 011 398 2 38089200.
Ind/Abst Index Foreign Leg. Per.

SP
COMUNIDADES EUROPEAS. **VFOAT** Ley Comunidades Europeas. 1985-. Spanish. **LC** K3; .O49.

US/0192-3854
CONDENSED CPA TAX REVIEW. **VAT** Condensed Certified Public Accountant Tax Review. 1st Ed. (1976)-. English. **LC** KF6369.3; .F47. **DD** 343/.73/052.

US/0890-3034
CONFIDENTIAL REPORT FOR ATTORNEYS. [Confid. rep. atty.]. **Added/Corp** Confidential Report for Attorneys (Firm). (19??)-. Periodical. English. Twenty-four times a year. $225.00. Neubauer & Association Inc., PO Box 1476, Oceanside CA 92051. **Tel** (619)721-3622, FAX (619)721-3683. **ED** Richard Neubauer. **DD** 340. cum. index ($125.00). **Ad Acc. Circ:** 11,000. available on an online database from LEXIS.

US/0099-0418
CONFLICTS OF LAW. **Main/Corp** Bay Area Review Course, Inc. English. an. Bay Area Review Course Inc, 5900 Wilshire Boulevard, Los Angeles CA 90036. **LC** KF412; .B35. **DD** 342/.73/042.

US/1047-1324
CONGRESS AND THE NATION. **See** Political Science.

US/1064-4679
CONGRESSIONAL MASTERFILE 2. (CONGRESSIONAL MASTERFILE 2 [COMPUTER FILE].). [Congr. masterfile 2]. **Added/Corp** Congressional Information Service. **VFOAT** Congressional Masterfile Two; Congressional Masterfile; CIS Congressional Masterfile 2. (19??)-. English. qt. Congressional Information Service Inc, 4520 East-West Highway, Suite 800, Bethesda MD 20814-3389. **Tel** (800)638-8380, (301)654-1550, FAX (301)654-4033, telex 292386 CIS UR. **LC** Z1223. **DD** 328.

US/0363-7239
CONGRESSIONAL RECORD (DAILY ED.). ***Ceased.*** (CONGRESSIONAL RECORD : PROCEEDINGS AND DEBATES OF THE ... CONGRESS.). [Congr. rec.]. **Main/Corp** United States. Congress. 43rd Congress (1873)-(19??). Academic Scholarly Publication. English. da. Superintendent of Documents, US Government Printing Office, Washington DC 20402. **Tel** (202)275-3328, FAX (202)786-2377. **LC** KF35. **DD** 328.73/02. **CODEN** CGLRB3. available on microfilm from University Microfilms International (UMI). Documents available from CASDDS. ***Continues** Congressional Globe.*
Ind/Abst Chem. Abstr.; Chem. Ind. Notes.

US/0364-7544
CONGRESSIONAL RECORD INDEX. (CONGRESSIONAL RECORD INDEX : PROCEEDINGS AND DEBATES OF THE ... CONGRESS.). [Congr. rec. index]. **Added/Corp** United States. Congress. Began With 43rd Congress (1873)-. Government Publication. English. ir (Daily when Congress is in session.). Included in price of subscription to Congressional Record. Superintendent of Documents, US Government Printing Office, Washington DC 20402. **Tel** (202)275-3328, FAX (202)786-2377. available on microfiche (Vols. for (1986-) distributed to depository libraries). ***Continues** Index to the Congressional Globe.*
Desc: Includes history of bills and resolutions.

US/0883-1947
CONGRESSIONAL RECORD (PERMANENT ED.). (CONGRESSIONAL RECORD : PROCEEDINGS AND DEBATES OF THE ... CONGRESS.). [Congr. rec.]. **Main/Corp** United States. Congress. (1873)-. Government Publication. English. da (when Congress is in session). $225.00 US; $281.25 other. Superintendent of Documents, US Government Printing Office, Washington DC 20402. **Tel** (202)275-3328, FAX (202)786-2377. **LC** KF35. **DD** 328.73/02. **NLM** KF 35 U58. available on microfilm and microfiche (Vols. for (June 16-21, 1980-) distributed to some depository libraries) from University Microfilms International (UMI). ***Continues** Congressional Globe.*
Desc: A verbatim report on Congressional debates and other proceedings. Each issue includes a Daily Digest that summarizes the proceedings for that day in each House and before each of their committees and subcommittees. The legislative program for that day is presented, and at the end of the week, the program for the following week.

US
CONGRESSIONAL RECORD [COMPUTER FILE] : PROCEEDINGS AND DEBATES OF THE ... CONGRESS. **Main/Corp** United States. Congress. **Added/Corp** United States. Government Printing Office. 99th Congress, 1st Session (Jan. 3, 1985 to Dec. 20, 1985) = Vol. 131-(1991)-. Government Publication. English. mo. $785.00. Superintendent of Documents, US Government Printing Office, Washington DC 20402. **Tel** (202)275-3328, FAX (202)786-2377. **LC** KF35; .D5.
Desc: Graphic materials and tables are not included on the CD-ROM. Includes section called "Daily Digest". System requirements: IBM compatible microcomputer with 640K memory or more; CD-ROM drive and MS-DOS CD-ROM extensions and device driver software 3.1 or higher; floppy or hard disk drive.

US
CONNECTICUT APPELLATE REPORTS. **Main/Corp** Connecticut. Appellate Court. **VFOAT** Appellate Reports. Vol. 1 (1983/1984)-. Periodical. English. ir. Price varies. Commission Official Legal Publisher, 111 Phoenix Avenue, Enfield CT 06082. **Tel** (203)741-3027. **LC** KFC3648; .A2. **DD** 348.741/043; 347.410843.

US/0010-6070
CONNECTICUT BAR JOURNAL. [Conn. bar j.]. **Added/Corp** State Bar Association of Connecticut. Connecticut Bar Association. **VFOAT** CBJ. Vol. 1, Jan. (1927)-. Periodical. English. Six times a year. $35.00. Connecticut Bar Association, 101 Corporate Place, Rocky Hill CT 06067. **Tel** (203)721-0025. **ED** William T. Barrante, PO Box 273, Watertown, CT 06795; Telephone: (203)879-5310. **DD** 347.05. Index available in last issue of volume--attached. cum. index. **Bk Rev. Ad Acc. Circ:** 11,300 (ctrl). available on microfiche from Williams S Hein & Co.
Desc: An association newsletter.
Ind/Abst Curr. Law Index (1980-); Fed. Tax Artic.; Index Leg. Period.; Law Office Inf. Serv. (1980-); Leg. Resour. Index (1980-); LegalTrac (1980-).

●US/1064-2382
CONNECTICUT ENVIRONMENTAL COMPLIANCE UPDATE. (CONNECTICUT ENVIRONMENTAL LAW LETTER.). [Pepe Hazard's Conn. environ. compliance update]. **Added/Corp** Pepe & Hazard. **VFOAT** Environmental Compliance Update. (Oct 1992)-. Periodical. English. mo. $107.00. M. Lee Smith Publishers and Printers, 162 4th Avenue North, PO Box 198867, Nashville TN 37219. **Tel** (615)242-7395, (800)274-6774, FAX (615)256-6601. **ED** James Thompson, Jr, Valerie Batialle, Andrew Davis, and Peter Hapke, (address) Pepe Hazard, Goodwin Square, Hartford, CT 06103-4302, (phone) 203-522-5175. **DD** 344.
Desc: Newsletter reporting the latest state specific environmental law developments that affect companies in that state.

US/0742-924X
CONNECTICUT INSURANCE LAW REVIEW, THE. [Conn. insur. law rev.]. (1981)-. Periodical. English. an. $15.00. Yules and Yules, PO Box 3597, Hartford CT 06103. **ED** Robert B. Yules. **LC** KFC3785; .A473. **DD** 346.746/0865; 347.4606865. Index available. **Bk Rev. Circ:** 2,000.
Desc: A review of the laws affecting the property/casualty and worker's compensation industry in Connecticut.

US/8750-0973
CONNECTICUT LAW JOURNAL. [Conn. law j.]. **Added/Corp** Connecticut. Superior Court. **VFOAT** Memoranda Filed in the Superior Court and Courts of Common Pleas of the State of Connecticut. Vol. 1 (Jan. 1935)-. Periodical. English. ir. $165.00. Commission on Official Legal Publications, 111 Phoenix Avenue, Enfield CT 06082. **Tel** (203)741-3027. **ED** J.J. Sweeney.

US/0010-6151
CONNECTICUT LAW REVIEW. [Conn. law rev.]. **Added/Corp** University of Connecticut. School of Law. Connecticut Law Review Association. Vol. 1, No. 1 (June 1968)-. Periodical. English. qt. $23.00. University of Connecticut / School of Law, 65 Elizabeth Street, Hartford CT 06105-2290. **Tel** (203)241-4607. **ED** Jennifer J. Barrett. **DD** 340. Index available. **Bk Rev. Ad Acc. Circ:** 1,600. available on microfilm and microfiche from University Microfilms International (UMI).
Desc: Publishes articles and casenotes on current legal topics by scholars, practitioners and students.
Ind/Abst Bowne Dig. Corp. Sec. Lawyers; Curr. Law Index (1980-); Fed. Tax Artic.; Index Leg. Period.; Leg. Resour. Index (1980-); LegalTrac (1980-).

US/0198-0289
CONNECTICUT LAW TRIBUNE, THE. (Nov. 4, 1975)-. Periodical. English. wk (52 issues). $355.00 corporations, $335.00 other. American Lawyer Media, L.P., 600 3rd Avenue, New York NY 10016. **Tel** (212)973-2800. **ED** Bruce S. Rogen. **LC** K3; .O524. **DD** 071/.46/3. cum. index. **Bk Rev. Ad Acc. Circ:** 1,800. available on microfiche. ***Absorbed** Connecticut Superior Court Reports.*
Desc: Publishes significant decisions of Connecticut courts and agencies, summaries of new legislation, and articles on developments affecting the legal profession.

US/0195-6809
CONNECTICUT LEGAL DIRECTORY, THE. 1977/78-. Directory. English. an. Legal Directories Publishing Company, 9111 Garland Road, PO Box 189000, Dallas TX 75218. **Tel** (214)321-3238, 800 447-5375. **LC** KF192.C6; C67. **DD** 340/.025/746.

US/0897-1234
CONNECTICUT PROBATE LAW JOURNAL, THE. [Conn. probate law j.]. **Added/Corp** Connecticut Probate Assembly. University of Bridgeport. School of Law. Vol. 1, No. 1 (Fall 1985)-. Periodical. English. sa. $25.00. Connecticut Probate Law Journal, University of Bridgeport, 303 University Avenue, Bridgeport CT 06601. **Tel** (203)576-4734. **LC** K3; .O525. **DD** 345.746/077; 347.460577.
Ind/Abst Index Leg. Period.; Leg. Resour. Index; LegalTrac (1989-).

US
CONNECTICUT REAL ESTATE LAW JOURNAL, THE. Vol. 1, No. 1 (Nov. 1982)-. Periodical. English. bm. Butterworth Heinemann / Woburn, MA, 225 Wildwood Avenue, Unit B, Woburn MA 01801. **Tel** (800)366-2665, FAX (617)928-2620, telex 880052. **LC** KFC3712.A15; C66. **DD** 346.74604/3/05; 347.46064305.

US/0749-131X
CONNECTICUT SCHOOL OF LAW ANNUAL. (CONNECTICUT SCHOOL LAW ANNUAL : CSLA.). [Conn. sch. law annu.]. **VFOAT** CSLA; C.S.L.A. English. an. $4.50 per copy. J F d'Angelo Editor, Connecticut School Law Annual, CCSU Foundation, 1615 Stanley Street, New Britain CT 06050. **ED** J F d'Angelo. **LC** KFC3990.A15; C66. **DD** 344.73/07/05; 347.304705.

US/1052-6714
CONNECTICUT SUPERIOR COURT REPORTS. ***Title Change.*** [Conn. Super. Court rep.]. **Added/Corp** Connecticut. Superior Court. Vol. 1 (1986)-(19??). Periodical. English. sa. American Lawyer Media, L.P., 600 3rd Avenue, New York NY 10016. **Tel** (212)973-2800. **LC** KFC3651; .C66. **DD** 348.746/046; 347.460846. ***Merged into** Connecticut Law Tribune.*
Desc: The full text of the Superior Court decisions digested weekly in the Tribune.

US/1047-8949
CONSOLIDATED RETURNS TAX REPORT. ***Ceased.*** [Consol. returns tax rep.]. **Added/Corp** Faulkner & Gray, Inc. Vol. 1, No. 1 Jan. (1990)-(199?). Periodical. English. mo. Faulkner & Gray Inc., 11 Penn Plaza, 17th Floor, New York NY 10001. **Tel** (212)967-7000, (800)535-8403. **DD** 343. available on microfilm and microfiche from University Microfilms International (UMI); available on an online database (file 485/Full-Text) from DIALOG.
Ind/Abst Account. Tax Datab. (Jan. 1991-Jun. 1992) [Full Txt.].

CN
CONSTITUTIONALLY SPEAKING. English. Nancy Allan, Department of Attorney-General, Room 104/Legislative Building, 450 Broadway, Winnipeg Manitoba R3C 0V8 Canada. **LC** KEM454.A13; C66. **DD** 342.7127/005; 347.12702005.

US/8755-7568
CONSTRUCTION AND DESIGN LAW DIGEST. (CONSTRUCTION AND DESIGN LAW DIGEST / COMPILED BY THE NATIONAL INSTITUTE OF CONSTRUCTION LAW, INC. (NICL).). [Constr. des. law dig.]. **Added/Corp** National Institute of Construction Law (U.S.) Michie Company. **VFOAT** CDLD. (July 1984)-. English. Eleven times a year. $550.00. Michie Company, PO Box 7587, Charlottesville VA 22906-7587. **Tel** (804)972-7600, (800)542-0957, FAX (800)643-1280. **LC** KF901.A75; C66. **DD** 343.
Desc: Comprehensive legal analysis of 1,500 plus construction and design cases each year in US. Includes expert critical commentary, practice tips and useful advice.

US/0148-933X
CONSTRUCTION & SURETY LAW DIVISION NEWSLETTER. **Main/Corp** New York State Bar Association. Construction & Surety Law Division. **VFOAT** Construction and Surety Newsletter. **VAT** Construction and Surety Law Division Newsletter. Newsletter. English. Free. New York State Bar Association, One Elk Street, Albany NY 12207. **Tel** (518)463-3200. **ED** Eugene Goldberg. **LC** KFN5230.B8; A493. **DD** 343/.747/078. **Circ:** 500 (ctrl).
Desc: Newsletter of section, current related legal issues and cases discussed dealing with construction law.

US
CONSTRUCTION CONTRACT MODIFICATIONS; COURSE MANUAL. **Added/Corp** Federal Publications Inc. (19??)-. English. an. Federal Publications Inc, 1120 20th Street Northwest, Washington DC 20036. **Tel** (202)337-7000, (800)922-4330, FAX (202)659-2233. **LC** KF865; .L482. **DD** 343/.73/078.

US
CONSTRUCTION CONTRACTS AND LITIGATION. ***Title Change.*** **Added/Corp** Practising Law Institute. (1987)-(19??). English. Practising Law Institute, 810 Seventh Avenue, New York NY 10019-5818. **Tel** (212)765-5700, FAX (212)581-4670 general correspondence, (212)265-4742 orders and billing inquiries. **LC** KF902.Z9; C673. **DD** 343.73/07869; 347.3037869. ***Continues*** *Construction Contracts.* ***Continued by*** *Drafting Construction Contracts & Handling Construction Litigation.*

UK/0269-0039
CONSTRUCTION INDUSTRY LAW LETTER. [Constr. ind. newsl.]. (1983)-. Periodical. English. mo (10 issues). £150.00. Legal Studies & Services Publ Ltd., 9-13 St. Andrew Street, London EC4A 3AE England. **Tel** 011 44 71 936-2016. **(Subscription address:** IBC Subscription Services, IBC House, Vickers Drive Weybridge, Surrey KT13 0XS England.**)** **DD** 349.203.

CN/0827-3480
CONSTRUCTION LAW LETTER. [Constr. law letter]. **Added/Corp** Build/Law Publications. Vol. 1 No. 1 (1984)-. Periodical. English. bm (6 issues). 120Can$ Canada; 135.00Can$ Other. Build Law Publications Inc., 253 College Street, Suite 286, Toronto Ontario M5T 1R5 Canada. **Tel** (416)395-0459. **ED** Paul Sandori. **DD** 343.71/07869005. Index available. cum. index. **Bk Rev. Circ:** 1,500. available on microfilm.
Desc: Summaries of court decisions and articles relating to construction law.
Ind/Abst Index Can. Leg. Period. Lit. (19??-19??).

CN/0824-2593
CONSTRUCTION LAW REPORTS. [Constr. law rep.]. Vol. 1, Pt. 1 (Oct./Nov. 1983)-. Periodical. English (French). ir. Carswell / Canada, 2075 Kennedy Road, Scarborough Ontario M1T 3V4 Canada. **Tel** (416)609-3800, (800)387-5164. **ED** Harvey J. Kirsh. **DD** 343.71/07869005. Index available. cum. index. **Ad Acc.**
Desc: Features all important construction law decisions from all Canadian jurisdictions, selected by experts in the field.
Ind/Abst Can. Legal Lit.; Index Can. Leg. Period. Lit.

UK/0950-3889
CONSTRUCTION LAW REPORTS (LONDON, ENGLAND). (CONSTRUCTION LAW REPORTS.). **VFOAT** ConLR. Vol. 1 (1985)-. English. ir. 3360.00Aus$. Butterworth & Co. Ltd. / Kent, England, Borough Green, Sevenoaks Kent TN15 8PH England. **Tel** 011 44 732-884567, FAX 011 44 732-885996. **LC** KD1641.A38; C66. **DD** 343.41/07869/0264; 3441.0378690264.
Desc: Gives systematic coverage of the cases decided by the Official Referees, who have in effect become the specialist court of the UK construction industry.

US/0272-0116
CONSTRUCTION LAWYER, THE. [Constr. lawyer]. **Added/Corp** American Bar Association. Forum Committee on the Construction Industry. Vol. 1 (Spring 1980)-. Periodical. English. qt. $40.00. American Bar Association, 750 North Lake Shore Drive, Chicago IL 60611. **Tel** (312)988-5522, (312)988-5241, FAX (312)988-5528, telex 270593. **LC** KF1950.A15; C65. **DD** 343.73/07869/0025; 347.30378690025. **Pr Rev. Circ:** 7,000 (ctrl).
Ind/Abst Curr. Law Index (1980-); Leg. Resour. Index (1980-); LegalTrac (1988-).

US
CONSTRUCTION LITIGATION LAW BULLETIN. **VFOAT** CLLB; C.L.L.B. Bulletin. English. mo. Pioneer Publishing Company, 131 Beverly Street, Boston MA 02114. **LC** KF901.A75; C668. **DD** 343.73/07869. available on microfilm and microfiche from University Microfilms International (UMI). ***Continues*** *Construction Litigation Bulletin, 0889-7638.*

US/0279-1102
CONSTRUCTION LITIGATION REPORTER. [Constr. litig. report.]. **Added/Corp** Litigation Research Group (San Francisco, Calif.). Vol. 1, No. 6 (Sept. 1980)-. English. mo. $330.00. Shepards McGraw-Hill Inc, 555 Middle Creek Parkway, PO Box 35300, Colorado Springs CO 80935-3530. **Tel** (719)488-3000, FAX (800)525-0053. **ED** Marc Schneier. **LC** KF901.A75; C67. **DD** 343.73/07869; 347.3037869. **Circ:** 875. ***Continues*** *Architects, Engineers & Contractors Litigation Reporter.*
Desc: Summaries of judicial and agency decisions in construction law together with articles discussing contemporary litigation topics.

UK/0963-6706
CONSTRUCTIONAL LAW. [Constr. law]. (1990)-. Periodical. English. bm. £60.00. Eclipse Publications Ltd, 18 20 Highbury Place, London N5 1QP England. **Tel** 011 44 71 354 5858. **DD** 344.1037869.

US/1058-3963
CONSUMER BANKRUPTCY NEWS. [Consum. bankruptcy news]. (1991)-. Periodical. English. bw. $265.00. LRP Publications, 747 Dresher Road, PO Box 980, Horsham PA 19044-0980. **Tel** (800)341-7874, (215)784-0860, FAX (215)784-9639, (215)784-0870. **ED** David Light. **DD** 346. available in Loose-leaf.
Desc: news and cases involving consumer bankruptcy. Provides articles, commentaries, and practice pointers to improve business.

●US/1068-1906
CONSUMER BANKRUPTCY NEWS DESK BOOK. [Consum. bankruptcy news desk book]. **VFOAT** CBN Desk Book. (1993)-. English. an. $76.00 (includes postage). LRP Publications, 747 Dresher Road, PO Box 980, Horsham PA 19044-0980. **Tel** (800)341-7874, (215)784-0860, FAX (215)784-9639, (215)784-0870. **DD** 346.
Desc: Compendium of articles, cases, indexes, and practice pointers that summarize the most significant developments in consumer bankruptcy law during the previous year.

US/0300-6034
CONSUMER CREDIT AND TRUTH-IN-LENDING COMPLIANCE REPORT. (Nov. 1969)-. Periodical. English. mo. $183.25 US and Canada; $252.45 other. Warren Gorham & Lamont Inc., Park Square Building, 31 St. James Avenue, Boston MA 02116-4112. **Tel** (617)423-2020, (800)950-1207, FAX (617)423-2026. **ED** Earl Phillips. **LC** KF1039.A15; C6. **[CCC].**
Desc: Focuses on the latest regulatory rulings and findings involving consumer lending and credit activity. Typical coverage includes articles on equal credit opportunity, truth-in-lending, debt collection practices and credit cards.

UK
CONSUMER LAW JOURNAL. (1993)-. English. Six times a year. £150.00 Europe; £157.00. Sweet & Maxwell Ltd., South Quay Plaza, 183 Marsh Wall, London E14 9FT England. **Tel** 011 44 264 342899, FAX 011 44 264 342723, telex 929089 ITPINF G.

US/1052-9632
CONSUMER PRODUCT LITIGATION REPORTER. [Consum. prod. litig. rep.]. (1990)-. Periodical. English. mo. $550.00. Andrews Publications Inc., 1646 West Chester Pike, PO Box 1000, Westtown PA 19395. **Tel** (610)399-6600, (800)345-1101, FAX (610)399-6610. **LC** KF1296.A59; C66. **DD** 346.7303/8/05; 347.3063805.
Desc: Provides comprehensive coverage of national product liability cases from the initial filing of complaints to final verdicts or settlements and on through the appeals process.

US/0191-8567
CONSUMER PROTECTION NEWSLETTER. ***Title Change.*** Newsletter. English. **LC** KF1602; .C66. **DD** 343/.73/07. ***Continued by*** *Consumer Protection Report (National Association of Attorneys General).*

US
CONSUMER PROTECTION REPORT / NATIONAL ASSOCIATION OF ATTORNEYS GENERAL. **See** Consumer Interests.

CN/0381-0925
CONTINUUM (DOWNSVIEW). (CONTINUUM.). [Continuum]. **Added/Corp** Osgoode Hall Law School. (June 1973)-(1990). Periodical. English. sa (Apr. and Nov.). Osgoode Hall Law School, 4700 Keele Street North, North York Ontario M3J 1P3 Canada. **Tel** (416)736-2100. **DD** 340/.07/11713541.

US/0190-3063
CONTRACT MANAGEMENT. [Contract manage.]. **Added/Corp** National Contract Management Association (U.S.). (19??)-. Periodical. English. mo. $72.00. National Contract Management Association, 1912 Woodford Road, Vienna VA 22180. **Tel** (703)448-9231, (800)344-8096. **ED** Terry Hoskins. **LC** KF842; .C66. **DD** 353.007/11/05. cum. index. **Bk Rev**, (Qty: 12 per year). **Ad Acc, Adv Mgr:** Lee Tapp, **Tel** (703)448-9231. ctrl circ. ***Continues*** *Newsletter (National Contract Management Association (U.S.)).*
Desc: Deals with current in-depth procurement issues presenting timely, substantive articles addressing current interests and needs of government and industry. Policy articles are balanced with basic 'how-to' articles.
Ind/Abst Bus. Index (1979-?).

US/0098-762X
CONTRACTS. **Main/Corp** Bay Area Review Course, Inc. English. an. Bay Area Review Course Inc, 5900 Wilshire Boulevard, Los Angeles CA 90036. **LC** KF801.Z9; B33. **DD** 346/.73/02.

US
CONTROLLED SUBSTANCES QUARTERLY. (1972)-. Periodical. English. qt. $176.00. Government Information Services / Virginia, 4301 North Fairfax Drive, Suite 875, Arlington VA 22203. **Tel** (703)528-1082, FAX (703)528-6060, telex RCA 263591 GIS UR.

UK/0010-8200
CONVEYANCER AND PROPERTY LAWYER, THE. [Conveyancer prop. lawyer]. Vol. 1, No. 1 (Sept. 1936)-. Periodical. English. Six times a year. £76.00 Europe; £80.00 other. Sweet & Maxwell Ltd., South Quay Plaza, 183 Marsh Wall, London E14 9FT England. **Tel** 011 44 264 342899, FAX 011 44 264 342723, telex 929089 ITPINF G. **ED** Carl Tullo. cum. index. **Bk Rev. Ad Acc. Circ:** 3,000. ***Continues*** *Conveyancer.*
Desc: A comprehensive approach to conveyancing and allied topics.
Ind/Abst Aust. Leg. Mon. Dig.; Index Leg. Period.; Leg. Resour. Index (1980-); LegalTrac (1980-).

US/0010-8839
CORNELL LAW FORUM (ITHACA, N.Y. : 1974). (CORNELL LAW FORUM.). [Cornell law forum]. **Added/Corp** Cornell Law School. Vol. 1, No. 1 (Jan. 1974)-. English. Three times a year. Cornell Law School, Myron Taylor Hall, Ithaca NY 14853. **Tel** (607)255-7477, FAX (607)255-7193. **ED** Dale Oesterle and Kathleen E. Rourke. **LC** KF292.C6914; A42. **DD** 340/.05. **Circ:** 8,000 (ctrl). available on microfilm and microfiche from University Microfilms International (UMI). ***Continues*** *Cornell Law Forum (Ithaca, N.Y. : 1949).*
Desc: Brief legal articles, news of school and alumni.
Ind/Abst Curr. Law Index (1980-); Leg. Resour. Index (1980-); LegalTrac (1980-).

US/0010-8847
CORNELL LAW REVIEW. [Cornell law rev.]. **Added/Corp** Cornell Law School. Vol. 53 (Nov. 1967)-. Periodical. English. bm (6 issues). $35.00 US & Canada; $39.00 other. Cornell Law School, Myron Taylor Hall, Ithaca NY 14853. **Tel** (607)255-7477, FAX (607)255-7193. **LC** K3; .O7. **DD** 340/.05. **NLM** W1 CO8597. **Bk Rev. Pr Rev. Circ:** 3,500 (ctrl). Documents available from The Genuine Article. ***Continues*** *Cornell Law Quarterly, 8755-2213.*
Ind/Abst ABC POL SCI (19??-1985); Bowne Dig. Corp. Sec. Lawyers; Commun. Abstr.; Crim. Penol. Police Sci. Abstr.; Curr. Contents Soc. Behav. Sci.; Curr. Law Index (1980-); Fed. Tax Artic.; Health Plan. Adminis.; Hospit. Health Admin. Index; Index Leg. Period.; Leg. Resour. Index (1980-); LegalTrac (1980-); PAIS Int. Print (1991-); Res. Alert [Full Cov.]; Soc. Sci. Cit. Index [Full Cov.]; Soc. Work Abstr. (?-?); Urban Aff. Abstr.

UK/0950-6209
CORPORATE BRIEFING. Added/Corp Legal Studies and Services Limited. (19??)-. Corporate Report. English. mo (10 issues). £145.00. Legal Studies & Services Publ Ltd., 9-13 St. Andrew Street, London EC4A 3AE England. **Tel** 011 44 71 936-2016. **(Subscription address:** IBC Subscription Services, IBC House, Vickers Drive Weybridge, Surrey KT13 0XS England.**) LC** KD1622; .C67. **DD** 343.41/07/05; 344.103705.

US/1061-8775
CORPORATE CONDUCT QUARTERLY. **See** Ethics.

US/0360-196X
CORRECTIONS COURT DIGEST, THE. English. mo. $20.00. Juridical Digests Institute, 1860 Broadway/Suite 1401, New York NY 10023. **LC** KF9728.A59. **DD** 344/.73/0356.

IT
CORRIERE GIURIDICO. (19??)-. Periodical. Italian. mo. L265000 Italy; L530000 other. IPSOA Editore SRL, Casella Postale 12055, Mastrangelo, 20120 Milan Italy. **Tel** 011 39 2 82476248. Index available (Included).

UK/0268-3784
COUNSEL : THE JOURNAL OF THE BAR OF ENGLAND & WALES. Added/Corp Senate of the Inns of Court and the Bar. General Council of the Bar (England and Wales). Vol. 1, No. 1 (Michaelmas 1985)-. Periodical. English. bm (6 issues). The General Council of the Bar, 3 Bedford Row, London WC1 4DB United Kingdom. **Tel** 011 44 71 2420082, FAX 011 44 4 86824117. **ED** Gavin Purves. **LC** K3; .O88. **DD** 347.42/05/05; 344.207505. **Bk Rev. Ad Acc. Circ:** 12,000.
Desc: A professional review of the English bar.

US/0271-2385
COUNSELING CLIENTS IN THE ENTERTAINMENT INDUSTRY. [Couns. clients entertain. ind.]. Periodical. English. an. Practising Law Institute, 810 Seventh Avenue, New York NY 10019-5818. **Tel** (212)765-5700, FAX (212)581-4670 general correspondence, (212)265-4742 orders and billing inquiries. **LC** KF390.E57; C66. **DD** 343.73/078791. Index available. cum. index. **Bk Rev.**
Desc: Paper-back course book.

BE
COUNTDOWN 1992. ***Title Change.*** **Added/Corp** American Chamber of Commerce in Belgium. EC Committee. **VFOAT** Countdown Nineteen Ninety Two. (1988)-(1992). English. qt. ***Continued by*** *Countdown 2000.*

US/0279-9626
COUNTY BAR UPDATE. [Cnty. bar update]. Vol. 1, No. 1 (Jan. 1981)-. Periodical. English. mo (except Aug.). $1.00 members with dues, $2.00 nonmembers. Los Angeles County Bar Association, PO Box 55020, Los Angeles CA 90055. **Tel** (213)896-6503, FAX (213)623-4328. **LC** KF200; .C65. **DD** 340/.06/079493.

UK
COUNTY COURT PRACTICE, THE. (1945)-. English. an. Butterworth & Co. Ltd. / Kent, England, Borough Green, Sevenoaks Kent TN15 8PH England. **Tel** 011 44 732-884567, FAX 011 44 732-885996. ***Formed by the union of*** *Annual County Court Practice* ***and*** *New County Court Practice.*

US/0093-3023
COURT DECISIONS AND LEGAL OPINIONS (SEATTLE). (COURT DECISIONS AND LEGAL OPINIONS, SUMMARIZED FOR WASHINGTON CITIES.). English. an. $2.00. Municipal Research Coun, 10517 NE 38th Pl, Kirkland WA 98033-7926. **LC** JS303.W2; A8 subser; KFW431. **DD** 342/.797/09.

US
COURT EXCELLENCE. English. Three times a year. $50.00. Council for Court Excellence, 1025 Vermont Avenue NW, Suite 510, Washington DC 20005. **Tel** (202)783-7736. **ED** Samuel F Harshen and Elizabeth H Paret. **Circ:** 2,000.

CN/0706-7178
COURT JUDGEMENT REPORT (NEW BRUNSWICK ED.). (COURT JUDGEMENT REPORT.). **VFOAT** Rapport sur Jugement de Cour. V. 1- March 1978-. Periodical. English (French). mo. $85.00. Kolectal-Info Ltd, 95A Botsford Street, Moncton New Brunswick E1C 4X2 Canada. **DD** 347/.715/077.

US/1063-0821
COURT MANAGEMENT & ADMINISTRATION REPORT. (THE COURT MANAGEMENT & ADMINISTRATION REPORT : THE NEWSLETTER FOR PROFESSIONALS IN JUSTICE SYSTEMS MANAGEMENT.). [Court manag. adm. rep.]. **VFOAT** CM&A; Court Management and Administration Report. Vol. 1, No. 1 (Jan. 1990)-. Newsletter. English. Eleven times a year. $145.00 US; $185.00 other. Greenwood Press Inc., PO Box 5007, Westport CT 06881-5007. **Tel** (203)226-3571, FAX (203)222-1502. **ED** Clifford P Kirsch. **DD** 347.
Desc: Provides timely and practical assistance to court executives who are responsible for a wide range of functions with the judicial system that include such varied duties as arranging for courthouse construction, prisoner transport, jury notification, fine administration, and case assignment.

US
COURT NEWS. Added/Corp California. Administrative Office of the Courts. (Jan. 1991)-. Periodical. English. bm (6 issues). Free on request. California Administrative Office of the Courts, 303 2nd Street South Tower, c/o D. Halperin, San Francisco CA 94107. **Tel** (415)396-9123, (415)396-9241. **LC** KFC958.A15; C68. ***Continues*** *A.O.C. Newsletter.*

AT
COURT STATISTICS, TASMANIA / AUSTRALIAN BUREAU OF STATISTICS. **See** Law-Abstracting, Bibliographies and Statistics.

CN/1180-1468
COURTLINK (VANCOUVER). (COURTLINK / LAW COURTS EDUCATION SOCIETY OF BRITISH COLUMBIA.). [Courtlink]. **Added/Corp** Law Courts Education Society of British Columbia. **VFOAT** Court Link. No. 1 (Spring 1990)-. Periodical. English. an. Free on request. Law Courts Education Society of British Columbia, 219 800 Smithe Street, Vancouver British Columbia V6Z 2E1 Canada. **Tel** (604)660-9870. **DD** 349.711.

US/0590-0301
COURTROOM MEDICINE. (1962)-. Monographic series. English. ir. Price varies per volume. Matthew Bender & Company Inc., 1275 Broadway, Albany NY 12204. **Tel** (800)833-9844, (518)487-3000. **DD** 340.

US/0544-4993
COURTS & CLE BULLETIN / THE MISSOURI BAR. Added/Corp Missouri Bar. **VAT** Courts and CLE Bulletin. Vol. 1 No. 1 (Aug. 1965)-. Periodical. English. mo. $20.00. Missouri Bar Association, 326 Monroe Street, Jefferson City MO 65101. **Tel** (314)635-4128. **LC** KF200; .C69.

●US/1062-2535
CPS EXPRESS. (CPS EXPRESS: A NEWS BULLETIN FROM THE NACS COPYRIGHT PERMISSIONS SERVICE.). [CPS express]. **Added/Corp** National Association of College Stores (U.S.) Copyright Permissions Service. **VAT** Copyright Permissions Service Express. March (1992)-. Bulletin. English. mo. Free. National Association of College Stores, 500 East Lorain Street, Oberlin OH 44074. **Tel** (216)775-7777. **DD** 346.

UK/0590-0441
CRACKNELL'S LAW STUDENT'S COMPANION. (1966)-. Periodical. English. ir. Butterworth & Co. Ltd. / Kent, England, Borough Green, Sevenoaks Kent TN15 8PH England. **Tel** 011 44 732-884567, FAX 011 44 732-885996. **(Subscription address:** Butterworth Heinemann Publishers, 225 Wildwood Avenue, Unit B, Woburn MA 01801.**) DD** 340.

US/0574-3869
CRAWFORD COUNTY LEGAL JOURNAL. Added/Corp Crawford County Bar Association. Crawford County Bar Association. Legal Publications Committee. Vol. 1 (1960/61)-. English. an. Crawford County Bar Association, New Wilmington PA 16142. **DD** 340.
Desc: Containing cases decided in the courts of the 13th judicial district of Pennsylvania.

●US/1062-807X
CREDIT UNION LEGAL LETTER. [Credit union leg. lett.]. **Added/Corp** Credit Union National Association. **VFOAT** Legal Letter. Vol. 1, No. 1 (Jan. 1992)-. Periodical. English. mo. $199.00. Credit Union National Association, PO Box 431, Madison WI 53701. **Tel** (608)231-4088, (800)356-9655, FAX (608)231-4370. **LC** KF1008.A15; C74. **DD** 346.73/0668; 347.306668.

US/0011-1155
CREIGHTON LAW REVIEW. [Creighton law rev.]. **Added/Corp** Creighton University. School of Law. Vol. 1, No. 1 (Spring 1968)-. Periodical. English. Four times a year (Feb., Apr., June, Dec.). $25.00. Creighton Law Review, 2133 California Street, Omaha NE 68178. **Tel** (402)280-2980, FAX (402)280-2244. **ED** Michael LeMax. **LC** K3; .R44. **DD** 340/.05. cum. index (1982). **Bk Rev. Ad Acc, Adv Mgr:** Ron Dowse, **Tel** (402)280-2988. **Circ:** 900 (ctrl). available on microfilm and microfiche from University Microfilms International (UMI).
Desc: Publishes articles by students, the bench, and the bar, covering a wide spectrum of legal topics.
Ind/Abst Bowne Dig. Corp. Sec. Lawyers; Curr. Law Index (1980-); Index Leg. Period.; Leg. Resour. Index (1980-); LegalTrac (1980-).

CN/0833-5737
CRIMINAL INJURIES COMPENSATION. **See** Law-Abstracting, Bibliographies and Statistics.

IT/0390-0657
CRITICA DEL DIRITTO. [Crit. diritto]. Vol. 1, No. 1 (Jan./April 1974)-. Italian. Three times a year. L70000 (one year), L100000 (two year) Italy; L140000 (one year), L200000 (two year) other. Sapere 2000 SRL, Via Turati 48, 00185 Rome Italy. **Tel** 011 39 6 730776.

IT
CRITICA GIUDIZIARIA. Yearly V. 1- Jan./Feb. 1976-. Periodical. Italian. $10.00. C.C.P.N. 10511400 Intestato A Casa Editrice Patron, Via Badini 12, 40127 Bologna Italy. **LC** K3; .R57.

US/1056-389X
CRITICAL LEGAL ISSUES. (CRITICAL LEGAL ISSUES : WORKING PAPER SERIES / WASHINGTON LEGAL FOUNDATION.). [Crit. legal issues]. **Added/Corp** Washington Legal Foundation. **VFOAT** Critical Legal Issues, Working Paper Series. (1985)-. Monographic series. English. $5.00 (single issue). **DD** 340.

US
CRIV SHEET, THE. **See** Library and Information Sciences.

UK
CROWN OFFICE DIGEST. (1988)-. English. Six times a year. £185.00 Europe; £195.00 other. Sweet & Maxwell Ltd., South Quay Plaza, 183 Marsh Wall, London E14 9FT England. **Tel** 011 44 264 342899, FAX 011 44 264 342723, telex 929089 ITPINF G.

DR
CUADERNOS JURIDICOS. Periodical. Spanish. Facultad de Ciencias Juridicas y Politcas, Universidad Nacional Pedro Herquez Urena, Edificio No 3, Locales 217 y 218, Campus, Autopista Duarte, Santo Domingo Dominican Republic. **LC** K3; .U2. **DD** 340/.097293.

CL
CUADERNOS JURIDICOS. 1- August 1977-. Periodical. Spanish. mo. Arzabispado de Santiago de Chile, Erasmo Escala 1822 Oficina 503, Santiago Chile. **LC** K3; .U19. **DD** 340/.0983.

US/0360-8298
CUMBERLAND LAW REVIEW. [Cumberland law rev.]. **Added/Corp** Cumberland School of Law. Vol. 6, (Spring 1975)-. Academic Scholarly Publication. English. Three times a year (varies). $24.00. Samford University, Box 2268, 800 Lakeshore Drive, Birmingham AL 35229. **Tel** (205)870-2757, FAX (205)870-2673. **ED** Jill Obersas. **LC** K3; .U45. **DD** 340/.05. Index available (3rd iss.). cum. index. **Bk Rev. Circ:** 1,500. available on microfilm and microfiche from University Microfilms International (UMI). ***Continues*** *Cumberland-Samford Law Review, 0045-9275.*
Desc: A scholarly legal periodical published three times per year which examines new developments in the legal field.
Ind/Abst Bowne Dig. Corp. Sec. Lawyers; Crim. Justice Abstr.; Curr. Law Index (1980-); Index Leg. Period.; Leg. Resour. Index (1980-); LegalTrac (1980-).

US/0590-3378
CUMBERLAND LAWYER, THE. Added/Corp Samford University, Birmingham, Alabama. Cumberland School of Law. Vol. 1 (1966)-. Periodical. English. sa. Free. Cumberland School of Law, 800 Lakeshore Drive, Room 305D, Birmingham AL 35229. **Tel** (205)870-2959. **ED** James N. Lewis Jr. **DD** 340. **Bk Rev. Circ:** 7,000 (ctrl).
Desc: Law-related materials of interest to graduates of Cumberland School of Law.

AT
CURRENT AUSTRALIAN AND NEW ZEALAND LEGAL LITERATURE INDEX. ***Ceased.*** **See** Law-Abstracting, Bibliographies and Statistics.

II
CURRENT CENTRAL LEGISLATION. Periodical. English. mo. Rs200.00 India; $62.50 US. Eastern Book Company, 34 Lalbagh, Lucknow 226 001 India. **Tel** 43171, 44328, 46517, telex 535 436 FAST IN. **ED** P L Malik and K K Malik. **DD** 348.54/022; 345.40822. Index available. cum. index. **Bk Rev. Ad Acc. Circ:** 4,000.
Desc: Contains central acts, ordinances, regulations, rules and notifications and also notifications of the Supreme Court of India.

CN/0382-5027
CURRENT INDEX TO COMMONWEALTH LEGAL PERIODICALS. ***Title Change.*** Vol. 1 (Sept. 1974)-?. Periodical. English. mo. Dalhousie University / Sir James Dunn Law Library, Faculty of Law, Halifax Nova Scotia B3H 3J5 Canada. **DD** 016.34/009171/241. ***Supersedes*** *Sir James Dunn Law Library. Current Materials.* ***Continued by*** *Index to Commonwealth Legal Periodicals, 0225-9036.*

US/0898-9451
CURRENT INDEX TO LEGAL PERIODICALS (SEATTLE, WASH.). **See** Law-Abstracting, Bibliographies and Statistics.

US/0883-0517

CURRENT ISSUES IN INTERNATIONAL SHIP FINANCE. (1984)-. English. Practising Law Institute, 810 Seventh Avenue, New York NY 10019-5818. **Tel** (212)765-5700, FAX (212)581-4670 general correspondence, (212)265-4742 orders and billing inquiries. **LC** K1188.B6; C88. **DD** 343/.0965; 342.3965. ***Continues*** *Current Issues in Ship Financing, 0883-0592.*

UK

CURRENT LAW CASE CITATOR. (1985)-. English. an. £480.00 Europe; £504.00 other Complete Current Law Subscription. Sweet & Maxwell Ltd., South Quay Plaza, 183 Marsh Wall, London E14 9FT England. **Tel** 011 44 264 342899, FAX 011 44 264 342723, telex 929089 ITPINF G. **ED** Kevan Norris. **LC** CURRENT ISSUES ONLY. **DD** 348/.42/047. **Circ:** 6,000 (ctrl). ***Continues in part*** *Current Law Citator.*
Desc: Indices of all case law developments since 1947.

UK

CURRENT LAW CITATOR. ***Title Change.*** (19??)-(19??). English. an. Sweet & Maxwell Ltd., South Quay Plaza, 183 Marsh Wall, London E14 9FT England. **Tel** 011 44 264 342899, FAX 011 44 264 342723, telex 929089 ITPINF G. ***Split into*** *Current Law Case Citator; Current Law Statute Citator* ***and*** *Current Law Legislation Citator.*

US/0196-1780

CURRENT LAW INDEX. **See** Law-Abstracting, Bibliographies and Statistics.

UK

CURRENT LAW LEGISLATION CITATOR. (1985)-. English. an. £480.00 Europe; £504.00 other Complete Current Law Subscription. Sweet & Maxwell Ltd., South Quay Plaza, 183 Marsh Wall, London E14 9FT England. **Tel** 011 44 264 342899, FAX 011 44 264 342723, telex 929089 ITPINF G. **LC** KD141; .C865. **DD** 348.41/027/05; 344.1082705. ***Continues in part*** *Current Law Citator.*

UK

CURRENT LAW MONTHLY DIGEST. **VFOAT** Current Law; Current Law ... Digest. (Jan. 1991)-. Periodical. English. mo. £260.00 Europe; £273.00 other. Sweet & Maxwell Ltd., South Quay Plaza, 183 Marsh Wall, London E14 9FT England. **Tel** 011 44 264 342899, FAX 011 44 264 342723, telex 929089 ITPINF G. ***Continues*** *Scottish Current Law* ***and*** *Current Law, 0011-362X.*

UK

CURRENT LAW, PART A. (1947)-. English. mo. £480.00 Europe; £504.00 other. Sweet & Maxwell Ltd., South Quay Plaza, 183 Marsh Wall, London E14 9FT England. **Tel** 011 44 264 342899, FAX 011 44 264 342723, telex 929089 ITPINF G.

UK

CURRENT LAW, PART B. (1947)-. English. ir. £340.00 Europe; £357.00 other. Sweet & Maxwell Ltd., South Quay Plaza, 183 Marsh Wall, London E14 9FT England. **Tel** 011 44 264 342899, FAX 011 44 264 342723, telex 929089 ITPINF G.

UK

CURRENT LAW, PART C. (1947)-. English. mo. £260.00 Europe; £273.00 other. Sweet & Maxwell Ltd., South Quay Plaza, 183 Marsh Wall, London E14 9FT England. **Tel** 011 44 264 342899, FAX 011 44 264 342723, telex 929089 ITPINF G.

UK

CURRENT LAW STATUTES ANNOTATED. **Added/Corp** Great Britain Laws, Statutes, etc. (1947)-. Periodical. English. Four times a year. £350.00 Europe; £368.00 other. Sweet & Maxwell Ltd., South Quay Plaza, 183 Marsh Wall, London E14 9FT England. **Tel** 011 44 264 342899, FAX 011 44 264 342723, telex 929089 ITPINF G.

●UK

CURRENT LAW WEEK. (1993)-. English. Forty-six times a year. £92.00 Europe; £97.00 other. Sweet & Maxwell Ltd., South Quay Plaza, 183 Marsh Wall, London E14 9FT England. **Tel** 011 44 264 342899, FAX 011 44 264 342723, telex 929089 ITPINF G.

US

CURRENT LEGAL FORMS. (19??)-. English. qt (4 issues). Matthew Bender & Company Inc., 1275 Broadway, Albany NY 12204. **Tel** (800)833-9844, (518)487-3000.

UK/0070-1998

CURRENT LEGAL PROBLEMS. [Curr. leg. probl.]. **Added/Corp** University College, London. Faculty of Laws. Vol. 1 (1948)-. English. ir. Price varies per volume. Oxford University Press, Walton Street, Oxford OX2 6DP England. **Tel** 011 44 865 56767, FAX 011 44 865 267773, telex 837330 OXPRES G. **(Subscription address:** Oxford University Press / USA, Journals Marketing Department, Oxford University Press, 2001 Evans Road, Cary NC 27513.**)** cum. index.
Ind/Abst Curr. Law Index (1980-); Index Leg. Period.; Leg. Resour. Index (1980-); LegalTrac (1980-).

BE/0772-1668

CURRENT LEGAL THEORY : INTERNATIONAL JOURNAL FOR DOCUMENTATION ON LEGAL THEORY. Vol. 1, No. 1-2 (1983)-. Periodical. English. sa. Fl100.00 (Subscription includes extra issues and access to online database.). Tilburg University Library, PO Box 90153, 5000 LE Tilburg Netherlands. **Tel** 011 31 13 662510, 354066, FAX 011 31 13 662996.

UK/0964-8461

CURRENT SENTENCING PRACTICE NEWS. [Curr. sentencing pract. news]. **VFOAT** Sentencing News. (1991)-. Periodical. English. qt. £75.00 Europe; £79.00 other. Sweet & Maxwell Ltd., South Quay Plaza, 183 Marsh Wall, London E14 9FT England. **Tel** 011 44 264 342899, FAX 011 44 264 342723, telex 929089 ITPINF G. **DD** 364.650942.

IE

CUSTOMS AND EXCISE TARIFF OF IRELAND. 1st Jan., 1963-. English. Government Publications, 4 5 Harcourt Road, Dublin 2 Ireland. **Tel** 011 353 1 6613111 Ext.4005. **LC** KDK1510.A329; .C87. ***Continues*** *Customs and Excise Tarrif.*

US/0162-6442

CUSTOMS BULLETIN AND DECISIONS. (CUSTOMS BULLETIN AND DECISION : REGULATIONS, RULINGS, DECISIONS, AND NOTICES CONCERNING CUSTOMS AND RELATED MATTERS OF THE UNITED STATES COURT OF CUSTOMS AND PATENT APPEALS AND THE UNITED STATES CUSTOMS COURT.). [Cust. bull. decis.]. **Added/Corp** U.S. Customs Service. United States. Customs Court. United States. Court of Customs and Patent Appeals. United States. Court of International Trade. United States. Court of Appeals (Federal Circuit). (19??)-. Government Publication. English. wk. $128.00 domestic; $160.00 other. Superintendent of Documents, US Government Printing Office, Washington DC 20402. **Tel** (202)275-3328, FAX (202)786-2377. **LC** KF6687.A2; T72. **DD** 353.0072/46. available on microfilm and microfiche from University Microfilms International (UMI). ***Continues*** *Customs Bulletin, 0011-4146.*
Desc: Contains regulations, rulings, decisions, and notices concerning Customs and related matters of the United States Court of Appeals for the Federal Circuit and the United States Court of International Trade.

US

CUSTOMS REGULATIONS OF THE UNITED STATES. **Main/Corp** United States. Customs Service. **Added/Corp** U.S. Customs Service. Office of Regulations & Rulings. (1???)-. Government Publication. English. ir (Supplementary material). $56.00 domestic; $70.00 other. Superintendent of Documents, US Government Printing Office, Washington DC 20402. **Tel** (202)275-3328, FAX (202)786-2377.
Desc: Contains regulations made and published for the purpose of carrying out customs laws administered by the United States Customs Service.

US/8750-944X

CYLA QUARTERLY. [CYLA q.]. **VAT** California Young Lawyers Association Quarterly. Vol. 1, No. 1 (Aug. 1984)-. Periodical. English. qt. Free. State Bar of California, 555 Franklin Street, San Francisco CA 94102. **Tel** (415)561-8200, FAX (415)561-8228. **Circ:** 38,000 (ctrl).
Desc: Features articles on current law topics; substantive law articles, and meeting announcements.

PL/0070-2471

CZASOPISMO PRAWNO-HISTORYCZNE. [Czas. praw.-hist.]. **Added/Corp** Poznanskie Towarzystwo Przyjaciol Nauk. Wydzial Historii i Nauk Spolecznych. Polska Akademia Nauk. **VFOAT** Annales d'Histoire du Droit. Vol. 1 (1948)-. Periodical. Polish (French). sa. **(Subscription address:** ARS Polona, PO Box 1001, 00068 Warsaw Poland.**)** ***Supersedes*** *Przewodnik Historyczno-Prawny.*
Ind/Abst Am. Hist. Life (1954-1974, 1979-).

US/0270-0506

D.C. CIRCUIT HANDBOOK. **VFOAT** Legal Times of Washington D.C. Circuit Handbook; District of Columbia Circuit Handbook. (1980)-. English. an. $50.00. Prentice-Hall Law and Business, 270 Sylvan Avenue, Englewood Cliffs NJ 07632. **Tel** (800)223-0231, (201)894-8538, FAX (201)894-8666.

US/0740-1744

D.C. CODE UPDATER. **VFOAT** DC Code Updater. English. mo. $275.00. Wilkes & Artis, 1666 K Street NW/Suite 1100, Washington DC 20006. **Tel** (202)457-7871. **ED** David W Lang. **LC** KFD1240; .D15. **DD** 348.753/028; 347.530828. **Circ:** 45.
Desc: Tracts current changes in the D.C. Code and the D.C. Municipal Regulations by title and subject number.

BL

D.O., DIARIO OFICIAL, ESTADO DO RIO DE JANEIRO. PARTE I. **Main/Corp** Rio de Janeiro (Brazil : State). Portuguese. $338.00. Rua Sao Jose, No 35/222/224, Rio de Janeiro Brazil. ***Continues*** *Diario Oficial do Estado do Rio de Janeiro. Parte I.*

BL

D.O., DIARIO OFICIAL, ESTADO DO RIO DE JANEIRO. PARTE III. **Main/Corp** Rio de Janeiro (Brazil : State). Portuguese. da. $223.00. Rua Sal Jose No 35/222/224, Rio de Janeiro Brazil. **Tel** (021)719-1122. Index available. cum. index. **Bk Rev. Ad Acc. Circ:** 20,000 (ctrl). ***Continues*** *Diario Oficial do Estado do Rio de Janeiro. Parte III.*

BL

D.O., DIARIO OFICIAL, ESTADO DO RIO DE JANEIRO. PARTE IV. **Main/Corp** Rio de Janeiro (Brazil : State). **VAT** Diario Oficial, Diario Oficial, Estado do Rio de Janeiro. Parte Cuatro. Periodical. Portuguese. $260. Imprensa Oficial do Estado do Rio de Janeiro, rua Marques de Olinda, 29 Centro Niterio, CEP 24.030 Rio de Janeiro Brazil. **Tel** 722.8955/719.1122. **DD** 340/.09815. ***Supersedes in part*** *Rio de Janeiro (Brazil : State). D.O. Diario Oficial, Estado do Rio de Janeiro. Partes IV e V.*

BL

D.O., DIARIO OFICIAL, ESTADO DO RIO DE JANEIRO. PARTE V. **Main/Corp** Rio de Janeiro (Brazil : State). Portuguese. 260.00. Imprensa Oficial do Estado do Rio de Janeiro, rua Marques de Olinda, 29 Centro Niterio, CEP 24.030 Rio de Janeiro Brazil. **Tel** 722.8955/719.1122. **Circ:** 24,000 (ctrl). ***Supersedes*** *Rio de Janeiro (Brazil : State). D.O. Diario Oficial, Estado do Rio de Janeiro. Partes IV e V.*

US/0740-1949

DAILY COURT REVIEW. (1983)-. Periodical. English. da (publ Monday through Friday except legal holidays). $195.00. Daily Court Review, PO Box 1889, Houston TX 77251-1889. **Tel** (713)528-5437, (713)869-5434, FAX (713)869-8887. **(Subscription telephone:** (713)869-5434**) ED** E. Milton Morin, Jr. (Daily Court Review's street address: 6807 Wynnwood, Houston, TX 77008-5023). cum. index. **Bk Rev. Ad Acc. Circ:** 2,100. available on CD-ROM.

US

DAILY JOURNAL DIRECTORY OF ATTORNEYS : LOS ANGELES AND ORANGE COUNTIES, THE. ***Title Change.*** **Added/Corp** Daily Journal (Firm). **VFOAT** Directory of Attorneys. (19??)-(19??). Directory. English. sa. Daily Journal Corporation, 915 East First Street, Los Angeles CA 90012. **Tel** (213)229-5300, FAX (213)680-3682. ***Continued by*** *California Lawyers Directory.*

US/0197-8055

DAILY RECORDER, THE. (1911)-. Periodical. English. da (260 issues). $167.00. Daily Journal Corporation, 915 East First Street, Los Angeles CA 90012. **Tel** (213)229-5300, FAX (213)680-3682. **ED** Steve Towns (Managing Editor). Index available. **Bk Rev**, (Qty: 5-7). **Photos**. **Ad Acc, Adv Mgr:** Laura Enright, **Tel** (916)444-2355. Full Page (B&W) $531.36. Half Page (B&W) $265.68. **Pub. Size:** Tabloid. **Wire Svcs.:** AP. **Circ:** 2,100 (ctrl). ***Formed by the union of*** *Sacramento Press-Journal.*
Desc: Legal and government newspaper.

US/0276-5926

DAILY REPORT (BAKERSFIELD, CALIF.), THE. (THE DAILY REPORT.). Periodical. English. da (Monday-Friday). The Daily Report, PO Box 637, Bakersfield CA 93302. **Tel** (805)322-3226, (805)322-9084. **ED** Gay Thurber. **Ad Acc.**

US/0360-9510

DAILY REPORTER (SIOUX CITY), THE. (THE DAILY REPORTER.). (19??)-. Periodical. English. da. $96.00. Sioux City Daily Reporter, 706 Pierce Street, Sioux City IA 51101. **Tel** (712)255-8829. **ED** Jeffrey S. Scotsky. **LC** K4; .A52. **DD** 340/.09777. **Ad Acc. Circ:** 500 (ctrl).
Desc: Includes court and commercial news.

US/0092-6884

DAILY TAX REPORT (WASHINGTON). (DAILY TAX REPORT.). **Added/Corp** Bureau of National Affairs (Washington, D.C.). (19??)-. Periodical. English. ir. $1,945.00. Bureau of National Affairs Inc., 9435 Key West Avenue, Rockville MD 20850. **Tel** (800)372-1033, (301)258-1033, FAX (301)948-5823. **(Subscription address:** 9435 Key West Avenue, Rockville MD 20850; telephone: FAX (301)948-5823**) ED** Rebecca Pearl. **LC** KF6289.A1; D3. **DD** 343/.73/04. **[CCC].**
Desc: A tax notification service that covers legislative, regulatory, judicial, and policy developments on a national basis, designed to give tax professionals rapid notification and comprehensive coverage of those developments.

US/1066-6095

DAILY WASHINGTON LAW REPORTER, THE. [Dly. Wash. law report.]. **Added/Corp** United States. Court of Appeals (District of Columbia Circuit)

United States. District Court (District of Columbia). (Sept. 1, 1959)-. Periodical. English. ir (250 issues per year). $200.80 Washington DC; $190.00 other. Washington Law Reporter, 1001 Connecticut Ave. NW, Suite 238, Washington DC 20036. **Tel** (202)331-1700. **LC** K4; .A523. **DD** 340. ***Continues*** *Washington Law Reporter.*

JA
DAITO HOGAKU. **Main/Corp** Daito Bunka Daigaku Hogakkai. **VFOAT** Journal of Law and Politics. Ed. 1974-. Japanese (Japanese). Daito Bunka Daigaku Hogakkai, 9-1 Takashimadaira 1 Itabashi-ku, Tokyo Japan. **LC** K4; .A524. **DD** 340/.0952.

●CN/1188-4258
DALHOUSIE JOURNAL OF LEGAL STUDIES. [Dalhous. j. leg. stud.]. **Added/Corp** Dalhousie University. Faculty of Law. Vol. 1, No. 1 (Spring 1992)-. Periodical. English. an. $25.00 institutions; $12.00 individuals. Dalhousie Journal of Legal Studies, 6061 University Avenue, Weldon Law Building, Halifax NS Canada B3H 4H9 Canada. **Tel** (902)424-3495, FAX (902)494-1316. **ED** Oliver Fulldauer. **DD** 340/.05. **Bk Rev**, (Qty: 6-10). **Ad Acc. Circ:** 500.
Ind/Abst Index Leg. Period. (1993-).

CN/0317-1663
DALHOUSIE LAW JOURNAL. [Dalhous. law j.]. **Added/Corp** Dalhousie University. Faculty of Law. Vol. 1 (Sept. 1973)-. Periodical. English (French). Carswell / Canada, 2075 Kennedy Road, Scarborough Ontario M1T 3V4 Canada. **Tel** (416)609-3800, (800)387-5164. **LC** K4; .A53. **DD** 340/.05.
Ind/Abst Can. Legal Lit.; Curr. Law Index (1980-); Index Can. Leg. Period. Lit.; Index Leg. Period.; Leg. Resour. Index (1980-); LegalTrac (1980-).

KU
DALIL AL-KUWAYT AL-YAWM / WIZARAT AL-TAKHTIT, MARKAZ AL-KUWAYT LIL-MALUMAT WA-AL-MIKRUFILM. **Main/Corp** Markaz Al-Kuwayt Lil-Malumat Wa-al-mikrufilm. Arabic. sa. 3.500KD (paperform), 5.000KD (microform). Ministry of Planning, Kuwait Information and Microfilm Center, PO Box 15-Safat, 13001 Safat Kuwait. **Tel** (965)2420331, telex KT 22468. cum. index. **Circ:** 1,000 (ctrl). available on microfilm.
Desc: Provides publishing and microfilming data of laws, degrees and ministerial issues. Supplemented by subject headings, names and agencies lists.

US
D&O BOOK. English. $125.00. Warren McVeigh & Griffin Inc, 1420 Bristol Street, Suite 220, Newport Beach CA 92660. **Tel** (714)752-1058, FAX (714)955-1929.

TZ
DAR ES SALAAM UNIVERSITY LAW JOURNAL. ***Title Change.*** **Main/Corp** Chuo Kikuu cha dar es Salaam. **Added/Corp** Dar es Salaam University Law Society. Denning Law Society. (1971)-(19??). Periodical. English. ir. Dar es Salaam School of Law, PO Box 35034, Dar es Salaam Tanzania. **LC** K4; .A75. **DD** 340/.09678. (n). **Ad Acc.** ctrl circ. ***Continues*** *Journal of the Denning Law Society.* ***Continued by*** *University of Dar es Salaam Law Journal.*

NE
DATA JURIDICA. (19??)-. Periodical. Dutch. mo. Fl240.00 Netherlands; $182.86 US. Libresso BV, Postbus 878, 7400 GA Deventer Netherlands. **Tel** 011 31 5700 47421. **ED** N.J. Troost. **LC** K4; .A78. Index available. cum. index. **Bk Rev. Ad Acc. Circ:** 700 (ctrl).
Desc: Review of legal literature; abstracts of books and magazine articles.

US/8755-2361
DATALINE (DALLAS, TEX.). (DATALINE.). [Dataline]. **VFOAT** Law School Computer Group Dataline. Vol. 1, No. 1-. Periodical. English. qt. $5.00. Law School Computer Group, Southern Methodist University School of Law, Dallas TX 75275. **LC** KF282.5.A15; D37. **DD** 340/.028/5.

GW
DATENSCHUTZ UND DATENSICHERUNG. (19??)-. Periodical. German. mo. DM356.00. Vieweg Publishing, PO Box 5829, D 65048 Wiesbaden Germany. **Tel** 011 49 611 160230, FAX 011 49 611 160229. **ED** Ing K. Rihaczer. **LC** K4; .A79. **DD** 342.43/0853; 344.302853. **Bk Rev. Ad Acc. Circ:** 2,300.
Desc: Deals with the interpretation of the law, the steps of following the BDGS and the problems attached to the brief information, original reports and empirical surveys.

US
DAUPHIN COUNTY REPORTS. **Added/Corp** Pennsylvania. Courts (Dauphin Co.). Dauphin County Bar Association. **VFOAT** Dauphin County Reporter. Vol. 1 (1898)-. English. **ED** G R Barnett. Each issue contains an index to its own contents (no volume index)--loose.
Desc: Beginning with 1917, the opinions, rules, and regulations of the Public Service Commission and the Workmens Compensation Board.

US
DC RULES OF PROFESSIONAL CONDUCT. English. Three times a year. $50.00. District of Columbia Bar, 1250 H Street Northwest, Sixth Floor, Washington DC 20005. **Tel** (202)737-4700, FAX (202)626-3471. Index available.

US/0011-7188
DE PAUL LAW REVIEW. [De Paul law rev.]. **Added/Corp** DePaul University. College of Law. **VFOAT** DePaul Law Review. Vol. 1, No. 1 (Autumn-Winter 1951)-. English. qt. $21.00. DePaul University, College of Law, 25 East Jackson Boulevard, Chicago IL 60604. **Tel** (312)341-8553. **LC** UNC. **Bk Rev**, (Qty: 0-1). **Circ:** 800 (ctrl).
Ind/Abst Curr. Law Index (1980-); Fed. Tax Artic.; Index Leg. Period.; Leg. Resour. Index (1980-); LegalTrac (1980-).

US/0147-3719
DEBTOR & CREDITOR. BENDER PAMPHLET EDITION. (DEBTOR & CREDITOR.). **Main/Corp** New York (State). **VAT** Debtor and Creditor. English. Matthew Bender & Company Inc., 1275 Broadway, Albany NY 12204. **Tel** (800)833-9844, (518)487-3000. **LC** KFN5364.A29; D4. **DD** 346/.747/077.

US
DECENCY REPORTER / CHILDREN'S LEGAL FOUNDATION. **Added/Corp** Children's Legal Foundation. Vol. 27, No. 1 (Summer 1990)-. Periodical. English. qt. Children's Legal Foundation, 2845 East Camelback Road, Phoenix AZ 85016. **LC** HV741; .C54. ***Continues*** *CLF Reporter.*

CN/1182-5316
DECISION - TRIBUNAL CANADIEN DU COMMERCE EXTERIEUR. (DECISION.). [Decis. - Trib. can. commer. exter.]. **Main/Corp** Tribunal Canadien du Commerce Exterieur. (1990)-. French. **DD** 343.71/087/02643.

US
DECISIONES DE PUERTO RICO. **Main/Corp** Puerto Rico. Supreme Court. Vol. 1- Sept. 25, 1899-. Spanish. ir. Equity Publishing Corporation, RR 1 Box 3, Orford NH 03777. **Tel** (603)637-5012, (800)637-5012. Each issue contains an index to its own contents (no volume index)--loose.

PR
DECISIONES DEL TRIBUNAL SUPREMO DE PUERTO RICO [COMPUTER FILE]. **Main/Corp** Puerto Rico. Supreme Court. Vols. 1 al 118- (1989)-. Periodical. English. qt. Compact Disc Technologies Corp., 421 Munoz Rivera Avenue, Midtown Plaza, Suite 106, Hato Rey Puerto Rico 00918.
Desc: System requirements: IBM PC or compatible; CD-ROM drive; MS-DOS CD-ROM extensions.

US
DECISIONS OF THE OCCUPATIONAL SAFETY AND HEALTH REVIEW BOARD. **Main/Corp** Alaska. Occupational Safety and Health Review Board. V. 1- 1976-. English. Occupational Safety and Health Review Board, Juneau AK 99801. **LC** KFA1535; .A556. **DD** 344/.798/046502646.

NQ
DECRETOS-LEYES Y LEYES DE LA REPUBLICA DE NICARAGUA. **Main/Corp** Nicaragua. 1985-. Spanish. ***Continues*** *Decretos-Leyes Para Gobierno de un Pais a Traves de una Junta de Gobierno de Reconstruccion Nacional.*

US/1047-8515
DEFAMATION & DISPARAGEMENT. **VFOAT** Defamation and Disparagement. (1990)-. Periodical. English. mo. $85.00. Miramar Publishing Company, 6133 Bristol Parkway, PO Box 3640, Culver City CA 90231. **Tel** (800)543-4116, (310)337-9717.

US/0011-751X
DEFENDER NEWSLETTER. **Added/Corp** National Legal Aid and Defender Association. Vol. 1 (Oct. 10, 1963)-. Periodical. English. American Bar Association, 750 North Lake Shore Drive, Chicago IL 60611. **Tel** (312)988-5522, (312)988-5241, FAX (312)988-5528, telex 270593. **DD** 362.

US/0011-7587
DEFENSE LAW JOURNAL. [Def. law j.]. Vol. 1 (1957)-. Periodical. English. Four times a year. $85.00. Michie Company, PO Box 7587, Charlottesville VA 22906-7587. **Tel** (804)972-7600, (800)542-0957, FAX (800)643-1280. **ED** R. Patterson. **LC** K4; .E33. **DD** 346.7303/23; 347.306323. Index available. cum. index. **Bk Rev.** available on microfilm and microfiche from University Microfilms International (UMI).
Desc: Articles on trial preparation and practice, products liability, medical and legal malpractice, workers' compensation, medical evidence, economists' testimony, settlement strategy and other topics of interest to defense, insurance and corporate lawyers.
Ind/Abst Curr. Law Index (1980-); Leg. Resour. Index (1980-); LegalTrac (1980-).

FI
DEFENSOR LEGIS; ORGAN FOR FINLANDS ADVOKAT-FORBUND. Vol. 1 (1920)-. Periodical. Finnish. Six times a year. Fmk335.00 Finland; Fmk370.00 other. Akateeminen Kirjakauppa, Keskuskatu 1, SF-00101 Helsinki Finland. **Tel** 011 358 0 12141. cum. index.
Ind/Abst Crim. Penol. Police Sci. Abstr.; Index Foreign Leg. Per.

US
DELAWARE CASE NAMES CITATOR. English. $40.00 (bound volume), $52.00 (cumulative supplements). Shepards McGraw-Hill Inc, 555 Middle Creek Parkway, PO Box 35300, Colorado Springs CO 80935-3530. **Tel** (719)488-3000, FAX (800)525-0053.

US/0193-4007
DELAWARE LAW MONTHLY, THE. [Del. law mon.]. Vol. 1, (Dec. 1978)-. Periodical. English. Twelve times a year. $350.00. The Delaware Law Monthly, PO Box 262, Wilmington DE 19899. **Tel** (302)475-7407. **ED** Charles M. Oberly III, Eileen F. Caulfield and Bartholomew J. Dalton. **LC** KFD57; .D44. **DD** 348/.751/046. **Ad Acc.**
Desc: Outlines recent Delaware Court opinions from all the major courts in the state, focusing heavily upon business and corporate opinions.

US/0735-6595
DELAWARE LAWYER. (DELAWARE LAWYER : A PUBLICATION OF DELAWARE BAR FOUNDATION.). [Del. lawyer]. **Added/Corp** Delaware Bar Foundation. Vol. 1, No. 1 (Spring 1982)-. Periodical. English. qt. $12.00. Suburban Marketing Associates, 201 North Walnut Street, Suite 1204, Wilmington DE 19800. **Tel** (302)656-8440. **ED** William E Wiggins. **LC** KF200; .D44. **DD** 340/.060751. **Bk Rev. Ad Acc. Circ:** 3,000.
Desc: Each issue covers a principal topic from varying viewpoints. Themes: environment, professional competence, lawyers in politics, and how the criminal justice system functions for lawyers and laymen.
Ind/Abst Curr. Law Index (1984-); Leg. Resour. Index (1984-); LegalTrac (1984-).

II
DELHI LAW REVIEW. **Added/Corp** University of Delhi. Faculty of Law. Vol. 1, (1972)-. English. University of Delhi Faculty of Law, New Delhi 110007 India. **LC** K4; .E4. **DD** 340/.0954. **Bk Rev. Ad Acc. Circ:** 200.
Desc: Current legal developments including issues of jurisprudential and philosophical nature in any branch of law.

GR
DELTION AUTOKINETISTIKES NOMOTHESIAS KAI NOMOLOGIAS. (1961)-. Greek, Modern. Twelve times a year. Dr2000.00. Dalianis, Patision 14 Stoa Phexe, Athens Greece. **Tel** 3823206. **ED** Maria Dalianis. Index available. cum. index. **Bk Rev. Ad Acc. Pr Rev. Acid Free. Circ:** 2,000 (ctrl).
Desc: Automobile law in Greece and abroad.

IT/0416-9565
DEMOCRAZIA E DIRITTO. [Democr. dir.]. (1960)-. Periodical. Italian. qt. L70000.00 Italy; L90000.00 other. Associazione CRS, Via della Vite 13, 00187 Rome Italy. **Tel** 011 39 6 6784101.

GW/0340-8590
DEMOKRATIE UND RECHT (KOLN). (DEMOKRATIE UND RECHT.). [Demokr. recht]. (1973)-. Periodical. German. qt. Demokratie und Recht, Sduelterblatt 58C, 2000 Hamburg 20 Germany. **DD** 340.
Ind/Abst Energy Res. Abstr.

UK/0269-1922
DENNING LAW JOURNAL, THE. [Denning law j.]. **Added/Corp** University of Buckingham. (1986)-. Periodical. English. an. £9.95 UK; $25.00 other. William W. Gaunt and Sons Inc, 3011 Gulf Drive, Gaunt Building, Holmes Beach FL 34217. **Tel** (800)942-8683, (813)778-5211. **ED** P.H. Pettit and C.G. Hall. **LC** K4; .E45. **DD** 349.42; 344.2. **Ad Acc.** ctrl circ.
Ind/Abst Index Leg. Period.; Leg. Resour. Index; LegalTrac (1986-).

US/0883-9409
DENVER UNIVERSITY LAW REVIEW. [Denver Univ. law rev.]. 1985-. Periodical. English. qt. $23.00 US; $28.00 other. University of Denver Law Review, 7039 East 18th Avenue, Denver CO 80220. **Tel** (303)871-6172. **ED** Sam Mitchell and Maureen Jaran. **LC** K4; .E5. **DD** 340. **Ad Acc. Circ:** 900 (ctrl). Documents available from The Genuine Article. ***Continues*** *Denver Law Journal, 0011-8834.*
Ind/Abst Bowne Dig. Corp. Sec. Lawyers; Curr. Contents Soc. Behav. Sci.; Curr. Law Index (1985-); Fed. Tax Artic.; Index Leg. Period.; Leg. Resour. Index (1985-); LegalTrac (1985-); PAIS Int. Print (1991-); Res. Alert [Select. Cov.]; Soc. Sci. Cit. Index [Select. Cov.].

US
DEPARTMENT OF JUSTICE FINANCIAL LITIGATION ANNUAL REPORT. **Main/Corp** United States. Dept. of Justice. **VFOAT** Financial Litigation Annual Report. (Dec. 1991)-. English. US

Law

Department of Justice, 10th Street & Constitution Avenue NW, Washington DC 20530. **Tel** (202)514-2000, FAX (202)633-4371.

US
DEPRECIATION AND CAPITAL PLANNING.
English. an. $119.00. Macmillan Publishing Company, 866 3rd Avenue, New York NY 10022. **Tel** (212)702-2000, (800)257-5755. **LC** KF6386. **DD** 343.7305/234. Index available. cum. index. **Circ**: 750.
Desc: One volume guide to sweeping tax laws involving depreciation and investment credit.

CK
DERECHO.
Spanish. Colegio de Abogados de Medellin, Apartado Nacional 3446, Medellin Colombia. **LC** K4; .E68.

CK
DERECHO.
Added/Corp Universidad de San Buenaventura de Cali. Facultad de Derecho. (1991)-. Periodical. Spanish. sa. **LC** K2; .O45. **Continues** Bonaventuriana Juridica.

AG
DERECHO COMPARADO.
No. 1- Dec. 1977-. Periodical. Spanish (summaries and/or abstracts in English and French). sa. Asociacion Argentina der Comp, Chacabuco 78, Piso Oficina 9, 1069 Buenos Aires Argentina. **LC** K4; .E714. **DD** 340/.2/05.

CK
DERECHO FINANCIERO.
Vol. 1- 2. Half 1975-. Spanish. Calle 35 No 4-89, Apartado Aereo 29677, Bogota Colombia. **LC** K4; .E72. **DD** 346/.861/0705.
Desc: Covers law and trade regulation.

MX
DERECHO PESQUERO / [ACADEMIA INTERNACIONAL DE DERECHO PESQUERO].
Added/Corp Academia Internacional de Derecho Pesquero. No. 1 (Oct. 1981)-. Periodical. Spanish. Academia Internacional de Derecho Pesquero, Dr Jimenez No 336-302, Mexico 06720 DF Mexico. **LC** K4; .E733. **DD** 343/.07692/05; 342.3769205.
Desc: Covers fishery law and legislation.

VE/0304-2820
DERECHO Y REFORMA AGRARIA; REVISTA.
[Derecho reforma agrar. rev.].
Added/Corp Universidad de Los Andes (Merida, Venezuela). Facultad de Derecho. Merida, Venezuela (City). Universidad de Los Andes. Centro de Jurisprudencia. Instituto Venezolano de Derecho Agrario y Estudios Rurales. Instituto Iberoamericano de Derecho Agrario y Reforma Agraria. Vol. 1 (1969)-. Spanish. an. $5.00. Instituto Derecho Reforma Agrario, Universite Andes, Avda Tulio Sebres 4, Merida Venezuela. **Tel** 011 58 74 528381. **ED** Ramon Vicente Casanova. **LC** K4; .E7. **Bk Rev. Circ**: 1,000 (ctrl).
Ind/Abst AGRICOLA; HAPI Hisp. Am. Period. Index.

US/0276-5675
DES LITIGATION REPORTER.
[DES litig. rep.]. **VFOAT** D.E.S. Litigation Reporter. **VAT** Diethylstilbestrol Litigation Reporter. (June 9, 1981)-. Periodical. English. mo. $800.00. Andrews Publications Inc., 1646 West Chester Pike, PO Box 1000, Westtown PA 19395. **Tel** (610)399-6600, (800)345-1101, FAX (610)399-6610. **ED** Leonard E. B. Andrews. **LC** KF1297.D7; A493. **DD** 346.7303/82; 347.306382. cum. index. ctrl circ.
Desc: Provides extensive coverage of rulings and strategies surrounding the litigation for damages allegedly caused by the anti-miscarriage drug diethylstilbestrol.

US/1058-4919
DESKBOOK ENCYCLOPEDIA OF AMERICAN SCHOOL LAW.
[Deskb. encycl. Am. sch. law]. **Added/Corp** Informational Research Systems (Washington, D.C.) Data Research, Inc. (Rosemount, Minn.). **VFOAT** Encyclopedia of American School Law. (1980/1981)-. English. an. $93.25. Data Research Inc., PO Box 490, Rosemount MN 55068. **Tel** (612)452-8267, (800)365-4900. **LC** KF4114; .D46. **DD** 344.73/07/02638; 347.304702638.
Desc: Encyclopedic compilation of federal and state court decisions in the field of school law.

II/0376-8287
DETAILED DEMAND FOR GRANTS OF LAW DEPARTMENT.
Main/Corp Jammu and Kashmir. Law Dept. English. Ranbir Government Press / Law, Jammu and Kashmir, Law Department, Jammu India. **DD** 354/.546/0088.

US
DETROIT COLLEGE OF LAW ALUMNI NEWS.
See College and School Publications-Alumni.

US/0099-135X
DETROIT COLLEGE OF LAW REVIEW.
[Detroit Coll. Law rev.]. **Added/Corp** Detroit College of Law. Detroit College of Law. Review. No. 1 (1975)-. Periodical. English. qt. $14.00. Detroit College of Law, 130 East Elizabeth Street, Detroit MI 48201. **Tel** (313)226-0100. **LC** K4; .E74. **DD** 340/.05. **Bk Rev. Ad Acc. Circ**: 930. **Continues** Detroit Law Review.

Ind/Abst Bowne Dig. Corp. Sec. Lawyers; Curr. Law Index (1980-); Fed. Tax Artic.; Index Leg. Period.; Leg. Resour. Index (1980-); LegalTrac (1980-).

US/0011-9652
DETROIT LAWYER, THE.
[Detroit lawyer]. **Added/Corp** Detroit Bar Association. Vol. 14, No. 1 (Jan. 1946)-. Periodical. English. ir (1-2 per year). $20.00. Detroit Bar Association, 2380 Penobscot Buliding, Detroit MI 48226. **Tel** (313)961-6120, FAX (313)965-0842. **LC** KF200; .D48. **DD** 340/.060774/34. **Ad Acc**. ctrl circ. **Continues** Detroit Bar Quarterly.
Desc: For Detroit bar association members and subscribing libraries; contains news about association activities.
Ind/Abst Fed. Tax Artic.; Law Office Inf. Serv.

US/0739-9480
DETROIT LEGAL NEWS (DAILY ED.).
(DETROIT LEGAL NEWS.). (Sept. 17, 1895)-. Periodical. English. da. $100.00. Detroit Legal News, 2001 West Lafayette, Detroit MI 48216. **Tel** (313)961-3949, FAX (313)961-7817. **ED** Eric Pope. **Bk Rev**, (Qty: 20). **Ad Acc. Circ**: 2,600 (ctrl). **Continues** Wayne County Legal News.
Desc: Information for the legal community in Michigan.

GW
DEUTSCHE RICHTERZEITUNG.
Vol. 28, No. 10 (Oct. 1950)-. Periodical. German. mo. DM96.40 Germany; DM106.00 other. Carl Heymanns Verlag KG, Luxemburger Strasse 449, D 50939 Cologne Germany. **Tel** 011 49 221 460100, telex 8 881 888. **Bk Rev. Ad Acc. Circ**: 12,500 (ctrl). **Continues** Deutsche Rechtspflege; **Absorbed** Justiz und Verwaltung.

GW/0940-1555
DEUTSCHE ZEITSCHRIFT FUER WIRTSCHAFTSRECHT. VFOAT
Wirtschaftsrecht; DWiR. (June 1991)-. Periodical. German. mo. DM996.00. Walter de Gruyter Inc., PO Box 303621, D 10728 Berlin Germany. **Tel** 011 49 30 260050, FAX 011 49 30 26005251.

GW
DEUTSCHES RECHT. Title Change.
Added/Corp Nationalsozialistischen Rechtswahrerbundes. (19??)-(19??). Periodical. German. wk. **Absorbed** Juristische Wochenschrift... . **Continued by** Neue Juristische Wochenschrift, 0341-1907.

GW/0012-1347
DEUTSCHES STEUERRECHT. See Public
Administration-Public Finance and Taxation.

GW/0012-1363
DEUTSCHES VERWALTUNGSBLATT.
(DEUTSCHES VERWALTUNGSBLATT : MIT VERWALTUNGSARCHIV.). [Dtsch. Verwaltungsbl.]. (1950)-. Periodical. German. bw. DM209.00. Carl Heymanns Verlag KG, Luxemburger Strasse 449, D 50939 Cologne Germany. **Tel** 011 49 221 460100, telex 8 881 888. **ED** Werner Hoppe. **Bk Rev. Ad Acc. Circ**: 3,650 (ctrl). **Continues** Reichsverwaltungsblatt; **Absorbed** Deutsche Verwaltung; Zeitschrift fuer Verwaltungsrecht.
Desc: Decisions and sentences, treatises and statements according to the German administration on law.
Ind/Abst Coal Abstr.; Energy Res. Abstr. (July 1977-); Index Foreign Leg. Per.; World Agric. Econ.

US/1063-9977
DEVELOPMENTS IN MENTAL HEALTH LAW.
[Dev. ment. health law]. **Added/Corp** University of Virginia. Institute of Law, Psychiatry & Public Policy. Vol. 1, No. 1 (Jan. 1981)-. Periodical. English. sa. Free (Va. residents), $10.00 (others). Institute of Law Psychiatry & Public Policy, Box 100, Blue Ridge Hospital, Charlottesville VA 22901. **Tel** (804)924-5435. **ED** Willis J Spaulding. **DD** 344. **Circ**: 3,200 (ctrl).
Desc: Provides in-depth analysis of constitutional and statutory issues in the mental health law field. Virginia legislative developments and judicial decisions are regularly featured.

SP
DIARI OFICIAL DE LA GENERALITAT DE CATALUNYA. Main/Corp
Catalonia (Spain). Catalan (Spanish). tw. 15.500ptas. Diari Oficial de la Generalitat de Catalunya, Palau de la Generalitat, Placa de St Jaume s-n, 08002 Barcelona Spain. **Tel** 93/318 80 12, FAX 315 21 80 GCDB E. (**Subscription address**: Entitat Autonoma del Diari Oficial i de Publicacions, Casa dels Canonges, C/ del Bisbe 4-6, 08002 Barcelona Spain) **DD** 349.46/7/05; 344.67005. Index available. cum. index. **Circ**: 8,200 (ctrl). available on microfiche; available on microfilm.
Desc: Legislation of parliament and government of Catalonia.

BL
DIARIO DA JUSTICA DO ESTADO DE MATO GROSSO.
Portuguese. da. Imprensa Oficial do Estado - IOMAT, Caixa Postal No 80, Cuiaba Mato Grosso Brazil. **DD** 349.81/72/05; 348.172005.

PO
DIARIO DA REPUBLICA. Main/Corp
Portugal. Portuguese. 16$00. Portugal, rua de d'Francisco Manuel de Melo 5, Lisbon Portugal. **Continues** Diario do Governo.

SF
DIARIO DA REPUBLICA. Main/Corp
Sao Tome and Principe. Portuguese. $330.00. Impr Nacional, Caixa Postal No 28, Sao Tome E Principe. **DD** 349.66/99305; 346.6993005.

GT
DIARIO DE CENTRO AMERICA. Main/Corp
Guatemala. Spanish. 18 Calle 6-72 Zona 1, Guatemala Guatemala. **DD** 340/.097281. **Continues** Guatemalteco.

BL
DIARIO OFICIAL DO MUNICIPIO.
Main/Corp Belem (Brazil). Portuguese. da. Imprensa Oficial do Estado S A Biblioteca, Rua de Mooca 1921, 03103 Sao Paulo Brazil. **LC** KHD9601.3; .A235.

BL
DIARIO OFICIAL, ESTADO DE SAO PAULO: DIARIO DA JUSTICA. Main/Corp
Sao Paulo, Brazil (State). (19??)-. Portuguese. Imprensa Oficial do Estado SA, Biblioteca, Rua da Mooca 1921, 03103 Sao Paulo Brazil. **DD** 340/.09816.

BL
DIARIO OFICIAL, ESTADO DE SAO PAULO : INEDITORIAIS. Main/Corp
Sao Paulo, Brazil (State). Portuguese. Cr$500.00. Rua da Mooca, 1921 CEP 03103-SP Sao Paulo Spain. **DD** 340/.09816.

BL
DIARIO OFICIAL, ESTADO DE SAO PAULO. PODER JUDICIARIO. Main/Corp
Sao Paulo (Brazil : State). Imprensa Oficial do Estado. Portuguese. ir. $5100. Imprensa Oficial do Estado, rua Maria Antonia 294, Sao Paulo Brazil. **DD** 348.81/61046; 348.1610846. **Continues** Diario Oficial, Estado de Sao Paulo. Diario da Justica.

●US/1063-7419
DICKINSON JOURNAL OF ENVIRONMENTAL LAW & POLICY.
(1992)-. Periodical. English. sa. $15.00. Dickinson's Journal of Environmental Law and Policy, 150 South College Street, Carlisle PA 17013. **Continues** Dickinson Journal of Environmental Law & Policy, 1063-7427.

US/0012-2459
DICKINSON LAW REVIEW. Added/Corp
Dickinson School of Law. Vol. 1 (Jan. 1897)-. Periodical. English. Four times a year. $35.00. Dickinson School of Law, 150 South College Street, Carlisle PA 17013. **Tel** (717)243-4611, (717)243-7883, FAX (717)243-4443. **DD** 347.05. Index available. cum. index. **Bk Rev. Ad Acc. Circ**: 1,800 (ctrl).
Desc: Publishing legal articles by outside authors and law school students.
Ind/Abst Bowne Dig. Corp. Sec. Lawyers; Curr. Law Index (1980-); Fed. Tax Artic.; Index Leg. Period.; Leg. Resour. Index (1980-); LegalTrac (1980-).

US
DICTA: A LAWYER'S MAGAZINE.
Periodical. English. mo. San Diego County Bar Association, 1333 7th Avenue, San Diego CA 92101. **Tel** (619)231-0781, FAX (619)338-0042.

US
DICTA : HARVARD LAW SCHOOL MAGAZINE. Added/Corp
Harvard Law School. Vol. 1 (Spring 1982)-. Periodical. English. Harvard Law School, Publications Center, Cambridge MA 02138. **Tel** (617)495-7984, (617)495-3694.

US/0417-4569
DICTA / NEWSLETTER FOR ATTORNEYS OF SAN DIEGO COUNTY.
(1952)-. Newsletter. English. mo. $30.00. San Diego County Bar Association, 1333 7th Avenue, San Diego CA 92101. **Tel** (619)231-0781, FAX (619)338-0042. **DD** 340. **Bk Rev**, (Qty: varies). **Ad Acc, Adv Mgr**: Jana Davis. **Circ**: 6,900.

US/0098-7395
DICTIONARY CATALOG OF THE COLUMBIA UNIVERSITY LAW LIBRARY. SUPPLEMENT. See Library and
Information Sciences.

FR/0998-4313
DICTIONNAIRE PERMANENT DROIT EUROPEEN DES AFFAIRES.
(1989)-. French. mo. 1700.00F. Editions Legislatives et Admin, 80 82 Avenue de la Marne, 92546 Montrouge Cedex France. **Tel** 011 33 1 40926868. **UDC** 341.176(4).

US
DIGEST, HOUSE AND SENATE BILLS AND RESOLUTIONS (SOUTH CAROLINA). Main/Corp
South Carolina. General Assembly. English. Legislative Information Systems, 112 Blatt Building, 1105 Pendleton Street, Columbia SC

Law

29201. **LC** KFS1815; .S68. **DD** 348.757/01; 347.579081. **Continues** South Carolina. General Assembly. Digest of Action on Bills and Resolutions.

US
DIGEST OF ACTS OF THE GENERAL ASSEMBLY OF VIRGINIA. Main/Corp Virginia.
General Assembly. Session 1980-. English. an. Commonwealth of Virginia Division of Legislative Automated Systems, PO Box 654, Richmond VA 23205. **LC** KFV2438; .V56. **DD** 348.755/026; 347.550826. **Continues** Virginia. Division of Legislative Services. Digest of Acts of Assembly.

US/0160-1377
DIGEST OF BILLS ENACTED BY THE GENERAL ASSEMBLY. Main/Corp Colorado.
General Assembly. (19??)-. English. an. Free. Office of Legislative Legal Services, State Capitol Building, Room 091, Denver CO 80203. **Tel** (303)866-2045. **LC** KFC1807; .D53. **DD** 348/.788/026.

US
DIGEST OF BILLS PASSED BY THE ... LEGISLATURE. 12th (Regular Session of 1984)-.
English. an. Legislative Reference Bureau - Hawaii, State Capitol, Honolulu HI 96813. **Tel** (800)587-0690, FAX (808)587-0699. **LC** KFH38; .H32. **Continues** Digest and Index of Laws Enacted, 0095-6619.

US/0090-175X
DIGEST OF CITY LAWS (SEATTLE, WASH.). (DIGEST OF CITY LAWS.). Main/Corp
Municipal Research and Services Center of Washington. English. Municipal Research Coun, 10517 NE 38th Pl, Kirkland WA 98033-7926. **LC** JS303.W2; A8 subser; KFW430. **DD** 352.0797 S; 342/.797/09.

US
DIGEST OF COMMISSION POLICIES AND COURT DECISIONS. WATER AND SEWER. Vol. 1, No. 1 (1970-1980)-. English. $100.00.
James J Konish, PO Box 385, Gainesville FL 32601. **ED** James J Konish. **LC** KFF289.A59; D53. **DD** 343.759/0924; 347.5903924. **Circ:** 50 (ctrl).
Desc: A digest or restatement of Florida utility regulation. Features capsule summaries of pertinent policy with citations to the source.

US/0272-832X
DIGEST OF COUNCIL BILLS - WISCONSIN. LEGISLATIVE COUNCIL.
Main/Corp Wisconsin. Legislative Council. English. Wisconsin Legislative Council, 147 North State Capitol, Madison WI 53702. **LC** KFW2415; .W57. **DD** 348.775/01; 347.75081. **Continues** Digest of Legislative Council Bills in the Legislature.

US/0516-9011
DIGEST OF COURT DECISIONS (NEW YORK, N.Y.). (DIGEST OF COURT DECISIONS.).
[Dig. court decis.]. Began with Mar. 15, 1973 issue. Periodical. English. qt. American Arbitration Association, 140 West 51st Street, New York NY 10020. **Tel** (212)484-4011, (212)484-4014, FAX (212)765-4874, telex 12463. **LC** KF9085.A59; D53. **DD** 346.73/07/0269; 347.30670269. **Continues in part** Arbitration Law, 0518-2611.

KE
DIGEST OF DECISIONS OF THE COURT.
Main/Corp Kenya. Court of Appeal. (Nov./Dec. 1977)-. Periodical. English. mo. Court of Appeal, Box 30187, Nairobi Kenya. **DD** 348.676/2046; 346.7620846. **Continues** Court of Appeal for East Africa. Digest of Decisions of the Court.

US/0160-0915
DIGEST OF ENACTMENTS, GENERAL ASSEMBLY. Main/Corp Ohio. Legislative Service
Commission. English. Ohio Legislative Service Commission, PO Box 301, Columbus OH 43216. **LC** KFO15; .L42. **DD** 348/.771/026.

US
DIGEST OF ENVIRONMENTAL LAW. Vol. 4, No. 12, (1991)-. Periodical. English. mo. $260.00.
Strafford Publications Inc., 590 Dutch Valley Road Northeast, Atlanta GA 30324. **Tel** (404)881-1141, (800)926-7926, FAX (404)881-0074. **LC** KF3775.A15; D53. **Continues** Digest of Environmental Law of Real Property.

US
DIGEST OF GENERAL LAWS ENACTED BY THE REGULAR SESSION AND SPECIAL SESSION OF THE FLORIDA LEGISLATURE. Main/Corp Florida. Legislature.
Joint Legislative Management Committee. Statutory Revision Division. 1978-. English. an. Statutory Revision Division, Room 726/The Capitol, Tallahassee FL 32304. **LC** KFF38; .L4. **DD** 348.759/026. **Continues** Digest of General Laws Enacted by the Regular Session of the Florida Legislature, 0364-8249.

KU
DIGEST OF KUWAIT OFFICIAL GAZETTE. Main/Corp Cultural & Publishing Bureau.
English. wk. Cultural & Publishing Bureau, PO Box 24582, Kuwait Kuwait. **DD** 348.53/67024; 345.3670824.

US/0093-4062
DIGEST OF MOTOR LAWS. Main/Corp
American Automobile Association. **Added/Corp** American Automobile Association. Traffic Safety Dept. American Automobile Association. Dept. of Public Relations. American Automobile Association. Legal Dept. (19??)-. English. an (Mar.). $10.20. American Automobile Association, 1000 AAA Drive, Heathrow FL 32746. **Tel** (407)444-7000. **LC** KF2210.Z95; A39. **DD** 343/.73/0944.

CN/1181-9006
DIGEST OF MUNICIPAL & PLANNING LAW, THE. [Dig. munic. plan. law]. Added/Corp
Carswell Company. **VFOAT** Digest of Municipal and Planning Law. Vol. 1, Issue 1 (Oct. 10, 1990)-. Periodical. English. mo. Carswell / Canada, 2075 Kennedy Road, Scarborough Ontario M1T 3V4 Canada. **Tel** (416)609-3800, (800)387-5164. **DD** 342.71/09.

US/0095-1161
DIGEST OF OREGON LAWS. (DIGEST OF OREGON LAWS, WITH TABLES.). Main/Corp Oregon.
Legislative Assembly. Legislative Counsel Committee. English. be. Oregon Legislative Assembly, Legislative Counsel Committee, S420 State Capital, Salem OR 97310. **LC** KFO2438; .L4. **DD** 348/.795/026.

US/0276-0150
DIGEST OF RICO INVESTIGATIONS.
(DIGEST OF RICO INVESTIGATIONS / U.S. DEPARTMENT OF JUSTICE, FEDERAL BUREAU OF INVESTIGATION.). **Added/Corp** United States. Federal Bureau of Investigation. **VAT** Digest of Racketeer Influenced and Corrupt Organizations Statute Investigations. (19??)-. English. Federal Bureau of Investigation, 10th Street and Pennsylvania Avenue NW, Washington DC 20535. **Tel** (202)324-3000, FAX (202)324-4705. **LC** KF9375.A59; D53. **DD** 345.73/05; 347.3055.

PE
DIRECTORIO DEL ABOGADO. Added/Corp
Colegio de Abogados de Lima. (1976)-. Spanish. an. Libreria Atlantida Oscar Cuenca J Martinez, Av Colmena 287, Lima Peru.

US/1046-0349
DIRECTORY / AMERICAN BAR ASSOCIATION. [Dir. - Am. Bar Assoc.]. Main/Corp
American Bar Association. **VFOAT** American Bar Association Directory. (19??)-. English. an (Oct.). Free on request. American Bar Association, 750 North Lake Shore Drive, Chicago IL 60611. **Tel** (312)988-5522, (312)988-5241, FAX (312)988-5528, telex 270593. **LC** KF190; .A54. **DD** 340. Index available. **Circ:** 12,000 (ctrl).
Desc: Lists the personnel making up the leadership of the American Bar Association. About 5,500 names are included, with addresses, telephone numbers, and electronic mailbox IDs.

US/0190-4787
DIRECTORY AND GUIDE - BUILDING CONSTRUCTION EMPLOYERS' ASSOCIATION OF CHICAGO, INC.
Main/Corp Building Construction Employers' Association of Chicago. **VFOAT** BCEA Directory. Directory. English. Building Construction Employers Association of Chicago, 228 North Lasalle Street, Chicago IL 60601. **LC** KFX1238.1.C64; B85. **DD** 344/.77311/018819.

US
DIRECTORY & HANDBOOK / STATE BAR OF GEORGIA. Main/Corp State Bar of
Georgia. **VFOAT** Directory and Handbook. (19??)-. Directory. English. State Bar of Georgia, 800 Hurt Building, 50 Hurt Plaza, Atlanta GA 30303. **Tel** (404)527-8700. **Formed by the union of** State Bar of Georgia. Directory - State Bar of Georgia, 1067-4861 **and** State Bar of Georgia. Handbook - State Bar of Georgia, 1067-4853.

CN/0821-4638
DIRECTORY / CANADIAN ASSOCIATION OF LAW LIBRARIES. See
Library and Information Sciences.

US/0093-1780
DIRECTORY - FEDERAL COMMUNICATIONS BAR ASSOCIATION. (DIRECTORY.). Main/Corp
Federal Communications Bar Association. **VFOAT** FCBA Directory. (19??)-. Directory. English. an. $1.00. Federal Communications Bar Association, 1815 H Street NW, Washington DC 20006. **LC** KF190; .F43. **DD** 343/.73/099402573.

US/0731-8766
DIRECTORY / FORUM COMMITTEE ON COMMUNICATIONS LAW. Main/Corp
American Bar Association. Forum Committee on Communications Law. (1981)-. English. American Bar Association, 750 North Lake Shore Drive, Chicago IL 60611. **Tel** (312)988-5522, (312)988-5241, FAX (312)988-5528, telex 270593. **LC** KF195.C573; A38. **DD** 343.73/099/025; 347.30399025.

US/0271-0196
DIRECTORY - FORUM COMMITTEE ON HEALTH LAW, AMERICAN BAR ASSOCIATION. Main/Corp American Bar
Association. Forum Committee on Health Law. (19??)-. English. American Bar Association, 750 North Lake Shore Drive, Chicago IL 60611. **Tel** (312)988-5522, (312)988-5241, FAX (312)988-5528, telex 270593. **LC** KF195.M43; A53. **DD** 340/.025/73.

US/0273-5180
DIRECTORY - FORUM COMMITTEE ON THE CONSTRUCTION INDUSTRY, AMERICAN BAR ASSOCIATION.
Main/Corp American Bar Association. Forum Committee on the Construction Industry. (19??)-. English. American Bar Association, 750 North Lake Shore Drive, Chicago IL 60611. **Tel** (312)988-5522, (312)988-5241, FAX (312)988-5528, telex 270593. **LC** KF195.C58; A43. **DD** 343.73/07869/0025; 347.30378690025.

US/0273-5172
DIRECTORY - FORUM COMMITTEE ON THE ENTERTAINMENT AND SPORTS INDUSTRIES. Main/Corp American Bar
Association. Forum Committee on the Entertainment and Sports Industries. **VFOAT** Forum on the Entertainment and Sports Industries Directory. (19??)-. English. American Bar Association, 750 North Lake Shore Drive, Chicago IL 60611. **Tel** (312)988-5522, (312)988-5241, FAX (312)988-5528, telex 270593. **LC** KF195.E58; A54. **DD** 340/.025/73.

GW/0376-8430
DIRECTORY - INTERNATIONAL ASSOCIATION OF LAW LIBRARIES.
Main/Corp International Association of Law Libraries. Directory. English. $5.00. International Association of Law Libraries, D 35 Marburg Universitatsstr, W-6200 Marburg Germany. **LC** Z675.L2; I56B. **DD** 026/.34/0025.

●US
DIRECTORY / NATIONAL ASIAN PACIFIC AMERICAN BAR ASSOCIATION. Main/Corp National Asian Pacific
American Bar Association. **VFOAT** NAPABA Directory. 1st Ed. (1992)-. Directory. English. Bernard C. Harris Publishing Company, 3 Barker Avenue, White Plains NY 10601. **Tel** (914)946-7500. **LC** WMLC 91/5120.

CN/0703-6426
DIRECTORY, OCCUPATIONAL SAFETY AND HEALTH LEGISLATION IN CANADA. [Dir., Occup. saf. health legis. Can.].
Added/Corp Canada. Labour Canada. Legislative Analysis. **VFOAT** Repertoire, Securite et Hygiene au Travail, Legislation au Canada. Vol. 1 (1977)-. English (French). an. price varies per volume. Labour Canada / Labour Standards National Headquarters, Ottawa Ontario K1A OJ2 Canada. **Tel** (819)997-3920. **LC** KE3365.A377; D57. **DD** 344.71/0465/02638; 347.10446502638. available on CD-ROM.

US/1055-8519
DIRECTORY OF AMERICAN INDIAN LAW ATTORNEYS. [Dir. Am. Indian law atty.].
(1991)-. Directory. English. $55.00. Native World Research & Publishing, 1620 Budd Court, Longmont CO 80501. **DD** 342.

US/0273-494X
DIRECTORY OF BAR ACTIVITIES.
Main/Corp American Bar Association. Division of Bar Services. (19??)-. English. American Bar Association, 750 North Lake Shore Drive, Chicago IL 60611. **Tel** (312)988-5522, (312)988-5241, FAX (312)988-5528, telex 270593. **LC** KF330.A15; A45. **DD** 340.060/073.

US/8756-1565
DIRECTORY OF BAR ASSOCIATIONS.
[Dir. bar assoc.]. **Added/Corp** American Bar Association. Division of Bar Services. (19??)-. English. an. American Bar Association, 750 North Lake Shore Drive, Chicago IL 60611. **Tel** (312)988-5522, (312)988-5241, FAX (312)988-5528, telex 270593. **LC** KF330.A15; D57. **DD** 340/.06/073.
Desc: A directory of state and local bar associations with over 300 members, including the president-elect and executive directors along with their addresses and phone numbers.

CN/0228-3395
DIRECTORY OF CANADIAN GRADUATE PROGRAMMES IN LAW. (DIRECTORY OF CANADIAN GRADUATE PROGRAMMES IN LAW / CANADIAN ASSOCIATION OF LAW TEACHERS.). [Dir. Can. grad. program. law]. **VFOAT** Annuaire des Programmes Canadiens d'Etudes Superieures en Droit. Began with 1st Ed., published in 1980. Directory. English (French). be. $7.00 per no. Osgoode Hall Law Journal, 4700 Keele Street, York University, Downsview Ontario M3J 2R5 Canada. **Tel** (416)736-5354. **LC** KE280; .D57. **DD** 340/.07/1171.

●US/1056-8735
DIRECTORY OF CONSTRUCTION LAW FIRMS, THE. (1991)-. Directory. English. HLK Global Communications, Inc., 8133 Leesburg Pike, Suite 700, Vienna VA 22182. ***Continues** CEMC/ENR Directory of Law Firms, 1045-6805.*

●US/1064-0355
DIRECTORY OF INTELLECTUAL PROPERTY ATTORNEYS. (DIRECTORY OF INTELLECTUAL PROPERTY ATTORNEYS / LAW & BUSINESS.). [Dir. intellect. prop. atty.]. **Added/Corp** Prentice Hall Law & Business (Firm). **VFOAT** Law & Business Directory of Intellectual Property Attorneys. (1993)-. Directory. English. an. $195.00. Prentice-Hall Law and Business, 270 Sylvan Avenue, Englewood Cliffs NJ 07632. **Tel** (800)223-0231, (201)894-8538, FAX (201)894-8666. **LC** KF3165.A3; D557. **DD** 346.7304/8/025; 347.30648025. ***Continues** Directory of Intellectual Property Lawyers and Patent Agents.*

US
DIRECTORY OF LAW LIBRARIES. See Library and Information Sciences.

CN/0383-8358
DIRECTORY OF LAW TEACHERS (MONTREAL). (DIRECTORY OF LAW TEACHERS. ANNUAIRE DES PROFESSEURS DE DROIT.). **Added/Corp** Association of Canadian Law Teachers. Canadian Association of Law Teachers. **VFOAT** Annuaire des Professeurs de Droit. (1971/72)-. English (French). an. 35.00Can$. Carswell / Canada, 2075 Kennedy Road, Scarborough Ontario M1T 3V4 Canada. **Tel** (416)609-3800, (800)387-5164. **LC** KE280.D575. **DD** 349.71/071/1; 347.1009711. ***Supersedes** Association of Canadian Law Teachers. Teachers' Directory., 0571-6187.*
Desc: Contains biographical information on most full time law teachers in Canada and some former teachers, as well as biographies of Associate members.

US/1045-3342
DIRECTORY OF LAWYER REFERRAL SERVICES (1976). (DIRECTORY OF LAWYER REFERRAL SERVICES.). **Added/Corp** American Bar Association. Standing Committee on Lawyer Referral Service. American Bar Association. Standing Committee on Lawyer Referral and Information Service. (Jan. 1976)-. Directory. English. an. $7.00. American Bar Association, 750 North Lake Shore Drive, Chicago IL 60611. **Tel** (312)988-5522, (312)988-5241, FAX (312)988-5528, telex 270593. **DD** 338. ***Continues** Directory of Lawyer Referral Services and Committees and Legal Aid and Defender Offices.*

US/0882-5033
DIRECTORY OF LEGAL EMPLOYERS (1985). (DIRECTORY OF LEGAL EMPLOYERS.). [Dir. leg. empl.]. **Added/Corp** National Association for Law Placement (U.S.). **VFOAT** NALP Directory of Employers. 6th Ed. (1985)-. Directory. English. an. Free to members: $120.00 (non-members). National Association for Law Placement, 1666 Connecticut Avenue, Suite 450, Washington DC 20009. **Tel** (202)667-1666, FAX (202)265-6735. **DD** 340. ***Continues** Directory of Employers.*

AT
DIRECTORY OF MEMBERS. Main/Corp Australasian Universities Law Schools Association. (19??)-. English. The Law Book Company Limited, 44-50 Waterloo Road, North Ryde New South Wales, 2113 Australia. **Tel** 011 61 2 8870177, FAX 011 61 2 8887240, telex ASBOOK 27445. **DD** 340/.07/1194.

US/0099-1643
DIRECTORY OF MEMBERS - STATE BAR OF ARIZONA. Main/Corp State Bar of Arizona. Directory. English. State Bar of Arizona, 363 North First Avenue, Phoenix AZ 85004. **Tel** (602)252-4804, FAX (602)271-4930. **LC** KF192.A73; S7. **DD** 340/.025/791.

US/0147-1325
DIRECTORY OF OFFICERS, COUNCIL, AND COMMITTEES. Main/Corp American Bar Association. Section of Real Property, Probate and Trust Law. (19??)-. English. an. American Bar Association, 750 North Lake Shore Drive, Chicago IL 60611. **Tel** (312)988-5522, (312)988-5241, FAX (312)988-5528, telex 270593. **LC** KF195.P75; A46. **DD** 346/.73/043062. ***Continues** American Bar Association. Section of Real Property, Probate, and Trust Law. Membership Directory, Officers and Committees.*

US/0092-9174
DIRECTORY OF SAN FRANCISCO ATTORNEYS. Added/Corp Bar Association of San Francisco. (19??)-. English. $35.00. Bar Association of San Francisco, 685 Market Street, Suite 700, San Francisco CA 94105. **Tel** (415)764-1600. **LC** KF193.S25; D57. **DD** 340/.025/79461. **Ad Acc. Circ:** 7,500.
Desc: The directory includes the addresses and telephone numbers for over 11,000 attorneys as well as those of all ASF law firm, Bay area courts, and legal associations in San Francisco.

●US/1062-0133
DIRECTORY OF STATE BAR PUBLIC SERVICE ACTIVITIES AND PROGRAMS. See Public Administration.

US/8756-1611
DIRECTORY OF THE NEW MEXICO BENCH AND BAR. Directory. English. an. $42.10 (per copy, non-members); $15.79 (per copy, non-profit organizations). State Bar of New Mexico, 1117 Stanford NE, PO Box 25883, Albuquerque NM 87125. **Tel** (505)842-6132. **ED** Cheryl Bruce. **LC** KF192.N43; S7. **DD** 340/.025789. Index available. cum. index. **Ad Acc. Circ:** 3,826 (ctrl). ***Continues** State Bar of New Mexico. Attorney Directory.*
Desc: Listing of New Mexico attorneys, judiciary, Bar committees and sections, governmental agencies, and other miscellaneous information listings.

US/0363-4930
DIRECTORY OF THE OFFICERS, BOARD OF MANAGERS, COMMITTEES AND SECTIONS AFFILIATED AND COOPERATING ORGANIZATIONS. Main/Corp Indiana State Bar Association (1916-). (19??)-. Directory. English. an. Indiana State Bar Association, 230 East Ohio Street, Indianapolis IN 46204. **LC** KF192.I5; I58. **DD** 340/06/2772.

US
DIRECTORY OF UNITED STATES PROBATION AND PRETRIAL SERVICES OFFICERS. Added/Corp United States. Administrative Office of the United States Courts. Probation Division. Directory. English. Probation Division, Administrative Office of the United States Courts, Washington DC 20544. **LC** HV9304; .D57. **DD** 364.6/3/02573. ***Continues** Directory of United States Probation Officers.*

US/0732-9857
DIRECTORY / SECTION OF TORT AND INSURANCE PRACTICE. [Dir. - Am. Bar Assoc., Sect. Tort Insur. Pract.]. **Main/Corp** American Bar Association. Tort and Insurance Practice Section. **VFOAT** Section of Tort and Insurance Practice Directory. (19??)-. English. American Bar Association, 750 North Lake Shore Drive, Chicago IL 60611. **Tel** (312)988-5522, (312)988-5241, FAX (312)988-5528, telex 270593. **LC** KF195.I5; A47. **DD** 340/.025/73.
Desc: Lists, officers, council, committees, and section members.

US/1067-4861
DIRECTORY - STATE BAR OF GEORGIA. *Title Change.* Main/Corp State Bar of Georgia. (1980)-(19??). Directory. English. an. State Bar of Georgia, 800 Hurt Building, 50 Hurt Plaza, Atlanta GA 30303. **Tel** (404)527-8700. **LC** KF192.G46; S85. **DD** 349.758/025. **Ad Acc. Circ:** 20,500 (ctrl). ***Supersedes in part** State Bar of Georgia. Handbook and Directory, 1067-4810. **Merged with** State Bar of Georgia. Handbook - State Bar of Georgia, 1067-4853 **to form** State Bar of Georgia. Directory & Handbook.*
Desc: Lists the names, addresses and telephone numbers of the members of the State Bar of Georgia. Also lists committees and related organizations.

US/0731-6496
DIRECTORY / THE YOUNG LAWYERS DIVISION OF THE AMERICAN BAR ASSOCIATION. Main/Corp American Bar Association. Young Lawyers Division. (1982)-. English. an. American Bar Association, 750 North Lake Shore Drive, Chicago IL 60611. **Tel** (312)988-5522, (312)988-5241, FAX (312)988-5528, telex 270593. **LC** KF325.26; .A4. **DD** 340/.06/073. ***Continues** American Bar Association. Young Lawyers Section. Directory.*

BL
DIREITO E AVESSO : BOLETIM DA NOVA ESCOLA JURIDICA BRASILEIRA. Added/Corp Nova Escola Juridica Brasileira. Vol. 1, No. 1, (Jan./June 1982)-. Bulletin. Portuguese. sa. Edicoes Nair Ltda, Caixa Postal 13-1957, CEP 70.259 Brasilia DF Brazil. **LC** K4; .I6917. **DD** 340/.05.

BL
DIREITO TRIBUTARIO. Portuguese. J Bushatsky, rua Riachuelo 195, Sao Paulo Brazil. **LC** K4; .I693.

IT/0012-3390
DIRITTO AEREO. *Suspended.* (1962)-Suspended (1991). Periodical. Italian. qt. L50000. Aldalberto Tempesta, Via Prisciano 8/4, Rome 00136 Italy. **Tel** (06)3450955. **Bk Rev. Ad Acc. Circ:** 500.
Desc: Devoted to air and space law and multimodal transport.

IT
DIRITTO AMMINISTRATIVO : RIVISTA TRIMESTRALE. (1993)-. Italian. qt. L70000 Italy; L105000 other. Giuffre Editore SPA, Via Busto Arsizio 40, 20151 Milan Italy. **Tel** 011 398 2 38089200. **ED** Leopoldo Mazzarolli, Umberto Pototschnig and Alberto Romano.
Desc: Strives to be a tool for wider and more frequent study of the basic problems linked to administrative law.

IT
DIRITTO & PRACTICA DEL LAVORO ORO. (19??)-. Periodical. Italian. L130000.00 Italy; L260000.00 other. IPSOA Editore SRL, Casella Postale 12055, Mastrangelo, 20120 Milan Italy. **Tel** 011 39 2 82476248.

IT/0391-6111
DIRITTO COMUNITARIO E DEGLI SCAMBI INTERNAZIONALI. [Diritto comunitario scambi int.]. Vol 14 (Jan./March 1975)-. Periodical. Multiple languages (French and Italian). 17.000. Edizioni Zara, Via Portillia 6, 43100 Parma Italy. **Tel** 011 39 521 45945. ***Continues** Diritto Negli Scambi Internazionali.*
Ind/Abst Index Foreign Leg. Per.

IT
DIRITTO DEGLI ITALIANI, IL. (1978)-. Periodical. Italian. Giuffre Editore SPA, Via Busto Arsizio 40, 20151 Milan Italy. **Tel** 011 398 2 38089200. **DD** 349.45/05.

IT
DIRITTO DEL COMMERCIO INTERNAZIONALE. VFOAT Giurisprudenza Commerciale; Pratica Internazionale e Diritto Interno. Vol. 1 (1987)-. Periodical. Italian. sa. L110000.00 Italy; L165000.00 other. Giuffre Editore SPA, Via Busto Arsizio 40, 20151 Milan Italy. **Tel** 011 398 2 38089200. **ED** Piero Bernardini, Michael Bonell, Franco Bonelli, Sergio Carbone, Antonio Crivellaro, Ugo Draetta, Andrea Giardina, Riccardo Luzzatto and Alberto Santa Mario.
Desc: All subjects which concern international trade are treated.

IT
DIRITTO DELLA REGIONE, IL. (19??)-. Periodical. Italian. bm (6 issues). L90000.00 Italy; L120000.00 other. Coord. Dipartimento per la Funzione Controllo, Rag Pellegrino v Longhena 6, 30175 Marghera-Mestre Italy. **Tel** 011 39 41 5495229, FAX 011 39 41 5495931. **(Subscription address:** Comp Editorial Veneta s.r.l., via CA Marcello 16, 30172 Mestre-Venezia Italy.**)**

IT
DIRITTO DELLE RADIODIFFUSIONI E DELLE TELECOMUNICAZIONI, IL. Added/Corp RAI--Radiotelevisione Italiana. (1969)-. Periodical. Italian. Three times a year. L70000 Italy; L95000 other. Nuova Eri Edizioni RAI, Via Arsenale 41, 10121 Turin Italy. **Tel** 011 39 11 8102238. Index available. **Bk Rev. Ad Acc. Circ:** 3,000 (ctrl).
Desc: All aspects of law concerning the distribution of radio and telecommunications in Italy and the world.

IT
DIRITTO DELL'ECONOMIA, IL. Added/Corp Unione Italiana delle Camere di Commercio, Industria, Artigianato e Agricoltura. (19??)-. Periodical. Italian. Four times a year. L100000.00 Italy; L150000.00 other. Giuffre Editore SPA, Via Busto Arsizio 40, 20151 Milan Italy. **Tel** 011 398 2 38089200. Index available. **Bk Rev. Ad Acc. Circ:** 1,500.
Desc: The chief aim of this journal is to make its contribution towards greater clarity in the increasingly interwoven and complex relationship between law and economy.

IT
DIRITTO DELL'IMPRESA. (1982)-. Periodical. Italian. tq. L75000 (institutions), L70000 (individuals) Italy; L110000 other. Edizioni Scientifiche Italiane, Via Chiatamone 7, 80121 Naples Italy. **Tel** 011 39 81 7645768, 011 39 81 7645443, FAX 011 39 81 7646477. **LC** K4; .I696. **DD** 343/.08; 342.38.

IT
DIRITTO DELL'INFORMAZIONE E DELL'INFORMATICA / RIVISTA QUADRIMESTRALE PROMOSSA DAL CENTRO DI INIZIATIVA GIURIDICA PIERO CALAMANDREI, IL. Added/Corp Centro di Iniziativa Giuridica Piero Calamandrei. Vol. 1,

Law

IT
No. 1 (Jan/April 1985)-. Periodical. Italian. Three times a year. L120000.00 Italy; L180000.00 other. Giuffre Editore SPA, Via Busto Arsizio 40, 20151 Milan Italy. **Tel** 011 398 2 38089200. **ED** Guido Alpa, Mario Bessone, Luca Boneschi, Corrado De Martini, Pietro Rescigno and Vincenzo Zeno-Zencovich.
Desc: Publishes articles, research studies, case law, collections of maxims, laws and bibliography, as well as reviews on media and informatics.
Ind/Abst Index Foreign Leg. Per.

IT
DIRITTO E GIURISPRUDENZA. (1???)-. Periodical. Italian. Four times a year. L90000 Italy; L100000.00 other. Casa Editrice Jovene, 109 Via Mezzocannone, 80134 Naples Italy. **Tel** 011 39 81 552-1274. **Continues** Dritto e Giurisprudenza.
Ind/Abst Index Foreign Leg. Per.

IT
DIRITTO E PRATICA NELL ASSICURAZIONE. **Title Change.** (1???)-(1993). Italian. qt. Giuffre Editore SPA, Via Busto Arsizio 40, 20151 Milan Italy. **Tel** 011 398 2 38089200. **ED** E. Pasanisi. Index available. **Ad Acc. Circ:** 3,700.
Continued by Diritto ed Economica dell Assicurazione.
Desc: The purpose of this periodical is to keep all those engaged in insurance fully informed about the most important juridical, technical and practical problems relating to insurance.

IT/0012-3447
DIRITTO E PRATICA TRIBUTARIA. [Dir. prat. tribut.]. Periodical. Italian. bm. L600000.00. Cedam Spa, Via Jappelli 5 6, 35121 Padua Italy. **Tel** 011 39 49 65667. **UDC** 34.

IT
DIRITTO E SOCIETA. Yearly Vol. 1 (1973)-. Periodical. Italian. qt. L150000 Italy; L210000 other. Cedam Spa, Via Jappelli 5 6, 35121 Padua Italy. **Tel** 011 39 49 65667. **LC** K4; .I697. **DD** 340/.115/05.

IT
DIRITTO E TECNICA DELLA CIRCOLAZIONE STRADALE E ASSICURAZIONE OBBLIGATORIA DI RCA. (19??)-. Periodical. Italian. L600000 Italy; L800000 Other. Cedam Spa, Via Jappelli 5 6, 35121 Padua Italy. **Tel** 011 39 49 65667.

IT
DIRITTO ECCLESIASTICO, IL. (19??)-. Italian. Four times a year. L130000.00 Italy; L195000.00 other. Giuffre Editore SPA, Via Busto Arsizio 40, 20151 Milan Italy. **Tel** 011 398 2 38089200. **ED** Sergio Bianconi.
Continues Diritto Ecclesiastico e Rassegna di Diritto Matrimoniale.
Desc: Covers the relations between church and state, with developments in legislation, doctrine, and civil and canon law.

IT/0012-3455
DIRITTO ECCLESIASTICO E RASSEGNA DI DIRITTO MATRIMONIALE, IL. **Title Change.** Vol. 82 (Jan./Mar. 1971)-(19??). Periodical. Italian. qt. Giuffre Editore SPA, Via Busto Arsizio 40, 20151 Milan Italy. **Tel** 011 398 2 38089200. **ED** Sergio Bianconi. Index available. **Bk Rev. Ad Acc. Circ:** 700. **Continues** Diritto Ecclesiastico. **Continued by** Diritto Ecclesiastico.
Desc: Publishes studies on relations between the state and the Catholic Church, with verdicts on matrimonial questions.
Ind/Abst Bibliogr. Mission.

IT/0394-8366
DIRITTO ED ECONOMIA. See Economics.

●IT
DIRITTO ED ECONOMIA DELL'ASSICURAZIONE. (1992)-. Italian. qt. L120000.00 Italy; L180000.00 other. Giuffre Editore SPA, Via Busto Arsizio 40, 20151 Milan Italy. **Tel** 011 398 2 38089200. **ED** Aurelio Candian and Sergio Paci.
Continues Diritto e Practica nell'Assicurazione.
Desc: Provides legal and economic information for those dealing with insurance problems.

IT/0391-5239
DIRITTO FALLIMENTARE E DELLE SOCIETA COMMERCIALI. [Diritto falliment. soc. commer.]. (1926)-. Periodical. Italian. bm. L220000 Itlay; L270000 other. Cedam Spa, Via Jappelli 5 6, 35121 Padua Italy. **Tel** 011 39 49 65667. **UDC** 34. Index available. **Pr Rev. Circ:** 2,500 (ctrl). **Continues** Diritto Fallimentare.

IT/0393-1315
DIRITTO PROCESSUALE AMMINISTRATIVO. [Diritto process. amm.]. Vol. 1, No. 1 (March 1983)-. Periodical. Italian. qt. L90000.00 Italy; L135000.00 other. Giuffre Editore SPA, Via Busto Arsizio 40, 20151 Milan Italy. **Tel** 011 398 2 38089200. **ED** Riccardo Villata.
Desc: Devoted to court proceedings in administrative cases and to related problems which, though dealt with to some extent by recent reforms, still contain much which is obscure and uncertain.

IT
DISINFESTAZIONE. (19??)-. Italian. bm (6 issues). L80000 Italy; L100000 Europe; L120000 other. MO ED CO SRL, Via Paolo DA Cannobio 9, 20122 Milan Italy. **Tel** 011 39 2 878724, 011 39 2 878577.

US
DISPUTE RESOLUTION FORUM. **Title Change. Added/Corp** National Institute for Dispute Resolution (U.S.). **VFOAT** DR Forum. (Dec. 1983)-(19??). Periodical. English. Five times a year. Dispute Resolution Forum, National Institute for Dispute Resolution, 1901 1st Street NW/Suite 200, Washington DC 20036. **Tel** (202)466-4764. **ED** William Drake, Robert Jones. **Bk Rev. Circ:** 6,500. **Continued by** Forum (Washington, D.C. : 1990), 1056-6937.
Desc: Serves as a medium for discussion and debate of the principle questions in the field of dispute resolution, with each edition focusing on a single subject.

●US/1074-8105
DISPUTE RESOLUTION JOURNAL. (DISPUTE RESOLUTION JOURNAL : OF THE AMERICAN ARBITRATION ASSOCIATION.). [Dispute resolut. j.]. **Added/Corp** American Arbitration Association. **VFOAT** Dispute Resolution Journal of the American Arbitration Association. Vol. 48, No. 4 (Dec. 1993)-. Periodical. English. qt. $55.00 US; $58.00 Canada & Pan America; $60.00 other. American Arbitration Association, 140 West 51st Street, New York NY 10020. **Tel** (212)484-4011, (212)484-4014, FAX (212)765-4874, telex 12463. **LC** K1; .R25. **DD** 380.12605. Documents available from UMI Article Clearinghouse. **Continues** Arbitration Journal, 0003-7893.
Ind/Abst ABI Inform Ondisc; Acad. Search (Dec. 1993-); Bus. Period. Index; Contents Curr. Leg. Period.; Index Leg. Period.; Int. Labour Doc.; Leg. Resour. Index; Manage. Contents; Soc. Sci. Cit. Index; Trade Ind. Index.

US/0741-3793
DISPUTE RESOLUTION PAPERS SERIES. **Added/Corp** American Bar Association. Special Committtee on Dispute Resolution. **VFOAT** Dispute Resolution Papers. (1982)-. Monographic series. English. ir. Price varies per volume. American Bar Association, 750 North Lake Shore Drive, Chicago IL 60611. **Tel** (312)988-5522, (312)988-5241, FAX (312)988-5528, telex 270593. **LC** UNC.

US/0731-4833
DISPUTE RESOLUTION PROGRAM DIRECTORY. **VFOAT** Dispute Resolution Directory. 1981-. Directory. English. $18.00. Special Committee on Dispute Resolution, American Bar Association, 1800 M Street NW/Suite 200, Washington DC 20036. **Tel** (202)331-2258. **ED** Larry Ray. **LC** KF9084.A15; D58. **DD** 347.73/9; 347.3079. **Circ:** 3,000.
Desc: A listing of dispute resolution programs with focus on median and on a list of resources.

US/0741-8442
DISPUTE RESOLUTION RESOURCE DIRECTORY. Jan. 1984-. Directory. English. an. $5.00. National Institute for Dispute Resolution, 1901 L Street NW/Suite 600, Washington DC 20036. **Tel** (202)466-4764. **ED** Robert Jones. **LC** KF9084.A15; D59. **DD** 347.73/9; 347.3079. **Circ:** 2,000.

US
DISPUTED PATERNITY PROCEEDINGS. Proceedings. English. ir. Matthew Bender & Company Inc., 1275 Broadway, Albany NY 12204. **Tel** (800)833-9844, (518)487-3000.

US/0748-1179
DISTRICT COUNCIL JOURNAL. See Public Administration.

US
DISTRICT COURT AND BMC ADVANCE SHEETS. (19??)-. Periodical. English. mo. $73.50. Lawyers Weekly Publications, 41 West Street, Boston MA 02111. **Tel** (617)451-7300, (800)444-5297.

NZ/0111-4239
DISTRICT COURT REPORTS. [Dist. court rep.]. **Added/Corp** New Zealand. District Court. (1988)-. English. ir. Price varies. Butterworth Ltd. / New Zealand, 33 35 Cumberland Place, Wellington New Zealand. **(Subscription address:** Butterworth Heinemann Publishers, 225 Wildwood Avenue, Unit B, Woburn MA 01801.**)** **LC** PAR. **[CCC]**. **Continues** New Zealand District Court Reports.

US
DISTRICT OF COLUMBIA CASE NAMES CITATOR. English. $70.00 (bound volume), $58.00 (cumulative supplements). Shepards McGraw-Hill Inc, 555 Middle Creek Parkway, PO Box 35300, Colorado Springs CO 80935-3530. **Tel** (719)488-3000, FAX (800)525-0053.

US
DISTRICT OF COLUMBIA CODE ENCYCLOPEDIA. English. West Publishing Company, 610 Opperman Drive, PO Box 64526, Eagan MN 55123-1308. **Tel** (612)687-5618, (800)328-9352, FAX (612)687-5388, (800)562-2329. **(Subscription telephone:** FAX (612)688-3570**)** **DD** 345/.22.

●US/1063-8601
DISTRICT OF COLUMBIA LAW REVIEW. [D.C. law rev.]. Vol. 1, No. 1 (Spring 1992)-. Periodical. English. sa. $20.00. DC School of Law, 719 13th Street NW, Law Review Office, Washington DC 20005. **DD** 340.

CU
DIVULGACION LEGISLATIVA. Spanish. qt. Ediciones Cubanas, Obispo 527, Altos ESQ Bernaza, CP 10100 Havana Cuba. **Tel** 011 632980, 631942, FAX 011 631011, telex 512337, 6540.

IT
DIZIONARIO GIURIDICO. (19??)-. Periodical. English (Italian). ir. Giuffre Editore SPA, Via Busto Arsizio 40, 20151 Milan Italy. **Tel** 011 398 2 38089200.

DK
DJF BLADET. **VFOAT** D.J.F. Bladet; D.J.F.-Bladet; DJF-Bladet. Jan. 8, 1982-. Periodical. Danish (English). bw. 300.00, free to members. Jurist Okonomforbundets Forlag, Gothersgade 133, 1123 Copenhagen Denmark. **Tel** 011 45 1 33142920. **LC** K4; .J63.

US/0895-1659
DOCKET, THE. [Docket]. **Added/Corp** National Association of Legal Secretaries (International). **VFOAT** NALS Docket. Periodical. English. bm. $20.00 US; $26.00 Canada (one year); $40.00 US; $52.00 Canada (two year). National Association of Legal Secretaries, 2250 East 73rd Street/ Suite 550, Tulsa OK 74136. **Tel** (918)493-3540. **LC** KF319; .D63. **DD** 349.73/05; 347.3005. **Continues** Nals Docket.

US/0078-317X
DOCKET SERIES. (1955)-. Monographic series. English. ir. Price varies per volume. Oceana Publications, Inc., 75 Main Street, Dobbs Ferry NY 10522. **Tel** (914)693-1320, FAX (914)693-0402.

US
DOCKET SHEET / SUPREME COURT OF THE UNITED STATES, THE. Main/Corp United States. Supreme Court. (Dec. 1959)-. Periodical. English. qt. Supreme Court of the United States, Washington DC 20543. available on microfiche (Vols. for 1985- distributed to depository libraries).

US/0739-3210
DOCKET (ST. PAUL, MINN.). (THE DOCKET : THE NEWSLETTER OF THE NATIONAL INSTITUTE FOR TRIAL ADVOCACY.). [Docket]. **Added/Corp** National Institute for Trial Advocacy (U.S.). (19??)-. Newsletter. English. qt. Free on request. National Institute for Trial Advocacy, Notre Dame Law School, Notre Dame IN 46556. **LC** KF8911.A3; D62. **DD** 347.73/504/05; 347.30750405.

UY
DOCTRINA Y LEGISLACION ADUANERA. (19??)-. Periodical. Spanish. $7.00. Ciudadela 1387 -Esc 2, Montevideo Uruguay. **LC** K4; .O37. **DD** 343/.895/05605.

PE
DOCTRINE JURIDIQUE BELGE. **Added/Corp** Universite de Liege. Faculte de Droit. (1986)-. French. **Continues in part** Annales de Droit de Liege, 0771-3029.

BL
DOCUMENTA. Portuguese. $180.00. Ministerio da Educacao e Cultura, Departmento de Documentacao e Divulgacao, Esplanada dos Ministerios Bloco H Terreo, Brasilia Brazil.

SP
DOCUMENTACION JURIDICA. No. 1- Jan./March 1974-. Spanish. qt. 1000ptas Spain; $20.00 US. Secretaria General Tecnica del Ministerio de Justicia, Gabinete de Documentacion Y Publicaciones, Calle Gran Via 76-8 C, 28013 Madrid Spain. **Tel** 2475892/2479833 MADRID, telex 22545. **LC** K4; .O38. **Circ:** 1,200. **Supersedes** Informacion Juridica.
Desc: Monographic issues about legislative changes prepared by the Department of Justice.
Ind/Abst Index Foreign Leg. Per.; Int. Labour Doc.

FR
DOCUMENTATION ORGANIQUE. French. wk. 1630.75F France; 2295.00F other. Inst Documentation Juridique et Fiscale, 11 rue de Teheran, 75008 Paris France. **Tel** 011 33 1 45625435.

SZ/1014-7063
DOCUMENTS DE DROIT SOCIAL - BUREAU INTERNATIONAL DU TRAVAIL. [Doc. droit soc. - Bur. int. trav.]. (1990)-. Periodical. French. tq. 85.00F. International Labour Office - ILO, Publications Sales Service, CH-1211 Geneva 22

Switzerland. **Tel** 011 41 22 7996111. **UDC** 341. **CODEN** NU051. ***Continues*** *Serie Legislative - Bureau International du Travail, 0378-5483.*

US
DOING BUSINESS IN CZECHOSLOVAKIA. **Added/Corp** Price Waterhouse (Firm). World Firm. **VFOAT** Czechoslovakia. (1991)-. English. Price Waterhouse & Company, 1177 Avenue of the Americas, New York NY 10020. **Tel** (212)596-7000.

US
DOING BUSINESS IN THE EUROPEAN COMMUNITY. **Added/Corp** Price Waterhouse (Firm). World Firm. (1991)-. English. Price Waterhouse & Company, 1177 Avenue of the Americas, New York NY 10020. **Tel** (212)596-7000. ***Continues*** *European Communities (Price Waterhouse (Firm)).*

US
DOING BUSINESS IN THE ISLE OF MAN. **Added/Corp** Price Waterhouse (Firm). **VFOAT** Isle of Man. 1st Ed. (June 1991)-. English. Price Waterhouse & Company, 1177 Avenue of the Americas, New York NY 10020. **Tel** (212)596-7000.

●US/1078-5108
DOING BUSINESS IN THE RUSSIAN FEDERATION. [Doing bus. Russ. Fed.]. **Added/Corp** Price Waterhouse (Firm). World Firm. **VFOAT** Russian Federation. (Jan. 1, 1994)-. English. Price Waterhouse & Company, 1177 Avenue of the Americas, New York NY 10020. **Tel** (212)596-7000. **LC** KLA78.B67; D65. **DD** 346.47/07/05; 344.706705. ***Continues*** *Doing Business in the Union of Soviet Socialist Republics, 1067-2982.*

CN/0836-5768
DOMINION LAW REPORTS. FOURTH SERIES, INDEX, ANNOTATIONS, TABLE OF CASES. [Dom. law rep., Fourth ser. index annot. table cases]. **VFOAT** Dominion Law Reports. Annotation Service and Index. Vols. 1/10 (1985)-. Periodical. English. an. $63.00 per issue. Dominion Law Reports, 240 Edward Street, Aurora Ontario M1S 1S5 Canada. **LC** KE132.3; .D66. **DD** 348.71/041. ***Continues*** *Dominion Law Reports. Annotation Service (Second and Third Series), 0316-652X.*

●US
DORSANEO & SOULES' TEXAS CODES AND RULES. CIVIL LITIGATION. **VFOAT** Dorsaneo and Soules' Texas Codes and Rules. Civil Litigation; Texas Codes and Rules. Civil Litigation; Civil Litigation. (1992/1993 Ed.)-. English. Matthew Bender & Company Inc., 1275 Broadway, Albany NY 12204. **Tel** (800)833-9844, (518)487-3000. **LC** KFT1728; .A193. **DD** 347.764/05; 347.64075. ***Continues*** *Dorsaneo's Texas Codes and Rules. Civil Litigation, 1064-7368.*

US/1064-7368
DORSANEO'S TEXAS CODES AND RULES. CIVIL LITIGATION. ***Title Change.*** [Dorsaneo's Tex. codes rules. Civil litig.]. **VFOAT** Texas Codes and Rules. Civil Litigation. (1991/1992 Ed.)-(1992). English. Matthew Bender & Company Inc., 1275 Broadway, Albany NY 12204. **Tel** (800)833-9844, (518)487-3000. **DD** 347. ***Continued by*** *Dorsaneo & Soules' Texas Codes and Rules. Civil Litigation.*

US
DRAFTING CONSTRUCTION CONTRACTS AND HANDLING CONSTRUCTION LITIGATION. English. an. $125.00. Practising Law Institute, 810 Seventh Avenue, New York NY 10019-5818. **Tel** (212)765-5700, FAX (212)581-4670 general correspondence, (212)265-4742 orders and billing inquiries. ***Continues*** *Construction Contracts and Litigation.*

US/0012-5938
DRAKE LAW REVIEW. [Drake law rev.]. **Added/Corp** Drake University. Law School. Vol. 1, No. 1 (Nov. 1951)-. Periodical. English. qt. $20.00. Drake Law Review, Drake University Law School, Des Moines IA 50311. **Tel** (515)271-2930. **DD** 347. **Ad Acc. Circ:** 1,700. available on an online database.
Ind/Abst Bowne Dig. Corp. Sec. Lawyers; Curr. Law Index (1980-); Fed. Tax Artic.; Index Leg. Period.; Leg. Resour. Index (1980-); LegalTrac (1980-); Soc. Plann. Policy Dev. Abstr.; Sociol. Abstr. (?-?).

RM
DREPTUL / UNIUNEA JURISTILOR DEMOCRATI DIN ROMANIA. **Added/Corp** Uniunea Juristilor Democrati din Romania. Vol. 1, No. 1/2 (1990)-. Periodical. Romanian. mo. DM316.00. Uniunea Juristilor Democrati din Romania, Redactia Revistei "Dreptul", B-dul Magheru, Nr. 22, 70158 Bucuresti Romania. **(Subscription address:** Kubon & Sagner, ABT Zeitschriftenimport, D 80328 Munich Germany.**)** **LC** K4; .R47. ***Continues*** *Revista Romana de Drept.*

US/0730-2568
DRINKING/DRIVING LAW LETTER. [Drink./driv. law lett.]. **VFOAT** Drinking, Driving Law Letter. Vol. 1, No. 1 (Jan. 15, 1982)-. Periodical. English. bw. $120.00. Clark Boardman Callaghan, 155 Pfingsten Road, Deerfield IL 60015. **Tel** (800)323-8067. **ED** Donald H. Nichols. **LC** KF2231.A15; D74. **DD** 345.73/0247; 347.305247. **Circ:** 2,500.
Desc: Summarizes literature and court opinions regarding driving while under the influence of intoxicating beverages.

US/0740-9788
DRIVER LICENSING LAWS ANNOTATED. SUPPLEMENT. **Main/Corp** United States. National Highway Traffic Safety Administration. **VFOAT** Driver Licensing Laws Annotated. Annual Supplement. 1981-. English. an. National Highway Traffic Safety Administration, 400 Seventh Street SW, Washington DC 20590.

FR/0991-2738
DROIT DE L'INFORMATIQUE ET DES TELECOMS. **See** Communication-Telecommunications.

FR
DROIT DES AFFAIRES EN GRANDE BRETAGNE. French. Editions Juridiques Associees, 26 rue Vercingetorix, 75014 Paris France. **Tel** 011 33 1 43350167.

FR
DROIT DES AFFAIRES PAR PAYS. French. ir. 1171.50F. Editions Juridiques Associees, 26 rue Vercingetorix, 75014 Paris France. **Tel** 011 33 1 43350167.

FR
DROIT DES AFFAIRES REGIME DES SOCIETES. French. 1072.50F. Editions Juridiques Associees, 26 rue Vercingetorix, 75014 Paris France. **Tel** 011 33 1 43350167.

FR
DROIT DES ENTREPRISES. ASSURANCES. French. ir. Editions Techniques, 141 rue de Javel, 75747 Paris Cedex 15 France. **Tel** 011 33 1 45589100.

CN/0835-9636
DROIT DISCIPLINAIRE EXPRESS. [Droit discip. express]. No. 1 (June 1987)-. Periodical. French. qt. Societe Quebecoise d'Information Juridique, 10 rue St Jacques Bureau 101, Montreal Quebec H2Y 1L3 Canada. **Tel** (514)842-8745, FAX (514)844-8984. **DD** 344.714/01712/02648.
Desc: Prints summaries of the most recent decisions and judgements made by the Quebec courts and judges.

FR/0184-5926
DROIT ET AFFAIRES INTERNATIONAL. [Droit aff. int.]. (1975)-. Periodical. French. sm. 1440.00F. Droit et Affaires, 71 rue du Faubourg St Honore, 75008 Paris France. **Tel** 42 66 6861, FAX 42 66 1316. **ED** Colette Mousset. **UDC** 34. Index available. **Ad Acc.** Full Page (B&W) 4000.00F. Half Page (B&W) 3000.00F. **Circ:** 400. ***Continues*** *Le Droit et les Affaires, 0012-6403.*

FR
DROIT ET CULTURES / REVUE SEMESTRIELLE ANTHROPOLOGIE ET D'HISTOIRE. **See** Anthropology.

FR/0769-3362
DROIT ET SOCIETE. [Droit soc.]. No. 1 (Aug. 1985)-. Periodical. French. Three times a year. 372.18F France; 400.00F others. Editions Juridiques Associees, 26 rue Vercingetorix, 75014 Paris France. **Tel** 011 33 1 43350167. **LC** K4; .R596. **DD** 340/.115.

PL/0070-7325
DROIT POLONAIS CONTEMPORAIN. ***Suspended.*** [Droit Pol. contemp.]. **Added/Corp** Instytut Nauk Prawnych (Polska Akademia Nauk). **VFOAT** Contemporary Polish Law. Vol. 1 (1963)-Vo. 29 No. 1/2. French (English and Russian). qt. Price on Request. **(Subscription address:** ARS Polona, PO Box 1001, 00068 Warsaw Poland.**)** **DD** 349.
Ind/Abst Index Foreign Leg. Per.

FR
DROITS : REVUE FRANCAISE DE THEORIE JURIDIQUE. **Added/Corp** Institut de Recherches Politiques, Aadministratives et Juridiques (France). (1985)-. Periodical. French. sa. 330.00F France; 385.00 other. Presses Universitaires de France, Department des Revues, 14 Avenue du Bois de l'Epine, BP 90, 91003 Evry Cedex France. **Tel** (1)60 77 82 05, FAX (1) 60 79 20 45, telex PUF 600 474 F. **LC** K4; .R64. **DD** 340/.1.
Ind/Abst Index Foreign Leg. Per.

US/0734-6166
DRUG LAW REPORT. (DRUG LAW REPORT / PREPARED UNDER THE AUSPICES OF NATIONAL ORGANIZATION FOR THE REFORM OF MARIJUANA LAWS.). [Drug law rep.]. **Added/Corp** National Organization for the Reform of Marijuana Laws (U.S.). Vol. 1, No. 1 (Jan.-Feb. 1983)-. Periodical. English. bm (6 issues). $150.00. Clark Boardman Callaghan, 155 Pfingsten Road, Deerfield IL 60015. **Tel** (800)323-8067. **LC** KF3890.A15; D78. **DD** 345.73/0277/05; 347.30527705. **Bk Rev.**
Desc: Legal reporting service covering law of illegal substance use.

IE/0332-3250
DUBLIN UNIVERSITY LAW JOURNAL. [Dubl. Univ. law j.]. **Added/Corp** Trinity College (Dublin, Ireland). (1976)-. English. an. Price varies. William W. Gaunt and Sons Inc, 3011 Gulf Drive, Gaunt Building, Holmes Beach FL 34217. **Tel** (800)942-8683, (813)778-5211. **LC** K4; .U23. **DD** 349.415/05; 344.15005.
Ind/Abst Index Leg. Period.; Leg. Resour. Index (1980-); LegalTrac (1984-).

US/1064-3958
DUKE ENVIRONMENTAL LAW & POLICY FORUM. [Duke environ. law policy forum]. **Added/Corp** Duke University. School of Law. **VFOAT** Duke Environmental Law and Policy Forum; Environmental Law & Policy Forum. **VAT** Duke Environmental Law and Policy Forum. Vol. 1 (1991)-. Periodical. English. an. $10.00. Duke University School of Law, 006 Law Towerview & Science Drive, Durham NC 27706. **Tel** (919)684-5966, FAX (919)684-3417. **LC** K4; .U58. **DD** 344.73/046/05; 347.3044605.
Desc: Covers environmental laws and policies.

US
DUKE JOURNAL OF GENDER LAW & POLICY. English. an (Published in July). $18.00 US; $22.00 other. Duke University School of Law, 006 Law Towerview & Science Drive, Durham NC 27706. **Tel** (919)684-5966, FAX (919)684-3417.

US/0012-7086
DUKE LAW JOURNAL. [Duke law j.]. **Added/Corp** Duke University. School of Law. Vol. 7 (1957)-. Periodical. English. bm. $36.00. Duke University School of Law, 006 Law Towerview & Science Drive, Durham NC 27706. **Tel** (919)684-5966, FAX (919)684-3417. **ED** John J. Hoffman. **LC** K4; .U63. **DD** 347. cum. index. **Bk Rev. Ad Acc. Pr Rev. Circ:** 1,400. Documents available from The Genuine Article. ***Continues*** *Duke Bar Journal.*
Desc: Administrative and general law reviews, comments and notes.
Ind/Abst Bowne Dig. Corp. Sec. Lawyers; Commun. Abstr. (?-?); Crim. Penol. Police Sci. Abstr.; Curr. Contents Soc. Behav. Sci.; Curr. Law Index (1980-); Fed. Tax Artic.; Health Plan. Adminis.; Hospit. Health Admin. Index; Index Leg. Period.; Leg. Resour. Index (1980-); LegalTrac (1980-); Res. Alert [Full Cov.]; Soc. Sci. Cit. Index [Full Cov.]; Urban Aff. Abstr.

US
DUKE LAW MAGAZINE. **Added/Corp** Duke University. School of Law. Office of the Dean. Vol. 1, No. 1 (Winter 1982)-. Periodical. English. sa. Free upon request. Duke University School of Law, 006 Law Towerview & Science Drive, Durham NC 27706. **Tel** (919)684-5966, FAX (919)684-3417. **LC** KF292.D854; A43. **DD** 340/.05.

CN/0706-8964
DUNHILL LIABILITY LOSS REPORT. **VFOAT** Dunhill Liability Loss Reports. (Oct. 1977)-. Periodical. English. Twelve times a year. 115.00Can$. Dunhill Research and Development Ltd, Drawer 520, Yarmouth Nova Scotia B5A 4B6 Canada. **DD** 346/.71/03202642.
Desc: In-depth articles and editorials dealing with all facts of negligence law.

CN/1180-9647
DUNHILL PERSONAL INJURY AND DEATH REPORTS. [Dunhill pers. inj. death rep.]. (Feb. 1990)-. Periodical. English. mo. Dunhill Research and Development Ltd, Drawer 520, Yarmouth Nova Scotia B5A 4B6 Canada. **DD** 346.7103/23/02642. ***Continues*** *Dunhill Personal Injury Awards Annotator., 0824-3611.*

US/0093-3058
DUQUESNE LAW REVIEW. [Duquesne law rev.]. **Added/Corp** Duquesne University. School of Law. Vol. 7, (1969)-. Academic Scholarly Publication. English. Four times a year (Seasonally). $20.00. Duquesne University School of Law, 900 Locust Street, Pittsburgh PA 15282. **Tel** (412)396-5020, (412)396-6283, (412)396-6186, FAX (412)296-6283. **ED** Linda Somerville. **LC** K4; .U65. **DD** 340/.05. Index available (4th iss. in (Summer)). cum. index. **Ad Acc. Circ:** 1,200 (ctrl). Documents available from Documents on Demand. ***Continues*** *Duquesne University Law Review, 0012-7213.*
Desc: The review publishes scholarly writings dealing with current legal topics.
Ind/Abst Bowne Dig. Corp. Sec. Lawyers; Coal Abstr.; Crim. Justice Abstr.; Curr. Law Index (1980-); Energy Inf. Abstr.; Environ. Abstr.; Fed. Tax Artic.; Index Leg. Period.; Leg. Resour. Index (1980-); LegalTrac (1980-); Writ. Am. Hist.

II
DVIVEDI'S ANNUAL DIGEST FOR MADHYA PRADESH. 1970-. English. Law Journal Publications, Jayendraganj, Gwalior 1 India. **Tel** (0751)22340. **ED** Harihat Nivas Dvivedi. **DD** 347/.54/010264.

US
DWELLING CONSTRUCTION UNDER THE UNIFORM BUILDING CODE.
Main/Corp International Conference of Building Officials. **Added/Corp** International Conference of Building Officials. International Conference of Building Officials. Dwelling House Construction Under the Uniform Building Code. (19??)-. English. ir (Published every three years). $11.00 (members) of ICBO; $14.70 (non-members). ICBO Evaluation Service Inc., 5360 South Workman Mill Road, Whittier CA 90601. **Tel** (213)699-0541, FAX (213)692-3853.
Desc: Designed primarily for use in home building and apprentice training.

US/0889-0234
DWI JOURNAL. (DWI JOURNAL : LAW & SCIENCE.). [DWI j.]. **VFOAT** Driving While Intoxicated Journal. Vol. 1, No. 1 (Mar./Apr. 1986)-. Periodical. English. mo. $255.00 (one year), $387.00 (two year). Whitaker Newsletter, PO Box 340, 313 South Avenue, Suite 202, Fanwood NJ 07023-0340. **Tel** (201)889-6336, FAX (201)889-6339. **(Subscription address:** Whitaker Newsletters, PO Box 192, Fanwood, NJ 07023-0192**) ED** John Tarantino and Joel Whitaker (managing editor). **LC** KF2231.A15; D85. **DD** 345.73/0247; 347.305247. **Bk Rev**.
Desc: Hands-on guide for defense attorneys who handle DWI/DUI cases. Case studies, motions, litigation tips, BrAC/BAC fallability, and appellate decisions.

US
EALS NEWSLETTER : THE NEWSLETTER OF THE EAST ASIAN LEGAL STUDIES PROGRAM AT HARVARD LAW SCHOOL. **Main/Corp** Harvard Law School. East Asian Legal Studies Program. **VAT** East Asian Legal Studies Newsletter. Vol. 1, No. 1 (Sept. 1990)-. Newsletter. English. mo.

US/1055-4157
EARLY CHILDHOOD LAW AND POLICY REPORTER. (EARLY CHILDHOOD LAW AND POLICY REPORTER.). [Early child. law policy report.]. (1991)-. Periodical. English. Twelve times a year. $395.00. LRP Publications, 747 Dresher Road, PO Box 980, Horsham PA 19044-0980. **Tel** (800)341-7874, (215)784-0860, FAX (215)784-9639, (215)784-0870. **(Subscription address:** LRP Publications, PO Box 980, Horsham PA 19044.**) DD** 346.
Desc: Developed especially for persons interested in preschool and early intervention services. Contains federal and state judicial decisions including US Department of Education policy rulings, letters of finding, and memoranda, as well as state administrative decisions.

US/0098-9479
EARTHBOND. V. 4- Feb. 1975-. Periodical. English. mo. Migrant Legal Action Program, 1910 K Street NW, Washington DC 20006. **LC** KF3580.A4; M5. **DD** 344/.73/01544. ***Continues** MLAP Monthly Report.*

UK
EAST EUROPEAN BUSINESS LAW / FINANCIAL TIMES. See Business.

US
EAST-WEST JOINT VENTURE NEWS. (19??)-. Government Publication. English. qt. $80.00. United Nations Publications, 2 United Nations Plaza, Room DC2 0853, Department 007C, New York NY 10017. **Tel** (212)963-8303, (800)253-9646. **(Subscription address:** United Nations Publications, Subscription Office, PO Box 361, Birmingham AL 35201-0361.**)**
Desc: A newsletter of new laws permitting foreign enterprises to establish joint ventures with domestic enterprises and to set up fully owned subsidiaries in the six European CMEA countries.

TZ/0012-8678
EASTERN AFRICA LAW REVIEW. V. 1- Apr. 1968-. Periodical. English. Three times a year. University of Dar Es Salaam Faculty of Law, PO Box 35093, Dar Es Salaam Tanzania. **Tel** 53611. **LC** K5; .A8. **DD** 340/.05.

II
EASTERN LAW REPORTS. Pt. 1 (Aug. 9, 1982)-. English. Eastern Law House Pvt Ltd, 54 Ganesh Chunder Avenue, Calcutta 700013 India. **Tel** 011 91 33 274989, FAX 011 91 33 943333. **DD** 348.54/1042; 345.410842.

US/1049-6459
EC BRIEF. (EC BRIEF / IBLF EUROPEAN INFORMATION SERVICE ; PRODUCED BY THE INTERNATIONAL BUSINESS LAW FIRM P.C. AND BUTTERWORTH LAW PUBLISHERS, LTD.). [EC brief]. **Added/Corp** IBLF European Information Service. International Business Law Firm P.C. Butterworth Law Publishers. **VAT** European Communities Brief. (1990)-. Periodical. English. wk. £250.00. Butterworth & Co. Ltd. / Kent, England, Borough Green, Sevenoaks Kent TN15 8PH England. **Tel** 011 44 732-884567, FAX 011 44 732-885996. **DD** 341.
Desc: Covers the official activity of the European Community, including secondary legislation and discussion documents on proposed legislation.

UK/0965-0717
EC FOOD LAW. [EC Food Law]. **VFOAT** European Community Food Law. (1992)-. Periodical. English. mo. £285.00 UK; £300.00 other, includes binder and indexes;. Agra Europe London Limited, 25 Frant Road, Tunbridge Wells, Kent TN2 5JT England. **Tel** 011 44 892 533813. **DD** 341.7592. Index available (free).

US/0424-2068
ECCLESIASTICAL COURT DIGEST, THE. V. 1- Jan. 1963-. Periodical. English. mo. $15.00. Juridical Digests Institute, 1860 Broadway/Suite 1401, New York NY 10023.

UK/0956-618X
ECCLESIASTICAL LAW JOURNAL : THE JOURNAL OF THE ECCLESIASTICAL LAW SOCIETY. **Added/Corp** Ecclesiastical Law Society. No. 1 (July 1987)-. Periodical. English. Twice a year (Jan. & July). £26.50. University of Newcastle upon Tyne, 22 24 Windsor Terrace, Newcastle Tyne NE1 7RU England. **Tel** 011 44 91 2226000. **LC** K5; .C35. **DD** 262.9/05.
Ind/Abst Index Leg. Period.

CN/0227-1141
ECHO DE LA COUR. [Echo cour, Dist. judic. Terrebonne]. **VFOAT** Court House Echo. April 1977-. Periodical. English (French). mo. Court Echo Newspaper, Suite 222/1400 Sauve Street West, Montreal Quebec H4N 1C5 Canada. **DD** 348.714/048.

UK/0929-2233
EDI LAW REVIEW, THE. English. qt. $320.00. Graham & Trotman Ltd, Sterling House, 66 Wilson Road, London SW1V 1DE England. **Tel** 44 71 8211123. **ED** Rob E. van Esch, Corien Prins. **Pr Rev. Acid Free.**
Desc: Provides a forum for discussing the legal aspects and consequences of electronic data interchange (EDI).

UK/0953-9964
EDUCATION AND THE LAW. See Education.

CN/0838-2875
EDUCATION LAW JOURNAL. [Educ. law j.]. **VFOAT** Education Law. Vol. 1, No. 1 (May 1988)-. Periodical. English (French). an. 140.00Can$ Canada. Carswell / Canada, 2075 Kennedy Road, Scarborough Ontario M1T 3V4 Canada. **Tel** (416)609-3800, (800)387-5164. **ED** Greg M Dickinson. **DD** 344.71/07/05. **Bk Rev. Ad Acc.**
Desc: A national journal covering legal issues concerned with the practice and administration of all levels of education in Canada.
Ind/Abst Can. Legal Lit.; Index Can. Leg. Period. Lit. (1992-).

US/0013-1741
EDUCATIONAL FREEDOM. (EDUCATIONAL FREEDOM / EEF.). **Added/Corp** Educational Freedom Foundation (U.S.). (19??)-. Periodical. English. Twice a year. $7.00. Educational Freedom Foundation, 110 East Rose, St Louis MO 63119. **Tel** (314)963-9170. **ED** Daniel D. McGarry. **LC** KF4124.A15; E35. **DD** 344.73/07/05; 347.304705. **Bk Rev**. ctrl circ.

CN/0849-4800
EDULAW SCHOOL NEWSLETTER. ***Title Change.*** [EduLaw sch. newsl.]. **Added/Corp** EduLaw Corporation. Vol. 1, issue 1 Sept. (1989)-Vol. 3, No. 10 June (1992)-. Newsletter. English. Ten times a year. Edulaw Corporation, 58 Willow Park Green Southeast, Calgary Alta T2J 3L1 Canada. **Tel** (403)278-2243, FAX (403)271-7388. **DD** 349.71/07. ***Continued by** EduLaw for Canadian Schools, 1193-7319.*

GW
EDV RECHT. (19??)-. German. ir. DM49.80. Erich Schmidt Verlag GmbH, Postfach 304240, D 10724 Berlin Germany. **Tel** 011 49 30 25008525.

UK
EEC COMPETITION LAW HANDBOOK. English. an. £60.00. Sweet & Maxwell Ltd., South Quay Plaza, 183 Marsh Wall, London E14 9FT England. **Tel** 011 44 264 342899, FAX 011 44 264 342723, telex 929089 ITPINF G.

CN/0384-062X
EGALE, L'. (1976)-. Periodical. English (French). L'Egale, PO Box 6471 Station A, Toronto Ontario M5W 1X3 Canada. **DD** 346/.71/013.
Desc: A journal of women and the law.

JA
EHS LAW BULLETIN SERIES, JAPAN. **Main/Corp** Japan. Laws, Statutes, etc. **VAT** Eibun Horei Sha Law Bulletin Series, Japan. (19??)-. Monographic series. English. ir. Eibun Horei Sha, 18 14 4-chome Higashi Nakano, Nakano-ku Tokyo Japan.

US/1056-7585
EIKENBURG & STILES' TEXAS ENVIRONMENTAL LAW LETTER. ***Title Change.*** [Eikenburg & Stiles' Texas environ. law lett.]. **Added/Corp** Eikenburg & Stiles (Firm). **VFOAT** Texas Environmental Law Letter. **VAT** Eikenburg and Stiles' Texas Environmental Law Letter. Vol. 1, No. 1 (July 1991)-(19??). Periodical. English. mo. M. Lee Smith Publishers and Printers, 162 4th Avenue North, PO Box 198867, Nashville TN 37219. **Tel** (615)242-7395, (800)274-6774, FAX (615)256-6601. **ED** Neil Mitchell and Adam Goodman, (address)Eikenburg and Stiles, 1100 First City National Bank Building, Houston, TX 77002-6501, (phone) 713-652-2144. **DD** 344. ***Continued by** Texas Environmental Compliance Update, 1075-2595.*
Desc: Newsletter reporting the latest state specific environmental law developments that affect companies in that state.

US/0364-118X
ELC. **Main/Corp** Education Law Center. **VAT** Education Law Center. V. 1- Winter 1975/76-. Periodical. English. qt. Education Law Center, 605 Broad Street/Suite 800, Newark NJ 07102. **LC** KF4102; .E3. **DD** 344/.749/07105.

US/1047-7055
ELDERLAW REPORT, THE. [Elderlaw rep.]. **VFOAT** Elder Law Report. Vol. 1, No. 1 (1989)-. Periodical. English. mo. $119.00. Little Brown & Company, 34 Beacon Street, Boston MA 02108. **Tel** (617)227-0730, (800)759-0190. **LC** KF390.A4; E43. **DD** 346.7301/3; 347.30613. **NLM** W1; EL288.

US/0145-8124
ELECTION ADMINISTRATION REPORTS. See Political Science.

IT
ELENCO DEI PROTESTI CAMBIARI ELEVATI E DEI FALLIMENTI DICHIARATI IN PROVINCIA DI BARI NELLA ... . Periodical. Italian. mo. Camera di Commercio Industria e Agricoltura, Via Emanuele Filiberto 3, 12100 Cuneo Italy. **LC** WMLC L 83/7564. ***Continues** Elenco dei Protesti Cambiari e dei Fallimenti in Provincia di Bari Nel Mesa di.*

IT
ELENCO UFFICIALE DEI PROTESTI CAMBIARI. ROMA. Italian. sm. L300000. Camera Comm Ind Art Agr Uff Pubbl, Via C Colombo 112, 00186 Rome Italy. **Tel** 011 39 6 57007597.

IT
ELENCO UFFICIALE DEI PROTESTI CAMBIARI. VERCELLI. Italian. bm. L57000. Camera Com Ind Art Agr Vercel, Piazza Risorgimento 12, 13100 Vercelli Italy. **Tel** 011 39 161 5981.

NE/0256-4467
ELLIS (ENGLISH EDITION). (ELLIS : EUROPEAN LEGAL LITERATURE INFORMATION SERVICE.). [Ellis]. **Added/Corp** Europe Data (Firm) European Law Centre. **VFOAT** European Legal Literature Information Service. Vol. 1, No. 1 (Sept. 1985)-. Periodical. English. an. $180.00. Kluwer Law and Taxation Publishers, Staverenstraat 32015, PO Box 23, 7400 GA Deventer Netherlands. **Tel** 011 31 5700 47261. **(Subscription address:** North America: Kluwer Law & Taxation, 675 Massachusetts Avenue, Cambridge, MA 02139; Phone: (617)354-0140**) ED** R. Hainebach. **LC** KJE901; .E44. **DD** 016.3494/05; 016.344005. **UDC** 014.3. Index available. cum. index. **Circ:** 200.
Desc: Yearbook with abstracts concerning developments on European law.

BL
EMENTARIO DE JURISPRUDENCIA DO TRIBUNAL DE JUSTICA DO ESTADO DO RIO DE JANEIRO. **Main/Corp** Rio de Janeiro (Brazil : State). Tribunal de Justica. Yearly V. 1, (1980)-. Portuguese. an. Editora Liber Juris Ltda, rua da Assembleia 36, 2O Andar, Rio de Janeiro RJ Brazil. **DD** 348.81/53043; 348.1530843.

BL
EMENTARIO DO TIT. **Main/Corp** Sao Paulo (Brazil : State). Tribunal de Impostos e Taxas. **VAT** Ementario do Tribunal de Impostos E Taxas. 1969/74-. Portuguese. an. Tribunal de Impostos e Taxas, Secretaria da Fazenda do Estado de Sao Paulo, Palacio Clovis Ribeiro Av Rangel Pestana 300, 9 Andar, Sao Paulo Brazil CEP 01091. **Tel** 55-011-35-9527, FAX 55-011-239-1014. **Circ:** 12,000 (ctrl).
Desc: Digests of judgements adjudicated at Sao Paulo Tax Court.

BL
EMENTARO DA LEGISLACAO ESTADUAL. **Main/Corp** Para (Brazil : State). Vol. 1 (1947/57)-. Portuguese. DSG/DISA Setor de Comunicacoes Altos, 66000 Belem Brazil. **DD** 348/.811/028.

US/1042-2978
EMERGENCY DEPARTMENT LAW. (EMERGENCY DEPARTMENT LAW / BNA.). [Emerg. dep. law]. **Added/Corp** Bureau of National Affairs (Washington, D.C.). Vol. 1, No. 1 (Feb. 16, 1989)-. Periodical. English. sm (24 issues per year). $300.00. Business Publishers Inc., 951 Pershing Drive, Silver Spring MD 20910-4464. **Tel** (301)587-6300, (800)274-0122, FAX (301)585-9075. **ED** William H. Feldman. **LC** KF3826.E5; A134. **DD** 344.73/03218/05; 347.304321805. **[CCC].**
Desc: News and analysis of malpractice and other legal issues as they affect urgent care facilities. Pertains to doctors, health professionals, hospital administrators, and lawyers.

US/1059-6631
EMF KEEPTRACK. (EMF KEEPTRACK / COMPILED BY RESEARCH & RECORD SERVICES.). [EMF keeptrack]. **Added/Corp** Central Maine Power Company. Research & Record Services. **VFOAT** EMF Keep Track. **VAT** Electric and Magnetic Fields Keeptrack. (1988)-. Periodical. English. bw. $400.00. Enter for Energy Information, 83 Edison Drive, Augusta ME 04330. **Tel** (207)626-9555, 800 947-8765, FAX (207)623-9384. **ED** Elizabeth S. Brooks. **DD** 343.
Desc: A compilation of legislative, regulatory, research and media news concerning electric and magnetic fields.

US/0094-4076
EMORY LAW JOURNAL. [Emory law j.]. **Added/Corp** Emory University. School of Law. Vol. 23 (Winter 1974)-. English. qt. $30.00 US; $34.00 other. Emory University School of Law, 1804 North Decatur Road, 3rd Floor, Atlanta GA 30322. **Tel** (404)727-6830, FAX (404)727-6820. **LC** K10; .O885. **DD** 340/.05. available on microfilm and microfiche from University Microfilms International (UMI). ***Continues*** *Journal of Public Law.*
Ind/Abst ABC POL SCI (19??-1985); Bowne Dig. Corp. Sec. Lawyers; Commun. Abstr. (?-?); Curr. Law Index (1980-); Fed. Tax Artic.; Index Leg. Period.; Leg. Resour. Index (1980-); LegalTrac (1980-).

US/1063-097X
EMPLOYEE TERMINATIONS LAW BULLETIN (1991). **See** Economics-Labor.

US/8755-0695
EMPLOYER'S GUIDE TO LAW SCHOOLS. [Empl. guide law sch.]. **Added/Corp** National Association for Law Placement (U.S.). (1984)-. English. an (May). $40.00 (members of the Natl. Association for Law Placement); $80.00 (nonmembers). National Association for Law Placement, 1666 Connecticut Avenue, Suite 450, Washington DC 20009. **Tel** (202)667-1666, FAX (202)265-6735. **DD** 340. ***Continues*** *Employers' Guide to NALP Member ABA-Approved Law Schools.*

UK
EMPLOYMENT LAW LINE. (19??)-. Periodical. English. ir. £523.15. Croner Publ Ltd, Croner House, London Road, Kingston upon Thames, Surrey KT2 6SR England. **Tel** 011 44 81 5473333, FAX 081 547-2637.

IT
ENCICLOPEDIA DEL DIRITTO. (19??)-. Monographic series. Italian. ir. Price varies per volume. Giuffre Editore SPA, Via Busto Arsizio 40, 20151 Milan Italy. **Tel** 011 398 2 38089200.

UK
ENCYCLOPEDIA OF CONSUMER LAW. (1980)-. English. £125.00 Europe; £131.00 other. Sweet & Maxwell Ltd., South Quay Plaza, 183 Marsh Wall, London E14 9FT England. **Tel** 011 44 264 342899, FAX 011 44 264 342723, telex 929089 ITPINF G.

US
ENCYCLOPEDIA OF GEORGIA LAW. English. an. $1,140. Harrison Company Publishers, 3110 Crossing Park, PO Box 7500, Norcross GA 30091-7500. **Tel** (800)241-3561, (404)447-9150.

UK/0142-2952
ENCYCLOPEDIA OF HIGHWAY LAW AND PRACTICE. [Encycl. highw. law pract.]. **VFOAT** Encyclopedia of Highway Law and Practice. Release. (1965)-. English. Three times a year. £340.00. Sweet & Maxwell Ltd., South Quay Plaza, 183 Marsh Wall, London E14 9FT England. **Tel** 011 44 264 342899, FAX 011 44 264 342723, telex 929089 ITPINF G. **(Subscription address:** International Thompson Publisher Servies Ltd., Sub. Dept., North Way Andover, Hampshire SP10 5BE United Kingdom.**)**

UK
ENCYCLOPEDIA OF PLANNING LAW AND PRACTICE. (19??)-. English. £236.00 Europe; £248.00 other. Sweet & Maxwell Ltd., South Quay Plaza, 183 Marsh Wall, London E14 9FT England. **Tel** 011 44 264 342899, FAX 011 44 264 342723, telex 929089 ITPINF G.
Desc: A fully comprehensive and authoritative statement of the law and practice relating to planning, comprising all the relevant primary and secondary sources with annotations.

UK/0142-2987
ENCYCLOPEDIA OF U.K. AND EUROPEAN PATENT LAW. [Encycl. U.K. Eur. pat. law]. **VFOAT** Encyclopedia of U.K. and European Patent Law. Release. (1977)-. English. sa. £165.00 Europe; £173.00 other. Sweet & Maxwell Ltd., South Quay Plaza, 183 Marsh Wall, London E14 9FT England. **Tel** 011 44 264 342899, FAX 011 44 264 342723, telex 929089 ITPINF G.

FR
ENCYCLOPEDIE JURIDIQUE. Monographic series. French. Price varies per volume. Dalloz, 35 rue Tournefort, 75240 Paris Cedex 05 France. **Tel** 011 33 1 40515434 or 40515454, FAX 45 87 37 48, telex 206 446 F.
Desc: This is a complete transcript of all current legislation and of the most significant judicial decisions, divided into areas of public and private law.

US/0270-9163
ENERGY LAW JOURNAL. [Energy law j.]. **Added/Corp** Federal Energy Bar Association. Vol. 1 (1980)-. Periodical. English. sa. $26.50 Washington, D.C. residents, $25.00 other US; $36.00 Canada; $42.00 other. Federal Energy Bar Association, 1350 Connecticut Ave. N.W., Suite 300, Washington DC 20036. **Tel** (202)223-5625, FAX (202)833-5596. **LC** K5; .N47. **DD** 346.7304/679/05. Index available (bound in first issue). cum. index. **Bk Rev**, (Qty: 1-2). **Ad Acc, Adv Mgr:** Brian O'Neill, **Tel** (202)986-8000. **Circ:** 2,200 (ctrl). available on microfiche from University Microfilms International (UMI).
Desc: Original material of interest to the legal profession.
Ind/Abst Curr. Law Index (1982-); Index Leg. Period.; INIS Atomindex [Micro.]; Int. Aerosp. Abstr.; J. Plan. Lit.; Leg. Resour. Index (1982-); LegalTrac (1982-).

US/0149-5550
ENERGY LEGISLATIVE SERVICE. Periodical. English. sm. McGraw Hill Publishing Company, Inc., 1221 Avenue of the Americas, New York NY 10020. **Tel** (212)512-6410, (800)525-5003, FAX (212)512-6111. **LC** KF2120.A15; E53. **DD** 343/.73/092.

UK
ENTERTAINMENT AND MEDIA LAW REPORTS. (1993)-. English. Six times a year. £205.00 Europe; £215.00 other. Sweet & Maxwell Ltd., South Quay Plaza, 183 Marsh Wall, London E14 9FT England. **Tel** 011 44 264 342899, FAX 011 44 264 342723, telex 929089 ITPINF G.

US/0732-1880
ENTERTAINMENT AND SPORTS LAWYER : PUBLICATION OF THE FORUM COMMITTEE ON THE ENTERTAINMENT AND SPORTS INDUSTRIES, THE. [Entertain. sports lawyer]. **Added/Corp** American Bar Association. Forum Committee on the Entertainment and Sports Industries. Vol. 1, No. 1 (Spring 1982)-. Periodical. English. qt (4 issues). $40.00. American Bar Association, 750 North Lake Shore Drive, Chicago IL 60611. **Tel** (312)988-5522, (312)988-5241, FAX (312)988-5528, telex 270593. **ED** Richard J. Greenstone. **LC** KF4290.A15; E57. **DD** 344.73/099; 347.30499. **Bk Rev. Circ:** 6,000.
Desc: Newsletter for attorneys specializing in the entertainment and sports industries.
Ind/Abst Curr. Law Index (1984-); Leg. Resour. Index (1984-); LegalTrac (1980-1989); SPORT Discus.

US/0883-2455
ENTERTAINMENT LAW & FINANCE. [Entertain. law finance]. **VFOAT** Entertainment Law and Finance. Vol. 1, No. 1 (Apr. 1985)-. Periodical. English. mo. $185.00. Leader Publications, 345 Park Avenue South, New York NY 10010. **Tel** (800)888-8300 ext. 6170, (212)545-6170, FAX (212)696-1848. **LC** KF4290.A15; E573. **DD** 344.73/097; 347.30497. ***Continues*** *Entertainment Legal News, 0747-8593.*

US/0270-3831
ENTERTAINMENT LAW REPORTER. [Entertain. law report.]. Vol. 1 (June 1, 1979)-. Periodical. English. mo. $175.00. Entertainment Law Reporter, 2210 Wilshire Boulevard/Suite 311, Santa Monica CA 90403. **Tel** (213)736-1089. **ED** Lionel S. Sobel. **LC** KF4290.A59; E57. **DD** 344.73/099. Index available (free). **Bk Rev. Ad Acc. Circ:** 900.
Desc: Legal developments in motion pictures, television, radio, music, sports, and the arts.

UK/0959-3799
ENTERTAINMENT LAW REVIEW. [Entertain. law rev.]. (1990)-. Periodical. English. Six times a year. £230.00 Europe; £242.00 other. Sweet & Maxwell Ltd., South Quay Plaza, 183 Marsh Wall, London E14 9FT England. **Tel** 011 44 264 342899, FAX 011 44 264 342723, telex 929089 ITPINF G. **DD** 338.47.
Ind/Abst Leg. Resour. Index; LegalTrac (1990-).

US/1047-4137
ENTERTAINMENT LITIGATION REPORTER. [Entertain. litig. rep.]. (May 9, 1989)-. Periodical. English. mo. $700.00. Andrews Publications Inc., 1646 West Chester Pike, PO Box 1000, Westtown PA 19395. **Tel** (610)399-6600, (800)345-1101, FAX (610)399-6610. **ED** Bob Sullivan. **LC** KF4290.A59; E575. **DD** 344.73/097. Index available. cum. index. **Circ:** 50 (ctrl).
Desc: Provides comprehensive coverage of litigation involving films, television, cable, stage and other media.

BE/0772-5310
ENTREPRISE ET LE DROIT, L'. **VFOAT** L'Entreprise et le Droit. (1984)-. Periodical. Multiple languages (French and Dutch). Four times a year. 1590.00F. Nationale Confed Bouwbedruf, Lombardstr 34-42, 1000 Brussels Belgium. **Tel** 32 2 5104611.

GW/0425-1288
ENTSCHEIDUNGEN DER OBERLANDESGERICHTE IN ZIVILSACHEN EINSCHLIESSLICH DER FREIWILLIGEN GERICHTSBARKEIT. **VFOAT** OLGZ. Entscheidungen der Oberlandesgerichte in Zivilsachen Einschliesslich der Freiwilligen Gerichtsbarkeit. (1965)-. Periodical. German. qt. DM163.20 Germany; DM164.40 other. CH Beck Verlagsbuchhandlung, D 80791 Munich Germany. **Tel** 011 49 89 381891. **UDC** 347(094.9).

GW/0340-8779
ENTSCHEIDUNGEN DER OBERVERWALTUNGSGERICHTE FUER DAS LAND NORDRHEIN-WESTFALEN IN MUENSTER SOWIE FUER DIE LANDER NIEDERSACHSEN UND SCHLESWIG-HOLSTEIN IN LUENEBURG. [Entscheid. Oberverwalt.ger. Land Nordrh.-Westf. Muenst. Land. Niedersachs. Schlesw.-Holst. Luenebg.]. **VFOAT** OVGE. Entscheidungen der Oberverwaltungsgerichte fuer das Land Nordrhein-Westfalen in Muenster Sowie fuer die Lander Niedersachsen und Schleswig-Holstein in Lueneburg. (1951)-. Periodical. German. ir. Aschendorffsche Verlagsbuchhandlung, Postfach 1124, D-48135 Muenster Germany. **Tel** 011 49 251 690132, telex 08-92 830 WN MS D. **UDC** 342(094.9)(430.1-43.23/.36). Index available. cum. index. **Circ:** 1,000 (ctrl).

GW
ENTSCHEIDUNGEN DES BUNDESGERICHTSHOFES IN ZIVILSACHEN. **Main/Corp** Germany (West) Bundesgerichtshof. Vol. 1 (1951)-. German. ir. Carl Heymanns Verlag KG, Luxemburger Strasse 449, D 50939 Cologne Germany. **Tel** 011 49 221 460100, telex 8 881 888. cum. index. ***Supersedes*** *Germany. Reichsgericht. Entscheidungen des Reichsgerichts in Zivilsachen.*

GW/0423-250X
ENTSCHEIDUNGEN DES BUNDESPATENTGERICHTS. [Entscheid. Bundespatentger.]. (1962)-. German. ir. DM90.00. Carl Heymanns Verlag KG, Luxemburger Strasse 449, D 50939 Cologne Germany. **Tel** 011 49 221 460100, telex 8 881 888. **UDC** 347.771/.772(094.9). Index available.
Desc: Decisions in patent law.

GW/0433-7646
ENTSCHEIDUNGEN DES BUNDESVERFASSUNGSGERICHTS. **Main/Corp** Germany (West). Bundesvarfassungsgericht. Vol. 1 (1952)-. German. ir. DM64.00. JCB Mohr / Paul Siebeck, Postfach 2040, D 72010 Tuebingen Germany. **Tel** 011 49 7071 9230, FAX 011 49 7071 51104, telex 7/262872 mohr d. **ED** members of the Germany Federal Constitutional Court. cum. index. **Acid Free.**

GW/0013-9106
ENTSCHEIDUNGEN DES BUNDESVERWALTUNGSGERICHT. **Main/Corp** Germany (Federal Republic, 1949-). Bundesverwaltungsgericht. (19??)-. Periodical. German. ir. DM68.00. Carl Heymanns Verlag KG, Luxemburger Strasse 449, D 50939 Cologne Germany. **Tel** 011 49 221 460100, telex 8 881 888.

GE
ENTSCHEIDUNGEN DES PREUSSISCHEN OBERVERWALTUNGSGERICHTS. HRSG. VON JEBENS ... UND VON MEYEREN. **Main/Corp** Prussia. Oberverwaltungsgericht. (1877)-. German. ir. Carl Heymanns Verlag KG, Luxemburger Strasse 449, D 50939 Cologne Germany. **Tel** 011 49 221 460100, telex 8 881 888.

GW
ENTSCHEIDUNGEN IN ARBEITSRECHTSSACHEN. **Main/Corp** Germany (Democratic Republic, 1949-). Oberstes Gericht. German. 13.00. Staatsverlag der Deutschen, Demokratischen Republik, Berlin Germany. **DD** 348/.431/041.

UK
ENVIRONMENT LAW BRIEF. English. Ten times a year. £95.00. Legal Studies & Services Publ Ltd., 9-13 St. Andrew Street, London EC4A 3AE England. **Tel** 011 44 71 936-2016.

GR
EPHEMERIS HELLENON NOMIKON. **VFOAT** Greek Lawyers' Journal. Periodical. Greek, Modern. mo. Arsake 6, Athens 10504 Greece. **Tel** 3247791. **ED** A S Izacharopoulos. **LC** K5; .P56. **Bk Rev.** ***Continues*** *Ephemeris Ton Hellinon Nomikon.* **Ind/Abst** Index Foreign Leg. Per.

CY/0254-6396
EPITHEORESE KYPRIAKOU DIKAIOU. [Epitheor. kupr. dikaiou]. **VFOAT** Cyprus Law Review. (1983)-. Periodical. English (Greek, Modern). qt. **LC** K5; .P575. **DD** 349.5645/05; 345.645005. **Ind/Abst** Index Foreign Leg. Per.

US/0194-3839
EQUIPMENT LEASING. ***Title Change.*** **Main/Corp** Practising Law Institute. English. Practising Law Institute, 810 Seventh Avenue, New York NY 10019-5818. **Tel** (212)765-5700, FAX (212)581-4670 general correspondence, (212)265-4742 orders and billing inquiries. **LC** KF946.Z9; N48. **DD** 346.7304/7. ***Continued by*** *Basics of Equipment Leasing.*

US/0743-247X
EQUITABLE DISTRIBUTION JOURNAL. (EQUITABLE DISTRIBUTION JOURNAL / NATIONAL LEGAL RESEARCH GROUP, INC.). **Added/Corp** National Legal Research Group. Vol. 1, No. 1 (Jan. 1984)-. Periodical. English. Twelve times a year. $105.00. National Legal Research Group Inc, PO Box 7187, Charlottesville VA 22906. **Tel** (800)727-6574, (804)977-5690, FAX (804)295-4667. **LC** KF532.7.A15; E68. **DD** 346.7304/0269; 347.30640269. **Desc:** Covers the law of equitable distribution of property upon divorce.

SP/0561-4473
ESTADISTICAS JUDICIALES DE ESPANA. **See** Law-Abstracting, Bibliographies and Statistics.

UK
ESTATES GAZETTE. DIGEST OF LAND AND PROPERTY CASES. (1902)-. Periodical. English. Fifty-two times a year. $98.00 UK; $146.00 others. Estates Gazette Ltd, 151 Wardour Street, London W1V 4BN England. **Tel** 011 44 71 437 0141. available on an online database (files 771,772,799/Full-Text) from DIALOG.

CN
ESTIMATES. PART III, DEPARTMENT OF JUSTICE CANADA, CANADIAN UNITY INFORMATION OFFICE PROGRAM. **Main/Corp** Canada. **VFOAT** Budget des Depenses. Partie III, Ministere de la Justice Canada, Programme du Centre d'Information sur l'Unite Canadienne. (19??)-. English (French). $3.00 Canada; $3.60 other. Canada Communication Group Publishers, Order Processing, Ottawa Ontario K1A 0S9 Canada. **Tel** (819)956-4800, (819)956-4802. **LC** KE4752.A72; C36. **DD** 354.71008/8.

CN
ESTIMATES. PART III, FEDERAL COURT OF CANADA. **Main/Corp** Canada. **VFOAT** Budget des Depenses. Partie III, La Cour Federale du Canada. (19??)-. English (French). $3.00 Canada; $3.60 other. Canada Communication Group Publishers, Order Processing, Ottawa Ontario K1A 0S9 Canada. **Tel** (819)956-4800, (819)956-4802. **LC** KE8265.A72; C36. **DD** 347.71/01/0681; 347.10710681.

CN
ESTIMATES. PART III, LAW REFORM COMMISSION OF CANADA. **Main/Corp** Canada. **VFOAT** Budget des Depenses. Partie III, Commission de Reforme du Droit du Canada. (19??)-. English (French). $3.00 Canada; $3.60 other. Canada Communication Group Publishers, Order Processing, Ottawa Ontario K1A 0S9 Canada. **Tel** (819)956-4800, (819)956-4802. **LC** KE430.A72; C364. **DD** 354.71008/8.

CN
ESTIMATES. PART III, RESTRICTIVE TRADE PRACTICES COMMISSION OF CANADA. **Main/Corp** Canada. **VFOAT** Budget des Depenses. Partie III, Commission sur les Pratiques Restrictives du Commerce du Canada. (19??)-. English (French). $3.00 Canada; $3.60 other. Canada Communication Group Publishers, Order Processing, Ottawa Ontario K1A 0S9 Canada. **Tel** (819)956-4800, (819)956-4802. **LC** KE1639.A2; C364. **DD** 354.710082.

CN
ESTIMATES. PART III, SOLICITOR GENERAL CANADA. **Main/Corp** Canada. **VFOAT** Budget des Depenses. Partie III, Solliciteur General Canada. (19??)-. English (French). $6.00 Canada; $7.20 other. Canada Communication Group Publishers, Order Processing, Ottawa Ontario K1A 0S9 Canada. **Tel** (819)956-4800, (819)956-4802. **LC** KE8813.A72; C36. **DD** 354.71008/8. ***Continues*** *Canada. Estimates. Part III, Solicitor General Secretariat.*

CN
ESTIMATES. PART III, SUPREME COURT OF CANADA. **Main/Corp** Canada. **VFOAT** Budget des Depenses. Partie III, Cour Supreme du Canada. (19??)-. English (French). $3.00 Canada; $3.60 other. Canada Communication Group Publishers, Order Processing, Ottawa Ontario K1A 0S9 Canada. **Tel** (819)956-4800, (819)956-4802. **LC** KE8244.A72; C36. **DD** 347.71/035/0681; 347.107350681.

CN
ESTIMATES. PART III, TARIFF BOARD. **Main/Corp** Canada. **VFOAT** Budget des Depenses. Partie III, Commission du Tarif. (19??)-. English (French). $3.00 Canada; $3.60 other. Canada Communication Group Publishers, Order Processing, Ottawa Ontario K1A 0S9 Canada. **Tel** (819)956-4800, (819)956-4802. **LC** KE6096.A72; C36. **DD** 354.0072/46.

CN
ESTIMATES. PART III, TAX REVIEW BOARD. **Main/Corp** Canada. **VFOAT** Budget de Depenses. Partie III, Commission de Revision de l'Impot. (19??)-. English (French). $3.00 Canada; $3.60 other. Canada Communication Group Publishers, Order Processing, Ottawa Ontario K1A 0S9 Canada. **Tel** (819)956-4800, (819)956-4802. **LC** KE5717.A72; C36. **DD** 354.0072/4.

CK/0014-1461
ESTUDIOS DE DERECHO. Vol. 1 (1952)-. Periodical. Spanish. sa. $26.00. Universidad de Antioquia / Medicina, Facultad de Medicina, 1226 Medellin Colombia. **Tel** 011 57 4 263-7954, 011 57 4 263-6446. **Ind/Abst** Am. Hist. Life (1969-1976); Index Foreign Leg. Per.; Int. Polit. Sci. Abstr.

SP/0423-4847
ESTUDIOS DE DEUSTO. [Estud. Deusto]. Vol. 1 (Jan. 1953)-. Periodical. Spanish. sa. **Ind/Abst** Am. Hist. Life (1964-1970).

BL
ESTUDOS DE DIREITO PUBLICO : EDP. **VFOAT** EDP; E.D.P.; Revista da Associacao dos Advogados da Prefeitura do Municipio de Sao Paulo. Yearly V. 1, No. 1, (Jan./June 1982)-. Periodical. Portuguese. Associacao dos Advogados da Prefeitura do Municipio de Sao Paulo, rua Maria Paula 96-6 O Andar, CEP 01319 Sao Paulo SP Brazil. **LC** K5; .S78. **DD** 342/.09/05; 342.2905.

BE
ETUDES DE LOGIQUE JURIDIQUE. (1966)-. Monographic series. Multiple languages (English, French and German). ir. Price varies per volume. Etablissements Emile Bruylant, 67 rue de la Regence, 1000 Brussels Belgium. **Tel** 011 32 2 5129845. **ED** CH Perelman.

IT
EUI WORKING PAPER. LAW / DEPARTMENT OF LAW, EUROPEAN UNIVERSITY INSTITUTE. **Added/Corp** European University Institute. Law Dept. **VFOAT** LAW; EUI Working Papers in Law. (1990)-. Monographic series. English (French). Price varies per volume. ***Continues in part*** *EUI Working Paper.*

GW/0937-7204
EUROPAISCHE ZEITSCHRIFT FUER WIRTSCHAFTSRECHT : EUZW. **VFOAT** EuZW; European Journal of Business Law; Revue Europeenne de Droit Economique. (April 10, 1990)-. German. Twenty-four times a year. Price varies. CH Beck Verlagsbuchhandlung, D 80791 Munich Germany. **Tel** 011 49 89 381891. **LC** KJE6411.3; .E87. **DD** 343.4/07/05; 344.03705.

GW/0531-2485
EUROPARECHT. [Europarecht]. Periodical. German. qt. DM125.00. Nomos Verlagsgesellschaft, Postfach 610, D-76484 Baden Baden Germany. **Tel** 011 49 7221 21040. **[CCC].** **Ind/Abst** Index Foreign Leg. Per.

US/1065-1055
EUROPE 92 (PORT WASHINGTON, N.Y.). (EUROPE 92.). [Eur. 92]. Vol. 1, Issue 1 (1990)-. Periodical. English. mo. $179.00. Europe 92, 37 Richards Road, Port Washington NY 11050. **DD** 341. available on an online database (file 636/Full-Text) from DIALOG. **Ind/Abst** PTS Newsl. Database [Full Txt.].

US/0093-5018
EUROPE : BASIC OIL LAWS AND CONCESSION CONTRACTS. ORIGINAL TEXTS. SUPPLELMENT. **Main/Corp** Petroleum Legislation, New York. (19??)-. English. qt. $6350.00. Barrows Company Inc., 116 East 66th Street, New York NY 10021. **Tel** (212)772-1199, (800)227-7697, FAX (212)288-7242, telex 4971238 BARROWS. **DD** 343/.73/077.

●UK/0964-0037
EUROPEAN CURRENT LAW : MONTHLY DIGEST. **Added/Corp** European Law Centre. (Jan. 1992)-. English. mo. £350.00 Europe; £368.00 other. Sweet & Maxwell Ltd., South Quay Plaza, 183 Marsh Wall, London E14 9FT England. **Tel** 011 44 264 342899, FAX 011 44 264 342723, telex 929089 ITPINF G. **LC** KJC30; .E97. **DD** 348/.4/026; 344.0826. ***Continues*** *European Law Digest, 0305-8476.*

UK/1350-4741
EUROPEAN FINANCIAL SERVICES LAW. (19??)-. English. Eleven times a year. $215.00. Graham & Trotman Ltd, Sterling House, 66 Wilson Road, London SW1V 1DE England. **Tel** 44 71 8211123.

NE/0929-0273
EUROPEAN JOURNAL OF HEALTH LAW. English. qt. $300.00. Martinus Nijhoff Publishers, Subsidiary of Kluwer Academic Publishers, Koraalrood 50, 2718 SC Zoetermeer Netherlands. **Tel** 011 31 79 684400. **ED** J.K.M. Gevers. **Desc:** Focuses on the development of health law in Europe. Includes discussions about ethical questions with legal implications, national legislation, court decisions and other relevant national material with international implications.

US/0929-1261
EUROPEAN JOURNAL OF LAW AND ECONOMICS. English. qt. $344.00. Kluwer Academic Publishers / Massachusetts, PO Box 358, Accord Station, Hingham MA 02018. **Tel** (617)871-6600. **ED** Jurgen G. Bakhaus. **Desc:** Publishes analytical studies of the impact of legal interventions into economic processes by legislators, courts and regulatory agencies, with an emphasis on European Community law and the comparative analysis of legal structures and the legal problem solutions in member states of the European Community.

●UK
EUROPEAN LAW JOURNAL. (1994)-. Academic Scholarly Publication. English. Three times a year. $147.00 North America; £95.00 other. Basil Blackwell Publishers Ltd, 108 Cowley Road, Oxford 0X4 1JF England. **Tel** 011 44 865 791100, FAX 011 44 865 791347, telex 837022 OXBOOK G. **(Subscription address:** Blackwell Publishers / UK, Marston Book Services, PO Box 87, Oxford OX2 0DT England.**)**

UK/0307-5400
EUROPEAN LAW REVIEW. [Eur. law rev.]. **VFOAT** Competition Law Checklist. Vol. 1 (Nov. 1975)-. Periodical. English. Six times a year. £210.00 Europe; £220.00 other. Sweet & Maxwell Ltd., South Quay Plaza, 183 Marsh Wall, London E14 9FT England. **Tel** 011 44 264 342899, FAX 011 44 264 342723, telex 929089 ITPINF G. **LC** K5; .U75. **DD** 341.24/2. available on microfilm and microfiche from University Microfilms International (UMI). **Ind/Abst** Aust. Leg. Mon. Dig.; Curr. Law Index (1980-); Index Foreign Leg. Per.; Index Leg. Period.; Leg. Resour. Index (1980-); LegalTrac (1980-).

●NE/1354-3725
EUROPEAN PUBLIC LAW. Vol. 1 (1995)-. English. qt. $386.00. Kluwer Academic Publishers, Postbus 322, 3300 AH Dordrecht, The Netherlands. **Tel** 011 (31) 78 524400, FAX 011 31 78 183273, telex 20083. **ED** Patrick Birkinshaw. **Desc:** Provides a detailed analysis of constitutional and administrative law at a crucial stage of European integration and legal development. Charts the emerging constitution of the European Community and the interplay between law and politics.

NE/0928-9801
EUROPEAN REVIEW OF PRIVATE LAW. **VFOAT** Revue Europeenne de Droit Prive; Europaische Zeitschrift fuer Privatrecht. Vol. 1, Nos. 1-2 (1993)-. Periodical. English (French and German). qt. $437.00. Martinus Nijhoff Publishers, Subsidiary of Kluwer Academic Publishers, Koraalrood 50, 2718 SC Zoetermeer Netherlands. **Tel** 011 31 79 684400. **ED** E. H. Hondius, M. E. Storme. **Desc:** Stresses the practical as well as academic importance of national private laws in an integrating Europe, in the face of the current emphasis placed on European Community Law.

BE/0014-3154
EUROPEAN TRANSPORT LAW. **VFOAT** Droit Europeen des Transports; Europaisches Transportrecht; Diritto Europeo dei Trasporti; Europees Vervoerrecht. Vol. 1, No 1 (1966)-. Periodical. English (French, German, Italian, Dutch and Spanish). Six times a year. 5,200F Belgium; 5,800F Europe; 6,200F other. European Transport Law, Maria Henriettalei 1, 2018 Antwerpen Belgium. **Tel** 011 32 3 2313655, FAX 011 32 3 2342380, telex 32 544. **ED** Robert Wyffels. **LC** K5; .U79. **DD** 343.4/093; 344.0393. Index available. **Bk Rev. Circ:** 900.

Law

SP

EUSKAL HERRIKO AGINTARITZAREN ALDIZKARIA / BOLETIN OFICIAL DEL PAIS VASCO. Main/Corp Pais Vasco (Spain). **VFOAT** Boletin Oficial del Pais Vasco. (19??)-. Basque (Spanish). 13800ptas. Duque de Wellington 2, Vitoria-Gasteiz Spain.

US

EVIDENCE. Main/Corp Bay Area Review Course, Inc. English. ir. Legal Book Corporation, 316 West 2nd Street, Los Angeles CA 90012. **Tel** (310)626-3494. **LC** KF8935.Z9; B38. **DD** 347/.73/6.

CN/0708-9031
EXCISE NEWS. Added/Corp Canada. Excise Technical Support Section. Canada. Excise Technical Information Section. **VFOAT** Nouvelles de l'Accise. No. 9 (May 1973)-. Periodical. English (French). Four times a year. Free. Canada Communication Group Publishers, Order Processing, Ottawa Ontario K1A 0S9 Canada. **Tel** (819)956-4800, (819)956-4802. **Circ:** 60,000. **Continues** Federal Sales Tax News, 0708-9023.
Desc: Newsletter containing information on Canadian federal sales and excise tax laws and on the administrative policy of the Department of National Revenue (Canada) regarding these laws.

US/0273-7612
EXECUTIVE COMPENSATION & TAXATION COORDINATOR. [Exec. compens. tax. coord.]. **Added/Corp** Research Institute of America. **VFOAT** Executive Compensation and Taxation Coordinator. **VAT** Executive Compensation and Taxation Coordinator. (19??)-. English. Twelve times a year. Research Institute of America, 117 East Stevens Avenue, Valhalla NY 10595. **Tel** (800)431-9025. **ED** James E. Cheeks. **DD** 343. [CCC].
Desc: Planning guidance to help structure successful compensation strategies.

US

EXECUTIVE ORDER. Main/Corp Connectiuct. Governor. English. Connecticut Governor's Office, Hartford CT 06115. **LC** KFC3634.A2; C64. **DD** 348/.746/01.

US

EXECUTIVE ORDER / EXECUTIVE DEPARTMENT, STATE OF CALIFORNIA. Main/Corp California. Executive Department. English. **LC** KFC34; .A234. **DD** 342.794/002636; 347.940202636.

US

EXECUTIVE ORDER - VIRGINIA. Main/Corp Virginia. Governor's Office. English. Commonwealth of Virginia, PO Box IB, Richmond VA 23201. **LC** KFV2434.A2; V54. **DD** 348/.755/01.

US/0891-0278
EXERCISE STANDARDS & MALPRACTICE REPORTER, THE. [Exerc. stand. malpract. report.]. **Added/Corp** Professional Reports Corporation. Vol. 1, No. 1 (Jan. 1987)-. Periodical. English. Six times a year. $39.95 US; $45.95 Canada; $49.95 other. Professional Reports Corporation, 4418 Belden Village Street Northwest, Canton OH 44718. **Tel** (216)492-6063, (800)336-0083, FAX (216)492-6176. **ED** David L. Herbert. **LC** KF2915.E95; A134. **DD** 344.73/017616137; 347.30417616137. **NLM** W1; EX204F. Index available. cum. index. **Bk Rev**. **Ad Acc**, **Adv Mgr:** Molly Romig. **Circ:** 700 (ctrl).
Desc: Focuses on current standards of practice for exercise, wellness and health promotion programs. Malpractice and professional concerns are examined in each issues.

US/0363-0919
EXPENSES AND APPROPRIATIONS OF THE MISSISSIPPI LEGISLATURE.
Added/Corp Mississippi. Auditor of Public Accounts. Mississippi. Office of the State Auditor. (19??)-. English. State Auditor of Public Accounts, PO Box 1060, Jackson MS 39205. **LC** HJ11; .M697. **DD** 328.762/0068/1.

US/1054-3473
EXPERIENCE : THE MAGAZINE OF THE SENIOR LAWYERS DIVISION, AMERICAN BAR ASSOCIATION.
[Experience]. **Added/Corp** American Bar Association. Senior Lawyers Division. Vol. 1, No. 1 (Fall 1990)-. Periodical. English. qt (4 issues). $20.00. American Bar Association, 750 North Lake Shore Drive, Chicago IL 60611. **Tel** (312)988-5522, (312)988-5241, FAX (312)988-5528, telex 270593. **LC** K5; .X86. **DD** 346.7301/3; 347.306/3. **Continues** Senior Lawyer, 0886-8255.

US/0737-8726
EXPERT AND THE LAW, THE. (THE EXPERT AND THE LAW : A PUBLICATION OF THE NATIONAL FORENSIC CENTER.). [Expert law]. Vol. 1, No. 1 (Dec. 7, 1981) -. Periodical. English. bm. $55.00. National Forensic Center, 17 Temple Terrace, Lawrenceville NJ 08649. **Tel** (609)883-0550, (800)526-5177, FAX (609)883-7622. **ED** Mark Wleckowski. **LC** KF8961.A15; E95. **DD** 347.73/67; 347.30767. **Bk Rev**. **Ad Acc**. **Circ:** 1,500 (ctrl).
Desc: The application of scientific medical and technical knowledge to litigation.
Ind/Abst NEXIS (1981-).

US/0277-0555
EXPERT WITNESS JOURNAL. (EXPERT WITNESS JOURNAL : ILLUSTRATES EI'S EXPERT WITNESS ASSISTANCE.). [Expert witn. j.]. **Added/Corp** Expertise Institute. (19??)-. Periodical. English. Twelve times a year. $95.00. Seak Inc., PO Box 729, East Falmouth MA 02541. **Tel** (508)548-7023, FAX (508)540-8304. **ED** Steven Bahitsky. **LC** KF8961.A15; E96. **DD** 347.73/66; 347.30766. **Bk Rev**. **Ad Acc**. ctrl circ. **Continues** Lawlab Journal.

BE

EXPLANATORY NOTES TO THE HARMONIZED SYSTEM. See Business-Commerce.

US

EXPORT ADMINISTRATION REGULATIONS. Main/Corp United States. Bureau of Export Administration. **VFOAT** US Export Administration Regulations; U.S. Export Administration Regulations. (Oct. 1988)-. Government Publication. English. an (Supplements for approximately one year). $87.00 US; $108.75 other. US Department of Commerce, 14th Street & Constitution Avenue NW, Washington DC 20230. **Tel** (202)482-2000, FAX (202)482-3772. **LC** KF1987.A329; Q45. **DD** 343.73/0878/05. **Continues** Export Administration Regulations, 0094-8411.
Desc: A compilation of official regulations and policies governing the export licensing of commodities and technical data.

US

EXPORTS UNDER THE CONCESSIONAL SALES PROGRAM : B.TITLE I, PUBLIC LAW 480. Added/Corp United States. Foreign Agricultural Service. (19??)-. Government Publication. English. US Department of Agriculture / Foreign Agricultural Service, 14th Street & Independence Avenue Southwest, Washington DC 20250. **Tel** (202)720-9445, FAX (202)720-7729. available on microfiche (Vols. for (April 1983-) distributed to depository libraries).

CN/1183-6792
EXPRESSION : BULLETIN DE L'ASSOCIATION DES JURISTES D'EXPRESSION FRANCAISE DE L'ONTARIO (AJEFO), L'. [Expr. - Assoc. juristes expr. fr. Ont.]. **Added/Corp** Association des Juristes d'Expression Francaise de l'Ontario. (May 1991)-. Bulletin. French. mo. 32.10Can$. Association des Juristes D'Expression Francaise de L'Ontario, 17 Rue Copernicus, Ottawa Ontario K1N 6N5 Canada. **DD** 340.

●CK/0121-6279
EXTERNADISTA : REVISTA DE LA UNIVERSIDAD EXTERNADO DE COLOMBIA. Added/Corp Universidad Externado de Colombia. No. 1 (July/Dec. 1992)-. Periodical. Spanish. sa. 4000Col$. Universidad Externado de Colombia, Departamento de Publicaciones, Calle 12, No. 0-46, Este, Apdo. Aereo 03414, Bogota, Colombia. **Tel** 341-2610, FAX 284-3769. **LC** K5; .X88. **Continues** Externado (Universidad Externado de Colombia).

CK

EXTERNADO (UNIVERSIDAD EXTERNADO DE COLOMBIA). Title Change. (EXTERNADO : REVISTA DE LA UNIVERSIDAD EXTERNADO DE COLOMBIA.). **Added/Corp** Universidad Externado de Colombia. **VFOAT** Revista de la Universidad Externado de Colombia. No. 1 (Oct. 1981)-(19??). Periodical. Spanish. La Universidad, Calle 12 No 1-17, Bogota Colombia. **LC** K5; .X88. **DD** 340/.05. **Continues** Revista de la Universidad Externado de Colombia. **Continued by** Externadista.

MM

EXTERNAL AFFAIRS SERVICE LIST. Main/Corp Malta. Ministry of Foreign Affairs. English. Ministry of Foreign Affairs / Malta, Palazzo Parisio, Merchanst Street, Valletta Malta. **LC** JX1802.7; .A35A. **DD** 354.45/8500892.

SP

F.J., REVISTA DE LA FACULTAD DE JURISPRUDENCIA Y CIENCIAS SOCIALES. Main/Corp Quito. Universidad Central. Facultad de Jurisprudencia y Ciencias Sociales. **VAT** Facultad de Jurisprudencia, Revista de la Facultad de Jurisprudencia y Ciencias Sociales. Periodical. Spanish. Facultad de Jurisprudencia y Ciencias Sociales, Casilla Postas 23-11, Quito Spain. **LC** K17; .U58.

CH

FA CHIH HSUEH KAN. VFOAT Law & Society. Periodical. Multiple languages (Chinese and German). $50.00 per copy, $1.50 US. Second Floor No. 509, Lane 6 Han-Chow South Road Sec, Taipei 100 Taiwan. **LC** K6; .A2.
Ind/Abst Soc. Work Abstr. (?-?).

CC

FA HSUEH TSA CHIH. VFOAT Law Magazine; Faxuezazhi; Faxue Zazhi. No. 1 (July 1980)-. Periodical. Chinese. bm. $5.60. **(Subscription address:** China International Book Trading Corporation, PO Box 399, Library Service Department, Beijing 100044 People's Republic of China.**)**

CC

FA HSUEH YEN CHIU. Added/Corp Chung-kuo She Hui ko Hsueh Chu Pan She. **VFOAT** Faxue Yanjiu; Studies in Law. No. 1 (1979)-. Periodical. Chinese (table of contents in English). bm. $17.22. **(Subscription address:** China International Book Trading Corporation, PO Box 399, Library Service Department, Beijing 100044 People's Republic of China.**)**
Ind/Abst Index Foreign Leg. Per.

US

FACTS AND FINDINGS. (FACTS AND FINDINGS : OFFICIAL PUBLICATION OF THE NATIONAL ASSOCIATION OF LEGAL ASSISTANTS INC.). (19??)-. Periodical. English. Four times a year. Free to members; $20.00 nonmembers. National Association of Legal Assistants, 1601 South Main, #300, Tulsa OK 74119. **Tel** (918)587-6828, FAX (918)582-6772.

PR

FACTUM : BOLETIN OFICIAL DEL COLEGIO DE ABOGADOS DE PUERTO RICO. Periodical. Spanish (English). qt. $10.00. Factum, Apartado 1900, San Juan, Puerto Rico 00903. **Tel** (809)721-3358. **ED** Juan R Deliz-Roman. **LC** KGV235.C65; A24. **DD** 340/.06/07295. **Bk Rev**. **Ad Acc**. **Circ:** 8,000 (ctrl).
Desc: An official publication of the Puerto Rico Bar Association. We accept articles that tends to promote and develop the discusion of today's law issues.

US/1069-921X
FAIR EMPLOYMENT PRACTICES GUIDELINES. See Business-Personnel Management.

IT/0394-2740
FALLIMENTO E LE ALTRE PROCEDURE CONCORSUALI, IL. VFOAT Fallimento. Vol. 1 (Jan./March 1979)-. Periodical. Italian. mo. L265000 Italy; L530000 other. IPSOA Editore SRL, Casella Postale 12055, Mastrangelo, 20120 Milan Italy. **Tel** 011 39 2 82476248.

UK/0967-7119
FAMILY MATTERS LONDON. (1993)-. English. Ten times a year. £75.00 Europe; £79.00 other. Sweet & Maxwell Ltd., South Quay Plaza, 183 Marsh Wall, London E14 9FT England. **Tel** 011 44 264 342899, FAX 011 44 264 342723, telex 929089 ITPINF G.
Ind/Abst Soc. Work Abstr. [Select. Cov.].

PH/0046-3272
FAR EASTERN LAW REVIEW. [Far East. law rev.]. **Added/Corp** Far Eastern University. Institute of Law. Vol. 4, No. 3 (Sept. 1956)-. Periodical. English. Twice a year. Far Eastern University of Manila / Institute of Law, PO Box 609, Manila Phillipines. available on microfilm and microfiche from University Microfilms International (UMI). **Continues** FEU Law Quarterly.
Ind/Abst Index Foreign Leg. Per.

US/1043-0547
FAULKNER & GRAY'S BANKRUPTCY LAW REVIEW. Ceased. [Faulkner & Gray's bankruptcy law rev.]. **Added/Corp** Faulkner & Gray, Inc. **VFOAT** Faulkner and Gray's Bankruptcy Law Review; Bankruptcy Law Review. Vol. 1, No. 1 (Spring 1989)-(19??). Periodical. English. qt. Faulkner & Gray Inc., 11 Penn Plaza, 17th Floor, New York NY 10001. **Tel** (212)967-7000, (800)535-8403. **ED** Robert J Murdich. **LC** K6; .A95. **DD** 346.73/078/05; 347.3067805. **Bk Rev**. **Ad Acc**. **Circ:** 1,500 (ctrl). available on microfilm and microfiche from University Microfilms International (UMI).
Ind/Abst Account. Tax Datab. (Winter 1991-) [Full Txt.].

US/0196-4194
FAYETTE LEGAL JOURNAL. Vol. 1 (1938)-. English. wk. $35.00. Fayette Legal Journal, 61 East Main Street, Uniontown PA 15401. **Tel** (412)430-1227. **DD** 348/.748/042.

US/0532-7091
FCL NEWSLETTER. See Public Administration.

US/0882-5041
FEDERAL AND STATE JUDICIAL CLERKSHIP DIRECTORY. Added/Corp National Association for Law Placement (U.S.). **VFOAT** Judicial Clerkship Directory. (1983)-. Directory. English. an. $35.00 members, $70.00 nonmembers. National Association for Law Placement, 1666 Connecticut Avenue, Suite 450, Washington DC 20009. **Tel** (202)667-1666, FAX (202)265-6735. **DD** 340. ***Continues*** *Judicial Clerkship Survey.*

US/1075-8534
FEDERAL BAR COUNCIL NEWS. (199?)-. English. Five times a year (Feb., Apr., June, Oct., Dec.). $7.50. Federal Bar Council, 145 East 49th Street, New York NY 10017. **Tel** (212)644-9771.

US/0279-4691
FEDERAL BAR NEWS & JOURNAL. [Fed. bar news j.]. **Added/Corp** Federal Bar Association. **VFOAT** Federal Bar News and Journal. Vol. 28, No. 9 (Sept. 1981)-. Academic Scholarly Publication. English. Ten times a year (Mar./Apr. and Nov./Dec. issues combined). $25.00 US; $35.00 other. Federal Bar Association, 1815 H Street Northwest, Suite 408, Washington DC 20006. **Tel** (202)638-0252, FAX (202)775-0295. **ED** Sally B. Pfund. **LC** K6; .E285. **DD** 349.73/05; 347.3005. Index available. cum. index (published every two years). **Bk Rev**, (Qty: 20-25). **Ad Acc, Adv Mgr:** Beth Kemper. **Circ:** 16,000. available on microfilm and microfiche from West Publishing; available on an online database from West Publishing. ***Formed by the union of*** *Federal Bar News (Washington, D.C. : 1953), 0014-9047* ***and*** *Federal Bar Journal, 0014-9039.*
Desc: A 48- to 56-page journal describing Federal Bar Association activities and various law topics of interest to the federal legal profession. It is directed solely toward issues affecting attorneys in federal practice. News columns offer rules/legislative updates, continuing education opportunities, Association activities. In-depth scholarly articles by leading experts discuss "hot" topics including civility, intellectual property, labor law. Regular features include book reviews, directories, cummulative indices, Annual Reports.
Ind/Abst Bowne Dig. Corp. Sec. Lawyers; Fed. Tax Artic.; Hum. Rights Intern. Rep.; Index Leg. Period.; Law Office Inf. Serv.; Leg. Resour. Index (1981-); LegalTrac (1981-).

US/0093-2108
FEDERAL CARRIERS CASES (CHICAGO). ***Ceased.*** (FEDERAL CARRIERS CASES.). **Main/Corp** Commerce Clearing House. **Added/Corp** United States. Interstate Commerce Commission. United States. Courts. (1940)-(Dec. 1992). English. Commerce Clearing House Inc., 4025 West Peterson Avenue, Chicago IL 60646-6085. **Tel** (312)583-8500, FAX (708)940-4600. **ED** A. E. Schechter. **LC** KF1091; .A513. **DD** 343/.73/093. cum. index.
Desc: Federal controls over motor and water carriers, freight forwarders.

US/1055-8195
FEDERAL CIRCUIT BAR JOURNAL, THE. [Fed. Circuit Bar j.]. **Added/Corp** United States. Court of Appeals (Federal Circuit) Federal Circuit Bar Association. Vol. 1, No. 1 (Spring 1991)-. Periodical. English. Four times a year. $30.00. Federal Circuit Bar Association, 1300 I Street Northwest, Suite 700, Washington DC 20005-3315. **LC** K6; .E286. **DD** 347.73/8/05; 347.307805.
Ind/Abst Index Leg. Period. (1992-).

●US/1067-4934
FEDERAL CLAIMS REPORTER. [Fed. claims report.]. **Added/Corp** West Publishing Company. United States. Court of Federal Claims. United States. Court of Appeals (Federal Circuit) United States. Supreme Court. No. 1 (Dec. 10, 1992)-. English. bw. $250.00. West Publishing Company, 610 Opperman Drive, PO Box 64526, Eagan MN 55123-1308. **Tel** (612)687-5618, (800)328-9352, FAX (612)687-5388, (800)562-2329. **DD** 348.73/44; 347.30844. ***Formed by the union of*** *United States Claims Court Reporter (Annual)* ***and*** *United States Claims Court Reporter.*

US
FEDERAL COMMUNICATIONS COMMISSION RULES AND REGULATIONS.--INDIVIDUAL PARTS. English. ir. Price varies. Rules Service Company, 7615 Standish Place, Rockville MD 20855. **Tel** (301)424-9402, FAX (301)762-7853.

US/0163-7606
FEDERAL COMMUNICATIONS LAW JOURNAL. [Fed. commun. law j.]. V. 30- Winter 1977-. Academic Scholarly Publication. English. ir (3 times per academic year). $20.00 US; $30.00 other. Federal Communications Law Journal, UCLA School of Law, 405 Hilgard Avenue, Los Angeles CA 90024. **Tel** (310)825-3712. **ED** Anita Larue. **LC** K6; .E29. **DD** 343/.73/099405. **Ad Acc. Circ:** 2,500 (ctrl). available on microfilm and microfiche from University Microfilms International (UMI). Documents available from UMI Article Clearinghouse. ***Continues*** *Federal Communications Bar Journal.*
Desc: The journal carries articles on broadcast communications, satellite telecommunications, and entertainment law. It is the oldest scholarly journal in the country, exclusively devoted to communications law and related fields.
Ind/Abst ABI/INFORM Glob. Ed.; ABI Inform Ondisc (Jan. 1985-); Commun. Abstr.; Curr. Law Index (1980-); Expand. Acad. Index (1992-); Index Leg. Period.; Leg. Resour. Index (1980-); LegalTrac (1980-); Newsp. Period. Abstr. (1989-).

US/0747-9700
FEDERAL CONTRACT DISPUTES. (May 1984)-. Periodical. English. mo. $285.00. Business Publishers Inc., 951 Pershing Drive, Silver Spring MD 20910-4464. **Tel** (301)587-6300, (800)274-0122, FAX (301)585-9075. **LC** KF846.3; .F43. **DD** 346.73/023/05; 347.3062305. **[CCC].**
Desc: Each issue brings you concise synopses of a dozen major decisions - from the courts, the Comptroller General, and the boards of contract appeals. In addition, each issue contains up to date summaries of the latest developments in federal procurement policy and practice, with expert commentary on current issues.

US/0014-9063
FEDERAL CONTRACTS REPORT. **Main/Corp** Bureau of National Affairs (Washington, D.C.). (Feb. 24 1964)-. Periodical. English. wk. $967.00. Bureau of National Affairs Inc., 9435 Key West Avenue, Rockville MD 20850. **Tel** (800)372-1033, (301)258-1033, FAX (301)948-5823. **(Subscription address:** 9435 Key West Avenue, Rockville MD 20850; telephone: FAX (301)948-5823**) ED** Sheila A Quigley. **LC** KF849.A1; B85. **DD** 346; 346/.73/023. **[CCC].** Index Available, published separately, free-automatically sent.
Desc: A reporting service providing comprehensive coverage of the latest significant developments affecting federal contracts and grants.

●US/1059-6828
FEDERAL COURT APPOINTMENTS REPORT. [Fed. court appointm. rep.]. Vol. 1, No. 1 Jan./Feb (1992)-. Periodical. English. Six times a year. $125.00 (one year). Want Publishing Company, 1511 K Street Northwest, Suite 635, Washington DC 20005. **Tel** (202)783-1887, FAX (202)393-5106. **ED** Robert Want. **DD** 347. available in Loose-leaf.

US/0428-111X
FEDERAL COURT CLERKS' NEWS, THE. [Fed. court clerks' news]. **Added/Corp** Federal Court Clerks Association. (19??)-. Periodical. English. bm. $12.00 Clerks, $6.00 Ch. Dep. Clerks, $1.20 Dep. Clerks. Federal Court Clerks Association, 120 Oriole Lane, La Platta MD 20646.

US/0741-692X
FEDERAL COURT MANAGEMENT STATISTICS. See Law-Abstracting, Bibliographies and Statistics.

CN/0227-0390
FEDERAL COURT OF APPEAL DECISIONS. [Fed. Court Appeal decis.]. **Added/Corp** Canada. Federal Court of Appeal. Western Legal Publications Ltd. **VFOAT** Canada Federal Court of Appeal Decision. (1981)-. Periodical. English. Twelve times a year. $150.00. Western Legal Publications Ltd., 301 One Alexander Street, Vancouver BC V6A 1B2 Canada. **Tel** (800)663-0422, (604)687-5671. **DD** 348.71/046.

UK
FEDERAL COURT OF CANADA SERVICE. English. ir. 400.00Can$. Butterworth & Company Ltd. / Canada, 75 Clegg Road, Markham Ontario L6G 1A1 Canada. **Tel** (905)479-2665, (800)668-6481.
Desc: Brings complete coverage of among other things the Federal Court Act, the Federal Court Rules, and the Federal Court Immigration Rules.

US/0734-9513
FEDERAL COURT PROCUREMENT DECISIONS. Vol. 1, No. 1 (Oct. 1982)-. Periodical. English. mo. $796.00 US; $826.00 other. Federal Publications Inc, 1120 20th Street Northwest, Washington DC 20036. **Tel** (202)337-7000, (800)922-4330, FAX (202)659-2233. **LC** KF845.A2; F43. **DD** 346.73/023/02643; 347.3062302643.

AT/0728-6082
FEDERAL COURT REPORTER. [Fed. Court report.]. (1982)-. Periodical. English. Twenty-six times a year (Every 2 wks.). 295.00Aus$ one year; 490.00Aus$two years. Law Press of Australia, GPO Box 3793, Sydney NSW 2001 Australia. **Tel** 011 61 2 3607788, FAX 011 61 2 3607838. **ED** Marion O'Halloran. **DD** 347.9402. Index available. cum. index. ctrl circ.

AT
FEDERAL COURT REPORTS, THE. **Main/Corp** Australia. Federal Court. **Added/Corp** Law Book Company. Vol. 1 (1984)-. English. 210.00Aus$ (renewals). The Law Book Company Limited, 44-50 Waterloo Road, North Ryde New South Wales, 2113 Australia. **Tel** 011 61 2 8870177, FAX 011 61 2 8887240, telex ASBOOK 27445.
Ind/Abst Aust. Leg. Mon. Dig.

●US/1065-9943
FEDERAL EEO UPDATE. [Fed. EEO update]. Vol. 1, No. 1 (Sept. 1992)-. Periodical. English. mo. $145.00. FPMI Communications Inc., 707 Fiber Street, Huntsville AL 35801. **Tel** (205)539-1850, FAX (205)539-0911, . **DD** 342.

US
FEDERAL FIFTH CIRCUIT CITATIONS. English. mo. $160.00 (2 bound volumes), $195.00 (cumulative supplements). Shepards McGraw-Hill Inc, 555 Middle Creek Parkway, PO Box 35300, Colorado Springs CO 80935-3530. **Tel** (719)488-3000, FAX (800)525-0053.

US/0730-5028
FEDERAL FINANCIAL REGULATORY DIGEST. [Fed. financ. regul. dig.]. English. mo. Capitol Reports Inc, 1750 Pennsylvania Avenue NW/Suite 1107, Washington DC 20006. **LC** KF1039.A15; F42. **DD** 346.73/073; 347.30673.

US
FEDERAL HEALTH MONITOR, THE. Periodical. English. mo. National Health Lawyers Association, 1120 Connecticut Street, Suite 950, Washington DC 20006. **Tel** (202)833-1100, FAX (202)833-1105.

US/1046-3631
FEDERAL INDEX (1985). ***Ceased.*** (FEDERAL INDEX.). [Fed. index]. **Added/Corp** National Standards Association (U.S.). Vol. 9, No. 1 (Jan. 1985)-(Dec. 1993). Periodical. English. mo. Federal Index Capital Services Inc., 1200 Quince Orchard Boulevard, Gaithersburg MD 20878. **LC** Z7165.U5; F42; JK1. **DD** 973. ***Continues*** *CSI Federal Index, 0738-6478.*

UK
FEDERAL INDUSTRIAL LAWS SERVICE. English. ir. Butterworth Heinemann Publishers, Linacre House, Jordan Hill, Oxford OX2 8DP England. **Tel** 011 44 865 310366.

US/0192-625X
FEDERAL JUDICIAL WORKLOAD STATISTICS. See Law-Abstracting, Bibliographies and Statistics.

US/0273-3641
FEDERAL LAW JOURNAL (OVIEDO). (THE FEDERAL LAW JOURNAL.). V. 1-. Periodical. English. $36.00. Federal Information News Service, 995 Westwood Square, Box 837, Oviedo FL 32765. **LC** K6; .E295. **DD** 349.73/05; 347.3005.

AT
FEDERAL LAW REPORTS (AUSTRALIA), THE. (THE FEDERAL LAW REPORTS : BEING REPORTS OF CASES DECIDED BY THE FEDERAL COURTS (OTHER THAN THE HIGH COURT), STATE COURTS EXERCISING FEDERAL JURISDICTION AND COURTS OF TERRITORIES.). **Added/Corp** Law Book Co. of Australasia. Law Book Company. Vol. 1 (1956-1961)-. English. $186.00. The Law Book Company Limited, 44-50 Waterloo Road, North Ryde New South Wales, 2113 Australia. **Tel** 011 61 2 8870177, FAX 011 61 2 8887240, telex ASBOOK 27445. **ED** Charles Sweeney.
Desc: Reports all the important decisions on federal law from the State Supreme Courts as well as decisions of the Territory Supreme Courts, the Family Court, and the federal tribunals.
Ind/Abst Aust. Leg. Mon. Dig.

AT/0067-205X
FEDERAL LAW REVIEW. [Fed. law rev.]. **Added/Corp** Australian National University. Faculty of Law. Vol. 1 (1964)-. Periodical. English. ir (4 issues). Price varies per volume. The Law Book Company Limited, 44-50 Waterloo Road, North Ryde New South Wales, 2113 Australia. **Tel** 011 61 2 8870177, FAX 011 61 2 8887240, telex ASBOOK 27445.
Ind/Abst APAIS, Aust. Public Aff. Inf. Ser. (1964-); Aust. Leg. Mon. Dig.; Curr. Law Index (1980-); Index Leg. Period.; Leg. Resour. Index (1980-); LegalTrac (1986-).

US
FEDERAL MERIT SYSTEMS DESK BOOK. English. an. $58.00 (postage included). LRP Publications, 747 Dresher Road, PO Box 980, Horsham PA 19044-0980. **Tel** (800)341-7874, (215)784-0860, FAX (215)784-9639, (215)784-0870.
Desc: Compact, affordable, and user-friendly source of MSPB decisions and commentary.

US/0888-269X
FEDERAL PAY AND BENEFITS REPORTER. See Public Administration-Civil Service.

US/0097-6326
FEDERAL REGISTER. [Fed. regist.]. **Added/Corp** United States. Office of the Federal

Register. United States. National Archives. Vol. 1 No. 1 (Mar. 14, 1936)-. Government Publication. English. da (except Saturday and Sunday and legal holidays). $490.00 US; $612.50 other. Superintendent of Documents, US Government Printing Office, Washington DC 20402. **Tel** (202)275-3328, FAX (202)786-2377. **LC** KF70; .A2. **DD** 353.005. **NLM** KF 70.A2 F292. **CODEN** FEREAC. Index available (monthly, $22.00 US; $27.50 other). available on CD-ROM (full-text) from Counterpoint Publishing; available on microfilm and microfiche from University Microfilms International (UMI); available on an online database. Documents available from CASDDS.
Desc: Provides a uniform system for making available to the public regulations and legal notices issued by Federal agencies. These include Presidential proclamations and Executive orders and Federal agency documents having general applicability and legal effect, documents required to be published by Act of Congress and other Federal agency documents of public interest.
Ind/Abst BioBusiness; Chem. Abstr.; Chem. Ind. Notes; Coal Abstr.; Foods Adlibra; Health Plan. Adminis.; Hospit. Health Admin. Index; Ind. Hyg. Dig.; INIS Atomindex [Micro.]; Int. Pharm. Abstr.; Iowa Drug Inf. Serv. (1971-); Lit. Pat. Abstr., Oilfield Chem. (1972-); Lit. Abstr., Catal. Catal.; Lit. Abstr., Health Environ.; Lit. Abstr., Pet. Refin. Petrochem.; Lit. Abstr., Pet. Substit.; Lit. Abstr., Transp. Storage; Text. Technol. Dig. (19??-199?).

US/0364-1406
FEDERAL REGISTER. **Added/Corp** United States. National Archives. United States. Office of the Federal Register. Vol. 1, No. 1 (Mar. 14, 1936)-. Government Publication. English. da. $444.00 US; $555.00 other. Superintendent of Documents, US Government Printing Office, Washington DC 20402. **Tel** (202)275-3328, FAX (202)786-2377.
Ind/Abst Aviat. Tradescan [Select. Cov.].

US
FEDERAL REGISTER HIGHLIGHTS NEWSLETTER. Newsletter. English. Twenty times a year. $50.00. National Clearinghouse for Legal Services, 205 West Monroe Street 2nd Floor, Chicago IL 60606. **Tel** (312)263-3830.

US/1066-5862
FEDERAL REGISTER MONITOR, THE. [Fed. regist. monit.]. (1987)-. Periodical. English. Twenty-four times a year. $190.00. Stockholder Consulting Service, PO Box 080260, Staten Island NY 10308. **Tel** (718)984-0900, FAX (718)984-5785. **ED** David W. Pitou. **DD** 353. **Circ:** 1,000 (ctrl).

US/0097-6326
FEDERAL REGISTER [MICROFORM]. **Added/Corp** United States. National Archives. United States. Office of the Federal Register. Vol. 1, No. 1 (Mar. 14, 1936)-. Government Publication. English. da. $444.00. Superintendent of Documents, US Government Printing Office, Washington DC 20402. **Tel** (202)275-3328, FAX (202)786-2377.

US
FEDERAL REGULATORY PROCESS : AGENCY PRACTICES & PROCEDURES. (19??)-. English. ir. $85.00. Prentice-Hall Law and Business, 270 Sylvan Avenue, Englewood Cliffs NJ 07632. **Tel** (800)223-0231, (201)894-8538, FAX (201)894-8666. cum. index.
Desc: Administrative case law and theory; includes tips for persuading an agency to make or change a decision, challenging agency actions in court, writing briefs, and seeking technical interpretative rulings.

US/0364-3581
FEDERAL RULES OF EVIDENCE NEWS. **Added/Corp** United States. Federal Rules of Evidence. Vol. 1 (Jan. 1976)-. Periodical. English. ir. Clark Boardman Callaghan, 155 Pfingsten Road, Deerfield IL 60015. **Tel** (800)323-8067. **LC** KF8931.A3; F4. **DD** 347/.73/605. **[CCC].**

US
FEDERAL SECURITIES ACT: PRIMARY SOURCE MANUAL. (19??)-. English. ir. Matthew Bender & Company Inc., 1275 Broadway, Albany NY 12204. **Tel** (800)833-9844, (518)487-3000.

US
FEDERAL SEVENTH CIRCUIT CITATIONS. English. mo. $180.00 (2 bound volumes), $225.00 (cumulative supplements). Shepards McGraw-Hill Inc, 555 Middle Creek Parkway, PO Box 35300, Colorado Springs CO 80935-3530. **Tel** (719)488-3000, FAX (800)525-0053.

US
FEDERAL TAX COORDINATOR 2D. LISTING OF CURRENT TAX ARTICLES. **Added/Corp** Research Institute of America, inc. **VFOAT** Listing of Current Tax Articles. (1977)-. English. mo. $1242.00. Research Institute of America, 117 East Stevens Avenue, Valhalla NY 10595. **Tel** (800)431-9025. **ED** James E Cheeks.
Desc: Thorough coverage of the entire body of federal tax law. Geared to the tax professional.

US/0737-8718
FEDERAL TAX COURSE (STUDENTS ED.). (FEDERAL TAX COURSE / PRENTICE HALL.). [Fed. tax course (Stud. ed.)]. **Added/Corp** Prentice-Hall, Inc. (1980)-. English. an. $52.50. Maxwell Macmillan Professional Business Division, 910 Sylvan Avenue, Englewood Cliffs NJ 07632-3310. **Tel** (800)431-9025. **(Subscription address:** Prentice Hall Inc, PO Box 801, Englewood Cliffs NJ 07632.**)** **LC** KF6289; .P75. **DD** 343.7304; 347.3034. ***Continues*** *Prentice-Hall Federal Tax Course (Students Edition).*
Desc: Analyzes income tax rules in light of accounting principles with special attention given to accounting angles involved in tax decisions.

US/0888-0522
FEDERAL TAX MANUAL. **See** Public Administration-Public Finance and Taxation.

US/1044-6648
FELA REPORTER AND RAILROAD LIABILITY MONITOR. [FELA report. railr. liabil. monit.]. **VAT** Federal Employers' Liability Act Reporter and Railroad Liability Monitor. (198?)-. Periodical. English. Twelve times a year. $385.00. M. Lee Smith Publishers and Printers, 162 4th Avenue North, PO Box 198867, Nashville TN 37219. **Tel** (615)242-7395, (800)274-6774, FAX (615)256-6601. **LC** KF1317.R2; A494. **DD** 3467303/22; 347.306322.

CN/0847-5261
FEMME ET LA LOI, LA. [Femme loi]. **Added/Corp** Nouveau-Brunswick. Direction Generale de la Condition Feminine. **VFOAT** Women and the Law. No 1 (Jan. 1990)-. Periodical. French. **DD** 346.715/10134/05.

BO
FICHERO DE JURISPRUDENCIA. **Added/Corp** Cochambamba, Bolivia. Universidad Mayor de San Simon. Spanish.

US/0747-6582
FIDELITY & SURETY NEWS : FSN. **Added/Corp** American Bar Association. Fidelity and Surety Law Committee. Michie Company. **VFOAT** FSN; F.S.N.; Fidelity and Surety News. (19??)-. Periodical. English. qt (4 issues). $125.00. American Bar Association, 750 North Lake Shore Drive, Chicago IL 60611. **Tel** (312)988-5522, (312)988-5241, FAX (312)988-5528, telex 270593. **DD** 346.

US
FIDUCIARY REPORTER. (1951)-. Periodical. English. mo. $60.00. Geo T. Bisel Company, 710 South Washington Square, Philadelphia PA 19106. **Tel** (800)247-3526.

US/0093-1381
FINAL REPORT - TEXAS LEGISLATIVE SERVICE. (FINAL REPORT, LEGISLATURE.). **Main/Corp** Texas Legislative Service. English. $25.00. Texas Legislative Service, PO Box 100, Austin TX 78767. **Tel** (512)476-7596. **LC** KFT1215; .T48. **DD** 348/.764/01. ctrl circ.
Desc: Summary of bills passed by the Texas legislature with effective dates. Appendices include bills passed by subjects, numerical listing, bills vetoed, bills passed by author, interim studies authorized, statutes amended or repealed, and totals page.

US
FINAL REPORTS OF INTERIM JOINT AND SPECIAL COMMITTEES. **Main/Corp** Kentucky. General Assembly. Legislative Research Commission. 1974/75-. English. an. Legislative Research Commission, State Capitol/Room 300, Frankfort KY 40601. **Tel** (502)564-8100. **LC** KFK1227; .A154 subser; KFK1220. **DD** 300/.9769 S; 328.769/07657/053. ***Continues*** *Joint Legislative Committees Final Report, ... Interim.*

US
FINAL TABLES AND INDEX TO LEGISLATIVE MEASURES. **Main/Corp** Oregon. Legislative Assembly. Legislative Counsel Committee. English. be. $10.00 approximately. Legislative Counsel Committee, S101 State Capital, Salem OR 97310. **Tel** (503)378-8148. **LC** KFO2412; .L43. **DD** 348/.795/028.

US/8750-6149
FINANCE AND COMMERCE (REGULAR DAILY ED.). (FINANCE AND COMMERCE.). [Finance commer.]. (18??)-. Periodical. English. ir (except Sundays, Mondays and holidays). $127.50. Credit Publishing Co, 615 South 7th Street, Minneapolis MN 55415. **Tel** (612)333-4244. **ED** Patrick Boulay. **DD** 330. **Ad Acc.** available on microfilm. ***Continues*** *Finance and Commerce of the Twin Cities;* ***Absorbed*** *Business Weekly; Register-Mirror.*

UK
FINANCIAL SERVICES LAW LETTER. **See** Business-Banking and Finance.

UK/0268-8433
FINANCIAL TIMES LAW REPORTS. (19??)-. Periodical. English. mo. **LC** KD1605.A38; F56. **DD** 346.41/07/05; 344.106705.
Ind/Abst Aust. Leg. Mon. Dig.

US/0896-8314
FIREHOUSE LAWYER MONTHLY NEWSLETTER. Newsletter. English. mo. $49.76. Quinlan Publishing Company, 23 Drydock Avenue, Boston MA 02210-2387. **Tel** (617)542-0048, (800)229-2084, FAX (617)345-9646. **LC** KF3976.A59; F57. **DD** 344.73/0537. **[CCC].** available on microfilm and microfiche from University Microfilms International (UMI).

FR/0750-8662
FISCALITE IMMOBILIERE. **See** Public Administration-Public Finance and Taxation.

UK
FLEET STREET REPORTS OF INDUSTRIAL PROPERTY CASES FROM THE COMMONWEALTH AND EUROPE. ***Title Change.*** **Added/Corp** European Law Centre. (1963)-(199?). Periodical. English. mo. Sweet & Maxwell Ltd., South Quay Plaza, 183 Marsh Wall, London E14 9FT England. **Tel** 011 44 264 342899, FAX 011 44 264 342723, telex 929089 ITPINF G. **LC** KD1365.A2; F54. **DD** 346/.4204/86. ***Continues*** *Fleet Street Patent Law Reports, 0141-9919.* ***Continued by*** *Fleet Street Reports.*
Desc: Covers patent laws and legislation pertaining to industrial property.

US/0098-874X
FLORIDA ADMINISTRATIVE WEEKLY. [Fla. adm. wkly.]. **Added/Corp** Florida. Division of Elections. Vol. 1 (Jan. 10, 1975)-. English. wk. $176.55 Florida; $165.00 other. Florida Department of State / Bureau of Administration Code, Room 1802, The Capitol, Tallahassee FL 32399-0250. **Tel** (904)488-8427. **ED** Liz Cloud. **LC** KFF36; .F55. **DD** 348/.759/01. **Ad Acc. Circ:** 3,000 (ctrl).
Desc: Contains information on proposed rule changes, a large bid section concerning public meetings, workshops and public hearings.

US
FLORIDA ATTORNEYS-SECRETARYS HANDBOOK. (19??)-. English. an. $64.00. Namar Communications, 4453 Lake Avenue South, Suite 202, Whitebear Lake MN 55110. **Tel** (612)426-0980, FAX (612)426-0849.

US/0164-6427
FLORIDA BAR CASE SUMMARY SERVICE, THE. ***Ceased.*** **Main/Corp** Florida Bar. ( )-(Aug. 1991). Periodical. English. wk. The Florida Bar / Legal Publishing Department, 650 Apalachee Parkway, Tallahassee FL 32399. **Tel** (904)561-5600, FAX (904)681-3859. **ED** Belinda H Miller. Index available. **Circ:** 1,200.
Desc: Provides summaries of selected opinions from the Florida Supreme Court and District Courts of Appeal.

US/0015-3915
FLORIDA BAR JOURNAL, THE. [FLA. bar j.]. **Added/Corp** Florida Bar. Vol. 27, No. 7 (July 1953)-. Periodical. English. Twelve times a year. $30.00 (one year), $70.00 (three years). The Florida Bar / Legal Publishing Department, 650 Apalachee Parkway, Tallahassee FL 32399. **Tel** (904)561-5600, FAX (904)681-3859. **ED** Judson H. Orrick. **LC** KF200; .F47. **DD** 340/.05. Index available. **Bk Rev. Ad Acc. Circ:** 43,500 (ctrl). available on microfilm and microfiche from University Microfilms International (UMI). ***Continues*** *Florida Law Journal.*
Desc: Contains how-to articles which strive to help advance the education, competence, ethical practice and public responsibility of lawyers. Official publication of The Florida Bar.
Ind/Abst Bowne Dig. Corp. Sec. Lawyers; Curr. Law Index (1980-); Fed. Tax Artic.; Highw. Res. Abstr.; Index Leg. Period.; Law Office Inf. Serv.; Leg. Resour. Index (1980-); LegalTrac (1980-).

US/0360-0114
FLORIDA BAR NEWS. **Main/Corp** Florida Bar. (19??)-. Periodical. English. sm. $12.00 (one year), $30.00 (three years). The Florida Bar / Legal Publishing Department, 650 Apalachee Parkway, Tallahassee FL 32399. **Tel** (904)561-5600, FAX (904)681-3859. **ED** Judson H Orrick. **LC** KF200; .F46. **DD** 340/.06/2759. **Ad Acc. Circ:** 43,500 (ctrl). available on microfilm and microfiche from University Microfilms International (UMI).
Desc: Official publication of the Florida Bar. General topics of interest, actions affecting the legal profession by the courts, legislature and the Board of Governors.
Ind/Abst Law Office Inf. Serv.

US/0744-981X
FLORIDA CASES REPORTED IN SOUTHERN REPORTER, SECOND SERIES. [Fla. cases rep. South. rep., second ser.]. **VFOAT** Florida Cases; West's Florida Cases. English. wk (except last week in Sept., and 1st week in Oct.). $60.00. West Publishing Company, 610 Opperman Drive, PO Box

64526, Eagan MN 55123-1308. **Tel** (612)687-5618, (800)328-9352, FAX (612)687-5388, (800)562-2329. **(Subscription telephone:** FAX (612)688-3570) **DD** 348.

US
FLORIDA DIGEST. English. ir. West Publishing Company, 610 Opperman Drive, PO Box 64526, Eagan MN 55123-1308. **Tel** (612)687-5618, (800)328-9352, FAX (612)687-5388, (800)562-2329. **(Subscription telephone:** FAX (612)688-3570)
Desc: Covers cases from state and federal courts.

US/1059-6275
FLORIDA JURY VERDICT REPORTER. (FLORIDA JURY VERDICT REPORTER : A PUBLICATION OF FLORIDA LEGAL PERIODICALS, INC.). [Fla. jury verdict report.]. **Added/Corp** Florida Legal Periodicals, Inc. **VFOAT** FJVR. Began July 2 (1981)-. Periodical. English. mo. $200.00. Florida Legal Periodicals Inc, PO Box 20728, 1333 North Adams Street, Tallahassee FL 32316. **LC** KFF195.A59; F55. **DD** 346.75903; 347.59063.

US
FLORIDA LAW OF TRUSTS. English. an. $77.95, $39.95 seperate pocket part supplement. Harrison Company Publishers, 3110 Crossing Park, PO Box 7500, Norcross GA 30091-7500. **Tel** (800)241-3561, (404)447-9150.

US/1045-4241
FLORIDA LAW REVIEW. [Fla. law rev.]. **Added/Corp** University of Florida. College of Law. Vol. 41, No. 1 (Winter 1989)-. Periodical. English. Five times a year. $30.00. University of Florida Law Review, College of Law, 115 Holland Hall, Gainesville FL 32611. **Tel** (904)392-2148. **ED** Vivien Payne. **LC** K25; .N6. **DD** 349.73/09759/05; 347.300975905. Index available (bound in last issue). **Bk Rev**, (Qty: 1). **Ad Acc. Circ:** 1,300. available on microfiche. ***Continues*** *University of Florida Law Review, 0041-9583.*
Ind/Abst Fed. Tax Artic.; Index Leg. Period.; Leg. Resour. Index; LegalTrac (1989-).

US/0274-8533
FLORIDA LAW WEEKLY, THE. Added/Corp Judicial and Administrative Research Associates. **VFOAT** FLW. (19??)-. Periodical. English. Fifty times a year (Weekly except August and Christmas week). $295.00 tax exempt, Florida; $315.65 other. JARA Inc., PO Box 4284, Tallahassee FL 32315. **Tel** (904)222-3171, FAX (904)222-7938. **ED** E Neil Young. **LC** KFF47.1; .F57. Index available. cum. index. **Circ:** 4,300 (ctrl).
Desc: Complete opinions- Florida Supreme Court and district courts of appeal within 1-10 days of filing. Index/tables each issues; cumulative indexes quarterly. Binders included.

US/0145-7829
FLORIDA LEGAL DIRECTORY, THE. [Fla. leg. dir.]. 1974/75-. Directory. English. an. $9.00. Legal Directories Publishing Company, 9111 Garland Road, PO Box 189000, Dallas TX 75218. **Tel** (214)321-3238, 800 447-5375. **LC** KF192.F54; F58. **DD** 340/.025/759.

US/0735-9071
FLORIDA REAL ESTATE BROKER & THE LAW, THE. **See** Real Estate.

US/0096-3070
FLORIDA STATE UNIVERSITY LAW REVIEW. [Fla. State Univ. law rev.]. **Main/Corp** Florida State University. College of Law. Vol. 1 (Winter 1973)-. Periodical. English. qt. $27.00 US; $29.00 other. Florida State University College of Law, Tallahassee FL 32306. **Tel** (904)644-0961. **ED** Dina A. Keever. **LC** K6; .L67. **DD** 340/.05. Index available. cum. index. **Bk Rev. Ad Acc. Circ:** 875.
Desc: Features articles by legal authorities, analyzing and critiquing major court decisions and legal developments affecting economic, political and social activities.
Ind/Abst Bowne Dig. Corp. Sec. Lawyers; Crim. Justice Abstr.; Curr. Law Index (1980-); Fed. Tax Artic.; Index Leg. Period.; Leg. Resour. Index (1980-); LegalTrac (1980-).

US
FLORIDA STATUTES. Main/Corp Florida. English. Florida Legislature, 111 West Madison Street, Room 716, Tallahassee FL 32399. **Tel** (904)922-0647.

US
FLORIDA STATUTES ANNOTATED. Main/Corp Florida. English. an. $1450.00. Harrison Company Publishers, 3110 Crossing Park, PO Box 7500, Norcross GA 30091-7500. **Tel** (800)241-3561, (404)447-9150. cum. index.

US
FLORIDA TAX REVIEW. (Oct. 15, 1992)-. English. ir (twelve to fourteen times per year). $125.00 domestic; $145.00 international. Tax Analysis, 6830 North Fairfax Drive, Arlington VA 22130. **Tel** (800)955-3444, FAX (703)533-4444. **ED** David M. Richardson (Editor's address: College of Law, University of Florida, Gainesville FL 32611, (904)392-1081). Index available. cum. index. **Bk Rev**, (Qty: one /issue). **Pr Rev.**
Desc: Discusses federal, state, and international tax law.

US/0893-0503
FLW FEDERAL. [FLW fed.]. **Added/Corp** Judicial and Administrative Research Associates. **VAT** Florida Law Weekly Federal. (1987)-. Periodical. English. wk (except two weeks in Aug. and Nov.). $278.20, non-tax exempt Florida residents; $260.00 other. JARA Inc., PO Box 4284, Tallahassee FL 32315. **Tel** (904)222-3171, FAX (904)222-7938. **ED** E Neil Young. **DD** 349. Index available. ctrl circ.

US/0148-026X
FOCUS (CHICAGO. 1977). (FOCUS.). **Added/Corp** American Bar Association. Fund for Public Education. American Bar Association. Fund for Public Education. (1977)-. Periodical. English. Twice a year. Free. American Bar Association, 750 North Lake Shore Drive, Chicago IL 60611. **Tel** (312)988-5522, (312)988-5241, FAX (312)988-5528, telex 270593. **ED** John Paul Ryan. **LC** KF200; .F63. **DD** 340/.06/273. **Bk Rev. Ad Acc. Circ:** 4,500 (ctrl).
Desc: Offers a forum of ideas, resources, analysis, and opinions on teaching about law in liberal arts and professional programs.

US
FOCUS ON LAW STUDIES : TEACHING ABOUT LAW IN THE LIBERAL ARTS. Added/Corp American Bar Association. Advisory Commission on College and University Nonprofessional Legal Studies. American Bar Association. Commission on College and University Nonprofessional Legal Studies. American Bar Association. Commission on College and University Legal Studies. Vol. 1, No. 1 (Fall 1985)-. Periodical. English. sa (2 issues). Free on request. American Bar Association, 750 North Lake Shore Drive, Chicago IL 60611. **Tel** (312)988-5522, (312)988-5241, FAX (312)988-5528, telex 270593. **LC** KF4245.5.L3; A134. **DD** 340/.07/1173.

US/0747-959X
FOCUS ON SPECIAL EDUCATION LEGAL PRACTICES. [Focus spec. educ. leg. pract.]. Periodical. English. qt. National Information Center for Handicapped Children and Youth, Box 1942, Washington DC 20013. **LC** KF4210.A15; F62. **DD** 344.73/0791/05; 347.30479105.
Desc: Covers articles on current research and relevant program information on specific topics in the disabilities field.

IT
FOGLIO ANNUNCI LEGALI ROMA. (19??)-. Italian. sw. L210924. Istituto Poligrafico Zecca Stato, Piazza Verdi 10, 00198 Rome Italy. **Tel** 011 39 6 85082307, 011 39 6 85082221.

IT
FOGLIO ANNUNZI LEGALI : IMPERIA. (19??)-. Italian. sw. Lit Centro Stampa Offset, Via F Airenti 2, 18100 Imperia Italy. **Tel** 011 39 183 64912.

IT
FOGLIO ANNUNZI LEGALI PROVINCIA DI BERGAMO. (19??)-. Italian. wk. Modulimpianti Snc Di C Innocenti, Via Leopardi 1 3, 24042 Capriate Gervasio Italy. **Tel** 011 39 2 90963632.

IT
FOGLIO ANNUNZI LEGALI : SAVONA. (19??)-. Italian. wk. L107100. Stediv Snc, Via Tiso da Campo S Piero 35, 35122 Padua Italy. **Tel** 011 39 49 8759166.

US/0198-7143
FOLIO. PUBLIC RELATIONS, THE. Added/Corp National Academy of Code Administration. (1979)-. Periodical. English. mo. $15.95. National Academy of Code Administration, 6861 Elm Street Road, Mclean VA 22101. **Tel** (703)821-8171. **LC** KF5701.A15; F64. **DD** 343.73/07869/005.

IT/0015-6221
FOOD AND AGRICULTURAL LEGISLATION. **See** Food and Food Industry.

●US/1064-590X
FOOD AND DRUG LAW JOURNAL. [Food drug law j.]. **Added/Corp** Food and Drug Law Institute (U.S.). Vol. 47, No. 1 (1992)-. Periodical. English. qt. $275.00. Food and Drug Law Institute, 1000 Vermont Avenue Northwest, Suite 1200, Washington DC 20005. **Tel** (202)371-1420, FAX (202)371-0649. **DD** 343. **NLM** W1; FO4044. **CODEN** FDLJES. **[CCC].** Documents available from The Genuine Article, Documents on Demand. ***Continues*** *Food, Drug, Cosmetic Law Journal, 0015-6361.*
Ind/Abst Curr. Contents, Agric. Biol. Environ. Sci.; Curr. Contents Soc. Behav. Sci.; Energy Inf. Abstr. (1992-); Environ. Abstr. (1992); Foods Adlibra; Index Leg. Period. (1992-); Leg. Resour. Index (?-?); Life Sci. Collect. (1992-); Res. Alert [Select. Cov.]; Soc. Sci. Cit. Index [Select. Cov.].

US/1053-9034
FOOD AND DRUG LAW REPORTS. ***Title Change.*** [Food drug law rep.]. **Added/Corp** Food and Drug Law Institute (U.S.). No. 1 (Nov. 1989)-(1993). English. mo. Food and Drug Law Institute, 1000 Vermont Avenue Northwest, Suite 1200, Washington DC 20005. **Tel** (202)371-1420, FAX (202)371-0649. **LC** KF3866.3; .F66. **DD** 344.73/0423/02648; 347.30442302648. **NLM** QV 33; AA1 F6. ***Continued by*** *Food and Drug Report, 1071-8869.*
Ind/Abst Foods Adlibra.

●US/1071-8869
FOOD AND DRUG REPORT. [Food drug rep.]. **Added/Corp** Food and Drug Law Institute (U.S.). Vol. 4, No. 8 (1993)-. Periodical. English. mo. $325.00. Food and Drug Law Institute, 1000 Vermont Avenue Northwest, Suite 1200, Washington DC 20005. **Tel** (202)371-1420, FAX (202)371-0649. **LC** KF3866.3; .F66. **DD** 344.73/0423/02648; 347.30442302648. **NLM** QV 33; AA1 F6. ***Continues*** *Food and Drug Law Reports, 1053-9034.*

US/1057-2759
FOOD, DRUG, COSMETIC, AND MEDICAL DEVICE LAW DIGEST. (FOOD, DRUG, COSMETIC, AND MEDICAL DEVICE LAW DIGEST : A PUBLICATION OF THE FOOD, DRUG, AND COSMETIC LAW SECTION.). [Food drug cosmet. med. device law dig.]. **Added/Corp** New York State Bar Association. Food, Drug, and Cosmetic Law Section. (19??)-. Periodical. English. New York State Bar Association, One Elk Street, Albany NY 12207. **Tel** (518)463-3200. **LC** KFN5630.A15; N48. **DD** 344.747/042/05; 347.47044205. ***Continues*** *Newsletter of the Food, Drug, and Cosmetic Law Section, 0742-4051.*
Ind/Abst Index Leg. Period. (1992-).

UK
FOOD LAW MONTHLY. English. mo. £105.00 UK; £120.00 other. Monitor Press, Rectory Road, Great Waldingfield, Sudbury Suffolk CO10 0TL United Kingdom. **Tel** 011 44 787 378607.
Ind/Abst Dairy Sci. Abstr.

US
FOR THE RECORD (PORTLAND, OR.). (FOR THE RECORD.). Periodical. English. mo. Oregon State Bar, 5200 Southwest Meadows Road, Lake Oswego OR 97035. **Tel** (503)620-0222 ext 340, (800)452-8260, FAX (503)684-1366. **ED** Randy Choy and Mary Gross. **LC** KF200; .F67. **DD** 340/.06/0795. **Ad Acc. Circ:** 9,500 (ctrl).

US/1064-1351
FOR YOUR INFORMATION (SAN DIEGO, CALIF.). **See** Library and Information Sciences.

US/1056-4128
FORDHAM ENTERTAINMENT, MEDIA & INTELLECTUAL PROPERTY LAW FORUM. ***Title Change.*** [Fordham entertain. media intellect. prop. law forum]. **Added/Corp** Fordham University. School of Law. **VFOAT** Fordham Entertainment, Media and Intellectual Property Law Forum; Entertainment, Media & Intellectual Property Law Forum; Entertainment, Media and Intellectual Property Law Forum. Vol. 1, No. 1 (Autumn 1990)-Vol. 3, No. 1 (Autumn 1993). Periodical. English. sa. Fordham University School of Law, 140 West 62nd Street, Room 35, New York NY 10023. **Tel** (212)636-6948. **LC** K6; .O725. **DD** 346.04/8; 342.648. ***Continued by*** *Fordham Intellectual Property, Media & Entertainment Law Journal.*
Ind/Abst Fed. Tax Artic.

●US
FORDHAM INTELLECTUAL PROPERTY, MEDIA & ENTERTAINMENT LAW JOURNAL. VFOAT Intellectual Property, Media & Entertainment Law Journal. (1993)-. English. Twice a year. $20.00. Fordham University School of Law, 140 West 62nd Street, Room 35, New York NY 10023. **Tel** (212)636-6948. ***Continues*** *Fordham Entertainment, Media & Intellectual Property Law Forum, 1056-4128.*

US/0015-704X
FORDHAM LAW REVIEW. (FORDHAM LAW REVIEW / EDITED BY FORDHAM LAW STUDENTS.). [Fordham law rev.]. **Added/Corp** Fordham University. School of Law. Vol. 1, No. 1 (Nov. 1914)-. Periodical. English. Seven times a year. $40.00 US; $50.00 others. Fordham University School of Law, 140 West 62nd Street, Room 35, New York NY 10023. **Tel** (212)636-6948. **Bk Rev. Ad Acc. Pr Rev. Circ:** 1,300 (ctrl). Documents available from The Genuine Article.
Desc: Collection of articles written by experts and students on wide-ranging legal topics.
Ind/Abst Bowne Dig. Corp. Sec. Lawyers; Commun. Abstr.; Crim. Justice Abstr.; Curr. Contents Soc. Behav. Sci.; Curr. Law Index (1980-); Fed. Tax Artic.; Index Leg. Period.; Leg. Resour. Index (1980-); LegalTrac (1980-); Res. Alert [Full Cov.]; Soc. Plann. Policy Dev. Abstr.; Soc. Sci. Cit. Index [Full Cov.]; Sociol. Abstr. (?-?); SportSearch.

US/0199-4646
FORDHAM URBAN LAW JOURNAL, THE. [Fordham urban law j.]. Vol. 1 (Summer 1972)-. Periodical. English. qt. $20.00. Fordham University School of Law, 140 West 62nd Street, Room 35, New York NY 10023. **Tel** (212)636-6948. **ED** Mark Lee and Elleen Shapiro Dunleavy. **LC** K6; .O73. **DD** 340/.05. Index available. cum. index. **Circ:** 1,500 (ctrl). available on

microfilm and microfiche from University Microfilms International (UMI).
Desc: Articles relating to urban law.
Ind/Abst Bowne Dig. Corp. Sec. Lawyers; Curr. Law Index (1980-); Index Leg. Period.; J. Plan. Lit.; Leg. Resour. Index (1980-); LegalTrac (1980-).

UK/1350-1771
FORENSIC LINGUISTICS: THE INTERNATIONAL JOURNAL OF LANGUAGE AND THE LAW. **See** Linguistics.

US/0192-3145
FORENSIC SERVICES DIRECTORY. [Forensic serv. dir.]. (1980)-. Directory. English. an. $98.00. National Forensic Center, 17 Temple Terrace, Lawrenceville NJ 08649. **Tel** (609)883-0550, (800)526-5177, FAX (609)883-7622. **ED** Betty S Lipscher. **LC** KF195.E96; F67. **DD** 363.2/5/02573. Index available. **Ad Acc. Circ:** 4,000.
Desc: The only directory devoted exclusively to experts, authorities and litigation consultants in all areas of expertise, criminal and civil. Contains approximately 5,000 experts and 1,500 associations to help in litigation; can be used to locate experts quickly and directly and identify experts and organizations who have specialized knowledge; includes the educational background training and experience of experts listed; indexes are complete and experts are located by subject, name or geographical location. Updates provided annually.

US
FORMAL OPINIONS - COMMITTEE ON PROFESSIONAL ETHICS, NEW YORK STATE BAR ASSOCIATION. **Main/Corp** New York State Bar Association. Committee on Professional Ethics. **Added/Corp** New York State Bar Association. Committee on Professional Ethics. Code of Professional Responsibility. No. 1 (Nov. 6, 1964)-. Periodical. English. ir. $6.00. New York State Bar Association, One Elk Street, Albany NY 12207. **Tel** (518)463-3200. Index Available, published separately, free-automatically sent.
Desc: Each volume includes an updated version of the New York State Bar Association Code of professional responsibility.

IT
FORMULARIO TRIBUTARIO ADEMPIMENTI E RICORSI. (19??)-. Periodical. Italian. sa. IPSOA Editore SRL, Casella Postale 12055, Mastrangelo, 20120 Milan Italy. **Tel** 011 39 2 82476248. Index available. cum. index. **Circ:** 3,000 (ctrl).
Desc: How to face and solve taxation problems.

CK/0121-0335
FORO DEL JURISTA. [Foro jurista]. (1986)-. Periodical. Spanish. sa. 10.00Col$. Camara de Comercio de Medellin, Apartado Aereo No. 1894, Medellin Colombia. **Tel** 5116111, FAX 2318648, telex 66768. **DD** 348.04. **Circ:** 1,000 (ctrl).
Desc: Publication of articles on commercial law.

IT/0015-783X
FORO ITALIANO, IL. (1876)-. Periodical. Italian. Twelve times a year. L394000 Italy; L472000 others. Zanichelli Editore SPA, via Irnerio 34, 40126 Bologna Italy. **Tel** 011 39 51 293263, telex 214885 ZANED I. **Bk Rev.**
Ind/Abst Index Foreign Leg. Per.

IT
FORO ITALIANO. MASSIMARIO, IL. Began in 1930. Periodical. Italian. Societa Editrice des Foro Italiano, Via Pietro Cossa 41, Rome Italy. **DD** 348/.45/041.

GW/0429-1603
FORSCHUNGEN ZUR NEUEREN PRIVATRECHTSGESCHICHTE. (1954)-. Monographic series. German. ir. Price varies per volume. Boehlau Verlag GmbH & Cie / Koeln, Theodor Heuss STR 76, D-51149 Cologne Germany. **Tel** 011 49 2203 307021, FAX 011 49 2203 307349. **(Subscription address:** BDK Buecherdienst GmBh, Postfach 900120, D 51111 Cologne Germany.**)**

US/0015-8097
FORT WORTH COMMERCIAL RECORDER. (1903)-. Periodical. English. da. $150.00. Fort Worth Commercial Recorder Jones Street, Ft Worth TX 76109. **Tel** (817)926-5351, FAX (817)926-5377. **ED** Genevieve Ratcliff. **LC** K6; .O74. **DD** 349.764/05; 347.6405. **Ad Acc. Circ:** 550.
Desc: Court and commercial business newspaper.

SW/0300-2055
FORTECKNING OVER ADVOKATER OCH ADVOKATBYRAER AR JAMIE STADGAR FOR SVERIGES ADVOKATSAMFUND. (FORTECKNING OVER ADVOKATER OCH ADVOKATBYRAER.). Swedish. Sveriges Advokatsamfund, Strandgatan 38, 27051 Skillinge Sweden. **Tel** 0414-30174, FAX 0414-14710.

US
FORUM (CHICAGO), THE. (FORUM.). **Added/Corp** American Bar Association. Section of Tort and Insurance Practice. American Bar Association. Section of Insurance, Negligence and Compensation Law. Vol. 16, No. 1 (Special Issue 1980)-. Periodical. English. qt. American Bar Association, 750 North Lake Shore Drive, Chicago IL 60611. **Tel** (312)988-5522, (312)988-5241, FAX (312)988-5528, telex 270593. ***Continues*** *The Forum.*
Ind/Abst Fed. Tax Artic.

US/0015-8305
FORUM (WASHINGTON, D.C.), THE. (FORUM.). [Forum]. **Added/Corp** Federal Bar Association. District of Columbia Chapter. (19??)-. Periodical. English. ir. $8.00. Federal Bar Association, 1815 H Street Northwest, Suite 408, Washington DC 20006. **Tel** (202)638-0252, FAX (202)775-0295. **ED** Paul A. Pumpian and Nancy E. Proulx. **Circ:** 4,000 (ctrl).
Ind/Abst Energy Res. Abstr. (Aug. 1982-).

US/1048-2768
FOURTH CIRCUIT AND DISTRICT OF COLUMBIA BANKRUPTCY COURT REPORTER, THE. [Fourth Circuit Dist. Columbia bankruptcy court report.]. **Added/Corp** Public Record Corporation. (1989)-. English. Six times a year. $316.00. The Public Record Corporation, PO Box 18186, 1666 Lafayette Street, Denver CO 80218. **Tel** (303)832-8262, (800)487-8262, FAX (303)861-5821. **DD** 346.
Desc: Information on bankruptcy courts at District of Columbia Fourth Circuit.

US/0889-3578
FOURTH CIRCUIT REVIEW (LOUISVILLE, KY.). (FOURTH CIRCUIT REVIEW : A TIMELY SUMMARY OF DECISIONS OF THE UNITED STATES COURT OF APPEALS FOR THE FOURTH CIRCUIT.). **Added/Corp** United States. Court of Appeals (4th Circuit). **VFOAT** 4th Circuit Review; FCR. (Oct. 7, 1985)-. English. bw. $245.00. Appellate Review, 500 Country Lane, Louisville KY 40207. **Tel** (502)897-5079. **ED** Pat Owen, Laura Huller. **LC** KF112 4th.1; .F684. **DD** 348.73/425; 347.308425. Index available. cum. index.
Desc: Verbatim digest of all Fourth Circuit Court of Appeals decisions with headnotes and index.

US
FRANCHISING BUSINESS AND LAW ALERT. **See** Education.

GW
FRANKFURTER WISSENSCHAFTLICHE BEITRAGE. RECHTS- UND WIRTSCHAFTSWISSENSCHAFTLICHE REIHE. **Added/Corp** Frankfurt am Main. Universitat. Wissenschaftliche Geselschaft. (1939)-. Monographic series. German. ir. Price varies per volume. Vittorio Klostermann, Frauenlobstrasse 22, D 60487 Frankfurt Germany. **Tel** 011 49 69 9708160.

US/0164-2820
FRANKLIN COUNTY LEGAL JOURNAL. V. 1- 1977/78-. English. Franklin County Legal Journal, 164 Lincoln Way East, Chambersburg PA 17201. **LC** KFP52.F7; F74. **DD** 348/.74844/043.
Desc: Containing reports of cases decided by the various divisions of the Franklin County branch of the Court of Common Pleas of the 39th Judicial District of Pennsylvania, and selected cases.

CN
FREE TRADE LAW REPORTER. (1989)-. Periodical. English. mo. 260.00Can$. CCH Canadian Ltd., 6 Garamond Court, Don Mills Ontario M3C 1Z5 Canada. **Tel** (416)441-2992, FAX (416)441-3418. **ED** Vida Vukadiniovic. **Bk Rev. Circ:** 1,000 (ctrl).
Desc: Provides expert commentary on key trade issues like the elimination of customs duties, tariff exemptions for trade in goods, customs matters like rules of origin and import/export restrictions. Includes complete text of the Canada/US Free Trade Agreement.

CN
FREEDOM OF INFORMATION SERVICE. English. an. 105.00Can$. Butterworth & Company Ltd. / Canada, 75 Clegg Road, Markham Ontario L6G 1A1 Canada. **Tel** (905)479-2665, (800)668-6481. **ED** Carl Dombek and Tom Riley. Index available. ctrl circ.
Desc: Annotated federal and provincial freedom of information by means of commentary, case digests, concordance and practical advice with specific emphasis on the Federal and Ontario Schemes.

US/1054-1950
FROM THE GYM TO THE JURY. (FROM THE GYM TO THE JURY / THE CENTER FOR SPORTS LAW AND RISK MANAGEMENT.). [Gym jury]. **Added/Corp** Center for Sports Law and Risk Management. Vol. 1, No. 1 (1989)-. Periodical. English. Five times a year (Jan., Mar., May, Aug., Nov.). $55.00 US; $61.00 other. Center of Sports Law and Risk Management, 6917 Wildglen Avenue, Dallas TX 75230. **Tel** (214)987-1766, FAX (214)891-6410. **ED** Ron Baron, Herb Appenzeken. **LC** KF3989.A15; F76. **DD** 344.73/099/05; 347.3049905. cum. index. ctrl circ.
Desc: Provides analysis of legal trends and litigation, as well as risk management strategies for the sports industry.

II
FROM THE LAWYERS COLLECTIVE. **Added/Corp** Lawyers Collective (Bombay, India). **VFOAT** Lawyers Collective; Lawyers. (198?)-. Periodical. English. mo. $60.00. Indira Jaising, 818, Stock Exchange Towers, Dalal Street, Bombay 400 0 23, India. **(Subscription address:** Prints India, 11 Darya Ganj, New Delhi 110002 India.**)**
Ind/Abst Hum. Rights Intern. Rep.

US/0734-1156
FROM THE STATE CAPITALS. PUBLIC HEALTH (1982). **See** Public Health and Safety.

US/1061-9690
FROM THE STATE CAPITALS. THE OUTLOOK FROM THE STATE CAPITALS. [From state cap., outlook state cap.]. **VFOAT** Outlook from the State Capitals. Vol. 45, No. 26 (Oct. 7, 1991)-. Periodical. English. wk. $21.50 (one year), $378.00 (two year) public and institutional libraries; $235.00 (one year), $420.00 (two year) other. Wakeman Walworth Inc., 300 North Washington Street #204, Alexandria VA 22314. **Tel** (703)549-8606. **LC** JK430; .F93. **DD** 328. ***Continues*** *From the State Capitals. General Trends, 0741-3475.*
Desc: A national round-up of state action on vital issues: abortion, environment, drug abuse, taxes. A great indicator of state trends in public policy.

US/0196-0016
FTC : WATCH. **Added/Corp** Washington Regulatory Reporting Group. Amolsch & Madden, Inc. **VAT** Federal Trade Commission : Watch. (July 5, 1976)-. Periodical. English. Twenty-two times a year. $614.00. Washington Regulatory Reporting Association, PO Box 356, Basye VA 22810. **Tel** (703)856-2216. **ED** Arthur Amolsch and Mimi Modden. **LC** KF1602; .F18. **DD** 343.73/08/05. **[CCC]. Bk Rev.** available on an online database (file 636/Full-Text) from DIALOG.
Desc: Covers the policies, programs, and personnel of the US Federal Trade Commission. Emphasis on in-depth, investigative reporting and political trends.
Ind/Abst PTS Newsl. Database [Full Txt.].

●US/1063-9209
FTCA NEWS. (FTCA NEWS : SUMMARY OF RECENT SIGNIFICANT FEDERAL TORT CLAIMS ACT CASES IN FEDERAL COURTS.). [FTCA news]. **VAT** Federal Tort Claims Act News. Vol. 1, No. 1 (Jan. 31, 1992)-. Periodical. English. mo. $175.00 (government), $195.00 (regular). Law Associates, Inc., 800 5th Avenue, Suite 305, Seattle WA 98104. **Tel** (907)278-2777, FAX (907)278-0338. **ED** Lynn Allingham. **DD** 340. Index available. cum. index.

JA
FUDOSAN ROPPO. **Main/Corp** Japan. **Added/Corp** Fudosan Horei Kenkukai. (19??)-. Periodical. Japanese. ¥2800. Kinensha, 9-6 Higashi Ueno 2, Taito-ku 110, Tokyo Japan.

US
FULTON COUNTY DAILY REPORT (ATLANTA). English. ir (253 issues). $535.00 (law firms with 10 or more lawyers for metro Atlanta, Georgia); $205.00 other. American Lawyer Media, L.P., 600 3rd Avenue, New York NY 10016. **Tel** (212)973-2800. **(Subscription address:** Fulton County Daily Report, 190 Pryor Street SW, Atlanta, GA 30303**)**

US/0732-4561
FUNDAMENTALS OF SECURED TRANSACTIONS. (FUNDAMENTALS OF SECURED TRANSACTIONS : ALI-ABA COURSE OF STUDY MATERIALS.). [Fundam. secur. trans.]. **Added/Corp** American Law Institute-American Bar Association Committee on Continuing Professional Education. **VFOAT** ALI-ABA Course of Study Materials; A.L.I.-A.B.A. Course of Study Materials. (19??)-. English. American Law Institute, 4025 Chestnut Street, Philadelphia PA 19104-3099. **Tel** (215)243-1661, (800)253-6397, FAX (215)243-1664. **LC** KF1050.Z9; F86. **DD** 346.73/074; 347.30674.

GW/0071-9919
FUNDHEFT FUER OFFENTLICHES RECHT. (1948)-. German. CH Beck Verlagsbuchhandlung, D 80791 Munich Germany. **Tel** 011 49 89 381891.

GW
FUNDHEFT FUER STEUERRECHT. (1949)-. Monographic series. German. an. Price varies per volume. CH Beck Verlagsbuchhandlung, D 80791 Munich Germany. **Tel** 011 49 89 381891.

GW
FUNDSTELLEN- UND INHALTSNACHWEIS ARBEITS- UND SOZIALRECHT. (19??)-. Periodical. English. sa. Verlag R S Shultz, Berger Strasse 8-10, Sehang 4, W-8136 Percha-Kempfenhausen Germany. **ED** F. Luber. **DD** 340/.0943.

Law

KU
FURANI'S DIGEST OF THE OFFICIAL GAZETTE AL KUWAIT AL YOUM. English. 135.00 Outside Kuwait. Furani's Translation and Advertising Company, PO Box 950, Safat Kuwait. **DD** 349.53/67/05; 345.367005.

●US
FUTURES INTERNATIONAL LAW LETTER. Vol. 12, No. 1 (Mar. 1992)-. Periodical. English. Twelve times a year. $285.00 (libraries), $305.00 (other). Commodities Law Press Association, 40 Broad Street, Suite 2000, New York NY 10004. **Tel** (212)612-9545. **ED** Richard A. Miller (editor's phone: (212)612-9500). **LC** KF1085.A15; C65. Index available. **Bk Rev. Continues** Commodities Law Letter, 0277-2930. **Desc:** Analysis of futures and derivatives law and regulations.

MX/0185-4356
GACETA INFORMATIVA DE LEGISLACION NACIONAL. Vol. 1, No. 1 (Jan./Feb. 1985). Periodical. Spanish. bm. $20,000 Mexico; $32.00 other. UNAM - Institute of Investigaciones Juridicas, Universidad Nacional Autonoma de Mexico, Ciudad Universitaria, Mario de la Cueva, 04510 Mexico DF Mexico. **Tel** 011 52 5 622-7461, 616-1784, FAX 011 52 5 665-2193. **ED** Eugenio Hurtado Marquez. **LC** KGF50; .G32. **Circ:** 1,000. **Continues** Legislacion y Jurisprudencia.
Desc: Dedicated to the Mexican federal and state legislation, systematized and analysed.

CK
GACETA JUDICIAL. Added/Corp Colombia. Corte Suprema de Justicia. Vol. 1 (1887)-. Spanish.

SP
GACETA JURIDICA DE LA CEE. Spanish. 19398.00ptas Spain; 18300.00ptas other. Ediciones Informatizadas SA, Francisco Gervas 7, 28100 Alcombendas Madrid Spain. **UDC** 34.

DR
GACETA OFICIAL - REPUBLICA DOMINICANA. Main/Corp Dominican Republic. (19??)-. Spanish. Direct General Rentas Internas, Santo Domingo Dominican Republic. **DD** 340/.097293. **Continues** Dominican Republic. Boletin Oficial.

US
GAO WORK INVOLVING TITLE V OF THE ENERGY POLICY AND CONSERVATION ACT OF 1975. Main/Corp United States. General Accounting Office. **VFOAT** Energy Policy and Conservation Act of 1975. **VAT** General Accounting Office Work Involving Title V of the Energy Policy and Conservation Act of 1975. 1977/78-. English. an. US General Accounting Office / District of Columbia, 441 G Street NW, Room 4528, Washington DC 20548. **Tel** (202)275-2812.

US/0148-9623
GARGOYLE (MADISON), THE. (THE GARGOYLE.). **Added/Corp** University of Wisconsin--Madison. Law School. (19??)-. Periodical. English. qt. The Gargoyle, University of Wisconsin-Madison Law School, Madison WI 53706. **Tel** (608)262-7856. **ED** Edward J. Reisner. **LC** KF292.W57; A724. **DD** 340/.07/1177584. **Circ:** 8,000.
Desc: Alumni magazine for University of Wisconsin Law School.

US/1054-4674
GAUER DISTINGUISHED LECTURE IN LAW AND PUBLIC POLICY, THE. [Gauer disting. lect. law public policy]. **Added/Corp** National Legal Center for the Public Interest. Vol. 1 (1991)-. Monographic series. English. National Legal Center Public Interest, 1000 16th Street NW, Suite 301, Washington DC 20036. **DD** 340.

II
GAUHATI LAW REPORTS. Periodical. English. mo. Rs320.00. GLR Publishing House, Sikaria Building/1st Floor, A T Road, Guwahati 781 001 India. **Tel** 26492. **ED** B P Saraf, B P Todi and Ashok K Saraf. **DD** 348.54/042/05; 345.4084205. Index available. cum. index. **Bk Rev. Ad Acc. Circ:** 2,000 (ctrl).

US/0093-1845
GAVEL (BISMARCK). (THE GAVEL.). English. mo. State Bar Association of North Dakota, University of North Dakota, School of Law, Grand Forks ND 58201. **Tel** (701)777-2941, FAX (701)777-2217. **LC** KF332.N6; S743. **DD** 340/.06/2784.

US/0363-5783
GAVEL (SACRAMENTO), THE. (THE GAVEL.). [Gavel]. **Added/Corp** California Jury Verdicts. (19??)-. Periodical. English. sm. $380.00 US and Canada. California Jury Verdicts, 2100 Watt Avenue, Suite 165, Sacramento CA 95825. **Tel** (916)485-4990. **LC** KFC52.S8; G38. **DD** 348/.794/044.

IV
GAZETTE DES TRIBUNAUX IVOIRIENS. Jan. 1982-. Periodical. French. mo. 12000.00. Gazette des Tribunaux Ivoiriens Maison des Juristes, 41 Boulevard Clozel, Abidjan Ivory Coast.

FR
GAZETTE DU PALAIS. French. mo. 1,435F France; 1,620F other. Gazette du Palais, 3 Boulevard du Palais, 75180 Paris Cedex 04 France.

NR
GAZETTE - KADUNA STATE OF NIGERIA. Main/Corp Kaduna, Nigeria (State). V. 10, No. 7 (Feb. 12, 1976)-. Periodical. English. wk. N12.00 overseas. Government Printer / Kaduna, Private Mail Bag 2020, Kaduna Nigeria. **DD** 340/.096695. **Continues** North-Central State of Nigeria. Gazette.

AT/1038-1872
GAZETTE - LAW SOCIETY OF THE AUSTRALIAN CAPITAL TERRITORY. (GAZETTE.). [Gaz. - Law Soc. Aust. Cap. Territ.]. (1992)-. Periodical. English. bm. 30.00Aus$. Law Society of Australian Capital Territory, GPO Box 932, Canberra City 2601 Australia. **Tel** 011 61 06 2475700, FAX 011 61 06 2473754. **DD** 349.94705. **Continues** Newsletter of the Law Society of the Australian Capital Territory, 0817-7066.

NR
GAZETTE - NIGER STATE OF NIGERIA. Main/Corp Niger State (Nigeria). English. N12.00. Government Printer / Nigeria, Private Mail Bag 48 Minna, Niger Nigeria. **DD** 349.669/5/05.

AT/0818-0148
GAZETTE OF LAW AND JOURNALISM. [Gaz. law journal.]. (1986)-. Periodical. English. Ten times a year. 195.00Aus$ one year; 340.00Aus$ two years. Gazette of Law & Journalism, GPO Box 2669, Syndey NSW 2001 Australia. **Tel** 011 61 2 3607788, FAX 011 61 2 3607838, telex 3607788. **ED** Richard Ackland. **DD** 343.940998. ctrl circ.
Desc: Defamation, contempt, legislation on broadcasting and print media. Important developments in media law policy.

CN/0703-5721
GAZETTE OFFICIELLE DU QUEBEC, PARTIE 2; LOIS ET REGLEMENTS. [Gaz. off. Que., Partie 2, Lois reglem.]. **Main/Corp** Quebec (Province). **VFOAT** Quebec Official Gazette, Part 2; Laws and Regulations. **VAT** Quebec Official Gazette. Part 2. Laws and Regulations. Vol. 105 (Jan. 6, 1973)-. Periodical. French (English). wk. 93.00Can$. Les Publications du Quebec, CP 1190, Outremont Quebec H2V 4S7 Canada. **Tel** (514)948-1222, (800)463-2100, FAX (514)278-3030. **Continues in part** Quebec (Province) Gazette Officielle du Quebec.

CN/0023-9364
GAZETTE - THE LAW SOCIETY OF UPPER CANADA. [Gaz. - Law Soc. Upper Can.]. **Main/Corp** Law Society of Upper Canada. Vol. 2 (March 1968)-. Periodical. English. Three times a year. 15.00Can$. Law Society of Upper Canada, 130 Queen Street West, Toronto M5H 2N6 Canada. **Tel** (416)947-3300, (416)947-3371, telex 065-28013. **(Subscription address:** Law Society Upper Canada Gazette, 65 Queen Street West, 17th Floor Honsberger, Toronto Ontario M5H 2M5 Canada.**)** **ED** John D. Honsberger. **DD** 340/.06/271. **Circ:** 21,000. **Continues** Law Society Gazette, 0315-5404.
Ind/Abst Can. Legal Lit.; Index Can. Leg. Period. Lit.; Leg. Resour. Index (1980-?).

UK
GAZETTE YEARBOOK. 1972-. English. 113 Chancery Lane, London WC2 England. **LC** KD345; .G3. **DD** 340/.05.

IT
GAZZETTA UFFICIALE DELLA REPUBBLICA ITALIANA. Main/Corp Italy. (1861)-. Periodical. Italian. da. L193000.00 Italy, L386000.00 other (part 1 E) L664000.00 Italy, L1328000.00 other (part 1 F). Istituto Poligrafico Zecca Stato, Piazza Verdi 10, 00198 Rome Italy. **Tel** 011 39 6 85082307, 011 39 6 85082221.

IT
GAZZETTA UFFICIALE : INDICE REPERTORIO ANNUALE CRONOLOGICO PER MATERIE. Italian. an. L70000 Italy; L140000 other. Istituto Poligrafico Zecca Stato, Piazza Verdi 10, 00198 Rome Italy. **Tel** 011 39 6 85082307, 011 39 6 85082221.

US
GENERAL AND SPECIAL LAWS OF THE STATE OF TEXAS. Main/Corp Texas. 43d- Legislature; 1934-. English. Secretary of State / Texas, PO Box 13824 Capitol Station, Austin TX 78711. **Tel** (512)463-5561. **LC** KFT1225; .A23. **DD** 347.764/023; 347.640723. **Continues in part** General Laws of the State of Texas; Special Laws of the State of Texas.

US/0887-7823
GENERAL AVIATION ACCIDENT REPORT. [Gen. aviat. accid. rep.]. (1983)-. Periodical. English. wk. $1500.00. Andrews Publications Inc., 1646 West Chester Pike, PO Box 1000, Westtown PA 19395. **Tel** (610)399-6600, (800)345-1101, FAX (610)399-6610. **DD** 387.
Desc: A critical source of information and potential business for attorneys, insurers, aviation salvage operators and industry executives.

US
GENERAL LAWS OF RHODE ISLAND. Main/Corp Rhode Island. (19??)-. English. ir. $850.00 (main volumes). Michie Company, PO Box 7587, Charlottesville VA 22906-7587. **Tel** (804)972-7600, (800)542-0957, FAX (800)643-1280.

US
GENERAL LEGAL PUBLICATIONS UNION LIST / COMPILED AND EDITED BY THE UNION LIST COMMITTEE; FRANCES G. DURAKO - CHAIRPERSON, SIMA DABIRASHTIANI, ELMO F. DATTALO, ROBERT E. DICKEY, AND BETH E. SMITH. Added/Corp Law Librarians' Society of Washington, D.C. Union List Committee. 1st Ed. (1991)-. English. **Continues** Union List of Legal Looseleafs, 1062-5941; Specialized Union List.

US/1061-7108
GENERAL PRACTICE SECTION DIRECTORY AND OPERATING MANUAL. Title Change. [Gen. Pract. Sect. dir. oper. man.]. **Main/Corp** American Bar Association. Section of General Practice. **VFOAT** General Practice Section Directory. (198?)-(19??). Directory. English. American Bar Association, 750 North Lake Shore Drive, Chicago IL 60611. **Tel** (312)988-5522, (312)988-5241, FAX (312)988-5528, telex 270593. **LC** KF190; .A547. **DD** 340. **Continues** General Practice Section Directory, 0741-0913. **Continued by** American Bar Association. Section of General Practice., 1061-7086.

US
GENERAL STATUTES OF CONNECTICUT. Main/Corp Connecticut. (1866)-. English. an (updates in Oct.). $345.50. Secretary of the State / Public Division, 30 Trinity Street, Hartford CT 06106. **Tel** (203)566-3606.

●US/1068-3801
GEORGE MASON INDEPENDENT LAW REVIEW. [George Mason indep. law rev.]. **Added/Corp** George Mason Independent Law Journal Association. George Mason University. School of Law. Vol. 1, No. 1 (Winter 1992)-. Periodical. English. Twice a year. $25.00 US; $35.00 other; $15.00 single copies. George Mason University School of Law, 3401 North Fairfax Drive, Room 321B, Arlington VA 22201. **Tel** (703)993-8161, FAX (703)993-8080. **ED** Heather K. Bardot. **LC** K7; .E624. **DD** 340/.71/1755295.

US/0741-8736
GEORGE MASON UNIVERSITY LAW REVIEW. [George Mason Univ. law rev.]. **Added/Corp** George Mason University. School of Law. Vol. 4, No. 1 (Spring 1981)- Vol. 14, No. 3 (Summer 1992). Periodical. English. sa. George Mason University School of Law, 3401 North Fairfax Drive, Room 321B, Arlington VA 22201. **Tel** (703)993-8161, FAX (703)993-8080. **ED** Bryan Beier. **LC** K12; .A9369. **DD** 340/.05. **Bk Rev. Ad Acc. Circ:** 500. **Continues** GMU Law Review, 0742-4752. **Continued by** George Mason University Law Review (Arlington, Va. : 1994).
Desc: Analysis of legal issues of current interest in general and administrative law issues in particular.
Ind/Abst Bowne Dig. Corp. Sec. Lawyers; Fed. Tax Artic.; Index Leg. Period.; Leg. Resour. Index (1981-?); LegalTrac (1980-?).

●US
GEORGE MASON UNIVERSITY LAW REVIEW. Added/Corp George Mason Law Journals Association. George Mason University. School of Law. **VFOAT** George Mason University School of Law-Law Review. Vol. 1 (Spring 1994)-. Periodical. English. Free. George Mason University School of Law, 3401 North Fairfax Drive, Room 321B, Arlington VA 22201. **Tel** (703)993-8161, FAX (703)993-8080. **(Subscription address:** George Mason Law Review, 3401 North Fairfax Drive, Arlington VA 22201.**) Continues** George Mason University Law Review, 0741-8736.

US/0016-8076
GEORGE WASHINGTON LAW REVIEW, THE. [George Washington law rev.]. V. 1 (Nov. 1932)-. Periodical. English. Six times a year. $30.00 US and Canada; $35.00 other. George Washington Law Review, 2008 G Street NW / 2nd Floor, Washington DC 20052. **Tel** (202)676-3868. **ED** Vicki Larson and Jonathan Ladd. **LC** K7; .E63. **DD** 347.05. Index available. **Bk Rev. Ad Acc. Pr Rev. Circ:** 2,500 (ctrl). Documents available from The Genuine Article.

Desc: Current trends and new developments in national legal issues with special emphasis on administrative, general constitutional, patent and corporate law.
Ind/Abst Bowne Dig. Corp. Sec. Lawyers; Commun. Abstr.; Crim. Justice Abstr.; Crim. Penol. Police Sci. Abstr.; Curr. Contents Phys. Chem. Earth Sci.; Curr. Law Index (1980-); Fed. Tax Artic.; Index Leg. Period.; Int. Aerosp. Abstr.; Leg. Resour. Index (1980-); LegalTrac (1980-); Res. Alert [Full Cov.]; Soc. Plann. Policy Dev. Abstr.; Soc. Sci. Cit. Index [Full Cov.]; Sociol. Abstr.; West. Hist. Q.

US/0891-4370
GEORGETOWN IMMIGRATION LAW JOURNAL. [Georget. immigr. law j.]. **Added/Corp** Georgetown University. Law Center. **VFOAT** GILJ. Vol. 1, No. 1 (Fall 1985)-. Periodical. English. qt. $30.00 US; $35.00 Other. Georgetown University Law Center, 600 New Jersey Avenue NW, Washington DC 20009. **Tel** (202)662-9468, FAX (202)662-9444. **LC** K7; .E64. **DD** 342. ***Continues*** *Georgetown University Law Center Immigration Law Reporter.*
Ind/Abst Index Leg. Period.; Leg. Resour. Index; LegalTrac (1980-).

US/1041-5548
GEORGETOWN JOURNAL OF LEGAL ETHICS, THE. [Georget. j. leg. ethics]. Vol. 1, No. 1 (Summer 1987)-. Periodical. English. qt. $35.00. Georgetown University Law Center, 600 New Jersey Avenue NW, Washington DC 20009. **Tel** (202)662-9468, FAX (202)662-9444. **LC** K7; .E644. **DD** 174/.3/0973. Index available (in Spring of each year).
Ind/Abst Index Leg. Period.; Leg. Resour. Index; LegalTrac (1980-).

US/0016-8092
GEORGETOWN LAW JOURNAL, THE. [Georget. law j.]. **Added/Corp** Georgetown University. School of Law. Georgetown University. Law Center. Vol. 1 (Nov. 1912)-. English. Seven times a year. $40.00 US; $50.00 other. Georgetown University Law Center, 600 New Jersey Avenue NW, Washington DC 20009. **Tel** (202)662-9468, FAX (202)662-9444. **ED** Philip A. Sechler. **DD** 349.73/05. Index available (In last issue of each volume). **Bk Rev. Ad Acc. Pr Rev. Circ:** 3,500. available on microfilm from University Microfilms International (UMI); available on an online database from WESTLAW; and LEXIS. Documents available from The Genuine Article.
Desc: Contains articles, notes, case comments and book reviews on a variety of topics pertaining to law.
Ind/Abst Arts Humanit. Citation Index [Select. Cov.]; Bowne Dig. Corp. Sec. Lawyers; Crim. Justice Abstr.; Curr. Contents Phys. Chem. Earth Sci.; Curr. Law Index (1980-); Fed. Tax Artic.; Index Leg. Period.; Leg. Resour. Index (1980-); LegalTrac (1980-); PAIS Int. Print (1991-); Res. Alert [Full Cov.]; Soc. Sci. Cit. Index [Full Cov.]; Urban Aff. Abstr.

US/8750-0515
GEORGIA ADVANCE SHEETS. Main/Corp Georgia. Court of Appeals. **VFOAT** Official Advance Sheets. Vol. 1, No. 1 (July 5, 1984)-. English. wk (52 issues). $299.00. Darby Printing Company, 6215 Purdue Drive, Atlanta GA 30336. **Tel** (404)344-2665, (800)848-2995. **ED** Bob Wilkinson. **Ad Acc. Circ:** 2,100.
Desc: Full text of official opinions of the Georgia Supreme Court and Court of Appeals, including research features such as table of cases, index, etc.

US/1047-9228
GEORGIA JOURNAL OF SOUTHERN LEGAL HISTORY, THE. [Ga. j. south. leg. hist.]. **Added/Corp** Georgia Legal History Foundation. **VFOAT** Southern Legal History. Vol. 1, No. 1 (Spring/Summer 1991)--. Periodical. English. Twice a year. $50.00 (law firms bar associations & corporations) $35.00 (others). Georgia Legal History Foundation, 705 Trailwood Lane, Marietta GA 30064. **Tel** (404)423-1511. **LC** K7; .E654. **DD** 349.75/05; 347.5005.

US/0884-1217
GEORGIA LAW LETTER. [Ga. law lett.]. **Added/Corp** Georgia Law Letter Publishers. (1985)-. Periodical. English. wk (published Mondays). $117.00. M. Lee Smith Publishers and Printers, 162 4th Avenue North, PO Box 198867, Nashville TN 37219. **Tel** (615)242-7395, (800)274-6774, FAX (615)256-6601. **LC** KFG57; .G43. **DD** 348.758/046; 347.580846.

US/0016-8300
GEORGIA LAW REVIEW (ATHENS, GA.: 1966). (GEORGIA LAW REVIEW.). [Georgia law rev.]. Vol. 1, No. 1 (Fall 1966)-. Periodical. English. qt. $22.50 US; $27.50 other. University of Georgia School of Law, Athens GA 30602. **Tel** (706)542-7060. **LC** K7; .E67. **Bk Rev.**
Ind/Abst Bowne Dig. Corp. Sec. Lawyers; Curr. Law Index (1980-); Fed. Tax Artic.; Index Leg. Period.; Leg. Resour. Index (1980-); LegalTrac (1980-); PAIS Int. Print (1991-).

US/0362-5931
GEORGIA LEGISLATIVE REVIEW. Added/Corp Southern Center for Studies in Public Policy. (1974)-. English. an. $15.00 institutions; $10.00 individuals. Clark Atlanta University, JP Brawley Drive and Fair Street SW, Atlanta GA 30314. **Tel** (404)880-8524, 880-8525. **LC** KFG15; .G46. **DD** 344/.758.

US/1040-4805
GEORGIA REAL ESTATE LAW LETTER. [Ga. real estate law lett.]. **Added/Corp** Georgia Law Letter Publishers. Vol. 1, No. 1 (Jan. 1988)-. Periodical. English. mo. $137.00 plus tax. M. Lee Smith Publishers and Printers, 162 4th Avenue North, PO Box 198867, Nashville TN 37219. **Tel** (615)242-7395, (800)274-6774, FAX (615)256-6601. **ED** Seth Weissman and Linda Curry, (address) Weissman, Nowack, Curry and Zaleon, P.C., 181 14th Street, 2nd Floor, Atlanta, GA 30309, (phone) 404-885-9215. **DD** 346.
Desc: Update on the most recent real estate laws in Georgia.

US
GEORGIA SCHOOL LAW REPORTER. English. Six times a year. $285.00 (includes postage). LRP Publications, 747 Dresher Road, PO Box 980, Horsham PA 19044-0980. **Tel** (800)341-7874, (215)784-0860, FAX (215)784-9639, (215)784-0870.
Desc: Reports on the following decisions: Georgia Board of Education decisions, State and Regional Hearing Officer decisions, Georgia Professional Practices Commission decisions, and other related court decisions.

US/0016-8416
GEORGIA STATE BAR JOURNAL. [Georgia state bar j.]. Vol. 1, No. 1 (Aug. 1964)-. Periodical. English. qt. $10.00. State Bar of Georgia, 800 Hurt Building, 50 Hurt Plaza, Atlanta GA 30303. **Tel** (404)527-8700. **ED** William L Bost Jr, 990 Hammond Dr, Suite 650, Atlanta, GA 30328, (404)393-2100. **LC** K7; .E73. Index available. **Ad Acc, Adv Mgr Tel** (404)527-8791. **Pr Rev. Circ:** 23,500 (ctrl). ***Continues*** *Georgia Bar Journal.*
Desc: Articles on substantive law and features written by Georgia attorneys.
Ind/Abst Curr. Law Index (1980-); Fed. Tax Artic.; Index Leg. Period.; Law Office Inf. Serv.; Leg. Resour. Index (1980-); LegalTrac (1980-).

US
GEORGIA STATE BAR NEWS. Main/Corp State Bar of Georgia. V. 1- Sept. 1975-. Periodical. English. bm. State Bar of Georgia, 800 Hurt Building, 50 Hurt Plaza, Atlanta GA 30303. **Tel** (404)527-8700. **LC** KF200; .S69. **DD** 340/.09758. **Ad Acc. Circ:** 19,600 (ctrl).
Desc: Newsletter containing bar association current events and listings for CLE and conferences and institutes.
Ind/Abst Law Office Inf. Serv.

US/8755-6847
GEORGIA STATE UNIVERSITY LAW REVIEW. [Ga. State Univ. law rev.]. **Added/Corp** Georgia State University. College of Law. Vol. 1, No. 1 (Fall 1984)-. Periodical. English. Four times a year. $25.00 US; $29.00 other. Georgia State University Law Review, PO Box 4037, College of Law, Atlanta GA 30302. **Tel** (404)651-2047, FAX (404)651-2092. **ED** Laure Story. **LC** K7; .E74. **DD** 349.758/05; 347.58005. Index available. cum. index. **Bk Rev. Circ:** 500 (ctrl).
Desc: Emphasis on Georgia legislation and case law.
Ind/Abst Curr. Law Index (1984-); Index Leg. Period.; Leg. Resour. Index (1984-); LegalTrac (1984-).

GW/0934-7062
GESCHMACKSMUSTERBLATT. [Geschmacksmusterblatt]. (1988)-. Periodical. German. bw. DM192.00. Wila Verlag fuer Wirstachaftswebung Wilhelm Lampl KG, Landsberger Str 191A, W-8000 Munich 21 Germany. **Tel** 089 5795 0, FAX 089 5706693, telex 5212943 WILA D. **UDC** 347.77. Index available. **Ad Acc.**
Desc: Publications according to the "Law of Protection of Designs".

GE/0232-4849
GESETZBLATT DER DEUTSCHEN DEMOKRATISCHEN REPUBLIC. SONDERDRUCK. ***Ceased.*** **Main/Corp** Germany (East). **VFOAT** Gesetzblatt Sonderdruck. Nr. ST 353 (1965)-?. Periodical. German. bw. Haufe Berlin, Otto Grotewohl Strasse 17, D-10117 Berlin Germany. **Tel** 011 49 30 2331989.

GW/0435-8600
GEWERBLICHER RECHTSSCHUTZ UND URHEBERRECHT. INTERNATIONALER TEIL. Added/Corp Deutschen Vereinigung fuer Gewerblichen Rechtsschutz und Urheberrecht. (1???)-. Periodical. German. mo. $450.00. VCH Gesellschaft GmbH, Postfach 101161, D 69451 Weinheim Germany. **Tel** 011 49 6201 606459, FAX 011 49 6201 606184. **(Subscription address:** VCH Publishers Inc., 303 Northwest 12th Avenue, Journals Department, Deerfield FL 33442.) **[CCC].** available on microfilm.
Ind/Abst Index Foreign Leg. Per.

US/0270-2908
GILBERT LAW SUMMARIES. CONFLICT OF LAWS. (CONFLICT OF LAWS.). [Gilbert law summ., Confl. laws]. 12th- Ed.; 1979-. English. $12.95. Law Distributors, 14415 South Main Street, Gardena CA 90248. **Tel** (310)321-3275, (800)421-1893, FAX (310)324-6381. **LC** KF412; .R87. **DD** 340/.9. ***Continues*** *Gilbert Law Summaries. Conflict of Laws, 0270-2908.*

US
GILBERT LAW SUMMARIES CONTRACTS. VFOAT Contracts. 9th Ed.; 1979-. English. Emanuel Law Outlines, 1865 Palmer Avenue, Larchmont NY 10538. **ED** M A Eisenberg. **LC** KF801.Z9; G53. **DD** 346.73/02. ***Continues*** *Contracts (Gardena, Calif.).*

●US/1065-2027
GIS LAW. [GIS law]. **Added/Corp** GIS Law and Policy Institute. **VAT** Geographic Information Systems Law. (1992)-. Periodical. English. Four times a year. $98.00. GIS Law and Policy Institute, 501 Nations Bank Building, Harrisonburg VA 22801. **Tel** (703)434-3307, FAX (703)434-3147. **ED** Bishop Dansby. **LC** KF5752.5.A15; G17. **DD** 342.73/0662/05; 347.30266205.
Desc: Contains articles on legal issues related to geographic information systems (GIS). The proliferation of GIS data in government raises issues of access, privacy and liability. Also, newly independent states and other developing nations are converting to the private ownership of land and free economies, giving rise to issues related to land information and land title registration.

IT
GIURISPRUDENZA AGRARIA ITALIANA. Reda Ramo Edit Agricoltori, Via di Tor Sapienza 172, 00155 Rome Italy. **Tel** 011 39 6 2280077.

IT
GIURISPRUDENZA ANNOTATA DI DIRITTO INDUSTRIALE. (1972)-. Italian. an. L26000. Giuffre Editore SPA, Via Busto Arsizio 40, 20151 Milan Italy. **Tel** 011 398 2 38089200. **DD** 343/.45/07.

IT
GIURISPRUDENZA : BANCA DATI LAVORO SU CD-ROM. (19??)-. Italian. qt. 580000L. IPSOA Editore SRL, Casella Postale 12055, Mastrangelo, 20120 Milan Italy. **Tel** 011 39 2 82476248.

IT
GIURISPRUDENZA DELLE IMPOSTE : RASSEGNA DELLE DECISIONI DI MASSIMA DELLA CORTE DI CASSAZIONE E DELLA COMMISSIONE CENTRALE DELLE IMPOSTE ... / ASSOCIAZIONE FRA LE SOCIETA ITALIANE PER AZIONI. Added/Corp Italy. Corte Suprema di Cassazione. Italy. Commissione Centrale delle Imposte. Associazione fra le Societa Italiane per Azioni. Vol. 27, No. 1 (1954)-. Italian. qt. L115000.00 Italy; L173000.00 other. Giuffre Editore SPA, Via Busto Arsizio 40, 20151 Milan Italy. **Tel** 011 398 2 38089200. **ED** Claudio Berliri. ***Continues*** *Giurisprudenza delle Imposte Dirette, di Registro e di Negoziazione.*
Desc: Consists of five parts. Three of which respectively concern income tax, taxes on business and local taxation; the fourth part is devoted to criminal law in this field while the fifth contains expositions of theory.

IT
GIURISPRUDENZA DI MERITO. (19??)-. Periodical. Italian. bm. L140000.00 Italy; L210000.00 other. Giuffre Editore SPA, Via Busto Arsizio 40, 20151 Milan Italy. **Tel** 011 398 2 38089200. **ED** Angelo Jammuzzi, Sabino Cassese, Guideppe De Luca, Franco Gallo, Agostino Gambino, Carmine Punzi, Stefano Rodota, and Vincenzo Scordamaglia. **Ad Acc. Circ:** 5,000.
Desc: Publishes rulings given by judges throughout Italy, accompanied by editorial and critical comment.

IT
GIURISPRUDENZA ITALIANA. Added/Corp Unione Tipografico-Editrice Torinese. Series 7a., Vol. 117 (1965)-. Italian. mo (12 issues). L285000. Unione Tipografico Ed Torinese, Corso Raffaello 28, 10125 Turin Italy. **Tel** 011 39 11 6529340. **LC** KKH19; .A351848. ***Continues*** *Giurisprudenza Italiana e la Legge Riunite.*

IT
GIURISPRUDENZA PIEMONTESE. Unione Induxtriale, Via Fanti 17, 10128 Turin Italy.

IT
GIURISPRUDENZA PREVIDENZIALE : BANCA DATI LAVORO SU CD-ROM. (19??)-. Italian. tq. 230000L. IPSOA Editore SRL, Casella Postale 12055, Mastrangelo, 20120 Milan Italy. **Tel** 011 39 2 82476248.

IT
GIUS - RASSEGNA DI GIURISPRUDENZA. (19??)-. Periodical. Italian. L290000 Italy; L580000 other. IPSOA Editore SRL, Casella Postale 12055, Mastrangelo, 20120 Milan Italy. **Tel** 011 39 2 82476248.

Law

IT
GIUSTIZIA CIVILE. MASSIMARIO ANNOTATO DELLA CASSAZIONE / A CURA DELLA DIREZIONE E REDEZIONE DELLA RIVISTA DI GIURISPRUDENZA. **Added/Corp** Italy. Corte Suprema di Cassazione. (1951)-. Periodical. Italian. Twelve times a year. L190000.00 Italy; L285000.00 other. Giuffre Editore SPA, Via Busto Arsizio 40, 20151 Milan Italy. **Tel** 011 398 2 38089200. **ED** Alfio Finocchiaro.
Desc: Provides maxims drawn from Supreme Court rulings on civil cases.

IT
GIUSTIZIA E COSTITUZIONE : RIVISTA TRIMESTRALE DELL'ASSOCIAZIONE DI STUDI GIURIDICI E COSTITUZIONALI. **Added/Corp** Associazione di Studi Giuridici e Costituzionali. (19??)-. Periodical. Italian. Four times a year. L70000 Italy; L80000 other. Nuove Ricerche SRL, Via Del Commercio 20/A, 60127 Ancona, Italy. **Tel** 011 39 71 897336.
Ind/Abst Foreign Lang. Index.

IT/0017-0658
GIUSTIZIA PENALE. [Giustizia penale]. (1895)-. Periodical. Italian. mo. L240000 Italy; L480000 other. Giustizia Penale, Via Giovanni Nicotera N 10, 00195 Rome, Italy. **Tel** 011 39 6 3215395. **UDC** 343. **CODEN** GUPN-A.

IT
GIUSTIZIA TRIBUTARIA E IMPOSTE DIRETTE. (19??)-. Italian. mo. L90000 Italy; L130000 other. Tipogr Tappini Editrice, Via Morandi 19, 06012 Citta Castello PG Italy. **Tel** 011 39 75 8558194.

US/0363-2423
GLENDALE LAW REVIEW. [Glendale law rev.]. **Added/Corp** Glendale University. College of Law. Vol. 1 (1976)-. English. ir. $9.00. Glendale Law Review, 220 North Glendale Avenue, Glendale CA 91206. **Tel** (818)247-0770. **LC** K7; .L46. **DD** 340/.0973. Index available. **Circ:** 500.
Desc: Interdisciplinary periodical on current and controversial issues.
Ind/Abst Curr. Law Index (1980-); Index Leg. Period.; Leg. Resour. Index (1980-); LegalTrac (1980-); PAIS Int. Print.

US/0363-0307
GOLDEN GATE UNIVERSITY LAW REVIEW. [Gold. Gate Univ. law rev.]. **Main/Corp** Golden Gate University. School of Law. V. 6- Fall 1975-. Periodical. English. Three times a year. $22.00. Golden Gate University, School of Law, 536 Mission Street, San Francisco CA 94105. **Tel** (415)442-7000 ext.7588. **ED** Maureen Sullivan, Carol Murphy, Lisa Croft, Michael Barnes, Beverly Saxon, Sheila Reed. **LC** K7; .O54. **DD** 340/.09794. **Bk Rev. Ad Acc.** **Circ:** 650. available on microfilm and microfiche from University Microfilms International (UMI). **Continues** *Golden Gate Law Review, 0098-6631.*
Desc: Concentrates on ninth circuit, women's legal issues, and general law.
Ind/Abst Bowne Dig. Corp. Sec. Lawyers; Curr. Law Index (1980-); Index Leg. Period.; Leg. Resour. Index (1980-); LegalTrac (1980-).

GW/0017-1956
GOLTDAMMER'S ARCHIV FUER STRAFRECHT. (19??)-. Periodical. German. Twelve times a year. $234.00. Dr. Alfred Huethig Verlag GmbH, Postfach 102869, D 69018 Heidelberg Germany. **Tel** 011 49 6221 489281. **(Subscription address:** Huethig Publishing Inc., 29 Macintosh Drive, Oxford CT 06478.**)**
Ind/Abst Index Foreign Leg. Per.

US/0046-6115
GONZAGA LAW REVIEW. [Gonzaga law rev.]. Vol. 1, No. 1 (Mar. 1966)-. Periodical. English. qt. $27.00 Washington residents; $25.00 other. Gonzaga University, School of Law, PO Box 3528, Spokane WA 99220. **Tel** (509)328-4220, (509)484-6481 ext 3715. **ED** Michael F McMahon, Bryce E Brown, Lauren E Winters, Stephen P McCleary, Reza Sadeghi, Elizabeth A Delay, Scott Bladek and Michelle D Dimond. **LC** K7; .O555. **DD** 340/.05. Index available. cum. index. **Bk Rev. Ad Acc. Circ:** 1,000 (ctrl).
Desc: A timely publication of recent developments in the legal field - particularly designed for the legal practitioners in Washington.
Ind/Abst Bowne Dig. Corp. Sec. Lawyers; Curr. Law Index (1980-); Fed. Tax Artic.; Index Leg. Period.; Leg. Resour. Index (1980-); LegalTrac (1982-).

US/0885-9868
GONZAGA SPECIAL REPORT. [Gonzaga spec. rep.]. **VFOAT** Gonzaga Special Report. Public Sector Labor Law; Public Sector Labor Law. Vol. 1 (1980)-. Periodical. English. $5.50. Gonzaga Public Sector Report, c/o Gonzaga Student Bar Association, Gonzaga University School of Law, Spokane WA 99202.

LC K7; .O56. **DD** 344.73/0189041353; 347. 304189041353.
Ind/Abst Leg. Resour. Index (1980-?).

UK
GORE-BROWNE ON COMPANIES. English. Six times a year. £165.00. Jordan & Sons Ltd, 21 St Thomas Street, Bristol BS1 6JS England. **Tel** 011 44 272 230600, FAX 0272 230063, telex 499119. **Circ:** 1,500 (ctrl). **Continues** *Secretarial Administration Releases.*
Desc: UK company law.

●**RU**
GOSUDARSTVO I PRAVO / INSTITUT GOSUDARSTVA I PRAVA, ROSSIISKAIA AKADEMIIA NAUK. **Added/Corp** Institut Gosudarstva i Prava (Rossiiskaia Akademiia Nauk). (1992)-. Periodical. Russian (summaries and/or abstracts in English; table of contents in English and French). mo. $134.00 US; $152.00 other. **(Subscription address:** Victor Kamkin, 4956 Boiling Brook Parkway, Rockville MD 20852.**)** **LC** K23; .O875. **Continues** *Sovetskoe Gosudarstvo i Pravo, 0038-5204.*
Ind/Abst Curr. Dig. Post Sov. Press.

GW
GOTTINGER RECHTSWISSENSCHAFTLICHE STUDIEN. **Added/Corp** Gottingen. Universitat. Rechts und Staatswissenschaftliche Fakultat. (1951)-. Monographic series. German. ir. Price varies per volume. Verlag Otto Schwartz & Company, Annastrasse 7, D 37075 Goettingen Germany. **Tel** 011 49 551 31051, 011 49 551 31052, FAX 011 49 551 372812.

US/0742-8901
GOVERNMENT CONTRACTS SECTION NEWSLETTER. Jan. 1984-. Newsletter. English. Federal Bar Association, 1815 H Street Northwest, Suite 408, Washington DC 20006. **Tel** (202)638-0252, FAX (202)775-0295. **LC** KF842; .G68. **DD** 346.73/023/05; 347.3062305. **Continues** *Government Contracts Council Newsletter, 0741-5311.*

US/0145-6598
GOVERNMENT CONTRACTS SERVICE. [Gov. contracts serv.]. (19??). English. Twenty-six times a year. $595.00. Procurement Associates, 733 North Dodsworth Avenue, Covina CA 91724. **Tel** (818)966-4576, FAX (818)915-1709. **ED** Paul R McDonald Sr. **LC** KF846.5; .G68. **DD** 346/.73/023. Index available.
Desc: Provides in-depth information on every aspect of the Government contracting process from the development of the requirement to the final close out of the contract.

US
GOWER FEDERAL SERVICE: MINING. **Main/Corp** Rocky Mountain Mineral Law Foundation. (1953)-. English. ir (6-8 issues per year). $540.00. Rocky Mountain Mineral Law Foundation, Porter Administration Building, 7039 East 18th Avenue, Denver CO 80220. **Tel** (303)321-8100, FAX (303)321-7657. Index available in last issue of volume--attached. cum. index. **Bk Rev,** (Qty: 1-3/year). **Circ:** 120. available on microfiche; available on an online database from WESTLAW.
Desc: Laws, federal regulations, and I.B.L.A. decisions related to mining.

US
GOWER FEDERAL SERVICE - MISCELLANEOUS LANDS DECISIONS SERVICE. **Added/Corp** United States. Interior Board of Land Appeals. Rocky Mountain Mineral Law Foundation. (1970)-. Periodical. English. Twelve times a year. $165.00. Rocky Mountain Mineral Law Foundation, Porter Administration Building, 7039 East 18th Avenue, Denver CO 80220. **Tel** (303)321-8100, FAX (303)321-7657. Index available. cum. index. **Circ:** 81 (ctrl). available on an online database from WESTLAW. **Continues** *Gower Federal Service. Consolidated Decisions.*
Desc: Decisions of the board of Land Appeals, Office of Hearings and Appeals, and Department of the Interior.

US/1061-3072
GPLLA NEWSLETTER. See *Library and Information Sciences.*

US
GRAND RAPIDS LEGAL NEWS. English. wk. $46.00 (one year). Grand Rapids Legal News, 840 Ottawa Avenue NW, Grand Rapids MI 49501. **Tel** (616) 454-9292, FAX (616) 454-9287.

US/0196-4593
GRANTS FOR RESEARCH ON LAW AND GOVERNMENT IN EDUCATION. See *Education.*

US
GRASSROOTS REPORT. English. Securities Industry Association, 120 Broadway/35th Floor, New York NY 10271. **Tel** (212)608-1500, FAX (212)608-1604. ctrl circ.

Desc: An update of legislative and political activities in Washington relevant to the industry. Sent to each member of the Grassroots network.

UK
GREAT BRITAIN LAW COMMISSION. WORKING PAPERS. (19??)-. English. ir. Price varies per volume. Her Majesty's Stationery Office, 51 Nine Elms Lane, London SW8 5DR England. **Tel** 011 44 71 873 8459, 011 44 71 873 8498, FAX 011 44 71 873 8499, 011 44 71 873 8456, telex 297138. **(Subscription address:** Her Majesty's Stationery Office, PO Box 276, Publications Centre, London SW8 5DT England.**)**

●**UK**
GREEN'S COURT PRACTICE BULLETIN. (1995)-. Bulletin. English. Six times a year. £74.00 Europe; £78.00 other. Sweet & Maxwell Ltd., South Quay Plaza, 183 Marsh Wall, London E14 9FT England. **Tel** 011 44 264 342899, FAX 011 44 264 342723, telex 929089 ITPINF G.

US
GREENS GEORGIA LAW OF EVIDENCE. English. an. $97.95. Harrison Company Publishers, 3110 Crossing Park, PO Box 7500, Norcross GA 30091-7500. **Tel** (800)241-3561, (404)447-9150.

●**UK**
GREEN'S PROPERTY LAW BULLETIN. (1993)-. Bulletin. English. Six times a year. £74.00 Europe; £78.00 other. Sweet & Maxwell Ltd., South Quay Plaza, 183 Marsh Wall, London E14 9FT England. **Tel** 011 44 264 342899, FAX 011 44 264 342723, telex 929089 ITPINF G.

●**UK**
GREEN'S REPARATION LAW BULLETIN. (1995)-. Bulletin. English. Six times a year. £74.00 Europe; £78.00 other. Sweet & Maxwell Ltd., South Quay Plaza, 183 Marsh Wall, London E14 9FT England. **Tel** 011 44 264 342899, FAX 011 44 264 342723, telex 929089 ITPINF G.

UK
GREENS WEEKLY DIGEST, CURRENT SCOTTISH CASE LAW. **Added/Corp** W. Green & Son. **VFOAT** Weekly Digest, Current Scottish Case Law; Current Scottish Case Law; G.W.D.; GWD; Greens Weekly Digest. (19??)-. English. Forty times a year. £105.00 Europe; £110.00 other. Sweet & Maxwell Ltd., South Quay Plaza, 183 Marsh Wall, London E14 9FT England. **Tel** 011 44 264 342899, FAX 011 44 264 342723, telex 929089 ITPINF G. **LC** KDC116.1; .G74.

CN/0822-7810
GRIEVANCE AND ADJUDICATION SECTION REPORTS / PUBLIC SERVICE ALLIANCE OF CANADA. **Main/Corp** Public Service Alliance of Canada. Grievance and Adjudication Section. Ser. 2, No. 2-. Periodical. English. Free. Public Service Alliance of Canada, 233 Gilmour Street, Ottawa Ontario K2P 0P1 Canada. **Tel** (613)560-4211. **DD** 342.71/068. **Continues** *Public Service Alliance of Canada. Report on Grievances Submitted to Adjudication, 0318-6296.*

GW
GRUNDGESETZ KOMMENTAR. (19??)-. German. ir. Price varies per volume. CH Beck Verlagsbuchhandlung, D 80791 Munich Germany. **Tel** 011 49 89 381891.

PE
GRUPO ANDINO : LEGISLACION ECONOMICA Y SOCIAL DE LOS PAISES MIEMBROS. **Main/Corp** Board of Cartagena Agreement. Spanish. mo. By request. Acuerdo de Cartagena, Centro de Documentacion, Apartado 18-1177, Lima 18 Peru. **Tel** 41 42 12, telex JUNAC 20104. Index available. cum. index. **Circ:** 15 (ctrl).
Desc: Abstracts of economic and social legislation from five member countries of the Andean group: Bolivia, Colombia, Ecuador, Peru, and Venezuela.

US
GUAM REPORTS : CONTAINING OPINIONS OF THE DISTRICT, SUPERIOR AND SUPREME COURTS. **Ceased. Added/Corp** Guam. District Court. Guam. Superior Court. Guam. Supreme Court. Vol. 1 (1955-1979)-(19??). Periodical. English. ir. Butterworth Legal Publishers / Salem, NH, 8 Industrial Way, Building C, Salem NH 03079. **Tel** (800)548-4001, (603)898-9664.

AG
GUIA PRACTICA DEL EXPORTADOR E IMPORTADOR. SUPLEMENTO. FASCICULO DE RESOLUCIONES DE CLASIFICACION. **VFOAT** Fasciculo de Resoluciones de Clasificacion. No. 1 (19??)-. Spanish. Lavalle 1125, P 3O of 8, 1048 Buenos Aires Argentina. **DD** 343.8205/6; 348.20356.

AG
GUIA PRACTICA DEL EXPORTADOR E IMPORTADOR Y PARA TODO HOMBRE DE NEGOCIOS. SUPLEMENTO DE LA SECCION INFORMATIVA. (19??)-. Spanish. Guia Practica del Exportador e Importador, Lavalle 1125, P 3 of 8, 1048 Buenos Aires Argentina. **Tel** 011 54 1 358533. **DD** 343.82/087; 348.20387.

GW
GUIDE DU DEPOSANT. English (German). an. Free. European Patent Office, Schottenfeldgasse 29, A 1060 Vienna Austria. **Tel** 011 43 1 52126543.

FR
GUIDE TO LEGISLATION ON RESTRICTIVE BUSINESS PRACTICES. ***Ceased.*** **VFOAT** Legislation on Restrictive Business Practices. (1967)-(1985). English. ir. OECD Publications and Information Center, 2 rue Andre-Pascal, 75775 Paris Cedex 16 France. **Tel** 011 33 1 45248167, US:(202)785-6323, FAX 011 33 1 45248500 OR 45248176, telex 620 160 OCDE. **(Subscription address:** US/2001 L Street NW, Suite 700, Washington, DC 20036**)** ***Continues*** *Guide to Legislation on Restrictive Business Practices. Europe and North America Trade.*

US/0271-6461
GUIDE TO RECORD RETENTION REQUIREMENTS. **Added/Corp** United States. Office of the Federal Register. **VFOAT** Guide to Record Retention Requirements in the Code of Federal regulations; Guide to Record Retention Requirements in the CFR; Record Retention Guide. (1955)-. English. ir. $25.00 (per copy). National Archives and Records Administration, Eighth Street and Pennsylvania Avenue NW, Washington DC 20408. **Tel** (202)523-3220. **(Subscription address:** Superintendent of Documents, US Government Printing Office, Washington DC 20402.**)** **LC** KF70; .G84.

●US/1064-7732
GUIDE TO TEXAS FRANCHISE TAX. [Guide Tex. franch. tax]. **Added/Corp** Texas Society of Certified Public Accountants. 1st Ed (Mar. 1992)-. English. $110.00. Practitioners Publishing Company, PO Box 901007, Fort Worth TX 76101-0966. **Tel** (800)323-8724, (817)332-3709. **DD** 343.

US/0148-0588
GUILD NOTES. **See** Political Science-Civil Rights.

GY
GUYANA LAW JOURNAL. V. 1-. Periodical. English. $6.00 per issue to students of institutions in the Caribbean, $10.00 per issue all other sales. Department of Political Science and Law, Box 841, Georgetown Guyana South Africa. **LC** K7; .U93. **DD** 349.88/1/05; 348.81005.

IS/0465-420X
HA-MAYAN. **Added/Corp** Mosad Yitshak Brayer Shel Pocale Agudat Yisrael (Jerusalem). Vol. 1 (1953)-. Periodical. Hebrew. Four times a year. $18.00. Ha Ma Yan, 26 Tsefanya Street, Jerusalem Israel.
Desc: News and information on the jewish law.

UK/0308-4388
HALSBURY'S LAWS OF ENGLAND ANNUAL ABRIDGEMENT. **VFOAT** Laws of England Annual Abridgment. (1974)-. English. an. £650.00 (complete set), price varies per individual volume. Butterworth & Co. Ltd. / Kent, England, Borough Green, Sevenoaks Kent TN15 8PH England. **Tel** 011 44 732-884567, FAX 011 44 732-885996. **ED** The Right Honorable Lord Hailsham. **LC** KD310; .H35. **DD** 340/.0941.
Desc: Consolidates all the material included in the previous year's issues of the Monthly Review.

UK
HALSBURY'S LAWS OF ENGLAND : CUMULATIVE SUPPLEMENT. (19??)-. English. an. £179.00. Butterworth & Co. Ltd. / Kent, England, Borough Green, Sevenoaks Kent TN15 8PH England. **Tel** 011 44 732-884567, FAX 011 44 732-885996.
Desc: Provides a thorough commentary on the Laws of England and Wales.

UK
HALSBURY'S LAWS OF ENGLAND MONTHLY REVIEW. **VFOAT** Laws of England Monthly Review. (19??)-. English. mo. Butterworth & Co. Ltd. / Kent, England, Borough Green, Sevenoaks Kent TN15 8PH England. **Tel** 011 44 732-884567, FAX 011 44 732-885996.
Desc: Provides a thorough commentary on the Laws of England and Wales.

UK
HALSBURY'S STATUTES OF ENGLAND AND WALES. English. wk. £3150.00. Butterworth & Co. Ltd. / Kent, England, Borough Green, Sevenoaks Kent TN15 8PH England. **Tel** 011 44 732-884567, FAX 011 44 732-885996. **ED** Andrew Davies. Index available. cum. index. **Ad Acc.** ctrl circ.
Desc: Comprises the statute law of England and Wales from the earliest times to the present day.

UK
HALSBURY'S STATUTORY INSTRUMENTS : BEING A COMPANION WORK TO HALSBURY'S STATUTES OF ENGLAND. **Main/Corp** Great Britain. (1951)-. English. mo. £1150.00. Butterworth & Co. Ltd. / Kent, England, Borough Green, Sevenoaks Kent TN15 8PH England. **Tel** 011 44 732-884567, FAX 011 44 732-885996. **ED** Lorena Sutherland.
Desc: Provides detailed and continually updated information on every statutory instrument of general application in force in England and Wales.

●CN/1188-4827
HAMILTON LAWYER. (THE HAMILTON LAWYER.). [Hamilt. lawyer]. **VFOAT** Hamilton Law Association News Magazine. (1992)-. Periodical. English. Nine times a year. $25.00. Hamilton Law Association, 50 Main Street East, Hamilton ONT L8N 1E9 Canada. **Tel** (905)522-1563, FAX (905)572-1188. **ED** Wendy Hearder-Moan (phone: (416)522-1563). **DD** 340.05. **Bk Rev**, (Qty: 5-10). **Ad Acc**, **Adv Mgr:** D. Sexton. **Circ:** 900. ***Continues*** *News Magazine - Hamilton Law Association, 0820-4799.*
Desc: News accomplishments and development of library , education programs, and professionals magazine.

US
HAMLINE JOURNAL OF PUBLIC LAW AND POLICY. **Added/Corp** Hamline University. School of Law. Hamline University. Master of Arts in Public Administration. Vol. 7, No. 1 (Spring 1986)-. Periodical. English. sa (Feb., June). $12.00. Hamline University School of Law, 1536 Hewitt Avenue, St Paul MN 55104. **Tel** (612)641-2350, FAX (612)641-2435. **ED** Suzanne Blankenship (editor's address: 18827 232nd Avenue, Big Lake, MN 55309; (612)263-8450). **LC** K8; .A634. **DD** 344..73/005; 347.304005. **Circ:** 1,000 (ctrl). ***Continues*** *Hamline Journal of Public Law, 0736-1033.*
Desc: Addresses issues of public law and policy considered by the executive, legislative, and judicial branches and administrative agencies. Constitutes an authoritative resource.
Ind/Abst Index Leg. Period.; Leg. Resour. Index; LegalTrac (1980-).

US/0198-7364
HAMLINE LAW REVIEW. [Hamline law rev.]. Vol. 1978, No. 1-. Periodical. English. Twice a year. $12.00. Hamline University School of Law, 1536 Hewitt Avenue, St Paul MN 55104. **Tel** (612)641-2350, FAX (612)641-2435. **LC** K8; .A636. **DD** 340/.05. **[CCC]**. cum. index. **Bk Rev. Ad Acc. Circ:** 1,200.
Desc: Comprised of articles, notes, comments, book reviews, and symposium projects focusing on particular fields of law.
Ind/Abst Bowne Dig. Corp. Sec. Lawyers; Crim. Justice Abstr.; Curr. Law Index (1980-); Index Leg. Period.; Leg. Resour. Index (1980-); LegalTrac (1980-).

UK
HAMLYN LECTURES, THE. 1st Series (1949)-. Monographic series. English. ir. Price varies per volume. Associated Book Publishers, North Way Andover, Hampshire SP10 5BE England. **Tel** 011 44 264 332424. **(Subscription address:** Sweet and Maxwell Limited, Cheriton House, Northway Andover, Hampshire SP10 5BE England.**)**
Desc: A series of lectures delivered by figures in the field of British law. The purpose is to further the knowledge among the general public of the British legal system.

JA/0438-4997
HANDAI HOGAKU. **VFOAT** Osaka Law Review. (1951)-. Periodical. Japanese. qt. $131.00. **(Subscription address:** Japan Publications Trading Company, Ltd., PO Box 5030, Tokyo International, Tokyo 100-31 Japan.**)**
Ind/Abst Index Foreign Leg. Per.

US/0149-0842
HANDBOOK - ALABAMA LAW INSTITUTE. **Main/Corp** Alabama Law Institute. English. Alabama Law Institute, PO Box 1425, University AL 35486. **Tel** (205)348-7411. **LC** KFA27.L38; A32. **DD** 340/.06/2761.

●US/1063-8253
HANDBOOK / ASSOCIATION OF AMERICAN LAW SCHOOLS. [Handb. - Assoc. Am. Law Sch.]. **Main/Corp** Association of American Law Schools. **VFOAT** AALS Handbook. **VAT** Association of American Law Schools Handbook. (1992)-. English. Association of American Law Schools, 1201 Connecticut Avenue NW, Suite 800, Washington DC 20036-2605. **DD** 340. ***Continues*** *Association Handbook, 1063-8245.*

UK
HANDBOOK OF RENT REVIEW. (1981)-. English. £180.00 (main work). Sweet & Maxwell Ltd., South Quay Plaza, 183 Marsh Wall, London E14 9FT England. **Tel** 011 44 264 342899, FAX 011 44 264 342723, telex 929089 ITPINF G.

US/0271-2571
HANDBOOK - OKLAHOMA BAR ASSOCIATION. **Main/Corp** Oklahoma Bar Association (1939-). English. an. Journal-Record Publishing Company, 621 North Robinson, Oklahoma City OK 73102. **ED** Blake Hogan. **LC** KF332.O4; O42197. **DD** 340/.06/0766. cum. index. **Ad Acc.** ctrl circ.

JA
HANREI JIHO. **VFOAT** Hanreijiho. No. 1 (1953)-. Periodical. Japanese. tm. $414.00. **(Subscription address:** Kyowa Book Company Inc., 1-38 Kanda Jinbo-Cho, Chiyoda-Ku Tokyo 101, Japan**)** cum. index.

JA
HANREI MINJI ROPPO ZENSHO / HENSHU, DAIICHI HOKI SHUPPAN KABUSHIKI KAISHA HENSHUBU. **Main/Corp** Japan. **VFOAT** Minji Roppo Zensho. 1982-. Japanese. an. ¥3800. Daiichi Hoki Shuppan Kabushiki Kaisha, 11-17 Minami Aoyama 2 Minato-ku, Tokyo-to 107 Japan.

JA
HANREI TAIMUZU. **VFOAT** Law Times Report. (1950)-. Periodical. Japanese. sm (24 issues). $498.00. **(Subscription address:** Japan Publications Trading Company, Ltd., PO Box 5030, Tokyo International, Tokyo 100-31 Japan.**)** cum. index. ***Continues*** *Hanrei Taimuzu (Tokyo, Japan : 1948).*

JA
HANREITSUKI ROPPO ZENSHO. **Main/Corp** Japan. **VFOAT** Roppo Zensho. (19??)-. Periodical. Japanese. ¥800. Kinensha, 9-6 Higashi Ueno 2, Taito-ku 110, Tokyo Japan.

US
HANSFORD & TILLEYS ALABAMA EQUITY. English. ir. $94.95, seperate part pocket supplement $28.95. Harrison Company Publishers, 3110 Crossing Park, PO Box 7500, Norcross GA 30091-7500. **Tel** (800)241-3561, (404)447-9150.

US
HANSON'S MANUAL OF EXAMINATION AND INSURANCE LAW HANDBOOK. **Added/Corp** Insurance License Bureau, Inc., Springfield, Il. (19??)-. English. ir. $16.00. Insurance License Bureau Inc, 414 East Monroe Street, PO Box 610, Springfield MD 62705. **Tel** (217)544-4833. **LC** KFI1385.Z9; I5. **DD** 346/.773/086076. ***Continues*** *Manual of Examination and Insurance Reference Guide for Illinois Insurance Agents and Brokers.*

CN/0849-262X
HARD ACT TO FOLLOW. ***Ceased.*** (A HARD ACT TO FOLLOW : NOTES ON ONTARIO SCHOOL LAW.). [Hard act foll.]. **Added/Corp** University of Toronto. Guidance Centre. Ontario Institute for Studies in Education. **VFOAT** Notes on Ontario School Law. (1973)-(19??). English. an. Guidance Center / The Ontario Institute for Studies in Education, 712 Gordon Baker Road, Toronto Ont M2H 3R7 Canada. **Tel** (416)502-1262, 800-668-6247, FAX (416)502-1101. **DD** 344.713/07/05.

US/1066-0925
HARMONIZED TARIFF SCHEDULE OF THE UNITED STATES. **See** Public Administration-Public Finance and Taxation.

US/0193-4872
HARVARD JOURNAL OF LAW & PUBLIC POLICY. [Harv. j. law public policy]. **Added/Corp** Harvard Society for Law and Public Policy. **VFOAT** Law and Public Policy. Vol. 1 (1978)-. Periodical. English. Three times a year (Feb., June & July). $32.50 US; $35.00 other. Harvard Law School, Publications Center, Cambridge MA 02138. **Tel** (617)495-7984, (617)495-3694. **ED** Jason Levine (editor's phone: (617)495-3105). **LC** K8; .A683. **DD** 340/.0973. **Bk Rev**, (Qty: 1 or 2). **Pr Rev. Circ:** 4,800. available on an online database from WESTLAW. Documents available from The Genuine Article, UMI Article Clearinghouse.
Desc: The second most widely circulated student edited law journal in the U.S,; publishes a wide range of articles on such topics as constitutional jurisprudence, federal securities laws, ethics in the judicial confirmation process, labor law, and energy policy.
Ind/Abst Bowne Dig. Corp. Sec. Lawyers; Commun. Abstr. (?-?); Crim. Justice Abstr.; Curr. Contents Soc. Behav. Sci.; Curr. Law Index (1980-); Expand. Acad. Index (1984-); Index Leg. Period.; J. Plan. Lit.; Leg. Resour. Index (1980-); LegalTrac (1980-); Newsp. Period. Abstr. (1992-); PAIS Int. Print; Public Aff. Inf. Serv. Bull.; Res. Alert [Full Cov.]; Soc. Sci. Cit. Index [Full Cov.].

US/0897-3393
HARVARD JOURNAL OF LAW & TECHNOLOGY. [Harv. j. law technol.]. **Added/Corp** Harvard Law School. **VFOAT** Harvard Journal of Law and Technology; Journal of Law and

Technology; Journal of Law & Technology. Vol. 1 (Spring 1988)-. English. sa. $35.00. Harvard Law School, Publications Center, Cambridge MA 02138. **Tel** (617)495-7984, (617)495-3694. **LC** K8; .A6827. **DD** 344.73/095/05; 347.304905.
Desc: Information on technology and law and biotechnology.
Ind/Abst Index Leg. Period.; Leg. Resour. Index; LegalTrac (1988-).

US/0017-808X
HARVARD JOURNAL ON LEGISLATION. [Harvard j. legis.]. **Added/Corp** Harvard Student Legislative Research Bureau. Vol. 1 Jan. (1964)-. Periodical. English. sa (Feb. & June). $24.00 US; $28.00 other. Harvard Law School, Publications Center, Cambridge MA 02138. **Tel** (617)495-7984, (617)495-3694. **ED** Nancy Young. **LC** K8; .A684. Index available (Free). cum. index. **Bk Rev. Ad Acc. Pr Rev. Circ:** 1,000 (ctrl). available on microfilm from University Microfilms International (UMI). Documents available from The Genuine Article. ***Continues** Selected Drafts.*
Desc: A student-edited journal on legislative reform. Presents detailed statements of how the law should be changed and proposes model acts for adoption by legislatures.
Ind/Abst ABC POL SCI; Bowne Dig. Corp. Sec. Lawyers; Curr. Contents Soc. Behav. Sci.; Curr. Law Index (1980-); Index Leg. Period.; Leg. Resour. Index (1980-); LegalTrac (1980-); PAIS Int. Print (1991-); Res. Alert [Full Cov.]; Soc. Sci. Cit. Index [Full Cov.].

US/0017-8101
HARVARD LAW RECORD. [Harvard law rec.]. **Added/Corp** Harvard Law School. Harvard Law School Record. Vol. 22, No. 1 (Feb. 2, 1956)-. Periodical. English. ir (20 issues). $30.00. Harvard Law School, Publications Center, Cambridge MA 02138. **Tel** (617)495-7984, (617)495-3694. **ED** Vincent Chang. **DD** 340. **Bk Rev. Ad Acc. Circ:** 11,000 (ctrl). ***Continues** Harvard Law School Record.*
Desc: General legal topics are covered.

US/0017-811X
HARVARD LAW REVIEW. [Harvard law rev.]. **Added/Corp** Harvard Law Review Publishing Association. Harvard Law Review Association. Vol. 1, No. 1 (Apr. 1887)-. English. Eight times a year. $40.00 (one year), $76.00 (two year), $108.00 (three year). Harvard Law Review Association, Gannett House, Cambridge MA 02138. **Tel** (617)495-4650. **LC** K8; .A69. **NLM** W1 HA635R. **CODEN** HALRAF. Index available. cum. index. **Bk Rev. Ad Acc. Pr Rev. Circ:** 7,500. available on CD-ROM; available on microfilm and microfiche from University Microfilms International (UMI). Documents available from The Genuine Article, UMI Article Clearinghouse.
Desc: Legal publication containing articles, book reviews, and notes.
Ind/Abst ABC POL SCI; ABI/INFORM Glob. Ed.; ABI Inform Ondisc (Nov. 1976-); Account. Index, Suppl.; Book Rev. Index; Bowne Dig. Corp. Sec. Lawyers; Crim. Justice Abstr.; Crim. Penol. Police Sci. Abstr.; Curr. Contents Soc. Behav. Sci.; Curr. Law Index (1980-); Expand. Acad. Index (1984-); Fed. Tax Artic.; Health Plan. Adminis.; Hospit. Health Admin. Index; Index Leg. Period.; Int. Bibliogr. Sociol.; Int. Polit. Sci. Abstr.; Leg. Resour. Index (1980-); LegalTrac (1980-); Manage. Contents (1974-); Newsp. Period. Abstr. (1989-); PAIS Int. Print (1991-); Public Aff. Inf. Serv. Bull.; Res. Alert [Full Cov.]; Soc. Sci. Cit. Index [Full Cov.]; Urban Aff. Abstr.

US/0270-1456
HARVARD WOMEN'S LAW JOURNAL. [Harv. women's law j.]. **Added/Corp** Harvard Law School. Vol. 1 (1978)-. English. an (Published in May). $15.00 US; $17.00 other. Harvard Law School, Publications Center, Cambridge MA 02138. **Tel** (617)495-7984, (617)495-3694. **ED** Ruth Borenstein. **LC** K8; .A75. **DD** 349.73/088042. Index available (Free). **Bk Rev.**
Desc: A student-edited journal devoted to the development of a feminist jurisprudence. Explores the impact of women on the law and the impact of the law on women.
Ind/Abst Altern. Press Index; Crim. Justice Abstr.; Curr. Law Index (1980-); Hum. Rights Intern. Rep.; Index Leg. Period.; Leg. Resour. Index (1980-); LegalTrac (1980-); Multicult. Educ. Abstr.; PAIS Int. Print; Sage Fam. Stud. Abstr. (?-?); Stud. Women Abstr.

UK
HARVEY INDUSTRIAL RELATIONS EMPLOYMENT LAW SERVICE. See Economics-Labor.

US/1061-6578
HASTINGS COMMUNICATIONS AND ENTERTAINMENT LAW JOURNAL (COMM/ENT). [Hastings commun. entertain. law j. Comm/Ent]. **Added/Corp** Hastings College of the Law. **VFOAT** Hastings Communications and Entertainment Law Journal; Comm/Ent; Hastings Comm/Ent L.J. Vol. 13, No. 1 (Fall 1990)-. Periodical. English. qt (Feb., April, June, Nov.). $23.00 US; $25.00 other. Hastings College of Law, 200 McAllister Street, San Francisco CA 94102. **Tel** (415)565-4816, (415)565-4738, FAX (415)565-4814. **ED** David Naby (editor's telephone: (415)565-4731). **LC** K3; .O38. **DD** 343.73/099/05; 347.3039905. Index available (every five years; included in price). **Bk Rev**, (Qty: 1-3 per year). **Ad Acc, Adv Mgr:** A. Kaba, **Tel** (415)565-4738. **Pr Rev. Circ:** 1,300. available on microfilm; available on microfiche; available on CD-ROM; available on an online database from WESTLAW. ***Continues** Comm/Ent (San Francisco, Calif.), 0193-8398.*
Desc: Specializing in a host of legal issues generally under communications and entertainment law, focusing on telecommunications, broadcasting, cable and nonbroadcast video, print media, defamation, advertising, the arts, sports, computers and high technology information services, copyright, patent, trademark, privacy, film obscenity and pornography, and other first-amendment issues.
Ind/Abst Commun. Abstr. (?-?); Curr. Law Index (1980-); Index Leg. Period.; Leg. Resour. Index; LegalTrac (1990-).

US/0017-8322
HASTINGS LAW JOURNAL. [Hastings law j.]. **Added/Corp** Hastings College of the Law. Vol. 2 (Fall 1950)-. Academic Scholarly Publication. English. Six times a year (Jan., March, April, July, Aug., Nov.). $28.00 US; $30.00 other. Hastings College of Law, 200 McAllister Street, San Francisco CA 94102. **Tel** (415)565-4816, (415)565-4738, FAX (415)565-4814. **ED** Johathan Demson (editor's telephone: (415)565-4727). **DD** 340. Index available. cum. index. **Bk Rev**, (Qty: 1-3). **Ad Acc, Adv Mgr:** A Kaba, **Tel** (415)565-4738. **Pr Rev. Circ:** 1,700. available on CD-ROM and an online database from WESTLAW; available on microfilm and microfiche from Williams S Hein & Co.; and University Microfilms International (UMI); available on an online database from WESTLAW; and LEXIS. Documents available from The Genuine Article. ***Continues** Hastings Journal (San Francisco, Calif.).*
Desc: Hastings' oldest law review strives to contribute to the advancement of knowledge in legal thinking through scholarly articles written by experts in the legal community.
Ind/Abst Bowne Dig. Corp. Sec. Lawyers; Crim. Justice Abstr.; Curr. Law Index (1980-); Fed. Tax Artic.; Index Leg. Period.; Leg. Resour. Index (1980-); LegalTrac (1980-); Res. Alert [Full Cov.]; Soc. Sci. Cit. Index [Full Cov.]; Urban Aff. Abstr.

US/1061-0901
HASTINGS WOMEN'S LAW JOURNAL. [Hastings women's law j.]. **Added/Corp** Hastings College of the Law. **VFOAT** Hastings Women's L.J. Vol. 1, No. 1 (Spring 1989)-. Periodical. English. sa. $25.00 US; $27.00 other. Hastings College of Law, 200 McAllister Street, San Francisco CA 94102. **Tel** (415)565-4816, (415)565-4738, FAX (415)565-4814. **ED** Robin Packel (editor's telephone: (415)565-4870). **LC** K8; .A87. **DD** 342.6762/0878; 346.76202878. **Bk Rev**, (Qty: 102 per year). **Ad Acc, Adv Mgr:** A Kaba, **Tel** (415)565-4738. **Pr Rev. Circ:** 600. available on CD-ROM and an online database from WESTLAW.
Desc: Committed to promoting scholarship in issues of concern common to all women, recognizing the unique concerns of communities that traditionally have been denied a voice, such as women of color, poor women, and lesbians.

US/1063-1585
HAWAII BAR JOURNAL (1992). (HAWAII BAR JOURNAL : AN OFFICIAL PUBLICATION OF THE HAWAII STATE BAR ASSOCIATION.). [Hawaii bar j.]. (1992)-. Periodical. English. mo. $30.00. Hawaii State Bar Association, PO Box 26, Honolulu HI 96810. **Tel** (808)537-1868, FAX (808)521-7936. **ED** Denise Winters. **DD** 340. **Ad Acc, Adv Mgr:** Brett Pruitt, **Tel** (808)521-1929. Full Page (B&W) $665.00. Half Page (B&W) $480.00. Full Page (Color) $1,175 (four color process). Half Page (Color) $990.00 (four color process). **Circ:** 5,500. ***Continues** Hawaii Bar News (Hawaii State Bar Association), 1054-8424.*
Desc: Official publication of the Hawaii State Bar association.
Ind/Abst Fed. Tax Artic.; Leg. Resour. Index.

US
HAWAII BAR JOURNAL MICROFORM. Vol. 1 (1963)-. Academic Scholarly Publication. English. sa. $12.00. Hawaii Bar Journal, PO Box 26, Honolulu HI 96810. **Tel** (808)524-0330. **ED** Edward C Kemper III. **LC** MICROFILM (O) 82/10069 . Index available. cum. index. **Bk Rev. Ad Acc. Circ:** 2,800 (ctrl). available on microfilm. ***Supersedes** Hawaii Bar News.*
Desc: Scholarly articles related to law.
Ind/Abst Index Leg. Period. (1980-); LegalTrac (1980-).

US/0147-1392
HAWAII LEGAL REPORTER. English. Seventeen times a year. $400.00 (one year), $720.00 (two year). Legal Pub Hawaii Inc, 1220 Kalama, Honolulu HI 96819. **Tel** 946-0920. **ED** Stephen I Okumura. **LC** KFH47; .H36. **DD** 348/.969/046. Index available. cum. index.
Desc: Summary and full text of selected Hawaii administrative agency and trial court decisions.

US/1048-9398
HAZARDOUS WASTE LITIGATION. [Hazard. waste litig.]. (1988)-. English. an. Practising Law Institute, 810 Seventh Avenue, New York NY 10019-5818. **Tel** (212)765-5700, FAX (212)581-4670 general correspondence, (212)265-4742 orders and billing inquiries. **DD** 346. ***Continues** Hazardous Waste Litigation After the RCRA and CERCLA Amendments.*

UK/0266-3597
HAZELL'S GUIDE AND THE BAR LIST. English. an. £24.00. R Hazell & Company, PO Box 39, Henley Thames, RG9 5UA England. **Tel** 11 44 491 641018. **ED** C G A Parker. Index available. **Ad Acc.**
Desc: Complete directory of all UK judiciary, all courts, all barristers and advocates.

●US/1064-7155
HBJ MILLER ACCOUNTANTS' LEGAL LIABILILTY. See Business-Accounting.

UK
HEADS LEGAL GUIDE. (19??)-. Periodical. English. qt. £131.20. Croner Publ Ltd, Croner House, London Road, Kingston upon Thames, Surrey KT2 6SR England. **Tel** 011 44 81 5473333, FAX 081 547-2637.

US/0897-3598
HEALTH ADVOCATE (MADISON, WIS.). See Medical Science and Technology.

NE
HEALTH & SAFETY CASE LAW INDEX. (19??)-. English. qt (4 issues). £195.10 UK. Croner Publ Ltd, Croner House, London Road, Kingston upon Thames, Surrey KT2 6SR England. **Tel** 011 44 81 5473333, FAX 081 547-2637.

US/0893-6099
HEALTH CARE LAW NEWSLETTER. (HEALTH CARE LAW NEWSLETTER / WEISSBURG AND ARONSON, INC.). [Health care law newsl.]. **Added/Corp** Matthew Bender (Firm) Weissburg and Aronson. Vol. 1, No. 1 (July 1986)-. English. Twelve times a year. Matthew Bender & Company Inc., 1275 Broadway, Albany NY 12204. **Tel** (800)833-9844, (518)487-3000. **LC** KF3821.A15; H37. **DD** 344.73/041; 347.30441. **NLM** W 32.5; AA1 H367. cum. index.
Ind/Abst Hospit. Health Admin. Index (1986-).

●US/1067-2214
HEALTH CARE REFORM WEEK. See Medical Science and Technology.

US/0148-5385
HEALTH FACILITIES COURT DIGEST, THE. V. 1- Jan. 1977-. Periodical. English. mo. $20.00. Juridical Digests Institute, 1860 Broadway/Suite 1401, New York NY 10023. **LC** KF3825.A59; H4. **DD** 344/.73/03211. **NLM** W1 HE335N.

US/0549-804X
HEALTH LAW BULLETIN. Added/Corp University of North Carolina at Chapel Hill. Institute of Government. No. 16 (Oct. 1968)-. Bulletin. English. ir. Price varies between $2.00-$3.00 per issue. Institute of Government, University of North Carolina at Chapel Hill, CB #3300 Knapp Building, Chapel Hill NC 27599-3330. **Tel** (919)966-4119, FAX (919)962-2707. **ED** Anne M Dellinger. ctrl circ. ***Continues** Public Health Bulletin, 0546-4455.*
Desc: Deals with a current legal issue in the health care field. It also reports the results of recent litigation and the effect of newly enacted legislation in North Carolina.

US
HEALTH LAW DIGEST / NATIONAL HEALTH LAWYERS ASSOCIATION. **Added/Corp** National Health Lawyers Association. Vol. 1, No. 1 (Jan. 1973)-. Periodical. English. Twelve times a year. $195.00 Comes with National Health Lawyers Association membership. National Health Lawyers Association, 1120 Connecticut Street, Suite 950, Washington DC 20006. **Tel** (202)833-1100, FAX (202)833-1105. **NLM** W1; HE402M. Index available. cum. index. **Circ:** 6,000 (ctrl). ***Continues** National Health Lawyers Association. Newsletter - National Health Lawyers Association.*
Ind/Abst Health Devices Alerts.

CN/0226-8841
HEALTH LAW IN CANADA. [Health law Can.]. **Added/Corp** Butterworth & Co. (Canada) Canadian Institute of Law and Medicine. Vol. 1, No. 1 (Spring 1980)-. Periodical. English. qt. 110.00Can$. Butterworth & Company Ltd. / Canada, 75 Clegg Road, Markham Ontario L6G 1A1 Canada. **Tel** (905)479-2665, (800)668-6481. **ED** Gilbert Sharpe. **LC** KE3646.A13; H4. **DD** 344.71/041; 347.10441. **NLM** W1 HE402T.
Desc: Focuses on how the law impinges on the day-to-day tasks of health-care professionals while also exploring the controversial ethical aspects of health law.
Ind/Abst Can. Legal Lit.; Curr. Law Index (1981-); Health Plan. Adminis.; Hospit. Health Admin. Index; Index Can. Leg. Period. Lit.; Leg. Resour. Index (1981-); LegalTrac (1980-).

Law

US/1043-6081
HEALTH LAW JOURNAL OF OHIO. [Health law j. Ohio]. Vol. 1, Issue 1 (July/Aug. 1989)-. Periodical. English. Six times a year. Banks-Baldwin Law Publishing Company, PO Box 1974, University Center, Cleveland OH 44106. **Tel** (216)721-7373. **LC** KFO360.A15; H43. **DD** 344.73/041/05; 347.3044105. *Continues Ohio Health Law Insider, 0893-8466.*

US/0163-3996
HEALTH LAW PROJECT LIBRARY BULLETIN. (LIBRARY BULLETIN.). **Added/Corp** University of Pennsylvania. Health Law Project. **VFOAT** Health Law Project Library Bulletin. (19??)-. Bulletin. English. mo. Free to active participants of HSA's in Pennsylvania, consumer organizations, individual consumers on restricted budgets, legislators, students, educational institutions, state governments, $9.00 all others. University of Pennsylvania / Health Law Project, 133 South 36th Street/Room 410, Philadelphia PA 19104. **LC** KF3821.A15; L5. **DD** 344.73/041/05. **NLM** W1 HE403.
Ind/Abst Health Plan. Adminis.; Hospit. Health Admin. Index (Apr. 1979-Apr. 1981).

US/0270-3343
HEALTH LAW VIGIL. *Ceased.* [Health law vigil]. Vol. 1 (June 23, 1978)-(Dec. 1988). Periodical. English. bw. American Hospital Association, 840 North Lake Shore Drive, Chicago IL 60611. **Tel** (312)280-6000, (800)242-2626. **ED** Azike A Ntephe. **DD** 344. **NLM** W1 HE403H. **Circ:** 4,000.
Desc: An analysis of law-related developments affecting hospitals and the health care field.
Ind/Abst Hospit. Health Admin. Index.

● US/1063-4061
HEALTH LAW WEEK. [Health law week]. **VFOAT** HLawWk. Vol. 1, No. 24 (June 19, 1992)-. Periodical. English. wk (48 issues). $647.00. Strafford Publications Inc., 590 Dutch Valley Road Northeast, Atlanta GA 30324. **Tel** (404)881-1141, (800)926-7926, FAX (404)881-0074. **ED** Nancy Johnson. **DD** 344. Index available (extra at cost of $64.50). cum. index. available in Loose-leaf.

US/0736-3443
HEALTH LAWYER, THE. [Health lawy.]. **Added/Corp** American Bar Association. Forum Committee on Health Law. Vol. 1, No. 1 (Summer 1982)-. Periodical. English. ir. $40.00. American Bar Association, 750 North Lake Shore Drive, Chicago IL 60611. **Tel** (312)988-5522, (312)988-5241, FAX (312)988-5528, telex 270593. **ED** Azike A. Ntephe. **LC** KF3821.A15; H39. **DD** 344.73/041/05; 347.3044105. **Circ:** 100.
Desc: Online bibliographic database devoted to recent developments in health law.

US/0145-4129
HEALTH LAWYERS NEWS REPORT. **Added/Corp** National Health Lawyers Association. (1971)-. English. mo. $50.00; Also comes with NHLA membership. National Health Lawyers Association, 1120 Connecticut Street, Suite 950, Washington DC 20006. **Tel** (202)833-1100, FAX (202)833-1105. **ED** Cynthia Barvin. **LC** KF3821.A15; H4. **DD** 344/.73/0405. **NLM** W1 HE405. **Circ:** 6,000 (ctrl).
Desc: Newsletter reporting on the latest developments in the health care field.
Ind/Abst Health Devices Alerts.

US/0899-8965
HEALTH LEGISLATION AND REGULATION. [Health legis. regul.]. **Added/Corp** Faulkner & Gray's Healthcare Information Center. **VFOAT** Health Legislation. Vol 12, No. 35 (Sept. 10, 1986)-. Periodical. English. wk (50 issues). $595.00. Faulkner & Gray Inc., 11 Penn Plaza, 17th Floor, New York NY 10001. **Tel** (212)967-7000, (800)535-8403. **LC** KF3821.A15; W38. **DD** 344.73041; 347.30441. **NLM** W1; HE4119. available on an online database (file 636/Full-Text) from DIALOG. Documents available from UMI Article Clearinghouse. *Continues Washington Report on Health Legislation & Regulation, 0740-7793.*
Ind/Abst Pharm. News Index (Nov. 1988-).

US/0892-7677
HEALTH SYSTEMS PLAN (HOUSTON, TEX.). (HEALTH SYSTEMS PLAN : PURSUANT TO THE NATIONAL HEALTH PLANNING AND RESOURCES DEVELOPMENT ACT OF 1974 (PUBLIC LAW 93-641) / HOUSTON-GALVESTON AREA COUNCIL, HEALTH SYSTEMS AGENCY, HEALTH SERVICE AREA 11.). **Main/Corp** Houston-Galveston Area Council. Health Systems Agency. **Added/Corp** United States. National Health Planning and Resources Development Act of 1974. **VFOAT** Health Systems Plan. Annual Implementation Plan. (1977)-. English. an. Health Systems Plan, 3701 West Alabama, PO Box 22777, Houston TX 77027. **NLM** W2; AT4 H8h.

US/0194-3049
HEALTH SYSTEMS REPORT ALMANAC ON FEDERAL HEALTH ISSUES, PROPOSALS, ADMINISTRATIVE ACTIONS, LEGISLATION, PUBLIC LAWS. 1978-. English. an. $105.00. Morris, Inc., 1345 Connecticutt Avenue, Washington DC 20036. **LC** KF3821.A15; H42. **DD** 344.73/041. **NLM** W1 HE589F.

US/0362-9929
HEARINGS AND REPORTS OF COMMITTEES OF THE CALIFORNIA LEGISLATURE : A LISTING. **Main/Corp** California. Legislature. Assembly. Office of Research. English. Sacramento Assembly Office of Research, 1116 Ninth Street, Sacramento CA 95814. **LC** KFC20; .R46. **DD** 016.328794/07/65. *Continues Hearings and Reports of Committees of the California Legislature: A Summary and Listing.*

US
HELLER AND HUNT LAW PRACTICE MANAGEMENT REPORT. **VFOAT** Law Practice Management; Heller and Hunt Management Report. Periodical. English. mo. $150.00. Butterworth Heinemann / Woburn, MA, 225 Wildwood Avenue, Unit B, Woburn MA 01801. **Tel** (800)366-2665, FAX (617)928-2620, telex 880052. **LC** KF318.A1; H45. **DD** 340/.068.

US
HENNEPIN LAWYER, THE. (1933)-. English. Six times a year. $20.00. Hennepin County Bar Association, 514 Nicollet Mall #350, Minneapolis MN 55402. **Tel** (612)340-0022. **ED** Nancy Klossner. **Ad Acc. Circ:** 5,300.
Desc: Articles to assist and educate lawyers about current issues and events relating to lawyers and changes in the laws.
Ind/Abst Fed. Tax Artic.; Law Office Inf. Serv.

CN/0824-6378
HENRY B. ZIMMER'S PROBLEMS & QUESTIONS IN CANADIAN TAXATION. [Henry B. Zimmer's probl. quest. Can. tax.]. **VAT** Problems & Questions in Canadian Taxation (Calgary); Problems and Questions in Canadian Taxation (Calgary). 1984-. English. an. $12.50 per vol. Henry B Zimmer's Problems & Questions in Canadian Taxation, c/o Cantax Seminars, 475-15055 5th Street SW, Calgary Alberta T2R 1K3 Canada. **DD** 343.7105/2. *Continues Problems & Questions in Canadian Taxation, 0824-6386.*

US/0885-2715
HIGH TECHNOLOGY LAW JOURNAL. [High technol. law j.]. **Added/Corp** University of California, Berkeley. School of Law. (Spring 1986)-. Periodical. English. sa (Apr., Oct.). $48.00. University of California Press, 2120 Berkeley Way, Berkeley CA 94720. **Tel** (510)642-4191, (510)642-3907, FAX (510)642-9917. **LC** K8; .I34. **DD** 344/.095/05; 342.49505. **[CCC].** available on microfilm and microfiche from University Microfilms International (UMI).
Ind/Abst Index Leg. Period.; Int. Bibliogr. Sociol.; Leg. Resour. Index; LegalTrac (1980-); PAIS Int. Print; UMI ABI/Inform--Bus. Period. Ondisc (Spring 1987-) [Full Txt.].

US/0742-0803
HIGHER EDUCATION LAW REPORT. English. mo. Law Offices of J. Andrew Usera, 4801 Mass. Avenue NW; Suite 400, Washington DC 20016. **LC** KF4225.A15; H53. **DD** 344.73/074/05; 347.3047405.

JA
HIKKEI GAKKO SHOROPPO. **Main/Corp** Japan. **VFOAT** Gakko Shoroppo. Japanese. ¥1200. Kyodo Shuppan, 5 Kanda Nishikicho 2 Chiyoda-ku, Tokyo 101 Japan. **ED** Sagara Lichi.

US
HINE'S INSURANCE COUNSEL. (19??)-. English. an. $20.00. Hine's Legal Directory Inc., PO Box 280, Glen Ellyn IL 60138. **Tel** (708)462-9670. **ED** James R. Collins. **LC** HG8525; .H66. **Ad Acc. Circ:** 8,000 (ctrl). *Continues Hine's Directory of Insurance Counsel, Railroad and Bank Counsel, Insurance Adjusters.*

JA/0073-2796
HITOTSUBASHI JOURNAL OF LAW & POLITICS. *See* Political Science.

JA
HO TO CHITSUJO. Periodical. Japanese. ¥1200. Sen'l Boeki Kaikan, 16-9 Uchi Kanda 2-chome, Chiyoda-ku Tokyo Japan. **LC** K8; .O18.

US/0091-4029
HOFSTRA LAW REVIEW. [Hofstra law rev.]. **Added/Corp** Hofstra University. School of Law. (1973)-. Academic Scholarly Publication. English. Four times a year. $26.00. Hofstra University, 109 Hofstra University Cultural Center, Hempstead NY 11550. **Tel** (516)463-5669. **LC** K8; .O45. **DD** 340/.05. Index available. **Bk Rev. Ad Acc. Circ:** 900.
Desc: Scholarly articles on legal and social issues.
Ind/Abst Bowne Dig. Corp. Sec. Lawyers; Crim. Justice Abstr.; Curr. Law Index (1980-); Energy Res. Abstr.; Fed. Tax Artic.; Index Leg. Period.; Leg. Resour. Index (1980-); LegalTrac (1980-).

US/1050-2076
HOFSTRA PROPERTY LAW JOURNAL. *Ceased.* [Hofstra prop. law j.]. **Added/Corp** Hofstra University. School of Law. Vol. 1 Spring (1988)-Vol. 6 No. 1 (1993). Periodical. English. Harwood Academic Publishers / New York, PO Box 786, Cooper Station, New York NY 10276. **Tel** (212)206-8900, (201)643-7500.

(**Subscription address:** International Publishers Distributor at one of the following addresses: 820 Town Center Drive, Langhorne, PA 19047; or PO Box 90, Reading Berkshire RG1 8JL UK; or Kent Ridge PO Box 1180, Singapore 9111, Republic of Singapore) **DD** 346. *Continues International Property Investment Journal, 0731-4639.*
Ind/Abst Fed. Tax Artic.; Index Leg. Period.; J. Plan. Lit.; Leg. Resour. Index (?-?).

JA
HOGAKU. **Added/Corp** Tohoku Daigaku. Hogakubu. **VFOAT** Journal of Law and Political Science. (Jan. 1932)-. Periodical. Japanese. bm (6 issues). $104.50.
(**Subscription address:** Japan Publications Trading Company, Ltd., PO Box 5030, Tokyo International, Tokyo 100-31 Japan.)

JA/0022-6815
HOGAKU KYOKAI ZASSHI. **Added/Corp** Hogaku Kyokai (Japan). **VFOAT** Hogaku Kyokai Zassi; Journal of the Jurisprudence Association. (1884)-. Periodical. Japanese (English; table of contents in English). Twelve times a year. $280.00. Japan Publications Inc, 150 Post Street, Suite 500, San Francisco CA 94108. **Tel** (415)772-5555. cum. index.
Ind/Abst Index Foreign Leg. Per.

JA
HOGAKU NO TOMO. English. mo. $120.50.
(**Subscription address:** Japan Publications Trading Company, Ltd., PO Box 5030, Tokyo International, Tokyo 100-31 Japan.)

JA/0387-2866
HOGAKU RONSO (KYOTO. 1919). (HOGAKU RONSO.). [Hogaku ronso]. **Added/Corp** Kyoto Daigaku. Hogakkai. Kyoto Teikoku Daigaku. Hoka Daigaku. Kyoto Teikoku Daigaku. Hogakkai. Kyoto Teikoku Daigaku. Hogakubu. **VFOAT** Kyoto Law Review; Hogakuronso. (1919)-. Japanese (table of contents in Multiple languages). mo. $160.00. (**Subscription address:** Kyowa Book Company, Inc., 1-38 Kanda Jinbo-Cho, Chiyoda-Ku tokyo 101, Japan) *Continues Kyoto Hogakkai Zasshi.*
Ind/Abst Am. Hist. Life (1954-1969); Index Foreign Leg. Per.

JA
HOGAKU SEMINA. **VFOAT** Hogaku Seminar. No. 1 (1956)-. Periodical. Japanese. mo. $199.50.
(**Subscription address:** Japan Publications Trading Company, Ltd., PO Box 5030, Tokyo International, Tokyo 100-31 Japan.)

JA/0009-6296
HOGAKU SHINPO. **VFOAT** Chuo Law Review. (1891)-. Periodical. Japanese (table of contents in English and German). mo.
Ind/Abst Index Foreign Leg. Per.

JA/0441-0351
HOGAKU ZASSHI. **VFOAT** Journal of Law and Politics of Osaka City University. (1954)-. Periodical. Multiple languages. qt. **DD** 340.
Ind/Abst Am. Hist. Life (1954-1957, 1969).

JA
HOKEI RON SHU: KENKYU KIYO. **Main/Corp** Shizuoka Daigaku. Hokei Tanki Daigakubu. **Added/Corp** Shizuoka Daigaku. Hokei Tanki Daigakubu. Kenkyu Kiyo. (19??)-. Periodical. Japanese. an. Shizuoka Daigaku Kyoyobu, 836 Oya, Shizuoka-shi 422 Japan. **LC** K23; .H55.

JA/0389-6498
HOKEI RONSO (MORIOKA, 1980). (HOKEI RONSO.). [Hokei ronso]. **Added/Corp** Iwate Kenritsu Morioka Tanki Daigaku. **VFOAT** Journal of Law and Economics; Journal of Law & Economics. (Dec. 1980)-. English (Japanese). an. Iwate Kenritsu Morioka Tanki Daigaku, 1-48 Sumiyoshicho, Morioakshi, Iwateken, 020 Japan. **Tel** 0196-23-2441. **LC** H8.J3; H62. **Circ:** 300-400. *Continues Morioka Tanki Daigaku Kenkyu Hokoku. Horitsu Keizai Hen.*
Desc: Overview on civilian control; mixed economy and method of public finance.
Ind/Abst ABC POL SCI (19??-19??).

JA
HOKEN ROPPO / HOKEN SEIDO KENKYUKAI HEN. **Main/Corp** Japan. Japanese. ¥4500. Sansei Shobo, 39-4 Minamidai 4 Tokyo-to Japan.

JA
HOKENGAKU ZASSHI. **Added/Corp** Nihon Hoken Gakkai. **VFOAT** Journal of Insurance Science. (19??)-. Periodical. Japanese. qt. $97.00. Nihon Hoken Gakkai, 6-5 Kanda Surugadai 3-chome, Chiyoda-ku, Tokyo Japan. (**Subscription address:** Maruzen Company Ltd., PO Box 5050, Import & Export Department, Tokyo 100 31 Japan.) **LC** K1241.A13; H64.

JA/0385-7255
HOKKAI GAKUEN DAIGAKU HOGAKKAI HOGAKU KENKYU. (HOGAKU KENKYU.). [Hokkai Gakuen Daigaku Hogakkai Hogaku kenkyu]. **Added/Corp** Hokkai Gakuen Daigaku. Hogakkai. Hokkai Gakuen Daigaku. Hogakubu. **VFOAT**

Hokkaigakuen Law Journal. Vol. 1 (1966)-. Periodical. Japanese. mo. $176.00. **(Subscription address:** Japan Publications Trading Company, Ltd., PO Box 5030, Tokyo International, Tokyo 100-31 Japan.**)** **LC** K8; .O46.
Ind/Abst Am. Hist. Life (1954-); Numis. Lit.

UK
HOLDSWORTH LAW REVIEW / UNIVERSITY OF BIRMINGHAM.
Added/Corp Holdsworth Club (University of Birmingham) University of Birmingham. Vol. 4, No. 2 (1977)-. English. Twice a year (Spring & Fall). University of Birmingham / England, Edgbaston, Center for Byzantine Ottoman, Greek Street, Birmingham B15 2TT England. **Tel** 011 44 21 414 5733, FAX 011 44 21 414 5726. **(Subscription address:** WM. W. Gaunt & Sons Inc, 3011 Gulf Drive, Gaunt Building, Holmes Beach FL 34217.**)** **ED** Jeremy McBride. **LC** K8; .O4693. **DD** 349.42/05; 344.2005. **Bk Rev. Ad Acc. Circ:** 300 (ctrl). ***Continues** Holdsworth.*
Desc: A general law journal aimed at academics, students and practitioners dealing with issues of English comparative and international law.

HK
HONG KONG LANDS TRIBUNAL LAW REPORTS, THE. **Main/Corp** Hongkong. Lands Tribunal. **Added/Corp** Hongkong. Lands Tribunal. Lands Tribunal Law Reports. Hongkong. Lands Tribunal. Law Reports. **VFOAT** Lands Tribunal Law Reports. (19??)-. English. ir. Price varies per volume. Hong Kong Government Information Service, Beaconsfield House, 4 Queens Road, Hong Kong Hong Kong. **Tel** 011 852 8428801 4, telex 61190 HKGIS. **DD** 346.512504/3/02648; 345.125064302648.

HK/0378-0600
HONG KONG LAW JOURNAL. [Hong Kong law j.]. Began in Jan. 1971. Periodical. English. ir. $77.00. Hong Kong Law Journal, 1030 Princes Building, Hong Kong Hong Kong. **Tel** 852-5-260318, FAX 852-5-8101731. **LC** K8.
Ind/Abst Aust. Leg. Mon. Dig.; Index Foreign Leg. Per.

CH
HONG KONG LAW REPORTS, THE.
Added/Corp Hongkong. District Court. (1953)-. Periodical. English. qt. HK$80.00. Hong Kong Government Information Service, Beaconsfield House, 4 Queens Road, Hong Kong Hong Kong. **Tel** 011 852 8428801 4, telex 61190 HKGIS. Index available. cum. index.

JA
HORITSU JIHO. **Added/Corp** Suehiro Kenkyujo. (Dec. 1929)-. Periodical. Japanese. mo (13 issues). $278.00. **(Subscription address:** Kyowa Book Company Inc., 1-38 Kanda Jinbo-Cho, Chiyoda-Ku Tokyo 101, Japan**)** cum. index.
Ind/Abst Index Foreign Leg. Per.

US/0734-0028
HOSPITAL CONTRACTS MANUAL. [Hosp. contracts man.]. **Added/Corp** Aspen Systems Corporation. Vol. 1 (1982)-. English. ir (2 supplements per year). $95.00. Aspen Publishers Inc., 7201 McKinney Circle, Frederick MD 21701. **Tel** (800)234-1660, (301)698-7100, FAX (301)251-5784, telex 5106014543. **(Subscription address:** Aspen Publishers Inc., PO Box 990, Frederick MD 21701.**)** **Bk Rev. Ad Acc.** ctrl circ.
Desc: Sample contract clauses, negotiating tips, a glossary of legal terms, alternative language, executive staff and trustee compensation guidelines, updated semi-annually.

US
HOSPITAL LAW MANUAL. ADMINISTRATORS VOLUME. **Added/Corp** Aspen Systems Corporation. Health Law Center. (1959)-. Periodical. English. qt. $675.00. Aspen Publishers Inc., 7201 McKinney Circle, Frederick MD 21701. **Tel** (800)234-1660, (301)698-7100, FAX (301)251-5784, telex 5106014543. **(Subscription address:** Aspen Publishers Inc., PO Box 990, Frederick MD 21701.**)**

US/0018-5728
HOSPITAL LAW MANUAL. ATTORNEYS VOLUME. **Added/Corp** Aspen Systems Corporation. Health Law Center. (1959)-. Periodical. English. qt. $775.00. Aspen Publishers Inc., 7201 McKinney Circle, Frederick MD 21701. **Tel** (800)234-1660, (301)698-7100, FAX (301)251-5784, telex 5106014543. **(Subscription address:** Aspen Publishers Inc., PO Box 990, Frederick MD 21701.**)** **NLM** WX 32 AA1 P6H.

US
HOSPITAL LAW MANUAL. NEWSLETTER AND QUARTERLY SUPPLEMENT. (19??)-. Periodical. English. qt. $875.00. Aspen Publishers Inc., 7201 McKinney Circle, Frederick MD 21701. **Tel** (800)234-1660, (301)698-7100, FAX (301)251-5784, telex 5106014543. **(Subscription address:** Aspen Publishers Inc., PO Box 990, Frederick MD 21701.**)**

US/1048-5201
HOSPITAL LITIGATION REPORTER. [Hosp. litig. report.]. (Jan. 1990)-. Periodical. English. mo. $294.00 (one year), $528.00 (two year). Strafford Publications Inc., 590 Dutch Valley Road Northeast, Atlanta GA 30324. **Tel** (404)881-1141, (800)926-7926, FAX (404)881-0074. **ED** Stephanie McEvily. **LC** KF3825.A15; H68. **DD** 346.73/031; 347.30631. **NLM** WX 33; AA1 H818h. Index available. cum. index.
Desc: Judicial decisions that concern or affect the hospital environment exclusively. Provides concise, comprehensive coverage of issues important to hospital attorneys and administrators, risk management professionals and others involved with hospital litigation.

US/0889-5414
HOSPITALITY LAW. [Hosp. law]. Vol. 1, No. 1 (July 1986)-. Periodical. English. mo. $197.00 US and Canada; $217.00 other. Magna Publications Inc, 2718 Dryden Drive, Madison WI 53704. **Tel** (800)433-0499, (608)246-3591, FAX (608)246-3597. **LC** KF2042.H6; A134. **DD** 343.73/0786479; 347.303786479. **[CCC]. Bk Rev.** ctrl circ.
Desc: A preventive-law information service for the hotel/motel industry, helping managers understand the legal environment in which they operate, and helping them reduce their risk of going to court.

US
HOUSE AND SENATE REPORTS ON PUBLIC BILLS (NUMBERED, UNBOUND). **Main/Corp** United States. Congress. (1789)-. Periodical. English.

US/0277-8491
HOUSING LAW BULLETIN. **Added/Corp** National Housing Law Project. Vol. 8, Issue 6 (Dec. 1978/Jan. 1979)-. Bulletin. English. Six times a year. $50.00. National Housing Law Project, 2201 Broadway Suite 815, Oakland CA 94612. **Tel** (510)251-9400. **ED** Katherine Castro. **LC** KF5722; .H68. **DD** 344.73/063635; 347.30463635. Index available. **Circ:** 1,500. ***Continues** Law Project Bulletin (National Housing Law Project).*
Desc: Articles on housing law issues, including judicial, statutory and regulatory developments relating to the development, maintenance and preservation of low-income housing.
Ind/Abst Urban Aff. Abstr.

UK
HOUSING LAW REPORTS. Vol. 1 (1981)-. English. bm (6 issues). £185.00 Europe; £194.00 other. Sweet & Maxwell Ltd., South Quay Plaza, 183 Marsh Wall, London E14 9FT England. **Tel** 011 44 264 342899, FAX 011 44 264 342723, telex 929089 ITPINF G. **LC** KD1175.A2; H68. **DD** 344.41/063635/05; 344.1046363505.

US/0279-3997
HOUSTON BAR BULLETIN. **Added/Corp** Houston Bar Association. (1942)-. Bulletin. English. mo. $6.00. Houston Bar Association of Texas, 1001 Fannin, Suite 1300, Houston TX 77002. **Tel** (713)759-1133, FAX (713)759-1710. **LC** KF200; .H67. **DD** 340.060764.

US/0018-6694
HOUSTON LAW REVIEW. (HOUSTON LAW REVIEW / UNIVERSITY OF HOUSTON.). [Houst. law rev.]. **Added/Corp** University of Houston. College of Law. Vol. 1, No. 1 (Spring 1963)-. Periodical. English. Five times a year (Jan., Mar., May, July, and Oct.). $26.00. Houston Law Review, University of Houston Law Center, University Park, Houston TX 77004. **Tel** (713)743-2247. **ED** Nicolas Evanoff. **LC** K8; .O9. **DD** 340. cum. index. **Ad Acc. Circ:** 1,200. available on microfilm and microfiche from University Microfilms International (UMI).
Desc: Publishes articles and commentaries that discuss legal issues of current interest.
Ind/Abst Bowne Dig. Corp. Sec. Lawyers; Crim. Justice Abstr.; Curr. Law Index (1980-); Fed. Tax Artic.; Index Leg. Period.; Leg. Resour. Index (1980-); LegalTrac (1980-); Soc. Work Abstr. (?-?).

US/0439-660X
HOUSTON LAWYER. [Houst. lawyer]. **Added/Corp** Houston Bar Association. Vol. 1, (Nov. 1963)-. Periodical. English. bm (Jan., Mar., May, July, Sept., Nov.). $19.50. Houston Bar Association of Texas, 1001 Fannin, Suite 1300, Houston TX 77002. **Tel** (713)759-1133, FAX (713)759-1710. **ED** Tara Shockley. **DD** 340. Index Bound in First Issue. cum. index. **Bk Rev**, (Qty: 20-30). **Ad Acc, Adv Mgr:** Lisa Kennedy, **Tel** (713)236-1048. **Circ:** 10,000 (ctrl).
Desc: Substantive legal articles, legal features, bar news.
Ind/Abst Law Office Inf. Serv.

US
HOW TO MANAGE YOUR LAW OFFICE. (19??)-. English. an. $82.50 (latest volume). Matthew Bender & Company Inc., 1275 Broadway, Albany NY 12204. **Tel** (800)833-9844, (518)487-3000. cum. index.

US/0018-6813
HOWARD LAW JOURNAL. [Howard law j.]. V. 1-. Periodical. English. qt. $22.00. Editorial and General Offices, Howard University, School of Law, 2900 Van Ness Street, Washington DC 20008. **Tel** (202)686-6570. **ED** Alice Thomas. Index available. cum. index. **Bk Rev. Ad Acc. Circ:** 700. available on an online database; available in microform.
Ind/Abst Crim. Penol. Police Sci. Abstr.; Curr. Law Index (1980-); Fed. Tax Artic.; High. Educ. Abstr. (1986-); Index Leg. Period.; Leg. Resour. Index (1980-); LegalTrac (1980-); PAIS Int. Print; Soc. Plann. Policy Dev. Abstr.; Sociol. Abstr.

US/0145-6083
HUGHES ESTATE, SUMMARY OF PROBATE PROCEEDINGS. V. 1- Apr. 1976-. Proceedings. English. Armadillo Publishing Company, PO Drawer 1415, La Porte TX 77571. **LC** KF759.H83; H8. **DD** 346/.73/056.

IO
HUKUM. Vol. 1 (1974)-. Indonesian. Yayasan Penelitian dan Pengembangan Hukum, Jln Kartanegara 51 Kebayoran Baru, Jakarta Indonesia.

IO
HUKUM DAN PEMBANGUNAN. Vol. 7, No. 2 (Mar. 1977)-. Periodical. Indonesian. $13.50. Fakultas Hukum Universitas, JL Cirebon 5, Jakarta Indonesia. **LC** K25; .N5637. ***Continues** Majalah Fakultas Hukum Universitas Indonesia.*

IO
HUKUM NASIONAL. Vol. 1, (1975)-. Indonesian. BPHN, Medan Merdeka Utara No 9, Jakarta Indonesia. **LC** K8; .U44. ***Supersedes** Hukum Nasional.*

US/0046-8185
HUMAN RIGHTS (CHICAGO, ILL.). (HUMAN RIGHTS : JOURNAL OF THE SECTION OF INDIVIDUAL RIGHTS AND RESPONSIBILITIES.). [Human rights]. **Added/Corp** American Bar Association. Section of Individual Rights and Responsibilities. Vol. 1, No. 1 (Aug. 1970)-. Periodical. English. tq (3 issues). $18.00. American Bar Association, 750 North Lake Shore Drive, Chicago IL 60611. **Tel** (312)988-5522, (312)988-5241, FAX (312)988-5528, telex 270593. **ED** Anthony Monahan. **LC** K8; .U45. **DD** 342/.73/085/05; 347.3028505. **Bk Rev. Ad Acc. Pr Rev. Circ:** 3,200 (ctrl). available on microfilm and microfiche from University Microfilms International (UMI). Documents available from The Genuine Article, UMI Article Clearinghouse. ***Absorbed** American Bar Association. Section of Individual Rights and Responsibilities Newsletter, 0572-3590 **and** American Bar Association. Section of Individual Rights and Responsibilities. Edited Proceedings.*
Desc: For lawyers interested in the practice of human rights and civil rights.
Ind/Abst Acad. Ind. [Computer File] (1992-); Acad. Search (Jan. 1992-); Curr. Contents Soc. Behav. Sci.; Expand. Acad. Index (1984-); Hum. Rights Intern. Rep.; Index Leg. Period.; INFO-SOUTH Abstr.; Law Office Inf. Serv.; Leg. Resour. Index (1980-); Mag. Search; Newsp. Period. Abstr. (1991-); PAIS Int. Print (1991-); Res. Alert [Full Cov.]; Soc. Sci. Source (Jan. 1992-); Soc. Sci. Cit. Index [Full Cov.]; Soc. Sci. Index; Soc. Sci. Index Fulltext (Fall 1988-) [Full Txt.].

HU
HUNGARIAN LAW REVIEW. **Added/Corp** Magyar Jogasz Szovetseg. Association of Hungarian Jurists. (1961)-. Periodical. English (French and Russian). sa. $18.00. Association of Hungarian Jurists. **(Subscription address:** Kultura, PO Box 149, H 1389 Budapest 62 Hungary.**)**
Ind/Abst Index Foreign Leg. Per.

MR
HUQUQUK. Periodical. Arabic. mo. 6.00MD single issue. Muhammad Al-Atlasi, 52 Shari Burdu 7, Al-Dar Al-Bayda Morocco. **LC** K8; .U48.

US/0749-0534
ICC REGISTER. (ICC REGISTER : A DAILY SUMMARY OF MOTOR CARRIER APPLICATIONS AND DECISIONS AND NOTES ISSUED BY THE INTERSTATE COMMERCE COMMISSION.). [ICC regist.]. **Added/Corp** United States. Interstate Commerce Commission. Office of the Secretary. **VFOAT** I.C.C. Register. **VAT** Interstate Commerce Commission Register. (Sept 30, 1984)-. Government Publication. English. da. $660.00 US; $825.00 other. Superintendent of Documents, US Government Printing Office, Washington DC 20402. **Tel** (202)275-3328, FAX (202)786-2377. **LC** KF2250; .I25. **DD** 343.73/093/02646; 347.3039302646.

US/0161-3367
ICE, INSIDE CODE ENFORCEMENT.
VFOAT Inside Code Enforcement. Periodical. English. $20.00. R.L. Sanderson, 327 South Lasalle Street, Chicago IL 60604. **LC** KF5701.A15; I2. **DD** 343/.73/078.

US
IDAHO CASE NAMES CITATOR. English. $40.00 (bound volume), $52.00 (cumulative supplements). Shepards McGraw-Hill Inc, 555 Middle Creek Parkway, PO Box 35300, Colorado Springs CO 80935-3530. **Tel** (719)488-3000, FAX (800)525-0053.

US/0019-1205
IDAHO LAW REVIEW. [Ida. law rev.]. Vol. 1- 1964-. Periodical. English. qt. $26.95. University of Idaho College of Law, Moscow ID 83843. **Tel** (208)885-7241. **ED** Steve Weeks. **LC** K9; .D3. **DD** 340/.0973. cum. index.

Ad Acc. Circ: 1,000.
Desc: General areas in the field of law with one issue devoted entirely to a yearly symposium with the topic varying each year.
Ind/Abst Bowne Dig. Corp. Sec. Lawyers; Curr. Law Index; Fed. Tax Artic.; Index Leg. Period.; Leg. Resour. Index (1980-); LegalTrac (1980-).

FR
IGD, INITIATION GENERALE AU DROIT. **Main/Corp** Centre de Formation Professionnelle et de Perfectionnement (France). **Added/Corp** Centre de Formation Professionnelle et de Perfectionnement (France) Initiation Generale au Droit, Formation Continue: Premiere Annee. **VFOAT** Initiation Generale au Droit, Formation Continue: Premiere Annee. (19??)-. French. Centre de Formation Professionnelle et de Perfectionnement, 8 rue des Bons-Enfants, 75056 Paris RP France. **DD** 349.44/02/02; 344.400202.

US/0884-0482
ILLINOIS APPELLATE REPORTS. (ILLINOIS APPELLATE REPORTS : OFFICIAL REPORTS OF THE ILLINOIS APPELLATE COURT / STEPHEN DAVIS PORTER, REPORTER OF DECISIONS.). [Ill. Appell. rep.]. **Main/Corp** Illinois. Appellate Court. **VFOAT** Illinois Appellate Court Reports. 3rd Ser. Vol. 24 (1975)-. English. $17.85. Legal Division Pantagraph Printing, PO Box 3366, Bloomington IL 61701. **Tel** (309)829-1071. **LC** KFI1248; .A2. ***Continues*** *Illinois. Appellate Court. Official Illinois Appellate Court Reports.*

US/0019-1876
ILLINOIS BAR JOURNAL. [Ill. bar j.]. **Added/Corp** Illinois State Bar Association. Illinois State Bar Association. Annual Report. (1931)-. Periodical. English. mo. $50.00 US; $53.00 other (nonprofit institutions & law libraries) $60.00 US; $63.00 others (all others). Illinois State Bar Association, 424 South Second, Springfield IL 62701. **Tel** (217)525-1760, FAX (217)525-0712. **ED** Mark S Mathewson. **LC** K9; .L47. **DD** 340.05. Index Available, published separately, free-automatically sent. cum. index. **Bk Rev.** **Ad Acc. Circ:** 31,000 (ctrl). ***Continues*** *Quarterly Bulletin (Illinois State Bar Association).*
Desc: Practical and analytical articles about Illinois law.
Ind/Abst Bowne Dig. Corp. Sec. Lawyers; Curr. Law Index (1980-); Fed. Tax Artic.; Highw. Res. Abstr.; Index Leg. Period.; Law Office Inf. Serv.; Leg. Resour. Index (1980-); LegalTrac (1980-).

US/8755-691X
ILLINOIS CONSTRUCTION LAW. Trade Publication. English. Professional Education Systems, 200 Spring Street, PO Box 1208, Eau Claire WI 54702. **Tel** (715)836-9700, (800)826-7155. **ED** Karen A Welch. **Ad Acc. Circ:** 200 (ctrl).
Desc: A manual which provides a summary of topics which are of concern to members of the construction industry and an introduction to mechanics' lien law.

●US/1059-5074
ILLINOIS ENVIRONMENTAL LAW LETTER. (ILLINOIS ENVIRONMENTAL LAW LETTER / GORDON & GLICKSON, AND ENSR CONSULTING AND ENGINEERING.). [Ill. environ. law lett.]. **Added/Corp** Gordon & Glickson, ENSR Consulting and Engineering. Vol. 1, No. 1 (Apr. 1992)-. Periodical. English. mo. $107.00. M. Lee Smith Publishers and Printers, 162 4th Avenue North, PO Box 198867, Nashville TN 37219. **Tel** (615)242-7395, (800)274-6774, FAX (615)256-6601. **ED** Sanford Stein, (address) Wildman, Harrold, Allen and Dixon, 225 West Wacker Drive Suite 3000, Chicago, IL 60606, (phone) 312-201-2000. **DD** 344.
Desc: Newsletter reporting the latest state specific environmental law developments that affect companies in that state.

US
ILLINOIS REGISTER. **Added/Corp** Illinois. Office of Secretary of State. Vol. 1, No. 15 (Oct. 1977)-. Periodical. English. wk. $290.00 all except federal, state and local governmental offices within the state of Illinois. Secretary of State Administration Code Unit, 288 Centennial Building, Springfield IL 62756. **Tel** (217)782-9786, FAX (217)524-0308. **LC** KFI1234.A2; I43. **DD** 348/.773/025. Index available. cum. index. **Circ:** 1,000. available on microfiche. ***Continues*** *Illinois Bulletin, 0148-8112.*
Desc: Rules promulgated by state agencies and all action taken on existing rules.

US/1058-5435
ILLINOIS REGISTER OF EXPERT WITNESSES, THE. **VFOAT** Expert Witnesses. (1991)-. English. $55.00.

US
ILLINOIS REGISTER [MICROFICHE]. **Added/Corp** Illinois. Office of Secretary of State. Began with: Vol. 1, No. 15 (Oct. 1977)-. Periodical. English. $200.00. Secretary of State Administration Code Unit, 288 Centennial Building, Springfield IL 62756. **Tel** (217)782-9786, FAX (217)524-0308. **LC** Microfiche (o) 91/10012. ***Continues*** *Illinois Bulletin, 0148-8112.*

US/0160-1199
ILLINOIS REPORTS. **Main/Corp** Illinois. Supreme Court. 2nd Ser. Vol. 57 (Mar. 1974)-(Jan. 1975)-. English. Legal Division Pantagraph Printing, PO Box 3366, Bloomington IL 61701. **Tel** (309)829-1071. **LC** KFI1245; .A213. **DD** 348/.773/043. ***Continues*** *Cases Argued and Determined in the Supreme Court of Illinois, 0160-1180.*

●US/1067-2338
ILLINOIS WORKERS' COMPENSATION LAW BULLETIN. [Ill. work. compens. law bull.]. **VFOAT** ILWCLB. (1993)-. Bulletin. English. Twenty-four times a year. $260.00. LRP Publications, 747 Dresher Road, PO Box 980, Horsham PA 19044-0980. **Tel** (800)341-7874, (215)784-0860, FAX (215)784-9639, (215)784-0870. **DD** 344.
Desc: Provides selected workers' compensation decisions and opinions from the Illinois INdustrial Commission and state appellate courts.

US/0897-6708
IMMIGRATION BRIEFINGS. [Immigr. brief.]. **Added/Corp** Federal Publications Inc. No. 88 (Jan. 1988)-. Periodical. English. mo. $349.80 Washington DC; $330.00 other. Federal Publications Inc, 1120 20th Street Northwest, Washington DC 20036. **Tel** (202)337-7000, (800)922-4330, FAX (202)659-2233. **LC** KF4802; .I463. **DD** 342.73/082/05; 347.3028205. **[CCC].** available on CD-ROM.
Ind/Abst Index Leg. Period.

US
IMMIGRATION LAW & BUSINESS NEWS. **VFOAT** Immigration Law and Business News. Vol. 1, No. 1 (1987)-. Periodical. English. mo. $200.00. Deutsch & Salberg, 1 East 57th Street, New York NY 10022. **Tel** (212)759-8373. **LC** KF480.2; .I467. **DD** 342.73/082; 347.30282.

US
IMMIGRATION LAW AND PROCEDURE. English. ir. Matthew Bender & Company Inc., 1275 Broadway, Albany NY 12204. **Tel** (800)833-9844, (518)487-3000.

US
IMMIGRATION LAW BULLETIN. **Added/Corp** National Center for Immigrants' Rights (U.S.). Vol. 1, No. 1, (Sept. 1979)-. Bulletin. English. ir. NCIR, 1544 West 8th Street, Los Angeles CA 90017.
Ind/Abst Hum. Rights Intern. Rep.

US/0731-5767
IMMIGRATION LAW REPORT. (IMMIGRATION LAW REPORT / PREPARED BY THE LAW FIRM OF FRIED, FRAGOMEN, DEL REY, BERNSEN & O'ROURKE.). [Immigr. law rep.]. **Added/Corp** Fried, Fragomen, Del Rey, Bernsen & O'Rourke. Clark Boardman Company. Fragomen, Del Rey & Bernsen. Vol. 1, No. 1 (May 1981)-. Periodical. English. Twenty-four times a year. $275.00. Clark Boardman Callaghan, 155 Pfingsten Road, Deerfield IL 60015. **Tel** (800)323-8067. **ED** Austin T. Fragamen Jr. **LC** KF4802; .I47. **DD** 342.73/082; 347.30282. **Bk Rev.**
Desc: A report on legal developments in the field of immigration.
Ind/Abst Hum. Rights Intern. Rep.

CN/0835-3808
IMMIGRATION LAW REPORTER (DON MILLS). (IMMIGRATION LAW REPORTER.). [Immigr. law report. (Don Mills).]. **VAT** Immigration Law Reporter (Agincourt). Vol. 1, Issue 1 (March 1985)-. Periodical. English. Fifteen times a year. Price varies. Carswell / Canada, 2075 Kennedy Road, Scarborough Ontario M1T 3V4 Canada. **Tel** (416)609-3800, (800)387-5164. **ED** Cecil L. Rotenberg. **LC** KE4454.A45; I46. **DD** 342.71/083/0264; 347.102830264. Index available. cum. index. **Ad Acc.**
Desc: Full text reports of Immigration Appeal Board decisions and all significant court decisions in immigration matters from all Canadian jurisdictions. Articles, annotations and case comments included.
Ind/Abst Can. Legal Lit.

US/0892-547X
IMMIGRATION POLICY & LAW. [Immigr. policy law]. **Added/Corp** Buraff Publications. **VFOAT** Immigration Policy and Law. Vol. 1, No. 1 (Feb. 26, 1987)-. Periodical. English. sm. $497.00 US, Canada and Mexico; $519.00 other. Buraff Publications Inc., 714 Church Street, Alexandria VA 22314. **Tel** (800)333-1291, (703)739-8500. **ED** David McIntyre. **LC** KF4802; .I48. **DD** 342.73/082; 347.30282. **[CCC].** Index available.

US/0162-4989
IMPACT (WASHINGTON). (IMPACT: A JOURNAL OF SAFETY LITIGATION NEWS FROM THE CENTER FOR AUTO SAFETY.). **Added/Corp** Center for Auto Safety. (19??)-. Periodical. English. Six times a year (Feb., Apr., June, Aug., Oct., Dec.). $75.00. Center for Auto Safety, 2001 South Street Northwest, Suite 410, Washington DC 20009-1160. **Tel** (202)328-7700. **ED** Debra Barclay. **LC** KF1297.A8; A134. **DD** 346/.73/038. Index available (Sept.). cum. index. **Circ:** 1,000.
Desc: Reporting on the auto safety work of IMPACT. Covers safety litigation, secret warranties, Crash tests, lemon laws, recalls and federal and state investigations.

IT
IMPOSTE LAVORO PREVIDENZA. **See** Economics-Labor.

BL
IMPOSTO DE RENDA. JURISPRUDENCIA / CAMARA SUPERIOR DE RECURSOS FISCAIS. 1.2-1-. Portuguese. Editora Resenha Tributaria Ltda, rua Quatinga 12, Sao Paulo Brazil. **LC** KHD4626.4; .I47. **DD** 343.8105/2/02648; 348. 1035202648.

BL
IMPOSTO DE RENDA NA FONTE : TABELAS PRATICAS. **Main/Corp** Brazil. Portuguese. Rua Quatinga 12, 04140 Sao Paulo Brazil. **DD** 343.8105/242.

FR
IMPRESSIONS. **Main/Corp** France. Parlement (1946-). Assemblee Nationale. **Added/Corp** France. Laws, Statutes, Etc. (Bills). (Nov. 28, 1946)-. French. Assemblee Nationale, 4 rue Louvois, Paris France. **DD** 348/.44/01.

CK
IMPUESTOS SUCESORIALES; REGIMEN LEGAL TRIBUTARIO. **Main/Corp** Colombia. **VFOAT** Regimen Legal Tributario. Periodical. Spanish. Editores y Distribuidores Asociados Ltda, Avenida Jimenez No 4-49, Apartado Aereo 14965, Bogota Colombia. **ED** Alejandro Restrepo Correa.

UK/0965-3597
IN COMPETITION. (1992)-. English. Ten times a year. £145.00 Europe; £152.00 other. Sweet & Maxwell Ltd., South Quay Plaza, 183 Marsh Wall, London E14 9FT England. **Tel** 011 44 264 342899, FAX 011 44 264 342723, telex 929089 ITPINF G.

US
IN FACT (MILWAUKEE, WIS.). (IN FACT : CITIZEN'S GOVERNMENTAL RESEARCH BUREAU BULLETIN.). **Added/Corp** Citizen's Governmental Research Bureau (Wis.) Public Policy Forum (Milwaukee, Wis.). Vol. 72, No. 7 (Sept. 29, 1984)-. Periodical. English. ir (Seven to nine issues per year). $50.00. Public Policy Forum, 633 West Wisconsin Avenue, Suite 406, Milwaukee WI 53202-1918. **Tel** (414)276-8240, FAX (414)276-9962. **ED** Jean B. Tyler. **Ad Acc. Circ:** 1,500. ***Continues*** *Bulletin (Citizen's Governmental Research Bureau (Wisconsin)).*
Desc: School and government financing, services, and staffing are evaluated.

IT
IN IURE PRAESENTIA. Vol. 1 (1975)-. Periodical. Italian (Italian). Twice a year. L60000.00 Italy; L90000.00 other. Giuffre Editore SPA, Via Busto Arsizio 40, 20151 Milan Italy. **Tel** 011 398 2 38089200. **ED** Vincenzo Panuccio.
Desc: Aims to provide a means for consultation and for updating readers on judicial proceedings, particularly in the area bordering on the Straits of Messina and within the socio-economic context of Southern Italy as a whole.

US/0897-1331
IN THE PUBLIC INTEREST (AMHERST, N.Y.). (IN THE PUBLIC INTEREST.). [In public interest]. **Added/Corp** State University of New York at Buffalo. Center for Public Interest Law. Vol. 1 No. 1 (Apr. 1980)-. Periodical. English. an. Free on request. Center for Public Interest Law, SUNY at Buffalo Faculty of Law, 118 O'Brian Hall, Amherst NY 14260. **Tel** (716)831-2000. **LC** K9; .N25. **DD** 340/.05.
Ind/Abst Altern. Press Index (199?-).

US/0736-8399
INA PROFESSIONAL LIABILITY BULLETIN, ATTORNEYS. **Added/Corp** INA Loss Control Services, Inc. **VFOAT** I.N.A. Professional Liability Bulletin, Attorneys; Professional Liability Bulletin, Attorneys; I.N.A. Professional Liability Bulletin for Attorneys; Professional Liability Bulletin for Attorneys; INA Professional Liability Bulletin for Attorneys. Vol. 1, No. 1 (Winter 1982)-. Bulletin. English. INA Loss Control Services Inc., 1600 Arch Street/PO Box 7728, Philadelphia PA 19101. **LC** KF313.A15; I5. **DD** 346.7303/3; 347.30633.

US/0736-8380
INA PROFESSIONAL LIABILITY BULLETIN, SCHOOLS. **Added/Corp** INA Loss Control Services, Inc. **VFOAT** I.N.A. Professional Liability Bulletin, Schools; Professional Liability Bulletin, Schools; I.N.A. Professional Liability Bulletin on Schools; Professional Liability Bulletin on Schools; INA Professional Liability Bulletin on Schools. (19??)-. Bulletin. English. INA Loss Control Services Inc., 1600 Arch Street/PO Box 7728, Philadelphia PA 19101. **LC** KF1309.A15; I5. **DD** 344.73/075; 347.30475.

Law

US/0270-2061
INCL JOURNAL. Main/Corp New York State Bar Association. Insurance, Negligence and Compensation Law Section. VAT Insurance, Negligence and Compensation Law Section Journal. Periodical. English. sa. $20.00. New York Bar Association, One Elk Street, Albany NY 12207. **Tel** (518)463-3200. **ED** Paul S Edelman. **LC** K14; .E964. **DD** 346.747/086. **Ad Acc. Circ:** 4,000 (ctrl). *Continues Journal of the Insurance, Negligence and Compensation Law Section, 0361-8471.*

CN/0527-7884
INCOME TAX ACT ... ANNOTATED. Main/Corp Canada. (1949)-. Periodical. English. an. Richard de Boo Ltd, 70 Richmond Street East, Toronto Ontario N5C 1M8 Canada. **Tel** (416)445-4940. **ED** H H Stikeman. **DD** 343/.71/05202638. *Continues Canada. Laws, Statutes, Etc. Income War Tax and Excess Profits Tax Act., 0316-8360.*

CN/0317-6150
INDEX COMMERCIAL, JUDICIAIRE, FINANCIER, L'. V. 1- Aug. 16, 1973-. Periodical. French. ir. $49.00. Information Judiciaire, Commerciale Et Financiere Inc., Bureau 305, 580 Est, AV. Grande Allee Quebec, Quebec G1R 2K2. **DD** 348/.714/048.

CN/0701-760X
INDEX OF CURRENT B.C. REGULATIONS. Main/Corp British Columbia. Registrar of Regulations. VAT Index of Current British Columbia Regulations. Vol. 1 (June 1977)-. Periodical. English. sa. 13.00Can$. Crown Publications Inc., 521 Fort Street, Victoria, British Columbia, V8W 1E7 Canada. **Tel** (604)386-4636, FAX (604)386-0221. **LC** KEB89; .B75. **DD** 348.711/028. *Continues Index of Current Regulations Filed under the Regulations Act, 1958, 0707-1086.*

US/0160-0656
INDEX OF LEGISLATION. Main/Corp North Carolina. General Assembly. English. University of North Carolina at Chapel Hill Institute of Government, CB 3330, Knapp Building, Chapel Hill NC 27599-3330. **Tel** (919)966-4119, FAX (919)962-0654. **LC** KFN7410; .G46. **DD** 348/.756/028.

US
INDEX OF LOCAL LAWS OF THE COUNTIES CITIES TOWNS AND VILLAGES BY SUBJECT AND BY MUNICIPALITY FILED DURING THE YEAR. 1980-. English. an. **LC** KFN5754; .I543. **DD** 348.747/028/05. *Formed by the union of Index of Local Laws of the Counties, Cities, Towns, and Villages by Municipality Filed During the Years and Index of Local Laws of the Counties, Cities, Towns, and Villages by Subject Filed During the Years.*

CN
INDEX OF PROCEEDINGS / CANADA. PARLIAMENT. STANDING JOINT COMMITTEE ON REGULATIONS AND OTHER STATUTORY INSTRUMENTS. Main/Corp Canada. Parliament. Standing Joint Committee on Regulations and other Statutory Instruments. Added/Corp Canada. Library of Parliament. Information and Technical Services Branch. VFOAT Index des Deliberations; Index. Proceedings. English (French). Canadian Government Publishing Center, Supply and Services Canada, Hull Quebec K1A 0S9 Canada. **Tel** (613)990-8116, telex 053-4296. **DD** 348.71/028/05; 347.1082805. *Continues Index / Standing Joint Committee on Regulations and other Statutory Instruments, Senate and House of Commons.*

IT/0392-2391
INDEX : QUADERNI CAMERTI DI STUDI ROMANISTICI. [Index. Quad. camerti studi romanistici]. VFOAT Quaderni Camerti di Studi Romanistici; Index: International Survey of Roman Law; International Survey of Roman Law. Vol. 1 (1970)-. Italian (English, French, German and Spanish). an. Casa Editrice Jovene, 109 Via Mezzocannone, 80134 Naples Italy. **Tel** 011 39 81 552-1274.

US/0149-1601
INDEX TO BILLS INTRODUCED IN UTAH LEGISLATIVE SESSION. [Index bills introd. Utah Legis. sess.]. English. an. Utah State Library Commission, 215 South 2nd Street West, Suite 16, Salt Lake City UT 84115. **LC** KFU15; .I53. **DD** 348/.792/028.

CN
INDEX TO CANADIAN LEGAL LITERATURE. Vol. 1 (1981)-. English. Carswell / Canada, 2075 Kennedy Road, Scarborough Ontario M1T 3V4 Canada. **Tel** (416)609-3800, (800)387-5164. **LC** KE1; .I53. **DD** 016.34971/05; 016.3471005.

CN/0316-8891
INDEX TO CANADIAN LEGAL PERIODICAL LITERATURE. See Law-Abstracting, Bibliographies and Statistics.

US/0731-440X
INDEX TO COURSE HANDBOOKS. (INDEX TO COURSE HANDBOOKS / PRACTISING LAW INSTITUTE.). Added/Corp Practising Law Institute. VFOAT Index to Course Handbooks PLI; Index to Course Handbooks P.L.I. (19??)-. English. an. $95.00. Practising Law Institute, 810 Seventh Avenue, New York NY 10019-5818. **Tel** (212)765-5700, FAX (212)581-4670 general correspondence, (212)265-4742 orders and billing inquiries. **LC** KF8; .I54. **DD** 349.73/016; 347.30016.

UK/0019-400X
INDEX TO FOREIGN LEGAL PERIODICALS. See Law-Abstracting, Bibliographies and Statistics.

UK
INDEX TO GOVERNMENT ORDERS IN FORCE 31ST DECEMBER ... . Main/Corp Great Britain. (196?)-. English. an. Her Majesty's Stationery Office, 51 Nine Elms Lane, London SW8 5DR England. **Tel** 011 44 71 873 8459, 011 44 71 873 8499, FAX 011 44 71 873 8499, 011 44 71 873 8456, telex 297138. (Subscription address: Her Majesty's Stationery Office, PO Box 276, Publications Centre, London SW8 5DT England.) *Continues Great Britain. Guide to Government Orders.*

US/0195-9492
INDEX TO GOVERNMENT REGULATION. [Index gov. regul.]. (19??)-. Periodical. English. mo. $680.00. Bureau of National Affairs Inc., 9435 Key West Highway, Rockville MD 20850. **Tel** (800)372-1033, (301)258-1033, FAX (301)948-5823. (Subscription telephone: FAX (301)948-5823) **ED** Inara Apinis. [CCC].
Desc: Provides references to laws and regulations affecting manufacture, processing, distribution, and control of chemicals contained in US code, code of Federal regulations or Federal Register.

II/0019-4034
INDEX TO INDIAN LEGAL PERIODICALS. Added/Corp Indian Law Institute. Vol. 1, No. 1 (Jan. 1963)-. English. Twice a year (Jan., July). $25.00. Indian Law Institute, Bhagwandass Road, New Delhi India. **Tel** 011 91 11 389429 or 389849. **ED** Upendra Bax. Index available. **Bk Rev. Ad Acc. Circ:** 150 (ctrl).
Desc: Index information for legal periodicals and includes author and subject indexes.

US
INDEX TO LAWS OF FLORIDA. SPECIAL AND LOCAL LAWS. English. an. International Press Cutting, PO Box 121, Allahabad 211001 India. **LC** KFF40; .I47. **DD** 348.759/028; 347.590828.

US/0019-4077
INDEX TO LEGAL PERIODICALS. See Law-Abstracting, Bibliographies and Statistics.

US/8756-2383
INDEX TO NEW JERSEY LEGAL DECISIONS. [Index N.J. leg. decis.]. VFOAT New Jersey Legal Decisions. English. New Jersey Education Association, PO Box 1211, 180 West State Street, Trenton NJ 08607. **Tel** (609)599-4561 ext. 208, FAX (609)599-1266. **LC** KFN2190.A59; I52. **DD** 344/.749/07/02648; 347. 4904702648.

US/0019-4093
INDEX TO PERIODICAL ARTICLES RELATED TO LAW. See Law-Abstracting, Bibliographies and Statistics.

US/0199-5626
INDEX TO RECENT NEW HAMPSHIRE CASES. (197?)-. Periodical. English. mo. New Hampshire Law, 18 Centre Street, Concord NH 03301. **Tel** (603)224-6942.

US/0198-9014
INDEX TO THE CODE OF FEDERAL REGULATIONS. [Index code fed. regul.]. Added/Corp Congressional Information Service. VFOAT Code of Federal Regulations. (1938/1976)-. Periodical. English. sa. $31.00. Superintendent of Documents, US Government Printing Office, Washington DC 20402. **Tel** (202)275-3328, FAX (202)786-2377. **LC** KF70.A34; I46. **DD** 348.73/25; 347.30825. **NLM** KF 70.A3 C6751.

CN/0703-2501
INDEXES TO ONTARIO MUNICIPAL BOARD APPLICATIONS DISPOSED OF... AND TO LAND COMPENSATION BOARD APPLICATIONS DISPOSED OF ... . VAT Ontario Municipal Board Index to Applications Disposed of (Monthly Edition). Began publication in Jan. 1974?. Periodical. English. mo. Law Society of Upper Canada, 130 Queen Street West, Toronto M5H 2N6 Canada. **Tel** (416)947-3300, (416)947-3371, telex 065-28013. **ED** L Heer. **DD** 346/.713/04502648.

II/0019-4301
INDIAN ADVOCATE. Added/Corp Bar Association of India. Vol. 1 (Apr./June 1961)-. English. Four times a year. $5.50 (latest edition). Bar Association of India, Chamber #93, Supreme Court Building, New Delhi India 110001.

II
INDIAN BAR REVIEW. Vol. 10 (1) (Jan.-Mar. 1983)-. Periodical. English. qt. Rs330.00 India; $25.00 US. Universal Book Traders, 80 Gokhale Market, Opp New Delhi Courts, New Delhi 110054 India. **Tel** 2911966. **ED** M H Beg, Y V Chandrachud, N N Mathur, V C Mishra, B P Samaiyar, Ranbir Singh Mahendra, K D Sood, N R Madhara Menm. **LC** K2; .A67. **DD** 349.54/05; 345.4005. Index available. **Bk Rev. Circ:** 700 (ctrl). *Continues Journal of the Bar Council of India.*
Desc: Critically examines every development in law, serves the goals of better legal education. Promotes socio-legal research and provide new insights into legal and judicial process.

II
INDIAN JUDGMENT REPORTER : IJR. VFOAT IJR; I.J.R. Periodical. English. mo. Rs195.00 India; $50.00 other. Indian Judgment Reporter, Hig-C-1613 Rajaji Puram, Lucknow-226107 India. **Tel** 53421. **ED** Rajesh Kumar Upadhyay. **DD** 348.54/044/05; 345.4084405. cum. index. **Bk Rev. Ad Acc. Circ:** 10,000.
Desc: Publish judgements of Supreme Court of India.

US/0097-1154
INDIAN LAW REPORTER. Added/Corp American Indian Lawyer Training Program. Vol. 1 (Jan 1974)-. Periodical. English. mo. $396.00. American Indian Lawyer Training Program Inc, 319 MacArthur Boulevard, Oakland CA 94610. **Tel** (510)834-9333, FAX (510)834-3836. **ED** Patricia M. Zell. **LC** KF8201.A3; I5. **DD** 342/.73/087. Index available. **Circ:** 650 (ctrl). available on microfilm and microfiche.
Desc: Information service summarizing and reporting current developments in Indian law from federal, tribal and state courts and administrative agencies.
Ind/Abst Hum. Rights Intern. Rep.

II
INDIAN LAW REPORTS, THE. English. Government of Karnataka, Director of Printing Stationery and Publications, Bangalore India. **DD** 348/.5487/043. *Continues Indian Law Reports.*

II
INDIAN LAW REPORTS; DELHI SERIES. English. mo. Rs120.00. Registrar / New Dehli, Delhi High Court of India, New Delhi India.

II/0970-7972
INDIAN SOCIO-LEGAL JOURNAL. Periodical. English. sa. Rs.50 India; $18.00 other. Indian Institute of Comparative Law, 6/146 Malviya Nagar, Jaipur 302017 India. **Tel** (0141)822-814. **ED** K B Agrawal. **LC** K9; .N365. **DD** 340/.115/0954. cum. index. **Circ:** 1,200 (ctrl).
Desc: A multidisciplinary publication dealing with the problems of law and society; it contains research papers from eminent jurists and sociologists of the world.

US/0744-9046
INDIANA CASES REPORTED IN NORTH EASTERN REPORTER, SECOND SERIES. [Indiana cases rep. North east. rep., second ser.]. VFOAT West's Indiana Cases; Ind. Cases. Began with 1-4 N.E. 2D issue. Periodical. English. wk (50 no. a year). West Publishing Company, 610 Opperman Drive, PO Box 64526, Eagan MN 55123-1308. **Tel** (612)687-5618, (800)328-9352, FAX (612)687-5388, (800)562-2329. (Subscription telephone: FAX (612)688-3570) **LC** PAR. **DD** 348.

US
INDIANA CODE. SUPPLEMENT. Main/Corp Indiana. Added/Corp Indiana. General Assembly. Legislative Council. (1978)-. English. an. Price varies. Indiana Legislative Service Agency, 302 State House, Indianapolis IN 46204. **Tel** (317)269-3550.

US/0445-8664
INDIANA DECISIONS AND LAW REPORTER. Periodical. English. wk. Bobbs Merrill Company Inc, 4300 West 62nd Street, Indianapolis IN 46268. **Tel** (804)295-6171.

US/1053-6183
INDIANA ENVIRONMENTAL LAW LETTER. Title Change. [Indiana environ. law lett.]. Added/Corp Barnes & Thornburg. (Jan 1991)-(199?). Periodical. English. mo. M. Lee Smith Publishers and Printers, 162 4th Avenue North, PO Box 198867, Nashville TN 37219. **Tel** (615)242-7395, (800)274-6774, FAX (615)256-6601. **ED** John Kyle (editor's address: Barnes and Thornburg, 11 South Meridian Street,

Indianapolis, IN 46204; phone (317)231-7284). **DD** 344. ***Continued by*** *Baker & Daniels' Indiana Environmental Compliance Update, 1067-4209.*
Desc: Newsletter reporting the latest state specific environmental law developments that affect Indiana.

US/0019-6665
INDIANA LAW JOURNAL (BLOOMINGTON). (INDIANA LAW JOURNAL.). [Indiana law j.]. **Added/Corp** Indiana State Bar Association (1916)- Indiana University. School of Law. Indiana University, Bloomington. School of Law. Vol. 1, (1926)-. Periodical. English. Four times a year (Seasonally). $27.00 (one year); $53.00 (two years); $78.00 (three years). Indiana Law Journal / Indiana University School of Law, Law Building 009, Bloomington IN 47405. **Tel** (812)855-5175, FAX (812)855-0555. **LC** K9; .N372. Index available (4th iss. (Fall)). **Bk Rev**, (Qty: 0-2). **Pr Rev. Circ:** 1,000. available on microfilm and microfiche from Fred B. Rothman and Company. Documents available from The Genuine Article. ***Continues*** *Indiana Law Journal (Crawfordsville, Ind.).*
Desc: These articles are by legal scholars, attorneys, judges, and IU law students. Articles and student notes are on topics of interest to the bench and bar. Concentration is upon legal articles, but other legally related topics are often included such as business articles, political science works, sociological studies, and scientific pieces with legal overtones.
Ind/Abst Bowne Dig. Corp. Sec. Lawyers (1980-); Crim. Justice Abstr.; Curr. Law Index (1980-); Fed. Tax Artic.; Index Leg. Period.; Leg. Resour. Index (1980-); LegalTrac (1980-); Res. Alert [Full Cov.]; Soc. Plann. Policy Dev. Abstr.; Soc. Sci. Cit. Index [Full Cov.]; Sociol. Abstr. (?-?); SportSearch.

US/0090-4198
INDIANA LAW REVIEW. [Indiana law rev.]. **Added/Corp** Indiana University. Indianapolis Law School. Indiana University School of Law-Indianapolis. Vol. 6 (1972)-. Periodical. English. qt. $25.00 US; $28.00 other. Indianapolis Law School, 735 West New York Street, Indianapolis IN 46202. **Tel** (317)264-4440, FAX (317)274-3955. **ED** Eric J. Graninger. **LC** K9; .N373. **DD** 340/.09772. Index available. **Bk Rev. Ad Acc. Circ:** 1,600 (ctrl). ***Continues*** *Indiana Legal Forum.*
Desc: Review and analysis of current developments in law.
Ind/Abst Bowne Dig. Corp. Sec. Lawyers; Curr. Law Index (1980-); Fed. Tax Artic.; Index Leg. Period.; Leg. Resour. Index (1980-); LegalTrac (1980-).

US/0193-1520
INDIANA REGISTER. Vol.1 (July 1, 1978). English. mo. $100.00. Legislative Services Agency, 302 State House, Indianapolis IN 46204. **Tel** (317)269-3550. **ED** Linda Miller. **Bk Rev**, (Qty: 12/y). **Circ:** 900.
Desc: Lists proposed and final rules of Indiana state agencies; also includes documents such as executive orders, opinions of the state attorney general, etc.

FR/1243-4671
INDICATEUR HORAIRES VILLE A VILLE. (1992)-. Periodical. French. sa. 93.00F France; 110.00F other. Bur de Vente Docs Tarifaires, 212 rue de Bercy, 75571 Paris Cedex 12 France. **Tel** 011 33 1 40196681, or -14. **UDC** 656.2(44). ***Continues*** *Indicateur Officiel Ville a Ville, 1164-7701.*

FR/1164-7701
INDICATEUR OFFICIEL VILLE A VILLE. ***Title Change.*** (1988)-(1992). Periodical. French. sa. Bur de Vente Docs Tarifaires, 212 rue de Bercy, 75571 Paris Cedex 12 France. **Tel** 011 33 1 40196681, or -14. **UDC** 656.2(44). ***Continues*** *Ville a Ville, 0182-3280.* ***Continued by*** *Indicateur Horaires Ville a Ville, 1243-4671.*

●DK
INDIGENOUS WORLD / INTERNATIONAL WORK GROUP FOR INDIGENOUS AFFAIRS. Added/Corp International Work Group for Indigenous Affairs. (1994)-. English. ir. International Work Group for Indigenous Affairs, Fiolstraede 10, DK-1171 Copenhagen K Denmark. **Tel** 011 45 1 33124724. **LC** GN380; .I95. ***Continues*** *Yearbook (International Work Group for Indigenous Affairs).*

UY
INDILEX. Jan./March 1974-. Spanish. $3.30. Polo Ltd, Avenida Garibaldi 2579, Montevideo Uruguay.

US/1055-520X
INDIVIDUAL WITH DISABILITIES EDUCATION LAW REPORT. [Individ. disabil. educ. law rep.]. Vol. 17, Suppl. 8 (Apr. 5, 1991)-. Periodical. English. bw (except July and Dec.). $860.00. LRP Publications, 747 Dresher Road, PO Box 980, Horsham PA 19044-0980. **Tel** (800)341-7874, (215)784-0860, FAX (215)784-9639, (215)784-0870. **(Subscription address:** LRP Publications, PO Box 980, Horsham PA 19044.**)** **DD** 344. **[CCC].** available on an online database from SpecialNet. ***Continues*** *Education for the Handicapped Law Report, 0744-4117.*
Desc: Reference source for special education law. Presents cases involving classroom discipline of students with special needs, mediation of disputes, development of effective IEPs, compliance with state standards, and more.

SA
INDUSTRIAL LAW JOURNAL, INCLUDING THE INDUSTRIAL LAW REPORTS. V. 1- May 1980-. Periodical. English. qt. R88.00 South Africa; $43.38 US. Juta & Company Ltd, PO Box 123, Kenwyn 7790 South Africa. **Tel** 711181. **ED** Halton Cheadle, Martin Brassby, Edwin Cameron, and Clive Thompson. cum. index. **Ad Acc. Circ:** 1,600 (ctrl).
Desc: Comments on and explains and evaluates new legislation also comments and explains recent decisions of the industrial courts.

CK
INFOLIOS. Main/Corp Colombia. Superintendencia de Notariado y Registro. Periodical. Spanish. $10.00. Superintendencia de Notariado y Registro Biblioteca, Calle 26 No 13-49 Interior 201 Piso A, Bogota Colombia. **LC** K14; .R58. **DD** 347/.861/016. ***Continues*** *SNR, Superintendencia de Notariado y Registro.*

IT/0390-0975
INFORMATICA E DIRITTO. [Inform. dir.]. Vol. 1- Jan./March 1975-. Spanish (summaries and/or abstracts in English, French and Italian). qt. $80.00. Editoriale e Finanziaria le Monnier Spa, Post Box 202, 50100 Firenze Italy. **Tel** 055-6813801. **LC** K9; .N43. **DD** 029/.9/34005. **Circ:** 1,500. Documents available from Ask*IEEE.
Ind/Abst Comput. Rev.; INSPEC (Jan./April 1982-); Soc. Plann. Policy Dev. Abstr.

NE
INFORMATIERECHT. ***Title Change.*** **Added/Corp** Vereniging voor Auteursrecht (Netherlands). Vol. 10, No. 1 (Feb. 1986)-(19??). Periodical. Dutch. bm. Libresso BV, Postbus 878, 7400 GA Deventer Netherlands. **Tel** 011 31 5700 47421. **ED** H. Cohen Jehoram, A. W. Hins and J. H. Spoor. **LC** K1; .U84. **Circ:** 800. ***Continues*** *Auteursrecht.* ***Continued by*** *Informatierecht AMI.*

NE
INFORMATIERECHT AMI. Added/Corp Vereniging voor Auteursrecht (Netherlands). (19??)-. Periodical. Dutch. Ten times a year. Fl115.15. Libresso BV, Postbus 878, 7400 GA Deventer Netherlands. **Tel** 011 31 5700 47421. **ED** H. Cohen Jehoram, A. W. Hins and J. H. Spoor. **LC** K1; .U84. **Circ:** 800. ***Continues*** *Informatierecht.*

US/0736-2765
INFORMATION BULLETIN - AMERICAN BAR ASSOCIATION. STANDING COMMITTEE ON SPECIALIZATION. (INFORMATION BULLETIN.). **Added/Corp** ABA Standing Committee on Specialization. (1976)-. Periodical. English. American Bar Association, 750 North Lake Shore Drive, Chicago IL 60611. **Tel** (312)988-5522, (312)988-5241, FAX (312)988-5528, telex 270593. **LC** KF297.A1; I53. **DD** 340/.023/73. **Ad Acc.**
Desc: State by state information on lawyer specialization.

AT/1031-6590
INFORMATION BULLETIN - CHILDREN'S COURT OF NEW SOUTH WALES. [Inf. bull. - Child. Court N. S. W.]. (1988)-. English. Twice a year. Free. Bidura Childrens Court, 357 Glebe Point road, R. Blackmore, Glebe 2037, Australia. **Tel** 11 61 2 6927132, FAX 11 61 2 5522568. **ED** R. D. Blackmore. **DD** 345.94408. cum. index. **Bk Rev. Circ:** 600 (ctrl).
Desc: News and information on the children's court in Australia.

US/0020-0115
INFORMATION LEGISLATIVE SERVICE (1969). (INFORMATION LEGISLATIVE SERVICES.). **Added/Corp** Pennsylvania School Boards Association. Vol. 7, No. 37 (Sept. 19, 1969)-. Periodical. English. wk (except during Thanksgiving and Christmas). $50.00 members, $150.00 nonmembers. Pennsylvania School Boards Association, 774 Limekiln Road, New Cumberland PA 17070. **Tel** (717)774-2331, FAX (717)774-0718. **ED** Lynn H. Mannion. **Circ:** 11,300 (ctrl). ***Continues*** *Information Legislative Service Report.*

GW
INFORMATIONEN ZUM STEUERRECHT. German. DM117.30. Verlagshaus Schmitt Gmbh & Co., Postfach 2653, D-4930 Detmold Germany. **Tel** 011 49 5231 983145.

GW/0174-2108
INFORMATIONSBRIEF AUSLANDERRECHT. [Inf.br. ausl.r.]. (1979)-. German. mo. Hermann Luchterhand Verlag, Postfach 2352, D 56513 Neuwied Germany. **Tel** 011 49 2631 8010. **LC** KK6050.A13; I53. **DD** 342.43/083; 344.30283.

BL
INFORMATIVO - ASSOCIACAO CATARINENSE DO MINISTERIO PUBLICO. Main/Corp Santa Catarina, Brazil. Ministerio Publico. Associacao Catarinense do Ministerio Publico. Portuguese. Rua General Bittencourt N 83, Santa Catarina Brazil.

PE
INFORMATIVO LEGAL RODRIGO. Began with March 1961 issue. Spanish. mo. S/4,700 Peru; $200.00 other. Asesores Financieros, Jr Pachacutec 1133 - Jesus Maria, Casilla 3218, Lima 100 Peru. **Tel** 240665, FAX 637300, telex 25622 PE LUCARO. **ED** Luis Carlos Rodrigo P. Index available. cum. index. **Bk Rev. Circ:** 650.
Desc: Publishes legal norms summarized and arranged. Contains chronological and thematic indexes, monthly and weekly. Answers written consultations, gives information and commented jurisprudence.

BL
INFORMATIVO MAI DE ENSINO DO ESTADO DE MINAS GERAIS. Jan. 1974-. Periodical. Portuguese. 120.00. Mai Arte E Criacas Ltda, rua Jose Lavarine 184 Santa Efigenia, Belo Horizonte Brazil.

CN/0381-131X
INFORMATOR (MONTREAL). (INFORMATOR.). English (French). an. $88.00. Editions De L'Homme, Suite 703, 59 St. Jacques Street, Montreal Quebec H2Y 1K9 Canada. **DD** 347.714/013.

IT/0394-9885
INFORMATORE GIURIDICO DELLE ATTIVITA SPORTIVE, L'. [Inf. giurid. attiv. sport.]. (1989)-. Periodical. Italian. qt. L50000.00. Medem Srl, Via Emilia Ovest 21 A, 42048 Rubiera RE Italy. **Tel** 011 39 522 62229. **UDC** 796 :34.

IT
INFORMATORE LEGISLATIVO (ITALY), L'. ***Ceased.*** **Main/Corp** Italy. Servizi Della Informazioni e Della Proprieta Letteraria, Artistica e Scientifica. Periodical. Italian. Via PO 14, Rome Italy. **DD** 348/.45/01.

IT
INFORMATORE PIROLA. (19??)-. Italian. Fifty times a year. L349000. Sole 24 Ore Libri, Via Parabiago 19, 20151 Milan Italy. **Tel** 011 39 2 66030288. **Ad Acc, Adv Mgr Tel** 02 3022.1. **Circ:** 14.500.

PR
INFORME ANUAL DEL DIRECTOR ADMINISTRATIVO DE LOS TRIBUNALES. ***Title Change.*** **Main/Corp** Puerto Rico. Office of Court Administration. **VFOAT** Informe Anual. (1953-19??). Spanish. ***Continued by*** *Puerto Rico. Office of Court Administration.; Informe Anual de la Rama Judicial.*

BO
INFORME DE LABORES ... Y APERTURA DEL ANO JUDICIAL / CORTE SUPERIOR DEL DISTRITO JUDICIAL DE CHUQUISACA. Main/Corp Bolivia. Corte Superior (Distrito Judicial de Chuquisaca). Spanish. an. **LC** KHC2539.C48; A153. **DD** 348.84/24/04405; 348.424084405.

UK
INLAND REVENUE PRACTICES & CONCESSIONS. **See** Public Administration-Public Finance and Taxation.

US/1069-0190
INQUIRY & ANALYSIS. [Inq. anal.]. **Added/Corp** Council of School Attorneys. **VFOAT** Inquiry and Analysis. (1979)-. Periodical. English. Six times a year. $60.00. National School Board Association, 1680 Duke Street, Alexandria VA 22314. **Tel** (703)838-6749, FAX (703)683-7590. **DD** 344.

US/1061-3390
INSIDER REPORTING AND LIABILITY UNDER SECTION 16 OF THE SECURITIES EXCHANGE ACT OF 1934. (INSIDER REPORTING AND LIABILITY UNDER SECTION 16 OF THE SECURITIES EXCHANGE ACT OF 1934 / BY PETER J. ROMEO.). [Insider rep. liabil. under Sect. 16 Secur. Exch. Act 1934]. **VFOAT** Peter Romeo's Comprehensive Section 16 Outline; Comprehensive Section 16 Outline. Began in Nov. (1986)-. Periodical. English. sa. $195.00 (comes with Peter Romeo Section 16, Treatise and Service). Executive Press, PO Box 21639, Concord CA 94521. **Tel** (510)685-5111. **DD** 346.

US/1043-8467
INSIGHT INTO COURTS. [Insight courts]. **Added/Corp** Georgetown University. Medical Center. Georgetown University. Law Center. Vol. 1, No. 1 (Apr. 1990)-. Periodical. English. bm. $245.00 US; $262.15 Canada; $260.00 other. **LC** KF3821.A15; I57. **DD**

344.73/041/05; 347.3044105.
Desc: For practicing attorneys providing detailed analyses, as well as expert legal opinion and commentary, on current litigation involving technical, scientific and medical issues.

UK/0950-2645
INSOLVENCY INTELLIGENCE. [Insolv. intell.]. (1988)-. Periodical. English. mo (10 issues per year). $215.00. Longman Group Ltd., Fourth Avenue, Longman House, Harlow Essex CM19 5SR England. **Tel** 011 44 279 429655, FAX 011 44 279 431059, telex 81259. **ED** Catherine Anderson. **DD** 344.10678. **[CCC].** Index available. cum. index. **Bk Rev. Ad Acc. Pr Rev. Circ:** 1,000. available on microfilm and microfiche from University Microfilms International (UMI).
Desc: A journal concentrating on the legal and financial aspects of the insolvency of companies and individuals.

UK
INSOLVENCY LAWYER. ***Ceased.*** (19??)-Vol. 9 (19??). English. Three times a year. John Wiley & Sons Ltd., Baffins Lane, Chichester West Sussex PO19 1UD England. **Tel** 0243 779777, FAX 0243 776128 BTG:JWP001, telex 86290 WIBOOKG. **(Subscription address:** John Wiley / Philadelphia, PO Box 7247, Philadelphia PA 19170.) **ED** Harry Rajak.
Desc: It reports on the activities of the association and provides comprehensive coverage and analysis of developments in the law affecting practitioners.

●UK
INSOLVENCY LAWYERS DIRECTORY / INSOLVENCY LAWYERS' ASSOCIATION. **Main/Corp** Insolvency Lawyers' Association (Great Britain). (1992)-. Directory. English. Chancery Law Publishing Ltd, 22 Eastcastle Street, London WQN 7PA England. **Tel** 44-71-323 3328, FAX 44-71-323 2386. **LC** KD340.B34; I57. **DD** 346.41/078/025; 344.10678025.

US/0146-7816
INSTITUTE OF JUDICIAL ADMINISTRATION REPORT. **Main/Corp** Institute of Judicial Administration. (19??)-. English. Institute of Judicial Administration, 1 Washington Square Village, New York NY 10012. **Tel** (212)598-7721. **LC** KF8732.A16; I53. **DD** 347/.73/13.

US/0887-7858
INSURANCE INDUSTRY LITIGATION REPORTER : THE NATIONAL JOURNAL OF RECORD OF INSURANCE LITIGATION. [Insur. ind. litig. report.]. (July 3, 1985)-. Periodical. English. sm. $825.00. Andrews Publications Inc., 1646 West Chester Pike, PO Box 1000, Westtown PA 19395. **Tel** (610)399-6600, (800)345-1101, FAX (610)399-6610. **ED** Leonard E. B. Andrews. **LC** KF1159; .I576. **DD** 346.73/086. cum. index. ctrl circ.
Desc: Reports on developments in litigation pertaining to the respective rights and obligations of insurance carriers and their policyholders.

US/0148-2688
INSURANCE LAW. **Main/Corp** New York (State). English. an. Matthew Bender & Company Inc., 1275 Broadway, Albany NY 12204. **Tel** (800)833-9844, (518)487-3000. **LC** KFN5290.A29; B46. **DD** 346/.747/086.

UK
INSURANCE LAW & PRACTICE. **See** Insurance.

US/0892-4422
INSURANCE LAW ANTHOLOGY. [Insur. law anthol.]. Vol. 1 (1986)-. English. an. $299.95. International Library Law Book Publishers, 101 Lakeforest Boulevard, Suite 270, Gaithersburg MD 20877. **Tel** (800)359-3349, (301)990-7755, FAX (301)990-7642. **ED** Alison P. Zabriskie. **LC** K9; .N74694. **DD** 346.73/086; 347.30686. Index available. cum. index. **Bk Rev.**
Desc: Contains insurance law review articles, in their entirety, from over 900 law review journals. Introduction and overview by highly respected experts in insurance law. Index by author, subject and leading cases.

AT/1030-2379
INSURANCE LAW JOURNAL (SYDNEY, N.S.W.). **See** Insurance.

UK
INSURANCE LAW REPORTS (HARLOW, ESSEX). (INSURANCE LAW REPORTS.). 1982-. Periodical. English. Three times a year. **LC** KD1855.A2; I57. **DD** 346.42/086/05; 344.2068605.

US/0744-1045
INSURANCE LITIGATION REPORTER. [Insur. litig. rep.]. **Added/Corp** Litigation Research Group (San Francisco, Calif.). Vol. 1, No. 1 (Sept. 1979)-. Periodical. English. mo. $335.00. Shepards McGraw-Hill Inc, 555 Middle Creek Parkway, PO Box 35300, Colorado Springs CO 80935-3530. **Tel** (719)488-3000, FAX (800)525-0053. **ED** John K. DiMugno. **LC** KF1159; .I58. **DD** 346.73/086/02638; 347.3068602638. **Circ:** 1,750. ***Continues*** *Insurance Liability Reporter, 0195-1858.*
Desc: Provides summaries and analyses of recent appellate decisions, trends and development of interest to the insurance lawyer and claims/risk manager.

US/0534-4638
INTER ALIA. **Added/Corp** State Bar of Michigan. Young Lawyers Section. Vol. 1 (Jan. 1963)-. Periodical. English. ir. State Bar of Michigan, 306 Townsend Street, Lansing MI 48933. **Tel** (517)372-9030. ***Supersedes*** *Michigan Young Lawyers News.*
Ind/Abst LegalTrac (1980-).

US/0092-6086
INTER ALIA (RENO). ***Title Change.*** (INTER ALIA.). [Inter alia]. **Added/Corp** State Bar of Nevada. Vol. 38 No. 2 (April 1973)-(1992). Periodical. English. qt. State Bar of Nevada, 1325 Airmotive Way, Suite 140, Reno NV 89502. **Tel** (702)329-4100, FAX (702)329-0522. **ED** Christine Cendagorta. **LC** K14; .E7. **DD** 340/05. Index available (published separately). cum. index. **Bk Rev**, (Qty: 12 per year). **Ad Acc, Adv Mgr:** C. Cendagorta, **Tel** (702)329-4100. **Circ:** 3,800 (ctrl). available on microfilm from University Microfilms International (UMI); available on an online database from WESTLAW. ***Continues*** *Nevada State Bar Journal, 0028-4092.* ***Merged with*** *Bar Letter, 1052-4541* ***to form*** *Nevada Lawyer, 1068-882X.*
Desc: Substantive law-related articles and features.
Ind/Abst Curr. Law Index (1980-); Law Office Inf. Serv.; Leg. Resour. Index (1980-).

CN/0715-4771
INTER-AMERICAN ARBITRATION. (INTER-AMERICAN ARBITRATION / INTER-AMERICAN COMMERCIAL ARBITRATION COMMISSION.). [Interam. arbitr.]. **VFOAT** I.A.C.A.C. Newsletter. **VAT** Inter-American Commercial Arbitration Commission Newsletter. No. 1 (1981)-. Periodical. English (Spanish, French and Portuguese). qt. 10.00Can$, Free to members. Canadian Arbitration Conciliation and Amicable Composition Centre, c/o Institute for International Cooperation, University of Ottawa, Ottawa Ontario K1N 6N5 Canada. **Tel** (613)232-1476, telex 0533338. **ED** L Kos-Rabcewicz-Zubkowski. **DD** 341.5/22. **Bk Rev. Ad Acc. Circ:** 350 (ctrl).
Desc: International, commercial arbitration and conciliation.

US/0886-7747
INTER-AMERICAN LEGAL MATERIALS / AMERICAN BAR ASSOCIATION, SECTION OF INTERNATIONAL LAW AND PRACTICE, INTER-AMERICAN LAW COMMITTEE. [IntAm. legal mater.]. **Added/Corp** American Bar Association. Committee on Inter-American Law. **VFOAT** Inter American Legal Materials. Vol. 1, No. 1 (Jan. 1983)-. Periodical. English. qt (4 issues). $71.00. American Bar Association, 750 North Lake Shore Drive, Chicago IL 60611. **Tel** (312)988-5522, (312)988-5241, FAX (312)988-5528, telex 270593. **LC** K9; .N7478. **DD** 349.8; 348.

US/0895-2523
INTERIM CASE CITATIONS TO THE RESTATEMENTS OF THE LAW. **Added/Corp** American Law Institute. American Law Institute. Restatement in the Courts. (July 1983 through June 1984)-. English. Twice a year. $65.00. American Law Institute, 4025 Chestnut Street, Philadelphia PA 19104-3099. **Tel** (215)243-1661, (800)253-6397, FAX (215)243-1664. **ED** Marianne M. Walker (Editor's Phone: (215)243-1600). **LC** KF395.A4; I58. **DD** 348.73/47; 347.30847. available on an online database from WESTLAW.
Desc: List of court cases that have cited the Restatements of the Law.

US
INTERIM REPORT TO THE ... LEGISLATURE. **Main/Corp** South Dakota. Legislature. State Legislative Research Council. English. an. State Legislative Research Council, State Capitol, 500 East Capitol, Pierre SD 57501. **LC** KFS3020; .S73. **DD** 348.783/01; 347.83081.

UK
INTERNATIONAL BANKING AND FINANCIAL LAW BULLETIN. Bulletin. English. mo. £300.00. Legal Studies & Services Publ Ltd., 9-13 St. Andrew Street, London EC4A 3AE England. **Tel** 011 44 71 936-2016.

CN/0843-4964
INTERNATIONAL BULLETIN OF LAW & MENTAL HEALTH. [Int. bull. law ment. health]. **Added/Corp** International Academy of Law and Mental Health. **VFOAT** Bulletin; International Bulletin of Law and Mental Health. Vol. 1, No. 1 (Spring 1989)-. Bulletin. English (summaries and/or abstracts in French). Twice a year (Varies). $20.00. International Academy of Law and Mental Health, 30 Saint Joseph Boulevard, Suite 520, Montreal QUE H2T 1G9 Canada. **Tel** (514)847-0782, FAX (514)843-5415. **DD** 344/.044. **NLM** W1; IN714. Index available (Vol. 2 (while supplies last)). **Bk Rev. Circ:** 400.

US/0893-2859
INTERNATIONAL COMPUTER LAW ADVISER. ***Title Change.*** [Int. comput. law advis.]. Vol. 1, No. 1 (Oct. 1986)-(199?). Periodical. English. mo. Law and Technology Press, PO Box 3280, Manhattan Beach CA 90266. **Tel** (310)372-1678. **ED** Michael D Scott. **LC** K564.C6; A155. **DD** 343/.078004; 342.378004. **[CCC].** Index available. **Bk Rev.** Documents available from Ask*IEEE. ***Formed by the union of*** *Scott Report on Computer Law, 1040-242X* ***and*** *International Review of Computers, Technology and the Law.* ***Continued by*** *International Computer Lawyer, 1067-6171.*
Desc: Reports on domestic and international legal problems.
Ind/Abst Comput. Lit. Index; Comput. Rev.; Data Process. Dig.; INSPEC (1986-).

●US/1067-6171
INTERNATIONAL COMPUTER LAWYER, THE. [Int. comput. lawyer]. Vol. 1, No. 1 (Nov./Dec. 1992)-. Periodical. English. Twelve times a year. $352.63 US; $406.88 other. Prentice-Hall Law and Business, 270 Sylvan Avenue, Englewood Cliffs NJ 07632. **Tel** (800)223-0231, (201)894-8538, FAX (201)894-8666. **LC** K564.C6; A1555. **DD** 343.099/9; 342.3999. **CODEN** ICOLE7. ***Continues*** *International Computer Law Adviser, 0893-2859.*

US/1057-5677
INTERNATIONAL CRIMINAL JUSTICE REVIEW. [Int. crim. justice rev.]. **Added/Corp** Georgia State University. College of Public and Urban Affairs. Vol. 1 (1991)-. Periodical. English. an. $18.00. Georgia State University Public and Urban Affairs, PO Box 4018, Atlanta GA 30302-4018. **Tel** (404)651-3515, FAX (404)651-2737. **DD** 364.

SZ/0020-6563
INTERNATIONAL DIGEST OF HEALTH LEGISLATION. [Int. dig. health legis.]. **Added/Corp** World Health Organization. Vol. 1, No. 1 (1948)-. Periodical. English (French). qt. $167.00 Surface Mail; $187.00 (airmail) Europe; $207.00 (airmail) other. World Health Organization, Distribution and Sales, 20 Avenue Appia, CH-1211 Geneva 27 Switzerland. **Tel** 011 41 22 7912111, FAX 011 41 22 7880401. **NLM** W2 MW6 I7. cum. index. Documents available from BIOSIS Document Express. ***Continues*** *Bulletin Mensuel de l'Office International d'Hygiene Publique, 0366-4465.*
Desc: Allows readers to follow worldwide developments in laws and regulations designed to protect public health and the human environment. In recent years, the Digest has also become a key reference to new AIDS legislation enacted throughout the world. Scope includes any new or amended legal text, whether national or international, that has a bearing on health protection or medical care.
Ind/Abst Biol. Abstr.; Dairy Sci. Abstr.; Food Sci. Technol. Abstr.; Health Plan. Adminis.; Int. Pharm. Abstr.; Leadscan; Maize Abstr.; Nutr. Abstr. Rev., Ser. A, Hum. Exp.; Nutr. Res. Newsl.; Life Sci. Collect.; Soyabean Abstr.

NE
INTERNATIONAL ENCYCLOPAEDIA OF LAWS. English. ir. Kluwer Law and Taxation Publishers, Staverenstraat 32015, PO Box 23, 7400 GA Deventer Netherlands. **Tel** 011 31 5700 47261.

NE
INTERNATIONAL ENCYCLOPEDIA FOR LABOUR LAW AND INDUSTRIAL RELATIONS. English. ir. Kluwer Law and Taxation Publishers, Staverenstraat 32015, PO Box 23, 7400 GA Deventer Netherlands. **Tel** 011 31 5700 47261.
Ind/Abst LABORDOC.

UK
INTERNATIONAL FINANCIAL LAW PRACTICE FILES. REGULATION REPORTS. English. mo. £745.00. Euromoney Publications PLC, Nestor House, Playhouse Yard, London EC4Z 5EX England. **Tel** 011 44 71 779 8888, FAX 011 44 71 779 8617, telex 290700 EUROMON G.

UK
INTERNATIONAL FRANCHISING & DISTRIBUTION LAW. English. qt. £100.00. Tolley Publishing Company Ltd, Tolley House, 2 Addiscombe Road, Croydon, Surrey CR9 5AF United Kingdom. **Tel** 011 44 81 6869141, FAX 011 44 81 6863155, 011 44 81 7600588.

NE
INTERNATIONAL HANDBOOK ON COMMERCIAL ARBITRATION. Dutch. Kluwer Law and Taxation Publishers, Staverenstraat 32015, PO Box 23, 7400 GA Deventer Netherlands. **Tel** 011 31 5700 47261.

UK
INTERNATIONAL INDIRECT LAW REPORT. (199?)-. Newsletter. English. £220.00 UK; $395.00 other. Euromoney Publications PLC, Nestor House, Playhouse Yard, London EC4Z 5EX England. **Tel** 011 44 71 779 8888, FAX 011 44 71 779 8617, telex 290700 EUROMON G.
Desc: Newsletter dealing with all aspects of indirect taxation. Areas covered include current value added tax, turnover and sales taxes, customs and excise duties, registration taxes for property, carbon and environmental taxes, trust taxes, credit taxes, accounting issues, on-going compliance requirements, airport and toll road taxes, tourist and hotel taxes, new indirect taxes.

UK
INTERNATIONAL INSOLVENCY REVIEW : JOURNAL OF THE INTERNATIONAL ASSOCIATION OF INSOLVENCY PRACTITIONERS. **Added/Corp** Insol International. **VFOAT** INSOL International Insolvency Review; INSOL International Review; A.IIR. (1993)-. Periodical. English (summaries and/or abstracts in French). sa. $195.00. John Wiley & Sons Ltd., Baffins Lane, Chichester West Sussex PO19 1UD England. **Tel** 0243 779777, FAX 0243 776128 BTG:JWP001, telex 86290 WIBOOKG. **(Subscription address:** John Wiley / Philadelphia, PO Box 7247, Philadelphia PA 19170.**)** **ED** Professor Ian Fletcher. ***Continues*** *INSOL International Insolvency Review, 1180-0518.*

●UK/0968-2090
INTERNATIONAL INSURANCE LAW REVIEW. (1993)-. English. mo. £305.00 Europe; £320.00 other. Sweet & Maxwell Ltd., South Quay Plaza, 183 Marsh Wall, London E14 9FT England. **Tel** 011 44 264 342899, FAX 011 44 264 342723, telex 929089 ITPINF G.

UK/0952-8059
INTERNATIONAL JOURNAL FOR THE SEMIOTICS OF LAW. **Added/Corp** International Association for the Semiotics of Law. **VFOAT** Revue Internationale de Semiotique Juridique. Vol. 1, No. 1- (1988)-. Periodical. English (French). Three times a year. $92.42 UK; $97.86 other. Deborah Charles Publications, 173 Mather Avenue, Liverpool L18 6JZ United Kingdom. **Tel** 011 44 51 724 2500. **(Subscription address:** WM W Gaunt & Sons Inc., 3011 Gulf Drive, Gaunt Building, Holmes Beach, FL 34217 (813-778-5211)**)** **ED** Eric Landowski. **Pr Rev.** Documents available from The Genuine Article.
Ind/Abst Curr. Contents Soc. Behav. Sci.; Res. Alert [Full Cov.]; Soc. Plann. Policy Dev. Abstr.; Soc. Sci. Cit. Index [Full Cov.].

UK/0967-0769
INTERNATIONAL JOURNAL OF LAW AND INFORMATION TECHNOLOGY. (Feb. 1993)-. English. tq. £99.00 UK and Europe; $190.00 other. Oxford University Press, Walton Street, Oxford OX2 6DP England. **Tel** 011 44 865 56767, FAX 011 44 865 267773, telex 837330 OXPRES G. **(Subscription address:** Oxford University Press / USA, Journals Marketing Department, Oxford University Press, 2001 Evans Road, Cary NC 27513.**)** **[CCC].**

US/0160-2527
INTERNATIONAL JOURNAL OF LAW AND PSYCHIATRY. [Int. j. law psych.]. Vol. 1 (Feb. 1978)-. Periodical. English. qt. $351.00 The Americas; £235.00 other. Pergamon Press, An Imprint of Elsevier Science Ltd., The Boulevard, Langford Lane, Kidlington, Oxford OX5 1GB United Kingdom. **Tel** 011 44 865 843000, 011 44 865 843699, FAX 011 44 865 843010. **(Subscription address:** Elsevier Science Ltd. Oxford Fulfillment Centre, PO Box 800, Kidlington, Oxford OX5 1DX United Kingdom.**)** **ED** David N. Weisstub. **LC** K9; .N847. **DD** 614/.19. **NLM** W1 IN769L. **[CCC].** **Pr Rev.** available on microfilm and microfiche from University Microfilms International (UMI). Documents available from The Genuine Article.
Ind/Abst Commun. Abstr.; Crim. Justice Abstr.; Crim. Penol. Police Sci. Abstr.; Curr. Contents Soc. Behav. Sci.; Curr. Law Index (1980-); EMBASE; Index Med.; Index Leg. Period.; Leg. Resour. Index (1980-); LegalTrac (1980-); Psychol. Abstr. (1978-); PsycINFO; PsycLit; Res. Alert [Full Cov.]; Soc. Plann. Policy Dev. Abstr.; Soc. Sci. Cit. Index [Full Cov.]; Sociol. Abstr.

US/0731-1265
INTERNATIONAL JOURNAL OF LEGAL INFORMATION. **See** Library and Information Sciences.

●UK/0969-5958
INTERNATIONAL JOURNAL OF THE LEGAL PROFESSION. Vol. 1 (1994)-. English. Three times a year. £118.00. Carfax Publishing Company, PO Box 25 Abingdon, Oxfordshire OX14 3UE England. **Tel** 011 44 235 555335, FAX (0279)31067, telex 817484. **(Subscription address:** US and Canada/ PO Box 2025, Dunnellon, FL 34430-2025; telephone:(904)489-6996**)** **ED** Avrom Sherr. available on microfiche.
Desc: Addresses the organization, structure, management and infrastructure of the legal professions of the common law and civil law world.

UK/0194-6595
INTERNATIONAL JOURNAL OF THE SOCIOLOGY OF LAW. [Int. j. sociol. law]. Vol. 7, No. 1 (Feb. 1979)-. Academic Scholarly Publication. English. qt (4 issues). $180.00. Academic Press Ltd., A Division of Harcourt Brace & Company Ltd., 24-28 Oval Road, London NW1 7DX England. **Tel** 071 267 4466, FAX 071 482 2293, 071 485 4752, telex 25775 ACPRES G. **(Subscription address:** Harcourt Brace & Company, Ltd., Foots Cray, High Street, Sidcup Kent DA14 5HP England.**)** **ED** C. Smart and S. Picciotto. **LC** K9; .N844. **DD** 340/.115/05. **[CCC].** **Bk Rev.** Documents available from The Genuine Article. ***Continues*** *International Journal of Criminology and Penology, 0306-3208.*
Desc: Adopts a critical stance toward the sociology of crime and law. Contributors from disciplines such as criminology, jurisprudence, sociology, history, and anthropology debate both issues of long-term theoretical importance and matters of more immediate political and social concern.
Ind/Abst Appl. Soc. Sci. Index Abstr. (1982, 1984, 1985-); Crim. Justice Abstr.; Crim. Justice Period. Index; Crim. Penol. Police Sci. Abstr.; Curr. Contents Soc. Behav. Sci.; Curr. Law Index (1980-); Int. Bibliogr. Sociol.; Leg. Resour. Index (1980-); LegalTrac (1980-); Psychol. Abstr. (1979-); PsycINFO; PsycLit; Res. Alert [Full Cov.]; Soc. Plann. Policy Dev. Abstr.; Soc. Sci. Cit. Index [Full Cov.]; Soc. Sci. Index; Sociol. Abstr. [Full Cov.].

US
INTERNATIONAL LAW FIRM MANAGEMENT. (19??)-. Periodical. English. bm. $450.00. Euromoney Publications PLC, Nestor House, Playhouse Yard, London EC4Z 5EX England. **Tel** 011 44 71 779 8888, FAX 011 44 71 779 8617, telex 290700 EUROMON G. **(Subscription address:** Euromoney Publications Plc. Perrymount Road Haywards Heath, West Sussex RH16 3DH England.**)**

UK
INTERNATIONAL LEGAL BOOKS IN PRINT. (1990)-. English. ir (2 volume set). $375.00. Bowker Saur Ltd., A Reed Reference Publishing Company, Part of Reed International PLC, 59-60 Grosvenor Street, London WIX 9DA England. **Tel** 011 44 71 4935841, FAX 011 44 71 4991590.
Desc: This comprehensive subject and title index of 20,000 major treatises is indispensable for research or acquisitions in the international law field.

US/1072-7795
INTERNATIONAL LEGAL STRATEGY : ILS. **VFOAT** ILS; Gekkan Kokusai Homu Senryaku. (199?)-. English. mo. $370.00. Journal Interworld, 1411 West 190th Street, Suite 355, Gardena CA 90248. **Tel** (310)323-8420. **ED** Kirk Sasaki. **Circ:** 3,000.

NE/0920-315X
INTERNATIONAL TAX ADVISOR, THE. ***Ceased.*** **VFOAT** ITA. Vol. 1, No. 1 (Aug. 1986)-Ceased (1990). Periodical. English. Six times a year. Kluwer Law and Taxation Publishers, Staverenstraat 32015, PO Box 23, 7400 GA Deventer Netherlands. **Tel** 011 31 5700 47261. **ED** T Goldsworth. **Bk Rev.** **Circ:** 500.
Desc: Covers developments and news in the taxation law area.

NE
INTERNATIONAL TRANSFER PRICING JOURNAL, THE. (19??)-. Periodical. English. tq. $260.00. International Bureau of Fiscal Documentation - IBFD Publications, PO Box 20237, 1000 HE Amsterdam The Netherlands. **Tel** 011 31 20-6267726, FAX 011 31 20-6228658, telex 13217 INTAX NL. **(Subscription address:** IBFD / International Bureau of Fiscal Documentation USA, Inc., 24 Hudson Street, Kinderhook NY 12106.**)**

●UK/0965-528X
INTERNATIONAL YEARBOOK OF LAW, COMPUTERS, AND TECHNOLOGY. **VFOAT** International Yearbook of Law, Computers & Technology. Vol. 6 (1992)-. Periodical. English. an. $198.00. Carfax Publishing Company, PO Box 25 Abingdon, Oxfordshire OX14 3UE England. **Tel** 011 44 235 555335, FAX (0279)31067, telex 817484. **[CCC].** ***Continues*** *Yearbook of Law, Computers, and Technology, 0269-3712.*

UK/0965-528X
INTERNATIONAL YEARBOOK OF LAW, COMPUTERS AND TECHNOLOGY. **See** Science and Technology.

US
INTERPRETER RELEASES. **Main/Corp** American Council for Nationalities Service. Vol. 36, No. 21 (June 1959)-. Periodical. English. Forty-eight times a year. $395.00 government agencies, public libraries, educational institutions & nonprofit organizations. Federal Publications Inc, 1120 20th Street Northwest, Washington DC 20036. **Tel** (202)337-7000, (800)922-4330, FAX (202)659-2233. **ED** Maurice Roberts. **Circ:** 2,100. available on CD-ROM. ***Continues*** *Common Council for American Unity. Interpreter Releases.*
Desc: A publication on immigration, naturalization and related matters. Indispensable for immigration lawyers and practitioners in the field.

US/0884-8394
INTERSTATE INFORMATION REPORT. (INTERSTATE INFORMATION REPORT / ATA.). [Interstate inf. rep.]. **Added/Corp** American Trucking Associations. Dept. of State Laws, Taxation, and Reciprocity. American Trucking Associations. Dept. of Interstate Cooperation. (19??)-. Periodical. English. mo. $60.00. American Trucking Association, 2200 Mill Road, Alexandria VA 22314. **Tel** (703)838-1772. **ED** Jan Balkin. **DD** 388. Index available. **Circ:** 1,800 (ctrl).
Desc: Digest of state legislation, regulatory activities and court cases which affect motor carriers in the trucking industry today.

AG
INVESTIGACION Y DOCENCIA / UNIVERSIDAD NACIONAL DE ROSARIO, FACULTAD DE DERECHO, CONSEJO ASESOR DE INVESTIGACIONES, CENTRO DE INVESTIGACIONES DE FILOSOFIA JURIDICA Y FILOSOFIA SOCIAL. **Added/Corp** Universidad Nacional de Rosario. Centro de Investigaciones de Filosofia Juridica y Filosofia Social. (19??)-. Periodical. Spanish. **LC** K9; .N94.
Ind/Abst Am. Hist. Life (1966).

●US/1075-4512
INVESTMENT LAWYER, THE. [Invest. lawyer]. Vol. 1, No. 1 (Apr. 1994)-. Periodical. English. Twelve times a year. $265.82. Prentice-Hall Law and Business, 270 Sylvan Avenue, Englewood Cliffs NJ 07632. **Tel** (800)223-0231, (201)894-8538, FAX (201)894-8666. **DD** 343.

US
IOMA'S MONTHLY REPORT ON PROPERTY CASUALTY RATES AND RATINGS. (19??)-. Periodical. English. mo. $195.00. Institute of Management and Administration, 29 West 35th Street, 5th Floor, New York NY 10001-2299. **Tel** (212)244-0360.

●US/1060-5924
IOMA'S REPORT ON CONTROLLING LAW FIRM COSTS. [IOMA's rep. control. law firm costs]. **Added/Corp** Institute of Management & Administration. **VFOAT** Report on Controlling Law Firm Costs. **VAT** Institute of Management & Administration's Report on Controlling Law Firm Costs. (1992)-. Periodical. English. mo. $175.00. Institute of Management and Administration, 29 West 35th Street, 5th Floor, New York NY 10001-2299. **Tel** (212)244-0360. **DD** 658. **[CCC].**

●US/1074-3898
IOMA'S REPORT ON MANAGING LITIGATION COSTS. **Added/Corp** Institute of Management and Administration. (1994)-. Periodical. English. mo. $275.00. Institute of Management and Administration, 29 West 35th Street, 5th Floor, New York NY 10001-2299. **Tel** (212)244-0360.

US
IOWA ADMINISTRATIVE BULLETIN. **Added/Corp** Iowa. Vol. 1 (June 14, 1978)-. English. bw. $221.00. Iowa State Printing Division, Grimes Building, Des Moines IA 50319. **Tel** (515)281-8789. **LC** KFI4236; .I68. **DD** 342.777/066.

US/0578-6533
IOWA ADVOCATE. English. sa. University of Iowa College of Law, Boyd Law Building Room 190, Iowa City IA 52242. **Tel** (319)335-9061, FAX (319)335-9019. **LC** KF292.I614; Z63. **DD** 340/.05.

US
IOWA CIVIL RIGHTS COMMISSION, CASE REPORTS. **See** Political Science-Civil Rights.

US/0360-7526
IOWA ELECTION HANDBOOK WITH ELECTION LAWS OF IOWA. **Main/Corp** Iowa. English. an. Box 1168, Cedar Rapids IA 52406. **LC** KFI4620.A29; I68. **DD** 342/.777/0702632.

US/0021-0552
IOWA LAW REVIEW. [Iowa law rev.]. **Added/Corp** University of Iowa. College of Law. Iowa State Bar Association. Proceedings. Vol. 11, No. 1 (Dec. 1925)-. Periodical. English. Five times a year (Jan., Mar., May, July, Oct.). $33.00. The University of Iowa, College of Law, 188 Boyd Law Building, Iowa City IA 52242-1113. **Tel** (319)335-9132 (319)335-9132, FAX (319)335-9054. **LC** K9; .O88. **DD** 349.777/05; 347.77005. Index available. cum. index. **Ad Acc.** **Pr Rev.** **Circ:** 2,200. Documents available from The Genuine Article. ***Continues*** *Iowa Law Bulletin.* ***Continued in part by***

Iowa Bar Review.
Ind/Abst Bowne Dig. Corp. Sec. Lawyers; Commun. Abstr. (?-?); Crim. Justice Abstr.; Crim. Penol. Police Sci. Abstr. (1980-); Curr. Contents Soc. Behav. Sci.; Curr. Law Index (1980-); Fed. Tax Artic.; Index Leg. Period.; Leg. Resour. Index (1980-); LegalTrac (1980-); PAIS Int. Print (1991-); Res. Alert [Full Cov.]; Soc. Sci. Cit. Index [Full Cov.].

US/1052-5327
IOWA LAWYER. [Iowa lawyer]. **Added/Corp** Iowa State Bar Association. Vol. 50, No. 8 (Aug. 1990)-. Periodical. English. mo. $5.00. Iowa State Bar Association, 521 East Locust, Des Moines IA 50309. **Tel** (515)243-3179. **LC** K9; .O86. **DD** 349.777/05; 347.77005. ***Continues*** *News Bulletin of the Iowa State Bar Association, 1043-0482.*

US
IOWA LAWYERS DIARY AND MANUAL. English. Lawyers Diary and Manual, 240 Mulberry Street, Newark NJ 07101. **LC** KF192.I55; I557. **DD** 340/.025/777.

US/0730-2479
IOWA LEGISLATIVE SERVICE. English. West Publishing Company, 610 Opperman Drive, PO Box 64526, Eagan MN 55123-1308. **Tel** (612)687-5618, (800)328-9352, FAX (612)687-5388, (800)562-2329. **(Subscription telephone:** FAX (612)688-3570**) LC** KFI4231. **DD** 348.777/022/05; 347.77082205.

IT/0029-6368
IP NUOVO DIRITTO. [Nuovo diritto]. (1939)-. Periodical. Italian. Nine times a year. L90000 Italy; L130000 other. Rassegna Giuridica Pratica, CP 11 171, 00141 Rome Italy. **Tel** 011 39 6 318345. **UDC** 34. ***Continues*** *La Pretura, 0393-9669.*

US/1059-1729
IR & R NEWS REPORT / SECTION OF INDIVIDUAL RIGHTS AND RESPONSIBILITIES. [IR R news rep.]. **Added/Corp** American Bar Association. Section of Individual Rights and Responsibilities. **VFOAT** IR&R News Report; IR and R News Report; Individual Rights and Responsibilities News Report. Vol. 1, No. 1 (Jan. 1990)-. English. sa (2 issues). $4.00. American Bar Association, 750 North Lake Shore Drive, Chicago IL 60611. **Tel** (312)988-5522, (312)988-5241, FAX (312)988-5528, telex 270593. **LC** KF4742; .I73. **DD** 342.73/085/05; 347.3028505.

●IE/0791-5403
IRISH JOURNAL OF EUROPEAN LAW. **Added/Corp** Irish Society for European Law. **VFOAT** European Law. Vol. 1, No. 1 & 2 (1992)-. English. Round Hall Press, Kill Lane, Blackrock County, Dublin Ireland. **Tel** 011 353 1 2892922, FAX 011 353 1 2893072. **ED** $95.00; 85.00p. **LC** K9; .R55. **DD** 349.4/05; 344.05. ***Continues*** *Journal of the Irish Society for European Law, 0332-4753.*

IE/0021-1273
IRISH JURIST, THE. [Ir. jurist]. New Ser. V. 1, Pt. 1 (Summer 1966)-. Periodical. English. sa. $55.00; 35.00p. Irish Jurist, University College, Dublin 2 Ireland. **ED** W N Osborough. **Bk Rev. Ad Acc. Circ:** 800. ***Continues*** *Irish Jurist, Together with Irish Jurist Reports.*
Desc: Modern Irish law explained and analysed by academic writers, laws of other countries similarly examined where relevant, legal history including Roman Law and Common Law but with a special emphasis on the history of law in Ireland.
Ind/Abst Index Leg. Period.; Leg. Resour. Index; LegalTrac (1990-).

IE/0021-1281
IRISH LAW TIMES AND SOLICITORS' JOURNAL, THE. [Ir. law times solicit. j.]. **VFOAT** Irish Law Times. No. 1 (Feb. 2, 1867)-. Periodical. English. mo. $245.00; 150.00p. Round Hall Press, Kill Lane, Blackrock County, Dublin Ireland. **Tel** 011 353 1 2892922, FAX 011 353 1 2893072. **DD** 349.415/05; 344.15005.

IE
IRISH REPORTS. (19??)-. English. sa. Incorporated Council of Law Reports, Law Library/Four Courts, Dublin 7 Ireland.

US/0148-1940
IRS LETTER RULINGS. **See** Public Administration-Public Finance and Taxation.

UK
IS IT IN FORCE? ... : A GUIDE TO THE COMMENCEMENT OF STATUTES PASSED SINCE ... / PREPARED BY BUTTERWORTHS EDITORIAL STAFF. **Added/Corp** Butterworths (Firm) Great Britain. Laws, Etc. (Halsbury). (19??)-. English. an. £62.00. Butterworth & Co. Ltd. / Kent, England, Borough Green, Sevenoaks Kent TN15 8PH England. **Tel** 011 44 732-884567, FAX 011 44 732-885996. **(Subscription address:** D & S Publishers, 2030 Calumet Street, Clearwater FL 34625.**) LC** KD142.6; .I8. **DD** 348.41/022; 344.10822.
Desc: Concise guide to the exact commencement dates of Acts of general application in England and Wales and General Synod Measures passed over the last quarter century.

CN/0827-441X
ISAAC PITBLADO LECTURES ... . (ISAAC PITBLADO LECTURES ... / UNDER THE JOINT SPONSORSHIP OF THE MANITOBA BAR ASSOCIATION, THE FACULTY OF LAW, UNIVERSITY OF MANITOBA [AND] THE LAW SOCIETY OF MANITOBA.). [Isaac Pitblado lect. ...]. **Added/Corp** Manitoba Bar Association. University of Manitoba. Faculty of Law. Law Society of Manitoba. **VFOAT** Isaac Pitblado Lectures. (1983)-. Monographic series. English. ir. Price varies per volume. Law Society of Manitoba, 101-219 Kennedy Street, Suite 201, Winnepeg Manitoba R3C 1S8 Canada. **Tel** (204)942-5571. **DD** 349.71/05. ***Continues*** *Isaac Pitblado Lectures on Continuing Legal Education, 0578-7726.*

US/1055-8705
ISBA NEWS. ***Title Change.*** [ISBA news]. **Added/Corp** Illinois State Bar Association. **VFOAT** News. **VAT** Illinois State Bar Association News. Vol. 31, No. 12 (Dec. 17, 1990)-(199?). English. sm. Illinois State Bar Association, 424 South Second, Springfield IL 62701. **Tel** (217)525-1760, FAX (217)525-0712. **LC** KF200; .I4. **DD** 340/.06/0773. ***Continues*** *Bar News, 0445-4200.* ***Continued by*** *ISBA Bar News, 1058-1863.*

●II
ISLAMIC AND COMPARATIVE LAW REVIEW. **Added/Corp** Jamia Hamdard. Dept. of Law. **VFOAT** Islamic & Comparative Law Review. Vol. 12, No. 1 (Summer 1992)-. Periodical. English. sa. $30.00. Jamia Hamdard, Department of Law, New Delhi, India. **(Subscription address:** Prints India, 11 Darya Ganj, New Delhi 110002 India.**) LC** K9; .S58. ***Continues*** *Islamic and Comparative Law Quarterly.*

IS/0021-2237
ISRAEL LAW REVIEW. [Isr. law rev.]. **Added/Corp** Hevrat Ketav Ha-et Ha-Yisreeli Le-mishpat. Universitah Ha-Ivrit Bi-Yerushalayim. Fakultah Le-mishpatim. Vol. 1- (Jan. 1966)-. Periodical. English. qt. $36.00 (add $10.00 for airmail postage) US. Hebrew University of Jerusalem / Faculty of Law, Mt Scopus POB 24100, Jerusalem 91240 Israel. **Tel** (02)882520, FAX (02)823042. Index available (published separately). **Bk Rev**, (Qty: 4-8). **Ad Acc. Circ:** 1,200. available on microfilm.
Desc: Contains articles on Jewish, international and comparative law, translations of case decisions and newly enacted laws.
Ind/Abst Index Foreign Leg. Per.; Int. Bibliogr. Sociol.; Int. Polit. Sci. Abstr.; Soc. Plann. Policy Dev. Abstr.; Sociol. Abstr.

US/8756-8160
ISSUES IN LAW & MEDICINE. [Issues law med.]. **Added/Corp** National Legal Center for the Medically Dependent & Disabled (U.S.) Horatio R. Storer Foundation. **VFOAT** Issues in Law and Medicine. Vol. 1, No. 1 (July 1985)-. Periodical. English. qt. $69.00 (one year), $120.00 (two year) US; $79.00(one year), $140.00 (two year) other. Issues in Law and Medicine, PO Box 1586, Terre Haute IN 47808. **Tel** (812)232-0103, FAX (812)232-0103. **ED** Barry Bostrom. **LC** KF480.A15; I87. **DD** 342.73/087; 347.30287. **NLM** W1; IS668T. **CODEN** ILAME3. **Bk Rev**, (Qty: 15-20). **Pr Rev. Acid Free. Circ:** 5,000 (ctrl). available on an online database (file 149/Full-Text) from DIALOG; WESTLAW; MEDLINE; and INFO ACCESS. Documents available from The Genuine Article, BIOSIS Document Express.
Desc: Focuses on medical and legal issues pertaining to medical treatment for the handicapped and disabled.
Ind/Abst Arts Humanit. Citation Index [Select. Cov.]; Biol. Abstr.; Crim. Justice Abstr.; Curr. Contents Soc. Behav. Sci.; Curr. Law Index; Except. Child Educ. Resour.; Health Index (1989-); Health Period. Database [Full Txt.]; Health Plan. Adminis.; Health Ref. Cent. (1987-) [Full Txt.] [Select. Cov.]; Hospit. Health Admin. Index; Index Med.; Index Leg. Period.; Int. Nurs. Index (July 1985-); Leg. Resour. Index (1985-); LegalTrac (1980-); PsycINFO; Res. Alert [Full Cov.]; Soc. Sci. Cit. Index [Full Cov.].

●UK
IT LAW TODAY. (Jan. 1993)-. Periodical. English. mo. Monitor Press, Rectory Road, Great Waldingfield, Sudbury Suffolk CO10 0TL United Kingdom. **Tel** 011 44 787 378607. ***Continues*** *Applied Computer and Communications Law, 0267-6621.*

●NE/0927-0523
ITALIAN STUDIES IN LAW : A REVIEW OF LEGAL PROBLEMS / EDITED BY THE ITALIAN ASSOCIATION OF COMPARATIVE LAW. **Added/Corp** Associazione Italiana di Diritto Comparato. Vol. 1 (1992)-. English (translations available in Italian). ir. $94.00. Martinus Nijhoff Publishers, Subsidiary of Kluwer Academic Publishers, Koraalrood 50, 2718 SC Zoetermeer Netherlands. **Tel** 011 31 79 684400. **(Subscription address:** Kluwer Academic Publishers, PO Box 253 Accord Station, Hingham, MA 02018, telephone: (617)871-6600**) LC** K9; .T3. **DD** 349.45/05; 344.505.

US/0198-7232
IT'S YOUR BUSINESS (ROCKVILLE CENTER). (IT'S YOUR BUSINESS.). **Added/Corp** Farnsworth Publishing Co. (19??)-. Periodical. English. ir. Farnsworth Publishing Company, 500 North Dearborn Street, Chicago IL 60610-4901. **Tel** (516)536-8400. **LC** KF6296.A15; I8. **DD** 343.7304/05.

UY
IUDAU. **Main/Corp** Instituto Uruguayo de Derecho de Arrendamientos Urbanos. **VFOAT** Revista del IUDAU. Began in 1975. Periodical. Spanish. an. Ediciones Juridicas Amalio, M Fernandez, 25 de Mayo 477, Planta Baja Oficina 11, Montevideo Uruguay. **Tel** 95-17-82. **ED** Juan Jacobo. **LC** K9; .N7467. **DD** 346/.895/04342. **Bk Rev**.
Desc: Contains doctrine and jurisprudence of urban leasings.

SP/0021-325X
IUS CANONICUM. **Added/Corp** Universidad de Navarra. Facultad de Derecho Canonico. Instituto Martin de Azpilcueta. Vol. 1 (Jan./June 1961)-. Periodical. Spanish (French, Italian, English and German). sa (Jan. and Jul.). $72.00 US. Servicio de Publicaciones de la Universidad de Navarra SA, Edificio Muga, Campus Universitario, 31008 Pamplona Spain. **Tel** 011 34 48 282700 ext. 2887. **ED** D. Tomas Rincon. **LC** K10; .U76. Index available (free). **Bk Rev. Ad Acc. Circ:** 1,000.
Desc: Contains scientific articles about Canon and ecclesiastic law, comments to sentences in the ecclesiastic tribunals and legal dispositions, etc.
Ind/Abst Bibliogr. Mission.; Canon Law Abstr.

GW
IUS COMMUNE. (19??)-. Monographic series. German. ir. Price varies per volume. Vittorio Klostermann, Frauenlobstrasse 22, D 60487 Frankfurt Germany. **Tel** 011 49 69 9708160. cum. index. **Ad Acc.**

GW
IUS COMMUNE. SONDERHEFTE. TEXTE UND MONOGRAPHIEN. Vol. 1 (1971)-. Monographic series. German. ir. Price varies per volume. Vittorio Klostermann, Frauenlobstrasse 22, D 60487 Frankfurt Germany. **Tel** 011 49 69 9708160.

IT
IUS ECCLESIAE : RIVISTA INTERNAZIONALE DI DIRITTO CANONICO. **Added/Corp** Centro Accademico Romano della Santa Croce. Vol. 1, No. 1 (1989)-. Italian (English, French, Latin and Spanish). sa. L100000.00 Italy; L140000.00 Europe; L170000.00 other. Giuffre Editore SPA, Via Busto Arsizio 40, 20151 Milan Italy. **Tel** 011 398 2 38089200. **ED** Juan Ignacio Arrieta. **LC** K9; .U7. **DD** 262.9/05.
Desc: The canon law review of the Roman Atheneum of the Holy Cross. Aims to contribute to scientific reflection on the juridical experience of the Church.

IT/0092-3524
IUSTITIA (BLOOMINGTON). (IUSTITIA.). [Iustitia]. **Added/Corp** Indiana University. School of Law. Indiana University, Bloomington. School of Law. Vol. 1 (April 1973)-. Periodical. English. qt. L60000.00 Italy; L90000.00 other. Giuffre Editore SPA, Via Busto Arsizio 40, 20151 Milan Italy. **Tel** 011 398 2 38089200. **ED** Sergio Cotta. **LC** K9; .U8. **DD** 340.1/15. Index available. **Bk Rev. Ad Acc. Circ:** 1,300.
Desc: Edited by the Union of Italian Catholic Jurists.
Ind/Abst Public Aff. Inf. Serv. Bull.

IT/0021-3241
IVRA. (IVRA; RIVISTA INTERNAZIONALE DI DIRITTO ROMANO E ANTICO.). **Added/Corp** Catania. Universita. Istituto di Diritto Romano. Palermo. Universita. Istituto di Diritto Romano. Italy. Consiglio Nazionale delle Ricerche. (1950)-. Periodical. Italian. ir. Casa Editrice Jovene, 109 Via Mezzocannone, 80134 Naples Italy. **Tel** 011 39 81 552-1274.
Desc: Covers Roman and ancient law.
Ind/Abst Index Foreign Leg. Per.

BU
IZVESTIIA NA INSTITUTA ZA PRAVNI NAUKI. **Main/Corp** Bulgarska Akademiia na Naukite, Sofia. Institut za Pravni Nauki. **VFOAT** Bulletin of the Institute of Law. (1954)-. Periodical. Bulgarian (summaries and/or abstracts in French and Russian). Izdatelstvo na Bulgarskata Akademiia Na Naukite, 6 Rouski Boulevard, Sofia Bulgaria. **Tel** FAX 80 13 41, telex 22267 HEMKIK. ***Supersedes in part*** *Izvestiia na Ikonomicheskiia i Pravniia Institut.*
Ind/Abst Index Foreign Leg. Per.

RU/0131-8039
IZVESTIIA VYSSHIKH UCHEBNYKH ZAVEDENII. PRAVOVEDENIE. **Added/Corp** Soviet Union. Ministerstvo Vysshego Obrazovaniia. Soviet Union. Ministerstvo Vysshego i Srednego Spetsialnogo Obrazovaniia. **VFOAT** Izvestiia Vuzov. Pravovedenie; Pravovedenie. (July 1957)-. Periodical. Russian (summaries and/or abstracts in English; table of contents in English, French, German and Spanish). bm. $85.00. St Petersburg State University / Izdatelstvo Leningradskogo Universiteta, Universitetskaia Nab 7/9,

199034 St Petersburg Russia. **Tel** 011 95 218-97-88, FAX 011 95 218-51-52, telex 121481. **(Subscription address:** Victor Kamkin, 4956 Boiling Brook Parkway, Rockville MD 20852.**)**
Ind/Abst Index Foreign Leg. Per.

UK/0264-3723
J.P. WEEKLY LAW DIGEST, THE.
Added/Corp Justice of the Peace Ltd. **VAT** Justice of the Peace Weekly Law Digest. (19??)-. English. wk. £35.20 UK; £38.20 other. Justice of the Peace Limited, Little London, Chichester West Sussex, PO19 1PG England. **Tel** 011 44 243 787841, FAX 011 44 243 779278. **LC** KD296; .J16. **DD** 348/.41/046. Index available. **Ad Acc.** ***Continues*** *Supplement ... to the Justice of the Peace and Local Government Review.*
Desc: Digest of cases decided, sentencing in the Magistrates' Court and the Crown Court, Parliamentary Intelligence, bills before Parliament and statutory instruments.

SA
JAARVERSLAG VAN DIE SUID-AFRIKAANSE REGSKOMMISSIE.
Main/Corp South Africa. Law Commission. **VFOAT** Annual Report of the South African Law Commission. 1974-. Multiple languages (Afrikaans and English). 1.40. The Government Printer, Bosman Street, Private Bag X85, Pretoria 0001 South Africa. **Tel** 012-323-9731, FAX 012-323-0009. **DD** 340/.3/0968.

II
JABALPUR LAW JOURNAL, THE.
Periodical. English. mo. Rs145.00. Law Journal Publications, Jayendraganj, Gwalior 1 India. **Tel** (0751)22340. **ED** Lokendra Gupta and Ashutosh Dvivedi. Index available. cum. index. **Circ:** 3,000.
Desc: Full text of decisions by high court of Madhya Pradesh and supreme court.

II
JABALPUR LEGAL QUARTERLY. VFOAT JLQ; J.L.Q.; J L Q. Vol. 1, No. 1 (Oct./Dec. 1980-). Periodical. English. qt. N C Beohar, 24 Bharat Society, Nagpur Road, Jabalput-1 India. **LC** K10; .A32. **DD** 349.54/05; 345.4005.

GW
JAHRBUCH DES SOZIALRECHTS DER GEGENWART. V. 1 (1979)-. German. an. Erich Schmidt Verlag GmbH, Postfach 304240, D 10724 Berlin Germany. **Tel** 011 49 30 25008525. **LC** KK3270.5.A63; J33. **DD** 344.43; 344.304. ***Continues*** *Sozialordnung der Gegenwart.*

GW
JAHRBUCH FUER AFRIKANISCHES RECHT. VFOAT Annuaire de Droit Africain; Yearbook of African Law. Vol. 1 (1980)-. English (French and German). an. C F Muller Juristischer Verlag GmbH, Heidelberg Germany. **DD** 349.6; 346.
Ind/Abst Index Foreign Leg. Per.

GW
JAHRBUCH FUER RECHTSSOZIOLOGIE & RECHTSTHEORIE. Westdeutscher Verlag GmbH, Postfach 5829, D 65048 Wiesbaden Germany. **Tel** 011 49 611 160220.

GW/0075-2886
JAHRESFACHKATALOG: RECHT, WIRTSCHAFT, STEUERN. (19??)-. German (English). an. DM45.11 Germany; DM48.50 others. Buchwerbung In Berlin GmbH, Luetzowstrasse 105 106, D 10785 Berlin Germany. **Tel** 011 49 30 2619257, 011 49 30 2614933. **Ad Acc. Circ:** 9,000.
Desc: Bibliography of new or recent publications corresponding the themes law, economics and tax.

JA
JAPAN LAW JOURNAL, THE. Added/Corp Survey Japan (Tokyo, Japan). Vol. 1 No. 1 (1987)-. Periodical. English. Six times a year. $100.00. **(Subscription address:** Japan Publications Trading Company, Ltd., PO Box 5030, Tokyo International, Tokyo 100-31 Japan.**) LC** K10; .A38. **DD** 349.52/05; 345.2005.

US/0747-9093
JD/MBA QUARTERLY. ***Ceased.*** [JD/MBA q.]. **VFOAT** J.D./M.B.A. Quarterly; JD, MBA Quarterly. Vol. 1, No. 1 (Winter 1984)-Ceased ?. Periodical. English. qt. National Association of JD/MBA Professionals, 2415 South 9th Street, Arlington VA 22204. **LC** KF299.J35; J35. **DD** 340/.023/73.

US/0272-0922
JD (WASHINGTON). (JD.). [JD]. **Added/Corp** General Conference of Seventh-Day Adventists. Office of the General Counsel. (1978)-. Periodical. English. an. Office of General Counsel, General Conference of Seventh-Day Adventists, 6940 Carroll Avenue, Takoma Park MD 20912. **LC** KF200; .J17. **DD** 347.30285205.
Desc: This include the directory of Seventh-Day Adventist attorneys.
Ind/Abst Seventh-Day Adventist Period. Index (19??-).

US/0092-170X
JEALOUS MISTRESS, THE. V. 1- July 1973-. English. $20.00. PO Box 487, Grapevine TX 76051. **LC** KF133; .J4. **DD** 348.73405.

US
JEFFERSON COUNTY LEGAL JOURNAL. (19??)-. Newspaper. English. Fifty-two times a year (Thurs.). $35.00 (one year). Jefferson County Bar Association, Room 204 Court House, Brookville PA 15825. **Tel** (814)849-8316. **ED** Heidi Ulrich Dennison (editor's address: 316 Main Street, Brookville PA 15825-1222; phone: (814)849-1237). **Ad Acc.**

US/0276-1432
JEWISH JURISPRUDENCE. [Jewish jurisprud.]. Vol. 1 (1980)-. Monographic series. English. ir. Price varies per volume. Harwood Academic Publishers / New York, PO Box 786, Cooper Station, New York NY 10276. **Tel** (212)206-8900, (201)643-7500. **ED** E. B. Quint and N. S. Hecht. **DD** 296.

NE/0169-8354
JEWISH LAW ANNUAL, THE. [Jew. law annu.]. **Added/Corp** International Association of Jewish Lawyers and Jurists. Oxford Centre for Postgraduate Hebrew Studies. Boston University. Institute of Jewish Law. Vol. 1, (1978)-. English. an. F65.00. Harwood Academic Publishers / New York, PO Box 786, Cooper Station, New York NY 10276. **Tel** (212)206-8900, (201)643-7500. **(Subscription address:** International Publishers Distributor at one of the following addresses: 820 Town Center Drive, Langhorne, PA 19047; or PO Box 90, Reading Berkshire RG1 8JL UK; or Kent Ridge PO Box 1180, Singapore 9111, Republic of Singapore**) ED** B. S. Jackson. **LC** K10; .E74. **DD** 296.1/8.
Desc: Reflects the place of Jewish law among the legal systems of the world. Includes historical, comparative and jurisprudential analyses, and conflict of law problems involving Jewish law.
Ind/Abst Old Testam. Abstr.

JA/0441-4225
JINBUN RONSHU / WASEDA DAIGAKU HOGAKKAI. Added/Corp Waseda Daigaku. Hogakkai. (1963)-. Japanese (Spanish, Russian, Chinese, English, German and French). Waseda Daigaku Hogakubu, c/o Waseda Daigaku, Shinjuku-ku Tokyo-to Japan. **Tel** 03-203-4141. **ED** Caseda Daigaku Hoakkai. **LC** AS552.W37; A26. Index available. **Circ:** 1,500 (ctrl).
Desc: Offers the full-time members of the Law School faculty specializing in the field of humanities an opportunity to publish the results of their researches. Copies of each issue distributed to the students and faculty members of the School of Law.

HU
JOGTUDOMANYI KOZLONY. Added/Corp Magyar Tudomanyos Akademia. Allam-es Jogtudomanyi Intezet. (1860)-. Periodical. Hungarian (summaries and/or abstracts in German, English and Russian). Twelve times a year. $65.00. Lapkiado Vallalat, Lenin Korut 9-11, 1073 Budapest 7, Hungary. **Tel** 222-408. **(Subscription address:** Kultura, PO Box 149, H 1389 Budapest 62 Hungary**) ED** Jozsef Halasz and Imre Voros.
Desc: Contains articles of all branches of the law and questions of state.
Ind/Abst Index Foreign Leg. Per.; Int. Bibliogr. Sociol.; Int. Polit. Sci. Abstr.

●US
JOHN MARSHALL JOURNAL OF COMPUTER & INFORMATION LAW, THE. Added/Corp John Marshall Law School (Chicago, Ill.) Center for Computer/Law. **VFOAT** John Marshall Journal of Computer and Information Law. Vol. 12, No. 3 (Oct. 1993)-. Periodical. English. qt. $97.50. John Marshall Law School / Illinois, 315 South Plymouth Court, Chicago IL 60604. **Tel** (312)987-1415. **LC** K10; .O338. ***Formed by the union of*** *Computer/Law Journal, 0164-8756* ***and*** *Software Law Journal, 0886-3628.*

US/0147-3689
JOHN MARSHALL LAW JOURNAL.
Added/Corp John Marshall Law School (Atlanta, Ga.). (Spring 1977)-. English. John Marshall Law School / Georgia, 105 Forest Avenue NE, Atlanta GA 30308. **LC** K10; .O35. **DD** 340/.05.

US/0270-854X
JOHN MARSHALL LAW REVIEW, THE.
Vol. 13, (Fall 1979)-. Periodical. English. Four times a year (Feb., May, Aug., Oct.). $18.00. John Marshall Law School / Illinois, 315 South Plymouth Court, Chicago IL 60604. **Tel** (312)987-1415. **LC** K10; .O34. **DD** 340/.05. **Bk Rev. Ad Acc. Circ:** 2,500 (ctrl). available on microfilm and microfiche from University Microfilms International (UMI). ***Continues*** *John Marshall Journal of Practice and Procedure.*
Desc: Articles, comments and casenotes on topics on the cutting edge of the law.
Ind/Abst Bowne Dig. Corp. Sec. Lawyers; Curr. Law Index (1980-); Fed. Tax Artic.; Highw. Res. Abstr.; Index Leg. Period.; Leg. Resour. Index (1980-); LegalTrac (1980-).

NE/0920-6280
JOURNAAL NV/BV. [J. NV/BV]. **VFOAT** Journaal Naamloze Vennootschappen/Besloten Vennootschappen. (1986)-. Periodical. Dutch. Three times a year. Fl106.15. Libresso BV, Postbus 878, 7400 GA Deventer Netherlands. **Tel** 011 31 5700 47421. **UDC** 347.72.

CN/0833-921X
JOURNAL BARREAU, LE. [J. Barreau]. Vol. 18, No. 9 (Sept. 1986)-. Periodical. French. sm. Free to members. Barreau du Quebec, 445 Boulevard St-Laurent, Montreal Quebec H2Y 3T8 Canada. **Tel** (514)954-3400, FAX (514)954-3478. **DD** 349.714/05. ***Continues*** *Le Journal du Barreau, 0833-921X.*

US/0730-4919
JOURNAL / CALIFORNIA TRIAL LAWYERS ASSOCIATION. [J. - Calif. Trial Lawyers Assoc.]. **Added/Corp** California Trial Lawyers Association. **VFOAT** CTLA Journal. (19??)-. Periodical. English. California Trial Lawyers Association, 1020 12th Street/4th Floor, Sacramento CA 95814. **LC** K3; .A436. **DD** 347.794/07/05; 347.9407705. ***Continues*** *California Trial Lawyers Journal, 0575-6316.*

BE
JOURNAL DE DROIT FISCAL. (19??)-. Periodical. French. bm (6 issues). 3300.00F. Etablissements Emile Bruylant, 67 rue de la Regence, 1000 Brussels Belgium. **Tel** 011 32 2 5129845. **LC** K10; .O8. **DD** 343/.493/0405. **Bk Rev. Ad Acc. Circ:** 1,000. ***Formed by the union of*** *Repertoire Fiscal; Journal Pratique de Droit Fiscal et Financier* ***and*** *Revue Fiscal.*
Desc: Covers legal doctrine and jurisprudence.

CN
JOURNAL DES DEBATS. INDEX.
Main/Corp Quebec (Province). Assemblee Nationale. 30. Legislature, 4. Session, (1976)-. French. ir. 10.00Can$. Assemblee Nationale Ministere Financiere, 5 Place Quebec Bureau 195, Quebec QUE G1R 5P3 Canada. **Tel** (418)643-2754. available on an online database. ***Continues*** *Quebec (Province). National Assembly. Journal des Debats. Index.*

BE
JOURNAL DES JUGES DE PAIX ET DE POLICE. Added/Corp Union Royale des Juges de Paix et de Police de Belgique. **VFOAT** Tijdschrift van de Vrede- en Politierechters; J.J.P.; T. Vred. (19??)-. Periodical. Dutch (French). mo. 4480.00F. S. A. Editions La Charte, Oude Gentweg 108, 8000 Bruges Belgium. **Tel** 050 33 12 35 - 4 lignee, FAX 050 34 34 68. **LC** KJK1583.A13; J68. Index available. cum. index. **Bk Rev.** ctrl circ. ***Continues*** *Journal de Juges des Paix, de Leur Suppleants, des Officiers du Ministere Public et des Greffiers.*

PH/0115-138X
JOURNAL - INTEGRATED BAR OF THE PHILIPPINES. [J. Integr. Bar Philipp.]. **Main/Corp** Integrated Bar of the Philippines. V. 1- June 1973-. Periodical. English. $6.00. Integrated Bar of the Phillippines, 955 Quezon Blvd. Extension, Quezon City Phillippines. **LC** K9; .N7475. **DD** 340/.09599.
Ind/Abst Hum. Rights Intern. Rep.; Index Philip. Period.

UK/0021-8553
JOURNAL OF AFRICAN LAW. [J. Afr. law]. **Added/Corp** University of London. School of Oriental and African Studies. (Spring 1957)-. Periodical. English. sa. £30.00 UK and Europe; $52.00 other. Oxford University Press, Walton Street, Oxford OX2 6DP England. **Tel** 011 44 865 56767, FAX 011 44 865 267773, telex 837330 OXPRES G. **(Subscription address:** Oxford University Press / USA, Journals Marketing Department, Oxford University Press, 2001 Evans Road, Cary NC 27513.**) ED** P. E. Slinn, S. Coldham and S. A. Poberts. **[CCC]**. Index available. cum. index. **Bk Rev. Ad Acc. Circ:** 700. available in microform.
Desc: Articles and book reviews on all aspects of law relating to Africa.
Ind/Abst Anthropol. Index; Curr. Law Index (1980-); Index Foreign Leg. Per.; Int. Bibliogr. Sociol.; Int. Polit. Sci. Abstr.; Leg. Resour. Index (1980-); LegalTrac (1980-); PAIS Int. Print (1991-?).

US/0745-9181
JOURNAL OF AGRICULTURAL TAXATION & LAW. ***Ceased.*** [J. agric. tax. law]. **VFOAT** Journal of Agricultural Taxation and Law. Vol. 5, No. 1 (Spring 1983)- Ceased with Vol. 14, No. 3 (1992). Periodical. English. qt. Warren Gorham & Lamont Inc., Park Square Building, 31 St. James Avenue, Boston MA 02116-4112. **Tel** (617)423-2020, (800)950-1207, FAX (617)423-2026. **ED** Keith G Meyer. **LC** K1; .G74. **DD** 343.73/076; 347.30376. ***Continues*** *Agricultural Law Journal, 0193-6190.*
Desc: Each issue brings you essential, on-target analysis and advice to help agribusiness clients achieve significant tax savings and avoid pitfalls regardless of economic conditions.
Ind/Abst Account. Tax Datab. (1987-Fall 1992);

Account. Art.; AGRICOLA [Full Cov.]; Curr. Law Index (1983-1992); Fed. Tax Artic.; Index Leg. Period.; Leg. Resour. Index (1983-1992); LegalTrac (1983-1992).

US/0021-8642
JOURNAL OF AIR LAW AND COMMERCE, THE. [J. air law commer.]. **Added/Corp** Southern Methodist University. School of Law. Air Law Institute (Chicago, Ill.) Northwestern University (Evanston, Ill.). School of Law. Northwestern University (Evanston, Ill.). School of Business. Northwestern University (Evanston, Ill.). Transportation Center. Vol. 10 (1939)-. Periodical. English. qt (Mar., June, Sept., Dec.). $32.00 US; $34.00 other. Journal of Air Law & Commerce, Southern Methodist University, Dallas TX 75275. **Tel** (214)768-2570, (214)768-2000, FAX (214)692-4330. **ED** Barbara Bell. **LC** K10; .O835. **DD** 629.13; 387.7. **Bk Rev. Circ:** 2,200 (ctrl). available on microfilm and microfiche from University Microfilms International (UMI). ***Continues** Journal of Air Law.*
Desc: Air law litigation and related litigation.
Ind/Abst Aviat. Tradescan [Full Cov.]; Bowne Dig. Corp. Sec. Lawyers; Crim. Penol. Police Sci. Abstr.; Curr. Law Index (1980-); Fed. Tax Artic.; Index Foreign Leg. Per.; Index Leg. Period.; Int. Aerosp. Abstr.; Int. Bibliogr. Sociol.; Leg. Resour. Index (1980-); LegalTrac (1980-).

US/1061-0553
JOURNAL OF ART & ENTERTAINMENT LAW. (JOURNAL OF ART & ENTERTAINMENT LAW / DEPAUL UNIVERSITY [AND] LAWYERS FOR THE CREATIVE ARTS.). [J. art entertain. law]. **Added/Corp** DePaul University. College of Law. Lawyers for the Creative Arts. **VFOAT** Journal of Art and Entertainment Law; DePaul-LCA Journal of Art and Entertainment Law. Vol. 1, No. 1 (Spring 1991)-. Periodical. English. sa. Depaul-LCA, Journal of Art & Entertainment Law, Depaul University College of Law, 25 East Jackson Boulevard, Chicago IL 60604. **LC** K10; .O843. **DD** 349.73/0247; 347.300247 2 20.

US/0733-5113
JOURNAL OF ARTS MANAGEMENT AND LAW, THE. ***Title Change.*** **See** The Arts-Performing Arts.

AT/1034-3040
JOURNAL OF BANKING AND FINANCE LAW AND PRACTICE. **See** Business-Banking and Finance.

US/1046-400X
JOURNAL OF CALIFORNIA TAXATION, THE. ***Ceased.*** [J. Calif. tax.]. Vol. 1, No. 1 (Fall 1989)-(19??). Periodical. English. qt. Faulkner & Gray Inc., 11 Penn Plaza, 17th Floor, New York NY 10001. **Tel** (212)967-7000, (800)535-8403. **ED** Lesli Laffie. **DD** 343. **Bk Rev. Ad Acc.** ctrl circ. available in microform from University Microfilms International (UMI); available on an online database (file 485/Full-Text) from DIALOG.
Ind/Abst Account. Tax Datab. (Winter 1991-Spring 1992) [Full Txt.].

UK/0955-4475
JOURNAL OF CHILD LAW, THE. Vol. 1, No. 1 (Oct./Dec. 1988)-. Periodical. English. qt. £75.00 UK; £84.00 other. Tolley Publishing Company Ltd, Tolley House, 2 Addiscombe Road, Croydon, Surrey CR9 5AF United Kingdom. **Tel** 011 44 81 6869141, FAX 011 44 81 6863155, 011 44 81 7600588.

US/1041-7567
JOURNAL OF CHINESE LAW. [J. Chin. law]. **Added/Corp** Columbia University. Center for Chinese Legal Studies. Columbia University. School of Law. Parker School of Foreign and Comparative Law. **VFOAT** Chung-Kuo Fa Yen Chiu Hsueh Kan. Vol. 1 No. 1 (Spring 1987)-. Periodical. English. sa. $18.00 US; $20.00 other. Journal of Chinese Law, 435 West 116th Street, Box C-10, New York NY 10027. **LC** K10; .O8547. **DD** 349.51/05; 345.1005.
Desc: Invites manuscripts on any topic of Chinese law.
Ind/Abst Index Foreign Leg. Per.; Index Leg. Period.; Int. Bibliogr. Sociol.; PAIS Int. Print (1991-).

US/0741-6075
JOURNAL OF CHRISTIAN JURISPRUDENCE. ***Suspended.*** (JOURNAL OF CHRISTIAN JURISPRUDENCE : A PUBLICATION OF THE O.W. COBURN SCHOOL OF LAW OF ORAL ROBERTS UNIVERSITY.). [J. Christ. jurisprud.]. **Added/Corp** Oral Roberts University. O.W. Coburn School of Law. (1980)-Suspended Vol. 8 (1990). Periodical. English. an. Oral Roberts University of Cobourn, School of Law, 7777 South Lewis, Tulsa OK 74171. **Tel** (918)495-6042. **ED** Florian Frederick Chess. **LC** K10; .O855. **DD** 261.5. **Bk Rev. Ad Acc. Circ:** 1,500 (ctrl).
Desc: Law journal concerned with legal issues confronting the Christian community and first amendment right of religious freedom.
Ind/Abst Curr. Law Index (1982-); Leg. Resour. Index (1982-); LegalTrac (1982-).

US/0093-8688
JOURNAL OF COLLEGE AND UNIVERSITY LAW, THE. [J. coll. univ. law]. **Added/Corp** National Association of College and University Attorneys (U.S.). Vol. 1 (Fall 1973)-. Periodical. English. qt. $40.00. Fred B. Rothman & Company, 10368 West Centennial Road, Littleton CO 80127. **Tel** (800)457-1986, (303)979-5657, FAX (303)978-1457, telex 87669. **ED** Laura F Rothstein. **LC** K10; .O856. **DD** 344/.73/07405. **Bk Rev. Ad Acc.** available on microfilm and microfiche from University Microfilms International (UMI). ***Supersedes** College Counsel.*
Desc: The only law review entirely devoted to the concerns of higher education in the United States.
Ind/Abst Contents Pages Educ.; Curr. Index J. Educ.; Curr. Law Index (1980-); High. Educ. Abstr. (1982-); Index Leg. Period.; Leg. Resour. Index (1980-); LegalTrac (1980-); SportSearch.

II/0022-0043
JOURNAL OF CONSTITUTIONAL AND PARLIAMENTARY STUDIES. [J. const. parliam. stud.]. **Added/Corp** Institute of Constitutional and Parliamentary Studies (New Delhi, India). Vol. 1 (Jan./Mar. 1967)-. Periodical. English. qt. $30.00. Institute of Constitutional and Parliamentary Studies, 18-21 Vithalbhai Patel House, Rafi Marg, New Delhi 1 India. **(Subscription address:** Prints India, 11 Darya Ganj, New Delhi, 110002 India, (Phone: 011 91 11 3268645)) **LC** JQ201; .J6. **DD** 320/.05. available on microfilm and microfiche from University Microfilms International (UMI).
Ind/Abst ABC POL SCI; Int. Bibliogr. Sociol.; Int. Polit. Sci. Abstr.

NE/0168-7034
JOURNAL OF CONSUMER POLICY. **See** Consumer Interests.

US/0882-1046
JOURNAL OF CONTEMPORARY HEALTH LAW AND POLICY, THE. [J. contemp. health law policy]. **Added/Corp** Columbus School of Law. Vol. 1, No. 1 (Spring 1985)-. Periodical. English. Twice a year. $15.00 (one year), $27.00 (two year). Catholic University of America / Columbus School of Law, Washington DC 20064. **Tel** (202)319-5732, FAX (202)319-4313. **ED** John Sten. **LC** K10; .O8575. **DD** 344.73/041; 347.30441. **NLM** W1; JO595T. Index available. cum. index. **Bk Rev. Ad Acc. Pr Rev. Circ:** 450 (ctrl). available on diskette; available on an online database from WESTLAW; and LEXIS.
Desc: Journal which discusses the issues confronting the legal, medical, and ethics profession.
Ind/Abst Health Plan. Adminis. (1985, 1986-); Index Leg. Period.; Leg. Resour. Index; LegalTrac (1980-).

US/0097-9937
JOURNAL OF CONTEMPORARY LAW. [J. contemp. law]. Vol. 1 (Winter 1974)-. Periodical. English. an. $10.00. University of Utah College of Law, Salt Lake City UT 84112. **Tel** (801)581-6833 or 581-4687. **LC** K10; .O858. **DD** 340/.05. **Bk Rev. Ad Acc. Circ:** 350 (ctrl). available on microfilm and microfiche from University Microfilms International (UMI).
Desc: Legal journal focusing on current and controversial legal issues.
Ind/Abst Bowne Dig. Corp. Sec. Lawyers (1982, 1983-); Curr. Law Index (1980-); Index Leg. Period.; Leg. Resour. Index (1980-); LegalTrac (1980-).

US/0896-5595
JOURNAL OF CONTEMPORARY LEGAL ISSUES. [J. contemp. legal issues]. **Added/Corp** University of San Diego. School of Law. Vol. 1, No. 1 (Fall 1987)-. Periodical. English. sa (2 issues). $24.00 (one year), $43.00 (two year), $60.00 (three year). Journal of Contemporary Legal Issues, San Diego University, School of Law, San Diego CA 92110. **Tel** (619)260-4600. **ED** Larry Alexander. **LC** K10; .O8582. **DD** 349.794/05; 347.94005. Index available. **Ad Acc. Circ:** 350.
Ind/Abst Index Leg. Period.; Leg. Resour. Index; LegalTrac (1988-).

AT/1030-7230
JOURNAL OF CONTRACT LAW. [J. contract law]. Vol. 1, No. 1 (July 1988)-. Periodical. English. Three times a year. 135.00Aus$. Butterworths Pty Ltd, 271-273 Lane Cove Road, PO Box 345, North Ryde NSW 2113 Australia. **Tel** 011 61 2 3354444, FAX 011 61 2 3354655. **LC** K10; .O8583. **DD** 346/.02/05; 342.6205. **Bk Rev.**
Desc: Discussion and analysis of issues confronting contract lawyers.
Ind/Abst Index Leg. Period.; Leg. Resour. Index; LegalTrac (1988-).

US/1052-2859
JOURNAL OF DISPUTE RESOLUTION. [J. dispute resolut.]. **Added/Corp** University of Missouri-Columbia. Center for the Study of Dispute Resolution. University of Missouri-Columbia. School of Law. (1988)-. Periodical. English. $18.00 (1 year), $30.00 (2 year) US; $20.00 (1 year), $35.00 (2 year) other. University of Missouri Columbia / Hulston, Hulston Hall Room 15, Columbia MO 65211. **Tel** (314)882-9682. **DD** 347. ***Continues** Missouri Journal of Dispute Resolution, 0748-0768.*
Ind/Abst Index Leg. Period.; J. Plan. Lit.; Leg. Resour. Index; LegalTrac (1987-).

UK/0264-6811
JOURNAL OF ENERGY & NATURAL RESOURCES LAW. [J. energy nat. resour. law]. **Added/Corp** University of Dundee. Centre for Petroleum and Mineral Law Studies. International Bar Association. Section on Energy and Natural Resources Law. **VFOAT** Journal of Energy and Natural Resources Law. Vol. 1, No. 1 (1983)-. Periodical. English. qt. $422.00. Kluwer Academic Publishers, Postbus 322, 3300 AH Dordrecht, The Netherlands. **Tel** 011 (31) 78 524400, FAX 011 31 78 183273, telex 20083. **ED** Thomas Walde and Alan Page. **LC** K10; .O85965. **DD** 343/.092; 342.392. **Bk Rev. Pr Rev. Acid Free.**
Desc: Provides comprehensive coverage of issues and events relevant to the law of energy and natural resources. Also provides authoritative analysis of all major issues in energy and natural resources law, with comprehensive coverage of legal developments, literature and research around the world. Each issue contains the following four sections: articles and notes; recent developments; bibliography; and book reviews.
Ind/Abst Aust. Leg. Mon. Dig.; Energy Inf. Abstr.; GeoRef; Index Leg. Period.; J. Plan. Lit.; Leg. Resour. Index; LegalTrac (1990-).

●US/1058-1367
JOURNAL OF ENVIRONMENTAL PERMITTING. **VFOAT** Environmental Permitting. Vol. 1, No. 1 (Winter 1991/92)-. English. qt. $159.00 US & Canada; $209.00 other. John Wiley & Sons, Inc., 605 Third Avenue, New York NY 10158-0012. **Tel** (212)850-6000, (212)850-6645, FAX (212)850-6088, telex 12-7063. **(Subscription address:** John Wiley & Sons Inc / New Jersey, PO Box 2575, Secaucus NJ 07096-2575.) **LC** K10; .O85996. **DD** 344.73/046; 347.30446. **[CCC].** Documents available from The Genuine Article.
Desc: Covers developments in air operating, water, and RCRA permits. Provides strategies for developing one system to obtain and maintain all environmental permits. Covers basic permitting issues, including technology assessment, data collection and management, engineering judgment precedents, federal, state, and local regulatory update, and enforcement trends.
Ind/Abst Res. Alert [Select. Cov.]; Soc. Sci. Cit. Index [Select. Cov.].

ET/0022-0914
JOURNAL OF ETHIOPIAN LAW. Vol. 1 (1964)-. Periodical. English (Amharic). sa. Haile Sellassie i University, Faculty of law, Addis Ababa Ethiopia.
Ind/Abst Index Foreign Leg. Per.

US/1046-4360
JOURNAL OF HEALTH AND HOSPITAL LAW : A PUBLICATION OF THE AMERICAN ACADEMY OF HOSPITAL ATTORNEYS OF THE AMERICAN HOSPITAL ASSOCIATION. [J. health hosp. law]. **Added/Corp** American Academy of Hospital Attorneys. **VFOAT** Health and Hospital Law. Vol. 21, No. 5 (May 1988)-. Periodical. English. mo. $135.00. DePaul University, College of Law, 25 East Jackson Boulevard, Chicago IL 60604. **Tel** (312)341-8553. **LC** KF3825.A59; H67. **DD** 344.73/03211; 347.3043211. **NLM** W1; JO6693. cum. index. **Circ:** 37,000. ***Continues** Hospital Law, 0193-9246.*
Ind/Abst Fed. Tax Artic.; Hospit. Health Admin. Index (May 1988-).

US/0361-6878
JOURNAL OF HEALTH POLITICS, POLICY AND LAW. [J. health polit. policy law]. **Added/Corp** Duke University. Dept. of Health Administration. Vol. 1 (Spring 1976)-. Academic Scholarly Publication. English. qt (4 issues). $96.00 (institutions), $48.00 (individuals) US; $108.00 (institutions), $60.00 (individuals) other. Duke University Press, PO Box 90660, Durham NC 27708-0660. **Tel** (919)687-3600, (919)688-5134 (orders), FAX (919)688-4574, telex 802829. **ED** Mark A. Peterson. **LC** RA395.A3; J68. **DD** 338.4/7/36210973. **NLM** W1 JO67BL. **CODEN** JHPLDN. **[CCC]. Bk Rev. Ad Acc. Pr Rev. Circ:** 1,800 (ctrl). available on microfilm and microfiche from University Microfilms International (UMI). Documents available from The Genuine Article, BIOSIS Document Express, UMI Article Clearinghouse.
Desc: Initiation, formulation, and implementation of health policy, drawing from politics, sociology, economics, public administration, law and ethics.
Ind/Abst ABI/INFORM Glob. Ed.; ABI Inform Ondisc (Spring 1986-); Biol. Abstr.; Cumul. Index Nurs. Allied Health Lit.; Curr. Contents Soc. Behav. Sci.; Curr. Law Index (1980-); EMBASE; Expand. Acad. Index (1992-); Hospit. Health Admin. Index; Hospit. Manage. Rev.; Hum. Resour. Abstr. (?-?); Index Med.; Int. Polit. Sci. Abstr.; Leg. Resour. Index (1980-); LegalTrac (1980-); Newsp. Period. Abstr. (1992-); PAIS Int. Print (1991-); Res. Alert [Full Cov.]; Sage Public Adm. Abstr.; Soc. Plann. Policy Dev. Abstr.; Soc. Sci. Cit. Index [Full Cov.]; Soc. Work Abstr. [Select. Cov.]; Sociol. Abstr.; Trop. Dis. Bull.

CN/0847-2971
JOURNAL OF HUMAN JUSTICE, THE. [J. hum. justice]. **Added/Corp** University of British Columbia. Dept. of Anthropology and Sociology. **VFOAT** Journal of the Human Justice Collective; JHJ. Vol. 1, No. 1 (Autumn 1989)-. Periodical. English. sa. 20.00Can$ individuals; 30.00Can$ institutions. Journal of Human Justice, P.O.Box 46108 Station G, Vancouver V6R 4C5 Canada. **Tel** (604)222-1740. **ED** Dr. B. MacLean. **LC** JC578; .J68. **DD** 340/.115/0971. **Bk Rev. Ad Acc. Circ:** 300.

AT/1036-7918
JOURNAL OF JUDICIAL ADMINISTRATION. **Added/Corp** Law Book Company. Australian Institute of Judicial Administration. Vol. 1, No. 1 (Aug. 1991)-. Periodical. English. qt. 185.00Aus$. The Law Book Company Limited, 44-50 Waterloo Road, North Ryde New South Wales, 2113 Australia. **Tel** 011 61 2 8870177, FAX 011 61 2 8887240, telex ASBOOK 27445.
Ind/Abst Aust. Leg. Mon. Dig.

PL/0075-4277
JOURNAL OF JURISTIC PAPYROLOGY, THE. **VFOAT** Rocznik Papirologii Prawniczej. Began with: Vol. 1, published in 1946. English (French and German). **(Subscription address:** ARS Polona, PO Box 1001, 00068 Warsaw Poland.**)**.

US/0733-2491
JOURNAL OF LAW AND COMMERCE, THE. [J. law commer.]. **Added/Corp** University of Pittsburgh. School of Law. Vol. 1 (1981)-. Periodical. English. Twice a year. $20.00. Journal of Law and Commerce, 3900 Forbes Avenue, University of Pittsburgh, Pittsburgh PA 15260. **Tel** (412)648-1359. **ED** Brian Vertz and Walter Hamberg. **LC** K10; .O8732. **DD** 346.73/07/05; 347.306705. **Bk Rev. Ad Acc. Circ:** 400 (ctrl).
Desc: The journal provides a central forum for scholarship elaborating and clarifying commercial law as it exists and as it is likely to develop.
Ind/Abst Bowne Dig. Corp. Sec. Lawyers; Curr. Law Index (1983-); Fed. Tax Artic.; Index Leg. Period.; Leg. Resour. Index (1983-); LegalTrac (1983-).

US/0022-2186
JOURNAL OF LAW & ECONOMICS, THE. [J. law econ.]. **Added/Corp** University of Chicago. Law School. **VAT** Journal of Law and Economics. Vol. 1 (Oct. 1958)-. Periodical. English. sa (2 issues). $41.00 institution, $27.00 individual, $16.00 student. University of Chicago Press / Journals Division, PO Box 37005, 5720 South Woodlawn, Chicago IL 60637. **Tel** (312)753-3347, FAX (312)753-0811. **(Subscription telephone:** (312)753-8083**) ED** Dennis W. Carlton, Sam Peltzman, Alan O. Sykes and Richard A. Epstein. **DD** 330.5. **CODEN** JLLEA7. **Pr Rev. Acid Free.** available on microfilm and microfiche from University Microfilms International (UMI). Documents available from The Genuine Article, UMI Article Clearinghouse.
Desc: Explores the complex relationships between law and economics, focusing on the influence of regulation and legal institutions on the operation of economic systems.
Ind/Abst ABC POL SCI; ABI/INFORM Glob. Ed.; ABI Inform Ondisc (April 1983-); Acad. Abstr. Full Text Elite (Jan. 1992-); Acad. Abstr. (Jan. 1992-); Acad. Search (Jan. 1992-); Am. Hist. Life (1963-); Bowne Dig. Corp. Sec. Lawyers; Coal Abstr.; Commun. Abstr.; Contents Pages Manage.; Curr. Contents Soc. Behav. Sci.; Curr. Law Index (1980-); Econ. Lit. Index; EMBASE; Energy Res. Abstr. (March 1981-); Expand. Acad. Index (1984-); Fed. Tax Artic.; Gen. BusinessFile (1992-); Index Leg. Period.; INFO-SOUTH Abstr.; Int. Labour Doc.; J. Econ. Lit.; Leg. Resour. Index (1980-); LegalTrac (1980-); Mag. Search; Newsp. Period. Abstr. (1991-); PAIS Int. Print; Res. Alert [Full Cov.]; Soc. Sci. Source (Jan. 1992-); Soc. Sci. Cit. Index [Full Cov.]; Soc. Sci. Index; Soc. Sci. Index Fulltext (Oct. 1988-) [Full Txt.]; UMI ABI/Inform--Bus. Period. Ondisc (Apr. 1987-) [Full Txt.]; West. Hist. Q.; World Agric. Econ.

US/0275-6072
JOURNAL OF LAW & EDUCATION. **See** Education-School Organization and Administration.

US
JOURNAL OF LAW AND EDUCATION / BRIGHAM YOUNG UNIVERSITY. ***Title Change.*** **Added/Corp** Brigham Young University. Dept. of Educational Leadership. J. Reuben Clark Law School. **VFOAT** Brigham Young University Journal of Law and Education; BYU Journal of Law and Education. (1992)-(Spring 1992). English. an. Brigham Young University / Law School Accounting, 358B JRCB, Provo UT 84602. **Tel** (801)378-6600, FAX (801)378-2188. ***Continued by*** *Brigham Young University Education and Law Journal.*

AT/0729-1485
JOURNAL OF LAW AND INFORMATION SCIENCE. [J. law inf. sci.]. **Added/Corp** New South Wales Institute of Technology. Faculty of Law. New South Wales Institute of Technology. Faculty of Mathematical and Computing Sciences. Vol. 1, No. 1 (1981)-. Periodical. English. Twice a year. 30.00Aus$ Australia; 35.00Aus$ other. University of Tasmania, PO Box 1214, Launceston 7250 Australia. **Tel** 011 61 3 243013, FAX 011 61 2 207623, telex 58150. **(Subscription address:** University of Tasmania / Law School, c/o David McGuire, Publications Manager, GPO Box 252C, Hobart Tasmania 7001 Australia.**) ED** Lynden Griggs and Gene Clark. **LC** K10; .O8733. **DD** 343.94/0999; 349.403999. **Bk Rev,** (Qty: varies). **Ad Acc, Adv Mgr:** David McGuire.
Desc: Deals with the increasing number of social and legal questions arising out of new scientific and technological developments in information science. Articles deal with computer crime, privacy law, legal text retrieval systems, informatics and law reform, control and audit of computer systems and liability for negligence and computer failures.
Ind/Abst Curr. Law Index (1984-); Index Leg. Period.; Leg. Resour. Index (1984-?); LegalTrac (1983-1986).

US/0749-2227
JOURNAL OF LAW & POLITICS. [J. law polit.]. **VFOAT** Journal of Law and Politics. Vol. 1, No. 1 (Fall 1983)-. Periodical. English. Four times a year. $36.00. University of Virginia / School of Law, North Grounds, Charlottesville VA 22903. **Tel** (804)924-0597. **ED** Charles Caldwell. **LC** K10; .O87315. **DD** 342/.005; 342.2005. **Bk Rev. Ad Acc. Circ:** 1,500.
Desc: Analyzes the interaction between law and politics, including regulation of political parties, campaign finance, relationship between executive, judicial legislative branches, state, and federal government.
Ind/Abst ABC POL SCI; Am. Hist. Life (1983-); Bowne Dig. Corp. Sec. Lawyers; Curr. Law Index (1984-); Index Leg. Period.; Leg. Resour. Index (1984-); LegalTrac (1983-); PAIS Int. Print (1991-).

US/0748-0814
JOURNAL OF LAW AND RELIGION, THE. [J. law relig.]. **Added/Corp** Hamline University. School of Law. Council on Religion and Law (U.S.). **VFOAT** Journal of Law & Religion. Vol. 1, No. 1 (Summer 1983)-. Periodical. English. sa (June, Nov.). $25.00 institutions, $15.00 individuals. Hamline University School of Law, 1536 Hewitt Avenue, St Paul MN 55104. **Tel** (612)641-2350, FAX (612)641-2435. **ED** M Failinger. **LC** K10; .O87333. **Bk Rev,** (Qty: varies). **Ad Acc, Adv Mgr:** J Matson, **Tel** (612)641-2082. **Circ:** 600 (ctrl). available on microfilm.
Desc: Interdisciplinary journal, published in law review format, presents articles which probe historical, theoretical, and practical ways in which religion, broadly defined, interacts with law.
Ind/Abst Curr. Law Index (1984, 1985, 1987-); Index Book Rev. Relig.; Index Leg. Period.; Leg. Resour. Index (1984-); LegalTrac (1983-); Relig. Index One Period.; Relig. Theol. Abstr.

UK/0263-323X
JOURNAL OF LAW AND SOCIETY. [J. law soc.]. Vol. 9, No. 1 (Summer 1982)-. Academic Scholarly Publication. English. Four times a year. £111.00 UK and Europe; $217.50 North America; £145.00 other. Basil Blackwell Publishers Ltd, 108 Cowley Road, Oxford 0X4 1JF England. **Tel** 011 44 865 791100, FAX 011 44 865 791347, telex 837022 OXBOOK G. **(Subscription address:** Blackwell Publishers / UK, Marston Book Services, PO Box 87, Oxford OX2 0DT England.**) ED** P A Thomas. **LC** K2; .R5. **DD** 340/.115/05. **[CCC]. Bk Rev. Ad Acc. Pr Rev.** available on microfilm and microfiche from University Microfilms International (UMI). Documents available from The Genuine Article. ***Continues*** *British Journal of Law and Society, 0306-3704.*
Desc: Devoted to the study of the interaction of law with other social forces.
Ind/Abst ABC POL SCI; Am. Hist. Life (1977-); Appl. Soc. Sci. Index Abstr.; Br. Humanit. Index; Commun. Abstr.; Crim. Justice Abstr.; Crim. Penol. Police Sci. Abstr.; Int. Bibliogr. Sociol.; Int. Polit. Sci. Abstr.; Leg. Resour. Index (1982-); LegalTrac (1986-); Res. Alert [Full Cov.]; Sage Public Adm. Abstr. (?-?); Sage Urban Stud. Abstr; Soc. Plann. Policy Dev. Abstr.; Soc. Sci. Cit. Index [Full Cov.]; Sociol. Abstr.; Stud. Women Abstr.

US/8756-6222
JOURNAL OF LAW, ECONOMICS & ORGANIZATION. [J. law econ. organ.]. **VFOAT** Journal of Law, Economics, and Organization; LEO. Vol. 1, No. 1 (Spring 1985)-. Periodical. English. sa (2 issues). $43.00 institutions, $28.00 individuals US; $51.00 institutions, $36.00 individuals other. Oxford University Press / New York, 200 Madison Avenue, New York NY 10016. **Tel** (212)679-7300, (919)677-0977, (800)451-7556, (800)445-9714, FAX (919)677-1303. **(Subscription address:** Oxford University Press / USA, Journals Marketing Department, Oxford University Press, 2001 Evans Road, Cary NC 27513.**) LC** K10; .O8734. **DD** 349.746/05; 347.46005. **[CCC].** available on microfilm and microfiche from University Microfilms International (UMI). Documents available from The Genuine Article.
Ind/Abst Bowne Dig. Corp. Sec. Lawyers (1985-); Curr. Contents Soc. Behav. Sci.; Curr. Law Index (1985-); Econ. Lit. Index (19??-); Int. Bibliogr. Sociol.; J. Econ. Lit.; Leg. Resour. Index (1985-); LegalTrac (1980-); Res. Alert [Full Cov.]; Soc. Sci. Cit. Index [Full Cov.].

●US/1073-1105
JOURNAL OF LAW, MEDICINE & ETHICS, THE. (THE JOURNAL OF LAW, MEDICINE & ETHICS : A JOURNAL OF THE AMERICAN SOCIETY OF LAW, MEDICINE & ETHICS.). [J. law med. ethics]. **Added/Corp** American Society of Law, Medicine & Ethics. **VFOAT** Journal of Law, Medicine and Ethics; JLME. Vol. 21, No. 1 (Spring 1993)-. Academic Scholarly Publication. English. qt (4 issues). $70.00. American Society of Law, Medicine and Ethics, 765 Commonwealth Avenue, 16th Floor, Boston MA 02215. **Tel** (617)262-4990, FAX (617)437-7596. **LC** KF3821.A15; L38. **DD** 344.73/041; 347.30441. **NLM** W1; JO739. **CODEN** JLAEEO. available in microform from University Microfilms International (UMI). ***Continues*** *Law, Medicine & Health Care, 0277-8459.*
Desc: Contains information on medical laws and legislation, nursing, medical ethics and delivery of health care.
Ind/Abst Acad. Abstr. (Jan. 1993-); Acad. Search (Jan. 1993-).

US/1072-0316
JOURNAL OF LEGAL ASPECTS OF SPORT. [J. legal asp. sport]. **Added/Corp** Society for the Study of Legal Aspects of Sport and Physical Activity. Vol. 1, No. 1 (Fall 1991)-. Periodical. English. sa. $65.00. Iowa State University Department of Health and Human Performance, PO Box 239, Ames IA 50011. **Tel** (515)294-8042, FAX (515)294-8740. **ED** Gary Gray. **DD** 344. **Bk Rev. Ad Acc. Pr Rev.** ***Continues*** *Legal Issues in Sports.*
Ind/Abst SPORT Discus.

US/0022-2208
JOURNAL OF LEGAL EDUCATION. [J. legal educ.]. **Added/Corp** Association of American Law Schools. **VFOAT** Legal Education. Vol. 1 (Autumn 1948)-. Periodical. English. qt. $30.00 US; $34.00 other. Case Western Reserve University / School of Law, 11075 East Boulevard, Cleveland OH 44106. **Tel** (216)368-3304, FAX (216)368-6144. **ED** Erik Jensen. **LC** K10; .O8735. **DD** 340/.071073. (included in last issue of each volume). cum. index. **Bk Rev,** (Qty: 4). **Pr Rev. Circ:** 750 (ctrl). available on microfilm and microfiche from WESTLAW; available on CD-ROM and an online database. Documents available from The Genuine Article.
Desc: The purpose is to foster a rich interchange of ideas and information about legal education and related matters.
Ind/Abst Arts Humanit. Citation Index [Select. Cov.]; Contents Pages Educ.; Curr. Contents Soc. Behav. Sci.; Curr. Index J. Educ.; Curr. Law Index (1980-); High. Educ. Abstr. (1979-); Index Leg. Period.; Law Office Inf. Serv.; Leg. Resour. Index (1980-); LegalTrac (1980-); Res. Alert [Full Cov.]; Soc. Sci. Cit. Index [Full Cov.].

UK/0144-0365
JOURNAL OF LEGAL HISTORY, THE. [J. legal hist.]. Vol. 1, No. 1 (May 1980)-. Periodical. English. Three times a year. $145.00. Frank Cass & Company Ltd, Newbury House, 890-900 Eastern Avenue, Newbury Park, Ilford, Essex IG2 7HH United Kingdom. **Tel** 011 44 81 599 8866, FAX 011 44 81 599 0984, telex 897719. **ED** Albert Kiralf. **LC** K10; .O8736. **DD** 340/.09. **Ad Acc, Adv Mgr:** Anne Kidson. available on microfilm and microfiche from University Microfilms International (UMI).
Desc: This journal publishes book reviews and articles on the history of the law of the British Isles and commonwealth and the USA, not necessarily limited to the common law tradition.
Ind/Abst Am. Hist. Life (1983-); Br. Humanit. Index; Curr. Law Index (1982-); Index Leg. Period. (1980-); Leg. Resour. Index (1982-); LegalTrac (1983-); Soc. Plann. Policy Dev. Abstr.; Sociol. Abstr.

US/0732-9113
JOURNAL OF LEGAL PLURALISM AND UNOFFICIAL LAW. [J. leg. plur. unoff. law]. **VFOAT** Journal of Legal Pluralism. No. 19 (1981)-. Periodical. English. ir. $26.00. Fred B. Rothman & Company, 10368 West Centennial Road, Littleton CO 80127. **Tel** (800)457-1986, (303)979-5657, FAX (303)978-1457, telex 87669. **ED** John Griffiths. **LC** K1; .F7. **DD** 340/.05. ***Continues*** *African Law Studies, 0002-0060.*
Ind/Abst Curr. Law Index (1980-); Index Foreign Leg. Per.; Index Leg. Period.; Leg. Resour. Index (1980-); LegalTrac (1983-); Soc. Plann. Policy Dev. Abstr.; Sociol. Abstr.

US/0047-2530
JOURNAL OF LEGAL STUDIES, THE. [J. legal stud.]. **Added/Corp** University of Chicago. Law School. Vol. 1 (Jan. 1972)-. Periodical. English. sa (January and June). $41.00 institution, $27.00 individual, $16.00 students. University of Chicago Press / Journals Division, PO Box 37005, 5720 South Woodlawn, Chicago IL 60637. **Tel** (312)753-3347, FAX (312)753-0811. **(Subscription telephone:** (312)753-8083**) ED** Geoffrey P. Miller and William M. Landes. **LC** K10; .O874. **DD** 340/.05. **Ad Acc. Pr Rev. Acid Free. Circ:** 2,300 (ctrl). available on microfilm and microfiche from University Microfilms International (UMI). Documents available from The Genuine Article.
Desc: Studies on contracts, property, torts and similar common law areas, from legal, economic, historical, or philosophical aspects.
Ind/Abst Bowne Dig. Corp. Sec. Lawyers; Crim. Justice Abstr.; Crim. Justice Period. Index; Curr. Contents Soc. Behav. Sci.; Curr. Law Index (1980-); Econ. Lit. Index (19??-); Fed. Tax Artic.; Index Leg. Period.; Int. Bibliogr. Sociol.; Int. Polit. Sci. Abstr.; J. Econ. Lit.; Leg. Resour. Index (1980-); LegalTrac (1980-); Res. Alert [Full Cov.]; Risk Abstr. (1980-); Soc. Plann. Policy Dev. Abstr.; Soc. Sci. Cit. Index [Full Cov.]; Sociol. Abstr.; Women Stud. Abstr.

US/0896-5811
JOURNAL OF LEGAL STUDIES EDUCATION, THE. [J. legal stud. educ.]. **Added/Corp** American Business Law Association.

VFOAT Legal Studies Education. Vol. 1 (Spring 1983)-. Periodical. English. sa. $12.00 US; $15.00 (includes postage) other. Abilene Christian University, PO Box 8177, ACU Station, Abilene TX 79699. **Tel** (915)674-2344, FAX (915)674-2202. **LC** KF279; .J68. **DD** 340.
Desc: Articles and book and media reviews relating to the legal studies profession, including related disciplines (business ethics, business and society and public policy).
Ind/Abst Leg. Resour. Index; LegalTrac (1990-).

PK
JOURNAL OF LEGAL THOUGHTS. Vol. 1, No. 1 (Jan. 1980)-. Periodical. English. Rs5.00. Journal of Legal Thoughts, c/o Department of Law, University of Dacca, Dacca 2 Bangladesh. **LC** K10; .O876. **DD** 349.549/2/05; 345.492005.

US/0146-9584
JOURNAL OF LEGISLATION. [J. legis.]. **Added/Corp** University of Notre Dame. Law School. Vol. 3 (1976)-. English. sa (Jan., July). $16.00 US, Canada, Mexico, & UK; $18.00 other. Notre Dame Law School, PO Box 486, Notre Dame IN 46556. **Tel** (219)239-5918, (219)255-2938. **ED** Vicent Sanchez. **LC** K14; .D13. **DD** 340/.0973. **Bk Rev. Ad Acc. Circ:** 1,800 (ctrl). available in microform from University Microfilms International (UMI). ***Continues*** *N.D. Journal of Legislation, 0360-4209.*
Desc: A student edited and published law review specializing in legislation, public policy, and regulatory affairs.
Ind/Abst ABC POL SCI; Coal Abstr.; Curr. Law Index (1980-); Energy Res. Abstr. (Jan. 1981-); Index Leg. Period.; Int. Polit. Sci. Abstr.; Leg. Resour. Index (1980-); LegalTrac (1980-); Sage Public Adm. Abstr. (?-?); Soc. Plann. Policy Dev. Abstr.; Work Relat. Abstr.

US/0892-9017
JOURNAL OF MINERAL LAW & POLICY. ***Title Change.*** [J. miner. law policy]. **Added/Corp** University of Kentucky. Mineral Law Center. **VFOAT** Journal of Mineral Law and Policy. Vol. 1, No. 1 (1985)-Vol. 7 No. 2 (1992). Periodical. English. sa. JML&P, 21 Law Building, University of Kentucky, College of Law, Lexington KY 40506-0048. **LC** K10.O8824. **DD** 343.73/00775; 347.030775. ***Continued by*** *Journal of Natural Resources & Environmental Law, 1070-4833.*
Ind/Abst Curr. Law Index (1985-); Index Leg. Period.; Leg. Resour. Index (1985-); LegalTrac (1980-).

CN/0840-7754
JOURNAL OF MOTOR VEHICLE LAW. [J. mot. veh. law]. Vol. 1, No. 1 (Jan. 1989)-. Periodical. English (French). Three times a year. 95.00Can$ Canada; $82.75 other. Carswell / Canada, 2075 Kennedy Road, Scarborough Ontario M1T 3V4 Canada. **Tel** (416)609-3800, (800)387-5164. **ED** Murray D Segal and Rick Libman. **DD** 343.71/0944. **Bk Rev. Ad Acc.**
Desc: A national journal covering issues relating to driving offences arising from both Canadian criminal and highway traffic law.
Ind/Abst Can. Legal Lit.; Index Can. Leg. Period. Lit.

US/0895-6219
JOURNAL OF PARALEGAL EDUCATION AND PRACTICE. (JOURNAL OF PARALEGAL EDUCATION AND PRACTICE / AMERICAN ASSOCIATION FOR PARALEGAL EDUCATION.). [J. paralegal educ. pract.]. **Added/Corp** American Association for Paralegal Education. Vol. 4, No. 1 (Oct. 1987)-. Periodical. English. an (Feb.). $25.00. American Association for Paralegal Education, PO Box 40244, Overland Park KS 66204. **Tel** (913)381-4458. **LC** KF320.L4; J68. **DD** 340/.023/73. ***Continues*** *Journal of Paralegal Education, 8755-7649.*

US/0148-2181
JOURNAL OF PENSION PLANNING AND COMPLIANCE. See Business-Investments.

●UK
JOURNAL OF PERSONAL INJURY LITIGATION. (1994)-. English. Six times a year. £125.00 Europe; £131.00 other. Sweet & Maxwell Ltd., South Quay Plaza, 183 Marsh Wall, London E14 9FT England. **Tel** 011 44 264 342899, FAX 011 44 264 342723, telex 929089 ITPINF G.

●US/1062-4546
JOURNAL OF PHARMACY & LAW, THE. See Pharmacy and Pharmacology.

●US/0967-2680
JOURNAL OF PRODUCTS AND TOXICS LIABILITY. [J. prod. toxics liabil.]. **VFOAT** Journal of Products & Toxics Liability. Vol. 15, No. 1 (1993)-. Periodical. English. Four times a year. $343.00 The Americas; £230.00 other. Pergamon Press, An Imprint of Elsevier Science Ltd., The Boulevard, Langford Lane, Kidlington, Oxford OX5 1GB United Kingdom. **Tel** 011 44 865 843000, 011 44 865 843699, FAX 011 44 865 843010. **(Subscription address:** Elsevier Science Ltd. Oxford Fulfillment Centre, PO Box 800, Kidlington, Oxford OX5 1DX United Kingdom.**)** **ED** Kenneth Ross. **LC** K10; .O8836. **DD** 346/.73/038. **NLM** W1; JO8442M. **CODEN** JPTLEW. Documents available from Article Express International, UMI Article Clearinghouse. ***Continues*** *Journal of Products Liability., 0363-0404.*
Desc: Original research papers from the legal as well as from technical fields such as engineering and medicine which are appropriate to the growing body of knowledge regarding product safety and liability. Topics range from the legal aspects of specified products, product groups, or broad issues in the prosecution or defense of products liability actions, to the analysis of accident causation, product failures, and technical sources of appropriate designs to minimize failure or encourage product safety.
Ind/Abst ABI/INFORM Glob. Ed.; ABI Inform Ondisc; Acad. Search (July 1993-); Bioeng. Abstr.; Consum. Index Prod. Eval. Inf. Source; Ei Page One; Eng. Index Annu.; Int. Aerosp. Abstr.; Leg. Resour. Index (?-?); Pollut. Abstr. Indexes; Trade Ind. Index (?-?).

US/0363-0404
JOURNAL OF PRODUCTS LIABILITY. ***Title Change.*** [J. prod. liabil.]. Vol. 1; (1977)-(19??). Periodical. English. qt. Pergamon Press Inc., 660 White Plains Road, Tarrytown NY 10591-5153. **Tel** (914)524-9200, FAX (914)333-2444, telex 13-7328. **(Subscription address:** UK/ Headington Hill Hall, Oxford OX3 0BW; Can/ 150 Consumers Road/Suite 104, Willowdale Ontario M2J 1P9; Aus-NZ/ POB 544, Potts Point NSW 2011**)** **ED** Kenneth Ross. **LC** K10. **DD** 346/.73/038. **NLM** W1 JO8443. **CODEN** JPLIDG. available on microfilm and microfiche from University Microfilms International (UMI); and Microfilms International Marketing Corp. Documents available from Article Express International, UMI Article Clearinghouse. ***Continued by*** *Journal of Products and Toxics Liability., 0967-2680.*
Ind/Abst ABI/INFORM Glob. Ed.; ABI Inform Ondisc (Spring 1978-); Bioeng. Abstr.; Bus. Index (1985-); Bus. Source (Jul. 1993-); Consum. Index Prod. Eval. Inf. Source; Curr. Law Index (1980-); Ei Page One; Eng. Index Annu.; Gen. BusinessFile (1985-); Gen. Period. Index (1985-); Health Saf. Sci. Abstr.; INFO-SOUTH Abstr.; Ins. Period. Index; Int. Aerosp. Abstr.; Leg. Resour. Index (1980-); LegalTrac (1980-); Mag. Search; Pollut. Abstr. Indexes; Trade Ind. Index (1981-).

AT/0810-9729
JOURNAL OF PROFESSIONAL LEGAL EDUCATION, THE. **Added/Corp** Australian Professional Legal Education Conference. Kuring-Gai College of Advanced Education. College of Law. Centre for Publication & Information. Vol. 1, No. 1 (June 1983)-. Periodical. English. sa. $42.50 Vol. 10. Centre for Publication and Information, College of Law, PO Box 2, St. Leonards NSW 2065 Australia. **Tel** 011 61 2 9657000. **(Subscription address:** North America: William W. Gaunt & Sons Inc., 3011 Gulf Drive, Gaunt Building, Holmes Beach, FL 34217**)** **LC** K10; .O8838. **DD** 340/.07/1194.
Ind/Abst Aust. Educ. Index (1986-); Aust. Leg. Mon. Dig.; Curr. Law Index (1983-); Leg. Resour. Index (1983-); LegalTrac (1983-).

US/1053-8445
JOURNAL OF PROGRESSIVE LEGAL THOUGHT. [J. progress. leg. thought]. **Added/Corp** National Lawyers Guild. FSU Chapter. Vol. 1, No. 1 (Autumn 1989)-. Periodical. English. Twice a year. Free. Florida State University College of Law, Tallahassee FL 32306. **Tel** (904)644-0961. **LC** K10; .O88385. **DD** 340/.05.
Ind/Abst Leg. Resour. Index; LegalTrac (1989-).

US/1041-3952
JOURNAL OF PROPRIETARY RIGHTS, THE. [J. propr. rights]. Vol. 1, No. 1 (Dec. 1988)-. Periodical. English. Twelve times a year. $298.38. Prentice-Hall Law and Business, 270 Sylvan Avenue, Englewood Cliffs NJ 07632. **Tel** (800)223-0231, (201)894-8538, FAX (201)894-8666. **LC** KF2972; .J68. **DD** 346.7304/8/05; 347.3064805.
Desc: Analyzes important trends in patent, trade secret, trademark and intellectual property law and helps intellectual property professionals solve practical problems.

US/0093-1853
JOURNAL OF PSYCHIATRY & LAW, THE. [J. psych. law]. **VFOAT** Psychiatry & Law. **VAT** Journal of Psychiatry and Law. Vol. 1 (Spring 1973)-. Academic Scholarly Publication. English. Four times a year. $45.00. Federal Legal Publications Inc, 157 Chambers Street, New York NY 10007. **Tel** (212)619-4949, FAX (212)608-3141. **ED** Gerald N. Epstein and Howard Nashel. **LC** K10; .O884. **DD** 614/.19. **NLM** W1 JO856H. **CODEN** JPSLAN. Index available. cum. index. **Ad Acc.** ctrl circ. available on microfilm and microfiche from University Microfilms International (UMI).
Ind/Abst Crim. Justice Abstr.; Crim. Penol. Police Sci. Abstr.; Curr. Law Index (1980-); EMBASE; Index Leg. Period.; Leg. Resour. Index (1980-); LegalTrac (1980-); Middle East Abstr. Index; Psychol. Abstr. (1973-); PsycINFO; PsycLit; Sage Fam. Stud. Abstr. (?-?); Sage Urban Stud. Abstr (?-?).

US/0362-062X
JOURNAL OF REPRINTS OF DOCUMENTS AFFECTING WOMEN. Vol. 1, No. 1 (July 1976)-. Periodical. English. qt. $60.00. Today Publication and News Services, National Press Building, Washington DC 20045. **LC** KF478.A45; J68. **DD** 342/.73/087.
Desc: Information on sex discrimination against women.

●UK
JOURNAL OF SOCIAL SECURITY LAW. (1994)-. English. Four times a year. £60.00 Europe; £63.00 other. Sweet & Maxwell Ltd., South Quay Plaza, 183 Marsh Wall, London E14 9FT England. **Tel** 011 44 264 342899, FAX 011 44 264 342723, telex 929089 ITPINF G.

US/0095-7577
JOURNAL OF SPACE LAW. [J. space law]. **Added/Corp** L.Q.C. Lamar Society of International Law. Vol. 1, (Spring 1973)-. English. Twice a year. $74.95 US; $79.95 other. Journal of Space Law, PO Box 308, University MS 38677. **Tel** (601)234-2391, FAX (601)232-7731. **ED** S. Gorove. **LC** JX1; .J63. **DD** 341.4/7. Index available. **Bk Rev. Ad Acc. Circ:** 2,000 (ctrl). available in microform.
Desc: Devoted to the legal problems of man's activities in outer space with attention to international, scientific and political aspects.
Ind/Abst Am. Bibliogr. Slavic East Europ. Stud.; Bowne Dig. Corp. Sec. Lawyers; Curr. Law Index (1980-); Index Leg. Period.; Int. Aerosp. Abstr.; Leg. Resour. Index (1980-); LegalTrac (1980-); PAIS Int. Print.

US/0515-2046
JOURNAL OF THE ACADEMY OF FLORIDA TRIAL LAWYERS. **Main/Corp** Academy of Florida Trial Lawyers. **VFOAT** AFTL Journal. No. 1 (July 1961)-. Periodical. English. Twelve times a year. $300.00. Academy of Florida Trial Lawyers, 218 South Monroe Street, Suite 400, Tallahassee FL 32301. **Tel** (904)224-9403. **ED** S. Victor Tipton, (editor's address: 606 Minnehaha Lane, Maitland, FL 32751, (407)647-1406). Index available (Current iss.). cum. index. **Ad Acc, Adv Mgr:** L. Garcia, **Tel** (904)224-9403. **Circ:** 4,500 (ctrl). available on diskette. ***Continues*** *Academy of Florida Trial Lawyers. AFTL Bulletin.*
Desc: Articles , news, and information exchanges with cases in all aspects of the law.

US/0022-8486
JOURNAL OF THE KANSAS BAR ASSOCIATION, THE. [J. Kans. Bar Assoc.]. **Main/Corp** Kansas Bar Association. Vol. 36, No. 2 (Summer 1967)-. Periodical. English. Ten times a year. $45.00. Kansas Bar Association, PO Box 1037, Topeka KS 66601. **Tel** (913)234-5696, FAX (913)234-3813. **ED** Patti Slider. **LC** K2; .A66. **DD** 340/.09781. Index available. cum. index. **Bk Rev. Ad Acc. Circ:** 5,300 (ctrl). available on microfilm and microfiche from University Microfilms International (UMI). ***Continues*** *Journal of the Kansas Bar Association. Bar Association of the State of Kansas.;* ***Absorbed*** *Kansas Barletter.*
Desc: Contains articles, reports, and practice aids of interest to the legal profession.
Ind/Abst Fed. Tax Artic.; Index Leg. Period.; Law Office Inf. Serv.; Leg. Resour. Index (1980-); LegalTrac (1980-).

UK/0458-8711
JOURNAL OF THE LAW SOCIETY OF SCOTLAND, THE. [J. Law Soc. Scotl.]. **Added/Corp** Law Society of Scotland. Vol. 1, No. 1 (Jan. 1956)-. Periodical. English. mo. £48.00. Law Society of Scotland, Law Society's Hall, 26 Drumsheugh Gardens, Edinburgh EH3 7YR Scotland. **Tel** 011 44 31 2267411, FAX 011 44 31 2252934. **ED** Joan N Aitken (editor's address: Shphard's Lodge, Gloickbea, Kiltarlity Inverness Shire IV4 7HR Scotland; editor's phone: 44 463 74369). Index available. **Bk Rev,** (Qty: 80). **Ad Acc, Adv Mgr:** N Kelly, **Tel** 44 31 2282792. **Circ:** 9,300. ***Absorbed*** *Conveyancing Review.*
Desc: News and articles regarding Scots Law.
Ind/Abst Curr. Law Index (1980-); Leg. Resour. Index (1980-); LegalTrac (1980-).

US/0196-7487
JOURNAL OF THE LEGAL PROFESSION, THE. [J. legal prof.]. (Spring 1976)-. English. an. $12.00 (add $2.00 for postage) US, (add $3.00 for postage) Canada, (add $4.00 for postage) other. University of Alabama School of Law, PO Box 870382, Tuscaloosa AL 35487. **Tel** (205)348-1175. **LC** K10; .O8958. **DD** 340/.05.
Ind/Abst Curr. Law Index (1980-); Index Leg. Period.; Leg. Resour. Index (1980-); LegalTrac (1980-).

US/0026-6485
JOURNAL OF THE MISSOURI BAR. [J. Mo. Bar]. **Added/Corp** Missouri Bar. **VFOAT** Journal of Missouri Bar. Vol. 1, No. 1 (Jan. 1945)-. Periodical. English. Six times a year. $12.00. The Missouri Bar, 326 Monroe, Jefferson City MO 65101. **Tel** (314)635-4128. **ED** Gary P. Toohey. **LC** KF200; .J685. **DD** 340/.05. Index available. **Ad Acc. Circ:** 17,600 (ctrl). available on microfilm and microfiche from University Microfilms International (UMI). ***Continues*** *Missouri Bar Journal.*
Desc: Articles legal in nature. Mostly 'bread and butter' articles for use by the lawyer in his everyday practice.
Ind/Abst Curr. Law Index (1980-); Fed. Tax Artic.; Index Leg. Period.; Law Office Inf. Serv.; Leg. Resour. Index (1980-); LegalTrac (1980-).

US/1049-5304
JOURNAL OF THE NEW YORK INSTITUTE OF LEGAL RESEARCH, THE. [J. N. Y. Inst. Leg. Res.]. **Added/Corp** New York Institute of Legal Research. Vol. 1, No. 1 (Feb. 1991)-. Periodical. English. bm. $95.00. New York Institute of Legal Research, PO Box 398, Yorktown Heights NY 10598-0398. **DD** 340.

US
JOURNAL OF THE SENATE, STATE OF FLORIDA. **Main/Corp** Florida. Legislature. Senate. 22nd Regular Session (1929)-. English. ir (During legislative sessions). Free to congressional staff; $10.00 others. Secretary of the State of Florida, The Capitol/Suite 404, Tallahassee FL 32301. **Tel** (904)487-5270. ***Continues*** *Florida. Legislature. Senate. Journal of the State Senate of Florida of the Session of ... .*

US/0888-2142
JOURNAL OF THE SUFFOLK ACADEMY OF LAW. [J. Suffolk Acad. Law]. **Added/Corp** Suffolk Academy of Law. Vol. 1, No. 1 (Winter 1980)-. Periodical. English. ir (numbered series). Price varies per volume. Suffolk Academy of Law, 340 Veterans Memorial Highway, Commack NY 11725. **Tel** (516)864-1666. **LC** K10; .O896. **DD** 349.747/05; 347.47005.
Ind/Abst Curr. Law Index (1982-); Leg. Resour. Index (1982-); LegalTrac (1982-).

CG
JOURNAL OFFICIEL. **Main/Corp** Zaire. French. sm. 28.40. Polais de Justice, Service du Journal Officiel, Kinshasa Zaire. **DD** 340/.0967/51. available on microfilm from New York Public Library. ***Continues*** *Moniteur Congolais.*

AE
JOURNAL OFFICIEL DE LA REPUBLIQUE ALGERIENNE DEMOCRATIQUE ET POPULAIRE. **Main/Corp** Algeria. **VFOAT** Jaridah Al-Rasmiyah. Vol 1. No. 1 (Oct. 26, 1962)-. Periodical. French (summaries and/or abstracts in Arabic). wk. Imprimerie Officielle Algeria, 7-9 et 13 Avenue Abdelkader-Benba, Alger Algeria. available on microfilm. ***Continues*** *Journal Officiel de l'Etat Algerien.*

SZ
JOURNAL OFFICIEL DE LA REPUBLIQUE ET CANTON DU JURA. **Main/Corp** Jura (Switzerland). French. wk. 40.00F Switzerland; $67.00 US. Journal Officiel de la Republique et Canton du Jura, Case Potale 135, 2900 Porrentruy 1 Switzerland. **Tel** 066/66 10 13, telex 93 11 85. **DD** 348.494/3026; 344.9430826. Index available. **Circ:** 3,200.
Desc: Publication of laws, decrees, ordinances, orders of the parliament, government and departments, official decisions of public administration, courts and municipalities.

FR
JOURNAL OFFICIEL DE LA REPUBLIQUE FRANCAISE. EDITION DES LOIS ET DECRETS : NUMERO COMPLEMENTAIRE. **Main/Corp** France. French. Direction des Journaux Officiels, 26 rue Desaix, 75727 Paris Cedex 15 France. **Tel** 011 33 1 40587500. **DD** 340/.0944.
Ind/Abst World Agric. Econ.

FR
JOURNAL OFFICIEL DE LA REPUBLIQUE FRANCAISE LES LOIS ET DECRETS. TABLES. French. mo. Direction des Journaux Officiels, 26 rue Desaix, 75727 Paris Cedex 15 France. **Tel** 011 33 1 40587500.

CF
JOURNAL OFFICIEL DE LA REPUBLIQUE POPULAIRE DU CONGO. **Main/Corp** Congo (Brazzaville). (1958)-. French. sw (104 issues). 6335.00CFAF Congo; 6840.00CFAF, $25.22 other. Imprimerie Nationale / Congo, Boite Postale 2087, Brazzaville Congo. **LC** Microfilm LL-02140 KRK.

FR
JOURNAL OFFICIEL. LOIS ET DECRETS. **Main/Corp** France. Periodical. French. da. Direction des Journaux Officiels, 26 rue Desaix, 75727 Paris Cedex 15 France. **Tel** 011 33 1 40587500.

PK
JOURNAL / PAKISTAN BAR COUNCIL. **Main/Corp** Pakistan Bar Council. **VFOAT** Pakistan Bar Kaunsil Jarnal. Vol. 1 (Jan. 1978)-. Periodical. English (Urdu). qt. 60.00, $12.00 US. Pakistan Bar Council, 1 Begum Road, Lahore Pakistan. **LC** K16; .A38. **DD** 349.549/1/05.

●US/1073-8800
JOURNAL / RHODE ISLAND BAR ASSOCIATION. [J. - Rhode Island Bar Assoc.]. **Added/Corp** Rhode Island Bar Association. **VFOAT** Rhode Island Bar Journal. (1993)-. Academic Scholarly Publication. English. mo (9 issues). $20.00. Rhode Island Bar Association, 115 Cedar Street, Providence RI 02903. **Tel** (401)421-5740, FAX (401)421-2703. **ED** Helen Desmond McDonald. **DD** 340. Index available (bound in June issue). **Bk Rev**, (Qty: 4). **Ad Acc**, **Adv Mgr:** Beth Bailey. **Circ:** 4,300 (ctrl). ***Continues*** *Rhode Island Bar Journal, 0556-8595.*
Ind/Abst Curr. Law Index; Fed. Tax Artic.; Law Office Inf. Serv.; Leg. Resour. Index; LegalTrac.

UK
JOWITT'S DICTIONARY OF ENGLISH LAW. English. ir. £135.00. Associated Book Publishers, North Way Andover, Hampshire SP10 5BE England. **Tel** 011 44 264 332424.

PR
JTS INFORMA. **VFOAT** J.T.S. Informa. Vol. 1, No. 1 (June 30, 1980)-. Periodical. Spanish. ir. Publicaciones JTS Inc, PO Box 4509, Old San Juan, Puerto Rico 00905. **LC** KGV70; .A24. **DD** 348.7295/041; 347.2950841.

US/0022-5800
JUDICATURE. [Judicature]. **Added/Corp** American Judicature Society. American Judicature Society. Annual Report of Executive Director. American Judicature Society. Annual Report. Vol. 50, (June/July (1966)-. Periodical. English. Six times a year (Feb., Apr., June, July, Oct., Dec.). $48.00 (one year); $55.00 (regular), $30.00 (age 30 or less), $125.00 (sustaining), $300.00 (sponsoring), $600.00 (contibuting) Comes with American Judicature Society membership. American Judicature Society, 25 East Washington Street, Suite 1600, Chicago IL 60602. **Tel** (312)558-6900, FAX (312)558-9175. **ED** David Richert. **LC** K10; .U3. Index available. **Bk Rev**, (Qty: 12). **Ad Acc**, **Adv Mgr:** David Richart, **Tel** (312)558-6900. **Pr Rev. Circ:** 24,000. available on microfilm and microfiche from University Microfilms International (UMI). Documents available from The Genuine Article. ***Continues*** *Journal of the American Judicature Society.*
Desc: The administration of justice and its improvement, including consideration of court organization operation and personnel.
Ind/Abst Acad. Search (July 1993-); Am. Hist. Life (1969-1974); Arts Humanit. Citation Index [Select. Cov.]; Bowne Dig. Corp. Sec. Lawyers; Crim. Justice Abstr.; Crim. Justice Period. Index (1980-); Curr. Contents Soc. Behav. Sci.; Curr. Law Index (1980-); Fed. Tax Artic.; Index Leg. Period.; INFO-SOUTH Abstr.; Law Office Inf. Serv. (1969-1974); Leg. Resour. Index (1980-); LegalTrac (1969-1974, 1979-); Mag. Search; PAIS Int. Print (1991-); Res. Alert [Full Cov.]; Soc. Plann. Policy Dev. Abstr.; Soc. Sci. Cit. Index [Full Cov.].

US/0148-4982
JUDICIAL FUNCTION OUTLINE. 1977-. English. an. The National Judicial College, Judicial College Building, University of Nevada Reno, Reno NV 89557. **Tel** (702)784-6747. **LC** KF8700.A59; J8. **DD** 347/.73/1.

US/0449-5519
JUDICIAL HIGHLIGHTS BULLETIN. V. 1-March 1970-. Bulletin. English. Pennsylvania Bar Association, PO Box 186, Harrisburg PA 17108. **Tel** (717)238-6715, FAX (717)238-7182. **LC** KFP81; .J84. **DD** 348/.748/046.

UK
JUDICIAL REVIEW. (1956)-. English. Three times a year. £52.00 Europe; £55.00 other. Sweet & Maxwell Ltd., South Quay Plaza, 183 Marsh Wall, London E14 9FT England. **Tel** 011 44 264 342899, FAX 011 44 264 342723, telex 929089 ITPINF G.

JA
JUMIN KIHON DAICHO ROPPO / JICHISHO GYOSEIKYOKU KANSHU. **Main/Corp** Japan. Began with 1971. Japanese. ¥2500. Nihon Kajo Shuppan Kabushiki, Kaisha 16-6 Minami Nagasaki 3 Toshima-ku, Tokyo-to 170-91 Japan.

GW/0170-1452
JURA : JURISTISCHE AUSBILDUNG. **VFOAT** Juristische Ausbildung. Vol. 1 (Jan. 1979)-. Periodical. German. mo. DM188.00. Walter de Gruyter Inc., PO Box 303421, D 10728 Berlin Germany. **Tel** 011 49 30 260050, FAX 011 49 30 26005251. **LC** K10; .U62. **DD** 349.43/05.

MX
JURIDICA. Spanish. an. $25,000 Mexico; $3.00 US; $4.00 other. Universidad Iberoamericana / Derecho - Law, Depto de Derecho Rev Juridica, Prol Paseo de la Reforma/880, Col Lomas de Santa Fe 01210 DF Mexico. **Tel** 011 52 5 570-7622. **ED** Jorge Gonzalez Chavez, Alejandra Serrano Manrique. **DD** 340/.098. Index available. cum. index. **Bk Rev**. **Pr Rev. Circ:** 1,000 (ctrl).
Desc: Covers all aspects of law. Occasionally one issue is devoted to a specific topic within law.

UK/0022-6785
JURIDICAL REVIEW, THE. [Jurid. rev.]. Vol. 1 (1889)-. Periodical. English. sa. £48.00. W Green & Son Ltd, St Giles Street, Edinburgh EH1 1PU Scotland. **Tel** 011 44 31 2254879, FAX 011 44 31 2252104. cum. index. available on microfilm from University Microfilms International (UMI).
Ind/Abst Index Leg. Period.; Leg. Resour. Index (1980-); LegalTrac (1980-).

US/0897-1277
JURIMETRICS (CHICAGO, ILL.). (JURIMETRICS.). [Jurimetrics]. **Added/Corp** American Bar Association. Section of Science and Technology. Arizona State University. College of Law. Arizona State University. Center for the Study of Law, Science, and Technology. **VFOAT** Jurimetrics Journal of Law, Science and Technology; Jurimetrics Journal. Vol. 19, No. 2 (Winter 1978)-. Periodical. English. qt (4 issues). $34.00. American Bar Association, 750 North Lake Shore Drive, Chicago IL 60611. **Tel** (312)988-5522, (312)988-5241, FAX (312)988-5528, telex 270593. **LC** K10; .U67. **DD** 344/.095/05; 342.49505. Documents available from Ask*IEEE. ***Continues*** *Jurimetrics Journal, 0022-6793.*
Ind/Abst Bowne Dig. Corp. Sec. Lawyers; Comput. Rev.; Crim. Justice Period. Index; Fed. Tax Artic.; Index Leg. Period.; INSPEC (Winter 1978-); Law Office Inf. Serv.; Leg. Resour. Index (1980-); LegalTrac (1980-).

US/0022-6807
JURIS. **Added/Corp** Duquesne University. School of Law. (1967)-. English. Three times a year (April, October, and December). Free. Duquesne University School of Law, 900 Locust Street, Pittsburgh PA 15282. **Tel** (412)396-5020, (412)396-6283, (412)396-6186, FAX (412)296-6283. **ED** Amy Haduch. **LC** K10; .U7. **DD** 340/.0973. **Bk Rev**. **Ad Acc**. **Circ:** 4,500 (ctrl).
Desc: Legal newsmagazine covering topics of current legal interest on local, statewide and national level.
Ind/Abst Fed. Tax Artic.

FR
JURIS-CLASSEUR : BAIL A LOYER. (19??)-. French. ir. Editions Techniques, 141 rue de Javel, 75747 Paris Cedex 15 France. **Tel** 011 33 1 45589100.

FR/0758-671X
JURIS-CLASSEUR COLLECTIVITES LOCALES. [Juris-classeur collectiv. locales]. (198?)-. French. 655.00F (updates). Editions Techniques, 141 rue de Javel, 75747 Paris Cedex 15 France. **Tel** 011 33 1 45589100. **UDC** 352.

FR/0750-8387
JURIS-CLASSEUR DE LA SECURITE SOCIALE. (1949)-. French. ir. 268.00F (updates). Editions Techniques, 141 rue de Javel, 75747 Paris Cedex 15 France. **Tel** 011 33 1 45589100. **UDC** 34:368.4.

FR
JURIS-CLASSEUR : DROIT COMMERCIAL. TRAITE DES SOCIETES. (19??)-. French. ir. 2350.00F. Editions Techniques, 141 rue de Javel, 75747 Paris Cedex 15 France. **Tel** 011 33 1 45589100.

US
JURIS NEWSLETTER. **Main/Corp** United States. Dept. of Justice. **VAT** Justice Retrieval and Inquiry System Newsletter. (Feb. 7, 1977)-. English. US Department of Justice, 10th Street & Constitution Avenue NW, Washington DC 20530. **Tel** (202)514-2000, FAX (202)633-4371. **LC** KF242.A1; J8. **DD** 340/.028/5.

US/0146-2709
JURIS QUAESITOR. V. 1- Fall 1976-. English (English). University of New Hampshire Student Press, Durham NH 03824. **LC** K10; .U725. **DD** 340/.05.

US/0162-3079
JURISDOCS. **Added/Corp** American Association of Law Libraries. Government Documents SIS. Vol. 1 (Sept. 1978)-. Periodical. English. Four times a year. Texas Southern University Law Library, 3201 Wheeler Street, Houston TX 77004. **Tel** (713)527-7125.
Ind/Abst Leg. Inf. Manage. Index (19??-).

CN/1180-341X
JURISELECTION (QUEBEC). (JURISELECTION / COMMISSION D'APPEL EN MATIERE DE LESIONS PROFESSIONNELLES.). [JuriSelection]. **Added/Corp** Quebec (Province). Commission d'Appel en Matiere de Lesions Professionnelles. **VFOAT** Decisions Recentes. (19??)-. Periodical. French. Twenty-six times a year (24 issues + 2 index updates in September and March). 25.00Can$. Comm Appel Mat Lesions Professionnelles, 1200 Avenue Bureau 350, McGill College, Montreal QUE H3B 4G7 Canada. **Tel** (514)873-7188. **DD** 344.714/021/02643. ***Continues*** *Commission d'Appel en Matiere de Lesions Professionnelles.*

CN/0835-0892
JURISFEMME (OTTAWA). (JURISFEMME / NATIONAL ASSOCIATION OF WOMEN AND THE LAW.). [Jurisfemme]. **Added/Corp** National Association

of Women and the Law. Vol. 7, No. 3 (Feb. 1987)-. Periodical. English (French). Four times a year. $30.00. National Association of Women & the Law, 604 1 Nicholas Street, Ottawa Ontario K1N 7B7 Canada. **DD** 342.71/0878. *Continues* National Association of Women and the Law. English and French., 0829-8289.
 Desc: Articles related to women in the legal profession and judicial system; includes child care, family law, equal rights, reproductive issues, criminal justice, income security, employment, and labor.

CN/0705-3061
JURISPRUDENCE EXPRESS. [Jurisprud. express]. **Added/Corp** Societe Quebecoise d'Information Juridique. (Oct. 14, 1977)-. Periodical. French. Fifty times a year. 315.00Can$. Societe Quebecoise d'Information Juridique, 10 rue St Jacques Bureau 101, Montreal Quebec H2Y 1L3 Canada. **Tel** (514)842-8745, FAX (514)844-8984. Index available. cum. index. **Ad Acc. Circ:** 536,000 (ctrl). available on microfiche.
 Desc: Reports summaries of more than 1100 decisions recently handed down by Supreme Court of Canada and other tribunals.

CN/0830-0380
JURISPRUDENCE LOGEMENT. [Jurisprud. logement]. **Added/Corp** Quebec (Province). Regie du Logement. No. 1 (1982)-. French. bm. 75.00Can$. SOQUIJ Societe Quebecoise Info Juridique, 276 rue Street, Jacques Suite 310, Montreal Quebec H2Y 1N3 Canada. **Tel** (514)842-8745. **LC** KEQ426.A49; C65. **DD** 346.71404/34/05; 347.140643405. *Continues* Quebec (Province). Regie du Logement. Decisions de la Regie du Logement, 0226-885X.

AG
JURISPRUDENCIA ARGENTINA. Spanish.
 Ind/Abst Index Foreign Leg. Per.

BL
JURISPRUDENCIA CATARINENSE. **Main/Corp** Santa Catarina (Brasil : State). Tribunal de Justica. V. 1- 3rd Quarter 1973-. Portuguese. qt. Santa Catarina Brazil Tribunal de Justica, Rua Duarte Schutel No 11, Caixa Postal 427, 88.000 Florianopolis Brazil.

SP
JURISPRUDENCIA DE SEGURIDAD SOCIAL Y SANIDAD. Periodical. Spanish. ir. $28.00. Servicio de Publicaciones Secretaria General Technica, Ministerio de Sanidad y Seguridad Social, Paseo Del Prado 18, Madrid 14 Spain. **DD** 344.46/0.

PR
JURISPRUDENCIA DEL TRIBUNAL SUPREMO DE PUERTO RICO. **Main/Corp** Puerto Rico. Supreme Court. **Added/Corp** Puerto Rico. Supreme Court. Reglamento del Tribunal Supremo de Puerto Rico. VFOAT JTS. (19??)-. Spanish. ir. $240.00. Jurisprudencia Tribun Sup Inc, PO Box 4509, Old San Juan, Puerto Rico 00905. **DD** 348.7295/041; 347.2950841.

GW
JURIST (BADEN-BADEN, GERMANY). (DER JURIST.). Periodical. German. wk. DM22.90 per month. Verlag Neue Wirtschaftsbriefe, Eschstrasse 22, D-44629 Herne Germany. **Tel** 011 49 2323 1410. **LC** K10; .U763. **DD** 349.43/05; 344.3005.

US/0022-6858
JURIST (WASHINGTON), THE. See Religion and Theology-Catholicism.

CN/0829-5476
JURISTE (MONCTON). See College and School Publications.

DK/0107-699X
JURISTEN / DANMARKS JURIST- OG KONOMFORBUND. **Added/Corp** Danmarks Jurist- Og Konomforbund. (19??)-. Periodical. Danish. kr290.00, Free (members). Jurist Okonomforbundets Forlag, Gothersgade 133, 1123 Copenhagen Denmark. **Tel** 011 45 1 33142920. **LC** K10; .U728. *Continues* Juristen & Konomen.
 Ind/Abst Index Foreign Leg. Per.

GW/0022-6882
JURISTENZEITUNG. [Juristenzeitung]. Vol. 6, (1951)-. Periodical. German. sm (24 issues). DM280.00. JCB Mohr / Paul Siebeck, Postfach 2040, D 72010 Tuebingen Germany. **Tel** 011 49 7071 9230, FAX 011 49 7071 51104, telex 7/262872 mohr d. **ED** Hans-Erich Brandner, Bernhard Grossfeld, Christian Starck, Rolf Sturner, and Ulrich Weber. **[CCC]**. **Bk Rev. Ad Acc. Circ:** 6,000. *Formed by the union of* Deutsche Rechts-Zeitschrift *and* Suddeutsche Juristen-Zeitung.
 Desc: A law journal containing contributions on current aspects of German law, legislation and jurisdiction.
 Ind/Abst Energy Res. Abstr. (April 1982-).

GW
JURISTISCHE ABHANDLUNGEN. Monographic series. German. ir. Price varies per volume. Vittorio Klostermann, Frauenlobstrasse 22, D 60487 Frankfurt Germany. **Tel** 011 49 69 9708160.

GW
JURISTISCHE ARBEITSBLATTER. VFOAT JA. Periodical. German. mo. Hermann Luchterhand Verlag, Postfach 2352, D 56513 Neuwied Germany. **Tel** 011 49 2631 8010. **LC** K10; .U74. **DD** 340/.0943.

AU/0022-6912
JURISTISCHE BLATTER. [J. Bl.]. VOL. 1-, NO.3 (MARCH 1872)-. Periodical. German. Twelve times a year. DM452.00. Springer-Verlag Wien, Sachsenplatz 4 6, PO Box 89, A-1201 Vienna Austria. **Tel** 011 43 1 3302415. (**Subscription address:** Springer Verlag New York Inc. / for North America, 44 Hartz Way, Secaucus NJ 07096.) **ED** M. Burgstaller, F. Bydlinski, P. Doralt, W. Kastner, H. R. Klecatsky, V. Liebscher, S. Morscher, P. Rummel, I. Seidl-Hohenveldern, and H. Torggler. **DD** 340/.09436. **CODEN** JUBLA7. **[CCC]**. *Absorbed* Gerichts-Zeitung.
 Desc: Prints articles on theoretical and practical problems from all area of Austrian jurisprudence. A detailed section on decisions documents the evolution of jurisprudential trends.
 Ind/Abst Index Foreign Leg. Per.

GW/0022-6920
JURISTISCHE RUNDSCHAU. (19??)-. Periodical. German. mo. $260.60. Walter de Gruyter Inc., PO Box 303421, D 10728 Berlin Germany. **Tel** 011 49 30 260050, FAX 011 49 30 26005251.
 Ind/Abst Index Foreign Leg. Per.

JA
JURISUTO. VFOAT Jurist. No. 1 (1952)-. Periodical. Japanese. Twenty-four times a year. $476.00. (**Subscription address:** Kyowa Book Company Inc., 1 38 Kanda Jinbocho Chiyoda-ku, Tokyo 101 Japan.) cum. index.
 Ind/Abst Index Foreign Leg. Per.

CN
JURY: A HANDBOOK OF LAW AND PROCEDURE, THE. English. ir. $95.00, $40.00 (updates). Butterworth & Company Ltd. / Canada, 75 Clegg Road, Markham Ontario L6G 1A1 Canada. **Tel** (905)479-2665, (800)668-6481. **ED** Balfour Der. Index available. **Pr Rev. Circ:** 272 (ctrl).
 Desc: Examines the role of the jury in a criminal trial. National in scope, it consists of materials derived from statutes, Rules of Court and Caselaw.

US
JURY (NEW YORK, N.Y.). (THE JURY : TECHNIQUES FOR THE TRIAL LAWYER.). 1983-. Periodical. English. an. Practising Law Institute, 810 Seventh Avenue, New York NY 10019-5818. **Tel** (212)765-5700, FAX (212)581-4670 general correspondence, (212)265-4742 orders and billing inquiries. **LC** KF8972.Z9; J83. **DD** 347.73/752.

US/0889-6003
JURY TRIALS AND TRIBULATIONS, INC. (JURY TRIALS AND TRIBULATIONS, INC. : [NEWSLETTER].). [Jury Trials Tribul. Inc.]. **Added/Corp** Jury Trials and Tribulations, Inc. (19??)-. Periodical. English. sm. $200.00. Jury Trials and Tribulations, 9100 South Dadeland Boulevard, Suite 400, Miami FL 33156. **Tel** (305) 670-9735, FAX (305) 661-2970. **DD** 342.

US/0888-0646
JURY VERDICTS WEEKLY. Vol. 1, No. 1 (1957)-. Periodical. English. Fifty-two times a year (Plus 2 indexes (Jan. & July)). $350.00 (without index); $540.00 (with index). Jury Verdicts Weekly Inc, 738 Montecito Center, Suite A, Santa Rosa CA 95405. **Tel** (707)539-5454, (800)445-6823, FAX (707)539-1839. **LC** KFC310.A59; J87. **DD** 346.79403; 347.94063. Index available.

PE
JUS. Vol. 1 (May 1974)-. Periodical. Spanish. L65.000 Italy; L101.000, $78.00 other. Editorial Jus, Paseo Colon 270 of 201, Lima Peru. **LC** K10; .U748.

GW/0022-6939
JUS. JURISTISCHE SCHULUNG. (JURISTISCHE SCHULUNG.). [JUS, Jurist. Schul.]. VFOAT JuS. Vol. 1 (Jan. 1961)-. Periodical. German. Twelve times a year. Price varies. CH Beck Verlagsbuchhandlung, D 80791 Munich Germany. **Tel** 011 49 89 381891.
 Ind/Abst Coal Abstr.; Energy Res. Abstr. (Nov. 1981-); Index Foreign Leg. Per.

BE/0775-0803
JUS MEDICUM. See Medical Science and Technology-Forensic Medicine, Medical Jurisprudence.

NO/0022-6971
JUSSENS VENNER. [Jussens venner]. Vol. 1 (1952)-. Periodical. Norwegian. bm. Kr495.00, $85.00. Scandinavian University Press, PO Box 2959 Toeyen, N 0608 Oslo 6 Norway. **Tel** 011 47 2 2575400, FAX 011 47 2 2575353, telex 71896 UROR N. (**Subscription address:** Scandinavian University Press, 200 Meacham Ave., Elmont NY 11003.) **ED** Filip Truyen and Soeren Wiig. **DD** 340. Index available. **Bk Rev. Ad Acc. Circ:** 4,000.
 Desc: A journal on the study of law. For students and lawyers in general.
 Ind/Abst Index Foreign Leg. Per.

CN/0824-281X
JUST CAUSE. [Just cause]. **Added/Corp** Canadian Legal Advocacy Information and Research Association of the Disabled. Vol. 1, No. 1 (Winter 1983)-. Periodical. English (French). Four times a year. 20.00Can$. Canadian Legal Advocacy Information and Research Association of the Disabled, PO Box 3553, Station C, Ottawa Ontario K1Y 4J7 Canada. **Tel** (613)230-8515. **ED** H. Wierenga. **DD** 346.7101/3. **Bk Rev. Circ:** 1,500.
 Desc: A journal of law and people with disabilities.
 Ind/Abst Can. Legal Lit.; Index Can. Leg. Period. Lit.

US/0738-6494
JUST COMPENSATION. (JUST COMPENSATION : A MONTHLY REPORT ON CONDEMNATION CASES.). Vol. 1 (1956)-. English. mo. $90.00. Just Compensation Inc, PO Box 5133, Sherman Oaks CA 91403. **Tel** (818)848-6765. **ED** Gideon Kanner. Index available. **Bk Rev.** ctrl circ.
 Desc: Reports on developments in the law of eminent domain and inverse condemnation.

●UK/1351-5756
JUSTICE OF THE PEACE & LOCAL GOVERNMENT LAW. See Public Administration.

UK/0141-5859
JUSTICE OF THE PEACE (CHICHESTER). *Title Change.* (JUSTICE OF THE PEACE.). [Justice peace]. (1971)-(1993). Periodical. English. wk. Justice of the Peace Limited, Little London, Chichester West Sussex, PO19 1PG England. **Tel** 011 44 243 787841, FAX 011 44 243 779278. **LC** K10; .U79. **DD** 347/.42/016. Index available. **Bk Rev. Ad Acc.** *Continues in part* Justice of the Peace and Local Government Review, 0022-703X. *Continued by* Justice of the Peace & Local Government Law.
 Desc: The oldest established legal journal to be published in the world, concerning the magistrates' court and the crown court.
 Ind/Abst Appl. Soc. Sci. Index Abstr.; Sage Race Relat. Abstr.

UK/0264-3731
JUSTICE OF THE PEACE REPORTS (CHICHESTER, WEST SUSSEX). (JUSTICE OF THE PEACE REPORTS.). **Added/Corp** Justice of the Peace Ltd. Vol. 147 (Jan. 1983)-. English. bw (26 times a year). £120.50 UK; £122.50 other. Justice of the Peace Limited, Little London, Chichester West Sussex, PO19 1PG England. **Tel** 011 44 243 787841, FAX 011 44 243 779278. **ED** Nicholas Tell. **LC** KD291; .J87. **DD** 348.41/041; 344.10841. Index available. cum. index. **Ad Acc.** *Continues* Justice of the Peace and Local Government Review Reports.
 Desc: Covers criminal law and procedure, domestic proceedings, coroners' law, consumer law, juvenile court, licensing law, local government law and road law.

US/0888-4315
JUSTICE PROFESSIONAL, THE. [Justice prof.]. Vol. 1, No. 2 (Fall 1986)-. Periodical. English. sa (Summer & Winter). $22.00 US; $28.00 other. Vande Vere Publishing, Ltd., PO Box 226, 8744 College Avenue, Berrien Springs MI 49103. **Tel** (616)695-3442, FAX (616)695-6515. **DD** 364. **Bk Rev. Ad Acc.**
 Ind/Abst Crim. Justice Abstr.; Crim. Penol. Police Sci. Abstr.

CN/0707-8501
JUSTICE (QUEBEC). *Ceased.* (JUSTICE : LE MAGAZINE DU MINISTERRE DE LA JUSTICE DE QUEBEC). **Added/Corp** Quebec (Province). Ministere de la Justice. (Mar.-Apr. 1979)-(May 1993). Periodical. French. mo (10 issues). Magazine Justice Inc., 1200 Route de L'Eglise, Bur 111, Sainte-Foy Quebec G1V 4M1 Canada. **Tel** (418)831-0790. **LC** KEQ1170.A72; J85. **DD** 345.714/05/05; 347.1405505.
 Ind/Abst Point Repere (1984-).

CN/1181-9243
JUSTICE RESEARCH NOTES. [Just. res. notes]. **Added/Corp** Canada. Dept. of Justice. Research and Development Directorate. VFOAT Notes de Recherche, Justice. No. 1 (Nov. 1990)-. Periodical. English (French). ir. Free on request. Research & Development Directorate, Dept. of Justice, Ottawa K1A 0H8 Canada. **Tel** (613)957-9609. **DD** 364.971/05.

Law

US/1056-8905
JUSTICE (WASHINGTON, D.C.).
(JUSTICE.). [Justice]. **Main/Corp** United States. Dept. of Justice. Vol. 1, No. 1 (Spring 1991)-. Periodical. English. sa. US Department of Justice, 10th Street & Constitution Avenue NW, Washington DC 20530. **Tel** (202)514-2000, FAX (202)633-4371. **LC** KF5106.A15; U56. **DD** 353.5/05.

US/0891-9224
JUSTICE WATCH / COMMITTEE FOR PUBLIC JUSTICE, INC. Suspended. [Justice watch]. Vol. 5, No. 1 (Feb. 1982)-?. Periodical. English. an (four no. a year). $32.00 (institutions), $12.00 (individuals). The Nation, 72 Fifth Avenue, New York NY 10011. **Tel** (212)242-8400. **LC** KF8700.A15; J87. **DD** 345.73/05; 347.3055. **Continues** Justice Department Watch.

AT/0157-5317
JUSTINIAN. [Justinian]. (1979)-. Periodical. English. Ten times a year (Except Jan. & July). 195.00Aus$ (ten issues); 320.00Aus$ (twenty issues). Rekata Pty Ltd, PO Box 2669, Sydney NSW 2001 Australia. **Tel** 011 61 2 3607788, FAX 011 61 2 3607838. **ED** Richard Ackland. **DD** 340.0994. ctrl circ.

UK
JUSTIS [COMPUTER FILE] : CELEX, OFFICIAL LEGAL DATABASE OF THE EUROPEAN COMMUNITIES. VFOAT JUSTIS CD-ROM; Celex. (19??)-. Periodical. English. qt. £1250.00 all except Benelux countries, Sweden, Hong Kong, Singapore, Malaysia, Israel, Germany, Austria, Switzerland and Italy (English edition). Context Limited, Tranley House, Tranley Mews Fleet, London NW3 2QW England. **Tel** 44 71 267 7055.
Desc: System requirements: IBM PC AT 286 or 386 or PS/2 or compatible, 450K, DOS 3.0 or higher, CD-ROM drive, MS-DOS CD-ROM extensions 2.1 or higher, Hercules monochrome, EGA or VGA monitor, hard disk.

GW
JUSTUF; DAS JURAMAGAZIN. Weimann Presse und Verlag, Hatschiergasse 21, W-5300 Bonn 1 Germany.

●US/1062-2926
JUVENILE AND FAMILY JUSTICE TODAY. (JUVENILE AND FAMILY JUSTICE TODAY: A PUBLICATION OF THE NATIONAL COUNCIL OF JUVENILE AND FAMILY COURT JUDGES.). [Juv. fam. justice today]. **Added/Corp** National Council of Juvenile and Family Court Judges. Vol. 1, No. 1 (Spring 1992)-. Periodical. English. Six times a year. $16.00 US & Canada; $21.00 other. National Council of Juvenile and Family Court Judges, PO Box 8978, Reno NV 89507. **Tel** (702)784-6012. **LC** KF9772; .J88. **DD** 347/.73/08; 347. **Continues** Juvenile and Family Court Newsletter, 0162-9859.

JA
KAISETSU KYOIKU ROPPO. Main/Corp Japan. (19??)-. Periodical. Japanese. ¥2000. Sanseido, 1 Kanda Jinbocho 1, Chiyoda-ku 101, Tokyo Japan.

JA/0388-886X
KANSAI UNIVERSITY REVIEW OF LAW AND POLITICS. Added/Corp Kansai Daigaku. Hogakubu. **VFOAT** Review of Law and Politics. No. 1, (Mar. 1980)-. Periodical. English (German and Italian). an. Exchange Department (LP), Kansai University Library, PO Box 50, Suita Osaka 564 Japan. **LC** K11; .A53. **DD** 340/.05.
Ind/Abst Int. Polit. Sci. Abstr.

US/1055-8942
KANSAS JOURNAL OF LAW & PUBLIC POLICY, THE. [Kans. j. law public policy]. **Added/Corp** University of Kansas. School of Law. Vol. 1, No. 1 (Summer 1991)-. Periodical. English. Three times a year. $30.00. University of Kansas School of Law, Kansas Journal of Law & Public Policy, Green Hall, Lawrence KS 66045. **DD** 343.

US
KANSAS LEGAL DIRECTORY, THE. (19??)-. English. an. $42.00. Legal Directories Publishing Company, 9111 Garland Road, PO Box 189000, Dallas TX 75218. **Tel** (214)321-3238, 800 447-5375. **ED** Patti Slider. **LC** KF192.K3; K35. **Ad Acc. Circ:** 5,300 (ctrl).
Desc: Contains a list of Kansas Bar Association members.

US
KANSAS STATUTES ANNOTATED. Main/Corp Kansas. (19??)-. Periodical. English. an. $42.35. Secretary of State / Kansas, Capitol Building/2nd Floor, Topeka KS 66612. **Tel** (913)296-2236.

II
KARNATAKA LAW JOURNAL. SUPPLEMENT, THE. Jan. 1974-. Periodical. English. mo. Kamataka Law Journal, Sri Bam No 4, Fourth Cross, Shankarapura Bangalore-4 India. **DD** 340/.095487.

IO
KATALOG PERATURAN PERUNDANG-UNDANGAN REPUBLIK INDONESIA. Indonesian. Pusat Dokumentasi Hukum, Fakultas Hukum, Universitas Indonesia, Jl Teuku Umar No 46, Jakarta Pusat Indonesia.

IS
KATIB (JERUSALEM). (AL-KATIB). **VFOAT** Kateb. (19??)-. Periodical. Arabic. $100.00. Al-Katib, SB 20489, Al-Quds Israel. **ED** A Al-Asad. **LC** AP95.A6; K315.

IO
KEADILAN. Periodical. Indonesian. 100 single issue. Senat Mahasiswa, Jalan Sagan 1/3, Yokyakarta Indonesia. **LC** K11; .E48.

DK
KENDELSER OM FAST EJENDOM.
Main/Corp Dansk Ingenirforening Voldgiftsret. **VFOAT** Voldfigtskendelser Efter Almindelige Betingelser. 1-1975-. Danish. Juristbundets Forlag, Gothersgade 133, 1123 Kobenhavn K Denmark.

JA
KENSETSUSHO SETCHI HO KANKEI HOREISHU / KENSETSU DAIJIN KANBO BUNSHOKA KANSHU. Main/Corp Japan. Japanese. ¥1150. Zenkoku Kajo Horei Shuppan Company Ltd., Dai 1 Zenkoku Biru 18 Saneicho, Shinjukuku Tokyoto 160 Japan.

RU
KENTAVR. (Oct./Dec. 1991)-. Periodical. Russian (table of contents in English, French, German and Spanish). Six times a year. $89.95. Izdatelstvo Pressa, Myasnitskaia 24, 101877 Moscow Russia. **Tel** 011 95 923 2122, FAX 011 95 200 2259. **(Subscription address:** East View Publications Inc., 3020 Harbor Lane North, Suite 110, Minneapolis MN 55447.**) LC** JN6598.K4; V6. **Continues** Voprosy Istorii KPSS (Moscow, R.S.F.S.R.), 0320-8907.
Ind/Abst Am. Hist. Life (1957-).

US/0164-9345
KENTUCKY BENCH & BAR. [Ky. bench bar]. **Added/Corp** Kentucky Bar Association (1971-). **VAT** Kentucky Bench and Bar. (Jan. 1975)-. Periodical. English. qt. $15.00. Kentucky Bar Association / Kentucky Bar Center, 514 West Main, Frankfurt KY 40601. **Tel** (502)564-3795, FAX (502)564-3225. **ED** Barbara Bonar. **LC** PAR. **DD** 340. Index available. cum. index. **Bk Rev Ad Acc.** Full Page (B&W) $1600.00. Half Page (B&W) $725.00. available on microfilm and microfiche from University Microfilms International (UMI). **Continues** Kentucky Bar Journal, 0362-6113.
Ind/Abst Curr. Law Index (1980-); Fed. Tax Artic.; Law Office Inf. Serv.; Leg. Resour. Index (1980-); LegalTrac (1980-).

US/0023-026X
KENTUCKY LAW JOURNAL. [KY. law j.]. Began in 1913. Periodical. English. qt. $28.00. Kentucky Law Journal, University of Kentucky, Lexington KY 40506-0048. **Tel** (606)257-4747, FAX (606)258-1061. **ED** Tom Halbleib. Index available. cum. index. **Bk Rev. Circ:** 1,300 (ctrl). available on microfiche; available on microfilm.
Desc: Articles, notes, comments, and book reviews analyzing legal issues.
Ind/Abst Bowne Dig. Corp. Sec. Lawyers; Crim. Penol. Police Sci. Abstr.; Curr. Law Index (1980-); Fed. Tax Artic.; Index Leg. Period.; Leg. Resour. Index (1980-); LegalTrac (1980-); PAIS Int. Print (1991-); Soc. Plann. Policy Dev. Abstr.; Sociol. Abstr.

US/1042-9212
KENTUCKY LAW SUMMARY. [Ky. law summ.]. (19??)-. English. Fifteen times a year. $159.00. Kentucky Law Summary, 449 Starks Building, Louisville KY 40202. **Tel** (502)583-2891. **DD** 342.
Desc: News and information on the laws and courts in Kentucky.

US/0145-658X
KENTUCKY LEGAL DIRECTORY, THE. [Ky. leg. dir.]. (19??)-. Directory. English. an. $44.00. Legal Directories Publishing Company, 9111 Garland Road, PO Box 189000, Dallas TX 75218. **Tel** (214)321-3238, 800 447-5375. **LC** KF192.K4; K46. **DD** 340/.025/769.

US/1058-3211
KENTUCKY RULES OF COURT. FEDERAL : INCLUDING AMENDMENTS RECEIVED THROUGH OCTOBER 1 ... . [Ky. rules court, Fed.]. **Added/Corp** West Publishing Company. (1991)-. English. West Publishing Company, 610 Opperman Drive, PO Box 64526, Eagan MN 55123-1308. **Tel** (612)687-5618, (800)328-9352, FAX (612)687-5388, (800)562-2329. **DD** 347. **Continues in part** Kentucky Rules of Court, State and Federal, 1058-5222.

US/1058-322X
KENTUCKY RULES OF COURT. STATE. (KENTUCKY RULES OF COURT. STATE : INCLUDING AMENDMENTS RECEIVED THROUGH OCTOBER 1 ...). [Ky. rules court, State]. **Added/Corp** West Publishing Company. (1991)-. English. West Publishing Company, 610 Opperman Drive, PO Box 64526, Eagan MN 55123-1308. **Tel** (612)687-5618, (800)328-9352, FAX (612)687-5388, (800)562-2329. **DD** 347. **Continues in part** Kentucky Rules of Court, State and Federal, 1058-5222.

KE
KENYA GAZETTE, THE. Main/Corp Kenya. English. Sh1200.00. Government Printer of Kenya, Box 30128, Nairobi Kenya. **Tel** 334075. **LC** J8; .B66. **DD** 354/.676/20005.

KE
KENYA HIGH COURT DIGEST. English. PO Box 30197, Nairobi Kenya. **DD** 348/.6762/046.

II
KERALA HIGH COURT NOTES, THE. Added/Corp India. High Court of Kerala. (19??)-. English. sm. Rs15.00. A. K. Avirah, c/o Law Times Press, Arnakulam India. **DD** 348/.5483/041.

IO
KERTHA PATRIKA. Periodical. English (Indonesian). Universitas Udayana, Kantor Pusat, Fakultas Hukum dan Pengetahuan Masyarakat, Jalan Panglima Besar Sudirman, Denpasar Indonesia. **LC** K11; .E74. **DD** 349.598/05.

CN/0229-9089
KEY PERSONNEL DIRECTORY (LAW SOCIETY OF ALBERTA). (KEY PERSONNEL DIRECTORY : A GENERAL PUBLIC INFORMATION PUBLICATION.). [Key pers. dir.]. **Main/Corp** Law Society of Alberta. Directory. English. Canadian Bar Association / Alberta Branch, 1830 540 5th Avenue Southwest, Calgary Alberta T2P 0M2 Canada. **Tel** (403)263-3707. **DD** 349.7123/06.

US
KEYES ENCYCLOPEDIC DICTIONARY OF PROCUREMENT LAW. English. Oceana Publications, Inc., 75 Main Street, Dobbs Ferry NY 10522. **Tel** (914)693-1320, FAX (914)693-0402. Index Available, published separately, free-automatically sent.

RU
KHOZIAISTVO I PRAVO. Added/Corp Soviet Union. Ministerstvo Iustitsii. Soviet Union. Gosudarstvennyi Arbitrazh. (1977)-. Periodical. Russian. mo. $110.95. Izdatelstvo Ekonomika, Berezhkovskaia Nab., 6, 121864 Moscow Russia. **(Subscription address:** East View Publications Inc., 3020 Harbor Lane North, Suite 110, Minneapolis MN 55447.**) LC** K11; .H69.
Ind/Abst Int. Labour Doc.; LABORDOC.

US/0733-8937
KINDEX. See Law-Abstracting, Bibliographies and Statistics.

UK/0453-8854
KINGSTON LAW REVIEW, THE. Ceased. [Kingst. law rev.]. Vol. 1 (1968)-Vol. 15 ( ). Periodical. English. sa. William W. Gaunt and Sons Inc, 3011 Gulf Drive, Gaunt Building, Holmes Beach FL 34217. **Tel** (800)942-8683, (813)778-5211. **LC** K11; .I5. **DD** 340/.0942.
Ind/Abst Curr. Law Index (1980-); Leg. Resour. Index (1980-); LegalTrac (1980-).

JA
KITAKYUSHU DAIGAKU HOSEI RONSHU. Added/Corp Kitakyushu Daigaku. Hogakkai. Kitakyushu Daigaku. Hosei Ronshu. **VFOAT** Hosei Ronshu; Journal of Law and Political Science; Kitakyushu Daigaku Hou-Sei Ronshu. (1974)-. Periodical. English (Japanese). qt. Kitakyushu Daigaku Hogakubu Kitakata, Kokura Minami-ku Japan. **LC** K11; .I55.

GW
KOLNER SCHRIFTEN ZUM EUROPARECHT. VFOAT Publications de Droit Europeen. Vol. 1 (1965)-. Monographic series. German (French). ir. Price varies per volume. Carl Heymanns Verlag KG, Luxemburger Strasse 449, D 50939 Cologne Germany. **Tel** 011 49 221 460100, telex 8 881 888.

SZ
KOMMENTAR ZUM SCHWEIZERISCHEN ZIVILGESETZBUCH. Main/Corp Switzerland. Laws, Statutes, Etc. (19??)-. Monographic series. German. ir. Price varies per volume. Schulthess Polygraphischer Verlag, Zwingliplatz 2, CH-8022 Zurich Switzerland. **Tel** 011 41 1 2519336.

RU
KOMMENTARII ARBITRAZHNOI PRAKTIKI. Added/Corp Vsesoiuznyi Nauchno-Issledovatelskii Institut Sovetskogo Zakonodatelstva (Soviet Union). (19??)-. Periodical. Russian. 0.44rub (single issue). Iuridicheskaia Literatura, K-64 Ulitsa Chkalova 38-40, Moscow Russia.

RU
KOMMENTARII SUDEBNOI PRAKTIKI ZA ... GOD / VSESOIUZNYI NAUCHNO-ISSLEDOVATELSKII INSTITUT SOVETSKOGO ZAKONODATELSTVA. Added/Corp Vsesoiuznyi Nauchno-Issledovatelskii Institut Sovetskogo Zakonodatelstva (Soviet Union). (19??)-. Russian. 0.60rub. K64 Ul Chkalova 38-40, Moscow Russia.

SW
KONSUMENTVERKETS FOERFATTNINGSSAMLING. Main/Corp Sweden. Added/Corp Sweden. Konsumentverket. (19??)-. Swedish. Konsumentverket, Box 503, 162 15 Vallingby Sweden. **DD** 343/.485/075.

KO/0377-0729
KOREAN JOURNAL OF COMPARATIVE LAW. Added/Corp Korean Research Institute of Comparative Law. (1973)-. English. an. $28.00. Korean Journal of Comparative Law, Suite 17/105 Hangang Mansion Apt, Yongsan-ku Seoul South Korea. **(Subscription address:** Korean Journal of Comparative Law, 1100 NE Campus Parkway, Seattle WA 98105.) **LC** K11; .O7. **DD** 340/.2/05.
Ind/Abst Index Foreign Leg. Per.

GW/0023-4834
KRITISCHE JUSTIZ. [Krit. Justiz]. Vol. 1 (1968)-. Periodical. German. qt. DM46.00 Germany; DM40.80 other. Nomos Verlagsgesellschaft, Postfach 610, D-76484 Baden Baden Germany. **Tel** 011 49 7221 21040. **LC** K11; .R57. **DD** 340/.0943. **[CCC]**.
Ind/Abst Crim. Penol. Police Sci. Abstr.; Energy Res. Abstr. (Nov. 1981-); Int. Polit. Sci. Abstr.

GW/0179-2830
KRITISCHE VIERTELJAHRESSCHRIFT FUER GESETZGEBUNG UND RECHTSWISSENSCHAFT. VFOAT KRITV. No. 1/2 (1986)-. Periodical. German. qt. J Schweitzer Verlag KG, Geibelstrasse 8, W-8000 Munchen 80 Germany. **Continues** Kritische Vierteljahrsschrift fur Gesetzgebung und Rechtswissenschaft.
Ind/Abst Index Foreign Leg. Per.

GW/0934-6724
KTS ZEITSCHRIFT FUER INSOLVENZRECHT : KONKURS, TREUHAND, SANIERUNG. VFOAT Zeitschrift fuer Insolvenzrecht; KTS. Vol. 50, No. 1 (March 1989)-. Periodical. German. Four times a year. DM198.00. Carl Heymanns Verlag KG, Luxemburger Strasse 449, D 50939 Cologne Germany. **Tel** 011 49 221 460100, telex 8 881 888. **Continues** Konkurs-, Treuhand- und Schiedsgerichtswesen.

CH
KUO LI TAI-WAN TA HSUEH FA HSUEH LUN TSUNG. VFOAT National Taiwan University Law Journal; Fa Hsueh Lun Tsung; Tai Ta Fa Hsueh Lun Tsung. (1971)-. Periodical. Chinese (French). sa. National Taiwan University - Law, Law Department, Taipei Taiwan.
Ind/Abst Index Foreign Leg. Per.

JA
KURASHI NO TAME NO HORITSU. Began in 1973. Japanese. an. ¥1800. Daiichi Hoki Shuppan Kabushiki Kaisha, 11-17 Minami Aoyama 2 Minato-ku, Tokyo-to 107 Japan. **ED** Wagatsuma Sakae Nakagawa Zennosuke, and Endo Hiroshi.

NE
KWARTAALBERICHT NIEUW BURGELIJK WETBOEK. Dutch. qt. Kluwer BV, Postbus 23, 7400 GA Deventer Netherlands. **Tel** 011 31 5700 33155, 011 31 5700 48999, FAX 011 31 5700 11504, telex 42829.

US
LA/C BUSINESS BULLETIN. Added/Corp Latin America/Caribbean Business Development Center (U.S.) United States. Agency for International Development. United States. International Trade Administration. **VAT** Latin America/Caribbean Business Bulletin. Vol. 1, No. 1 (Dec. 1990)-. Government Publication. English. mo. US Department of Commerce, 14th Street & Constitution Avenue NW, Washington DC 20230. **Tel** (202)482-2000, FAX (202)482-3772. **LC** HC121; .L2. **DD** 330.98/0038. **Continues** CBI Business Bulletin.

●US/1065-7576
LAB LAW REPORTER. [Lab law report.]. (1992)-. Periodical. English. bm. $95.00. MedicoLegal Associates, PO Box 740234, Arvada CO 80006. **Tel** (402)558-3143. **DD** 344.

IT/0023-6462
LABEO; RASSEGNA DI DIRETTO ROMANO. (1955)-. Periodical. Italian (English). Three times a year. L105000 Italy; L115000 other. Casa Editrice Jovene, 109 Via Mezzocannone, 80134 Naples Italy. **Tel** 011 39 81 552-1274.

US/0272-3778
LABORATORY REGULATION MANUAL. [Lab. regul. man.]. (197?)-. English. Four times a year. $675.00 US. Aspen Publishers Inc., 7201 McKinney Circle, Frederick MD 21701. **Tel** (800)234-1660, (301)698-7100, FAX (301)251-5784, telex 5106014543. **(Subscription address:** Aspen Publishers Inc., PO Box 990, Frederick MD 21701.) **ED** H. Robert Halper and Hope S. Foster. ctrl circ.
Desc: Covers existing or proposed state and federal laws and regulations affecting the operation of clinical laboratories.

US
LABORWATCH. See Business-Personnel Management.

US/0023-7078
LACKAWANNA JURIST. Added/Corp Lackawanna Bar Association. Vol. 1 (Dec. 14, 1888)-. Periodical. English. wk. Lackawanna Bar Association, Law Library Courthouse, Scranton PA 18501. **Tel** (717)344-2944. **ED** Marita E. Paparelli. Index available. cum. index. **Ad Acc**.

FI/0023-7353
LAKIMIES. (1903)-. Periodical. Finnish. bm. Suomalainen lakimiesyhdistys, Annankatu 16 B 42, 00120 Helsinki 12 Finland.
Ind/Abst Index Foreign Leg. Per.

FR
LAMY DEHOVE. See Food and Food Industry.

FR
LAMY DROIT COMMERCIAL. French. ir. 1650.00F. Editions Lamy SA, 187-189 Quai de Valmy, 75490 Paris Cedex 10 France. **Tel** 011 33 1 44721200, 011 33 1 44721212, FAX 011 33 1 44721395.

FR/0983-6802
LAMY DROIT DE L'INFORMATIQUE. Added/Corp Societe Lamy. **VFOAT** Droit de l'Informatique; Lamy Informatique. (1986)-. French. an. Editions Lamy SA, 187 189 Quai de Valmy, 75490 Paris Cedex 10 France. **Tel** 011 33 1 44721200 or, 44721212, telex 214.398. **LC** KJV333.C65; L36.
Desc: Regroups the total of juridical questions raised by the informatics, the telematics and the networks. A compilation of clauses for contracts, models of commented contracts, typed contracts arisen from of the practice, standard formules and printed forms.

FR
LAMY DROIT DU FINANCEMENT. French. ir. 1962.09F. Editions Lamy SA, 187-189 Quai de Valmy, 75490 Paris Cedex 10 France. **Tel** 011 33 1 44721200, 011 33 1 44721212, FAX 011 33 1 44721395.

FR
LAMY FISCAL. Main/Corp Societe Lamy. Added/Corp Services Lamy. Fiscal. (19??)-. French. ir. 1790.00F. Editions Lamy SA, 187-189 Quai de Valmy, 75490 Paris Cedex 10 France. **Tel** 011 33 1 44721200, 011 33 1 44721212, FAX 011 33 1 44721395.

FR
LAMY FORMULAIRES. REGROUPEMENT DROIT DE SOCIETES. French. ir. 1095.00F France; 1141.71F Europe; 1245.50F other. Editions Lamy SA, 187-189 Quai de Valmy, 75490 Paris Cedex 10 France. **Tel** 011 33 1 44721200, 011 33 1 44721212, FAX 011 33 1 44721395.

FR
LAMY SOCIAL. (19??)-. French. an. 1590.00F. Editions Lamy SA, 187-189 Quai de Valmy, 75490 Paris Cedex 10 France. **Tel** 011 33 1 44721200, 011 33 1 44721212, FAX 011 33 1 44721395.

FR
LAMY TRANSPORT (SOCIETE LAMY). (LAMY TRANSPORT.). French. Societe Lamy, 155 rue Legendre, Paris France. **Tel** (1)46.27.28.90, FAX 42.29.86.81, telex 650.790. **DD** 343.44/093; 344.40393. **Continues** Lamy Transport (Services Lamy).
Desc: Publishes everything about the regulation and juridical problems related to any kind international traffic. Informs about the changes on the area of types of contracts, coordination, Code of the road and social regimentation.

CN/1185-040X
LAND CLAIMS NEWSLETTER. [Land claims newsl.]. Added/Corp British Columbia. Ministry of Native Affairs. VFOAT Information Update. (Nov. 1990)-. Newsletter. English. **DD** 346.71104/32/08997.

CN/0704-5808
LAND COMPENSATION BOARD INDEX TO APPLICATIONS DISPOSED OF. English. an. 15.00Can$. Law Society of Upper Canada, 130 Queen Street West, Toronto M5H 2N6 Canada. **Tel** (416)947-3300, (416)947-3371, telex 065-28013. **ED** John D Honsberger. **DD** 343/.713/02502648. cum. index. **Circ:** 21,000.

CN/0380-4208
LAND COMPENSATION REPORTS. Vol. 1 (Nov. 1971)-. Periodical. English. ir. 111.00Can$. Canada Law Book Inc., 240 Edward Street, Aurora Ontario L4G 3S9 Canada. **Tel** (800)263-3269, (905)841-6472, FAX (905)841-5085. **ED** Arnold S. Weinrib. **LC** KE5175.A45; L36. **DD** 343.71/0252. **Bk Rev**. **LC** Acq.
Desc: A series designed for those concerned with the expropriation process in Canada whether at the local, regional, provincial or federal level.

US/1058-7012
LAND USE FORUM. Title Change. [Land use forum]. Added/Corp California Continuing Education of the Bar. **VFOAT** CEB Land Use Forum. Vol. 1, No. 1 (Fall 1991)-(1993). Periodical. English. qt. California Continuing Education of the Bar, 2300 Shattuck Avenue, Berkeley CA 94704. **Tel** (510)642-8000, (800)232-3444. **LC** K12; .A6. **DD** 346.79404/5; 347.940645. **Continued by** Land Use & Environment Forum, 1072-7973.

US/0094-7598
LAND USE LAW & ZONING DIGEST. [Land use law zoning dig.]. Added/Corp American Planning Association. American Society of Planning Officials. **VAT** Land Use Law and Zoning Digest. Vol. 26 (1974)-. English. Twelve times a year. $220.00; (additional subscriptions $75.00 each). American Planning Association, 1313 East 60th Street, Chicago IL 60637. **Tel** (312)955-9100, FAX (312)955-8312. **ED** Rodney L. Cobb. **LC** K30; .O5. **DD** 346/.73/04505. Index available. **Bk Rev. Circ:** 1,280. available on microfilm and microfiche from University Microfilms International (UMI). **Continues** Zoning Digest, 0084-5566.
Desc: Case abstracts, commentaries, statutes and other analysis of land use law.
Ind/Abst J. Plan. Lit.; Urban Aff. Abstr.

US/1064-0401
LAND USE LAW REPORT. [Land use law rep.]. **VFOAT** LULR. Vol. 19, No. 21 (Oct. 9, 1991)-. Periodical. English. bw (26 issues). $299.00 (includes Inside Interior). Business Publishers Inc., 951 Pershing Drive, Silver Spring MD 20910-4464. **Tel** (301)587-6300, (800)274-0122, FAX (301)585-9075. **DD** 346. **Continues** Land Use Planning Report, 0093-3864.

US/0271-5228
LANDLORD TENANT LAW BULLETIN. [Landlord tenant law bull.]. **VFOAT** LTLB; L.T.L.B. (1980)-. Bulletin. English. mo. $59.95. Quinlan Publishing Company, 23 Drydock Avenue, Boston MA 02210-2387. **Tel** (617)542-0048, (800)229-2084, FAX (617)345-9646. **LC** KF587.8; .L35. **DD** 346.7304/34; 347.306434. **[CCC]**. available on microfilm and microfiche from University Microfilms International (UMI).

US/0883-0746
LANDLORD VS. TENANT/NYC. VFOAT Landlord vs. Tenant NYC; Landlord vs. Tenant New York City. (May 1985)-. Periodical. English. mo. $318.00. Brownstone Publishers Inc, 149 Fifth Avenue, 16th Floor, New York NY 10100. **Tel** (212)473-8200, FAX (212)995-9205. **ED** George Schaeffer. **LC** KFX2022; .A45. **DD** 346.74704/34; 347.4706434. Index available.
Desc: Written primarily for landlords, managers, and attorneys. Describes recent cases in landlord/tenant law.

US
LARMAC CONSOLIDATED INDEX TO THE CONSTITUTION AND LAWS OF CALIFORNIA. VFOAT Larmac Consolidated Code and Court Rule Index; Index to California Laws. (1935)-. English. an. $79.00. Parker Publications, 2283 Cosmos Court, Carlsbad CA 92009. **Tel** (800)452-9873, (619)931-5979. **ED** Francis Franzin Verducci. **Circ:** 3,000.
Desc: One-volume index to all California codes, general laws and the State Constitution, with full text of California Rules of Court.

IT
LAVORO NELLA GIURISPRUDENZA, IL. (19??)-. Periodical. Italian. mo. L255000 Italy; L510000 other. IPSOA Editore SRL, Casella Postale 12055, Mastrangelo, 20120 Milan Italy. **Tel** 011 39 2 82476248.

AT
LAW ALMANAC. English. NSW Government Printing Office, PO Box 256, Regents Park2143 Australia. **Tel** 011 61 02 7438777, FAX 062 954455.

●US
LAW ALUMNI DIRECTORY, ST. MARY'S UNIVERSITY SCHOOL OF LAW. Main/Corp St. Mary's University (San Antonio, Tex.). School of Law. **VFOAT** St. Mary's University Law Alumni Directory. (1992)-. Directory. English. **LC** WMLC 91/3320.

US/0458-8428
LAW ALUMNI JOURNAL, THE. See College and School Publications-Alumni.

AU/0259-0816
LAW & ANTHROPOLOGY. (LAW & ANTHROPOLOGY : INTERNATIONALES JAHRBUCH FUER RECHTSANTHROPOLOGIE.). [Law anthropol.]. Added/Corp Universitat Wien. Institut fuer Kirchenrecht.

Arbeitsgruppe fuer Rechtsanthropologie und Inkulturationsforschung. **VFOAT** Law and Anthropology; Internationales Jahrbuch fuer Rechtsanthropologie. Vol. 1 (1986)-. English (German, Portuguese and Spanish). ir. Oesterr Ges Kirchenrecht, Freyung 6 2 4, A 1010 Vienna Austria. **LC** K12; .A855. **DD** 340/.115.
Ind/Abst Anthropol. Lit.

US/0023-9186
LAW AND CONTEMPORARY PROBLEMS. [Law contemp. probl.]. **Added/Corp** Duke University. School of Law. Vol. 1, No. 1 (Dec. 1933)-. Periodical. English. Four times a year. $45.00. Duke University School of Law, 006 Law Towerview & Science Drive, Durham NC 27706. **Tel** (919)684-5966, FAX (919)684-3417. **ED** John J. Hoffman. **LC** K12; .A9. **DD** 340/.05. Index available. **Ad Acc. Pr Rev. Circ:** 2,100. available on microfilm from Fred B. Rothman and Company. Documents available from The Genuine Article, UMI Article Clearinghouse.
Desc: Each issue is a symposium on a particular inter-disciplinary topic, with contributions by lawyers, academics in many disciplines, public officials, and law students.
Ind/Abst ABC POL SCI; Acad. Search (July 1993-); Appl. Soc. Sci. Index Abstr.; Bowne Dig. Corp. Sec. Lawyers; Coal Abstr.; Commun. Abstr. (?-?); Crim. Justice Abstr.; Crim. Justice Period. Index (-1989); Crim. Penol. Police Sci. Abstr. (1980-); Curr. Contents Soc. Behav. Sci.; Curr. Law Index (1980-); Expand. Acad. Index (1984-); Fed. Tax Artic.; Health Plan. Adminis.; Hospit. Health Admin. Index; Index Leg. Period.; INFO-SOUTH Abstr.; Int. Bibliogr. Sociol.; Int. Polit. Sci. Abstr.; J. Econ. Lit.; J. Plan. Lit.; Leg. Resour. Index (1980-); LegalTrac (1980-); Mag. Search; Middle East Abstr. Index; Newsp. Period. Abstr. (1991-); PAIS Int. Print (1991-); Res. Alert [Full Cov.]; Soc. Plann. Policy Dev. Abstr.; Soc. Sci. Source (Jul. 1993-); Soc. Sci. Cit. Index [Full Cov.]; Soc. Sci. Index; Soc. Sci. Index Fulltext (Winter 1988-) [Full Txt.]; Sociol. Abstr.; West. Hist. Q.

UK/0957-8536
LAW AND CRITIQUE. **Added/Corp** Critical Legal Studies Conference of the U.K. Vol. 1, No. 1 (Spring 1990)-. Periodical. English. sa. price varies per volume. Deborah Charles Publications, 173 Mather Avenue, Liverpool L18 6JZ United Kingdom. **Tel** 011 44 51 724 2500. **(Subscription address:** WM. W. Gaunt & Sons Inc, 3011 Gulf Drive, Gaunt Building, Holmes Beach FL 34217.**)** **CODEN** LACREI.
Ind/Abst Soc. Plann. Policy Dev. Abstr.

US
LAW AND ETHICS OF THE VETERINARY PROFESSION. English. $59.95. Priority Press Ltd, PO Box 306, Yardley PA 19067.
Desc: Ideal for use by veterinarians, animal owners, or attorneys interested in a synopsis of case and statutory law dealing with standards of care involving animals and veterinary medicine.

US/0738-2480
LAW AND HISTORY REVIEW. [Law hist. rev.]. **Added/Corp** Cornell Law School. American Society for Legal History. Vol. 1, No. 1 (Spring 1983)-. Periodical. English. sa. $50.00 (one year), $90.00 (two year), institutions; $35.00 (one year), individuals. University of Illinois Press, 1325 South Oak Street, Champaign IL 61820. **Tel** (217)333-0950, FAX (217)244-8082. **LC** K12; .A9137. **DD** 340/.05. **[CCC].** available on microfilm from University Microfilms International (UMI).
Ind/Abst Am. Hist. Life (1983-); Curr. Law Index (1984-); Index Leg. Period.; Leg. Resour. Index (1984-); LegalTrac (1983-).

US/0193-8290
LAW & HOUSING JOURNAL. [Law hous. j.]. **VAT** Law and Housing Journal. Vol. 5, No. 2, Fall (1977)-. English. an. Case Westen Reserve Law Student Service Association, 11075 East Boulevard, Cleveland OH 44106. **Tel** (216)851-6932. ***Continues** Law and Housing Newsletter, 0197-4793.*
Ind/Abst Curr. Law Index (1980-); Leg. Resour. Index (1980-?) [Full Txt.]; LegalTrac (1980-1983).

US/0147-7307
LAW AND HUMAN BEHAVIOR. [Law hum. behav.]. **Added/Corp** University of Virginia. School of Law. American Psychology-Law Society. Vol. 1 (1977)-. Periodical. English. Six times a year. $335.00 institutions, $54.00 individuals US; $390.00 institutions, $63.00 individuals other. Plenum Press, 233 Spring Street, New York NY 10013-1578. **Tel** (212)620-8000, (800)221-9369, FAX (212)463-0742, (212)807-1047, telex 23/421139. **ED** Ronald Roesch. **LC** K12; .A914. **DD** 340/.05. **NLM** W1 LA942. **CODEN** LHBEDM. **[CCC].** Index available. **Pr Rev.** available on microfilm and microfiche from University Microfilms International (UMI). Documents available from The Genuine Article, BIOSIS Document Express.
Desc: Multidisciplinary forum for articles and discussions of issues arising out of the relationship between human behavior and the law legal system and legal process.
Ind/Abst Biol. Abstr.; Commun. Abstr.; Crim. Justice Abstr.; Crim. Penol. Police Sci. Abstr.; Curr. Contents Soc. Behav. Sci.; Curr. Law Index (1980-); EMBASE; Index Leg. Period.; Leg. Resour. Index (1980-); LegalTrac (1980-); Psychol. Abstr. (1977-); PsycINFO; PsycLit; PsycScan: Appl. Psych.; Res. Alert [Full Cov.]; Soc. Plann. Policy Dev. Abstr.; Soc. Sci. Cit. Index [Full Cov.]; Sociol. Abstr.

US/0737-089X
LAW & INEQUALITY. [Law inequal.]. **Added/Corp** University of Minnesota. Law School. **VFOAT** Law and Inequality. Vol. 1 No. 1 (June 1983)-. Periodical. English. Three times a year. $18.00. University of Minnesota Law School, 299 19th Avenue South, Minneapolis MN 55455. **Tel** (612)625-8034. **ED** Dwight Penas. **LC** K12; .A86. **DD** 340/.05. **Bk Rev. Ad Acc. Circ:** 750.
Desc: Law and inequality. People's experience of systematic oppression and how law contributes to lack of power. Plus, how law might remedy group-based oppression.
Ind/Abst Curr. Law Index (1984-); Index Leg. Period.; Leg. Resour. Index (1984-); LegalTrac (1983-).

UK/0269-817X
LAW & JUSTICE. [Law justice]. **Added/Corp** Edmund Plowden Trust. **VAT** Law and Justice. No. 42 (1974)-. Periodical. English. Twice a year. £12.50 (individuals), £17.50 (institutions) UK; £13.50 (individuals), £18.50 (institutions) others. Edmund Plowden Trust, 100A Hazellville Road, London N19 3NA England. **Tel** 011 44 71 263 1501. **ED** M. Welstead (editor's address: The Mount, Eastgate, Hornton, Nr Banbury, Oxfordshire OX15 6BT England). **LC** K17; .U57. **DD** 340/.05. **Circ:** 250. ***Continues** Quis Custodiet?.*
Desc: Articles, casenotes, book reviews relating to current legal matters with Christian ethical implications.
Ind/Abst Canon Law Abstr.; Curr. Law Index (1981-); Leg. Resour. Index (1981-); LegalTrac (1980-).

US/0740-090X
LAW AND LEGAL INFORMATION DIRECTORY. [Law legal inf. dir.]. (1980)-. Directory. English. be. $320.00. Gale Research Inc., 835 Penobscot Building, Detroit MI 48226. **Tel** (800)877-GALE, (313)961-2242, FAX (313)961-6083, telex TWX 810-221-7086. **ED** Steven Wasserman and Jacqueline Wasserman O'Brien. **LC** KF190. **DD** 340/.025/73. **NLM** KF 190 L415.
Desc: Covers national and international organizations, bar associations, federal court system federal regulatory agencies, law schools, para-legal education, scholarships and grants, special libraries, research centers, legal periodical publications.

GW/0458-8460
LAW AND LEGISLATION IN THE GERMAN DEMOCRATIC REPUBLIC. ***Ceased.*** (Sept. 1959)-Ceased (Jan. 1989). Periodical. English. sa. Deutscher Judo Verband, Redaktion Ippon Segewaldweg 40, D 12557 Berlin Germany. **Tel** 011 49 711 210770, telex 051 678. **LC** K12; .A916. **DD** 349.431/05.
Ind/Abst Index Foreign Leg. Per.

US/0890-5037
LAW AND MENTAL HEALTH. ***Ceased.*** [Law ment. health]. (1985)-Ceased (Dec. 1990). Periodical. English. an. Pergamon Press Inc., 660 White Plains Road, Tarrytown NY 10591-5153. **Tel** (914)524-9200, FAX (914)333-2444, telex 13-7328. **(Subscription address:** UK/ Headington Hill Hall, Oxford OX3 0BW; Can/ 150 Consumers Road/Suite 104, Willowdale Ontario M2J 1P9; Aus-NZ/ POB 544, Potts Point NSW 2011**)** **ED** David N Weisstub. **DD** 344. **NLM** W1; LA943. **[CCC].**
Desc: Offers a comprehensive account of the major areas of research and practice in law and mental health.

NE/0167-5249
LAW AND PHILOSOPHY. [Law philos.]. Vol. 1, No. 1 (April 1982)-. Periodical. English. qt. $373.00. Kluwer Academic Publishers, Postbus 322, 3300 AH Dordrecht, The Netherlands. **Tel** 011 (31) 78 524400, FAX 011 31 78 183273, telex 20083. **ED** Alan Mabe. **LC** K12; .A919. **DD** 340/.1. **[CCC]. Bk Rev. Ad Acc. Pr Rev. Acid Free. Circ:** 900. available on microfilm and microfiche from University Microfilms International (UMI). Documents available from The Genuine Article.
Desc: A forum for the publication of work in law and philosophy which is of common interest to members of the two disciplines of jurisprudence and legal philosophy. It is open to all disciplines in both fields and to work in any of the major legal traditions - common law, civil law, or the socialist tradition.
Ind/Abst Acad. Search (July 1993-); Curr. Contents Soc. Behav. Sci.; Curr. Law Index (1983-); Index Leg. Period.; INFO-SOUTH Abstr.; J. Plan. Lit.; Leg. Resour. Index (1983-); LegalTrac (1983-); Mag. Search; Philos. Index; Res. Alert [Full Cov.]; Soc. Plann. Policy Dev. Abstr.; Soc. Sci. Cit. Index [Full Cov.]; Sociol. Abstr.

UK/0265-8240
LAW & POLICY. [Law policy]. **VFOAT** Law and Policy. Vol. 6, No. 1 (Jan. 1984)-. Academic Scholarly Publication. English. Four times a year. £89.50 UK and Europe; $136.00 North America; £111.00 other. Basil Blackwell Publishers Ltd, 108 Cowley Road, Oxford 0X4 1JF England. **Tel** 011 44 865 791100, FAX 011 44 865 791347, telex 837022 OXBOOK G. **(Subscription address:** Blackwell Publishers / UK, Marston Book Services, PO Box 87, Oxford OX2 0DT England.**)** **ED** Keith Hawkings, Thomas Headrick, and Errol Meidinger. **LC** K12; .A922. **DD** 340/.05. **CODEN** LAPOE6. **[CCC]. Ad Acc. Circ:** 800. available on microfilm and microfiche from University Microfilms International (UMI). ***Continues** Law & Policy Quarterly, 0164-0267.*
Desc: A multidisciplinary journal which critically analyses the role of law in the policy process.
Ind/Abst ABC POL SCI; Acad. Search (July 1993-); Am. Hist. Life (1983-); Crim. Justice Abstr.; INFO-SOUTH Abstr.; Int. Bibliogr. Sociol.; J. Plan. Lit.; Leg. Resour. Index (1984-); LegalTrac (1983-); Mag. Search; PAIS Int. Print (1991-); Sage Public Adm. Abstr.; Soc. Sci. Source (Jul. 1993-).

US/1062-7421
LAW AND POLITICS BOOK REVIEW. [Law polit. book rev.]. **Added/Corp** American Political Science Association. Law, Courts, and Judicial Process Section. (1991)-. Periodical. English. mo. Law and Politics Book Review, 2234 Asbury Avenue, Evanston IL 60201. **DD** 324.

US/0148-6136
LAW AND POPULATION PROGRAMME NEWSLETTER. **Added/Corp** Fletcher School of Law and Diplomacy. (Apr. 1972)-. Periodical. English. Tufts University / Law, The Fletcher School of Law Diplomacy, Medford MA 02155. **Tel** (617)623-3610, FAX (617)623-3610. **LC** K2000.A13; L37. **DD** 344.04/8.

US/0098-5961
LAW & PSYCHOLOGY REVIEW. [Law psychol. rev.]. **VAT** Law and Psychology Review. (Spring 1975)-. English. an. $14.00. University of Alabama School of Law, PO Box 870382, Tuscaloosa AL 35487. **Tel** (205)348-1175. **LC** K12; .A923. **DD** 340.1/9. **NLM** W1; LA945.
Ind/Abst Crim. Justice Abstr.; Crim. Penol. Police Sci. Abstr.; Index Leg. Period.; Leg. Resour. Index (1980-); LegalTrac (1982-); Psychol. Abstr. (1975-); PsycINFO; PsycLit; PsycScan: Appl. Psych.

US/1062-0680
LAW & SEXUALITY. **See** Homosexuality.

US/0897-6546
LAW & SOCIAL INQUIRY. (LAW & SOCIAL INQUIRY : JOURNAL OF THE AMERICAN BAR FOUNDATION.). [Law soc. inq.]. **Added/Corp** American Bar Foundation. **VFOAT** Law and Social Inquiry. Vol. 13, No. 1 (1988)-. Periodical. English. qt (4 issues). $59.00 institution, $36.00 individual, $29.00 college/university faculty and students. University of Chicago Press / Journals Division, PO Box 37005, 5720 South Woodlawn, Chicago IL 60637. **Tel** (312)753-3347, FAX (312)753-0811. **(Subscription telephone:** (312)753-8083**)** **ED** Arthur F. McEvoy, Elizabeth Mertz and Peter Siegelman. **LC** K1; .M39. **DD** 340/.115/05. **[CCC]. Ad Acc. Pr Rev. Acid Free.** available on microfilm and microfiche from University Microfilms International (UMI). Documents available from The Genuine Article. ***Continues** American Bar Foundation Research Journal, 0361-9486.*
Desc: Features both empirical and theoretical studies that make original contributions to the understanding of sociolegal processes.
Ind/Abst Crim. Justice Abstr. (199?-); Index Leg. Period. (1988-); Leg. Resour. Index (1980-1988) (19??-); LegalTrac (1988-); Res. Alert [Full Cov.]; Sage Public Adm. Abstr.; Soc. Plann. Policy Dev. Abstr.; Soc. Sci. Cit. Index [Full Cov.]; Sociol. Abstr. (1988-).

US/8755-7088
LAW & SOCIETY NEWSLETTER (DENVER, COLO.). (LAW & SOCIETY NEWSLETTER.). [Law soc. newsl.]. **Added/Corp** Law & Society Association. Law & Society Association Periodicals. **VFOAT** Law and Society Newsletter. (19??)-. Newsletter. English. comes with membership. Law and Society Association, University of Massachusetts, Hampshire House, Box 33615, Amherst MA 01003-3615. **Tel** (413)454-4617, FAX (413)545-1640. **LC** KF200; .L36. **DD** 340/.06.

II/0377-0869
LAW AND SOCIETY QUARTERLY. Periodical. English. $10.50. Centre for the Study of Law and Society, 20 Vithalbhai Patel House, Rafi Marg, New Delhi India. **LC** K12; .A924. **DD** 340.1/15/05. ***Continues** Law and Society Newsletter.*

US/0023-9216
LAW & SOCIETY REVIEW. [Law soc. rev.]. **Added/Corp** Law & Society Association. **VFOAT** Law and Society Review. Vol. 1, No. 1 (Nov. 1966)-. Periodical. English. qt. $102.00 US; $109.00 other. Law and Society Association, University of Massachusetts, Hampshire House, Box 33615, Amherst MA 01003-3615. **Tel** (413)454-4617, FAX (413)545-1640. **ED** Shari Diamond. **LC** K12; .A865. **DD** 340/.115/05. Index available. cum. index. **Bk Rev. Ad Acc. Pr Rev. Circ:** 2,400. available on microfilm and microfiche from University Microfilms International (UMI). Documents available from The Genuine Article, UMI Article Clearinghouse. ***Continues** Law & Society Association. Newsletter.*
Desc: Accepts articles concerning political, social and economic aspects of law.
Ind/Abst ABC POL SCI; Acad. Abstr. Full Text Elite (Jan. 1990-); Acad. Abstr. (Jan. 1990-); Acad. Ind. [Computer File] (1984-); Acad. Search (Jan. 1990-); Am. Hist. Life

(1972-); Anthropol. Lit.; Appl. Soc. Sci. Index Abstr.; Bowne Dig. Corp. Sec. Lawyers; Crim. Justice Abstr.; Crim. Penol. Police Sci. Abstr.; Curr. Contents Soc. Behav. Sci.; Curr. Law Index (1980-); Expand. Acad. Index (1984-); Highw. Res. Abstr.; Index Leg. Period.; INFO-SOUTH Abstr.; Int. Bibliogr. Sociol.; Leg. Resour. Index (1980-); LegalTrac (1980-); Mag. Search; Middle East Abstr. Index; Newsp. Period. Abstr. (1991-); PAIS Int. Print (1991-); Peace Res. Abstr. J. (1975-1977); Psychol. Abstr. (1983-); PsycINFO; PsycLit; Public Aff. Inf. Serv. Bull.; Recent. Publ. Artic.; Res. Alert [Full Cov.]; Sage Public Adm. Abstr.; Soc. Plann. Policy Dev. Abstr.; Soc. Sci. Source (Jul. 1990-); Soc. Sci. Cit. Index [Full Cov.]; Soc. Sci. Index; Soc. Sci. Index Fulltext (1988-) [Full Txt.]; Soc. Welf. Soc. Plan./Policy Soc. Dev.; Soc. Work Abstr. [Select. Cov.]; Sociol. Abstr. [Full Cov.]; U.S. Polit. Sci. Doc.; Urban Aff. Abstr.; Writ. Am. Hist.

US
LAW BOOKS IN PRINT / EDITED AND COMPILED BY J. MYRON JACOBSTEIN AND MEIRA G. PIMSLEUR. (1957)-. English. ir. $750.00. Glanville Publishers Inc, 75 Main Street, Dobbs Ferry NY 10522. **Tel** (914)693-1320, FAX (914)693-0402. **ED** Nicholas Triffin.
Desc: Interdisciplinary and law-related materials are included in such fields as political science, government, public administration, business and economics, science and medicine, environmental studies, international relations.

US/0886-0408
LAW BOOKS IN REVIEW. [Law books rev.]. (Spring/Summer 1974)-. Periodical. English. qt. $55.00. Glanville Publishers Inc, 75 Main Street, Dobbs Ferry NY 10522. **Tel** (914)693-1320, FAX (914)693-0402. **ED** Alden W Domizio. **LC** KF1; .A9. **DD** 340.
Desc: Journal of reviews of current publications in law and related fields.

US/0023-9240
LAW BOOKS PUBLISHED. [Law books publ.]. Vol. 1 (Jan./Apr. 1969)-. Periodical. English. qt. $150.00. Glanville Publishers Inc, 75 Main Street, Dobbs Ferry NY 10522. **Tel** (914)693-1320, FAX (914)693-0402. **LC** KF1; .L38. **DD** 016.34.

AT
LAW CALENDAR. Main/Corp Victoria, Australia. Law Dept. English. an. Free. Law Department, 221 Queen Street, Melbourne Victoria 3001 Australia. **Tel** 6036777, telex AA152158. **ED** C Bruce. **DD** 347/.945/013. **Bk Rev. Ad Acc.** ***Continues*** *Victoria, Australia. Law Calendar.*
Desc: An overview of the attorney general's department, Victoria, including personnel, addresses and time tables for Victorian courts 1987.

UK
LAW COMPUTERS AND ARTIFICIAL INTELLIGENCE. See Computers-Artificial Intelligence.

US
LAW DAY U.S.A. PLANNING GUIDE AND PROGRAM MANUAL. Main/Corp American Bar Association. **VFOAT** May 1, Law Day U.S.A. (1968)-. English. an. American Bar Association, 750 North Lake Shore Drive, Chicago IL 60611. **Tel** (312)988-5522, (312)988-5241, FAX (312)988-5528, telex 270593. ***Formed by the union of*** *Law Day U.S.A. Program Manual* ***and*** *Law Day U.S.A. Planning Guide for Bar Associations.*

●US/1061-9410
LAW FIRM BENEFITS. (1992)-. Periodical. English. mo. $155.00. Leader Publications, 345 Park Avenue South, New York NY 10010. **Tel** (800)888-8300 ext. 6170, (212)545-6170, FAX (212)696-1848. **ED** Patricia L. Johnson.

US
LAW FIRM MARKETING AND PROFIT REPORT. ***Ceased.*** (1993)-(19??). Periodical. English. bm. Institute of Management and Administration, 29 West 35th Street, 5th Floor, New York NY 10001-2299. **Tel** (212)244-0360. ***Absorbed*** *Law Firm Profit Report, 0895-9412; Attorneys Marketing Report, 0745-1369.*

US/1056-2028
LAW FIRM PARTNERSHIP REPORT. [Law firm partnersh. rep.]. (1991)-. Periodical. English. mo. $155.00. Leader Publications, 345 Park Avenue South, New York NY 10010. **Tel** (800)888-8300 ext. 6170, (212)545-6170, FAX (212)696-1848. **ED** Justine Jeffrey (editor's phone: (602)445-2775). **DD** 340. Index available.
Desc: Focuses on partnership issues of importance to high level law firm partners.

US/0895-9412
LAW FIRM PROFIT REPORT. ***Title Change.*** [Law firm profit rep.]. **VFOAT** Profit Report. Vol. 1, No. 1 (Jan. 1988)-(19??). Periodical. English. Six times a year. James Publishing Group, Inc., PO Box 25202, Santa Ana CA 92799. **Tel** (714)755-5450, FAX (714)556-4133. **ED** Kathy McCoy (editor's phone: (714)755-5461). **LC** KF315.A15; L38. **DD** 340/.068. **Ad Acc, Adv Mgr:** L Thinnes. ***Merged into*** *Law Firm Marketing and Profit Report.*
Desc: Covers law firm marketing and management.
Ind/Abst Law Office Inf. Serv.

US/1054-4054
LAW FIRMS YELLOW BOOK. See Encyclopedias and General Reference Books.

US
LAW FORUM SERIES. Monographic series. English. ir. Price varies per volume.

AT/0814-4788
LAW HANDBOOK - REDFERN LEGAL CENTRE. [Law handb. - Redfern Leg. Cent.]. (1983)-. English. tq. 40.45Aus$ (schools, libraries and government institutions); 44.95Aus$ other. Legal Services Commission South Australia, 82 Wakefield Street, Adelaide SA 5000, Australia. **Tel** 11 61 8 2050110. **DD** 349.944. **Circ:** 3,000. ***Continues*** *Legal Resources Book (NSW).*

US/0197-3886
LAW IN AMERICAN SOCIETY. [Law Am. soc.]. V. 1- May 1972-. Periodical. English. qt. $10.00. Law in American Society Foundation, 33 North La Salle Street, Suite 1700, Chicago IL 60602. **LC** K12; .A93634. **DD** 340./07/1073.

AT/0811-5796
LAW IN CONTEXT (BUNDOORA, VIC.). (LAW IN CONTEXT.). Vol. 1 (1983)-. Periodical. English. Twice a year (May, Aug.). $34.00 (individual); $43.50 (institution). LaTrobe University Press, LaTrobe University C A Day, Bundoora Victoria 3083 Australia. **Tel** 011 61 3 4791460, FAX (03)470 2011, telex AA 33143. **ED** M. Chanock. **LC** K12; .A936344. **DD** 340/.115. **Bk Rev. Ad Acc. Circ:** 450 (ctrl).
Desc: Law and legal-oriented articles.
Ind/Abst APAIS, Aust. Public Aff. Inf. Ser.; Index Leg. Period.

NE/0075-823X
LAW IN EASTERN EUROPE. Added/Corp Rijksuniversiteit te Leiden. Documentatie Bureau voor Oost-Europees Recht. No. 1 (1958)-. Monographic series. English. ir. Price varies per volume. Kluwer Academic Publishers, Postbus 322, 3300 AH Dordrecht, The Netherlands. **Tel** 011 (31) 78 524400, FAX 011 31 78 183273, telex 20083. **(Subscription address:** Kluwer Academic Publishers / US Subscriptions, PO Box 253, Accord Station, Hingham MA 02018.**) LC** KJC510.A15; L39. **DD** 349.47.
Ind/Abst Index Foreign Leg. Per.

JA/0458-8584
LAW IN JAPAN. [Law Jpn.]. **Added/Corp** Japanese American Society for Legal Studies. Vol. 1 (1967)-. Periodical. English. an. $7.50. University of Washington School of Law, Japanese American Society of Legal Studies, Seattle WA 98105. **Tel** (206)543-9302.
Ind/Abst Index Foreign Leg. Per.

CN/1185-2534
LAW INFORMANT, THE. [Law informant]. **Added/Corp** McGraw-Hill Ryerson Ltd. School Division. Vol. 1, No. 1 (Mar. 1990)-. Periodical. English. $33.95 per year. McGraw-Hill Ryerson Limited, 330 Progress Avenue, Scarborough, Ontario M1P 2Z5 Canada. **DD** 349.71/05.

AT/0023-9267
LAW INSTITUTE JOURNAL. (LAW INSTITUTE JOURNAL : THE OFFICIAL ORGAN OF THE LAW INSTITUTE OF VICTORIA.). [Law Inst. j.]. **Added/Corp** Law Institute of Victoria. Queensland Law Society. Vol. 1, No. 1 (July 1, 1927)-. Periodical. English. Eleven times a year. 83.00Aus$ Australia; $128.30 others. Law Institute of Victoria, 470 Bourke Street, Melbourne Victoria 3000 Australia. **Tel** 011 61 3 6079311, FAX 011 61 3 6079451. **ED** Martha Schiel. **DD** 347.05. **[CCC].** Index Available, published separately, free-automatically sent. cum. index. **Bk Rev,** (Qty: 200). **Ad Acc, Adv Mgr:** B. Holt, **Tel** (03)6079345. **Circ:** 10,000. available on microfilm and microfiche from University Microfilms International (UMI).
Desc: Articles on all aspects of law and reviews of judgments.
Ind/Abst Aust. Leg. Mon. Dig.; Curr. Law Index (1980-); Index Leg. Period.; Leg. Resour. Index (1980-); LegalTrac (1980-).

TH
LAW JOURNAL OF MARUT BUNNAG INTERNATIONAL LAW OFFICE. Main/Corp Marut Bunnag International Law Office. English. Marut Bunnag International Law Office, Bangkok Insurance Building/2nd Floor, 302 Silom Road, Bangkok Thailand. **LC** K12; .A93636. **DD** 340/.09593. ***Continues*** *Law Journal.*

AT/0816-4800
LAW JOURNAL / QUEENSLAND INSTITUTE OF TECHNOLOGY. Added/Corp Queensland Institute of Technology. Queensland University of Technology. **VFOAT** Queensland Institute of Technology Law Journal; QLD. Institute of Technology Law Journal; QIT Law Journal. Vol. 1 (1985)-. English. Four times a year. **(Subscription address:** William W. Gaunt & Sons Inc., 3011 Gulf Drive, Gaunt Building, Holmes Beach, FL 34217**) LC** K12; .A93638. **DD** 349.94; 349.4.
Ind/Abst Leg. Resour. Index; LegalTrac (1980-).

AT
LAW JOURNAL QUEENSLAND UNIVERSITY OF TECHNOLOGY. English. an. 15.00Aus$. Queensland University of Technology / School of Accountancy, GPO Box 2434, Brisbane 4001 Australia. **Tel** 011 61 7 8642663.
Ind/Abst Aust. Leg. Mon. Dig.; Index Leg. Period.

US/0883-0959
LAW LETTER & JOURNAL. (LAW LETTER & JOURNAL / VIRGINIA TRIAL LAWYERS ASSOCIATION.). [Law lett. j.]. **VFOAT** Law Letter and Journal. Vol. 1, No. 1 (Jan. 1984)-. Periodical. English. ir (seven issues per year). Virginia Trial Lawyers Association, PO Box 5127, Charlottesville VA 22905. **LC** KFV2938.A1; L38.

UK/0023-9275
LAW LIBRARIAN (LONDON). See Library and Information Sciences.

UK/0268-8336
LAW LIBRARY INFORMATION REPORTS. See Library and Information Sciences.

US/0023-9283
LAW LIBRARY JOURNAL. See Library and Information Sciences.

US/0457-2483
LAW LIBRARY LIGHTS. See Library and Information Sciences.

US/0147-1376
LAW LIBRARY NEWSLETTER. See Library and Information Sciences.

US/0148-0553
LAW LINES. See Library and Information Sciences.

US/0277-8459
LAW, MEDICINE & HEALTH CARE. ***Title Change.*** [Law, med. health care]. **Added/Corp** American Society of Law and Medicine. **VFOAT** Law, Medicine and Health Care. Vol. 9, No. 4 (Sept. 1981)-(1993). Periodical. English. qt. American Society of Law, Medicine and Ethics, 765 Commonwealth Avenue, 16th Floor, Boston MA 02215. **Tel** (617)262-4990, FAX (617)437-7596. **ED** Barry Furrow. **LC** KF3821.A15; L38. **DD** 344.73/04105; 347.3044105. **NLM** W1 LA946. **[CCC]. Bk Rev. Ad Acc. Circ:** 9,000. available on microfilm and microfiche from University Microfilms International (UMI). Documents available from UMI Article Clearinghouse. ***Formed by the union of*** *Medicolegal News, 0097-0085* ***and*** *Nursing Law & Ethics, 0270-6636.* ***Continued by*** *The Journal of Law, Medicine & Ethics, 1073-1105.*
Desc: Provides the reader with practical reference information on topics of current concern in the medicolegal field.
Ind/Abst Acad. Abstr. Full Text Elite (Jan. 1992-); Acad. Abstr. (Jan. 1992-Dec. 1992); Acad. Ind. [Computer File] (1984-); Acad. Search (Jan. 1992-Dec. 1992); Cumul. Index Nurs. Allied Health Lit.; Curr. Law Index (1981-); Expand. Acad. Index (1982-); Health Index (1992-); Health Period. Database; Health Plan. Adminis.; Health Ref. Cent. (Jan. 1989-) [Full Cov.]; Health Source (Jul. 1990-); Hospit. Health Admin. Index; Hospit. Manage. Rev. (19??-19??); Index Leg. Period.; INFO-SOUTH Abstr.; Int. Nurs. Index; Int. Pharm. Abstr.; Leg. Resour. Index (1981-); LegalTrac (1982-); Mag. Search; Newsp. Period. Abstr. (1989-); PAIS Int. Print (1991-); Psychol. Abstr. (1984-); PsycINFO; PsycLit; Soc. Plann. Policy Dev. Abstr.; Sociol. Abstr.

UK
LAW NOTES (LONDON, ENGLAND). ***Ceased.*** (LAW NOTES.). Vol. 4, Part 1 (Jan. 1885)-(June 1994). Periodical. English. Twelve times a year. Blackstone Press Limited, 9 15 Aldine Street, London W12 8AW England. **Tel** 011 44 71 081 740 1173, FAX 011 44 71 081 743 2292. **DD** 340/.05. cum. index. ***Continues*** *Gibson's Law Notes.*
Ind/Abst LegalTrac (1980-1983).

CN/0841-2626
LAW NOW. [Law now]. **Added/Corp** University of Alberta. Legal Resource Centre. Vol. 13, No. 4 (Dec./Jan. 1988/1989)-. Periodical. English. Ten times a year (monthly with July/Aug. and Dec./Jan. issues combined). 19.00Can$ Canada; 45.00Can$ other. Legal Resource Centre, 10049-81 Avenue, University of Alberta Ext., Edmonton Alberta T6E 1W7 Canada. **Tel** (403)492-5732. **ED** Marsha Mildon. **DD** 349.7123/05. **Bk Rev,** (Qty: Varies). **Ad Acc. Circ:** 2,500 (ctrl). ***Continues*** *Resource News (University of Alberta. Legal Resource Centre), 0228-0779.*
Desc: A magazine designed to provide information to Albertans about the law and law-related activities and resources.

US
LAW OF LENDER LIABILITY. English. ir. $135.00 US; $175.50 other. Warren Gorham & Lamont Inc., Park Square Building, 31 St. James Avenue, Boston

MA 02116-4112. **Tel** (617)423-2020, (800)950-1207, FAX (617)423-2026.
Desc: Comprehensive examination of lender liability law and of the issues that arise at every stage of the loan relationship. This treatise analyzes the various common law and statutory theories under which lenders may be held liable to their borrowers and explains the elements of each cause of action and the defenses available to lenders. Case summaries are organized by court and jurisdiction.

US
LAW OF LIABILITY INSURANCE. English. ir. $320.00. Matthew Bender & Company Inc., 1275 Broadway, Albany NY 12204. **Tel** (800)833-9844, (518)487-3000. **ED** Rowland H Long.

US
LAW OF MODERN COMMERCIAL PRACTICES, THE. **See** Business-Commerce.

US
LAW OF OIL AND GAS LEASES. (19??)-. English. ir. Matthew Bender & Company Inc., 1275 Broadway, Albany NY 12204. **Tel** (800)833-9844, (518)487-3000.

US/0733-6233
LAW OF THE HANDICAPPED : REPORTER AND COMMENTATOR, THE. [Law handicap.: report. commentat.]. Vol. 1 (1982)-. Periodical. English. bm. $18.00. RM Weiner, 142 Leahy Street, Jericho NY 11753. **Tel** (516)222-1744. **ED** Richard M Weiner and Tapper Bragg. **LC** KF480.A15; L38. **DD** 346.7301/3; 347.30613. **Bk Rev. Circ:** 1,000.
Desc: Current legal materials, articles, and cases concerning the law of the handicapped.

US/1056-5698
LAW OFFICE AUTOMATOR, THE. [Law off. autom.]. Vol. 1, No. 1 (Mar. 1990)-. Periodical. English. mo. $35.00. Adkins Computer Engineering Services, PO Box 2187, Gainesville FL 32602. **DD** 651.

US/1055-128X
LAW OFFICE COMPUTING. [Law off. comput.]. (Winter 1991)-. Periodical. English. bm. $72.00 US; $85.00 other. James Publishing Group, Inc., PO Box 25202, Santa Ana CA 92799. **Tel** (714)755-5450, FAX (714)556-4133. **LC** K12; .A93649. **DD** 340/.068. **[CCC].**
Ind/Abst Leg. Resour. Index; LegalTrac (1991-).

US/0458-8630
LAW OFFICE ECONOMICS AND MANAGEMENT. **See** Business-General Management.

US
LAW OFFICE EMPLOYMENT BULLETIN. COMPLIANCE AND LITIGATION. (19??)-. Bulletin. English. mo. $135.00. Leader Publications, 345 Park Avenue South, New York NY 10010. **Tel** (800)888-8300 ext. 6170, (212)545-6170, FAX (212)696-1848.

US/0739-5132
LAW OFFICE GUIDE IN COMPUTERS. ***Ceased.*** (LAW OFFICE GUIDE IN COMPUTERS : LOGIC.). [Law office guide comput.]. **VFOAT** L.O.G.I.C.; LOGIC. Vol. 1, No. 1 (Oct. 1983)-?. Periodical. English. bm. 3315 Sacramento, Suite 407, San Francisco CA 94118. **Tel** (415)923-1747. **ED** Rey Montez. **LC** KF320.A9; L395. **DD** 651.8/4/024344. Index available. cum. index. **Bk Rev. Circ:** 4,000 (ctrl).
Desc: Lawyer's consumer publication reviewing and rating computer hardware and software designed for law firms.

US/0164-5390
LAW OFFICE INFORMATION SERVICE. ***Ceased.*** **See** Law-Abstracting, Bibliographies and Statistics.

US/0883-0525
LAW OFFICE MANAGEMENT (1981). (LAW OFFICE MANAGEMENT.). [Law off. manage.]. 1981-. English. an. Practising Law Institute, 810 Seventh Avenue, New York NY 10019-5818. **Tel** (212)765-5700, FAX (212)581-4670 general correspondence, (212)265-4742 orders and billing inquiries. **LC** KF318.Z9; L38. ***Continues*** *Law Office Management and Administration, 0883-0533.*

US/0735-4843
LAW OFFICE MANAGEMENT & ADMINISTRATION REPORT. [Law off. manage. adm. rep.]. **Added/Corp** Institute for Office Management and Administration (U.S.). **VFOAT** Law Office Management and Administration Report. (1983)-. Periodical. English. mo. $295.00. Institute of Management and Administration, 29 West 35th Street, 5th Floor, New York NY 10001-2299. **Tel** (212)244-0360. **ED** David L. Foster. **LC** KF318.A1; L393. **DD** 651/.934/005. **[CCC].** Index available.
Desc: Publication covering all topics of interest to those managing law offices, including personnel, automation, financial management, insurance, professional news, meetings, etc.
Ind/Abst Law Office Inf. Serv.

CN/0843-7076
LAW OFFICE MANAGEMENT JOURNAL. [Law off. manage. j.]. Vol. 1, No. 1 (Aug. 1989)-. Periodical. English (French). Three times a year. 95.00Can$ Canada; $82.75 other. Carswell / Canada, 2075 Kennedy Road, Scarborough Ontario M1T 3V4 Canada. **Tel** (416)609-3800, (800)387-5164. **ED** Donna Wannop. **DD** 340/.068. **Bk Rev. Ad Acc.**
Desc: A practical information tool providing strategies and techniques for increasing the operating efficiency and profitability of a law firm.
Ind/Abst Can. Legal Lit.

US/1047-6482
LAW OFFICE TECHNOLOGY REVIEW. **See** Computers.

CN/0829-2094
LAW PRACTICE MANAGEMENT. [Law pract. manage.]. Vol. 1, No. 1 (June 1985)-. Periodical. English. mo. $125.00. Carswell / Canada, 2075 Kennedy Road, Scarborough Ontario M1T 3V4 Canada. **Tel** (416)609-3800, (800)387-5164. **DD** 340/.068.
Ind/Abst Leg. Resour. Index; LegalTrac (1990-).

US/1045-9081
LAW PRACTICE MANAGEMENT (CHICAGO, ILL.). (LAW PRACTICE MANAGEMENT.). [Law pract. manage.]. **Added/Corp** American Bar Association. Section of Law Practice Management. Vol. 16, No. 1 (Jan./Feb. 1990)-. Periodical. English. Eight times a year. $48.00. American Bar Association, 750 North Lake Shore Drive, Chicago IL 60611. **Tel** (312)988-5522, (312)988-5241, FAX (312)988-5528, telex 270593. **LC** KF315.A15; L4. **DD** 340/.068. **CODEN** LPMAEK. available on microfilm and microfiche from University Microfilms International (UMI). Documents available from Ask*IEEE. ***Continues*** *Legal Economics, 0360-1439.*
Ind/Abst INSPEC (Jan./Feb. 1992-); PAIS Int. Print (1991-).

UK/0023-933X
LAW QUARTERLY REVIEW, THE. [Law q. rev.]. Vol. 1, No. 1 (Jan. 1885)-. Periodical. English. Four times a year. £70.00 Europe; £74.00 other. Sweet & Maxwell Ltd., South Quay Plaza, 183 Marsh Wall, London E14 9FT England. **Tel** 011 44 264 342899, FAX 011 44 264 342723, telex 929089 ITPINF G. **DD** 340/.05. cum. index. available on microfilm and microfiche from University Microfilms International (UMI).
Ind/Abst Aust. Leg. Mon. Dig.; Br. Humanit. Index; Crim. Penol. Police Sci. Abstr.; Curr. Law Index; Index Leg. Period.; Leg. Resour. Index (1980-); LegalTrac (1980-).

II
LAW REFERENCER, THE. Periodical. English. $10.00. 35 Lawyer's Chambers, Supreme Court, New Delhi 110001 India. cum. index.
Desc: A digest of cases decided by the highest courts of Australia, Canada, England, India, Pakistan, U.S.A..

●US/1065-9285
LAW-RELATED CD-ROM UPDATE. (1993)-. Periodical. English. Three times a year. $45.00. Infosources Publishing, 140 Norma Road, Teaneck NJ 07666. **Tel** (201)836-7072, FAX (201)836-7072.

UK
LAW RELATING TO TRADE DESCRIPTIONS. (19??)-. English. ir. £195.00. Butterworth & Co. Ltd. / Kent, England, Borough Green, Sevenoaks Kent TN15 8PH England. **Tel** 011 44 732-884567, FAX 011 44 732-885996.

US/1052-4649
LAW REPORTER (WASHINGTON, D.C.). (LAW REPORTER / THE ASSOCIATION OF TRIAL LAWYERS OF AMERICA.). [Law report.]. **Added/Corp** Association of Trial Lawyers of America. **VFOAT** ATLA Law Reporter; ATLA L. Rep. Vol. 28, No. 5 (June 1985)-. Periodical. English. mo. $135.00. Association of Trial Lawyers of America, 1050 31st Street Northwest, Washington DC 20007. **Tel** (800)424-2725 ext. 307, FAX (202)298-6849. **LC** KF294.A8; A3. **DD** 346.7303/23/0269; 347.3063230269. available on microfilm and microfiche from University Microfilms International (UMI). ***Continues*** *ATLA Law Reporter, 0364-8125.*

UK/0264-1097
LAW REPORTS. CHANCERY DIVISION (1972). (THE LAW REPORTS. CHANCERY DIVISION, AND ON APPEAL THEREFROM IN THE COURT OF APPEAL, AND DECISIONS IN THE COURT OF PROTECTION.). [Law rep., Chancery Div.]. **Added/Corp** Great Britain. High Court of Justice. Chancery Division. Great Britain. Court of Appeal. Great Britain. Court of Protection. Incorporated Council of Law Reporting for England and Wales. **VFOAT** Chancery Division, and on Appeal Therefrom in the Court of Appeal, and Decisions in the Court of Protection. (1977)-. English. an (bound volume; l). £40.00. Incorporated Council of Law Reporting for England and Wales, 3 Stone Buildings, Lincoln's Inn, London WC2A 3XN England. **Tel** (071)242-6471, FAX (071)831-5247. ***Continues*** *Law Reports. Chancery Division and Cases in Lunacy, and on Appeal Therefrom in the Court of Appeal, 0264-1097.*

UK/0264-1135
LAW REPORTS. HOUSE OF LORDS. (THE LAW REPORTS. HOUSE OF LORDS, AND JUDICIAL COMMITTEE OF THE PRIVY COUNCIL, AND PEERAGE CASES.). [Law rep. House Lords]. **Added/Corp** Great Britain. Parliament. House of Lords. Great Britain. Privy Council. Judicial Committee. Incorporated Council of Law Reporting for England and Wales. **VFOAT** House of Lords, and Judicial Committee of the Privy Council, and Peerage Cases. (1955)-. English. an (bound volume; l). £40.00. Incorporated Council of Law Reporting for England and Wales, 3 Stone Buildings, Lincoln's Inn, London WC2A 3XN England. **Tel** (071)242-6471, FAX (071)831-5247. ***Continues*** *Law Reports of the Incorporated Council of Law Reporting. House of Lords, Judicial Committee of the Privy Council, and Peerage Cases.*

UK/0265-1238
LAW REPORTS. INDEX, THE. [Law rep., Index]. **Added/Corp** Incorporated Council of Law Reporting for England and Wales. **VFOAT** Index; Law Reports Index. (19??)-. English. an. comes with Weekly Law Reports. Incorporated Council of Law Reporting for England and Wales, 3 Stone Buildings, Lincoln's Inn, London WC2A 3XN England. **Tel** (071)242-6471, FAX (071)831-5247. **ED** Carol Ellis and Hilary Jellie. **LC** KD285; .L39. **DD** 348.41/048; 344.10848. ***Continues*** *Law Reports, Weekly Law Reports, and Restrictive Practices Reports. Consolidated Index.*

NR
LAW REPORTS OF NIGERIA, THE. Vol. 1 (1978)-. English. Butterworth Heinemann Publishers, Linacre House, Jordan Hill, Oxford OX2 8DP England. **Tel** 011 44 865 310366. **DD** 348.669/041; 346.690841.
Desc: The majority of decisions are from the Supreme Court of Nigeria.

UK
LAW REPORTS. QUEEN'S BENCH DIVISION, AND ON APPEAL THEREFROM IN THE COURT OF APPEAL, AND DECISIONS IN THE COURT OF APPEAL CRIMINAL DIVISION AND EMPLOYMENT APPEAL TRIBUNAL, THE. 1977-. English. an. £40.00. Incorporated Council Law Reports, Stone Buildings, Lincoln Inn, London WC2A 3XN England. **Tel** (01)242-6471, FAX (01)831-5247. ***Continues*** *Law Reports. Queen's Bench Division, and on appeal Therefrom in the Court of Appeal, and Decisions in the Court of Appeal Criminal Division.*

UK
LAW REVIEW. (1990)-. English. Twelve times a year. £305.00 Europe; £320.00 other. Sweet & Maxwell Ltd., South Quay Plaza, 183 Marsh Wall, London E14 9FT England. **Tel** 011 44 264 342899, FAX 011 44 264 342723, telex 929089 ITPINF G.

US/0734-1938
LAW REVIEW JOURNAL. [Law rev. j.]. **Added/Corp** Legal Institute. (1978)-. Periodical. English. tq (3 issues). $9.75. Legal Institute, 3250 Wilshire Boulevard, Suite 1000, Los Angeles CA 90010. **Tel** (213)487-6268. **LC** KF250; .L38. **DD** 340/.05. Index available (Free). **Bk Rev. Ad Acc. Circ:** 200 (ctrl).
Desc: Focuses on the production and management of law reviews.

US/0042-5117
LAW REVIEW (WELLINGTON). (VICTORIA UNIVERSITY OF WELLINGTON LAW REVIEW.). [Law rev.]. **Added/Corp** Victoria University of Wellington. Law Faculty. **VFOAT** Law Review. Vol. 2, No. 3 (Oct. 1957)-. Periodical. English. ir. 44.00NZ$ New Zealand; 52.00NZ$ Australia; 68.00NZ$ other. William W. Gaunt and Sons Inc, 3011 Gulf Drive, Gaunt Building, Holmes Beach FL 34217. **Tel** (800)942-8683, (813)778-5211. **LC** K26; .I25. **DD** 340/.05. cum. index. ***Continues*** *Victoria University College Law Review.*
Ind/Abst Curr. Law Index (1980-); Index Leg. Period.; Leg. Resour. Index (1980-); LegalTrac (1980-).

US/0741-1170
LAW SCHOOL ADMINISTRATOR'S JOURNAL. (LAW SCHOOL ADMINISTRATOR'S JOURNAL : A LEGAL INSTITUTE PROJECT.). [Law sch. adm. j.]. Vol. 1, Issue 1-. Periodical. English. Three times a year. $9.75. Legal Institute, 3250 Wilshire Boulevard, Suite 1000, Los Angeles CA 90010. **Tel** (213)487-6268. **ED** Herman B Lancaster. **LC** KF273; .L4. **DD** 340/.07/1173. Index available. **Bk Rev. Ad Acc. Circ:** 200 (ctrl).
Desc: Covers information useful in legal education administration.

US/0737-2590
LAW SCHOOL JOURNAL. [Law school j.]. **Added/Corp** Legal Institute. Vol. 1, Issue 1 (1980)-. Periodical. English. Three times a year. $9.75. Legal Institute, 3250 Wilshire Boulevard, Suite 1000, Los

Angeles CA 90010. **Tel** (213)487-6268. **ED** Herman B. Lancaster. **LC** KF283; .L37. **DD** 340/.07/1173. **Bk Rev. Circ:** 200.
Desc: Provides information about succeeding in law school, about bar exams, and law careers.

US/0529-097X
LAW SCHOOL RECORD. [Law Sch. rec.]. **Main/Corp** University of Chicago. Law School. **VFOAT** University of Chicago Law School Record. No. 1 (Autumn 1951)-. English. sa. $35.00. William S. Hein & Company Inc., 1285 Main Street, Buffalo NY 14209. **Tel** (716)882-2600, (800)828-7571, FAX (716)883-8100, telex 91-209 WM S HEIN BUF. available on microfilm and microfiche from University Microfilms International (UMI). **Ind/Abst** Leg. Resour. Index; LegalTrac (1980-).

US/0737-1152
LAW SCHOOL TRANSCRIPT, THE. (THE LAW SCHOOL TRANSCRIPT / UNIVERSITY OF MISSOURI-COLUMBIA SCHOOL OF LAW.). Began in 1977. Periodical. English. University of Missouri Columbia / Hulston, Hulston Hall Room 15, Columbia MO 65211. **Tel** (314)882-9682. **LC** KF292.M5914; A44. **DD** 340/.07/1177829.

US/0892-7073
LAW SEMINAR JOURNAL. [Law semin. guide]. 1987-. Periodical. English. mo. $96.00. PO Box 2764, Wilmington DE 19805. **LC** KF275.A15; L37. **DD** 340/.07/073.
Desc: Contains information on thousands of law and law-related seminars.

AT/0157-8952
LAW SOCIETY BULLETIN. [Law Soc. bull.]. **Added/Corp** Law Society of South Australia. (1967)-. Bulletin. English. Eleven times a year. 66.00Aus$. Law Society of South Australia, GPO Box 2066, Adelaide SA 5001 Australia. **Tel** 011 61 8 2319972. **DD** 349.942305. **Ind/Abst** Aust. Leg. Mon. Dig.

AT
LAW SOCIETY JOURNAL (SYDNEY, N.S.W. : 1982). (LAW SOCIETY JOURNAL : THE OFFICIAL JOURNAL OF THE LAW SOCIETY OF NEW SOUTH WALES.). **Added/Corp** Law Society of New South Wales. Vol. 20, No. 8 (Sept. 1982)-. Periodical. English. Eleven times a year. 90.00Aus$ Australia; 110.00Aus$ other. Law Society of New South Wales, 170 Phillip Street, Sydney New South Wales, 2000 Australia. **Tel** 011 61 2 2200333, 011 61 2 2200289, FAX 011 61 2 231 5809, telex 73063. **ED** Bob Campbell. **DD** 340/.06/0944. Index available. cum. index. **Bk Rev. Ad Acc, Adv Mgr:** John Tottrup. **Circ:** 12,400 (ctrl). ***Continues*** *Journal of the Law Society of N.S.W.*
Desc: Legal journal primarily to inform members of the profession.
Ind/Abst Aust. Leg. Mon. Dig.; Curr. Law Index (1982-); Leg. Resour. Index (1982-); LegalTrac (1980-).

UK/0262-1495
LAW SOCIETY'S GAZETTE. [Law Soc. gaz.]. (1903)-. Periodical. English. Forty-six times a year (The last issue of each month as the Guardian Gazette). £72.00 UK, £97.00 others (surface mail); £114.00 Europe, £137.00 others (airmail). Law Society SVCS Ltd., 113 Chancery Lane, London WC2A 1PL England. **Tel** 011 44 71 242 122226, FAX 011 44 71 831 0869, telex 261203. **ED** Ms. Sheila Pratt. Index available (Bound in July/Dec. iss. #46). **Bk Rev. Ad Acc, Adv Mgr:** M. Manning, **Tel** 071 320 5852. ctrl circ.

NZ
LAW TALK (WELLINGTON, N.Z.). (LAW TALK : NEWSLETTER OF THE NEW ZEALAND LAW SOCIETY.). **VFOAT** Lawtalk. Newsletter. English. sm. 60.00NZ$ New Zealand; 70.00NZ$ (airmail) Australia and South Pacific; 95.00NZ$ (airmail) North America and Asia; 100.00NZ$ (airmail) South America, Europe, Africa, and Middle East. New Zealand Law Society, Box 5041, 26 Waring Taylor Street, Wellington 1 New Zealand. **Tel** (04)727837, FAX (04)737-909. **ED** A J McLeod. **DD** 340/.06/0931. **Bk Rev. Ad Acc. Circ:** 7,000 (ctrl).
Desc: Commentary on matters pertinent to members of New Zealand Law Society.

UK/0306-9400
LAW TEACHER, THE. [Law teach.]. **Added/Corp** Association of Law Teachers (Great Britain). (1971)-. Periodical. English. Three times a year. £37.00 Europe; £39.00 other. Sweet & Maxwell Ltd., South Quay Plaza, 183 Marsh Wall, London E14 9FT England. **Tel** 011 44 264 342899, FAX 011 44 264 342723, telex 929089 ITPINF G. **LC** K12; .A9374. **DD** 340/.05. **[CCC]**. ***Continues*** *Journal of the Association of Law Teachers, 0044-9628.*
Ind/Abst Curr. Law Index (1980-); Leg. Resour. Index (1980-); LegalTrac (1983-).

US/0741-1197
LAW TEACHER'S JOURNAL. (LAW TEACHER'S JOURNAL : A LEGAL INSTITUTE PROJECT.). [Law teach. j.]. Vol. 1, Issue 1-. Periodical. English. Three times a year. $9.75. Legal Institute, 3250 Wilshire Boulevard, Suite 1000, Los Angeles CA 90010. **Tel** (213)487-6268. **ED** Herman B Lancaster. **LC** KF273; .L42. **DD** 340/.07/073. Index available. **Bk Rev. Ad Acc. Circ:** 200 (ctrl).
Desc: Provides information about teaching law.

US/1071-9121
LAW TECHNOLOGY PRODUCT NEWS. (1993)-. Periodical. English. ir. Free on request. New York Law Publishing Company, 345 Park Avenue South, New York NY 10010. **Tel** (212)741-8300, (800)888-8300.

SI
LAW TIMES, THE. Began with July 1966. English. an. $12.00. University of Singapore Law Club, Kentridge, Singapore 0511 Republic of Singapore. **Tel** 7756666. **(Subscription address:** Wm W Gaunt and Sons Inc, 3011 Gulf Drive, Holmes Beach, FL 34217-2199**) ED** Boon Chinaun. **LC** K12; .A9376. **DD** 349.595/7/05. **Ad Acc. Circ:** 700.
Desc: Articles from Singapore judges, lawyers, and students on aspects of our legal system. Also foreign contributions concerning topical issues in law today.

UK
LAW UNDER REVIEW : QUARTERLY BULLETIN OF LAW REFORM PROJECTS. No. 1 (March 1987)-. Bulletin. English. qt. Law Commission Conquest House, 37-38 John Street, Theobalds Road, London WC1N2BQ England. **Tel** 011 44 71 242 0561.

CN/0824-4421
LAW UNION NEWS (TORONTO). (THE LAW UNION NEWS.). [Law Union news]. **Added/Corp** Law Union of Ontario. (1974)-. Periodical. English. Four times a year. $25.00. Law Union of Ontario, 489 College Street, Suite 303, Toronto Ontario M6G 1A5 Canada. **Tel** (416)927-9662. **DD** 349.713/05.

US/0190-5252
LAW WEEK'S SUMMARY & ANALYSIS OF CURRENT LAW. **VAT** Law Week's Summary and Analysis of Current Law. (19??)-. Periodical. English. wk. $159.00. Bureau of National Affairs Inc., 9435 Key West Avenue, Rockville MD 20850. **Tel** (800)372-1033, (301)258-1033, FAX (301)948-5823. **(Subscription address:** 9435 Key West Avenue, Rockville MD 20850; telephone: FAX (301)948-5823**) ED** Gregory R Pease. **[CCC].**
Desc: Summary of the most important legal developments during the past week, with an index and table of cases. It is Section 1 of BNA's U.S. Law Week.

AT
LAWASIA. **Main/Corp** Law Association for Asia and the Western Pacific. V. 1-5 (Dec. 1969-1974); N.S. Vol. 1 (1979)-. English. ir. price varies per volume. University of Technology, Sydney, PO Box 123, City Camp, Broadway, N.S.W. 2007, Australia. **Tel** 011 61 2 330 1990, FAX 011 61 2 330 1551. **LC** K12; .A926. **DD** 340/.05.
Ind/Abst Index Foreign Leg. Per.

US/0737-8971
LAWMARK. [Lawmark]. **VFOAT** Law Mark. Vol. 1, No. 1-. Periodical. English. mo. Howard M Markman, PO Box 177, Northfield NJ 08225.

AM
LAWS OF ANGUILLA. **Main/Corp** Anguilla. (1971-1973)-. English. **LC** KGJ7008; .A235. **DD** 348.7297/3; 347.2973.

AQ
LAWS OF ANTIGUA AND BARBUDA. **Main/Corp** Antigua and Barbuda. (19??)-. English. an. Antigua & Barbuda Government Publications, G.P.O., St. John's Antigua & Barbuda. **LC** KGK8; .A23. **DD** 348.7297/4022; 347.29740822. ***Continues*** *Laws, Etc. Laws of Antigua.*

US
LAWS OF FLORIDA. **Main/Corp** Florida. English. Florida Legislature, 111 West Madison Street, Room 716, Tallahassee FL 32399. **Tel** (904)922-0647.

US
LAWS OF MEXICO. English. $370.00 (US); $407.00 (other). Foreign Tax Law Publishers Inc., PO Box 2189, Ormond Beach FL 32175-2189. **Tel** (904)253-5785, FAX (904)257-3003.

US
LAWS OF PUERTO RICO ANNOTATED. **Main/Corp** Puerto Rico. English. an. Equity Publishing Corporation, RR 1 Box 3, Orford NH 03777. **Tel** (603)637-5012, (800)637-5012.

AM
LAWS OF ST. CHRISTOPHER, NEVIS & ANGUILLA. **Main/Corp** Saint Kitts-Nevis-Anguilla. **VFOAT** Laws of Saint Christopher, Nevis & Anguilla. (19??)-. English. **LC** KGW2008; .A23. **DD** 348.7297/3022; 347.29730822.

SZ
LAWS OF THE GAME AND UNIVERSAL GUIDE FOR REFEREES. **Main/Corp** Football Association International Federation. English. 5.00F. Hitzigweg 11, 8032 Zurich Switzerland. **LC** GV943.4; .F65A. **DD** 796.33/4/02022.

US/0148-4494
LAWS RELATED TO THE DEPARTMENT OF SOCIAL SERVICES, PASSED DURING THE LEGISLATIVE SESSION. **Main/Corp** Michigan. English. Department of Social Services / Michigan, 300 South Capitol Avenue, Lansing MI 48026. **LC** HV86 B .M536 subser; KFM4549. **DD** 361/.9774 S; 344/.774/03.

US
LAWS RELATING TO FIRES AND FIREMEN, STATE OF CALIFORNIA. **Main/Corp** California. English. California Department of General Services Document Section, PO Box 20191, Sacramento CA 95820. **DD** 352.3. **UDC** 351.78:614.84(794).

US
LAWS RELATING TO THE MINNESOTA PUBLIC SCHOOL SYSTEM. **Main/Corp** Minnesota. (18??)-. English. an. $22.70 Minnesota residents; $21.50 others. Minnesota Documents, 117 University Avenue, St Paul MN 55155. **Tel** (612)297-3000, (800)657-3757, FAX (612)296-2265.

US/0160-1326
LAWS RELATING TO THE PRACTICE OF OPTOMETRY, WITH RULES AND REGULATIONS. **Main/Corp** California. English. California Department of Consumer Affairs, 1020 North Street, Room 510, Sacramento CA 95814. **Tel** (916)445-4465, FAX (916)443-1601. **LC** KFC546.5.O6; A295. **DD** 346/.794/041.

TR
LAWYER, THE. **VFOAT** Digest of Cases with Editorial Notes; Law Reports. V. 1- Oct./Dec. 1977-. Periodical. English. $40.00. Trinidad and Tobago Bar Association, Treasurer, Sydney R R Martineau, Chambers, 13A Pembroke Street, Port of Spain Trinidad and Tobago. **DD** 349.7298/3/05.
Desc: Includes separately paged section: The Lawyer, digest of cases with editorial notes. (Vol. 1 No. 1 called Law Reports).

UK
LAWYER. (19??)-. Periodical. English. wk (50 issues). £50.00 UK; £75.00 Europe; £110.00 other. Centaur Communications Ltd., St Giles House, 50 Poland Street, London W1V 4AX England. **Tel** 011 44 71 439 4222, FAX 011 44 71 734 6748, telex 261352.

US/0276-6108
LAWYER DIRECTORY (ROCKVILLE, MD.). (LAWYER DIRECTORY / BAR ASSOCIATION OF MONTGOMERY COUNTY, MARYLAND.). **VFOAT** Bar Association of Montgomery County Lawyer Directory. Directory. English. $1.00. Lawyer Directory, 17 West Jefferson Street/Suite 105, Rockville MD 20850. **LC** KF193.M65; L38. **DD** 349.752/84/025; 347.52840025.

US
LAWYER GUIDE & DIRECTORY, LOS ANGELES COUNTY. **VFOAT** Los Angeles County Lawyer Guide. 1st Ed. (1978)-. English. ir. Lawyer Guide & Directory Publishing Company, 7045 Hawthorne Avenue, Los Angeles CA 90028. **LC** KF193.L65; L3. **DD** 340/.025/79493.

US/0739-1706
LAWYER HIRING & TRAINING REPORT. **VFOAT** Lawyer Hiring and Training Report; Hiring & Training Report; Hiring and Training Report. Vol. 4, No. 1 (June 1983)-. Periodical. English. Twelve times a year. $168.18 nonprofit organizations; $303.80 other. Prentice-Hall Law and Business, 270 Sylvan Avenue, Englewood Cliffs NJ 07632. **Tel** (800)223-0231, (201)894-8538, FAX (201)894-8666. **LC** KF276.5.A15; L38. **DD** 340/.07/073. Index available. **Bk Rev.** ***Continues*** *Henning CLE Reporter, 0276-5004.*
Desc: Gives a systematic way to run the most productive and cost-effective recruitment and productivity program. Provides detailed information on state-of-the-art methods used by other firms, companies and government agencies.

IE/0791-7481
LAWYER INTERNATIONAL. English. mo (10 issues). $749.00. Lafferty Publications Ltd. / Dublin, Tower Ida Centre Pearse St., Dublin 2 Ireland. **Tel** 011 353 1 6718022, FAX 01-718520.

US/0890-7765
LAWYER REFERRAL NETWORK. (LAWYER REFERRAL NETWORK / PUBLISHED BY THE STANDING COMMITTEE ON LAWYER REFERRAL AND INFORMATION SERVICE, AMERICAN BAR ASSOCIATION.). **Added/Corp** American Bar Association. Standing Committee on Lawyer Referral and Information Service. Vol. 1, No. 1 (Spring 1986)-. Periodical. English. qt. American Bar Association, 750 North Lake Shore Drive, Chicago IL 60611. **Tel** (312)988-5522, (312)988-5241, FAX (312)988-5528, telex 270593. **LC** KF338; .L39. **DD** 349.73/023; 347.30023. ***Continues*** *LRIS Newsletter.*

US/0091-0430
LAWYER-TO-LAWYER CONSULTATION PANEL. 1st- Ed.; 1973-. English. an. 800 Caxton Building, Cleveland OH 44115. **LC** KF190; .L362. **DD** 340/.025/73.

US/0278-9817
LAWYER'S ALERT. ***Title Change.*** [Lawyer's alert]. Vol. 1, No. 1 (Oct. 19, 1981)-(19??). Periodical. English. wk. Lawyers Weekly Publications, 41 West Street, Boston MA 02111. **Tel** (617)451-7300, (800)444-5297. **ED** J. Edward Pawlick. **LC** K12; .A955. **DD** 349.73/05; 347.3005. **Bk Rev. Ad Acc. Circ:** 8,439. ***Continued by*** *Lawyer's Weekly USA, 1069-7837.*
Desc: Guide to new cases and trends in areas of the law with advice and ideas from legal experts.

US/0277-9544
LAWYER'S ALMANAC, THE. [Lawyer's alm.]. (1981/1982)-. English. an. $103.08. Prentice-Hall Law and Business, 270 Sylvan Avenue, Englewood Cliffs NJ 07632. **Tel** (800)223-0231, (201)894-8538, FAX (201)894-8666. **LC** KF190; .L3625. **DD** 349.73/025; 347.30025.
Desc: Offers an encyclopedic compilation of facts, figures, names and statistics on lawyers, law practice, the courts and government operations.

US
LAWYERS AND THE ARTS COMMITTEE NEWSLETTER / AMERICAN BAR ASSOCIATION, YOUNG LAWYERS DIVISION. ***Title Change.*** **Added/Corp** American Bar Association. Young Lawyers Division. Lawyers and the Arts Committee. (1992)-(199?). Newsletter. English. sa (2 issues). American Bar Association, 750 North Lake Shore Drive, Chicago IL 60611. **Tel** (312)988-5522, (312)988-5241, FAX (312)988-5528, telex 270593. **LC** KF4288.A15; L38. **DD** 344.73/097/05; 347.3049705. ***Continues*** *Lawyers for the Arts Newsletter.* ***Continued by*** *Arts, Entertainment & Sports Law News.*
Desc: Journal for lawyers regarding the arts community as related to the law.

US
LAWYERS' ARBITRATION LETTER. Vol. 1, (1973)-. Periodical. English. an. $30.00. American Arbitration Association, 140 West 51st Street, New York NY 10020. **Tel** (212)484-4011, (212)484-4014, FAX (212)765-4874, telex 12463. **ED** Laura Buckley. Index available. cum. index. ***Continues in part*** *Lawyers' Arbitration Letter; Arbitration Law, 0518-2611.*
Desc: Features in-depth articles on topics primarily directed to attorneys. Each letter discusses the case history and developments in a certain area of dispute resolution, such as arbitration and the common law, the enforceability of partial final awards, consolidation, confidentiality and immunity and international arbitration.

US/0898-9966
LAWYER'S BRIEF, THE. [Lawyer's brief]. **Added/Corp** Business Laws, inc. (1971)-. Periodical. English. sm. $398.00. Business Laws Inc., 11630 Chillicothe Road, Chesterland OH 44026. **Tel** (216)729-7996, (800)759-0929, FAX (216)729-0645. **LC** K12; .A956. **DD** 349.73/05; 347.3005. **[CCC].**

US
LAWYERS DIARY AND MANUAL INCLUDING BAR DIRECTORY OF NEW JERSEY. ***Title Change.*** **VFOAT** Bar Directory of New Jersey. (19??)-(19??). English. an (Nov.). Skinder Strauss Associates, PO Box 50, Newark NJ 07101. **Tel** (800)444-4041, (201)642-1440, FAX (201)642-4280. **LC** KF192.N4; L35. **DD** 340/.025/749. **Ad Acc, Adv Mgr:** Bergamo. ***Continued by*** *New Jersey Lawyers Diary and Manual, 1053-1955.*

UK/0967-6562
LAWYERS' EUROPE. [Lawyers' Eur.]. (1990)-. Periodical. English. qt. £40.00. Butterworth & Co. Ltd. / Kent, England, Borough Green, Sevenoaks Kent TN15 8PH England. **Tel** 011 44 732-884567, FAX 011 44 732-885996. **ED** Simon Holmes, Robert Strivens. **DD** 341.094. ***Continues*** *Law Society's Solicitors' European Group Journal.*
Desc: Publication of the Solicitors' European Group.

UK
LAWYERS' EUROPE. English. qt. £48.00 UK; $95.00 other. John Wiley & Sons Ltd., Baffins Lane, Chichester West Sussex PO19 1UD England. **Tel** 0243 779777, FAX 0243 776128 BTG:JWP001, telex 86290 WIBOOKG. **(Subscription address:** North, South and Central America/ John Wiley & Sons, Inc., Subscription Department, 605 Third Avenue, New York, NY 10158-0012, USA; telephone: (212)850-6645; FAX: (212)850-6021**)** **ED** Simon Holmes and Robert Strivens.
Desc: It provides articles on all areas of EC law and other legal issues throughout Europe.

UK
LAWYERS FACT BOOK. English. Three times a year. £110.00 UK; £120.00 other. Gee & Company Limited, 183 Marsh Wall, South Quay Plaza, London E14 9FS England. **Tel** 011 44 71 538 5386, FAX 071 538 8623.

US
LAWYERS' GUIDE TO MEDICAL PROOF. 1966-. English. an. Matthew Bender & Company Inc., 1275 Broadway, Albany NY 12204. **Tel** (800)833-9844, (518)487-3000. Index Available, published separately, free-automatically sent.

US
LAWYERS JOB BULLETIN BOARD. Bulletin. English. Twelve times a year. $30.00. Federal Bar Association, 1815 H Street Northwest, Suite 408, Washington DC 20006. **Tel** (202)638-0252, FAX (202)775-0295. **ED** Maragret Simon. **Circ:** 300.
Desc: Job listings for attorneys in federal practice.

US/0896-7075
LAWYERS' LIABILITY REVIEW. [Lawyers' liabil. rev.]. **VFOAT** LLR. (Feb. 1986)-. English. Twelve times a year. $325.00 one year; $575.00 two years; $900.00 three years. Timeline Publishing Company, PO Box 1435, Bellvue WA 98009. **Tel** (800)444-7714 or (206)462-7714, FAX (206)462-0411. **LC** KF313.A15; L375. **DD** 346.7303/3; 347.30633. cum. index. available on an online database from Bulletin Board.
Desc: Case notes and briefs news covering the full range of topics within the subject areas of legal malpractice, professional responsibility and ethics.

US/8755-5891
LAWYER'S MEDICAL DIGEST. [Lawyers' med. dig.]. **VFOAT** LMD. Vol. 1, No. 1 (July 1984)-. Periodical. English. mo. $129.00. Clark Boardman Callaghan, 155 Pfingsten Road, Deerfield IL 60015. **Tel** (800)323-8067. **ED** Steven Babitsky. **LC** RA1001; .L38. **DD** 610/.5. Each issue contains an index to its own contents (no volume index)--loose. **Circ:** 700.
Desc: Summarizes and indexes articles appearing in medical journals.

US/0732-0922
LAWYER'S MICROCOMPUTER, THE. ***Title Change.*** Vol. 1, No. 1 (April 1982)-(1992). Periodical. English. mo. RPW Publishing Corporation, PO Box 1108, Lexington SC 29071-0729. **Tel** (803)359-9954, FAX (803)957-8226. **LC** KF320.A9; L398. **DD** 651.8/4/024344. ***Continued by*** *Lawyer's PC.*

US/1044-7660
LAWYER'S MONTHLY CATALOG. [Lawyer's mon. cat.]. No. 1 (1989)-. Catalog. English. bm. $230.00. Ward & Associates, 317 South Division, Suite 66, Ann Arbor MI 48104. **Tel** (313)665-3520, FAX (313)665-7880. **LC** Z1223.Z7; L34. **DD** 016. ***Continues in part*** *National Legal Bibliography. Part 2, Government Documents from Official and Commercial Sources, 0887-106X.*

US/1049-7978
LAWYERS MONTHLY CATALOG, ANNUAL. [Lawyers mon. cat. annu.]. (1990)-. Catalog. English. $295.00. William S. Hein & Company Inc., 1285 Main Street, Buffalo NY 14209. **Tel** (716)882-2600, (800)828-7571, FAX (716)883-8100, telex 91-209 WM S HEIN BUF. **DD** 016. ***Continues in part*** *National Legal Bibliography, Annual, 1057-1825.*

US/0740-0942
LAWYER'S PC, THE. [Lawyer's PC]. **VFOAT** LPC. **VAT** Lawyer's Personal Computer. Vol. 1, No. 1 (Sept. 1, 1983)-. Periodical. English. sm (24 issues). $105.00. Shepards McGraw-Hill Inc, 555 Middle Creek Parkway, PO Box 35300, Colorado Springs CO 80935-3530. **Tel** (719)488-3000, FAX (800)525-0053. **ED** Robert P. Wilkins. **LC** KF320.A9; L42. **DD** 340/.028/5416. **Bk Rev. Ad Acc. Circ:** 4,000. ***Continues*** *The Lawyer's Microcomputer, 0732-0922.*
Desc: Newsletter written for lawyers by lawyers using personal computers.
Ind/Abst Comput. Lit. Index; Law Office Inf. Serv.

UK
LAWYER'S REMEMBRANCER. (19??)-. English. an. £18.50. Butterworth & Co. Ltd. / Kent, England, Borough Green, Sevenoaks Kent TN15 8PH England. **Tel** 011 44 732-884567, FAX 011 44 732-885996.

UK/0142-7490
LAWYER'S REMEMBRANCER. [Lawyer's remembr.]. (1969)-. English. an. £17.50. Butterworth & Co. Ltd. / Kent, England, Borough Green, Sevenoaks Kent TN15 8PH England. **Tel** 011 44 732-884567, FAX 011 44 732-885996. **ED** Julian Roskams. **DD** _a348.42005. ***Continues*** *Lawyer's Remembrancer and Pocket Book.*
Desc: Provides indispensable information with a day-to-day diary section for forward planning.

US/0272-7161
LAWYERS TITLE NEWS. [Lawyers title news]. **Added/Corp** Lawyers Title Insurance Corporation. (Aug. 1937)-. Periodical. English. bm (6 issues). Lawyers Title Insurance Company, 6630 West Broad Street, Richmond VA 23230. **Tel** (804)281-6700. **LC** UNC.

US/0732-4901
LAWYERS WEEKLY GUIDEBOOK. (1979)-. English. an. Massachusetts Lawyers Weekly, 30 Court Square, Boston MA 02108. **Tel** (617)227-6034, FAX (617)227-8824. **LC** KFM2477; .L38. **DD** 349.744/05; 347.44005. ***Continues*** *Lawyers Weekly Guide to Massachusetts Courts and Lawyers.*

CN/0830-0151
LAWYERS WEEKLY (SCARBOROUGH). (THE LAWYERS WEEKLY.). [Lawyers wkly.]. **Added/Corp** Butterworth & Co. (Canada). Vol. 6, No. 1 (May 2, 1986)-. Periodical. English. ir (48 issues per year). $160.00 US; $180.00 other. The Lawyers Weekly, 423 Queen Street West/Suite 201, Toronto Ontario M5V 2A5 Canada. **Tel** (416)598-5211, FAX (416)598-5656. **(Subscription address:** Butterworth & Co Ltd., 75 Clegg Road, Markham Ontario, L6G 1A1 Canada (416-479-2665)**)** **ED** D M Fitz-James. **DD** 349.713/05. Index available. cum. index. **Bk Rev. Ad Acc. Circ:** 37,500 (ctrl). available on microfilm from University Microfilms International (UMI). ***Continues*** *Ontario Lawyers Weekly, 0822-5745.*
Desc: A newspaper of legal affairs, jurisprudence and features of interest to lawyers and the legal community.

●US/1069-7837
LAWYER'S WEEKLY USA. [Lawyer's wkly. USA]. **VFOAT** LWUSA. Issue 93-1 (April 12, 1993)-. Periodical. English. bw (26 issues). $89.00. Lawyers Weekly Publications, 41 West Street, Boston MA 02111. **Tel** (617)451-7300, (800)444-5297. **DD** 349. ***Continues*** *Lawyer's Alert, 0278-9817.*

US/1056-1226
LAWYER'S WORD : A NEWSLETTER FOR LAWYERS USING MICROSOFT WORD AND OTHER MICROSOFT PRODUCTS, THE. ***Ceased.*** **See** Computers-Software.

US
LDRC 50-STATE SURVEY / PREPARED BY LEADING MEDIA ATTORNEYS AND LAW FIRMS IN ALL FIFTY STATES AND THE U.S. TERRITORIES. **Added/Corp** Libel Defense Resource Center. **VFOAT** L.D.R.C. 50-State Ssurvey; LDRC Fifty-State Survey; Current Developments in Media Libel and Invasion of Privacy law; Libel Defense Resource Center 50-State Survey. Vol. 1, (1982)-. English. an. $118.50. Libel Defense Resource Center, 404 Park Avenue South, 16th Floor, New York NY 10017. **Tel** (212)889-2306, FAX (212) 689-3315. **ED** Henry R. Kaufman. **LC** KF1266.Z95; L3.
Desc: Current developments in media libel and invasion of the privacy law.

US/0737-8130
LDRC BULLETIN. (LDRC BULLETIN / LIBEL DEFENSE RESOURCE CENTER.). [LDRC bull.]. **Added/Corp** Libel Defense Resource Center. **VFOAT** L.D.R.C. Bulletin. **VAT** Libel Defense Resource Center Bulletin. (19??)-. Bulletin. English. qt. $100.00. Libel Defense Resource Center, 404 Park Avenue South, 16th Floor, New York NY 10017. **Tel** (212)889-2306, FAX (212) 689-3315. **LC** KF1266.A15; L35. **DD** 346.7303/4/02648; 347.3063402648.

US/0733-4303
LEADER'S EQUIPMENT LEASING NEWSLETTER. [Leader's Equip. leasing newsl.]. **VFOAT** Equipment Leasing Newsletter. (Jan. 1982)-. Newsletter. English. mo. $275.00. Leader Publications, 345 Park Avenue South, New York NY 10010. **Tel** (800)888-8300 ext. 6170, (212)545-6170, FAX (212)696-1848. **ED** Herbert S. Schlagman. **DD** 338. cum. index. **Circ:** 700.
Desc: Reports and analyzes developments in equipment leasing industry in areas of tax, accounting, bankruptcy, finance including legislative and judicial proposals.

US/1047-2827
LEADER'S EUROPE 1992 LAW & STRATEGY. ***Title Change.*** [Lead. Eur. 1992 law strategy]. **VFOAT** Leader's Europe 1992 Law and Strategy; Leader's Europe 1992; Leader's Europe Nineteen Ninety-Two Law and Strategy; Europe 1992 Law & Strategy. Vol. 1, No. 1 (December 1989)-(1992). Periodical. English. mo. Leader Publications, 345 Park Avenue South, New York NY 10010. **Tel** (800)888-8300 ext. 6170, (212)545-6170, FAX (212)696-1848. **LC** KJE6411.3; .L43. **DD** 349.4/05; 344.05. ***Continued by*** *Leader's European Market Law Report.*

●US
LEADER'S EUROPEAN MARKET LAW REPORT. **VFOAT** European Market Law Report. Vol. 4, No. 1 (Jan. 1993)-. Periodical. English. mo. $190.00. Leader Publications, 345 Park Avenue South, New York NY 10010. **Tel** (800)888-8300 ext. 6170, (212)545-6170, FAX (212)696-1848. **LC** KJE6411.3; .L43. **DD** 349.4/05; 344.05. ***Continues*** *Leader's Europe 1992 Law & Strategy.*

US/0738-0186
LEADER'S LEGAL TECH NEWSLETTER. [Leader's legal tech newsl.]. **VFOAT** Legal Tech Newsletter; Legal Tech. Vol. 1, No. 1 (Apr. 1983)-. Newsletter. English. mo. $185.00. Leader Publications, 345 Park Avenue South, New York NY

10010. **Tel** (800)888-8300 ext. 6170, (212)545-6170, FAX (212)696-1848. **LC** KF320.A9; L425. **DD** 340/.068. cum. index.
Desc: Reports on automating corporate or firm law offices; includes product reviews, new technology applications, analyses of firm uses of computers and evaluations.

US/0733-513X
LEADER'S PRODUCT LIABILITY LAW AND STRATEGY. **VFOAT** Product Liability Law and Strategy; Product Liability. Vol. 5, No. 7 (Jan. 1987)-. Periodical. English. mo. $185.00. Leader Publications, 345 Park Avenue South, New York NY 10010. **Tel** (800)888-8300 ext. 6170, (212)545-6170, FAX (212)696-1848. **ED** Margaret Knox. **LC** KF1296.A15; L4. **DD** 346.7303/82/05; 347.30638205. cum. index. **Bk Rev**. ctrl circ. ***Continues*** *Leader's Product Liability Newsletter*.
Desc: Reports on judicial, legislative, and regulatory developments in product liability law. Includes verdicts, settlements, decisions, and advice on legal strategy by eminent practitioners.

US/0147-3190
LECOURT. V. 1- Spring 1976-. Periodical. English (English). qt. $24.00. **LC** K87; .L43. **DD** 029/.9/34.

CN/0714-8216
LECTURE FAITE. (LECTURE FAITE : BULLETIN DE LA FEDERATION DES NOTAIRES DU QUEBEC.). [Lect. faite]. V. 1, No. 1, Aug. 15, 1980)-. Bulletin. French. mo. Free. Federation Des Notaires Du Quebec, 82328, Rue St. Denis, Montreal Quebec H2P 2G8. **DD** 347.714/016. ctrl circ.

UK
LEGAL 500 : THE MAJOR LAW FIRMS IN ENGLAND, WALES AND SCOTLAND, THE. **VFOAT** Legal Five Hundred. 1988-. English. an. Legalease Ltd, 28 33 Cato Street, London W1H 5HS England. **Tel** 011 44 71 396 9292. **ED** John M Pritchard.

UK/0266-3953
LEGAL ACTION. (LEGAL ACTION : THE BULLETIN OF THE LEGAL ACTION GROUP.). [Legal action]. (Jan. 1984)-. Bulletin. English. mo. £59.00. Legal Action Group, 242-244 Pentonville Road, London N1 9UN England. **Tel** 44 71 8332931, FAX 44 71 8376094. **ED** Roger Smith. **LC** KD3000.A13; L43. **DD** 344.42/005. Index available (bound in Jan. issue). **Bk Rev**, (Qty: 7-10). **Ad Acc. Circ:** 5,500. available on microfilm from University Microfilms International (UMI). ***Continues*** *LAG Bulletin, 0306-7963*.
Desc: Articles on welfare law (housing, employment, social security, family and childcare, immigration, crime and police, legal aid, disability, prisoners rights, etc., for legal professionals and law advisors. Also news and features to keep readers in touch with developments in legal debates.
Ind/Abst Curr. Law Index (1984-); Hum. Rights Intern. Rep.; Leg. Resour. Index (1984-?); LegalTrac (1983-1989).

AT
LEGAL ACTION IN NEW SOUTH WALES. **Main/Corp** SIB Publishing Company. (19??)-. English. SIB Publishing Company, 11/44 Bridge Street, Sydney Australia. **DD** 346.944/077/0269.

US/8756-7768
LEGAL ADVISOR, THE. [Leg. advis.]. **VFOAT** Advisor. Vol. 1, No. 1 (July 1984)-. Periodical. English. mo. $138.00. Learning Associates International, 145 East Center Street, PO Box 3000, Provo UT 84603-3000. **ED** Richard J Allen. **LC** K12; .E26. **DD** 349.73/05.

US
LEGAL ALERT. English. ir. $50.00 (nonmembers), $35.00 (members) US and Canada; (add $12.00 postage) other. Securities Industry Association, 120 Broadway/35th Floor, New York NY 10271. **Tel** (212)608-1500, FAX (212)608-1604.
Desc: A flash publication to alert SIA members to significant compliance and legal developments that may require their immediate attention.

US/0190-2350
LEGAL ASPECTS OF MEDICAL PRACTICE. [Leg. asp. med. pract.]. **Added/Corp** American College of Legal Medicine. Vol. 5, No. 9 (Sept. 1977)-. Academic Scholarly Publication. English. Four times a year. $139.00 US; $175.00 other. Shugar Publishing Inc., 32 Mill Road, West Hampton Beach NY 11978. **Tel** (516)288-4404, FAX (516)288-4435. **LC** KF3821.A15; J6. **DD** 344/.73/041. **NLM** W1 LE448J. **[CCC]**. Index available in last issue of volume--attached. **Bk Rev**. **Ad Acc**. available on microfilm and microfiche from University Microfilms International (UMI). ***Continues*** *Journal of Legal Medicine, 0093-1748*.
Desc: Covers medical laws and legislation.
Ind/Abst Curr. Law Index (1980-); EMBASE; Energy Res. Abstr. (Aug. 1982-); Health Devices Alerts; Highw. Res. Abstr.; Leg. Resour. Index (1980-); LegalTrac (1980-).

US/0191-8516
LEGAL ASPECTS OF PHARMACY PRACTICE. **Added/Corp** Professional Communications Associates. Merrell-National Laboratories. Vol. 1 (Sept. 1978)-. Periodical. English. bm. Professional Communications Associates, 625 North Michigan Avenue, Chicago IL 60611. **LC** KF2915.P4; A134. **DD** 344/.73/042.

US/0883-0924
LEGAL ASPECTS OF PSYCHIATRIC PRACTICE. [Leg. asp. psychiatr. pract.]. **Added/Corp** Sieber & McIntyre. Publishing Division. Vol. 1, No. 1 (Aug. 1984)-. Periodical. English. bm. $30.00. Sieber & McIntyre Inc., The Publishing Division, 625 North Michigan Avenue / Suite 800, Chicago IL 60611. **LC** KF2910.P75; A134. **DD** 344.73/041; 347.30441.

US/1051-3663
LEGAL ASSISTANT TODAY (1990). (LEGAL ASSISTANT TODAY.). [Leg. assist. today]. Vol. 7, No. 5 (May/June 1990)-. Periodical. English. bm. $47.98 US; $62.98 other. James Publishing Group, Inc., PO Box 25202, Santa Ana CA 92799. **Tel** (714)755-5450, FAX (714)556-4133. **DD** 340. available on microfilm and microfiche from University Microfilms International (UMI). ***Continues*** *Legal Professional, 1045-6686*.
Ind/Abst Leg. Inf. Manage. Index (1990-).

●US/1062-8959
LEGAL ASSISTANT'S NOTEBOOK (NORTHERN CALIFORNIA ED.), THE. (THE LEGAL ASSISTANT'S NOTEBOOK.). [Legal assist. noteb.]. (1992)-. English. $70.00. ASAP Publications / California, 1081 Camino del Rio South, Suite 222, San Diego CA 92108. **Tel** (619)297-2727, FAX (619)297-2770. **DD** 347.

●US/1062-8940
LEGAL ASSISTANT'S NOTEBOOK. VOL. 1, SOUTHERN CALIFORNIA ED, THE. (1992)-. English. $70.00. ASAP Publications / California, 1081 Camino del Rio South, Suite 222, San Diego CA 92108. **Tel** (619)297-2727, FAX (619)297-2770.

US/0272-1961
LEGAL ASSISTANTS: UPDATE. **Added/Corp** American Bar Association. Vol. 1 (1980)-. English. Three times a year. $18.00. American Bar Association, 750 North Lake Shore Drive, Chicago IL 60611. **Tel** (312)988-5522, (312)988-5241, FAX (312)988-5528, telex 270593. **ED** Roger A. Larson. **LC** KF320.L4; L45. **DD** 340/.023/73. **Circ:** 5,000 (ctrl).
Desc: Reports on current trends and activities within the legal assistant profession. Directed to legal assistants, legal assistant educators, prospective students, lawyers, and generally those working in a legal environment.

US/0149-1695
LEGAL BRIEFS FOR EDITORS, PUBLISHERS, AND WRITERS. V. 1- June 1977-. Periodical. English. $48.00. McGraw Hill Publishing Company, Inc., 1221 Avenue of the Americas, New York NY 10020. **Tel** (212)512-6410, (800)525-5003, FAX (212)512-6111. **LC** KF2750.A15; L4. **DD** 343/.73/0998.

US/0730-952X
LEGAL BRIEFS FOR THE CONSTRUCTION INDUSTRY. ***Ceased.*** **VFOAT** Legal Briefs. Vol. 7, No. 20 (Oct. 26, 1981)-Ceased Vol. 18, No. 14. Periodical. English. sm. McGraw Hill Publishing Company, Inc., 1221 Avenue of the Americas, New York NY 10020. **Tel** (212)512-6410, (800)525-5003, FAX (212)512-6111. ***Continues*** *Legal Briefs for Architects, Engineers and Contractors*.

UK/0958-4609
LEGAL BUSINESS. [Legal bus.]. (1990)-. Periodical. English. mo (10 issues). $495.00. Legalease Ltd, 28 33 Cato Street, London W1H 5HS England. **Tel** 011 44 71 396 9292. **ED** John Pritchard. **DD** 340.02341. **Bk Rev**. **Ad Acc. Circ:** 5,500 (ctrl).
Desc: Commentator on commercial law firms and their clients. Each issue contains facts explaining the law business and analyzes its key payers.

US/0145-2851
LEGAL CIRCLE, THE. English. Constitutional Rights Foundation, Chicago Project, 25 East Jackson, Room 1612, Chicago IL 60604. **LC** KF9223.A15; L4. **DD** 345/.773/05.

US
LEGAL CONSIDERATIONS IN DENTISTRY. Vol. 1, No. 1 (Mar. 1980)-. Periodical. English. qt. Legal Considerations in Dentistry, Continuing Professional Education, 625 North Michigan Avenue, Chicago IL 60611. **LC** KF2910.D3; A134. **DD** 344.73/0413. **NLM** WU 33 AA1 L4.

AT
LEGAL DATE. (19??)-. English. ir (Mar., May, July and Sept.). 45.00Aus$. Warringal Productions, 114 Argyle Street, Fitzroy 3065 Australia. **Tel** 011 61 03 4160200, FAX 011 61 03 4160402. **(Subscription address:** Warringal Publications, PO Box 336, Fitzroy 3065 Australia.)
Desc: Provides years 11 and 12 teachers and students of legal studies with comment and material on legal topics within the areas of the individual and the law, the law in operation, making changes in the law and the attainment of justice.

US/0741-5036
LEGAL DIRECTORY OF WASHINGTON STATE. [Leg. dir. Wash. State]. 1984-. Directory. English. an. $14.95. Vector Associates, PO Box 6215, Bellevue WA 98008. **LC** KF192.W37; L44. **DD** 340/.025/797.

US
LEGAL EAGLE, THE. Apr. 1972-. Periodical. English. mo. New Jersey State Bar Association, 1 Constitution Square, New Brunswick NJ 08901. **Tel** (908)249-5000, FAX (908)249-2815. **LC** KF200; .L4. **DD** 340/.06/2749.

US/1063-9888
LEGAL EDGE, THE. (THE LEGAL EDGE : THE VALUE OF LAW FIRM MARKETING.). [Leg. edge]. **Added/Corp** Coulter King, Ltd. Coulter King O'Neill (Firm). Vol. 1, No. 1 (July-Aug. 1987)-. Periodical. English. bm. $145.00. Coulter King Ltd., Two Oliver Street, Eighth Floor, Boston MA 02109. **Tel** (617)482-1310, FAX (617)482-6528. **ED** Silvia L. Coulter. **DD** 338. Index available (Additional $3.00). cum. index. **Ad Acc. Circ:** 100.

AT/1033-2839
LEGAL EDUCATION REVIEW. **Added/Corp** University of Sydney. Faculty of Law. Vol. 1, No. 1 (1989)-. Periodical. English. sa. 35.00Aus$ Australia; 40.00Aus$ other. Legal Education Review, University of Sydney Law, 173 Phillip, Sydney NSW 2000 Australia. **Tel** 61-2-232-5944.
Ind/Abst Index Leg. Period.; Leg. Resour. Index; LegalTrac (1989-).

UK/0024-0362
LEGAL EXECUTIVE, THE. **Added/Corp** Institute of Legal Executives (Great Britain). Vol. 1, (Jan. 1963)-. Periodical. English. Twelve times a year. £30.00 UK; £36.72 other. IPA Limited, Kempston Manor, Kempston Bedford MK42 7AB England. **Tel** 011 44 234 840022. **ED** Stephen Mayson. Index available. **Bk Rev**. **Ad Acc. Circ:** 16,000 (ctrl).
Desc: Articles on law reform; educational information for students of the Institute; general institute news and views, book reviews, classified and display advertising.

US/0887-1183
LEGAL HANDBOOK FOR ARCHITECTS, ENGINEERS AND CONTRACTORS. [Leg. handb. archit. eng. contract.]. (1985)-. English. an. Clark Boardman Callaghan, 155 Pfingsten Road, Deerfield IL 60015. **Tel** (800)323-8067. **ED** Albert Dib. **LC** KF902; .L44. **DD** 343.73/078624; 347.30378624.

II/0377-0907
LEGAL HISTORY. [Leg. hist.]. Vol. 1 (Jan. 1975)-. Periodical. English. qt. $50.00. K K Roy Private Ltd, PO Box 10210, 55 Gariahat Road, Calcutta 700019 India. **Tel** 91 33-474872, 91 33-475069. **ED** K. K. Roy. **LC** K12; .E3. **DD** 340/.09. **Bk Rev**. **Ad Acc. Circ:** 2,000.
Desc: Covers all facets of the history of law and institutions and antecedents in law of all countries.
Ind/Abst Am. Hist. Life (1975-).

US/0747-9298
LEGAL INFORMATION MANAGEMENT INDEX. **See** Law-Abstracting, Bibliographies and Statistics.

US
LEGAL INFORMATION MANAGEMENT REPORTS. Vol. 1, No. 1 (Winter 1989)-. Periodical. English. Four times a year. $57.75 Massachusetts; $55.00 others in US & Canada; $60.00 other. Legal Information Services, Box 67, Newton Highlands MA 02161. **Tel** (508)443-4087. **ED** Elyse H. Fox. Index available.
Desc: Devoted to one topic in legal information management or law librarianship.
Ind/Abst Leg. Inf. Manage. Index.

CN/0225-2287
LEGAL INFORMATION SERVICE - NATIVE LAW CENTRE. (LEGAL INFORMATION SERVICE.). [Legal inf. serv. - Nativ. Law Centre]. No. 1- May 1979 -. Periodical. English. ir. Native Law Centre, University of Saskatchewan, Diefenbaker Center, Saskatoon Saskatchewan S7N 0W0 Canada. **Tel** (306)966-6189. **ED** Zandra MacEachern. **DD** 346.7101/3. **Circ:** 200.
Desc: Reports dealing with various native law topics and issues of particular interest to native people and practitioners in the field of native law.

IR
LEGAL INFORMATION SERVICE (TEHRAN, IRAN). (LEGAL INFORMATION SERVICE.). Periodical. English. wk. **LC** K12; .E32. **DD** 340/.05.

US/0277-495X
LEGAL INTELLIGENCER, THE. [Leg. intell.]. Vol. 1 (Dec. 2, 1843)-. Periodical. English. da (260 issues per year). $265.00 (one year), $450.00 (two year). Legal Communications Ltd, 1617 JFK Boulevard, Suite 960, Philadelphia PA 19103. **Tel** (215)563-2700, (800)722-7670, FAX (215)563-4911. **ED** Brian R Harris. Index available. cum. index. **Bk Rev. Ad Acc. Circ:** 10,000. available on microfilm. ***Continues** Philadelphia Legal Intelligencer.*
Desc: Trial lists, court verdicts, news of interest to the bar. Paper of record for the Philadelphia legal community.
Ind/Abst Law Office Inf. Serv.

US/0741-417X
LEGAL INVESTIGATOR, THE. (THE LEGAL INVESTIGATOR : THE OFFICIAL JOURNAL OF THE NATIONAL ASSOCIATION OF LEGAL INVESTIGATORS, INC.). English. qt. $35.00. National Association of Legal Investigators, PO Box 3158, Baton Rouge LA 70821. **ED** Julius Bombet. **LC** KF8936; .L43. **DD** 363.2/5/0973. **Bk Rev. Ad Acc. Circ:** 500 (ctrl).
Desc: Devoted to articles about legal investigations, legal photography and other subjects of interest to legal investigators, detectives and private investigators.

UK/0950-4206
LEGAL JOURNALS INDEX. Added/Corp Legal Information Resources Ltd. **VFOAT** Journals Index. Vol. 1 (1986)-. Periodical. English. mo (12 issues). $825.00 (Vol.9, 1994). Legal Information Resources Ltd, Elphin House, 1 New Road, West Yorkshire HX7 5DZ England. **Tel** 011 44 422 886277, . **(Subscription address:** William W. Gaunt & Sons Inc., Gaunt Building, 3011 Gulf Drive, Holmes Beach FL 34217-2199**) ED** Christine Miskin. **LC** K33; .L45. **DD** 016.34.005. cum. index. **Acid Free.**
Desc: Indexes all case reports and articles appearing in more than 175 British legal journals.

US
LEGAL LC SUBJECT HEADINGS -WEEKLY LISTS. (19??)-. English. qt (4 updates a year). $55.00. Fred B. Rothman & Company, 10368 West Centennial Road, Littleton CO 80127. **Tel** (800)457-1986, (303)979-5657, FAX (303)978-1457, telex 87669.

US/0148-2750
LEGAL MALPRACTICE REVIEW. June/July 1977-. Periodical. English. bm. West Publishing Company, 610 Opperman Drive, PO Box 64526, Eagan MN 55123-1308. **Tel** (612)687-5618, (800)328-9352, FAX (612)687-5388, (800)562-2329. **LC** KF313.A15; L44. **DD** 346/.73/033.

US/1043-7355
LEGAL MANAGEMENT. (LEGAL MANAGEMENT : THE JOURNAL OF THE ASSOCIATION OF LEGAL ADMINISTRATORS.). [Legal manage.]. **Added/Corp** Association of Legal Administrators. Vol. 8, No. 1 (Jan.- Feb. 1989)-. Periodical. English. bm. Free. Association of Legal Administrators, 175 East Hawthorn Parkway, Vernon Hills IL 60061. **Tel** (708)816-1212. **LC** KF318.A1; L43. **DD** 340/.068. **CODEN** LEMAEB. ***Continues** Legal Administrator (Glenview, Ill. : 1982), 0745-0532.*
Ind/Abst Leg. Inf. Manage. Index (19??-); Leg. Resour. Index (1982-); LegalTrac (1989-).

US/0192-6152
LEGAL MEMORANDUM (RESTON), A. (A LEGAL MEMORANDUM.). **Main/Corp** National Association of Secondary School Principals (U.S.). (19??)-. Periodical. English. ir. $95.00 (membership). National Association of Secondary School Principals / NASSP, 1904 Association Drive, Reston VA 22091-1537. **Tel** (703)860-0200, (800)253-7746, FAX (703)476-5432. **ED** Thomas F. Koerner. **LC** KF4102; .N38. **DD** 344.73/07; 347.3047. **Circ:** 43,000 (ctrl).
Desc: Provides discussions on legal issues affecting school administrators.

US/0739-5183
LEGAL NEWSLETTER (WASHINGTON, D.C.). (LEGAL NEWSLETTER / SECRETARIAT FOR LEGAL AFFAIRS.). [Legal newsl.]. **Added/Corp** Organization of American States. Secretariat for Legal Affairs. Nos. 1 and 2 (Jan./Aug. 1982)-. English. Three times a year. $12.00. Organization of American States, 19th Street & Constitution Avenue NW, Suite 300, Washington DC 20006. **Tel** (202)458-6256. **LC** KDZ1103; .L44. **DD** 340/.05.

US
LEGAL NOTES. English. Municipal Research Coun, 10517 NE 38th Pl, Kirkland WA 98033-7926. **LC** JS303.W2. **DD** 352.

US/0093-397X
LEGAL NOTES FOR EDUCATION. **Added/Corp** Informational Research Systems (Washington, D.C.) Data Research, Inc. (Rosemount, Minn.). Vol. 1, No. 1 (Apr. 1973)-. Periodical. English. mo. $108.00. Data Research Inc., PO Box 490, Rosemount MN 55068. **Tel** (612)452-8267, (800)365-4900. **LC** KF4119.A1; L43. **DD** 344/.73/0705. Index available.
Desc: School law.

US/0094-0623
LEGAL NOTES FOR INSURANCE. [Leg. notes insur.]. **Added/Corp** Informational Research Systems. Data Research, Inc. Vol. 1 (July 1973)-. Periodical. English. mo. $106.00. Data Research Inc., PO Box 490, Rosemount MN 55068. **Tel** (612)452-8267, (800)365-4900. **LC** KF1164.A1; L43. **DD** 346/.73/08605. Index available.
Desc: Covers information on insurance law.

US/1056-1137
LEGAL OPINION LETTER / WASHINGTON LEGAL FOUNDATION. [Leg. opin. lett.]. **Added/Corp** Washington Legal Foundation. (1991)-. Periodical. English. Washington Legal Foundation, 1705 N Street NW, Washington DC 20036. **DD** 340.

US/0272-7129
LEGAL OPINIONS OF THE OFFICE OF GENERAL COUNSEL - UNITED STATES. DEPT. OF HOUSING AND URBAN DEVELOPMENT. Main/Corp United States. Dept. of Housing and Urban Development. Office of General Counsel. 1977-. Government Publication. English. an. US Department of Housing and Urban Development, 451 Seventh Street SW, Washington DC 20401. **Tel** (202)708-0980, FAX (202)708-0299. **LC** KF5726.A2; H684. **DD** 346.7304/5; 347.30645.

CN/0840-190X
LEGAL PERSPECTIVES. *Suspended.* (LEGAL PERSPECTIVES / LEGAL SERVICES SOCIETY, SCHOOLS PROGRAM.). [Leg. perspect.]. **Added/Corp** British Columbia. Legal Services Society. Schools Program. Vol. 12, No. 1 (Oct. 1987)-(Sept. 1994). Periodical. English. Five times a year. Legal Society Services, 1140 West Pender Street, Suite 300, Vancouver British Columbia V6E 4G1 Canada. **Tel** (604)660-4600. **DD** 349.71/0712711. ***Continues** Newsletter (British Columbia. Legal Services Society. Schools Program)., 0706-1927.*

US/1056-196X
LEGAL PUBLISHER, THE. See Publishing.

US/0000-1333
LEGAL PUBLISHING PREVIEW. *Ceased.* [Leg. publ. preview]. **Added/Corp** R.R. Bowker Company. Vol. 1, Issue 1 (Nov./Dec. 1989)-Vol. 4, No. 6 (Dec. 1992). Periodical. English. bm. R R Bowker, A Reed Reference Publishing Company, Part of Reed International PLC, PO Box 31, 121 Chanlon Drive, New Providence NJ 07974. **Tel** (908)464-6800, (800)521-8110, FAX (908)665-6688, telex 138-755. **LC** KF6; .B69. **DD** 016.34. ***Continues** Bowker's Legal Publishing Preview, 0000-1279.*
Ind/Abst Book Rev. Index; Leg. Inf. Manage. Index (1989-).

US/1051-533X
LEGAL QUARTERLY DIGEST OF MINE SAFETY AND HEALTH DECISIONS. [Leg. q. dig. mine saf. health decis.]. **Added/Corp** Crowell & Moring. **VFOAT** Mine Regulation Reporter Legal Quarterly Digest of Mine Safety and Health Decisions. (Jan./Mar. 1990)-. English. Four times a year. $325.00. Legal Publication Services, 1818 North Veitch, Arlington VA 22201. **Tel** (703)276-9796, FAX (703)243-3562. **ED** Ellen Smith and Melanie Aclander. Index available. cum. index. **Circ:** 170 (ctrl). available via fax; available on diskette.
Desc: Digest of mine safety and health decisions from the Federal Mine Safety and Health Review Commission, district courts and courts of appeal. Copies of full decisions are also available by fax or on computer disk.

US/0270-319X
LEGAL REFERENCE SERVICES QUARTERLY. [Legal ref. serv. q.]. Vol. 1, No. 1 (Spring 1981)-. Periodical. English. qt. $115.00 US; $161.00 other. The Haworth Press Inc, 10 Alice Street, Binghamton NY 13904-1580. **Tel** (607)722-5857, (800)3-HAWORTH, FAX (607)722-1424. **ED** Robert Berring (editor's address: Law Librarian and Professor of Law, Boalt Hall, University of California, School of Law, Berkeley, CA 94720). **LC** K12; .E357. **DD** 340/.072073. **CODEN** LRSQD9. **Bk Rev. Ad Acc. Pr Rev. Acid Free. Circ:** 1,003. available on microfilm and microfiche from University Microfilms International (UMI). Documents available from Ask*IEEE, Haworth Document Delivery Service.
Desc: Practical and informative journal continues to enhance the knowledge of law librarians about the continuously expanding volume of legal materials and its utility in legal research. Concise and current, it meets the needs of the law librarian and the reference librarian, who must deal with the increasing number of questions that involve the law.
Ind/Abst Index Leg. Period.; Index Period. Artic. Relat. Law (19??-19??); Inf. Instruc. Technol.; Inf. Sci. Abstr.; INSPEC (Summer 1982-); Leg. Inf. Manage. Index; Leg. Resour. Index; LegalTrac (1984-); Libr. Inf. Sci. Abstr.; Libr. Lit.; PAIS Int. Print (1991-).

US
LEGAL REFORMER, THE. Added/Corp HALT, Inc. Vol. 9, No. 1 (Oct./Dec. 1988)-. Periodical. English. qt. $15.00. Halt, 201 Mass. Avenue NE, Suite 319, Washington DC 20002. ***Continues** Americans for Legal Reform.*

US/8756-2006
LEGAL REGISTER, METROPOLITAN WASHINGTON, THE. [The Leg. regist. metrop. Wash.]. **VFOAT** Legal Register. (1980)-. English. an. $14.25. Legal Register Publishing Company, 1200 18th Street NW/Suite 210, Washington DC 20036-2506. **Tel** (202)659-9240. **ED** A I Robinson. **DD** 340. **Ad Acc. Circ:** 17,000 (ctrl). ***Continues** Legal Register for the District of Columbia.*
Desc: Directory of lawyers, courts, government agencies, US, state, and local for Washington DC, suburban Maryland, and Northern Virginia.

AT/0159-2483
LEGAL REPORTER, THE. Added/Corp Australia. High Court. (19??)-. English. Twenty times a year. 345.00Aus$ (Australia), 375.00Aus$ (other). Scribe Pty Ltd, GPO Box 1807, Canberra ACT 2601 Australia. **Tel** 011 61 6 2471069. **DD** 347.94/035/02648; 349.4073502648. **[CCC].**
Ind/Abst Aust. Leg. Mon. Dig.

US
LEGAL RESEARCH AND LAW LIBRARY MANAGEMENT. SUPPLEMENT / JULIUS J. MARKE, RICHAD SLOANE. VFOAT Supplement to Legal Research and Law Library Management. (1985)-. English. be. Law Journal Seminars Press, 111 Eighth Avenue/Suite 900, New York NY 10011. **Tel** (212)741-8300, (800)888-8300 Ext. 565, FAX (212)741-3985. ***Continues** Marke, Julius J. Supplement to Legal Research and Law Library Management.*

US/0146-0382
LEGAL RESEARCH JOURNAL. [Leg. res. j.]. **Added/Corp** Legal Institute. Vol. 1 (1976)-. English. Three times a year. $9.75. Legal Research Journal, H. Lancaster, 3250 Wilshire Boulevard, Suite 1000, Los Angeles CA 90010. **Tel** (213)487-6268. **ED** Herman B. Lancaster. **LC** KF240; .L42. **DD** 340/.07/2073. **Bk Rev. Circ:** 200.
Desc: Focuses on the art and issues of legal research.
Ind/Abst Bibliogr. Mission. (1980-); Curr. Law Index (1980-); Leg. Resour. Index (1980-); LegalTrac (1980-).

CN/0835-6009
LEGAL RESEARCH UPDATE. [Leg. res. update]. **Added/Corp** Canadian Law Information Council. Legal Research Network (Society). Vol. 1, No. 1 (Feb. 1986)-. Periodical. English. Four times a year. 60.00Can$. Legal Research Update, T-D Bank Tower, Suite 4700, Toronto Ontario M5K 1E6 Canada. **Tel** (416)601-7939, FAX (416)868-1790. **ED** Martin Felsky. **DD** 340/.07/2071. **Bk Rev**, (Qty: 4). **Circ:** 200.

US/1050-3056
LEGAL RESEARCHER'S DESK REFERENCE, THE. [Legal res. desk ref.]. (1990)-. English. be. $54.00. Infosources Publishing, 140 Norma Road, Teaneck NJ 07666. **Tel** (201)836-7072, FAX (201)836-7072. **ED** Arlene L Eis. **LC** Z675.L2; L3832. **DD** 340. ***Continues** Lawyer's Diary and Desk Reference.*

US/0272-9296
LEGAL RESOURCE INDEX. See Law-Abstracting, Bibliographies and Statistics.

US
LEGAL SECTION PROCEEDINGS / THE ... ANNUAL MEETING OF THE LEGAL SECTION OF THE AMERICAN COUNCIL OF LIFE INSURANCE. See Insurance.

CN/0225-5391
LEGAL SHOCK. [Leg. shock]. **VFOAT** Legal Shock - Without Prejudice - A Search for Justice Under God. V. 1- Jan. 1980-. Periodical. English. mo. $12.00. Legal Shock, PO Box 284, Station G, Toronto Ontario M4M 3G7 Canada. **DD** 261.5.

US/0894-5993
LEGAL STUDIES FORUM, THE. [Leg. stud. forum]. **Added/Corp** American Legal Studies Association. Vol. 9, No. 1 (1985)-. Periodical. English. qt. $50.00. American Legal Studies Association, 341 Cushing Hall, NE University, Boston MA 02115. **Tel** (617)373-5211, FAX (617)437-4691. **LC** K1; .M45. **DD** 344. ***Continues** American Legal Studies Association. ALSA Forum, 0162-7937.*
Ind/Abst Leg. Resour. Index; LegalTrac (1984-).

UK/0261-3875
LEGAL STUDIES (LONDON. 1981). (LEGAL STUDIES : THE JOURNAL OF THE SOCIETY OF PUBLIC TEACHERS OF LAW.). [Legal stud.]. **Added/Corp** Society of Public Teachers of Law (London, England). **VFOAT** Journal of the Society of Public Teachers of Law. Vol. 1, No. 1 (1981)-. Academic Scholarly Publication. English. Three times a year. £44.00. Butterworth & Co. Ltd. / Kent, England, Borough

Law

Green, Sevenoaks Kent TN15 8PH England. **Tel** 011 44 732-884567, FAX 011 44 732-885996. **ED** J. A. Andrews. **LC** K12; .E3575. **DD** 340/.05. *Continues Journal of the Society of Public Teachers of Law.*
Desc: Carries major articles of scholarly interest contributed by leading authorities in the UK, US and elsewhere and appeals to a broad spectrum of academic readers.
Ind/Abst Curr. Law Index (1982-); Index Leg. Period.; Leg. Resour. Index (1982-); LegalTrac (1982-).

CN/0229-5393
LEGAL SUPPORT STAFF NEWSLETTER. **VAT** Legal Secretary's Newsletter (1980). Vol. 7, No. 6 (Oct. 1980)-. Periodical. English. Twelve times a year. Moore Publishing Ltd., 3390 West 41st Avenue, Vancouver British Columbia V6N 3E4 Canada. **Tel** (604)261-0066. **DD** 651/.934. *Continues Legal Secretary's Newsletter, 0318-8396.*

UK/1352-3252
LEGAL THEORY. Vol. 1 (1995)-. Academic Scholarly Publication. English. qt. $100.00 US, Canada & Mexico; £62.00 other. Cambridge University Press, The Edinburgh Building, Shaftesbury Road, Cambridge CB2 2RU United Kingdom. **Tel** 011 44 223 312393, FAX 011 44 223 325959. **(Subscription address:** Cambridge University Press / North America, 110 Midland Avenue, Port Chester NY 10573.) **ED** Larry Alexander, Jules Coleman and Frederick Schauer. **Pr Rev.**
Desc: Draws contributions not only from academic law, but also from a wide range of related disciplines in the humanities and social sciences, including philosophy, political science, economics, history and sociology. Topics fall mainly into the catagories of analytical and normative jurisprudence, doctrinal theory, policy analyses of legal doctrines and critical theories of law.

US/0732-7536
LEGAL TIMES. [Leg. times]. Vol. 4, No. 38 (Mar. 1, 1982)-. Periodical. English. wk (except last week in Aug. and Dec.). $525.00 (law firms with 20 or partners); $205.00 other. American Lawyer Media, L.P., 600 3rd Avenue, New York NY 10016. **Tel** (212)973-2800. **(Subscription address:** Legal Times, 1730 M Street Northwest, Suite 802, Washington DC 20036.) **ED** Eric Effron. **LC** K12; .E358. **DD** 340/.05. **Bk Rev**. **Ad Acc**. **Circ:** 10,000. available on microfilm; available on microfiche. *Continues Legal Times of Washington (1978), 0162-7295.*
Desc: Covers law, lobbying, and politics in the nation's capital. Articles on the Justice Department and other federal agencies, the Supreme Court, Congress, lobbying, and law practice regularly picked up by the national media.
Ind/Abst Bowne Dig. Corp. Sec. Lawyers (1982-); Curr. Lit. Fam. Plan. (Mar. 1, 1982-199?); Leg. Resour. Index (1982-); LegalTrac (1982-); NEXIS (March 1, 1982-); Trade Ind. Index.

US/0898-9427
LEGAL VIDEO REVIEW. [Leg. video rev.].
Added/Corp Social Law Library (Boston, Mass.). Lawrence R. Cohen Media Library. Vol. 1, No. 1 (May 1985)-. Periodical. English. bm. $125.00. The Social Law Library, 1200 Court House, Boston MA 02108. **Tel** (617)720-0294, FAX (617)523-2458. **DD** 340. Index available (free). cum. index. **Bk Rev**. **Circ:** 150 (ctrl).
Desc: Review recent videotapes on law-related subject for law schools and law firms.

US/0732-4529
LEGAL WRITING JOURNAL. [Leg. writ. j.].
Added/Corp Legal Institute. Vol. 1 Issue 1 (1980)-. Periodical. English. Three times a year (Mar., July, Nov.). $9.75. Legal Research Journal, H. Lancaster, 3250 Wilshire Boulevard, Suite 1000, Los Angeles CA 90010. **Tel** (213)487-6268. **ED** Herman B. Lancaster. **LC** KF250; .L43. **DD** 808/.06634. **Bk Rev**. **Circ:** 200.
Desc: Covers information about the art and techniques of legal communication.

US
LEGAL WRITING : THE JOURNAL OF THE LEGAL WRITING INSTITUTE.
Added/Corp Legal Writing Institute. University of Puget Sound. School of Law. **VFOAT** Journal of the Legal Writing Institute. Vol. 1 (Fall 1991)-. Periodical. English. Three times a year. $22.00. Seattle University / Law Review, 950 Broadway Plaza, Tacoma WA 98402-4470. **Tel** (206)591-2995, FAX (206)591-6313. Index available. cum. index. **Bk Rev**, (Qty: 1). **Pr Rev. Circ:** 500 (ctrl). available on an online database from LEXIS.
Desc: Law review articles and essays.

CU/0138-7669
LEGALIDAD SOCIALISTA : BOLETIN DE INFORMACION JURIDICA EDITADO POR LA FISCALIA GENERAL DE LA REPUBLICA. **Added/Corp** Cuba. Fiscalia General de la Republica. (19??)-. Periodical. Spanish. qt. $15.00 North and South America; $16.00 Europe; $18.00 other. Ediciones Cubanas, Obispo 527, Altos ESQ Bernaza, CP 10100 Havana Cuba. **Tel** 011 632980, 631942, FAX 011 631011, telex 512337, 6540. **LC** K12; .E3586. **DD** 349.7291/05; 347.291/005.
Desc: Presents different aspects of juridicial character

and nature, with the purpose of contributing to the technical improvement and modernization of lawyers, especially fiscal lawyers.

IT
LEGALITA E GIUSTIZIA. **Added/Corp** Edizioni Scientifiche Italiane. (1973)-. Periodical. Italian. qt. L120000 institutions Italy, 95000 individuals Italy; 140000 other. Edizioni Scientifiche Italiane, Via Chiatamone 7, 80121 Naples Italy. **Tel** 011 39 81 7645768, 011 39 81 7645443, FAX 011 39 81 7646477. **LC** K12; .E3588.

ZA
LEGALITY : A JOURNAL OF THE UNIVERSITY OF ZAMBIA LAW ASSOCIATION. Periodical. English. University of Zambia, PO Box 32379, Lusaka Zambia. **Tel** 213221, telex ZA 44370. **LC** K12; .E359. **DD** 349.6894/05; 346.894005. *Continues Law Bulletin (University of Zambia. Law Association).*

US
LEGALTRAC [COMPUTER FILE]. See Law-Abstracting, Bibliographies and Statistics.

IT
LEGGI, LE. (19??)-. Italian. sm (24 issues). L200000.00 Italy; L250000.00 other. Zanichelli Editore Spa, Via Irnerio 34, 40126 Bologna Italy. **Tel** 011 39 51 293263.

IT
LEGGI D'ITALIA. (19??)-. Italian. mo. IST Geografico de Agostini, Via Giovanni Da Verrazano 15, 28100 Novara Italy.

IT
LEGGI NUOVE. Ceased. (19??)-(Dec. 1994). Italian. Pirola Editore, CP 10444, Via Parabiago 19, 20151 Milan Italy. **Tel** 011 39 2 3022888. **Ad Acc**, **Adv Mgr Tel** 02 3022.1. **Circ:** 4,300.

IT
LEGGI PER LA CASA. Italian. ir. L180000.00. Edilizia Popolare SRL, Quadrato della Concordia 9, 00144 Rome Italy. **Tel** 011 39 6 5925693, 94 OR 95.

IT
LEGGI REGIONALI TOSCANA. Societa Pistoiese di Storia Patria, Cas Postale 339, 51100 Pistoia Italy.

FR/0751-9478
LEGIPRESSE. (LEGIPRESSE : REVUE DE DROIT DE LA COMMUNICATION.). (19??)-. Periodical. French. Ten times a year. 1909.89F. Victoires Editions, 38 rue Croix des Petits Champs, 75001 Paris France. **Tel** 011 33 1 42600193. **UDC** 34:07.

BL
LEGIS BANCOS INFORMATIVO CVM / COMISSAO DA VALORES MOBILIARIOS. **VFOAT** Legisbancos. Informativo CVM. Portuguese. Legis Bancos Editora Ltda, rue Santa Luzia 799 190, Andar Grupo 1902 CEP 20.030, 23666 Palm BR Rio de Janeiro RJ Brazil. **DD** 346.81/0666; 348.106666.

BL
LEGIS BANCOS INFORMATIVO. IMPOSTO DE RENDA : IR. **Main/Corp** Brazil. **VFOAT** IR; I.R.; Legis Bancos I.R. Informativo, Imposto de Renda; Legis Bancos IR Informativo, Imposto de Renda. Periodical. Portuguese. sa. Legis Bancos Editora Ltda, rue Santa Luzia 799 190, Andar Grupo 1902 CEP 20.030, 23666 Palm BR Rio de Janeiro RJ Brazil. **LC** KHD4582; .B7. **DD** 343.8105/2/05; 348.1035205.

BL
LEGISLACAO DE ENSINO DE 1O. E 2O. GRAUS. FEDERAL. **Main/Corp** Brazil. **VFOAT** Legislacao de Ensino de Primeiro e Segundo Graus. Portuguese. an. **LC** KHD3572.A27; B7. **DD** 344.81/07/05; 348.104705.

BL
LEGISLACAO DO DISTRITO FEDERAL. Main/Corp Distrito Federal, Brazil. V. 1- 1960/62-. Portuguese. Senado Federal Centro Grafico, Procuradoria-Geral do Distrito Federal, Edificio Brasilia 8 Andar Sector Bancario Sur, Brasilia Brazil.

BL
LEGISLACAO DO ESTADO DE MATO GROSSO DO SUL / SECRETARIA DE ADMINISTRACAO. **Main/Corp** Mato Grosso do Sul (Brazil). Vol. 1 (1979)-. Portuguese. Secreatria de Administracao, Av 31 de Marco 559 Ed Erpe, 2O Andar, 79.100 Campo Grande MS Brazil. **DD** 348.81/72026; 348.1720826.

BL
LEGISLACAO DO ESTADO DO RIO DE JANEIRO. Main/Corp Rio de Janeiro (State). Portuguese. Secretaria de Estado de Justica,

Departamento Geral de Documentacao, Divisao de Divulgacao, Av Mal Floriano 227 ZC-05, Rio de Janeiro Brazil. cum. index.

BL/0100-378X
LEGISLACAO DO ESTADO DO RIO DE JANEIRO / SECRETARIA DE ESTADO DE JUSTICA, DIVISAO DE DIVULGACAO. **Main/Corp** Rio de Janeiro (Brasil : State). Vol. 1 (1975)-. Portuguese. an. Avenida Erasmo Braga, 118 - 9O Andar, Rio de Janeiro ZC-P Brazil. **LC** KHD8103.7; .R56. **DD** 348.81/026; 348.10826.

BL
LEGISLACAO FEDERAL E MARGINALIA. **Main/Corp** Brazil. (19??)-. Portuguese. Thirty-six times a year. $990.70. Lex S A Editora, rua Machado de Assis 57, 01406 Sao Paulo Brazil. **Tel** 011 55 11 355888, FAX 011 55 11 5759138. **DD** 348.81/024; 348.10824. Index available. cum. index. **Circ:** 16,000 (ctrl).
Desc: Laws, decrees, constitutional amendments, and resolutions.

VE
LEGISLACION VENEZOLANA. **Main/Corp** Venezuela. Spanish. an. **ED** A R Brewer-Carias and G Burgueno Alvarez. **LC** KHW35; .A23. **DD** 348.87/02/05.

IO
LEGISLATIEF. Indonesian. mo. Rp1000. Biro DPRD Propinsi Jawa Timur, Km 1 Jl Pahlawan No 18, Surabaya Indonesia.

US/0095-8220
LEGISLATION CHECK LIST. English. an. Illinois State Bar Association, 424 South Second, Springfield IL 62701. **Tel** (217)525-1760, FAX (217)525-0712. **LC** KFI1215; .L43. **DD** 348/.773/01.

CN/1183-062X
LEGISLATION (SCARBOROUGH). (LEGISLATION.). [Legislation]. **Added/Corp** Carswell Legal Publications. **VFOAT** Legislation; Canadian Current Law Legislation; C.C.L. Legislation. No. 1 (Jan. 25, 1991)-. English (summaries and/or abstracts in French). Six times a year. 495.00Can$ Comes with Canadian Current Law. Carswell / Canada, 2075 Kennedy Road, Scarborough Ontario M1T 3V4 Canada. **Tel** (416)609-3800, (800)387-5164. *Continues in part Canadian Current Law (1988), 0835-9768.*

US
LEGISLATIVE ALERT. English. Securities Industry Association, 120 Broadway/35th Floor, New York NY 10271. **Tel** (212)608-1500, FAX (212)608-1604.
Desc: A timely publication sent to the Grassroots network when a key congressional vote is imminent. "Alerts" encourage members to contact their congressmen and senators and urge support or opposition to the legislation.

US/0160-1245
LEGISLATIVE APPROPRIATIONS REPORT. **Main/Corp** Nevada. Legislative Counsel Bureau. Division of Fiscal Analysis. English. be. Legislative Counsel Bureau, Legislative Building, Capitol Complex, Carson City NV 89710. **LC** HJ11; .N346B. **DD** 353.9/793/00722.

US
LEGISLATIVE BULLETIN, THE. Bulletin. English. Pennsylvania Chamber Business Industry, 222 North Third Street, Harrisburg PA 17101. **Tel** (717)255-3252.

US/0740-4204
LEGISLATIVE BULLETIN - ASSOCIATION OF WASHINGTON CITIES. (LEGISLATIVE BULLETIN.). **Added/Corp** Association of Washington Cities. (19??)-. English. ir. free. Association of Washington Cities, 1076 South Franklin Street, Olympia WA 98501. **Tel** (206)753-4137. **LC** KFW431.A15; L44. **DD** 348.797/026; 347.970826. **Circ,** 2,500 (ctrl). *Continues Legislative Digest (Association of Washington Cities).*

US/0426-570X
LEGISLATIVE BULLETIN - FLORIDA. **Main/Corp** Florida Education Association. **Added/Corp** Florida. Legislature. No. 1 (April 10, 1959)-. Bulletin. English. ir. Florida Education Association, 208 West Pensacola Street, Tallahassee FL 32301. **Tel** (904)224-1161. **DD** 370.

US/0739-0130
LEGISLATIVE BULLETIN / OHIO CITIZENS' COUNCIL. **Added/Corp** Ohio Citizens' Council. (19??)-. Bulletin. English. wk (weekly during legislative seesion/after that publishes only as needed). $27.00 (members), $54.00 nonmembers. Ohio United Way, 16 East Broad Street, 8th Floor, Columbus OH 43215. **Tel** (614)224-8146, FAX (614)224-6597. **ED** Judith T Bird. cum. index.

Law

US/0363-2121
LEGISLATIVE FISCAL REPORT (CARSON CITY). (LEGISLATIVE FISCAL REPORT.). **Main/Corp** Nevada. Legislative Counsel Bureau. English. Legislative Counsel Bureau, Legislative Building, Capitol Complex, Carson City NV 89710. **LC** HJ11; .N346A. **DD** 353.9/793/00722.

US
LEGISLATIVE HISTORY OF CAB REGULATIONS. Main/Corp United States. Civil Aeronautics Board. **VAT** Legislative History of Civil Aeronautics Board Regulations. Periodical. English. Civil Aeronautics Board, 1825 Connecticut Avenue NW, Washington DC 20428. **Tel** (202)673-5174.

US/0732-6394
LEGISLATIVE HISTORY OF TITLES I-XX OF THE SOCIAL SECURITY ACT. [Legis. hist. Titles I-XX Soc. Secur. Act]. **VFOAT** Legislative History, Titles I-XX of the Social Security Act. Vol. 18 (1977-1978)- = 95th Congress-. English. Social Security Administration, 6401 Security Boulevard, Baltimore MD 21235. **Tel** (410)965-8822, FAX (410)966-1463. **LC** KF3644.522.A14; L43. **DD** 344.73/023/0262; 347.304230262. **Continues** Legislative History of Titles II, XVI, and XVIII of the Social Security Act.

US
LEGISLATIVE MANUAL, STATE OF NEVADA. Added/Corp Nevada. Legislature. Legislative Counsel Bureau. (19??)-. English. be. $25.00. Legislative Council Bureau, 401 South Carson Street, Carson City NV 89710. **Tel** (702)885-5627. **Continues** Legislative Manual of the Nevada Legislature.

US
LEGISLATIVE MEMORANDUM. Main/Corp New York Civil Liberties Union. **VFOAT** NYCLU. No. 1- ; 1966-. Periodical. English. New York Civil Liberties Union York NY 10036-6503, 132 West 43rd Street, New York NY 10036. **Tel** (212)944-9800 ext.562.

US/8756-0054
LEGISLATIVE NETWORK FOR NURSES. [Legis. Netw. Nurses]. **VFOAT** LNN. (Sept. 19, 1984)-. Periodical. English. Twenty-four times a year. $240.00. Business Publishers Inc., 951 Pershing Drive, Silver Spring MD 20910-4464. **Tel** (301)587-6300, (800)274-0122, FAX (301)585-9075. **ED** Hurdis Griffith and Nancy Sharp. **NLM** W1; LE450. **[CCC]**. **Ad Acc**. **Circ:** 500.
Desc: Published to keep health professionals informed on legislative and regulatory issues affecting health care delivery.
Ind/Abst Cumul. Index Nurs. Allied Health Lit.

US
LEGISLATIVE REPORT - COUNCIL ON BLACK MINNESOTANS. Main/Corp Council on Black Minnesotans. 1981-. English. be. Council on Black Minnesotans, 504 Rice Street, St Paul MN 55103. **LC** E185.93.M55; C68B.

CN/0709-5333
LEGISLATIVE REPORT (EDMONTON). (LEGISLATIVE REPORT.). **Added/Corp** Alberta Chamber of Commerce. Vol. 1 (Oct. 23, 1978)-. Periodical. English. ir (6 to 8 times per year). 125.00Can$. Alberta Chamber of Commerce, 2105 TD Tower Edmonton Center, Edmonton Alberta T5J 2Z1 Canada. **Tel** (403)425-4180, FAX (403)429-1061, telex 037-43172. **DD** 328.7123/07/7. **Circ:** 400 (ctrl).

US
LEGISLATIVE REPORT / MICHIGAN COUNCIL FOR THE ARTS. Main/Corp Michigan Council for the Arts. English. an. Michigan Council for the Arts, 1200 16th Avenue, Detroit MI 48226. **LC** NX24.M5; M5314. **DD** 353.97740085/4.

US/0145-8604
LEGISLATIVE REVIEW. Main/Corp Montana. Legislature. Legislative Council. English. be. $6.00. Legislative Council - Alaska, State Capitol, Juneau AK 99811. **Tel** (406)444-3064. **LC** KFM9015; .L43. **DD** 348/.786/01. Index available. available on microfiche.
Desc: Covers numerical list of bills, joint resolutions and simple resolutions passed by the Montana legislature in regular session.

US/0730-2649
LEGISLATIVE REVIEW ACTIVITY - UNITED STATES. CONGRESS. SENATE. COMMITTEE ON LABOR AND HUMAN RESOURCES. **Title Change.** (LEGISLATIVE REVIEW ACTIVITY : REPORT OF THE COMMITTEE ON LABOR AND HUMAN RESOURCES, UNITED STATES SENATE, DURING THE ... CONGRESS PURSUANT TO SECTION 136 OF THE LEGISLATIVE REORGANIZATION ACT OF 1946, AS AMENDED BY THE LEGISLATIVE REORGANIZATION ACT OF 1970.). **Main/Corp** United States. Congress. Senate. Committee on Labor and Human Resources. 96th (1979-80)-(198?). English. be. **LC** KF30.8; .L342. **DD** 344.73; 347.304. **NLM** WA 33; A U5. available on microfiche (Vols. for (1979-80)- distributed to some depository libraries).

Continues United States. Congress. Senate. Committee on Human Resources. Legislative Review Activity. **Continued by** United States. Congress. Senate. Committee on Human Resources. Report on Legislative Activities of the Committee on Labor and Human Resources, United States Senate During the ... Congress ... .

US/0739-7690
LEGISLATIVE STATUS REPORT (NATIONAL ASSOCIATION OF COMMUNITY HEALTH CENTERS). (LEGISLATIVE STATUS REPORT : A PUBLICATION OF THE NATIONAL ASSOCIATION OF COMMUNITY HEALTH CENTERS, INC.). [Legis. status rep. - Natl. Assoc. Commun. Health Cent.]. **Added/Corp** National Association of Community Health Centers. (197?)-. English. **NLM** W1 LE459.

US/8755-4410
LEGISLATIVE STATUS REPORT - UNITED STATES. VETERANS ADMINISTRATION. (LEGISLATIVE STATUS REPORT / VETERANS ADMINISTRATION.). **Main/Corp** United States. Periodical. English. mo. US Veterans Administration / Washington DC, 810 Vermont Avenue Southwest, Washington DC 20420. **Tel** (202)393-2124.

US
LEGISLATIVE SUMMARY - CONNECTICUT. DEPT. ON AGING. Main/Corp Connecticut. Dept. on Aging. English. an. Department on Aging, 175 Main Street, Hartford CT 06106-1818. **LC** KFC3950.A35; A3973. **DD** 344.746/03263.

US/0147-9644
LEGISLATIVE SUMMARY - DEPARTMENT OF COMMUNITY AND REGIONAL AFFAIRS, DIVISION OF COMMUNITY AND RURAL DEVELOPMENT. (LEGISLATIVE SUMMARY.). [Legis. summ. - Dep. Community Reg. Aff. Div. Community Rural Dev.]. **Main/Corp** Alaska. Division of Community and Rural Development. V. 1- Jan. 24, 1977-. Periodical. English. bw. Alaska Department of Community & Regional Affairs, Pouch B, Juneau AK 99811. **LC** KFA1207; .C65. **DD** 348/.798/026.

CN/0711-9682
LEGISLATURE OF ONTARIO DEBATES. OFFICIAL REPORT (HANSARD). STANDING COMMITTEE ON REGULATIONS AND OTHER STATUTORY INSTRUMENTS. (LEGISLATURE OF ONTARIO DEBATES / STANDING COMMITTEE ON REGULATIONS AND OTHER STATUTORY INSTRUMENTS.). [Legis. Ont. debates, Off. rep. (Hansard), Standing Comm. Regul. Other Statut. Instrum.]. **Main/Corp** Ontario. Legislative Assembly. Standing Committee on Regulations and Other Statutory Instruments. No. I-1, 1st Session, 32nd Parliament (Nov. 9, 1981)-. English. $15.00 per session. Sessional Subscription Service Print Procurement Section, Ministry of Government Services, 8th Floor/Ferguson Block, Parliament Buildings, Toronto Ontario M7A 1N8 Canada. **DD** 328.713/02.

IT
LEGISLAZIONE ITALIANA, LA. (19??)-. Italian. an. L240000.00 Italy; L360000.00 other. Giuffre Editore SPA, Via Busto Arsizio 40, 20151 Milan Italy. **Tel** 011 398 2 38089200. **ED** Renato Borruso. **LC** KKH11; .I86. **DD** 348.45/026; 344.50826.

IT
LEGISLAZIONE PENALE. Unione Tipografico Ed Torinese, Corso Raffaello 28, 10125 Turin Italy. **Tel** 011 39 11 6529340.

IT
LEGISLAZIONE PENALE TRIBUTARIA. (19??)-. Periodical. Italian. tq. IPSOA Editore SRL, Casella Postale 12055, Mastrangelo, 20120 Milan Italy. **Tel** 011 39 2 82476248. Index available (Included).

US/8756-5587
LEGISLETTER. [LegisLetter]. **Added/Corp** Tennessee Bar Association. Tennessee. General Assembly. **VFOAT** TBA Legisletter. (Dec. 19, 1983)-. Periodical. English. ir (3 or 4 per year). $6.00. Tennessee Bar Association, c/o Mary Tucker, 3622 West End Evenue, Nashville TN 37205. **Tel** (615)383-7421, (800)899-6993, FAX (615)297-8058. **LC** KFT31; .L43. **DD** 349.768/05; 347.68005.

US/8755-9021
LESBIAN-GAY LAW NOTES. [Lesbian/gay law notes]. **Added/Corp** Bar Association for Human Rights of Greater New York (N.Y.). **VFOAT** Lesbian Gay Law Notes. (1984)-. Periodical. English. mo (except Aug.). $30.00. Lesbian and Gay Law Association of New York, 799 Broadway, Room 340, New York NY 10003. **Tel** (212)353-9118. **ED** Professor Arthur Leonard (Editor's Address: c/o New York Law School, 57 Worth Street, New York, NY 10013, editor's phone:

(212)431-2156). **LC** KF4754.5.A15; L47. **DD** 342.73/087; 347.30287. Index available. **Circ:** 1,000 (ctrl). **Continues** Law Group Notes.
Desc: Comprehensive monthly update of developments in lesbian and gay law.

LO/0255-6472
LESOTHO LAW JOURNAL. Added/Corp National University of Lesotho. Faculty of Law. Vol. 1, No. 1 (1985)-. Periodical. English. an. William W. Gaunt and Sons Inc, 3011 Gulf Drive, Gaunt Building, Holmes Beach FL 34217. **Tel** (800)942-8683, (813)778-5211. **LC** K12; .E76. **DD** 349.681/605; 346.816005.
Ind/Abst Index Foreign Leg. Per.

●US/1065-9072
LETTER OF CREDIT LAW AND ANNOTATIONS. (1992)-. Periodical. English. mo. $295.00. JW3 Information Services, 515 Lincoln Avenue, #300, Pittsburgh PA 15202.

US/0882-9950
LEVERAGED LEASING. Added/Corp Practising Law Institute. (19??)-. English. Practising Law Institute, 810 Seventh Avenue, New York NY 10019-5818. **Tel** (212)765-5700, FAX (212)581-4670 general correspondence, (212)265-4742 orders and billing inquiries. **LC** KF946.Z9; L49. **DD** 346.7304/7; 347.30647.

BL
LEX : COLETANEA DE LEGISLACAO E JURISPRUDENCIA. Portuguese. Cr$3,340. Lex Editora, Caixa Postal 12.888, CEP 04106 Sao Paulo Brazil. **Tel** 549-0122. cum. index. **Circ:** 8,418 (ctrl).

CE
LEX (COLOMBO, SRI LANKA). (LEX.). 1983-. English (Sinhalese). an. Law Students' Union, Sri Lanka Law College, Sri Lanka Colombo Ceylon. **DD** 349.549/3/05 345.493005.

BE/0771-5102
LEX-INTERDOC. Added/Corp Interdoc (Organization). **VFOAT** Lex Interdoc. Vol. 1, No. 1 (1st Quarter 1984)-. Periodical. English. qt. Lex-Interdoc, rue de la Montagne 34 Bte 11, B-1000 Brussels Belgium. **LC** KJC79.A13; L49.

BL
LEX, JURISPRUDENCIA DO SUPREMO TRIBUNAL FEDERAL. Main/Corp Brazil. Supremo Tribunal Federal. Portuguese. mo. Cr$344.00. Lex Editora, Caixa Postal 12.888, CEP 04106 Sao Paulo Brazil. **Tel** 549-0122. **DD** 348.81/041. **Circ:** 3,500 (ctrl).

IT/0024-1598
LEX; LEGISLAZIONE ITALIANA. Italian. wk. L225.00 Italy; L237.50 other. Unione Tipografico Ed Torinese, Corso Raffaello 28, 10125 Turin Italy. **Tel** 011 39 11 6529340.

PN
LEX (PANAMA, PANAMA). (LEX : REVISTA DEL COLEGIO NACIONAL DE ABOGADOS DE PANAMA.). Periodical. Spanish (Spanish). El Colegio / Panama, Apartado Postal 4792, Panama 5 Republic de Panama. **LC** K12; .E915. **DD** 340/.05.

AG
LEY, REVISTA JURIDICA PARAGUAYA, LA. VFOAT Revista Juridica Paraguaya: La Ley. V. 1, Jan./March 1978-. Periodical. Spanish. qt. La Ley SA, Tucuman 1471, 1050 Buenos Aires Argentina. **Tel** 011 54 1 495481, 011 54 1 495489. **LC** K12; .E92. **DD** 349.892/05.

CL
LEYES ... APROBADAS BAJO LA CONSTITUCION DE 1980. Main/Corp Chile. Spanish. ir. Editorial Juridica de Chile / Santiago, Casilla Postal 4256, Santiago Chile. **Tel** 011 56 2 2049900. **LC** KHF35; .A215. **DD** 348.83/022/05. **Continues** Decretos Leyes Dictados por la Junta de Gobierno de la Republica de Chile.

UY
LEYES PROMULGADAS. Main/Corp Uruguay. **VFOAT** Decretos del Poder Ejectivo. Spanish. sa. Presidencia de la Republica Centro de Difusion e Informacion, Plaza Independencia 776, Montevideo Uruguay. **DD** 348/.895/026.

US/0360-3156
LGA BILL OF PARTICULARS. Main/Corp Local Government Attorneys of Virginia. **VAT** Local Government Attorneys of Virginia Bill of Particulars. V. 1- June 1975-. English. mo. 207 Minor Hall, University of Virginia, Charlottesville VA 22903. **LC** KFV2830.A59; R8. **DD** 342/.755/09.

US/0193-3388
LIABILITY LEDGER. Periodical. English. mo. $135.00. Federal-State Reports Inc, 5203 Leesburg Pike, Ste 1201, Arlington VA 22041. **Tel** (703)379-0222. **LC** KF1296.A15; L5. **DD** 346/.73/038.

US
LIABILITY OF ATTORNEYS AND ACCOUNTANTS FOR SECURITIES TRANSACTIONS / BY ROBERT J. HAFT.
See Business-Accounting.

CN/1187-4945
LIAISON - CANADIAN ASSOCIATION OF LEGAL ASSISTANTS.
(LIAISON.). [Liaison - Can. Assoc. Leg. Assist.]. **Added/Corp** Canadian Association of Legal Assistants. **VFOAT** Liaison. No. 2 (June 1991)-. Periodical. English (French). qt. Canadian Association of Legal Assistants, PO Box 967, Station B, Montreal Quebec H3B 3K5 Canada. **DD** 340. ***Continues*** *Newsletter (Canadian Association of Legal Assistants)., 0836-6616.*

CN/1187-4945
LIAISON - CANADIAN ASSOCIATION OF LEGAL ASSISTANTS.
(LIAISON.). [Liaison - Can. Assoc. Leg. Assist.]. **Added/Corp** Association Canadienne des Adjoints Juridiques. **VFOAT** Liaison. No 2 (Jun 1991)-. Periodical. French (English). qt. Association Canadienne des Adjoints Juridiques, CP 967, Succursale B, Montreal Quebec H3B 3K5 Canada. **DD** 340. ***Continues*** *Bulletin (Association Canadienne des Adjoints Juridiques)., 0836-6616.*

FR/0294-8176
LIAISONS SOCIALES. LEGISLATION SOCIALE.
(1946)-. Periodical. French. tw. Liaisons Sociales, 1 Avenue E Belin, F 92856 Rueil Mal France. **Tel** 011 33 1 41299872. **UDC** 36.
Ind/Abst LABORDOC.

US/0147-8729
LIAS NEWSLETTER.
VFOAT Law in American Society Newsletter. V. 1- Mar. 1977-. Newsletter. English. qt. $10.00. Law in American Society Foundation, 33 North La Salle Street, Suite 1700, Chicago IL 60602. **LC** KF200; .L15. **DD** 340/.07/1073.

AG
LIBERACION Y DERECHO.
V. 1- Jan./April 1974-. Periodical. Spanish. Three times a year. $12.00 single issue. Universidad Nacional y Popular de Buenos Aires, Avda Figueroa Alcorta 2263, Buenos Aires Argentina. **LC** K12; .I22.

US
LIBERIAN CODE OF LAWS OF ... : ADOPTED BY THE LEGISLATURE OF THE REPUBLIC OF LIBERIA .... .
Main/Corp Liberia. Vol. 1 (1956)-. English. ir. Cornell University Press, 124 Roberts Place, Ithaca NY 14853. **Tel** (607)277-2338.

US/0091-9055
LICENSED ATTORNEYS OF NORTH DAKOTA.
[Licens. atty. N. D.]. **VFOAT** Directory : Licensed Attorneys of North Dakota. English. Bismarck State Bar Board, State Capitol, Bismarck ND 58501. **LC** KF192.N69; L5. **DD** 340/.025/784.

US/1056-9057
LICENSEE EVENT REPORT (LER) COMPILATION.
Ceased. [Licens. event rep. (LER) compil.]. **VFOAT** LER Compilation. (1982)-(19??). Periodical. English. mo. Nuclear Regulatory Commission, 1717 H Street NW, Washington DC 20555. **Tel** (301)492-7000. **DD** 621. available on microfiche (Vols. for July 1984- distributed to depository libraries).
Desc: Contains summaries of License Event Report (LER) operational information submitted to the NRC by nuclear powerplant licensees in accordance with Federal Regulations. Summaries are arranged alphabetically by facility name and chronologically by event data for each facility, with components, system, and keyword indexes following the summaries.

US/0742-5120
LICENSING, COUNTERSIGNING, AND SURPLUS LINE LAWS FOR THE 50 STATES, DISTRICT OF COLUMBIA, PUERTO RICO, AND THE VIRGIN ISLANDS.
Added/Corp National Underwriter Company. (19??)-. English. an. $21.95. National Underwriter Company, 505 Gest Street, Cincinnati OH 45203-0874. **Tel** (513)721-2140, (800)543-0874. **LC** KF1165; .L53. **DD** 346.73/086; 347.30686.
Desc: Access to information on resident and non-resident requirements for property and casualty or life, accident and health insurance.

US/0889-9320
LICENSING INTERNATIONAL.
[Licens. int.]. Periodical. English. bm. WFC Inc, Sandra Wainer, 3000 Hadley Road, South Plainfield NJ 07080. **Tel** (201)769-1160, FAX (201)769-1171.

UK
LICENSING LAWS OF NEW SOUTH WALES. LIQUOR ACT & REGULATIONS.
(19??)-. English. Butterworth & Co. Ltd. / Kent, England, Borough Green, Sevenoaks Kent TN15 8PH England. **Tel** 011 44 732-884567, FAX 011 44 732-885996.

UK/0959-8421
LICENSING REVIEW.
[Licens. rev.]. (1990)-. Periodical. English. Four times a year (Jan., Apr., July, Oct.). £72.00. Benedict Books, PO Box 900, Hemel Hempstead Herts HP3 ORJ England. **Tel** 011 44 81 442 834 900, FAX 011 44 81 442 834 901. **ED** Peter Coulson. **DD** 344.1037864795. Index available. cum. index. **Bk Rev. Circ:** 300 (ctrl).
Desc: Specialist journal in the area of licensing law and administration.

US/0047-4606
LIFE COMPANY TAX NEWSLETTER.
V. 1- March 1970-. Newsletter. English. qt. $30.00. Candidate Press, 4225 Office Parkway, Dallas TX 75204. **ED** T G Nash and J B Reid Jr. **LC** K12; .I29. **DD** 343/.73/052.

US/0163-0652
LIMITED PARTNERS LETTER.
Periodical. English. mo. $36.00. Prologue Press Inc, PO Box 1146, Menlo Park CA 94026. **Tel** (415)321-9111. **ED** Arnold Rudoff. **LC** KF6452.A15; L55. **DD** 346.7306/62/05.

US/0024-368X
LINCOLN LAW REVIEW (SAN FRANCISCO, CALIF.).
(LINCOLN LAW REVIEW.). [Linc. law rev.]. **Added/Corp** Lincoln University (San Francisco, Calif.). Law School. Vol. 1, No. 1 (Dec. 1965)-. Periodical. English. sa (Jan and Aug.). $15.00. Lincoln University / California, 2160 Lundy Avenue, San Jose CA 95131. **Tel** (408)434-0727. **DD** 340/.05. cum. index. **Bk Rev. Ad Acc. Circ:** 450 (ctrl). available on microfilm and microfiche from University Microfilms International (UMI).
Desc: Concerns the discipline of law.
Ind/Abst Bowne Dig. Corp. Sec. Lawyers (1980-); Curr. Law Index (1980-); Index Leg. Period.; Leg. Resour. Index (1980-); LegalTrac (1980-).

US
LISP NEWS.
Added/Corp American Association of Law Libraries. Legal Information Service to the Public Special Interest Section. **VAT** Legal Information Service to the Public News. Vol. 1, No. 1 (Winter 1989)-. Periodical. English. qt. American Association of Law Libraries, 53 West Jackson Boulevard, Suite 940, Chicago IL 60604. **Tel** (312)939-4764, FAX (312)431-1097, telex ABA7603.
Ind/Abst Leg. Inf. Manage. Index (19??-).

UK
LIST OF STATUTORY INSTRUMENTS.
Added/Corp Great Britain. Laws, Etc. (Statutory Instruments). (1948)-. Periodical. English. mo. £32.50. Her Majesty's Stationery Office, 51 Nine Elms Lane, London SW8 5DR England. **Tel** 011 44 71 873 8459, 011 44 71 873 8499, FAX 011 44 71 873 8499, 011 44 71 873 8456, telex 297138. **(Subscription address:** Her Majesty's Stationery Office, PO Box 276, Publications Centre, London SW8 5DT England.**)** ***Continues*** *Great Britain. Stationery Office. List of Statutory Rules and Orders.*

SP
LISTA DE SENORES COLEGIADOS.
Main/Corp Ilustre Colegio de Abogados de Oviedo. (19??)-. Spanish. Palacio de Justicia, Plaza Porlier No 5, Oviedo Spain.

SP
LISTA DE SENORES COLEGIADOS, GUIA JUDICIAL Y ADMINISTRATIVA.
Main/Corp Illustre Colegio Provincial de Abogados de Lerida. Spanish. Illustre Colegio Provincial de Abogados de Lerida, Avenida Caudillo 11 10, Lerida Spain. **DD** 340/.025/4674.

UY
LISTA NACIONAL DE ARGENTINA.
Main/Corp Asociacion Latinoamericana de Libre Comercio. (19??)-. Spanish. Asociacion Latinoamericana de Libre Comercio, Cebollati 1461 Casilla de Correo 577, Montevideo Uruguay. **Tel** 40.11.21/28, telex ALADI UY 32 6944. **DD** 343/.82/056.

US
LITIGATION.
VFOAT Litigation Handbook. Government Publication. English. US Department of Housing and Urban Development, 451 Seventh Street SW, Washington DC 20401. **Tel** (202)708-0980, FAX (202)708-0299.

US/0097-9813
LITIGATION.
[Litigation]. **Added/Corp** American Bar Association. Section of Litigation. Vol. 1 (Winter 1975)-. Periodical. English. qt (4 issues). $40.00. American Bar Association, 750 North Lake Shore Drive, Chicago IL 60611. **Tel** (312)988-5522, (312)988-5241, FAX (312)988-5528, telex 270593. **ED** William Pannill. **LC** K12; .I68. **DD** 347/.73/705. ctrl circ. available on microfilm and microfiche from University Microfilms International (UMI).
Desc: For lawyers who try cases and judges who decide them; discussion regarding how justice may be reached through advocacy.
Ind/Abst Curr. Law Index (1980-); Index Leg. Period.; Law Office Inf. Serv.; Leg. Resour. Index (1980-?); LegalTrac (1980-1989).

US/8756-4548
LITIGATION AND ADMINISTRATIVE PRACTICE SERIES.
[Litig. adm. pract. ser.]. **Added/Corp** Practising Law Institute. (19??)-. Monographic series. English. ir. $825.00. Practising Law Institute, 810 Seventh Avenue, New York NY 10019-5818. **Tel** (212)765-5700, FAX (212)581-4670 general correspondence, (212)265-4742 orders and billing inquiries. **(Subscription address:** Practising Law Institute, Source Code GBY4, 810 Seventh Avenue, New York NY 10019.**)** **DD** 342.

US/1055-4084
LITIGATION APPLICATIONS.
[Litig. appl.]. **Added/Corp** American Bar Association. Section of Law Practice Management. Litigation Interest Group. (1989)-. Periodical. English. qt (4 issues). $65.00. American Bar Association, 750 North Lake Shore Drive, Chicago IL 60611. **Tel** (312)988-5522, (312)988-5241, FAX (312)988-5528, telex 270593. **DD** 658. ***Continues*** *Litigation Applications User Group News.*

UK/0263-2160
LITIGATION (CHICHESTER, ENGLAND).
(LITIGATION.). Vol. 1, No. 1, (1981)-. Periodical. English. Eight times a year. £50.75 UK; £52.80 other. Barry Rose Law Periodicals Ltd., Little London, Chichester West Sussex PO19 1PG England. **Tel** 011 44 243 787841, 011 44 243 783637, FAX 011 44 243 779174, 011 44 243 779278. **Bk Rev. Ad Acc.**
Desc: A journal covering personal injuries, civil practice and procedure, landlord and tenent, matrimonial law, employment law, commercial law, and practice noter-up.

US/1072-9984
LITIGATION COMMITTEE NEWSLETTER.
VFOAT ABA Litigation Committee Newsletter (Fall 1992-). (198?)-. English. tq (3 issues). $15.00. American Bar Association, 750 North Lake Shore Drive, Chicago IL 60611. **Tel** (312)988-5522, (312)988-5241, FAX (312)988-5528, telex 270593.

US/8756-4491
LITIGATION COURSE HANDBOOK SERIES.
[Litig. course handb. ser.]. **Main/Corp** Practising Law Institute. No. 1-. English. ir. $775.00. Practising Law Institute, 810 Seventh Avenue, New York NY 10019-5818. **Tel** (212)765-5700, FAX (212)581-4670 general correspondence, (212)265-4742 orders and billing inquiries. **DD** 347.

UK/0268-0653
LITIGATION LETTER.
[Litig. lett.]. (1981)-. Periodical. English. mo (10 issues). £105.00. Legal Studies & Services Publ Ltd., 9-13 St. Andrew Street, London EC4A 3AE England. **Tel** 011 44 71 936-2016. **(Subscription address:** IBC Subscription Services, IBC House Vickers Drive, Weybridge, Surrey KT13 OXS England**)**

US/0147-9970
LITIGATION NEWS.
[Litig. news]. **Added/Corp** American Bar Association. Section of Litigation. Vol. 1 (Oct. 1975)-. Periodical. English. qt (4 issues). Free to members of Section of Litigation. American Bar Association, 750 North Lake Shore Drive, Chicago IL 60611. **Tel** (312)988-5522, (312)988-5241, FAX (312)988-5528, telex 270593. **LC** KF200; .L57. **DD** 345/.73/075.
Ind/Abst Curr. Law Index (1980-); Leg. Resour. Index (1980-?); LegalTrac (1980-1988).

●US/1061-3625
LITIGATION SERVICES RESOURCE DIRECTORY.
(1992)-. Directory. English. John Wiley & Sons, Inc., 605 Third Avenue, New York NY 10158-0012. **Tel** (212)850-6000, (212)850-6645, FAX (212)850-6088, telex 12-7063. **(Subscription address:** John Wiley & Sons / England, Baffins Lane, Chichester, West Sussex PO19 1UD England.**)**

●UK
LITIGATOR, THE.
(1994)-. English. Six times a year. £130.00 Europe; £136.00 other. Sweet & Maxwell Ltd., South Quay Plaza, 183 Marsh Wall, London E14 9FT England. **Tel** 011 44 264 342899, FAX 011 44 264 342723, telex 929089 ITPINF G.

BL
LITIS.
Yearly V. 1- Oct. 1974-. Periodical. Portuguese. Rua Sao Salvador 31, Apt C-01 ZC-01, Rio de Janeiro Brazil. **LC** K12; .I688.

LI
LITUANISTIKA V SSSR: PRAVO.
Added/Corp Lietuvos TSR Mokslu Akademija. Visuomenes Mokslu Informacijos Sektorius. **VFOAT** Pravo. No. 1 (1978)-. Periodical. Russian. 0.45rub single issue. Akademiia Nauk Litevskoi SSR, Lietuvos Tsr Mokslu Akademija Visuomenes Mokslu, Informacijos Sektorius Vilnius Lithuanian SSR 232600, Lenin Avenue 3, Vilnius Lithuanian.

UK/0144-932X
LIVERPOOL LAW REVIEW, THE.
[Liverp. law rev.]. Vol. 1, (Autumn 1979)-. Periodical. English. sa. £35.00 (add £2.00 postage) UK; (add £4.00 postage) other. Deborah Charles Publications, 173 Mather Avenue,

Liverpool L18 6JZ United Kingdom. **Tel** 011 44 51 724 2500. **(Subscription address:** US/ W Gaunt, 3011 Gulf Drive, Holmes Beach, FL 34217-2199**) LC** K12; .I73. **DD** 349.41/05; 344.1005. Index available. **Bk Rev. Ad Acc. Pr Rev.** available on microfilm and microfiche from University Microfilms International (UMI).
Desc: A journal of contemporary legal issues.
Ind/Abst Curr. Law Index (1980-); Index Leg. Period.; Leg. Resour. Index (1980-); LegalTrac (1980-).

LH
LJZ : LIECHTENSTEINISCHE JURISTEN-ZEITUNG. VFOAT Liechtensteinische Juristen-Zeitung; Liechtensteinische Entscheidungssammlung (LES). Vol. 1, No. 1/2 (Oct. 1980)-. Periodical. German. qt. 100.00F. Liechtensteinisches Landgericht, Aeulestrasse 70, FI-9490 Vaduz Liechtenstein. **LC** K12; .J9. **DD** 348.436/48. ***Continues*** *Entscheidungen der Liechtensteinischen Gerichtshofe von ... .*
Ind/Abst Index Foreign Leg. Per.

UK/0268-9669
LLOYD'S PROFESSIONAL LIABILITY TODAY. [Lloyd's prof. liabil. today]. **VFOAT** Professional Liability Today. (1986)-. Periodical. English. mo. £175.00. Lloyd's of London Press Ltd, Sheepen Place, Colchester, Essex, CO3 3LP England. **Tel** 011 44 206 772113, US: (212)529-9500, US: (800)955-6937, FAX 011 44 206 772880, US: (212)529-9826, telex 987321 LLOYDS G. **(Subscription address:** Lloyd's of London Press Inc. / North America, 611 Broadway, Suite 308, New York NY 10012.**) ED** Stuart Ashworth. **DD** 368.012. **Bk Rev. Ad Acc. Circ:** 325.
Desc: This journal advises on law, insurance, and practical means to avoid and minimize liability. Each month, contributors report on and interpret developments in the law and claims practice. The same legal principles apply to all professions.

AT
LOCAL GOVERNMENT APPEALS TRIBUNAL REPORTS OF NEW SOUTH WALES, THE. Main/Corp New South Wales. Local Government Appeals Tribunal. Vol. 1 (1972/1973)-. English. ir. 130.00Aus$. The Law Book Company Limited, 44-50 Waterloo Road, North Ryde New South Wales, 2113 Australia. **Tel** 011 61 2 8870177, FAX 011 61 2 8887240, telex ASBOOK 27445. **DD** 346.94404/5.
Desc: Reports cases relating to environmental control, local government, valuation of land, compensation, town planning, and powers and duties of statutory authorities from the High Court and the Supreme Courts of the States and Territories.
Ind/Abst Aust. Leg. Mon. Dig.

US/0362-5729
LOCAL GOVERNMENT LAW BULLETIN. Added/Corp University of North Carolina at Chapel Hill. Institute of Government. (1975)-. Bulletin. English. ir. $2.00-$3.00 per issue. Institute of Government, University of North Carolina at Chapel Hill, CB #3300 Knapp Building, Chapel Hill NC 27599-3330. **Tel** (919)966-4119, FAX (919)962-2707. **ED** David M Lawrence. **LC** KFN7830.A15; L6. **DD** 342/.756/09. ctrl circ.
Desc: Discusses legislation of interest to North Carolina Local Government Officials.
Ind/Abst Index Philip. Period. (-199?).

●UK/1351-5764
LOCAL GOVERNMENT REVIEW REPORTS. Vol. 157, No. 47 (Saturday Nov. 20, 1993)-. Periodical. English. wk. £168.80 UK; £177.80 other. Barry Rose Law Periodicals Ltd., Little London, Chichester West Sussex PO19 1PG England. **Tel** 011 44 243 787841, 011 44 243 783637, FAX 011 44 243 779174, 011 44 243 779278. ***Continues*** *Local Government Review.*
Desc: Includes lands tribunal cases, planning appeal decisions, law reports, ombudsman cases.

US
LOCATE: LAW OFFICE COMPUTER APPLICATIONS TECHNIQUES AND EQUIPMENT. Added/Corp Arthur Young & Company. American Bar Association. Section of Economics of Law Practice. **VFOAT** Law Office Computer Applications Techniques and Equipment; Directory of Law Office Computer Software. (1981)-. English. an. $69.95. American Bar Association, 750 North Lake Shore Drive, Chicago IL 60611. **Tel** (312)988-5522, (312)988-5241, FAX (312)988-5528, telex 270593. **LC** KF320.A9; L63. **DD** 651.8/4/024344.

CN/0318-4447
LOIS DU QUEBEC. (STATUTES OF QUEBEC.). [Lois Que.]. **Main/Corp** Quebec (Province). (1969)-. Periodical. English (French). ir. Price varies per volume. Les Publications du Quebec, CP 1190, Outremont Quebec H2V 4S7 Canada. **Tel** (514)948-1222, (800)463-2100, FAX (514)278-3030. **DD** 348/.714/022. **Bk Rev.** ctrl circ. ***Continues*** *Statuts de la Province de Quebec, 0318-4455.*
Desc: The English edition of the title 'Lois du Quebec' - Laws of Quebec.

CN/1184-7484
LOIS DU TRAVAIL. [Lois trav.]. **Main/Corp** Quebec (Province). **Added/Corp** Centre de Documentation Juridique du Quebec. Canada. **VFOAT** Canada Labour Code; Labour Laws. (1990)-. Periodical. English. sa. Wilson & Lafleur Ltd., 40 Rue Notre Dame East, Montreal, Quebec H2Y 1B9 Canada. **Tel** (514)875-6326, FAX (514)875-8356. **DD** 344.714/01/02632.

US/0889-602X
LOOKING OUT FOR YOUR LEGAL RIGHTS. [Look. out your leg. rights]. **Added/Corp** Legal Services of New Jersey. (198?)-. Periodical. English. Ten times a year. $8.00. Legal Services of New Jersey, PO Box 1357, Edison NJ 08818. **Tel** (908)572-9100, FAX (908)572-0066. **ED** Susan K. Perger. **LC** KFN1881; .L56. **DD** 349.749/05; 347.49005. Index available. **Circ:** 9,000.
Desc: Legal education newsletter covering legal rights of New Jersey residents, with an emphasis on the low-income community.

US/0362-5575
LOS ANGELES DAILY JOURNAL, THE. (THE LOS ANGELES DAILY JOURNAL AND THE LOS ANGELES NEWS.). [Los Angel. dly. j.]. **VFOAT** Los Angeles News. (1888)-. Newspaper. English. ir (260 issues). $357.00 (print), $799.00 (microfilm). Daily Journal Corporation, 915 East First Street, Los Angeles CA 90012. **Tel** (213)229-5300, FAX (213)680-3682. **ED** T. Sumner Robinson, Stephen R. Trovsdale. Index available. **Photos. Ad Acc, Adv Mgr:** Nell Fields. Full Page (B&W) $3321.00. Half Page (B&W) $1660.50. Full Page (Color) $3671.00. Half Page (Color) $2010.50. **Circ:** 17,500 (ctrl). available on microfilm.
Ind/Abst Leg. Resour. Index (1980-); LegalTrac (1980-).

US/0162-2900
LOS ANGELES LAWYER. [Los Angel. lawyer]. **Added/Corp** Los Angeles County Bar Association. Vol. 1, (Mar. 1978)-. Academic Scholarly Publication. English. mo (except combined Aug./Sept. issue). $28.00 US; $40.00 Canada, Mexico & Pan American countries; $42.00 other. Los Angeles County Bar Association, PO Box 55020, Los Angeles CA 90055. **Tel** (213)896-6503, FAX (213)623-4328. **ED** Sam Lipsman. **LC** KF200; .L67. **DD** 340/.06/279493. Index available. **Bk Rev. Ad Acc. Circ:** 21,500. available on microfilm from University Microfilms International (UMI). ***Continues*** *Los Angeles Bar Journal, 0362-837X.*
Desc: Official magazine of the Los Angeles County Bar Association. Features consumer opinion and scholarly legal articles, with profiles of Association programs and projects, tax tips, practice tips and a calendar.
Ind/Abst Calif. Period. Index (19??-); Calif. Period. Microfi. (19??-); Curr. Law Index (1980-); Law Office Inf. Serv. (1980-); Leg. Resour. Index (1980-); LegalTrac (1980-).

US/0459-8881
LOUISIANA BAR JOURNAL. [LA. bar j.]. V. 1- July 1953-. Periodical. English. bm. Louisiana State Bar Association, 210 Okeefe Avenue, Suite 600, New Orleans LA 70112. **Tel** (504)522-9172. **LC** KF200; .L68. ***Supersedes*** *Louisiana Bar.*
Ind/Abst Curr. Law Index (1980-1982); Fed. Tax Artic.; Index Leg. Period.; Law Office Inf. Serv.; Leg. Resour. Index (1980-1982); LegalTrac (1991-).

US/0745-4589
LOUISIANA CASES REPORTED IN SOUTHERN REPORTER, SECOND SERIES. Main/Corp Louisiana. Supreme Court. **VFOAT** West's Louisiana Cases; Southern Reporter Louisiana Cases. 182 So. 2nd- 1966-. English. wk. $65.00. West Publishing Company, 610 Opperman Drive, PO Box 64526, Eagan MN 55123-1308. **Tel** (612)687-5618, (800)328-9352, FAX (612)687-5388, (800)562-2329. **(Subscription telephone:** FAX (612)688-3570**) LC** KFL47; .A34. **DD** 345/.42.

US/0024-6859
LOUISIANA LAW REVIEW. [LA. law rev.]. **Added/Corp** Louisiana State University and Agricultural and Mechanical College. Law School. Louisiana State University (Baton Rouge, La.). Law School. Vol. 1 (Nov. 1938)-. Periodical. English. Six times a year (Sept., Nov., Jan., Mar., May, July). $42.00. LSU Law Center, Paul M. Herbert Law Center, Room 192, Baton Rouge LA 70803-1012. **Tel** (504)388-1683, FAX (504)388-5773. **ED** Daniel Joseph Shapiro. **LC** K12; .O863. Index available. cum. index. **Bk Rev. Ad Acc, Adv Mgr:** M. Pourcian. **Pr Rev. Circ:** 1,500. available on microfilm and microfiche from University Microfilms International (UMI). Documents available from The Genuine Article.
Desc: Includes legal articles, commentaries on legislation or cases, and book reviews.
Ind/Abst Bowne Dig. Corp. Sec. Lawyers; Curr. Contents Soc. Behav. Sci.; Curr. Law Index (1980-); Fed. Tax Artic.; Index Leg. Period.; INIS Atomindex [Micro.]; Leg. Resour. Index (1980-); LegalTrac (1980-); Res. Alert [Full Cov.]; Soc. Sci. Cit. Index [Full Cov.].

US/0278-4734
LOUISIANA LEGAL DIRECTORY, THE. (THE LOUISIANA LEGAL DIRECTORY : OFFICIAL DIRECTORY OF THE LOUISIANA STATE BAR ASSOCIATION.). 1980-. Directory. English. an. Legal Directories Publishing Company, 9111 Garland Road, PO Box 189000, Dallas TX 75218. **Tel** (214)321-3238, 800 447-5375. **LC** KF192.L8; L68. **DD** 349.763/025; 347.630025. ***Continues in part*** *Arkansas, Louisiana, and Mississippi Legal Directory.*

US/0098-8545
LOUISIANA REGISTER. Added/Corp Louisiana. Dept. of the State Register. (Jan. 1975)-. English. Twelve times a year. $113.30 Louisiana; $110.00 other. Louisiana Office of the State Register, PO Box 94095, Baton Rouge LA 70804. **Tel** (504)342-5015. **ED** Suzanne McAndrew. **LC** KFL34.A2; L68. **DD** 348/.763/01. Index available. cum. index. **Circ:** 800.
Desc: State government rules and regulations.

US/0890-8605
LOUISVILLE LAW EXAMINER. Added/Corp University of Louisville. School of Law. (19??)-. Periodical. English. Six times a year. Free on request. Louisville Law Examiner, School of Law, University of Louisville, Louisville KY 40292. **Tel** (502)588-6398. **LC** KF292.L674; A45. **DD** 340/.07/1176944. **Bk Rev. Ad Acc. Circ:** 4,500 (ctrl).

NO/0024-6980
LOV OG RETT. (1???)-. Norwegian. Ten times a year (ten issues per year). Kr640.00 $115.00. Scandinavian University Press, PO Box 2959 Toeyen, N 0608 Oslo 6 Norway. **Tel** 011 47 2 2575400, FAX 011 47 2 2575353, telex 71896 UROR N. **(Subscription address:** Scandinavian University Press, 200 Meacham Ave., Elmont NY 11003.**) ED** Anders Bratholm. Index available. **Bk Rev. Ad Acc. Circ:** 5,000.
Desc: The main professional journal for legal matters in Norway.
Ind/Abst Index Foreign Leg. Per.

US/1065-3678
LOW-INCOME HOUSING TAX CREDIT ADVISOR. [Low-income hous. tax credit advis.]. **Added/Corp** Dworbell Inc. Business Communication Services. National Housing and Rehabilitation Association (U.S.). **VFOAT** Low Income Housing Tax Credit Advisor; Tax Credit Advisor. Vol. 1, No. 1 (July 1990)-. Periodical. English. mo. $269.00. Dworbell Inc., 1726 18th Street Northwest, Washington DC 20009. **Tel** (202)328-9171. **ED** Andre Shashaty. **DD** 343. **Circ:** 500.

US/1041-5114
LOYOLA CONSUMER LAW REPORTER. [Loyola consum. law rep.]. **Added/Corp** Loyola University of Chicago. School of Law. Vol. 1, No. 1 (Fall 1988)-. Periodical. English. qt. $12.00. Loyola University / Chicago School of Law, 1 East Pearson Street, Chicago IL 60611. **Tel** (312)915-7174. **LC** KF1602; .L69. **DD** 343.73/071/05; 347.3037105.
Ind/Abst PAIS Int. Print.

US/0740-9370
LOYOLA ENTERTAINMENT LAW JOURNAL. ***Title Change.*** [Loyola entertain. law j.]. **Added/Corp** Loyola of Los Angeles School of Law. **VFOAT** Loyola of Los Angeles Entertainment Law Journal. Vol. 2 (1982)-(1992). Periodical. English. Twice a year. Loyola of Los Angeles, 1441 West Olympic Boulevard, Los Angeles CA 90015. **Tel** (213)736-1403. **ED** Greg Schenz (Editor's Phone: (213)736-1403). **LC** K5; .N8. **DD** 344.73/099; 347.30499. **Circ:** 350. ***Continues*** *Entertainment Law Journal (Loyola of Los Angeles School of Law), 0273-4249.* ***Continued by*** *Loyola of Los Angeles Entertainment Law Journal.*
Desc: Current review of recent developments in entertainment law.
Ind/Abst Index Leg. Period.; Leg. Resour. Index (1982-); LegalTrac (1984-).

US/0192-9720
LOYOLA LAW REVIEW. [Loyola law rev.]. Vol. 1, No. 1 (May 1941)-. Periodical. English. qt. $20.00 US; $22.00 other. Loyola University of the South, Box 58, New Orleans LA 70118. **Tel** (504)861-5558. **ED** Jerry Speir. Index available. cum. index. **Bk Rev. Ad Acc. Circ:** 1,200.
Desc: Provides the advancement of legal education and scholarship. Analysis of noteworthy cases.
Ind/Abst Bowne Dig. Corp. Sec. Lawyers; Curr. Law Index (1980-); Fed. Tax Artic.; Index Leg. Period.; Leg. Resour. Index (1980-); LegalTrac (1980-).

●US
LOYOLA OF LOS ANGELES ENTERTAINMENT LAW JOURNAL. **See** The Arts.

US/0147-9857
LOYOLA OF LOS ANGELES LAW REVIEW. [Loyola Los Angel. law rev.]. Began with Jan. 1972 issue. Periodical. English. qt. $40.00. Loyola University of Los Angeles / School of Law, 1441 West Olympic Boulevard, Los Angeles CA 90015. **Tel** (213)736-1125. **LC** K12; .O9. **DD** 340/.05. **Bk Rev. Ad Acc. Circ:** 625. ***Continues*** *Loyola University of Los*

Angeles Law Review.
Ind/Abst Bowne Dig. Corp. Sec. Lawyers; Crim. Justice Abstr.; Curr. Law Index (1980-); Fed. Tax Artic.; Index Leg. Period.; Leg. Resour. Index (1980-); LegalTrac (1979-).

US/0024-7081
LOYOLA UNIVERSITY OF CHICAGO LAW JOURNAL. [Loyola Univ. Chicago law j.].
Main/Corp Loyola University of Chicago. School of Law. **VFOAT** Loyola University Law Journal. V. 1 (Winter 1970)-. Periodical. English. qt. $18.00. Loyola University / Chicago School of Law, 1 East Pearson Street, Chicago IL 60611. **Tel** (312)915-7174. **LC** K12; .O88. **DD** 340/.05. Index available in last issue of volume--attached. cum. index. **Bk Rev**. **Ad Acc**. **Circ**: 95,000 (ctrl).
 Desc: The publication informs control engineers of automatic control and data-handling systems through the practical application of instrumentation and new analytical and system design
 Ind/Abst Curr. Law Index (1980-); Fed. Tax Artic.; Index Leg. Period.; Leg. Resour. Index (1980-); LegalTrac (1980-).

US/0274-9319
LPBA JOURNAL. [LPBA j.]. **Main/Corp**
Lawyer-Pilots Bar Association. **Added/Corp** Lawyer-Pilots Bar Association. Journal. **VAT** Lawyer Pilots Bar Association Journal. Vol. 1 (Mar./Apr. 1980)-. Periodical. English. mo (Except July and August). $60.00. Lawyer Pilot Bar Association, 500 E Street SW, Suite 930, Washington DC 20024. **Tel** (202)863-1000. **LC** KF2400.A15; L38. **DD** 343.73/097/05; 347.3039705. **Supersedes** Legal Eagles News, 0024-0354.

US/0740-2554
LRB SUMMARIES (KEW GARDENS, QUEENS, NEW YORK, N.Y.). (LRB SUMMARIES : SUMMARIES OF EVERY IMMIGRATION AND NATURALIZATION OPINION OF FEDERAL COURTS.). [LRB summ.]. **VFOAT** L.R.B. Summaries. Periodical. English. mo $30.00. Legal Research Bureau, PO Box 374, Kew Gardens NY 11415. **LC** KF4814; .L7. **DD** 342.73/082/02648; 347. 3028202648.

US/0734-0990
LRE PROJECT EXCHANGE. **Added/Corp**
ABA Special Committee on Youth Education for Citizenship. **VFOAT** L.R.E. Project Exchange. **VAT** Law-Related Education Project Exchange. Vol. 1, No. 1 (Spring 1981)-. Periodical. English. ir (2-3 issues). Free on request. American Bar Association, 750 North Lake Shore Drive, Chicago IL 60611. **Tel** (312)988-5522, (312)988-5241, **FAX** (312)988-5528, telex 270593. **LC** KF4208.5.L3; A134. **DD** 340/.07/1273.
 Desc: Packed full of help for lawyers who volunteer to teach youngsters about law and the legal process.

US/0731-9711
LRE REPORT. [LRE rep.]. **Added/Corp** ABA Special Committee on Youth Education for Citizenship. **VFOAT** L.R.E. Report. **VAT** Law-Related Education Report. Vol. 1, No. 1 (Winter 1980)-. Periodical. English. Three times a year. Free on request. American Bar Association, 750 North Lake Shore Drive, Chicago IL 60611. **Tel** (312)988-5522, (312)988-5241, **FAX** (312)988-5528, telex 270593. **LC** KF4208.5.L3; A135. **DD** 344.73/074; 347.30474.

II
LUCKNOW LAW TIMES. Began with Jan. 1960 issue. Periodical. English. mo $60.00. Eastern Book Company, 34 Lalbagh, Lucknow 226 001 India. **Tel** 43171, 44328, 46517, telex 535 436 FAST IN ED P L Malik and K K Malik. Index available. cum. index. **Bk Rev**. **Ad Acc**. **Circ**: 6,000.
 Desc: Contains acts, ordinances, rules and notifications of the central and U.P. governments, notifications of the Allahabad High Court, Supreme Court of India, Central and U.P. Board of Revenue and Allahabad Bar Council.

NE/0548-1937
MAANDSTATISTIEK POLITIE EN JUSTITIE. **Title Change**. See Law-Abstracting, Bibliographies and Statistics.

US/0024-9289
MACOMB COUNTY LEGAL NEWS.
Added/Corp Michigan. Circuit Court. (Macomb County). (19??)-. Newspaper. English. Fifty-two times a year. $28.00. The Macomb County Legal News, PO Box 707, 67 Cass Avenue, Mt Clemens MI 48046. **Tel** (313)469-4510.

II
MADHYA PRADESH WEEKLY NOTES.
Added/Corp India. Madhya Pradesh High Court. **VFOAT** M.P. Weekly Notes. (19??)-. English. Law Journal Publications, Jayendraganj, Gwalior 1 India. **Tel** (0751)22340. **ED** Shri Lokendra Gupta. **DD** 348.54/3046; 345.430846. Index available. cum. index. **Circ**: 5,000.
 Desc: Short notes on cases decided by high court of Madhya Pradesh and supreme court.

II
MADRAS LAW JOURNAL, THE. Vol. 1 (1891)-. Periodical. English. mo.
Ind/Abst Index Foreign Leg. Per.

UG
MAGISTRATE (KAMPALA, UGANDA).
(THE MAGISTRATE : JOURNAL OF THE UGANDA MAGISTRATES' ASSOCIATION.). Vol. 1, No. 1 (Mar. 1972)-. Periodical. English.

HU/0025-0147
MAGYAR JOG (MAGYAR JOGASZ SZOVETSEG : 1982). (MAGYAR JOG : MJ.).
VFOAT MJ; M.J. Periodical. Hungarian. mo. Magyar Jogasz Szovetseg, Szalay Utca 16, Budapest V Hungary. **LC** K13; .A366. **Continues** Magyar Jog Es Kulfoldi Jogi Szemle.

II
MAHARASHTRA BAR COUNCIL JOURNAL. **Main/Corp** Bar Council of Maharashtra. Periodical. English. 12.00. Bar Council of Maharashtra, High Court Extension 32, Bombay India. **DD** 340/.0954792.

US/0885-9973
MAINE BAR JOURNAL. [Me. bar j.].
Added/Corp Maine State Bar Association. Vol. 1, No. 1 (Jan. 1986)-. Periodical. English. Six times a year (Jan., Mar., May, July, Sept., Nov.). $30.00 Comes with Maine State Bar Association Membership. Maine State Bar Association, 124 State Street, PO Box 788, Augusta ME 04332. **Tel** (207)622-7523. **LC** KF200; .M27. **DD** 340/.06/0741. available on microfiche. **Continues** Bar Bulletin (Augusts, ME.), 0738-0364.
 Ind/Abst Index Leg. Period.; Leg. Resour. Index; LegalTrac (1980-).

US/0025-0651
MAINE LAW REVIEW (1963). (MAINE LAW REVIEW.). [Maine law rev.]. **Added/Corp** University of Maine. College of Law. Maine Law Review Association. University of Maine School of Law. **VFOAT** University of Maine Law Review. Vol. 1, No. 1 (Apr. 1908)-. Periodical. English. Twice a year (Jan. & July). $25.00. University of Maine School of Law, 246 Deering Avenue, Portland ME 04102. **Tel** (207)780-4357. **ED** Liz Wallace. **LC** K13; .A4. **DD** 340/.05. Each issue contains an index to its own contents (no volume index)--loose. available on microfilm and microfiche from University Microfilms International (UMI). **Absorbed** University of Maine Law Review.
 Ind/Abst Fed. Tax Artic.; Index Leg. Period.; Leg. Resour. Index (1980-); LegalTrac (1980-).

CN
MAITRES. **Ceased**. **Added/Corp** Barreau du Quebec. Corporation de Service. Vol. 1, No 1 (Jan. 1989)-Vol. 4, No. 6 (June 1992). Periodical. French. mo. **LC** KEQ160.A2; M35. **DD** 349.714/05; 347.14005.

CN/0842-9960
MAITRES (MONTREAL). **Ceased**. (MAITRES). [Maitres]. **Added/Corp** Barreau du Quebec. Corporation de Service. Vol. 1, No 1 (Jan. 1989)-(1992). Periodical. French. ir. Free for members. **DD** 349.714/05.
 Ind/Abst Index Can. Leg. Period. Lit. (1992-).

IO
MAJALAH FAKULTAS HUKUM UNIVERSITAS AIRLANGGA. **Added/Corp**
Universitas Airlangga. Fakultas Hukum. Vol. 1, No. 1, (Apr./June 1980)-. Periodical. English (Indonesian). bm. Universitas Airlangga Fakultas Hukum, Jalan Darmawangsa Dalam Selatan, Surabaya 60286 Indonesia. **Tel** 031 41228. **ED** S.S. Rangkuti. **LC** K13; .A46. **DD** 349.598/05; 345.98005. **Bk Rev**. **Ad Acc**. **Circ**: 750.

UA
MAJALLAT KULLIYAT AL-SHARIAH.
Main/Corp Jamiat Al-Qarawiyin. Kulliyat Al-Shariah. Periodical. Arabic. Jamiat Al-Qarawiyin Kullyat Al-Shariah, PO Box 1728, Al-Atlas Fas, Al-Maghrib United Arab Republic Egypt. **DD** 340.5/9/05.

CN/0228-7838
MAL DE BLOCS. (LE MAL DE BLOCS : BULLETIN DE L'ASSOCIATION DES LOCATAIRES DE LONGUEUIL.). [Mal blocs]. No. 1 (Oct./Nov. 79)-. Bulletin. French. bm. Free. L'Association Le Mal de Blocs, Suite 102/832 Chemin Chambly, Longueuil Quebec J4H 3M1 Canada. **DD** 346.71404/34.

SI/0025-1283
MALAYAN LAW JOURNAL (BILINGUAL ED.). (THE MALAYAN LAW JOURNAL.). [Malayan law j.]. (July 1932)-. Periodical. English (Malay). Twenty-four times a year. 555.00Aus$. Butterworths Asia, (A subsidiary of Reed International (Singapore) Pte. Ltd.), 3 Shenton Way, Number 1403, Singapore 0106 Republic of Singapore. **Tel** 011 65 2203684, FAX 011 65 2255026. **ED** Stephen J. Stout. **DD** 349.595; 347.05. Index available. cum. index. **Bk Rev**. **Ad Acc**. **Circ**: 1,500. **Continued in part by** Singapore Law Reports, 0218-3161.
 Desc: Law reporter of court cases for Singapore, Malaysia and Brunei.
 Ind/Abst Aust. Leg. Mon. Dig.; Index Foreign Leg. Per.

US/0094-6133
MALPRACTICE DIGEST. **Added/Corp** St. Paul Fire and Marine Insurance Company. Professional Liability Risk Management Dept. (19??)-. English. ir. Professional Liability Risk Management, 385 Washington Street, St Paul MN 55102. **LC** KF1289.A73; M3. **DD** 346/.73/03305.

US/0193-6166
MALPRACTICE PREVENTION FOR HOSPITALS. **Added/Corp** David Karp Associates. Vol. 1 (Jan. 1979)-. Periodical. English. David Karp Associates, 24 Fremont Road, San Rafael CA 94902. **LC** KFC6173.A15; M34. **DD** 346/.794/033.

US/0276-0495
MALPRACTICE PREVENTION FOR PHYSICIANS. **Added/Corp** David Karp Associates. (19??)-. Periodical. English. David Karp Associates, 24 Fremont Road, San Rafael CA 94902. **LC** KF2905.3.A15; M34. **DD** 346.7303/32; 347.306332.

US/0739-6031
MALPRACTICE PREVENTION REPORTER. [Malpract. prev. rep.]. **Added/Corp**
Duke Nordlinger Stern & Associates. Vol. 1, No. 1 (1983)-. Periodical. English. Four times a year (Jan., Apr., July, Oct.). $45.00. Duke Nordlinger Stern & Associates Inc, 385 Bayview Drive Northeast, St Petersburg FL 33704-2430. **Tel** (800)237-8903 or 894-4000, FAX (813)894-1040. **ED** Duke Nordlinger Stern. **LC** KF318; .M24. **DD** 346.7303/3; 347.30633. Index Bound in First Issue (Each vol., price included). cum. index. **Bk Rev**, (Qty: 1-2). **Pr Rev**. **Circ**: 35,000.
 Desc: Systems, procedures and techniques for preventing legal malpractice. Includes forms, annotated claims, digests, reviews and bibliographies.

US/0738-1026
MALPRACTICE REPORTER, THE. (THE MALPRACTICE REPORTER : MPR.). [Malpract. rep.]. **VFOAT** MPR; M.P.R.; Malpractice Reporter. (19??)-. Periodical. English. Ten times a year. $128.00 (one year), $235.00 (two years), $325.00 (three years). Malpractice Reporter, 332 Bleecker Street/ Neil Fabricant, New York NY 10014. **Tel** (212)989-8303, (212)406-2405, FAX (212)406-9855. **LC** KF2905.3.A15; M345. **DD** 346.7303/32/05; 347.30633205. **Circ**: 1,200.
 Desc: Comprehensive reporting for the medical, legal and health service communities on medical malpractice, drugs and devices.
 Ind/Abst Hospit. Manage. Rev.

US/0738-1018
MALPRACTICE REPORTER. ANESTHESIOLOGY, THE. (THE MALPRACTICE REPORTER. ANESTHESIOLOGY : MPR.). [Malpract. rep., Anesth.]. **VFOAT** Anesthesiology; MPR; M.P.R.; Malpractice Reporter. (19??)-. Periodical. English. Ten times a year. $128.00 US/ $140.00 other. Malpractice Reporter, 332 Bleecker Street/ Neil Fabricant, New York NY 10014. **Tel** (212)989-8303, (212)406-2405, FAX (212)406-9855. **ED** Neil Fabricant. **LC** KF2910.A53; A495. **DD** 346.7303/32; 347.306332. **Bk Rev**. **Ad Acc**. **Circ**: 2,500 (ctrl).
 Desc: Comprehensive reporting for the medical, legal, health services and insurance communities on medical malpractice, drugs and devices.

US/0738-1956
MALPRACTICE REPORTER. HOSPITALS, THE. (THE MALPRACTICE REPORTER. HOSPITALS : MPR.). [Malpract. rep., Hosp.]. **VFOAT** Hospitals; MPR; M.P.R.; Malpractice Reporter. (19??)-. Periodical. English. Ten times a year. $128.00 US; $140.00 other. Malpractice Reporter, 332 Bleecker Street/ Neil Fabricant, New York NY 10014. **Tel** (212)989-8303, (212)406-2405, FAX (212)406-9855. **ED** Neil Fabricant. **LC** KF3825.3.A59; M34. **DD** 346.7303/1; 347.30631. **Bk Rev**. **Ad Acc**. **Circ**: 2,500 (ctrl).
 Desc: Comprehensive reporting for the medical, legal and health service community on medical malpractice, drugs and devices.

US/0738-1948
MALPRACTICE REPORTER. OB/GYN, THE. (THE MALPRACTICE REPORTER. OB/GYN : MPR.). [Malpract. rep., OB/GYN]. **VFOAT** OB/GYN; O.B./G.Y.N.; MPR; M.P.R.; Malpractice Reporter. (19??)-. Periodical. English. Ten times a year. $128.00 US; $140.00 other. Malpractice Reporter, 332 Bleecker Street/ Neil Fabricant, New York NY 10014. **Tel** (212)989-8303, (212)406-2405, FAX (212)406-9855. **LC** KF2910.G943; A495. **DD** 346.7303/32; 347.306332.
 Desc: Reporting of medical malpractice issues.

US/0749-3495
MALPRACTICE REPORTER. PODIATRY, THE. (THE MALPRACTICE REPORTER. PODIATRY : MPR.). [Malpract. rep., Podiatry]. **VFOAT** MPR; M.P.R.; Podiatry. Vol. 1, No. 1 (July/Aug. 1984)-. Periodical. English. Ten times a year. $128.00 US; $140.00 other. Malpractice Reporter, 332 Bleecker Street/ Neil Fabricant, New York NY 10014. **Tel** (212)989-8303, (212)406-2405, FAX (212)406-9855. **ED** Natalie Kaplan. **DD** 346. **Pr Rev**. **Circ**: 1500.
 Desc: Comprehensive reporting for the medical, legal and health service communities on medical malpractice, drugs and devices.

US
MALPRACTICE REPORTER. SURGERY : MPR, THE. VFOAT Surgery; MPR. Vol. 6, No. 3 (June/July 1987)-. Periodical. English (English). Ten times a year. $128.00. Malpractice Reporter, 332 Bleecker Street/ Neil Fabricant, New York NY 10014. **Tel** (212)989-8303, (212)406-2405, FAX (212)406-9855. **ED** Natalie Kaplan. **LC** KF2905.3.A59; M34. **DD** 346.7303/32/05; 347.30633205. **Circ:** 2,500. ***Continues*** *Malpractice Reporter. Surgeon's, 0738-1964.*
Desc: Medical malpractice publications reporting for surgeons, lawyers, health administrators and the insurance communities.

US/1042-4091
MANAGED CARE LAW OUTLOOK. [Manag. care law outl.]. **VFOAT** Managed Care Law. Vol. 1, No. 1 (Jan. 1989)-. Periodical. English. mo. $398.00. Capitol Publications, 1101 King Street, Suite 444, Alexandria VA 22314. **Tel** (703)683-4100, (800)655-5597. **(Subscription address:** Capitol Publications, PO Box 1453, Alexandria, VA 22313**) LC** PAR. **DD** 344.73/022; 347.30422. **NLM** W1; MA57JK. **[CCC].** available on an online database (files 16,636/Full-Text) from DIALOG.
Ind/Abst PTS Newsl. Database [Full Txt.].

US/0893-8911
MANHATTAN LAWYER. ***Ceased.*** [Manhattan lawyer]. Vol. 1, No. 1 (May 11, 1987)-Ceased (Dec. 1991). Periodical. English. wk. American Lawyer Media, L.P., 600 3rd Avenue, New York NY 10016. **Tel** (212)973-2800. **ED** Steven Brill. **LC** K13; .A496. **DD** 340. **Circ:** 35,000.
Desc: Covers court news and gives information on the business of practicing law. Solo practitioners as well as corporate lawyers are the targeted audience.

CN/0380-0008
MANITOBA DECISIONS, CIVIL AND CRIMINAL CASES. (1975)-. English. mo. 275.00Can$. Western Legal Publications Ltd., 301 One Alexander Street, Vancouver BC V6A 1B2 Canada. **Tel** (800)663-0422, (604)687-5671. **DD** 348/.7127/048. cum. index.
Desc: Digests of all available civil and criminal decisions from the Manitoba Court of Appeal, Court of Queen's Bench and County Courts filed by subjects.

CN/0076-3861
MANITOBA LAW JOURNAL (1966). (MANITOBA LAW JOURNAL.). [Manit. law j.]. **Added/Corp** Manitoba Law School. University of Manitoba. Faculty of Law. Vol. 2 (1966)-. Periodical. English (French). Three times a year. $30.00. University of Manitoba / Rosbon Hall, Rosbon Hall, Winnipeg Manitoba R3T 2N2 Canada. **Tel** (204)474-6159, FAX (204)275-5540. **ED** L. Yvette Creft. **LC** K13; .A5. **DD** 349.7127/05. **Bk Rev. Ad Acc, Adv Mgr:** J. Epp. **Pr Rev. Circ:** 450. ***Continues*** *Manitoba Law School Journal. Manitoba Law School, 0381-5587;* ***Absorbed*** *Manitoba Bar News News, 0025-2212.*
Desc: A student organized law journal that is chiefly but not exclusively devoted to the work of Manitoba writers and issues of significance in the province.
Ind/Abst Can. Legal Lit. (1980-); Curr. Law Index (1980-); Index Can. Leg. Period. Lit.; Index Leg. Period.; Leg. Resour. Index (1980-); LegalTrac (1980-).

CN/0713-7109
MANITOBA REPORTS (FREDERICTON, N.B. : BOUND CUMULATION). (MANITOBA REPORTS.). [Manit. rep.]. 2nd Ser., V. 1 (1979)-. Periodical. English. $65.00 each volume. Maritime Law Book Ltd, PO Box 302, Fredericton New Brunswick, E3B 4Y9 Canada. **Tel** (506)453-9921, (800)561-0220. **DD** 348.7127/043. ***Continues*** *Manitoba Reports, 0713-7109.*

CN
MANITOBA STATUTES AND RULES OF COURT JUDICIALLY CONSIDERED, INCLUDING ALL AMENDMENTS TO THE STATUTES AND RULES SINCE THE LAST CONSOLIDATIONS IN EACH CASE. **VFOAT** Western Weekly Reports. 1954/56-. English. Carswell / Canada, 2075 Kennedy Road, Scarborough Ontario M1T 3V4 Canada. **Tel** (416)609-3800, (800)387-5164. **LC** KEM60; .M36. **DD** 348.7127/026; 347.1270826.

CL
MANUAL DE CONSULTAS TRIBUTARIAS / ASSOCIACION NACIONAL DE INSPECTORES DE IMPUESTOS INTERNOS. Spanish. mo. Ediciones Tecnicas Tributarias Ltda, Casilla 3571, Santiago de Chile. **DD** 343.8305/2/05; 348.3035205.

US
MANUAL FOR COMPLEX AND MULTIDISTRICT LITIGATION. **Main/Corp** Federal Judicial Center. (19??)-. English. ir. Matthew Bender & Company Inc., 1275 Broadway, Albany NY 12204. **Tel** (800)833-9844, (518)487-3000.

US
MANUAL FOR THE USE OF THE LEGISLATURE OF THE STATE OF NEW YORK. **Main/Corp** New York (State). Dept. of State. 1840-. English. an. Department of State / New York, 162 Washington Avenue, Albany NY 12231. **Tel** (518)474-6957. **LC** JK3430; .A25. **DD** 320.9/747.

US
MANUAL. NEW YORK BUILDING LAWS. **Main/Corp** New York Society of Architects. **Added/Corp** New York Society of Architects. Yearbook. 1st Ed. (1911)-. English. tw. $145.50. New York Society of Architects, 275 Seventh Avenue, 15th Floor, New York NY 10001. **Tel** (212)675-6646. **Bk Rev. Ad Acc. Circ:** 3,000 (ctrl).
Desc: NYC building codes, housing maintenance, multiple dwelling laws, and updating service.

UK/0267-534X
MANX LAW REPORTS. (THE MANX LAW REPORTS.). [Manx law rep.]. (19??)-. English. an. Law Reports International, Trinity College, Oxford OX1 3BH England. **Tel** 011 44 865 279883, FAX 011 44 865 279911. **ED** A. Milner. **LC** KDG27; .A516. **DD** 348.427/9046; 344.2790846. Index available. cum. index. **Circ:** 200.
Desc: Edited court reports from the Isle of Man.

US/0745-8959
MARIN COUNTY COURT REPORTER. **VFOAT** Court Reporter. (19??)-. Periodical. English. da (260 issues). $93.00. Daily Journal Corporation, 915 East First Street, Los Angeles CA 90012. **Tel** (213)229-5300, FAX (213)680-3682. **ED** Gerald L. Salzman. Index available. **Bk Rev. Ad Acc.**

US/0893-7788
MARKETING FOR LAWYERS. [Mark. lawyers]. **VFOAT** Marketing for Lawyers Newsletter. Vol. 1, No. 1 (May 1987)-. Newsletter. English. mo. $175.00. Leader Publications, 345 Park Avenue South, New York NY 10010. **Tel** (800)888-8300 ext. 6170, (212)545-6170, FAX (212)696-1848. **LC** KF316.5.A15; M37. **DD** 349.73/0688; 347.300688.
Ind/Abst Law Office Inf. Serv.

US/0025-3987
MARQUETTE LAW REVIEW. [Marquette law rev.]. **Added/Corp** Marquette University. Law School. Vol. 1 (Dec. 1916)-. Periodical. English. qt. $20.00. Marquette University / Law School, 1103 West Wisconsin Avenue, Milwaukee WI 53233. **Tel** (414)288-7090, (414)288-5815. **ED** Colin M. Lancaster, (414)288-5143. Index available (bound in last issue). cum. index. **Bk Rev. Ad Acc. Circ:** 1,600 (ctrl).
Desc: Critical analysis of developing areas of the law. Includes student articles and lead articles by prominent attorneys and scholars. Emphasis on Wisconsin law.
Ind/Abst Bowne Dig. Corp. Sec. Lawyers; Crim. Justice Abstr.; Curr. Law Index (1980-); Fed. Tax Artic.; Index Leg. Period.; Leg. Resour. Index (1980-); LegalTrac (1980-); PAIS Int. Print (1991-).

US/1057-6029
MARQUETTE SPORTS LAW JOURNAL. (MARQUETTE SPORTS LAW JOURNAL : JOURNAL OF THE NATIONAL SPORTS LAW INSTITUTE.). [Marquette sports law j.]. **Added/Corp** National Sports Law Institute (U.S.). Vol. 1, No. 1 (Fall 1990)-. Periodical. English. sa. $25.00. Marquette University / Law School, 1103 West Wisconsin Avenue, Milwaukee WI 53233. **Tel** (414)288-7090, (414)288-5815.
Ind/Abst Index Leg. Period. (1992-); Leg. Resour. Index; LegalTrac (1990-).

US/1051-5518
MARTINDALE-HUBBELL BAR REGISTER, THE. [Martindale-Hubbell bar regist.]. **VFOAT** Martindale-Hubbell Bar Register of Preeminent Lawyers in the United States, Canada, and Other Countries; Martindale Hubbell Bar Register; Bar Register; Bar Register of Preeminent Lawyers in the United States, Canada, and other Countries. (1990)-. Periodical. English. an. $145.00. Martindale-Hubbell, A Reed Reference Publishing Company, Part of Reed International PLC, 121 Chanlon Road, New Providence NJ 07974. **Tel** (800)526-4902, (908)464-6800, FAX (908)464-3553, telex 138755. **LC** KF190; .B37. **DD** 340/.025. ***Continues*** *Bar Register, 0277-3848.*
Desc: Provides listings for over 7,000 members of the bar, as designated by their fellow lawyers. Supplies contact information on each partnership, plus names of members of the firm and major clients represented. Source of information on today's leading attorneys and law firms.

US
MARTINDALE-HUBBELL CANADIAN LAW DIRECTORY. (19??)-. Directory. English. $75.00. Martindale-Hubbell, A Reed Reference Publishing Company, Part of Reed International PLC, 121 Chanlon Road, New Providence NJ 07974. **Tel** (800)526-4902, (908)464-6800, FAX (908)464-3553, telex 138755.

●US
MARTINDALE-HUBBELL DISPUTE RESOLUTION DIRECTORY. **Added/Corp** American Arbitration Association. (Oct. 1994)-. Directory. English. an (Oct.). $85.00. Martindale-Hubbell, A Reed Reference Publishing Company, Part of Reed International PLC, 121 Chanlon Road, New Providence NJ 07974. **Tel** (800)526-4902, (908)464-6800, FAX (908)464-3553, telex 138755.
Desc: Provides listings of professionals participating in dispute resolution, Code of Professional Responsibility, profiles of non-profit dispute resolution organizations and government agency sources.

US
MARTINDALE-HUBBELL INTERNATIONAL LAW DIRECTORY. **Added/Corp** Martindale-Hubbell (Firm). **VFOAT** Martindale Hubbell International Law Directory. 123rd year (1991)-. Directory. English. an. $155.00 (combined set). Martindale-Hubbell, A Reed Reference Publishing Company, Part of Reed International PLC, 121 Chanlon Road, New Providence NJ 07974. **Tel** (800)526-4902, (908)464-6800, FAX (908)464-3553, telex 138755. **LC** K68; .M37. **DD** 340/.025. ***Separated from*** *Martindale-Hubbell Law Directory, 0191-0221.*
Desc: Listing of international attorneys, with information on lawyers and law firms in Canada and over 100 countries from Afghanistan to Zimbabwe.

US
MARTINDALE-HUBBELL LAW DIGEST. **Added/Corp** Martindale-Hubbell (Firm). **VFOAT** Martindale Hubbell Law Digest; United States Law Digest; Canadian & International Law Digest, Uniform Acts, A.B.A. Codes; Canadian and International Law Digest, Uniform Acts, A.B.A. Codes. (1991)-. Periodical. English. ir. Martindale-Hubbell, A Reed Reference Publishing Company, Part of Reed International PLC, 121 Chanlon Road, New Providence NJ 07974. **Tel** (800)526-4902, (908)464-6800, FAX (908)464-3553, telex 138755. **LC** KF190; .M3. **DD** 348/.026; 342.826. ***Separated from*** *Martindale-Hubbell Law Directory, 0191-0221.* ***Continued in part by*** *Martindale-Hubbell International Law Digest.*

US/0191-0221
MARTINDALE-HUBBELL LAW DIRECTORY (PRINT). (MARTINDALE-HUBBELL LAW DIRECTORY.). [Martindale-Hubbell law dir.]. **Added/Corp** Martindale-Hubbell Law Directory, Inc. Martindale-Hubbell, Inc. Martindale-Hubbell (Firm). **VFOAT** Martindale Hubbell Law Directory; Law Directory. 63rd Year (1931)-. Periodical. English. an. $305.00. Martindale-Hubbell, A Reed Reference Publishing Company, Part of Reed International PLC, 121 Chanlon Road, New Providence NJ 07974. **Tel** (800)526-4902, (908)464-6800, FAX (908)464-3553, telex 138755. **LC** KF190; .H813. **[CCC].** available on an online database from LEXIS; and NEXIS; available on CD-ROM. ***Formed by the union of*** *Martindale's American Law Directory* ***and*** *Hubbell's Legal Directory.* ***Continued in part by*** *Martindale-Hubbell Law Digest; Martindale-Hubbell International Law Directory.*
Desc: Contains information on lawyers of the United States, Canada, and other countries of the world as well as authoritative digests of laws.

US/0199-0926
MARYLAND ADVANCE REPORTS. [Md. adv. rep.]. **Main/Corp** Maryland. Court of Appeals. **VFOAT** Cases Adjudged in the Court of Appeals of Maryland. English. wk (except 1st and last week of Sept.). West Publishing Company, 610 Opperman Drive, PO Box 64526, Eagan MN 55123-1308. **Tel** (612)687-5618, (800)328-9352, FAX (612)687-5388, (800)562-2329. **(Subscription telephone:** FAX (612)688-3570**) DD** 348. ***Continues*** *Advance Reports, Maryland Reports, Maryland Appellate Reports.*

US/0025-4177
MARYLAND BAR JOURNAL, THE. [Md. bar j.]. **Added/Corp** Maryland State Bar Association. Vol. 1 (Oct. 1968)-. Periodical. English. bm. $25.00. Maryland State Bar Association, 520 West Fayette Street, Baltimore MD 21201. **Tel** (410)685-7878, (800)492-1964. **ED** N. Polvinale. **LC** K13; .A7. **DD** 340/.062/752. **Ad Acc. Circ:** 11,000 (ctrl).
Desc: Evolves around law and law related ideas. Includes new legislation and current events relating to law.
Ind/Abst Index Leg. Period.; Law Office Inf. Serv.; Leg. Resour. Index; LegalTrac (1990-).

US
MARYLAND JOURNAL OF CONTEMPORARY LEGAL ISSUES. **Added/Corp** University of Maryland at Baltimore. School of Law. Vol. 1, Issue 1 (Spring 1990)-. Periodical. English. sa. $18.50. Maryland Journal of Contemporary Law, 500 West Baltimore Street, Baltimore MD 21201. **Tel** (410)706-6744. ***Continues*** *Maryland Law Forum, 0163-4380.*

US/0025-4282
MARYLAND LAW REVIEW (1936). (MARYLAND LAW REVIEW.). [MD. law rev.]. Vol. 1, No.

1 (Dec. 1936)-. English. Four times a year. $30.00. University of Maryland School of Law, 500 West Baltimore Street, Baltimore MD 21201. **Tel** (410)706-6744. **LC** K13; .A74. cum. index. **Bk Rev**. **Ad Acc**. **Circ:** 2,200. available on microfilm and microfiche from University Microfilms International (UMI).
Desc: Deals with all law topics. Publishes articles on specific topics, case analyses of critical cases and a general survey of developments in Maryland law.
Ind/Abst Bowne Dig. Corp. Sec. Lawyers; Curr. Law Index (1980-); Fed. Tax Artic.; Index Leg. Period.; Leg. Resour. Index (1980-); LegalTrac (1980-); PAIS Int. Print.

US
MARYLAND LAWYERS' MANUAL. **Added/Corp** Maryland State Bar Association. (19??)-. English. sa. $37.00 members of the State Bar Association; $60.00 other. Maryland State Bar Association, 520 West Fayette Street, Baltimore MD 21201. **Tel** (410)685-7878, (800)492-1964. **ED** Michael Ruby. **LC** KF192.M36; M3. **DD** 340/.025/752. **Ad Acc**. **Circ:** 15,500 (ctrl).
Desc: Directory of Maryland attorneys.

US/0360-2834
MARYLAND REGISTER. Vol.1 (Oct. 17, 1974)-. English. bw. $90.00 (surface mail) $160.00 (1st class). Maryland Division of State Documents, PO Box 2249, Annapolis MD 21404. **Tel** (410)974-2486. **ED** Robert J Colborn Jr. **LC** KFM1234.A2; M37. **DD** 348/.752/025. Index available. cum. index. **Bk Rev**. **Ad Acc**. **Circ:** 2,500 (ctrl).
Desc: State rules and regulations, state contract bids and awards, executive orders, legislative information, legislative bills, administrative rules of courts of appeal.

US/0047-6099
MARYLAND RESEARCHER, THE. Began with July 1970 issue. Periodical. English. mo. National Legal Research Group Inc, PO Box 7187, Charlottesville VA 22906. **Tel** (800)727-6574, (804)977-5690, FAX (804)295-4667. **LC** KFM1257; .M35. **DD** 348.752/026.

US
MASSACHUSETTS ADMINISTRATIVE LAW LIBRARY ON CD-ROM [COMPUTER FILE] / SOCIAL LAW LIBRARY. **Added/Corp** Social Law Library (Boston, Mass.). Disc 89-001 (July 1989)-. Periodical. English. qt. $1000.00. The Social Law Library, 1200 Court House, Boston MA 02108. **Tel** (617)720-0294, FAX (617)523-2458.

US
MASSACHUSETTS ATTORNEY DISCIPLINE REPORTS : DECISIONS OF THE SUPREME JUDICIAL COURT OF MASSACHUSETTS / COMPILED BY BOARD OF BAR OVERSEERS. **Main/Corp** Massachusetts. Supreme Judicial Court. **Added/Corp** Massachusetts. Board of Bar Overseers. Vol. 1 (Sept. 1974/Dec. 1979)-. English. an. $70.00. Butterworth Heinemann / Woburn, MA, 225 Wildwood Avenue, Unit B, Woburn MA 01801. **Tel** (800)366-2665, FAX (617)928-2620, telex 880052. **LC** KFM2476.5.A2; A497. **DD** 347.744/0504; 347.40447504.

US/0744-818X
MASSACHUSETTS DECISIONS REPORTED IN NORTH EASTERN REPORTER, SECOND SERIES. [Mass. decis. rep. North East. rep., second ser.]. **VFOAT** West's Massachusetts Decisions. Began publication in 1937. Periodical. English. wk. West Publishing Company, 610 Opperman Drive, PO Box 64526, Eagan MN 55123-1308. **Tel** (612)687-5618, (800)328-9352, FAX (612)687-5388, (800)562-2329. **(Subscription telephone:** FAX (612)688-3570) **DD** 348.

US/0199-5235
MASSACHUSETTS DISCRIMINATION LAW REPORTER. (MDLR/MASSACHUSETTS DISCRIMINATION LAW REPORTER.). **Added/Corp** Massachusetts Commission Against Discrimination. Vol. 1 (1979)-. Periodical. English. mo. $273.00 Massachusetts; $260.00 other. New England Legal Publishers, PO Box 425, Weston MA 02193. **Tel** (617)891-6200. **ED** Joseph Ambash. Each issue contains an index to its own contents (no volume index)--loose. cum. index. **Bk Rev**. **Circ:** 100.
Desc: Contains digests and the full text of decisions issued by the Massachusetts Commission Against Discrimination, as well as court decisions involving the Commission.

US/0163-1411
MASSACHUSETTS LAW REVIEW. [Mass. law rev.]. V. 63- Jan./Feb. 1978-. Academic Scholarly Publication. English. qt. $25.00 US; $40.00 other. Massachusetts Bar Association, 20 West Street, Boston MA 02111. **Tel** (617)542-3602. **LC** K13; .A78. **DD** 349.744/05; 347.44005. cum. index. **Ad Acc**. **Circ:** 21,000 (ctrl). available on microfilm and microfiche from University Microfilms International (UMI). ***Continues*** *Massachusetts Law Quarterly.*
Desc: Scholarly legal publication.
Ind/Abst Curr. Law Index (1980-); Index Leg. Period.; Law Office Inf. Serv.; Leg. Resour. Index (1980-); LegalTrac (1980-).

US/0738-369X
MASSACHUSETTS LAWYERS DIARY AND MANUAL : INCLUDING BAR DIRECTORY. **VFOAT** Lawyers Diary and Manual. (19??)-. Directory. English. an (Oct.). $35.00. Skinder Strauss Associates, PO Box 50, Newark NJ 07101. **Tel** (800)444-4041, (201)642-1440, FAX (201)642-4280. **ED** Richard Lurie. **LC** KF192.M38; L35. **DD** 340/.025/744. **Ad Acc, Adv Mgr:** N. Bergamo. **Circ:** 20,000. ***Continues*** *Lawyers Diary and Manual.*

US/0196-7509
MASSACHUSETTS LAWYERS WEEKLY. [Mass. lawyers wkly.]. **VFOAT** Lawyers Weekly. (1972)-. Periodical. English. wk. $259.00. Lawyers Weekly Publications, 41 West Street, Boston MA 02111. **Tel** (617)451-7300, (800)444-5297. **ED** Robert Ambrogi. **LC** K13; .A79. **DD** 349.744/05. Index available. **Ad Acc**. **Circ:** 10,000. available on microfilm from University Microfilms International (UMI).
Desc: Covers court opinions, summaries, bar association news, judges, courtroom assignments, front page news on the legal profession, seminar listings, and court announcements on new rules.

US/0195-5845
MASSACHUSETTS LEGAL DIRECTORY, WITH RHODE ISLAND SECTION. **VFOAT** Massachusetts Legal Directory. 1977/78-. Directory. English. an. Legal Directories Publishing Company, 9111 Garland Road, PO Box 189000, Dallas TX 75218. **Tel** (214)321-3238, 800 447-5375. **LC** KF192.M38; M37. **DD** 340/.025/744.

US
MASSACHUSETTS REGISTER (BOSTON, MASS. 1976). (MASSACHUSETTS REGISTER.). [Mass. regist.]. **Added/Corp** Massachusetts. Secretary of the Commonwealth. Massachusetts. Office of the Secretary of State. Issue No. 1 (Apr. 4, 1976)-. English. Fifty-two times a year. $300.00. Commonwealth of Massachusetts, State House, Boston MA 02133. **Tel** (617)727-2834. **(Subscription address:** Commonwealth Massachusetts Bookstore, State House Room 116, Secretary of State, Boston MA 02133.**)** **LC** KFM2436; .M35. **DD** 348/.744/025. cum. index. **Circ:** 750 (ctrl).

US/8750-8516
MASSCITIZEN. (MASSCITIZEN : THE QUARTERLY REPORT OF THE MASSACHUSETTS PUBLIC INTEREST RESEARCH GROUP.). [Masscitizen]. **Added/Corp** Massachusetts Public Interest Research Group. **VFOAT** Mass Citizen. **VAT** Massachusetts Citizen. (1981)-. Periodical. English. qt. comes with Mass Public Interest Research Group membership. Masspirg, Publications Department, 29 Temple Place, Boston MA 02111. **Tel** (617)292-4800. **ED** Kathleen Traphager. **DD** 328. **Circ:** 90,000 (ctrl).
Desc: A report to members of the Massachusetts Public Interest Research Group.

IT
MASSIMARIO DEL FORO ITALIANO; RACOLTA DELLE MASSIME DELLE SENTENZE DELLA CASSAZIONE CIVILE, IL. (19??)-. Periodical. Italian. mo. L172000 Italy; L206000 other. Zanichelli Editore Spa, Via Irnerio 34, 40126 Bologna Italy. **Tel** 011 39 51 293263.

IT/0025-4940
MASSIMARIO DELLA GIURISPRUDENZA ITALIANA. [Massim. Giurisprud. ital.]. (1931)-. Periodical. Italian. mo. L160.000 Italy; L240.000 other. Unione Tipografico Ed Torinese, Corso Raffaello 28, 10125 Turin Italy. **Tel** 011 39 11 6529340. **UDC** 34.

IT/0392-6354
MASSIMARIO PENALE COMPLETO DELLA CORTE SUPREMA DI CASSAZIONE. [Massim. penale completo Corte Suprema Cassaz.]. (1949)-. Periodical. Italian. mo. L68000 Italy; L136000 other. Edizioni Progresso, Via Mazzocchi 175, 81055 S Maria Capua Vetere Italy. **Tel** 011 39 823 846553. **UDC** 34.

IT
MATERIALI PER UNA STORIA DELLA CULTURA GIURIDICA. **Main/Corp** Genoa. Universita. Istituto di Filosofia del Diritto. (1971)-. Italian. sa. L70000.00 Italy; L120000.00 (surface mail), L140000.00 (airmail) other. Societa Editrice il Mulino, Strada Maggiore 37, 40125 Bologna Italy. **Tel** 011 39 51 256011, FAX 011 39 51 256034. **ED** Compiler: 1971- G. Tarello.

MF
MAURITIUS LAW REVIEW / REVUE DE DROIT, DE DOCTRINE, ET DE JURISPRUDENCE MAURICIENNE. **Added/Corp** University of Mauritius. Dept. of Law. **VFOAT** Revue de Droit, de Doctrine, et de Jurisprudence Mauricienne; Revue de Droit et de Jurisprudence Mauricienne. Vol. 1, No. 1 (Aug. 1977)-. Periodical. English (French). ir. Dept. of Law / Maritius, University of Maritius. **LC** K13; .A85. **DD** 340/.05.

NE/0005-8335
MBB : BELASTINGBESCHOUWINGEN. **See** Public Administration-Public Finance and Taxation.

US
MCGEORGE MAGAZINE / UNIVERSITY OF THE PACIFIC, MCGEORGE SCHOOL OF LAW. **Main/Corp** McGeorge School of Law. English. an. McGeorge School of Law, 3401 Fifth Avenue, Sacramento CA 95817. **Tel** (916)739-7171. **LC** KF292.M314; A435. **DD** 340/.05. **Circ:** 65,000 (ctrl). ***Continues*** *McGeorge, 0737-9188.*
Desc: Publication features topics on legal education, both national and international in scope.
Ind/Abst Law Office Inf. Serv.

US
MCKINNEY'S SESSION LAWS OF NEW YORK. **Main/Corp** New York (State). **VFOAT** Laws of New York. (1951)-. English. an. West Publishing Company, 610 Opperman Drive, PO Box 64526, Eagan MN 55123-1308. **Tel** (612)687-5618, (800)328-9352, FAX (612)687-5388, (800)562-2329. **LC** KFN5025; .M3. ***Continues*** *New York (State). General Laws of the State of New York.*

US/0735-4436
MD/PC. (MD/PC : MEDICAL LAW AND PRACTICE MANAGEMENT.). [MD/PC]. **Added/Corp** Biomedical Information Corporation. **VFOAT** Medical Law and Practice Management; M.D./P.C. Vol. 1, No. 1 (1981)-. Periodical. English. Biomedical Information Corporation, 800 Second Avenue, New York NY 10017. **Tel** (212)262-9662. **LC** KF3821.A15; M38. **DD** 344.73/041; 347.30441.

US/1040-0192
MEALEY'S LITIGATION REPORT. ASBESTOS PROPERTY ACTIONS. [Mealey's litig. rep., Asbestos prop. actions]. **Added/Corp** Mealey Publications. **VFOAT** Asbestos Property Actions. Vol. 1, Issue 1 (Oct. 7, 1988)-. Periodical. English. sm. $795.00. Mealey Publications, PO Box 446, Wayne PA 19087-0446. **Tel** (215)688-6566, FAX (215)688-7552. **LC** KF3964.A73; A1365. **DD** 344.73/0218/05; 347.30421805. **[CCC].**

US/1049-5347
MEALEY'S LITIGATION REPORT. REINSURANCE. [Mealey's litig. rep., Reinsur.]. **Added/Corp** Mealey Publications. **VFOAT** Reinsurance; Mealey's Litigation Report. Reinsurance. Vol. 1, Issue #1 (May 10, 1990)-. Periodical. English. Twenty-four times a year. $850.00. Mealey Publications, PO Box 446, Wayne PA 19087-0446. **Tel** (215)688-6566, FAX (215)688-7552. **ED** Susan A. Winchurch. **LC** KF1236.A15; M4. **DD** 346.73/086/0264; 347.306860264. **[CCC].** Index available. cum. index.
Desc: Focuses on the field of reinsurance law.

US/0886-0122
MEALEY'S LITIGATION REPORT. TOBACCO. ***Title Change.*** [Mealey's litig. rep., Tob.]. **Added/Corp** Mealey Publications. **VFOAT** Tobacco. Vol. 1, Issue 1 (Jan. 1986)-(19??). Periodical. English. mo. Mealey Publications, PO Box 446, Wayne PA 19087-0446. **Tel** (215)688-6566, FAX (215)688-7552. **ED** Michael P. Mealey and W. Thomas Hagy. **LC** KF1297.T63; A496. **DD** 346.7303/82; 347.306382. **[CCC].** Index available. cum. index. **Bk Rev**. ***Absorbed by*** *Mealey's Litigation Reports Toxic Torts.*
Desc: Editorial and document coverage of tobacco product liability litigation throughout the United States.

●US/1068-5405
MEALEY'S LITIGATION REPORTS. AMERICANS WITH DISABILITIES ACT. [Mealey's litig. rep., Am. disabil. act]. **Added/Corp** Mealey Publications. United States. Americans with Disabilities Act of 1990. **VFOAT** Americans with Disabilities Act. Vol. 1, Issue #1 (Feb. 1993)-. Periodical. English. mo. $450.00. Mealey Publications, PO Box 446, Wayne PA 19087-0446. **Tel** (215)688-6566, FAX (215)688-7552. **DD** 344.

US/0742-4647
MEALEY'S LITIGATION REPORTS. ASBESTOS. [Mealey's litig. rep., Asbestos]. **Added/Corp** Mealey Publications. **VFOAT** Asbestos. (Feb. 10, 1984)-. Periodical. English. sm. $925.00. Mealey Publications, PO Box 446, Wayne PA 19087-0446. **Tel** (215)688-6566, FAX (215)688-7552. **ED** Pamela J. Craft. **LC** KF3964.A73; A136. **DD** 344.73/021; 347.30421. **[CCC].** Index available. cum. index.
Desc: Complete coverage of health and property damage claims involving asbestos.

US/0893-1011
MEALEY'S LITIGATION REPORTS. BAD FAITH. [Mealey's litig. rep., Bad faith]. **Added/Corp** Mealey Publications. **VFOAT** Bad Faith; Mealey's

Litigation Report. Bad Faith. Vol. 1, Issue 1 (May 1987)-. Periodical. English. sm. $795.00. Mealey Publications, PO Box 446, Wayne PA 19087-0446. **Tel** (215)688-6566, FAX (215)688-7552. **ED** Michael P. Mealey and W. Thomas Hagy. **LC** KF1301.5.I58; M43. **DD** 346.73/086; 347.30686. **[CCC]**. Index available. cum. index. **Bk Rev**.
Desc: Editorial and document coverage of national litigation concerning bad faith insurance claims.

US/1057-1000
MEALEY'S LITIGATION REPORTS. BANKING INSOLVENCY. ***Title Change.*** **See** Business-Banking and Finance.

●US/1067-0246
MEALEY'S LITIGATION REPORTS. BREAST IMPLANTS. [Mealey's litig. rep., Breast implants]. **Added/Corp** Mealey Publications. **VFOAT** Breast Implants. Vol. 1, Issue #1 (Nov. 9, 1992)-. Periodical. English. sm. $695.00. Mealey Publications, PO Box 446, Wayne PA 19087-0446. **Tel** (215)688-6566, FAX (215)688-7552. **LC** KF1297.B74; A134. **DD** 346.7303/8/02638; 347.3063802638.

●US/1068-414X
MEALEY'S LITIGATION REPORTS. D&O LIABILITY. [Mealey's litig. rep., D&O liabil.]. **Added/Corp** Mealey Publications. **VFOAT** D & O Liability; D and O Liability. **VAT** Directors & Officers Liability; Directors and Officers Liability. Vol. 3, Issue #15 (Jan. 6, 1993)-. Periodical. English. sm. $750.00 North America; $846.00 other. Mealey Publications, PO Box 446, Wayne PA 19087-0446. **Tel** (215)688-6566, FAX (215)688-7552. **DD** 346.

US/8755-9005
MEALEY'S LITIGATION REPORTS. INSURANCE. [Mealey's litig. rep., Insur.]. **Added/Corp** Mealey Publications. **VFOAT** Insurance; Mealey's Litigation Report. Insurance. (Nov. 1984)-. Periodical. English. Forty-eight times a year. $1375.00. Mealey Publications, PO Box 446, Wayne PA 19087-0446. **Tel** (215)688-6566, FAX (215)688-7552. **ED** W. Thomas Hagy. **LC** KF1147; .M4. **DD** 346.73/086/05; 347.3068605. **[CCC]**. Index available. cum. index.
Desc: Document and editorial coverage of declaratory judgment actions involving insurance coverage for latent property damage and personal injury claims.

US/1043-8416
MEALEY'S LITIGATION REPORTS. INSURANCE INSOLVENCY. [Mealey's litig. rep., Insur. insolv.]. **Added/Corp** Mealey Publications. **VFOAT** Insurance Insolvency. Vol. 1, Issue No. 1 (June 7, 1989)-. Periodical. English. sm (2 issues per month). $795.00. Mealey Publications, PO Box 446, Wayne PA 19087-0446. **Tel** (215)688-6566, FAX (215)688-7552. **ED** Susan A. Winchurch. **LC** KF1535.I58; A496. **DD** 016.34673/078; 016.34730678. **[CCC]**. Index available. cum. index. available on diskette.
Desc: Covers legal and financial implications of insurer insolvencies.

●US/1065-9390
MEALEY'S LITIGATION REPORTS. INTELLECTUAL PROPERTY. [Mealey's litig. rep., Intellect. prop.]. **Added/Corp** Mealey Publications. **VFOAT** Litigation Reports. Intellectual Property; Intellectual Property; Mealy's Litigation Report. Intellectual Property. Vol. 1, Issue #1 (Oct. 5, 1992)-. English. sm. $750.00. Mealey Publications, PO Box 446, Wayne PA 19087-0446. **Tel** (215)688-6566, FAX (215)688-7552. **LC** KF2972; .M4. **DD** 346.7304/8/05; 347.3064805.

US/1059-4116
MEALEY'S LITIGATION REPORTS. LEAD. [Mealey's litig. rep., Lead]. **Added/Corp** Mealey Publications. **VFOAT** Litigation Reports. Lead; Lead. Vol. 1, Issue #1 (Oct. 3, 1991)-. Periodical. English. sm. $650.00. Mealey Publications, PO Box 446, Wayne PA 19087-0446. **Tel** (215)688-6566, FAX (215)688-7552. **LC** KF3964.L43; A135. **DD** 344.73/0472; 347.304472. **[CCC]**.

●US/1070-4043
MEALEY'S LITIGATION REPORTS. PATENTS. [Mealey's litig. rep., Pat.]. **Added/Corp** Mealey Publications. **VFOAT** Patents. Vol. 1, Issue #1 (June 14, 1993)-. Periodical. English. sm. $450.00. Mealey Publications, PO Box 446, Wayne PA 19087-0446. **Tel** (215)688-6566, FAX (215)688-7552. **LC** KF3109; .M39. **DD** 346.7304/86; 347.306486.

US/1070-4035
MEALEY'S LITIGATION REPORTS. PREMISES LIABILITY. (MEALEY'S LITIGATION REPORTS. PREMISES LIABILITY : COVERING NEGLIGENT SECURITY & SUPERVISION LAWSUITS ARISING FROM THIRD-PARTY CRIME.). [Mealey's litig. rep., Premises liabil.]. **Added/Corp** Mealey Publications. **VFOAT** Premises Liability. Vol. 1, Issue #1 (June 11, 1993)-. Periodical. English. sm. $650.00. Mealey Publications, PO Box 446, Wayne PA 19087-0446. **Tel** (215)688-6566, FAX (215)688-7552. **LC** KF1287.A59; M4. **DD** 346.7303/2; 347.30632.

●US/1064-1475
MEALEY'S LITIGATION REPORTS. TOXIC TORTS. [Mealey's litig. rep. Toxic torts]. **Added/Corp** Mealey Publications. **VFOAT** Litigation Reports. Toxic Torts; Toxic Torts. Vol. 1, Issue #1 (Apr. 2, 1992)-. English. sm. $695.00. Mealey Publications, PO Box 446, Wayne PA 19087-0446. **Tel** (215)688-6566, FAX (215)688-7552. **LC** KF1301.H39; A134. **DD** 346.7303/8; 347.30638. ***Absorbed*** *Measley's Litigation Reports Tobacco.*

FR/1246-7391
MEDECINE ET DROIT. **See** Medical Science and Technology.

●US/1065-965X
MEDIA AND THE LAW (GREENWICH, CONN.). **See** Communication-Broadcasting.

US/0736-1750
MEDIA LAW NOTES. (MEDIA LAW NOTES : NEWSLETTER FOR THE LAW DIVISION OF AEJ & THE MASS COMMUNICATIONS LAW SECTION OF AALS.). [Media law notes]. **Added/Corp** Association for Education in Journalism. Law Division. Association of American Law Schools. Mass Communications Law Section. (197?)-. Newsletter. English. qt. $12.00. AEJMC / South Carolina, University of South Carolina, 1621 College Street, J McGill, Columbia SC 29208. **LC** KF2750.A15; M4. **DD** 343.73/099/05; 347.3039905. **Circ:** 500 (ctrl). ***Continues*** *Tortfeasor.*
Ind/Abst Curr. Law Index (1980-); Leg. Resour. Index (1980-?); LegalTrac (1982-).

US/0148-1045
MEDIA LAW REPORTER. [Media law report.]. **Main/Corp** Bureau of National Affairs (Washington, D.C.). (Jan. 1977)-. Periodical. English. wk. $933.00. Bureau of National Affairs Inc., 9435 Key West Avenue, Rockville MD 20850. **Tel** (800)372-1033, (301)258-1033, FAX (301)948-5823. **(Subscription address:** 9435 Key West Avenue, Rockville MD 20850; telephone: FAX (301)948-5823**)** **ED** Cynthia J Bolbach. **LC** KF2750; .A513. **DD** 343/.73/0994. **[CCC]**. **Circ:** 1,200 (ctrl).
Desc: A reference service containing the full-text of federal and state court decisions and selected agency rulings affecting newspapers, magazines, radio, television, film and other media.

US/0145-5583
MEDICAL DIRECTORY (WATERVILLE). **See** Medical Science and Technology-Physicians and Medical Personnel.

AT
MEDICAL FRAUD AND OVERSERVICING / THE PARLIAMENT OF THE COMMONWEALTH OF AUSTRALIA, JOINT COMMITTEE OF PUBLIC ACCOUNTS. **Added/Corp** Australia. Parliament. Joint Committee of Public Accounts. **VFOAT** Minutes of Evidence, Medical Fraud and Overservicing. Vol. 1 (July 1982)-. Periodical. English. ir. **LC** HD7102.A8; M42. **DD** 364.1/63.

US/0098-4833
MEDICAL LAW LETTER FOR PHYSICIANS, SURGEONS & HEALTH PROFESSIONALS, THE. **VAT** The Medical Law Letter for Physicians, Surgeons, and Health Professionals. Periodical. English. mo. $60.00. Physicians Medical Law Letter Inc, 133 East 73rd Street, New York NY 10021. **LC** KF1289.A15; M4. **DD** 346/.73/033.

UK/0957-9346
MEDICAL LAW REPORTS. [Med. law rep.]. (1989)-. English. Ten times a year. £110.00 UK; £125.00 others. Business & Medical Publications Limited, Saxeway Business Centre, Chartridge Lane, Chesham, Bucks HP5 2SH England. **Tel** 011 44 494 792621, FAX 011 44 494 793098, telex 86402. **ED** Geoffrey Hall. **DD** 342.441. Index available. **Bk Rev**. **Ad Acc**, **Adv Mgr:** J. Arcker, **Tel** 011 44 494 79262.
Desc: All about medical law reports.

●UK/0967-0742
MEDICAL LAW REVIEW. **Added/Corp** King's College (University of London). Centre of Medical Law and Ethics. Vol. 1, No. 1 (Spring 1993)-. Periodical. English. tq. £80.00 UK and Europe; $150.00 other. Oxford University Press, Walton Street, Oxford OX2 6DP England. **Tel** 011 44 865 56767, FAX 011 44 865 267773, telex 837330 OXPRES G. **(Subscription address:** Oxford University Press / USA, Journals Marketing Department, Oxford University Press, 2001 Evans Road, Cary NC 27513.**)** **ED** Ian Kennedy and Andrew Grubb. **NLM** W1; ME361T. **[CCC]**. **Circ:** 2000.

US/0732-9636
MEDICAL LIABILITY MONITOR. [Med. liabil. monit.]. Vol. 6, No. 9 (Sept. 1981)-. Periodical. English. Twelve times a year. $150.00. Malpractice Lifeline Inc, PO Box 9011, Winnetka IL 60093. **Tel** (312)441-6474. **ED** Carol B. Golin. **NLM** W1 ME366M. **Bk Rev**. **Circ:** 500. ***Continues*** *Malpractice Lifeline, 0361-8412.*
Desc: Newsletter reporting medical liability news; claims, severity, insurance availability and cost, legal aspects, legislation, risk management, audience, physicians, hospitals, insurers, attorneys, risk managers policy makers.

US/0199-1833
MEDICAL LIABILITY REPORTER. [Med. liabil. report.]. **Added/Corp** Litigation Research Group (San Francisco, Calif.). Vol. 1 (Sept. 1979)-. Periodical. English. mo. $295.00. Shepards McGraw-Hill Inc, 555 Middle Creek Parkway, PO Box 35300, Colorado Springs CO 80935-3530. **Tel** (719)488-3000, FAX (800)525-0053. **ED** Kevin Bushnell. **LC** KF2905.3.A59; M4. **DD** 346.7303/32/02648. **NLM** W1; ME366P. cum. index. **Circ:** 825.
Desc: Opinions and case summaries for attorneys who practice litigation in the healthcare industry.

●US/1067-1269
MEDICAL LITIGATION ALERT. [Med. litig. alert]. (1992)-. Periodical. English. mo (12 issues). $250.00. Jury Verdict Review Publications Inc., 24 Commerce Street/Suite 1722, Newark NJ 07102. **Tel** (201)624-1665. **DD** 344.

US/0893-8229
MEDICAL MALPRACTICE DEFENSE REPORTER, THE. ***Ceased.*** [Med. malpract. def. report.]. **VFOAT** Reporter. Vol. 1, No. 1 (Sept. 1987)-(19??). Periodical. English. qt. Professional Reports Corporation, 4418 Belden Village Street Northwest, Canton OH 44718. **Tel** (216)492-6063, (800)336-0083, FAX (216)492-6176. **ED** Molly J. Romig. **LC** KF2905.3.A15; M433. **DD** 346.7303/32/05; 347.30633205. Index available. cum. index. **Bk Rev**. **Ad Acc**. **Pr Rev**. **Circ:** 100.
Desc: Designed for medical malpractice carriers and their attorneys. It provides current case and legislation information, trends of practice recommendations and expert witness information.

US/0747-8925
MEDICAL MALPRACTICE LAW & STRATEGY. [Med. malpract. law strategy]. **VFOAT** Medical Malpractice Law and Strategy; Medical Malpractice. (1983)-. Periodical. English. mo. $185.00. Leader Publications, 345 Park Avenue South, New York NY 10010. **Tel** (800)888-8300 ext. 6170, (212)545-6170, FAX (212)696-1848. **ED** Cynthia Cooper. **LC** KF2905.3.A15; M435. **DD** 346.7303/32/05; 347.30633205. **NLM** W 32.5; AA1 M388. cum. index.
Desc: Reports on judicial and legislative developments in medical malpractice law; includes verdicts, settlements, articles on negotiation and litigation strategy by practitioners.

US/0277-7266
MEDICAL MALPRACTICE LITIGATION. English. Practising Law Institute, 810 Seventh Avenue, New York NY 10019-5818. **Tel** (212)765-5700, FAX (212)581-4670 general correspondence, (212)265-4742 orders and billing inquiries. **LC** KF2905.3.Z9; M4. **DD** 346.7303/32; 347.306332.

US/0882-8555
MEDICAL MALPRACTICE LITIGATION REPORTER. ***Title Change.*** [Med. malpract. litig. report.]. (April 2, 1985)-(19??). Periodical. English. sm. Andrews Publications Inc., 1646 West Chester Pike, PO Box 1000, Westtown PA 19395. **Tel** (610)399-6600, (800)345-1101, FAX (610)399-6610. **ED** Leonard E B Andrews. **LC** KF2905.3.A59; M43. **DD** 346.7303/32; 347.306332. ctrl circ. ***Absorbed by*** *Medical Malpractice OB/GYN Litigation Reporter, 1056-4098.*
Desc: Provides information on the latest medical malpractice, obstetrical and gynecological-related litigation.

US/0885-744X
MEDICAL MALPRACTICE PREVENTION. ***Suspended.*** [Med. malpract. prev.]. (1986)-(1994). Periodical. English. bm. $60.00 US; $24.00 medical students, $75.00 other. World Medical Communications Organizations, 7 Ridgedale Avenue, Cedar Knolls NJ 07927. **Tel** (201)455-1121. **ED** Donald W Aaronson. **DD** 346. Index available. **Bk Rev**. **Ad Acc**. **Circ:** 85,000 (ctrl).
Desc: Medical malpractice case histories with medical lessons to be learned.

US/0888-658X
MEDICAL MALPRACTICE VERDICTS, SETTLEMENTS & EXPERTS. [Med. malpract. verdicts, settl. experts]. **VFOAT** Medical Malpractice Verdits, Settlements, and Experts. Vol. 1, No. 1 (June 1985)-. Periodical. English. mo. M. Lee Smith Publishers and Printers, 162 4th Avenue North, PO Box 198867, Nashville TN 37219. **Tel** (615)242-7395, (800)274-6774, FAX (615)256-6601. **LC** KF2905.3.A59; M45. **DD** 346.7303/32; 347.306332. **NLM** W 32.5; AA1 M39.
Ind/Abst Health Devices Alerts.

US
MEDICAL PRACTICE FOR TRIAL LAWYERS. English. an. $99.95. Harrison Company Publishers, 3110 Crossing Park, PO Box 7500, Norcross GA 30091-7500. **Tel** (800)241-3561, (404)447-9150.

●US/1061-4192
MEDICAL RECORD RISKS, CLAIMS & LITIGATION. **VFOAT** Claims & Litigation; Medical Record Risks. (1992)-. Periodical. English. mo (12 issues). $250.00 US; $336.00 other. Cox Publications, PO Box 20316, Billings MT 59104-0316. **Tel** (406)256-8822.

US/0161-3251
MEDICAL TRIAL TECHNIQUE QUARTERLY ANNUAL. 1954/55-. English. an. Clark Boardman Callaghan, 155 Pfingsten Road, Deerfield IL 60015. **Tel** (800)323-8067. **NLM** W1 ME5279. cum. index.

US/1060-5355
MEDICARE AND MEDICAID LAW REPORTER. ***Ceased.*** [Medicare Medicaid law report.]. (Jan. 1992)-(1994). English. Fifty times a year. $695.00 (includes postage). LRP Publications, 747 Dresher Road, PO Box 980, Horsham PA 19044-0980. **Tel** (800)341-7874, (215)784-0860, FAX (215)784-9639, (215)784-0870. **DD** 346.
Desc: Designed to meet the legal research needs of attorneys practicing Medicare and Medicaid law and others interested in these issues.

JA
MEIJI DAIGAKU KEIJI HAKUBUTSUKAN MOKUROKU. **Main/Corp** Meiji Daigaku. Keiji Hakubutsukan. No. 1 (1952)-. Japanese. Meiji Daigaku Keiji Hakubutsukan Iinkai, 1 Kanda Surugakai 1, Chiyoda-ku, Tokyo Japan. **LC** Z3306; .M44A.

JA
MEIJI DAIGAKU KEIJI HAKUBUTSUKAN NEMPO. **Main/Corp** Meiji Daigaku, Tokyo. Meiji Hakubutsukan. Japanese. 1 Kanda Surugadai 1 Chiyoda-ku, Tokyo Japan. **LC** DS803; .M44A.

AT/0254-0657
MELANESIAN LAW JOURNAL. [Melanes. law j.]. Vol. 1, No. 1 (Dec. 1970)-. English. sa. 47.00Aus$ except for Canada. Law Book Company Ltd, 44 50 Waterloo Road, North Ryde 2113 Australia. **Tel** 61 2 8870177. **LC** K13; .E335. **DD** 340/.05.
Ind/Abst Aust. Leg. Mon. Dig.; Index Foreign Leg. Per.; Int. Bibliogr. Sociol.; Leg. Resour. Index (1980-); LegalTrac (1980-).

AT/0025-8938
MELBOURNE UNIVERSITY LAW REVIEW. [Melb. Univ. law rev.]. **Added/Corp** Melbourne University Law Review Association. **VFOAT** MULR; M.U.L.R. (July 1957)-. English. sa. Law Book Company Ltd, 44 50 Waterloo Road, North Ryde 2113 Australia. **Tel** 61 2 8870177. **LC** K13; .E34. **DD** 340/.05. ***Continues*** *Res Judicatae.*
Ind/Abst APAIS, Aust. Public Aff. Inf. Ser. (1963-); Aust. Leg. Mon. Dig.; Index Leg. Period.; Leg. Resour. Index; LegalTrac (1980-).

US/0538-446X
MEMBERSHIP DIRECTORY - INTERNATIONAL ASSOCIATION OF ASSESSING OFFICERS (1977). **See** Public Administration-Public Finance and Taxation.

US
MEMBERSHIP DIRECTORY - OREGON STATE BAR. **Main/Corp** Oregon State Bar. Directory. English. an. $15.00 members, $25.00 nonmembers. Oregon State Bar, 5200 Southwest Meadows Road, Lake Oswego OR 97035. **Tel** (503)620-0222 ext 340, (800)452-8260, FAX (503)684-1366. **LC** KF192.O7; O72. ***Continues*** *Lawyers' Deskbook and Directory, 0272-9725.*

FR
MEMENTO PRATIQUE FRANCIS LEFEBVRE : AGRICULTURE. French. 15 rue Viete, 75017 Paris France. **DD** 343.44/076/05; 344.4037605.

FR
MEMENTO PRATIQUE FRANCIS LEFEBVRE: FISCAL. (1976)-. French. an. Editions Francis Lefebvre, 5 rue Jacques Bingen, F-75854 Paris Cedex 17 France. **Tel** (1)47 63 12 60, FAX 46 22 72 66, telex 649 470 F. **DD** 343.4404. ***Continues*** *Memento Pratique du Contribuable.*
Desc: Information on legislation.

FR
MEMOIRES DE LA SOCIETE POUR L'HISTOIRE DU DROIT ET DES INSTITUTIONS DES ANCIENS PAYS BOURGUIGNONS, COMTOIS ET ROMANDS. **Main/Corp** Societe pour l'Histoire du Droit et des Institutions des Anciens Pays Bourguignons, Comtois et Romands, Dijon. **Added/Corp** Societe pour l'Histoire du Droit et des Institutions des Anciens Pays Bourguignons, Comtois et Romands. No. 1 (1932/1933)-. French. an. 120.00F. Memoires de la Societe pour l'Histoire du Droit et des Institutions, 4 BD Gabrielle, MME Chevrier, 21000 Dijon France. **Tel** 011 33 80 395000. cum. index.

CK
MEMORIA DEL ... FORO NACIONAL DE NOTARIADO Y REGISTRO. **Main/Conf** Foro Nacional de Notariado y Registro. Spanish. **LC** KHH250.A15; F67. **DD** 347.861/016; 348.610716.

US/0047-6714
MEMPHIS STATE UNIVERSITY LAW REVIEW. [Memphis State Univ. law rev.]. **VFOAT** Memphis State Law Review. V. 1, No. 1 (Fall 1970)-. Academic Scholarly Publication. English. qt. $18.00. Memphis State University / School of Law, Memphis TN 38152. **Tel** (901)678-2078. **LC** K24; .E47. **DD** 340/.05. Index available. cum. index. **Ad Acc. Circ:** 900. available on microfilm and microfiche from University Microfilms International (UMI); available on microfilm from WESTLAW. ***Continues*** *Memphis State University Law Commentary, 0543-4467.*
Desc: Scholarly legal journal including works by students, faculty, and legal professionals. Concentrating primarily on regional law.
Ind/Abst Bowne Dig. Corp. Sec. Lawyers; Curr. Law Index (1980-); Index Leg. Period.; Leg. Resour. Index (1980-); LegalTrac (1980-).

US/0883-7902
MENTAL AND PHYSICAL DISABILITY LAW REPORTER. [Ment. phys. disabil. law report.]. **VFOAT** MPDLR. Vol. 8, No. 1 (Jan./Feb. 1984)-. Periodical. English. bm (6 issues). $249.00. American Bar Association, 750 North Lake Shore Drive, Chicago IL 60611. **Tel** (312)988-5522, (312)988-5241, FAX (312)988-5528, telex 270593. **(Subscription address:** American Bar Association / Washington D.C., Comm. Mental, 1800 M Street Northwest, Washington DC 20036.) **ED** John W. Parry. **LC** KF480.A15. **DD** 344.73/044; 347.30444. **NLM** W1; ME9228J. Index available (bound in last issue). cum. index. **Bk Rev. Circ:** 1,500. ***Continues*** *Mental Disability Law Reporter, 0147-3700.*
Desc: Summarizes case law, legislative and regulatory developments affecting mentally and physically disabled persons, their service providers, friends and families.
Ind/Abst Crim. Justice Abstr.; Curr. Law Index (1984-); Leg. Resour. Index (1984-); LegalTrac (1984-); Psychol. Abstr. (1976-); PsycINFO; PsycLit.

US/0889-017X
MENTAL HEALTH LAW NEWS. [Ment. health law news]. Vol. 1, No. 1 (Jan. 1986)-. Periodical. English. mo. $89.00. Interwood Publications, 3 Interwood Place, PO Box 20241, Cincinnati OH 45220. **Tel** (513)221-3715. **ED** Frank J. Bardack. **LC** KF2910.P75; A496. **DD** 344.73/044; 347.30444.
Desc: Summaries of court cases in mental health law including: mental health malpractice, commitment, appropriate treatment, patient rights, consent, insanity defense, patient danger to community.

US/0741-5141
MENTAL HEALTH LAW REPORTER. [Ment. health law report.]. **Added/Corp** Capitol Publications, inc. Vol. 1, No. 1 (May 1983)-. Periodical. English. mo. $234.00. Business Publishers Inc., 951 Pershing Drive, Silver Spring MD 20910-4464. **Tel** (301)587-6300, (800)274-0122, FAX (301)585-9075. **LC** KF480.A15; M43. **DD** 345.73/04; 347.3054. **[CCC].**
Desc: Brings you 10 full pages of the news you need to know about mental health law: malpractice litigation; patient-therapist confidentiality; the insanity defense; and social security admistrative case law. Also administrative you the most timely, focused, and thorough information on the legal issues that concern you.

US/0164-2650
MENTAL HYGIENE LAW (NEW YORK). (MENTAL HYGIENE LAW.). **Main/Corp** New York (State). Laws, Statutes, etc. English. an. Matthew Bender & Company Inc., 1275 Broadway, Albany NY 12204. **Tel** (800)833-9844, (518)487-3000. **LC** KFN5620.A29; M46. **DD** 344/.747/044.
Desc: Covers mental health law.

US/0098-8111
MENTAL RETARDATION AND THE LAW. English. ir. President's Committee on Mental Retardation, 330 Independence Avenue Southwest, Washington DC 20201. **Tel** (202)245-7634. **ED** Lawrence A Kane, Julius Cohen, Phyliss Brown and George N Bouthilet. **LC** KF480.A59; M46. **DD** 344/.73/0323. **NLM** W1 ME936JF. **Circ:** 2,000.
Desc: Papers presented at the second national conference on legal rights for citizens with mental retardation.

US/0025-987X
MERCER LAW REVIEW. [Mercer law rev.]. **Added/Corp** Walter F. George School of Law. Vol. 1, No. 1 (Fall 1949)-. Periodical. English. Four times a year (Jan., Apr., June, Aug.). $40.00. Mercer University / School of Law, School of Law, Macon GA 31207. **Tel** (912)752-2622, FAX (912)752-2259. **ED** Robert Weber (phone: (912)752-2624). **DD** 340/.05. Index available (4th iss. of each Vol.). **Ad Acc, Adv Mgr:** Jonathan Martin, **Tel** (912)752-2624. **Circ:** 1,600 (ctrl). available on microfilm, microfiche, and CD-ROM from University Microfilms International (UMI).
Desc: Legal periodical in which editorial revisions are made.
Ind/Abst Bowne Dig. Corp. Sec. Lawyers; Crim. Justice Abstr.; Curr. Law Index (1980-); Fed. Tax Artic.; Index Leg. Period.; Leg. Resour. Index (1980-); LegalTrac (1980-).

CN/0821-3690
MEREDITH MEMORIAL LECTURES (1975). (MEREDITH MEMORIAL LECTURES / THE FACULTY OF LAW, MCGILL UNIVERSITY.). [Meredith meml. lect.]. **VFOAT** Conferences Memorial Meredith. 1975-. Periodical. French (English). an. 6.00Can$. Wilson & Lafleur Ltd., 40 Rue Notre Dame East, Montreal, Quebec H2Y 1B9 Canada. **Tel** (514)875-6326, FAX (514)875-8356. **DD** 346.71/066. ***Continues*** *W. C. J. Meredith Memorial Lectures, 0509-5166.*
Ind/Abst Can. Legal Lit.; Index Can. Leg. Period. Lit.

US/1063-3014
MERRILL'S ILLINOIS LEGAL TIMES. [Merrill's Ill. leg. times]. **VFOAT** Illinois Legal Times. Vol. 1, No. 1 (May 1987)-. Periodical. English. Twelve times a year. $48.00. Illinois Legal Times, 222 Merchandise Mart Place, Suite 1513, Chicago IL 60654. **Tel** (312)644-4378, FAX (312)644-0765. **ED** Kelly Fox. **LC** K13; .E374. **DD** 349.773; 347.73. **Ad Acc, Adv Mgr:** Chuck Carman. ctrl circ. available on an online database from LEXIS; and WESTLAW.
Desc: Articles and columns deal with how to manage a law firm or practice. The publication routinely addresses strategic planning, marketing, law office technology, qualtity of life and associate training.
Ind/Abst Law Office Inf. Serv.

US/0197-7458
METADATA'S LEGALGRAM FOR THE COMMUNICATIONS INDUSTRY. **VFOAT** Metadata's Legalgram; Legalgram for the Communications Industry. Vol. 1, No. 1 (Apr. 8, 1980)-. Periodical. English. sm. $137.00. Metadata, PO Box 585, Locust NJ 07760. **Tel** (212)687-3836. **LC** KF2750.A15; M47. **DD** 343.73/099/05; 347.3039905.
Desc: Each issue includes a separate section with title: MetaData's legalnotes.

US/0897-2281
METROPOLITAN NEWS-ENTERPRISE. **See** Newspapers.

US/1058-5702
MEXICO TRADE AND LAW REPORTER. **See** Business-Commerce.

US/0196-7649
MICHIGAN APPELLATE DIGEST. **Added/Corp** Michigan Court of Appeals. (19??)-. Periodical. English. mo (11 issues). $225.00. Michigan Appellate Digest, 600 Washington Square Building, Lansing MI 48933. **Tel** (517)373-3869. **LC** KFM4248.1; .M53. **DD** 348.774/046.

US/0164-3576
MICHIGAN BAR JOURNAL, THE. [Mich. Bar j.]. **Added/Corp** State Bar of Michigan. Vol. 58 (Jan. 1979)-. Periodical. English. mo. $35.00 US. State Bar of Michigan, 306 Townsend Street, Lansing MI 48933. **Tel** (517)372-9030. **ED** Nancy F. Brown (editor's telephone: (517)372-9030 ext. 3050). **LC** KF200; .M5. **DD** 349.73/05. cum. index. **Bk Rev. Ad Acc, Adv Mgr:** Mary Stowell, **Tel** (517)372-9030 ext. 3035. **Circ:** 28,200. available on microfilm and microfiche from University Microfilms International (UMI). ***Continues*** *Journal (State Bar of Michigan), 0162-5101.*
Desc: Includes substantive law articles as well as organization business.
Ind/Abst Curr. Law Index (1980-); Fed. Tax Artic.; Highw. Res. Abstr.; Index Leg. Period.; Law Office Inf. Serv.; Leg. Resour. Index (1980-); LegalTrac (1980-).

US/0026-2234
MICHIGAN LAW REVIEW. [Mich. law rev.]. **Added/Corp** University of Michigan. Law School. University of Michigan. Dept. of Law. Vol. 1, No. 1 (June 1902)-. Academic Scholarly Publication. English. Eight times a year. $40.00 US; $46.00 other. Michigan Law Review Association, Hutchins Hall, Ann Arbor MI 48109. **Tel** (313)763-5870, FAX (313)764-8309. **ED** Jenne Moldovan. **LC** K13; .I35. **DD** 340/.05. **NLM** W1 MI216. cum. index. **Bk Rev**, (Qty: 6). **Ad Acc. Pr Rev. Circ:** 3,000 (ctrl). available in microform; available in print from Williams S Hein & Co.; available on an online database from WESTLAW; LEXIS; and (file 15/Full-Text) DIALOG. Documents available from The Genuine Article, UMI Article Clearinghouse.
Desc: A scholarly legal publication.
Ind/Abst ABI/INFORM Glob. Ed.; ABI Inform Ondisc (Aug. 1972-); Account. Index, Suppl.; Arts Humanit. Citation Index [Select. Cov.]; Bowne Dig. Corp. Sec. Lawyers; Crim. Justice Abstr.; Curr. Contents Soc. Behav. Sci.; Curr. Law Index (1980-); Econ. Lit. Index; Expand. Acad. Index (1989-); Fed. Tax Artic.; Health Plan. Adminis.; Hospit. Health Admin. Index; Index Leg. Period.; J. Econ. Lit.; Leg. Resour. Index (1980-); LegalTrac (1980-); Manage. Contents (1974-); Newsp.

Period. Abstr. (1989-); PAIS Int. Print (1991-); Public Aff. Inf. Serv. Bull.; Res. Alert [Full Cov.]; Soc. Sci. Cit. Index [Full Cov.]; SportSearch; Urban Aff. Abstr.; Writ. Am. Hist.

US/0897-618X
MICHIGAN LAWYERS WEEKLY. [Mich. lawyers wkly.]. **VFOAT** Lawyers Weekly. Vol. 1, No. 1 (Nov. 17, 1986)-. Newspaper. English. Fifty-two times a year. $225.00. Michigan Lawyers Weekly, 333 South Washington Square, Suite 300, Lansing MI 48933. **Tel** (800)678-5297, (517)374-6200, FAX (517)374-6222. **ED** Edward Wesoloski. **LC** K13; .I353. **DD** 349.73/09774/05; 347.300977405. Index available. **Ad Acc. Circ:** 5,000 (ctrl).
Desc: Provides summaries of court opinions and up-to-date legal information.

US/1059-2105
MICHIGAN MUNICIPAL LEAGUE AND MICHIGAN ASSOCIATION OF MUNICIPAL ATTORNEYS MONOGRAPH SERIES. **Added/Corp** Michigan Municipal League. Michigan Association of Municipal Attorneys. **VFOAT** Drafting Enacting and Maintaining Local Ordinances. (1991)-. Monographic series. English. sa. $25.00 (members), $40.00 (non-members). Michigan Municipal League, PO Box 1487, Ann Arbor MI 48106. **Tel** (313)662-3246.

US/0892-3124
MICHIGAN REGISTER. [Mich. regist.]. **Main/Corp** Michigan. Legislative Council. **Added/Corp** Michigan. Legislative Service Bureau. Michigan. Michigan Administrative Code. No. 1 (Jan. 1984)-. Periodical. English. mo. $50.00. Michigan Department of Management and Budget, PO Box 30026, Lansing MI 48909. **Tel** (517)373-5644. **LC** KFM4236; .M53. **DD** 342.774/066; 347.740266.

US/0899-2460
MICHIGAN TAX LAWYER. [Mich. tax lawyer]. **Added/Corp** State Bar of Michigan. Taxation Section. (1988)-. Periodical. English. qt. State Bar of Michigan, 306 Townsend Street, Lansing MI 48933. **Tel** (517)372-9030. **LC** KFM4670.A15; M5. **DD** 343.77404/05 /A 347.7303405. ***Continues** Michigan Tax Law Journal, 0273-9984.*
Ind/Abst Leg. Resour. Index; LegalTrac (1988-).

US/0738-6753
MIDWEST AGRICULTURAL LAW JOURNAL. [Midwest agric. law j.]. Vol. 1, No. 1 (Oct./Nov. 1983)-. Periodical. English. bm. $75.00. Mason Publishing Company, 289 East 5th Street, St Paul MN 55101-1904. **LC** KF1681.A15; M53. **DD** 343.77/076/05; 347.7037605.
Desc: Covers agricultural laws and legislation.

US/0360-5094
MIDWESTERN ADVOCATE. Periodical. English. mo. Midwestern Advocate, 1536 Hewitt Avenue, St Paul MN 55104. **LC** KF292.M56414; A45. **DD** 340/.05.

US
MIFFLIN COUNTY LEGAL JOURNAL. v. 1- ; 1961-. English. ir. William Gaunt and Sons Inc, 3011 Gulf Drive, Holmes Beach FL 33510. **LC** KFP52.M5.

NE
MILIEU AANSPRAKELIJKHEID. **See** Environmental Issues-Conservation and Natural Resources.

UK
MILLER PRODUCT LIABILITY SAFETY ENCYCLOPEDIA. (19??)-. English. Fifteen times a year. Price varies per issue. Butterworth & Co. Ltd. / Kent, England, Borough Green, Sevenoaks Kent TN15 8PH England. **Tel** 011 44 732-884567, FAX 011 44 732-885996.

US/0148-3242
MILWAUKEE LAWYER, THE. ***Ceased.*** **Added/Corp** Milwaukee Bar Association. Vol. 1 (Fall 1976)-(19??). Periodical. English. qt. Milwaukee Bar Association, 610 East Wisconsin Avenue, Milwaukee WI 53202-4604. **Tel** (414)274-6760. **ED** Arthur J Harrington and Alyson K Sloan. **LC** KF200; .M53. **DD** 340/.06/277595. **Ad Acc. Circ:** 5,000. ***Supersedes** MBA Gavel.*
Desc: All articles are law related and most written by attorneys or judges.
Ind/Abst Law Office Inf. Serv.

US/1040-8223
MINE REGULATION REPORTER. [Mine regul. rep.]. Vol. 1, No. 1 (Oct. 14, 1988)-. Periodical. English. Twenty-five times a year. $785.00 US; $815.00 other. Pasha Publications Inc., 1616 North Fort Myer Drive, Suite 1000, Arlington VA 22209. **Tel** (800)424-2908, (703)528-1244, FAX (703)528-3742, (703)528-1253. **LC** KF3574.M5; A136. **DD** 343.73/0775/05; 347.30377505. **CODEN** MRREEE. **[CCC].** available on an online database (file 636/Full-Text) from DIALOG. ***Formed by the union of** Surface Mining Reporter, 0739-4020 **and** Mine Safety & Health Reporter, 0192-4745.*
Ind/Abst PTS Newsl. Database [Full Txt.].

US/0897-6694
MINERAL LAW NEWSLETTER. (MINERAL LAW NEWSLETTER / ROCKY MOUNTAIN MINERAL LAW FOUNDATION.). [Miner. law newsl.]. **Added/Corp** Rocky Mountain Mineral Law Foundation. Vol. 1, No. 1 (1984)-. Newsletter. English. qt. $30.00 (law school members); $60.00 (other). Rocky Mountain Mineral Law Foundation, Porter Administration Building, 7039 East 18th Avenue, Denver CO 80220. **Tel** (303)321-8100, FAX (303)321-7657. **ED** John S. Lowe and Mark S. Squillace. **DD** 346. **Pr Rev. Circ:** 450. available in hardback.
Desc: Thirty-six reporters representing 22 states and Canada report on current judicial, legislative, and regulatory developments in natural resources law. Coverage also includes federal courts and agencies, Congress, natural gas litigation, environmental issues, ethics, and significant finance and tax developments. State coverage includes Alabama, Alaska, Arizona, Arkansas, California, Colorado, Idaho, Kansas, Louisiana, Mississippi, Montana, Nebraska, Nevada, New Mexico, North Dakota, Oklahoma, Oregon, South Dakota, Texas, utah, Washington, and Wyoming.

US/0897-0122
MINERAL LAW SERIES. [Miner. law ser.]. **Added/Corp** Rocky Mountain Mineral Law Foundation. No. 1 (1988)-. Monographic series. English. Price varies per volume. Rocky Mountain Mineral Law Foundation, Porter Administration Building, 7039 East 18th Avenue, Denver CO 80220. **Tel** (303)321-8100, FAX (303)321-7657. **DD** 346.
Ind/Abst Leg. Resour. Index; LegalTrac (1988-).

CN/0821-0799
MINI-RECUEIL DE RENSEIGNEMENTS FISCAUX. [Mini-recueil de renseignements fiscaux]. French (English). an. Free. Mini-Recueil de Renseignements Fiscaux, Coopers & Lybrand, 1170 Peel Street, Montreal Quebec H3B 4T2 Canada. **DD** 343.7105/2/05. ctrl circ.

US/0418-4432
MINIMIS, DE. Began with May 1966 issue. English (English). McGeorge School of Law, 3401 Fifth Avenue, Sacramento CA 95817. **Tel** (916)739-7171. **LC** KF292.M314; A424. **DD** 340/.07/1179454.

US/0540-2239
MINNESOTA LAW ALUMNI NEWS. **See** College and School Publications-Alumni.

US/0026-5535
MINNESOTA LAW REVIEW. [Minn. law rev.]. **Added/Corp** University of Minnesota. Law School. Minnesota State Bar Association. Minnesota State Bar Association. Proceedings of the Minnesota State Bar Association. Vol. 1, No. 1 (Jan. 1917)-. Periodical. English. Six times a year. $30.00. University of Minnesota Law School, 229 19th Avenue South, Minneapolis MN 55455. **Tel** (612)625-8034. **LC** K13; .I55. cum. index. **Pr Rev.** Documents available from The Genuine Article.
Ind/Abst ABC POL SCI (19??-19??); Bowne Dig. Corp. Sec. Lawyers; Curr. Law Index (1980-); Fed. Tax Artic.; Index Leg. Period.; Leg. Resour. Index (1980-); LegalTrac (1980-); Res. Alert [Full Cov.]; Soc. Sci. Cit. Index [Full Cov.].

US/0749-0224
MINNESOTA LEGAL DIRECTORY, THE. [Minn. legal dir.]. 1982-1983-. Directory. English. an. Legal Directories Publishing Company, 9111 Garland Road, PO Box 189000, Dallas TX 75218. **Tel** (214)321-3238, 800 447-5375. **LC** KF192.M55; M56. **DD** 340/.025/776. ***Continues in part** Minnesota, Nebraska, North Dakota and South Dakota Legal Directory.*

US
MINNESOTA MOTOR VEHICLE LAW. **Main/Corp** Minnesota. English. ir. Masson SA, Avenue Beauregard 12, CH-1701 Fribourg Switzerland. **Tel** 011 41 37 249585, FAX 011 41 37 247559, telex 942658 SEMI CH. **(Subscription address:** 7A Boulevard de Perolles, CH-1701 Fribourg Switzerland**)**

US/0278-7628
MINNESOTA REAL ESTATE LAW JOURNAL. Vol. 1, No. 1 (Nov./Dec. 1981)-. Periodical. English. bm. $65.00. Butterworth Heinemann / Woburn, MA, 225 Wildwood Avenue, Unit B, Woburn MA 01801. **Tel** (800)366-2665, FAX (617)928-2620, telex 880052. **LC** KFM5512.A15; M56. **DD** 346.7304/3/05; 347.3064305.

US
MINNESOTA'S JOURNAL OF LAW AND POLITICS. English. mo. $29.00. BRJG Publishing Corporation, 10 South 5th Street, Minneapolis MN 55402. **Tel** (612)338-3828.

IT
MINORE GIUSTIZIA. (19??)-. Italian. qt. L64000 Italy; L90000 other. Franco Angeli Riviste SRL, Viale Monza 106, 20127 Milan Italy. **Tel** 011 39 2 2827651, 011 39 2 289562.

KO
MINSA PALLYE YONGU / MINSA PALLYE YONGUHOE PYON. **See** Political Science-Civil Rights.

CN/0710-6327
MINUTES OF PROCEEDINGS AND EVIDENCE OF THE SPECIAL COMMITTEE ON REGULATORY REFORM. [Minutes proc. evid. Spec. Comm. Regul. Reform]. **Main/Corp** Canada. Parlement. Chambre des Communes. Comite Special sur la Reforme de la Reglementation. **VFOAT** Proces-Verbaux et Temoignages du Comite Special sur la Reforme de la Reglementation. Issue No. 1 (Sept. 16, 1980)-. Proceedings. Multiple languages (English and French). Receiver General for Canada / Ottawa, Canada Comm Group Publishing, Ottawa Ontario K1A 0S9 Canada. **Tel** (819)956-4802, (800)661-2868. **DD** 348.71/025.

CN/0228-0825
MINUTES OF PROCEEDINGS AND EVIDENCE OF THE STANDING COMMITTEE ON MANAGEMENT AND MEMBERS' SERVICES. ***Title Change.*** [Minutes proc. evid. Standing Comm. Manage. Memb. Serv.]. **Main/Corp** Canada. Parlement. Chambre des Communes. Comite Permanent de la Gestion et des Services aux Deputes. **VFOAT** Proces-Verbaux et Temoignages du Comite Permanent de la Gestion et des Services aux Deputes. 31st Parliament, 1st Session, Issue No. 1 (Oct. 24, 1979/Nov. 14, 1979)-(19??). Proceedings. French (English). Imprimeur de la Reine pour le Canada, c/o Receiver General for Canada, Ottawa Ontario K1A 0S9 Canada. **DD** 328.71/0731. ***Continued by** Canada. Parlement. Chambre des Communes. Comite Permanent de la Gestion de la Chambre. Minutes of Proceedings and Evidence of the Standing Committee on House Management, 1187-2462.*

CN/0825-012X
MINUTES OF PROCEEDINGS AND EVIDENCE OF THE SUB-COMMITTEE ON INDIAN WOMEN AND THE INDIAN ACT OF THE STANDING COMMITTEE ON INDIAN AFFAIRS AND NORTHERN DEVELOPMENT. [Minutes proc. evid. Sub-comm. Indian Women Indian Act Standing Comm. Indian Aff. North. Dev.]. **Main/Corp** Canada. Parliament. House of Commons. Sub-Committee on Indian Women and the Indian Act. **VFOAT** Indian Women and the Indian Act; Proces-Verbaux et Temoignages du Sous-Comite sur les Femmes Indiennes et la Loi sur les Indienes du Comite Permanent des Affaires Indiennes et du Developpement du Nord Canadien; Indian Women and Indian Act. Issue No. 1 (Sept. 1/8, 1982)-. English (French). Canada Communication Group Publishers, Order Processing, Ottawa Ontario K1A 0S9 Canada. **Tel** (819)956-4800, (819)956-4802. **LC** KE7722.W6; A2445. **DD** 342.71/0872; 347.102872.

CN/0315-7253
MINUTES OF PROCEEDINGS OF THE ANNUAL CONFERENCE - ASSOCIATION OF SUPERINTENDENTS OF INSURANCE OF THE PROVINCES OF CANADA. [Minutes proc. annu. conf. - Assoc. Supt. Insur. Prov. Can.]. **Main/Corp** Association of Superintendents of Insurance of the Provinces of Canada. (1927)-. Proceedings. English. an (Mar.). 25.00can$. Association of Superintendents of Insurance of the Provinces of Canada, 555 Yonge Street, 6th Floor, Toronto Ontario M4Y 1Y7 Canada. **DD** 346/.71/08606171.

FR/1163-1651
MISE A JOUR EN DROIT D'AUTEUR, LA. (1991)-. Periodical. French. Five times a year. 240.00F France; $65.00 US; £48.00 other. Masson SA, Avenue Beauregard 12, CH-1701 Fribourg Switzerland. **Tel** 011 41 37 249585, FAX 011 41 37 247559, telex 942658 SEMI CH. **UDC** 347.77/.78.

US
MISSISSIPPI CODE 1972, ANNOTATED : ADOPTED AS THE OFFICIAL CODE OF THE STATE OF MISSISSIPPI BY THE 1972 SESSION OF THE LEGISLATURE. **Main/Corp** Mississippi. (1972)-. English. an. must order direct. Harrison Company Publishers, 3110 Crossing Park, PO Box 7500, Norcross GA 30091-7500. **Tel** (800)241-3561, (404)447-9150. cum. index.

US/0277-1152
MISSISSIPPI COLLEGE LAW REVIEW. [Miss. Coll. law rev.]. **Main/Corp** Mississippi College. School of Law. **Added/Corp** Mississippi College. Law review. Mississippi. Attorney General's Office. Opinions. Vol. 1 (June 1978)-. Periodical. English. sa. $20.00 US; $22.00 other. Mississippi College Law Review, 151 East Griffith Street, Jackson MS 39201. **Tel** (601)353-3908. **ED** Aileen McNeill. **LC** K13; .I776. **DD** 340/.09762. Index available. cum. index. **Bk Rev. Ad Acc.** ctrl circ.

Desc: A student publication dealing with timely subjects in the law. Primarily Mississippi and Fifth-Circuit oriented.
Ind/Abst Curr. Law Index (1980-); Index Leg. Period.; Leg. Resour. Index (1980-); LegalTrac (1980-).

US/0026-6280
MISSISSIPPI LAW JOURNAL. [Miss. law j.]. **Added/Corp** University of Mississippi. School of Law. Mississippi State Bar Association. Mississippi State Bar. Mississippi State Bar. Junior Bar Section. Vol. 1 (July 1928)-. Periodical. English. Three times a year (Jan., Apr., Oct.). $35.00. Mississippi Law Journal, PO Box 146, University MS 38677. **Tel** (601)232-7361. **ED** Joh Healy. **LC** K13; .I78. **DD** 349.762/05. Index available (Bound in 3rd issue). cum. index (10 yr index published separately). **Bk Rev. Ad Acc. Circ:** 1,000.
Desc: Publishes articles, comments, recent decisions, and book reviews in all areas of law. Contributors include academicians, attorneys, and law students.
Ind/Abst Bowne Dig. Corp. Sec. Lawyers; Curr. Law Index (1980-); Fed. Tax Artic.; Index Leg. Period.; Leg. Resour. Index (1980-); LegalTrac (1980-).

US
MISSISSIPPI LAW JOURNAL. CUMULATIVE TEN-YEAR INDEX FOR VOLUMES 41-50. **Added/Corp** University of Mississippi. School of Law. Mississippi State Bar Association. Mississippi State Bar. Mississippi State Bar. Junior Bar Section. Vol. 1 (July 1928)-. Periodical. English. Three times a year. $25.00. Mississippi Law Journal, PO Box 146, University MS 38677. **Tel** (601)232-7361. **ED** Betty Whittington Maynard. cum. index. **Bk Rev. Ad Acc. Circ:** 1,800 (ctrl).
Desc: Publishes articles, comments, recent decision, and book reviews in all areas of law. Contributions include academicians, attorneys, and law students.

US/0462-8551
MISSISSIPPI LAWYER, THE. [Miss. lawyer]. **Added/Corp** Mississippi State Bar. Vol. 1, No. 1 (Jan. 1954)-. Periodical. English. bm. Mississippi Lawyer, PO Box 2168, Jackson MS 39205. **Tel** (601)948-4471. **LC** KF200; .M55. **DD** 340/.06/0762.
Ind/Abst Fed. Tax Artic.

US/0738-2235
MISSISSIPPI LEGAL DIRECTORY, THE. Directory. English. an. £15.00. Legal Directories Publishing Company, 9111 Garland Road, PO Box 189000, Dallas TX 75218. **Tel** (214)321-3238, 800 447-5375. **LC** KF192.M57; M57. **DD** 349.762/025; 347.620025. ***Continues in part*** *Arkansas, Louisiana and Mississippi Legal Directory.*

US
MISSOURI BAR BULLETIN. Bulletin. English. Missouri Bar Association, 326 Monroe Street, Jefferson City MO 65101. **Tel** (314)635-4128.

US/0745-7642
MISSOURI CASES REPORTED IN SOUTH WESTERN REPORTER, SECOND SERIES. [Mo. cases rep. South west. rep., second ser.]. **Main/Corp** Missouri. Supreme Court. **VFOAT** West's Missouri Cases. English. wk. $65.00. West Publishing Company, 610 Opperman Drive, PO Box 64526, Eagan MN 55123-1308. **Tel** (612)687-5618, (800)328-9352, FAX (612)687-5388, (800)562-2329. **(Subscription telephone:** FAX (612)688-3570**) DD** 348. ***Continues*** *Missouri Decisions Reported in South Western Reporter, Second Series.*

US
MISSOURI JUDICIAL REPORT. **Main/Corp** Missouri. Office of State Courts Administrator. FY 1981/1982-. English. an. Office of State Courts Administrator, 1105 Rear Southwest Boulevard, Jefferson City MO 65101. **Tel** (314)751-3585. **LC** KFM7871; .J8. **DD** 347.778/013/05; 347.78071305. **Circ:** 600. ***Continues*** *Missouri. Office of State Courts Administrator. Annual Statistical Report, 0731-4000.*
Desc: Includes caseload information, a year in review section, a description of Missouri's court system and information on judicial qualifications and selection in general.

US
MISSOURI LAW FINDER. 1983 Ed.-. English. an. West Publishing Company, 610 Opperman Drive, PO Box 64526, Eagan MN 55123-1308. **Tel** (612)687-5618, (800)328-9352, FAX (612)687-5388, (800)562-2329. **(Subscription telephone:** FAX (612)688-3570**) LC** KFM7861; .M58. **DD** 348.778/028; 347.780828.

US/0026-6604
MISSOURI LAW REVIEW. [Miss. law rev.]. V. 1-Jan. 1936-. English. qt. $20.00. University of Missouri Columbia / Hulston, Hulston Hall Room 15, Columbia MO 65211. **Tel** (314)882-9682. **ED** Dan Conlisk. **LC** K13; .I85. cum. index. **Bk Rev. Ad Acc. Circ:** 1,200. ***Supersedes*** *Law Series.*
Desc: Publish articles, case notes and comments concerning all areas of law for use by legal practitioners, law students and law professors.
Ind/Abst Bowne Dig. Corp. Sec. Lawyers; Curr. Law Index (1980-); Fed. Tax Artic.; Index Leg. Period.; Leg. Resour. Index (1980-); LegalTrac (1980-); PAIS Int. Print (1991-).

US
MISSOURI LEGAL DIRECTORY, THE. Directory. English. an. $29.42. Legal Directories Publishing Company, 9111 Garland Road, PO Box 189000, Dallas TX 75218. **Tel** (214)321-3238, 800 447-5375. **LC** KF192.M58; M55. **DD** 340/.025/778.

US/0149-2942
MISSOURI REGISTER. [Mo. regist.]. **Main/Corp** Missouri. Office of the Secretary of State. Vol. 1 (May 3, 1976)-. Periodical. English. sm. $56.00. Missouri Register, Secretary of State Administrative Rules Division, 301 West High Street, Jefferson City MO 65102. **Tel** (314)751-4015. **ED** Carolan Underwood. **LC** KFM7834.A2; S4. **DD** 348/.778/025. **Circ:** 850.
Desc: Rules on agriculture, medicine, business, environment, education, conservation, housing, professional registration, mental health, medicare, aging, drugs, and law enforcement, affecting Missouri citizens.

GW
MITTEILUNGEN - ARBEITSGEMEINSCHAFT FUR JURISTISCHES BIBLIOTHEKS- (GERMANY). **Main/Corp** Arbeitsgemeinschaft fur Juristisches Bibliotheks- und Dokumentationswesen (Germany). German. Mittelweg 187, 2 Hamburg 13 Germany.

FR/0026-9719
MOCI; MONITEUR DU COMMERCE INTERNATIONAL, LE. [MOCI, Monit. commer. int.]. **Added/Corp** Centre Francais du Commerce Exterieur. **VFOAT** MOCI; Moniteur du Commerce Exterieur. New Series, No. 1-2 (Oct. 1972)-. Periodical. French. Fifty-two times a year (Mon.). 1,910F France; 2,280.00F others. Librairie de Commerce International, 24 Boulevard de l'Hopital, 75005 Paris Cedex 05 France. **Tel** 011 33 1 40733000, FAX 011 33 43364798, telex 206 811. Index available. **Bk Rev. Ad Acc. Circ:** 15,000 (ctrl). ***Continues*** *Moniteur du Commerce International.*
Ind/Abst Infomat Int. Bus.; PAIS Int. Print (1991-); PROMT.

CE
MODERN LAW REPORTS, EMBODYING CASES DECIDED BY THE SUPREME COURT OF THE REPUBLIC OF SRI LANKA. **Main/Corp** Sri Lanka. Sresthadhikaranaya. V. 1 (July 1975)-. Multiple languages (English and Sinhalese). Rs2.50. C L Perera, 29/12 Visaka Road 4, Colombo Sri Lanka Ceylon. **DD** 348/.5493/041.

UK/0026-7961
MODERN LAW REVIEW. (THE MODERN LAW REVIEW.). [Mod. law rev.]. Vol. 1 (June 1937)-. Academic Scholarly Publication. English. bm. £57.50 UK & Europe; $92.00 North America; £59.50 other. Basil Blackwell Publishers Ltd, 108 Cowley Road, Oxford 0X4 1JF England. **Tel** 011 44 865 791100, FAX 011 44 865 791347, telex 837022 OXBOOK G. **(Subscription address:** Blackwell Publishers / UK, Marston Book Services, PO Box 87, Oxford OX2 0DT England.**) ED** Simon Roberts. **LC** K13; .O27. **[CCC].** Index available. cum. index. **Bk Rev. Ad Acc. Circ:** 3,000. available on microfilm and microfiche from University Microfilms International (UMI).
Desc: An academic journal of law as a social science.
Ind/Abst Aust. Leg. Mon. Dig.; Br. Humanit. Index; Crim. Penol. Police Sci. Abstr.; Curr. Law Index (1980-); Index Leg. Period.; Int. Bibliogr. Sociol.; Int. Polit. Sci. Abstr.; Leg. Resour. Index (1980-); LegalTrac (1980-); School Organ. Manage. Abstr.

JA
MOHAN ROPPO. **Main/Corp** Japan. (1971)-. Periodical. Japanese. Sanseido, 1 Kanda Jinbocho 1, Chiyoda-ku 101, Tokyo Japan. ***Continues*** *Mohan Roppo Zensho.*

AT/0311-3140
MONASH UNIVERSITY LAW REVIEW. [Monash Univ. law rev.]. **Main/Corp** Monash University. Faculty of Law. Vol. 1, Aug. (1974)-. Periodical. English. sa. 30.00Aus$. Monash University Law Review, Monash University, Faculty of Law, Clayton Victoria 3168 Australia. **Tel** 011 61 3 5653374. **ED** Julienne Baron, Gregg Bosmans. **LC** K13; .O5. **DD** 340/.0994. Index available. **Bk Rev**, (Qty: 2). **Ad Acc. Pr Rev. Circ:** 500 (ctrl). available on microfilm and microfiche from University Microfilms International (UMI).
Desc: Primarily focuses on Australian legal issues, with articles by professionals, academicians and students; includes book reviews and case notes.
Ind/Abst APAIS, Aust. Public Aff. Inf. Ser. (1976-); Aust. Leg. Mon. Dig.; Curr. Law Index (1980-); Index Leg. Period.; Leg. Resour. Index (1980-); LegalTrac (1976-, 1980).

GW/0340-1812
MONATSSCHRIFT FUER DEUTSCHES RECHT. Vol. 1 (April 1947)-. Periodical. German. Twelve times a year. DM240.47 Germany; DM268.00 others. Verlag Dr. Otto Schmidt KG, Postfach 511026, D 50946 Cologne Germany. **Tel** 011 49 221 93738450. **ED** K. Mittelstein. **[CCC].** Index available. **Bk Rev. Ad Acc. Circ:** 7,100.
Ind/Abst Index Foreign Leg. Per.

CN/0828-4989
MONDE JURIDIQUE, LE. [Monde jurid.]. Vol. 1, No. 1 (Autumn 1984)-. Periodical. French (English). Ten times a year. $30.00. Le Monde Juridique, 381 Boul Richelieu, Saint-Basile-Le-Grand Quebec J0L 1S0 Canada. **Tel** (514)658-5983, FAX (514)288-4137, telex 286-9283. **ED** Andre Gagnon. **DD** 349.714. **Bk Rev. Ad Acc. Circ:** 16,507 (ctrl).
Desc: The legal profession with news about the law, how it is practiced, trends and features concerning major firms, small firms and lawyers and notaries and judges in Quebec, Canada and the world and court management.
Ind/Abst Index Can. Leg. Period. Lit.

IT
MONDO GIUDIZIARIO, IL. (April 1946)-. Periodical. Italian. wk. L170000.00. Il Mondo Giudiziario, Viale Angelico 90, 00195 Rome Italy. **Tel** 011 39 6 3721071, 011 39 6 3701541, FAX 011 39 6 3250961. Index available. cum. index. **Bk Rev**, (Qty: 30). **Ad Acc. Circ:** 5,400.

US/1050-4826
MONEY LAUNDERING LAW REPORT. [Money laund. law rep.]. Vol. 1, No. 1 (Aug. 1990)-. Periodical. English. mo. $195.00. Leader Publications, 345 Park Avenue South, New York NY 10010. **Tel** (800)888-8300 ext. 6170, (212)545-6170, FAX (212)696-1848. **ED** John K. Villa (editor's phone:(202)434-5117). **DD** 345. Index available.
Desc: Covers legal developments of interest to bankers and white-collar crime and money laundering practitioners.

US
MONITEUR BELGE. BELGISCH STAATSBLAD. **Main/Corp** Belgium. **Added/Corp** Belgium. Belgisch Staatsblad. **VFOAT** Belgisch Staatsblad. (1831)-. Newspaper. Multiple languages (Dutch and French). ir (299 per year). 3045.66F Belgium; 12345.66F other. Moniteur Belge, rue de Louvain 40-42, 1000 Brussels Belgium. **Tel** 011 32 2 5120026. **LC** Microfilm LL-02131KJM. Index available (free). **Ad Acc.**
Desc: Columns cover laws, decrees, government decisions, official announcements, legal publications, job vacancies, judicial decisions and sentences.

PL
MONITOR POLSKI : DZIENNIK URZEDOWY RZECZYPOSPOLITEJ POLSKIEJ. **Main/Corp** Poland. **Added/Corp** Poland. Rada Ministrow. **VFOAT** Dziennik Urzedowy Rzeczypospolitej Polskiej. (1918)-. Polish. ir. $75.00. **(Subscription address:** ARS Polona, PO Box 1001, 00068 Warsaw Poland.**)**
Desc: Provides information on legislation.

SZ
MONOGRAPH: LEGAL AND ADMINISTRATIVE SERIES. **Main/Corp** European Broadcasting Union. **VFOAT** EBU Monograph:; Legal and Administrative Series; Monograph: Legal and Administrative Series; EBU Monograph: Legal and Administrative Series. No. 4 (196?)-. Monographic series. English (French). ir. Price varies per volume. European Broadcasting Union, Case Postal 67, CH-1218 Geneva Switzerland. **Tel** 011 41 22 7172111. **Bk Rev. Circ:** 4,000. ***Continues*** *Legal Monograph, 0531-2841.*
Desc: Series of monographs on administrative and legal aspects of radio and television broadcasting.

US
MONOGRAPH SERIES. **Main/Corp** American Bar Association. Section of Litigation. No. 1 (1976)-. Monographic series. English. ir. Price varies per volume. American Bar Association, 750 North Lake Shore Drive, Chicago IL 60611. **Tel** (312)988-5522, (312)988-5241, FAX (312)988-5528, telex 270593.

US/0275-0791
MONROE LEGAL REPORTER. ***Suspended.*** Vol. 1 (1938/39)-Suspended with Vol. 25/26 (1976)-. English. wk. William W. Gaunt and Sons Inc, 3011 Gulf Drive, Gaunt Building, Holmes Beach FL 34217. **Tel** (800)942-8683, (813)778-5211. **DD** 348.747/88044.

US
MONTANA CASE NAMES CITATOR. English. $40.00 (1 bound volume), $48.00 (cumulative supplements). Shepards McGraw-Hill Inc, 555 Middle Creek Parkway, PO Box 35300, Colorado Springs CO 80935-3530. **Tel** (719)488-3000, FAX (800)525-0053.

US
MONTANA CODE ANNOTATED. **Main/Corp** Montana. **Added/Corp** Montana. Office of Code Commissioner. (1978)-. English. ir. $290.00. Montana Legislative Council, State Capitol/Room 138, Helena MT 59620-1706. **Tel** (406)444-3064, FAX (406)444-3036. **LC** KFM9029; .M66. **Circ:** 3,200. available on microfilm.
Desc: Annotations to titles 1-90 of the MCA statute

text-supplemental materials used in interpreting what has happened to the statutes, i.e. case notes, attorney general opinions, supreme court decisions.

US
MONTANA CODE ANNOTATED STATUTES TEXT. English. be. $360.00. Montana Legislative Council, State Capitol/Room 138, Helena MT 59620-1706. **Tel** (406)444-3064, FAX (406)444-3036. **ED** Mary Ellen Randall. **Circ:** 6,000. available on microfilm and microfiche; available on CD-ROM and an online database.
Desc: Case laws, Attorney General's opinions, etc., pertaining to the laws as recorded in the Montana Code Annotated statute text.

US/0026-9972
MONTANA LAW REVIEW. [Mont. law rev.]. **Added/Corp** University of Montana (Missoula). School of Law. Montana State University (Missoula). Law School Association. Vol. 1, No. 1 (Spring 1940)-. Periodical. English. Twice a year. $25.00 US; $26.00 other. University of Montana School of Law, Missoula MT 59812. **Tel** (406)243-2023, FAX (406)243-2576. **ED** Page Carroccia and James Conwell. **DD** 340. Index Available, published separately, free-automatically sent. cum. index. **Ad Acc. Circ:** 3,000. available on microfiche from Williams S Hein & Co.; available on an online database from WESTLAW. ***Absorbed** Proceedings of the Montana Bar Association, 0272-8281.* ***Continued in part by** Montana Bar Association Bulletin.*
Desc: Legal publication with primary emphasis on issues of Montana law.
Ind/Abst Bowne Dig. Corp. Sec. Lawyers; Curr. Law Index (1980-); Fed. Tax Artic.; Index Leg. Period.; Leg. Resour. Index (1980-); LegalTrac (1980-).

US
MONTANA LAW WEEK. English. wk. $265.00. Online Communications, Box 1236, Helena MT 59624. **Tel** (406)443-5202.

US/0276-3788
MONTANA LAWYER, THE. **Added/Corp** State Bar of Montana. (19??)-. Periodical. English. Ten times a year (except July and Aug.). $25.00. State Bar of Montana, PO Box 577, Helena MT 59624. **Tel** (406)442-7660, FAX (406)447-6179.

US
MONTANA SUPREME COURT PREVIEWS. English. mo. $100.00. Online Communications, Box 1236, Helena MT 59624. **Tel** (406)443-5202.

US
MONTGOMERY COUNTY LAW REPORTER. V. 1- 1885-. English. an. Montgomery Bar Association, 100 West Airy Street, Norristown PA 19401. **LC** KFP52.M65; M6. Each issue contains an index to its own contents (no volume index)--loose.

II
MONTHLY LAW DIGEST, THE. English. mo. Rs30.00 each issue. Monthly Law Digest Office, Katchery Road, Lahore Pakistan. **DD** 348.549/1046.

US
MOORE'S MANUAL; FEDERAL PRACTICE FORMS. English. Matthew Bender & Company Inc., 1275 Broadway, Albany NY 12204. **Tel** (800)833-9844, (518)487-3000.

US
MOOT COURT CASEBOOK. **Added/Corp** New York University. School of Law. Moot Court Board. (197?)-. English. Six times a year. $50.00. New York University School of Law, 110 West Third Street, New York NY 10012. **Tel** (212)998-6540, (212)998-6560, FAX (212)995-4032.

CN/0709-5341
MOTOR VEHICLE REPORTS. (1979)-. English (French). ir. 120.00Can$. Carswell / Canada, 2075 Kennedy Road, Scarborough Ontario M1T 3V4 Canada. **Tel** (416)609-3800, (800)387-5164. **ED** Murray D. Segal. **LC** KE2112.A45; M67. **DD** 343.71/0946/05; 347.10394605; 345.71/0247/02643. Index available. cum. index. **Ad Acc.**
Desc: Features all important decisions in motor vehicle law from all Canadian jurisdictions.
Ind/Abst Aust. Leg. Mon. Dig.; Can. Legal Lit.; Index Can. Leg. Period. Lit.

US/0195-7511
MOVING FORCE. V. 1- May 10, 1979-. English. $48.00 for 5 Issues, $78.00 for 10 Issues. Communications Law Publishers, 1819 H Street North West, Washington DC 20036. **LC** KF2265 .A15; M68. **DD** 343.73/09483.

BL
MP. **Main/Corp** Parana, Brazil (State). Ministerio Publico. **VAT** Ministerio Publico. Vol. 1 (1972)-. Portuguese. Ministerio Publico, Palacio da Justica 60 Andar (Centro Civico), 80000 Parama Brazil.

CN/0704-0377
MPS IN THE NEWS. **VAT** Members of Parliament in the News. Vol. 1, No. 1 (Sept. 18, 1977)-. Periodical. English. bw. Free to all MPS, $6.25 Others. Tuk-Metaphor Clipping Division, Toronto Ontario M5W 1G7 Canada. **DD** 328.71/073.

US/1051-9661
MRO ALERT. [MRO alert]. **VAT** Medical Review Officer Alert. Vol. 1, No. 1 (July 1990)-. Periodical. English. Ten times a year. $245.00. MRO Alert, PO Box 12873, Research Triangle Park NC 27709. **Tel** (919)489-9588, FAX (919)490-1010. **ED** Theodore Shults (editor's address: 6320 Quadrangle #340, Chapel Hill NC 27514). **DD** 344. Index available. cum. index.

US/0884-1667
MSBA IN BRIEF. (MSBA IN BRIEF / MINNESOTA STATE BAR ASSOCIATION.). [MSBA brief]. **Added/Corp** Minnesota State Bar Association. **VAT** Minnesota State Bar Association in Brief. Vol. 1, No. 1 (Oct. 1985)-. Periodical. English. mo. $15.00. Minnesota State Bar Association, 514 Nicollet Hall, Suite 300, Minneapolis MN 55402. **Tel** (612)333-1183, (800)882-6722, FAX (612)333-4927. **ED** Judson Haverkamp and Richard Ericson. **LC** KF200; .M75. **DD** 340/.06/0776. **Ad Acc. Circ:** 13,000.
Desc: News of the Minnesota State Bar Association and of the legal profession in Minnesota.

●US/1066-1085
MSL LAW REVIEW. **Added/Corp** Massachusetts School of Law at Andover. **VFOAT** Massachusetts School of Law at Andover Law Review. (1993)-. Periodical. English. qt. Free (1st issue). Massachusetts School of Law at Andover, 500 Federal Street, Andover MA 01810. **Tel** (508)681-0800.

US/1065-0091
MSPB ALERT. [MSPB alert]. **VFOAT** Alert. (Jan 1991)-. Periodical. English. mo. $125.00 (regular subscribers); $95.00 (federal labor & employee relations update). FPMI Communications Inc., 707 Fiber Street, Huntsville AL 35801. **Tel** (205)539-1850, FAX (205)539-0911, . **DD** 344.

US/0277-0911
MSRB REPORTS. (MSRB REPORTS / MUNICIPAL SECURITIES RULEMAKING BOARD.). [MSRB rep.]. **Added/Corp** Municipal Securities Rulemaking Board. **VFOAT** M.S.R.B. Reports; Reports. **VAT** Municipal Securities Rulemaking Board Reports. (1981)-. Periodical. English. mo. Free on request. Municipal Securities Rulemaking Board, 1818 N Street Northwest, Suite 800, Washington DC 20036. **Tel** (202)223-9347. **LC** KF6775.A15; M83. **DD** 346.73/0922; 347.306922. ***Continues** Municipal Securities Rulemaking Board Reports.*

US
MTLA QUARTERLY. **Added/Corp** Michigan Trial Lawyers Association. Vol. 25, No. 1 (Mar. 1991)-. Periodical. English. bm. ***Continues** MTLA Newsletter.*

UK
MULTIMEDIA BUSINESS AND LAW INTERNATIONAL. **See** Business.

US/0273-0057
MULTINATIONAL CORPORATION REGULATORY GUIDEBOOK, THE. ***Title Change.*** [Multinatl. corp. regul. guideb.]. **VFOAT** International Organizations Monitoring Service. English. an. International Business-Government Counsellors Inc, 1625 Eye Street NW, Washington DC 20006. **LC** K1322; .M84. **DD** 346/.07; 342.67. ***Continued by** International Organizations Regulatory Guidebook.*

US/0098-4671
MULTISTATE BAR REVIEW MANUAL. 1972-. English. Multi-State Media, Inc., 8 Cottage Place, White Plains NY 10601. **LC** KF388; .M84. **DD** 340/.0973.

US/0160-1334
MULTISTATE BAR REVIEW SERIES. **Main/Corp** Multistate Legal Studies, Inc. Vol. 1 (1977)-. English. $6.50 single issue. Multistate Legal Studies, Inc., PO Box 9330, Wilmington DE 19809. **LC** KF388; .M85. **DD** 340/.076.

CN/0702-7206
MUNICIPAL AND PLANNING LAW REPORTS. [Munic. plann. law rep.]. **VFOAT** Municipal and Planning Law Reports. Vol. 1 (Dec. 1976)-. Periodical. English (French). mo. 120.00Can$. Carswell / Canada, 2075 Kennedy Road, Scarborough Ontario M1T 3V4 Canada. **Tel** (416)609-3800, (800)387-5164. **ED** Stanley K. Makuch. **DD** 346/.71/04502642. Index available. cum. index. **Ad Acc.**
Desc: Full text of reports of all significant municipal law decisions of the courts and planning tribunals from all Canadian jurisdictions. Articles, annotations and case coments are included.
Ind/Abst Can. Legal Lit.; Curr. Law Index (1981-Dec. 1984); Index Can. Leg. Period. Lit.; Leg. Resour. Index (1981-Dec. 1984); LegalTrac (1981-1984).

US/0027-3449
MUNICIPAL ATTORNEY, THE. [Munic. atty.]. **Added/Corp** National Institute of Municipal Law Officers (U.S.). Vol. 1 (Oct. 1959)-. Periodical. English. bm. $25.00. National Institute of Municipal Law Officers, 1000 Connecticut Avenue NW/Suite 800, Washington DC 20036. **Tel** (202)466-5424. **LC** K13; .U53. **DD** 340/.05. ***Absorbed** Municipal Law Journal; National Institute of Municipal Law Officers (U.S.) Municipal Law Court Decisions; Municipal Ordinance Review; Municipal Law Docket; NIMLO's Congressional News; Municipalities in the United States Supreme Court.*
Desc: A sounding board for municipal attorneys to exchange ideas and to profit from each other's experiences and expertise through publication and exposure.
Ind/Abst Curr. Law Index (1980-); Leg. Resour. Index (1980-?); LegalTrac (1980-1988); Urban Aff. Abstr.

US/0277-6294
MUNICIPAL ATTORNEYS' OPINIONS. [Munic. atty. opin.]. V. 1-. English. ir. National Institute of Municipal Law Officers, 1000 Connecticut Avenue NW/Suite 800, Washington DC 20036. **Tel** (202)466-5424.

US
MUNICIPAL CODE OF CHICAGO. **Main/Corp** Chicago. Ordinances, etc. (19??)-. Periodical. English. an. Book Publishing Company, 201 Westlake Avenue North, Seattle WA 98109. **Tel** (206)343-5700. **ED** Sylvia J. Youpel. Index available. **Ad Acc. Circ:** 2,500.

US/0027-3503
MUNICIPAL LAW COURT DECISIONS. **Main/Corp** National Institute of Municipal Law Officers, Washington, D.C. **VFOAT** NIMLO Municipal Law Court Decisions. **VAT** National Institute of Municipal Law Officers Municipal Law Court Decisions. V. 1- 1942-. Periodical. English. bm. National Institute of Municipal Law Officers, 1000 Connecticut Avenue NW/Suite 800, Washington DC 20036. **Tel** (202)466-5424.
Desc: Gives concise digests of court decisions on municipal problems.

US/0196-5778
MUNICIPAL LAW SECTION NEWSLETTER. **Main/Corp** New York State Bar Association. Municipal Law Section. V. 1- Jan. 1978-. Newsletter. English. bm. Free. New York State Bar Association, One Elk Street, Albany NY 12207. **Tel** (518)463-3200. **ED** Lester D Steinman. **LC** KFN5752.A15; N48. **DD** 342.747/09. **Circ:** 1,200 (ctrl).
Desc: Section newsletter. Current legal issues dealing with municipal law matters.

US/0278-1301
MUNICIPAL LITIGATION REPORTER. [Munic. litig. rep.]. **Added/Corp** Legal Research Services. Vol. 1, Issue 1 (June 1981)-. Periodical. English. mo (12 issues). $342.00 (one year), $597.00 (two year). Strafford Publications Inc., 590 Dutch Valley Road Northeast, Atlanta GA 30324. **Tel** (404)881-1141, (800)926-7926, FAX (404)881-0074. **LC** KF5304.A75; M85. **DD** 342.73/09/02638; 347.302902638. Index available (free). cum. index.
Desc: Legal developments, case reports and key trends in litigation involving local government. Provides concise, comprehensive coverage of issues important to municipal attorneys and others involved with local government litigation.

II/0377-757X
MUNICIPALITIES AND CORPORATION CASES. English. mo. Rs80.00. International Law Book Company Gate, Delhi-6 India. **DD** 342/.54/09.

US
MUNICIPALITIES IN THE UNITED STATES SUPREME COURT. Periodical. English. National Institute of Municipal Law Officers, 1000 Connecticut Avenue NW/Suite 800, Washington DC 20036. **Tel** (202)466-5424. **LC** KF5304.A75; M86. **DD** 342.73/09. ***Continues in part** Municipal Law Docket, 0148-3366.*
Desc: A newsletter whose schedule corresponds with Supreme Court action, provides a synopsis and status of every case which impacts municipalities on the Supreme Court's docket.

US/0145-5044
N.J. STATE BAR ASSOCIATION. **Main/Corp** New Jersey State Bar Association. **VFOAT** State Bar Advocate. **VAT** New Jersey State Bar Association Advocate. V. 1- June 1976-. English. New Jersey State Bar Association, 1 Constitution Square, New Brunswick NJ 08901. **Tel** (908)249-5000, FAX (908)249-2815. **LC** KF200; .N425. **DD** 340/.06/2749.

US
N.Y. COUNTY LAWYER / NEW YORK COUNTY LAWYERS' ASSOCIATION. **VFOAT** NY County Lawyer. **VAT** New York County Lawyer. Sept. 1981-. Periodical. English. mo. New York County Lawyers Association, 14 Vesey Street, New York NY 10007. **Tel** (212)267-6646. **LC** KF200; .V45. **DD** 340/.060747. ***Continues** Vesey Street Letter.*

GW
NACHSCHLAGEWERK DES BUNDESARBEITSGERICHTS. Periodical. German. ir. CH Beck Verlagsbuchhandlung, D 80791 Munich Germany. **Tel** 011 49 89 381891. **ED** Alfred Hueck.

UK
NAPF PENSIONS LEGISLATION SERVICE. English. £180.00. Butterworth & Co. Ltd. / Kent, England, Borough Green, Sevenoaks Kent TN15 8PH England. **Tel** 011 44 732-884567, FAX 011 44 732-885996. **ED** John Quarrell.

•US
NARCOTICS ENFORCEMENT & PREVENTION DIGEST. See Drug Abuse and Alcoholism.

US/8755-8289
NARCOTICS LAW BULLETIN. [Narc. law bull.]. (19??)-. Bulletin. English. mo. $58.75. Quinlan Publishing Company, 23 Drydock Avenue, Boston MA 02210-2387. **Tel** (617)542-0048, (800)229-2084, FAX (617)345-9646. **LC** KF3890.A59; N37. **DD** 344.73/0545; 347.304545. **[CCC]**. available on microfilm and microfiche from University Microfilms International (UMI).
Ind/Abst Crim. Justice Period. Index.

US/0739-862X
NARF LEGAL REVIEW, THE. (THE NARF LEGAL REVIEW / NATIVE AMERICAN RIGHTS FUND.). [NARF leg. rev.]. **Added/Corp** Native American Rights Fund. **VAT** Native American Rights Fund Legal Review. Vol. 9, No. 2 (Summer 1983)-. Periodical. English. Twice a year. Free. Native American Rights Fund, NARF, 1506 Broadway, Boulder CO 80302. **Tel** (303)447-8760. **ED** Ray Ramirez. **LC** KF8201.A3; N37. **DD** 346.7301/3; 347.30613. **Bk Rev. Circ:** 30,000. ***Continues*** *Announcements - Native American Rights Fund, 0197-2073.*
Desc: Reports on legal and legislative issues on Native American rights.

US/0161-4290
NASBA DIGEST OF STATE ACCOUNTANCY LAWS AND STATE BOARD REGULATIONS. (DIGEST OF STATE ACCOUNTANCY LAWS AND STATE BOARD REGULATIONS / NASBA.). **Main/Corp** National Association of State Boards of Accountancy. **Added/Corp** National Association of State Boards of Accountancy. American Institute of Certified Public Accountants. **VAT** National Association of State Boards of Accountancy Digest of State Accountancy Laws and State Board Regulations. (19??)-. English. ir (approx. every other year). $30.85. American Institute of Certified Public Accountants, Harborside Financial Center, 201 Plaza 3, Jersey City NJ 07311. **Tel** (201)938-3333, (800)862-4272. **(Subscription address:** American Institute of CPA's, PO Box 1003, Order Department, New York NY 10108.**)** **LC** KF2920.Z95; N3. **DD** 344/.73/01761657.

US/0891-9291
NASH & CIBINIC REPORT, THE. See Public Administration.

US
NASHVILLE RECORD, THE. See Business.

US/0197-0968
NASSAU COUNTY BAR ASSOCIATION ANNUAL DIRECTORY. **Main/Corp** Bar Association of Nassau County, N.Y. Directory. English. an. Bar Association of Nassau County, 15th and West Streets, Mineola NY 11501. **Tel** (516)288-5400. ***Continues*** *Nassau County Bar Directory, 0197-095X.*

US/0733-3285
NATIONAL AND FEDERAL LEGAL EMPLOYMENT REPORT, THE. [Natl. fed. leg. employ. rep.]. Vol. 3, No. 2 (Aug. 1982)-. Periodical. English. mo. $147.20. Federal Reports, PO Box 3709 Georgetown Station, Washington DC 20007. **Tel** (202)393-3311, FAX (202)393-1553. **LC** KF299.G6; F43. **DD** 331.12/4134973/05; 331.12413473/005. **Circ:** 5,000 (ctrl). ***Continues*** *Federal Legal Employment Report, 0198-036X.*
Desc: Listing of attorney and law-related job opportunities with the US Government and other public/private employees in the US and abroad.

US/0272-6025
NATIONAL ASSOCIATION FOR LAW PLACEMENT MEMBERSHIP DIRECTORY. **Main/Corp** National Association for Law Placement (U.S.). **Added/Corp** National Association for Law Placement (U.S.) Membership Directory. (19??)-. Directory. English. an. $100.00 (non-members); $10.00 (members), free on request. National Association for Law Placement, 1666 Connecticut Avenue, Suite 450, Washington DC 20009. **Tel** (202)667-1666, FAX (202)265-6735. **LC** KF297.A1; N38. **DD** 340/.025/73.

US/0741-0115
NATIONAL BAR ASSOCIATION MAGAZINE. (NATIONAL BAR ASSOCIATION MAGAZINE / NBA.). [Natl. Bar Assoc. mag.]. **Added/Corp** National Bar Association. **VFOAT** NBA Magazine; NBA National Bar Association Magazine. Vol. 1, No. 1 (Summer 1983)-. Periodical. English. bm. $60.00. National Bar Association, 1225 11th Street Northwest, Washington DC 20001. **Tel** (202)842-3900, FAX (202)289-6170. **ED** Maurice Foster. **LC** KF200; .N37. **DD** 349.73/05; 347.3005. **Bk Rev. Ad Acc, Adv Mgr:** H. Carter. **Circ:** 16,000. available on microfilm and microfiche.

US
NATIONAL BAR BULLETIN, THE. Bulletin. English. bm. Free upon request, $20.00 libraries. National Bar Association, 1225 11th Street Northwest, Washington DC 20001. **Tel** (202)842-3900, FAX (202)289-6170. **LC** KF200; .N38. **DD** 340/.06/273. **Bk Rev. Ad Acc. Circ:** 10,500 (ctrl).

US/0896-0194
NATIONAL BLACK LAW JOURNAL. [Natl. Black law j.]. **Added/Corp** University of California, Los Angeles. School of Law. Vol. 10, No. 1 (Winter 1987)-. Periodical. English. Three times a year. $18.00 (individuals), $25.00 (institutions). University of California at Los Angeles / School of Law, Los Angeles CA 90024. **Tel** (310)825-7941. **LC** K2; .L3. **DD** 340.5. Index available. **Bk Rev. Ad Acc. Circ:** 5,000 (ctrl). available on microfilm and microfiche from University Microfilms International (UMI). Documents available from UMI Article Clearinghouse. ***Continues*** *Black Law Journal, 0045-2181.*
Desc: Publishes articles addressing legal issues of relevance to blacks and other minority communities. Past article subjects include desegregation, civil rights, affirmative action, police abuse and apartheid.
Ind/Abst Crim. Justice Abstr.; Expand. Acad. Index (1984-); Index Leg. Period. (1987-); Leg. Resour. Index (1987-); LegalTrac (1980-); Newsp. Period. Abstr. (1989-).

US/0095-2028
NATIONAL COLLEGE OF THE STATE JUDICIARY. English. an. The National Judicial College, Judicial College Building, University of Nevada Reno, Reno NV 89557. **Tel** (702)784-6747. **LC** KF270; .N37. **DD** 347/.73/1407152.

US/1062-5631
NATIONAL CONFERENCE OF BAR FOUNDATIONS' FOUNDATION FORUM. [Natl. Conf. Bar Found. found. forum]. **Added/Corp** National Conference of Bar Foundations (U.S.). **VFOAT** Foundation Forum; NCBF's Ffoundation Forum. (1991)-. Periodical. English. qt. $12.00 (non-members), Free (members). National Conference of Bar Foundation, c/o Division for Bar Services, 541 North Fairbanks Court, Chicago IL 60611-3314. **DD** 340. ***Continues*** *NCBF Newsletter.*

US/1054-9471
NATIONAL DIRECTORY OF COURTS OF LAW, THE. [Natl. dir. courts law]. (1991)-. Directory. English. be. $90.00. Information Resources Press, 1110 North Glebe Road, Suite 550, Arlington VA 22201. **Tel** (703)558-8270. **LC** KF8700.A19; N363. **DD** 347.73/1/025; 347.3071025.

US/1053-7902
NATIONAL DIRECTORY OF REAL ESTATE ATTORNEYS, THE. [Natl. dir. real estate atty.]. **VFOAT** NDREA. (1991)-. Directory. English. $395.00. Kurt Allen Communications, 733 Bishop Street, Suite 170-218, Honolulu HI 96813. **LC** KF195.P75; N38. **DD** 340/.025/73.

US/0271-1133
NATIONAL DIRECTORY OF SHORTHAND REPORTERS. [Natl. dir. shorth. report.]. Directory. English. National Directory of Shorthand Reporters, Bank of Idaho, PO Box 1758, Boise ID 83701. **LC** KF8700.A19; N37. **DD** 347.73/16.

US/1053-1084
NATIONAL DISABILITY LAW REPORTER. (1990)-. Periodical. English. Twenty-four times a year. $675.00. LRP Publications, 747 Dresher Road, PO Box 980, Horsham PA 19044-0980. **Tel** (800)341-7874, (215)784-0860, FAX (215)784-9639, (215)784-0870. **(Subscription address:** LRP Publications, PO Box 980, Horsham PA 19044.**)**
Desc: Designed to meet the research needs of professionals involved with the legal aspects of disability rights. Provides information needed to conduct conclusive research, make decisions, and formulate positions and policies.

US
NATIONAL FINANCING LAW DIGEST. (19??)-. English. mo. $260.00. Strafford Publications Inc., 590 Dutch Valley Road Northeast, Atlanta GA 30324. **Tel** (404)881-1141, (800)926-7926, FAX (404)881-0074.

AT/1037-6615
NATIONAL HIV/AIDS LEGAL LINK NEWSLETTER. (1990)-. Periodical. English. Four times a year (Mar., June, Sept., Dec.). 25.00Aus$ (individuals), 50.00Aus$ (institutions) Comes with Australian Federation of AIDS Organisations membership. AFAO Legal Project, PO Box H274, Australia Square Sydney 2000 Australia. **Tel** 011 61 02 2312111, FAX 011 61 02 2312092. **ED** Michael Alexander. **Bk Rev. Ad Acc. Circ:** 500.
Desc: News and information about the laws and policy of HIV/AIDS in the Australia, Asia and the Pacific region.

US/0743-7927
NATIONAL INSURANCE LAW REVIEW. [Natl. insur. law rev.]. **Added/Corp** National Insurance Law Service. (Winter 1984)-. Periodical. English. qt. $125.00. National Insurance Law Service, 21625 Prairie Street, PO Box 2507, Chatsworth CA 91311. **Tel** (818)998-8830, (800)423-5910. **LC** K14; .A8677. **DD** 346.73/086/05; 347.3068605. ***Continues*** *National Insurance Law Review Service, 0147-8532.*

US/0897-2222
NATIONAL JEWISH LAW REVIEW. ***Suspended.*** [Natl. Jew. law rev.]. **Added/Corp** National Jewish Law Students' Network. Vol. 1 (1986)-Suspended (Vol.5). Periodical. English. an. National Jewish Law Students Network, 3 Miriam Lane, Monsey NY 10952. **Tel** (914)352-2980, FAX (212)818-9662. **LC** K14; .A854. **DD** 349.73/089924; 347.30089924.
Ind/Abst Index Leg. Period.; Leg. Resour. Index; LegalTrac (1980-).

US/0162-7325
NATIONAL LAW JOURNAL, THE. [Natl. law j.]. Vol. 1 (Aug. 7, 1978)-. Periodical. English. wk. $124.00 US; $144.00 other. New York Law Publishing Company, 345 Park Avenue South, New York NY 10010. **Tel** (212)741-8300, (800)888-8300. **(Subscription address:** National Law Journal, Agency Department, Boulder CO 80306-8034.**)** **LC** K14; .A858. **DD** 340/.0973. **Circ:** 40,000. available on microfilm and microfiche from University Microfilms International (UMI). Documents available from UMI Article Clearinghouse, Documents on Demand.
Ind/Abst Bibliogr. Mission. (1980-); Bowne Dig. Corp. Sec. Lawyers; Energy Inf. Abstr.; Environ. Abstr.; Expand. Acad. Index (1984-); Leg. Inf. Manage. Index (19??-); Leg. Resour. Index (1980-); LegalTrac (1980-); Newsp. Period. Abstr. (1991-); NEXIS (1983-); Trade Ind. Index.

US/0276-7546
NATIONAL LAW REVIEW REPORTER. [Natl. law rev. rep.]. Began with Oct./Nov. 1979 issue. Periodical. English. bm. $100.00. National Law Review Reporter, 67 Park Avenue, New York NY 10016. **LC** K14; .A859. **DD** 349.73/05,347.3005.

II
NATIONAL LAW SCHOOL JOURNAL. **Added/Corp** National Law School of India. **VFOAT** NLSJ. Vol. 1 (1989)-. English. an. $14.00. Bharat Law House Pvt. Ltd., New Delhi, India. **(Subscription address:** Prints India, 11 Darya Ganj, New Delhi 110002 India.**)** **LC** K14; .A86775. **DD** 349.54/05; 345.4005.

US
NATIONAL LAWYER'S GUILD PRACTITIONER. (19??)-. English. qt (4 issues). $30.00. National Lawyers Guild, Box 673, Berkeley CA 94701. **Tel** (510)848-0599. Index available (extra at $23.95). ***Continues*** *Guild Practitioner.*

US/0275-9233
NATIONAL LEGAL CENTER NEWS. Periodical. English. qt. Free. National Legal Center Public Interest, 1000 16th Street NW, Suite 301, Washington DC 20036. **LC** KF299.P8; N37. **DD** 349.73/05,347.3005.

AT/0813-9741
NATIONAL LEGAL EAGLE. [Natl. leg. eagle]. (1983)-. English. qt. $15.00. Law Society of New South Wales, 170 Phillip Street, Sydney New South Wales, 2000 Australia. **Tel** 011 61 2 2200333, 011 61 2 2200289, FAX 011 61 2 231 5809, telex 73063. **ED** Donna Bain. **DD** 340.05. **Ad Acc. Circ:** 500. ***Continues*** *Legal Eagle, 0313-8046.*

US/1055-1069
NATIONAL LEGAL EXCHANGE. [Natl. leg. exch.]. **VFOAT** Legal Exchange. Vol. 3, No. 3 (April 1988)-. Periodical. English. mo. Chrysalis Publishers Inc, 9744 Wilshire Boulevard/Suite 205, Beverly Hills CA 90212. **DD** 340. ***Formed by the union of*** *Legal Exchange. Los Angeles; Legal Exchange. Bay Area* ***and*** *Legal Exchange. New York.*

US/1052-309X
NATIONAL MEDICAL-LEGAL JOURNAL. [Natl. med., legal j.]. **Added/Corp** Medical-Legal Consulting Institute. **VFOAT** National Medical Legal Journal. Vol. 1, No. 1 (3rd Quarter 1990)-. Periodical. English. qt. $30.00. Medical-Legal Consulting Institute, PO Box 27087, Houston TX 77227. **Tel** (713)961-3078. **LC** K14; .A86777. **DD** 344.73/041/05; 347.3044105. **NLM** W1; NA527.
Ind/Abst Cumul. Index Nurs. Allied Health Lit.; Health Plan. Adminis.

CN/0315-2286
NATIONAL (OTTAWA). (NATIONAL.). [National]. **Added/Corp** Canadian Bar Association. Canadian Bar Foundation. Vol. 1 (Jan. 1974)-Vol. 19, No. 5, (Summer 1992); Vol. 1 (Oct. 1992)-. English (French). Eleven times a year. 35.00Can$ Canada; 48.00Can$ other. MacLean Hunter Ltd. Business Publishers / Canada, Box 9100, Station A, Toronto ONT M5W 1A5 Canada. **Tel** (416)946-8420, (800)567-0444. **(Subscription address:** Indas, 35 Riviera Drive, Building 17, Markham Ontario L3R 8N4 Canada.**)** **DD** 340/.06/271. Index available. **Bk Rev. Circ:** 600. ***Formed by the union of*** *Canadian Bar Association. Journal, 0591-0919* ***and*** *Canadian Bar Bulletin, 0045-4443;* ***Absorbed*** *Ontario Bar News, 0317-4603.*
Desc: A journal addressing the legal, financial and management issues and policies affecting charities and foundations and their legal and financial advisors in Canada.
Ind/Abst Law Office Inf. Serv.

US/1058-482X
NATIONAL PARALEGAL REPORTER. (NATIONAL PARALEGAL REPORTER / NATIONAL FEDERATION OF PARALEGAL ASSOCIATIONS.). [Natl. paralegal report.]. **Added/Corp** National Federation of Paralegal Associations. (19??)-. Periodical. English. qt (Jan., Apr., Jul., Oct.). $20.00. National Paralegal Reporter, PO Box 33108, Kansas City MO 64114. **Tel** (816)941-4000, FAX (816)941-2725. **DD** 348.

US/1058-482X
NATIONAL PARALEGAL REPORTER. (NATIONAL PARALEGAL REPORTER : OFFICIAL PUBLICATION OF NATIONAL FEDERATION OF PARALEGAL ASSOCIATIONS.). [Natl. paralegal report.]. **Added/Corp** National Federation of Paralegal Associations (U.S.). (197?)-. Periodical. English. qt (Jan., Apr., July, Oct.). $20.00 (one year), $35.00 (two year). The National Federation of Paralegals, PO Box 33108, Kansas City MO 64114. **Tel** (816)941-4000, FAX (816)941-2725. **ED** Sandra Peterson, (503)243-2300. **DD** 348. **Bk Rev. Ad Acc. Circ:** 19,000 (ctrl).
Desc: Articles pertaining to current issues in the paralegal profession. Published primarily for paralegals / legal assistants, this magazine offers information about legislation, career opportunities, ways to improve research skills and to improve performance in this profession.

US/0363-8340
NATIONAL PROPERTY LAW DIGESTS. [Natl. prop. law dig.]. (19??)-. Periodical. English. mo. $380.00. Strafford Publications Inc., 590 Dutch Valley Road Northeast, Atlanta GA 30324. **Tel** (404)881-1141, (800)926-7926, FAX (404)881-0074. **LC** KF567.8; .N38. **DD** 346/.73/04302648. cum. index.

CN/0317-641X
NATIONAL REPORTER (FREDERICTON, N.B. : BOUND CUMULATION). (NATIONAL REPORTER.). Vol. 1 (1974)-. Periodical. English. ir. $64.00 per vol. Maritime Law Book Ltd, PO Box 302, Fredericton New Brunswick, E3B 4Y9 Canada. **Tel** (506)453-9921, (800)561-0220. **DD** 348.71/041.

US
NATIONAL REPORTER ON LEGAL ETHICS AND PROFESSIONAL RESPONSIBILITY. (1982)-. Periodical. English. Ten times a year. $730.00. University Publications of America, 4520 East West Highway 800, Bethesda MD 20814. **Tel** (800)638-8380, (301)654-1550.

US
NATIONAL SECURITY LAW REPORT / AMERICAN BAR ASSOCIATION, STANDING COMMITTEE ON LAW AND NATIONAL SECURITY. **Added/Corp** American Bar Association. Standing Committee on Law and National Security. Vol. 13, No. 10 (Oct. 1991)-. Periodical. English. mo. Free on request. American Bar Association, 750 North Lake Shore Drive, Chicago IL 60611. **Tel** (312)988-5522, (312)988-5241, FAX (312)988-5528, telex 270593. **LC** KF4850.A15; N37. **DD** 342.73/0418; 347.302418. ***Continues*** *Intelligence Report (Chicago, Ill.), 0736-2773.*

US/0742-4388
NATIONAL TORT LAW DIGESTS. [Nat. tort law dig.]. Vol. 1 No. 1-. English. mo. $96.00. National Tort Law Digests, Inc., Suite 308, 1301 20th Street NW, Washington DC 20036. **LC** KF1247.8; .N37. **DD** 346.7303/02648; 347.306302648.
Desc: Summary: Selected briefs of recent nationally significant decisions ... .

CN
NATIONAL TRADE & TARIFF SERVICE. (19??)-. English. ir. Price varies. Butterworth & Company Ltd. / Canada, 75 Clegg Road, Markham Ontario L6G 1A1 Canada. **Tel** (905)479-2665, (800)668-6481. ***Continues*** *Canadian Customs and Excise Reports.*

●US/1066-7733
NATIONAL TRIAL LAWYER (FLORIDA ED.). (NATIONAL TRIAL LAWYER.). [Natl. trial lawyer]. **VFOAT** Trial Lawyer. (1992)-. Periodical. English. Six times a year (Jan., Mar., May., July, Sept., Nov.). $30.00 one year; $58.00 two years; $86.00 three years. Trial Lawyer Publications Inc, 212 East Vine Street, Millville NJ 08332. **Tel** (609)825-9099, (800)331-9000, FAX (609)825-5959. **ED** Stephen C. Rubino and Brad X. Terry, (phone: (609)825-9099). **DD** 347. **Bk Rev. Ad Acc, Adv Mgr:** Par Haffert. **Circ:** 2,400 (ctrl).
Desc: An independent and open forum for the free exchange of information and opinions for attorneys interested in litigation. Coverage ranges widely from technical information to the human issues affecting practitioners. Editors and contributers are free to present articles on subjects relevant to lawyers.

US/1049-684X
NATIONAL TRIAL LAWYER (NATIONAL ED.). (NATIONAL TRIAL LAWYER.). [Natl. trial lawyer]. **VFOAT** Trial Lawyer; NTL. (19??)-. Periodical. English. Six times a year (Jan., Mar., May, July, Sept., Nov.). $30.00 one year; $58.00 two years; $86.00 three years. Trial Lawyer Publications Inc, 212 East Vine Street, Millville NJ 08332. **Tel** (609)825-9099, (800)331-9000, FAX (609)825-5959. **ED** Stephen C. Rubino (editor's address: P.O. Box 1217, Millville, N.J. 08332-8217). **LC** K14; .A8678. **DD** 347.73/7/05; 347.307705. Index available. cum. index. **Bk Rev. Ad Acc. Circ:** 4,000.
Desc: An independent and open forum for the free exchange of information and opinions for attorneys interested in litigation. Coverage ranges widely from technical information to the human issues affecting practitioners. Editors and contributors are free to present articles on the subjects relevant to lawyers, such as travel, health, trial techniques, and litigation.

●US/1060-9210
NATIONAL TRIAL LAWYER (NEW YORK ED.). (NATIONAL TRIAL LAWYER.). [Natl. trial lawyer]. **VFOAT** NTL; Trial Lawyer. Vol. 1, Issue 1 (Jan. 1992)-. Periodical. English. Six times a year (Jan., Mar., May, July, Sept., Nov.). $30.00 one year; $58.00 two years; $86.00 three years. Trial Lawyer Publications Inc, 212 East Vine Street, Millville NJ 08332. **Tel** (609)825-9099, (800)331-9000, FAX (609)825-5959. **ED** Stephen C. Rubino and Brad X. Terry. **LC** K14; .A8645. **DD** 347.747/07/05; 347.4707705. Index available. cum. index. **Bk Rev. Ad Acc, Adv Mgr:** Pat Haffert, **Tel** (800)331-9000. **Circ:** 2,600.
Desc: An independent and open forum for the free exchange of information and opinions for attorneys interested in litigation. Coverage ranges widely from technical information to the human issues affecting practitioners. Editors and contributers are free to present articles on subjects relevant to lawyers.

US/1052-3413
NATURAL GAS LAWYER'S JOURNAL, THE. (THE NATURAL GAS LAWYER'S JOURNAL / LEGAL SECTION, AMERICAN GAS ASSOCIATION.). [Nat. gas lawyer's j.]. **Added/Corp** American Gas Association. Legal Section. (198?)-. Periodical. English. an. American Gas Association / Virginia, 1515 Wilson Boulevard, Arlington VA 22209. **Tel** (703)841-8400, (703)841-8559, FAX (703)841-8697. **DD** 346.
Ind/Abst Gas Abstr.; Index Leg. Period.; Leg. Resour. Index; LegalTrac (1980-).

US
NCALRI NEWSLETTER. **See** Agriculture.

US/0733-1851
NCBL NOTES. (NCBL NOTES / NATIONAL CONFERENCE OF BLACK LAWYERS.). [NCBL notes]. **Added/Corp** National Conference of Black Lawyers (U.S.). **VFOAT** N.C.B.L. Notes. **VAT** National Conference of Black Lawyers Notes. (19??)-. Periodical. English. Four times a year. $35.00 institutions; $15.00 individuals. National Conference of Black Lawyers, 126 West 119th Street, New York NY 10026. **Tel** (212)864-4000.

US
NEBRASKA DIGEST. **Added/Corp** Nebraska. Courts. United States. Courts. West Publishing Company. (1855)-. English. West Publishing Company, 610 Opperman Drive, PO Box 64526, Eagan MN 55123-1308. **Tel** (612)687-5618, (800)328-9352, FAX (612)687-5388, (800)562-2329. **DD** 345.32.
Desc: Covers Nebraska reports and North western reporter as well as Nebraska cases decided in Supreme Court of the United States, Circuit Court of Appeals and Federal circuit and district court.

●US/1062-953X
NEBRASKA LAW NEWSLETTER. [Neb. law newsl.]. (1992)-. Newsletter. English. qt. Free on request. Damman Legal Research, PO Box 30412, Lincoln NE 68503. **Tel** (800)538-3101. **DD** 340.

US/0047-9209
NEBRASKA LAW REVIEW. [Neb. law rev.]. **Added/Corp** Nebraska State Bar Association. University of Nebraska (Lincoln Campus). College of Law. Vol. 20 (Mar. 1941)-. Periodical. English. qt (Feb., May, Aug., Nov.). $32.00 (outside Nebraska). University of Nebraska / College of Law, Lincoln NE 68583-0903. **Tel** (402)472-1267. **ED** Sheree Strom Carson (Editor's phone: 472-1267). **LC** K14; .E25. Each issue contains an index to its own contents (no volume index)--loose. cum. index. **Bk Rev. Ad Acc, Adv Mgr:** Jane Kemper. **Circ:** 1,250. available cn an online database; available in hardback. ***Continues*** *Nebraska Law Bulletin, 0196-4089.*
Desc: Topics in law of general interest to both practicing attorneys and law school faculty.
Ind/Abst Bowne Dig. Corp. Sec. Lawyers; Crim. Justice Abstr.; Curr. Law Index (1980-); Fed. Tax Artic.; Index Leg. Period.; Leg. Resour. Index (1980-); LegalTrac (1980-).

US/0748-2744
NEBRASKA LEGAL DIRECTORY, THE. [Neb. legal dir.]. **Added/Corp** Legal Directories Publishing Company. **VFOAT** Legal Directory. (1983)-. Directory. English. an (Nov.). $20.00. Legal Directories Publishing Company, 9111 Garland Road, PO Box 189000, Dallas TX 75218. **Tel** (214)321-3238, 800 447-5375. **LC** KF192.N39; N38. **DD** 349.782/025; 347.820025. ***Continues in part*** *Minnesota, Nebraska, North Dakota and South Dakota Legal Directory.*

NE/0167-7594
NEDERLANDS INTERNATIONAAL PRIVATRECHT : REPERTORIUM OP VERDRAGENRECHT, WETGEVING, RECHTSPRAAK EN LITERATUUR. **Added/Corp** T.M.C. Asser Instituut. (19??)-. Periodical. Dutch. Three times a year. Fl90.00. T M C Asser Instituut, Postbus 30461, 2500 GL S-Gravenhage The Netherlands. **Tel** (70)42 03 00, FAX (07)42 03 59, telex 34273 ASSER NL. **ED** Mathilde Sumampouw, K Boele-Woelki, L M B Veraart. Index available. cum. index. **Bk Rev. Circ:** 300.
Desc: Contains documentation in the field of Netherlands International Private Law, including law of treaties, legislation, judicial decisions and literature.

NE
NEDERLANDS JURISTENBLAD : TEVENS ORGAAN DER NED. JURISTEN VEREENIGING. **Added/Corp** Nederlands Juristen-Vereniging. Vol. 23 No. 1 (Jan. 3, 1948)-. Periodical. Dutch. Forty-two times a year. F269.00. W. E. J. Tjeenk Willink, Box 25, 8000 AA Zwolle Netherlands. **Tel** 011 31 38 228819, 011 31 38 211444. **(Subscription address:** Libresso BV, Postbus 23, 7400 GA Deventer, Netherlands**)** ***Continues*** *Nederlandsch Juristenblad.*
Ind/Abst Crim. Penol. Police Sci. Abstr.; Index Foreign Leg. Per.

ET
NEGARIT GAZETA. **Main/Corp** Ethiopia. Multiple languages (Amharic and English).

US/0748-4526
NEGOTIATION JOURNAL. **See** Political Science.

US/0548-1546
NELSON'S LAW OFFICE DIRECTORY. [Nelson's law off. dir.]. **Main/Corp** Nelson Company. (1968)-. Directory. English. an. $23.00 (non-listees only). The Nelson Company, PO Box 309, Hopkins MN 55343. **ED** Robert J. Nelson. **LC** KF190; .N4. **DD** 340/.065.
Desc: A list of the law offices in the United States that have received the top rating in legal ability, diligence and integrity by their fellow lawyers.

NP
NEPAL MISCELLANEOUS SERIES. Vol. 1/77 (Jan. 25, 1977)-. English. ir. Rs900.00 Nepal, Rs600.00 India, $50.00 other countries. Regmi Research Pvt Ltd, Lazimpat, Kathmandu Nepal. **ED** Mahesh C. Regmi.
Desc: Consolidated texts of laws and regulations.

●US/1063-9829
NETWORK 2D. (NETWORK 2D : COMPUTERS & TECHNOLOGY IN THE PRACTICE OF LAW FROM THE ABA LAW PRACTICE MANAGEMENT SECTION.). [Netw. 2d]. **Added/Corp** American Bar Association. Section of Law Practice Management. Vol. 1, No. 1 (Aug. 1992)-. Periodical. English. qt (4 issues). $65.00. American Bar Association, 750 North Lake Shore Drive, Chicago IL 60611. **Tel** (312)988-5522, (312)988-5241, FAX (312)988-5528, telex 270593. **DD** 340.

GW/0341-1907
NEUE JURISTISCHE WOCHENSCHRIFT. [Neue jurist. Wochenschr.]. **Added/Corp** Deutscher Anwaltsverein. Bundesrechtsanwaltskammer. **VFOAT** NJW, Neue Juristische Wochenschrift. (1947)-. Periodical. German. wk. DM306.00. CH Beck Verlagsbuchhandlung, D 80791 Munich Germany. **Tel** 011 49 89 381891. ***Continues*** *Neue Juristische.*
Ind/Abst Coal Abstr.; Energy Res. Abstr. (Oct. 1974-); Index Foreign Leg. Per.

GW/0028-3231
NEUE JUSTIZ. **Added/Corp** Germany (Territory under Allied occupation, 1945-1955. Russian Zone). Deutsche Justizverwaltung. Germany (East). Ministerium der Justiz. Germany (Democratic Republic). Oberstes Gericht. Germany (Democratic Republic). Staatsanwaltschaft. Vol. 1 (Jan. 1947)-. Periodical. German. mo. DM117.20. Nomos Verlagsgesellschaft, Postfach 610, D-76484 Baden Baden Germany. **Tel** 011

49 7221 21040. cum. index.
Ind/Abst Crim. Penol. Police Sci. Abstr.; Index Foreign Leg. Per.

US/1058-4706
NEUROLAW LETTER, THE. [Neurolaw lett.]. (1991)-. Periodical. English. mo. $96.00. HDI Publishers, 5626 Weeping Willow, Houston TX 77092. **Tel** (713)682-8700, FAX (713)681-9595. **ED** J. Sherrod Taylor J. D. (phone: (706)323-7711). **DD** 344. Index available. cum. index. **Bk Rev**, (Qty: 10).
Desc: Devoted solely to covering the issues important to professional active in brain and spinal cord injury law and litigation. Provides practical information of immediate use concerning: expert testimony, depositions, the litigation process, marketing services to attorneys, and features case and literature reviews.

●US/1068-882X
NEVADA LAWYER. (NEVADA LAWYER : OFFICIAL PUBLICATION OF THE STATE BAR OF NEVADA.). [Nev. lawyer]. **Added/Corp** State Bar of Nevada. Vol. 1, No. 1 (Jan. 1993)-. Periodical. English. Twelve times a year. $40.00. State Bar of Nevada, 1325 Airmotive Way, Suite 140, Reno NV 89502. **Tel** (702)329-4100, FAX (702)329-0522. **ED** Christine Cendagorta. **DD** 349. Index available. cum. index. **Bk Rev**, (Qty: 8-12). **Ad Acc, Adv Mgr:** C. Cendagonla, **Tel** (702)329-4100. **Pr Rev. Circ:** 4,000 (ctrl). available on microfilm from Williams S Hein & Co.; available on an online database from WESTLAW. ***Formed by the union of*** *Bar Letter, 1052-4541* ***and*** *Inter Alia, 0092-6086.*

US/0744-8902
NEVADA LEGAL NEWS. [Nev. leg. news]. (19??)-. Periodical. English. da (except Sat.-Sun. and holidays). $25.00 (1 month), $60.00 (3 mos.), $110.00 (6 mos.). Nevada Legal News, PO Box 1720, Las Vegas NV 89125. **Tel** (702)382-2747. **ED** Ruby Reed. **LC** K14; .E69. **DD** 349.793/05; 347.93005. **Ad Acc. Circ:** 300.

CN/0713-8989
NEW BRUNSWICK REPORTS (1969). (NEW BRUNSWICK REPORTS.). [N.B. rep.]. Began with V. 1 (1969). Periodical. English (French). mo. 550.00Can$ Canada; $450.00 US. Maritime Law Book Ltd, PO Box 302, Fredericton New Brunswick, E3B 4Y9 Canada. **Tel** (506)453-9921, (800)561-0220. **DD** 348.715/043. Index available. cum. index.
Desc: Law reports on New Brunswick courts.

US
NEW ENGLAND LAW LIBRARY CONSORTIUM UNION CATALOG. CD-ROM. Catalog. English (French, German and Spanish). sa. $995.00 US and Canada; $1015.00 other. New England Law Library Consortium, Langdell Hall, Cambridge MA 02138. **Tel** (617)495-9918. **Bk Rev. Circ:** 50.

US/0028-4823
NEW ENGLAND LAW REVIEW. [New Engl. law rev.]. **Added/Corp** New England School of Law. Vol. 4, No. 2 (Spring 1969)-. English. Four times a year (Feb., Apr., Sept., Nov.). $20.00. New England Law Review, 154 Stuart Street, Boston MA 02116. **Tel** (617)451-0010 ext 237-294-311, FAX (617)422-7385. **ED** Joe Stanton, Elizabeth Delfs and Minique Govsie. **Bk Rev. Circ:** 2,000 (ctrl). available on microfilm from University Microfilms International (UMI); available on an online database from WESTLAW. ***Continues*** *Portia Law Journal, 0196-5646.*
Desc: Legal articles written by legal scholars on matters of current importance in the legal community.
Ind/Abst Bowne Dig. Corp. Sec. Lawyers; Curr. Law Index (1980-); Fed. Tax Artic.; Index Leg. Period.; Leg. Resour. Index (1980-); LegalTrac (1980-); PAIS Int. Print (1991-).

●US/1069-3181
NEW EUROPE LAW REVIEW. [New Eur. law rev.]. **Added/Corp** Benjamin N. Cardozo School of Law. Vol. 1, No. 1 (Winter 1992)-. Periodical. English. tq. $22.00. Benjamin N Cardozo School of Law, Yeshiva University, 55 5th Avenue, Room 121, New York NY 10003. **Tel** (212)790-0292. **DD** 341.

US/0548-4928
NEW HAMPSHIRE BAR JOURNAL. [N.H. bar j.]. **Added/Corp** New Hampshire Bar Association. Bar Association of the State of New Hampshire. Vol. 1 (1958)-. Academic Scholarly Publication. English. qt. $40.00. New Hampshire Bar Association, 112 Pleasant Street, Concord NH 03301. **Tel** (603)224-6942. **ED** Virginia M. Guiser. **LC** UNC. **Bk Rev. Ad Acc. Circ:** 2,900. ***Absorbed*** *Proceedings of the Bar Association of the State of New Hampshire at its annual meeting.*
Desc: Scholarly articles on legal subjects of interest to New Hampshire attorneys.
Ind/Abst Curr. Law Index (1980-); Fed. Tax Artic.; Index Leg. Period.; Leg. Resour. Index (1980-); LegalTrac (1980-).

US/1051-4023
NEW HAMPSHIRE BAR NEWS. VFOAT NHBN. Vol. 1, No. 1 (June 6, 1990)-. Periodical. English. sm. $60.00. New Hampshire Bar Association, 112 Pleasant Street, Concord NH 03301. **Tel** (603)224-6942. **LC** KF200; .N42. **DD** 340/.09742. ***Continues*** *New Hampshire Law Weekly, 0362-1073.*

US/0730-6210
NEW HAMPSHIRE LAW DIRECTORY & DAYBOOK. VFOAT New Hampshire Law Directory and Daybook. Directory. English. an. $16.25. New Hampshire Law Directory and Daybook, 795 Elm Street, Manchester NH 03101. **LC** KF192.N395; N48. **DD** 349.742/025; 347.420025.

US
NEW HAMPSHIRE REPORTS. CURRENT CASES, THE. Main/Corp New Hampshire. Supreme Court. Periodical. English. ir. Equity Publishing Corporation, RR 1 Box 3, Orford NH 03777. **Tel** (603)637-5012, (800)637-5012. Index Available Received separately--bound from publisher.

US
NEW HAMPSHIRE REVISED STATUTES ANNOTATED. Main/Corp New Hampshire. (19??)-. Periodical. English. ir. $45.00. Butterworth Legal Publishers / Salem, NH, 8 Industrial Way, Building C, Salem NH 03079. **Tel** (800)548-4001, (603)898-9664.

US
NEW HAMPSHIRE RULEMAKING REGISTER. Added/Corp New Hampshire. Office of Legislative Services. Administrative Procedures Division. **VFOAT** Rulemaking Register. Vol. 1, No. 1 (Apr. 10, 1981)-. English. wk. $60.00. Office of Legislative Services Division, Room 109 State House, Concord NH 03301. **Tel** (603)271-3680. **LC** KFN1236; .N48. **DD** 348.742/025; 347.420825.

US
NEW HAMPSHIRE SELECTED MOTOR VEHICLE AND BOATING LAWS. Main/Corp New Hampshire. **VFOAT** New Hampshire Motor Vehicle and Boating Laws; N.H. Motor Vehicle and Boating Laws. (1990)-. Periodical. English. an. $40.00. Butterworth Legal Publishers / Salem, NH, 8 Industrial Way, Building C, Salem NH 03079. **Tel** (800)548-4001, (603)898-9664. **LC** KFN1497.A29; N48. **DD** 343.74209/44/05; 347.420394405. ***Continues*** *New Hampshire. New Hampshire Motor Vehicle Laws and Related Laws, 1050-5776.*

US
NEW JERSEY COURT RULES. English. an (pub. in Sept.). $54.38. Gann Law Books, 1 Washington Park Suite 1500, Newark NJ 07102. **Tel** (201)268-1200.

US/0279-8557
NEW JERSEY EDUCATION LAW REPORT, THE. (198?)-. Periodical. English. mo. $192.00 (one year), $380.00 (two year). Whitaker Newsletter, PO Box 340, 313 South Avenue, Suite 202, Fanwood NJ 07023-0340. **Tel** (201)889-6336, FAX (201)889-6339. **(Subscription address:** Whitaker Newsletters, PO Box 192, Fanwood, NJ 07023-0192**) ED** Irving Evers. **[CCC]. Bk Rev.**
Desc: Latest administrative rulings by the Commissioner of Education and PERC on unit bargaining, tenure, seniority rights, and special education.

US/0028-5803
NEW JERSEY LAW JOURNAL, THE. [N. J. law j.]. **VFOAT** New Jersey Law Journal and New Jersey Law News. Vol. 1, No. 1 (Jan. 1878)-. Periodical. English. wk. $272.00. American Lawyer Media, L.P., 600 3rd Avenue, New York NY 10016. **Tel** (212)973-2800. **(Subscription address:** New Jersey Law Journal, PO Box 20081, Newark, NJ 07101**) ED** Bruce G Rosen. Index available. cum. index. **Ad Acc. Circ:** 11,700. available on microfilm from University Microfilms International (UMI). ***Absorbed*** *New Jersey Law News.*
Desc: It contains recent state judicial and administrative decisions in digest form, complete text of state legislation, commentary on legal developments contributed by experts in the field, as well as journalism focusing on the courts, judges, lawyers and the business of legal practice in New Jersey.
Ind/Abst Fed. Tax Artic.; Leg. Resour. Index (1980-); LegalTrac (1980-).

US/0195-0983
NEW JERSEY LAWYER (MAGAZINE). (NEW JERSEY LAWYER.). [N.J. lawyer]. **Added/Corp** New Jersey State Bar Association. No. 88 (Aug. 1979)-. Periodical. English. Eight times a year. New Jersey State Bar Association, 1 Constitution Square, New Brunswick NJ 08901. **Tel** (908)249-5000, FAX (908)249-2815. **ED** Mary Ann Shive. **LC** KF200; .B354. **DD** 349.749/05. Index available. cum. index. **Bk Rev. Ad Acc. Circ:** 18,300 (ctrl). ***Continues*** *Bar Journal (Trenton, N.J.), 0162-1211.*
Desc: Practical information about law office management and substantive law in New Jersey.
Ind/Abst Curr. Law Index (1980-Dec. 1985); Index Leg. Period.; Leg. Resour. Index (1980-Dec. 1985); LegalTrac (1980-1985).

US/1053-1955
NEW JERSEY LAWYERS DIARY AND MANUAL. (NEW JERSEY LAWYERS DIARY AND MANUAL : INCLUDING BAR DIRECTORY OF NEW JERSEY.). [N.J. lawyers diary man.]. **VFOAT** Bar Directory of New Jersey. (19??)-. Periodical. English. an (Dec.). $53.00. Skinder Strauss Associates, PO Box 50, Newark NJ 07101. **Tel** (800)444-4041, (201)642-1440, FAX (201)642-4280. **LC** KF192.N4; L35. **DD** 340/.025749. **Ad Acc, Adv Mgr:** Bergamo. **Circ:** 45,000 (ctrl). ***Continues*** *Lawyers Diary and Manual Including Bar Directory of New Jersey.*

US/0271-8448
NEW JERSEY LEGISLATIVE INDEX. See Law-Abstracting, Bibliographies and Statistics.

US/0735-4010
NEW JERSEY MUNICIPAL LAW NEWS. VFOAT Municipal Law News. Vol. 1, No. 1 (Jan. 1982)-. Periodical. English. sa. $20.00. G & W Legal Publications Inc, PO Box 6791, Lawrenceville NJ 08648. **Tel** (609)394-1910. **ED** Lewis Goldshore and Marsha Wolf. **LC** KFN2231.A15; N47. **DD** 342.749/09; 347.49029. **Circ:** 300.

●US/1070-6364
NEW JERSEY RULES OF COURT. (NEW JERSEY RULES OF COURT : STATE AND FEDERAL.). [N.J. rules court]. **Added/Corp** New Jersey. Supreme Court. United States. Supreme Court. (1993)-. English. an. **LC** KFN2329; .A196. **DD** 347/.749/05. ***Continues*** *Rules Governing the Courts of the State of New Jersey, 1969 Revision, as Amended, 0193-967X.*

US/0146-7603
NEW JERSEY SCHOOL LAW DECISIONS (INDEX). (NEW JERSEY SCHOOL LAW DECISIONS.). English. New Jersey Education Association, PO Box 1211, 180 West State Street, Trenton NJ 08607. **Tel** (609)599-4561 ext. 208, FAX (609)599-1266. **LC** KFN2190.A59; N48. **DD** 344/.749/0702646.

US
NEW JERSEY SESSION LAW SERVICE. Added/Corp West Publishing Company. (19??)-. Periodical. English. ir. West Publishing Company / St. Paul, 50 West Kellogg Boulevard, St. Paul MN 55172. **Tel** (800)328-9352.

US
NEW JERSEY STATUTES - TITLE 18A EDUCATION. English. an. $43.29 (with tax), $41.00 (tax exempt). Gann Law Books, 1 Washington Park Suite 1500, Newark NJ 07102. **Tel** (201)268-1200.

US/1051-8746
NEW JERSEY TRIAL LAWYER, THE. [N. J. trial lawyer]. **Added/Corp** Association of Trial Lawyers of America--New Jersey. **VFOAT** Trial Lawyer. Vol. 1, Issue 1 (1987)-. Periodical. English. Six times a year (Jan., Mar., May, July, Sept., Nov.). $30.00 one year; $58.00 two years; $86.00 three yeasr. Trial Lawyer Publications Inc, 212 East Vine Street, Millville NJ 08332. **Tel** (609)825-9099, (800)331-9000, FAX (609)825-5959. **ED** Stephen C. Rubino and Brad X. Terry. **LC** KFN2338.A15; N49. **DD** 347.749/07; 347.49077. Index available. cum. index. **Bk Rev. Ad Acc, Adv Mgr:** Pat Haffert. **Circ:** 4,200.
Desc: An independent and open forum for the free exchange of information and opinions for attorneys interested in litigation. Coverage ranges widely from technical information to the human issues affecting practitioners.

UK/0264-8121
NEW LAW FOR SURVEYORS. See Real Estate.

UK/0306-6479
NEW LAW JOURNAL, THE. [New law j.]. Vol. 116, No. 5205 (Oct. 28, 1965)-. Periodical. English. wk. £105.00. Butterworth & Co. Ltd. / Kent, England, Borough Green, Sevenoaks Kent TN15 8PH England. **Tel** 011 44 732-884567, FAX 011 44 732-885996. **ED** James Morton. **LC** K14; .E89. **DD** 348.41/026; 344.10826. **[CCC]. Bk Rev.** ***Formed by the union of*** *Law Times (London, England)* ***and*** *Law Journal (London, England : 1866).*
Desc: In addition to regular features there are major articles on different aspects of the law and legal practice contributed by leading experts. These are backed by comprehensive news coverage of the latest developments in the law, litigation, police powers, practice directions and by editorial comment on issues of moment, letters page book reviews, and selected case reports and precedents.
Ind/Abst Appl. Soc. Sci. Index Abstr.; Aust. Leg. Mon. Dig.; Crim. Penol. Police Sci. Abstr.; Curr. Law Index (1980-); Index Leg. Period.; Leg. Resour. Index (1980-); LegalTrac (1980-); Soc. Plann. Policy Dev. Abstr.; Sociol. Abstr. (?-?).

US/0028-6214
NEW MEXICO LAW REVIEW. [N.M. law rev.]. **Added/Corp** University of New Mexico. School of Law. Vol. 1, No. 1 (Jan. 1971)-. Periodical. English. Three times a year. $28.00. University of New Mexico School of Law, 1117 Stanford NE, Albuquerque NM 87131. **Tel** (505)277-4820, 277-8659. **LC** K14; .E9. **DD** 340/.05. cum. index. **Ad Acc. Circ:** 700.
Desc: A survey of general law and New Mexico law.

Ind/Abst Bowne Dig. Corp. Sec. Lawyers; Curr. Law Index (1980-); Fed. Tax Artic.; Index Leg. Period.; Leg. Resour. Index (1980-); LegalTrac (1980-).

US
NEW MEXICO LAWYER. English. mo. $35.00 (one year); $59.00 (two year). New Mexico Legal Press, PO Box 907, Albuquerque NM 87103. **Tel** (505) 243-7995.

US/0951-547X
NEW MEXICO REAL ESTATE LAW REPORTER. English. Butterworth Heinemann / Woburn, MA, 225 Wildwood Avenue, Unit B, Woburn MA 01801. **Tel** (800)366-2665, FAX (617)928-2620, telex 880052. **ED** Jamie Fuller. Index available.

UK
NEW PROPERTY CASES. (19??)-. Academic Scholarly Publication. English. ir (approximately every week). £550.00 UK. New Law Publishing, Brookfield House, Portnall Rise, Wentworth, Surrey GU25 4JZ England. **Tel** 011 44 344 843696.

AT/0312-1674
NEW SOUTH WALES LAW REPORTS. **Added/Corp** New South Wales. Supreme Court. New South Wales. Land and Valuation Court. New South Wales, Australia. Land and Valuation Court. (1971)-. English. ir. Price varies. The Law Book Company Limited, 44-50 Waterloo Road, North Ryde New South Wales, 2113 Australia. **Tel** 011 61 2 8870177, FAX 011 61 2 8887240, telex ASBOOK 27445. **ED** J. D. Heydon and N. J. Haxton. **DD** 348/.944/041. ***Supersedes** State Reports, New South Wales; **Absorbed** Land and Valuation Court Reports of New South Wales.*
Desc: The authorised reports of the Supreme Court of New South Wales containing, where appropriate, important decisions from other Courts and Commissions such as the Land and Environment Court and the District Court.
Ind/Abst Aust. Leg. Mon. Dig.

US
NEW YORK CITY CHARTER AND ADMINISTRATIVE CODE, ANNOTATED. **Main/Corp** New York (City). Charters. Periodical. English. an. Williams Press Inc, PO Box 4025, Albany NY 12204. **Tel** (518)434-1141.
Desc: Includes recodified New York City charter, building, housing maintenance, electrical and plumbing codes, real property assessment, social services, street and highways and city employees.

US/1043-0628
NEW YORK CIVIL MOTION CITATOR. [N. Y. civ. motion cit.]. (1980)-. English. an. $180.00. Moran Publishing Company, PO Box 310, 150 Islip Avenue, Suite 6, Islip NY 11751. **Tel** (800)832-1900, (516)581-1930, FAX (516)581-8937. **ED** Russell F. Moran. **LC** KFN6012.A53; N49. **DD** 347.747/072; 347.470772. Index available. cum. index. **Bk Rev. Circ:** 500.

US/0896-4122
NEW YORK EDUCATION LAW REPORT. [N. Y. educ. law rep.]. (198?)-. Periodical. English. mo. $130.00 (one year), $250.00 (two year). Whitaker Newsletter, PO Box 340, 313 South Avenue, Suite 202, Fanwood NJ 07023-0340. **Tel** (201)889-6336, FAX (201)889-6339. **(Subscription address:** Whitaker Newsletters, PO Box 192, Fanwood, NJ 07023-0192**) ED** Fred Rossi. **LC** PAR. **DD** 371. **[CCC]. Bk Rev.**
Desc: Abstracts of decisions by the Commissioner of Education and PERB on teacher tenure, special education, unit bargaining, and labor issues.

US/0738-1697
NEW YORK JURY VERDICT REPORTER (METROPOLITAN ED.), THE. (THE NEW YORK JURY VERDICT REPORTER.). [N. Y. jury verdict report.]. **VFOAT** Jury Verdict Reporter. (1981)-. Periodical. English. wk (50 issues). $325.50 Westbury, NY; $324.75 New York City, Bronx, Kings, New York, Queens, and Richmond counties; $300.00 other. Moran Publishing Company, PO Box 310, 150 Islip Avenue, Suite 6, Islip NY 11751. **Tel** (800)832-1900, (516)581-1930, FAX (516)581-8937. **ED** Russell F. Moran. **DD** 348. **Ad Acc, Adv Mgr:** Karen Hertz. **Circ:** 900. ***Absorbed** New York Jury Verdict Reporter (Upstate edition).*

US/0028-7326
NEW YORK LAW JOURNAL. [N. Y. law j.]. (March 26, 1888)-. Newspaper. English. da (except Sat., Sun., and holidays). $465.00. New York Law Publishing Company, 345 Park Avenue South, New York NY 10010. **Tel** (212)741-8300, (800)888-8300. **ED** Charles Kiley. Index available. **Bk Rev. Ad Acc. Circ:** 16,000. available on microfilm and microfiche from University Microfilms International (UMI).
Desc: Legal publication.
Ind/Abst Bowne Dig. Corp. Sec. Lawyers; Curr. Lit. Fam. Plan. (19??-199?); Fed. Tax Artic.; Law Office Inf. Serv.; Leg. Inf. Manage. Index (19??-); Leg. Resour. Index (1980-); LegalTrac (1980-); N. Y. Law J. Dig.-Annot. (1937-).

US/0745-4406
NEW YORK LAW JOURNAL DIGEST-ANNOTATOR. **See** Law-Abstracting, Bibliographies and Statistics.

US/0145-448X
NEW YORK LAW SCHOOL LAW REVIEW. [N.Y. Law sch. law rev.]. **Main/Corp** New York Law School. Vol. 22 (1976)-. Periodical. English. qt. $30.00. New York Law School, 57 Worth Street, New York NY 10013. **Tel** (212)431-2109. **LC** K14; .E933. **DD** 340/.0973. available on microfilm and microfiche from University Microfilms International (UMI). ***Continues** New York Law Forum, 0028-7318.*
Ind/Abst Bowne Dig. Corp. Sec. Lawyers; Curr. Law Index (1980-); Fed. Tax Artic.; Index Leg. Period.; Leg. Resour. Index (1980-); LegalTrac (1980-); PAIS Int. Print (1991-).

US
NEW YORK LAWYERS DIARY AND MANUAL. **VFOAT** Bar Directory of the State of New York. (19??)-. English. an (Nov. of the prior year). $47.00. Skinder Strauss Associates, PO Box 50, Newark NJ 07101. **Tel** (800)444-4041, (201)642-1440, FAX (201)642-4280.

US/0275-7346
NEW YORK LAWYER'S LETTER. [N.Y. lawyer's lett.]. (1950)-. Periodical. English. ir (48 issues a year). $105.00 (one year). Doran Publications Inc, Northway 10 Executive Park, Ballston Lake NY 12019. **Tel** (518)877-7492. **ED** Robert F. Doran. **DD** 340. **Circ:** 1,000.
Desc: Report of court cases and legislation of interest to New York attorneys.

US/0193-7693
NEW YORK NO-FAULT ARBITRATION REPORTS. **Added/Corp** American Arbitration Association. **VFOAT** No-Fault Arbitration Reports. **VAT** New York No Fault Arbitration Reports. Vol. 1 (Jan. 1977)-. Periodical. English. mo. $90.00. American Arbitration Association, 140 West 51st Street, New York NY 10020. **Tel** (212)484-4011, (212)484-4014, FAX (212)765-4874, telex 12463. **ED** Roger Mooney. Index available. **Circ:** 650 (ctrl).
Desc: Summaries of actual no-fault arbitration awards including master cases.

US/0545-6339
NEW YORK SCHOOL DISTRICT LAW LETTER, THE. [N.Y. sch. dist. law lett.]. **Added/Corp** New York State Association of School Attorneys. **VFOAT** School District Law Letter. Vol. 1 (1957)-. Periodical. English. sm. $72.00 (one year). Doran Publications Inc, Northway 10 Executive Park, Ballston Lake NY 12019. **Tel** (518)877-7492. **ED** Patricia A Fitzpatrick. **DD** 344. Index available (publ separately). **Circ:** 1,000 (ctrl).
Desc: A publication reporting cases and legislation affecting education in New York State.

US/0028-7547
NEW YORK STATE BAR JOURNAL. [N.Y. state bar j.]. **Added/Corp** New York State Bar Association. New York State Bar Association. Bulletin. Vol. 1 (Mar. 1928)-. Periodical. English. Eight times a year. $16.00. New York State Bar Association, One Elk Street, Albany NY 12207. **Tel** (518)463-3200. **ED** Eugene C. Gerhart. **LC** K14; .E963. **DD** 349.747/05; 347.47005. Index available. **Bk Rev. Ad Acc. Circ:** 48,000 (ctrl). available on microfilm and microfiche from University Microfilms International (UMI). ***Continues** New York State Bar Bulletin, 0743-4014.*
Desc: Articles and other material of general interest to the legal (and related) profession.
Ind/Abst Bowne Dig. Corp. Sec. Lawyers; Crim. Justice Period. Index; Curr. Law Index (1980-); Fed. Tax Artic.; Index Leg. Period.; Law Office Inf. Serv.; Leg. Resour. Index (1980-); LegalTrac (1980-); PAIS Int. Print (1991-).

US
NEW YORK STATE BOARD OF ELECTIONS FORMAL OPINION / STATE OF NEW YORK, STATE BOARD OF ELECTIONS. **Main/Corp** New York (State). State Board of Elections. **VFOAT** N.Y.S. Board of Elections Formal Opinion; NYS Board of Elections Formal Opinion; State Board of Elections Formal Opinion; State Board of Elections Opinion. No. 6 (1982)-. English. New York State Board of Elections, 99 Washington Avenue, Albany NY 12210. **LC** KFN5710; .A556. **DD** 342.747/07; 347.47027. ***Continues** New York (State). State Board of Elections. Formal Opinion, 0271-4736.*

US/0028-7636
NEW YORK STATE LAW DIGEST. [N. Y. state law dig.]. **Added/Corp** New York State Bar Association. No. 1 (March 1965)-. Periodical. English. mo. $32.00. New York State Bar Association, One Elk Street, Albany NY 12207. **Tel** (518)463-3200. **ED** David D. Siegel. **LC** UNC. **Circ:** 44,000 (ctrl). available on microfilm from University Microfilms International (UMI). ***Continues** Lawyer Service Letter.*

Desc: A digest summarizing and analyzing recent New York and federal court cases and legislation of importance to New York practising attorneys.

US/0737-5891
NEW YORK STATE TAX MONITOR. **VFOAT** Tax Monitor. Vol. 1, No. 1 (Sept. 1983)-. Periodical. English. Twelve times a year. $195.00. Law Planning Reports Ltd, 19 West 36th Street, New York NY 10018. **Tel** (212)307-1300. **LC** KFN5860.A15; N48. **DD** 343.74704/05; 347.4703405.

US
NEW YORK TAX LAW. **Main/Corp** New York (State). **VFOAT** Tax Law & Regulations. 1977-. English. an. Matthew Bender & Company Inc., 1275 Broadway, Albany NY 12204. **Tel** (800)833-9844, (518)487-3000.

US/0028-7881
NEW YORK UNIVERSITY LAW REVIEW (1950). (NEW YORK UNIVERSITY LAW REVIEW.). [N.Y. Univ. law rev.]. **Added/Corp** New York University. School of Law. Vol. 25, No. 1 (Jan. 1950)-. Periodical. English. Six times a year. $35.00. New York University School of Law, 110 West Third Street, New York NY 10012. **Tel** (212)998-6540, (212)998-6560, FAX (212)995-4032. **LC** K14; .E974. Index available in last issue of volume--attached. **Bk Rev. Ad Acc. Pr Rev. Circ:** 3,000 (ctrl). Documents available from The Genuine Article, The Genuine Article, UMI Article Clearinghouse. ***Continues** New York University Law Quarterly Review.*
Ind/Abst Bowne Dig. Corp. Sec. Lawyers; Commun. Abstr.; Crim. Justice Abstr.; Curr. Contents Soc. Behav. Sci.; Curr. Law Index (1980-); Expand. Acad. Index (1984-); Fed. Tax Artic.; Highw. Res. Abstr.; Index Leg. Period.; Int. Bibliogr. Sociol.; Int. Polit. Sci. Abstr.; Leg. Resour. Index (1980-); LegalTrac (1980-); Newsp. Period. Abstr. (1988-); Res. Alert [Full Cov.]; Soc. Sci. Cit. Index [Full Cov.].

US/0048-7481
NEW YORK UNIVERSITY REVIEW OF LAW AND SOCIAL CHANGE. (REVIEW OF LAW AND SOCIAL CHANGE.). [N.Y. Univ. rev. law soc. changee]. **Main/Corp** New York University. Vol. 1 (1971)-. Periodical. English. qt. $24.00 US; $28.00 other. New York University School of Law, 110 West Third Street, New York NY 10012. **Tel** (212)998-6540, (212)998-6560, FAX (212)995-4032. **LC** K14.E97. **DD** 301.1/15. **Bk Rev. Circ:** 800. available on microfilm and microfiche from University Microfilms International (UMI).
Desc: Publishes works that deal with issues of law and social policy which look for legal solutions to problems of social inequity.
Ind/Abst Bowne Dig. Corp. Sec. Lawyers; Crim. Justice Abstr.; Curr. Law Index (1980-); Index Leg. Period.; Leg. Resour. Index (1980-); LegalTrac (1980-); PAIS Int. Print (1991-).

NZ/0110-1277
NEW ZEALAND ADMINISTRATIVE REPORTS : NZAR. **VFOAT** NZAR. (1976)-. English. ir. Butterworth Heinemann / Woburn, MA, 225 Wildwood Avenue, Unit B, Woburn MA 01801. **Tel** (800)366-2665, FAX (617)928-2620, telex 880052. **LC** LAW . **DD** 342.931/06. **[CCC].**

US/0028-8373
NEW ZEALAND LAW JOURNAL, THE. (THE NEW ZEALAND LAW JOURNAL : NZLJ.). [N. Z. law j.]. **VFOAT** NZLJ. Began with: Vol. 4, No. 1 (March 6, 1928). Periodical. English. mo. $176.00 US. Butterworth & Co. Ltd. / Kent, England, Borough Green, Sevenoaks Kent TN15 8PH England. **Tel** 011 44 732-884567, FAX 011 44 732-885996. **ED** Pat Downey. **[CCC].** Index Available, published separately, free-automatically sent. cum. index. Documents available from UMI Article Clearinghouse. ***Continues** Butterworths Fortnightly Notes.*
Ind/Abst ABI/INFORM Glob. Ed.; Aust. Leg. Mon. Dig.; Curr. Law Index (1980-); Index Leg. Period.; Leg. Resour. Index (1980-); LegalTrac (1980-).

NZ
NEW ZEALAND LAW SOCIETY'S NEWS SHEET, THE. **Main/Corp** New Zealand Law Society. English. sm. 90.00NZ$. New Zealand Law Society, Box 5041, 26 Waring Taylor Street, Wellington 1 New Zealand. **Tel** (04)727837, FAX (04)737-909. **ED** S R Mazengorb. **DD** 340/.09931. **Bk Rev. Ad Acc. Circ:** 6,100.

NZ/0114-0655
NEW ZEALAND RECENT LAW REVIEW. **Added/Corp** Legal Research Foundation (University of Auckland). **VFOAT** Recent Law Review; NZ Recent Law Review. (March 1989)-. English. Four times a year. 180.00NZ$. Legal Research Foundation, PO Box 741, Auckland 1 New Zealand. **Tel** 011 64 9 3099540, FAX 011 64 9 3737473. **ED** Paul Rishworth. **LC** K14; .N988. **DD** 349.93/05; 349.3005. Index available (Bound in Dec. issue). **Ad Acc. Circ:** 900 (ctrl). ***Continues** New Zealand Recent Law.*
Desc: Provides critical analysis of recent and pending developments in New Zealand law.
Ind/Abst Index Leg. Period.

Law

NZ/0549-0618
NEW ZEALAND UNIVERSITIES LAW REVIEW. [N. Z. univ. law rev.]. Vol. 1 (1963)-. Periodical. English. sa (2 issues). 65.00NZ$; $40.00 other. Oxford University Press / New Zealand, PO Box 11-149 Ellerslie, Auckland 5 New Zealand. **Tel** 011 64 9 5233134. **(Subscription address:** William W. Gaunt & Sons, Inc. / North America Subscriptions, 3011 Gulf Drive, Gaunt Building, Holmes Beach FL 34217.) **[CCC].**
Ind/Abst Aust. Leg. Mon. Dig.; Index Leg. Period.; Leg. Resour. Index (1980-); LegalTrac (1980-).

US
NEWBERG ON CLASS ACTIONS. **Added/Corp** Shepard's Inc. of Colorado Springs. Vol. 1 (1977)-. English. ir. $525.00. Shepards McGraw-Hill Inc, 555 Middle Creek Parkway, PO Box 35300, Colorado Springs CO 80935-3530. **Tel** (719)488-3000, FAX (800)525-0053. Index available in last issue of volume--attached. **Bk Rev**. **Ad Acc**.
Desc: Since its 1977 publication it has been the leading authority for class action law and litigation consulted by lawyers and judges nationwide.

CN/0715-4755
NEWFOUNDLAND & PRINCE EDWARD ISLAND REPORTS (BOUND CUMULATION). (NEWFOUNDLAND & PRINCE EDWARD ISLAND REPORTS.). [Nfld. P.E.I. rep.]. **Added/Corp** Newfoundland. Court of Appeal. Prince Edward Island. Court of Appeal. Law Society of Newfoundland. Law Society of Prince Edward Island. Vol. 1 (1971)-. English. ir. $75.00 per volume U.S. Maritime Law Book Ltd, PO Box 302, Fredericton New Brunswick, E3B 4Y9 Canada. **Tel** (506)453-9921, (800)561-0220. **DD** 348.717/043. Index available. cum. index.
Desc: Law reports-Newfoundland and Prince Edward Island Courts.

CN/0028-8888
NEWFOUNDLAND GAZETTE, THE. [Nfld. gaz.]. (1???)-. Periodical. English. wk. 75.00Can$. Newfoundland Gazette, PO Box 8700, St John's Newfoundland A1B 4J6 Canada. **Tel** (709)576-3649, FAX (709)576-3627, telex 016-4197. **ED** David C. B. Dawe. Index available. cum. index. **Circ:** 1,300 (ctrl). available on microfilm from Toronto Micromedia; and New York Public Library; available on microfilm and microfiche from University Microfilms International (UMI).
Desc: Includes legal notices, subordinate legislation, and statutory notices.

US
NEWS AND VIEWS (WASHINGTON, D.C.). (NEWS AND VIEWS / PROBATION DIVISION.). **Added/Corp** United States. Administrative Office of the United States Courts. Probation Division. United States. Administrative Office of the United States Courts. Probation and Pretrial Services Division. (19??)-. Periodical. English. bw. Administrative Office of the United States Courts, 811 Vermont Avenue NW, Room 655, Washington DC 20544. **LC** HV9304; .N56. **DD** 364.6/3/097305.

US
NEWS BRIEFS : A PUBLICATION OF THE LOUISIANA STATE BAR ASSOCIATION. **Main/Corp** Louisiana State Bar Association. Vol. 22, No. 1 (Apr.-May 1979)-. Periodical. English. Louisiana State Bar Association, 210 Okeefe Avenue, Suite 600, New Orleans LA 70112. **Tel** (504)522-9172. **Continues** LSBA News.

US/0198-702X
NEWS BULLETIN - ARKANSAS BAR ASSOCIATION. **Main/Corp** Arkansas Bar Association. Bulletin. English. bm. Newspublications Assistant, Arkansas Bar Association, 400 West Markham Street, Little Rock AR 72201. **Tel** (501)375-4605. **ED** Ruth Williams. **LC** KF200; .A7. **DD** 340/.06/0767. **Circ:** 3,400 (ctrl).
Desc: A legal news service for members of the Arkansas Bar association.
Ind/Abst Law Office Inf. Serv.

CE
NEWS LETTER - BAR ASSOCIATION OF SRI LANKA. **Main/Corp** Bar Association of Sri Lanka. No. 1 (Aug. 1975)-. Periodical. English. qt. Bar Association of Sri Lanka, 129 Hulftsdorp Street, Colombo 12 Sri Lanka Ceylon. **Tel** 547134. **ED** A P Niles and Ronald Perera. **DD** 340/.06/25493. **Bk Rev**. **Ad Acc**. **Circ:** 2,500 (ctrl).

US/0149-0737
NEWS MEDIA & THE LAW, THE. [News media law]. **Added/Corp** Reporters Committee for Freedom of the Press. **VAT** News Media and the Law. Vol. 1 (Oct. 1977)-. Periodical. English. qt (Jan., Apr., July, Oct.). $25.00. News Media & The Law, 1735 I Street NW/Suite 504, Washington DC 20006. **Tel** (202)466-6313, FAX (202)466-6313. **ED** Jane E. Kirtley and Robert S. Becker. **LC** KF2750.A15; N48. **DD** 343/.73/0998. Index available. cum. index. **Circ:** 3,000. available on microfilm and microfiche from University Microfilms International (UMI). Documents available from UMI Article Clearinghouse. **Supersedes** Press Censorship Newsletter.
Desc: Publishes analysis of court decisions, federal and state legislation, and events that affect the news media's ability to gather and disseminate news.
Ind/Abst Curr. Law Index (1982-); Expand. Acad. Index (1992-); Hum. Rights Intern. Rep.; Leg. Resour. Index (1982-); LegalTrac (1982-); Newsp. Period. Abstr. (1992-).

US/0896-5633
NEWSLETTER (AMERICAN ACADEMY OF PSYCHIATRY AND THE LAW). See Medical Science and Technology-Psychiatry.

US/0732-2771
NEWSLETTER - ASSOCIATION OF AMERICAN LAW SCHOOLS. SECTION ON WOMEN IN LEGAL EDUCATION. (NEWSLETTER-SECTION ON WOMEN IN LEGAL EDUCATION.). [Newsl. - Assoc. Am. Law Schools, Sect. Women Legal Educ.]. **Main/Corp** Association of American Law Schools. Section on Women in Legal Education. Newsletter. English. Section on Women in Legal Education, Brooklyn Law School, 250 Joralemon, Brooklyn NY 11201.

US/0197-4815
NEWSLETTER - ASSOCIATION OF LAW LIBRARIES OF UPSTATE NEW YORK. See Library and Information Sciences.

AT/0311-5984
NEWSLETTER / AUSTRALIAN LAW LIBRARIANS' GROUP. *Title Change.* See Library and Information Sciences.

US
NEWSLETTER / HARVARD WOMEN'S LAW ASSOCIATION. **Added/Corp** Harvard Women's Law Association. (1990)-. Newsletter. English.

US
NEWSLETTER - ILLINOIS STATE BAR ASSOCIATION. **Main/Corp** Illinois State Bar Association. Section on Individual Rights and Responsibilities. V. 1- Aug. 1972-. Newsletter. English. ir. $38.00 (for one newsletter subscription), $8.00 (for each additional newsletter subscription). Illinois State Bar Association & Responsibilities, 424 South Second, Springfield IL 62701. **Tel** (217)525-1760. **ED** Patrick J Hughes Jr. **LC** KF4749.A1; I44. **DD** 323.4/0973. **Circ:** 550.

CN/0229-2181
NEWSLETTER (INTERNATIONAL OMBUDSMAN INSTITUTE). (NEWSLETTER / INTERNATIONAL OMBUDSMAN INSTITUTE.). [Newsl. - Int. Ombudsman Inst.]. **Added/Corp** International Ombudsman Institute. Vol. 1, No. 1 (Jan. 1979)-. Newsletter. English. ir (Approx. 3-4 times a year.). 10.00Can$. International Ombudsman Institute, University of Alberta, Faculty of Law, Edmonton, Alberta T6G 2H5 Canada. **Tel** (403)492-3196. **ED** Linda Reif. **DD** 350.9/1. **Circ:** 200.
Ind/Abst Hum. Rights Intern. Rep.

CN/0715-3465
NEWSLETTER - LAW SOCIETY OF ALBERTA. (NEWSLETTER / LAW SOCIETY OF ALBERTA, CANADIAN BAR ASSOCIATION, ALBERTA BR.). [Newsl. - Law Soc. Alta.]. **Main/Corp** Law Society of Alberta. **Added/Corp** Canadian Bar Association. Alberta Branch. **VAT** Newsletter - Canadian Bar Association, Alberta Br. (1976)-. Newsletter. English. bm. Free on request. Canadian Bar Association / Alberta Branch, 1830 540 5th Avenue Southwest, Calgary Alberta T2P 0M2 Canada. **Tel** (403)263-3707. **LC** KE361.A43; A25. **DD** 340/.06/27123.

US
NEWSLETTER - MID-AMERICA ASSOCIATION OF LAW LIBRARIES. See Library and Information Sciences.

US/0197-2707
NEWSLETTER-STATE, COURT, AND COUNTY LAW LIBRARIES SECTION. See Library and Information Sciences.

US/0094-2251
NEWSLETTER - VIRGINIA STATE BAR. YOUNGER MEMBERS CONFERENCE. (NEWSLETTER.). **Main/Corp** Virginia State Bar. Younger Members Conference. Vol. 1, (Oct. 1973)-. Newsletter. English. Virginia State Bar, 801 East Main Street, Ross Building #1000, Richmond VA 23219. **Tel** (804)924-3416. **LC** KF200; .V57. **DD** 340/.05.

US/0276-203X
NEWSNOTES - CENTER FOR LAW AND EDUCATION (U.S.). (NEWSNOTES / CENTER FOR LAW AND EDUCATION, INC.). **Added/Corp** Center for Law and Education (U.S.). No. 1, (July 1979)-. Periodical. English. Four times a year. Free. Center for Law & Education Inc., 955 Massachusetts Avenue, Suite 3A, Cambridge MA 02139. **Tel** (617)876-6611, FAX (617)876-0203. **ED** Sharon Schumack. **LC** KF4102; .N48. **DD** 344.73/07. **Circ:** 5,000.
Desc: Newsletter on education advocacy. Includes noteworthy legal developments, reports on local advocacy efforts and useful resources.

BE/0772-5183
NIEUWSBRIEF - LIGA VOOR MENSENRECHTEN. [Nieuwsbr. - Liga mensenrechten]. (1982)-. Periodical. Dutch. mo. **UDC** 342.711001.
Ind/Abst Hum. Rights Intern. Rep.

NR
NIGERIAN BAR JOURNAL. - . Periodical. English. sa. $6.50. Nigerian Bar Association, Ozumba Mbadiwe Street, PMB 12610, Lagos Nigeria. **Tel** 01 610783 or 01 610778.
Ind/Abst Index Foreign Leg. Per.

NR/0189-207X
NIGERIAN CURRENT LAW REVIEW : THE JOURNAL OF THE NIGERIAN INSTITUTE OF ADVANCED LEGAL STUDIES. **Added/Corp** Nigerian Institute of Advanced Legal Studies. (Jan. 1982)-. Periodical. English. an. $80.00. University of Lagos / Nigerian Institute of Advanced Legal Studies, University of Lagos Campus, PMB 12820, Lagos Nigeria. **Tel** 821752/3, FAX 825558, telex 27506 NAILS NG. **ED** M.A. Ajomo. **LC** K14; .I357. **DD** 349.669/05; 346.69005. Index available. **Bk Rev**. **Ad Acc**. **Circ:** 2,000 (ctrl).
Desc: Carries a digest of legislation, both federal and state; also notes some important judicial decisions from superior courts. Carries comments by experts on any legislation or judicial decision thought necessary, and also carries learned articles on current important matters. Publishes reviews of newly published law books.

NR/0078-0774
NIGERIAN LAW JOURNAL, THE. [Niger. law j.]. Vol. 1, No. 1 (Nov. 1964)-. Periodical. English. an. Oceana Publications, Inc., 75 Main Street, Dobbs Ferry NY 10522. **Tel** (914)693-1320, FAX (914)693-0402. **DD** 340/.05.
Ind/Abst Index Foreign Leg. Per.

JA
NIHON KYOIKUHO GAKKAI NEMPO. **Main/Corp** Nihon Kyoikuho Gakkai. **VFOAT** Educational Law Review. Issue No. 1- 1972-. Japanese (summaries and/or abstracts in English; table of contents in English). ¥1000. Nihon Kyoikuho Gakkai, 2-17 Kanda Jimbocho Chiyoda-ku, Tokyo Japan. **LC** K14; .I39.

GW/0934-8778
NJW-COR COMPUTERREPORT : DER NEUEN JURISTISCHEN WOCHENSCHRIFT : INFORMATIONSMANAGEMENT AND BUROORGANISATION IN DER JUSTISCHEN PRAXIS. **VFOAT** Computerreport der Neuen Juristischen Wochenschrift; NJW-CoR Computerreport; A.Neue juristische Wochenschrift Computerreport. 1/88 (Sept./Oct. 1988)-. Periodical. German. bm. CH Beck Verlagsbuchhandlung, D 80791 Munich Germany. **Tel** 011 49 89 381891. **(Subscription address:** CH Beck Verlagsbuchhandlung, Wilhelmstrasse 9, D 80801 Munich Germany.**)**

US
NOCALL NEWSLETTER / NORTHERN CALIFORNIA ASSOCIATION OF LAW LIBRARIES. See Library and Information Sciences.

JA
NOGYO ROPPO. **Main/Corp** Japan. **Added/Corp** Japan. Norinsho. Gakuyo Shobo. (1976)-. Periodical. Japanese. ¥2800. Gakuyo Shobo, 7-5 Fujimi 1 Chiyoda-ku, Tokyo 102 Japan. *Continues* Nogyo Shoroppo.

US/0890-2208
NOLO NEWS. (NOLO NEWS : PEOPLE'S SELF-HELP LAW). [Nolo news]. Vol. 1, No. 1 (Summer 1981)-. Periodical. English. Four times a year. $12.00 (two years) US; $30.00 (two years) other. Nolo Press, 950 Parker Street, Berkeley CA 94710. **Tel** (415)549-1976, FAX (415)548-5902. **ED** Barbara Kate Repa. **LC** K14; .043. **DD** 349.73/05; 347.3005. **[CCC].** Bk Rev, (Qty: 40). **Circ:** 100,000.
Desc: Aims to keep readers up-to-date on law changes that affect Nolo books and to provide practical legal information to readers for use in everyday life.

US/0047-8997
NOLPE NOTES. [NOLPE notes]. **Main/Corp** National Organization on Legal Problems of Education. **VAT** National Organization on Legal Problems of Education notes. (196?)-. Periodical. English. mo. comes with membership. National Organization on Legal Problems of Education, 3601 Southwest 29th Street, Suite 223, Topeka KS 66614. **Tel** (913)273-3550, FAX (913)273-2001. **ED** Thomas N. Jones. **DD** 344. **Bk Rev. Circ:** 2,500 (ctrl).
Desc: Education law case digests and summaries.

GR
NOMIKO VEMA. Added/Corp Dikegorikos Syllogos Athenon. (19??)-. Periodical. Greek, Modern. ir (approximately 12 per year). Dr12000.00 Greece; Dr15000.00 other. President of Lawyers Association, Akadimias and Mavromichali 2, Athens 106 79 Greece. **Tel** 011 30 1 3611830. **LC** K14; .O46. ***Continues*** *Nomikon Vema.*
Ind/Abst Index Foreign Leg. Per.

BL
NOMOS (FORTALEZA, BRAZIL). (NOMOS.). **Added/Corp** Universidade Federal do Ceara. Departamento de Direito Publico. (1978)-. Periodical. Portuguese (Portuguese). an. $5.00. Curso de Mestrado em Direito da UFC, Praca Clovis Bevilacqua, s/n, 60035-180 Fortaleza - CE Brazil. **Tel** 55 85 231 4334, FAX 55 85 261 6765. **ED** Willis S. Guerra Filho. **LC** K14; .O48. **DD** 349.81/05; 348.1005. **Bk Rev**, (Qty: 2). **Ad Acc. Pr Rev.** ctrl circ.
Desc: Review of the post-graduate courses at the Federal University of Ceara's Law Faculty. Contains articles of the professors and students, as well as other related institutions in Brazil.

IT
NOMOS (ROME, ITALY). (NOMOS.). (1988)-. Periodical. Italian. Four times a year. L77000.00 Italy; L121000.00 other. Istituto Poligrafico Zecca Stato, Piazza Verdi 10, 00198 Rome Italy. **Tel** 011 39 6 85082307, 011 39 6 85082221. **LC** K14; .O484.

NO/0029-1315
NORDISK DOMSSAMLING. [Nord. domssaml.]. (1959)-. Periodical. Multiple languages (Danish, Norwegian and Swedish). qt. Kr520.00, $92.00. Scandinavian University Press, PO Box 2959 Toeyen, N 0608 Oslo 6 Norway. **Tel** 011 47 2 2575400, FAX 011 47 2 2575353, telex 71896 UROR N. **(Subscription address:** Scandinavian University Press, 200 Meacham Ave., Elmont NY 11003.**)** **ED** Ole Agersnap, Ole Roos, Gudmundur Jonsson, Trond Dolva, and Bjoern Bernhard. **DD** 345. Index available. **Ad Acc. Circ:** 1,000.
Desc: A collection of verdicts passed by the Supreme Courts in areas of legal cooperation in the Nordic countries.

PE
NORMAS LEGALES. Vol. 1 (June 1942)-. Periodical. Spanish. Twice a year. Normas Legales, Calle Orbegoso 338, Trujillo Peru. **Tel** 257509, telex 43078 PE ICETRU. **ED** Franco Chico Colugna. Index available. cum. index. **Bk Rev. Ad Acc. Pr Rev.** available on diskette.

US/0549-7434
NORTH CAROLINA CENTRAL LAW JOURNAL. [North Carol. Centr. law j.]. **Added/Corp** North Carolina Central University. School of Law. Vol. 2, No. 1 (Spring 1970)-. Periodical. English. Twice a year. $12.00 US; $14.00 other. NC Central University School of Law, Box 19678, Durham NC 27707. **Tel** (919)682-8078. **ED** Wayne Hamilton. **LC** UNC. **DD** 340/.05. cum. index. **Bk Rev. Circ:** 700. ***Continues*** *North Carolina College Law Journal.*
Desc: Open forum for the publication of any appropriately documented legal writing concerning new or evolving areas of the law and problems facing minorities.
Ind/Abst Bowne Dig. Corp. Sec. Lawyers; Crim. Justice Abstr.; Curr. Law Index (1980-); Index Leg. Period.; Leg. Resour. Index (1980-); LegalTrac (1980-).

US/0549-7450
NORTH CAROLINA COURT OF APPEALS REPORTS. Main/Corp North Carolina. Court of Appeals. V. 1- Spring session 1968-. English. North Carolina Judicial Department, PO Box 2448, Raleigh NC 27602. **LC** KFN7448; .A2. **DD** 348/.756/043.

US/0883-7783
NORTH CAROLINA LAW MONITOR, THE. ***Ceased.*** [N. C. law monit.]. **Added/Corp** State Capital Services, Inc. **VFOAT** Law Monitor. Vol. 1, No. 1 (Mar. 8, 1985)-(19??). Periodical. English. sm. State Capital Services Inc, 3600 Glenwood Avenue, Raleigh NC 27612-4945. **Tel** (919)787-7086. **LC** KFN7457; .N63. **DD** 348.756/048; 347.560848. **Circ:** 1,000 (ctrl). ***Absorbed*** *North Carolina Case Reporter.*
Desc: A summary of North Carolina appellate court decisions.

US/0029-2524
NORTH CAROLINA LAW REVIEW. [North Carol. law rev.]. **Added/Corp** University of North Carolina (1793-1962). School of Law. North Carolina Law Review Association. University of North Carolina at Chapel Hill. School of Law. Vol. 1 (June 1922)-. Periodical. English. Six times a year. $32.00 US; $36.00 other. University of North Carolina Law School, CB 3380 Van Heche Wettach Hall, Chapel Hill NC 27599. **Tel** (919)962-3926. **LC** K14; .O694. **DD** 345.32. Index available. cum. index. **Bk Rev. Ad Acc. Circ:** 2,000 (ctrl).
Desc: Articles, comments, and notes analyzing current legal problems and significant new developments in the law.
Ind/Abst Bowne Dig. Corp. Sec. Lawyers; Curr. Law Index; Fed. Tax Artic.; Index Leg. Period.; Leg. Resour. Index (1980-); LegalTrac (1980-); Ocean. Abstr.; PAIS Int. Print (1991-).

US/1041-1747
NORTH CAROLINA LAWYERS WEEKLY. [N. C. lawyers wkly.]. **VFOAT** Lawyers Weekly. Vol. 1, No. 1, Mar. 28 (1988)-. Periodical. English. wk. $238.50. Lawyers Weekly, 107 Fayetteville Street Mall, Raleigh NC 27601. **Tel** (800) 876-5297, FAX (919)829-8088. **ED** Michael J. Dayton. **DD** 340. **Ad Acc, Adv Mgr:** Laura Price. Full Page (B&W) $1237.00. Half Page (B&W) $687.00. Full Page (Color) $1577.00. Half Page (Color) $1024.00. **Circ:** 4,000 (ctrl).

US
NORTH CAROLINA REGISTER, THE. Added/Corp North Carolina. Office of Administrative Hearings. Vol. 1, Issue 1 (Apr. 15, 1986)-. Periodical. English. Twenty-four times a year. $111.30 North Carolina (includes 6 percent state tax); $105.00 other. Office of Administrative Hearings, PO Drawer 27447, Raleigh NC 27611. **Tel** (919)733-2691. **LC** KFN7436; .N67. **DD** 348.756/025; 347.560825. cum. index.

US/0048-0665
NORTH CAROLINA RESEARCHER, THE. Began May 1970. Periodical. English. mo. $95.00. The Research Group Inc, PO Box 7187, Charlottesville VA 22906. **LC** KFN7457; .N65. **DD** 348.756/048.

US/1058-255X
NORTH CAROLINA RULES OF COURT. FEDERAL. (NORTH CAROLINA RULES OF COURT. FEDERAL : INCLUDING AMENDMENTS RECEIVED THROUGH SEPTEMBER 15 ...). [North Carol. rules court, Fed.]. **Added/Corp** West Publishing Company. (19??)-. English. West Publishing Company, 610 Opperman Drive, PO Box 64526, Eagan MN 55123-1308. **Tel** (612)687-5618, (800)328-9352, FAX (612)687-5388, (800)562-2329. **LC** KF8816; .A1967. **DD** 347.73/051/09756; 347.3075109756. ***Continues in part*** *North Carolina Rules of Court, with Amendments Received to ..., 0732-281X.*

US/1058-2568
NORTH CAROLINA RULES OF COURT. STATE. (NORTH CAROLINA RULES OF COURT. STATE : INCLUDING AMENDMENTS RECEIVED THROUGH SEPTEMBER 15 ...). [North Carol. rules court, State]. **Added/Corp** West Publishing Company. (19??)-. English. West Publishing Company, 610 Opperman Drive, PO Box 64526, Eagan MN 55123-1308. **Tel** (612)687-5618, (800)328-9352, FAX (612)687-5388, (800)562-2329. **LC** KF8816; .A1968. **DD** 347.73/051/09756; 347.3075109756. ***Continues in part*** *North Carolina Rules of Court, with Amendments Received to ..., 0732-281X.*

US/1047-5524
NORTH CAROLINA STATE BAR NEWSLETTER, THE. [North Carol. State Bar newsl.]. **Added/Corp** North Carolina State Bar. Vol. 6, No. 4 (1981)-. Newsletter. English. qt. $6.00 (non-members). North Carolina State Bar, PO Box 25908, Raleigh NC 27611. **Tel** (919)828-4620. **LC** KF200; .N66. **DD** 340/.06/0756. ***Continues*** *North Carolina Bar Newsletter, 0193-6646.*
Ind/Abst Leg. Resour. Index (1981-?); LegalTrac (1980-1984).

US/0164-6850
NORTH CAROLINA STATE BAR QUARTERLY. Added/Corp North Carolina State Bar. North Carolina State Bar. Council. Vol. 25, No. 1 (1978)-. Periodical. English. qt. $10.00. North Carolina State Bar, PO Box 25908, Raleigh NC 27611. **Tel** (919)828-4620. **ED** Jennifer White. **LC** KF200; .N65. **DD** 340/.060756. **Bk Rev. Ad Acc. Circ:** 11,000 (ctrl). ***Continues*** *North Carolina Bar, 0048-0657.*
Desc: Contains material relating to the practice of law.
Ind/Abst Curr. Law Index (1980-); Leg. Resour. Index (1980-); LegalTrac (1980-).

US/0748-2752
NORTH DAKOTA AND SOUTH DAKOTA LEGAL DIRECTORY, THE. [N.D. S.D. legal dir.]. **Added/Corp** Legal Directories Publishing Company. **VFOAT** South Dakota Legal Directory; Legal Directory. (1983)-. English. an (Nov.). $20.00. Legal Directories Publishing Company, 9111 Garland Road, PO Box 189000, Dallas TX 75218. **Tel** (214)321-3238, 800 447-5375. **LC** KF192.N69; .N57. **DD** 340/.025/783. ***Continues in part*** *Minnesota, Nebraska, North and South Dakota Legal Directory.*

US
NORTH DAKOTA CASE NAMES CITATOR. English. $40.00 (1 bound volume), $52.00 (cumulative supplements). Shepards McGraw-Hill Inc, 555 Middle Creek Parkway, PO Box 35300, Colorado Springs CO 80935-3530. **Tel** (719)488-3000, FAX (800)525-0053.

US/0362-1812
NORTH DAKOTA JUDICIAL NEWS. English. Bismarck Supreme Court, State Capitol, Bismarck ND 58505. **LC** KFN9108.A15; N67. **DD** 347/.784/005.

US/0029-2745
NORTH DAKOTA LAW REVIEW. [N. D. law rev.]. **Added/Corp** University of North Dakota. School of Law. State Bar Association of North Dakota. (Jan. 1951)-. Periodical. English. qt. $18.00. University of North Dakota, Grand Forks ND 58202. **Tel** (701)777-2941. **ED** Tamara Yon. Index available. cum. index. **Bk Rev. Circ:** 2,300. available on microfiche and CD-ROM. ***Continues*** *North Dakota Bar Briefs.*
Desc: Compilation of legal articles and reviews of recent court cases.
Ind/Abst Bowne Dig. Corp. Sec. Lawyers; Curr. Law Index (1980-); Fed. Tax Artic.; Index Leg. Period.; Leg. Resour. Index (1980-); LegalTrac (1980-).

US
NORTHAMPTON COUNTY REPORTER, THE. Added/Corp Pennsylvania. Courts (Northampton County). Pennsylvania. Courts. Northampton County Bar Association. **VFOAT** Northampton County Reports. (1887)-. Newspaper. English. Fifty-two times a year. $50.00. Northampton County Bar Association, 155 South Ninth Street, Easton PA 18042. **Tel** (215)258-6333. Each issue contains an index to its own contents (no volume index)--loose.

●US/1056-2508
NORTHERN CALIFORNIA LEGAL RESOURCE MANUAL. (1992)-. English. $65.00. ASAP Publications / California, 1081 Camino del Rio South, Suite 222, San Diego CA 92108. **Tel** (619)297-2727, FAX (619)297-2770.

US/0734-1490
NORTHERN ILLINOIS UNIVERSITY LAW REVIEW. [North. Ill. Univ. law rev.]. **Added/Corp** Northern Illinois University. College of Law. Vol. 1, No. 1 (Winter 1980)-. Periodical. English. Three times a year. $18.00. Northern Illinois University Law Review, Northern Illinois University, Dekalb IL 60115. **Tel** (815)753-0619. **ED** Philip C. Fontana (Managing Editor). **LC** K14; .O74. **DD** 349.773/05; 347.73005. **Bk Rev. Ad Acc. Circ:** 300. available in microform (back issues from William S Hein). ***Continues*** *Lewis University Law Review.*
Desc: Review of current federal, state, and agency law, focusing on impact and analysis of recent court decisions.
Ind/Abst Bowne Dig. Corp. Sec. Lawyers; Curr. Law Index (1980-); Fed. Tax Artic.; Index Leg. Period.; Leg. Resour. Index (1980-); LegalTrac (1980-).

IE
NORTHERN IRELAND LAW REPORTS, THE. Jan. 1925-. Periodical. English. qt. £25.00. Inc Council Law Reporting, Royal Courts of Justice, Belfast BT1 3JX Northern Ireland. **Tel** 0232 235111. **ED** W D Trimble. Index available. cum. index. **Ad Acc. Circ:** 700.
Desc: Reports of cases argued and determined in the Supreme Courts in Northern Ireland.

IE/0029-3105
NORTHERN IRELAND LEGAL QUARTERLY, THE. [North. Irel. leg. q.]. **Added/Corp** Incorporated Law Society of Northern Ireland. Vol. 1 (Nov. 1936)-. Periodical. English. qt. 47.50p. Queens University of Belfast / SLS Legal Publications, Belfast BT7 1NN, Northern Ireland. **Tel** 011 353 232 245133 Ext 3597, FAX 011 353 247895. **ED** Dr. Peter Ingram. **LC** K14; .O75. **Ad Acc, Adv Mgr:** Patricia McCann. **Circ:** 550.
Desc: A general journal on topics of journal, with special attention paid to the law of Northern Ireland.
Ind/Abst Curr. Law Index (1980-); Index Leg. Period.; Leg. Resour. Index (1980-); LegalTrac (1980-).

US/0198-8549
NORTHERN KENTUCKY LAW REVIEW. [North. KY. law rev.]. **Added/Corp** Salmon P. Chase College of Law. Vol. 3, No. 2 (1976)-. Periodical. English. Three times a year (April, Aug., Dec.). $15.00. North Kentucky University / Law School, Nunn Hall, Highland KY 41076. **Tel** (606)572-5444. **ED** Marla Merdinger. **LC** K14; .O753. **DD** 340/.05. **Bk Rev. Circ:** 1,200. available on microfilm and microfiche from University Microfilms

International (UMI). **Continues** Northern Kentucky State Law Forum, 0198-8530.
Desc: Casenotes and comments on general law topics.
Ind/Abst Bowne Dig. Corp. Sec. Lawyers; Crim. Justice Abstr.; Curr. Law Index (1980-); Index Leg. Period.; Leg. Resour. Index (1980-); LegalTrac (1980-); PAIS Int. Print; Public Aff. Inf. Serv. Bull.; Soc. Work Abstr. (?-?).

NW
NORTHERN MARIANA ISLANDS REPORTS : CASES ARGUED AND DETERMINED IN THE SUPREME COURT OF THE COMMONWEALTH OF THE NORTHERN MARIANA ISLANDS.
Added/Corp Northern Mariana Islands. Supreme Court. **VFOAT** NMI Reports. Vol. 1 (1990)-. English.

US/0194-0015
NORTHERN NEW ENGLAND LEGAL DIRECTORY, MAINE, NEW HAMPSHIRE, AND VERMONT, THE.
1977/78-. Directory. English. an. $14.00. Legal Directories Publishing Company, 9111 Garland Road, PO Box 189000, Dallas TX 75218. **Tel** (214)321-3238, 800 447-5375. **LC** KF190; .N64. **DD** 340/.025/74.

AT
NORTHERN TERRITORY LEGISLATION.
(19??)-. Periodical. English. ir. 275.00Aus$. Northern Territory Government Information Center, GPO Box 1046, Darwin Northern Territory 5794 Australia. **Tel** 011 61 89 897928, FAX 011 61 89 897972. **(Subscription address:** Receiver of Territory Monies, 13 Smith Street, GPO Box 1046, Darwin NT 0801 Australia.) Index available.
Desc: Northern Territory regulations.

US/0735-5505
NORTHERNTIER LEGAL JOURNAL.
Vol. 1, No. 1 (Jan. 9, 1982)-. Periodical. English. wk. $10.00. Tioga County Bar Association, c/o George C Williams, 3 Pearl Street, Wellboro PA 16901. **LC** K14; .O755. **DD** 349.748/56/05; 347.4856005.

US/0887-4301
NORTHROP UNIV. LAW J. AEROSP., BUS. TAX. Ceased.
(NORTHROP UNIVERSITY LAW JOURNAL OF AEROSPACE, BUSINESS AND TAXATION.). [Northrop Univ. law j. aerosp. bus. tax.]. Vol. 6 (1985)-Vol. 8 (?). Periodical. English. an. Northrop University, Law Journal of Aerospace Business and Taxation, 5800 West Arbor Vitae Street, Los Angeles CA 90045. **Tel** (310)337-4411. **LC** K14; .O757. **DD** 346.7304/692. **Bk Rev. Ad Acc. Continues** Northrop University Law Journal of Aerospace, Energy and the Environment, 0196-1489.
Ind/Abst Curr. Law Index (?-?); Index Leg. Period. (?-?); LegalTrac (1980-).

CN/0824-3433
NORTHWEST TERRITORIES REPORTS.
[Northwest Territ. rep.]. **VFOAT** N.W.T.R. **VAT** Northwest Territories Law Reports. Pt. 1 (Sept. 1983)-. Periodical. English. Four times a year. 105.00Can$ Canada; 91.50Can$ other. Carswell Publications, 2330 Midland Avenue, Agincourt Ontario M1S 1P7 Canada. **Tel** (416)291-8421. **ED** Mark A Aitken, Sheldon B Tate, Sandra A Aitken, Gerald P Stang, Linda M Tarras, Linda J Wall, Edward W Gullberg. **DD** 348.719/2/042. Index available. cum. index. **Ad Acc.**
Desc: Consists of cases and digests of available judgments of the courts in the Northwest Territories.

CN/0824-3433
NORTHWEST TERRITORIES REPORTS.
[Northwest Territ. rep.]. (1983)-. English. Carswell Company Ltd, 2075 Kennedy Road, Scarborough Ontario M1T 3V4 Canada. **DD** 348.719/2/043.

US
NORTHWESTERN REPORTER CASE NAMES CITATOR.
English. $300.00 (5 bound volumes), $85.00 (cumulative supplements). Shepards McGraw-Hill Inc, 555 Middle Creek Parkway, PO Box 35300, Colorado Springs CO 80935-3530. **Tel** (719)488-3000, FAX (800)525-0053.

US/0029-3571
NORTHWESTERN UNIVERSITY LAW REVIEW.
[Northwest. Univ. law rev.]. **Added/Corp** Northwestern University (Evanston, Ill.). School of Law. Vol. 47, No. 1 (Mar./April 1952)-. Periodical. English. Four times a year. $35.00 US; $38.00 other. Northwestern University School of Law, 357 East Chicago Avenue, Chicago IL 60611-3069. **Tel** (312)503-8467, FAX (312)503-0132. **(Subscription address:** Fred B. Rothman & Co. / for back issues, 10368 West Centennial Road, Littleton CO 80127.) **ED** Carole A. Cheney. **LC** K14; .O77. **DD** 340/.05. Index available. **Bk Rev. Pr Rev. Circ:** 1,300. available on microfiche; available on microfilm; available on phonorecord. Documents available

from The Genuine Article. **Continues** Illinois Law Review (1939).
Desc: Publishes a variety of articles, from traditional legal scholarship to interdisciplinary scholarship relating to the law. Review essays are also published.
Ind/Abst ABC POL SCI; Bowne Dig. Corp. Sec. Lawyers; Curr. Contents Soc. Behav. Sci.; Curr. Law Index (1980-); Educ. Adm. Abstr. (?-?); Fed. Tax Artic.; Hum. Resour. Abstr. (?-?); Index Leg. Period.; Leg. Resour. Index (1980-); LegalTrac (1980-); PAIS Int. Print (1991-); Res. Alert [Full Cov.]; Sage Public Adm. Abstr.; Soc. Plann. Policy Dev. Abstr.; Soc. Sci. Cit. Index [Full Cov.]; Sociol. Abstr.

LU
NOTES / COUR DE JUSTICE DES COMMUNANTES EUROPEENES, DIRECTION RECHERCHE, DOCUMENTATION ET BIBLIOTHEQUE.
Main/Corp Court of Justice of the European Communities. Direction Recherche, Documentation, et Bibliotheque. **VFOAT** Notes aux Arrets. (198?)-. French. Office for Official Publications of the European Communities, 2 Rue Mercier, 2985 Luxembourg Luxembourg. **Tel** 011 352 499281, FAX 011 352 488573.

US
NOTICIAS (HISPANIC NATIONAL BAR ASSOCIATION).
(NOTICIAS.). (1985)-. Periodical. English. qt. **Continues** HNBA Noticias.
Ind/Abst Am. Hist. Life (1963-1973); Trop. Dis. Bull.

IT
NOTIZIARIO DEL CONSIGLIO REGIONALE DELLA LIGURIA. Main/Corp
Liguria (Italy). Consiglio Regionale. Yearly V. 1- July 1973-. Italian. mo. Consiglio Regionale Della Liguria, Mura Santa Chiara 3, 16128 Genova Italy.

IT/0392-4335
NOTIZIARIO DI GIURISPRUDENZA DEL LAVORO.
[Not. giurisprud. lav.]. (1961)-. Periodical. Italian. bm. L120000.00. Assn Sindacale Aziende Credito, Via Paisiello 5, 00198 Rome Italy. **Tel** 011 39 6 854591. **UDC** 34.
Desc: Jurisprudence cases concerning labor matters.

IT
NOTIZIARIO GIURIDICO REGIONALE.
Main/Corp Unione Degli Industriali Della Provincia di Torino. Vol. 1, (Sept./Oct. 1971)-. Periodical. Italian. Twelve times a year. L70000 Italy; L140000 other. Ediesse / Rome, Via Dei Frentani 4A, 00185 Rome Italy. **Tel** 011 39 6 44870286, 44870288, FAX 011 39 6 4481260. **LC** K25; .N38. **DD** 342/.45/0905.

IT
NOTIZIARIO IAP.
Italian. bm. Free. Ist Autodisciplina Pubblic, Via Larga 15, 20122 Milan Italy. **Tel** 011 39 2 58303975.

IT
NOTIZIARIO LEGISLATIVO DEGLI UFFICI FISCALI E AMMINISTRATIVI DELLO STATO.
(19??)-. Italian. mo. L295000.00. Notiziario Legislativo Uffici Fiscali e Amministrativi dello Stato, CP 7246, 00162 Rome Nomentano Italy. **Tel** 011 39 6 8608920.

US/0883-3648
NOTRE DAME JOURNAL OF LAW, ETHICS & PUBLIC POLICY.
[Notre Dame j. law ethics public policy]. **Added/Corp** Thos. J. White Center on Law & Government. **VFOAT** Journal of Law, Ethics, and Public Policy; Journal of Law, Ethics & Public Policy. **VAT** Notre Dame Journal of Law, Ethics, and Public Policy. Vol. 1, Inaugural Issue (1984)-. Periodical. English. Twice a year. $16.00. Thomas J. White Center, Notre Dame Law School, Notre Dame IN 46556. **Tel** (219)631-5913. **ED** Patrick Henry. **LC** K14; .O796. **DD** 340/.112/05. **Ad Acc. Circ:** 1,000 (ctrl). available on microfiche (from William S Heim and Co. Inc.).
Desc: Application of religious teaching and philosophy to law and public policy issues.
Ind/Abst Crim. Justice Abstr.; Index Leg. Period.; Leg. Resour. Index; LegalTrac (1980-); PAIS Int. Print (1991-); Sage Public Adm. Abstr.; Soc. Plann. Policy Dev. Abstr.

US/0745-3515
NOTRE DAME LAW REVIEW, THE.
[Notre Dame law rev.]. **Added/Corp** University of Notre Dame. Law School. Vol. 58, No. 1 (Oct. 1982)-. Periodical. English. Five times a year. $28.00 (one year), $52.00 (two year), $75.00 (three year). Notre Dame Law School, PO Box 486, Notre Dame IN 46556. **Tel** (219)239-5918, (219)255-2938. **ED** Anthony J. Bellia, Jr. **LC** K14; .O797. **DD** 340/.05. Index available. **Bk Rev. Ad Acc. Circ:** 1,200 (ctrl). available on microfilm and microfiche from University Microfilms International (UMI). Documents available from The Genuine Article. **Continues** Notre Dame Lawyer, 0029-4535.

Desc: Articles and book reviews by judges, lawyers, law professors and students analyzing current and emerging legal issues and developments.
Ind/Abst Am. Bibliogr. Slavic East Europ. Stud.; Bowne Dig. Corp. Sec. Lawyers; Crim. Justice Abstr.; Crim. Justice Period.; Curr. Contents Soc. Behav. Sci.; Curr. Law Index (1982-); Fed. Tax Artic.; Index Leg. Period.; Leg. Resour. Index (1982-); LegalTrac (1982-); PAIS Int. Print (1991-); Res. Alert [Select. Cov.]; Soc. Sci. Cit. Index [Select. Cov.]; Abr. Cathol. Period. Lit. Index; Cathol. Period. Lit. Index.

US/0894-0657
NOTRE DAME STUDIES IN LAW AND CONTEMPORARY ISSUES.
[Notre Dame stud. law contemp. issues]. (1985)-. Monographic series. English. ir. Price varies per volume. University of Notre Dame Press, PO Box 635, South Bend IN 46624. **Tel** (219)239-6349, (800)677-3232, FAX (219)239-8148. **DD** 300.

US/1049-0248
NOVA LAW REVIEW.
[Nova law rev.]. Vol. 11, No. 1 (Fall 1986)-. Periodical. English. Three times a year. $20.00. Nova University Law Center, 3100 SW 9th Avenue, Ft Lauderdale FL 33315. **Tel** (305)467-0309. **LC** K14; .O83. **DD** 349.759/05. **Bk Rev. Ad Acc. Circ:** 1,000. **Continues** Nova Law Journal, 0149-6204.
Desc: All topical issues of current legal problems explored in intellectual, stimulating analysis.
Ind/Abst Index Leg. Period.; LegalTrac (1986-).

CN/0316-6325
NOVA SCOTIA LAW NEWS. Added/Corp
Nova Scotia Barristers' Society. Vol. 1 (June 1974)-. Periodical. English. Six times a year. 60.00Can$. Nova Scotia Barristers Society, 1475 Hollis Street, Halifax NS B3J 3M4 Canada. **Tel** (902)422-1491, FAX (902)429-4869. **ED** Helen I MacDonnell. **LC** KE361.N6; A25. **DD** 340/.09716. Index available. cum. index. **Ad Acc. Circ:** 1,800 (ctrl).
Desc: Digests of decisions of Nova Scotia courts, articles of interest to lawyers' digests of new Nova Scotia legislation.
Ind/Abst Can. Legal Lit.; Index Can. Leg. Period. Lit. (19??-19??).

CN
NOVA SCOTIA REAL PROPERTY PRACTICE MANUAL.
English. sa. 140.00Can$. Butterworth & Company Ltd. / Canada, 75 Clegg Road, Markham Ontario L6G 1A1 Canada. **Tel** (905)479-2665, (800)668-6481. **ED** Charles W. MacIntosh. Index available. **Pr Rev. Circ:** 186 (ctrl).
Desc: Comprehensive treatment of practice and procedure of Nova Scotia and Real Property Law with forms and checklists.

CN/0048-0983
NOVA SCOTIA REPORTS (FREDERICTON).
(NOVA SCOTIA REPORTS.). [N.S. rep.]. Vol. 1 1965/69)-V. 5 (1965/69; 2nd Series, V. 1 (1970)-. Periodical. English. $75.00 per vol. Maritime Law Book Ltd, PO Box 302, Fredericton New Brunswick, E3B 4Y9 Canada. **Tel** (506)453-9921, (800)561-0220. **DD** 348.716/043.

RU
NOVAIA INOSTRANNAIA LITERATURA PO OBSHCHESTVENNYM NAUKAM: GOSUDARSTVO I PRAVO. Title Change.
Added/Corp Institut Nauchnoi Informatsii po Obshchestvennym Naukam (Akademiia Nauk SSSR). **VFOAT** Gosudarstvo i Pravo. (1976)-(1992). Academic Scholarly Publication. Multiple languages (Russian and Multiple languages). mo. Izdatelstvo Nauka / Akademiia Nauk, Publishing House of the Russian Academy of Sciences, Leninskii Porspekt 14, 117901 Moscow Russia. **Tel** 011 95 954-21-53, FAX 011 95 938-21-44, telex 411964. **ED** S. O. Shevtsova and B. L. Polunin. **LC** K38; .N68. **Continues** Novaia Literatura po Gosudarstvu I Pravu za Rubezhom. **Merged with** Novaia Otechestvennaia Literatura po Obshchestvennym Naukam. Gosudarstvo i Pravo **to form** Novaia Literatura po Sotsialnym i Gumanitarnym Naukam. Gosudarstvo i Pravo.

●RU
NOVAIA LITERATURA PO SOTSIALNYM I GUMANITARNYM NAUKAM. GOSUDARSTVO I PRAVO / ROSSIISKAIA AKADEMIIA NAUK, INSTITUT NAUCHNOI INFORMATSII PO OBSHCHESTVENNYM NAUKAM. See
Political Science.

RU
NOVAIA OTECHESTVENNAIA LITERATURA PO OBSHCHESTVENNYM NAUKAM. GOSUDARSTVO I PRAVO. Title Change.
Added/Corp Institut Nauchnoi Informatsii po

Obshchestvennym Naukam (Rossiiskaia Akademiia Nauk). **VFOAT** Gosudarstvo i Pravo. (1992)-(1992). Academic Scholarly Publication. Russian. mo. Izdatelstvo Nauka / Akademiia Nauk, Publishing House of the Russian Academy of Sciences, Leninskii Porspekt 14, 117901 Moscow Russia. **Tel** 011 95 954-21-53, FAX 011 95 938-21-44, telex 411964. **(Subscription address:** East View Publications Inc., 3020 Harbor Lane North, Suite 110, Minneapolis MN 55447.**)** **LC** K38; .N683. ***Continues*** *Novaia Sovetskaia Literatura po Obshchestvennym Naukam: Gosudarstvo i Pravo.* ***Merged with*** *Novaia Inostrannaia Literatura po Obshchestvennym Naukam. Gosudarstvo i Pravo* ***to form*** *Novaia Literatura po Sotsialnym i Gumanitarnym Naukam. Gosudarstvo i Pravo.*

BL
NOVAS TABELAS DO IMPOSTO DE RENDA PARA ... ASSALARIADOS E NAO-ASSALARIADOS. Portuguese. an. **LC** KHD4630; .N68. **DD** 343.8105/2/0212; 348.103520212.

SP
NOVELA POLICIACA. $4.90. Ediciones Acervo, Julio Verne 5-7, Barcelona 6 Spain. **UDC** 34.

BU
NOVOTO V TEORIIATA I SOTSIALNATA PRAKTIKA. DURZHAVA I PRAVO. **Added/Corp** Druzhestvo Georgi Kirkov. Republikanski Suvet. **VFOAT** Durzhava i Pravo. (19??)-. Monographic series. Bulgarian. ir. Price varies per volume. **LC** K14; .O87.
Ind/Abst Index Foreign Leg. Per.

CN/0229-690X
NOW AND THEN (DOWNSVIEW). (NOW AND THEN : A NEWSLETTER FOR THOSE INTERESTED IN HISTORY AND LAW.). [Now and then]. Oct. 1979-. Newsletter. English. ir. $15.48. Society of History & Law in Canada, York University, Osgoode Hall, Law School, Downsview Ontario M3J 2R5 Canada. **Tel** (416)667-2100. **DD** 349.71/05.

US/1071-2267
NRC CALENDAR, THE. [NRC cal.]. **VAT** Nuclear Regulatory Commission Calendar. (19??)-. Periodical. English. wk. $600.00. Southern Technical Services Inc. (STS), 3 Metro Center, Suite 610, Bethesda MD 20814. **Tel** (301)652-2500, FAX (301)652-0338. **ED** Deann E. Jackson. **DD** 343.
Desc: Contains summaries of important US Nuclear Regulatory Commission, Advisory Committee on Reactor Safeguards and NRC staff meetings. Provides dates and agenda for upcoming NRC, ACRS and staff meetings.

US/0362-8833
NRECA--APPA LEGAL REPORTING SERVICE. **Main/Corp** National Rural Electric Cooperative Association. **Added/Corp** American Public Power Association. NRECA--APPA Legal Reporting Service. **VAT** National Rural Electric Cooperative--American Public Power Association Legal Reporting Service. (1975)-. Periodical. English. mo (12 issues). $145.00. National Rural Electric Cooperative Association, 1800 Massachusetts Avenue Northwest, Washington DC 20036. **Tel** (202)857-9500, FAX (202)857-4863. **ED** William T. Crisp. **LC** KF2125.A15; N37. **DD** 343/.73/092. Index available. **Bk Rev. Circ:** 1,500. ***Continues*** *National Rural Electric Cooperative Association. NRECA Legal Reporting Service.*
Desc: Editorial, electric utility legal cases, and announcements of electric utility legal seminars.

US
NSBA NEWS MICROFORM. **VAT** Nebraska State Bar Association News. Periodical. English. ir. Nebraska State Bar Association, 635 South 14th Street, Lincoln NE 68508.

US/0277-7460
NSCLC WASHINGTON WEEKLY. **Main/Corp** National Senior Citizens Law Center (U.S.). **VAT** National Senior Citizens Law Center Washington Weekly. 1974-. Periodical. English. wk. National Senior Citizens Law Center National Council of Senior Citizens Law Center, 1815 H Street NW, 351700, 1331 F Street Northwest, Washington Washington DC DC 20006 20004. **Tel** (202)887-5280, (202)347-8800, FAX , , telex , . **ED** Carla J Reimann. **Ad Acc. Circ:** 1,800 (ctrl).

FR/0304-341X
NUCLEAR LAW BULLETIN. [Nucl. law bull.]. **Added/Corp** OECD Nuclear Energy Agency. European Nuclear Energy Agency. (1968)-. English (French). sa (June and Dec.). $44.00. OECD Publications and Information Center, 2 rue Andre-Pascal, 75775 Paris Cedex 16 France. **Tel** 011 33 1 45248167, US:(202)785-6323, FAX 011 33 1 45248500 OR 45248176, telex 620 160 OCDE. **(Subscription address:** OECD Publications Center, 2001 L Street, Suite 700, Washington DC 20036.**)** **NLM** W1 NU124. Index available. cum. index. **Bk Rev. Circ:** 1,200. Documents available from Documents on Demand.
Desc: Presents information on legislative activities, administrative decisions, international organizational activities and agreements regarding nuclear law.
Ind/Abst Energy Inf. Abstr.; Energy Res. Abstr.; Environ. Abstr.; PAIS Int. Print (1991-); Public Aff. Inf. Serv. Bull.

FR/0304-3428
NUCLEAR LAW BULLETIN. (BULLETIN DE DROIT NUCLEAIRE.). **Added/Corp** OECD Nuclear Energy Agency. (19??)-. Periodical. French. sa (published in June and Dec.). $42.00. OECD Publications and Information Center, 2 rue Andre-Pascal, 75775 Paris Cedex 16 France. **Tel** 011 33 1 45248167, US:(202)785-6323, FAX 011 33 1 45248500 OR 45248176, telex 620 160 OCDE. **(Subscription address:** OECD Publications Center, 2001 L Street, Suite 700, Washington DC 20036.**)** **LC** K2; .U43. **DD** 343/.0925; 342.3925.

US/1056-487X
NUNC PRO TUNC. (NUNC PRO TUNC : A QUARTERLY NEWSLETTER OF THE GEORGIA LEGAL HISTORY FOUNDATION, INC.). [Nunc pro tunc]. **Added/Corp** Georgia Legal History Foundation. Vol. 4, No. 1 (Mar. 1990)-. Newsletter. English. qt. $35.00 (libraries). Georgia Legal History Foundation, Inc., 568 State Office Annex, 244 Washington Street SW, Atlanta GA 30334. **DD** 340. ***Continues*** *Georgia Legal History Foundation Newsletter.*

IT/0392-7059
NUOVA RASSEGNA DI LEGISLAZIONE DOTTRINA E GIURISPRUDENZA. [Nuova rass. legis. dottrina giurisprud.]. (1927)-. Periodical. Italian. Twenty-four times a year. L54000 Italy; L56000 other. Noccioli, Via E Fermi 24, 50019 Sesto Fiorent Fi Italy. **Tel** 011 39 55 310316. **UDC** 3.

IT/0391-3740
NUOVE LEGGI CIVILI COMMENTATE. [Nuove leggi civili comment.]. (1978)-. Periodical. Italian. bm. L310000.00. Cedam Spa, Via Jappelli 5 6, 35121 Padua Italy. **Tel** 011 39 49 65667. **UDC** 34. **Circ:** 7,000.

US/0196-6790
NURSE, THE PATIENT & THE LAW, THE. **VAT** Nurse, the Patient and the Law. (1977)-. Periodical. English. bm. $100.00 US; $125.00 Canada; $140.00 other. Cox Publications, PO Box 20316, Billings MT 59104-0316. **Tel** (406)256-8822. **ED** Meridith B Cox. **LC** KFC615.A15; N87. **DD** 344.794/041/05. Index available. **Bk Rev**, (Qty: 4). **Ad Acc, Adv Mgr:** S Berntson. **Pr Rev. Circ:** 1,500.
Desc: Devoted exclusively to nursing law and risk management. You'll find articles and cases to help you keep current with nursing law decision and risk management date in the sections: Risk Management Perspectives, In-Service Topics and Management Risks. This journal is peer reviewed and is registered with the Copyright Clearance Center. It is indexed in Cumulative Index to Nursing and Allied Health Literature.
Ind/Abst Cumul. Index Nurs. Allied Health Lit.

US/8756-6060
NUTRITION LEGISLATION NEWS. [Nutr. leg. news]. 1st Session, Issue No. 1 (Mar. 15, 1985)-. Periodical. English. ir (twice monthly, minimum of 18 times a year). $150.00 (one year) $250.00 (two year) US; $175.00 (one year) $300.00 (two year) other. Nutrition Legislation Service, PO Box 75035, Washington DC 20013. **Tel** (202)488-8879, FAX (202)554-3116. **ED** Lenora Moragne. **DD** 343. **NLM** W1; NU888D.
Desc: Report of US Government activities covering the Senate, the House of Representatives and the four reach arms of government: the Congressional Budget Office, the Congressional Research Service of the Library of Congress, the General Accounting Office, and the Office of Technology Assessment.

CN/0029-7585
OBITER DICTA (1963). ***Ceased.*** (OBITER DICTA.). **Added/Corp** Osgoode Hall Law School. Legal and Literary Society. (1???)-(1???). Periodical. English. bw. Osgoode Hall Law School, 4700 Keele Street North, North York Ontario M3J 1P3 Canada. **Tel** (416)736-2100. **ED** Karen Villenevve, Grant Murray Frank Bernhardt and John Mooran. **Bk Rev. Ad Acc.** ctrl circ. ***Continues*** *Osgoode Hall Obiter Dicta.*
Desc: Topical articles about local and legal affairs. Movie reviews, book reviews, forum for the exchange and expression ideas about law.
Ind/Abst Curr. Law Index (1981-); Leg. Resour. Index (1981-?); LegalTrac (1980-1989).

CN/0711-7639
OBJECTION. [Objection]. No. 1 (Feb. 1982)-. Periodical. French. qt. $10.00. Centre d'Information Juridique, CP 301, Succursale N, Montreal Quebec H2Y 3M4. **DD** 349.714/05.

US/0195-1696
OBSCENITY LAW BULLETIN. **Added/Corp** National Obscenity Law Center (U.S.). Vol. 1, No. 1 (Jan. 1977)-. Periodical. English. Six times a year (Feb., April, July, Aug., Oct., and Dec.). $15.00. Morality in Media Inc., 475 Riverside Drive, New York NY 10115. **Tel** (212)870-3232. **ED** Paul J. McGeady. **LC** KF9444.A15; O27. **DD** 344.73/0547/05; 347.30454705. **Circ:** 900 (ctrl).
Desc: Current information on obscenity legislation and obscenity law decisions for use of prosecutors and other interested parties and libraries.

US/0886-4306
OBSERVER (NEW YORK, N.Y. : 1985). ***Title Change.*** (THE OBSERVER.). [Observer]. (1985)-?. Periodical. English. qt. Columbia Law School, 435 West 116th Street, Box A-27, New York NY 10027. **LC** KF292.C6; A728. **DD** 340/.07/117471. ***Continues*** *Columbia Law Alumni Observer, 0093-304X.* ***Continued by*** *Columbia Law Observer, 1050-1290.*

RU
OBSHCHESTVENNYE NAUKI V ROSSII. SERIIA 4, GOSUDARSTVO I PRAVO / ROSSIISKAIA AKADEMIIA NAUK, INSTITUT NAUCHNOI INFORMATSII PO OBSHCHESTVENNYM NAUKAM. ***Title Change.*** **Added/Corp** Institut Nauchnoi Informatsii po Obshchestvennym Naukam (Rossiiskaia Akademiia Nauk). **VFOAT** Gosudarstvo i Pravo. (1992)-(1992). Academic Scholarly Publication. Russian (table of contents in English). bm. Izdatelstvo Nauka / Akademiia Nauk, Publishing House of the Russian Academy of Sciences, Leninskii Porspekt 14, 117901 Moscow Russia. **Tel** 011 95 954-21-53, FAX 011 95 938-21-44, telex 411964. **LC** K15; .B8. ***Continues*** *Obshchestvennye Nauki v SSSR. Seriia 4, Gosudarstvo i Pravo, 0202-2060.* ***Split into*** *Sotsialnye i Gumanitarnye Nauki. Seriia 4, Gosudarstvo i Pravo. Otechestvennaia Literatura* ***and*** *Sotsialnye i Gumanitarnye Nauki. Seriia 4, Gosudarstvo i Pravo. Zarubezhnaia Literatura.*

RU
OBSHCHESTVENNYE NAUKI ZA RUBEZHOM. SERIIA 4: GOSUDARSTVO I PRAVO. **Added/Corp** Akademiia Nauk SSSR. Institut Nauchnoi Informatsii i Fundamentalnaia Biblioteka po Obshchestvennym Naukam. **VFOAT** Gosudarstvo I Pravo. **VAT** Obshchestvennye Nauki za Rubezhom. Seriia Chetyre : Gosudarstvo I Pravo. (1973)-. Academic Scholarly Publication. Russian. mo. $99.95. Izdatelstvo Nauka / Akademiia Nauk, Publishing House of the Russian Academy of Sciences, Leninskii Porspekt 14, 117901 Moscow Russia. **Tel** 011 95 954-21-53, FAX 011 95 938-21-44, telex 411964. **(Subscription address:** East View Publications Inc., 3020 Harbor Lane North, Suite 110, Minneapolis MN 55447.**)** **LC** K15; .B83.

BU/0204-8523
OBSHTESTVO I PRAVO. **Added/Corp** Bulgaria. Ministerstvo na Pravosudieto. Suiuz na Iuristite v Bulgariia. (Oct. 1979)-. Periodical. Bulgarian. mo. DM110.00. Suiuz Na Iuristite v Bulgaria, Ul Zhdanov No, 1000 Sofia Bulgaria. **(Subscription address:** Kubon & Sagner, ABT Zeitschriftenimport, D 80328 Munich Germany.**)** **LC** K15; .B85.

US
OCCASIONAL PAPERS. **Main/Corp** University of Chicago. Law School. Vol. 1 (1971)-. English. ir. $30.00; Comes also with Law School Record. William S. Hein & Company Inc., 1285 Main Street, Buffalo NY 14209. **Tel** (716)882-2600, (800)828-7571, FAX (716)883-8100, telex 91-209 WM S HEIN BUF. **DD** 340. cum. index. **Circ:** 7,000 (ctrl). available in microform.
Desc: Reprinted papers written by members of the law school faculty.

CN/0383-9656
OCCASIONAL REPORT - LAW SOCIETY OF UPPER CANADA. **Main/Corp** Law Society of Upper Canada. No. 1, (Jan. 30, 1976)-. Periodical. English. Law Society of Upper Canada, 130 Queen Street West, Toronto M5H 2N6 Canada. **Tel** (416)947-3300, (416)947-3371, telex 065-28013. **(Subscription address:** Law Society of Upper Canada Gazette, 65 Queen Street West, 17th Floor, Honsberger Toronto ONT M5H 2M5 Canada**)** **DD** 340/.09713.

CN/0706-5019
OCCUPATIONAL HEALTH AND SAFETY LAW. **Added/Corp** Business Law Reporting Services. Vol. 1 (Apr. 1977)-. Periodical. English. mo. 340.00Can$. Business Law Reporting Ltd, PO Box 1762, Main Post Office, Kingston Ontario K7L 5J6 Canada. **Tel** (905)372-1156. **ED** Mark R. Sabourin. **DD** 344/.71/046502632.
Desc: Full text loose-leaf service containing all Canadian occupational safety and health legislation.

Law

US/0737-1268
OCCUPATIONAL SAFETY AND HEALTH LAW. [Occup. saf. health law]. Began with 1978. English. an. Practising Law Institute, 810 Seventh Avenue, New York NY 10019-5818. **Tel** (212)765-5700, FAX (212)581-4670 general correspondence, (212)265-4742 orders and billing inquiries. **NLM** WA 33 AA1 O16.

CN/0842-4136
OCLA-LINK. See Library and Information Sciences.

US/1055-3304
O'DWYER'S FARA REPORT. *Title Change.* See Business.

US
O'DWYER'S WASHINGTON REPORT. See Business.

BB
OECS LAW REPORTS, THE. Added/Corp O.E.C.S. (Organization) U.W.I. / U.S. AID Caribbean Justice Improvement Project. **VFOAT** Organisation of Eastern Caribbean States Law Reports. Vol. 1 (1991)-. English. $60.00. University of the West Indies / Cave Hill Campus, PO Box 64, Bridgetown Barbados. **Tel** (809)425-1310, FAX (809)424-1788, telex WB 2257. **ED** Nicholas Huerpool, Cecil Hewlett. Index available. **Circ:** 300.
Desc: Contains a selection of cases decided in the Superior Courts of the Organisation of Eastern Caribbean States over the last forty years.

US/0730-3815
OF COUNSEL (NEW YORK, N.Y.). (OF COUNSEL.). [Of couns.]. Vol. 1, No. 1 (Jan. 1982)-. Periodical. English. Twenty-four times a year. $352.63. Prentice-Hall Law and Business, 270 Sylvan Avenue, Englewood Cliffs NJ 07632. **Tel** (800)223-0231, (201)894-8538, FAX (201)894-8666. **ED** Larry Smith. **LC** KF300.A1; O33. **DD** 340/.023/73. **Bk Rev. Ad Acc. Circ:** 1,000. *Absorbed* The Profitable Lawyer, 0743-5401.
Desc: A management report for larger law firms and corporate law departments. Helps firm managers solve financial, business and practice problems.
Ind/Abst Law Office Inf. Serv.

US/0743-3085
OF SUBSTANCE. (OF SUBSTANCE / BY THE LEGAL ACTION CENTER.). **Added/Corp** Legal Action Center. (1987)-. Periodical. English. bm. $44.95. Legal Action Center, 153 Waverly Place, New York NY 10014. **Tel** (212)243-1313. ctrl circ.

GW/0029-859X
OFFENTLICHE VERWALTUNG, DIE. [Off. Verwalt.]. Vol. 1; (Oct. 1948)-. Periodical. German. sm. DM335.00. W Kohlhammer Verlag GMBH, Postfach 800430, D70549 Stuttgart Germany. **Tel** 011 49 711 78631. **[CCC]**.
Desc: Journal for law affecting public bodies administrative service.
Ind/Abst Coal Abstr.; Energy Res. Abstr. (April 1979-); Index Foreign Leg. Per.; Int. Polit. Sci. Abstr.

US/0093-0229
OFFICIAL BRAND LAWS (LINCOLN). (OFFICIAL BRAND LAWS GOVERNING REGISTRATION, INVESTIGATION, INSPECTION AND RULES AND REGULATIONS OF THE NEBRASKA BRAND COMMITTEE.). **Main/Corp** Nebraska. **Added/Corp** Nebraska. Secretary of State. Nebraska. Brand Committee. Rules and regulations. (19??)-. English. Nebraska Secretary of State, 2300 State Capital Building, Lincoln NE 68509. **Tel** (402)471-2554. **LC** KFN246.A29; O3. **DD** 343/.782/076.

US/0747-6965
OFFICIAL CODE OF GEORGIA ANNOTATED. ADVANCE INFORMATION SERVICE. (OFFICIAL CODE OF GEORGIA ANNOTATED. ADVANCE ANNOTATION SERVICE.). **Added/Corp** Georgia. Laws, etc. (Official Code of Georgia Annotated) Michie Company. **VFOAT** Official Code of Georgia Annotated. Advance Annotations; Advance Annotation Service; Georgia Advance Annotation Service. (198?)-. English. an. $80.00. Michie Company, PO Box 7587, Charlottesville VA 22906-7587. **Tel** (804)972-7600, (800)542-0957, FAX (800)643-1280. ctrl circ.

US
OFFICIAL COMPILATION OF THE CODES, RULES AND REGULATIONS OF THE STATE OF NEW YORK. Main/Corp New York (State). **Added/Corp** New York (State). Dept. of State. Vol. 1 (Apr. 30, 1945)-. English. qt. Lenz & Riecker Inc., 1 Columbia Place, Albany NY 12207. **Tel** (518)436-8647.

US/0279-1005
OFFICIAL DECISIONS, OPINIONS AND RELATED MATTERS OF THE PUBLIC EMPLOYMENT RELATIONS BOARD OF THE STATE OF NEW YORK. Main/Corp New York (State). Public Employment Relations Board. **VFOAT** New York PERB Reports; Official Decisions, Opinions and Related Matters of the Public Employment Relations Board of the State of New York. **VAT** New York Public Employment Relations Board Reports. (1968)-. English. mo. $315.00 (includes postage). LRP Publications, 747 Dresher Road, PO Box 980, Horsham PA 19044-0980. **Tel** (800)341-7874, (215)784-0860, FAX (215)784-9639, (215)784-0870. **ED** Matthew McNaly. **LC** KFN5568.P8; A4962. Index available. cum. index. **Circ:** 500.
Desc: Abstracts and full-text of all NY Public Employment Relations Board and related court decisions. Complete indexing, cite tracker, statute tracker, citator, articles, and parallel database.

US
OFFICIAL DIRECTORY - NEW JERSEY STATE BAR ASSOCIATION. Main/Corp New Jersey State Bar Association. 1972/73-. Directory. English. an. New Jersey State Bar Association, 1 Constitution Square, New Brunswick NJ 08901. **Tel** (908)249-5000, FAX (908)249-2815. **LC** KF192.N4; N495. **DD** 340/.06/2749. ctrl circ. *Continues* Directory - New Jersey State Bar Association.
Desc: Directory of New Jersey State Bar Association.

NR
OFFICIAL GAZETTE - EAST CENTRAL STATE OF NIGERIA. Main/Corp East Central State (Nigeria). (19??)-. English. $15.00. **DD** 340./096694.

US/0886-3342
OFFICIAL GUIDE TO U.S. LAW SCHOOLS, THE. See Education-Higher Education.

LU/0378-5041
OFFICIAL JOURNAL OF THE EUROPEAN COMMUNITIES: DEBATES OF THE EUROPEAN PARLIAMENT. See Public Administration.

LU/0378-6978
OFFICIAL JOURNAL OF THE EUROPEAN COMMUNITIES : LEGISLATION. [Off. j. Eur. Commun., L, Legis.]. Vol. 16, (Jan. 1, 1973)-. English. ir. £400.00 UK; 425.00p Ireland. Office for Official Publications of the European Communities, 2 Rue Mercier, 2985 Luxembourg Luxembourg. **Tel** 011 352 499281, FAX 011 352 488573. **DD** 340/.094.
Desc: Consists of 2 related series, the L (legislation) and the C (information and notices), a supplement and an annex. The L series contains all the legislative acts and regulations whose publication is obligatory under the EC treaties, as well as other acts, and the C series covers the complete range of Community information other than legislation.
Ind/Abst Chem. Bus. Bull.; Chem. Bus. NewsBase (1987-); Chem. Bus. Update; Coal Abstr.; Int. Packag. Abstr.

US/0896-1077
OFFICIAL OPINIONS FROM THE SUPREME JUDICIAL COURT OF MASSACHUSETTS EDITION. (OFFICIAL OPINIONS FROM THE SUPREME JUDICIAL COURT OF MASSACHUSETTS.). [Off. opin. Supreme Judic. Court Mass. ed.]. **Main/Corp** Massachusetts. Supreme Judicial Court. **Added/Corp** Massachusetts. Supreme Judicial Court. Massachusetts Reports. **VFOAT** Official Opinions from the Supreme Judicial Court of Massachusetts edition; Official Opinions. 392 Mass. (May 25, 1984)-. Periodical. English. wk. $110.00. Darby Printing Company, 6215 Purdue Drive, Atlanta GA 30336. **Tel** (404)344-2665, (800)848-2995. **DD** 347. Each issue contains an index to its own contents (no volume index)--loose. *Continues* Massachusetts. Supreme Judicial Court. Advance Sheet Opinions. Section 1.

CN
OFFICIAL REPORT OF DEBATES OF THE LEGISLATIVE ASSEMBLY. Main/Corp British Columbia. Legislative Assembly. **VFOAT** Debates of the Legislative Assembly (Hansard). Periodical. English. ir. 138.00Can$ (daily issues), 41.50Can$ (paper bound issues at end of session). Crown Publications Inc., 521 Fort Street, Victoria, British Columbia, V8W 1E7 Canada. **Tel** (604)386-4636, FAX (604)386-0221. Index available.

US/0364-0973
OFFICIAL REPORTS OF THE SUPREME COURT. [Off. rep. Supreme Court]. **Main/Corp** United States. Supreme Court. **VFOAT** United States Reports. (19??)-. Government Publication. English. ir. Superintendent of Documents, US Government Printing Office, Washington DC 20402. **Tel** (202)275-3328, FAX (202)786-2377. **DD** 348.
Ind/Abst Fed. Tax Artic.

UK
OFFSHORE LICENCE REPORT. See Petroleum and Natural Gas.

US
OGDEN'S REVISED CALIFORNIA REAL PROPERTY LAW. English. IAS Publications Office / University of California, 223 Fulton Street, 3rd Floor, Berkeley CA 94720. **Tel** (415)642-7189. cum. index.

US/0742-9266
OHIO BAR REPORTS. (OHIO BAR REPORTS : REPORTS OF CASES ARGUED AND DETERMINED IN ALL COURTS IN OHIO : ALSO CONTAINING THE SUMMARIES OF CIVIL AND CRIMINAL CASES FROM OHIO'S COURTS OF APPEALS AS APPEARED IN THE JULY-SEPTEMBER ISSUES OF THE OHIO STATE BAR ASSOCIATION REPORT MAGAZINE.). [Ohio Bar rep.]. **Added/Corp** Ohio. Supreme Court. Vol. 1 (July/Sept. 1982)-. English. Law Abstract Publishing Company, 71 East Elm Street, PO Box 564, Norwalk OH 44857. **ED** William C Moore. **LC** KFO47.A33; O35. **DD** 348.771/044/05; 347.71084405. cum. index.

US/0274-7294
OHIO DISTRICT COURT REVIEW.
Added/Corp United States. District Court (Ohio : Northern District) United States. District Court (Ohio : Southern District). Vol. 1 (1980)-. Periodical. English. mo. $245.00. Anadem Inc, 3620 North High Street, Columbus OH 43214. **Tel** (614)262-2539, (800)633-0055. **ED** Mike Cheadle. **LC** KF128.O36; O36. **DD** 348.73/26; 347.30826. Index available.
Desc: Digests unreported civil decisions of Ohio Federal District Court Judges, Magistrates, and Bankruptcy Judges.

US
OHIO LAWYER (COLUMBUS, OHIO : 1987). (OHIO LAWYER.). Vol. 1, No. 1 (Jan./Feb. 1987)-. Periodical. English. bm. $24.00. Ohio State Bar Association, Ohio Legal Center, 33 West Eleventh Avenue, Columbus OH 43201. **Tel** (614)421-2121. **ED** Kate Hagan. **LC** PAR. **Ad Acc. Circ:** 22,000 (ctrl). *Absorbed in part* Summary Judgement : A Publication for Members of the Ohio State Bar Association.
Desc: Contains the latest information about issues affecting the practice of law. Examines legal trends and issues through feature articles.
Ind/Abst Law Office Inf. Serv.

US/0163-0008
OHIO MONTHLY RECORD. (Feb. 1977)-. English. Twelve times a year. Banks-Baldwin Law Publishing Company, PO Box 1974, University Center, Cleveland OH 44106. **Tel** (216)721-7373. **Bk Rev. Ad Acc.**
Desc: An easy-to-use companion service updating the Ohio Administrative Code. Following each month, subscribers receive all administrative agency rules adopted, amended, or rescinded.

US
OHIO MOTOR VEHICLE LAWS. Main/Corp Ohio. **Added/Corp** Ohio. Dept. of Highway Safety. (1988)-. English. an. $15.95. Gould Publications / Florida, 1333 North 1792, Longwood FL 32750-3724. **Tel** (407)695-9500, 800 847-6502. **LC** KFO297.A29; O5. **DD** 343/.771/0946. **Bk Rev. Ad Acc.**
Desc: Contains the traffic laws of Ohio.

US/0094-534X
OHIO NORTHERN UNIVERSITY LAW REVIEW. [Ohio North. Univ. law rev.]. **Added/Corp** Claude W. Pettit College of Law. Vol. 1 (1973)-. English. Four times a year (Jan., Mar., May, Nov.). $20.00. Ohio Northern University Law School, PO Box 153, Ada OH 45810. **Tel** (419)772-2248, FAX (419)772-1932. **ED** John Melvin. **LC** K15; .H55. **DD** 340/.05. **Bk Rev.** (Qty: 4). **Ad Acc. Pr Rev. Circ:** 1,200 (ctrl). available on microfiche; available on microfilm; available in microform. *Supersedes* Ohio Northern University Intramural Law Review.
Desc: This review contains articles on a recent supreme court decision current legal issues.
Ind/Abst Bowne Dig. Corp. Sec. Lawyers; Curr. Law Index (1980-); Fed. Tax Artic.; Index Leg. Period.; Leg. Resour. Index (1980-); LegalTrac (1980-).

US
OHIO OFFICIAL REPORTS. Main/Corp Ohio. Courts. English. ir. Law Abstract Publishing Company, 71 East Elm Street, PO Box 564, Norwalk OH 44857.

US/0744-9607
OHIO OFFICIAL REPORTS. ADVANCE SHEETS. (OHIO OFFICIAL REPORTS.). [Ohio off. rep., Adv. sheets]. **Added/Corp** Ohio. Attorney General's Office. Anderson Publishing Co. (Cincinnati, Ohio) West Publishing Company. **VFOAT** Ohio Official Reports. Advance Sheets. Vol. 1, No. 1, New Series (July 12, 1982)-. English. wk. $115.00. West Publishing Company, 610 Opperman Drive, PO Box 64526, Eagan MN 55123-1308. **Tel** (612)687-5618, (800)328-9352, FAX (612)687-5388, (800)562-2329. **DD** 348. **Ad Acc.**

US
OHIO PROBATE CODE, ANNOTATED. **Main/Corp** Ohio. English. Banks-Baldwin Law Publishing Company, PO Box 1974, University Center, Cleveland OH 44106. **Tel** (216)721-7373. **(Subscription address:** Banks-Baldwin Law Publishing Company, University Center, PO Box 1974, Cleveland, OH 44106-9990) **LC** KFO144.A29; O34. **DD** 346.77105/2/02632. ***Continues*** *Ohio Revised Probate Code Annotated, Amended.*

US/0744-8376
OHIO STATE BAR ASSOCIATION REPORT (1981). (OHIO STATE BAR ASSOCIATION REPORT.). [Ohio State Bar Assoc. rep.]. **Added/Corp** Ohio State Bar Association. Vol. 54 No. 44 (Nov. 16 1981)-. Periodical. English. Fifty times a year. $135.00. Ohio State Bar Association, 1700 Lakeshore Drive, PO Box 16562, Columbus OH 43204. **Tel** (614)487-2050, FAX (614)421-7650. **ED** William C. Moore. **LC** KF200; .O36. **DD** 340/.06/0771. Index available. **Ad Acc. Circ:** 22,000 (ctrl). available on microfiche. ***Continues*** *Ohio State Bar Association (Series), 0199-0322.*
Desc: Full text opinions and summaries of opinions from all courts serving Ohio. Specialized features on Ohio legislation and rules for attorneys, classified and display ads.
Ind/Abst Curr. Law Index (1980-); Fed. Tax Artic.; Law Office Inf. Serv.; Leg. Resour. Index (1981-?); LegalTrac (1980-1989).

US/1046-4344
OHIO STATE JOURNAL ON DISPUTE RESOLUTION. [Ohio State j. dispute resolut.]. **Added/Corp** Ohio State University. College of Law. **VFOAT** Journal on Dispute Resolution. Vol. 1, No. 1 (Fall 1985)-. Periodical. English. Twice a year (May, Dec.). $25.00. OSU Development Fund, 1659 North High Street, Ohio State University, Columbus OH 43210. **Tel** (614)292-7170. **ED** Yvonne Schlosberg. **LC** K15; .H57. **DD** 347.771/09; 347.71079. **Bk Rev. Ad Acc. Circ:** 500.
Desc: Contains journal articles and abstracts of articles published in other journals which cover current developments in alternative dispute resolution.
Ind/Abst Index Leg. Period.; Leg. Resour. Index; LegalTrac (1985-).

US/0048-1572
OHIO STATE LAW JOURNAL. [Ohio State law j.]. Vol.9 (Winter 1948)-. Periodical. English. Five times a yearFive times a year. $35.00 US; $40.00 other. Ohio State Law Journal University / College of Law, 55 West 12th Street, Columbus OH 43210. **Tel** (614)292-6892. **ED** D Gerow. **LC** K15; .H58. **DD** 340/.05. cum. index. **Bk Rev. Ad Acc. Circ:** 2,000 (ctrl). available on microfilm and microfiche from University Microfilms International (UMI). ***Continues*** *Ohio State University Law Journal.*
Desc: Welcomes the submission of unsolicited manuscripts for possible publication.
Ind/Abst Bowne Dig. Corp. Sec. Lawyers; Curr. Law Index (1980-); Fed. Tax Artic.; Index Leg. Period.; Leg. Resour. Index (1980-); LegalTrac (1980-); PAIS Int. Print (1991-).

●US/1062-3817
OHIO UST CLAIMS DIGEST. [Ohio UST claims dig.]. **VAT** Ohio Underground Storage Tank Claims Digest. (1992)-. Periodical. English. qt. $125.00. Ohio Ust Claims Digest, 71 East Wilson Bridge Road, Suite A-5, Worthington OH 43085. **DD** 346.

US
OIL AND GAS LAW. English. an. $700.00. Matthew Bender & Company Inc., 1275 Broadway, Albany NY 12204. **Tel** (800)833-9844, (518)487-3000.

UK/0263-5070
OIL & GAS (OXFORD, OXFORDSHIRE). (OIL & GAS : LAW AND TAXATION REVIEW.). **VFOAT** O.G.L.T.R.; Oil and Gas; Oil and Gas Law and Taxation Review; Oil & Gas Law and Taxation Review; OGLTR. No. 1 (July 1982)-. Periodical. English. Twelve times a year. £410.00 Europe; £430.00 other. Sweet & Maxwell Ltd., South Quay Plaza, 183 Marsh Wall, London E14 9FT England. **Tel** 011 44 264 342899, FAX 011 44 264 342723, telex 929089 ITPINF G. **ED** Brenda Wackitchie. **LC** K3911.2; .O35. **DD** 343/.0772; 342.3772. Index available. **Bk Rev. Ad Acc. Circ:** 400 (ctrl).
Desc: For legal and tax advisers working in this current period of extreme market turbulence, which has led to both major adjustments to the activities of oil companies and pressures to alter the fiscal regime under which they work.

US/1055-9175
OIL SPILL U.S. LAW REPORT. (OIL SPILL U.S. LAW REPORT : LEGISLATION, LITIGATION, REGULATIONS & ENFORCEMENT ACTIONS FROM CUTTER INFORMATION CORP.). [Oil spill U. S. law rep.]. Vol. 1, No. 1 (Mar. 1991)-. Periodical. English. mo. $997.00 North America; $1250.00 other (full service). Cutter Information Corporation, 37 Broadway, Arlington MA 02174-5539. **Tel** (617)648-8700, (800)964-5118, FAX (617)648-8707, (617)648-1950, telex 650 100 9891. **DD** 344. **[CCC].** available on an online database (file 636/Full-Text) from DIALOG.
Ind/Abst PTS Newsl. Database [Full Txt.].

NE
OJCD. (19??)-. English. Four times a year. £695.00. ELLIS Publications, PO Box 1059, 6201 BB Maastricht Netherlands. **Tel** 011 31 04457 2275, FAX 011 31 04457 2148.
Desc: Full text oriented CD-ROM covering legislation, proposed legislation, case law, parliamentary documents and information and notices as published in the Official and Journal, European Court Reports, and other official documents and publications.

JA
OKINAWA HOGAKU. **VFOAT** Journal of the Association of Law, The Okinawa Kokusai University. 1973 Ed.-. Japanese (Japanese). Okinawa Kokusai Daigaku Hogakai, 276-2 Aza Ginowan, Okinawa-ken, Ginowan Japan. **LC** K15. **DD** 340/.0952.

US/0030-1655
OKLAHOMA BAR JOURNAL, THE. [Okla. bar j.]. **Added/Corp** Oklahoma Bar Association (1939-) Oklahoma. Supreme Court. Oklahoma. Court of Appeals. Oklahoma. Court of Criminal Appeals. **VFOAT** OBA Journal. **VAT** Oklahoma Bar Association Journal. Vol. 50, No. 1 (Jan. 6, 1979)-. Periodical. English. Forty-eight times a year (Weekly except Aug.). $25.00. Oklahoma Bar Association, PO Box 53036, Oklahoma City OK 73125. **Tel** (405)524-2365. **ED** Martha M. Snow. **LC** KF200; .J68. Index available (December). **Bk Rev,** (Qty: 48). **Ad Acc. Circ:** 13,500. available on microfilm and microfiche from University Microfilms International (UMI). ***Continues*** *Journal (Oklahoma Bar Association (1939-)).*
Desc: Articles on substantive areas of the law.
Ind/Abst Curr. Law Index (1980-1986); Fed. Tax Artic.; Law Office Inf. Serv.; Leg. Resour. Index (1980-1985)(1980-); LegalTrac (1980-1985).

US/0364-9458
OKLAHOMA CITY UNIVERSITY LAW REVIEW. [Oklahoma City Univ. law rev.]. **Main/Corp** Oklahoma City University. Vol. 1 (Spring 1976)-. English. Three times a year. $18.00. Oklahoma City University, Northwest 23rd at North Blackwelder, Oklahoma City OK 73106. **Tel** (405)521-5280. **LC** K15; .K54. **DD** 340/.05. Index available. cum. index. **Bk Rev. Ad Acc. Circ:** 700.
Desc: First two issues of each volume are general subjects. The last issue of each volume is a symposium.
Ind/Abst Curr. Law Index (1980-); Index Leg. Period.; Leg. Resour. Index (1980-); LegalTrac (1980-).

US/1065-9587
OKLAHOMA COURT RULES AND PROCEDURE. FEDERAL. [Okla. court rules proced., Fed.]. **Added/Corp** West Publishing Company. (1990)-. English. West Publishing Company, 610 Opperman Drive, PO Box 64526, Eagan MN 55123-1308. **Tel** (612)687-5618, (800)328-9352, FAX (612)687-5388, (800)562-2329. **DD** 347. ***Continues in part*** *Oklahoma Court Rules and Procedure, 1045-1781.*

US/0747-2986
OKLAHOMA DECISIONS REPORTED IN PACIFIC REPORTER, SECOND SERIES. ***Title Change.*** [Okla. decis. rep. Pac. rep. second ser.]. **VFOAT** Oklahoma Decisions; West's Oklahoma Decisions. English. wk (50 issues a year). West Publishing Company, 610 Opperman Drive, PO Box 64526, Eagan MN 55123-1308. **Tel** (612)687-5618, (800)328-9352, FAX (612)687-5388, (800)562-2329. **(Subscription telephone:** FAX (612)688-3570) **DD** 348. ***Continued by*** *West's Oklahoma Decisions, 1041-6730.*

●US/1066-1123
OKLAHOMA EMPLOYMENT LAW LETTER. (OKLAHOMA ENVIROMENT LAW LETTER.). [Okla. employ. law lett.]. **Added/Corp** Doerner, Stuart, Saunders, Daniel & Anderson (Firm). (1993)-. Periodical. English. mo. $95.00. M. Lee Smith Publishers and Printers, 162 4th Avenue North, PO Box 198867, Nashville TN 37219. **Tel** (615)242-7395, (800)274-6774, FAX (615)256-6601. **DD** 344.

US/0030-1752
OKLAHOMA LAW REVIEW. [Oklahoma law rev.]. **Added/Corp** University of Oklahoma. School of Law. University of Oklahoma. College of Law. Vol. 1 (May 1948)-. Academic Scholarly Publication. English. Four times a year (Mar., June, Sept., Dec.). $25.00. Oklahoma Law Review, 300 Timberdell Road, Norman OK 73069. **Tel** (405)325-5191, FAX (405)325-6282. **ED** Philip A. Schovanec. **DD** 347.05. Index available in last issue of volume--attached. cum. index. **Bk Rev,** (Qty: 1). **Ad Acc, Adv Mgr:** Michael Waters. **Circ:** 1,250. available on microfilm.
Desc: A scholarly legal journal with articles covering a wide range of national and state legal issues.
Ind/Abst Account. Index, Suppl.; Bowne Dig. Corp. Sec. Lawyers; Curr. Law Index (1980-); Fed. Tax Artic.; Index Leg. Period.; Leg. Resour. Index (1980-); LegalTrac (1980-).

US
OKLAHOMA LEGAL DIRECTORY, THE. (1956)-. Directory. English. an. Legal Directories Publishing Company, 9111 Garland Road, PO Box 189000, Dallas TX 75218. **Tel** (214)321-3238, 800 447-5375. **LC** KF192.O38; O4. **DD** 340/.025/766.

US/0741-8612
OKLAHOMA REGISTER, THE. **Added/Corp** Oklahoma. Dept. of Libraries. Legislative Reference Division. Vol. 1, No. 1 (Nov. 1983)-. Periodical. English. sm (24 issues). $150.00. Office of Administrative Rules, 418 Will Rogers Building, PO Box 73152, Oklahoma City OK 73152. **Tel** (405)521-4911. **ED** Peggy Coe. **LC** KFO1236; .O45. **DD** 348.766/025/05; 347.66082505. **Circ:** 300. ***Continues*** *Oklahoma Gazette, 0030-1728.*
Desc: Oklahoma administrative rules.

KO
OLLON CHUNGJAE. **VFOAT** Press Arbitration Quarterly. Periodical. Korean. qt. Ollon Chungjae Wiwonhoe, 1 L-ka Uijo-ro, Chung-ku, Seoul South Korea.

CN/0710-538X
OMBUDSMAN JOURNAL, THE. [Ombudsman j.]. **Added/Corp** International Ombudsman Institute. No. 1 (Sept. 1981)-. Periodical. English. an (late fall). $40.00. International Ombudsman Institute, University of Alberta, Faculty of Law, Edmonton, Alberta T6G 2H5 Canada. **Tel** (403)492-3196. **LC** K15; .M38. **DD** 342.71/0667; 347.102667.
Ind/Abst Leg. Resour. Index; LegalTrac (1988-).

CN/0714-6132
OMBUDSMAN OFFICE PROFILES / INTERNATIONAL OMBUDSMAN OFFICE PROFILES. [Ombudsman off. profiles]. English. an. $40.00. Ombudsman Office Profiles, International Ombudsman Institute Faculty of Law, University of Alberta, Edmonton Alberta T6G 2H5 Canada. **Tel** (403)432-3196. **ED** Randall E Ivany. **DD** 342/.0667/025. **Bk Rev. Circ:** 450 (ctrl). ***Absorbed*** *Ombudsman and Other Complaint Handling Systems Survey, 0711-0383.*
Desc: General legislation and description of offices throughout the world, including terms of office, current Ombudsman, staff, budget, complaints handled.

AT/1030-9837
ON THE RECORDS. [On record]. (1987)-. Periodical. English. Four times a year (Mar., June, Sept., Dec.). 25.00Aus$. NSW Community Legal Centres, 245 Chalmers Street, Secret Suite 1, Redfern 2016 Australia. **Tel** 011 61 2 6982401, FAX 011 61 2 3182031. **DD** 347.944017. **Circ:** 400 (ctrl).
Desc: A newsletter listing news and activities of the NSW Community Legal Centres.

US/0733-639X
ONE ON ONE (ALBANY, N.Y.). (ONE ON ONE : NEWSLETTER OF THE GENERAL PRACTICE SECTION OF THE NEW YORK STATE BAR ASSOCIATION.). [One one]. **Added/Corp** New York State Bar Association. General Practice Section. (19??)-. Newsletter. English. Three times a year. New York State Bar Association, One Elk Street, Albany NY 12207. **Tel** (518)463-3200. **ED** Vincent Alexander and Alan Scheinkman. **LC** KF200; .O63. **DD** 349.747/05; 347.47005. **Ad Acc. Circ:** 4,200 (ctrl).
Desc: Articles of interest to the general legal practitioners in New York.

CN/0827-3308
ONTARIO APPEAL CASES (BOUND CUMULATION). (ONTARIO APPEAL CASES.). [Ont. appeal cases]. **Added/Corp** Ontario. Court of Appeal. Ontario. Divisional Court. Vol. 1 (1984)-. Periodical. English. ir. $58.00 (per volume, includes the advance parts and the bound cum. edition) U.S. Maritime Law Book Ltd, PO Box 302, Fredericton New Brunswick, E3B 4Y9 Canada. **Tel** (506)453-9921, (800)561-0220. **LC** KEO117.6; .O58. **DD** 348.713/043; 34.130843. Index available. cum. index.
Desc: Law reports of the Ontario Court of Appeals.

CN/0030-2937
ONTARIO GAZETTE, THE. [Ont. gaz.]. **Main/Corp** Ontario. **Added/Corp** Ontario. Ministry of Government Services. **VFOAT** Gazette de l'Ontario. Vol. 1, (March 7, 1868)-. Periodical. English (summaries and/or abstracts in French). Fifty-two times a year. $13.16 depository libraries; $123.16 others. Ontario Gazette, 50 Grosvenor Street, Toronto ONT M7A 1N8 Canada. **Tel** (416)326-5310. **LC** J2; .O5. **CODEN** ONGAE9. available on microfiche from Micromedia Limited; available on microfilm and microfiche from University Microfilms International (UMI). ***Continues*** *Upper Canada Gazette.*

●CN/1195-3136
ONTARIO LANDLORD AND TENANT LEGISLATION. (1993)-. English. an. 40.00Can$. Canada Law Book Inc., 240 Edward Street, Aurora Ontario L4G 3S9 Canada. **Tel** (800)263-3269, (905)841-6472, FAX (905)841-5085.
Desc: Covers relevant legislation regulating Ontario landlords and tenants.

CN/0845-4825
ONTARIO LAWYER'S PHONE BOOK, THE. [Ont. lawyer's phone book]. **Added/Corp** Canada Law Book Inc. (1988)-. Directory. English. an. 39.00Can$. Canada Law Book Inc., 240 Edward Street, Aurora Ontario L4G 3S9 Canada. **Tel** (800)263-3269, (905)841-6472, FAX (905)841-5085. **DD** 340.025/713. **Ad Acc.** ***Continues*** *Lawyer's Phone Book, 0317-8668.*
Desc: Lists every individual lawyer and law office in Ontario complete with telephone number, street address and postal code.

CN/1195-0188
ONTARIO MUNICIPAL ACT. (ONTARIO MUNICIPAL ACT, R.S.O. 1990, C. M.45.). (1992)-. English. an. 35.00Can$. Canada Law Book Inc., 240 Edward Street, Aurora Ontario L4G 3S9 Canada. **Tel** (800)263-3269, (905)841-6472, FAX (905)841-5085.
Desc: Portable edition of the Ontario Municipal Act, R.S.O. 1990, c.M.45.

CN/0318-7527
ONTARIO MUNICIPAL BOARD REPORTS. **Main/Corp** Ontario. Municipal Board. Vol. 1 (1973)-. English. ir. 111.00Can$. Canada Law Book Inc., 240 Edward Street, Aurora Ontario L4G 3S9 Canada. **Tel** (800)263-3269, (905)841-6472, FAX (905)841-5085. **ED** John G. Chipman, Ian James Lord, Roger T. Beaman. **LC** KEO866.4; .M86. **DD** 342.713/09/0264; 342/.713/0902646. **Bk Rev. Ad Acc.**
Desc: Reports leading Ontario Municipal Board decisions as well as relevant cabinet decisions and court judgements.
Ind/Abst Can. Legal Lit.

●CN/1195-017X
ONTARIO PLANNING ACT. (ONTARIO PLANNING ACT, R.S.O. 1990, C. P.13.). [Ont. Plan. Act]. **Main/Corp** Ontario. **Added/Corp** Canada Law Book Inc. **VFOAT** Ontario Planning Act. (1992)-. English. an. 29.00Can$. Canada Law Book Inc., 240 Edward Street, Aurora Ontario L4G 3S9 Canada. **Tel** (800)263-3269, (905)841-6472, FAX (905)841-5085. **DD** 346.71304/5/02632.
Desc: Portable edition of the Ontario Planning Act, R.S.O. 1990, c. P.13.

●CN/1195-3152
ONTARIO REAL ESTATE LEGISLATION. [Ont. real estate legis.]. **Added/Corp** Canada Law Book Inc. (1993)-. English. an. 60.00Can$. Canada Law Book Inc., 240 Edward Street, Aurora Ontario L4G 3S9 Canada. **Tel** (800)263-3269, (905)841-6472, FAX (905)841-5085. **DD** 346.71304/3/0263.
Desc: Source for all relevant statutes and regulations involved in Ontario real estate transactions.

CN/0030-3089
ONTARIO REPORTS (1963). (ONTARIO REPORTS.). [Ont. rep.]. **Added/Corp** Law Society of Upper Canada. (Jan. 11, 1963)-. Periodical. English. ir. 70.00Can$. Butterworth & Company Ltd. / Canada, 75 Clegg Road, Markham Ontario L6G 1A1 Canada. **Tel** (905)479-2665, (800)668-6481. ***Continues*** *Ontario Reports (1931);* ***Supersedes*** *Ontario Reports and Ontario Weekly Notes, 0380-1640.*

●CN/1191-159X
ONTARIO SMALL CLAIMS COURT PRACTICE. (ONTARIO SMALL CLAIMS COURT PRACTICE/ MARVIN A. ZUKER.). [Ont. small claims court pract.]. (1992)-. English. Carswell / Canada, 2075 Kennedy Road, Scarborough Ontario M1T 3V4 Canada. **Tel** (416)609-3800, (800)387-5164. **DD** 347.713/4. ***Continues*** *Small Claims Court Practice in the Ontario Court (General Division)., 1191-1581.*

●CN/1189-3419
ONTARIO'S ACCESS AND PRIVACY LEGISLATION, AN ANNOTATION. [Ont. access. priv. legis. annot.]. **Added/Corp** Ontario. Management Board of Cabinet. Secretariat. Jan. 1, (1992)-. Periodical. English. ir. **DD** 342.713/0662.

US
OPINION. **Added/Corp** New York (State). State University, Buffalo. School of Law. (19??)-. Newspaper. English. bw. $15.00. University of New York at Buffalo Law School, 724 O'Brian Hall, Amherst NY 14260. **Tel** (716)636-2147. **ED** Daniel Ibarrondo. **Bk Rev. Ad Acc. Circ:** 2,500 (ctrl).
Desc: Contains news and features articles concerning UB Law School, its students, the legal community and profession.

US/0743-7668
OPINIONS OF THE NEW YORK STATE COMPTROLLER. [Opin. N.Y. State Comptrol.]. **Main/Corp** New York (State). Comptroller's Office. English. mo. Lenz & Riecker Inc., 1 Columbia Place, Albany NY 12207. **Tel** (518)436-8647. **LC** KFN5752; .A556. **DD** 342.747/09/026; 347.47029026. ***Continues*** *Opinions of the Comptroller Relating to Municipal Government.*

US/1048-2199
ORALL NEWSLETTER. **See** Library and Information Sciences.

US/0897-5698
ORANGE COUNTY LAWYER. [Orange Cty. lawyer]. **Added/Corp** Orange County Bar Association. Vol. 1, No. 1 (Jan. 1988)-. Periodical. English. Twelve times a year. $36.00. Orange County Bar Association, 601 Civic Center Drive West, Santa Ana CA 92701-4002. **Tel** (714)541-6222. **ED** Winston Frost. **LC** KF200; .O7. **DD** 340. **Bk Rev,** (Qty: 2). **Ad Acc, Adv Mgr:** Susan Serpa, **Tel** (714)222-4782. **Circ:** 6,000 (ctrl). ***Continues*** *Bulletin (Orange County Bar Association), 0279-9243.*
Desc: The focus of the magazine is the legal community in Orange County.

US/1060-2585
ORANGE COUNTY REPORTER (SANTA ANA, CALIF.). (ORANGE COUNTY REPORTER.). **Added/Corp** Daily Journal (Firm). **VFOAT** Reporter. (May 12, 1921)-. Newspaper. English. da. $72.00. Daily Journal Corporation, 915 East First Street, Los Angeles CA 90012. **Tel** (213)229-5300, FAX (213)680-3682.

IT/0393-4012
ORATORI DEL GIORNO, GLI. [Oratori giorno]. (1927)-. Periodical. Italian. mo. L30000 regular; L45000 sustaining; L85000 special. Oratori del Giorno, V Colli Farnesina 144, 00194 Rome Italy. **Tel** 011 39 6 36306176, 36301773, FAX 011 39 6 36304174. **UDC** 8.085. **Bk Rev. Ad Acc. Circ:** 2000.

CN/0227-3268
ORDERS IN COUNCIL (OTTAWA). (ORDERS IN COUNCIL.). **VFOAT** Weekly Listing of Federal Cabinet Orders in Council. V. 1- Mar. 21, 1980-. Periodical. English. wk (when cabinet meets). $212.81. Carswell / Canada, 2075 Kennedy Road, Scarborough Ontario M1T 3V4 Canada. **Tel** (416)609-3800, (800)387-5164. **ED** Kathryn Blackett. **DD** 348.71/028. **Circ:** 300 (ctrl).
Desc: Provides all weekly descriptive listings of privy council orders when Federal Cabinet meets. Includes regulations, appointments, FIRA decisions, ministerial orders and proclamations.

US
ORDINANCE LAW ANNOTATIONS. **Added/Corp** Shepard's Citations, Inc. Shepard's, Inc. of Colorado Springs. Shepard's/McGraw-Hill. **VFOAT** Shepard's Ordinance Law Annotations. (1969)-. English. ir. $1050.00 (15 bound volumes). Shepards McGraw-Hill Inc, 555 Middle Creek Parkway, PO Box 35300, Colorado Springs CO 80935-3530. **Tel** (719)488-3000, FAX (800)525-0053.

JA
ORDINANCES. **Main/Corp** Seychelles. Laws, Statutes, etc. English. qt. $46.50. **(Subscription address:** Japan Publications Trading Company, Ltd., PO Box 5030, Tokyo International, Tokyo 100-31 Japan.**)**

US/0733-2475
OREGON BARS. (OREGON BARS : BUTTERWORTH ADVANCE REPORT SERIES.). **VFOAT** Oregon B.A.R.S.; Butterworth Advance Report Series. **VAT** Oregon Butterworth Advance Report Series. Vol. 8, No. 12 (June 11, 1982)-. Periodical. English. bw. $90.00. Butterworth Heinemann / Woburn, MA, 225 Wildwood Avenue, Unit B, Woburn MA 01801. **Tel** (800)366-2665, FAX (617)928-2620, telex 880052. **ED** Ray Krontz. **Circ:** 300 (ctrl). ***Continues*** *Oregon Appellate Reporter Service, 0273-9666.*
Desc: Summarizes judicial opinions handed down by the Oregon Supreme Court, Court of Appeals, and Tax Court.

●US/1068-6622
OREGON COMPREHENSIVE INDEX. (OREGON COMPREHENSIVE INDEX : A TOPICAL INDEX FOR OREGON REVISED STATUTES AND OREGON REVISED STATUTES ANNOTATED / PREPARED BY THE EDITORIAL STAFF OF THE PUBLISHER.). [Or. compr. index]. **Added/Corp** Butterworth Legal Publishers. (1992)-. English. be. Butterworth Legal Publishers / Salem, NH, 8 Industrial Way, Building C, Salem NH 03079. **Tel** (800)548-4001, (603)898-9664. **LC** KFO2430 1953; .A43 1983 Suppl. **DD** 348.795/028; 347.950828. ***Continues*** *Comprehensive Index to Oregon Statutes, 1060-2844.*

US/0196-2043
OREGON LAW REVIEW. [Oregon law rev.]. **Added/Corp** University of Oregon. School of Law. Oregon Bar Association. Oregon State Bar. Vol. 1 (Apr. 1921)-. Periodical. English. Four times a year. $20.00. University of Oregon / Law, 201 Law Center, Eugene OR 97403. **Tel** (503)346-3881, 346-3844, FAX (503)346-1564. **ED** Karen O'Connor. **LC** K15; .R39. **DD** 349.795/05. Index available (4th iss.). cum. index. **Bk Rev,** (Qty: seldom). **Ad Acc, Adv Mgr:** Julie Martil, **Tel** (503)346-1551. **Circ:** 1,000 (ctrl). available on an online database from WESTLAW.
Desc: Articles and comments on current legal issues of national interest as well as issues specific to Oregon and the Pacific Northwest.
Ind/Abst Bowne Dig. Corp. Sec. Lawyers; Curr. Law Index (1980-); Fed. Tax Artic.; Index Leg. Period.; Leg. Resour. Index (1980-); LegalTrac (1980-).

US/0148-379X
OREGON LEGISLATION. **Main/Corp** Oregon State Bar. Committee on Continuing Legal Education. English. Oregon State Bar, 5200 Southwest Meadows Road, Lake Oswego OR 97035. **Tel** (503)620-0222 ext 340, (800)452-8260, FAX (503)684-1366. **LC** KFO2415; .O73. **DD** 348/.795/01.

US
OREGON RULES OF COURT. FEDERAL. **Added/Corp** West Publishing Company. (1990)-. English. West Publishing Company, 610 Opperman Drive, PO Box 64526, Eagan MN 55123-1308. **Tel** (612)687-5618, (800)328-9352, FAX (612)687-5388, (800)562-2329. ***Continues in part*** *Oregon Rules of Court, 8756-3614.*

US
OREGON RULES OF COURT. STATE. **Added/Corp** West Publishing Company. (1990)-. English. West Publishing Company, 610 Opperman Drive, PO Box 64526, Eagan MN 55123-1308. **Tel** (612)687-5618, (800)328-9352, FAX (612)687-5388, (800)562-2329. ***Continues in part*** *Oregon Rules of Court, 8756-3614.*

US/0030-4816
OREGON STATE BAR BULLETIN, THE. (OREGON STATE BAR BULLETIN.). [Or. State Bar bull.]. **Added/Corp** Oregon State Bar. **VFOAT** Bulletin. Vol. 1, No. 1 (July 1941)-. Periodical. English. Twenty-two times a year. $45.00. Oregon State Bar, 5200 Southwest Meadows Road, Lake Oswego OR 97035. **Tel** (503)620-0222 ext 340, (800)452-8260, FAX (503)684-1366. **ED** Paul Nickell. **LC** KF200; .O733. **DD** 340/.025/795. **Ad Acc, Adv Mgr:** Art Greisser. **Circ:** 12,500. ***Continues*** *Oregon State Bar Bulletin (1935), 0030-4816.*
Desc: Covers legal trends and news of substantive law.
Ind/Abst Law Office Inf. Serv.

US/0734-0966
... OREGON STATE BAR ECONOMIC SURVEY, THE. **VFOAT** Oregon State Bar ... Economic Survey Results. English. **LC** KF301.5.O7; O74. **DD** 331.2/81349795.

PY
ORGANIZACION LABOR. **Main/Corp** Organizacion Labor. Spanish. Organizacion Labor, El Paraguayo Independiente No 741.

IT
ORIENTAMENTI DELLA GIURISPRUDENZA DEL LAVORO. (19??)-. Italian. Four times a year. L150000.00. Assoservizi, Via Chiaravalle 8 10, 20122 Milan Italy. **Tel** 011 39 2 58304888.

US/0094-7776
OSAHRC REPORTS. **Main/Corp** United States. Occupational Safety and Health Review Commission. V. 1- Apr. 28, 1971/Dec. 4, 1972-. English. $14.10. Occupational Safety and Health Review Commission, 1825 K Street NW, Washington DC 20006. **Tel** (202)634-7943. **LC** KF3568.3.A2; O256. **DD** 344/.73/0465. **NLM** W2 A O60.

SA
OSAR/OSALL. **See** Library and Information Sciences.

CN
OSGOODE HALL LAW JOURNAL. **Added/Corp** Osgoode Hall Law School. Legal and Literary Society. Vol. 1 (June 1958)-. Periodical. English. Four times a year. 40.00Can$. Osgoode Hall Law Journal, 4700 Keele Street, York University, Downsview Ontario M3J 2R5 Canada. **Tel** (416)736-5354. **ED** John D. McCamus. **LC** K15; .S45. **Bk Rev. Ad Acc. Circ:** 1,000 (ctrl).
Desc: The journal is a forum for the exchange and expression of ideas about law, both practical and theoretical. The criterion of publication is quality and originality.
Ind/Abst Bowne Dig. Corp. Sec. Lawyers; Can. Legal Lit.; Curr. Law Index (1980-); Index Can. Leg. Period. Lit.; Index Leg. Period.; Leg. Resour. Index (1980-); LegalTrac (1980-).

CN/0030-6185
OSGOODE HALL LAW JOURNAL (1960). (OSGOODE HALL LAW JOURNAL.). [Osgoode Hall law j.]. **Added/Corp** Osgoode Hall Law School. Legal and Literary Society. Osgoode Hall Law School. Vol. 2 (Apr. 1960)-. Periodical. English. Four times a year. 40.00Can$ (individuals), 60.00Can$ (institutions). Osgoode Hall Law Journal, 4700 Keele Street, York University, Downsview Ontario M3J 2R5 Canada. **Tel** (416)736-5354. **ED** John

D. McCamus, and Beverley Stone (Managing Editor). **LC** K15; .S45. **[CCC]**. ***Continues*** *Osgoode Hall Law School Journal., 0380-1683.*
Desc: The journal primary aim is to publish research that will further our understanding of the law. Its aims, in particular, to publish articles relating to the law that present new theoretical generalizations, report empirical findings, or address the policy implications of current research.
Ind/Abst Index Can. Leg. Period. Lit.; Index Leg. Period.; Leg. Resour. Index (1980-).

AU/0029-9251
OSTERREICHISCHE JURISTEN-ZEITUNG. (1946)-. Periodical. German. Twenty-six times a year. S1,940.00. Manzsche Verlagsbuchhandlung, Kohlmarkt 16 Postfach 163, A 1014 Vienna Austria. **Tel** 011 43 222 5316171. Index available. **Bk Rev. Ad Acc. Circ:** 3,600 (ctrl).
Desc: Articles treating actual judicial themes. Decisions of Austraian appeals and supreme courts on private law, criminal law, constitutional law and administrative law.
Ind/Abst Index Foreign Leg. Per.

AU
OSTERREICHISCHES ANWALTSBLATT. Added/Corp Osterreichischer Rechtsanwaltskammertag. (19??)-. Periodical. German. mo. S1650.00. Manzsche Verlagsbuchhandlung, Kohlmarkt 16 Postfach 163, A 1014 Vienna Austria. **Tel** 011 43 222 5316171. **LC** K15; .E89.

AU
OSTERREICHISCHES RECHT DER WIRTSCHAFT. V. 1, No. 1, (Sept. 1983)-. Periodical. German. mo. S670.00. Verlag Orac GmbH & Co., Schoenbrunner Str 59 61, A-1050 Vienna Austria. **Tel** 011 43 1 5130651. **LC** K15; .S6. **DD** 343.436/08/05; 344.3603805. Index available. **Bk Rev. Ad Acc. Circ:** 12,500.
Desc: Essays and reviews on economic law (taxation, constitutional development, public and private law), reviews on jurisdiction and legislation, book reviews.

GW/0030-6444
OSTEUROPA-RECHT. [Osteur.-Recht]. **Added/Corp** Deutsche Gesellschaft fuer Osteuropakunde. **VAT** Osteuropa Recht. (Mar. 1955)-. Periodical. German (English). qt. DM44.40. DVA Deutsche Verlagsanstalt, Neckarstrasse 121, D-70190 Stuttgart Germany. **Tel** 011 49 711 26310. **(Subscription address:** Zenit Pressevertrieb GmbH, Postfach 810640, D 70523 Stuttgart Germany) **[CCC].**
Ind/Abst Index Foreign Leg. Per.; LABORDOC.

NZ/0078-6918
OTAGO LAW REVIEW. [Otago law rev.]. **Added/Corp** Otago Law Review Trust Board. Otago University Law Students' Association. Vol. 1 (Aug. 1965)-. Periodical. English. William W. Gaunt and Sons Inc, 3011 Gulf Drive, Gaunt Building, Holmes Beach FL 34217. **Tel** (800)942-8683, (813)778-5211. **LC** K15; .T3. **DD** 340/.05.
Ind/Abst Index Leg. Period.; Leg. Resour. Index (1980-); LegalTrac (1980-).

CK
OTRO DERECHO, EL. Added/Corp Instituto Latinoamericano de Servicios Legales Alternativos. No. 1 (Aug 1988)-. Periodical. Spanish. Three times a year. $20.00 (Latin America & Caribbean); $30.00 other. ILSA - Instituto Latinoamericano de Servicios Legales Alternativos, PO Box 077844, Bogota Colombia. **Tel** 011 57 1 2455995, 011 57 1 2884437, FAX 011 57 1 2884854. **LC** K15; .T76. **DD** 349.8/05; 348.005.
Ind/Abst Hum. Rights Intern. Rep.

CN/0048-2331
OTTAWA LAW REVIEW. [Ottawa law rev.]. **Added/Corp** University of Ottawa. Common Law Section. Vol. 1 (1966)-. Periodical. English (French). Three times a year (Feburary, June, and October). 30.00Can$. Ottawa Law Review for Canada, University of Ottawa, Law Faculty, 57 Louis Pasteur, Ottawa ONT K1N 6N5 Canada. **Tel** (613)564-2919, FAX 9613)564-9800. **ED** Steve Winder. **LC** K15; .T83. **DD** 340.0971. Index available. **Bk Rev. Ad Acc. Circ:** 500 (ctrl).
Desc: Legal articles, comments, recent developments and book reviews, of current interest to academics and practicing lawyers.
Ind/Abst Can. Legal Lit.; Curr. Law Index (1980-); Index Can. Leg. Period. Lit.; Index Leg. Period.; Leg. Resour. Index (1980-); LegalTrac (1980-); PAIS Int. Print (1991-).

UK
OVERSEAS FOOD LEGISLATION MANUAL. **See** Food and Food Industry.

US
OVERVIEW OF LEGISLATION IN THE SESSION OF THE ILLNOIS GENERAL ASSEMBLY, AN. Main/Corp Illinois. Legislative Council. (19??)-. English. Illinois Legislative Council, 222 S College/3rd Floor, Springfield IL 62704. **LC** KFI1215; .L44. **DD** 348/.773/01.

UK/0143-6503
OXFORD JOURNAL OF LEGAL STUDIES. [Oxf. j. leg. stud.]. **Added/Corp** University of Oxford. Faculty of Law. Vol. 1, No. 1 (Spring 1981)-. Periodical. English. qt. £70.00 UK and Europe; $130.00 other. Oxford University Press, Walton Street, Oxford OX2 6DP England. **Tel** 011 44 865 56767, FAX 011 44 865 267773, telex 837330 OXPRES G. **(Subscription address:** Oxford University Press / USA, Journals Marketing Department, Oxford University Press, 2001 Evans Road, Cary NC 27513.) **ED** P. M. North. **LC** K15; .X47. **DD** 340/.05. **[CCC].** Index available. **Bk Rev. Ad Acc.** available on microfilm and microfiche from University Microfilms International (UMI).
Desc: Emphasis on matters of theory and on broad issues arising from the relationship of law to other disciplines, drawing on Oxford's particular strength in legal philosophy and socio-legal matters. Articles cover comparative and international law, EEC law, legal history and philosophy and interdisciplinary material from, e.g. the fields of economics and sociology.
Ind/Abst Aust. Leg. Mon. Dig.; Curr. Law Index (1985-); Index Leg. Period.; Leg. Resour. Index (1985-); LegalTrac (1982-).

US
OYEZ REVIEW. **See** College and School Publications.

NR
OYO STATE OF NIGERIA GAZETTE. Main/Corp Oyo State (Nigeria). V. 1- April 1, 1976-. English. wk. N12.00. Oyo State of Nigeria, Government Printer, Ibadan Nigeria. **DD** 340/.096692.

FR/0758-802X
P.J.R. PRAXIS JURIDIQUE ET RELIGION. **See** Religion and Theology.

US/0272-2410
PACE LAW REVIEW. [Pace law rev.]. Vol. 1, No. 1 (1980)-. Periodical. English. Three times a year. $20.00 US; $22.00 other. Pace University / School of Law, 78 North Broadway, White Plains NY 10603. **Tel** (914)422-4000, (914)422-4271, FAX (914)422-4139. **LC** K16; .A23. **DD** 349.747/05; 347.47005. Index available. **Bk Rev. Ad Acc. Circ:** 500 (ctrl).
Desc: A publication comprised of both professional and student articles; addresses current legal issues. All articles are appropriately footnoted to provide easy access to information.
Ind/Abst Bowne Dig. Corp. Sec. Lawyers; Curr. Law Index (1982-); Index Leg. Period.; Leg. Resour. Index (1982-); LegalTrac (1980-).

US/0030-8757
PACIFIC LAW JOURNAL. [Pac. law j.]. **Added/Corp** McGeorge School of Law. Vol. 1, (Jan. 1970)-. Periodical. English. Four times a year (Jan., Apr., July, Oct.). $20.00. McGeorge School of Law, 3401 Fifth Avenue, Sacramento CA 95817. **Tel** (916)739-7171. Index available. **Circ:** 3,300 (ctrl).
Desc: Professional periodical devoted to scholar, legal analysis and commentary as well as in-depth reporting of California legislation.
Ind/Abst Bowne Dig. Corp. Sec. Lawyers; Crim. Justice Abstr.; Curr. Law Index (1980-); Fed. Tax Artic.; Index Leg. Period.; Leg. Resour. Index (1980-); LegalTrac (1980-).

US
PAGE'S OHIO REVISED CODE, ANNOTATED, CONTAINING THE TEXT OF THE OFFICIAL OHIO REVISED CODE, EFFECTIVE OCT. 1, 1953 CURRENT MATERIAL. Main/Corp Ohio. English. an (Published in March). $385.00. Anderson Publishing, 2035 Reading Road, Cincinnati OH 45202. **Tel** (513)421-4142, (800)582-7295, FAX (513)562-8116. **(Subscription address:** Anderson Publishing Company, PO Box 1576, Cincinnati OH 45201.**)**

PK
PAKISTAN LAW JOURNAL. Periodical. English (Urdu). mo. Rs340.00 Pakistan; $40.00 US. Punjab Council, 13 Fane Road, Lahore Pakistan. **Tel** 54344. **ED** Tariq Masood and M Bachir Chaudhri. **DD** 340/.095491. Index available. cum. index. **Ad Acc. Circ:** 4,200.
Desc: Important judgements and decisions of the Superior Courts and articles or speeches by leaders of the judiciary.

PK
PAKISTAN SUPREME COURT CASES. Added/Corp Pakistan. Supreme Court. (19??)-. English. $20.00. Pakistan Supreme Court Cases, 1 Turner Road Near High Court, Lahore Pakistan. **DD** 348.549/1044; 345.4910844.

PK
PAKISTAN SUPREME COURT REPORTS, THE. Main/Corp Pakistan. Supreme Court. **VFOAT** P.S.C.R.; PSCR. (1956)-. English.

US/0884-8785
PALM BEACH REVIEW. VFOAT Review. (19??)-. Periodical. English. dada (Mon.-Fri.). Price varies for law firms. American Lawyer Media, L.P., 600 3rd Avenue, New York NY 10016. **Tel** (212)973-2800. **(Subscription address:** Palm Beach Review, PO Box 66, West Palm Beach FL 33402) ***Continues*** *Palm Beach Review and Business Record, 0199-0969.*

UK/0961-8295
PALMER'S IN COMPANY. [Palmer's co.]. (1991)-. Periodical. English. Ten times a year. £115.00 Europe; £121.00 other. Sweet & Maxwell Ltd., South Quay Plaza, 183 Marsh Wall, London E14 9FT England. **Tel** 011 44 264 342899, FAX 011 44 264 342723, telex 929089 ITPINF G. **DD** 344.10666. ***Continues*** *Palmer's Company Law. Reporter, 0950-7841.*

US/0739-1978
PANEL DISCUSSION SERIES. [Panel discuss. ser.]. Began with: Topic 1, issued in 1982. Monographic series. English. Price varies per volume. Special Committee on Dispute Resolution, American Bar Association, 1800 M Street NW/Suite 200, Washington DC 20036. **Tel** (202)331-2258. **DD** 347.

PL/0031-0980
PANSTWO I PRAWO. (PANSTWO I PRAWO : ORGAN ZRZESZENIA PRAWNIKOW DEMOKRATOW W POLSCE.). [Panst. prawo]. **Added/Corp** Zrzeszenie Prawnikow Demokratow w Polsce. Zrzeszenie Prawnikow Demokratow (Poland) Zrzeszenie Prawnikow Polskich. Polska Akdemia Nauk. Komitet Nauk Prawnych. Instytut Nauk Prawnych (Polska Akademia Nauk) Instytut Panstwa i Prawa (Polska Akademia Nauk). **VFOAT** State and Law. Vol. 1, No. 1 (1946)-. Periodical. Polish (summaries and/or abstracts in English, French and Russian). mo. $144.00. **(Subscription address:** ARS Polona, PO Box 1001, 00068 Warsaw Poland.) cum. index.
Ind/Abst Am. Hist. Life (1955-1984); Index Foreign Leg. Per.; Int. Bibliogr. Sociol.

IO
PANTA-RHEI. VFOAT Edisi Pertama. Vol. 1 June 1975-. Periodical. Indonesian (Indonesian). Senat Mahasiswa Fak Hakum and Peng Masyarajat, Universitas Sumatera Utara, Jalan Universitas 4, Medan Indonesia. **LC** K16; .A56. **DD** 340/.09598.

US
PAPER BOOK OF THE DELTA THETA PHI LAW FRATERNITY, INTERNATIONAL. Added/Corp Delta Theta Phi Law Fraternity, International. Vol. 89, No. 1 (Winter 1984)-. Periodical. English. qt. Delta Theta Phi Law Fraternity International Inc, 666 High Street, Worthington OH 43085-4106. **Tel** (614)888-2600. cum. index. ***Continues*** *Paper Book of the Delta Theta Phi Law Fraternity.*

CN/0715-4534
PAPERS PRESENTED AT THE MID-WINTER MEETING OF THE ALBERTA BRANCH OF THE CANADIAN BAR ASSOCIATION. ***Ceased.*** (PAPERS PRESENTED AT THE ... ANNUAL MID-WINTER MEETING OF THE ALBERTA BRANCH OF THE CANADIAN BAR ASSOCIATION.). **Main/Corp** Canadian Bar Association. Alberta Branch. Mid-Winter Meeting. **VAT** Mid-Winter Meeting - Canadian Bar Association, Alberta Branch. (1981)-(199?). English. an. **DD** 349.7123. ***Continues*** *Selected Papers Presented at the Mid-Winter Meeting of the Alberta Branch, Canadian Bar Association, 0711-2025.*

US
PAPERS USED AT THE ANNUAL EXAMINATIONS IN LAW HELD AT HARVARD UNIVERSITY. Main/Corp Harvard Law School. (19??)-. English. an. $10.25. Harvard Law School, Publications Center, Cambridge MA 02138. **Tel** (617)495-7984, (617)495-3694.

AT/0085-4689
PAPUA NEW GUINEA LAW REPORTS. [Papua N. Guin. law rep.]. (1971/1972)-. English. an. 165.00Aus$. The Law Book Company Limited, 44-50 Waterloo Road, North Ryde New South Wales, 2113 Australia. **Tel** 011 61 2 8870177, FAX 011 61 2 8887240, telex ASBOOK 27445. **(Subscription address:** Law Book Company, 35 Mitchell, North Sydney NSW 2060 Australia) **ED** N J Haxton. Index available. ***Continues*** *Papua and New Guinea Law Reports.*
Desc: Provides leading cases from the Supreme Court of Justice and the National Court of Justice of Papua, New Guinea. Catchwords and headnotes are provided for each case.
Ind/Abst Aust. Leg. Mon. Dig.

BL
PARA FISCAL : ORGAO OFICIAL DA ASSOCIACAO DOS FISCAIS DE TRIBUTOS ESTADUAIS DO PARA. Periodical. Portuguese. mo. Ed Para-Fiscal, Rua Dom

Pedro I No 273, Dro I No 273 CEP 66000 Belem Para Brazil. **LC** KHD7677.A15; P37. **DD** 343.81/1504/05; 348.11503405.

US/0146-2954
PARA-LEGAL UPDATE. ***Suspended.*** **Main/Corp** National Legal Assistant Conference Center. **VAT** Para Legal Update. Vol. 1- Oct. 1976-?. English. qt. $15.00. National Legal Assistant Conference, 2444 Wilshire Boulevard, Suite 301, Santa Monica CA 90403. **Tel** (310)453-1941. **ED** Joseph E Deering Jr. **LC** KF320.L4; N37. **DD** 340/.023. **Bk Rev. Ad Acc. Circ:** 2,000.
Desc: Ideas for improvement and increased job satisfaction for legal assistants. Also updates law and procedures for legal assistants (paralegals)

US/0739-3601
PARALEGAL, THE. ***Suspended.*** [Paralegal]. Vol. 1, No. 1 (Jan./Feb. 1983)-?. Periodical. English. bm. $30.00 US; $50.00 (first class mail), $75.00 (airmail) other. Paralegal Publishing Group, PO Box 406, Solebury PA 18963. **Tel** (215)297-8333, FAX (215)297-8358. **ED** William Cameron. **LC** KF320.L4; P37. **DD** 340/.023/73. **Bk Rev. Ad Acc. Circ:** 29,500.
Desc: Circulated among Personnel who are practising paralegals, attorneys, paralegal educators, paralegal associations, law librarians, court personnel and paralegal schools.

US/0196-6138
PARKER DIRECTORY OF CALIFORNIA ATTORNEYS. (1980)-. English. an (Nov.). $28.50 (two volume set without revised editions); $40.00 (two volume set with revised editions). Parker Publications, 2283 Cosmos Court, Carlsbad CA 92009. **Tel** (800)452-9873, (619)931-5979. **ED** Mary Redondo. **LC** KF192.C3; P35. **DD** 340/.025/794. **Bk Rev. Ad Acc. Circ:** 65,000 (ctrl). available on labels. ***Continues*** *Parker Directory of Attorneys, 0079-0044.*
Desc: Lists of attorneys, firms, court reporters and courts alphabetically by county (only in state of California). Also includes a certified specialist section, a preferred practice section and an expert witness section.

AT/0312-6862
PARLIAMENT OF WESTERN AUSTRALIA DIGEST, THE. Main/Corp Western Australia. Parliament. (1973)-. English. Government Printer / Parliament House, Harvest Terra, Perth Western Australia, 6000 Australia. **DD** 348/.941/01.

US/0892-4805
PARTNER'S REPORT. [Partn. rep.]. **Added/Corp** Institute for Office Management and Administration (U.S.). Issue 87-5 (May 1987)-. Periodical. English. Twelve times a year. $245.00. Institute of Management and Administration, 29 West 35th Street, 5th Floor, New York NY 10001-2299. **Tel** (212)244-0360. **LC** KF300.A1; P37. **DD** 338.7/6134. **[CCC].**
Desc: A brief for law firm owners.

BE/0031-2614
PASICRISIE BELGE. RECUEIL GENERAL DE LA JURISPRUDENCE DES COURS ET TRIBUNAUX. Periodical. French. ir. 17000.00F. Etablissements Emile Bruylant, 67 rue de la Regence, 1000 Brussels Belgium. **Tel** 011 32 2 5129845. **ED** Emile Bruylant. **Circ:** 1,100.
Desc: Covers jurisprudence.

BE
PASINOMIE : COLLECTION COMPLETE DES LOIS, ARRETES ET REGLEMENTS GENERAUX... . Main/Corp Belgium. Periodical. French. ir. 9500.00F. Etablissements Emile Bruylant, 67 rue de la Regence, 1000 Brussels Belgium. **Tel** 011 32 2 5129845. **Circ:** 475.
Desc: Collection of laws of Belgium with preparation and discussion of texts.

US/0737-7630
PASSPORT TO LEGAL UNDERSTANDING. (PASSPORT TO LEGAL UNDERSTANDING : THE NEWSLETTER ON PUBLIC EDCUATION PROGRAMS AND MATERIALS.). **Added/Corp** American Bar Association. Commission on Public Understanding about the Law. Vol. 1, No. 1 (Winter 1983)-. Periodical. English. sa (2 issues). Free on request. American Bar Association, 750 North Lake Shore Drive, Chicago IL 60611. **Tel** (312)988-5522, (312)988-5241, FAX (312)988-5528, telex 270593. **ED** Cynthia Canary. **LC** KF298; .P28. **DD** 349.73/07; 347.3007. **Bk Rev. Circ:** 10,000 (ctrl).
Desc: Legal education analysis for the general public.

US
PATENT LAW ANNUAL. See Copyright, Intellectual Property.

US/0147-6173
PATENT OFFICE EXAMINATION REVIEW COURSE. Main/Corp Practising Law Institute. Periodical. English. an. $450.00. Practising Law Institute, 810 Seventh Avenue, New York NY 10019-5818. **Tel** (212)765-5700, FAX (212)581-4670 general correspondence, (212)265-4742 orders and billing inquiries. **LC** KF3120.Z9; N47. **DD** 346/.73/0486.

US
PATENT OFFICE RULES AND PRACTICES. See Copyright, Intellectual Property.

US/0730-5524
PATIENT CARE LAW. (19??)-. Periodical. English. bm. $275.00 (also comes with Action Kit for Hospital Law complete package). Action Kit for Hospital Law, 4614 5th Avenue, Pittsburgh PA 15213. **Tel** (800)245-1205, (412)687-8275. **ED** John Horty. **LC** KF3821.A15; P38. **DD** 344.73/041/05; 347.3044105. **Circ:** 500 (ctrl).
Desc: A legal reference for nurses that discusses recent court cases, statutes and regulations and includes a reference manual and bi-monthly newsletters.

US
PATIENTS RIGHTS REPORTER. (19??)-. English. qt. $60.00. Cox Publications, PO Box 20316, Billings MT 59104-0316. **Tel** (406)256-8822. **ED** Meridith B. Cox. ***Continues*** *Patients Rights in California, 0736-2544.*

US
PBA BRIEF. Main/Corp Pennsylvania Bar Association. V. 23, No. 2- March 1978-. Periodical. English. mo. 100 South Street, PO Box 186, Harrisburg PA 17108. ***Continues*** *Pennsylvania Bar Brief.*

FR/0336-1551
PENANT. [Penant]. **VFOAT** Revue de Droit des Pays d'Afrique. Vol. 72, No. 692 (June/Aug. 1962)-. Periodical. French. qt. 650.00F. Editions d'IENA, 17 rue Thiers France. **Tel** 011 33 1 39763993. **LC** K18; .E5. ***Continues*** *Recueil Penant.*
Ind/Abst Index Foreign Leg. Per.; Int. Labour Doc.; Int. Polit. Sci. Abstr.; Irr. Drain. Abstr.; LABORDOC.

US/8755-0342
PENNSYLVANIA BAR ASSOCIATION LAWYERS DIRECTORY. Added/Corp Pennsylvania Bar Association. **VFOAT** Pennsylvania Lawyers Directory; Lawyers Directory. (1982)-. Directory. English. an (Jan.). $42.00. Pennsylvania Bar Association, PO Box 186, Harrisburg PA 17108. **Tel** (717)238-6715, FAX (717)238-7182. **ED** Marcy Mallory. **Ad Acc, Adv Mgr:** Leonard and Associates, **Tel** (215)675-9133. **Circ:** 3,000. ***Continues*** *Pennsylvania Lawyers Almanac.*
Desc: Alpha listing of all attorneys licensed to practice in Pennsylvania. Also contains state and federal court listings.

US/0196-2051
PENNSYLVANIA BAR ASSOCIATION QUARTERLY. [PA. Bar Assoc. q.]. **Main/Corp** Pennsylvania Bar Association. **Added/Corp** Pennsylvania Bar Association. Quarterly. Vol. 1 (June 1929)-. Periodical. English. qt (Jan., Apr., July, Oct.). $20.00. Pennsylvania Bar Association, PO Box 186, Harrisburg PA 17108. **Tel** (717)238-6715, FAX (717)238-7182. **ED** Louis Del Duca. **LC** K16; .E47. **DD** 340/.06/0748. **Circ:** 27,000 (ctrl).
Desc: Provides highlights of significant developments in Pennsylvania law.
Ind/Abst Curr. Law Index (1980-); Fed. Tax Artic.; Index Leg. Period.; Law Office Inf. Serv.; Leg. Resour. Index (1980-); LegalTrac (1980-).

US/0162-2137
PENNSYLVANIA BULLETIN (HARRISBURG). (PENNSYLVANIA BULLETIN.). **Added/Corp** Pennsylvania. General Assembly. Legislative Reference Bureau. (1970)-. Bulletin. English. wk. $65.00. Legislative Reference Bureau - Pennsylvania, Main Capitol Building, Room 641, Harrisburg PA 17120. **ED** Mary Jane Phelps. **LC** KFP36; .P46. Index available. cum. index. **Circ:** 13,000 (ctrl). available on microfilm.
Desc: Official rules, regulations, and related documents of state agencies; analogous to Federal register.

US/0893-9691
PENNSYLVANIA EDUCATION LAW REPORT. [Pa. educ. law rep.]. (1987)-. Periodical. English. mo. $114.00. Whitaker's Legal Newsletter, 313 South Avenue, Fanwood NJ 07023. **Tel** (908)889-6336. **LC** KFP390.A15; P46. **DD** 344.748/07/05; 347.4804705.
Desc: Recent rulings by the Secretary of Education and PERB on staff and administrative classification, special education, and other issues.

US/0092-3605
PENNSYLVANIA JUVENILE COURT DISPOSITIONS. See Law-Abstracting, Bibliographies and Statistics.

US/0741-5540
PENNSYLVANIA LAW FINDER. 1983 Ed.-. English. West Publishing Company, 610 Opperman Drive, PO Box 64526, Eagan MN 55123-1308. **Tel** (612)687-5618, (800)328-9352, FAX (612)687-5388, (800)562-2329. **(Subscription telephone:** FAX (612)688-3570**) LC** KFP61; .P38. **DD** 348.748/028; 347.480828.

US/1065-0962
PENNSYLVANIA LAW JOURNAL (1992). ***Title Change.*** (PENNSYLVANIA LAW JOURNAL : THE WEEKLY NEWSPAPER FOR THE LEGAL PROFESSION.). [Pa. law j.]. **Added/Corp** Pennsylvania. Commonwealth Court. Vol. 15, No. 25 (June 29, 1992)-(1994). Periodical. English. wk. Legal Communications Ltd., 1617 John F Kennedy Boulevard, Suite 960, Philadelphia PA 19103. **LC** K16; .E48. **DD** 340/.09748. ***Continues*** *Pennsylvania Law Journal-Reporter, 0279-8166.* ***Continued by*** *Pennsylvania Law Weekly, 1075-8801.*

US/0279-8166
PENNSYLVANIA LAW JOURNAL-REPORTER. ***Title Change.*** [Pa. law j.-report.]. **VFOAT** Pennsylvania Law Journal Reporter. (19??-1992). Periodical. English. wk. Packard Press Corporation, One Penn Center at Suburban Station, 1617 John F Kennedy Boulevard, Philadelphia PA 19103. **Tel** (215)563-2700, FAX (215)563-4911. **ED** Brian R Harris and Fred Maher. **LC** K16; .E48. **DD** 340. Index available. **Bk Rev. Ad Acc. Circ:** 10,000. available on microfilm. ***Continues*** *Pennsylvania Law Journal (Philadelphia, Pa. : 1977), 0160-8495.* ***Continued by*** *Pennsylvania Law Journal (Philadelphia, Pa. : 1992), 1065-0962.*
Desc: Recent developments in Pennsylvania law and the practice of law in Pennsylvania. Digests of all significant decisions from county, state and federal courts in Pennsylvania.
Ind/Abst Law Office Inf. Serv.; Leg. Resour. Index (1980-); LegalTrac (1980-).

US/0193-4821
PENNSYLVANIA LAWYER, THE. Added/Corp Pennsylvania Bar Association. (Feb. 1979)-. Periodical. English. Six times a year (Jan., Mar., May, July, Sept., Nov.). $20.00. Pennsylvania Bar Association, PO Box 186, Harrisburg PA 17108. **Tel** (717)238-6715, FAX (717)238-7182. **ED** Marcy C. Mallory. **LC** KF200; .P43. **DD** 340/.09748. **Ad Acc, Adv Mgr:** Leonard and Associates, **Tel** (215)675-9133. **Circ:** 27,000 (ctrl).
Desc: The flagship publication of Pennsylvania Bar Association.
Ind/Abst Law Office Inf. Serv.

●US/1067-2400
PENNSYLVANIA PERSONAL INJURY REPORTER. (1993)-. Periodical. English. sm. $275.00. LRP Publications, 747 Dresher Road, PO Box 980, Horsham PA 19044-0980. **Tel** (800)341-7874, (215)784-0860, FAX (215)784-9639, (215)784-0870. ***Continues*** *Pennsylvania Trial Lawyers Association. Personal Injury Reporter.*
Desc: Provides information on the latest decisions on such topics as medical malpractice, motor vehicle law, workers' compensation, and products liability handed down by Pennsylvania's Supreme, Superior, Commonwealth and trial courts and the Third Circuit.

US/0745-8037
PENNSYLVANIA REPORTER. (PENNSYLVANIA REPORTER, COVERING CASES REPORTED IN ATLANTIC REPORTER, SECOND SERIES.). [Pa. report.]. **VFOAT** West's Pennsylvania Reporter. 1A. 2D-2A. 2D-. English. wk. $65.00. West Publishing Company, 610 Opperman Drive, PO Box 64526, Eagan MN 55123-1308. **Tel** (612)687-5618, (800)328-9352, FAX (612)687-5388, (800)562-2329. **(Subscription telephone:** FAX (612)688-3570**) DD** 345.42.

US/0048-3249
PENNSYLVANIA RESEARCHER, THE. ***Ceased.*** Periodical. English. mo. National Legal Research Group Inc, PO Box 7187, Charlottesville VA 22906. **Tel** (800)727-6574, (804)977-5690, FAX (804)295-4667. **LC** KFP57; .P43. **DD** 348/.748/026.

US
PENNSYLVANIA SCHOOL LAWS & RULES ANNOTATED. VFOAT Pennsylvania School Laws and Rules Annotated. (1990)-. English. an. Banks-Baldwin Law Publishing Company, PO Box 1974, University Center, Cleveland OH 44106. **Tel** (216)721-7373. **LC** KFP390.A29; P46.

US
PENNSYLVANIA TAX HANDBOOK. VFOAT Prentice-Hall Pennsylvania Tax Handbook. (19??)-. English. an. Prentice-Hall Law and Business, 270 Sylvan Avenue, Englewood Cliffs NJ 07632. **Tel** (800)223-0231, (201)894-8538, FAX (201)894-8666. **LC** KFP470; .P46. **DD** 343.74804; 347.48034.

US/1052-9640
PENSION FUND LITIGATION REPORTER. (PENSION FUND LITIGATION REPORTER : THE MONTHLY JOURNAL OF RECORD OF LITIGATION INVOLVING BENEFIT PLAN FIDUCIARIES.). [Pension fund litig. rep.]. (Jan. 1990)-. English. mo. $700.00. Andrews Publications Inc., 1646 West Chester Pike, PO Box 1000, Westtown PA 19395. **Tel** (610)399-6600, (800)345-1101, FAX (610)399-6610. **LC** KF3512; .A516. **DD** 344.73/01252/02648; 347.304125202648.
Desc: Be amoung the first to know of developments in state and federal courts in actions brought by the PBGC,

Labor Department, employees and beneficiaries involving such issues as withdrawal liability, asset reversion, breach of duty and illegal transfers.

US/1042-9433
PENSION HANDBOOK. [Pension handb.]. **Added/Corp** Prentice-Hall, Inc. Information Services Division. **VFOAT** Prentice Hall's Pension Handbook; Pension Reform Handbook. (1988)-. English. an. $54.50. Macmillan Publishing Company, 100 Front Street, Box 500, Riverside NJ 08075-7500. **Tel** (800)257-5755, (609)461-6500, FAX (609)461-7070. **LC** KF6449; .P46. **DD** 343.7305/24; 347.303524.

US/0092-430X
PEPPERDINE LAW REVIEW. [Pepperdine law rev.]. **Added/Corp** Pepperdine University. School of Law. Vol. 1 (1973)-. Periodical. English. Four times a year (Feb., Mar., May, Dec.). $24.00. Pepperdine University, School of Law / Law Review, Malibu CA 90265. **Tel** (213)456-4764. **LC** K16; .E65. **DD** 340/.05. **Circ:** 650 (ctrl). available on microfilm and microfiche from University Microfilms International (UMI).
Desc: Current legal issues and analysis of cases.
Ind/Abst Bowne Dig. Corp. Sec. Lawyers; Crim. Justice Abstr.; Curr. Law Index (1980-); Index Leg. Period.; Leg. Resour. Index (1980-); LegalTrac (1980-).

IS
PERAKLIT, HA-. **VFOAT** Hapraklit. (19??)-. Periodical. Hebrew. qt. $25.00. Lishkat Orkhe Ha Din, PO Box 14152, Tel Aviv Israel. **LC** K16; .E68.

IO
PERATURAN DAERAH DAERAH ISTIMEWA YOGYAKARTA. **Main/Corp** Yogyakarta, Indonesia (Daerah Istimewa). (19??)-. Indonesian.

US/1049-3964
PERFECT LAWYER, THE. **See** Computers-Word Processing.

US
PERIODICAL SUBSCRIPTION PLAN B (INCLUDES REPORT, STATE COURT JOURNAL, SURVEY OF JUDICIAL SALARIES, AND ANNUAL REPORT). (19??)-. English. ir. $35.00. National Center for State Courts, 300 Newport Avenue, PO Box 8798, Williamsburg VA 23185. **Tel** (804)253-2000, FAX (804)220-0449.

NE
PERIODIEK WOORDENBOEK VAN ADMINISTRATIEVE EN GERECHTELIJKE BESLISSINGEN. Dutch. qt. 60.65. Uitgeverij Fed BV, Postbus 23 Netherlands. **LC** K16; .E69.

UK
PERSONAL AND MEDICAL INJURIES LAW LETTER. English. Legal Studies & Services Publ Ltd., 9-13 St. Andrew Street, London EC4A 3AE England. **Tel** 011 44 71 936-2016.

UK/1351-3850
PERSONAL INJURY LAW AND MEDICAL REVIEW. (19??)-. English. qt. £93.00 UK; £95.00 other. Barry Rose Law Periodicals Ltd., Little London, Chichester West Sussex PO19 1PG England. **Tel** 011 44 243 787841, 011 44 243 783637, FAX 011 44 243 779174, 011 44 243 779278.
Desc: Seeks to promote and support the debate and the dissemination of current issues affecting medical and legal jurisprudence.

US/1047-8566
PERSONAL INJURY NEWSLETTER. [Pers. inj. newsl.]. Vol. 1 (1958)-. Periodical. English. bw. Matthew Bender & Company Inc., 1275 Broadway, Albany NY 12204. **Tel** (800)833-9844, (518)487-3000. **LC** KF8925.P4; P38. **DD** 346.

US/0048-3435
PERSONAL INJURY RESEARCHER, THE. Periodical. English. mo. $42.00. The Research Group Inc, PO Box 7187, Charlottesville VA 22906. **LC** KF1256.A75; P47. **DD** 346/.73/032.

US
PERSONAL INJURY REVIEW. **Added/Corp** Matthew Bender (Firm). (1987)-. English. ir. Matthew Bender & Company Inc., 1275 Broadway, Albany NY 12204. **Tel** (800)833-9844, (518)487-3000. **LC** KF8925.P4; P4. **DD** 346.7303/23/0269; 347.3063230269. **NLM** W1; PE845D. ***Continues*** *Personal Injury Deskbook, 0736-640X.*
Ind/Abst Leg. Resour. Index (1987-?); LegalTrac (1980-1991).

●US/1067-2427
PERSONAL INJURY VERDICT REVIEWS. [Pers. inj. verdict rev.]. **Added/Corp** LRP Publications (Firm). Vol. 1, Issue 1 (Jan. 13, 1993)-. Periodical. English. sm. $385.00. LRP Publications, 747 Dresher Road, PO Box 980, Horsham PA 19044-0980. **Tel** (800)341-7874, (215)784-0860, FAX (215)784-9639, (215)784-0870. **(Subscription address:** LRP Publications, PO Box 980, Horsham PA 19044.**)** **DD** 346. ***Formed by the union of*** *Personal Injury Verdict Reviews. Trucking, Railroad & Marine Lines, 0749-6591; Personal Injury Verdict Reviews. Media and Government, 0749-6567; Personal Injury Verdict Reviews. Utilities, Construction & Industry, 0749-6559; Personal Injury Verdict Reviews. Consumer Products, 8755-5182; Personal Injury Verdict Reviews. Vehicular Negligence, 8755-5190; Personal Injury Verdict Reviews. Transportation Products, 8755-5204; Personal Injury Verdict Reviews. Professional Negligence, 8755-5212; Personal Injury Verdict Reviews. Physician & Hospital Negligence, 8755-5220; Personal Injury Verdict Reviews. Retailing, Banking, and Other Service Establishments, 0749-6583; Personal Injury Verdict Reviews. Public & Private Passenger Services, 8755-5239; Personal Injury Verdict Reviews. Food, Lodging, Sports & Entertainment Facilities, 8755-5255; Personal Injury Verdict Reviews. Personal Liability, 8755-5247* ***and*** *Personal Injury Verdict Reviews. Commercial & Industrial Products, 8755-5263.*
Desc: Contains a feature article, backed by nationwide case examples, which analyzes significant trends in personal injury jury verdicts.

US/0749-6567
PERSONAL INJURY VERDICT REVIEWS. MEDIA AND GOVERNMENT. ***Title Change.*** **VFOAT** Media and Government. (1983)-(199?). Periodical. English. qt. Jury Verdict Research Inc, 30700 Bainbridge Road #H, Cleveland OH 44139-2291. **Tel** (800)321-6910. **LC** KF1256.A75; P475. **DD** 346.7303/23/05; 347.30632305. ***Continues in part*** *Verdict Reports, 0092-2293.* ***Merged with*** *Personal Injury Verdict Reviews ...* ***to form*** *Personal Injury Verdict Reviews, 1067-2427.*

US/8755-5220
PERSONAL INJURY VERDICT REVIEWS. PHYSICIAN & HOSPITAL NEGLIGENCE. ***Title Change.*** **Added/Corp** Jury Verdict Research, Inc. **VFOAT** Physician & Hospital Negligence; Physician and Hospital Negligence. Issue 1 (Sept. 1983)-(199?). Periodical. English. qt. Jury Verdict Research Inc, 30700 Bainbridge Road #H, Cleveland OH 44139-2291. **Tel** (800)321-6910. **LC** KF1256.A75; P477. ***Continues in part*** *Jury Verdict Research, Inc. Verdict Reports, 0092-2293.* ***Merged with*** *Personal Injury Verdict Reviews ...* ***to form*** *Personal Injury Verdict Reviews, 1067-2427.*

US/0749-6583
PERSONAL INJURY VERDICT REVIEWS. RETAILING, BANKING, AND OTHER SERVICE ESTABLISHMENTS. ***Title Change.*** **Added/Corp** Jury Verdict Research, Inc. **VFOAT** Retailing, Banking, and Other Service Establishments. (1983)-(199?). Periodical. English. qt. Jury Verdict Research Inc, 30700 Bainbridge Road #H, Cleveland OH 44139-2291. **Tel** (800)321-6910. **LC** KF1256.A75; P48. **DD** 346.7303/23/05; 347.30632305. ***Continues in part*** *Verdict Reports, 0092-2293.* ***Merged with*** *Personal Injury Verdict Reviews ...* ***to form*** *Personal Injury Verdict Reviews, 1067-2427.*

US/0749-6591
PERSONAL INJURY VERDICT REVIEWS. TRUCKING, RAILROAD & MARINE LINES. ***Title Change.*** **Added/Corp** Jury Verdict Research, Inc. Jury Verdict Research, Inc. **VFOAT** Trucking, Railroad & Marine Lines; Trucking, Railroad, and Marine Lines. (1983)-(199?). Periodical. English. qt. Jury Verdict Research Inc, 30700 Bainbridge Road #H, Cleveland OH 44139-2291. **Tel** (800)321-6910. **LC** KF1256.A75; P485. **DD** 346.7303/23/05; 347.30632305. ***Continues in part*** *Verdict Reports, 0092-2293.* ***Merged with*** *Personal Injury Verdict Reviews ...* ***to form*** *Personal Injury Verdict Reviews, 1067-2427.*

US/8755-6413
PERSONAL INJURY VERDICT SURVEY. ALABAMA EDITION. [Pers. inj. verdict surv., Ala. ed.]. **Added/Corp** Jury Verdict Research, Inc. **VFOAT** Alabama Verdict Survey. (19??)-. Periodical. English. an. $33.00. LRP Publications, 747 Dresher Road, PO Box 980, Horsham PA 19044-0980. **Tel** (800)341-7874, (215)784-0860, FAX (215)784-9639, (215)784-0870. **DD** 346. **Bk Rev. Circ:** 250 (ctrl).
Desc: Provides the most recent analysis of statewide personal injury verdicts to assist in counseling clients and developing case strategies. Provides summaries of recent verdicts, million-dollar verdict activity, and more.

US/8755-6618
PERSONAL INJURY VERDICT SURVEY. ALASKA EDITION. [Pers. inj. verdict surv., Alsk. ed.]. **Added/Corp** Jury Verdict Research, Inc. **VFOAT** Alaska Verdict Survey. (19??)-. Periodical. English. an. $33.00 (includes postage). LRP Publications, 747 Dresher Road, PO Box 980, Horsham PA 19044-0980. **Tel** (800)341-7874, (215)784-0860, FAX (215)784-9639, (215)784-0870. **DD** 346. **Bk Rev. Circ:** 250 (ctrl).
Desc: Provides the most recent analysis of statewide personal injury verdicts to assist in counseling clients and developing case strategies. Provides summaries of recent verdicts, million-dollar verdict activity, and more.

US/8755-6774
PERSONAL INJURY VERDICT SURVEY. ARIZONA EDITION. [Pers. inj. verdict surv., Ariz. ed.]. **Added/Corp** Jury Verdict Research, Inc. **VFOAT** Arizona Verdict Survey. (19??)-. Periodical. English. an. $33.00 (includes postage). LRP Publications, 747 Dresher Road, PO Box 980, Horsham PA 19044-0980. **Tel** (800)341-7874, (215)784-0860, FAX (215)784-9639, (215)784-0870. **DD** 346. **Bk Rev. Circ:** 250 (ctrl).
Desc: Provides the most recent analysis of statewide personal injury verdicts to assist in counseling clients and developing case strategies. Provides summaries of recent verdicts, million-dollar verdict activity, and more.

US/8755-6782
PERSONAL INJURY VERDICT SURVEY. ARKANSAS EDITION. [Pers. inj. verdict surv., Ark. ed.]. **Added/Corp** Jury Verdict Research, Inc. **VFOAT** Arkansas Verdict Survey. (19??)-. Periodical. English. an. $33.00 (includes postage). LRP Publications, 747 Dresher Road, PO Box 980, Horsham PA 19044-0980. **Tel** (800)341-7874, (215)784-0860, FAX (215)784-9639, (215)784-0870. **DD** 346. **Bk Rev. Circ:** 250 (ctrl).
Desc: Provides the most recent analysis of statewide personal injury verdicts to assist in counseling clients and developing case strategies. Provides summaries of recent verdicts, million-dollar verdict activity, and more.

US/8755-6790
PERSONAL INJURY VERDICT SURVEY. CALIFORNIA EDITION. [Pers. inj. verdict surv., Calif. ed.]. **Added/Corp** Jury Verdict Research, Inc. **VFOAT** California Verdict Survey. (19??)-. Periodical. English. an. $33.00 (includes postage). LRP Publications, 747 Dresher Road, PO Box 980, Horsham PA 19044-0980. **Tel** (800)341-7874, (215)784-0860, FAX (215)784-9639, (215)784-0870. **DD** 346. **Bk Rev. Circ:** 250 (ctrl).
Desc: Provides the most recent analysis of statewide personal injury verdicts to assist in counseling clients and developing case strategies. Provides summaries of recent verdicts, million-dollar verdict activity, and more.

US/8755-6731
PERSONAL INJURY VERDICT SURVEY. COLORADO EDITION. [Pers. inj. verdict surv., Colo. ed.]. **Added/Corp** Jury Verdict Research, Inc. **VFOAT** Colorado Verdict Survey. (19??)-. Periodical. English. an. $33.00 (includes postage). LRP Publications, 747 Dresher Road, PO Box 980, Horsham PA 19044-0980. **Tel** (800)341-7874, (215)784-0860, FAX (215)784-9639, (215)784-0870. **DD** 346. **Bk Rev. Circ:** 250 (ctrl).
Desc: Provides the most recent analysis of statewide personal injury verdicts to assist in counseling clients and developing case strategies. Provides summaries of recent verdicts, million-dollar verdict activity, and more.

US/8755-6596
PERSONAL INJURY VERDICT SURVEY. CONNECTICUT EDITION. [Pers. inj. verdict surv., Conn. ed.]. **Added/Corp** Jury Verdict Research, Inc. **VFOAT** Connecticut Verdict Survey. (19??)-. Periodical. English. an. $33.00 (includes postage). LRP Publications, 747 Dresher Road, PO Box 980, Horsham PA 19044-0980. **Tel** (800)341-7874, (215)784-0860, FAX (215)784-9639, (215)784-0870. **DD** 346. **Bk Rev. Circ:** 250 (ctrl).
Desc: Provides the most recent analysis of statewide personal injury verdicts to assist in counseling clients and developing case strategies. Provides summaries of recent verdicts, million-dollar verdict activity, and more.

US/8755-6529
PERSONAL INJURY VERDICT SURVEY. DELAWARE EDITION. [Pers. inj. verdict surv., Del. ed.]. **Added/Corp** Jury Verdict Research, Inc. **VFOAT** Delaware Verdict Survey. (19??)-. Periodical. English. an. $33.00 (includes postage). LRP Publications, 747 Dresher Road, PO Box 980, Horsham PA 19044-0980. **Tel** (800)341-7874, (215)784-0860, FAX (215)784-9639, (215)784-0870. **DD** 346. **Bk Rev. Circ:** 250 (ctrl).
Desc: Provides the most recent analysis of statewide personal injury verdicts to assist in counseling clients and developing case strategies. Provides summaries of recent verdicts, million-dollar verdict activity, and more.

US/8755-6723
PERSONAL INJURY VERDICT SURVEY. FLORIDA EDITION. [Pers. inj. verdict surv., Fla. ed.]. **Added/Corp** Jury Verdict Research, Inc. **VFOAT** Florida Verdict Survey. (19??)-. Periodical. English. an. $33.00 (includes postage). LRP Publications, 747 Dresher Road, PO Box 980, Horsham PA 19044-0980. **Tel** (800)341-7874, (215)784-0860, FAX (215)784-9639, (215)784-0870. **DD** 346. **Bk Rev. Circ:** 250 (ctrl).
Desc: Provides the most recent analysis of statewide personal injury verdicts to assist in counseling clients and developing case strategies. Provides summaries of recent verdicts, million-dollar verdict activity, and more.

US/8755-6758
PERSONAL INJURY VERDICT SURVEY. GEORGIA EDITION. (PERSONAL INJURY VERDICT SURVEY. GEORGIA EDITION.). [Pers. inj.

verdict surv., Ga. ed.]. **Added/Corp** Jury Verdict Research, Inc. **VFOAT** Georgia Verdict Survey. (19??)-. Periodical. English. an. $33.00. LRP Publications, 747 Dresher Road, PO Box 980, Horsham PA 19044-0980. **Tel** (800)341-7874, (215)784-0860, FAX (215)784-9639, (215)784-0870. **(Subscription address:** LRP Publications, PO Box 980, Horsham PA 19044.**)** **DD** 346. **Bk Rev. Circ:** 250 (ctrl).
Desc: Provides the most recent analysis of statewide personal injury verdicts to assist in counseling clients and developing case strategies. Provides summaries of recent verdicts, million-dollar verdict activity, and more.

US/8755-674X
PERSONAL INJURY VERDICT SURVEY. HAWAII EDITION. [Pers. inj. verdict surv., Hawaii ed.]. **Added/Corp** Jury Verdict Research, Inc. **VFOAT** Hawaii Verdict Survey. (19??)-. Periodical. English. an. $33.00 (includes postage). LRP Publications, 747 Dresher Road, PO Box 980, Horsham PA 19044-0980. **Tel** (800)341-7874, (215)784-0860, FAX (215)784-9639, (215)784-0870. **DD** 346. **Bk Rev. Circ:** 250 (ctrl).
Desc: Provides the most recent analysis of statewide personal injury verdicts to assist in counseling clients and developing case strategies. Provides summaries of recent verdicts, million-dollar verdict activity, and more.

US/8755-6693
PERSONAL INJURY VERDICT SURVEY. IDAHO EDITION. [Pers. inj. verdict surv., Ida. ed.]. **Added/Corp** Jury Verdict Research, Inc. **VFOAT** Idaho Verdict Survey. (19??)-. Periodical. English. an. $33.00 (includes postage). LRP Publications, 747 Dresher Road, PO Box 980, Horsham PA 19044-0980. **Tel** (800)341-7874, (215)784-0860, FAX (215)784-9639, (215)784-0870. **DD** 346. **Bk Rev. Circ:** 250 (ctrl).
Desc: Provides the most recent analysis of statewide personal injury verdicts to assist in counseling clients and developing case strategies. Provides summaries of recent verdicts, million-dollar verdict activity, and more.

US/8755-6685
PERSONAL INJURY VERDICT SURVEY. ILLINOIS EDITION. [Pers. inj. verdict surv., Ill. ed.]. **Added/Corp** Jury Verdict Research, Inc. **VFOAT** Illinois Verdict Survey. (19??)-. Periodical. English. an. $33.00 (includes postage). LRP Publications, 747 Dresher Road, PO Box 980, Horsham PA 19044-0980. **Tel** (800)341-7874, (215)784-0860, FAX (215)784-9639, (215)784-0870. **DD** 346. **Bk Rev. Circ:** 250 (ctrl).
Desc: Provides the most recent analysis of statewide personal injury verdicts to assist in counseling clients and developing case strategies. Provides summaries of recent verdicts, million-dollar verdict activity, and more.

US/8755-6715
PERSONAL INJURY VERDICT SURVEY. INDIANA EDITION. [Pers. inj. verdict surv., Indiana ed.]. **Added/Corp** Jury Verdict Research, Inc. **VFOAT** Indiana Verdict Survey. (19??)-. Periodical. English. an. $33.00 (includes postage). LRP Publications, 747 Dresher Road, PO Box 980, Horsham PA 19044-0980. **Tel** (800)341-7874, (215)784-0860, FAX (215)784-9639, (215)784-0870. **DD** 346. **Bk Rev. Circ:** 250 (ctrl).
Desc: Provides the most recent analysis of statewide personal injury verdicts to assist in counseling clients and developing case strategies. Provides summaries of recent verdicts, million-dollar verdict activity, and more.

US/8755-6669
PERSONAL INJURY VERDICT SURVEY. IOWA EDITION. [Pers. inj. verdict surv., Iowa ed.]. **Added/Corp** Jury Verdict Research, Inc. **VFOAT** Iowa Verdict Survey. (19??)-. Periodical. English. an. $33.00 (includes postage). LRP Publications, 747 Dresher Road, PO Box 980, Horsham PA 19044-0980. **Tel** (800)341-7874, (215)784-0860, FAX (215)784-9639, (215)784-0870. **DD** 346. **Bk Rev. Circ:** 250 (ctrl).
Desc: Provides the most recent analysis of statewide personal injury verdicts to assist in counseling clients and developing case strategies. Provides summaries of recent verdicts, million-dollar verdict activity, and more.

US/8755-6677
PERSONAL INJURY VERDICT SURVEY. KANSAS EDITION. [Pers. inj. verdict surv., Kans. ed.]. **Added/Corp** Jury Verdict Research, Inc. **VFOAT** Kansas Verdict Survey. (19??)-. Periodical. English. an. $33.00 (includes postage). LRP Publications, 747 Dresher Road, PO Box 980, Horsham PA 19044-0980. **Tel** (800)341-7874, (215)784-0860, FAX (215)784-9639, (215)784-0870. **DD** 346. **Bk Rev. Circ:** 250 (ctrl).
Desc: Provides the most recent analysis of statewide personal injury verdicts to assist in counseling clients and developing case strategies. Provides summaries of recent verdicts, million-dollar verdict activity, and more.

US/8755-6707
PERSONAL INJURY VERDICT SURVEY. KENTUCKY EDITION. [Pers. inj. verdict surv., Ky. ed.]. **Added/Corp** Jury Verdict Research, Inc. **VFOAT** Kentucky Verdict Survey. (19??)-. Periodical. English. an. $33.00 (includes postage). LRP Publications, 747 Dresher Road, PO Box 980, Horsham PA 19044-0980. **Tel** (800)341-7874, (215)784-0860, FAX (215)784-9639, (215)784-0870. **DD** 346. **Bk Rev. Circ:** 250 (ctrl).
Desc: Provides the most recent analysis of statewide personal injury verdicts to assist in counseling clients and developing case strategies. Provides summaries of recent verdicts, million-dollar verdict activity, and more.

US/8755-6820
PERSONAL INJURY VERDICT SURVEY. LOUISIANA EDITION. [Pers. inj. verdict surv., La. ed.]. **Added/Corp** Jury Verdict Research, Inc. **VFOAT** Louisiana Verdict Survey. (19??)-. Periodical. English. an. $33.00 (includes postage). LRP Publications, 747 Dresher Road, PO Box 980, Horsham PA 19044-0980. **Tel** (800)341-7874, (215)784-0860, FAX (215)784-9639, (215)784-0870. **DD** 346. **Bk Rev. Circ:** 250 (ctrl).
Desc: Provides the most recent analysis of statewide personal injury verdicts to assist in counseling clients and developing case strategies. Provides summaries of recent verdicts, million-dollar verdict activity, and more.

US/8755-6545
PERSONAL INJURY VERDICT SURVEY. MAINE EDITION. [Pers. inj. verdict surv., Me. ed.]. **Added/Corp** Jury Verdict Research, Inc. **VFOAT** Maine Verdict Survey. (19??)-. Periodical. English. an. $33.00 (includes postage). LRP Publications, 747 Dresher Road, PO Box 980, Horsham PA 19044-0980. **Tel** (800)341-7874, (215)784-0860, FAX (215)784-9639, (215)784-0870. **DD** 346. **Bk Rev. Circ:** 250 (ctrl).
Desc: Provides the most recent analysis of statewide personal injury verdicts to assist in counseling clients and developing case strategies. Provides summaries of recent verdicts, million-dollar verdict activity, and more.

US/8755-6537
PERSONAL INJURY VERDICT SURVEY. MARYLAND EDITION. [Pers. inj. verdict surv., Md. ed.]. **Added/Corp** Jury Verdict Research, Inc. **VFOAT** Maryland Verdict Survey. (19??)-. Periodical. English. an. $33.00 (includes postage). LRP Publications, 747 Dresher Road, PO Box 980, Horsham PA 19044-0980. **Tel** (800)341-7874, (215)784-0860, FAX (215)784-9639, (215)784-0870. **DD** 346. **Bk Rev. Circ:** 250 (ctrl).
Desc: Provides the most recent analysis of statewide personal injury verdicts to assist in counseling clients and developing case strategies. Provides summaries of recent verdicts, million-dollar verdict activity, and more.

US/8755-2809
PERSONAL INJURY VERDICT SURVEY MASSACHUSETTS EDITION. [Pers. inj. verdict surv., Mass. ed.]. (19??)-. English. an. $33.00 (includes postage). LRP Publications, 747 Dresher Road, PO Box 980, Horsham PA 19044-0980. **Tel** (800)341-7874, (215)784-0860, FAX (215)784-9639, (215)784-0870. **DD** 346.
Desc: Provides the most recent analysis of statewide personal injury verdicts to assist in counseling clients and developing case strategies. Provides summaries of recent verdicts, million-dollar verdict activity, and more.

US/8755-6499
PERSONAL INJURY VERDICT SURVEY. MICHIGAN EDITION. [Pers. inj. verdict surv., Mich. ed.]. **Added/Corp** Jury Verdict Research, Inc. **VFOAT** Michigan Verdict Survey. (19??)-. Periodical. English. an. $33.00 (includes postage). LRP Publications, 747 Dresher Road, PO Box 980, Horsham PA 19044-0980. **Tel** (800)341-7874, (215)784-0860, FAX (215)784-9639, (215)784-0870. **DD** 346. **Bk Rev. Circ:** 250 (ctrl).
Desc: Provides the most recent analysis of statewide personal injury verdicts to assist in counseling clients and developing case strategies. Provides summaries of recent verdicts, million-dollar verdict activity, and more.

US/8755-6502
PERSONAL INJURY VERDICT SURVEY MINNESOTA EDITION. [Pers. inj. verdict surv., Minn. ed.]. **VFOAT** Minnesota Verdict Survey. (19??)-. Periodical. English. an. $33.00 (includes postage). LRP Publications, 747 Dresher Road, PO Box 980, Horsham PA 19044-0980. **Tel** (800)341-7874, (215)784-0860, FAX (215)784-9639, (215)784-0870. **DD** 346.
Desc: Provides the most recent analysis of statewide personal injury verdicts to assist in counseling clients and developing case strategies. Provides summaries of recent verdicts, million-dollar verdict activity, and more.

US/8755-6480
PERSONAL INJURY VERDICT SURVEY. MISSISSIPPI EDITION. [Pers. inj. verdict surv., Miss. ed.]. **Added/Corp** Jury Verdict Research, Inc. **VFOAT** Mississippi Verdict Survey. (19??)-. Periodical. English. an. $33.00. LRP Publications, 747 Dresher Road, PO Box 980, Horsham PA 19044-0980. **Tel** (800)341-7874, (215)784-0860, FAX (215)784-9639, (215)784-0870. **DD** 346. **Bk Rev. Circ:** 250 (ctrl).
Desc: Provides the most recent analysis of statewide personal injury verdicts to assist in counseling clients and developing case strategies. Provides summaries of recent verdicts, million-dollar verdict activity, and more.

US/8755-6472
PERSONAL INJURY VERDICT SURVEY. MISSOURI EDITION. [Pers. inj. verdict surv., Mo. ed.]. **Added/Corp** Jury Verdict Research, Inc. **VFOAT** Missouri Verdict Survey. (19??)-. Periodical. English. an. $33.00 (includes postage). LRP Publications, 747 Dresher Road, PO Box 980, Horsham PA 19044-0980. **Tel** (800)341-7874, (215)784-0860, FAX (215)784-9639, (215)784-0870. **DD** 346. **Bk Rev. Circ:** 250 (ctrl).
Desc: Provides the most recent analysis of statewide personal injury verdicts to assist in counseling clients and developing case strategies. Provides summaries of recent verdicts, million-dollar verdict activity, and more.

US/8755-6464
PERSONAL INJURY VERDICT SURVEY. MONTANA EDITION. [Pers. inj. verdict surv., Mont. ed.]. **Added/Corp** Jury Verdict Research, Inc. **VFOAT** Montana Verdict Survey. (19??)-. Periodical. English. an. $33.00. LRP Publications, 747 Dresher Road, PO Box 980, Horsham PA 19044-0980. **Tel** (800)341-7874, (215)784-0860, FAX (215)784-9639, (215)784-0870. **DD** 346. **Bk Rev. Circ:** 250 (ctrl).
Desc: Provides the most recent analysis of statewide personal injury verdicts to assist in counseling clients and developing case strategies. Provides summaries of recent verdicts, million-dollar verdict activity, and more.

US/8755-6642
PERSONAL INJURY VERDICT SURVEY. NEBRASKA EDITION. [Pers. inj. verdict surv., Neb. ed.]. **Added/Corp** Jury Verdict Research, Inc. **VFOAT** Nebraska Verdict Survey. (19??)-. Periodical. English. an. $33.00 (includes postage). LRP Publications, 747 Dresher Road, PO Box 980, Horsham PA 19044-0980. **Tel** (800)341-7874, (215)784-0860, FAX (215)784-9639, (215)784-0870. **DD** 346. **Bk Rev. Circ:** 250 (ctrl).
Desc: Provides the most recent analysis of statewide personal injury verdicts to assist in counseling clients and developing case strategies. Provides summaries of recent verdicts, million-dollar verdict activity, and more.

US/8755-6588
PERSONAL INJURY VERDICT SURVEY NEVADA EDITION. [Pers. inj. verdict surv., Nev. ed.]. (19??)-. English. an. $33.00 (includes postage). LRP Publications, 747 Dresher Road, PO Box 980, Horsham PA 19044-0980. **Tel** (800)341-7874, (215)784-0860, FAX (215)784-9639, (215)784-0870. **DD** 346.
Desc: Provides the most recent analysis of statewide personal injury verdicts to assist in counseling clients and developing case strategies. Provides summaries of recent verdicts, million-dollar verdict activity, and more.

US/8755-6391
PERSONAL INJURY VERDICT SURVEY. NEW HAMPSHIRE EDITION. [Pers. inj. verdict surv., N.H. ed.]. **Added/Corp** Jury Verdict Research, Inc. **VFOAT** New Hampshire Verdict Survey. (19??)-. Periodical. English. an. $33.00 (includes postage). LRP Publications, 747 Dresher Road, PO Box 980, Horsham PA 19044-0980. **Tel** (800)341-7874, (215)784-0860, FAX (215)784-9639, (215)784-0870. **DD** 346. **Bk Rev. Circ:** 250 (ctrl).
Desc: Provides the most recent analysis of statewide personal injury verdicts to assist in counseling clients and developing case strategies. Provides summaries of recent verdicts, million-dollar verdict activity, and more.

US/8755-2825
PERSONAL INJURY VERDICT SURVEY NEW JERSEY EDITION. [Pers. inj. verdict surv., N.J. ed.]. (19??)-. English. an. $33.00 (includes postage). LRP Publications, 747 Dresher Road, PO Box 980, Horsham PA 19044-0980. **Tel** (800)341-7874, (215)784-0860, FAX (215)784-9639, (215)784-0870. **DD** 346.
Desc: Provides the most recent analysis of statewide personal injury verdicts to assist in counseling clients and developing case strategies. Provides summaries of recent verdicts, million-dollar verdict activity, and more.

US/8755-6375
PERSONAL INJURY VERDICT SURVEY. NEW MEXICO EDITION. [Pers. inj. verdict surv., N.M. ed.]. **Added/Corp** Jury Verdict Research, Inc. **VFOAT** New Mexico Verdict Survey. (19??)-. Periodical. English. an. $33.00 (includes postage). LRP Publications, 747 Dresher Road, PO Box 980, Horsham PA 19044-0980. **Tel** (800)341-7874, (215)784-0860, FAX (215)784-9639, (215)784-0870. **DD** 346. **Bk Rev. Circ:** 250 (ctrl).
Desc: Provides the most recent analysis of statewide personal injury verdicts to assist in counseling clients and developing case strategies. Provides summaries of recent verdicts, million-dollar verdict activity, and more.

US/8755-6383
PERSONAL INJURY VERDICT SURVEY. NEW YORK EDITION. [Pers. inj. verdict surv., N.Y. ed.]. **Added/Corp** Jury Verdict Research, Inc. **VFOAT** New York Verdict Survey. (19??)-. Periodical. English. an. $33.00 (includes postage). LRP Publications, 747 Dresher Road, PO Box 980, Horsham PA 19044-0980. **Tel** (800)341-7874, (215)784-0860, FAX (215)784-9639, (215)784-0870. **DD** 346. **Bk Rev. Circ:** 250 (ctrl).
Desc: Provides the most recent analysis of statewide

personal injury verdicts to assist in counseling clients and developing case strategies. Provides summaries of recent verdicts, million-dollar verdict activity, and more.

US/8755-6359
PERSONAL INJURY VERDICT SURVEY. NORTH CAROLINA EDITION. [Pers. inj. verdict surv., N.C. ed.]. **Added/Corp** Jury Verdict Research, Inc. **VFOAT** North Carolina Verdict Survey. (19??)-. Periodical. English. an. $33.00 (includes postage). LRP Publications, 747 Dresher Road, PO Box 980, Horsham PA 19044-0980. **Tel** (800)341-7874, (215)784-0860, FAX (215)784-9639, (215)784-0870. **DD** 346. **Bk Rev. Circ:** 250 (ctrl).
Desc: Provides the most recent analysis of statewide personal injury verdicts to assist in counseling clients and developing case strategies. Provides summaries of recent verdicts, million-dollar verdict activity, and more.

US/8755-6812
PERSONAL INJURY VERDICT SURVEY. NORTH DAKOTA EDITION. [Pers. inj. verdict surv., N.D. ed.]. **Added/Corp** Jury Verdict Research, Inc. **VFOAT** North Dakota Verdict Survey. (19??)-. Periodical. English. an. $33.00 (includes postage). LRP Publications, 747 Dresher Road, PO Box 980, Horsham PA 19044-0980. **Tel** (800)341-7874, (215)784-0860, FAX (215)784-9639, (215)784-0870. **DD** 346. **Bk Rev. Circ:** 250 (ctrl).
Desc: Provides the most recent analysis of statewide personal injury verdicts to assist in counseling clients and developing case strategies. Provides summaries of recent verdicts, million-dollar verdict activity, and more.

US/8755-6367
PERSONAL INJURY VERDICT SURVEY. OHIO EDITION. [Pers. inj. verdict surv., Ohio ed.]. **Added/Corp** Jury Verdict Research, Inc. **VFOAT** Ohio Verdict Survey. (19??)-. Periodical. English. an. $33.00 (includes postage). LRP Publications, 747 Dresher Road, PO Box 980, Horsham PA 19044-0980. **Tel** (800)341-7874, (215)784-0860, FAX (215)784-9639, (215)784-0870. **DD** 346. **Bk Rev. Circ:** 250 (ctrl).
Desc: Provides the most recent analysis of statewide personal injury verdicts to assist in counseling clients and developing case strategies. Provides summaries of recent verdicts, million-dollar verdict activity, and more.

US/8755-6405
PERSONAL INJURY VERDICT SURVEY. OKLAHOMA EDITION. [Pers. inj. verdict surv., Okla. ed.]. **Added/Corp** Jury Verdict Research, Inc. **VFOAT** Oklahoma Verdict Survey. (19??)-. Periodical. English. an. $33.00 (includes postage). LRP Publications, 747 Dresher Road, PO Box 980, Horsham PA 19044-0980. **Tel** (800)341-7874, (215)784-0860, FAX (215)784-9639, (215)784-0870. **DD** 346. **Bk Rev. Circ:** 250 (ctrl).
Desc: Provides the most recent analysis of statewide personal injury verdicts to assist in counseling clients and developing case strategies. Provides summaries of recent verdicts, million-dollar verdict activity, and more.

US/8755-6766
PERSONAL INJURY VERDICT SURVEY. OREGON EDITION. [Pers. inj. verdict surv., Or. ed.]. **Added/Corp** Jury Verdict Research, Inc. **VFOAT** Oregon Verdict Survey. (19??)-. Periodical. English. an. $33.00 (includes postage). LRP Publications, 747 Dresher Road, PO Box 980, Horsham PA 19044-0980. **Tel** (800)341-7874, (215)784-0860, FAX (215)784-9639, (215)784-0870. **DD** 346. **Bk Rev. Circ:** 250 (ctrl).
Desc: Provides the most recent analysis of statewide personal injury verdicts to assist in counseling clients and developing case strategies. Provides summaries of recent verdicts, million-dollar verdict activity, and more.

US/8755-6804
PERSONAL INJURY VERDICT SURVEY. PENNSYLVANIA EDITION. [Pers. inj. verdict surv., Pa. ed.]. **Added/Corp** Jury Verdict Research, Inc. **VFOAT** Pennsylvania Verdict Survey. (19??)-. Periodical. English. an. $33.00 (includes postage). LRP Publications, 747 Dresher Road, PO Box 980, Horsham PA 19044-0980. **Tel** (800)341-7874, (215)784-0860, FAX (215)784-9639, (215)784-0870. **DD** 346. **Bk Rev. Circ:** 250 (ctrl).
Desc: Provides the most recent analysis of statewide personal injury verdicts to assist in counseling clients and developing case strategies. Provides summaries of recent verdicts, million-dollar verdict activity, and more.

US/8755-2817
PERSONAL INJURY VERDICT SURVEY RHODE ISLAND. [Pers. inj. verdict surv., R.I.]. (19??)-. English. an. $33.00 (includes postage). LRP Publications, 747 Dresher Road, PO Box 980, Horsham PA 19044-0980. **Tel** (800)341-7874, (215)784-0860, FAX (215)784-9639, (215)784-0870. **DD** _a346.
Desc: Provides the most recent analysis of statewide personal injury verdicts to assist in counseling clients and developing case strategies. Provides summaries of recent verdicts, million-dollar verdict activity, and more.

US/8755-6448
PERSONAL INJURY VERDICT SURVEY. SOUTH CAROLINA EDITION. [Pers. inj. verdict surv., S.C. ed.]. **Added/Corp** Jury Verdict Research, Inc. **VFOAT** South Carolina Verdict Survey. (19??)-. Periodical. English. an. $33.00 (includes postage). LRP Publications, 747 Dresher Road, PO Box 980, Horsham PA 19044-0980. **Tel** (800)341-7874, (215)784-0860, FAX (215)784-9639, (215)784-0870. **DD** 346. **Bk Rev. Circ:** 250 (ctrl).
Desc: Provides the most recent analysis of statewide personal injury verdicts to assist in counseling clients and developing case strategies. Provides summaries of recent verdicts, million-dollar verdict activity, and more.

US/8755-6456
PERSONAL INJURY VERDICT SURVEY. SOUTH DAKOTA EDITION. [Pers. inj. verdict surv., S.D. ed.]. **Added/Corp** Jury Verdict Research, Inc. **VFOAT** South Dakota Verdict Survey. (19??)-. Periodical. English. an. $33.00 (includes postage). LRP Publications, 747 Dresher Road, PO Box 980, Horsham PA 19044-0980. **Tel** (800)341-7874, (215)784-0860, FAX (215)784-9639, (215)784-0870. **DD** 346. **Bk Rev. Circ:** 250 (ctrl).
Desc: Provides the most recent analysis of statewide personal injury verdicts to assist in counseling clients and developing case strategies. Provides summaries of recent verdicts, million-dollar verdict activity, and more.

US/8755-643X
PERSONAL INJURY VERDICT SURVEY. TENNESSEE EDITION. [Pers. inj. verdict surv., Tenn. ed.]. **Added/Corp** Jury Verdict Research, Inc. **VFOAT** Tennessee Verdict Survey. (19??)-. Periodical. English. an. $33.00 (includes postage). LRP Publications, 747 Dresher Road, PO Box 980, Horsham PA 19044-0980. **Tel** (800)341-7874, (215)784-0860, FAX (215)784-9639, (215)784-0870. **DD** 346. **Bk Rev. Circ:** 250 (ctrl).
Desc: Provides the most recent analysis of statewide personal injury verdicts to assist in counseling clients and developing case strategies. Provides summaries of recent verdicts, million-dollar verdict activity, and more.

US/8755-6421
PERSONAL INJURY VERDICT SURVEY. TEXAS EDITION. [Pers. inj. verdict surv., Tex. ed.]. **Added/Corp** Jury Verdict Research, Inc. **VFOAT** Texas Verdict Survey. (19??)-. Periodical. English. an. $33.00 (includes postage). LRP Publications, 747 Dresher Road, PO Box 980, Horsham PA 19044-0980. **Tel** (800)341-7874, (215)784-0860, FAX (215)784-9639, (215)784-0870. **DD** 346. **Bk Rev. Circ:** 250 (ctrl).
Desc: Provides the most recent analysis of statewide personal injury verdicts to assist in counseling clients and developing case strategies. Provides summaries of recent verdicts, million-dollar verdict activity, and more.

US/8755-6650
PERSONAL INJURY VERDICT SURVEY. UTAH EDITION. [Pers. inj. verdict surv., Utah ed.]. **Added/Corp** Jury Verdict Research, Inc. **VFOAT** Utah Verdict Survey. (19??)-. Periodical. English. an. $33.00 (includes postage). LRP Publications, 747 Dresher Road, PO Box 980, Horsham PA 19044-0980. **Tel** (800)341-7874, (215)784-0860, FAX (215)784-9639, (215)784-0870. **DD** 346. **Bk Rev. Circ:** 250 (ctrl).
Desc: Provides the most recent analysis of statewide personal injury verdicts to assist in counseling clients and developing case strategies. Provides summaries of recent verdicts, million-dollar verdict activity, and more.

US/8755-6626
PERSONAL INJURY VERDICT SURVEY. VERMONT EDITION. [Pers. inj. verdict surv., Vt. ed.]. **Added/Corp** Jury Verdict Research, Inc. **VFOAT** Vermont Verdict Survey. (19??)-. Periodical. English. an. $33.00 (includes postage). LRP Publications, 747 Dresher Road, PO Box 980, Horsham PA 19044-0980. **Tel** (800)341-7874, (215)784-0860, FAX (215)784-9639, (215)784-0870. **DD** 346. **Bk Rev. Circ:** 250 (ctrl).
Desc: Provides the most recent analysis of statewide personal injury verdicts to assist in counseling clients and developing case strategies. Provides summaries of recent verdicts, million-dollar verdict activity, and more.

US/8755-657X
PERSONAL INJURY VERDICT SURVEY. VIRGINIA EDITION. [Pers. inj. verdict surv., Va. ed.]. **Added/Corp** Jury Verdict Research, Inc. **VFOAT** Virginia Verdict Survey. (19??)-. Periodical. English. an. $33.00 (includes postage). LRP Publications, 747 Dresher Road, PO Box 980, Horsham PA 19044-0980. **Tel** (800)341-7874, (215)784-0860, FAX (215)784-9639, (215)784-0870. **DD** 346. **Bk Rev. Circ:** 250 (ctrl).
Desc: Provides the most recent analysis of statewide personal injury verdicts to assist in counseling clients and developing case strategies. Provides summaries of recent verdicts, million-dollar verdict activity, and more.

US/8755-6510
PERSONAL INJURY VERDICT SURVEY. WASHINGTON, D.C. EDITION. [Pers. inj. verdict surv., Wash. D.C. ed.]. **Added/Corp** Jury Verdict Research, Inc. **VFOAT** Washington, D.C. Verdict Survey. (19??)-. Periodical. English. an. $33.00 (includes postage). LRP Publications, 747 Dresher Road, PO Box 980, Horsham PA 19044-0980. **Tel** (800)341-7874, (215)784-0860, FAX (215)784-9639, (215)784-0870. **DD** 346. **Bk Rev. Circ:** 250 (ctrl).
Desc: Provides the most recent analysis of statewide personal injury verdicts to assist in counseling clients and developing case strategies. Provides summaries of recent verdicts, million-dollar verdict activity, and more.

US/8755-6553
PERSONAL INJURY VERDICT SURVEY. WASHINGTON EDITION. [Pers. inj. verdict surv., Wash. ed.]. **Added/Corp** Jury Verdict Research, Inc. **VFOAT** Washington Verdict Survey. (19??)-. Periodical. English. an. $33.00 (includes postage). LRP Publications, 747 Dresher Road, PO Box 980, Horsham PA 19044-0980. **Tel** (800)341-7874, (215)784-0860, FAX (215)784-9639, (215)784-0870. **DD** 346. **Bk Rev. Circ:** 250 (ctrl).
Desc: Provides the most recent analysis of statewide personal injury verdicts to assist in counseling clients and developing case strategies. Provides summaries of recent verdicts, million-dollar verdict activity, and more.

US/8755-6561
PERSONAL INJURY VERDICT SURVEY. WEST VIRGINIA EDITION. [Pers. inj. verdict surv., W. Va. ed.]. **Added/Corp** Jury Verdict Research, Inc. **VFOAT** West Virginia Verdict Survey. (19??)-. Periodical. English. an. $33.00 (includes postage). LRP Publications, 747 Dresher Road, PO Box 980, Horsham PA 19044-0980. **Tel** (800)341-7874, (215)784-0860, FAX (215)784-9639, (215)784-0870. **DD** 346. **Bk Rev. Circ:** 250 (ctrl).
Desc: Provides the most recent analysis of statewide personal injury verdicts to assist in counseling clients and developing case strategies. Provides summaries of recent verdicts, million-dollar verdict activity, and more.

US/8755-660X
PERSONAL INJURY VERDICT SURVEY. WISCONSIN EDITION. [Pers. inj. verdict surv., Wis. ed.]. **Added/Corp** Jury Verdict Research, Inc. **VFOAT** Wisconsin Verdict Survey. (19??)-. Periodical. English. an. $33.00 (includes postage). LRP Publications, 747 Dresher Road, PO Box 980, Horsham PA 19044-0980. **Tel** (800)341-7874, (215)784-0860, FAX (215)784-9639, (215)784-0870. **DD** 346. **Bk Rev. Circ:** 250 (ctrl).
Desc: Provides the most recent analysis of statewide personal injury verdicts to assist in counseling clients and developing case strategies. Provides summaries of recent verdicts, million-dollar verdict activity, and more.

US/8755-6634
PERSONAL INJURY VERDICT SURVEY. WYOMING EDITION. [Pers. inj. verdict surv., Wyo. ed.]. **Added/Corp** Jury Verdict Research, Inc. **VFOAT** Wyoming Verdict Survey. (19??)-. Periodical. English. an. $33.00 (includes postage). LRP Publications, 747 Dresher Road, PO Box 980, Horsham PA 19044-0980. **Tel** (800)341-7874, (215)784-0860, FAX (215)784-9639, (215)784-0870. **DD** 346. **Bk Rev. Circ:** 250 (ctrl).
Desc: Provides the most recent analysis of statewide personal injury verdicts to assist in counseling clients and developing case strategies. Provides summaries of recent verdicts, million-dollar verdict activity, and more.

US/0149-6131
PERSONAL LIABILITY DIGEST. V. 1- Feb. 1978-. Periodical. English. qt. $18.00. Center for the Study of Civil Liberties and Civil Rights, PO Box 477, Montgomery AL 36101. **Tel** (205)288-9055. **LC** KF1306.A2; A496. **DD** 342/.73/068.

CN/0821-5510
PERSONAL PROPERTY SECURITY ACT. [Pers. prop. secur. act cases]. Vol. 1 (1977/81)-. English. ir. Law Society of Upper Canada, 130 Queen Street West, Toronto M5H 2N6 Canada. **Tel** (416)947-3300, (416)947-3371, telex 065-28013. **ED** Richard H. McLaren. **LC** KE1042.A45; P47. **DD** 346.71/074/0264; 347.106740264.

NE
PERSONEEL STATUUT : ORGAN VAN DE NEDERLANDSE VERENIGING VAN AMBTENAREN VAN DE BURGERLIJKE STAND (NEVABS), HET. Periodical. Dutch. bm. Nederlandse Vereniging Van Ambtenaren Van de Burgerlijke Stand, Herrengracht 531-537, 1017 BV Amsterdam Netherlands.

CN/0824-1902
PERSONNES C.L.E.F. ***Ceased.*** (PERSONNES C.L.E.F. / CENTRE DE REFERENCE DE LA DOCUMENTATION JURIDIQUE DE LANGUE FRANCAISE EN MATIERE DE COMMON LAW.). [Pers. C.L.E.F.]. **VAT** Personnes Common Law en Francais. (1984)-(199?). French. an. Centre de Reference de la Documentation Juridique de Langue Francaise en Matiere de Common Law, 161 Laurier Avenue West/5th Floor, Ottawa Ontario K1P 5J2 Canada. **Tel** (613)236-9766. **ED** Gerald Levesque. **DD** 340.5/7/02571.

Law

Ad Acc. Circ: 1,000.
 Desc: French language directory of Canada. Common Law: names and addresses.

US/0743-6475
PERSPECTIVE (ALBANY, N.Y. 1983).
(PERSPECTIVE : THE NEWSLETTER OF THE YOUNG LAWYERS SECTION.). **Main/Corp** New York State Bar Association. Young Lawyers Section. (198?)-. Newsletter. English. qt. New York State Bar Association, One Elk Street, Albany NY 12207. **Tel** (518)463-3200. **ED** Carl L Bucki. **LC** KF200; .N46. **DD** 349.747/05; 347.47005. **Ad Acc. Circ:** 5,000 (ctrl). **Continues** New York State Bar Association. Young Lawyers Section. Young Lawyers Section Newsletter, 0733-8066.

US/0888-9732
PERSPECTIVE (MADISON, WIS.).
(PERSPECTIVE.). [Perspective]. Vol. 1, No. 1 (April 1986)-. Periodical. English. mo. $158.00. Magna Publications Inc, 2718 Dryden Drive, Madison WI 53704. **Tel** (608)433-0499, (608)246-3591, FAX (608)246-3597. **LC** KF4225.A15; P47. **DD** 344.73/074; 347.30474. [CCC].
 Desc: Provides campus administrator with guidelines for keeping their school out of court. It covers past and future legal issues affecting students, faculty and the public, notes current cases of significance and reviews key cases in depth.

●US
PERSPECTIVE : TEACHING LEGAL RESEARCH AND WRITING. Added/Corp
West Publishing Company. Vol. 1, No. 1 (Aug. 1992)-. Periodical. English. Three times a year. West Publishing Company, 610 Opperman Drive, PO Box 64526, Eagan MN 55123-1308. **Tel** (612)687-5618, (800)328-9352, FAX (612)687-5388, (800)562-2329.

US/1062-1083
PERSPECTIVES - AMERICAN BAR ASSOCIATION. COMMISSION ON WOMEN IN THE PROFESSION.
(PERSPECTIVES : A NEWSLETTER FOR AND ABOUT WOMEN LAWYERS.). [Perspect. - Am. Bar Assoc., Comm. Women Prof.]. **Added/Corp** American Bar Association. Commission on Women in the Profession. Vol. 1, No. 1 Fall (1991)-. Newsletter. English. sa (2 issues). $14.00. American Bar Association, 750 North Lake Shore Drive, Chicago IL 60611. **Tel** (312)988-5522, (312)988-5241, FAX (312)988-5528, telex 270593. **DD** 340.

US/0160-4422
PERSPECTIVES IN LAW & PSYCHOLOGY. VFOAT Law & Psychology. VAT
Perspectives in Law and Psychology. Vol. 1 (1977)-. Monographic series. English. ir. Price varies per volume. Plenum Press, 233 Spring Street, New York NY 10013-1578. **Tel** (212)620-8000, (800)221-9369, FAX (212)463-0742, (212)807-1047, telex 23/421139. **NLM** W1 PE871AS.

US/0887-7815
PHARMACEUTICAL LITIGATION REPORTER. [Pharm. litig. report.]. (July 1985)-.
Periodical. English. mo. $750.00. Andrews Publications Inc., 1646 West Chester Pike, PO Box 1000, Westtown PA 19355. **Tel** (610)399-6600, (800)345-1101, FAX (610)399-6610. **ED** Leonard E. B. Andrews. **LC** KF1297.D7; A496. **DD** 346.7303/82. cum. index. ctrl circ.
 Desc: Covers legal developments in cases involving pharmaceuticals and medical devices. The lawsuits covered range from product liability suits to copyright infringement, from wrongful death to FDA approval. Pre-trial, trial and appeal proceedings, as well as settlements and class action lawsuits, are thoroughly reported.

US/0149-1717
PHARMACY LAW DIGEST. (1965)-. English.
sa $69.50 (loose-leaf edition) US; $87.00 (loose-leaf edition) other. Facts and Comparisons Inc, 111 West Port Plaza, Suite 400, St Louis MO 63146-3098. **Tel** (314)878-2515, (800)223-0554, FAX (314)878-5563. **ED** Joseph L. Fink, III. **LC** KF2915.P4; K33. **DD** 344/.73/041. **NLM** QV 32 AA1 K2P.
 Desc: Covers all pharmaceutical jurisprudence for students and practitioners.

●US/0145-3491
PHILADELPHIA BAR REPORTER.
Added/Corp Philadelphia Bar Association. Vol. 22, No. 1 (Jan. 18, 1993). Periodical. English. Twenty-one times a year (Except July, Aug., Dec.) $60.00 Comes with Philadelphia Bar Association Membership. Philadelphia Bar Association, 1101 Market Street, 1 Reading Center, Philadelphia PA 19107. **Tel** (215)238-6300, FAX (215)238-1267. **Continues** Retainer.

PH
PHILIPPINE CASE LAW. Main/Corp
Philippines. Supreme Court. English. mo. Rex Book Store, 856 Nicanor Reyes Sr St, Manila Philippines. **DD** 348.599/041; 345.990841.

PH
PHILIPPINE LAW AND JURISPRUDENCE. Added/Corp Philippines.
Supreme Court. Philippines. Court of Appeals. Current Events Digest, inc. **VFOAT** Philjur. Vol. 1 (Nov./Dec. 1977)-. Periodical. English. bm. $240.00, $20.00 (per copy). Current Events Digest Inc, 1223 Vergara & Pax, Quiapo Manila Philippine Islands. **Tel** 46-16-56, 47-28-23. **ED** Arturo M. de Castro. **DD** 348.599/046. **Circ:** 1,000 (ctrl).
 Desc: Complete Philippine Supreme Court decisions, selected appellate courts cases digests, laws of general applications, and annotations, syllabi of Supreme Court cases.

PH/0031-7721
PHILIPPINE LAW JOURNAL. Vol. 1 (Aug.
1914)-. Periodical. English. qt. $20.00 US. University of Philippines College of Law, Room 208 210, Second Floor Palma Hall, Diliman Quezon City, Philippines. **Tel** 011 63 2 982471 ext. 6901, FAX 6 32 97 67 85. **ED** Eloisa Palazo. Index available. **Bk Rev. Ad Acc. Circ:** 4 (ctrl).
 Ind/Abst Hum. Rights Intern. Rep.; Index Foreign Leg. Per.; Index Philip. Period.; Soc. Plann. Policy Dev. Abstr.; Sociol. Abstr. (?-?).

PH
PHILIPPINE LAW REPORT, THE.
Added/Corp University of the Philippines. Law Center. (19??)-. Periodical. English. mo. $13.50. University of the Philippines Law Center, Diliman Quezon City Philippines. **DD** 348/.599/041.

PH
PHILIPPINE SUPREME COURT REPORTS ANNOTATED / COMPILED, ANNOTATED AND EDITED BY THE EDITORIAL STAFF OF THE CENTRAL LAWBOOK PUBLISHING CO., INC.
Added/Corp Philippines. Supreme Court. **VFOAT** Supreme Court Reports Annotated; SCRA. Vol. 25 (Sept./Oct. 31, 1968)-. English. **Continues** Supreme Court Reports, Annotated.

US
PIRACY, COUNTERFEITING AND INFRINGEMENT REPORT. (19??)-. English.
Twelve times a year. $160.00. Prentice-Hall Law and Business, 270 Sylvan Avenue, Englewood Cliffs NJ 07632. **Tel** (800)223-0231, (201)894-8538, FAX (201)894-8666.

US
PIRSIG ON MINNESOTA PLEADING.
(19??)-. Periodical. English. $194.00. Butterworth Legal Publishers / Salem, NH, 8 Industrial Way, Building C, Salem NH 03079. **Tel** (800)548-4001, (603)898-9664.

US/0032-0331
PITTSBURGH LEGAL JOURNAL.
Added/Corp Allegheny County Bar Association. (1853)-. Periodical. English. Twelve times a year. $35.00. Pittsburgh Legal Journal, 400 Koppers Building, Pittsburgh PA 15219-2011. **Tel** (412)261-6255, FAX (412)281-6558. **ED** Frederick N. Egler, James I. Smith and Julie Shannon. **LC** KFP52.P5; P5. **DD** 348.748/043/05; 347.48084305. Index available. cum. index. **Ad Acc. Circ:** 6,300 (ctrl).
 Desc: Covers law information.
 Ind/Abst Fed. Tax Artic.; Law Office Inf. Serv.

US
PLACEMENT BULLETIN - ASSOCIATION OF AMERICAN LAW SCHOOLS. Main/Corp Association of American Law
Schools. Bulletin. English. bm. $6.00. One Dupont Circle, Suite 370, Washington DC 20036.

US/0738-114X
PLANNING & ZONING NEWS. See Housing
and Urban Development.

US/0091-4053
PLANNING LEGISLATION IN NEW YORK STATE. Main/Corp New York (State). Office
of Planning Coordination. English. Office of Planning Coordination, 488 Broadway, Albany NY 12207. **LC** KFN5810.A73; P55. **DD** 346/.747/045.

US
PLANNING, ZONING, AND DEVELOPMENT LAWS. Main/Corp California.
Added/Corp California. Office of Planning and Research. **VFOAT** State of California Planning, Zoning, and Development Laws. (198?)-. English. an. $10.00. Office of Planning and Research, 1400 Tenth Street, Sacramento CA 95814. **Tel** (916)322-2318. **LC** KFC811.A29; C34. **DD** 346.79404/5/02632; 347.94064502632. **Continues** Laws, etc. State of California Planning, Zoning, and Development Laws.

CN/0715-4224
PLEA. PUBLIC LEGAL EDUCATION ASSOCIATION OF SASKATCHEWAN.
(THE PLEA.). [PLEA, Public Leg. Educ. Assoc. Sask.]. **Added/Corp** Public Legal Education Association of Saskatchewan. **VAT** Public Legal Education Association of Saskatchewan. (1980)-. Periodical. English. Four times a year. Free on request. Public Legal Education Association of Saskatchewan, 210 220 3rd Avenue South, Saskatoon Saskatchewan S7K 1M1 Canada. **Tel** (306)653-1868. **DD** 349.7124/07.

US/0196-6782
PLEADER, THE. Added/Corp NDTLA. (19??)-.
Periodical. English. North Dakota Trial Lawyers Association, PO Box 2359, Bismarck ND 58501. **LC** KF200; .P55. **DD** 347.784/07/05.

US/0479-0219
PLI NEWS. Main/Corp Practising Law Institute. VAT
Practising Law Institute News. (19??)-. English. sw. Practising Law Institute, 810 Seventh Avenue, New York NY 10019-5818. **Tel** (212)765-5700, FAX (212)581-4670 general correspondence, (212)265-4742 orders and billing inquiries.
 Desc: Conducts over 250 seminars and publishes more than 400 specialized law books, and audio and video cassette programs. Satellite telecasts and an increasing production of video and audio cassettes characterize PLI's efforts to satisfy the diverse needs of this nation's lawyers.

US
PLL NEWSLETTER. See Library and Information
Sciences.

AT
POLEMIC. Added/Corp Sydney University Law
Society. Vol. 1 (May 1990)-. Periodical. English. Three times a year (Feb., June, Sept.). 30.00Aus$ (institutions); 15.00Aus$ (individuals). Polemic Committee, c/o Sydney University Law Society, 173/175 Philip Street/Level 3, Sydney 2000 Australia. **Tel** 011 61 02 2259204, FAX 011 61 02 2215635. **Bk Rev. Ad Acc. Pr Rev.**
 Desc: Sociological journal examining the broader ramifications of law. For example, the extent of human rights in Australian law.

US/0197-2596
POLICY AND PROCEDURES HANDBOOK. [Policy and proc. handb.]. Main/Corp
American Bar Association. **Added/Corp** American Bar Association. ABA Policy and Procedures Handbook. **VFOAT** ABA Policy and Procedures Handbook. (19??)-. English. an. Free on request. American Bar Association, 750 North Lake Shore Drive, Chicago IL 60611. **Tel** (312)988-5522, (312)988-5241, FAX (312)988-5528, telex 270593. **LC** KF325; .A395. **DD** 340/.06/073.

PL
POLISH SOCIOLOGY OF LAW NEWSLETTER, THE. Newsletter. English. Polish
Sociological Association, Section on the Sociology of Law, UL Nowy Swait 72, 00-330 Warszawa Poland. **LC** K16; .0433. **DD** 340/.115/05.

US/0196-1179
POLYGRAPH LAW REPORTER. V. 1- Sept.
1978-. Periodical. English. qt. $28.00. American Polygraph Association, PO Box 1061, Severna Park MD 21146. **Tel** (410)647-0936. **ED** Norman Ansley. **LC** KF9666.A15; P64. **DD** 345.73/052. **Circ:** 3,300.
 Desc: Reporting service on current cases, regulations and statutes. It also updates reference: The Law and the Polygraph: A Compilation of Polygraph Case Law and Statutory Law.

KO
POMMU YONGU. Added/Corp Pommu Yonsuwon
(Korea). (19??)-. Korean. Pommu Yonsuwon, 164 Uman-dong, Suwon-si Korea.

US/0739-0203
PONTIAC-OAKLAND COUNTY LEGAL NEWS. (PONTIAC-OAKLAND COUNTY LEGAL
NEWS : OFFICIAL NEWSPAPER OF THE OAKLAND COUNTY COURTS / COUNTY OF OAKLAND, MICHIGAN.). **Added/Corp** Oakland County (Mich.). **VFOAT** Legal News. (19??)-. Periodical. English. Fifty-two times a year. $45.00 Oakland County; $52.00 elsewhere Michigan; $60.00 other. Pontiac-Oakland County Legal News, PO Box 430238, Pontiac MI 48343. **Tel** (313)338-4567, FAX (313)338-4240. **ED** Nancy L. Howarth. **Bk Rev. Ad Acc. Circ:** 1,447 (ctrl).
 Desc: Credit data, court dockets, legal notices, vital statistics, and new businesses, with features of interest to the legal, business and financial readership.

KO
POPCHO. VFOAT Bup Jo; Lawyers Association
Journal. Periodical. Korean. mo. Popcho Hyophoe, 77 Sejong-ro, Jongro-ku, Seoul South Korea.

KO
POPHAK. VFOAT Seoul Law Journal. (1959)-.
Periodical. Korean. qt. Korean Law Research Institute, San 56-1 Sinlim Dong Gwang Gu, Seoul 151 Korea.

CN/0837-9831
PORTRAIT DE LA FISCALITE DES PARTICULIERS AU QUEBEC, STATISTIQUES / REDIGE PAR LE MINISTERE DU REVENU DU QUEBEC.
[Portrait fisc. part. Que. stat.]. **VFOAT** Portrait de la Fiscalite des Particuliers au Quebec. 11E Ed.,

(1983/1985)-. French. **DD** 343.71305/2/021. ***Continues*** *Statistiques Fiscales des Particuliers du Quebec, 0382-358X.*

US
POSTAL LAWS AND REGULATIONS OF THE UNITED STATES OF AMERICA.
Ceased. **VFOAT** Postal Laws & Regulations of the USA. (19??)-(19??). English. T Wierenga, PO Box 2007, Holland MI 49423. **LC** KF2661.9; .P67. **DD** 343.73/0992/0263; 347.3039920263.

US/0192-9801
POTOMAC LAW REVIEW. [Potom. law rev.]. **Added/Corp** Potomac School of Law. Vol. 1 (Fall 1978)-. Periodical. English. sa. $6.00. Potomac School of Law, 2600 Virginia Avenue NW, Washington DC 20037. **LC** K16; .O68. **DD** 340/.05.
Ind/Abst Curr. Law Index (1980-); Leg. Resour. Index (1980-); LegalTrac (1980-).

UK
PRACTICAL LAW FOR COMPANIES.
English. Eleven times a year. £195.00 Europe; £245.00 other (airmail). Legal & Commercial Publishing, PO Box 672, London SW11 5PQ England. **Tel** 011 41 71 7382303, FAX 011 41 71 9785452. **ED** Robert Dow, Susan Fairlie, and Christopher Millerchip. Index available (published separately). **Ad Acc.**

US/0032-6429
PRACTICAL LAWYER, THE. [Pract. lawyer]. **Added/Corp** American Law Institute-American Bar Association Committee on Continuing Professional Education. American Law Institute. Committee on Continuing Legal Education. (1954)-. Periodical. English. Eight times a year. $35.00. American Law Institute, 4025 Chestnut Street, Philadelphia PA 19104-3099. **Tel** (215)243-1661, (800)253-6397, FAX (215)243-1664. **ED** Mark T. Carroll (phone: (215)243-1604). **LC** K16; .R22. Index available (Dec. iss.). cum. index. **Bk Rev**, (Qty: 4 per year). **Ad Acc**, **Adv Mgr:** K. Lawner, **Tel** (215)243-1659. **Pr Rev. Circ:** 7,938. available in microform; available on an online database from WESTLAW; available on microfilm and microfiche.
Desc: Contains articles on current legal issues, legal practice, and law office management.
Ind/Abst Account. Tax Datab. (1974-) [Full Txt.]; Bowne Dig. Corp. Sec. Lawyers; Curr. Law Index (1980-); Fed. Tax Artic.; Index Leg. Period.; Law Office Inf. Serv.; Leg. Resour. Index (1980-); LegalTrac (1980-).

US/0092-248X
PRACTICAL LAWYER'S LAW OFFICE MANAGEMENT MANUAL, THE. No. 3-1972-. English. American Law Institute, 4025 Chestnut Street, Philadelphia PA 19104-3099. **Tel** (215)243-1661, (800)253-6397, FAX (215)243-1664. **LC** KF318.A1; P7. **DD** 340/.068. ***Continues*** *Practical Lawyer. Law Office Manual.*

US/1047-6261
PRACTICAL LITIGATOR, THE. [Pract. litig.]. **Added/Corp** American Law Institute-American Bar Association Committee on Continuing Professional Education. **VFOAT** Litigator. Vol. 1, No. 1 (Jan. 1990)-. Periodical. English. Six times a year (Jan., Mar., May, July, Sept., Nov.). $35.00. American Law Institute, 4025 Chestnut Street, Philadelphia PA 19104-3099. **Tel** (215)243-1661, (800)253-6397, FAX (215)243-1664. **ED** Mark T. Carroll (phone: (215)243-1604). **LC** K16; .R222. **DD** 347.73/7/05; 347.307705. Index available (Nov. iss.). cum. index. **Ad Acc**, **Adv Mgr:** Kathy Lawner, **Tel** (215)243-1659. **Pr Rev. Circ:** 2,108.
Desc: Articles for lawyers on improving their litigation skills.
Ind/Abst Account. Tax Datab. (Jan. 1992-) [Full Txt.]; Index Leg. Period. (1992-).

US/8756-0372
PRACTICAL REAL ESTATE LAWYER, THE. [Pract. real estate lawyer]. **Added/Corp** American Law Institute-American Bar Association Committee on Continuing Professional Education. Vol. 1, No. 1 (Jan. 1985)-. Periodical. English. Six times a year (Jan., Mar., May, July, Sept., Nov.). $35.00. American Law Institute, 4025 Chestnut Street, Philadelphia PA 19104-3099. **Tel** (215)243-1661, (800)253-6397, FAX (215)243-1664. **ED** Mark T. Carroll (phone: (215)243-1604). **LC** KF566.A3; P73. **DD** 346.7304/3/05; 347.3064305. Index available (Nov. iss.). cum. index. **Ad Acc**, **Adv Mgr:** K. Lawner, **Tel** (215)243-1659. **Pr Rev. Circ:** 5,229.
Desc: Articles for lawyers on real property law issues, with practical, how-to-do-it orientation.
Ind/Abst Account. Tax Datab. (Jan. 1992-) [Full Txt.]; Index Leg. Period.; Leg. Resour. Index; LegalTrac (1980-).

US
PRACTICAL SKILLS COURSE. **Main/Corp** Oregon State Bar. Committee on Continuing Legal Education. Periodical. English. Oregon State Bar, 5200 Southwest Meadows Road, Lake Oswego OR 97035. **Tel** (503)620-0222 ext 340, (800)452-8260, FAX (503)684-1366. **LC** KFO2481; .O75. **DD** 349.795.

US/0890-4898
PRACTICAL TAX LAWYER, THE. [Pract. tax lawyer]. **Added/Corp** American Law Institute-American Bar Association Committee on Continuing Professional Education. American Bar Association. Section of Taxation. Vol. 1, No. 1 (Fall 1986)-. Periodical. English. Four times a year (Feb., May, Aug., Nov.). $27.50 (members ABA Tax section); $35.00 (non-members). American Law Institute, 4025 Chestnut Street, Philadelphia PA 19104-3099. **Tel** (215)243-1661, (800)253-6397, FAX (215)243-1664. **ED** Mark T. Carroll (phone: (215)243-1604). **LC** K16; .R225. **DD** 343.7304/05; 347.303405. Index available (Aug. iss.). cum. index. **Ad Acc**, **Adv Mgr:** K. Lawner, **Tel** (215)243-1659. **Pr Rev. Circ:** 3,201.
Desc: Professional journal for tax attorneys. Publishes course study materials on taxation, trial techniques, business and commercial transactions, labor laws, federal legislation, investments, criminal law, family law, law office management, and the Uniform Commercial Code.
Ind/Abst Account. Tax Datab. (1986-) [Full Txt.]; Account. Art.; Fed. Tax Artic.; Index Leg. Period.; Leg. Resour. Index; LegalTrac (1980-).

UK
PRACTICAL TAX PLANNING AND PRECEDENTS. **See** Public Administration-Public Finance and Taxation.

●US/1064-7724
PRACTITIONERS 5500 DESKBOOK.
[Pract. 5500 deskb.]. **Added/Corp** Practitioners Publishing Company. **VFOAT** Practitioners Fifty-Five Hundred Deskbook.; Practitioners Fifty Five Hundred Deskbook; Practitioners Five Thousand Five Hundred Deskbook. 1st Ed. (Mar. 1992)-. English. an. $125.00. Practitioners Publishing Company, PO Box 901007, Fort Worth TX 76101-0966. **Tel** (800)323-8724, (817)332-3709. **LC** KF6425; .P7. **DD** 343.7305/24; 347.303524.

UK/0961-0804
PRACTITIONERS' CHILD LAW BULLETIN. [Pract. child law bull.]. **VFOAT** Longman Practitioners' Child Law Bulletin. (1989)-. Periodical. English. £89.00. Longman Group Ltd., Fourth Avenue, Longman House, Harlow Essex CM19 5SR England. **Tel** 011 44 279 429655, FAX 011 44 279 431059, telex 81259. ***Continues*** *Practitioners' Child Law Journal, 0954-6421.*

BN
PRAVNA MISAO. V. 1- Jan./Feb. 1969-. Serbo-Croatian (Roman). bm. **(Subscription address:** Jugoslovenska Knjiga, PO Box 36, YU 11001 Belgrade Yugoslovia.**)** **LC** K16; .R29. ***Supersedes*** *Narodna Uprava.*

●XR/1210-0900
PRAVNI PRAXE. **Added/Corp** Czech Republic. Ministerstvo Spravedlnosti. (1993)-. Periodical. Czech. mo. ***Continues*** *Pravo a Zakonnost.*

XR
PRAVNIK (PRAGUE, CZECHOSLOVAKIA). (PRAVNIK / PRAVNICKA JEDNOTA V PRAZE.). **Added/Corp** Pravnicka Jednota v Praze. Jednota Ceskoslovenskych Pravniku. Czechoslovakia. Pravnicky Ustav. Ustav Prava CSAV. Ustav Statu a Prava CSAV. (1961)-. Periodical. Czech (summaries and/or abstracts in Russian and English). Twelve times a year. $120.40. Institute for State & Law of the Czechoslovakia / Academy of Sciences in Prague, Narodni TR 18, Prague 1 Czechoslovakia Republic. **ED** Josef Blahoz. Index available. **Bk Rev. Circ:** 3,800.
Desc: A theoretical scientific journal dealing with all aspects of the science of the state and law.
Ind/Abst Index Foreign Leg. Per.

XO
PRAVNY OBZOR : CASOPIS USTAVU STATU A PRAVA SLOVENKEJ AKADEMIE VIED. **Added/Corp** Slovenska Akademia Vied. Ustav Statu a Prava. (19??)-. Periodical. Slovak. Ten times a year. DM259.00 Germany; DM319.00. Veda, Publishing House of the Slovak Academy of Sciences, Klemensova 19, 814 30 Bratislava Slovakia. **Tel** (7)583-15. **(Subscription address:** Kubon & Sagner, ABT Zeitschriftenimport, D 80328 Munich Germany.**)** **ED** Jan Azud.
Desc: An important tool in all legal matters. In wide use with lawyers, national committees and organisations.
Ind/Abst Geogr. Abstr. Human Geogr.; Index Foreign Leg. Per.

CS
PRAVO A ZALONNOST. ***Title Change.*** **Added/Corp** Czech Republic (Czechoslovakia). Ministerstvo Spravedlnosti. (1990)-(1992). Periodical. Czech. mo. Washington State Gambling Commission, Olympia WA 98504. **LC** K23; .O24. ***Continues*** *Socialisticka Zakonnost.* ***Continued by*** *Pravni Praxe.*

PL
PRAWO I ZYCIE : ORGAN ZRZESZENIA PRAWNIKOW POLSKICH. **Added/Corp** Zrzeszenie Prawnikow Polskich. (1956)-. Periodical. Polish. wk. $78.00. **(Subscription address:** ARS Polona, PO Box 1001, 00068 Warsaw Poland.**)** **LC** .P25.

PL/1230-2856
PRAWO PRZEDSIEBIORCY. (1991)-. Periodical. Polish. Twenty-six times a year. Price on Request. **(Subscription address:** ARS Polona, PO Box 1001, 00068 Warsaw Poland.**)** **UDC** 347. **CODEN** 342.9.

US/0741-1162
PRE-LAW JOURNAL. (PRE-LAW JOURNAL : A LEGAL INSTITUTE PROJECT.). [Pre-law j.]. **Added/Corp** Legal Institute. **VFOAT** Pre Law Journal; PreLaw Journal. (1982)-. Periodical. English. Three times a year. $9.75. Legal Institute, 3250 Wilshire Boulevard, Suite 1000, Los Angeles CA 90010. **Tel** (213)487-6268. **ED** Herman B. Lancaster. **LC** KF287; .P73. **DD** 340/.07/1173. cum. index. **Bk Rev. Ad Acc. Circ:** 200 (ctrl).
Desc: Provides information of assistance in deciding to attend law school and in doing well in law school.

UK
PRECEDENTS FOR THE CONVEYANCER. (1970)-. English. Four times a year. £130.00 Europe; £137.00 other. Sweet & Maxwell Ltd., South Quay Plaza, 183 Marsh Wall, London E14 9FT England. **Tel** 011 44 264 342899, FAX 011 44 264 342723, telex 929089 ITPINF G. **ED** Carol Tullo. **Circ:** 3,000 (ctrl).
Desc: New precedents with practical emphasis issued for the conveyancer.

CI
PREGLED SUDSKE PRAKSE. 1- 1972-. Serbo-Croatian (Roman). Narodne Novine, Ratkajev Prolaz BR 4, Zagreb Croatia.

US/0747-878X
PRELAW ADVISER'S KIT. [Prelaw advis. kit]. English. Association of American Law Schools, 1201 Connecticut Avenue NW, Suite 800, Washington DC 20036-2605. **LC** KF285; .P74. **DD** 340/.07/1173.

US/1055-730X
PREMISES LIABILITY REPORT. [Premises liabil. rep.]. Vol. 1, No. 1 (March 1991)-. Periodical. English. mo. $187.00. Strafford Publications Inc., 590 Dutch Valley Road Northeast, Atlanta GA 30324. **Tel** (404)881-1141, (800)926-7926, FAX (404)881-0074. **DD** 346.

US/0276-6094
PREPARATION OF ANNUAL DISCLOSURE DOCUMENTS. English. an. Practising Law Institute, 810 Seventh Avenue, New York NY 10019-5818. **Tel** (212)765-5700, FAX (212)581-4670 general correspondence, (212)265-4742 orders and billing inquiries. **LC** KF1449; .P74. **DD** 346.73/0666; 347.306666. ***Continues*** *Preparation of Annual Documents Disclosure, 0884-691X.*

US/1062-1687
PREPARING A TOXIC TORT CASE FOR TRIAL. [Prep. toxic tort case trial]. **Added/Corp** Practising Law Institute. (1991)-. English. Practising Law Institute, 810 Seventh Avenue, New York NY 10019-5818. **Tel** (212)765-5700, FAX (212)581-4670 general correspondence, (212)265-4742 orders and billing inquiries. **DD** 346. ***Continues*** *Preparation and Trial of a Toxic Tort Case, 1044-3274.*

US/0882-9748
PREPARING PERSONAL INJURY CASES FOR TRIAL. [Prep. pers. injury cases trial]. English. Practising Law Institute, 810 Seventh Avenue, New York NY 10019-5818. **Tel** (212)765-5700, FAX (212)581-4670 general correspondence, (212)265-4742 orders and billing inquiries. **LC** KF8900; .P74. **DD** 346.7303/33/0269.

US/0882-715X
PRESERVATION LAW REPORTER.
[Preserv. law rep.]. **Added/Corp** National Trust for Historic Preservation in the United States. Vol. 1, No. 1 (Jan. 1982)-. Periodical. English. Twelve times a year. $90.00 (nonmembers), $50.00 (members). National Trust for Historic Preservation, 1785 Massachusetts Avenue Northwest, Washington DC 20036. **Tel** (202)673-4035. **ED** Harrison B. Wetherill Jr. **LC** KF4310.A15; P73. **DD** 344.73/094/05; 347.3049405. **Bk Rev. Pr Rev. Circ:** 500 (ctrl).
Desc: Loose-leaf reporting service. Law of historic preservation and rehabilitation. Tax incentives, easements, financing, litigation, zoning and land use.

US/0734-1660
PREVENTIVE LAW REPORTER. [Prev. law rep.]. **Added/Corp** National Center for Preventive Law (U.S.). Vol. 1, No. 1 (July 1982)-. Periodical. English. Four times a year (Mar., Jun., Sep., Dec.). $65.00 US & Canada; $80.00 other. National Center of Preventive Law Inc, 1900 Olive Street, Denver CO 80220. **Tel** (303)871-6099, FAX (303)871-6001. **ED** Diane

Burkhardt. **LC** KF300.A1; P74. **DD** 346.7303/05; 347.306305. Index available. cum. index. **Bk Rev**, (Qty: 4). ***Continues*** *Preventive Law Newsletter, 0555-0963.*
Desc: Techniques and ideas for avoiding disputes and minimizing liability exposure through appropriate planning and counseling.
Ind/Abst Curr. Law Index (1984-); Leg. Resour. Index (1984-); LegalTrac (1983-).

US/0363-0048
PREVIEW OF UNITED STATES SUPREME COURT CASES. **Added/Corp** American Bar Association. Public Education Division. Association of American Law Schools. American Law Institute-American Bar Association Committee on Continuing Professional Education. Joint Committee on Continuing Legal Education (U.S.). (Dec. 7, 1973)-. English. Twelve times a year. $130.00 (one copy). American Bar Association, 750 North Lake Shore Drive, Chicago IL 60611. **Tel** (312)988-5522, (312)988-5241, FAX (312)988-5528, telex 270593. **ED** Barbara Kate Repa. **LC** KF4547.8; .P7. **DD** 348/.73/413. Index available. **Circ:** 4,000.
Desc: Features articles analyzing every case orally argued before the Supreme Court.

BL
PRIMEIRA INSTANCIA. No. 1- 1973-. Portuguese. Associacao dos Magistrados de Primeira Instancia, Esplanada dos Ministerios, Bloco 6 - 7 Andar, Brasilia Brazil.

US
PRIMER SERIES FOR HEALTH CARE PROFESSIONALS. **Added/Corp** Saul, Ewing, Remick & Saul. Health Law Group. No. 1 (1985)-. Monographic series. English. ir. Price varies per volume. LRP Publications, 747 Dresher Road, PO Box 980, Horsham PA 19044-0980. **Tel** (800)341-7874, (215)784-0860, FAX (215)784-9639, (215)784-0870. **NLM** W1; PR523E.
Desc: Explains general legal principles for health care professionals.

US
PRINCIPLES OF CIVIL SERVICE LAW / BY ROBERT G. VAUGHN ; UNDER THE SPONSORSHIP OF THE NATIONAL CIVIL SERVICE LEAGUE. **Added/Corp** National Civil Service League. (19??)-. English. ir. Matthew Bender & Company Inc., 1275 Broadway, Albany NY 12204. **Tel** (800)833-9844, (518)487-3000. cum. index.

US/0190-8146
PRIVACY ACT ISSUANCES ... COMPILATION. Began with 1976. English. an. Office of the Federal Register, National Archives and Records Service, Washington DC 20408. **LC** KF5753.A329; F4. **DD** 342/.73/085.

US/1063-7222
PRIVACY TIMES. [Priv. times]. (1981)-. Periodical. English. sm. $275.00 US and Canada; $300.00 Europe and Asia. Privacy Times, PO Box 21501, Washington DC 20009. **Tel** (202)829-3660. **ED** Evan Hendricks. **DD** 323.
Desc: Newsletter on privacy and freedom of information law. Emphasis on legislative and judicial actions and industry developments.

UK
PRIVATE CLIENT BUSINESS. (1992)-. English. bm. £125.00 Europe; £131.00 other. Sweet & Maxwell Ltd., South Quay Plaza, 183 Marsh Wall, London E14 9FT England. **Tel** 011 44 264 342899, FAX 011 44 264 342723, telex 929089 ITPINF G.

US/0890-121X
PRIVATE EDUCATION LAW REPORT. [Priv. educ. law rep.]. **Added/Corp** Data Research, Inc. (Rosemount, Minn.). (1986)-. Periodical. English. Twelve times a year. $97.00. Data Research Inc., PO Box 490, Rosemount MN 55068. **Tel** (612)452-8267, (800)365-4900. **LC** KF4220.A15; P73. **DD** 344.73/072; 347.30472. Index available.
Desc: Covers information on education law.

US/0738-6958
PRIVATE SECURITY CASE LAW REPORTER. [Priv. secur. case law report.]. (19??)-. Periodical. English. ir (monthly with 10 issues). $267.00 (one year), $474.00 (two year). Strafford Publications Inc., 590 Dutch Valley Road Northeast, Atlanta GA 30324. **Tel** (404)881-1141, (800)926-7926, FAX (404)881-0074. **ED** R. Keegan Federal and Jennifer Fogleman Vaughan. **LC** KF5399.5.P7; A495. **DD** 345.73/052; 347.30552. Index available (extra at cost of $62.00). cum. index.
Desc: The security professional's digest of state and federal appellate court decisions, including the range of issues affecting private security and loss prevention operations and policymaking. Includes insights and trend analysis by nation's leading security expert.

US/0093-8858
PRO SE. Periodical. English. sm. $25.00. Pro, 79 Dartmouth Street No 2, Boston MA 02116. **LC** KF4758.A73; P76. **DD** 346/.73/013.

US
PROBATE COUNSEL, THE. 1st- Ed.; 1941-. English. an. Royal Publishing Company Inc, PO Box 2241, Palm Beach FL 33480. **Tel** (407)588-9773. **ED** R A Sfraga. **Circ:** 1,500 (ctrl).
Desc: Listings by state, of law firms dealing in probate law. Also contains digest of probate laws, abstract and title company and real estate appraisal firms.

US/0737-3112
PROBATE LAW JOURNAL. (PROBATE LAW JOURNAL / NATIONAL COLLEGE OF PROBATE JUDGES AND BOSTON UNIVERSITY SCHOOL OF LAW.). [Probate law j.]. **Added/Corp** Boston University. School of Law. National College of Probate Judges (U.S.). Vol. 4, No. 3 (1982)-. Periodical. English. Three times a year. $25.00. Boston University School of Law, 765 Commonwealth Avenue, Boston MA 02215. **Tel** (617)353-3157, (617)353-3115. **ED** Faye G. Yoffa Stone. **LC** K16; .R573. **DD** 346.7305/2/05; 347.3065205. Index available. cum. index. **Bk Rev. Ad Acc. Circ:** 1,000. ***Continues*** *National College of Probate Judges Probate Journal.*
Desc: Probate and family law tax, matters pertaining to trusts and estates, property settlements in divorce, constitutional rights in commitments, rights, and refusals of treatment.
Ind/Abst Index Leg. Period.; Leg. Resour. Index; LegalTrac (1983-).

US/0094-999X
PROBATE LAWYER, THE. [Probate lawyer]. V. 1- Summer 1974-. English. an. Prices varies. American College of Probate Counsel, 2716 Ocean Park Boulevard/#1080, Santa Monica CA 90405. **Tel** (310)450-2033. **ED** Regis W Campfield. **LC** KF765.A73; P7. **DD** 346.7305/2/05; 347.3065205. Index available. ctrl circ.
Ind/Abst Curr. Law Index (1980-); Leg. Resour. Index (1980-); LegalTrac (1980-).

US/0362-4773
PROBATE REPORTER. Periodical. English. qt. Connecticut Probate Assembly, City Hall PO Box 388, Meriden CT 06450. **LC** KFC3744.A15; P76. **DD** 346/.746/0505.

PL
PROBLEMY PRAWA PRZEWOZOWEGO / WNIWERSYTET SLASKI. 1-. Periodical. Polish (summaries and/or abstracts in English and Russian). Uniwersytet Slaski, Ul Bankowa 14, 40-007 Katowice Poland. **Tel** 59-69-15, FAX 48 32 599-506, telex 0315584 USKPL. **LC** K16; .R5785.

IT
PROCEDURE REVISIONE FISCALE IMPOSTA VALORE AGGIUNTO. (19??)-. Periodical. Italian. sa. L97000. IPSOA Editore SRL, Casella Postale 12055, Mastrangelo, 20120 Milan Italy. **Tel** 011 39 2 82476248. Index available (Included). cum. index. **Circ:** 3,600 (ctrl).
Desc: Audit on V.A.T. taxation.

US
PROCEEDINGS - AMERICAN BAR ASSOCIATION. SECTION OF INSURANCE, NEGLIGENCE AND COMPENSATION LAW. **Main/Corp** American Bar Association. Section of Insurance, Negligence and Compensation Law. (195?)-. Proceedings. English. American Bar Association, 750 North Lake Shore Drive, Chicago IL 60611. **Tel** (312)988-5522, (312)988-5241, FAX (312)988-5528, telex 270593. ***Continues*** *American Bar Association. Section of Insurance Law. Proceedings.*
Ind/Abst Fed. Tax Artic.

US/0065-9045
PROCEEDINGS / AMERICAN LAW INSTITUTE. [Proc. - Am. Law Inst.]. **Main/Corp** American Law Institute. **VFOAT** Annual Meeting. Vol. 1 (February 23, 1923)-. Proceedings. English. an. $80.75. American Law Institute, 4025 Chestnut Street, Philadelphia PA 19104-3099. **Tel** (215)243-1661, (800)253-6397, FAX (215)243-1664. **ED** Michael Greenwald. **DD** 340. **Circ:** 300.
Desc: Yearly transcript of the American Law Institute's annual meeting, its annual report and other information on the Institute's activities.

US/0069-5831
PROCEEDINGS / COLLOQUIUM ON THE LAW OF OUTER SPACE. **Added/Corp** International Astronautical Federation. International Institute of Space Law. **VFOAT** Proceedings of the ... Colloquium on the Law of Outer Space. (1958)-. English. ir. Price varies per volume. American Institute of Aeronautics & Astronautics, 370 l'Enfant Promenade Southwest, Washington DC 20024-2518. **Tel** (202)646-7400, FAX (202)646-7508, telex 204792 AIAA UR. **DD** 341.520631.
Desc: Proceedings of International Institute of Space Law and the International Astronautical Federation annual colloquiums. Original papers on domestic and space law, property, nuclear power sources and more.

US/0733-6098
PROCEEDINGS OF THE ANNUAL INSTITUTE - EASTERN MINERAL LAW FOUNDATION (U.S.). ANNUAL INSTITUTE. (PROCEEDINGS OF THE ... ANNUAL INSTITUTE / EASTERN MINERAL LAW FOUNDATION.). [Proc. Annu. Inst. - East. Miner. Law Found. (U.S.), Annu. Inst.]. **Main/Corp** Eastern Mineral Law Foundation (U.S.). Annual Institute. 1st (Mar. 6/7, 1980)-. Proceedings. English. an. Matthew Bender & Company Inc., 1275 Broadway, Albany NY 12204. **Tel** (800)833-9844, (518)487-3000. **LC** KF1819.A2; E37. **DD** 343.73/077; 347.30377.
Ind/Abst GeoRef; Index Leg. Period.; Leg. Resour. Index; LegalTrac (1980-).

US/0895-1578
PROCEEDINGS OF THE ... ANNUAL INSTITUTE OF OIL AND GAS LAW AND TAXATION. [Proc. annu. Inst. Oil Gas Law Tax.]. **Main/Conf** Institute on Oil and Gas Law and Taxation. 11th-. Proceedings. English. an. Matthew Bender & Company Inc., 1275 Broadway, Albany NY 12204. **Tel** (800)833-9844, (518)487-3000. **LC** KF1849.A2; S6. **DD** 343.73/077; 346.30377. cum. index. ***Continues*** *Proceedings of the Annual Institute on Oil and Gas Law and Taxation as it Affects the Oil and Gas Industry.*
Ind/Abst Fed. Tax Artic.; Index Leg. Period.; Leg. Resour. Index.

US/0161-4002
PROCEEDINGS OF THE ANNUAL INSTITUTE ON SECURITIES LAWS AND REGULATIONS. **Main/Conf** Institute on Securities Laws and Regulations. **Main/Corp** Institute on Securities Laws and Regulations. 1st- 1977-. Proceedings. English. an. Matthew Bender & Company Inc., 1275 Broadway, Albany NY 12204. **Tel** (800)833-9844, (518)487-3000. **LC** KF1439.A2; I57. **DD** 346/.73/0666.

CN/0318-4900
PROCEEDINGS OF THE ... ANNUAL MEETING / UNIFORM LAW CONFERENCE OF CANADA. [Proc. annu. meet. Unif. Law Conf. Can.]. **Main/Corp** Uniform Law Conference of Canada. Meeting. **VAT** Conference sur l'Uniformisation des lois au Canada. (Aug. 1977)-. Proceedings. English (French). Free. Uniform Law Conference of Canada, 622 Hochelaga Street, Ottawa Ontario K1K 2E9 Canada. **Tel** (613)747-1695. **DD** 348.71/01. **Circ:** 400 (ctrl). ***Continues*** *Uniform Law Conference of Canada. Meeting. Proceedings of the ... Annual Meeting of the Uniform Law Conference of Canada.*
Desc: Law reform.
Ind/Abst Index Can. Leg. Period. Lit.

LU
PROCEEDINGS OF THE COURT OF JUSTICE AND OF THE COURT OF FIRST INSTANCE OF THE EUROPEAN COMMUNITIES. **Main/Corp** Court of Justice of the European Communities. **Added/Corp** Court of First Instance of the European Communities. Information Service of the Court of Justice of the European Communities. No. 19 (Sept. 1990)-. Proceedings. English (translations available in French). wk. Free on request. Office for Official Publications of the European Communities, 2 Rue Mercier, 2985 Luxembourg Luxembourg. **Tel** 011 352 499281, FAX 011 352 488573. **LC** KJE924.3; .P76. **DD** 341.5/5. ***Continues*** *Court of Justice of the European Communities. Proceedings of the Court of Justice of the European Communities.*
Desc: Summary of judgments, opinions, oral proceedings and new cases.

US/0730-3009
PROCEEDINGS OF THE INSTITUTE ON PLANNING, ZONING, AND EMINENT DOMAIN. [Proc. Inst. Plan. Zoning Eminent Domain]. **Main/Conf** Institute on Planning, Zoning, and Eminent Domain. **Added/Corp** Southwestern Legal Foundation. (Dec. 7-9, 1970)-. English. an. $80.00. Matthew Bender & Company Inc., 1275 Broadway, Albany NY 12204. **Tel** (800)833-9844, (518)487-3000. **LC** KF5692.A5; I53. **DD** 346.7304/5; 347.30645. ***Formed by the union of*** *Proceedings of the Institute on Planning and Zoning, 0537-9814* ***and*** *Proceedings of the ... Institute on Eminent Domain (1966).*
Ind/Abst Curr. Law Index (1980-); Index Leg. Period.; Leg. Resour. Index (1980-); LegalTrac.

AT/0813-8230
PROCEEDINGS OF THE NEW SOUTH WALES SOCIETY FOR COMPUTERS AND THE LAW. [Proc. N. S. W. Soc. Comput. Law]. **Added/Corp** New South Wales Society for Computers and the Law. (1983)-. Proceedings. English. an. £35.00 (individuals); £125.00 (institutions). Society for Computers & Law, 10 Hurle Crescent, Clifton Bristol BS8 2TA England. **Tel** 011 44 272 237393. **DD** 340.0285.
Ind/Abst Aust. Leg. Mon. Dig.

Law

US
PROCEEDINGS - PUBLIC LAW SECTION OF THE STATE BAR OF CALIFORNIA. Main/Corp State Bar of California. Public Law Section. Proceedings. English. an. State Bar of California, 555 Franklin Street, San Francisco CA 94102. Tel (415)561-8200, FAX (415)561-8228. LC KFC678.A75; S82. DD 342.794/005; 347.940205.

FR
PROCES CAHIERS D'ANALYSE POLITIQUE ET JURIDIQUE. French. sa. 198.00F. Centre d'Epistemologie Juridique et Politique, Univ de Lyon, 2-1 rue Raulin, 69355 Lyon Cedex 07 France.

EC
PROCESOS. Added/Corp Corporacion Editora Nacional (Quito, Ecuador). (1991)-. Periodical. Spanish. sa. Corporacion Editora Nacional, Roca 230 Y Tamayo, Apartado Postal 17-12-00886, Quito Ecuador.

CN
PROCESS. V. 1- Jan. 1975-. Periodical. English. mo. Ind/Abst Dairy Sci. Abstr.; Nutr. Abstr. Rev., Ser. A, Hum. Exp.

LE/0032-9649
PROCHE-ORIENT, ETUDES JURIDIQUES. VFOAT Sharq Al-Adna, Dirasat Fi Al-Qanun; Sharq Al-Adna, Dirasat Fi Al-Huquq. (Jan./April 1967)-. Periodical. French (French). Three times a year. LC K16; .R583. Continues Etudes de Droit Libanais. Ind/Abst Index Foreign Leg. Per.

AT
PROCTOR. English. mo (except Jan.). 60.00Aus$ Australia; 90.00Aus$ other. Queensland Law Society Inc, 179 Ann Street, GPO Box 1785, Brisbane QLD 4001 Australia. Tel 011 61 7 2335888, FAX 011 61 7 2335999, telex 44137. ED Susan Addison. Index available. Ad Acc. Circ: 4,800 (ctrl).
Ind/Abst Aust. Leg. Mon. Dig.

SP
PROCURADORES. Added/Corp Junta Nacional de la Junta Nacional de los Ilustres Colegios de Procuradores de Espana. (19??)-. Spanish. ir. Procuradores, Arturo Soria 241, 28033 Madrid Spain. Tel 1 457 97 59, FAX 1 457 95 73. DD 340/.0946.

UK
PRODUCT LIABILITY INTERNATIONAL. Added/Corp Lloyd's (Firm). Vol. 1 (Jan. 1979)-. Periodical. English. mo (12 issues). £150.00. Lloyd's of London Press Ltd, Sheepen Place, Colchester, Essex, CO3 3LP England. Tel 011 44 206 772113, US: (212)529-9500, US: (800)955-6937, FAX 011 44 206 772880, US: (212)529-9826, telex 987321 LLOYDS G. (Subscription address: Lloyd's of London Press Inc. / North America, 611 Broadway, Suite 308, New York NY 10012.) ED J. Stuart Ashworth. LC K16; .R585. DD 341.7/54. Bk Rev. Ad Acc. Circ: 650.
Desc: Provides a unique, monthly update on international product liability and product safety for manufacturers, insurers, and lawyers. Reports on the latest developments in product liability together with feature articles, comment and analysis. Has an established reputation for reliable news and opinions.

US/0164-9574
PRODUCT LIABILITY TRENDS. Ceased. Added/Corp Research Group, Inc. (Charlottesville, Va.). Vol. 1 (Aug. 1977)- Vol. 17, No. 8 (1992). Periodical. English. mo. National Legal Research Group Inc, PO Box 7187, Charlottesville VA 22906. Tel (800)727-6574, (804)977-5690, FAX (804)295-4667. LC K953.A13; P76. DD 346.03/8.

US/0192-5075
PRODUCT LIABILITY UPDATE. English. Practising Law Institute, 810 Seventh Avenue, New York NY 10019-5818. Tel (212)765-5700, FAX (212)581-4670 general correspondence, (212)265-4742 orders and billing inquiries. ED R J Phelan. LC KF1296.Z9; P7. DD 346/.73/038.

US/0094-5463
PRODUCT SAFETY & THE LAW. Periodical. English. mo. $30.00. Man & Manager, 87 Terminal Drive, Plainview NY 11803. LC KF3945.A73; P73. DD 344/.73/04205.

US/0272-1767
PRODUCTS LIABILITY AND TRANSPORTATION LEGAL DIRECTORY. [Prod. liabil. transp. legal dir.]. (1978/79)-. English. an. Products Liability and Transportation Legal Directory, 8396 Mississippi Street, Merrillville IN 46410. LC KF195.T7; T7. DD 346.7303/82/025; 347.306382025. Continues Transportation and Products Legal Directory, 0092-6175.

US/0162-122X
PRODUCTS LIABILITY REPORTS. [Prod. liabil. rep.]. Main/Corp Commerce Clearing House. (1963)-. Periodical. English. bw. $655.00. Commerce Clearing House Inc., 4025 West Peterson Avenue, Chicago IL 60646-6085. Tel (312)583-8500, FAX (708)940-4600.

AU
PRODUKTHAFTUNG AKTUELL : PH. VFOAT PH. (1988)-. Periodical. German. bm. S320.00. Oesterreichischen Akademie Wissenschaften, Dr. Ignaz Seipel Platz 2, A-1010 Vienna Austria. Tel 011 43 1 51581. LC K16; .R587.

US/1042-5675
PROFESSIONAL LAWYER : PL / SPECIAL COORDINATING COMMITTEE ON PROFESSIONALISM, AMERICAN BAR ASSOCIATION CENTER FOR PROFESSIONAL RESPONSIBILITY, THE. [Prof. lawyer]. Added/Corp Center for Professional Responsibility (American Bar Association). Special Coordinating Committee on Professionalism. VFOAT PL. Vol. 1, No. 1 (Spring 1989)-. Periodical. English. qt (4 issues). $25.00. American Bar Association, 750 North Lake Shore Drive, Chicago IL 60611. Tel (312)988-5522, (312)988-5241, FAX (312)988-5528, telex 270593. DD 340.

US/0275-0503
PROFESSIONAL LIABILITY. [Prof. liabil.]. No. 1 (Jan. 1981)-. Periodical. English. mo. $120.00. Stainbrook and Levine, Inc., 1852 Columbia Road NW, Suite 540, Washington DC 20009. LC KF1289.A15; P76. DD 346.7303/32/05; 347.30633205.

US/0145-3505
PROFESSIONAL LIABILITY REPORTER. [Prof. liabil. report.]. Added/Corp Litigation Research Group (San Francisco, Calif.) Shepard's/McGraw-Hill. (19??)-. Periodical. English. mo. $320.00. Shepards McGraw-Hill Inc, 555 Middle Creek Parkway, PO Box 35300, Colorado Springs CO 80935-3530. Tel (719)488-3000, FAX (800)525-0053. ED William Jordan. LC KF1289.A59; P74. DD 346/.73/033. Index available. cum. index. Circ: 850.
Desc: Covers the liability of and successful defenses against the imposition of liability on accountants, attorneys, real estate brokers, architects, securities brokers and dealers, corporate directors and officers, judges, and trustees.

US/0744-7817
PROFESSIONAL MONITOR / MICHIGAN ASSOCIATION OF THE PROFESSIONS, THE. Vol. 16, No. 18 Apr./May 1982. Periodical. English. mo (except July and September). $22.00. Michigan Association of the Professions, 530 W Ionia Street/Suite A, Lansing MI 48933. Tel (517)484-1024. ED William D Dansby. Bk Rev. Ad Acc. Circ: 650 (ctrl). Continues Legislative Monitor, 0279-8743.
Desc: Provides news of and for the association's affiliated professions, certified public accountants, dentists, medical doctors, optometrists, lawyers, veterinarians, psychologists, engineers, land surveyors, and school administrators.

UK/0267-078X
PROFESSIONAL NEGLIGENCE. Title Change. [Prof. neglig.]. Vol. 1, No. 1 (Jan./Feb. 1985)-(199?). Periodical. English. bm. Tolley Publishing Company Ltd, Tolley House, 2 Addiscombe Road, Croydon, Surrey CR9 5AF United Kingdom. Tel 011 44 81 6869141, FAX 011 44 81 6863155, 011 44 81 7600588. LC KD1978.A13; P76. DD 346.4103/3; 344.10633. NLM W1; PR593. Continued by Tolley's Professional Negligence.
Desc: A journal of liability, ethics and discipline.
Ind/Abst Leg. Resour. Index; LegalTrac (1980-).

US/1051-3744
PROFESSIONAL NEGLIGENCE LAW REPORTER. [Prof. neglig. law rep.]. VFOAT PNLR. (Feb. 1990)-. Periodical. English. Ten times a year. $95.00 (members), $155.00 (nonmembers). Association of Trial Lawyers of America, 1050 31st Street Northwest, Washington DC 20007. Tel (800)424-2725 ext. 307, FAX (202)298-6849. ED Cathy G Kruvant. LC KF1289.A59; A85. DD 346.7303/3; 347.30633. Index available. Ad Acc. Circ: 2,000. Continues ATLA Professional Negligence Law Reporter, 1043-0393.
Desc: Digest of opinions, verdicts, settlements and trends in the law dealing with litigation of professional negligence cases.

US/0362-8531
PROFESSIONAL RESPONSIBILITY. Main/Corp Bay Area Review Course, Inc. 1976-. English. Bay Area Review Course Inc, 5900 Wilshire Boulevard, Los Angeles CA 90036. LC KF306.Z9; B38. DD 174/.3/0973. Continues Bay Area Review Course, Inc. Legal Ethics.

US/0743-5401
PROFITABLE LAWYER, THE. Title Change. [Profit. lawyer]. Vol. 1, No. 1 (July/Aug. 1984)-. Periodical. English. mo (10 issues). Prentice-Hall Law and Business, 270 Sylvan Avenue, Englewood Cliffs NJ 07632. Tel (800)223-0231, (201)894-8538, FAX (201)894-8666. ED Larry Smith. LC KF318.A1; P76. DD 340/.068. Bk Rev. Circ: 800. Absorbed by Of Counsel, 0730-3815.
Desc: Information and ideas on how to run a firm efficiently and profitably.

UK
PROPERTY LAW BULLETIN. (19??)-. Periodical. English. Ten times a year. $190.30. Longman Group Ltd., Fourth Avenue, Longman House, Harlow Essex CM19 5SR England. Tel 011 44 279 429655, FAX 011 44 279 431059, telex 81259. ED John Samson, William Taylor, and Patrick Soares. LC KD822; .P76. DD 346.4104/3; 344.10643. Index available. Ad Acc.
Desc: Digest of articles and court decisions affecting property.

UK
PROPERTY, PLANNING, AND COMPENSATION REPORTS. VFOAT Law Reports. Property, Planning, and Compensation Reports. 51, Pt. 1 (Jan./Feb. 1986)-. Periodical. English. Ten times a year. £250.00 Europe; £262.00 other. Sweet & Maxwell Ltd., South Quay Plaza, 183 Marsh Wall, London E14 9FT England. Tel 011 44 264 342899, FAX 011 44 264 342723, telex 929089 ITPINF G. LC KD826.A2; P7. DD 346.4104/5; 344.10645. available on microfilm and microfiche from University Microfilms International (UMI). Continues Property and Compensation Reports, 0033-1295.

MY
PROPOSED LEGISLATIVE PROGRAM - DEPARTMENT OF THE INTERIOR. Main/Corp United States. Department of the Interior. VFOAT Department of the Interior Proposed Legislative Program. (1960)-. Periodical. English. Continues Preliminary Legislative Program - Department of the Interior.

IT
PROPOSTE E DISEGNI LEGGE. (19??)-. Italian. Libreria Camera Dei Deputati, Via Uffici Del Vicario 17, 00186 Rome Italy. Tel 011 39 6 67603715.

CK
PROYECTO DE PRESUPUESTO. SECTOR CENTRAL. Main/Corp Colombia. Direccion General del Presupuesto. VFOAT Sector Central. (1978)-. Spanish. an. LC KHH4560.A22; C64. DD 343.861/034/05; 348.61033405. Continues Colombia, Proyecto de Presupuesto.

GW
PROZESSRECHTLICHE ABHANDLUNGEN. Monographic series. German. ir. Price varies per volume. Carl Heymanns Verlag KG, Luxemburger Strasse 449, D 50939 Cologne Germany. Tel 011 49 221 460100, telex 8 881 888.

AG/0326-2774
PRUDENTIA IURIS. Added/Corp Pontificia Universidad Catolica Argentina Santa Maria de los Buenos Aires. Facultad de Derecho y Ciencias Politicas. (1980)-. Periodical. Spanish. Twice a year. Universit Catolica Argentina, Derecho & Ciencias, Moreno 371, 1116 Buenos Aires Argentina. Tel 011 54 1 8124224. LC K16; .R83.

US/1062-3523
PSYCHIATRY MALPRACTICE PROTECTOR. Ceased. See Medical Science and Technology-Psychiatry.

●US/1076-8971
PSYCHOLOGY, PUBLIC POLICY, AND LAW. See Psychology.

US/0735-4703
PUBLIC ADMINISTRATOR AND THE COURTS, THE. See Public Administration.

US/0893-2573
PUBLIC AND LOCAL ACTS OF THE LEGISLATURE OF THE STATE OF MICHIGAN. [Public local acts Leg. State Mich.]. Main/Corp Michigan. Added/Corp Michigan. Dept. of State. Michigan. Compilation Commission. Michigan. Legislative Service Bureau. (1933)-. English. an. Michigan Department of Management and Budget, PO Box 30026, Lansing MI 48909. Tel (517)373-5644. LC KFM4225; .A25. DD 348.774/022. Index available (Bound in all issues). ctrl circ. Formed by the union of Michigan. Public Acts of the Legislature of the State of Michigan Passed at the Regular Session and Michigan. Local Acts of the Legislature of the State of Michigan Passed at the Regular Session.
Desc: Laws enacted by the Michigan Legislature for a particular year.

US/0360-7704
PUBLIC AND SPECIAL ACTS. Main/Corp Connecticut. Vol. 36 (Feb. Session 1972)-. Government Publication. English. an. $97.52 Connecticut; $90.00 other. Secretary of the State / Public Division, 30 Trinity Street, Hartford CT 06106. Tel (203)566-3606. LC KFC3625; .P8. DD 348/.746/022. Index available.

Formed by the union of Public Acts Passed by the General Assembly *and* Special Acts and Resolutions of the State of Connecticut.

US/0033-3441
PUBLIC CONTRACT LAW JOURNAL. [Public contract law j.]. **Added/Corp** American Bar Association. Section of Public Contract Law. Vol. 1, No. 1 (July 1967)-. English. qt (4 issues). $20.00. American Bar Association, 750 North Lake Shore Drive, Chicago IL 60611. **Tel** (312)988-5522, (312)988-5241, FAX (312)988-5528, telex 270593. **ED** Matthew S. Sinchak. **LC** K16; .U17. **DD** 346/.73/023/05; 347.3062305. **Ad Acc.** ctrl circ. available on microfilm and microfiche from University Microfilms International (UMI).
Desc: Articles on all phases of federal, state, local procurement and grant law by leading authorities.
Ind/Abst Bowne Dig. Corp. Sec. Lawyers; Curr. Law Index (1980-); Index Leg. Period.; Leg. Resour. Index (1980-); LegalTrac (1980-).

US/0569-3314
PUBLIC CONTRACT NEWSLETTER. [Public contract newsl.]. **Added/Corp** American Bar Association. Section of Public Contract Law. (1965)-. Periodical. English. qt (4 issues). Free on request. American Bar Association, 750 North Lake Shore Drive, Chicago IL 60611. **Tel** (312)988-5522, (312)988-5241, FAX (312)988-5528, telex 270593. **LC** KF849.A1; P8. **DD** 346/.73/023.
Ind/Abst Curr. Law Index (1980-); Leg. Resour. Index (1980-); LegalTrac (1980-).

US
PUBLIC EMPLOYEE TERMINATIONS LAW BULLETIN. **See** Economics-Labor.

UK
PUBLIC GENERAL ACTS AND GENERAL SYNOD MEASURES, THE. **See** Public Administration.

US/1058-384X
PUBLIC INTEREST LAW REVIEW, THE. [Public interest law rev.]. **Added/Corp** National Legal Center for the Public Interest. (1991)-. Periodical. English. ir. $29.95. Carolina Academic Press, 700 Kent Street, Durham NC 27701. **Tel** (919)489-7486. **LC** K16; .U198. **DD** 342.73/0662; 347.302662.

US/0732-0264
PUBLIC LAND LAW REVIEW, THE. [Public land law rev.]. **Added/Corp** University of Montana (Missoula). School of Law. Vol. 1, No. 1 (Spring 1980)-. English. an. $20.00. University of Montana School of Law, Missoula MT 59812. **Tel** (406)243-2023, FAX (406)243-2576. **LC** K16; .U214. **DD** 333.1/05. **Bk Rev. Circ:** 550 (ctrl).
Desc: Publishes articles, notes and comments involving legal issues surrounding public lands, natural resources and Indian law.
Ind/Abst Curr. Law Index (1980-); Index Leg. Period.; Leg. Resour. Index (1980-); LegalTrac (1984-).

UK/0033-3565
PUBLIC LAW. [Public law]. (1956)-. English. Four times a year. £82.00 Europe; £86.00 other. Sweet & Maxwell Ltd., South Quay Plaza, 183 Marsh Wall, London E14 9FT England. **Tel** 011 44 264 342899, FAX 011 44 264 342723, telex 929089 ITPINF G. **LC** K16; .U22. available on microfilm and microfiche from University Microfilms International (UMI). ***Absorbed*** *British Journal of Administrative Law.*
Ind/Abst Index Leg. Period.; Int. Bibliogr. Sociol.; Leg. Resour. Index (1980-); LegalTrac (1980-).

AT/1034-3024
PUBLIC LAW REVIEW. Vol. 1, No. 1 (Apr. 1990)-. Periodical. English. qt (4 issues). 210.00Aus$. The Law Book Company Limited, 44-50 Waterloo Road, North Ryde New South Wales, 2113 Australia. **Tel** 011 61 2 8870177, FAX 011 61 2 8887240, telex ASBOOK 27445. **(Subscription address:** Wm. W. Gaunt & Sons, Inc., 3011 Gulf Drive, Gaunt Building, Holmes Beach, FL 34217**) ED** Cheryl Saunders and Greg Craven. Index available. cum. index. **Circ:** 300.
Desc: Deals with the framework of law and practice within which government operates. While the primary focus of the review is Australia and New Zealand, its coverage also to the Asia-Pacific region.
Ind/Abst Aust. Leg. Mon. Dig.

US
PUBLIC LAWS. **Main/Corp** United States. **Added/Corp** United States. Office of the Federal Register. **VFOAT** Slip Laws. (1???)-. Government Publication. English. ir. $156.00 US; $195.00 other. Superintendent of Documents, US Government Printing Office, Washington DC 20402. **Tel** (202)275-3328, FAX (202)786-2377.
Desc: A public law, often referred to as a slip law, is the initial publication of a Federal law upon enactment and is printed as soon as possible after approval by the President. Some legislative history references appear on each new law.

US
PUBLIC LAWS OF THE STATE OF RHODE ISLAND AND PROVIDENCE PLANTATIONS PASSED AT THE GENERAL ASSEMBLY. **Main/Corp** Rhode Island. English. an. Secretary of State / Rhode Island, State House, Providence RI 02903. **Tel** (401)277-2000. **ED** Stephen Cicilline. Each issue contains an index to its own contents (no volume index)--loose. **Circ:** 310.
Desc: Contains the public laws, private acts and resolutions passed by the General Assembly that year. Published at the end of the year.

●UK/0963-8245
PUBLIC PROCUREMENT LAW REVIEW. No. 1 (1992)-. English. bm (6 issues). £175.00 Europe; £184.00 other. Sweet & Maxwell Ltd., South Quay Plaza, 183 Marsh Wall, London E14 9FT England. **Tel** 011 44 264 342899, FAX 011 44 264 342723, telex 929089 ITPINF G. **LC** K16; .U226. **DD** 346.4/023; 344.0623.

CN/0822-1790
PUBLIC SERVICE STAFF RELATIONS BOARD DECISIONS. [Public Serv. Staff Relat. Board decis.]. **Main/Corp** Canada. Public Service Staff Relations Board. **VFOAT** PSSRB Decisions; Decisions de la Commission des Relations de Travail dans la Fonction Publique. **VAT** Recueil de Decisions de la CRTFP. Jan. 1, 1982/June 30, 1982-. English (French). sa. Canada Communication Group Publishers, Order Processing, Ottawa Ontario K1A 0S9 Canada. **Tel** (819)956-4800, (819)956-4802. **LC** KE3240.F4; A4636. **DD** 344.71/01890413540002648; 347.1041890413540002648.

US/0095-5086
PUBLIC UTILITIES LAW ANTHOLOGY. Vol. 1 (1974)-. Periodical. English. sa (May and Oct.). $299.90. International Library Law Book Publishers, 101 Lakeforest Boulevard, Suite 270, Gaithersburg MD 20877. **Tel** (800)359-3349, (301)990-7755, FAX (301)990-7642. **ED** Allison P. Zabriskie. **LC** KF2094.A1; P8. **DD** 343/.73/0905. Index available. cum. index. **Bk Rev.**
Desc: Covers public utilities law review articles, by year, selected from over 900 law review journals. Introduction and overview by highly respected experts in Public Utilities Law. Indexed by subject, author, and leading cases.

CL/0577-8573
PUBLICACIONES - CHILE. UNIVERSIDAD, SANTIAGO. SEMINARIO DE DERECHO PUBLICO. **Main/Corp** Chile. Universidad, Santiago. Seminario de Derecho Publico. (1959)-. Periodical. Spanish. Editorial Universitaria SA de Chile, Casilla 10220, Santiago Chile. **Tel** 011 56 2 223-4555. **DD** 340.

UK
PUBLICATIONS, LIST OF MEMBERS AND RULES / SELDEN SOCIETY. **Main/Corp** Selden Society. English. ir (two-three issues per year). £19.00 UK; $50.00 US; £21.00 other. Selden Society, Faculty of Law, Queen Mary College, Mile End Road, London E1 4NS England. **Tel** 011 44 71 9755136, FAX 011 44 71 9818733, telex 893750. **Circ:** 2,000.

US
PUBLICATIONS OF THE CONSORTIUM FOR COMPARATIVE LEGISLATIVE STUDIES. ***Ceased.*** **Main/Corp** Consortium for Comparative Legislative Studies. **VFOAT** Comparative Legislative Studies Series. (19??)-(19??). Monographic series. English. ir. Duke University Press, PO Box 90660, Durham NC 27708-0660. **Tel** (919)687-3600, (919)688-5134 (orders), FAX (919)688-4574, telex 802829.

UK
PUBLICATIONS OF THE SELDEN SOCIETY, THE. **Main/Corp** Selden Society, London. (1887)-. English. an. £19.00 UK; $50.00 North America; £21.00 other. Selden Society, Faculty of Law, Queen Mary College, Mile End Road, London E1 4NS England. **Tel** 011 44 71 9755136, FAX 011 44 71 9818733, telex 893750. **ED** J. M. Baker. **LC** Z6459; .S46. Index available. **Circ:** 2,000.

US/0555-6392
PUBLISHING, ENTERTAINMENT, ADVERTISING AND ALLIED FIELDS LAW QUARTERLY. [Publ. entertain. advert. allied fields law q.]. **VFOAT** P.E.A.L.; PEAL. Vol. 1 No. 1 (June 1961)-. Periodical. English. qt. Clark Boardman Callaghan, 155 Pfingsten Road, Deerfield IL 60015. **Tel** (800)323-8067. **ED** A D Choka. **LC** K16; .U27. **DD** 659.2/934973. cum. index. available on microfilm and microfiche from University Microfilms International (UMI).
Ind/Abst Curr. Law Index (1980-); Leg. Resour. Index (1980-?); LegalTrac (1980-1982).

US/1071-2623
Q-DEX (LISLE, ILL.). (Q-DEX : A QUICK INDEX TO INDUSTRIAL COMMISSION DECISIONS, ILLINOIS.). [Q-DEX]. **VFOAT** Q DEX. (19??)-. English. Twice a year (Apr., Nov.). $310.00. Damien Corporation, 645 Crest Lane, Lisle IL 60532. **Tel** (708)963-4750, FAX (708)963-4855. **ED** Nancy Nyhan. **DD** 346.

IT
QUADERNI DEL DIRITTO DEL LAVORO. Italian. sa. L150.00 Italy; 225.00 other. Unione Tipografico Ed Torinese, Corso Raffaello 28, 10125 Turin Italy. **Tel** 011 39 11 6529340.

IT
QUADERNI DI DIRITTO DEL LAVORO E RELAZIONI INDUSTRIALI. (19??)-. Italian. sa. L150000 Itlay; L225000 other. Unione Tipografico Ed Torinese, Corso Raffaello 28, 10125 Turin Italy. **Tel** 011 39 11 6529340.

IT
QUADERNI FIORENTINI PER LA STORIA DEL PENSIERO GIURIDICO MODERNO. (1972)-. Italian (French, German, Spanish and English). an. L9000 (latest issue). Giuffre Editore SPA, Via Busto Arsizio 40, 20151 Milan Italy. **Tel** 011 398 2 38089200. **Ad Acc.** ctrl circ.

IT
QUADERNI MONOTEMATICI DI DIRITTO TRIBUTARIO. Italian. Ten times a year. L119600.00. Editoriale Tributaria Italiana, Viale Mazzini 25, 00195 Rome Italy. **Tel** 011 39 6 87130300.

US/0362-3564
QUAERE (MINNEAPOLIS). (QUAERE.). Began with Oct. 1974 issue. Periodical. English. ir (eight no. a year). $5.00. Quaere Inc, Fraser Hall, University of Minnesota, Minneapolis MN 55455. **LC** KF292.M5714; A46. **DD** 340/.09776.

UK/0961-1452
QUANTUM LONDON. (QUANTUM.). [Quantum Lond.]. (1990)-. English. bm (6 issues). £75.00 Europe; £79.00 other. Sweet & Maxwell Ltd., South Quay Plaza, 183 Marsh Wall, London E14 9FT England. **Tel** 011 44 264 342899, FAX 011 44 264 342723, telex 929089 ITPINF G. **DD** 344.206323.

US/0736-0142
QUARTERLY / CHRISTIAN LEGAL SOCIETY. [Q. - Christ. Legal Soc.]. **Added/Corp** Christian Legal Society. **VFOAT** Christian Legal Society Quarterly. Vol. 2, No. 2 (Spring 1981)-. Periodical. English. qt. $20.00 (one year), $35.00 (two year), $50.00 (three year) US; $22.52 (one year), $40.04 (two year), $57.56 (three year) Canada; $26.22 (one year), $47.44 (two year), $68.66 (three year) other. Christian Legal Society, 4208 Evergreen Lane, Suite 222, Annandale VA 22003. **Tel** (703)642-1070, FAX (703)642-1075. **ED** Karen Heal. **LC** KF200; .C46. **DD** 344/.09; 342.49. **Bk Rev**, (Qty: 12). **Circ:** 5,000 (ctrl). available on microfilm from University Microfilms International (UMI). ***Continues*** *Christian Legal Society Quarterly, 0275-6765.*
Desc: Professional journal containing articles of interest to Christian lawyers, judges and law students.
Ind/Abst Leg. Resour. Index (1981-).

US/0020-8752
QUARTERLY / INTERNATIONAL SOCIETY OF BARRISTERS. **Added/Corp** International Society of Barristers. **VFOAT** International Society of Barristers Quarterly. Vol. 1, No. 1 (Jan. 1966)-. Periodical. English. Four times a year (Jan., Apr., July, Aug.). $10.00. International Society of Barristers, 3586 East Huron River Drive, Ann Arbor MI 48104-4238. **Tel** (313)557-3933. **ED** John W. Reed (University of Michigan Law School, Ann Arbor, MI 48109-1215; telephone: (313)763-0165; FAX: (313)764-8309). **LC** K9; .N87. Index available (bound in issue). cum. index. **Circ:** 700.
Desc: Concerns litigation and trial advocacy. Includes topics of the courts, the jury, trial lawyers, and the adversary system.

US
QUARTERLY LAW NOTES AND ALUMNI NEWS. **Main/Corp** University of San Diego. School of Law. Fall 1975-. Periodical. English. qt. University of San Diego School of Law, 5998 Alcala Park, San Diego CA 92110. **Tel** (619)260-4531. ***Continues in part*** *San Diego, Calif. University. School of Law. Alumni Newsletter.*

US/0048-6302
QUEENS BAR BULLETIN. [Queens bar bull.]. **Added/Corp** Queens County Bar Association. (1950)-. Bulletin. English. bm. $2.50. Queens County Bar Association, 90-35-148th Street, Jamaica NY 11435. **LC** KF200; .Q43. **DD** 340/.06/0747243. ***Continues*** *Queens County Bar Association Bulletin.*
Ind/Abst Fed. Tax Artic.

US/0730-9724
QUEENS COLLEGE LAW JOURNAL. **Added/Corp** Queens College (New York, N.Y.). Bench and Bar Association. Vol. 1, (Spring 1976)-. Periodical. English. an. Queens College, Political Science Department, 65-30 Kissena Boulevard, Flushing NY 11367. **Tel** (718)520-7000.

CN/0316-778X
QUEEN'S LAW JOURNAL. [Queen's law j.]. **Added/Corp** Queen's University (Kingston, Ont.). Faculty of Law. **VFOAT** Labour Law Under the Charter. Vol. 1 (Mar. 1971)-. English. Twice a year. 45.00Can$. Queens's University / Faculty of Law, Kingston Ontario K7L 3N6 Canada. **Tel** (613)547-5803, (613)545-2220. **LC** K17; .U34. **DD** 340/.05. **Bk Rev**. **Ad Acc**. **Circ:** 900. ***Supersedes*** *Queen's Intramural Law Journal, 0048-6310.*
Desc: An academic journal publishing articles and book reviews of legal interest.
Ind/Abst Can. Legal Lit.; Curr. Law Index (1980-); Index Can. Leg. Period. Lit.; Index Leg. Period.; Leg. Resour. Index (1980-); LegalTrac (1980-).

AT
QUEENSLAND LAND COURT REPORTS. **Main/Corp** Queensland. Land Court. Vol. 1 (1974)-. English. an (July). 84.00Aus$. Land Administration Commission, PO Box 40, Sunmap Centre, Woolloonga QLD 4102 Australia. **Tel** 011 61 7 8963224. **DD** 343./943/025/0269. Index available. **Circ:** 150 (ctrl). ***Continues*** *Crown Lands Law Reports.*
Desc: Significant decisions and judgements of the Land Court Land Appeal Court dealing with valuation of land for rental, rating and acquisition purposes.
Ind/Abst Aust. Leg. Mon. Dig.

AT/0726-0784
QUEENSLAND LAW REPORTER. [Qld. law rep.]. (1976)-. Periodical. English. wk. **DD** 346.943.
Ind/Abst Aust. Leg. Mon. Dig.

AT/0313-4253
QUEENSLAND LAW SOCIETY JOURNAL, THE. [Queensl. Law Soc. j.]. **Main/Corp** Queensland Law Society. Vol. 1 (July 1971)-. Periodical. English. bm (6 issues). 80.00Aus$ Australia; 135.00Aus$ other. Queensland Law Society Inc, 179 Ann Street, GPO Box 1785, Brisbane QLD 4001 Australia. **Tel** 011 61 7 2335888, FAX 011 61 7 2335999, telex 44137. **LC** K17; .U33. **DD** 349.943/05. Index available (published separately). **Ad Acc**, **Adv Mgr:** Gail Baker, **Tel** same as publisher. **Circ:** 4,800 (ctrl). available on microfilm from University Microfilms International (UMI).
Desc: Deals with substansive legal matters and provides practitioners with a permanent reference work on important and topical issues.
Ind/Abst Aust. Leg. Mon. Dig.; Curr. Law Index (1980-); Leg. Resour. Index (1980-); LegalTrac (1980-).

AT/0312-1658
QUEENSLAND LAWYER, THE. **VFOAT** Queensland Lawyer, Reports; Queensland Lawyer and Reports. Vol. 1 (Feb. 1973)-. Periodical. English. bm. $124.00. The Law Book Company Limited, 44-50 Waterloo Road, North Ryde New South Wales, 2113 Australia. **Tel** 011 61 2 8870177, FAX 011 61 2 8887240, telex ASBOOK 27445. **ED** Bernard Cairns. **DD** 348/.943/044. **Ad Acc**. ***Continues*** *Queensland Justice of the Peace and Report.*
Desc: Articles on Queensland law. Incorporates decisions of Queensland District Court.
Ind/Abst Aust. Leg. Mon. Dig.

AT/0727-095X
QUEENSLAND PLANNING LAW REPORTS. [Qld. plann. law rep.]. **VFOAT** Q.P.L.R. (1981)-. Periodical. English. Four times a year (Feb., May, Aug., Nov.). 225.00Aus$. Printacular Printing & Publishing, 661 Mains Road, MacGregor QLD 4109 Australia. **Tel** 07 343 5853. **DD** 346.943045. ***Continues*** *Planner. Local Government Report, 0727-0968.*
Desc: A magazine about planning law.
Ind/Abst Aust. Leg. Mon. Dig.

AT
QUEENSLAND REPORTS. **VFOAT** Queensland Law Journal; Queensland Law Reporter. (1902)-. English. bm. $265.00. The Law Book Company Limited, 44-50 Waterloo Road, North Ryde New South Wales, 2113 Australia. **Tel** 011 61 2 8870177, FAX 011 61 2 8887240, telex ASBOOK 27445. **ED** J S Douglas. Index available. ***Continues*** *Queensland Law Journal Reports.*
Desc: Reports of the decisions of the Supreme Court of Queensland.
Ind/Abst Aust. Leg. Mon. Dig.

US/0736-2846
QUINLAN PRIVATE TRUCK LAW REPORT, THE. **VFOAT** Private Truck Law Report. Vol. 1, No. 1 Jan.-Mar. 1982. English. qt. William A Quinlan, 3045 Riva Road, Riva MD 21140. **LC** KF2265.A15; Q56. **DD** 343.73/09483/05; 347.303948305.

●US/1073-8606
QUINNIPIAC LAW REVIEW. (1994)-. English. Four times a year. $32.00. Quinnipiac College School of Law, 303 University Avenue, Bridgeport CT 06604. **Tel** (203)576-4068. ***Continues*** *Bridgeport Law Review, 1066-8411.*

FR
QUOTIDIEN JURIDIQUE. (19??)-. Periodical. French. ir (156 issues). 310.00F. Le Quotidien Juridique, 2 rue Seguier, 75006 Paris France. **Tel** 43 29 80 60.

IT
RACCOLTA ATTI NORMATIVI. Italian. ir. L240000 Italy; L480000 other. Istituto Poligrafico Zecca Stato, Piazza Verdi 10, 00198 Rome Italy. **Tel** 011 39 6 85082307, 011 39 6 85082221. ***Continues*** *Raccolta Ufficiale Decreti.*

IT
RACCOLTA SISTEMATICA DI GIURISPRUDENZA COMMENTATA. (1963)-. Monographic series. Italian. ir. Price varies per volume. Raccolta Sistematica di Cedam, Via Jappelli 5, Padova 1 Italy.

IT
RACCOLTA UFFICIALE DELLE SENTENZE E ORDINANZE. **Main/Corp** Italy. Corte Costituzionale. (1956)-. Italian. ir. L25000.00. Corte Constituzionale Ufficio, Piazza del Quirinale 41, 00187 Rome Italy. **Tel** 011 39 6 4698206.

UN/0485-8573
RADIANSKE PRAVO. (19??)-. Periodical. Ukrainian. mo. $97.00. Izdatelstvo Naukova Dumka / Ukrainian Academy of Sciences, Vladimirskaia Ulitsa 54, 252601 Kiev Ukraine. **Tel** 225-63-66, telex 131376. **(Subscription address:** Victor Kamkin, 4956 Boiling Brook Parkway, Rockville MD 20852.**)**
Ind/Abst Index Foreign Leg. Per.

IT/1120-1762
RAGIUSAN. RASSEGNA GIURIDICA DELLA SANITA. [Ragiusan, Rass. giurid. sanit.]. **VFOAT** Rassegna Giuridica Della Sanita. (1984)-. Periodical. Italian. mo (10 issues). L650000.00. Sipis, Viale Parioli 77, 00197 Rome Italy. **Tel** 011 39 6 8073368. **UDC** 351.83. Index available. cum. index. **Bk Rev**. **Ad Acc**. **Pr Rev**. ctrl circ. available on diskette.

US
RAINMAKER'S REVIEW, THE. English. qt. $70.00. Shepards McGraw-Hill Inc, 555 Middle Creek Parkway, PO Box 35300, Colorado Springs CO 80935-3530. **Tel** (719)488-3000, FAX (800)525-0053.
Desc: A law office marketing publication that offers growth strategies concerning ethics, diversification, selecting clients and more.

II/0377-7723
RAJASTHAN LAW WEEKLY, THE. **Main/Corp** India. Rajasthan High Court. English (Hindi). wk. $60.00. P R Sharma, Maan Bhawan/1st Floor, Ratanada Road, Jodhpur 342 001 India. **Tel** 23023. **ED** D V Kalia and B B L Mathur. **DD** 348/.544/043. Index available. cum. index. **Bk Rev**. **Ad Acc**. **Circ:** 3,200.

II
RAJASTHAN STATE CURRENT STATUTES. Periodical. English. mo. 45.00. Rajasthan State Current Statutes, High Court Road, Jodhpur (Raj) India. **DD** 348.54/4022/05; 345.44082205.

CN/0703-0762
RAPPORT ANNUEL - COMMISSION DES SERVICES JURIDIQUES. (RAPPORT ANNUEL.). **Main/Corp** Commission des Services Juridiques. Began in 1975. French. an. 2 Complexe Desjardins, Tour de l'Est Bureau 1404, Montreal Quebec H5B 1B3 Canada. **LC** KEQ180.A13; C65. **DD** 354.7140084/5. ***Continues*** *Legal Services Commission. Rapport Annuel, 0703-0762.*

CN
RAPPORT ANNUEL - MINISTERE DE LA JUSTICE. **Main/Corp** Quebec (Province). Dept. of Justice. 1967-. French. Editeur Officiel du Quebec, 1283 Boul Charest Ouest, Quebec Quebec G1N 2C9 Canada. **LC** KEQ787.A72; J887. **DD** 354.714065.

CN/0822-7829
RAPPORTS DE LA SECTION DES GRIEFS ET DE L'ARBITRAGE. (RAPPORTS DE LA SECTION DES GRIEFS ET DE L'ARBITRAGE / PUBLIC SERVICE ALLIANCE OF CANADA). [Rapp. Sect. griefs arbitr.]. **Main/Corp** Alliance de la Fonction Publique du Canada. Section des Griefs et de l'Arbitrage. (1979)-. Periodical. French. Free. Alliance de la Fonction Publique du Canada, 233 rue Gilmore, Ottawa Ontario K2P 0P1 Canada. **DD** 342.71/068. ***Continues*** *Alliance de la Fonction Publique du Canada. Disposition d'un Gief Sumis a u Cnseil d'Abitrage., 0318-630X.*

IT
RASSEGNA DELL AVVOCATURA DELLO STATO. (19??)-. Italian. bm (6 issues). L52000 Italy; L104000 other. Istituto Poligrafico Zecca Stato, Piazza Verdi 10, 00198 Rome Italy. **Tel** 011 39 6 85082307, 011 39 6 85082221.

IT/0033-9512
RASSEGNA DI DIRITTO PUBBLICO. Periodical. Italian. qt. Libreria Scientifica Editrice, Corso Umberto 34, Naples Italy.

IT
RASSEGNA FORENSE. **Added/Corp** Consiglio Nazionale Forense (Italy). Year 1 (Jan./Mar. 1968)-. Italian. qt. L60000.00 Italy; L90000.00 other. Giuffre Editore SPA, Via Busto Arsizio 40, 20151 Milan Italy. **Tel** 011 398 2 38089200. **ED** Edilberto Ricciardi.
Desc: Publishes theoretical material and articles on subjects of present-day interest, and also all decisions taken on disciplinary questions by the Forensic Council and the most important pronouncements of the Court of Cassation on matters concerning the legal profession in its work.

IT
RASSEGNA GIURIDICA DELL ENERGIA ELETTRICA. (19??)-. Italian. Four times a year. L110000.00 Italy; L165000.00 other. Giuffre Editore SPA, Via Busto Arsizio 40, 20151 Milan Italy. **Tel** 011 398 2 38089200. **ED** Giovanni Gentile.
Desc: Essentially concerned with the legal aspects of the field of electricity, and more in general with that of energy as a whole.

UK
RATING AND VALUATION REPORTER. Periodical. English. ir (11 issues per year). £72.00 UK; $150.00 US. Rating Publishing Ltd, 2 Paper Buildings, Temple London EC4 England. **Tel** 0483-233571. **ED** Christopher Lewsley. Index available. cum. index. **Bk Rev**. **Ad Acc**. ***Continues*** *Rating and Income Tax.*
Desc: Law reports and articles for those particularly interested in rating, land valuation and compensation.

UK
RATING APPEALS. (19??)-. English. Eleven times a year. £90.00. Rating Publishing Ltd, 2 Paper Buildings, Temple London EC4 England. **Tel** 0483-233571. **ED** Christopher Lewsley. **LC** KD5534.A38; R37. **DD** 343/.42/05402648. Index available. **Bk Rev**. **Ad Acc**.
Desc: For professional valuers of land and those interested in local taxation.

UK/0952-1917
RATIO JURIS. Vol. 1, No. 1 (March 1988)-. Academic Scholarly Publication. English. Three times a year. £100.00 UK and Europe; $200.00 North America; £118.00 other. Basil Blackwell Publishers Ltd, 108 Cowley Road, Oxford 0X4 1JF England. **Tel** 011 44 865 791100, FAX 011 44 865 791347, telex 837022 OXBOOK G. **(Subscription address:** Blackwell Publishers / UK, Marston Book Services, PO Box 87, Oxford OX2 0DT England.**)** **ED** Enrico Paltaro. **LC** K18; .A93. **DD** 340/.1/05. **CODEN** RAJUEQ. **[CCC]**. cum. index. **Ad Acc**. **Circ:** 800. available on microfilm and microfiche from University Microfilms International (UMI).
Desc: A journal of jurisprudence and legal philosophy providing a truly international forum for the communication of ideas about law and legal questions.
Ind/Abst Index Leg. Period.; Leg. Resour. Index; LegalTrac (1988-).

US/8755-8815
RAZA LAW JOURNAL, LA. [Raza law j.]. **Added/Corp** University of California, Berkeley. School of Law. **VFOAT** Raza Law Journal. Vol. 1, No. 1 (Spring 1983)-. English. sa (Jan., July). $30.00. University of California Press, 2120 Berkeley Way, Berkeley CA 94720. **Tel** (510)642-4191, (510)642-3907, FAX (510)642-9917. **ED** Students of Boalt Hall School of Law, Univ. of California, Berkeley. **LC** K18; .A95. **DD** 349.73/0896873; 347.30089686. **[CCC]**. **Bk Rev**. **Circ:** 250 (ctrl).
Desc: Investigates Hispanic social and legal issues.
Ind/Abst Curr. Law Index (1984-); Leg. Resour. Index (1984-); LegalTrac (1984-).

GW/0936-5893
RDE. RECHT DER ELEKTRIZITATSWIRTSCHAFT. **See** Energy.

US
READER SERVICES LAW LIBRARIAN. **See** Library and Information Sciences.

UK
READERS PAYE : PII HANDBOOK. **See** Public Administration-Public Finance and Taxation.

US/0270-7683
REAL ESTATE & THE LAW. **See** Real Estate.

US/0548-7366
REAL ESTATE LAW AND PRACTICE COURSE HANDBOOK SERIES. [Real estate law pract. course handb. ser.]. **Main/Corp** Practising Law Institute. (1968)-. Monographic series. English. ir. $450.00. Practising Law Institute, 810 Seventh Avenue, New York NY 10019-5818. **Tel** (212)765-5700, FAX (212)581-4670 general correspondence, (212)265-4742 orders and billing inquiries. **(Subscription address:** Practising Law Institute, Source Code GBY4, 810 Seventh Avenue, New York NY 10019.**)** **DD** 346.
Desc: Current trends, developments, and problems in real estate law and practice.

US/0048-6868
REAL ESTATE LAW JOURNAL. [Real estate law j.]. **Added/Corp** Warren, Gorham & Lamont, Inc. Vol. 1 (1972)-. Periodical. English. qt. $141.50 US; $219.45 other. Warren Gorham & Lamont Inc., Park Square Building, 31 St. James Avenue, Boston MA 02116-4112.

Tel (617)423-2020, (800)950-1207, FAX (617)423-2026. **ED** Jerome G. Rose, Peter F. Knopp and Alvin L. Arnold. **LC** K18; .E14. **DD** 346/.73/04305. **[CCC].** available on microfilm and microfiche from University Microfilms International (UMI). Documents available from UMI Article Clearinghouse.
Desc: Devoted to the continuing practical concerns of real estate law professionals. Draws upon the expertise of leading real estate attorneys, tax specialists, financial experts, and government officials.
Ind/Abst ABI/INFORM Glob. Ed.; ABI Inform Ondisc (Summer 1976-); Gen. BusinessFile (1992-); Index Leg. Period.; J. Plan. Lit.; Leg. Resour. Index (1980-); LegalTrac (1980-); PAIS Int. Print.

US/0162-752X
REAL ESTATE LAW REPORT. **Added/Corp** Warren, Gorham & Lamont, Inc. Vol. 1 (June 1971)-. Periodical. English. mo. $124.48 US and Canada; $179.00 other. Warren Gorham & Lamont Inc., Park Square Building, 31 St. James Avenue, Boston MA 02116-4112. **Tel** (617)423-2020, (800)950-1207, FAX (617)423-2026. **ED** Ross Lloyd. **LC** KF570; .R39. **DD** 346/.73/04305. **[CCC].** Index available (bound in last issue). available in microform from University Microfilms International (UMI).
Desc: Legislative changes, precedent-setting court decisions, and governmental rulings and regulations. Delivers information on significant legal and tax developments in clear, jargon-free language.

US
REAL ESTATE LICENSE LAW AND RULES AND REGULATIONS. **Added/Corp** Detroit Board of Realtors. Michigan. Dept. of Licensing and Regulation. Michigan. Laws, Statutes, Etc. (19??)-. English. $5.00. **LC** KFM4482.R4; R42. **DD** 346.77404/37.

US
REAL PROPERTY. **Main/Corp** Bay Area Review Course, Inc. English. an. Bay Area Review Course Inc, 5900 Wilshire Boulevard, Los Angeles CA 90036. **LC** KF570.Z9; B35. **DD** 346/.73/043.

US/0198-893X
REAL PROPERTY (GARDENA). (REAL PROPERTY.). 10th Ed. (1979)-. English. ir. $14.95. Law Distributors, 14415 South Main Street, Gardena CA 90248. **Tel** (310)321-3275, (800)421-1893, FAX (310)324-6381. **LC** KF570.Z9; R88. **DD** 346.7304/3. ***Continues** Real Property, 0198-893X.*

US
REAL PROPERTY LAW, REAL PROPERTY ACTIONS AND PROCEEDINGS LAW, AND RELATED MISCELLANEOUS STATUTES, AS AMENDED. **Main/Corp** New York (State). **Added/Corp** New York (State). Real Property Actions and Proceedings Law. New York (State). Weed RPL-RPAPL. **VFOAT** Warren's Weed RPL-RPAPL. (1968)-. Proceedings. English. Matthew Bender & Company Inc., 1275 Broadway, Albany NY 12204. **Tel** (800)833-9844, (518)487-3000. **LC** KFN5140.A29; R4. **DD** 346.7304/3/02632.

US/0898-1698
REAL PROPERTY LAW REPORTER. [Real prop. law report.]. **Added/Corp** California Continuing Education of the Bar. **VFOAT** CEB Real Property Law Reporter. (Dec. 1977)-. Periodical. English. Eight times a year. $175.00. California Continuing Education of the Bar, 2300 Shattuck Avenue, Berkeley CA 94704. **Tel** (510)642-8000, (800)232-3444. **ED** Roger Bernhardt, Noel Ellis and Jo Sherlin. **LC** KFC140.A15; R43. **DD** 346.79404/3/05; 347.94064305. Index available (free). **Pr Rev.** ***Continues** California Real Property Law Reporter, 0146-7530.*
Desc: Articles and summaries of court opinions and legislation designed to keep attorneys up to date with recent developments in California real property law. Analysis and practice tips included.

CN/0703-4687
REAL PROPERTY REPORTS. [Real prop. rep.]. V. 1- Mar. 1977-. Periodical. English (French). mo. 64.50Can$. Carswell / Canada, 2075 Kennedy Road, Scarborough Ontario M1T 3V4 Canada. **Tel** (416)609-3800, (800)387-5164. **ED** Sirje Sellers. **DD** 346/.71/04302642. Index available. cum. index. **Ad Acc.**
Desc: Features all important decisions in real property law from all Canadian jurisdictions selected by experts in the field.
Ind/Abst Can. Legal Lit.; Curr. Law Index (1980-Dec. 1985); Index Can. Leg. Period. Lit.; Leg. Resour. Index (1980-Dec. 1985); LegalTrac (1981-1985).

US
REAL PROPERTY SECTION NEWS. **Main/Corp** Utah State Bar. Real Property Section. Vol. 1 (1974)-. Periodical. English. bm. 203 Kearns Building, Salt Lake City UT 84101. **LC** KFU112.A73; U8. **DD** 346/.792/04305.

SA/0250-0329
REBUS, DE. **Added/Corp** Association of Law Societies of the Republic of South Africa. (19??)-. Periodical. Afrikaans (English). Twelve times a year. R150.00 South Africa; R100.00 other. Association of Law Societies of the Republic of South Africa, PO Box 36626, Menlo Park 0102 South Africa. **Tel** 011 27 12 3423330 9. **ED** Phillip van der Merwe. **LC** K18; .E16. **DD** 349.68/05; 346.8005. **Bk Rev. Ad Acc. Circ:** 10,850 (ctrl). ***Continues** DR, De Rebus.*
Desc: Publishes articles on law and practice, finance, professional news, office administration, new books, practical aids and other matters related to legal practice.

US/0890-8451
RECALL/REGULATORY ANALYSIS. **VFOAT** Recall Regulatory Analysis. Vol. 1, No. 1 (Aug. 1986)-. Periodical. English. Twelve times a year. $295.00 US; $320.00 other. Recall/Regulatory Analysis, PO Box 6353, Silver Spring MD 20916. **Tel** (301)460-8821. **ED** William McVicker. **DD** 343.
Desc: Presentation and commentary on new regulations and regulations affecting industries regulated by the US Food and Drug Administration.

NP
RECENT LAWS OF NEPAL. **Added/Corp** Legal Research Associates. Vol. 1, No. 1 (Jan./Feb. 1989)-. Periodical. English (translations available in Nepali). bm. $66.00 Nepal; $84.00 other. Legal Research Associates / Kathmandu, Post Box 828, Kathmandu Nepal. **Tel** 011 977 1 272534, FAX 011 977 1 272866. **ED** Dhruba Bar Singh Thapa. **LC** KPK1.85; .R43. **DD** 348.5496/022; 345.4960822. **Circ:** 100.

US/0899-0662
RECENT TITLES IN LAW FOR THE SUBJECT SPECIALIST. AGRICULTURE, ANIMAL, AND FOOD LAW. [Recent titles law subj. spec., Agric. anim. food law]. **Added/Corp** Ward & Associates. **VFOAT** Agriculture, Animal, and Food Law. Vol. 5, No. 1 (Jan.-March 1988)-. English. qt. $85.00 US. Ward & Associates, 317 South Division, Suite 66, Ann Arbor MI 48104. **Tel** (313)665-3520, FAX (313)665-7880. **LC** K3870.A12; N38. **DD** 016.343/076; 016.342376. Index available (Bound in all issues). **Bk Rev.** ***Continues** National Legal Bibliography. Subject Area List. Agriculture, Animal and Food Law, 8755-7959.*
Desc: Current awareness service and bibliography of recently published titles in subject area.

US/0899-0883
RECENT TITLES IN LAW FOR THE SUBJECT SPECIALIST. COMMUNICATION LAW. [Recent titles law subj. spec., Commun. law]. **Added/Corp** Ward & Associates. **VFOAT** Communication Law. Vol. 5, No. 1 (Jan./Mar. 1988)-. English. Four times a year. $85.00. Ward & Associates, 317 South Division, Suite 66, Ann Arbor MI 48104. **Tel** (313)665-3520, FAX (313)665-7880. **LC** K4240.A12; N38. **DD** 016.343/09945; 016.34239945. ***Continues** National Legal Bibliography. Subject Area List. Communication Law, 8755-7975.*

US/0899-0867
RECENT TITLES IN LAW FOR THE SUBJECT SPECIALIST. CONTRACT LEASE, AND SALES LAW. [Recent titles law subj. spec., Contract lease sales law]. **VFOAT** Contract, Lease, and Sales Law. Vol. 5, No. 1 (Jan.-March 1988)-. English. qt. $85.00. Ward & Associates, 317 South Division, Suite 66, Ann Arbor MI 48104. **Tel** (313)665-3520, FAX (313)665-7880. **LC** K840.A1; N38. **DD** 016.346/02. ***Continues** National Legal Bibliography. Subject Area List. Contract, Lease, and Sales Law, 8755-7991.*

US/0899-0859
RECENT TITLES IN LAW FOR THE SUBJECT SPECIALIST. COPYRIGHT AND ENTERTAINMENT LAW. [Recent titles law subj. spec., Copyr. entertain. law]. **VFOAT** Copyright and Entertainment Law. Vol. 5, No. 1 (Jan.-Mar. 1988)-. English. qt. $85.00. William S. Hein & Company Inc., 1285 Main Street, Buffalo NY 14209. **Tel** (716)882-2600, (800)828-7571, FAX (716)883-8100, telex 91-209 WM S HEIN BUF. **DD** 016. ***Continues** National Legal Bibliography. Subject Area List. Copyright and Entertainment Law, 8755-8009.*

US/0899-0824
RECENT TITLES IN LAW FOR THE SUBJECT SPECIALIST. ENTERPRISE ORGANIZATION. [Recent titles law subj. spec., Enterp. organ.]. **Added/Corp** Ward & Associates. **VFOAT** Enterprise Organization. Vol. 5, No. 1 (Jan./Mar. 1988)-. English. qt. $85.00. Ward & Associates, 317 South Division, Suite 66, Ann Arbor MI 48104. **Tel** (313)665-3520, FAX (313)665-7880. **LC** K1301.A12; N38. **DD** 016.346/065; 016.342665; 016. ***Continues** National Legal Bibliography. Subject Area List. Enterprise Organization, 8755-8033.*

US/0899-0816
RECENT TITLES IN LAW FOR THE SUBJECT SPECIALIST. EVIDENCE, PRATICE, AND PROCEDURE. [Recent titles law subj. spec., Evid. pract. proced.]. **Added/Corp** Ward & Associates. **VFOAT** Evidence, Practice, and Procedure. Vol. 5, No. 1 (Jan.-Mar. 1988)-. English. qt. $85.00. Ward & Associates, 317 South Division, Suite 66, Ann Arbor MI 48104. **Tel** (313)665-3520, FAX (313)665-7880. **LC** K2201; .N38. **DD** 016.347/05; 016.34275. ***Continues** National Legal Bibliography. Subject Area List. Evidence, Practice, and Procedure, 8755-8041.*

US/0899-0778
RECENT TITLES IN LAW FOR THE SUBJECT SPECIALIST. MEDICINE AND HEALTH LAW. [Recent titles law subj. spec., Med. health law]. **VFOAT** Medicine and Health Law. Vol. 5, No. 1 (Jan.-Mar. 1988)-. English. qt. $85.00. Ward & Associates, 317 South Division, Suite 66, Ann Arbor MI 48104. **Tel** (313)665-3520, FAX (313)665-7880. **LC** K3601.A12; N38. **DD** 016. **NLM** ZW 32.6; R295. ***Continues** National Legal Bibliography. Subject Area List. Medicine and Health Law, 8755-8084.*

US
RECENT TITLES IN LAW FOR THE SUBJECT SPECIALIST. MUNICIPAL AND ADMINISTRATIVE LAW, AND POLITICS. English. William S. Hein & Company Inc., 1285 Main Street, Buffalo NY 14209. **Tel** (716)882-2600, (800)828-7571, FAX (716)883-8100, telex 91-209 WM S HEIN BUF.

US/0899-0697
RECENT TITLES IN LAW FOR THE SUBJECT SPECIALIST. PROPERTY (REAL AND CHATTEL), AND CONSTRUCTION LAW. **VFOAT** Property (Real and Chattel), and Construction Law. Vol. 5, No. 1 (Jan./Mar. 1988)-. English. Four times a year. $85.00. Ward & Associates, 317 South Division, Suite 66, Ann Arbor MI 48104. **Tel** (313)665-3520, FAX (313)665-7880. **DD** 016. ***Continues** National Legal Bibliography. Subject Area List. Property (Real and Chattel) and Construction Law, 8755-8114.*

US/0899-0751
RECENT TITLES IN LAW FOR THE SUBJECT SPECIALIST. TECHNOLOGY AND DESIGN PROTECTION. [Recent titles law subj. spec., Technol. des. prot.]. **VFOAT** Technology and Design Protection. Vol. 5, No. 1 (Jan./Mar. 1988)-. English. qt. $85.00. Ward & Associates, 317 South Division, Suite 66, Ann Arbor MI 48104. **Tel** (313)665-3520, FAX (313)665-7880. **DD** 016. ***Continues** National Legal Bibliography. Subject Area List. Technology and Design Protection, 8755-8149.*

US/0899-0743
RECENT TITLES IN LAW FOR THE SUBJECT SPECIALIST. TORTS, LIABILITY, AND INDEMNITY. [Recent titles law subj. spec. Torts liabil. indemn.]. **VFOAT** Torts, Liability, and Indemnity. Vol. 5, No. 1 (Jan.-Mar. 1988)-. English. qt. $85.00. William S. Hein & Company Inc., 1285 Main Street, Buffalo NY 14209. **Tel** (716)882-2600, (800)828-7571, FAX (716)883-8100, telex 91-209 WM S HEIN BUF. **DD** 016. ***Continues** National Legal Bibliography. Subject Area List. Torts, Liability, and Indemnity, 8755-8157.*

US/0899-0735
RECENT TITLES IN LAW FOR THE SUBJECT SPECIALIST. TRADE REGULATION AND ECONOMICS. [Recent titles law subj. spec., Trade regul. econ.]. **VFOAT** Trade Regulation and Economics. Vol. 5, No. 1 (Jan.-Mar. 1988)-. Periodical. English. Four times a year. $85.00. Ward & Associates, 317 South Division, Suite 66, Ann Arbor MI 48104. **Tel** (313)665-3520, FAX (313)665-7880. **DD** 016. ***Continues** National Legal Bibliography. Subject Area List. Trade Regulation and Economics, 8755-8165.*

SZ
RECHT (BERN, SWITZERLAND). (RECHT.). (1983)-. Periodical. German. Four times a year. 89.00F Switzerland; 110.00F other. Staempfli & Cie SA, Postfach 8326, CH-3001 Bern Switzerland. **Tel** 011 41 31 3006666, telex 031 911 515 EDMZ CH. **DD** 349.494/05; 344.94005.

GW/0171-712X
RECHT DER ELEKTRIZITATSWIRTSCHAFT. ***Title Change.*** **See** Energy.

GW/0340-7926
RECHT DER INTERNATIONALEN WIRTSCHAFT. **VFOAT** RIW/AWD-Recht der Internationalen Wirtschaft. (Jan. 1975)-. Periodical. German. Twelve times a year. DM616.20. Verlag Recht und Wirtschaft GmbH, Postfach 105960, D 69049 Heidelberg Germany. **Tel** 011 49 6221 9061. **LC** K1; .U767. **DD** 343.43/087/05; 344.3038705. **[CCC].** Index Available, published separately, free-automatically sent. cum. index. ***Continues** Aussenwirtschaftsdienst des Betriebs-Beraters.*
Ind/Abst Index Foreign Leg. Per.; World Agric. Econ.

Law

GW/0034-1312
RECHT DER JUGEND UND DES BILDUNGSWESEN. (19??)-. Academic Scholarly Publication. German. Four times a year. DM175.70. Hermann Luchterhand Verlag, Postfach 2352, D 56513 Neuwied Germany. **Tel** 011 49 2631 8010. **ED** Ingo Richter. **LC** K18; .E23. **DD** 344.43/07/05; 344.304705. **[CCC]. Bk Rev. Ad Acc.** *Continues Recht der Jugend.*
Desc: Scholarly journal covering West German law and administration in the field of education. A forum for interaction between jurists, teachers, social scientists and administrators.

AU
RECHT DER SCHULE. (19??)-. Periodical. German. qt. S180.00. Manzsche Verlagsbuchhandlung, Kohlmarkt 16 Postfach 163, A 1014 Vienna Austria. **Tel** 011 43 222 5316171. **ED** Viktor Keller. **LC** K18; .E24. **DD** 344.436/07/05; 344.304705. Index available. **Bk Rev.**
Desc: Covers educational law and legislation.

GW
RECHT DER WOHNUNGSWIRTSCHAFT. Periodical. German. mo. 84.00. J. Schweitzer Verlag, Zeppelinallee 43, Postfach 97 01 48, D 60325 Frankfurt Germany. **Tel** 011 39 69 793009 0, FAX 011 39 69 793009 48. **LC** KK6786.A13; R43.

NE
RECHT EN KRITIEK. 1975-. Dutch. 20.00. Utigave Sun, Biileveldsingel 9, Nijmegen Netherlands. **LC** K18; .E26.

GW/0486-1485
RECHT IN OST UND WEST. [Recht Ost West]. **Added/Corp** Vereinigung Freiheitlicher Juristen. Institut fuer Ostrecht. Vol. 1, (Mar. 1957)-. Periodical. German. Nine times a year. DM158.00. Berlin Verlag Arno Spitz GmbH, Pacelliallee 5, D 14195 Berlin Germany. **Tel** 011 49 30 8326232, FAX 011 49 30 8316249. **(Subscription address:** Nomos Verlagsgesellschaft GmbH, Waldseestr. 3-5, D 76530 Baden-Baden Germany.) **LC** K18; .E27. **DD** 349.43/05; 344.305. Index Available in first issue of next volume--attached. cum. index. **Bk Rev. Ad Acc. Circ:** 1,000.
Desc: Features documentation of important legal texts, a chronicle of legislative developments in East European states, and more.
Ind/Abst Am. Hist. Life; Coal Abstr.; Index Foreign Leg. Per.

GW/0341-7050
RECHT UND GESELLSCHAFT (MUNCHEN). (RECHT UND GESELLSCHAFT.). Vol. 1- ; Oct. 1971-. German. 10.80. CH Beck Verlagsbuchhandlung, D 80791 Munich Germany. **Tel** 011 49 89 381891. **LC** K18; .E29.

GW/0344-7871
RECHT UND POLITIK. (1965)-. Periodical. German. qt. DM76.00. Berlin Verlag Arno Spitz GmbH, Pacelliallee 5, D 14195 Berlin Germany. **Tel** 011 49 30 8326232, FAX 011 49 30 8316249. **(Subscription address:** Nomos Verlagsgesellschaft GmbH, Waldseestr. 3-5, D 76530 Baden-Baden Germany.) **ED** Rudolf Wassermann, Ernst Zivier. **UDC** 340.134. **CODEN** 351/354:6 011.1. Index available. cum. index. **Bk Rev. Ad Acc. Circ:** 1,200.
Desc: Working in the area where political science, politics and legal practice overlap, the journal deals with the actual problems and the background of administration and jurisdiction.

GW/0343-9771
RECHT UND SCHADEN. VFOAT R und S; R + S. (19??)-. Periodical. German. ir. Verlag Information Ambs GmbH, Postfach 208, D 97828 Kippenheim Germany. **Tel** 011 49 7825 7114. **LC** K18; .E295. **DD** 346.4303; 344.3063. Index available. cum. index. **Bk Rev. Ad Acc. Circ:** 2,300.
Desc: Includes insurance against damage, rules and regulations, compensation, identification and laws concerning insurance.

NE
RECHTSGELEERD MAGAZIN THEMIS. (1939)-. Periodical. Dutch. bm. Fl129.00. W. E. J. Tjeenk Willink, Box 25, 8000 AA Zwolle Netherlands. **Tel** 011 31 38 228819, 011 31 38 211444. **(Subscription address:** Libresso BV, Postbus 23, 7400 GA Deventer Netherlands.)
Ind/Abst Index Foreign Leg. Per.

GW/0723-1180
RECHTSHISTORISCHES JOURNAL. [Rechtshist. J.]. (1982)-. German (English and French). an. DM70.00. Loewenklau Gesellschaft EV, Altkoenigstr 10, W-6000 Frankfurt 1 Germany.

BE
RECHTSKUNDIG WEEKBLAD. Vol. 1, No. 1 (1931)-. Periodical. Dutch. Forty-three times a year. 4250F. Maklu Uitgevers NV, Somerstraat 13-15, 2018 Antwerp Belgium. **Tel** 011 32 3 2312900, FAX 011 32 3 2332659.
Ind/Abst Index Foreign Leg. Per.

NE
RECHTSPRAAK VAN DE WEEK. Kluwer BV, Postbus 23, 7400 GA Deventer Netherlands. **Tel** 011 31 5700 33155, 011 31 5700 48999, FAX 011 31 5700 11504, telex 42829.

NE
RECHTSPRAAK VREEMDELINGENRECHT / [NEDERLANDS CENTRUM BUITENLANDERS]. Added/Corp Nederlands Centrum Buitenlanders. (1977)-. Dutch. **DD** 342.492/083; 344.920283.

GW/0931-6183
RECHTSPRECHUNG FRANKFURT. (RECHTSPRECHUNG.). [Rechtsprechung Frankf.]. (1986)-. Monographic series. German. ir. Price not set by publisher at time of publication. Vittorio Klostermann, Frauenlobstrasse 22, D 60487 Frankfurt Germany. **Tel** 011 49 69 9708160. **UDC** 34.038.

GW
RECHTSPRECHUNG ZUM WIEDERGUTMACHUNGSRECHT. (Nov. 1949)-. Periodical. German. qt. DM68.00. CH Beck Verlagsbuchhandlung, D 80791 Munich Germany. **Tel** 011 49 89 381891. Index available in last issue of volume--attached.

GW
RECHTSPRECHUNGSKARTEI GEWERBLICHER RECHTSSCHUTZ. (19??)-. German. Carl Heymanns Verlag KG, Luxemburger Strasse 449, D 50939 Cologne Germany. **Tel** 011 49 221 460100, telex 8 881 888.
Desc: Commercial legal protection.

GW/0034-1398
RECHTSTHEORIE. [Rechtstheorie]. Vol. 1 (1970)-. Periodical. German. Four times a year. DM174.30 Germany; DM178.40 others. Duncker und Humblot Verlag, Postfach 410329, D-12113 Berlin Germany. **Tel** 011 49 30 79000612, 011 49 30 79000613. **ED** W. Krawietz. **LC** K18; .E35. **DD** 340/.1/05. **[CCC].** Index available in last issue of volume--attached. **Bk Rev. Ad Acc. Circ:** 600.
Desc: Theory of law, journal of logic, methodology, and sociology of the law.
Ind/Abst Philos. Index.

FR
RECOMMENDATIONS AND RESOLUTIONS / COUNCIL OF EUROPE, COMMITTEE OF MINISTERS. Main/Corp Council of Europe. Committee of Ministers. (1979)-. English. an. Free on request. Council of Europe / Group Pact ED, Pharmacopoeia BP 907, 67029 Strasbourg Cedex 01 France. **Tel** 011 33 88 412036, FAX 011 33 88 41277181, telex 880388. *Continues Council of Europe. Committee of Ministers. Resolutions.*

US
RECOMMENDATIONS FOR LEGISLATIVE CONSIDERATION ON PUBLIC EDUCATION IN TEXAS. Main/Corp Texas. Education Agency. English. be. Texas Education Agency, Publications Distribution, 1701 North Congress Avenue, Austin TX 78701-1494. **Tel** (512)463-9734, (512)463-9000. **LC** KFT1590; .A837. **DD** 344.764/071; 347.640471.

US
RECOMMENDATIONS OF THE WEST VIRGINIA BOARD OF EDUCATION FOR LEGISLATIVE ACTION. Main/Corp West Virginia. State Board of Education. English. an. West Virginia Board of Education, Executive Offices, Charleston WV 25305. **Tel** (304)348-2699. **ED** Carolyne Spangler. **LC** KFW1590; .A835. **DD** 344.754/073; 347.540473. **Circ:** 1,000 (ctrl).

US/0004-5837
RECORD OF THE ASSOCIATION OF THE BAR OF THE CITY OF NEW YORK, THE. [Rec. Assoc. Bar City New York]. **Main/Corp** Association of the Bar of the City of New York. Vol. 1 (Feb. 1946)-. English. Eight times a year. $60.00. Association of the Bar of the City of New York, 42 West 44th Street, New York NY 10036. **Tel** (212)382-6650, FAX (212)768-8630. **ED** Lilou Irvine. Index available. cum. index. **Ad Acc. Circ:** 21,000 (ctrl). available on microfilm and microfiche from University Microfilms International (UMI).
Desc: Legal reports, legal lectures, and legal bibliographies.
Ind/Abst Crim. Justice Abstr.; Fed. Tax Artic.; Index Leg. Period.; Leg. Inf. Manage. Index (19??-); Leg. Resour. Index; LegalTrac (1980-).

US/0145-8566
RECORD (WASHINGTON, D.C. : 1975). (RECORD / FEDERAL ELECTION COMMISSION.). Publication began with Sept. 1975. Periodical. English. mo. Free. US Federal Election Commission, 999 E Street NW, Washington DC 20463. **Tel** (800)424-9530. **ED** Louise Wides. **LC** KF4885.A15; E5. **DD** 342/.73/07. Index available. cum. index. **Bk Rev. Circ:** 13,237 (ctrl).
Desc: Summarizes all commission actions that occurred the previous month. Summaries include advisory opinions, upcoming reports, audits, statistics, and court cases.

US/0362-6121
RECORDER, THE. VFOAT San Francisco Law Journal. English. da. $150.00. Am-Law California Corporation, 99 South Van Ness Avenue/Suite 200, San Francisco CA 94103. **Tel** (415)621-5400, FAX (415)626-0857. **ED** Av Goldstein. **LC** MICROFILM LL-010 K18. **Ad Acc.** ctrl circ. available in microform (and wire service).

US
RECORDER (SAN FRANCISCO, CALIF.).
See Newspapers.

US/1055-2863
RECORDS OF WILLS, SURROGATES COURT, STATEN ISLAND, NEW YORK (RICHMOND COUNTY). [Rec. wills surrog. court Staten Is. N. Y. (Richmond Cty.)]. Vol. 1 (1991)-. English. $12.00 (single issue). Name Game Enterprises, 4204 South Conklin Street, Spokane WA 99203-6235. **Tel** (509)747-4903. **DD** 346.

US/0743-5649
RECREATION AND PARKS LAW REPORTER. (RECREATION AND PARKS LAW REPORTER : RPLR.). [Recreat. parks law report.]. **Added/Corp** National Recreation and Park Association. **VFOAT** RPLR; R.P.L.R. Vol. 1, No. 1 (1st Quarter 1984)-. Periodical. English. qt. $50.00 members, $100.00 nonmembers. National Recreation and Park Association, 2775 South Quincy Street, Suite 300, Arlington VA 22206. **Tel** (703)820-4940, (703)578-5564, FAX (703)671-6772. **LC** KF5638.A59; R42. **DD** 346.7304/6783; 347.30646783. available on microfilm from University Microfilms International (UMI).
Ind/Abst SPORT Discus.

FR
RECUEIL ANNUEL DES PAGES JURIDIQUES DE LA VIE OUVRIERE. French. an. 50.00F. Sogedil, 146 rue du FG Poissonniere, 75010 Paris France.

FR
RECUEIL DALLOZ SIREY. 6 Jan. 1965-. Periodical. French. wk. 740.00F France; 880.00F other. Dalloz, 35 rue Tournefort, 75240 Paris Cedex 05 France. **Tel** 011 33 1 40515434 or 40515454, FAX 45 87 37 48, telex 206 446 F. **ED** Andre Dunes. Index available. cum. index. *Formed by the union of Recueil Dalloz and Recueil Sirey.*
Desc: Flash section informs on essential decisions; chronicles offer commentary on recent legislative rulings; principle laws, degrees and instructions are transcribed. Includes general bibliography.
Ind/Abst Index Foreign Leg. Per.; Int. Labour Doc.

FR/0034-1835
RECUEIL DALLOZ SIREY DE DOCTRINE, DE JURISPRUDENCE ET DE LEGISLATION. VFOAT Recueil Dalloz Sirey. (19??)-. Periodical. French. Forty-Four times a year. 1280.00F France; 1600.00F other. Dalloz, 35 rue Tournefort, 75240 Paris Cedex 05 France. **Tel** 011 33 1 40515434 or 40515454, FAX 45 87 37 48, telex 206 446 F. **LC** KJV112; .R43. **[CCC].** *Continues Recueil Dalloz.*

CN/0704-2035
RECUEIL DE DROIT FISCAL QUEBECOIS. [Recl. droit fisc. que.]. **Added/Corp** Societe Quebecoise d'Information Juridique. Service des Publications. (1977)-. Periodical. French. an. SOQUIJ Societe Quebecoise Info Juridique, 276 rue Street, Jacques Suite 310, Montreal Quebec H2Y 1N3 Canada. **Tel** (514)842-8745. **DD** 343.71404/02643. **Circ:** 800.
Desc: Reports on all judgements handed down by various courts concerning fiscal matters.

CN/0832-8943
RECUEIL DE DROIT IMMOBILIER. [Recl. droit immob.]. **Added/Corp** Societe Quebecoise d'Information Juridique. Vol. 1 (1986)-. Periodical. French. qt. $119.71. Societe Quebecoise d'Information Juridique, 10 rue St Jacques Bureau 101, Montreal Quebec H2Y 1L3 Canada. **Tel** (514)842-8745, FAX (514)844-8984. **DD** 346.71404/3/02648.
Ind/Abst Can. Legal Lit.

LU
RECUEIL DE LA JURISPRUDENCE DE LA COUR. Main/Corp Court of Justice of the European Communities. 1958-. French. Etablissements Emile Bruylant, 67 rue de la Regence, 1000 Brussels Belgium. **Tel** 011 32 2 5129845. **(Subscription address:** Office des Publications Officielles des Communautes Europeennes, rue Mercier 2, 2985 Luxembourg Belgium)

Law

FR/0583-8282
RECUEIL DE MEMOIRES ET TRAVAUX PUBLIE PAR LE SOCIETE D'HISTOIRE DU DROIT ET DES INSTITUTIONS DES ANCIENS PAYS DE DROIT ECRIT.
Added/Corp Societe d'Histoire du Droit et des Institutions des Anciens Pays de Droit Ecrit. Faculte de Droit et des Sciences Economiques de Montpellier. (19??)-. Monographic series. Multiple languages (French, English, Italian and Spanish). ir. Price varies per volume. Universite Paul Valery, BP 5043 Route de Mende, 34032 Montpellier, Cedex 1 France. **Tel** 11 33 67 142000, FAX 011 33 67 142052. **(Subscription address:** Universite de Montpellier, Ihapde 39 rue de l'Universite, 34060 Montpellier Cedex France.**)**

CN/1183-0271
RECUEIL EN MATIERE DE PROTECTION DU TERRITOIRE AGRICOLE. [Recl. matiere prot. territ. agric.]. **Added/Corp** Societe Quebecoise d'Information Juridique. Commission de Protection du Territoire Agricole du Quebec. (1990)-. Periodical. French. qt. **DD** 346.71404/676. **Continues** Commission de Protection du Territoire Agricole du Quebec. Decisions., 0827-1925.

CN/0832-8935
RECUEIL EN RESPONSABILITE ET ASSURANCE. [Recl. responsab. assur.]. **Added/Corp** Societe Quebecoise d'Information Juridique. Vol. 1 (1986)-. Periodical. French. Four times a year. 199.00Can$. Societe Quebecoise d'Information Juridique, 10 rue St Jacques Bureau 101, Montreal Quebec H2Y 1L3 Canada. **Tel** (514)842-8745, FAX (514)844-8984. **DD** 346.71403.
Ind/Abst Can. Legal Lit.

SZ
RECUEIL OFFICIEL DES LOIS FEDERALES. Main/Corp Switzerland. (Jan. 12, 1988)-. Periodical. French. wk. 109.50F. Jordi SA, CP 96, 3123 Belp Switzerland. **Tel** 011 41 31 8190142.
Continues Recueil des Lois Federales.

CN/0830-0402
RECUEILS DE JURISPRUDENCE DU QUEBEC. COUR PROVINCIALE, COUR DES SESSIONS DE LA PAIX, TRIBUNAL DE LA JEUNESSE. [Recl. jurisprud. Que., Cour prov., Cour sess. paix, Trib. jeun.]. **Added/Corp** Quebec (Province). Cour Provinciale. Quebec (Province). Cour des Sessions de la Paix. Quebec (Province). Tribunal de la Jeunesse. Societe Quebecoise d'Information Juridique. **VFOAT** Cour Provinciale, Cour des Sessions de la Paix, Tribunal de la Jeunesse. **VAT** Recueils de Jurisprudence. Cour Provinciale. Cour des Sessions de la Paix. Tribunal de la Jeunesse. (19??)-. French (summaries and/or abstracts in English). Eleven times a year. 180.00Can$. SOQUIJ Societe Quebecoise Info Juridique, 276 rue Street, Jacques Suite 310, Montreal Quebec H2Y 1N3 Canada. **Tel** (514)842-8745. **LC** KEQ110; .A227.
Continues Recueils de Jurisprudence du Quebec. Cour Provinciale, Cour des Sessions de la Paix, Cour de Bien-Etre Social.
Desc: Reproduces entire text of most important decisions of provincial courts, justice of peace courts, and youth courts of Canada.

US
REDFEARN'S WILLS AND ADMINISTRATION OF ESTATES IN GEORGIA. English. ir. $329.95, $64.95 seperate pocket part supplement. Harrison Company Publishers, 3110 Crossing Park, PO Box 7500, Norcross GA 30091-7500. **Tel** (800)241-3561, (404)447-9150.

AT
REFORM. Added/Corp Australia. Law Reform Commission. (Jan. 1976)-. Periodical. English. qt. 12.00Aus$. Australian Law Reform Commission, GPO Box 3708, Sydney New South Wales 2001 Australia. **Tel** (02) 2311733. **ED** Barry Hunt. **DD** 340/.3/0994. Index available. cum. index. **Bk Rev. Circ:** 3,000 (ctrl). available on microfilm.
Desc: A regular bulletin of law reform news, views and information.
Ind/Abst Aust. Leg. Mon. Dig.

US/0034-317X
REGAN REPORT ON HOSPITAL LAW, THE. Vol. 8, No. 3 (June 1967)-. Periodical. English. mo. $48.00. Medica Press Inc, 10 Dorrance Street, Suite 500, Providence RI 02903. **Tel** (401)421-4747. **ED** A. David Tammelleo. **NLM** W1 RE172CR. **[CCC].** ctrl circ. available on microfilm and microfiche from University Microfilms International (UMI). **Continues** Regan Report.
Desc: Reporting court cases on hospital law with legal lessons from actual court decisions.

US/0034-3188
REGAN REPORT ON MEDICAL LAW. Vol. 1 (1968)-. Periodical. English. mo. $48.00. Medica Press Inc, 10 Dorrance Street, Suite 500, Providence RI 02903. **Tel** (401)421-4747. **ED** A. David Tammelleo. **NLM** W1 RE172CT. **[CCC].** ctrl circ. available on microfilm and microfiche from University Microfilms International (UMI); available on microfiche (16mm) from Copyright Clearance Center.
Desc: Reporting court cases on medical law and medical malpractice with legal lessons from actual court decisions.

US/0034-3196
REGAN REPORT ON NURSING LAW, THE. [Regan rep. nursing law]. Vol. 1 (June 1960)-. Periodical. English. mo. $48.00. Medica Press Inc, 10 Dorrance Street, Suite 500, Providence RI 02903. **Tel** (401)421-4747. **ED** A. David Tammelleo. **NLM** W1 RE172D. **[CCC].** Index available. ctrl circ. available on microfilm and microfiche from Copyright Clearance Center; and University Microfilms International (UMI).
Desc: Reports court cases on nursing law with legal lessons from actual court decisions.
Ind/Abst Cumul. Index Nurs. Allied Health Lit.; Int. Nurs. Index.

US/1056-3962
REGENT UNIVERSITY LAW REVIEW. [Regent Univ. law rev.]. **Added/Corp** Regent University. School of Law. Vol. 1, No. 1 (Spring 1991)-. Periodical. English. Twice a year. $12.50. Regent University School of Law, 1000 Regent University Drive, Virginia Beach VA 23464-9800. **Tel** (804)579-4333, (804)579-3900. **LC** K18; .E554. **DD** 349.73/05; 347.3005.
Ind/Abst Index Leg. Period. (1992-).

US
REGISTER / SOUTH DAKOTA, LEGISLATIVE RESEARCH COUNCIL.
Added/Corp South Dakota. Legislature. State Legislative Research Council. **VFOAT** South Dakota Register. (19??)-. Periodical. English. wk. Legislative Research Council, State Capitol Building, 500 East Capitol, Pierre SD 57501. **Tel** (605)773-3251. **LC** KFS3036; .S68. **DD** 348/.783/028. **Continues** South Dakota Register, 0191-1104.

US/0147-9091
REGULATORY ALERT. Main/Corp Research Institute of America, Inc. Periodical. English. wk. Research Institute of America, 117 East Stevens Avenue, Valhalla NY 10595. **Tel** (800)431-9025. **LC** KF1600.A15; R4. **DD** 343/.73/07.

US/1065-1896
REGULATORY UPDATE (PHILADELPHIA, PA.). (REGULATORY UPDATE : GOVERNMENT REGULATIONS RELATED TO PLASTICS INDUSTRY.). [Regul. update]. (19??)-. Periodical. English. mo. $95.00 US; $105.00 other. Regulatory Update, One Franklin Town Boulevard, Philadelphia PA 19103. **Tel** (215)567-7235. **ED** Lewis B. Weisfeld. **DD** 343. available on an online database.

●CN/1196-5266
REID'S ADMINISTRATIVE LAW. [Reid's adm. law]. Vol. 2, No. 1 (Sept. 1992)-. English. ir. $272.00 per year. Carswell / Canada, 2075 Kennedy Road, Scarborough Ontario M1T 3V4 Canada. **Tel** (416)609-3800, (800)387-5164. **DD** 342.71/06/0264.
Formed by the union of Reid's Administrative Law Letter, 1183-708X **and** Reid's Digest of Administrative Law, 1191-5447.

CN/1183-708X
REID'S ADMINISTRATIVE LAW LETTER.
Title Change. [Reid's adm. law lett.]. **VFOAT** Administrative Law Letter. Vol. 1, No. 1 (July/Aug. 1991)-(199?). Periodical. English. Ten times a year. Carswell / Canada, 2075 Kennedy Road, Scarborough Ontario M1T 3V4 Canada. **Tel** (416)609-3800, (800)387-5164. **DD** 342.71/06/05. **Merged with** Reid's Digest of Administrative Law, 1191-5447 **to form** Reid's Administrative Law, 1196-5266.

UK
REINSURANCE LAW. (19??)-. Periodical. English. ir. £474.55. Croner Publ Ltd, Croner House, London Road, Kingston upon Thames, Surrey KT2 6SR England. **Tel** 011 44 81 5473333, FAX 081 547-2637.

UK/0961-7264
REINSURANCE LAW REPORTS. [Reinsur. law reports]. (1991)-. English. Ten times a year. £130.00 UK; £145.00 others. Business & Medical Publications Limited, Saxeway Business Centre, Chartridge Lane, Chesham, Bucks HP5 2SH England. **Tel** 011 44 494 792621, FAX 011 44 494 793098, telex 86402. **ED** Geoffrey Hall. **DD** 342.686. Index available. cum. index. **Bk Rev. Ad Acc, Adv Mgr:** J. Arcker, **Tel** 011 44 494 79262.
Desc: About the reinsurance law reports.

BL
RELATORIO DA GESTAO DA DIRETORIA DO INSTITUTO DOS ADVOGADOS DO RIO GRANDE DO SUL. Main/Corp Instituto dos Advogados do Rio Grande do sul. Diretoria. (19??)-. Periodical. Portuguese. Travessa Engenheiro Acilino de Carvalho 21, Edificio el Cairo 60 Andar, Porto Alegre Brazil.

IT
RELAZIONE DELLA CORTE DEI CONTI AL PARLAMENTO SULLA GESTIONE FINANZIARIA DEGLI ENTI SOTTOPOSTI A CONTROLLO IN APPLICAZIONE DELLA LEGGE 21 MARZO 1958, N. 259. Italian. **DD** 342.45/0664; 344.502664.

US/0098-7999
REMEDIES. [Remedies]. **Main/Corp** Bay Area Review Course, Inc. English. Bay Area Review Course Inc, 5900 Wilshire Boulevard, Los Angeles CA 90036. **LC** KF9010.Z9; B38. **DD** 347/.73/77.

FR
REPERTOIRE DU NOTARIAT DEFRENOIS. (19??)-. Periodical. French. Twenty-two times a year. 700.00F France; 920.00F other. Repertoire Notariat Defrenois, 83 Ave Denfert Rochereau, 75014 Paris France. **Tel** 011 33 1 43548020. **DD** 347/.44/016.

CN/0704-9730
REPERTOIRE LEGISLATIF DE L'ASSEMBLEE DU QUEBEC. (REPERTOIRE LEGISLATIF DE L'ASSEMBLEE NATIONALE DU QUEBEC.). **Main/Corp** Quebec (Province). Assemblee Nationale. 1977-. French. an. Editeur Officiel du Quebec, 1283 Boul Charest Ouest, Quebec Quebec G1N 2C9 Canada. **LC** KEQ72; .Q42. **DD** 348.714/026; 347.140826.

IT
REPERTORIO 4 CODICI TRIBUTARI. (19??)-. Periodical. Italian. bm. L198.000. IPSOA Editore SRL, Casella Postale 12055, Mastrangelo, 20120 Milan Italy. **Tel** 011 39 2 82476248. Index available (Included). cum. index. **Circ:** 5,000 (ctrl). available on CD-ROM.
Desc: Fiscal index.

IT/0394-6347
REPERTORIO DEL FORO ITALIANO; LEGISLAZIONE, BIBLIOGRAFIA, GIURISPRUDENZA. (1971)-. Italian. an (published in July). Zanichelli Editore Spa, Via Irnerio 34, 40126 Bologna Italy. **Tel** 011 39 51 293263.

IT
REPERTORIO GENERALE DELLA GIURISPRUDENZA ITALIANA. Vol. 71 (Jan./Dec. 1969)-. Italian. an. Licosa Spa, PO Box 552, 50125 Florence Italy. **Tel** 011 39 55 645415. **Continues** Repertorio Generale Annuale della Giurisprudenza Italiana.

CN/0317-1604
REPORT / ALBERTA LAW REFORM INSTITUTE. No. 53 (June 1989)-. English. Alberta Law Reform Institute, 402 Law Centre, University of Alberta, Edmonton Alberta T6G 2H5 Canada. **Tel** (403)492-5291, (403)492-3374, FAX (403)492-1790.
Continues Report (University of Alberta. Institute of Law Research and Reform).

US/0732-0736
REPORT - CINCINNATI BAR ASSOCIATION. (REPORT / THE CINCINNATI BAR ASSOCIATION.). **Added/Corp** Cincinnati Bar Association. (19??)-. Periodical. English. Ten times a year. $20.00. Cincinnati Bar Association, 35 East Seventh Street, 8th Floor, Cincinnati OH 45202. **Tel** (513)381-0528. **LC** KF200; .C48. **DD** 340/.06/077178.
Continues CBA Report, 0091-5475.

US
REPORT - COUNCIL ON LEGAL EDUCATION FOR PROFESSIONAL RESPONSIBILITY. Main/Corp Council on Legal Education for Professional Responsibility. Vol. 1-9/68-12/70-. Periodical. English. be. Council on Legal Education for Professional Responsibility, 280 Park Avenue, New York NY 10017.
Ind/Abst LegalTrac (Jan. 1980-Dec. 1980).

US
REPORT / DISTRICT OF COLUMBIA. PUBLIC DEFENDER SERVICE. BOARD OF TRUSTEES. Main/Corp District of Columbia. Public Defender Service. Board of Trustees. No. 1 (1970/1971)-. English. an. Free. Public Defender Service, 451 Indiana Avenue NW, Washington DC 20001. **Tel** (202)628-1200. **Continues** Report / District of Columbia. Legal Aid Agency.

US/0742-5317
REPORT - FEDERAL BAR ASSOCIATION. SECTION OF TAXATION. (REPORT / SECTION OF TAXATION.). [Rep. - Fed. Bar Assoc., Sect. Tax.]. Winter 1984-. Periodical. English. qt. $23.00 US; $25.00 other. Federal Bar Association, 1815 H Street Northwest, Suite 408, Washington DC 20006. **Tel** (202)638-0252, FAX (202)775-0295. **ED** Lynn P Weidberg. **LC** KF6272; .R45. **DD** 343.7304/05; 347.303405. **Bk Rev. Ad Acc. Circ:**

Law

15,500. *Continues* Council on Taxation Report.
Desc: Each issue focuses on a given topic or concern to those who practice or who have interest in federal law and adjudication.

US/0731-1168
REPORT FOR ... / UNITED STATES ATTORNEY, NORTHERN DISTRICT OF ILLINOIS. **Main/Corp** United States. Attorney (Illinois : Northern District). English. an. US Department of Justice / Chicago, Office of the US Attorney, Northern District of Illinois, Chicago IL 60604. **LC** KF8700; .A837. **DD** 353.008/8.

II
REPORT - KERALA, INDIA (STATE). LEGISLATIVE ASSEMBLY. BUSINESS ADVISORY COMMITTEE. **Main/Corp** Kerala, India (State). Legislative Assembly. Business Advisory Committee. English. India Legislative Assembly, Kerala Business Advisory Committee, Trivandrum India. **DD** 348/.5483/01.

US
REPORT OF AMERICAN BAR FOUNDATION, THE. **Main/Corp** American Bar Foundation. (1988)-. English. ir. American Bar Association, 750 North Lake Shore Drive, Chicago IL 60611. **Tel** (312)988-5522, (312)988-5241, FAX (312)988-5528, telex 270593. *Continues* American Bar Foundation. Annual Report, 0569-3438.

US/0094-7148
REPORT OF CASES DETERMINED IN THE SUPREME COURT AND COURT OF APPEALS OF THE STATE OF NEW MEXICO. **Main/Corp** New Mexico. Supreme Court. **VFOAT** New Mexico Reports. V. 78- 1967/68-. English. West Publishing Company, 610 Opperman Drive, PO Box 64526, Eagan MN 55123-1308. **Tel** (612)687-5618, (800)328-9352, FAX (612)687-5388, (800)562-2329. **(Subscription telephone:** FAX (612)688-3570) **LC** KFN3645; .A2. **DD** 348/.789/043. *Continues* Report of Cases Determined in the Supreme Court of the State of New Mexico.

US
REPORT OF FINDINGS AND RECOMMENDATIONS / STATUTORY REVISION COMMITTEE (COLORADO). **Main/Corp** Colorado. General Assembly. Statutory Revision Committee. Began with 1978 V. English. an. **LC** KFC1827.S73; A328. **DD** 340/.3/09786. available on microfiche (from Colorado State Depositories).

II
REPORT OF THE COMMITTEE ON RULES. **Main/Corp** West Bengal. Legislature. Legislative Assembly. Committee on Rules. (Mar. 1974)-. English. **DD** 328.54/14/05.

UK
REPORT OF THE COMMONWEALTH MAGISTRATES' CONFERENCE. **Main/Conf** Commonwealth Magistrates' Conference. **Added/Corp** Commonwealth Magistrates' Association. (19??)-. English. Commonwealth Magistrates Association, 28 Fitzroy Square, London W1P 6DD England. **Tel** 01-387-4889, telex 937400 ONECOM-G. **DD** 347.01. **Circ:** 500.

UK
REPORT OF THE COUNCIL AND ABSTRACT OF THE ACCOUNTS / SELDEN SOCIETY. **Main/Corp** Selden Society. English. an. Selden Society, Faculty of Law, Queen Mary College, Mile End Road, London E1 4NS England. **Tel** 011 44 71 9755136, FAX 011 44 71 9818733, telex 893750. **ED** V. Tunkel. **Circ:** 1,700 (ctrl). *Continues* Report of the Council / Selden Society.

US
REPORT OF THE PROCEEDINGS OF THE ANNUAL MEETING OF THE ... MISSOURI BAR ASSOCIATION. Title Change. **Main/Corp** Missouri Bar Association. Vol. 1 (1881)-. Proceedings. English. *Continued by* Missouri Bar Journal.

US
REPORT OF THE SELECT COMMITTEE ON INSURANCE RATES, REGULATION AND RECODIFICATION OF THE INSURANCE LAW. **Main/Corp** New York (State). Legislature. Select Committee on Insurance Rates, Regulation and Recodification of the Insurance Law. 1974-. English. New York Legislature, Albany NY 12236. **LC** KFN5010.6; .I587. **DD** 346/.747/086. *Continues* Report of the Joint Legislative Committee on Insurance Rates, Regulation and Recodification of the Insurance Law.

IT
REPORT OF THE SESSION OF THE JOINT ECE/CODEX ALIMENTARIUS GROUP OF EXPERTS ON STANDARDIZATION OF QUICK FROZEN FOODS. **Main/Corp** Joint ECE/Codex Alimentarius Group of Experts on Standardization of Quick Frozen Foods. **VAT** Report of the Session of the Joint Economic Commission For Europe/Codex Alimentarius Group of Experts on Standardization of Quick Frozen Foods. English. Joint ECE/Codex Alimentarius Group of Experts on Standardization of Quick Frozen Foods, Via Delle Terme di Caracalla, Rome 00100 Italy. **LC** TP372.3; .J63A. **DD** 341.7/547/56640285.

CN
REPORT OF THE STANDING JOINT COMMITTEE OF THE SENATE AND OF THE HOUSE OF COMMONS ON REGULATIONS AND OTHER STATUTORY INSTRUMENTS. **Main/Corp** Canada. Parliament. Standing Joint Committee on Regulations and Other Statutory Instruments. **Added/Corp** Canada. Parliament. Standing Joint Committee on Regulations and other Statutory Instruments. Rapport du Comite Mixte Permanent du Senat et de la Chambre des Communes des Reglements et Autres Textes Reglementaires. **VFOAT** Rapport du Comite Mixte Permanent du Senat et de la Chambre des Communes des Reglements et Autres Textes Reglementaires. 2d Session, 30th Parliament (1976/1977)-. Periodical. English (French). Canada Communication Group Publishers, Ottawa Ontario K1A 0S9 Canada. **Tel** (819)956-4800, (819)956-4802. **LC** KE5024.A2; R43. **DD** 348/.71/01. *Continues in part* Canada. Parliament. Standing Joint Committee on Regulations and Other Statutory Instruments. Minutes of Proceedings and Evidence of the Standing Joint Committee on Regulations and Other Statutory Instruments, 0317-6770.

US/0363-0692
REPORT ON ADMINISTRATIVE ADJUDICATION OF TRAFFIC INFRACTIONS. (REPORT ON ADMINISTRATIVE ADJUDICATION OF TRAFFIC INFRACTIONS : HIGHWAY SAFETY ACT OF 1973 (SECTION 222).). Began with 1975. English. an. US Department of Transportation / National Highway Traffic Safety Administration, 400 7th Street SW, Washington DC 20590. **LC** KF2232; .A878. **DD** 343/.73/09460269.

US
REPORT ON APPLICATIONS FOR ORDERS AUTHORIZING OR APPROVING THE INTERCEPTION OF WIRE, ORAL, OR ELECTRONIC COMMUNICATIONS (WIRETAP REPORT) FOR THE PERIOD ... . **VFOAT** Wiretap Report. English. an. Statistical Analysis and Reports Division, Administrative Office of the United States Courts, Washington DC 20544. *Continues* Report on Applications for Orders Authorizing or Approving the Interception of Wire or Oral Communications for the Period.

BE
REPORT ON COMPETITION POLICY. **Main/Corp** Commission of the European Communities. (19??)-. English. an. $45.00. Her Majesty's Stationery Office, 51 Nine Elms Lane, London SW8 5DR England. **Tel** 011 44 71 873 8459, 011 44 71 873 8499, FAX 011 44 71 873 8499, 011 44 71 873 8456, telex 297138. **(Subscription address:** US: UNIPUB, 4611 F Assembly Drive, Lanham, MD 20706) **LC** HF1532.92; .C6a. **DD** 341.7/54.
Desc: Gives a general view of the anti-trust policy followed during the past year. Includes general competition policy, policy toward enterprises, state aids, and the development on concentration, competition, and competitiveness.

US/0270-4331
REPORT ON KANSAS LEGISLATIVE INTERIM STUDIES TO THE LEGISLATURE. **Main/Corp** Kansas. Legislature. Legislative Coordinating Council. English. Legislative Research Department, Statehouse/Room 545-N, Topeka KS 66612. **LC** KFK20; .L437. **DD** 347.81081.

US
REPORT, SURVEY OF METROPOLITAN JUVENILE COURTS / NATIONAL CENTER FOR STATE COURTS. **Main/Corp** National Center for State Courts. **Added/Corp** National Center for State Courts. Survey of Metropolitan Juvenile Courts. Vol. 1, No. 1 (Apr. 1980)-. English. National Center for State Courts, 300 Newport Avenue, PO Box 8798, Williamsburg VA 23185. **Tel** (804)253-2000, FAX (804)220-0449. **LC** KF9787; .N34. **DD** 345.73/081/05; 347.3058105.

US/0889-5090
REPORTER (O'FALLON, ILL.), THE. (THE REPORTER.). (19??)-. English. wk (52 issues). $27.50. The Reporter / O'Fallon, 612 East State Street, O'Fallon IL 62269. **Tel** (618)632-3643. **LC** K18; .E7. **DD** 349.773/86/05; 347.7386005.

US/8756-2057
REPORTER ON HUMAN REPRODUCTION AND THE LAW. [Report. hum. reprod. law]. (19??)-. English. Three times a year. $75.00. Legal Medical Studies, Box 8219 John F. Kennedy Station, Boston MA 02114. **Tel** (617)723-9040. **ED** Patricia Patterson-Kindregan. **DD** 344. Index available. cum. index. **Bk Rev**, (Qty: 6). **Circ:** 300.
Desc: Provides information on such subjects as abortion, artificial insemination, contraception, surrogate motherhood, medical malpractice and product liability issues affecting human reproduction.

US/8755-7509
REPORTER ON THE LEGAL PROFESSION. [Report. leg. prof.]. **Added/Corp** Legal-Medical Studies, Inc. (1979)-. English. Four times a year. $120.00. Legal Medical Studies, Box 8219 John F. Kennedy Station, Boston MA 02114. **Tel** (617)723-9040. **ED** C. Kindregan. **LC** KF300.A1; R46. **DD** 347.73/0504/05; 347.30750405. Index available. cum. index. **Bk Rev**, (Qty: 10). **Circ:** 500.
Desc: A major resource for information on the practice of law. Provides a regular, cumulative and comprehensive reference to reported cases involving lawyer discipline, admission to the bar, fee issues, legal malpractice and related matters.

US/0484-4610
REPORTER (PATERSON), THE. (THE REPORTER.). Periodical. English. mo. **LC** KF200; .R43. **DD** 340/.09749.
Ind/Abst LegalTrac (1980-).

IT
REPORTORIO GENERALE ANNUALE GIURISPRUDENZA ITALIANA. Utet Ed Giuridica, Via Corte d'Appello 6, 10122 Turin Italy. **Tel** 011 39 11 530406.

US
REPORTS OF CASES ARGUED AND DETERMINED IN THE COURTS OF APPEALS OF OHIO. **Added/Corp** West Publishing Company. **VFOAT** Ohio Appellate Reports 3D; Ohio Official Reports. Ohio Appellate Reports 3D. 3rd Ser.Vol. 61 (1991)-. English. West Publishing Company, 610 Opperman Drive, PO Box 64526, Eagan MN 55123-1308. **Tel** (612)687-5618, (800)328-9352, FAX (612)687-5388, (800)562-2329. **LC** KFO48; .A2. **DD** 348.771/047. *Continues in part* Ohio Official Reports (Cincinnati, Ohio).

US
REPORTS OF CASES ARGUED AND DETERMINED IN THE SUPERIOR COURT, APPELLATE DIVISION, CHANCERY DIVISION, LAW DIVISION, AND IN THE COUNTY COURTS OF THE STATE OF NEW JERSEY. **Main/Corp** New Jersey. Superior Court. V. 1- 1948-. English. West Publishing Company, 610 Opperman Drive, PO Box 64526, Eagan MN 55123-1308. **Tel** (612)687-5618, (800)328-9352, FAX (612)687-5388, (800)562-2329. **(Subscription telephone:** FAX (612)688-3570) **DD** 345.42.

US
REPORTS OF CASES ARGUED AND DETERMINED IN THE SUPREME COURT OF OHIO. **Main/Corp** Ohio. Supreme Court. **Added/Corp** West Publishing Company. **VFOAT** Ohio State Reports 3D; Ohio Official Reports. Ohio State Reports 3D. 3rd Vol. 61 (June-Sept. 1991)-. English. West Publishing Company, 610 Opperman Drive, PO Box 64526, Eagan MN 55123-1308. **Tel** (612)687-5618, (800)328-9352, FAX (612)687-5388, (800)562-2329. **LC** KFO45; .A2. **DD** 348.771/048; 347.710848. *Continues in part* Ohio Official Reports (Cincinnati, Ohio).

US/0731-2954
REPORTS OF CASES ARGUED AND DETERMINED IN THE TAX COURT OF NEW JERSEY. [Rep. cases arg. determ. Tax Court N. J.]. **VFOAT** New Jersey Tax Court Reports. Vol. 1-. English. ir. West Publishing Company, 610 Opperman Drive, PO Box 64526, Eagan MN 55123-1308. **Tel** (612)687-5618, (800)328-9352, FAX (612)687-5388, (800)562-2329. **(Subscription telephone:** FAX (612)688-3570) **LC** KFN2270; .A517. **DD** 343.74904/02642; 347. 4903402642.

LU/0378-7591
REPORTS OF CASES BEFORE THE COURT OF JUSTICE AND THE COURT OF FIRST INSTANCE. **Added/Corp** Court of Justice of the European Communities. Court of First

Instance of the European Communities. **VFOAT** Reports. (1990)-. English. ir. Price varies per volume. Office for Official Publications of the European Communities, 2 Rue Mercier, 2985 Luxembourg Luxembourg. **Tel** 011 352 499281, FAX 011 352 488573. **LC** KJE924.5; .R472. ***Continues*** *Court of Justice of the European Communities. Reports of Cases before the Court, 0378-7591.*
Desc: Cases heard before the Court of Justice and the Court of First Instance, comprising the report for the hearing, the conclusion of the Advocate General and the text of the judgment.

US/0276-9581
REPORTS OF CASES DECIDED IN THE APPELLATE DIVISION OF THE SUPREME COURT, STATE OF NEW YORK. **Main/Corp** New York (State). Supreme Court. Appellate Division. **VFOAT** Appellate Division Reports, Supreme Court, New York. V. 1-286, 1896-1955; 2nd Series, V. 1- 1956-. English. ir (five-six issues per year). $119.00-142.00. The Lawyers Co-Operative Publishing Company, Aqueduct Building, Rochester NY 14694. **Tel** (800)527-4030. **LC** KFN5048; .A22. **DD** 345.42; 345.412. Index available in last issue of volume--attached. available on microfiche.
Desc: Only official set of reports in the state of New York for the appellate division.

US/0279-9413
REPORTS OF MASSACHUSETTS APPELLATE DIVISION (MONTHLY). (REPORTS OF MASSACHUSETTS APPELLATE DIVISION.). [Rep. Mass. Appell. Div.]. **Added/Corp** Massachusetts. Municipal Court (Boston) Massachusetts. District Court. Appellate Division. (1980)-. Periodical. English. an. $50.00. Lawyers Weekly Publications, 41 West Street, Boston MA 02111. **Tel** (617)451-7300, (800)444-5297. **ED** Paul E. Lamoureux. ***Continues*** *Official Opinions from the Supreme Judicial Court of Massachusetts and the Appeals Court* ***and*** *Official Opinions from the Appellate Divisions of the District Court Department and the Boston Municipal Court.*

●US
REPORTS OF MISCELLANEOUS CASES ARGUED AND DETERMINED IN THE COURTS OF OHIO: OTHER THAN THE SUPREME COURT AND THE COURTS OF APPEALS OF OHIO. **Added/Corp** West Publishing Company. **VFOAT** Ohio Miscellaneous 2d; Ohio Official Reports. Ohio Miscellaneous 2d. 2nd ser., Vol. 61 (1992)-. English. West Publishing Company, 610 Opperman Drive, PO Box 64526, Eagan MN 55123-1308. **Tel** (612)687-5618, (800)328-9352, FAX (612)687-5388, (800)562-2329. ***Continues in part*** *Ohio Official Reports (Cincinnati, Ohio).*

UK
REPORTS OF PATENT, DESIGN AND TRADE MARK CASES (LONDON, ENGLAND : 1964). (REPORTS OF PATENT, DESIGN AND TRADE MARK CASES.). **Added/Corp** Great Britain. Patent Office. Great Britain. Patent Office. Illustrated Official Journal (Patents). **VFOAT** Reports of Patent, Design, Trade Mark and Other Cases. (1964)-. English. ir. £158.50. Patent Office / United Kingdom, Unit 6 / Nine Mile Point, Cwmfelinfach Cross Keys, Newport Gwent NP1 7HZ S Wales England. **Tel** 011 44 633 246161. **LC** KD1365.A2; G7. ***Continues*** *Reports of Patent, Design, Trade Mark, and Other Cases.*

US/8755-6294
REPORTS OF THE UNITED STATES TAX COURT. (REPORTS OF THE UNITED STATES TAX COURT / ELLA C. THOMAS, REPORTER.). [Rep. U. S. Tax Court]. **Main/Corp** United States. Tax Court. **VFOAT** United States Tax Court Reports. Vol. 54 (Jan. 1, 1970 to Sept. 30, 1970)-. Periodical. English. ir. Claitors Law Books, 3165 South Acadian, Baton Rouge LA 70808. **Tel** (504)344-0476, (800)274-1403. **(Subscription address:** Claitors Law Books and Publ. Division, PO Box 261333, Baton Rouge LA 70826.**)** **ED** R.G. Claitor. **LC** KF6280.A2; T37. **DD** 343.7304/02642; 347.303402642. ***Continues*** *Reports of the Tax Court of the United States ..., 8755-6111.*
Desc: Official court decisions of the Tax Court of the US.

US
REPORTS ON PUBLIC BILLS (BOUND) (HOUSE AND SENATE). **Main/Corp** United States. Congress. (1789)-. Government Publication. English. ir. $2,069.00 (per session of congress) US; $2,586.25 (per session of congress) other. Superintendent of Documents, US Government Printing Office, Washington DC 20402. **Tel** (202)275-3328, FAX (202)786-2377.

US/0040-0017
REPORTS - UNITED STATES. TAX COURT. (REPORTS / UNITED STATES TAX COURT.). [Rep. - U. S., Tax Court]. **Main/Corp** United States. Tax Court. Vol. 1, No. 1 (Oct. 22, 1942)-. Government Publication. English. mo. $29.00; US; $36.25 other. Superintendent of Documents, US Government Printing Office, Washington DC 20402. **Tel** (202)275-3328, FAX (202)786-2377. **LC** HJ10; .H263118. **DD** 343.7304/02642; 347.303402642.
Desc: A consolidation of decisions for a month.

US/0276-7627
REPRESENTING PROFESSIONAL ATHLETES AND TEAMS. **Added/Corp** Practising Law Institute. (19??)-. English. an. Practising Law Institute, 810 Seventh Avenue, New York NY 10019-5818. **Tel** (212)765-5700, FAX (212)581-4670 general correspondence, (212)265-4742 orders and billing inquiries. **LC** KF3989.Z9; R39. **DD** 344.73/099; 347.30499.

AT
REPRINTED ACTS OF THE PARLIAMENT OF WESTERN AUSTRALIA. **Main/Corp** Western Australia. Laws, Statutes, etc. (1939)-. English. ir. 300.00Aus$ Australia; 240.00Aus$ other. NSW Government Printing Office, PO Box 256, Regents Park2143 Australia. **Tel** 011 61 02 7438777, FAX 062 954455.

BB
REPUBLIC OF TRINIDAD AND TOBAGO CONSOLIDATED INDEX OF PUBLIC ACTS & SUBSIDIARY LEGISLATION TO ... / COMPILED AT THE FACULTY OF LAW LIBRARY, UNIVERSITY OF THE WEST INDIES, BARBADOS. **Added/Corp** University of the West Indies (Cave Hill, Barbados). Faculty of Law. Library. Great Britain. British Development Division in the Caribbean. **VFOAT** Consolidated Index of Public Acts & Subsidiary Legislation To ... . (Jan. 1991)-. English. William W. Gaunt and Sons Inc, 3011 Gulf Drive, Gaunt Building, Holmes Beach FL 34217. **Tel** (800)942-8683, (813)778-5211. **LC** KGX10.5; .R47. **DD** 348.72983/028/05; 347.2983082805. ***Continues*** *Republic of Trinidad and Tobago Consolidated Index of Statutes and Subsidiary Legislation to ... .*

US/0557-9295
RES GESTAE (INDIANAPOLIS, IND.). (RES GESTAE.). **Added/Corp** Indiana State Bar Association (1916-). (1956)-. Periodical. English. ir. Yale Book Company Ltd, 34 Butternut Street, Toronto, 6 Ontario Canada. **LC** KF332.I5; I537. **DD** 340/.062/772.
Ind/Abst Curr. Law Index (1980-); Fed. Tax Artic.; Index Leg. Period.; Law Office Inf. Serv.; Leg. Resour. Index (1980-); LegalTrac (1980-).

SA
RES PUBLICA. No. 1- Feb. 1975-. Afrikaans (Afrikaans). Departement Staatsreg dn Regsfilosofie, Universiteit Van Die Ovx, Postbus 339, Bloemfontein South Africa. **LC** K18; .E83.
Ind/Abst Int. Polit. Sci. Abstr.

US
RESEARCH CONTRIBUTIONS OF THE AMERICAN BAR FOUNDATION. (19??)-. English. ir. Free on request. American Bar Association, 750 North Lake Shore Drive, Chicago IL 60611. **Tel** (312)988-5522, (312)988-5241, FAX (312)988-5528, telex 270593. **ED** Bette Sikes. **Bk Rev. Circ:** 500 (ctrl).
Desc: Reprints of articles published in professional journals written by American Bar Foundation staff members or affiliated scholars.
Ind/Abst Law Office Inf. Serv.

US/0193-5895
RESEARCH IN LAW AND ECONOMICS. [Res. law econ.]. Vol. 1 (1979)-. Monographic series. English. ir. $73.25. JAI Press Inc., 55 Old Post Road, Suite 2, PO Box 1678, Greenwich CT 06836-1678. **Tel** (203)661-7602, FAX (203)661-0792. **ED** Richard O. Zerbe Jr. **LC** K18; .E835. **DD** 330/.05. **[CCC].**
Ind/Abst Curr. Law Index (1980-); Leg. Resour. Index (1980-); LegalTrac (1980-).

US/0898-0179
RESEARCH IN LAW AND POLICY STUDIES. [Res. law policy stud.]. Vol. 1 (1987)-. English. an. $73.25. JAI Press Inc., 55 Old Post Road, Suite 2, PO Box 1678, Greenwich CT 06836-1678. **Tel** (203)661-7602, FAX (203)661-0792. **ED** Stuart Nagel. **LC** K18; .E836. **DD** 347.73; 347.307.

US/0163-9994
RESEARCH INSTITUTE LAWYERS TAX ALERT, THE. **Main/Corp** Research Institute of America, Inc. **VFOAT** Lawyers Tax Alert. Periodical. English. mo. $48.00. Research Institute of America, 117 East Stevens Avenue, Valhalla NY 10595. **Tel** (800)431-9025. **LC** KF6352; .R47. **DD** 343.7304/05.

US
RESEARCH INSTITUTE MASTER FEDERAL TAX MANUAL WITH FEDERAL TAX COORDINATOR 2D REFERENCES. ***Title Change.*** **Added/Corp** Research Institute of America, inc. **VFOAT** Master Federal Tax Manual; RIA ... Master Federal Tax Manual; Research Institute Master Federal Tax Manual. (1982)-(1992). English. Research Institute of America, 117 East Stevens Avenue, Valhalla NY 10595. **Tel** (800)431-9025. **LC** KF6272; .M37. **DD** 343.7304; 347.3034. ***Continues*** *Master Federal Tax Manual, 0734-7103.* ***Merged with*** *Federal Tax Handbook, 0749-212X* ***to form*** *RIA Federal Tax Handbook.*

US/0413-768X
RESEARCH PUBLICATION (COLORADO. GENERAL ASSEMBLY. LEGISLATIVE COUNCIL). (RESEARCH PUBLICATION - COLORADO. GENERAL ASSEMBLY. LEGISLATIVE COUNCIL.). Began publication in 1951. Periodical. English. ir. Colorado General Assembly, 30 State Capital Building, Denver CO 80203. **LC** KFC1820; .L4.

IT
RESOCONTI DELLE GIUNTE E DELLE COMMISSIONI. TIPO II. Italian. tw. L220.00. Libreria del Senato Repubblica, Via del Teatro Valle 37, 00186 Rome Italy. **Tel** 011 39 67062505.
Desc: Summary of discussions in the italian senate committees.

SA/0486-5588
RESPONSA MERIDIANA. **Added/Corp** University of Cape Town. Student Law Society. University of Stellenbosch. Student Law Society. (Aug. 1964)-. Periodical. English (Afrikaans). an (Sept.). $12.00. Responsa Meridiana, University of Stellenbosch, Faculty of Law, Stellenbosch F600 South Africa. **Tel** 011 2721 698531. **ED** K. Idensohn. **LC** K18; .E88. **DD** 340/.0968. **Ad Acc. Pr Rev. Circ:** 600 (ctrl).
Desc: Essays on legal topics, written by law students.
Ind/Abst Index Foreign Leg. Per.

IT
RESPONSABILITA CIVILE E PREVIDENZA. (19??)-. Periodical. Italian. bm. L120000.00 Italy; L180000.00 other. Giuffre Editore SPA, Via Busto Arsizio 40, 20151 Milan Italy. **Tel** 011 398 2 38089200. **ED** Gianguido Scalfi. **Bk Rev. Ad Acc. Circ:** 5,500.
Desc: Publishes a well-coordinated and complete collection of juridical views concerning civil liability, state insurance and other forms of insurance.

US/0484-5765
RESTATEMENT, THE. **Added/Corp** Cincinnati. University. School of Law. (1958)-. Periodical. English. University of Cincinnati / College of Law, Room 300, Cincinnati OH 45221. **Tel** (513)556-5101.

US
RESTATEMENT OF THE LAW SECOND: TRUSTS / SUBMITTED TO THE MEMBERS BY THE COUNCIL. **Main/Corp** American Law Institute. Tentative Draft No. 2 (Apr. 1, 1955)-. English. ir. American Law Institute, 4025 Chestnut Street, Philadelphia PA 19104-3099. **Tel** (215)243-1661, (800)253-6397, FAX (215)243-1664. ***Continues*** *American Law Institute. Restatement of the Law Continued: Agency, Conflict of Laws, Trusts.*

CN/0225-2651
RESUMES DES DECISIONS RECENTES RENDUES PAR LA COMMISSION D'APPEL DE L'IMMIGRATION. **See** Emigration and Immigration.

US/0735-8520
RETAIL SECURITY DIGEST. Vol. 1, No. 1 (Jan. 1981)-. English. Law Offices of Robert L Barry, 3937th Avenue/Suite 2220, New York NY 10001. **LC** KF2005.A15; R48. **DD** 345.73/0268; 347.305268.

US/0145-3491
RETAINER, THE. ***Title Change.*** **Added/Corp** Philadelphia Bar Association. Vol. 1, No. 5 (Feb. 1, 1972)-(1992). Periodical. English. Twenty-six times a year. Philadelphia Bar Association, 1101 Market Street, 1 Reading Center, Philadelphia PA 19107. **Tel** (215)238-6300, FAX (215)238-1267. **LC** KF200; .R45. **DD** 340/.09748. ***Continues*** *New Philadelphia Lawyer.* ***Continued by*** *Philladelphia Bar Reporter.*
Ind/Abst Law Office Inf. Serv.

DK/0105-1121
RETFRD ARHUS. (RETFAERD.). [Retfrd Arhus]. (1976)-. Periodical. Danish. qt. Kr415.00, $71.00. Scandinavian University Press, PO Box 2959 Toeyen, N 0608 Oslo 6 Norway. **Tel** 011 47 2 2575400, FAX 011 47 2 2575353, telex 71896 UROR N. **(Subscription address:** Scandinavian University Press, 200 Meacham Ave., Elmont NY 11003.**)** **ED** Mette Hartlev, Poul Carstensen, Anders von Koskull, Pia Letto-Vanamo, Hans-Peter Graver, Ulf Stridbeck, and Hakan Gustafsson. **DD** 340.
Desc: Covers law and justice, seeing law in the perspective of politics, economics, ecology and culture.

NO
RETTENS GANG. **Main/Corp** Norske Advokatforening. Norwegian. Norske Advokatforening, Kirkegaten 26 1, Oslo Norway.

UK/0963-1046
REVENUE LONDON. (1991)-. English. Ten times a year. £95.00 Europe; £100.00 other. Sweet & Maxwell Ltd., South Quay Plaza, 183 Marsh Wall, London E14 9FT England. **Tel** 011 44 264 342899, FAX 011 44 264 342723, telex 929089 ITPINF G.

US/1051-1741
REVIEW OF BANKING & FINANCIAL SERVICES, THE. [Rev. bank. fin. serv.]. **Added/Corp** Standard and Poor's Corporation. **VFOAT** Review of Banking and Financial Services; Banking & Financial Services; Banking and Financial Services. Vol. 5, No. 1 (Jan. 4, 1989)-. Periodical. English. Twenty-two times a year (twice monthly except monthly issues in July and August). $525.00. Standard & Poor's Corporation, 25 Broadway, New York NY 10004. **Tel** (212)208-8775. **DD** 346. ***Continues*** *Review of Financial Services Regulation, 0897-1196.*

PL/0860-8156
REVIEW OF COMPARATIVE LAW, THE. [Rev. comp. law]. **Added/Corp** Katolicki Uniwersytet Lubelski. Vol. 1 (1988)-. Periodical. English (German). ir. $6.00. Katolickiego Uniwersytetu Lubelskiego, Towrzystwo Naukowe Kul, Ul Chopina 29, Lublin Poland. **(Subscription address:** ARS Polona, PO Box 1001, 00068 Warsaw Poland.**) LC** K18; .E94. **DD** 340/.2/05; 342.005.

GH/0034-6578
REVIEW OF GHANA LAW. [Rev. Ghana law]. **Added/Corp** Council for Law Reporting. Vol. 1 (May 1969)-. Periodical. English. Three times a year. $15.00. Council for Law Reporting, PO Box M 165, Accra Ghana. **(Subscription address:** Steven Withan Enterprises, 33 Haddo House, Haddo Street, London SE 10 England.**) LC** K18; .E95. **DD** 340/.05.
Ind/Abst Index Foreign Leg. Per.

US/0163-8831
REVIEW OF LEGAL EDUCATION IN THE UNITED STATES, A. (A REVIEW OF LEGAL EDUCATION IN THE UNITED STATES; LAW SCHOOLS AND BAR ADMISSION REQUIREMENTS.). [Rev. leg. educ. U. S.]. **Main/Corp** American Bar Association. Section of Legal Education and Admissions to the Bar. (1977)-. English. an. $192.95 (latest edition). American Bar Association, 750 North Lake Shore Drive, Chicago IL 60611. **Tel** (312)988-5522, (312)988-5241, FAX (312)988-5528, telex 270593. **LC** KF265; .A53. **DD** 340/.07/1173. ***Continues*** *Law Schools and Bar Admission Requirements in the United States, 1046-3178.*

US/0734-4015
REVIEW OF LITIGATION, THE. [Rev. litig.]. Vol. 1, No. 1 (Winter 1980)-. Periodical. English. Three times a year. $20.00 US; $23.00 other. Review of Litigation, University of Texas, Law School, 727 East 26th Street, Austin TX 78705. **Tel** (512)471-1106. **ED** David Klingler (editor's telephone: (512)471-4386). **LC** K18; .E96. **DD** 347.73/05; 347.30705. **Bk Rev. Ad Acc. Circ:** 900. available on microfilm from University Microfilms International (UMI).
Desc: A national law journal reviewing issues of interest to the practising litigator.
Ind/Abst Curr. Law Index (1981-); Index Leg. Period.; Leg. Resour. Index (1981-); LegalTrac (1980-).

US/0884-2426
REVIEW OF SECURITIES & COMMODITIES REGULATION, THE. [Rev. secur. & commod. regul.]. **Added/Corp** Standard and Poor's Corporation. **VFOAT** Review of Securities and Commodities Regulation; Securities & Commodities Regulation. Vol. 18, No. 1 (Jan. 9, 1985)-. Periodical. English. Twenty-two times a year (semi-monthly except one issue published in Jul. and Aug.). $590.00. Standard & Poor's Corporation, 25 Broadway, New York NY 10004. **Tel** (212)208-8775. **LC** KF1432; .R48. **DD** 346.73/092/05; 347.3069205. ***Continues*** *Review of Securities Regulation, 0034-6756.*
Desc: Devoted to continuous discussion and analysis of regulations governing the purchase and sale of securities and commodities. Each issue focuses on one or two aspects of law and regulation, and makes sense of regulations and court decisions in terms of everyday practice.
Ind/Abst Curr. Law Index (1980-); Leg. Resour. Index (1980-); LegalTrac (1985-).

AT
REVIEW / REMUNERATION TRIBUNAL. **Main/Corp** Australia. Remuneration Tribunal. (19??)-. Government Publication. English. an. Australian Government Publishing Service, GPO Box 84, Canberra ACT 2601 Australia. **Tel** 011 61 6 2954411, FAX 011 61 6 2954455. **DD** 342.94/0686/0264; 349.4026860264.

SP/0213-1137
REVISATA DE DERECHO PROCESAL. **Added/Corp** Editoriales de Derecho Reunidas. No. 1 (1985)-. Periodical. Spanish. Three times a year. 8100ptas Spain; 8500ptas others. Edersa Editoriales de Derecho, Reunidas SA Valverde 32 1, 28004 Madrid Spain. **Tel** 011 34 1 5210246, 011 34 1 5229849.

US
REVISED CODE OF AMERICAN SAMOA. CUMULATIVE SUPPLEMENT. **Main/Corp** American Samoa. Laws, Statues, etc. English. ir. Equity Publishing Corporation, RR 1 Box 3, Orford NH 03777. **Tel** (603)637-5012, (800)637-5012.

US
REVISED STATUTES OF NEBRASKA, 1943. **Main/Corp** Nebraska. Vol. 1 (1944)-. Monographic series. English. ir. Nebraska Supreme Court Publishing, 1207 State Capitol, Lincoln NE 68509. **Tel** (402)471-4436. Index available.

BL
REVISTA BRASILEIRA DE DIREITO PROCESSUAL. V. 1- 1st Quarter 1975-. Portuguese. Editora Vitoria Artes Graficas Universitaria de Direito, rua Benjamin Constant, 117-10 Andar Salas 1A 5 01005, Sao Paulo Brazil. **LC** K19; .B73. **DD** 347/.81/005.

CL
REVISTA CHILENA DE DERECHO. **Added/Corp** Universidad Catolica de Chile. Escuela de Derecho. (1974)-. Spanish. Three times a year. $60.00. Universidad Catolica de Chile Facultad de Derecho, Casilla 114D, Santiago Chile. **Tel** 011 56 2 744041, FAX 011 56 2 2232779. **LC** K19; .C48. **DD** 340/.0983. Index available. **Bk Rev. Pr Rev. Circ:** 700.
Desc: First hand theoretical and empirical legal studies on Chilean and comparative judicial systems, with judicial and administrative decisions, reports of legal experts and transportation of statutes.

CL/0716-5447
REVISTA CHILENA DE HISTORIA DEL DERECHO. [Rev. chil. hist. derecho]. Began in 1959?. Periodical. Spanish. ir. $25.00 per volume. Editorial Juridica de Chile / Santiago, Casilla Postal 4256, Santiago Chile. **Tel** 011 56 2 2049900. **Circ:** 500.
Ind/Abst Am. Hist. Life (1959-).

CU
REVISTA CUBANA DE DERECHO. ***Ceased.*** **Added/Corp** Instituto Cubano del Libro. (19??)-(1992). Periodical. Spanish (summaries and/or abstracts in English, French and Russian). qt. Ediciones Cubanas, Obispo 527, Altos ESQ Bernaza, CP 10100 Havana Cuba. **Tel** 011 632980, 631942, FAX 011 631011, telex 512337, 6540. **LC** K19; .C82. Index available. **Bk Rev. Circ:** 20,000 (ctrl).
Desc: A publication dedicated to those who, in one way or another, work in the field of the juridical sciences. It also helps to publicize the most important laws decreed by the Cuban government and state.
Ind/Abst Index Foreign Leg. Per.

BL
REVISTA DA ASSOCIACAO DOS MAGISTRADOS, PARANA. **Main/Corp** Associacao dos Magistrados do Parana. Portuguese. Rua Alferes Poli 1658, Curitiba Brazil. **LC** K1; .M67. **DD** 340/.0981.

BL
REVISTA DA FACULDADE DE DIREITO DE PORTO ALEGRE. **Main/Corp** Rio Grande do Sul, Brazil (State). Universidade Federal. Faculdade de Direito. Began in 1949. Portuguese. Universidade Federal do Rio Grande do Sul / Joao Pessoa, Av Joao Pessoa S/N, Porto Alegre 90.000 Brazil. **LC** K19; .D143.

BL
REVISTA DA FACULDADE DE DIREITO DE SAO PAULO. **Added/Corp** Universidade de Sao Paulo. Faculdade de Direito. (1897)-. Portuguese. Universidade de Sao Paulo / Direito, Faculdade de Direito, Sao Paulo Brazil.
Ind/Abst Index Foreign Leg. Per.

BL
REVISTA DA PROCURADORIA GERAL DO ESTADO. **Main/Corp** Ceara (Brazil : State). Procuradoria Geral do Estado. Portuguese. Procuradoria Geral do Estado Centro de Estudos e Treinamento, rua Silva Paulet 324 E 334, Fortaleza Brazil. **DD** 349.81/31/05; 348.131005.

BL
REVISTA DA PROCURADORIA GERAL DO ESTADO DE SAO PAULO. **Main/Corp** Sao Paulo, Brazil (State). Procuradoria Geral. 1- 1971-. Portuguese. sa. Rua Alvaris Mechedo, N 18/7th Floor, CEP 01501, Sao Paulo SP Brazil. **Tel** (011)377999, telex 1122617 BRPGDA BR. **LC** K23; .A66. Index available. cum. index. **Bk Rev. Circ:** 2,000 (ctrl).

BL
REVISTA DA PROCURADORIA GERAL DO ESTADO (MATO GROSSO DO SUL (BRAZIL). PROCURADORIA GERAL DO ESTADO). (REVISTA DA PROCURADORIA GERAL DO ESTADO.). No. 1 (1979)-. Periodical. Portuguese. Avenue Afonso Pena 2968, Mato Grosso do Sul Cep 79.100, Campo Grande Brazil. **LC** K19; .D15. **DD** 349.81/72/05; 348.172005.

CL
REVISTA DE CIENCIAS SOCIALES (UNIVERSIDAD DE VALPARAISO. FACULTAD DE CIENCIAS JURIDICAS, ECONOMICAS Y SOCIALES). (REVISTA DE CIENCIAS SOCIALES : PUBLICACION DE LA FACULTAD DE CIENCIAS JURIDICAS, ECONOMICAS Y SOCIALES.). **Added/Corp** Universidad de Valparaiso. Facultad de Ciencias Juridicas, Economicas y Sociales. No. 17 (Second Semester, 1980)-. Spanish. sa. $15.00 Chile; $62.00 other. Universidad de Valparaiso / Facultad de Derecho, 211 Sr. Salas, Valparaiso Chile. **Tel** 011 56 32 213071. **LC** K19; .D26. **DD** 300/.5. ***Continues*** *Revista de Ciencias Sociales (Universidad de Chile. Sede Valparaiso. Facultad de Ciencias Juridicas, Economicas, y Sociales).*

EC
REVISTA DE DERECHO. Spanish. Corporacion de Estudios y Publicaciones, Apartado de Correos 1287, Quito Ecuador. **LC** K19; .D323.

AG/0327-2265
REVISTA DE DERECHO ADMINISTRATIVO. [Rev. derecho adm.]. Vol. 1, No. 1 (May/Aug. 1989)-. Periodical. Spanish. Three times a year. $90.00. Depalma SRL, Talcahuano 494, 1013 Buenos Aires Argentina. **Tel** 011 54 1 407306, 461815, FAX 011 54 1 406913. **ED** Juan Carlos Cassagne. Index available. cum. index. **Bk Rev.** ctrl circ.
Desc: Covers administrative law, public law and rights, administrative organization, public services, administrative contracts, responsibility of the state, etc.

SP/0214-4042
REVISTA DE DERECHO AMBIENTAL. [Rev. derecho ambient.]. (1988)-. Periodical. Spanish. Twice a year. 5000ptas. Revista de Derecho Ambiental, Apartado 4164, 30080 Murcia Spain. **Tel** 011 34 68 824064. **UDC** 349.6.

SP
REVISTA DE DERECHO FINANCIERO Y DE HACIENDA PUBLICA. **Added/Corp** Spain. Laws, Statutes, etc. Vol. 1 (June 1951)-. Periodical. Spanish. bm. 12100ptas Spain; 13000ptas other. Edersa Editoriales de Derecho, Reunidas SA Valverde 32 1, 28004 Madrid Spain. **Tel** 011 34 1 5210246, 011 34 1 5229849. **LC** K19; .D36.

SP
REVISTA DE DERECHO PRIVADO; PUBLICACION MENSUAL PARA EL ESTUDIO DE LAS CUESTIONES PRACTICAS DEL DERECHO ESPANOL, CIVIL, MERCANTIL, ETC. (Oct 15, 1913)-. Periodical. Spanish. Twelve times a year. 13500ptas Spain; 16000ptas other. Edersa Editoriales de Derecho, Reunidas SA Valverde 32 1, 28004 Madrid Spain. **Tel** 011 34 1 5210246, 011 34 1 5229849. **ED** Felipe Clemente de Diego, J.M. Navarro de Palencia.
Ind/Abst Index Foreign Leg. Per.

CL
REVISTA DE DERECHO PROCESAL. **Added/Corp** Chile. Universidad, Santiago. Departamento de Derecho Procesal. (1971)-. Spanish. ir. Price varies. Editorial Juridica de Chile / Santiago, Casilla Postal 4256, Santiago Chile. **Tel** 011 56 2 2049900. **LC** K19; .D463.

SP
REVISTA DE DERECHO PROCESAL IBEROAMERICANA. Periodical. Spanish. Edersa Editoriales de Derecho, Reunidas SA Valverde 32 1, 28004 Madrid Spain. **Tel** 011 34 1 5210246, 011 34 1 5229849.
Ind/Abst Index Foreign Leg. Per.

●UY
REVISTA DE DERECHO PUBLICO. **Added/Corp** Fundacion de Cultura Universitaria. No. 1 (Mar. 1992)-. Periodical. Spanish. sa. Fundacion de Cultura Universitaria, 25 de Mayo, 568 Casilla 1155, 11000 Montevideo Uruguay. **Tel** 011 598 2 961152.

VE
REVISTA DE DERECHO PUBLICO. (19??)-. Periodical. Spanish. Bs2.800. Editorial Juridica Venezolana, Av. Francisco de Miranda, Edif. Galipan entra C, piso 3, Letra "D", Apartado 17598, Caracas 1015-A Venezuela. **Tel** 951 14 45. **ED** Allan R. Brewer-Carias. **LC** K19; .D528.

PR/0034-7930
REVISTA DE DERECHO PUERTORRIQUENO. [Rev. derecho puertorriq.]. **Added/Corp** Universidad Catolica de Puerto Rico. Escuela de Derecho. No. 1 (Sept. 1961)-. Periodical. Spanish (English). Three times a year. $15.00. Catholic University of Puerto Rico, Revista de Derecho Puertorriqueno, Ponce Puerto Rico 00731. **Tel** (809)841-2000. **DD** 349. Index available. cum. index. **Bk**

Law

Rev. Circ: 700 (ctrl).
Desc: Publishes local, national and international law articles. Also makes jurisprudence, legislative and bibliographic commentaries.
Ind/Abst Curr. Law Index (1980-); Index Leg. Period.; Leg. Resour. Index (1980-); LegalTrac (1980-).

SP
REVISTA DE DERECHO URBANISTICO.
Spanish. ir. 5000ptas. Revista de Derecho Urbanistico, Dr Esquerdo 47, Madrid 28 Spain. **Tel** 011 34 1 5746411.

PE/0034-7949
REVISTA DE DERECHO Y CIENCIAS POLITICAS. [Rev. derecho cienc. polit.].
Added/Corp Universidad Nacional Mayor de San Marcos. Departamento Academico de Derecho y Ciencias Politicas. (1936)-. Periodical. Spanish. tq. **LC** K19; .D49.
Ind/Abst Am. Hist. Life (1966-1970).

PY
REVISTA DE DERECHO Y JURISPRUDENCIA.
Began with No. 1 in Oct. 1970. Spanish. mo. Gs1,800.00. Calle Azara, 180 Casi Independencia Nacional, Oficina 110, Asuncion Paraguay. **DD** 349.892; 348.92.

CL
REVISTA DE DERECHO Y JURISPRUDENCIA Y GACETA DE LOS TRIBUNALES. (1979). *Title Change.* (1979)-?.
Periodical. Spanish. Editorial Juridica de Chile / Santiago, Casilla Postal 4256, Santiago Chile. **Tel** 011 56 2 2049900. **LC** KHF72; .A23. **DD** 348.83/041; 348.30841. *Continues* Revista de Derecho, Jurisprudencia y Ciencias Sociales y Gaceta de Los Tribunales, 0716-0119. *Continued by* Revista de Derecho y Jurisprudencia.
Ind/Abst Index Foreign Leg. Per.

CL
REVISTA DE DERECHO Y JURISPRUDENCIA Y GACETA DE LOS TRIBUNALES (1981).
(1981)-. Spanish. qt. Editorial Juridica de Chile / Santiago, Casilla Postal 4256, Santiago Chile. **Tel** 011 56 2 2049900. *Continues* Revista de Derecho Y Jurisprudencia.

BL
REVISTA DE DIREITO AGRARIO.
Yearly V. 1- 2nd Quarter 1973-. Periodical. Portuguese. Cr$35.00. Incra, Setor Bamcario Sul-Ed Bnde-14 Andar, Brasilia Brazil. **LC** K19; .D573.

BL
REVISTA DE DIREITO DA PROCURADORIA-GERAL DA JUSTICA DO ESTADO DO RIO DE JANEIRO.
Main/Corp Rio de Janeiro (State). Procuradoria-Geral da Justica. Vol. 1 (Mar./July 1975)-. Periodical. Portuguese. Three times a year. Procuradoria-Geral da Justica, Av Nilo Pecanha 12 30 Andar Sala 308 ZC-P, 20 000 Rio de Janeiro Brazil. **LC** K22; .I4.

BL
REVISTA DE DIREITO MUNICIPAL.
Periodical. Portuguese. Revista Juridica, rua dos Andradas 1270, 7O Andar, Porto Alegre Brazil. **LC** K19; .D656. **DD** 342.81/09.

BL/0034-8015
REVISTA DE DIREITO PUBLICO. [Rev. direito publico]. Vol. 1 (July/Sept. 1967)-.
Periodical. Portuguese. Four times a year. Editora Revista dos Tribunais, rua Conde do Pinhal 78, 01501 Sao Paulo SP Brazil. **Tel** 011 55 11 372433. **LC** K19; .D662. **DD** 340. cum. index.

BL/0101-8868
REVISTA DE DOUTRINA E JURISPRUDENCIA / TRIBUNAL DE JUSTICA DO DISTRITO FEDERAL E DOS TERRITORIOS.
Periodical. Portuguese. Three times a year. 50.00. Tribunal de Justica do Distrito Federal e dos Territorios, Palacio da Justica Praca do Buriti Sala 249, Brasilia DF Brazil. **Tel** (061)226-1009. **LC** KHD6706; .A23. **DD** 348.81/041; 348.10841. **Circ:** 3,000 (ctrl).
Desc: Appellate court decisions and sentences by judges of the first degree and judicial studies.

CL/0716-5455
REVISTA DE ESTUDIOS HISTORICO-JURIDICOS. [Rev. estud. hist.-jurid.].
Vol. 1, (1976)-. Spanish. an. $40.00 US. Ediciones Universitarias de Valparaiso, Casilla 1415, Valparaiso Chile. **Tel** 011 56 31 252900. **ED** Alejandro Guzman. **LC** K19; .D723. **Bk Rev. Circ:** 500 (ctrl).
Desc: Academic magazine of essays and studies over history and law from the point of view of researching.
Ind/Abst Am. Hist. Life (1976-).

AG
REVISTA DE HISTORIA DEL DERECHO.
Added/Corp Instituto de Investigaciones de Historia del Derecho. (1973)-. Spanish. an. $25.00. Instituto de Investigaciones de Historia del Derecho, Ave de Mayo 1437 Piso 1RO A, 1085 Buenos Aires Argentina. **Tel** 011 54 1 3815625. **LC** K19; .D726. **DD** 340/.0982. Index available. **Circ:** 700.

BL/0034-835X
REVISTA DE INFORMACAO LEGISLATIVA. [Rev. inf. legis.]. Added/Corp
Brazil. Congresso Nacional. Senado Federal. **VFOAT** A.R. Inf. Legisl. Vol. 1 (March 1964)-. Periodical. Portuguese. qt. Subsecretaria de Edicoes Tecnicas, Senado Federal, Anexo 1, 70160 Brasilia DF Brazil. **CODEN** RINLE7.
Ind/Abst PAIS Int. Print.

MX
REVISTA DE INVESTIGACIONES JURIDICAS.
Yearly Vol. 1, No. 1 (19??)-. Periodical. Spanish. Excuela Libre de Derecho Inst de Investigaciones Juridicas, Dr Vertiz No 12, Mexico 7 D F Mexico. **LC** K19; .D737. **DD** 349.72/05. *Supersedes* Revista Juridica de la Escuela Libre de Derecho.
Ind/Abst Index Foreign Leg. Per.

BL
REVISTA DE JURISPRUDENCIA DO TRIBUNAL DE JUSTICA DE MATO GROSSO DO SUL / RESPONSABILIDADE DE COMISSAO TECNICA PERMANENTE DE BIBLIOTECA E PUBLICACOES. Main/Corp
Mato Grosso do sul (Brazil). Tribunal de Justica. Year 1, No. 1 (1st Quarterly 1979)-. Portuguese. Grafica e Papelaria Brasilia Ltda, rua 14 de Julho No 2536, Campo Grande Brazil. **DD** 348.81/72043; 348.1720843.

BL
REVISTA DE JURISPRUDENCIA DO TRIBUNAL DE JUSTICA DO ESTADO DE SAO PAULO. Main/Corp
Sao Paulo (Brazil : State). Tribunal de Justica. Portuguese. Tribunal de Justica / Sao Paula, Brazil, Praca Clovis Bevilacqua 351 - 60 - Conj 601, Sao Paulo 01018 Brazil.

PE
REVISTA DE JURISPRUDENCIA FISCAL.
VFOAT Jurisprudencia Fiscal. Vol. 75 (July 1975)-. Spanish. sa. S/4,000.00. Editorial de Derecho Tributario, Bolognesi 508 - Barranco, Lima Peru. **DD** 343.8504/05; 348.503405. *Continues* Revista Mensual de Jurisprudencia Fiscal.

UY
REVISTA DE JURISPRUDENCIA Y DOCTRINA.
Vol. 1, No. 1 (19??)-. Periodical. Spanish. qt. Secretaria de Publicaciones del Ministerio de Justicia, Av 18 de Julio 1865, Montevideo Republica Oriental del Uruguay. **LC** K19; .D755. **DD** 349.895/05; 348.95005.

SP
REVISTA DE LA CORTE ESPANOLA DE ARBITRAJE. Added/Corp
Spain. Corte Espanola de Arbitraje. Consejo Superior de las Camaras Oficiales de Comercio, Industria y Navegacion de Espana. Vol. 1 (1984)-. Periodical. Spanish (English, French and Italian). an. Consejo Superior de las Camaras Oficiales de Comercio, Industria y Navegacion de Espana, Claudio Coello 19, 28001 Madrid Spain. **Tel** 011 34 1 5753400. **(Subscription address:** Civitas, C Ignacio Ellacuria 3, 28107 Madrid Spain.**)**

MX
REVISTA DE LA ESCUELA DE DERECHO Y CIENCIAS SOCIALES.
Main/Corp Hermosillo, Mexico. Universidad de Sonora. Escuela de Derecho y Ciencias Sociales. **VFOAT** Revista de la Escuela de Derecho de la Universidad de Sonora. Vol. 1 (July/Dec. 1975)-. Spanish. Universidad de Sonora, Hermosillo Sonora Mexico. **LC** K8; .E7. **DD** 340/.0972.

VE
REVISTA DE LA FACULTAD DE CIENCIAS JURIDICAS Y POLITICAS.
No. 58 (1976)-. Periodical. Spanish. an. B$45.00. Universidad de Central Venezuela, Caracas Venezuela. **LC** K19; .D767. **DD** 349.87/05; 348.7005. *Continues* Revista de la Facultad de Derecho (Caracas, Venezuela).
Ind/Abst Int. Polit. Sci. Abstr.

VE
REVISTA DE LA FACULTAD DE DERECHO. Main/Corp
Caracas. Universidad Santa Maria. Facultad de Derecho. **Added/Corp** Universidad Santa Maria. Facultad de Derecho. No. 1 (Jan.-March 1972)-. Periodical. Spanish. tq. $15.00. Univesity Catolica Andres Bello, Apartado 29068, Caracas 1021 Venezuela. **Tel** 011 58 2 4429511. **LC** K3; .A68.
Ind/Abst LABORDOC.

MX
REVISTA DE LA FACULTAD DE DERECHO. Added/Corp
Universidad Autonoma de San Luis Potosi. Facultad de Derecho. Periodical. Spanish. Escuela de Derecho de la Universidad Autonoma de San Luis Potosi, Av Cuahutemoc y Tomasa Estevez, San Luis Potosi SLP Mexico. **LC** K19; .D766. **DD** 349.72/05; 347.2005. *Continues* Revista de la Escuela de Derecho.

SP
REVISTA DE LA FACULTAD DE DERECHO DE LA UNIVERSIDAD COMPLUTENSE. Added/Corp
Universidad Complutense de Madrid. Facultad de Derecho. (19??)-. Periodical. Spanish. Three times a year. 3500ptas. Universidad Complutense / Facultad de Derecho, 28040 Madrid Spain. **Tel** 011 31 1 3549418. **LC** K25; .N54. **DD** 340/.0946. Index available. cum. index. **Bk Rev. Pr Rev.** ctrl circ. *Continues* Revista de la Facultad de Derecho de Madrid.
Desc: Publishes articles about law written by lawyers and professors, presenting various subjects.

MX/0185-1810
REVISTA DE LA FACULTAD DE DERECHO DE MEXICO. [Rev. Fac. Derecho Mex.]. Main/Corp
Universidad Nacional Autonoma de Mexico. Facultad de Derecho. (1951)-. Periodical. Spanish. Three times a year. $50.00. Tesoreria de la Unam, Ciudad Universitaria, Mexico 20 DF Mexico. **Tel** 011 52 5 5488180. **Bk Rev. Ad Acc. Circ:** 2,000 (ctrl). *Continues* Escuela Nacional de Jurisprudencia (Mexico). Revista de la Escuela Nacional de Jurisprudencia.
Desc: Contains information on doctrinal essays, traditional law documents, book reviews, and general information of law events.
Ind/Abst Am. Hist. Life (1971-1976, 1979-); Index Foreign Leg. Per.; Int. Polit. Sci. Abstr.

AG/0325-9471
REVISTA DE LA FACULTAD DE DERECHO : PUBLICACION DE LA FACULTAD DE DERECHO DE LA UNIVERSIDAD NACIONAL DE ROSARIO. Main/Corp
Revista de la Facultad de Derecho (Rosario, Argentina). V. 1, No. 1, (June 1981)-. Periodical. Spanish. Cordoba 2020, Rosario COD Postal 20000 Republica Argentina. **LC** K19; .D7667. **DD** 340/.05.

PO
REVISTA DE LEGISLACAO E DE JURISPRUDENCIA. Added/Corp
Portugal. Laws, Statutes, etc. (1868)-. Portuguese. ir. Coimbra Editora Lda., Rua do Arnado, Apartado 101, 3002 Coimbra Codex Portugal. **Tel** 011 351 39 23372, 25459. **ED** Joao De Matos Antunes Varela. **LC** K19; .D77. cum. index. **Bk Rev. Ad Acc. Circ:** 3,400 (ctrl).
Desc: All matters related to legislation and jurisprudence.

PR/0010-0579
REVISTA DEL COLEGIO DE ABOGADOS DE PUERTO RICO. [Rev. Col. Abog. P.R.]. Added/Corp
Colegio de Abogados de Puerto Rico. Vol. 15, No. 1 (Nov. 1954)-. Periodical. Spanish (English). Three times a year. $30.00. Colegio D Abogados Puerto Rico, Apartado 1900, San Juan 00936 Puerto Rico. **Tel** (809)721-3358. **DD** 349.7295; 347.295. *Continues* Revista de Derecho, Legislacion y Jurisprudence del Colegio de Abogados de Puerto Rico.
Ind/Abst Curr. Law Index (1980-); Index Leg. Period.; Leg. Resour. Index (1980-); LegalTrac (1980-).

AG/0326-0763
REVISTA DEL DERECHO INDUSTRIAL.
Vol. 1 No. 1 (Jan./Apr. 1979)-. Periodical. Spanish. Three times a year (Mar., June, Oct.). $75.00. Depalma SRL, Talcahuano 494, 1013 Buenos Aires Argentina. **Tel** 011 54 1 407306, 461815, FAX 011 54 1 406913. **ED** Manuel A. Laquis. **LC** K19; .D87. **DD** 346.04/8; 342.648. Index available. cum. index (Every 5 years). **Bk Rev. Pr Rev. Circ:** 1,200 (ctrl).
Desc: Includes author's and inventor's rights, trade marks, technology transfer, and enterprise's law.

PE
REVISTA DEL FORO.
Vol. 1 (June 1914)-. Periodical. Spanish. ir. **LC** K19; .D88. **DD** 349.85/05.
Ind/Abst Index Foreign Leg. Per.; PAIS Int. Print.

CK
REVISTA DEL INSTITUTO COLOMBIANO DE DERECHO PROCESAL.
Vol. 1, No. 1-. Periodical. Spanish. Three times a year. **LC** K19; .D893. **DD** 347.861/05; 348.61075.

AG/0325-061X
REVISTA DEL INSTITUTO DE HISTORIA DEL DERECHO RICARDO LEVENE. [Rev. Inst. Hist. Derecho Ricardo Levene]. Main/Corp
Instituto de Historia del Derecho Ricardo Levene. No.1 (1949)-. Spanish. an.
Ind/Abst Am. Hist. Life (1958-1972).

VE/0506-5798
REVISTA DEL MINISTERIO DE JUSTICIA. [Rev. Minist. justicia]. Main/Corp
Venezuela. Ministerio de Justicia. Yearly V. 1- April/June 1952-. Periodical. Spanish. qt. Free. Republica De

Law

Veneuela, Ministerio De Justicia, PISO 10, Torre Sur, Edificio Lincoln, Sabana Grande Apartado Postal 2084 Venezuela.

VE
REVISTA DEL MINISTERIO PUBLICO : ORGANO DE DIVULGACION DEL MINISTERIO PUBLICO DE LA REPUBLICA DE VENEZUELA. VFOAT Ministerio Publico. Periodical. Spanish. Three times a year. **LC** K26; .E47. **DD** 349.87/05; 348.705. *Continues* Ministerio Publico (Venezuela. Ministerio Publico).

MX
REVISTA DEL PODER JUDICIAL DEL ESTADO DE TLAXCALA. No. 1- Jan./Mar. 1978-. Periodical. Spanish. Palacio de Justica, Plaza de la Constitucion No 23, Tlaxcala Tlax Mexico. **LC** K19; .D9. **DD** 340/.09724.

BL
REVISTA DO INSTITUTO DE DIREITO DA ENERGIA. Main/Corp Minas Gerais, Brazil. Universidade Catolica. Instituto de Diretito da Energia. Portuguese. Instituto de Diretito da Energia, Avenida Dom Jose Gaspar 500, Belo Horizonte Brazil. **LC** K13; .I524. **DD** 343/.81/092.

BL/0100-1752
REVISTA DO INSTITUTO DOS ADVOGADOS BRASILEIROS. Main/Corp Instituto dos Advogados Brasileiros. Yearly V. 1- (No. 1-); July/Sept. 1966-. Portuguese. ir. Av Marechal Camara 210/5 Andar. **LC** K9; .N7464.

BL
REVISTA DO MINISTERIO PUBLICO DE PERNAMBUCO. Began in 1972. Portuguese. Associacao do Ministerio Publico de Pernambuco, rua Diario de Pernambuco 28-2 Andar, Recife Brazil. **LC** K19; .D936.

AG
REVISTA DO TRIBUNAL DE CONTAS DO MUNICIPIO DO RIO DE JANEIRO. Periodical. Portuguese. Tribunal de Contas do Municipio do Rio de Janeiro, Avenida Presidente Wilson 210/7O, Andar Castelo RJ Brazil. **LC** KHD9816; .A77. **DD** 343.81/5303/05; 348.103305.

BL
REVISTA DO TRIBUNAL DE JUSTICA. Main/Corp Sergipe, Brazil (State). Tribunal de Justica. Jan. 1975-. Periodical. Portuguese. Tribunal de Justica / Aracaju, Brazil, Praca Olimpio Campos 736, Aracaju Brazil. **DD** 340/.09814.

AG/0430-1420
REVISTA - FEDERACION ARGENTINA DE COLEGIOS DE ABOGADOS. Main/Corp Federacion Argentina de Colegios de Abogados. Vol. 1 (1968)-. Spanish. **DD** 340.

BL
REVISTA FORENSE. Vol. 1 (1904)-. Periodical. Portuguese. **LC** K19.
Ind/Abst Index Foreign Leg. Per.

SP
REVISTA GENERAL DE DERECHO. Periodical. Spanish.
Ind/Abst Index Foreign Leg. Per.

SP/0210-8518
REVISTA GENERAL DE LEGISLACION Y JURISPRUDENCIA. VFOAT Revista de Legislacion y Jurisprudencia. Periodical. Spanish.
Ind/Abst Index Foreign Leg. Per.

CU
REVISTA JURIDICA. Main/Corp Cuba. Fiscalia General de la Republica. 1979-. Spanish. Fiscalia General de la Republica, San Rafael No 3, Habana 2 Cuba. **DD** 347.7291/005; 347.29107005. *Continues* Cuba. Fiscalia General de la Republica. Revista de Informacion Juridica.

AG
REVISTA JURIDICA ARGENTINA LA LEY. Vol. 1 (Jan./Feb./March 1936)-. Periodical. Spanish. qt. La Ley SA, Tucuman 1471, 1050 Buenos Aires Argentina. **Tel** 011 54 1 495481, 011 54 1 495489. Each issue contains an index to its own contents (no volume index)--loose.
Ind/Abst Index Foreign Leg. Per.

CU/0864-0831
REVISTA JURIDICA (CUBA. MINISTERIO DE JUSTICIA. DEPTO. DE DIVULGACION). (REVISTA JURIDICA.). Began in 1983?. Periodical. Spanish (table of contents in English, German and Russian). qt. $18.00 North America; $21.00 South America; $24.00 other. Ediciones Cubanas, Obispo 527, Altos ESQ Bernaza, CP 10100 Havana Cuba. **Tel** 011 632980, 631942, FAX 011 631011, telex 512337, . 6540. **LC** K19; .J6927.

Desc: Covers the historical precedents of the Cuban notary, with special emphasis on the metamorphosis that it undergoes from the time of the revolution.

BL
REVISTA JURIDICA (CURITIBA, BRAZIL). (REVISTA JURIDICA.). Added/Corp Faculdade de Direito de Curitiba. Diretorio Academico Clotario Portugal. Vol. 1, No. 1, (Nov. 1981)-. Periodical. Portuguese. **DD** 340/.05.

SP
REVISTA JURIDICA DE CATALUNYA. (19??)-. Spanish. Four times a year. 8500ptas. Colegio Abogados Barcelona, C Mallorca 283, 08037 Barcelona, Spain. **Tel** 011 34 3 4872814. **Bk Rev. Circ:** 5,500.

PR/0886-2516
REVISTA JURIDICA DE LA UNIVERSIDAD DE PUERTO RICO. [Rev. jurid. Univ. P. R.]. Main/Corp University of Puerto Rico (Rio Piedras Campus). School of Law. Added/Corp Puerto Rico. Supreme Court. VFOAT Revista Juridica. Vol. 1 (Mar. 1932)-. Periodical. Spanish (English). qt. $30.00 Puerto Rico; $34.00 other. Revista Juridica de la Universidad de Puerto Rico, Escuela de Derecho, Rio Piedras, Puerto Rico 00931. **Tel** (809)764-2443, (809)764-3550. **ED** Anibelle Sloan (editor's address: Revista Juridica UPR PO Box 23349 San Juan PR 00931-3349; editor's phone: (809)764-0000 ext. 3840). **DD** 347.05; 349.7295. **Bk Rev**, (Qty: 1 or 2). **Ad Acc**, **Adv Mgr:** same as editor. **Circ:** 1,000 (ctrl). available on microfiche from Williams S Hein & Co.
Ind/Abst Index Leg. Period.; Leg. Resour. Index; LegalTrac (1980-).

PR/0041-851X
REVISTA JURIDICA DE LA UNIVERSIDAD INTERAMERICANA DE PUERTO RICO. [Rev. jurid. Univ. Interam. P. R.]. Added/Corp Inter American University of Puerto Rico. Facultad de Derecho. Vol. 1, No. 1 (Jan./March 1964)-. Periodical. Spanish. Three times a year. $20.00. Interamerican University, PO Box 70351, San Juan PR 00936-8351. **Tel** (809)751-1912 ext. 2073. **ED** Cesar Vazquez. **DD** 340/.05. Index available. cum. index. **Circ:** 1,000 (ctrl).
Desc: Publishes a forum open to the free discussion of topics on law that are of general interest.
Ind/Abst Crim. Penol. Poiice Sci. Abstr.; Curr. Law Index (1980-); Index Leg. Period.; Leg. Resour. Index (1980-); LegalTrac (1980-).

PE
REVISTA JURIDICA DEL PERU. *Ceased.* (19??)-(1992). Periodical. Spanish. qt. Julio Ayasta Gonzalez, Lampa 1115 of 905, Lima Peru. **Tel** 27-7854 246698. **ED** Julio Ayasta Gonzalez. **Bk Rev. Ad Acc.**
Ind/Abst Index Foreign Leg. Per.

BL
REVISTA JURIDICA DO MINISTERIO PUBLICO CATARINENSE. Added/Corp Santa Catarina (Brazil : State). Ministerio Publico Catarinense. (19??)-. Periodical. Portuguese. an. Ministerio Publico Catarinense, Praca XV de Novembro No 6, 88.000 Florianopolis SC Brazil. **LC** K19; .J697.

BL
REVISTA JURIDICA LEMI. EDICAO NACIONAL. Periodical. Portuguese. Editoria Lemi, rua Pecanha 402, Caixa Postal, Belo Horizonte Brazil. **DD** 349.81/05. *Continues* Legislacao Mineira; *Absorbed* Revista Juridica Lemi. Edicao Mensal; Sao Paulo.

BL
REVISTA JURIDICA LEMI. LEGISLACAO ESTADUAL. MINAS GERAIS. Main/Corp Minas Gerais (Brazil). VFOAT Revista Juridica L.E.M.I. Legislacao Estadual. Minas Gerais. (19??)-. Periodical. Portuguese. sm. Editora Lemi SA, Caixa Postal 1890, Belo Horizonte 30.000 Brazil. **LC** KHD7503.25; .M56.

SP
REVISTA JURISDICCION CONTENCIOSO ADMINISTRATIVA. Spanish. mo. 7075.00ptas Spain; 9000.00ptas other. Edersa Editoriales de Derecho, Reunidas SA Valverde 32 1, 28004 Madrid Spain. **Tel** 011 34 1 5210246, 011 34 1 5229849.

MX
REVISTA MEXICANA DE JUSTICIA. Added/Corp Mexico. Ministerio Publico Federal. (19??)-. Periodical. Spanish. Consejo Editorial, San Juan de Letran, 9 Piso, 13 Mexico DF Mexico. **LC** K19; .M38. **DD** 349.72/05; 347.2005.

PE
REVISTA PERUANA DE DERECHO DE LA EMPRESA. (198?)-. Periodical. Spanish. bm. $100.00. Asesorandina S R Ltda, Av Salaverry 674 OF 403, Casilla 11-0059 Lima Peru. **Tel** 237730, FAX (14)424585, telex 20339 CP. **ED** Alonso Morales Acosta. **LC** K19; .P43. **DD** 346.85/065; 348.50665. Index available. cum. index. **Bk Rev. Ad Acc. Pr Rev. Circ:** 1,000 (ctrl).

Desc: Each issue is devoted to one theme relevant to business law. Articles are by specialists in banking, finance, credit and legislation; covers new laws, international ramifications and offers analyses.
Ind/Abst Int. Labour Doc.; LABORDOC.

BL
REVISTA - PROCURADORIA GERAL DO ESTADO. Main/Corp Bahia, Brazil (State). Procuradoria Geral do Estado. V. 1- 1976-. Portuguese. Procuradoria Geral do Estado, Travessa da Ajuda No 2 - 20 Andar, Salvador Brazil. **LC** K2; .A45. **DD** 340/.09814.

UY
REVISTA TRIBUTARIA. V. 1- July/August 1974-. Spanish. bm. Editorial Amalio M Fernandez, 25 de Mayo 477 P Baja, OF 11, Montevideo Uruguay. **Tel** 951782 OR 952684. **ED** Jorge Rosetto. **DD** 343/.895/0405. **Bk Rev.**
Desc: Contains doctrines, jurisprudence and legislation related to financial and taxation law.

BL
REVISTA - UNIVERSIDADE DE UBERLANDIA FACULDADE DE DIREITO. Main/Corp Universidade de Uberlandia Faculdade de Direito. V. 1- 1st Semester 1972-. Portuguese. 25.00 single issue. Universidade de Uberlandia, Faculdade de Direito, Av Joao Pinheiro 556, 38400 Uberlandia Brazil. **LC** K25; .N56.

UY
REVISTA URUGUAYA DE DERECHO PROCESAL. Added/Corp Fundacion de Cultura Universitaria. (1975)-. Periodical. Spanish. Four times a year. Fundacion de Cultura Universitaria, 25 de Mayo, 568 Casilla 1155, 11000 Montevideo Uruguay. **Tel** 011 598 2 961152. **ED** Enrique Vescovi. **LC** K19; .U79. **DD** 347/.895/05. Index available. cum. index. **Bk Rev. Pr Rev. Circ:** 1,000.

FR/0035-0672
REVUE ADMINISTRATIVE, LA. See Public Administration.

AE/0035-0699
REVUE ALGERIENNE DES SCIENCES JURIDIQUES, ECONOMIQUES ET POLITIQUES. [Rev. alger. sci. jurid. econ. polit.]. Added/Corp Jamiat Al-Jazair. Institut de Droit, des Sciences Politiques et Administratives. Jamiat Al-Jazair. Faculte de Droit et des Sciences Economiques. Jamiat Al-Jazair. Institut des Sciences Economiques. Jamiat Al-Jazair. Mahad Al-Huquq Wa-Al-Ulum Al-Idariyah. Algeria. Journal Officiel de Republique Algerienne Democratic Ed Populaire. VFOAT Majallah Al-Jazairiyah Lil-Ulum Al-Qanuniyah, Al-Iqtisadiyah Wa-Al-Siyasiyah. Vol. 1 (Jan. 1964)-. Periodical. French. qt. Institut de Droit, Des Sciences Politiques et Administratives, Alger Algeria. **LC** K21; .A4. **DD** 349.65/05. cum. index. *Supersedes* Revue Algerienne, Tunisienne et Marocaine de Legislation et de Jurisprudence.
Ind/Abst Int. Bibliogr. Sociol.

CN/0226-7284
REVUE AUTOCHTONE. [Rev. autochtone]. VFOAT Native Review. V. 1- July 1979-. Periodical. French (English). J Lagarde, Rural Route 2, Ile du Grand Calumet Quebec J0X 1J0 Canada. **DD** 342.714/0872.

UV/0773-8439
REVUE BURKINABE DE DROIT. [Rev. burkinabe droit]. No. 7 (Jan. 1985)-. Periodical. French. sa. 50.00CFAF. Ecole Superieur de Droit, Universite de Ouagadougou, BP 7021, Ouagadougou Burkina Faso. **LC** K21; .B87. *Continues* Revue Voltaique de Droit, 0771-663X.
Ind/Abst Index Foreign Leg. Per.

CM
REVUE CAMEROUNAISE DE DROIT. VFOAT Cameroon Law Review. Periodical. French (summaries and/or abstracts in English). 1600. **LC** K21; .C28. **DD** 340/.05.

BE/0035-0966
REVUE CRITIQUE DE JURISPRUDENCE BELGE. Vol. 1 (1947)-. Periodical. French. four times a year. 5269.00F. Etablissements Emile Bruylant, 67 rue de la Regence, 1000 Brussels Belgium. **Tel** 011 32 2 5129845. cum. index. **Circ:** 1,675.
Desc: Commentary on Belgian law.
Ind/Abst Index Foreign Leg. Per.

FR/0180-9869
REVUE DE DROIT IMMOBILIER. French. qt. 610.00F France; 740.00F other. Dalloz, 35 rue Tournefort, 75240 Paris Cedex 05 France. **Tel** 011 33 1 40515434 or 40515454, FAX 45 87 37 48, telex 206 446 F.

BE
REVUE DE DROIT INTELLECTUAL L'INGENIEUR-CONSEIL. See Copyright, Intellectual Property.

FR
REVUE DE DROIT RURAL. French. mo (July/Aug. & Sept./Oct. issues combined). 680.00F. Les Editions Techniques et Economiques, 3 rue Soufflot, 75005 Paris France. **Tel** 33 1 46341030, FAX 33 1 46345583, telex 260 717 F.
Ind/Abst Dairy Sci. Abstr.; Maize Abstr.; Seed Abstr.; Wheat Barley Trit. Abstr.; World Agric. Econ.

CN/0317-9656
REVUE DE DROIT (SHERBROOKE). (REVUE DE DROIT.). [Rev. droit]. V. 1- 1970-. French (English). sa. 26.00Can$. Universite de Sherbrooke / Droit - Law, Faculte de Droit - Faculty of Law, 2500 Boul de Universite, Sherbrooke Quebec J1K 2R1 Canada. **Tel** (819)821-7508. **LC** K21. **DD** 340/.05. **Bk Rev. Ad Acc. Circ:** 2,000 (ctrl). available in microform.
Desc: General review of law: public law, commercial law, civil law and criminal law.
Ind/Abst Can. Legal Lit.; Index Foreign Leg. Per.; Index Leg. Period.; Leg. Resour. Index (1980-?); Point Repere (1983-).

BE
REVUE DE DROIT SOCIAL. VFOAT Tijdschrift voor Sociaal Recht. (1962)-. Periodical. French (Dutch). Six times a year. 3200.00F. Maison F Larcier SA, 39 rue des Minimes, B-1000 Bruxelles Belgium. **Tel** 011 32 2 512-4712, 512-9679. **(Subscription address:** Access / France, Fond Dean Paques, 4 B1348, Louvain la Neuve Belgium.**)** Index available. **Bk Rev.**
Ind/Abst Int. Bibliogr. Sociol.

CN/0317-9656
REVUE DE DROIT [FRENCH EDITION] (SHERBROOKE). (REVUE DE DROIT.). [Rev. droit]. **Added/Corp** Universite de Sherbrooke. Faculte de Droit. Vol. 1 (1970)-. French (English and French). be. Universite de Sherbrooke / Droit - Law, Faculte de Droit - Faculty of Law, 2500 Boul de Universite, Sherbrooke Quebec J1K 2R1 Canada. **Tel** (819)821-7508. **LC** K21; .D298. **DD** 340/.05.
Ind/Abst Index Leg. Period. (?-?); Leg. Resour. Index (1980-); LegalTrac (1980-); Point Repere (1983-).

FR/0048-7937
REVUE DE JURISPRUDENCE COMMERCIALE. [R. jurisprud. commer.]. **VFOAT** Revue de Jurisprudence Commerciale, Ancien Journal des Agrees; Journal des Agrees; Revue de Jurisprudence Commerciale, Journal des Agrees. (1957)-. Periodical. French. mo (July/Aug. and Sept./Oct. issues combined). 783.55F France; 950.00F other. Revue de Jurisprudence Commerciale, 77 rue Royale, 78000 Versailles France. **Tel** 011 33 1 39504497. **UDC** 347.7.

FR
REVUE DE LA RECHERCHE JURIDIQUE, DROIT PROSPECTIF / PUBLIEE PAR LA FACULTE DE DROIT ET DE SCIENCE POLITIQUE D'AIX-MARSEILLE. Added/Corp Faculte de Droit et de Science Politique d'Aix-Marseille. **VFOAT** Revue de la Recherche Juridique. (1976)-. Periodical. French. Four times a year. 400.00F France; 450.00F other. Reg d'Recettes Presses Univ d'Aix Marsielle, 3 Ave R Schuman, 13628 Aix en Provence France. **Tel** 011 33 42172800, FAX 011 33 42172903. **LC** K21; .D425. **DD** 349.44/05; 344.4005. ***Continues*** *Revue de Droit Prospectif, 0396-3667.*

FR/0556-7440
REVUE DE L'ARBITRAGE. Added/Corp Comite Francais de L'Arbitrage. (1955)-. Periodical. French. Four times a year. 430.00F France; 500.00F other. Litec Service Abonnements, 6 Rue Victor Cousin, 75005 Paris France. **Tel** 011 33 1 46332237, FAX 46.33.50.32. **ED** Philippe Fouchard. **LC** K21; .D44. **Bk Rev.** ctrl circ.
Desc: Covers arbitration and award.

FR
REVUE DES SOCIETES. JOURNAL DES SOCIETES. VFOAT Journal des Societes. Vol. 93 (Jan./March 1975)-. Periodical. French. Four times a year. 535.00F (France); 640.00F (other). Dalloz, 35 rue Tournefort, 75240 Paris Cedex 05 France. **Tel** 011 33 1 40515434 or 40515454, FAX 45 87 37 48, telex 206 446 F. ***Formed by the union of*** *Revue des Societes; Journal des Societes* ***and*** *Civiles et Commerciales.*
Desc: Presents documentation authored by judges, lawyers and professors for the use of students and teachers. Each number gives principal legislation of the quarter accompanied by ministerial responses, important decisions followed by notes and articles on basic scholarship and current events.

FR
REVUE D'HISTOIRE DES FACULTES DE DROIT ET DE LA SCIENCE JURIDIQUE. Added/Corp Societe pour l'Histoire des Facultes de Droit et de la Science Juridique (France). No. 4 (1987)-. French. an. Societe pour l'Histoire des Facultes de Droit et de la Science Juridique, 10 Avenue Pierre Larousse, 92241 Malakoff Cedex France. ***Continues*** *Annales d'Histoire des Facultes de Droit, 0765-4847.*

FR/0989-7925
REVUE D'HISTOIRE DES FACULTES DE DROIT ET DE LA SCIENCE JURIDIQUE. (1987)-. Periodical. French. an. 176.30F France; 206.30F other. Societe Histoire Facultes Droit, 10 Ave Pierre Larousse, 92241 Malakoff Cedex France. **(Subscription address:** Societe Histoire Facultes Droit, LJDJ 26 rue Vercingetorix, 75014 Paris France.**) UDC** 93 : 34.

CN/0383-669X
REVUE DU BARREAU, LA. [Rev. barreau]. **Added/Corp** Barreau du Quebec. Vol. 29, No 7 (Sept. 1969)-. Periodical. French (English). Twice a year. 19.80Can$ Quebec; 16.95Can$ others in Canada; 22.80Can$ others. Barreau du Quebec, 445 Boulevard St-Laurent, Montreal Quebec H2Y 3T8 Canada. **Tel** (514)954-3400, FAX (514)954-3478. **DD** 340/.09714. Index available. cum. index. **Bk Rev. Ad Acc. Circ:** 14,000. available on microfilm. ***Continues*** *Barreau du Quebec. Revue du Barreau du Quebec., 0005-6065.*
Desc: Covers in the areas of civil, criminal and commercial law. Comments on the jurisprudence, civil rights and administrative law.
Ind/Abst Can. Legal Lit.; Index Can. Leg. Period. Lit.; Index Foreign Leg. Per.; Index Leg. Period. (1992-); Leg. Resour. Index (1980-?); LegalTrac (1981-1987); Point Repere (1983-).

CN/0383-669X
REVUE DU BARREAU. (LA REVUE DU BARREAU.). [Rev. barreau]. **Added/Corp** Barreau du Quebec. (1969)-. Periodical. French (English). qt. 19.80Can$. Barreau du Quebec, 445 Boulevard St-Laurent, Montreal Quebec H2Y 3T8 Canada. **Tel** (514)954-3400, FAX (514)954-3478. ***Continues*** *Revue du Barreau du Quebec, 0005-6065.*

CN/0035-2632
REVUE DU NOTARIAT, LA. [Rev. notar.]. **Added/Corp** Board of Notaries of the Province of Quebec. Chambre des Notaires du Qu,ebec. Board of Notaries of Quebec. (Aug. 15, 1898)-. Periodical. French (English). qt. 40.00Can$ Canada; 45.00Can$ other. Revue Du Notariat, 630 Boulevard Rene Levesque Ouest, Montreal QUE H3B 1T6 Canada. **Tel** (514)879-1793. **ED** Roger Comtois. **Ad Acc. Circ:** 4,045.
Ind/Abst Can. Legal Lit.; Index Can. Leg. Period. Lit.; Index Foreign Leg. Per.; LegalTrac (1980-1987); Point Repere (1983-).

FR/0775-3209
REVUE EUROPEENNE DE DROIT DE LA CONSOMMATION. (1986)-. Periodical. French. qt. 1050.00F. Editions Lamy SA, 187-189 Quai de Valmy, 75490 Paris Cedex 10 France. **Tel** 011 33 1 44721200, 011 33 1 44721212, FAX 011 33 1 44721395. **UDC** 340.5 (4).

FR
REVUE FIDUCIAIRE. INFORMATION HEBDOMADAIRES. VFOAT Informations Hebdomadaires. (19??)-. Periodical. French. Fifty-two times a year. 602.35F France; 965.00F others. Revue Fiduciaire, 100 rue la Fayette, 75485 Paris Cedex 10 France. **Tel** 011 33 1 48408044. **ED** Jean de la Villeguerin. **LC** K21; .F5. **DD** 343/.44/0405. Index available. cum. index. **Ad Acc. Circ:** 160,000. ***Continues*** *Revue Fiduciaire. Feuillets Hebdomadaires d'Information.*
Desc: Covers tax, law, social security, labour law and accounting.

CN/0035-3086
REVUE GENERALE DE DROIT. [Rev. gen. droit]. V. 1- 1970-. French (English). ir (4 times a year). $33.27. Wilson & Lafleur Ltd., 40 Rue Notre Dame East, Montreal, Quebec H2Y 1B9 Canada. **Tel** (514)875-6326, FAX (514)875-8356. **ED** Ernest Caparros. cum. index. **Bk Rev.** ***Supersedes*** *Justinien, 0449-4504.*
Ind/Abst Can. Legal Lit.; Curr. Law Index (1980-); Index Can. Leg. Period. Lit.; Index Foreign Leg. Per.; Index Leg. Period.; Leg. Resour. Index (1980-); LegalTrac (1980-).

BE
REVUE GENERALE DE FISCALITE. VFOAT R.G.F.; RGF. (19??)-. Periodical. French. mo. 12076.00F. C E D Samsom, Koutervel 14, B 1831 Diegem Belgium. **Tel** 011 32 2 7231111, FAX (02)7231191, telex CEDSAM 64 130. **DD** 343.49304/05; 344.9303405. Index available.
Desc: General financial, fiscal and revenue taxes information according to Belgian legislation.

FR
REVUE GENERALE DE L'AIR ET DE L'ECSPACE. Vol. 27, No. 1 (1964)-. French. qt. 75.00. Editions Internationales, Cheque Postal Editions Internationales 1568-87, Paris France. **LC** K21; .G46. **DD** 343.09/7/05. ***Continues*** *Revue Generale de l'Air.*

FR/0035-3280
REVUE HISTORIQUE DE DROIT FRANCAIS ET ETRANGER. [Rev. hist. droit fr. etrang.]. **Added/Corp** Centre National de la Recherche Scientifique (France). Vol. 1 (1922)-. Periodical. French. qt. 650.00F (France); 720.00F (other). Dalloz, 35 rue Tournefort, 75240 Paris Cedex 05 France. **Tel** 011 33 1 40515434 or 40515454, FAX 45 87 37 48, telex 206 446 F. **ED** Georges Daux. **[CCC].** ***Continues*** *Nouvelle Revue Historique de Droit Francais et Etranger.*
Desc: Steering committee comprised of professors at the University of Paris who are experts in law, economics and social sciences.
Ind/Abst Am. Hist. Life (1955-); Index Foreign Leg. Per.; Numis. Lit.

BE
REVUE INTERDISCIPLINAIRE D'ETUDES JURIDIQUES. Added/Corp Facultes Universitaires Saint-Louis. Seminaire Interdisciplinaire d'Etudes Juridiques. (1978)-. French. sa. 1000.00F (institutions), 800.00F (individuals) Belgium; 1200.00F (institutions), 900.00F (individuals) other. Facultes Universite Saint Louis ASBL, BD du Jardin Botanique 43, 1000 Brussels Belgium. **Tel** 011 32 2 2117894.

BE
REVUE INTERNATIONALE DES DROITS DE L'ANTIQUITE. 3E SERIE. Vol. 1 (1954)-. French. an. 1000.00F. Office Internationale des Periodiques, Kouterveld 14, B 1831 Diegem Belgium. **Tel** 011 32 2 7231158. ***Continues*** *Archives d'Histoire du Droit Oriental, Revue International des Droits de l'Antiquite.*
Ind/Abst Index Foreign Leg. Per.

CN/0845-9401
REVUE JURIDIQUE DES ETUDIANTS ET ETUDIANTES DE L'UNIVERSITE LAVAL, LA. [Rev. jurid. etud. etud. Univ. Laval]. (1989)-. French. an. 20.00Can$ (per no.). **DD** 349.714/05. ***Continues*** *Revue Juridique des Etudiants de l'Universite Laval, 0832-848X.*
Ind/Abst Can. Legal Lit.; Index Can. Leg. Period. Lit.

BD
REVUE JURIDIQUE DU BURUNDI. Added/Corp Societe d'Etudes Juridiques du Burundi. Vol. 1, No. 1, (March 1980)-. Periodical. French. qt. 800.00 US and Canada. Societe d'Etudes Juridiques du Burundi A S B L, BP 1010, Bujumbura Burundi. **LC** K21; .J79. **DD** 340/.05.

FR/0985-2549
REVUE JURIDIQUE DU CENTRE QUEST. [Rev. jurid. Centre Ouest]. **Added/Corp** Universite d'Orleans. Faculte de Droit, d'Economie et de Gestion. No. 1 (1988)-. Periodical. French. Twice a year. 300.00F. Faculte de Droit d'Economie et de Gestion d'Orleans, Rue de Blois, BP 6739, 45067 Orleans Cedex 2 France. Index available. cum. index. **Circ:** 1,800.

NR
REVUE JURIDIQUE DU RWANDA. IGAZETI ISOBANURA AMATEGEKO MU RWANDA. VFOAT Igazeti Isobanura Amategeko mu Rwanda. (19??)-. French (Ruanda). Three times a year (Jan., May, & Sept.). $25.00 Rwanda; $50.00 others. Universite National du Rwanda, Faculte de Droit, BP 1690, Gikondo Kigali Rwanda Africa. **Tel** 73142. **LC** K21; .J8. **DD** 340/.0967/571. Index available. **Bk Rev. Ad Acc. Circ:** 1,000.
Ind/Abst Index Foreign Leg. Per.

CG
REVUE JURIDIQUE DU ZAIRE. Added/Corp Societe d'Etudes Juridiques du Katanga. Societe d'Etudes Juridiques du Shaba. (1924)-. Periodical. French. Three times a year. $10.00. Societe d'Etudes Juridiques du Zaire, Universite de Lubumbashi, BP 510, Lubumbashi Zaire. **LC** K21; .J84. **DD** 340/.096751. ***Continues*** *Revue Juridique du Congo.*

CG
REVUE JURIDIQUE DU ZAIRE; DROIT ECRIT ET DROIT COUTUMIER. (1924)-. Periodical. French. Three times a year. $46.00. Societe d'Etudes Juridique d'Zaire, Secretariat General, BP 5502, Kinshasa Gombe Zaire. **ED** Dibunda Kabuinji. **Bk Rev. Ad Acc. Circ:** 1,000 (ctrl).
Desc: Includes written law and customary law, studies of judicial doctrine, notes and comments of Zaire, Central Africa.
Ind/Abst Index Foreign Leg. Per.

FR/0035-3574
REVUE JURIDIQUE ET POLITIQUE, INDEPENDANCE ET COOPERATION. [Rev. jurid. polit. indep. coop.]. **Added/Corp** Institut international de Droit d'Expression Francaise. Institut International de Droit d'Expression Francaise. Bulletin. Vol. 18 (Jan./March 1964)-. French. Three times a year. 786.72F France; 830.00F others. Editions d'Iena, 17 rue Thiers, Box Postale 2, 78110 le Vesinet France. **Tel** 011 33 1 39763993. **LC** K21; .J85. Index available in last issue of volume--attached. ***Continues*** *Revue Juridique et Politique d'Outre-Mer.*
Ind/Abst Index Foreign Leg. Per.; Int. Labour Doc.; Int. Polit. Sci. Abstr.; LABORDOC; PAIS Int. Print.

MR/0251-4761
REVUE JURIDIQUE, POLITIQUE, ET ECONOMIQUE DU MAROC. (AL-MAJALLAH AL-MAGHRIBIYAH LIL-QANUN WA-AL-SIYASAH WA-AL-IQTISAD.). [Rev. jurid. polit. econ. Maroc]. **Added/Corp** Jamiat Muhammad al-Khamis. Kulliyat al-Ulum al-Qanuniyah wa-al-Iqtisadiyah wa-al-Ijtimaiyah (Rabat, Morocco). **VFOAT** RJPEM; R.J.P.E.M. (1976)-. Periodical. Arabic (French). sa. Faculte des Sciences Juridiques, Economiques et Sociales de Rabat, Blvd. des Nations Unies, BP 721, Rabat-Agdal, Morocco. **LC** K13; .A4715.
Ind/Abst PAIS Int. Print.

CN/0556-7963
REVUE JURIDIQUE THEMIS (1970). (REVUE JURIDIQUE THEMIS / PUBLIE PAR LES ETUDIANTS EN DROIT DE L'UNIVERSITE DE MONTREAL.). [Rev. jurid. Themis]. **Added/Corp** Universite de Montreal. Faculte de Droit. **VFOAT** Themis. (1970)-. Periodical. French (English). Three times a year. 36.00Can$ (unbound); 34.00Can$ (bound). Editions Themis, University of Montreal, Faculty of Law, PO Box 6128 SUCC-A Centre-Ville, Montreal Que H3C 3J7 Canada. **Tel** (514)739-9945, FAX (514)343-2199. **LC** K21; .J86. **DD** 349.714/05; 347.14005. cum. index. **Ad Acc, Adv Mgr:** M. Joubert. **Circ:** 1,700 (ctrl). available on microfilm and microfiche from University Microfilms International (UMI). ***Supersedes*** *Revue Juridique Themis de l'Universite de Montreal, 0380-8327.*
Desc: Specifically concentrated on areas of Quebec civil and commercial law. Includes articles on international law, criminal law and studies of the Quebec and Canadian Charters.
Ind/Abst Can. Legal Lit.; Curr. Law Index (1980-); Index Can. Leg. Period. Lit.; Index Foreign Leg. Per.; Index Leg. Period.; Leg. Resour. Index (1980-); LegalTrac (1980-); Point Repere (1983-).

CN/0556-7963
REVUE JURIDIQUE THEMIS (1970). (REVUE JURIDIQUE THEMIS.). [Rev. jurid. Th,emis]. **VFOAT** Themis. (1970)-. Periodical. French (English). tq. 36.00Can$. Editions Themis, University of Montreal, Faculty of Law, PO Box 6128 SUCC-A Centre-Ville, Montreal Que H3C 3J7 Canada. **Tel** (514)739-9945, FAX (514)343-2199. **DD** 349.714/05; 347.14005. **Ad Acc, Adv Mgr:** M. Joubert. ctrl circ. ***Continues*** *Revue Juridique Themis de l'Universite de Montreal., 0380-8327.*

CN/0035-3604
REVUE LEGALE. Vol. 1 (1869)-. Periodical. French. Five times a year. 100.00Can$. Wilson & Lafleur Ltd., 40 Rue Notre Dame East, Montreal, Quebec H2Y 1B9 Canada. **Tel** (514)875-6326, FAX (514)875-8356.

FR
REVUE PRACTIQUE DE DROIT SOCIAL. (19??)-. Periodical. French. mo. 370.00F France; 520.00F other. Editions de la Vie Ouvriere, 33 rue Bouret, 75168 Paris Cedex 19 France. **Tel** 011 33 1 40403636, FAX 42 09 97 36, telex LAVEO 21114 GF. **ED** Lavie Ouvriere. ctrl circ.
Desc: Social law and jurisprudence.
Ind/Abst LABORDOC.

BE
REVUE PRATIQUE DES SOCIETES CIVILES & COMMERCIALES. French. ir. Etablissements Emile Bruylant, 67 rue de la Regence, 1000 Brussels Belgium. **Tel** 011 32 2 5129845.

SG/0035-4112
REVUE SENEGALAISE DE DROIT. (1967)-. Periodical. French. sa.
Ind/Abst Index Foreign Leg. Per.

FR/0035-4317
REVUE TRIMESTRIELLE DE DROIT EUROPEEN (COURT OF JUSTICE OF THE EUROPEAN COMMUNITIES). (REVUE TRIMESTRIELLE DE DROIT EUROPEEN.). [Rev. trimest. droit eur.]. **Added/Corp** Court of Justice of the European Communities. Vol. 16 No. 2 (April/June 1980)-. Periodical. French. qt. 600.00F (France); 780.00F (other). Dalloz, 35 rue Tournefort, 75240 Paris Cedex 05 France. **Tel** 011 33 1 40515434 or 40515454, FAX 45 87 37 48, telex 206 446 F. **ED** Roger Houin and Claude-Albert Colliard. **LC** K21; .T695. **DD** 349.4/05; 344.005. **[CCC].** ***Continues*** *Revue de Droit Europeen.*
Ind/Abst PAIS Int. Print; World Agric. Econ.

TI
REVUE TUNISIENNE DE DROIT. **Added/Corp** Jamiah al-Tunisiyah. Kulliyat al-Huquq wa-al-Ulum al-Siyasiyah wa-al-Iqtisadiyah. Markaz al-Dirasat wa-al-Buhuth wa-al-Nashr. Jamiat al-Huquq wa-al-Iqtisad wa-al-Tasarruf bi-Tunis. Markaz al-Dirasat wa-al-Buhuth wa-al-Nashr. **VFOAT** Majallah al-Qanuniyah al-Tunisiyah. (19??)-. French (Arabic). Twelve times a year. 15TD. Centre d'Etude et de Recherche et de Publications / Faculte de Droit, 1060 Tunis Tunisia.
Ind/Abst Index Foreign Leg. Per.

US/0556-8595
RHODE ISLAND BAR JOURNAL. ***Title Change.*** [R.I. bar j.]. **Added/Corp** Rhode Island Bar Association. Vol. 1, No. 1 (Oct. 1952)-(19??). Periodical. English. mo (Oct. - June). Rhode Island Bar Association, 115 Cedar Street, Providence RI 02903. **Tel** (401)421-5740, FAX (401)421-2703. **ED** Helen Desmond McDonald. **DD** 340/.05. Index available. **Bk Rev**, (Qty: 4). **Ad Acc, Adv Mgr:** Beth Bailey. **Circ:** 4,300 (ctrl). ***Continued by*** *Journal (Rhode Island Bar Association), 1073-8800.*
Ind/Abst Curr. Law Index (1980-19??); Fed. Tax Artic.; Law Office Inf. Serv.; Leg. Resour. Index (1980-?); LegalTrac (1980-1985).

US
RHODE ISLAND CASE NAMES CITATOR. English. $40.00 (1 bound volume), $52.00 (cumulative supplements). Shepards McGraw-Hill Inc, 555 Middle Creek Parkway, PO Box 35300, Colorado Springs CO 80935-3530. **Tel** (719)488-3000, FAX (800)525-0053.

US/0279-0882
RHODE ISLAND LAWYERS WEEKLY. **VFOAT** Lawyers Weekly. (198?)-. Periodical. English. wk. $224.00. Lawyers Weekly Publications, 41 West Street, Boston MA 02111. **Tel** (617)451-7300, (800)444-5297. **LC** K22; .H6. **DD** 349.745; 347.45. ***Continues*** *Rhode Island Lawyers News, 0274-6158.*

US/0893-8245
RISK MANAGEMENT REPORTER FOR THE HEALTH CARE PROFESSIONAL, THE. (1990)-. Periodical. English. qt. $59.95. Professional Reports Corporation, 4418 Belden Village Street Northwest, Canton OH 44718. **Tel** (216)492-6063, (800)336-0083, FAX (216)492-6176.

US/1062-2624
RISK MANAGER'S LAW ALERT. ***Ceased.*** (RISK MANAGER'S LAW ALERT : PRACTICAL INFORMATION FOR HEALTH CARE PROFESSIONALS.). [Risk manag. law alert]. Vol. 1, No. 1 (May 1992)-(1994). Periodical. English. mo. Aspen Publishers Inc., 7201 McKinney Circle, Frederick MD 21701. **Tel** (800)234-1660, (301)698-7100, FAX (301)251-5784, telex 5106014543. **ED** Audrey L. Covner, RN, JD. **DD** 610. **NLM** W1; RI285G. available in Loose-leaf.
Desc: Designed to serve as a resource for health care risk managers on legal and legislative matters relevant to their area of practice. Contains information about recent court decisions and includes notes explaining the impact of these cases for risk managers.

IT
RIVISTA DEI DOTTORI COMMERCIALISTI. (19??)-. Italian. Six times a year. L140000.00 Italy; L210000.00 other. Giuffre Editore SPA, Via Busto Arsizio 40, 20151 Milan Italy. **Tel** 011 398 2 38089200. **ED** Angelo Provasoli.
Desc: Contributes to the development of economics in the field of business, also of company, accounting and fiscal law.

IT
RIVISTA DEL CONSIGLIO, LA. (19??)-. Italian. Four times a year. L40000.00 Italy; L60000.00 other. Giuffre Editore SPA, Via Busto Arsizio 40, 20151 Milan Italy. **Tel** 011 398 2 38089200. **ED** Michele Saponara.
Desc: Official organ of the Milan Ordine degli Avvocati e Procuratori. Provides a link between the order and its lawyer members.

IT
RIVISTA DEL NOTARIATO. (19??)-. Italian. Six times a year. L140000.00 Italy; L210000.00 other. Giuffre Editore SPA, Via Busto Arsizio 40, 20151 Milan Italy. **Tel** 011 398 2 38089200. **ED** Matilde Atlante.
Desc: Surveys a wide area of public and private law that may concern the work of a notary.

IT
RIVISTA DELLA CORTE DEI CONTI. Istituto Poligrafico Zecca Stato, Piazza Verdi 10, 00198 Rome Italy. **Tel** 011 39 6 85082307, 011 39 6 85082221.

IT
RIVISTA DELL'ARBITRATO / ASSOCIAZIONE ITALIANA PER L'ARBITRATO. **Added/Corp** Associazione Italiana per l'Arbitrato. Vol. 1, No. 1 (1991)-. Periodical. Italian (French and Spanish; summaries and/or abstracts in English). qt. L100000.00 Italy; L160000.00 other. Giuffre Editore SPA, Via Busto Arsizio 40, 20151 Milan Italy. **Tel** 011 398 2 38089200. **ED** Elio Fazzalari. **LC** K22; .I52. ***Continues*** *Rassegna dell'Arbitrato, 0033-9415.*
Desc: Contains a section dealing with doctrine, a section with both Italian and international case law, reviews on doctrine and case law, and a section containing documentation and information.

IT/0391-8696
RIVISTA DI DIRITTO AGRARIO MILANO. [Riv. dir. agr. Milano]. (1922)-. Periodical. Italian. qt. L110000.00 Italy; L165000.00 other. Giuffre Editore SPA, Via Busto Arsizio 40, 20151 Milan Italy. **Tel** 011 398 2 38089200. **UDC** 351.823.1.
Desc: Covers agrarian law.

IT/0035-6123
RIVISTA DI DIRITTO EUROPEO. (1961)-. Periodical. Italian (English and French). qt. L880000 Italy; 176000 other. Istituto Poligrafico Zecca Stato, Piazza Verdi 10, 00198 Rome Italy. **Tel** 011 39 6 85082307, 011 39 6 85082221. cum. index.
Ind/Abst Index Foreign Leg. Per.

IT
RIVISTA DI DIRITTO PROCESSUALE. Periodical. Italian. qt. L160000 Italy; L220000 other. Cedam Spa, Via Jappelli 5 6, 35121 Padua Italy. **Tel** 011 39 49 65667.
Ind/Abst Index Foreign Leg. Per.

IT
RIVISTA DI DIRITTO SPORTIVO. (19??)-. Italian. Four times a year. L50000.00 Italy; L75000.00 other. Giuffre Editore SPA, Via Busto Arsizio 40, 20151 Milan Italy. **Tel** 011 398 2 38089200. **ED** Arrigo Gattai.
Desc: Deals exclusively with legal matters concerning sports. Organ of the Comitato Olimpico Nazionale Italiano.

IT/1121-4074
RIVISTA DI DIRITTO TRIBUTARIO. [Riv. diritto tribut.]. (1990)-. Periodical. Italian. mo. L200000.00 Italy; L300000.00 other. Giuffre Editore SPA, Via Busto Arsizio 40, 20151 Milan Italy. **Tel** 011 398 2 38089200. **ED** Gaspare Falsitta and Augusto Fantozzi. **UDC** 340.336.
Desc: Contains sections dealing with doctrine, case law, legislation and administrative procedures.

IT
RIVISTA DI GIURISPRUDENZA TRIBUTARIA. (19??)-. Periodical. Italian. mo. L240000 Italy; L480000 other. IPSOA Editore SRL, Casella Postale 12055, Mastrangelo, 20120 Milan Italy. **Tel** 011 39 2 82476248.

IT
RIVISTA DI GIUSTIZIA AMMINISTRATIVA DELLA LOMBARDIA. ***Ceased.*** (19??)-(Jan. 1992). Italian. Edi Asga, Via Lovanio 5, 20121 Milan Italy.

IT
RIVISTA DI LEGISLAZIONE FISCALE. Rivista Legislazione Fiscale, Piazza Cola di Rienzo 69, 00192 Rome Italy.

IT
RIVISTA DI STORIA DEL DIRITTO ITALIANO. Vol. 1 (Jan./Apr. 1928)-. Italian. an. Biblioteca Patetta Facolta, University of Torina, Via S Ottavio 20, 10124 Turin Italy. **Tel** 001 39 11 885821. **LC** K22; .I76.

IT
RIVISTA GIURIDICA DEGLI UFFICI DI CONCILIAZIONE. (19??)-. Italian. bm (6 issues). L50000. Ceda, Via Prampolini 13, 42027 Montecchio Emilia Italy. **Tel** 011 39 522 864544.

IT
RIVISTA GIURIDICA DELL'EDILIZIA. (19??)-. Periodical. Italian. bm. L170000.00 Italy; L255000.00 other. Giuffre Editore SPA, Via Busto Arsizio 40, 20151 Milan Italy. **Tel** 011 398 2 38089200. **ED** Massimo Severo Giannini, Giuseppe Guarino, Lino Salis and Maria Alessandra Sandulli. **LC** KKH3067.A13; R58.
Desc: Provides a specialized and exhaustive review of legislation, administrative practice and jurisprudence related to urban planning and building.

IT/0394-834X
RIVISTA GIURIDICA DI POLIZIA LOCALE. [Riv. giurid. poliz. locale]. (1984)-. Periodical. Italian. bm (6 issues). L185000.00. Maggioli Editore, Casella Postale 290, 47037 Rimini, Italy. **Tel** 011 39 541 628666, FAX 011 39 541 742217. **UDC** 352.

IT
RIVISTA GIURIDICA DI URBANISTICA. No. 1 (Jan./March 1985)-. Periodical. Italian. qt. L160000 Italy; L118000 other. Maggioli Editore, Casella Postale 290, 47037 Rimini, Italy. **Tel** 011 39 541 628666, FAX 011 39 541 742217. **LC** K22; .I799.

IT/0394-0942
RIVISTA GIURIDICA SARDA. [Riv. giurid. sarda]. (1986)-. Periodical. Italian. tq. L100000.00 Italy; L150000.00 other. Giuffre Editore SPA, Via Busto Arsizio 40, 20151 Milan Italy. **Tel** 011 398 2 38089200. **ED** Luigi Concas, Angelo Luminoso, Paolo Fois, Costantino Murgia and Fausto Satta. **UDC** 34.
Desc: Offers a picture of the case law produced by Sardinian judges in the various branches of private and criminal law.

IT/0035-6727
RIVISTA INTERNAZIONALE DI FILOSOFIA DEL DIRITTO. Vol. 1 (Jan./March 1921)-. Periodical. Italian. qt. L90000.00 Italy; L135000.00 other. Giuffre Editore SPA, Via Busto Arsizio 40, 20151 Milan Italy. **Tel** 011 398 2 38089200. **ED**

Sergio Cotta. **LC** K22; .I82. cum. index. **Ad Acc. Circ:** 800.
Desc: This is the only Italian journal dealing with philosophy of law.
Ind/Abst Index Foreign Leg. Per.; Philos. Index.

IT/1120-5695
RIVISTA INTERNAZIONALE DIRITTO COMUNE. Multiple languages (Italian, English, French and German). an. L28000 (individuals), L40000 (institutions). Il Cigno Galileo Galilei, P Za de Ricci 129, 00186 Rome Italy.

IT
RIVISTA ITALIANA DI DIRITTO PUBBLICO COMUNITARIO. (1991)-. Italian. qt. L150000.00 Italy; L225000.00 other. Giuffre Editore SPA, Via Busto Arsizio 40, 20151 Milan Italy. **Tel** 011 398 2 38089200. **ED** Mario Chiti and Guido Greco. **LC** K22; .I87. **DD** 349.4/05; 344.05.
Desc: Contains reports on constitutional and administrative development underway in the Italian judicial system and in the most important member countries of the European Community.

IT
RIVISTA PENALE. Casa Editrice La Tribuna, Via Don Minzoni 51, 29100 Piacenza Italy. **Tel** 011 39 523 759015, 011 39 523 759020.

IT
RIVISTA PENALE ECONOMIA. (19??)-. Italian. Four times a year. L150000 (institutions), L125000 (individuals) Italy; L180000 other. Edizioni Scientifiche Italiane, Via Chiatamone 7, 80121 Naples Italy. **Tel** 011 39 81 7645768, 011 39 81 7645443, FAX 011 39 81 7646477.

IT
RIVISTA TRIMESTRALE DI DIRITTO E PROCEDURA CIVILE. Vol. 1 (1947)-. Periodical. Italian. Four times a year. L140000.00 Italy; L210000.00 other. Giuffre Editore SPA, Via Busto Arsizio 40, 20151 Milan Italy. **Tel** 011 398 2 38089200. **ED** Federico Carpi and Umberto Romagnoli. Index Available, published separately, free-automatically sent. cum. index. **Bk Rev. Ad Acc. Circ:** 3,000.
Desc: The continuously widening scope of this journal towards branches of law not strictly of a private nature, merely reflects the evolution of Italian juridical culture.
Ind/Abst Index Foreign Leg. Per.

IT
RIVISTA TRIMESTRALE DI DIRITTO PENALE DELL'ECONOMIA. Vol. 1, (1988)-. Periodical. Italian. Four times a year. L180000 Italy; L250000 other. Cedam Spa, Via Jappelli 5 6, 35121 Padua Italy. **Tel** 011 39 49 65667. **LC** K22; .I93. **Circ:** 1,200.

UK
ROAD TRAFFIC INDICATOR. (1994)-. Newsletter. English. Three times a year. £50.00 Europe; £52.00 other. Sweet & Maxwell Ltd., South Quay Plaza, 183 Marsh Wall, London E14 9FT England. **Tel** 011 44 264 342899, FAX 011 44 264 342723, telex 929089 ITPINF G.

●RU
ROSSIISKAIA IUSTITSIIA. Added/Corp Russia (Federation). Administratsiia Prezidenta. Russia (Federation). Ministerstvo Iustitsii. Russia (Federation). Verkhovnyi Sud. (1994)-. Periodical. Russian. mo. **(Subscription address:** East View Publications Inc., 3020 Harbor Lane North, Suite 110, Minneapolis MN 55447.**)** **LC** K23; .O9. ***Continues** Sovetskaia Iustitsiia (Moscow, R.S.F.S.R. : 1957).*
Ind/Abst Index Foreign Leg. Per.

UK
ROUFF & ROPER REGISTERED CONVEYANCING. (1991)-. English. ir. £195.00 (main work). Sweet & Maxwell Ltd., South Quay Plaza, 183 Marsh Wall, London E14 9FT England. **Tel** 011 44 264 342899, FAX 011 44 264 342723, telex 929089 ITPINF G.

CN
ROYAL GAZETTE. Main/Corp Nova Scotia. (19??)-. Periodical. English. Fifty-two times a year. 80.84Can$. Office of the Royal Gazette Department of Government Services, Finance and Administration, 14th Floor/Maritime Center, PO Box 54, Halifax Nova Scotia B3J 2L4 Canada. **Tel** (902)424-8575, FAX (902)424-0500. **ED** Susan MacIsaac. **LC** J2; .N8. Index available. cum. index. **Circ:** 600 (ctrl). available on microfilm from New York Public Library; and Micromedia Limited.
Desc: Official government record of cabinet proclamations, orders-in-council, regulations and non-government legal notices.

US
RULES AND REGULATIONS. Main/Corp United States. Federal Communications Commission. (19??)-. English. ir. Rules Service Company, 7615 Standish Place, Rockville MD 20855. **Tel** (301)424-9402, FAX (301)762-7853.

US/0362-1103
RULES AND REGULATIONS OF THE NEW YORK STATE THRUWAY AUTHORITY. Main/Corp New York State Thruway Authority. 1974-. English. New York State Thruway Authority, 200 Southern Boulevard, PO Box 189, Albany NY 12201. **LC** KFN5788.A39; N48. **DD** 343/.747/0946. ***Continues** Rules and Regulations for the Use and Occupancy of the Thruway System.*

US
RULES AND REGULATIONS - SOUTH CAROLINA. RESIDENTIAL HOME BUILDERS COMMISSION. Main/Corp South Carolina. Residential Home Builders Commission. 1976-. English. 2221 Devine Street, Suite 312, Columbia SC 29205.

US
RULES AND REGULATIONS / UNITED STATES NUCLEAR REGULATORY COMMISSION. Main/Corp United States. Nuclear Regulatory Commission. **VFOAT** United States Nuclear Regulatory Commission Rules and Regulations. (197?)-. Government Publication. English. ir. $422.00 US; $527.50 other. Superintendent of Documents, US Government Printing Office, Washington DC 20402. **Tel** (202)275-3328, FAX (202)786-2377. ***Continues** Atomic Energy Commission. Rules and Regulations.*
Desc: Information on law concerning nuclear reactors.

II/0485-9383
RULES COMPENDIUM UNDER CENTRAL ACTS. Main/Corp Rajasthan, India. **Added/Corp** Rajasthan, India. Law Dept. (1963)-. Periodical. English. Government of India Press / General Manager, Minto Road, New Delhi India.

US
RULES OF COURT. (19??)-. Periodical. English. ir. Lawyers Weekly Publications, 41 West Street, Boston MA 02111. **Tel** (617)451-7300, (800)444-5297.

US
RULES UPDATES. (19??)-. Periodical. English. ir (5 to 7 per year). $42.40. Lawyers Weekly Publications, 41 West Street, Boston MA 02111. **Tel** (617)451-7300, (800)444-5297.

US
RULINGS ENFORCEMENT ACTIONS, ADVISORY OPINIONS / STATE ETHICS COMMISSION. Main/Corp Massachusetts State Ethics Commission. (198?)-. English. ir (two or five times per year). Free. Massachusetts State Ethics Commission, 1 Ashburton Place, Room 619, Boston MA 12108. **Tel** (617)727-0060. **LC** KFM2806; .A555. **DD** 342.744/0684/02648; 347.440268402648. ***Continues** Massachusetts State Ethics Commission. State Ethics Commission Enforcement Actions, Advisory Opinions, 0898-946X.*

●US/1061-1940
RUSSIAN POLITICS AND LAW. [Russ. polit. law]. Vol. 31, No. 1 (Summer 1992)-. Periodical. English (translations available in Russian). bm. $520.00 US; $571.00 other. M. E. Sharpe Inc., 80 Business Park Drive, Armonk NY 10504. **Tel** (914)273-1800, (800)541-6563, FAX (914)273-2106. **LC** K22; .U78. **DD** 348. Documents available from The Genuine Article. ***Continues** Soviet Law and Government, 0038-5530.*
Ind/Abst Curr. Contents Soc. Behav. Sci.; Res. Alert [Full Cov.]; Soc. Sci. Cit. Index [Full Cov.].

US/0277-318X
RUTGERS LAW JOURNAL. [Rutgers law j.]. **Added/Corp** Rutgers School of Law, Camden (N.J.). Vol. 12, No. 1 (Fall 1980)- LVol. 24 (1993)- Vol. 24 No. 2 (Winter 1993)-. Periodical. English. Four times a year (Within seasons of the year). $22.50 US & Canada; $27.50 other. Rutgers University / Law, School of Law, 5th and Penn Streets, Camden NJ 08102. **Tel** (609)964-9101, FAX (609)225-6487. **ED** Donna E. Correll. **LC** K22; .U8. **DD** 349.73/05; 347.3005. Index Available in last issue of each volume--loose separately paged. cum. index. **Bk Rev. Ad Acc. Circ:** 1,200 (ctrl). ***Continues** Rutgers Camden Law Journal, 0036-0449.*
Desc: Professional and student legal scholarship and book reviews.
Ind/Abst Bowne Dig. Corp. Sec. Lawyers; Crim. Justice Abstr.; Curr. Law Index (1980-); Fed. Tax Artic.; Index Leg. Period.; Leg. Resour. Index (1980-); LegalTrac (1985-).

US/0036-0465
RUTGERS LAW REVIEW. [Rutgers law rev.]. **Added/Corp** Rutgers Law School (Newark, N.J.). **VFOAT** Civil Rights Developments. Vol. 3 (Feb. 1949)-. Periodical. English. qt. $30.00 US; $35.00 other. Rutgers Law School, 15 Washington Street, 14th Floor, Newark NJ 07102. **Tel** (201)648-5549. **ED** Patricia Cullen. **Bk Rev**, (Qty: 2-4). **Ad Acc, Adv Mgr:** Brenda McDonough. **Circ:** 1,000 (ctrl). Documents available from The Genuine Article. ***Continues** Rutgers University Law Review.*
Ind/Abst Bowne Dig. Corp. Sec. Lawyers; Crim. Justice Abstr.; Curr. Contents Soc. Behav. Sci.; Curr. Law Index (1980-); Fed. Tax Artic.; Hum. Resour. Abstr. (?-?); Index Leg. Period.; Leg. Resour. Index (1980-); LegalTrac (1980-); Res. Alert [Select. Cov.]; Sage Fam. Stud. Abstr. (?-?); Sage Public Adm. Abstr. (?-?); Soc. Sci. Cit. Index [Select. Cov.]; Urban Aff. Abstr.

AT/0818-3236
S.A. LAW LIBRARIANS BULLETIN. **See** Library and Information Sciences.

FR/0038-7282
S.P.E.L.D - INFORMATION. (S.P.E.L.D - INFORMATION : DROIT ECONOMIE POLITIQUE SCIENCES SOCIALES ET HUMAINES ERUDITION.). [S.P.E.L.D - inf.]. **Added/Corp** Societe de Promotion a l'Etranger du Livre de Droit, Sciences Economiques, Sociales et Humaines. (19??)-. Periodical. French (English and German). qt (4 issues). 90.00F France; $15.00 US. SPELD Information, 6 rue Victor-Cousin, 75005 Paris France. **Tel** 011 33 1 46336910. **Circ:** 7,000.
Desc: Future books, and new publications in law, economics, political, and social sciences.

SA/1015-0099
SA MERCANTILE LAW JOURNAL / SA TYDSKRIF VIR HANDELSREG. Added/Corp University of South Africa. Faculty of Law. **VFOAT** SA Tydskrif vir Handelsreg; SA Merc LJ. **VAT** South Africa Mercantile Law Journal. Vol. 1, No. 1 (1989)-. Periodical. English (Afrikaans). Three times a year. R144.00. Juta Subscription Services, PO Box 14373, Kenwyn 7790 South Africa. **Tel** 011 27 21 7975101, FAX (021)761-5010, telex 523072 SA. ***Continues** Moderne Besigheidsreg.*

SA/0258-6568
SA PUBLIEKREG. VFOAT SA Public Law; SA Publiekreg/Public Law. **VAT** Suid-Arikaanse Publiekreg; South African Public Law. Vol. 1 (June 1986)-. Periodical. Afrikaans (English). be (May and November). $30.00. University of South Africa, PO Box 392, Pretoria 0001 South Africa. **Tel** 011 27 12 4298468, FAX 011 (27)12 429 3321, telex (59)350068+. **ED** D. San Wyk. **LC** K23; .A25. **DD** 344.68; 346.804. Index available. **Circ:** 400.
Desc: An established biennual legal periodical containing topical articles, comments and features on all aspects of South African public law, including environmental law.

US/0486-8161
SACRAMENTO NEWSLETTER, THE. (19??)-. Newsletter. English. wk. $60.00. The Sacramento Newsletter, 1714 Capitol Avenue, Sacramento CA 95814. **Tel** (916)444-2840. **ED** Gary L. Queale. **Circ:** 2,000 (ctrl).
Desc: Comprehensive weekly report on California legislation in state and local government. Reports and provides insight into current and proposed legislation.

US/0036-3030
SAINT LOUIS UNIVERSITY LAW JOURNAL. [St. Louis Univ. law j.]. **Main/Corp** St. Louis University. School of Law. Vol. 1, No. 4 (Winter 1951)-. Periodical. English. Four times a year. $25.00 US; $27.00 other. St Louis University Law, 3700 Lindell Boulevard, St Louis MO 63108. **Tel** (314)658-3964, FAX (314)658-3946. **ED** Stanley Rice; Telephone: (314)658-3933. Index available in last issue of volume--attached. **Bk Rev**, (Qty: 2-3). **Ad Acc, Adv Mgr:** Mark Boatman. ctrl circ. ***Continues** Intramural Law Review (Saint Louis, Mo.).*
Ind/Abst Bowne Dig. Corp. Sec. Lawyers; Crim. Justice Abstr.; Curr. Law Index (1980-); Fed. Tax Artic.; Index Leg. Period.; Leg. Resour. Index (1980-); LegalTrac (1980-).

US/0898-8404
SAINT LOUIS UNIVERSITY PUBLIC LAW REVIEW. [St. Louis Univ. public law rev.]. **Added/Corp** St. Louis University. School of Law. Thomas J. White Family Center of Public Law and Government of the Saint Louis University School of Law. **VFOAT** Public Law Review. (1986)-. Periodical. English. Twice a year (Jan., & May). $20.00 US; $25.00 other. Saint Louis University School of Law, 3700 Lindell Boulevard, c/o Susie Lee, Saint Louis MO 63108. **Tel** (314)658-3964, FAX (314)658-3966. **LC** K16; .U224. **DD** 342.73; 347.302. Index available. **Bk Rev. Ad Acc. Circ:** 750. ***Continues** Public Law Forum, 0738-5390.*
Desc: Covers public law issues including: housing, ethics, medical technology and its legal impacts, international, economic, and industrial law issues, constitutional and criminal law.
Ind/Abst Index Leg. Period.; Leg. Resour. Index; LegalTrac (1986-); PAIS Int. Print; Sage Public Adm. Abstr.

SZ
SAMMLUNG DER EIDGENOSSISCHEN GESETZE. Main/Corp Switzerland. (1850)-. Periodical. German (French and Italian). wk. 80.00F. Staempfli & Cie SA, Postfach 8326, CH-3001 Bern Switzerland. **Tel** 011 41 31 3006666, telex 031 911 515 EDMZ CH. Index available. cum. index. **Bk Rev.** ctrl circ.
Desc: Concerned with Swiss law.

GW/0080-5823
SAMMLUNG GELTENDER STAATSANGEHARIGKEITSGESETZE. (1949)-. Monographic series. German. ir. Price varies per volume. Hermann Luchterhand Verlag, Postfach 2352, D 56513 Neuwied Germany. **Tel** 011 49 2631 8010. **(Subscription address:** Luchterhand Verlagsauslieferng, Postfach 2352, D 56513 Neuwied Germany.**)**

●US/1073-676X
SAN DIEGO JUSTICE JOURNAL. [S. Diego justice j.]. **Added/Corp** Western State University College of Law. **VFOAT** WSU San Diego Justice Journal. Vol. 1, No. 1 (Winter 1993)-. Periodical. English. sa. $9.00 (per issue). Western State University College of Law, 2121 San Diego Avenue, San Diego CA 92110. **Tel** (619)298-3111. **DD** 345. ***Continues*** *Criminal Justice Journal, 0145-4226.*

US/0036-4037
SAN DIEGO LAW REVIEW, THE. [San Diego law rev.]. **Added/Corp** University of San Diego. School of Law. Vol. 1 (Jan. 1964)-. Periodical. English. qt. $25.00. University of San Diego School of Law, 5998 Alcala Park, San Diego CA 92110. **Tel** (619)260-4531. **DD** 349.794/05; 347.94005. Index available. cum. index. **Bk Rev. Ad Acc. Circ:** 1,000 (ctrl). Documents available from UMI Article Clearinghouse.
Desc: Immigration, tax law, Pacific Rim, open topics.
Ind/Abst ABI/INFORM Glob. Ed.; ABI Inform Ondisc (Dec. 1976-); Bowne Dig. Corp. Sec. Lawyers; Curr. Law Index (1980-); Fed. Tax Artic.; Index Leg. Period.; Leg. Resour. Index (1980-); LegalTrac (1980-).

US/0744-9348
SAN FRANCISCO ATTORNEY, THE. [San Franc. atty.]. **Added/Corp** Bar Association of San Francisco. Vol. 8, No. 3 (April 1982)-. English. bm (Feb., Apr., Jun., Aug., Oct., Dec.). $26.00. Bar Association of San Francisco, 685 Market Street, Suite 700, San Francisco CA 94105. **Tel** (415)764-1600. **LC** KF200; .B74. **DD** 340/.06/0794. ***Continues*** *Brief/Case (San Francisco, Calif. : 1974), 0520-9633.*
Ind/Abst Fed. Tax Artic.

US/0744-3072
SAN FRANCISCO BARRISTER. Vol. 1, No. 1 (Jan./Feb. 1982)-. Periodical. English. mo. San Francisco Barrister, 685 Market Street, San Francisco CA 94105. **LC** KF200; .S23. **DD** 340/06/079461. ***Continues*** *Barristers' Bailiwick, 0279-4314.*
Ind/Abst Fed. Tax Artic.

US/1059-2636
SAN FRANCISCO DAILY JOURNAL (1990). (SAN FRANCISCO DAILY JOURNAL.). [San Franc. dly. j.]. Vol. 96, No. 102 (May 21, 1990)-. Newspaper. English. da. $357.00 (print); $799.00 (microfilm). Daily Journal Corporation, 915 East First Street, Los Angeles CA 90012. **Tel** (213)229-5300, FAX (213)680-3682. **ED** Dirk Olin and Steve Ball (Managing Editor). **DD** 340. **Photos. Ad Acc, Adv Mgr:** Linda Hubbell, **Tel** (415)252-0500. Full Page (B&W) $1,151.28. Half Page (B&W) $575.64. **Pub. Size:** Standard. **Wire Svcs.:** AP. available in microform from Data Microfilming Corporation. ***Continues*** *San Francisco Banner Daily Journal.*

US/1055-422X
SAN JOAQUIN AGRICULTURAL LAW REVIEW. [San Joaquin agric. law rev.]. **Added/Corp** San Joaquin College of Law. **VFOAT** Agricultural Law Review. Vol. 1, No. 1 (1991)-. English. an. $12.00. San Joaquin College of Law, 3385 East Shields Avenue, Fresno CA 93726. **Tel** (209)225-4953. **LC** K23; .A517. **DD** 343.73/076; 347.30376. **Bk Rev**, (Qty: 1). **Circ:** 500.

IO
SANGKAKALA PERADILAN. Indonesian. 450. Ikatan Hakim Indonesia, Djl Siliwangi 151, Semaraney Indonesia. **LC** K23; .A53.

US/0882-3383
SANTA CLARA COMPUTER AND HIGH-TECHNOLOGY LAW JOURNAL. [Santa Clara comput. high-technol. law j.]. **Added/Corp** University of Santa Clara. School of Law. **VFOAT** Santa Clara Computer and High Technology Law Journal. Vol. 1, No. 1 (Jan. 1985)-. Periodical. English. sa. $40.00. Santa Clara Computer High Tech, Santa Clara University, Santa Clara CA 95053. **Tel** (408)554-4197. **LC** K23; .A55. **DD** 343.73/07800164; 347.3037800164 #2 19. **Bk Rev.**
Desc: Provides articles, essays and analysis of current legal developments in the fields of high technology, computers, intellectual property, and licensing.
Ind/Abst Curr. Law Index (1985-); Index Leg. Period.; Leg. Resour. Index (1985-); LegalTrac (1980-).

US/0146-0315
SANTA CLARA LAW REVIEW. [Santa Clara law rev.]. **Added/Corp** University of Santa Clara. School of Law. Vol. 16 (1975)-. Periodical. English. Four times a year. $40.00. Santa Clara Law Review, Santa Clara Unversity, School of Law, Santa Clara CA 95053. **Tel** (408)554-4074. **ED** Christine Nakagawa. **LC** K23; .A56. **DD** 340/.09794. Index available. cum. index. **Bk Rev**, (Qty: 4). **Circ:** 20,000 (ctrl). ***Continues*** *Santa Clara Lawyer.*
Desc: Articles, comments, case notes and book reviews on subjects of interest to the legal community.
Ind/Abst Bowne Dig. Corp. Sec. Lawyers; Curr. Law Index (1980-); Fed. Tax Artic.; Index Leg. Period.; Leg. Resour. Index (1980-); LegalTrac (1980-).

CN/0319-7999
SASKATCHEWAN DECISIONS, CIVIL AND CRIMINAL CASES. (1975)-. English. mo. 290.00Can$. Western Legal Publications Ltd., 301 One Alexander Street, Vancouver BC V6A 1B2 Canada. **Tel** (800)663-0422, (604)687-5671. **DD** 348/.7124/048. cum. index.
Desc: Comprehensive digests of civil and criminal decisions from Saskatchewan Court of Appeal, Court of Queen's Bench and District Courts of Saskatchewan.

CN/0036-4916
SASKATCHEWAN LAW REVIEW. [Sask. law rev.]. **Added/Corp** University of Saskatchwan. College of Law. Vol. 32 (April 1967)-. Periodical. English. Twice a year. 26.00Can$. University of Saskatchewan College of Law, Saskatoon Saskatchewan S7N 0W0 Canada. **Tel** (306)966-5897, FAX (306)966-5900. **ED** Tim Quigley (Editor's Phone: (306)966-5884). cum. index (up to 1990). **Bk Rev. Circ:** 1,800 (ctrl). ***Continues*** *Saskatchewan Bar Review, 0380-8564.*
Desc: Prints articles, case comments and book reviews of interest to Saskatchewan and Canadian practitioners and academics.
Ind/Abst Can. Legal Lit.; Curr. Law Index (1980-); Energy Res. Abstr. (June 1982-); Hum. Rights Intern. Rep.; Index Can. Leg. Period. Lit.; Index Leg. Period.; Leg. Resour. Index (1980-); LegalTrac (1980-).

CN/0713-7095
SASKATCHEWAN REPORTS. [Sask. rep.]. **Added/Corp** Saskatchewan. Court of Appeal. Canada. Supreme Court. Issue 1 (Dec. 15, 1979)-. English. ir (Publishes six or nine times). 124.00Can$ (latest volume). Maritime Law Book Ltd, PO Box 302, Fredericton New Brunswick, E3B 4Y9 Canada. **Tel** (506)453-9921, (800)561-0220. **DD** 348.7124/043.
Desc: Contains all information of judgements of the Saskatchewan Court of Appeal, plus selected judgements from other courts, and judgements of the Supreme Court of Canada as well for other related cases.

US
SCALL NEWSLETTER / SOUTHERN CALIFORNIA ASSOCIATION OF LAW LIBRARIES. See Library and Information Sciences.

GW/0036-6250
SCHOFFE, DER. Vol. 1- ; June 1954-. Periodical. German. mo. Deutscher Judo Verband, Redaktion Ippon Segewaldweg 40, D 12557 Berlin Germany. **Tel** 011 49 711 210770, telex 051 678. **DD** 347.431/0752; 344.3107752. Index available in last issue of volume--attached.

CN/0833-0875
SCHOOL LAW COMMENTARY. [Sch. law comment.]. Vol. 1, No. 1 (Sept. 1986)-. Periodical. English. mo (10 issues). $64.95. School Law Commentary, PO Box 48645, Vancouver BC V7X 1A3 Canada. **Tel** (604)924-1171. **DD** 344.71/07/05.

US/0891-5474
SCHOOL LAW NEWSLETTER (VERNON, TEX.), THE. (THE SCHOOL LAW NEWSLETTER.). [Sch. law newsl.]. (19??)-. Newsletter. English. Three times a year. $36.00 (two years). School Law Newsletter, PO Box 199, Ranger TX 76470. **Tel** (817)647-3300. **ED** Dr. Joe Mills. **LC** KF4102; .S36. **DD** 344.73/07/05; 347.304705.

US/1059-4094
SCHOOL LAW REPORTER. [Sch. law report.]. **Added/Corp** National Organization on Legal Problems of Education. Vol. 28, No. 5, May (1987)-. Periodical. English. mo. $75.00 US; $80.00 Canada; $85.00 other. National Organization on Legal Problems of Education, 3601 Southwest 29th Street, Suite 223, Topeka KS 66614. **Tel** (913)273-3550, FAX (913)273-2001. **ED** Reynolds C Seitz. **LC** KF4114; .N35. **DD** 344/.73/07. **Bk Rev. Circ:** 2,500 (ctrl). ***Continues*** *Nolpe School Law Reporter, 0364-9547.*
Desc: Education law case digests and summaries.

●US
SCHOOL LAW / WASHINGTON STATE SCHOOL DIRECTORS' ASSOCIATION. **Added/Corp** Washington State School Directors' Association. **VFOAT** School Law Digest; WSSDA School Law Digest. (Jan. 1992)-. Periodical. English. mo. **LC** KFW390.A15; S36. ***Continues*** *School Law Digest.*

US/0890-1236
SCHOOLS ADVOCATE, THE. [Sch. advocate]. Vol. 1, No. 1, (June 1986)-. Periodical. English. mo. $175.00. Kinghorn Press Inc., 12280 Sar/Sunnyvale Road, Suite 209, Saratoga CA 95070. **Tel** (408)253-9585, FAX (408)253-0230. **ED** Eric Hermstoe. **LC** KF4210.A15; S36. **DD** 344.73/0791; 347.304791. (June). cum. index.
Desc: Emphasizes legal advice to schools.

GW
SCHRIFTEN ZUM DEUTSCHEN UND EUROPAISCHEN ZIVIL, -HANDELS- UND PROZESSRECHT. (1956)-. Monographic series. German. ir. Price varies per volume. Verlag E & W Gieseking GmbH, Postfach 130120, Deckerstrasse 30, D-33544 Bielefeld 13 Germany. **Tel** 011 49 521 14674.

GW
SCHRIFTEN ZUM OFFENTLICHEN RECHT. (1958)-. Monographic series. German. ir. Price varies per volume. Duncker und Humblot Verlag, Postfach 410329, D-12113 Berlin Germany. **Tel** 011 49 30 79000612, 011 49 30 79000613.

GW
SCHRIFTEN ZUM PROZESSRECHT. (19??)-. Monographic series. German. ir. Price varies per volume. Duncker und Humblot Verlag, Postfach 410329, D-12113 Berlin Germany. **Tel** 011 49 30 79000612, 011 49 30 79000613.

GW
SCHRIFTEN ZUR RECHTSGESCHICHTE. No. 1, (1970)-. Monographic series. German. ir. Price varies per volume. Duncker und Humblot Verlag, Postfach 410329, D-12113 Berlin Germany. **Tel** 011 49 30 79000612, 011 49 30 79000613.

GW
SCHRIFTEN ZUR RECHTSTHEORIE. Monographic series. German. ir. Price varies per volume. Duncker und Humblot Verlag, Postfach 410329, D-12113 Berlin Germany. **Tel** 011 49 30 79000612, 011 49 30 79000613.
Desc: Contributions to theories of law, morals and ethics.

GW
SCHRIFTENREIHE. **Main/Corp** Berlin. Freie Universitat. Institut fur Rechtssoziologie und Rechtstatsachenforschung. German. ir. Duncker und Humblot Verlag, Postfach 410329, D-12113 Berlin Germany. **Tel** 011 49 30 79000612, 011 49 30 79000613.

SZ
SCHWEIZERISCHE ZEITSCHRIFT FUER WIRTSCHAFTSRECHT. **VFOAT** Revue Suisse de Droit des Affaires; Swiss Review of Business Law. (1990)-. German. bm. Schulthess Polygraphischer Verlag, Zwinglipatz 2, CH-8022 Zurich Switzerland. **Tel** 011 41 1 2519336. **LC** K23; .C39. ***Continues*** *Schweizerische Aktiengesellschaft.*

SZ
SCHWEIZERISCHES PRIVATRECHT. (19??)-. Periodical. German. ir. Price varies per volume. Helbing & Lichtenhahn Verlag, Freie Strasse 82, CH-4051 Basel Switzerland. **Tel** 011 41 61 2721116.

SZ
SCHWEIZERISCHES ZENTRALLBLATT FUER STAATS- UND VERWALTUNGSRECHT. (19??)-. Periodical. German. mo. 128.00F. Orell Fuessli Zeitschriften, Dietzingerstrasse 3, PF 8036, CH 8036 Zurich Switzerland. **Tel** 044 41 1 4667711. ***Continues*** *Schweizerisches Zentralblatt fur Staats- und Gemeindeverwaltung.*
Desc: Information on administrative law.

PO
SCIENTIA IURIDICA. (July/Sept. 1951)-. Portuguese. ir. Livraria Cruz, Rua D Diogo de Sousa 127-133, 4700 Braga Portugal.

UK/0264-8717
SCOLAG : SCOTTISH LEGAL ACTION GROUP BULLETIN. [SCOLAG, Scott. Legal Action Group]. **Added/Corp** Scottish Legal Action Group. **VFOAT** Bulletin of the Scottish Legal Action Group; Scottish Legal Action Group Bulletin. No. 1 (Oct. 1975)-. Bulletin. English. mo. SCOLAG, 40 Perth Road, Dundee DD1 4LN Scotland.
Ind/Abst Leg. Resour. Index; LegalTrac (1980-).

UK/0036-908X
SCOTS LAW TIMES, THE. **Added/Corp** Scotland. Laws, Statutes, etc. (May 20, 1893)-. English. Forty times a year. £358.00 Europe; £376.00 other. Sweet & Maxwell Ltd., South Quay Plaza, 183 Marsh Wall, London E14 9FT England. **Tel** 011 44 264 342899, FAX 011 44 264 342723, telex 929089 ITPINF G.
Ind/Abst Leg. Resour. Index.

UK/0036-908X
SCOTS LAW TIMES; LYON COURT REPORTS, THE. **VFOAT** Lyon Court Reports. (1955)-. English. W Green & Son Ltd, St Giles Street, Edinburgh EH1 1PU Scotland. **Tel** 011 44 31 2254879, FAX 011 44 31 2252104.

UK/0036-908X
SCOTS LAW TIMES; NOTES OF RECENT DECISIONS, THE. **Added/Corp** Scotland. Courts. (1960)-. English. an. W Green & Son Ltd, St Giles Street, Edinburgh EH1 1PU Scotland. **Tel** 011 44 31 2254879, FAX 011 44 31 2252104.

UK/0036-908X
SCOTS LAW TIMES; REPORTS, THE. (1895/96)-. English. an. W Green & Son Ltd, St Giles Street, Edinburgh EH1 1PU Scotland. **Tel** 011 44 31 2254879, FAX 011 44 31 2252104.

UK/0036-908X
SCOTS LAW TIMES; SCOTTISH LAND COURT REPORTS, THE. **VFOAT** Scottish Land Court Reports. (1964)-. English. an. W Green & Son Ltd, St Giles Street, Edinburgh EH1 1PU Scotland. **Tel** 011 44 31 2254879, FAX 011 44 31 2252104. ***Continues*** *Scottish Land Court Reports.*

UK/0036-908X
SCOTS LAW TIMES; SHERIFF COURT REPORTS, THE. **VFOAT** Sheriff Court Reports. (1922)-. English. an. W Green & Son Ltd, St Giles Street, Edinburgh EH1 1PU Scotland. **Tel** 011 44 31 2254879, FAX 011 44 31 2252104.

UK/0036-908X
SCOTS LAW TIMES; THE LANDS TRIBUNAL FOR SCOTLAND REPORTS, THE. **Added/Corp** Scotland. Lands Tribunal for Scotland. **VFOAT** Lands Tribunal for Scotland Reports. (1971)-. English. Forty times a year (Fridays and weekly when court is in session). £330.00 UK; £380.00 other. W Green & Son Ltd, St Giles Street, Edinburgh EH1 1PU Scotland. **Tel** 011 44 31 2254879, FAX 011 44 31 2252104. **ED** Peter A Nicholson. Index available. cum. index. **Bk Rev**. **Ad Acc. Circ:** 2,000 (ctrl).
Desc: A comprehensive and authoritative law reporting service combined with up-to-date news and comment on all matters of interest to the legal profession in Scotland.
Ind/Abst LegalTrac (1980-).

UK
SCOTTISH CURRENT LAW YEAR BOOK. ***Title Change.*** (1948)-(199?). English. an. W Green & Son Ltd, St Giles Street, Edinburgh EH1 1PU Scotland. **Tel** 011 44 31 2254879, FAX 011 44 31 2252104. ***Continued by*** *Current Law.*

UK/0080-8083
SCOTTISH LAW DIRECTORY FOR ..., THE. (1892)-. Directory. English. an. £32.00 UK; £45.50 US. T & T Clark Ltd., 59 George Street, Edinburgh EH2 2LQ Scotland. **Tel** 011 44 31 2254703, FAX 011 44 31 2204260. **ED** Elizabeth Thompson. Index available. **Ad Acc, Adv Mgr:** Raylene Davidson, **Tel** 011 44 31 225 4703. **Acid Free. Circ:** 4,000. Documents available from BLDSC.
Desc: A list of legal practitioners published by the authority of the Law Society of Scotland. Regular features include latest professional lists of the Faculty of Advocates and Chartered Accountants. Complete lists of solicitor-Advocates and solicitor's accredited by the Law Society of Scotland as specialists in by Scottish legal firms. Information on Scottish courts, central and local governments, branches of Building Societies, insurance companies, banks and estate agents, messengers-at-arms, Sheriff Officers, Licensing Boards and Surveyors.

UK/0036-9314
SCOTTISH LAW GAZETTE, THE. [Scott. law gaz.]. **Added/Corp** Scottish Law Agents Society. Council. Vol. 1, No. 1 (Mar. 1933)-. Periodical. English. qt (Mar., June, Sept., Dec.). £16.00. Scottish Law Agents Society, 3 Albyn Pl, c/o R M Sinclair Secy, Edinburgh EH2 4NQ Scotland. **Tel** (011-44-31)225-7515, FAX (001-44-31)220-1083. **ED** Dr. Enid Marshall. **Bk Rev**. **Ad Acc, Adv Mgr:** Derek Flyn. **Circ:** 2,300 (ctrl).
Desc: This publication includes articles dealing with European law, special cases, Parliament, taxation, Scottish Law Commission, employment and other relevant areas.

UK/0144-8196
SCOTTISH PLANNING LAW & PRACTICE. ***Title Change.*** [Scott. plann. law pract.]. **Added/Corp** Law Society of Scotland. Planning Exchange. **VFOAT** Scottish Planning Law and Practice. No. 1 (Sept. 1980)-(1993). Periodical. English. Three times a year. Planning Exchange, 186 Bath Street, Glasgow G2 4HG Scotland. **Tel** 011 44 41 3328541. **ED** Tony Burton. **LC** KDC446.A13; S25. **DD** 346.41104/5; 344.110645. cum. index. **Bk Rev**. **Ad Acc. Circ:** 8,000. ***Continued by*** *Scottish Planning & Environmental Law.*
Ind/Abst Geogr. Abstr. Human Geogr. (?-?).

US/1049-5177
SCRIBES JOURNAL OF LEGAL WRITING, THE. (THE SCRIBES JOURNAL OF LEGAL WRITING : AN OFFICIAL PUBLICATION OF SCRIBES, THE AMERICAN SOCIETY OF WRITERS ON LEGAL SUBJECTS.). [Scribes j. legal writing]. **Added/Corp** Scribes. **VFOAT** SJLW. Vol. 1 (1990)-. English. an. $25.00. Scribes, PO Box 7206 WFU Reynold A Stat, Winston Salem NC 27109. **Tel** (919)759-5440. **LC** K23; .S37. **DD** 808/.06634; 808.
Ind/Abst Index Leg. Period. (1992-).

US/0095-1005
SEARCH AND SEIZURE LAW REPORT. [Search seiz. law rep.]. **Added/Corp** Clark Boardman Company. Vol. 1, (Nov. 1973)-. English. Eleven times a year (With 1 combined iss.). $165.00. Clark Boardman Callaghan, 155 Pfingsten Road, Deerfield IL 60015. **Tel** (800)323-8067. **ED** A. Weinstein. **LC** KF9630.A73; S4. **DD** 345/.73/052. **Bk Rev**. available on microfilm and microfiche from University Microfilms International (UMI).
Ind/Abst Crim. Justice Period. Index; Curr. Law Index (1982-); Leg. Resour. Index (1982-); LegalTrac (1982-).

●CN/1188-6137
SEARCH AND SEIZURE LAW REPORTER, THE. [Search Seizure Law Report.]. **Added/Corp** Amicus Legal Publishing Co. Vol. 1, Issue 1 (May 1992)-. Periodical. English. mo. $195.00 per year. Amicus Legal Publishing Co., 39 Tamarack Drive, Thornhill Ontario L3T 4W2 Canada. **DD** 345.71.

●US
SEATTLE UNIVERSITY LAW REVIEW. (Fall 1994)-. English. ir. $22.00. Seattle University / Law Review, 950 Broadway Plaza, Tacoma WA 98402-4470. **Tel** (206)591-2995, FAX (206)591-6313. Index available. ***Continues*** *University of Puget Sound Law Review, 0161-0708.*

PH
SEC QUARTERLY BULLETIN, THE. **Main/Corp** Philippines. Securities and Exchange Commission. Bulletin. English. qt (March, June, September and December). P120.00. Securities & Exchange Commission, Box 104, Greenhills Metro Manila Philippines. **Tel** 78-09-31 LOC. 254. **ED** Angelita A Ledesma. **DD** 346/.599/066605.

US/0145-8744
SEC SPEAKS IN ..., THE. [SEC speaks]. **VFOAT** S.E.C. Speaks in ... . **VAT** Securities and Exchange Commission Speaks. English. Practising Law Institute, 810 Seventh Avenue, New York NY 10019-5818. **Tel** (212)765-5700, FAX (212)581-4670 general correspondence, (212)265-4742 orders and billing inquiries. **LC** KF1440; .S453. **DD** 346.73/092; 347.30692. ***Continues*** *United States. Securities and Exchange Commission. SEC Speaks, 0145-8744.*

US/0746-5254
SECOND CIRCUIT DIGEST. ***Title Change.*** **Added/Corp** Federal Bar Council. United States. Circuit Court (2nd Circuit). (197?)-(199?). English. mo (10 issues). Federal Bar Council, 145 East 49th Street, New York NY 10017. **Tel** (212)644-9771. ctrl circ. ***Continued by*** *Federal Bar Council News, 1075-8534.*

US/0277-2361
SECTION OF TAXATION NEWSLETTER / ABA. [Sect. tax. newsl.]. **Added/Corp** American Bar Association. Section of Taxation. **VFOAT** Newsletter. Vol. 1, No. 1 (Fall 1981)-. Newsletter. English. qt (4 issues). $15.00. American Bar Association, 750 North Lake Shore Drive, Chicago IL 60611. **Tel** (312)988-5522, (312)988-5241, FAX (312)988-5528, telex 270593. **LC** KF6272; .S42. **DD** 343.7304/05; 347.303405.

UK
SECURITIES AND CAPITAL MARKETS LAW REPORTS. (199?)-. Periodical. English. Ten times a year. £395.00 UK; $595.00 other. Euromoney Publications PLC, Nestor House, Playhouse Yard, London EC4Z 5EX England. **Tel** 011 44 71 779 8888, FAX 011 44 71 779 8617, telex 290700 EUROMON G. **(Subscription address:** Euromoney Publications Plc, Perrymount Road Haywards Heath, West Sussex RH16 3DH England.**)**
Desc: Written for those using the national and international securities markets. Provides information on changes in the regulatory environment, issuing securities, listing and trading of securities, on-going compliance and taxation of securities and mergers and acquisitions.

US
SECURITIES & INSIDER TRADING LITIGATION REPORTER. (Feb. 12, 1987)-. English. sm (24 issues). $1250.00. Andrews Publications Inc., 1646 West Chester Pike, PO Box 1000, Westtown PA 19395. **Tel** (610)399-6600, (800)345-1101, FAX (610)399-6610. **LC** KF1073.I5; A497. **DD** 345.73/0268.
Desc: Provides coverage of civil and criminal actions involving insider trading and other types of stock price manipulation.

US/1042-3184
SECURITIES ARBITRATION. [Secur. arbitr.]. **Added/Corp** Practising Law Institute. (1988)-. English. an. $80.00. Practising Law Institute, 810 Seventh Avenue, New York NY 10019-5818. **Tel** (212)765-5700, FAX (212)581-4670 general correspondence, (212)265-4742 orders and billing inquiries. **LC** KF1070.Z9; S42. **DD** 346.73/0926; 347.306926.

US/8756-209X
SECURITIES REGULATION LAW ALERT. ***Ceased.*** [Secur. regul. law alert]. Vol. 17, No. 10 (1984)-Vol. 20, No. 4 (1987). Periodical. English. sm. Warren Gorham & Lamont Inc., Park Square Building, 31 St. James Avenue, Boston MA 02116-4112. **Tel** (617)423-2020, (800)950-1207, FAX (617)423-2026. **LC** KF1066.A3; S43. **DD** 346.73/092/05; 347.3069205. ***Continues*** *Securities Regulation and Transfer Report, 0037-0673.*

US/0097-9554
SECURITIES REGULATION LAW JOURNAL. [Secur. regul. law j.]. Vol. 1 (Spring 1973)-. English. qt (4 issues). $183.25 US & Canada; $271.45 other. Warren Gorham & Lamont Inc., Park Square Building, 31 St. James Avenue, Boston MA 02116-4112. **Tel** (617)423-2020, (800)950-1207, FAX (617)423-2026. **ED** S. James Rosenfeld. **LC** K23; .E28. **DD** 346/.73/09205. **[CCC]**. cum. index. **Pr Rev**. available on microfilm and microfiche from University Microfilms International (UMI). Documents available from The Genuine Article, UMI Article Clearinghouse.
Desc: Offers incisive analysis and in-depth advice through articles and features by noted practitioners and scholars helping you to keep up with the constant changes in the law, rules, and regulations.
Ind/Abst ABI/INFORM Glob. Ed.; ABI Inform Ondisc (Winter 1982-); Account. Tax Datab. (1974-); Bowne Dig. Corp. Sec. Lawyers; Bus. Index (1985-); Curr. Law Index (1980-); Gen. BusinessFile (1985-); Gen. Period. Index (1985-); Index Leg. Period.; Leg. Resour. Index (1980-); LegalTrac (1980-); Res. Alert [Full Cov.]; Soc. Sci. Cit. Index [Full Cov.].

US
SECURITIES REGULATION (NEW YORK, N.Y.). ***Title Change.*** (SECURITIES REGULATION.). 1st Ed. (1979)-2nd Ed. (1981). English. Law Distributors, 14415 South Main Street, Gardena CA 90248. **Tel** (310)321-3275, (800)421-1893, FAX (310)324-6381. **LC** KF1440; .G55. **DD** 346.73/092. ***Continued by*** *Gilbert Law Summaries. Securities Regulation.*

BL
SELECAO DE PARECERES E ESTUDOS DA COORDENACAO DE LEGISLACAO E NORMAS DE ENSINO. **Main/Corp** Brazil. Coordenacao de Legislacao e Normas de Ensino. **Added/Corp** Brazil. Departamento de Ensino Supletivo. (19??)-. Portuguese. Departamento de Documentacao e Divulgacao, Brasilia Brazil. **DD** 344/.81/079167.

NR
SELECTED JUDGEMENTS OF THE HIGH COURT OF LAGOS STATE. **Main/Corp** Lagos State (Nigeria). High Court. **VFOAT** High Court of Lagos State Selected Judgements. (July 1972)-. English. High Court Law Library, High Court of Lagos State, Tefawa Balewa Square, Lagos Nigeria. ***Continues*** *Selected Judgements (Lagos State (Nigeria)). High Court, 0331-0418.*

NR
SELECTED JUDGEMENTS OF THE OGUN STATE HIGH COURT / OGUN STATE OF NIGERIA. **Main/Corp** Ogun State (Nigeria). High Court. English. an. N5.00. Chief Registrar's Office, High Court of Justice, Abeokuta Nigeria. **DD** 348.669/2043; 346.6920848.

US/0537-9342
SELECTED LIST OF ACQUISITIONS CATALOGED. (SELECTED LIST OF ACQUISITIONS CATALOGED - INSTITUTE OF JUDICIAL ADMINISTRATION, LIBRARY.). **Main/Corp** Institute of Judicial Administration. Library. English. qt. Free. Institute of Judicial Administration, 1 Washington Square Village, New York NY 10012. **Tel** (212)598-7721. **ED** Margaret L Shaw. **LC** KF4; .I55. **DD** 016.34/00973. **Bk Rev. Circ:** 12,000 (ctrl).
Desc: A newsletter about Institute of Judicial Administration activities and news in the field of judicial administration.

SZ
SEMAINE JUDICIAIRE, LA. (Feb. 17, 1879)-. Periodical. French. wk. Banque Hypothecaire, Case Postale 428, 1211 Geneve 3 Switzerland. cum. index.

FR
SEMAINE JURIDIQUE, LA. (1924)-. Periodical. French. wk (52 issues). 1050.00F. Editions Techniques, 141 rue de Javel, 75747 Paris Cedex 15 France. **Tel** 011 33 1 45589100.
Ind/Abst Index Foreign Leg. Per.

US/0740-9834
SENATE ELECTION LAW GUIDEBOOK. [Senate elect. law guideb.]. 1980-. English. be. US Federal Election Commission, 999 E Street NW, Washington DC 20463. **Tel** (800)424-9530. **LC** KF4913; .A247. **DD** 342.73/055; 347.30255. available on microfiche (Vols. for (1980-) distributed to some

depository libraries). ***Formed by the union of*** *Election Law Guidebook* ***and*** *Senate Campaign Information, 0162-590X.*

US/1050-3250
SENIOR LAW REPORT. ***Title Change.*** [Sr. law rep.]. (June 1, 1989)-(1993). Periodical. English. sm. CD Publications, 8204 Fenton Street, Silver Spring MD 20910. **Tel** (800)666-6380, (301)588-6380, FAX (301)588-6385. **DD** 362. ***Merged into*** *Aging News Alert.*

SP
SENTENCIAS EN APELACION DE LAS AUDIENCIAS PROVINCIALES EN MATERIA CIVIL Y PENAL. **Main/Corp** Spain. Tribunal Supremo. Secretaria Tecnica. Spanish. an. 4000ptas Spain; $60.00 US. Ministerio de Justicia, Centro de Publicaciones, Gran via 76-8, 28013 Madrid Spain. **Tel** 011 34 1 5475422. **DD** 347.46. **Circ:** 3,000 (ctrl).
Desc: Judgements and decisions of all the Spanish "audiencias provinciales" (appeal courts) in relation with the first instance judges decisions which have been appealed.

IT
SENTENZE DELLA CORTE COSTITUZIONALE NEL ..., LE. **Main/Corp** Italy. Coret Costituzionale. 1979-. Italian. an. 5.000.

JA
SERIES OF PROMINENT JUDGEMENTS OF THE SUPREME COURT UPON QUESTIONS OF CONSTITUTIONALITY. **Main/Corp** Japan. Saiko Saibansho. No. 1-. Japanese. Supreme Court of Japan, 4 2 Hayabusa Cho, Chiyoda-ku Tokyo 102 Japan. **DD** 342/.52/002643.

II
SERVICES LAW REPORTER. Pt. 1- Jan. 1967-. Periodical. English. Jagjit Singh Chawla, Kothi No 108-B Sector 27-A, Chandigarh India. **DD** 349/.54/04.

AS
SESSION LAWS AND DIGEST. **Main/Corp** American Samoa. **Added/Corp** American Samoa. Legislature. American Samoa. Legislative Reference Bureau. (19??)-. English (Austronesian). American Reference Bureau, Fagatogo American Samoa. **DD** 348.96/13022.

US
SESSION LAWS OF THE STATE OF SOUTH DAKOTA. **Main/Corp** South Dakota. **VFOAT** Laws of South Dakota; Session Laws of South Dakota; South Dakota Session Laws. (1981)-. English. an. State Publishing Company, South Dakota Secretary of State, Pierre SD 57501. **Tel** (605)224-7323. available on microfiche. ***Continues*** *South Dakota. Session Laws of South Dakota.*

US
SESSION LAWS OF THE VIRGIN ISLANDS. **Main/Corp** Virgin Islands of the United States. (1955)-. English. ir. $43.50. Butterworth Legal Publishers / Salem, NH, 8 Industrial Way, Building C, Salem NH 03079. **Tel** (800)548-4001, (603)898-9664.

US/1059-4310
SETON HALL JOURNAL OF SPORT LAW. [Seton Hall j. sport law]. **Added/Corp** Seton Hall University. School of Law. **VFOAT** Journal of Sport Law. Vol. 1, No. 1 (1991)-. Periodical. English. Twice a year. $20.00 US; $24.00 other. Seton Hall University School of Law, One Newark Center, Newark NJ 07102. **Tel** (201)642-8811. **ED** John Tortora. **DD** 344. **Bk Rev. Pr Rev. Circ:** 350 (ctrl). available on an online database from LEXIS; and WESTLAW.
Desc: Strives to establish a dialogue between the legal, educational, and professional community with the sports related industries.
Ind/Abst Index Leg. Period. (1992-); SPORT Discus.

US/0586-5964
SETON HALL LAW REVIEW. [Seton Hall law rev.]. **Added/Corp** Seton Hall University. School of Law. (Spring 1970)-. Periodical. English. Four times a year. $30.00. Seton Hall University School of Law, One Newark Center, Newark NJ 07102. **Tel** (201)642-8811. **LC** K23; .E85. **DD** 340/.05. Index Available in last issue of each volume--loose separately paged. cum. index. **Bk Rev. Ad Acc.** ***Continues*** *Seton Hall Law Journal, 0742-6127.*
Desc: Ideas in all aspects of the law with an emphasis on New Jersey.
Ind/Abst Bowne Dig. Corp. Sec. Lawyers; Crim. Justice Abstr.; Curr. Law Index (1980-); Fed. Tax Artic.; Index Leg. Period.; Leg. Resour. Index (1980-); LegalTrac (1980-).

US/0361-8951
SETON HALL LEGISLATIVE JOURNAL. [Seton Hall legis. j.]. **Added/Corp** Seton Hall University. School of Law. Vol. 1 (1975)-. English. Twice a year. $20.00. Seton Hall University School of Law, One Newark Center, Newark NJ 07102. **Tel** (201)642-8811. **LC** K23; .E84. **DD** 340/.09749. **Bk Rev. Ad Acc. Circ:** 1,200 (ctrl).
Desc: Detailed analysis of current legislation written by legislators and experts in the field of law.
Ind/Abst Curr. Law Index (1980-); Index Leg. Period.; Leg. Resour. Index (1980-); LegalTrac (1980-).

IT/0392-7253
SETTIMANA GIURIDICA, LA. [Settim. giurid.]. (1960)-. Periodical. Italian. wk. L420000 Italy; L630000 other. Casa Editrice Italedi, Piazza Cavour 19, 00193 Rome Italy. **Tel** 011 39 6 3210803. **UDC** 34.

US/0747-9387
SEVENTH CIRCUIT DIGEST. (SEVENTH CIRCUIT DIGEST / UNITED STATES COURT OF APPEALS FOR THE SEVENTH CIRCUIT.). Began in 1976. English. ir. Bar Association of the Seventh Federal Circuit, Sidley & Austin, One First National Plaza, Chicago IL 60603. **ED** H Helsinger.

UK/0307-3343
SHAW'S DIRECTORY OF COURTS IN ENGLAND AND WALES. (1972)-. Directory. English. an. Shaw and Sons Ltd., Shaway House, 21 Bourne Park / Bourne Road, Crayford Kent, DA1 4BZ England. **Tel** 011 44 322 550676, FAX 011 44 322 550553. **ED** Gordon Morris. **LC** KD7302.3; .S47. **DD** 347/.42/02025. Index available. **Ad Acc.** ***Continues*** *Shaw's Directory of Magistrates' Courts and Crown Courts, 0085-6061.*

UK
SHAW'S DIRECTORY OF COURTS IN THE UNITED KINGDOM. (19??)-. Directory. English. an (Oct.). £29.00. Shaw and Sons Ltd., Shaway House, 21 Bourne Park / Bourne Road, Crayford Kent, DA1 4BZ England. **Tel** 011 44 322 550676, FAX 011 44 322 550553. **ED** Gordon Morris. Index available (bound in issue). **Ad Acc, Adv Mgr:** Crispin Williams. **Circ:** 3,500.
Desc: This directory is essential to every court and legal office, takes account of all changes in staff, sitting of courts, addresses, court code numbers and telephone numbers each year. Prison establishments, Crown courts, county courts, magistrate's courts, other courts of summary jurisdiction and and the Crown Prosecution Service are fully covered.

US/0080-9233
SHEPARD'S ACTS AND CASES BY POPULAR NAMES, FEDERAL AND STATE. [Shepard's acts cases pop. names fed. state]. **Added/Corp** Shepard's/McGraw-Hill. Shepard's, Inc. of Colorado Springs. Shepard's Citations, Inc. **VFOAT** Acts and Cases by Popular Names, Federal and State. (1968)-. English. an (4 cumulative supplements per year). $489.00 (3 bound volumes); $217.00 (supplements). Shepards McGraw-Hill Inc, 555 Middle Creek Parkway, PO Box 35300, Colorado Springs CO 80935-3530. **Tel** (719)488-3000, FAX (800)525-0053. **DD** 348. ***Formed by the union of*** *Table of Fed eral and State Cases by Popular Names* ***and*** *Table of Federal Acts by Popular Names or Short Titles.*
Desc: Acts are listed alphabetically by their popular names and followed by references to the United States Code and United States Statutes at large or to the specific state codes or session laws.

US
SHEPARD'S ALABAMA CASE NAMES CITATOR. **Added/Corp** Shepard's/McGraw-Hill. **VFOAT** Alabama Case Names Citator. 1st Ed. (1986)-. Periodical. English. ir (4 supplements per year). $75.00 (bound volume), $83.00 (cumulative supplements per year). Shepards McGraw-Hill Inc, 555 Middle Creek Parkway, PO Box 35300, Colorado Springs CO 80935-3530. **Tel** (719)488-3000, FAX (800)525-0053.
Desc: Index to all the recent cases in the state. Provides plaintiff/defendant and reverse defendant/plaintiff listings.

US/0730-3572
SHEPARD'S ALABAMA CITATIONS. [Shepard's Ala. cit.]. **Added/Corp** Shepard's Citations, Inc. Shepard's/McGraw-Hill. **VFOAT** Alabama Citations. (19??)-. Periodical. English. bm. $520.00 (4 bound volumes), $347.00 (cumulative supplements). Shepards McGraw-Hill Inc, 555 Middle Creek Parkway, PO Box 35300, Colorado Springs CO 80935-3530. **Tel** (719)488-3000, FAX (800)525-0053. **DD** 348.

●US
SHEPARD'S ALABAMA CODE CITATIONS. **Added/Corp** Shepard's/McGraw-Hill. Vol. 1, No. 1 (July 1992)-. English. mo. $120.00. Shepards McGraw-Hill Inc, 555 Middle Creek Parkway, PO Box 35300, Colorado Springs CO 80935-3530. **Tel** (719)488-3000, FAX (800)525-0053.

US/1056-8980
SHEPARD'S ALABAMA EXPRESS CITATIONS. [Shepard's Ala. express cit.]. **Added/Corp** Shepard's/McGraw-Hill. **VFOAT** Alabama Express Citations. (1991)-. English. sm. $149.00. Shepards McGraw-Hill Inc, 555 Middle Creek Parkway, PO Box 35300, Colorado Springs CO 80935-3530. **Tel** (719)488-3000, FAX (800)525-0053. **DD** 348.

US/1052-5696
SHEPARD'S ALASKA CASE NAMES CITATOR. [Shepard's Alsk. case names cit.]. **Added/Corp** Shepard's/McGraw-Hill. **VFOAT** Alaska Case Names Citator. (1988)-. English. sa. $75.00 (one bound volume), $63.00 (cumulative supplements). Shepards McGraw-Hill Inc, 555 Middle Creek Parkway, PO Box 35300, Colorado Springs CO 80935-3530. **Tel** (719)488-3000, FAX (800)525-0053. **DD** 348.

US/0488-6097
SHEPARD'S ALASKA CITATIONS. [Shepard's Alsk. cit.]. **Added/Corp** Shepard's/McGraw-Hill. (19??)-. English. bm. $150.00 (bound volume), $232.00 (cumulative supplements). Shepards McGraw-Hill Inc, 555 Middle Creek Parkway, PO Box 35300, Colorado Springs CO 80935-3530. **Tel** (719)488-3000, FAX (800)525-0053. **DD** 348.
Desc: Gives every citing reference to the statute in question ever made by appellate courts.

US
SHEPARD'S ARIZONA CASE NAMES CITATOR. **Added/Corp** Shepard's/McGraw-Hill. **VFOAT** Arizona Case Names Citator. 1st Ed. (1986)-. Periodical. English. $75.00 (bound volume), $83.00 (cumulative supplements). Shepards McGraw-Hill Inc, 555 Middle Creek Parkway, PO Box 35300, Colorado Springs CO 80935-3530. **Tel** (719)488-3000, FAX (800)525-0053.
Desc: Index to all the recent cases in the state. Provides plaintiff/defendant and reverse defendant/plaintiff listings.

US/0730-3629
SHEPARD'S ARIZONA CITATIONS. [Shepard's Ariz. cit.]. **Added/Corp** Shepards Citations, Inc. Frank Shepard Company Shepard's Inc. of Colorado Springs. Shepard's Mc/Graw-Hill. (1918)-. Periodical. English. bm. $405.00 (3 bound volumes), $332.00 (cumulative supplements). Shepards McGraw-Hill Inc, 555 Middle Creek Parkway, PO Box 35300, Colorado Springs CO 80935-3530. **Tel** (719)488-3000, FAX (800)525-0053. **DD** 348.
Desc: Gives every citing reference to the statute in question ever made by your appellate courts.

US/1055-2510
SHEPARD'S ARIZONA EXPRESS CITATIONS. [Shepard's Ariz. express cit.]. **Added/Corp** Shepard's/McGraw-Hill. **VFOAT** Arizona Express Citations. Vol. 1, No. 1 (Nov. 25, 1990)-. Periodical. English. mo. $140.00. Shepards McGraw-Hill Inc, 555 Middle Creek Parkway, PO Box 35300, Colorado Springs CO 80935-3530. **Tel** (719)488-3000, FAX (800)525-0053. **DD** 348.

US
SHEPARD'S ARKANSAS CASE NAMES CITATOR. **Added/Corp** Shepard's/McGraw-Hill. **VFOAT** Arkansas Case Names Citator. 1st Ed. (1986)-. Periodical. English. $75.00 (bound volume), $83.00 (cumulative supplements). Shepards McGraw-Hill Inc, 555 Middle Creek Parkway, PO Box 35300, Colorado Springs CO 80935-3530. **Tel** (719)488-3000, FAX (800)525-0053.
Desc: Index to all the recent cases in the state. Provides plaintiff/defendant and reverse defendant/plaintiff listings.

US/0730-3637
SHEPARD'S ARKANSAS CITATIONS. [Shepard's Ark. cit.]. **Added/Corp** Shepard's/McGraw-Hill. **VFOAT** Arkansas Citations. (1915)-. Periodical. English. Twelve times a year. $540.00 (4 bound volumes), $347.00 (cumulative supplements). Shepards McGraw-Hill Inc, 555 Middle Creek Parkway, PO Box 35300, Colorado Springs CO 80935-3530. **Tel** (719)488-3000, FAX (800)525-0053. **DD** 348.
Desc: Gives every citing reference to the statute in question ever made by your appellate courts.

US
SHEPARD'S ATLANTIC REPORTER CITATIONS (ADVANCE SHEET EDITION). (SHEPARD'S ATLANTIC REPORTER CITATIONS.). **Added/Corp** Shepard's Citations, Inc. Vol. 1 (Mar. 1956)-. Periodical. English. ir. $945.00 (9 bound volumes), $400.00 (cumulative supplements). Shepards McGraw-Hill Inc, 555 Middle Creek Parkway, PO Box 35300, Colorado Springs CO 80935-3530. **Tel** (719)488-3000, FAX (800)525-0053. **DD** 345.
Desc: Gives you every state and federal citation to every reporter case as cited anywhere throughout the entire National Reporter System.

US/1048-0587
SHEPARD'S BANKRUPTCY CASE NAMES CITATOR. [Shepard's bankruptcy case names cit.]. **Added/Corp** Shepard's/McGraw-Hill. **VFOAT** Bankruptcy Case Names Citator. (1989)-. English. bm. $85.00 (bound volume), $68.00 (sumulative supplements). Shepards McGraw-Hill Inc, 555 Middle Creek Parkway, PO Box 35300, Colorado Springs CO 80935-3530. **Tel** (719)488-3000, FAX (800)525-0053. **DD** 346.
Desc: Features bankruptcy citations by case name.

US/0730-1936
SHEPARD'S BANKRUPTCY CITATIONS. [Shepard's bankruptcy cit.]. **Added/Corp** Shepard's/McGraw-Hill. (1980)-. Periodical. English. $596.00 (4 bound volumes), $350.00 (cumulative supplements). Shepards McGraw-Hill Inc, 555 Middle Creek Parkway, PO Box 35300, Colorado Springs CO 80935-3530. **Tel** (719)488-3000, FAX (800)525-0053. **DD** 346.

US/1048-0757
SHEPARD'S CALIFORNIA CASE NAMES CITATOR. [Shepard's Calif. case names cit.]. **Added/Corp** Shepard's/McGraw-Hill. **VFOAT** California Case Names Citator. (1985)-. English. qt. $150.00 (2 bound volumes), $98.00 (cumulative supplements). Shepards McGraw-Hill Inc, 555 Middle Creek Parkway, PO Box 35300, Colorado Springs CO 80935-3530. **Tel** (719)488-3000, FAX (800)525-0053. **DD** 348.

US/0730-3661
SHEPARD'S CALIFORNIA CITATIONS (1919). (SHEPARD'S CALIFORNIA CITATIONS). [Shepard's Calif. cit.]. **Added/Corp** Shepard's/McGraw-Hill. Shepard's Inc. of Colorado Springs. Shepard's Citations, Inc. Frank Shepard Company. (1919)-. English. $1598.00 (17 bound volumes), $347.00 (cumulative supplements). Shepards McGraw-Hill Inc, 555 Middle Creek Parkway, PO Box 35300, Colorado Springs CO 80935-3530. **Tel** (719)488-3000, FAX (800)525-0053. **DD** 348. available on CD-ROM from the publisher. ***Continues*** *Shepard's California Citations and Annotations.*

US/1055-9469
SHEPARD'S CALIFORNIA CONSTRUCTION LAW REPORTER. [Shepard's Calif. constr. law report.]. **VFOAT** California Construction Law Reporter. Vol. 1, No. 1 (Feb. 1991)-. Periodical. English. mo. $195.00. Shepards McGraw-Hill Inc, 555 Middle Creek Parkway, PO Box 35300, Colorado Springs CO 80935-3530. **Tel** (719)488-3000, FAX (800)525-0053. **ED** James Acret. **DD** 343. Index available (Looseleaf format).
Desc: Current coverage of California construction law. Includes case summaries, legislative and regulatory summaries, and statutory developments and practice pointers. Also includes coverage of California construction liability insurance and property insurance.

US/1053-8283
SHEPARD'S CALIFORNIA EXPRESS CITATIONS. [Shepard's Calif. express cit.]. **Added/Corp** Shepard's/McGraw-Hill. **VFOAT** California Express Citations. (1990)-. English. sm. $220.00. Shepards McGraw-Hill Inc, 555 Middle Creek Parkway, PO Box 35300, Colorado Springs CO 80935-3530. **Tel** (719)488-3000, FAX (800)525-0053. **DD** 348.

US/0559-7781
SHEPARD'S CALIFORNIA REPORTER CITATIONS. [Shepard's Calif. rep. cit.]. **Added/Corp** Shepard's/McGraw-Hill. **VFOAT** California Reporter Citations. (19??)-. English. mo. $448.00 (2 bound volumes), $358.00 (cumulative supplements). Shepards McGraw-Hill Inc, 555 Middle Creek Parkway, PO Box 35300, Colorado Springs CO 80935-3530. **Tel** (719)488-3000, FAX (800)525-0053. **DD** 348.
Desc: Gives you every state and federal citation to every reporter case as cited anywhere throughout the entire national reporter system.

US/1047-9163
SHEPARD'S CITATIONS FOR ANNOTATIONS. (SHEPARD'S CITATIONS FOR ANNOTATIONS : CUMULATIVE SUPPLEMENT.). [Shepard's cit. annot.]. **Added/Corp** Shepard's/McGraw-Hill. Vol. 1, No. 1 (Nov. 1989)-. English. qt. $200.00 (2 bound volumes), $167.00 (cumulative supplements). Shepards McGraw-Hill Inc, 555 Middle Creek Parkway, PO Box 35300, Colorado Springs CO 80935-3530. **Tel** (719)488-3000, FAX (800)525-0053. **DD** 348.

US/0730-465X
SHEPARD'S CODE OF FEDERAL REGULATIONS CITATIONS. [Shepard's Code fed. regul. cit.]. **Added/Corp** Shepard's/McGraw-Hill. (1979)-. English. an. $350.00 (bound volume), $185.00 (bound supplement). Shepards McGraw-Hill Inc, 555 Middle Creek Parkway, PO Box 35300, Colorado Springs CO 80935-3530. **Tel** (719)488-3000, FAX (800)525-0053. **DD** 348.
Desc: This comprehensive research system shows citations to the Code of Federal Regulations to presidential proclamations, presidential executive orders and reorganization plans.

US/1052-5653
SHEPARD'S COLORADO CASE NAMES CITATOR. [Shepard's Colo. case names cit.]. **Added/Corp** Shepard's/McGraw-Hill. **VFOAT** Colorado Case Names Citator. (1984)-. English. qt. $80.00 (1 bound volume), $82.00 (cumulative supplements). Shepards McGraw-Hill Inc, 555 Middle Creek Parkway, PO Box 35300, Colorado Springs CO 80935-3530. **Tel** (719)488-3000, FAX (800)525-0053. **DD** 348.

US/0730-2096
SHEPARD'S COLORADO CITATIONS. [Shepard's Colo. cit.]. **Added/Corp** Shepard's/McGraw-Hill. **VFOAT** Colorado Citations. Cases and Statutes. (19??)-. English. ir. $320.00 (bound volume), $332.00 (cumulative supplements). Shepards McGraw-Hill Inc, 555 Middle Creek Parkway, PO Box 35300, Colorado Springs CO 80935-3530. **Tel** (719)488-3000, FAX (800)525-0053. **DD** 348.
Desc: Gives you every citing reference to the statute in question ever made by your appellate courts.

US/1056-4217
SHEPARD'S COLORADO EXPRESS CITATIONS. [Shepard's Colo. express cit.]. **Added/Corp** Shepard's/McGraw-Hill. **VFOAT** Colorado Express Citations. Vol. 1, No. 1 (Feb. 10, 1991)-. English. mo. $125.00. Shepards McGraw-Hill Inc, 555 Middle Creek Parkway, PO Box 35300, Colorado Springs CO 80935-3530. **Tel** (719)488-3000, FAX (800)525-0053. **DD** 348.

US
SHEPARD'S CONNECTICUT CASE NAMES CITATOR. **Added/Corp** Shepard's/McGraw-Hill. **VFOAT** Connecticut Case Names Citator. 1st Ed. (1985)-. Periodical. English. $80.00 (bound volume), $82.00 (cumulative supplements). Shepards McGraw-Hill Inc, 555 Middle Creek Parkway, PO Box 35300, Colorado Springs CO 80935-3530. **Tel** (719)488-3000, FAX (800)525-0053.
Desc: Index to all the recent cases in the state. Provides plaintiff/defendant and reverse defendant/plaintiff listings.

US/0730-3688
SHEPARD'S CONNECTICUT CITATIONS. [Shepard's Conn. cit.]. **Added/Corp** Shepard's Citations, Inc. Shepard's/McGraw-Hill. **VFOAT** Connecticut Citations. (1973)-. English. qt. $420.00 (3 bound volumes), $337.00 (cumulative supplements). Shepards McGraw-Hill Inc, 555 Middle Creek Parkway, PO Box 35300, Colorado Springs CO 80935-3530. **Tel** (719)488-3000, FAX (800)525-0053. **DD** 348.

US/1055-9507
SHEPARD'S CONNECTICUT EXPRESS CITATIONS. [Shepard's Conn. express cit.]. **Added/Corp** Shepard's/McGraw-Hill. **VFOAT** Connecticut Express Citations. (1990)-. English. mo. $125.00. Shepards McGraw-Hill Inc, 555 Middle Creek Parkway, PO Box 35300, Colorado Springs CO 80935-3530. **Tel** (719)488-3000, FAX (800)525-0053. **DD** 348.

US/0730-5869
SHEPARD'S DELAWARE CITATIONS. [Shepard's Del. cit.]. **Added/Corp** Shepard's Citations, Inc. Shepard's/McGraw-Hill. (19??)-. English. Three times a year. $180.00 (bound volume), $232.00 (cumulative supplements). Shepards McGraw-Hill Inc, 555 Middle Creek Parkway, PO Box 35300, Colorado Springs CO 80935-3530. **Tel** (719)488-3000, FAX (800)525-0053. **DD** 348.
Desc: Gives you every citing reference to the statute in question ever made by your appellate courts.

US
SHEPARD'S DISTRICT OF COLUMBIA CITATIONS. **Added/Corp** Shepard's Citations, Inc. **VFOAT** District of Columbia Citations. 1st Ed. (1968)-. English. $180.00 (bound volume), $342.00 (cumulative supplements). Shepards McGraw-Hill Inc, 555 Middle Creek Parkway, PO Box 35300, Colorado Springs CO 80935-3530. **Tel** (719)488-3000, FAX (800)525-0053.
Desc: Gives you every citing reference to the statute in question ever made by your appellate courts.

●US/1060-7625
SHEPARD'S EVIDENCE CITATIONS. [Shepard's evid. cit.]. **Added/Corp** Shepard's/McGraw-Hill. **VFOAT** Evidence Citations. (1991)-. English. qt. $399.00 (3 bound volumes), $201.00 (cumulative supplements). Shepards McGraw-Hill Inc, 555 Middle Creek Parkway, PO Box 35300, Colorado Springs CO 80935-3530. **Tel** (719)488-3000, FAX (800)525-0053. **DD** 348.

US/1048-0331
SHEPARD'S FEDERAL CASE NAMES CITATOR, DISTRICT OF COLUMBIA CIRCUIT CASES. [Shepard's fed. case names cit. Dist. Columbia circuit cases]. **Added/Corp** Shepard's/McGraw-Hill. **VFOAT** Federal Case Names Citator, District of Columbia Circuit Cases. (1988)-. English. qt. $75.00 (1 bound volume), $70.00 (cumulative supplements). Shepards McGraw-Hill Inc, 555 Middle Creek Parkway, PO Box 35300, Colorado Springs CO 80935-3530. **Tel** (719)488-3000, FAX (800)525-0053. **DD** 348.

US/1048-0250
SHEPARD'S FEDERAL CASE NAMES CITATOR, EIGHTH CIRCUIT CASES. [Shepard's fed. case names cit. eighth circuit cases]. **Added/Corp** Shepard's/McGraw-Hill. **VFOAT** Federal Case Names Citator, Eighth Circuit Cases. (1988)-. English. qt. $75.00 (1 bound volume), $60.00 (cumulative supplements). Shepards McGraw-Hill Inc, 555 Middle Creek Parkway, PO Box 35300, Colorado Springs CO 80935-3530. **Tel** (719)488-3000, FAX (800)525-0053. **DD** 348.

US
SHEPARD'S FEDERAL CASE NAMES CITATOR, ELEVENTH CIRCUIT CASES. **Added/Corp** Shepard's/McGraw-Hill. 1st Ed., Pt. 1 (1987)-. Periodical. English. $114.00 (1 bound volume), $70.00 (cumulative supplements). Shepards McGraw-Hill Inc, 555 Middle Creek Parkway, PO Box 35300, Colorado Springs CO 80935-3530. **Tel** (719)488-3000, FAX (800)525-0053.

US/1048-0102
SHEPARD'S FEDERAL CASE NAMES CITATOR, FIFTH CIRCUIT CASES. [Shepard's fed. case names cit. fifth circuit cases]. **Added/Corp** Shepard's/McGraw-Hill. **VFOAT** Federal Case Names Citator, Fifth Circuit Cases. (1987)-. English. qt. $160.00 (2 bound volumes), $195.00 (cumulative supplements). Shepards McGraw-Hill Inc, 555 Middle Creek Parkway, PO Box 35300, Colorado Springs CO 80935-3530. **Tel** (719)488-3000, FAX (800)525-0053. **DD** 348.

US
SHEPARD'S FEDERAL CASE NAMES CITATOR, FIRST CIRCUIT CASES. **Added/Corp** Shepard's/McGraw-Hill. **VFOAT** Federal Case Names Citator, First Circuit Cases. 1st Ed. (1987)-. Periodical. English. qt. $75.00 (1 bound volume), $64.00 (cumulative supplements). Shepards McGraw-Hill Inc, 555 Middle Creek Parkway, PO Box 35300, Colorado Springs CO 80935-3530. **Tel** (719)488-3000, FAX (800)525-0053.

US/1048-0099
SHEPARD'S FEDERAL CASE NAMES CITATOR, FOURTH CIRCUIT CASES. [Shepard's fed. case names cit. fourth circuit cases]. **Added/Corp** Shepard's/McGraw-Hill. **VFOAT** Federal Case Names Citator, Fourth Circuit Cases. (1988)-. English. qt. $75.00 (1 bound volume), $60.00 (cumulative supplements). Shepards McGraw-Hill Inc, 555 Middle Creek Parkway, PO Box 35300, Colorado Springs CO 80935-3530. **Tel** (719)488-3000, FAX (800)525-0053. **DD** 348.

US
SHEPARD'S FEDERAL CASE NAMES CITATOR : NINTH CIRCUIT CASES. **Added/Corp** Shepard's/McGraw-Hill. **VFOAT** Federal Case Names Citator : Ninth Circuit Cases. 1st Ed. (1987)-. Periodical. English. ir. $75.00 (bound volume), $70.00 (cumulative supplements). Shepards McGraw-Hill Inc, 555 Middle Creek Parkway, PO Box 35300, Colorado Springs CO 80935-3530. **Tel** (719)488-3000, FAX (800)525-0053.
Desc: Index to all the recent cases in the ninth circuit. Provides plaintiff/defendant and reverse defendant/plaintiff listings.

US
SHEPARD'S FEDERAL CASE NAMES CITATOR, SECOND CIRCUIT CASES. **Added/Corp** Shepard's/McGraw-Hill. **VFOAT** Federal Case Names Citator, Second Circuit Cases. 1st Ed. (1987)-. English. qt. $114.00 (2 bound volumes), $74.00 (cumulative supplements). Shepards McGraw-Hill Inc, 555 Middle Creek Parkway, PO Box 35300, Colorado Springs CO 80935-3530. **Tel** (719)488-3000, FAX (800)525-0053.

US/1048-0242
SHEPARD'S FEDERAL CASE NAMES CITATOR, SEVENTH CIRCUIT CASES. [Shepard's fed. case names cit. seventh circuit cases]. **Added/Corp** Shepard's/McGraw-Hill. **VFOAT** Federal Case Names Citator, Seventh Circuit Cases. (1987)-. English. qt. $75.00 (1 bound volume), $75.00 (cumulative supplements). Shepards McGraw-Hill Inc, 555 Middle Creek Parkway, PO Box 35300, Colorado Springs CO 80935-3530. **Tel** (719)488-3000, FAX (800)525-0053. **DD** 348.

US/1048-0234
SHEPARD'S FEDERAL CASE NAMES CITATOR, SIXTH CIRCUIT CASES. [Shepard's fed. case names cit. sixth circuit cases]. **Added/Corp** Shepard's/McGraw-Hill. **VFOAT** Federal Case Names Citator, Sixth Circuit Cases. (1987)-. English. qt. $75.00 (1 bound volume), $60.00 (cumulative supplements). Shepards McGraw-Hill Inc, 555 Middle Creek Parkway, PO Box 35300, Colorado Springs CO 80935-3530. **Tel** (719)488-3000, FAX (800)525-0053. **DD** 348.

Law

US
SHEPARD'S FEDERAL CASE NAMES CITATOR, TENTH CIRCUIT CASES. **Added/Corp** Shepard's/McGraw-Hill. **VFOAT** Federal Case Names Citator, Tenth Circuit Cases. 1st Ed. (1987)-. Periodical. English. $75.00 (1 bound volume), $70.00 (cumulative supplements). Shepards McGraw-Hill Inc, 555 Middle Creek Parkway, PO Box 35300, Colorado Springs CO 80935-3530. **Tel** (719)488-3000, FAX (800)525-0053.

US/1048-0080
SHEPARD'S FEDERAL CASE NAMES CITATOR, THIRD CIRCUIT CASES. [Shepard's fed. case names cit. third circuit cases]. **Added/Corp** Shepard's/McGraw-Hill. **VFOAT** Federal Case Names Citator, Third Circuit Cases. (1988)-. English. qt. $75.00 (1 bound volume), $60.00 (cumulative supplements). Shepards McGraw-Hill Inc, 555 Middle Creek Parkway, PO Box 35300, Colorado Springs CO 80935-3530. **Tel** (719)488-3000, FAX (800)525-0053. **DD** 348.

US/1048-034X
SHEPARD'S FEDERAL CIRCUIT CASE NAMES CITATOR. [Shepard's fed. circuit case names cit.]. **Added/Corp** Shepard's/McGraw-Hill. **VFOAT** Federal Circuit Case Names Citator. (1989)-. English. qt. $75.00 (1 bound volume), $60.00 (cumulative supplements). Shepards McGraw-Hill Inc, 555 Middle Creek Parkway, PO Box 35300, Colorado Springs CO 80935-3530. **Tel** (719)488-3000, FAX (800)525-0053. **DD** 348.

US/0730-7039
SHEPARD'S FEDERAL CIRCUIT TABLE. [Shepard's fed. circuit table]. **Added/Corp** Shepard's/McGraw-Hill. **VFOAT** Federal Circuit Table; Federal Circuit Identification Table. (198?)-. English. $180.00 (bound volume), $81.00 (cumulative supplements). Shepards McGraw-Hill Inc, 555 Middle Creek Parkway, PO Box 35300, Colorado Springs CO 80935-3530. **Tel** (719)488-3000, FAX (800)525-0053. **DD** 347.
Desc: Identifies by circuit or district any citing pages published in the Federal Reporter Second Series, Federal Supplement and Federal Rules Decisions.

US/0730-4633
SHEPARD'S FEDERAL CITATIONS. [Shepard's Fed. cit.]. **Added/Corp** Shepard's Citations, Inc. **VFOAT** Federal Citations. (19??)-. English. mo. $2470.00 (26 bound volumes), $365.00 (cumulative supplements). Shepards McGraw-Hill Inc, 555 Middle Creek Parkway, PO Box 35300, Colorado Springs CO 80935-3530. **Tel** (719)488-3000, FAX (800)525-0053. **DD** 348. Continues Shepard's Citations of all Cases in the Federal Reporter Which have had a Subsequent Citation.
Desc: Complete compilation of citations to federal courts of appeal and district courts.
Ind/Abst Curr. Lit. Fam. Plan. (19??-199?).

US/0746-312X
SHEPARD'S FEDERAL ENERGY LAW CITATIONS (QUARTERLY). (SHEPARD'S FEDERAL ENERGY LAW CITATIONS.). [Shepard's fed. energy law cit.]. **Added/Corp** Shepard's/McGraw-Hill. **VFOAT** Federal Energy Law Citations. Vol. 1, No. 1 (April 1983)-. English. qt. $300.00 (bound volume), $202.00 (cumulative supplements). Shepards McGraw-Hill Inc, 555 Middle Creek Parkway, PO Box 35300, Colorado Springs CO 80935-3530. **Tel** (719)488-3000, FAX (800)525-0053. **DD** 346.
Desc: Gives you a valuable new reference source to case and statutory energy laws.

US/0094-9531
SHEPARD'S FEDERAL LAW CITATIONS IN SELECTED LAW REVIEWS. [Shepard's fed. law cit. sel. law rev.]. **Added/Corp** Shepard's Citations, Inc. Shepard's, Inc. of Colorado Springs. Shepard's/McGraw-Hill. **VFOAT** Federal Law Citations in Selected Law Reviews. Vol. 1 (Mar. 1974)-. English. ir (6 cumulative supplements per year). $140.00 (bound volume), $226.00 (cumulative supplements). Shepards McGraw-Hill Inc, 555 Middle Creek Parkway, PO Box 35300, Colorado Springs CO 80935-3530. **Tel** (719)488-3000, FAX (800)525-0053. **LC** KF105.2; .S425. **DD** 348/.73/47.
Desc: A citation system showing citations in articles in selected leading reviews to the opinions of the United States Supreme Court Reports.

US/1053-5799
SHEPARD'S FEDERAL MERIT SYSTEMS CITATIONS. Ceased. [Shepard's fed. merit syst. cit.]. **VFOAT** Federal Merit Systems Citations. (1990)-Final Supplement (Dec. 1992). English. qt. Shepards McGraw-Hill Inc, 555 Middle Creek Parkway, PO Box 35300, Colorado Springs CO 80935-3530. **Tel** (719)488-3000, FAX (800)525-0053. **DD** 348.
Desc: Covers Federal Merit Systems Protection Board decisions, pertinent federal court cases and relevant provisions from the United States Code and Code of Federal Regulations.

US/0732-7722
SHEPARD'S FEDERAL OCCUPATIONAL SAFETY AND HEALTH CITATIONS. [Shepard's fed. occup. saf. health cit.]. **Added/Corp** Shepard's/McGraw-Hill. Vol. 1, No. 1 (Nov. 1981)-. Periodical. English. qt. $130.00 (bound volume), $227.00 (cumulative supplements). Shepards McGraw-Hill Inc, 555 Middle Creek Parkway, PO Box 35300, Colorado Springs CO 80935-3530. **Tel** (719)488-3000, FAX (800)525-0053. **LC** KF3568.15; .S47. **DD** 344.73/0465/02646; 347.30446502646.
Desc: Provides citations to federal cases, administrative decisions and statutes dealing with occupational safety and health.

US/0732-7714
SHEPARD'S FEDERAL TAX CITATIONS. [Shepard's fed. tax cit.]. **Added/Corp** Shepard's/McGraw-Hill. **VFOAT** Federal Tax Citations. (1981)-. English. ir (3 cumulative supplements and 3 advance sheets per year). $990.00 (12 bound volumes), $317.00 (cumulative supplements). Shepards McGraw-Hill Inc, 555 Middle Creek Parkway, PO Box 35300, Colorado Springs CO 80935-3530. **Tel** (719)488-3000, FAX (800)525-0053. **DD** 343. cum. index.
Desc: Includes features such as cross-references, citations to statutory laws, citations to treasury regulations, citations to all federal tax cases including US Tax Court regular and memorandum decisions.

US/0730-4714
SHEPARD'S FEDERAL TAX LOCATOR. Ceased. **VFOAT** Federal Tax Locator. Vol. 1 (1974)-(1991). English. qt (4 cumulative supplements per year). Shepards McGraw-Hill Inc, 555 Middle Creek Parkway, PO Box 35300, Colorado Springs CO 80935-3530. **Tel** (719)488-3000, FAX (800)525-0053.
Desc: Complete index to all the current sources of law relating to federal taxation.

US/1048-096X
SHEPARD'S FLORIDA CASE NAME CITATOR. [Shepard's Fla. case names cit.]. **Added/Corp** Shepard's/McGraw-Hill. **VFOAT** Florida Case Names Citator. (1985)-. English. Six times a year. $219.00 (3 bound volumes), $122.00 (cumulative supplements). Shepards McGraw-Hill Inc, 555 Middle Creek Parkway, PO Box 35300, Colorado Springs CO 80935-3530. **Tel** (719)488-3000, FAX (800)525-0053. **DD** 348.
Desc: Index to all the recent cases in the state. Provides plaintiff/defendant and reverse defendant/plaintiff listings.

US/0730-3718
SHEPARD'S FLORIDA CITATIONS. [Shepard's Fla. cit.]. **Added/Corp** Shepard's/McGraw-Hill. **VFOAT** Florida Citations. Cases and Statutes. (19??)-. Periodical. English. ir. $750.00 (6 bound volumes), $357.00 (cumulative supplements). Shepards McGraw-Hill Inc, 555 Middle Creek Parkway, PO Box 35300, Colorado Springs CO 80935-3530. **Tel** (719)488-3000, FAX (800)525-0053. **DD** 348. cum. index. ctrl circ. available on an online database from LEXIS; and WESTLAW.
Desc: A compilation of Citations to Florida Reports and Supplement, Report of the Attorney General of Florida and the Southern Reporter, as well as every citing reference to relating statutes in question.

US/1050-9100
SHEPARD'S FLORIDA EXPRESS CITATIONS. [Shepard's Fla. express cit.]. **Added/Corp** Shepard's/McGraw-Hill. **VFOAT** Express Citations. Vol. 1, No. 1 (Mar. 8, 1990)-. Periodical. English. sm. $149.00. Shepards McGraw-Hill Inc, 555 Middle Creek Parkway, PO Box 35300, Colorado Springs CO 80935-3530. **Tel** (719)488-3000, FAX (800)525-0053. **DD** 348.

US/8750-1074
SHEPARD'S GEORGIA CASE NAME CITATOR. (198?)-. Periodical. English. qt. $192.00 (3 bound volumes), $88.00 (cumulative supplements). Shepards McGraw-Hill Inc, 555 Middle Creek Parkway, PO Box 35300, Colorado Springs CO 80935-3530. **Tel** (719)488-3000, FAX (800)525-0053. **DD** 348.
Desc: Handy index to all the recent cases in the state. Provides plaintiff/defendant and reverse defendant/plaintiff listings.

US/0730-3742
SHEPARD'S GEORGIA CITATIONS. [Shepard's Ga. cit.]. **Added/Corp** Shepard's/McGraw-Hill. **VFOAT** Georgia Citations. (19??)-. English. bm. $875.00 (7 bound volumes), $352.00 (cumulative supplements). Shepards McGraw-Hill Inc, 555 Middle Creek Parkway, PO Box 35300, Colorado Springs CO 80935-3530. **Tel** (719)488-3000, FAX (800)525-0053. **DD** 348. available on CD-ROM from the publisher.

US
SHEPARD'S GEORGIA CODE CITATIONS. (199?)-. English. mo. $120.00. Shepards McGraw-Hill Inc, 555 Middle Creek Parkway, PO Box 35300, Colorado Springs CO 80935-3530. **Tel** (719)488-3000, FAX (800)525-0053.

US/1058-9732
SHEPARD'S GEORGIA EXPRESS CITATIONS. [Shepard's Ga. express cit.]. **Added/Corp** Shepard's/McGraw-Hill. **VFOAT** Georgia Express Citations. (1991)-. English. sm (24 issues). $149.00. Shepards McGraw-Hill Inc, 555 Middle Creek Parkway, PO Box 35300, Colorado Springs CO 80935-3530. **Tel** (719)488-3000, FAX (800)525-0053. **DD** 348.

US/1052-5920
SHEPARD'S HAWAII CASE NAMES CITATOR. [Shepard's Hawaii case names cit.]. **Added/Corp** Shepard's/McGraw-Hill. **VFOAT** Hawaii Case Names Citator. (1988)-. English. sa. $75.00 (bound volume), $58.00 (cumulative supplements). Shepards McGraw-Hill Inc, 555 Middle Creek Parkway, PO Box 35300, Colorado Springs CO 80935-3530. **Tel** (719)488-3000, FAX (800)525-0053. **DD** 348.

US/0730-5885
SHEPARD'S HAWAII CITATIONS. [Shepard's Hawaii cit.]. **Added/Corp** Shepard's/McGraw-Hill. **VFOAT** Hawaii Citations. (19??)-. English. Six times a year. $180.00 (bound volume), $247.00 (cumulative supplements). Shepards McGraw-Hill Inc, 555 Middle Creek Parkway, PO Box 35300, Colorado Springs CO 80935-3530. **Tel** (719)488-3000, FAX (800)525-0053. **DD** 348.
Desc: Gives you every citing reference to the statute in question ever made by your appellate courts.

US/0730-5893
SHEPARD'S IDAHO CITATIONS. [Shepard's Ida. cit.]. **Added/Corp** Shepard's/McGraw-Hill. **VFOAT** Idaho Citations. Cases and Statutes. (19??)-. Periodical. English. ir. $300.00 (bound volume), $232.00 (cumulative supplements). Shepards McGraw-Hill Inc, 555 Middle Creek Parkway, PO Box 35300, Colorado Springs CO 80935-3530. **Tel** (719)488-3000, FAX (800)525-0053. **DD** 348.
Desc: Gives you every citing reference to the statute in question ever made by your appellate courts.

US
SHEPARD'S ILLINOIS CASE NAMES CITATOR. **Added/Corp** Shepard's/McGraw-Hill. **VFOAT** Illinois Case Names Citator. 1st Ed. (1985)-. Periodical. English. Six times a year. $150.00 (2 bound volumes), $108.00 (cumulative supplements). Shepards McGraw-Hill Inc, 555 Middle Creek Parkway, PO Box 35300, Colorado Springs CO 80935-3530. **Tel** (719)488-3000, FAX (800)525-0053.
Desc: Index to all the recent cases in the state. Provides plaintiff/defendant and reverse defendant/plaintiff listings.

US/0730-3904
SHEPARD'S ILLINOIS CITATIONS. [Shepard's Ill. cit.]. **Added/Corp** Shepard's/McGraw-Hill. **VFOAT** Illinois Citations. (19??)-. English. bm. $990.00 (3 bound volumes), $317.00 (cumulative supplements). Shepards McGraw-Hill Inc, 555 Middle Creek Parkway, PO Box 35300, Colorado Springs CO 80935-3530. **Tel** (719)488-3000, FAX (800)525-0053. **DD** 348. available on CD-ROM from the publisher.
Desc: Gives you every citing reference to the statute in question ever made by your appellate courts.

US/1057-3380
SHEPARD'S ILLINOIS EXPRESS CITATIONS. [Shepard's Ill. express cit.]. **Added/Corp** Shepard's/McGraw-Hill. **VFOAT** Illinois Express Citations. (1991)-. Periodical. English. sm (24 issues). $174.00. Shepards McGraw-Hill Inc, 555 Middle Creek Parkway, PO Box 35300, Colorado Springs CO 80935-3530. **Tel** (719)488-3000, FAX (800)525-0053. **DD** 348.

US/1053-1769
SHEPARD'S ILLINOIS TORT REPORTER. [Shepard's Ill. tort rep.]. **Added/Corp** Shepard's/McGraw-Hill. **VFOAT** Illinois Tort Reporter. Vol. 1, No. 1 (Aug. 1990)-. Periodical. English. mo. $150.00. Shepards McGraw-Hill Inc, 555 Middle Creek Parkway, PO Box 35300, Colorado Springs CO 80935-3530. **Tel** (719)488-3000, FAX (800)525-0053. **ED** Ralph Brill. **LC** KFI1395.A15; S46. **DD** 346.77303/05; 347.7306305.
Desc: Features summaries and analysis of important Illinois tort cases, legislative and regulatory updates, short descriptions of interesting law review articles, tables, indexes, and a cumulative annual index make your subscription an ever-growing research system.

US
SHEPARD'S IMMIGRATION AND NATURALIZATION CITATIONS. **Added/Corp** Shepard's/McGraw-Hill. **VFOAT** Immigration and Naturalization Citations. 1st Ed. (1982)-. English. Four times a year. $140.00 (bound volume), $190.00 (cumulative supplements). Shepards McGraw-Hill Inc, 555 Middle Creek Parkway, PO Box 35300, Colorado Springs CO 80935-3530. **Tel** (719)488-3000, FAX (800)525-0053.

US/1052-5939
SHEPARD'S INDIANA CASE NAMES CITATOR. [Shepard's Indiana case names cit.]. **Added/Corp** Shepard's/McGraw-Hill. **VFOAT** Indiana Case Names Citator. (1985)-. English. bm. $75.00 (bound volume), $93.00 (cumulative supplements). Shepards McGraw-Hill Inc, 555 Middle Creek Parkway, PO Box 35300, Colorado Springs CO 80935-3530. **Tel** (719)488-3000, FAX (800)525-0053. **DD** 348.

US/0730-3831
SHEPARD'S INDIANA CITATIONS. [Shepard's Indiana cit.]. **Added/Corp** Shepard's/McGraw-Hill. **VFOAT** Indiana Citations. (19??)-. English. qt (4 cumulative supplements). $520.00 (4 bound volumes), $337.00 (cumulative supplements). Shepards McGraw-Hill Inc, 555 Middle Creek Parkway, PO Box 35300, Colorado Springs CO 80935-3530. **Tel** (719)488-3000, FAX (800)525-0053. **DD** 348.
Desc: Gives you every citing reference to the statute in question ever made by your appellate courts.

●US/1071-961X
SHEPARD'S INDIANA EXPRESS CITATIONS. [Shepard's Indiana express cit.]. **Added/Corp** Shepard's/McGraw-Hill. Vol. 1, No. 1 (June 7, 1993)-. English. sm (24 issues). $149.00. Shepards McGraw-Hill Inc, 555 Middle Creek Parkway, PO Box 35300, Colorado Springs CO 80935-3530. **Tel** (719)488-3000, FAX (800)525-0053. **DD** 341.

US/1048-082X
SHEPARD'S INSURANCE LAW CITATIONS. ***Ceased.*** [Shepard's insur. law cit.]. **VFOAT** Insurance Law Citations. (1988)-Final Supplement (April 1993). English. qt. Shepards McGraw-Hill Inc, 555 Middle Creek Parkway, PO Box 35300, Colorado Springs CO 80935-3530. **Tel** (719)488-3000, FAX (800)525-0053. **DD** 346. Index available. cum. index.
Desc: Contains citations to cases and statutes compiled and analyzed from the area of insurance law.

US
SHEPARD'S IOWA CASE NAMES CITATOR. **Added/Corp** Shepard's/McGraw-Hill. **VFOAT** Iowa Case Names Citator. 1st Ed. (1985)-. Periodical. English. $80.00 (bound volume), $83.00 (cumulative supplements). Shepards McGraw-Hill Inc, 555 Middle Creek Parkway, PO Box 35300, Colorado Springs CO 80935-3530. **Tel** (719)488-3000, FAX (800)525-0053.
Desc: Index to all the recent cases in the state. Provides plaintiff/defendant and reverse defendant/plaintiff listings.

US/0730-3866
SHEPARD'S IOWA CITATIONS. [Shepard's Iowa cit.]. **Added/Corp** Shepard's/McGraw-Hill. Shepard's, Inc. of Colorado Springs. **VFOAT** Iowa Citations. (1909)-. English. mo. $456.00. Shepards McGraw-Hill Inc, 555 Middle Creek Parkway, PO Box 35300, Colorado Springs CO 80935-3530. **Tel** (719)488-3000, FAX (800)525-0053. **DD** 348.

US/1052-5955
SHEPARD'S KANSAS CASE NAMES CITATOR. [Shepard's Kans. case names cit.]. **Added/Corp** Shepard's/McGraw-Hill. **VFOAT** Kansas Case Names Citator. Vol. 1, No. 1 (May 1985)-. English. Four times a year. $80.00 (bound volume), $78.00 (cumulative supplements). Shepards McGraw-Hill Inc, 555 Middle Creek Parkway, PO Box 35300, Colorado Springs CO 80935-3530. **Tel** (719)488-3000, FAX (800)525-0053. **DD** 348.
Desc: Index to all the recent cases in the state. Provides plaintiff/defendant and reverse defendant/plaintiff listings.

US/0730-3947
SHEPARD'S KANSAS CITATIONS. [Shepard's Kan. cit.]. **Added/Corp** Shepard's/McGraw-Hill. Shepard's Citations, Inc. **VFOAT** Kansas Citations. (19??)-. English. mo. $399.00 (3 bound volumes), $317.00 (cumulative supplements). Shepards McGraw-Hill Inc, 555 Middle Creek Parkway, PO Box 35300, Colorado Springs CO 80935-3530. **Tel** (719)488-3000, FAX (800)525-0053. **DD** 348.

●US/1069-0506
SHEPARD'S KANSAS EXPRESS CITATIONS. [Shepard's Kans. express cit.]. **Added/Corp** Shepard's/McGraw-Hill. **VFOAT** Kansas Express Citations. Vol. 1, No. 1 (Feb. 14, 1993)-. English. sm. $165.00 (cumulative supplements). Shepards McGraw-Hill Inc, 555 Middle Creek Parkway, PO Box 35300, Colorado Springs CO 80935-3530. **Tel** (719)488-3000, FAX (800)525-0053. **DD** 348.

US
SHEPARD'S KENTUCKY CASE NAMES CITATOR. **Added/Corp** Shepard's/McGraw-Hill. **VFOAT** Kentucky Case Names Citator. 1st Ed. (1986)-. Periodical. English. Four times a year. $75.00 (bound volume), $83.00 (cumulative supplements). Shepards McGraw-Hill Inc, 555 Middle Creek Parkway, PO Box 35300, Colorado Springs CO 80935-3530. **Tel** (719)488-3000, FAX (800)525-0053.
Desc: Index to all the recent cases in the state. Provides plaintiff/defendant and reverse defendant/plaintiff listings.

US/0730-3971
SHEPARD'S KENTUCKY CITATIONS. [Shepard's Ky. cit.]. **Added/Corp** Shepard's/McGraw-Hill. **VFOAT** Kentucky Citations. Cases and Statutes. (19??)-. English. Twelve times a year. $468.00 (4 bound volumes), $347.00 (cumulative supplements). Shepards McGraw-Hill Inc, 555 Middle Creek Parkway, PO Box 35300, Colorado Springs CO 80935-3530. **Tel** (719)488-3000, FAX (800)525-0053. **DD** 348.
Desc: Gives you every citing reference to the statute in question ever made by your appellate courts.

US/1058-9600
SHEPARD'S KENTUCKY EXPRESS CITATIONS. [Shepard's Ky. express cit.]. **Added/Corp** Shepard's/McGraw-Hill. **VFOAT** Kentucky Express Citations. Vol. 1, No. 1 (July 1, 1991)-. Periodical. English. mo. $140.00. Shepards McGraw-Hill Inc, 555 Middle Creek Parkway, PO Box 35300, Colorado Springs CO 80935-3530. **Tel** (719)488-3000, FAX (800)525-0053. **DD** 348.

US/0582-9887
SHEPARD'S LAW REVIEW CITATIONS. [Shepard's law rev. cit.]. **Added/Corp** Shepard's Citations, Inc. Shepard's, Inc. of Colorado Springs. Shepard's/McGraw-Hill. **VFOAT** Law Review Citations. (1968)-. Periodical. English. $300.00 (3 bound volumes), $282.00 (cumulative supplements). Shepards McGraw-Hill Inc, 555 Middle Creek Parkway, PO Box 35300, Colorado Springs CO 80935-3530. **Tel** (719)488-3000, FAX (800)525-0053. **DD** 340.
Desc: Law review articles which often treat developing areas of law, are a good source of 'in-point' cases. To locate such authorities and to expand research in this area, this citator is an ideal tool.

US/1048-0773
SHEPARD'S LOUISIANA CASE NAMES CITATOR. [Shepard's La. case names cit.]. **Added/Corp** Shepard's/McGraw-Hill. **VFOAT** Louisiana Case Names Citator. (1985)-. English. bm. $328.00 (4 bound volumes), $108.00 (cumulative supplements). Shepards McGraw-Hill Inc, 555 Middle Creek Parkway, PO Box 35300, Colorado Springs CO 80935-3530. **Tel** (719)488-3000, FAX (800)525-0053. **DD** 348.

US/0730-4005
SHEPARD'S LOUISIANA CITATIONS. [Shepard's La. cit.]. **Added/Corp** Shepard's/McGraw-Hill. **VFOAT** Louisiana Citations. (19??)-. English. mo. $762.00 (6 bound volumes), $317.00 (cumulative supplements). Shepards McGraw-Hill Inc, 555 Middle Creek Parkway, PO Box 35300, Colorado Springs CO 80935-3530. **Tel** (719)488-3000, FAX (800)525-0053. **DD** 348.

US/1052-5971
SHEPARD'S MAINE CASE NAMES CITATOR. [Shepard's Me. case names cit.]. **Added/Corp** Shepard's/McGraw-Hill. **VFOAT** Maine Case Names Citator. (1988)-. English. sa. $75.00 (bound volume), $58.00 (cumulative supplements). Shepards McGraw-Hill Inc, 555 Middle Creek Parkway, PO Box 35300, Colorado Springs CO 80935-3530. **Tel** (719)488-3000, FAX (800)525-0053. **DD** 348.

US/0730-5923
SHEPARD'S MAINE CITATIONS. [Shepard's Me. cit.]. **Added/Corp** Shepard's/McGraw-Hill. Shepard's, Inc. of Colorado Springs. Shepard's Citations, Inc. **VFOAT** Maine Citations. (19??)-. English. Six times a year. $180.00 (bound volume), $257.00 (cumulative supplements). Shepards McGraw-Hill Inc, 555 Middle Creek Parkway, PO Box 35300, Colorado Springs CO 80935-3530. **Tel** (719)488-3000, FAX (800)525-0053. **DD** 349.
Desc: Gives you every citing reference to the statute in question ever made by your appellate courts.

US
SHEPARD'S MANUAL OF FEDERAL PRACTICE / EDITORIAL STAFF, EDITOR IN CHIEF, RUDOLPH W. FISCHER ... [ET AL.]. **Added/Corp** Shepard's, Inc. of Colorado Springs. English. $210.00 (3 volumes), $53.00 (1993 pocket part). Shepards McGraw-Hill Inc, 555 Middle Creek Parkway, PO Box 35300, Colorado Springs CO 80935-3530. **Tel** (719)488-3000, FAX (800)525-0053. **ED** Richard Givens. **Bk Rev**. **Ad Acc**.
Desc: Completely revised and updated guide to litigation on the federal level.

US
SHEPARD'S MARYLAND CASE NAMES CITATOR. **Added/Corp** Shepard's/McGraw-Hill. **VFOAT** Maryland Case Names Citator. 1st Ed. (1985)-. Periodical. English. $80.00 (bound volume), $82.00 (cumulative supplements). Shepards McGraw-Hill Inc, 555 Middle Creek Parkway, PO Box 35300, Colorado Springs CO 80935-3530. **Tel** (719)488-3000, FAX (800)525-0053.
Desc: Handy index to all the recent cases in the state. Provides plaintiff/defendant and reverse defendant/plaintiff listings.

US/0730-403X
SHEPARD'S MARYLAND CITATIONS. [Shepard's Md. cit.]. **Added/Corp** Shepard's/McGraw-Hill. **VFOAT** Maryland Citations. (19??)-. Periodical. English. mo. $390.00 (3 bound volumes), $357.00 (cumulative supplements). Shepards McGraw-Hill Inc, 555 Middle Creek Parkway, PO Box 35300, Colorado Springs CO 80935-3530. **Tel** (719)488-3000, FAX (800)525-0053. **DD** 348.

●US
SHEPARD'S MARYLAND CODE CITATIONS. (1992)-. English. mo. $120.00. Shepards McGraw-Hill Inc, 555 Middle Creek Parkway, PO Box 35300, Colorado Springs CO 80935-3530. **Tel** (719)488-3000, FAX (800)525-0053.

●US/1072-1622
SHEPARD'S MARYLAND EXPRESS CITATIONS. [Shepard's Md. express cit.]. **Added/Corp** Shepard's/McGraw-Hill. **VFOAT** Maryland Express Citations. (1993)-. English. sm (24 issues). $149.00. Shepards McGraw-Hill Inc, 555 Middle Creek Parkway, PO Box 35300, Colorado Springs CO 80935-3530. **Tel** (719)488-3000, FAX (800)525-0053. **DD** 348.

US
SHEPARD'S MASSACHUSETTS CASE NAMES CITATOR. **Added/Corp** Shepard's/McGraw-Hill. **VFOAT** Massachusetts Case Names Citator. 1st Ed. (1985)-. Periodical. English. Six times a year. $75.00 (bound volume), $88.00 (cumulative supplements). Shepards McGraw-Hill Inc, 555 Middle Creek Parkway, PO Box 35300, Colorado Springs CO 80935-3530. **Tel** (719)488-3000, FAX (800)525-0053.
Desc: Index to all the recent cases in the state. Provides plaintiff/defendant and reverse defendant/plaintiff listings.

US/0730-4064
SHEPARD'S MASSACHUSETTS CITATIONS. [Shepard's Mass. cit.]. **Added/Corp** Shepard's/McGraw Hill. **VFOAT** Massachusetts Citations. (19??)-. English. mo. $500.00 (4 bound volumes), $337.00 (cumulative supplements). Shepards McGraw-Hill Inc, 555 Middle Creek Parkway, PO Box 35300, Colorado Springs CO 80935-3530. **Tel** (719)488-3000, FAX (800)525-0053. **DD** 348. available on CD-ROM from the publisher.

US/1053-5780
SHEPARD'S MASSACHUSETTS EXPRESS CITATIONS. [Shepard's Mass. express cit.]. **Added/Corp** Shepard's/McGraw-Hill. **VFOAT** Massachusetts Express Citations. Vol. 1, No. 1 (Aug. 6, 1990)-. Periodical. English. sm (24 issues). $149.00. Shepards McGraw-Hill Inc, 555 Middle Creek Parkway, PO Box 35300, Colorado Springs CO 80935-3530. **Tel** (719)488-3000, FAX (800)525-0053. **DD** 348.

US/1048-0846
SHEPARD'S MEDICAL MALPRACTICE CITATIONS. [Shepard's med. malpract. cit.]. **Added/Corp** Shepard's/McGraw-Hill. **VFOAT** Medical Malpractice Citations. (1988)-. English. qt. $120.00 (bound volume), $235.00 (cumulative supplements). Shepards McGraw-Hill Inc, 555 Middle Creek Parkway, PO Box 35300, Colorado Springs CO 80935-3530. **Tel** (719)488-3000, FAX (800)525-0053. **DD** 346. Index available. cum. index.
Desc: Citations to cases and statutes compiled and analyzed from the area of medical malpractice.

US/1048-0684
SHEPARD'S MICHIGAN CASE NAMES CITATOR. [Shepard's Mich. case names cit.]. **Added/Corp** Shepard's/McGraw-Hill. **VFOAT** Michigan Case Names Citator. Vol. 1, No. 1 (Oct. 1985)-. English. Six times a year. $150.00 (2 bound volumes), $88.00 (cumulative supplements). Shepards McGraw-Hill Inc, 555 Middle Creek Parkway, PO Box 35300, Colorado Springs CO 80935-3530. **Tel** (719)488-3000, FAX (800)525-0053. **DD** 348.
Desc: Index to all the recent cases in the state. Provides plaintiff/defendant and reverse defendant/plaintiff listings.

US/0730-4102
SHEPARD'S MICHIGAN CITATIONS. [Shepard's Mich. cit.]. **Added/Corp** Shepard's/McGraw-Hill. **VFOAT** Michigan Citations. (19??)-. Periodical. English. bm. $600.00 (5 bound volumes), $357.00 (cumulative supplements). Shepards McGraw-Hill Inc, 555 Middle Creek Parkway, PO Box 35300, Colorado Springs CO 80935-3530. **Tel** (719)488-3000, FAX (800)525-0053. **DD** 348.
Desc: Gives you every citing reference to the statute in question ever made by your appellate courts.

●US/1065-8815
SHEPARD'S MICHIGAN EXPRESS CITATIONS. [Shepard's Mich. express cit.]. **Added/Corp** Shepard's/McGraw-Hill. **VFOAT** Michigan Express Citations. (1992)-. English. sm (24 issues). $145.00. Shepards McGraw-Hill Inc, 555 Middle Creek Parkway, PO Box 35300, Colorado Springs CO 80935-3530. **Tel** (719)488-3000, FAX (800)525-0053. **DD** 348.

US
SHEPARD'S MINNESOTA CASE NAMES CITATOR. **Added/Corp** Shepard's/McGraw-Hill. **VFOAT** Minnesota Case Names Citator. 1st Ed. (1986)-. Periodical. English. $80.00 (bound volume), $83.00 (cumulative supplements). Shepards McGraw-Hill Inc, 555 Middle Creek Parkway, PO Box 35300, Colorado Springs CO 80935-3530. **Tel** (719)488-3000, FAX (800)525-0053.
Desc: Index to all the recent cases in the state. Provides plaintiff/defendant and reverse defendant/plaintiff listings.

US/0730-4145
SHEPARD'S MINNESOTA CITATIONS. [Shepard's Minn. cit.]. **Added/Corp** Shepard's/McGraw-Hill. **VFOAT** Minnesota Citations. Cases and Statutues. (19??)-. Periodical. English. $420.00 (3 bound volumes), $302.00 (cumulative supplements). Shepards McGraw-Hill Inc, 555 Middle Creek Parkway, PO Box 35300, Colorado Springs CO 80935-3530. **Tel** (719)488-3000, FAX (800)525-0053. **DD** 348.
Desc: Gives you every citing reference to the statute in question ever made by your appellate courts.

●US/1068-4077
SHEPARD'S MINNESOTA EXPRESS CITATIONS. [Shepard's Minn. express cit.]. **Added/Corp** Shepard's/McGraw Hill. **VFOAT** Minnesota Express Citations. (1993)-. English. sm. $149.00. Shepards McGraw-Hill Inc, 555 Middle Creek Parkway, PO Box 35300, Colorado Springs CO 80935-3530. **Tel** (719)488-3000, FAX (800)525-0053. **DD** 348.

US
SHEPARD'S MISSISSIPPI CASE NAMES CITATOR. **Added/Corp** Shepard's/McGraw-Hill. **VFOAT** Mississippi Case Names Citator. 1st Ed. (1986)-. Periodical. English. Four times a year. $75.00 (bound volume), $83.00 (cumulative supplements). Shepards McGraw-Hill Inc, 555 Middle Creek Parkway, PO Box 35300, Colorado Springs CO 80935-3530. **Tel** (719)488-3000, FAX (800)525-0053.
Desc: Index to all the recent cases in the state. Provides plaintiff/defendant and reverse defendant/plaintiff listings.

US/0488-6119
SHEPARD'S MISSISSIPPI CITATIONS. [Shepard's Miss. cit.]. **Added/Corp** Shepard's Citations, Inc. Shepard's, Inc. of Colorado Springs. Shepard's/McGraw-Hill. **VFOAT** Mississippi Citations. Vol. 25 No. 3 (Feb. 1957)-. English. $310.00 (2 bound volumes), $302.00 (cumulative supplements). Shepards McGraw-Hill Inc, 555 Middle Creek Parkway, PO Box 35300, Colorado Springs CO 80935-3530. **Tel** (719)488-3000, FAX (800)525-0053. **DD** 348. ***Continues*** *Shepard's Mississippi Citations, 0488-6119.*
Desc: Gives you every citing reference to the statute in question ever made by your appellate courts.

US
SHEPARD'S MISSOURI CASE NAMES CITATOR. **Added/Corp** Shepard's/McGraw-Hill. **VFOAT** Missouri Case Names Citator. 1st Ed. (1986)-. Periodical. English. Six times a year. $75.00 (bound volume), $82.00 (cumulative supplements). Shepards McGraw-Hill Inc, 555 Middle Creek Parkway, PO Box 35300, Colorado Springs CO 80935-3530. **Tel** (719)488-3000, FAX (800)525-0053.
Desc: Index to all the recent cases in the state. Provides plaintiff/defendant and reverse defendant/plaintiff listings.

US/0730-417X
SHEPARD'S MISSOURI CITATIONS. [Shepard's Mo. cit.]. **Added/Corp** Shepard's/McGraw-Hill. Shepard's Citations, Inc. **VFOAT** Missouri Citations. (19??)-. English. mo. $625.00 (5 bound volumes), $337.00 (cumulative supplements). Shepards McGraw-Hill Inc, 555 Middle Creek Parkway, PO Box 35300, Colorado Springs CO 80935-3530. **Tel** (719)488-3000, FAX (800)525-0053.

US/1053-6892
SHEPARD'S MISSOURI EXPRESS CITATIONS. [Shepard's Mo. express cit.]. **Added/Corp** Shepard's/McGraw-Hill. **VFOAT** Missouri Express Citations. Vol. 1, No. 1 (Aug. 13, 1990)-. English. sm. $149.00. Shepards McGraw-Hill Inc, 555 Middle Creek Parkway, PO Box 35300, Colorado Springs CO 80935-3530. **Tel** (719)488-3000, FAX (800)525-0053. **DD** 348.

US/0730-5931
SHEPARD'S MONTANA CITATIONS. [Shepard's Mont. cit.]. **Added/Corp** Shepard's Citations, Inc. Shepard's, Inc. of Colorado Springs. Shepard's/McGraw-Hill. **VFOAT** Montana Citations. (1913)-. English. Six times a year. $150.00 (bound volume), $257.00 (cumulative supplements). Shepards McGraw-Hill Inc, 555 Middle Creek Parkway, PO Box 35300, Colorado Springs CO 80935-3530. **Tel** (719)488-3000, FAX (800)525-0053. **DD** 348.
Desc: Gives you every citing reference to the statute in question ever made by your appellate courts.

US/1052-6315
SHEPARD'S NEBRASKA CASE NAMES CITATOR. [Shepard's Neb. case names cit.]. **Added/Corp** Shepard's/McGraw-Hill. **VFOAT** Nebraska Case Names Citator. (1988)-. English. sa. $75.00 (1 bound volume), $62.00 (cumulative supplements). Shepards McGraw-Hill Inc, 555 Middle Creek Parkway, PO Box 35300, Colorado Springs CO 80935-3530. **Tel** (719)488-3000, FAX (800)525-0053. **DD** 348.

US/0730-594X
SHEPARD'S NEBRASKA CITATIONS. [Shepard's Neb. cit.]. **Added/Corp** Shepard's/McGraw-Hill. **VFOAT** Nebraska Citations. Cases and Statutes. (19??)-. English. Six times a year. $300.00 (2 bound volumes), $237.00 (cumulative supplements). Shepards McGraw-Hill Inc, 555 Middle Creek Parkway, PO Box 35300, Colorado Springs CO 80935-3530. **Tel** (719)488-3000, FAX (800)525-0053. **DD** 348.
Desc: Gives you every citing reference to the statute in question ever made by your appellate courts.

US/1052-6307
SHEPARD'S NEVADA CASE NAMES CITATOR. [Shepard's Nev. case names cit.]. **Added/Corp** Shepard's/McGraw-Hill. **VFOAT** Nevada Case Names Citator. (1988)-. English. sa. $75.00 (1 bound volume), $62.00 (cumulative supplements). Shepards McGraw-Hill Inc, 555 Middle Creek Parkway, PO Box 35300, Colorado Springs CO 80935-3530. **Tel** (719)488-3000, FAX (800)525-0053. **DD** 348.

US/0730-5974
SHEPARD'S NEVADA CITATIONS. [Shepard's Nev. cit.]. **Added/Corp** Shepard's/McGraw-Hill. **VFOAT** Nevada Citations. (19??)-. English. Six times a year. $180.00 (bound volume), $257.00 (cumulative supplements). Shepards McGraw-Hill Inc, 555 Middle Creek Parkway, PO Box 35300, Colorado Springs CO 80935-3530. **Tel** (719)488-3000, FAX (800)525-0053. **DD** 348.
Desc: Gives you every citing reference to the statute in question ever made by your appellate courts.

US
SHEPARD'S NEW HAMPSHIRE CASE NAMES CITATOR. **Added/Corp** Shepard's/McGraw-Hill. **VFOAT** New Hampshire Case Names Citator. 1st Ed. (1986)-. Periodical. English. Six times a year. $180.00 (bound volume), $252.00 (cumulative supplements). Shepards McGraw-Hill Inc, 555 Middle Creek Parkway, PO Box 35300, Colorado Springs CO 80935-3530. **Tel** (719)488-3000, FAX (800)525-0053.
Desc: Index to all the recent cases in the state. Provides plaintiff/defendant and reverse defendant/plaintiff listings.

US/0730-5982
SHEPARD'S NEW HAMPSHIRE CITATIONS. [Shepard's N. H. cit.]. **Added/Corp** Shepard's/McGraw-Hill. Frank Shepard Company Shepard's Citations, Inc. Shepard's, Inc. of Colorado Springs. (19??)-. English. Six times a year. $180.00 (bound volume), $252.00 (cumulative supplements). Shepards McGraw-Hill Inc, 555 Middle Creek Parkway, PO Box 35300, Colorado Springs CO 80935-3530. **Tel** (719)488-3000, FAX (800)525-0053. **DD** 348.
Desc: Gives you every citing reference to the statute in question ever made by your appellate courts.

US
SHEPARD'S NEW JERSEY CASE NAMES CITATOR. **Added/Corp** Shepard's/McGraw-Hill. **VFOAT** New Jersey Case Names Citator. 1st Ed. (1984)-. Periodical. English. Six times a year. $150.00 (2 bound volumes), $88.00 (cumulative supplements). Shepards McGraw-Hill Inc, 555 Middle Creek Parkway, PO Box 35300, Colorado Springs CO 80935-3530. **Tel** (719)488-3000, FAX (800)525-0053.
Desc: Index to all the recent cases in the state. Provides plaintiff/defendant and reverse defendant/plaintiff listings.

US/0730-420X
SHEPARD'S NEW JERSEY CITATIONS. [Shepard's N. J. cit.]. **Added/Corp** Shepard's/McGraw-Hill. **VFOAT** New Jersey Citations. (19??)-. Periodical. English. Six times a year. $720.00 (6 bound volumes), $362.00 (cumulative supplements). Shepards McGraw-Hill Inc, 555 Middle Creek Parkway, PO Box 35300, Colorado Springs CO 80935-3530. **Tel** (719)488-3000, FAX (800)525-0053. cum. index. ctrl circ. available on an online database.
Desc: Gives you every citing reference to the statute in question ever made by your appellate courts, as well as citations to cases reported in New Jersey Reports, law journals, law reports and the Atlantic Reporter.

US/1060-3697
SHEPARD'S NEW JERSEY EXPRESS CITATIONS. [Shepard's N.J. express cit.]. **Added/Corp** Shepard's/McGraw-Hill. **VFOAT** New Jersey Express Citations. (1991)-. English. sm (24 issues). $149.00. Shepards McGraw-Hill Inc, 555 Middle Creek Parkway, PO Box 35300, Colorado Springs CO 80935-3530. **Tel** (719)488-3000, FAX (800)525-0053. **DD** 340.

US/1055-8667
SHEPARD'S NEW JERSEY INSURANCE LAW & REGULATION REPORTER. [Shepard's N. J. insur. law regul. rep.]. **VFOAT** New Jersey Insurance Law & Regulation Reporter; New Jersey Insurance Law and Regulation Reporter. Vol. 1, No. 1 (Feb. 1991)-. Periodical. English. mo. $325.00. Shepards McGraw-Hill Inc, 555 Middle Creek Parkway, PO Box 35300, Colorado Springs CO 80935-3530. **Tel** (719)488-3000, FAX (800)525-0053. **ED** Davis Howard. **DD** 346.
Desc: Provides current coverage of New Jersey insurance law. Includes summaries, commentaries and analysis of judicial decisions, legislative actions, rulings, regulations and bulletins.

US
SHEPARD'S NEW MEXICO CASE NAMES CITATOR. **Added/Corp** Shepard's/McGraw-Hill. **VFOAT** New Mexico Case Names Citator. 1st Ed. (1986)-. Periodical. English. Twice a year. $75.00 (bound volume), $62.00 (cumulative supplements). Shepards McGraw-Hill Inc, 555 Middle Creek Parkway, PO Box 35300, Colorado Springs CO 80935-3530. **Tel** (719)488-3000, FAX (800)525-0053.
Desc: Index to all the recent cases in the state. Provides plaintiff/defendant and reverse defendant/plaintiff listings.

US/0730-6008
SHEPARD'S NEW MEXICO CITATIONS. [Shepard's N. M. cit.]. **Added/Corp** Shepard's/McGraw-Hill. (19??)-. English. Six times a year. $180.00 (bound volume), $257.00 (cumulative supplements). Shepards McGraw-Hill Inc, 555 Middle Creek Parkway, PO Box 35300, Colorado Springs CO 80935-3530. **Tel** (719)488-3000, FAX (800)525-0053. **DD** 348.
Desc: Gives you every citing reference to the statute in question ever made by your appellate courts.

US
SHEPARD'S NEW YORK COURT OF APPEALS CASE NAMES CITATOR. **Added/Corp** Shepard's/McGraw-Hill. New York (State). Court of Appeals. **VFOAT** New York Court of Appeals Case Names Citator. 1st Ed. (1986)-. English. Six times a year. $75.00 (bound volume), $72.00 (cumulative supplements). Shepards McGraw-Hill Inc, 555 Middle Creek Parkway, PO Box 35300, Colorado Springs CO 80935-3530. **Tel** (719)488-3000, FAX (800)525-0053.
Desc: Index to all the recent cases in the state. Provides plaintiff/defendant and reverse defendant/plaintiff listings.

US/0730-4277
SHEPARD'S NEW YORK COURT OF APPEALS CITATIONS. [Shepard's N. Y. Court of Appeals cit.]. **Added/Corp** Frank Shepard Company. Shepard's Citations, Inc. Shepard's Inc. of Colorado Springs. Shepard's/McGraw-Hill. **VFOAT** New York Court of Appeals Citations. (194?)-. English. Six times a year. $1060.00 (10 bound volumes), $187.00 (cumulative supplements). Shepards McGraw-Hill Inc, 555 Middle Creek Parkway, PO Box 35300, Colorado Springs CO 80935-3530. **Tel** (719)488-3000, FAX (800)525-0053. **DD** 348.
Desc: Gives you every citing reference to the statute in question ever made by your appellate courts.

US/1046-7092
SHEPARD'S NEW YORK MISCELLANEOUS CASE NAMES CITATOR. [Shepard's N. Y. misc. case names cit.]. (198?)-. Periodical. English. bm. $140.00 (2 bound volumes), $88.00 (cumulative supplements). Shepards McGraw-Hill Inc, 555 Middle Creek Parkway, PO Box 35300, Colorado Springs CO 80935-3530. **Tel** (719)488-3000, FAX (800)525-0053. **DD** 348.

US/0730-4269
SHEPARD'S NEW YORK MISCELLANEOUS CITATIONS. [Shepard's N. Y. misc. cit.]. **Added/Corp** Frank Shepard Company. Shepard's Citations, Inc. Shepard's Inc. of Colorado Springs. Shepard's/McGraw Hill. **VFOAT** New York Miscellaneous Citations. (1942)-. English. Six times a year. $399.00 (3 bound volumes), $187.00 (cumulative supplements). Shepards McGraw-Hill Inc, 555 Middle Creek Parkway, PO Box 35300, Colorado Springs CO 80935-3530. **Tel** (719)488-3000, FAX (800)525-0053.
Desc: Gives you every citing reference to the statute in question ever made by your appellate courts.

US/0730-4242
SHEPARD'S NEW YORK STATUTE CITATIONS. [Shepard's N. Y. statute cit.]. **Added/Corp** Shepard's/McGraw-Hill. Frank Shepard Co. Shepard's Citations, Inc. Shepard's, Inc. of Colorado

Springs. (1940)-. Periodical. English. Six times a year. $826.00 (7 bound volumes), $207.00 (cumulative supplements). Shepards McGraw-Hill Inc, 555 Middle Creek Parkway, PO Box 35300, Colorado Springs CO 80935-3530. **Tel** (719)488-3000, FAX (800)525-0053. **DD** 348.
Desc: Gives you every citing reference to the statute in question ever made by your appellate courts.

●US/1061-7906
SHEPARD'S NEW YORK STATUTE EXPRESS CITATIONS. [Shepard's N.Y. statute express cit.]. **Added/Corp** Shepard's McGraw-Hill. (1992)-. Periodical. English. sm. $115.00. Shepards McGraw-Hill Inc, 555 Middle Creek Parkway, PO Box 35300, Colorado Springs CO 80935-3530. **Tel** (719)488-3000, FAX (800)525-0053. **DD** 348.

US/0730-4234
SHEPARD'S NEW YORK SUPPLEMENT CITATIONS. [Shepard's N. Y. suppl. cit.]. **Added/Corp** Frank Shepard Company. Shepard's Citations, Inc. Shepard's, Inc. of Colorado Springs. Shepard's/McGraw-Hill. (1940)-. Periodical. English. mo. $1155.00 (11 bound volumes), $345.00 (cumulative supplements). Shepards McGraw-Hill Inc, 555 Middle Creek Parkway, PO Box 35300, Colorado Springs CO 80935-3530. **Tel** (719)488-3000, FAX (800)525-0053. **DD** 348.
Desc: Gives you every citing reference to the statute in question ever made by your appellate courts.

●US/1061-7914
SHEPARD'S NEW YORK SUPPLEMENT EXPRESS CITATIONS. [Shepard's N. Y. suppl. express cit.]. **Added/Corp** Shepard's/McGraw-Hill. (1992)-. English. sm. $220.00. Shepards McGraw-Hill Inc, 555 Middle Creek Parkway, PO Box 35300, Colorado Springs CO 80935-3530. **Tel** (719)488-3000, FAX (800)525-0053. **DD** 348.

US/1048-079X
SHEPARD'S NEW YORK SUPREME COURT APPELLATE DIVISION CASE NAMES CITATOR. [Shepard's N. Y. Supreme Court Appell. Div. case names cit.]. **Added/Corp** Shepard's/McGraw-Hill. **VFOAT** New York Supreme Court Appellate Division Case Names Citator. (1986)-. English. Six times a year. $272.00 (4 bound volumes), $92.00 (cumulative supplements). Shepards McGraw-Hill Inc, 555 Middle Creek Parkway, PO Box 35300, Colorado Springs CO 80935-3530. **Tel** (719)488-3000, FAX (800)525-0053. **DD** 348.

US
SHEPARD'S NEW YORK SUPREME COURT CITATIONS. **Added/Corp** Frank Shepard Company Shepard's Citations, Inc. Shepard's, Inc. of Colorado Springs. Shepard's/McGraw-Hill. **VFOAT** New York Supreme Court Citations. Vol. 1 (1942)-. English. ir. $944.00 (8 bound volumes), $187.00 (cumulative supplements). Shepards McGraw-Hill Inc, 555 Middle Creek Parkway, PO Box 35300, Colorado Springs CO 80935-3530. **Tel** (719)488-3000, FAX (800)525-0053.
Desc: Gives you every citing reference to the statute in question ever made by your appellate courts.

US
SHEPARD'S NORTH CAROLINA CASE NAMES CITATOR. **Added/Corp** Shepard's/McGraw-Hill. **VFOAT** North Carolina Case Names Citator. 1st Ed. (1985)-. Periodical. English. Six times a year. $85.00 (bound volume), $88.00 (cumulative supplements). Shepards McGraw-Hill Inc, 555 Middle Creek Parkway, PO Box 35300, Colorado Springs CO 80935-3530. **Tel** (719)488-3000, FAX (800)525-0053.
Desc: Index to all the recent cases in the state. Provides plaintiff/defendant and reverse defendant/plaintiff listings.

US/0730-2126
SHEPARD'S NORTH CAROLINA CITATIONS. [Shepard's N. C. cit.]. **Added/Corp** Shepard's/McGraw-Hill. **VFOAT** North Carolina Citations. (1957)-. English. mo. $500.00 (4 bound volumes), $342.00 (cumulative supplements). Shepards McGraw-Hill Inc, 555 Middle Creek Parkway, PO Box 35300, Colorado Springs CO 80935-3530. **Tel** (719)488-3000, FAX (800)525-0053. **DD** 348.
Desc: Gives you every citing reference to the statute in question ever made by your appellate courts.

US/1060-7633
SHEPARD'S NORTH CAROLINA EXPRESS CITATIONS. [Shepard's N.C. express cit.]. **Added/Corp** Shepard's/McGraw-Hill. **VFOAT** North Carolina Express Citations. (1991)-. English. sm (24 issues). $149.00. Shepards McGraw-Hill Inc, 555 Middle Creek Parkway, PO Box 35300, Colorado Springs CO 80935-3530. **Tel** (719)488-3000, FAX (800)525-0053. **DD** 348.

●US/1069-9511
SHEPARD'S NORTH CAROLINA STATUTES CITATIONS. [Shepard's N.C. statut. cit.]. **Added/Corp** Shepard's/McGraw-Hill. Vol. 1, No. 1 (Sept. 1992)-. English. mo. $120.00. Shepards McGraw-Hill Inc, 555 Middle Creek Parkway, PO Box 35300, Colorado Springs CO 80935-3530. **Tel** (719)488-3000, FAX (800)525-0053. **DD** 349.

US/0730-6016
SHEPARD'S NORTH DAKOTA CITATIONS. [Shepard's N.D. cit.]. **Added/Corp** Frank Shepard Company. Shepard's Citations, Inc. Shepard's, Inc. of Colorado Springs. Shepard's/McGraw-Hill. **VFOAT** North Dakota Citations. 4th Ed. (1947)-. English. Six times a year. $150.00 (bound volume), $252.00 (cumulative supplements). Shepards McGraw-Hill Inc, 555 Middle Creek Parkway, PO Box 35300, Colorado Springs CO 80935-3530. **Tel** (719)488-3000, FAX (800)525-0053. **DD** 348. ***Continues in part*** *Shepard's Dakota Citations and Key Number Annotations.*
Desc: Gives you every citing reference to the statute in question ever made by your appellate courts.

US/0730-1979
SHEPARD'S NORTHEASTERN REPORTER CITATIONS. [Shepard's northeast. report. cit.]. **Added/Corp** Shepard's Citations, Inc. Frank Shepard Company. Shepard's Inc. of Colorado Springs. Shepard's/McGraw-Hill. **VFOAT** Shepard's North Eastern Reporter Citations; Northeastern Reporter Citations. (1909)-. English. mo. $990.00 (10 bound volumes), $400.00 (cumulative supplements). Shepards McGraw-Hill Inc, 555 Middle Creek Parkway, PO Box 35300, Colorado Springs CO 80935-3530. **Tel** (719)488-3000, FAX (800)525-0053. **DD** 348.
Desc: Gives you every state and federal citation to every reporter case as cited anywhere throughout the entire national reporter system.

US/0730-4706
SHEPARD'S NORTHWESTERN REPORTER CITATIONS. [Shepard's northwest. report. cit.]. **Added/Corp** Shepard's/McGraw-Hill. Frank Shepard Company Shepard's Citations, Inc. Shepard's Inc. of Colorado Springs. **VFOAT** Shepard's North Western Reporter Citations; Northwestern Reporter Citations. (1922)-. English. mo. $960.00 (10 bound volumes), $400.00 (cumulative supplements). Shepards McGraw-Hill Inc, 555 Middle Creek Parkway, PO Box 35300, Colorado Springs CO 80935-3530. **Tel** (719)488-3000, FAX (800)525-0053. **DD** 348. ***Continues*** *Shepard's Citations of all Cases in the Northwestern Reporter.*
Desc: Gives you every state and federal citation to every reporter case as cited anywhere throughout the entire national reporter system.

US
SHEPARD'S OHIO CASE NAMES CITATOR. **Added/Corp** Shepard's/McGraw-Hill. **VFOAT** Ohio Case Names Citator. 1st Ed. (1985)-. Periodical. English. Six times a year. $80.00 (bound volume), $88.00 (cumulative supplements). Shepards McGraw-Hill Inc, 555 Middle Creek Parkway, PO Box 35300, Colorado Springs CO 80935-3530. **Tel** (719)488-3000, FAX (800)525-0053.
Desc: Index to all the recent cases in the state. Provides plaintiff/defendant and reverse defendant/plaintiff listings.

US/0730-4293
SHEPARD'S OHIO CITATIONS. [Shepard's Ohio cit.]. **Added/Corp** Shepard's/McGraw-Hill. Shepard's Citations, Inc. **VFOAT** Ohio Citations. Cases and Statutes Supplement. 5th Ed. (1975)-. English. Six times a year. $896.00 (8 bound volumes), $357.00 (cumulative supplements). Shepards McGraw-Hill Inc, 555 Middle Creek Parkway, PO Box 35300, Colorado Springs CO 80935-3530. **Tel** (719)488-3000, FAX (800)525-0053. **DD** 348.

US/1050-9119
SHEPARD'S OHIO EXPRESS CITATIONS. [Shepard's Ohio express cit.]. **Added/Corp** Shepard's/McGraw-Hill. **VFOAT** Express Citations. Vol. 1, No. 1 (Mar. 1, 1990)-. Periodical. English. sm. $149.00. Shepards McGraw-Hill Inc, 555 Middle Creek Parkway, PO Box 35300, Colorado Springs CO 80935-3530. **Tel** (719)488-3000, FAX (800)525-0053. **DD** 348.

US
SHEPARD'S OKLAHOMA CASE NAMES CITATOR. **Added/Corp** Shepard's/McGraw-Hill. **VFOAT** Oklahoma Case Names Citator. 1st Ed. (1986)-. Periodical. English. Four times a year. $75.00 (bound volume), $83.00 (cumulative supplements). Shepards McGraw-Hill Inc, 555 Middle Creek Parkway, PO Box 35300, Colorado Springs CO 80935-3530. **Tel** (719)488-3000, FAX (800)525-0053.
Desc: Index to all the recent cases in the state. Provides plaintiff/defendant and reverse defendant/plaintiff listings.

US/0730-4323
SHEPARD'S OKLAHOMA CITATIONS. [Shepard's Okla. cit.]. **Added/Corp** Shepard's/McGraw-Hill. **VFOAT** Oklahoma Citations. (1957)-. English. bm. $399.00 (3 bound volumes), $347.00 (cumulative supplements). Shepards McGraw-Hill Inc, 555 Middle Creek Parkway, PO Box 35300, Colorado Springs CO 80935-3530. **Tel** (719)488-3000, FAX (800)525-0053. **DD** 348.
Desc: Gives you every citing reference to the statute in question ever made by your appellate courts.

US/1054-903X
SHEPARD'S OKLAHOMA EXPRESS CITATIONS. [Shepard's Okla. express cit.]. **Added/Corp** Shepard's/McGraw-Hill. **VFOAT** Oklahoma Express Citations. Vol. 1, No. 1 (Oct. 16, 1990)-. Periodical. English. mo. $125.00. Shepards McGraw-Hill Inc, 555 Middle Creek Parkway, PO Box 35300, Colorado Springs CO 80935-3530. **Tel** (719)488-3000, FAX (800)525-0053. **DD** 348.

US
SHEPARD'S OREGON CASE NAMES CITATOR. **Added/Corp** Shepard's/McGraw-Hill. **VFOAT** Oregon Case Names Citator. 1st Ed. (1986)-. Periodical. English. Four times a year. $75.00 (bound volume), $83.00 (cumulative supplements). Shepards McGraw-Hill Inc, 555 Middle Creek Parkway, PO Box 35300, Colorado Springs CO 80935-3530. **Tel** (719)488-3000, FAX (800)525-0053.
Desc: Index to all the recent cases in the state. Provides plaintiff/defendant and reverse defendant/plaintiff listings.

US/0730-4358
SHEPARD'S OREGON CITATIONS. [Shepard's Or. cit.]. **Added/Corp** Shepard's/McGraw-Hill. **VFOAT** Oregon Citations. (19??)-. Periodical. English. bm (6 issues). $399.00 (3 bound volumes), $342.00 (cumulative supplements). Shepards McGraw-Hill Inc, 555 Middle Creek Parkway, PO Box 35300, Colorado Springs CO 80935-3530. **Tel** (719)488-3000, FAX (800)525-0053. **DD** 348.

●US/1069-7853
SHEPARD'S OREGON EXPRESS CITATIONS. [Shepard's Or. express cit.]. **Added/Corp** Shepard's/McGraw-Hill. Vol. 1, No. 1 (Apr. 1, 1993)-. Periodical. English. sm. $165.00. Shepards McGraw-Hill Inc, 555 Middle Creek Parkway, PO Box 35300, Colorado Springs CO 80935-3530. **Tel** (719)488-3000, FAX (800)525-0053. **DD** 348.

US
SHEPARD'S PACIFIC REPORTER CITATIONS; A COMPILATION OF CITATIONS TO ALL CASES REPORTED IN THE PACIFIC REPORTER. [COMPILED BY THE PUBLISHERS EDITORIAL STAFF]. **Added/Corp** Shepard's Citations, Inc. Shepard's, Inc. of Colorado Springs. (19??)-. English. mo. $1089.00 (11 bound volumes), $400.00 (cumulative supplements). Shepards McGraw-Hill Inc, 555 Middle Creek Parkway, PO Box 35300, Colorado Springs CO 80935-3530. **Tel** (719)488-3000, FAX (800)525-0053.

US
SHEPARD'S PENNSYLVANIA CASE NAMES CITATOR. **Added/Corp** Shepard's/McGraw-Hill. **VFOAT** Pennsylvania Case Names Citator. 1st Ed. (1985)-. Periodical. English. Six times a year. $195.00 (3 bound volumes), $102.00 (cumulative supplements). Shepards McGraw-Hill Inc, 555 Middle Creek Parkway, PO Box 35300, Colorado Springs CO 80935-3530. **Tel** (719)488-3000, FAX (800)525-0053.
Desc: Index to all the recent cases in the state. Provides plaintiff/defendant and reverse defendant/plaintiff listings.

US/0730-4382
SHEPARD'S PENNSYLVANIA CITATIONS. [Shepard's Pa. cit.]. **Added/Corp** Shepard's/McGraw-Hill. **VFOAT** Pennsylvania Citations. (19??)-. Periodical. English. Six times a year. $990.00 (9 bound volumes), $357.00 (cumulative supplements). Shepards McGraw-Hill Inc, 555 Middle Creek Parkway, PO Box 35300, Colorado Springs CO 80935-3530. **Tel** (719)488-3000, FAX (800)525-0053. **DD** 348.

US/1057-8161
SHEPARD'S PENNSYLVANIA EXPRESS CITATIONS. [Shepard's Pa. express cit.]. **Added/Corp** Shepard's/McGraw-Hill. **VFOAT** Pennsylvania Express Citations. (1991)-. English. sm (24 issues). $165.00. Shepards McGraw-Hill Inc, 555 Middle Creek Parkway, PO Box 35300, Colorado Springs CO 80935-3530. **Tel** (719)488-3000, FAX (800)525-0053. **DD** 348.
Desc: Provides the latest analyzed citations to Pennsylvania cases, Pennsylvania statutes, and the Pennsylvania Constitution.

US
SHEPARD'S PRODUCTS LIABILITY CITATIONS. [Shepard's prod. liabil. cit.]. (198?)-. English. qt. $270.00 (bound volume), $270.00 (cumulative supplements). Shepards McGraw-Hill Inc, 555 Middle Creek Parkway, PO Box 35300, Colorado Springs CO 80935-3530. **Tel** (719)488-3000, FAX (800)525-0053.
Desc: Easy-to-find, clear listing of case names and dates on every page. Plus a case name table listing cases alphabetically with both the plaintiff's and defendant's name.

US/1052-6641
SHEPARD'S PUERTO RICO CASE NAMES CITATOR. [Shepard's P. R. case names cit.]. **Added/Corp** Shepard's/McGraw-Hill. **VFOAT** Puerto Rico Case Names Citator. (1988)-. English. sa. $70.00 (1 bound volume), $63.00 (cumulative supplements). Shepards McGraw-Hill Inc, 555 Middle Creek Parkway, PO Box 35300, Colorado Springs CO 80935-3530. **Tel** (719)488-3000, FAX (800)525-0053. **DD** 348.

US/0730-6261
SHEPARD'S PUERTO RICO CITATIONS. [Shepard's P.R. cit.]. **Added/Corp** Shepard's McGraw-Hill. Shepard's Citations, Inc. Shepard's Inc. of Colorado Springs. **VFOAT** Puerto Rico Citations. (1968)-. Periodical. English. Six times a year. $150.00 (bound volume), $237.00 (cumulative supplements). Shepards McGraw-Hill Inc, 555 Middle Creek Parkway, PO Box 35300, Colorado Springs CO 80935-3530. **Tel** (719)488-3000, FAX (800)525-0053. **DD** 349.
Desc: Gives you every citing reference to the statute in question ever made by your appellate courts.

US/0730-4641
SHEPARD'S RESTATEMENT OF THE LAW CITATIONS. **Added/Corp** Shepard's McGraw-Hill. Shepard's, Inc. of Colorado Springs. **VFOAT** Restatement of the Law Citations. (1976)-. English. bm (6 issues). $150.00 (bound volume), $267.00 (cumulative supplements). Shepards McGraw-Hill Inc, 555 Middle Creek Parkway, PO Box 35300, Colorado Springs CO 80935-3530. **Tel** (719)488-3000, FAX (800)525-0053. **DD** 348.
Desc: Covers citations to the American Law Institute's Restatement of the Law.

US/0730-6024
SHEPARD'S RHODE ISLAND CITATIONS. [Shepard's Rhode Island cit.]. **Added/Corp** Shepard's Citations, Inc. Shepard's/McGraw Hill. Shepard's Inc. of Colorado Springs. Frank Shepard Company. (1915)-. Periodical. English. Six times a year. $180.00 (bound volume), $257.00 (cumulative supplements). Shepards McGraw-Hill Inc, 555 Middle Creek Parkway, PO Box 35300, Colorado Springs CO 80935-3530. **Tel** (719)488-3000, FAX (800)525-0053. **DD** 348.
Desc: Gives you every citing reference to the statute in question ever made by your appellate courts.

US
SHEPARD'S SOUTH CAROLINA CASE NAMES CITATOR. **Added/Corp** Shepard's/McGraw-Hill. **VFOAT** South Carolina Case Names Citator. 1st Ed. (1986)-. Periodical. English. Four times a year. $75.00 (bound volume), $83.00 (cumulative supplements). Shepards McGraw-Hill Inc, 555 Middle Creek Parkway, PO Box 35300, Colorado Springs CO 80935-3530. **Tel** (719)488-3000, FAX (800)525-0053.
Desc: Index to all the recent cases in the state. Provides plaintiff/defendant and reverse defendant/plaintiff listings.

US/0730-6059
SHEPARD'S SOUTH CAROLINA CITATIONS. [Shepard's S. C. cit.]. **Added/Corp** Shepard's/McGraw-Hill. Shepard's Citations, Inc. Shepard's, Inc. of Colorado Springs. **VFOAT** South Carolina Citations. (1926)-. English. bm. $310.00 (2 bound volumes), $307.00 (cumulative supplements). Shepards McGraw-Hill Inc, 555 Middle Creek Parkway, PO Box 35300, Colorado Springs CO 80935-3530. **Tel** (719)488-3000, FAX (800)525-0053. **DD** 348.

US/0730-6032
SHEPARD'S SOUTH DAKOTA CITATIONS. [Shepard's S. D. cit.]. **Added/Corp** Shepard's Citations, Inc. Frank Shepard Company. Shepard's Inc. of Colorado Springs. Shepard's Mc/Graw-Hill. **VFOAT** South Dakota Citations. (1947)-. Periodical. English. Six times a year. $150.00 (bound volume), $257.00 (cumulative supplements). Shepards McGraw-Hill Inc, 555 Middle Creek Parkway, PO Box 35300, Colorado Springs CO 80935-3530. **Tel** (719)488-3000, FAX (800)525-0053. **DD** 348. ***Continues in part*** *Shepard's Dakota Citations and Key Number Annotations.*
Desc: Gives you every citing reference to the statute in question ever made by your appellate courts.

US/0730-4692
SHEPARD'S SOUTHEASTERN REPORTER CITATIONS. [Shepard's southeast. report. cit.]. **Added/Corp** Shepard's/McGraw-Hill. Frank Shepard Company. Shepard's Citations, Inc. Shepard's, Inc. of Colorado Springs. **VFOAT** Shepard's South Eastern Reporter Citations; Southeastern Reporter Citations. (1921)-. English. mo. $720.00 (6 bound volumes), $400.00 (cumulative supplements). Shepards McGraw-Hill Inc, 555 Middle Creek Parkway, PO Box 35300, Colorado Springs CO 80935-3530. **Tel** (719)488-3000, FAX (800)525-0053. **DD** 348.
Desc: Gives you every state and federal citation to every reporter case as cited anywhere throughout the entire national reporter system.

US/0730-1944
SHEPARD'S SOUTHERN REPORTER CITATIONS. [Shepard's south. report. cit.]. **Added/Corp** Frank Shepard Company. Shepard's Citations, Inc. Shepard's, Inc. of Colorado Springs. Shepard's/McGraw-Hill. **VFOAT** Southern Reporter Citations. (1907)-. English. mo. $798.00 (7 bound volumes), $400.00 (cumulative supplements). Shepards McGraw-Hill Inc, 555 Middle Creek Parkway, PO Box 35300, Colorado Springs CO 80935-3530. **Tel** (719)488-3000, FAX (800)525-0053. **DD** 348.
Desc: Gives you every state and federal citation to every reporter case as cited anywhere throughout the entire national reporter system.

US/0730-1952
SHEPARD'S SOUTHWESTERN REPORTER CITATIONS. [Shepard's southwest. report. cit.]. **Added/Corp** Frank Shepard Company. Shepard's Citations, Inc. Shepard's, Inc. of Colorado Springs. Shepard's/McGraw-Hill. **VFOAT** Shepard's South Western Reporter Citations; Southwestern Reporter Citations. (1908)-. English. mo. $1080.00 (8 bound volumes), $400.00 (cumulative supplements). Shepards McGraw-Hill Inc, 555 Middle Creek Parkway, PO Box 35300, Colorado Springs CO 80935-3530. **Tel** (719)488-3000, FAX (800)525-0053. **DD** 348.
Desc: Gives you every state and federal citation to every reporter case as cited anywhere throughout the entire national reporter system.

US/1052-6668
SHEPARD'S TENNESSEE CASE NAMES CITATOR. [Shepard's Tenn. case names cit.]. **Added/Corp** Shepard's/McGraw-Hill. **VFOAT** Tennessee Case Names Citator. (1985)-. English. bm (three cumulative supplements per year). $90.00 (bound volume), $88.00 (cumulative supplements). Shepards McGraw-Hill Inc, 555 Middle Creek Parkway, PO Box 35300, Colorado Springs CO 80935-3530. **Tel** (719)488-3000, FAX (800)525-0053. **DD** 348.
Desc: Index to all the recent cases in the state. Provides plaintiff/defendant and reverse defendant/plaintiff listings.

US/0730-4439
SHEPARD'S TENNESSEE CITATIONS. [Shepard's Tenn. cit.]. **Added/Corp** Shepard's/McGraw-Hill. **VFOAT** Tennessee Citations. (1971)-. English. bm (6 issues). $320.00 (bound volumes), $347.00 (cumulative supplements). Shepards McGraw-Hill Inc, 555 Middle Creek Parkway, PO Box 35300, Colorado Springs CO 80935-3530. **Tel** (719)488-3000, FAX (800)525-0053. **DD** 348.
Desc: Gives you every citing reference to the statute in question ever made by your appellate courts.

US
SHEPARD'S TENNESSEE CODE CITATIONS. English. mo. $120.00. Shepards McGraw-Hill Inc, 555 Middle Creek Parkway, PO Box 35300, Colorado Springs CO 80935-3530. **Tel** (719)488-3000, FAX (800)525-0053.

●US/1067-2591
SHEPARD'S TENNESSEE EXPRESS CITATIONS. [Shepard's Tenn. express cit.]. **Added/Corp** Shepard's/McGraw-Hill. **VFOAT** Tennessee Express Citations. Vol. 1, No. 1 (Nov. 10, 1992)-. Periodical. English. sm. $145.00. Shepards McGraw-Hill Inc, 555 Middle Creek Parkway, PO Box 35300, Colorado Springs CO 80935-3530. **Tel** (719)488-3000, FAX (800)525-0053. **DD** 348.

US/8750-1120
SHEPARD'S TEXAS CASE NAMES CITATOR. [Shepard's Tex. case names cit.]. (198?)-. Periodical. English. Six times a year. $168.00 (2 bound volumes), $108.00 (cumulative supplements). Shepards McGraw-Hill Inc, 555 Middle Creek Parkway, PO Box 35300, Colorado Springs CO 80935-3530. **Tel** (719)488-3000, FAX (800)525-0053. **DD** 348.
Desc: Index to all the recent cases in the state. Provides plaintiff/defendant and reverse defendant/plaintiff listings.

US/0730-4463
SHEPARD'S TEXAS CITATIONS. [Shepard's Texas cit.]. **Added/Corp** Shepard's/McGraw-Hill. **VFOAT** Texas Citations. (19??)-. English. bm (6 issues). $1062.00 (9 bound volumes), $337.00 (cumulative supplements). Shepards McGraw-Hill Inc, 555 Middle Creek Parkway, PO Box 35300, Colorado Springs CO 80935-3530. **Tel** (719)488-3000, FAX (800)525-0053. **DD** 348. available on CD-ROM from the publisher.

US/1056-8204
SHEPARD'S TEXAS EXPRESS CITATIONS. [Shepard's Tex. express cit.]. **Added/Corp** Shepard's/McGraw-Hill. **VFOAT** Texas Express Citations. Vol. 1, No. 1 (Mar. 6, 1991)-. Periodical. English. sm (24 issues). $174.00. Shepards McGraw-Hill Inc, 555 Middle Creek Parkway, PO Box 35300, Colorado Springs CO 80935-3530. **Tel** (719)488-3000, FAX (800)525-0053. **DD** 348.

US/1048-1273
SHEPARD'S UNIFORM COMMERCIAL CODE CASE CITATIONS. [Shepard's Unif. Commer. Code case cit.]. **Added/Corp** Shepard's/McGraw-Hill. **VFOAT** Uniform Commercial Code Case Citations. Vol. 1, No. 1 (Jan. 1989)-. English. qt. $520.00 (4 bound volumes), $190.00 (cumulative supplements). Shepards McGraw-Hill Inc, 555 Middle Creek Parkway, PO Box 35300, Colorado Springs CO 80935-3530. **Tel** (719)488-3000, FAX (800)525-0053. **DD** 346.
Desc: Gives you access to any type of commercial transaction, commercial paper, sales, or secured transaction.

US/0745-5925
SHEPARD'S UNIFORM COMMERCIAL CODE CITATIONS. (SHEPARD'S UNIFORM COMMERCIAL CODE CITATIONS : A COMPILATION OF CITATIONS TO THE UNIFORM COMMERCIAL CODE.). [Shepard's Unif. commer. code cit.]. **Added/Corp** Shepard's/McGraw-Hill. **VFOAT** Uniform Commercial Code Citations; Uniform Commercial Code. (198?)-. English. Three times a year. $400.00 (2 bound volumes), $275.00 (cumulative supplements). Shepards McGraw-Hill Inc, 555 Middle Creek Parkway, PO Box 35300, Colorado Springs CO 80935-3530. **Tel** (719)488-3000, FAX (800)525-0053. **DD** 346.
Desc: Commercial Code of all 50 states.

US/0582-9909
SHEPARD'S UNITED STATES ADMINISTRATIVE CITATIONS. [Shepard's U.S. adm. cit.]. **Added/Corp** Shepard's Citations, Inc. Shepard's, Inc. of Colorado Springs. Shepard's/McGrw-Hill. (Jan. 1967)-. English. Three times a year. $550.00 (5 bound volumes), $256.00 (cumulative supplements). Shepards McGraw-Hill Inc, 555 Middle Creek Parkway, PO Box 35300, Colorado Springs CO 80935-3530. **Tel** (719)488-3000, FAX (800)525-0053. **DD** 345.
Desc: Comprehensive system showing citations to decisions and orders of federal administrative departments, courts, boards and commissions.

US
SHEPARD'S UNITED STATES CITATIONS. **Added/Corp** United States. Supreme Court. Frank Shepard Company Shepard's Citations, Inc. Shepard's, Inc. of Colorado Springs. Shepard's/McGraw-Hill. 5th Ed. (1943)-. English. bm. $3080.00 (35 bound volumes), $330.00 (cumulative supplements). Shepards McGraw-Hill Inc, 555 Middle Creek Parkway, PO Box 35300, Colorado Springs CO 80935-3530. **Tel** (719)488-3000, FAX (800)525-0053. ***Continues*** *Shepard's United States Citations and Annotations.*
Desc: Provides a comprehensive system of legal research covering decisions of the US Supreme Court and statutes enacted by Congress.

US/0730-2061
SHEPARD'S UNITED STATES CITATIONS. CASES. **Added/Corp** Shepard's/McGraw-Hill. Periodical. English. $2700.00 (27 bound volumes), $215.00 (cumulative supplements). Shepards McGraw-Hill Inc, 555 Middle Creek Parkway, PO Box 35300, Colorado Springs CO 80935-3530. **Tel** (719)488-3000, FAX (800)525-0053.

US
SHEPARD'S UNITED STATES CITATIONS: STATUTES. **Added/Corp** Frank Shepard Company Shepard's Citations, Inc. Shepard's, Inc. of Colorado Springs. Shepard's/McGraw-Hill. 5th Ed. (1943)-. Periodical. English. $832.00 (8 bound volumes), $210.00 (cumulative supplements). Shepards McGraw-Hill Inc, 555 Middle Creek Parkway, PO Box 35300, Colorado Springs CO 80935-3530. **Tel** (719)488-3000, FAX (800)525-0053. ***Continues in part*** *Shepard's United States Citations and Annotations.*
Desc: A compilation of citations to the United States Constitution, United States code, United States statutes at large, United States treaties and other international agreements, and general orders.

US/0582-9917
SHEPARD'S UNITED STATES PATENTS AND TRADEMARKS CITATIONS. [Shepard's U. S. pat. trademarks cit.]. **Added/Corp** Shepard's/McGraw-Hill. Shepard's Citations, Inc. Shepard's, Inc. of Colorado Springs. (1968)-. English. Three times a year. $990.00 (10 bound volumes), $317.00 (cumulative supplements). Shepards McGraw-Hill Inc, 555 Middle Creek Parkway, PO Box 35300, Colorado Springs CO 80935-3530. **Tel** (719)488-3000, FAX (800)525-0053. **DD** 346.
Desc: Shows citations to the United States patents, trademarks and copyrights as well as to court decisions, administrative regulations relating to patents, and trademarks and copyrights.

US
SHEPARD'S UNITED STATES SUPREME COURT CASE NAMES CITATOR. **Added/Corp** Shepard's/McGraw-Hill. United States. Supreme Court. Official Reports of the

Supreme Court. **VFOAT** United States Supreme Court Case Names Citator. 1st Ed. (1987)-. Periodical. English. mo. $114.00 (2 bound volumes), $100.00 (cumulative supplements). Shepards McGraw-Hill Inc, 555 Middle Creek Parkway, PO Box 35300, Colorado Springs CO 80935-3530. **Tel** (719)488-3000, FAX (800)525-0053.
Desc: The case names and citations appear in United States Reports Lawyer's Edition, United States Supreme Court Reports Lawyer's Edition, and the United States Supreme Court Reports Second Series.

US/0730-6091
SHEPARD'S VERMONT CITATIONS. [Shepard's Vt. cit.]. **Added/Corp** Shepard's/McGraw-Hill. Frank Shepard Company. Shepard's Citations, Inc. Shepard's, Inc. of Colorado Springs. **VFOAT** Vermont Citations. (19??)-. English. Six times a year. $150.00 (1 bound volume), $252.00 (cumulative supplements). Shepards McGraw-Hill Inc, 555 Middle Creek Parkway, PO Box 35300, Colorado Springs CO 80935-3530. **Tel** (719)488-3000, FAX (800)525-0053. **DD** 348.
Desc: Gives you every citing reference to the statute in question ever made by your appellate courts.

US/1052-6676
SHEPARD'S VIRGINIA CASE NAMES CITATOR. [Shepard's Va. case names cit.]. **Added/Corp** Shepard's/McGraw-Hill. **VFOAT** Virginia Case Names Citator. (1985)-. English. sa. $75.00 (1 bound volume), $82.00 (cumulative supplements). Shepards McGraw-Hill Inc, 555 Middle Creek Parkway, PO Box 35300, Colorado Springs CO 80935-3530. **Tel** (719)488-3000, FAX (800)525-0053. **DD** 348.

US/0730-4498
SHEPARD'S VIRGINIA CITATIONS. [Shepard's Va. cit.]. **Added/Corp** Shepard's/McGraw-Hill. **VFOAT** Virginia Citations. (1958)-. English. bm. $300.00 (2 bound volumes), $327.00 (cumulative supplements). Shepards McGraw-Hill Inc, 555 Middle Creek Parkway, PO Box 35300, Colorado Springs CO 80935-3530. **Tel** (719)488-3000, FAX (800)525-0053. **DD** 348.

●US
SHEPARD'S VIRGINIA CODE CITATIONS. (1992)-. English. mo. $120.00. Shepards McGraw-Hill Inc, 555 Middle Creek Parkway, PO Box 35300, Colorado Springs CO 80935-3530. **Tel** (719)488-3000, FAX (800)525-0053.

US/1060-4774
SHEPARD'S VIRGINIA EXPRESS CITATIONS. [Shepard's Va. express cit.]. **Added/Corp** Shepard's/McGraw-Hill. **VFOAT** Virginia Express Citations. Vol. 1, No. 1 (Sept. 1991)-. English. mo. $125.00. Shepards McGraw-Hill Inc, 555 Middle Creek Parkway, PO Box 35300, Colorado Springs CO 80935-3530. **Tel** (719)488-3000, FAX (800)525-0053. **DD** 348.

US
SHEPARD'S WASHINGTON CASE NAMES CITATOR. **Added/Corp** Shepard's/McGraw-Hill. **VFOAT** Washington Case Names Citator. 1st Ed. (1985)-. Periodical. English. Six times a year. $75.00 (bound volume), $82.00 (cumulative supplements). Shepards McGraw-Hill Inc, 555 Middle Creek Parkway, PO Box 35300, Colorado Springs CO 80935-3530. **Tel** (719)488-3000, FAX (800)525-0053.
Desc: Index to all the recent cases in the state. Provides plaintiff/defendant and reverse defendant/plaintiff listings.

US/0730-4528
SHEPARD'S WASHINGTON CITATIONS. [Shepard's Wash. cit.]. **Added/Corp** Shepard's/ McGraw-Hill. **VFOAT** Washington Citations. Cases and Statutes. (19??)-. English. mo. $460.00 (4 bound volumes), $337.00 (cumulative supplements). Shepards McGraw-Hill Inc, 555 Middle Creek Parkway, PO Box 35300, Colorado Springs CO 80935-3530. **Tel** (719)488-3000, FAX (800)525-0053. **DD** 348.
Desc: Gives you every citing reference to the statute in question ever made by your appellate courts.

●US/1066-1298
SHEPARD'S WASHINGTON EXPRESS CITATIONS. [Shepard's Wash. express cit.]. **VFOAT** Washington Express Citations. (1992)-. Periodical. English. sm. $145.00. Shepards McGraw-Hill Inc, 555 Middle Creek Parkway, PO Box 35300, Colorado Springs CO 80935-3530. **Tel** (719)488-3000, FAX (800)525-0053. **DD** _a348.

US/1052-6684
SHEPARD'S WEST VIRGINIA CASE NAMES CITATOR. [Shepard's W. Va. case names cit.]. **Added/Corp** Shepard's/McGraw-Hill. **VFOAT** West Virginia Case Names Citator. (1988)-. English. sa. $75.00 (1 bound volume), $83.00 (cumulative supplements). Shepards McGraw-Hill Inc, 555 Middle Creek Parkway, PO Box 35300, Colorado Springs CO 80935-3530. **Tel** (719)488-3000, FAX (800)525-0053. **DD** 348.

US/0730-4579
SHEPARD'S WEST VIRGINIA CITATIONS. [Shepard's W. V. cit.]. **Added/Corp** Shepard's/McGraw-Hill. (19??)-. English. Six times a year. $300.00 (2 bound volumes), $262.00 (cumulative supplements). Shepards McGraw-Hill Inc, 555 Middle Creek Parkway, PO Box 35300, Colorado Springs CO 80935-3530. **Tel** (719)488-3000, FAX (800)525-0053. **DD** 348.

US/1052-5718
SHEPARD'S WISCONSIN CASE NAMES CITATOR. (SHEPARD'S WISCONSIN CASE NAMES CITATOR : WISCONSIN CASES.). [Shepard's Wis. case names cit.]. **Added/Corp** Shepard's/McGraw-Hill. **VFOAT** Wisconsin Case Names Citator. Vol. 1, No. 1 (June 1984)-. English. Six times a year. $80.00 (1 bound volume), $88.00 (cumulative supplements). Shepards McGraw-Hill Inc, 555 Middle Creek Parkway, PO Box 35300, Colorado Springs CO 80935-3530. **Tel** (719)488-3000, FAX (800)525-0053. **DD** 348.

US
SHEPARD'S WISCONSIN CITATIONS. **Added/Corp** Shepard's, Inc. of Colorado Springs. Shepard's Citations, Inc. **VFOAT** Wisconsin Citations. (19??)-. English. mo. $399.00 (3 bound volumes), $342.00 (cumulative supplements). Shepards McGraw-Hill Inc, 555 Middle Creek Parkway, PO Box 35300, Colorado Springs CO 80935-3530. **Tel** (719)488-3000, FAX (800)525-0053.
Desc: Gives you every citing reference to the statute in question ever made by your appellate courts.

US/1055-4629
SHEPARD'S WISCONSIN EXPRESS CITATIONS. [Shepard's Wis. express cit.]. **Added/Corp** Shepard's/McGraw-Hill. **VFOAT** Wisconsin Express Citations. Vol. 1, No. 1 (Nov. 25, 1990)/(1991)-. English. sm (24 issues). $149.00. Shepards McGraw-Hill Inc, 555 Middle Creek Parkway, PO Box 35300, Colorado Springs CO 80935-3530. **Tel** (719)488-3000, FAX (800)525-0053. **DD** 348.
Desc: Provides the latest analyzed citations to Wisconsin cases, Wisconsin statutes, and the Wisconsin Constitution.

US/0730-6105
SHEPARD'S WYOMING CITATIONS. [Shepard's Wyo. cit.]. **Added/Corp** Frank Shepard Company. Shepard's, Inc. of Colorado Springs. Shepard's Citations, Inc. Shepard's/McGraw-Hill. (1918)-. Periodical. English. sa. $150.00 (1 bound volume), $187.00 (cumulative supplements). Shepards McGraw-Hill Inc, 555 Middle Creek Parkway, PO Box 35300, Colorado Springs CO 80935-3530. **Tel** (719)488-3000, FAX (800)525-0053. **DD** 348.

US/0037-377X
SHINGLE, THE. **Added/Corp** Philadelphia Bar Association. Vol. 1 (Jan. 1938)-. Periodical. English. Four times a year (Mar., June, Sept., Dec.). $10.70. Philadelphia Bar Association, 1101 Market Street, 1 Reading Center, Philadelphia PA 19107. **Tel** (215)238-6300, FAX (215)238-1267. **ED** Nancy L. Hebble. **LC** K23; .H5. **Bk Rev. Ad Acc, Adv Mgr Tel** (215)238-6342. **Circ:** 14,000 (ctrl).
Desc: Law-related articles, news features, profiles, opinion pieces, humor, travel, and interviews. Directed to the membership of the Philadelphia Bar Association.
Ind/Abst Fed. Tax Artic.; Law Office Inf. Serv.

JA/0287-069X
SHOKEN IHO. [Shoken shuho]. Began in 1953. Academic Scholarly Publication. Japanese. an. Shobo Kenkyujo, 14-1 Nakahara 3-chome Mitakashi, Tokyo-to Japan. **LC** TH9111; .S55. **CODEN** SSSKD7. Documents available from CASDDS.
Ind/Abst Chem. Abstr. (1953-1982).

JA
SHOROPPO. **Main/Corp** Japan. (1949)-. Periodical. Japanese. an. ¥16.00. Yuhikaku Publishing Company Ltd., 2-17 Kanda Jinbocho, Chiyoda-ku, Tokyo 101 Japan. **Tel** 03 2641311.

JA
SHUSHO NEMPO - HOMUSHO HOMU TOSHOKAN. **Main/Corp** Japan. Homusho. Homu Toshokan. Multiple languages (Japanese, English, French and German). Homu Daijin Kambo Shiho Hosei Chosabu, 1-1 Kasumigaseki 1, Chiyoda-ku Tokyo 100 Japan. **LC** K40; .J3.

US
SIA WASHINGTON REPORT. English. Free (one copy per firm), $25.00 (additional subscriptions), $40.00 (nonmembers). Securities Industry Association, 120 Broadway/35th Floor, New York NY 10271. **Tel** (212)608-1500, FAX (212)608-1604.
Desc: Informs members of legislative and regulatory developments in Washington pertinent to our industry.

US/0199-6177
SIGNIFICANT SEC FILINGS REPORTER. [Signif. SEC filings report.]. **VAT** Significant Securities and Exchange Commission Filings Reporter. (19??)-. English. mo. $1060.00 Washington, D.C. residents (sales tax included); $1000.00 other. Washington Service Bureau Inc., 655 15th Street Northwest, Suite 270, Washington DC 20005. **Tel** (800)955-5219, (202)508-0600. **ED** Peggy Marsili. **[CCC].** Index available. cum. index. **Circ:** 300.
Desc: Indexes and abstracts; significant and unusual proxy statements; registration statements; and Williams Act filings from the Securities and Exchange Commission.

US/0882-181X
SIMON GREENLEAF LAW REVIEW : A PUBLICATION OF THE SIMON GREENLEAF SCHOOL OF LAW, THE. [Simon Greenleaf law rev.]. Vol. 1 (Academic Year 1981-82)-. Periodical. English. an. $7.00. The Simon Greenleaf School of Law, 3855 East La Palma Avenue, Anaheim CA 92807-1721. **LC** K23; .I75. **DD** 261.5.
Ind/Abst Curr. Law Index (1981-); Leg. Resour. Index (1981-); LegalTrac (1980-); Relig. Theol. Abstr.

UK
SIMON'S TAXES. (19??)-. English. mo. £645.00. Butterworth & Co. Ltd. / Kent, England, Borough Green, Sevenoaks Kent TN15 8PH England. **Tel** 011 44 732-884567, FAX 011 44 732-885996. Index available. cum. index. **Ad Acc.** ctrl circ.
Desc: Information on tax law.

SI/0218-2173
SINGAPORE JOURNAL OF LEGAL STUDIES. **Added/Corp** National University of Singapore. Faculty of Law. **VFOAT** SJLS; S.J.L.S. (July 1991)-. Periodical. English. sa. $50.00. University of Singapore / Faculty of Law, Kent Ridge, Singapore 0511 Singapore. **Tel** 011 65 7756666. ***Continues*** *Malaya Law Review, 0542-335X.*
Ind/Abst PAIS Int. Print.

●SI/0218-3161
SINGAPORE LAW REPORTS, THE. **Added/Corp** Singapore Academy of Law. (Jan. 3, 1992)-. Periodical. English. Twenty-four times a year. $395.00 US. Butterworths Asia, (A subsidiary of Reed International (Singapore) Pte. Ltd.), 3 Shenton Way, Number 1403, Singapore 0106 Republic of Singapore. **Tel** 011 65 2203684, FAX 011 65 2255026. **LC** KPP2.23; .A2. **DD** 348.5957/042; 345.9570842. ***Separated from*** *Malayan Law Journal, 0025-1283.*

SI/0080-9705
SINGAPORE LAW REVIEW. **Added/Corp** University of Singapore Law Society. Vol. 1 (1969)-. Periodical. English. an. $12.00. University of Singapore Law Club, Kentridge, Singapore 0511 Republic of Singapore. **Tel** 7756666. **(Subscription address:** WM. W. Gaunt & Sons Inc, 3011 Gulf Drive, Gaunt Building, Holmes Beach FL 34217.**)** **LC** K23; .I77. **DD** 349.595/7/05. **Bk Rev. Ad Acc. Circ:** 1,000. ***Absorbed*** *ME Judice.*
Desc: Articles from Singapore judges, lawyers, and students on aspects of the legal system. Also foreign contributions concerning topical issues in law today.
Ind/Abst Index Foreign Leg. Per.

SI
SINGAPORE'S JUDICIAL & LEGAL DIRECTORY. **VFOAT** Singapore's Judicial and Legal Directory. Directory. English. Legal Publications Pte Ltd, 206 Colombo Court, 0617 Singapore.

US/0889-356X
SIXTH CIRCUIT REVIEW. [Sixth Circuit Rev.]. **VFOAT** 6th Circuit Review; SCR. (197?)-. Periodical. English. Twenty-four times a year. $245.00. Appellate Review, 500 Country Lane, Louisville KY 40207. **Tel** (502)897-5079. **ED** Pat Owen, Sue Simon. **DD** 340. Index Available, published separately, free-automatically sent.
Desc: Verbatim digest of all Sixth Circuit Court of Appeals decisions with headnotes and index.

NO/0333-2810
SKATTERETT. **VFOAT** Skatte Rett. Vol. 1, (1982)-. Periodical. Norwegian. qt. Kr625.00, $103.00. Scandinavian University Press, PO Box 2959 Toeyen, N 0608 Oslo 6 Norway. **Tel** 011 47 2 2575400, FAX 011 47 2 2575353, telex 71896 UROR N. **(Subscription address:** Scandinavian University Press, 200 Meacham Ave., Elmont NY 11003.**)** **ED** Ole Gjems-Onstad. **LC** K23; .K38. **DD** 343.48104/05; 344.8103405. Index available. **Bk Rev. Ad Acc. Circ:** 2,500.
Desc: A professional journal for legal matters in Norway.

US
SLIP OPINION / SUPREME COURT OF THE UNITED STATES. **Main/Corp** United States. Supreme Court. (1???)-. Government Publication. English. ir. $218.00 US; $272.50 other. Superintendent of Documents, US Government Printing Office, Washington DC 20402. **Tel** (202)275-3328, FAX (202)786-2377.
Desc: All the Supreme Court's decisions as announced by the bench.

●YU
SLUZBENI LIST SAVEZNE REPUBLIKE JUGOSLAVIJE. **Main/Corp** Yugoslavia. **VFOAT** Sluzbeni List SRJ. (27 Apr. 1992)-. Serbo-Croatian (Cyrillic) (Serbo-Croatian (Roman)). **LC** J7.T9; .A22. ***Continues*** *Yugoslavia. Laws, Etc.; Sluzbeni List Socijalisticke Federativne Republike Jugoslavije.*

US/0887-2481
SMALL LAW OFFICE MANAGEMENT REPORT. [Small law off. manage. rep.]. **Added/Corp** Institute for Office Management and Administration (U.S.). Issue 86-4 (April 1986)-. Periodical. English. mo. $195.00. Institute of Management and Administration, 29 West 35th Street, 5th Floor, New York NY 10001-2299. **Tel** (212)244-0360. **LC** KF318.A1; S63. **DD** 340/.068.

●US/1066-1271
SMU LAW REVIEW. (SMU LAW REVIEW : A PUBLICATION OF SOUTHERN METHODIST UNIVERSITY SCHOOL OF LAW.). [SMU law rev.]. **Added/Corp** Southern Methodist University. School of Law. **VAT** Southern Methodist University Law Review. Vol. 46, No. 1 (Summer 1992)-. Periodical. English. Five times a year. $36.00 US; $43.00 other. Southern Methodist University / School of Law, 130 Storey Hall, Dallas TX 75275. **Tel** (214)768-2594. **LC** K23; .O85. **DD** 340/.05. ***Continues*** *Southwestern Law Journal, 0038-4836.*
Ind/Abst Index Leg. Period.

US
SMU LAW SCHOOL STUDY, AN. Main/Corp Dallas. Southern Methodist University. School of Law. (19??)-. English. ir. Southern Methodist University / English, Department of English, c/o Theresa Enos, Dallas TX 75275. **Tel** (214)692-2945.

US/0272-765X
SOCIAL ACTION & THE LAW. *Ceased.* [Soc. action law]. **VAT** Social Action and The Law. Vol. 1 (March 1973)-Vol. 12. Periodical. English. qt. Center for Responsive Psychology, Brooklyn College, Brooklyn NY 11210. **Tel** (718)780-5960. **ED** Justin L Anderson. **LC** K23; .O23. **DD** 349.73/05; 347.3005. Index available. cum. index. **Bk Rev. Ad Acc. Circ:** 1,000 (ctrl).
Desc: A journal presenting social science findings to law professionals.
Ind/Abst Curr. Law Index (1981-); Leg. Resour. Index (1981-); LegalTrac (1981-); PsycINFO (?-?); Soc. Plann. Policy Dev. Abstr.; Sociol. Abstr. (?-?).

●UK/0964-6639
SOCIAL & LEGAL STUDIES. VFOAT Social and Legal Studies. Vol. 1, No. 1 (Mar. 1992)-. Periodical. English. qt. £95.00. Sage Publications Ltd., 6 Bonhill Street, London EC2A 4PU, UK. **Tel** 071 374 0645, FAX 071 374 8741, telex 296207 SAGE G. **CODEN** SLSTEK. **Acid Free.**

UK/0954-3635
SOCIALIST LAWYER. See Political Science-Socialism, Communism, Anarchism, Utopianism.

PE
SOCIEDAD Y DERECHO. (Jan. 1974)-. Spanish. qt. Jiron Huancavelica No 470-OF 308, Lima Peru. **LC** K23; .O25.

IT
SOCIETA / ITALY, LE. (19??)-. Italian. ir. Giuffre Editore SPA, Via Busto Arsizio 40, 20151 Milan Italy. **Tel** 011 398 2 38089200.

IT/0390-0851
SOCIOLOGIA DEL DIRITTO. [Sociol. diritto]. **Added/Corp** Centro Nazionale di Prevenzione e Difesa Sociale. Commissione Permanente di Sociologia del Diritto. (1974)-. Italian. qt. L87000 Italy; L120000 other. Franco Angeli Riviste SRL, Viale Monza 106, 20127 Milan Italy. **Tel** 011 39 2 2827651, 011 39 2 289562. **ED** Renato Treves. **LC** K23; .O26.
Ind/Abst Soc. Plann. Policy Dev. Abstr.; Sociol. Abstr. [Full Cov.].

US/0897-2680
SOFTWARE LAW BULLETIN, THE. [Softw. law bull.]. (Jan. 1988)-. Bulletin. English. Ten times a year. $297.00. Andrews Publications Inc., 1646 West Chester Pike, PO Box 1000, Westtown PA 19395. **Tel** (610)399-6600, (800)345-1101, FAX (610)399-6610. **LC** KF390.5.C6; A497. **DD** 342. **[CCC].** Index available (free).
Desc: Scans the major computer databases looking for the words "software" or "computer program". We then tell our readers about what we found.

US/0886-3628
SOFTWARE LAW JOURNAL. *Title Change.* [Softw. law j.]. **Added/Corp** Center for Computer/Law. Vol. 1, No. 1 (Fall 1985)-(1993). Periodical. English. qt. Center for Computer Law, 4010 Palos Verdes Drive N, Suite 105, Rolling Hills Est. CA 90274. **Tel** (310)544-7372. **LC** K23; .O35. **DD** 343.73/07800164; 347.3037800164. **[CCC].** ***Merged with*** *Computer/Law Journal, 0164-8756* ***to form*** *John Marshall Journal of Computer & Information Law.*
Ind/Abst ACM Guide Comput. Lit.; Comput. Lit. Index; Comput. Rev.; Data Process. Dig.; Gen. BusinessFile (1992-); Index Leg. Period.; Leg. Resour. Index; LegalTrac (1980-).

US/1048-521X
SOFTWARE TAXATION LETTER. [Softw. tax. lett.]. **VFOAT** Software Taxation Reporter. Vol. 1, No. 1 (Feb. 1990)-. Periodical. English. Ten times a year. $260.00 North America; $297.00 other. Kutish Publications, PO Box 113, Wayne PA 19087. **Tel** (215)975-9619, FAX (215)975-9623. **DD** 343. **[CCC].**

US/8756-1107
SOFTWHERE. LEGAL. See Computers-Software.

US
SOLAR LAW : CUMULATIVE SUPPLEMENT / PRESENT AND FUTURE : WITH PROPOSED FORMS. SANDY F. KRAEMER. VFOAT Solar Law Cumulative Supplement. (1980)-. English. ir. $95.00 (bound volume), $65.00 (1993 pocket part). Shepards McGraw-Hill Inc, 555 Middle Creek Parkway, PO Box 35300, Colorado Springs CO 80935-3530. **Tel** (719)488-3000, FAX (800)525-0053. **ED** Sandy Kraemer. **Bk Rev. Ad Acc.**
Desc: Tailored for attorneys who represent local government, builders, developers, and consumers.

UK
SOLICITORS' AND BARRISTERS' DIRECTORY AND DIARY, THE. (1984)-. Directory. English. an (Sept.). £45.00 UK; £55.00 others. Waterlow Directories, Paulton House, 8 Shepherdess Walk, London N17 LB England. **Tel** 011 44 71 49000049. **LC** KD336; .S64. **DD** 340/.025/41. ***Formed by the union of*** *Bar List of the United Kingdom* ***and*** *Solicitors' Diary.*

UK/0038-1047
SOLICITORS' JOURNAL (LONDON, ENGLAND : 1928). (THE SOLICITOR'S JOURNAL.). [Solicit. j.]. Vol. 72, No. 1 (Jan. 7, 1928)-. Periodical. English. wk. £58.00 UK; $97.00 US; £63.00 other. Solicitors Journal, 21-27 Lambs Conduit Street, London WC1N 3NJ England. **Tel** 01-242 2548. **ED** Neville D Vandyk and Julian Harris. **LC** K23; .O4. **DD** 340/.05. **[CCC]. Bk Rev. Ad Acc. Circ:** 6,000. available on microfilm and microfiche from University Microfilms International (UMI). ***Continues*** *Solicitors' Journal and Weekly Reporter.*
Desc: Magazine on United Kingdom and international law.
Ind/Abst Aust. Leg. Mon. Dig.; Can. Legal Lit.; Curr. Law Index (1980-); Index Leg. Period.; Leg. Resour. Index (1980-); LegalTrac (1980-).

CN/0821-5383
SOLICITORS' LIABILITY INDEX. [Solicit. liabil. index]. English. an. $15.00 each volume. British Columbia Law Library Foundation, 800 Smith Street, Vancouver British Columbia V6Z 2E1 Canada. **DD** 346.7103/3.

BP
SOLOMON ISLANDS LAW REPORTS, THE. Added/Corp Solomon Islands. High Court. University of the South Pacific. Institute of Pacific Studies. University of the South Pacific. Pacific Law Unit. (1981)-. Periodical. English. an. $100.00. Solomon Islands Law Reports, PO Box 521, Registrar High Court, Honiara Solomon Islands. **Tel** 011 677 21632, FAX 011 677 22702. **DD** 348.93/5/026; 349.350826.

US
SOMERSET LEGAL JOURNAL. Added/Corp Pennsylvania. Courts. Somerset County Bar Association, Somerset, Pa. Vol. 1 (Mar. 1, 1920)-. Periodical. English. Fifty-two times a year (Published on Fridays). $40.00. Somerset County Bar Association, PO Box 501, Somerset PA 15501. **Tel** (814)445-4021, FAX (814)445-4944. **ED** Mark Persun. **Ad Acc. Circ:** 250.
Desc: Contains the decision of the Courts of the 16th Judicial District, and other cases of particular interest, legal advertisements and other related topics.

●CN/1193-414X
SOMMAIRE - SYNDICAT DE L'ASSOCIATION DES JURISTES DE L'ETAT. (LE SOMMAIRE.). [Somm. - Synd. Assoc. juristes Etat]. **Added/Corp** Syndicat de l'Association des Juristes de l'Etat. Vol. 1, No 1 (Jan. 1992)-. Periodical. French. mo. Free to members. Syndicat de l'Association des Juristes de l'Etat, Bureau 340, 20 Rue St.-Jean, Quebec, Quebec G1R 1N6 Canada. **DD** 331.88. ***Continues*** *Sommaire (Syndicat des Avocats et Notaires de la Fonction Publique)., 1187-760X.*

●RU
SOTSIALNYE I GUMANITARNYE NAUKI. SERIIA 4, GOSUDARSTVO I PRAVO. OTECHESTVENNAIA LITERATURA / ROSSIISKAIA AKADEMIIA NAUK, INSTITUT NAUCHNOI INFORMATSII PO OBSHCHESTVENNYM NAUKAM. Added/Corp Institut Nauchnoi Informatsii po Obshchestvennym Naukam (Rossiiskaia Akademiia Nauk). **VFOAT** Gosudarstvo i Pravo. (1993)-. Academic Scholarly Publication. Russian. qt. Izdatelstvo Nauka / Akademiia Nauk, Publishing House of the Russian Academy of Sciences, Leninskii Porspekt 14, 117901 Moscow Russia. **Tel** 011 95 954-21-53, FAX 011 95 938-21-44, telex 411964. **(Subscription address:** East View Publications Inc., 3020 Harbor Lane North, Suite 110, Minneapolis MN 55447.**) LC** K15; .B8. ***Continues in part*** *Obshchestvennye Nauki v Rossii. Seriia 4, Gosudarstvo i Pravo, 0202-2060.*

●RU
SOTSIALNYE I GUMANITARNYE NAUKI. SERIIA 4, GOSUDARSTVO I PRAVO. ZARUBEZHNAIA LITERATURA / ROSSIISKAIA AKADEMIIA NAUK, INSTITUT NAUCHNOI INFORMATSII PO OBSHCHESTVENNYM NAUKAM. Added/Corp Institut Nauchnoi Informatsii po Obshchestvennym Naukam (Rossiiskaia Akademiia Nauk). **VFOAT** Gosudarstvo i Pravo. (1993)-. Academic Scholarly Publication. Russian. qt. Izdatelstvo Nauka / Akademiia Nauk, Publishing House of the Russian Academy of Sciences, Leninskii Porspekt 14, 117901 Moscow Russia. **Tel** 011 95 954-21-53, FAX 011 95 938-21-44, telex 411964. **(Subscription address:** East View Publications Inc., 3020 Harbor Lane North, Suite 110, Minneapolis MN 55447.**) LC** K15; .B8. ***Continues in part*** *Obshchestvennye Nauki v Rossii. Seriia 4, Gosudarstvo i Pravo, 0202-2060.*

CN/0712-5836
SOUNDS ABOUT SUNDAY (1981). *Ceased.* (SOUNDS ABOUT SUNDAY.). [Sounds Sunday]. **Added/Corp** Lord's Day Alliance of Canada. (1981)-(Summer 1992). Periodical. English. sa. People for Sunday Association of Canada, Box 457, Islington Ontario M9A 4X4 Canada. **DD** 344.71/012574. ctrl circ. ***Continues*** *Sunday Update News, 0711-219X.*

US/0730-1154
SOURCE BOOK OF AMERICAN STATE LEGISLATION, THE. (THE SOURCE BOOK OF AMERICAN STATE LEGISLATION / DEVELOPED BY THE ... COMMITTEE ON ALEC'S SUGGESTED STATE LEGISLATION, AMERICAN LEGISLATIVE EXCHANGE COUNCIL.). 1980-. English. be. $25.00. ALEC, 214 Massachusetts Avenue NE/#400, Washington DC 20002. **Tel** (202)547-4646, FAX (202)547-8142. **ED** William C Myers and Kymberly S Messersmith. **LC** KF165; .S9. **DD** 348.73/2/05; 347.320805. Index available. cum. index. **Circ:** 10,000 (ctrl). ***Continues*** *Suggested State Legislation (Washington, D.C.).*
Desc: All model proposals featured in the source book are the product of ALEC's unique joint committees, the state legislator task forces and private sector coordinating councils. The bipartisan committees comprised of over 200 state legislators and private sector leaders worked in tandem to select and develop model proposals.

SA/0038-2388
SOUTH AFRICAN LAW JOURNAL. Added/Corp Law Society of the Cape of Good Hope. Vol. 18 (1901)-. Periodical. English. Four times a year (Feb., May, Aug., Nov.). R146.00 South Africa; R175.00 other. Juta Subscription Services, PO Box 14373, Kenwyn 7790 South Africa. **Tel** 011 27 21 7975101, FAX (021)761-5010, telex 523072 SA. **LC** K23; .O7. **DD** 349.68/05; 346.8005. Index Available, published separately, free-automatically sent. cum. index. ***Continues*** *Cape Law Journal.*
Ind/Abst Aust. Leg. Mon. Dig.; Index Foreign Leg. Per.

SA
SOUTH AFRICAN LAW REPORTS; TRANSLATION OF AFRIKAANS PASSAGES IN REPORTED CASES, THE. Added/Corp South Africa. Supreme Court. South Africa. Courts. (19??)-. English. Twelve times a year. R629.40 South Africa & Transkei; R693.39 other. Juta Subscription Services, PO Box 14373, Kenwyn 7790 South Africa. **Tel** 011 27 21 7975101, FAX (021)761-5010, telex 523072 SA. **ED** D. S. Fisher. **Circ:** 5,570 (ctrl). available in bound issues.
Desc: Official reports of the South African law courts from 1947 including index table of cases overruled, considered, and discussed cases.

SA/0038-2752
SOUTH AFRICAN TAX CASES, INCLUDING DECISIONS OF THE SUPREME COURT OF SOUTH AFRICA, THE HIGH COURT OF ZIMBABWE AND THE SPECIAL COURTS FOR HEARING INCOME TAX APPEALS. Main/Corp South Africa. Supreme Court. **Added/Corp** South Africa. Special Courts for Housing Income Tax Appeals. Rhodesia, Southern. High Court. Vol. 1, Pt. I (1925)-. English (Afrikaans). Eight times a year (Approximately every 6 weeks). R211.40. Juta Subscription Services, PO Box 14373, Kenwyn 7790 South Africa. **Tel** 011 27 21 7975101, FAX (021)761-5010, telex 523072 SA. **ED** J. Silke, J. Cavvadas, G. Goncalves, M. M. Corbett. cum. index. **Circ:** 3,500. available on CD-ROM.
Desc: Official reports of special court for hearing income tax appeals. Also significant cases from all countries in southern Africa on income tax, estate duty, etc.
Ind/Abst Index Foreign Leg. Per.

AT/0049-1470
SOUTH AUSTRALIAN STATE REPORTS, THE. Main/Corp South Australia. Supreme Court. Vol. 1 (1971)-. English. mo. $192.00. The

Law Book Company Limited, 44-50 Waterloo Road, North Ryde New South Wales, 2113 Australia. **Tel** 011 61 2 8870177, FAX 011 61 2 8887240, telex ASBOOK 27445. **ED** Elliott Johnston. Index available in last issue of volume--attached. ***Continues** The South Australian Law Reports.*
Desc: Reports of the Supreme Court of South Australia.
Ind/Abst Aust. Leg. Mon. Dig.

US/0743-2453
SOUTH CAROLINA APPELLATE DIGEST, THE. **Added/Corp** National Legal Research Group. Vol. 1, No. 1 (Jan. 6, 1984)-. Periodical. English. Twenty-six times a year. $85.00. National Legal Research Group Inc, PO Box 7187, Charlottesville VA 22906. **Tel** (800)727-6574, (804)977-5690, FAX (804)295-4667. **LC** KFS1857; .S67.

US/0038-3104
SOUTH CAROLINA LAW REVIEW. [S. C. law rev.]. **Added/Corp** South Carolina Bar Association. University of South Carolina. School of Law. Vol. 15, No. 1 (1963)-. Periodical. English. qt (seasonal). $35.00. University of South Carolina Law Revie, University of South Carolina, School of Law, Columbia SC 29208. **Tel** (803)777-5874, FAX (803)777-2368. **ED** David Rothstein, (editor's address: University of South Carolina, Room 401, phone: (803)777-3426). **DD** 340/.05. Index available. cum. index. **Ad Acc.** ctrl circ. ***Continues** South Carolina Law Quarterly, 0276-9441.*
Ind/Abst Bowne Dig. Corp. Sec. Lawyers; Curr. Law Index (1980-); Fed. Tax Artic.; Index Leg. Period.; Leg. Resour. Index (1980-); LegalTrac (1980-).

US/1044-4238
SOUTH CAROLINA LAWYER. [S. C. lawyer]. Vol. 1, No. 1 (July/Aug. 1989)-. Periodical. English. bm. $18.00. South Carolina Bar, PO Box 608, 950 Taylor Street, Columbia SC 29202. **Tel** (803)799-6653. **ED** Robert P Wilkins. **LC** K23; .O725. **DD** 349.757/05. **Ad Acc. Circ:** 6,000 (ctrl).
Desc: Focuses on legal issues and state and national court rulings affecting South Carolina law.

US
SOUTH CAROLINA STATE REGISTER. **Added/Corp** South Carolina Legislative Council. Vol. 1 (Mar. 18, 1977)-. English. mo. $95.00. South Carolina State Register, PO Box 11489, Columbia SC 29211. **Tel** (803)758-2145. **ED** Lynn P. Bartlett. **LC** KFS1836; .S68. **DD** 348.757/01.
Desc: A publication of notices, hearings, proposed, final and emergency regulations promulgated by state agencies pursuant to the South Carolina Administrative Procedures Act.

US
SOUTH DAKOTA CASE NAMES CITATOR. English. $40.00 (1 bound volume), $48.00 (cumulative supplements). Shepards McGraw-Hill Inc, 555 Middle Creek Parkway, PO Box 35300, Colorado Springs CO 80935-3530. **Tel** (719)488-3000, FAX (800)525-0053.

US
SOUTH DAKOTA COURTS : THE STATE OF THE JUDICIARY AND ... ANNUAL REPORT OF THE SOUTH DAKOTA UNIFIED JUDICIAL SYSTEM. **Main/Corp** South Dakota. Supreme Court. Office of the Court Administrator. **VFOAT** State of the Judiciary; Annual Report of the South Dakota Unified Judicial System. (1991)-. Periodical. English. **LC** KFS3570; .A86. **DD** 347.783/01. ***Continues** Benchmark.*

US/0038-3325
SOUTH DAKOTA LAW REVIEW. [S. D. law rev.]. **Added/Corp** University of South Dakota. School of Law. Vol. 1 (Spring 1956)-. Academic Scholarly Publication. English. Three times a year. $24.00 US; $28.00 other. South Dakota Law Review, 414 East Clark Street, University of South Dakota, Vermillion SD 57069. **Tel** (605)677-5646. **ED** Laura Schmitt. **LC** K23; .O735. **DD** 340/.09783. Index available. **Bk Rev**, (Qty: Varies). **Ad Acc. Circ:** 1,200 (ctrl).
Desc: A scholarly legal journal. Publishes articles of both national and state interest and specializes in agricultural law.
Ind/Abst Bowne Dig. Corp. Sec. Lawyers; Curr. Law Index (1980-); Fed. Tax Artic.; Index Leg. Period.; Leg. Resour. Index (1980-); LegalTrac (1980-).

US/0362-2738
SOUTH DAKOTA LEGISLATIVE MANUAL. **Main/Corp** South Dakota. Legislature. **VFOAT** South Dakota Manual. (19??)-. English. be. $5.00 (two-year). South Dakota Legislative Mailing, 701 E Sioux Avenue, Pierre SD 57501. **Tel** (605)773-4935. **LC** JK6531. Index available (Bound in all issues).

US/0191-1104
SOUTH DAKOTA REGISTER. ***Title Change.*** **Added/Corp** South Dakota Code Commission. (19??)-(19??). Periodical. English. wk. Legislative Research Council, State Capitol Building, 500 East Capitol, Pierre SD 57501. **Tel** (605)773-3251. **ED** Thomas R. Vickerman. **LC** KFS3036; .S68. **DD** 348/.783/028. **Circ:** 330 (ctrl). ***Continued by** Register (Pierre, S.D.).*
Desc: Contains synopses of proposed rules filed with code counsel and adopted rules, executive orders and appointments, and Supreme Court rules filed with Secretary of State.

UK/0967-4136
SOUTH PACIFIC LAW REPORTS. [South Pac. law rep.]. (1991)-. English. an. $100.00 US. Oxford University Press / New Zealand, PO Box 11-149 Ellerslie, Auckland 5 New Zealand. **Tel** 011 64 9 5233134. **(Subscription address:** North America/ William W. Gaunt & Sons, Inc., 3011 Gulf Drive, Gaunt Building, Holmes Beach, FL 34217; telephone: (813)778-5211**)**

US/1052-343X
SOUTH TEXAS LAW REVIEW. [South Tex. law rev.]. **Added/Corp** South Texas College of Law. Vol. 27, No. 1 (Spring 1986)-. Periodical. English. Four times a year (Seasonally). $37.14 Texas (includes 6.15% sales tax); $35.18 others. South Texas Law Review, 1303 San Jacinto, Houston TX 77002. **Tel** (713)646-1848. **ED** Charles Aris (phone: (713)659-8040 ext. 1672). **LC** K23; .O74. **DD** 349.764/05; 347.64005. Index available. **Bk Rev.** ***Continues** South Texas Law Journal, 0038-3546.*
Ind/Abst Bowne Dig. Corp. Sec. Lawyers; Fed. Tax Artic.; Index Leg. Period.; Leg. Resour. Index (1986-); LegalTrac (1986-).

US/1045-0459
SOUTHEASTERN REGULATORY ALERT. ***Ceased.*** (SOUTHEAST REGULATORY ALERT : A MONTHLY NEWSLETTER ON ENERGY AND COMMUNICATIONS REGULATIONS IN ALABAMA, FLORIDA, GEORGIA, MISSISSIPPI, NORTH CAROLINA, SOUTH CAROLINA & TENNESSEE.). [Southeast. regul. alert]. Vol. 1, No. 1 (July 1989)-Vol. 4 No. 4 (Oct. 1992). Periodical. English. mo. Word Merchants Inc., PO Box 440755, Kennesaw GA 30144. **Tel** (404)422-2543, FAX (404)422-0227. **ED** Bill Shipp, (phone: (404)984-0151). **DD** 343.

US
SOUTHEASTERN REPORTER CASE NAMES CITATOR. English. $240.00 (4 bound volumes), $85.00 (cumulative supplements). Shepards McGraw-Hill Inc, 555 Middle Creek Parkway, PO Box 35300, Colorado Springs CO 80935-3530. **Tel** (719)488-3000, FAX (800)525-0053.

US/0038-3910
SOUTHERN CALIFORNIA LAW REVIEW. [South. Calif. law rev.]. Vol. 1, No. 1 (Nov. 1927)-. Periodical. English. bm. $30.00. Southern California Law Review, USC Law Center Room 330, University Park CA 90089. **Tel** (213)740-8475, 740-9244. **ED** Peter M Juzwiak. **LC** K23; .O76. **DD** 340/.05. Index Available, published separately, free-automatically sent. cum. index. **Bk Rev. Ad Acc. Pr Rev. Circ:** 2,053 (ctrl). available on microfilm. Documents available from The Genuine Article.
Ind/Abst Bowne Dig. Corp. Sec. Lawyers; Curr. Law Index (1980-); Fed. Tax Artic.; Index Leg. Period.; Int. Polit. Sci. Abstr.; Leg. Resour. Index (1980-); LegalTrac (1980-); Res. Alert [Full Cov.]; Sage Public Adm. Abstr.; Soc. Sci. Cit. Index [Full Cov.]; Urban Aff. Abstr.

●US/1056-2494
SOUTHERN CALIFORNIA LEGAL RESOURCE MANUAL. (1992)-. English. $65.00. ASAP Publications / California, 1081 Camino del Rio South, Suite 222, San Diego CA 92108. **Tel** (619)297-2727, FAX (619)297-2770.

US/0145-3432
SOUTHERN ILLINOIS UNIVERSITY LAW JOURNAL. [South. Ill. Univ. law j.]. **Main/Corp** Southern Illinois University at Carbondale. School of Law. May 1976-. English. qt. $18.00. Southern Illinois University / Carbondale - Law, School of Law, Carbondale IL 62901. **Tel** (618)536-7711. **ED** Tom Wilson. **LC** K23; .O78. **DD** 340/.05. Index available. **Bk Rev. Ad Acc. Circ:** 800. available on microfilm and microfiche from University Microfilms International (UMI).
Desc: Published lead articles, case notes, and comments on legal topics of general interest.
Ind/Abst Bowne Dig. Corp. Sec. Lawyers; Curr. Law Index (1980-); Index Leg. Period.; Leg. Resour. Index (1980-); LegalTrac (1980-).

US/1056-2184
SOUTHERN LAW JOURNAL (ABILENE, TEX.). (SOUTHERN LAW JOURNAL.). **Added/Corp** Southern Business Law Association. (1992)-. Periodical. English. $15.00. Southern Business Law Association, PO Box 8335, Abilene TX 79699.

US/0361-0861
SOUTHERN SCHOOL LAW DIGEST. **Added/Corp** Southern Region School Boards Research and Training Center. (19??)-. English. mo. $55.00. Louisiana School Boards Association, 7912 Summa Avenue, Baton Rouge LA 70809. **Tel** (504)769-3191. **LC** KF4114; .S68. **DD** 344/.75/0702648.

US/0099-1465
SOUTHERN UNIVERSITY LAW REVIEW. [South. Univ. law rev.]. **Main/Corp** Southern University and A & M College. School of Law. Vol. 1 (Fall 1974)-. Periodical. English. sa. $10.00. Southern University, School of Law, Southern Branch PO, Baton Rouge LA 70813. **Tel** (504)771-2223. **LC** K12; .O86. **DD** 340/.09763. **Bk Rev. Ad Acc.**
Desc: Ideas in the areas of law: criminal and civil.
Ind/Abst Bowne Dig. Corp. Sec. Lawyers; Curr. Law Index (1980-); Fed. Tax Artic.; Index Leg. Period.; Leg. Resour. Index (1980-); LegalTrac (1980-).

US/0038-4836
SOUTHWESTERN LAW JOURNAL. ***Title Change.*** [Southwest. law j.]. **Added/Corp** Southern Methodist University. School of Law. Southwestern Legal Foundation. Vol. 2, No. 1 (Spring 1948)-Vol. 54, No. 4 (Spring 1992). Periodical. English. ir. Southern Methodist University / School of Law, 130 Storey Hall, Dallas TX 75275. **Tel** (214)768-2594. **ED** John Lindgren. **LC** K23; .O85. **DD** 340/.05. cum. index. **Circ:** 1,200. ***Continues** Texas Law and Legislation. **Continued by** SMU Law Review, 1066-1271.*
Desc: Leading articles and student notes and comments covering timely subjects in Texas, national and international law.
Ind/Abst Bowne Dig. Corp. Sec. Lawyers; Curr. Law Index (1980-); Fed. Tax Artic.; Index Leg. Period.; Leg. Resour. Index (1980-); LegalTrac (1980-).

US/0886-3296
SOUTHWESTERN UNIVERSITY LAW REVIEW. [Southwest. Univ. law rev.]. **VFOAT** Southwestern Nevada Law Review. Vol. 3, No. 1 (Spring 1971)-. Periodical. English. qt. $22.00 US; $27.00 other. SW University School of Law, 675 South Westmoreland Avenue, Los Angeles CA 90005. **Tel** (310)738-6744. **LC** K12; .O83. **DD** 340/.05. cum. index. **Bk Rev. Circ:** 870. ***Continues** Southwestern Law Review.*
Desc: A student edited publication comprised of legal articles written by jurists, practitioners, legal scholars and law students.
Ind/Abst Bowne Dig. Corp. Sec. Lawyers; Curr. Law Index (1980-); Index Leg. Period.; Leg. Resour. Index (1980-); LegalTrac (1980-).

RU/0131-6761
SOVETSKAJA JUSTICIJA. ***Title Change.*** (SOVETSKAIA IUSTITSIIA.). [Sov. justicija]. **Added/Corp** Russian S.F.S.R. Ministerstvo Iustitsii. Russian S.F.S.R. Verkhovnyi Sud. (1957)-(1993). Periodical. Russian. sm. **(Subscription address:** East View Publications Inc., 3020 Harbor Lane North, Suite 110, Minneapolis MN 55447.**)** **LC** LAW; K23; .O9. available on microfilm from University Microfilms International (UMI). ***Continues in part** Sotsialisticheskaia Zakonnost. **Continued by** Rossiiskaia Iustitsiia.*
Ind/Abst Index Foreign Leg. Per.

RU/0038-5204
SOVETSKOE GOSUDARSTVO I PRAVO. ***Title Change.*** [Sov. gos. pravo]. **Added/Corp** Institut Gosudarstva i Prava (Akademiia Nauk SSSR). (1939)-(1992). Periodical. Russian (summaries and/or abstracts in English; table of contents in English). mo. **(Subscription address:** Victor Kamkin, 4956 Boiling Brook Parkway, Rockville MD 20852.**)** **LC** K23; .O875. **DD** 349.47/09; 344.7009. available on microfilm from University Microfilms International (UMI). ***Continues** Sovetskoe Gosudarstvo. **Continued by** Gosudarstvo i Pravo.*
Ind/Abst Am. Hist. Life (1954-1956, 1968-); Index Foreign Leg. Per.; Int. Bibliogr. Sociol.; Int. Labour Doc.; Int. Polit. Sci. Abstr.; LABORDOC; Soc. Plann. Policy Dev. Abstr.; Sociol. Abstr.

US/0038-5530
SOVIET LAW AND GOVERNMENT. ***Title Change.*** [Sov. law gov.]. Vol. 1 (Summer 1962)-Vol. 30 (Spring 1992). Periodical. English (translations available in Russian). bm. M. E. Sharpe Inc., 80 Business Park Drive, Armonk NY 10504. **Tel** (914)273-1800, (800)541-6563, FAX (914)273-2106. **ED** Nils H Wessell. **DD** 348.47. **Bk Rev. Ad Acc. Pr Rev. Circ:** 350 (ctrl). available on microfilm and microfiche from University Microfilms International (UMI). ***Continued by** Russian Politics and Law, 1061-1940.*
Desc: Studies from a wide variety of Soviet sources on the interactions of law, government, and society in the USSR.
Ind/Abst Index Period. Artic. Relat. Law; Int. Polit. Sci. Abstr.; PAIS Int. Print (?-?); SportSearch.

US/8756-3746
SPECIAL EDUCATION AND THE HANDICAPPED. ***Title Change.*** [Spec. educ. handicap.]. (198?)-(19??). Periodical. English. mo. Data Research Inc., PO Box 490, Rosemount MN 55068. **Tel** (612)452-8267, (800)365-4900. **DD** 344. Index available. ***Continued by** Special Education Law Update.*
Desc: Special education law.

US
SPECIAL EDUCATION LAW UPDATE. (19??)-. Periodical. English. mo. $117.00. Data Research Inc., PO Box 490, Rosemount MN 55068. **Tel** (612)452-8267, (800)365-4900. ***Continues** Special Education and the Handicapped.*

US
SPECIAL EDUCATOR ... DESK BOOK, THE. (1991)-. Periodical. English. an. $58.50. LRP Publications, 747 Dresher Road, PO Box 980, Horsham PA 19044-0980. **Tel** (800)341-7874, (215)784-0860, FAX (215)784-9639, (215)784-0870.
Desc: Desk reference providing a summation to special education judicial case law for the previous year.

US
SPECIAL LAWS ENACTED BY THE REGULAR SESSION OF THE LEGISLATIVE ASSEMBLY, THE. Main/Corp Oregon. **VFOAT** Oregon Special Laws. English. Legislative Counsel Committee, S101 State Capital, Salem OR 97310. **Tel** (503)378-8148. **LC** KFO2425; .A24. **DD** 348.795/024; 347.950824.

CN/0316-5310
SPECIAL LECTURES OF THE LAW SOCIETY OF UPPER CANADA. [Spec. lect. Law Soc. Up. Can.]. **Main/Corp** Law Society of Upper Canada. Began in 1950. English. an. R De Boo, 81 Curlew Drive, Don Mills Ontario M3A 3P7 Canada. **LC** KE16; .S67. **DD** 340/.09713.
Ind/Abst Can. Legal Lit.; Index Can. Leg. Period. Lit.

US/0194-8237
SPIDELL'S CALIFORNIA TAXLETTER. Main/Corp Spidell Publishing Inc. **VFOAT** California Taxletter. (197?)-. Periodical. English. Twelve times a year. $97.00 (one year), $177.00 (two years), $247.00 (three years). Spidell Publishing Inc, 1110 North Gilbert Street, Anaheim CA 92801. **Tel** (714)776-7850, FAX (714)776-9906. **ED** Robert A. Spidell. **Circ:** 6,000 (ctrl).
Desc: Provides a review and analysis of new California tax laws and tax law changes and interpretations.

CN/0700-8279
SPOKESWOMAN FOR ABORTION LAW REPEAL. Began publication in 1972?. Periodical. English. 0.15Can$ each number. Spokeswoman, PO Box 5673 Station A, Toronto Ontario M5W 1P1 Canada.

US/0733-0669
SPORTS AND THE COURTS. [Sports courts]. (1980)-. Periodical. English. Five times a year. $40.00. Sports and the Courts, PO Box 2836, Winston Salem NC 27102. **Tel** (910)725-7700, FAX (910)725-6777. **ED** C. Thomas Ross. **LC** KF4166.A59; S66. **DD** 344.73/075; 347.30475. Index available (published separately). **Circ:** 2,000.
Desc: Reports current legal cases in sports, physical education, and recreation with editorial comment for administrators, coaches, and physical educators.
Ind/Abst SPORT Discus.

US/0195-8623
SPORTS LAW REPORTER. Vol. 1 (May 1978)-. Periodical. English. mo. $45.00 students, $75.00 others. Sports Law Reporter, PO Box 664, Scarsdale NY 10583. **LC** KF3989.A59; S66. **DD** 344.73/099.
Desc: Current cases and decisions in the law of sports.

US/0893-8210
SPORTS, PARKS & RECREATION LAW REPORTER, THE. [Sports parks recreat. law report.]. **Added/Corp** Professional Reports Corporation. **VFOAT** Reporter. Vol. 1, No. 1 (June 1987)-. Periodical. English. qt. $49.95. Professional Reports Corporation, 4418 Belden Village Street Northwest, Canton OH 44718. **Tel** (216)492-6063, (800)336-0083, FAX (216)492-6176. **ED** David L. Herbert. **LC** KF1290.S66; A136. **DD** 346.7303/22; 347.306322. Index available. cum. index. **Bk Rev. Ad Acc, Adv Mgr:** Molly Romig. **Pr Rev. Circ:** 200.
Desc: Current developments in legislation, trends and actual pending cases and standards information. Legislation, verdicts and original articles will be featured in each issue.

CE
SRI LANKA ATTORNEY-AT-LAW, THE. V. 1 (Aug. 1974)-. English. Rs2.50 each issue. Institute of Legal Executives of Sri Lanka, 54 3/2 Australia Lanka Ceylon. **DD** 340/.095493.

II
SRINAGAR LAW JOURNAL. Vol. 1 (July 1979)-. English. mo. Rs150.00. SLJ Publications, Court Road, Srinagar 190001 India. **Tel** 31065. **ED** H. Ishtiaq Hussain. **LC** K23; .R55. **DD** 349.54/05. Index available. **Bk Rev. Ad Acc. Circ:** 800.

US/1049-0299
ST. JOHN'S JOURNAL OF LEGAL COMMENTARY. [St. John's j. legal comment.]. **Added/Corp** St. John's University (New York, N.Y.). School of Law. **VFOAT** Journal of Legal Commentary. Vol. 1, Issue 1 (1985)-. Periodical. English. Twice a year. $18.50. St. John's Journal Legal Commentary, St. John's University School of Law, Jamaica NY 11439. **Tel** (718)990-6688. **ED** John Ivanac. **LC** K23; .A32. **DD** 349.747/05; 347.47005. available on an online database from WESTLAW.
Ind/Abst Index Leg. Period.; Leg. Resour. Index; LegalTrac (1988-).

US/0036-2905
ST. JOHN'S LAW REVIEW. [St. John's law rev.]. **Added/Corp** St. John's University (New York, N.Y.). School of Law. **VFOAT** Saint John's Law Review. Vol. 1, No. 1 (Dec. 1926)-. Periodical. English. qt. $24.00. St Johns University, Law Review Association, Grand Central & Utopia Parkways, Jamaica NY 11432. **Tel** (718)990-6654, FAX (718)990-6649. **ED** Paul V Majkowski (editor's address: 20 IU Willets Road, Albertson NY 11507; editor's phone: (718)990-1950). **LC** K23; .A33. **DD** 340/.05. Index available (bound in fourth issue). **Circ:** 2,500.
Desc: A journal devoted to timely legal problems and survey of New York practice.
Ind/Abst Bowne Dig. Corp. Sec. Lawyers; Curr. Law Index (1980-); Fed. Tax Artic.; Index Leg. Period.; Leg. Resour. Index (1980-); LegalTrac (1980-).

US/0581-3344
ST. LOUIS BAR JOURNAL. [St. Louis bar j.]. **Added/Corp** Bar Association of Metropolitan St. Louis. Vol. 1, (May 1950)-. Periodical. English. Four times a year. $12.00. Bar Association Metropolitan St Louis, One Mercantile Center, Suite 3600, St Louis MO 63101. **Tel** (314)421-4134. **DD** 342.
Ind/Abst Fed. Tax Artic.; Law Office Inf. Serv.

US
ST. LOUIS DAILY RECORD. (18??)-. Periodical. English. da. $288.63 one year. St. Louis Daily Record, PO Box 88910, St Louis MO 63188. **Tel** (314)421-1880. **ED** Will Connighan. **LC** Microfilm LL-011 K23. **Ad Acc, Adv Mgr Tel** (314)_421-1880. **Circ:** 3,200 (ctrl). available on microfilm from University Microfilms International (UMI).
Desc: New suits filed, bankruptcies, mechanic's liens, foreclosures, transfers of property, marriages and bid notices. Legal newspaper for credit information, business leads and more.

US/0581-3441
ST. MARY'S LAW JOURNAL. [St. Mary's law j.]. **Added/Corp** St Mary's University (San Antonio, Tex.). **VAT** Saint Mary's Law Journal. Vol. 1 (Spring 1969)-. Academic Scholarly Publication. English. Four times a year (Jan., Mar., May, Oct.). $25.00. St. Marys University School of Law, One Camino Santa Maria, San Antonio TX 78228-8604. **Tel** (210)436-3439, FAX (210)436-3756. **ED** D. Todd Smith. **LC** K23; .A35. **DD** 340/.05. Index available (Bound in 4th iss. (May)). cum. index. **Bk Rev. Ad Acc. Circ:** 1,600. available on an online database from WESTLAW.
Desc: Devoted to the study of scholarly material of practical value to students and members of the legal community.
Ind/Abst Bowne Dig. Corp. Sec. Lawyers; Curr. Law Index (1980-); Index Leg. Period.; Leg. Resour. Index (1980-); LegalTrac (1980-).

●US/1065-318X
ST. THOMAS LAW REVIEW. [St. Thomas law rev.]. **Added/Corp** Saint Thomas University (Miami, Fla.). School of Law. **VAT** Saint Thomas Law Review. Vol. 4 (Spring 1992)-. Periodical. English. Twice a year. $20.00. St. Thomas Law Review, 16400 Northwest 32nd Avenue, St. Thomas University, Miami FL 33054. **Tel** (305)623-2373. **LC** K23; .A37. **DD** 340/.05. ***Continues*** *St. Thomas Law Forum, 1044-8942.*
Ind/Abst Index Leg. Period.

●US/1061-3447
STANFORD LAW ALUM. [Stanford law alum]. **Added/Corp** Stanford University.School of Law. No. 1 (Spring 1992)-. Periodical. English. Free. Stanford Law School, Crown Quadrangle 42, Stanford CA 94305-8610. **Tel** (415)723-4421, FAX (415)725-0253. **DD** 378.

US/1044-4386
STANFORD LAW & POLICY REVIEW. [Stanford law pol. rev.]. **Added/Corp** Stanford University. School of Law. **VFOAT** Stanford Law and Policy Review. Vol. 1, No. 1 (Fall 1989)-. Periodical. English. Twice a year. $43.00. Stanford Law School, Crown Quadrangle 42, Stanford CA 94305-8610. **Tel** (415)723-4421, FAX (415)725-0253. **ED** Susan Brienza. **LC** H97; .S74. **DD** 320/.6/097305. **Ad Acc. Circ:** 5,000.
Ind/Abst Leg. Resour. Index; LegalTrac (1989-); PAIS Int. Print.

US/0038-9765
STANFORD LAW REVIEW. [Stanford law rev.]. **Added/Corp** Stanford University. School of Law. Vol. 1 (Nov. 1948)-. Periodical. English. Six times a year. $35.00. Stanford University School of Law, Crown Quadrangle 42, Stanford CA 94305. **Tel** (415)723-4421. **LC** K23; .T3. **DD** 347.05. **NLM** W1 ST165. cum. index. **Pr Rev. Circ:** 2,600. Documents available from The Genuine Article, UMI Article Clearinghouse. ***Continues*** *Stanford Intramural Law Review.*
Ind/Abst ABC POL SCI; Bowne Dig. Corp. Sec. Lawyers; Crim. Justice Abstr.; Curr. Contents Soc. Behav. Sci.; Curr. Law Index (1980-); Expand. Acad. Index (1984-); Fed. Tax Artic.; Health Plan. Adminis.; Hospit. Health Admin. Index; Index Leg. Period.; Leg. Resour. Index (1980-); LegalTrac (1980-); Newsp. Period. Abstr. (1992-); PAIS Int. Print; Res. Alert [Full Cov.]; Soc. Sci. Cit. Index [Full Cov.]; Women Stud. Abstr.

US/0585-0576
STANFORD LAWYER. [Stanf. lawyer]. **Added/Corp** Stanford University. School of Law. (1966)-. Periodical. English. Twice a year (May & Nov.). Free. Stanford Law School, Crown Quadrangle 42, Stanford CA 94305-8610. **Tel** (415)723-4421, FAX (415)725-0253. **ED** Constance Hellyer. **DD** 340. Index available. **Ad Acc. Circ:** 8,000 (ctrl). available on microfiche (from Wm. S. Hein and Company).
Desc: Published for Stanford Law School alumni, faculty, students, staff, and friends. Topics include law and legal education, politics, news of the school, and alumni news.
Ind/Abst Curr. Law Index (1980-); Leg. Resour. Index (1980-); LegalTrac (1980-).

US/1066-1972
STANLEY & KILCULLEN'S FEDERAL INCOME TAX LAW. [Stanley Kilcullen's fed. income tax law]. **VFOAT** Stanley and Kilcullen's Federal Income Tax Law; Federal Income Tax Law. (19??)-. English. an. $90.00 US; $117.00 other. Warren Gorham & Lamont Inc., Park Square Building, 31 St. James Avenue, Boston MA 02116-4112. **Tel** (617)423-2020, (800)950-1207, FAX (617)423-2026. **LC** KF6369; .S733. **DD** 343.7305/2; 347.30352.

US
STATE BAR SECTION REPORT. GENERAL PRACTICE. Main/Corp State Bar of Texas. English. State Bar of Texas, PO Box 12487, Capitol Station, Austin TX 78711. **Tel** (512)463-1411. **LC** KF200; .S76. **DD** 347.764/0504/05.

US/1065-6839
STATE CONSTITUTIONAL COMMENTARIES AND NOTES. [State const. comment. notes]. **Added/Corp** Edward McNall Burns Center for State Constitutional Studies. Vol. 1, No. 1 (Fall 1989)-. Periodical. English. Four times a year. $12.00 (individuals), $15.00 (institutions). Rutgers State University / Burn Center, Hickman Hall, Douglas Campus Box 270, New Brunswick NJ 08903. **Tel** (908)932-6995, FAX (908)932-7170. **ED** Stanley H. Friedelbaum. **LC** K23; .T33. **DD** 342.73/02/05; 347.302205.
Desc: Contains timely contributions from academic reporters throughout the United States.
Ind/Abst PAIS Int. Print.

US
STATE COURT CASELOAD STATISTICS, ADVANCE REPORT. **See** Law-Abstracting, Bibliographies and Statistics.

US/0145-3076
STATE COURT JOURNAL. [State court j.]. **Added/Corp** National Center for State Courts. Vol. 1 (Winter 1977)-. Periodical. English. Four times a year (Feb., May, Aug., Nov.). $24.00 (one year); $50.00 Comes with National Center for State Courts Periodical Plan or National Center for State Courts Associates Program Membership. National Center for State Courts, 300 Newport Avenue, PO Box 8798, Williamsburg VA 23185. **Tel** (804)253-2000, FAX (804)220-0449. **ED** Madelyn McRae. **LC** KF8732.A15; S73. **DD** 347/.73/3. Index available. **Bk Rev. Circ:** 2,000 (ctrl). available on microfilm and microfiche from University Microfilms International (UMI).
Desc: A leading national journal of opinion and practice in the field of state court management. Also features articles by experts in the field of court improvement.
Ind/Abst Crim. Justice Abstr.; Crim. Justice Period. Index; Curr. Law Index (1980-); Law Office Inf. Serv.; Leg. Resour. Index (1980-); LegalTrac (1980-).

US/0363-1362
STATE JUDICIARY NEWS. Added/Corp Council of State Governments. Conference of Chief Justices. Conference of State Court Administrators. Vol. 1 (May 1975)-. Periodical. English. **LC** KF8736.A15; S8. **DD** 347/.73/105.

US/0276-7651
STATE LAWS AND PUBLISHED ORDINANCES, FIREARMS. Added/Corp United States. Bureau of Alcohol, Tobacco, and Firearms. (1980)-. Government Publication. English. an. Superintendent of Documents, US Government Printing Office, Washington DC 20402. **Tel** (202)275-3328, FAX (202)786-2377. **LC** KF3941.Z95; S83. ***Continues*** *Firearms, State Laws and Published Ordinances.*

US/0362-4579
STATE LAWS GOVERNING BOXING AND WRESTLING IN CALIFORNIA, WITH RULES AND REGULATIONS. Main/Corp California. **Added/Corp** California. State Athletic Commission. (19??)-. English. ir. State Athletic Commission, 1021 O Street, Room A-153, Sacramento CA 95814. **LC** KFC645.A29; S7. **DD** 344/.794/099. ***Continues*** *Rules, Regulations and Law Regulating Boxing and Wrestling Matches in California.*

Law

US
STATE LEGAL ISSUES QUARTERLY.
English. qt (Jan., Apr., July, Oct.). $50.00. Federation of Tax Administrators, 444 North Capital Street Northwest, Suite 334, Washington DC 20001. **Tel** (202)624-5890.

US/0735-8733
STATE LEGISLATIVE REPORT. See Public Administration.

US/0891-8341
STATE NURSING LEGISLATION QUARTERLY. Ceased. [State nurs. legis. q.].
Added/Corp American Nurses' Association. Center for Research. National Council of State Boards of Nursing (U.S.). Vol. 3, No. 4 (Winter 1985)-Vol. 11, No. 4. Periodical. English. Four times a year (Mar., June, Sept., Dec.). National Council of State Boards of Nursing Inc, 676 North Saint Clair Street, Suite 550, Chicago IL 60611. **Tel** (312)787-6555. **LC** KF2915.N8; Z957. **DD** 344.73/0414/05; 347.30441405. **NLM** W1; ST314YC. **Continues** State Legislative Report (Kansas City, Mo.), 8756-5994.
Ind/Abst Cumul. Index Nurs. Allied Health Lit. (Winter 1985-); Int. Nurs. Index (Winter 1985-).

US
STATE OF LOUISIANA, ACTS OF THE LEGISLATURE. Main/Corp Louisiana. **VFOAT** Acts, State of Louisiana. 1955-. English. an. Acts of Legislature, Box 44125, Baton Rouge LA 70804. **Tel** (504)922-0415. **LC** KFL25; .A24. **DD** 348.763/023. **Circ:** 1,400. **Continues** Laws, etc. Acts of the Legislature, State of Louisiana.

US
STATE REPORTER. English. wk. $215.00. State Reporter Publishing Co., PO Box 749, Helena MT 59624. **Tel** (406)449-8889. **ED** Shauna Thomas. Index available. cum. index. available on an online database from MONTLAW.
Desc: A prompt and accurate reporting of the full text of the opinions of the Montana Supreme Court.

US
STATE REPORTER OF EDUCATION LAW. See Education.

US
STATEMENT OF THE LAWS OF ARGENTINA IN MATTERS AFFECTING BUSINESS. (19??)-. English (Spanish). ir. $10.00. Organization of American States, 19th Street & Constitution Avenue NW, Suite 300, Washington DC 20006. **Tel** (202)458-6256.

US
STATEMENT OF THE LAWS OF MEXICO IN MATTERS AFFECTING BUSINESS. (19??)-. English (Spanish). ir. $10.00. Organization of American States, 19th Street & Constitution Avenue NW, Suite 300, Washington DC 20006. **Tel** (202)458-6256.

US
STATEVIEW. English. Securities Industry Association, 120 Broadway/35th Floor, New York NY 10271. **Tel** (212)608-1500, FAX (212)608-1604.
Desc: A discussion of key legislative and regulatory issues on the state level which are of particular significance to our industry.

US/0740-8277
STATISTICAL REPORT - EXECUTIVE OFFICE FOR U.S. ATTORNEYS. See Law-Abstracting, Bibliographies and Statistics.

US/0731-6992
STATISTICAL SUMMARY OF THE COLORADO JUDICIARY. See Law-Abstracting, Bibliographies and Statistics.

II
STATISTICS OF CIVIL COURTS IN THE STATE OF TAMIL NADU FOR THE YEAR ... . Title Change. See Law-Abstracting, Bibliographies and Statistics.

UK
STATISTICS ON THE OPERATION OF THE PREVENTION OF TERRORISM LEGISLATION. (19??)-. English. qt. Free. Planning and Management Unit, 40 Wellesley Road, #1834 Lunar HS, Croydon, Surrey CR0 9YD England. **Tel** 011 44 81 760-2850.

GW
STATISTIK UBER NS-PROZESSE. See Law-Abstracting, Bibliographies and Statistics.

PO/0253-0600
STATISTIQUES DE LA JUSTICE : CONTINENT ET ILES ADJACENTES. See Law-Abstracting, Bibliographies and Statistics.

FR
STATISTIQUES DIVERSES. See Law-Abstracting, Bibliographies and Statistics.

BE/0775-311X
STATISTIQUES JUDICIAIRES. See Law-Abstracting, Bibliographies and Statistics.

CN/0704-609X
STATUS OF BILLS REPORT. Ceased.
Main/Corp Canada. Parliament. **VFOAT** Rapport sur le Statut des Bills. 30th Parliament, 2nd Session-?. English (French). ir (when Parliament is in session). Canadian Law Information Council / Ottawa, 161 Laurier Avenue West, 5th Floor Ottawa, Ontario K1P 5J2 Canada. **Tel** (613)236-9766. **DD** 348/.71/01. **Circ:** 220.
Desc: Provides the name and number of each federal bill and the dates of successive readings and proclamation as the legislation proceeds through parliament.

AT
STATUTE LAW OF TASMANIA, THE.
Main/Corp Tasmania. **Added/Corp** Tasmania. Office of the Parliamentary Counsel. **VFOAT** Tasmanian Statutes. (1981)-. English. an. **DD** 348.946/022; 349.460822.
Continues Tasmania. Laws, Etc. Acts of the Parliament of Tasmania.

UK/0144-3593
STATUTE LAW REVIEW. [Statute law rev.].
Added/Corp Statute Law Society. (Spring 1980)-. Periodical. English. tq. £66.00 UK and Europe; $123.00 other. Oxford University Press, Walton Street, Oxford OX2 6DP England. **Tel** 011 44 865 56767, FAX 011 44 865 267773, telex 837330 OXPRES G. **(Subscription address:** Oxford University Press / USA, Journals Marketing Department, Oxford University Press, 2001 Evans Road, Cary NC 27513.**) ED** J. N. Bates. **LC** K23; .T34. **DD** 348.41/022/05; 344.10822005. **[CCC].** **Bk Rev**. **Ad Acc**. **Circ:** 400. available on microfilm and microfiche from University Microfilms International (UMI).
Desc: Covers the legislative process of the use of legislation as an instrument of public policy and the drafting and interpretation of new legislation.
Ind/Abst Aust. Leg. Mon. Dig.; Curr. Law Index (1982-); Index Leg. Period.; Int. Bibliogr. Sociol.; Leg. Resour. Index (1982-); LegalTrac (1980-).

●US/1061-0014
STATUTES & DECISIONS. (STATUTES & DECISIONS : THE LAWS OF THE USSR AND ITS SUCCESSOR STATES.). [Statut. decis.]. **VFOAT** Statutes and Decisions. Vol. 28, No. 2 Winter (1991/1992)-. Periodical. English (translations available in Russian). bm. $587.00 US; $646.00 other. M. E. Sharpe Inc., 80 Business Park Drive, Armonk NY 10504. **Tel** (914)273-1800, (800)541-6563, FAX (914)273-2106. **LC** K23; .O9. **DD** 347.4705; 344.70705. **Continues** Soviet Statutes & Decisions, 0038-5840.
Ind/Abst PAIS Int. Print (?-?).

US
STATUTES GOVERNING MUNICIPAL PLANNING AND ZONING. Main/Corp Connecticut. 1976-. English. 1179 Main Street, Hartford CT 06101. **LC** KFC4058.A29; S7. **DD** 346/.746/045.
Supersedes Selected Compilation of Connecticut Laws Concerning Planning and Zoning.

CN/0823-3489
STATUTES OF ALBERTA. [Statutes Alta.].
Main/Corp Alberta. **VFOAT** Statutes of Alberta (1981). (1981)-. Periodical. English. Alberta Government, 11510 Kingsway, Edmonton Alberta T5G 2Y5 Canada. **DD** 348.7123/022. **Continues** Alberta. Laws, etc. Statutes of the Province of Alberta, 0709-146X.

CN/0226-1219
STATUTES OF NEW BRUNSWICK. [Statut. N.B.]. **Main/Corp** New Brunswick. **VFOAT** Lois du Nouveau-Brunswick. Periodical. English (French). an. 290.00Can$. Queens Printer, PO Box 6000, Fredericton New Brunswick E3B 5H1 Canada. **Tel** (506)453-2520, (506)453-2506. **Circ:** 1,000.
Desc: Statutes of New Brunswick in loose-leaf format. Updates mailed to subscribers twice yearly.

NZ
STATUTES OF NEW ZEALAND (1947), THE. (THE STATUTES OF NEW ZEALAND.).
Main/Corp New Zealand. **VFOAT** New Zealand Statutes. (1947)-. English. an. Government Printing Office / New Zealand, 10 Mulgrave Street, Wellington New Zealand. **Tel** 011 64 4 4737211, FAX 011 64 4 734943, telex GOVPRINT NZ 31320. **Continues** New Zealand. Laws, Statutes, Etc. Statutes of the Dominion of New Zealand.

CN/0840-2043
STATUTES OF SASKATCHEWAN. [Statut, Sask.]. **Main/Corp** Saskatchewan. 20th Legislature, 3rd Session (1983-84)-. English. ir. Office of the Queens Printer / Saskatchewan, 1874 Scarth Street, Eighth Floor, Regina Saskatchewan S4P 3V7 Canada. **Tel** (306)787-6894. **ED** Sharlene Taylor. **DD** 348.7124/023. ctrl circ. **Continues** Saskatchewan. Statutes of the Province of Saskatchewan, 0229-8600.

CN
STATUTES OF THE PROVINCE OF MANITOBA. Main/Corp Manitoba. Laws, Statutes, etc. English (French). an. Queens Printer Statutory Publishing, 200 Vaughn Street, Winnipeg Manitoba R3C 1T5 Canada. **Tel** (204)945-3102. **Circ:** 1,500 (ctrl).
Desc: Permanent record of government and public workers.

CN
STATUTES OF THE PROVINCE OF NEWFOUNDLAND. Main/Corp Newfoundland.
VFOAT Statutes of Newfoundland. (1976)-. English. an. Office of the Queens Printer / Newfoundland, Confederation Building East Block, St John's Newfoundland A1B 4J6 Canada. **Tel** (709)729-3649, FAX (709)576-3627. **ED** David C.B. Dawe. Index available. cum. index. **Circ:** 1,000 (ctrl). **Continues** Newfoundland. Laws, etc. **and** Statutes of Newfoundland.
Desc: Contains all acts as passed by the Legislature of the province.

CN/0823-4949
STATUTES OF THE YUKON TERRITORY. (STATUTES OF THE YUKON TERRITORY PASSED BY THE LEGISLATURE OF THE YUKON TERRITORY IN THE YEAR ...). [Statut. Yukon Territ.]. **Main/Corp** Yukon Territory. **Added/Corp** Yukon Territory. Legislative Assembly. **VFOAT** Statutes of the Yukon Passed by the Legislature of the Yukon Territory in the Year ... . (1982)-. Periodical. English. ir. 14.00Can$. Government of Yukon, Box 2703 Queens Priter, Whitehorse Yukon Territory Y1A 2C6 Canada. **Tel** (403)667-5783, FAX (403)667-2958, telex 036-8 260. **LC** KEY39; .A23. **DD** 348.719/1/02205; 347.191082205. Index available. cum. index. **Circ:** 659 (ctrl). **Continues** Statutes of the Yukon Territory Passed By the Yukon Council in the Year ... .

CN/1185-9652
STATUTORY PUBLICATIONS, PRICE LIST - MANITOBA. OFFICE OF THE QUEEN'S PRINTER (ENGLISH EDITION).
(STATUTORY PUBLICATIONS, PRICE LIST / QUEEN'S PRINTER). [Statut. pub. price list - Manit., Off. Queen's Print.]. **Main/Corp** Manitoba. Office of the Queen's Printer. **Added/Corp** Manitoba. Manitoba Culture, Heritage and Citizenship. **VFOAT** Publications Officielles, Liste des Prix. **VAT** Publications Officielles, Liste des Prix - Manitoba. Imprimeur de la Reine. (June 1991)-. Periodical. English (French). Three times a year. **DD** 016.3487127/02.

CN/1185-9652
STATUTORY PUBLICATIONS, PRICE LIST - MANITOBA. OFFICE OF THE QUEEN'S PRINTER (FRENCH EDITION).
(STATUTORY PUBLICATIONS, PRICE LIST / QUEEN'S PRINTER). [Statut. pub. price list - Manit., Off. Queen's Print.]. **Main/Corp** Manitoba. Imprimeur de la Reine. **Added/Corp** Manitoba. Culture, Patrimoine et Citoyennete Manitoba. **VFOAT** Publications Officielles, Liste des Prix. (June 1991)-. Periodical. French (English). Three times a year. **DD** 016.3487127/02.

NZ
STATUTORY REGULATIONS. Main/Corp New Zealand. Laws, Statutes. English. wk. 300.00NZ$. Government Printing Office / New Zealand, 10 Mulgrave Street, Wellington New Zealand. **Tel** 011 64 4 4737211, FAX 011 64 4 734943, telex GOVPRINT NZ 31320.
Desc: Issued under the authority of an Act of Parliament detailing procedures, etc., as necessary.

US/0739-9731
STETSON LAW REVIEW. [Stetson law rev.].
Added/Corp John B. Stetson University. College of Law. Vol. 8, No. 1 (Fall 1978)-. Periodical. English. Three times a year (Feb., May, Oct.). $25.00. Stetson Law Review, 1401 61st Street South, St Petersburg FL 33707. **Tel** (813)345-1121 Ext. 257, FAX (813)345-8973. **ED** Carl Brice. **LC** K23; .T4. **DD** 340/.05. cum. index. **Bk Rev**, (Qty: varies). **Ad Acc**, **Adv Mgr Tel** (813)343-1344. ctrl circ. available on an online database from WESTLAW.
Continues Stetson Intermural Law Review, 0145-5842.
Ind/Abst Bowne Dig. Corp. Sec. Lawyers; Curr. Law Index (1980-); Index Leg. Period.; Leg. Resour. Index (1980-); LegalTrac (1980-).

GW
STEUERBERATER RECHTSHANDBUCH / DEUTSCHER STEUERBERATERVERBAND E.V. See Public Administration-Public Finance and Taxation.

UK
STONE'S JUSTICES' MANUAL. (19??)-. English. an (April). $135.00. Butterworth & Co. Ltd. / Kent, England, Borough Green, Sevenoaks Kent TN15 8PH England. **Tel** 011 44 732-884567, FAX 011 44 732-885996. **ED** Anthony Draycott. Index available. **Circ:** 10,000. **Continues** Stone Justice Manual; Being the Yearly Justices' Practice for 18.

US
STORRS LECTURES ON JURISPRUDENCE. (19??)-. Monographic series. English. ir. Price varies per volume. Yale University Press, PO Box 209040, New Haven CT 06520. **Tel** (203)432-0940, (800)987-7323, FAX (203)432-0948.

GW
STRAFRECHTLICHE ABHANDLUNGEN, NEUE FOLGE. (1968)-. Monographic series. German. ir. Price varies per volume. Duncker und Humblot Verlag, Postfach 410329, D-12113 Berlin Germany. **Tel** 011 49 30 79000612, 011 49 30 79000613.

YU/0039-2138
STRANI PRAVNI ZIVOT / INSTITUT ZA UPOREDNO PRAVO. **Added/Corp** Institut za Uporedno Pravo (Belgrade, Serbia). **VFOAT** Serija D. (19??)-. Periodical. Serbo-Croatian (Roman). Four times a year. **(Subscription address:** Jugoslovenska Knjiga, PO Box 36, YU 11001 Belgrade Yugoslovia.**)**

GW/0175-4467
STREIT. (1983)-. Academic Scholarly Publication. German. Four times a year. DM68.00. Streit, Hamburger Strasse 181, D-28205 Bremen, Germany. **Tel** 011 49 421 490079, FAX 011 49 421 440914. **UDC** 396.342.722-055.2(430.1). Index available (published separately). cum. index. **Bk Rev**, (Qty: 4-10). **Circ:** 1300.
Desc: A German feminist law journal.

UK
STROUD'S JUDICIAL DICTIONARY OF WORDS & PHRASES. (19??)-. English. ir. £120.00 (each volume). Sweet & Maxwell Ltd., South Quay Plaza, 183 Marsh Wall, London E14 9FT England. **Tel** 011 44 264 342899, FAX 011 44 264 342723, telex 929089 ITPINF G.

US/0196-9773
STUDENT GUIDE TO: GRADUATE LAW STUDY PROGRAMS. (STUDENT GUIDE TO GRADUATE LAW STUDY PROGRAMS.). [Stud. guide: grad. law study programs]. **Added/Corp** New England School of Law. Suffolk University. Law School. **VFOAT** Graduate Law Study Programs. 12th Ed. (1980)-. English. ir. $19.00. New England School of Law, 46 Church Street, Attention NEJCCC, Boston MA 02116. **Tel** (617)422-7238, FAX (617)422-7451. **ED** Ellen Wayne and Betsy McCombs. **LC** K100.A4; S88. **DD** 340/.07/11. **Ad Acc.** ctrl circ. ***Continues*** *Directory of Graduate Law Programs, 0070-5608.*
Desc: Listing of graduate law study programs available throughout the world; includes curriculum and program information.

US/0197-6656
STUDENT GUIDE TO: SUMMER LAW STUDY PROGRAMS. [Stud. guide: Summer law study programs]. **Added/Corp** New England School of Law. Suffolk University. Law School. **VFOAT** Summer Law Study Programs. 7th- Ed. (1980)-. English. be. $17.50. New England School of Law, 46 Church Street, Attention NEJCCC, Boston MA 02116. **Tel** (617)422-7238, FAX (617)422-7451. **ED** Ellen Wayne and Betsy McCombs. **LC** KF266; .S8. **DD** 340/.07/1173. **Ad Acc.** ctrl circ. ***Continues*** *Directory of Summer Law Programs.*
Desc: Listing of law summer programs available throughout the world including program and curriculum information.

US/0039-274X
STUDENT LAWYER (CHICAGO. 1972). (STUDENT LAWYER.). [Stud. lawyer]. Vol. 1 (Sept. 1972)-. Periodical. English. mo. $22.00. American Bar Association, 750 North Lake Shore Drive, Chicago IL 60611. **Tel** (312)988-5522, (312)988-5241, FAX (312)988-5528, telex 270593. **ED** Lizanne Poppens. **LC** K23; .T8. **DD** 340/.05. **Ad Acc. Circ:** 40,000 (ctrl). available on microfilm and microfiche from University Microfilms International (UMI). ***Continues*** *Student Lawyer Journal (Chicago, ILL. : 1967).*
Desc: For law students, covering sociolegal issues and practical, professional topics.
Ind/Abst Curr. Law Index (1980-); Fed. Tax Artic.; Law Office Inf. Serv.; Leg. Resour. Index (1980-); LegalTrac (1980-).

US/0160-3825
STUDENT PRESS LAW CENTER REPORT. (REPORT - STUDENT PRESS LAW CENTER.). [Stud. Press Law Cent. rep.]. **Main/Corp** Student Press Law Center. **VFOAT** SPLC Report. (197?)-. Periodical. English. Three times a year (Jan., May, Sept.). $15.00. Student Press Law Center, 1735 Eye Street Northwest, Suite 504, Washington DC 20006. **Tel** (202)466-5242, FAX (202)466-6326. **ED** Michelle L. Breidenbach. **LC** KF4165.A15; S8. **DD** 344/.73/0793. **Circ:** 4,000.
Desc: Summarizes current issues and cases in student press law. It explains and analyzes complex legal issues most often confronted by student journalists and offers advice on how to avoid legal problems. Major court and legislative actions are highlighted.

MW
STUDENTS LAW JOURNAL. Periodical. English. Chancellor College, PO Box 280, Zomba Malawi. **LC** K23; .T82. **DD** 349.6897/05; 346.897005.

IT/0039-3010
STUDI SENESI NEL CIRCOLO GIURIDICO DELLA R. UNIVERSITA. **Main/Corp** Universita di Siena. Circolo Giuridico. (1???)-. Italian. Three times a year. L60000 Italy; L100000 others. Industries Grafica Pistolesi, via Pantaneto 107-109, 53100 Siena Italy. **Tel** 011 39 577 222498, FAX 011 39 577 222498. **ED** Professor Paolo Nard. Index available. cum. index. **Bk Rev.** ctrl circ.

NE
STUDIA ET DOCUMENTA AD IURA ORIENTIS ANTIQUI PERTINENTIA. Vol. 1 (1936)-. Monographic series. German (English). ir. Price varies per volume. E. J. Brill, Postbus 9000, 2300 PA Leiden Netherlands. **Tel** 011 31 71 312624, FAX 011 31 71 317532, telex 39296 BRILL NL.

PL
STUDIA IURIDICA SILESIANA / UNIWERSYTET SLASKI. 1(1976)-. Periodical. English (French, German, Polish and Russian). ir. Uniwersytet Slaski, Ul Bankowa 14, 40-007 Katowice Poland. **Tel** 59-69-15, FAX 48 32 599-506, telex 0315584 USKPL. **LC** K23; .T85. **DD** 340/.05.
Desc: Contains articles about different problems and theory of law.

PL/0039-3312
STUDIA PRAWNICZE. [Stud. praw.]. **Added/Corp** Instytut Nauk Prawnych (Polska Akademia Nauk). Instytut Panstwa i Prawa (Polska Akademia Nauk). Vol. 2 (1963)-. Periodical. Polish. qt. $54.00. **(Subscription address:** ARS Polona, PO Box 1001, 00068 Warsaw Poland.**) DD** 349.438/05; 344.38/05. ***Continues*** *Zeszyty Prawnicze.*

IT
STUDIE ET DOCUMENTA HISTORIAE ET IURIS. **Added/Corp** Pontificia Universita Lateranense. Pontificium Istitutum Utriusque Iuris. Vol. 1 (1935)-. Italian (English, French, German and Latin). an. L140000.00 Italy; L160000.00 other. Pontificia Universita Lateranense, Piazza S Giovanni Laterano 4, 00120 Citta del Vaticano. **Tel** 011 39 6 69886401, FAX 011 39 6 69886103. Index available in last issue of volume--attached.
Ind/Abst Bibliogr. Mission.; Index Foreign Leg. Per.

GW
STUDIEN ZUM INTERNATIONALEN ROHSTOFFRECHT. **VFOAT** Studies in Transnational Law of Natural Resources. Vol. 1 (1977)-. Monographic series. German. Price varies per volume. Alfred Metzner Verlag, Zeppelinallee 43, POB 970148, W-6000 Frankfurt 1 Germany. **Tel** 011 49 69 793009 0.

UK/0263-8630
STUDIES IN LAW AND PRACTICE FOR HEALTH SERVICE MANAGEMENT. [Stud. law pract. health serv. manage.]. 1978-. Monographic series. English. Price varies per volume. **ED** W A J Farndale. **DD** 344. **NLM** W1 ST92X. ***Continues*** *Case Studies on Law and Practice for Health Service Management, 0143-9278.*

SW/0348-1964
STUDIES OF LAW IN SOCIAL CHANGE AND DEVELOPMENT. **Added/Corp** Nordiska Afrikainstitutet. International Legal Centre. (1977)-. Monographic series. English. ir. Price varies per volume. Holmes and Meier Publishers Inc, 160 Broadway, Suite 900 East Wing, New York NY 10038. **Tel** (212)374-0100.

RM/0039-4041
STUDII DE DREPT ROMANESC / ACADEMIA ROMANA, INSTITUTUL DE CERCETARI JURIDICE. **Added/Corp** Institutul de Cercetari Juridice (Academia Romana). Vol. 1, No. 1 (Oct./Dec. 1989)-. Periodical. Romanian (table of contents in English and French). qt. $110.00. **(Subscription address:** Orion Press SRL, SPL Independentei 202-A, Bucharest 6 Romania.**) LC** K23; .T856. ***Continues*** *Studii si Cercetari Juridice.*

US/0192-673X
SUBCONTRACTING. (SUBCONTRACTING; COURSE MANUAL.). **Added/Corp** Federal Publications Inc. (19??)-. English. an. Federal Publications Inc, 1120 20th Street Northwest, Washington DC 20036. **Tel** (202)337-7000, (800)922-4330, FAX (202)659-2233. **LC** KF869.3; .S82. **DD** 346/.73/023.

CN/0713-8954
SUBJECT MATTER INDEX TO PUBLIC AND PRIVATE STATUTES OF NEW BRUNSWICK. [Subj. matter index public priv. statut. N.B.]. Pt. 1 (1971)-. English. an. Maritime Law Book Ltd, PO Box 302, Fredericton New Brunswick, E3B 4Y9 Canada. **Tel** (506)453-9921, (800)561-0220. **LC** KEN62; .N48. **DD** 348.715/028; 347.150828.

US/0039-4696
SUFFOLK UNIVERSITY LAW REVIEW. [Suffolk Univ. law rev.]. **Main/Corp** Suffolk University. Law School. Vol. 1 (Spring 1967)-. Periodical. English. qt (Mar., June, Sept., Dec.). $18.00. Suffolk University / Law, School of Law, 41 Temple Street, Boston MA 02114. **Tel** (617)573-8000, 573-8610. **LC** UNC. Each issue contains an index to its own contents (no volume index)--loose. cum. index. **Bk Rev. Circ:** 1,200.
Desc: Reviews of cases and legal principles which are of interest to the practitioner.
Ind/Abst Bowne Dig. Corp. Sec. Lawyers; Curr. Law Index (1980-); Fed. Tax Artic.; Index Leg. Period.; Leg. Resour. Index (1980-); LegalTrac (1980-).

US/0196-318X
SUFFOLK UNIVERSITY LAW SCHOOL ALUMNI DIRECTORY. **See** College and School Publications-Alumni.

US/0070-1157
SUGGESTED STATE LEGISLATION (1965). (SUGGESTED STATE LEGISLATION / THE COUNCIL OF STATE GOVERNMENTS.). **Added/Corp** Council of State Governments. Committee on Suggested State Legislation. Council of State Governments. Committee of State Officials on Suggested State Legislation. Vol. 24 (1965)-. English. an (Dec.). $30.00 US; $35.00 other. Council of State Governments, PO Box 11910, Iron Works Pike, Lexington KY 40578-1910. **Tel** (800)800-1910, (606)231-1850. **(Subscription address:** Council of State Governments, PO Box 2167, Lexington, KY 40595**) LC** KF165; .C68. **DD** 349.73; 347.309. **Circ:** 5,000. ***Continues*** *Program of Suggested State Legislation.*
Desc: Source of legislative ideas and drafting assistance.

US
SULLIVAN'S LAW DIRECTORY FOR THE STATE OF ILLINOIS. 75th Annual Ed. (1951/1952)-. English. an (Sept.). $40.50. Sullivan's Law Directory Inc., PO Box 643, Barrington IL 60011. **Tel** (708)381-2750, FAX (708)381-7240. **LC** KF192.I4; S9. **DD** 340/.025/773. ***Continues*** *Sullivan's Law Directory.*

IO
SULUH HUKUM YUSTITIA. **Added/Corp** Universitas Kristen Indonesia. Lembaga Bantuan Hukum & Research. (197?)-. Periodical. Indonesian (summaries and/or abstracts in English). Jln Diponegoro 86, Jakarta Indonesia. **LC** K10; .U818. ***Continues*** *Justitia.*

CN/0319-3667
SUMMARY - ALBERTA SECURITIES COMMISSION. **Main/Corp** Alberta Securities Commission. (April 1975)-. Proceedings. English. wk. 300.00Can$. Alberta Securities Commission, 10025 Jasper Avenue, 21st Floor, Edmonton Alberta T5J 3Z5 Canada. **Tel** (403)427-5201, FAX (403)422-0777, telex 037-2701. **DD** 346/.7123/0666. **Circ:** 250 (ctrl).
Desc: Account of proceedings brought before the Alberta Securities Commission.

US/0738-1972
SUMMARY JUDGEMENT. (SUMMARY JUDGMENT : A PUBLICATION FOR MEMBERS OF THE OHIO STATE BAR ASSOCIATION.). **Added/Corp** Ohio State Bar Association. Vol. 1, No. 1 (Nov. 1982)-?. Periodical. English. bm. Ohio State Bar Association, Ohio Legal Center, 33 West Eleventh Avenue, Columbus OH 43201. **Tel** (614)421-2121. **LC** KF200; .S85. **DD** 340/.06/0771. ***Continues*** *2 Minute News.* ***Continued in part by*** *Ohio Lawyer (Columbus, Ohio : 1987).*

US
SUMMARY OF ACTION. **Main/Corp** American Bar Association. House of Delegates. (19??)-. English. an. American Bar Association, 750 North Lake Shore Drive, Chicago IL 60611. **Tel** (312)988-5522, (312)988-5241, FAX (312)988-5528, telex 270593. **LC** KF325.135; .A4. **DD** 340/.06/273.

US
SUMMARY OF ACTION TAKEN BY THE HOUSE OF DELEGATES OF THE AMERICAN BAR ASSOCIATION. **Main/Corp** American Bar Association. House of Delegates. **VFOAT** Summary of Action of the House of Delegates. (1975)-. English. an. $7.00. American Bar Association, 750 North Lake Shore Drive, Chicago IL 60611. **Tel** (312)988-5522, (312)988-5241, FAX (312)988-5528, telex 270593. **LC** KF325; .A626. **DD** 340/.06/073. Index available in last issue of volume--attached. ***Continues*** *American Bar Association. Summary of Action and Reports to the House of Delegates, 0092-0797.*

US/0363-2687
SUMMARY OF ACTIVITIES - MENTAL HEALTH LAW PROJECT. **Main/Corp** Mental Health Law Project. Periodical. English. be. Free (donors), $25.00 other. Mental Health Law Project, 2021 L Street NW/Suite 800, Washington DC 20036. **Tel** (202)467-5730, FAX (202)467-5736. **ED** Lee Carty. **LC** KF480.A15; M4. **DD** 344/.73/044. **Bk Rev. Circ:** 6,000

(ctrl).
Desc: Reports on work by non-profit public-interest organizations representing people with mental disabilities.

US
SUMMARY OF ALASKA LEGISLATION.
Main/Corp Alaska. Legislature. Legislative Affairs Agency. English. an. Legislative Affairs Agency, Pouch Y, State Capitol, Juneau AK 99811. **LC** KFA1215; .L4. **DD** 348.798/01; 347.98081. ***Continues*** *Summary of Alaska Legislation.*

US
SUMMARY OF CALIFORNIA LAW.
Added/Corp Bancroft-Whitney Company. Periodical. English. Bancroft-Whitney Company, 301 Brannon Street, San Francisco CA 94107.

US/0095-2796
SUMMARY OF ELECTION LAWS ENACTED BY THE LEGISLATIVE ASSEMBLY - OREGON.
Main/Corp Oregon. English. Elections Division, State Capitol/Room 122, Salem MA 97310. **LC** KFO2820; .A472. **DD** 342/.795/0702638.

US/0098-759X
SUMMARY OF ENACTMENTS.
Main/Corp Ohio. General Assembly. Legislative Service Commission. English. an. Ohio Legislative Service Commission, PO Box 301, Columbus OH 43216. **LC** KFO15; .L43. **DD** 348/.771/01. ***Continues*** *Ohio. Legislative Service Commission. Legislation.*

US
SUMMARY OF ENACTMENTS - TEXAS. LEGISLATURE. LEGISLATIVE COUNCIL.
Main/Corp Texas. Legislature. Legislative Council. English. Texas Legislative Council, PO Box 12128 Capitol Station, Austin TX 78711. **LC** KFT1215; .L437. **DD** 348.764/023.

US
SUMMARY OF HIV/AIDS LAWS FROM THE ... STATE LEGISLATIVE SESSIONS, A.
Added/Corp George Gund Foundation. Robert Wood Johnson Foundation. George Washington University. AIDS Policy Center. **VFOAT** Summary of HIV/AIDS Laws from the ... State Legislative Session. (1990)-. English. **NLM** W 32; AA1 S955. ***Continues*** *Summary of AIDS Laws from the ... Legislative Sessions.*

US
SUMMARY OF LEGISLATION.
Main/Corp Nevada. Legislative Counsel Bureau. Research Division. English. Legislative Counsel Bureau, Legislative Building, Capitol Complex, Carson City NV 89710. **LC** KFN615; .L437. **DD** 348.793/026; 347.930826.

US/0740-9427
SUMMARY OF LEGISLATIVE ACTIVITIES - UNITED STATES. CONGRESS. HOUSE. COMMITTEE ON PUBLIC WORKS AND TRANSPORTATION.
(SUMMARY OF LEGISLATIVE ACTIVITIES / COMMITTEE ON PUBLIC WORKS AND TRANSPORTATION, U.S. HOUSE OF REPRESENTATIVES.). [Summary of legislative activities - United States. Congress. House. Committee on Public Works and Transportation]. **Main/Corp** United States. Congress. House. Committee on Public Works and Transportation. English. be. US House of Representatives / Committee on Public Works and Transportation, Washington DC. **LC** KF4997.P8; A248. **DD** 328.73/0765.

US/0093-9226
SUMMARY OF PUBLIC ACTS (HARTFORD).
(SUMMARY OF PUBLIC ACTS - CONNECTICUT. GENERAL ASSEMBLY. OFFICE OF LEGISLATIVE RESEARCH.). **Main/Corp** Connecticut. General Assembly. Office of Legislative Research. English. Connecticut General Assembly, State Capital, Hartford CT 06115. **LC** KFC3615; .G45. **DD** 348/.746/026.

US/0148-625X
SUMMARY OF SELECTED LEGISLATION RELATED TO THE HANDICAPPED, A.
[Summ. sel. legis. relat. handicap.]. **Main/Corp** United States. Dept. of Health, Education and Welfare. 1963/67-. Government Publication. English. US Department of Education, 400 Maryland Avenue SW, Room 4181, Washington DC 20202. **Tel** (202)401-1576, FAX (202)272-5447. **LC** KF3738; .A374. **DD** 344/.73/0324.

US/0081-931X
SUMMARY OF STATE LAWS AND REGULATIONS RELATING TO DISTILLED SPIRITS.
[Summ. state laws regul. relat. distill. spirits]. **Added/Corp** Distilled Spirits Council of the U.S. Distilled Spirits Institute. **VFOAT** Summary of State Laws & Regulations Relating to Distilled Spirits. (19??)-. English. ir. $14.00. Distilled Spirits Council of the United States, 1250 Eye Street Northwest, Suite 900, Washington DC 20005. **Tel** (202)628-3544. **LC** KF3920; .D5. **DD** 343.73/0786631; 347.303786631. ***Continues*** *Summary of State Liquor Control Laws and Regulations Relating to Distilled Spirits as of ... .*

US/1061-0146
SUMMARY REPORTER.
(SUMMARY REPORTER : SUMMARIES OF KEY DEVELOPMENTS IN MINNESOTA LAW.). [Summ. report.]. **Added/Corp** Minnesota State Bar Association. Vol. 1, No. 1 (Oct. 22, 1991)-. Periodical. English. Fifty-one times per year. $365.00. Finance & Commerce, 615 South 7th Street, Minneapolis MN 55415. **Tel** (612)333-4248. **DD** 348.

US/0738-1921
SUMMER LEGAL EMPLOYMENT GUIDE.
(SUMMER LEGAL EMPLOYMENT GUIDE / BY THE EDITORS OF THE NATIONAL AND FEDERAL LEGAL EMPLOYMENT REPORT.). **Added/Corp** American Bar Association. Law Student Division. Federal Reports (Firm). (1983)-. English. an. $18.00. Federal Reports, PO Box 3709 Georgetown Station, Washington DC 20007. **Tel** (202)393-3311, FAX (202)393-1553. **LC** KF287; .S93. **DD** 331.12/4134. ***Continues*** *Summer Federal Legal Employment Guide, 0278-6737.*

US
SUPPLEMENT TO ATTORNEY'S GUIDE TO TRADE SECRETS.
Added/Corp California Continuing Education of the Bar. **VFOAT** Trade Secrets. (19??)-. English. ir. California Continuing Education of the Bar, 2300 Shattuck Avenue, Berkeley CA 94704. **Tel** (510)642-8000, (800)232-3444.

US
SUPPLEMENT TO CAMPAIGN FINANCE LAW.
Main/Corp Library of Congress. Congressional Research Service. American Law Division. **VFOAT** Campaign Finance Law; Analysis of Federal and State Campaign Finance Law. 1979-. English. be. US Federal Election Commission, 999 E Street NW, Washington DC 20463. **Tel** (800)424-9530.

US/0199-5030
SUPREME COURT BULLETIN (MANCHESTER, N.H.).
(SUPREME COURT BULLETIN.). [Supreme Court bull.]. (197?)-. Periodical. English. ir (When court is in session in Oct. thru July). $32.00. Haleridge Publishing, PO Box 370, Windham NH 03087. **Tel** (603)889-7231. **ED** David R. Armstrong. Index available. cum. index. **Ad Acc. Circ:** 2,500.
Desc: Contains opinions of the US Supreme Court as they are handed down.

II
SUPREME COURT CASES, THE.
Main/Corp India (Republic). Supreme Court. English. sm. Rs480.00 India; $76.00 (surface mail), $130.00 (airmail) US. Eastern Book Company, 34 Lalbagh, Lucknow 226 001 India. **Tel** 43171, 44328, 46517, telex 535 436 FAST IN. **ED** Surendra Malik and P L Malik. **DD** 348.54/046. Index available. **Bk Rev. Ad Acc. Circ:** 6,000.
Desc: Contains reports of both reportable and non-reportable cases of the Supreme Court of India.

PH
SUPREME COURT DECISIONS : SUBJECT INDEX AND DIGESTS.
1977-. English. University of the Philippines Law Center, Diliman Quezon City Philippines. **DD** 348.599/044.

PH
SUPREME COURT DOCTRINES.
1975-. English. Rex Printing Company, 84 P Florentine Street, Quezon City Philippines. **DD** 348/.599/041.

US/0736-9921
SUPREME COURT ECONOMIC REVIEW.
See Economics.

II
SUPREME COURT JOURNAL, THE.
V. 1- 1937-. Periodical. English. bw. 76.00. Post Box 604, Madras-600004 India. Index Available, published separately, free-automatically sent.

US/0893-9640
SUPREME COURT LAW JOURNAL.
[Supreme Court law j.]. Vol. 1, (Oct. 18, 1984)-. Periodical. English. Fifty-two times a year (Monday). $78.00. Supreme Court Law Journal, Drawer 1076, Ridgefield CT 06877. **LC** K23; .U667. **DD** 340/.05.
Desc: National legal newspaper of record for the US Supreme Court and lower statutory courts; editorial emphasis is on the commercial impact of court and legislative proceedings.

CN/0228-0108
SUPREME COURT LAW REVIEW, THE.
[Supreme Court law rev.]. **VFOAT** New Constitution and The Charter of Rights. Vol. 1 (1980)-. Periodical. English (French). ir. 165.00Can4. Butterworth Heinemann / Woburn, MA, 225 Wildwood Avenue, Unit B, Woburn MA 01801. **Tel** (800)366-2665, FAX (617)928-2620, telex 880052. **LC** K23; .U67. **DD** 347.71/035/05; 347.1073505.
Desc: Offers sytematic analysis of the Supreme Court of Canada's key decisions and critical examinations of the Court's performance in reaching them.
Ind/Abst Can. Legal Lit.; Curr. Law Index (1982-); Index Can. Leg. Period. Lit.; Index Leg. Period.; Leg. Resour. Index (1982-); LegalTrac (1980-).

PK
SUPREME COURT MONTHLY REVIEW, THE.
V. 1- Jan. 1968-. Periodical. English. mo. 36.00. 1/5 Edward Road, Lahore Pakistan. **LC** PAKISTAN 5 1968-. **DD** 349/.549/04.

CN/0709-5600
SUPREME COURT OF CANADA DECISIONS. CIVIL AND CRIMINAL CASES.
Main/Corp Canada. Supreme Court. (1978)-. English. mo. 125.00Can$. Western Legal Publications Ltd., 301 One Alexander Street, Vancouver BC V6A 1B2 Canada. **Tel** (800)663-0422, (604)687-5671. **DD** 348/.71/041. Index available.
Desc: Digest of facts, ratio, and obiter dicta of all judgements of the Supreme Court of Canada.

US/0892-810X
SUPREME COURT RECORD.
[Supreme Court rec.]. **Added/Corp** United States. Supreme Court. (1986)-. Periodical. English. Forty-Four times a year. $96.00. Haleridge Publishing, PO Box 370, Windham NH 03087. **Tel** (603)889-7231. **ED** Robert Gillmore. **LC** KF101; .S86. **DD** 348.73/413/05; 347.3084105. Index available. cum. index. **Ad Acc. Circ:** 2,800.
Desc: Full texts of every Supreme Court opinion each day when opinions are handed down.

II
SUPREME COURT REPORTS.
Main/Corp India. Supreme Court. English. Twelve times a year. **(Subscription address:** Prints India, 11 Darya Ganj, New Delhi 110002 India.**)**

US/0081-9557
SUPREME COURT REVIEW, THE.
[Supreme Court rev.]. **Added/Corp** University of Chicago. Law School. (1960)-. Periodical. English. an. $45.00. University of Chicago Press / Book Department, 11030 South Langley Avenue, Chicago IL 60628. **Tel** (800)621-2736, (312)568-1550, FAX (312)753-0811, telex 23933. **ED** Philip B. Kurland, Gerhard Casper and Dennis J. Hutchinson. **LC** KF4546; .S9. **DD** 347.9973. **Circ:** 2,500. available on microfilm and microfiche from University Microfilms International (UMI). Documents available from The Genuine Article, UMI Article Clearinghouse.
Desc: Provides a survey of the quality and implications of the court's decisions, both past and present.
Ind/Abst ABC POL SCI; Curr. Law Index (1980-); Expand. Acad. Index (1984-); Index Leg. Period.; Int. Polit. Sci. Abstr.; Leg. Resour. Index (1980-); LegalTrac (1980-); Newsp. Period. Abstr. (1989-); Res. Alert [Full Cov.].

US/1054-2701
SUPREME COURT YEARBOOK, THE.
[Supreme Court yearb.]. (1990)-. English. an (Nov./Dec.). $31.95 (hardcover), $22.95 (softcover). Congressional Quarterly Inc., 1414 22nd Street Northwest, Washington DC 20037. **Tel** (202)887-8500, (800)432-2250 ext. 621, FAX (202)728-1863. **LC** KF8741.A152; S87. **DD** 347.73/2605.

US/0271-2792
SURVEY OF LAW.
[Surv. law]. **Added/Corp** American Bar Association. Section of General Practice. (1979)-. Periodical. English. an. American Bar Association, 750 North Lake Shore Drive, Chicago IL 60611. **Tel** (312)988-5522, (312)988-5241, FAX (312)988-5528, telex 270593. **LC** KF178; .S95. **DD** 349.73/05.
Ind/Abst Curr. Law Index (1982-); Leg. Resour. Index (1982-?); LegalTrac (1980-1985).

US/0360-7372
SURVEY OF LAW REVIEWS.
V. 1- Summer 1974-. English. qt. $20.00. Legal Information Services - Virginia, Data Solutions Corporation, 6849 Old Dominion Drive, McLean VA 22101. **LC** KF8; .S9. **DD** 340/.05.

MY/0217-3239
SURVEY OF MALAYSIAN LAW.
[Surv. Malays. law]. **Added/Corp** Universiti Malaya. Fakulti Undang-Undang. (1977)-. English. an. Malaysian Law Journal Pte Ltd, 3 Shenton Way 14-03, Shenton House, Singapore 0106 Singapore. **Tel** 011 65 2203684, telex RS 28904 MLJLAW. **(Subscription address:** Butterworth Legal Publishers, PO Box 93643, Chicago IL 93643.**) ED** A. Krishnan. **DD** 349.595; 345.95.
Desc: Contains various aspects of Malayan laws by law academicians on criminal justice, administrative, commercial, company, constitutional, contract, equity, trusts, evidence, family, Islamic law, etc.

US/0098-714X
SURVEY OF PHARMACY LAW.
Added/Corp National Association of Boards of Pharmacy. (1942)-. Periodical. English. an. National Association Boards of Pharmacy, 700 Busse Highway, Park Ridge IL 60068. **Tel** (708)698-6227. **NLM** QV 32 AA1 S9.

US/1044-0011
S'VARA (NEW YORK, N.Y.).
Suspended. **See** Philosophy.

SW/0039-6591
SVENSK JURISTTIDNING. Added/Corp Sweden. Courts. (1916)-. Periodical. Swedish. Ten times a year. Kr352.00. Iustus Forlag AB, Ostra Agatan 9, S 75322 Uppsala Sweden. **Tel** 011 46 18 693091. cum. index.
Ind/Abst Selec. Coop. Index Manage. Period.

US
SWALL BULLETIN. See Library and Information Sciences.

AT/0082-0512
SYDNEY LAW REVIEW, THE. [Syd. law rev.]. **Added/Corp** University of Sydney. Faculty of Law. Vol. 1, No. 1 (April 1953)-. Periodical. English. qt. price varies per volume. The Law Book Company Limited, 44-50 Waterloo Road, North Ryde New South Wales, 2113 Australia. **Tel** 011 61 2 8870177, FAX 011 61 2 8887240, telex ASBOOK 27445. **Bk Rev.**
Desc: Journal of the University of Sydney law faculty. Includes articles and case notes.
Ind/Abst APAIS, Aust. Public Aff. Inf. Ser. (1963-); Aust. Leg. Mon. Dig.; Curr. Law Index (1980-); Index Leg. Period.; Leg. Resour. Index (1980-); LegalTrac (1980-).

US
SYLLABUS. (SYLLABUS / AMERICAN BAR ASSOCIATION, SECTION OF LEGAL EDUCATION AND ADMISSIONS TO THE BAR.). **Added/Corp** American Bar Association. Section of Legal Education and Admissions to the Bar. Vol. 12, No. 4 (Nov. 1981)-. Periodical. English. qt. $15.00. American Bar Association, 750 North Lake Shore Drive, Chicago IL 60611. **Tel** (312)988-5522, (312)988-5241, FAX (312)988-5528, telex 270593. **ED** Susan K. Boyd. **LC** KF200; .L43. **DD** 340/.07/1173. **Bk Rev. Circ:** 5,000. available in microform from University Microfilms International (UMI). ***Continues*** *Legal Education Newsletter.*
Desc: Articles on legal education and bar admissions.
Ind/Abst LegalTrac (1981-1988).

US/0093-0520
SYNOPSIS OF LAWS ENACTED BY THE STATE OF MARYLAND. Main/Corp Maryland. State Dept. of Legislative Reference. **Added/Corp** Baltimore (Md.). Dept. of Legislative Reference. Maryland. General Assembly. State Dept. of Legislative Reference. (19??)-. English. an. State Department of Legislative Reference, 90 State Circle, Room G 17, Annapolis MD 21401. **Tel** (301)841-3884. **LC** KFM1238; .S96. **DD** 348/.752/7326. Index available. **Circ:** 600.
Desc: Synopsis of bills passed and vetoed each session and table of sections of code affected.

US/1042-0169
SYNTHESIS (ASHEVILLE, N.C.). (SYNTHESIS: LAW AND POLICY IN HIGHER EDUCATION.). [Synthesis]. **VFOAT** Law and Policy in Higher Education. Vol. 1, No. 1 (Jan. 1989)-. Periodical. English. qt. $67.50. College Administration Publications Inc, 830D Fairview Road, PO Box 15898, Asheville NC 28813. **Tel** (704)277-8777. **ED** Gary Pavela. **LC** KF4225.A15; S95. **DD** 344.73/07684/05; 347.304768405. ctrl circ.
Desc: Providing an analysis and commentary on a single law and policy issue of concern to today's higher education administrators and faculty.

US/0039-7938
SYRACUSE LAW REVIEW. [Syracuse law rev.]. **Added/Corp** Syracuse University. College of Law. Vol. 1 (Spring 1949)-. Academic Scholarly Publication. English. qt. $24.00 US; $35.00 other. Syracuse University / Law, College of Law, Ernest I. White Hall, Syracuse NY 13244-1030. **Tel** (315)443-3680, FAX (315)443-9568. **LC** K23; .Y7. **DD** 340/.09747. Index available. **Ad Acc. Circ:** 2,000 (ctrl). Documents available from The Genuine Article.
Desc: Covers New York law and scholarly aspects of the legal profession. A help in practice, research, and conversation.
Ind/Abst Bowne Dig. Corp. Sec. Lawyers; Crim. Penol. Police Sci. Abstr.; Curr. Contents Soc. Behav. Sci.; Curr. Law Index (1980-); Fed. Tax Artic.; Index Leg. Period.; Leg. Resour. Index (1980-); LegalTrac (1980-); Res. Alert [Select. Cov.]; Women Stud. Abstr.

CN/0841-8195
TALL NEWSLETTER (1984). See Library and Information Sciences.

US/0149-9718
TAR, TENNESSEE ADMINISTRATIVE REGISTER. NOTICE SECTION. Main/Corp Tennessee. State Dept. Administrative Procedure Division. **VFOAT** Tennessee Administrative Register. Notice Section. **VAT** Tennessee Administrative Register. Tennessee Administrative Register. Notice Section. Periodical. English. mo. $10.00. Tennessee Secretary State Publishers, James K. Polk Building, Suite 500, Nashville TN 37243. **Tel** (615)741-2650, FAX (615)741-1278. **ED** Richard Arnold. **LC** KFT36; .A35.

HU/0231-2522
TARSADALOMKUTATAS. See Social Sciences.

AT/0085-7106
TASMANIAN REPORTS, THE. Added/Corp Council of Law Reporting of Tasmania. Tasmania. Supreme Court. (1979)-. English. ir. The Law Book Company Limited, 44-50 Waterloo Road, North Ryde New South Wales, 2113 Australia. **Tel** 011 61 2 8870177, FAX 011 61 2 8887240, telex ASBOOK 27445. **DD** 348.946/048; 349.460848. ***Continues*** *Tasmanian State Reports.*
Ind/Abst Aust. Leg. Mon. Dig.

AT
TASMANIAN STATE REPORTS, THE. Added/Corp Tasmania. Supreme Court. Tasmania. Mining Board. (1905)-. English. ir. 39.50Aus$. The Law Book Company Limited, 44-50 Waterloo Road, North Ryde New South Wales, 2113 Australia. **Tel** 011 61 2 8870177, FAX 011 61 2 8887240, telex ASBOOK 27445. **ED** F. D. Cumbrae-Stewart.
Desc: Contain cases determined in the Supreme Court of Tasmania.

II/0039-9965
TAX AFFAIRS. Began in 1960. Periodical. English. Practical Tax Publishers, D-75 Anand Niketan, New Delhi 110021 India. **LC** K24. **DD** 343/.54/0405.

US
TAX DIGEST (CORAL GABLES, FLA.). (TAX DIGEST.). **VFOAT** Tax Savings Digest. Periodical. English. $124.00. HMD Inc, 159 Madeira Avenue, Coral Gables FL 33134. **LC** KF6296.A15; T35. **DD** 343.7304/05.

UK
TAX DIGEST (LONDON, ENGLAND). (TAX DIGEST.). **Added/Corp** Institute of Chartered Accountants in England and Wales. (19??)-. Periodical. English. Twelve times a year. £185.00. Institute of Chartered Accountants, 399 Silbury Boulevard, Central Milton, Keynes Bucks MK9 2HL England. **Tel** 011 41 71 920 8100, telex 727530. **LC** KD5352; .T39. **DD** 343.4104/05; 344.103405.

●US/1062-7308
TAX DIGEST (SANTA BARBARA, CALIF.). (TAX DIGEST.). [Tax dig.]. (Winter 1991/92)-. Periodical. English. qt. $9.00. Robert Dozier, Tax Digest, 515 Arrellaga Street #14, Santa Barbara CA 93103. **DD** 343.

US/1043-0873
TAX EXEMPT FINANCING. [Tax exempt financ.]. **Added/Corp** Practising Law Institute. (1988)-. English. an. $70.00. Practising Law Institute, 810 Seventh Avenue, New York NY 10019-5818. **Tel** (212)765-5700, FAX (212)581-4670 general correspondence, (212)265-4742 orders and billing inquiries. **LC** KF6383.Z9; T37. **DD** 343.7305/23; 347.303523. Index available. **Pr Rev.**

US
TAX EXEMPTIONS (OLYMPIA, WASH.). (TAX EXEMPTIONS.). English. Department of Revenue / Washington, Olympia WA 98504. **LC** KFW472; .A877. **DD** 343.79705/23; 347.9703523.

US/0892-4430
TAX LAW ANTHOLOGY. *Ceased.* (1992)-(19??). English. International Library Law Book Publishers, 101 Lakeforest Boulevard, Suite 270, Gaithersburg MD 20877. **Tel** (800)359-3349, (301)990-7755, FAX (301)990-7642. **ED** Donald J. Hoyes. Index available. **Bk Rev.**
Desc: US tax law review articles selected from over 900 law review journals. Articles are printed in their entirety. Indexed by subject, author, leading cases.

US/0040-0041
TAX LAW REVIEW. [Tax law rev.]. **Added/Corp** New York University. School of Law. Vol. 1 (Oct./Nov. 1945)-. Periodical. English. qt (Feb., May, Aug., Nocv.). $107.75 US and Canada; $168.25 other. Warren Gorham & Lamont Inc., Park Square Building, 31 St. James Avenue, Boston MA 02116-4112. **Tel** (617)423-2020, (800)950-1207, FAX (617)423-2026. **ED** Deborah H. Schenk. **[CCC].** available on microfilm and microfiche from University Microfilms International (UMI). Documents available from UMI Article Clearinghouse.
Ind/Abst ABI/INFORM Glob. Ed.; ABI Inform Ondisc (Fall 1974-); Account. Tax Datab. (Fall 1974-Summer 1987); Account. Art.; Bowne Dig. Corp. Sec. Lawyers; Curr. Law Index (1980-); Fed. Tax Artic.; Index Leg. Period.; Leg. Resour. Index (1980-); LegalTrac (1980-).

US/0040-005X
TAX LAWYER : BULLETIN OF THE SECTION OF TAXATION, AMERICAN BAR ASSOCIATION, THE. [Tax lawyer]. **Added/Corp** American Bar Association. Section of Taxation. Vol. 21, No. 1 (Fall 1967)-. Bulletin. English. qt (4 issues). $83.00. American Bar Association, 750 North Lake Shore Drive, Chicago IL 60611. **Tel** (312)988-5522, (312)988-5241, FAX (312)988-5528, telex 270593. **ED** Albert C. O'Neil. **LC** K24; .A92. **DD** 343.7304/05; 347.303405. cum. index. **Ad Acc.** ctrl circ. Documents available from UMI Article Clearinghouse, UMI Article Clearinghouse. ***Continues*** *Bulletin of the Section of Taxation, American Bar Association.*
Desc: Articles and student notes and comments pertaining to taxation.
Ind/Abst ABI/INFORM Glob. Ed.; ABI Inform Ondisc (Spring 1973-); Account. Tax Datab. (Spring 1973-); Account. Art.; Bowne Dig. Corp. Sec. Lawyers; Fed. Tax Artic.; Index Leg. Period.; Law Office Inf. Serv.; Leg. Resour. Index (1980-); LegalTrac (1980-).

US/8755-0369
TAX LITERATURE REPORT. *Ceased.* [Tax. lit. rep.]. No. 1 (Jan. 13, 1984)-Ceased Issue 46. English. wk. Symposia Press Inc, PO Box 418. **DD** 343.

US/8755-0628
TAX MANAGEMENT REAL ESTATE JOURNAL. [Tax Manage. real estate j.]. **Added/Corp** Tax Management Inc. **VFOAT** Real Estate Journal. Vol. 1, No. 1 Nov./Dec (1984)-. Periodical. English. Six times a year. $495.00. Bureau of National Affairs Inc., 9435 Key West Avenue, Rockville MD 20850. **Tel** (800)372-1033, (301)258-1033, FAX (301)948-5823. **ED** Glenn Davis. **LC** KF6535.A15; T39. **DD** 343. **[CCC].** available on microfilm and microfiche from University Microfilms International (UMI); available on an online database (file 485/Full-Text) from DIALOG.
Desc: Journal providing coverage of judicial, legislative, and administrative developments in the real estate tax area.
Ind/Abst Account. Tax Datab. (1984-) [Full Txt.]; Leg. Resour. Index; LegalTrac (1984-).

NE/0040-0076
TAX NEWS SERVICE. Main/Corp International Bureau of Fiscal Documentation. (Jan. 15, 1965)-. English. wk. $375.00. International Bureau of Fiscal Documentation - IBFD Publications, PO Box 20237, 1000 HE Amsterdam The Netherlands. **Tel** 011 31 20-6267726, FAX 011 31 20-6228658, telex 13217 INTAX NL. **LC** K4456.2; .I57. **DD** 343.04/05. **Bk Rev. Ad Acc.** ctrl circ. available on an online database.
Desc: Reports changes and developments in taxation around the world which are considered to be of more than purely domestic interest.

US/1058-3971
TAX NOTES INTERNATIONAL WEEKLY NEWS. (TAX NOTES INTERNATIONAL WEEKLY NEWS : TAX NEWS FROM AROUND THE GLOBE.). [Tax notes int. wkly. news]. **Added/Corp** Tax Analysts (Firm : U.S.). **VFOAT** Weekly News. Vol. 1, No. 1 Sept. 2 (1991)-. Periodical. English. wk. $149.00. Tax Analysts, 6830 North Fairfax Drive, Arlington VA 22213. **Tel** (703)533-4400, (800)955-3444. **LC** K4471.2; .T37. **DD** 343.05/2605; 342.352605.

CN/0821-0764
TAX PLANNING CHECKLIST. Added/Corp Coopers & Lybrand (Firm). (1978)-. English (French). an (Fall). Free. Currie Coopers and Lybrand, 145 King Street West, 24th Floor, Toronto Ontario M5H 1V8 Canada. **Tel** (416)869-1130. **DD** 343.7105/23. **Circ:** 25,000 (ctrl).
Desc: Checklist of various Canadian income tax tips and traps for individuals and corporations.

US/0279-7046
TAX PREPARERS LIABILITY SERVICE. [Tax prep. liabil. serv.]. (198?)-. Periodical. English. mo. $150.00. Research Institute of America, 117 East Stevens Avenue, Valhalla NY 10595. **Tel** (800)431-9025. **ED** James E. Cheeks. **[CCC].**
Desc: Protects against federal, state, and civil liability.

NZ/0110-0246
TAX REPORTS, NEW ZEALAND. Added/Corp New Zealand. Privy Council. Judicial Committee. New Zealand. Court of Appeal. New Zealand. Supreme Court. **VFOAT** Butterworths Taxation Service. Vol. 1 (1975)-. Periodical. English. ir. Butterworth Ltd. / New Zealand, 33 35 Cumberland Place, Wellington New Zealand. **DD** 343.93104/02642. **[CCC]. *Formed by the union of*** *Decisions - New Zealand Taxation Board of Review* ***and*** *Australasian Tax Reports.*
Desc: Authentic reports of tax cases decided by Judicial Committee of the Privy Council, Court of Appeal, Supreme Court and the official reports of the taxation review authorities.

US/0742-888X
TAX SHELTER ANALYST. Vol. 1, No. 1 (Jan. 1984)-. Periodical. English. mo. $144.00. Tax Shelter Analyst, 10076 Boca Entrada Boulevard, Boca Raton FL 33433-5897. **Tel** (407)483-2600. **ED** Mark M Ford. **LC** KF6415.A15; T38. **DD** 343.7305/23; 347.303523.

US/0161-178X
TAXATION FOR LAWYERS. [Tax. lawyers]. **Added/Corp** Tax Research Group (U.S.). Vol. 1 (July/Aug. 1972)-. Periodical. English. bm (6 issues). $115.98 US and Canada; $186.95 other. Warren Gorham & Lamont Inc., Park Square Building, 31 St. James Avenue, Boston MA 02116-4112. **Tel** (617)423-2020, (800)950-1207, FAX (617)423-2026. **LC** K24; .A95. **DD** 343/.73/0405. **[CCC].** available on microfilm and microfiche from University Microfilms International (UMI).
Desc: Designed to help the lawyer in general practice, develop and maintain up-to-date tax awareness in legal matters that affect his everyday practice.

Ind/Abst Account. Tax Datab. (1974-); Account. Art.; Curr. Law Index (1980-); Fed. Tax Artic.; Leg. Resour. Index (1980-); LegalTrac (1980-).

II
TAXATION LAW REPORTS, THE. Vol. 1 (Apr. 1971)-. English. mo. $115.00. All India Reporter Ltd, Medows HS Nagindas/Master Road, Bombay 400 023 India. **(Subscription address:** Prints India, 11 Darya Ganj, New Delhi 110002 India.**)**

US/0040-0203
TAXES INTERPRETED. **Added/Corp** Alexander Hamilton Institute (U.S.) Phillips Publishing, Inc. (July 16, 1962)-. Periodical. English. Twenty-six times a year. $147.00 (one year), $264.00 (two years). Gersten Savage Kaplowitz Sime, 575 Lexington Avenue, New York NY 10022. **Tel** (212)752-9700. **ED** Michael Savage. **DD** 343.7304/05; 347.303405. Index Available, published separately, free-automatically sent. ***Absorbed*** *Tax Barometer, 0039-9981.*

AT
TAXPAYER: ANNUAL TAXATION SUMMARY. **See** Public Administration-Public Finance and Taxation.

BR
TAYA YEI YA SA SAUNG. Burmese (Burmese). Taya Yon-Chok, Chief Court, Yankonmyo Burma.

UK
TEACHER'S LEGAL GUIDE. **See** Education-Teaching and Curriculum.

US/0195-4857
TECHNICAL SERVICES LAW LIBRARIAN. **See** Library and Information Sciences.

IS
TEL AVIV UNIVERSITY STUDIES IN LAW. **Main/Corp** Universitat Tel-Aviv. Fakultah Le-Mishpatim. Vol. 1 (1975)-. English. an. Price varies. Tel Aviv University, Faculty of Law, PO Box 39296, Tel Aviv 69978 Israel. **Tel** 011 972 3 420361. **ED** Nili Cohen. **LC** K24; .E4. **DD** 340/.095694. **Ad Acc.**
Ind/Abst Index Foreign Leg. Per.

CN/0822-451X
TELE-C.L.E.F. ***Title Change.*** [Tele-C.L.E.F.]. **Added/Corp** Centre de Reference de la Documentation Juridique de Langue Francaise en Matiere de "Common Law". No 1 (Jan. 1983)-(19??). Periodical. French. qt. Centre de Reference de la Documentation Juridique de Langue Francaise en Matiere de Common Law, 161 Laurier Avenue West/5th Floor, Ottawa Ontario K1P 5J2 Canada. **Tel** (613)236-9766. **ED** Chantal Lacasse. **DD** 340.5/7/0971. **Bk Rev. Ad Acc. Circ:** 1,000. ***Continued by*** *La CLEF.*
Desc: A publication on common law in Canada.

UK
TELLING AND DUXBURY : PLANNING LAW AND PROCEDURE. English. an. Butterworth & Co. Ltd. / Kent, England, Borough Green, Sevenoaks Kent TN15 8PH England. **Tel** 011 44 732-884567, FAX 011 44 732-885996.
Desc: Includes all relevant case law and the effect of the increasing EC and governmental influence brought to bear upon planning law.

IT
TEMI ROMANA. Italian. Three times a year. L50000.00. Tipogr Tappini Editrice, Via Morandi 19, 06012 Citta Castello PG Italy. **Tel** 011 39 75 8558194.

FR
TEMOIGNAGES ET DOSSIER. French. qt. 50.00F. Freres des Hommes, 45 Bis Rue de la Glaciere, 75013 Paris France. **Tel** 011 33 43251818.

US/0899-8086
TEMPLE LAW REVIEW. [Temple law rev.]. Vol. 61, No. 1 (Spring 1988)-. Periodical. English. qt. $22.00 US; $23.00 other. Temple Law Review, 1719 North Broad Street, Philadelphia PA 19122. **Tel** (215)787-7868. **ED** Thomas Doyle and John Larocca. **LC** K24; .E44. **Bk Rev. Ad Acc. Circ:** 2,000. Documents available from The Genuine Article. ***Continues*** *Temple Law Quarterly (Philadelphia, PA. : 1946), 0040-2974.*
Desc: Practitioner and student written scholarly articles on important, current cases and legal issues with a focus on conflicts between circuits and Pennsylvania law.
Ind/Abst Curr. Contents Soc. Behav. Sci.; Index Leg. Period.; Leg. Resour. Index; LegalTrac (1988-); Res. Alert [Select. Cov.]; Soc. Sci. Cit. Index [Select. Cov.].

US/0742-4329
TENNESSEE ATTORNEYS DIRECTORY. **Added/Corp** M. Lee Smith Publishers & Printers. (1982)-. Directory. English. an. $34.00. M. Lee Smith Publishers and Printers, 162 4th Avenue North, PO Box 198867, Nashville TN 37219. **Tel** (615)242-7395, (800)274-6774, FAX (615)256-6601. **ED** Joseph White. **LC** KF192.T4; T46. **DD** 340/.025/768. **Ad Acc. Circ:** 2,000 (ctrl).
Desc: A complete, accurate, and easy-to-use listing of all Tennessee attorneys and law firms.

US/0194-1259
TENNESSEE ATTORNEYS MEMO. (19??)-. Periodical. English. wk. $327.00 (firm); $297.00 (sole practioner). M. Lee Smith Publishers and Printers, 162 4th Avenue North, PO Box 198867, Nashville TN 37219. **Tel** (615)242-7395, (800)274-6774, FAX (615)256-6601.

US/0497-2325
TENNESSEE BAR JOURNAL. [Tenn. Bar j.]. **Main/Corp** Tennessee Bar Association. **Added/Corp** Tennessee Bar Association. Tennessee Bar Association. Journal. Vol. 1, (Feb. 1965)-. Periodical. English. Six times a year (Jan., Mar., May, July, Sept., Nov.). $35.00. Tennessee Bar Association, c/o Mary Tucker, 3622 West End Evenue, Nashville TN 37205. **Tel** (615)383-7421, (800)899-6993, FAX (615)297-8058. **DD** 340. **Ad Acc. Circ:** 6,200 (ctrl).
Desc: Publishes mostly substantive law articles, especially those specifically relating to Tennessee.
Ind/Abst Curr. Law Index (1980-); Fed. Tax Artic.; Index Leg. Period.; Law Office Inf. Serv.; Leg. Resour. Index (1980-); LegalTrac (1980-).

US/0747-7074
TENNESSEE CODE ANNOTATED ADVANCE ANNOTATION SERVICE. (TENNESSEE CODE ANNOTATED ADVANCE ANNOTATION SERVICE / PREPARED BY THE EDITORIAL STAFF OF THE PUBLISHER.). **Added/Corp** Tennessee. Laws, etc. (Code : 1956). Michie Company. **VFOAT** Advance Annotation Service. Vol. 1, No. 1 (Dec. 1981)-. Periodical. English. ir. $37.50. Michie Company, PO Box 7587, Charlottesville VA 22906-7587. **Tel** (804)972-7600, (800)542-0957, FAX (800)643-1280.
Desc: Annotations to Tennessee and federal cases.

US/1042-3168
TENNESSEE ENVIRONMENTAL LAW LETTER. [Tenn. environ. law lett.]. (February 1989)-. Periodical. English. mo. $177.00 plus tax. M. Lee Smith Publishers and Printers, 162 4th Avenue North, PO Box 198867, Nashville TN 37219. **Tel** (615)242-7395, (800)274-6774, FAX (615)256-6601. **ED** Andrew Goddard and Scott Thomas, (address) Bass, Berry and Sims, Suite 2700, First American Center, Nashville, TN 37238, (phone) 615-742-6224. **DD** 344.
Desc: Newsletter reporting the latest state specific environmental law developments that affect companies in that state.

US
TENNESSEE JUDICIAL NEWSLETTER. **Added/Corp** University of Tennessee, Knoxville. Public Law Institute. University of Tennessee, Knoxville. College of Law. **VFOAT** Judicial Newsletter. Vol. 11, No. 1 (1984)-. Newsletter. English. qt. $24.00 (individuals), $19.00 (per person, groups of 50 or more), $14.00 (per person, groups of 100 or more). Public Law Institute, 1505 West Cumberland Avenue, Knoxville TN 37916. **Tel** (615)974-6691. **ED** Eric J Morrison. **LC** KFT562.A15; J8. **DD** 345.768/05/05; 347.6805505. Index available. **Ad Acc. Circ:** 450. ***Continues*** *Judicial Newsletter / University of Tennessee (Knoxville). College of Law, 0163-2078.*
Desc: Features articles on substantive trends in Tennessee law as well as summaries of recent state and federal decisions.

US/1059-5082
TENNESSEE LAW ENFORCEMENT BULLETIN. **See** Law-Law Enforcement and Criminology.

US/0040-3288
TENNESSEE LAW REVIEW. [Tenn. law rev.]. Vol. 1 (Nov. 1922)-. Academic Scholarly Publication. English. qt. $20.00 US and Canada; $22.00 other. Tennessee Law Review Association Inc, 1505 W Cumberland Avenue, Knoxville TN 37916. **Tel** (615)974-4464. **LC** K24; .E5. **DD** 349.768. Index available. cum. index. **Bk Rev. Ad Acc. Circ:** 1,500.
Desc: Scholarly journal analyzing decisions and statutes of interest to the region and the nation.
Ind/Abst Curr. Law Index (1980-); Fed. Tax Artic.; Index Leg. Period.; Leg. Resour. Index (1980-); LegalTrac (1980-).

US
TENNESSEE LEGISLATIVE RECORD. **Added/Corp** Tennessee. General Assembly. Tennessee. Office of Legislative Services. (1955)-. Periodical. English. ir (during the legislative session). Tennessee Legislative Record, G 3 State Capitol, Nashville TN 37219. **Tel** (615)741-3511. **Circ:** 525 (ctrl).
Desc: Abstracts of bills, joint resolutions and resolutions in numerical order with sponsors, companion bill numbers were applicable, and latest disposition at time of publication.

US/0164-4130
TENNESSEE LEGISLATIVE RESEARCHER. **Added/Corp** Research Group, Inc. (Charlottesville, Va.). (March 1974)-. Periodical. English. The Research Group Inc, PO Box 7187, Charlottesville VA 22906. **LC** KFT7; .T46. **DD** 348.768/046.

●US
TENNESSEE PUBLIC ACTS : SUMMARIES OF INTEREST TO MUNICIPAL OFFICIALS. **Added/Corp** University of Tennessee (System). Municipal Technical Advisory Service. Tennessee Municipal League. **VFOAT** Summaries of Interest to Municipal Officials. (1992)-. English. **LC** KFT38; .O87. **DD** 348.768/023; 347.680823. ***Continues*** *Summary of ... Public Acts of Interest to Tennessee Officials.*

US/1059-5090
TENNESSEE REAL ESTATE LAW LETTER. [Tenn. real estate law lett.]. **Added/Corp** M. Lee Smith Publishers & Printers. **VFOAT** Real Estate Law Letter. Vol. 1, No. 1, Sept. (1983)-. Periodical. English. mo. $92.00 plus tax. M. Lee Smith Publishers and Printers, 162 4th Avenue North, PO Box 198867, Nashville TN 37219. **Tel** (615)242-7395, (800)274-6774, FAX (615)256-6601. **ED** C. Dewees Berry, (address) Bass, Berry and Sims, 2700 First American Center, Nashville, TN 37238, (phone) 615-742-6200. **LC** KFT112.A59; T46. **DD** 346.76804/3; 347.680643.
Desc: Monthly issues include analysis of real property appellate court decisions, statutes, and administrative rulings. Also included are summaries of new federal decisions, statutes, and rules.

US/0163-2604
TENNESSEE RESEARCHER (CHARLOTTESVILLE), THE. (THE TENNESSEE RESEARCHER.). Periodical. English. mo. $66.00. Research Group Inc, PO Box 7187, Charlottesville VA 22906. **LC** KFT57; .T44. **DD** 348.768/046; 347.680846.

IT
TESTO UNICO CODICE PENALE DELL IMPRESA. (19??)-. Periodical. Italian. tq. IPSOA Editore SRL, Casella Postale 12055, Mastrangelo, 20120 Milan Italy. **Tel** 011 39 2 82476248. Index available (Included).

IT
TESTO UNICO IMPOSTE DIRETTE. (19??)-. Periodical. Italian. ir. L316.800. IPSOA Editore SRL, Casella Postale 12055, Mastrangelo, 20120 Milan Italy. **Tel** 011 39 2 82476248. cum. index. **Ad Acc. Pr Rev. Circ:** 12,000 (ctrl). available on CD-ROM.
Desc: All Italian law-taxation on IRPEF-IRPEG-ILOR since 1988.

IT
TESTO UNICO LEGISLAZIONE PENALE TRIBUTARIA. (19??)-. Periodical. Italian. qt. IPSOA Editore SRL, Casella Postale 12055, Mastrangelo, 20120 Milan Italy. **Tel** 011 39 2 82476248. Index available (Included).

US/0040-4187
TEXAS BAR JOURNAL. [Texas bar j.]. Vol. 1 (Jan. 1938)-. Periodical. English. Eleven times a year (not Aug.). $12.00 (one year). Texas Bar Journal, Box 12487 Capitol Station, Austin TX 78711. **Tel** (512)463-1522, FAX (512)463-1475. **ED** Kelley Jones, Melinda Smith. **LC** K24; .E9. **DD** 340/.09764. Index available. **Bk Rev. Ad Acc. Circ:** 53,000 (ctrl). available on microfilm and microfiche from University Microfilms International (UMI).
Desc: News of the State Bar of Texas, Texas judiciary, and attorneys. Features on interesting Texan lawyers, issues facing the legal profession. Legal articles, humor column, obituaries of state bar members.
Ind/Abst Bowne Dig. Corp. Sec. Lawyers; Curr. Law Index (1980-); Fed. Tax Artic.; Index Leg. Period.; Law Office Inf. Serv.; Leg. Resour. Index (1980-); LegalTrac (1980-).

US/0270-529X
TEXAS BRIEFCASE SHEPARD'S. **Added/Corp** Shepard's Citations, Inc. Shepard's, Inc. of Colorado Springs. **VFOAT** Shepard's Texas Briefcase Citations. (19??)-. Periodical. English. qt. $112.00. Shepards McGraw-Hill Inc, 555 Middle Creek Parkway, PO Box 35300, Colorado Springs CO 80935-3530. **Tel** (719)488-3000, FAX (800)525-0053. **LC** KFT1259; .T47. **DD** 348.764/047; 347.640847.

US/0266-0814
TEXAS EVIDENCE REPORTER. Vol. 1, No. 1 (May 1984)-. English. bm. $72.00. Butterworth Heinemann / Woburn, MA, 225 Wildwood Avenue, Unit B, Woburn MA 01801. **Tel** (800)366-2665, FAX (617)928-2620, telex 880052. **ED** Gilbert T Adams Jr and Richard J Clarkson. **LC** KFT1740.A15; T49. **DD** 347.764/06/05; 347.6407605. Index available. cum. index. **Circ:** 400.
Desc: Digest of Texas evidence decisions with feature articles and reports on the Texas legal community.

US/0266-0806
TEXAS HEALTH LAW REPORTER. ***Ceased.*** [Tex. health law report.]. **Added/Corp** Butterworth Legal Publishers (Austin, Tex.). Vol. 1, No. 1 (Apr. 1984)-Vol. 10, No. 3. Periodical. English. bm. Butterworth Heinemann / Woburn, MA, 225 Wildwood Avenue, Unit B, Woburn MA 01801. **Tel** (800)366-2665, FAX (617)928-2620, telex 880052. **ED** David M Davis. **LC**

KFT1560.A15; T49. **DD** 344.764/041/05; 347.64044105. Index available. cum. index. **Circ:** 200.
Desc: Digests of Texas Health Law court decisions, feature articles and reportage on Texas Legal Community.

US/0264-6307
TEXAS INSURANCE LAW REPORTER. [Tex. insur. law report.]. Vol. 1, No. 1 (June 1983)-. Periodical. English. an. $84.00. Butterworth Heinemann / Woburn, MA, 225 Wildwood Avenue, Unit B, Woburn MA 01801. **Tel** (800)366-2665, FAX (617)928-2620, telex 880052. **ED** Michael R Knox and Robert O Lamb. **LC** KFT1385.A15; T49. **DD** 346.764/086/05; 347.64068605. Index available. cum. index. **Circ:** 400.
Desc: Feature articles and digests of Texas Appellate Court cases on insurance issues. Contains updates on cases previously reported.

●US/1058-5427
TEXAS JOURNAL OF WOMEN AND THE LAW. **See** Women's Interests.

US
TEXAS JUDICIAL SYSTEM ANNUAL REPORT FISCAL YEAR. **See** Law-Abstracting, Bibliographies and Statistics.

US/0040-4411
TEXAS LAW REVIEW. [Tex. law rev.]. **Added/Corp** Texas Bar Association. Proceedings of the Annual Meeting. State Bar of Texas. Proceedings of the Annual Meeting. University of Texas. School of Law. Texas Law Review Association. Vol. 1 (Dec. 1922)-. Proceedings. English. Seven times a year. $32.00. University of Texas School of Law, 727 East 26th Street 2101, Austin TX 78705. **Tel** (512)471-1106. **ED** Eric J.R. Nichols. **LC** K24; .E93. **DD** 340. cum. index. **Pr Rev.** **Circ:** 2,100. available on microfilm and microfiche from University Microfilms International (UMI). Documents available from The Genuine Article, UMI Article Clearinghouse.
Desc: Articles, comments, notes and book reviews on current legal topics.
Ind/Abst ABC POL SCI; ABI/INFORM Glob. Ed.; ABI Inform Ondisc (Dec. 1976-); Arts Humanit. Citation Index [Select. Cov.]; Bowne Dig. Corp. Sec. Lawyers; Crim. Justice Abstr.; Curr. Contents Soc. Behav. Sci.; Curr. Law Index (1980-); Fed. Tax Artic.; Index Leg. Period.; Leg. Resour. Index (1980-); LegalTrac (1980-); Res. Alert [Full Cov.]; Sage Public Adm. Abstr. (?-?); Soc. Sci. Cit. Index [Full Cov.].

US/0267-8306
TEXAS LAWYER, THE. [Tex. lawyer]. **Added/Corp** Butterworth Legal Publishers. Vol. 1, No. 1 (April 3, 1985)-. Periodical. English. wk (except last two weeks in Dec.). $530.00 law firms with 21 or more lawyers, $180.00 other. American Lawyer Media, L.P., 600 3rd Avenue, New York NY 10016. **Tel** (212)973-2800. **(Subscription address:** Texas Lawyer, 400 South Record Street, Suite 1400, Dallas, TX 75202**)** **ED** Mark Obbie. **LC** K24; .E87. **DD** 349.764/05; 347.64005. **[CCC].** **Ad Acc.** **Circ:** 10,000. available on microfiche.
Desc: Digests of Texas appellate court decisions, feature articles and reportage on Texas legal community.

US/0731-9088
TEXAS LAWYER'S CIVIL DIGEST. **Added/Corp** State Bar of Texas. Vol. 19, No. 1 (Jan. 4, 1982)-. Periodical. English. Fifty times a year (Mon.). $35.00. State Bar of Texas Digest, PO Box 12487, Austin TX 78711. **Tel** (512)463-1522. **LC** KFT1257; .T454. **DD** 348.764/046; 347.640846. ***Continues*** *Texas Lawyer's Weekly Digest, 0098-8987.*

US
TEXAS LEGAL DIRECTORY. (19??)-. English. an (Oct.). $40.00. Legal Directories Publishing Company, 9111 Garland Road, PO Box 189000, Dallas TX 75218. **Tel** (214)321-3238, 800 447-5375. **LC** KF192.T45; T43. **DD** 340/.025/764.

US
TEXAS OFFICIAL FEES. English. Hart Graphics Inc, PO Box 968, Austin TX 78767. **LC** KFT1745.Z9; T49. **DD** 347.764/077.

US/0264-4770
TEXAS PERSONAL INJURY LAW REPORTER. [Tex. pers. inj. law report.]. Vol. 1, No. 1 (May 1983)-. Periodical. English. an. $84.00. Butterworth Heinemann / Woburn, MA, 225 Wildwood Avenue, Unit B, Woburn MA 01801. **Tel** (800)366-2665, FAX (617)928-2620, telex 880052. **ED** Frank R Southers. **LC** KFT1397.P3; A137. **DD** 346.76403/23; 347.6406323. Index available. cum. index. **Circ:** 400.
Desc: Feature articles and digests of Texas Appellate Court decisions on personal injury issues.

US/0267-8896
TEXAS REAL ESTATE LAW REPORTER. [Tex. real estate law report.]. **VFOAT** Reporter. Vol. 1, No. 1 (June 1985)-. Periodical. English. bm. $84.00. Butterworth Heinemann / Woburn, MA, 225 Wildwood Avenue, Unit B, Woburn MA 01801. **Tel** (800)366-2665, FAX (617)928-2620, telex 880052. **ED** Charles J Jacobus. Index available. cum. index. **Circ:** 600.
Desc: Digest of Texas real estate decisions with feature articles and reports on the Texas legal community.

US/0882-021X
TEXAS SCHOOL ADMINISTRATOR'S LEGAL DIGEST. [Tex. sch. adm. leg. dig.]. **VFOAT** Legal Digest. (1984)-. Periodical. English. Ten times a year (Except July & Dec.). $85.00. Texas School Administrator's Legal Digest, PO Box 13855 NT Station, Denton TX 76203-3855. **Tel** (817)382-7212, FAX (817)382-7212. **ED** Jackie Lain (editor's address: PO Box 2156, Austin, TX 78768-2156, phone: (512)454-6864). **DD** 344. Index Bound in First Issue. cum. index. **Circ:** 1,000.
Desc: Designed to keep administrators, board members and school attorneys abreast of legal developments in the field of school law.

US/0362-6334
TEXAS SCHOOL LAW BULLETIN. **Main/Corp** Texas. **VFOAT** Texas Public School Law Bulletin. (1976)-. Bulletin. English. be. Price varies per volume. Texas Education Agency, Publications Distribution, 1701 North Congress Avenue, Austin TX 78701-1494. **Tel** (512)463-9734, (512)463-9000. **DD** 344/.764/071. Each issue contains an index to its own contents (no volume index)--loose.

US/0275-4444
TEXAS SCHOOL LAW NEWS (AUSTIN, TEX. : 1980). (TEXAS SCHOOL LAW NEWS.). Vol. 1, No. 1 (Mar. 16, 1980)-. Periodical. English. Eleven times a year. $98.00. Texas School Law News, 9600 Great Hills Trail, Suite 300, Austin TX 78759. **Tel** (512)345-8928. **ED** Eric Schulze. **Circ:** 850 (ctrl). ***Continues*** *Texas School Law News, 0275-4444.*
Desc: Latest developments on legal issues and public education in Texas.

US/0492-973X
TEXAS SUPREME COURT JOURNAL, THE. **Main/Corp** Texas. Supreme Court. V. 1- Sept. 14, 1957-. English. $54.86. Box 12132 Capitol Station, Austin TX 78711. **LC** KFT1245; .A34. **DD** 348.764/044. ***Supersedes*** *Texas Supreme Court Reporter.*

US/0564-6197
TEXAS TECH LAW REVIEW. [Tex. tech law rev.]. **VFOAT** Law Review. Vol. 1, No. 1 (Fall 1969)-. Periodical. English. qt. $32.00. Texas Tech Law Review, Texas Tech School of Law, Lubbock TX 79409-0004. **Tel** (806)742-3789. **ED** Gary Sanders. **LC** K24; .E95. **DD** 340/.05. Index available in last issue of volume--attached. cum. index. **Ad Acc.** **Circ:** 1,400.
Desc: Concentrates generally on Texas related articles. Publishes the 'Fifth Circuit Symposium' which is professionally authored survey of decisions in each area of law during the preceding year.
Ind/Abst Bowne Dig. Corp. Sec. Lawyers; Curr. Law Index (1980-); Index Leg. Period.; Leg. Resour. Index (1980-); LegalTrac (1980-).

FR
TEXTES D'INTERET GENERAL. **Main/Corp** France. **Added/Corp** France. Direction des Journaux Officiels. France. Journal Officiel. (19??)-. French. Twenty-six times a year. 304.00F France; 835.00F other. Direction des Journaux Officiels, 26 rue Desaix, 75727 Paris Cedex 15 France. **Tel** 011 33 1 40587500. **DD** 340/.0944.

US
THOMAS M. COOLEY LAW REVIEW. **Added/Corp** Thomas M. Cooley Law School. Vol. 8, No. 1 (Hilary Term 1991)-. Periodical. English. Three times a year. $20.00. Thomas Cooley Law School, 217 South Capital Avenue, PO Box 13038, Lansing MI 48901. **Tel** (517)371-5140 ext. 535, FAX (517)334-5748. **ED** William Durr. ***Continues*** *Cooley Law Review, 0733-3501.*
Ind/Abst Index Leg. Period.

US/0749-1646
THURGOOD MARSHALL LAW REVIEW. [Thurgood Marshall law rev.]. **VFOAT** Law Review. Vol. 7, No. 1 (Fall 1981)-. Periodical. English. sa. $9.00. Thurgood Marshall Law Review, Business Manager, 3100 Cleburne Avenue, Box 45, Houston TX 77004. **Tel** (713)527-7011. **LC** K24; .E88. **DD** 340/.05. **Bk Rev.** **Ad Acc.** available on microfilm and microfiche from University Microfilms International (UMI). ***Continues*** *Texas Southern University Law Review, 0092-3559.*
Ind/Abst Bowne Dig. Corp. Sec. Lawyers; Fed. Tax Artic.; Index Leg. Period.; Leg. Resour. Index; LegalTrac (1980-).

SW
TIDSKRIFT FOR RATTSSOCIOLOGI. **VFOAT** Rattssociologi. Vol. 1 1983/84 No. 1-. Periodical. Swedish (English). qt. Kr140.00 Sweden; $30.00, $50.00 (airmail) US. Tidskrift for Rattssociologi, Bredgatan 4, S-222 21 Lund Sweden. **Tel** 046-10 88 10. **ED** Antionette Hetzler. **LC** K24; .I29. **DD** 340/.115/05. Index available. cum. index. **Bk Rev.** **Ad Acc.** **Circ:** 300.
Desc: Publishes articles of theoretical and empirical interest to the sociology of law.

FI/0040-6953
TIDSKRIFT (SUOMEN LAINOPILLINEN YHDISTYS). (TIDSKRIFT / UTGIVEN AV JURIDISKA FORENINGEN I FINLAND.). (18??)-. Periodical. Danish (English and Swedish). Juridiska Foreningen i, Helsinki 13 Finland. **LC** K24; .I27.
Ind/Abst Selec. Coop. Index Manage. Period.

NO/0040-7143
TIDSSKRIFT FOR RETTSVIDENSKAP. [Tidsskr. rettsvidensk.]. **Added/Corp** Stangske Stiftelse (Oslo, Norway) Norske Sakfrerforening. Vol. 1 (1888)-. Periodical. Norwegian. Five times a year. Kr465.00, $89.00. Scandinavian University Press, PO Box 2959 Toeyen, N 0608 Oslo 6 Norway. **Tel** 011 47 2 2575400, FAX 011 47 2 2575353, telex 71896 UROR N. **(Subscription address:** Scandinavian University Press, 200 Meacham Ave., Elmont NY 11003.**)** **ED** Birger Stuevold Lassen and Magnus Aarbakke. **LC** K24; .I3. **Bk Rev.** **Ad Acc.** **Circ:** 2,300.
Desc: Scientific journal of law and legal matters.
Ind/Abst Am. Hist. Life (1969-1974).

BE/0771-0704
TIJDSCHRIFT RECHTSDOCUMENTATIE. [Tijdsch. rechtsdoc.]. (1980)-. Periodical. Dutch. Ten times a year. 6150F. Kluwer Edn Juridiques Belgique, Blvd E Bockstael 230, 1020 Brussels Belguim. **Tel** 011 32 2 7232111. **ED** R. de Corte. **Bk Rev.** **Ad Acc.** **Circ:** 2,200 (ctrl).
Desc: Reference review that informs every important change in law last month.

NA
TIJDSCHRIFT VOOR ANTILLIAANS RECHT, JUSTICIA / UITGEVER STICHTING TIJDSCHRIFT VOOR ANTILLIAANS RECHT, JUSTICIA. Periodical. Dutch (English and Spanish). qt. Fl75.00 Netherlands; $45.00 US. Stichting Tijdschrift voor Antilliaans Recht, Jan Noorduynweg 111, Curacao Netherlands Antilles. **Tel** 84422, FAX 85465. **LC** K24; .I366. Index available. **Bk Rev.** **Ad Acc.** **Circ:** 600. ***Formed by the union of*** *Tijdschrift voor Antilliaans Recht and Justicia (Oranjestad, Aruba).*
Desc: Contains articles on jurisprudence, legislation and other law-related subjects.
Ind/Abst Index Foreign Leg. Per.

NE/0167-1359
TIJDSCHRIFT VOOR ARBITRAGE. [Tijdschr. arbitr.]. (1980)-. Periodical. Dutch. bm (6 issues). Fl91.50. Kluwer BV, Postbus 23, 7400 GA Deventer Netherlands. **Tel** 011 31 5700 33155, 011 31 5700 48999, FAX 011 31 5700 11504, telex 42829. **Bk Rev.** **Ad Acc.** **Circ:** 900.

BE/0040-7437
TIJDSCHRIFT VOOR BESTUURSWETENCHAPPEN EN PUBLEKRECHT. [Tijdschr. Bestuurswet. Publiek Recht]. (1951)-. Periodical. Dutch (English). Twelve times a year. $3000.00F EEC Countries; $3500.00F other. Tijdschrift Voor Bestuursweten, G Mercatorlaan 28, B 1780 Wenmel Belgium. **Tel** 011 32 2 2694109, FAX 011 32 2 2701319. **ED** T. B. P. C/O P. Berckx, (phone: (011) 32 2 2694109). **UDC** 501. Index Available Received separately--bound from publisher. **Bk Rev.** **Ad Acc**, **Adv Mgr:** P. Berckx, **Tel** 011 32 2 2694109. **Circ:** 2,000 (ctrl). available on an online database, CD-ROM, magnetic tape, and microfilm from University Microfilms International (UMI). ***Continues*** *Tijdschrift Voor Bestuurswetenschappen, 0773-6401.*

NE/0040-7585
TIJDSCHRIFT VOOR RECHTSGESCHIEDENIS. (TIJDSCHRIFT VOOR RECHTSGESCHIEDENIS. REVUE D'HISTOIRE DU DROIT. THE LEGAL HISTORY REVIEW.). [Tijdschr. rechtsgeschiedenis]. **VFOAT** Revue d'Histoire du Droit; The Legal History Review; Legal History Review. Vol. 1 (1918)-. Academic Scholarly Publication. Dutch (French and English). qt. $352.00. Martinus Nijhoff Publishers, Subsidiary of Kluwer Academic Publishers, Koraalrood 50, 2718 SC Zoetermeer Netherlands. **Tel** 011 31 79 684400. **(Subscription address:** Kluwer Academic Publishers / Netherlands, PO Box 322, 3300 AH Dordrecht Netherlands.**)** **LC** K24; .I43. **DD** 340/.05. **CODEN** TIREES. **[CCC].** cum. index. **Pr Rev.** **Acid Free.** available on microfilm and microfiche from University Microfilms International (UMI).
Desc: Set up to stimulate in its own country a scholarly interest in the history of law, and to create at the same time an international center of co-operation in this field.
Ind/Abst Am. Hist. Life (1954-); Index Foreign Leg. Per. (1954-).

●NE/0926-874X
TILBURG FOREIGN LAW REVIEW. **Added/Corp** Katholieke Universiteit Brabant. Vol. 1, No. 1 (Sept. 1991)-. Periodical. English. Four times a year. $55.00 US: F65.00 others. Tilburg University, PO Box 90153, Room B 1008, 5000 Le Tilburg Netherlands. **Tel** 011 31 13 662121, FAX 011 31 13 663143. **ED** W. van der Wolf (phone: 013-662821). **LC** K24; .I46. **DD** 340/.2; 342. Index Bound in First Issue (Each year in Sept.). cum.

index. **Bk Rev**. **Ad Acc**. **Circ:** 2,000 (ctrl).
Desc: News and information on foreign and comparative law.

UK/0958-0441
TIMES LAW REPORTS. (1990)-. English. Twelve times a year. £110.00 UK; £115.00 others. T & T Clark, 59 George Street, Edinburgh EH2 2LQ England. **Tel** 011 44 31 2254703. **ED** Iain Sutherland. Index available. cum. index. **Circ:** 1,600 (ctrl).

US
TIMESHARING LAW REPORTER (WASHINGTON, D.C. : 1987). (TIMESHARING LAW REPORTER.). **Added/Corp** Land Development Institute. American Resort and Residential Development Association. National TimeSharing Council. (198?)-. Periodical. English. bm. $195.00 university libraries, state supreme courts & their libraries; $225.00 other. Land Development Institute Ltd, 1401 16th Street Northwest, Washington DC 20036. **Tel** (202)232-2144, FAX (202)232-4757. **ED** Stuart Marshall Bloch and William B Ingersoll. **LC** KF598.A15; T55. **DD** 346.7304/32; 347.306432. Index available. **Circ:** 250 (ctrl). ***Continues*** *Timesharing Law Reporter Briefs, 0738-6923.*
Desc: News on federal, state and local laws regarding timesharing and related court and administrative decisions.

US
TML LEGISLATIVE REPORT. Main/Corp Texas Municipal League. **VAT** Texas Municipal League Legislative Report. (19??)-. Periodical. English. ir. Texas Municipal League, 211 East Seventh, Suite 1020, Austin TX 78701. **Tel** (512)478-6601.

US/0887-7831
TOBACCO INDUSTRY LITIGATION REPORTER. [Tob. ind. litig. report.]. (Dec 13, 1985)-. Periodical. English. mo. $675.00. Andrews Publications Inc., 1646 West Chester Pike, PO Box 1000, Westtown PA 19395. **Tel** (610)399-6600, (800)345-1101, FAX (610)399-6610. **ED** Leonard E. B. Andrews. **LC** KF1297.T63; A498. **DD** 346.7303/82. cum. index. ctrl circ.
Desc: Provides nationwide coverage of litigation involving the tobacco industry. Follows new and ongoing suits involving personal injury and wrongful death allegedly associated with tobacco use, current state and federal tobacco related legislation, the ongoing issue of smoke in the workplace, public and privately funded studies on tobacco use and other current developments related to the tobacco industry.

PR
TOGA, LA. Spanish. Colegio de Abogados de Puerto Rico, Apartado 1900, San Juan Puerto Rico. **DD** 340/.06/27295.

IT
TOGA VERDE : DIRITTO E AMBIENTE. Italian. qt. L24000 (individuals), L48000 (institutions). Coop Energia Domani, Via XII Gennaio 9, 90141 Palermo Italy. **Tel** 011 39 91 329638.

UK
TOLLEY'S CAPITAL ALLOWANCES. English. an (November). £27.95. Tolley Publishing Company Ltd, Tolley House, 2 Addiscombe Road, Croydon, Surrey CR9 5AF United Kingdom. **Tel** 011 44 81 6869141, FAX 011 44 81 6863155, 011 44 81 7600588. **ED** Patrick Noakes and Alan Dolton.
Desc: Provides comprehensive and up-to-date coverage of the Capital Allowances Act 1990, as well as other related law. Includes provisions of the Finance Act 1991 regarding such matters as toll roads and the capital goods scheme for VAT. Includes full reference to relevant case law and Inland Revenue practices and concessions.

UK
TOLLEY'S CAPITAL GAINS TAX / DAVID G. YOUNG, DAVID R. HARRIS. Added/Corp Tolley Publishing Company. (1979)-. English. an (Sept.). £28.95. Tolley Publishing Company Ltd, Tolley House, 2 Addiscombe Road, Croydon, Surrey CR9 5AF United Kingdom. **Tel** 011 44 81 6869141, FAX 011 44 81 6863155, 011 44 81 7600588. **ED** Patrick Noakes and Stephen Savory. **LC** KD5550; .T64. **DD** 343.4105/245/05; 344.103524505.
Desc: Covers deduction of trading losses against chargeable gains and changes to private residence relief.

UK
TOLLEY'S CAPITAL TRANSFER TAX. 1979-80-. English. an. $16.78 US. Tolley Publishing Company Ltd, Tolley House, 2 Addiscombe Road, Croydon, Surrey CR9 5AF United Kingdom. **Tel** 011 44 81 6869141, FAX 011 44 81 6863155, 011 44 81 7600588. **ED** Jane Scollen. **LC** KD5560; .T64. **DD** 343.4105/3/05; 344.1035305.
Desc: A comprehensive guide to capital transfer tax since its introduction in 1974. The book covers relevant legislation, statements by the revenue and other official bodies in the United Kingdom.

UK/0305-893X
TOLLEY'S INCOME TAX. **See** Public Administration-Public Finance and Taxation.

UK
TOLLEY'S JOURNAL OF MEDIA LAW AND PRACTICE. VFOAT Media Law and Practice. Vol. 12, No. 3 (Oct. 1991)-. Periodical. English. Four times a year (Jan., Apr., July, Oct.). £100.00 UK; £108.00 others. Tolley Publishing Company Ltd, Tolley House, 2 Addiscombe Road, Croydon, Surrey CR9 5AF United Kingdom. **Tel** 011 44 81 6869141, FAX 011 44 81 6863155, 011 44 81 7600588. **LC** K10; .O882. **DD** 343/.099/05; 342.39905. ***Continues*** *Journal of Media Law and Practice, 0144-0373* ***and*** *Advertising & Marketing Law & Practice.*

UK
TOLLEY'S LAW DATA. English. ir. £7.95. Tolley Publishing Company Ltd, Tolley House, 2 Addiscombe Road, Croydon, Surrey CR9 5AF United Kingdom. **Tel** 011 44 81 6869141, FAX 011 44 81 6863155, 011 44 81 7600588.

UK
TOLLEY'S PRACTICAL VAT. English. mo. £95.00. Tolley Publishing Company Ltd, Tolley House, 2 Addiscombe Road, Croydon, Surrey CR9 5AF United Kingdom. **Tel** 011 44 81 6869141, FAX 011 44 81 6863155, 011 44 81 7600588.
Desc: Coverage on all VAT matters, including news, practical advice and articles by leading VAT experts. Contains summaries of VAT Tibunals, High Court judgments, appeals and European Court decisions with expert commentary.

UK
TOLLEY'S PROFESSIONAL NEGLIGENCE. VFOAT Professional Negligence. (199?)-. Periodical. English. qt. Tolley Publishing Company Ltd, Tolley House, 2 Addiscombe Road, Croydon, Surrey CR9 5AF United Kingdom. **Tel** 011 44 81 6869141, FAX 011 44 81 6863155, 011 44 81 7600588. **LC** KD1978.A13; P76. **DD** 346.4103/3; 344.10633. ***Continues*** *Professional Negligence, 0267-078X.*

UK
TOLLEY'S TAX CASES. Began with Vol. for 1976. English. an (March). £25.95. Tolley Publishing Company Ltd, Tolley House, 2 Addiscombe Road, Croydon, Surrey CR9 5AF United Kingdom. **Tel** 011 44 81 6869141, FAX 011 44 81 6863155, 011 44 81 7600588. **ED** Alan Dolton and Glyn Saunders. **LC** KD5356.3; .G77. **DD** 343.4104/02648; 344.103402648.
Desc: Contains concise reports of more than 2,500 tax cases relevant to UK legislation as of January 1991, cross-referenced to earlier case law. Gives a narrative and numerical summary of 1990 decisions and relevant Irish tax cases.

UK
TOLLEY'S TAXATION IN THE REPUBLIC OF IRELAND / BY NIGEL A.D. LAMBERT LLM, BARRISTER & ERIC L. HARVEY, FCA AITI. Added/Corp Tolley Publishing Company. (19??)-. English. an (September). £25.95. Tolley Publishing Company Ltd, Tolley House, 2 Addiscombe Road, Croydon, Surrey CR9 5AF United Kingdom. **Tel** 011 44 81 6869141, FAX 011 44 81 6863155, 011 44 81 7600588. **ED** Glyn Saunders and Stephen Savory. **LC** KDK1443; .T64. **DD** 343.41704/05; 344.1703405.
Desc: Covers all the important legislative provisions as well as double taxation relief agreements with the UK. Provides expert guidance and advice with Deloitte & Touche of Dublin as acting consultant. Contains a special chapter devoted to summarising over 180 Irish tax cases.

US
TOPICAL ISSUES IN PROCUREMENT SERIES. **See** Business-Purchasing.

UK/0265-9735
TOPICAL LAW. ***Ceased.*** **Added/Corp** Polytechnic of North London. Dept. of Law. (1974)-(1993). Periodical. English. sa. Department of Law, Polytechnic of North London, Ladbroke House, 62/66 Highbury Grove, London N5 2AD England. **ED** C. Champness. **LC** K24; .O68. **DD** 349.42/05; 344.2005. **Bk Rev**. **Circ:** 140.
Desc: A general law review, articles frequently explain the role of various law. Related offices, public and private.

CN
TOPICAL LAW REPORTS. (CANADIAN TRADE LAW REPORTER.). (1989)-. Periodical. English. mo. 335.00Can$ Canada. CCH Canadian Ltd., 6 Garamond Court, Don Mills Ontario M3C 1Z5 Canada. **Tel** (416)441-2992, FAX (416)441-3418. **ED** Vida Vukadinovic. **Bk Rev**. **Circ:** 600 (ctrl).
Desc: Coverage of the Legislation Governing Trade. Explains the Customs Act, Customs Tariff, Special Import Measures Act, Export and Import Permits Act, Access to Information Act, Canadian Charter to Rights and Freedoms, and all applicable regulations and guidelines pertaining to this legislation.

CN/0317-588X
TORONTO LEGAL DIRECTORY. VFOAT Toronto Legal Directory (Metropolitan List) and Tariff Guide. (1925)-. Periodical. English. an. $55.00 (Vol. 29). University of Toronto Press, 5201 Dufferin Street, Downsview Ontario M3H 5T8 Canada. **Tel** (416)667-7781, (416)667-7782, FAX (416)667-7803. **DD** 340/.025/713541.

US/0885-856X
TORT & INSURANCE LAW JOURNAL. [Tort insur. law j.]. **Added/Corp** American Bar Association. Tort and Insurance Practice Section. **VFOAT** Tort and Insurance Law Journal. Vol. 21, No. 1 (Fall 1985)-. Periodical. English. qt (4 issues). $23.00. American Bar Association, 750 North Lake Shore Drive, Chicago IL 60611. **Tel** (312)988-5522, (312)988-5241, FAX (312)988-5528, telex 270593. **LC** K6; .O75. **DD** 346.73/086/05; 347.3068605. available on microfilm and microfiche from University Microfilms International (UMI). ***Continues*** *Forum (Chicago, Ill.), 0015-8356.*
Ind/Abst Bowne Dig. Corp. Sec. Lawyers; Curr. Law Index (1980-); Index Leg. Period.; Ins. Period. Index; Leg. Resour. Index (1980-); LegalTrac (1985-).

US/0094-7849
TORT LAW LETTER, THE. No. 1- Sept. 1973-. English. mo. $10.00. Benchmark Publications, Box 487, Chapel Hill NC 27514. **LC** KF1287.8; .T67. **DD** 346/.73/0305.

US/0098-7611
TORTS. [Torts]. **Main/Corp** Bay Area Review Course, Inc. English. an. Bay Area Review Course Inc, 5900 Wilshire Boulevard, Los Angeles CA 90036. **LC** KF1250.Z9; B38. **DD** 346/.73/03.

US/8756-7326
TOURO LAW REVIEW. [Touro law rev.]. **Added/Corp** Touro College. School of Law. Vol. 1, No. 1 (Spring 1985)-. Periodical. English. tq. $21.00. Touro College, Fuchsberg Law Center, 300 Nassau Road, Huntington NY 11743. **Tel** (516)421-2244. **ED** Stacey Levin (editor's telephone: (516)421-2244 ext. 404). **LC** K24; .O73. **DD** 349.747/05; 347.47005. **Bk Rev**. ctrl circ.
Ind/Abst Curr. Law Index (1985-); Index Leg. Period.; Leg. Resour. Index (1985-); LegalTrac (1980-).

CN/0824-2801
TOUTE JUSTICE (OTTAWA, ONT.), EN. (EN TOUTE JUSTICE.). [En toute justice]. Vol. 1, No 1 (Winter 1983)-. Periodical. French (English). qt. 20.00Can$. Association Canadienne d'Assistance Juridique d'Information et de Recherche des Handicapes, C P 3553 Succursale C, Ottawa Ontario K1Y 4J7 Canada. **Tel** (613)230-8515. **ED** H Wierenga. **DD** 346.7101/3. **Bk Rev**. **Circ:** 500.
Desc: A journal of law and people with disabilities.
Ind/Abst Can. Legal Lit.

AT/0040-9995
TOWN-PLANNING AND LOCAL GOVERNMENT GUIDE, THE. **See** Housing and Urban Development.

AT/0818-044X
TRADE PRACTICES COMMISSION BULLETIN. [Trade Pract. Comm. bull.]. **Added/Corp** Australia. Trade Practices Commission. (1986)-. Bulletin. English. Six times a year. 50.00Aus$. Trade Practices Commission, PO Box 19, Belconnen ACT 2616 Australia. **Tel** 011 61 62 641166, FAX 011 61 62 642803 515093, telex 62526. **ED** Alana Woods. **DD** 343.940723. Index available. cum. index. **Circ:** 800.
Desc: Provides an comprehensive summary of trade practices law during the reporting period.

US/8756-1492
TRADE SECRET LAW REPORTER. [Trade secret law rep.]. Vol. 1, No. 1 (May 1985)-. Periodical. English. mo. $187.00. Law and Technology Press, PO Box 3280, Manhattan Beach CA 90266. **Tel** (310)372-1678. **LC** KF3197.A15; T73. **DD** 343.73/072; 347.30372. **[CCC].**
Ind/Abst Comput. Rev.

US/0893-3030
TRAFFIC LAW REPORTS. [Traffic law rep.]. Vol. 1, No. 1 (Jan. 1987)-. Periodical. English. mo. $115.00 US and Canada; $135.00 other. Knehans Miller Publications, PO Box 88, Warrensburg MO 64093. **Tel** (816)429-1102. **ED** Dane C Miller. **LC** KF2226.A3; T73. **DD** 343.7309/46/05; 347.30394605. Index available. cum. index.
Desc: In-depth summaries, often with verbatim excerpts, periodic professional articles, and thorough indexing by subject and jurisdiction of all federal and state appellate court decisions dealing with all aspects of traffic enforcement and administration.

FR
TRAITEMENTS, SOLDES ET INDEMNITES DES FONCTIONNAIRES A COMPTER DU ... / JOURNAL OFFICIEL DE LA REPUBLIQUE FRANCAISE. VFOAT Traitements des Fonctionnaires. French. 48F. Direction des Journaux Officiels, 26 rue Desaix, 75727 Paris Cedex 15 France. **Tel** 011 33 1 40587500. **LC** LAW . **DD** 342.44/0686; 344.402686.

US/0049-450X
TRANSPORTATION LAW JOURNAL, THE. [Transp. law j.]. Vol. 1 (Feb. 1969)-. Periodical. English. sa. $15.00 US; $20.00 other. University of

Denver Law School, 7039 East 18th Avenue, Foote Hall, Denver CO 80220. **Tel** (303)871-6223. **ED** Paul S Dempsey. **LC** K24; .R29. **DD** 343/.73/093. Index available. cum. index. **Bk Rev. Ad Acc. Circ:** 1,200. available on microfilm and microfiche from University Microfilms International (UMI).
Desc: Publishes articles on national and international regulatory issues for the legal scholar, practising lawyers and other transportation practitioners.
Ind/Abst Curr. Law Index (1980-); Index Leg. Period.; J. Plan. Lit.; Leg. Resour. Index (1980-); LegalTrac (1980-); PAIS Int. Print.

GW/0174-559X
TRANSPORTRECHT. [Transportrecht]. Periodical. German (German). bm. DM234.00 (add DM19.80 for postage) Germany; add DM22.50 postage other. Alfred Metzner Verlag, Zeppelinallee 43, POB 970148, W-6000 Frankfurt 1 Germany. **Tel** 011 49 69 793009 0. **LC** K24; .R287. **DD** 343.43/093/05; 344.3039305. ***Continues*** *Transport + Speditionsrecht.*

FR
TRAVAUX DE L'ASSOCIATION HENRI CAPITANT DES AMIS DE LA CULTURE JURIDIQUE FRANCAISE. Added/Corp Association Henri Capitant des Amis de la Culture Juridique Francaise. **VFOAT** Travaux de l'Association Henri Capitant. Vol. 14 (1961/62)-. Monographic series. French. an. Price varies per volume. Editions Economica, 49 rue Hericart, 75015 Paris France. **LC** K555; .T73. ***Continues*** *Travaux de l'Association Henri Capitant pour la Culture Juridique Francaise.*

US/0191-7684
TRAWICK'S FLORIDA PRACTICE AND PROCEDURE. VFOAT Florida Practice and Procedure. (1978)-. English. an. $59.95 subscribers, $64.95 other. Harrison Company Publishers, 3110 Crossing Park, PO Box 7500, Norcross GA 30091-7500. **Tel** (800)241-3561, (404)447-9150. **LC** KFF530; .T73. **DD** 347/.759/05. ***Continues*** *Florida Practice and Procedure, 0191-7676.*

●US/1062-5364
TRENDS IN HEALTH CARE, LAW & ETHICS. See Ethics.

US/0893-6773
TRENDS IN LAW LIBRARY MANAGEMENT AND TECHNOLOGY. See Library and Information Sciences.

US/0098-8995
TRENDS IN LEGAL SERVICES. English. mo. Editorial Services / Washington DC, 1523 L Street NW, Washington DC 20005. **LC** KF300.A1; T73. **DD** 340/.0973.

US/0041-2538
TRIAL. (TRIAL / THE AMERICAN TRIAL LAWYERS ASSOCIATION.). [Trial]. **Added/Corp** American Trial Lawyers Association. Public Affairs & Education Committee. American Trial Lawyers Association. National Committee on Public Affairs. American Trial Lawyers Association. Vol. 1, No. 1 (Dec. 1964)-. Periodical. English. mo. $48.00 (one year); $80.00 (two year). Association of Trial Lawyers of America, 1050 31st Street Northwest, Washington DC 20007. **Tel** (800)424-2725 ext. 307, FAX (202)298-6849. **ED** Betty Yeary. **LC** KF8911.A3; T73. **DD** 347.73/7; 347.3077. **[CCC].** Index available. cum. index. **Bk Rev. Ad Acc. Circ:** 73,000. available on microfilm and microfiche from University Microfilms International (UMI). Documents available from The Genuine Article, UMI Article Clearinghouse. ***Continues*** *PI & E Bulletin.*
Desc: Educational information on lawyers, policy and trial techniques for plaintiff's lawyers.
Ind/Abst Acad. Search (July 1993-); Arts Humanit. Citation Index [Select. Cov.]; Crim. Justice Abstr.; Crim. Justice Period. Index; Curr. Contents Soc. Behav. Sci.; Curr. Law Index (1980-); Expand. Acad. Index (1984-); Fed. Tax Artic.; Highw. Res. Abstr.; Index Leg. Period.; INFO-SOUTH Abstr.; Law Office Inf. Serv.; Leg. Inf. Manage. Index (19??-199?); Leg. Resour. Index (1980-); LegalTrac (1980-); Newsp. Period. Abstr. (1989-); Res. Alert [Select. Cov.]; Soc. Sci. Source (Jul. 1993-); Soc. Sci. Cit. Index [Select. Cov.]; Soc. Sci. Index; Soc. Sci. Index Fulltext (Oct. 1988-) [Full Txt.]; SportSearch.

US/0743-412X
TRIAL ADVOCATE QUARTERLY. [Trial advocate q.]. **Added/Corp** Florida Defense Lawyers Association. Vol. 1, No. 1 (Dec. 1981)-. Academic Scholarly Publication. English. Four times a year. $35.00. Fred B. Rothman & Company, 10368 West Centennial Road, Littleton CO 80127. **Tel** (800)457-1986, (303)979-5657, FAX (303)978-1457, telex 87669. **ED** Michael L. Richmond. **LC** KFF538.A1; T74. **DD** 347.759/07/05; 347.5907705. Index available (Free). cum. index. **Bk Rev. Pr Rev. Circ:** 1,700 (ctrl).
Desc: Scholarly articles and recent cases of interest to attorneys representing defendants in civil litigation, to judges, and to all concerned with the development of tort law.
Ind/Abst Curr. Law Index (1984-); Leg. Resour. Index (1984-); LegalTrac (1983-).

US/0564-2108
TRIAL AND TORT TRENDS. VFOAT Belli Seminar. English. an. **ED** M M Belli. **DD** 347.5. ***Continues in part*** *National Association of Claimants' Compensation Attorneys. Annual Convention.*
Desc: Partial proceedings of the National Convention of the National Association of Claimants Compensation Attorneys.

US/0732-5959
TRIAL BAR NEWS (SAN DIEGO, CALIF.). (TRIAL BAR NEWS / SAN DIEGO TRIAL LAWYERS ASSOCIATION.). [Trial bar news]. **Added/Corp** San Diego Trial Lawyers Association. Attorney Referral Service. **VFOAT** S.D.T.L.A. Trial Bar News; SDTLA Trial Bar News. (19??)-. Periodical. English. Ten times a year. $35.00. San Diego Trial Lawyers Association, 1305 7th Avenue, Suite 110, San Diego CA 92101. **Tel** (619)696-1166. **LC** KFC1025.A15; T74. **DD** 347.794/07; 347.94077.

US
TRIAL COURT REPORTER / OFFICE OF THE CHIEF ADMINISTRATIVE JUSTICE, THE TRIAL COURT, THE. English. Office of the Chief, Administrative Justice, 2 Center Plaza/9th Floor, Boston MA 02108. **Tel** (617)742-8383. **LC** KFM2915; .A88. **DD** 347.744/01/05; 347.4407105.

US/0160-7308
TRIAL DIPLOMACY JOURNAL. [Trial dipl. j.]. **Added/Corp** Court Practice Institute (U.S.). Vol. 1 (Spring 1978)-. Periodical. English. bm. $108.00 US; $132.00 other. John Wiley & Sons, Inc., 605 Third Avenue, New York NY 10158-0012. **Tel** (212)850-6000, (212)850-6645, FAX (212)850-6088, telex 12-7063. **(Subscription address:** John Wiley & Sons Inc / New Jersey, PO Box 2575, Secaucus NJ 07096-2575.**) ED** John F. Romano, Esq. and Rodney G. Romano, Esq. **LC** KF8911.A3; T74. **DD** 347/.73/705. **Bk Rev. Ad Acc. Circ:** 1,600. available on microfilm and microfiche from University Microfilms International (UMI).
Desc: Covers all aspects of trial practice- from preparation through summation including discussions of a broad variety of substansive legal issues.
Ind/Abst Crim. Justice Period. Index (-1989); Curr. Law Index (1980-); Leg. Resour. Index (1980-); LegalTrac (1980-).

US/0041-2546
TRIAL LAWYER'S GUIDE, THE. [Trial lawyer's guide]. (1957)-. English. qt. $140.00. Clark Boardman Callaghan, 155 Pfingsten Road, Deerfield IL 60015. **Tel** (800)323-8067. **ED** John Kennelly. **LC** K24.R46. **DD** 347.9. Index available. cum. index. available on microfilm and microfiche from University Microfilms International (UMI).
Desc: Contains practical articles on topics of interest to trial lawyers.
Ind/Abst Curr. Law Index (1980-); Index Leg. Period.; Leg. Resour. Index (1980-); LegalTrac (1980-).

US/0041-2554
TRIAL LAWYERS QUARTERLY. [Trial lawyers q.]. **Added/Corp** New York State Trial Lawyers Association. New York State Association of Trial Lawyers. Vol. 1 (Summer 1964)-. Periodical. English. Four times a year. $25.00. New York State Association of Trial Lawyers, 132 Nassau Street, Suite 200, New York NY 10038. **Tel** (212)349-5890. **LC** K24; .R48. **DD** 346/.747/032. available on microfilm and microfiche from University Microfilms International (UMI). ***Supersedes*** *Plaintiff's Advocate.*
Ind/Abst Index Leg. Period.; Leg. Resour. Index; LegalTrac (1980-).

US
TRIAL LAWYERS SECTION DIGEST. Added/Corp New York State Bar Association. Trial Lawyers Section. Periodical. English. qt. New York State Bar Association, One Elk Street, Albany NY 12207. **Tel** (518)463-3200. **LC** KFN5995.A1; T75. **DD** 347.747/07/05; 347.4707705. ***Continues*** *Trial Lawyers Section Newsletter, 0276-1009.*

US
TRIAL OF ACCIDENT CASES. (19??)-. English. sa. Matthew Bender & Company Inc., 1275 Broadway, Albany NY 12204. **Tel** (800)833-9844, (518)487-3000.

US/0887-4212
TRIAL TACTICS AND TECHNIQUES. ***Ceased.*** [Trial tactics tech. newsl.]. No. 1, May (1986)-?. Periodical. English. mo. John Wiley & Sons, Inc., 605 Third Avenue, New York NY 10158-0012. **Tel** (212)850-6000, (212)850-6645, FAX (212)850-6088, telex 12-7063. **(Subscription address:** John Wiley & Sons / England, Baffins Lane, Chichester, West Sussex PO19 1UD England.**) LC** KF8911.A3; T75. **DD** 347.73/7/05.

US/0747-1378
TRIAL TALK. (TRIAL TALK / COLORADO TRIAL LAWYERS ASSOCIATION.). [Trial talk]. **Main/Corp** Colorado Trial Lawyers Association. (19??)-. Periodical. English. mo. $24.00. Colorado Trial Lawyers Association, 1818 Sherman 370, Denver CO 80203-1158. **Tel** (303)831-1192. **ED** John Carroll. **LC** K24; .O448. **DD** 347.788/07/05; 347.8807705. **Ad Acc. Circ:** 1,500 (ctrl).
Desc: Articles of legal and medical interest of concern to trial attorneys in the fields of personal injury, commercial, criminal and domestic relations.

BL
TRIBUNA DA JUSTICA. SUPLEMENTO DE JURISPRUDENCIA. (19??)-. Periodical. Portuguese. wk. Hemeron Editora SA, Avenida Aclimacao No 226, CEP 01531, Sao Paulo Brazil. **LC** KHD72; .A243. **DD** 348.81/041/05; 348.1084105.

BL
TRIBUNA DO ADVOGADO. Added/Corp Ordem dos Advogados do Brasil. Conselho Seccional do Estado do Rio de Janeiro. (19??)-. Periodical. Portuguese. Twelve times a year. Ordem dos Advogados do Brasil, Avenida Marechal Camara 186-7 Andar, 20020 Rio de Janeiro Brazil. **Tel** 44 21 240-8852. **DD** 340/.06/2815.

BE
TRIBUNAUX CORRECTIONNELS, COURS D'APPEL, CONSEILS DE GUERRE ET COUR MILITAIRE. See Law-Abstracting, Bibliographies and Statistics.

DR
TRIBUTACION. Periodical. Spanish. qt. Departamento de Ingresos y Deuda Publica, Oficina Nacional de Presupuesto, Av Mexico Esq Leopoldo, Navarro 4To Piso, Santo Domingo Dominican Republic. **LC** K24; .R52. **DD** 343.804/05.

IO
TRISAKTI. Vol. 1- Jan. 1976-. Periodical. Indonesian. Kampus Kompleks Barat, Jalan Kiai Tapa Jakarta-Barat, Jakarta Indonesia. **LC** K24; .R58.

●CN/1188-7702
TRUDEL, NADEAU INFO. [Trudel Nadeau info]. **Added/Corp** Trudel, Nadeau, Lesage, Cleary, Lariviere et Associes, Avocats. (May 1992)-. Periodical. French. qt. Limited free distribution. Trudel, Nadeau, Lesage, Cleary, Lariviere et Associes Avocats, Bureau 2500, CP 993, Succursale Place du Parc, Montreal Quebec H2W 2N1 Canada. **DD** 344.714/01.

US
TRUST INDENTURE ACT OF 1939 RELEASE. Main/Corp United States. Securities and Exchange Commission. **Added/Corp** United States. Laws, Statutes, etc. Trust Indenture Act of 1939. (Jan. 23, 1940)-. English. ir. Securities and Exchange Commission / Washington, 450 Fifth Street NW, Washington DC 20549. **Tel** (202)272-3100.

US
TRUSTS. Main/Corp Bay Area Review Course, Inc. English. an. Bay Area Review Course Inc, 5900 Wilshire Boulevard, Los Angeles CA 90036. **LC** KF730.Z9; B35. **DD** 346/.73/059.

GW/0082-6731
TUBINGER RECHTSWISSENSCHAFTLICHE ABHANDLUNGEN. (1961)-. Monographic series. German. ir. Price varies per volume. JCB Mohr / Paul Siebeck, Postfach 2040, D 72010 Tuebingen Germany. **Tel** 011 49 7071 9230, FAX 011 49 7071 51104, telex 7/262872 mohr d.

US/0041-3992
TULANE LAW REVIEW. [Tulane law rev.]. **Added/Corp** Tulane Law Review Association. Tulane Law School. Vol. 4 (Dec. 1929)-. Periodical. English. Six times a year (Feb., Mar., May, June, Nov., Dec.). $35.00 US; $40.00 other. Tulane Law Review Association, Tulane University, Joseph Merrick Jones Hall, 6801 Freret Street, New Orleans LA 70118. **Tel** (504)865-5973. **ED** Thomas G. Macauley. **LC** K24; .U4. Index available. cum. index. **Bk Rev. Ad Acc. Circ:** 2,061. available on microfilm and microfiche from University Microfilms International (UMI). ***Continues*** *Southern Law Quarterly.*
Desc: Coverage of civil and comparative law.
Ind/Abst ABC POL SCI (19??-19??); Am. Bibliogr. Slavic East Europ. Stud.; Bowne Dig. Corp. Sec. Lawyers; Curr. Law Index (1980-); Fed. Tax Artic.; Index Leg. Period.; Leg. Resour. Index (1980-); LegalTrac (1980-).

US
TULANE LAW REVIEW. TEN YEAR INDEX VOLUMES 46-55. Added/Corp Tulane Law Review Association. Tulane University. School of Law. Vol. 4 (Dec. 1929)-. Periodical. English. ir. Tulane Law Review Association, Tulane University, Joseph Merrick Jones Hall, 6801 Freret Street, New Orleans LA 70118. **Tel** (504)865-5973. cum. index. ***Continues*** *Southern Law Quarterly.*

US
TULANE LAWYER. Added/Corp Tulane Law School. Vol. 1 (Spring 1979)-. Periodical. English. qt. $5.00. Tulane University School of Law, 6801 Freret Street, New Orleans LA 70118. **Tel** (504)865-5990. **ED**

Morris Ardoin. cum. index. **Bk Rev. Ad Acc. Pr Rev. Circ:** 7,000 (ctrl).
Desc: Magazine for alumni and friends of Tulane Law School with occasional articles of general interest.

US/0041-4050
TULSA LAW JOURNAL. [Tulsa law j.]. **Added/Corp** University of Tulsa. College of Law. University of Tulsa. School of Law. **VFOAT** University of Tulsa Law Journal. Vol. 1, No. 1 (Jan. 1964)-. Periodical. English. Four times a year. $23.00 US; $26.00 other. University of Tulsa / College of Law, 3120 East 4th Place, Tulsa OK 74104. **Tel** (918)631-2431, FAX (918)631-3556, telex 497543 INFOSVC TU TUL. (bound in third issue - $10.00). cum. index. **Ad Acc. Circ:** 650 (ctrl).
Ind/Abst Fed. Tax Artic.; Index Leg. Period.; Leg. Resour. Index (1980-); LegalTrac (1980-).

CH
TUNG WU FA LU HSUEH PAO. **VFOAT** Soochow Law Review. V. 1- ; 1976-. Periodical. Chinese (English). sa. N$500.00 Taiwan; $14.00 US. Tung Wu Ta Hsueh, 56 Kueiyang Street/Section 1, Taipei 100 Taiwan. **Tel** (02)8819471. (**Subscription address:** Library of Soochow University, Wai Shung Hsi, Shih Lin, Taipei Taiwan 111 Republic of China) **LC** K24; .U44. **Bk Rev. Circ:** 500 (ctrl).

FI/0355-2187
TUOMIOISTUIMISSA KASITELLYT RIKOS- , SIVIILI- JA HALLINTOOIKEUDELLISET ASIAT. See Law-Abstracting, Bibliographies and Statistics.

FI
TUOMIOISTUINTEN TUTKIMAT RIKOKSET. See Law-Abstracting, Bibliographies and Statistics.

IT
TUTTI GLI ATTI PARLAMENTARI. (19??)-. Italian. sw. L1485000. Libreria del Senato Repubblica, Via del Teatro Valle 37, 00186 Rome Italy. **Tel** 011 39 67062505.

SA
TYDSKRIF VIR DIE SUID-AFRIKAANSE REG. Added/Corp Randse Afrikaanse Universiteit. Fakulteit Regsgeleerdheid. **VFOAT** Journal of South African Law. (March 1976)-. Periodical. Afrikaans (English). Four times a year. R148.00. Juta Subscription Services, PO Box 14373, Kenwyn 7790 South Africa. **Tel** 011 27 21 7975101, FAX (021)761-5010, telex 523072 SA. **ED** J.C. Sonnekus. **LC** K24; .Y38. Index available. cum. index. **Bk Rev. Circ:** 1,100 (ctrl).
Desc: Journal containing articles on all subjects pertaining to South African law with the emphasis on articles regarding law practice in South Africa.
Ind/Abst Index Foreign Leg. Per.

SA/0258-252X
TYDSKRIF VIR REGSWETENSKAP. [Tydskr. regswet.]. Periodical. Afrikaans (summaries and/or abstracts in English). 20.00. Fakulteit van Regsgeleerdheid, Universiteit van die Oranje-Vrystaat, Postbus 339, Bloemfontein South Africa. **Tel** (051)70711. **ED** D C du Tort. **LC** K24; .Y4. **DD** 340/.0968. **Bk Rev. Ad Acc. Circ:** 2,000.
Desc: Devoted to original research in law, general juridical articles on law and practice, critical reviews, discussion of case law and legislation of South Africa.

US/0197-4564
U.C. DAVIS LAW REVIEW. [U.C. Davis law rev.]. **Main/Corp** University of California, Davis. School of Law. **VFOAT** University of California, Davis, Law Review. Vol. 13, (Winter 1979/80)-. Academic Scholarly Publication. English. Four times a year. $30.00. Regents of the University of California / Law, School of Law, Davis CA 95616. **Tel** (916)752-2551, FAX (916)752-4704. **ED** Alice Trujillo (phone: (916)752-2551). **LC** K3; .A42. **DD** 349.794/05. Index available. **Bk Rev**, (Qty: varies). **Ad Acc, Adv Mgr:** A. Trujillo. **Circ:** 700. available on microfiche from WESTLAW; available on microfilm from LEXIS; available on an online database from NEXIS. ***Continues*** *University of California, Davis, School of Law UCD Law Review.*
Desc: Scholarly legal journal with academic and professional articles dealing with contemporary legal issues.
Ind/Abst Bowne Dig. Corp. Sec. Lawyers; Crim. Justice Abstr.; Index Leg. Period.; Leg. Resour. Index; LegalTrac (1980-).

US/1055-0801
U.S. CONSTITUTION REVIEW, THE. [U. S. Const. rev.]. **Added/Corp** Institute for Constitutional Research. Vol. 1, No. 1 (Jan./Feb. 1991)-. Periodical. English. bm. $12.00. Institute for Constitutional Research, PO Box 2408, Monterey CA 93942. **DD** 342.

US/0742-1087
U.S. DISTRICT COURT FEDERAL FILINGS ALERT. ***Ceased.*** **VFOAT** Federal Filings Alert. **VAT** United States District Court Federal Filings Alert. Vol. 6, No. 1 (Jan. 14, 1980)-Ceased (1988). Periodical. English. wk. Want Publishing Company, 1511 K Street Northwest, Suite 635, Washington DC 20005. **Tel** (202)783-1887, FAX (202)393-5106. **ED** Robert S Want. **Circ:** 1,200. ***Continues*** *U.S. District Court Current Filings Alert.*
Desc: Reports on new cases in selected areas of the law filed in federal courts around the country.

US/0041-560X
U-T LAWYER, THE. Added/Corp Tennessee. University. College of Law. Vol. 1 (Fall 1962)-. Periodical. English. sa. University of Tennessee College of Law, 1505 West Cumberland Avenue, Knoxville TN 37916.

US/1062-7693
UCC BULLETIN. Added/Corp Pike and Fischer, Inc. Callaghan and Company. **VAT** Uniform Commercial Code Bulletin. No. 1 (Apr. 1991)-. Bulletin. English. mo. Clark Boardman Callaghan, 155 Pfingsten Road, Deerfield IL 60015. **Tel** (800)323-8067. ***Absorbed*** *Current Material Highlights for Uniform Commercial Code Reporting Service;* ***Continues*** *UCC Bulletin, 1062-7693.*

US/0041-5650
UCLA LAW REVIEW. [UCLA law rev.]. **Main/Corp** University of California, Los Angeles. School of Law. **Added/Corp** University of California, Los Angeles. School of Law. Law Review. **VFOAT** University of California Los Angeles Law Review. **VAT** University of California at Los Angeles Law Review. Vol. 1 (Dec. 1953)-. Academic Scholarly Publication. English. Six times a year. $30.00 US; $33.00 other. UCLA Law Review, 405 Hilgard Avenue, Los Angeles CA 90024. **Tel** (310)825-4929, FAX (310)206-6489. **LC** K25; .C152. **DD** 340.05. Index available in last issue of volume--attached. **Ad Acc, Adv Mgr:** Brian Hofstra. **Pr Rev. Circ:** 1,600. available on microfilm from Fred B. Rothman and Company; available on an online database from WESTLAW; and LEXIS. Documents available from The Genuine Article, UMI Article Clearinghouse. ***Supersedes*** *UCLA Intramural Law Review.*
Desc: A scholarly journal publishing work by law students, law faculty, and lawyers regarding issues of general interest in the law.
Ind/Abst ABI/INFORM Glob. Ed.; ABI Inform Ondisc (Oct. 1976-); Bowne Dig. Corp. Sec. Lawyers; Commun. Abstr. (?-?); Curr. Contents Soc. Behav. Sci.; Curr. Law Index (1980-); Fed. Tax Artic.; Index Leg. Period.; Leg. Resour. Index (1980-); LegalTrac (1980-); PAIS Int. Print; Res. Alert [Full Cov.]; Soc. Sci. Cit. Index [Full Cov.]; Women Stud. Abstr.

US/0884-0768
UCLA PACIFIC BASIN LAW JOURNAL. [UCLA Pac. Basin law j.]. **Added/Corp** University of California, Los Angeles. School of Law. **VFOAT** Pacific Basin Law Journal. **VAT** University of California, Los Angeles Pacific Basin Law Journal. Vol. 1, No. 1 (Winter 1982)-. Academic Scholarly Publication. English. sa. $25.00 US and Canada; $29.00 other. Regents of University of California / UCLA Law School, 405 Hilgard Avenue, Los Angeles CA 90024. **Tel** (213)206-6174. **ED** Andrew Ruff. **LC** K25; .C57. **DD** 340/.05. **Bk Rev. Ad Acc. Circ:** 500.
Desc: Scholarly articles and commentaries on various legal issues affecting the nations which constitute the Pacific Basin Rim.
Ind/Abst Curr. Law Index (1983-); Index Leg. Period.; Leg. Resour. Index (1983-); LegalTrac (1980-); PAIS Int. Print.

US
UCLA WOMEN'S LAW JOURNAL. Added/Corp University of California, Los Angeles. School of Law. Vol. 1, No. 1 (Spring 1991)-. Periodical. English. $15.00 (regular), $25.00 (institution). UCLA School of Law, 405 Hilgard Avenue, Los Angeles CA 90024. **Tel** (310)825-3712.

UG
UGANDA LAW FOCUS, THE. V. 1- Oct. 1972-. English. an. SH500.00. Law Den Center, PO Box 7117, Kampala Uganda. **Tel** 532881/4. **ED** Mr Malinga, Mrs Bossa and Mr Wante. **LC** K25; .G35. **DD** 340/.05. **Circ:** 2,000 (ctrl).
Desc: A detailed analysis of cases of the High Court of Uganda.

DK
UGESKRIFT FOR RETSVAESEN. (1862)-. Danish.
Ind/Abst Index Foreign Leg. Per.

UK
UK OIL & GAS LAW. English. sa. £275.00 Europe; £289.00 other. Sweet & Maxwell Ltd., South Quay Plaza, 183 Marsh Wall, London E14 9FT England. **Tel** 011 44 264 342899, FAX 011 44 264 342723, telex 929089 ITPINF G.

US/0047-7575
UMKC LAW REVIEW. [UMKC law rev.]. **Added/Corp** University of Missouri--Kansas City. **VFOAT** U.M.K.C. Law Review. **VAT** University of Missouri, Kansas City, Law Review. Vol. 35, No. 1 (Winter 1967)-. Periodical. English. qt. $25.00 US; $27.00 other. University of Missouri at Kansas City, 5100 Rockhill Road, Kansas City MO 64110. **Tel** (816)235-1168. **LC** K11; .A54. **DD** 349.778/05; 347.78005. ***Continues*** *University of Missouri at Kansas City Law Review, 0737-0636.*
Ind/Abst Bowne Dig. Corp. Sec. Lawyers; Curr. Law Index (1980-); Fed. Tax Artic.; Index Leg. Period.; Leg. Resour. Index (1980-); LegalTrac (1980-).

GW/0341-8669
UMSATZSTEUER-RUNDSCHAU (COLOGNE, GERMANY : 1986). (UMSATZSTEUER-RUNDSCHAU : UR.). **VFOAT** Umsatzsteure Rundschau; UR. (19??)-. Periodical. German. mo (12 issues). DM171.33 Germany; DM202.00 other. Verlag Dr Otto Schmidt KG, Unter den Ulman 96/98, D 50968 Cologne Germany. **Tel** 011 49 221 9373801. **LC** KK7290.A13; U47. **DD** 343.4305/5; 344.30355. **[CCC]**. Index available. **Bk Rev. Ad Acc. Circ:** 4,200. ***Continues*** *Rundschau fuer Umsatzsteuer (Cologne, Germany : 1983). Rundschau fuer Umsatzsteuer, 0341-2733.*
Desc: Information of the value-added tax.

CN/0836-6632
UNB LAW JOURNAL. [UNB law j.]. **VFOAT** Revue de Droit UN-B; Revue de Droit de UN-B; University of New Brunswick Law Journal; Revue de Droit de l'Universite du Nouveau-Brunswick. Vol. 35 (1986)-. English (French). ir. Carswell / Canada, 2075 Kennedy Road, Scarborough Ontario M1T 3V4 Canada. **Tel** (416)609-3800, (800)387-5164. **ED** Linda Hill. **DD** 349.71/05. Index available. cum. index. **Bk Rev. Ad Acc. Circ:** 2,000 (ctrl). available in microform from University Microfilms International (UMI); available on microfilm. ***Continues*** *University of New Brunswick Law Journal, 0077-8141.*
Ind/Abst Curr. Law Index; Index Can. Leg. Period. Lit.

US/0503-1966
UNIFORM COMMERCIAL CODE LAW LETTER, THE. Added/Corp Management Reports, Inc. Warren, Gorham & Lamont, Inc. Vol. 1 (Mar. 1967)-. Periodical. English. mo. $183.25 US and Canada; $252.45 other. Warren Gorham & Lamont Inc., Park Square Building, 31 St. James Avenue, Boston MA 02116-4112. **Tel** (617)423-2020, (800)950-1207, FAX (617)423-2026. **ED** Thomas M. Quinn. **[CCC].**
Desc: This newsletter helps those involved with commercial law keep up with key changes and trends in today's regulatory environment.

US/0501-1183
UNIFORM COMMERCIAL CODE REPORTING SERVICE. VFOAT U.C.C. Reporting Service; UCC Reporting Service. Vol. 1-Vol. 42 2nd Ser. Vol. 1 (1965)-. English. ir. Clark Boardman Callaghan, 155 Pfingsten Road, Deerfield IL 60015. **Tel** (800)323-8067. **LC** KF885; .A45 Suppl. **DD** 347.70973.

US
UNION LIST OF LEGAL PERIODICALS, DISTRICT OF COLUMBIA AREA. Main/Corp Law Librarians' Society of Washington, D. C. (19??)-. English. ir. $115.00 (non-members), $100.00 (members). Hogan and Hartson Law Firm, 815 Connecticut Avenue Northwest, Washington DC 20006. **Tel** (202)331-5799.

US/0566-0785
UNITED STATES ATTORNEYS BULLETIN. (UNITED STATES ATTORNEYS BULLETIN / U.S. DEPARTMENT OF JUSTICE, EXECUTIVE OFFICE FOR UNITED STATES ATTORNEYS.). [U.S. atty. bull.]. Bulletin. English. bw. US Department of Justice, 10th Street & Constitution Avenue NW, Washington DC 20530. **Tel** (202)514-2000, FAX (202)633-4371. **LC** KF127; .U5. **DD** 348/.73/26.

US
UNITED STATES ATTORNEYS' MANUAL. Added/Corp United States. Dept. of Justice. (1976)-. Government Publication. English. ir. Price varies per volume. Superintendent of Documents, US Government Printing Office, Washington DC 20402. **Tel** (202)275-3328, FAX (202)786-2377.

US/8755-5980
UNITED STATES CLAIMS COURT DIGEST. ***Title Change.*** [U. S. Claims Court dig.]. **Added/Corp** United States. Claims Court. West Publishing Company. No. 1 (Aug. 1983)-No. 26 (Jan. 1993). English. mo. West Publishing Company, 610 Opperman Drive, PO Box 64526, Eagan MN 55123-1308. **Tel** (612)687-5618, (800)328-9352, FAX (612)687-5388, (800)562-2329. (**Subscription address:** FAX (612)688-3570) **LC** KF125.C51; U49. **DD** 348.73/415/05; 347.3084105. ***Continued by*** *United States Federal Claims Digest.*

US
UNITED STATES CLAIMS COURT REPORTER. ***Title Change.*** **Added/Corp** West Publishing Company. United States. Claims Court. United States. Court of Appeals (Federal Circuit) United States. Supreme Court. Vol. 1 (1983)-(1992). English. West Publishing Company, 610 Opperman Drive, PO Box 64526, Eagan MN 55123-1308. **Tel** (612)687-5618, (800)328-9352, FAX (612)687-5388, (800)562-2329. **LC** KF125.C5; U55. **DD** 348.73/44; 347.30844. ***Merged with*** *United States Claims Court Reporter, 0740-8080* ***to form*** *Federal Claims Reporter, 1067-4934.*

US
UNITED STATES CODE ANNOTATED.
(1927)-. Periodical. English. ir. West Publishing Company, 610 Opperman Drive, PO Box 64526, Eagan MN 55123-1308. **Tel** (612)687-5618, (800)328-9352, FAX (612)687-5388, (800)562-2329. **DD** 345.21. Index Available Received separately--bound from publisher. cum. index.

US/0094-2553
UNITED STATES JUDICIAL REPORTER.
Ceased. English. ir. US Judicial Reporter, PO Box 541, Harrisburg PA 17018. **LC** KF105.1; .U5. **DD** 348/.73/44.

US/0148-8139
UNITED STATES LAW WEEK, THE.
Added/Corp Bureau of National Affairs (Washington, D.C.). **VFOAT** U.S. Law Week. Vol. 1, No. 1 (Sept. 5, 1933)-. Periodical. English. ir (50 issues). $780.00 (surface mail). Bureau of National Affairs Inc., 9435 Key West Avenue, Rockville MD 20850. **Tel** (800)372-1033, (301)258-1033, FAX (301)948-5823. **ED** Gregory R. Pease. **[CCC]. *Continues*** *United States Weekly Law Journal.*
Desc: A weekly notification and reference service providing complete, up-to-date information about all significant court decisions, rulings, regulations, and interpretations in state and federal law.
Ind/Abst Curr. Lit. Fam. Plan. (19??-199?); Predicasts F&S Index, U. S. Annu. Ed.

US
UNITED STATES LAWYERS REFERENCE DIRECTORY.
(1967)-. English. ir. Legal Directories Publishing Company, 9111 Garland Road, PO Box 189000, Dallas TX 75218. **Tel** (214)321-3238, 800 447-5375. **LC** KF190; .U5. **DD** 340/.025/73.

US/0891-6845
UNITED STATES REPORTS.
(UNITED STATES REPORTS..., CASES ADJUDGED IN THE SUPREME COURT AT...). [U. S. rep.]. **Main/Corp** United States. Supreme Court. **VFOAT** Cases Adjudged in the Supreme Court at ... and Rules Announced; Cases Adjudged in the Supreme Court at ... . Vol. 108 (Oct. Term 1882... Oct. Term 1883)-. English. ir. Superintendent of Documents, US Government Printing Office, Washington DC 20402. **Tel** (202)275-3328, FAX (202)786-2377. **LC** KF101; .A212. **DD** 348. ***Continues*** *United States Reports, Supreme Court.*

US
UNITED STATES SUPREME COURT RECORDS AND BRIEFS INDEX.
Main/Corp Information Handling Services. Library and Education Division. **VFOAT** Records and Briefs Index. (1974)-. English. an. PO Box 1154, Englewood CO 80110.

US/0162-8372
UNIVERSITY OF ARKANSAS AT LITTLE ROCK LAW JOURNAL.
[Univ. Ark. Little Rock law j.]. **Added/Corp** University of Arkansas at Little Rock. School of Law. **VFOAT** UALR Law Journal; Law Journal. (1978)-. Academic Scholarly Publication. English. qt. $15.00. U A L R School of Law, 400 West Markham Street, Little Rock AR 72201-1418. **Tel** (501)371-1144. **ED** Scott J. Lancaster and Pamela G. Alan Perkins. **LC** K25; .N5676. **DD** 340/.09767. (Published in last issue). cum. index. **Bk Rev. Ad Acc. Circ:** 4,500 (ctrl).
Desc: Scholarly law publication with particular emphasis on areas of interest to Arkansas lawyers.
Ind/Abst Bowne Dig. Corp. Sec. Lawyers (19??-); Curr. Law Index (1980-); Index Leg. Period. (19??-); Leg. Resour. Index (1980-); LegalTrac (1980-).

US/0091-5440
UNIVERSITY OF BALTIMORE LAW REVIEW.
[Univ. Baltimore law rev.]. **Main/Corp** University of Baltimore. School of Law. (Winter 1971)-. English. sa. $15.00. University of Baltimore Law Review, 1420 North Charles Street, Baltimore MD 21201. **Tel** (410)837-4489. **LC** K2; .A46. **DD** 340/.05. Index available (bound in all issues). **Bk Rev. Ad Acc. Circ:** 1,500.
Desc: Law review focusing on both, national and Maryland issues and trends.
Ind/Abst Bowne Dig. Corp. Sec. Lawyers (19??-); Curr. Law Index (1980-); Index Leg. Period. (19??-); Leg. Resour. Index (1980-); LegalTrac (1980-).

CN/0068-1849
UNIVERSITY OF BRITISH COLUMBIA LAW REVIEW.
[Univ. B.C. law rev.]. **Main/Corp** University of British Columbia. **Added/Corp** University of British Columbia. Faculty of Law. University of British Columbia. Law Undergraduate Society. University of British Columbia. Law review. **VFOAT** U. B. C. Law Review. Vol. 1 (March 1959)-. Periodical. English. sa. 35.00Can$ Canada; 40.00Can$ other. University of British Columbia Faculty of Law, Room 165 1822 E. Mall, Vancouver BC V6T 1Z1 Canada. **Tel** (604)822-3066. ***Supersedes*** *University of British Columbia Legal Notes, 0497-2910.*
Ind/Abst Can. Legal Lit. (19??-); Curr. Law Index (1980-); Index Can. Leg. Period. Lit. (19??-); Index Leg. Period. (19??-); Leg. Resour. Index (1980-); LegalTrac (1980-); PAIS Int. Print (19??-).

US/0041-9494
UNIVERSITY OF CHICAGO LAW REVIEW, THE.
[Univ. Chic. law rev.]. **Main/Corp** University of Chicago. Law School. **Added/Corp** University of Chicago. Law School. Law Review. Vol. 1 (May 1933)-. Periodical. English. Four times a year. $35.00. University of Chicago Law School, 1111 East 60th Street, Chicago IL 60637. **Tel** (312)962-9593. **LC** K25; .N568. **DD** 347.05. **CODEN** UCLRA2. **Bk Rev. Ad Acc. Pr Rev. Circ:** 2,100. Documents available from The Genuine Article, UMI Article Clearinghouse.
Desc: Contains articles and book reviews by eminent legal authorities as well as comments by students on current legal problems.
Ind/Abst ABC POL SCI; ABI/INFORM Glob. Ed.; ABI Inform Ondisc (Fall 1976-); Bowne Dig. Corp. Sec. Lawyers; Crim. Justice Abstr.; Curr. Contents Soc. Behav. Sci.; Curr. Law Index (1980-); Expand. Acad. Index (1984-); Fed. Tax Artic.; Index Leg. Period.; Leg. Resour. Index (1980-); LegalTrac (1980-); Newsp. Period. Abstr. (1989-); Res. Alert [Full Cov.]; Soc. Sci. Cit. Index [Full Cov.]; Urban Aff. Abstr.

US/0892-5593
UNIVERSITY OF CHICAGO LEGAL FORUM.
[Univ. Chic. leg. forum]. **VFOAT** Legal Forum. (1986)-. Periodical. English. ir. University of Chicago Law School, 1111 East 60th Street, Chicago IL 60637. **Tel** (312)962-9593. **DD** 340/.05. Documents available from The Genuine Article.
Ind/Abst Curr. Contents Soc. Behav. Sci. (19??-); Index Leg. Period. (19??-); Res. Alert (19??-) [Full Cov.]; Soc. Sci. Cit. Index [Select. Cov.].

US/0009-6881
UNIVERSITY OF CINCINNATI LAW REVIEW.
[Univ. Cincinnati law rev.]. **Main/Corp** University of Cincinnati. College of Law. **VFOAT** Cincinnati Law Review. Vol. 1 (Jan. 1927)-. Periodical. English. qt. $25.00 US; $30.00 other. University of Cincinnati / College of Law, Room 300, Cincinnati OH 45221. **Tel** (513)556-5101. **ED** Michael Scheier. **LC** K25; .N569. **Bk Rev. Ad Acc. Circ:** 1,100 (ctrl). Documents available from The Genuine Article.
Desc: Lead articles, comments and case notes all relating to law.
Ind/Abst Arts Humanit. Citation Index [Select. Cov.]; Bowne Dig. Corp. Sec. Lawyers (19??-); Curr. Contents Soc. Behav. Sci. (19??-); Curr. Law Index (1980-); Fed. Tax Artic. (19??-); Index Leg. Period. (19??-); Leg. Resour. Index (1980-); LegalTrac (1980-); Res. Alert (19??-) [Select. Cov.]; Soc. Sci. Cit. Index [Select. Cov.].

US/0041-9516
UNIVERSITY OF COLORADO LAW REVIEW.
[Univ. Colo. law rev.]. **Main/Corp** University of Colorado (Boulder Campus). School of Law. **Added/Corp** University of Colorado (Boulder Campus). School of Law. Law Review. Vol. 35 (Fall 1962)-. Periodical. English. qt. $29.00 US and Canada; $32.50 other. University of Colorado Law Review, 290 Fleming Law Building, Campus Box 401, Boulder CO 80309. **Tel** (303)492-6145, FAX (303)492-1200. **ED** Jody Harper. **LC** K25; .N5695. **DD** 347.05. **Bk Rev. Ad Acc. Circ:** 800 (ctrl). available on microfilm from WESTLAW; available on an online database from LEXIS. ***Continues*** *Rocky Mountain Law Review.*
Desc: As well as general law topics, at least one issue of the four each year is devoted to natural resources topic.
Ind/Abst Bowne Dig. Corp. Sec. Lawyers; Curr. Law Index (1980-); Fed. Tax Artic.; Index Leg. Period.; Leg. Resour. Index (1980-); LegalTrac (1980-); Sel. Water Resour. Abstr.

TZ
UNIVERSITY OF DAR ES SALAAM LAW JOURNAL.
Added/Corp Dar es Salaam University Law Society. **VFOAT** DULJ; Dar es Salaam University Law Journal; A.D.U.L.J. (19??)-. Periodical. English. an. Dar es Salaam School of Law, PO Box 35034, Dar es Salaam Tanzania. **ED** E.B. Kasimbazi. **LC** K4; .A75. **DD** 340/.09678. ***Continues*** *Chuo Kikuu Cha Dar es Salaam. Dar es Salaam University Law Journal.*

US/0162-9174
UNIVERSITY OF DAYTON LAW REVIEW.
[Univ. Dayton law rev.]. **Main/Corp** University of Dayton. Law School. (1976)-. Periodical. English. Three times a year (Mar., Jun., Dec.). $17.50. University of Dayton Law Review, 300 College Park, Dayton OH 45469. **Tel** (513)229-3642. **ED** Robert Windus and Walt A. Linscott. **LC** K4; .A9. **DD** 340/.05. **Bk Rev. Ad Acc. Circ:** 1,000. ***Continues*** *University of Dayton Intramural Law Review, 0363-2148.*
Desc: General coverage of all areas of law, with special emphasis on Ohio legislation and judicial decisions.
Ind/Abst Bowne Dig. Corp. Sec. Lawyers (19??-); Curr. Law Index (1980-); Index Leg. Period. (19??-); Leg. Resour. Index (1980-); LegalTrac (1980-).

US/1058-4323
UNIVERSITY OF DETROIT MERCY LAW REVIEW.
[Univ. Detroit Mercy law rev.]. **Added/Corp** University of Detroit Mercy. School of Law. Vol. 69, Issue 1 (Fall 1991)-. Periodical. English. qt. $17.00 US & Canada; $19.00 other. University of Detroit, 651 East Jefferson Avenue, Detroit MI 48226. **Tel** (313)596-0200, (313)596-0238. **LC** K25; .N58. **DD** 349. Index available (in October).
Ind/Abst Index Leg. Period. (19??-); Sage Public Adm. Abstr. (19??-).

US/1047-8035
UNIVERSITY OF FLORIDA JOURNAL OF LAW AND PUBLIC POLICY.
(UNIVERSITY OF FLORIDA JOURNAL OF LAW AND PUBLIC POLICY : JL & PP.). [Univ. Fla. j. law public policy]. **Added/Corp** University of Florida. College of Business Administration. **VFOAT** Journal of Law and Public Policy; JL & PP; JL and PP. Vol. 1 (1987)-. English. Twice a year (Spring and Fall). $24.00. Journal of Law and Public Policy, 115 Holland Hall, University of Florida, Gainesville FL 32611. **Tel** (904)392-7139. **ED** Stephen R. Prescott. **LC** K25; .N597. **DD** 340/.05. **Bk Rev**, (Qty: varies). **Ad Acc, Adv Mgr:** Keith Riffardi, **Tel** (904)373-7139. **Pr Rev. Circ:** 1,000. available on an online database from WESTLAW.
Desc: School which is devoted to analysis of the society and public policy significance of current legal trends.
Ind/Abst Index Leg. Period.

US/0502-6679
UNIVERSITY OF FLORIDA LAW CENTER NEWS, THE.
Added/Corp Florida. University, Gainesville. Law Center Association. Vol. 1 (March 1964)-. English. University of Florida Law Center Association, PO Box 14412, Gainesville FL 32604. **Tel** (904)392-9586. **DD** 340.

US
UNIVERSITY OF FLORIDA LAWYER : MAGAZINE OF THE UNIVERSITY OF FLORIDA COLLEGE OF LAW.
Spring 1984-. Periodical. English. Three times a year. Free to alumni and friends of the UF College of Law. University of Florida Law Center Association, PO Box 14412, Gainesville FL 32604. **Tel** (904)392-9586. **ED** Denise Stobbie. **Circ:** 11,000 (ctrl). ***Continues*** *Law Center News.*
Desc: Magazine of the University of Florida College of Law.

GH/0041-9605
UNIVERSITY OF GHANA LAW JOURNAL.
Added/Corp University of Ghana. School of Law. (1964)-. Periodical. English. ir. Sam Woode Ltd., PO Box 12719, Accra North Ghana. **Tel** 011 220257. **ED** Akua Kuenyehia. **Bk Rev. Ad Acc. Circ:** 1,000 (ctrl). ***Continues*** *Legon Law Journal.*
Desc: Articles range from discussion of Ghanaian law, through discussion of African and third world legal issues to contributions on general legal theory.
Ind/Abst Index Foreign Leg. Per. (19??-).

US/0271-9835
UNIVERSITY OF HAWAII LAW REVIEW.
[Univ. Hawaii law rev.]. **Main/Corp** University of Hawaii at Manoa. School of Law. (Fall 1979)-. Periodical. English. ir. $16.00 US; $17.00 other. University Hawaii, Research Corporation, 2515 Dole Street, Honolulu HI 96822. **Tel** (808)956-6554. **ED** Rexford Reynolds. **LC** K25; .N62. **DD** 349.969/05. **Bk Rev. Ad Acc. Pr Rev. Circ:** 500.
Desc: Focus on Hawaii Law, Pacific Asian affairs, water use, and land use.
Ind/Abst Bowne Dig. Corp. Sec. Lawyers (19??-); Curr. Law Index (1980-); Index Leg. Period. (19??-); Leg. Resour. Index (1980-); LegalTrac (1980-).

NR
UNIVERSITY OF IFE (NIGERIA) LAW REPORTS, THE.
Main/Corp University of Ife. 1971-. English. qt. $38.50. University of IFE Periodicals Department, Ile-Ife Nigeria. **DD** 348/.669/046.

US/0276-9948
UNIVERSITY OF ILLINOIS LAW REVIEW.
[Univ. Ill. law rev.]. **VFOAT** Law Review. (1981)-. Academic Scholarly Publication. English. qt. $30.00. University of Illinois / Law, 74 Law Building, 504 East Pennsylvania Avenue, Champaign IL 61820. **Tel** (217)333-3156, (217)333-1000. **LC** K25; .N63. **DD** 349.73/05; 347.3005. **Ad Acc. Pr Rev. Circ:** 1,500 (ctrl). available on microfilm and microfiche from University Microfilms International (UMI). Documents available from The Genuine Article. ***Continues*** *University of Illinois Law Forum, 0041-963X.*
Desc: Scholarly legal periodical with national and international focus but mindful of Illinois practitioner needs.
Ind/Abst Arts Humanit. Citation Index [Select. Cov.]; Bowne Dig. Corp. Sec. Lawyers (19??-); Crim. Justice Abstr. (19??-); Curr. Law Index (1980-); Fed. Tax Artic. (19??-); Index Leg. Period. (19??-); Leg. Resour. Index (1981-); LegalTrac (1980-); Res. Alert (19??-) [Full Cov.]; Soc. Sci. Cit. Index (19??-) [Full Cov.].

US/0083-4025
UNIVERSITY OF KANSAS LAW REVIEW.
[Univ. Kans. law rev.]. **Main/Corp** University of Kansas. School of Law. **Added/Corp** University of Kansas. School of Law. Law Review. **VFOAT** Kansas Law Review. Vol. 1, (Nov. 1952)-. Periodical. English. Four times a year (Feb., May, July, Oct.). $32.55 Kansas;

$31.00 other. University of Kansas Law Review, 510 Green Hall, Lawrence KS 66045. **Tel** (913)864-3463. **ED** Sharon Stallbaumer (phone: (913)864-3463). **LC** K25; .N64. **DD** 340. cum. index. **Circ:** 1,300. available on microfilm. ***Absorbed** Kansas Criminal Procedure Review.*
Desc: An academic journal that provides analysis and updates in all areas of the law.
Ind/Abst Bowne Dig. Corp. Sec. Lawyers; Curr. Law Index (1980-); Fed. Tax Artic.; Index Leg. Period.; Leg. Resour. Index (1980-); LegalTrac (1980-).

US/1051-2225
UNIVERSITY OF MIAMI ENTERTAINMENT & SPORTS LAW REVIEW.
[Univ. Miami entertain. sports law rev.]. **Added/Corp** University of Miami. School of Law. **VFOAT** University of Miami Entertainment and Sports Law Review; Entertainment & Sports Law Review. Vol. 6, No. 1 & 2 (1989)-. Periodical. English. ir. Peter Lang Publishing, 62 West 45th Street, 4th Floor, New York NY 10036. **Tel** (212)764-1471, (800)770-5264, telex 6973364 PLNY. **ED** Michael R. Hanrahan. **DD** 344. **Bk Rev. Ad Acc. Circ:** 300 (ctrl). ***Continues** Entertainment & Sports Law Journal, 8756-3991.*
Desc: Articles on many diverse topics arising in sports and entertainment Law.
Ind/Abst Index Leg. Period. (19??-); Leg. Resour. Index (19??-); LegalTrac (1989-).

US/0041-9818
UNIVERSITY OF MIAMI LAW REVIEW.
[Univ. Miami law rev.]. **Added/Corp** University of Miami. School of Law. Vol. 12 (Fall 1957)-. Periodical. English. ir. University of Miami School of Law, 1311 Miller Drive, 460 Law Library, PO Box 248087, Coral Gables FL 33124. **Tel** (305)284-2464, FAX (305)284-2349. Index available. cum. index. **Ad Acc. Circ:** 2,000 (ctrl). available on microfilm and microfiche from University Microfilms International (UMI). ***Continues** Miami Law Quarterly.*
Ind/Abst Bowne Dig. Corp. Sec. Lawyers (19??-); Crim. Justice Abstr. (19??-); Curr. Law Index (1980-); Fed. Tax Artic. (19??-); Index Leg. Period. (19??-); Leg. Resour. Index (1980-); LegalTrac (1980-); PAIS Int. Print (19??-); Soc. Plann. Policy Dev. Abstr. (19??-); Sociol. Abstr. (19??-).

US/0363-602X
UNIVERSITY OF MICHIGAN JOURNAL OF LAW REFORM.
[Univ. Mich. j. law reform]. **Main/Corp** University of Michigan. Law School. (1972)-. Periodical. English. qt. $31.00. University of Michigan Law School, S-324 Legal Research Building, Ann Arbor MI 48109. **Tel** (313)763-2195, (313)763-6100. **ED** Maureen A. Bishop. **LC** K16; .R68. **DD** 340/.05. **Bk Rev. Ad Acc. Circ:** 1,000 (ctrl). available in microform. ***Continues** Journal of Law Reform, 0033-1546.*
Desc: Legal periodical focusing on law reform, drafting model statutes, constitutional reform and empirical research.
Ind/Abst Bowne Dig. Corp. Sec. Lawyers (19??-); Crim. Justice Abstr. (19??-); Curr. Law Index (1980-); Index Leg. Period. (19??-); Leg. Resour. Index (1980-); LegalTrac (1980-); PAIS Int. Print (19??-).

US/0540-2239
UNIVERSITY OF MINNESOTA LAW SCHOOL NEWS.
Added/Corp Minnesota University. Law School. Vol. 1, (1951)-. Periodical. English. qt. University of Minnesota Law School, 229 19th Avenue South, Minneapolis MN 55455. **Tel** (612)625-8034. **DD** 340.

AT/0313-0096
UNIVERSITY OF NEW SOUTH WALES LAW JOURNAL, THE.
[Univ. N. S. W. law j.]. **Added/Corp** University of New South Wales. Faculty of Law. **VFOAT** New South Wales Law Journal; UNSW Law Journal; U.N.S.W. Law Journal. (June 1975)-. Periodical. English. Twice a year. 50.00Aus$. University of New South Wales Law Journal, Faculty of Law, PO Box 1, Kensington New South Wales 2033 Australia. **Tel** 011 61 2 6972222, FAX 011 61 2 6627698. **ED** Wanda Lander, Anna Golovsky, and Rhoda Yung. **LC** K25; .N67. **DD** 349.944/05; 349.4405. Index available. **Bk Rev**, (Qty: 2-3/yr). **Ad Acc, Adv Mgr:** Rhoda Yung, **Tel** 011 61 2 6972237. **Pr Rev. Circ:** 700.
Desc: Both a thematic issue centering around a topic of current legal interest and a general issue published each year.
Ind/Abst APAIS, Aust. Public Aff. Inf. Ser. (1976-); Aust. Leg. Mon. Dig.; Curr. Law Index (1980-); Index Leg. Period.; Leg. Resour. Index (1980-); LegalTrac (1980-).

US/0041-9907
UNIVERSITY OF PENNSYLVANIA LAW REVIEW.
[Univ. PA. law rev.]. **Main/Corp** University of Pennsylvania. Law School. **Added/Corp** University of Pennsylvania. Law School. (1945)-. Periodical. English. ir. University of Pennsylvania / Law Review, 3400 Chestnut Street / 14, Philadelphia PA 19104. **Tel** (215)898-7060. **LC** K25; .N69. **DD** 340/.09748. **Bk Rev. Ad Acc. Pr Rev. Circ:** 2,000. Documents available from The Genuine Article, UMI Article Clearinghouse. ***Continues** University of Pennsylvania Law Review and American Law Register, 0749-9833.*
Desc: Publishes unsolicited articles that in any way relate to the law. We assume our readership will include students, academics, and practitioners.
Ind/Abst ABC POL SCI (19??-); Bowne Dig. Corp. Sec. Lawyers (19??-); Crim. Penol. Police Sci. Abstr. (19??-); Curr. Contents Soc. Behav. Sci. (19??-); Curr. Law Index (1980-); Expand. Acad. Index (1984-); Fed. Tax Artic. (19??-); Index Leg. Period. (19??-); Leg. Resour. Index (1980-); LegalTrac (1980-); Newsp. Period. Abstr. (1988-); Res. Alert (19??-) [Full Cov.]; Soc. Sci. Cit. Index (19??-) [Full Cov.].

US/0041-9915
UNIVERSITY OF PITTSBURGH LAW REVIEW.
[Univ. Pittsbg. law rev.]. **Main/Corp** University of Pittsburgh. School of Law. **Added/Corp** University of Pittsburgh. School of Law. Law review. Vol. 1 (Mar. 1935)-. Periodical. English. qt. $25.00. University of Pittsburgh Law Review, 3900 Forbes Avenue, Pittsburgh PA 15260. **Tel** (412)648-1354. **ED** Luke Bergstron. **LC** K25; .N7. Index available. cum. index. **Ad Acc. Pr Rev. Circ:** 1,200 (ctrl). available on microfiche; available on microfilm; available in microform. Documents available from The Genuine Article.
Desc: Publication of articles of current general interest to the legal community.
Ind/Abst Bowne Dig. Corp. Sec. Lawyers; Commun. Abstr.; Curr. Contents Soc. Behav. Sci.; Curr. Law Index (1980-); Fed. Tax Artic.; Index Leg. Period.; Leg. Resour. Index (1980-); LegalTrac (1980-); Res. Alert [Full Cov.]; Soc. Sci. Cit. Index [Full Cov.]; Women Stud. Abstr.

US/0161-0708
UNIVERSITY OF PUGET SOUND LAW REVIEW.
Title Change. [Univ. Puget Sound law rev.]. **Main/Corp** University of Puget Sound. School of Law. (1977)-(1994). Periodical. English. Three times a year. Seattle University / Law Review, 950 Broadway Plaza, Tacoma WA 98402-4470. **Tel** (206)591-2995, FAX (206)591-6313. **LC** K24; .A24. **DD** 340/.05. Index available. cum. index. **Bk Rev. Circ:** 1,000 (ctrl). available on microfilm. ***Continued by** Seattle University Law Review.*
Desc: Law review.
Ind/Abst Bowne Dig. Corp. Sec. Lawyers (?-?); Crim. Justice Abstr. (?-?); Curr. Law Index (1980-?); Index Leg. Period. (?-?); Leg. Resour. Index (1980-); LegalTrac (1980-).

AT/0083-4041
UNIVERSITY OF QUEENSLAND LAW JOURNAL, THE.
[Univ. Qld. law j.]. **Added/Corp** University of Queensland. Law School. **VFOAT** Law Journal. Vol. 1, No. 1 (Dec. 1948)-. English. an. 25.00Aus$ (individuals), 27.50Aus$ (institutions) Australia; 38.00Aus$ (airmail) other. University of Queensland Press, PO Box 42, St Lucia Queensland 4067 Australia. **Tel** 011 61 7 3652127, FAX 011 61 7 3651988, telex UNIVQLD AA40315. **LC** UNC. available on microfilm and microfiche from University Microfilms International (UMI).
Ind/Abst APAIS, Aust. Public Aff. Inf. Ser. (1963-); Aust. Leg. Mon. Dig.; Curr. Law Index (1980-); Index Leg. Period.; Leg. Resour. Index (1980-); LegalTrac (1980-).

US/0566-2389
UNIVERSITY OF RICHMOND LAW REVIEW.
[Univ. Richmond law rev.]. **Main/Corp** University of Richmond. **Added/Corp** T. C. Williams School of Law. University of Richmond. Law Review. Vol. 3 (1968)-. Periodical. English. Five times a year. $30.00. TC Williams School of Law, University of Richmond, Richmond VA 23173. **Tel** (804)289-8216. **ED** M. Eldridge Blanton III. **LC** K25; .I35. **DD** 340/.0973. Index available. cum. index. **Bk Rev. Ad Acc. Circ:** 1,200 (ctrl). ***Continues** University of Richmond Law Notes.*
Desc: Offers a survey of the changes in Virginia Law.
Ind/Abst Bowne Dig. Corp. Sec. Lawyers; Curr. Law Index (1980-); Fed. Tax Artic.; Index Leg. Period.; Leg. Resour. Index (1980-); LegalTrac (1980-).

US/0042-0018
UNIVERSITY OF SAN FRANCISCO LAW REVIEW.
[Univ. San Francisco law rev.]. **Main/Corp** University of San Francisco. School of Law. **Added/Corp** University of San Francisco. School of Law. Law Review. (1966)-. Periodical. English. qt. $30.00. University of San Francisco Law Review, 2130 Fulton Street, San Francisco CA 94117. **Tel** (415)666-6154, FAX (415)666-6433. **DD** 340.05. **Bk Rev. Circ:** 1,000 (ctrl). available on microfiche from Xerox; available on an online database from WESTLAW.
Desc: Legal journal with articles by attorneys and law students- edited by law review members.
Ind/Abst Bowne Dig. Corp. Sec. Lawyers; Curr. Law Index (1980-); Fed. Tax Artic.; Hum. Rights Intern. Rep.; Index Leg. Period.; Leg. Resour. Index (1980-); LegalTrac (1980-).

AT/0082-2108
UNIVERSITY OF TASMANIA LAW REVIEW.
[Univ. Tasman. law rev.]. **Added/Corp** University of Tasmania. Law School. University of Tasmania. Faculty of Law. Vol. 2, No. 1 (Nov. 1964)-. Periodical. English. Twice a year. 30.00Aus$ Australia; 35.00Aus$ other. University of Tasmania, PO Box 1214, Launceston 7250 Australia. **Tel** 011 61 3 243013, FAX 011 61 2 207623, telex 58150. **(Subscription address:** University of Tasmania / Law School, c/o David McGuire, Publications Manager, GPO Box 252C, Hobart Tasmania 7001 Australia.**) ED** M. Tsamenyi. **LC** K25; .N733. **DD** 340/.05. Index available. cum. index. **Bk Rev. Ad Acc. Pr Rev. Circ:** 500. available on microfilm and microfiche from University Microfilms International (UMI). ***Continues** Tasmanian University Law Review.*
Desc: Publishes articles on a wide range of legal subjects.
Ind/Abst APAIS, Aust. Public Aff. Inf. Ser. (1970-); Aust. Leg. Mon. Dig.; Curr. Law Index (1980-); Index Leg. Period.; Leg. Resour. Index (1980-); LegalTrac (1980-); PAIS Int. Print.

US/0042-0190
UNIVERSITY OF TOLEDO LAW REVIEW, THE.
(UNIVERSITY OF TOLEDO LAW REVIEW.). [Univ. Toledo law rev.]. **Main/Corp** University of Toledo. College of Law. **Added/Corp** University of Toledo. College of Law. Law review. **VFOAT** Toledo Law Review. Vol. 1 (Winter 1969)-. Academic Scholarly Publication. English. qt (Mar., June, Sept., Dec.). $16.00. University of Toledo, 2801 West Bancroft Street, Toledo OH 43606. **Tel** (419)537-2962. **LC** K24; .O4. **DD** 340/.09771. Index available in last issue of volume--attached. **Bk Rev. Circ:** 700 (ctrl). ***Supersedes** Student Law Journal, 0585-458X.*
Desc: Scholarly discussion of current legal problems. Articles by legal scholars, professionals and students.
Ind/Abst Bowne Dig. Corp. Sec. Lawyers; Curr. Law Index (1980-); Fed. Tax Artic.; Index Leg. Period.; Leg. Resour. Index (1980-); LegalTrac (1980-).

CN/0381-1638
UNIVERSITY OF TORONTO FACULTY OF LAW REVIEW.
[Univ. Tor. Fac. Law rev.]. Vol. 31 (Aug. 1973)-. English. sa. Carswell / Canada, 2075 Kennedy Road, Scarborough Ontario M1T 3V4 Canada. **Tel** (416)609-3800, (800)387-5164. **LC** K24; .O7. **DD** 340/.05. **[CCC]. *Continues** Faculty of Law Review, 0381-162X.*
Ind/Abst Can. Legal Lit. (19??-); Curr. Law Index (1980-); Index Can. Leg. Period. Lit. (19??-); Index Leg. Period. (19??-); Leg. Resour. Index (1980-); LegalTrac (1980-).

CN/0042-0220
UNIVERSITY OF TORONTO LAW JOURNAL, THE.
[Univ. Tor. law j.]. **Added/Corp** University of Toronto. Faculty of Law. Vol. 1 (1935)-. Periodical. English (French). qt (Jan., Apr., July, Oct.). $63.00. University of Toronto Press, 5201 Dufferin Street, Downsview Ontario M3H 5T8 Canada. **Tel** (416)667-7781, (416)667-7782, FAX (416)667-7803. **ED** S. Waddams. **LC** K25; .N74. **[CCC].** Index available. **Bk Rev. Ad Acc. Circ:** 600 (ctrl). available on microfilm and microfiche from University Microfilms International (UMI).
Desc: The subject of the journal is the law in its widest sense- as a complex of ideas and doctrines, the illumination of which is achieved through an interdisciplinary consideration of theory, of the economics and sociology of law, and of its history.
Ind/Abst Can. Legal Lit.; Curr. Law Index (1980-); Index Can. Leg. Period. Lit.; Index Leg. Period.; Leg. Resour. Index (1980-); LegalTrac (1980-); PAIS Int. Print; Soc. Plann. Policy Dev. Abstr.; Sociol. Abstr.

US/0504-3972
UNIVERSITY OF VIRGINIA LAW SCHOOL FOUNDATION ANNUAL REPORT, THE.
(ANNUAL REPORT - UNIVERSITY OF VIRGINIA LAW SCHOOL FOUNDATION.). **Main/Corp** University of Virginia Law School Foundation. English. an. University of Virginia Law, School Foundation, PO Box 3668, Charlottesville VA 22903. **LC** KF292.V572; U6. **DD** 340/.07/11755481.

AT/0042-0328
UNIVERSITY OF WESTERN AUSTRALIA LAW REVIEW.
[Univ. West. Aust. law rev.]. **VFOAT** Western Australia Law Review. (1960)-. Periodical. English. sa. University of Western Australia / University Bookshop, PO Box 656, Nedlands WA 6009 Australia. **Tel** 011 61 9 3802069. **LC** K25; .N765. **DD** 340. Each issue contains an index to its own contents (no volume index)--loose. **Bk Rev. Circ:** 800. ***Continues** Annual Law Review.*
Ind/Abst APAIS, Aust. Public Aff. Inf. Ser. (1963-); Aust. Leg. Mon. Dig. (19??-); Curr. Law Index (1980-); Index Leg. Period. (19??-); Leg. Resour. Index (1980-); LegalTrac (1980-).

II
UNREPORTED JUDGEMENTS, THE.
Main/Corp India. Supreme Court. English. sm. Rs35.00. 861 Chopasani Road, Sardarpura Jodhpur India. **DD** 348/.54/044.

UK
UP AGAINST THE LAW.
Added/Corp Up Against the Law Collective. (19??)-. English. **LC** KD654.A13; U6. **DD** 347/.41.

US/1041-4789
UPDATE (ANNAPOLIS, MD.).
(UPDATE / DEPARTMENT OF LEGISLATIVE REFERENCE.). [Update]. **Added/Corp** Maryland. General Assembly. State Dept. of Legislative Reference. (198?)-. English. Free. Department of Legislative Reference, 90 State Circle, Annapolis MD 21401. **Tel** (410)841-3870. **ED** William Somerville. **LC** KFM1220; .U63. **DD** 349.752/05;

347.52005. **Circ:** 500.
Desc: Publishes short and concise documents relating to issues of current legislative interest geared to state level.

US
UPDATE - FOOD AND DRUG LAW INSTITUTE. (19??)-. Periodical. English. qt. $30.00. Food and Drug Law Institute, 1000 Vermont Avenue Northwest, Suite 1200, Washington DC 20005. **Tel** (202)371-1420, FAX (202)371-0649.

US/0147-8648
UPDATE ON LAW-RELATED EDUCATION. [Update law-relat. educ.]. **Added/Corp** ABA Special Committee on Youth Education for Citizenship. **VFOAT** Update on Law Related Education. Vol. 1 (Spring 1977)-. Periodical. English. Three times a year. $25.00. American Bar Association, 750 North Lake Shore Drive, Chicago IL 60611. **Tel** (312)988-5522, (312)988-5241, FAX (312)988-5528, telex 270593. **ED** Charles J. White. **LC** KF4208.5.L3; A138. **DD** 340/.07/1073. **Bk Rev. Ad Acc. Circ:** 3,000.
Desc: Ideas for teaching children about law.
Ind/Abst Curr. Index J. Educ.; Curr. Law Index (1980-); Educ. Index; Leg. Resour. Index (1980-?); LegalTrac (1980-1989); SportSearch.

US/0739-4004
UPDATE ON STATE LEGISLATION. (19??)-. Periodical. English. ir (published during legislation). $95.00. Ed Silverbrand and Associates, 1100 North Street 1-E, Sacramento CA 95814. **Tel** (916)444-5773, (916)442-1380, FAX (916)442-2098. **ED** Ed Silverbrand. **LC** KFC20; .U6. **DD** 348.794/043/05; 347.94084305. **Circ:** 150 (ctrl).
Desc: Provides commentary on the education and political scene in California, and summaries of lelgislation affecting California schools.

US
UPDATED WISCONSIN SCHOOL LAWS. (19??)-. English. $95.00 Wisconsin Association of School Boards or Wisconsin School Attorneys Association members tax exempt; $110.00 non-members exempt; $100.23 members non-exempt; $116.05 non-members non-exempt. Wisconsin Association of School Boards, 122 West Washington, Madison WI 53703. **Tel** (608)257-2622, FAX (608)257-8386. **ED** Ken Cole.

XV
URADNI LIST REPUBLIKE SLOVENIJE. **Main/Corp** Slovenia. Vol.1 No. 1 (June 25 1991)-. Slovenian. **LC** J7.T9; S622. ***Continues*** *Uradni List Republike Slovenije.*

US/0042-0905
URBAN LAWYER, THE. [Urban lawyer]. **Added/Corp** American Bar Association. Section of Local Government Law. Vol. 1 (Spring 1969)-. Periodical. English. qt (4 issues). $49.95. American Bar Association, 750 North Lake Shore Drive, Chicago IL 60611. **Tel** (312)988-5522, (312)988-5241, FAX (312)988-5528, telex 270593. **LC** K25; .R32. **DD** 342/.73/0905. **Pr Rev.** available on microfilm and microfiche from University Microfilms International (UMI). Documents available from The Genuine Article.
Ind/Abst Curr. Contents Soc. Behav. Sci.; Curr. Law Index (1980-); Educ. Adm. Abstr.; Environ. Period. Bibliogr.; Fed. Tax Artic.; Index Leg. Period.; J. Plan. Lit.; Leg. Resour. Index (1980-); LegalTrac (1980-); Res. Alert [Full Cov.]; Sage Urban Stud. Abstr; Soc. Sci. Cit. Index [Full Cov.]; Urban Aff. Abstr.

US/0195-7686
URBAN, STATE AND LOCAL LAW NEWSLETTER. ***Title Change.*** [Urban state local law newsl.]. **Added/Corp** American Bar Association. Section of Urban, State and Local Government Law. Vol. 2 (Winter 1979)-(1993). Newsletter. English. qt (4 issues). American Bar Association, 750 North Lake Shore Drive, Chicago IL 60611. **Tel** (312)988-5522, (312)988-5241, FAX (312)988-5528, telex 270593. **LC** KF5300; .S7. **DD** 342.73/09/05. ***Continues*** *State, Local, and Urban Law Newsletter, 0163-2922.* ***Continued by*** *State & Local Law News.*
Ind/Abst Curr. Law Index (1980-?); Leg. Resour. Index (1980-?); LegalTrac (1984-?).

US
US SUPREME COURT PETITIONS & BRIEFS. TAX LAW SERIES. English. ir. $295.00. Law Reprints Publications, 5442 30th Street Northwest, Washington DC 20015. **Tel** (202)362-8502, (800)356-0671. **ED** Bart Sigerson. Index available. ctrl circ.

XR
USTREDNI VESTNIK CESKE SOCIALISTICKE REPUBLIKY. **Main/Corp** Czech Socialist Republic, (Czechoslovakia). Czech. kcs16.00. Ministerstvo Spravedlnosti CSR Upraze, Czechoslavakia.

XO
USTREDNY VESTNIK SLOVENSKEJ SOCIALISTICKEJ REPUBLIKY. **Main/Corp** Slovak Socialist Republic (Czechoslovakia). Slovak. 16.00. Ministerstvo Spravodlivosti Slovenskej Socialistickej Republiky, Suvorovova Ul 16, Bratislava Slovakia.

US/0897-9227
UTAH ADVANCE REPORTS. [Utah adv. rep.]. **Added/Corp** Utah. Supreme Court. Issue No. 1 (Jan. 14, 1985)-. English. bw. $159.00. Code Company, PO Box 1471, Provo UT 84603. **Tel** (801)364-2633, (800)255-5294. **DD** 348.

US/0091-9691
UTAH BAR JOURNAL. [Utah bar j.]. Vol. 1, No. 1 (Aug./Sept. 1988)-. Periodical. English. mo. Free to members, $20.00 nonmembers. Utah State Bar, 645 S 200 E, Salt Lake City UT 84111. **LC** KF200; .U83. **DD** 340/.05. ***Continues*** *Utah Bar Journal, 0091-9691.*
Ind/Abst Leg. Resour. Index.

US/0145-8558
UTAH BAR LETTER. ANNUAL ROSTER OF ACTIVE RESIDENT UTAH ATTORNEYS. **VFOAT** Annual Roster of Active Resident Utah Attorneys. English. an. Utah State Bar, 645 S 200 E, Salt Lake City UT 84111. **LC** KF192.U8; U8. **DD** 340/.25/792.

US
UTAH CASE NAMES CITATOR. English. $40.00 (1 bound volume), $52.00 (cumulative supplements). Shepards McGraw-Hill Inc, 555 Middle Creek Parkway, PO Box 35300, Colorado Springs CO 80935-3530. **Tel** (719)488-3000, FAX (800)525-0053.

US/0147-3581
UTAH JUDICIAL BRIEFS. **Main/Corp** Utah. Office of the State Court Administrator. V. 1- July 1975-. Periodical. English. qt. Utah Office of the State Court, 250 East Broadway, Suite 240, Salt Lake City UT 84111. **LC** KFU510.5.A3; A136. **DD** 347.792/013/05.

US/0042-1448
UTAH LAW REVIEW. [Utah law rev.]. Vol. 1, No. 1 (1949)-V. 9, No. 4 (Winter 1965); (1966)-. Periodical. English. qt. $25.00. University of Utah College of Law, Salt Lake City UT 84112. **Tel** (801)581-6833 or 581-4687. **LC** K25; .T34. **DD** 340/.05. cum. index. **Bk Rev. Ad Acc. Circ:** 1,000. available on microfilm and microfiche from University Microfilms International (UMI).
Desc: Legal related articles.
Ind/Abst Bowne Dig. Corp. Sec. Lawyers (19??-); Curr. Law Index (1980-); Fed. Tax Artic. (19??-); Index Leg. Period. (19??-); Leg. Resour. Index (1980-); LegalTrac (1980-); West. Hist. Q. (19??-).

US/0737-9277
UTAH STATE BAR DIRECTORY. **Main/Corp** Utah Sate Bar. Directory. English. Utah State Bar, 645 S 200 E, Salt Lake City UT 84111. **LC** KF192.U8; U83. **DD** 340/.025792.

US/0882-4738
UTAH STATE BULLETIN. (UTAH STATE BULLETIN / PREPARED BY THE OFFICE OF ADMINISTRATIVE RULES, DEPARTMENT OF ADMINISTRATIVE SERVICES.). [Utah state bull.]. **Added/Corp** Utah. Office of Administrative Rules. Utah. Utah Administrative Code. No. 85-9 (May 1, 1985)-. Bulletin. English. sm. $145.00. Legislative Printing / Utah, 419 State Capitol, Salt Lake City UT 84114. **Tel** (801)538-1103. **ED** Ken Hansen. **LC** KFU440.A73; S7. **DD** 348.792/025; 347.920825. ***Continues*** *Utah. State Archives and Records Service. State of Utah Bulletin, 0886-9650.*
Desc: The official noticing publication of the executive branch of Uah State Government.

US/1053-0258
UTILITIES INDUSTRY LITIGATION REPORTER. (1989)-. Periodical. English. sm (24 issues). $750.00. Andrews Publications Inc., 1646 West Chester Pike, PO Box 1000, Westtown PA 19395. **Tel** (610)399-6600, (800)345-1101, FAX (610)399-6610. **ED** Ronald V. Baker. **LC** KF2089; .U85. **DD** 343.73/09/05. **Ad Acc.**
Desc: Provides comprehensive national coverage of the many types of litigation stemming from the generation and distribution of energy by publicly and privately owned utilities.

UK/0960-2356
UTILITIES LAW REVIEW. Vol. 1, Issue 1 (Spring 1990)-. Periodical. English. Four times a year. $300.00. John Wiley & Sons Ltd., Baffins Lane, Chichester West Sussex PO19 1UD England. **Tel** 0243 779777, FAX 0243 776128 BTG:JWP001, telex 86290 WIBOOKG. **(Subscription address:** John Wiley / Philadelphia, PO Box 7247, Philadelphia PA 19170.**)** **LC** K25; .U86. **DD** 343.4109/05; 344.103905. **CODEN** ULAWET.
Desc: Provides detailed and expert commentary, update and analysis on every relevant aspect of the law as it develops.

BB
UWI STUDENT'S LAW REVIEW. **Main/Corp** University of the West Indies, Cave Hill, Barbados. Law Faculty. **Added/Corp** University of the West Indies (Cave Hill, Barbados). Faculty of Law. Student's Law Review. **VAT** University of the West Indies Student's Law Review. Vol. 1 (May 1976)-. English. an. 8.000Bar$ Barbados; $4.00 US. University of the West Indies / Cave Hill Campus, PO Box 64, Bridgetown Barbados. **Tel** (809)425-1310, FAX (809)424-1788, telex WB 2257. **LC** K25; .N734. **DD** 340/.09729. **Bk Rev. Ad Acc. Circ:** 200.
Desc: A student-produced journal, with assistance and guidance from the law faculty, comprised of articles of a legal and quasi-legal nature.

US/0899-7446
UWLA LAW REVIEW. (UWLA LAW REVIEW / UNIVERSITY OF WEST LOS ANGELES, SCHOOL OF LAW.). [UWLA law rev.]. **Added/Corp** University of West Los Angeles. School of Law. **VFOAT** University of West Los Angeles Law Review. Vol. 14 (1982)-. English. an (Mar.). $25.00. University of West Los Angeles / School of Law, 1155 West Arbor Vitae Street, Inglewood CA 90301. **Tel** (310)215-3339. **ED** Abby Friedman, Maggie Blackwell and Modeline Clark. **LC** K25; .N76. **DD** 340/.05. **Bk Rev.** ctrl circ. ***Continues*** *University of West Los Angeles Law Review, 0083-4068.*
Ind/Abst Index Leg. Period. (1982-); Leg. Resour. Index (1982-?).

US/0042-2363
VALPARAISO UNIVERSITY LAW REVIEW. [Valparaiso Univ. law rev.]. **Main/Corp** Valparaiso University. School of Law. **Added/Corp** Valparaiso University. School of Law. Law Review. (Fall 1966)-. Periodical. English. Three times a year. $20.00 US; $22.00 other. Valparaiso University / School of Law, Valparaiso IN 46383. **Tel** (219)465-7895. **ED** Robert Null (editor's phone: (219)465-7805). **LC** K26; .A4. **DD** 340/.09772/98. **Bk Rev,** (Qty: 1/year). **Circ:** 500.
Desc: A general law review accepting most types of articles; specializes in jurisprudential topics.
Ind/Abst Bowne Dig. Corp. Sec. Lawyers; Curr. Law Index (1980-); Fed. Tax Artic.; Index Leg. Period.; Leg. Resour. Index (1980-); LegalTrac (1980-); PAIS Int. Print.

US/0042-2533
VANDERBILT LAW REVIEW. [Vanderbilt law rev.]. Vol. 1 (Dec. 1947)-. Periodical. English. Six times a year (January, March, April, May, October, November). $28.00 US; $30.00 other. Vanderbilt Law Review, Vanderbilt University School of Law, Nashville TN 37240. **Tel** (615)322-4766. **ED** Andrew B. Nace. **LC** K26; .A58. **DD** 340/.5. Index available (Bound in last issue). cum. index. **Bk Rev. Ad Acc. Pr Rev. Circ:** 1,400. available on microfilm and microfiche from University Microfilms International (UMI); available on an online database from WESTLAW; and LEXIS. Documents available from The Genuine Article.
Desc: The Review follows the customary law review format, containing articles and book reviews by eminent writers and scholars.
Ind/Abst Bowne Dig. Corp. Sec. Lawyers (19??-); Commun. Abstr. (?-?); Crim. Justice Abstr. (19??-); Curr. Contents Soc. Behav. Sci. (1980-); Curr. Law Index (1980-); Fed. Tax Artic. (19??-); Index Leg. Period. (19??-); Leg. Resour. Index (1980-); LegalTrac (1980-); Res. Alert (19??-) [Full Cov.]; Soc. Sci. Cit. Index (19??-) [Full Cov.]; Urban Aff. Abstr. (19??-).

UK
VAUGHAN : LAW OF THE EUROPEAN COMMUNITIES SERVICE. English. £685.00. Butterworth & Co. Ltd. / Kent, England, Borough Green, Sevenoaks Kent TN15 8PH England. **Tel** 011 44 732-884567, FAX 011 44 732-885996. **ED** David Vaughan.
Desc: Comprehensive lists of core EC legislation, giving detailed references to the Official Journal and listing amendments to legislation where appropriate.

RU
VEDOMOSTI SEZDA NARODNYKH DEPUTATOV ROSSIISKOI FEDERATSII I VERKHOVNOGO SOVETA ROSSIISKOI FEDERATSII. ***Ceased.*** **Added/Corp** Russia (Federation). Sezd Narodnykh Deputatov. Russia (Federation). Verkhovnyi Sovet. Vol. 3, No 6, (Feb. 6, 1992)-(1993). Periodical. Russian. wk. $149.95. **(Subscription address:** East View Publications Inc., 3020 Harbor Lane North, Suite 110, Minneapolis MN 55447.**)** **LC** J400.R9; H47. ***Continues*** *Vedomosti Sezda Narodnykh Deputatov RSFSR i Verkhovnogo Soveta RSFSR, 0868-4944.*

US
VEHICLE AND TRAFFIC LAW. **Main/Corp** New York (State). **Added/Corp** New York (State). Dept. of Motor Vehicles. **VFOAT** Vehicle & Traffic Law. (1960)-. English. an. $8.95. Looseleaf Law Publications Inc, 41-23 150th Street, Flushing NY 11355. **Tel** (718)359-5559. **Ad Acc.** ctrl circ. ***Continues*** *New York State Vehicle and Traffic Law with Appendix, 0197-2057.*

US/1041-0740
VERDICTS, SETTLEMENTS & TACTICS. (VERDICTS, SETTLEMENTS & TACTICS : A PERSONAL INJURY LITIGATION REPORTER.). [Verdicts settl. tactics]. **VFOAT** Verdicts, Settlements and Tactics. Vol. 9 [i.e. Vol. 8], No. 9 (Sept. 1988)-. Periodical. English. mo. $340.00. Shepards McGraw-Hill Inc, 555 Middle Creek Parkway, PO Box 35300, Colorado Springs CO 80935-3530. **Tel** (719)488-3000, FAX (800)525-0053. **ED** William Jordan. **LC** KF1256.A75;

V47. **DD** 346.7303/23/02638; 347.30632302638. ***Formed by the union of*** *Verdicts & Settlements, 0744-5733* ***and*** *Trial Practice Newsletter.*
Desc: Covers all types of liability cases involving personal injury and trial tactics.

GW
VERMOEGENSTEUER-HAUPTVERANLAGUNG, DIE.
Main/Corp Germany (Federal Republic, 1949-). (19??)-. German. IDW Verlag GmbH, Postfach 320580, D-40420 Duesseldorf Germany. **Tel** 011 49 211 45610119. **DD** 343/.43/05402632.

US/0748-4925
VERMONT BAR JOURNAL & LAW DIGEST, THE.
(THE VERMONT BAR JOURNAL & LAW DIGEST / VERMONT BAR ASSOCIATION.). [Vt. bar j. law dig.]. **Added/Corp** Vermont Bar Association. **VFOAT** Vermont Bar Journal and Law Digest; Journal & Law Digest; Journal and Law Digest. Vol. 9, No. 3 (June 1983)-. Periodical. English. Six times a year. $35.00 (one year), $60.00 (two years). Vermont Bar Association, PO Box 100, Montpelier VT 05601. **Tel** (802)223-2020, FAX (802)223-1573. **ED** Phyllis A. Andrews. **Bk Rev**, (Qty: 30). **Ad Acc. Circ:** 2,000 (ctrl). ***Continues*** *Vermont Bar, 0193-7073.*
Desc: Journal featuring law articles and case digests of interest to Vermont legal community.

US
VERMONT CASE NAMES CITATOR.
English. $40.00 (1 bound volume), $52.00 (cumulative supplements). Shepards McGraw-Hill Inc, 555 Middle Creek Parkway, PO Box 35300, Colorado Springs CO 80935-3530. **Tel** (719)488-3000, FAX (800)525-0053.

US/0145-2908
VERMONT LAW REVIEW.
[Vt. law rev.]. (1976)-. English. ir. $15.00. Vermont Law Review, Vermont Law School, South Royalton VT 05068. **Tel** (802)763-8303. **LC** K26; .E76. **DD** 340/.09743. **Circ:** 1,000.
Desc: General law school publication with emphasis on current legal developments nationwide.
Ind/Abst Bowne Dig. Corp. Sec. Lawyers (19??-); Curr. Law Index (1980-); Index Leg. Period. (19??-); Leg. Resour. Index (1980-); LegalTrac (1980-).

US
VERMONT REPORTS CURRENT CASE SERVICE.
English. ir. $46.00. Butterworth Legal Publishers / Salem, NH, 8 Industrial Way, Building C, Salem NH 03079. **Tel** (800)548-4001, (603)898-9664.

US
VERMONT REPORTS CURRENT CASE STUDIES.
English. ir (3 supplements per year). $41.00 (Vol. 158). Butterworth Legal Publishers / Salem, NH, 8 Industrial Way, Building C, Salem NH 03079. **Tel** (800)548-4001, (603)898-9664.

US
VERMONT STATUTES ANNOTATED.
Main/Corp Vermont. (19??)-. English. an. $75.00 (includes supplements). Butterworth Legal Publishers / Salem, NH, 8 Industrial Way, Building C, Salem NH 03079. **Tel** (800)548-4001, (603)898-9664.

GW
VEROEFFENTLICHUNGEN DER VEREINIGING DER DEUTSCHEN STAATSRECHTSLEHRER.
(19??)-. German. an. Vol. 52 DM150.00. Walter de Gruyter Inc., PO Box 303421, D 10728 Berlin Germany. **Tel** 011 49 30 260050, FAX 011 49 30 26005251.

GW
VEROFFENTLICHUNGEN.
Main/Corp Germany (West). Bundesaufsichtsamt fuer das Versicherungswesen. (19??)-. German. ir. DM72.00. Bundesaufsichtsamt Bersicherun, Ludwigkirchplatz 3-4 ABT Z 4, D 10719 Berlin Germany. **Tel** 011 49 30 8893240, FAX 011 49 30 8893494, telex 01 83554. Index available. cum. index. **Bk Rev. Circ:** 2,800 (ctrl). ***Continues*** *Germany (West). Bundesaufsichtsamt fuer das Versicherungs- und Bausparwesen. Veroffentlichungen.*

SZ
VEROFFENTLICHUNGEN DER SCHWEIZERISCHEN KARTELLKOMMISSION.
Main/Corp Switzerland. Schweizerische Kartellkommission. **VFOAT** Publications de la Commission Suisse des Cartels. V. 1- ; 1966-. Multiple languages. qt. Orell Fuessli Zeitschriften, Dietzingerstrasse 3, PF 8036, CH 8036 Zurich Switzerland. **Tel** 044 41 1 4667711.

SA
VERSLAE VAN DIE GEKOSE KOMITEE OOR DIE MORATORIUMWYSIGINGSWETSONTWERP. REPORTS OF THE SELECT COMMITTEE ON THE MORATORIUM AMENDMENT BILL.
Main/Corp South Africa. Parliament. House of Assembly. Select Committee on the Moratorium Amendment Bill. **Added/Corp** South Africa. Parliament. House of Assembly. Select Committee on the Moratorium Amendment Bill. Reports of the Select Committee on the Moratorium Amendment Bill. **VFOAT** Reports of the Select Committee on the Moratorium Amendment Bill. (19??)-. Afrikaans (English). R1.35. Government Printer / South Africa, Bosman Street, Private Bag X85, Pretoria 0001 South Africa. **Tel** 011 27 12 3239731 Ext. 262. **DD** 346.68/077.

SA
VERSLAE VAN DIE GEKOSE KOMITEE VOOR DIE BOSWETSONTWERP.
Main/Corp South Africa. Parliament. House of Assembly. Select Committee on the Forest Bill. **VFOAT** Reports of the Select Committee on the Forest Bill. Afrikaans (English). Government Printer / South Africa, Bosman Street, Private Bag X85, Pretoria 0001 South Africa. **Tel** 011 27 12 3239731 Ext. 262. **DD** 346.6804/675.

NE
VERSLAG - COMMISSIE WET OP HET CONSUMPTIEF GELDKREDIET.
Main/Corp Netherlands (Kingdom, 1815-). Commissie Wet op het Consumptief Geldkrediet. 1973/75-. Dutch. Commissie Wet Ophet Consumptief Geldkrediet, Staatsuitgeverij, S-Gravenhage Netherlands. **DD** 346/.492/073.

GW/0042-4501
VERWALTUNGSARCHIV.
(1892)-. Periodical. German. qt. DM140.00 Germany; $98.44 other. Carl Heymanns Verlag KG, Luxemburger Strasse 449, D 50939 Cologne Germany. **Tel** 011 49 221 460100, telex 8 881 888. Index available. **Ad Acc. Circ:** 2,800.
Ind/Abst Index Foreign Leg. Per. (19??-).

GW
VERWALTUNGSRECHTSPRECHUNG IN DEUTSCHLAND.
(19??)-. Periodical. German. mo. $106.65. CH Beck Verlagsbuchhandlung, D 80791 Munich Germany. **Tel** 011 49 89 381891.

GW/0174-6162
VERWALTUNGSWIRT, DER.
[Verwaltungswirt]. **VFOAT** DVW. Der Verwaltungswirt. (1984)-. Periodical. German. bm (6 issues). DM55.00. Dr. Alfred Huethig Verlag GmbH, Postfach 102869, D 69018 Heidelberg Germany. **Tel** 011 49 6221 489281. **(Subscription address:** Huethig Publishing Inc., 29 Macintosh Drive, Oxford CT 06478.**) UDC** 656.811:35.083(430.1).

RU
VESTNIK MORKOVSKOGO UNIVERSITETA. SERIIA XI : PRAVO.
Main/Corp Moskovskii Gosudarstvennyi Universitet Im. M.V. Lomonosova. **VFOAT** Pravo. (1977)-. Periodical. Russian. bm. $119.95. Izdatelstvo Moskovskogo Universiteta, K-9 Ulitsa Gertsena 5/7, Moscow Russia. **Tel** (301)881-5973. **(Subscription address:** East View Publications Inc., 3020 Harbor Lane North, Suite 110, Minneapolis MN 55447.**) LC** K13; .O7. ***Supersedes*** *Vestnik. Seriia XII: Pravo.*
Ind/Abst Index Foreign Leg. Per.; Int. Labour Doc.

US/1046-3429
VETERANS ADVOCATE (WASHINGTON, D.C.), THE.
(THE VETERANS ADVOCATE.). [Veterans advocate]. **Added/Corp** National Veterans Legal Services Project (U.S.). Vol. 1, No. 1 (Sept. 1989)-. Periodical. English. Ten times a year. $50.00. National Veterans Legal Services Project, 2001 S Street Northwest, Suite 610, Washington DC 20009. **Tel** (202)265-8305, FAX (202)328-0063. **ED** Mary E. Cadette. **LC** KF7702; .V46. **DD** 343.73/011/05; 347.3031105. Index available. **Circ:** 1,500.
Desc: Concerned with issues in veterans law and advocacy; offers timely information on changes in VA laws, regulations, and procedures. Covers current developments in matters related to veterans benefits.

AT
VICTORIAN ACCIDENT COMPENSATION PRACTICE GUIDE.
English. bm (6 issues). 700.00Aus$. CCH Australia Ltd, PO Box 230, North Ryde New South Wales, 2113 Australia. **Tel** 011 61 02 888 2555, FAX 011 61 02 888 7324.

AT/0159-3285
VICTORIAN BAR NEWS.
[Vic. Bar news]. (1971)-. Periodical. English. qt. **DD** _a340.09945.
Ind/Abst Aust. Leg. Mon. Dig.

AT/0505-4435
VICTORIAN REPORTS.
[Vic. rep.]. **Main/Corp** Victoria. Supreme Court. **Added/Corp** Council of Law Reporting in Victoria. (Jan. 1957)-. Periodical. English. mo. Butterworths Pty Ltd, 271-273 Lane Cove Road, PO Box 345, North Ryde NSW 2113 Australia. **Tel** 011 61 2 3354444, FAX 011 61 2 3354655. ***Continues*** *Victoria. Supreme Court. Victorian Law Reports.*
Desc: Comprehensive record of Victorian superior court decisions from 1846 to the present.
Ind/Abst Aust. Leg. Mon. Dig.

US/0741-5125
VIDEO LAW MONTHLY.
See Communication.

US
VIDEO TRIAL REPORT.
Ceased. (19??)-(1993). English. ir. American Lawyer Media, L.P., 600 3rd Avenue, New York NY 10016. **Tel** (212)973-2800.

US/0277-4844
VIEW FROM SPRINGFIELD.
See Public Administration.

US/0148-8015
VILLAGE LAW.
Main/Corp New York (State). English. ir. Matthew Bender & Company Inc., 1275 Broadway, Albany NY 12204. **Tel** (800)833-9844, (518)487-3000. **LC** KFN5758.5.A29; B46.

US/0042-6229
VILLANOVA LAW REVIEW.
[Villanova law rev.]. (1956)-. Periodical. English. ir. $25.00. Villanova University School of Law, Villanova PA 19085. **Tel** (215)519-7053. **LC** K26; .I56. **Bk Rev. Ad Acc. Circ:** 1,600 (ctrl).
Desc: Articles, essays and book reviews addressing significant recent developments in American law with emphasis on law in Pennsylvania and the third circuit court of appeals.
Ind/Abst Bowne Dig. Corp. Sec. Lawyers (19??-); Crim. Justice Abstr. (19??-); Curr. Law Index (1980-); Fed. Tax Artic. (19??-); Index Leg. Period. (19??-); Leg. Resour. Index (1980-); LegalTrac (1980-); Soc. Plann. Policy Dev. Abstr. (19??-); Sociol. Abstr. (19??-).

●US
VIRGIN ISLANDS COURT RULES ANNOTATED.
(1992)-. English. **LC** KGZ9; .V57.

US
VIRGIN ISLANDS REPORTS.
Added/Corp United States. District Court (Virgin Islands). Vol. 1 (1959)-. English. an. $80.00. Butterworth Legal Publishers / Salem, NH, 8 Industrial Way, Building C, Salem NH 03079. **Tel** (800)548-4001, (603)898-9664.

US
VIRGIN ISLANDS RULES AND REGULATIONS. VIRGIN ISLANDS REGISTER.
Main/Corp Virgin Islands of the United States. Laws, Statutes, etc. English. ir. $30.00. Equity Publishing Corporation, RR 1 Box 3, Orford NH 03777. **Tel** (603)637-5012, (800)637-5012.

US/0360-3857
VIRGINIA BAR ASSOCIATION JOURNAL, THE.
Main/Corp Virginia Bar Association. Vol. 1 (Jan. 1975)-. Periodical. English. Four times a year (Jan., Apr., July, Oct.). $30.00. Bess C. Wendell, 3849 West Weyburn Road, Richmond VA 23235. **ED** Charles E. Friend, (editor's address: 322 Scotland Street, Williamsburg, VA 23185, phone: (804)229-8846). **LC** KF200; .V53. **DD** 340/.09755. **Bk Rev**, (Qty: (varies)). **Circ:** 5,500.
Desc: Contains articles on topical legal issues, recent court rulings changes in federal and state laws, and the association activities.
Ind/Abst Curr. Law Index (1981-); Leg. Resour. Index (1981-); LegalTrac (1980-).

US/0196-5174
VIRGINIA CONTINUING LEGAL EDUCATION BULLETIN.
Bulletin. English. mo. School of Law, University of Virginia, Charlottesville VA 22901. **LC** KF275.A15; V57. **DD** 349.755/05; 347.5505. ***Continues*** *Virginia Continuing Legal Education, 0193-6654.*

US
VIRGINIA COURT OF APPEALS REPORTS.
Main/Corp Virginia. Court of Appeals. Vol. 1 (Jan. 1, 1985)-. English. Supreme Court of Virginia, Office of the Executive Secretary, 100 North 9th Street/3rd Floor, Richmond VA 23219. **Tel** (804)786-6455. **LC** KFV2448; .A2. **DD** 348.755/046.

US/8750-3247
VIRGINIA LAW REPORTS.
[Va. law rep.]. **Main/Corp** Virginia. 1 VLR, Pt. 5 (Feb. 1, 1986)-. English. bm (22 no. a year). $175.00. Virginia Reports Reprints, 14031 Steeplestone Rd., Midlothian VA 23113-6416. **LC** KFV2445; .A33. **DD** 348.755/048; 347.550848. ***Continues*** *Opinions of the Supreme Court of Virginia, 0745-0060.*

US/0042-6601
VIRGINIA LAW REVIEW.
[VA. law rev.]. Vol. 1 (Oct. 1913)-. Periodical. English. ir (eight times a year). $40.00. University of Virginia / School of Law, North Grounds, Charlottesville VA 22903. **Tel** (804)924-0597. **LC** K26. **DD** 349.755/05. **CODEN** VLIBAD. cum. index. **Bk Rev. Ad Acc. Pr Rev. Circ:** 2,200 (ctrl). Documents available from The Genuine Article, UMI Article Clearinghouse. ***Absorbed*** *Virginia Law Register.*
Desc: Published by students of the University of Virginia School of Law, covering all areas of legal scholarship.
Ind/Abst ABC POL SCI (19??-1984); ABI/INFORM Glob. Ed.; ABI Inform Ondisc (Dec. 1976-); Account. Art.; Am. Hist. Life (1966-1967); Bowne Dig. Corp. Sec. Lawyers; Crim. Justice Abstr.; Curr. Law Index (1980-); Fed. Tax

Artic.; Index Leg. Period.; Leg. Resour. Index (1980-); LegalTrac (1980-); PAIS Int. Print; Res. Alert [Full Cov.]; Soc. Sci. Cit. Index [Full Cov.].

US/0042-661X
VIRGINIA LAW WEEKLY. Added/Corp University of Virginia. Dept. of Law. University of Virginia. School of Law. Vol. 1; (May 27, 1948)-. Periodical. English. ir (Twenty-eight times a year). $25.00. Virginia Law Weekly, University of Virginia School of Law, Charlottesville VA 22901. **Tel** (804)924-3070. **ED** Michael Weiss. **LC** UNC. **Ad Acc. Circ:** 1,300.
Desc: Student weekly devoted to coverage of school issues in current legal developments, law and education, etc.

US/0899-9473
VIRGINIA LAWYER. [Va. lawyer]. Vol. 36, No. 12 (June 1988)-. Periodical. English. mo. $3.50 members; $12.00 other. Virginia State Bar, 801 East Main Street, Ross Building #1000, Richmond VA 23219. **Tel** (804)924-3416. **LC** KF200; .V55. **DD** 349.755/05. ***Continues*** *Virginia Bar News.*

US/1060-4065
VIRGINIA LEGAL DESKBOOK : THE COMMON SENSE APPROACH. [Va. legal deskb.]. **VFOAT** Virginia Legal Desk Book. (1991)-. English. an. $60.00. Common Sense Inc., 7210 Hull St., Suite 112, Richmond VA 23235. **Tel** (804)276-7533. **LC** KFV2477; .V474. **DD** 349.755; 347.55.

US
VIRGINIA LEGAL STUDIES. English. ir. University Press of Virginia, PO Box 3608, Charlottesville VA 22903. **Tel** (804)924-3469. **ED** R Lillich. ctrl circ.
Desc: Various topics of importance in legal studies, international as well as American, dealt with in monographs. Most have more than one contributor.

US
VIRGINIA REGISTER OF REGULATIONS, THE. Added/Corp Virginia Code Commission. **VFOAT** Virginia Register. Vol. 1, Issue 1 (Oct. 15, 1984)-. Periodical. English. Twenty-six times a year. Free on request to public libraries in Virginia; $100.00 others. Virginia Code Commission, 910 Capitol Street, Richmond VA 23219. **Tel** (804)786-3591. **LC** KFV2436; .V57. **DD** 348.755/01; 347.55081. Index available. cum. index.
Desc: Includes text, both proposed and adopted, of all regulations, plus other information concerning the Virginia state government.

US/0049-6499
VIRGINIA RESEARCHER (CHARLOTTESVILLE VA). (THE VIRGINIA RESEARCHER.). Periodical. English. mo. $99.00. National Legal Research Group Inc, PO Box 7187, Charlottesville VA 22906. **Tel** (800)727-6574, (804)977-5690, FAX (804)295-4667. **LC** KFV2457; .V575. **DD** 348.755/043/05.
Desc: Digests of cases of the Virginia Supreme Court, the Virginia Court of Appeals, and federal cases arising in Virginia.

US/0735-9004
VIRGINIA TAX REVIEW. [Va. tax rev.]. **Added/Corp** Virginia Tax Review Association. Vol. 1, No. 1 (Spring 1981)-. Periodical. English. qt. $45.00. University of Virginia / School of Law, North Grounds, Charlottesville VA 22903. **Tel** (804)924-0597. **ED** Paul Quinn. **LC** K26; .I75. **DD** 343.7305/05; 347.303505. **Ad Acc. Circ:** 1,000. Documents available from UMI Article Clearinghouse.
Desc: Publishes articles by distinguished academics and tax law practitioners, as well as student authors, on a variety of current tax topics of interest to the profession.
Ind/Abst ABI/INFORM Glob. Ed. (19??-); ABI Inform Ondisc (Winter 1983-); Account. Tax Datab. (Winter 1983-); Account. Art. (19??-); Bowne Dig. Corp. Sec. Lawyers (19??-); Curr. Law Index (1983-); Fed. Tax Artic. (19??-); Gen. BusinessFile (1992-); Index Leg. Period. (19??-); Leg. Resour. Index (1983-); LegalTrac (1980-).

US/0507-1348
VIRGINIAS, MARYLAND, DELAWARE AND DISTRICT OF COLUMBIA LEGAL DIRECTORY, THE. (19??)-. English. an (June). $42.00. Legal Directories Publishing Company, 9111 Garland Road, PO Box 189000, Dallas TX 75218. **Tel** (214)321-3238, 800 447-5375. **LC** KF190; .V5. **DD** 340/.025/75.

PH
VITAL LEGAL DOCUMENTS IN THE NEW PEOPLE'S GOVERNMENT. **Main/Corp** Philippines. **Added/Corp** Philippines. President (1986- : Aquino) Central Book Supply, Inc. **VFOAT** Vital Legal Documents in the New government. Vol. 99 (1986)-. English. Central Book Supply Inc, Alemar's Building, 769 Rizal Avenue, Manila Philippines. **DD** 348.599/025; 345.990825. ***Continues*** *Philippine Presidential Decrees and Other Vital Legal Documents.*

US/0883-573X
VOICE (EAST LANSING, MICH.). See Education.

SZ
VOLK + RECHT : ORGAN DER DEMOKRATISCHEN JURISTEN DER SCHWEIZ. VFOAT Volk und Recht. Periodical. German. ir. 12.00F. DJS Volk + Recht, Postfach 1308, 4001 Basel Switzerland. **DD** 349.494/05; 344.94005.

US/0043-003X
WAKE FOREST LAW REVIEW. [Wake Forest law rev.]. (1970)-. Periodical. English. qt. $21.00. Wake Forest University, School of Law, PO Box 7206 Reynolda Station, Winston-Salem NC 27109. **Tel** (919)759-5439. **LC** K27; .A36. **DD** 340/.05. (Bound in Dec. issue). cum. index. **Bk Rev. Ad Acc. Circ:** 1,900 (ctrl). Documents available from UMI Article Clearinghouse. ***Continues*** *Intramural Law Review (Winston-Salem, N.C.).*
Desc: A comprehensive, updating publication which addresses and explains topics of current interest in the legal profession.
Ind/Abst ABI/INFORM Glob. Ed. (19??-); ABI Inform Ondisc (Jan. 1988-); Bowne Dig. Corp. Sec. Lawyers (19??-); Crim. Justice Abstr. (19??-); Curr. Law Index (1980-); Fed. Tax Artic. (19??-); Index Leg. Period. (19??-); Leg. Resour. Index (1980-); LegalTrac (1979-).

US/0363-9517
WARRANTY WATCH. English. Federal State Reports Inc, PO Box 986 Courthouse Station, Arlington VA 22216. **LC** KF919.C6; A138. **DD** 343/.73/08.

US/0043-0420
WASHBURN LAW JOURNAL. [Washburn law j.]. **Added/Corp** Washburn University of Topeka. School of Law. Vol. 1 (Winter 1960)-. Periodical. English. Three times a year. Price varies. Washburn University of Topeka, School of Law, Topeka KS 66621. **Tel** (913)231-1010. **ED** Marta Linenberger. **LC** K27; .A75. **DD** 340. Index available (bound in last issue). cum. index. **Circ:** 2,000.
Desc: A publication on current legal issues.
Ind/Abst Bowne Dig. Corp. Sec. Lawyers; Crim. Penol. Police Sci. Abstr.; Curr. Law Index (1980-); Fed. Tax Artic.; Index Leg. Period.; Leg. Resour. Index (1980-); LegalTrac (1980-).

US/0278-7652
WASHBURN UNIVERSITY SCHOOL OF LAW ALUMNI DIRECTORY. See College and School Publications-Alumni.

US/0043-0463
WASHINGTON AND LEE LAW REVIEW. [Wash. Lee law rev.]. **Added/Corp** Washington and Lee University. School of Law. Vol. 1 (Fall 1939)-. English. qt. $32.50. Washington & Lee University, School of Law Lewis Hall, Lexington VA 24450. **Tel** (703)463-8566, FAX (703)463-8945. **LC** K27; .A77. (Bound in last issue). cum. index. **Ad Acc. Circ:** 2,000 (ctrl). available on microfilm and microfiche from University Microfilms International (UMI).
Desc: Scholarly publication of notes and comments on various areas of the law and the implications of new decisions and areas of law that affect the legal profession.
Ind/Abst Account. Tax Datab. (1979-) [Full Txt.]; Bowne Dig. Corp. Sec. Lawyers (19??-); Curr. Law Index (1980-); Fed. Tax Artic. (19??-); Index Leg. Period. (19??-); Leg. Resour. Index (1980-); LegalTrac (1980-).

US
WASHINGTON COUNTY REPORTS. **Added/Corp** Washington County Bar Association (Pa.). (1922)-. English. wk. $26.50. Washington County Bar Association, 523 Washington Trust Building, Washington PA 15301. **Tel** (412)225-6710.

US/1052-8385
WASHINGTON COURT RULES. FEDERAL. [Wash. court rules, Fed.]. (1989)-. English. an. West Publishing Company, 610 Opperman Drive, PO Box 64526, Eagan MN 55123-1308. **Tel** (612)687-5618, (800)328-9352, FAX (612)687-5388, (800)562-2329. **(Subscription telephone:** FAX (612)688-3570) **DD** 347. ***Continues in part*** *Washington Court Rules.*

US/1052-8377
WASHINGTON COURT RULES. STATE. [Wash. court rules, State]. (1989)-. English. an. West Publishing Company, 610 Opperman Drive, PO Box 64526, Eagan MN 55123-1308. **Tel** (612)687-5618, (800)328-9352, FAX (612)687-5388, (800)562-2329. **(Subscription telephone:** FAX (612)688-3570) **DD** 347. ***Continues in part*** *Washington Court Rules.*

US/0195-959X
WASHINGTON CREDIT LETTER DIGEST. Main/Corp Capitol Reports, Inc. Periodical. English. mo. $96.00. Capitol Reports Inc, 1750 Pennsylvania Avenue NW/Suite 1107, Washington DC 20006. **LC** KF1039.A15; C36. **DD** 346.73/073.

US/0195-9581
WASHINGTON CREDIT LETTER PRIVACY REPORT. *Suspended.* Main/Corp Capitol Reports, Inc. Periodical. English. mo. $120.00. Capitol Reports Inc, 1750 Pennsylvania Avenue NW/Suite 1107, Washington DC 20006. **LC** KF1039.A15; C37. **DD** 346.73/073.

US/0889-5724
WASHINGTON CRIME NEWS SERVICES' CRIMINAL JUSTICE DIGEST. *Title Change.* [Wash. Crime News Serv. crim. justice dig.]. **Added/Corp** Washington Crime News Services. **VFOAT** Criminal Justice Digest. Vol. 4, No. 3 (Mar. 1985)-(Jan. 1995). Periodical. English. mo. Washington Crime News Services, 3918 Prosperity Avenue, Suite 318, Fairfax VA 22031-3334. **Tel** (703)573-1600, (800)422-9267, FAX (703)573-1604. **DD** 364. ***Continues*** *Criminal Justice Journal (Annandale, Va.).* ***Absorbed by*** *CJ Management and Training Digest.*
Desc: A comprehensive management journal for the criminal justice administrator. Each month, authors address such complex issues as staff management, productivity, office automation, intelligence functions, computerization, manpower utilization, deployment and management of financial resources.

US/0194-1291
WASHINGTON DRUG LETTER (WASHINGTON. 1979). See Pharmacy and Pharmacology.

US/0043-0617
WASHINGTON LAW REVIEW (1967). (WASHINGTON LAW REVIEW.). [Wash. law rev.]. **Added/Corp** University of Washington. School of Law. Vol. 43 (1967)-. Academic Scholarly Publication. English. qt. $26.00 US; $30.00 other. Washington Law Review Association, University of Washington Law School, Condon Hall JB-20, Seattle WA 98195. **Tel** (206)543-6335. **ED** Anrea Oakley and Pete Ramels. Index available. cum. index. **Bk Rev. Ad Acc. Pr Rev. Circ:** 1,850 (ctrl). Documents available from The Genuine Article. ***Continues*** *University of Washington. School of Law. University of Washington Law Review, 0190-6186.*
Desc: A scholarly journal published by the law students of the University of Washington School of Law.
Ind/Abst Bowne Dig. Corp. Sec. Lawyers; Crim. Justice Abstr.; Curr. Contents Soc. Behav. Sci.; Curr. Law Index (1980-); Fed. Tax Artic.; Index Leg. Period.; Leg. Resour. Index (1980-); LegalTrac (1980-); Res. Alert [Full Cov.]; Soc. Sci. Cit. Index [Full Cov.].

US/0890-8761
WASHINGTON LAWYER, THE. [Wash. lawyer]. **Added/Corp** District of Columbia Bar. Vol. 1, No. 1 (Sept./Oct. 1986)-. Periodical. English. bm. $20.00. District of Columbia Bar, 1250 H Street Northwest, Sixth Floor, Washington DC 20005. **Tel** (202)737-4700, FAX (202)626-3471. **LC** KF200; .W36. **DD** 340/.060753. **Ad Acc, Adv Mgr:** Maureen Muller, **Tel** ext. 205. ctrl circ. ***Continues*** *District Lawyer, 0147-7943.*
Ind/Abst Leg. Resour. Index (1986-); LegalTrac (1981-).

US/0516-9968
WASHINGTON LETTER (AMERICAN BAR ASSOCIATION). (WASHINGTON LETTER.). **Added/Corp** American Bar Association. Governmental Affairs Group. American Bar Association. Governmental Relations Office. (19??)-. Periodical. English. wk. $30.00 (nonmember), $25.00 (member of ABA). American Bar Association, 750 North Lake Shore Drive, Chicago IL 60611. **Tel** (312)988-5522, (312)988-5241, FAX (312)988-5528, telex 270593. **ED** Rhonda J. McMillion. **LC** KF200; .W37. **DD** 348.73/46; 340. **Circ:** 5,000 (ctrl).
Desc: An update on legislation in Congress of interest to the legal profession.

US/0741-9295
WASHINGTON LOBBYISTS & LAWYERS DIRECTORY, THE. [Washington lobby. lawyers dir.]. **Added/Corp** Amward Publications. **VFOAT** Washington Lobbyists and Lawyers Directory. (1981)-. English. an. $34.50. Communications Services, PO Box 137 Benjamin Franklin Station, Washington DC 20044. **ED** Ed Zuckerman. **LC** KF195.L6; W36. **DD** 328,73/078/025753. ***Continues*** *Washington Lobbyists/Lawyers Directory, 0741-9295.*

US
WASHINGTON PROPERTY LAW REPORTER. VFOAT Property Law Reporter. Periodical. English. Butterworth Heinemann / Woburn, MA, 225 Wildwood Avenue, Unit B, Woburn MA 01801. **Tel** (800)366-2665, FAX (617)928-2620, telex 880052.

US/0889-8162
WASHINGTON REPORTS. 2D SERIES. [Wash. rep., 2d ser.]. **Main/Corp** Washington (State). Supreme Court. **VFOAT** Cases Determined in the Supreme Court of Washington; Rules of Court; Official Rules of Court. Vol. 1 (Oct. 19, 1939)-. English. bw (with additional issues in Jan., July, and Aug.). Court Reports, Temple of Justice Avenue 05, Olympia WA 98504. **Tel** (206)357-2155. **ED** Reporter: v. 1- S. D. Williams. - July 1986- Richard F. Jones. **LC** KFW45; .A212. **DD** 348. cum. index. ***Supersedes*** *Washington (State). Supreme Court. Cases Determined in the Supreme Court of Washington.*

US/0199-1507
WASHINGTON SERVICE BUREAU SUPREME COURT BRIEF SERVICE. SECURITIES. *Ceased.* Main/Corp Washington Service Bureau. **VFOAT** Supreme Court Brief Service.

Securities. (19??)-(19??). Periodical. English. wk. Washington Service Bureau Inc., 655 15th Street Northwest, Suite 270, Washington DC 20005. **Tel** (800)955-5219, (202)508-0600.

US/0886-5213
WASHINGTON STATE BAR NEWS.
[Wash. State Bar news]. **Added/Corp** Washington State Bar Association. Vol. 1, No. 1 (March 1947)-. Periodical. English. Twelve times a year. $25.97 Washington State (includes 8.2% sales tax); $24.00 other. Washington State Bar Association, 2001 6th Avenue / #500, Seattle WA 98121-2599. **Tel** (206)448-0441. **ED** Lindsay Thompson (editor's phone: (206)727-8215). **DD** 340. Index available in last issue of volume--attached. cum. index. **Bk Rev**. **Ad Acc**. **Circ:** 20,000 (ctrl).
Desc: Legal articles and notices of interest to Washington lawyers.
Ind/Abst Index Leg. Period.; Leg. Resour. Index; LegalTrac (1980-).

US/8756-0801
WASHINGTON UNIVERSITY JOURNAL OF URBAN AND CONTEMPORARY LAW.
[Wash. Univ. j. urban contemp. law]. **Added/Corp** Washington University (Saint Louis, Mo.). School of Law. **VFOAT** Journal of Urban and Contemporary Law. Vol. 24 (1983)-. Periodical. English. sa. $20.00 US; $21.00 other. Washington University School of Law, Campus Box 1120, One Brookings Drive, St Louis MO 63130-4899. **Tel** (314)935-6436, (314)935-6422, FAX (314)935-6493. **ED** Ted Bowling and David Knieriem. **LC** K25; .R26. **DD** 346.7304/5/05; 347.3064505. cum. index. **Bk Rev**. **Ad Acc**. **Circ:** 900. available on microfiche. ***Continues*** *Urban Law Annual, 0566-3377.*
Desc: Law review that publishes articles discussing recent legal developments in topics affecting the urban community. For example: zoning, housing, environment, energy, transportation, and education.
Ind/Abst Bowne Dig. Corp. Sec. Lawyers; Curr. Law Index (1984-); Index Leg. Period.; J. Plan. Lit.; Leg. Resour. Index (1984-); LegalTrac (1982-); PAIS Int. Print; Public Aff. Inf. Serv. Bull.

US/0043-0862
WASHINGTON UNIVERSITY LAW QUARTERLY.
[Wash. Univ. law q.]. **Main/Corp** Washington University (Saint Louis, MO.). School of Law. Vol. 22 (1936/37)-. Periodical. English. qt. $24.00. Washington University School of Law, Campus Box 1120, One Brookings Drive, St Louis MO 63130-4899. **Tel** (314)935-6436, (314)935-6422, FAX (314)935-6493. **ED** Kelly Riley and John Voorhees. **LC** K23; .A34. **DD** 349.73/05. Index available (Free). cum. index. **Bk Rev**. **Ad Acc**. **Circ:** 1,100. ***Continues*** *St. Louis Law Review, 0271-2849.*
Desc: Student and professional-written articles on current legal issues in a wide range of subject areas.
Ind/Abst Bowne Dig. Corp. Sec. Lawyers (19??-); Crim. Justice Abstr. (19??-); Curr. Law Index (1980-); Fed. Tax Artic. (19??-); Index Leg. Period. (19??-); Leg. Resour. Index (1980-); LegalTrac (1980-).

US/0043-1621
WAYNE LAW REVIEW.
[Wayne law rev.]. **Added/Corp** Wayne University. Law School. Wayne State University. Law School. Vol. 1, No. 1 (Winter 1954)-. Periodical. English. Four times a year. $28.00. Wayne State University / School of Law, 468 West Ferry, Detroit MI 48202. **Tel** (313)577-3939. Index available in last issue of volume--attached. **Bk Rev**, (Qty: 1/year). **Ad Acc**. **Circ:** 1,100 (ctrl).
Ind/Abst Bowne Dig. Corp. Sec. Lawyers; Curr. Law Index (1980-); Fed. Tax Artic.; Index Leg. Period.; Leg. Resour. Index (1980-); LegalTrac (1980-).

US/0272-1201
WBA NEWSLETTER (BOSTON, MASS.).
(WBA NEWSLETTER.). [WBA newsl.]. **Main/Corp** Women's Bar Association of Massachusetts. **Added/Corp** Women's Bar Association of Massachusetts. Newsletter. **VAT** Women's Bar Association newsletter. Vol. 1, No. 2 (Feb. 1980)-. Periodical. English. bm. $15.00. Womens Bar Association, 191 Monsen Road, Concord MA 01742. **Tel** (617)227-0986, (617)369-0487. **LC** KF200; .W65. **DD** 340/.06/0744. ***Continues*** *Women's Bar Association Newsletter, 0272-121X.*

CN/1180-2588
WCAT IN FOCUS.
(WCAT IN FOCUS : THE NEWSLETTER OF THE WORKERS' COMPENSATION APPEALS TRIBUNAL OF ONTARIO.). [WCAT focus]. **Main/Corp** Ontario. Workers' Compensation Appeals Tribunal. **VFOAT** Gros Plan sur le TAAT. **VAT** Workers' Compensation Appeals Tribunal in Focus; Gros Plan sur la Tribunal d'Appel des Accidents du Travail. Vol. 1, No. 1 (Apr. 1990)-. Newsletter. English (French). qt. **DD** 344.713/021/0269.

●US/1061-2564
WE THE PEOPLE (WASHINGTON, D.C.: 1992).
(WE THE PEOPLE.). [We people]. **Added/Corp** Congressional Institute. Vol. 1, No. 1 (Jan./Feb. 1992)-. Periodical. English. bm. We The People, 316 Pennsylvania Avenue, SE # 403, Washington DC 20003-1147. **DD** 328.

NE
WEEKBLAD VOOR FISCAL RECHT.
Kluwer BV, Postbus 23, 7400 GA Deventer Netherlands. **Tel** 011 31 5700 33155, 011 31 5700 48999, FAX 011 31 5700 11504, telex 42829.

US/0092-2560
WEEKLY CALIFORNIA CITATOR.
English. wk. $100.00. Marshall F Johnson, 2528 5th Avenue, Sacramento CA 95818. **LC** KFC59; .W4. **DD** 348/.794/047.

UK
WEEKLY LAW REPORTS.
Added/Corp Incorporated Council of Law Reporting for England and Wales. Great Britain. Parliament. House of Lords. Gold Coast (Colony). Constitution. Great Britain. Courts. (Jan. 2, 1953)-. Periodical. English. wk (except Sept.). £1956.00 UK; £215.00 other. Incorporated Council of Law Reporting for England and Wales, 3 Stone Buildings, Lincoln's Inn, London WC2A 3XN England. **Tel** (071)242-6471, FAX (071)831-5247. **ED** Carol Ellis, Hilary Jellie and Robert Williams. cum. index. **Ad Acc**. ***Continues*** *Weekly Notes.*
Desc: Contains decisions in the House of Lords, the Privy Council, the Supreme Court of Judicature, Assize Courts and Ecclesiastical Courts.
Ind/Abst Aust. Leg. Mon. Dig.

US
WEEKLY LEGISLATIVE SUMMARY.
Added/Corp Empire State Chamber of Commerce. (19??)-. Periodical. English. ir. University of North Carolina Institute of Government CB, 3330 Knapp Building, Chapel Hill NC 27599. **Tel** (919)966-4119.

US/0161-2972
WEEKLY REGULATORY MONITOR, THE.
Main/Corp Washington Monitor. Periodical. English. wk. $300.00. The Washington Monitor, 1301 Pennsylvania Avenue NW/Suite 1000, Washington DC 20004. **Tel** (202)347-7757, FAX (202)628-3430. **(Subscription address:** 104 5th Avenue, New York, NY 10011**)** **LC** KF5406.A15; W36. **DD** 342/.73/0605.

US
WEEKLY WRAP-UP / MINNESOTA HOUSE OF REPRESENTATIVES.
Main/Corp Minnesota. Legislature. House of Representatives. **VFOAT** Minnesota House of Representatives Weekly Wrap-Up. Periodical. English. wk. Minnesota House of Representatives Information Office, Room 9/State Capitol, St Paul MN 55155. **LC** KFM5415; .M55. **DD** 342.776/00262; 347.76020262. ***Continues*** *Minnesota. Legislature. House of Representatives. Weekly News Wrap-Up.*

CN/0702-8989
WELDON TIMES, THE.
V. 1- April 1976-. Periodical. English. ir. Free. Dalhousie Law School, Dalhousie University, Halifax Nova Scotia B3H 4H9 Canada. **Tel** (902)424-6552. **DD** 340/.07/1171622. ctrl circ.

JM/0253-7370
WEST INDIAN LAW JOURNAL.
[West Indian law j.]. **Added/Corp** Council of Legal Education. (Oct. 1977)-. Periodical. English. Twice a year. $80.00. Council of Legal Education, PO Box 231, Kingston 7 Jamaica West Indies. **Tel** (809)927-1235. **ED** William A. Roper. **LC** K27; .E74. **DD** 340/.09729. **Bk Rev**. **Ad Acc**. **Circ:** 700 (ctrl). ***Supersedes*** *Jamaica Law Journal.*
Desc: Legal and quasi-legal articles primarily related to the Commonwealth Caribbean and secondarily to countries with a common law tradition.
Ind/Abst Curr. Law Index (1980-); Index Leg. Period.; Leg. Resour. Index (1980-); LegalTrac (1980-).

US/0043-3268
WEST VIRGINIA LAW REVIEW.
[West VA. law rev.]. **Added/Corp** West Virginia University. College of Law. Vol. 52 (Dec. 1949)-. Periodical. English. qt (Jan., Apr., June, Nov.). $27.00. West Virginia Law Review, West Virginia University, College of Law, Morgantown WV 26506. **Tel** (304)293-5306. **ED** John D. Moore. **LC** K27; .E8. **DD** 340/.06/0754. cum. index. **Bk Rev**. **Ad Acc**. **Circ:** 1,200. available on microfilm and microfiche from University Microfilms International (UMI); available on an online database from WESTLAW. ***Continues*** *West Virginia Law Quarterly and the Bar.*
Desc: Legal issues relevant to West Virginia and the nation with one issue dedicated to coal related topics.
Ind/Abst Bowne Dig. Corp. Sec. Lawyers; Coal Abstr.; Curr. Law Index (1980-); Fed. Tax Artic.; Index Leg. Period.; Leg. Resour. Index (1980-); LegalTrac (1980-).

US
WEST VIRGINIA REGISTER : RULES OF GOVERNMENTAL AGENCIES / SECRETARY OF STATE'S OFFICE, ADMINISTRATIVE LAW DIVISION.
Added/Corp West Virginia. Office of the Secretary of State. Administrative Law Division. (May 1983)-. Periodical. English. Fifty-two times a year. $250.00. Secretary of State / West Virginia, State Capital Administrative Law Division, Charleston WV 25305. **Tel** (304)345-4000. **ED** Judy Cooper (phone: (304)558-6000). **LC** KFW1236; .W47. **DD** 348.754/025; 347.540825. Index available. **Circ:** 165.

US/0161-1909
WEST VIRGINIA STATE BAR CONTINUING LEGAL EDUCATION BULLETIN.
Main/Corp West Virginia State Bar. **Added/Corp** West Virginia State Bar. Continuing legal education bulletin. (1977)-. Periodical. English. mo. $10.00 (non-members), $4.00 (members). West Virginia State Bar Association, E-400 State Capitol, Charleston WV 25305. **Tel** (304)346-8414. **LC** KF200; .W45. **DD** 340/.9754.

US/0364-3425
WEST VIRGINIA STATE BAR JOURNAL.
Ceased. **Main/Corp** West Virginia State Bar. Vol. 1 (Oct. 1975)-(1984). English. qt. West Virginia State Bar Association, E-400 State Capitol, Charleston WV 25305. **Tel** (304)346-8414. **LC** KF200; .W47. **DD** 340/.09754. ***Continues*** *West Virginia State Bar News.*
Ind/Abst Law Office Inf. Serv.

US/0746-1844
WESTCHESTER BAR JOURNAL.
(WESTCHESTER BAR JOURNAL / WESTCHESTER COUNTY BAR ASS'N.). Vol. 10, No. 3 (Summer 1983)-. Academic Scholarly Publication. English. qt. $8.00. Westchester County Bar Association, 199 Main Street, White Plains NY 10601. **Tel** (914)761-3707. **ED** Frank D Arcuri. **Bk Rev**. **Ad Acc**. **Circ:** 2,500 (ctrl). ***Continues*** *Westchester Bar Topics (1976).*
Desc: The official publication of the Westchester County Bar Association and is issued for the purpose of presenting scholarly articles to its members.

US/0049-7274
WESTCHESTER LAW JOURNAL.
(19??)-. Newspaper. English. wk. $40.00. Westchester Law Journal Inc., 175 Main Street, White Plains NY 10601. **LC** K27; .E83. **DD** 349.747/277/05; 347.47277005. **Ad Acc**. **Circ:** 200.

AT/0727-2022
WESTERN AUSTRALIA IN BRIEF.
(BRIEF.). [West. Aust. brief]. (1979)-. English. mo (11 issues per year). 45.00Aus$. Law Society of Western Australia, GPO Box A35, Perth WA 6000 Australia. **Tel** 11 61 481 0548. **ED** Rob Meadows. **DD** 319.41. **Bk Rev**, (Qty: 11). **Ad Acc**, **Adv Mgr:** Tony Stevens. ctrl circ.

AT/0083-8764
WESTERN AUSTRALIAN REPORTS.
Added/Corp Council of Law Reporting of Western Australia. Western Australia. Supreme Court. **VFOAT** W. A. Reports. (1960)-. English. be. The Law Book Company Limited, 44-50 Waterloo Road, North Ryde New South Wales, 2113 Australia. **Tel** 011 61 2 8870177, FAX 011 61 2 8887240, telex ASBOOK 27445. **(Subscription address:** Law Book Company, Australia Level 7 132 Arthur St., N Sydney NSW 2060 Australia.**)** **ED** K. J. Martin. ***Continues*** *Western Australian Law Reports.*
Desc: These reports are the authorised Law Reports of the Supreme Court of Western Australia.
Ind/Abst Aust. Leg. Mon. Dig. (19??-).

US/0896-2189
WESTERN LEGAL HISTORY.
(WESTERN LEGAL HISTORY : THE JOURNAL OF THE NINTH JUDICIAL CIRCUIT HISTORICAL SOCIETY.). [West. legal hist.]. (1988)-. Periodical. English. Twice a year (July, Dec.). $25.00 US; $35.00 other (Comes with Ninth Judicial Circuit Historical Society Membership). Ninth Judicial Circuit Historical Society, 125 South Grand Avenue, Pasadena CA 91105. **Tel** (818)795-0266, FAX (818)405-7018. **ED** Bradley B. Williams, Ph. D. **LC** K27; .E8525. **DD** 349.78. **Bk Rev**, (Qty: 10-12). **Pr Rev. Circ:** 2,000.
Desc: An illustrated journal that publishes scholarship in all areas of western American legal history. Articles, book reviews, reprints, and analyses of source documents, and oral histories explore, interpret, and describe the influential roles the law and courts have played in the history of the western states.
Ind/Abst Am. Hist. Life (1988-); Index Leg. Period.; Leg. Resour. Index; LegalTrac (1988-); West. Hist. Q.

US/0190-6593
WESTERN NEW ENGLAND LAW REVIEW.
[West. New Engl. law rev.]. **Added/Corp** Western New England College. School of Law. Vol. 1 (Apr. 1978)-. Academic Scholarly Publication. English. Twice a year (Spring and Fall). $10.00. Western New England College, 1215 Wilbraham Road, Springfield MA 01119. **Tel** (413)782-1463 Ext 463. **ED** Patricia A. McCullough. **LC** K27; .E853. **DD** 340/.09744. Index available. cum. index. **Bk Rev**. **Circ:** 1,000 (ctrl).
Desc: A scholarly legal journal with contributions by the student and outside authors.
Ind/Abst Bowne Dig. Corp. Sec. Lawyers; Curr. Law Index (1980-); Index Leg. Period.; Leg. Resour. Index (1980-); LegalTrac (1980-).

US/0362-8892
WESTERN STATE UNIVERSITY LAW REVIEW.
[West. State Univ. law rev.]. Vol. 2, No. 2 (Spring 1975)-. English. Twice a year (June & Sept.).

$20.00. Western State University / College of Law, 1111 North State College Boulevard, Fullerton CA 92631. **Tel** (714)871-1820. **ED** Jeannette Rodriguez. **LC** K12; .A9368. **DD** 340/.05. **Bk Rev**, (Qty: Approx. 10). **Ad Acc, Adv Mgr:** Debora Paul. ***Continues*** *Western State Law Review, 0360-9901.*
Ind/Abst Bowne Dig. Corp. Sec. Lawyers; Crim. Justice Abstr.; Curr. Law Index (1980-); Fed. Tax Artic.; Index Leg. Period.; Leg. Resour. Index (1980-); LegalTrac (1980-).

US/0734-9904
WESTERN TAX. Vol. 1, No. 1 (Sept. 1982)-. Periodical. English. mo. $100.00. Butterworth Heinemann / Woburn, MA, 225 Wildwood Avenue, Unit B, Woburn MA 01801. **Tel** (800)366-2665, FAX (617)928-2620, telex 880052. **LC** KF6750.A15; W47. **DD** 343.7304/05; 347.303405.

CN/0049-7525
WESTERN WEEKLY REPORTS. V. 1- Nov. 18, 1911-. Periodical. English. wk. 102.00Can$ Canada; 88.75Can$ other. Carswell / Canada, 2075 Kennedy Road, Scarborough Ontario M1T 3V4 Canada. **Tel** (416)609-3800, (800)387-5164. **ED** Laura M Wright. Index available. cum. index. **Ad Acc.** available on an online database from QL Systems Ltd. ***Absorbed*** *Western Law Reporter (Canada) and Index-Digest.* **Desc:** Complete coverage of decisions of the Courts of Western Canada and appeals to the Supreme Court of Canada.

US
WEST'S ANNOTATED CALIFORNIA CODES. **Main/Corp** California. 1954-. English. West Publishing Company, 610 Opperman Drive, PO Box 64526, Eagan MN 55123-1308. **Tel** (612)687-5618, (800)328-9352, FAX (612)687-5388, (800)562-2329. **(Subscription telephone:** FAX (612)688-3570**)** **LC** KFC30.5. **DD** 345/.2/2.

US
WEST'S ARIZONA DIGEST 2D LAW FINDER. ***Title Change.*** **Added/Corp** West Publishing Company. **VFOAT** West's Arizona Digest Second Law Finder; Arizona Digest 2d Law Finder; Arizona Digest Second Law Finder. (1991) Ed.-(1992) Ed. English. West Publishing Company, 610 Opperman Drive, PO Box 64526, Eagan MN 55123-1308. **Tel** (612)687-5618, (800)328-9352, FAX (612)687-5388, (800)562-2329. **LC** KFA2461; .W47. ***Continued by*** *West's Arizona Law Finder.*

●US
WEST'S ARIZONA LAW FINDER. **Added/Corp** West Publishing Company. **VFOAT** Arizona Law Finder. (1993) Ed.-. English. ***Continues*** *West's Arizona Digest 2d Law Finder.*

US
WEST'S ATLANTIC DIGEST 2D. **Added/Corp** United States. Courts. West Publishing Company. **VFOAT** Atlantic Digest 2D. Vol. 1 (1968)-. Periodical. English. West Publishing Company, 610 Opperman Drive, PO Box 64526, Eagan MN 55123-1308. **Tel** (612)687-5618, (800)328-9352, FAX (612)687-5388, (800)562-2329. **(Subscription telephone:** FAX (612)688-3570**)** **LC** KF135.A7; W4. **DD** 345/.5/2.

US/8750-2623
WEST'S CALIFORNIA REPORTER. [West's Calif. report.]. **Added/Corp** West Publishing Company. California. Supreme Court. **VFOAT** California Reporter. Vol. 1 (1960)-. English. wk. West Publishing Company, 610 Opperman Drive, PO Box 64526, Eagan MN 55123-1308. **Tel** (612)687-5618, (800)328-9352, FAX (612)687-5388, (800)562-2329. **LC** KFC47; .C32. **DD** 348/.794/043. ***Continues*** *California Reporter, Covering Cases Reported in Pacific Reporter.*

US/0741-5346
WEST'S EDUCATION LAW DIGEST. **Added/Corp** West Publishing Company. **VFOAT** Education Law Digest. (March 1983)-. Periodical. English. West Publishing Company, 610 Opperman Drive, PO Box 64526, Eagan MN 55123-1308. **Tel** (612)687-5618, (800)328-9352, FAX (612)687-5388, (800)562-2329. **LC** KF4110.3; .W47. **DD** 344.73/07/02648; 347.304702648.

US/0744-8716
WEST'S EDUCATION LAW REPORTER. [West's educ. law report.]. **VFOAT** Education Law Reporter. Vol. 1, No. 1 (Jan. 14, 1982)-. Periodical. English. bw (with 5 to 6 cumulations yearly). West Publishing Company, 610 Opperman Drive, PO Box 64526, Eagan MN 55123-1308. **Tel** (612)687-5618, (800)328-9352, FAX (612)687-5388, (800)562-2329. **LC** KF4110.A2; W47. **DD** 344.73/07/02648; 347.304702648.
Ind/Abst Curr. Index J. Educ. (March 1990); Educ. Index (19??-).

US
WEST'S EDUCATION LAW REPORTER. SPECIAL PAMPHLET / NATIONAL ASSOCIATION OF COLLEGE AND UNIVERSITY ATTORNEYS. **Added/Corp** National Association of College and University Attorneys (U.S.). **VFOAT** Education Law Reporter. Special Pamphlet.; Special Pamphlet. (Sept. 23, 1982)-. Periodical. English. bw. National Association of College and University Attorneys, 1 Dupont Circle, Washington DC 20036. **Tel** (303)979-5657. ***Absorbed*** *College Law Digest, 0045-737X.*

US/0162-2005
WEST'S FEDERAL CASE NEWS. [West's Federal. case news]. **Added/Corp** United States. Supreme Court. West Publishing Company. Vol. 1 (Jan. 1978)-. English. wk. West Publishing Company, 610 Opperman Drive, PO Box 64526, Eagan MN 55123-1308. **Tel** (612)687-5618, (800)328-9352, FAX (612)687-5388, (800)562-2329. **LC** KF127; .W46. **DD** 348/.73/46.

US
WEST'S FEDERAL FORMS. 1952-. English. West Publishing Company, 610 Opperman Drive, PO Box 64526, Eagan MN 55123-1308. **Tel** (612)687-5618, (800)328-9352, FAX (612)687-5388, (800)562-2329. **(Subscription telephone:** FAX (612)688-3570**)** **DD** 347.93.

US/1048-4906
WEST'S FEDERAL RULES DECISIONS. (WEST'S FEDERAL RULES DECISIONS : OPINIONS, DECISIONS AND RULINGS INVOLVING THE FEDERAL RULES OF CIVIL PROCEDURE AND FEDERAL RULES OF CRIMINAL PROCEDURE.). [West's fed. rules decis.]. **Added/Corp** West Publishing Company. **VFOAT** Federal Rules Decisions. Vol. 117 (1988)-. English. ir. West Publishing Company, 610 Opperman Drive, PO Box 64526, Eagan MN 55123-1308. **Tel** (612)687-5618, (800)328-9352, FAX (612)687-5388, (800)562-2329. **LC** KF8830; .W47. **DD** 347.73/051/02643; 347.3075102643. ***Continues*** *Federal Rules Decisions, 0886-3644.*
Ind/Abst Index Leg. Period. (1988-); Leg. Resour. Index (1988-); LegalTrac (1987-).

US/0749-1034
WEST'S FEDERAL TAX MANUAL WITH WESTLAW. [West's fed. tax man. WESTLAW]. **VFOAT** Federal Tax Manual with Westlaw. 1985 Ed.-. English. an. West Publishing Company, 610 Opperman Drive, PO Box 64526, Eagan MN 55123-1308. **Tel** (612)687-5618, (800)328-9352, FAX (612)687-5388, (800)562-2329. **(Subscription telephone:** FAX (612)688-3570**)** **DD** 343. ***Continues*** *West's Federal Tax Guide with Westlaw, 0749-095X.*

US/0277-5158
WEST'S FEDERAL TAX SYSTEM. [West's fed. tax syst.]. **VFOAT** Federal Tax System. 1981-1, No. 1 (Jan. 15, 1981)-. English. wk. $150.00. West Publishing Company, 610 Opperman Drive, PO Box 64526, Eagan MN 55123-1308. **Tel** (612)687-5618, (800)328-9352, FAX (612)687-5388, (800)562-2329. **(Subscription telephone:** FAX (612)688-3570**)** **LC** KF6272; .W47. **DD** 343.7304/05; 347.303405.

US/8750-2615
WEST'S ILLINOIS DECISIONS. [West's Ill. decis.]. **VFOAT** Illinois Decisions. 1 ILL. Dec.- Nov. 30, 1976-. English. ir (50 no. a year). $97.50. West Publishing Company, 610 Opperman Drive, PO Box 64526, Eagan MN 55123-1308. **Tel** (612)687-5618, (800)328-9352, FAX (612)687-5388, (800)562-2329. **(Subscription telephone:** FAX (612)688-3570**)** **LC** KFI1247; .A34. **DD** 348/.773/044.

US
WEST'S INDIANA DIGEST 2D LAW FINDER. **Added/Corp** West Publishing Company. **VFOAT** Indiana Digest 2d Law Finder; West's Indiana Digest Second Law Finder; Indiana Digest Second Law Finder; Indiana Digest Law Finder. (1991)-. English. West Publishing Company, 610 Opperman Drive, PO Box 64526, Eagan MN 55123-1308. **Tel** (612)687-5618, (800)328-9352, FAX (612)687-5388, (800)562-2329.

US/0148-1991
WEST'S LOUISIANA SESSION LAW SERVICE. **Main/Corp** Louisiana. **VFOAT** Louisiana Session Law Service. English. West Publishing Company, 610 Opperman Drive, PO Box 64526, Eagan MN 55123-1308. **Tel** (612)687-5618, (800)328-9352, FAX (612)687-5388, (800)562-2329. **(Subscription telephone:** FAX (612)688-3570**)** **LC** KFL25; .W4. **DD** 348/.763/022.

US
WEST'S LOUISIANA STATUTES ANNOTATED. **Main/Corp** Louisiana. V. 1- 1951-. Periodical. English. West Publishing Company, 610 Opperman Drive, PO Box 64526, Eagan MN 55123-1308. **Tel** (612)687-5618, (800)328-9352, FAX (612)687-5388, (800)562-2329. **(Subscription telephone:** FAX (612)688-3570**)** **DD** 345.22.

US
WEST'S MCKINNEY'S FORMS. **Added/Corp** West Publishing Company. (1964)-. English. bm. West Publishing Company, 610 Opperman Drive, PO Box 64526, Eagan MN 55123-1308. **Tel** (612)687-5618, (800)328-9352, FAX (612)687-5388, (800)562-2329. **DD** 347.93. Each issue contains an index to its own contents (no volume index)--loose.

US/1053-5322
WEST'S MISSISSIPPI CASES REPORTED IN SOUTHERN REPORTER, SECOND SERIES. [West's Miss. cases rep. South. report. second ser.]. **Added/Corp** West Publishing Company. Mississippi. Supreme Court. **VFOAT** West's Mississippi Cases; Southern Reporter, Mississippi Cases. (1988)-. English. West Publishing Company, 610 Opperman Drive, PO Box 64526, Eagan MN 55123-1308. **Tel** (612)687-5618, (800)328-9352, FAX (612)687-5388, (800)562-2329. **LC** KFM6645; .A21. **DD** 348.762/046/05; 347.62084605. ***Continues*** *Mississippi Cases Reported in Southern Reporter, Second Series.*

US
WEST'S NEW HAMPSHIRE DIGEST, 1760 TO DATE, COVERING CASES FROM STATE AND FEDERAL COURTS. **VFOAT** New Hampshire Digest. V. 1- 1951-. English. West Publishing Company, 610 Opperman Drive, PO Box 64526, Eagan MN 55123-1308. **Tel** (612)687-5618, (800)328-9352, FAX (612)687-5388, (800)562-2329. **(Subscription telephone:** FAX (612)688-3570**)** **DD** 345.32. cum. index.

US
WEST'S NEW JERSEY DIGEST. **Added/Corp** New Jersey. Courts. United States. Courts. West Publishing Company. **VFOAT** New Jersey Digest. (1954)-. English. ir. West Publishing Company, 610 Opperman Drive, PO Box 64526, Eagan MN 55123-1308. **Tel** (612)687-5618, (800)328-9352, FAX (612)687-5388, (800)562-2329. **DD** 345.32. cum. index.

US/1048-3624
WEST'S NEW YORK SUPPLEMENT. [West's N. Y. suppl.]. **Added/Corp** West Publishing Company. New York (State). Court of Appeals. **VFOAT** New York Supplement. (1988)-. English. wk. West Publishing Company, 610 Opperman Drive, PO Box 64526, Eagan MN 55123-1308. **Tel** (612)687-5618, (800)328-9352, FAX (612)687-5388, (800)562-2329. **LC** KFN5045; .A333. **DD** 348.747/046; 347.470846. ***Continues*** *New York Supplement. Second Series, 8750-264X.*

US/1041-6730
WEST'S OKLAHOMA DECISIONS. (WEST'S OKLAHOMA DECISIONS : CASES DECIDED IN THE SUPREME COURT, COURT OF CRIMINAL APPEALS, COURT OF APPEALS, AND COURT ON THE JUDICIARY.). [West's Okla. decis.]. **Added/Corp** Oklahoma. Supreme Court. West Publishing Company. **VFOAT** Oklahoma Decisions. (1988)-. English. West Publishing Company, 610 Opperman Drive, PO Box 64526, Eagan MN 55123-1308. **Tel** (612)687-5618, (800)328-9352, FAX (612)687-5388, (800)562-2329. **LC** KFO1247; .A2. **DD** 348.766/046; 347.660846. ***Continues*** *Oklahoma Decisions Reported in Pacific Reporter, Second Series, 0747-2986.*

US
WEST'S OREGON CASES REPORTED IN PACIFIC REPORTER, SECOND SERIES. **Added/Corp** West Publishing Company. **VFOAT** Oregon Cases Reported in Pacific Reporter, Second Series; Oregon Cases; West's Oregon Cases. (198?)-. English. wk. West Publishing Company, 610 Opperman Drive, PO Box 64526, Eagan MN 55123-1308. **Tel** (612)687-5618, (800)328-9352, FAX (612)687-5388, (800)562-2329. **(Subscription telephone:** FAX (612)688-3570**)** ***Continues*** *Oregon Cases Reported in Pacific Reporter, Second Series, 0747-2994.*

US/0746-1526
WEST'S PERSONAL INJURY NEWS. [West's pers. inj. news]. **VFOAT** Personal Injury News. Vol. 1, No. 1 (Mar. 8, 1983)-. Periodical. English. bw. $80.00. West Publishing Company, 610 Opperman Drive, PO Box 64526, Eagan MN 55123-1308. **Tel** (612)687-5618, (800)328-9352, FAX (612)687-5388, (800)562-2329. **(Subscription telephone:** FAX (612)688-3570**)** **LC** KF1256.A53; W47. **DD** 346.7303/23; 347.306323.

US
WEST'S RHODE ISLAND DIGEST, 1783 TO DATE. **VFOAT** Rhode Island Digest. 1952-. English. West Publishing Company, 610 Opperman Drive, PO Box 64526, Eagan MN 55123-1308. **Tel** (612)687-5618, (800)328-9352, FAX (612)687-5388, (800)562-2329. **(Subscription telephone:** FAX (612)688-3570**)** **DD** 345.32. cum. index.

US
WEST'S SOCIAL SECURITY REPORTING SERVICE. SOCIAL SECURITY CASES FROM U.S. SUPREME COURT, U.S. COURT OF APPEALS, U.S. DISTRICT COURTS, U.S. CLAIMS COURT, U.S. BANKRUPTCY COURTS, STATE APPELLATE COURTS. **VFOAT** Social Security Cases from U.S. Supreme Court,

U.S. Court of Appeals, U.S. District Courts, U.S. Claims Court, U.S. Bankruptcy Courts, State Appellate Courts; Cases; West's Social Security Reporting Service. Cases. 1-. English. West Publishing Company, 610 Opperman Drive, PO Box 64526, Eagan MN 55123-1308. **Tel** (612)687-5618, (800)328-9352, FAX (612)687-5388, (800)562-2329. **(Subscription telephone:** FAX (612)688-3570**)**

US/1048-3780
WEST'S SOUTH WESTERN REPORTER. [West's south west. report.]. **Added/Corp** West Publishing Company. **VFOAT** South Western Reporter. (1988)-. English. wk. West Publishing Company, 610 Opperman Drive, PO Box 64526, Eagan MN 55123-1308. **Tel** (612)687-5618, (800)328-9352, FAX (612)687-5388, (800)562-2329. **LC** KF135.S7; S612. **DD** 348/76/046; 347.60846. cum. index. ***Continues*** *Southwestern Reporter, 8750-2682.*

US/1048-3799
WEST'S SOUTHERN REPORT. [West's south. rep.]. **Added/Corp** West Publishing Company. **VFOAT** Southern Reporter. (1988)-. English. wk. West Publishing Company, 610 Opperman Drive, PO Box 64526, Eagan MN 55123-1308. **Tel** (612)687-5618, (800)328-9352, FAX (612)687-5388, (800)562-2329. **LC** KF135.S8; S612. **DD** 348.75/046; 347.50846. ***Continues*** *Southern Reporter. Second Series. Cases Argued and Determined in the Courts of Alabama, Florida, Louisiana, Mississippi, 8750-2690.*

●US
WEST'S TAX LAW DICTIONARY. **Added/Corp** West Publishing Company. **VFOAT** Tax Law Dictionary. (1992)-. English. an. West Publishing Company, 610 Opperman Drive, PO Box 64526, Eagan MN 55123-1308. **Tel** (612)687-5618, (800)328-9352, FAX (612)687-5388, (800)562-2329.

US
WEST'S VETERANS APPEALS REPORTER. See Military and Defense.

US
WEST'S WYOMING DIGEST, A DIGEST OF WYOMING LEGAL AUTHORITIES, STATE AND FEDERAL. **VFOAT** Wyoming Digest. V. 1- 1956-. English. West Publishing Company, 610 Opperman Drive, PO Box 64526, Eagan MN 55123-1308. **Tel** (612)687-5618, (800)328-9352, FAX (612)687-5388, (800)562-2329. **(Subscription telephone:** FAX (612)688-3570**)** **DD** 345.42; 345.412. cum. index.

GW/0042-9678
WGO MONATSHEFTE FUER OSTEUROPAISCHES RECHT. [WGO. Monatsh. osteur. Recht]. Vol. 9 (1967)-. Periodical. German. bm. DM196.00. CF Muller Juristischer Verlag, Verlagsgr Huethig PF 102869, D 69018 Heidelberg Germany. **(Subscription address:** Huethig Publishing Inc., 29 Macintosh Drive, Oxford CT 06478.**)** **LC** K27; .G16. ***Continues*** *WGO.*
Ind/Abst Index Foreign Leg. Per.

US/0195-7643
WHITTIER LAW REVIEW. [Whittier law rev.]. **Added/Corp** Whittier College (Whittier, Calif.). School of Law. Vol. 1, No. 1 (1978)-. Periodical. English. Four times a year. $21.00. Whittier College / School of Law, 5353 West Third Street, Los Angeles CA 90020. **Tel** (213)938-3621 Ext. 232. **ED** Aram Dobalian (editor's phone: (213)938-3621 Ext. 231). **LC** K27; .H57. **DD** 349.794/05. cum. index. **Ad Acc, Adv Mgr:** T. Jeha. ctrl circ. available on an online database from WESTLAW.
Desc: Articles dealing with contemporary issues in the legal field. Topics range from American constitutional law to copyright and business law.
Ind/Abst Bowne Dig. Corp. Sec. Lawyers; Crim. Justice Abstr.; Curr. Law Index (1980-); Index Leg. Period.; Leg. Resour. Index (1980-); LegalTrac (1980-).

US/0278-6478
WHO'S WHO AMONG AMERICAN LAW STUDENTS. [Who's who among Am. law stud.]. **Added/Corp** University Publishing Bureau. 1st Ed. (1982)-. English. an. $35.00. Summa Publishing Bureau, 5670 Lincoln Drive, Edina MN 55436. **Tel** (612)933-1139. **ED** Joanne R. Desotelle. **LC** KF266; .W5. **DD** 349.73/025 B; 347.30025 B.

US/0162-7880
WHO'S WHO IN AMERICAN LAW. **Added/Corp** Marquis-Who's Who, Inc. 1st Ed. (1978)-. English. be. $249.95. Marquis Who's Who, A Reed Reference Publishing Company, Part of Reed International PLC, 121 Chanlon Road, New Providence NJ 07974. **Tel** (908)464-6800, (800)521-8110, FAX (908)665-6688, telex 138 755. **LC** KF372; .W48. **DD** 340/.092/2; B. **[CCC].** available on magnetic tape and CD-ROM.
Desc: Biographical reference directory including sketches of leading attorneys, judges, educators and other top legal professionals.

AT
WICKS SUBJECT INDEX TO COMMONWEALTH LEGISLATION. **Added/Corp** Australia. Laws, Etc. (Acts of the Australian Parliament, 1901-1973). English. an. $52.00. The Law Book Company Limited, 44-50 Waterloo Road, North Ryde New South Wales, 2113 Australia. **Tel** 011 61 2 8870177, FAX 011 61 2 8887240, telex ASBOOK 27445. ***Continues*** *Subject Index to the Acts of the Australian Parliament.*

●US/1064-5012
WIDENER JOURNAL OF PUBLIC LAW. [Widener j. public law]. **Added/Corp** Widener University. School of Law. **VFOAT** Journal of Public Law. (1992)-. Periodical. English. sa (Mar., Nov.). $32.00 US; $38.00 other. Widener University School of Law, 3800 Vartan Way, Harrisburg PA 17110. **Tel** (717)541-3965, FAX (717)541-3966. **ED** Bruce Grabow. **LC** K27; .I32. **DD** 342.73/06; 347.3026. **Circ:** 250.
Desc: Includes articles on public law, Pennsylvania administrative law, and legislature digest.

US/0191-9822
WILLAMETTE LAW REVIEW. [Willamette law rev.]. **Added/Corp** Willamette University. College of Law. Vol. 15, (Winter 1978)-. Academic Scholarly Publication. English. Four times a year (Jan., Mar., May, July). $22.00. Willamette University, College of Law, 250 Winter Street, Salem OR 97301. **Tel** (503)370-6300. **ED** Edwin Budge. **LC** K27; .I4. **DD** 340/.05. **Ad Acc, Adv Mgr:** Chris, **Tel** (503)370-6300 Ext. 4343. **Pr Rev. Circ:** 1,000. ***Continues*** *Willamette Law Journal.*
Desc: A scholarly publication which provides a timely forum for the discussion of legal issues and related legal problems.
Ind/Abst Bowne Dig. Corp. Sec. Lawyers; Curr. Law Index (1980-); Fed. Tax Artic.; Index Leg. Period.; Leg. Resour. Index (1980-); LegalTrac (1980-).

●US/1065-8254
WILLIAM AND MARY BILL OF RIGHTS JOURNAL, THE. (THE WILLIAM AND MARY BILL OF RIGHTS JOURNAL : A STUDENT PUBLICATION OF THE MARSHALL-WYTHE SCHOOL OF LAW.). [William Mary Bill Rights j.]. **Added/Corp** Marshall-Wythe School of Law. Marshall-Wythe School of Law. Institute of Bill of Rights Law. **VFOAT** William & Mary Bill of Rights Journal; Bill of Rights Journal. Vol. 1, Issue 1 (Spring 1992)-. Periodical. English. Twice a year. $20.00. Marshall-Wythe School of Law, College of William and Mary, PO Box 8795, Williamsburg VA 23187-8795. **Tel** (804)221-3860. **LC** K27; .I44. **DD** 342. ***Continues*** *The Colonial Lawyer, 0884-4429.*
Ind/Abst Index Leg. Period. (1993-).

US/0043-5589
WILLIAM AND MARY LAW REVIEW. [William Mary law rev.]. V. 1- 1957-. Periodical. English. qt. $28.00 US; $30.00 other. William & Mary Law Review, Marshall Wythe School of Law, Williamsburg VA 23185. **Tel** (804)253-4430. **ED** Tracey Nelson. **LC** K27; .I45. **DD** 349.755/05. Index available. cum. index. **Bk Rev. Ad Acc. Circ:** 800. ***Continues*** *William and Mary Review of Virginia Law (Williamsburg, VA. : 1949).*
Ind/Abst Acad. Search (July 1993-); Bowne Dig. Corp. Sec. Lawyers; Curr. Law Index (1980-); Fed. Tax Artic.; Index Leg. Period.; INFO-SOUTH Abstr.; Leg. Resour. Index (1980-); LegalTrac (1980-); Mag. Search; PAIS Int. Print.

US/0270-272X
WILLIAM MITCHELL LAW REVIEW. [William Mitchell law rev.]. **Added/Corp** William Mitchell College of Law. Vol. 1 (1974)-. Periodical. English. Four times a year. $24.00. William Mitchell College of Law, 875 Summit, St Paul MN 55105. **Tel** (612)290-6305. **LC** K27; .I47. **DD** 340/.5. **Bk Rev. Ad Acc. Circ:** 1,900 (ctrl).
Desc: Articles by known authors regarding current legal issues.
Ind/Abst Bowne Dig. Corp. Sec. Lawyers; Crim. Justice Abstr.; Curr. Law Index (1980-); Index Leg. Period.; Leg. Resour. Index (1980-); LegalTrac (1980-).

CN/0838-3596
WINDSOR REVIEW OF LEGAL AND SOCIAL ISSUES. [Windsor rev. leg. soc. issues]. **Added/Corp** University of Windsor. Faculty of Law. **VFOAT** Revue des Affaires Juridiques et Sociales--Windsor. Vol. 1 (1989)-. English (summaries and/or abstracts in French). an. $10.00. University of Windsor Faculty of Law, Windsor Ontario, N9B 3P4 Canada. **Tel** (519)253-4232 ext. 2926. **ED** Andrew Pinto. **DD** 349.71/05. **Bk Rev.** ***Continues*** *Canadian Community Law Journal, 0704-0857.*
Desc: This publication is a multi-disciplinary law journal that examines legal and social issues that affect the Canadian community.
Ind/Abst Can. Legal Lit.; Index Can. Leg. Period. Lit. (1992-).

CN/0710-0841
WINDSOR YEARBOOK OF ACCESS TO JUSTICE, THE. [Windsor yearb. access justice]. **Added/Corp** University of Windsor. Faculty of Law. **VFOAT** Access to Justice; Recueil Annuel de Windsor d'Acces a la Justice. Vol. 1 (1981)-. English (French; summaries and/or abstracts in French). an. 25.00Can$ US & Canada; 27.50Can$ other. University of Windsor Faculty of Law, Windsor Ontario, N9B 3P4 Canada. **Tel** (519)253-4232 ext. 2926. **ED** W.A. Bogart. **LC** K27; .I53. **DD** 347/.005; 342.7005. Index available. cum. index. **Bk Rev. Pr Rev.**
Desc: An international, interdisciplinary and independently refereed journal focusing upon either issues of access to justice or justice itself.
Ind/Abst Can. Legal Lit.; Curr. Law Index; Index Can. Leg. Period. Lit. (1981-); Index Foreign Leg. Per.; Index Leg. Period. (1981-); Leg. Resour. Index; LegalTrac (1980-); Soc. Plann. Policy Dev. Abstr.

GW
WIRTSCHAFTSWISSENSCHAFTLICHE UND WIRTSCHAFTSRECHTLICHE UNTERSUCHUNGEN. See Economics.

US
WISCONSIN ADMINISTRATIVE REGISTER. **Added/Corp** Wisconsin. Revisor of Statutes. No. 1 (Jan. 1956)-. English. sm. $45.00. Wisconsin Department of Administration, 101 South Webster Street, PO Box 7864, Madison WI 53702. **Tel** (608)266-1651. **ED** Gary L. Poulson. **Circ:** 7,500.
Desc: Provides information as to proposed administrative rules.

US
WISCONSIN COURT RULES AND PROCEDURE. FEDERAL. **Added/Corp** West Publishing Company. (1989)-. English. West Publishing Company, 610 Opperman Drive, PO Box 64526, Eagan MN 55123-1308. **Tel** (612)687-5618, (800)328-9352, FAX (612)687-5388, (800)562-2329. ***Continues in part*** *Wisconsin Court Rules and Procedure ..., State and Federal, 0731-1907.*

US
WISCONSIN COURT RULES AND PROCEDURE. STATE. **Added/Corp** West Publishing Company. (1989)-. English. West Publishing Company, 610 Opperman Drive, PO Box 64526, Eagan MN 55123-1308. **Tel** (612)687-5618, (800)328-9352, FAX (612)687-5388, (800)562-2329. ***Continues in part*** *Wisconsin Court Rules and Procedure ..., State and Federal, 0731-1907.*

US/0043-650X
WISCONSIN LAW REVIEW. [Wis. l. rev.]. **Added/Corp** University of Wisconsin--Madison. Law School. University of Wisconsin. Law School. (Oct. 1920)-. Academic Scholarly Publication. English. Six times a year. $30.00. University of Wisconsin Law School, 975 Bascom Mall, Madison WI 53706-1399. **Tel** (608)262-3877, FAX (608)262-5485. **ED** Kevin M. Kelly. **LC** K27; .I8. **DD** 349.775/05. **[CCC].** Index available. cum. index. **Bk Rev. Ad Acc. Pr Rev. Circ:** 2,000 (ctrl). available on microfilm and microfiche from University Microfilms International (UMI). Documents available from The Genuine Article.
Desc: Scholarly law journal perhaps with historical or sociological tones.
Ind/Abst Bowne Dig. Corp. Sec. Lawyers; Crim. Justice Abstr.; Curr. Contents Soc. Behav. Sci.; Curr. Law Index (1980-); Fed. Tax Artic.; Index Leg. Period.; Int. Bibliogr. Sociol.; Leg. Resour. Index (1980-); LegalTrac (1980-); PAIS Int. Print; Res. Alert [Full Cov.]; Soc. Plann. Policy Dev. Abstr.; Soc. Sci. Cit. Index [Full Cov.]; Sociol. Abstr.; SportSearch.

US
WISCONSIN LEGAL DIRECTORY, THE. **Added/Corp** Legal Directories Publishing Company. (1932)-. English. an. $25.00. Legal Directories Publishing Company, 9111 Garland Road, PO Box 189000, Dallas TX 75218. **Tel** (214)321-3238, 800 447-5375. **LC** KF192.W57; W58.

US/0746-150X
WISCONSIN REPORTER. (WISCONSIN REPORTER : COVERING CASES REPORTED IN NORTH WESTERN REPORTER, SECOND SERIES.). [Wisconsin rep.]. **VFOAT** West's Wisconsin Reporter; West's Official Wisconsin Reporter. English. wk. $80.00. West Publishing Company, 610 Opperman Drive, PO Box 64526, Eagan MN 55123-1308. **Tel** (612)687-5618, (800)328-9352, FAX (612)687-5388, (800)562-2329. **(Subscription telephone:** FAX (612)688-3570**)** **DD** 348.

US/0145-6628
WISCONSIN SESSION LAWS. **Main/Corp** Wisconsin. **Added/Corp** Wisconsin. Laws, Statutes, Etc. Laws of Wisconsin. **VFOAT** Laws of Wisconsin. (1911)-. English. be. $65.55. Wisconsin Department of Administration, 101 South Webster Street, PO Box 7864, Madison WI 53702. **Tel** (608)266-1651. **LC** KFW2425; .A213. **DD** 348/.775/022. ***Continues*** *Wisconsin. Laws, Statutes, Etc. Laws of Wisconsin.*

US
WISCONSIN STATUTES. **Main/Corp** Wisconsin. English. ir. $95.00 (hard cover), $84.00 (soft cover). Wisconsin Department of Administration, 101 South Webster Street, PO Box 7864, Madison WI 53702. **Tel** (608)266-1651.

US/1052-3421
WISCONSIN WOMEN'S LAW JOURNAL. [Wis. women's law j.]. Vol. 1 (Spring 1985)-. Academic Scholarly Publication. English. an. $15.00 (institutions), $8.00 (individuals). University of Wisconsin Law School, 975 Bascom Mall, Madison WI 53706-1399. **Tel** (608)262-3877, FAX (608)262-5485. **LC** K27; .I84. **DD** 342.73/0878/05. **Circ:** 450.
Desc: An alternative forum to traditional law reviews for scholarly research and discussion of legal issues as they affect women in all areas of their lives.
Ind/Abst Index Leg. Period.

GW
WISSENSCHAFT UND GEGENWART. JURISTISCHE REIHE. Issue 1- 1969-. Periodical. German. ir. Vittorio Klostermann, Frauenlobstrasse 22, D 60487 Frankfurt Germany. **Tel** 011 49 69 9708160.

GW/0443-6976
WISSENSCHAFTSRECHT, WISSENSCHAFTSVERWALTUNG, WISSENSCHAFTSFORDERUNG. Vol. 1, (Feb. 1968)-. Periodical. German. Three times a year. DM175.00. JCB Mohr / Paul Siebeck, Postfach 2040, D 72010 Tuebingen Germany. **Tel** 011 49 7071 9230, FAX 011 49 7071 51104, telex 7/262872 mohr d. **ED** Christian Flamig, Otto Kimminich, Dieter Leuze, Wolfgang Lower, Ernst-Joachim Meusel, Hans-Heinricht Rupp, Hermann-Josef Schuster, and Friedrich Graf Stenbock-Fermor, Hartmut Kruger. **Bk Rev. Circ:** 600.
Desc: Endeavours to help university administrators, lawyers, judges, legislators, scholars and the interested public in understanding the legal and administrative problems of modern research and teaching on the university level.

US
WITTENBERG'S PRODUCTS LIABILITY: THE LAW IN MISSISSIPPI. English. be. $32.95, $10.95 seperate pocket part supplement. Harrison Company Publishers, 3110 Crossing Park, PO Box 7500, Norcross GA 30091-7500. **Tel** (800)241-3561, (404)447-9150.

AU/0933-2766
WOHNRECHTLICHE BLAETTER. [Wohnrechtl. Bl.]. (1988)-. Periodical. German. Twelve times a year. $187.00. Springer-Verlag Wien, Sachsenplatz 4 6, PO Box 89, A-1201 Vienna Austria. **Tel** 011 43 1 3302415. **(Subscription address:** Springer Verlag New York Inc. / for North America, 44 Hartz Way, Secaucus NJ 07096.) **[CCC].**

US/1047-4633
WOMBLE, CARLYLE, SANDRIDGE & RICE'S NORTH CAROLINA ENVIRONMENTAL LAW LETTER. [Womble, Carlyle, Sandridge Rice's N. C. environ. law lett.]. **Added/Corp** Womble, Carlyle, Sandridge & Rice (Firm). **VFOAT** Womble, Carlyle, Sandridge and Rice's North Carolina Environmental Law letter; North Carolina Environmental Law Letter. Vol. 1, No. 1 (May 1990)-. Periodical. English. mo. $137.00. M. Lee Smith Publishers and Printers, 162 4th Avenue North, PO Box 198867, Nashville TN 37219. **Tel** (615)242-7395, (800)274-6774, FAX (615)256-6601. **ED** Howard Grubbs and Martin Holton, III, (address) 2400 Wachovia Building, Winston-Salem, NC 27199-2301, (phone) 919-721-3600. **DD** 344.
Desc: Newsletter reporting the latest state specific environmental law developments that affect the companies in that state.

CN/0847-5253
WOMEN AND THE LAW (FREDERICTON). (WOMEN AND THE LAW.). [Women law]. **Added/Corp** New Brunswick. Women's Directorate. No. 1 (Jan. 1990)-. Periodical. English. **DD** 346.71501/5/05.

US/0741-4102
WOMEN & THE LAW REPORT. [Women law rep.]. **VFOAT** Women and the Law Report. Vol. 1, No. 1 (Mar. 1983)-. Periodical. English. mo. Newsletter Services Inc, 9700 Philadelphia Court, Lanham MD 20706. **Tel** (800)345-2611. **LC** KF477.A15; W64. **DD** 342.73/0878/05; 347.30287805.

US/0095-1188
WOMEN LAW REPORTER. Sept. 1, 1974-. Periodical. English. sm. $275.00. Women Law Reporter Inc, 5141 Massachusetts Avenue, Washington DC 20016. **LC** KF4758.A15; W65. **DD** 346/.73/013.

US/0043-7468
WOMEN LAWYERS' JOURNAL. [Women lawyers' j.]. **Added/Corp** National Association of Women Lawyers. Women Lawyers' Club (U.S.) Women Lawyers' Association (U.S.). Vol. 1, No. 1 (May 1911)-. Academic Scholarly Publication. English. qt. $16.00. National Association of Women Lawyers, 750 North Lake Shore Drive, Chicago IL 60611. **Tel** (312)988-6186. **ED** Claire E. Morrison. **DD** 340. **Bk Rev. Ad Acc. Circ:** 1,600. available on microfilm and microfiche from University Microfilms International (UMI).
Desc: Covers women in law, education and promotion; women's legal issues; and current general legal issues.
Ind/Abst Crim. Justice Period. Index; Curr. Law Index (1980-Summer 1986); Fed. Tax Artic.; Leg. Resour. Index (1980-Summer 1986); LegalTrac (1980-1991).

US/0736-9433
WOMEN'S LEGAL DEFENSE FUND NEWSLETTER, THE. **VFOAT** W.L.D.F. Newsletter; WLDF Newsletter. Newsletter. English. Three times a year. Free. Women's Legal Defense Fund, 2000 P Street NW/Suite 400, Washington DC 20036. **Tel** (202)887-0364. **ED** A Pauley. **LC** KF477.A15; W65. **DD** 346.7301/34/0269; 347. 3061340269. **Circ:** 2,000 (ctrl).
Desc: Updates on sex discrimination employment law and family law from a feminist perspective, and information on women's legal defense fund activities.

US/0085-8269
WOMEN'S RIGHTS LAW REPORTER. [Women's rights law report.]. V. 1- July/Aug. 1971-. English. qt. $15.00 (students); $20.00 (individuals); $40.00 (institutions). Women's Rights Law Reporter, 15 Washington Street, Newark NJ 07102. **Tel** (201)648-5320. **LC** KF478.A45; W6. **DD** 346/.73/013. **Bk Rev. Ad Acc. Circ:** 1,200 (ctrl). available on microfilm and microfiche from University Microfilms International (UMI).
Desc: Oldest specialized legal journal in U.S. dealing with laws and cases affecting women. Designed as a forum for ideas, criticism, debate and analysis for the feminist and legal communities.
Ind/Abst Altern. Press Index; Crim. Justice Abstr.; Curr. Law Index (1980-); Index Leg. Period.; Leg. Resour. Index (1980-); LegalTrac (1980-); Multicult. Educ. Abstr.; PAIS Int. Print; Soc. Plann. Policy Dev. Abstr.; Sociol. Abstr.; Stud. Women Abstr.; Women Stud. Abstr.

US/1070-3896
WORDPERFECT FOR THE LAW OFFICE. [WordPerfect law off.]. Vol. 1, No. 1 (Mar./April 1993)-. Periodical. English. bm. $72.00 US; $77.00 other. James Publishing Group, Inc., PO Box 25202, Santa Ana CA 92799. **Tel** (714)755-5450, FAX (714)556-4133. **DD** 005.

UK
WORDS & PHRASES LEGALLY DEFINED. English. ir. £260.00. Butterworth & Co. Ltd. / Kent, England, Borough Green, Sevenoaks Kent TN15 8PH England. **Tel** 011 44 732-884567, FAX 011 44 732-885996. **ED** John Saunders. **Ad Acc.**
Desc: 4 volumes and a supplement defining words and phrases legally.

US/1050-9836
WORKERS' COMPENSATION LAW REVIEW. [Work. compens. law rev.]. **VFOAT** Workers' Compensation. Vol. 11 (1988)-. English. an. $55.00. William S. Hein & Company Inc., 1285 Main Street, Buffalo NY 14209. **Tel** (716)882-2600, (800)828-7571, FAX (716)883-8100, telex 91-209 WM S HEIN BUF. **ED** William Moran. **LC** K27; .O7. **DD** 344.73/021/05; 347.3042105. **Circ:** 400 (ctrl). ***Continues*** *Workmen's Compensation Law Review, 0094-3436.*
Desc: Primary emphasis is on specific timely areas in each volume.

AT
WORKERS' COMPENSATION LEGISLATION IN AUSTRALIA / DEPARTMENT OF SOCIAL SECURITY. **Added/Corp** Australia. Dept. of Social Security. (1980)-. English. sa. Department of Social Security, PO Box 1, Woden Australian Capital Territory 2606 Australia. **Tel** (062)750000, FAX 574045. **DD** 344.94/021; 349.40421. **Circ:** 1,500 (ctrl). ***Continues*** *Conspectus of Workers Compensation Legislation in Australia.*
Desc: Comparison of workers' compensation legislations in states and territories as well as federally.

AT
WORKERS' COMPENSATION REPORTS. ***Suspended.*** **Main/Corp** New South Wales. Workers' Compensation Commission. Vol. 1 (1926/27)-?. English. ir. NSW Government Printing Office, PO Box 256, Regents Park2143 Australia. **Tel** 011 61 02 7438777, FAX 062 954455. **LC** HD7816.A82.
Ind/Abst Aust. Leg. Mon. Dig. (-19??).

CN/0708-2827
WORKING PAPER (LAW REFORM COMMISSION OF CANADA). (WORKING PAPER - LAW REFORM COMMISSION OF CANADA.). [Work pap. - Law Reform Comm. Can.]. **VFOAT** Document de Travail. No. 1-. Monographic series. English (French). Price varies per volume. Law Reform Commission of Canada, 130 Albert Street/7th Floor, Ottawa Ontario K1A 0L6 Canada. **DD** 340/.3/0971.

US/1056-4683
WORKPLACE AND THE LAW, THE. **See** Economics-Labor.

US/1054-7312
WORKPLACE INJURY REPORTER. **See** Economics-Labor.

US/1071-9067
WORKSHOPS FOR LEGAL ASSISTANTS. BANKRUPTCY. (WORKSHOPS FOR LEGAL ASSISTANTS. BANKRUPTCY.). [Workshops legal assist., Bankruptcy]. **Added/Corp** Practising Law Institute. **VFOAT** Bankruptcy. (1991)-. English. an. Practising Law Institute, 810 Seventh Avenue, New York NY 10019-5818. **Tel** (212)765-5700, FAX (212)581-4670 general correspondence, (212)265-4742 orders and billing inquiries. **DD** 346. ***Continues in part*** *Legal Assistants, 0730-3068.*

US/1071-9059
WORKSHOPS FOR LEGAL ASSISTANTS. EMPLOYEE BENEFITS. [Workshops legal assist., Empl. benefits]. **Added/Corp** Practising Law Institute. **VFOAT** Employee Benefits. (1991)-. English. Practising Law Institute, 810 Seventh Avenue, New York NY 10019-5818. **Tel** (212)765-5700, FAX (212)581-4670 general correspondence, (212)265-4742 orders and billing inquiries. **LC** KF6410.Z9; W675. **DD** 340/.023/73. ***Continues in part*** *Legal Assistants, 0730-3068.*

UK/0963-4894
WORLD FOOD REGULATION REVIEW. **See** Food and Food Industry.

US
WORLD LEGAL DIRECTORY. **Added/Corp** World Peace Through Law Center. (1974)-. Directory. English. World Peace Through Law Center, 1000 Connecticut Avenue NW, Suite 202, Washington DC 20036. **Tel** (202)466-5428, FAX (202)452-8540, telex 440456. **DD** 340/.025. ***Continues*** *World Law Directory.*

NE
WPNR, WEEKBLAD VOOR PRIVAATRECHT, NOTARIAAT EN REGISTRATIE. **Added/Corp** Koninklijke Notariele Broederschap. **VFOAT** Weekblad voor Privaatrecht, Notariaat en Registratie. (19??)-. Periodical. Dutch (English, French and German). wk. Fl185.00. T Hoenstraat 5, Postbox 96827, 2509 JE, S-Gravenhage The Netherlands. **Tel** 070-469697, FAX 070-453226. **ED** A L Mouissault. **DD** 348/.492/046. Index available. **Bk Rev. Ad Acc. Circ:** 3,500 (ctrl). ***Continues*** *Weekblad voor Privaatrecht, Notaris-Ambt en Registratie.*
Ind/Abst Index Foreign Leg. Per.

US
WRIT, THE. Periodical. English. sa. Ohio Northern University, Robertson-Evans Bldg., Suite 229, Ada OH 45810. **ED** Michael J Biddinger. **Circ:** 4,300 (ctrl).
Desc: News about alumni and law school activities.

US/0198-8107
WRIT (WASHINGTON), THE. (THE WRIT.). Vol. 1 No. 1 (Winter 1980)-. Periodical. English. qt. $6.00. The Writ, 640 14th Place Northeast, Washington DC 20002. **LC** K27; .R555. **DD** 349.73/05; 347.3005.

US
WRONGFUL DEATH ACTIONS: THE LAW IN ALABAMA. English. an. $32.95, $25.95 seperate pocket part supplement. Harrison Company Publishers, 3110 Crossing Park, PO Box 7500, Norcross GA 30091-7500. **Tel** (800)241-3561, (404)447-9150.

US
WYOMING CASE NAMES CITATOR. English. $40.00 (1 bound volume), $52.00 (cumulative supplements). Shepards McGraw-Hill Inc, 555 Middle Creek Parkway, PO Box 35300, Colorado Springs CO 80935-3530. **Tel** (719)488-3000, FAX (800)525-0053.

US/1043-9366
YALE JOURNAL OF LAW AND FEMINISM. [Yale j. law fem.]. **Added/Corp** Yale Law School. Vol. 1, No. 1 (Spring 1989)-. Periodical. English. Twice a year. $28.00 (institutions), $16.00 (individuals) US; add $10.00 postage other. Yale Law School, PO Box 208215, New Haven CT 06520. **Tel** (203)432-7652, FAX (203)432-2592. **LC** K29; .A365. **DD** 342.73/0878/05; 347.30287805. **Bk Rev. Ad Acc.**
Ind/Abst Index Leg. Period.; Leg. Resour. Index; LegalTrac (1989-).

US/1041-6374
YALE JOURNAL OF LAW & THE HUMANITIES. [Yale j. law humanit.]. **VFOAT** Yale Journal of Law and the Humanities. Vol. 1, No. 1 (Dec. 1988)-. Periodical. English. sa. $30.00. Yale Journal of Law & the Humanities, 401A Yale Station, New Haven CT 06520. **ED** Lawrence Douglas, James Tourtelott and Elizabeth Wilkins. **LC** K29; .A36. **DD** 340/.05.
Ind/Abst Leg. Resour. Index.

US/0741-9457
YALE JOURNAL ON REGULATION. [Yale j. regul.]. Vol. 1, No. 1 (1983)-. Academic Scholarly Publication. English. sa. $20.00 (individuals), $30.00 (institutions). Yale Law School, PO Box 208215, New Haven CT 06520. **Tel** (203)432-7652, FAX (203)432-2592. **LC** K29; .A37. **DD** 343.73/07/05; 347.303705. Index available. **Bk Rev. Ad Acc. Circ:**

1,500. Documents available from Documents on Demand.
Desc: A forum for the scholarly discussion and debate of regulatory issues and administrative law.
Ind/Abst Bowne Dig. Corp. Sec. Lawyers; Commun. Abstr. (?-?); Curr. Law Index (1983-); Econ. Lit. Index; Energy Inf. Abstr.; Environ. Abstr.; Index Leg. Period.; J. Econ. Lit.; Leg. Resour. Index (1983-); LegalTrac (1980-1984); PAIS Int. Print; Urban Aff. Abstr.

US/0740-8048
YALE LAW & POLICY REVIEW. [Yale law policy rev.]. **VFOAT** Yale Law and Policy Review. Vol. 1, No. 1 (Fall 1982)-. Periodical. English. sa. $16.00 (individuals), $25.00 (institutions) US, (add $10.00 for postage) other. Yale Law School, PO Box 208215, New Haven CT 06520. **Tel** (203)432-7652, FAX (203)432-2592. **LC** K29; .A38. **DD** 340/.05. Index available. **Bk Rev. Ad Acc. Circ:** 500.
Desc: Interdisciplinary forum for discussion of legal and policy issues.
Ind/Abst Bowne Dig. Corp. Sec. Lawyers; Curr. Law Index (1984-); Index Leg. Period.; Leg. Resour. Index (1984-); LegalTrac (1983-).

US/0044-0094
YALE LAW JOURNAL, THE. [Yale law j.]. **Added/Corp** Yale Law School. Vol. 1 (Oct. 1891)-. Periodical. English. Eight times a year. $40.00 US; $46.00 other. Yale Law Journal, 401 A Yale Station, New Haven CT 06520. **Tel** (203)432-1622, FAX (203)432-2592. **LC** K29; .A4. **DD** 340/.05. **CODEN** YALJAB. Index available. **Bk Rev. Ad Acc. Pr Rev. Circ:** 4,500 (ctrl). available on an online database (file 15/Full-Text) from DIALOG. Documents available from The Genuine Article, UMI Article Clearinghouse.
Desc: Articles, student notes and book reviews dealing with current legal topics.
Ind/Abst ABC POL SCI; ABI/INFORM Glob. Ed.; ABI Inform Ondisc (Nov. 1976-); Book Rev. Index; Bowne Dig. Corp. Sec. Lawyers; Crim. Justice Abstr.; Crim. Penol. Police Sci. Abstr.; Curr. Contents Soc. Behav. Sci.; Curr. Law Index (1980-); Econ. Lit. Index; Expand. Acad. Index (1984-); Fed. Tax Artic.; Index Leg. Period.; Int. Bibliogr. Sociol.; Int. Polit. Sci. Abstr.; J. Econ. Lit.; Leg. Resour. Index (1980-); LegalTrac (1980-); Newsp. Period. Abstr. (1989-); PAIS Int. Print; Res. Alert [Full Cov.]; Soc. Sci. Cit. Index [Full Cov.]; Urban Aff. Abstr.

US/0513-1391
YALE LAW REPORT. Added/Corp Yale Law School Association. Vol. 1 (1954)-. Periodical. English. Twice a year. $12.00. Yale Law School, PO Box 208215, New Haven CT 06520. **Tel** (203)432-7652, FAX (203)432-2592. **ED** Catherine Iino. **LC** KF292.Y3; A75. **DD** 340/.09746/8. **Bk Rev. Circ:** 10,000 (ctrl). ***Continues*** *Alumni Newsletter (Yale Law School Association).*
Desc: Articles on legal issues by and news about faculty, students, and alumni.

CN/0318-4935
YEAR BOOK OF THE CANADIAN BAR ASSOCIATION AND THE MINUTES OF PROCEEDINGS OF THE ... ANNUAL MEETING, THE. ***Title Change.*** [Yearb. Can. Bar Assoc. minutes proc. annu. meet.]. **Main/Corp** Canadian Bar Association. **Added/Corp** Canadian Bar Association. Meeting. **VFOAT** Annuaire de l'Association du Barreau Canadien et le Proces-Verbal de sa ... Assemblee Annuelle; Proceedings of the Canadian Bar Association. 28th (1946)-(19??). Proceedings. English (French). an. Canadian Bar Association, Suite 902 50 O'Connor Street, Ottawa Ontario K1P 6L2 Canada. **Tel** (613)237-2925. **DD** 340/.06/271. ***Continues*** *Canadian Bar Association. Council. Proceedings of the Council of the Canadian Bar Association, 0318-4919.* ***Continued by*** *Proceedings of the Annual Meeting of the Conference of Commissioners on Uniformity of Legislation in Canada, 0318-4897.*
Ind/Abst Index Can. Leg. Period. Lit.

US/0548-8729
YEARBOOK - NEW YORK COUNTY LAWYERS' ASSOCIATION. Main/Corp New York County Lawyers' Association. 1909-. English. an. New York County Lawyers Association, 14 Vesey Street, New York NY 10007. **Tel** (212)267-6646. **ED** Jan Levy. **Ad Acc. Circ:** 10,000 (ctrl).
Desc: Lists members, officers, past officers, directors, past and present, committees, by-laws of New York County Lawyers' Association.

UK
YEARBOOK OF EUROPEAN LAW. Vol. 1, (1981)-. Periodical. English. an. £85.00 - £95.00 (depending on Volume number). Oxford University Press, Walton Street, Oxford OX2 6DP England. **Tel** 011 44 865 56767, FAX 011 44 865 267773, telex 837330 OXPRES G. **(Subscription address:** Oxford University Press / USA, Journals Marketing Department, Oxford University Press, 2001 Evans Road, Cary NC 27513.**) LC** K29; .E174. **DD** 349.4/05; 344.005. Each issue contains an index to its own contents (no volume index)--loose.
Ind/Abst Index Foreign Leg. Per.

US
YEARBOOK OF PROCUREMENT ARTICLES. Vol. 1 (1961)-. English. an. Federal Publications Inc, 1120 20th Street Northwest, Washington DC 20036. **Tel** (202)337-7000, (800)922-4330, FAX (202)659-2233. **DD** 340. cum. index.

CN/0318-4935
YEARBOOK OF THE CANADIAN BAR ASSOCIATION AND THE MINUTES OF PROCEEDINGS OF THE ... ANNUAL MEETING, THE. ***Title Change.*** [Yearb. Can. Bar Assoc. minutes proc. annu. meet.]. **Main/Corp** Association du Barreau Canadien. **VFOAT** Yearbook of the Canadian Bar Association and the Minutes of Proceedings of the ... Annual Meeting.; Annuaire de l'Association du Barreau Canadien et le Proces-Verbal de sa ... Assemblee Annuelle; Proceedings of the Canadian Bar Association. (1946)-(19??). Proceedings. French (English). **DD** 340/.06/271. ***Supersedes*** *Canadian Bar Association. Proceedings of the Council of the Canadian Bar Association, 0318-4919.* ***Continued by*** *Proceedings of the Annual Meeting of the Conference of Commissioners on Uniformity of Legislation in Canada., 0318-4897.*
Ind/Abst Index Can. Leg. Period. Lit. (19??-1992).

FI
YLEISISSA ALIOIKEUKSISSA SYYTETYT JA TUOMITUT. See Law-Abstracting, Bibliographies and Statistics.

US/0731-1109
YOU & THE LAW. Added/Corp Research Institute of America, Inc. National Institute of Business Management. National Business Institute (New York, N.Y.). **VFOAT** You and the Law. (Jan. 9, 1978)-. Newsletter. English. mo. $125.00 US; $135.00 Canada. National Institute of Business Management, Inc., 1101 King Street, Alexandria VA 22134. **Tel** (800)543-2051, (703)548-3885, (800)543-2049, FAX (703)549-0182. **(Subscription address:** National Institute of Business Management, PO Box 25337, Alexandria VA 22313.**) ED** Dan Moscowitz. **LC** KF889.A1; Y68. **DD** 349.73/05; 347.3005. ***Continues*** *Your Business and the Law, 0093-3503.*

US/0147-6777
YOUNG LAWYERS NEWSLETTER. Newsletter. English. ir. Illinois State Bar Association, 424 South Second, Springfield IL 62701. **Tel** (217)525-1760, FAX (217)525-0712. **ED** Norma Sutton. **LC** KF200; .Y68. **DD** 340/.06/2773.

US/0094-0399
YOUR SCHOOL & THE LAW. [Your sch. law]. **VFOAT** Your School and the Law. (1972)-. Newsletter. English. mo. $160.00. LRP Publications, 747 Dresher Road, PO Box 980, Horsham PA 19044-0980. **Tel** (800)341-7874, (215)784-0860, FAX (215)784-9639, (215)784-0870. **(Subscription address:** LRP Publications, PO Box 980, Horsham PA 19044.**) ED** Kim A. Putnam. **LC** KF4102; .Y68. **DD** 344.73/07/05; 347.304705. **Bk Rev. Ad Acc.** ***Absorbed*** *Athletic Director and Coach.*
Desc: Cases involving schools and school officials. Serves as a primer to help readers spot and avoid potentially litigous situations.

US
YOUTH COURT REPORT / MISSISSIPPI DEPARTMENT OF YOUTH SERVICES. 1980-. Periodical. English. an. Mississippi Department of Youth Services, 301 North Lamar 410, Jackson MS 39201-1404. **LC** KFM6671.55; .M57. **DD** 345.762/081. ***Continues*** *Mississippi Youth Court Statistics.*

YU/0350-2252
YUGOSLAV LAW. [Yugosl. law]. **Added/Corp** Savez Udruzenja Pravnika Jugoslavije. Institut za Uporedno Pravo (Belgrade, Serbia). **VFOAT** Droit Yougoslave. (Jan./April 1975)-. Periodical. English (French). Four times a year. $40.00. Union of Jurist Associations of Yugoslavia, Institut za Uporedno Pravo, Terazije 41, 11000 Belgrade Yugoslavia. **(Subscription address:** Mladost Export Import, PO Box 1028, Ilica 30, 41000 Zagreb Croatia.**) LC** K29; .U34. **DD** 340/.09497. available on microfilm and microfiche from University Microfilms International (UMI). ***Supersedes*** *New Yugoslav Law, 0028-7946.*
Ind/Abst Index Foreign Leg. Per.

●US/1060-6092
ZA ZAGOLOVKAMI. Added/Corp Russian Information Services. (1992)-. Periodical. English (Russian). mo. $175.00 (libraries), $225.00 (other) US; $190.00 (libraries), $250.00 other Non-US. Russian Information Services, 89 Main Street, Box 2, Montpelier VT 05602. **Tel** (802)223-4955, FAX (802)223-6105. **ED** Paul Richardson. Index available. cum. index.
Desc: A monthly compendium of all laws of Russia relating to foreign trade and investment.

RU/0869-4400
ZAKON : ZHURNAL DLIA DELOVYKH LIUDEI. (19??)-. Periodical. Russian (table of contents in English). mo. $172.95. **(Subscription address:** East View Publications Inc., 3020 Harbor Lane North, Suite 110, Minneapolis MN 55447.**) LC** KLA911.3; .Z34.
Desc: Information on commercial law, business enterprises, and foreign investments.

ZA
ZAMBIA LAW JOURNAL. Added/Corp University of Zambia. School of Law. Vol. 1 No. 1 (1969)-. English. an. Price varies. University of Zambia, PO Box 32379, Lusaka Zambia. **Tel** 213221, telex ZA 44370. **(Subscription address:** Law Reports International, Trinity College, African Law Reports, c/o Dr. Milner, Oxford OX1 3BH England.**) LC** K30; .A5. **DD** 340/.05.

ZA
ZAMBIA LAW REPORTS. English. Council of Law Reporting, General Editor, Zambia Law Reports, PO Box RW67, Lusaka Zambia. **DD** 348/.6894/041.
Desc: Contains selected judgments of the Court of Appeal for Zambia, and other courts.

CI
ZBORNIK PRAVNOG FAKULTETA U ZAGREBU. Main/Corp Zagreb. Univerzitet. Pravni Fakultet. **VFOAT** Recueil des Travaux de la Faculte de Droit de l'Universite de Zagreb; Collected Papers of the University of Zagreb Law School; Zbornik Pravnog Fakulteta u Zagrebu. (1948)-. Periodical. Serbian (English, German and French). bm. 65.00 Din. Pravni Fakultet u Zagrebu, TRG Marsala Tita 14, Zagreb Croatia. **Tel** 011 38 41 42922217. **ED** Stanko Petkovic. Index available. ctrl circ.
Desc: Collected papers of the University of Zagreb Law School.
Ind/Abst Crim. Penol. Police Sci. Abstr.; Index Foreign Leg. Per.

GW/0323-4045
ZEITSCHRIFT DER SAVIGNY-STIFTUNG FUER RECHTSGESCHICHTE. GERMANISTISCHE ABTEILUNG. [Z. Savigny-Stift. Rechtsgesch., Ger. Abt.]. **Added/Corp** Savigny-Stiftung. Vol. 1 (1880)-. German (English, French, Italian and Spanish). an (Sept.). DM1876.00. Boehlau Verlag GmbH & Cie / Koeln, Theodor Heuss STR 76, D-51149 Cologne Germany. **Tel** 011 49 2203 307021, FAX 011 49 2203 307349. **(Subscription address:** Minerva Wissenschaftl Buchhdlg, Sachsenplatz 4 6, Postfach 88, A 1201 Vienna Austria.**)** Index available in last issue of volume--attached. cum. index. ***Continues in part*** *Zeitschrift fuer Rechtsgeschichte.*
Ind/Abst Canon Law Abstr.; Index Foreign Leg. Per.

GW/0323-4142
ZEITSCHRIFT DER SAVIGNY-STIFTUNG FUER RECHTSGESCHICHTE. KANONISTISCHE ABTEILUNG. [Z. Savigny-Stift. Rechtsgesch., Kanon. Abt.]. **Added/Corp** Savigny-Stiftung. (1911)-. German (English, French, Italian and Spanish). an. DM1806.00. Boehlau Verlag GmbH & Co KG, Sachsenplatz 4 6 PF 87, A 1201 Vienna Austria. **Tel** 011 43 222 3302427. **(Subscription address:** Minerva Wissenschaftl Buchhdlg, Sachsenplatz 4 6, Postfach 88, A 1201 Vienna Austria.**) ED** Knut W. Norr, Martin Heckel and Paul Mikal. Index available in last issue of volume--attached. cum. index. **Bk Rev. Ad Acc.** ***Continues in part*** *Zeitschrift fuer Rechtsgeschichte.*
Desc: This german journal cover the history of Canon law. Covers the research work from the roots up to recent legacy.
Ind/Abst Index Foreign Leg. Per.

AU
ZEITSCHRIFT DER SAVIGNY-STIFTUNG FUER RECHTSGESCHICHTE. ROMANISTISCHE ABTEILUNG. Added/Corp Savigny-Stiftung. Vol. 1 (1880)-. German. an. S2464.00 Volume 110. Boehlau Verlag GmbH & Co KG, Sachsenplatz 4 6 PF 87, A 1201 Vienna Austria. **Tel** 011 43 222 3302427. **ED** Theo Mayer-Maly and Dieter Norr. Index available in last issue of volume--attached. cum. index. **Bk Rev. Ad Acc.** ***Continues in part*** *Zeitschrift fuer Rechtsgeschichte.*
Desc: German speaking journal in the history of Roman and antique law. It covers research work from the very roots up to modern legacy in the field of Roman law and origins.
Ind/Abst Index Foreign Leg. Per.

SZ/0044-2127
ZEITSCHRIFT DES BERNISCHEN JURISTENVEREINS. Main/Corp Bernischer Juristenverein. **VFOAT** Revue de la Societe des Juristes Bernois. (1864)-. Periodical. German. mo. 65.00F Switzerland; 79.00F other. Staempfli & Cie SA, Postfach 8326, CH-3001 Bern Switzerland. **Tel** 011 41 31 3006666, telex 031 911 515 EDMZ CH. **[CCC].** ***Continues*** *Zeitschrift fuer Vaterlandisches Recht.*
Ind/Abst Index Foreign Leg. Per.

GW
ZEITSCHRIFT FUER AUSLANDERRECHT UND AUSLANDERPOLITIK : ZAR. VFOAT ZAR; Z.A.R. (1981)-. Periodical. German. Four times a year. DM128.00 Germany; DM132.60 others. Nomos

Law

Verlagsgesellschaft, Postfach 610, D-76484 Baden Baden Germany. **Tel** 011 49 7221 21040. **LC** K30; .E266. **DD** 342.43/083; 344.30283.

GW/0044-2437
ZEITSCHRIFT FUER DAS GESAMTE HANDELSRECHT UND WIRTSCHAFTSRECHT. Vol. 124 (1961/62)-.
Periodical. German. Six times a year. DM290.10 Germany; DM302.10 other. Verlag Recht und Wirtschaft GmbH, Postfach 105960, D 69049 Heidelberg Germany. **Tel** 011 49 6221 9061. **[CCC].** available on microfilm from University Microfilms International (UMI). **Continues** *Zeitschrift fur das Gesamte Handelsrecht und Konkursrecht.*
Ind/Abst Index Foreign Leg. Per.

GW/0179-4051
ZEITSCHRIFT FUER GESETZGEBUNG : ZG. Ceased. VFOAT ZG. Vol. 1 (1986)-Vol. 9.
Periodical. German. qt. CH Beck Verlagsbuchhandlung, D 80791 Munich Germany. **Tel** 011 49 89 381891. **LC** K30; .E55.
Ind/Abst ARTbibliogr. Mod.

GW/0340-8329
ZEITSCHRIFT FUER LUFT- UND WELTRAUMRECHT. [Z. Luft- Weltraumr.].
Added/Corp Universitat Koln. Institut fuer Luft- und Weltraumrecht. **VFOAT** German Journal of Air and Space Law; Revue Allemande de Droit Aerien et Spatial. Vol. 24, No. 2 (June 1975)-. Periodical. German (English and French). qt. DM228.00. Carl Heymanns Verlag KG, Luxemburger Strasse 449, D 50939 Cologne Germany. **Tel** 011 49 221 460100, telex 8 881 888. **LC** K30; .E6. **DD** 343.09/7/05. **[CCC].** Index available. **Bk Rev. Ad Acc. Circ:** 600 (ctrl). **Continues** *Zeitschrift fur Luftrecht und Weltraumrechtsfragen.*
Desc: Treatises statements and sentences to the legal problems of aviation security, space activities and emerging international law. Recent publications on the air and space law.
Ind/Abst Energy Res. Abstr. (Aug. 1982-); Index Foreign Leg. Per.; Int. Aerosp. Abstr.

AU/0250-6459
ZEITSCHRIFT FUER NEUERE RECHTSGESCHICHTE. [Z. Neuere Rechtsgesch.]. (1979)-. Periodical. German. sa. S885.00.
Manzsche Verlagsbuchhandlung, Kohlmarkt 16 Postfach 163, A 1014 Vienna Austria. **Tel** 011 43 222 5316171. **ED** W Brauneder. **LC** K30; .E643. **DD** 340/.09.
Ind/Abst Am. Hist. Life (1987-).

GW/0173-0568
ZEITSCHRIFT FUER SCHADENSRECHT : ZFS / HERAUSGEGEBEN VON DEN RECHTSANWAELTEN ALFRED FLEISCHMANN, HANAU ... [ET AL.].
VFOAT ZfS. No. 1, Issue 1 (Jan. 1980)-. Periodical. German. mo. DM138.88. Deutscher Anwaltverlag GmbH, Bocholder Strasse 259, D 45356 Essen Germany. **LC** KK1610.A13; Z43. **DD** 346.4303/05; 344.306305.

SZ/0084-540X
ZEITSCHRIFT FUER SCHWEIZERISCHES RECHT. VFOAT Revue de Droit Suisse; Rivista di Diritto Svizzero; Revue der Gerichtspraxis im Gebiete des Bundescivilrechts; Revue de la Jurisprudence en Maitiere de Droit Civil Federal. Vol. 1-22 (1852/82)-. Periodical. German (French).
Helbing & Lichtenhahn AG, Freie Strasse 82, CH-4051 Basel Switzerland. cum. index.

GW/0342-3468
ZEITSCHRIFT FUER ZIVILPROZESS. Vol. 1 (1879)-. Periodical. German. qt. DM198.00. Carl Heymanns Verlag KG, Luxemburger Strasse 449, D 50939 Cologne Germany. Tel 011 49 221 460100, telex 8 881 888. ED M. C. Fritz Baur und Dieter Leipold. Index available. Bk Rev. Ad Acc. Circ: 1,000 (ctrl).
Desc: Treatises and decisions on civil action.
Ind/Abst Index Foreign Leg. Per.

SZ
ZEITSCHRIFT FUR GESETZGEBUNG UND RECHTSPRECHUNG IN GRAUBUNDEN. 82/1 (March 1982)-. Periodical. German. qt. 38.00F students, 48.00F others. Arcas Verlag, Werkstrasse 2, 7000 Chur Switzerland. LC K30; .E548. DD 349.494/705.

PL
ZESZYTY NAUKOWE INSTYTUTU BADANIA PRAWA SADOWEGO.
Main/Corp Instytut Badania Prawa Sadowego. (19??)-. German (Polish and Russian). sa. Price on Request. **(Subscription address:** ARS Polona, PO Box 1001, 00068 Warsaw Poland.**).**

GW
ZFBR, ZEITSCHRIFT FUER DEUTSCHES UND INTERNATIONALES BAURECHT.
Added/Corp Deutsche Gesellschaft fuer Baurecht. Institut fuer Deutsches und Internationales Baurecht (Bonn, Germany). **VFOAT** Zeitschrift fuer deutsches und Internationales Baurecht. (Oct. 1978)-. Periodical. German. bm (6 issues). DM246.00 Germany; DM274.00 other. Bauverlag GmbH, Postfach 1460, D 65173 Wiesbaden Germany. **Tel** 011 49 6123 7000, FAX 011 49 6123 700122. **ED** G. Watzke and W. Sofker. **DD** 343.43/07869. **Bk Rev. Ad Acc. Circ:** 2,000.
Desc: Gives detailed information and authoritative analysis on the current state and latest developments in public, private, and international building law including the relevant jurisdiction.

UN/0130-884X
ZIBRANNIA POSTANOV URIADU UKRAINY. Main/Corp Ukraine. Kabinet Ministriv. VFOAT Sobranie Postanovlenii Pravitelstva Ukrainy. (199?)-. Periodical. Ukrainian (Russian). Six times a year. $299.95. (Subscription address: East View Publications Inc., 3020 Harbor Lane North, Suite 110, Minneapolis MN 55447.) LC KLP17; .U37.

RH
ZIMBABWE LAW REVIEW. Vol. 1 & 2 (1983/84)-. Periodical. English. sa. University of Zimbabwe / Department of Law, PO Box MP 167, Mount Pleasant, Harare Zimbabwe. Tel 011 263 0 303211 ext. 1813, FAX 011 263 4 303273. LC K30; .I45. DD 349.6891/05. Continues Zimbabwe Law Journal.
Ind/Abst Index Foreign Leg. Per.

GW/0342-3476
ZLR, ZEITSCHRIFT FUER DAS GESAMTE LEBENSMITTELRECHT. [ZLR, Z. Gesamte Lebensm.R.]. VFOAT Zeitschrift fuer das Gesamte Lebensmittelrecht. (19??)-. Periodical. German (summaries and/or abstracts in English and French). Six times a year. DM364.49 Germany; DM399.00 other. Deutscher Fachverlag GmbH, Verlagsgruppe, D 60264 Frankfurt Germany. Tel 011 49 69 75951001, telex 411 862. ED Sabine Klamroth (editor's address: Lessingstrasse 24, 6900 Heidelberg West Germany). LC K30; .L13. Index available. Bk Rev. Ad Acc. Circ: 800 (ctrl).
Ind/Abst Int. Packag. Abstr.

GW
ZOLL UND HANDELSINFORMATION. (19??)-. German. ir. Bundesstelle fuer Aussenhandelsinformation, Agrippastr 87 93, D 50676 Cologne Germany. Tel 011 49 221 2057316, FAX 011 49 221 2057212.

GW
ZOLLDIENST. Main/Corp Bundesstelle fur Aussenhandelsinformation (Germany). German. Bundesstelle fuer Aussenhandelsinformation, Agrippastr 87 93, D 50676 Cologne Germany. Tel 011 49 221 2057316, FAX 011 49 221 2057212. LC K4600; .G47.

US/0731-5791
ZONING AND PLANNING LAW HANDBOOK. Added/Corp Clark Boardman Company. (1981)-. English. an. $85.00. Clark Boardman Callaghan, 155 Pfingsten Road, Deerfield IL 60015. Tel (800)323-8067. ED Noah G Gordon. LC KF5697.A152; Z66. DD 346.7304/5; 347.30645. Index available. Bk Rev.
Ind/Abst Curr. Law Index; Leg. Resour. Index (?-?).

US/0161-8113
ZONING AND PLANNING LAW REPORT. Added/Corp Clark Boardman Company. Vol. 1 (Nov. 1977)-. Periodical. English. Eleven times a year. $195.00. Clark Boardman Callaghan, 155 Pfingsten Road, Deerfield IL 60015. Tel (800)323-8067. ED F. Strom and N. Gordon. LC KF5697.A15; B6. DD 346/.73/045. cum. index. Bk Rev.
Ind/Abst Curr. Law Index (1984-); Leg. Resour. Index (1984-); LegalTrac (1981-); Urban Aff. Abstr.

ABSTRACTING, BIBLIOGRAPHIES AND STATISTICS

CN/0701-0524
ACQUISITIONS LIST - CENTRE OF CRIMINOLOGY LIBRARY, UNIVERSITY OF TORONTO. Main/Corp University of Toronto. Centre of Criminology. Library. (1975)-. Periodical. English. Twice a year (Published in Spring and Fall). 13.00Can$. University of Toronto Centre of Criminology, 130 St George Street/Room 8001, Toronto Ontario M5S 1A1 Canada. Tel (416)978-7124, FAX (416)978-4195. ED Jane Gladstone. DD 016.364. Circ: 200.
Desc: List catalogued books and reports plus newly acquired uncataloged materials added to the criminology library collection.

BE
ACTIVITE DES COURS ET TRIBUNAUX. STATISTIQUES DIVERSES. French. an. 85F Belgium; 135F other. Institut National de Statistique / Belgium, rue de Louvain, 44, Centre Albert, 8e Etage, 1000 Brussels Belgium. Tel 011 32 2 5486211. Bk Rev. Ad Acc. Circ: 350 (ctrl).
Desc: Court statistics.

UK/0264-6552
ADMINISTRATION OF JUSTICE STATISTICS ... ESTIMATES. 1983-84-. English. an. £9.00. Chartered Institute of Public Finance and Accountancy, 2 3 Robert Street, London WC2N 6BH England. Tel 011 44 1 895 8823. LC KD7122.5.A13; A36. DD 347.41/013; 344.10713.

II
ADMINISTRATION REPORT OF THE CIVIL COURTS STATISTICS FOR THE YEAR ... . Added/Corp Tamil Nadu (India). VFOAT Statistics of Civil Courts in the State of Tamil Nadu for the Year ... . (19??)-. English. DD 347.54/82013; 345.4820713. Continues Statistics of Civil Courts in the State of Tamil Nadu for the Year ... .

CN/0715-2973
ADULT CORRECTIONAL SERVICES IN CANADA. (ADULT CORRECTIONAL SERVICES IN CANADA / STATISTICS CANADA, CANADIAN CENTRE FOR JUSTICE STATISTICS.). [Adult correct. serv. Can.]. Added/Corp Canadian Centre for Justice Statistics. VFOAT Services Correctionnels Pour Adultes au Canada. (1981/1982)-. English (French). an. 39.00Can$ Canada; $47.00 US; $55.00 other. Statistics Canada, Publications Sales & Services, Main Building Room 1710, Ottawa Ontario K1A 0T6 Canada. Tel (613)951-5078, (800)267-6677, FAX (613)951-1584, telex 053-3585. LC HV9504; .A38. DD 364.6/0971. Formed by the union of Correctional Services in Canada, 0711-6802 and Services Correctionnels au Canada.

FR
ANNUAIRE STATISTIQUE DE LA JUSTICE. 1978-. French. an. Documentation Francaise, 29 Quai Voltaire, 75344 Paris Cedex 7 France. Tel 011 33 1 40157000, FAX 011 33 1 40157230, telex 204 826 DOCFRAN. DD 347.44/013; 344.40713. available on microfiche.

US/0098-1834
ANNUAL REPORT - CRIMINAL COURT OF THE CITY OF NEW YORK. Main/Corp New York (City). Criminal Court. 1962-. English. an. LC KFX2007.3; .C7. DD 345/.7471/01. Formed by the union of New York (N.Y.). City Magistrates' Courts. Annual Report and New York (N.Y.). Court of the Special Sessions. Annual Report of the Calendar Year ... .

US
ANNUAL STATISTICAL REPORT OF PENNSYLVANIA COUNTY PRISONS AND JAILS / DIVISION OF PLANNING AND RESEARCH. Title Change. Added/Corp Pennsylvania. Bureau of Correction. Division of Planning and Research. Pennsylvania. Bureau of Correction. Division of Finance, Planning, and Research. Pennsylvania. Dept. of Corrections. Division of Finance, Planning & Research. (19??)-?. Statistical Publication. English. an. Pennsylvania Bureau of Correction, PO Box 598, Camp Hill PA 17011. LC HV8358; .P4b. DD 365/.9748. Continued by County Prison and Jail Statistical Report.

US/0193-9300
ATTORNEYS' DIRECTORY OF SAN DIEGO COUNTY. Added/Corp San Diego County Bar Association. VFOAT Attorneys' Directory. (19??)-. Directory. English. an. $15.00. San Diego Daily Transcript, 2131 3rd Avenue, PO Box 85469, San Diego CA 92138. Tel (619)232-4381 Ext. 207. ED Melanie J. Potter. LC KF193.S24; A87. DD 340/.025/79498. Index available. Ad Acc. Circ: 15,000. available on labels; available on a computer list.
Desc: Directory listing of attorneys in San Diego County. The listing includes business firms, addresses, phone numbers, years admitted to bar, universities attended and areas of expertise. Also includes information on court records and various legal organizations.

AT/0004-9646
AUSTRALIAN LEGAL MONTHLY DIGEST. (19??)-. Abstracting/Indexing Service. English. Twelve times a year. 495.00Aus$. The Law Book Company Limited, 44-50 Waterloo Road, North Ryde New South Wales, 2113 Australia. Tel 011 61 2 8870177, FAX 011 61 2 8887240, telex ASBOOK 27445. ED P. Leslie and K. Krust. Index available. Circ: 3,500 (ctrl).
Desc: Comprehensive summary of developments in the law - reported case law, statutes and delegated legislation, articles, etc., from all Australian jurisdictions, both state and federal.
Ind/Abst Aust. Leg. Mon. Dig.

AT/0813-2364
AUSTRALIAN PRISONERS. Added/Corp Australian Institute of Criminology. (1982)-. English. an. $10.00. Australian Institute of Criminology, 4 Marcus Clarke Street, Canberra ACT 2601 Australia. Tel 011 61 6 2740200, FAX 011 61 6 2740260, telex 61340. LC HV9872; .A97. DD 364.3/0994/021. Circ: 200.
Desc: Statistics of prison figures for Australian territories.

US/0360-2745
BIBLIOGRAPHIC GUIDE TO LAW. (1975)-. English. an (Mar.). $360.00. Macmillan Publishing Company, 100 Front Street, Box 500, Riverside NJ 08075-7500. **Tel** (800)257-5755, (609)461-6500, FAX (609)461-7070. **LC** K38; .B52. **DD** 016.34. ***Supersedes*** *Law Book Guide, 0000-0353; Law Book Guide, 0146-3861.*

NE
BIBLIOGRAPHIE DE LA COUR INTERNATIONALE DE JUSTICE / PREPAREE PAR LA BIBLIOTHEQUE DE LA COUR. **Added/Corp** International Court of Justice. Library. **VFOAT** Bibliography of the International Court of Justice. No. 19 (1966)-. French (English). an. United Nations Publishers Geneva, Palais des Nations, C115 Services Ventes, CH-1211 Geneva 10 Switzerland. **Tel** 011 41 227988400, 7985850. **LC** Z6464.Z9; .B42; JX1971.6. **DD** 016.3415/52. ***Continues*** *International Court of Justice. Bibliography of the International Court of Justice.*

GW
BIBLIOGRAPHIE JURISTISCHER FESTSCHRIFTEN UND FESTSCHRIFTENBEITRAGE : DEUTSCHLAND, SCHWEIZ, OSTERREICH. **VFOAT** Bibliography of Legal Festschriften : Titles and Contents : Germany, Switzerland, Austria; Bibliography of Legal Festschriften. (1864-1944)-. German (English). ir. DM160.00. Berlin Verlag, Arno Spitz, Pacellialle 5, D 14195 Berlin Germany. **Tel** 011 49 30 8326232, FAX 030/8316249. **ED** Helmut Dau. **LC** KJC158.5; .B53. **DD** 016.34943. Index available. **Ad Acc. Circ:** 600.
Desc: Bibliography of legal festschriften dedicated to academic jurists in Austria, Germany, and Switzerland. Listed by names of the honoured persons, book titles, and celebrated occasion.

SZ
BIBLIOGRAPHIE : STAAT UND RECHT. Began in 1972. Periodical. German. sm. Deutscher Judo Verband, Redaktion Ippon Segewaldweg 40, D 12557 Berlin Germany. **Tel** 011 49 711 210770, telex 051 678.

GW/0006-1468
BIBLIOGRAPHIE : STAAT UND RECHTDER DEUTSCHEN DEMOKRATISCHEN REPUBLIK. ***Ceased.*** Periodical. German. sm. Akademie fuer Staats und Rechtswissenschaft der DDR, Informationszentrum Staat und Recht, Augues-Bebel-Str. 89, 1502 Potsdam-Babelsberg, Germany. **LC** WMLC L 83/3062. **Circ:** 8,000.
Desc: Articles in the field of state law and legislation.

US/0067-7329
BIBLIOGRAPHY ON FOREIGN AND COMPARATIVE LAW, A. (A BIBLIOGRAPHY ON FOREIGN AND COMPARATIVE LAW / COMPILED AND ANNOTATED BY CHARLES SZLADITS.). [Bibliogr. foreign comp. law]. **Added/Corp** Parker School of Foreign and Comparative Law. **VFOAT** Szladits' Bibliography on Foreign and Comparative Law; Szladits' Bibliography on Foreign and Comparative Law. (April 1, 1953)-. Bibliography. English. ir. Price varies. Oceana Publications, Inc., 75 Main Street, Dobbs Ferry NY 10522. **Tel** (914)693-1320, FAX (914)693-0402. **LC** K38; .B53. **DD** 016.34.

US/0749-5706
BIBLIOGRAPHY SERIES - UNITED STATES. DEPT. OF JUSTICE. (BIBLIOGRAPHY SERIES / U.S. DEPARTMENT OF JUSTICE.). [Bibliogr. ser. - U. S., Dep. Justice]. No. 1-. Bibliography. English. Price varies per volume. US Department of Justice, 10th Street & Constitution Avenue NW, Washington DC 20530. **Tel** (202)514-2000, FAX (202)633-4371. **DD** 340.

MX
BOLETIN BIBLIOGRAFICO DISTRITO FEDERAL (MEXICO). (BOLETIN BIBLIOGRAFICO / INSTITUTO DE FORMACION PROFESSIONAL, CENTRO DE DOCUMENTACION E INFORMACION.). Spanish. Centro de Documentacion E Informacion del Instituto de Formacion Profesional Nihos Heroes, # 61 Y Dr Lavista Col Doctores, Mexico DF Mexico. **LC** Z5703.3; .B64; HV6005.

US/0000-0752
BOWKER'S LAW BOOKS AND SERIALS IN PRINT. [Bowker's law books ser. print]. **Added/Corp** R.R. Bowker Company. **VFOAT** Law Books and Serials in Print. (1985)-. English. an. $650.00 (3 volume set). R R Bowker, A Reed Reference Publishing Company, Part of Reed International PLC, PO Box 31, 121 Chanlon Drive, New Providence NJ 07974. **Tel** (908)464-6800, (800)521-8110, FAX (908)665-6688, telex 138-755. **LC** KF1; .L39. **DD** 016.34/005. ***Continues*** *Law ... Information, 0000-0701.*
Desc: With over 60,000 titles intended exclusively for legal professionals, this unmatched bibliographic guide lists virtually every available legal resource (books, serials, microfiche, audio and video cassettes, software, and online databases). Includes 23,000 descriptive annotations which provide expert guidance on selecting the right sources for every research need.

US/0896-906X
BOWNE DIGEST FOR CORPORATE & SECURITIES LAWYERS. [Bowne dig. corp. secur. lawyers]. **VFOAT** Bowne Digest for Corporate and Securities Lawyers; Digest for Corporate and Securities Lawyers; Digest for Corporate & Securities Lawyers; Bowne Digest. Vol. 1, No. 11 (Nov. 1987)-. Abstracting/Indexing Service. English. mo. Brumberg Publications, 124 Harvard Street, Suite 3, Brookline MA 02146-6432. **Tel** (617)734-1979. **ED** Bruce Brumberg and Susan Koffman. **LC** KF1396; .A27. **DD** 346.73/066/02638; 347.3066602638. Index available. **Bk Rev.** ctrl circ. available on an online database from NEWSNET. ***Continues*** *Abstracts of Legal Periodicals (Corporate & Securities Ed.), 0894-2447.*
Desc: Abstracts current articles from more than 240 legal periodicals on corporate and securities law.

US/0742-7271
BULLETIN (UNITED STATES. BUREAU OF JUSTICE STATISTICS). (BULLETIN / BUREAU OF JUSTICE STATISTICS.). [Bull. - U. S., Bur. Justice Stat.]. **Added/Corp** United States. Bureau of Justice Statistics. **VFOAT** Bureau of Justice Statistics Bulletin. (Feb. 1981)-. Bulletin. English. Eight times a year. Free on request. National Criminal Justice Reference Services / NCJRS, Box 6000, 1600 Research Boulevard, Rockville MD 20850. **Tel** (301)251-5500. **ED** Tom Heiter. **LC** HV9278; .B84. **DD** 364.6/3/0973. ctrl circ. available on microfiche.
Ind/Abst Crim. Justice Abstr.

US
BUREAU OF JUSTICE STATISTICS ANNUAL REPORT / U.S. DEPARTMENT OF JUSTICE, BUREAU OF JUSTICE STATISTICS. **Main/Corp** United States. Bureau of Justice Statistics. (19??)-. Statistical Publication. English. an. Free on request. Bureau of Justice Statistics, Department of Justice, 633 Indiana Avenue NW/11th Floor, Washington DC 20531. **Tel** (202)724-7774. **LC** HV7245; .B85a. **DD** 364/.973021.

CN/0824-0337
CANADIAN CRIME STATISTICS. (CANADIAN CRIME STATISTICS / STATISTICS CANADA, CANADIAN CENTRE FOR JUSTICE STATISTICS.). [Can. crime stat.]. **Added/Corp** Canadian Centre for Justice Statistics. **VFOAT** Statistique de la Criminalite du Canada. (1983)-. English (French). an. 42.00Can$ Canada; $51.00 US; $59.00 other. Statistics Canada, Publications Sales & Services, Main Building Room 1710, Ottawa Ontario K1A 0T6 Canada. **Tel** (613)951-5078, (800)267-6677, FAX (613)951-1584, telex 053-3585. **LC** HV7315; .A43. **DD** 364.1/0971/021. ***Continues*** *Crime and Traffic Enforcement Statistics., 0702-6625.*
Desc: Provides in-depth statistical summaries of criminal incidents reported by Canada's law enforcement agencies.

CN
CANADIAN LAW SYMPOSIA INDEX. (19??)-. English. Twice a year (midyear cumulation may be skipped). 400.00Can$. Special Libraries Cataloging, 4493 Lindholm Road RR1, Victoria BC V9B 5T7 Canada. **Tel** (604)474-3361, FAX (604)474-3362. **ED** J. McRee Elrod. **Circ:** 25.

CN/0832-9257
CANADIAN LEGAL LITERATURE. **Added/Corp** Carswell Legal Publications. **VFOAT** Documentation Juridique au Canada; Canadian Current Law Index to Canadian Legal Literature; Index to Canadian Legal Literature; C.C.L. Canadian Legal Literature. **VAT** Canadian Current Law Canadian Legal Literature. No. 1 (Feb. 28, 1991)-. Abstracting/Indexing Service. English (French). bm. $525 (includes subscription to: Jurisprudence (Scarborough, Ont.), and Legislation (Scarborough, Ont.). Carswell / Canada, 2075 Kennedy Road, Scarborough Ontario M1T 3V4 Canada. **Tel** (416)609-3800, (800)387-5164. ***Continues in part*** *Canadian Current Law (1988), 0835-9768.*

US
CASELOAD STATISTICAL REPORT ... FOR SUPREME COURT OF ALABAMA, COURT OF CRIMINAL APPEALS, COURT OF CIVIL APPEALS, CIRCUIT COURTS, DISTRICT COURTS. Statistical Publication. English. an. Administrative Office of Courts, 817 South Court Street, Montgomery AL 36104. **LC** KFA510; .A832 SUPPL. **DD** 347.761/01; 347.61071.

US/0092-3419
CATALOGUE - NATIONAL INDIAN LAW LIBRARY. (CATALOGUE.). [Cat. - Natl. Indian Law Libr.]. **Main/Corp** National Indian Law Library. V. 1 (1973/74)-. English. ir (issued every five years). $75.00. National Indian Law Library, Native American Rights Fund, 1522 Broadway, Boulder CO 80302-6296. **Tel** (303)447-8760. **LC** KF8201.A1; N38. **DD** 016.342/701/087. Index available. **Circ:** 1,000 (ctrl).
Desc: An index to legal materials on Indian Law of the National Indian Law Library.

US/0000-1058
CODE OF FEDERAL REGULATIONS INDEX. [Code fed. regul. index]. **VFOAT** CFR Index. (1988)-. English. an (with three supplements each year). $550.00. R R Bowker, A Reed Reference Publishing Company, Part of Reed International PLC, PO Box 31, 121 Chanlon Drive, New Providence NJ 07974. **Tel** (908)464-6800, (800)521-8110, FAX (908)665-6688, telex 138-755. **ED** Lucille Boorstein. **LC** KF70.A34; C6 Suppl. **DD** 349.73; 347.3. **[CCC]. Pr Rev.**
Desc: Index to Code of Federal Regulations by title, topic, and several tables.

US/0897-7852
COMPREHENSIVE INDEX, CALIFORNIA CODE OF REGULATIONS. [Compr. index Calif. code regul.]. **Added/Corp** University Microfilms International. **VFOAT** California Code of Regulations. (1988)-. English. ir. $370.00. University Microfilms International, 300 North Zeeb Road, Ann Arbor MI 48106-1346. **Tel** (313)761-4700, (800)521-0600 Exts. 2490, 2491, FAX (313)973-1540. **LC** KFC35 1972; .A223 Suppl. **DD** 348.794/025; 347.940825. ***Continues*** *Comprehensive Index, California Administrative Code, 0731-0676.*

FR
COMPTE GENERAL DE L'ADMINISTRATION DE LA JUSTICE PENALE / MINISTERE DE LA JUSTICE. **Main/Corp** France. Ministere de la Justice. French. 150F. Documentation Francaise, 29 Quai Voltaire, 75344 Paris Cedex 7 France. **Tel** 011 33 1 40157000, FAX 011 33 1 40157230, telex 204 826 DOCFRAN. **LC** HV7348; .A32A. **DD** 364/.944/0212.

US
CORRECTIONAL POPULATIONS IN THE UNITED STATES / U.S. DEPT. OF JUSTICE, BUREAU OF JUSTICE STATISTICS. **Added/Corp** United States. Bureau of Justice Statistics. (1985)-. English. National Criminal Justice Reference Services / NCJRS, Box 6000, 1600 Research Boulevard, Rockville MD 20850. **Tel** (301)251-5500. **LC** HV9465; .C67. **DD** 365/.6/0973021. ***Formed by the union of*** *Capital Punishment, 0191-3220* ***and*** *Prisoners in State and Federal Institutions on ..., 0148-5288.*

AT
COURT STATISTICS, TASMANIA / AUSTRALIAN BUREAU OF STATISTICS. **Added/Corp** Australian Bureau of Statistics. Tasmanian Office. (1980)-. English. an. 11.20Aus$. Australian Bureau of Statistics, PO Box 10, Belconnen Australian Capital Territory, 2616 Australia. **Tel** 011 61 6 2527911, FAX 011 61 6 2516009. **DD** 345.946/00212; 349.460500212. ***Continues in part*** *Public Justice, Tasmania.*
Desc: Shows criminal offenses finalized by type of offense, outcomes by type and age of defendant.

US
CRIME AND JUSTICE ANNUAL REPORT. **VFOAT** Crime and Justice. (1984)-. English. an. New York Division of Criminal Services, Office of Justice Systems, Executive Park Tower, Stuyvesant Plaza, Albany NY 12203. **Tel** (518)457-8381. **LC** HV7282; .A22A. **DD** 364/.9747. ***Continues*** *New York State Crime and Justice Annual Report.*
Desc: A collection of data concerning crimes and arrests in New York State.

US
CRIME AND JUVENILE DELINQUENCY : A BIBLIOGRAPHIC GUIDE TO THE DOCUMENTS UPDATE. **Main/Corp** Microfilming Corporation of America. English. an. Microfilming Corporation of America, 21 Harristown Road, Glen Rock NJ 07452. **LC** Z5703.5.U5; M53A; HV6789. **DD** 016.364/973.

US
CRIME IN ARKANSAS. Began in 1974. English. an. Arkansas Crime Information Center, One Capitol Mall, Little Rock AR 72201. **LC** HV6793.A8; C74. **DD** 364/.9767.

US
CRIME IN COLORADO / COLORADO BUREAU OF INVESTIGATION. **Added/Corp** Colorado Bureau of Investigation. (1976)-. English. an. **LC** HV6793.C6; C74. **DD** 364/.9788.

US
CRIME IN CONNECTICUT. English. an. Connecticut Department of Public Safety, Division of State Police, Uniform Crime Reporting Program, 294 Cology Street, Meridan CT 06450. **Tel** (203)238-6575. **LC**

HV7936.C88; C745. **DD** 364/.9746/05. **Circ:** 600.
Desc: Statistical summary of reported crime in Connecticut.

US
CRIME IN FLORIDA. **Added/Corp** Florida. Uniform Crime Reports and Statistics Bureau. Florida. Division of Criminal Justice Information Systems. (19??)-. English. an. Free on request. Florida Department of Law Enforcement, PO Box 1489, VCR Special Services Bureau, Tallahassee FL 32302. **Tel** (904)488-5221. **LC** CURRENT ISSUES ONLY. ***Continues*** *Florida. Dept. of Criminal Law Enforcement. Uniform Crime Reports, State of Florida.*

US/0146-9029
CRIME IN HAWAII. **Main/Corp** Hawaii Criminal Justice Statistical Analysis Center. Uniform Crime Reporting Division. 1975-. English. an. PO Box 2560, Honolulu HI 96804. **LC** HV7260.5; .A34A. **DD** 364/.9969.

US
CRIME IN LOUISIANA. **Main/Corp** Louisiana. Criminal Justice Information System Division. English. an. Louisiana Criminal Justice, Information System Division, 1885 Wooddale Boulevard/Room 502, Baton Rouge LA 70806. **LC** HV7268; .A17A. **DD** 364/.9763.

US/0148-6292
CRIME IN MAINE (ANNUAL). (CRIME IN MAINE.). [Crime Me.]. 1975-. Periodical. English. an. Department of Public Safety / Maine, 36 Hospital Street, Augusta ME 04330. **LC** HV6793.M3; C74. **DD** 364/.9741.

US/0160-7103
CRIME IN MONTANA. **Main/Corp** Montana. Criminal Justice Data Center. 1974-. English. an. Montana Board of Crime Control, 1336 Helena Avenue, Helena MT 59601. **LC** HV7276; .A34B. **DD** 364/.9786. ***Continues*** *Montana: Arrests, Offenses, 0361-414X.*

US
CRIME IN SOUTH CAROLINA. **Added/Corp** South Carolina. Law Enforcement Division. (19??)-. English. an (Spring). $5.75. South Carolina Law Enforcement Division, PO Box 21398, Uniformcrime RPT, Columbia SC 29221. **Tel** (803)737-9000. **LC** HV7290; .A33. **DD** 364/.9757.

US
CRIME IN TEXAS. **Main/Corp** Texas. Dept. of Public Safety. English. Department of Public Safety / Texas, PO Box 4087, 5805 North Lamar Boulevard, Austin TX 78773. **Tel** (512)465-2138. **LC** HV7293; .A38A. **DD** 364.1/09764.

US/0743-1872
CRIME LABORATORY DIGEST. (CRIME LABORATORY DIGEST / U.S. DEPARTMENT OF JUSTICE, FEDERAL BUREAU OF INVESTIGATION.). [Crime lab. dig.]. **Added/Corp** FBI Laboratory. American Society of Crime Laboratory Directors. (19??)-. Periodical. English. qt. Free on request. Forensic Science Research and Training Center, FBI Academy, Room 326, Quantico VA 22135. **Tel** (703)640-1126. **ED** Barry L. Brown and Denise K. Bennett. **LC** HV8073; .C692. **DD** 363.2/56/0973. cum. index. **Pr Rev. Circ:** 3,000 (ctrl). Documents available from The Genuine Article.
Desc: Contains technical articles in the forensic sciences.
Ind/Abst Curr. Contents Clin. Med.; Res. Alert [Select. Cov.]; SCISEARCH; Soc. Sci. Cit. Index [Select. Cov.].

●US
CRIME STATE RANKINGS. (CRIME STATE RANKINGS. CRIME IN THE 50 UNITED STATES.). (1994)-. English. an. $43.95. Morgan Quitno Corporation, PO Box 1656, 512 East 9th Street, Lawrence KS 66044. **Tel** (800)457-0742, (913)841-3534, FAX (913)841-3534.
Desc: Contains up-to-date collection of state information from a wide variety of federal, state and private sources.

CN/0833-5737
CRIMINAL INJURIES COMPENSATION. (CRIMINAL INJURIES COMPENSATION / STATISTICS CANADA, SOCIAL SECURITY SECTION, HEALTH DIVISION [AND] CANADIAN CENTRE FOR JUSTICE STATISTICS [AND] DEPARTMENT OF JUSTICE, POLICY, PROGRAMS AND RESEARCH BRANCH.). [Crim. inj. compens.]. **Added/Corp** Statistics Canada. Social Security Section. Canadian Centre for Justice Statistics. Canada. Dept. of Justice. Policy, Programs and Research Branch. **VFOAT** Indemnisation des Victimes d'Actes Criminels. (1986)-. English (French). ir. 25.00Can$ Canada; $26.50 other. Statistics Canada, Publications Sales & Services, Main Building Room 1710, Ottawa Ontario K1A 0T6 Canada. **Tel** (613)951-5078, (800)267-6677, FAX (613)951-1584, telex 053-3585. **DD** 362.8/8/0971. ***Continues*** *Criminal Injuries Compensation, Social Security, Provincial Programs., 0828-3044.*
Desc: With extensive analysis and numerous charts, this publication draws a national profile of Canada's criminal injuries compensation programs.

US/0146-9177
CRIMINAL JUSTICE ABSTRACTS. **Added/Corp** National Council on Crime and Delinquency. **VFOAT** Crime and Delinquency Literature. Vol. 9 (March 1977)-. Abstracting/Indexing Service. English. qt (Mar., Jun., Sep., Dec.). $150.00 (one year), $270.00 (two year), $360.00 (three year) US and Canada; $165.00 (one year) (air freight included) other. Willow Tree Press, PO Box 249, Monsey NY 10952. **Tel** (914)354-9139, FAX (914)362-8376. **ED** Richard Allinson. **LC** HV6001; .C67. **DD** 364. **NLM** Z 5118.C9 I51. cum. index. **Bk Rev. Ad Acc. Circ:** 1,000 (ctrl). available in microform from Williams S Hein & Co.; available on CD-ROM from the publisher; available on microfilm from University Microfilms International (UMI); available on an online database from WESTLAW. ***Continues*** *Crime and Delinquency Literature, 0037-1327.*
Desc: Contains approximately 1,600 in-depth abstracts of the most important books, journal articles, and reports published worldwide, plus literature reviews.
Ind/Abst Crim. Justice Abstr.; Crim. Justice Period. Index; Crim. Penol. Police Sci. Abstr.

US/0145-5818
CRIMINAL JUSTICE PERIODICAL INDEX. [Crim. justice period. index]. (19??)-. Abstracting/Indexing Service. English. Three times a year. $307.00 US; $319.00 Canada; $399.00 other. University Microfilms International, 300 North Zeeb Road, Ann Arbor MI 48106-1346. **Tel** (313)761-4700, (800)521-0600 Exts. 2490, 2491, FAX (313)973-1540. **ED** Millie Atkins. **LC** Z5118.C9; C74; HV8138. **DD** 016.364/0973.
Desc: A subject author index to over 100 US, British, and Canadian journals covering criminal law, police studies, corrections and security.

UK
CRIMINAL STATISTICS, ENGLAND AND WALES. **Added/Corp** Great Britain. Home Dept. Great Britain. Home Office. (19??)-. English. an. Her Majesty's Stationery Office, 51 Nine Elms Lane, London SW8 5DR England. **Tel** 011 44 71 873 8459, 011 44 71 873 8499, FAX 011 44 71 873 8499, 011 44 71 873 8456, telex 297138. **(Subscription address:** Her Majesty's Stationery Office, PO Box 276, Publications Centre, London SW8 5DT England.**)**

UK
CRIMINAL STATISTICS, ENGLAND AND WALES. SUPPLEMENTARY TABLES. VOL. 1, PROCEEDINGS IN MAGISTRATES' COURTS. **VFOAT** Proceedings in Magistrates' Courts. 1980-. Proceedings. English. an. £18.75. Home Office, Queen Anne's Gate, Room 137 Edit, London SW1H 9AT England. **Tel** 011 44 71 273 3762, FAX 011 44 71 273 2568. **LC** HA1131; .A3 SUPPL. **DD** 312/.46/0942.

UK
CRIMINAL STATISTICS, ENGLAND AND WALES. SUPPLEMENTARY TABLES. VOL. 3, TABLES BY POLICE FORCE AREAS AND SOME COURT AREAS. **VFOAT** Tables by Police Force Areas and Some Court Areas. 1980-. English. an. £18.75. Home Office, Queen Anne's Gate, Room 137 Edit, London SW1H 9AT England. **Tel** 011 44 71 273 3762, FAX 011 44 71 273 2568. **LC** HA1131; .A3 SUPPL. 3. **DD** 312/.46/0942. available on microfilm.

NE/0168-9029
CRIMINALITEIT EN STRAFRECHTSPELEGING. **VFOAT** Criminality and Criminal Justice. (1983)-. Dutch. an. Fl32.00. Centraal Bureau voor de Statistiek, AFD ALG Zaken, Postbus 959, 2270 AZ Voorburg Netherlands. **Tel** 011 31 70 3373800, FAX 011 31 038 7429, telex 32692 CBS NL. ***Absorbed*** *Justitiele Statistiek; Criminele Statistiek; Toepassing der Wegenverkeerswet; Statistiek Jeugdcriminaliteit.*

●NE/0928-8759
CRIMINOLOGY, PENOLOGY AND POLICE SCIENCE ABSTRACTS. **Added/Corp** Criminologica Foundation. Vol. 32, No. 1 (Jan./Feb. 1992)-. Abstracting/Indexing Service. English. bm. $480.00 Americas; Fl865.00 others. Kugler Publications BV / Amsterdam, PO Box 11188, 1001 GD Amsterdam Netherlands. **Tel** 011 31 20 6278070. **(Subscription address:** Kugler Publications, PO Box 1498, New York, NY 10009**)** **NLM** Z 5703.4.C73; C929. ***Formed by the union of*** *Criminology & Penology Abstracts, 0166-6231* ***and*** *Police Science Abstracts, 0166-6282.*
Desc: Contains information on the etiology of crime and juvenile delinquency, the control and treatment of offenders, criminal procedure, the administration of justice and forensic and police sciences, including forensic medicine.

SP
CUADERNOS DE BIBLIOGRAFIA ESPANOLA. SERIE A : DERECHO. **VFOAT** Cuadernos de Bibliografia Espanola de Articulos de Revistas Serie A - Derecho. V. 1- Jan./March 1974-. Spanish. Direccion General de Archivos y Bibliotecas, Vitruvio 4, Madrid Spain.

AT
CURRENT AUSTRALIAN AND NEW ZEALAND LEGAL LITERATURE INDEX. ***Ceased.*** (Jan. 1973)-(19??). Abstracting/Indexing Service. English. qt. The Law Book Company Limited, 44-50 Waterloo Road, North Ryde New South Wales, 2113 Australia. **Tel** 011 61 2 8870177, FAX 011 61 2 8887240, telex ASBOOK 27445. **ED** Gwenda Fisher. **DD** 016.34/009931.
Desc: Arranged alphabetically by subject, listing articles, case notes and comments, professional practice notes, committee reports, editorials, letters, books and book reviews which have been published in Australian and New Zealand periodicals.
Ind/Abst Aust. Leg. Mon. Dig.

US/0898-9451
CURRENT INDEX TO LEGAL PERIODICALS (SEATTLE, WASH.). (CURRENT INDEX TO LEGAL PERIODICALS.). [Curr. index leg. period.]. **Added/Corp** Marian Gould Gallagher Law Library. (1968)-. English. wk. $75.00. Gallagher Law Library, 212 Condon Hall, JB 20, Seattle WA 98105. **Tel** (206)543-4097. **DD** 340. Index available. **Circ:** 2,350. available on diskette.
Desc: A subject-defined listing of contents of newly published periodicals. Precedes the Index to Legal Periodicals in currency.

US/0196-1780
CURRENT LAW INDEX. [Curr. law index]. **Added/Corp** Information Access Corporation. Vol. 1 (Jan. 1980)-. Abstracting/Indexing Service. English. mo. $546.00 (nonmember), $444.00 (member) US; $635.00 (nonmember), $533.00 (member) other. Information Access Company, 362 Lakeside Drive, Foster City CA 94404. **Tel** (800)227-8431. **(Subscription address:** Information Access Company, PO Box 61000, Department 1851, San Francisco CA 84161.**)** **LC** K33; .C87. **DD** 340/.16. **[CCC].**
Desc: Guide to legal periodicals of the US, Canada, UK, Australia and New Zealand.

US/0011-3859
CURRENT PUBLICATIONS IN LEGAL AND RELATED FIELDS. [Curr. publ. leg. relat. fields]. **Added/Corp** American Association of Law Libraries. Fred B. Rothman & Co. Vol. 1, No. 1 (Apr. 15, 1953)-. Periodical. English. Nine times a year (Except June, July, and Sept.). $125.00. Fred B. Rothman & Company, 10368 West Centennial Road, Littleton CO 80127. **Tel** (800)457-1986, (303)979-5657, FAX (303)978-1457, telex 87669. **DD** 340; 016. cum. index. **Bk Rev.**
Desc: A bibliographic source containing a listing of books and materials in law and related fields.

US/0731-8189
CURRENT TREATY INDEX. (CURRENT TREATY INDEX / COMPILED BY IGOR I. KAVASS AND ADOLF SPRUDZS.). [Curr. treaty index]. (1982)-. Directory. English. sa. $98.00. W S Hein & Company Inc, 1285 Main Street, Buffalo NY 14209-1987. **ED** Igor I. Kavass, A. Sprudzs. **LC** JX236.5; .C87. **DD** 341/.0264/73. **Circ:** 400. ***Absorbed*** *United States International Treaties Today, Unpublished and Unnumbered Treaties Index, 1050-9445.*
Desc: Treaties and other international acts published in slip form and not yet appearing in the bound UST series.

IT/0419-4632
DIZIONARIO BIBLIOGRAFICO DELLE RIVISTE GIURIDICHE ITALIANE. (1957)-. Italian. Giuffre Editore SPA, Via Busto Arsizio 40, 20151 Milan Italy. **Tel** 011 398 2 38089200. **DD** 349; 016. ***Continues*** *Dizionario Bibliografico delle Riviste Giuridiche Italiane su Leggi Vigenti.*

CK
ESTADISTICA DE CRIMINALIDAD. **VFOAT** Criminalidad. Statistical Publication. Spanish. Policia Nacional de Colombia, Carrera 25 No 10-41, Bogota Colombia. **LC** HV7335; .A4.

SP/0561-4473
ESTADISTICAS JUDICIALES DE ESPANA. **Main/Corp** Spain. Instituto Nacional de Estadistica. (1959)-. Statistical Publication. Spanish. ir. 1200ptas. Instituto Nacional Estadistico Spain, Paseo de la Castellana 183, 28046 Madrid Spain. **Tel** 011 34 1 583 9100. ***Supersedes*** *Estadistica de los Tribunales Tutelares de Menores; Estadistica Penal de Espana; Estadistica Penitenciaria* ***and*** *Estadistica Judicial Civil y de lo Contencioso-Administrativo.*

US/0741-692X
FEDERAL COURT MANAGEMENT STATISTICS. 1983-. English. an. Administrative Office of the United States Courts, 811 Vermont Avenue NW, Room 655, Washington DC 20544. **LC** KF180; .A337. **DD** 347/.73/2/00212; 347.30720212. available on microfiche (Vols. for (1983-) distributed to depository libraries). ***Continues*** *Management Statistics for United States Courts, 0099-0434.*

US/0192-625X
FEDERAL JUDICIAL WORKLOAD STATISTICS. (FEDERAL JUDICIAL WORKLOAD STATISTICS / PREPARED BY THE ADMINISTRATIVE OFFICE OF THE UNITED STATES COURTS, STATISTICAL ANALYSIS AND REPORTS DIVISION.). **Added/Corp** United States. Administrative Office of the United States Courts. Statistical Analysis and Reports Division. United States. Administrative Office of the United States Courts. **VFOAT** Federal Judicial Workload Statistics for the Twelve-Month Period Ended ...; Federal Judicial Workload Statistics During the Twelve-Month Period Ending .... (19??)-. Statistical Publication. English. qt. Administrative Office of the United States Courts, 811 Vermont Avenue NW, Room 655, Washington DC 20544. **LC** KF180; .A354. **DD** 347/.73/13.

US
GRENADA CONSOLIDATED INDEX OF STATUTES AND SUBSIDIARY LEGISLATION TO ... . **VFOAT** Consolidated Index of Statutes and Subsidiary Legislation to ... . English. an. $20.00. Faculty of Law Library, PO Box 64, Bridgetown Barbados. **Tel** (813)778-5211. **ED** Clifford Hammett. **LC** KGR4010.5; .G74. **DD** 348.7298/45028. **Bk Rev**. **Ad Acc**. **Circ:** 250.
Desc: Contains titles of current laws in the territory concerned with references to the amendments to and subsidiary legislation made under each statute.

US
GUYANA CONSOLIDATED INDEX TO STATUTES AND SUBSIDIARY LEGISLATION TO 1ST JAN. ... . English. an. $20.00. Faculty of Law Library, PO Box 64, Bridgetown Barbados. **Tel** (813)778-5211. **ED** Clifford Hammett. **LC** KHN52; .G89. **DD** 348.88/1028. **Bk Rev**. **Ad Acc**. **Circ:** 250.
Desc: Contains titles of current laws in the territory concerned with references to the amendments to and subsidiary legislation made under each statute.

US/0732-9849
ILLINOIS UNIFORM CRIME REPORTS USER'S GUIDE UPDATE. (ILLINOIS UNIFORM CRIME REPORTS USER'S GUIDE UPDATE FOR ... DATA.). [Ill. unif. crime rep. user's guide update]. English. an. Statistical Analysis Center, Illinois Law Enforcement Commission, 120 South Riverside Plaza, Chicago IL 60606. **LC** HV6793.I3; I57. **DD** 364.1/09773.

US/0192-2602
INDEX-DIGEST - UNITED STATES DEPARTMENT OF THE INTERIOR, OFFICE OF HEARINGS AND APPEALS. (INDEX-DIGEST / UNITED STATES DEPARTMENT OF THE INTERIOR, OFFICE OF HEARINGS AND APPEALS [AND] OFFICE OF THE SOLICITOR.). **Main/Corp** United States. Dept. of the Interior. Office of Hearings and Appeals. **Added/Corp** United States. Dept. of the Interior. Office of the Solicitor. **VFOAT** Index Digest. (Jan./March 1971)-. Government Publication. English. ir. Department of the Interior, 1849 C Street Northwest, Washington DC 20240. **Tel** (202)343-3171, FAX (202)208-5048. **LC** KF5500.A57; I65. **DD** 346/.73/04402646. ***Continues*** *United States. Dept. of the Interior. Office of the Solicitor. Index-Digest.*
Desc: Covers all the published and all the important published decisions and opinions of the Department of the Interior.

CN/0832-9257
INDEX TO CANADIAN LEGAL LITERATURE (LIBRARY ED.). (INDEX TO CANADIAN LEGAL LITERATURE.). [Index Can. leg. lit.]. **VFOAT** Index a la Documentation Juridique au Canada. (1985)-. Periodical. English (French). Three times a year. 325.00Can$ Canada; $282.70 other. Carswell Publications, 2330 Midland Avenue, Agincourt Ontario M1S 1P7 Canada. **Tel** (416)291-8421. **ED** Louis P Mirando. **DD** 016.34971. Index available. cum. index. available on an online database.
Desc: A periodical index and a bibliography providing complete listing of Canadian articles, monographs, book reviews, case comments and annotations on legal subjects.

CN/0316-8891
INDEX TO CANADIAN LEGAL PERIODICAL LITERATURE. **Added/Corp** Canadian Association of Law Libraries. (1965)-. Abstracting/Indexing Service. English. Four times a year. 140.00Can$. Index Canadian Legal Periodical Literature, PO Box 386 NDG Station, Montreal Quebec H4A 3P7 Canada. **Tel** (514)484-8763. **DD** 016.34/005. cum. index. **Circ:** 500.
Desc: Completely indexes 110 Canadian legal periodical titles and articles from more than 50 Canadian periodicals and law reports.

UK/0019-400X
INDEX TO FOREIGN LEGAL PERIODICALS. [Index foreign legal period.]. **Added/Corp** University of London. Institute of Advanced Legal Studies. American Association of Law Libraries. **VFOAT** Index to Foreign Legal Periodicals and Collections of Essays. Vol. 1 (Feb. 1960)-. Abstracting/Indexing Service. English. qt. $520.00. University of California Press, 2120 Berkeley Way, Berkeley CA 94720. **Tel** (510)642-4191, (510)642-3907, FAX (510)642-9917. **ED** Thomas Reynolds. **DD** 016.3405. **Circ:** 600. available on microfilm and microfiche from University Microfilms International (UMI).
Desc: This publications indexes over 365 business periodicals internationally.

US/0019-4077
INDEX TO LEGAL PERIODICALS. [Index leg. period.]. **Added/Corp** American Association of Law Libraries. **VFOAT** Index to Legal Periodicals and Law Library Journal. (Jan. 1908)-. Abstracting/Indexing Service. English. mo (except Sept., with annual cumulations). $245.00 US and Canada; $265.00 other. H W Wilson Company, 950 University Avenue, Bronx NY 10452. **Tel** (800)367-6770, (718)588-8400, FAX (718)590-1617, telex 4990003 HWILSON. **ED** Stephen Rosen. **LC** K9; .N32. **DD** 016.34705. **NLM** ZKA 38 I381. Index available. cum. index. ctrl circ. available on an online database from WESTLAW; LEXIS; and WILSONLINE; available on CD-ROM from WILSONDISC; available on diskette from WILSONSEARCH; available on magnetic tape from WILSONTAPE.
Desc: Author and subject index to legal periodicals published in the US and Canada, Great Britain, Ireland, Australia, and New Zealand. Includes a table of cases under both the plaintiff's and the defendant's name and a table of statutes by jurisdiction.

US/0019-4077
INDEX TO LEGAL PERIODICALS. CD-ROM. English. mo. $1495.00. H W Wilson Company, 950 University Avenue, Bronx NY 10452. **Tel** (800)367-6770, (718)588-8400, FAX (718)590-1617, telex 4990003 HWILSON. **ED** Stephen Rosen. Index available. cum. index. ctrl circ. available on diskette from WILSONSEARCH; available on magnetic tape from WILSONTAPE; available in print; available on an online database from WILSONLINE.
Desc: Author and subject index to legal periodicals published in the U.S. and Canada, Great Britain, Ireland, Australia and New Zealand. Includes a table of cases under both the plaintiffs and defendants name and a table of statutes by jurisdiction.

US/0019-4093
INDEX TO PERIODICAL ARTICLES RELATED TO LAW. [Index per. artic. relat. law]. Vol. 1 (Sept. 1958)-. Abstracting/Indexing Service. English. Four times a year. $75.00. Glanville Publishers Inc, 75 Main Street, Dobbs Ferry NY 10522. **Tel** (914)693-1320, FAX (914)693-0402. **ED** Roy M. Mersky, J. Myron Jacobstein and Donald J. Dunn. **DD** 340. cum. index (from 1958-1988). **Ad Acc**. **Circ:** 600 (ctrl).
Desc: Geared to the increasing interaction of law and other disciplines: political science, sociology, psychology, medicine and international relations. Serves as a ready-reference to non-legal periodical articles related to law and selected from journals not included in the Current Law Index to Foreign Legal Periodicals, Index to Legal Periodicals, Legal Resource Index or LegalTrac.
Ind/Abst Energy Res. Abstr. (Sept. 1980-).

US
INDEX TO THE ABSTRACTS ON CRIME AND JUVENILE DELINQUENCY, AN. **VFOAT** Abstracts on Crime and Juvenile Delinquency. (1984)-. English. ir. University Microfilms International, 300 North Zeeb Road, Ann Arbor MI 48106-1346. **Tel** (313)761-4700, (800)521-0600 Exts. 2490, 2491, FAX (313)973-1540. ***Continues*** *Microfilming Corporation of America. Abstracts on Crime and Juvenile Delinquency: an Index to the Microform Collection, 0164-1654.*

SP
INDICE ESPANOL DE CIENCIAS SOCIALES. SERIE C, DERECHO. **Added/Corp** Instituto de Informacion y Documentacion en Ciencias Sociales y Humanidades (Spain). **VFOAT** Derecho. Vol. 7 (1983)-. Spanish. ir. 5500.00ptas. Consejo Superior Investigacion Cientificas (CSIC), Vitruvio 8, 28006 Madrid Spain. **Tel** 011 34 1 5612833, FAX 011 34 1 4113077, telex 42182. available on CD-ROM. ***Continues in part*** *Indice Espanol de Ciencias Sociales, 0211-1373.*

CN/0715-271X
JURISTAT. [Juristat]. **Added/Corp** Canadian Centre for Justice Statistics. **VAT** Juristat Service Bulletin. Vol. 1, No. 1, (1981)-. Periodical. English (French). ir. 60.00Can$ Canada; $72.00 US; $84.00 other. Statistics Canada, Publications Sales & Services, Main Building Room 1710, Ottawa Ontario K1A 0T6 Canada. **Tel** (613)951-5078, (800)267-6677, FAX (613)951-1584, telex 053-3585. **DD** 363.2/0971.
Desc: Each issue provides an analysis and detailed statistics on a different aspect of the justice system.

NE/0168-5783
JUSTICIELE KINDERBESCHERMING. **Main/Corp** Netherlands (Kingdom, 1815-). Central Bureau voor de Statistiek. Hoofdafdeling Statistieken Van Criminaliet en Rechtspleging. **VFOAT** Statistics of Judicial Child Protection. Dutch. 8.95. Centraal Bureau voor de Statistiek, AFD ALG Zaken, Postbus 959, 2270 AZ Voorburg Netherlands. **Tel** 011 31 70 3373800, FAX 011 31 038 7429, telex 32692 CBS NL.

US
JUVENILE COURT STATISTICS. **Main/Corp** United States. Office of Youth Development. (19??)-. English. Office of Youth Development, Washington DC 20201. **LC** HV9091; .U53a. **DD** 345/.73/08.

US
JUVENILE COURT STATISTICS AND ADOPTION PETITIONS IN KANSAS. **Main/Corp** Kansas. State Dept. of Social Welfare. English. an. Kansas State Department of Social Welfare, Topeka KS 66620. **LC** HV9093.K2; A3. **DD** 364.36/09781.

US/0091-3278
JUVENILE COURT STATISTICS (WASHINGTON). (JUVENILE COURT STATISTICS.). **Main/Corp** National Center for Juvenile Justice. **Added/Corp** National Center for Social Statistics. United States. Children's Bureau. United States. Office of Juvenile Delinquency and Youth Development. United States. Office of Youth Development. National Institute for Juvenile Justice and Delinquency Prevention. United States. Office of Juvenile Justice and Delinquency Prevention. National Center for Juvenile Justice. (192?)-. English. an. Free. National Center for Juvenile Justice, 701 Forbes Avenue, Pittsburgh PA 15219. **Tel** (412)227-6950. **(Subscription address:** National Criminal Justice Reference Services, Juvenile Justice Clearinghouse, Box 6000, Rockville, MD 20850**)** **LC** KF184; .O353. **DD** 345.73/081; 347.30581. ***Continues*** *Juvenile Court Statistics, 0091-3278.*
Desc: National estimates and detailed descriptions of the delinquency and status offense cases processed by juvenile courts.

GW/0453-3283
KARLSRUHER JURISTISCHE BIBLIOGRAPHIE. Vol. 1 (1965)-. Bibliography. German. mo. CH Beck Verlagsbuchhandlung, D 80791 Munich Germany. **Tel** 011 49 89 381891. **LC** K11; .A7.

US/0733-8937
KINDEX. [Kindex]. **Added/Corp** National Center for Juvenile Justice. Vol. 1 (1975)-. English. an. $45.00. National Center for Juvenile Justice, 701 Forbes Avenue, Pittsburgh PA 15219. **Tel** (412)227-6950. **ED** Linda Szymanski and Terrence Finnegan. **LC** K33; .K56. **DD** 016.346/73/013. **Ad Acc**. **Circ:** 150. Documents available from the publisher, the publisher.
Desc: Cumulative bibliographical index of articles from 500 legal periodicals classified under 200 juvenile justice subject categories.

US/0164-5390
LAW OFFICE INFORMATION SERVICE. ***Ceased.*** [Law off. inf. serv.]. **Added/Corp** American Bar Association. Section of Economics of Law Practice. Institute of Continuing Legal Education (Mich.). Vol. 1 (July 1978)-Vol. 15 (April 1993). Abstracting/Indexing Service. English. qt. University of Michigan / Institute of Continuing Legal Education, 1020 Greene Street, Ann Arbor MI 48109-1444. **Tel** (313)764-0533, FAX (313)763-2412. **ED** Austin G. Anderson and Barbara Concannon. **LC** KF318.A1; L39. **DD** 016.658/91/34. Index available. **Circ:** 500.
Desc: Bibliography covering more than 80 subject areas and listing articles from more than 130 journals in the law office economics field. Also includes five different indexes.
Ind/Abst Curr. Law Index (1980-); Leg. Resour. Index (1980-?).

US/0094-6516
LEGAL BIBLIOGRAPHIC DATA SERVICE : WEEKLY SUBJECT LISTING. English. wk. Information Dynamics Corporation, 80 Main Street, Reading MA 01867. **DD** 016.34.

US/0741-1189
LEGAL BIBLIOGRAPHY JOURNAL. (LEGAL BIBLIOGRAPHY JOURNAL : A LEGAL INSTITUTE PROJECT.). [Legal bibliogr. j.]. **Added/Corp** Legal Institute. Vol. 1, Issue 1 (1983)-. Bibliography. English. Three times a year. $9.75. Legal Institute, 3250 Wilshire Boulevard, Suite 1000, Los Angeles CA 90010. **Tel** (213)487-6268. **ED** Herman B Lancaster. Index available. **Bk Rev**. **Ad Acc**. **Circ:** 200 (ctrl).
Desc: Focuses on information about law materials.

US/0883-1297
LEGAL INFORMATION ALERT. [Leg. info. alert]. (1984)-. Periodical. English. Ten times a year (Monthly with July/Aug. and Nov./Dec. issues combined). $149.00 US; $169.00 other. Alert Publications Inc, 399 West Fullerton Parkway, Chicago IL 60614. **Tel** (312)525-7594, FAX (312)525-7015. **ED** Donna Tuke Heroy. **LC** KF240; .L415. **DD** 349.73/072; 347.30072.

[CCC]. Index available. **Bk Rev. Ad Acc.** available on an online database. ***Continues*** *U.S. Law Library Alert, 0278-5854.*
Ind/Abst Leg. Inf. Manage. Index; Leg. Resour. Index; LegalTrac (1991-).

US/0747-9298
LEGAL INFORMATION MANAGEMENT INDEX. [Leg. inf. manage. index]. **Added/Corp** Fox Information Consultants. Vol. 1, No. 1 (Jan./Feb. 1984)-. Abstracting/Indexing Service. English. bm (with annual cumulations). $123.90 Massachusetts; $118.00 others. Legal Information Services, Box 67, Newton Highlands MA 02161. **Tel** (508)443-4087. **ED** Elyse H. Fox. **LC** Z675.L2; L46. **DD** 026/.34. cum. index.
Desc: Indexes articles and reviews appearing in over 90 periodicals published throughout the world relating to law librarianship and legal information management.

US/0275-4088
LEGAL LOOSELEAFS IN PRINT. [Leg. looseleafs print]. (1981)-. English. an. $93.00. Infosources Publishing, 140 Norma Road, Teaneck NJ 07666. **Tel** (201)836-7072, FAX (201)836-7072. **ED** Arlene L Eis. **LC** KF1; .S73. **DD** 016.34973; 016.3473. **[CCC].** cum. index. **Ad Acc. Circ:** 1,000.
Desc: The only bibliography of loose leafs, listing and indexing by subject and publisher, about 3,500 titles by 320 publishers, giving detailed bibliographic information on each title.

US/8755-416X
LEGAL NEWSLETTERS IN PRINT. [Leg. newsl. print]. (1985)-. English. an. $85.00. Infosources Publishing, 140 Norma Road, Teaneck NJ 07666. **Tel** (201)836-7072, FAX (201)836-7072. **ED** Arlene L Eis. **LC** KF1; .L44. **DD** 016.34/005. **[CCC]. Ad Acc. Circ:** 1,000.
Desc: Lists and describes 1,600 newsletters and newsletter-reporters that are law-related. Publisher and subject indexes included.

US
LEGAL PERIODICALS IN ENGLISH. Vol. 1 (1976)-. English. Five times a year. $525.00. Glanville Publishers Inc, 75 Main Street, Dobbs Ferry NY 10522. **Tel** (914)693-1320, FAX (914)693-0402. **ED** Eugene M. Wypyski. ***Continues*** *Morse's Checklist of Anglo-American Legal Periodicals.*
Desc: Catalogs all legal periodicals published in the English language.

US/0272-9296
LEGAL RESOURCE INDEX. [Leg. resour. index]. **Added/Corp** Information Access Corporation. American Association of Law Libraries. (June 1980)-. Abstracting/Indexing Service. English. ir. $3232.00. Information Access Company, 362 Lakeside Drive, Foster City CA 94404. **Tel** (800)227-8431. **(Subscription address:** Information Access Company, PO Box 61000, Department 1851, San Francisco CA 84161.**) DD** 340. available on an online database.
Desc: Contains comprehensive indexing for over 990 key law journals, bar association publications and numerous legal newspapers. Provides coverage of all legal specialities and subject areas such as copyright law, real property, international trade, labor law, criminal justice, civil rights, and law office management.

US
LEGALTRAC [COMPUTER FILE]. (19??)-. Abstracting/Indexing Service. English. mo. $3,500 (with one workstation), $5500.00 (with two to four workstations) basic subscription; $4500.00 (with one workstation), $7500.00 (with two workstations), $8500.00 (with three workstations), $9500.00 (with four workstations) basic subscription with InfoTrac Enhanced Workstation. Information Access Company, 362 Lakeside Drive, Foster City CA 94404. **Tel** (800)227-8431.
Desc: Provides indexing to over 1000 legal publications. Indexes come from all major law reviews, Bar association journals, seven legal newspapers, and specialty publications.

NE/0548-1937
MAANDSTATISTIEK POLITIE EN JUSTITIE. ***Title Change.*** **Main/Corp** Netherlands. Centraal Bureau Voor de Statistiek. **Added/Corp** Netherlands (Kingdom, 1915-). Centraal Bureau voor de Statistiek. Monthly Bulletin of Judicial Statistics. Netherlands. Centraal Bureau voor de Statistiek Maandstatistiek van Rechtswezen, Politie en Branden. Netherlands. Centraal Bureau voor de Statistiek Monthly Statistical Bulletin of Justice, Police and Fires. **VFOAT** Monthly Bulletin of Judicial Statistics; Monthly Statistical Bulletin of Justice, Police and Fires. Vol. 1 (Jan. 1957)-(199?). Dutch. mo (12 issues). SDU Uitgeverij, Postbus 20014, Christoffel Plan, 2500 EA Den Haag Netherlands. **Tel** 011 31 70 3789911. ***Supersedes*** *Netherlands (Kingdom, 1815-). Centraal Bureau voor de Statistiek. Criminele Politiele Statistiek.* ***Continued by*** *Kwartaalbericht Rechtsbescherming en Veiligheid, 0921-819X.*

NE/0169-9385
MAANDSTATISTIEK RECHTSBESCHERMING EN VEILIGHEID. **Added/Corp** Netherlands. Centraal Bureau voor de Statistiek. **VFOAT** Monthly Bulletin on Justice and Security Statistics. Vol. 30, No. 1 (Jan. 1986)-. Dutch. mo. Centraal Bureau voor de Statistiek, AFD ALG Zaken, Postbus 959, 2270 AZ Voorburg Netherlands. **Tel** 011 31 70 3373800, FAX 011 31 038 7429, telex 32692 CBS NL. **LC** HV7354; .A473a. ***Continues*** *Maandstatistiek Politie, Justitie en Brandweer.*

US/0271-8448
NEW JERSEY LEGISLATIVE INDEX. [N.J. legis. index]. **Added/Corp** New Jersey. Legislature. **VFOAT** Legislative Index. (1913)-. English. Twelve times a year (During the legislative sessions). $275.00. Legislative Index of New Jersey, PO Box 236, Somerville NJ 08876. **Tel** (908)526-9100, FAX (908)526-9102. **ED** Patsy Hawley. **LC** KFN1810; .N48. **DD** 328. Index available. cum. index. **Circ:** 1,000.
Desc: Synopsis and up-to-date standing of each bill, index by topic and by the name of each bill.

US/0277-0512
NEW YORK LAW FINDER. [New York law finder]. 1979-. English. an. West Publishing Company, 610 Opperman Drive, PO Box 64526, Eagan MN 55123-1308. **Tel** (612)687-5618, (800)328-9352, FAX (612)687-5388, (800)562-2329. **(Subscription telephone:** FAX (612)688-3570**) LC** KFN5061; .N482. **DD** 348.747/028; 347.470828.
Desc: Indexes McKinney's Consolidated laws of New York and pertinent sections of 26 other titles issued by West, included United States Code annotated, Corpusjuris secundum, and various topics.

US/0745-4406
NEW YORK LAW JOURNAL DIGEST-ANNOTATOR. [N. Y. law j. dig.-annot.]. **VFOAT** New York Law Journal Digest Annotator. Vol. 46, No. 11 (Nov. 1982)-. Abstracting/Indexing Service. English. mo (with hardcover annual compilation). $395.00 (includes index), $290.00 (without index). New York Law Journal, 345 Park Avenue South, New York NY 10010. **Tel** (800)888-8300 ext. 565. **ED** Cathy Seidner. **DD** 348. cum. index. **Circ:** 800. ***Continues*** *Clark's Digest-Annotator.*
Desc: A digest of all lower court cases reported in full in the New York Law Journal, with indexing of all the journal's columns, articles and special sections.

US
OHIO COURTS ... SUMMARY. **VFOAT** Ohio Courts. Began with 1960. English. an. Ohio Supreme Court, Office of the Administrative Director, 30 East Broad Street, Columbus OH 43215. **LC** KFO71; .A3. **DD** 347/.771/01.

UK
ORIGINAL STATISTICS, ENGLAND AND WALES. SUPPLEMENTARY TABLES. VOL. 2, PROCEEDINGS IN THE CROWN COURT. **VFOAT** Proceedings in the Crown Court. 1980-. Proceedings. English. an. £12.75. Home Office, Queen Anne's Gate, Room 137 Edit, London SW1H 9AT England. **Tel** 011 44 71 273 3762, FAX 011 44 71 273 2568. **LC** HA1131.A3; SUPPL 2. **DD** 312/.46/0942.

US/0092-3605
PENNSYLVANIA JUVENILE COURT DISPOSITIONS. English. an. Juvenile Court Judges' Commission, Juvenile Statistics Division, PO Box 1234, Federal Square Station, Harrisburg PA 17108. **Tel** (717)532-1149. **ED** John Lemmon. **LC** KFP71.55; .P46. **DD** 345.748/08; 347.48058. **Circ:** 600.
Desc: Overview of Juvenile Court operations in Pennsylvania. Data represents dispositional information submitted to the Commonwealth's Juvenile Courts on delinquency cases on an annual basis.

UK
POLICE FORCE STATISTICS. **Main/Corp** Chartered Institute of Public Finance and Accountancy. English. £1.00. Chartered Institute of Public Finance and Accountancy, 2 3 Robert Street, London WC2N 6BH England. **Tel** 011 44 1 895 8823. **LC** HV8195; .C46A. **DD** 363.2/0942.

UK
POLICE STATISTICS ACTUALS. **Added/Corp** Chartered Institute of Public Finance and Accountancy. Statistical Information Service. (19??)-. English. an. £2.50. Chartered Institute of Public Finance and Accountancy, 2 3 Robert Street, London WC2N 6BH England. **Tel** 011 44 1 895 8823. **LC** HV8196.A2; P64. **DD** 363.2/0942.

UK
POLICE STATISTICS (CHARTERED INSTITUTE OF PUBLIC FINANCE AND ACCOUNTANCY. STATISTICAL INFORMATION SERVICE). (POLICE STATISTICS.). English. an. **LC** HV8195.A2; P63. **DD** 363.2/0941.

FI/0355-2160
POLIISIN TIETOON TULLUT RIKOLLISUUS. **VFOAT** Brottslighet Som Kommit Till Polisens Kannedom; Criminality Known to the Police. English (Finnish and Swedish). an. Tilastokeskus, PL 504, Annankatu 44, 00101 Helsinki Finland. **Tel** 358-0-17341, FAX 358-0-17342474, telex 1002111 TILASTO SF. **LC** HA1448.F4 subser; HV7355.3.

PL/0551-3855
POLSKA BIBLIOGRAFIA PRAWNICZA / POLSKA AKADEMIA NAUK, INSTYTUT PANSTWA I PRAWA. **VFOAT** Bibliographie Juridique Polonaise. French. an. 340.00. Panstwowe Wydawn Naukowe, Miodowa 10, PO Box 391, 00251 Warsaw Poland. **DD** 016.349438; 016.34438.

KO
POMJOE PUNSOK (SEOUL, KOREA : 1983). (POMJOE PUNSOK.). **VFOAT** Analytical Report on Crime. '83-Year 1/4-. Korean (Korean). qt. **LC** HV7377.5; .A43.

CN/0317-3828
PROBATION & PAROLE STATISTICS (REGINA). (PROBATION & PAROLE STATISTICS.). [Probat. parole stat.]. **Main/Corp** Saskatchewan. Dept. of Social Services. Planning and Evaluation Division. 1973/74-?. Periodical. English. an. Department of Social Services / Saskatchewan Canada, 2210 Albert Street, Regina Saskatchewan S4P 2Y3 Canada. **LC** HV9309.S3; S26A. **DD** 364.6/3/097124. ***Continues*** *Probation & Parole Statistics, 0317-3828.*

UK/0264-6544
PROBATION SERVICE STATISTICS ... ESTIMATES. ***Title Change.*** **Added/Corp** Chartered Institute of Public Finance and Accountancy. Statistical Information Service. (1984)-(1992). English. an. Chartered Institute of Public Finance and Accountancy, 2 3 Robert Street, London WC2N 6BH England. **Tel** 011 44 1 895 8823. **LC** HV9346.A5; P763. **DD** 364.6/3/0942. ***Merged with*** *Probation Service Statistics ... Actuals, 0140-8291* ***to form*** *Probation Service Statistics ... Estimates and ... Actuals.*

●UK
PROBATION SERVICE STATISTICS ... ESTIMATES AND ... ACTUALS. **Added/Corp** Chartered Institute of Public Finance and Accountancy. Statistical Information Service. (1993)-. Statistical Publication. English. an. £47.00. Chartered Institute of Public Finance and Accountancy, 2 3 Robert Street, London WC2N 6BH England. **Tel** 011 44 1 895 8823. ***Formed by the union of*** *Probation Service Statistics ... Estimates, 0264-6544* ***and*** *Probation Service statistics ... Actuals, 0140-8291.*

UK/0265-573X
PROBATION STATISTICS, ENGLAND AND WALES / HOME OFFICE. **Added/Corp** Great Britain. Home Office. (19??)-. English. an (Nov.). £7.50. Home Office, Queen Anne's Gate, Room 137 Edit, London SW1H 9AT England. **Tel** 011 44 71 273 3762, FAX 011 44 71 273 2568. **LC** HV9649.E5; G74a. ***Continues*** *Great Britain. Home Office. Probation and After-Care Statistics, England and Wales.*

US/0550-6387
PROCEEDINGS IN THE MUNICIPAL COURTS. **Main/Corp** New Jersey. Administrative Office of the Courts. Proceedings. English. an. Proceedings in the Municipal Courts, State House Annex, Trenton NJ 08625. **LC** KFN1871; .A35. **DD** 345/.749/0247.

SZ
RECHTSBIBLIOGRAPHIE. **VFOAT** Law Bibliography. German. an. Studio Verlag, Postfach CH-8023, Zurich Switzerland. **ED** N M Cerutti. **LC** K38; .R42. **DD** 016.349436; 016.34436.

BL
RELATORIO ESTATISTICO (SALVADOR, BRAZIL). (RELATORIO ESTATISTICO / SECRETARIA DA SEGURANCA PUBLICA, POLICIA CIVIL DA BAHIA.). (19??)-. Portuguese. **LC** HV8184.B33; R45. **DD** 3545.81/420074/06.

BL
RELATORIO ESTATISTICO - SERVICO DE ESTATISTICA POLICIAL E CRIMINAL. **Main/Corp** Bahia, Brazil (State). Servico de Estatistica Policial e Criminal. (19??)-. Portuguese. an. **LC** HV7333.B33; B34A. **DD** 364/.98142/0212.

US
REPORT OF THE STATISTICAL COMMISSION. ECONOMIC AND SOCIAL COUNCIL, UNITED NATIONS. **Main/Corp** United Nations. Economic and Social Council. Statistical Commission. **VFOAT** Report to the Economic and Social

Law —Abstracting, Bibliographies and Statistics

Council on the ... Session of the Commission. 1st Session (Jan. 27/Feb. 7, 1947)-. Statistical Publication. English. ir. United Nations Publications, 2 United Nations Plaza, Room DC2 0853, Department 007C, New York NY 10017. **Tel** (212)963-8303, (800)253-9646. **LC** JX1977; .A2 E/264, etc. **DD** 310.611.

CN/0822-7616
RESUMES DE JURISPRUDENCE PENALE DU QUEBEC. [Resumes jurisprud. penale Que.]. Vol. 1, No. 1 (1983)-. Periodical. French. sm. 145.00Can$. Editions Yvon Blais, Case Postale 180, Cowansville Quebec J2K 3H6 Canada. **Tel** (514)263-1086, (800)363-3047, FAX (514)263-9256. **ED** Alain Dubois and Philip Scheider. **DD** 345.714/002643. Index available. **Bk Rev**. **Ad Acc**. **Circ**: 800.
Desc: Abstract of recent judgements in criminal law in Quebec and Canada.

US/0145-2436
SELECTED STATISTICS ON THE OFFICE OF ATTORNEY GENERAL.
Main/Corp National Association of Attorneys General. Committee on the Office of Attorney General. English. Congressional Education Associates, 302 East Capital Street NE, Washington DC 20002. **LC** KF5107.Z9; N33. **DD** 353.9.

AT/0725-654X
SENTENCING STATISTICS, HIGHER CRIMINAL COURTS, VICTORIA.
Added/Corp Victoria. Law Dept. Research Section. (19??)-. English. an. Research Section, Law Department, 271 William Street Australia. **LC** HV8708; .S45. **DD** 364.6/5/09945.

US/0360-3431
SOURCEBOOK OF CRIMINAL JUSTICE STATISTICS. **Added/Corp** United States. Bureau of Justice Statistics. Criminal Justice Research Center. Michael J. Hindelang Criminal Justice Research Center. United States. National Criminal Justice Information and Statistics Service. (1973)-. English. an (Sept.). $6.00. National Criminal Justice Reference Services / NCJRS, Box 6000, 1600 Research Boulevard, Rockville MD 20850. **Tel** (301)251-5500. **LC** HV7245; .N37b. **DD** 364/.973. Index available. **Circ**: 9,500 (ctrl). available on microfiche.
Desc: Data from 153 sources in an easy-to-read, comprehensive format. Covers criminal justice system characteristics, public attitudes, offenses, arrests, court processing and persons under correctional supervision. Index, annotated bibliography of sources, 400-plus tables.
Ind/Abst Predicasts Forecasts.

US/0275-5157
SOURCES OF COMPILED LEGISLATIVE HISTORIES. (SOURCES OF COMPILED LEGISLATIVE HISTORIES : A BIBLIOGRAPHY OF GOVERNMENT DOCUMENTS, PERIODICAL ARTICLES, AND BOOKS.). [Sources compil. legis. hist.]. 1979-. Bibliography. English. ir. Fred B. Rothman & Company, 10368 West Centennial Road, Littleton CO 80127. **Tel** (800)457-1986, (303)979-5657, FAX (303)978-1457, telex 87669. **ED** Nancy P Johnson. **Bk Rev**.
Desc: Lists sources of compiled legislative histories, bibliography of government documents, periodical articles and books, 1st Congress thru 96th Congress.

US
STATE COURT CASELOAD STATISTICS, ADVANCE REPORT.
Added/Corp United States. National Criminal Justice Information and Statistics Service. (1975)-. English. an. $100.00. National Center for State Courts, 300 Newport Avenue, PO Box 8798, Williamsburg VA 23185. **Tel** (804)253-2000, FAX (804)220-0449.

US/0096-3208
STATE OF NORTH CAROLINA UNIFORM CRIME REPORT. **Main/Corp** North Carolina. Police Information Network. **VFOAT** Crime in North Carolina; North Carolina Uniform Crime Report. Jan.-Dec. 1973-. English. an. Police Information Network, 111 East North Street, Raleigh NC 27601. **LC** HV7283; .A3A. **DD** 364/.9756.

US/0093-4186
STATISTICAL COMPILATION - ADMINISTRATIVE OFFICE OF THE COURTS (ANNAPOLIS). (STATISTICAL COMPILATION.). **Main/Corp** Maryland. Administrative Office of the Courts. (19??)-. Statistical Publication. English. mo. Administrative Office of the Courts / Maryland, Court of Appeals Building, PO Box 431, Baltimore MD 21401. **LC** KFM1271; .A3. **DD** 347/.752/013.

US/0097-7667
STATISTICAL DATA ON PERSONS RELEASED FROM PAROLE BY DISCHARGE AND VIOLATION. **Main/Corp** Virginia. Dept. of Corrections. (19??)-. Statistical Publication. Virginia Department of Corrections, 6900 Atmore Drive, Richmond VA 23225. **Tel** (804)674-3119, FAX (804)674-3587. **LC** HV7296; .H252a. **DD** 364.6/2/09755. **Continues** Virginia. Dept. of Welfare and Institutions. Statistical Data on Persons Released from Parole by Discharge and Violation.

UK
STATISTICAL INFORMATION SERVICE : POLICE FORCE AND REGIONAL CRIME SQUAD STATISTICS, ACTUALS.
Main/Corp Chartered Institute of Public Finance and Accountancy. Statistical Publication. English. £1.20 each. **LC** HV8195.A2; C45A.

US
STATISTICAL PAPERS - UNITED NATIONS. STATISTICAL OFFICE.
Main/Corp United Nations. Statistical Office. Ser. A (1949)-. Statistical Publication. English. ir. United Nations Publications, 2 United Nations Plaza, Room DC2 0853, Department 007C, New York NY 10017. **Tel** (212)963-8303, (800)253-9646. **LC** JX1977; .A2; HA13; .U5. **DD** 310.82.

US/0740-8277
STATISTICAL REPORT - EXECUTIVE OFFICE FOR U.S. ATTORNEYS.
(STATISTICAL REPORT / UNITED STATES ATTORNEY'S OFFICE.). [Stat. rep. - Exec. Off. U. S. Atty.]. **Main/Corp** Executive Office for U.S. Attorneys. 1978/79-. Statistical Publication. English. an. US Department of Justice, 10th Street & Constitution Avenue NW, Washington DC 20530. **Tel** (202)514-2000, FAX (202)633-4371. **LC** KF180; .J86. **DD** 347.73/13; 347.30713. available on microfiche (Vols. for Fiscal Year 1982- distributed to depository libraries). **Continues** United States Attorney's Offices Statistical Report, 0162-668X.

US/0098-2016
STATISTICAL REPORT - STATE OF NEW YORK OFFICE OF COURT ADMINISTRATION. **Main/Corp** New York (State). Office of Court Administration. Statistical Publication. English. Office of Court Administration, 270 Broadway, New York NY 10007. **LC** KFN5070; .O33. **DD** 347/.747/013.

AT
STATISTICAL REVIEW OF CRIME.
Added/Corp Victoria. Police Dept. (19??)-. Statistical Publication. English. ir. Victorian Police, Government Printer, PO Box 203, North Melbourne Victoria Australia. **LC** HV7396; .A4. **DD** 364/.9945.

US/0731-6992
STATISTICAL SUMMARY OF THE COLORADO JUDICIARY. **Added/Corp** Colorado. Office of the State Court Administrator. (July 1978 to June 30, 1979)-. Statistical Publication. English. an. Colorado State Judicial Department, 1301 Pennsylvania Street, Suite 300, Denver CO 80203-2416. **Tel** (303)837-3613, FAX (303)831-1814. **LC** KFC1871; .S75. **DD** 347.788/013; 347.880713.

II
STATISTICS OF CIVIL COURTS IN THE STATE OF TAMIL NADU FOR THE YEAR
... . **Title Change.** 1971-. English. an. **DD** 347.54/82013; 345.4820713. **Continues** Administration Report of the Civil Courts Statistics. **Continued by** Administration Report of the Civil Courts Statistics for the Year ... .

GW
STATISTIK UBER NS-PROZESSE.
Added/Corp VVN--Bund der Antifaschisten. (19??)-. Periodical. German. mo. Prasidium der VVN-Bund der Antifaschisten, Rossestrasse 4, 6 Frankfurt Main Germany. **DD** 341.6/9.

BE
STATISTIQUE CRIMINELLE DE LA BELGIQUE. **Added/Corp** Institut National de Statistique (Belgium). (1944)-. French. an. 125F Belgium; 175F other. Institut National de Statistique / Belgium, rue de Louvain, 44, Centre Albert, 8e Etage, 1000 Brussels Belgium. **Tel** 011 32 2 5486211. **LC** HV7353; .A33. **DD** 304/.9493/0212. **Bk Rev**. **Ad Acc**. **Circ**: 350 (ctrl).
Desc: Statistics about criminality.

FR
STATISTIQUES CRIMINELLES INTERNATIONALES. (STATISTIQUES CRIMINELLES INTERNATIONALES. INTERNATIONAL CRIME STATISTICS.). [Stat. crim. int.]. **Main/Corp** International Criminal Police Organization. **Added/Corp** International Criminal Police Organization. General Secretariat. **VFOAT** International Crime Statistics; International Criminal Statistics; Estadisticas Internacionales de Delincuencia. (1952)-. French (Arabic, English and Spanish). an. 120.00F. International Criminal Police Organization, 50 Qvai Achille Lignon, 69006 Lyon France. **Tel** 011 33 72 447000. **LC** HV6208; .I57a. **DD** 364/.021/2.

PO/0253-0600
STATISTIQUES DE LA JUSTICE : CONTINENT ET ILES ADJACENTES.
[Stat. justice, Cont. iles adjac.]. **Main/Corp** Portugal. Instituto Nacional de Estatistica. Servicos Centrais. **VFOAT** Estatisticas da Justica : Continente e Ilhas Adjacentes. Portuguese (French). be. **DD** 347/.469/0130212.

FR
STATISTIQUES DIVERSES. **Added/Corp** Institut National de Statistique (Belgium). (19??)-. French. an. 85.00F France; 135.00F other. CNGP INSEE - Institut National de la Statistique et des Estudes Economiques, BP 2718, 1 rue V Auriol, F 80027 Amiens Cedex 1 France. **Tel** 011 33 22 927322. **DD** 347.493/013; 344.930713. **Bk Rev**. **Ad Acc**. **Circ**: 350 (ctrl).
Desc: Law and court statistics.

BE/0775-311X
STATISTIQUES JUDICIAIRES. [Stat. judic.]. **Main/Corp** Belgium. Institut National de Statistique. (1969)-. Monographic series. French. ir. Price varies per volume. Institut National de Statistique / Belgium, rue de Louvain, 44, Centre Albert, 8e Etage, 1000 Brussels Belgium. **Tel** 011 32 2 5486211. **DD** 342. **Bk Rev**. **Ad Acc**. **Circ**: 350 (ctrl).
Desc: Statistics about the courts' activities, law and criminality.

US/0273-3692
SUBJECT INDEX TO THE ILLINOIS REGISTER, WITH TABLES. 1977/78-. Periodical. English. Illinois Eyes, Inc., 33 North Lasalle Street, Chicago IL 60602. **ED** T Kearley. **LC** KFI1234.A2; I43 SUPPL. **DD** 348.773/025; 347.730825.

US/0085-7092
TARLTON LAW LIBRARY LEGAL BIBLIOGRAPHY SERIES. **Main/Corp** Tarlton Law Library. Bibliography. English. ir. Price varies per volume. Tarlton Law Library, University of Texas at Austin School of Law, 727 East 26th Street, Austin TX 78705-5799. **Tel** (512)471-7726. **Circ**: 40. **Continues** Tarlton Law Library Legal Bibliography, 0363-0730.
Desc: Legal bibliographies on various subjects.

US
TEXAS JUDICIAL SYSTEM ANNUAL REPORT FISCAL YEAR. **Main/Corp** Texas Judicial Council. **Added/Corp** Texas. Office of Court Administration. **VFOAT** Texas Judicial System Annual Report; Texas Judicial Council Annual Report; Office of Court Administration Annual Report. 56th (1984)-. English. Texas Judicial System Annual Report of Statistical and other Data, 1414 Colorado Street/Suite 600, PO Box 12066, Austin TX 78711. **Continues** Texas Judicial System Annual Report of Statistical and Other Data for Calendar Year ... .
Desc: Issues for 1984-1989 include the report of the Texas Office of Court Administration.

US
TEXAS JUVENILE PROBATION STATISTICAL REPORT : STATISTICAL AND OTHER DATA ON THE JUVENILE JUSTICE SYSTEM IN TEXAS FOR CALENDAR YEARS ... ABBREVIATED.
1980-81-. Statistical Publication. English. an. **LC** HV9105.T44; T5. **DD** 364.6/3/09764.

US/0897-389X
TRAVEL & TOURISM LAW BIBLIOGRAPHY. [Travel tour. law bibliogr.]. **VFOAT** Travel and Tourism Law Bibliography. Bibliography. English. qt. IFTTA, 693 Sutter Street/6th Floor, San Francisco CA 94102. **LC** KF2042.T75; A128. **DD** 016.34373/07891/05.

BE
TRIBUNAUX CORRECTIONNELS, COURS D'APPEL, CONSEILS DE GUERRE ET COUR MILITAIRE. French. an. 85F Belgium; 135F other. Institut National de Statistique / Belgium, rue de Louvain, 44, Centre Albert, 8e Etage, 1000 Brussels Belgium. **Tel** 011 32 2 5486211.

DD 347.493/013; 344.930713. **Bk Rev. Ad Acc. Circ:** 350 (ctrl).
Desc: Court statistics.

FI/0355-2187
TUOMIOISTUIMISSA KASITELLYT RIKOS- , SIVIILI- JA HALLINTOOIKEUDELLISET ASIAT. **Main/Corp** Finland. Tilastokeskus. **VFOAT** Vid Domstolarna Handlagda Kriminalcivil- Och Forvaltningsrattsliga Mal Och Arenden; Criminal, Civil and Administrative Cases Concluded in Courts. Finnish (Swedish; summaries and/or abstracts in Swedish and English). an. Tilastokeskus, PL 504, Annankatu 44, 00101 Helsinki Finland. **Tel** 358-0-17341, FAX 358-0-17342474, telex 1002111 TILASTO SF. **LC** HA1448; .F4 subser. **DD** 314.897 S 347.4897/013; 314.897 344.8970713.

FI
TUOMIOISTUINTEN TUTKIMAT RIKOKSET. **Main/Corp** Finland. Tilastokeskus. **VFOAT** Vid Domstolar Rannsakade Brott; Criminal Cases Tried by the Courts; Rikollisuus. English (Finnish and Swedish). Tilastokeskus, PL 504, Annankatu 44, 00101 Helsinki Finland. **Tel** 358-0-17341, FAX 358-0-17342474, telex 1002111 TILASTO SF. **LC** HA1448; .F4 subser. ***Continues*** *Tuomioistuinten Tutkimat Rikokset.*

US/0360-9146
UNIFORM CRIME REPORT FOR THE STATE OF MICHIGAN. **Main/Corp** Michigan. Dept. of State Police. **VFOAT** Crime in Michigan ... Uniform Crime Report. (1973)-. English. an. Michigan Department of State Police, 714 South Harrison Road, East Lansing MI 48823. **LC** HV6793.M5; A33. **DD** 364/.9774. ***Continues*** *Michigan State Police. Uniform Crime Report.*
Ind/Abst Stat. Ref. Index.

US/0095-5752
UNIFORM CRIME REPORTS, COMMONWEALTH OF PENNSYLVANIA. **Main/Corp** Pennsylvania. State Police. Bureau of Research and Development. **VFOAT** Crime in Pennsylvania. 1973-. English. an. Bureau of Research and Development, Pennsylvania State Police, Harrisburg PA 17101. **LC** HV7288; .A37A. **DD** 364/.9748.

US/0082-7592
UNIFORM CRIME REPORTS FOR THE UNITED STATES. **Added/Corp** United States Bureau of Investigation. United States. Dept. of Justice. Division of Investigation. United States. Federal Bureau of Investigation. **VFOAT** Crime in the United States; Crime in U.S.; Crime in the U.S. Vol. 1, No. 1 (Aug. 1930)-. Government Publication. English. an. Price varies per volume. Superintendent of Documents, US Government Printing Office, Washington DC 20402. **Tel** (202)275-3328, FAX (202)786-2377. **LC** HV6787; .A3. available on microfilm and microfiche from University Microfilms International (UMI). ***Continues*** *Uniform Crime Reports for the United States and Its Possessions.*
Ind/Abst Predicasts Forecasts.

US/0548-5851
UNIFORM CRIME REPORTS, STATE OF NEW JERSEY. (UNIFORM CRIME REPORTS, STATE OF NEW JERSEY / ARTHUR J. SILLS (ATTORNEY GENERAL, STATE OF NEW JERSEY) ... [ET AL.].). **Added/Corp** New Jersey. Office of the Attorney General. New Jersey. Division of State Police. Uniform Crime Reporting Unit. **VFOAT** Crime in New Jersey; Uniform Crime Report. (1967)-. Periodical. English. an. Free on request. State Police of New Jersey, Uniform Crime Reporting, Box 7086, West Trenton NJ 08625-0068. **Tel** (609)882-2000. **LC** HV9475.N5; U54. **DD** 364/.9749.

US
UNION LIST OF LEGISLATIVE HISTORIES. **Added/Corp** Law Librarians' Society of Washington, D.C. Legislative History Committee. 1st ed. (1950)-. English. ir. $82.50. Fred B. Rothman & Company, 10368 West Centennial Road, Littleton CO 80127. **Tel** (800)457-1986, (303)979-5657, FAX (303)978-1457, telex 87669.
Desc: This publication provides the user with a listing of the holdings of the libraries in Washington, DC area that have compiled in-house legislative histories on various legislative matters.

US
VITAL STATISTICS IN CORRECTIONS. **Added/Corp** American Correctional Association. (1984)-. English. ir. $18.00 (nonmembers), $14.40 (members of ACA). American Correctional Association, 8025 Laurel Lakes Court, Laurel MD 20707-5075. **Tel** (301)206-5100, (800)222-5646, FAX (301)206-5061. **ED** Diana Travisono. **LC** HV8482; .A38. **DD** 365/.973/021. **Bk Rev. Ad Acc. Circ:** 2,000. available on microfiche. ***Continues*** *Correctional Personnel Compensation and Benefits.*
Desc: Provides statistical information on salaries, benefits, education, training of correctional staff in the US, and statistics on many other areas of corrections. Also provides information about fiscal, populations, incarceration rates, etc.

US
WISCONSIN CRIMINAL JUSTICE INFORMATION, CRIME AND ARRESTS. **Main/Corp** Wisconsin. Crime Information Bureau. (1969)-. English. an. **LC** HV7299; .A25. **DD** 3641.9775.

FI
YLEISISSA ALIOIKEUKSISSA SYYTETYT JA TUOMITUT. **VFOAT** Vid de Allmanna Underratterna Atalade Och Domda. Finnish (Swedish). an. Government Printing Centre, PO Box 516, SF-00101 Helsinki 10 Finland. **LC** JN7399.A5; T54 subser.

BANKING LAW

US/0191-0280
ALI-ABA COURSE OF STUDY : BANK DEFENSE OF NEGOTIABLE INSTRUMENT CASES : MATERIALS. **VAT** American Law Institute-American Bar Association Court of Study. Bank Defense of Negotiable Instrument Cases: Materials. English. an. American Law Institute, 4025 Chestnut Street, Philadelphia PA 19104-3099. **Tel** (215)243-1661, (800)253-6397, FAX (215)243-1664. **LC** KF957.Z9; A14. **DD** 346/.73/096.

US/0271-356X
ALI-ABA COURSE OF STUDY. BANKING AND COMMERCIAL LENDING LAW : MATERIALS. **Main/Conf** ALI-ABA Course of Study: Banking and Commercial Lending Law. **VFOAT** Banking and Commercial Lending Law: Materials. **VAT** American Law Institute, American Bar Association Course of Study. Banking and Commercial Lending Law: Materials. English. an. American Law Institute, 4025 Chestnut Street, Philadelphia PA 19104-3099. **Tel** (215)243-1661, (800)253-6397, FAX (215)243-1664. **LC** KF1035.Z9; A15. **DD** 346.73/082.

US/0191-1570
ALI-ABA COURSE OF STUDY. POSTGRADUATE COURSE IN FEDERAL SECURITIES LAW: MATERIALS. **Main/Conf** ALI-ABA Course of Study : Post-Graduate Course in Federal Securities Law. **Added/Corp** American Law Institute-American Bar Association Committee on Continuing Professional Education. University of Wisconsin--Madison. **VFOAT** Postgraduate Course in Federal Securities Law: Materials. **VAT** American Law Institute-American Bar Association Course of Study. Postgraduate Course in Federal Securities Law: Materials. (19??)-. English. an. price varies per volume. American Law Institute, 4025 Chestnut Street, Philadelphia PA 19104-3099. **Tel** (215)243-1661, (800)253-6397, FAX (215)243-1664. **LC** KF1440; .A184. **DD** 346/.73/0666.

US
AMERICAN BANK ATTORNEYS. (19??)-. English. sa. $200.00. Capron Publishing Corporation, PO Box 711, Wellesley MA 02181. **Tel** (617)235-0800. **ED** Alyssa G. Murphy. **Ad Acc.**
Desc: Listing of lawyers and law firms representing bank counsels; for U.S., Canada, and foreign

US/0736-5659
AMERICAN BANKERS ASSOCIATION BANKING LITERATURE INDEX. [Am. Bank. Assoc. bank. lit. index]. **Added/Corp** American Bankers Association. **VFOAT** Banking Literature Index; A.B.A. Banking Literature Index; ABA Banking Literature Index. Vol. 1, No. 1 (July 1982)-. Periodical. English. mo. $155.00 (non-members), $105.00 (members) US; $165.00 (non-members), $115.00 (members) other. American Bankers Association, 1120 Connecticut Avenue Northwest, Washington DC 20036. **Tel** (202)663-5221, , FAX (202)828-4544. **(Subscription telephone:** (202)663-7667**)** **ED** Aubrey Nye Hamilton (editor's phone: (202)663-5227). **LC** Z7164.F5; A53; HG1501. **DD** 016.3321. Index available. cum. index. **Circ:** 400+.
Desc: A subject index to current periodical articles on banking trends, topics, issues and operations. Includes references to 175 newsletters, newspapers, journals and magazines.

US/0027-9048
AMERICAN BANKRUPTCY LAW JOURNAL, THE. [Am. Bankruptcy Law J.]. **Added/Corp** National Conference of Bankruptcy Judges (U.S.) National Conference of Referees in Bankruptcy (U.S.). **VFOAT** Referee's Journal National Conference of Bankruptcy Judges. Vol. 45, No. 1 (Winter 1971)-. Periodical. English. qt. $50.00 US; $56.50 other. American Bankruptcy Law, 8929 Laurel Hurst, Ft Wayne IN 46835. **Tel** (219)486-6574, FAX (219)486-6474. **ED** Joe Lee. **LC** K1; .M38. **DD** 346.73/078/05; 347.3067805. **Bk Rev. Pr Rev. Circ:** 3,200. available on microfilm and microfiche from University Microfilms International (UMI). Documents available from The Genuine Article. ***Continues*** *Journal of the National Conference of Referees in Bankruptcy, 0197-2669.*

Ind/Abst Bowne Dig. Corp. Sec. Lawyers; Curr. Contents Soc. Behav. Sci.; Curr. Law Index (1980-); Fed. Tax Artic.; Index Leg. Period.; Leg. Resour. Index (1980-); LegalTrac (1980-); Res. Alert [Full Cov.]; Soc. Sci. Cit. Index [Full Cov.].

US/1059-3969
ANDREWS' PROFESSIONAL LIABILITY LITIGATION REPORTER. [Andrews' prof. liability litig. report.]. **Added/Corp** Andrews Publications (Firm). **VFOAT** Professional Liability Litigation Reporter. Vol. 1, No. 1 (Sept. 1991)-. Periodical. English. mo. $600.00. Andrews Publications Inc., 1646 West Chester Pike, PO Box 1000, Westtown PA 19395. **Tel** (610)399-6600, (800)345-1101, FAX (610)399-6610. **LC** KF1289.A59; A53. **DD** 346.7303/3; 347.30633.
Desc: This publication focuses on lawsuits filed against attorneys, investment bankers, financial advisors, rating services, accountants and other financial professionals facing liability in this fast growing area of law.

US
ANNOTATED MANUAL OF STATUTES AND REGULATIONS. **Main/Corp** United States. Federal Home Loan Bank Board. Periodical. English. bm. Federal Home Loan Bank Board, 1700 G Street Northwest, Washington DC 20552. **Tel** (202)377-6904.

US
ANNUAL BANKRUPTCY LITIGATION INSTITUTE. **Main/Corp** Bankruptcy Litigation Institute. **Added/Corp** Law & Business, Inc. **VFOAT** Bankruptcy Litigation Institute. (1981)-. English. an. Prentice-Hall Law and Business, 270 Sylvan Avenue, Englewood Cliffs NJ 07632. **Tel** (800)223-0231, (201)894-8538, FAX (201)894-8666. **LC** KF1527; .B27. **DD** 346.73/078/0269; 347.306780269.

US/1051-1539
ANNUAL INSTITUTE, SECURITIES ACTIVITIES OF BANKS. (ANNUAL INSTITUTE, SECURITIES ACTIVITIES OF BANKS : [PAPERS].). [Annu. Inst. Secur. Act. Banks]. **Added/Corp** Prentice Hall Law & Business (Firm). **VFOAT** Securities Activities of Banks. 6th (1986)-. English. an. $95.00. Prentice-Hall Law and Business, 270 Sylvan Avenue, Englewood Cliffs NJ 07632. **Tel** (800)223-0231, (201)894-8538, FAX (201)894-8666. **LC** KF975; .A56. **DD** 346.73/082; 347.30682. ***Continues*** *Annual Seminar, Securities Activities of Banks, 0743-1295.*

CN/0703-2625
ANNUAL REPORT. SUPERINTENDENT OF BANKRUPTCY (OTTAWA). (ANNUAL REPORT, SUPERINTENDENT OF BANKRUPTCY.). **Main/Corp** Canada. Bankruptcy Branch. **VFOAT** Rapport Annuel, Surintendant des Faillites; Rapport Annuel, Surintendant des Faillites (Ottawa). (1975/76)-. English (French). an. Free. Consumer and Corporate Affairs, Place du Portage, Ottawa-Hull Ontario K1A OC9 Canada. ***Continues*** *Canada. Bankruptcy Branch. Report of the Superintendent of Bankruptcy, 0576-0828.*

US/0739-2451
ANNUAL REVIEW OF BANKING LAW. (ANNUAL REVIEW OF BANKING LAW / CENTER FOR BANKING LAW STUDIES, BOSTON UNIVERSITY SCHOOL OF LAW.). [Annu. rev. bank. law]. **Added/Corp** Boston University. Center for Banking Law Studies. Vol. 1 (1982)-. English. an. $125.00. Butterworth Heinemann / Woburn, MA, 225 Wildwood Avenue, Unit B, Woburn MA 01801. **Tel** (800)366-2665, FAX (617)928-2620, telex 880052. **(Subscription address:** Butterworth Legal Publishers, PO Box 93643, Chicago IL 93643.**)** **LC** K1; .N53. **DD** 346.73/082; 347.30682. available on an online database.
Ind/Abst Curr. Law Index (1980-); Index Leg. Period.; Leg. Resour. Index (1980-); LegalTrac (1984-).

US/0270-1464
ANNUAL SURVEY OF BANKRUPTCY LAW. [Annu. surv. bankruptcy law]. 1st (1979)-. English. an. Clark Boardman Callaghan, 155 Pfingsten Road, Deerfield IL 60015. **Tel** (800)323-8067. **LC** K1; .N54. **DD** 346.73/078.

TU
BANKA VE TICARET HUKUKU DERGISI. Turkish. 40.00. Batider, Banka ve Ticaret Hukuku Arastrma Enstitusu, Hukuk Fakultesi, Cebeci/Ankara, Ankara Turkey. **LC** K2; .A56.
Ind/Abst Index Foreign Leg. Per.

US/0005-5433
BANKERS LETTER OF THE LAW, THE. (19??)-. Periodical. English. mo. $193.00 US; $265.00 other. Warren Gorham & Lamont Inc., Park Square Building, 31 St. James Avenue, Boston MA 02116-4112. **Tel** (617)423-2020, (800)950-1207, FAX (617)423-2026. **ED** Robert Volk. **[CCC].**
Desc: A timely monthly alert designed to keep bank attorneys up-to-date on the latest rulings involving federal and state banking cases.

US
BANKING AND COMMERCIAL LENDING LAW : RESOURCE MATERIALS. **VFOAT** Resource Materials--Banking and Commercial Lending

Law. Vol. 1; 1980-. English. an. American Law Institute, 4025 Chestnut Street, Philadelphia PA 19104-3099. **Tel** (215)243-1661, (800)253-6397, FAX (215)243-1664. **LC** KF1035.Z9; B35. **DD** 346.73/073.

CN/0832-8722
BANKING & FINANCE LAW REVIEW. [Bank. finance law rev.]. **VFOAT** Banking and Finance Law Review. Vol. 1, No. 1 (Oct. 1986)-. Periodical. English. Three times a year. 113.25Can$. Carswell / Canada, 2075 Kennedy Road, Scarborough Ontario M1T 3V4 Canada. **Tel** (416)609-3800, (800)387-5164. **ED** Benjamin Geva. **LC** K2; .A563. **DD** 346.71/082/05; 347.1068205. **Bk Rev. Ad Acc.**
Desc: Provides discussion and insight into issues and problems which confront both the legal and financial communities in Canada.
Ind/Abst Bowne Dig. Corp. Sec. Lawyers; Can. Legal Lit.; Leg. Resour. Index; LegalTrac (1980-).

US
BANKING ATTORNEY, THE. No. 91-28 (July 19, 1991)-. Periodical. English. wk. $650.00. American Banker, Concourse Level, 1 State Street Plaza, New York NY 10004. **Tel** (212)803-8200, (800)221-1809. ***Continues*** *Thrift Attorney.*

US/0737-2159
BANKING LAW ANTHOLOGY. [Bank. law anthol.]. Vol. 1 (1983)-. Periodical. English. an. $299.95. International Library Law Book Publishers, 101 Lakeforest Boulevard, Suite 270, Gaithersburg MD 20877. **Tel** (800)359-3349, (301)990-7755, FAX (301)990-7642. **ED** Donald J. Hoyes. **LC** K2; .A57. **DD** 346.73/082; 347.30682. Index available. **Bk Rev. Pr Rev.**
Desc: Presents banking law review articles by year, printed in their entirety, selected from over 900 US law review journals. Introduction and overview written by highly respected experts in banking law. Indexed by author, subject and leading cases.

US/1065-1004
BANKING LAW BRIEFS : BLB. [Bank. law briefs]. **VFOAT** BLB. (19??)-. Periodical. English. sm (2 per month). $67.00. Banking Law Briefs, P.O.Box 426 Lenox Station, New York NY 10021. **Tel** (212)472-0917. **DD** 332. Index available. cum. index.
Desc: Recent developments in commercial banking law.

US/0005-5506
BANKING LAW JOURNAL, THE. [Bank. law j.]. Vol. 1, No. 1 (May 15, 1889)-. Periodical. English. bm. $136.75 US and Canada; $212.95 other. Warren Gorham & Lamont Inc., Park Square Building, 31 St. James Avenue, Boston MA 02116-4112. **Tel** (617)423-2020, (800)950-1207, FAX (617)423-2026. **ED** Peter Knopp. **DD** 346.73/082/05; 347.3068205. **[CCC].** available on microfilm and microfiche from University Microfilms International (UMI). Documents available from The Genuine Article, UMI Article Clearinghouse. ***Absorbed*** *Business Law Journal; Bankers Magazine, 0730-4080.* ***Continued in part by*** *Bankers Magazine (New York, N.Y. : 1964), 0730-4080.*
Desc: An authoratative guide to the latest developments in banking law. Covers every area of major interest to bankers and bank attorneys with practical material for bank counsel to use.
Ind/Abst ABI/INFORM Glob. Ed. (Jan. 1981-); ABI Inform Ondisc (Jan. 1981-); Account. Tax Datab. (Jan. 1981-); Bowne Dig. Corp. Sec. Lawyers (1974-); Curr. Contents Soc. Behav. Sci.; Curr. Law Index (1980-); Gen. BusinessFile (1992-); Index Leg. Period.; Leg. Resour. Index (1980-); LegalTrac (1980-); PAIS Int. Print (1991-); Res. Alert [Full Cov.]; Soc. Sci. Cit. Index [Full Cov.].

US/0271-6909
BANKING LAW JOURNAL DIGEST. 3rd Ed. (1889/1924)-. English. ir. $125.00 US; $162.50 other. Warren Gorham & Lamont Inc., Park Square Building, 31 St. James Avenue, Boston MA 02116-4112. **Tel** (617)423-2020, (800)950-1207, FAX (617)423-2026. ***Continues*** *Digest of the Banking Law Journal.*
Desc: A classified digest of legal decisions published in The Banking Law Journal.

US/0198-9251
BANKING LAW: NEW YORK BANKING LAW. Main/Corp New York (State). **Added/Corp** Matthew Bender (Firm) New York (State). Law, Statutes, etc. New York Banking Law. (19??)-. English. ir. Price varies. Matthew Bender & Company Inc., 1275 Broadway, Albany NY 12204. **Tel** (800)833-9844, (518)487-3000. **LC** KFN5250.A333; A193. **DD** 346.747/082/02632.

US/0742-3942
BANKING LAW REPORT. (BANKING LAW REPORT / BLI.). [Bank. law rep.]. Vol. 1, No. 1 (Mar. 1984)-. Periodical. English. mo. Free to members, $120.00 others. Executive Enterprises, 22 West 21st Street, New York NY 10010-6990. **Tel** (800)332-8804, FAX (212)645-8689. **LC** KF967; .B367. **DD** 346.73/082/05; 347.3068205.

US/0898-7998
BANKING LAW REVIEW. ***Ceased.*** [Bank. law rev.]. Vol. 1, No. 1 (Summer 1988)-(19??0. Periodical. English. qt. Faulkner & Gray Inc., 11 Penn Plaza, 17th Floor, New York NY 10001. **Tel** (212)967-7000, (800)535-8403. **ED** Pamela Goett. **LC** KF967; .B368. **DD** 346.73/082; 347.30682. **Bk Rev. Ad Acc. Circ:** 1,000 (ctrl). available on microfilm and microfiche from University Microfilms International (UMI); available on an online database (files 15,485) from DIALOG.
Ind/Abst Account. Tax Datab. (Winter 1991-) [Full Txt.]; Index Leg. Period. (1992-).

US/0094-7555
BANKING LEGISLATION IN THE CONGRESS. Main/Corp American Bankers Association. English. American Bankers Association, 1120 Connecticut Avenue Northwest, Washington DC 20036. **Tel** (202)663-5221, , FAX (202)828-4544. **LC** KF969.78; .A4. **DD** 346/.73/082.

US
BANKING LEGISLATION IN THE ... SESSION, ... CONGRESS. Main/Corp American Bankers Association. Federal Legislative Committee. English. an.

US/1059-1257
BANKING POLICY REPORT. [Bank. policy rep.]. **Added/Corp** Secura Group. **VFOAT** Banking Policy. Vol. 10, No. 7 (Apr. 1, 1991)-. Periodical. English. Twenty-four times a year. $374.33. Prentice-Hall Law and Business, 270 Sylvan Avenue, Englewood Cliffs NJ 07632. **Tel** (800)223-0231, (201)894-8538, FAX (201)894-8666. **LC** KF967; .B365. **DD** 346. ***Continues*** *Banking Expansion Reporter, 0730-689X.*
Desc: Covers the impact of government, legal, and regulatory decisions on banks. Provides special insights into the supervisory process, examination policy, loan loss provisions, capital requirements and enforcement proceedings.

US/0892-1377
BANKING REGULATOR. ***Ceased.*** [Bank. regul.]. ( )-(Sept. 1988). Periodical. English. wk. Reports Publications, PO Box 1992, Wilmington DE 19899. **DD** 346.

US
BANKRUPTCY COUNSELLOR. Vol. 1, No. 1 (Jan. 4, 1988)-. Periodical. English. Twenty-four times a year. $345.00. Counsellor Publications, Inc., PO Box 19070, Alexandria VA 22320. **Tel** (703)684-9156. **ED** Gregory Lee. **LC** KF1507; .B347. **DD** 346.73/078/05; 347.3067805. Index available in last issue of volume--attached. cum. index.
Desc: A newsletter providing a short analytical article, summaries of significant recently handed down bankruptcy decisions, and highlights of precedential laws in the bankruptcy field.

US/0098-7336
BANKRUPTCY COURT DECISIONS. Added/Corp Corporate Reorganization Reporter, Inc. (1974)-. Newsletter. English. Fifty times a year. $780.00. LRP Publications, 747 Dresher Road, PO Box 980, Horsham PA 19044-0980. **Tel** (800)341-7874, (215)784-0860, FAX (215)784-9639, (215)784-0870. **ED** Newell Blair. **LC** KF1519; .B34. **DD** 346/.73/07802643. **[CCC].** Index available. cum. index. **Circ:** 1,410.
Desc: Provides coverage of bankruptcy decisions, as well as news and developments in the bankruptcy field.

US/0890-7862
BANKRUPTCY DEVELOPMENTS JOURNAL. [Bankruptcy dev. j.]. **Added/Corp** Emory University. School of Law. Southeastern Bankruptcy Law Institute. Vol. 1 No. 1 (1984)-. Periodical. English. Twice a year (April, Sept.). $32.00. Emory University School of Law, 1804 North Decatur Road, 3rd Floor, Atlanta GA 30322. **Tel** (404)727-6830, FAX (404)727-6820. **ED** Michelle Caron, 1722 North Decatur Road, Atlanta, GA, (404)727-3630. **LC** K2; .A59. **DD** 346.73/078; 347.30678. **Circ:** 1500.
Ind/Abst Gen. BusinessFile (1992-); Index Leg. Period.; Leg. Resour. Index; LegalTrac (1984-).

US/0882-4924
BANKRUPTCY LAW HANDBOOK. [Bankruptcy law handb.]. (1985)-. English. an. $60.00. Clark Boardman Callaghan, 155 Pfingsten Road, Deerfield IL 60015. **Tel** (800)323-8067. **ED** Richard I Aaron. **LC** KF1524; .B355. **DD** 346.73/078; 347.30678.

US/0744-7671
BANKRUPTCY LAW LETTER. [Bankruptcy law lett.]. Vol. 1, No. 1 (Jan. 1981)-. Periodical. English. mo. $156.50 US; $218.65 other. Warren Gorham & Lamont Inc., Park Square Building, 31 St. James Avenue, Boston MA 02116-4112. **Tel** (617)423-2020, (800)950-1207, FAX (617)423-2026. **ED** Richard D. Holper and David Meider. **LC** KF1507; .B35. **DD** 346.73/078/05; 347.3067805. **[CCC].**
Desc: Provides insights and practical alternatives to help solve client's complex problems. Each issue has in-depth coverage of the latest cases interpreting the Bankruptcy Code; analysis of new federal and state statues; expert commentary on planning and drafting techniques; bankruptcy code nuances; and review of Uniform Commercial Code cases and their effect on the Bankruptcy Code.

US/0747-8917
BANKRUPTCY STRATEGIST, THE. [Bankruptcy strateg.]. Vol. 1, No. 1 (Nov. 1983)-. Periodical. English. mo. $225.00. Leader Publications, 345 Park Avenue South, New York NY 10010. **Tel** (800)888-8300 ext. 6170, (212)545-6170, FAX (212)696-1848. **ED** Herbert S. Schlagman. **LC** KF1507; .B36. **DD** 346.73/078/05; 347.3067805. cum. index.
Desc: Reports on legislative and judicial developments in bankruptcy law; includes articles on pretrial and trial strategy, as well as accounting and financial issues.

US/8756-6079
BANKS IN INSURANCE REPORT. [Banks insur. rep.]. **Added/Corp** Banking Law Institute (New York, N.Y.). Vol. 1, No. 1 (May 1985)-. Periodical. English. mo. $345.00 US & Canada; $395.00 other. John Wiley & Sons, Inc., 605 Third Avenue, New York NY 10158-0012. **Tel** (212)850-6000, (212)850-6645, FAX (212)850-6088, telex 12-7063. **(Subscription address:** John Wiley & Sons Inc / New Jersey, PO Box 2575, Secaucus NJ 07096-2575.**) ED** Jane G. Bensahel. **LC** KF1167.A15; B36. **DD** 346.73/0821/05; 347.3060405. **[CCC].** Index available. **Ad Acc.** available on microfiche; available on microfilm; available in microform.
Desc: What, who and how-to's of bank expansion into insurance. Covers legally legislative, regulatory developments, business strategies and selling tactics.

US/0891-0634
BNA'S BANKING REPORT. [BNA's bank. rep.]. **Added/Corp** Bureau of National Affairs (Washington, D.C.). **VFOAT** Banking Report. **VAT** Bureau of National Affairs' Banking Report. Vol. 48, No. 1 (Jan. 5, 1987)-. Periodical. English. wk. $1004.00. Bureau of National Affairs Inc., 9435 Key West Avenue, Rockville MD 20850. **Tel** (800)372-1033, (301)258-1033, FAX (301)948-5823. **(Subscription address:** 9435 Key West Avenue, Rockville MD 20850; telephone: FAX (301)948-5823**) ED** Susan Webster. **LC** KF967; .W37. **DD** 346.73/082/05; 347.3068205. **[CCC].** ***Continues*** *Washington Financial Reports, 0511-3172.*
Desc: An information service covering the major developments from Washington affecting financial institutions and their competitors.
Ind/Abst NEXIS.

US/1044-7474
BNA'S BANKRUPTCY LAW REPORTER. [BNA's bankruptcy law report.]. **Added/Corp** Bureau of National Affairs (Washington, D.C.). **VFOAT** Bankruptcy Law Reporter. **VAT** Bureau of National Affairs' Bankruptcy Law Reporter. Vol. 1, No. 1 (July 27, 1989)-. Periodical. English. wk. $844.00. Bureau of National Affairs Inc., 9435 Key West Avenue, Rockville MD 20850. **Tel** (800)372-1033, (301)258-1033, FAX (301)948-5823. **ED** Wendell Yee. **LC** KF1507; .B63. **DD** 346.73/078/05; 347.3067805. **[CCC].**
Desc: Covers various areas of bankruptcy law.

PO
BOLETIM SEMESTRAL / BANCO DE PORTUGAL, DELEGACAO REGIONAL DOS ACORES. No. 1 (June 1983)-. Bulletin. Portuguese. sa. 380$00. Banco de Portugal, Departamento de Estatistica e Estudos Economicos, Rua Febo Moniz 4, 1100 Lisbon Portugal. **Tel** 52 35 59, FAX 52 38 41, telex 165540 BAGAL P. **LC** HG188.A95; B64. **DD** 332/.09469.

CK
BOLETIN / BANCO DE LA REPUBLICA, JUNTA DIRECTIVA. Added/Corp Banco de Republica (Colombia). Junta Directiva. (Sept 9 1991)-. Spanish. ***Continues*** *Boletin (Colombia. Junta Monetaria).*

SP/0210-3737
BOLETIN ECONOMICO / BANCO DE ESPANA. [Bol. econ. - Banco Esp.]. **Added/Corp** Banco de Espana. (1979)-. Periodical. Spanish. mo (11 issues). Banco de Espana, Alcala 50, 28014 Madrid Spain. **Tel** 011 34 1 4469055, 011 34 1 3385072. **LC** HC381; .B64. **DD** 330.946/005. ***Absorbed*** *Evolucion Monetaria.*

US/0739-652X
BROKEN BENCH REVIEW. ***Suspended.*** [Broken bench rev.]. **VFOAT** BBR; B.B.R. Vol. 1, No. 1 (Nov. 1981)-Suspended with Vol. 8 (1991). Periodical. English. qt. $72.00. Whitman Publishing Company, 10 Water Street, Box 573, Lebanon NH 03766. **Tel** (603)448-2600. **ED** J E Yacos. **LC** KF1519; .B76. **DD** 346.73/078/02638; 347. 3067802638. Index available. **Bk Rev. Ad Acc.**
Desc: Business bankruptcies and reorganizations in the federal courts. Significant recent developments and trends.

●US/1067-618X
BURAFF'S LITIGATION REPORTS. BANK LAWYER LIABILITY. [Buraff's litig. rep., Bank lawyer liabil.]. **VFOAT** Litigation Reports. Bank Lawyer Liability.; Bank Lawyer Liability. Vol. 1, No. 37 (Jan. 8, 1993)-. Periodical. English. wk. $745.00. LRP Publications, 747 Dresher Road, PO Box 980, Horsham PA 19044-0980. **Tel** (800)341-7874, (215)784-0860, FAX (215)784-9639, (215)784-0870. **DD** 346. ***Continues*** *Bank Lawyer Liability Report.*

US/0007-6899
BUSINESS LAWYER, THE. **See** Law-Corporate Law.

US/0733-4613
BUSINESS REORGANIZATIONS UNDER THE BANKRUPTCY CODE. (BUSINESS REORGANIZATIONS UNDER THE BANKRUPTCY CODE : ALI-ABA COURSE OF STUDY MATERIALS.). **VFOAT** ALI-ABA Course of Study Materials; A.L.I.-A.B.A. Course of Study Materials. Periodical. English. sa. American Law Institute, 4025 Chestnut Street, Philadelphia PA 19104-3099. **Tel** (215)243-1661, (800)253-6397, FAX (215)243-1664. **LC** KF1544.Z9; B895. **DD** 346.73/06626.

UK/0269-2694
BUTTERWORTHS JOURNAL OF INTERNATIONAL BANKING AND FINANCIAL LAW. [Butterworths j. int. bank. fianc. law]. **Added/Corp** Butterworths (Firm). **VFOAT** Journal of International Banking and Financial Law. Vol. 1, No. 1 (June 1986)-. Periodical. English. mo. 1270.00Aus$. Butterworth & Co. Ltd. / Kent, England, Borough Green, Sevenoaks Kent TN15 8PH England. **Tel** 011 44 732-884567, FAX 011 44 732-885996. **ED** Josephine McAfee. **LC** K2; .U85. **DD** 341.7/51. **[CCC].** Index available. **Ad Acc.**
Desc: A journal of up-to-date news and comment from all the major financial centres in the world. Contributors are professionals with knowledge of the international banking system and financial markets.

CN/0068-8347
CANADIAN BANKRUPTCY REPORTS. [Can. bankruptcy rep.]. **VFOAT** Canadian Bankruptcy Reports Annotated; Recueil de Jurisprudence Canadienne en Droit de la Faillite. Vol. 1-38, (1920-1960);New Series Vol. 1-80 (1960-1990);3rd Series, Vol. 1 (1991)-. Periodical. English (French). Three times a year. 120.00Can$. Carswell / Canada, 2075 Kennedy Road, Scarborough Ontario M1T 3V4 Canada. **Tel** (416)609-3800, (800)387-5164. **ED** Carl H. Morawetz, David E. Baird, and Yoine J. Goldstein. Index available. cum. index. **Ad Acc.**
Desc: Series of bankruptcy reports which includes all important decisions across Canada.
Ind/Abst Curr. Law Index (1980-Dec. 1985); Index Can. Leg. Period. Lit.; Leg. Resour. Index (1980-Dec. 1985); LegalTrac (1981-1985).

US/0748-562X
CHAPTER 11 REPORTER. ***Title Change.*** [Chapter 11 report.]. **VFOAT** Chapter Eleven Reporter. Vol. 1, No. 1 (Aug. 1983)-(19??). Periodical. English. mo. Business Laws Inc., 11630 Chillicothe Road, Chesterland OH 44026. **Tel** (216)729-7996, (800)759-0929, FAX (216)729-0645. **LC** KF1544.A15; C48. **DD** 346.73/06626/05. ***Continued by*** *Bankruptcy and Commercial Law Advisor.*

US
CHAPTER ELEVEN THEORY AND PRACTICE. (19??)-. English. $775.00. LRP Publications, 747 Dresher Road, PO Box 980, Horsham PA 19044-0980. **Tel** (800)341-7874, (215)784-0860, FAX (215)784-9639, (215)784-0870.
Desc: Provides legal analysis of the Chapter 11 program.

US
CLAIMS MANAGEMENT. (19??)-. English. $50.00. LRP Publications, 747 Dresher Road, PO Box 980, Horsham PA 19044-0980. **Tel** (800)341-7874, (215)784-0860, FAX (215)784-9639, (215)784-0870.

US/0099-1848
COLLIER BANKRUPTCY CASES. Vol. 1 (Sept. 1974)-. English. Twenty-six times a year. $375.00. Matthew Bender & Company Inc., 1275 Broadway, Albany NY 12204. **Tel** (800)833-9844, (518)487-3000. **LC** KF1515.A2; C6. **DD** 346/.73/07802648.

US
COLLIER BANKRUPTCY MANUAL. (19??)-. English. ir. Matthew Bender & Company Inc., 1275 Broadway, Albany NY 12204. **Tel** (800)833-9844, (518)487-3000.

US
COLLIER ON BANKRUPTCY. (19??)-. Periodical. English. ir. Matthew Bender & Company Inc., 1275 Broadway, Albany NY 12204. **Tel** (800)833-9844, (518)487-3000.

US/0732-1023
COMMERCIAL FINANCE, FACTORING, AND OTHER ASSET-BASED LENDING. English. Practising Law Institute, 810 Seventh Avenue, New York NY 10019-5818. **Tel** (212)765-5700, FAX (212)581-4670 general correspondence, (212)265-4742 orders and billing inquiries. **LC** KF1050.Z9; C593. **DD** 346.73/074; 347.30674.

CN/0832-7688
COMMERCIAL INSOLVENCY REPORTER. [Commer. insolv. report.]. **Added/Corp** Butterworths (Firm). Vol. 1, No. 1 (Aug. 1987)-. Periodical. English. bm. 195.00Can$. Butterworth & Company Ltd. / Canada, 75 Clegg Road, Markham Ontario L6G 1A1 Canada. **Tel** (905)479-2665, (800)668-6481. **LC** KE1492; .C66. **DD** 346.71/078/05; 347.1067805.
Desc: Intended to provide timely insights into, and analysis of, developments in the law and other matters affecting commercial insolvency in Canada.

US
COMPACT BANKRUPTCY CODE & RULES. (19??)-. English. an. $41.00. LRP Publications, 747 Dresher Road, PO Box 980, Horsham PA 19044-0980. **Tel** (800)341-7874, (215)784-0860, FAX (215)784-9639, (215)784-0870.

US
CONSUMER AND COMMUNITY AFFAIRS HANDBOOK / BOARD OF GOVERNORS OF THE FEDERAL RESERVE SYSTEM. **Added/Corp** Board of Governors of the Federal Reserve System (U.S.). (19??)-. Periodical. English. mo. $75.00. Board of Governors of the Federal Reserve System, Mail Stop 127, Washington DC 20551. **Tel** (202)452-3244 or 3245.

US
CONSUMER CREDIT AND OTHER RETAIL BANKING DEVELOPMENTS. (1986)-. English. an. Practising Law Institute, 810 Seventh Avenue, New York NY 10019-5818. **Tel** (212)765-5700, FAX (212)581-4670 general correspondence, (212)265-4742 orders and billing inquiries. **LC** KF1040.Z9; C65. **DD** 346.73/073. ***Continues*** *Consumer Credit, 0098-048X.*

US/0732-863X
CONSUMER DEBTORS AND THE BANKRUPTCY CODE. (CONSUMER DEBTORS AND THE BANKRUPTCY CODE : ALI-ABA COURSE OF STUDY, MATERIALS / COSPONSORED BY THE UNIVERSITY OF ARKANSAS, SCHOOL OF LAW.). **Added/Corp** University of Arkansas, Fayetteville. School of Law. American Law Institute-American Bar Association Committee on Continuing Professional Education. **VFOAT** ALI-ABA Course of Study, Materials. (19??)-. English. an. American Law Institute, 4025 Chestnut Street, Philadelphia PA 19104-3099. **Tel** (215)243-1661, (800)253-6397, FAX (215)243-1664. **LC** KF1526; .C659. **DD** 346.73/078; 347.30678.

US
CONSUMER FINANCE LAW BULLETIN. **Added/Corp** National Consumer Finance Association. Law Forum. Vol. 4, No. 4 (Dec. 1950)-. Periodical. English. mo. $95.00. American Financial Services Association, 919 18th Street Norhtwest, Washington DC 20006. **Tel** (202)296-5544. ***Continues*** *National Consumer Finance Association. Law Forum. Bulletin of the Law Forum.*

US/0883-4555
CONSUMER FINANCE LAW QUARTERLY REPORT. **Added/Corp** Conference on Consumer Finance Law (U.S.). **VFOAT** Quarterly Report. Vol. 38, No. 3 (Summer 1984)-. Periodical. English. Four times a year. $50.00. Conference Consumer Finance Law, 200 East Randolph Drive, Suite 7300, Chicago IL 60601. **Tel** (312)861-1400, FAX (312)565-0832. **ED** Alvin C. Harrell. **LC** KF1039.A15; C63. **DD** 346.73/073; 347.30673. **Ad Acc.** ***Continues*** *Personal Finance Law Quarterly Report, 0362-6342.*
Desc: Resource journal for banking institutions and their counsel.
Ind/Abst Leg. Resour. Index; LegalTrac (1984-).

US/0197-7172
CONTROL OF BANKING. (CONTROL OF BANKING / PRENTICE-HALL.). [Control. bank.]. **Added/Corp** Prentice-Hall, Inc. **VFOAT** Prentice-Hall Control of Banking. (19??)-. English. bw (26 issues). $300.00. Maxwell Macmillan Professional Business Division, 910 Sylvan Avenue, Englewood Cliffs NJ 07632-3310. **Tel** (800)431-9025. ***Continues*** *Prentice-Hall, Inc. Federal Control of Banking.*

US/0883-055X
CURRENT DEVELOPMENTS IN BANKRUPTCY AND REORGANIZATION. English. Practising Law Institute, 810 Seventh Avenue, New York NY 10019-5818. **Tel** (212)765-5700, FAX (212)581-4670 general correspondence, (212)265-4742 orders and billing inquiries. **LC** KF1524.3; .C86. **DD** 346.73/078; 347.30678.

US/0093-1829
DEVELOPMENTS IN CORPORATE, BANKING, AND SECURITIES LAW. **See** Law-Corporate Law.

US/0892-4198
DISTRESSED REAL ESTATE LAW ALERT. ***Ceased.*** [Distressed real estate law alert]. Vol. 1, No. 1 (May-June 1987)-(Jan. 1994). English. bm. Clark Boardman Callaghan, 155 Pfingsten Road, Deerfield IL 60015. **Tel** (800)323-8067. **LC** KF1507; .D57. **DD** 346.73/078. available in microform.

US/0887-7807
FAILED BANK AND THRIFT LITIGATION REPORTER. Vol. 1 (1986)-. English. sm. $825.00. Andrews Publications Inc., 1646 West Chester Pike, PO Box 1000, Westtown PA 19395. **Tel** (610)399-6600, (800)345-1101, FAX (610)399-6610. **LC** KF971.3; .F35. **DD** 346.73/082/05.
Desc: Provides national coverage of suits spawned by bank and thrift failures. Coverage includes suits by federal regulators to recoup money from former bank and thrift officers, insurers and noteholders, as well as investor suits challenging the regulators' actions. Also follows criminal prosecutions of bank and thrift officials.

US/1055-9485
FAILED LBO LITIGATION REPORTER. [Failed LBO litig. report.]. **Added/Corp** Andrews Publications, Inc. **VAT** Failed Leveraged Buyout Litigation Reporter. (Oct. 1990)-. Periodical. English. mo. $700.00. Andrews Publications Inc., 1646 West Chester Pike, PO Box 1000, Westtown PA 19395. **Tel** (610)399-6600, (800)345-1101, FAX (610)399-6610. **LC** KF1544.A53; F35. **DD** 346.73/06626; 347.3066626.
Desc: Be among the first to know about developments in a rapidly emerging area of bankruptcy law that includes such issues as fraudulent conveyance, claims trading, conduit liability, creditor rights and employee actions.

US
FDIC ENFORCEMENT DECISIONS. **Added/Corp** Federal Deposit Insurance Corporation. Prentice-Hall, Inc. Information Services Division. **VAT** Federal Deposit Insurance Corporation Enforcement Decisions. Vol. 1 (1988)-. English. Twelve times a year. $444.85. Prentice-Hall Law and Business, 270 Sylvan Avenue, Englewood Cliffs NJ 07632. **Tel** (800)223-0231, (201)894-8538, FAX (201)894-8666. **LC** KF1023; .A554. **DD** 346.73/082; 347.30682.

US
FEDERAL RESERVE ACT OF 1913, WITH AMENDMENTS AND LAWS RELATING TO BANKING, THE. **Main/Corp** United States. 1920- Ed. English. US Government Printing Office, Washington DC 20402. **DD** 332.11.

US
FERC REPORT, THE. (Sept. 12, 1988)-. English. bw. $196.00 US; $221.00 other. United Communications Group, 11300 Rockville Pike, Suite 1100, Rockville MD 20852. **Tel** (301)816-8950 ext. 223, FAX (301)816-8945.

US
FINANCE AND COMMERCE. English. Credit Publishing Co, 615 South 7th Street, Minneapolis MN 55415. **Tel** (612)333-4244. ***Formed by the union of*** *Finance and Commerce (Minneapolis, Minn. : Criminal/Tax Appellate Ed.)* ***and*** *Finance and Commerce (Minneapolis, Minn. : Civil Appellate Ed.).*

US/0883-2447
FINANCIAL SERVICES LAW REPORT. ***Title Change.*** [Financ. serv. law rep.]. **Added/Corp** Leader Publications, Inc. Vol. 1 No. 1 (May 1985)-(199?). Periodical. English. Twenty-six times a year. Phillips Business Information, Inc., 1201 Seven Locks Road, Potomac MD 20854. **Tel** (301)424-3338, (800)777-5006, FAX (301)309-3847. **LC** KF967; .F56. **DD** 346.73/082; 347.30682. cum. index. ***Continued by*** *Financial Services Report, 0894-7260.*
Desc: Covers national and state-by-state developments in the banking field. Information stems from Congress, the state legislatures and banking commissions, the courts, the bank board, the OCC, the FDIC and the SEC. Includes analyses of business and legal strategies.

US/0889-9274
FORECLOSURE LAW BULLETIN. ***Ceased.*** (July 1985)-Ceased ?. Bulletin. English. mo. Pioneer Publishing Company, 131 Beverly Street, Boston MA 02114. **LC** KF697.F6; A494. **DD** 346.7304/364. available on microfilm and microfiche from University Microfilms International (UMI).

US
FUNDAMENTALS OF BANKRUPTCY LAW : ALI-ABA COURSE OF STUDY, MATERIALS. **VFOAT** ALI-ABA Course of Study, Materials. English. American Law Institute, 4025 Chestnut Street, Philadelphia PA 19104-3099. **Tel** (215)243-1661, (800)253-6397, FAX (215)243-1664. **LC** KF1524.3; .F86.

US/0891-611X
GARLAND'S BANKRUPTCY BULLETIN. ***Ceased.*** [Garland's bankruptcy bull.]. **VFOAT** Bankruptcy Bulletin. Vol. 1, Issue 1 (1987)-?. Bulletin. English. bm. Garland Publishing Inc, 1000A Sherman Avenue, Hamden CT 06514. **Tel** 800-627-6273, (203)281-4487. **LC** KF1507; .G37. **DD** 346.73/078.

US
GETTING INJURED WORKERS BACK TO WORK. (19??)-. English. $171.50. LRP Publications, 747 Dresher Road, PO Box 980, Horsham PA 19044-0980. **Tel** (800)341-7874, (215)784-0860, FAX (215)784-9639, (215)784-0870.

JA
GINKO TORIHIKI SHOROPPO / HAYASHI RYOHEI ... HOKA HENSHU. Japanese. 2800. Kinyu Zaisei Jijo Kenkyukai, 19 Minami Notomachi, Shinjuku-ku, Tokyo-to Japan.

US/0199-9990
GOVERNMENT RELATIONS STATUS REPORT. **Main/Corp** American Bankers Association. (19??)-. English. American Bankers Association, 1120 Connecticut Avenue Northwest, Washington DC 20036. **Tel** (202)663-5221, , FAX (202)828-4544. **(Subscription telephone:** (202)663-7667**)** **LC** KF967; .A54. **DD** 346.73/082.

VE
GUIBANCA. Spanish. Avada, Las Acacoas, Esp Sabana Grande, Edif Arismendi, Letra B, Ofic 304, Piso 3, Sabana Grande, Caracas Venezuela. **LC** HG185.V4; G84. **DD** 332.1/025/87. ***Continues*** *Guia Nacional de Bancos, Companias de Seguros, Entidades de Ahorro y Prestamo, Sociedades Financieras.*

US
ILLINOIS WORKERS' COMP LAW BULLETIN. (19??)-. English. $260.00. LRP Publications, 747 Dresher Road, PO Box 980, Horsham PA 19044-0980. **Tel** (800)341-7874, (215)784-0860, FAX (215)784-9639, (215)784-0870.

CN/0821-0012
INSOLVENCY BULLETIN. (INSOLVENCY BULLETIN / ISSUED BY THE OFFICE OF THE SUPERINTENDENT OF BANKRUPTCY.). [Insolv. bull.]. **Added/Corp** Canada. Office of the Superintendent of Bankruptcy. Canada. Consumer and Corporate Affairs Canada. **VFOAT** Bulletin sur l'Insolvabilite; Faillite et Insolvabilite. (1981)-. Bulletin. French (English). mo. **DD** 346.71/078. ***Continues in part*** *Canada. Bureau des Corporations. Bulletin, Canada Corporations, Bankruptcy and Insolvency., 0382-3288.*
Ind/Abst Index Can. Leg. Period. Lit. (1992-).

UK/0267-0771
INSOLVENCY LAW & PRACTICE. [Insolv. law pract.]. **Added/Corp** Frank Cass & Co. **VFOAT** Insolvency Law and Practice. Vol. 1, No. 1 (Jan./Feb. 1985)-. Periodical. English. bm. £139.00. Tolley Publishing Company Ltd, Tolley House, 2 Addiscombe Road, Croydon, Surrey CR9 5AF United Kingdom. **Tel** 011 44 81 6869141, FAX 011 44 81 6863155, 011 44 81 7600588. **LC** KD2142; .I57. **DD** 346.41/078/05; 344.1067805.
Ind/Abst Leg. Resour. Index; LegalTrac (1980-).

UK
INTERNATIONAL BANKING AND FINANCIAL LAW. Vol. 10, No. 1 (June 1991)-. Periodical. English. mo. $283.00. Longman Group Ltd., Fourth Avenue, Longman House, Harlow Essex CM19 5SR England. **Tel** 011 44 279 429655, FAX 011 44 279 431059, telex 81259. ***Continues*** *International Banking Law, 0263-8185.*

UK/0267-937X
JOURNAL OF INTERNATIONAL BANKING LAW. [J. int. bank. law]. **VFOAT** International Banking Law. Vol. 1, Issue 1 (1986)-. Periodical. English. Twelve times a year. £305.00 Europe; £320.00 other. Sweet & Maxwell Ltd., South Quay Plaza, 183 Marsh Wall, London E14 9FT England. **Tel** 011 44 264 342899, FAX 011 44 264 342723, telex 929089 ITPINF G. **LC** K10; .O8686. **DD** 341.7/51. **[CCC].** Index available. **Bk Rev. Ad Acc.**
Desc: Providing the practitioner with both a worldwide digest of cases, developments in legislation, regulations and news as well as in depth articles on banking and securities law.

US/1064-0371
LAW & BUSINESS DIRECTORY OF BANKRUPTCY ATTORNEYS. [Law bus. dir. bankruptcy atty.]. **Added/Corp** Prentice Hall Law & Business (Firm). **VFOAT** Law and Business Directory of Bankruptcy Attorneys; Directory of Bankruptcy Attorneys. (1988)-. Directory. English. an. $244.13. Prentice-Hall Law and Business, 270 Sylvan Avenue, Englewood Cliffs NJ 07632. **Tel** (800)223-0231, (201)894-8538, FAX (201)894-8666. **ED** Linda Deegan. **LC** KF195.B35; L38. **DD** 340/.025/73. Index available. available on an online database from WESTLAW; and LEXIS. ***Continues*** *Directory of Bankruptcy Attorneys.*
Desc: Provides detailed profiles of firms. Includes attorney profiles, firm profiles, foreign language index, and firm index. Provides complete information on Bankruptcy Courts and the US Trustee System.

US
LAW OF BANK DEPOSITS, COLLECTIONS, AND CREDIT CARDS, THE. (19??)-. English. an. $115.00 US; $149.50 other. Warren Gorham & Lamont Inc., Park Square Building, 31 St. James Avenue, Boston MA 02116-4112. **Tel** (617)423-2020, (800)950-1207, FAX (617)423-2026.

US
LAWS RELATING TO STATE BANKS AND TRUST COMPANIES, SAVINGS BANKS, INDUSTRIAL BANKS, SAVINGS BANK LIFE INSURANCE, BUILDING OR SAVINGS AND LOAN ASSOCIATIONS. **Main/Corp** Connecticut. English. be. Connecticut State Office Building, Hartford CT 06103. **DD** 332.109746. Index available in last issue of volume--attached.

US/1049-376X
LEGAL BULLETIN - UNITED STATES LEAGUE OF SAVINGS INSTITUTIONS. (LEGAL BULLETIN.). [Legal bull. - U. S. Leag. Sav. Inst.]. **Added/Corp** United States League of Savings Institutions. Vol. 49, No. 1 (Jan. 1983)-. Bulletin. English. ir. United States League of Savings Associations, 111 East Wacker Drive, Chicago IL 60601. **Tel** (312)644-3100. **LC** KF1004.A15; L44. **DD** 346.73/08221; 347.3068221. cum. index. ***Continues*** *Legal Bulletin (United States League of Savings Associations).*
Ind/Abst Fed. Tax Artic.

US/0547-7794
LEGAL BULLETIN (WASHINGTON). (LEGAL BULLETIN - NATIONAL SAVINGS AND LOAN LEAGUE.). **Main/Corp** National Savings and Loan League. Bulletin. English. National Savings and Loan League, 1101 15th Street NW, Washington DC 20005. **LC** KF1009.A73; N38. **DD** 346/.73/082. ***Continues*** *National League of Insured Savings Associations. Legal Bulletin.*

US/0147-9490
LEGAL NOTES (WASHINGTON). (LEGAL NOTES.). **Main/Corp** National Savings and Loan League. English. National Savings and Loan League, 1101 15th Street NW, Washington DC 20005. **LC** KF1009.A15; N35. **DD** 346/.73/073.

US/1045-1463
LENDER LIABILITY LAW REPORT. [Lend. liabil. law rep.]. **Added/Corp** Warren, Gorham & Lamont, Inc. Vol. 1, No. 1 (July 1987)-. Periodical. English. mo. $183.25 US and Canada; $252.45 other. Warren Gorham & Lamont Inc., Park Square Building, 31 St. James Avenue, Boston MA 02116-4112. **Tel** (617)423-2020, (800)950-1207, FAX (617)423-2026. **ED** Helen Davis Chaitman and Peter Knopp, (212)971-5000. **LC** KF1035.A59; L46. **DD** 346.73/0821753; 347.306821753. **[CCC]. Pr Rev. Circ:** 2300 (ctrl).
Desc: Contains a summary of the previous month's court activities relating to lender liability suits and articles analyzing court decisions and new legislation. These also provide suggestions for developing protective mechanisms for lenders and means of defending borrower suits.

US/1042-5764
LENDER LIABILITY LITIGATION REPORTER. [Lend. liabil. litig. report.]. (Oct 14, 1988)-. Periodical. English. mo. $700.00. Andrews Publications Inc., 1646 West Chester Pike, PO Box 1000, Westtown PA 19395. **Tel** (610)399-6600, (800)345-1101, FAX (610)399-6610. **ED** Kathy Knaub. **LC** KF1301.5.B36; L463. **DD** 346.7303/1/02638 3063102638. Index available. cum. index. **Circ:** 100.
Desc: Covers the latest, often precedent-setting cases, involving allegations of fraudulent banking practices on the parts of both lenders and borrowers.

US/0898-7645
LENDER LIABILITY NEWS. [Lend. liabil. news]. (1988)-. Periodical. English. sm. $597.00 US, Canada and Mexico; $619.00 other. Buraff Publications Inc., 714 Church Street, Alexandria VA 22314. **Tel** (800)333-1291, (703)739-8500. **ED** Corby Anderson. **LC** KF1035.A15; L46. **DD** 346.73/073/05. **[CCC].**
Desc: Newsletter on liability issues facing lenders in all areas, from fraud to breach of fiduciary duty to environmental cleanup. Covers litigation, legislation and regulation, and new industry practices (how lenders are reducing their exposure in negotiating, administering and enforcing loan agreements).

US/0098-891X
LENDING LAW FORUM, THE. [Lend. law forum]. V. 1 (June 1975)-. English. bm. $43.20. Lending Law Forum, 921 Westover Road, Wilmington DE 19807-2980. **Tel** (516)799-4003. **ED** William M Aukamp. **LC** K12; .E5. **DD** 346/.73/07305.
Desc: This newsletter covers legal developments in the field of commercial and consumer lending.
Ind/Abst Curr. Law Index (1980-1983); Leg. Resour. Index (1980-1983); LegalTrac (1980-1983).

US/0733-0049
LENDING TRANSACTIONS AND THE BANKRUPTCY REFORM ACT. [Lend. trans. Bankruptcy Reform Act]. **Added/Corp** Practising Law Institute. (1978)-. English. Practising Law Institute, 810 Seventh Avenue, New York NY 10019-5818. **Tel** (212)765-5700, FAX (212)581-4670 general correspondence, (212)265-4742 orders and billing inquiries. **LC** KF1524.3; .L45. **DD** 346.73/078; 347.30678.

US/8756-1522
LOAN OFFICERS LEGAL ALERT. [Loan off. legal alert]. **Added/Corp** Banking Law Institute (New York, N.Y.). Vol. 1, No. 1 (Feb. 1985)-. Periodical. English. mo. $180.00 US & Canada; $230.00 other. Executive Enterprises Publications Company Inc, 22 West 21st Street, 10th Floor, PO Box 10088, New York NY 10010-6990. **Tel** (212)645-7880, (800)332-8804, FAX (212)675-4883. **(Subscription address:** John Wiley & Sons Inc / New Jersey, PO Box 2575, Secaucus NJ 07096-2575.**)** **ED** Jane G. Bensahel. **LC** KF1035.A15; L63. **DD** 346.73/0821753; 347.306821753. **[CCC].** Index available. **Ad Acc.** available on microfiche; available on microfilm; available in microform.
Desc: Designed for bank lending officers who need to know the practical legal issues at their institution's policies and procedures in commercial lending. Alerts loan officers to common and not-so-common legal considerations in commercial lending with brief, pointed anecdotes drawn from real cases.

CN/1187-452X
MINUTES OF PROCEEDINGS AND EVIDENCE OF THE SUB-COMMITTEE ON FINANCIAL INSTITUTIONS LEGISLATION OF THE STANDING COMMITTEE ON FINANCE. [Minutes proc. evid. Sub-Comm. Financ. Inst. Legis. Standing Comm. Finance]. **Main/Corp** Canada. Parliament. House of Commons. Sub-Committee on Financial Institutions Legislation. **VFOAT** Financial Insitutions Legislation; Proces-Verbaux et Temoignages du Sous-Comite sur la Legislation sur les Institutions Financieres du Comite Permanent des Finances. 34th Parliament, 3rd Session, Issue No. 1 (Oct. 7, 1991)-. Proceedings. English (French). **DD** 346.71/08/0262.

US
MISSOURI WORKERS' COMP LAW REPORTER. (19??)-. English. $475.00. LRP Publications, 747 Dresher Road, PO Box 980, Horsham PA 19044-0980. **Tel** (800)341-7874, (215)784-0860, FAX (215)784-9639, (215)784-0870.

US/1046-3070
MONEY LAUNDERING ALERT. [Money laund. alert]. Vol. 1, No. 1 (July 1989)-. Periodical. English. Twelve times a year. $295.00 US; $540.00 other. Money Laundering Alert, PO Box 011390, Miami FL 33101. **Tel** (305)530-1652, (800)232-3652, FAX (305)530-9434. **ED** Charles Intriago and Kimberely K. Young, (editor's address: 1401 Brierell Avenue, Suite 570, Miami, FL 33131, phone: (305)530-0500). **LC** KF1030.R3; A135. **DD** 345.7302/68; 347.305268. **[CCC]. Ad Acc.** available on an online database (files 16,636/Full-Text) from DIALOG.
Desc: A leading source on the Bank Secrecy Act and money laundering laws. Provides information that interprets and explains key enforcement worldwide.
Ind/Abst PROMT [Full Txt.]; PTS Newsl. Database [Full Txt.].

CN/0822-1081
NATIONAL BANKING LAW REVIEW. [Nati. bank. law rev.]. (Sept. 1982)-. Periodical. English. Six times a year. 165.00Can$. Butterworth & Company Ltd. / Canada, 75 Clegg Road, Markham Ontario L6G 1A1 Canada. **Tel** (905)479-2665, (800)668-6481. **ED** Lazar Sarna. **DD** 346.71/082/05. Index available. cum. index. **Bk Rev.**
Desc: Provides institutional lenders, their clients and their legal counsel with up-to-date information regarding current legal trends affecting the banking industry.
Ind/Abst Can. Legal Lit.; Index Can. Leg. Period. Lit.

US/0275-0252
NATIONAL BANKRUPTCY REPORTER. [Natl. bankruptcy report.]. (1972)-. Periodical. English. wk (52 issues). $1800.00. Andrews Publications Inc., 1646 West Chester Pike, PO Box 1000, Westtown PA 19395. **Tel** (610)399-6600, (800)345-1101, FAX (610)399-6610. **ED** Richard H. Groves. **DD** 332. **Bk Rev. Ad Acc.** ctrl circ.
Desc: Provides a detailed list of recent business bankruptcies, usually within two weeks of filing. Reports all pertinent data from the original court petition, including the name of the company, principals and their addresses, description of the business, amount of assets, liabilities and secured debt, and the date and place of the bankruptcy filing. Bankruptcies in manufacturing, wholesale and retail sales, real estate and various service businesses are among those reported in the publication.

CN/0829-2019
NATIONAL CREDITOR/DEBTOR REVIEW. [Natl. credit./debt. rev.]. Vol. 1 No. 1 (Oct./Dec. 1985)-. Periodical. English. qt. 140.00Can$. Butterworth & Company Ltd. / Canada, 75 Clegg Road, Markham Ontario L6G 1A1 Canada. **Tel** (905)479-2665, (800)668-6481. **DD** 346.71/077/05.
Desc: Analyzes developments and cases dealing with the complex field of creditor-debtor relations.
Ind/Abst Can. Legal Lit.

CN/0822-2584
NATIONAL INSOLVENCY REVIEW. [Natl. insolv. rev.]. Vol. 1, No. 1 (Nov./Dec. 1983)-. Periodical.

Law —Banking Law

English. bm. 180.00Can$. Butterworth & Company Ltd. / Canada, 75 Clegg Road, Markham Ontario L6G 1A1 Canada. **Tel** (905)479-2665, (800)668-6481. **ED** Lazar Sarna. **DD** 346.71/078/05. Index available. cum. index. **Bk Rev**.
Desc: Law comments on solvency and bankruptcy matters.
Ind/Abst Can. Legal Lit.; Index Can. Leg. Period. Lit. (19??-).

US
NORTON BANKRUPTCY LAW AND PRACTICE. English. Clark Boardman Callaghan, 155 Pfingsten Road, Deerfield IL 60015. **Tel** (800)323-8067.

US
PRACTICAL GUIDE TO THE BANKRUPTCY REFORM ACT. (19??)-. English. an. $110.00. Prentice-Hall Law and Business, 270 Sylvan Avenue, Englewood Cliffs NJ 07632. **Tel** (800)223-0231, (201)894-8538, FAX (201)894-8666.

US
QUARTERLY BUSINESS FAILURES. **Added/Corp** Dun & Bradstreet Corporation. Economic Analysis Dept. **VFOAT** Dun & Bradstreet Record of Business Closings; U.S. Business Failures Quarterly Report. Vol. 28, No. 1 (1st Quarter 1986)-. Periodical. English. Four times a year (Jan., Apr., July, Oct.). $40.00. Dun & Bradstreet / New York, 299 Park Avenue, 24th Floor, New York NY 10171. **Tel** (212)593-4173. **Continues** Quarterly Business Failures Report.

US/0899-0891
RECENT TITLES IN LAW FOR THE SUBJET SPECIALIST. BANKING, FINANCE (INCLUDING SECURITIES), AND INVESTMENT. [Recent titles law subj. spec., Bank. finance (incl. secur.) investm.]. **Added/Corp** Ward & Associates. **VFOAT** Banking, Finance (Including Securities), and Investment. Vol. 5, No. 1 (Jan.-Mar. 1988)-. Periodical. English. qt. $85.00. Ward & Associates, 317 South Division, Suite 66, Ann Arbor MI 48104. **Tel** (313)665-3520, FAX (313)665-7880. **LC** K1066.A12; N38. **DD** 016.346/082; 016.342682. Index available (Bound in all issues). **Continues** National Legal Bibliography. Subject Area List. Banking, Finance (Including Securities) and Investment, 8755-7967.

IT
RIVISTA DI DIRITTO ED ECONOMIA VALUTARIA. Yearly Vol. 1979 - Issue 1. Periodical. Italian. qt. L100000. Societa Editrice Edizioni Giuridico-Scientifiche, Via Donizetti 37, 20122 Milan Italy. **LC** K22; .I645. **DD** 343.45/032/05; 344.5033205.

IT
RIVISTA DIRITTO FINANZIARIO E SCIENZA DELLE FINANZE. (19??)-. Italian. Four times a year. L100000.00 Italy; L150000.00 other. Giuffre Editore SPA, Via Busto Arsizio 40, 20151 Milan Italy. **Tel** 011 398 2 38089200. **ED** Enrico Allorio and Emilio Gerelli.
Desc: Offers a complete and updated overview of the economy, techniques and laws of finance. Publishes essays on the public economy, financial techniques, and policies for dealing with present-day situations, as well as scientifically valid contributions on the various technical and practical aspects of the new fiscal legislation, concentrating on the more recent jurisprudence concerning taxation laws.
Ind/Abst Int. Bibliogr. Sociol.

US
SEC GUIDELINES, RULES, AND REGULATIONS. **Added/Corp** Prentice-Hall, Inc. **VFOAT** SEC Guidelines, Rules & Regulations. (198?)-. English. an. $54.95. Warren Gorham & Lamont Inc., Park Square Building, 31 St. James Avenue, Boston MA 02116-4112. **Tel** (617)423-2020, (800)950-1207, FAX (617)423-2026. **LC** KF1434.599; .S43. **DD** 346.73/0666; 347.306666.

US
SECURED CREDITORS AND LESSORS UNDER THE BANKRUPTCY REFORM ACT. 1990. English. an. $55.00 (softcover). Practising Law Institute, 810 Seventh Avenue, New York NY 10019-5818. **Tel** (212)765-5700, FAX (212)581-4670 general correspondence, (212)265-4742 orders and billing inquiries. **ED** Patrick A Murphy. **LC** KF1526; .S37. **DD** 346.73/078; 347.30678.

US/0037-0665
SECURITIES REGULATION & LAW REPORT. **Added/Corp** Bureau of National Affairs (Washington, D.C.). **VAT** Securities Regulation and Law Report. (June 4, 1969)-. English. Fifty-two times a year. $1016.00. Bureau of National Affairs Inc., 9435 Key West Avenue, Rockville MD 20850. **Tel** (800)372-1033, (301)258-1033, FAX (301)948-5823. **ED** Susan Raleigh Jenkins. **LC** KF1439.A1; S38. **DD** 346/.73/09205. **[CCC]**.
Desc: Covers the latest securities and commodities activity at the federal and state levels, including developments from Congress, the Administration, SEC,

CFTC, banking regulations, FASB, professional associations, the courts and industry. Contains full text of selected regulations, opinions and legislation.

US
SHEPARD'S BANKING LAW CITATIONS. Ceased. Added/Corp Shepard's/McGraw-Hill. Ist Ed. (1988)-(Jan. 1993). English. Shepards McGraw-Hill Inc, 555 Middle Creek Parkway, PO Box 35300, Colorado Springs CO 80935-3530. **Tel** (719)488-3000, FAX (800)525-0053.

US/0884-8629
STATE BANKING, CREDIT UNION, AND SAVINGS, AND LOAN ASSOCIATION LEGISLATION. [State bank. credit union sav. loan assoc. legis.]. Periodical. English. sa. American Bankers Association, 1120 Connecticut Avenue Northwest, Washington DC 20036. **Tel** (202)663-5221, , FAX (202)828-4544. **(Subscription telephone:** (202)663-7667) **LC** KF975.Z95; S72. **DD** 346.73/082; 347.30682.

US/0895-2736
TEXAS BANKRUPTCY COURT REPORTER, THE. [Tex. bankruptcy court report.]. **Added/Corp** Public Record Corporation. Vol. 1, Issue 1 (Jan. 1987)-. Periodical. English. bm. $296.00. The Public Record Corporation, PO Box 18186, 1666 Lafayette Street, Denver CO 80218. **Tel** (303)832-8262, (800)487-8262, FAX (303)861-5821. **DD** 346.
Desc: Information on the Texas bankruptcy courts.

GW/0342-6971
WERTPAPIER-MITTLEILUNGEN. TEIL 4. ZEITSCHRIFT FUER WIRTSCHAFTS- UND BANKRECHT. (ZEITSCHRIFT FUER WIRTSCHAFTS- UND BANKRECHT.). [Wertpap.-Mitt., Tl. 4, Z. Wirtsch.- Bankr.]. (1977)-. Periodical. German. wk. DM1240.20. Boersen Zeitung/Wertpapier, Postfach 110932, D-60044 Frankfurt Germany. **Tel** 011 49 69 2732187. **DD** 346.43/07. **Continues** Wertpapier-Mitteilungen. Teil 4. Wirtschafts-, Wertpapier-, und Bankrecht, 0342-698X.

US/0199-5782
WEST'S BANKRUPTCY REPORTER. **VFOAT** Bankruptcy Reporter. V. 1 (Jan. 1980)-. English. sm. $75.00. West Publishing Company, 610 Opperman Drive, PO Box 64526, Eagan MN 55123-1308. **Tel** (612)687-5618, (800)328-9352, FAX (612)687-5388, (800)562-2329. **(Subscription telephone:** FAX (612)688-3570) **LC** KF1515.A2; W47. **DD** 346.73/078/02642.

US
WORKERS COMP INSURANCE AND LAW. See Insurance.

US
WORKERS' COMP YEARBOOK. (19??)-. English. $62.00. LRP Publications, 747 Dresher Road, PO Box 980, Horsham PA 19044-0980. **Tel** (800)341-7874, (215)784-0860, FAX (215)784-9639, (215)784-0870.

US
WORKERS COMPENSATION CASE MANAGEMENT. (19??)-. English. $18.50. LRP Publications, 747 Dresher Road, PO Box 980, Horsham PA 19044-0980. **Tel** (800)341-7874, (215)784-0860, FAX (215)784-9639, (215)784-0870.

US
WORKERS COMPENSATION HEALTH CARE COST CONTAINMENT. (19??)-. English. ir. $63.00. LRP Publications, 747 Dresher Road, PO Box 980, Horsham PA 19044-0980. **Tel** (800)341-7874, (215)784-0860, FAX (215)784-9639, (215)784-0870.

US
WORKERS COMPENSATION STRATEGIES FOR LOWERING COSTS. (19??)-. English. $41.00. LRP Publications, 747 Dresher Road, PO Box 980, Horsham PA 19044-0980. **Tel** (800)341-7874, (215)784-0860, FAX (215)784-9639, (215)784-0870.

GW/0723-9416
ZEITSCHRIFT FUER WIRTSCHAFTSRECHT. **VFOAT** Z.I.P.; ZIP. Vol. 4, No. 1 (Jan. 20, 1983)-. Periodical. German. Twenty-six times a year. DM631.00. Kommunikationsforum Recht Wirtschaft Steuern Zuverlassig Informativ Praxisorientiert ZIP, Aachener Str 217 Tagungs Verlag, D 50931 Cologne Germany. **Tel** 011 49 221 4008818. **LC** K9; .N685. **DD** 346.43/078/05; 344.3067805. **Continues** Zeitschrift fuer Wirtschaftsrecht und Insolvenzpraxis.
Ind/Abst Index Foreign Leg. Per.

CIVIL LAW

SP/0213-7100
ACTUALIDAD CIVIL. [Actual. civil]. (1985)-. Periodical. Spanish. wk. 40000ptas. Actualidad Editorial SA, Calle Aragoneses 7, 28100 Alcobendas Madrid Spain. **Tel** 011 34 1 6616284. **UDC** 347. **Bk Rev**.

SP/1130-7390
ACTUALIDAD CIVIL. LEGISLACION. [Actual. civ., Legis.]. (1990)-. Periodical. Spanish. wk. 28000.00ptas. Actualidad Editorial SA, Calle Aragoneses 7, 28100 Alcobendas Madrid Spain. **Tel** 011 34 1 6616284. **UDC** 347. **Bk Rev. Continues** Actualidad Civil. Monografia de Legislacion, 0213-5833.

CN/0704-0288
ADVOCATES' QUARTERLY. (ADVOCATES' QUARTERLY : A CANADIAN JOURNAL FOR PRACTITIONERS OF CIVIL LITIGATION.). [Advocates' q.]. Vol. 1, (Sept. 1977)-. Periodical. English. qt. 108.00Can$. Canada Law Book Inc., 240 Edward Street, Aurora Ontario L4G 3S9 Canada. **Tel** (800)263-3269, (905)841-6472, FAX (905)841-5085. **ED** Garry D. Watson. **LC** K1; .D866. **DD** 347.71/05/05; 347.107505.
Desc: Features timely and informative articles as well as carefully considered notes on procedural and evidentiary problems, and more.
Ind/Abst Can. Legal Lit.; Curr. Law Index (1980-); Index Leg. Period.; Leg. Resour. Index (1980-); LegalTrac (1980-).

US/0191-2011
ALI-ABA COURSE OF STUDY. CLASS AND DERIVATIVE ACTIONS AND OTHER MULTIPARTY COMPLEX LITIGATION : MATERIALS. **VAT** American Law Institute-American Bar Association Course of Study. Class and Derivation Actions and Other Multiparty Complex Litigation: Materials. English. American Law Institute, 4025 Chestnut Street, Philadelphia PA 19104-3099. **Tel** (215)243-1661, (800)253-6397, FAX (215)243-1664. **LC** KF8896.Z9; A15. **DD** 347/.73/5.

CN/0705-1360
ALL-CANADA WEEKLY SUMMARIES. (1977)-. Periodical. English. ir. 150.00Can$ (parts and bound volume). Canada Law Book Inc., 240 Edward Street, Aurora Ontario L4G 3S9 Canada. **Tel** (800)263-3269, (905)841-6472, FAX (905)841-5085. **ED** Patricia V. Selden, Michael J. Cowle, Elliot R. Citron. **DD** 340/.0971. **Bk Rev**. **Ad Acc**.
Desc: National, civil law summary service that covers every province and territory in Canada. A reporting service, keeping abreast of changes on a weekly basis.

US
AMERICAN JURISPRUDENCE PLEADING AND PRACTICE FORMS ANNOTATED. (AMERICAN JURISPRUDENCE PLEADING AND PRACTICE FORMS ANNOTATED; A COMPREHENSIVE, CAREFULLY COMPILED AND EDITED COLLECTION OF PLEADING AND PRACTICE FORMS, INCLUDING JURY INSTRUCTIONS, KEYED TO THE SUBSTANTIVE LAW IN AMERICAN JURISPRUDENCE 2D AND DESIGNED TO PROVIDE DEPENDABLE FORMS FOR ALL TYPES OF PLEADING AND PROCEDURAL STEPS IN JUDICIAL AND ADMINISTRATIVE PROCEEDINGS.). **Added/Corp** Bancroft-Whitney Company. (1956)-. Periodical. English. ir. Lawyers Cooperative Publishing Company, Aqueduct Building, Rochester NY 14694. **Tel** (800)527-0430, (716)546-5530. **DD** 347.92.

SP
ANUARIO DE DERECHO CIVIL. **Added/Corp** Consejo Superior de Investigaciones Cientificas (Spain). Instituto Nacional de Estudios Juridicos. (1948)-. Spanish. Four times a year (Mar., June, Sept., Dec.). 6400.00ptas Spain; 7300.00ptas other. Ministerio de Justicia Centro, Publicaciones, Gran Via 76 8, 28013 Madrid Spain. **Tel** 011 34 1 5475422. **Ind/Abst** Index Foreign Leg. Per.

GW/0003-8997
ARCHIV FUER DIE CIVILISTISCHE PRAXIS. Vol. 1, (1818)-. Periodical. German. bm (6 issues). DM236.00. JCB Mohr / Paul Siebeck, Postfach 2040, D 72010 Tuebingen Germany. **Tel** 011 49 7071 9230, FAX 011 49 7071 51104, telex 7/262872 mohr d. **ED** Wolfgang Grunsky, Manfred Lieb, and Dieter Medicus. **[CCC]**. cum. index. **Bk Rev**. **Ad Acc**. **Circ:** 1,100.
Desc: Deals with all aspects of German civil law.
Ind/Abst Index Foreign Leg. Per.

UK
ATKIN'S ENCYCLOPAEDIA OF COURT FORMS IN CIVIL PROCEEDINGS. Proceedings. English. Price varies per volume. Butterworth & Co. Ltd. / Kent, England, Borough Green, Sevenoaks Kent TN15 8PH England. **Tel** 011 44 732-884567, FAX 011 44 732-885996. **ED** Sir Jack I. H. Jacob. Index available.

Desc: Reference source for those engaged in litigation work. Eaxh issue contains fully annotated precedents with cross-references and explanatory text. Covers all stages of proceedings from the beginning to the enforcement of judgements.

NZ/0067-0510
AUCKLAND UNIVERSITY LAW REVIEW.
[Auckl. Univ. law rev.]. **Added/Corp** Auckland University Law Students' Society. Vol. 1, No. 1 (1968)-. English. an (4 issues per volume/volume covers 4 years). 25.00NZ$ New Zealand; 35.00NZ$ Australia and South Pacific; $25.00 other. University of Auckland / Law School, 9 Eden Crescent, Private Bag 92019, Auckland New Zealand. **Tel** 011 64 9 3737599 Ext. 5634, FAX 011 64 9 3737440. **LC** K1; .U25. **DD** 340/.05. Index available (index in final number of each volume). **Bk Rev**, (Qty: varies). **Ad Acc. Circ:** 1,500.
Desc: Law, both civil and criminal, especially common law and the law relating to New Zealand.
Ind/Abst Curr. Law Index (1980-); Index Leg. Period.; Leg. Resour. Index (1980-); LegalTrac (1980-).

US/1052-4541
BAR LETTER - STATE BAR OF NEVADA.
Title Change. **See** Law.

BL
CADERNOS DE DIREITO PRIVADO.
v. 1-. Periodical. Portuguese. Departamento de Direito Privado da Faculdade de Direito da Universidade Federal Fluminese, R President Pedreira, No 54, Niteroi Brazil. **LC** K3; .A35. **DD** 346.81/005.

CN/0701-1733
CANADIAN CASES ON THE LAW OF TORTS.
[Can. cases law torts]. (1976/77)-. English (French). ir. 125.00Can$. Carswell / Canada, 2075 Kennedy Road, Scarborough Ontario M1T 3V4 Canada. **Tel** (416)609-3800, (800)387-5164. **ED** John Irvine. **LC** KE1232.A45; C363. **DD** 346.7103; 347.1063. Index available. cum. index. **Ad Acc.**
Desc: Features all important decisions in tort law from all Canadian jurisdictions selected by experts in the field.
Ind/Abst Can. Legal Lit.; Curr. Law Index (1981-Dec. 1984); Index Can. Leg. Period. Lit.; Leg. Resour. Index (1981-Dec. 1984); LegalTrac (1981-1984).

CN/0706-5388
CARSWELL'S PRACTICE CASES.
[Carswell's pract. cases]. **VFOAT** C.P.C. Vol. 1-50, (July 1976)-(1985); 2nd Series, Vol. 1-50, (1985)-(Feb. 1992); 3rd Series, Vol. 1 (Mar. 1992)-. Periodical. English. ir. Carswell / Canada, 2075 Kennedy Road, Scarborough Ontario M1T 3V4 Canada. **Tel** (416)609-3800, (800)387-5164. **ED** Michael McGowan. **LC** KEO1115.8; C37. **DD** 347/.71/0502648. Index available. cum. index. **Ad Acc.**
Desc: Features important decisions on practice in civil proceedings from all Canadian common law jurisdictions and all court levels selected by experts in the field.
Ind/Abst Can. Legal Lit.; Curr. Law Index (1981-1985); Index Can. Leg. Period. Lit.; Leg. Resour. Index (1981-1985); LegalTrac (1981-1985).

US
CIVIL CODE (CALIFORNIA).
VFOAT West's California Codes. 1978-. Periodical. English. an. Civil Code, 50 West Kellogg Boulevard, St Paul MN 55102.

UK/0261-9261
CIVIL JUSTICE QUARTERLY.
[Civil justice q.]. **Added/Corp** University of Birmingham. Institute of Judicial Administration. Vol. 1 (Jan. 1982)-. Periodical. English. Four times a year. £90.00 Europe; £95.00 other. Sweet & Maxwell Ltd., South Quay Plaza, 183 Marsh Wall, London E14 9FT England. **Tel** 011 44 264 342899, FAX 011 44 264 342723, telex 929089 ITPINF G. **ED** Carol Tullo. **LC** K3; .I92. **DD** 347/.05/05; 342.7505. **Bk Rev. Ad Acc. Circ:** 500. available on microfilm and microfiche from University Microfilms International (UMI).
Desc: A practical forum for debate and discussion in matters of litigation practice and procedure.
Ind/Abst Aust. Leg. Mon. Dig.; Curr. Law Index (1984-); Index Leg. Period.; Leg. Resour. Index (1984-); LegalTrac (1984-).

US/0748-7657
CIVIL LAW OPINIONS OF THE JUDGE ADVOCATE GENERAL, UNITED STATES AIR FORCE.
Main/Corp United States. Air Force. Judge Advocate General. Vol. 1 (1961/1977)-. English. ir (approx. every four years). Judge Advocate General, Department of the Air Force, The Pentagon, Washington DC 20330. **Tel** (202)694-4075. **LC** KF7405; .A558. **DD** 343.73/0184; 347.303184. Index available. ctrl circ.
Desc: Compilation of selected civil and administrative law opinions of the Judge Advocate General of the US Air Force.

US/0199-0802
CIVIL LITIGATION REPORTER.
(CIVIL LITIGATION REPORTER / CEB, CALIFORNIA CONTINUING EDUCATION OF THE BAR.). **Added/Corp** California Continuing Education of the Bar. **VFOAT** CEB Civil Litigation Reporter. **VAT** California Education of the Bar Civil Litigation Reporter. Vol. 1 (July 1979)-. Periodical. English. Eight times a year. $175.00. California Continuing Education of the Bar, 2300 Shattuck Avenue, Berkeley CA 94704. **Tel** (510)642-8000, (800)232-3444. **LC** KFC995.A1; C35. **DD** 347.794/05/05; 347.9407505. Index available.
Desc: Features articles providing timely coverage of important developments in civil litigation practice.

US
CIVIL PRACTICE ANNUAL OF NEW YORK.
Main/Corp New York (State). 1923-. English. an. Matthew Bender & Company Inc., 1275 Broadway, Albany NY 12204. **Tel** (800)833-9844, (518)487-3000.

US
CIVIL PRACTICE LAW & RULES OF THE STATE OF NEW YORK : CPLR.
Main/Corp New York (State). **VFOAT** CPLR; Civil Practice Law and Rules of the State of New York. (1967/68)-. English. an. Gould Publications, 199/300 State Street, Binghamton NY 13901. **Tel** (607)724-3000, FAX (607)723-4285. **LC** KFN5990; .A195. **DD** 347.747/05.
Desc: Presents the Civil Practice Law and Rules, Chapter 8 of the Consolidated Laws of New York, plus official forms, sections of the New York Constitution, Judiciary Law, N.Y.C. Civil Court Act, and other selected pertinent sections of New York laws.

US/0099-1244
CIVIL PROCEDURE.
Main/Corp Bay Area Review Course, Inc. English. an. Bay Area Review Course Inc, 5900 Wilshire Boulevard, Los Angeles CA 90036. **LC** KF8841; .B38. **DD** 347/.73/5.

US/0884-0032
CIVIL RICO REPORT.
[Civil RICO rep.]. **VFOAT** BNA Civil RICO Report. **VAT** Civil Racketeer Influenced and Corrupt Organizations Act Report. Vol. 1, No. 1 (June 5, 1985)-. Periodical. English. wk (50 issues). $795.00 US, Canada and Mexico; $817.00 other. Buraff Publications Inc., 714 Church Street, Alexandria VA 22314. **Tel** (800)333-1291, (703)739-8500. **(Subscription telephone:** FAX (301)948-5823) **ED** Corby Anderson. **LC** KF9375.A15; C58. **DD** 345.73/02; 347.3052. **[CCC].**
Desc: A newsletter on civil litigation under the Racketeer Influenced and Corrupt Organizations Act: case summaries, new RICO suits being filed, new plaintiff strategies, defense tactics, legislation, the latest interpretations of RICO provisions, and more.

FR
CODE CIVIL.
Main/Corp France. **Added/Corp** Dalloz (Firm). French. an. Jurisprudence Generale Dalloz, 11 rue Soufflot, 75240 Cedex 05 Paris France. **LC** KJV444.21804.A5; F73. **DD** 346.44; 344.406.

●CN/1187-2861
COMPAGNIES, SOCIETES PAR ACTIONS ET FAILLITE.
[Cie. soc. actions faill.]. **Added/Corp** Ecole des Hautes Etudes Commerciales (Montreal, Quebec) Wilson & Lafleur Martel Limitee. (1991/92)-. French. be. Wilson & Lafleur Ltd., 40 Rue Notre Dame East, Montreal, Quebec H2Y 1B9 Canada. **Tel** (514)875-6326, FAX (514)875-8356. **DD** 346.714/07/02632. ***Continues*** *Compagnies, Societes Commerciales et Faillite., 0837-0222.*

US
COOK COUNTY JURY VERDICT REPORTER.
English. ir. $285.00. Cook County Jury Verdict, 415 North State Street, Chicago IL 60610. **Tel** (312)644-7800. Index available. available on an online database.
Desc: Summaries of civil jury verdicts for cases tried in Cook County Illinois.

CN/0316-1234
COURS DE PERFECTIONNEMENT DU NOTARIAT.
[Cours perfect. notar.]. **Added/Corp** Chambre des Notaires du Quebec. No. 1 (1975)-. Periodical. French. ir (1 or 2 per year). 40.00Can$. Chambre des Notaires du Quebec, 630 Boul Ouest Dorchester, Montreal Quebec H3B 1T6 Canada. **Tel** (514)879-1793, FAX (514)879-1923. **DD** 346/.714/0024349. ***Continues*** *Cours de Perfectionnement.*
Ind/Abst Can. Legal Lit.; Index Can. Leg. Period. Lit.

US/0748-7592
CURRENT PROBLEMS IN FEDERAL CIVIL PRACTICE.
[Curr. probl. fed. civ. pract.]. Periodical. English. Practising Law Institute, 810 Seventh Avenue, New York NY 10019-5818. **Tel** (212)765-5700, FAX (212)581-4670 general correspondence, (212)265-4742 orders and billing inquiries. **LC** KF8840; .C86. **DD** 347.73/5; 347.3075.

US/0895-0016
DEFENSE COUNSEL JOURNAL.
(DEFENSE COUNSEL JOURNAL / INTERNATIONAL ASSOCIATION OF DEFENSE COUNSEL.). [Def. couns. j.]. **Added/Corp** International Association of Defense Counsel. Vol. 54, No. 1 (Jan. 1987)-. Academic Scholarly Publication. English. qt (4 issues). $55.00 US; $61.00 other. International Association of Defense Counsel, 20 North Wacker Drive/Suite 3100, Chicago IL 60606. **Tel** (312)368-1494, FAX (312)368-1854. **ED** R. Crawford Morris and Richard B. Allen. **LC** K9; .N7469. **DD** 346.73/086/05; 347.3068605. Index available in last issue of volume--attached. cum. index. **Bk Rev**, (Qty: 12). **Circ:** 4,000 (ctrl). available on microfiche from Williams S Hein & Co.; available on CD-ROM from University Microfilms International (UMI). Documents available from UMI Article Clearinghouse. ***Continues*** *Insurance Counsel Journal, 0020-465X.*
Desc: Devoted to news and scholarly articles dealing with developments in tort law and defense of civil litigation.
Ind/Abst ABI/INFORM Glob. Ed.; ABI Inform Ondisc (Jan. 1984-); Gen. BusinessFile (1992-); Index Leg. Period.; INIS Atomindex [Micro.]; Ins. Period. Index; Leg. Resour. Index; LegalTrac (1987-).

US/0191-877X
DEFENSE MANUAL.
Added/Corp Law Enforcement Legal Defense Center (Evanston, Ill.). **VFOAT** Law Enforcement Legal Defense Manual; Legal Defense Manual. (Sept. 1978)-. Periodical. English. qt. $98.00 US; $100.00 other. Law Enforcement Legal Defence Manual, 421 Ridgewood Avenue, Glen Ellyn IL 60137-4900. **Tel** (708)858-6392, FAX (708)858-6392. **ED** James P. Manak. **LC** KF1307.A73; A395. **DD** 347.735; 347.3075. Index available. **Ad Acc. Pr Rev. Circ:** 1,000. available on microfilm and microfiche from University Microfilms International (UMI). ***Continues*** *Americans for Effective Law Enforcement. AELE Law Enforcement Legal Defense Manual, 0092-2552.*
Desc: Founded for the public and private safety sectors including prosecutors; county counsel; municipal attorneys; police legal advisors; and fire, police, and sheriff personnel who have an interest in civil litigation involving state, county, and municipal public safety agencies. Written from a pro-law enforcement perspective.

IS/0070-4903
DINE ISRAEL.
Added/Corp Universitat Tel-Aviv. Fakultah le-Mishpatim. Bet Midrash le-Mishpatim. **VFOAT** Dine Israel. (1970)-. English (Hebrew). an. $40.00. Tel Aviv University / Law, Faculty of Law, Tel Aviv 69978 Israel. **Tel** 11 972 3 420361, telex 342171. **ED** Aaron Kirschenbaum. **LC** K4; .I69.
Desc: Comprehensive study of Jewish civil law in the light of equity, from the dogmatic, the historical, the analytic-jurisprudential, and the comparative perspectives.

CN/0012-5350
DOMINION LAW REPORTS.
[Dom. law rep.]. **Added/Corp** Canada. Courts. Canada. Supreme Court. Canada. Exchequer Court. Canada Law Book Limited. Vol. 1 (1912)-Vol. 70 (1922); 1923, Vol. 1-1955, Vol. 5; 2nd Ser., Vol. 1 (1956)- Vol. 70 (1968); 3rd Ser., Vol. 1 (1969)-Vol. 150 (1984); 4th Ser., Vol. 1 (1984)-. English. wk. 115.00Can$. Canada Law Book Inc., 240 Edward Street, Aurora Ontario L4G 3S9 Canada. **Tel** (800)263-3269, (905)841-6472, FAX (905)841-5085. **ED** J. Bruce Dunlop. **DD** 348.71/046. **Bk Rev. Ad Acc.**
Desc: National series of law reports. Leading civil case decisions from all Common Law provinces and Supreme Court of Canada are reported.

FR
DROIT INTERNATIONAL PRIVE : TRAVAUX DU COMITE FRANCAIS DE DROIT INTERNATIONAL PRIVE.
Added/Corp Comite Francais de Droit International Prive. (1975-1977)-. Periodical. French. ir (when published, published every 2 years). Editions du CNRS, 22 rue Saint Armand, F 75015 Paris France. **Tel** 011 33 1 45075050. **LC** K7001; .D76. **DD** 340.9. **Circ:** 1,500. ***Continues*** *Travaux du Comite Francais de Droit International Prive.*
Desc: Articles by the French Committee on International Civil Law, with thoughts on judicial practice in civil and commercial matters.

US/0886-621X
FEDERAL LITIGATOR.
Vol. 1, No. 1 (Jan. 1986)-. Periodical. English. ir (10 times a year). $290.00. Shepards McGraw-Hill Inc, 555 Middle Creek Parkway, PO Box 35300, Colorado Springs CO 80935-3530. **Tel** (719)488-3000, FAX (800)525-0053. **ED** Neil M. Levy and Jeffrey S. Brand. **LC** KF8840.A2; .F425. **DD** 342.73/066; 347.30266. Index available. cum. index.
Desc: Reports and analyzes major federal rules and practice cases from the supreme court, circuit and district courts. Comprehensive coverage of federal discovery, evidence and appellate practice.

US/0745-2306
FEDERAL LOCAL COURT RULES.
[Fed. local court rules]. **Main/Corp** United States. District Courts. (1964)-. English. ir. $175.00. Clark Boardman Callaghan, 155 Pfingsten Road, Deerfield IL 60015. **Tel** (800)323-8067. **DD** 347.

US/1058-8604
FLORIDA JURY VERDICT REVIEW AND ANALYSIS.
[Fla. jury verdict rev. anal.]. Vol. 1, Issue 1 (Dec. 1990)-. Periodical. English. mo (12 issues). $250.00. Jury Verdict Review Publications Inc., 24 Commerce Street/Suite 1722, Newark NJ 07102. **Tel** (201)624-1665. **DD** 347.

US/0015-6884
FOR THE DEFENSE (MILWAUKEE, WIS.). (FOR THE DEFENSE.). [For def.]. **Added/Corp** International Association of Insurance Counsel. Defense Research Institute. **VFOAT** F.T.D.; FTD. Vol. 1, No. 1 (March 1960)-. Periodical. English. mo. $50.00 plaintiff attorneys or organizations, except Defense Research & Trial Lawyer Association Corporate members; $20.00 University Law Libraries. Defense Research Institute, 750 North Lakeshore Drive, Suite 500, Chicago IL 60611. **Tel** (312)944-0575, FAX (312)944-2003. **ED** Davidson Ream. **LC** KF8911.A3; F67. **DD** 347.73/7; 347.3077. **Circ:** 28,000 (ctrl).
Desc: Developments in the law, and advice on legal practice techniques, for lawyers concerned with the defense of tort and insurance matters.
Ind/Abst Ind. Hyg. Dig.; Leg. Resour. Index (1980-); LegalTrac (1981-).

US/1049-4766
GEORGE MASON UNIVERSITY CIVIL RIGHTS LAW JOURNAL. [George Mason Univ. civ. rights law j.]. **Added/Corp** George Mason University. School of Law. **VFOAT** Geo Mason U CRLJ; Geo. Mason U. C.R.L.J.; Civil Rights Law Journal. Vol. 1, No. 1 (Spring 1990)-. Periodical. English. sa. $10.00 (single issue, institution), $7.00 (single issue, individual), $4.00 (single issue, student). George Mason University School of Law, 3401 North Fairfax Drive, Room 321B, Arlington VA 22201. **Tel** (703)993-8161, FAX (703)993-8080. **LC** K7; .E625. **DD** 342.73/085; 347.30285.
Ind/Abst Index Leg. Period.; Leg. Resour. Index; LegalTrac (1990-).

IT/0017-0631
GIUSTIZIA CIVILE. (1951)-. Periodical. Italian. mo. L280000.00 Italy; L420000.00 other. Giuffre Editore SPA, Via Busto Arsizio 40, 20151 Milan Italy. **Tel** 011 398 2 38089200. **ED** Vittorio Sgroi.
Desc: Offers a complete picture of civil law in its widest sense and includes decisions made by the Constitutional Court, by the ordinary and administrative magistracy and by the EEC Court of Justice.

US
HANDBOOK OF CIVIL PROCEDURE. (19??)-. Periodical. English. ir. $109.81. Lawyers Weekly Publications, 41 West Street, Boston MA 02111. **Tel** (617)451-7300, (800)444-5297.

US/0018-991X
IJA REPORT. **Main/Corp** Institute of Judicial Administration. Began with Oct. 1968 issue. Periodical. English. qt. 40 Washington Square South, New York NY 10012. **LC** KF8732.A16; I5. **DD** 347/.73/13.

US/8756-8969
ILLINOIS CODE OF CIVIL PROCEDURE AND COURT RULES. [Ill. code civ. proced. court rules]. 1983-. English. an. West Publishing Company, 610 Opperman Drive, PO Box 64526, Eagan MN 55123-1308. **Tel** (612)687-5618, (800)328-9352, FAX (612)687-5388, (800)562-2329. **(Subscription telephone:** FAX (612)688-3570**)** **LC** KFI1729; .A195. **DD** 347.773/05; 347.73075. ***Continues*** *Illinois Practice Act and Rules.*

US/0890-7315
INSIDE LITIGATION. [Inside litig.]. (Nov. 1986)-. Periodical. English. Twelve times a year. $320.08. Prentice-Hall Law and Business, 270 Sylvan Avenue, Englewood Cliffs NJ 07632. **Tel** (800)223-0231, (201)894-8538, FAX (201)894-8666. **LC** KF8911.A3; I57. **DD** 347.73/7; 347.3077.
Desc: Journalistic report on litigation strategy and procedure. Also analyzes attorney fee awards, including bankruptcy fee awards.

IT
ITALIAN YEARBOOK OF CIVIL PROCEDURE. (1991)-. English. ir. Giuffre Editore SPA, Via Busto Arsizio 40, 20151 Milan Italy. **Tel** 011 398 2 38089200. **LC** KKH1701.3; .I83. **DD** 347.45/05; 344.5075.

BL
JURISCIVEL DO S.T.F. **VFOAT** Revista Jurischvel do S.T.F. V. 1- June 1972-. Portuguese. Cultural Distribuidora de Livros, rua Sergipe No 1 466, Sao Joaquim da Barra Brazil.

BL
JURISPRUDENCIA BRASILEIRA. 1-. Monographic series. Portuguese. Price varies per volume. Jurua Editora, Av Visconde de Guarapuava, 2435-10 Andar, CEP 80.000, Curitiba Parana Brazil. **LC** KHD387.A48; J87. **DD** 349.81/05; 348.1005.

US/1062-2470
LAW & BUSINESS DIRECTORY OF LITIGATION ATTORNEYS. (LAW & BUSINESS DIRECTORY OF LITIGATION ATTORNEYS / IN COOPERATION WITH THE AMERICAN BAR ASSOCIATION'S SECTION OF LITIGATION.). [Law Bus. dir. litig. atty.]. **Added/Corp** Prentice Hall Law & Business (Firm) American Bar Association. Section of Litigation. **VFOAT** Law and Business Directory of Litigation Attorneys; Directory of Litigation Attorneys. (1990)-. English. an. $390.60. Prentice-Hall Law and Business, 270 Sylvan Avenue, Englewood Cliffs NJ 07632. **Tel** (800)223-0231, (201)894-8538, FAX (201)894-8666. **LC** KF195.L53; L39. **DD** 349.73/025; 347.30025.

US
LOUISIANA CIVIL CODE. Began in 1980. English. an. $18.00. West Publishing Company, 610 Opperman Drive, PO Box 64526, Eagan MN 55123-1308. **Tel** (612)687-5618, (800)328-9352, FAX (612)687-5388, (800)562-2329. **(Subscription telephone:** FAX (612)688-3570**)** **LC** KFL30.5.W4; A296. **DD** 346.763/002632.

US
LOUISIANA CIVIL LAW AND PROCEDURE NEWSLETTER. (197?)-. Newsletter. English. Twenty-six times a year. $90.00. LA Civil Law & Procedure Newsletter, 330 Sunset Boulevard, Baton Rouge LA 70808. **Tel** (504)769-1362.

US/1050-852X
MASSACHUSETTS, CONNECTICUT, RHODE ISLAND VERDICT REPORTER, THE. [Mass. Conn. R. I. verdict report.]. **VFOAT** Verdict Reporter; Mass, Conn, RI Verdict Reporter. (1989)-. Periodical. English. mo (12 iussues). $245.00. Judicial Advisory Services, Inc., PO Box 99704, Louisville KY 40299. **Tel** (800)445-3165, (502)266-6161, FAX (502)266-6060. **ED** Chris C. Wakild. **DD** 347. **Circ:** 300.
Desc: Contains summaries of civil jury verdict trials.

US
MERIT SYSTEMS PROTECTION BOARD SERVICE. INCLUDES INDEX DIGEST AND ANALYSIS OF DECISIONS. (Nov. 1984)-. English. Twelve times a year. $320.00. Hawkins Publishing Company, PO Box 480, Mayo MD 21106. **Tel** (410)798-1677. available in Loose-leaf.
Desc: Analysis of decisions of the Merit Systems Protection Board, the Federal and U.S. Supreme Courts relating to the Civil Service Reform Act of 1978.

US/0899-904X
MICHIGAN TRIAL REPORTER, THE. (THE MICHIGAN TRIAL REPORTER : MTR.). [Mich. trial report.]. **VFOAT** MTR. (1988)-. Periodical. English. mo (12 issues). $265.00. Judicial Advisory Services, Inc., PO Box 99704, Louisville KY 40299. **Tel** (800)445-3165, (502)266-6161, FAX (502)266-6060. **ED** Chris C. Wakild. **DD** 348. **Circ:** 300.
Desc: Contains summaries of civil jury verdict trials.

JA
MINSHOHO ZASSHI. (1935)-. Periodical. Japanese. mo. $238.00. **(Subscription address:** Kyowa Book Company Inc., 1-38 Kanda Jinbo-Cho, Chiyoda-Ku Tokyo 101, Japan**)**

US/0887-2899
NATIONAL JURY VERDICT REVIEW AND ANALYSIS, THE. [Natl. jury verdict rev. anal.]. **Added/Corp** Jury Verdict Review Publications, Inc. Vol. 1, Issue 1 (Dec. 1985)-. Periodical. English. Twelve times a year. $275.00. Jury Verdict Review Publications Inc., 24 Commerce Street/Suite 1722, Newark NJ 07102. **Tel** (201)624-1665. **ED** Lisa Marchant Weitzman. **LC** KF1247.8; .N36. **DD** 346.7303; 347.3063.
Desc: A nationwide review of state and federal civil jury verdicts with professional analysis and commentary.

US/0886-2540
NEW ENGLAND JURY VERDICT REVIEW AND ANALYSIS. [N. Engl. jury verdict rev. anal.]. **Added/Corp** Jury Verdict Review Publications, Inc. (1985)-. Periodical. English. Twelve times a year. $275.00. Jury Verdict Review Publications Inc., 24 Commerce Street/Suite 1722, Newark NJ 07102. **Tel** (201)624-1665. **LC** KF1247.8; .N48. **DD** 346.7403; 347.4063.

US/8750-8060
NEW JERSEY JURY VERDICT REVIEW AND ANALYSIS. [N. J. jury verdict rev. anal.]. **Added/Corp** Jury Verdict Review (Firm). **VFOAT** N.J. Jury Verdict Review & Analysis. (19??)-. Periodical. English. Twelve times a year. $275.00. Jury Verdict Review Publications Inc., 24 Commerce Street/Suite 1722, Newark NJ 07102. **Tel** (201)624-1665. Index available.

US/0276-8127
NEW MEXICO CIVIL TRIAL REPORTER. (Jan./Feb. 1980)-. Periodical. English. bm. New Mexico Civil Trial Reporter, PO Box 826, Albuquerque NM 87103.

US
NEW YORK CIVIL PRACTICE. **Main/Corp** New York (State). English. ir. Matthew Bender & Company Inc., 1275 Broadway, Albany NY 12204. **Tel** (800)833-9844, (518)487-3000.

US
NEW YORK ... CPLR REDBOOK. **Main/Corp** New York (State). **VFOAT** New York ... C.P.L.R. Redbook; C.P.L.R; CPLR. (1979)-. Periodical. English. an. Matthew Bender & Company Inc., 1275 Broadway, Albany NY 12204. **Tel** (800)833-9844, (518)487-3000. **LC** KFN5990; .A196. **DD** 347.747/05; 347.47075. ***Continues*** *New York (State). Civil Practice Law and Rules.; CPLR Including all ... Amendments Enacted by the Regular Session of the ... Legislature and Promulgated by the Judicial Conference.*

US/8750-8044
NEW YORK STATE JURY VERDICT REVIEW AND ANALYSIS. [N. Y. State jury verdict rev. anal.]. **Added/Corp** Jury Verdict Review Publications, Inc. Vol. 1, No. 1 (Dec. 1983)-. Periodical. English. Twelve times a year. $275.00. Jury Verdict Review Publications Inc., 24 Commerce Street/Suite 1722, Newark NJ 07102. **Tel** (201)624-1665. **LC** KFN5311.A59; .N48. **DD** 346.74803/23; 347.4806323.
Desc: A monthly statewide review of New York Supreme and Federal District Court civil jury verdicts with commentary by Ira J. Zrin, Esq.

GW/0179-4043
NJW-RECHTSPRECHUNGS-REPORT, ZIVILRECHT. [NJW-Rechtsprech.-Rep. Ziv.r.]. **VFOAT** NJW-RR. Vol. 1, No. 1 (Jan. 30, 1986)-. Periodical. German. Twenty-four times a year. DM501.20 Germany; DM508.40 others. CH Beck Verlagsbuchhandlung, D 80791 Munich Germany. **Tel** 011 49 89 381891. **LC** KK40; .N59.

FR
NOUVEAU CODE DE PROCEDURE CIVILE ET CODE DE PROCEDURE CIVILE. **Main/Corp** France. **VFOAT** Code de Procedure Civile; Nouveau Code de Procedure Civile. Began with 1976 Vol. French. an. 130.00F. Dalloz, 35 rue Tournefort, 75240 Paris Cedex 05 France. **Tel** 011 33 1 40515434 or 40515454, FAX 45 87 37 48, telex 206 446 F. **DD** 347.44/02632; 344.407502632. ***Continues*** *Code de Procedure Civile. Code de Procedure Civile Annote d'Apres la Doctrine et la Jurisprudence, avec Renvois aux Publications Dalloz.*
Desc: Prints texts of civil laws for the past year. Information on employer obligations, contracts, leaves, temporary employment, etc.

IT
NUOVA GIURISPRUDENZA CIVILE COMMENTATA, LA. **Added/Corp** CEDAM. Vol. 1, No. 1 (Jan./Feb. 1985)-. Periodical. Italian. bm. L220000 Itlay; L320000 other. Cedam Spa, Via Jappelli 5 6, 35121 Padua Italy. **Tel** 011 39 49 65667. **LC** KKH496.3; .N86.

US
OHIO CIVIL PRACTICE, PROCEDURE, AND FORMS. **Main/Corp** Ohio. English. ir. Anderson Publishing, 2035 Reading Road, Cincinnati OH 45202. **Tel** (513)421-4142, (800)582-7295, FAX (513)562-8116.

US
PARTNERSHIP TAXATION. **Added/Corp** Practising Law Institute. (19??)-. English. ir. $195.00 (4 volumes), $60.00 (1993 supplement) regular edition; $36.00 (2 volumes student edition) for students only. Shepards McGraw-Hill Inc, 555 Middle Creek Parkway, PO Box 35300, Colorado Springs CO 80935-3530. **Tel** (719)488-3000, FAX (800)525-0053. **LC** KF6452.Z9; P37. **DD** 343.7306/62; 347.303662.

US/1062-1822
PENNSYLVANIA CIVIL APPELLATE REPORTER. ***Ceased.*** [Pa. civil appell. report.]. **Added/Corp** Andrews Publications, Inc. **VFOAT** Civil Appellate Reporter. (1992)-(199?). Periodical. English. sm (24 issues). Andrews Publications Inc., 1646 West Chester Pike, PO Box 1000, Westtown PA 19395. **Tel** (610)399-6600, (800)345-1101, FAX (610)399-6610. **DD** 348.
Desc: Important decisions regarding Pennsylvania civil law as interpreted by the state's three appellate courts and the Third Circuit U.S. Court of Appeals.

US/8750-8052
PENNSYLVANIA JURY VERDICT REVIEW AND ANALYSIS. [Pa. jury verdict rev. anal.]. Vol. 1, Issue 1 (Sept. 15, 1982)-. Periodical. English. mo (12 issues). $250.00. Jury Verdict Review Publications Inc., 24 Commerce Street/Suite 1722, Newark NJ 07102. **Tel** (201)624-1665. **LC** KFP197.P3; A496. **DD** 346.74803/23; 347.4806323.

SP/0211-4526
PERSONA Y DERECHO. [Pers. derecho]. **Added/Corp** Universidad de Navarra. Facultad de Derecho. Vol. 1 (1974)-. Spanish (English, German, Italian, French and Portuguese). sa (2 issues). $46.00 (latest volume). Servicio de Publicaciones de la Universidad de Navarra SA, Edificio Muga, Campus Universitario, 31008 Pamplona Spain. **Tel** 011 34 48 282700 ext. 2887. **ED** Javier Hervada. **LC** K16; .E698. **DD** 346/.01/2; 342.612. Index available (free). **Bk Rev. Pr Rev. Circ:** 500.
Desc: Aim is to offer studies on basic themes of law and to contribute to the dissemination of human values in today's society.
Ind/Abst Bibliogr. Mission.

Law —Constitutional Law

US/1045-9677
PERSONAL INJURY DEFENSE REPORTER. [Pers. injury def. report.]. Vol. 1, No. 1 (Feb. 1985)-. Periodical. English. mo. Matthew Bender & Company Inc., 1275 Broadway, Albany NY 12204. **Tel** (800)833-9844, (518)487-3000. **LC** KF8925.P4; A136. **DD** 346.7303/23; 347.306323.

CN/0229-6632
PRAIRIE WEED. See Biology-Botany.

●UK/1068-316X
PSYCHOLOGY, CRIME & LAW. See Psychology.

IT
QUADRIMESTRE. Ceased. VFOAT Rivista di Diritto Privato. No. 1 (1984)-(Dec. 1993). Periodical. Italian. Three times a year. Giuffre Editore SPA, Via Busto Arsizio 40, 20151 Milan Italy. **Tel** 011 398 2 38089200.

IT/0393-182X
RASSEGNA DI DIRITTO CIVILE. [Rass. diritto civ.]. (1980)-. Periodical. Italian. qt. L180000 (institutions), L120000 (individuals) Italy; L220000 other. Edizioni Scientifiche Italiane, Via Chiatamone 7, 80121 Naples Italy. **Tel** 011 39 81 7645768, 011 39 81 7645443, FAX 011 39 81 7646477. **UDC** 347.

US/0147-135X
REAL PROPERTY LAW SECTION NEWSLETTER. See Real Estate.

FR
RECUEIL PERIODIQUE DES JURIS-CLASSEURS : DROIT CIVIL. French. ir. 850.00. Editions Techniques, 141 rue de Javel, 75747 Paris Cedex 15 France. **Tel** 011 33 1 45589100. **Continues** Juris-Classeurs. Droit Civil.

IT
REPERTORIO GIUSTIZIA CIVILE. (19??)-. Italian. an. Giuffre Editore SPA, Via Busto Arsizio 40, 20151 Milan Italy. **Tel** 011 398 2 38089200.

VE
REVISTA DE DERECHO PRIVADO (CARACAS, VENEZUELA). (REVISTA DE DERECHO PRIVADO.). VFOAT Derecho Privado. Yearly V. 1, No. 1 (Jan./March 1983)-. Periodical. Spanish. qt. $45.00. Apartado de Correos No 60379, Caracas 106 Venezuela. **LC** K19; .D449. **DD** 346.87/005; 348.706005.

BL
REVISTA DE DIREITO CIVIL. (July/Sept 1977)-. Periodical. Portuguese. qt. $80.00. Editora Revista dos Tribunais, rua Conde do Pinhal 78, 01501 Sao Paulo SP Brazil. **Tel** 011 55 11 372433. **ED** R. Limongi Franca. **LC** K19; .D578. **DD** 346/.81. Bk Rev. Ad Acc. Circ: 5,000.
Desc: Jurisprudence commentaries and leading articles for civil jurisdiction.

BL
REVISTA DE PROCESSO. Year 1 (Jan./March 1976)-. Periodical. Portuguese. qt. Editora Revista dos Tribunais, rua Conde do Pinhal 78, 01501 Sao Paulo SP Brazil. **Tel** 011 55 11 372433. **ED** Alvaro Malheiros. **LC** K19; .D84. **DD** 347/.81/05. Bk Rev. Ad Acc. Circ: 5,000.
Desc: Jurisprudence commentaries and leading articles for lawsuit (civil, penal, and labor).

CN/0822-5117
REVUE DE DROIT JUDICIAIRE. [Rev. droit judic.]. **Added/Corp** Groupe de Recherche en Droit Judiciaire. VFOAT RDJ; R.D.J. Vol. 1, No. 1 (1983)-. Periodical. English (French). Five times a year. 155.40Can$. Wilson & Lafleur Ltd., 40 Rue Notre Dame East, Montreal, Quebec H2Y 1B9 Canada. **Tel** (514)875-6326, FAX (514)875-8356. **ED** Hubert Reid. **LC** KEQ110; .A23. **DD** 348.714/043/05; 347.14084305. Bk Rev. Circ: 1,000 (ctrl). **Continues** Rapports de Pratique de Quebec, 0384-6970.
Desc: Reports of jurisprudence on application of the civil procedure code of Quebec.
Ind/Abst Index Can. Leg. Period. Lit.

IT
REVUE DE DROIT UNIFORME. [Rev. droit unif.]. **Added/Corp** International Institute for the Unification of Private Law. VFOAT Uniform Law Review. (1973)-. Periodical. Multiple languages (English and French). sa. $45.00. Unidroit, via Panisperna 28, 00184 Rome Italy. **Tel** 011 39 6 6841372. **DD** 340.9. Index available. **Formed by the union of** Jurisprudence de Droit Uniforme **and** Unification du Droit.
Ind/Abst Index Foreign Leg. Per.

FR/0397-9873
REVUE TRIMESTRIELLE DE DROIT CIVIL (PARIS, FRANCE : 1980). (REVUE TRIMESTRIELLE DE DROIT CIVIL.). (April-June 1980)-. Periodical. French. Four times a year. 535.00F (France); 650.00F (other). Dalloz, 35 rue Tournefort, 75240 Paris Cedex 05 France. **Tel** 011 33 1 40515434 or 40515454, FAX 45 87 37 48, telex 206 446 F. **LC** K21; .D316. **DD**

346.44; 344.406. [CCC]. cum. index. **Continues** Revue de Droit Civil.
Ind/Abst Index Foreign Leg. Per.

IT
RIVISTA CRITICA DEL DIRITTO PRIVATO. **Added/Corp** Societa Editrice il Mulino. Vol. 1, No. 1 (March 1983)-. Periodical. Italian. qt. L100000 Italy; L110000 other. Casa Editrice Jovene, 109 Via Mezzocannone, 80134 Naples Italy. **Tel** 011 39 81 552-1274. **LC** K22; .I465.

IT/0035-6093
RIVISTA DI DIRITTO CIVILE. Vol. 1 (1955)-. Periodical. Italian. bm. L170000 Italy; L240000 other. Cedam Spa, Via Jappelli 5 6, 35121 Padua Italy. **Tel** 011 39 49 65667. **LC** K22; .I58. **DD** 346/.005. Index Available published separately, bound from publisher, free-automatically sent. cum. index.
Ind/Abst Index Foreign Leg. Per.

JA
SAISHIN TOKI ROPPO / TODA SHUZO KANSHU. Main/Corp Japan. (19??)-. Japanese. ir. ¥3000. Akatsuki Shuppan Kabushiki Kaisha, 20 Kanda Jinbo-cho 2, Chiyoda-ku, Tokyo-to Japan.

GW
SCHRIFTEN ZUM BURGERLICHEN RECHT. (1969)-. Monographic series. German. ir. Price varies per volume. Duncker und Humblot Verlag, Postfach 410329, D-12113 Berlin Germany. **Tel** 011 49 30 79000612, 011 49 30 79000613.
Desc: Contributions to civil law.

UK/0951-0443
SCOTTISH CIVIL LAW REPORTS. English. qt. £70.00. Law Society of Scotland, Law Society's Hall, 26 Drumsheugh Gardens, Edinburgh EH3 7YR Scotland. **Tel** 011 44 31 2267411, FAX 011 44 31 2252934. **ED** A Graham Johnston. Index available. cum. index. Circ: 600.

US
SETTLEMENTS BY CATEGORY. English. mo. $60.00. Cook County Jury Verdict, 415 North State Street, Chicago IL 60610. **Tel** (312)644-7800. available on an online database.
Desc: Out of court settlements in civil cases filed throughout the state of Illinois.

US
SPEAKERS' OUTLINES, FEDERAL PRACTICE AND PROCEDURE. VFOAT Federal Practice and Procedure. 1981-. English. Missouri Bar Association, 326 Monroe Street, Jefferson City MO 65101. **Tel** (314)635-4128. **LC** KF8841; .S65. **DD** 347.73/5; 347.3075.

US/1071-7625
SUCCESSFUL RESTRUCTURINGS. [Success. restruct.]. **Added/Corp** LRP Publications (Firm). Vol. 1, Issue 1 (Apr. 29, 1993)-. Periodical. English. sm. $355.00. LRP Publications, 747 Dresher Road, PO Box 980, Horsham PA 19044-0980. **Tel** (800)341-7874, (215)784-0860, FAX (215)784-9639, (215)784-0870. **DD** 346.
Desc: Updates in the turnaround and insolvency market.

US
TEGLAND'S LITIGATION TODAY. VFOAT Litigation Today. Issue No. 1 (Feb. 1987)-. English. mo (12 issues per year). $130.00. KB Tegland, PO Box 12189, Bothwell WA 98012. **Tel** (206)486-8860. **ED** Karl B. Tegland. **LC** KFW530.A1; T44. **DD** 347.797/05; 347.97075. Index available. Circ: 500.
Desc: Information on civil procedure, evidence, and appellate procedure.

●US/1062-5887
TEMPLE POLITICAL & CIVIL RIGHTS LAW REVIEW. See Political Science-Civil Rights.

BE/0775-2814
TIJDSCHRIFT VOOR BELGISCH BURGERLIJK RECHT : TBBR. VFOAT TBBR; RGDC; Revue Generale de Droit Civil Belge. (Sept./Oct. 1987)-. Periodical. Dutch (French). bm (6 issues). 4650.00F. E Story Scientia, 228 Boulevard E Brockstael, 1020 Brussels Belgium. **Tel** 011 32 2 4223911. **ED** O. Lefebore. **LC** KJK496; .T55. Index available. Ad Acc. Circ: 1,450.
Ind/Abst Index Foreign Leg. Per.

BE
TIJDSCHRIFT VOOR PRIVAATRECHT. Vol. 1 (1964)-. Periodical. Dutch (summaries and/or abstracts in English, French and German). qt. 4000.00F. Kluwer Edn Juridiques Belgique, Blvd E Bockstael 230, 1020 Brussels Belguim. **Tel** 011 32 2 7232111. **(Subscription address:** Distybo, Santvoortbeeklan 21 25, 2100 Deurne Antwerpen Belgium) **ED** M. Storme. **LC** K24; .I38. Bk Rev. Circ: 1,800 (ctrl).
Desc: Law
Ind/Abst Index Foreign Leg. Per.

US/1045-8891
TULANE CIVIL LAW FORUM. Title Change. [Tulane civil law forum]. **Added/Corp** Tulane Law School.

VFOAT Tulane Law Forum. Vol. 1, Issue 1 (1973)-Vol. 6/7, Issued (1992). Monographic series. English. ir. Tulane University School of Law, 6801 Freret Street, New Orleans LA 70118. **Tel** (504)865-5990. **DD** 349. available on microfilm and microfiche from University Microfilms International (UMI). **Continued by** Tulane European and Civil Law Forum.
Ind/Abst Index Leg. Period.

US
TULANE EUROPEAN AND CIVIL LAW FORUM. (19??)-. English. an. $20.00 US; $25.00 others. Tulane University School of Law, 6801 Freret Street, New Orleans LA 70118. **Tel** (504)865-5990.

US
URBAN RING EDITION. English. ir. $500.00. Cook County Jury Verdict, 415 North State Street, Chicago IL 60610. **Tel** (312)644-7800. Index available. available on an online database.
Desc: Summaries of civil jury verdicts and settlements for cases filed throughout the state of Illinois.

CN/0827-4266
WEEKLY DIGEST OF CIVIL PROCEDURE, THE. [Wkly. dig. civ. proced.]. Vol. 1, Pt. 1 (Jan. 18, 1985)-. Periodical. English. Forty times a year. 350.00Can$. Carswell / Canada, 2075 Kennedy Road, Scarborough Ontario M1T 3V4 Canada. **Tel** (416)609-3800, (800)387-5164. **ED** Heather Stone. **DD** 347.713/05/02648.
Desc: Summaries of cases relating to civil procedure from the Ontario, Supreme and Federal Courts of Canada.

CONSTITUTIONAL LAW

BE
ADMINISTRATION PUBLIQUE. Main/Corp Institut Belge des Sciences Administratives. Vol. 1 (Sept. 1976)-. Periodical. French. Fourteen times a year. 4500.00F. Administration Publique, 98 rue Saint Bernard, 1060 Brussels Belgium. **Tel** 322 5365938, telex LAWBRU 61287. **ED** Jacques Putzeys. **DD** 342/.493/06. Index available. Bk Rev. Ad Acc. Circ: 600.
Desc: Summarizes most important decisions pronounced by Belgian and European jurisdictions on public and administrative law.

US/0149-3272
ADMINISTRATIVE LAW (GARDENA). Title Change. (ADMINISTRATIVE LAW.). 1st Ed. (1971)-(19??). English. Gilbert Law Summaries, 14415 South Main Street, Gardena CA 90248. **LC** KF5402.Z9; R87. **DD** 342/.73/066. **Continued by** Gilbert Law Summaries. Administrative Law.

US/1052-2913
ADMINISTRATIVE LAW JOURNAL (WASHINGTON, D.C.), THE. (THE ADMINISTRATIVE LAW JOURNAL.). [Adm. law j.]. **Added/Corp** Washington College of Law. Vol. 1, No. 1 (Summer 1987)-. Periodical. English. qt (four issues per year). $15.00 alumni, $20.00 other. Washington College of Law, 4410 Massachusetts Avenue NW, Washington DC 20016. **Tel** (202)885-2652, FAX (202)885-1039. **LC** K1; .D55. **DD** 342.73/06; 347.3026.
Ind/Abst Index Leg. Period.; LegalTrac (1987-).

US/0567-9494
ADMINISTRATIVE LAW NEWS (AMERICAN BAR ASSOCIATION. SECTION OF ADMINISTRATIVE LAW : 1974). (THE ADMINISTRATIVE LAW NEWS.). [Adm. law news]. **Added/Corp** American Bar Association. Section of Administrative Law. Vol. 1 (Oct. 1974)-. Periodical. English. qt. American Bar Association, 750 North Lake Shore Drive, Chicago IL 60611. **Tel** (312)988-5522, (312)988-5241, FAX (312)988-5528, telex 270593. **Continues** Administrative Law News (American Bar Association. Section on Administration Law : 1961).
Ind/Abst Leg. Resour. Index (1980-?); LegalTrac (1980-).

US/0742-9673
ADMINISTRATIVE LAW NOTES / SECTION ON ADMINISTRATIVE LAW, FEDERAL BAR ASSOCIATION. Periodical. English. ir. Federal Bar Association, 1815 H Street Northwest, Suite 408, Washington DC 20006. **Tel** (202)638-0252, FAX (202)775-0295. **LC** KF5401.A15; A34. **DD** 342.73/0605; 347.302605.

CN/0824-2615
ADMINISTRATIVE LAW REPORTS (TORONTO). (ADMINISTRATIVE LAW REPORTS.). [Adm. law rep.]. Vol. 1 Pt. 1 (Oct./Nov. 1983)-. Periodical. English (French). ir. Price varies. Carswell / Canada, 2075 Kennedy Road, Scarborough Ontario M1T 3V4 Canada. **Tel** (416)609-3800, (800)387-5164. **ED** David J. Mullan. **DD** 342.71/0664/02642. Index available. cum. index. Ad Acc.

Desc: Features all important decisions in administrative law from all Canadian jurisdictions selected by experts in the field. Includes cases on the availability of and grounds for judicial review of decisions of administrative tribunals, delegation of legislative powers, and remedies on judicial review.
Ind/Abst Index Can. Leg. Period. Lit.

US/0001-8368
ADMINISTRATIVE LAW REVIEW. [Adm. law rev.]. **Added/Corp** American Bar Association. Section of Administrative Law. Vol. 13 (Fall 1960)-. Periodical. English. qt (4 issues). $35.00. American Bar Association, 750 North Lake Shore Drive, Chicago IL 60611. **Tel** (312)988-5522, (312)988-5241, FAX (312)988-5528, telex 270593. cum. index. **Ad Acc. Pr Rev.** ctrl circ. Documents available from The Genuine Article, UMI Article Clearinghouse. ***Continues*** *Administrative Law Bulletin.*
Ind/Abst Bowne Dig. Corp. Sec. Lawyers; Crim. Justice Abstr. (1974-); Curr. Contents Soc. Behav. Sci.; Curr. Law Index (1980-); Expand. Acad. Index (1984-); Fed. Tax Artic.; Index Leg. Period.; Leg. Resour. Index (1980-); LegalTrac (1980-); Newsp. Period. Abstr. (1988-); Res. Alert [Full Cov.]; Soc. Sci. Cit. Index [Full Cov.]; Trade Ind. Index (1981-?).

US
ADMINISTRATIVE LAW TREATISE. (19??)-. English. ir. $395.00. Little Brown & Company, 34 Beacon Street, Boston MA 02108. **Tel** (617)227-0730, (800)759-0190. cum. index.

US
ANNIVERSARY REPORT. Main/Corp California. Office of Administrative Laws. 4th (1980/1984)-. English. an. Office of Administrative Law, 1414 K Street/Suite 600, Sacramento CA 95814. ***Continues*** *Annual Report / California. Office of Administrative Law.*

FR
ANNUAIRE INTERNATIONAL DE JUSTICE CONSTITUTIONNELLE / GROUPEMENT D'ETUDES ET DE RECHERCHES SUR LA JUSTICE CONSTITUTIONNELLE. Added/Corp Groupement d'Etudes et de Recherches sur la Justice Constitutionnelle (France). (1985)-. French. an. Editions Economica, 49 rue Hericart, 75015 Paris France. **Tel** 011 33 1 45781292. **(Subscription address:** Le Diffuseur G Vermette, PO Box 85, 1501 Ampere, Boucherville Quebec J4B 6G4 Canada.**) LC** K1; .N524.

US/0197-1239
ANNUAL REPORT - AMERICAN CIVIL LIBERTIES UNION. See Political Science-Civil Rights.

CL
ANUARIO DE DERECHO ADMINISTRATIVO. 1- 1975/76-. Periodical. Spanish. Ediciones Revista de Derecho Publico, Universidad de Chile, Bernarda Morin 435, Santiago Chile. **LC** K1; .N915. **DD** 342/.83/06.

GW/0003-8911
ARCHIV DES OFFENTLICHEN RECHTS. [Arch. off. Rechts]. (1911)-. Periodical. German. qt. DM208.00. JCB Mohr / Paul Siebeck, Postfach 2040, D 72010 Tuebingen Germany. **Tel** 011 49 7071 9230, FAX 011 49 7071 51104, telex 7/262872 mohr d. **ED** Peter Badura, Konrad Hesse, and Peter Lerche. **LC** JA14; .A67. **DD** 320/.05. **[CCC]. Bk Rev. Ad Acc. Circ:** 1,200. ***Continues*** *Archiv fuer Offentliches Recht.*
Desc: Deals with all aspects of public law (mainly German).
Ind/Abst ABC POL SCI; Index Foreign Leg. Per.; Int. Polit. Sci. Abstr.

US/0743-0310
BENCHMARK (WASHINGTON, D.C.). ***Suspended.*** (BENCHMARK : A BIMONTHLY REPORT ON THE CONSTITUTION AND THE COURTS.). [Benchmark]. V. 1, No. 1 (Jan./Feb. 1984)-Vol. 4, No. 5 (198?). Periodical. English. qt. $18.00, $16.00 (students), $20.00 (institutions) US; $26.00, $24.00 (students), $28.00 (institutions) other. Benchmark, PO Box 15449, Washington DC 20003. **Tel** (804)492-4922. **ED** James McClellan. **LC** KF4546.A3; B46. **DD** 342.73/005; 347.302005. **Ad Acc.**
Desc: Journal of opinion reporting on political and legal activities affecting the Constitution and the courts; critically examines judicial decisions on individual liberty, religion, and the family, property rights, the free enterprise system and national security.
Ind/Abst LegalTrac (1984-).

US/0160-7731
BILL OF RIGHTS IN ACTION. See Political Science-Civil Rights.

SP
BOLETIN DE JURISPRUDENCIA CONSTITUCIONAL : BJC. Added/Corp Spain. Cortes Generales. Servicio de Estudios. **VFOAT** BJC; B.J.C. (May 1981)-. Periodical. Spanish. mo. Cortes Generales / Congreso Diputado Publicaciones, Floridablanca, 28014 Madrid Spain. **Tel** 011 34 1 4295193, 011 34 1 4292577.

IT/0444-9266
BOLLETTINO DI INFORMAZIONI COSTITUZIONALI E PARLAMENTARI. NUOVA SERIE. Main/Corp Italy. Parlamento. Camera Dei Deputati. Segretariato Generale. (19??)-. Periodical. Italian. qt. L50000. Camera Deputati-Uff Stampa Pub, Piazza del Parlamento 24, 00100 Rome Italy. **Tel** (06)67179307. Index available. **Circ:** 1,000.
Desc: Parliamentary procedure, constitutional law; papers and original documents on both subjects.

GW
BVR, BERNISCHE VERWALTUNGSRECHTSPRECHUNG. **VFOAT** Bernische Verwaltungsrechtsprechung; Jurisprudence Administrative Bernoise; JAB, Jurisprudence Administrative Bernoise. Periodical. German (summaries and/or abstracts in French). ir. 58.00. Genossenschafts-Buchdruckerie AG, 3000 Bern 16 Switzerland. **DD** 348/.4945/025.

CN/0835-6742
CANADIAN JOURNAL OF ADMINISTRATIVE LAW & PRACTICE. [Can. j. adm. law pract.]. **VFOAT** Canadian Journal of Administrative Law and Practice; Administrative Law & Practice. Vol. 1, No. 1 (Sept. 1987)-. Periodical. English (French). Three times a year. 98.00Can$ Canada; 85.50Can$ other. Carswell / Canada, 2075 Kennedy Road, Scarborough Ontario M1T 3V4 Canada. **Tel** (416)609-3800, (800)387-5164. **ED** Michael I Jeffery. **LC** K3; .A494. **DD** 342.71/0. **Bk Rev. Ad Acc.**
Desc: A national journal providing in-depth discussion of administrative law issues. Covers the role of tribunals, boards and commissions in the Canadian administrative process.
Ind/Abst Can. Legal Lit.; Index Can. Leg. Period. Lit. (1992-).

CN/0715-4860
CANADIAN RIGHTS REPORTER. SECOND SERIES. See Political Science-Civil Rights.

IT/0008-7424
CASSAZIONE PENALE : RIVISTA MENSILE DI GIURISPRUDENZA. (19??)-. Italian. mo. L280000.00 Italy; L420000.00 other. Giuffre Editore SPA, Via Busto Arsizio 40, 20151 Milan Italy. **Tel** 011 398 2 38089200. **ED** Giorgio Lattanzi.
Desc: Provides full and systematically set out information on verdicts given by the Supreme Court on criminal matters and trial procedures, with significant decisions by the Constitutional Court and by the trial courts.

SP/0210-8461
CIVITAS. REVISTA ESPANOLA DE DERECHO ADMINISTRATIVO. (REVISTA ESPANOLA DE DERECHO ADMINISTRATIVO.). [Civitas, Rev. esp. derecho adm.]. Vol. 1 (April/June 1974)-. Periodical. Spanish. qt. Editorial Civitas SA, Igancio Ellacuria 3, 28017 Madrid Spain. **Tel** 011 34 1 7253156.

FR
CODE ADMINISTRATIF. Main/Corp France. 1. Ed. French. 148.00F. Dalloz, 35 rue Tournefort, 75240 Paris Cedex 05 France. **Tel** 011 33 1 40515434 or 40515454, FAX 45 87 37 48, telex 206 446 F. Index available.
Desc: All laws in the field reproduced and annotated. Easy access due to index system.

SZ/0010-6623
CONSTITUTIONAL AND PARLIAMENTARY INFORMATION. **Main/Corp** Inter-Parliamentary Union. **Added/Corp** Association of Secretaries General of Parliaments. (1948)-. Periodical. English (French). qt. 40.00F. Association of Secretaries General of Parliaments, 126 rue de l'Universite, 75355 Paris France. **LC** JF8; .I5. Index available. cum. index. **Bk Rev. Circ:** 1,500 (ctrl). ***Continues*** *Constitutional and Parliamentary Information.*
Ind/Abst Int. Labour Doc.; PAIS Int. Print.

US/0742-7115
CONSTITUTIONAL COMMENTARY. [Const. comment.]. **Added/Corp** University of Minnesota. Law School. Vol. 1, No. 1 (Winter 1984)-. Periodical. English. sa. $18.00. University of Minnesota Law School, 229 19th Avenue South, Minneapolis MN 55455. **Tel** (612)625-8034. **ED** Dan Farber and Dave Bryden. **LC** K3; .O528. **DD** 342.73; 347.302. **Bk Rev. Circ:** 700. Documents available from UMI Article Clearinghouse.
Desc: A journal for lawyers, political scientists, and historians interested in constitutional law.
Ind/Abst Bowne Dig. Corp. Sec. Lawyers; Curr. Law Index (1984-); Expand. Acad. Index (1992-); Index Leg. Period.; Leg. Resour. Index (1984-); LegalTrac (1984-); Newsp. Period. Abstr. (1989-).

CN/0847-3889
CONSTITUTIONAL FORUM. (CONSTITUTIONAL FORUM / CENTER FOR CONSTITUTIONAL STUDIES.). [Const. forum]. **Added/Corp** University of Alberta. Centre for Constitutional Studies. **VFOAT** Forum Constitutionnel. Vol. 1, No. 1 (Oct. 1989)-. Periodical. English (French). Four times a year. $35.00 (includes Points of View). Alberta Law Review, University of Alberta, Faculty of Law, Edmonton Alberta T6G 2H5 Canada. **Tel** (403)492-5681, FAX (403)492-4924. **ED** David Schneiderman, (phone: (403)492-8281). **LC** KE4212; .C66. **DD** 342.71/005; 347.105. Index available. cum. index. **Bk Rev. Ad Acc, Adv Mgr:** Christine Urouhart. **Pr Rev. Circ:** 1,200.
Desc: Publishes case comments, essays and updates on recent constitutional developments. It is designed to fill a gap in our national discourse on the constitution.
Ind/Abst Index Can. Leg. Period. Lit. (1992-).

US/0098-7638
CONSTITUTIONAL LAW. Main/Corp Bay Area Review Course, Inc. English. an. Bay Area Review Course Inc, 5900 Wilshire Boulevard, Los Angeles CA 90036. **LC** KF4550.Z9; B37. **DD** 342/.73.

US
CONSTITUTIONAL LAW JOURNAL / SETON HALL LAW SCHOOL. Added/Corp Seton Hall University. School of Law. **VFOAT** Seton Hall Constitutional Law Journal. Vol. 1, No. 1 (Fall/Winter 1990)-. Periodical. English. sa. Seton Hall University School of Law, One Newark Center, Newark NJ 07102. **Tel** (201)642-8811. ***Continues*** *Constitutional Law Journal (Newark, N.J.).*
Ind/Abst Index Leg. Period.; Leg. Resour. Index; LegalTrac (1990-).

US/1043-4062
CONSTITUTIONAL POLITICAL ECONOMY. [Const. polit. econ.]. **Added/Corp** George Mason University. Center for Study of Public Choice. **VFOAT** CPE. Vol. 1, No. 1 (Winter 1990)-. Periodical. English. Three times a year. $65.00. George Mason University / Georges Hall, Fairfax VA 22030. **Tel** (703)993-2329, FAX (703)993-2323. **ED** J. Buchanan, V. Vanberg, R. Wagner. **LC** HB73; .C66. **DD** 330/.05. Index available. cum. index. **Bk Rev**, (Qty: 15). **Ad Acc, Adv Mgr:** V Vauberg. **Pr Rev. Circ:** 560.
Desc: Forum for papers in constitutional analysis, an approach that tries to integrate the institutional dimension, the study of political, legal and moral institutions-into economic analysis. Publishes contributions from the various social sciences, philosophy and law.
Ind/Abst Econ. Lit. Index.

UK/0269-2511
CONSTITUTIONAL REFORM : THE QUARTERLY REVIEW. ***Ceased.*** Vol. 1, No. 1 (Spring 1986)-?. Periodical. English. qt. Constitutional Reform Centre, 60 Chandos Place, London WC2N 4HG England. **Tel** (01)240 1719. **ED** Hilary Muggridge. Index available. **Circ:** 2,000 (ctrl).
Desc: News and features on constitutional issues.

US/0572-8274
CONSTITUTIONS OF THE UNITED STATES, NATIONAL AND STATE. **Main/Corp** Columbia University. Legislative Drafting Research Fund. (1962)-. English. Twice a year. $750.00. Oceana Publications, Inc., 75 Main Street, Dobbs Ferry NY 10522. **Tel** (914)693-1320, FAX (914)693-0402. **DD** 342.

US/1057-5812
DECISIONS OF THE OFFICE OF ADMINISTRATIVE LAW JUDGES AND OFFICE OF ADMINISTRATIVE APPEALS. [Decis. Office Adm. Law Judges Office Adm. Appeals]. **Main/Corp** United States. Dept. of Labor. Office of Administrative Law Judges. **Added/Corp** United States. Dept. of Labor. Office of Administrative Appeals. Vol. 1, No. 1 (Jan./Feb. 1987)-. Government Publication. English. bm. $29.00; US; $36.25; other. Superintendent of Documents, US Government Printing Office, Washington DC 20402. **Tel** (202)275-3328, FAX (202)786-2377. **LC** KF3312.A2; U55. **DD** 344.73/01/02642; 347.304102642.

PO
DIREITO ADMINISTRATIVO (COIMBRA, PORTUGAL). (DIREITO ADMINISTRATIVO.). Yearly V. 1, No. 1, (Jan./Feb. 1980)-. Periodical. Portuguese. Centelha Promocao do Livro, SARL, Apartado 241, 3003 Coimbra Portugal. **DD** 342.469/06/0; 344.6902605.

US/0148-5997
DOCKET REPORT - CENTER FOR CONSTITUTIONAL RIGHTS. Main/Corp Center for Constitutional Rights (New York, N.Y.). (19??)-. English. an. Center for Constitutional Rights, 835 Broadway, New York NY 10003. **Tel** (212)674-3303.
Ind/Abst Hum. Rights Intern. Rep.

II
ELECTION ARCHIVES AND INTERNATIONAL POLITICS. See Public Administration.

FR
ETUDES ET DOCUMENTS - CONSEIL D'ETAT. **Main/Corp** France. Conseil d'Etat. No. 1 (1947)-. French. an.
Ind/Abst Index Foreign Leg. Per.

AT/0728-6082
FEDERAL COURT REPORTER. See Law.

US/0194-4800
FLORIDA ADMINISTRATIVE LAW REPORTS. **Added/Corp** Judicial and Administrative Research Associates. **VFOAT** FALN. (1979)-. Periodical. English. bw. $495.00. Florida Administrative Law Reports, PO Box 385, Gainesville FL 32602. **Tel** (904)375-8036. **ED** James Konish. **LC** KFF440; .A513. **DD** 348/.759/025. Index available. cum. index. ctrl circ. available on an online database from NETLAW.
Desc: A publication of all contested hearings of nearly every agency in Florida.

IT
FORO AMMINISTRATIVO (ANNUAL). (IL FORO AMMINISTRATIVO.). (19??)-. Italian. mo. L280000.00 Italy; L420000.00 other. Giuffre Editore SPA, Via Busto Arsizio 40, 20151 Milan Italy. **Tel** 011 398 2 38089200. **ED** E. Cannada Bartoli and Riccardo Chieppa. **DD** 342.45/0664; 344.502664. Index available. **Bk Rev. Ad Acc.** ***Continues*** *Foro Amministrativo e Delle Acque Pubbliche (Annual).*
Desc: Articles on jurisprudence and administrative law.

US/0899-7225
FREE SPEECH YEARBOOK. [Free speech yearb.]. **Added/Corp** Speech Communication Association. Speech Communication Association. Commission on Freedom of Speech. (1970)-. English. an. Speech Communication Association, 5105 Backlick Road, Building E, Annandale VA 22003. **Tel** (703)750-0533, FAX (703)914-9471. **LC** K6; .R44. **DD** 323.44/3/097305. available on microfilm and microfiche from University Microfilms International (UMI). ***Continues*** *Yearbook of the Committee on Freedom of Speech of the Speech Association of America, 0584-8679.*
Ind/Abst Index Leg. Period.

IT/0436-0222
GIURISPRUDENZA COSTITUZIONALE. **Added/Corp** Italy. Laws, Statutes, Etc. Italy. Corte di Cassazione. Vol. 1 (1956)-. Periodical. Italian. Six times a year. L300000.00 Italy; L450000.00 other. Giuffre Editore SPA, Via Busto Arsizio 40, 20151 Milan Italy. **Tel** 011 398 2 38089200. **ED** Leopoldo Elia. **DD** 342. Index available. **Bk Rev. Ad Acc. Circ:** 2,400.
Desc: Contains all the verdicts of the Supreme Court, and articles on jurisprudence.
Ind/Abst Index Foreign Leg. Per.

JA
GYOSEI KANKEI HANREI KAISETSU / GOSEI HANREI KENKYUKAI HEN. Japanese. ¥4950. Gyosei Corporation Ltd., 4-2 Nishi Goken-cho, Shinjuku-Ku Tokyo 162 Japan. **Tel** 33269-4145, FAX 33268-2315.

NE
HARTMANS TIJDSCHRIFT VOOR STUDERENDEN OPENBAAR BESTUUR. ***Title Change.*** Dutch. mo. Samson Bedrijfsinformatie, Postbus 4, 2400 HA Alphen Rij Netherlands. **Tel** 011 31 1 72066633. ***Continues*** *Hartmans Tijdschrift Ter Beoefening Van Het Administratief Recht.* ***Continued by*** *Openbaar Bestuur.*

US/0094-5617
HASTINGS CONSTITUTIONAL LAW QUARTERLY. [Hastings constit. law q.]. **Added/Corp** Hastings College of the Law. Vol. 1 (Spring 1974)-. Periodical. English. qt (4 issues). $23.00 US; $25.00 other. Hastings College of Law, 200 McAllister Street, San Francisco CA 94102. **Tel** (415)565-4816, (415)565-4738, FAX (415)565-4814. **ED** Ted Franklin (editor's telephone: (415)565-4726). **LC** K8; .A8. **DD** 342/.73/005. **Bk Rev**, (Qty: 1-3 per year). **Ad Acc, Adv Mgr:** A Kaba, **Tel** (415)565-4738. **Pr Rev. Circ:** 1,200. available on CD-ROM and an online database from WESTLAW; available on microfilm and microfiche from Williams S Hein & Co.
Desc: The oldest law journal devoted to constitutional law. Publishes articles in legal scholarship on topics significant to current developments in constitutional law.
Ind/Abst Bowne Dig. Corp. Sec. Lawyers; Crim. Justice Abstr.; Curr. Law Index (1980-); Index Leg. Period. (1980-); Leg. Resour. Index; LegalTrac (1980-).

SP/0211-9560
HERRI-ARDURALARITZAZKO EUSKAL ALDIZKARIA. **VFOAT** Revista Vasca de Administracion Publica. 1 (Iraila-Abendua 1981)-. Periodical. Basque (Spanish). Three times a year. $24.00. Instiuto Vasco de Administracion Publica, Onati Guipuzcoa Spain. **LC** K8; .E73. **DD** 342.46/606; 344.66026.

US/0735-0821
JOURNAL OF THE NATIONAL ASSOCIATION OF ADMINISTRATIVE LAW JUDGES. [J. Natl. Assoc. Adm. Law Judges]. **Added/Corp** National Association of Administrative Law Judges (U.S.). (Spring 1981)-. Academic Scholarly Publication. English. Twice a year (Apr., Oct.). $20.00. National Association of Administrative Law Judges, 300 Newport Avenue, Williamsburg VA 23187-8798. **Tel** (312)793-1118, FAX (312)793-1119. **ED** Edward Schoenbaum (phone: (217)524-2184). **LC** KF5421.A15; J68. **DD** 342.73/066/05; 347.3026605. Index available (Oct. iss. ($10.00)). cum. index. **Bk Rev**, (Qty: 2). **Ad Acc, Adv Mgr:** E. Schoenbaum, **Tel** (217)524-2184. **Pr Rev. Circ:** 600 (ctrl). available on microfiche (through William S Hein Company) from Williams S Hein & Co.
Desc: A scholarly review of developments in administrative law, from the point of view of administrative law judges.
Ind/Abst Curr. Law Index (1984-); Leg. Resour. Index (1984-); LegalTrac (1984-).

US/0194-4010
LANDMARK BRIEFS AND ARGUMENTS OF THE SUPREME COURT OF THE UNITED STATES : CONSTITUTIONAL LAW. **Main/Corp** United States. Supreme Court. (1975)-. English. an. University Publications of America, 4520 East West Highway 800, Bethesda MD 20814. **Tel** (800)638-8380, (301)654-1550. **ED** P.B. Kurland and G. Casper. **LC** KF101.8; .K87. **DD** 342.73/00264.

●UK
LAW REPORTS OF THE COMMONWEALTH. (1993)-. English. qt. Professional Books Ltd, 46 Milton Trading Estate, Abingdon Oxford OX14 4SY England. **LC** K528; .L39. **DD** 348/.048/09171241; 342.84809171241. ***Formed by the union of*** *Law Reports of the Commonwealth. Commercial Law Reports, 0952-1046; Law Reports of the Commonwealth. Constitutional and Administrative Law Reports, 0951-0699* ***and*** *Law Reports of the Commonwealth. Criminal Law Reports.*

UK/0951-0699
LAW REPORTS OF THE COMMONWEALTH. CONSTITUTIONAL AND ADMINISTRATIVE LAW REPORTS. ***Title Change.*** [Law rep. Commonw., Const. adm. law rep.]. **VFOAT** Constitutional and Administrative Law Reports. (1985)-(1992). English. an. Professional Books Ltd, 46 Milton Trading Estate, Abingdon Oxford OX14 4SY England. **LC** K3150.A495; L39. **DD** 342/.009171/241. ***Merged with*** *Law Reports of the Commonwealth. Commercial Law Reports, 0952-1046* ***and*** *Law Reports of the Commonwealth. Criminal Law Reports* ***to form*** *Law Reports of the Commonwealth.*

US
MODERN CONSTITUTIONAL LAW. 1969-. English. an. $41.00. Lawyers Co-Operative Publishing Company, Aqueduct Building, Rochester NY 14694. **Tel** (800)527-4030. Index available in last issue of volume--attached.

CN/1181-9340
NATIONAL JOURNAL OF CONSTITUTIONAL LAW. [Natl. j. const. law]. **VFOAT** Revue Nationale de Droit Constitutionnel. Vol. 1, No. 1 (Mar. 1991)-. Periodical. French (English). Three times a year. Carswell / Canada, 2075 Kennedy Road, Scarborough Ontario M1T 3V4 Canada. **Tel** (416)609-3800, (800)387-5164. **DD** 342.71/005.
Ind/Abst Index Can. Leg. Period. Lit. (1992-).

CN/1181-9340
NATIONAL JOURNAL OF CONSTITUTIONAL LAW. **VFOAT** Revue Nationale de Droit Constitutionnel; NJCL. Vol. 1, No. 1 (Mar. 1991)-. Periodical. English (French). Three times a year. $150.65 per bound volume including parts service. $122.15, parts only. Carswell / Canada, 2075 Kennedy Road, Scarborough Ontario M1T 3V4 Canada. **Tel** (416)609-3800, (800)387-5164. **LC** K14; .A86773. **DD** 342.71; 347.102.

US
NEW JERSEY ADMINISTRATIVE REPORTS. **Added/Corp** New Jersey. Office of Administrative Law. Vol. 1 (1982)-. English. qt. $454.00. Barclays Law Publishers, 400 Oyster Point Boulevard, South San Francisco CA 94080. **Tel** (800)888-3600, (415)244-6611, FAX (415)244-0408. **LC** KFN2240; .A556. **DD** 342.749/06/02642; 347.4902602642. Index Available in last issue of each volume--loose separately paged. cum. index.

NR
NIGERIAN CONSTITUTIONAL LAW REPORTS. **VFOAT** NCLR; N.C.L.R. Vol. 1 (1981)-. English. an. Nigerian Law Publications, 28 Sabiu-Ajose Crescent, Suru-Lere Lagos State Nigeria. **DD** 342.669/00264; 346.690200264.

CN/0576-3835
PROCEEDINGS OF THE STANDING SENATE COMMITTEE ON LEGAL AND CONSTITUTIONAL AFFAIRS. (PROCEEDINGS OF THE STANDING SENATE COMMITTEE ON LEGAL AND CONSTITUTIONAL AFFAIRS. DELIBERATIONS DU COMITE SENATORIAL PERMANENT DES AFFAIRES JURIDIQUES ET CONSTITUTIONNELLES.). **Main/Corp** Canada. Parliament. Senate. Standing Committee on Legal and Constitutional Affairs. **VFOAT** Deliberations du Comite Senatorial Permanent des Affaires Juridiques et Constitutionnelles. **VAT** Proceedings of the Senate Committee on Legal and Constitutional Affairs. (Feb. 13 1969)-. Proceedings. English (French). ir. 2.50Can$ (single issue) Canada; 3.00Can$ (single issue) other. Canada Communication Group Publishers, Order Processing, Ottawa Ontario K1A 0S9 Canada. **Tel** (819)956-4800, (819)956-4802. ***Absorbed*** *Canada. Parlement. Senat. Comite Permanent des Aaffaires Juridiques et Cconstitutionnelles. Deliberations du Comite Seneatorial Permanent des Affaires Juridiques et Constitutionnelles., 0576-3827.*

IT
QUADERNI COSTITUZIONALI. (19??)-. Periodical. Italian. tq. L80000.00 Italy; L120000.00 (surface mail), L140000.00 (airmail) other. Societa Editrice il Mulino, Strada Maggiore 37, 40125 Bologna Italy. **Tel** 011 39 51 256011, FAX 011 39 51 256034. **DD** 342.45; 344.502.
Ind/Abst PAIS Foreign Lang. Index (1987-); PAIS Int. Print.

IT/0486-0373
RASSEGNA PARLAMENTARE. **Added/Corp** Istituto per la Documatazione e Gli Studi Legislativi. (1959)-. Periodical. Italian. qt. L30000 Italy; L63000 other. Istituto Doc Legislativa Palazzo Grazioli, Via del Plebissito 102, 00186 Rome Italy. **Tel** 39 6 6793449. **Bk Rev. Ad Acc. Circ:** 2,000 (ctrl).
Desc: Parliamentary and constitutional law.

US/0899-0875
RECENT TITLES IN LAW FOR THE SUBJECT SPECIALIST. CONSTITUTIONAL LAW, HUMAN RIGHTS, AND CITIZENSHIP. (RECENT TITLES IN LAW FOR THE SUBJECT SPECIALIST. CONSTITUTIIONAL LAW, HUMAN RIGHTS, AND CITIZENSHIP.). [Recent titles law subj. spec., Const. law human rights citizensh.]. **VFOAT** Constitutional Law, Human Rights, and Citizenship. Vol. 5, No. 1 (Jan.-Mar. 1988)-. English. qt. $85.00. William S. Hein & Company Inc., 1285 Main Street, Buffalo NY 14209. **Tel** (716)882-2600, (800)828-7571, FAX (716)883-8100, telex 91-209 WM S HEIN BUF. **DD** 016. ***Continues*** *National Legal Bibliography. Subject Area List. Constitutional Law, Human Rights and Citizenship, 8755-7983.*

GW
RECHT IM AMT, DAS. Vol. 1 (April 1954)-. Periodical. German. mo. Hermann Luchterhand Verlag, Postfach 2352, D 56513 Neuwied Germany. **Tel** 011 49 2631 8010.

FR/0753-0759
RECUEIL DES ACTES ADMINISTRATIFS DE LA PREFECTURE DE LA REUNION. **Main/Corp** Reunion (Region). Prefecture. **VFOAT** Recueil des Actes Administratifs. French. mo. 20F. Imprimerie Departementale Cour du Secretariat General, 2 EME Bureau Avenue de la Victoire, 97-488 Saint-Denis Reunion. **DD** 348.69/81045/05; 346.981084505. ***Continues*** *Reunion (Region). Prefecture. Recueil des Actes Administratifs.*

US/0275-3529
RELIGIOUS FREEDOM REPORTER. (RELIGIOUS FREEDOM REPORTER : A SERVICE OF THE CENTER FOR LAW AND RELIGIOUS FREEDOM.). [Relig. freedom rep.]. **Added/Corp** Christian Legal Society. Center for Law and Religious Freedom. **VFOAT** RFR. Vol. 1, No. 1 (Jan. 1981)-. Periodical. English. mo. $125.00 (one year), $220.00 (two year), $300.00 (three year). Church & State Resource Center, PO Box 505, Campbell University, Buies Creek NC 27506. **Tel** (910)893-1804, FAX (910)893-1805. **ED** Lynn R. Buzzard. **LC** KF4783.A59; R44. **DD** 342.73/0852/02648; 347.30285202648. Index available in last issue of volume--attached (December). cum. index. **Bk Rev. Circ:** 300.
Desc: Provides coverage of pending and decided state and federal cases, new state and federal legislation and regulation, law review articles, books and other resources related to religious freedom, church-state law, and collateral issues. Includes indexes by state, case name and topic.
Ind/Abst Leg. Resour. Index; LegalTrac (1990-).

Law —Constitutional Law

BL/0034-7191
REVISTA BRASILEIRA DE ESTUDOS POLITICOS. See Political Science.

SP/0210-7562
REVISTA DE DERECHO POLITICO.
Added/Corp Universidad Nacional de Educacion a Distancia. (19??)-. Periodical. Spanish. Four times a year. 5347ptas Spain; 6000ptas other;. Libreria Marcial Pons, Tamayo y Baus 7, 28004 Madrid Spain. **Tel** 011 34 1 3194254. **LC** K19; .D447. **DD** 342.46/005; 344.602005. cum. index.
Ind/Abst Int. Polit. Sci. Abstr.; PAIS Int. Print.

SP/0214-6185
REVISTA DEL CENTRO DE ESTUDIOS CONSTITUCIONALES. (1988)-. Spanish. qt. 4500ptas Spain; $59.00 (airmail) other. Centro de Estudios Constitucionales, Calle Fuencarial 45 6A, 28071 Madrid Spain. **Tel** 011 34 1 5325069, 011 34 1 5316430.
Ind/Abst Int. Bibliogr. Sociol.

SP/0211-5743
REVISTA ESPANOLA DE DERECHO CONSTITUCIONAL. [Rev. esp. derecho const.].
Added/Corp Centro de Estudios Constitucionales. Vol. 1, No. 1 (Jan./April 1981)-. Periodical. Spanish. Three times a year. $59.00. Centro de Estudios Constitucionales, Calle Fuencarial 45 6A, 28071 Madrid Spain. **Tel** 011 34 1 5325069, 011 34 1 5316430. **LC** K19; .E82. **DD** 342.46/005; 344.602005.
Ind/Abst Int. Polit. Sci. Abstr.

UY/0256-0151
REVISTA URUGUAYA DE DERECHO CONSTITUCIONAL Y POLITICO. [Rev. urug. derecho const. polit.]. Vol. 1, No. 1 (June/July 1984)-. Spanish. bm. Revista Uruguaya de Derecho, Reconquista 338 Apartado 705, Montevideo Uruguay. **Tel** 951853. **LC** K19; .U78. **DD** 342.895/005; 348.950205.

UY
REVISTA URUGUAYA DE ESTUDIOS ADMINISTRATIVOS. Vol. 1 (Jan./June 1977)-. Periodical. Spanish. sa. ACALI Editorial Ltda, Montevideo Uruguay. **LC** K19; .U8. **DD** 342.895/06.

DM
REVUE BENINOISE DE SCIENCES JURIDIQUES ET ADMINISTRATIVES.
Periodical. French. Universite Nationale du Benin, B P No 526, Cotonou Republique Populaire du Benin Dahomey. **LC** K21; .B43. **DD** 349.66/83/05; 346.683005.

UK/1105-1590
REVUE EUROPEENNE DE DROIT PUBLIC. Added/Corp Universite de Paris I: Pantheon-Sorbonne. ERASMUS (Organization). **VFOAT** European Review of Public Law; Eur. Zeitschrift des Offentl. Rechts; Rivista Europea di Diritto Pubblico; REDP/ERPL. **VAT** REDP ERPL. Vol. 1 No. 1 (Summer 1989)-. Periodical. English (French, German and Italian). Twice a year (Summer & Winter). Price varies. Esperia Publications Ltd., 38D Orsett Terrace Bayswater, London W2 6AJ England. **LC** K21; .E96. **DD** 349.4/05; 344.005.
Ind/Abst PAIS Int. Print (1991-).

FR/0763-1219
REVUE FRANCAISE DE DROIT ADMINISTRATIF. No. 1 (Jan./Feb. 1985)-. Periodical. French. bm. 670.00F (France); 775.00F (other). Dalloz, 35 rue Tournefort, 75240 Paris Cedex 05 France. **Tel** 011 33 1 40515434 or 40515454, FAX 45 87 37 48, telex 206 446 F. [CCC].
Ind/Abst Index Foreign Leg. Per.; Int. Polit. Sci. Abstr.

FR
REVUE FRANCAISE DE DROIT CONSTITUTIONNEL. VFOAT Droit Constitutionnel. (1990)-. Periodical. French. qt. 510.00F France; 580.00 other. Presses Universitaires de France, Department des Revues, 14 Avenue du Bois de l'Epine, BP 90, 91003 Evry Cedex France. **Tel** (1)60 77 82 05, FAX (1) 60 79 20 45, telex PUF 600 474 F.

IT/0557-1464
RIVISTA TRIMESTRALE DI DIRITTO PUBBLICO. (1951)-. Periodical. Italian. Four times a year. L140000.00 Italy; L210000.00 other. Giuffre Editore SPA, Via Busto Arsizio 40, 20151 Milan Italy. **Tel** 011 398 2 38089200. **ED** Giovanni Miele and Massimo Serero Giammimi. **Bk Rev. Ad Acc. Circ:** 2,100.
Desc: The magazine publishes the most significant contribution from all the branches of public law and administrative science.
Ind/Abst Index Foreign Leg. Per.; Int. Bibliogr. Sociol.

US/0749-6613
SECTION OF ADMINISTRATIVE LAW DIRECTORY. Main/Corp American Bar Association. Section of Administrative Law. (19??)-. English. an. American Bar Association, 750 North Lake Shore Drive, Chicago IL 60611. **Tel** (312)988-5522, (312)988-5241, FAX (312)988-5528, telex 270593. **LC** KF195.A4; A45.

DD 342.73/06/025; 347.3026025. **Continues** American Bar Association. Section of Administrative Law. Directory, 0569-308X.

XR/0139-6005
SPRAVNI PRAVO. [Sprav. pravo]. Began in 1968. Periodical. Czech. ir (8 no. a year). **LC** K23; .P7. **DD** 342.437/06; 344.37026.
Ind/Abst Energy Res. Abstr. (July 1979-).

GW/0038-884X
STAAT, DER. [Staat]. (1962)-. Periodical. German. qt. DM158.30 Germany; DM162.40 other. Duncker und Humblot Verlag, Postfach 410329, D-12113 Berlin Germany. **Tel** 011 49 30 79000612, 011 49 30 79000613. **[CCC].** Index Available, published separately, free-automatically sent.
Ind/Abst Energy Res. Abstr. (July 1981-); Index Foreign Leg. Per.; Int. Polit. Sci. Abstr.

US
STATE CONSTITUTIONAL LAW - CASES AND MATERIALS. (19??)-. English. ir. $30.00 (main volumes); $7.00 (supplement only). Advisory Committee of Intergovernment Relations, 800 K Street Northwest, Suite 450, S Building, Washington DC 20575. **Tel** (202)653-5640.

GR
SYNTAGMA, TO. VFOAT Constitution; Verfassung. Vol. 1, No. 1 (Jan./Feb. 1975)-. Periodical. Greek, Modern. qt. $35.00. Solonos 69, Athens Greece.

US
TEXAS ELECTION LAW, INCLUDING POLITICAL CALENDER, CONSTITUTIONAL PROVISIONS, ELECTION CODE, AND STATUTES.
Main/Corp Texas. (19??)-. English. Hart Graphics Inc, PO Box 968, Austin TX 78767. **LC** KFT1620.A29; T49. **DD** 342.746/07.

IT
TRIBUNALI AMMINISTRATIVI REGIONALI, I. Yearly V. 1- Jan. 1975-. Periodical. Italian. mo. L50000. Casa Editrice Italedi, Piazza Cavour 19, 00193 Rome Italy. **Tel** 011 39 6 3210803.

GW/0506-7286
VERFASSUNG UND RECHT IN UBERSEE. [Verfass. recht Ubersee]. Vol. 1 (1968)-. Periodical. German. qt. DM118.00 Germany; DM122.40 other. Nomos Verlagsgesellschaft, Postfach 610, D-76484 Baden Baden Germany. **Tel** 011 49 7221 21040. **ED** Brun-Otto Bryde, Philip Kunig, and Karl-Andreas Hernekamp. **DD** 342/.005. **[CCC].** Index available. **Bk Rev. Ad Acc.**
Ind/Abst Index Foreign Leg. Per.; Int. Bibliogr. Sociol.; Int. Polit. Sci. Abstr.

GW
VERZEICHNIS RHEINLAND-PFALZISCHER RECHTS- UND VERWALTUNGSVORSCHRIFTEN.
German. an. DM15.00. Ministerium der Justiz, Ernst-Ludwig-Strasse 3, W-6500 Mainz Germany. **LC** KKC616.A24; V47. **DD** 342.43/43/06; 344.343026.

US
WISCONSIN ADMINISTRATIVE LAW DIGEST, THE. (19??)-. English. an. Law Reporter Company, 209 Michigan Avenue, PO Box 270, Crystal Falls MI 49920-1312. **Tel** (906)875-6970. **LC** KFW2840.A59; W57. **DD** 342.775/06/02638; 347.7502602638.

AU
ZEITSCHRIFT FUER VERWALTUNG.
(1976)-. Periodical. German. Six times a year. S3100.00. Verlag Orac GmbH & Co., Schoenbrunner Str 59 61, A-1050 Vienna Austria. **Tel** 011 43 1 5130651. **ED** Heinz-Peter Rill. **DD** 342/.436/0605. **Bk Rev. Ad Acc. Circ:** 5,000 (ctrl).
Desc: Essays on administrative law and its application, review and index of jurisdiction.

CORPORATE LAW

US
ABA SECTION OF TAXATION ANNUAL ADVANCED STUDY SESSIONS, ADVANCED TAX PLANNING FOR CLOSELY HELD BUSINESS : ALI-ABA COURSE OF STUDY, MATERIALS. VFOAT A.B.A. Section of Taxation Annual Advanced Study Sessions, Advanced Tax Planning for Closely Held Business; Advanced Tax Planning for Closely Held Business; ALI-ABA Course of Study, Materials. English. an. American Law Institute, 4025 Chestnut Street, Philadelphia PA 19104-3099. **Tel** (215)243-1661, (800)253-6397, FAX (215)243-1664. **LC** KF6484.Z9; A23. **DD** 343.7306/7; 347.30367.

US/0895-9544
ACCA DOCKET. (ACCA DOCKET : JOURNAL OF THE AMERICAN CORPORATE COUNSEL ASSOCIATION.). [ACCA docket]. **Added/Corp** American Corporate Counsel Association. **VAT** American Corporate Counsel Association Docket. (198?)-. Corporate Report. English. Six times a year (Jan., Mar., May, July, Sept., Dec.). $125.00. American Corporate Counsel Association, 1225 Connecticut Avenue Northwest, Suite 302, Washington DC 20036. **Tel** (202)296-4523, (202)296-4522, FAX (202)331-7454. **ED** Deneen Stambone. **DD** 346. **Bk Rev. Ad Acc. Adv Mgr:** Jeffrey Logel, **Tel** (202)296-4522. **Pr Rev. Circ:** 10,000. available on an online database from WESTLAW.
Desc: Issues of import to in-house counsel.

US/0883-4407
ACQUISITIONS AND MERGERS IN A TROUBLED ENVIRONMENT. *Title Change.* [Acquis. mergers]. **Added/Corp** Practising Law Institute. (19??)-(19??). English. an. Practising Law Institute, 810 Seventh Avenue, New York NY 10019-5818. **Tel** (212)765-5700, FAX (212)581-4670 general correspondence, (212)265-4742 orders and billing inquiries. **LC** KF1477.Z9; A273. **DD** 346.73/06626; 347.3066626. Index available. **Continued by** Acquisitions and Mergers in a Troubled Environment.

UK
ADMINISTRATOR (LONDON, ENGLAND). (ADMINISTRATOR.). **Added/Corp** Institute of Chartered Secretaries and Administrators. Vol. 2, No. 1 (Jan. 1982)-. Periodical. English. Eleven times a year. £34.00 UK; £45.00 other. Institute of Chartered Secretaries & Administrators, 16 Park Crescent, London W1N 4AH England. **Tel** 011 44 71 5804741, FAX 011 44 71 3231132, telex 268350. **Continues** Professional Administration.

US/0191-1651
ALI-ABA COURSE OF STUDY. ADVANCED BUSINESS TAX PLANNING : MATERIALS. VAT American Law Institute-American Bar Association Course of Study. Advanced Business Tax Planning: Materials. English. American Law Institute, 4025 Chestnut Street, Philadelphia PA 19104-3099. **Tel** (215)243-1661, (800)253-6397, FAX (215)243-1664. **LC** KF6450.Z9; A214. **DD** 343/.73/068.

US
ALI-ABA COURSE OF STUDY. ADVANCED TAX PLANNING FOR THE CLOSELY HELD BUSINESS : MATERIALS. Main/Conf I-ABA Course of Study: Advanced Tax Planning for the Closely Held Business. **Added/Corp** American Law Institute-American Bar Association Committee on Continuing Professional Education. Utah State Bar. Tax Section. (19??)-. English. American Law Institute, 4025 Chestnut Street, Philadelphia PA 19104-3099. **Tel** (215)243-1661, (800)253-6397, FAX (215)243-1664. **LC** PAR.

US/0193-6905
ALI-ABA COURSE OF STUDY. BUSINESS TAX PLANNING : MATERIALS. VFOAT ALI-ABA Course of Study. Advanced Business Tax Planning. **VAT** American Law Institute-American Bar Association Course of Study. Business Tax Planning: Materials. Periodical. English. American Law Institute, 4025 Chestnut Street, Philadelphia PA 19104-3099. **Tel** (215)243-1661, (800)253-6397, FAX (215)243-1664. **LC** KF6450.Z9; A215. **DD** 343/.73/066.

US/0190-9665
ALI-ABA COURSE OF STUDY. BUSINESS WORKOUTS: MATERIALS.
Main/Corp ALI-ABA Course of Study: Business Workouts. **Added/Corp** American Law Institute-American Bar Association Committee on Continuing Professional Education. Emory University. School of Law. ALI-ABA Course of Study: Business Workouts. Business Workouts: Materials. **VFOAT** Business Workouts: Materials. **VAT** American Law Institute-American Bar Association Course of Study. Business Workouts: Materials. (19??)-. English. American Law Institute, 4025 Chestnut Street, Philadelphia PA 19104-3099. **Tel** (215)243-1661, (800)253-6397, FAX (215)243-1664. **LC** KF1544.Z9; A17. **DD** 346/.73/077.

US/0191-2178
ALI-ABA COURSE OF STUDY. FRAUD, INSIDE INFORMATION, AND FIDUCIARY DUTY UNDER RULE 10B-5 :
MATERIALS. VAT American Law Institute-American Bar Association Course of Study. Fraud, Inside Information, and Fiduciary Duty under Rule 10B-5: Materials. English. American Law Institute, 4025 Chestnut Street, Philadelphia PA 19104-3099. **Tel** (215)243-1661, (800)253-6397, FAX (215)243-1664. **LC** KF9369; .A93. **DD** 345/.73/026.

US/0271-1370
ALI-ABA COURSE OF STUDY. QUALIFIED PLANS, INSURANCE, AND PROFESSIONAL CORPORATIONS : MATERIALS. **VAT** American Law Institute, American Bar Association Course of Study. Qualified Plans, Insurance, and Professional Corporations: Materials. English. an. American Law Institute, 4025 Chestnut Street, Philadelphia PA 19104-3099. **Tel** (215)243-1661, (800)253-6397, FAX (215)243-1664. **LC** KF3512.Z9; A15. **DD** 343.7305/2; 347.30352.

US/0190-9355
ALI-ABA COURSE OF STUDY. TAX AND BUSINESS PLANNING FOR THE SMALL BUT GROWING BUSINESS : MATERIALS. **VAT** American Law Institute-American Bar Association Course of Study. Tax and Business Planning for the Small but Growing Business: Materials. English. American Law Institute, 4025 Chestnut Street, Philadelphia PA 19104-3099. **Tel** (215)243-1661, (800)253-6397, FAX (215)243-1664. **LC** KF6491.Z9; A18. **DD** 343/.73/068.

US/0191-2399
ALI-ABA COURSE OF STUDY. THE ECONOMICS OF ANTITRUST : MATERIALS. **VAT** American Law Institute-American Bar Association Course of Study. The Economics of Antitrust: Materials. English. American Law Institute, 4025 Chestnut Street, Philadelphia PA 19104-3099. **Tel** (215)243-1661, (800)253-6397, FAX (215)243-1664. **LC** HD2731; .A17A. **DD** 338.4/7/343072.

US/0191-3697
ALI-ABA SYMPOSIUM. REGIONAL SYMPOSIUM ON THE STRUCTURE AND GOVERNANCE OF CORPORATIONS : MATERIALS. **VAT** American Law Institute-American Bar Association Symposium. Regional Symposium on the Structure and Governance of Corporations: Materials. English. American Law Institute, 4025 Chestnut Street, Philadelphia PA 19104-3099. **Tel** (215)243-1661, (800)253-6397, FAX (215)243-1664. **LC** KF1414.3; A18. **DD** 346/.73/066.

US/0736-3613
ALTERNATIVES TO THE HIGH COST OF LITIGATION. (ALTERNATIVES TO THE HIGH COST OF LITIGATION / LAW & BUSINESS INC. / CENTER FOR PUBLIC RESOURCES.). **Added/Corp** Center for Public Resources (New York, N.Y.). **VFOAT** Alternatives. Vol. 1, No. 1 (Jan. 1983)-. Periodical. English. Twelve times a year. $175.00. Center for Public Resources, 366 Madison Avenue, New York NY 10017. **Tel** (212)949-6490, FAX (212)949-8859. **ED** Deborah Jacobs. **LC** KF9084.A15; A44. **DD** 347.73/77; 347.30777. **Bk Rev. Circ:** 4,000 (ctrl).
Desc: Information on Alternative Dispute Resolution of Business disputes.

US/0002-7766
AMERICAN BUSINESS LAW JOURNAL. [Am. Bus. Law J.]. **Added/Corp** American Business Law Association. (1963)-. Periodical. English. Four times a year (Feb., May, Aug., Nov.). $28.00 (institutions); (individuals must order membership). American Business Law Journal, C/O G. J. Naples, Marquette University, Straz Hall, Milwaukee WI 53233. **Tel** (414)288-7331. **ED** Michael Phillips. **LC** K1; .M4. **DD** 346.73/07/05; 347.306705. **CODEN** ABLJAN. Index available. cum. index. **Bk Rev. Ad Acc. Pr Rev. Circ:** 2,300 (ctrl). available on microfilm and microfiche from University Microfilms International (UMI). Documents available from The Genuine Article, UMI Article Clearinghouse. ***Continues*** *American Business Law Association. Bulletin - American Business Law Association.*
Desc: Articles address contemporary legal problems related to business such as contracts, anti-trust and 'whistle-blowers'.
Ind/Abst ABI/INFORM Glob. Ed.; ABI Inform Ondisc (Winter 1972-); Acad. Ind. [Computer File] (1992-); Acad. Search (Jan. 1994-); Bowne Dig. Corp. Sec. Lawyers; Bus. ASAP (1992-) [Full Txt.]; Bus. Index (1985-); Bus. Period. Index; Bus. Source (Jul. 1993-); Curr. Contents Soc. Behav. Sci.; Curr. Law Index (1980-); Expand. Acad. Index (1984-); Fed. Tax Artic.; Gen. BusinessFile (1985-); Gen. Period. Index (1985-); Index Leg. Period.; INFO-SOUTH Abstr.; Leg. Resour. Index (1980-); LegalTrac (1980-); Mag. Search; Newsp. Period. Abstr. (1991-); Res. Alert [Full Cov.]; Risk Abstr. (19??-19??); Soc. Sci. Cit. Index [Full Cov.]; Trade Ind. Index (1981-?); Wilson Bus. Abstr.

US/0887-1337
ANALYSIS OF KEY SEC NO-ACTION LETTERS. [Anal. key SEC no-action lett.]. **Added/Corp** United States. Securities and Exchange Commission. Haft, Robert J. Key SEC No-Action Letters. **VFOAT** Key SEC No-Action Letters. **VAT** Analysis of Key Securities and Exchange Commission No Action Letters. (1985/86)-. English. an. $97.50. Clark Boardman Callaghan, 155 Pfingsten Road, Deerfield IL 60015. **Tel** (800)323-8067. **ED** Robert J Haft. **LC** KF1439; .A79. **DD** 346.73/0666; 347.306666.

US/1059-3969
ANDREWS' PROFESSIONAL LIABILITY LITIGATION REPORTER. **See** Law-Banking Law.

US/0194-1127
ANNUAL ADVANCED ANTITRUST WORKSHOP. **Main/Corp** Advanced Antitrust Workshop. 1970-. English. an. Practising Law Institute, 810 Seventh Avenue, New York NY 10019-5818. **Tel** (212)765-5700, FAX (212)581-4670 general correspondence, (212)265-4742 orders and billing inquiries. **LC** KF1649.3; .A34. **DD** 343.73/072.

US/0739-1323
ANNUAL FORUM - AMERICAN BAR ASSOCIATION. FORUM COMMITTEE ON FRANCHISING. ANNUAL FORUM. (ANNUAL FORUM / FORUM COMMITTEE ON FRANCHISING.). [Annu. forum - Am. Bar Assoc., Forum Comm. Franch., Annu. Forum]. **Main/Corp** American Bar Association. Forum Committee on Franchising. Annual Forum. (19??)-. English. an. American Bar Association, 750 North Lake Shore Drive, Chicago IL 60611. **Tel** (312)988-5522, (312)988-5241, FAX (312)988-5528, telex 270593. **LC** KF2023.A75; A44. **DD** 343.73/0887; 347.303887.

US/0195-3680
ANNUAL INSTITUTE FOR CORPORATE COUNSEL. **Main/Corp** Institute for Corporate Counsel. 1st-. English. an. Practising Law Institute, 810 Seventh Avenue, New York NY 10019-5818. **Tel** (212)765-5700, FAX (212)581-4670 general correspondence, (212)265-4742 orders and billing inquiries. **LC** KF1425.Z9; I57. **DD** 346.73/0664. Index available. cum. index. **Bk Rev.**

US
ANNUAL INSTITUTE ON ACQUISITIONS & TAKEOVERS : [PROCEEDINGS]. **VFOAT** Annual Institute on Acquisitions and Takeovers; Acquisitions & Takeovers; Acquisitions and Takeovers. (19??)-. English. an. $47.25. Prentice-Hall Law and Business, 270 Sylvan Avenue, Englewood Cliffs NJ 07632. **Tel** (800)223-0231, (201)894-8538, FAX (201)894-8666. **LC** KF1477.Z9; I565. **DD** 346.73/06626; 347.3066626.

US/0271-3489
ANNUAL LICENSING LAW AND BUSINESS INSTITUTE. [Annu. Licens. Law Bus. Inst.]. **Main/Corp** Licensing Law and Business Institute. 1st- 1979-. English. an. Clark Boardman Callaghan, 155 Pfingsten Road, Deerfield IL 60015. **Tel** (800)323-8067. **LC** KF3145.A75; L45. **DD** 346.7304/8.

AT
ANNUAL REPORT FOR THE YEAR ... / COMMISSIONER FOR CORPORATE AFFAIRS. **Main/Corp** Tasmania. Corporate Affairs Office. 1st (1982/1983)-. English. an. **LC** HD2930.Z8; T377a. **DD** 354.9460082.

CN
ANNUAL REPORT FOR THE YEAR ENDED MARCH 31 ... / RESTRICTIVE TRADE PRACTICES COMMISSION (CANADA). **Main/Corp** Canada. Restrictive Trade Practices Commission. 1981-. English. an. **LC** KE1639.A2; R473. **DD** 354.710082.

AT/0314-0520
ANNUAL REPORT / TRADE PRACTICES COMMISSION. **Main/Corp** Australia. Trade Practices Commission. (19??)-. Government Publication. English. an. Australian Government Publishing Service, GPO Box 84, Canberra ACT 2601 Australia. **Tel** 011 61 6 2954411, FAX 011 61 6 2954455. **DD** 354.940082/6.

US
ANTITRUST ADVISOR. **Added/Corp** Shepard's, Inc. of Colorado Springs. Shepard's/McGraw-Hill. 1st Ed. (1971)-. English. ir. $95.00 (Vol. 1), $42.00 (1991 pocket part). Shepards McGraw-Hill Inc, 555 Middle Creek Parkway, PO Box 35300, Colorado Springs CO 80935-3530. **Tel** (719)488-3000, FAX (800)525-0053. **Bk Rev. Ad Acc.**
Desc: Includes complete discussion of the Sherman Act, the Clayton Act, the Robinson-Patman Act and the Federal Trade Commission Act organized to help practitioners.

US
ANTITRUST & COMMERCE REPORT. **Added/Corp** National Association of Attorneys General. **VFOAT** Antitrust and Commerce Report. (July 1983)-. Periodical. English. mo. $145.00. National Association of Attorneys General, 444 North Capitol Street, Suite 339, Washington DC 20001. **Tel** (202)434-8000. **LC** KF1650; .A58. **DD** 343.73/072; 347.30372. ***Continues*** *Antitrust Report (National Association of Attorneys General).*

US/0003-6021
ANTITRUST & TRADE REGULATION REPORT. (BNA ANTITRUST & TRADE REGULATION REPORT.). **Main/Corp** Bureau of National Affairs (Washington, D.C.). **VFOAT** Antitrust and Trade Regulation Report; B.N.A. Antitrust and Trade Regulation Report. **VAT** Bureau of National Affairs Antitrust and Trade Regulation Report. Vol. 1 (July 1961)-. English. wk (except the Thursday after Labor Day and the last Thursday in December). $1020.00. Bureau of National Affairs Inc., 9435 Key West Avenue, Rockville MD 20850. **Tel** (800)372-1033, (301)258-1033, FAX (301)948-5823. **(Subscription address:** 9435 Key West Avenue, Rockville MD 20850; telephone: FAX (301)948-5823**) ED** Sheldon B Richman. **[CCC].** available on an online database (file 655/Full-Text) from DIALOG.
Desc: Covers significant competition and deceptive trade practice law developments on the federal, state and international levels.

US/0003-603X
ANTITRUST BULLETIN. [Antitrust bull.]. Vol. 1 (April 1955)-. Bulletin. English. qt (published seasonally). $85.00. Federal Legal Publications Inc, 157 Chambers Street, New York NY 10007. **Tel** (212)619-4949, FAX (212)608-3141. **ED** William Curran. **LC** K1; .N9. **DD** 343.73/072/05. **CODEN** ATBUAU. Index available. cum. index. **Bk Rev. Ad Acc. Pr Rev. Circ:** 4,000. available on microfilm and microfiche from University Microfilms International (UMI); available on an online database (file 648/Full-Text) from DIALOG. Documents available from UMI Article Clearinghouse, UMI Article Clearinghouse.
Desc: The only professional journal including domestic and foreign antitrust legal issues and industrial organization economics.
Ind/Abst ABI/INFORM Glob. Ed.; ABI Inform Ondisc (Winter 1974-); Acad. Search (July 1993-); Account. Art.; Bowne Dig. Corp. Sec. Lawyers; Bus. ASAP (1992-) [Full Txt.]; Bus. Index (1985-); Bus. Source (Jul. 1993-); Contents Recent Econ. J.; Curr. Law Index (1980-); Econ. Lit. Index; Gen. BusinessFile (1985-); Gen. Period. Index (1985-); Index Leg. Period.; INFO-SOUTH Abstr.; J. Econ. Lit.; Leg. Resour. Index (1980-); LegalTrac (1980-); Mag. Search; PAIS Int. Print; Selec. Coop. Index Manage. Period; Trade Ind. Index (1981-?).

US/0162-7996
ANTITRUST (CHICAGO, ILL.). (ANTITRUST.). [Antitrust]. **Added/Corp** American Bar Association. Section of Antitrust Law. Vol. 1, No. 1 (Fall 1986)-. Periodical. English. Three times a year. $30.00. American Bar Association, 750 North Lake Shore Drive, Chicago IL 60611. **Tel** (312)988-5522, (312)988-5241, FAX (312)988-5528, telex 270593. **LC** KF1632; .A56. **DD** 343.73/072; 347.30372. ***Continues*** *Antitrust, 0162-7996.*
Ind/Abst Leg. Resour. Index (1980-?); PAIS Int. Print.

US
ANTITRUST DIVISION MANUAL. **Main/Corp** United States. Dept. of Justice. Antitrust Division. (1979)-. Government Publication. English. ir. $40.00. Superintendent of Documents, US Government Printing Office, Washington DC 20402. **Tel** (202)275-3328, FAX (202)786-2377.
Desc: A guide to the operating policies and procedures of the Antitrust Division of the United States Department of Justice. Devoted to the suggested methods of conducting investigations and litigation that the division has employed in the past.

US/0891-8546
ANTITRUST FREEDOM OF INFORMATION LOG. [Antitrust freedom inf. log]. **Added/Corp** Washington Regulatory Reporting Associates. **VFOAT** FTC Watch, Antitrust Freedom of Information Log. **VAT** Federal Trade Commission Watch, Antitrust Freedom of Information Log. (1986)-. Periodical. English. Forty-six times a year. $335.00. Washington Regulatory Reporting Association, PO Box 356, Basye VA 22810. **Tel** (703)856-2216. **LC** KF1632; .A565. **DD** 343.73/0721/05; 347.30372105. **[CCC].** available on an online database (file 636/Full-Text) from DIALOG.
Desc: A summary of Freedom Information Act requests received by the Antitrust Division of the Department of Justice. Each entry lists the name and address of the person requesting information, the information control number, the date the information was filed, and the subject of the file.
Ind/Abst PTS Newsl. Database [Full Txt.].

US/0003-6048
ANTITRUST LAW & ECONOMICS REVIEW. [Antitrust law econ. rev.]. **VAT** Antitrust Law and Economics Review. Vol. 1 (July/Aug. 1967)-. Periodical. English. Four times a year. $98.50. Antitrust Law and Economic Review Inc., PO Box 3532, Vero Beach FL 32964. **Tel** FAX (407)461-6007. **LC** K1.; N912. Documents available from UMI Article Clearinghouse.
Ind/Abst ABI/INFORM Glob. Ed.; ABI Inform Ondisc (Winter 1970); Acad. Search (July 1992-); Bus. Index; Bus. Period. Index (1980-); Bus. Source (Jul. 1993-); Contents Recent Econ. J.; Curr. Law Index; Gen. BusinessFile; Gen. Period. Index; Index Leg. Period.; INFO-SOUTH Abstr.; Leg. Resour. Index (1974-); LegalTrac; Mag. Search; PAIS Int. Print; Wilson Bus. Abstr.

US/0738-5919
ANTITRUST LAW HANDBOOK. **Added/Corp** Clark Boardman Company. **VFOAT** Antitrust Law Hand Book. (1984)-. English. an. $85.00. Clark Boardman Callaghan, 155 Pfingsten Road, Deerfield IL 60015. **Tel** (800)323-8067. **LC** KF1632.5; .A57. **DD** 343.73/072; 347.30372.

US/0003-6056
ANTITRUST LAW JOURNAL. [Antitrust law j.]. **Added/Corp** American Bar Association. Section of Antitrust Law. **VFOAT** A.B.A. Antitrust L.J.; ABA Antitrust LJ. (1966)-. Periodical. English. Three times a year. $30.00. American Bar Association, 750 North Lake Shore Drive, Chicago IL 60611. **Tel** (312)988-5522, (312)988-5241, FAX (312)988-5528, telex 270593. **LC** K1; .M388. cum. index. available on an online database (file 648/Full-Text) from DIALOG. ***Continues** Section of Antitrust Law.*
Ind/Abst Bus. ASAP (1992-) [Full Txt.]; Bus. Index (1985-); Fed. Tax Artic.; Gen. BusinessFile (1985-); Index Leg. Period.; Leg. Resour. Index (1980-); LegalTrac (1980-); Trade Ind. Index (1981-?).

US
ANTITRUST LAWS AND TRADE REGULATION. English. bm. $455.00. Matthew Bender & Company Inc., 1275 Broadway, Albany NY 12204. **Tel** (800)833-9844, (518)487-3000.

US/1057-8919
ANTITRUST REPORT (WASHINGTON, D.C. 1991). (ANTITRUST REPORT.). [Antitrust rep.]. **Added/Corp** National Association of Attorneys General. Vol. 18, No. 1 (Dec. 1990/Jan. 1991)-. Periodical. English. bm. National Association of Attorneys General, 444 North Capitol Street, Suite 339, Washington DC 20001. **Tel** (202)434-8000. **LC** KF1650; .A58. **DD** 343.73/027; 347.30372. ***Continues** Antitrust & Commerce Report.*

AT/0310-1053
AUSTRALIAN BUSINESS LAW REVIEW. [Aust. bus. law rev.]. Vol. 1 (Mar. 1973)-. Periodical. English. bm. 195.00Aus$ (volume 20, 1992). The Law Book Company Limited, 44-50 Waterloo Road, North Ryde New South Wales, 2113 Australia. **Tel** 011 61 2 8870177, FAX 011 61 2 8887240, telex ASBOOK 27445. **ED** Jeff Waincymer and Robert Baxt. **LC** K1; .U77. **DD** 346/.94/0705. **CODEN** ABRVDO. available on microfilm and microfiche from University Microfilms International (UMI). Documents available from UMI Article Clearinghouse.
Desc: Commentary on all major areas of commercial law and business practice.
Ind/Abst ABI/INFORM Glob. Ed.; ABI Inform Ondisc (Feb. 1980-); APAIS, Aust. Public Aff. Inf. Ser. (1973-); Aust. Leg. Mon. Dig.; Curr. Law Index (1980-); Gen. BusinessFile (1992-); Index Leg. Period.; Leg. Resour. Index (1980-); LegalTrac (1980-); UMI ABI/Inform--Bus. Period. Ondisc (Aug. 1987-) [Full Txt.].

AT
AUSTRALIAN COMPANY LAW CASES. **Added/Corp** CCH Australia Limited. (1???)-. English. an. 645.00Aus$. CCH Australia Ltd, PO Box 230, North Ryde New South Wales, 2113 Australia. **Tel** 011 61 02 888 2555, FAX 011 61 02 888 7324. **DD** 346.94/066. cum. index.
Desc: Provides reports of Australian company law, securities industry and futures industry decisions plus selected cases of importance from overseas jurisdictions.
Ind/Abst Aust. Leg. Mon. Dig.

AT/0313-8445
AUSTRALIAN COMPANY LAW REPORTS. ***Title Change.*** [Aust. co. law rep.]. Vol. 1 (1976)-(19??). English. an. Butterworths Pty Ltd, 271-273 Lane Cove Road, PO Box 345, North Ryde NSW 2113 Australia. **Tel** 011 61 2 3354444, FAX 011 61 2 3354655. **ED** W.E. Paterson and H.H. Ednie. **DD** 346.94/066/02648; 349.4066602648. ***Continued by** Australian Corporations and Securities Reports.*
Ind/Abst Aust. Leg. Mon. Dig. (?-19??).

AT/1033-7466
AUSTRALIAN CORPORATIONS AND SECURITIES REPORTS. **VFOAT** ACSR. Vol. 1 Pt. 1 (Feb. 9, 1990)-. Periodical. English. ir. 218.00Aus$. Butterworths Pty Ltd, 271-273 Lane Cove Road, PO Box 345, North Ryde NSW 2113 Australia. **Tel** 011 61 2 3354444, FAX 011 61 2 3354655. Index available. **Pr Rev.** ***Continues** Australian Company Law Reports, 0313-8445.*
Ind/Abst Aust. Leg. Mon. Dig.

AT/1037-4124
AUSTRALIAN JOURNAL OF CORPORATE LAW. **Added/Corp** University of Canberra. Centre for National Corporate Law Research. Vol. 1, No. 1 (1991)-. Periodical. English. Three times a year. 140.00Aus$. Butterworths Pty Ltd, 271-273 Lane Cove Road, PO Box 345, North Ryde NSW 2113 Australia. **Tel** 011 61 2 3354444, FAX 011 61 2 3354655.
Desc: Focuses on the system of corporate regulation in Australia, its development and reform.
Ind/Abst Index Leg. Period. (1992-).

IT/0392-257X
BIBLIOGRAFIA IDG. A, DIRITTO COMMERCIALE. [Bibliogr. IDG, A, Diritto commerc.]. **Added/Corp** Istituto per la Documentazione Giuridica. **VFOAT** Diritto Commerciale. (1979)-. Italian. an. L9,000. Giuffre Editore SPA, Via Busto Arsizio 40, 20151 Milan Italy. **Tel** 011 398 2 38089200. **DD** 016.34645/07; 016.3445067.

FR
BIBLIOTHEQUE DE DROIT COMMERCIAL. Vol. 1 (1961)-. Periodical. French. 22 rue Soufflot, Paris 75005 France.
Desc: Offers titles on such topics as corporation organization and function, bankruptcy, copyright, and non-fulfillment of commercial contracts.

US/0896-906X
BOWNE DIGEST FOR CORPORATE & SECURITIES LAWYERS. **See** Law-Abstracting, Bibliographies and Statistics.

UK/0269-0535
BRITISH COMPANY CASES. **Added/Corp** CCH Editions Limited. (1990)-. English. CCH Editions Ltd., Telford Road, Bicester, Oxfordshire OX6 OXD England. **Tel** 011 44 86 925 3300. ***Continues** British Company Law Cases, 0269-0535.*

UK
BRITISH COMPANY LAW & PRACTICE. English. ir. CCH Editions Ltd., Telford Road, Bicester, Oxfordshire OX6 OXD England. **Tel** 011 44 86 925 3300.

US/0887-4751
BROWARD REVIEW. (198?)-. Periodical. English. da. Price varies for law firms. American Lawyer Media, L.P., 600 3rd Avenue, New York NY 10016. **Tel** (212)973-2800. **(Subscription address:** Broward Review, PO Box 14366, Ft. Lauderdale FL 33302**)** ***Continues** Broward Review and Business Record.*

UK
BUCKLEY ON THE COMPANIES ACTS. English. an. £400.00. Butterworth & Co. Ltd. / Kent, England, Borough Green, Sevenoaks Kent TN15 8PH England. **Tel** 011 44 732-884567, FAX 011 44 732-885996. **ED** Sir Leonard Hoffman.
Desc: Reference source on company law. Expands the coverage of relevant legislation, containing the fully-annotated text of not only the Companies Acts but of other Acts such as the Insolvency Act 1986 and more.

US/0885-1034
BUSINESS ACCOUNTING FOR LAWYERS NEWSLETTER / PRACTISING LAW INSTITUTE. [Bus. acc. lawyers newsl.]. **VFOAT** Business Accounting for Lawyers. Vol. 1, No. 1 (May 1984)-. Newsletter. English. Eight times a year. $110.00. Practising Law Institute, 810 Seventh Avenue, New York NY 10019-5818. **Tel** (212)765-5700, FAX (212)581-4670 general correspondence, (212)265-4742 orders and billing inquiries. **ED** Samuel P Gunther. **LC** KF1357.A15; B87. **Circ:** 3,500 (ctrl).

US/0193-4414
BUSINESS ADVOCATE, THE. [Bus. advocate]. Periodical. English. mo. $28.00. US Chamber of Commerce, 1615 H Street NW, Washington DC 20062. **Tel** (800)638-6582, (800)352-1450, FAX (202)887-3430. **ED** Al Holzinger. **LC** KF1409; .B87. **DD** 346.73/066. **Circ:** 200,000.
Desc: Provides in-depth details on regulatory and legislative issues and pending actions that could affect your livelihood.

US/0746-3669
BUSINESS ADVOCATE (WASHINGTON, D.C. : 1983), THE. (THE BUSINESS ADVOCATE : A U.S. CHAMBER OF COMMERCE PUBLICATION.). [Bus. advocate]. Vol. 1, No. 1 (Sept. 26, 1983)-. Periodical. English. bw. The Business Advocate, 4940 Nicholson Street, Kensington MD 20895. **LC** HC101; .W29. **DD** 330.973/005. available on microfilm from University Microfilms International (UMI). ***Continues** Washington Report (Chamber of Commerce of the United States), 0043-0714.*

CN/0825-4982
BUSINESS & THE LAW. [Bus. law]. **Added/Corp** Richard De Boo Limited. **VAT** Business and the Law. Vol 1, No. 1 (April 1984)-. Periodical. English. mo. $136.50 (latest edition). Carswell / Canada, 2075 Kennedy Road, Scarborough Ontario M1T 3V4 Canada. **Tel** (416)609-3800, (800)387-5164. **DD** 346.71/07/05. ***Absorbed** Canada-U.S. Trade (Don Mills, North York, Ont.), 0840-6278.*
Ind/Abst Can. Legal Lit.; Index Can. Leg. Period. Lit.

UK
BUSINESS LAW BRIEF. ***Title Change.*** (Jan. 1984)-(19??). Periodical. English. mo. Financial Times England, 8 16 Great New Street, London EC4A 3BN England. **Tel** 011 44 71 353 0305, 353 1040, FAX 011 44 353 0846. **ED** A. H. Hermann. **DD** 346.4/07/05; 344.06705. Index available. cum. index. **Bk Rev.** available on an online database (files 16,636/Full-Text) from DIALOG. ***Formed by the union of** European Law Letter; Eurolaw Commercial Intelligence **and** Commercial Law Reports; **Continues** European Law Newsletter. **Continued by** Business Law Europe.*
Desc: Reports on new judgements, the organization of courts and their procedures, events affecting the legal profession, changes in financial laws affecting banks and insurance groups.
Ind/Abst PROMT (?-?) [Full Txt.]; PTS Newsl. Database (?-?) [Full Txt.].

GW
BUSINESS LAW EUROPE. (19??)-. Periodical. English. bw (26 issues). $585.00 North and South America. European Law Press, Vogelweideplatz 10, D 81677 Munich Germany. **Tel** 011 49 89 4706998. **(Subscription address:** Transnational Juris Publ Inc. / North & South America Subscriptions, 1 Bridge Street, Irvington-on-Hudson NY 10533.**)** **LC** KJE2041.3; .B87. **DD** 346.4/07/05; 344.06705.

UK
BUSINESS LAW HANDBOOK. (19??)-. Periodical. English. tq. £304.50. Croner Publ Ltd, Croner House, London Road, Kingston upon Thames, Surrey KT2 6SR England. **Tel** 011 44 81 5473333, FAX 081 547-2637. **ED** David Johnston.
Desc: Covers the main legal subject areas of company law, employment law, business contracts, intellectual property, and competition law in the United Kingdom.

US/1047-2819
BUSINESS LAW JOURNAL (CORAL GABLES, FLA.), THE. (THE BUSINESS LAW JOURNAL.). [Bus. law j.]. **Added/Corp** University of Miami. School of Law. Business Law Society. Vol. 1, No. 1 (Spring 1990)-. Periodical. English. sa. $25.00 US; $30.00 other. University of Miami School of Law, 1311 Miller Drive, 460 Law Library, PO Box 248087, Coral Gables FL 33124. **Tel** (305)284-2464, FAX (305)284-2349. **LC** K2; .U76. **DD** 346.73/07/05; 347.306705.

US
BUSINESS LAW MONOGRAPHS. Vol. 1 (1984)-. Monographic series. English. qt. Price varies per volume. Matthew Bender & Company Inc., 1275 Broadway, Albany NY 12204. **Tel** (800)833-9844, (518)487-3000. **LC** KF1414.A1; B87. **DD** 346.73/066; 34730666.

US/0277-1713
BUSINESS LAW REPORTER. Vol. 1, No. 1 (Aug. 1981)-. Periodical. English. mo. $150.00. Shepards McGraw-Hill Inc, 555 Middle Creek Parkway, PO Box 35300, Colorado Springs CO 80935-3530. **Tel** (719)488-3000, FAX (800)525-0053. **LC** KF884; .B87. **DD** 346.73/07/02648; 347.306702648.

CN/0703-5551
BUSINESS LAW REPORTS. [Bus. law rep.]. V. 1- April 1977-. Periodical. English (French). mo. 102.00Can$ Canada; 88.75Can$ other. Carswell / Canada, 2075 Kennedy Road, Scarborough Ontario M1T 3V4 Canada. **Tel** (416)609-3800, (800)387-5164. **ED** George C Glover. **LC** KE915.8; .B8. **DD** 346/.71/07. Index available. cum. index. **Ad Acc.**
Desc: Features all important decisions in corporate, commercial and business law from all Canadian jurisdictions selected by experts in the field.
Ind/Abst Can. Legal Lit.; Curr. Law Index (1980-Dec. 1984); Index Can. Leg. Period. Lit.; Leg. Resour. Index (1980-Dec. 1984); LegalTrac (1981-1984).

UK
BUSINESS LAW REVIEW. Vol. 1, Jan. (1980)-. Periodical. English. mo. $255.00. Graham & Trotman Ltd, Sterling House, 66 Wilson Road, London SW1V 1DE England. **Tel** 44 71 8211123. **ED** Susan Nicholas. **LC** KD1622; .B87. **DD** 346.41/07. Index available. cum. index. **Bk Rev.** **Ad Acc.** **Circ:** 1,000. available in microform from University Microfilms International (UMI).
Desc: Provides information services for the business lawyer. Concise articles and detailed summaries of recent developments are combined to present a practical magazine for all those dealing with business law on a day-to-day basis.
Ind/Abst Leg. Resour. Index; LegalTrac (1980-1981).

UK/0143-6295
BUSINESS LAW REVIEW LONDON. (BUSINESS LAW REVIEW.). [Bus. law rev. Lond.]. **VFOAT** BLR. Business Law Review. (1980)-. English. mo (11 times per year). $255.00. Graham & Trotman Ltd, Sterling House, 66 Wilson Road, London SW1V 1DE England. **Tel** 44 71 8211123. **ED** Susan Nicholas. **Pr Rev.** **Acid Free.** available on microfilm and microfiche from University Microfilms International (UMI).
Desc: Concise articles and detailed summaries of recent developments are combined to present a practical magazine for all those dealing with business law on a day to day basis. Each month four or five articles are devoted to practical aspects of business law. Infobank features recent developments in business law; Eurobrief monitors European community legislation directives.

US/1054-0326
BUSINESS LAW SECTION NEWSLETTER. [Bus. Law Sect. newsl.]. **Added/Corp** New York State Bar Association. Business

Law Section. Vol. 13, No. 2 Summer (1989)-. Newsletter. English. Free to section members. New York State Bar Association, One Elk Street, Albany NY 12207. **Tel** (518)463-3200. **LC** KFN5225.A15; B3. **DD** 346.73/07/05; 347.306705. ***Continues*** *Banking, Corporation & Business Law Newsletter, 0148-3684.*

●US/1059-9436
BUSINESS LAW TODAY / THE MAGAZINE OF THE ABA SECTION OF BUSINESS LAW. [Bus. law today]. **Added/Corp** American Bar Association. Section of Business Law. Vol. 1, No. 1 (Mar/Apr. 1992)-. Periodical. English. bm (6 issues). $28.00. American Bar Association, 750 North Lake Shore Drive, Chicago IL 60611. **Tel** (312)988-5522, (312)988-5241, FAX (312)988-5528, telex 270593. **LC** KF872; .B87. **DD** 346.73/07/05; 347.306705. ***Continues*** *Business Lawyer Update, 0884-1977.*

US/0007-6899
BUSINESS LAWYER, THE. (THE BUSINESS LAWYER : A BULLETIN OF THE SECTION ON CORPORATION, BANKING, AND MERCANTILE LAW, AMERICAN BAR ASSOCIATION.). [Bus. lawyer.]. **Added/Corp** American Bar Association. Section of Corporation, Banking, and Mercantile Law. American Bar Association. Section of Corporation, Banking, and Business Law. (1946)-. Bulletin. English. qt (4 issues). $40.00. American Bar Association, 750 North Lake Shore Drive, Chicago IL 60611. **Tel** (312)988-5522, (312)988-5241, FAX (312)988-5528, telex 270593. cum. index. **Bk Rev. Ad Acc. Pr Rev. Circ:** 60,000 (ctrl). Documents available from The Genuine Article, UMI Article Clearinghouse.
Ind/Abst ABI/INFORM Glob. Ed.; ABI Inform Ondisc (April 1973-); Account. Art.; Bowne Dig. Corp. Sec. Lawyers; Bus. ASAP (1992-) [Full Txt.]; Bus. Index (1985-); Curr. Contents Soc. Behav. Sci.; Curr. Law Index (1980-); Fed. Tax Artic.; Gen. BusinessFile (1985-); Index Leg. Period.; Law Office Inf. Serv.; Leg. Resour. Index (1980-); LegalTrac (1980-); PAIS Int. Print; Res. Alert [Full Cov.]; Soc. Sci. Cit. Index [Full Cov.].

US/0884-1977
BUSINESS LAWYER UPDATE, THE. ***Title Change.*** [Bus. lawyer update]. **Added/Corp** American Bar Association. Section of Corporation, Banking and Business Law. Vol. 5, No. 6 (July/Aug. 1985)-Vol. 12, No. 3 (Jan./Feb. 1992). Periodical. English. bm. American Bar Association, 750 North Lake Shore Drive, Chicago IL 60611. **Tel** (312)988-5522, (312)988-5241, FAX (312)988-5528, telex 270593. **LC** KF872; .B87. **DD** 346.73/07/05; 347.306705. ***Continues*** *Business Law Memo, 0271-9045.* ***Continued by*** *Business Law Today, 1059-9436.*

US/0094-2502
BUSINESS REGULATION LAW REPORT: WAGE AND PRICE CONTROL. **Added/Corp** Wage and Price Controls Institute. (19??)-. English. sm. $60.00. Warren Gorham & Lamont Inc., Park Square Building, 31 St. James Avenue, Boston MA 02116-4112. **Tel** (617)423-2020, (800)950-1207, FAX (617)423-2026. **LC** KF6067.A73; B87. **DD** 343/.73/07.

US/0897-9979
BUSINESS TAX REPORT. [Bus. tax rep.]. Vol. 1, No. 1 (Feb. 12, 1988)-. Periodical. English. bw. $385.00. Tax Management Inc / Washington DC, 1231 25th Street NW, Washington DC 20037. **Tel** (202)452-4556, (800)372-1033, FAX (202)452-4096, telex 285656 BNAI WSH. **(Subscription address:** 9435 Key West Avenue, Rockville MD 20850**) ED** Glenn B Davis. **LC** KF6450.A15; B86. **DD** 343.7306/8/05. Index available. cum. index. **Circ:** 240.
Desc: A service designed for the financial executive who needs to keep abreast of tax issues and developments. Includes tax news stories, analysis of tax issues, tax planning tips and ideas, and a calendar of upcoming meetings and conferences in the tax field.

UK
BUTTERWORTHS COMPANY LAW CASES. **Added/Corp** Butterworths (Firm). **VFOAT** Company Law Cases. (1983)-. English. bm. £145.00. Butterworth & Co. Ltd. / Kent, England, Borough Green, Sevenoaks Kent TN15 8PH England. **Tel** 011 44 732-884567, FAX 011 44 732-885996. **ED** D. D. Prentice and Mary Stokes. Index available. **Circ:** 1,050.
Desc: A comprehensive series of specialised law reports which covers all UK cases of relevance and practical importance to company lawyers.

UK
C.M.L.R. ANTITRUST REPORTS. **Added/Corp** European Law Centre. **VFOAT** CMLR Antitrust Reports; Antitrust Reports; Common Market Law Reports Antitrust Reports. Pt. 1 (Jan. 1991)-. Periodical. English. mo. £250.00 Europe; £262.00 other. Sweet & Maxwell Ltd., South Quay Plaza, 183 Marsh Wall, London E14 9FT England. **Tel** 011 44 264 342899, FAX 011 44 264 342723, telex 929089 ITPINF G. **LC** KJE6456.A7; C66. **DD** 343.4/0721; 344.03721. ***Continues*** *Common Market Law Reports Antitrust Supplement, 0953-4423.*

US/0892-2349
CALIFORNIA BUSINESS LAW PRACTITIONER. (CALIFORNIA BUSINESS LAW PRACTITIONER : A GUIDE TO CURRENT PRACTICE.). [Calif. bus. law pract.]. **Added/Corp** California Continuing Education of the Bar. Vol. 1, No. 1 (Spring 1986)-. Periodical. English. qt. $175.00. California Continuing Education of the Bar, 2300 Shattuck Avenue, Berkeley CA 94704. **Tel** (510)642-8000, (800)232-3444.
Desc: Reflecting the day-to-day concerns of working lawyers, the topics chosen for coverage show you the practical consequences of changes in the law, explain how to put new strategies to use, and fill in the gaps where information on a subject has been scarce.

US/0199-669X
CALIFORNIA BUSINESS LAW REPORTER. **Added/Corp** California Continuing Education of the Bar. **VFOAT** California Continuing Education of the Bar; CEB California Business Law Reporter. Vol. 1 (Jan. 1980)-. Periodical. English. Six times a year. $175.00. California Continuing Education of the Bar, 2300 Shattuck Avenue, Berkeley CA 94704. **Tel** (510)642-8000, (800)232-3444. **ED** Hale Kronenberg. **LC** KFC337.A15; C35. **DD** 346.794/065; 347.940665. Index available. **Pr Rev.**
Desc: Emphasizes how new developments relate to, or change, the prior law and how they can be used in your practice, what new forms you should use, what advice to give a client, what pitfalls to avoid and how recent developments might affect other areas of law.

US/0360-0955
CALIFORNIA COMMISSIONER OF CORPORATIONS CURRENT OFFICIAL OPINIONS ISSUED PURSUANT TO THE CORPORATE SECURITIES LAW OF 1968. **Main/Corp** California. Dept. of Corporations. **Added/Corp** California. Laws, Statutes, Etc. Corporate Securities Law of 1968. (19??)-. English. $312.00 (13 volume set of Opinions and 1969-1971 Policy Letters), $75.00 (Update service). California Continuing Education of the Bar, 2300 Shattuck Avenue, Berkeley CA 94704. **Tel** (510)642-8000, (800)232-3444. **LC** KFC350; .A553. **DD** 346/.794/09202646.
Desc: Includes opinions, a subject index and a list of citations.

CN/0317-6649
CANADA BUSINESS CORPORATIONS ACT WITH REGULATIONS. 1st- Ed.; 1975-. Periodical. English. CCH Canadian Ltd., 6 Garamond Court, Don Mills Ontario M3C 1Z5 Canada. **Tel** (416)441-2992, FAX (416)441-3418. **DD** 346/.71/06602633.

CN/0848-4686
CANADA CORPORATIONS BULLETIN. (CANADA CORPORATIONS BULLETIN / BUREAU OF CORPORATE AFFAIRS.). [Can. corp. bull.]. **Added/Corp** Canada. Bureau of Corporate Affairs. **VFOAT** Bulletin des Societes Canadiennes. Vol. 15, No. 11 (Nov. 1985)-. Bulletin. English (French). mo. 250.00Can$. Micromedia Limited, 20 Victoria Street, Toronto Ontario M5C 2N8 Canada. **Tel** (416)362-5211, (800)387-2689, FAX (416)362-6161, telex 06524668. **LC** HG4090; .A145. **DD** 338.7/4/0971. ***Continues*** *Bulletin, Canada Corporations (Ottawa, Ont.), 0821-0004.*

CN/1180-4823
CANADA-U.S. BUSINESS LAW REVIEW. ***Ceased.*** [Can./U.S. bus. law rev.]. **VFOAT** Revue de Droit Commercial Canada-Etats-Unis; Canada-United States Business Law Review. **VAT** Canada/United States Business Law Review. Vol. 4, No. 1 (July 1990)-(1993). Periodical. English (summaries and/or abstracts in French). Three times a year. Carswell / Canada, 2075 Kennedy Road, Scarborough Ontario M1T 3V4 Canada. **Tel** (416)609-3800, (800)387-5164. **LC** K18; .E953. **DD** 341.7/5/05. ***Continues*** *Review of International Business Law, 0835-2399.*
Ind/Abst Index Can. Leg. Period. Lit. (1992-); Leg. Resour. Index; LegalTrac (1990-).

CN/0319-3322
CANADIAN BUSINESS LAW JOURNAL, THE. [Can. bus. law j.]. **VFOAT** Revue Canadienne du Droit de Commerce. Vol. 1, No. 1 (Sept. 1975)-. Periodical. English (French). Three times a year (plus bound volume consolidating the issues). 115.00Can$. Canada Law Book Inc., 240 Edward Street, Aurora Ontario L4G 3S9 Canada. **Tel** (800)263-3269, (905)841-6472, FAX (905)841-5085. **ED** Jacob S. Ziegel. **LC** K3; .A4922. **DD** 346.71/07/05; 347.106705. Documents available from UMI Article Clearinghouse, UMI Article Clearinghouse.
Desc: Banking, consumer law, products liability, securities regulation, taxation, real estate and trade regulation are some of the areas considered. Also provides coverage of current legislation, case law and policy developments.
Ind/Abst ABI/INFORM Glob. Ed.; ABI Inform Ondisc (March 1980-); Bowne Dig. Corp. Sec. Lawyers; Bus. Index (1985-); Can. Legal Lit. (1975-); Can. Period. Index (March 1980-); Curr. Law Index (1980-); Gen. BusinessFile (1985-); Index Can. Leg. Period. Lit.; Index Leg. Period.; Leg. Resour. Index (1980-); LegalTrac (1980-).

CN/0835-9245
CANADIAN CORPORATE LAW REPORTER. ***Ceased.*** [Can. corp. law report.]. Vol. 1, No. 1 (Nov. 1987)-Ceased (Sept. 1991). Corporate Report. English. bm. Butterworth & Company Ltd. / Canada, 75 Clegg Road, Markham Ontario L6G 1A1 Canada. **Tel** (905)479-2665, (800)668-6481. **ED** Vern Krishna. **DD** 346.71/06.
Desc: Analysis of legislative and judicial developments in corporate law.

BB/1013-9230
CARIBBEAN LAW AND BUSINESS. **Added/Corp** Caribbean Law Institute. Vol. 1, No. 1 (Apr. 1989)-. Periodical. English. Three times a year (Apr., Sept., Dec.). $42.00 Caribbean Commerical Law Reporter; $51.00 Caribbean Law and Business. Caribbean Law Institute, University of West Indies, Faculty of Law, Box 64, Bridgetown, Barbados. **Tel** 809 425 1310, FAX 809 424 4138. **(Subscription address:** Caribbean Law Institute: Florida State University, College of Law, Tallahassee, FL 32306 (telephone: (904) 641-2045, (904) 644-7731)**) ED** Velma Newton. **LC** K3; .A698. **DD** 346.729/07/05; 347.2906705. Index available. **Bk Rev. Ad Acc. Circ:** 400.
Desc: Contains digests of cases decided in Commonwealth Caribbean courts, lists of legislation for all the territories, news of legal and business developments, case commentaries, articles of legal and commercial interests.

US
CIS LAW REPRINTS. TRADE REGULATION SERIES : THE SUPREME COURT OF THE UNITED STATES PETITIONS AND BRIEFS. **VFOAT** Congressional Information Service Law Reprint. Trade Regulation Series; Trade Regulation Series; Supreme Court of the United States Petitions and Briefs. Vol. 18, No. 1 (1984/85)-. English. ir. Congressional Information Service Inc, 4520 East-West Highway, Suite 800, Bethesda MD 20814-3389. **Tel** (800)638-8380, (301)654-1550, FAX (301)654-4033, telex 292386 CIS UR. ***Continues*** *BNA's Law Reprints. Trade Regulation Series, 0275-6978.*

US
CIVIL RICO LITIGATION REPORTER. (March 1987)-. English. mo. $800.00. Andrews Publications Inc., 1646 West Chester Pike, PO Box 1000, Westtown PA 19395. **Tel** (610)399-6600, (800)345-1101, FAX (610)399-6610. **LC** KF9375.A59; R33. **DD** 345.73/02; 347.3052. cum. index. ***Continues*** *Racketeering Litigation Reporter, 0887-7874.*
Desc: Provides in-depth coverage of issues surrounding the continued evolution of the RICO Act from a sporadically used organized crime deterrent to a powerful weapon deployed in a diverse range of legal situations.

US/0884-0032
CIVIL RICO REPORT. **See** Law-Civil Law.

US/0898-0721
COLUMBIA BUSINESS LAW REVIEW. [Columbia bus. law rev.]. **Added/Corp** Columbia University. School of Law. Vol. 1, No. 1 (1986)-. Periodical. English. Three times a year. $45.00 US; $60.00 others. Columbia University School of Law, 435 West 116th Street, New York NY 10027. **Tel** (212)854-4398, (212)854-3742. **(Subscription address:** Columbia Business Law Review, Box B-26, 435 West 116th Street, New York NY 10027.**) LC** K3; .O3465. **DD** 346.73/07/05; 347.306705. **Bk Rev.** ctrl circ.
Ind/Abst Bowne Dig. Corp. Sec. Lawyers; Index Leg. Period.; Leg. Resour. Index; LegalTrac (1980-).

US/0888-8000
COMMERCIAL LAW BULLETIN (CHICAGO, ILL.). (COMMERCIAL LAW BULLETIN.). [Commer. law bull.]. **Added/Corp** Commercial Law League of America. **VFOAT** Bulletin. (Jan./Feb. 1986)-. Bulletin. English. bm. $45.00 (journal only), $120.00 (combined with Commercial Law Journal) US; $50.00 (journal only), $135.00 (combined with Commercial Law Bulletin) other. Commercial Law League of America, 150 North Michigan Avenue, Suite 600, Chicago IL 60601. **Tel** (312)781-2000, FAX (312)781-2010. **ED** Linda Saghir. **LC** KF872; .C66. **DD** 346.73/07/05; 347.306705. available on microfilm and microfiche from University Microfilms International (UMI). Documents available from UMI Article Clearinghouse. ***Separated from*** *Commercial Law Journal, 0010-3055.*
Ind/Abst ABI/INFORM Glob. Ed.; ABI Inform Ondisc (November 1987); UMI ABI/Inform--Bus. Period. Ondisc [Full Txt.].

CN/0832-235X
COMMERCIAL LAW DIGEST. ***Ceased.*** [Commer. law dig.]. **Added/Corp** Carswell Legal Publications. Issue 1 (Jan. 16, 1987)-(199?). Periodical. English. bw. Carswell Publications, 2330 Midland Avenue, Agincourt Ontario M1S 1P7 Canada. **Tel** (416)291-8421. **ED** Sharon J Sims. **LC** KE916.22; .C66. **DD** 346.71/07/02648; 347.106702648. Index available. cum. index.
Desc: Summaries of cases relating to commercial transactions and corporation law from Canada's common law jurisdictions

US/0277-3643
COMMERCIAL LAW. GOLD BOOK. BENDER PAMPHLET EDITION. NEW YORK UNIFORM COMMERCIAL CODE, GENERAL OBLIGATIONS LAW.
(COMMERCIAL LAW.). **Main/Corp** New York (State). **VFOAT** Commercial Law UCC-GOL. English. an. Matthew Bender & Company Inc., 1275 Broadway, Albany NY 12204. **Tel** (800)833-9844, (518)487-3000. **LC** KFN5225.A29; C65. **DD** 346.747/07; 347.47067.
Desc: Includes General Obligations Law

US/0010-3055
COMMERCIAL LAW JOURNAL. [Commer. law j.]. **Added/Corp** Commercial Law League of America. Vol. 35, No. 8 (Aug. 1930)-. Periodical. English. qt. $75.00 (journal only), $120.00 (combined with Commercial Law Bulletin) US; $85.00 (journal only), $135.00 (combined with Commercial Law Journal). Commercial Law League of America, 150 North Michigan Avenue, Suite 600, Chicago IL 60601. **Tel** (312)781-2000, FAX (312)781-2010. **ED** Linda Saghir. **DD** 346. cum. index. **Ad Acc.** available on microfilm and microfiche from University Microfilms International (UMI). ***Continues*** *Commercial Law League Journal.* ***Continued in part by*** *Commercial Law Bulletin.*
Ind/Abst Account. Art.; Fed. Tax Artic.; Gen. BusinessFile (1992-); Index Leg. Period. (1980-); Leg. Resour. Index (1974-); LegalTrac (1980-); UMI ABI/Inform--Bus. Period. Ondisc [Full Txt.].

UK/0141-7258
COMMERCIAL LAWS OF EUROPE.
[Comm. laws Eur.]. **Added/Corp** European Law Centre. Vol. 1 (April 1978)-. Periodical. English (Multiple languages). Twelve times a year. £360.00 Europe; £378.00 other. Sweet & Maxwell Ltd., South Quay Plaza, 183 Marsh Wall, London E14 9FT England. **Tel** 011 44 264 342899, FAX 011 44 264 342723, telex 929089 ITPINF G. **ED** Lusia Ten Kate. **DD** 346.4/07. **Ad Acc.**
Desc: Full text in English plus original language of laws from countries of Western Europe together with their legislative histories, explanatory notes and other essential information.

●CN/1187-2861
COMPAGNIES, SOCIETES PAR ACTIONS ET FAILLITE. See Law-Civil Law.

AT/0729-2775
COMPANY AND SECURITIES LAW JOURNAL. [Co. secur. law j.]. Vol. 1, No. 1 (Aug. 1982)-. Periodical. English. Eight times a year. 280.00Aus$ (renewals). The Law Book Company Limited, 44-50 Waterloo Road, North Ryde New South Wales, 2113 Australia. **Tel** 011 61 2 8870177, FAX 011 61 2 8887240, telex ASBOOK 27445. **ED** Sally Sievers and Robert Baxt. Documents available from UMI Article Clearinghouse.
Desc: Provides a clear and practical picture of a range of subjects including company law, take-overs and public securities, proprietary companies and insolvency.
Ind/Abst ABI/INFORM Glob. Ed.; APAIS, Aust. Public Aff. Inf. Ser.; Aust. Leg. Mon. Dig.; Index Leg. Period.; Leg. Resour. Index; LegalTrac (1990-).

II
COMPANY LAW DIGEST (NEW DELHI, INDIA). (COMPANY LAW DIGEST.). Periodical. English. qt. Rs75.00. Company Law Digest, ASAF Ali Road, PO Box 7071, New Delhi 110 002 India. **Tel** 619264. **ED** S S Kumar. **DD** 346.54/066/05 345.4066605. **Bk Rev. Ad Acc. Circ:** 10,000 (ctrl).

II/0970-3640
COMPANY LAW JOURNAL. ANNUAL REVIEW, THE. (1986)-. English. Rs150.00. Company Law Journal, 66/2230 Gurdwara Road Karol Bagh, PO No 2693, New Delhi 11005 India. **Tel** 572-0687/573-0440.

II
COMPANY LAW JOURNAL (NEW DELHI, INDIA). (THE COMPANY LAW JOURNAL.). Periodical. English. mo. Rs500.00 India; $104.00 US. Company Law Journal, 66/2230 Gurdwara Road Karol Bagh, PO No 2693, New Delhi 11005 India. **Tel** 572-0687/573-0440. **ED** L M Sharma. **DD** 346.54/066/05; 345.4066605. Index available. cum. index. **Bk Rev. Ad Acc. Circ:** 2,100.
Desc: Indian corporate laws: practice and procedure, acts and bills of Indian parliament, rules notifications circulars by government, and reports of Indian/English superior courts.

●UK
COMPANY LAW MONITOR. (1993)-. English. Twelve times a year. £160.00 UK; £182.00 others. Monitor Press, Rectory Road, Great Waldingfield, Sudbury Suffolk CO10 0TL United Kingdom. **Tel** 011 44 787 378607. ***Continues*** *Corporate Legal Letter, 0141-4852.*

UK/0144-1027
COMPANY LAWYER, THE. [Co. lawyer]. Vol. 1 (1980)-. Periodical. English. mo. $275.00 US and Canada. Longman Group Ltd., Fourth Avenue, Longman House, Harlow Essex CM19 5SR England. **Tel** 011 44 279 429655, FAX 011 44 279 431059, telex 81259. **LC** K3; .O397. **DD** 346.41/066/05. **[CCC].** Index available (bound in last issue).
Ind/Abst Leg. Resour. Index (1980-); LegalTrac (1981-).

II/0010-4027
COMPANY NEWS AND NOTES.
Added/Corp India. Dept. of Company Law Administration. Research and Statistics Division. India. Company Law Division. India. Dept. of Revenue. India. Company Law Board. Directorate of Research Statistics. India. Company Law Board. Research and Statistics Division. India. Dept. of Company Affairs. **VFOAT** Company News & Notes. (Oct. 1, 1962)-. Periodical. English. mo. $85.00. Department of Compnay Law Administration, Research and Statistics Division, New Delhi, India. **(Subscription address:** Prints India, 11 Darya Ganj, New Delhi 110002 India.**) DD** 338.3. ***Absorbed*** *Quarterly Blue Book on Joint Stock Companies in India.*

UK/0309-703X
COMPANY SECRETARY'S REVIEW.
Added/Corp Tolley Publishing Company. (19??)-. Periodical. English. Twenty-six times a year. £119.00. Tolley Publishing Company Ltd, Tolley House, 2 Addiscombe Road, Croydon, Surrey CR9 5AF United Kingdom. **Tel** 011 44 81 6869141, FAX 011 44 81 6863155, 011 44 81 7600588. **ED** Gail Moss. **LC** KD2072; .C65. **DD** 346.41/066/05; 344.1066605. **Bk Rev. Ad Acc. Circ:** 8,500 (ctrl).
Desc: Concise, thorough updating on developments in company law, accounting, property, pensions, insurance, health and safety, and taxation. Highlights key future dates, from the implementation of new legislation and regulations to conferences and seminars. Contains law reports which summarise and explain relevant Court and Tribunal decisions.
Ind/Abst Manage. Market. Abstr.

UK
COMPARATIVE LAW YEARBOOK OF INTERNATIONAL BUSINESS. Added/Corp Center for International Legal Studies. Vol. 12 (1990)-. English. ***Continues*** *Comparative Law Yearbook, 0169-0728.*
Ind/Abst Am. Bibliogr. Slavic East Europ. Stud.

UK
COMPETITION LAW IN THE EUROPEAN COMMUNITIES. Added/Corp Centre for Legal and Business Information. (19??)-. Periodical. English. Twelve times a year. Price varies. Monitor Press, Rectory Road, Great Waldingfield, Sudbury Suffolk CO10 0TL United Kingdom. **Tel** 011 44 787 378607. **ED** Bryan Harris. **DD** 341.7/53. Index available. cum. index. ctrl circ.
Desc: For the specialist lawyer or legal advisor in companies or organizations that need to be informed about the complex decisions and regulations emanating from the common market.

FR
COMPETITION POLICY IN OECD COUNTRIES. Added/Corp Organisation for Economic Co-Operation and Development. **VAT** Competition Policy in Organisation for Economic Co-Operation and Development Countries. (1984)-. English. an. $40.00. OECD Publications and Information Center, 2 rue Andre-Pascal, 75775 Paris Cedex 16 France. **Tel** 011 33 1 45248167, US:(202)785-6323, FAX 011 33 1 45248500 OR 45248176, telex 620 160 OCDE. **(Subscription address:** OECD Publications Center, 2001 L Street, Suite 700, Washington DC 20036.**) LC** K3856.A13; C66. **DD** 343/.072; 342.372. ***Continues*** *Organisation for Economic Co-Operation and Development. Annual Reports on Competition Policy in OECD Member Countries.*
Desc: Describes the main developments in competition policy and law enforcement in this field in OECD countries.

IT
CONTRATTO E IMPRESA. (1986)-. Periodical. Italian. tq. L170000 Italy; L240000 other. Cedam Spa, Via Jappelli 5 6, 35121 Padua Italy. **Tel** 011 39 49 65667.

US/0737-4046
CORPORATE ACQUISITIONS, MERGERS, AND DIVESTITURES. [Corp. acquis. mergers divest.]. **Added/Corp** Prentice-Hall, Inc. Information Services Division. Vol. 1, No. 1 (May 1983)-. English. ir. $354.00. Warren Gorham & Lamont Inc., Park Square Building, 31 St. James Avenue, Boston MA 02116-4112. **Tel** (617)423-2020, (800)950-1207, FAX (617)423-2026. **DD** 346.

US/1041-3871
CORPORATE ANALYST, THE. [Corp. anal.]. Vol. 1, No. 1 (Nov. 1988)-. Corporate Report. English. qt. $135.00. Business Laws Inc., 11630 Chillicothe Road, Chesterland OH 44026. **Tel** (216)729-7996, (800)759-0929, FAX (216)729-0645. **LC** K3; .O715. **DD** 346.73/066/05; 347.3066605. **[CCC].**

AT
CORPORATE & BUSINESS LAW JOURNAL. Added/Corp University of Adelaide. Corporate and Business Law Centre. **VFOAT** Corporate and Business Law Journal; CBLJ. Vol. 1, No. 1 & 2 (Nov. 1988)-. Periodical. English. sa. 40.00Aus$. University of Adelaide / Law School, Helen Creeper, Adelaide SA 5005 Australia. **Tel** 011 61 8 3034440. **LC** K3; .O713. **DD** 346.94/06/05; 349.406605.
Ind/Abst Index Leg. Period.

US/0160-4732
CORPORATE AND PERSONAL TAXATION IN THE ARAB WORLD. English. $12.50. Corporate & Personal Taxation in the Arab World, Subscription Department, Harvard Square, Box 92, Cambridge MA 02138. **DD** 343.05/2/09174927.

US/0731-650X
CORPORATE CAPITAL TRANSACTIONS COORDINATOR. See Business-Accounting.

US/0193-4880
CORPORATE COUNSEL, THE. Vol. 3, No. 2 (March/April 1978)-. Corporate Report. English. bm (6 issues). $450.00. Executive Press, PO Box 21639, Concord CA 94521. **Tel** (510)685-5111. **ED** Jesse M. Brill and Michael Gettelman. **LC** KF1397; .C65. **DD** 346/.73/06605. Index available. cum. index.
Desc: Recognized as the leading practical publication in the field for corporate and securities lawyers.
Ind/Abst Bowne Dig. Corp. Sec. Lawyers.

US/0886-327X
CORPORATE COUNSEL REVIEW. [Corp. couns. rev.]. V. 1- Oct. 1978-. Corporate Report. English. qt. Houston Bar Association, 1001 Fannin Street, Suite 1300, Houston TX 77002. **Tel** (713)759-1133. **LC** K3; .O72. **DD** 346.73/066/05.
Ind/Abst Curr. Law Index (1980-); Leg. Resour. Index (1980-); LegalTrac (1981-).

US
CORPORATE COUNSEL : STATE BAR SECTION REPORT. Main/Corp State Bar of Texas. Corporate Counsel Section. V. 1- Nov. 1975-. Corporate Report. English. State Bar of Texas, PO Box 12487, Capitol Station, Austin TX 78711. **Tel** (512)463-1411. **LC** KFT1413.A15; S83. **DD** 346.764/066.

US/0888-5877
CORPORATE COUNSELLOR, THE. [Corp. couns.]. Vol. 1, No. 1 (June 1986)-. Corporate Report. English. mo. $230.00. Leader Publications, 345 Park Avenue South, New York NY 10010. **Tel** (800)888-8300 ext. 6170, (212)545-6170, FAX (212)696-1848. **ED** Herbert S. Schlagman. **LC** KF1425.A15; C67. **DD** 346.73/066; 347.30666.
Desc: For the corporation lawyer.

US/0589-784X
CORPORATE COUNSEL'S ANNUAL.
Began publication in 1966. Corporate Report. English. Matthew Bender & Company Inc., 1275 Broadway, Albany NY 12204. **Tel** (800)833-9844, (518)487-3000.

US/0898-9907
CORPORATE COUNSEL'S INTERNATIONAL ADVISER. See Law-International Law.

US/0898-9923
CORPORATE COUNSEL'S MONITOR.
[Corp. couns. monit.]. **Added/Corp** Business Laws, inc. No. 1 (Sept. 15, 1986)-. Corporate Report. English. mo. $285.00. Business Laws Inc., 11630 Chillicothe Road, Chesterland OH 44026. **Tel** (216)729-7996, (800)759-0929, FAX (216)729-0645. **LC** KF1397; .C653. **DD** 346.73/066; 347.30666. **[CCC].**

US/0897-1617
CORPORATE COUNSEL'S QUARTERLY. [Corp. couns. q.]. **Added/Corp** Business Laws, inc. Vol. 1, No. 1 (Oct. 1984)-. Corporate Report. English. qt. $165.00. Business Laws Inc., 11630 Chillicothe Road, Chesterland OH 44026. **Tel** (216)729-7996, (800)759-0929, FAX (216)729-0645. **LC** K3; .O724. **DD** 346.73/066/05; 347.3066605. **[CCC].**
Ind/Abst Leg. Resour. Index; LegalTrac (1980-).

US/0892-4848
CORPORATE CRIMINAL LIABILITY REPORTER. ***Ceased.*** [Corp. crim. liabil. report.]. Vol. 1, No. 1 (1986)-?. Corporate Report. English. qt. Federal Litigators Group, c/o Gregory Nicolaysen, 8530 Wilshire Boulevard/Suite 404, Beverly Hills CA 90211. **Tel** (310)854-5135. **ED** Gregory Nicolaysen. **LC** KF9236.5.A15; C67. **DD** 345.73/0268/05; 347.30526805. **Circ:** 650.
Desc: Articles on substantive areas of corporate crime enforcement, prosecution and legislative updates.

US
CORPORATE EXECUTIVE, THE. (1975)-. Periodical. English. ir (5 issues). $375.00; $750.00

(combined with Corporate Counsel). Executive Press, PO Box 21639, Concord CA 94521. **Tel** (510)685-5111. **LC** KF1397; .C65. **DD** 346.73/066; 347.30666.

●US/1067-6163
CORPORATE GOVERNANCE ADVISOR, THE. [Corp. gov. advis.]. **Added/Corp** Prentice Hall Law & Business (Firm). **VFOAT** Corporate Governance. Vol. 1, No. 1 (Oct./Nov. 1992)-. Periodical. English. Six times a year. $244.13. Prentice-Hall Law and Business, 270 Sylvan Avenue, Englewood Cliffs NJ 07632. **Tel** (800)223-0231, (201)894-8538, FAX (201)894-8666. **LC** KF1423.A15; C67. **DD** 346.73/06642; 347.3066642.

UK
CORPORATE LEGAL LETTER, THE. *Title Change*. **Added/Corp** Centre for Legal and Business Information. (19??)-(19??). Periodical. English. Twelve times a year. Monitor Press, Rectory Road, Great Waldingfield, Sudbury Suffolk CO10 0TL United Kingdom. **Tel** 011 44 787 378607. **LC** KD2072; .C67. **DD** 346.41/066/05. Index available. ctrl circ. *Continued by Company Law Monitor, 0969-3831.*
Desc: Provides a distillation of all major relevant cases, statutes and regulations, including those from the EEC, that effect companies. Covers employment, monopolies and mergers, corporation tax, property, advertising and commercial law.

US
CORPORATE LEGAL TIMES. Vol. 1, No. 1 (Fall 1991)-. Periodical. English. Twelve times a year. $95.00 (one year), $190.00 (three year). Giant Steps Publishing Corporation, 222 Merchandise Mart Plaza, Suite 1513, Chicago IL 60654. **Tel** (312)644-4378. **LC** KF1425.A15; C676. **DD** 346.73/066; 347.30666. **Bk Rev**. **Ad Acc**. **Circ:** 40,000 (ctrl). available on an online database from LEXIS.
Desc: A national magazine that gives general counsel and in-house attorneys information on legal and business issues to help them better manage a corporate law departments.

US/0887-7793
CORPORATE OFFICERS & DIRECTORS LIABILITY LITIGATION REPORTER. [Corp. off. dir. liabil. litig. report.]. (1985)-. Periodical. English. sm. $850.00. Andrews Publications Inc., 1646 West Chester Pike, PO Box 1000, Westtown PA 19395. **Tel** (610)399-6600, (800)345-1101, FAX (610)399-6610. **ED** Leonard E. B. Andrews. **LC** KF1423.A59; C68. **DD** 346.73/06642. cum. index. ctrl circ.
Desc: Provides comprehensive, nationwide coverage of merger and acquisition-related litigation. Also covers the latest legal developments in the areas of director and officer insurance disputes, ERISA duty, insider trading and disclosure, mismanagement, ESOP's and new legislation.

US/0010-8995
CORPORATE PRACTICE COMMENTATOR. [Corp. pract. commentat.]. Vol. 1 (May 1959)-. Periodical. English. ir. $180.00. Clark Boardman Callaghan, 155 Pfingsten Road, Deerfield IL 60015. **Tel** (800)323-8067. **ED** F.H. O'Neal. **LC** K3; .O73. **DD** 346. cum. index.
Desc: A collection of informative articles written on all aspects of corporate law in one convenient source.
Ind/Abst Acad. Search (Jan. 1994-); Account. Tax Datab. (1986-); Bus. Index (1985-1990); Curr. Law Index (1980-); Fed. Tax Artic.; Gen. BusinessFile (1985-1990); Law Office Inf. Serv.; Leg. Resour. Index (1980-?); LegalTrac (1980-1990).

US/0162-5691
CORPORATE PRACTICE SERIES. [Corp. pract. ser.]. **Added/Corp** Bureau of National Affairs (Washington, D.C.). No. 1 (1978)-. Monographic series. English. wk. $1,389.00. Bureau of National Affairs Inc., 9435 Key West Avenue, Rockville MD 20850. **Tel** (800)372-1033, (301)258-1033, FAX (301)948-5823. **(Subscription address:** 9435 Key West Avenue, Rockville MD 20850; telephone: FAX (301)948-5823) **ED** Larry Lempert. **LC** KF1397; .C654. **DD** 343.73/07/05; 347.303705. **[CCC]**.
Desc: A corporate law reference service organized into a series of portfolios written by legal experts, with a weekly newsletter.

US/0886-0475
CORPORATE PRACTICE SERIES. BNA'S CORPORATE COUNSEL WEEKLY. [Corp. pract. ser. BNA's corp. couns. wkly.]. **Added/Corp** Bureau of National Affairs (Washington, D.C.). **VFOAT** BNA'S Corporate Council Weekly. **VAT** Bureau of National Affairs' Corporate Council Weekly. Vol. 1, No. 1 (Jan. 8, 1986)-. Periodical. English. wk. $562.00. Bureau of National Affairs Inc., 9435 Key West Avenue, Rockville MD 20850. **Tel** (800)372-1033, (301)258-1033, FAX (301)948-5823. **ED** Larry Lempert. **LC** KF1397; .C655. **DD** 346.73/066/05; 347.3066605. **[CCC]**. Index available. *Continues Corporate Practice Series. Washington Memorandum, 0883-5489.*
Desc: A roundup of the latest developments in law that affect business, including coverage of the courts, federal regulatory agencies, the executive branch, states and professional associations.

US/0045-8597
CORPORATION JOURNAL, THE. [Corp. j.]. **Added/Corp** Corporation Trust Company. Vol. 2 (19??)-. English. ir. C T Corporation System, 1633 Broadway, New York NY 10019. **LC** KF1397; .C66. **DD** 346.73/066; 347.30666. available on microfilm and microfiche from University Microfilms International (UMI). *Continues Corporation Trust Company Journal.*

US/0147-1619
CORPORATION LAW AND TAX REPORT (1975). *Ceased*. (CORPORATION LAW AND TAX REPORT.). (May 1975)-(May 1986). Periodical. English. sm. Warren Gorham & Lamont Inc., Park Square Building, 31 St. James Avenue, Boston MA 02116-4112. **Tel** (617)423-2020, (800)950-1207, FAX (617)423-2026. **LC** KF1397; .C67. **DD** 346/.73/06605. *Continues Corporation Counsel's Law and Tax Report.*

US
CORPORATION LAWS OF OHIO. **Added/Corp** Blackford, Jason C. Ohio Corporation Law and Practice. (1991)-. English. Banks-Baldwin Law Publishing Company, PO Box 1974, University Center, Cleveland OH 44106. **Tel** (216)721-7373.

US/0099-1236
CORPORATIONS. **Main/Corp** Bay Area Review Course, Inc. English. an. Bay Area Review Course Inc, 5900 Wilshire Boulevard, Los Angeles CA 90036. **LC** KF1414.3; .B3. **DD** 346/.73/066.

US/0070-1467
CREDIT MANUAL OF COMMERCIAL LAWS. (CREDIT MANUAL OF COMMERCIAL LAWS FOR...). [Credit man. commer. laws]. **Added/Corp** National Association of Credit Men (U.S.). National Association of Credit Management. **VFOAT** War Edition of Credit Manual of Commercial Laws. (19??)-. English. an. $66.50 (NACM Members); $81.00 (non-members). National Association of Credit Management, 8815 Centre Park Drive, Suite 200, Columbia MD 21045-2158. **Tel** (410)740-5560, FAX (410)740-5574. **DD** 346. cum. index. **Bk Rev**, **(Qty:** 1). **Circ:** 4,500. *Continues Credit Manual of Commercial Laws with Diary.*
Desc: Easy-to-use reference work. Covers all aspects of commercial law. Includes most recent rules and legislation enacted by Congress and state legislatures.

US/1042-5756
DELAWARE CORPORATE LITIGATION REPORTER. [Del. corp. litig. report.]. (Nov. 5, 1986)-. Periodical. English. sm (24 issues). $850.00. Andrews Publications Inc., 1646 West Chester Pike, PO Box 1000, Westtown PA 19395. **Tel** (610)399-6600, (800)345-1101, FAX (610)399-6610. **LC** KFD213.A59; D45. **DD** 346.751/066; 347.510666.
Desc: The legal battle involving Paramount Communications, Time Inc., and Warner Communications underscores the importance (and the difficulty) of following all the fast-moving, multifaceted corporate litigation in Delaware's state and federal courts.

US/0884-1683
DELAWARE CORPORATION LAW UPDATE (EXECUTIVE EDITION). (DELAWARE CORPORATION LAW UPDATE.). [Del. corp. law update]. Vol. 1, No. 1 (Aug. 15, 1985)-. Periodical. English. Twelve times a year. $475.00. Andrews Publications Inc., 1646 West Chester Pike, PO Box 1000, Westtown PA 19395. **Tel** (610)399-6600, (800)345-1101, FAX (610)399-6610. **LC** KFD213.A59; D453. **DD** 346.751/066/02638.
Desc: In-depth analysis of the changes in case law emerging from the recent corporate decisions of Delaware's state and federal courts. Summaries provide factual and legal points and the supporting citations and statutes from every reported and unreported opinion involving corporate law issues and outline the major issues. Also provides a calendar of capsule summaries of newly issued opinions to be examined in the next issue and a list of the newest corporate law cases to be filed in Delaware Chancery Court.

US/0364-9490
DELAWARE JOURNAL OF CORPORATE LAW, THE. [Del. j. corp. law]. **Added/Corp** Widener College. Delaware Law School. Vol. 1 (1976)-. Periodical. English. Three times a year (Jan., July, Sep.). $50.00 US; $77.40 (includes postage) other. Widener University School of Law, 3800 Vartan Way, Harrisburg PA 17110. **Tel** (717)541-3965, FAX (717)541-3966. **ED** Blaine Phillips, Jr. **LC** K4; .E38. **DD** 346/.751/06605. Index available. cum. index. **Bk Rev**. **Ad Acc**, **Adv Mgr:** B Glassman. **Circ:** 1,100 (ctrl). available on an online database from WESTLAW.
Desc: Law journal with corporate focus; antitrust, banking, commercial, securities and general corporate law.
Ind/Abst Bowne Dig. Corp. Sec. Lawyers; Curr. Law Index (1980-); Gen. BusinessFile (1992-); Index Leg. Period.; Leg. Resour. Index (1980-); LegalTrac (1980-).

US/1049-6122
DEPAUL BUSINESS LAW JOURNAL. [DePaul bus. law j.]. **Added/Corp** DePaul University. College of Law. Vol. 1, No. 1 (Spring 1989)-. Periodical. English. sa. $20.00 US; $22.00 other. DePaul Business Law Journal, DePaul University, Room 500, Chicago IL 60614. **Tel** (312)362-6178. **ED** Robert Christie. **LC** K4; .E65. **DD** 346. **Ad Acc**. available on an online database from WESTLAW.
Ind/Abst Index Leg. Period.; Leg. Resour. Index; LegalTrac (1989-).

US/0093-1829
DEVELOPMENTS IN CORPORATE, BANKING, AND SECURITIES LAW. Summer 1972-. English. State Bar of Georgia, 800 Hurt Building, 50 Hurt Plaza, Atlanta GA 30303. **Tel** (404)527-8700. **LC** KFG210.A73; D48. **DD** 346/.758/066.

CN/0315-811X
DIGEST BUSINESS & LAW JOURNAL. No. 1 (July 26, 1971)-. Periodical. English. wk. 255.00Can$ (one year), 425.00Can$ (two year). Digest Business & Law Journal, 826 Erin Street, Winnipeg Manitoba R3G 2W4 Canada. **Tel** (204)775-8918, FAX (204)788-4322. **ED** Walter G Bowden. **Bk Rev**. **Ad Acc**. **Circ:** 2,000 (ctrl).
Desc: Contains listings for credit references and real estate sales.

US/0272-1198
DIRECTORY - FORUM COMMITTEE ON FRANCHISING. **Main/Corp** American Bar Association. Forum Committee on Franchising. (19??)-. English. American Bar Association, 750 North Lake Shore Drive, Chicago IL 60611. **Tel** (312)988-5522, (312)988-5241, FAX (312)988-5528, telex 270593. **LC** KF195.F73; A45. **DD** 349.73/025.

UK
DIRECTORY OF MEMBERS - INTERNATIONAL BAR ASSOCIATION, SECTION ON BUSINESS LAW. **Main/Corp** International Bar Association. Section on Business Law. Directory. English. be. International Bar Association, 2 Harewood Place, Hanover Square, London W1R 9HB England. **Tel** 011 44 71 629-1206, FAX 011 44 71 409 0456, telex 8812664 INBAR G. **LC** K70.C65; I53. **DD** 346.07/06/21. **Circ:** 8,500 (ctrl).

US/0273-3633
DONNELLEY SEC HANDBOOK. [Donnelley SEC handb.]. **Main/Corp** R.R. Donnelley and Sons Company. Financial Printing Division. **VAT** Donnelley Securities and Exchange Commission Handbook. (Feb. 1974)-. English. ir. $29.95. R R Donnelley & Sons Company, 1050 17th Street, Suite 2400, Denver CO 80265. **LC** KF1433.99; .D65. **DD** 346.73/0666; 347.306666.

US/0272-1589
EAST ASIAN EXECUTIVE REPORTS. [East Asian exec. rep.]. Vol. 1 (Sept. 1979)-. Periodical. English. mo. $195.00 (public and educational libraries), $455.00 other US; $205.00 (public and educational libraries), $465.00 other. International Executive Reports, 717 D Street NW/Suite 300, Washington DC 20004-2807. **Tel** (202)628-6900, FAX (202)628 6618, telex 440462 MEER UI. **ED** William Hearn. **DD** 346.5/07. **[CCC]**. Index available. **Bk Rev**. **Ad Acc**. **Circ:** 600 (ctrl). available on microfilm and microfiche from University Microfilms International (UMI); available on an online database (file 15/Full-Text) from DIALOG; IBEX; and NEXIS. Documents available from UMI Article Clearinghouse.
Desc: Publication covering the financial, legal and practical aspects of conducting business in the Far East.
Ind/Abst ABI/INFORM Glob. Ed.; ABI Inform Ondisc (Jan. 1988-); Bus. Index (1985-); Curr. Law Index; Gen. BusinessFile (1985-); Index Period. Artic. Relat. Law; Leg. Resour. Index (1983-); LegalTrac (1983-); NEXIS (Sept. 1979-); UMI ABI/Inform--Bus. Period. Ondisc [Full Txt.].

UK
EAST EUROPEAN BUSINESS LAW. English. mo. 3,940F. Financial Times Business Information Ltd., Tower House, Southampton Street, London WC2E 7HA England. **Tel** 011 44 71 353 1040.

NE
EC CORPORATE TAX LAW. (1992)-. English. sa. $745.00. International Bureau of Fiscal Documentation - IBFD Publications, PO Box 20237, 1000 HE Amsterdam The Netherlands. **Tel** 011 31 20-6267726, FAX 011 31 20-6228658, telex 13217 INTAX NL. **(Subscription address:** IBFD / International Bureau of Fiscal Documentation USA, Inc., 24 Hudson Street, Kinderhook NY 12106.)
Desc: Detailed commentary on EC direct tax measures. Includes texts, related information and other documentation.

UK/0959-6941
EUROPEAN BUSINESS LAW REVIEW. Vol. 1, No. 1 Sept. (1990)-. Periodical. English. Eleven times a year (11 issues per year). $255.00. Graham & Trotman Ltd, Sterling House, 66 Wilson Road, London SW1V 1DE England. **Tel** 44 71 8211123. **ED** Susan Nicholas and Laurence Gormley. **LC** K5; .U715. **DD**

346.4/0705; 344.06705. cum. index. **Bk Rev. Pr Rev. Acid Free. Circ:** 250. available on microfilm and microfiche from University Microfilms International (UMI). **Desc:** Provides authoritative, practical and succinct coverage of key developments in European business law within the European community as well as EFTA countries (the forthcoming European Economic Area), and Central and Eastern Europe. Business law developments within the individual countries are carefully monitored, but the primary emphasis of the journal is reporting and interpretation of issues of transnational legal significance within Europe.

UK/0141-7266
EUROPEAN COMMERCIAL CASES. [Eur. commer. cases]. **Added/Corp** European Law Centre. Vol. 1 (April 1978)-. Periodical. English. bm (6 issues). £350.00 Europe; £368.00 other. Sweet & Maxwell Ltd., South Quay Plaza, 183 Marsh Wall, London E14 9FT England. **Tel** 011 44 264 342899, FAX 011 44 264 342723, telex 929089 ITPINF G. **DD** 341.7/54. Index available. cum. index. **Ad Acc. Circ:** 200 (ctrl). **Desc:** Reports on commercial matters in the countries of Europe.

US/1065-6235
EUROPEAN COMMUNITY BUSINESS LAW. HANDBOOK. (1992)-. English. West Publishing Company, 610 Opperman Drive, PO Box 64526, Eagan MN 55123-1308. **Tel** (612)687-5618, (800)328-9352, FAX (612)687-5388, (800)562-2329.

●US/1065-6227
EUROPEAN COMMUNITY BUSINESS LAW. SOURCEBOOK. (1992)-. English. West Publishing Company, 610 Opperman Drive, PO Box 64526, Eagan MN 55123-1308. **Tel** (612)687-5618, (800)328-9352, FAX (612)687-5388, (800)562-2329.

UK/0144-3054
EUROPEAN COMPETITION LAW REVIEW : ECLR. VFOAT ECLR; E.C.L.R. Vol. 1, No. 1 (1980)-. Periodical. English. Eight times a year. £230.00 Europe; £242.00 other. Sweet & Maxwell Ltd., South Quay Plaza, 183 Marsh Wall, London E14 9FT England. **Tel** 011 44 264 342899, FAX 011 44 264 342723, telex 929089 ITPINF G. **ED** Julian Maitland-Walker. **DD** 343.4/072; 344.0372. **Circ:** 500 (ctrl). **Desc:** Update of developments in national jurisdictions in the European community and other major trading nations. **Ind/Abst** Index Foreign Leg. Per.

US/1043-3082
EXECUTIVE ACTION REPORT. [Exec. action rep.]. Periodical. English. wk. $282.00 US; $367.00 other. Macmillan Publishing Company, 866 3rd Avenue, New York NY 10022. **Tel** (212)702-2000, (800)257-5755. **LC** KF1397; .E94. **DD** 658.4/005. **Circ:** 1,500. ***Continues*** *Prentice-Hall Executive Action Report.* **Desc:** Analyses and recommendations concerning current developments, practical tax-saving ideas, impact of labor and personnel relations.

●CN/1195-3144
FEDERAL AND ONTARIO INSOLVENCY LEGISLATION. (1993)-. English. an. 65.00Can$. Canada Law Book Inc., 240 Edward Street, Aurora Ontario L4G 3S9 Canada. **Tel** (800)263-3269, (905)841-6472, FAX (905)841-5085. **Desc:** Federal and provincial legislation regulating bankruptcy and insolvency.

US/0891-7515
FEDERAL TRADE COMMISSION DECISIONS. [Fed. Trade Comm. decis.]. **Main/Corp** United States. Federal Trade Commission. **Added/Corp** United States. Federal Trade Commission. Rules and Publications Section. United States. Federal Trade Commission. Rules and Publications Branch. United States. Federal Trade Commission. Editorial/Publishing Services Branch. United States. Federal Trade Commission. Division of Administrative Services. Publishing Section. United States. Federal Trade Commission. Information Management Branch. Vol. 1 (March 16, 1915 to June 30, 1919)-. Government Publication. English. Four times a year. $40.00. Superintendent of Documents, US Government Printing Office, Washington DC 20402. **Tel** (202)275-3328, FAX (202)786-2377. **LC** HD2775; .F7. **DD** 343.73/07/02646; 347.303702646.

US/0887-0942
FEDERATION OF INSURANCE & CORPORATE COUNSEL QUARTERLY. **See** Insurance.

US/0162-1122
FOOD DRUG COSMETIC LAW REPORTS (RX EDITION). (FOOD DRUG COSMETIC LAW REPORTS.). [Food drug cosmet. law rep.]. **Main/Corp** Commerce Clearing House. (19??)-. Periodical. English. wk. $2,025.00. Commerce Clearing House Inc., 4025 West Peterson Avenue, Chicago IL 60646-6085. **Tel** (312)583-8500, FAX (708)940-4600. **ED** A. E. Schechter. **NLM** WA 697 C734F. **Ind/Abst** Int. Pharm. Abstr.

US/8756-8888
FORENSIC ACCOUNTING REVIEW. [Forensic account. rev.]. (198?)-. Periodical. English. mo. $125.00. Computer Protection System Inc., 150 North Main Street, Plymouth MI 48170. **Tel** (313)459-8787, FAX (313)459-2720. **ED** Jack Bologna. **LC** HV8079.W47; F67. **DD** 658. **Bk Rev.** ***Continues*** *Corporate Fraud Digest.* **Desc:** Provides digests of current incidents of corporate fraud. Various items of interest are specifically addressed throughout the year and include such items as insider trading, embezzlement, bank fraud, commercial bribery, and legislation.

US/8756-7962
FRANCHISE LAW JOURNAL. [Franch. law j.]. **Added/Corp** American Bar Association. Forum Committee on Franchising. Vol. 4, No. 1 (Summer 1984)-. Periodical. English. qt (4 issues). $50.00. American Bar Association, 750 North Lake Shore Drive, Chicago IL 60611. **Tel** (312)988-5522, (312)988-5241, FAX (312)988-5528, telex 270593. **LC** KF2023.A15; A45. **DD** 343.73/084/05; 347.3038405. ***Continues*** *Journal of the Forum Committee on Franchising, 0732-1910.* **Ind/Abst** Curr. Law Index (1984-); Gen. BusinessFile (1992-); Leg. Resour. Index (1984-); LegalTrac (1984-).

US/0739-8239
FRANCHISE LEGAL DIGEST. (FRANCHISE LEGAL DIGEST / INTERNATIONAL FRANCHISE ASSOCIATION.). [Franch. legal dig.]. **Added/Corp** International Franchise Association. (198?)-. Periodical. English. Four times a year. $195.00. International Franchise Association, 1350 New York Avenue Northwest, Suite 900, Washington DC 20005. **Tel** (202)628-8000, telex 323175. **ED** Neil A Simon and Herbert A Hedden. **LC** KF2023.A15; F7. **DD** 343.73/0887; 347.303887. **Bk Rev. Ad Acc. Circ:** 1,000 (ctrl). ***Continues*** *Current Legal Digest, 0361-8390.* **Desc:** Articles reviewing current domestic and international legal and legislative developments concerning franchising and the implications of these developments for franchisors and franchisees.

US
FRANCHISING (NEW YORK, N.Y.). See Business-Retail.

IT
GIURISPRUDENZA COMMERCIALE. 1 (Jan./Feb. 1974)-. Italian. bm. L200000.00 Italy; L300000.00. Giuffre Editore SPA, Via Busto Arsizio 40, 20151 Milan Italy. **Tel** 011 398 2 38089200. **ED** Pier Giusto Jaeger. **Ad Acc. Circ:** 5,300. **Desc:** This journal is mainly intended for practitioners. The first part contains articles on topical subjects. The second part publishes the latest and most important decisions.

US
GOING INTERNATIONAL, INTERNATIONAL TRADE FOR THE NONSPECIALIST : ALI-ABA COURSE OF STUDY, MATERIALS. VFOAT ALI-ABA Course of Study, Materials; International Trade for the Nonspecialist. English. American Law Institute, 4025 Chestnut Street, Philadelphia PA 19104-3099. **Tel** (215)243-1661, (800)253-6397, FAX (215)243-1664. **LC** KF390.B8; G64. **DD** 343.73/087; 347.30387.

US/0434-2593
GOVERNMENT CONTRACTS CITATOR. (1958)-. Periodical. English. qt. $780.00 US; $810.00 other. Federal Publications Inc, 1120 20th Street Northwest, Washington DC 20036. **Tel** (202)337-7000, (800)922-4330, FAX (202)659-2233. **DD** 351.

UK
GREEN'S BUSINESS LAW BULLETIN. (1993)-. Bulletin. Six times a year. £74.00 Europe; £78.00 other. Sweet & Maxwell Ltd., South Quay Plaza, 183 Marsh Wall, London E14 9FT England. **Tel** 011 44 264 342899, FAX 011 44 264 342723, telex 929089 ITPINF G.

GW
GRUNDLAGEN UND PRAXIS DES WIRTSCHAFTSRECHTS. (1964)-. Monographic series. German. ir. Price varies per volume. Erich Schmidt Verlag GmbH, Postfach 304240, D 10724 Berlin Germany. **Tel** 011 49 30 25008525. **Desc:** Foundations of business law.

US/1076-3376
HOW TO PREPARE AN INITIAL PUBLIC OFFERING. [How prep. initial public offer.]. **Added/Corp** Practising Law Institute. (19??)-. Periodical. English. $70.00. Practising Law Institute, 810 Seventh Avenue, New York NY 10019-5818. **Tel** (212)765-5700, FAX (212)581-4670 general correspondence, (212)265-4742 orders and billing inquiries. **LC** KF1440; .H69. **DD** 346.73/092; 347.30692.

US/0736-0150
INSIDE (ALBANY, N.Y.). (INSIDE : NEWSLETTER OF THE CORPORATE COUNSEL SECTION OF THE NEW YORK STATE BAR ASSOCIATION.). **VFOAT** Inside Newsletter. Vol. 1, No. 1 (Mar. 1982)-. Newsletter. English. qt. New York State Bar Association, One Elk Street, Albany NY 12207. **Tel** (518)463-3200. **ED** Terrence J Gallagher. **LC** KFN5345.A15; I57. **DD** 346.747/066/05; 34747066605. **Ad Acc. Circ:** 1,200 (ctrl).

US/0894-3524
INSIGHTS (CLIFTON, N.J.). (INSIGHTS.). **VFOAT** In Sights. Vol. 1, No. 1 (July 1987)-. Periodical. English. Twelve times a year. $405.79. Prentice-Hall Law and Business, 270 Sylvan Avenue, Englewood Cliffs NJ 07632. **Tel** (800)223-0231, (201)894-8538, FAX (201)894-8666. **LC** KF1397; .I57. **DD** 346.73/066/05; 347.3066605. **Desc:** Covers substantive law developments in corporate and securities law on the state, national, and international levels. Transactions, office practice, court decisions, behind the scenes SEC and regulatory developments are all analyzed and interpreted by corporate lawyers in firms, corporations, government and academia.

US/0898-5170
INSURANCE ANTITRUST & TORT REFORM REPORT. ***Title Change.*** [Insur. antitrust tort reform rep.]. **VFOAT** Insurance Antitrust and Tort Reform Report. (1988)-(19??). English. sm. Mealey Publications, PO Box 446, Wayne PA 19087-0446. **Tel** (215)688-6566, FAX (215)688-7552. **ED** Scott Jacobs. **LC** KF1246.A3; M43. **DD** 346.7303/05; 347.306305. **[CCC].** Index available. ***Continues*** *Mealey's Litigation Reports. National Tort Reform, 0888-3114.* ***Continued by*** *Mealey's Litigation Reports. Punitive Damages & Tort Reform, 1055-307X.* **Desc:** Covers antitrust litigation against insurance companies and federal and state initiatives to revise tort laws.

UK/0958-5214
INTERNATIONAL COMPANY AND COMMERCIAL LAW REVIEW. [Int. co. commer. law rev.]. (1990)-. Periodical. English. mo. £295.00. Sweet & Maxwell Ltd., South Quay Plaza, 183 Marsh Wall, London E14 9FT England. **Tel** 011 44 264 342899, FAX 011 44 264 342723, telex 929089 ITPINF G. **DD** 342.67.

UK/0961-5326
INTERNATIONAL CORPORATE LAW. [Int. Corp. law]. (1990)-. English. mo (10 issues). $405.00. Euromoney Publications PLC, Nestor House, Playhouse Yard, London EC4Z 5EX England. **Tel** 011 44 71 779 8888, FAX 011 44 71 779 8617, telex 290700 EUROMON G. **(Subscription address:** Euromoney Publications PLC, Perrymount Road, Haywards Heath, West Sussex RH16 3DH England**)** **DD** 341.753. ***Absorbed*** *Environment Risk.* **Desc:** For in-house lawyers and senior executives in industry and commerce. Expert articles covering a wide range of commercial law developments are supplemented by special features addressing professional issues of particular importance to in-house counsel.

UK/0262-6969
INTERNATIONAL FINANCIAL LAW REVIEW. [Int. financ. law rev.]. (May 1982)-. Periodical. English. mo. £380.00 UK; $675.00 US. Euromoney Publications PLC, Nestor House, Playhouse Yard, London EC4Z 5EX England. **Tel** 011 44 71 779 8888, FAX 011 44 71 779 8617, telex 290700 EUROMON G. **ED** Josephine Carr. **LC** K9; .N825. **DD** 346/.07; 342.67. Index available. **Bk Rev. Ad Acc.** Documents available from UMI Article Clearinghouse. ***Continues*** *International Contract, 0258-8056.* **Desc:** Articles written by experts in the field on areas of national laws that affect cross border financing transactions for both banks and companies. **Ind/Abst** ABI/INFORM Glob. Ed.; ABI Inform Ondisc (Sept. 1983-); Bowne Dig. Corp. Sec. Lawyers; Contents Pages Manage.; Index Foreign Leg. Per.; Index Period. Artic. Relat. Law; PAIS Int. Print (1991-).

US/1041-3855
INTERNATIONAL QUARTERLY (CHESTERLAND, OHIO). (INTERNATIONAL QUARTERLY.). Vol. 1, No. 1 (Jan. 1989)-. Periodical. English. qt. $153.00. Business Laws Inc., 11630 Chillicothe Road, Chesterland OH 44026. **Tel** (216)729-7996, (800)759-0929, FAX (216)729-0645. **LC** K9; .N863. **DD** 346/.07; 342.67. **[CCC].**

CN/0826-9505
INTERPRETATION BULLETIN / ALBERTA TREASURY, CORPORATE TAX ADMINISTRATION. [Interpret. bull. - Alta. Treas., Corp. Tax Admin.]. **Main/Corp** Alberta. Corporate Tax Administration. Bulletin. English. ir. Free. Alberta Treasury/Corporate Tax Administration, 9811-109 Street, Edmonton Alberta T5K 2L5 Canada. **Tel** (403)427-0712, telex 037-43237 (403)422-5284. **LC** KEA513.A72; C675. **DD** 343.712306/7/05; 347.123076705. **Circ:** 4,000. **Desc:** Published to aid the interpretation of the Alberta Corporate Income Tax Act.

US/0747-9484
INVESTMENT COMPANIES (NEW YORK, N.Y. 1983). ***Title Change.*** (INVESTMENT COMPANIES : AN INDUSTRY IN TRANSITION.).

[Investm. co.]. **Added/Corp** Practising Law Institute. (1983)-(1992). English. Practising Law Institute, 810 Seventh Avenue, New York NY 10019-5818. **Tel** (212)765-5700, FAX (212)581-4670 general correspondence, (212)265-4742 orders and billing inquiries. **LC** KF1078.Z9; I575. **DD** 346.73/092; 347.30692. Index available. **Pr Rev.** available on videocassette. ***Continued by*** *Investment Company Regulation, 1071-8265.*
Desc: Information on corporate and securities law.

US/0731-8278
INVESTMENT COMPANIES REREGULATION AND THE CHANGING ROLE OF OUTSIDE DIRECTORS.
(INVESTMENT COMPANIES REREGULATION AND THE CHANGING ROLE OF OUTSIDE DIRECTORS : ALI-ABA COURSE OF STUDY MATERIALS.). Dec. 11-12, 1980-. English. American Law Institute, 4025 Chestnut Street, Philadelphia PA 19104-3099. **Tel** (215)243-1661, (800)253-6397, FAX (215)243-1664. **LC** KF1078; .A92. **DD** 346.73/0666; 347.306666. ***Continues*** *Investment Companies, the Changing Role of Outside Directors, 0190-5880.*

●US/1071-8265
INVESTMENT COMPANY REGULATION. [Invest. co. regul.]. **Added/Corp** Practising Law Institute. (1993)-. Academic Scholarly Publication. English. an. Practising Law Institute, 810 Seventh Avenue, New York NY 10019-5818. **Tel** (212)765-5700, FAX (212)581-4670 general correspondence, (212)265-4742 orders and billing inquiries. **LC** KF1078.Z9; I575. **DD** 346.73/092; 347.30692. available on videocassette. ***Continues*** *Investment Companies (Practising Law Institute), 0747-9484.*
Desc: Information on corporate and securities law.

UK/0021-9460
JOURNAL OF BUSINESS LAW, THE. [J. bus. law]. **VFOAT** Business Law. (1957)-. English. Six times a year. £95.00 Europe; £100.00 other. Sweet & Maxwell Ltd., South Quay Plaza, 183 Marsh Wall, London E14 9FT England. **Tel** 011 44 264 342899, FAX 011 44 264 342723, telex 929089 ITPINF G. **ED** Alan Wells. **LC** K10; .O85. **DD** 346/.07/05. **[CCC].** cum. index. **Bk Rev. Ad Acc. Circ:** 2,500. available on microfilm and microfiche from University Microfilms International (UMI).
Desc: Indicates trends in the development of business law as well as making a contribution to the knowledge and understanding of foreign law required for international trade.
Ind/Abst Aust. Leg. Mon. Dig. (1974, 1981, 1982, 1985, 1986-); Contents Recent Econ. J.; Curr. Law Index (1980-); Index Leg. Period.; J. Plan. Lit.; Leg. Resour. Index (1980-); LegalTrac (1980-); Selec. Coop. Index Manage. Period.

US/1052-3405
JOURNAL OF CORPORATE DISCLOSURE AND CONFIDENTIALITY.
Ceased. [J. corp. discl. confid.]. **VFOAT** Corporate Disclosure and Confidentiality. (1989)-(1992). Periodical. English. qt. Garland Publishing Inc, 1000A Sherman Avenue, Hamden CT 06514. **Tel** 800-627-6273, (203)281-4487. **LC** K10; .O8586. **DD** 346. ***Continues*** *Corporate Information and Privacy Reporter, 0892-4317.*
Ind/Abst Index Leg. Period. (?-?).

●AT/1038-2410
JOURNAL OF CORPORATE MANAGEMENT, THE. [J. corp. manag.]. (1992)-. Periodical. English. Eleven times a year (Except Jan.). 30.00Aus$ Australia; 65.00Aus$ other. Institute Corporate Managers, Secretaries and Administrators Ltd., GPO Box 1594, Sydney NSW 2001 Australia. **Tel** 011 61 02 2235744, FAX 011 61 02 2327174. **ED** P. W. Walford (phone: (02)223-5744). **DD** 658.400994. Index available (Each iss.). **Bk Rev. Ad Acc, Adv Mgr Tel** (02)223-5744. **Pr Rev. Circ:** 10,131 (ctrl). available on magnetic tape, and microfilm; available on CD-ROM and an online database. ***Continues*** *The Professional Administrator, 0707-3054* ***and*** *Corporate Management (Sydney), 1034-0408.*
Desc: This magazine presents news, articles, and regular updates on corporate law, changing of the workforce, strategies, employment law, environment law, trade practices, taxation law, and superannuation.

US/0360-795X
JOURNAL OF CORPORATION LAW, THE. [J. corp. law]. **Added/Corp** University of Iowa. College of Law. Vol. 1, (Fall 1975)-. Academic Scholarly Publication. English. Four times a year (Apr., July, Sept., Dec.). $25.00 US; $27.00 other. University of Iowa College of Law, Boyd Law Building Room 190, Iowa City IA 52242. **Tel** (319)335-9061, FAX (319)335-9019. **ED** Dan Christenser. **LC** K10; .O859. **DD** 346/.73/06605. Index available (bound with 4th issue of each volume). cum. index. **Bk Rev. Ad Acc. Circ:** 900 (ctrl). available on microfilm.
Desc: We publish scholarly articles in the fields of corporations law, securities law, tax law, commercial and banking law, and labor law.
Ind/Abst Acad. Search (Jan. 1993-); Bowne Dig. Corp. Sec. Lawyers; Bus. Source (July 1993-); Curr. Law Index (1980-); Fed. Tax Artic.; Gen. BusinessFile (1992-); Gen. Period. Index (1985-); Index Leg. Period.; INFO-SOUTH Abstr.; Leg. Resour. Index (1980-); LegalTrac (1980-); Mag. Search; PAIS Int. Print (1991-).

US/0022-4243
JOURNAL OF REPRINTS FOR ANTITRUST LAW AND ECONOMICS, THE. Vol. 1 (Summer 1969)-. English. sa. $55.00. Federal Legal Publications Inc, 157 Chambers Street, New York NY 10007. **Tel** (212)619-4949, FAX (212)608-3141. **ED** Gerald N Epstein and Howard Nashel. **LC** K10; .O89. **DD** 340. cum. index.
Desc: Articles on the subject of antitrust law and economics reprinted from major law reviews and economic journals.

FR
LAMY COMMERCIAL. (19??)-. French. 155 rue Legendre, 75850 Paris Cedex 17 France. **DD** 343.44/072/02632; 344.4037202632.

FR
LAMY PROTECTION SOCIALE. (19??)-. French. an. 1450.00F. Editions Lamy SA, 187-189 Quai de Valmy, 75490 Paris Cedex 10 France. **Tel** 011 33 1 44721200, 011 33 1 44721212, FAX 011 33 1 44721395. Index available. available with charts.

FR
LAMY SOCIETIES COMMERCIALES. **VFOAT** Societes Commerciales. (1987)-. French. an. Editions Lamy SA, 187-189 Quai de Valmy, 75490 Paris Cedex 10 France. **Tel** 011 33 1 44721200, 011 33 1 44721212, FAX 011 33 1 44721395. **LC** KJV2999; .L36. ***Continues*** *Lamy Societes.*

●US/1065-7428
LATIN AMERICAN LAW & BUSINESS REPORT. [Latin Am. law bus. rep.]. **Added/Corp** WorldTrade Executive, Inc. **VFOAT** Latin American Law and Business Report. (1992)-. Periodical. English. mo. $445.00 US; $475.00 other. WorldTrade Executive Incorporated, PO Box 761, Concord MA 01742. **Tel** (508)287-0301, FAX (508)287-0302. **LC** KG101.B87; L38. **DD** 346.8/065; 348.0665.

US/0272-4065
LAW & BUSINESS DIRECTORY OF CORPORATE COUNSEL. (DIRECTORY OF CORPORATE COUNSEL.). [Law Bus. dir. corp. couns.]. **Added/Corp** Law & Business, Inc. Prentice Hall Law & Business (Firm). **VFOAT** Law & Business Directory of Corporate Counsel. **VAT** Law and Business Directory of Corporate Counsel. (1980/1981)-. English. an. $390.60. Prentice-Hall Law and Business, 270 Sylvan Avenue, Englewood Cliffs NJ 07632. **Tel** (800)223-0231, (201)894-8538, FAX (201)894-8666. **ED** Robert J. Fox. **LC** KF195.C6; D57. **DD** 340/.025/73. **Circ:** 5,000.
Desc: Provides up-to-date, comprehensive information on the organization and personnel of the nation's corporate and nonprofit law departments.

US/0023-9208
LAW AND POLICY IN INTERNATIONAL BUSINESS. [Law policy intern. bus.]. **Added/Corp** Georgetown University. Law Center. Law and Policy in International Business Association. Vol. 1 (Winter 1969)-. Periodical. English. qt. $35.00. Georgetown University Law Center, 600 New Jersey Avenue NW, Washington DC 20009. **Tel** (202)662-9468, FAX (202)662-9444. **LC** K12; .A92. **DD** 343/.73/087. available on microfilm and microfiche from University Microfilms International (UMI). Documents available from UMI Article Clearinghouse.
Ind/Abst ABI/INFORM Glob. Ed.; ABI Inform Ondisc (1985); Account. Art.; Am. Bibliogr. Slavic East Europ. Stud. (1980-); Bowne Dig. Corp. Sec. Lawyers; Bus. ASAP (1992-) [Full Txt.]; Bus. Index (1985-); Curr. Law Index (1980-); Fed. Tax Artic.; Gen. BusinessFile (1985-); Index Foreign Leg. Per. (1974-); Index Leg. Period.; Leg. Resour. Index (1980-); LegalTrac (1980-); Manage. Contents (1974-); PAIS Int. Print (1991-); Public Aff. Inf. Serv. Bull.

UK/0954-2809
LAW FOR BUSINESS. [Law bus.]. (1988)-. Periodical. English. Ten times a year. £149.00 UK; £169.00 other. Wallace Publishing, 161 Chertsey Road, Twickenham Middlesex TW1 1EP England. **Tel** 011 44 81 8914747, FAX (081)892 2289. **ED** Jean Campbell. **DD** 344.2. Index available. cum. index. **Pr Rev. Circ:** 500.
Desc: Covers the full range of practical legal and tax problems which members of the business community are likely to encounter in commercial and industrial situations.

UK/0952-1046
LAW REPORTS OF THE COMMONWEALTH. COMMERCIAL LAW REPORTS. ***Title Change.*** [Law rep. Commonw., Commer. law rep.]. **VFOAT** Commercial Law Reports. (1985)-(1992). English. an. Butterworth & Co. Ltd. / Kent, England, Borough Green, Sevenoaks Kent TN15 8PH England. **Tel** 011 44 732-884567, FAX 011 44 732-885996. **LC** K1004.23; .L39. **DD** 346/.07/0917124102642; 342.670917124102642. ***Merged with*** *Law Reports of the Commonwealth. Criminal Law Reports* ***and*** *Law Reports of the Commonwealth. Constitutional and Administrative Law Reports, 0951-0699* ***to form*** *Law Reports of the Commonwealth.*

US/1061-7272
LAWYER'S REGISTER INTERNATIONAL BY SPECIALTIES AND FIELDS OF LAW INCLUDING A DIRECTORY OF CORPORATE COUNSEL. [Lawyer's regist. int. spec. fields law incl. dir. corp. couns.]. **Added/Corp** Lawyer's Register Publishing Company. **VFOAT** Lawyer's Register International. 10th Ed. (1991)-. Directory. English. an (Sept.). $119.50. Lawyers Register Publishing Company, 28790 Chagrin Boulevard, Suite 140, Cleveland OH 44122. **Tel** (216)591-1492, FAX (216)591-0265. **ED** Shirley Phfer. **LC** KF190; .L369. **DD** 349.73/025; 347.3025. **Ad Acc. Pr Rev. Circ:** 3,500. ***Continues*** *Lawyer's Register by Specialties and Fields of Law, 0163-3147.*

CN/0712-841X
LEGAL ALERT. [Leg. alert]. **VFOAT** Canadian Senior Executives' Legal Alert. Vol. 1, No. 1 (1982)-. Periodical. English (French). mo. 275.00Can$ (one year), 449.00Can$ (two years). Insight Press, 55 University Avenue, Suite 1700, Toronto Ontario M5J 2V6, Canada. **Tel** (416)777-1363, (416)777-2020, FAX (416)777-1292. **DD** 346.71/066/024658. cum. index. **Bk Rev. Ad Acc.** ctrl circ.

US/0270-3424
LEGAL CONNECTION; CORPORATIONS & LAW FIRMS, THE. ***Ceased.*** [Legal connect., Corp. law firms]. **VAT** Legal Connection. Corporations and Law Firms. (1979)-(19??). English. an. The Data Financial Press, PO Box 801, Menlo Park CA 94025. **Tel** (415)321-4553. **LC** KF195.C6; L43. **DD** 346.73/066/025.

US
LEGAL REQUIREMENTS FOR BUSINESS RECORDS. English. qt (4 issues). $730.00 (federal requirements), $485.00 (state requirements), $1215.00 (federal and state requirements). Information Requirements Clearinghouse, 5600 South Quebec Street, Suite 250C, Englewood CO 80111. **Tel** (303)721-7500, FAX (303)721-8849.

US/0162-5764
LICENSING LAW AND BUSINESS REPORT. [Licens. law bus. rep.]. Vol. 1 (May 1978)-. Periodical. English. Six times a year (Jan., Mar., May, July, Sept., Nov.). $205.00. Clark Boardman Callaghan, 155 Pfingsten Road, Deerfield IL 60015. **Tel** (800)323-8067. **ED** Steven Z. Szczepanski. **LC** KF3145.A15; L5. **DD** 343/.73/07. **CODEN** LLBRDL.
Ind/Abst Curr. Law Index (1982-); Leg. Resour. Index (1982-?); LegalTrac (1982-1989).

US/0739-1889
LIMITED OFFERING EXEMPTIONS: REGULATION D. (LIMITED OFFERING EXEMPTIONS, REGULATION D / BY J. WILLIAM HICKS.). [Ltd. offer. exempt.: Regul. D]. (1983)-. English. an (Aug.). $97.50. Clark Boardman Callaghan, 155 Pfingsten Road, Deerfield IL 60015. **Tel** (800)323-8067. **ED** J. William Hicks. **LC** KF1659.A152; L56. **DD** 346.73/0652; 347.306652.

US/0196-3317
LITIGATING AN ANTITRUST CASE. English. Practising Law Institute, 810 Seventh Avenue, New York NY 10019-5818. **Tel** (212)765-5700, FAX (212)581-4670 general correspondence, (212)265-4742 orders and billing inquiries. **LC** KF9066.A5; L56. **DD** 343.73/072/0269.

US
LOUISIANA CORPORATE NEWSLETTER. V. 1- Apr. 1972-. Newsletter. English. sa. Louisiana State Bar Association, 210 Okeefe Avenue, Suite 600, New Orleans LA 70112. **Tel** (504)522-9172. **LC** KFL213.A73; L68. **DD** 346/.73/066.

US/0748-3120
MAINE BUSINESS AND EMPLOYMENT LAW. **VFOAT** Maine Business & Employment Law. (198?)-. Periodical. English. mo. $89.00. Northern New England Law Publishers, PO Box 89, Portland ME 04112. **Tel** (207)773-2240. **LC** KFM331.A15; M35.

US
MARSH'S CALIFORNIA CORPORATION LAW. (19??)-. English. ir (supplements). Prentice-Hall Law and Business, 270 Sylvan Avenue, Englewood Cliffs NJ 07632. **Tel** (800)223-0231, (201)894-8538, FAX (201)894-8666.
Desc: Covers recent statutory, regulatory and case law developments relevant to California corporate law practice.

US/1055-307X
MEALEY'S LITIGATION REPORTS. PUNITIVE DAMAGES & TORT REFORM.
See Insurance.

Law —Corporate Law

FR
MEMENTO PRATIQUE FRANCIS LEFEBVRE: SOCIETES COMMERCIALES. (19??)-. French. an. Editions Francis Lefebvre, 5 rue Jacques Bingen, F-75854 Paris Cedex 17 France. **Tel** (1)47 63 12 60, FAX 46 22 72 66, telex 649 470 F. **DD** 346.44/066; 344.40666. Index available. cum. index. *Continues Memento Pratique des Societes Commerciales.*

NZ
MERCANTILE GAZETTE. (1981)-. Periodical. English. bw. $27.00. D N Adams Ltd, 8 Sheffield Crescent, Christchurch 5 New Zealand. **LC** HF4030.5; .A23. **DD** 658.8/009931. *Continues New Zealand Mercantile Gazette.*

US/0899-9651
MICHIGAN BUSINESS LAW JOURNAL, THE. [Mich. bus. law j.]. **Added/Corp** State Bar of Michigan. Corporation, Finance, and Business Law Section. (198?)-. Periodical. English. qt (4 issues). $20.00. State Bar of Michigan, 306 Townsend Street, Lansing MI 48933. **Tel** (517)372-9030. **ED** Harvey W. Berman (editor's telephone: (313)761-3780). **LC** KFM4413.A15; M53. **DD** 346.774/07/05; 347.7406705. *Continues State Bar of Michigan. Corporation, Finance, and Business Law Section. Journal - Corporation, Finance, & Business Law Section, 0274-7812.*
Ind/Abst Leg. Resour. Index; LegalTrac (1988-).

US
MODERN TECHNIQUES IN STRUCTURING PARTNERSHIP AGREEMENTS. **Added/Corp** Prentice Hall Law & Business (Firm). **VFOAT** Structuring Partnership Agreements; Annual Institute, Modern Techniques in Structuring Partnership Agreements. (1989)-. English. an. $225.00. Prentice-Hall Law and Business, 270 Sylvan Avenue, Englewood Cliffs NJ 07632. **Tel** (800)223-0231, (201)894-8538, FAX (201)894-8666. **LC** KF1380.Z9; S79. **DD** 346.73/0682; 347.306682. *Continues Structuring Partnership Agreements.*

PH/0115-1657
MONTHLY BUSINESS & TAX BULLETIN. VAT Monthly Business and Tax Bulletin. Bulletin. English. 45.00. Tax Quarterly of the Phillippines, Suite 506, Shurdut Building, Intramuros, PO Box 100, Manila Philippines. **DD** 343/.599/0405.

BL
MUNICIPIO PAULISTA : ASPECTOS JURIDICOS. **Main/Corp** Sao Paulo (Brazil : State). Procuradoria de Assistencia Juridica Aos Municipios Municipios. Portuguese. Procuradoria de Assistencia Juridica Aos Municipios, 272- 4 E 5 Andares, Sao Paulo Brazil. cum. index.

US/1048-6550
NATIONAL SURVEY OF CORPORATE LAW DEPARTMENTS COMPENSATION AND ORGANIZATION PRACTICES. [Natl. surv. corp. law dep. compens. organ. pract.]. **Added/Corp** Association of the Bar of the City of New York. Committee on Corporate Law Departments. Arthur Young & Company. (19??)-. English. an. $495.00. Committee Corporate / Law Departments, 787 7th Avenue, Room 1748, New York NY 10019. **Tel** (212)773-5145. **LC** KF1425.A15; N38. **DD** 658.1/2.

US/0149-323X
NATIONAL TAX TRAINING PROGRAM : TAX PRACTICE FUNDAMENTALS FOR NONTAX PROFESSIONALS. **Main/Corp** Ernst & Ernst. **VFOAT** Tax Practice Fundamentals for Nontax Professionals. English. an. 1300 Union Commerce Building, 925 Euclid Avenue, Cleveland OH 44115. **LC** KF6450; .E76. **DD** 343/.73/067.

US
NEW YORK CORPORATION LAW ... WHITEBOOK, WHITE CORPORATION LAW : BUSINESS CORPORATION LAW, NOT-FOR-PROFIT CORPORATION LAW, SELECTIONS FROM RELATED STATUTES AS AMENDED BY THE ... REGULAR LEGISLATIVE SESSION THROUGH ... . **Main/Corp** New York (State). **Added/Corp** Matthew Bender (Firm). **VFOAT** Whitebook; White Corporation Law; White Corporation Law BCL-NPCL. (1991)-. English. Matthew Bender & Company Inc., 1275 Broadway, Albany NY 12204. **Tel** (800)833-9844, (518)487-3000. *Continues Whitebook, White's New York Corporations.*

US
NEW YORK LAWS AFFECTING CORPORATIONS. **Main/Corp** New York (State). **Added/Corp** Prentice Hall Legal & Financial Services. 72nd Ed. (Revised to Sept. 1, 1991)-. English. *Continues New York (State). New York Laws Affecting Corporations and Foreign Limited Partnerships.*

US/0270-0662
NEWS FROM THE HILL (WASHINGTON). (NEWS FROM THE HILL.). **Added/Corp** Legislative Research International. (19??)-. Periodical. English. Twelve times a year. $48.00. Legislative Research International, PO Box 1511, Washington DC 20013. **ED** Alice Cherian.
Desc: Specifically designed to report new federal legislative developments (selected) relating to international business including export, import and foreign investment.

US/0196-3228
NORTHWESTERN JOURNAL OF INTERNATIONAL LAW & BUSINESS. [Northwest. j. int. law bus.]. **Added/Corp** Northwestern University (Evanston, Ill.). School of Law. VAT Northwestern Journal of International Law and Business. Vol. 1 (Spring 1979)-. Periodical. English. Three times a year. $30.00 US / $33.00 other. Northwestern University School of Law, 357 East Chicago Avenue, Chicago IL 60611-3069. **Tel** (312)503-8467, FAX (312)503-0132. **LC** K14; .O76. **Bk Rev**. **Ad Acc**. **Circ:** 500. available on microfiche; available on microfilm; available on phonorecord; available on an online database (file 15/Full-Text) from DIALOG. Documents available from UMI Article Clearinghouse.
Desc: Focuses on private international law and business.
Ind/Abst ABI/INFORM Glob. Ed.; Account. Art.; Bowne Dig. Corp. Sec. Lawyers; Curr. Law Index (1980-); Fed. Tax Artic.; Index Leg. Period.; Leg. Resour. Index (1980-); LegalTrac (1980-); PAIS Int. Print (1991-).

CN/0316-6481
ONTARIO BUSINESS CORPORATIONS ACT WITH REGULATIONS (CCH CANADIAN). (ONTARIO BUSINESS CORPORATIONS ACT WITH REGULATIONS.). [Ont. bus. corp. act reg. - CCH Can.]. **Main/Corp** Ontario. 1st-Ed.; 1971-. Periodical. English. an. CCH Canadian Ltd., 6 Garamond Court, Don Mills Ontario M3C 1Z5 Canada. **Tel** (416)441-2992, FAX (416)441-3418. **DD** 346/.713/06602633.

PL
ORZECZNICTWO GOSPODARCZE. **Added/Corp** Instytut Przwa PrzedsiÖebiorstw. (1991)-. Polish. qt. Price on Request. (**Subscription address:** ARS Polona, PO Box 1001, 00068 Warsaw Poland.)

AU/0379-4407
OZW, OESTERREICHISCHE ZEITSCHRIFT FUER WIRTSCHAFTSRECHT. **Added/Corp** Institut fuer Angewandte Sozial- und Wirtschaftsforschung (Vienna, Austria). **VFOAT** OZW; Oesterreichische Zeitschrift fuer Wirtschaftsrecht. (19??)-. Periodical. German. qt. S370.00, (add S35.00 for postage). Wilhelm Braumueller, Servitengasse 5, A 1092 Vienna, Austria. **Tel** 011 43 1 3191482, 3191159. **LC** K15; .E15. **DD** 346.07/05.

US/0749-0607
PARKER'S BUSINESS STATUTES AND SECURITIES RULES OF TEXAS. *Title Change*. **Main/Corp** Texas. **Added/Corp** Parker & Son Publications, Inc. **VFOAT** Business Statutes and Securities Rules of Texas; Texas Business Statutes & Securities Rules; Parker's Business Statutes. (19??)-(198?). English. an. **LC** KFT1405.A29; P37. **DD** 346.764/065; 347.640665. *Continued by Texas. Texas Business Statutes and Securities Rules, 1069-8434.*

US/0272-8621
PATENT ANTITRUST. See Copyright, Intellectual Property.

US
PENNSYLVANIA ASSOCIATIONS CODE AND RELATED MATERIALS. **Added/Corp** Pennsylvania. Associations Code. **VFOAT** Associations Code and Related Materials. (1991)-. English. West Publishing Company, 610 Opperman Drive, PO Box 64526, Eagan MN 55123-1308. **Tel** (612)687-5618, (800)328-9352, FAX (612)687-5388, (800)562-2329. **LC** KFP210.A29; P46. **DD** 346.748/066; 347.480666.

US
PERSONAL INJURY LAW DEFENSE BULLETIN : A NEWSLETTER FOR DEFENSE COUNSEL, INSURANCE AND CORPORATE CLAIMS MANAGEMENT, THE. **VFOAT** Defense Bulletin. (1987)-. Newsletter. English. mo. Free to people on mailing list. 21300 Lawland Court, Germantown MD 20876. **Tel** (301)353-1829.

US/1060-4081
PROCEEDINGS OF THE BUSINESS LAW SECTION ANNUAL MEETING. [Proc. Bus. Law Sect. annu. meet.]. **Main/Corp** New York State Bar Association. Business Law Section. Meeting. (Jan. 19, 1989)-. Proceedings. English. New York State Bar Association, One Elk Street, Albany NY 12207. **Tel** (518)463-3200. **DD** 340. *Continues Proceedings of the Banking, Corporation and Business Law Section.*

US/0192-5547
PROTECTING THE CORPORATE OFFICER AND DIRECTOR FROM LIABILITY. English. an. Practising Law Institute, 810 Seventh Avenue, New York NY 10019-5818. **Tel** (212)765-5700, FAX (212)581-4670 general correspondence, (212)265-4742 orders and billing inquiries. **ED** J F Johnston. **LC** KF1423.Z9; P76. **DD** 346/.73/0664.

US
PROXY STATEMENTS. English. mo (10 issues). $975.00. Jefren Publishing Company, 1513 Auburn Avenue, Rockville MD 20850. **Tel** (301)279-7082. **ED** Howard E. Deutch. Index available. cum. index.

PL/0137-5490
PRZEGLAD USTAWODAWSTWA GOSPODARCZEGO. **VFOAT** Economic Legislation Review; Obzor Khoziaistvennogo Zakonodatel'stva. (1948)-. Polish (English and Russian). mo. $90.00. (**Subscription address:** ARS Polona, PO Box 1001, 00068 Warsaw Poland.)

AE
RAPPORT DE SYNTHESE (CHAMBRE FRANCAISE DE COMMERCE ET D'INDUSTRIE EN ALGERIE). (RAPPORT DE SYNTHESE.). **Added/Corp** Chambre Francaise de Commerce et d'Industrie en Algerie. (19??)-. French. an. Chambre Francaise de Commerce et d'Industrie en Algerie, Algiers Algeria. **LC** HC815.A1; R36. **DD** 330.965/005.

GW
RECHT DER WIRTSCHAFT, DAS. (19??)-. German. ir. Erich Schmidt Verlag GmbH, Postfach 304240, D 10724 Berlin Germany. **Tel** 011 49 30 25008525. **ED** P. Erlinghagen. **Bk Rev**. **Ad Acc**. ctrl circ. *Continues Rechtsarchiv der Wirtschaft.*
Desc: Covers business law.

FR
REPERTOIRE DE DROIT COMMERCIAL. (1972)-. French. ir. 3500.00F. Dalloz, 35 rue Tournefort, 75240 Paris Cedex 05 France. **Tel** 011 33 1 40515434 or 40515454, FAX 45 87 37 48, telex 206 446 F. **ED** Jean Hemard.
Desc: Of interest to legal, commercial and administrative professionals, as well as accounting and personnel officials, this is an encyclopedia of French business law in 5 vols. and 1986 up date.

US/0276-6639
REPRESENTING PUBLICLY TRADED CORPORATIONS. English. an. Practising Law Institute, 810 Seventh Avenue, New York NY 10019-5818. **Tel** (212)765-5700, FAX (212)581-4670 general correspondence, (212)265-4742 orders and billing inquiries. **LC** KF1440; .R45. **DD** 346.73/066; 347.30666.

UY
REVISTA DE DERECHO COMERCIAL Y DE LA EMPRESA. V. 1-. Periodical. Spanish. $20.00. 25 de Mayo 555, ESC 303-304, Montevideo Uruguay. **LC** K19; .D345. **DD** 346.07/05. *Supersedes Revista de Derecho Comercial.*

SP
REVISTA DE DERECHO MERCANTIL. (Jan./Feb. 1946)-. Periodical. Spanish. Four times a year. Revista de Derecho Mercantil, Conde de Aranda 7 2 Derecha, 28001 Madrid Spain. **Tel** 011 34 1 5753432. **LC** K19; .D42.
Ind/Abst Index Foreign Leg. Per.

AG/0556-6428
REVISTA DEL DERECHO COMERCIAL Y DE LAS OBLIGACIONES. (19??)-. Periodical. Spanish. ir (2 issues). $140.00. Depalma SRL, Talcahuano 494, 1013 Buenos Aires Argentina. **Tel** 011 54 1 407306, 461815, FAX 011 54 1 406913. **ED** Hector Camara and Alfredo M. di Iorio. **LC** K19; .D868. **DD** 346.82/07/05; 348.206705. Index available. cum. index. **Bk Rev**. **Pr Rev**. **Circ:** 2,500 (ctrl).
Desc: Commercial law and jurisprudence. Includes bibliography, magazine reviews, news on meetings and bank law.

BE
REVUE DE DROIT COMMERCIAL BELGE. **VFOAT** Tijdschrift Voor Belgisch Handelsrecht. Vol. 16 (Jan. 1983)-. Periodical. Dutch (French). Ten times a year. 3350F. Kluwer Edn Juridiques Belgique, Blvd E Bockstael 230, 1020 Brussels Belguim. **Tel** 011 32 2 7232111. **ED** I. Verougstraete. Index available. **Bk Rev**. **Ad Acc**. ctrl circ. *Continues Jurisprudence Commerciale de Belgique.*
Desc: Informs readers of latest news in field of commercial law. Includes articles and notes which are both scientific and practical.

FR/0295-5830
REVUE DE DROIT DES AFFAIRES INTERNATIONALES. **VFOAT** International Business Law Journal; R.D.A.I. (1985)-. Periodical.

English. ir (8 issues per year). $397.00. Kluwer Law and Taxation Publishers, Staverenstraat 32015, PO Box 23, 7400 GA Deventer Netherlands. **Tel** 011 31 5700 47261. **(Subscription address:** Kluwer Law & Taxation, 675 Massachusetts Avenue, Cambridge MA 02139.**) UDC** 341.5.
Desc: Fills the need for a high quality journal which provides up-to-date information in the fields of international business law, finance, and taxation. Reports on new developments of the law in research, events, practices and trends in international business.
Ind/Abst PAIS Int. Print.

FR/0220-9896
REVUE DE LA CONCURRENCE ET DE LA CONSOMMATION. Added/Corp France. Direction Generale de la Concurrence et de la Consommation. France. Direction Generale de la Concurrence, de la Consommation et de la Repression des Fraudes. (197?)-. Periodical. French. Six times a year. 215.48F. Documentation Francaise, 29 Quai Voltaire, 75344 Paris Cedex 7 France. **Tel** 011 33 1 40157000, FAX 011 33 1 40157230, telex 204 826 DOCFRAN. **(Subscription address:** Documentation Francaise, 124 rue Henri Barbusse, 93308 Aubervilliers Cedex France.**) LC** KJV5595.A15; R48.

FR
REVUE INTERNATIONALE DE LA CONCURRENCE. VFOAT International Review of Competition Law. Periodical. English (French). 2 rue Fabert, 75007 Paris France. **LC** K21; .I56. **DD** 343/.072/05; 342.37205. ***Continues** Communication (Ligue Internationale Contre la Concurrence d'Eloyale).*

FR/0244-9358
REVUE TRIMESTRIELLE DE DROIT COMMERCIAL ET DE DROIT ECONOMIQUE. (Jan./Mar. 1980)-. Periodical. French. Four times a year. 550.00F (France); 660.00F (other). Dalloz, 35 rue Tournefort, 75240 Paris Cedex 05 France. **Tel** 011 33 1 40515434 or 40515454, FAX 45 87 37 48, telex 206 446 F. **ED** Roger Houin. **LC** K21; .T69. **DD** 346.44/07/05; 344.406705. **[CCC]. *Continues*** *Revue Trimestrielle de Droit Commercial.*
Ind/Abst Index Foreign Leg. Per.

US/0889-0641
RICO LAW REPORTER. (RICO LAW REPORTER : A BI-MONTHLY JOURNAL OF CIVIL RICO LAW AND PRACTICE.). [RICO law report.]. **VAT** Racketeer Influenced and Corrupt Organization Act Law Reporter. Vol. 1, No. 6 (May 1985)-. Periodical. English. bm. $1352.50 District of Columbia; $1275.00 other. Law Reporters, 1519 Connecticut Avenue Northwest, Suite 200, Washington DC 20036. **Tel** (202)462-5755. **LC** KF9375.A15; R53. **DD** 345.73/02; 347.3052. ***Continues*** *RICO Litigation Reporter.*

IT/0035-5887
RIVISTA DEL DIRITTO COMMERCIALE E DEL DIRITTO GENERALE DELLE OBBLIGAZIONI. Vol. 1 (1903)-. Periodical. Italian. bm. L135000 Italy; $170.00 other. Piccin Nuova Libraria, Via Altinate 107, 35121 Padua Italy. **Tel** 39 49 655566, FAX 39 49 8750693. **ED** Prof. Berardino (editor's phone: 39 49 66791132). Index available (bound in last issue). cum. index. **Pr Rev.**
Ind/Abst Index Foreign Leg. Per.

IT/0035-6018
RIVISTA DELLE SOCIETA. (19??)-. Periodical. Italian. bm. L140000.00 Italy; L210000.00 other. Giuffre Editore SPA, Via Busto Arsizio 40, 20151 Milan Italy. **Tel** 011 398 2 38089200. **ED** Giuseppe Auletta. Index available. **Bk Rev. Ad Acc. Circ:** 5,300.
Desc: Deals with the problems of joint stock companies.
Ind/Abst Index Foreign Leg. Per.

●US/1064-637X
RUSSIA AND COMMONWEALTH BUSINESS LAW REPORT. [Russ. commonw. bus. law rep.]. Vol. 2, Issue 15 (Feb. 24, 1992)-. Periodical. English. sm. $970.00 US, Canada and Mexico; $992.00 other. Buraff Publications Inc., 714 Church Street, Alexandria VA 22314. **Tel** (800)333-1291, (703)739-8500. **LC** KLA78.B67; S64. **DD** 346.47/07/05; 344.706705. ***Continues** Russian Commonwealth Business Law Report, 1065-2868.*

US/1065-2868
RUSSIAN COMMONWEALTH BUSINESS LAW REPORT. ***Title Change.*** [Russ. Commonw. bus. law rep.]. (1992). Periodical. English. sm. Buraff Publications Inc., 714 Church Street, Alexandria VA 22314. **Tel** (800)333-1291, (703)739-8500. **LC** KLA78; .B67564. **DD** 346.47/07; 344.7067. ***Continues** Soviet Business Law Report, 1050-3730.* ***Continued by** Russia and Commonwealth Business Law Report, 1064-637X.*

GW
SCHWERPUNKTE DES KARTELLRECHTS. Main/Corp Forschungsinstitut fur Wirtschaftsverfassung und Wettbewerb (Cologne, Germany). German. **LC** HB41; .F22 subser.

UK/0308-1176
SCOTS MERCANTILE LAW STATUTES. Main/Corp Great Britain. (19??)-. English. an. W Green & Son Ltd, St Giles Street, Edinburgh EH1 1PU Scotland. **Tel** 011 44 31 2254879, FAX 011 44 31 2252104. **LC** KDC495.A29; S3. **DD** 346/.411/07.

US/0273-0685
SECURITIES AND FEDERAL CORPORATE LAW REPORT. (SECURITIES AND FEDERAL CORPORATE LAW REPORT / AUTHORED AND EDITED BY HAROLD S. BLOOMENTHAL.). [Secur. Fed. corp. law rep.]. Vol. 1, No. 1 (Jan. 1979)-. English. Eleven times a year. $195.00. Clark Boardman Callaghan, 155 Pfingsten Road, Deerfield IL 60015. **Tel** (800)323-8067. **ED** Harold Bloomenthal. **LC** KF1432; .S42. **DD** 346.73/0666; 347.306666.
Desc: A reporting service for lawyers.
Ind/Abst Curr. Law Index (1982-); Leg. Resour. Index (1982-); LegalTrac (1981-).

US/0731-5805
SECURITIES LAW HANDBOOK / BY HAROLD S. BLOOMENTHAL. [Secur. law handb.]. **Added/Corp** Clark Boardman Company. (1978)-. English. an. $120.00 (latest edition). Clark Boardman Callaghan, 155 Pfingsten Road, Deerfield IL 60015. **Tel** (800)323-8067. **ED** Harold S. Bloomenthal. **LC** KF1439; .B544. **DD** 346.73/0666; 347.306666. **Circ:** 2,700.
Desc: An overview and update of American securities law and important developments.

US/0080-8474
SECURITIES LAW REVIEW. [Secur. law rev.]. (1969)-. English. an. $97.50. Clark Boardman Callaghan, 155 Pfingsten Road, Deerfield IL 60015. **Tel** (800)323-8067. **LC** KF1066.A32; S4. **DD** 346.
Desc: Anthology of articles published in previous year on federal securities and corporate law.
Ind/Abst Curr. Law Index (1980-); Leg. Resour. Index (1980-); LegalTrac (1980-).

US/0742-3802
SEMI-ANNUAL REPORT OF THE INSPECTOR GENERAL, U.S. SMALL BUSINESS ADMINISTRATION. (SEMI-ANNUAL REPORT OF THE INSPECTOR GENERAL, U.S. SMALL BUSINESS ADMINISTRATION : PURSUANT TO PUBLIC LAW 95-452.). **Main/Corp** United States. Small Business Administration. Office of Inspector General. (April/Sept. 1979)-. English. sa. Office of Inspector General, United States Small Business Administration, 409 Third Street SW, 7th Floor, Washington DC 20416. **Tel** (202)205-6580. **LC** HD2346.U5; U57C. **DD** 353.9982/048/06. **Circ:** 500 (ctrl). available on microfiche (Vols. for (April 1-Sept. 30, 1986-) distributed to depository libraries).

CN
SHAREHOLDER REMEDIES IN CANADA. English. an. 195.00Can$. Butterworth & Company Ltd. / Canada, 75 Clegg Road, Markham Ontario L6G 1A1 Canada. **Tel** (905)479-2665, (800)668-6481. **ED** Dennis Peterson. Index available. **Pr Rev. Circ:** 396 (ctrl).
Desc: An examination of all statutory provisions and common law principles governing the rights and remedies of shareholders and other corporate stakeholders in Canada.

US/8750-1104
SHEPARD'S CORPORATION LAW CITATIONS. ***Ceased.*** [Shepard's corp. law cit.]. **Added/Corp** Shepard's/McGraw-Hill. Vol. 1, No. 1 (Mar. 1984)-Final Supplement (Dec. 1992). English. qt. Shepards McGraw-Hill Inc, 555 Middle Creek Parkway, PO Box 35300, Colorado Springs CO 80935-3530. **Tel** (719)488-3000, FAX (800)525-0053. **DD** 346.
Desc: An up-to-date timesaving comprehensive citation system. Provides coverage of federal court corporation cases reported in the United States Supreme Court.

US
SHEPARD'S CORPORATION LAW CITATIONS : A COMPILATION OF CITATIONS TO DECISIONS OF THE UNITED STATES SUPREME COURT, LOWER FEDERAL COURTS, AND STATE COURTS IN CORPORATION CASES, TO CORPORATION PROVISIONS OF STATE CODES, AND TO THE MODEL BUSINESS CORPORATION ACT. ***Ceased.*** 1st Ed (1983)-(1992). English. Prentice-Hall Law and Business, 270 Sylvan Avenue, Englewood Cliffs NJ 07632. **Tel** (800)223-0231, (201)894-8538, FAX (201)894-8666.

US/8750-1112
SHEPARD'S PARTNERSHIP LAW CITATIONS. ***Ceased.*** [Shepard's partnersh. law cit.]. **Added/Corp** Shepard's/McGraw-Hill. (198?)-Final Supplement (Jan. 1993). English. qt. Shepards McGraw-Hill Inc, 555 Middle Creek Parkway, PO Box 35300, Colorado Springs CO 80935-3530. **Tel** (719)488-3000, FAX (800)525-0053. **DD** 346.
Desc: The only source available in this specialized field with in-depth coverage from formation to dissolution of a partnership.

US/0883-9395
SOCIAL RESPONSIBILITY, BUSINESS, JOURNALISM, LAW, MEDICINE. [Soc. responsib.: bus. journal. law med.]. **Added/Corp** Washington and Lee University. **VFOAT** Social Responsibility; Business, Journalism, Law, Medicine. Vol. 10 (1984)-. English. Washington Lee University, Box 722, Lexington VA 24450. **Tel** (703)463-8765, FAX (703)463-8945. **LC** BJ1725; .S65. **DD** 174. **NLM** W1; SO126. ***Continues** Social Responsibility, Journalism, Law, Medicine, 0732-9938.*
Ind/Abst Leg. Resour. Index; LegalTrac (1980-).

BL
SOCIEDADES POR ACOES. Study 5-. Periodical. Portuguese. Editora Resenha Universitaria, rua Quatinga 12-3 Andar, 04140 Sao Paulo Brazil. **LC** K23; .O254. **DD** 346/.81/06605.

IT
SOCIETA, LE. Vol. 1, No. 1 (Jan. 31, 1982)-. Periodical. Italian. mo. L285000.00 Italy; L570000.00 other. IPSOA Editore SRL, Casella Postale 12055, Mastrangelo, 20120 Milan Italy. **Tel** 011 39 2 82476248.

US/1055-4580
SOVIET LAW & BUSINESS NEWS. [Sov. law bus. news]. **VFOAT** Soviet Law and Business News. Vol. 1 No. 1 Feb. (1991)-. Periodical. English. sm. $885.00. **DD** 338.
Ind/Abst Leg. Resour. Index; LegalTrac (1991-).

US/0148-0901
SPERRY LAWYER, THE. [Sperry lawyer]. V. 1- Spring 1977-. Periodical. English. Three times a year. Sperry Rand Corporation, 1290 Avenue of the Americas, New York NY 10016. **LC** K23; .P47. **DD** 340/.05.

US/1078-313X
STOCKHOLDERS & CREDITORS NEWS SERVICE CONCERNING ASBESTOS BANKRUPTCIES. [Stockhold. credit. news serv. concern. asbestos bankruptcies]. **Added/Corp** Andrews Publications, Inc. **VFOAT** Stockholders and Creditors News Service Concerning Asbestos bankruptcies; S&CNS re Asbestos Bankruptcies; Asbestos Bankruptcies. July 19, (1993)-. English. sm. $1300.00. Andrews Publications Inc., 1646 West Chester Pike, PO Box 1000, Westtown PA 19395. **Tel** (610)399-6600, (800)345-1101, FAX (610)399-6610. **DD** 346. ***Formed by the union of** Stockholders & Creditors News Service Concerning Hillsborough Holdings Corporation, 1053-0215* ***and** Stockholders & Creditors News Service Concerning Johns-Manville Corporation, Et Al., 1042-5780.*
Desc: Summarizes and reprints documents filed in Hillsborough's Chapter 11 bankruptcy proceedings before Judge Alexander L. Paskay in Tampa, Florida.

US/1042-5772
STOCKHOLDERS & CREDITORS NEWS SERVICE CONCERNING LTV CORPORATION, ET AL. [Stockhold. credit. news serv. concern. LTV Corp. et al.]. **Added/Corp** Andrews Publications, Inc. **VFOAT** Stockholders and Creditors News Service Concerning LTV Corporation, et al.; Stockholders & Creditors News Service re. LTV Corp., et al. (198?)-. Periodical. English. sm (24 issues). $1350.00. Andrews Publications Inc., 1646 West Chester Pike, PO Box 1000, Westtown PA 19395. **Tel** (610)399-6600, (800)345-1101, FAX (610)399-6610. **LC** KF228.L78; S76. **DD** 343.73/078669142; 347.30378669142.
Desc: Summarizes and reprints documents filed in LTV's Chapter 11 bankruptcy proceeding before U.S. Bankruptcy Judge Burton R. Lifland in New York.

US
STUDY OF FEDERAL TAX LAW. CASES AND MATERIALS. TAXATION OF BUSINESS ENTERPRISES, THE. **Added/Corp** Commerce Clearing House. **VFOAT** Cases and Materials. Taxation of Business Enterprises; Taxation of Business Enterprises. (19??)-. English. an. $56.50. Commerce Clearing House Inc., 4025 West Peterson Avenue, Chicago IL 60646-6085. **Tel** (312)583-8500, FAX (708)940-4600. ***Continues** Study of Federal Tax Law. Taxation of Business Enterprises.*

US
STUDY OF FEDERAL TAX LAW. TAXATION OF BUSINESS ENTERPRISES, THE. ***Title Change.*** **Added/Corp** Commerce Clearing House. **VFOAT** Taxation of Business Enterprises. (1987/1988)-(199?). English. Commerce Clearing House Inc., 4025 West Peterson Avenue, Chicago IL 60646-6085. **Tel** (312)583-8500, FAX (708)940-4600. **LC** KF6450.A7; T39. **DD** 343.7305/268; 347.3035268. ***Continues** Study of Federal Tax Law. Income Tax. Business Enterprises, 0738-1352.* ***Continued by** Study of Federal Tax Law. Cases and Materials. Taxation of Business Enterprises.*

US
SYNOPSIS OF BOILER AND PRESSURE VESSEL LAW RULES AND REGULATIONS. (19??)-. English. Three times a year. $130.00 non-members, $120.00 members. Uniform Boiler & Pressure Vessels, 308 North Evergreen Road, Suite 240, Louisville KY 40243. **Tel** (502)244-6029, FAX (502)244-6030.

US/8756-5412
TAX, SEC, AND ACCOUNTING ASPECTS OF CORPORATE ACQUISITIONS. [Tax SEC account. asp. corp. acquis.]. **VAT** Tax, Securities and Exchange Commission, and Accounting Aspects of Corporate Acquisitions. English. Practising Law Institute, 810 Seventh Avenue, New York NY 10019-5818. **Tel** (212)765-5700, FAX (212)581-4670 general correspondence, (212)265-4742 orders and billing inquiries. **LC** KF6499.M4; T39. **DD** 343. ***Continues*** *Tax and Accounting Aspects of Corporate Reorganizations, 0883-4474.*

US
TAXATION OF CORPORATE LIQUIDATIONS. $119.00. Macmillan Publishing Company, 866 3rd Avenue, New York NY 10022. **Tel** (212)702-2000, (800)257-5755. **LC** KF6499.D5. **DD** 343.7305/236. Index available. cum. index.
Desc: Describes liquidation alternatives and compliance.

NE
TAXES AND INVESTMENT IN THE MIDDLE EAST. See Public Administration-Public Finance and Taxation.

NE
TAXES AND INVESTMENT IN THE MIDDLE EAST. SUPPLEMENT. No. 1 (1978)-. English. qt. $630.00 (includes two binders and four supplements). International Bureau of Fiscal Documentation - IBFD Publications, PO Box 20237, 1000 HE Amsterdam The Netherlands. **Tel** 011 31 20-6267726, FAX 011 31 20-6228658, telex 13217 INTAX NL. **(Subscription address:** IBFD / International Bureau of Fiscal Documentation USA, Inc., 24 Hudson Street, Kinderhook NY 12106.**)**

US/0271-1923
TEXAS ANTITRUST BULLETIN. Main/Corp State Bar of Texas. Antitrust and Trade Regulation Section. **VFOAT** State Bar Section Report. V. 1- Jan. 1977-. Bulletin. English. qt. State Bar of Texas, PO Box 12487, Capitol Station, Austin TX 78711. **Tel** (512)463-1411. **LC** KFT1431.A15; S7. **DD** 343.764/072/05.

US/1069-8434
TEXAS BUSINESS STATUTES AND SECURITIES RULES. [Tex. bus. statut. secur. rules]. **Main/Corp** Texas. **VFOAT** Business Statutes and Securities Rules of Texas; Texas Business Statutes & Securities Rules; Texas Business Statutes. (1990)-. English. Parker Publications, 2283 Cosmos Court, Carlsbad CA 92009. **Tel** (800)452-9873, (619)931-5979. **LC** KFT1405.A29; P37. **DD** 346.764/065; 347.640665. ***Continues*** *Texas. Parker's Business Statutes and Securities Rules of Texas.*

US/1045-5191
TRADE CASES. ***Ceased.*** (TRADE CASES / CCH.). [Trade cases]. **Added/Corp** Commerce Clearing House. **VFOAT** CCH Trade Cases. (1932)-(Jan. 1993). English. sa. Commerce Clearing House Inc., 4025 West Peterson Avenue, Chicago IL 60646-6085. **Tel** (312)583-8500, FAX (708)940-4600. **ED** A. E. Schechter. **DD** 380.1681522.
Desc: Court decisions and decrees on antitrust and Federal Trade Commission law published in compact bound volumes.

AT/0818-044X
TRADE PRACTICES COMMISSION BULLETIN. See Law.

US
TRADE SECRETS. English. ir. Matthew Bender & Company Inc., 1275 Broadway, Albany NY 12204. **Tel** (800)833-9844, (518)487-3000.

●UK/1352-061X
TRADING LAW AND TRADING LAW REPORTS. VFOAT Trading Law and Trading Law Reports. (1994)-. Periodical. English. Six times a year. £63.40 UK; £65.00 other. Barry Rose Law Periodicals Ltd., Little London, Chichester West Sussex PO19 1PG England. **Tel** 011 44 243 787841, 011 44 243 783637, FAX 011 44 243 779174, 011 44 243 779278. **ED** Susan Singleton. **LC** KD2200.A38; T735. **Bk Rev**, (Qty: 18). **Ad Acc, Adv Mgr:** Mrs. Curtis. ***Continues*** *Trading Law Reports.*
Desc: Articles covering the law relating to competition, restrictive trade practices, monopolies, merges, international trade, trade descriptions and more.

UK
TRADING LAW REPORTS. ***Title Change.*** (Jan. 1983)-(199?). Periodical. English. qt. Barry Rose Law Periodicals Ltd., Little London, Chichester West Sussex PO19 1PG England. **Tel** 011 44 243 787841, 011 44 243 783637, FAX 011 44 243 779174, 011 44 243 779278. **ED** G Stephenson. **LC** KD2200.A38; T7. **DD** 343.41/08; 344.1038. Index available. ***Continued by*** *Trading Law and Trading Law Reports.*
Desc: Covers judgements within the High Court Queen's Bench Division, Court of Justice of the European Communities and The House of Lords.

US/1045-8905
TRANSNATIONAL LAWYER, THE. See Law-International Law.

US/0041-672X
UNIFORM COMMERCIAL CODE LAW JOURNAL. [Unif. commer. code law j.]. Vol. 1, No. 1 (Summer 1968)-. Periodical. English. qt (4 issues). $141.50 US and Canada; $219.45 other. Warren Gorham & Lamont Inc., Park Square Building, 31 St. James Avenue, Boston MA 02116-4112. **Tel** (617)423-2020, (800)950-1207, FAX (617)423-2026. **ED** Louis P. del Luca. **LC** K25; .N37. **DD** 347.7. **CODEN** UCCLA7. **[CCC].** available on microfilm and microfiche from University Microfilms International (UMI). Documents available from UMI Article Clearinghouse.
Desc: Continuous coverage of the laws of commercial and consumer secured lending, sales, and negotiable instruments.
Ind/Abst ABI/INFORM Glob. Ed.; ABI Inform Ondisc (Winter 1980-); Acad. Search (Jan. 1994-); Bus. Index (1985-); Gen. BusinessFile (1985-); Gen. Period. Index (1985-); Index Leg. Period.; INFO-SOUTH Abstr.; Leg. Resour. Index (1980-); LegalTrac (1980-); Mag. Search; Trade Ind. Index (1981-?).

US/0891-9895
UNIVERSITY OF PENNSYLVANIA JOURNAL OF INTERNATIONAL BUSINESS LAW. [Univ. Pa. j. int. bus. law]. **Added/Corp** University of Pennsylvania. Law School. **VFOAT** Journal of International Business Law. Vol. 9, No. 1 (1987)-. Periodical. English. Four times a year (Jan., Apr., July, Oct.). $27.50. University of Pennsylvania / Journal of International Business Law, 3400 Chestnut Street, Philadelphia PA 19104. **Tel** (215)898-6869, FAX (215)898-6619. **LC** K10; .O857. **DD** 346/.066/05; 342.66605. **Pr Rev.** available on microfilm from University Microfilms International (UMI). Documents available from The Genuine Article. ***Continues*** *Journal of Comparative Business and Capital Market Law, 0167-9333.*
Ind/Abst Bowne Dig. Corp. Sec. Lawyers; Curr. Contents Soc. Behav. Sci.; Gen. BusinessFile (1992-); Index Leg. Period.; Leg. Resour. Index; LegalTrac (1980-); Res. Alert [Full Cov.]; Soc. Sci. Cit. Index [Full Cov.].

US/0735-8350
WASHINGTON BUSINESS LAW REPORTER. VFOAT Business Law Reporter. Vol. 1, No. 1 Nov.-Dec. 1982. Periodical. English. bm. $42.60. Butterworth Heinemann / Woburn, MA, 225 Wildwood Avenue, Unit B, Woburn MA 01801. **Tel** (800)366-2665, FAX (617)928-2620, telex 880052. **LC** KFW152.A15; W37. **DD** 346.797/07; 347.97067.

US/0164-4610
WASHINGTON SERVICE BUREAU SUPREME COURT BRIEF SERVICE. ANTITRUST AND SECURITIES. Main/Corp Washington Service Bureau. **VFOAT** Supreme Court Brief Service. Antitrust and Securities. (19??)-. English. wk. Washington Service Bureau Inc., 655 15th Street Northwest, Suite 270, Washington DC 20005. **Tel** (800)955-5219, (202)508-0600.

GW/0172-049X
WETTBEWERB IN RECHT UND PRAXIS : WRP. Added/Corp Zentrale zur BekÈampfung Unlauteren Wettbewerbs (Frankfurt am Main, Germany). **VFOAT** WRP. (19??)-. Periodical. German. Twelve times a year. DM620.56 Germany; DM648.00 other. Deutscher Fachverlag GmbH, Verlagsgruppe, D 60264 Frankfurt Germany. **Tel** 011 49 69 75951001, telex 411 862. **ED** Jabine Klamroth. **LC** KK6456.A13; W48. **DD** 343.43/072/05; 344.3037205. **Bk Rev. Ad Acc. Circ:** 1,800 (ctrl). ***Continues*** *Wettbewerb in Recht und Praxis mit Kartellrecht.*
Desc: Competition, premium and discount law, trade mark law and their significance for competition, antitrust law, advertising law and international competition law.
Ind/Abst Index Foreign Leg. Per.

US
WHITE, NEW YORK CORPORATIONS: BCL, N-PCL AND RELATED STATUTES. Main/Corp New York (State). **Added/Corp** New York (State). New York Corporations: BCL, N-PCL and Related Statutes. New York (State). Whitebook. (19??)-. English. an. Matthew Bender & Company Inc., 1275 Broadway, Albany NY 12204. **Tel** (800)833-9844, (518)487-3000. **LC** KFN5340.A29; B46. **DD** 346/.747/066.

GW/0512-6320
WIRTSCHAFTSRECHT. Added/Corp Germany (East). Ministerrat. Arbeitsgruppe Fur Staats und Wirtschaftsrecht. (1970)-. Periodical. German (English and Russian; table of contents in English and Russian). Twice a year. DM133.20. Verlag die Wirtschaft Berlin, Am Friedrichshain 22, D 10407 Berlin Germany. **Tel** 011 49 30 42870. **ED** Claus Treufeldt. Index available. **Bk Rev**, (Qty: 50-70). **Ad Acc, Adv Mgr:** Mr. Kassner, **Tel** (030)4287323. ctrl circ. ***Supersedes*** *Vertagssystem.*
Desc: Monthly journal for commercial law, especially addressed to lawyers, legal advisers, scientists and students of law.

AU/0930-3855
WIRTSCHAFTSRECHTLICHE BLAETTER : WBL. VFOAT WBL. (Jan. 1987)-. Periodical. German. mo. Comes with Juristische Blaetter. Springer-Verlag GmbH & Company KG, Heidelberger Platz 3, D 14197 Berlin Germany. **Tel** 011 49 30 8207223, FAX 011 49 30 8214091, telex 183 319 SPBLN D. **(Subscription address:** Springer Verlag New York Inc. / for North America, 44 Hartz Way, Secaucus NJ 07096.**) [CCC].**

SZ/1011-4548
WORLD COMPETITION. [World compet.]. **VFOAT** Law and Economics Review; World Competition Law and Economics Review. No. 31 (Oct. 1987)-. Periodical. English. Four times a year. 330.00F. Werner Publishing Company Ltd., PO Box 5134, CH 1211 Geneva 11 Switzerland. **Tel** 011 41 22 3103422. **LC** K21; .S85. **DD** 343/.0721/05; 342.372105. **[CCC].** ***Continues*** *Swiss Review of International Competition Law.*
Desc: Research journal in the field of international competition law and economics as well as covering international trade regulations.
Ind/Abst PAIS Int. Print; World Agric. Econ.

NE
YEARBOOK : COMMERCIAL ARBITRATION. Added/Corp International Council for Commercial Arbitration. **VFOAT** Commercial Arbitration. (1976)-. English. an. $130.00 North America; Fl240.00 other. Kluwer Law and Taxation Publishers, Staverenstraat 32015, PO Box 23, 7400 GA Deventer Netherlands. **Tel** 011 31 5700 47261. **(Subscription address:** Kluwer Law & Taxation, 675 Massachusetts Avenue, Cambridge MA 02139.**) ED** Pieter Sanders. **LC** K2400.A53; Y4. **DD** 346.07/0269. **Bk Rev. Ad Acc.** ctrl circ.
Desc: The foremost guide to commercial arbitration law and practice throughout the world.

GW
ZEITSCHRIFT FUER UNTERNEHMENS- UND GESELLSCHAFTSRECHT. Vol. 1 (Jan. 1972)-. Periodical. German. qt (Jan., Apr., July, Oct.). $226.10. Walter de Gruyter Inc., PO Box 303421, D 10728 Berlin Germany. **Tel** 011 49 30 260050, FAX 011 49 30 26005251. **LC** K30; .E73. **DD** 346/.43/06605.
Ind/Abst Index Foreign Leg. Per.

CRIMINAL LAW

US
ADVANCED CRIMINAL TRIAL TACTICS FOR PROSECUTION AND DEFENSE / PRACTISING LAW INSTUTUTE. English. an. Practising Law Institute, 810 Seventh Avenue, New York NY 10019-5818. **Tel** (212)765-5700, FAX (212)581-4670 general correspondence, (212)265-4742 orders and billing inquiries. **LC** KF9656.Z9; A37. **DD** 354.73/07; 347.3057.

CN/0715-3155
ALBERTA SASKATCHEWAN MANITOBA CRIMINAL DECISIONS. [Alta., Sask., Manit. crim. decis.]. **VFOAT** Alberta Saskatchewan Manitoba Criminal Conviction Decisions. 1978-. English. an. $115.50. Western Legal Publications Ltd., 301 One Alexander Street, Vancouver BC V6A 1B2 Canada. **Tel** (800)663-0422, (604)687-5671. **DD** 345.71/002648. Index available. available on an online database (from CAN/LAW Database).
Desc: Digests of criminal conviction decisions made available by the Courts of Appeal and Courts of Queen's Bench of Alberta, Saskatchewan, and Manitoba indexed by subject.

US
ALCOHOL SERVER LIABILITY : A COMPILATION OF DRAM SHOP AND RELATED STATUTES AND JUDICIAL RULINGS. VFOAT Compilation of Dram Shop and Related Statutes and Judicial Rulings. 6th Ed. (Aug. 1986)-. English. an. NABCA, 4216 King Street West, Alexandria VA 22302. ***Continues*** *Compilation of Dram Shop Statutes and Judicial Rulings, 0749-0860.*
Desc: A comprehensive nation-wide compilation of dram shop laws and related statutes and judicial rulings.

II
ALL INDIA CRIMINAL LAW REPORTER. English. mo. 70.00. Manager All India Criminal Law Reporter, Kothi No 108-B Sector 27-A, Chandigarh India. **DD** 345.46/002648; 344.605002648.

US/0164-0364
AMERICAN CRIMINAL LAW REVIEW, THE. [Am. Crim. Law Rev.]. **Added/Corp** American Bar Association. Section of Criminal Justice. American Bar Association. Section of Criminal Law. Vol. 10 (July 1971)-. Periodical. English. qt. $30.00 US; $38.00 Other. Georgetown University Law Center, 600 New Jersey Avenue NW, Washington DC 20009. **Tel** (202)662-9468, FAX (202)662-9444. **LC** K1; .M43. **DD** 345/.73/005. **Pr Rev.** available on microfilm and microfiche from University Microfilms International (UMI). Documents available from The Genuine Article, UMI Article Clearinghouse. ***Continues*** *American Criminal Law Quarterly, 0002-8118.*
Ind/Abst Crim. Justice Abstr.; Crim. Justice Period. Index (1980-); Crim. Penol. Police Sci. Abstr.; Curr. Contents Soc. Behav. Sci.; Curr. Law Index (1980-); Expand. Acad. Index (1984-); Index Leg. Period.; Leg. Resour. Index (1980-); LegalTrac (1980-); Newsp. Period. Abstr. (1989-); Res. Alert [Full Cov.]; Soc. Sci. Cit. Index [Full Cov.].

US/0092-2315
AMERICAN JOURNAL OF CRIMINAL LAW. [Am. j. crim. law]. **Added/Corp** University of Texas at Austin. School of Law. Vol. 1 (Feb. 1972)-. Periodical. English. Three times a year (Jan., June and Sept.). $20.00 US; $23.00 other. University of Texas School of Law, 727 East 26th Street 2101, Austin TX 78705. **Tel** (512)471-1106. **ED** John L. Williams (512)471-9200. **LC** K1; .M44. **DD** 345/.73/005. Index available. **Bk Rev. Circ:** 750 (ctrl). available on microfilm and microfiche from University Microfilms International (UMI).
Desc: The journal serves as a national forum on all aspects of criminal jurisprudence.
Ind/Abst Crim. Justice Abstr.; Crim. Justice Period. Index; Crim. Penol. Police Sci. Abstr.; Curr. Law Index (1980-); Index Leg. Period.; Leg. Resour. Index (1980-); LegalTrac (1980-); Sage Urban Stud. Abstr.

US
AMERICAN SERIES OF FOREIGN PENAL CODES. Vol. 1 (1960)-. Monographic series. English. ir. Price varies per volume. Fred B. Rothman & Company, 10368 West Centennial Road, Littleton CO 80127. **Tel** (800)457-1986, (303)979-5657, FAX (303)978-1457, telex 87669. **ED** Edward M. Wise. **Bk Rev.**
Desc: English translation of foreign penal codes.

CN/1197-8538
ANNOTATED ONTARIO RULES OF CRIMINAL PRACTICE. (ANNOTATED ONTARIO RULES OF CRIMINAL PRACTICE / MURRAY D. SEGAL, RICK LIBMAN.). [Annot. Ont. rules crim. pract.]. **VFOAT** Rules of Criminal Practice. (199?)-. English. an. 70.00Can$. Carswell / Canada, 2075 Kennedy Road, Scarborough Ontario M1T 3V4 Canada. **Tel** (416)609-3800, (800)387-5164. **DD** 345.713/05/02632. ***Continues*** *Segal, Murray D., 1949- Annotated Rules of Criminal Practice.*

CN/1184-0293
ANNOTATED TREMEEAR'S CRIMINAL CODE. (CRIMINAL ANNOTATIONS.). [Annot. Tremeear's Crim. Code]. **Main/Corp** Canada. **VFOAT** Tremeear's Criminal Code; Annotated Tremeear's Criminal Code. (1990)-. Periodical. English. **ED** Editors, 1990- : David Watt and Michelle K. Fuerst. **LC** KE8804.519.A18; T74. **DD** 345.71/002632. ***Continues*** *Tremeear's Criminal Code and Miscellaneous Statutes, 0226-1987.*

US/0093-8653
ANNUAL PUBLIC DEFENDERS' WORKSHOP. (ANNUAL PUBLIC DEFENDERS' WORKSHOP HANDBOOK.). **Main/Corp** Public Defenders' Workshop. English. an. Public Defenders' Workshop, 810 Seventh Avenue, New York NY 10019. **LC** KF9646.A73; P8. **DD** 345/.73/05.

US
ANNUAL REPORT OF THE PROSECUTOR COUNCIL (TEXAS). **Main/Corp** Texas. Prosecutor Council. (1981)-. English. an. Texas Law Center, Office of Court Administration, 1414 Colorado Street, PO Box 12066, Austin TX 78711. **LC** KFT1777; .A86. **DD** 353.9764008/8. ***Continues*** *Annual Report of the Texas Prosecutors Council.*

CN/0821-7912
ANNUAL REVIEW OF CRIMINAL LAW. [Annu. rev. crim. law.]. **VFOAT** Criminal Law. (1982)-. English. an. price varies per volume. Carswell / Canada, 2075 Kennedy Road, Scarborough Ontario M1T 3V4 Canada. **Tel** (416)609-3800, (800)387-5164. **LC** KE8807.7; .G64. **DD** 345.71; 347.105. **Circ:** 1,000.
Desc: Summarizes and distills important developments in Canadian criminal law, practice and evidence. Includes an overview of trends in judicial interpretation of the Charter.

UK/0961-4249
ARCHBOLD NEWS. [Archbold News]. (1991)-. Periodical. English. Ten times a year. £75.00 Europe; £79.00 other. Sweet & Maxwell Ltd., South Quay Plaza, 183 Marsh Wall, London E14 9FT England. **Tel** 011 44 264 342899, FAX 011 44 264 342723, telex 929089 ITPINF G. **DD** 344.205.

FR
ARCHIVES DE POLITIQUE CRIMINELLE. **Added/Corp** Centre de Recherches de Politique Criminelle (France). No. 1 (1975)-. French. an (Apr.). 160.00F. Editions A Pedone, 13 rue Soufflot, 75005 Paris France. **Tel** 011 33 1 43540597. **LC** K1; .R43. **DD** 345/.005.
Ind/Abst PAIS Int. Print.

NZ/0067-0510
AUCKLAND UNIVERSITY LAW REVIEW. See Law-Civil Law.

AT
AUSTRALIAN CRIMINAL REPORTS, THE. **Added/Corp** Law Book Company. Vol. 1, Pt. 1 (Aug. 1980)-. English. 225.00Aus$. The Law Book Company Limited, 44-50 Waterloo Road, North Ryde New South Wales, 2113 Australia. **Tel** 011 61 2 8870177, FAX 011 61 2 8887240, telex ASBOOK 27445. **ED** Fiori Rinaldi. **DD** 345.94/002642; 349.405002642.
Desc: Keeps criminal law specialists and general practitioners alike up to date with all the cases, not only from their own jurisdictions, but also from other courts of the States and Territories.
Ind/Abst Aust. Leg. Mon. Dig.

CN/0709-2598
B. C. CROWN COUNSEL NEWSLETTER. **VAT** British Columbia Crown Counsel Newsletter. V. 1- 1979-. Newsletter. English. Crown Counsel Association, 420-700 West Georgia Street, Vancouver BC V7Y 1C6. **DD** 345.71/05.

IT/0392-2596
BIBLIOGRAFIA IDG. C, DIRITTO E PROCEDURA PENALE. [Bibliogr. IDG, C, Diritto procedura penale]. **VFOAT** Diritto e Procedura Penale. 1979-. Italian. an. L9000. Casa Editrice Giuffre, via Statuto 2, 20121 Milan Italy. **LC** KKH3791.2; .B55.

US/0892-9033
CALIFORNIA DUI REPORT. [Calif. DUI rep.]. **VAT** California Driving Under the Influence Report. Vol. 1, No. 1 (May 1987)-. Periodical. English. Twelve times a year. $99.00. Courtroom Compendiums, PO Box 705, Woodland Hills CA 91365. **Tel** (818)884-9039. **ED** James Scott Bell. **DD** 343. Index available. cum. index. **Bk Rev. Circ:** 350.
Desc: For California judges and lawyers and law enforcement on drunk driving law, science and information.

CN/0008-3348
CANADIAN CRIMINAL CASES (BOUND CUMULATION). (CANADIAN CRIMINAL CASES.). [Can. crim. cases]. Vol. 1 (1963)-New Ser., Vol. 5 (1970); 2nd Ser. Vol. 1 (1971)-2nd Ser. Vol. 70 (183); 3rd Ser., Vol. 1 (1983)-. Periodical. English. ir. 115.00Can$ (weekly paper parts & bound volume), 97.00Can$ (bound volume). Canada Law Book Inc., 240 Edward Street, Aurora Ontario L4G 3S9 Canada. **Tel** (800)263-3269, (905)841-6472, FAX (905)841-5085. **ED** Edward L. Greenspan. **DD** 345.71/002642. cum. index. **Bk Rev. Ad Acc.** ***Absorbed*** *Canadian Criminal Cases. Annotation Service, 0380-2582.*
Desc: National series of law reports containing full text of all important decisions rendered in criminal and quasi-criminal cases from all Canadian courts and jurisdictions.

US/0736-8240
CASE COMMENTARIES AND BRIEFS. (CASE COMMENTARIES AND BRIEFS / NATIONAL DISTRICT ATTORNEYS ASSOCIATION.). [Case comment. briefs]. **Added/Corp** National District Attorneys Association. Vol. 1, No. 1 (July 1981)-. Periodical. English. Ten times a year. Free to members of the National District Attorneys Association. National District Attorneys Association / Virginia, 99 Canal Center Plaza, Suite 510, Alexandria VA 22314. **Tel** (703)549-9222. **LC** KF9614; .C37. **DD** 345.73/05/02648; A 347.305502648. **Circ:** 7,000 (ctrl).

US/0890-8400
CASE DIGEST (SACRAMENTO, CALIF.). (CASE DIGEST / CALIFORNIA DISTRICT ATTORNEYS ASSOCIATION.). [Case dig.]. **Added/Corp** California District Attorney's Association. (197?)-. Periodical. English. Twenty-four times a year. $150.00. California District Attorneys Association, 1414 K Street, Suite 3000, Sacramento CA 95814-3929. **Tel** (916)443-2017. **DD** 345.

US/0744-9488
CHAMPION (HOUSTON, TEX.), THE. (THE CHAMPION : THE OFFICIAL NEWS REPORT OF THE NATIONAL ASSOCIATION OF CRIMINAL DEFENSE LAWYERS.). [Champion]. **Added/Corp** National Association of Criminal Defense Lawyers (U.S.). (19??)-. Periodical. English. Ten times a year (monthly except Jan. & Sept.). $40.00 University Law Libraries; $75.00 private subscriptions. National Association of Criminal Defense Lawyers, 1110 Vermont Avenue NW, Suite 1150, Washington DC 20005. **Tel** (202)872-8688, FAX (202)331-8269. **LC** KF9602; .C47. **DD** 345.73/05/05; 347.305505.

US
CIS LAW REPRINTS. CRIMINAL LAW SERIES : THE SUPREME COURT OF THE UNITED STATES PETITIONS AND BRIEFS. **VFOAT** Supreme Court of the United States Petitions and Briefs. Criminal Law Series. Vol. 16, No. 1 (1984/85)-. English. ir. Congressional Information Service Inc, 4520 East-West Highway, Suite 800, Bethesda MD 20814-3389. **Tel** (800)638-8380, (301)654-1550, FAX (301)654-4033, telex 292386 CIS UR. ***Continues*** *BNA's Law Reprints. Criminal Law Series.*

US/0882-0244
CJ INTERNATIONAL. See Law-Law Enforcement and Criminology.

FR
CODE PENAL. **Main/Corp** France. **VFOAT** Code Penal et Code de Justice Militaire, Armee de Terre; Code Penal et Code de Justice Militaire, Armee de Terre, Armee de Mer. (1931)-. French. an. Jurisprudence Generale Dalloz, 11 rue Soufflot, 75240 Cedex 05 Paris France.

CN/0317-3585
COMMUNITY EDUCATION SERIES. Began publication in 1972?. Monographic series. English. Price varies per volume. John Howard Society of Ontario, 168 Isabella Street, Toronto Ontario M4Y 1P6 Canada. **DD** 345/.71.

BS
CRIM. COMMITTAL. **Main/Corp** Botswana. High Court. (19??)-. English. Botswana Government High Court, PO Box 87, Government Printer, Gaborone Botswana. **DD** 348/.681/94.

UK/0070-1521
CRIMINAL APPEAL REPORTS, THE. **Main/Corp** Great Britain. Court of Appeal. (19??)-. English. Six times a year (2 volumes per year). £220.00 Europe; £230.00 other. Sweet & Maxwell Ltd., South Quay Plaza, 183 Marsh Wall, London E14 9FT England. **Tel** 011 44 264 342899, FAX 011 44 264 342723, telex 929089 ITPINF G. **LC** KD7865.A2; C7. **DD** 345/.41/002643. ***Continues*** *Great Britain. Court of Criminal Appeals. Criminal Appeal Reports.*
Ind/Abst Aust. Leg. Mon. Dig.

UK/0144-3321
CRIMINAL APPEAL REPORTS (SENTENCING), THE. **Main/Corp** Great Britain. Court of Appeal. Vol. 1 (1979)-. English. Four times a year. £145.00 Europe; £152.00 other. Sweet & Maxwell Ltd., South Quay Plaza, 183 Marsh Wall, London E14 9FT England. **Tel** 011 44 264 342899, FAX 011 44 264 342723, telex 929089 ITPINF G. **ED** Santha Rasaih. **Bk Rev. Ad Acc. Circ:** 700.
Desc: A series of law reports devoted solely to matters of sentencing.

US/0731-082X
CRIMINAL DEFENSE NEWSLETTER. (CRIMINAL DEFENSE NEWSLETTER / STATE APPELLATE DEFENDER OFFICE, LEGAL RESOURCES PROJECT.). Began with Nov. 1977 issue. Newsletter. English. mo. $35.00. State Appellate Defender, Office Legal Resources Project 1200-6th Avenue, Detroit MI 48226. **Tel** (313)256-2814. **ED** Dawn Van Hoek. **LC** KFM4775; .C75. **DD** 345.774/05044/05; 347. 7405504405. Index available. cum. index. **Bk Rev. Circ:** 1,500 (ctrl).
Desc: Contains articles on various criminal issues, new legislation, summaries of recent criminal cases, practice notes and news of interest to criminal defense attorneys.

US/0045-9038
CRIMINAL JUSTICE NEWSLETTER (NEW YORK, N.Y.). (CRIMINAL JUSTICE NEWSLETTER.). [Crim. justice newsl.]. **Added/Corp** Institute of Judicial Administration National Council on Crime and Delinquency. **VFOAT** CJN. Vol. 1 (June 1970)-. Newsletter. English. Twenty-four times a year. $198.00. Pace Publications / New York, PO Box 2972, Grand Central Station, New York NY 10163. **Tel** (212)685-5450, FAX (212)679-4701. **LC** K3; .R48. **DD** 345/.73/0505.
Ind/Abst Leg. Resour. Index (1980-?); LegalTrac (1980-1988).

US/0092-3907
CRIMINAL JUSTICE QUARTERLY, THE. ***Suspended.*** **Added/Corp** New Jersey. Division of Criminal Justice. Appellate Section. (19??)-Vol. 10.

English. qt. Free. Editor Division of Criminal Justice Appellate Section, 7 Glenwood Avenue, East Orange NJ 07017. **LC** K3; .R49. **DD** 345/.73/0505.
Ind/Abst Crim. Justice Abstr.

US
CRIMINAL LAW. **Main/Corp** New York (State). **VFOAT** Criminal Law P.L.-C.P.L.; Criminal Law C.P.L.-P.L.; Criminal Law Pamphlet; Criminal Law PL-CPL; Criminal Law CPL-PL. English. an. Matthew Bender & Company Inc., 1275 Broadway, Albany NY 12204. **Tel** (800)833-9844, (518)487-3000. **LC** KFN6100.A29; .N48. **DD** 345.747; 347.4705.

US/0011-1317
CRIMINAL LAW BULLETIN. [Crim. law bull.]. Vol. 1 (Feb. 1965)-. Periodical. English. bm. $139.25 US and Canada; $216.20 other. Warren Gorham & Lamont Inc., Park Square Building, 31 St. James Avenue, Boston MA 02116-4112. **Tel** (617)423-2020, (800)950-1207, FAX (617)423-2026. **ED** Fred Cohen. **LC** K3; .R5. **DD** 343. **[CCC]**. available on microfilm and microfiche from University Microfilms International (UMI).
Desc: Delivers comprehensive coverage of criminal procedures from arrest to appeal; state and federal constitutional issues; specific crimes; and other related proceedings.
Ind/Abst Crim. Justice Abstr.; Crim. Justice Period. Index; Curr. Law Index (1980-); Index Leg. Period.; Leg. Resour. Index (1980-); LegalTrac (1980-).

US/0093-4674
CRIMINAL LAW COMMENTATOR (NEW YORK). (CRIMINAL LAW COMMENTATOR.). Periodical. English. bm. $15.00. Federal Legal Publications Inc, 157 Chambers Street, New York NY 10007. **Tel** (212)619-4949, FAX (212)608-3141.

US
CRIMINAL LAW DIGEST. (1970)-. Periodical. English. ir. $120.00 US; $156.00 other. Warren Gorham & Lamont Inc., Park Square Building, 31 St. James Avenue, Boston MA 02116-4112. **Tel** (617)423-2020, (800)950-1207, FAX (617)423-2026.

CN/0824-7544
CRIMINAL LAW DIGEST. SUPPLEMENT (TORONTO 1982). (CRIMINAL LAW DIGEST. SUPPLEMENT.). [Crim. law dig., Suppl.]. (1982)-. English. an. Warren Gorham & Lamont Inc., Park Square Building, 31 St. James Avenue, Boston MA 02116-4112. **Tel** (617)423-2020, (800)950-1207, FAX (617)423-2026. **DD** 345.71/002648. ***Continues** Criminal Law Digest. Cumulative Supplement (Toronto, Ont.), 0712-1407.*

US/1046-8374
CRIMINAL LAW FORUM. [Crim. law forum]. **Added/Corp** Society for the Reform of Criminal Law. Rutgers School of Law, Camden (N.J.). Vol. 1, No. 1 (Autumn 1989)-. Periodical. English. Three times a year. $45.00 US & Canada; $50.00 others. Rutgers University School of Law, 5th and Penn Streets, Camden NJ 08102. **Tel** (609)964-9101, FAX (609)757-6487. **ED** Madeline Sann, (phone: (609)757-6352). **LC** K3; .R515. **DD** 345/.005. Index available. cum. index. **Bk Rev. Ad Acc. Pr Rev. Circ:** 850. available on an online database from WESTLAW.
Desc: The goal of this journal is to advance criminal law theory, practice and reform on both the domestic and international level. It features original articles, conference papers, book reviews, audience, chief justices, law commissioners and attorneys general throughout the Commonwealth government. Information on attorneys, state and federal justices of appeal, and legislators in the U.S., and university and government law libraries in some three dozen countries across Africa, Europe, Asia, Pacific Rim, and the Western Hemisphere.
Ind/Abst Appl. Soc. Sci. Index Abstr.; Crim. Justice Abstr.; Crim. Justice Period. Index; Crim. Penol. Police Sci. Abstr.; Curr. Law Index; Index Leg. Period. (1992-); Leg. Resour. Index; LegalTrac (1989-); PAIS Int. Print (1991-).

II/0011-1325
CRIMINAL LAW JOURNAL. (19??)-. Periodical. English. mo. $144.00. All India Reporter Ltd, Medows HS Nagindas/Master Road, Bombay 400 023 India. **(Subscription address:** Prints India, 11 Darya Ganj, New Delhi 110002 India.)
Ind/Abst LegalTrac (1980-).

AT/0314-1160
CRIMINAL LAW JOURNAL. [Crim. law j.]. **Added/Corp** Law Book Company. Vol. 1, No. 1 (Feb. 1977)-. Periodical. English. bm (6 issues). 195.00Aus$. The Law Book Company Limited, 44-50 Waterloo Road, North Ryde New South Wales, 2113 Australia. **Tel** 011 61 2 8870177, FAX 011 61 2 8887240, telex ASBOOK 27445. **ED** Paul Byrne. **LC** K3; .R52. **DD** 349.405005. Index available. **Ad Acc.**
Desc: Provides lawyers throughout Australia with up-to-date analyses of the latest developments in law through articles, case notes and reviews.
Ind/Abst APAIS, Aust. Public Aff. Inf. Ser. (1977-); Aust. Leg. Mon. Dig.; Curr. Law Index (1980-); Index Leg. Period.; Leg. Resour. Index (1980-).

US/0098-8049
CRIMINAL LAW (LOS ANGELES, CALIF.). (CRIMINAL LAW.). [Crim. law]. **Main/Corp** Bay Area Review Course, Inc. (19??)-. English. Legal Book Corporation, 316 West 2nd Street, Los Angeles CA 90012. **Tel** (310)626-3494. **LC** KF9219.3; B38. **DD** 345/.73.

US/0888-7012
CRIMINAL LAW NEWSLETTER (SAN JOSE, CALIF.). (CRIMINAL LAW NEWSLETTER.). [Crim. law newsl.]. (19??)-. Newsletter. English. bw. $327.00. La Jolla Legal Publications, 5580 La Jolla Boulevard, Suite 116, La Jolla CA 92037. **Tel** (619)581-9444. **DD** 345.

US/0145-7322
CRIMINAL LAW OUTLINE. **Added/Corp** National College of the State Judiciary. (19??)-. English. an. $12.00. National Judicial College, Judicial Building, University of Nevada Reno, Reno NV 89557. **ED** George B. Richter. **LC** KF9210.3; .G73. **DD** 345/.73. **Circ:** 6,000.
Desc: Annotated outline of criminal law and procedure confined to federal constitutional laws; emphasis on 4th, 5th, 6th, and 8th amendments and miscellaneous due process problems.

CN/0011-1333
CRIMINAL LAW QUARTERLY (TORONTO). (THE CRIMINAL LAW QUARTERLY.). [Crim. law q.]. Vol. 1 (May 1958)-. Periodical. English. Four times a year. 108.00Can$. Canada Law Book Inc., 240 Edward Street, Aurora Ontario L4G 3S9 Canada. **Tel** (800)263-3269, (905)841-6472, FAX (905)841-5085. **ED** Alan W. Mewett. cum. index.
Desc: Combines informed commentary on current issues with thought-provoking editorials and articles. Each issue features a section devoted exclusively to criminal appeals in the Supreme Court of Canada which takes into account recent judgements and appeals inscribed for hearing or reserved, and notices of appeal filed or leave granted.
Ind/Abst Can. Legal Lit.; Crim. Justice Abstr.; Crim. Justice Period. Index; Curr. Law Index (1980-); Index Leg. Period.; Leg. Resour. Index (1980-); LegalTrac (1980-); Soc. Plann. Policy Dev. Abstr.; Sociol. Abstr. (?-?).

US/0011-1341
CRIMINAL LAW REPORTER, THE. **Added/Corp** Bureau of National Affairs (Washington, D.C.). Vol. 1 (April 19, 1967)-. English. ir (49 issues). $661.00. Bureau of National Affairs Inc., 9435 Key West Avenue, Rockville MD 20850. **Tel** (800)372-1033, (301)258-1033, FAX (301)948-5823. **(Subscription telephone:** FAX (301)948-5823) **ED** Robert L Goebes. **LC** KF9615; .C7. **DD** 343/.0973. **[CCC]**.
Desc: A notification service providing coverage of court decisions, federal legislative activities, and administrative developments in the field of criminal law.
Ind/Abst Crim. Justice Period. Index.

UK/0011-135X
CRIMINAL LAW REVIEW (LONDON, ENGLAND). (THE CRIMINAL LAW REVIEW.). [Crim. law rev.]. (Jan. 1954)-. Periodical. English. Twelve times a year. £96.00 Europe; £101.00 other. Sweet & Maxwell Ltd., South Quay Plaza, 183 Marsh Wall, London E14 9FT England. **Tel** 011 44 264 342899, FAX 011 44 264 342723, telex 929089 ITPINF G. **ED** J. Belford. **LC** K3; .R55. **[CCC]**. cum. index. **Bk Rev. Ad Acc. Pr Rev. Circ:** 6,000. available on microfilm from University Microfilms International (UMI). Documents available from The Genuine Article.
Desc: A wide range of articles by experts in criminal law for everyone involved in the practical problems of the criminal process.
Ind/Abst Aust. Leg. Mon. Dig.; Br. Humanit. Index; Crim. Justice Abstr.; Crim. Penol. Police Sci. Abstr.; Curr. Contents Soc. Behav. Sci.; Index Leg. Period.; Int. Bibliogr. Sociol.; Leg. Resour. Index (1980-?); Res. Alert [Full Cov.]; Soc. Sci. Cit. Index [Full Cov.].

US/0192-3323
CRIMINAL LAW REVIEW (NEW YORK, N.Y. : 1979). (CRIMINAL LAW REVIEW.). **Added/Corp** Clark Boardman Company. (1979)-. English. an. Clark Boardman Callaghan, 155 Pfingsten Road, Deerfield IL 60015. **Tel** (800)323-8067. **LC** K3; .R56. **DD** 345.73/005; 347.305005.
Desc: A compilation of articles published in the previous year.
Ind/Abst Curr. Law Index (1980-); Leg. Resour. Index (1980-); LegalTrac (1980-).

UK/0956-7429
CRIMINAL LAWYER, THE. [Crim. lawyer]. (1989)-. English. £45.00. Butterworth & Co. Ltd. / Kent, England, Borough Green, Sevenoaks Kent TN15 8PH England. **Tel** 011 44 732-884567, FAX 011 44 732-885996. **ED** James Morton. **DD** 344.205.
Desc: Designed specifically for the busy criminal law practitioner, and provides news and information in a practical and easily assimilated form.

US/0099-1228
CRIMINAL PROCEDURE. [Crim. proced.]. **Main/Corp** Bay Area Review Course, Inc. English. Legal Book Corporation, 316 West 2nd Street, Los Angeles CA 90012. **Tel** (310)626-3494. **LC** KF9619.3; .B38. **DD** 345/.73/05.

US/0743-4626
CRIMINAL PROCEDURE HANDBOOK. (CRIMINAL PROCEDURE HANDBOOK / BY JAMES G. CARR.). [Crim. proced. handb.]. **Added/Corp** Clark Boardman Company. (1984)-. English. an. $80.00. Clark Boardman Callaghan, 155 Pfingsten Road, Deerfield IL 60015. **Tel** (800)323-8067. **ED** James G Carr. **LC** KF9602.5; .C75. **DD** 345.73/05; 347.3055. **Circ:** 2,800.
Desc: Survey of state, federal, and U.S. Supreme Court cases relating to criminal procedure. Commentary by the Honorable James G Carr.

CN/0383-9494
CRIMINAL REPORTS. [Crim. rep.]. **VFOAT** Recueil de Jurisprudence en Droit Criminel; Criminal Reports, Canada. (1946)-. Periodical. English (French). sm. 110.00Can$. Carswell / Canada, 2075 Kennedy Road, Scarborough Ontario M1T 3V4 Canada. **Tel** (416)609-3800, (800)387-5164. **ED** Don Stuart. Index available. cum. index. **Ad Acc.**
Desc: Features fast, accurate reporting of judgments covering criminal offences, and evidence from every court level.
Ind/Abst Can. Legal Lit. (1980-); Curr. Law Index (1980-Dec. 1988); Index Can. Leg. Period. Lit.; Leg. Resour. Index (1980-Dec. 1988); LegalTrac (1981-1985).

CN/0703-4687
CRIMINAL REPORTS FOURTH SERIES. Vol. 1 (1991)-. Periodical. English. sm. $108.00 per bound volume, including parts. Carswell / Canada, 2075 Kennedy Road, Scarborough Ontario M1T 3V4 Canada. **Tel** (416)609-3800, (800)387-5164.

US/0732-0930
CRIMINAL TRIAL MANUAL, CALIFORNIA. SUPPLEMENT. English. bm. Hanford Publishing Company, 1525 Oregon Pike, Suite 901, Lancaster PA 17601. **Tel** (717)392-1133.

US/0732-7293
CRIMINAL TRIAL MANUAL. MARYLAND. (19??)-. English. qt. $220.00. Hanford Publishing Company, 1525 Oregon Pike, Suite 901, Lancaster PA 17601. **Tel** (717)392-1133.

US/0732-7285
CRIMINAL TRIAL MANUAL. NEW JERSEY. (19??)-. English. ir. $220.00. Hanford Publishing Company, 1525 Oregon Pike, Suite 901, Lancaster PA 17601. **Tel** (717)392-1133.

CN/0319-8510
CROWN'S NEWSLETTER. May 1972-. Newsletter. English. mo. Ontario Crown Attorneys Association, Crown's Newsletter, c/o Kenneth Chasse Court House, Toronto Ontario M5G 1V1 Canada. **LC** KE8802; .C76. **DD** 345/.71/005.
Ind/Abst Can. Legal Lit.

US/0882-9853
CUYAHOGA CRIMINAL DEFENSE LAWYERS ASSOCIATION NEWSLETTER. **Added/Corp** Cuyahoga Criminal Defense Lawyers Association. **VFOAT** CCDLA Newsletter. Vol. 7, No. 1 (Fall 1984)-. Newsletter. English. qt. Cuyahoga Criminal Defense Lawyers Association, Greene & Hennenberg Company LPA, 801 Bond Court Building, Cleveland OH 44114. **LC** KFO575.A15; C89. **DD** 345.771/05/05; 347.7105505. ***Continues** Cuyahoga County Criminal Courts Bar Association Newsletter.*

US/0270-3432
DEFENDER (COLUMBUS), THE. (THE DEFENDER.). [Defender]. **Added/Corp** Ohio Public Defenders Association. (19??)-. Periodical. English. mo. The Defender, Room 519/8 East Long Street, Columbus OH 43215. **LC** KFO578.A15; D42. **DD** 345.771/01.

NE
DELIKT EN DELINKWENT. (Nov. 1970)-. Periodical. Dutch. Ten times a year. Fl299.00. Uitgeverij Gouda Quint BV, Antwoordnummer 47, 6800 BV Arnhem Netherlands. **Tel** 011 31 85 454762. **(Subscription address:** Libresso BV, Postbus 23, 7400 GA Deventer Netherlands.) **LC** K4; .E42. **Circ:** 1,700. ***Supersedes** Tijdschrift voor Strafrecht.*
Ind/Abst Crim. Penol. Police Sci. Abstr.; Index Foreign Leg. Per.

IT
DIFESA PENALE, LA. Vol. 1, No. 1 (Apr./June 1983)-. Periodical. Italian. Four times a year. L110000. Edizioni Bucalo SNC, Casella Postale 51, 04100 Latina Italy. **Tel** 011 39 773 623226. **LC** K4; .I67. **DD** 345.45/05044; 344.5055044. Index available. **Bk Rev. Ad Acc.**

US
DISTRICT ATTORNEY NEWSLETTER (NEW YORK, N.Y.). (DISTRICT ATTORNEY NEWSLETTER / DISTRICT ATTORNEYS ASSOCIATION OF THE STATE OF NEW YORK.). **Added/Corp** District Attorneys Association of the State of

New York. Vol. 1, No. 1 (Jan. 1973)-. Periodical. English. ir. New York State District, 215 East 161st Street, Bronx NY 10451.

AG
DOCTRINA PENAL. Suspended. Vol. 1, No. 1 (1978)-Vol. B (1992). Periodical. Spanish. Four times a year. $120.00. Depalma SRL, Talcahuano 494, 1013 Buenos Aires Argentina. **Tel** 011 54 1 407306, 461815, FAX 011 54 1 406913. **ED** Ricardo C. Nunez, Carlos A. Tozzini. **LC** K4; .O36. **DD** 345/.005; 342.5005. Index available. cum. index. **Bk Rev**. **Pr Rev. Circ:** 2,000 (ctrl).
Desc: Covers penal law and criminology, including doctrines, jurisprudence and legislation, with a bibliography, magazine reviews and information on symposia, meetings, etc.

US
FLORIDA POLICE ADVISOR. English. Twelve times a year. $24.00. Cumberland Publications Inc., 1322 Southeast Third Avenue, Fort Lauderdale FL 33316. **Tel** (305)462-3273.

XXU
FLORIDA POLICE INFORMANT. Title Change. Vol. 1, (Mar. 1977)-(1993). Periodical. English. mo. **LC** KFF575.A15; F47. **DD** 345/.759/0505. **Continued by** Florida Police Advisor.

US/0091-1011
FOR THE DEFENSE (AUSTIN). (FOR THE DEFENSE.). Periodical. English. qt. National Association Criminal Defense Lawyers, PO Box 12964, Austin TX 78711. **LC** K6; .O7. **DD** 345/.73/07505.

US/0164-6931
FORUM (NORTH HOLLYWOOD). (FORUM.). **Added/Corp** California Attorneys for Criminal Justice. **VFOAT** CACJ Forum; CACJ/Forum. (19??)-. Periodical. English. qt (Mar., June, Sept., Dec.). $25.00. California Attorneys for Criminal Justice, 10551 Jefferson Boulevard, Culver City CA 90232. **Tel** (310)204-0502, FAX (310)204-0502. **ED** Larry Gibbs. **LC** KFC1102.A15; F67. **DD** 345.794/05/05. Index Available published separately, bound from publisher, free-automatically sent. cum. index. **Bk Rev**, (Qty: 4). **Ad Acc, Adv Mgr:** Mary Warner. **Circ:** 2,700 (ctrl).
Desc: For criminal defense lawyers.
Ind/Abst Calif. Period. Index (19??-); Calif. Period. Microfi. (19??-).

US/0884-1632
GEORGIA CRIMINAL TRIAL PRACTICE / BY WILLIAM W. DANIEL. [Ga. crim. trial pract.]. **VFOAT** Criminal Trial Practice. (1984)-. English. ir. $89.95. Harrison Company Publishers, 3110 Crossing Park, PO Box 7500, Norcross GA 30091-7500. **Tel** (800)241-3561, (404)447-9150. **LC** KFG575; .D35. **DD** 345.758/05; 347.58055. Index available.

US
GILBERT CRIMINAL LAW AND PROCEDURE OF NEW YORK. Main/Corp New York (State). **VFOAT** Criminal Law and Procedure of New York; Gilbert Criminal Law and Procedure. 53rd Ed. (1970)-. English. an. Matthew Bender & Company Inc., 1275 Broadway, Albany NY 12204. **Tel** (800)833-9844, (518)487-3000. Index Available in last issue of each volume--loose separately paged. **Continues** New York (State). Gilbert Criminal Law and Practice of New York.

US/0193-7200
GILBERT LAW SUMMARIES. CRIMINAL LAW. (CRIMINAL LAW.). 11th- Ed.; 1979-. English. $13.95. Law Distributors, 14415 South Main Street, Gardena CA 90248. **Tel** (310)321-3275, (800)421-1893, FAX (310)324-6381. **LC** KF9219.3; .R88. **DD** 345/.73; 347.305. **Continues** Criminal Law, 0193-7170.

US/0193-8010
GILBERT LAW SUMMARIES: CRIMINAL PROCEDURE. (CRIMINAL PROCEDURE.). 9th- Ed.; 1979-. English. $11.50. Law Distributors, 14415 South Main Street, Gardena CA 90248. **Tel** (310)321-3275, (800)421-1893, FAX (310)324-6381. **LC** KF9619.3; .R87. **DD** 345.73/05. **Continues** Criminal Procedure, 0193-922X.

●NE/0928-9313
GLOBAL JOURNAL ON CRIME AND CRIMINAL LAW. See Law-Law Enforcement and Criminology.

US/1045-1625
GOULD'S CRIMINAL LAW HANDBOOK OF NEW YORK. [Gould's crim. handb. N. Y.]. **Main/Corp** New York (State). **VFOAT** Criminal Law Handbook of New York; Criminal Law Handbook. English. an. $21.95. Gould Publications, 199/300 State Street, Binghamton NY 13901. **Tel** (607)724-3000, FAX (607)723-4285. **LC** KFN6100.A29; N49. **DD** 345.747/005.
Desc: The complete New York Penal Law and New York Criminal Procedure Law, New York Correction Law, and selected pertinent sections of New York laws, comprehensive Crimes Classification Charts, Sentencing Guides and selected Criminal Jury Instructions.

UK
GREEN'S CRIMINAL LAW BULLETIN. (1993)-. Bulletin. English. Six times a year. £74.00 Europe; £78.00 other. Sweet & Maxwell Ltd., South Quay Plaza, 183 Marsh Wall, London E14 9FT England. **Tel** 011 44 264 342899, FAX 011 44 264 342723, telex 929089 ITPINF G.

US/0363-0463
HAWAII PROSECUTOR-PUBLIC DEFENDER NEWSLETTER. Newsletter. English. mo. 119 Merchant Street, Room 400, Honolulu HI 96813. **LC** KFH575.A15; H38. **DD** 345/.969/05.

US/0047-0554
IACP LAW ENFORCEMENT LEGISLATION AND LITIGATION REPORT. Main/Corp International Association of Chiefs of Police. Legislative Research Unit. (19??)-. Periodical. English. mo. $21.00. Law Enforcement Legal Review, 421 Ridgewood Avenue, Suite 100, Glen Ellyn IL 60137-4900. **Tel** (708)858-6392, FAX (708)858-6392. **LC** K9; .N755. **DD** 345/.73/005. available on microfilm from University Microfilms International (UMI).
Ind/Abst Crim. Justice Period. Index (-1989).

IE/0791-539X
IISH CIMINAL LW JURNAL. Vol. 1, No. 1 (June 1991)-. Periodical. English. sa. $80.00; 55.00p. Round Hall Press, Kill Lane, Blackrock County, Dublin Ireland. **Tel** 011 353 1 2892922, FAX 011 353 1 2893072.

US
ILLINOIS CRIMINAL LAW AND PROCEDURE. Main/Corp Illinois. **Added/Corp** West Publishing Company. Illinois. Laws, etc. (Illinois revised statutes). (19??)-. English. an. $16.95. Gould Publications / Florida, 1333 North 1792, Longwood FL 32750-3724. **Tel** (407)695-9500, 800 847-6502. **LC** KFI1761.A29; I44. **DD** 345.773; 347.7305.

US
INDIANA CRIMINAL LAW REVIEW. Vol. 1 Oct. (1978)-. Periodical. English. bm. Free. Indiana Criminal Law Review, 200 Franklin Street, Porter IN 46304. **Bk Rev**. **Ad Acc. Circ:** 350 (ctrl).
Desc: Review of criminal law and procedure and articles pertaining to the same subject.

IT/0019-7084
INDICE PENALE, L'. (19??)-. Periodical. Italian. Three times a year. L130000 Italy; L180000 other. Cedam Spa, Via Jappelli 5 6, 35121 Padua Italy. **Tel** 011 39 49 65667. **LC** K9; .N374. **Bk Rev. Circ:** 1,300.

US
INFORMATION PAMPHLET - CALIFORNIA. DEPT. OF JUSTICE. Main/Corp California. Dept. of Justice. English. California Department of Justice, PO Box 13427, 1515 K Street, Second Floor, Sacramento CA 95814. **Tel** (916)324-5080. **LC** KFC1100.A73; J88. **DD** 345/.794.

US
IOWA CRIMINAL LAW BULLETIN. Added/Corp Iowa. Criminal Appeals Division. Iowa. Criminal Appeals and Research Division. (19??)-. Periodical. English. mo. $7.00. Iowa Department of Justice, Hoover State Office Building, Des Moines IA 50319. **ED** Roxann M. Ryan and Ann Brenden. **LC** KFI4761.A59; I58. **DD** 345.777/002648. Index available. cum. index. **Circ:** 650.

US/0091-4169
JOURNAL OF CRIMINAL LAW & CRIMINOLOGY. (THE JOURNAL OF CRIMINAL LAW & CRIMINOLOGY / NORTHWESTERN UNIVERSITY SCHOOL OF LAW.). [J. crim. law criminol.]. **Added/Corp** Northwestern University (Evanston, Ill.). School of Law. **VFOAT** Journal of Criminal Law and Criminology. Vol. 64 (March 1973)-. Periodical. English. Four times a year. $35.00 US; $38.00 other. Northwestern University School of Law, 357 East Chicago Avenue, Chicago IL 60611-3069. **Tel** (312)503-8467, FAX (312)503-0132. **(Subscription address:** Fred B. Rothman & Co. / for back issues, 10368 West Centennial Road, Littleton CO 80127.) **LC** K10; .O8593. **DD** 364/.05. **NLM** W1 JO611N. **CODEN** JCRLA. Each issue contains an index to its own contents (no volume index)--loose. **Bk Rev**. **Ad Acc**. **Pr Rev. Circ:** 3,000. available on phonorecord; available in microform from University Microfilms International (UMI). Documents available from The Genuine Article, UMI Article Clearinghouse, CASDDS. **Continues in part** Journal of Criminal Law, Criminology and Police Science, 0022-0205.
Ind/Abst ABC POL SCI; Acad. Ind. [Computer File] (1992-); Acad. Search (Jan. 1993-); Appl. Soc. Sci. Index Abstr. (1980-); Chem. Abstr.; Crim. Justice Abstr.; Crim. Justice Period. Index; Crim. Penol. Police Sci. Abstr. (1973-1981); Curr. Contents Soc. Behav. Sci.; Curr. Law Index (1980-); EMBASE; Expand. Acad. Index (1984-); Index Leg. Period.; INFO-SOUTH Abstr.; Int. Bibliogr. Sociol.; Leg. Resour. Index (1980-); LegalTrac (1980-); Mag. Search; Newsp. Period. Abstr. (1990-); Psychol. Abstr. (1973-1981); Res. Alert [Full Cov.]; Soc. Sci. Source (Jul. 1993-); Soc. Sci. Cit. Index [Full Cov.]; Soc. Sci. Index; Soc. Sci. Index Fulltext (Winter 1988-) [Full Txt.].

US/0091-4169
JOURNAL OF CRIMINAL LAW & CRIMINOLOGY. [MICROFILM], THE. [J. crim. law criminol.]. **Added/Corp** Northwestern University (Evanston, Ill.). School of Law. **VAT** Journal of Criminal Law and Criminology. Vol. 64 (Mar. 1973)-. Academic Scholarly Publication. English. qt. $35.00. Fred B. Rothman & Company, 10368 West Centennial Road, Littleton CO 80127. **Tel** (800)457-1986, (303)979-5657, FAX (303)978-1457, telex 87669. **LC** Microfilm 057. **CODEN** JCRLA. Index available. available in print. Documents available from CASDDS. **Continues in part** Journal of Criminal Law, Criminology & Police Science, 0022-0205; Journal of Police Science and Administration, 0090-9084.
Ind/Abst Chem. Abstr.; Crim. Justice Period. Index; INFO-SOUTH Abstr.; Psychol. Abstr.

UK/0022-0183
JOURNAL OF CRIMINAL LAW (HERTFORD). (THE JOURNAL OF CRIMINAL LAW.). [J. crim. law]. Vol. 1, No. 1 (Jan. 1937)-. Periodical. English. qt. Pageant Publishing, 5 Turners Road, London NW11 6TD England. **Tel** 011 44 81 455 3703. **(Subscription address:** World-Wide Subscription Services, Unit 4, Gibbs Reed Farm Pashley Road, Ticehurst TN5 7HE England.) **[CCC]**. Index Available, published separately, free-automatically sent. **Ad Acc**. **Pr Rev**. available in microform from Kraus Microform.
Desc: Criminal law in practice and trends in legislation.
Ind/Abst Appl. Soc. Sci. Index Abstr.; Crim. Justice Abstr.; Crim. Penol. Police Sci. Abstr.; Curr. Law Index (1980-); Int. Bibliogr. Sociol.; Leg. Resour. Index (1980-); LegalTrac (1980-).

YU
JUGOSLOVENSKA REVIJA ZA KRIMINOLOGIJU I KRIVICNO PRAVO. Added/Corp Jugoslovensko Udruzenje za Krivicno Pravo i Kriminologiju. Institut za Kriminoloska i Kriminalisticka Istrazivanja (Yugoslavia) Institut za Kriminoloska i Socioloska Istrazivanja. (19??)-. Periodical. Serbo-Croatian (Roman) (summaries and/or abstracts in English, French and Russian). qt. $18.00 Yugoslavia; $40.00 other. Jugoslovensko Udruzenje Za Kri, Grananicka 18, YU 1100 Belgrad Yugoslavia.
Ind/Abst Index Foreign Leg. Per.

BL
JURISPRUDENCIA BRASILEIRA CRIMINAL. Vol. 1-. Periodical. Portuguese. $2940. Jurua Editora, Av Visconde de Guarapuava, 2435-10 Andar, CEP 80.000, Curitiba Parana Brazil. **LC** KHD5402.A48; J87. **DD** 345.81/002648; 348.105002648.

NE
JUSTITIELE VERKENNINGEN. Dutch. **LC** K10; .U82. **DD** 345/.492/005.
Ind/Abst Crim. Penol. Police Sci. Abstr.

JA
KOTO SAIBANSHO KEIJI SAIBAN SOKUHO SHU / HOMU DAIJIN KANBO SHIHO HOSEI CHOSABU HEN. 1986-. Japanese. ¥2500. Hosokai 1-1 Kasumigaseki 1 Chiyoda-ku, Tokyo-to 100 Japan.

US/1070-9967
LAW ENFORCEMENT LEGAL REVIEW. [Law enforc. leg. rev.]. **Added/Corp** International Association of Chiefs of Police. National District Attorneys Association. No. 79 (Jan. 1979)-. Periodical. English. bm (6 issues). $78.00. Law Enforcement Legal Review, 421 Ridgewood Avenue, Suite 100, Glen Ellyn IL 60137-4900. **Tel** (708)858-6392, FAX (708)858-6392. **ED** James P. Manak. **LC** KF9614; .I54. **DD** 345.73/05; 347.3055. Index available. cum. index. **Ad Acc**. **Pr Rev. Circ:** 500. **Continues** International Association of Chiefs of Police. IACP Law Enforcement Legal Review.

US/0145-6571
LAW OFFICER'S BULLETIN, THE. Added/Corp Bureau of National Affairs (Washington, D.C.). (19??)-. Bulletin. English. bw. $140.00. Bureau of National Affairs Inc., 9435 Key West Avenue, Rockville MD 20850. **Tel** (800)372-1033, (301)258-1033, FAX (301)948-5823. **(Subscription address:** 9435 Key West Avenue, Rockville MD 20850; telephone: FAX (301)948-5823) **ED** Robert L Goebes. **LC** KF9202; .L38. **DD** 345/.73/005. **[CCC]**.
Desc: Provides an update of court decisions, Justice Department proposals and congressional actions involving law enforcement officers, describing the legal reasoning and explaining the impact on the law enforcement community.
Ind/Abst Crim. Justice Period. Index.

UK
LAW REPORTS OF THE COMMONWEALTH. CRIMINAL LAW REPORTS. Title Change. VFOAT Criminal Law Reports. (1985)-(1992). Periodical. English. an. Butterworth & Co. Ltd. / Kent, England, Borough Green,

Sevenoaks Kent TN15 8PH England. **Tel** 011 44 732-884567, FAX 011 44 732-885996. **LC** K5014.23; .L39. **DD** 345/.00171241; 342.500171241. ***Merged with*** *Law Reports of the Commonwealth. Commercial Law Report, 0952-1046* ***and*** *Law Reports of the Commonwealth. Constitutional and Administrative Law Reports, 0951-0699* ***to form*** *Law Reports of the Commonwealth.*

US/0092-1505
LEGISLATIVE REPORTER (LINCOLN). ***Ceased.*** (LEGISLATIVE REPORTER.). (19??)-(19??). Periodical. English. wk. Commission on Law Enforcement and Criminal Justice, State Capitol Building, Lincoln NE 68509. **LC** KFN562.A73; L4. **DD** 345/.782/0505.

US/0094-5439
MAINE PROSECUTOR BULLETIN, THE. Nov. 1973-. Bulletin. English. mo. Law & Legislative Ref Library, State House Station 43, Augusta ME 04330. **Tel** (207)289-1110. **LC** KFM575.A73; M34. **DD** 345/.741/0505.

CN/0527-7892
MARTIN'S ANNUAL CRIMINAL CODE. **Main/Corp** Canada. (1957)-. Periodical. English. an. 62.00Can$. Canada Law Book Inc., 240 Edward Street, Aurora Ontario L4G 3S9 Canada. **Tel** (800)263-3269, (905)841-6472, FAX (905)841-5085. **ED** Edward L. Greenspan. **DD** 345/.71. ***Supersedes*** *Canada. [Criminal Code]. The Criminal Code of Canada.*
Desc: Includes a table of cases, a table of concordance, the Criminal Code and Forms, the Canada Evidence Act, the Food and Drugs Act, the Narcotic Control Act, the Young Offenders Act and Forms, the Canadian Charter of Rights and Freedoms, and Forms of Charges under the Criminal Code.

●CN/1188-9640
MARTIN'S ONTARIO CRIMINAL PRACTICE. [Martin's Ont. crim. pract.]. **Added/Corp** Canada Law Book Inc. (1992/1993)-. English. an. 37.50Can$. Canada Law Book Inc., 240 Edward Street, Aurora Ontario L4G 3S9 Canada. **Tel** (800)263-3269, (905)841-6472, FAX (905)841-5085. **ED** Edward L. Greenspan. **DD** 345.713/05.
Desc: Guide to the completely revised Ontario rules of criminal practice.

CN/0710-1805
MARTIN'S RELATED CRIMINAL STATUTES. (MARTIN'S RELATED CRIMINAL STATUTES ... / WITH ANNOTATIONS BY EDWARD L. GREENSPAN.). [Martin's relat. crim. stat.]. **Main/Corp** Canada. (1980)-. English. an. 57.00Can$. Canada Law Book Inc., 240 Edward Street, Aurora Ontario L4G 3S9 Canada. **Tel** (800)263-3269, (905)841-6472, FAX (905)841-5085. **ED** Edward L. Greenspan. **DD** 345.71.
Desc: Collection of the most significant federal non-Criminal Code penal statutes.

US/0748-2957
MARYLAND PROSECUTOR, THE. Periodical. English. Five times a year. Free. D Broccolino State's Attorneys Coordinator, 500 West Baltimore Street, Baltimore MD 21201. **Tel** (410)328-6334. **ED** Dario J Broccolino. **LC** KFM1777.A15; M37. **DD** 345.752/005; 347.5205005. Index available. **Bk Rev**. **Ad Acc. Circ:** 1,000 (ctrl).

US
MISSOURI'S PUBLIC DEFENDER AND APPOINTED COUNSEL PROGRAMS. **Main/Corp** Missouri. Public Defender Commission. 1978/79-. English. an. Public Defender Commission, 1105 Rear Southwest Boulevard, Jefferson City MO 65101. **LC** KFM8377; .A865. **DD** 345.778/01. ***Continues*** *Public Defender & Appointed Counsel Programs.*

US/0590-0875
MONOGRAPH SERIES - CRIMINAL LAW EDUCATION AND RESEARCH CENTER. **Main/Corp** New York University. Criminal Law Education and Research Center. Monographic series. English. ir. Price varies per volume. New York University School of Law, 110 West Third Street, New York NY 10012. **Tel** (212)998-6540, (212)998-6560, FAX (212)995-4032. **CODEN** CLEMA.

US
NDAA BULLETIN / NATIONAL DISTRICT ATTORNEYS ASSOCIATION. ***Title Change.*** **Added/Corp** National District Attorneys Association. **VAT** National District Attorneys Association Bulletin. Vol. 6, No. 2 (May/June 1987)-Vol. 11, No. 6 (Nov./Dec. 1992). Bulletin. English. bm. National District Attorneys Association / Virginia, 99 Canal Center Plaza, Suite 510, Alexandria VA 22314. **Tel** (703)549-9222. **ED** Jean Holt. **LC** KF9640.A15; C36. **DD** 345.73/01; 347.3051. **Bk Rev. Circ:** 7,000 (ctrl). ***Continues*** *Capital Perspective, 0278-9027.* ***Absorbed by*** *Prosecutor, 0027-6383.*

GW/0934-9200
NEUE KRIMINALPOLITIK. **VFOAT** NK. (1988)-. Periodical. German. qt. DM68.00 Germany; DM70.00 other. Nomos Verlagsgesellschaft, Postfach 610, D-76484 Baden Baden Germany. **Tel** 011 49 7221 21040. **LC** HV6022.G3; N48.

US
NEW HAMPSHIRE CRIMINAL CODE : R.S.A. TITLE LXII, AS AMENDED THROUGH JULY 1975. **Main/Corp** New Hampshire. **Added/Corp** Equity Publishing Corporation. English. ir. Equity Publishing Corporation, RR 1 Box 3, Orford NH 03777. **Tel** (603)637-5012, (800)637-5012. cum. index.

US
NEW STATUTES AFFECTING THE CRIMINAL LAW. **Main/Corp** California. Legislature. Assembly. Committee on Criminal Justice. English. an. $7.85. Joint Publications, State Capitol, Box 942849, Sacramento CA 94249-0001. **Tel** (916)445-4874. **ED** Larry Stirling. **LC** KFC10.8; .C726. **DD** 345.794/002632. **Circ:** 300.

US/0271-6283
NEW YORK STATE CRIMINAL LAW REVIEW. (NEW YORK STATE CRIMINAL LAW REVIEW / BUREAU OF PROSECUTION AND DEFENSE SERVICES.). **Added/Corp** New York (State). Bureau of Prosecution and Defense Services. New York (State). Bureau of Prosecution Services. New York (State). Division of Criminal Justice Services. Office of Legal Services. **VFOAT** Criminal Law Review. (197?)-. Periodical. English. Six times a year. Free on request. New York Bureau of Prosecution and Defense Services, New York State Division of Criminal Justice, Albany NY 12203. **Tel** (518)453-6930. **LC** KFN6155.A59; N49. **DD** 345.747/05/05; 347.4705505.

CN/0715-5980
NEWSLETTER (CRIMINAL LAWYERS' ASSOCIATION (TORONTO, ONT.)). (NEWSLETTER / CRIMINAL LAWYERS' ASSOCIATION.). [Newsl. - Crim. Lawyers' Assoc.]. Newsletter. English. Six times a year. $45.00. Criminal Lawyers Association, 149 Gerrard Street E, Toronto Ontario M5A 2E4 Canada. **Tel** 960-1071. **ED** Michael Lomer. **DD** 345/.00971. **Bk Rev**. **Ad Acc.** ctrl circ.
Desc: Articles of interest to practising members of the criminal defense bar.

GW
NSTZ : NEUE ZEITSCHRIFT FUER STRAFRECHT. **VFOAT** N.ST.Z.; Neue Zeitschrift fur Strafrecht. (19??)-. Periodical. German. mo. CH Beck Verlagsbuchhandlung, D 80791 Munich Germany. **Tel** 011 49 89 381891. **LC** KK7972; .N73. **DD** 345.43/005; 344.305005.
Ind/Abst Index Foreign Leg. Per.

US/0748-5891
OHIO APPELLATE DECISIONS INDEX. CRIMINAL CASES. **Added/Corp** Banks-Baldwin Law Publishing Company. (1982)-. English. qt. $137.00. Banks-Baldwin Law Publishing Company, PO Box 1974, University Center, Cleveland OH 44106. **Tel** (216)721-7373. **LC** KFO561.A54; O36. **DD** 345.771/01/02648; 347.7105102648. cum. index.

US
POINT OF VIEW. Periodical. English. qt. Free. Alameda County District Attorneys Office, 1225 Fallon Street, Oakland CA 94612. **Tel** (510)272-6222. **ED** John J Meehan. **LC** KFC1100.A15; P6. **DD** 345/.794/005. cum. index. **Circ:** 3,500.
Desc: Discussion of current appellate court rulings and analysis of effect upon existing law. Guidelines presented for assistance of trial courts, attorneys and law enforcement.

UK/0953-4377
PRISON REPORT. [Prison rep.]. (1987)-. Periodical. English. qt. £15.00 (individual), £20.00 (institution), £8.00 (unemployed). Prison Reform Trust, 59 Caledonian Road, London NI 9BU England. **Tel** 011 44 71 2789815. **DD** 364.60941.

PL
PROBLEMY PRAWA KARNEGO. 1-. Polish. Z40.00. Uniwersytet Slaski, Ul Bankowa 14, 40-007 Katowice Poland. **Tel** 59-69-15, FAX 48 32 599-506, telex 0315584 USKPL. **LC** K16; .R578.

US/0092-5977
PROGRAM MATERIALS FOR SEMINAR FOR GEORGIA DISTRICT ATTORNEYS. (PROGRAM MATERIALS.). **Added/Corp** Institute of Continuing Legal Education in Georgia. Georgia Center for Continuing Education. (19??)-. English. University of Georgia / Institute of Continuing Education in Georgia, School of Law, Law Building, Athens GA 30601. **LC** KFG561.A73; S4. **DD** 345/.758/05.

US/0027-6383
PROSECUTOR, THE. (THE PROSECUTOR : JOURNAL OF THE NATIONAL DISTRICT ATTORNEYS ASSOCIATION.). [Prosecutor]. **Added/Corp** National District Attorneys Association. Vol. 3, No. 4 (July-Aug. 1967)-. Periodical. English. Six times a year (Feb., Apr., June, Aug., Oct., Dec.). $55.00 Comes with National District Attorneys Association membership. National District Attorneys Association / Virginia, 99 Canal Center Plaza, Suite 510, Alexandria VA 22314. **Tel** (703)549-9222. **LC** K16; .R66. **DD** 345/.73/01. available on microfilm from University Microfilms International (UMI). ***Continues*** *NDAA (Series);* ***Absorbed*** *NDAA Bulletin.*
Ind/Abst Crim. Justice Abstr.; Curr. Law Index (1980-); Leg. Resour. Index (1980-); LegalTrac (1980-).

US/0098-8774
PROSECUTORS' BULLETIN, THE. **Main/Corp** Wisconsin. Dept. of Justice. Bulletin. English. Department of Justice, 819 North 6th Street/Room 520, Milwaukee WI 53203. **LC** KFW2961; .A84. **DD** 345/.775/01.

SW
PROSECUTORS' NOTES. English. an. The Chief Legal Adviser Attention: Senior Legal Adviser/P J Mears, Police National Headquarter, Private Bag, Wellington New Zealand. **Tel** 749-499. **ED** Paul Mears. **DD** 345.931/01; 349.31051. **Circ:** 200 (ctrl).
Desc: Recent law and practical guidance on prosecuting in criminal courts.

IT
QUESTIONE GIUSTIZIA. **Added/Corp** Magistratura Democratica. Vol. 1, No. 1 (1982)-. Periodical. Italian. Three times a year. L108000 Italy; L150000 other. Franco Angeli Riviste SRL, Viale Monza 106, 20127 Milan Italy. **Tel** 011 39 2 2827651, 011 39 2 289562.

US/0899-0840
RECENT TITLES IN LAW FOR THE SUBJECT SPECIALIST. CRIMINAL LAW, PROCEDURE AND CRIMINOLOGY. [Recent titles law subj. spec., Crim. law proced. crim.]. **VFOAT** Criminal Law, Procedure and Criminology. Vol. 5, No. 1 (Jan.-Mar. 1988)-. English. qt. $85.00. William S. Hein & Company Inc., 1285 Main Street, Buffalo NY 14209. **Tel** (716)882-2600, (800)828-7571, FAX (716)883-8100, telex 91-209 WM S HEIN BUF. **DD** 016. ***Continues*** *National Legal Bibliography. Subject Area List. Criminal Law, Procedure, and Criminology, 8755-8017.*

SZ
RECHTSPRECHUNG IN STRAFSACHEN. **Added/Corp** Schweizerische Kriminalistische Gesellschaft. **VFOAT** Bulletin de Jurisprudence Penale. (19??)-. Multiple languages (French and German). qt. 44.00F Switzerland; 48.00F other. Staempfli & Cie SA, Postfach 8326, CH-3001 Bern Switzerland. **Tel** 011 41 31 3006666, telex 031 911 515 EDMZ CH. **ED** F. Clerc. **DD** 345/.494/002638. **Circ:** 1,800.

US/0093-2159
REPORT OF THE OFFICE OF THE PUBLIC DEFENDER FOR THE STATE OF MARYLAND. (REPORT.). [Rep. Off. Public Def. State Md.]. **Main/Corp** Maryland. Office of the Public Defender. 1st- 1972-. English. Central Offices, 800 Equitable Building, Baltimore MD 21202. **LC** KFM1778.A73; O3. **DD** 345/.752/01.

CN/0822-7616
RESUMES DE JURISPRUDENCE PENALE DU QUEBEC. **See** Law-Abstracting, Bibliographies and Statistics.

SP
REVISTA DE DERECHO PENAL (FUNDACION DE CULTURA UNIVERSITARIA). (REVISTA DE DERECHO PENAL.). No. 1 (July 1980)-. Periodical. Spanish. Three times a year. $35.00. Fundacion de Cultura Universitaria, 25 de Mayo, 568 Casilla 1155, 11000 Montevideo Uruguay. **Tel** 011 598 2 961152. **LC** K19; .D445. **DD** 345.895/005; 348.9505005.

UY
REVISTA DEL INSTITUTO URUGUAYO DE DERECHO PENAL. V. 1, No. 1; Jan./July 1980-. Spanish. Editorial Amalio M Fernandez, 25 de Mayo 477 P Baja, OF 11, Montevideo Uruguay. **Tel** 951782 OR 952684. **ED** Milton Cairoli Martinez. **LC** K19; .D895. **DD** 345.895/005; 348.9505005. **Bk Rev**.
Desc: Contains doctrines, jurisprudence and legislation of criminal law.

BL
REVISTA INTERAMERICANA DE DIREITO PROCESSUAL PENAL. Portuguese (Spanish). Monetary Authority of Singapore, 10 Shenion Way, PO Box 52, Singapore 9001 Singapore. **Tel** 011 65 2255577, FAX 011 65 2299491. **LC** K19; .I45. **DD** 345.81/05/05.

MX/0034-9992
REVISTA MEXICANA DE DERECHO PENAL. No. 1-25, 1961-1963. Periodical. Spanish. Procuradoria General de Justicia del Distrito Federal, Avenida Ninos Heroes y Dr, Liceaga Mexico 7 D F Mexico.

FR/0035-1733
REVUE DE SCIENCE CRIMINELLE ET DE DROIT PENAL COMPARE. **Added/Corp** Universite de Paris. Institut de Criminologie. Universite de

Paris. Institut de Droit Compare. Centre Francais de Droit Compare. Universite de Droit, d'Economie et de Sciences Sociales de Paris. Institut de Criminologie. Universite de Droit, d'Economie et de Sciences Sociales de Paris. Institut de Droit Compare. Vol 1 (Jan./Mar. 1936)-. Periodical. French. Four times a year. 590.00F (France); 725.00F (other). Dalloz, 35 rue Tournefort, 75240 Paris Cedex 05 France. **Tel** 011 33 1 40515434 or 40515454, FAX 45 87 37 48, telex 206 446 F. **ED** Mireille Delmus-Marty. **LC** K21; .D54. **DD** 345.44/005. **[CCC].** Index available in last issue of volume--attached. **Bk Rev.**
Desc: Offers information on crimes, their prevention and punishment, as well as crime detection and its related technologies.
Ind/Abst Crim. Justice Abstr.; Crim. Penol. Police Sci. Abstr.; Index Foreign Leg. Per.; Int. Bibliogr. Sociol.; PAIS Int. Print.

FR/0223-5404
REVUE INTERNATIONALE DE DROIT PENAL / DIRIGEE PAR J.A. ROUX, L. HUGUENEY, H. DONNEDIEU DE VABRES. **Added/Corp** International Association of Penal Law. **VFOAT** International Review of Penal Law. (1924)-. Periodical. French (English). Four times a year. 327.01F France; 345.00F other. Editions Eres, 11 rue des Alouettes, Ramonville St. Agne France. **Tel** 011 33 61 751576.
Ind/Abst Crim. Justice Abstr.; Index Foreign Leg. Per.; PAIS Int. Print.

IT
RIVISTA ITALIANA DI DIRITTO E PROCEDURA PENALE. New Series, Year 1 (1958)-. Periodical. Italian. Four times a year. L160000.00 Italy; L240000.00 other. Giuffre Editore SPA, Via Busto Arsizio 40, 20151 Milan Italy. **Tel** 011 398 2 38089200. **LC** K22; .I84. **Bk Rev. Ad Acc. Circ:** 3,100. ***Formed by the union of*** *Rivista Italiana di Dritto Penale* ***and*** *Rivista di Diritto Processuale Penale.*
Desc: Provides doctrine and jurisprudence applied to current topics, information on legislation, and more.
Ind/Abst Index Foreign Leg. Per.

GW
SCHRIFTEN ZUM STRAFRECHT. (19??)-. Monographic series. German. ir. Price varies per volume. Duncker und Humblot Verlag, Postfach 410329, D-12113 Berlin Germany. **Tel** 011 49 30 79000612, 011 49 30 79000613.
Desc: Contributions to criminal law.

US/0363-0978
SHEPARD'S CRIMINAL JUSTICE CITATIONS. [Shepard's crim. justice cit.]. **Added/Corp** Shepard's Citations, Inc. Shepard's/McGraw-Hill. **VFOAT** Criminal Justice Citations. Vol. 1 (Nov. 1975)-. Periodical. English. Four times a year. $172.00. Shepards McGraw-Hill Inc, 555 Middle Creek Parkway, PO Box 35300, Colorado Springs CO 80935-3530. **Tel** (719)488-3000, FAX (800)525-0053. **LC** KF9610.5; .S5. **DD** 345/.73/0502638.
Desc: Citations since 1972 to ABA's standards relating to the administration of criminal justice.

UK
SMITH & HOGAN : CRIMINAL LAW - CASES AND MATERIALS. English. an. Butterworth & Co. Ltd. / Kent, England, Borough Green, Sevenoaks Kent TN15 8PH England. **Tel** 011 44 732-884567, FAX 011 44 732-885996.
Desc: Addresses the elements of crime, causation, ommissions, fault, proof, incitement, etc.

SA/1011-8527
SOUTH AFRICAN JOURNAL OF CRIMINAL JUSTICE. [S. Afr. j. crim. justice]. **VFOAT** Suid-Afrikaanse Tydskrif vir Strafregspleging; SACJ; SAS. Vol. 1, No. 1 (1988)-. Periodical. Afrikaans (English). Three times a year (Apr., Aug., Nov.). R143.55 (South Africa, Transkei, Venda, Bophuthatswana, Ciskei); R130.50 (Africa); R152.25 (other). **(Subscription address:** Juta Subscription Services, PO Box 14373, Kenwyn 7790 South Africa, Tel. 27 21 7975101**)** ***Continues*** *Suid-Afrikaanse Tydskrif vir Strafreg en Kriminologie, 0258-2511.*
Ind/Abst Crim. Justice Abstr. (199?-).

GW/0720-1605
STRAFVERTEIDIGER. Vol. 1 No. 1 (Feb. 1981)-. Periodical. German. Twelve times a year. DM310.50. Hermann Luchterhand Verlag, Postfach 2352, D 56513 Neuwied Germany. **Tel** 011 49 2631 8010. **LC** K23; .T73. **DD** 345.43/05044/05; 344.305504405.

AT/1037-9177
SUMMARY OF CRIMINAL COURT PROCEEDINGS, WESTERN AUSTRALIA. (1991/1992)-. English. an. 18.40Aus$. Australian Bureau of Statistics, PO Box 10, Belconnen Australian Capital Territory, 2616 Australia. **Tel** 011 61 6 2527911, FAX 011 61 6 2516009. ***Formed by the union of*** *Court Statistics: Higher Criminal Courts, Western Australia; Court Statistics: Courts of Petty Sessions, Western Australia* ***and*** *Court Statistics: Children's Courts, Western Australia.*
Desc: Contains data on criminal matters finalized in the Western Australia Higher Courts, Courts of Petty Session, and Children's Courts.

PE
TEMAS DE DERECHO PENAL / LUIS A. BRAMONT ARIAS. (19??)-. Periodical. Spanish. **LC** KHQ5402.Z9; B7. **DD** 345.85; 348.505.

US/1055-1913
TEXAS CRIMINAL LAW AND MOTOR VEHICLE HANDBOOK. [Tex. crim. law motor veh. handb.]. **Added/Corp** Gould Publications of Texas. **VFOAT** Criminal Law and Motor vehicle Handbook; Tx. Criminal and Vehicle Handbook; Tx. Criminal & Vehicle Handbook; A.Texas criminal law & motor vehicle handbook. (19??)-. English. an. $15.95 US; $20.95 other. Gould Publications / Florida, 1333 North 1792, Longwood FL 32750-3724. **Tel** (407)695-9500, 800 847-6502. **LC** KFT1761.A29; T496. **DD** 345.764/0247; 347.6405247.
Desc: Presentation of the Texas Penal Code, Code of Criminal Procedure, Rules of Criminal Evidence, Rules of Appellate Procedure, Vehicle Laws, and related statutes.

IT
TOMMASO NATALE, IL. Vol. 1- Jan./April 1973-. Italian. Via Maqueda 172, Palermo 90100 Italy. **LC** K24; .O45. **DD** 345/.45/0505.

US/0093-7932
UTAH PROSECUTOR, THE. English. Statewide Association of Prosecutors of Utah, 530 East Fifth South, Suite 202, Salt Lake City UT 84102. **LC** KFU577.A73; U85. **DD** 345/.792/01.

US/0364-2232
VOICE FOR THE DEFENSE. **Added/Corp** Texas Criminal Defense Lawyers Association. (19??)-. Periodical. English. mo. $10.00 (individuals), $36.00 (members), $100.00 (attorneys who are not members). Texas Criminal Defense Lawyers Association, 600 West 13th Street, Suite A, Austin TX 78701. **Tel** (512)478-2514. **LC** KF9602; .V64. **DD** 345/.73/0505.

●RU
VSEMIRNYI UGOLOVNYI ARKHIV. (1992)-. Periodical. Russian. bm.

CN/0703-1319
WEEKLY CRIMINAL BULLETIN. Vol. 1 (1977)-. Periodical. English. wk. 177.00Can$. Canada Law Book Inc., 240 Edward Street, Aurora Ontario L4G 3S9 Canada. **Tel** (800)263-3269, (905)841-6472, FAX (905)841-5085. **ED** Marc Rosenberg and Chris Buhr. **DD** 345.71/00264.
Desc: A comprehensive summary, on a weekly basis, of all available criminal judgements handed down by Canadian courts.

US/8750-2607
WEST'S CRIMINAL LAW NEWS. [West's crim. law news]. **VFOAT** Criminal Law News. Vol. 1, No. 1 (May 2, 1984)-. Periodical. English. wk. $157.50. West Publishing Company, 610 Opperman Drive, PO Box 64526, Eagan MN 55123-1308. **Tel** (612)687-5618, (800)328-9352, FAX (612)687-5388, (800)562-2329. **(Subscription telephone:** FAX (612)688-3570**) LC** KF9210.3; .W47. **DD** 345.73.

GW/0721-6890
WISTRA. **VFOAT** W.I.S.T.R.A. Vol. 1, 82/1 (15. Jan. 1982)-. Periodical. German. Nine times a year. DM322.00 Germany; DM332.00 other. Verlag CF Mueller, Verlags GS, D-69018 Heidelberg Germany. **Tel** 011 49 6221 4890. **(Subscription address:** Heidelberger Verlagsservice, Postfach 102869, D 69121 Heidelberg, Germany**) ED** Erich Samson and Wolfgang Joecks. **LC** K27; .I87. **DD** 349.43/05; 344.3005. Index available. cum. index. **Bk Rev. Ad Acc. Circ:** 1,000.

II/0377-6719
YEARLY ALL INDIA CRIMINAL DIGEST. 1971-. English. an. Rs150.00. The Law Book Company Pvt Ltd, 18B Sardar Patel Marg, Civil Lines, PO Box 1004, 211 001 Allahabad India. **Tel** 011 91 532 602415. **ED** Rakesh Bagga. **DD** 345/.54/002648. Index available. cum. index. **Circ:** 2,000 (ctrl).
Desc: Contains digest of the criminal cases of the Supreme Court and of all the high courts of India.

GW/0084-5310
ZEITSCHRIFT FUER DIE GESAMTE STRAFRECHTSWISSENSCHAFT. **VFOAT** Mitteilungsblatt der Fachgruppe Strafrecht in der Gesellschaft fuer Rechtsvergleichung. Vol. 1 (1881)-. Periodical. German. qt. $271.40. Walter de Gruyter Inc., PO Box 303421, D 10728 Berlin Germany. **Tel** 011 49 30 260050, FAX 011 49 30 26005251. **LC** K30; .E5. **DD** 345/.005; 342.5005. cum. index.
Ind/Abst Crim. Justice Abstr. (199?-); Index Foreign Leg. Per.

ENVIRONMENTAL LAW

●US/1066-1131
ALABAMA ENVIRONMENTAL COMPLIANCE UPDATE. [Ala. environ. compliance update]. **Added/Corp** Sirote & Permutt, P.C. (Firm). (1993)-. Periodical. English. mo. $137.00. M. Lee Smith Publishers and Printers, 162 4th Avenue North, PO Box 198867, Nashville TN 37219. **Tel** (615)242-7395, (800)274-6774, FAX (615)256-6601. **DD** 344.

US/0192-0820
ALI-ABA COURSE OF STUDY. ENVIRONMENTAL LAW: MATERIALS. **Main/Conf** I-ABA Course of Study: Environmental Law. **Added/Corp** American Law Institute-American Bar Association Committee on Continuing Professional Education. Environmental Law Institute. Smithsonian Institution. **VFOAT** Environmental Law: Materials. **VAT** American Law Institute-American Bar Association Course of Study. Environmental Law: Materials. (19??)-. English. an. $150.00 (two volume set). American Law Institute, 4025 Chestnut Street, Philadelphia PA 19104-3099. **Tel** (215)243-1661, (800)253-6397, FAX (215)243-1664. **LC** KF3775.Z9; A12. **DD** 346/.73/046.

US/0191-166X
ALI-ABA COURSE OF STUDY. ENVIRONMENTAL LITIGATION : MATERIALS. **VAT** American Law Institute-American Bar Association Course of Study. Environmental Litigation: Materials. English. American Law Institute, 4025 Chestnut Street, Philadelphia PA 19104-3099. **Tel** (215)243-1661, (800)253-6397, FAX (215)243-1664. **LC** KF3775.Z9; A1433. **DD** 344/.73/0460269.

US/0191-2038
ALI-ABA COURSE OF STUDY : OIL SPILLS AND THE LAW : MATERIALS. **VAT** American Law Institute-American Bar Association Course of Study. Oil Spills and the Law: Materials. English. American Law Institute, 4025 Chestnut Street, Philadelphia PA 19104-3099. **Tel** (215)243-1661, (800)253-6397, FAX (215)243-1664. **LC** KF3790.Z9; A16. **DD** 344/.73/0463.

US/0191-4073
ALI-ABA COURSE OF STUDY. WATER AND AIR POLLUTION: MATERIALS. **Main/Conf** I-ABA Course of Study: Water and Air Pollution. **Added/Corp** American Law Institute-American Bar Association Committee on Continuing Professional Education. Environmental Law Institute. **VFOAT** Water and Air Pollution: Materials. **VAT** American Law Institute-American Bar Association Course of Study. Water and Air Pollution: Materials. (19??)-. English. American Law Institute, 4025 Chestnut Street, Philadelphia PA 19104-3099. **Tel** (215)243-1661, (800)253-6397, FAX (215)243-1664. **LC** KF3790.Z9; A18. **DD** 344/.73/0463.

AG/0326-422X
AMBIENTE Y RECURSOS NATURALES : REVISTA DE DERECHO, POLITICA Y ADMINISTRACION. V. 1, No. 1 (Jan.-Mar. 1984)-. Periodical. Spanish (summaries and/or abstracts in English). qt. $100.00. Editorial La Ley, Tucuman 1471, 1050 Buenos Aires, Argentina. **Tel** 49-5481-9, telex 22088 CARTE AR. **ED** Pedro Tarak. **LC** K1; .M37. **DD** 344.82/046/05. **Circ:** 1,500.
Ind/Abst Life Sci. Collect.

CN/1188-021X
ANNUAL REPORT / ENVIRONMENTAL APPEAL BOARD. [Annu. rep. - B.C., Environ. Appeal Board]. **Main/Corp** British Columbia. Environmental Appeal Board. (July 1, 1990/June 30, 1991)-. English. **DD** 354.7110082/321.

CN/0317-3526
ANNUAL REPORT - ENVIRONMENTAL CONTROL COUNCIL. (ANNUAL REPORT - ENVIRONMENTAL CONTROL COUNCIL (NOVA SCOTIA).). **Main/Corp** Nova Scotia. Environmental Control Council. 1973-. English. an. Howe Building, PO Box 2107, Halifax Nova Scotia B3J 3B7 Canada. **LC** HC120.E5; N68A. **DD** 354/.716/0077.
Desc: Covers environmental protection and environmental law.

AT
ANNUAL REPORT - VICTORIA, AUSTRALIA. ENVIRONMENT PROTECTION AUTHORITY. **Main/Corp** Victoria, Australia. Environment Protection Authority. 1st (1971/72)-. English. an. Free. Melbourne Government Printer, 232 Victoria Parade, East Melbourne 3002 Australia. **Tel** 03 628 5777, FAX 03 628 5631. **ED** Brian Robinson. **DD** 354/.945/008232. ctrl circ.
Desc: Retails policy, procedures and current areas of interest to the authority. A summary of the years activities and results is also included.

VE
ANUARIO DE DERECHO AMBIENTAL. **Added/Corp** Venezuela. Ministerio del Ambiente y de los Recursos Naturales Renovables. Consultoria Juridica. (1977)-. Spanish. Editorial Juridica Venezolana, Av. Francisco de Miranda, Edif. Galipan entra C, piso 3, Letra "D", Apartado 17598, Caracas 1015-A Venezuela. **Tel** 951 14 45. **LC** K1; .N9154. **DD** 344/.87/046.

●US/1067-4209
BAKER & DANIELS' INDIANA ENVIRONMENTAL COMPLIANCE UPDATE. [Baker Daniels Indiana environ. compliance update]. **Added/Corp** Baker & Daniels (Firm). **VFOAT** Baker and Daniels' Indiana Environmental Compliance Update; Indiana Environmental Compliance Update. (1993)-. Periodical. English. mo. $107.00. M. Lee Smith Publishers and Printers, 162 4th Avenue North, PO Box 198867, Nashville TN 37219. **Tel** (615)242-7395, (800)274-6774, FAX (615)256-6601. **ED** John Kyle (editor's address: Barnes and Thornburg, 11 South Meridian Street, Indianapolis, IN 46204; phone (317)231-7284). **DD** 344. ***Continues** Indiana Environmental Law Letter, 1053-6183.*
Desc: Newsletter reporting the latest state specific environmental law developments that affect Indiana.

GW
BERICHTE / UMWELTBUNDESAMT. **Added/Corp** Germany. Umweltbundesamt. (199?)-. Monographic series. German (summaries and/or abstracts in English). Erich Schmidt Verlag GmbH, Postfach 304240, D 10724 Berlin Germany. **Tel** 011 49 30 25008525. **LC** TD186.5.G3; G47a. **DD** 363.7/00943. ***Continues** Berichte (Germany (West). Umweltbundesamt), 0171-1911.*
Ind/Abst GeoRef.

US/1052-813X
BNA CALIFORNIA ENVIRONMENT REPORTER. (BNA CALIFORNIA ENVIRONMENT REPORTER / THE BUREAU OF NATIONAL AFFAIRS, INC.). [BNA Calif. environ. reprt.]. **Added/Corp** Bureau of National Affairs, (Washington, D.C.). **VFOAT** California Environment Reporter. **VAT** Bureau of National Affairs California Environment Reporter. Vol. 1, No. 1 (Nov. 12, 1990)-. Periodical. English. bw. $522.00. Bureau of National Affairs Inc., 9435 Key West Avenue, Rockville MD 20850. **Tel** (800)372-1033, (301)258-1033, FAX (301)948-5823. **LC** KFC610.A15; B63. **DD** 333. **[CCC].** available on an online database (file 655/Full-Text) from DIALOG.

IT
BOLLETTINO DEI CHIMICI IGIENISTI. PARTE LEGISLATIVA. REPUBBLICA ITALIANA. **Added/Corp** Unione Italiana Chimici Igienisti. Vol. 35 (Feb. 1984)-. Periodical. Italian. Sixteen times a year. L300000. Societa Editorial Farmaceutico, Via Ausonio 12, 20123 Milan Italy. **Tel** 011 39 2 89404545. **Ad Acc.** ***Continues in part** Unione Italiana Chimici Igienisti dei Laboratori Provinciali. Bollettino dei Chimici dell Unione Italiana dei Laboratori Provinciali.*

US/0190-7034
BOSTON COLLEGE ENVIRONMENTAL AFFAIRS LAW REVIEW. [Boston Coll. environ. aff. law rev.]. **Main/Corp** Boston College. Law School. **Added/Corp** Boston College. Law School. Environmental Affairs Law Review. **VFOAT** Environmental Affairs Law Review. Vol. 7 (1978)-. Academic Scholarly Publication. English. qt. $23.00 US; $26.00 other. Boston College Law School, 885 Centre Street, Newton Centre MA 02159. **Tel** (617)552-8550, FAX (617)552-2615. **LC** K5; .N83. **DD** 344.73/046/05. **CODEN** BCERDX. Index available. cum. index. **Ad Acc. Circ:** 1,200. available on microfilm and microfiche from University Microfilms International (UMI). Documents available from BIOSIS Document Express, UMI Article Clearinghouse, Documents on Demand. ***Continues** Environmental Affairs, 0046-2225.*
Desc: A student publication whose policy is to present a balanced, multi-disciplinary forum for the analysis of environmental issues. Included are scholarly articles from experts in law, politics, sciences and economics.
Ind/Abst Acad. Search (July 1993-); AGRICOLA [Select. Cov.]; AQUAREF; Biol. Abstr.; Coal Abstr.; Crim. Justice Abstr.; Curr. Law Index (1980-); Energy Res. Abstr. (1979-); Environ. Abstr.; Environ. Period. Bibliogr.; Expand. Acad. Index (1984-); GeoRef; Health Saf. Sci. Abstr.; Index Leg. Period.; INFO-SOUTH Abstr.; J. Plan. Lit.; Leg. Resour. Index (1980-); LegalTrac (1980-); Newsp. Period. Abstr. (1990-); Ocean. Abstr.; PAIS Int. Print (1991-); Life Sci. Collect.; Pollut. Abstr. Indexes; Risk Abstr.; Soc. Sci. Source (Jul. 1993-); Soc. Sci. Index; Soc. Sci. Index Fulltext (Winter 1987-) [Full Txt.].

FR
BULLETIN OFFICIEL DU MINISTERE DE L'ENVIRONNEMENT ET DU CADRE DE VIE ET DU MINISTERE DES TRANSPORTS. **Main/Corp** France. Ministere de l'Environnement et du Cadre de Vie. **Added/Corp** France. Ministere des Transports. Bulletin Officiel. (19??)-. French. an. 126.00F France; 258.00F other. Direction des Journaux Officiels, 26 rue Desaix, 75727 Paris Cedex 15 France. **Tel** 011 33 1 40587500. **DD** 344.44/046; 344.40446.

US/1061-365X
CALIFORNIA ENVIRONMENTAL LAW REPORTER. [Calif. environ. law report.]. **Added/Corp** Matthew Bender (Firm). **VFOAT** Environmental Law Reporter. Vol. 1, Issue 1 (1991)-. Periodical. English. sm. $350.00. Matthew Bender & Company Inc., 1275 Broadway, Albany NY 12204. **Tel** (800)833-9844, (518)487-3000. **ED** Bill Ryan. **LC** K3; .A4324. **DD** 344.794/04605; 347.94044605. available in Loose-leaf.

US/1053-4938
CALIFORNIA WATER LAW & POLICY REPORTER. [Calif. water law policy report.]. **Added/Corp** Shepard's/McGraw-Hill. **VFOAT** California Water Law and Policy Reporter. Vol. 1, No. 1 (Oct. 1990)-. Periodical. English. mo. $295.00. Shepards McGraw-Hill Inc, 555 Middle Creek Parkway, PO Box 35300, Colorado Springs CO 80935-3530. **Tel** (719)488-3000, FAX (800)525-0053. **LC** KFC790.A15; C35. **DD** 346.79404/91/005; 347.9406491005.
Desc: In-depth legal analysis of current case law. Provides complete coverage of EPA, SWRCB, FWS, NMFS and all relevant state, district, federal and industry organizations' activities.

CN/0707-7874
CANADIAN ENVIRONMENTAL LAW REPORTS. (CANADIAN ENVIRONMENTAL LAW REPORTS, NEW SERIES.). [Can. environ. law rep.]. **VFOAT** Rapports Canadiens du Droit de l'Environnement. Vol. 1, Pt. 1 (Dec. 1986)-. Periodical. English (French). bm. $88.00. Canadian Environmental Law Reports New Series, 2330 Midland Avenue, Agincourt Ontario M1S 1P7 Canada. **DD** 344.71/046/02642. **[CCC].** ***Continues** Canadian Environmental Law Reports, 0707-7874.*

US/0889-0633
CHEMICAL WASTE LITIGATION REPORTER. [Chem. waste litig. report.]. Vol. 11, No. 1 (Dec. 1985)-. Periodical. English. mo. $1749.00 Washington DC; $1650.00 US. Law Reporters, 1519 Connecticut Avenue Northwest, Suite 200, Washington DC 20036. **Tel** (202)462-5755. **LC** KF3945.A59; C48. **DD** 344.73/04622; 347.3044622. ***Continues** Chemical & Radiation Waste Litigation Reporter, 0731-8839.*

US/1040-1024
CITIZEN AGENDA. [Citiz. agenda]. **VAT** United States Public Interest Research Group Citizen Agenda. Periodical. English. qt. $25.00. U.S. Public Interest Research Group PIRG, 215 Pennsylvania Avenue SE, Washington DC 20003. **Tel** (202)546-9707. **DD** 363.
Desc: Articles cover legislation and lawsuits.

●US/1074-7729
CLEAN AIR ACT COMPLIANCE GUIDE UPDATE. **Added/Corp** Business & Legal Reports (Firm). (1994)-. Periodical. English. mo. $429.00. Business & Legal Reports, 39 Academy Street, Madison CT 06443. **Tel** (203)245-7448, (800)727-5257, FAX (203)245-2559.

US
CODE OF FEDERAL REGULATIONS. 18, CONSERVATION OF POWER AND WATER RESOURCES. **Added/Corp** United States. Office of the Federal Register. **VFOAT** Conservation of Power and Water Resources; CFR. N18, Power and Water Resources. (19??)-. English. an. Superintendent of Documents, US Government Printing Office, Washington DC 20402. **Tel** (202)275-3328, FAX (202)786-2377. available on microfiche.
Desc: Special edition of the Federal Register, containing a codification of documents.

US
CODE OF FEDERAL REGULATIONS. 50, WILDLIFE AND FISHERIES. **Added/Corp** United States. Office of the Federal Register. **VFOAT** Wildlife and Fisheries; CFR. 50, Wildlife and Fisheries. (19??)-. English. an. Superintendent of Documents, US Government Printing Office, Washington DC 20402. **Tel** (202)275-3328, FAX (202)786-2377. available on microfiche.
Desc: Special edition of the Federal Register, containing a codification of documents.

US/0361-6673
COLLECTION OF LEGAL OPINIONS, A. **Main/Corp** United States. Environmental Protection Agency. Office of General Counsel. Vol. 1 (Dec. 1970/1973)-. English. an. US Environmental Protection Agency / Office of Public Affairs, 401 M Street SW, Washington DC 20460. **LC** KF3775; .A552. **DD** 344/.73/04602646.

●US/1072-057X
COLORADO ENVIRONMENTAL COMPLIANCE UPDATE. (1993)-. Periodical. English. mo. $137.00. M. Lee Smith Publishers and Printers, 162 4th Avenue North, PO Box 198867, Nashville TN 37219. **Tel** (615)242-7395, (800)274-6774, FAX (615)256-6601.

US/1050-0391
COLORADO JOURNAL OF INTERNATIONAL ENVIRONMENTAL LAW AND POLICY. [Colo. j. int. environ. law policy]. **Added/Corp** University of Colorado, Boulder. School of Law. Vol. 1, No. 1 (Summer 1990)-. Periodical. English. sa (2 issues). $35.00 (institutions); $20.00 (individuals). University Press of Colorado, PO Box 849, Niwot CO 80544. **Tel** (303)530-5337, FAX (303)530-5306. **ED** Alexandra Andrews. **LC** K3; .O3459. **DD** 341.7/62. Documents available from Documents on Demand.
Desc: Provides a forum for an in-depth analyses of legal and public-policy implications relating to problems facing the global environment. It also examines proposals that aim to manage and resolve international environmental concerns and offers a concise annual overview of the activities conducted by the major international environmental organizations.
Ind/Abst Environ. Abstr.; Geogr. Abstr. Phys. Geogr.; Index Leg. Period.; Int. Dev. Abstr.; Leg. Resour. Index; LegalTrac (1990-); PAIS Int. Print (1991-).

US/0098-4582
COLUMBIA JOURNAL OF ENVIRONMENTAL LAW. [Columbia j. environ. law]. **Added/Corp** Columbia University. School of Law. Vol. 1 (Fall 1974)-. Periodical. English. sa. $30.00 US; $40.00 other. Columbia University School of Law / Box B-28, 435 West 116th Street, New York NY 10027. **Tel** (212)663-8717, FAX (212)854-1915. **ED** Robert Magnanim. **LC** K3; .O347. **DD** 344/.73/04605. **CODEN** CJELE8. **[CCC].** Index available. **Bk Rev. Ad Acc. Circ:** 650. available in microform. Documents available from Documents on Demand.
Desc: Publishes articles, notes, comments, and book reviews on subjects of importance to the environmental-legal community.
Ind/Abst Bowne Dig. Corp. Sec. Lawyers; Curr. Law Index (1980-); Environ. Abstr.; Index Leg. Period.; J. Plan. Lit.; Leg. Resour. Index (1980-); LegalTrac (1980-); Pollut. Abstr. Indexes; Rev. Agric. Entomol.; West. Hist. Q.; Wildl. Rev. (19??-199?).

●US/1060-2976
DAILY ENVIRONMENT REPORT. [Dly. environ. rep.]. **Added/Corp** Bureau of National Affairs (Washington, D.C.). **VFOAT** DEN. (1992)-. Periodical. English. da. $2,900. Bureau of National Affairs Inc., 9435 Key West Avenue, Rockville MD 20850. **Tel** (800)372-1033, (301)258-1033, FAX (301)948-5823. **LC** KF3775.A15; D35. **DD** 344.73/04605; 347.3044605. **[CCC].**

US/8755-9013
ECOLOGICAL ILLNESS LAW REPORT. ***Suspended.*** [Ecol. illn. law rep.]. **VFOAT** E.I.L.R.; EILR. Vol. 1, No. 1 (Nov./Dec. 1982)-?. Periodical. English. qt. $30.00 US, (add $10.00 for postage) other. Ecological Illness Law Report, PO Box 1796, Evanston IL 60204-1796. **Tel** (312)256-3730. **ED** Earon S Davis. **DD** 363. Index available. **Bk Rev. Ad Acc. Circ:** 1,200 (ctrl). ***Continues** Ecological Health Law Report.*
Desc: News journal on chemically induced illnesses, legal cases and governmental actions affecting those made ill at work, outdoors and/or indoors. For both professionals and laymen.

US/0046-1121
ECOLOGY LAW QUARTERLY. [Ecol. law. q.]. **Added/Corp** University of California, Berkeley. School of Law. Vol. 1 (Winter 1971)-. Periodical. English. qt (Feb., May, Aug., Nov.). $29.00 (individuals), $48.00 (institutions), $21.00 (students) US. University of California Press, 2120 Berkeley Way, Berkeley CA 94720. **Tel** (510)642-4191, (510)642-3907, FAX (510)642-9917. **ED** Robert Perlmutter (Editor-in-Chief) and Eric M. Albritton (Managing Editor). **LC** K5; .C64. **DD** 344/.73/04605. **[CCC].** Index available. cum. index. **Bk Rev. Ad Acc. Pr Rev. Circ:** 1300 (ctrl). available on microfilm and microfiche from University Microfilms International (UMI). Documents available from The Genuine Article, Documents on Demand.
Desc: Publishes articles on a range of environmental law topics.
Ind/Abst Bowne Dig. Corp. Sec. Lawyers; Coal Abstr.; Curr. Contents Soc. Behav. Sci.; Curr. Law Index (1980-); EMBASE; Energy Res. Abstr. (Oct. 1974-); Environ. Abstr.; Environ. Period. Bibliogr.; GeoRef; Health Saf. Sci. Abstr.; Index Leg. Period.; INIS Atomindex [Micro.]; Int. Dev. Abstr. (?-?); J. Plan. Lit.; Leg. Resour. Index (1980-); LegalTrac (1980-); PAIS Int. Print (1991-); Life Sci. Collect.; Pollut. Abstr. Indexes; Res. Alert [Full Cov.]; Risk Abstr.; Sage Public Adm. Abstr. (?-?); Sage Urban Stud. Abstr; Soc. Sci. Cit. Index [Full Cov.]; West. Hist. Q.

US
ENVIROACTION : ENVIRONMENTAL DIGEST OF THE NATIONAL WILDLIFE FEDERATION. **Added/Corp** National Wildlife Federation. **VFOAT** Enviro Action; National Wildlife Federation's Enviroaction. Vol. 9, No. 1 (Mar. 1991)-. Periodical. English. National Wildlife Federation / Washington, 1400 16th Street Northwest, Washington DC

20036. **Tel** (800)432-6564, (202)797-6800. ***Continues*** *National Wildlife Federation's Conservation ..., 0736-9522.*

US/0013-9211
ENVIRONMENT REPORTER. [Environ. rep.]. **Added/Corp** Bureau of National Affairs (Washington, D.C.). Vol. 1 (May 1970)-. Periodical. English. wk. $2,179.00. Bureau of National Affairs Inc., 9435 Key West Avenue, Rockville MD 20850. **Tel** (800)372-1033, (301)258-1033, FAX (301)948-5823. **(Subscription address:** 9435 Key West Avenue, Rockville MD 20850; telephone: FAX (301)948-5823**)** **ED** Wallis E McClain Jr. **[CCC].**
Desc: A notification and reference service covering the full-spectrum of legislative, administrative, judicial, industrial, and technological developments affecting pollution control and environmental protection.
Ind/Abst Abstr. Bull. Inst. Pap. Sci. Tech.

US/1044-7695
ENVIRONMENTAL & LAND USE ADMINISTRATIVE LAW REPORTS (ER FALR). [Environ. land use adm. law report. ER FALR]. **VFOAT** Environmental and Land Use Administrative Law Reporter (ER FALR); ER FALR. (1989)-. English. wk. $583.00 Florida; $550.00 other. Florida Administrative Law Reports, PO Box 385, Gainesville FL 32602. **Tel** (904)375-8036. **DD** 344.

AT/0813-300X
ENVIRONMENTAL AND PLANNING LAW JOURNAL. Vol. 1, No. 1 (April 1984)-. Periodical. English. bm (6 issues). 225.00Aus$. The Law Book Company Limited, 44-50 Waterloo Road, North Ryde New South Wales, 2113 Australia. **Tel** 011 61 2 8870177, FAX 011 61 2 8887240, telex ASBOOK 27445. **ED** Gerry Bates. **LC** K5; .N84. **DD** 344.94/046/05; 349.4044605. **CODEN** EPLJEX. Index available. **Bk Rev. Ad Acc. Circ:** 430.
Desc: Provides a broad and detailed coverage of developments, issues and problems that occur in environmental and planning law.
Ind/Abst AESIS Q.; APAIS, Aust. Public Aff. Inf. Ser.; Aust. Leg. Mon. Dig.; Environ. Period. Bibliogr.; Index Leg. Period.; J. Plan. Lit.

CN
ENVIRONMENTAL APPROVALS IN CANADA : PRACTICE AND PROCEDURE. English. an. 140.00Can$. Butterworth & Company Ltd. / Canada, 75 Clegg Road, Markham Ontario L6G 1A1 Canada. **Tel** (905)479-2665, (800)668-6481. **ED** Michael I. Jeffery. Index available. **Pr Rev. Circ:** 466 (ctrl).
Desc: Discusses all aspects of the process from pre-hearing activity and public participation to the elements of the hearing itself. It also provides an overview of the environmental legislation in each province and territory.

US/1040-6026
ENVIRONMENTAL CLAIMS JOURNAL. [Environ. claims j.]. Vol. 1, No. 1 (Autumn 1988)-. Periodical. English. qt. $180.00 US & Canada; $230.00 other. John Wiley & Sons, Inc., 605 Third Avenue, New York NY 10158-0012. **Tel** (212)850-6000, (212)850-6645, FAX (212)850-6088, telex 12-7063. **(Subscription address:** John Wiley & Sons Inc / New Jersey, PO Box 2575, Secaucus NJ 07096-2575.**)** **LC** K5; .N844. **DD** 346.7303/05; 347.306305. **[CCC].** available on microfilm and microfiche from University Microfilms International (UMI). Documents available from The Genuine Article.
Desc: A journal for attorneys in private practice and corporations, hospital administrators, government and municipal employees, and insurers containing information on complex legal, technical, and insurance issues surrounding environmental claims.
Ind/Abst Index Leg. Period. (1992-); PAIS Int. Print (1991-); Res. Alert [Select. Cov.]; Sage Urban Stud. Abstr; Soc. Sci. Cit. Index [Select. Cov.].

US
ENVIRONMENTAL COMPLIANCE AND LITIGATION STRATEGY. (19??)-. Periodical. English. mo. $195.00. Leader Publications, 345 Park Avenue South, New York NY 10010. **Tel** (800)888-8300 ext. 6170, (212)545-6170, FAX (212)696-1848.

US/1066-2553
ENVIRONMENTAL COMPLIANCE (MADISON, CONN.). (ENVIRONMENTAL COMPLIANCE.). [Environ. compliance]. **Added/Corp** Business & Legal Reports (Firm). Issue No. 101 (Apr. 1990)-. Periodical. English. mo. $595.00. Business & Legal Reports, 39 Academy Street, Madison CT 06443. **Tel** (203)245-7448, (800)727-5257, FAX (203)245-2559. **DD** 363.

CN/1187-0125
ENVIRONMENTAL COMPLIANCE REPORT, THE. [Environ. compliance rep.]. **Added/Corp** Southam Business Information and Communications Group. **VFOAT** Environmental Compliance Report. Vol. 7, No. 10 (Oct. 1990)-. Periodical. English. mo. 299.00Can$ Canada; 319.00Can$ other. Southam Information and Technology Group Inc., 1450 Don Mills Road, Don Mills Ontario M3B 2X7 Canada. **Tel** (416)445-6641, (800)668-2374, FAX (416)442-2261. **DD** 344.71/046/05. ***Continues*** *Monthly Report (Southam Business Information and Communications Group), 0824-7528.*
Ind/Abst PTS Newsl. Database [Full Txt.].

US/1041-3863
ENVIRONMENTAL COUNSELOR, THE. [Environ. couns.]. **Added/Corp** Business Laws, Inc. (Aug. 1988)-. Periodical. English. mo. $245.00. Business Laws Inc., 11630 Chillicothe Road, Chesterland OH 44026. **Tel** (216)729-7996, (800)759-0929, FAX (216)729-0645. **LC** KF3775.A15; E53. **DD** 344.73/046/05; 347.3044605. **[CCC].**

US/0731-5732
ENVIRONMENTAL FORUM (WASHINGTON, D.C.), THE. (THE ENVIRONMENTAL FORUM.). [Environ. forum]. (May 1982)-. Periodical. English. mo. $75.00 (organizations), $50.00 (non-profit organizations). Environmental Law Institute, 1616 P Street NW/Suite 200, Washington DC 20036. **Tel** (800)433-5120, (202)939-3844, FAX (202)328-5002. **ED** Morris A. Ward. **LC** KF3775.A15; E54. **DD** 363.7/00973. **Bk Rev. Circ:** 2,000.
Desc: Feature and analysis coverage of timely environmental pollution control, and natural resources public policies, for professionals in the field (lawyers, engineers, public administrators, etc).
Ind/Abst Curr. Law Index (1984-); Environ. Period. Bibliogr. (?-?); Leg. Resour. Index (1984-); LegalTrac (1980-); PAIS Int. Print (1991-); Urban Aff. Abstr. (?-?).

CN/0847-2068
ENVIRONMENTAL LAW ALERT. [Environ. law alert]. No. 1 (Oct. 1989)-. Newsletter. English. bm. 115.00Can$. Canada Law Book Inc., 240 Edward Street, Aurora Ontario L4G 3S9 Canada. **Tel** (800)263-3269, (905)841-6472, FAX (905)841-5085. **ED** Robert Fishlock, Johnathan Kahn. **DD** 344.71/046/05.
Desc: Sets out the environmental facts affecting corporations, businesses, natural resource companies and municipalities. Covers everything from chemical spill liability to sewage seepage.

●UK/1067-6058
ENVIRONMENTAL LAW AND MANAGEMENT. (1993)-. Periodical. English. bm. $325.00. John Wiley & Sons Ltd., Baffins Lane, Chichester West Sussex PO19 1UD England. **Tel** 0243 779777, FAX 0243 776128 BTG:JWP001, telex 86290 WIBOOKG. **(Subscription address:** John Wiley / Philadelphia, PO Box 7247, Philadelphia PA 19170.**)** **ED** Malcolm Forster and David Hughes. ***Continues*** *Land Management and Environmental Law Report, 0955-6354.*
Desc: Review of current developments in environmental law, including international issues, European Community law, the law in major Commonwealth jurisdictions and the USA, UK law and practice concerning the environmental media, and UK and EC case law.

US
ENVIRONMENTAL LAW AND PRACTICE. English. an. Practising Law Institute, 810 Seventh Avenue, New York NY 10019-5818. **Tel** (212)765-5700, FAX (212)581-4670 general correspondence, (212)265-4742 orders and billing inquiries. **LC** KF3775.Z9; E52. **DD** 344.73/046; 347.30446.

US/1054-8297
ENVIRONMENTAL LAW ANTHOLOGY. [Environ. law anthol.]. Vol. 1 (1990/1991)-. Periodical. English. an. $199.95. International Library Law Book Publishers, 101 Lakeforest Boulevard, Suite 270, Gaithersburg MD 20877. **Tel** (800)359-3349, (301)990-7755, FAX (301)990-7642. **ED** Alison P. Zabriskie. **LC** K5; .N855. **DD** 344.73/04605; 347.3044605. Index available. cum. index. **Bk Rev**, (Qty: 1). **Pr Rev.**
Desc: Contains environment law review articles selected from over 900 US law review journals. Articles are printed in their entirety.

US
ENVIRONMENTAL LAW CITATIONS. English. $250.00 (2 bound volumes), $227.00 (cumulative supplements). Shepards McGraw-Hill Inc, 555 Middle Creek Parkway, PO Box 35300, Colorado Springs CO 80935-3530. **Tel** (719)488-3000, FAX (800)525-0053.

US/0147-7714
ENVIRONMENTAL LAW HANDBOOK. [Environ. law handb.]. **Added/Corp** Government Institutes. (19??)-. English. ir. $72.00. Government Institutes Inc., 4 Research Place, Suite 200, Rockville MD 20850. **Tel** (301)921-2300, 921-2355, FAX (301)251-0638. **LC** KF3775; .E473. **DD** 344/.73/046.
Desc: Offers current compliance information on environmental law fundamentals, enforcement and liabilities. Written by eleven respected environmental attorneys.

US/1045-599X
ENVIRONMENTAL LAW JOURNAL OF OHIO. ***Title Change.*** [Environ. law j. Ohio]. **VFOAT** ELJO. Vol. 1, Issue 1 (Sept./Oct. 1989)-(19??). Periodical. English. bm. Banks-Baldwin Law Publishing Company, PO Box 1974, University Center, Cleveland OH 44106. **Tel** (216)721-7373. **LC** KFO354.A15; E58. **DD** 344.771/046/05; 347.71044605. ***Continued by*** *Ohio Environmental Monthly, 1063-9594.*

●US/1064-2129
ENVIRONMENTAL LAW NEWS (SAN FRANCISCO, CALIF.). (ENVIRONMENTAL LAW NEWS : A PUBLICATION OF THE ENVIRONMENTAL LAW SECTION OF THE STATE BAR OF CALIFORNIA.). [Environ. law news]. **Added/Corp** State Bar of California. Environmental Law Section. Vol. 1, No. 1 (Spring 1992)-. Periodical. English. State Bar of California, 555 Franklin Street, San Francisco CA 94102. **Tel** (415)561-8200, FAX (415)561-8228. **DD** 341.

US/0163-545X
ENVIRONMENTAL LAW NEWSLETTER. ***Title Change.*** [Environ. law newsl.]. Newsletter. English. qt. State Bar of Texas, PO Box 12487, Capitol Station, Austin TX 78711. **Tel** (512)463-1411. **ED** Jimmy Hall (editor's address: 602 West 11th Street, Austin, TX 78701). **LC** KFT1554.A15; E58. **DD** 344/.764/04605. **Bk Rev.** ctrl circ. ***Continued by*** *Environmental Law Journal.*

US/0046-2276
ENVIRONMENTAL LAW (PORTLAND, ORE.). (ENVIRONMENTAL LAW. NORTHWESTERN SCHOOL OF LAW OF LEWIS AND CLARK COLLEGE.). [Environ. law]. **Added/Corp** Northwestern School of Law. Vol. 1, (Spring 1970)-. Periodical. English. Four times a year (Jan., Apr., July, Oct.). $24.00. Northwestern School of Law, 10015 Southwest, Terwilliger Boulevard, Portland OR 97219. **Tel** (503)244-1181 Ext. 700, FAX (503)246-8542. **LC** K5; .N85. **DD** 344.73/046/05; 347.3044605. Index available (4th iss. in (Oct.).). **Bk Rev**, (Qty: varies). **Ad Acc. Pr Rev. Circ:** 900. available on microfilm and microfiche from University Microfilms International (UMI); available on an online database from LEXIS; and WESTLAW. Documents available from Documents on Demand.
Desc: The topics of the discussions run the gamut from in depth analyses of recent cases to more abstract discussions of the latest pollution prevention theories. We strive to provide the practitioner with practical, helpful articles, while continuing to lead the way in environmental thinking.
Ind/Abst EMBASE; Energy Inf. Abstr.; Environ. Abstr.; Environ. Period. Bibliogr.; Expand. Acad. Index (1984-); Fish Rev.; GeoRef; Index Leg. Period.; Int. Aerosp. Abstr.; J. Plan. Lit.; Leg. Resour. Index (1980-?); LegalTrac (1980-); Life Sci. Collect.; Wildl. Rev.

US/0046-2284
ENVIRONMENTAL LAW REPORTER. (ENVIRONMENTAL LAW REPORTER : A PROJECT OF THE ENVIRONMENTAL LAW INSTITUTE.). [Environ. law report.]. **Added/Corp** Environmental Law Institute. Vol. 1, No. 1 (Jan. 1971)-. Periodical. English. mo. $995.00. Environmental Law Institute, 1616 P Street NW/Suite 200, Washington DC 20036. **Tel** (800)433-5120, (202)939-3844, FAX (202)328-5002. **ED** Barry Breen. **LC** KF3775.A6; E5. Index available. cum. index. **Circ:** 1,300. available on microfiche. Documents available from Documents on Demand.
Desc: Reporting service - 6 loose-leaf volume - 12 monthly releases - 12 issues of news and analysis - updates issued weekly. Keeps you informed of major judicial, legislative and regulatory developments. Provides quick access to all major federal environmental statutes and regulations.
Ind/Abst Curr. Law Index (1980-); Environ. Abstr.; Environ. Period. Bibliogr.; Leg. Resour. Index (1980-); LegalTrac (1980-); PAIS Int. Print (1991-).

AT/1035-6150
ENVIRONMENTAL LAW REPORTER SYDNEY. (1983)-. Periodical. English. bw. $170.00 US; $255.00 other. Environmental Law Association, GPO Box 2144, Sydney 2001 Australia. **Tel** 011 61 2 9491760. Index available. **Circ:** 450. ***Continues*** *Environmental Law Reporter of NSW, 0727-0666.*
Desc: Presents decisions of importance in environmental law from the planning and environment courts and tribunals in all Australian states.

UK
ENVIRONMENTAL LAW REPORTS. (1993)-. English. Four times a year. £150.00 Europe; £158.00 other. Sweet & Maxwell Ltd., South Quay Plaza, 183 Marsh Wall, London E14 9FT England. **Tel** 011 44 264 342899, FAX 011 44 264 342723, telex 929089 ITPINF G.

US/8756-9280
ENVIRONMENTAL LAW SECTION JOURNAL. (ENVIRONMENTAL LAW SECTION JOURNAL / NEW YORK STATE BAR ASSOCIATION.). [Environ. Law Sect. j.]. **Added/Corp** New York State Bar Association. Environmental Law Section. (198?)-. Periodical. English. Four times a year. $35.00 US; $45.00 other. New York State Bar Association, One Elk Street, Albany NY 12207. **Tel** (518)463-3200. **ED** Kevin Reilly. **LC** KFN5610.A15; N48. **DD** 344.747/046/05; 347.47044605. **Bk Rev. Ad Acc, Adv Mgr:** Mary Beth

Martin. **Circ:** 1,850 (ctrl). ***Continues*** *Newsletter (New York State Bar Association. Environmental Law Section), 0736-7104.*

US
ENVIRONMENTAL LAW SYMPOSIUM. **Added/Corp** American Bar Association. Tort and Insurance Practice Section. Vol. 1 (1981)-. Periodical. English. an. Masson Publishing Company, 366 Wacouta Street, St Paul MN 55101. **ED** Peter W Schroth. **LC** K5; .N86. **DD** 344/.046; 342.446.

US/0748-8769
ENVIRONMENTAL LAW (WASHINGTON D.C.). (ENVIRONMENTAL LAW.). [Environ. law]. **Added/Corp** American Bar Association. Standing Committee on Environmental Law. (Winter 1978)-. Periodical. English. sa (2 issues). $15.00 institutions. American Bar Association, 750 North Lake Shore Drive, Chicago IL 60611. **Tel** (312)988-5522, (312)988-5241, FAX (312)988-5528, telex 270593. **ED** Elissa C. Lichtenstein and Courtney Leyendecker. **LC** KF3775.A15; E55. **DD** 344.73/046/05; 347.3044605. **Bk Rev. Pr Rev. Circ:** 5,000 (ctrl). Documents available from UMI Article Clearinghouse. ***Continues*** *Environmental Law Newsletter.*
Desc: Features articles on current law and policy issues. Summaries of ABA environmental law activities, book and conference notices.
Ind/Abst AESIS Q.; Leg. Resour. Index (1980-); Newsp. Period. Abstr. (1989-).

US
ENVIRONMENTAL LEGISLATION. Periodical. English. wk. University of Pittsburgh / 228 Parran Hall, Pittsburgh PA 15260.

US/0362-5400
ENVIRONMENTAL LEGISLATION REPORTER. ***Ceased.*** **Added/Corp** Virginia Water Resources Research Center. No. 1 (Jan. 9, 1976)-(19??). Periodical. English. wk. Virginia Water Resources Research Center, 617 North Main Street, Blacksburg VA 24060. **Tel** (703)961-5624, FAX (703)231-6673. **LC** KFV2754.A15; E5. **DD** 344/.755/04605.

UK
ENVIRONMENTAL LIABILITY. (1993)-. English. Six times a year. £195.00 Europe; £205.00 other. Sweet & Maxwell Ltd., South Quay Plaza, 183 Marsh Wall, London E14 9FT England. **Tel** 011 44 264 342899, FAX 011 44 264 342723, telex 929089 ITPINF G.

US/1041-8172
ENVIRONMENTAL MANAGEMENT REVIEW (ROCKVILLE, MD.). (ENVIRONMENTAL MANAGEMENT REVIEW.). [Environ. manage. rev.]. **Added/Corp** Government Institutes. No. 10 (4th Quarter 1988)-. Periodical. English. Four times a year. $198.00. Government Institutes Inc., 4 Research Place, Suite 200, Rockville MD 20850. **Tel** (301)921-2300, 921-2355, FAX (301)251-0638. **LC** KF3775.A15; E57. **DD** 344.73/046/05; 347.3044605. **Circ:** 300. Documents available from Documents on Demand. ***Continues*** *Environmental Management Report, 0889-4663.*
Desc: Selected papers from the more than 100 environmental seminars and courses which government institutes present yearly. Covers a broad range of environmental compliance topics.
Ind/Abst Environ. Abstr.

US/0887-9753
ENVIRONMENTAL MANAGER'S COMPLIANCE ADVISOR, THE. [Environ. manager's compliance advis.]. **Added/Corp** Bureau of Law & Business, Inc. Business & Legal Reports (Firm). (198?)-. Periodical. English. sm. $269.95. Business & Legal Reports, 39 Academy Street, Madison CT 06443. **Tel** (203)245-7448, (800)727-5257, FAX (203)245-2559. **LC** KF3775.A15; E58. **DD** 344.73/046/05; 347.3044605. **[CCC].** ***Continues*** *Hazardous Materials/Hazardous Waste Legal Reporter.*

SZ/0378-777X
ENVIRONMENTAL POLICY AND LAW. [Environ. policy and law]. Vol. 1 (June 1975)-. Periodical. English. Six times a year. Fl436.00. IOS Press, Van Diemenstraat 94, 1013 CN Amsterdam Netherlands. **Tel** 011 31 20 6382189, FAX 011 31 20 620 3419. **ED** W. E. Burhenne & and M. Jahnke. **DD** 344.04/6/05. **[CCC].** available on microfilm and microfiche from University Microfilms International (UMI). Documents available from Documents on Demand.
Desc: Created to encourage and develop the exchange of information and experience on all legal, administrative and policy matters relevant to the human and natural environment.
Ind/Abst AGRICOLA; Aquat. Sci. Fish. Abstr. (Computer File); Ecol. Abstr. (?-?); EMBASE; Energy Inf. Abstr.; Energy Res. Abstr. (July 1977-); Environ. Abstr.; Environ. Period. Bibliogr. (?-?); Geogr. Abstr. Human Geogr.; GeoRef; Health Saf. Sci. Abstr.; Int. Dev. Abstr.; Int. Polit. Sci. Abstr.; J. Plan. Lit.; Ocean. Abstr.; PAIS Int. Print (1991-?); Life Sci. Collect.; Pollut. Abstr. Indexes; Risk Abstr. (19??-19??).

US
ENVIRONMENTAL PROTECTION : THE LEGAL FRAMEWORK / FRANK F. SKILLERN. (1981)-. English. ir. New sales not available for the main volume; pocket parts still available for $55.00 (Nov. 1992 ed.). Shepards McGraw-Hill Inc, 555 Middle Creek Parkway, PO Box 35300, Colorado Springs CO 80935-3530. **Tel** (719)488-3000, FAX (800)525-0053. cum. index. **Bk Rev.**
Desc: Extensive analysis of current law as it affects environmental issues.

US/1056-3164
ENVIRONMENTAL REGULATORY ADVISOR. [Environ. regul. advis.]. **Added/Corp** J.J. Keller & Associates. Vol. 1, No. 1 (May 1991)-. Periodical. English. Twelve times a year. $98.85. J. J. Keller & Associates, PO Box 548, Neenah WI 54957-0368. **Tel** (800)558-5011, (414)722-2848. **LC** KF3775.A15; E594. **DD** 344.73/046; 347.30446. ***Continues*** *Hazardous Substances Advisor, 0196-3767.*

US
ENVIRONMENTAL RIGHTS AND REMEDIES. CUMULATIVE SUPPLEMENT. Began with 1973-1976. English. an. **ED** Steven G Davison and Bernard S Cohen.

US/0736-573X
ENVIRONMENTAL STATUTES. **Main/Corp** United States. **Added/Corp** Government Institutes. (1979)-. English. an. $63.00 (hardcover), $53.00 (softcover). Government Institutes Inc., 4 Research Place, Suite 200, Rockville MD 20850. **Tel** (301)921-2300, 921-2355, FAX (301)251-0638. **LC** KF3775.A29; U55. **DD** 344.73/046; 347.30446. Index available.
Desc: The new edition continues to be the most complete and up-to-date source of all major environmental laws you can find anywhere. This manual includes U.S. Code Citations throughout and an alphabetical index for ease of reference.

US/0193-6387
ENVIRONS (DAVIS). (ENVIRONS.). Periodical. English. Environmental Law Society, King Hall, University of California, Davis CA 95616. **LC** KFC610.A15; E58. **DD** 344/.794/046.

US
EPA ADMINISTRATIVE LAW REPORTER. (19??)-. Periodical. English. mo (11 issues). $850.00. Law Reporters, 1519 Connecticut Avenue Northwest, Suite 200, Washington DC 20036. **Tel** (202)462-5755.

FR
ETAT DE L'ENVIRONNEMENT (PARIS, FRANCE). (L'ETAT DE L'ENVIRONNEMENT / MINISTERE DE L'ENVIRONNEMENT.). Began with 1976/77 Vol. French. an. Documentation Francaise, 29 Quai Voltaire, 75344 Paris Cedex 7 France. **Tel** 011 33 1 40157000, FAX 011 33 1 40157230, telex 204 826 DOCFRAN. **LC** HC280.E5; E85. **DD** 333.7/0944.

UK/1353-3525
EUROPEAN ENVIRONMENT LAW. (19??)-. Periodical. English. £475.00 UK & Europe; £550.00 Other. Agra Europe London Limited, 25 Frant Road, Tunbridge Wells, Kent TN2 5JT England. **Tel** 011 44 892 533813.

●UK/0966-1646
EUROPEAN ENVIRONMENTAL LAW REVIEW. [Eur. environ. law rev.]. (1992)-. Periodical. English. mo (11 issues per year). $215.00. Graham & Trotman Ltd, Sterling House, 66 Wilson Road, London SW1V 1DE England. **Tel** 44 71 8211123. **ED** E. Bramwell. **DD** 341.762. **Bk Rev. Pr Rev. Acid Free.**
Desc: Brings comprehensive coverage of developments in environmental law throughout the whole of Europe. A Pan-European network of expert correspondents covers news from the European community as well as from the national jurisdictions of each European state, both inside and outside the EC, together with additional reports on the activities of international organizations such as the OECD and the UN. Important developments in the US will also be covered. The journal provides a complete information service on every aspect of environmental law - including the legal issues relating to land, air, fresh water, oceans, noise, waste management, dangerous substances and nature conservation.

US/1048-4078
FEDERAL FACILITIES ENVIRONMENTAL JOURNAL. [Fed. facil. environ. j.]. Vol. 1, No. 1 (Spring 1990)-. Periodical. English. qt. $159.00 US & Canada; $209.00 other. John Wiley & Sons, Inc., 605 Third Avenue, New York NY 10158-0012. **Tel** (212)850-6000, (212)850-6645, FAX (212)850-6088, telex 12-7063. **(Subscription address:** John Wiley & Sons Inc / New Jersey, PO Box 2575, Secaucus NJ 07096-2575.**)** **ED** Jane G. Bensahely. **LC** K6; .E294. **DD** 344.73/046/05; 347.3044605. **[CCC].** Index available. **Ad Acc.** available in microform.
Desc: Provides answers to compliance questions, including case studies of agency/ contractor solutions to current problems and recommendations for avoiding future problems. Analysis of latest actions by federal and state agencies also covered.

●US/1064-1874
FLORIDA ENVIRONMENTAL COMPLIANCE UPDATE. [Fla. environ. compliance update]. (Sept 1992)-. Periodical. English. mo. $147.00. M. Lee Smith Publishers and Printers, 162 4th Avenue North, PO Box 198867, Nashville TN 37219. **Tel** (615)242-7395, (800)274-6774, FAX (615)256-6601. **ED** Sidney Ansbacher, (address) Brant, Moore, Sapp, MacDonald and Wells, 50 North Laura, Suite 3100, Jacksonville, Fl 32202, (phone) 904-353-3100. **DD** 344. ***Continues*** *Holland & Knight's Florida Environmental & Land Use Newsletter, 1047-4641.*
Desc: Newsletter reporting the latest state specific environmental law developments that affect companies in that state.

UK
GARNER'S ENVIRONMENTAL LAW. (19??)-. English. ir. £88.00. Butterworth & Co. Ltd. / Kent, England, Borough Green, Sevenoaks Kent TN15 8PH England. **Tel** 011 44 732-884567, FAX 011 44 732-885996. ***Continues*** *Garner's Control of Pollution.*

US/1042-1858
GEORGETOWN INTERNATIONAL ENVIRONMENTAL LAW REVIEW. [Georget. int. environ. law rev.]. **Added/Corp** Environmental Law Institute. Georgetown University. Law Center. Vol. 1, Issue 1 (Spring 1988)-. Periodical. English. Three times a year (Fall, Spring, Summer). $35.00. Georgetown University Law Center, 600 New Jersey Avenue NW, Washington DC 20009. **Tel** (202)662-9468, FAX (202)662-9444. **LC** K7; .E642. **DD** 341.7/62/05.

US/1044-2324
GEORGIA ENVIRONMENTAL LAW LETTER. [Ga. environ. law lett.]. **Added/Corp** Georgia Law Letter Publishers. Vol. 1, No. 1 (July 1989)-. English. mo. $147.00 (tax included). M. Lee Smith Publishers and Printers, 162 4th Avenue North, PO Box 198867, Nashville TN 37219. **Tel** (615)242-7395, (800)274-6774, FAX (615)256-6601. **ED** Jean Tolman, (address) Arnall Golden and Gregory, 55 Park Place NE, Suite 400, Atlanta, GA 30335, (phone)404-527-4719. **LC** KFG354.A15; G46. **DD** 344.758/04605; 347.58044605.
Desc: Newsletter reporting the latest state specific environmental law developments that affect companies in that state.

●UK
GREEN'S ENVIRONMENTAL LAW BULLETIN. (1994)-. Bulletin. English. Six times a year. £99.00 Europe; £104.00 other. Sweet & Maxwell Ltd., South Quay Plaza, 183 Marsh Wall, London E14 9FT England. **Tel** 011 44 264 342899, FAX 011 44 264 342723, telex 929089 ITPINF G.

CN
GUIDE TO ENVIRONMENTAL LEGISLATION IN ONTARIO. an. 43.00Can$. Southam Information and Technology Group Inc., 1450 Don Mills Road, Don Mills Ontario M3B 2X7 Canada. **Tel** (416)445-6641, (800)668-2374, FAX (416)442-2261.

US/0884-3775
HAZARDOUS WASTE AND TOXIC TORTS. ***Title Change.*** (HAZARDOUS WASTE AND TOXIC TORTS : LAW AND STRATEGY.). **VFOAT** Hazardous Waste and Toxic Torts Law & Strategy. Vol. 1, No. 1 (June 1985)-(19??). Periodical. English. mo. Leader Publications, 345 Park Avenue South, New York NY 10010. **Tel** (800)888-8300 ext. 6170, (212)545-6170, FAX (212)696-1848. **LC** KF3945.A15; H392. **DD** 344.73/0462/0269; 347.3044620269; 355. ***Continued by*** *Environmental Compliance Litigation.*
Desc: Offers reports of legislative and regulatory rulings, and a recap of opinions, verdicts and settlements. Also presents what new statutes are brewing in Washington and around the country, perspectives on insurance issues, and advice from experienced attorneys on trial tactics and strategies.

US/0275-0244
HAZARDOUS WASTE LITIGATION REPORTER. [Hazard. waste litig. rep.]. (1980)-. Periodical. English. sm. $850.00. Andrews Publications Inc., 1646 West Chester Pike, PO Box 1000, Westtown PA 19395. **Tel** (610)399-6600, (800)345-1101, FAX (610)399-6610. **ED** Leonard E. B. Andrews. **LC** KF3946.A59; H39. **DD** 344.73/04622; 347.3044622. cum. index. ctrl circ.
Desc: Covers federal, state, private party and citizens lawsuits against hazardous waste generators, transporters and past and present waste facility owners/operators.

US/1059-468X
HAZARDOUS WASTE STRATEGIES UPDATE. (HAZARDOUS WASTE STRATEGIES UPDATE : NEW APPROACHES TO REMEDIATION AND LIABLITY ISSUES.). [Hazard. waste strateg. update]. Vol. 2, No. 1 (1990)-. English. Four times a year.

$125.00. Shepards McGraw-Hill Inc, 555 Middle Creek Parkway, PO Box 35300, Colorado Springs CO 80935-3530. **Tel** (719)488-3000, FAX (800)525-0053. **ED** Robert Steinberg and James Miller. **DD** 363. ***Continues*** *RCRA and Superfund Quarterly.*
Desc: Provides cutting-edge strategies for remediation and litigation. Each issue gives you innovative remediation strategies, descriptions and analysis of all pertinent case law, and up-to-date statutory and regulatory developments.

US/0147-8257
HELR. THE HARVARD ENVIRONMENTAL LAW REVIEW. (THE HARVARD ENVIRONMENTAL LAW REVIEW : HELR.). [HELR, Harvard environ. law rev.]. **VFOAT** HELR; H.E.L.R. Vol. 1 (1976)-. Academic Scholarly Publication. English. sa (Feb. &June). $24.00 US; $28.00 other. Harvard Law School, Publications Center, Cambridge MA 02138. **Tel** (617)495-7984, (617)495-3694. **LC** K8; .A682. **DD** 344.7304/6; 347.30446. Index available (Free). **Bk Rev**. Documents available from The Genuine Article, Documents on Demand.
Desc: Scholarly articles on current topics in environmental law.
Ind/Abst Coal Abstr.; Curr. Contents Soc. Behav. Sci.; Curr. Law Index (1980-); Energy Inf. Abstr.; Energy Res. Abstr. (Aug. 1980-); Environ. Abstr.; Environ. Period. Bibliogr.; Health Saf. Sci. Abstr.; Index Leg. Period.; INIS Atomindex [Micro.]; J. Plan. Lit.; Leg. Resour. Index (1980-); LegalTrac (1980-); Ocean. Abstr.; PAIS Int. Print; Pollut. Abstr. Indexes; Res. Alert [Full Cov.]; Soc. Sci. Cit. Index [Full Cov.].

US/0882-6765
HOFSTRA ENVIRONMENTAL LAW DIGEST. [Hofstra environ. law dig.]. Vol. 1, No. 2, Fall (1984)-. Periodical. English. sa. $8.00. Hofstra Environmental Law Society, Hofstra University, School of Law, Hempstead NY 11550. **Tel** (516)560-5007. **ED** Donald Campbell. **LC** KF3775.A59; E49. **DD** 344.73/046/05. **Bk Rev. Ad Acc. Circ:** 500. ***Continues*** *Environmental Law Digest.*
Desc: Digest provides reviews and analyses of significant developments in the field of environmental law and litigation.

US/1047-4641
HOLLAND & KNIGHT'S FLORIDA ENVIRONMENTAL & LAND USE LETTER. ***Title Change.*** [Holland Knight's Fla. environ. land use lett.]. **Added/Corp** Holland & Knight (Firm). **VFOAT** Holland and Knight's Florida Environmental and Land Use Letter; Florida Environmental & Land Use Letter; Florida Environmental and Land Use Letter. Vol. 1, No. 1 (Feb. 1990)-(1992). Periodical. English. mo. Florida Environmental and Land Use Letter, 800 North Magnolia Avenue, POB 1526, Orlando FL 32802. **LC** KFF354.A15; H65. **DD** 344.759/046; 347.590446. ***Continued by*** *Florida Environmental Compliance Update, 1064-1874.*

AT/1030-3847
IMPACT SYDNEY, 1986. [Impact Syd., 1986]. (1986)-. Newsletter. English. qt. 55.00Aus$. Environmental Defenders Office Ltd., 280 Pitt Street, 8th Floor Suite 82, Sydney NSW 2000 Australia. **Tel** 011 61 2 2613599, FAX 011 61 2 2677548. **DD** 344.94046. **Bk Rev. Circ:** 500.

US/0192-3773
INDEX TO TITLE 40 OF THE CODE OF FEDERAL REGULATIONS : PROTECTION OF ENVIRONMENT. VAT Index to Title Forty of the Code of Federal Regulations: Protection of Environment. 1978-. English. be. Information Resources Press / Washington DC, 2100 M Street NW, Washington DC 20037. **LC** KF3775.A3697; I52. **DD** 344/.73/04602638.

US/1061-916X
INDIANA ENVIRONMENTAL RULES. [Ind. environ. rules]. (1991)-. English. $39.95. Cromer, Eaglesfield, and Maher, 1500 Market Tower, 10 West Market Street, Indianapolis IN 46204-2968. **DD** 344.

US/1061-7957
INDIANA ENVIRONMENTAL STATUTES. [Ind. environ. statut.]. **Main/Corp** Indiana. (1991)-. English. $39.95. Cromer, Eaglesfield, and Maher, 1500 Market Tower, 10 West Market Street, Indianapolis IN 46204-2968. **LC** KFI3354.A336; A195. **DD** 344.772/046/0263205; 347.7204460263205.

US/0894-0533
INDOOR POLLUTION LAW REPORT. ***Title Change.*** [Indoor pollut. law rep.]. **Added/Corp** Cadwalader, Wickersham & Taft. Environmental Law Group. Vol. 1, No. 1 (June 1987)-(19??). Periodical. English. mo. Leader Publications, 345 Park Avenue South, New York NY 10010. **Tel** (800)888-8300 ext. 6170, (212)545-6170, FAX (212)696-1848. **LC** KF3812.A15; I53. **DD** 344.73/046342; 347.30446342. ***Absorbed by*** *Environmental Compliance Litigation.*

US
INSIDE EPA'S CLEAN AIR REPORT. **VFOAT** Clear Air Report. (1990)-. English. bw. $375.00 US and Canada; $425.00 other. Inside Washington Publishers, PO Box 7167, Benjamin Franklin Station, Washington DC 20044. **Tel** (703)416-8500, (800)424-9068.

US/0894-6655
INSIDE EPA'S ENVIRONMENTAL POLICY ALERT. [Inside EPA's envir. policy alert]. **VFOAT** Environmental Policy Alert. Vol. 1, No. 1 (June 20, 1984)-. Periodical. English. bw. $510.00. Inside Washington Publishers, PO Box 7167, Benjamin Franklin Station, Washington DC 20044. **Tel** (703)416-8500, (800)424-9068. **LC** KF3775.A15; I57. **DD** 344.73/046; 347.30446. **NLM** W1; IN4576M.

US/1049-6149
INSIDE EPA'S SUPERFUND REPORT. [Inside EPA's superfund rep.]. **VFOAT** Superfund Report Newswatch; Superfund Report. Vol. 1, No. 1 (Feb. 1987)-. Periodical. English. bw. $480.00. Inside Washington Publishers, PO Box 7167, Benjamin Franklin Station, Washington DC 20044. **Tel** (703)416-8500, (800)424-9068. **LC** KF1299.H39; A135. **DD** 346.7303/2; 347.30632. **NLM** W1; IN45766.

US/0149-8738
INTERNATIONAL ENVIRONMENT REPORTER. CURRENT REPORT. **Added/Corp** Bureau of National Affairs (Washington, D.C.). **VFOAT** Current Report; Current Reports; IER. Current Reports. Vol. 1 (Jan. 1978)-. Periodical. English. bw. $1,645.00. Bureau of National Affairs Inc., 9435 Key West Avenue, Rockville MD 20850. **Tel** (800)372-1033, (301)258-1033, FAX (301)948-5823. **(Subscription address:** 9435 Key West Avenue, Rockville MD 20850; telephone: FAX (301)948-5823) **ED** Marlon Allen. **LC** TD169; .I573. **DD** 614.7/05. **[CCC]**. Index available. cum. index.
Desc: A four-binder information and reference service covering international environmental law and developing policy in the major industrial nations.

GW
INTERNATIONAL ENVIRONMENTAL LAW. MULTILATERAL TREATIES. English (German and French). Twice a year. DM290.00. Erich Schmidt Verlag GmbH, Postfach 304240, D 10724 Berlin Germany. **Tel** 011 49 30 25008525.

CN/0820-3458
INTERVENOR : NEWSLETTER OF THE CANADIAN ENVIRONMENTAL LAW ASSOCIATION. [Intervenor]. **Added/Corp** Canadian Environmental Law Association. (1986)-. Newsletter. English. bm. 20.00Can$ (1 year), 38.00Can$ (2 year), 54.00Can$ (3 year) Canada; 18.00Can$ (1 year) student; 22.00Can$ (1 year) US; 25.00Can$ (1 year) other. Canadian Environmental Law Association, 517 College Street, Suite 401, Toronto Ontario M6G 4A2 Canada. **Tel** (416)960-2284, FAX (416)960-9392. **ED** Jill Cameron-Huff. **DD** 344.71/046/05. cum. index. **Bk Rev**, (Qty: 6/yr). ctrl circ. ***Continues*** *The CELA Newsletter, 0707-7866.*
Desc: Environmental law reform issues and environmental legislation commentary. Environmental advocacy and citizen action updates.
Ind/Abst Can. Legal Lit.

US/1053-377X
JOURNAL OF ENERGY, NATURAL RESOURCES & ENVIRONMENTAL LAW. **VFOAT** Journal of Energy, Natural Resources and Environmental Law; JENREL. Vol. 11, No. 1 (1990)-. Periodical. English. sa. $10.00. University of Utah College of Law, Salt Lake City UT 84112. **Tel** (801)581-6833 or 581-4687. **ED** Frederick S. Etheridge. **LC** K10; .O8597. **DD** 346.7304/6/05. **Bk Rev. Ad Acc. Circ:** 400 (ctrl). ***Continues*** *Journal of Energy Law & Policy, 0275-9926.*
Ind/Abst Energy Inf. Abstr.; INIS Atomindex [Micro.]; Leg. Resour. Index; LegalTrac (1990-); PAIS Int. Print.

UK/0952-8873
JOURNAL OF ENVIRONMENTAL LAW. Vol. 1, No. 1 (1989)-. Periodical. English. sa. £56.00 UK and Europe; $102.00 other. Oxford University Press, Walton Street, Oxford OX2 6DP England. **Tel** 011 44 865 56767, FAX 011 44 865 267773, telex 837330 OXPRES G. **(Subscription address:** Oxford University Press / USA, Journals Marketing Department, Oxford University Press, 2001 Evans Road, Cary NC 27513.) **ED** Richard Macrory. **LC** K10; .O8598. **DD** 344.41/046; 344.10446. **CODEN** JELAEI. **[CCC]. Bk Rev. Ad Acc. Pr Rev.** available on microfilm and microfiche. Documents available from The Genuine Article.
Desc: Appraisals of current and emerging concepts, policies, control, waste management, biotechnology, regulation of hazardous substances, and international regimes for common natural resources.
Ind/Abst Index Leg. Period. (1992-); Res. Alert [Select. Cov.]; SCISEARCH; Soc. Sci. Cit. Index [Select. Cov.].

US/1049-0280
JOURNAL OF ENVIRONMENTAL LAW AND LITIGATION. [J. environ. law litig.]. **Added/Corp** University of Oregon. School of Law. **VFOAT** Journal of Environmental Law & Litigation; Environmental Law and Litigation; Envtl. Law & Litigation; Envtl. Law and Litigation. Vol. 1 (1986)-. English. sa. $16.00. Journal of Environmental Law, University of Oregon Law School, Eugene OR 97403. **Tel** (503)346-3891. **ED** Katherine Buntinz. **LC** K10; .O8599. **DD** 344.73/046; 347.30446. **Bk Rev. Ad Acc, Adv Mgr:** Derek Snelling. **Circ:** 650.
Ind/Abst Index Leg. Period.; Leg. Resour. Index; LegalTrac (1980-).

CN/1181-7534
JOURNAL OF ENVIRONMENTAL LAW AND PRACTICE. [J. environ. law pract.]. **VFOAT** J.E.L.P.; JELP. Vol. 1, No. 1 (Sept. 1990)-. Periodical. English. sa. $101.30. Carswell Company Ltd, 2075 Kennedy Road, Scarborough Ontario M1T 3V4 Canada.
Ind/Abst Index Can. Leg. Period. Lit. (1992-).

US/0892-4880
JOURNAL OF LAND USE & ENVIRONMENTAL LAW. [J. land use environ. law]. **VFOAT** Journal of Land Use and Environmental Law. Vol. 1, No. 1 (Winter 1985)-. Periodical. English. sa. $28.00. Journal of Land Use & Environmental Law, FSU College of Law, Tallahassee FL 32306. **Tel** (904)644-4240. **LC** K10; .O8727. **DD** 346.75904/5; 347.590645. cum. index. **Ad Acc.** Documents available from Documents on Demand.
Ind/Abst Curr. Law Index (1984-); Environ. Abstr.; Environ. Period. Bibliogr.; Index Leg. Period.; J. Plan. Lit.; Leg. Resour. Index (1984-); LegalTrac (1980-).

●US/1070-4833
JOURNAL OF NATURAL RESOURCES & ENVIRONMENTAL LAW. (JOURNAL OF NATURAL RESOURCES & ENVIRONMENTAL LAW /MINERAL LAW CENTER, UNIVERSITY OF KENTUCKY, COLLEGE OF LAW.). [J. nat. resour. environ. law]. **Added/Corp** University of Kentucky. Mineral Law Center. **VFOAT** Journal of Natural Resources and Environmental Law. Vol. 8, No. 1 (1992)-. Periodical. English. Twice a year (July & Dec.). $15.00. Journal of Natural Resources & Environmental Law, 21 Law Building,, University of Kentucky, College of Law, Lexington KY 40506. **Tel** (606)257-1161. **DD** 343. ***Continues*** *Journal of Mmineral Law & Policy, 0892-9017.*

UK/0307-4870
JOURNAL OF PLANNING AND ENVIRONMENT LAW. [J. plann. environ. law]. **VFOAT** Journal of Planning & Environment Law. (1973)-. Periodical. English. mo. £105.00 Europe; £110.00 other. Sweet & Maxwell Ltd., South Quay Plaza, 183 Marsh Wall, London E14 9FT England. **Tel** 011 44 264 342899, FAX 011 44 264 342723, telex 929089 ITPINF G. **LC** K10; .O883. **DD** 346/.42/045. available on microfilm and microfiche from University Microfilms International (UMI). ***Continues*** *Journal of Planning and Property Law, 0022-376X.*
Ind/Abst Appl. Soc. Sci. Index Abstr.; Archit. Period. Index (1973-); Avery Index Archit. Period. Suppl. Colum. Univ. (Feb. 1990); Br. Archaeol. Bibliogr.; Coal Abstr.; Curr. Law Index (1980-); Energy Res. Abstr. (Jan. 1981-); Fish Rev.; Geogr. Abstr. Human Geogr. (?-?); Leg. Resour. Index (1980-); LegalTrac (1980-); PAIS Int. Print (1991-); Sage Urban Stud. Abstr.

JA
KANKYO KOGAI NENKAN. Japanese. ¥950. Gakuyo Shobo, 7-5 Fujimi 1 Chiyoda-ku, Tokyo 102 Japan.

US/1057-4174
KANSAS-IOWA ENVIRONMENTAL LAW LETTER. [Kans.-Iowa environ. law lett.]. **Added/Corp** Armstrong, Teasdale, Schlafly, Davis & Dicus. **VFOAT** Kansas Iowa Environmental Law Letter. Vol. 1, No. 1 (July 1991)-. Periodical. English. mo. $107.00. M. Lee Smith Publishers and Printers, 162 4th Avenue North, PO Box 198867, Nashville TN 37219. **Tel** (615)242-7395, (800)274-6774, FAX (615)256-6601. **DD** 344. ***Continues in part*** *Midwest Environmental Law Letter, 1049-9350.*

US/0023-7612
LAND AND WATER LAW REVIEW. Vol. 1 (1966)-. Periodical. English. sa. $18.00 US; $19.00 other. Land and Water Law Review, University of Wyoming, College of Law, University Station, Box 3035, Laramie WY 82071. **Tel** (307)766-2251. **ED** Lynette Boomgaarden. **LC** MICROFILM (O) 83/10016 . **DD** 344/.787/0636361. Index available. **Circ:** 2,500. available on microfilm and microfiche from University Microfilms International (UMI). Documents available from Documents on Demand. ***Absorbed*** *Wyoming Law Journal.*
Desc: Development of land, water, and natural resources law. Surveys important developments in Wyoming case law and statutory law.
Ind/Abst Aquat. Sci. Fish. Abstr. (Computer File); Curr. Law Index (1980-); Energy Inf. Abstr.; Environ. Abstr.; Fed. Tax Artic.; GeoRef; Index Leg. Period.; INIS Atomindex [Micro.]; J. Plan. Lit.; Leg. Resour. Index (1980-); LegalTrac (1980-); Life Sci. Collect.; Pollut. Abstr. Indexes; West. Hist. Q.

UK/0955-6354
LAND MANAGEMENT AND ENVIRONMENTAL LAW REPORT : LME LAW REPORT. ***Title Change.*** [Land manage. environ. law rep.]. **VFOAT** LME Law Report. Vol. 1, No. 1 (May/June 1989)-(19??). Periodical. English. Six times a year. John Wiley & Sons Ltd., Baffins Lane, Chichester West Sussex PO19 1UD England. **Tel** 0243 779777, FAX 0243 776128 BTG:JWP001, telex 86290 WIBOOKG. **(Subscription address:** North, South and Central America/ John Wiley & Sons, Inc., PO Box 7247-8491, Philadelphia, PA 19170-8491**) ED** Malcolm Forster. **DD** 340. **CODEN** LMEREA. **[CCC].** available on microfilm and microfiche from University Microfilms International (UMI). ***Continued by*** *Environmental Law and Management, 1067-6058.*
Desc: Provides comprehensive coverage of developments in environmental law as they occur. The journal covers not only pollution of water, soil, atmosphere, noise control, public health, etc., but also agriculture, forestry and rural development, minerals and water resources, access to the countryside, land taxation, etc.
Ind/Abst Curr. Aware. Biol. Sci., CABS; Environ. Period. Bibliogr.; World Agric. Econ.

●US/1072-7973
LAND USE & ENVIRONMENT FORUM. [Land use environ. forum]. **Added/Corp** Continuing Education of the Bar--California. **VFOAT** Land Use and Environment Forum. Vol. 2, No. 4 (Fall 1993)-. English. qt. $225.00. California Continuing Education of the Bar, 2300 Shattuck Avenue, Berkeley CA 94704. **Tel** (510)642-8000, (800)232-3444. **LC** K12; .A6. **DD** 346.79404/5; 347.940645. ***Continues*** *Land Use Forum, 1058-7012.*
Desc: Resource for land use and environmental professionals. Provides information on the law and policy analysis.

US/0192-8309
LAND USE & ENVIRONMENT LAW REVIEW. [Land use environ. law rev.]. **Added/Corp** Clark Boardman Company. **VFOAT** Land Use and Environment Law Review. (1978)-. English. an. $85.00. Clark Boardman Callaghan, 155 Pfingsten Road, Deerfield IL 60015. **Tel** (800)323-8067. **LC** KF3790.A2; E5. ***Continues*** *Environment Law Review, 0071-0830.*
Ind/Abst Coal Abstr.; Curr. Law Index (1980-); GeoRef; Leg. Resour. Index (1980-?); LegalTrac (1980-1988).

●US/1064-0363
LAW & BUSINESS DIRECTORY OF ENVIRONMENTAL ATTORNEYS. [Law bus. dir. environ. atty.]. **Added/Corp** Prentice Hall Law & Business (Firm). **VFOAT** Directory of Environmental Attorneys; Law and Business Directory of Environmental Attorneys. (1992)-. English. an. $211.58. Prentice-Hall Law and Business, 270 Sylvan Avenue, Englewood Cliffs NJ 07632. **Tel** (800)223-0231, (201)894-8538, FAX (201)894-8666. **LC** KF195.E6; L39. **DD** 344.73/046/02573; 347.3044602573.

US
LAWS OF THE STATE OF NEBRASKA PERTAINING TO THE GAME AND PARKS COMMISSION. **Main/Corp** Nebraska. **VFOAT** Nebraska Game Laws. English. an. Game and Parks Commission, 2200 North 33rd Street/Box 30370, Lincoln NE 68503. **LC** KFN453.A29; G34. **DD** 344/.782/099. ***Continues*** *Laws of the Game, Forestation and Parks Commission of State of Nebraska.*

US
LEGAL COMPILATION. (LEGAL COMPILATION : STATUTES AND LEGISLATIVE HISTORY, EXECUTIVE ORDERS, REGULATIONS, GUIDELINES AND REPORTS.). **Added/Corp** United States. Environmental Protection Agency. (Jan. 1973)-. English. US Environmental Protection Agency, 401 M Street SW, Washington DC 20460. **Tel** (202)755-9163. **LC** KF3775; .L42. **DD** 344/.73/046.
Desc: Compilation of legal authority under which the U. S. Environmental Protection Agency operates.

●AT/1039-7213
LOCAL GOVERNMENT AND ENVIRONMENTAL REPORTS OF AUSTRALIA, THE. See Public Administration.

AT/0076-0242
LOCAL GOVERNMENT REPORTS OF AUSTRALIA, THE. ***Title Change.*** See Public Administration.

US
LOUISIANA COASTAL LAW. **VFOAT** LCL Report. No. 1- Sept. 1971-. Periodical. English. Free. National Network Early Language Learn, 1118 22nd Street Northwest, Washington DC 20037. **Tel** (202)429-9292, FAX (202)659-5641. **(Subscription address:** Sea Grant Legal Program, Newsletter Subscriptions, 170 Law Center, LSU, Baton Rouge, LA 70803-1018**) Circ:** 2,000.

●US/1066-1115
LOUISIANA ENVIRONMENTAL COMPLIANCE UPDATE. [La. environ. compliance update]. **Added/Corp** M. Lee Smith Publishers & Printers. (1993)-. Periodical. English. mo. $137.00. M. Lee Smith Publishers and Printers, 162 4th Avenue North, PO Box 198867, Nashville TN 37219. **Tel** (615)242-7395, (800)274-6774, FAX (615)256-6601. **DD** 344.

●US/1062-7960
MARYLAND ENVIRONMENTAL LAW LETTER. [Md. environ. law lett.]. **Added/Corp** Piper & Marbury. (May 1992)-. Periodical. English. mo. $137.00. M. Lee Smith Publishers and Printers, 162 4th Avenue North, PO Box 198867, Nashville TN 37219. **Tel** (615)242-7395, (800)274-6774, FAX (615)256-6601. **ED** Deborah Jennings and William Toole, (address) Piper and Marbury, Charles Center South, 36 South Charles Street, Baltimore, MD 21201-3010, (phone)410-539-2530. **DD** 344.
Desc: Newsletter reporting the latest state specific environmental law developments that affect companies in that state.

●US/1064-2374
MASSACHUSETTS ENVIRONMENTAL COMPLIANCE UPDATE. [Mass. environ. compliance update]. **Added/Corp** M. Lee Smith Publishers & Printers. McGregor & Shea, P.C. (Firm). **VFOAT** Environmental Compliance Update. (Oct 1992)-. Periodical. English. mo. $107.00. M. Lee Smith Publishers and Printers, 162 4th Avenue North, PO Box 198867, Nashville TN 37219. **Tel** (615)242-7395, (800)274-6774, FAX (615)256-6601. **ED** Gregor I. McGregor, (address) McGregor and Shea, 141 Tremont Street, Suite 200, Boston, MA, (phone) 617-338-6464. **DD** 344.
Desc: Newsletter reporting the latest state specific environmental law developments that affect companies in that state.

US/1050-897X
MEALEY'S EUROPEAN ENVIRONMENTAL LAW REPORT. [Mealey's Eur. environ. law rep.]. **Added/Corp** Mealey Publications. **VFOAT** European Environmental Law Report. Vol. 1, Issue 1 (Aug. 8, 1990). Periodical. English. sm. $650.00 US, Canada, and Mexico; $746.00 other. Mealey Publications, PO Box 446, Wayne PA 19087-0446. **Tel** (215)688-6566, FAX (215)688-7552. **ED** John T. Hayes. **LC** KJC6242.A52; M43. **DD** 346.404/6; 344.0646. **[CCC].** Index available. cum. index.
Desc: Coverage of environmental laws, directives and regulations, and litigation for those doing business in Europe.

US/0897-3407
MEALEY'S LITIGATION REPORTS. SUPERFUND. [Mealey's litig. rep., Superfund]. **Added/Corp** Mealey Publications. **VFOAT** Litigation Reports. Superfund; Superfund. Vol. 1, Issue No. 1 (April 1988)-. Periodical. English. sm. $795.00. Mealey Publications, PO Box 446, Wayne PA 19087-0446. **Tel** (215)688-6566, FAX (215)688-7552. **ED** Edie Scott. **LC** KF1299.H39; A494. **DD** 346.7303/8; 347.30638. **[CCC].** Index available. cum. index. available on diskette.
Desc: Covers litigation and regulation concerning all sites on Superfund's National Priority List.

●US/1073-9459
MICHIGAN ENVIRONMENTAL COMPLIANCE UPDATE. (MICHIGAN ENVIRONMENTAL COMPLIANCE UPDATE / HONIGMAN, MILLER, SCHWARTZ, AND COHN.). [Mich. environ. compliance update]. **Added/Corp** Honigman, Miller, Schwartz, and Cohn. Vol. 4, No. 10 (Jan. 1994)-. Periodical. English. mo. $137.00. M. Lee Smith Publishers and Printers, 162 4th Avenue North, PO Box 198867, Nashville TN 37219. **Tel** (615)242-7395, (800)274-6774, FAX (615)256-6601. **DD** 344. ***Continues*** *Michigan Environmental Law Letter, 1046-9192.*

US/1046-9192
MICHIGAN ENVIRONMENTAL LAW LETTER. ***Title Change.*** [Mich. environ. law lett.]. Vol. 1, No. 1 (Apr. 1990)-(199?). Periodical. English. mo. M. Lee Smith Publishers & Printers, PO Box 198867, Nashville TN 37219. **Tel** (615)242-7395. **ED** Joseph Polito, Robert Hykan, and Arthur Siegal. **DD** 344. ***Continued by*** *Michigan Environmental Compliance Update, 1073-9459.*

●US/1072-916X
MINNESOTA ENVIRONMENTAL COMPLIANCE UPDATE. (MINNESOTA ENVIRONMENTAL COMPLIANCE UPDATE / OPPENHEIMER, WOLFF & DONNELLY.). [Minn. environ. compliance update]. **Added/Corp** Oppenheimer, Wolff & Donnelly. **VFOAT** Environmental Compliance Update. (1994)-. Periodical. English. mo. $137.00. M. Lee Smith Publishers and Printers, 162 4th Avenue North, PO Box 198867, Nashville TN 37219. **Tel** (615)242-7395, (800)274-6774, FAX (615)256-6601. **DD** 344.

US
MISSOURI ENVIRONMENTAL COMPLIANCE UPDATE. (19??)-. English. mo. $137.00. M. Lee Smith Publishers and Printers, 162 4th Avenue North, PO Box 198867, Nashville TN 37219. **Tel** (615)242-7395, (800)274-6774, FAX (615)256-6601. ***Continues*** *Missouri Environmental Law Letter, 1057-4166.*

US/1057-4166
MISSOURI ENVIRONMENTAL LAW LETTER. ***Title Change.*** [Mo. environ. law lett.]. **Added/Corp** Armstrong, Teasdale, Schlafly, Davis & Dicus. Vol. 1, No. 1 (July 1991)-(19??). Periodical. English. mo. M. Lee Smith Publishers and Printers, 162 4th Avenue North, PO Box 198867, Nashville TN 37219. **Tel** (615)242-7395, (800)274-6774, FAX (615)256-6601. **DD** 344. ***Continues in part*** *Midwest Environmental Law Letter, 1049-9350.* ***Continued by*** *Missouri Environmental Compliance Update.*

US
NATIONAL ENVIRONMENTAL ENFORCEMENT JOURNAL. **Added/Corp** National Association of Attorneys General. United States. Environmental Protection Agency. Office of Enforcement and Compliance Monitoring. United States. Environmental Protection Agency. Office of Solid Waste and Emergency Response. Vol. 1, No. 1 (May 1986)-. Periodical. English. mo (11 issues). $195.00, $95.00 government, libraries, non-profit rate. National Association of Attorneys General, 444 North Capitol Street, Suite 339, Washington DC 20001. **Tel** (202)434-8000. **ED** Cynthia H. Evans. **LC** KF3775.A59; N37. **DD** 344.73/046/05; 347.3044605. **Bk Rev. Ad Acc. Circ:** 500 (ctrl). ***Continues*** *Environmental Protection Report, 0739-7887.*
Desc: Covers state environment litigation: hazardous waste, air pollution, water pollution, nuclear waste, land use, right to know, energy litigation, etc.

US/0164-0712
NATIONAL WETLANDS NEWSLETTER. [Natl. wetlands newsl.]. **Added/Corp** Environmental Law Institute. National Wetlands Technical Council (U.S.). Vol. 1, Nov. (1978)-. Newsletter. English. bm. $48.00. Environmental Law Institute, 1616 P Street NW/Suite 200, Washington DC 20036. **Tel** (800)433-5120, (202)939-3844, FAX (202)328-5002. **ED** Nicole Veilleux. **DD** 344. Index available. cum. index. **Bk Rev.** Documents available from Documents on Demand.
Desc: Newsletter that keeps you completely up-to-date on all federal and state wetlands law policies and programs. Written specifically for persons concerned with the future of wetlands or floodplains.
Ind/Abst Environ. Abstr.; Environ. Period. Bibliogr.; GeoRef; J. Plan. Lit.; PAIS Int. Print (1991-).

US/0736-9522
NATIONAL WILDLIFE FEDERATION'S CONSERVATION. ***Title Change.*** [Natl. Wildl. Fed. conserv.]. **Added/Corp** National Wildlife Federation. Vol. 1, No. 1 (Jan. 28, 1983)-(199?). Periodical. English. National Wildlife Federation / Washington, 1400 16th Street Northwest, Washington DC 20036. **Tel** (800)432-6564, (202)797-6800. **LC** S930; .N38. **DD** 333.7/2/0973. ctrl circ. available on microfilm and microfiche from University Microfilms International (UMI). ***Continues*** *Conservation Report, 0010-6488.* ***Continued by*** *EnviroAction.*

GW
NATUR + I.E. UND RECHT. **VFOAT** Natur und Recht. (Jan. 1979)-. Periodical. German. Ten times a year. DM432.00 Europe; DM428.00 other. Blackwell Wissenschafts-Verlag, Kurfuerstendamm 57, D 10707 Berlin Germany. **Tel** 011 49 30 32790623, 011 49 30 32790624, FAX 011 49 30 327 90610. **ED** C. Carlsen. **LC** KK6242.A13; N37. **DD** 344.43/046/05; 344.3044605. Index available. cum. index. **Bk Rev. Ad Acc. Circ:** 2,500.
Desc: Reports on all laws with regard to protection of nature.

US/0882-3812
NATURAL RESOURCES & ENVIRONMENT. [Nat. resour. environ.]. **Added/Corp** American Bar Association. Section of Natural Resources Law. **VFOAT** Natural Resources and Environment. Vol. 1, No. 1 (Winter 1985)-. Periodical. English. qt (4 issues). $23.00. American Bar Association, 750 North Lake Shore Drive, Chicago IL 60611. **Tel** (312)988-5522, (312)988-5241, FAX (312)988-5528, telex 270593. **LC** K14; .A8679. **DD** 346.7304/4; 347.30644. Documents available from Documents on Demand. ***Continues*** *Natural Resources Lawyer, 0028-0747.*
Ind/Abst Bowne Dig. Corp. Sec. Lawyers; Energy Inf. Abstr.; Environ. Abstr.; Fish Rev. (Jan. 1989-July 1992); For. Prod. Abstr. (1991-); For. Abstr.; Index Leg. Period.; Index Period. Artic. Relat. Law (19??-19??); Leg. Resour. Index; LegalTrac (1985-); Wildl. Rev. (Jan. 1989-July 1992).

US/1045-0580
NATURAL RESOURCES, ENERGY, AND ENVIRONMENTAL LAW. [Nat. resour., energy, environ. law]. **Added/Corp** American Bar

Association. Section of Natural Resources, Energy, and Environmental Law. University of Tulsa. National Energy Law & Policy Institute. (1988)-. English. an. $39.95. American Bar Association, 750 North Lake Shore Drive, Chicago IL 60611. **Tel** (312)988-5522, (312)988-5241, FAX (312)988-5528, telex 270593. **LC** K14; .A8687. **DD** 346.7304/4; 347.30644. ***Continues*** *Natural Resources Law, 0882-7680.*

US/0028-0739
NATURAL RESOURCES JOURNAL. [Nat. resour. j.]. **Added/Corp** University of New Mexico. School of Law. Vol. 1 (March 1961)-. Academic Scholarly Publication. English. qt. $32.00. University of New Mexico School of Law, 1117 Stanford NE, Albuquerque NM 87131. **Tel** (505)277-4820, 277-8659. **ED** Albert E. Utton. **LC** K14; .A868. **CODEN** NRJOAB. cum. index. **Bk Rev. Ad Acc. Pr Rev. Circ:** 1,700. Documents available from The Genuine Article, UMI Article Clearinghouse, Petroleum Abstracts Document Delivery Service, Documents on Demand.
Desc: An international, interdisciplinary forum devoted to the study of natural and environmental resources. The emphasis is on research directly related to public policy.
Ind/Abst ABC POL SCI; AESIS Q.; AGRICOLA [Select. Cov.]; AQUAREF; Book Rev. Index; Bowne Dig. Corp. Sec. Lawyers; Coal Abstr.; Contents Pages Manage.; Curr. Contents Soc. Behav. Sci.; Curr. Law Index (1980-); Ecol. Abstr.; Econ. Lit. Index; EMBASE; Energy Inf. Abstr.; Energy Res. Abstr. (April 1974-); Environ. Abstr.; Environ. Period. Bibliogr.; Expand. Acad. Index (1992-); Fed. Tax Artic.; Fish Rev.; Geogr. Abstr. Human Geogr.; Index Leg. Period.; Int. Bibliogr. Sociol.; Int. Dev. Abstr.; J. Econ. Lit.; J. Plan. Lit.; Leg. Resour. Index (1980-); LegalTrac (1980-); Middle East Abstr. Index; Newsp. Period. Abstr. (1992-); PAIS Int. Print (1991-); Life Sci. Collect.; Pet. Abstr.; Res. Alert [Full Cov.]; Risk Abstr.; Soc. Sci. Cit. Index [Full Cov.]; West. Hist. Q.; Wildl. Rev.

●US/1060-9954
NEW JERSEY ENVIRONMENTAL LAW LETTER. [N.J. environ. law lett.]. Vol. 1, No. 1 (1992)-. Periodical. English. mo. $107.00. M. Lee Smith Publishers and Printers, 162 4th Avenue North, PO Box 198867, Nashville TN 37219. **Tel** (615)242-7395, (800)274-6774, FAX (615)256-6601. **ED** Gail Allyn, William Hyatt, Jr, and Robert Rose, (address) Pitney, Hardin, Kipp, and Szuch, 200 Campus Drive, Florham, NJ 07932, (phone)201-966-6300. **DD** 344.
Desc: Newsletter reporting the latest state specific environmental law developments that affect the companies in that state.

US/1065-1888
NEW YORK BUSINESS ENVIRONMENT. [N.Y. bus. environ.]. **VFOAT** NYBE. (198?)-. Periodical. English. bw. $500.00. New York Business Environment, 6 Sevilla Drive, Clifton Park NY 12065. **Tel** (518)383-1471, FAX (518)371-7419. **ED** C.D. Bassett. **DD** 338. Index available. cum. index. **Bk Rev**, (Qty: 4). ctrl circ.

US
NEW YORK ENVIRONMENTAL COMPLLIANCE UPDATE. English. mo. $147.00. M. Lee Smith Publishers and Printers, 162 4th Avenue North, PO Box 198867, Nashville TN 37219. **Tel** (615)242-7395, (800)274-6774, FAX (615)256-6601.

US
NEW YORK LAND REPORT : A PROJECT OF THE NEW YORK LAND INSTITUTE. ***Ceased.*** Vol. 1, (March 1980)-?. Periodical. English. mo. NYLARD Institute, c/o R Nichols, 315 19th Street, Watervliet NY 12189. **Tel** (518)465-7412. **ED** Ilene Wagner. Index available. cum. index. **Circ:** 100 (ctrl).
Desc: NYS environmental and land use Case Law summaries. Reprints of Administrative Proceedings of NYS Department of Environmental Conservation and Opinions of NYS Attorney General. Articles on land use, planning and environmental issues.

●US/1061-8651
NEW YORK UNIVERSITY ENVIRONMENTAL LAW JOURNAL. [N.Y. Univ. environ. law j.]. **Added/Corp** New York University. **VFOAT** Environmental Law Journal. (1992)-. Periodical. English. Twice a year. $15.00 US; $18.00 other. New York University School of Law, 110 West Third Street, New York NY 10012. **Tel** (212)998-6540, (212)998-6560, FAX (212)995-4032. **LC** K14; .E972. **DD** 344.73/046; 347.30446.
Ind/Abst Index Leg. Period. (1993-).

CN/1188-2565
NEWS BRIEF - ENVIRONMENTAL LAW CENTRE (EDMONTON). (NEWS BRIEF / ENVIRONMENTAL LAW CENTRE.). [News brief - Environ. Law Cent.]. **Added/Corp** Environmental Law Centre (Alta.). Vol. 6, No. 4 (1991)-. Periodical. English. qt. 25.00Can$ non-profit environmental organizations; 120.00Can$ other. Environmental Law Centre, Suite 201 10350 124 Street, Edmonton ALTA T5N 3V9 Canada. **Tel** (403)482-4891, FAX (403)488-6779. **DD** 344.7123/046/05. ***Continues*** *Newsletter (Environmental Law Centre (Alta.))., 0826-581X.*

CN/0715-4275
NEWSLETTER / WEST COAST ENVIRONMENTAL LAW RESEARCH FOUNDATION. [Newsl. - West Coast Environ. Law Res. Found.]. **Added/Corp** West Coast Environmental Law Research Foundation. **VFOAT** WCELRF Newsletter. **VAT** West Coast Environmental Law Research Foundation Newsletter. (197?)-. Newsletter. English. Twelve times a year. 20.00Can$. West Coast Environmental Law Research Foundation, 1012-207 West Hastings Street, Vancouver BC V6B 1H7 Canada. **Tel** (604)684-7378, FAX (604)684-1312. **ED** William Andrews. **DD** 344.71/046. **Bk Rev. Ad Acc. Circ:** 1,200 (ctrl).
Desc: Environmental legal issues including newsbriefs, case comments and book reviews.

CN/0715-7983
NORTHERN DECISIONS. ***Ceased.*** [North decis.]. Vol. 1, No. 1 (15 Apr. 1983)-Vol. 7, No. 22 (?). English. bw. Canadian Arctic Resources Committee, 1 Nicholas Street Suite 412, Ottawa ONT K1N 7B7 Canada. **Tel** (613)241-7379, FAX (613)236-7379. **ED** Ann Ray. **LC** KE5110.A13; N67. **DD** 354.710082/3. Index available. cum. index. **Circ:** 175 (ctrl).
Desc: Newsletter released 22 times a year dealing with regulatory and policy decisions north of 60 degrees.

US
NRDC NEWSLINE. **Added/Corp** Natural Resources Defense Council. **VFOAT** N.R.D.C. Newsline. Vol. 1, No. 1 (1983)-. Periodical. English. Five times a year. Natural Defense Resources Council, 40 West 20th Street, 11th Floor, New York NY 10011. **Tel** (212)727-2700. **ED** Catherine A. Dold. **Circ:** 80,000. ***Continues*** *NRDC News.*
Desc: Reports on activities of the Natural Resources Defense Council, a public interest, environmental law firm.

US/0360-7690
NUCLEAR REGULATION REPORTS. [Nucl. regul. rep.]. **Main/Corp** Commerce Clearing House. **Added/Corp** U.S. Nuclear Regulatory Commission. No. 1 (Aug. 1, 1975)-. English. wk. $2640.00. Commerce Clearing House Inc., 4025 West Peterson Avenue, Chicago IL 60646-6085. **Tel** (312)583-8500, FAX (708)940-4600. **ED** A. E. Schechter. **LC** KF2138.A6; C67. **DD** 343/.73/092.
Desc: Publishes rules for development, production, licensing, processing and use of nuclear energy and its by-products and waste disposal.

●US/1063-9594
OHIO ENVIRONMENTAL MONTHLY. [Ohio environ. mon.]. **VFOAT** OEM. Vol. 1, Issue 1 (Oct. 1992)-. Periodical. English. mo. $65.00. Banks-Baldwin Law Publishing Company, PO Box 1974, University Center, Cleveland OH 44106. **Tel** (216)721-7373. **DD** 344. ***Continues*** *Environmental Law Journal of Ohio, 1045-599X.*

●CN/1195-163X
ONTARIO ENVIRONMENTAL LEGISLATION. (1993)-. English. an. 49.00Can$. Canada Law Book Inc., 240 Edward Street, Aurora Ontario L4G 3S9 Canada. **Tel** (800)263-3269, (905)841-6472, FAX (905)841-5085.
Desc: Portable consolidation of Ontario environmental Acts and regulations.

US
OUTLINE OF RCRA CERCLA. (19??)-. Periodical. English. sa. $165.00 (nonsubscribers, Chemical Waste Litigation Reporter); $60.00 (subscribers) (one issue). Law Reporters, 1519 Connecticut Avenue Northwest, Suite 200, Washington DC 20036. **Tel** (202)462-5755.
Desc: Covers the Resource Conservation and Recovery Act and Comprehensive Environmental Response, Compensation, and Liability Act amendments.

US/0738-6206
PACE ENVIRONMENTAL LAW REVIEW. [Pace environ. law rev.]. Vol. 1, No. 1, (1983)-. Periodical. English. sa. $17.00 US; $19.00 other. Pace University / School of Law, 78 North Broadway, White Plains NY 10603. **Tel** (914)422-4000, (914)422-4271, FAX (914)422-4139. **ED** Alex Desevo, (914)422-4116. **LC** K16; .A225. **DD** 344.73/046/05; 347.3044605. **Bk Rev. Circ:** 200.
Desc: Provides a forum for the discussion of critical issues in the field.
Ind/Abst Curr. Law Index (1985-); Index Leg. Period.; Leg. Resour. Index (1985-); LegalTrac (1983-).

●US/1072-9143
PENNSYLVANIA ENVIRONMENTAL COMPLIANCE UPDATE. (PENNSYLVANIA ENVIRONMENTAL COMPLIANCE UPDATE / DECHERT, PRICE & RHOADS.). [Pa. environ. compliance update]. **Added/Corp** Dechert, Price & Rhoads. **VFOAT** Environmental Compliance Update. (1994)-. Periodical. English. mo. $137.00. M. Lee Smith Publishers and Printers, 162 4th Avenue North, PO Box 198867, Nashville TN 37219. **Tel** (615)242-7395, (800)274-6774, FAX (615)256-6601. **DD** 344.

US/1046-6568
PENNSYLVANIA ENVIRONMENTAL LAW LETTER. [Pa. environ. law lett.]. (1989)-. English. mo. $300.00. Andrews Publications Inc., 1646 West Chester Pike, PO Box 1000, Westtown PA 19395. **Tel** (610)399-6600, (800)345-1101, FAX (610)399-6610. **LC** KFP354.A15; P46. **DD** 344.73/0462/0974805; 347.3044620974805.
Desc: Provides Pennsylvania attorneys and their clients, waste generators and haulers, municipalities, counties, insurers, landfill owners and operators, environmental action groups and concerned and/or injured citizens with news of legal developments from state and federal courts, the state Department of Environmental Resources and the federal Environmental Protection Agency.

US/1048-4647
PERRY'S ENVIRONMENT AND THE LAW DIGEST. **VFOAT** Environment and the Law Digest. (1991)-. Periodical. English. sm. $275.00. LPA Publications, Box 3194, Oak Ridge TN 37831-3194.

US/1052-4355
PORTER, WRIGHT, MORRIS & ARTHUR'S OHIO ENVIRONMENTAL LAW LETTER. [Porter Wright Morris Arthur's Ohio environ. law lett.]. **Added/Corp** Porter, Wright, Morris & Arthur. **VFOAT** Ohio Environmental Law Letter. (Nov 1990)-. Periodical. English. mo. $137.00. M. Lee Smith Publishers and Printers, 162 4th Avenue North, PO Box 198867, Nashville TN 37219. **Tel** (615)242-7395, (800)274-6774, FAX (615)256-6601. **ED** Martin Seltzer, Robert Brubaker and Jeffrey McNealey, (address) 41 South High Street, 30th Floor, Columbus, OH 43215-3406, (phone) 614-227-2000. **DD** 344.
Desc: Newsletter reporting the latest state specific environmental law developments that affect companies in that state.

US/0886-747X
PROCEEDINGS OF THE ANNUAL INSTITUTE - ROCKY MOUNTAIN MINERAL LAW INSTITUTE. (PROCEEDINGS OF THE ... ANNUAL INSTITUTE.). [Proc. annu. inst. - Rocky Mt. Miner. Law Inst.]. **Main/Corp** Rocky Mountain Mineral Law Institute. **Added/Corp** Rocky Mountain Mineral Law Foundation. 16th (July 9-11, 1970)-. English. an. $130.00 (non-member), $85.00 (member of the Rocky Mountain Law Foundation). Rocky Mountain Mineral Law Foundation, Porter Administration Building, 7039 East 18th Avenue, Denver CO 80220. **Tel** (303)321-8100, FAX (303)321-7657. **LC** KF1819.A2; R6. **DD** 343.73/0775; 347.303775. (published separately). cum. index. **Circ:** 900. ***Continues*** *Rocky Mountain Mineral Law Institute. Annual, 0557-1987.*
Desc: Covers mining law, natural gas, and petroleum law and legislation.
Ind/Abst GeoRef; Index Leg. Period.; Leg. Resour. Index (1980-); LegalTrac (1980-).

US/0895-5042
PROP. 65 NEWS. [Prop. 65 News]. **Added/Corp** California Council for Environmental and Economic Balance. **VFOAT** Prop. Sixty-five News; Prop. 65. **VAT** Proposition Sixty-five News. Vol. 1, No. 1 (July 1987)-. Periodical. English. Twelve times a year. $295.00. American Environment Institute, 45 Belden Street, 3rd Floor, San Francisco CA 64104. **Tel** (415)544-0111. **ED** Shane Ahern. **DD** 351. Index available. cum. index. **Bk Rev**, (Qty: 1). **Ad Acc. Pr Rev. Circ:** 1,000 (ctrl).

US/0148-6489
PUBLIC LAND AND RESOURCES LAW DIGEST, THE. [Public land resour. law dig.]. **Added/Corp** Rocky Mountain Mineral Law Foundation. Vol. 8 (Fall 1970)-. Periodical. English. sa. $15.00 law school members; $29.50 other. Rocky Mountain Mineral Law Foundation, Porter Administration Building, 7039 East 18th Avenue, Denver CO 80220. **Tel** (303)321-8100, FAX (303)321-7657. **ED** Patrick Martin and Adrien Phillips. **LC** K16; .U2. **DD** 343/.73/02505. **[CCC].** Index available (published separately). cum. index. **Pr Rev. Circ:** 400. available in hardback. Documents available from Documents on Demand. ***Continues*** *Rocky Mountain Mineral Law Review.*
Desc: The Digest indexes all significant legal periodical literature relating to natural resources law, including international issues, public lands, mining, oil and gas, outer continental shelf, water, timber, grazing, and natural resources environmental law. In addition, important leading articles are reprinted or referenced.
Ind/Abst Coal Abstr.; Energy Inf. Abstr.; Energy Res. Abstr. (July 1979-); Environ. Abstr.; GeoRef; J. Plan. Lit.; West. Hist. Q.

US
QUARTERLY NEWSLETTER - STANDING COMMITTEE ON ENVIRONMENTAL LAW. **Main/Corp** American Bar Association. Standing Committee on Environmental Law. (Fall 1975)-. Newsletter. English. qt. Included with membership. American Bar Association, 750 North Lake Shore Drive, Chicago IL 60611. **Tel** (312)988-5522, (312)988-5241, FAX (312)988-5528, telex 270593. **ED** Elissa C. Lichtenstein. **LC** KF200; .A43. **DD** 344/.73/04605. **Bk Rev. Circ:** 2,400. ***Continues***

American Bar Association. Special Committee on Environmental Law. Quarterly Newsletter.
Desc: Articles on current environmental law topics; book and conference notices; updates on American Bar Association environmental law activities.
Ind/Abst LegalTrac (1980-1988).

US/0899-0689
RECENT TITLES IN LAW FOR THE SUBJECT SPECIALIST. RESOURCE, ENVIRONMENTAL, AND ENERGY LAW. [Recent titles law subj. spec., Resour. environ. energy law]. **VFOAT** Resource, Environmental, and Energy Law. Vol. 5, No. 1 (Jan.-Mar. 1988)-. English. Four times a year. $85.00. Ward & Associates, 317 South Division, Suite 66, Ann Arbor MI 48104. **Tel** (313)665-3520, FAX (313)665-7880. **LC** K3581; .N38. **DD** 016. ***Continues*** *National Legal Bibliography. Subject Area List. Resource, Environmental and Energy Law, 8755-8122.*

US/0194-0376
REGULATORY REPORTER. (REGULATORY REPORTER / INTERAGENCY REGULATORY LIAISON GROUP.). Began with V. 1, Apr. 1979. English. sa. US Environmental Protection Agency / Regulatory Development Work Group, 401 M Street SW, Washington DC 20460. **LC** KF3958; .A855. **DD** 344.73/0472/05. **NLM** QV 33 AA1 R344.

CN/0714-5918
RESOURCES - CANADIAN INSTITUTE OF RESOURCES LAW. (RESOURCES : THE NEWSLETTER OF THE CANADIAN INSTITUTE OF RESOURCES LAW.). [Resour. - Can. Inst. Resour. Law]. **Added/Corp** Canadian Institute of Resources Law. No. 1 (May 1982)-. Newsletter. English (French). Four times a year. Free on request. Canadian Institute of Resources Law, 430 BioSciences Building, The University of Calgary, 2500 University Drive NW, Calgary Alberta T2N 1N4 Canada. **Tel** (403)220-3200, FAX (403)282-6182. **ED** Nancy Money. **DD** 346.7104/67/05. **Circ:** 6,200 (ctrl).
Desc: Offers timely comments on current resources law issues along with information about the Canadian Institute of Resources Law, its publications, and programs.
Ind/Abst AESIS Q.; Can. Legal Lit.

●UK/0962-8797
REVIEW OF EUROPEAN COMMUNITY AND INTERNATIONAL ENVIRONMENTAL LAW. **Added/Corp** Foundation for International Environmental Law and Development. **VFOAT** Review of European Community and International Environmental Law; RECIEL. Vol. 1, Issue 1 (1992)-. Academic Scholarly Publication. English. qt. $211.00 North America; £136.00 other. Basil Blackwell Publishers Ltd, 108 Cowley Road, Oxford 0X4 1JF England. **Tel** 011 44 865 791100, FAX 011 44 865 791347, telex 837022 OXBOOK G. **(Subscription address:** Blackwell Publishers / UK, Marston Book Services, PO Box 87, Oxford OX2 0DT England.) **[CCC].**

FR
REVUE JURIDIQUE DE L'ENVIRONNEMENT. **Added/Corp** Societe Francaise pour le Droit de l'Environnement. **VFOAT** RJE; R.J.E. (1976)-. Periodical. French. Five times a year. 520.00F France; 580.00F other. Revue Juridique de l'Environnement, 143 rue Francois Perrin, 87000 Limoges France. **Tel** 011 33 55 343222, FAX 011 33 55 505784. **LC** K21; .J78. **DD** 344/.046/05; 342.44605.
Ind/Abst Index Foreign Leg. Per.; Int. Polit. Sci. Abstr.

IT
RIVISTA GIURIDICA DELL'AMBIENTE. **Added/Corp** Istituto di Studi e Documentazione per il Territorio (Italy). Vol. 1, No. 1 (April 1986)-. Periodical. Italian. Six times a year. L110000.00 Italy; L165000.00 other. Giuffre Editore SPA, Via Busto Arsizio 40, 20151 Milan Italy. **Tel** 011 398 2 38089200. **ED** Achille Cutrera and Stefano Nespor. **LC** K22; .I798.
Desc: Contains original contributions and articles with discussion of legal theory and verdicts on matters related to the protection of the environment.

US/0093-4631
SELECTED LIST OF FEDERAL LAWS AND TREATIES RELATING TO SPORT FISH AND WILDLIFE. **Main/Corp** United States. Bureau of Sport Fisheries and Wildlife. English. $0.20. Bureau of Sport Fisheries & Wildlife, Washington DC 20240. **LC** KF5640; .A3693. **DD** 346/.73/04695.

US/1059-5414
SHEPARD'S CALIFORNIA ENVIRONMENTAL LAW & REGULATION REPORTER. [Shepard's Calif. environ. law regul. report.]. **Added/Corp** Shepard's/McGraw-Hill. **VFOAT** California Environmental Law & Regulation Reporter; California Environmental Law and Regulation Reporter; Shepard's California Environmental Law and Regulation Reporter. Vol. 1, No. 1 (Mar. 1991)-. Periodical. English. mo. $285.00. Shepards McGraw-Hill Inc, 555 Middle Creek Parkway, PO Box 35300, Colorado Springs CO 80935-3530. **Tel** (719)488-3000, FAX (800)525-0053. **ED** Rafael Barnardino. **LC** KFC610.A15; S54. **DD** 344.794/046/05; 347.94044605. Index available. available in Loose-leaf.
Desc: Provides current coverage of California environmental law. Includes case summaries, legislative and regulatory summaries, lead articles, a subject matter index, and a table of cases.

●US/1068-235X
SHEPARD'S CLEAN AIR ACT REPORTER. [Shepard's Clean Air Act report.]. **VFOAT** Shepard's Clean Air Act. Vol. 1, No. 1 (May 1992)-. Periodical. English. mo. $275.00. Shepards McGraw-Hill Inc, 555 Middle Creek Parkway, PO Box 35300, Colorado Springs CO 80935-3530. **Tel** (719)488-3000, FAX (800)525-0053. **ED** Edward McGrath, James Spensley, David Grady. **DD** 344.
Desc: Current coverage of federal EPA rulemaking required to be undertaken by the Clean Air Act and litigation over proposed rules.

US/1068-5804
SHEPARD'S ENVIRONMENTAL LIABILITY, ENFORCEMENT & PENALTIES REPORTER. [Shepard's environ. liabil. enforc. penal. report.]. **Added/Corp** Shepard's McGraw/Hill. **VFOAT** Environmental Liability, Enforcement & Penalties Reporter; Environmental Liability, Enforcement and Penalties Reporter; Shepard's Environmental Liability, Enforcement and Penalties Reporter. (199?)-. Periodical. English. mo. $295.00. Shepards McGraw-Hill Inc, 555 Middle Creek Parkway, PO Box 35300, Colorado Springs CO 80935-3530. **Tel** (719)488-3000, FAX (800)525-0053. **DD** 346. ***Continues*** *Shepard's Environmental Liability in Commercial Transactions Reporter, 1054-4771.*
Desc: Covers environmental liability issues of interest to lawyers, in-house counsel, consultants, and lenders who counsel business, commerical and real estate clients. Keeps subscribers appraised of current environmental law and regulations which can affect business transactions and operations.

US/1054-4771
SHEPARD'S ENVIRONMENTAL LIABILITY IN COMMERCIAL TRANSACTIONS REPORTER. ***Title Change.*** [Shepard's environ. liabil. comm. trans. report.]. **Added/Corp** Shepard's/McGraw-Hill. **VFOAT** Environmental Liability in Commercial Transactions Reporter. Vol. 1, No. 1 (Nov. 1990)-(199?). Periodical. English. mo. Shepards McGraw-Hill Inc, 555 Middle Creek Parkway, PO Box 35300, Colorado Springs CO 80935-3530. **Tel** (719)488-3000, FAX (800)525-0053. **ED** Edward McGrath. **LC** KF1298.A59; S48. **DD** 346.7303/8; 347.30638. ***Continued by*** *Shepard's Environmental Liability, Enforcement & Penalties Reporter, 1068-5804.*
Desc: Each issue features case digests, federal and state legislative and regulatory updates, news and events, and compliance articles. It keeps you on top of CER-CLA and RCRA cases, insurance coverage, power producer, and D liability, judicial review, successor liability, asbestos and hazardous waste cases, air and water pollution, and more.

●US/1070-213X
SHEPARD'S ENVIRONMENTAL REGULATION SUMMARIES. [Shepard's environ. regul. summ.]. **Added/Corp** Shepard's/McGraw-Hill. **VFOAT** Environmental Regulation Summaries; ERS. Vol. 1, No. 1 (May 15, 1993)-. Periodical. English. sm. $345.00. Shepards McGraw-Hill Inc, 555 Middle Creek Parkway, PO Box 35300, Colorado Springs CO 80935-3530. **Tel** (719)488-3000, FAX (800)525-0053. **ED** Richard J. Ludeman. **DD** 344.
Desc: Contains concise and timely summaries of the latest environmental notices and regulations from all federal agencies as they appear in the Federal Register along with a monthly datadisk containing the cumulative summaries for the calendar year.

US/8756-7059
SPEER'S DIGEST OF TOXIC SUBSTANCES STATE LAW. (SPEER'S DIGEST OF TOXIC SUBSTANCES STATE LAW : ... TRENDS, SUMMARIES & FORECASTS.). [Speer's dig. toxic subst. state law]. **VFOAT** Toxic Substances State Law; Speer's Digest. 1983/84 Ed.-. English. Strategic Assessments Inc, 5000 Butte Street/Suite 132, Boulder CO 80301. **LC** KF3958.Z95; S68. **DD** 344.73/046; 347.30446.

US/0892-7138
STANFORD ENVIRONMENTAL LAW JOURNAL. [Stanf. environ. law j.]. **Added/Corp** Stanford Environmental Law Society. **VFOAT** Journal. Vol. 6 (1986-1987)-. English. Twice a year (Jan. & May). $33.00. Stanford University School of Law, Crown Quadrangle 42, Stanford CA 94305. **Tel** (415)723-4421. **LC** K23; .T215. **DD** 344.73/046; 347.30446. **Circ:** 500 (ctrl). ***Continues*** *Stanford Environmental Law Annual, 0197-7873.*
Desc: Consists of student articles on topics of current interest in environmental law.
Ind/Abst Index Leg. Period. (1987-); Leg. Resour. Index; LegalTrac (1986-).

US/1054-2604
STATE ENVIRONMENT REPORT. ***Title Change.*** [State environ. rep.]. **Added/Corp** Business Publishers. Vol. 10, No. 19 (September 1990)-(1992). Periodical. English. wk (mailed every Wed.). Business Publishers Inc., 951 Pershing Drive, Silver Spring MD 20910-4464. **Tel** (301)587-6300, (800)274-0122, FAX (301)585-9075. **DD** 344. **[CCC].** ***Continues*** *State Regulation Report, 0276-2870.* ***Absorbed by*** *Air Water Pollution Report, 0002-2608.*
Desc: Provides timely warnings of regulations and enforcement actions that can save your company thousands (or millions) in fines and lost business.

US/0885-2987
TEMPLE ENVIRONMENTAL LAW & TECHNOLOGY JOURNAL. [Temple environ. law technol. j.]. **Added/Corp** Temple University. School of Law. **VFOAT** Temple Environmental Law and Technology Journal. Vol. 3 (1984)-. Periodical. English. sa (June and Dec.). Temple University School of Law, 1719 North Broad Street, Philadelphia PA 19122. **Tel** (215)204-1610. **LC** K24; .E43. **DD** 344.73/046; 347.30446. ***Continues*** *Outlook Environmental Law Journal.*
Ind/Abst Index Leg. Period.; Leg. Resour. Index; LegalTrac (1980-).

●US/1075-2595
TEXAS ENVIRONMENTAL COMPLIANCE UPDATE. (TEXAS ENVIRONMENTAL COMPLIANCE UPDATE / BICKERSTAFF, HEATH & SMILEY, L.L.P.). [Tex. environ. compliance update]. **Added/Corp** Bickerstaff, Heath & Smiley, L.L.P. (1994)-. Periodical. English. mo. $137.00. M. Lee Smith Publishers and Printers, 162 4th Avenue North, PO Box 198867, Nashville TN 37219. **Tel** (615)242-7395, (800)274-6774, FAX (615)256-6601. **DD** 344. ***Continues*** *Eikenburg & Stiles' Texas Environmental Law Letter, 1056-7585.*

US/1055-2561
TEXAS INDUSTRY ENVIRONMENTAL ALERT. [Tex. Ind. Environ. Alert]. **Added/Corp** Environmental Compliance Reporter, Inc. **VFOAT** Environmental Alert. (1988)-. Periodical. English. Twenty-two times a year. $345.00. Environmental Compliance Reporter, 3154-B College Drive, Suite 522, Baton Rouge LA 70808. **Tel** (504)383-3937. **LC** KFT1554.A15; T49. **DD** 344.764/046/05; 347.64044605. available on an online database (files 16,636/Full-Text) from DIALOG.

NE/0165-1137
TIJDSCHRIFT VOOR MILIEU EN RECHT. [Tijdschr. milieu recht]. **Added/Corp** Stichting Natuur en Milieu. **VFOAT** Milieu en Recht. (1974)-. Periodical. Dutch. mo. Fl113.00. Libresso BV, Postbus 878, 7400 GA Deventer Netherlands. **Tel** 011 31 5700 47421. **LC** K24; .I376. **DD** 344/.492/04605.
Ind/Abst EMBASE.

US/0737-8513
TOXIC CHEMICALS LITIGATION REPORTER. [Toxic chem. litig. report.]. (May 16, 1983)-. Periodical. English. sm. $850.00. Andrews Publications Inc., 1646 West Chester Pike, PO Box 1000, Westtown PA 19395. **Tel** (610)399-6600, (800)345-1101, FAX (610)399-6610. **ED** Leonard E. B. Andrews. **LC** KF3958.A59; T68. **DD** 344.73/0424/02638; 347. 30442402638. (free). cum. index. ctrl circ.
Desc: Covers recent developments in suits alleging personal injuries or property damage from exposure to toxic chemicals.

US/0883-0576
TOXIC SUBSTANCES CONTROL ACT. (TOXIC SUBSTANCES CONTROL ACT (TSCA) : REPORT TO CONGRESS FOR FISCAL YEAR ... - U.S. ENVIRONMENTAL PROTECTION AGENCY.). [Toxic Subst. Control Act]. **Main/Corp** United States. Environmental Protection Agency. **VFOAT** Toxic Substances Control Act (T.S.C.A). (1981)-. English. an. US Environmental Protection Agency, 401 M Street SW, Washington DC 20460. **Tel** (202)755-9163. **LC** KF3958; .A84. **DD** 344.73/0424; 347.304424. ***Continues*** *Administration of the Toxic Substances Control Act.*

US/0887-7394
TOXICS LAW REPORTER. (TOXICS LAW REPORTER / THE BUREAU OF NATIONAL AFFAIRS, INC.). [Toxics law report.]. **Added/Corp** Bureau of National Affairs (Washington, D.C.). Vol. 1, No. 1 (June 11, 1986)-. Periodical. English. wk. $1340.00. Bureau of National Affairs Inc., 9435 Key West Avenue, Rockville MD 20850. **Tel** (800)372-1033, (301)258-1033, FAX (301)948-5823. **ED** William Harris Frank. **LC** KF1246.A3; T69. **DD** 346.7303/8; 347.30638. **CODEN** TLREEF. **[CCC].**
Desc: Covers legal developments concerning toxic tort and hazardous waste lawsuits and related insurance issues. Includes litigation under the Comprehensive Environmental Response, Compensation, and Liability Act (Superfund), the Resource Conversation and Recovery Act (RCRA), developments in tort law reform and pertinent state cases and legislation.

US
TREATISE ON ENVIRONMENTAL LAW. English. ir. Matthew Bender & Company Inc., 1275 Broadway, Albany NY 12204. **Tel** (800)833-9844, (518)487-3000. Index Available, published separately, free-automatically sent.

US/1047-6857
TULANE ENVIRONMENTAL LAW JOURNAL. [Tulane environ. law j.]. **Added/Corp** Tulane Law School. Tulane Environmental Law Society. Vol. 1 (Spring 1988)-. Periodical. English. Tulane University School of Law, 6801 Freret Street, New Orleans LA 70118. **Tel** (504)865-5990. **LC** K24; .U38. **DD** 344.73/046/05; 347.3044605.
Ind/Abst Index Leg. Period.; Leg. Resour. Index; LegalTrac (1988-).

US/0733-401X
UCLA JOURNAL OF ENVIRONMENTAL LAW & POLICY. [UCLA j. environ. law policy]. **VFOAT** U.C.L.A. Journal of Environmental Law & Policy; Journal of Environmental Law & Policy; Journal of Environmental Law and Policy; Journal of Environmental Law. **VAT** University of California, Los Angeles Journal of Environmental Law and Policy; UCLA Journal of Environmental Law and Policy. Vol. 1, No. 1 (Fall 1980)-. Academic Scholarly Publication. English. sa. $15.00. University of California at Los Angeles / UCLA Law School, 405 Hilgard Avenue, RM 1444 Law Building, Los Angeles CA 90024. **Tel** (310)206-9103. **ED** Roy Ogden. **LC** K25; .C55. **DD** 344.73/046/05; 347.3044605. **Circ:** 300.
Desc: Supply forum for scholarly discussion concerning the environment and other related topics.
Ind/Abst Curr. Law Index (1982-); Environ. Period. Bibliogr.; Fish Rev. (Jan. 1989-July 1992); Index Leg. Period.; J. Plan. Lit.; Leg. Resour. Index (1982-); LegalTrac (1980-); PAIS Int. Print; Wildl. Rev. (Jan. 1989-July 1992).

US/1062-6212
UNIVERSITY OF BALTIMORE JOURNAL OF ENVIRONMENTAL LAW. [Univ. Baltim. j. environ. law]. **Added/Corp** University of Baltimore. School of Law. **VFOAT** Journal of Environmental Law. Vol. 1, No. 1 (Summer 1991)-. Periodical. English. sa. $15.00. University of Baltimore School of Law, 1420 North Charles Street, Baltimore MD 21201. **Tel** (410)837-4655. **DD** 344. ***Continues*** *Environmental Perspectives (Baltimore, Md.).*
Ind/Abst Environ. Period. Bibliogr. (19??-); Index Leg. Period. (1992-).

US/1049-2631
VILLANOVA ENVIRONMENTAL LAW JOURNAL, THE. [Villanova environ. law j.]. **Added/Corp** Villanova University. School of Law. Vol. 1, Issue 1 (1990)-. Periodical. English. sa. $22.00. Villanova University School of Law, Villanova PA 19085. **Tel** (215)519-7053. **DD** 344.
Desc: Dedicated to reviewing various environmental topics including criminal enforcement, hazardous waste, pollutants, national and international policy concerns, and environment dispute resolution.
Ind/Abst Index Leg. Period. (1992-); Leg. Resour. Index; LegalTrac (1990-).

●US/1068-9516
VIRGINIA ENVIRONMENTAL COMPLIANCE UPDATE. (1993)-. English. mo. $137.00. M. Lee Smith Publishers and Printers, 162 4th Avenue North, PO Box 198867, Nashville TN 37219. **Tel** (615)242-7395, (800)274-6774, FAX (615)256-6601.

US/1045-5183
VIRGINIA ENVIRONMENTAL LAW JOURNAL. [Va. environ. law j.]. **Added/Corp** Virginia Environmental Law Journal Association. University of Virginia. School of Law. Vol. 8, No. 2 (Spring 1989)-. Periodical. English. sa. $32.00 US & Canada; $48.00 other. University of Virginia / School of Law, North Grounds, Charlottesville VA 22903. **Tel** (804)924-0597. **LC** K26; .I67. **DD** 344.73/046/05; 347.3044605. Documents available from Documents on Demand. ***Continues*** *Virginia Journal of Natural Resources Law, 0748-8122.*
Desc: Devoted to addressing contemporary issues in environmental law.
Ind/Abst Environ. Abstr. (19??-); Index Leg. Period. (19??-); Leg. Resour. Index (19??-); LegalTrac (19??-).

●US/1072-0596
WASHINGTON ENVIRONMENTAL COMPLIANCE UPDATE. (1993)-. English. mo. $137.00. M. Lee Smith Publishers and Printers, 162 4th Avenue North, PO Box 198867, Nashville TN 37219. **Tel** (615)242-7395, (800)274-6774, FAX (615)256-6601.

US
WEEKLY BULLETIN. **Added/Corp** United States. Congress. Environmental and Energy Study Conference. **VFOAT** ESC Weekly Bulletin; E.S.C. Weekly Bulletin. (198?)-. Bulletin. English. wk. $215.00 US; $430.00 other. Environmental and Energy Study Institute, 122 C Street Northwest, Suite 700, Washington DC 20001. **Tel** (202)628-1400, FAX (202)628-1825. **(Subscription address:** National Technical Information Service, 5285 Port Royal Road, Springfield, VA 22161) ***Continues*** *United States. Congress. Environmental Study Conference. Weekly Bulletin - Environmental Study Conference.*

US/0737-2795
WILLIAM MITCHELL ENVIRONMENTAL LAW JOURNAL. ***Suspended.*** [William Mitchell environ. law j.]. Vol. 1, No. 1 (May 1983)-?. English. an. $6.00. William Mitchell Environmental Law Society, 875 Summit Avenue, St Paul MN 55105. **LC** K27; .I465. **DD** 344/.046/05; 342.44605.

●US/1072-9151
WISCONSIN ENVIRONMENTAL COMPLIANCE UPDATE. (WISCONSIN ENVIRONMENTAL COMPLIANCE UPDATE / DEWITT, PORTER.). [Wis. environ. compliance update]. **Added/Corp** DeWitt, Porter (Firm). **VFOAT** Environmental Compliance Update. (1994)-. English. mo. $137.00. M. Lee Smith Publishers and Printers, 162 4th Avenue North, PO Box 198867, Nashville TN 37219. **Tel** (615)242-7395, (800)274-6774, FAX (615)256-6601. **DD** 344.

GW/0931-0983
ZEITSCHRIFT FUER UMWELTPOLITIK & UMWELTRECHT. **VFOAT** Zeitschrift fur Umweltpolitik und Umweltrecht; Journal of Environmental Law and Policy. Vol. 8, No. 4 (Dec. 1985)-. Periodical. German. qt. DM192.00. Deutscher Fachverlag GmbH, Verlagsgruppe, D 60264 Frankfurt Germany. **Tel** 011 49 69 75951001, telex 411 862. **LC** HC79.E5; Z44. ***Continues*** *Zeitschrift fur Umweltpolitik, 0343-7167.*
Ind/Abst PAIS Int. Print.

ESTATE PLANNING

US/0732-8184
ABA SECTION OF TAXATION ANNUAL ADVANCED STUDY SESSIONS. SELECTED PROBLEMS AND TECHNIQUES IN ESTATE PLANNING. (ABA SECTION OF TAXATION ANNUAL ADVANCED STUDY SESSIONS, SELECTED PROBLEMS AND TECHNIQUES IN ESTATE PLANNING : ALI-ABA COURSE OF STUDY MATERIALS / JOINTLY PRESENTED BY THE ABA SECTION OF TAXATION AND ALI-ABA.). **Added/Corp** American Bar Association. Section of Taxation. American Law Institute-American Bar Association Committee on Continuing Professional Education. **VFOAT** A.B.A. Section of Taxation Annual Advanced Study Sessions, Selected Problems and Techniques in Estate Planning; Selected Problems and Techniques in Estate Planning; ALI-ABA Course of Study Materials; A.L.I.-A.B.A. Course of Study Materials. **VAT** American Bar Association Section of Taxation Annual Advanced Study Sessions, Selected Problems and Techniques in Estate Planning. (19??)-. English. an. American Law Institute, 4025 Chestnut Street, Philadelphia PA 19104-3099. **Tel** (215)243-1661, (800)253-6397, FAX (215)243-1664. **LC** KF6585; .A115. **DD** 343.7305/3; 347.30353.

US/0732-7579
ADVANCED WILL DRAFTING. English. an. Practising Law Institute, 810 Seventh Avenue, New York NY 10019-5818. **Tel** (212)765-5700, FAX (212)581-4670 general correspondence, (212)265-4742 orders and billing inquiries. **LC** KF755.Z9; A37. **DD** 346.7305/4; 347.30654.

US/0191-412X
ALI-ABA COURSE OF STUDY : ABA SECTION OF TAXATION, ADVANCED STUDY SESSIONS, ADVANCED ESTATE PLANNING TECHNIQUES : MATERIALS. **Main/Conf** ALI-ABA Course of Study: Advanced Estate Planning Techniques. **VAT** American Law Institute-American Bar Association Course of Study. American Bar Association Section of Taxation, Advanced Study Sessions, Advanced Estate Planning Techniques: Materials. English. American Law Institute, 4025 Chestnut Street, Philadelphia PA 19104-3099. **Tel** (215)243-1661, (800)253-6397, FAX (215)243-1664. **LC** KF6585; .A12. **DD** 343/.73/053.

US/0191-8249
ALI-ABA COURSE OF STUDY. ABA SECTION OF TAXATION, ADVANCED STUDY SESSIONS, ESTATE AND INCOME TAX PLANNING FOR EXECUTIVES AND SMALL BUSINESS OWNERS : MATERIALS. **VAT** American Law Institute-American Bar Association Course of Study. American Bar Association Section of Taxation, Advanced Study Sessions, Estate and Income Tax Planning for Executives and Small Business Owners: Materials. English. American Law Institute, 4025 Chestnut Street, Philadelphia PA 19104-3099. **Tel** (215)243-1661, (800)253-6397, FAX (215)243-1664. **LC** KF6369.8.E9; A14. **DD** 343/.73/068.

US/0271-3578
ALI-ABA COURSE OF STUDY : ABA SECTION OF TAXATION, ANNUAL ADVANCED STUDY SESSIONS, BUSINESS AND ESTATE PLANNING WITH LIFE AND DISABILITY INSURANCE : MATERIALS. **VAT** American Law Institute, American Bar Association Course of Study. American Bar Association Section of Taxation, Annual Advanced Study Sessions, Business and Estate Planning with Life and Disability Insurance: Materials. English. an. American Law Institute, 4025 Chestnut Street, Philadelphia PA 19104-3099. **Tel** (215)243-1661, (800)253-6397, FAX (215)243-1664. **LC** KF1175.Z9; A13. **DD** 346.73/08632.

US/0271-3551
ALI-ABA COURSE OF STUDY. BASIC ESTATE AND GIFT TAXATION: MATERIALS. **Main/Conf** I-ABA Course of Study: Basic Estate and Gift Taxation. **Added/Corp** State Bar of Arizona. **VFOAT** Basic Estate and Gift Taxation: Materials. **VAT** American Law Institute, American Bar Association Course of Study. Basic Estate and Gift Taxation: Materials. (19??)-. English. an. $80.00. American Law Institute, 4025 Chestnut Street, Philadelphia PA 19104-3099. **Tel** (215)243-1661, (800)253-6397, FAX (215)243-1664. **LC** KF6572.Z9; A14. **DD** 343.7305/3.
Desc: Information on inheritance and transfer tax laws.

US/0270-7594
ALI-ABA COURSE OF STUDY. ESTATE PLANNING FOR RETIRING OR DYING CLIENTS : MATERIALS. **VAT** American Law Institute-American Bar Association Course of Study. Estate Planning for Retiring or Dying Clients: Materials. English. an. American Law Institute, 4025 Chestnut Street, Philadelphia PA 19104-3099. **Tel** (215)243-1661, (800)253-6397, FAX (215)243-1664. **LC** KF750.Z9; A13. **DD** 346.7305/2.

US/0271-3543
ALI-ABA COURSE OF STUDY. ESTATE PLANNING FOR THE CLOSELY HELD BUSINESS : MATERIALS. **VAT** American Law Institute, American Bar Association Course of Study. Estate Planning for the Closely Held Business: Materials. English. an. American Law Institute, 4025 Chestnut Street, Philadelphia PA 19104-3099. **Tel** (215)243-1661, (800)253-6397, FAX (215)243-1664. **LC** KF6491.Z9; A14. **DD** 343.7306/7.

US/0191-8656
ALI-ABA COURSE OF STUDY. ESTATE PLANNING IN DEPTH : MATERIALS. **VAT** American Law Institute-American Bar Association Course of Study. Estate Planning In Depth: Materials. English. American Law Institute, 4025 Chestnut Street, Philadelphia PA 19104-3099. **Tel** (215)243-1661, (800)253-6397, FAX (215)243-1664. **LC** KF6585; .A14. **DD** 343/.73/053.

US/0270-9694
ALI-ABA COURSE OF STUDY. ESTATE PLANNING : MATERIALS. **VAT** American Law Institute-American Bar Association Course of Study. Estate Planning. Materials. English. an. American Law Institute, 4025 Chestnut Street, Philadelphia PA 19104-3099. **Tel** (215)243-1661, (800)253-6397, FAX (215)243-1664. **LC** KF6585; .A127. **DD** 346.7305/2.

US/0190-9584
ALI-ABA COURSE OF STUDY : ESTATE PLANNING UNDER THE NEW ESTATE AND GIFT TAX LAW : MATERIALS. **VAT** American Law Institute-American Bar Association Course of Study. Estate Planning under the New Estate and Gift Tax Law. Materials. English. American Law Institute, 4025 Chestnut Street, Philadelphia PA 19104-3099. **Tel** (215)243-1661, (800)253-6397, FAX (215)243-1664. **LC** KF6572.Z9; A15. **DD** 343/.73/053.

US/0732-8850
ANNUAL NOTRE DAME ESTATE PLANNING INSTITUTE. (ANNUAL NOTRE DAME ESTATE PLANNING INSTITUTE : PROCEEDINGS.). **Main/Corp** Notre Dame Estate Planning Institute. Vol. 2 (Sept. 15-16, 1977)-. Proceedings. English. an. $49.00. Clark Boardman Callaghan, 155 Pfingsten Road, Deerfield IL 60015. **Tel** (800)323-8067. **ED** R W Campfield. **LC** KF6584.A2; N67. **DD** 343.7305/3; 347.30353. ***Continues*** *Notre Dame Estate Planning Institute. Proceedings, 0278-1840.*
Ind/Abst Curr. Law Index (1980-); Leg. Resour. Index (1980 ?); LegalTrac (Jan. 1980 Dec. 1980).

US/0363-8456
BULLETIN INDEX-DIGEST SYSTEM. SERVICE TWO. ESTATE AND GIFT TAX. (BULLETIN INDEX-DIGEST SYSTEM. SERVICE 2, ESTATE AND GIFT TAX / DEPARTMENT OF THE

TREASURY, INTERNAL REVENUE SERVICE.). **Added/Corp** United States. Internal Revenue Service. **VFOAT** Estate & Gift Tax; Estate and Gift Tax; Service 2 Estates and Gift Taxes. (19??)-. Bulletin. English. an (cumulative supplements). $19.00. Claitors Law Books, 3165 South Acadian, Baton Rouge LA 70808. **Tel** (504)344-0476, (800)274-1403. **(Subscription address:** Claitors Law Books, PO Box 3333, Baton Rouge, LA 70821**) LC** KF6571.A65; I5. **DD** 343/.73/053.
Desc: Contains the Finding List and Digests for all permanent tax matters published in the Internal Revenue Bulletin-Estate and Gift Taxes.

US
CLOSELY HELD BUSINESS, THE. **Added/Corp** Practising Law Institute. **VAT** Closely Held Business. (1991)-. English. Practising Law Institute, 810 Seventh Avenue, New York NY 10019-5818. **Tel** (212)765-5700, FAX (212)581-4670 general correspondence, (212)265-4742 orders and billing inquiries. **LC** KF6484.Z9; P56. **DD** 343.7305/267; 347.3035267. ***Continues*** *Planning for the Closely Held Business, 1044-6958.*

CN/0848-2489
CONGRES - ASSOCIATION DE PLANIFICATION FISCALE ET FINANCIERE. (CONGRES / APFF.). [Congr. - Assoc. planif. fisc. financ.]. **Main/Corp** Association de Planification Fiscale et Financiere. Congres. **Added/Corp** Association de Planification Fiscale et Financiere. (1988)-. French. Free to members. Association De Planification Fiscale Et Financiere, Bureau 300, 445 Boul., Saint-Laurent Montreal, Quebec H2V 2V7 Canada. **DD** 343.71405/3. ***Continues*** *Congres, 0713-7486.*

US/1044-7911
ESTATE & FINANCIAL PLANNERS ALERT. ***Title Change.*** (ESTATE & FINANCIAL PLANNERS ALERT / THE RESEARCH INSTITUTE OF AMERICA, INC.). [Estate financ. plan. alert]. **Added/Corp** Research Institute of America, Inc. **VFOAT** Estate and Financial Planners Alert. Vol. 14, No. 7 (July 1989)-(199?). Periodical. English. mo. Research Institute of America, 117 East Stevens Avenue, Valhalla NY 10595. **Tel** (800)431-9025. **DD** 343. ***Continues*** *Estate Planning & Taxation Coordinator. Estate Planners Alert, 0163-9986.* ***Continued by*** *Estate Planners Alert (Englewood, N.J. : 1994), 1076-819X.*

●US/1076-819X
ESTATE PLANNER'S ALERT (1994). (ESTATE PLANNER'S ALERT.). [Estate planner's alert]. **Added/Corp** Research Institute of America. Vol. 19, No. 3 (March 1994)-. Periodical. English. mo. Research Institute of America, 117 East Stevens Avenue, Valhalla NY 10595. **Tel** (800)431-9025. **DD** 343. ***Continues*** *Estate & Financial Planners Alert, 1044-7911.*

US/0423-4596
ESTATE PLANNERS QUARTERLY. Vol. 1 (Mar. 1952)-. Periodical. English. qt. $190.00. Farnsworth Publishing Company, 500 North Dearborn Street, Chicago IL 60610-4901. **Tel** (516)536-8400. **ED** Stuart A Monroe. **LC** HG179; .E8. **Circ:** 5,000.
Desc: A supplemented 2-volume loose-leaf service containing individually bound reports by field experts in areas of financial and estate planning.
Ind/Abst Fed. Tax Artic.

US/0273-7027
ESTATE PLANNING & CALIFORNIA PROBATE REPORTER. (ESTATE PLANNING & CALIFORNIA PROBATE REPORTER / CALIFORNIA CONTINUING EDUCATION OF THE BAR.). **Added/Corp** California Continuing Education of the Bar. **VFOAT** CEB Estate Planning & California Probate Reporter. **VAT** Estate Planning and California Probate Reporter. Vol. 1, No. 1 (Oct. 1980)-. Periodical. English. bm. $125.00. California Continuing Education of the Bar, 2300 Shattuck Avenue, Berkeley CA 94704. **Tel** (510)642-8000, (800)232-3444. **ED** Edward Halbach. **LC** KFC195.A15; E88.
Desc: Features practice-oriented articles; digests of the latest developments (including legislation and court cases); extensive editorial comments analyzing the significance of developments; and more.

US/0195-1238
ESTATE PLANNING & TAXATION COORDINATOR. [Estate plan. tax. coord.]. **Added/Corp** Research Institute of America. **VAT** Estate Planning and Taxation Coordinator. (197?)-. English. ir. Research Institute of America, 117 East Stevens Avenue, Valhalla NY 10595. **Tel** (800)431-9025. **ED** James E. Cheeks. **DD** 343. **[CCC].**
Desc: Shows the practitioner how to develop, implement and follow through on every estate planning situation.

US/0014-1224
ESTATE PLANNING CHECKLISTS AND FORMS. Periodical. English. qt. Institute for Business Planning Inc, Subscription Service Center, IBP Plaza, Englewood Cliffs NJ 07632.

US/0014-1216
ESTATE PLANNING (ENGLEWOOD CLIFFS, N.J.). (ESTATE PLANNING.). **Main/Corp** Institute for Business Planning, Inc. (19??)-. English. bm. $141.75 US and Canada; $219.45 other. Warren Gorham & Lamont Inc., Park Square Building, 31 St. James Avenue, Boston MA 02116-4112. **Tel** (617)423-2020, (800)950-1207, FAX (617)423-2026.
Ind/Abst Bus. Index (1985-); Curr. Law Index; Gen. BusinessFile (1985-); Leg. Resour. Index (?-?); LegalTrac (1980-).

US/0278-4009
ESTATE PLANNING (LOS ANGELES, CALIF.). (ESTATE PLANNING.). [Estate plann.]. **Added/Corp** University of California, Los Angeles. School of Law. California Continuing Education of the Bar. (198?)-. English. an. $95.00. California Continuing Education of the Bar, 2300 Shattuck Avenue, Berkeley CA 94704. **Tel** (510)642-8000, (800)232-3444. **LC** KF750.A2; E85. **DD** 343.7305/3; 347.30353. ***Continues*** *Annual Estate Planning Institute (Sacramento, Calif.), 0887-4662.*
Desc: Emphasizing family and business estate planning, the authors intensively analyze advanced-level estate planning concepts.
Ind/Abst Leg. Resour. Index (1981-).

US/0098-2873
ESTATE PLANNING REVIEW. **Added/Corp** Commerce Clearing House. (1974)-. Periodical. English. ir. Commerce Clearing House Inc., 4025 West Peterson Avenue, Chicago IL 60646-6085. **Tel** (312)583-8500, FAX (708)940-4600. **ED** Sidney Kess and Bertil Westlin. **LC** KF746.A3; E87. **DD** 346/.73/052.
Desc: Covers new estate planning developments and cases. Real-life facts and figures show how to keep estate taxes at 'legal vows'.

US/0094-1794
ESTATE PLANNING (TAMPA). (ESTATE PLANNING.). [Estate plann.]. Vol. 1 (Autumn 1973)-. Periodical. English. bm. $141.75 US and Canada; $219.45 other. Warren Gorham & Lamont Inc., Park Square Building, 31 St. James Avenue, Boston MA 02116-4112. **Tel** (617)423-2020, (800)950-1207, FAX (617)423-2026. **LC** KF750.A1; E83. **DD** 346/.73/05205. **[CCC].** available on microfilm and microfiche from University Microfilms International (UMI). Documents available from UMI Article Clearinghouse.
Desc: Provides a complete, current picture of opportunities in estate planning and family asset management. Each issue offers analysis of recent tax developments and legal decisions.
Ind/Abst ABI/INFORM Glob. Ed.; ABI Inform Ondisc (Fall 1973-); Account. Tax Datab. (Fall 1973-); Account. Art.; Fed. Tax Artic.; Leg. Resour. Index (1980-?); Trade Ind. Index (1981-).

US
ESTATE TAX TECHNIQUES. English. an. Matthew Bender & Company Inc., 1275 Broadway, Albany NY 12204. **Tel** (800)833-9844, (518)487-3000.

CN/0840-7886
ESTATES & TRUSTS JOURNAL. [Estates trusts j.]. **VFOAT** Estates and Trusts Journal. Vol. 9, No. 1 (Dec. 1988)-. Periodical. English. Four times a year. 97.00Can$. Canada Law Book Inc., 240 Edward Street, Aurora Ontario L4G 3S9 Canada. **Tel** (800)263-3269, (905)841-6472, FAX (905)841-5085. **ED** Barry S. Corbin. **DD** 346.7105/2. ***Continues*** *Estates and Trusts Quarterly, 0381-8888.*
Desc: Features new insights and approaches to legislative change as well as practical solutions in the drafting of wills and trusts.
Ind/Abst Can. Legal Lit.; Leg. Resour. Index (1980-?).

CN/0706-5655
ESTATES & TRUSTS REPORTS. [Estates trusts rep.]. (1977)-. Periodical. English (French). ir. 125.00Can$. Carswell / Canada, 2075 Kennedy Road, Scarborough Ontario M1T 3V4 Canada. **Tel** (416)609-3800, (800)387-5164. **ED** T.G. Youdan. **DD** 346'.71'0502642. Index available. cum. index. **Ad Acc.**
Desc: Features all important decisions in estates and jurisdictions selected by experts in the field.
Ind/Abst Can. Legal Lit.; Curr. Law Index (1980-); Index Can. Leg. Period. Lit.; Leg. Resour. Index (1980-?); LegalTrac (Jan. 1980-Dec. 1980).

US/0164-1255
FUNDAMENTAL CONCEPTS OF ESTATE ADMINISTRATION. **Added/Corp** Practising Law Institute. (1976)-. English. Practising Law Institute, 810 Seventh Avenue, New York NY 10019-5818. **Tel** (212)765-5700, FAX (212)581-4670 general correspondence, (212)265-4742 orders and billing inquiries. **LC** KF6585; .F85. **DD** 343/.73/053.

US/0733-0057
FUNDAMENTAL CONCEPTS OF ESTATE PLANNING. [Fundam. concepts estate plann.]. 1976-. English. an. Practising Law Institute, 810 Seventh Avenue, New York NY 10019-5818. **Tel** (212)765-5700, FAX (212)581-4670 general correspondence, (212)265-4742 orders and billing inquiries. **LC** KF750.Z9; F86. **DD** 343.7305/3; 347.30352.

US
INSTITUTE ON ESTATE PLANNING. 1st- ; 1967-. English. ir. Matthew Bender & Company Inc., 1275 Broadway, Albany NY 12204. **Tel** (800)833-9844, (518)487-3000.
Ind/Abst Curr. Law Index (1980-); Index Leg. Period.; Leg. Resour. Index (1980-); LegalTrac (1980-).

US/1044-9418
JOURNAL OF TAXATION OF ESTATES & TRUSTS, THE. ***Ceased.*** [J. tax. estates trusts]. **VFOAT** Taxation of Estates & Trusts; Taxation of Estates and Trusts; Journal of Taxation of Estates and Trusts. Vol. 1, No. 4 (Summer 1989)-(19??). Periodical. English. qt. Faulkner & Gray Inc., 11 Penn Plaza, 17th Floor, New York NY 10001. **Tel** (212)967-7000, (800)535-8403. **ED** Alice V Benson. **LC** KF6449.A15; J68. **DD** 343.7305/3/05; 347.3035305. **Bk Rev. Ad Acc. Circ:** 2,500 (ctrl). available in microform from University Microfilms International (UMI); available on an online database (files 15,485/Full-Text) from DIALOG. ***Continues*** *Journal of Taxation of Trusts & Estates, 1040-7839.*
Ind/Abst Account. Tax Datab. (Winter 1991-Spring 1992) [Full Txt.].

US/0733-4184
NEWS FROM DRAFTING WILLS AND TUST AREEMENTS. [News Draft. wills trust agreem.]. **VFOAT** News from DWTA. (Apr. 16, 1982)-. Periodical. English. ir. Comes with Drafting Wills and Trust Agreements Annual Update Service. Shepards McGraw-Hill Inc, 555 Middle Creek Parkway, PO Box 35300, Colorado Springs CO 80935-3530. **Tel** (719)488-3000, FAX (800)525-0053. **ED** Robert P. Wilkins. **LC** KF748.1; .W55 Suppl. **DD** 346.7305/4/05; 347.3065405. **Circ:** 3,000.
Desc: Provides the attorney with an efficient, easy-to-use estate planning system from the gathering of information to the execution of high quality documents.

US
PAGE ON THE LAW OF WILLS, INCLUDING PROBATE, WILL CONTESTS, EVIDENCE, TAXATION, CONFLICTS, ESTATE PLANNING, FORMS, AND STATUTES RELATING TO WILLS. English. an. Anderson Publishing, 2035 Reading Road, Cincinnati OH 45202. **Tel** (513)421-4142, (800)582-7295, FAX (513)562-8116.

US/0734-4406
POST MORTEM ESTATE PLANNING. English. an. Practising Law Institute, 810 Seventh Avenue, New York NY 10019-5818. **Tel** (212)765-5700, FAX (212)581-4670 general correspondence, (212)265-4742 orders and billing inquiries. **LC** KF6585; .P67. **DD** 343.7305/3; 347.30353.

US/0192-3889
PRACTICAL WILL DRAFTING. 1971-. English. an. Practising Law Institute, 810 Seventh Avenue, New York NY 10019-5818. **Tel** (212)765-5700, FAX (212)581-4670 general correspondence, (212)265-4742 orders and billing inquiries. **LC** KF755.Z9; P7. **DD** 346/.73/054.

US/0164-0372
PROBATE AND PROPERTY (CHICAGO, ILL. : 1987). (PROBATE AND PROPERTY : THE MAGAZINE OF THE REAL PROPERTY, PROBATE AND TRUST LAW SECTION OF THE AMERICAN BAR ASSOCIATION.). [Probate prop.]. **Added/Corp** American Bar Association. Section of Real Property, Probate and Trust Law. Vol. 1, No. 1 (Jan./Feb. 1987)-. Periodical. English. bm (6 issues). $40.00. American Bar Association, 750 North Lake Shore Drive, Chicago IL 60611. **Tel** (312)988-5522, (312)988-5241, FAX (312)988-5528, telex 270593. **ED** Robert P. Wilkins. **LC** KF566.A3; P76. **DD** 346.73/05/2/05; 347.3065205. **Ad Acc. Circ:** 33,000. ***Continues*** *Probate and Property, 0164-0372.*
Desc: For lawyers who devote a large part of their practice to real estate law or laws dealing with wills, trusts, and estates. Provides lawyers with up-to-date practical information that they can apply to legal questions raised by their clients.
Ind/Abst Law Office Inf. Serv.

US/1044-7423
PROBATE PRACTICE REPORTER. [Probate pract. report.]. **Added/Corp** Shepard's/McGraw-Hill. Vol. 1, No. 1 (Jan. 1989)-. Periodical. English. mo. $260.00. Shepards McGraw-Hill Inc, 555 Middle Creek Parkway, PO Box 35300, Colorado Springs CO 80935-3530. **Tel** (719)488-3000, FAX (800)525-0053. **ED** F. Ladson Boyle and Alan Medlin. **LC** KF765.A59; P76. **DD** 346.7305/2/02638; 347.3065202638.
Desc: Brings expert analyses of the most significant probate cases from across the nation and presents them for fast reading. Each issue includes an insightful article by a guest columnist, a recent articles section briefly describing journal articles of interest, and more.

US/0034-0855
REAL PROPERTY, PROBATE AND TRUST JOURNAL. Added/Corp American Bar Association. Section of Real Property, Probate and Trust Law. Vol. 1 (Spring 1966)-. Academic Scholarly Publication. English. qt (4 issues). $23.00. American Bar Association, 750 North Lake Shore Drive, Chicago IL 60611. **Tel** (312)988-5522, (312)988-5241, FAX (312)988-5528, telex 270593. **ED** Jean A. Mortland. **LC** K18; .E15. ctrl circ. available on microfilm and microfiche from University Microfilms International (UMI). *Absorbed Newsletter of the Section of Real Property, Probate and Trust Law; Absorbed in part American Bar Association. Section of Real Property, Probate and Trust Law. Proceedings. Superseded in part by Probate and Property, 0164-0372.*
Desc: Scholarly articles in the fields of estate planning, trust law and real property law.
Ind/Abst Account. Tax Datab. (1974-) [Full Txt.]; Curr. Law Index (1980-); Fed. Tax Artic.; Index Leg. Period.; Leg. Resour. Index (1980-); LegalTrac (1980-).

US
REDFEARN'S WILLS AND ADMINISTRATION OF ESTATES IN FLORIDA. English. ir. $159.95, $49.95 seperate pocket part supplement. Harrison Company Publishers, 3110 Crossing Park, PO Box 7500, Norcross GA 30091-7500. **Tel** (800)241-3561, (404)447-9150.

US/0145-5079
REPORT OF ANNUAL SEMINAR ON ESTATE PLANNING. Main/Conf Seminar on Estate Planning. **Added/Corp** University of Kentucky. Office of Continuing Legal Education. Kentucky Bar Association (1971-). (19??)-. English. an. **LC** KFK1340.A75; S45. **DD** 343/.769/053.

US/0272-264X
RESOURCE MATERIALS : ESTATE PLANNING IN DEPTH. Main/Conf ALI-ABA Course of Study: Estate Planning in Depth. **VFOAT** Estate Planning in Depth, Resource Materials. 1st Ed.- 1972-. English. American Law Institute, 4025 Chestnut Street, Philadelphia PA 19104-3099. **Tel** (215)243-1661, (800)253-6397, FAX (215)243-1664. **LC** KF750.Z9; A145. **DD** 343.7305/3; 347.30353.

US/0147-9229
REVIEW OF TAXATION OF INDIVIDUALS, THE. Ceased. [Rev. tax. individ.]. Vol. 1 (Winter 1977)-(1992). Periodical. English. qt. Warren Gorham & Lamont Inc., Park Square Building, 31 St. James Avenue, Boston MA 02116-4112. **Tel** (617)423-2020, (800)950-1207, FAX (617)423-2026. **ED** James Halpern. **LC** K18; .E99. **DD** 343/.73/04. available on microfilm and microfiche from University Microfilms International (UMI). Documents available from UMI Article Clearinghouse.
Desc: This unique journal covers every aspect of tax planning for highly compensated individuals. It provides practice-tested guidance on everything from income and estate planning to closely held businesses.
Ind/Abst ABI/INFORM Glob. Ed.; ABI Inform Ondisc (Spring 1978-); Account. Tax Datab. (Spring 1978-); Bus. Index (1985-); Curr. Law Index (1980-); Fed. Tax Artic.; Gen. BusinessFile (1985-); Gen. Period. Index (1985-); Index Leg. Period.; INFO-SOUTH Abstr.; Leg. Resour. Index (1980-); LegalTrac (1980-); Mag. Search.

US/0708-5079
REVUE DE PLANIFICATION FISCALE ET SUCCESSORALE. [Rev. planif. fisc. successor.]. **Added/Corp** Association Quebecoise de Planification Successorale. Vol. 1 (Mar. 1979)-. Periodical. French. qt. comes with membership. NFTA / Winrock International, Route 3, Box 376, Morrilton AR 72110. **Tel** (501)727-5435. **DD** 343/.714/04.
Ind/Abst Index Can. Leg. Period. Lit.

US/1056-1218
SHEPARD'S ELDER CARE/LAW NEWSLETTER. [Shepard's elder care/law newsl.]. **Added/Corp** Shepard's/McGraw-Hill. **VFOAT** Shepard's Elder Care Law Newsletter; Elder Care/Law Newsletter; Elder Care Law Newsletter. (Mar. 15, 1991)-. Newsletter. English. mo. $125.00. Shepards McGraw-Hill Inc, 555 Middle Creek Parkway, PO Box 35300, Colorado Springs CO 80935-3530. **Tel** (719)488-3000, FAX (800)525-0053. **ED** Robert Wilkins. **LC** KF390.A4; S48. **DD** 346.3701/3; 347.30613.
Desc: More than just an estate planning newsletter, this product provides coverage of all legal issues relating to the elderly, including age discrimination, litigation affecting the elderly, and right to die questions.

JA
SOZOKUZEIHO ENSHU, RIRON TO KEISAN. (19??)-. Periodical. Japanese. ¥1600. Zeimu Keiri Kyokai, 5-13 Shimo Ochiai 2-chome Shinjuku-ku, Tokyo 161 Japan. *Continues Shirasaki, Asakichi: Enshu Sozokuzeiho.*

US/0194-8822
TAX, FINANCIAL AND ESTATE PLANNING FOR THE OWNER OF A CLOSELY-HELD CORPORATION. Ceased. Vol. 1- May 1979-?. Periodical. English. mo. Panel Publishers, A Division of Aspen Publishers, Inc., 7201 McKinney Circle, PO Box 990, Frederick MD 21705-9727. **Tel** (800)638-8437. **ED** Tom Whitehall. **LC** KF6457; .T38. **DD** 343.7306/7. **Bk Rev**. **Ad Acc**. **Circ:** 2,000 (ctrl).
Desc: The closely held corporation is a remarkably easy-to-use loose-leaf service that delivers a unique system of answering every tax question concerning closely held corporations and their owners.

US/0886-3547
TAX MANAGEMENT ESTATES, GIFTS, AND TRUSTS JOURNAL. [Tax Manage. estates gifts trusts j.]. Vol. 9, No. 1 (Jan./Feb. 1984). Periodical. English. bm. $129.00 (public libraries), $146.00 (other libraries), $128.00 (federal government), $129.00 (state and local governments). Tax Management Inc / Washington DC, 1231 25th Street NW, Washington DC 20037. **Tel** (202)452-4556, (800)372-1033, FAX (202)452-4096, telex 285656 BNAI WSH. **(Subscription address:** 9435 Key West Avenue Rockville MD 20850) **ED** Glenn Davis. **LC** KF6571.A15; E8. **DD** 343.7305/3/05; 347.3035305. **[CCC].** Index available. cum. index. **Circ:** 1,350. available on microfilm and microfiche from University Microfilms International (UMI); available on an online database (files 15,485/Full-Text) from DIALOG. Documents available from UMI Article Clearinghouse. *Continues Estates, Gifts and Trusts Journal, 0364-9253.*
Desc: Journal of practical guidance and timely review of current developments in estates, gifts and trusts.
Ind/Abst ABI/INFORM Glob. Ed.; ABI Inform Ondisc (Jan. 1988-); Account. Tax Datab. (1976-) [Full Txt.]; Leg. Resour. Index (198?-); LegalTrac (1980-); UMI ABI/Inform--Bus. Period. Ondisc (Jan. 1988-) [Full Txt.].

CN/0384-9201
TAXATION (DON MILLS). See Public Administration-Public Finance and Taxation.

US
TAXATION OF ESTATES, GIFTS, AND TRUSTS : CASES AND MATERIALS. See Public Administration-Public Finance and Taxation.

US/1048-2121
TAXLINE (CINCINNATI, OHIO). See Public Administration-Public Finance and Taxation.

US/0041-3682
TRUSTS & ESTATES. (TRUSTS AND ESTATES.). [Trusts estates]. Vol. 68, No. 1 (Jan. 1939)-. Periodical. English. Thirteen times a year. $75.00. Argus Business, 6151 Powers Ferry Road, Atlanta GA 30339. **Tel** (404)995-2500, (800)233-3359. **(Subscription address:** Sunbelt Fulfillment Services, PO Box 41369, Nashville, TN 37204 USA; telephone: (615)377-3322, (800)888-5139) **ED** Richard H. Gamble. **LC** HG4341; .T8. **DD** 332. **CODEN** TRUSB9. **[CCC].** Index available. cum. index. **Circ:** 12,033. available on microfilm and microfiche from University Microfilms International (UMI); available on an online database (files 15,485,648/Full-Text) from DIALOG. Documents available from UMI Article Clearinghouse. *Continues Trust Companies.*
Ind/Abst ABI/INFORM Glob. Ed.; ABI Inform Ondisc (Sept. 1971-); Acad. Search (July 1993-); Account. Tax Datab. (Sept. 1971-) [Full Txt.]; Account. Art.; Bus. ASAP (1992-) [Full Txt.]; Bus. Index (1985-); Bus. Period. Index; Bus. Source (Jul. 1993-); Curr. Law Index (1980-); Fed. Tax Artic.; Gen. BusinessFile (1985-); Gen. Period. Index (1985-); Index Leg. Period.; INFO-SOUTH Abstr.; Ins. Period. Index; Law Office Inf. Serv.; Leg. Resour. Index (1980-); LegalTrac (1980-); Mag. Search; PAIS Int. Print; Stat. Ref. Index; Trade Ind. Index [Full Txt.]; UMI ABI/Inform--Bus. Period. Ondisc (Jan. 1987-) [Full Txt.]; Wilson Bus. Abstr.

US
WILLS. Main/Corp Bay Area Review Course, Inc. English. an. Bay Area Review Course Inc, 5900 Wilshire Boulevard, Los Angeles CA 90036. **LC** KFC201.Z9; B37. **DD** 346/.794/054.

CN/0824-1406
WILLS FOR ALBERTA. [Wills Alta.]. 2nd Ed. (Aug. 1977)-. English. ir. $6.50. International Self-Counsel Press, Head and Editorial Office, 1481 Charlotte Road, Vancouver British Columbia V7J 1H1 Canada. **Tel** (604)986-3947. **ED** Ruth Wilson. **DD** 346.712305/4. *Continues Wills and Probate Procedure, 0824-1392.*

FAMILY LAW

US/0887-896X
ABA JUVENILE & CHILD WELFARE LAW REPORTER. [ABA juv. child welf. law report]. **Added/Corp** National Legal Resource Center for Child Advocacy and Protection (U.S.). **VFOAT** ABA Juvenile and Child Welfare Law Reporter; Juvenile and Child Welfare Law Reporter; Juvenile & Child Welfare Law Reporter. **VAT** American Bar Association Juvenile and Child Welfare Law Reporter. Vol. 5, No. 1 (Mar. 1986)-. Periodical. English. mo. $199.00 institution. American Bar Association, 750 North Lake Shore Drive, Chicago IL 60611. **Tel** (312)988-5522, (312)988-5241, FAX (312)988-5528, telex 270593. **ED** Robert Horowitz. **LC** KF479.A59; A23. **DD** 346.7301/35; 347.306135. Index available. cum. index (for Volumes 5 and 6). **Bk Rev**. **Circ:** 600. *Continues National Juvenile Law Reporter.*
Desc: Case citations of law pertaining to child welfare, juvenile justice and rights of families and children. Also Supreme Court decisions, legislative and legal ethics.

US/0732-3565
ADVANCES IN LAW AND CHILD DEVELOPMENT. Ceased. [Adv. law child dev.]. Vol. 1 (1982)-Vol. 1 (19??). English. ir. Jessica Kingsley Publishers, 118 Pentonville Road, London N1 9JN England. **Tel** 011 44 71 833 2307, FAX 011 44 71 837 2917. **(Subscription address:** Taylor & Francis Inc., 1900 Frost Road, Suite 101, Bristol PA 19007-1598.) **ED** R.L. Sprague. **LC** K1; .D8. **DD** 346.7301/35; 347.306135. **NLM** W1 AD654F.
Ind/Abst Psychol. Abstr. (1982-).

US/0891-6330
AMERICAN JOURNAL OF FAMILY LAW. [Am. j. fam. law]. Vol. 1, No. 1 (Spring 1987)-. Periodical. English. qt. $120.00 US; $136.00 other. John Wiley & Sons, Inc., 605 Third Avenue, New York NY 10158-0012. **Tel** (212)850-6000, (212)850-6645, FAX (212)850-6088, telex 12-7063. **(Subscription address:** John Wiley & Sons Inc / New Jersey, PO Box 2575, Secaucus NJ 07096-2575.) **ED** Laura E. Shapiro, Esq. **LC** K1; .M442. **DD** 346. **Bk Rev**. **Ad Acc**. **Circ:** 800.
Desc: Provides articles and features on current family law issues. The journal is practice-oriented and filled with new ideas and practical family law tips.
Ind/Abst Index Leg. Period.; Leg. Resour. Index; LegalTrac (1980-).

US/0190-7395
ANNUAL ADVANCED FAMILY LAW COURSE. Main/Corp State Bar of Texas. Professional Development Program. **VFOAT** Advanced Family Law Course. English. an. State Bar of Texas, PO Box 12487, Capitol Station, Austin TX 78711. **Tel** (512)463-1411. **LC** KFT1294; .S83. **DD** 346/.764/015.

US
ANNUAL REPORT, FISCAL YEAR ... / STATE OF CONNECTICUT, SUPERIOR COURT, FAMILY DIVISION. Main/Corp Connecticut. Superior Court. Family Division. 1978/79-. English. an. **LC** KFC3694.5; .A874. **DD** 346.74601/5/0269; 347. 4606150269.

US
ANNUAL REPORT / NEW YORK STATE ASSEMBLY, COMMITTEE ON CHILDREN & FAMILIES. Main/Corp New York (State). Legislature. Assembly. Standing Committee on Children and Families. 1983-. Periodical. English. an. **LC** KFN5603; .A244. **DD** 353.974784/7. *Continues New York (State). Legislature. Assembly. Standing Committee on Child Care. Annual Report.*

AT/0817-623X
AUSTRALIAN JOURNAL OF FAMILY LAW. [Aust. j. fam. law]. Vol. 1, No. 1 (Aug. 1986)-. Periodical. English. Three times a year. 130.00Aus$. Butterworths Pty Ltd, 271-273 Lane Cove Road, PO Box 345, North Ryde NSW 2113 Australia. **Tel** 011 61 2 3354444, FAX 011 61 2 3354655. **ED** Peter Nygh. **LC** K1; .U775. **DD** 346.9401/5/05; 349.4061505.
Desc: Forum for the discussion of important issues in family law, such as child custody and maintenance, property settlements, de facto relationships and artificial conception.
Ind/Abst Aust. Leg. Mon. Dig.; Index Leg. Period.

US/0882-7842
CALIFORNIA FAMILY LAW MONTHLY. [Calif. fam. law mon.]. **Added/Corp** Matthew Bender (Firm). Vol. 1 No. 1 (Aug. 1984)-. Periodical. English. mo. $160.00. Matthew Bender & Company Inc., 1275 Broadway, Albany NY 12204. **Tel** (800)833-9844, (518)487-3000. **ED** Steven Revell. **LC** KFC115.A15; C35. **DD** 346.79401/5/05; 347.94061505.
Desc: Analysis of new California court cases and statutes relating to family law matters such as divorce, community property, etc.

US/0164-7040
CALIFORNIA FAMILY LAW REPORT. [Calif. fam. law rep.]. **VFOAT** CFLR (1977)-. Periodical. English. mo. $285.00. California Family Law Report, 107 Caledonia Street East, Sausalito CA 94965. **Tel** (415)332-9000.
Desc: Covers domestic relations.

US
CALIFORNIA LAWS FOR PSYCHOTHERAPISTS. Main/Corp California. (1980)-. English. an. $23.95. Legal Books Distributors, 4247 Whitesight Street, Los Angeles CA 90063. **Tel** (213)526-7110. **LC** KFC31; .H37. **DD** 349.794/024616.

CN/0832-6983
CANADIAN FAMILY LAW QUARTERLY. [Can. fam. law q.]. **Added/Corp** Carswell Legal Publications. **VFOAT** Family Law Quarterly. Vol. 1, No. 1

(Aug. 1986)-. Periodical. English. Three times a year. 135.00Can$. Carswell / Canada, 2075 Kennedy Road, Scarborough Ontario M1T 3V4 Canada. **Tel** (416)609-3800, (800)387-5164. **ED** James G. McLeod. **LC** K3; .C36. **DD** 346.7101/5/05; 347.1061505. **Bk Rev.** ctrl circ.
Desc: A national journal focusing on topics of practical interest to all family law practitioners
Ind/Abst Can. Legal Lit.; Index Can. Leg. Period. Lit.; Leg. Resour. Index; LegalTrac (1980-).

CN/0704-1225
CANADIAN JOURNAL OF FAMILY LAW.
[Can. j. fam. law]. **VFOAT** Revue Canadienne de Droit Familial. Vol. 1, No. 1 (Jan. 1978)-. Periodical. English (French). Twice a year (Apr., Sept.). 50.00Can$ Canada; 60.00Can$ others. University of British Columbia Faculty of Law, Room 165 1822 E. Mall, Vancouver BC V6T 1Z1 Canada. **Tel** (604)822-3066. **LC** K3; .A495. **DD** 346.7101/5/05; 347.1061505. **NLM** W1 CA586W. **Bk Rev.** available on microfilm and microfiche from University Microfilms International (UMI). Documents available.
Ind/Abst Can. Index (?-?); Can. Legal Lit.; Crim. Justice Abstr.; Crim. Justice Period. Index (-1989); Curr. Law Index (1980-); Index Leg. Period.; Leg. Resour. Index (1980-); LegalTrac (1980-); Linguist. Lang. Behav. Abstr.; Sage Fam. Stud. Abstr.; Soc. Plann. Policy Dev. Abstr.; Soc. Work Abstr. (?-?); Sociol. Abstr.

US/0884-8076
CHILD SUPPORT REPORT.
(CHILD SUPPORT REPORT / NATIONAL CHILD SUPPORT ENFORCEMENT REFERENCE CENTER.). [Child support rep.]. **Added/Corp** National Child Support Enforcement Reference Center (U.S.) United States. Office of Child Support Enforcement. Vol. 1, No. 1 (Jan. 1979)-. Periodical. English. ir. Office of Child Support Enforcement, 370 L'Enfant Promenade SW, Mail Stop OCSE-RC, Washington DC 20447. **LC** HV741; .C49. **Bk Rev. Circ:** 10,000 (ctrl).
Desc: Presents information on child support enforcement programs, policies and regulations at federal, state and local levels.

US/0278-7210
CHILDREN'S LEGAL RIGHTS JOURNAL.
[Child. leg. rights j.]. **Added/Corp** Children's Legal Rights Information and Training Program. Vol. 1, No. 1 (July/Aug 1979)-. Periodical. English. qt. $60.00. William S. Hein & Company Inc., 1285 Main Street, Buffalo NY 14209. **Tel** (716)882-2600, (800)828-7571, FAX (716)883-8100, telex 91-209 WM S HEIN BUF. **ED** Robert Horowitz. **LC** KF479.A15; C46. **DD** 346.7301/35/05; 347.30613505. Index available (free). **Ad Acc. Circ:** 550 (ctrl).
Desc: Provides insight into the relationship between the professional and the child in such areas as: child abuse and neglect, foster care, child custody and adoption, juvenile delinquency, delinquency status offenses, medical care, mental health and mental retardation, education for the handicapped child and student's rights.
Ind/Abst Crim. Justice Abstr.; Curr. Law Index (1981-); Except. Child Educ. Resour.; Index Leg. Period.; Leg. Resour. Index (1981-); LegalTrac (1981-).

US/1077-8519
CHITTY'S LAW JOURNAL AND FAMILY LAW REVIEW.
[Chitty's law j. fam. law rev.]. **VFOAT** Chitty's Law Journal. (198?)-. Periodical. English. Jonah Publications Ltd. Inc, 558 Pleasant Street, 3rd Floor, New Bedford MA 02740. **Tel** (508)994-5515. **DD** 340. ***Formed by the union of*** *Chitty, Robert Michael Willes, 1893- Chitty's Law Journal, 0009-4889* ***and*** *Family Law Review, 0705-1131.*
Ind/Abst Index Can. Leg. Period. Lit.

US
CONNECTICUT FAMILY LAW CITATIONS : A REFERENCE GUIDE TO CONNECTICUT FAMILY LAW DECISIONS.
Added/Corp Butterworth Legal Publishers. Issue 1 (1984)-. Periodical. English. Butterworth Heinemann / Woburn, MA, 225 Wildwood Avenue, Unit B, Woburn MA 01801. **Tel** (800)366-2665, FAX (617)928-2620, telex 880052. **LC** KFC3694.A54; C66. **DD** 346.74601/5/02648; 347.46061502648.

US/0737-920X
CONNECTICUT FAMILY LAW JOURNAL, THE.
(THE CONNECTICUT FAMILY LAW JOURNAL / THE CONNECTICUT CHAPTER OF THE AMERICAN ACADEMY OF MATRIMONIAL LAWYERS.). [Conn. fam. law j.]. Vol. 1, No. 1 (Oct. 1982)-. Periodical. English. bm. $59.95. Butterworth Heinemann / Woburn, MA, 225 Wildwood Avenue, Unit B, Woburn MA 01801. **Tel** (800)366-2665, FAX (617)928-2620, telex 880052. **LC** KFC3700.A15; C66. **DD** 346.74601/5/05; 347.46061505.

AG
CUADERNOS DE FAMILIA.
Vol. 1, No. 1 (July/Sept. 1981)-. Periodical. Spanish. qt. $12.00. Abeledo-Perrot Sociedad Anonima Editora e Impresora, Lavalle 1280, 1048 Buenos Aires Argentina. **Tel** 40 6126, 382 2848, FAX 40 5156. **LC** KHA480.A15; C8. **DD** 346.8201/5/05; 348.2061505. Index available.

IT
DIRITTO DI FAMIGLIA E DELLE PERSONE.
(1972)-. Italian. qt. L130000.00 Italy; L196000.00 other. Giuffre Editore SPA, Via Busto Arsizio 40, 20151 Milan Italy. **Tel** 011 398 2 38089200. **ED** Vincenzo Lojacono. **Bk Rev. Ad Acc. Circ:** 2,600.
Desc: This journal deals with the most diverse rulings of jurisprudence and doctrine on the many problems arising in family law.

US/1050-141X
DIVORCE LITIGATION.
(DIVORCE LITIGATION : CUSTODY, PROPERTY, SUPPORT.). [Divorce litig.]. **Added/Corp** National Legal Research Group. Vol. 1, No. 1 (April 1989)-. Periodical. English. Twelve times a year. $145.00. National Legal Research Group Inc, PO Box 7187, Charlottesville VA 22906. **Tel** (800)727-6574, (804)977-5690, FAX (804)295-4667. **LC** KF531.A3; D58. **DD** 346.7301/66/05; 347.30616605. Index available (In January, annually the following year.). available on microfilm from University Microfilms International (UMI). ***Continues*** *Equitable Distribution Reporter, 0274-8614;* ***Absorbed*** *Community Property Journal, 0196-4453.*
Ind/Abst Leg. Resour. Index; LegalTrac (1989-).

US/0730-6555
DIVORCE TAXATION.
[Divorce tax.]. (Feb. 25, 1982)-. English. mo. $499.95 US and Canada; $679.45. Warren Gorham & Lamont Inc., Park Square Building, 31 St. James Avenue, Boston MA 02116-4112. **Tel** (617)423-2020, (800)950-1207, FAX (617)423-2026. **DD** 343.

US/0895-8858
DOMESTIC VIOLENCE LAW BULLETIN.
Ceased. [Domest. violence law bull.]. Ceased (Dec. 1988). Bulletin. English. mo. Quinlan Publishing Company, 23 Drydock Avenue, Boston MA 02210-2387. **Tel** (617)542-0048, (800)229-2084, FAX (617)345-9646. **LC** KF9320.A59; D66. **DD** 345.73/025553.

US/0273-3560
FAIRSHARE.
VFOAT Fair Share. (19??)-. Periodical. English. Twelve times a year. $157.33. Prentice-Hall Law and Business, 270 Sylvan Avenue, Englewood Cliffs NJ 07632. **Tel** (800)223-0231, (201)894-8538, FAX (201)894-8666. **ED** Ronald L. Brown. **LC** KF506.A3; F34. **DD** 346.7301/63/05; 347.30616305. **Bk Rev. Circ:** 1,200.
Desc: Provides the latest information on approaches, techniques, and precedents used by leading lawyers to solve the financial and economic questions at the heart of equitable distribution divorce practice today.
Ind/Abst Fed. Tax Artic.

GW/0937-2180
FAMILIE UND RECHT : FUR.
VFOAT FuR. (Feb. 1990)-. Periodical. German. Six times a year. DM160.80. Hermann Luchterhand Verlag, Postfach 2352, D 56513 Neuwied Germany. **Tel** 011 49 2631 8010.

US/0163-710X
FAMILY ADVOCATE.
[Fam. advocate]. **Added/Corp** American Bar Association. Section of Family Law. Vol. 1, No. 1 (Summer 1978)-. Periodical. English. qt (4 issues). $37.50. American Bar Association, 750 North Lake Shore Drive, Chicago IL 60611. **Tel** (312)988-5522, (312)988-5241, FAX (312)988-5528, telex 270593. **LC** KF501.A3; F33. **DD** 346/.73/01505. **Bk Rev. Ad Acc. Circ:** 20,000 (ctrl). available on microfilm and microfiche from University Microfilms International (UMI). ***Continues*** *Family Law Newsletter, 0427-9638.*
Ind/Abst Curr. Law Index (1980-); Law Office Inf. Serv.; Leg. Resour. Index (1980-); LegalTrac (1980-).

US/1047-5699
FAMILY AND CONCILIATION COURTS REVIEW.
[Fam. concil. courts rev.]. **Added/Corp** Association of Family and Conciliation Courts. **VFOAT** Conciliation Courts Review. Vol. 27, No. 1 (July 1989)-. Periodical. English. qt (Jan., Apr., Julu, Oct.). $123.00. SAGE Periodical Press, 2455 Teller Road, Thousand Oaks CA 91320. **Tel** (805)499-0721, FAX (805)499-0871, telex 100799. **ED** Hugh McIsaac (Family Services, Multnomah County Circuit Court, Portland, Oregon). **LC** K3; .A43. **DD** 346.01/66/05; 342/616605. **CODEN** FCCREY. Index available. cum. index. **Bk Rev. Ad Acc. Pr Rev. Acid Free. Circ:** 1,200. ***Continues*** *Conciliation Courts Review, 0588-9774.*
Desc: For judges, attorneys, mediators and mental health and human services professionals concerned with the improvement of all aspects of family court.
Ind/Abst PAIS Int. Print (1991-?); Psychol. Abstr. (1981-); PsycINFO; PsycLit; Sage Fam. Stud. Abstr.

UK/0952-8199
FAMILY COURT REPORTER.
Added/Corp Justice of the Peace Ltd. **VFOAT** FCR; F.C.R. (1987)-. Periodical. English. wk. £92.00 UK; £101.00 other. Justice of the Peace Limited, Little London, Chichester West Sussex, PO19 1PG England. **Tel** 011 44 243 787841, FAX 011 44 243 779278. **ED** C. T. Latham. **LC** KD750; .A514. **DD** 346.41/015/0264; 344.1061560264. Index available. **Ad Acc.**
Desc: Series of law reprints with comments.

●CN/1189-4245
FAMILY JUSTICE BULLETIN.
[Fam. justice bull.]. **Added/Corp** British Columbia. Ministry of Attorney General. Vol. 1, No. 1 (Apr. 1992)-. Bulletin. English. **DD** 346.71101.

US/0099-1988
FAMILY LAW. BENDER PAMPHLET EDITION.
(FAMILY LAW.). **Main/Corp** New York (State). English. Matthew Bender & Company Inc., 1275 Broadway, Albany NY 12204. **Tel** (800)833-9844, (518)487-3000. **LC** KFN5115.A29; F34. **DD** 346/.747/015.

UK/0014-7281
FAMILY LAW (CHICHESTER).
(FAMILY LAW.). [Fam. law]. Vol. 1, No. 1 (Jan./Feb. 1971)-. English. mo. £75.00. Family Law, 21 St. Thomas Street, Bristol BS1 6JS England. **Tel** 011 44 0272 230600, FAX 011 44 0272 230063, telex 449119. **ED** M M McColl, E A Walsh. **LC** K6; .A43. **DD** 346.4101/5/05; 344.1061505. Index available. cum. index. **Bk Rev. Ad Acc. Circ:** 4,000 (ctrl).
Desc: Essential information on the latest developments in every branch of the law relating to the family.
Ind/Abst Appl. Soc. Sci. Index Abstr.; Leg. Resour. Index (1980-); LegalTrac (1980-); Stud. Women Abstr.

US/0014-729X
FAMILY LAW QUARTERLY.
[Fam. law q.]. **Added/Corp** American Bar Association. Section of Family Law. Vol. 1, No. 1 (March 1967)-. Periodical. English. qt (4 issues). $39.50. American Bar Association, 750 North Lake Shore Drive, Chicago IL 60611. **Tel** (312)988-5522, (312)988-5241, FAX (312)988-5528, telex 270593. **ED** Timothy B. Walker. **LC** K6; .A437. Index available. cum. index. **Bk Rev. Pr Rev. Circ:** 16,000. available on microfilm and microfiche from University Microfilms International (UMI). Documents available from The Genuine Article. ***Continues*** *American Bar Association. Section of Family Law. Proceedings of the Section, 0270-1685.*
Desc: Including regular coverage of judicial decisions, legislation, taxation, summaries of state and local bar association projects.
Ind/Abst Crim. Justice Period. Index; Curr. Contents Soc. Behav. Sci.; Curr. Law Index (1980-); Fed. Tax Artic.; Index Leg. Period.; Leg. Resour. Index (1980-); LegalTrac (1980-); Res. Alert [Full Cov.]; Soc. Sci. Cit. Index [Full Cov.]; Women Stud. Abstr.

US/0148-7922
FAMILY LAW REPORTER, THE.
[Fam. law rep.]. **Added/Corp** Bureau of National Affairs (Washington, D.C.). Vol. 1 (Nov. 12, 1974)-. Periodical. English. wk. $581.00. Bureau of National Affairs Inc., 9435 Key West Avenue, Rockville MD 20850. **Tel** (800)372-1033, (301)258-1033, FAX (301)948-5823. **(Subscription address:** 9435 Key West Avenue, Rockville MD 20850; telephone: FAX (301)948-5823**) ED** Randy P Auerbach. **LC** KF501.A3; F3. **DD** 346/.73/01505. **[CCC].**
Desc: A notification and reference service dealing with all significant state and federal developments in the field of family law.
Ind/Abst Crim. Justice Period. Index; Curr. Lit. Fam. Plan. (19??-199?).

AT
FAMILY LAW REPORTS (SYDNEY, N.S.W.).
(FAMILY LAW REPORTS : INCORPORATING FAMILY LAW NOTES / REPORTERS: M.H. COOPER ... [ET AL.]). Vol. 1 (1976)-. Periodical. English. ir. 125.00Aus$ (bound volumes and monthly advance parts). Butterworths Pty Ltd, 271-273 Lane Cove Road, PO Box 345, North Ryde NSW 2113 Australia. **Tel** 011 61 2 3354444, FAX 011 61 2 3354655. cum. index. ***Absorbed*** *Family Law Notes.*
Desc: Presents judgements from the Family Court and all other superior courts in which matters relating to family law are considered.
Ind/Abst Aust. Leg. Mon. Dig.

US/0149-1431
FAMILY LAW REVIEW.
[Fam. law rev.]. V. 9, No. 2- July 1977-. Periodical. English. qt. New York State Bar Association, One Elk Street, Albany NY 12207. **Tel** (518)463-3200. **LC** KFN5115.A15; N4. **DD** 346. **Bk Rev. Circ:** 3,500 (ctrl). ***Continues*** *Family Law Section Newsletter, 0148-3692.*
Desc: Section newsletter-current section information and family law issues discussed.
Ind/Abst Can. Legal Lit.; LegalTrac (1980-).

US
FAMILY LAW TRIAL SUMMARIES.
V. 1, No. 1 (June 15, 1982)-. Periodical. English. mo. $65.00. Family Law Trial Summaries, 2554 Lincoln Boulevard/Suite 211, Marina Del Rey CA 90291. **LC** KFC1199.L62; P423. **DD** 346.794/930166/02648; 347. 94930616602648.

●UK
GREEN'S FAMILY LAW BULLETIN.
(1993)-. Bulletin. Six times a year. £74.00 Europe; £78.00 other. Sweet & Maxwell Ltd., South Quay Plaza, 183

Marsh Wall, London E14 9FT England. **Tel** 011 44 264 342899, FAX 011 44 264 342723, telex 929089 ITPINF G.

US/0276-6272
GUARDIANSHIP NEWS. (19??)-. Periodical. English. Ten times a year (Except Jan. & July). $48.00. Christian & Robertson Publishers, 85 Pine Grove Road, PO Box 674, Amherst MA 01004. **Tel** (413)253-7383. **LC** KF553.A15; G83. **DD** 346.7301/8/05; 347.3061805.

US
HANDBOOK OF MASSACHUSETTS FAMILY LAW. (19??)-. Periodical. English. an. $37.50. Lawyers Weekly Publications, 41 West Street, Boston MA 02111. **Tel** (617)451-7300, (800)444-5297.

US/1061-6489
HANDBOOK ON LOUISIANA FAMILY LAW. [Handb. La. fam. law]. **VFOAT** Louisiana Family Law. (1991)-. English. West Publishing Company, 610 Opperman Drive, PO Box 64526, Eagan MN 55123-1308. **Tel** (612)687-5618, (800)328-9352, FAX (612)687-5388, (800)562-2329. **LC** KFL94; .H36. **DD** 346.76301/5; 347.630615.

CN
INCOME TAX AND FAMILY LAW HANDBOOK. English. an. 140.00Can$. Butterworth & Company Ltd. / Canada, 75 Clegg Road, Markham Ontario L6G 1A1 Canada. **Tel** (905)479-2665, (800)668-6481. **ED** Mary Lou Benotto. **Pr Rev.**
Desc: Includes easy-to-read tables showing the after-tax monthly income of spouses paying support and spouses receiving support.

NE/0927-5568
INTERNATIONAL JOURNAL OF CHILDREN'S RIGHTS, THE. English. qt. Fl308.00 (postage included). Martinus Nijhoff Publishers, Subsidiary of Kluwer Academic Publishers, Koraalrood 50, 2718 SC Zoetermeer Netherlands. **Tel** 011 31 79 684400. **ED** Michael Freeman and Geraldine Van Bueren. **Bk Rev. Pr Rev. Acid Free.**
Desc: The focus of the journal is directed both to critical scholarship and practical policy development. Articles are published from the perspective of the widest range of those disciplines which contribute to a greater understanding of children's rights and the impact of these on the concept and development of childhood. The aim is on furthering children's rights in all parts of the world deploying the insights and methodologies of all relevant disciplines, including law, legal and political theory, psychology, psychiatry, educational theory, sociology, social administration and social work, health, social anthropology, economics, theology and history.

UK/0950-4109
INTERNATIONAL JOURNAL OF LAW AND THE FAMILY. Vol. 1, No. 1 April (1987)-. Periodical. English. Three times a year. £60.00 UK and Europe; $115.00 other. Oxford University Press, Walton Street, Oxford OX2 6DP England. **Tel** 011 44 865 56767, FAX 011 44 865 267773, telex 837330 OXPRES G. **(Subscription address:** Oxford University Press / USA, Journals Marketing Department, Oxford University Press, 2001 Evans Road, Cary NC 27513.**) ED** John Eekelaar and Robert Dingwall. **LC** K9; .N848. **DD** 346.01/5/05; 342.615005. **CODEN** IJLFEN. **[CCC]. Bk Rev. Ad Acc.** available on microfilm and microfiche from University Microfilms International (UMI).
Desc: Theoretical analysis of family law; sociological literature concerning the family which is of special interest to law and legal policy; literature in related disciplines, such as medicine, psychology, and demography, which is of special relevance to law and the family.
Ind/Abst Appl. Soc. Sci. Index Abstr.; Index Leg. Period.; PAIS Int. Print (1991-); Sage Fam. Stud. Abstr.; Soc. Plann. Policy Dev. Abstr.

US/1050-2556
JOURNAL OF DIVORCE & REMARRIAGE. See Family and Marriage.

US/0022-1066
JOURNAL OF FAMILY LAW. ***Title Change.*** (JOURNAL OF FAMILY LAW / UNIVERSITY OF LOUISVILLE SCHOOL OF LAW.). [J. fam. law]. **Added/Corp** University of Louisville. School of Law. Vol. 1 No. 1 (Spring 1961)-Vol. 30 No. 4 (1991-92). Periodical. English. qt. University of Louisville School of Law, Louisville KY 40292. **Tel** (502)852-6396. **LC** K10; .086. **DD** 346.7301/5/05; 347.3061505. cum. index. **Pr Rev.** available on microfilm and microfiche from University Microfilms International (UMI). Documents available from The Genuine Article, Documents on Demand. ***Continued by*** *University of Louisville Journal of Family Law.*
Ind/Abst Acad. Search (Jan. 1994-); Crim. Justice Abstr.; Crim. Justice Period. Index (1980-); Curr. Law Index (1980-); Energy Inf. Abstr.; Environ. Abstr.; Fed. Tax Artic.; Index Leg. Period.; INFO-SOUTH Abstr.; Int. Bibliogr. Sociol.; Leg. Resour. Index (1980-); LegalTrac (1980-); Mag. Search; PsycINFO; PsycLit; Res. Alert [Full Cov.]; Sage Fam. Stud. Abstr. (?-?); Soc. Plann. Policy Dev. Abstr.; Soc. Work Abstr. [Select. Cov.]; Sociol. Abstr.; Women Stud. Abstr.

US/0160-2098
JOURNAL OF JUVENILE LAW. [J. juv. law]. **Added/Corp** La Verne College. Law Center. University of La Verne. College of Law. (June 1977)-. Periodical. English. sa. $12.00. Laverne College Law Center, 1950 3rd Street, Laverne CA 91750. **Tel** (818)593-1848. **LC** K10; .O872. **DD** 345/.73/08. **Bk Rev. Ad Acc.**
Desc: A law review limited to discussions of how various laws impact juveniles.
Ind/Abst Crim. Justice Abstr.; Curr. Law Index (1980-); Index Leg. Period.; Leg. Resour. Index (1980-); LegalTrac (1980-).

UK/0141-8033
JOURNAL OF SOCIAL WELFARE & FAMILY LAW. **VFOAT** Journal of Social Welfare and Family Law. No. 1 (1991)-. Periodical. English. Four times a year. $140.00 US & Canada; £78.00 UK; £82.00 Other. Routledge, 11 New Fetter Lane, London EC4P 4EE England. **Tel** 071 583 9855, FAX 071 842 2298. **(Subscription address:** Kinokuniya Company Ltd., 38-1 Sakuragaoka 5, chome Setagaya-ku, Tokyo 156 Japan.**) LC** K10; .O895. **DD** 344.41/03/05. **NLM** W1; JO889BG. **CODEN** JSWLEY. available on microfilm from University Microfilms International (UMI). ***Continues*** *Journal of Social Welfare Law, 0141-8033.*
Ind/Abst Leg. Resour. Index; LegalTrac (1991-); PAIS Int. Print; Sage Fam. Stud. Abstr.

US/0882-6714
JOURNAL OF THE AMERICAN ACADEMY OF MATRIMONIAL LAWYERS, THE. [J. Am. Acad. Matrim. Lawyers]. **Added/Corp** American Academy of Matrimonial Lawyers. University of Wisconsin--Madison. Law School. Vol. 1, No. 1 (Spring 1985)-. English. an (June). $15.00 (per issues); $25.00 (two issues). American Academy of Matrimonial Lawyers, 150 North Michigan Avenue, Suite 2040, Chicago IL 60601. **Tel** (312)263-6477. **LC** K10; .O89575. **DD** 346.7301/5/05; 347.3061505.
Ind/Abst Index Leg. Period.; Leg. Resour. Index; LegalTrac (1980-).

US/0888-9120
JUSTICE FOR CHILDREN. ***Ceased.*** [Justice child.]. Vol. 1, No. 1 (1985)-Vol 2, No. 3 ( ). Periodical. English. qt. Justice for Children, PO Box 42266, Washington DC 20015. **Tel** (202)686-1035. **ED** Janet L Dinsmore. **DD** 346. **Bk Rev. Circ:** 1,000 (ctrl).
Desc: Policies and programs affecting abused and delinquent children. Aimed at juvenile justice and child welfare reform.

US/0161-7109
JUVENILE & FAMILY COURT JOURNAL. [Juv. fam. court j.]. **Added/Corp** National Council of Juvenile and Family Court Judges. **VAT** Juvenile and Family Court Journal. Vol. 29, No. 2 (May 1978)-. Periodical. English. qt (Jan., June, Sept., Dec.). $40.00 US and Canada; $46.00 other; $144.00 combined subscription with Juvenile and Family Law Digest. National Council of Juvenile and Family Court Judges, PO Box 8978, Reno NV 89507. **Tel** (702)784-6012. **ED** Cheri L Briggs. **LC** K10; .U84. **CODEN** JFCJD6. cum. index. **Pr Rev. Circ:** 3,000 (ctrl). available on microfilm. Documents available from The Genuine Article. ***Continues*** *Journal of Juvenile & Family Courts, 0162-0525.*
Desc: Forum of articles centering on juvenile justice issues, usually in the form of several topics per issue. Occasionally, the journal will explore a single topic of current interest to juvenile justice professionals.
Ind/Abst Crim. Justice Abstr.; Crim. Penol. Police Sci. Abstr.; Curr. Contents Soc. Behav. Sci.; Curr. Law Index (1980-); Leg. Resour. Index (1980-); LegalTrac (1980-); Res. Alert [Select. Cov.]; Soc. Sci. Cit. Index [Select. Cov.]; Soc. Work Abstr. [Select. Cov.].

US/0162-9859
JUVENILE AND FAMILY COURT NEWSLETTER. ***Title Change.*** **Added/Corp** National Council of Juvenile and Family Court Judges. Vol. 8 (Feb. 1978)-(199?). Newsletter. English. bm. National Council of Juvenile and Family Court Judges, PO Box 8978, Reno NV 89507. **Tel** (702)784-6012. **ED** Rene Chilton. **LC** KF9772; .J88. **DD** 347/.73/08. **Bk Rev. Ad Acc. Circ:** 2,500 (ctrl). ***Continues*** *Juvenile Court Newsletter.* ***Continued by*** *Juvenile and Family Justice Today, 1062-2926.*
Desc: Concerned with the field of juvenile justice and delinquency. Recurring features include coverage of organizational and membership activities, council programs, and results of studies in the field.

US/0279-2257
JUVENILE AND FAMILY LAW DIGEST. [Juv. fam. law dig.]. **Added/Corp** National Council of Juvenile and Family Court Judges. **VFOAT** Juvenile & Family Law Digest. Vol. 13, No. 7 (July 1981)-. Periodical. English. mo. $120.00 US & Canada; $130.00 other; $144.00 combined subscription with Juvenile and Family Court Journal. National Council of Juvenile and Family Court Judges, PO Box 8978, Reno NV 89507. **Tel** (702)784-6012. **ED** Lindsay G Arthur. **LC** KF9776.3; .J88. **DD** 346.7301/35; 347.306135. Index available. cum. index. **Circ:** 2,500 (ctrl). available in microform from University Microfilms International (UMI). ***Continues*** *Juvenile Law Digest, 0162-5055.*
Desc: A law digest presenting the most recent and precedent setting cases in the juvenile and family courts across the nation.
Ind/Abst Crim. Justice Period. Index.

US/0362-918X
JUVENILE COURT REPORT (LINCOLN). ***Title Change.*** (JUVENILE COURT REPORT.). **Main/Corp** Nebraska Commission on Law Enforcement and Criminal Justice. (1977)-(198?). English. Nebraska Commission on Law Enforcement and Criminal Justice, 301 Centennial Mall South, PO Box 94946, Lincoln NE 68509. **LC** HV7277; .A273. **DD** 364.36/09782. ***Continues*** *Nebraska Commission on Law Enforcement and Criminal Justice. Statistical Analysis Center. Juvenile Court Report, 0362-918X.* ***Continued by*** *Nebraska Juvenile Court Report, 1070-8316.*

US/0095-697X
JUVENILE LAW NEWSLETTER. July 1972-. Newsletter. English. mo. National Juvenile Law Center, 3642 Lindell Boulevard, St. Louis MO 63108. **LC** KF479.A73; J88. **DD** 345/.73/08.

US/0276-9603
JUVENILE LAW REPORTS. Vol. 1 (July 1979)-. Periodical. English. mo. $115.00 US and Canada; $135.00 other. Knehans Miller Publications, PO Box 88, Warrensburg MO 64093. **Tel** (816)429-1102. **ED** Dane C Miller. Index available. cum. index. **Bk Rev. Ad Acc. Circ:** 300 (ctrl).
Desc: In-depth summaries, often with verbatim excerpts, and thorough subject/jurisdiction indexing of all federal and state appellate court decisions dealing with all aspects of juvenile justice and welfare.

UK/0265-1211
LAW REPORTS. CHANCERY DIVISION, FAMILY DIVISION. (THE LAW REPORTS. CHANCERY DIVISION, FAMILY DIVISION.). [Law rep., Chancery Div. Fam. Div.]. **Added/Corp** Great Britain. High Court of Justice. Chancery Division. Great Britain. High Court of Justice. Family Division. Incorporated Council of Law Reporting for England and Wales. **VFOAT** Chancery Division, Family Division; Chancery and Family. (19??)-. Periodical. English. mo. £120.00. Incorporated Council Law Reports, Stone Buildings, Lincoln Inn, London WC2A 3XN England. **Tel** (01)242-6471, FAX (01)831-5247. **ED** Carol Ellis and Alan Bray. Index available. **Ad Acc.**

UK/0264-1119
LAW REPORTS. FAMILY DIVISION. (THE LAW REPORTS. FAMILY DIVISION, AND ON APPEAL THEREFROM IN THE COURT OF APPEAL, AND DECISIONS IN THE ECCLESIASTICAL COURTS.). [Law rep., Fam. Div.]. **Added/Corp** Great Britain. High Court of Justice. Family Division. Great Britain. Court of Appeal. Incorporated Council of Law Reporting for England and Wales. **VFOAT** Family Division, and on Appeal Therefrom in the Court of Appeal, and Decisions in the Ecclesiastical Courts. (1972)-. Periodical. English. ir. £57.00 UK; £60.00 other. Incorporated Council of Law Reporting for England and Wales, 3 Stone Buildings, Lincoln's Inn, London WC2A 3XN England. **Tel** (071)242-6471, FAX (071)831-5247. ***Continues*** *Law Reports. Probate, Divorce, and Admiralty Division, and on Appeal Therefrom in the Court of Appeal, and Decisions in the Ecclesiastical Courts.*

US
MASSACHUSETTS FAMILY LAW JOURNAL, THE. Vol. 1, No. 1 (Apr. 1983)-. Periodical. English. bm. $65.00. Butterworth Heinemann / Woburn, MA, 225 Wildwood Avenue, Unit B, Woburn MA 01801. **Tel** (800)366-2665, FAX (617)928-2620, telex 880052. **LC** KFM2494.A15; M37. **DD** 346.74401/5/05; 347.44061505.

II
MATRIMONIAL LAW REPORTER, THE. English. Rs40.00. Matrimonial Law Reporter, 33/34 Gohale Mkt, Delhi 110006 India. **DD** 346.5401/6/02642.

US/0736-4881
MATRIMONIAL STRATEGIST, THE. [Matrim. strateg.]. **Added/Corp** Leader Publications, Inc. Vol. 1, No. 1 (Feb. 1983)-. Periodical. English. mo. $165.00. Leader Publications, 345 Park Avenue South, New York NY 10010. **Tel** (800)888-8300 ext. 6170, (212)545-6170, FAX (212)696-1848. **ED** Robert K. Collins (editor's phone: (212)564-3700. **LC** KF531.A3; M37. **DD** 346.7301/66/05; 347.30616605. Index available (bound in issue). **Bk Rev. Ad Acc, Adv Mgr:** Nancy Gedder, **Tel** (212)741-8300.
Desc: Strategy and new pieces for the divorce lawyer.

US/0739-4098
MEDIATION QUARTERLY. (MEDIATION QUARTERLY : JOURNAL OF THE ACADEMY OF FAMILY MEDIATORS.). [Mediat. Q.]. **Added/Corp** Academy of Family Mediators (U.S.). **VFOAT** Mediation Quarterly Series. No. 1 (Sept. 1983)-. Periodical. English. qt. $82.00 institutions; $49.00 individuals. Jossey Bass Inc., 350 Sansome Street, San Francisco CA 94104. **Tel** (415)433-1767, FAX (415)433-0499. **ED** Peter R. Maida. **LC** KF9084.A15; M45. **DD** 347.73/9/05; 347.307905. **Circ:** 550 (ctrl). available on microfilm and microfiche from University Microfilms International (UMI).
Desc: Discusses techniques, applications, research, and

theory of mediation as an alternative to litigation and a tool for resolving family-related conflicts.
Ind/Abst Index Period. Artic. Relat. Law; Psychol. Abstr. (1983-); PsycINFO; PsycLit; Sage Fam. Stud. Abstr. (?-?); Soc. Plann. Policy Dev. Abstr.

US/0278-761X
MINNESOTA FAMILY LAW JOURNAL. [Minn. fam. law j.]. Vol. 1, No. 1 (Nov. 1981)-. Periodical. English. ir. Butterworth Heinemann / Woburn, MA, 225 Wildwood Avenue, Unit B, Woburn MA 01801. **Tel** (800)366-2665, FAX (617)928-2620, telex 880052. **LC** KFM5494.A15; M56. **DD** 346.77601/5/05.

US/1049-6319
NEW YORK FAMILY LAW UPDATE. [N. Y. fam. law update]. **Added/Corp** New York Family Law Institute. Vol. 1, No. 1 (May 7, 1990)-. Periodical. English. wk. $190.00 law school libraries; $87.50 state court libraries. New York Family Law Institute, 32 S Monsey Road, Box 774, Monsey NY 10952. **Tel** (914)426-3930. **DD** 347. cum. index. **Circ:** 250 (ctrl).
Desc: Reporting current developments in New York matrimonial and family law (decisional and statutory law) for lawyers, judges and related professionals.

CN/0824-4669
ONTARIO ANNOTATED FAMILY LAW SERVICE (BOUND EDITION). (ONTARIO ANNOTATED FAMILY LAW SERVICE.). [Ont. annot. fam. law serv.]. (197?)-. English. ir. 330.00Can$. Butterworth & Company Ltd. / Canada, 75 Clegg Road, Markham Ontario L6G 1A1 Canada. **Tel** (905)479-2665, (800)668-6481. **(Subscription address:** Butterworth Heinemann Publishers, 225 Wildwood Avenue, Unit B, Woburn MA 01801.) **ED** Donna M. Ford. **DD** 346.71301/5/02638.
Desc: Provides up-to-date information on Ontario and federal family law statutes and regulations complete with legislative history, forms and case law annotations.

CN/0835-636X
ONTARIO FAMILY LAW REPORTER. [Ont. fam. law report.]. Vol. 1, Issue 1 (July 1987)-. Periodical. English. mo. 190.00Can$. Butterworth & Company Ltd. / Canada, 75 Clegg Road, Markham Ontario L6G 1A1 Canada. **Tel** (905)479-2665, (800)668-6481. **DD** 346/71301/5/02642. cum. index. ***Continues*** *Family Law Reform Reporter, 0706-5647.*
Desc: Offers lengthy digests of key unreported decisions on all aspects of family law.

AU
OSTERREICHISCHE AMTSVORMUND, DER. **Added/Corp** Verein der Amtsvormunder Osterreichs. (19??)-. Periodical. German. Six times a year. S60.00. Verein der Amtsvormunder Osterreichs, Alserbachstrasse 41, Postfach 28, 1091 Vienna Austria. **Tel** (0222)343600. **LC** K15; .S77. **Bk Rev. Ad Acc. Circ:** 10,000 (ctrl).
Desc: The one and only journal for youth, family, marriage and official guardians affairs and the positions of the dedicated law.

●US
PRACTICE UNDER THE CALIFORNIA FAMILY CODE : DISSOLUTION, LEGAL SEPARATION, NULLITY. (1994)-. English. $120.00. California Continuing Education of the Bar, 2300 Shattuck Avenue, Berkeley CA 94704. **Tel** (510)642-8000, (800)232-3444. **ED** M. Dee Samuels, Frederick Mandabach. ***Continues*** *Practice under the California Family Law Act.*

US/0148-9763
PRACTICING FAMILY LAWYER, THE. v. 1- Spring 1977-. Periodical. English. qt. $37.00. The Practicing Family Lawyer Inc, 3711 Long Beach Boulevard, PO Box 7888, Long Beach CA 90807. **LC** KFC115.A15; P7.

US/0899-0808
RECENT TITLES IN LAW FOR THE SUBJECT SPECIALIST. FAMILY LAW AND SOCIAL WELFARE. (RECENT TITLES IN LAW FOR THE SPECIALIST. FAMILY LAW AND SOCIAL WELFARE.). [Recent titles law subj. spec., Fam. law soc. welf.]. **VFOAT** Family Law and Social Welfare. Vol. 5, No. 1 (Jan.-Mar. 1988)-. Periodical. English. qt. $85.00. William S. Hein & Company Inc., 1285 Main Street, Buffalo NY 14209. **Tel** (716)882-2600, (800)828-7571, FAX (716)883-8100, telex 91-209 WM S HEIN BUF. **DD** 016. ***Continues*** *National Legal Bibliography. Subject Area List. Family Law and Social Welfare, 8755-805X.*

CN/0832-8927
RECUEIL DE DROIT DE LA FAMILLE. [Recl. droit fam.]. **Added/Corp** Societe Quebecoise d'Information Juridique. Vol. 1 (1986)-. Periodical. French. Four times a year (Mar., May, Sept., Nov.). 160.00Can$ (latest edition). Societe Quebecoise d'Information Juridique, 10 rue St Jacques Bureau 101, Montreal Quebec H2Y 1L3 Canada. **Tel** (514)842-8745, FAX (514)844-8984. **DD** 346.71401/5/02648.
Ind/Abst Can. Legal Lit.

CN/0317-4859
REPORTS OF FAMILY LAW. [Rep. fam. law]. **Added/Corp** Carswell Company. (1971)-. Periodical. English (French). ir. $118.00. Carswell / Canada, 2075 Kennedy Road, Scarborough Ontario M1T 3V4 Canada. **Tel** (416)609-3800, (800)387-5164. **ED** James G. McLeod. **DD** 346/.71/01502642. Index available. cum. index. **Ad Acc.**
Desc: A series introduced to coincide with provincial family law legislation.
Ind/Abst Can. Legal Lit.; Curr. Law Index (1980-); Index Can. Leg. Period. Lit.; Leg. Resour. Index (1980-?); LegalTrac (1981-).

BE
REVUE TRIMESTRIELLE DE DROIT FAMILIAL. (1978)-. French. qt. 3000F Belgium; (add 400F postage) Europe; (add 400F surface mail, 700F airmail postage) other. De Boeck Wesmael SA, Fond Jean Paques 4, 1348 Louvain La Neuve Belgium. **Tel** 011 32 10 482509, FAX 32 (0) 2 6273650. cum. index.

US/0890-5355
TENNESSEE FAMILY LAW LETTER. [Tenn. fam. law lett.]. **VFOAT** Family Law Letter. Vol. 1, No. 1 (Nov. 1986)-. Periodical. English. mo. $80.00. M. Lee Smith Publishers and Printers, 162 4th Avenue North, PO Box 198867, Nashville TN 37219. **Tel** (615)242-7395, (800)274-6774, FAX (615)256-6601. **LC** KFT94.A59; T46. **DD** 346.76801/5/05; 347.68061505. Index available. cum. index. ctrl circ.

US/0743-9342
TEXAS FAMILY LAW REPORTER. [Tex. fam. law rep.]. Vol. 1, No. 1 (Aug. 1983)-. Periodical. English. mo. $120.00. Matthew Bender & Company Inc., 1275 Broadway, Albany NY 12204. **Tel** (800)833-9844, (518)487-3000.

NE
TIJDSCHRIFT VOOR FAMILIE- EN JEUGDRECHT. **Added/Corp** Vereniging Familie- en Jeugdrecht (Netherlands). **VFOAT** Familie- en Jeugdrecht. (Jan. 1979)-. Periodical. Dutch. Eleven times a year. $50.00. W. E. J. Tjeenk Willink, Box 25, 8000 AA Zwolle Netherlands. **Tel** 011 31 38 228819, 011 31 38 211444. **LC** K24; .I373. Index available. **Bk Rev. Ad Acc.** ctrl circ.

●US
UNIVERSITY OF LOUISVILLE JOURNAL OF FAMILY LAW. **Added/Corp** University of Louisville. School of Law. International Society on Family Law. **VFOAT** Journal of Family Law. Vol. 31, No. 1 (Winter Issue 1992-93)-. Periodical. English. Four times a year (Feb., May, Aug., Nov.). $30.00. University of Louisville School of Law, Louisville KY 40292. **Tel** (502)852-6396. **LC** K10; .086. **DD** 346.7301/5/05; 347.3061505. **CODEN** UJFLE7. Documents available from Documents on Demand. ***Continues*** *Journal of Family Law, 0022-1066.*
Ind/Abst Curr. Law Index; Energy Inf. Abstr.; Environ. Abstr.; Index Leg. Period.; Leg. Resour. Index; Soc. Sci. Cit. Index [Full Cov.]; Sociol. Abstr.; Women Stud. Abstr.

US/0739-4179
WASHINGTON MEMO. [Wash. memo - Alan Guttmacher Inst.]. **Added/Corp** Alan Guttmacher Institute. Planned Parenthood-World Population (U.S.). (1968)-. Periodical. English. Twenty times a year. $45.00 (institutions), $35.00 (individuals) US; $60.00 others. Alan Guttmacher Institute, 120 Wall Street, New York NY 10005. **Tel** (212)248-1111, FAX (212)248-1951.
Desc: Delivers information and insights on reproductive health policy development. Includes such issues as: the impact of health care reform on family planning clinics; debates over abortion rights and the introduction of RU 486; teenage pregnancy, STD and HIV prevention initiatives; US population assistance to developing nations; and research into infertility and new contraceptives.

CN/0713-7907
WEEKLY DIGEST OF FAMILY LAW. [Wkly. dig. fam. law]. **Added/Corp** Carswell Legal Publications. Issue No. 1 (Jan. 4, 1982)-. Periodical. English. Fifty times a year. Carswell / Canada, 2075 Kennedy Road, Scarborough Ontario M1T 3V4 Canada. **Tel** (416)609-3800, (800)387-5164. **ED** Brenda-Jean Currie. **LC** PAR. **DD** 346.7101/5/02648. Index available. cum. index.
Desc: Contains case summaries of all available family law and young offenders judgments from courts across Canada.

US
WOMEN'S ADVOCATE (NEW YORK, N.Y.). (THE WOMEN'S ADVOCATE : NEWSLETTER OF THE NATIONAL CENTER ON WOMEN AND FAMILY LAW.). **Added/Corp** National Center on Women and Family Law (U.S.). (19??)-. Periodical. English. bm (Jan., Mar., May, July, Sep., Nov.). $30.00. National Center on Women & Family Law, 799 Broadway, Room 402, New York NY 10003. **Tel** (212)674-8200, FAX (212)533-5104. **ED** Laurie Woods. **Bk Rev**, (Qty: 20). **Circ:** 3,700.
Desc: This newsletter discusses legal developments and emerging trends in such areas as domestic violence, intrafamaily custody, child support, wife supports, the rights of single mothers, divorce, child-snatching, rape, incest, and legal safeguards for older women.

US/0882-8520
YOUTH LAW NEWS. [Youth law news]. **Added/Corp** National Center for Youth Law (U.S.). (198?)-. Periodical. English. Six times a year. $95.00 (institutions), $40.00 (individuals). National Center for Youth Law, 114 Sansome Street, Suite 900, San Francisco CA 94104. **Tel** (415)543-3307. **ED** Marcia Henry. **LC** KF3731.A3; Y68. **DD** 344.73/0327/05; 347.30432705. Index available (pubd seperately and is free). cum. index. **Bk Rev**, (Qty: 4/yr). **Circ:** 2,500.
Desc: Journal of the national center for youth law, providing by-monthly coverage of significant legal developments affecting poor children throughout the country.

GW/0044-2410
ZEITSCHRIFT FUER DAS GESAMTE FAMILIENRECHT. Vol. 9 (Jan. 1967)-. Periodical. German. Twenty-six times a year. DM270.00 Germany; DM300.00 others. Verlag E & W Gieseking GmbH, Postfach 130120, Deckerstrasse 30, D-33544 Bielefeld 13 Germany. **Tel** 011 49 521 14674. **[CCC]. *Continues*** *EHE und Familie in Privaten und Offentlichen Recht.*
Ind/Abst Index Foreign Leg. Per.

GW/0176-6449
ZENTRALBLATT FUER JUGENDRECHT. Periodical. German. mo. Carl Heymanns Verlag KG, Luxemburger Strasse 449, D 50939 Cologne Germany. **Tel** 011 49 221 460100, telex 8 881 888. **LC** KK1192.A13; Z46. **DD** 346.4301/35/05. ***Continues*** *Zentralblatt fur Jugendrecht und Jugendwohlfahrt.*
Ind/Abst Crim. Penol. Police Sci. Abstr.

INTERNATIONAL LAW

US/0567-5111
ABOGADA INTERNACIONAL. THE INTERNATIONAL WOMAN LAWYER, LA. **Added/Corp** International Federation of Women Lawyers. **VFOAT** International Woman Lawyer. First issued in (1953)-. Periodical. Spanish. an. $1.00. International Federation of Women Lawyers, 815 Broadway, Brooklyn NY 11206. **Tel** (212)227-8339.
Ind/Abst Hum. Rights Intern. Rep.

HU
ACTA JURIDICA HUNGARICA / HUNGARIAN JOURNAL OF LEGAL STUDIES. **Added/Corp** Magyar Tudomanyos Akademia. **VFOAT** Hungarian Journal of Legal Studies. Vol. 33, No. 1/2 (1991)-. Academic Scholarly Publication. English. Four times a year. $92.00. Akademiai Kiado, Publishing House of the Hungarian Academy of Sciences, Prielle Kornelia u. 19-35, H-1117 Budapest Hungary. **Tel** 011 36 1 1811991, FAX 011 36 1 1811991, telex 22-6228 AKNYO H. **LC** K1; .C67. ***Continues*** *Acta Juridica.*
Ind/Abst Foreign Lang. Index (1991-); PAIS Bull. (1991-); PAIS Foreign Lang. Index (1991-); Public Aff. Inf. Serv. Bull. (1991-).

FR/1011-923X
ACTUALITES COMMUNAUTAIRES. [Actual. communaut.]. (1986)-. Periodical. French. Eleven times a year. 734.57F France; 750.00F other. Juridictionnaires Joly, 1 Av Franklin D. Roosevelt, F 75008 Paris France. **Tel** 011 33 1 42254740, FAX 011 33 1 45638939. **UDC** 33(4). ***Continues*** *Notes d'Informations Communautaires, 0339-6460.*

GW
AFRICAN INTERNATIONAL ORGANIZATION DIRECTORY, AND AFRICAN PARTICIPATION IN OTHER INTERNATIONAL ORGANIZATIONS. 1st Ed. (1984/85)-. Directory. English (French). ir. K.G. Saur Verlag KG, A Reed Reference Publishing Company, Part of Reed International PLC, Ortlerstrasse 8, D 81373 Munich Germany. **Tel** 011 49 89 769020, FAX 011 49 89 76902150, telex 5212067-SAUR-D. **LC** JX1995; .A444. **DD** 341.2/025/6.

UK/0954-8890
AFRICAN JOURNAL OF INTERNATIONAL AND COMPARATIVE LAW. **Added/Corp** African Society of International and Comparative Law. **VFOAT** Revue Africaine de Droit International et Compare. Vol. 1, Pt. 1 (March 1989)-. Periodical. English (French). qt (Mar., June, Oct., Dec.). £60.00. African Society of International and Comparative Law, Aberdeen House 22 Highbury Grove, London N5 2EA England. **Tel** 011 44 71 7040610. **LC** K1; .F68. **DD** 340/.2; 342.

UK/1011-663X
AFRICAN JOURNAL OF INTERNATIONAL LAW, THE. **Added/Corp** International Society of African Lawyers. **VFOAT** Journal

Africain de Droit International. Vol. 1, No. 1 (Summer 1988)-. Periodical. English (French). ir. Price varies. International Society of African Lawyers, 9 Stone Building, Lincolns Inns, London WC2 3TA England. **(Subscription address:** WM. W. Gaunt & Sons Inc, 3011 Gulf Drive, Gaunt Building, Holmes Beach FL 34217.) **LC** K1; .F69. **DD** 341/.05.
Ind/Abst Hum. Rights Intern. Rep.

CN/0847-9798
AGIR (MONTREAL). (AGIR.). [Agir]. **Added/Corp** Amnistie Internationale. Section Canadienne Francophone. Vol. 10, No 1 (Apr. 1989)-. Periodical. French. Four times a year (Mar., June, Sept., Dec.). 30.00Can$. Amnistie Internationale, 6250 Boulevard Monk, Montreal Quebec H4E 3H7 Canada. **Tel** (514)766-9766, FAX (514)766-2088, telex 055/60543. **DD** 364.1/3/05. **Bk Rev**, (Qty: 1-2). **Circ:** 30,000. ***Continues*** *Communications (Amnistie Internationale. Section Canadienne Francophone)., 0226-3556.*

US/0898-1663
AILA MONTHLY MAILING. [AILA mon. mail.]. **Added/Corp** American Immigration Lawyers Association. **VFOAT** Monthly Mailing. **VAT** American Immigration Lawyers Association Monthly Mailing. (198?)-. English. Eleven times a year. $195.00. American Immigration Lawyers Association, 1400 I Street Northwest, Suite 1200, Washington DC 20005. **Tel** (202)371-9377. **LC** KF4802; .A38. **DD** 342.73/082; 347.30282.
Desc: Digest of immigration related cases, legislation and regulations.

US
AMERICAN BAR, THE CANADIAN BAR, THE INTERNATIONAL BAR, THE. English. an. $180.00. Forster Long Inc, 3280 Ramos Circle, Sacramento CA 95827. **Tel** (916)362-3276, FAX 916362-5643. **ED** Marie Hough. **Circ:** 33,000 (ctrl).
Desc: Professional directory of lawyers of the world containing over 64,000 lawyers annually investigated with regard to legal ability, character and diligence.

US/0002-919X
AMERICAN JOURNAL OF COMPARATIVE LAW, THE. [Am. j. comp. law]. **Added/Corp** American Association for the Comparative Study of Law. Vol. 1 (Winter/Spring 1952)-. Periodical. English. qt. $30.00. American Journal of Comparative Law, 327 Boalt Hall, University of California, Berkeley CA 94720. **Tel** (510)643-6115. **ED** John G. Fleming. **LC** K1; .M439. **DD** 341. Index available in last issue of volume--attached. cum. index. **Pr Rev.** available on microfilm and microfiche from University Microfilms International (UMI). Documents available from The Genuine Article.
Ind/Abst ABC POL SCI; Am. Bibliogr. Slavic East Europ. Stud.; Bowne Dig. Corp. Sec. Lawyers; Crim. Penol. Police Sci. Abstr.; Curr. Contents Soc. Behav. Sci.; Curr. Law Index (1980-); Fed. Tax Artic.; Index Foreign Leg. Per.; Index Leg. Period.; Int. Labour Doc.; LABORDOC; Leg. Resour. Index (1980-); LegalTrac (1980-); PAIS Int. Print (1991-); Res. Alert [Full Cov.]; Soc. Sci. Cit. Index [Full Cov.]; U.S. Polit. Sci. Doc.; Women Stud. Abstr.

US/0002-9300
AMERICAN JOURNAL OF INTERNATIONAL LAW, THE. [Am. j. int. law]. **Added/Corp** American Society of International Law. Vol. 1 (Jan. 1907)-. Periodical. English. Four times a year (Jan., Apr., July, Oct.). $120.00 US; $135.00 other. American Society of International Law, 2223 Massachusetts Avenue Northwest, Washington DC 20008-2864. **Tel** (202)939-6000, FAX (202)797-7133. **ED** Theodor Meron and Detlev F. Vogts. **LC** JX1; .A6. **DD** 341.05. **[CCC].** Index available (bound in Oct. issue). cum. index. **Bk Rev. Ad Acc. Circ:** 8,000. available on microfilm and microfiche from University Microfilms International (UMI); available on CD-ROM from University Microfilms International (UMI). Documents available from The Genuine Article, UMI Article Clearinghouse. ***Absorbed*** *Proceedings of the American Society of International Law at its Annual Meeting, 0272-5045.* ***Superseded in part by*** *Proceedings of the Annual Meeting - American Society of International Law, 0272-5037.*
Desc: Articles, editorials, judicial decisions and book reviews provide an indispensable source of current thought, trends and material affecting international law and regulations for the layman and the professional.
Ind/Abst ABC POL SCI; Acad. Abstr. Full Text Elite (July 1990-); Acad. Abstr. (July 1990-); Acad. Search (July 1990-); Account. Art.; Am. Hist. Life (1954-1973); Am. Bibliogr. Slavic East Europ. Stud.; Bowne Dig. Corp. Sec. Lawyers; Bus. Source (Jul. 1990-); Curr. Contents Soc. Behav. Sci.; Curr. Law Index (1980-); Expand. Acad. Index (1984-); Hum. Rights Intern. Rep.; Index Foreign Leg. Per. (1954-); Index Leg. Period.; INFO-SOUTH Abstr.; Int. Labour Doc.; Int. Polit. Sci. Abstr. (1980-); J. Plan. Lit.; Leg. Inf. Manage. Index; Leg. Resour. Index (1980-); LegalTrac (1954-, 1980); Mag. Search; Middle East Abstr. Index; Newsp. Period. Abstr. (1989-); PAIS Int. Print (1991-); Peace Res. Abstr. J. (1967-1970); Res. Alert [Full Cov.]; Soc. Sci. Source (Jul. 1990-); Soc. Sci. Cit. Index [Full Cov.]; Soc. Sci. Index; Soc. Sci. Index Fulltext (Oct. 1988-) [Full Txt.]; U.S. Polit. Sci. Doc. (1954-).

US/0888-630X
AMERICAN UNIVERSITY JOURNAL OF INTERNATIONAL LAW AND POLICY, THE. [Am. Univ. j. int. law policy]. **VFOAT** Journal of International Law and Policy. Vol. 1 (Summer 1986)-. Periodical. English. qt. $22.00 US; $25.00 other. Washington College of Law, 4410 Massachusetts Avenue NW, Washington DC 20016. **Tel** (202)885-2652, FAX (202)885-1039. **ED** Charles Cole. **LC** JX1; .A75. **DD** 341/.05. **Ad Acc. Pr Rev. Circ:** 900.
Desc: A unique journal focusing on the development of important Washington-based organizations, private international law, public international law, and comparative international law.
Ind/Abst Index Leg. Period.; Leg. Resour. Index; LegalTrac (1980-).

BB
ANGUILLA CONSOLIDATED INDEX OF STATUTES AND SUBSIDIARY LEGISLATION TO ... . **Added/Corp** University of the West Indies (Cave Hill, Barbados). Faculty of Law. University of the West Indies (Cave Hill, Barbados). Faculty of Law. Library. **VFOAT** Consolidated Index of Statutes and Subsidiary Legislation to ... . (19??)-. English. an. $20.00. Faculty of Law Library, PO Box 64, Bridgetown Barbados. **Tel** (813)778-5211. **ED** Clifford Hammett. **LC** KGJ7010.5; .A54. **DD** 348.7297/3028; 347.29730828. **Bk Rev. Ad Acc. Circ:** 250.
Desc: Contains titles of current laws in the territory concerned with references to the amendments to and subsidiary legislation made under each statute.

CN/0701-158X
ANNALS OF AIR AND SPACE LAW. [Ann. Air Space Law]. **VFOAT** Annales de Droit Aerien et Spatial. V. 1- 1976-. English (French). an. $55.00 (Vol. 1-4), $67.00 (Vol. 5-15), $870.00 (set). Centre for Research of Air and Space Law, McGill University, 3690 Peel Street, Montreal Quebec H3A 1W9 Canada. **Tel** (514)398-3544, FAX (514)398-4659. **ED** Nicolas M Matte. **LC** K1; .N5. **DD** 341.45/05. Index available. cum. index. **Bk Rev. Circ:** 1,000 (ctrl).
Desc: Gathers articles of worldwide prominent scholars, practitioners and other specialists in air and space law. It deals with topics of current interest and problems of growing concern related to emerging air and space activities.
Ind/Abst Can. Legal Lit.; Curr. Law Index (1980-); Index Can. Leg. Period. Lit.; Index Foreign Leg. Per.; Index Leg. Period.; Leg. Resour. Index (1980-); LegalTrac (1980-).

FR/0066-2658
ANNUAIRE DE LEGISLATION FRANCAISE ET ETRANGERE / PUBLIE PAR LE CENTRE FRANCAIS DE DROIT COMPAREE. ***Ceased.*** **Added/Corp** Centre Francais de Droit Compare. Centre National de la Recherche Scientifique (France) Centre National de la Recherche Scientifique (France). Service de Recherches Juridiques Comparatives. Centre National de la Recherche Scientifique (France). Institut de Recherches Juridiques Comparatives. New Series Vol. 5 (Yearly 1956)-(199?). French. an. Les Presses du CNRS, 22 rue Saint Amand, 75015 Paris France. **Tel** 45 33 16 00, telex 200 356 F. **Circ:** 1,500. ***Continues*** *Annuaire de Legislation Etrangere.*
Desc: The evolution of law in different countries seen through legislation in France and elsewhere.

FR
ANNUAIRE DE L'INSTITUT DE DROIT INTERNATIONAL. **Main/Corp** Institute of International Law. **Added/Corp** Institute of International Law. Yearbook. **VFOAT** Annuaire; Yearbook. (1877)-. French. ir. Price varies per volume. Editions A Pedone, 13 rue Soufflot, 75005 Paris France. **Tel** 011 33 1 43540597.

NE/0071-3139
ANNUAIRE EUROPEEN. **Added/Corp** Council of Europe. **VFOAT** European Yearbook. Vol. 1 (1955)-. English (French). an. Fl29.95. Martinus Nijhoff Publishers, Subsidiary of Kluwer Academic Publishers, Koraalrood 50, 2718 SC Zoetermeer Netherlands. **Tel** 011 31 79 684400. **ED** A Kiss and J G Lammers. **LC** JN3; .A5. **DD** 341.24/2. **NLM** JN 3 A615.
Desc: Aims to maintain intellectual and friendly attenders and alumni of the Hague Academy of International Law. Attempts to develop international consciousness.
Ind/Abst Index Foreign Leg. Per.

FR/0066-3085
ANNUAIRE FRANCAIS DE DROIT INTERNATIONAL. [Annu. fr. droit int.]. **Added/Corp** Centre National de la Recherche Scientifique (France) Hague Academy of International Law. Groupe Francais des Anciens Auditeurs. Faculte de Droit et des Sciences Economiques de Paris. Universite de Droit, d'Economie et de Sciences Sociales de Paris. Vol. 1 (1955)-. Monographic series. French. an. price varies per volume. Editions du CNRS, 22 rue Saint Armand, F 75015 Paris France. **Tel** 011 33 1 45075050. **(Subscription address:** CNRS Editions, 20-22 rue Saint Amand, c/o Mme. Bodet, 75015 Paris France.) **LC** JX21; .A63. **Circ:** 1,500.
Desc: Legal analyses of international events, treaties and judicial rulings. Focuses on such topics as human rights, actions of the United Nations, the nuclear arms race, and international crimes.
Ind/Abst Index Foreign Leg. Per.; Int. Labour Doc.; Int. Polit. Sci. Abstr.; LABORDOC.

US/0078-6403
ANNUAL REPORT OF THE SECRETARY GENERAL TO THE GENERAL ASSEMBLY. (ANNUAL REPORT.). **Main/Corp** Organization of American States. Secretary General. **Added/Corp** Organization of American States. General Secretariat. **VFOAT** Annual Report of the Secretary General - Organization of American States. (19??)-. English. an. Organization of American States, 19th Street & Constitution Avenue NW, Suite 300, Washington DC 20006. **Tel** (202)458-6256. **LC** F1402.A4; S4. **DD** 341.187. **NLM** W1 OR663FH.

US
ANNUAL REPORT / UNICEF. **Main/Corp** UNICEF. English. an. UNICEF / New York, 866 United Nations Plaza, New York NY 10017. **LC** HV1; .U62A. **DD** 341.7/66. **NLM** W2; MU8 U3u.

US/0739-5353
ANNUAL REPORT - UNITED STATES. FOREIGN CLAIMS SETTLEMENT COMMISSION. ***Title Change.*** (ANNUAL REPORT / FOREIGN CLAIMS SETTLEMENT COMMISSION OF THE UNITED STATES.). [Annu. rep. - U. S., Foreign Claims Settlement Comm.]. **Main/Corp** United States. Foreign Claims Settlement Commission. **VFOAT** F.C.S.C. Ann. Rep.; FCSC Ann. Rep. (1981)-(198?). English. an. Foreign Claims Settlement Commission, 1111 20th Street NW, Washington DC 20579. **LC** KF6074; .A84. **DD** 346.7303/6/0264; 347.306360264. available on microfiche (Vols. for (1985) - distributed to depository libraries). ***Continues*** *United States. Foreign Claims Settlement Commission. Annual Report to the Congress for the Period ..., 0565-5587.* ***Continued by*** *United States. Foreign Claims Settlement Commission. Annual Report to Congress for ... .*

US/1040-824X
ANNUAL REVIEW OF OCEAN AFFAIRS--LAW & POLICY, MAIN DOCUMENTS. (ANNUAL REVIEW OF OCEAN AFFAIRS : LAW AND POLICY, MAIN DOCUMENTS / COMPILED AND EDITED BY THE UNITED NATIONS OFFICE FOR OCEAN AFFAIRS AND THE LAW OF THE SEA.). [Annu. rev. ocean aff.--Law policy main doc.]. **Added/Corp** United Nations. Office for Ocean Affairs and the Law of the Sea. UNIFO Publishers. United Nations. Division for Ocean Affairs and the Law of the Sea. **VFOAT** Law of the Sea : Annual Review of Ocean Affairs. (1985-1987)-. Government Publication. English. an. $75.00. United Nations Publications, 2 United Nations Plaza, Room DC2 0853, Department 007C, New York NY 10017. **Tel** (212)963-8303, (800)253-9646. **LC** JX4408; .A56. **DD** 341.7/566.
Desc: Gives and overview of developments and outlines the activities of the Office of Ocean Affairs and the Law of the Sea in its efforts for protection and preservation.

US
ANNUAL SUMMARY OF LAWS AND REGULATIONS RELATING TO THE CONTROL OF NARCOTIC DRUGS. **Main/Corp** United Nations. Commission on Narcotic Drugs. (1947)-. English. United Nations / Commission on Narcotic Drugs, New York NY 10017. **Tel** (212)754-8302. **LC** JX1977; .A2. **DD** 614.3; 178.8.
Desc: Some years accompanied by Corrigenda.

IT/0003-5149
ANNUARIO DI DIRITTO COMPARATO E DI STUDI LEGISLATIVI. (ANNUARIO DI DIRITTO COMPARATO E DI STUDI LEGISLATIVI / A CURA DEL PROF. SALVATORE GALGANO.). [Annu. dir. comp. studi legis.]. **VFOAT** Collana della Ricostruzione dell'Annuarion di Diritto Comparato e di Studi Legislativi; Yearbook of Comparative Law and Legislative Studies. Vol. 1 (1927)-. Italian (English, French and German). Twice a year. L90000. Maggioli Editore, Casella Postale 290, 47037 Rimini, Italy. **Tel** 011 39 541 628666, FAX 011 39 541 742217.
Ind/Abst Index Foreign Leg. Per.

AT/1034-361X
ANTARCTIC AND SOUTHERN OCEANS LAW AND POLICY OCCASIONAL PAPERS. [Antarct. s. oceans law policy occas. pap.]. **VFOAT** ASOLP Occasional Papers. (1989)-. Monographic series. English. ir. 25.00Aus$ Australia; 30.00Aus$ other. University of Tasmania, PO Box 1214, Launceston 7250 Australia. **Tel** 011 61 3 243013, FAX 011 61 2 207623, telex 58150. **(Subscription address:** University of Tasmania / Law School, c/o David McGuire, Publications Manager, GPO Box 252C, Hobart Tasmania 7001 Australia.) **DD** 341.29. **Ad Acc, Adv Mgr:** David McGuire.
Desc: Series aimed at encouraging research and providing a forum for public discussion of law and policy issues relating to the Antarctic and southern oceans.

BB
ANTIGUA & BARBUDA CONSOLIDATED INDEX TO STATUTES AND SUBSIDIARY LEGISLATION TO ... . **Added/Corp** University of the West Indies (Cave Hill, Barbados). Faculty of Law. Library. **VFOAT** Consolidated Index of Statutes and Subsidiary Legislation to ...; Antigua and Barbuda Consolidated Index of Statutes and Subsidiary Legislation to ... . (19??)-. English. an. $20.00. Faculty of Law Library, PO Box 64, Bridgetown Barbados. **Tel** (813)778-5211. **ED** Clifford Hammett. **LC** KGK10.5; .A55. **DD** 348.7297/4028; 347.29740828. **Bk Rev. Ad Acc. Circ:** 250. ***Continues*** *Antiqua Consolidated Index of Statutes and Subsidiary Legislation to ... .*
Desc: Contains titles of current laws in the territory concerned with references to the amendments to and subsidiary legislation made under each statute.

SP/0212-0747
ANUARIO DE DERECHO INTERNACIONAL. ***Suspended.*** [Anu. derecho int.]. Began 1974-Suspended. Academic Scholarly Publication. Spanish. an. 2500ptas Spain; $30.00 US. Ediciones Universidad de Navarra SA, Plaza Los Sauces, Apartado 396, 31080 Baranain Pamplona Spain. **Tel** (48)25 68 50, FAX (948)173650, telex 37917 UNAV E. **ED** Jose Antonio Corriente Cordoba. **LC** JX9; .A59. **Bk Rev. Ad Acc. Circ:** 100 (ctrl).
Desc: Scholarly publication whose objective is to offer to law professionals and to the general public interested in international law a series of studies, chronicles and documentation of current interest and serious practical usefulness.
Ind/Abst Index Foreign Leg. Per.

SP/0570-4316
ANUARIO HISPANO-LUSO-AMERICANO DE DERECHO INTERNACIONAL. [Anu. hisp.-luso-am. derecho int.]. Vol. 1 (1959)-. Spanish. ir. **LC** JX84; .A56.
Ind/Abst Index Foreign Leg. Per.

US
ANUARIO JURIDICO INTERAMERICANO. ***Suspended.*** **VFOAT** Inter-American Juridical Yearbook; Annuaire Juridique Interamericain. (1948)-(1986). Multiple languages (English, French, Portuguese and Spanish). Organization of American States, 19th Street & Constitution Avenue NW, Suite 300, Washington DC 20006. **Tel** (202)458-6256.
Ind/Abst Index Foreign Leg. Per.

•UK/0965-7053
ARBITRATION AND DISPUTE RESOLUTION LAW JOURNAL, THE. [Arbitr. disput. resolut. law j.]. (1992)-. Periodical. English. qt. £81.00. Lloyd's of London Press Ltd, Sheepen Place, Colchester, Essex, CO3 3LP England. **Tel** 011 44 206 772113, US: (212)529-9500, US: (800)955-6937, FAX 011 44 206 772880, US: (212)529-9826, telex 987321 LLOYDS G. **(Subscription address:** Lloyd's of London Press Inc. / North America, 611 Broadway, Suite 308, New York NY 10012.) **ED** Andrew Burr. **DD** 342.79. **Bk Rev. Circ:** 250. available in bound issues.
Desc: Strives to answer the need for a practical and authoritative regular information source to keep those involved abreast of developments, from major legislative changes to particular commercial problems. Feature articles provide discussion of on-going problems as well as an analysis of topical issues. Case notes cover all commercial areas, including insurance, construction, engineering etc. The information section reports on current developments, the activities of arbital and dispute resolution organizations and forthcoming events.

UK/0957-0411
ARBITRATION INTERNATIONAL. [Arbitr. int.]. **Added/Corp** Chartered Institute of Arbitrators (Great Britain) London Court of International Arbitration. Vol. 1, No. 1 (April 1985)-. Periodical. English. qt. $426.00. Graham & Trotman Ltd, Sterling House, 66 Wilson Road, London SW1V 1DE England. **Tel** 44 71 8211123. **ED** Jan Paulsson, Anthony Guest, V. Veeder, Ronald Goodman, and Rhidian Thomas. **LC** K1; .R248. **DD** 341.5/22. **Bk Rev. Pr Rev. Acid Free.**
Desc: Designed to meet the needs of lawyers and others engaged in the development and widespread application of international arbitration as a means of international commercial dispute resolution.

GW/0003-892X
ARCHIV DES VOLKERRECHTS. [Arch. Volkerr.]. Vol. 1, (July 1948)-. Periodical. German (English). qt. DM272.00. JCB Mohr / Paul Siebeck, Postfach 2040, D 72010 Tuebingen Germany. **Tel** 011 49 7071 9230, FAX 011 49 7071 51104, telex 7/262872 mohr d. **ED** Ingo von Munch, Otto Kimminich, Philip Kunig and Walter Rudolf. **LC** JX5; .A58. **[CCC].** cum. index. **Bk Rev. Ad Acc. Circ:** 800.
Desc: Publishing analysis, comments, reports and court decisions on international public law.
Ind/Abst ABC POL SCI; Am. Hist. Life (1973-); Index Foreign Leg. Per.; Int. Bibliogr. Sociol.; Int. Polit. Sci. Abstr.

FR/0181-009X
ARES (LYON, FRANCE). (ARES.). Vol. 1 (1977)-. French. Three times a year. Presses Universite de Grenoble, BP 47, 38040 Grenoble, Cedex 9 France. **Tel** 011 33 76 825651, 825652. **LC** JX1952; .A7826. **DD** 355/.03.

US/0743-6963
ARIZONA JOURNAL OF INTERNATIONAL AND COMPARATIVE LAW. [Ariz. j. int. comp. law]. **VFOAT** Revista de Derecho Internacional y Comparado de Arizona. Vol. 1, No. 1-. Periodical. English (Spanish and Portuguese). sa. $38.50 (per vol.), $272.00 (set). University of Arizona College of Law, Tucson AZ 85721. **Tel** (602)621-5593. **ED** Kenneth Love. **LC** K1; .R477. **DD** 340/.05. **Bk Rev. Ad Acc. Circ:** 250. available in microform.
Desc: Articles authored by legal scholars, lawyers, and law students that provide practical and comparative information on legal matters pertaining to the United States and Latin America.
Ind/Abst Curr. Law Index (1982-); Index Leg. Period.; Leg. Resour. Index (1982-); LegalTrac (1982-); PAIS Int. Print.

US/0196-125X
ARMS CONTROL TODAY. (ARMS CONTROL TODAY : A PUBLICATION OF THE ARMS CONTROL ASSOCIATION.). [Arms control today]. **Added/Corp** Arms Control Association (Washington, D.C.). (1974)-. Periodical. English. Ten times a year. $20.00 (students), $40.00 (members); $40.00 (individuals), $50.00 (institutions) US; $50.00 others. Arms Control Association, 1726 M Street Northwest, Suite 201, Washington DC 20036. **Tel** (202)463-8270, FAX (202)463-8273. **ED** John Schulz. **LC** JX1974; .A76928. **DD** 327.1/74/05. Each issue contains an index to its own contents (no volume index)--loose. cum. index (missed in 1992). **Bk Rev**, (Qty: 8-10). **Ad Acc, Adv Mgr:** Tom Pfieffer. **Circ:** 5,000. Documents available from UMI Article Clearinghouse. ***Continues*** *ACA Newsletter.*
Desc: Deals with the latest developments in arms control negotiations and national security. Provides updates on the nuclear arsenals of the superpowers.
Ind/Abst Expand. Acad. Index (1992-); Newsp. Period. Abstr. (1992-); PAIS Int. Print (1991-); Sage Public Adm. Abstr.

NE/0928-432X
ASIAN YEARBOOK OF INTERNATIONAL LAW. **Added/Corp** Foundation for the Development of International Law in Asia. Vol. 1 (1991)-. English. an. Martinus Nijhoff Publishers, Subsidiary of Kluwer Academic Publishers, Koraalrood 50, 2718 SC Zoetermeer Netherlands. **Tel** 011 31 79 684400. **(Subscription address:** Kluwer Academic Publishers / US Subscriptions, PO Box 253, Accord Station, Hingham MA 02018.) **LC** JX21; .A85. **DD** 341/.095. **Pr Rev.**
Desc: Covers Asian views and preactices in international law.

BE
ASPECTS & DOCUMENTS. **See** Business-Banking and Finance.

AT/0811-9260
AUSTRALIAN INTERNATIONAL LAW NEWS. (AUSTRALIAN INTERNATIONAL LAW NEWS / INTERNATIONAL LAW ASSOCIATION (AUSTRALIAN BRANCH).). [Aust. int. law news]. **Added/Corp** International Law Association. Australian Branch. New South Wales Institute of Technology. Faculty of Law. (July 1983)-. Periodical. English. Twice a year. $33.64. **(Subscription address:** William W. Gaunt & Sons Inc., 3011 Gulf Drive, Gaunt Building, Holmes Beach, FL 34217)

AT
AUSTRALIAN TREATY SERIES. **Main/Corp** Australia. **Added/Corp** Australia. Dept. of Foreign Affairs and Trade. Monographic series. English. Price varies per volume. Australian Bureau of Statistics, PO Box 10, Belconnen Australian Capital Territory, 2616 Australia. **Tel** 011 61 6 2527911, FAX 011 61 6 2516009. **LC** JX1165.9; .A3. **DD** 341/.0264/94. ***Continues*** *Treaty Series.*
Ind/Abst Aust. Leg. Mon. Dig.

AT/0084-7658
AUSTRALIAN YEAR BOOK OF INTERNATIONAL LAW, THE. [Aust. yearb. int. law]. **Added/Corp** Australian National University. Faculty of Law. **VFOAT** Year Book of International Law. (1965)-. English. an. $170.00. Centre for International and Public Law, Australian National University, Canberra ACT 0200 Australia. **Tel** 011 61 6 2490454, FAX 011 61 6 2572886. **(Subscription address:** Bibliotech, GPO Box 4, Canberra, ACT 2601 Australia) **ED** Philip Alston and Don Greg, (06)249-0454. **LC** JX3091; .A9. **DD** 341/.05. **Bk Rev**, (Qty: 10). **Circ:** 800 (ctrl).
Desc: Articles for, and Australian government pratice in international law; also case and legislation notes from Australia on international law.
Ind/Abst Index Foreign Leg. Per.; Index Leg. Period.; Leg. Resour. Index (1980-); LegalTrac (1980-1984).

AU/0942-010X
AUSTRIAN JOURNAL OF PUBLIC AND INTERNATIONAL LAW 1991. [Austrian j. public int. law 1991]. **VFOAT** Osterreichische Zeitschrift fur Offentliches Recht und Volkerrecht (1991); AJPIL. Austrian Journal of Public and International Law. (1991)-. Periodical. Multiple languages. Four times a year. DM464.00. Springer-Verlag Wien, Sachsenplatz 4 6, PO Box 89, A-1201 Vienna Austria. **Tel** 011 43 1 3302415. **(Subscription address:** Springer Verlag New York Inc. / for North America, 44 Hartz Way, Secaucus NJ 07096.) ***Continues*** *Osterreichische Zeitschrift fur Offentliches Recht und Volkerrecht, 0378-3073.*

BB
BARBADOS CONSOLIDATED INDEX TO STATUTES AND SUBSIDIARY LEGISLATION TO ... . **Added/Corp** University of the West Indies (Cave Hill, Barbados). Faculty of Law. Library. (19??)-. English. an. $20.00. Faculty of Law Library, PO Box 64, Bridgetown Barbados. **Tel** (813)778-5211. **ED** Clifford Hammett. **LC** KGL1010.5; .B37. **DD** 348.7298/1028; 347.29810828. **Bk Rev. Ad Acc. Circ:** 250.
Desc: Contains titles of current laws in the territory concerned with references to the amendments to and subsidiary legislation made under each statute.

US/0067-4419
BASIC FACTS ABOUT THE UNITED NATIONS. **Main/Corp** United Nations. Dept. of Public Information. (19??)-. Government Publication. English. ir. $5.00. United Nations Publications, 2 United Nations Plaza, Room DC2 0853, Department 007C, New York NY 10017. **Tel** (212)963-8303, (800)253-9646. **LC** JX1977.A37; B3. **DD** 341.23/05. ***Continues*** *Basic Facts about the United Nations, 0067-4419.*
Desc: Provides a general introduction to the role and functions of the United Nations and its related agencies, highligting and outlinig the main objectives and achievements of the Organization.

GW
BEITRAEGE ZUM INTERNATIONALEN WIRTSCHAFTSRECHT UND ATOMENERGIERECHT. **See** Economics-International Economics.

GW
BEITRAGE ZUM AUSLANDISCHEN UND INTERNATIONALEN PRIVATRECHT. (19??)-. Monographic series. German. ir. Price varies per volume. Walter de Gruyter Inc., PO Box 303421, D 10728 Berlin Germany. **Tel** 011 49 30 260050, FAX 011 49 30 26005251. **(Subscription address:** US and Canada/ 200 Saw Mill River Road, Hawthorne, NY 10532)

US
BELIZE CONSOLIDATED INDEX OF STATUTES AND SUBSIDIARY LEGISLATION TO ... . **VFOAT** Consolidated Index of Statutes and Subsidiary Legislation to ... . 1st Jan. 1984-. English. an. $20.00. Faculty of Law Library, PO Box 64, Bridgetown Barbados. **Tel** (813)778-5211. **ED** Clifford Hammett. **LC** KGA52; .B45. **DD** 348.7282/028. **Bk Rev. Ad Acc. Circ:** 250.
Desc: Contains titles of current laws in the territory concerned with references to the amendments to and subsidiary legislation made under each statute.

US/0067-8562
BILATERAL STUDIES IN PRIVATE INTERNATIONAL LAW. No. 1, (1951)-. Monographic series. English. ir. Price varies per volume. Oceana Publications, Inc., 75 Main Street, Dobbs Ferry NY 10522. **Tel** (914)693-1320, FAX (914)693-0402.

SP/0212-5617
BLE. BOLETIN DE LEGISLACION EXTRANJERA. [BLE, Bol. legis. extranj.]. **VFOAT** Boletin de Legislacion Extranjera (1981). (1981)-. Periodical. Spanish. bm (6 double issues per year). 8250ptas. Cortes Generales / Congreso Diputado Publicaciones, Floridablanca, 28014 Madrid Spain. **Tel** 011 34 1 4295193, 011 34 1 4292577. **UDC** 34. **Circ:** 1500 (ctrl). ***Continues*** *Boletin de Legislacion Extranjera, 0212-5609.*

MX/0041-8633
BOLETIN MEXICANO DE DERECHO COMPARADO. [Bol. Mex. derecho comp.]. **Added/Corp** Universidad Nacional Autonoma de Mexico. Instituto de Investigaciones Juridicas. Vol. 1, No. 1 (Jan./Feb. 1968)-. Periodical. Spanish. Three times a year (Apr., Aug., Dec.). $45.00. UNAM - Institute of Investigaciones Juridicas, Universidad Nacional Autonoma de Mexico, Ciudad Universitaria, Mario de la Cueva, 04510 Mexico DF Mexico. **Tel** 011 52 5 622-7461, 616-1784, FAX 011 52 5 665-2193. **ED** Eugenio Hurtado Marquez. Index available (Published separately). cum. index. **Bk Rev. Ad Acc. Circ:** 1,000 (ctrl). ***Continues*** *Boletin del Instituto de Derecho Comparado de Mexico.*
Desc: Specialized juridical journal for one part existing of the Mexican and foreign doctrine for the other part giving

reviews of books and periodicals.
Ind/Abst ABC POL SCI; Hum. Rights Intern. Rep.; Index Foreign Leg. Per.; Int. Polit. Sci. Abstr.

US/0277-5778
BOSTON COLLEGE INTERNATIONAL AND COMPARATIVE LAW REVIEW. [Boston College int. comp. law rev.]. **Added/Corp** Boston College. Law School. Vol. 2, No. 2 (1979)-. Periodical. English. Twice a year. $11.00 US; $14.00 other. Boston College Law School, 885 Centre Street, Newton Centre MA 02159. **Tel** (617)552-8550, FAX (617)552-2615. **ED** Edward G. McAnoney. **LC** K2; .O77. **DD** 340/.05. **Bk Rev. Ad Acc. Circ:** 500. ***Continues*** *Boston College International and Comparative Law Journal, 0161-2832.*
Desc: All areas of international and comparative law are dealt with.
Ind/Abst ABC POL SCI; Am. Bibliogr. Slavic East Europ. Stud.; Bowne Dig. Corp. Sec. Lawyers; Curr. Law Index (1982-); Index Leg. Period.; Leg. Resour. Index (1982-); LegalTrac (Jan. 1982-Feb. 1982); PAIS Int. Print (1991-).

US/0276-3583
BOSTON COLLEGE THIRD WORLD LAW JOURNAL. [Boston Coll. Third World law j.]. **Added/Corp** Boston College. Law School. **VFOAT** Third World Law Journal. Vol. 1, No. 1 (Spring 1980)-. Academic Scholarly Publication. English. Twice a year (Jan. & July). $11.00 US; $14.00 other. Boston College Law School, 885 Centre Street, Newton Centre MA 02159. **Tel** (617)552-8550, FAX (617)552-2615. **ED** Remsen M. Kinne. **LC** K2; .O84. **DD** 340/.09172/4. Index available. **Bk Rev. Circ:** 300. available on an online database from WESTLAW.
Desc: A forum for scholarly legal works comparing and analyzing the legal systems in developing countries and the position of those countries in the global community.
Ind/Abst Curr. Law Index (1982-); Index Foreign Leg. Per.; Index Leg. Period.; Leg. Resour. Index (1982-); LegalTrac (1983-); PAIS Int. Print (1991-).

US/0737-8947
BOSTON UNIVERSITY INTERNATIONAL LAW JOURNAL. [Boston Univ. int. law j.]. **Added/Corp** Boston University. School of Law. **VFOAT** International Law Journal. Vol. 1, Issue 1 (Spring 1982)-. Periodical. English. Twice a year. $25.00. Boston University School of Law, 765 Commonwealth Avenue, Boston MA 02215. **Tel** (617)353-3157, (617)353-3115. **ED** Lawrence R. Moon. **LC** K2; .O85. **DD** 340/.05. **Bk Rev. Ad Acc. Circ:** 350.
Desc: Provides articles and reviews on current issues in international law.
Ind/Abst Bowne Dig. Corp. Sec. Lawyers; Curr. Law Index (1984-); Index Leg. Period.; Leg. Resour. Index (1984-); LegalTrac (1982-).

UK/0524-627X
BRITISH INSTITUTE STUDIES IN INTERNATIONAL & COMPARATIVE LAW. **Added/Corp** British Institute of International and Comparative Law. British Institute Studies in International and Comparative Law. Vol. 1 (1964)-. Monographic series. English. be. Free on request. British Institute International & Comparative Law, Charles Clore HS-17 Russel Square, London WC1B 5DR England. **Tel** 011 44 71 636 5802.

BB
BRITISH VIRGIN ISLANDS CONSOLIDATED INDEX OF STATUTES AND SUBSIDIARY LEGISLATION TO ... . **Added/Corp** University of the West Indies (Cave Hill, Barbados). Faculty of Law. Library. **VFOAT** Consolidated Index of Statutes and Subsidiary Legislation to ... . (19??)-. English. an. $20.00. Faculty of Law Library, PO Box 64, Bridgetown Barbados. **Tel** (813)778-5211. **ED** Clifford Hammett. **LC** KGL4010.5; .B75. **DD** 348.7297/25028; 347.297250828. **Bk Rev. Ad Acc. Circ:** 250.
Desc: Contains titles of current laws in the territory concerned with references to the amendments to and subsidiary legislation made under each statute.

UK/0068-2691
BRITISH YEAR BOOK OF INTERNATIONAL LAW, THE. [Br. year book int. law]. **Added/Corp** Royal Institute of International Affairs. British Institute of International Affairs. **VFOAT** British Yearbook of International Law. Vol. 1 (1921)-. English. an. £75.00 - £90.00 (depending on Volume number). Oxford University Press, Walton Street, Oxford OX2 6DP England. **Tel** 011 44 865 56767, FAX 011 44 865 267773, telex 837330 OXPRES G. **(Subscription address:** Oxford University Press / USA, Journals Marketing Department, Oxford University Press, 2001 Evans Road, Cary NC 27513.**)** **ED** Ian Brownlie and D.W. Bowett. **LC** JX21; .B7. **DD** 341/.05. cum. index. **Bk Rev.**
Desc: Contains surveys of decisions of British courts, the Court of Justice of the EEC and the European Convention on Human Rights on questions of international law.
Ind/Abst Curr. Law Index (1980-); Index Foreign Leg. Per.; Index Leg. Period.; Int. Polit. Sci. Abstr.; Leg. Resour. Index (1980-); LegalTrac (1980-).

US/0740-4824
BROOKLYN JOURNAL OF INTERNATIONAL LAW. [Brooklyn j. int. law]. **Added/Corp** Brooklyn Law School. Vol. 1 (Spring 1975)-. English. Three times a year. $15.00 US; $18.00 other. Brooklyn Law School, 250 Joralemon Street, Brooklyn NY 11201. **Tel** (718)780-7971. **ED** Brian Ross and Heather Cooper. **LC** JX1; .B76. **DD** 341/.05. **Bk Rev. Circ:** 350.
Desc: Covers international law, international trade, and international relations.
Ind/Abst Curr. Law Index (1980-); Fed. Tax Artic.; Index Leg. Period.; Leg. Resour. Index (1980-); LegalTrac (1980-).

CN/1184-8774
BULLETIN DE LA SDIE. (BULLETIN DE LA SDIE / SOCIETE DE DROIT INTERNATIONAL ECONOMIQUE, CANADA). [Bull. SDIE]. **Added/Corp** Societe de Droit International Economique. **VFOAT** Bulletin de la Societe de Droit International Economique; Societe de Droit International Economique, Bulletin. **VAT** SDIE Bulletin. Vol. 3, No 2 (Spring 1990)-. Bulletin. French (summaries and/or abstracts in English). qt. Free. Societe de Droit International Economique, 5me Etage, 445 Boulevard St-Laurent, Montreal, Quebec H2Y 3T8 Canada. **DD** 341.7/5/05. ***Continues*** *Information SDIE., 0838-9667.*

FR
BULLETIN D'INFORMATION SUR LES ACTIVITES JURIDIQUES AU SEIN DU CONSEIL DE L'EUROPE ET DANS LES ETATS MEMBRES : BULLETIN D'INFORMATION DE LA DIRECTION DES AFFAIRES JURIDIQUES DU CONSEIL DE L'EUROPE. **Added/Corp** Council of Europe. Directorate of Legal Affairs. **VFOAT** Bulletin d'Information de la Direction des Affaires Juridiques du Conseil de l'Europe. (19??)-. Bulletin. French. Manhattan Publishing Company, PO Box 650, Croton-on-Hudson NY 10520. **Tel** (914)271-5194. **DD** 349.4/05; 344/.005.

LU/0423-7846
BULLETIN - EUROPEAN PARLIAMENT. (BULLETIN.). **Main/Corp** European Parliament. Bulletin. English. European Parliament, PO Box 1601, Luxembourg Luxembourg. **LC** JN32; .E9A. **DD** 341.24/2.

UK/0007-4969
BULLETIN OF LEGAL DEVELOPMENTS. **Added/Corp** British Institute of International and Comparative Law. No. 1 (Jan. 1966)-. Bulletin. English. sm. $190.00. British Institute of International and Comparative Law, Charles Clore House, 17 Russell Square, London WC1B 5DR England. **Tel** 011 44 71 636-5802, FAX 011 44 71 323-2016. **ED** D. Chalmers and S. M. Beckwith. Index Available, published separately, free-automatically sent. cum. index. **Circ:** 350.
Desc: News of developments in law worldwide and internationally.

US
BULLETIN ON CURRENT RESEARCH IN SOVIET AND EAST EUROPEAN LAW. (Feb. 1970)-. Bulletin. English. Three times a year. University of Toronto / Peter Solomon, 130 St. George Street, Suite 14335, Toronto Ontario M5S 1A1 Canada. **Tel** (416)978-3330. **DD** 340/.07/2047.

CN/0317-6460
BULLETIN - UNITED NATIONS ASSOCIATION IN CANADA. **Main/Corp** United Nations Association in Canada. (May 1975)-. Bulletin. English (French). Four times a year. 20.00Can$. United Nations Association in Canada, 63 Sparks Street / Suite 808, Ottawa Ontario K1P 5A6 Canada. **Tel** (613)232-5751. **DD** 341.23/06/271.

NZ/0110-070X
BUTTERWORTHS CURRENT LAW. **Added/Corp** Butterworths of New Zealand Ltd. (1969)-. English. bw. Butterworth Heinemann / Woburn, MA, 225 Wildwood Avenue, Unit B, Woburn MA 01801. **Tel** (800)366-2665, FAX (617)928-2620, telex 880052. **(Subscription address:** Butterworth Heinemann, 80 Montvale Avenue, Stoneham, MA 02180**)** **ED** Andrew Marshall. **DD** 340/.09931. **[CCC]**. Index available. cum. index. **Bk Rev. Ad Acc. Pr Rev.** ctrl circ.
Desc: Publication containing Acts of Parliament, regulations, rules, bills before Parliament and their progress, decisions of courts and administrative tribunals, articles in periodicals and important English and Australian cases.

US
CALIFORNIA INTERNATIONAL PRACTITIONER, THE. **Added/Corp** State Bar of California. International Law Section. **VFOAT** International Practitioner. Vol. 1, No. 1 (1989/1990)-. Periodical. English. sa. Free to all members of the International Law Section. State Bar of California, 555 Franklin Street, San Francisco CA 94102. **Tel** (415)561-8200, FAX (415)561-8228.
Ind/Abst Index Leg. Period. (1992-).

US/0886-3210
CALIFORNIA WESTERN INTERNATIONAL LAW JOURNAL. [Calif. West. int. law j.]. **Added/Corp** California Western School of Law. Vol. 1 (Fall 1970)-. Periodical. English. ir (2 issues per year). $20.00 US; $25.00 Other. California Western School of Law, 225 Cedar Street, San Diego CA 92101. **Tel** (619)239-0391, (800)225-4252, FAX (619)696-9999. **ED** Michael P Fitzgerald and John J Gorski. **LC** JX1; .C25. **DD** 341/.05. **Bk Rev. Ad Acc. Circ:** 600 (ctrl). available in microform; available on an online database.
Desc: Concentrates on public and private international law, with a wide score of issues within these broad categorizations.
Ind/Abst Am. Bibliogr. Slavic East Europ. Stud.; Bowne Dig. Corp. Sec. Lawyers; Curr. Law Index; Index Leg. Period.; Leg. Resour. Index (1980-); LegalTrac (1980-); Peace Res. Abstr. J. (1972-1979, 1982-1985).

UK
CAMBRIDGE STUDIES IN INTERNATIONAL AND COMPARATIVE LAW. Vol. 1 (1946)-. Monographic series. English. ir. Price varies per volume. Cambridge University Press, The Edinburgh Building, Shaftesbury Road, Cambridge CB2 2RU United Kingdom. **Tel** 011 44 223 312393, FAX 011 44 223 325959. **(Subscription address:** North America/ Cambridge University Press, 40 West 20th Street, New York, NY 10011-4211; telephone: (212)924-3900**)**

US/0163-6391
CANADA-UNITED STATES LAW JOURNAL. [Can.-U. S. law j.]. **Added/Corp** Canada-United States Law Institute. **VAT** Canada United States Law Journal. Vol. 1 (1978)-. Periodical. English (French). an. $15.00. Case Western Reserve University / School of Law, 11075 East Boulevard, Cleveland OH 44106. **Tel** (216)368-3304, FAX (216)368-6144. **ED** Saleh S. Awadallah. **LC** K3; .A48. **DD** 349.71/05. **Ad Acc. Circ:** 350. available on CD-ROM from WESTLAW; available on microfiche; available on microfilm; available on an online database.
Desc: Articles on comparative aspects of United States and Canadian law, and international law affecting both nations.
Ind/Abst Index Can. Leg. Period. Lit.; Index Leg. Period.; Leg. Resour. Index (1980-); LegalTrac (1980-); PAIS Int. Print.

CN/0008-3003
CANADIAN BAR REVIEW, THE. [Can. Bar rev.]. **Added/Corp** Canadian Bar Association. **VFOAT** Revue du Barreau Canadien. Vol. 1, (Jan. 1923)-. Periodical. English (French). Four times a year (Mar., June, Sept., Dec.). 100.00Can$ one year. Canadian Bar Association, Suite 902 50 O'Connor Street, Ottawa Ontario K1P 6L2 Canada. **Tel** (613)237-2925. **ED** A. J. McClean. cum. index. **Bk Rev. Ad Acc. Circ:** 34,000 (ctrl).
Desc: Contains articles by eminent Canadian legal scholars on a broad range of legal issues.
Ind/Abst Bus. Index (1979-?); Can. Index (?-?); Can. Legal Lit.; Crim. Justice Abstr.; Curr. Law Index (1980-); Index Can. Leg. Period. Lit.; Index Leg. Period.; Leg. Resour. Index (1980-); LegalTrac (1980-).

CN/0382-8662
CANADIAN WORLD FEDERALIST (1975). (CANADIAN WORLD FEDERALIST.). **Added/Corp** World Federalists of Canada. Vol. 1 (May 1975)-. Periodical. English (French). Three times a year (Apr., June, Oct.). 12.00Can$. World Federalists of Canada, 145 Spruce Street, Suite 207, Ottawa Ontario K1R 6 P1 Canada. **Tel** (613)232-0647. **ED** Fergus Watt. **DD** 341.2. **Bk Rev**, (Qty: 3). **Circ:** 2,500.
Desc: Provides examinations and reports of latest developments leading to stronger international law, federalism (global and regional) and stronger UN. News of local, national, international people's movements for world federalism.
Ind/Abst Peace Res. Abstr. J. (1961-1968).

CN/0069-0058
CANADIAN YEARBOOK OF INTERNATIONAL LAW. (THE CANADIAN YEARBOOK OF INTERNATIONAL LAW / ANNUAIRE CANADIEN DE DROIT INTERNATIONAL.). [Can. yearb. int. law]. **Added/Corp** International Law Association. Canadian Branch. **VFOAT** Annuaire Canadien de Droit International. Vol. 1 (1963)-. Periodical. English (French). an. $99.00 US; $101.25 other. University of British Columbia Press, 6344 Memorial Road, Vancouver British Columbia V6T 1Z2 Canada. **Tel** (604)228-3259, FAX (604)228-6083. **ED** C.B. Bourne. **LC** JX21; .C3. **DD** 341/.05. **Bk Rev. Circ:** 1,000 (ctrl). available on CD-ROM from Fred B. Rothman and Company.
Desc: An authoritative survey of important and topical issues in international law including recent legal and policy changes of countries and of multinational organizations.
Ind/Abst Am. Bibliogr. Slavic East Europ. Stud.; Can. Legal Lit.; Curr. Law Index; Index Can. Leg. Period. Lit.; Index Foreign Leg. Per.; Index Leg. Period.; Int. Bibliogr. Sociol.; Int. Polit. Sci. Abstr.; Leg. Resour. Index (1980-); LegalTrac (1980-).

US/0008-7254
CASE WESTERN RESERVE JOURNAL OF INTERNATIONAL LAW. [Case West. Reserve j.int. law]. **Added/Corp** Franklin Thomas Backus School of Law. **VFOAT** Journal of International Law. Vol. 1, No. 1 (Fall 1968)-. Academic Scholarly Publication. English. Three times a year. $20.00 North America; $22.00 other. Case Western Reserve University / School of Law, 11075 East Boulevard, Cleveland OH 44106. **Tel** (216)368-3304, FAX (216)368-6144. **ED** James P Merriman and John G Beck. **LC** JX1; .C3. **DD** 341/.05. **NLM** W1 CA901S. **Circ:** 500. available on microfilm. Documents available from UMI Article Clearinghouse.
Desc: A scholarly journal of international law composed of articles by experts, student notes, recent developments, book reviews and conferences.
Ind/Abst ABI/INFORM Glob. Ed. (1984-); ABI Inform Ondisc (1980-); Account. Art.; Am. Bibliogr. Slavic East Europ. Stud.; Curr. Law Index (1980-); Fed. Tax Artic.; Hum. Rights Intern. Rep.; Index Foreign Leg. Per.; Index Leg. Period.; Int. Labour Doc.; Leg. Resour. Index (1980-); LegalTrac (1980-); PAIS Int. Print (1991-?).

US/1043-4852
CATALOG OF NEW FOREIGN AND INTERNATIONAL LAW TITLES. [Cat. new foreign int. law titles]. Vol. 1, No. 1 (Jan./Feb. 1989)-. Catalog. English. bm. $248.00. Ward & Associates, 317 South Division, Suite 66, Ann Arbor MI 48104. **Tel** (313)665-3520, FAX (313)665-7880. **LC** K40; .C38. **DD** 016.34/005. ***Continues*** *National Legal Bibliography. Part 2, Government Documents From Official and Commercial Sources, 0887-106X.*

BB
CAYMAN ISLANDS CONSOLIDATED INDEX OF STATUTES AND SUBSIDIARY LEGISLATION TO ... . **Added/Corp** University of the West Indies (Cave Hill, Barbados). Faculty of Law. Library. **VFOAT** Consolidated Index of Statutes and Subsidiary Legislation to ... . (19??)-. English. an. $20.00. Faculty of Law Library, PO Box 64, Bridgetown Barbados. **Tel** (813)778-5211. **ED** Clifford Hammett. **LC** KGM10.5; .C39. **DD** 348.7292/1029; 347.29210828. **Bk Rev. Ad Acc. Circ:** 250.
Desc: Contains titles of current laws in the territory concerned with references to the amendments to and subsidiary legislation made under each statute.

US/0731-0854
CHINESE YEARBOOK OF INTERNATIONAL LAW AND AFFAIRS. [Chin. yearb. int. law aff.]. **Added/Corp** Chung-kuo kuo Chi fa Hsueh hui. Occasional Papers/Reprints Series in Contemporary Asian Studies. **VFOAT** Chinese Yearbook. Vol. 1 (1981)-. English (Chinese). an (Oct. or Nov.). $24.00. Chinese Yearbook International Law Affairs, 500 West Baltimore Street, Baltimore MD 21201. **Tel** (410)328-3870. **ED** Hungdah Chiu and Chih-yu Wu. **LC** JX18; .C48a. **DD** 341/.05. Index available. **Bk Rev. Circ:** 1,000. ***Continues*** *Annals of the Chinese Society of International Law.*
Desc: Articles and current development on Republic of China's (Taiwan) trade, investment and human rights situation. Chinese contemporary practice and judicial decision relating to international law, reviews and others.
Ind/Abst Index Foreign Leg. Per.; Int. Polit. Sci. Abstr.

INT/1013-5235
CHRONIQUE DES NATIONS UNIES. [Chron. N.U.]. (1982)-. Government Publication. French. qt (Mar., June, Sept., Dec.). $20.00. United Nations Publications, 2 United Nations Plaza, Room DC2 0853, Department 007C, New York NY 10017. **Tel** (212)963-8303, (800)253-9646. **CODEN** NU001. ***Continues*** *Chronique Mensuelle - ONU, 0251-1843.*

HT
CHRONIQUE JUDICIAIRE D'HAITI, LA. (Oct. 1980)-. Periodical. French (English). Twelve times a year. $24.00 US. La Chronique Judiciaire d'Haiti, PO Box 1453, Port au Prince Haiti. **Tel** 011 509 1 29203, 011 509 1 59206. **ED** Lucien LaCarriere. **LC** K3; .H73. **DD** 349.7294/05; 347.294/005. **Bk Rev. Ad Acc. Circ:** 10,000 (ctrl).
Desc: Articles from Haitian scholars on laws in the country, current problems and analysis.

CC
CHUNG-KUO KUO CHI FA NIEN KAN / CHUNG-KUO KUO CHI FA HSUEH HUI PIEN CHI. **VFOAT** Chinese Yearbook of International Law. 1982-. Chinese. an. RMBY3.00. Chung-Kuo Tui Wai Fan I Chu, Pan Kung SSU, Beijing, People's Republic of China. **LC** JX18; .C49. **DD** 341/.05.
Ind/Abst Index Foreign Leg. Per.

US/0010-1931
COLUMBIA JOURNAL OF TRANSNATIONAL LAW. [Columbia j. transnatl. law]. **Added/Corp** Columbia Journal of Transnational Law Association. Columbia Society of International Law. Vol. 3 (Fall 1964)-. Periodical. English. Three times a year. $29.50 US & Canada; $32.50 other. Columbia University School of Law, 435 West 116th Street, New York NY 10027. **Tel** (212)854-4398, (212)854-3742. **ED** Douglas Doetsch. **DD** 341/.05. cum. index. **Bk Rev. Ad Acc. Pr Rev. Circ:** 1,000. Documents available from The Genuine Article. ***Continues*** *International Law Bulletin, 0734-3272.*
Desc: Dedicated to the concept of transnational law including both civil and criminal aspects, what we know as public and private international law, and which involves individual states, corporations or other groups.
Ind/Abst ABC POL SCI (19??-19??); Acad. Search (July 1993-); Account. Art. (1968-1978, 19??-); Am. Hist. Life (1968-1978); Am. Bibliogr. Slavic East Europ. Stud.; Bowne Dig. Corp. Sec. Lawyers; Bus. Source (Jul. 1993-); Curr. Contents Soc. Behav. Sci.; Curr. Law Index (1980-); Fed. Tax Artic.; Index Foreign Leg. Per. (1970-1991); Index Leg. Period.; INFO-SOUTH Abstr.; Int. Polit. Sci. Abstr. (1980-); Leg. Resour. Index (1980-); LegalTrac (1968-1978, 1980-); Res. Alert [Full Cov.]; Soc. Sci. Cit. Index [Full Cov.].

US
COMMERCIAL LAWS OF THE WORLD. CLASS C. (19??)-. English. Twenty-six times a year. Comes with Foreign Tax Law Publishers membership; $1100.00 (membership). Foreign Tax Law Publishers Inc., PO Box 2189, Ormond Beach FL 32175-2189. **Tel** (904)253-5785, FAX (904)257-3003. **ED** S. Yanaura. Index available. **Pr Rev. Circ:** 500 (ctrl). available on diskette.
Desc: 100 countries in 33 volumes -- all translated into English -- not a digest -- most countries include the complete texts of the companies act and/or commercial code. Some countries include civil law provision affecting commercial transactions. Kept up to date by monthly looseleaf supplements. (Supplementation is more frequent in some cases).

BB
COMMONWEALTH OF DOMINICA CONSOLIDATED INDEX OF STATUTES AND SUBSIDIARY LEGISLATION TO ... . **Added/Corp** University of the West Indies (Cave Hill, Barbados). Faculty of Law. Library. **VFOAT** Consolidated Index of Statutes and Subsidiary Legislation to ... . (19??)-. English. an. $20.00. Faculty of Law Library, PO Box 64, Bridgetown Barbados. **Tel** (813)778-5211. **ED** Clifford Hammett. **LC** KGP2010.5; .C65. **DD** 348.7298/41028; 347.298410828. **Bk Rev. Ad Acc. Circ:** 250.
Desc: Contains titles of current laws in the territory concerned with references to the amendments to and subsidiary legislation made under each statute.

CN/0226-3556
COMMUNICATIONS - AMNISTIE INTERNATIONALE, SECTION CANADIENNE. ***Title Change.*** [Commun. - Amnistie int., Sept. can.]. **Main/Corp** Amnesty International Canada. **VFOAT** Bulletin Mensuel. Vol. 1 (Oct. 1979)-(19??). Periodical. French. Six times a year. Amnistie Internationale, 6250 Boulevard Monk, Montreal Quebec H4E 3H7 Canada. **Tel** (514)766-9766, FAX (514)766-2088, telex 055/60543. **DD** 364.1/3/05. ***Continued by*** *AGIR, 0847-9798.*

SA/0010-4051
COMPARATIVE AND INTERNATIONAL LAW JOURNAL OF SOUTHERN AFRICA, THE. [Comp. int. law. j. south. Afr.]. **VFOAT** Tydskrif vir Regsvergelyking en Internasionale Reg van Suidelik Afrika; Jornal de Direito Comparativo e Internacional Para os Paises do Sul da Africa; Journal de Droit Compare et International des Pays de l'Afrique Australe; Zeitschrift fur Rechtsvergleichung und Internationales Recht des Sudlichen Afrika. Vol. 1 March 1968-. Periodical. English. Three times a year. $60.00. Institute of Foreign and Comparative Law, University of South Africa, PO Box 392, Pretoria 0001 South Africa. **Tel** 11 27 12 4298468, telex (59) 350068. **ED** J Joubert. **LC** K3; .O4. **DD** 340/.068; 341. Index available. cum. index. **Bk Rev. Ad Acc. Circ:** 500 (ctrl).
Desc: Presents contributions and facts on foreign laws, African in particular; private and public international law; constitutional law; and recent developments in southern Africa.
Ind/Abst Index Foreign Leg. Per.; Int. Bibliogr. Sociol.

UK/0068-2160
COMPARATIVE LAW SERIES. **Main/Corp** British Institute of International and Comparative Law. Monographic series. English. ir. Price varies per volume. British Institute of International and Comparative Law, Charles Clore House, 17 Russell Square, London WC1B 5DR England. **Tel** 011 44 71 636-5802, FAX 011 44 71 323-2016.

US/0897-1218
CONNECTICUT JOURNAL OF INTERNATIONAL LAW. [Conn. j. int. law]. **Added/Corp** Connecticut Journal of International Law Association. University of Connecticut. School of Law. **VFOAT** Connecticut Journal of Int'l Law. Vol. 1 (1985/86)-. Periodical. English. ir. $20.00 (US); $25.00 (other). University of Connecticut / School of Law, 65 Elizabeth Street, Hartford CT 06105-2290. **Tel** (203)241-4607. **ED** Mary Margaret Scharf. **LC** JX1; .C624. **DD** 341/.05. **Bk Rev. Ad Acc. Circ:** 700.
Desc: Provides an innovative international forum for the publication of articles, book reviews and commentary by scholars and practitioners . Student notes, comments and recent developments are also included.
Ind/Abst Index Leg. Period.; Leg. Resour. Index; LegalTrac (1980-).

AT
CONSULAR LIST / DEPARTMENT OF FOREIGN AFFAIRS AND TRADE. (19??)-. Government Publication. English. Six times a year. 40.00Aus$. Australian Government Publishing Service, GPO Box 84, Canberra ACT 2601 Australia. **Tel** 011 61 6 2954411, FAX 011 61 6 2954455. ***Continues*** *Consular, Trade, and Other Official Representatives in Australia.*

HK
CONSULAR POSTS, OFFICIALLY RECOGNIZED REPRESENTATIVES AND BODIES ESTABLISHED UNDER THE SINO-BRITISH JOINT DECLARATION / HONG KONG. **Main/Corp** Hong Kong. (July 1988)-. Periodical. English. ir. HK$25.00. Hong Kong Government Information Service, Beaconsfield House, 4 Queens Road, Hong Kong Hong Kong. **Tel** 011 852 8428801 4, telex 61190 HKGIS. ***Continues*** *Hong Kong. Consular Posts and Officially Recognized Representatives.*

AT
CONSULAR, TRADE, AND OTHER OFFICIAL REPRESENTATIVES IN AUSTRALIA / DEPARTMENT OF FOREIGN AFFAIRS. ***Title Change.*** **Added/Corp** Australia. Dept. of Foreign Affairs. **VFOAT** Consular, Trade, and Other Official Representatives List. (19??)-(19??). English. Australian Bureau of Statistics, PO Box 10, Belconnen Australian Capital Territory, 2616 Australia. **Tel** 011 61 6 2527911, FAX 011 61 6 2516009. **LC** JX1875; .A15213. **DD** 351.8/92/0994. ***Continues*** *Consular and Trade Representatives in Australia.* ***Continued by*** *Consular List / Department of Foreign Affairs and Trade.*
Desc: A list of Consular Posts and Trade Delegations in all states of Australia and the staff with consular status at these posts.

US/0010-8812
CORNELL INTERNATIONAL LAW JOURNAL. [Cornell int. law j.]. **Added/Corp** Cornell Society of International Law. Vol. 1 (Spring 1968)-. English. Three times a year. $25.00 US; $28.00 other. Cornell International Law, Cornell University, Ithaca NY 14853. **Tel** (607)255-9666. **ED** Paul D. Callister. **LC** JX1; .C63. **DD** 341/.05. cum. index. **Bk Rev. Pr Rev. Circ:** 1,400. Documents available from The Genuine Article.
Desc: Student-edited publication dealing with legal problems of international dimensions. Includes student comments on recent developments in international law and notes on unresolved problems facing the international legal community.
Ind/Abst Am. Bibliogr. Slavic East Europ. Stud.; Crim. Penol. Police Sci. Abstr. (1980-); Curr. Law Index; Index Foreign Leg. Per.; Index Leg. Period.; Leg. Resour. Index (1980-); LegalTrac (1980-); PAIS Int. Print (1991); Res. Alert [Full Cov.]; Soc. Sci. Cit. Index [Full Cov.].

US/0898-9907
CORPORATE COUNSEL'S INTERNATIONAL ADVISER. [Corp. couns. int. advis.]. **Added/Corp** Business Laws, inc. **VFOAT** International Adviser. No. 1 (June 1985)-. Corporate Report. English. mo. $285.00 US; $360.00 other. Business Laws Inc., 11630 Chillicothe Road, Chesterland OH 44026. **Tel** (216)729-7996, (800)759-0929, FAX (216)729-0645. **LC** K3943.A13; C67. **DD** 341.7/54. **[CCC].** cum. index.

UY
CUADERNO DE DERECHO INTERNACIONAL PRIVADO. **Added/Corp** Fundacion de Cultura Universitaria. (1975)-. Monographic series. Spanish. ir. Price varies per volume. Fundacion de Cultura Universitaria, 25 de Mayo, 568 Casilla 1155, 11000 Montevideo Uruguay. **Tel** 011 598 2 961152. **LC** K13; .U15. **DD** 340.9.

US/1063-7443
CUSTOMS RECORD. [Cust. rec.]. (1988)-. Periodical. English. wk. $495.00. International Business Reports, PO Box 1009, Falls Church VA 22041. **Tel** (703)998-2927, FAX (703)998-0019. **ED** Edward Kemp. **DD** 343. **Circ:** 450. available on an online database.
Desc: Concise, comprehensive and timely coverage of customs activity, including customs service private rulings, new regulations, court case tracking system, and congressional activity.

US/0196-2035
DENVER JOURNAL OF INTERNATIONAL LAW AND POLICY. [Denver j. int. law policy]. **VFOAT** Journal of International Law and Policy. V. 1 (Fall 1971)-. English. sa. $23.00 US; $25.00 other. University of Denver Law School, 7039 East 18th Avenue, Foote Hall, Denver CO 80220. **Tel** (303)871-6223. **LC** JX1; .D38. **DD** 341/.05. available on microfilm and microfiche from University Microfilms

Law—International Law

International (UMI). Documents available from Documents on Demand.
Ind/Abst Account. Art.; Am. Bibliogr. Slavic East Europ. Stud.; Bowne Dig. Corp. Sec. Lawyers; Coal Abstr.; Curr. Law Index (1980-); Environ. Abstr.; Fed. Tax Artic.; Index Foreign Leg. Per.; Index Leg. Period.; Int. Polit. Sci. Abstr.; Leg. Resour. Index (1980-); LegalTrac (1980-); PAIS Int. Print (1991-); Peace Res. Abstr. J. (1976-1983).

GW
DEUTSCHE RECHTSPRECHUNG AUF DEM GEBIETE DES INTERNATIONALEN PRIVATRECHTS, DIE. (19??)-. Periodical. German. an. Walter de Gruyter Inc., PO Box 303421, D 10728 Berlin Germany. **Tel** 011 49 30 260050, FAX 011 49 30 26005251.
Desc: Covers legal decisions.

NE
DEVELOPMENTS IN INTERNATIONAL LAW. Vol. 1 (1979)-. Monographic series. English. ir. Price varies per volume. Kluwer Academic Publishers, Postbus 322, 3300 AH Dordrecht, The Netherlands. **Tel** 011 (31) 78 524400, FAX 011 31 78 183273, telex 20083. **Pr Rev.**

US/0887-283X
DICKINSON JOURNAL OF INTERNATIONAL LAW. [Dickinson j. int. law]. **Added/Corp** Dickinson School of Law. Vol. 2, No. 2 (Spring 1984)-. Periodical. English. Three times a year. $25.00. Dickinson School of Law, 150 South College Street, Carlisle PA 17013. **Tel** (717)243-4611, (717)243-7883, FAX (717)243-4443. **LC** K4; .I65. **DD** 341/.05. **Continues** Dickinson International Law Annual, 1052-3618.
Ind/Abst Index Leg. Period.; Leg. Resour. Index; LegalTrac (1984-).

FR
DICTIONNAIRE DU MARCHE COMMUN. (19??)-. French. qt. 3933.65F. Juridictionnaires Joly, 1 Av Franklin D. Roosevelt, F 75008 Paris France. **Tel** 011 33 1 42254740, FAX 011 33 1 45638939.

US/0095-3369
DIGEST OF UNITED STATES PRACTICE IN INTERNATIONAL LAW. **Added/Corp** United States. Dept. of State. Office of the Legal Adviser. (1973)-. Government Publication. English. an. Superintendent of Documents, US Government Printing Office, Washington DC 20402. **Tel** (202)275-3328, FAX (202)786-2377. **ED** Prepared by: Arthur W. Rovine, 1973-1974; Eleanor C. McDowell, 1975-1976; John A. Boyd, 1977; Marian L. Nash, 1978-. **LC** JX21; .R68. **DD** 341/.0973.

GR
DIKAIO KAI POLITIKE (THESSALONIKE, GREECE : 1982). (DIKAIO KAI POLITIKE.). **VFOAT** Law and Politics. 1 (Jan.-April 1982)-. Periodical. Greek, Modern. Three times a year. $70.00 Europe, $90.00 US. Paratiritis Publishing House, 15 Al Stavrou Str, Thessaloniki Greece. **ED** A. Manesis and D. Tsatsos. **Bk Rev. Ad Acc. Circ:** 3,000 (ctrl).
Desc: Law problems including international law, and their relationship with the social and politic conditions.

CE
DIPLOMATIC, CONSULAR AND OTHER REPRESENTATION IN THE DEMOCRATIC SOCIALIST REPUBLIC OF SRI LANKA. **Main/Corp** Sri Lanka. Rajya Araksake Ha Videsa Katayutu Amatyamsaya. **VFOAT** Sri Lanka Prajatantrika Samajavadi Janarajaye Rajya Tantrika, Konsal Ha Sesu Niyojama. 1979-. English. an. Rs7.75. Government Publications Bureau, PO Box 500, Colombo Sri Lanka. **LC** JX1859.S75; S75A. **DD** 351.8/92/095493. **Continues** Diplomatic, Consular and Other Representation in the Republic of Sri Lanka.

US/0012-3099
DIPLOMATIC LIST (WASHINGTON). (DIPLOMATIC LIST.). [Dipl. list]. **Added/Corp** United States. Dept. of State. (1???)-. Government Publication. English. qt. $8.50 domestic; $10.65 other. Superintendent of Documents, US Government Printing Office, Washington DC 20402. **Tel** (202)275-3328, FAX (202)786-2377. **LC** JX1705; .A22. **DD** 353.
Desc: List of foreign diplomats in and around Washington, DC.

US/0736-0959
DIPLOMATIC REGISTER AND DESK REFERENCE. [Dipl. regist. desk ref.]. Periodical. English. sa. $299.95. Spex International, 51 East 42nd Street, New York NY 10017. **LC** JX1705; .A145. **DD** 351.8/92/0973.

●RU
DIPLOMATICHESKII VESTNIK. **Added/Corp** Russia (Federation). Ministerstvo Inostrannykh del. No 1 (Jan. 15, 1992)-. Periodical. Russian. Twenty-four times a year. $189.95. **(Subscription address:** East View Publications Inc., 3020 Harbor Lane North, Suite 110, Minneapolis MN 55447.) **LC** JX1808; .A4a. **Continues** Vestnik Ministerstva Vneshnikh Snoshenii SSSR.
Desc: Information on the Russian diplomatic and consular services.

US/0270-4552
DIRECT INVESTMENT LAW REPORT. [Dir. investm. law rep.]. Vol. 1, No. 1 (Apr. 1980)-. Periodical. English. mo. $175.00 US and Canada, $195.00 elsewhere. Transnational Investments, Ltd., 1101 Conn. Avenue NW, Suite 600, Washington DC 20036. **LC** KF1575.A15; D57. **DD** 346.73/07/05; 347.306705.

LU
DIRECTORY OF COMMUNITY LEGISLATION IN FORCE AND OTHER ACTS OF THE COMMUNITY INSTITUTIONS. **Added/Corp** Office for Official Publications of the European Communities. 5th Ed. (1984)-. Directory. English (Danish, Dutch, French, Greek, Modern and German, Italian). an. £80.00 UK; 85.00p Ireland. Office for Official Publications of the European Communities, 2 Rue Mercier, 2985 Luxembourg Luxembourg. **Tel** 011 352 499281, FAX 011 352 488573. **(Subscription address:** Moniteur Belg Belg Straatsblad, Rue de Louvain 40 42, 1000 Brussels Belgium) **LC** KJE920.5; .D57. **DD** 341.24/22. **Continues** Register of Current Community Legal Instruments.
Desc: Covers binding instruments of secondary legislation arising out of the Treaties establishing the three Communities, other legislation, and agreements between the Communities and non-member countries.

US/0148-7345
DIRECTORY OF OPPORTUNITIES IN INTERNATIONAL LAW. **Added/Corp** John Bassett Moore Society of International Law. (1968)-. English. ir (Publishes every two years). $20.00 (two years). John Bassett Moore Society of International Law, University of Virginia, School of Law, Charlottesville VA 22901. **Tel** (804)924-3087. **ED** Elizabeth E. Q. Harris. **LC** KF195.I54; D48. **DD** 331.7/61/341025.
Desc: A guide to the possibilities for employment and other opportunities in this field.

BE/0591-1745
DIRECTORY OF THE COMMISSION OF THE EUROPEAN COMMUNITIES. **Title Change. Main/Corp** Commission of the European Communities. (19??)-(May 1993). Directory. English. Four times a year. Office for Official Publications of the European Communities, 2 Rue Mercier, 2985 Luxembourg Luxembourg. **Tel** 011 352 499281, FAX 011 352 488573. **(Subscription address:** UNIPUB, 4611 F Assembly Drive, Lanham MD 20706.) **LC** HC240.A1; C624a. **DD** 341.24/22/025. **Continued by** Commission of the European Communities. Directory of the European Commission.

●LU
DIRECTORY OF THE EUROPEAN COMMISSION. **Main/Corp** Commission of the European Communities. (Dec. 1993)-. Directory. English. sa. Office for Official Publications of the European Communities, 2 Rue Mercier, 2985 Luxembourg Luxembourg. **Tel** 011 352 499281, FAX 011 352 488573. **LC** HC240.A1; C624a. **DD** 341.24/22/025. **Continues** Commission of the European Communities. Directory of the Commission of the European Communities, 0591-1745.

IQ/0303-1594
DIRECTORY OF THE UNITED NATIONS ORGANIZATION AND SPECIALIZED AGENCIES IN IRAQ. **VFOAT** Dalil Al-Uman Al-Muttahida Fi Al-Iraq. Directory. English. United Nations den Programme, POB 2048, Alwiyah Baghdad Iraq. **LC** JX1977.2.I7; D55. **DD** 341.23/567.

US/0191-8621
DIRECTORY OF USSR MINISTRY OF FOREIGN AFFAIRS OFFICIALS. (DIRECTORY OF USSR MINISTRY OF FOREIGN AFFAIRS OFFICIALS / DIRECTORATE OF INTELLIGENCE). **Added/Corp** United States. Central Intelligence Agency. Directorate of Intelligence. United States. Central Intelligence Agency. National Foreign Assessment Center (U.S.). **VFOAT** Directory of U.S.S.R. Ministry of Foreign Affairs Officials. **VAT** Directory of Union of Soviet Socialist Republics Ministry of Foreign Affairs Officials. (19??)-. Directory. English. ir. $11.00. Documents Expediting Project, Exchange and Gift Division, Library of Congress, Washington DC 20540. **Tel** (202)707-9527. **LC** JX1807; .A16. **DD** 354.47008/92. available on microfiche (Vols. for (1983-) distributed to depository libraries).

FR
DOC. - COUNCIL OF EUROPE, PARLIAMENTARY ASSEMBLY. **Main/Corp** Council of Europe. Parliamentary Assembly. English (English and French). Council of Europe / Group Pact ED, Pharmacopoeia BP 907, 67029 Strasbourg Cedex 01 France. **Tel** 011 33 88 412036, FAX 011 33 88 41277181, telex 880388. **LC** JN22; .D63. **DD** 341.24/2. **Continues** Council of Europe. Consultative Assembly. Doc.

BE
DOCUMENTATION JURIDIQUE ETRANGERE. **Title Change. Added/Corp** Belgium. Service d'etudes et de Documentation Juridique Internationale. Belgium. Service de Legislation Etrangere. Volume 1 (1949)-(19??). Periodical. French. mo. **Absorbed** Belgium. Service de Legislation Etrangere. Textes Legislatifs Etrangers. **Continued by** Documentation Juridique Internationale.

CN/0714-931X
DOCUMENTS JURIDIQUES INTERNATIONAUX. [Doc. jurid. int.]. **Added/Corp** Societe Quebecoise de Droit International. Vol. 1 (Sept. 1982)-. Periodical. French (English). ir. 48.00Can$. Documents Juridiques Internationaux, Editions Themis Inc, CP 6128 Succ A, Montreal Quebec H3C 3J7 Canada. **Tel** (514)739-9945, FAX (514)343-2199. **DD** 341/.05. Index available. cum. index. ctrl circ.

FR/0252-0656
DOCUMENTS, WORKING PAPERS - COUNCIL OF EUROPE, PARLIAMENTARY ASSEMBLY. [Doc. work. pap. - Counc. Eur., Parliam. Assem.]. **Main/Corp** Council of Europe. Parliamentary Assembly. **VFOAT** Documents de Seance - Conseil de l'Europe, Assemblee Parlementaire. Sess. 26- Pt. 2- V. 3- Sept. 24/30, 1974-. English (French). ir. $26.00 (per volume). Manhattan Publishing Company, PO Box 650, Croton-on-Hudson NY 10520. **Tel** (914)271-5194. **LC** JN22; .A35. **DD** 341.24/2. Index available. **Continues** Council of Europe. Consultative Assembly. Documents.

GW
DOKUMENTE - INSTITUT FUER INTERNATIONALE ANGELEGENHEITEN DER UNIVERSITAT HAMBURG. Ceased. **Main/Corp** Hamburg. Universitat. Institut fur Internationale Angelegenheiten. **Added/Corp** Universitat Kiel. Institut fur Internationales Recht. Universitat Gottingen. Institut fur Volkerrecht. (19??)-(19??). Multiple languages (English, French, German and Spanish). Hermann Luchterhand Verlag, Postfach 2352, D 56513 Neuwied Germany. **Tel** 011 49 2631 8010. **LC** JX77; .H25. **Continues** Universitat Hamburg. Forschungsstelle fur Volkerrecht und Auslandisches Offentliches Recht. Dokumente.

BE
DROIT DE LA COMMUNAUTE ECONOMIQUE EUROPEENNE. (19??)-. French. ir. Editions University de Bruxelles, Avenue Paul Heger 26, B-1050 Bruxelles Belgium. **Tel** 32 2 642 3789, 3799, FAX 32 2 642 3794, telex 23069 UNILIB. **(Subscription address:** Centre Export Livre Francais, 9 rue de Toul, 75012 Paris France.) **ED** Michel Waelbroeck, Jean-Victor Lovis, Daniel Vignes and Jean-Louis Dewoust.
Desc: Covers international law in Europe.

FR/0247-9788
DROIT ET CULTURES : CAHIERS DU CENTRE DE RECHERCHE DE L'U.E.R. DE SCIENCES JURIDIQUES. No. 1-. Periodical. French. Twice a year. 270.00F. 2 rue de Rouen, 92001 Nanterre France. **LC** K4; .R593. **DD** 340/.2; 342.

US/1053-6736
DUKE JOURNAL OF COMPARATIVE & INTERNATIONAL LAW. [Duke j. comp. int. law]. **Added/Corp** Duke University. School of Law. **VFOAT** Duke Journal of Comparative and International Law. Vol. 1991, No. 1 (1991)-. Periodical. English. sa (Published in June & Dec.). $20.00. Duke University School of Law, 006 Law Towerview & Science Drive, Durham NC 27706. **Tel** (919)684-5966, FAX (919)684-3417. **ED** John J. Hoffman. **LC** K4; .U6. **DD** 341/.05. **Ad Acc. Circ:** 285. **Continues** Duke International and Comparative Law Annual, 1054-691X.
Desc: Addresses issues in public and private international law, comparative law, and select topics in foreign law; the December issue is devoted to European Economic Law.
Ind/Abst Index Leg. Period. (1992-).

US/0272-1589
EAST ASIAN EXECUTIVE REPORTS. See Law-Corporate Law.

NE/0925-4641
EEC NEWSLETTER. [EEC newsl.]. **VFOAT** European Economic Community Newsletter. (1990)-. Periodical. English. Five times a year. $200.00. Kluwer Law and Taxation Publishers (Mass.), 675 Massachusetts Avenue, Cambridge MA 02139. **Tel** (617) 354-0140. **UDC** 347.96. **Continues** EEC Newletter.
Desc: Presents a systematic analysis of important legal developments within the European Community.

UA/0013-239X
EGYPTE CONTEMPORAINE, L'. See Economics.

US/1052-2840
EMORY INTERNATIONAL LAW REVIEW. [Emory int. law rev.]. **Added/Corp** Emory University. School of Law. Vol. 4, No. 1 (Spring 1990)-. Periodical. English. sa. $20.00 US; $22.00 other. Emory University School of Law, 1804 North Decatur Road, 3rd Floor, Atlanta GA 30322. **Tel** (404)727-6830, FAX (404)727-6820. **LC** K5; .M63. **DD** 341/.05. ***Continues*** *Emory Journal of International Dispute Resolution, 0897-0564.*
Ind/Abst Index Leg. Period.; Leg. Resour. Index; LegalTrac (1990-).

NE
EURIDICA. (19??)-. Dutch. ir (10 issues). Fl650.00. Euroforum Uitgeverij, Postbus 845, 5600 AV Eindhoven Netherlands. **Tel** 011 31 40 608811.

UK/0950-7361
EUROPEAN COMMUNITIES LEGISLATION : CURRENT STATUS. [Eur. communities legis. curr. status]. **VFOAT** Current Status. (1987)-. English. an. 1130.00Can$. Butterworth & Company Ltd. / Canada, 75 Clegg Road, Markham Ontario L6G 1A1 Canada. **Tel** (905)479-2665, (800)668-6481.
Desc: Provides an efficient, accurate and rapid way into and around the growing maze of EC legislation.

IT/0938-5428
EUROPEAN JOURNAL OF INTERNATIONAL LAW. **Added/Corp** European University Institute. **VFOAT** Journal Europeen de Droit International; EJIL. Vol. 1, No. 1/2 (1990)-. Periodical. English (French). Four times a year. £38.00 Europe; £42.00. Sweet & Maxwell Ltd., South Quay Plaza, 183 Marsh Wall, London E14 9FT England. **Tel** 011 44 264 342899, FAX 011 44 264 342723, telex 929089 ITPINF G. **LC** K5; .U725. **DD** 341/.05.
Desc: Provides readers with a varied selection of articles, all contributed by experts in their field on: discussions and analyses of theory and practice of international law; topical developments in general international law; the legal dimension of the EC's role in world affairs; legislative, judicial and international trade measures in the world environment affecting the EC.

US/0251-690X
EVERYONE'S UNITED NATIONS. [Everyone's U.N.]. **Added/Corp** United Nations. Dept. of Public Information. (1979)-. Government Publication. English. ir. $14.95. United Nations Publications, 2 United Nations Plaza, Room DC2 0853, Department 007C, New York NY 10017. **Tel** (212)963-8303, (800)253-9646. **LC** JX1977.A37; E9. **DD** 341.23. Each issue contains an index to its own contents (no volume index)--loose. ***Continues*** *Everyman's United Nations, 0071-3244.*
Desc: Basic history book describing the structure and activities of the United Nations since its founding in 1945. Specialized agencies related to the United Nations are also covered.

GW/0176-7771
FINANZ-RUNDSCHAU FUER EINKOMMENSTEUER UND KORPERSCHAFTSTEUER : FR. **VFOAT** FR. (19??)-. Periodical. German. sm. DM286.00 (includes supplement). Verlag Dr Otto Schmidt KG, Unter den Ulman 96/98, D 50968 Cologne Germany. **Tel** 011 49 221 9373801. **LC** KK7163.A13; F56. ***Continues*** *Finanz-Rundschau.*

FR
FISCALITE AFRICAINE: REVUE DU DROIT DES AFFAIRES AFRICAINES. French. ir. 7257.21F France; 7220.00F French speaking Africa and Europe; 7310.00F other. Editions FFA, 51 rue Louis Blanc Cedex 75, 92037 Paris La Defns 1 France. **Tel** 011 33 1 46936901, FAX 011 33 1 47880096, telex 615200.

US/0747-9395
FORDHAM INTERNATIONAL LAW JOURNAL. [Fordham int. law j.]. **Added/Corp** Fordham University. School of Law. Vol. 4 No. 1 (1980)-. Periodical. English. qt. $20.00 (one year), $50.00 (two year) US; $25.00 (one year), $65.00 (two year) other. Fordham University School of Law, 140 West 62nd Street, Room 35, New York NY 10023. **Tel** (212)636-6948. **LC** JX1; .F57. **DD** 341/.05. Index available. cum. index. **Bk Rev. Ad Acc. Circ:** 450 (ctrl). ***Continues*** *Fordham International Law Forum, 0741-1944.*
Ind/Abst Curr. Law Index (1980-); Index Leg. Period.; Leg. Resour. Index (1980-); LegalTrac (1980-).

US/0095-7291
FOREIGN TAX LAW BI-WEEKLY BULLETIN. **Added/Corp** Foreign Tax Law Association. (19??)-. Bulletin. English. Twenty-six times a year. $125.00. Foreign Tax Law Publishers Inc., PO Box 2189, Ormond Beach FL 32175-2189. **Tel** (904)253-5785, FAX (904)257-3003. **ED** Sondra Yanaura. **DD** 343.04/05. Index available. **Bk Rev. Circ:** 5,000 (ctrl).
Desc: Covers comparative tax and commercial law, synopses of foreign laws, conducting business abroad, new and proposed laws, investment, labor and social security laws (all foreign).

US
FORIEGN LAW. CURRENT SOURCES OF CODES AND BASIC LEGISLATION IN JURISDICTIONS OF THE WORLD. English. ir. $225.00 (per volume); $600.00 (per set). Fred B. Rothman & Company, 10368 West Centennial Road, Littleton CO 80127. **Tel** (800)457-1986, (303)979-5657, FAX (303)978-1457, telex 87669.

SZ/0340-0255
FRIEDENSWARTE, DIE. (DIE FRIEDENS-WARTE.). [Friedenswarte]. Vol. 1 (1899)-. German. ir. DM50.00. Berlin Verlag Arno Spitz GmbH, Pacelliallee 5, D 14195 Berlin Germany. **Tel** 011 49 30 8326232, FAX 011 49 30 8316249. **ED** Ferenc Majoros. **LC** JX1903; .F7. **Bk Rev. Ad Acc. Circ:** 500. ***Continues*** *Waffen Nieder.*
Desc: Serves as a forum for the discussion of contemporary theoretical and practical problems of international law. It is devoted to the maintenance of peace by means of diplomacy and multilaterality.
Ind/Abst Am. Hist. Life (1954-1962).

●BE/1021-2353
FRONTIER-FREE EUROPE / COMMISSION OF THE EUROPEAN COMMUNITIES, DIRECTORATE-GENERAL FOR AUDIOVISUAL MEDIA, INFORMATION, COMMUNICATION AND CULTURE. See Economics-Economic History, Conditions.

US/0748-4305
GEORGE WASHINGTON JOURNAL OF INTERNATIONAL LAW AND ECONOMICS, THE. [George Washington j. int. law econ.]. **Added/Corp** George Washington University. National Law Center. Vol. 16, No. 1 (1981)-. Periodical. English. Three times a year (Jan., May, Sept.). $23.00 US; $25.00 other. National Law Center, George Washington University, 2008 G Street Northwest, Washington DC 20052. **Tel** (202)676-3847. **ED** Jeff Wolfson. **LC** K10; .O87. **DD** 341.7/5/05. Index available (Bound in last issue of each volume). **Bk Rev**, (Qty: Approx. 6). **Ad Acc. Circ:** 750. available on microfilm and microfiche from University Microfilms International (UMI). Documents available from The Genuine Article. ***Continues*** *Journal of International Law and Economics, 0022-2003.*
Desc: Discuss problems international in scope of having an impact on the nation's legal, economic, or financial policy.
Ind/Abst Account. Art.; Am. Bibliogr. Slavic East Europ. Stud.; Curr. Contents Soc. Behav. Sci.; Fed. Tax Artic.; Gen. BusinessFile (1992-); Int. Bibliogr. Sociol.; Res. Alert [Full Cov.]; Soc. Sci. Cit. Index [Full Cov.]; UMI ABI/Inform--Bus. Period. Ondisc (1987-) [Full Txt.].

US
GEORGE WASHINGTON JOURNAL OF INTERNATIONAL LAW AND ECONOMICS, THE. Vol. 16, No. 1 (1981)-. Periodical. English. Three times a year. $20.00. National Law Center, George Washington University, 2008 G Street Northwest, Washington DC 20052. **Tel** (202)676-3847. **ED** H Stuart Irvin. **LC** MICROFILM (O) 83/10000 . Index available. **Bk Rev. Circ:** 1,500. Documents available from UMI Article Clearinghouse, UMI Article Clearinghouse. ***Continues*** *Journal of International Law and Economics.*
Desc: Articles and student-written notes on areas of interest in international law and comparative law.
Ind/Abst ABI/INFORM Glob. Ed.; ABI Inform Ondisc (1981-); Curr. Law Index (1980-); Index Foreign Leg. Per.; Index Leg. Period.; Leg. Resour. Index (1980-); LegalTrac (1980-); PAIS Int. Print.

US/0360-6082
GEORGETOWN INTERNATIONAL REVIEW. Vol. 1 (1975)-. English. qt (Winter, Spring, Summer, Autumn). $25.00 (individuals), $53.00 (institutions), $20.00 (students) US and Canada, add $9.00 (surface mail), $18.00 (airmail) for postage other. Center for Strategic and International Studies, 1800 K Street NW / Suite 520, Washington DC 20006. **Tel** (202)887-0200 Ext. 306. **(Subscription address:** MIT Press Journals, 55 Hayward Street, Cambridge, MA 02142-9902**)** **ED** Stanton Burnett, Walter Laqueur, Brad Roberts. **LC** JX1; .G46. **DD** 327/.05. **Ad Acc. Circ:** 3,500. available on microfilm.
Desc: Probes beneath the headlines for foreign and defense policies that are both pragmatic and creative. Contributors are drawn from across the US and overseas to reflect diverse political and professional perspectives.

US/0046-578X
GEORGIA JOURNAL OF INTERNATIONAL AND COMPARATIVE LAW, THE. [Ga. j. int. comp. law]. Vol. 1 (Fall 1970)-. Periodical. English. Three times a year. $15.00 US; $17.00 other. University of Georgia School of Law, Athens GA 30602. **Tel** (706)542-7060. **LC** K7; .E65. **DD** 341/.05. Index available. cum. index. **Ad Acc.** available in microform from University Microfilms International (UMI).
Desc: A legal periodical which informs the legal community on subjects relevant to the practice of international law.
Ind/Abst Curr. Law Index (1980-); Index Foreign Leg. Per.; Index Leg. Period.; Leg. Resour. Index (1980-); LegalTrac (1980-); PAIS Int. Print (1991-).

GW/0344-3094
GERMAN YEARBOOK OF INTERNATIONAL LAW. [Ger. yearb. int. law]. **Added/Corp** Universitaet Kiel. Institut fuer Internationales Recht. **VFOAT** Jahrbuch fuer Internationales Recht. Vol. 19 (1976)-. Periodical. English (French and German). an. DM247.50. Duncker und Humblot Verlag, Postfach 410329, D-12113 Berlin Germany. **Tel** 011 49 30 79000612, 011 49 30 79000613. **LC** JX21; .J33. **DD** 341/.05. **[CCC].** ***Continues*** *Jahrbuch fur Internationales Recht.*
Ind/Abst Acad. Search (July 1993-); Am. Hist. Life (1955-1989); INFO-SOUTH Abstr.; Int. Polit. Sci. Abstr.

●NE/0928-9313
GLOBAL JOURNAL ON CRIME AND CRIMINAL LAW. See Law-Law Enforcement and Criminology.

US/1060-0884
GLOBAL JUSTICE. See Political Science-International Relations.

NE
GROTIANA (1980). (GROTIANA.). **Added/Corp** Grotiana Foundation. Vol. 1 (1980)-. English (French and German). an. FL80.00 (institutions and libraries), Fl65.00 (individuals) Netherlands; Fl90.00 (institutions and libraries), Fl75.00 (individuals) other. Van Gorcum & Company BV, PO Box 43, NL 9400 AA Assen Netherlands. **Tel** 011 31 5920 46846, FAX 011 31 5920 72064. **ED** A C Eyffinger. **LC** JX18; .G76. **DD** 341/.05. **Bk Rev. Ad Acc. Circ:** 400 (ctrl).
Desc: The journal intends to be a forum for exchanges concerning the philosophical, ethical and legal fundamentals of the search for an international order.

US/0736-5713
GUIDE TO THE UNITED STATES TREATIES IN FORCE, A. [Guide U. S. treaties force]. **Added/Corp** United States. Treaties in Force. (1982)- Edition. English. an. $147.50. William S. Hein & Company Inc., 1285 Main Street, Buffalo NY 14209. **Tel** (716)882-2600, (800)828-7571, FAX (716)883-8100, telex 91-209 WM S HEIN BUF. **ED** I. I. Kavass and A. Sprudzs. **LC** JX236.5; .G84. **DD** 341/.0264/73.

●US/1061-7345
GULF WAR CLAIMS REPORTER. **Added/Corp** International Law Institute (Washington, D.C.). (1992)-. Periodical. English. qt. $120.00. Dixon & Dixon, International Law Institute, 615 New Hampshire Avenue NW, Washington DC 20009.

NE
HAGUE YEARBOOK OF INTERNATIONAL LAW / ANNUAIRE DE LA HAYE DE DROIT INTERNATIONAL. **Added/Corp** Hague Academy of International Law. Association of Attenders and Alumni. **VFOAT** Annuaire de la Haye de Droit International. Vol. 1 (1988)-. English (French). an. Kluwer Academic Publishers, Postbus 322, 3300 AH Dordrecht, The Netherlands. **Tel** 011 (31) 78 524400, FAX 011 31 78 183273, telex 20083. **(Subscription address:** Kluwer Academic Publishers / US Subscriptions, PO Box 253, Accord Station, Hingham MA 02018.**)** **LC** JX18; .H33. **DD** 341/.05. ***Continues*** *Hague Academy of International Law. Association of Attenders and Alumni. Annuaire de l'A.A.A.*

NE
HAGUE-ZAGREB-GHENT : ESSAYS ON THE LAW OF INTERNATIONAL TRADE. sa. Fl130. Maklu Publishers, PO Box 960, 7301 BE Apeldoorn The Netherlands. **Tel** (0)55-220625, FAX (0)55-225694. **ED** C. C. A. Voskuil and J. A. Wade. **Circ:** 150.
Desc: Facilitates the exchange of legal information to stimulate discussion between scholars and institutions in the Dutch, Yugoslavian, and Belgian legal systems.

US/0017-8063
HARVARD INTERNATIONAL LAW JOURNAL. [Harvard int. law j.]. Vol. 8 (Winter 1967)-. English. sa (Feb. & June). $24.00 US; $28.00 other. Harvard Law School, Publications Center, Cambridge MA 02138. **Tel** (617)495-7984, (617)495-3694. **ED** John Barquin. **LC** JX1; .H37. **DD** 341/.05. Index available (Free). **Bk Rev. Pr Rev.** available on microfilm and

microfiche from University Microfilms International (UMI). Documents available from The Genuine Article. *Continues* Harvard International Law Club Journal.
Desc: Student-edited journal of international law; publishes articles and notes on matters of current interest to lawyers practicing international law.
Ind/Abst ABC POL SCI; Am. Bibliogr. Slavic East Europ. Stud.; Bowne Dig. Corp. Sec. Lawyers; Curr. Contents Soc. Behav. Sci.; Curr. Law Index (1980-); Fed. Tax Artic.; Hum. Rights Intern. Rep.; Index Foreign Leg. Per.; Index Leg. Period.; Leg. Resour. Index (1980-); LegalTrac (1980-); PAIS Int. Print (1991-); Res. Alert [Full Cov.]; Soc. Sci. Cit. Index [Full Cov.].

US/0149-9246
HASTINGS INTERNATIONAL AND COMPARATIVE LAW REVIEW. [Hastings int. comp. law rev.]. **Added/Corp** Hastings College of the Law. Vol. 1,(Winter 1977)-. Periodical. English. qt. $23.00 US; $25.00 other. Hastings College of Law, 200 McAllister Street, San Francisco CA 94102. **Tel** (415)565-4816, (415)565-4738, FAX (415)565-4814. **ED** Brian Keating (editor's telephone: (415)565-4730). **LC** K8; .A84. **DD** 341/.05. Index available (every five years). cum. index. **Bk Rev**, (Qty: 1-3). **Ad Acc**, **Adv Mgr:** A Kava, **Tel** (415)565-4738. **Pr Rev. Circ:** 1,000. available on CD-ROM and an online database from WESTLAW; available on microfilm and microfiche from Fred B. Rothman and Company.
Desc: Publishes articles by law professors and practitioners addressing timely issues in public and private international law.
Ind/Abst ABC POL SCI; Curr. Law Index (1980-); Index Leg. Period.; Leg. Resour. Index (1980-); LegalTrac (1980-); PAIS Int. Print; Peace Res. Abstr. J. (1977-1983).

JA
HIKAKU HOSEI. **VFOAT** Journal of the Kinki University Comparative Law and Politics Institute. 1972-. Periodical. Japanese (Japanese). Kinki Daigaku Hikakuho Seiji Kenkyujo, 4-1 Kowakae 3-chome, Higashi Osaka Japan. **LC** K8; .I46.

UK
HOLDSWORTH LAW REVIEW / UNIVERSITY OF BIRMINGHAM. See Law.

TZ
HOTUBA YA WAZIRI WA MAMBO YA NJE. **Main/Corp** Tanzania. Wizara ya Mambo ya Nje. Swahili (Swahili). an. **LC** JX1865.T362; T36A. *Continues* Hotuba ya Waziri wa Mambo ya Nchi za Nje ... .

US/0194-1879
HOUSTON JOURNAL OF INTERNATIONAL LAW. [Houst. j. int. law]. Vol. 1 (Spring 1978)-. Periodical. English. Three times a year. $18.00 US; $20.00 other. Houston Journal of International Law, University of Houston, Law Center, BLB Suite 29, Houston TX 77204. **Tel** (713)743-2212. **ED** Bradley W Paulson. **LC** JX1; .H68. **DD** 341/.05. Index available. cum. index. **Bk Rev. Circ:** 600 (ctrl).
Desc: Discussions of recent developments in international law including public international law, international business, tax and trade.
Ind/Abst Curr. Law Index (1980-); Hum. Rights Intern. Rep.; Index Leg. Period.; Leg. Resour. Index (1980-); LegalTrac (1980-).

GW/0174-4704
HUMAN RIGHTS LAW JOURNAL : HRLJ. **VFOAT** HRLJ. Vol. 1 (1980)-. Academic Scholarly Publication. English. qt. DM286.00 (add DM16.80 postage) Germany; £98.00 (add £5.75 postage) Europe; $192.00 (add $15.60 postage-libraries), (add $21.60 postage-regular) US; $192.00 (add $32.60 postage) Canada; £98.00 (add £16.75 postage) other. N P Engel Verlag, Gutenbergstrasse 29, D-77694 Kehl Germany. **Tel** 011 49 7851 2463, FAX 011 49 7851 4234, telex 753 560. **ED** Thomas Buergenthal. **LC** K8; .U454. **DD** 341.4/81/05. cum. index. **Ad Acc**. *Absorbed* Human Rights Review.
Desc: Scholarly articles, decisions and reports (international, constitutional and supreme court decisions), documentations and pending proceedings.
Ind/Abst Hum. Rights Intern. Rep.; Int. Polit. Sci. Abstr.; Leg. Resour. Index; LegalTrac (1980-); PAIS Int. Print (1991-).

FR/1017-284X
ICC INTERNATIONAL COURT OF ARBITRATION BULLETIN, THE. **Added/Corp** International Chamber of Commerce. Court of Arbitration. **VAT** Internation Chamber of Commerce International Court of Arbitration Bulletin. Vol. 1, No. 1 (June 1990)-. Bulletin. English (French). Twice a year. $75.00. International Chamber of Commerce, 38 Cours Albert 1 ER, 75009 Paris France. **Tel** 011 33 49532828, FAX 011 33 1 45623456, telex 650770. **ED** Jean Francois Bourdue. **Bk Rev. Pr Rev.**

US/0258-3690
ICSID REVIEW. [ICSID rev.]. **Added/Corp** International Centre for Settlement of Investment Disputes. **VFOAT** Foreign Investment Law Journal; ICSID Review, Foreign Investment Law Journal. **VAT** International Centre for Settlement of Investment Disputes Review. Vol. 1, No. 1 (Spring 1986)-. Periodical.

English. Twice a year (April, October). $50.00 US; $54.80 Canada and Mexico; $58.90 other. Johns Hopkins University Press, 2715 North Charles Street, Baltimore MD 21218-4319. **Tel** (410)516-6987, FAX (410)516-6968. **ED** Ibrahim F.I. Shihata. **LC** K9; .C75. **DD** 346/.07/05; 342.6705. [CCC]. **Ad Acc**. available on microfilm and microfiche from University Microfilms International (UMI).
Desc: Devoted to foreign investment law. Offers legal and business professionals a review of domestic law, investment treaties, contractual trends and resolutions of investment disputes. Includes articles, comments, cases, documents, and bibliographies pertinent to investment law and international business transactions.
Ind/Abst Index Foreign Leg. Per.; PAIS Int. Print (1991-).

US/1052-3391
ILSA JOURNAL OF INTERNATIONAL LAW. [ILSA j. int. law]. **Added/Corp** International Law Students Association. **VAT** International Law Students Association Journal of International Law. Vol. 11 (Winter 1987)-. Periodical. English. an. $9.00. International Law Students Association, 2223 Massachusetts Avenue Northwest, Washington DC 20008. **Tel** (202)939-6000. **LC** JX1; .A86a. **DD** 341.05. *Continues* Association of Student International Law Societies. ASILS International Law Journal, 0161-1402.
Desc: Includes exclusively student-written articles by association members in the international and comparative law fields. Also includes the annual Jessup Competition materials.
Ind/Abst Index Leg. Period.; Leg. Resour. Index; LegalTrac (1987-).

CN
INDEX : CANADA TREATY SERIES. **VFOAT** Index: Recueil des Traites du Canada. 1960-. Periodical. Multiple languages (English and French). an. 0.35Can$ per number. **DD** 341.0266/71. *Formed by the union of* Index to Treaty Series *and* Index au Recueils des Traites.

US
INDEX TO RESOLUTIONS OF THE GENERAL ASSEMBLY. **Added/Corp** United Nations. General Assembly. Resolutions Adopted by the General Assembly. United Nations. Dag Hammarskjold Library. Documentation Division. (1946/70)-. Government Publication. English. an. $3.50. United Nations Publications, 2 United Nations Plaza, Room DC2 0853, Department 007C, New York NY 10017. **Tel** (212)963-8303, (800)253-9646. **LC** JX1977; .A2 subser. **DD** 300/.8 S; 341.23/01/6.
Desc: Index of all resolutions made by the General Assembly, the deliberate organ of the United Nations.

II
INDIAN JOURNAL OF COMPARATIVE LAW. **Added/Corp** Kerala Law Institute. (197?)-. Periodical. English. sa. Rs365.10 US; Rs257.00 India. Indian Journal of Comparative Law, Kerala Law Institute, Kerala India 64315. **LC** K9; .N355. **DD** 340/.2; 342.

II/0019-5294
INDIAN JOURNAL OF INTERNATIONAL LAW, THE. **Added/Corp** Indian Society of International Law. Vol. 1, No. 1 (July 1960)-. English. qt. $50.00. Indian Society of International Law, 7-8 Scindia H/Kasturba Gandhi M, New Delhi 110001 India. (**Subscription address:** Prints India, 11 Darya Ganj, New Delhi 110002 India.) **LC** JX18; .I5.
Ind/Abst Hum. Rights Intern. Rep.; Index Foreign Leg. Per.

US/1061-4982
INDIANA INTERNATIONAL & COMPARATIVE LAW REVIEW. [Indiana int. comp. law rev.]. **Added/Corp** Indiana University School of Law-Indianapolis. Vol. 1, No. 1 (Spring 1991)-. Periodical. English. Twice a year. $15.00 US; $21.00 other. Indiana International and Comparative Law Review, Indiana University, 735 W New York Street, Indianapolis IN 46202. **Tel** (317)274-4440. **ED** Scott Chinn. **LC** K9; .N368. **DD** 341/.05.
Ind/Abst Index Leg. Period. (1992-).

FR/0252-0877
INFORMATION BULLETIN ON LEGAL ACTIVITIES WITHIN THE COUNCIL OF EUROPE AND IN MEMBER STATES. [Inf. bull. leg. act. Counc. Eur. memb. states]. **Main/Corp** Council of Europe. Directorate of Legal Affairs. No. 1 (June 1978)-. Periodical. English. Twice a year. Manhattan Publishing Company, PO Box 650, Croton-on-Hudson NY 10520. **Tel** (914)271-5194. **LC** KJE112; .I54. **DD** 341/.24/2. *Formed by the union of* Council of Europe. Exchange of Information Between the Member States on their Legislative Activity and Regulations; Newsletter on Legislative Activities *and* Legal Cooperation in Europe.

NE/0925-9872
INFORMATION TECHNOLOGY AND THE LAW: AN INTERNATIONAL BIBLIOGRAPHY. Bibliography. English. sa. Fl284.00 (postage included). Martinus Nijhoff Publishers, Subsidiary of Kluwer Academic Publishers, Koraalrood 50, 2718 SC Zoetermeer Netherlands. **Tel** 011 31 79

684400. **ED** Costantino Ciampi, Rosa Maria Di Giorgi, Elio Famelli, Roberta Nannucci, Giuseppe Trivisonno. **Pr Rev. Acid Free**. available on microfilm and microfiche from University Microfilms International (UMI). Documents available from Ask*IEEE. *Continues* Informatica e Diritto: Bibliografia Internazionale.
Desc: The international character of the bibliography merits separate consideration. In the first place, the journal is international because it documents literature of world wide importance on legal information science and computer law. Furthermore, it is directed toward scholars and experts in all countries represented in it. Finally, the bibliographical analysis is carried out with the cooperation of various national documentation centers, qualified to cover all the most important geographical areas.
Ind/Abst INSPEC.

US/0747-6574
INFORMATIVO JURIDICO (WASHINGTON D.C.). (INFORMATIVO JURIDICO / SUBSECRETARIA DE ASUNTOS JURIDICOS.). [Inf. jurid.]. Nos. 1 & 2 (Jan./Aug. 1982)-. Spanish. Three times a year. $12.00. General Secretariat of the Organization of American States, 1889 F Street NW, Washington DC 20006. **Tel** (202)789-6284. **ED** Christian Garcia-Godoy. **LC** KDZ1103; .I54. **DD** 341.24/5/05. **Circ:** 600.
Desc: International law and legal developments within the Interamerican System (Latin America, the Caribbean and the United States).

●US/1078-2028
INTER-AMERICAN TRADE AND INVESTMENT LAW. See Business-Commerce.

UK/0020-5893
INTERNATIONAL AND COMPARATIVE LAW QUARTERLY, THE. [Int. comp. law q.]. **Added/Corp** British Institute of International and Comparative Law. Society of Comparative Legislation. Vol. 1 (Jan. 1952)-. Periodical. English. Four times a year (Jan., Apr., July, Oct.). $125.00 US & Canada; £65.00 (one year) surface mail; £70.00 (one year) airmail. British Institute of International and Comparative Law, Charles Clore House, 17 Russell Square, London WC1B 5DR England. **Tel** 011 44 71 636-5802, FAX 011 44 71 323-2016. **ED** Hazel Fox. **DD** 340.05. Index available. cum. index. **Bk Rev. Ad Acc. Pr Rev. Circ:** 2,500. Documents available from The Genuine Article. *Formed by the union of* International Law Quarterly *and* Journal of Comparative Legislation and International Law; *Absorbed* Transactions for the Year (Grotius Society).
Desc: Public and private international law, comparative law, European law and Commonwealth law.
Ind/Abst ABC POL SCI; Aust. Leg. Mon. Dig.; Bowne Dig. Corp. Sec. Lawyers; Curr. Law Index (1980-); Highw. Res. Abstr.; Index Foreign Leg. Per.; Index Leg. Period.; Int. Polit. Sci. Abstr.; LABORDOC; Leg. Inf. Manage. Index; Leg. Resour. Index (1980-); LegalTrac (1980-); PAIS Int. Print (1991-); Res. Alert [Full Cov.]; Soc. Sci. Cit. Index [Full Cov.]; West. Hist. Q.

US/0886-0114
INTERNATIONAL ARBITRATION REPORT. [Int. arbitr. rep.]. **Added/Corp** Mealey Publications. Vol. 1, Issue 1 (Jan. 1986)-. Periodical. English. mo. $600.00 US; $648.00 other. Mealey Publications, PO Box 446, Wayne PA 19087-0446. **Tel** (215)688-6566, FAX (215)688-7552. **ED** Michael P. Mealey and Pamela J. Craft. **LC** K2400.A13; I57. **DD** 341.5/22. [CCC]. Index available. cum. index. **Bk Rev. Desc:** Editorial and document coverage of commercial arbitration disputes and court orders concerning arbitration worldwide.

UK/0143-7453
INTERNATIONAL BAR NEWS (LONDON, ENGLAND). (INTERNATIONAL BAR NEWS.). [Int. bar news]. **Added/Corp** International Bar Association. (May 1980)-. Periodical. English. Five times a year. International Bar Association, 2 Harewood Place, Hanover Square, London W1R 9HB England. **Tel** 011 44 71 629-1206, FAX 011 44 71 409 0456, telex 8812664 INBAR G. **ED** Ruth Elden. **LC** K110.I47; A2. **DD** 340/.06. **Ad Acc. Circ:** 9,000. *Continues in part* International Bar Journal, 0047-0589.
Desc: Membership news and conference proceedings.

UK/0309-7676
INTERNATIONAL BUSINESS LAWYER. [Int. bus. lawyer]. **Added/Corp** International Bar Association. Section on Business Law. (1973)-. Periodical. English. mo. £130.00. International Bar Association, 2 Harewood Place, Hanover Square, London W1R 9HB England. **Tel** 011 44 71 629-1206, FAX 011 44 71 409 0456, telex 8812664 INBAR G. **ED** Ruth Eldon. **LC** K9; .N757. **DD** 346.07/05. Index available. cum. index. **Bk Rev. Ad Acc. Circ:** 10,000 (ctrl).
Desc: International law and practice relating to business, commercial and corporate law.
Ind/Abst Bowne Dig. Corp. Sec. Lawyers; Coal Abstr.; Curr. Law Index (1980-); Index Foreign Leg. Per.; Leg. Resour. Index (1980-); LegalTrac (1980-).

UK/0265-1416
INTERNATIONAL CONSTRUCTION LAW REVIEW, THE. [Int. constr. law rev.]. Vol. 1, Pt. 1 (Oct. 1983)-. Periodical. English. qt (Jan., Apr., Jul. and Oct.). £134.00. Lloyd's of London Press Ltd, Sheepen Place, Colchester, Essex, CO3 3LP England. **Tel** 011 44 206 772113, US: (212)529-9500, US: (800)955-6937, FAX 011 44 206 772880, US: (212)529-9826, telex 987321 LLOYDS G. **(Subscription address:** Lloyd's of London Press Inc. / North America, 611 Broadway, Suite 308, New York NY 10012.**) ED** Humphrey Lloyd, David Wrightman, Stuart Ashworth. **LC** K9; .N8155. **DD** 343/.07869/005; 342.37869005. Index available. cum. index. **Bk Rev. Circ:** 400.
Desc: Meets the requirements of those involved in the legal and commercial aspects of international construction. Contains case notes from all parts of the world, correspondents' reports on current developments and in-depth articles on a wide range of topics. Features information on conferences, book reviews and a regular annual index.
Ind/Abst Index Leg. Period.; Leg. Resour. Index; LegalTrac (1991-).

US/0899-7799
INTERNATIONAL CONTRACT ADVISER. [Int. contract advis.]. (1988)-. Periodical. English. mo. $250.00. Kluwer Law and Taxation Publishers (Mass.), 675 Massachusetts Avenue, Cambridge MA 02139. **Tel** (617) 354-0140. **DD** 341.
Desc: Provides a welcome and unique source of "hands-on" international business advice. Each issues contains articles on current international business topics with a strong slant toward contract negotiating and drafting advice.

US
INTERNATIONAL COURT OF JUSTICE. **Main/Corp** United Nations. Office of Public Information. (19??)-. Government Publication. English. ir. price vaires per volume. United Nations Publications, 2 United Nations Plaza, Room DC2 0853, Department 007C, New York NY 10017. **Tel** (212)963-8303, (800)253-9646.
Desc: Contains a brief explanation of the aims, functions and organization of the World Court.

SA/0897-5086
INTERNATIONAL FREEDOM FOUNDATION. ***Title Change.* See** Economics-International Economics.

NE
INTERNATIONAL GENEVA YEARBOOK. (1988)-. Monographic series. English. ir. Price varies per volume. Verlag Peter Lang AG, Jupiterstrasse 15, CH-3000 Bern 15 Switzerland. **Tel** 011 41 31 9411122, FAX 011 41 31 321131. **LC** JX1995; .I524. **DD** 341.2. ***Continues*** *International Geneva.*

NE/0927-3522
INTERNATIONAL JOURNAL OF MARINE AND COASTAL LAW, THE. English. qt. $626.00. Martinus Nijhoff Publishers, Subsidiary of Kluwer Academic Publishers, Koraalrood 50, 2718 SC Zoetermeer Netherlands. **Tel** 011 31 79 684400. **ED** D. Freestone and G. Mangone. **Pr Rev. Acid Free.** ***Absorbed*** *Marine Policy Reports, 0735-5912.*
Desc: Covers all aspects of the law of estuarine and coastal management. It publishes major articles and contains a vigorous section devoted to current legal developments, providing up to date information on international treaties and case law, national statute law, national court decisions, and other aspects of national state practice.

UK/0953-8186
INTERNATIONAL JOURNAL OF REFUGEE LAW. [Int. j. refug. law]. **Added/Corp** Oxford University Press. Vol. 1, No. 1 (Jan. 1989)-. Periodical. English. qt. £66.00 UK and Europe; $125.00 other. Oxford University Press, Walton Street, Oxford OX2 6DP England. **Tel** 011 44 865 56767, FAX 011 44 865 267773, telex 837330 OXPRES G. **(Subscription address:** Oxford University Press / USA, Journals Marketing Department, Oxford University Press, 2001 Evans Road, Cary NC 27513.**) ED** Guy S. Goodwin-Gill. **LC** K9; .N8495. **DD** 342/.083; 342.283. **[CCC].** available on microfilm and microfiche from University Microfilms International (UMI).
Ind/Abst Hum. Rights Intern. Rep.; Index Leg. Period. (1992-); Sage Public Adm. Abstr.

NE/0927-5908
INTERNATIONAL JOURNAL ON GROUP RIGHTS. English. qt. Fl322.00 (postage included). Martinus Nijhoff Publishers, Subsidiary of Kluwer Academic Publishers, Koraalrood 50, 2718 SC Zoetermeer Netherlands. **Tel** 011 31 79 684400. **ED** Yonah Alexander. **Bk Rev. Pr Rev. Acid Free.**
Desc: An interdisciplinary publication on the legal political, and related problems involved in the existence and rights of groups within society. By groups, the reference is to clearly recognizable segments of society, defined by spontaneous and rather constant factors, such as religion, race, culture, or language.

US/0047-0813
INTERNATIONAL LAW NEWS, THE. [Int. law news]. **Added/Corp** American Bar Association. Section of International Law. American Bar Association. Section of International and Comparative Law. Vol. 1 (Jan. 1972)-. English. qt (4 issues). Free on request to members. American Bar Association, 750 North Lake Shore Drive, Chicago IL 60611. **Tel** (312)988-5522, (312)988-5241, FAX (312)988-5528, telex 270593. **ED** Gerold W. Libby. **LC** JX1; .I57. **DD** 341/.05. **Circ:** 12,000 (ctrl).
Desc: Current items of interest for members of the Section of International Law and Practice, ABA, including law notes, committee activity reports, meetings/conference information and new publications.
Ind/Abst Curr. Law Index (1980-Dec. 1985); Leg. Resour. Index (1980-Dec. 1985); LegalTrac (1980-1985).

GW
INTERNATIONAL LAW OF ARMS CONTROL. English (German). ir. DM0.25 (per page). Berlin Verlag Arno Spitz, Pacelliallee 5, W-100 Berlin 33 Germany. **ED** Gundolf Fahl.
Desc: This collection contains all international treaties on arms control, beginning with the Red Cross Convention of 1925, in addition are surveys of others signataries, charts of delivery systems and other military data.

US/1041-3405
INTERNATIONAL LAW PRACTICUM. [Int. law pract.]. **Added/Corp** New York State Bar Association. International Law and Practice Section. Vol. 1, No. 1 (Spring 1988)-. Periodical. English. Twice a year (Apr., & Oct.). Free (members of New York State Bar Association); $65.00 (non-members); Comes with the New York International Law Review Membership). New York State Bar Association, One Elk Street, Albany NY 12207. **Tel** (518)463-3200. **ED** Ronald David Gleenberg. **LC** K1001.2; .I56. **DD** 341.7/54. **Bk Rev. Ad Acc. Pr Rev. Circ:** 2,000 (ctrl). ***Continues*** *International Trade & Transaction Committee Newsletter.*
Desc: Articles on international law issues to aid the general practitioner in the international law area.
Ind/Abst Leg. Resour. Index; LegalTrac (1990-).

II
INTERNATIONAL LAW REPORTER, THE. Periodical. English. mo. $8.00. Kishan Lal Chopra, 590 Sector 7-B Urban Estate, Faridabad India. **LC** JX18; .I53. **DD** 341/.05.

UK/0309-0671
INTERNATIONAL LAW REPORTS. [Int. law rep.]. (1950)-. English. ir. $154.00. Grotius Publications Ltd, PO Box 115, Cambridge CB3 9BP England. **Tel** 011 44 223 323410. **ED** Editors: (1950-1957), Hersch Lauterpacht; (1958)- E. Lauterpacht. **LC** JX68; .A65. ***Continues*** *Annual Digest and Reports of Public International Law Cases.*

US/0020-7810
INTERNATIONAL LAWYER, THE. [Int. lawyer]. **Added/Corp** American Bar Association. Section of International Law. American Bar Association. Section of International and Comparative Law. Vol. 1 (Oct. 1966)-. English. qt (4 issues). $31.00. American Bar Association, 750 North Lake Shore Drive, Chicago IL 60611. **Tel** (312)988-5522, (312)988-5241, FAX (312)988-5528, telex 270593. **LC** JX1; .I63. **DD** 341/.05. **Bk Rev. Ad Acc.** ctrl circ. ***Formed by the union of*** *American Bar Association. Section of International and Comparative Law. Proceedings* ***and*** *Section of International and Comparative Law Bulletin.*
Ind/Abst Am. Bibliogr. Slavic East Europ. Stud.; Bowne Dig. Corp. Sec. Lawyers; Curr. Law Index; Fed. Tax Artic.; Index Foreign Leg. Per.; Index Leg. Period.; Leg. Inf. Manage. Index; Leg. Resour. Index (1980-); LegalTrac (1980-).

US/0738-9728
INTERNATIONAL LAWYERS' NEWSLETTER. [Int. lawyers' newsl.]. (Fall 1979)-. Newsletter. English. bm. $90.00 (includes annual index). Kluwer Law and Taxation Publishers (Mass.), 675 Massachusetts Avenue, Cambridge MA 02139. **Tel** (617) 354-0140. **ED** Carol Emory and Arthur Kroos. **LC** K120.A2; I58. **DD** 340/.05. **[CCC].** Index available. cum. index. **Bk Rev. Circ:** 1,500.
Desc: A unique periodical of practical information directed to the interest of international business lawyers. Articles focus on the basic issues of recurring legal problems, as well as on specialty areas. It also offers business travel tips, salary survey, a calendar of upcoming conference, reviews on new publication and products of relevance, a listing of current job openings for international lawyers, etc.

US/0020-7829
INTERNATIONAL LEGAL MATERIALS. [Int. leg. mater.]. **Added/Corp** American Society of International Law. Vol. 1, No. 1 (Aug. 1962)-. English. Six times a year (Jan., Mar., May, July, Sept., Nov.). $170.00 US; $190.00 other. American Society of International Law, 2223 Massachusetts Avenue Northwest, Washington DC 20008-2864. **Tel** (202)939-6000, FAX (202)797-7133. **ED** Marilou M. Righini. **LC** JX68; .I5. **DD** 341/.1. **[CCC].** Index available (bound in Nov. issue). cum. index. **Ad Acc. Circ:** 2,800 (ctrl). available on microfiche from WESTLAW; LEXIS; and Williams S Hein & Co.
Desc: A full text of treaties, laws, and court decisions used throughout the world by scholars and practitioners of international law and politics.
Ind/Abst ABC POL SCI; Curr. Law Index (1980-Dec. 1985); Leg. Resour. Index (1980-Dec. 1985)(1980-); LegalTrac (1982-); Middle East Abstr. Index; PAIS Int. Print (1991-).

US
INTERNATIONAL LEGAL PERSPECTIVES. **Added/Corp** Northwestern School of Law. (198?)-. Periodical. English. sa. $15.00. Northwestern School of Law, 10015 Southwest, Terwilliger Boulevard, Portland OR 97219. **Tel** (503)244-1181 Ext. 700, FAX (503)246-8542. **ED** Karen Read and Kathy Fritz. **Bk Rev**, (Qty: 2). ctrl circ. available on an online database; available on microfilm. Documents available.
Ind/Abst LegalTrac (1988-).

UK/0309-7684
INTERNATIONAL LEGAL PRACTITIONER. [Int. leg. pract.]. **Added/Corp** International Bar Association. Section on General Practice. Vol. 4 (I) (Jan. 1979)-. Periodical. English. qt. £65.00. International Bar Association, 2 Harewood Place, Hanover Square, London W1R 9HB England. **Tel** 011 44 71 629-1206, FAX 011 44 71 409 0456, telex 8812664 INBAR G. **(Subscription address:** International Bar Association, PO Box 217, Subscription Dept., Maidstone Kent ME16 9LT England; Telephone: 071 005260**) ED** Ruth Eldon. **LC** K110.I47; A22. **DD** 340/.05. Index available. **Bk Rev. Ad Acc. Circ:** 2,500. ***Continues in part*** *International Bar Journal, 0047-0589.*
Desc: General legal practice.

US
INTERNATIONAL LITIGATION : A GUIDE TO JURISDICTION PRACTICE & STRATEGY. (19??)-. English. an. $95.00. Prentice-Hall Law and Business, 270 Sylvan Avenue, Englewood Cliffs NJ 07632. **Tel** (800)223-0231, (201)894-8538, FAX (201)894-8666.

UK/0958-9767
INTERNATIONAL LITIGATION PROCEDURE. Vol. 1, Issue 1 (1990)-. English. mo. £275.00 Europe; £289.00 other. Sweet & Maxwell Ltd., South Quay Plaza, 183 Marsh Wall, London E14 9FT England. **Tel** 011 44 264 342899, FAX 011 44 264 342723, telex 929089 ITPINF G.
Desc: Reports regularly, cases concerning transnational litigation and strives to be solely devoted to procedural issues arising out of litigation with a foreign element.

UK
INTERNATIONAL MEDIA LAW. VFOAT IML; I.M.L. Vol. 1, No. 1 (Oct. 1982)-. Periodical. English. mo. £95.00 UK; $165.00 US; £99.00 other. 21/27 Lamb's Conduit Street, London WCIN 3NJ England. **LC** K4240.A13; I57. **DD** 341.7/57. available on microfilm and microfiche from University Microfilms International (UMI).

US
INTERNATIONAL ORGANIZATIONS REGULATORY GUIDEBOOK, THE. (1981)-. English. International Business-Government Counsellors Inc, 1625 Eye Street NW, Washington DC 20006. ***Continues*** *Multinational Corporation Regulatory Guidebook, 0273-0057.*

US
INTERNATIONAL PRACTITIONER'S NOTEBOOK. Began with: No. 8 (Nov. 1979). Periodical. English. qt. American Branch of the International Law Association, 14 Wall Street, New York NY 10005. ***Continues*** *Practitioner's Notebook.*

PL
INTERNATIONAL PROTECTION OF INDUSTRIAL PROPERTY. **Added/Corp** Uniwersytet im. Adama Mickiewicza w Poznaniu. Vol. 1 (1978)-. Periodical. English. Z50.00. **(Subscription address:** ARS Polona, PO Box 1001, 00068 Warsaw Poland.**) LC** K9; .N86. **DD** 341.7/58/09438.

US/1041-3855
INTERNATIONAL QUARTERLY (CHESTERLAND, OHIO). **See** Law-Corporate Law.

BE
INTERNATIONAL REVIEW OF CONTEMPORARY LAW. ***Suspended.*** (1982)-(19??). Periodical. English. sa. Aijd Revue Deoit Contempora, 263 Avenue Albert, 1180 Brussels Belgium. **LC** JX3; .R24. **DD** 341/.05. ***Continues*** *Review of Contemporary Law.*
Ind/Abst Hum. Rights Intern. Rep.

US/0144-8188
INTERNATIONAL REVIEW OF LAW AND ECONOMICS. **See** Economics-International Economics.

US/0896-3010
INTERNATIONAL SECURITIES REGULATION REPORT. [Int. sec. regul. rep.]. Vol. 1, No. 1 (Dec. 23, 1987)-. Periodical. English. sm. $795.00 North America; $817.00 other. LRP Publications, 747 Dresher Road, PO Box 980, Horsham PA 19044-0980. **Tel** (800)341-7874, (215)784-0860, FAX (215)784-9639, (215)784-0870. **(Subscription telephone:** FAX (301)948-5823) **ED** William H Feldman. **DD** 341.
Desc: Provides information on regulation of international securities trading, new links among markets, and cooperation among governments in enforcing securities laws.

II/0020-8817
INTERNATIONAL STUDIES (SAHIBABAD). (INTERNATIONAL STUDIES.). [Int. stud.]. **Added/Corp** Indian School of International Studies. Jawaharlal Nehru University. School of International Studies. Vol. 1 (July 1959)-. Periodical. English. qt (Jan., April, July, Oct.). $95.00. SAGE Periodical Press, 2455 Teller Road, Thousand Oaks CA 91320. **Tel** (805)499-0721, FAX (805)499-0871, telex 100799. **ED** Anirudha Gupta. **LC** JX18; .I55. Index available. **Ad Acc.** available on microfilm and microfiche from University Microfilms International (UMI).
Desc: Indian research journal in the field of international affairs and area studies.
Ind/Abst ABC POL SCI (19??-1985); Am. Hist. Life (1965-1969, 1973-1979); Int. Bibliogr. Sociol.; Int. Polit. Sci. Abstr.; Middle East Abstr. Index; Peace Res. Abstr. J. (1969).

US/0074-896X
INTERNATIONAL TAX AGREEMENTS. **See** Public Administration-Public Finance and Taxation.

US
INTERNATIONAL TAX AGREEMENTS / UNITED NATIONS, DEPARTMENT OF ECONOMIC AFFAIRS, FISCAL DIVISION. **Added/Corp** United Nations. United Nations. Dept. of Economic Affairs. Fiscal Division. United Nations. Dept. of Economic and Social Affairs. Fiscal and Financial Branch. United Nations. Dept. of Economic and Social Affairs. **VFOAT** World Guide to International Tax Agreements. (1948)-. Government Publication. English. ir. $10.00. United Nations Publications, 2 United Nations Plaza, Room DC2 0853, Department 007C, New York NY 10017. **Tel** (212)963-8303, (800)253-9646. ***Continues*** *League of Nations. Double Taxation and Fiscal Evasion.*
Desc: Loose-leaf series covering all types of international taxation agreements on income and fortune, moveable capital, commercial, industrial, and agricultural enterprises, or maritime and air transport enterprises.

US/0741-4269
INTERNATIONAL TAX & BUSINESS LAWYER. [Int. tax bus. lawyer]. **Added/Corp** University of California, Berkeley. School of Law. **VFOAT** International Tax and Business Lawyer. Vol. 1, No. 1 (Summer 1983)-. Periodical. English. sa (Feb., Aug.). $43.00 US; $46.00 other. University of California Press, 2120 Berkeley Way, Berkeley CA 94720. **Tel** (510)642-4191, (510)642-3907, FAX (510)642-9917. **ED** Greg Vamos. **LC** K9; .N885. **DD** 341.7/5/05. **[CCC]. Bk Rev. Circ:** 500. available on microfilm from University Microfilms International (UMI).
Ind/Abst Bowne Dig. Corp. Sec. Lawyers; Curr. Law Index (1980-); Index Foreign Leg. Per.; Index Leg. Period.; Leg. Contents, LC; Leg. Resour. Index (1980-); LegalTrac (1983-); PAIS Int. Print (1991-).

GW/0020-9503
INTERNATIONALES RECHT UND DIPLOMATIE. ***Ceased.*** **See** Political Science-International Relations.

GW
IPRAX : PRAXIS DES INTERNATIONALEN PRIVAT- UND VERFAHRENSRECHTS. **VFOAT** I.Prax; Praxis des Internationalen Privat- und Verfahrensrechts. Vol. 1, (1981)-. Periodical. German. bm (Jan., Mar., May, July, Sept., Nov.). DM208.00; DM226.00 other. Ernst und Werner Gieseking, Deckerstrasse 30, Postfach 130 120, 4800 Bielefeld 13 Germany. **LC** K9; .P7. **DD** 340.9/05.
Ind/Abst Index Foreign Leg. Per.

UK
IRAN-UNITED STATES CLAIMS TRIBUNAL REPORTS. **Main/Corp** Iran-United States Claims Tribunal. **VFOAT** Iran-U.S. Claims Tribunal Reports. Vol. 1 (1981/82)-. English. Three times a year. $158.00 (per volume). Grotius Publications Ltd, PO Box 115, Cambridge CB3 9BP England. **Tel** 011 44 223 323410. **ED** M Mac Glashan. **LC** JX233.I7; I72A. **DD** 341.5/22/026873055. Index available. cum. index. **Ad Acc.**
Desc: The only complete and fully indexed report of this unique and important tribunal. These reports are essential for all governments and law libraries.

US/0277-2922
IRANIAN ASSETS LITIGATION REPORTER. [Iran. assets litig. rep.]. (1980)-. Periodical. English. mo. $2300.00. Andrews Publications Inc., 1646 West Chester Pike, PO Box 1000, Westtown PA 19395. **Tel** (610)399-6600, (800)345-1101, FAX (610)399-6610. **ED** Leonard E. B. Andrews. **LC** JX238.I7; I7. **DD** 341.5/5. cum. index. ctrl circ.
Desc: Provides comprehensive coverage of the Iran-U.S. Claims Tribunal in The Hague, including reporting on several major oil company claims pending before the Tribunal.

IT
ITALIAN YEARBOOK OF INTERNATIONAL LAW, THE. V. 1- 1975-. English. an. Oceana Publications, Inc., 75 Main Street, Dobbs Ferry NY 10522. **Tel** (914)693-1320, FAX (914)693-0402. **LC** JX7; .I82. **DD** 341/.05.
Ind/Abst Index Foreign Leg. Per.

GW/0021-3993
JAHRBUCH FUER INTERNATIONALES RECHT. ***Title Change.*** **Added/Corp** Hamburg. Universitat. Forschungsstelle fur Volkerrecht und Auslandisches Offentliches Recht. Kiel. Universitat. Institut fur Internationales Recht. **VFOAT** German Yearbook of International Law. (1948)-(199?). German (English and German). an. Duncker und Humblot Verlag, Postfach 410329, D-12113 Berlin Germany. **Tel** 011 49 30 79000612, 011 49 30 79000613. **ED** J Delbiuck, W Fiedler and W A Kewluig. ***Continued by*** *German Yearbook of International Law, 0344-3094.*
Desc: Yearbook of international law.
Ind/Abst Am. Hist. Life (1955-1975); Index Foreign Leg. Per.

GW/0075-2746
JAHRBUCH FUER OSTRECHT. **Added/Corp** Institut fur Ostrecht. Vol. 1 (April 1960)-. Periodical. German. ir. DM86.00. Deutscher Bundes-Verlag GmbH, Postfach 12 03 80, W-5300 Bonn 1 Germany. **LC** K10; .A35.
Desc: Publication of eastern law, analyses, reports, comparisons of laws, translations, documents and discussions on eastern European laws. Forum for the complete German and international research on Eastern Europe.
Ind/Abst Index Foreign Leg. Per.; Int. Bibliogr. Sociol.

BB
JAMAICA CONSOLIDATED INDEX OF STATUTES AND SUBSIDIARY LEGISLATION TO ... . **Added/Corp** University of the West Indies (Cave Hill, Barbados). Faculty of Law. Library. **VFOAT** Consolidated Index of Statutes and Subsidiary Legislation to ... . (19??)-. English. an. $20.00. Faculty of Law Library, PO Box 64, Bridgetown Barbados. **Tel** (813)778-5211. **ED** Clifford Hammett. **LC** KGT10.5; .J35. **DD** 348.7292/028; 347.2920828. **Bk Rev. Ad Acc. Circ:** 250.
Desc: Contains titles of current laws in the territory concerned with references to the amendments to and subsidiary legislation made under each statute.

JA/0448-8806
JAPANESE ANNUAL OF INTERNATIONAL LAW, THE. **Added/Corp** International Law Association. Japan Branch. No. 1 (1957)-. Periodical. English. an. ¥7500.00 Japan; ¥10620.00 other. Yushodo Booksellers Ltd, 29 San EI Cho Shinjuku Ku, Tokyo 160 Japan. **Tel** 011 81 3 33571411. **LC** JX21; .J37. **DD** 341.058.
Ind/Abst Index Foreign Leg. Per.

MY/0126-6322
JERNAL UNDANG-UNDANG. [J. undang-undang]. **Added/Corp** Universiti Malaya. Fakulti Undang-Undang. **VFOAT** Journal of Malaysian and Comparative Law; JMCL. Vol. 1 (May 1974)-. Periodical. English (Malay). sa. $8.50 Malaysia and Singapore; $19.50 other. University of Malaya Faculty of Law, Pantari Valley, 59100 Kuala Lumpur Malaysia. **Tel** 011 60 3 7560022 ext. 428. **LC** K10; .E7. **DD** 340/.09595.
Ind/Abst Index Foreign Leg. Per.

FR/0021-8170
JOURNAL DU DROIT INTERNATIONAL. [J. droit int.]. No. 1/2 (1915)-. Periodical. French. Four times a year. 749.26F France; 910.00F other. Editions Techniques, 141 rue de Javel, 75747 Paris Cedex 15 France. **Tel** 011 33 1 45589100. **ED** B. Goldman and P. Kahn. **Bk Rev.** ***Continues*** *Journal du Droit International Prive et de la Jurisprudence Comparee.*
Ind/Abst Index Foreign Leg. Per.; Int. Labour Doc.; Int. Polit. Sci. Abstr.; PAIS Int. Print (1991-).

SZ/0255-8106
JOURNAL OF INTERNATIONAL ARBITRATION. [J. int. arbitr.]. Vol. 1, No. 1 (Apr. 1984)-. Periodical. English. qt. 370.00F. Werner Publishing Company Ltd., PO Box 5134, CH 1211 Geneva 11 Switzerland. **Tel** 011 41 22 3103422. **LC** K10; .O8685. **DD** 341.5/22. **[CCC].**
Desc: Research periodical for all those concerned with international arbitration, whether academics, practitioners, or scholars. Discusses the current and most important questions raised by international arbitration as a means of solving business, investment and economic disputes between parties from all over the world.
Ind/Abst Index Foreign Leg. Per.; Index Leg. Period.; Leg. Resour. Index; LegalTrac (1989-); PAIS Int. Print (1991-).

●US/1067-8182
JOURNAL OF TRANSNATIONAL LAW & POLICY. (JOURNAL OF TRANSNATIONAL LAW & POLICY / FLORIDA STATE UNIVERSITY.). [J. transnatl. law policy]. **Added/Corp** Florida State University. College of Law. **VFOAT** Journal of Transnational Law and Policy; Florida State University Journal of Transnational Law & Policy. Vol. 1, No. 1 (Summer 1992)-. Periodical. English. an. $8.00 US; $10.00 other. Florida State University College of Law, Tallahassee FL 32306. **Tel** (904)644-0961. **LC** K10; .O897. **DD** 341/.05. **Ad Acc. Circ:** 600.

FR
JOURNEES DE LA SOCIETE DE LEGISLATION COMPAREE. Vol. 1- 1979-. French. an. 320.00F. Societe de Legislation Comparee, 28 rue Saint-Guillaume, 75007 Paris France. **Tel** (+33)1-45 44 44 67, FAX (1)45 49 41 65. **LC** K555; .J68. **DD** 340/.2. Index available. cum. index. **Circ:** 500. ***Continues*** *Journees Juridiques.*
Desc: Publication including all papers presented to legal bilateral symposiums regularly organized by the Society of Comparative Legislation with 15 different countries.
Ind/Abst Index Foreign Leg. Per.

US
JUDGEMENTS OF THE UNITED NATIONS ADMINISTRATIVE TRIBUNAL. **Main/Corp** United Nations. Administrative Tribunal. No. 1/70 (1950/1957)-. Government Publication. English. ir. $60.00. United Nations Publications, 2 United Nations Plaza, Room DC2 0853, Department 007C, New York NY 10017. **Tel** (212)963-8303, (800)253-9646. **LC** JX1977; .A2. **DD** 341.137.
Desc: Claims and appeals by individuals against the Secretary General of the United Nations and the United Nations Joint Staff Pension Board and subsequent judgements of the United Nations Administrative Tribunal.

YU/0022-6084
JUGOSLOVENSKA REVIJA ZA MEUNARODNO PRAVO. **Added/Corp** Jugoslovensko Udruzenje za Meunarodno Pravo. Vol. 1 (1954)-. Periodical. Multiple languages (Serbo-Croatian (Roman), English and French). Three times a year. $57.00. **(Subscription address:** Jugoslovenska Knjiga, PO Box 36, YU 11001 Belgrade Yugoslovia.) **LC** JX18; .J83.
Ind/Abst Index Foreign Leg. Per.

FR
JURIS-CLASSEUR DE DROIT COMPARE. (19??)-. French. sa. Editions Techniques, 141 rue de Javel, 75747 Paris Cedex 15 France. **Tel** 011 33 1 45589100.

FR/0750-8239
JURIS-CLASSEUR DE DROIT INTERNATIONAL. [Juris-classeur droit int.]. **VFOAT** Droit International (Juris-Classeur). (195?)-. French. Editions Techniques, 141 rue de Javel, 75747 Paris Cedex 15 France. **Tel** 011 33 1 45589100. **UDC** 341.

IT/0022-6963
JUS GENTIUM. Vol. 1 (1949)-. Italian (French, English and Spanish). Twice a year. L50000. Jus Gentium, Casella Postale 410, 1-00100 Rome Centro Italy. **Tel** 011 39 6 6869012. **ED** Giovanni Scarangella Arpino. cum. index. **Bk Rev. Ad Acc.**
Ind/Abst Index Foreign Leg. Per.

US/0023-0790
KEY OFFICERS OF FOREIGN SERVICE POSTS. [Key off. foreign serv. posts]. **Added/Corp** Foreign Affairs Document and Reference Center (U.S.) United States. Dept. of State. (19??)-. Government Publication. English. sa. $5.00 domestic; $6.25 other. Superintendent of Documents, US Government Printing Office, Washington DC 20402. **Tel** (202)275-3328, FAX (202)786-2377. **LC** JX1705; .A255. **DD** 353.
Desc: Lists key officers at Foreign Service posts-the Chiefs and Deputy Chiefs of Missions, the Senior officers of the political, economic, commercial, and consular sections of the post, and the agricultural attache. It also lists all embassies, legations, and consulates general.

UK/0075-6040
KIME'S INTERNATIONAL LAW DIRECTORY. [Kime's int. law dir.]. **VFOAT** International Law Directory; Kime's International Law Directory and Telegraphic Code. (1892)-. Directory. English. an (November). £48.00. Longman Law Tax and Finance, 21 27 Lambs Conduit St., London WC1N 3NJ England. **Tel** 011 44 712422548. **ED** James Matthews. **DD** 340/.025.

Desc: List of legal practitioners in principal cities throughout the world; also legal information for each country.

JA
KOKUSAI JOYAKUSHU. Began in 1950. Japanese. ¥2200. Yuhikaku Publishing Company Ltd., 2-17 Kanda Jinbocho, Chiyoda-ku, Tokyo 101 Japan. **Tel** 03 2641311. **ED** Yokota Kisaburo and Takano Yuichi. **LC** JX178; .J3K64.

JA/0023-2866
KOKUSAIHO GAIKO ZASSHI. Added/Corp Kokusaiho Gakkai (Japan). **VFOAT** Journal of International Law and Diplomacy. Vol. 1 (1912)-. Periodical. Japanese (summaries and/or abstracts in English). bm. $120.00. **(Subscription address:** Kyowa Book Company Inc., 1 38 Kanda Jinbocho Chiyoda-ku, Tokyo 101 Japan.**)** ***Continues*** *Kokusaiho Zasshi.*
Ind/Abst Am. Hist. Life (1953-1958); Index Foreign Leg. Per.

GW
KONSULARISCHE VERTRETUNGEN UND ANDERE VERTRETUNGEN IN DER BUNDESREPUBLIK DEUTSCHLAND UND BERLIN (WEST). Main/Corp Germany (West). Auswartiges Amt. German. VWV Verlag fur Wirtschaft und Verwaltung GmbH, Korberstrasse 15, Frankfurt Am Main 50 Germany. **LC** JX1795; .A227. ***Continues*** *Konsularischen Vertretungen in der Bundesrepublik Deutschland und im Land Berlin.*

BG
LAW AND INTERNATIONAL AFFAIRS. v. 1- Jan. 1975-. Periodical. English. sa. $6.00. Bangladesh Institute of Law and International Affairs, 501 Ehanmondi Residential Area Road No 7, Dacca 5 Bangladesh. **LC** K12; .A915. **DD** 340/.095492.

GW/0341-6151
LAW AND STATE. ***Ceased.*** Vol. 1 (1970)-(19??). Periodical. English (translations available in German). Twice a year. Institut fuer Wissenschaftliche Zusammenarbeit / Education, Landhausstr 18, D-72074 Tuebingen, Germany. **Tel** 011 49 7071 5066. **ED** Karl-Heinz W. Bechtold. **LC** K12; .A9244. **DD** 349.43/05; 344.3005. ctrl circ.
Ind/Abst Hum. Rights Intern. Rep.

US/0080-2808
LAW OF THE SEA INSTITUTE: OCCASIONAL PAPERS. See Earth Sciences-Oceanography.

UK/0959-0889
LAWYERS IN EUROPE. (Jan./Feb. 1990)-. Periodical. English. Ten times a year (monthly except Jan. and Aug.). $395.00 US; £150.00 other. Lawyers in Europe Ltd., 11 Vine Hill, London EC1N 8YY, England. **Tel** 44 71 8338550, FAX 44 f71 8335934. **ED** Tina Coccough. **Bk Rev. Ad Acc, Adv Mgr:** M R Cane. **Pr Rev. Circ:** 4,000.
Desc: Aimed at all lawyers, whether based within Europe or beyond, who have clients with cross-European border requirements.

NE/0377-0915
LEGAL ISSUES OF EUROPEAN INTEGRATION. Added/Corp Universiteit van Amsterdam. Europa Instituut. (1974)-. Periodical. English. Twice a year (Jan. & Sept.). Price varies. Kluwer Law and Taxation Publishers, Staverenstraat 32015, PO Box 23, 7400 GA Deventer Netherlands. **Tel** 011 31 5700 47261. **(Subscription address:** Kluwer Law & Taxation, 675 Massachusetts Avenue, Cambridge MA 02139.**) ED** D. J. Gylstra, R. H. Lauwoars and E. L. M. Volker. **LC** K12; .E33. **DD** 341.24/2. Index available. **Circ:** 750.
Desc: Designed to provide information on international aspects of taxation. It covers direct/indirect taxation in European countries and gives topical reviews of EEC taxation developments.
Ind/Abst Index Foreign Leg. Per.; PAIS Int. Print (1991-).

AU/0074-1868
LEGAL SERIES. Main/Corp International Atomic Energy Agency. (1959)-. Monographic series. English. ir. Price varies per volume. International Atomic Energy Agency / IAEA, Wagramerstrasse 5, PO Box 100, A-1400 Vienna Austria. **Tel** 011 43 1 2360 ext. 2530, FAX 011 43 1 234564. **(Subscription address:** UNIPUB, 4611 F Assembly Drive, Lanham MD 20706.**)**

NE/0922-1565
LEIDEN JOURNAL OF INTERNATIONAL LAW. Added/Corp Leiden Journal of International Law Foundation. Rijksuniversiteit te Leiden. Faculteit der Rechtsgeleerdheid. Vol. 1, No. 1 (May 1988)-. Periodical. English. ir. Leiden Journal of International Law Foundation, PO Box 9520, 2300 Leiden The Netherlands. **Tel** 011 31 71 277664. **(Subscription address:** WM. W. Gaunt & Sons Inc, 3011 Gulf Drive, Gaunt Building, Holmes Beach FL 34217.**) LC** JX18; .L45. **DD** 341/.05.

TZ
LIST OF DIPLOMATIC AND CONSULAR MISSIONS, TRADE AND INTERNATIONAL ORGANIZATIONS / [ISSUED BY PROTOCOL DIVISION, MINISTRY OF FOREIGN AFFAIRS]. Added/Corp Tanzania. Protocol Division. **VFOAT** List of Diplomatic Missions, Consular Missions, Trade and International Organizations. (19??)-. English. sa. 40. Ministry of Foreign Affairs / Tanzania, Protocol Division, PO Box 9000, Dar Es Salaam Tanzania. **LC** JX1873.T3; T34a. **DD** 351.8/92/097678. ***Continues*** *Tanzania. Protocol Division. Diplomatic Missions, Consular Missions, Trade and International Organizations, 0376-8392.*

QA
LIST OF DIPLOMATIC CORPS - QATAR. PROTOCOL DEPT. Main/Corp Qatar. Protocol Dept. English. Qatar Protocol Department, PO Box 250, Doha Qatar. **LC** JX1859.Q3; Q37A. **DD** 351/.892.

FI
LIST OF MEMBERS - WORLD PEACE COUNCIL. Main/Corp World Council of Peace. English. Information Centre of the World Peace Council, Lonnrotinkatu 25 A 5 KRS, PO Box 1811, 00180 Helsinki 18 Finland. **LC** JX1907; .W669. **DD** 327.1/72/0601.

SP
LISTA DEL CUERPO DIPLOMATICO. Main/Corp Spain. Ministerio de Asuntos Exteriores. Spanish. **LC** JX1819; .A3.
Desc: List of foreign diplomats in Madrid.

UA
LISTE DIPLOMATIQUE - DEPARTEMENT DU PROTOCOLE. Main/Corp Egypt. Departement du Protocole. French. **LC** JX1863; .A1565. **DD** 351/.892.

UA
LISTE DU CORPS DIPLOMATIQUE AU CAIRE. English. Republique Arabe Unie, Ministere des Affaires, Le Caire Egypt. **LC** JX1863; .A1575.

SG
LISTE DU CORPS DIPLOMATIQUE - REPUBLIQUE DU SENEGAL. Main/Corp Senegal. French. Imprimerie Nationale / France, BP 514, 59505 Douai Cedex France. **Tel** 011 33 27 937090. **LC** JX1873.S4; S45A. **DD** 351/.892. ***Continues*** *Liste Diplomatique et Consulaire.*

LU
LISTE OVER MDEDOKUMENTER. Main/Corp European Parliament. **VFOAT** Numerisches Verzeichnis der Sitzungsdokumente; Numerical List of Working Documents. French. **LC** JN32; .N86. **DD** 341.24/24. ***Continues*** *Numerical List of Working Documents.*

UK
LONDON DIPLOMATIC LIST / FOREIGN OFFICE, THE. Added/Corp Great Britain. Foreign Office. Great Britain. Foreign and Commonwealth Office. (19??)-. Periodical. English. sa. £3.95. Her Majesty's Stationery Office, 51 Nine Elms Lane, London SW8 5DR England. **Tel** 011 44 71 873 8459, 011 44 71 873 8499, FAX 011 44 71 873 8499, 011 44 71 873 8456, telex 297138. **(Subscription address:** Her Majesty's Stationery Office, PO Box 276, Publications Centre, London SW8 5DT England.**) LC** JX1783; .A14. ***Continues*** *Alphabetical List of the Foreign Embassies and Legations in London.*

US/0277-5417
LOYOLA OF LOS ANGELES INTERNATIONAL AND COMPARATIVE LAW JOURNAL. [Loyola Los Angel. int. comp. law j.]. **Added/Corp** Loyola of Los Angeles School of Law. **VFOAT** International and Comparative Law Journal. Vol. 4 (1981)-. Periodical. English. Three times a year. $35.00. Loyola of Los Angeles / California, 1441 West Olympic Boulevard, Los Angeles CA 90015. **Tel** (213)736-1405. **ED** Mark Kaufman (editor's phone: (213)736-1000). **LC** K12; .O89. **DD** 340/.05. Index available. cum. index. **Bk Rev. Ad Acc. Circ:** 300 (ctrl). ***Continues*** *Loyola of Los Angeles International and Comparative Law Annual, 0277-5409.*
Desc: Select articles on international legal issues.
Ind/Abst Curr. Law Index (1981-); Index Leg. Period.; Leg. Resour. Index (1981-); LegalTrac (1983-); PAIS Int. Print (1991-).

US/0884-9331
MARYLAND JOURNAL OF INTERNATIONAL LAW AND TRADE. [Md. j. int. law trade]. **Added/Corp** University of Maryland at Baltimore. School of Law. **VFOAT** MD. Journal of International Law & Trade. Vol. 8, No. 1 (Spring/Summer 1984)-. Periodical. English. sa. $10.00 (students), $12.00 US; $14.00 other. University of Maryland School of Law, 500 West Baltimore Street, Baltimore MD 21201. **Tel** (410)706-6744. **LC** K9; .N893. **DD** 341.7/54. ***Continues*** *International Trade Law Journal, 0360-5833.*
Ind/Abst Index Leg. Period.; Leg. Resour. Index (1984-); LegalTrac (1984-).

CN/0024-9041
MCGILL LAW JOURNAL. (MCGILL LAW JOURNAL. REVUE DE DROIT DE MCGILL.). [McGill law j.]. **Added/Corp** McGill University. Faculty of Law. McGill University. Law Undergraduate Society. **VFOAT** Revue de Droit de McGill. Vol. 1 (Autumn 1952)-. Periodical. English (French). qt. 55.00Can$ US. McGill Law Journal Revue Droit Magill, 3644 Peel Street, Montreal Quebec H3A 1W9 Canada. **Tel** (514)398-7397. **ED** Mark Phillies. cum. index. **Bk Rev. Ad Acc. Circ:** 2,000 (ctrl).
Desc: Topics include comparative private law, legal, theory, public international law and constitutional law.
Ind/Abst Can. Legal Lit.; Crim. Penol. Police Sci. Abstr.; Curr. Law Index (1980-); Index Can. Leg. Period. Lit.; Index Leg. Period.; Leg. Resour. Index (1980-); LegalTrac (1980-); Sage Race Relat. Abstr.

US/0742-4655
MEALEY'S LITIGATION REPORTS. IRANIAN CLAIMS. ***Ceased.*** [Mealey's litig. rep., Iran. claims]. **Added/Corp** Mealey Publications. **VFOAT** Iranian Claims; Mealey's Litigation Report. Iranian Claims. (1984)-(1991). Periodical. English. sm. Mealey Publications, PO Box 446, Wayne PA 19087-0446. **Tel** (215)688-6566, FAX (215)688-7552. **ED** Michael P. Mealey and Pamela J. Craft. **LC** JX238.I7; M43. **DD** 341.6/7/026873055. Index available. cum. index.
Desc: Coverage and texts of litigation and arbitration between United States and Iranian companies and entities.

NE
MEDEDELINGEN VAN DE NEDERLANDSE VERENIGING VOOR INTERNATIONAAL RECHT. Main/Corp Nederlandse Vereniging Voor Internationaal Recht. No. 1 (1910)-. Dutch (English). ir. Kluwer BV, Postbus 23, 7400 GA Deventer Netherlands. **Tel** 011 31 5700 33155, 011 31 5700 48999, FAX 011 31 5700 11504, telex 42829. **Circ:** 500 (ctrl).

US/1052-2867
MICHIGAN JOURNAL OF INTERNATIONAL LAW. [Mich. j. int. law]. **Added/Corp** University of Michigan. Law School. **VFOAT** Journal of International Law. Vol. 10, No. 1 (Winter 1989)-. Periodical. English. ir. Price varies. Michigan Journal of International Law, South 275 Legal Research Building, Ann Arbor MI 48109. **Tel** (313)763-6100. **DD** 341. ***Continues*** *Michigan Yearbook of International Legal Studies, 8756-0615.*
Ind/Abst Index Leg. Period.; Leg. Resour. Index (1989-); LegalTrac (1989-); PAIS Int. Print.

US/0271-0498
MIDDLE EAST EXECUTIVE REPORTS. [Middle East exec. rep.]. Vol. 1, No. 1 (Sept. 1978)-. Periodical. English. mo. $482.00 Washington D.C. excluding libraries, $455.00 US excluding libraries, $195.00 libraries, $465.00 other. International Executive Reports, 717 D Street NW/Suite 300, Washington DC 20004-2807. **Tel** (202)628-6900, FAX (202)628 6618, telex 440462 MEER UI. **ED** Colin MacKinnon. **DD** 346.56/07; 345.6067. **[CCC].** Index available. **Bk Rev. Ad Acc. Circ:** 1,200 (ctrl). available on an online database from IBEX; and NEXIS. Documents available from UMI Article Clearinghouse, UMI Article Clearinghouse.
Desc: Publication covering the financial, legal and practical aspects of conducting business in the Middle East.
Ind/Abst ABI/INFORM Glob. Ed. (19??-); ABI Inform Ondisc (Jan. 1988-); Bus. Index (1985-); Curr. Law Index (19??-); Gen. BusinessFile (1985-); Index Period. Artic. Relat. Law (19??-); Leg. Resour. Index (1983-); LegalTrac (1983-); Middle East Abstr. Index (1983-); NEXIS (Sept. 1978-).

TU
MILLETLERARAS HUKUK VE MILLETLERARAS OZEL HUKUK BULTENI : MHB. VFOAT MHB. (1981)-. Periodical. Turkish. sa. **LC** JX18; .M54.

BB
MONTSERRAT CONSOLIDATED INDEX OF STATUTES AND SUBSIDIARY LEGISLATION TO 1ST JANUARY .... . Added/Corp University of the West Indies (Cave Hill, Barbados). Faculty of Law. Library. **VFOAT** Consolidated Index of Statutes and Subsidiary Legislation to 1st January .... . (19??)-. English. an. $20.00. Faculty of Law Library, PO Box 64, Bridgetown Barbados. **Tel** (813)778-5211. **ED** Clifford Hammett. **LC** KGT2010.5; .M66. **DD** 348.7297/5028; 347.29750828. **Bk Rev. Ad Acc. Circ:** 250.
Desc: Contains titles of current laws in the territory concerned with references to the amendments to and subsidiary legislation made under each statute.

US
MULTILATERAL TREATIES DEPOSITED WITH THE SECRETARY-GENERAL. Added/Corp United Nations. Secretary-General. (1981)-. Government

Publication. English. an. $75.00. United Nations Publications, 2 United Nations Plaza, Room DC2 0853, Department 007C, New York NY 10017. **Tel** (212)963-8303, (800)253-9646. **LC** JX171; .U372a. **DD** 341/.0262. ***Continues*** *Multilateral Treaties in Respect of Which the Secretary-General Performs Depository Functions. Lists of Signatures, Ratifications, Accessions, etc.*
Desc: Lists country ratifications of treaties and other international instruments.

UK
MULTILATERAL TREATIES : INDEX AND CURRENT STATUS. CUMULATIVE SUPPLEMENT. (1984)-. Academic Scholarly Publication. English. an. £20.00 UK; $45.00 North America; £20.00 other. University of Nottingham Department of Law, Nottingham NG7 2RD England. **Tel** 011 44 602484842, FAX 011 44 602420825. **(Subscription address:** M. J. Bowman, University of Nottingham Treaty Centre, Department of Law, Nottingham University. Notts. NG7 2RD UK**) ED** M. J. Bowman and D. J. Harris. Index available. cum. index. **Circ:** 400 (ctrl).
Desc: The main volume contains comprehensive status information on around 1,000 of the major multilateral conventions/treaties and is updated by an annual supplement.

US/0149-0818
MULTINATIONAL INDUSTRIAL RELATIONS SERIES. **See** Economics-Labor.

US/0377-7588
NAMIBIA BULLETIN. **Added/Corp** United Nations. (1973)-. Government Publication. English. qt. United Nations Publications, 2 United Nations Plaza, Room DC2 0853, Department 007C, New York NY 10017. **Tel** (212)963-8303, (800)253-9646. **LC** JX1977.2.A45; N35. **DD** 341.23/68/8.

BE
NATO HANDBOOK, THE. **Main/Corp** North Atlantic Treaty Organization. **Added/Corp** North Atlantic Treaty Organization. Information Service. **VFOAT** NATO Hand Book. **VAT** North Atlantic Treaty Organization Handbook. (Nov. 1967)-. English. ir. Free on request. US Department of State, 2201 C Street NW, Room 5819, Washington DC 20520. **Tel** (202)647-9859. **LC** JX1393; .N6122. **DD** 341.24/3. ***Continues*** *North Atlantic Treaty Organization. North Atlantic Treaty Organization.*

NE/0165-070X
NETHERLANDS INTERNATIONAL LAW REVIEW. [Neth. int. law rev.]. **Added/Corp** T.M.C. Asser Instituut. **VFOAT** N.I.L.R.; NILR. Vol. 22 (1975)-. Periodical. English (French). tq. $451.00. Martinus Nijhoff Publishers, Subsidiary of Kluwer Academic Publishers, Koraalrood 50, 2718 SC Zoetermeer Netherlands. **Tel** 011 31 79 684400. **ED** P Morris. **LC** JX18; .N47. **DD** 341/.05. **CODEN** NILRE5. **Bk Rev. Ad Acc. Pr Rev. Acid Free.** ***Continues*** *Nederlands Tijdschrift voor Internationaal Recht, 0028-2138.*
Desc: Features reports on judicial decisions involving private international law.
Ind/Abst Crim. Penol. Police Sci. Abstr.; Index Foreign Leg. Per.; Int. Labour Doc.

NE
NETHERLANDS INTERNATIONAL LAW REVIEW, INDEX. English. Fl210.00, $119.50. Martinus Nijhoff Publishers, Subsidiary of Kluwer Academic Publishers, Koraalrood 50, 2718 SC Zoetermeer Netherlands. **Tel** 011 31 79 684400. **LC** JX18 .N47. **DD** 341/.05.

NE/0167-6768
NETHERLANDS YEARBOOK OF INTERNATIONAL LAW. **Added/Corp** T.M.C. Asser Instituut. Vol. 1 (1970)-. English. an. Fl412.00 (postage included); price includes subscription to Netherlands International Law Review. Martinus Nijhoff Publishers, Subsidiary of Kluwer Academic Publishers, Koraalrood 50, 2718 SC Zoetermeer Netherlands. **Tel** 011 31 79 684400. **LC** JX21; .N45. cum. index.
Ind/Abst Index Foreign Leg. Per.; Int. Polit. Sci. Abstr.

US/0738-2812
NEW HAVEN STUDIES IN INTERNATIONAL LAW AND WORLD PUBLIC ORDER, THE. (1986)-. Monographic series. English. ir. Price varies per volume. Kluwer Academic Publishers / Massachusetts, PO Box 358, Accord Station, Hingham MA 02018. **Tel** (617)871-6600. **LC** UNC. **DD** 341. Index available. **Circ:** 700.
Desc: Contains new books and reprints on international law and public order.

US/1050-9453
NEW YORK INTERNATIONAL LAW REVIEW. [N. Y. int. law rev.]. **Added/Corp** New York State Bar Association. International Law and Practice Section. Vol. 1, No. 1 (Winter 1987/1988)-. Periodical. English. Twice a year (Jan., July). Free (members of the New York State Bar Association); $65.00 (non-members). New York State Bar Association, One Elk Street, Albany NY 12207. **Tel** (518)463-3200. **ED** Ronald David Greenberg. **LC** K14; .E92. **DD** 341. **Bk Rev. Ad Acc. Pr Rev. Circ:** 2,000 (ctrl).
Desc: Substantive articles on international law issues and book reviews.
Ind/Abst Index Leg. Period.; Leg. Resour. Index; LegalTrac (1990-).

US
NEW YORK LAW SCHOOL JOURNAL OF INTERNATIONAL AND COMPARATIVE LAW. **Added/Corp** New York Law School. **VFOAT** Journal of International and Comparative Law. Vol. 4, No. 1 (1983)-. Periodical. English. Three times a year. $22.00. New York Law School, 57 Worth Street, New York NY 10013. **Tel** (212)431-2109. **LC** K14; .E935. **DD** 341/.05. ***Continues*** *Journal of International and Comparative Law, 0740-6177.*
Ind/Abst Index Leg. Period.; Leg. Resour. Index; LegalTrac (1981-); PAIS Int. Print.

US/0028-7873
NEW YORK UNIVERSITY JOURNAL OF INTERNATIONAL LAW & POLITICS. [N.Y. Univ. j. int. law polit.]. **Main/Corp** New York University International Law Society. **Added/Corp** New York University. School of Law. New York University. International Law Society. Journal of International Law & Politics. **VFOAT** Journal of International Law and Politics. **VAT** New York University Journal of International Law and Politics. Vol. 1 (April 1968)-. Periodical. English. qt. $26.00. New York University School of Law, 110 West Third Street, New York NY 10012. **Tel** (212)998-6540, (212)998-6560, FAX (212)995-4032. **ED** Arunas Gudaitis. **LC** JX1; .N45. **DD** 341/.05. Index available. cum. index. **Bk Rev. Pr Rev. Circ:** 800. available in microform from University Microfilms International (UMI); available on audiocassette.
Ind/Abst ABC POL SCI; Am. Hist. Life (1971-); Bowne Dig. Corp. Sec. Lawyers; Curr. Law Index (1980-); Index Foreign Leg. Per.; Index Leg. Period.; Int. Bibliogr. Sociol.; Leg. Resour. Index (1980-); LegalTrac (1980-); PAIS Int. Print (1991-).

NZ/0110-148x
NEW ZEALAND LAW REPORTS, THE. **Added/Corp** Council of Law Reporting for New Zealand. New Zealand. Court of Appeal. New Zealand. Supreme Court. New Zealand. Court of Arbitration. New Zealand. Court of Review. New Zealand. Privy Council. Judicial Committee. New Zealand. Workers' Compensation Court. New Zealand. Land Sales Court. (1883)-. English. an. Butterworths Pty Ltd, 271-273 Lane Cove Road, PO Box 345, North Ryde NSW 2113 Australia. **Tel** 011 61 2 3354444, FAX 011 61 2 3354655.
Desc: Official law report series for New Zealand, published under statutory authority.

US/1049-7803
NEWSLETTER / AMERICAN SOCIETY OF INTERNATIONAL LAW. [Newsl. - Am. Soc. Int. Law]. **Added/Corp** American Society of International Law. **VFOAT** ASIL Newsletter. (Oct.-Nov.-Dec. 1987)-. English. Five times a year. $20.00 US; $25.00 other. American Society of International Law, 2223 Massachusetts Avenue Northwest, Washington DC 20008-2864. **Tel** (202)939-6000, FAX (202)797-7133. **LC** KF200; .N469. **DD** 341/.06/073. ***Continues*** *ASIL Newsletter.*

UK/0308-2482
NEWSLETTER - BRITISH INSTITUTE OF INTERNATIONAL AND COMPARATIVE LAW. **Main/Corp** British Institute of International and Comparative Law. No. 2 (Oct. 1973)-. Periodical. English. qt. British Institute of International and Comparative Law, Charles Clore House, 17 Russell Square, London WC1B 5DR England. **Tel** 011 44 71 636-5802, FAX 011 44 71 323-2016. **LC** JX31; .B715. **DD** 340/.05. ***Continues*** *British Institute of International and Comparative Law. Quarterly Newsletter.*

US/8755-7428
NONVIOLENT ACTIVIST, THE. (THE NONVIOLENT ACTIVIST : THE MAGAZINE OF THE WAR RESISTERS LEAGUE.). [Nonviolent act.]. **Added/Corp** War Resisters League. (Dec. 1984)-. Periodical. English. Six times a year (Jan., Mar., May, July., Sept., Nov.). $25.00 (institutions); $15.00 (individuals). Nonviolent Activist, 339 Lafayette Street, New York NY 10012. **Tel** (212)228-0450, FAX (212)228-6193. **ED** Sharon Seidenstein. **LC** JX1901; .N5. **DD** 327.1/72/05. Index available. cum. index. **Bk Rev. Ad Acc. Circ:** 20,000. available on microfilm. ***Continues*** *WRL News, 0042-9791.*
Desc: Pacifist journal exploring issues of nonviolence, disarmament, feminism, international relations, and more.
Ind/Abst Altern. Press Index; Hum. Rights Intern. Rep.

NE/0902-7351
NORDIC JOURNAL OF INTERNATIONAL LAW. **VFOAT** Acta Scandinavica Juris Gentium; Nordisk Tidsskrift for International Ret. Vol. 55 No. 1/2 (1986)-. Periodical. Danish (English, Norwegian and Swedish). qt. $286.00. Kluwer Academic Publishers, Postbus 322, 3300 AH Dordrecht, The Netherlands. **Tel** 011 (31) 78 524400, FAX 011 31 78 183273, telex 20083. **LC** JX18; .N6. ***Continues*** *Nordisk Tidsskrift for International Ret, 0029-151X.*
Ind/Abst Hum. Rights Intern. Rep.; Index Foreign Leg. Per.

DK
NORDISK TIDSSKRIFT FOR INTERNATIONAL RET. PUBLIKATIONSSERIE. **VFOAT** Acta Scandinavica Juris Gentium. Publikationsserie. No. 1-. Monographic series. Danish. ir. Price varies per volume. Krohns Bogtrykkeri, Sct Peders Strae de 45, 1453 Copenhagen K Denmark. **Tel** (1)152166. **ED** Isi Foighel, Allan Philip and Bengt Broms. **Bk Rev. Ad Acc. Circ:** 1,000.
Desc: Publishes qualified articles of both dogmatic and critical character of importance to the Nordic countries.

US/0743-1759
NORTH CAROLINA JOURNAL OF INTERNATIONAL LAW AND COMMERCIAL REGULATION. (NORTH CAROLINA JOURNAL OF INTERNATIONAL LAW AND COMMERCIAL REGULATION.). [N.C. j. int. law commer. regul.]. **Added/Corp** North Carolina International Law and Commercial Regulation Association. **VFOAT** NC J. Int'l L. & Comm. Reg.; N.C. J. Int'l L. & Comm. Reg. Vol. 2. No. 1 (Winter 1977)-. Periodical. English. Three times a year. $21.00 US; $25.00 other. University of North Carolina School of Law, CB 3380, Chapel Hill NC 27599. **Tel** (919)962-4402, FAX (919)962-1193. **ED** Michael Grubb. **LC** K10; .O869. **DD** 341.7/54/05. Index available. cum. index. **Bk Rev. Ad Acc. Circ:** 900 (ctrl). ***Continues*** *Journal of International Law and Commercial Regulation, 0160-113X.*
Desc: Dedicated to coverage of current legal issues in international transaction law and public international law.
Ind/Abst Curr. Law Index (1980-); Index Leg. Period.; Leg. Resour. Index (1980-); LegalTrac (1980-).

LU/0378-6986
OFFICIAL JOURNAL OF THE EUROPEAN COMMUNITIES : INFORMATION AND NOTICES. [Off. j. Eur. Commun., C, Inf. not.]. Vol. 16, (Jan. 15, 1973)-. Periodical. English. da. $45.00. Office for Official Publications of the European Communities, 2 Rue Mercier, 2985 Luxembourg Luxembourg. **Tel** 011 352 499281, FAX 011 352 488573. **(Subscription address:** UNIPUB, 4611 F Assembly Drive, Lanham MD 20706.**) LC** JN15; .O36. **DD** 341.24/2.
Desc: Consists of 2 related series, the L (legislation) and the C (information and notices), a supplement and an annex. The L series contains all the legislative acts and regulations whose publication is obligatory under the EC treaties, as well as other acts, and the C series covers the complete range of Community information other than legislation.
Ind/Abst Chem. Bus. Bull.; Chem. Bus. NewsBase (1987-); Chem. Bus. Update; Coal Abstr.; LABORDOC.

●US
PACE INTERNATIONAL LAW REVIEW. **Added/Corp** Pace University. School of Law. **VFOAT** International Law Review. Vol. 5 (1993)-. Periodical. English. an. $15.00. Pace University / School of Law, 78 North Broadway, White Plains NY 10603. **Tel** (914)422-4000, (914)422-4271, FAX (914)422-4139. ***Continues*** *Pace Yearbook of International Law, 1052-3448.*
Ind/Abst Index Leg. Period.

US/1052-3448
PACE YEARBOOK OF INTERNATIONAL LAW. ***Title Change.*** [Pace yearb. int. law]. **Added/Corp** Pace University. School of Law. Vol. 1, No. 1 (1989)-Vol. 4 (1992). English. an. Pace University / School of Law, 78 North Broadway, White Plains NY 10603. **Tel** (914)422-4000, (914)422-4271, FAX (914)422-4139. **DD** 341. ***Continued by*** *Pace International Law Review.*
Ind/Abst Index Leg. Period.

CY
PALESTINE YEARBOOK OF INTERNATIONAL LAW, THE. **Added/Corp** Shaybani Society of International Law. Vol. 1 (1984)-. English. an. $75.00. Al Shaybani Society of International Law, PO Box 4247, Nicosia Cyprus. **Tel** 011 357 21 441021. **LC** JX18; .P3. **DD** 341.2/9/095694. **Bk Rev. Circ:** 4,000.
Ind/Abst Index Foreign Leg. Per.

PH/0115-8805
PHILIPPINE YEARBOOK OF INTERNATIONAL LAW, THE. **Added/Corp** Philippine Society of International Law. University of the Philippines. Legal Resources Center. University of the Philippines. Law Center. Vol. 1 (1966/1968)-. English. $23.00. Philippine Society of International Law, UP Law Complex Bocobo Hall, Quezon City 1101 Philippines. **Tel** 011 63 2 977137. **LC** JX18; .P45. ***Continues*** *Philippine International Law Journal.*
Ind/Abst Index Foreign Leg. Per.; Index Philip. Period. (-199?).

NE
PLEADINGS OF THE INTERNATIONAL COURT OF JUSTICE SERIES.
Government Publication. English. ir. United Nations Publications, 2 United Nations Plaza, Room DC2 0853, Department 007C, New York NY 10017. **Tel** (212)963-8303, (800)253-9646.

PL/0554-498X
POLISH YEARBOOK OF INTERNATIONAL LAW, THE.
[Pol. yearb. int. law]. **Added/Corp** Polski Instytut Spraw Miqedzynarodowych. Instytut Nauk Prawnych (Polska Akademia Nauk) International Law Association. Polish Branch. Instytut Panstwa i Prawa (Polska Akademia Nauk). **VFOAT** Annuaire Polonais de Droit International. 1 (1966/1967)-. English (French). an. $38.00. **(Subscription address:** ARS Polona, PO Box 1001, 00068 Warsaw Poland.**)** **LC** JX21; .P64. **DD** 341/.05.
Ind/Abst Index Foreign Leg. Per.

PL
PROBLEMY PRAWNE HANDLU ZAGRANICZNEGO.
Periodical. Polish (summaries and/or abstracts in French and Russian). ir. varies. Uniwersytet Slaski, Ul Bankowa 14, 40-007 Katowice Poland. **Tel** 59-69-15, FAX 48 32 599-506, telex 0315584 USKPL. **(Subscription address:** CHZ Ars Polona, Krakowskie Przedmiescie 7, skr pocztowa 1001, 00 950 Warszawa Polska**)** **ED** Naczelny Redaktor. **Bk Rev. Pr Rev. Circ:** 1,000.
Desc: Comprises studies, articles, casenotes, materials and book reviews on international private and commercial law and international procedure.

CN/0317-9087
PROCEEDINGS OF THE ANNUAL CONFERENCE - CANADIAN COUNCIL ON INTERNATIONAL LAW.
[Proc. annu. conf. - Can. Counc. Int. Law]. **Main/Corp** Canadian Council on International Law. **Added/Corp** Conseil Canadien de Droit International. Travaux du Congres Annuel. **VFOAT** Travaux du Congres Annuel - Conseil Canadien de Droit International. (1972)-. Proceedings. English (French; summaries and/or abstracts in French). an. 17.00Can$. Canadian Council on International Law, 236 Metcalfe Street, Ottawa Ontario K2P 1R3 Canada. **Tel** (613)235-0442. **DD** 341. **Bk Rev. Ad Acc. Circ:** 300 (ctrl).
Ind/Abst Can. Legal Lit.; Index Foreign Leg. Per.

US/0272-5037
PROCEEDINGS OF THE ANNUAL MEETING - AMERICAN SOCIETY OF INTERNATIONAL LAW.
[Proc. annu. meet. - Am. Soc. Int. Law]. **Main/Corp** American Society of International Law. **VFOAT** Proceedings of the Anniversary Convocation. (1974)-. Proceedings. English. an (December). $60.00 US; $70.00 other. American Society of International Law, 2223 Massachusetts Avenue Northwest, Washington DC 20008-2864. **Tel** (202)939-6000, FAX (202)797-7133. **ED** John Lawrence Hargrove. **DD** 341. **[CCC].** Index available (bound in all issues). **Ad Acc. Circ:** 2,700. available on microfilm and microfiche from University Microfilms International (UMI). ***Supersedes in part*** *American Journal of International Law, 0002-9300.*
Desc: Covers proceedings regarding the meetings of the Society.
Ind/Abst Am. Hist. Life (1974-); Curr. Law Index (1980-); Index Leg. Period.; Leg. Resour. Index (1980-); LegalTrac (1980-).

GW/0340-7349
PUBLIC INTERNATIONAL LAW.
[Public int. law]. **Added/Corp** Max-Planck-Institut fuer Auslandisches Offentliches Recht und Volkerrecht. Vol. 1 (1975)-. English (Multiple languages). Twice a year. DM160.00. Springer-Verlag GmbH & Company KG, Heidelberger Platz 3, D 14197 Berlin Germany. **Tel** 011 49 30 8207223, FAX 011 49 30 8214091, telex 183 319 SPBLN D. **(Subscription address:** Springer Verlag New York Inc. / for North America, 44 Hartz Way, Secaucus NJ 07096.**)** **ED** R. Bernhardt, K. Doehring, and J.A. Frowein. **LC** Z6461; .P83; JX3091. **DD** 016.341. **CODEN** PILAEA. **[CCC]. Bk Rev.** available on microfilm from University Microfilms International (UMI).
Desc: Aims are to enable the reader to follow the literature with regard to developments in specialized areas, and to facilitate through its computer-produced index the retrieval of literature from the whole field of public international law.

EC
PUBLICACIONES - QUITO. UNIVERSIDAD CENTRAL DEL ECUADOR.
Main/Corp Quito. Universidad Central del Ecuador. Vol. 1 (1951)-. Spanish. Universidad Central del Ecuador, Quito Ecuador. **DD** 340/.09866.

US
PUBLICACIONES Y CONFERENCIAS : INFORME TRIMESTRAL - DEPARTAMENTO DE PUBLICACIONES Y CONFERENCIAS.
Main/Corp Organization of American States. Dept. of Publications and Conferences. **Added/Corp** Organization of American States. Dept. of Publications and Conferences. Publications and Conferences: Quarterly Report - Department of Publications and Conferences. **VFOAT** Publications and Conferences Quarterly Report - Department of Publications and Conferences. (19??)-. Multiple languages (English and Spanish). ir. Organization of American States, 19th Street & Constitution Avenue NW, Suite 300, Washington DC 20006. **Tel** (202)458-6256. **LC** F1402; .A169 subser. **DD** 341.24/5 S; 341.24/5.

FR
PUBLICATIONS DE LA COUR EUROPEENNE DES DROITS DE L'HOMME SERIE A, ARRETS ET DECISIONS.
Main/Corp European Court of Human Rights. **VFOAT** Arrets et Decisions; Judgements and Decisions; Publications of the European Court of Human Rights. Series Judgements and Decisions. Monographic series. French (English). ir. Price varies per volume. Carl Heymanns Verlag KG, Luxemburger Strasse 449, D 50939 Cologne Germany. **Tel** 011 49 221 460100, telex 8 881 888. **(Subscription address:** Manhattan Publishing Company, PO Box 650, Croton-on-Hudson NY 10520**)** **LC** KJC5132.A52; E88. **DD** 341.4/84.
Desc: The official records of the 23 democratic countries of Western Europe.

GW/0033-7250
RABELS ZEITSCHRIFT FUER AUSLANDISCHES UND INTERNATIONALES PRIVATRECHT.
[Rabels Z. ausl. int. Privatr.]. **Added/Corp** Max-Planck-Institut fuer Auslandisches und Internationales Privatrecht. (1961)-. Periodical. German (French; summaries and/or abstracts in English). qt. DM244.00. JCB Mohr / Paul Siebeck, Postfach 2040, D 72010 Tuebingen Germany. **Tel** 011 49 7071 9230, FAX 011 49 7071 51104, telex 7/262872 mohr d. **ED** Ulrich Drobnig, Hein Kotz, and Ernst-Joachim Mestmacker. **LC** K1; .U753. **[CCC].** cum. index. **Bk Rev. Ad Acc. Circ:** 1,050. ***Continues*** *Zeitschrift fuer Auslandisches und Internationales Privatrecht.*
Desc: Areas of specific interest are comparative and foreign civil law, the conflict of laws, the law of international transactions and the unification of law, including the law of the European Community.
Ind/Abst Index Foreign Leg. Per.

RU
RAZORUZHENIE, VELENIE VREMENI.
Vol. 1 (1983)-. Periodical. Russian. 0.45rub single issue. **LC** JX1974.7; .R39.

RM
RECHERCHES SUR L'HISTOIRE DES INSTITUTIONS ET DU DROIT.
Main/Corp Association d'Histoire Comparative des Institutions et du Droit de la Republique Socialiste de Roumaine. (1977)-. Periodical. French. Editura Academia Republicii Socialiste Romania, Calea Victoriei Nr 125, R-79717 Bucuresti Romania. **Tel** telex 10376 PRSFI R. **LC** K1; .S78. **DD** 340/.2/05.

GW
RECHT ZOLL UND VERFAHREN.
(19??)-. German. mo. DM119.70. Bundesstelle fuer Aussenhandelsinformation, Agrippastr 87 93, D 50676 Cologne Germany. **Tel** 011 49 221 2057316, FAX 011 49 221 2057212. Index available. **Bk Rev. Circ:** 300.

NE
RECUEIL DES ARRETS, AVIS CONSULTATIFS ET ORDONNANCES / COUR INTERNATIONALE DE JUSTICE.
Main/Corp International Court of Justice. **VFOAT** Reports of Judgments, Advisory Opinions, and Orders. (1947)-. English (French). ir. United Nations Publishers Geneva, Palais des Nations, C115 Services Ventes, CH-1211 Geneva 10 Switzerland. **Tel** 011 41 227988400, 7985850. **LC** JX1971.6; .A244.
Desc: Contains the reports of the decisions of the International Court of Justice. Each decision is published as soon as given.

NE/0169-5436
RECUEIL DES COURS - ACADEMIE DE DROIT INTERNATIONAL.
(RECUEIL DES COURS.). [Recl. cours - Acad. Droit Int.]. **Added/Corp** Hague Academy of International Law. **VFOAT** Collected Courses of the Hague Academy of International Law. Vol. 1 (1923)-. Monographic series. French (English). ir (5 or 6 per year). Price varies per volume. Kluwer Academic Publishers, Postbus 322, 3300 AH Dordrecht, The Netherlands. **Tel** 011 (31) 78 524400, FAX 011 31 78 183273, telex 20083. **(Subscription address:** Kluwer Academic Publishers / US Subscriptions, PO Box 253, Accord Station, Hingham MA 02018.**)** **LC** JX74; .H3. cum. index.
Ind/Abst Index Foreign Leg. Per.; Int. Labour Doc.

BE
RECUEIL DES LOIS, DECRETS, ET ARRETES / ROYAUME DE BELGIQUE.
Main/Corp Belgium. **VFOAT** Verzameling der Wetten, Decreten, en Besluiten. (19??)-. Dutch (French). wk. Moniteur Belge, rue de Louvain 40-42, 1000 Brussels Belgium. **Tel** 011 32 2 5120026. ***Continues*** *Belgium. [Law, etc.]. Recueil des Lois et Arretes Royaux de Belgique.*

IT
RELAZIONE PROVVISORIA DEL CONSIGLIO DIRETTIVO PER L'ANNO.
Main/Corp Societa Italiana per l'Organizzazione Internazionale. Consiglio Direttivo. Italian. Palazzetto di Venezia, Via S Marco 3, Rome Italy. **LC** JX1908.I8; S64A. **DD** 341.2/06/045.

US
REPERTOIRE OF THE PRACTICE OF THE SECURITY COUNCIL.
Main/Corp United Nations. Dept of Political and Security Council Affairs. (1946)-. Government Publication. English. an. price varies per volume. United Nations Publications, 2 United Nations Plaza, Room DC2 0853, Department 007C, New York NY 10017. **Tel** (212)963-8303, (800)253-9646. **LC** JX1977; .A2. **DD** 341.135.
Desc: An analytical indexed presentation of the practices and procedures of the Security Council since 1946. Texts of decisions on disputes and situations are accompanied by historical case summaries of the relevant chain of proceedings.

UK/0074-6738
REPORT OF THE ... CONFERENCE / THE INTERNATIONAL LAW ASSOCIATION.
[Rep. conf. - Int. Law Assoc.]. **Main/Corp** International Law Association. Conference. **VFOAT** Compte Rendu de la ... Conference. 17th (Oct. 1st-4th, 1895)-. Proceedings. English. be. £74.00. International Law Association, 17 Russell Square, Charles Clor House, London WC1B 5DR England. **Tel** 011 44 71 323 2978. cum. index. ctrl circ. ***Continues*** *Association for the Reform and Codification of the Law of Nations. Conference. Report of the ... Conference.*
Desc: Contains reports of the international committees submitted, a record of discussions at Conference working sessions, and substantive resolutions passed.
Ind/Abst Index Foreign Leg. Per.

XE
REPORT OF THE UNITED NATIONS VISITING MISSION TO THE TRUST TERRITORY OF THE PACIFIC ISLANDS.
Main/Corp United Nations. Trusteeship Council. Periodical. English. United Nations Publications / Marshall Islands, The Office of the President, Republic of the Marshall Islands, Majuro Marshall Islands 96960. **Tel** (212)754-8302. **LC** JX4021; .U385. **DD** 354.965. ***Continues*** *Report on the Trust Territory of the Pacific Islands, Collected Works.*

US
REPORT ON THE WORK OF ITS SESSIONS - UNITED NATIONS. COMMISSION ON INTERNATIONAL TRADE LAW.
Main/Corp United Nations. Commission on International Trade Law. English. United Nations / Commission on International Trade Law, New York NY 10017. **Tel** (212)754-8302. **LC** JX1977; .A41 subser. **DD** 341.7/54.

US
REPORT - UNITED NATIONS' COUNCIL FOR NAMIBIA.
Main/Corp United Nations. Council for Namibia. English. an. $3.00. United Nations for Namibia, Sales Section/Room A 3315, New York NY 10017. **LC** JX1977; .A2 subser. **DD** 341.23/68/8.

US/0251-7833
REPORTS OF INTERNATIONAL ARBITRAL AWARDS - UNITED NATIONS.
(REPORTS OF INTERNATIONAL ARBITRAL AWARDS.). [Rep. int. arbitral awards - U. N.]. **Main/Corp** United Nations. Office of Legal Affairs. **Added/Corp** International Court of Justice. Registry. United Nations. Legal Dept. United Nations. Codification Division. **VFOAT** Recueil des Sentences Arbituales. Vol. 1 (1948)-. Government Publication. English (French). an. price varies per volume. United Nations Publications, 2 United Nations Plaza, Room DC2 0853, Department 007C, New York NY 10017. **Tel** (212)963-8303, (800)253-9646. **LC** JX1991; .A25.
Desc: A systematic collection of international arbitral awards.

US/0252-7014
RESOLUTIONS AND DECISIONS ADOPTED BY THE GENERAL ASSEMBLY DURING ITS ... SESSION - UNITED NATIONS.
(RESOLUTIONS AND DECISIONS ADOPTED BY THE GENERAL ASSEMBLY.). [Resolut. decis. adopt. by Gen. Assem. during its sess. - U. N.]. **Main/Corp** United Nations. General Assembly. (19??)-. Government Publication. English. ir. Price varies per volume. United Nations Publications, 2 United Nations Plaza, Room DC2 0853, Department 007C, New York NY 10017. **Tel** (212)963-8303, (800)253-9646. **LC** JX1977; .A41 subser; JX1977. **DD** 300/.8S; 341.23/22/026.

SZ/0020-6393
REVIEW (INTERNATIONAL COMMISSION OF JURISTS (1952-)). (THE REVIEW / INTERNATIONAL COMMISSION OF JURISTS.). [Rev. - Int. Comm. Jurists]. No. 1 (March 1969)-. Periodical. English (French and Spanish). sa. 20.00F surface mail; 23.00F airmail. International Commission of Jurists, 26 Chemin Joinville, PO Box 160, CH 1216 Geneva Switzerland. **Tel** 011 41 22 7884747. **ED** Niall Macdermot. **LC** K9; .N787. **DD** 340/.05. **Circ:** 10,000. available on diskette. ***Formed by the union of*** *Bulletin of the International Commission of Jurists* ***and*** *Journal of the International Commission of Jurists.*
Desc: Concerns human rights and the rule of law worldwide.
Ind/Abst Curr. Law Index (1980-); Hum. Rights Intern. Rep.; Index Foreign Leg. Per.; Index Period. Artic. Relat. Law; Int. Polit. Sci. Abstr.; Leg. Resour. Index (1980-); LegalTrac (1982-); PAIS Int. Print (1991-).

●NE/0925-9880
REVIEW OF CENTRAL AND EAST EUROPEAN LAW. **Added/Corp** Rijksuniversiteit te Leiden. Documentatie Bureau voor Oost-Europees Recht. Vol. 18, No. 1 (1992)-. Periodical. English. bm. $561.00. Martinus Nijhoff Publishers, Subsidiary of Kluwer Academic Publishers, Koraalrood 50, 2718 SC Zoetermeer Netherlands. **Tel** 011 31 79 684400. **ED** F.J.M. Feldbrugge. **LC** K18; .E98. **DD** 340/.091717. **CODEN** RCELEM. **Pr Rev. Acid Free. *Continues*** *Review of Socialist Law, 0165-0300.*
Desc: Focuses mainly on legal developments in Central and East Europe, and in particular on the increasing integration of this part of the world into a pan-European framework. Emphasis will be given to practical aspects of law.

BL
REVISTA DE DIREITO DO COMERCIO DAS RELACOES INTERNACIONAIS. **VFOAT** Revue du Droit du Commerce et des Relations Internationales; International Law, Trade, and Relations Journal; RDCRI. Vol. 1 (1989)-. Periodical. Portuguese (English and French; summaries and/or abstracts in English and French). ir. $15.00 Brazil; $27.00 US; $26.00 (sea mail), $29.00 (air mail) South America; $27.00 (sea mail), $30.00 (air mail) other. Editora Forense Universitaria, Rua Visconde Silva 32, 22271 Botafofo RJ Brazil. **Tel** (021)286-1475, FAX (021)286-1185. **ED** Luiz Olavo Batista. **LC** K19; .D9313. **DD** 346/.07/05; 342.7005. Index available. **Circ:** 2,000.
Desc: The international law trade and relations journal publishes articles dealing with matters related to those subjects and notes about their recent evolution of general interest.

BO
REVISTA DIPLOMATICA E INTERNACIONAL. Began in 1966. Spanish. Casilla 1598, La Paz Boliva. **LC** JX9; .R546. **DD** 327/.2/05.
Ind/Abst Am. Hist. Life (1954-1958).

SP/0034-9380
REVISTA ESPANOLA DE DERECHO INTERNACIONAL. [Rev. esp. derecho int.]. **Added/Corp** Instituto Francisco de Vitoria. Instituto de Ciencias Juridicas (Spain). Departamento Francisco de Vitoria. Vol. 1, No. 1 (1948)-. Periodical. Spanish. tq. 3500ptas Spain; 5500ptas other. Consejo Superior Investigacion Cientificas (CSIC), Vitruvio 8, 28006 Madrid Spain. **Tel** 011 34 1 5612833, FAX 011 34 1 4113077, telex 42182. **LC** JX9; .R548.
Desc: Contains articles, documents, and bibliographic notes on international public and private law and on Spanish jurisprudence in the field.
Ind/Abst Index Foreign Leg. Per.; Int. Polit. Sci. Abstr.

BE/0035-0788
REVUE BELGE DE DROIT INTERNATIONAL. (REVUE BELGE DE DROIT INTERNATIONAL : PUBLICATION SEMESTRIELLE DU CENTRE DE DROIT INTERNATIONAL ET DE SOCIOLOGIE APPLIQUEE AU DROIT INTERNATIONAL DE L'UNIVERSITE LIBRE DE BRUXELLES ET DU CENTRE DE DROIT INTERNATIONAL DE L'UNIVERSITE CATHOLIQUE DE LOUVAIN.). [Rev. belg. droit int.]. **Added/Corp** Universite Libre de Bruxelles. Centre de Droit International. Universite Catholique de Louvain (1835-1969). Centre de Droit International. Universite Catholique de Louvain (1970-). Centre de Droit International. Societe Belge de Droit International. **VFOAT** Belgian Review of International Law. (1965)-. Periodical. Multiple languages (French, English and Dutch). sa. 3113.00F. Etablissements Emile Bruylant, 67 rue de la Regence, 1000 Brussels Belgium. **Tel** 011 32 2 5129845. **LC** JX3; .R25. **DD** 341/.05. Index available in last issue of volume--attached. **Bk Rev. Ad Acc. Circ:** 1,000.
Desc: Belgian journal of international law, doctrine and legislation.
Ind/Abst Index Foreign Leg. Per.; Int. Bibliogr. Sociol.; Int. Polit. Sci. Abstr.; PAIS Int. Print.

FR/0035-0958
REVUE CRITIQUE DE DROIT INTERNATIONAL PRIVE. Vol. 1 (Jan./Feb. 1905)-. Periodical. French. Four times a year. 675.00F (France); 770.00F (other). Dalloz, 35 rue Tournefort, 75240 Paris Cedex 05 France. **Tel** 011 33 1 40515434 or 40515454, FAX 45 87 37 48, telex 206 446 F. **ED** Flenri Batiffol and Philippe Francescakis. **LC** JX6002. **[CCC].** Index available in last issue of volume--attached. cum. index.
Desc: Covers topics relating to the part of law administered between citizens on an international level, and which are concerned with definition, regulation and enforcement of rights where both rights and obligation devolve upon private citizens.
Ind/Abst Index Foreign Leg. Per.

FR
REVUE DE DROIT DES AFFAIRES INTERNATIONALES. INTERNATIONAL BUSINESS LAW JOURNAL. **VFOAT** International Business Law Journal. No. 4 (1985)-. Periodical. French (summaries and/or abstracts in English). Eight times a year. 1750.00F France; 2000.00F other. Forum Europeen Communication, 47 rue Chardon Lagache, 75016 Paris France. **Tel** 011 33 1 4525117, FAX 011 33 1 42885037. **LC** K10; .O78. ***Continues*** *Journal de Droit des Affaires Internationales.*
Desc: News and information on the international trade law and list the problems of international taxation and international finances.
Ind/Abst Index Foreign Leg. Per.

SZ/0035-1091
REVUE DE DROIT INTERNATIONAL, DE SCIENCES DIPLOMATIQUES ET POLITIQUES. **VFOAT** International Law Review; The International Law Review. 1.- Vol. July, 1923-. Periodical. French (English, German and Italian). qt. 180.00F Switzerland and North America; 190.00F other. Revue de Droit International, Case Postale 138, CH-1211 Geneve 12 Switzerland. **Tel** 22/29.87.55, FAX 22/29.22.06, telex 427.019. **ED** C L Heinbach. **LC** JX3; .R37. Index available. ctrl circ.
Desc: Articles of law, international law and political science in French, English, German and/or Italian.

BE/0775-4663
REVUE DE DROIT INTERNATIONAL ET DE DROIT COMPARE. [Rev. droit int. droit comp.]. **Added/Corp** Institut Belge de Droit Compare. (1949)-. Periodical. French. qt. 3373.00F. Etablissements Emile Bruylant, 67 rue de la Regence, 1000 Brussels Belgium. **Tel** 011 32 2 5129845. **LC** K21; .D383. **Bk Rev. Ad Acc. Circ:** 750. ***Continues*** *Revue Trimestrielle (Institut Belge de Droit Compare), 0775-4655.*
Desc: Journal of international law and comparative law; doctrine and legislation.
Ind/Abst Index Foreign Leg. Per.

FR/0035-2578
REVUE DU DROIT PUBLIC ET DE LA SCIENCE POLITIQUE EN FRANCE ET A L'ETRANGER. [Rev. droit public sci. polit. Fr.etrang.]. Vol. 1 (1894)-. Periodical. French. Six times a year. 597.45F France; 640.00F others. Editions Juridiques Associees, 26 rue Vercingetorix, 75014 Paris France. **Tel** 011 33 1 43350167. **ED** F. Larnaude. **LC** JA11; .R5. **[CCC].** cum. index.
Ind/Abst Int. Bibliogr. Sociol.; PAIS Int. Print.

UA/0080-259X
REVUE EGYPTIENNE DE DROIT INTERNATIONAL. [Rev. egypt. droit int.]. **Added/Corp** Jamiyah al-Misriyah lil-Qanun al-Dawli. **VFOAT** Majallah Al-Misriyah Lil-Qanun Al-Dawli. Vol. 1 (1945)-. Arabic (English and French). an. $26.00 Egypt; $50.00 other. Society Egyptienne Droit International, 16 Avenue Ramses, Cairo Egypt. **Tel** 011 20 2 48162. **ED** Waheed Raafat. **LC** JX3; .R53. cum. index. **Bk Rev.**
Desc: Covers international law and relations.
Ind/Abst ABC POL SCI (19??-1984)(19 -1984); Index Foreign Leg. Per.; Int. Polit. Sci. Abstr.; Middle East J. (?-?).

FR/0373-6156
REVUE GENERALE DE DROIT INTERNATIONAL PUBLIC. [Rev. gen. droit int. public]. Began in 1894. Periodical. French. qt. $160.00. Editions A Pedone, 13 rue Soufflot, 75005 Paris France. **Tel** 011 33 1 43540597. **LC** JX3; .R56. Index available. cum. index. **Bk Rev.**
Ind/Abst Index Foreign Leg. Per.; Int. Labour Doc.; Int. Polit. Sci. Abstr.; LABORDOC; PAIS Int. Print.

GR/0035-3256
REVUE HELLENIQUE DE DROIT INTERNATIONAL. [Rev. hell. droit int.]. **Added/Corp** Hellenikon Institouton Diethnous kai Allodapou Dikaiou. (Jan./March 1948)-. French (English and German). ir. Hellenic Institute of International Foreign Law, Solonos Street 73, Athens 106 79 Greece. **Tel** 011 30 1 3615646.
Ind/Abst Index Foreign Leg. Per.

FR/0035-3337
REVUE INTERNATIONALE DE DROIT COMPARE. [Rev. int. droit comp.]. Vol. 1, No. 1-2 (Jan./June 1949)-. Periodical. French. Four times a year. 545.00F France; 645.00F other. Societe de Legislation Comparee, 28 rue Saint-Guillaume, 75007 Paris France. **Tel** (+33)1-45 44 44 67, FAX (1)45 49 41 65. **ED** M. Xavier Blanc-Jouvan. **LC** K21; .I555. **DD** 340/.2/05. Index available. cum. index. **Bk Rev. Ad Acc. Circ:** 1600. ***Absorbed*** *Bulletin de la Societe de Legislation Comparee.*
Ind/Abst ABC POL SCI; Am. Hist. Life (1955-1956, 1964-); Index Foreign Leg. Per.; Int. Polit. Sci. Abstr.; PAIS Int. Print.

CN/0828-9999
REVUE QUEBECOISE DE DROIT INTERNATIONAL. [Rev. que. droit int.]. **Added/Corp** Societe Quebecoise de Droit International. Quebec (Province). Ministere des Relations Internationales. Quebec (Province). Ministere de la Justice. No. 1 (1984)-. French. sa. 60.00Can$. Societe Quebecoise de Droit Internationale, Universite Montreal Faculty of Law, PO Box 6128 Station A, Montreal Quebec H3C 3J7 Canada. **Tel** (514)-343-6124. **DD** 341. **Ad Acc.** ctrl circ.
Ind/Abst Index Can. Leg. Period. Lit.; Index Foreign Leg. Per.; Index Leg. Period.

IT/0035-6158
RIVISTA DI DIRITTO INTERNAZIONALE. Vol. 1, No. 1 (Jan./Feb. 1906)-. Periodical. Italian. qt. L110000.00 Italy; L165000.00 other. Giuffre Editore SPA, Via Busto Arsizio 40, 20151 Milan Italy. **Tel** 011 398 2 38089200. **ED** Roberto Ago, Gaetano Arangio-Ruiz, Francesco Capotorti, Benedetto Conforti, Luigi Ferrari Bravo, Giorgio Gaja, Riccardo Monaco, Giuseppe Sperduti, Vincenzo Starace, and Piero Ziccardi. Index available. **Bk Rev. Ad Acc. Circ:** 800.
Desc: Deals with public and private international law.
Ind/Abst Index Foreign Leg. Per.

IT/0035-6174
RIVISTA DI DIRITTO INTERNAZIONALE PRIVATO E PROCESSUALE. [Riv. diritto int. priv. process.]. Vol. 1 (1965)-. Periodical. Multiple languages. qt. L160000 Itlay; L240000 other. Cedam Spa, Via Jappelli 5 6, 35121 Padua Italy. **Tel** 011 39 49 65667. Index available in last issue of volume--attached.
Ind/Abst Index Foreign Leg. Per.

BB
SAINT CHRISTOPHER AND NEVIS CONSOLIDATED INDEX OF STATUTES AND SUBSIDIARY LEGISLATION TO ... . **Added/Corp** University of the West Indies (Cave Hill, Barbados). Faculty of Law. Library. **VFOAT** Consolidated Index of Statutes and Subsidiary Legislation to ... . (19??)-. English. an. $20.00. Faculty of Law Library, PO Box 64, Bridgetown Barbados. **Tel** (813)778-5211. **ED** Clifford Hammett. **LC** KGW2010.5; .S24. **DD** 348.7297/3028; 347.29730828. **Bk Rev. Ad Acc. Circ:** 250.
Desc: Contains titles of current laws in the territory concerned with references to the amendments to and subsidiary legislation made under each statute.

BB
SAINT LUCIA CONSOLIDATED INDEX OF STATUTES AND SUBSIDIARY LEGISLATION TO ... . **VFOAT** Consolidated Index of Statutes and Subsidiary Legislation to ... . (19??)-. English. an. $20.00. Faculty of Law Library, PO Box 64, Bridgetown Barbados. **Tel** (813)778-5211. **ED** Clifford Hammett. **LC** KGW3010.5; .S24. **DD** 348.7297/25028. **Bk Rev. Ad Acc. Circ:** 250.
Desc: Contains titles of current laws in the territory concerned with references to the amendments to and subsidiary legislation made under each statute.

BB
SAINT VINCENT AND THE GRENADINES CONSOLIDATED INDEX OF STATUTES AND SUBSIDIARY LEGISLATION TO ... . **Added/Corp** University of the West Indies (Cave Hill, Barbados). Faculty of Law. Library. Saint Vincent and the Grenadines. Ministry of Legal Affairs. **VFOAT** Consolidated Index of Statutes and Subsidiary Legislation to ... . (19??)-. English. an. $20.00. Faculty of Law Library, PO Box 64, Bridgetown Barbados. **Tel** (813)778-5211. **ED** Clifford Hammett. **LC** KGW5010.5; .S25. **DD** 348.7298/44028; 347.298440828. **Bk Rev. Ad Acc. Circ:** 250.
Desc: Contains titles of current laws in the territory concerned with references to the amendments to and subsidiary legislation made under each statute.

SW/0085-5944
SCANDINAVIAN STUDIES IN LAW. **Added/Corp** Stockholm. Universitetet. Juridiska Fakulteten. (1957)-. Periodical. English. an. Almqvist & Wiksell International, PO Box 4627, S-11691 Stockholm Sweden. **Tel** 011-46-8-6408800. **ED** F. Schmidt. Each issue contains an index to its own contents (no volume index)--loose.
Ind/Abst Index Foreign Leg. Per.

SZ
SCHWEIZERISCHE ZEITSCHRIFT FUER INTERNATIONALES UND EUROPAISCHES RECHT. **Added/Corp** Schweizerische Vereinigung fuer Internationales Recht. **VFOAT** Revue Suisse de Droit International et de Droit

Europeen; Rivista Svizzera di Diritto Internazionale e di Diritto Europeo; Swiss Review of International and European Law; SZIER; RSDIE; SRIEL. (1991)-. Periodical. French (German). ir. 190.00F. Schulthess Polygraphischer Verlag, Zwingliplatz 2, CH-8022 Zurich Switzerland. **Tel** 011 41 1 2519336. ***Continues*** *Schweizerisches Jahrbuch fuer Internationales Recht.*

NE
SEW. **Added/Corp** Belgische Vereniging voor Europees Recht. Nederlandse Vereniging voor Europees Recht. **VAT** Sociaal-Economische Wetgeving. (19??)-. Periodical. Dutch. Twelve times a year. Fl209.25. W. E. J. Tjeenk Willink, Box 25, 8000 AA Zwolle Netherlands. **Tel** 011 31 38 228819, 011 31 38 211444. **ED** P.J.G. Kapteyn. Index available. cum. index. **Bk Rev. Ad Acc. Circ:** 1,000. ***Continues*** *Sociaal-Economische Wetgeving. Europa/Benelux/Nederland.*
Desc: Specializes in law and economics.

NE
SEW TIJDSCHRIFT VOOR EUROPEES EN ECONOMISCH RECHT. Dutch. mo. Fl180.00. W. E. J. Tjeenk Willink, Box 25, 8000 AA Zwolle Netherlands. **Tel** 011 31 38 228819, 011 31 38 211444. **(Subscription address:** Libresso BV, Postbus 23, 7400 GA Deventer Netherlands; telephone: 011 31 5700 47333 or 33155**)** Index available (bound in last issue).

SA/0379-8895
SOUTH AFRICAN YEARBOOK OF INTERNATIONAL LAW. [S. Afr. yearb. int. law]. **Added/Corp** University of South Africa. Verloren van Themaat Centre for International Law. **VFOAT** Suid-Afrikaanse Jaarboek vir Volkereg. Vol. 1, (1975)-. English. an (Feb.). $55.00. University of South Africa, PO Box 392, Pretoria 0001 South Africa. **Tel** 011 27 12 4298468, FAX 011 (27)12 429 3321, telex (59)350068+. **ED** D. H. Van Wyk. **LC** JX21; .S59. **DD** 341/.05. Each issue contains an index to its own contents (no volume index)--loose. **Bk Rev. Circ:** 500.
Desc: Articles, case discussions, book reviews, notes and comments on international law, with particular reference to the Republic of South Africa and the international community.
Ind/Abst Index Foreign Leg. Per.

RU/0584-5335
SOVETSKII EZHEGODNIK MEZHDUNARODNOGO PRAVA / SOVETSKAIA ASSOTSIATSIIA MEZHDUNARODNOGO PRAVA. ***Ceased.*** **Added/Corp** Sovetskaia Assotsiatsiia Mezhdunarodonogo Prava. **VFOAT** Soviet Year-Book of International Law. (1958)-(19??). Russian (summaries and/or abstracts in English, French and German; table of contents in Chinese, French, English and German). ir. Izdatelstvo Nauka / Akademiia Nauk, Publishing House of the Russian Academy of Sciences, Leninskii Porspekt 14, 117901 Moscow Russia. **Tel** 011 95 954-21-53, FAX 011 95 938-21-44, telex 411964. **(Subscription address:** East View Publications Inc., 3020 Harbor Lane North, Suite 110, Minneapolis MN 55447.**) LC** JX21; .S6.
Ind/Abst Index Foreign Leg. Per.

UK/0963-7036
SOVIET & EASTERN EUROPEAN REPORT. [Sov. East. Eur. rep.]. **VFOAT** Soviet and Eastern European Report. (198?)-. English. mo. £225.00. Interforum Services Ltd., 565 Fulham Road, London SW6 1E5 England. **Tel** 011 41 71 3869322, FAX 011 41 71 3818914. **ED** John Goldsworth. **DD** 338.947. **Bk Rev. Pr Rev.**
Desc: Legal and economic background of doing business in Soviet Union, Poland, Czechoslavakia, Hungary, Romania, Bulgaria, Yugoslavia and Albania.

UK
STANDING ORDERS OF THE HOUSE OF COMMONS. **Main/Corp** Great Britain. Parliament. House of Commons. (18??)-. English. ir. Her Majesty's Stationery Office, 51 Nine Elms Lane, London SW8 5DR England. **Tel** 011 44 71 873 8459, 011 44 71 873 8499, FAX 011 44 71 873 8499, 011 44 71 873 8456, telex 297138. **(Subscription address:** Her Majesty's Stationery Office, PO Box 276, Publications Centre, London SW8 5DT England.**) LC** JN685.

US/0731-5082
STANFORD JOURNAL OF INTERNATIONAL LAW. [Stanford j. int. law]. **Added/Corp** Stanford University. School of Law. Vol. 16 (Summer 1980)-. Periodical. English. Twice a year. Price varies. Stanford University School of Law, Crown Quadrangle 42, Stanford CA 94305. **Tel** (415)723-4421. **(Subscription address:** Stanford Law School, Crown Quadrangle 14, Stanford CA 84305.**) ED** Susan Williams. **LC** JX1; .S7. **DD** 341/.05. **Bk Rev. Ad Acc. Circ:** 500. Documents available from The Genuine Article. ***Continues*** *Stanford Journal of International Studies, 0081-4326.*
Ind/Abst ABC POL SCI; Crim. Justice Abstr.; Curr. Contents Soc. Behav. Sci.; Curr. Law Index (1980-); Index Foreign Leg. Per.; Index Leg. Period.; Index Period. Artic. Relat. Law (19??-19??); Int. Polit. Sci. Abstr.; Leg. Resour. Index (1980-); LegalTrac (1980-); Middle East Abstr. Index; PAIS Int. Print; Res. Alert [Full Cov.]; Soc. Sci. Cit. Index [Full Cov.].

US/1057-0551
STUDIES IN TRANSNATIONAL LEGAL POLICY. [Stud. transnatl. leg. policy]. **Added/Corp** American Society of International Law. (1972)-. Monographic series. English. ir. Price varies per volume. American Society of International Law, 2223 Massachusetts Avenue Northwest, Washington DC 20008-2864. **Tel** (202)939-6000, FAX (202)797-7133. **DD** 341.
Desc: Deals with various topics of international law varying from international investment, trade, monetary reform to international telecommunications, terrorism, and UN systems.

US/0886-2648
SUFFOLK TRANSNATIONAL LAW JOURNAL. ***Title Change.*** [Suffolk transnatl. law j.]. **Added/Corp** Suffolk University. Law School. Vol. 1 (1977)-Vol. 15, No. 2 (Spring 1992). Periodical. English. sa. Suffolk University Law School, 41 Temple Street, Boston MA 02114. **Tel** (617)573-8000. **LC** K23; .U34. **DD** 340. ***Continued by*** *Suffolk Transnational Law Review.*
Ind/Abst Index Leg. Period.; Leg. Resour. Index (1980-?); LegalTrac (1980-?).

●US/0886-2648
SUFFOLK TRANSNATIONAL LAW REVIEW. [Suffolk transnatl. law r.]. **Added/Corp** Suffolk University. Law School. **VFOAT** Suffolk Transnational Law Journal. Vol. 16, No. 1 (Fall 1992)-. Periodical. English. Twice a year (Fall & Spring). $18.00. Suffolk Transnational Law Review, 41 Temple Street, Boston MA 02114. **Tel** (617)573-8000. **ED** Amy Moss, Production Editor, (phone: (617)573-8610). **DD** 340. **Bk Rev.** ***Continues*** *Suffolk Transnational Law Journal, 0886-2648.*

US/0250-6319
SUMMARY OF THE DECISIONS TAKEN AT THE MEETINGS AND TEXTS OF THE RESOLUTIONS APPROVED. (SUMMARY OF THE DECISIONS TAKEN AT THE MEETINGS AND TEXTS OF THE RESOLUTIONS APPROVED / ORGANIZATION OF AMERICAN STATES, PERMANENT COUNCIL.). **Main/Corp** Organization of American States. Permanent Council. (1971)-. English. ir. Organization of American States, 19th Street & Constitution Avenue NW, Suite 300, Washington DC 20006. **Tel** (202)458-6256. **LC** KDZ1171.A4; O74. **DD** 341.24/5. ***Continues*** *Organization of American States. Council. Decisions Taken at the Meetings of the Council of the Organization of American States.*

US/0093-0709
SYRACUSE JOURNAL OF INTERNATIONAL LAW AND COMMERCE. [Syracuse j. int. law commer.]. **Added/Corp** Syracuse University. College of Law. Vol. 1, (Oct. 1972)-. Periodical. English. an. $10.00. Syracuse University / Law, College of Law, Ernest I. White Hall, Syracuse NY 13244-1030. **Tel** (315)443-3680, FAX (315)443-9568. **LC** JX1; .S94. **DD** 341/.05. **Ad Acc. Circ:** 600. available on microfilm and microfiche from University Microfilms International (UMI). Documents available from UMI Article Clearinghouse.
Ind/Abst ABI/INFORM Glob. Ed.; ABI Inform Ondisc (Winter 1979/1980-); Curr. Law Index (1980-); Index Leg. Period.; Leg. Resour. Index (1980-); LegalTrac (1980-); UMI ABI/Inform--Bus. Period. Ondisc (Fall 1987-) [Full Txt.].

LU/0776-8508
TARGET 92 / COMMISSION OF THE EUROPEAN COMMUNITIES, DIRECTORATE-GENERAL INFORMATION, COMMUNICATIONS, CULTURE. ***Title Change.*** **See** Economics-Economic History, Conditions.

US
TAX LAWS OF THE WORLD. CLASS B. **See** Public Administration-Public Finance and Taxation.

SZ/0898-5081
TAX TREATY NETWORKS. [Tax treaty netw.]. 1st Ed. (1988/89)-. English. ir. Worldwide Information Inc, PO Box 786, Cooper Station, New York NY 10276. **LC** K4475.4; .T375. **DD** 341.48/44/026.

US/0889-1915
TEMPLE INTERNATIONAL AND COMPARATIVE LAW JOURNAL. [Temple int. comp. law j.]. **Added/Corp** Temple University. School of Law. **VFOAT** International and Comparative Law Journal. Vol. 1, No. 1 (Fall 1985)-. Periodical. English. sa (Spring & Fall). $14.00 US: $16.00 other. Temple University School of Law, 1719 North Broad Street, Philadelphia PA 19122. **Tel** (215)204-1610. **ED** Ute Joas. **LC** K24; .E434. **DD** 340/.2; 342. cum. index. **Bk Rev. Pr Rev. Circ:** 300 (ctrl).
Ind/Abst Index Leg. Period.; Leg. Resour. Index; LegalTrac (1980-).

US/0163-7479
TEXAS INTERNATIONAL LAW JOURNAL. [Tex. int. law j.]. **Added/Corp** University of Texas at Austin. School of Law. Vol. 7, No. 1 (Summer 1971)-. Periodical. English. Three times a year. $25.00 US; $28.00 other. Texas International Law Journal, 727 East 26th Street, Suite 2101, Austin TX 78705. **Tel** (512)471-1106. **ED** Laura Ferguson and Cindy Degitz. **LC** JX1; .T48. **DD** 341/.05. Index available. cum. index. **Bk Rev. Ad Acc. Circ:** 800 (ctrl). available on microfilm from University Microfilms International (UMI). ***Continues*** *Texas International Law Forum.*
Desc: Journal of articles, student works, and book reviews in the various fields of transnational law. Also includes coverage of domestic law with international implications.
Ind/Abst Account. Art.; Am. Bibliogr. Slavic East Europ. Stud.; Curr. Law Index (1980-); Fed. Tax Artic.; Index Foreign Leg. Per.; Index Leg. Period.; Leg. Resour. Index (1980-); LegalTrac (1980-).

US/0895-5018
THIRD WORLD LEGAL STUDIES. [Third world legal stud.]. **Added/Corp** International Third World Legal Studies Association. Valparaiso University. School of Law. **VFOAT** TWLS. (1982)-. English. an. $7.00 Third World countries; $20.00 others Comes with International Third World Legal Studies Association membership. International Third World Legal Studies Association, Valparaiso University, School of Law, Valparaiso IN 46383. **Tel** (219)465-7838, FAX (219)465-7872. **ED** Samuel O. Gyandah, Paul Brietake and Jack Hiller. **LC** K24; .H57. **DD** 340/.09172/4. **Circ:** 500.
Desc: News and information on international law.
Ind/Abst Index Foreign Leg. Per.; Leg. Resour. Index (1985-); LegalTrac (1980-).

●NE/0926-874X
TILBURG FOREIGN LAW REVIEW. **See** Law.

US/1046-3445
TOURO JOURNAL OF TRANSNATIONAL LAW. [Touro j. transnatl. law]. **Added/Corp** Jacob D. Fuchsberg Law Center. Vol. 1, No. 1 (Fall 1988)-. Periodical. English. Twice a year (Oct., June). $15.00. Touro College Fuchsberg Law Center, 300 Nassau Road, Huntington NY 11743. **Tel** (516)421-2244. **ED** Bryan Salamore. **LC** K24; .O725. **DD** 340/.05. **Bk Rev**, (Qty: 2). **Ad Acc, Adv Mgr:** Sean Conway, **Tel** (516)421-2244 Ext. 508. **Circ:** 1,800. available on an online database from WESTLAW.
Ind/Abst Am. Bibliogr. Slavic East Europ. Stud.; Leg. Resour. Index; LegalTrac (1988-).

UK/0262-9240
TRADING LAW. ***Title Change.*** Vol. 1, No. 1 (1981)-Vol. 10, No. 4 (Oct./Dec. 1993). Periodical. English. qt. Barry Rose Law Periodicals Ltd., Little London, Chichester West Sussex PO19 1PG England. **Tel** 011 44 243 787841, 011 44 243 783637, FAX 011 44 243 779174, 011 44 243 779278. **ED** Graham Stephenson. **LC** KD2200.A13; T73. **DD** 343.41/08; 344.1038. Index available. **Bk Rev. Ad Acc.** ***Merged with*** *Trading Law Reports; Trading Law & Trading Law Reports.*
Desc: Information on all developments affecting trading law such as consumer law, fair trading law, product liability, contract law, unfair and misleading advertisement, monopolies and mergers, food labeling, patents, etc.
Ind/Abst ARTbibliogr. Mod. (1982-).

US/1058-1006
TRANSNATIONAL LAW & CONTEMPORARY PROBLEMS : A JOURNAL OF THE UNIVERSITY OF IOWA COLLEGE OF LAW. [Transnatl. law contemp. probl.]. **Added/Corp** University of Iowa. College of Law. **VFOAT** Transnational Law and Contemporary Problems; TLCP. Vol. 1, No. 1 (Spring 1991)-. Periodical. English. sa. $22.00. University of Iowa College of Law, Boyd Law Building Room 190, Iowa City IA 52242. **Tel** (319)335-9061, FAX (319)335-9019. **ED** Susan Crawford (Phone: (319)335-9736). **LC** K24; .R286. **DD** 341. **Ad Acc. Circ:** 250 (ctrl).
Desc: Provides the international and comparative law community matters of interest and innovation not commonly found in other journals and reviews. Each issues focuses on a contemporary forum of transnational significance in a symposium format.
Ind/Abst Index Leg. Period. (1992-); Leg. Resour. Index; LegalTrac (1991-).

US/1045-8905
TRANSNATIONAL LAWYER, THE. [Transnatl. lawyer]. **Added/Corp** McGeorge School of Law. Vol. 1, No. 1 (Spring 1988)-. English. sa. Transnational Lawyer, 3200 5th Avenue, Sacramento CA 95817. **DD** 341.
Ind/Abst J. Plan. Lit.; Leg. Resour. Index; LegalTrac (1988-).

SZ/0376-6403
TRANSNATIONAL PERSPECTIVES. ***Ceased.*** [Transnatl. perspect.]. (1974)-Vol. 15. English. Three times a year. Transnational Perspectives, CP 161, CH-1211 Geneva 16 Switzerland. **ED** Rene Wadlow. **LC** JX1901; .T7. **DD** 341.2/05. **Bk Rev. Circ:** 5,000. ***Formed by the union of*** *World Federalist* ***and*** *Contact.*
Desc: Covers international relations, peace, conflict resolution, and development.
Ind/Abst Int. Dev. Abstr. (?-?); Peace Res. Abstr. J. (1975-1976, 1978-1980).

SZ/0082-6030
TRAVAUX DE JURIDICTION INTERNATIONALE. (1959)-. Monographic series. French. ir. Price varies per volume. Librairie Droz SA, 11 rue Massot BP 389, CH 1211 Geneva 12 Switzerland. **Tel** 011 41 22 3466666, FAX 011 41 22 472391.

FR
TRAVAUX DU COMITE FRANCAIS DE DROIT INTERNATIONAL PRIVE. Main/Corp Comite Francais de Droit International Prive. Vol. 1 (1934)-. French. ir. 180.09F. Editions A Pedone, 13 rue Soufflot, 75005 Paris France. **Tel** 011 33 1 43540597. **LC** JX6012; .C6. **DD** 341.506244.
Ind/Abst Index Foreign Leg. Per.

SA
TREATY SERIES. Main/Corp South Africa. **VFOAT** Verdragreeks. Monographic series. Afrikaans (English). Price varies per volume. Government Printer / South Africa, Bosman Street, Private Bag X85, Pretoria 0001 South Africa. **Tel** 011 27 12 3239731 Ext. 262. **LC** JX1040.A58. **DD** 341.268.

US/0379-8267
TREATY SERIES - UNITED NATIONS. (TREATY SERIES / UNITED NATIONS / RECUEIL DES TRAITES / NATIONS UNIES.). [Treaty ser. - U.N.]. **Main/Corp** United Nations. **Added/Corp** United Nations. **VFOAT** Recueil des Traites. Vol. 1 (1946-1947)-. Government Publication. English (French). ir. $25.00. United Nations Publications, 2 United Nations Plaza, Room DC2 0853, Department 007C, New York NY 10017. **Tel** (212)963-8303, (800)253-9646. **LC** JX170; .U35. **DD** 341.2. cum. index. available on microfilm from Trans-Media; available on microfiche from Law Library Microform Consortium; and Unifo. ***Continues*** *Treaty Series.*
Desc: The text of every treaty and international agreement entered into by any member state of the United Nations.

BB
TURKS AND CAICOS ISLANDS CONSOLIDATED INDEX OF STATUTES AND SUBSIDIARY LEGISLATION TO ... / COMPILED AT THE FACULTY OF LAW LIBRARY, UNIVERSITY OF THE WEST INDIES, BARBADOS. Added/Corp University of the West Indies (Cave Hill, Barbados). Faculty of Law. Library. (19??)-. English. $20.00 each index. Faculty of Law Library, PO Box 64, Bridgetown Barbados. **Tel** (813)778-5211. **ED** Clifford Hammett. **LC** KGY10.5; .T87. **DD** 348.7296/1028; 347.29610828. **Circ:** 200.
Desc: Contains titles of current laws in the territory concerned with references to the amendments to and subsidiary legislation made under each statute.

US/1014-6539
U.N. OBSERVER & INTERNATIONAL REPORT. [U. N. obs. int. rep.]. **VFOAT** U.N. Observer and international Report. **VAT** United Nations Observer and International Report. Vol. 1, (1978)-. Periodical. English. Twelve times a year. $79.00 North America; $95.00 other. Tres Publications Inc., 1004 Cinta Court, Virginia Beach VA 23454. **Tel** (804)491-1016, FAX (804)491-0532. **ED** Ted Morello, (phone: (212)751-3657). Index available. cum. index. **Circ:** 2,500 (ctrl).
Desc: Report on UN agenda & world overview in relation to United Nations.

AT/1033-1891
UNESCO AUSTRALIA / AUSTRALIAN NATIONAL COMMISSION FOR UNESCO. Added/Corp Australian National Commission for Unesco. **VAT** United Nations Educational, Scientific and Cultural Organization Australia. Vol. 1, No. 1 (Apr. 1989)-. Periodical. English. Twice a year. Free. Australia National Commission Unesco, Administrative Building, Parkes ACT 2600 Australia. **Tel** 06 6162 83 2896. **LC** AS4.U825; A857. **DD** 341.7/67/05. ***Continues*** *Newsletter (Australian National Commission for Unesco : 1985), 0725-5756.*

NP
UNESCO BULLETIN. Main/Corp Nepal. National Commission for UNESCO. (19??)-. Government Publication. Multiple languages (English and Nepali). ir. United Nations Publications, 2 United Nations Plaza, Room DC2 0853, Department 007C, New York NY 10017. **Tel** (212)963-8303, (800)253-9646. **LC** AS4.U825; N342a. **DD** 341.7/67.

US/0082-8297
UNITED NATIONS JURIDICAL YEARBOOK. [U.N. jurid. yearb.]. **Main/Corp** United Nations. (1962)-. Government Publication. English. an. price varies per volume. United Nations Publications, 2 United Nations Plaza, Room DC2 0853, Department 007C, New York NY 10017. **Tel** (212)963-8303, (800)253-9646. **LC** JX1977.A1; U54. **DD** 341.23/05.
Desc: Documentary texts of treaties and other materials concerning the legal status and activities of the United Nations and related inter-governmental organizations.

US
UNITED NATIONS LAW REPORTS. Vol. 1 (Sept. 1966)-. Periodical. English. mo. $95.00 US. Walker and Company, 435 Hudson Street, New York NY 10014. **Tel** (212)727-8300. **ED** John Carey.
Desc: Extracts from a wide range of United Nation documents of legal significance.

US/0082-8300
UNITED NATIONS LEGISLATIVE SERIES. (19??)-. Government Publication. English. ir. Price varies per volume. United Nations Publications, 2 United Nations Plaza, Room DC2 0853, Department 007C, New York NY 10017. **Tel** (212)963-8303, (800)253-9646.
Desc: Includes compilations of legal texts submitted by governments on selected topics.

LE
UNITED NATIONS RESOLUTIONS ON PALESTINE AND ARAB-ISRAELI CONFLICT. 1975- . English. Institute for Palestine Studies, PO Box 7164, Beirut Lebanon. **Tel** 01 - 814174, 01 - 312512. **LC** JX1977.2.P34; U57. **DD** 341.23/5694. **Circ:** 3,000.
Desc: Includes all pertinent resolutions on the Palestine question passed by the United Nations and its subsidiary organs during the year.

LE
UNITED NATIONS RESOLUTIONS ON PALESTINE AND THE ARAB-ISRAELI CONFLICT. (QARARAT AL-UMAM AL-MUTTAHIDAH BI-SHAN FILASTIN WA-AL-SIRA AL-ARABI-AL-ISRAILI.). Began with Vol. for 1975. Arabic. an. £L15.00. Shari Anis Al-Nusuli Mutafarri Min Shari Firdan, Beirut Lebanon. **LC** JX1977.2.P34; H3312 1975 SUPPL.

US/0898-2929
UNITED NATIONS RESOLUTIONS. SERIES 2, RESOLUTIONS AND DECISIONS OF THE SECURITY COUNCIL. (RESOLUTIONS AND DECISIONS OF THE SECURITY COUNCIL.). [U. N. resolut., 2 Resolut. decis. Secur. Counc.]. **Main/Corp** United Nations. Security Council. **VFOAT** Resolutions et Decisions du Conseil de Securite; United Nations Resolutions. Series II, Resolutions and Decisions of the Security Council; United Nations Resolutions. Series 2, Security Council. Vol. 1 (1946)-. English (French). ir. $50.00. Oceana Publications Inc, 75 Main Street, Dobbs Ferry NY 10522. **Tel** (914)693-1320, FAX (914)693-0402, telex (914)693-81007105640834. **ED** Dusan J Djonovich. **LC** JX1977; .A515A. **DD** 341. **Bk Rev. Pr Rev. Circ:** 350 (ctrl).
Desc: This multi-volume series provides a unified, comprehensively indexed collection of the security council resolutions.

US/1015-2199
UNITED NATIONS SYSTEM OF ORGANIZATIONS ... AND DIRECTORY OF SENIOR OFFICIALS. (UNITED NATIONS SYSTEM OF ORGANIZATIONS.). [U. N. syst. organ. dir. sen. off.]. **Added/Corp** United Nations. Office of Secretariat Services for Economic and Social Matters. United Nations. Office for Inter-Agency Affairs and Co-Ordination. United Nations. Administrative Committee on Coordination. Secretariat. **VFOAT** United Nations System of Organizations and Directory of Senior Officials. (19??)-. English. an. **LC** JX1977.8.O35; U543. **DD** 354.1/2.

US/0740-9540
UNITED STATES COURT OF INTERNATIONAL TRADE REPORTS. (UNITED STATES COURT OF INTERNATIONAL TRADE REPORTS : CASES ADJUDGED IN THE UNITED STATES COURT OF INTERNATIONAL TRADE.). [U.S. Court Int. Trade rep.]. **Main/Corp** United States. Court of International Trade. Vol. 1 (Nov. 1980-June 1981)-. English. ir. Superintendent of Documents, US Government Printing Office, Washington DC 20402. **Tel** (202)275-3328, FAX (202)786-2377. **LC** KF6655.A2; U54. **DD** 347.73/28; 347.30728. ***Continues*** *United States Customs Court Reports.*

US/0083-3487
UNITED STATES TREATIES AND OTHER INTERNATIONAL AGREEMENTS. [U. S. treaties other int. agreem.]. **Main/Corp** United States. **Added/Corp** United States. Dept. of State. (1950)-. English. ir. Superintendent of Documents, US Government Printing Office, Washington DC 20402. **Tel** (202)275-3328, FAX (202)786-2377. **LC** JX231; .A34. **DD** 341.273. ***Continues in part*** *United States. Laws, etc. United States Statutes at Large.*

US/0884-1756
UNIVERSITY OF MIAMI INTER-AMERICAN LAW REVIEW, THE. [Univ. Miami inter-Am. law rev.]. **VFOAT** Inter-American Law Review. Vol. 16, No. 1 (Spring 1984)-. Academic Scholarly Publication. English. Three times a year. $20.00 US; $22.00 other. Inter-American Law Review, University of Miami Law School, PO Box 248087, Coral Gables FL 33124. **Tel** (305)284-6887, FAX (305)284-2349. **ED** Sarah B Clasby (305)284-5562. **LC** K12; .A95. cum. index. **Ad Acc. Circ:** 1,000 (ctrl). available on microfilm. ***Continues*** *Lawyer of the Americas, 0023-9445.*
Desc: A valuable source of information regarding recent legal developments in the Western Hemisphere and around the globe. It publishes scholarly articles, comments and casenotes dealing with Inter American and international law, immigration and search and seizure. Provides an account of the major legal and legally-related developments of current interest to residents of the Western Hemisphere.
Ind/Abst Account. Art.; Curr. Law Index (1984-); Index Foreign Leg. Per.; Index Leg. Period.; Leg. Resour. Index (1984-); LegalTrac (1984-).

US/0090-2594
VANDERBILT JOURNAL OF TRANSNATIONAL LAW. [Vanderbilt j. transnatl. law]. **Added/Corp** Vanderbilt University. School of Law. Vol. 5 (Winter 1971)-. Periodical. English. ir (Five times per year). $23.00. Vanderbilt Journal of Transnational Law, Vanderbilt University School of Law, 21st Avenue South, Nashville TN 37240. **Tel** (615)322-2284. **LC** JX1; .V35. **DD** 341/.05. Index available (Free). cum. index. **Bk Rev. Ad Acc. Circ:** 1,000 (ctrl). available on microfilm and microfiche from University Microfilms International (UMI). ***Continues*** *Vanderbilt International, 0042-2525.*
Desc: Designed to serve the interests of the practitioner and the theoretician; examines legal events and trends that transcend national boundaries.
Ind/Abst Account. Art. (19??-); Am. Bibliogr. Slavic East Europ. Stud. (19??-); Bowne Dig. Corp. Sec. Lawyers (19??-); Curr. Law Index (1980-); Fed. Tax Artic. (19??-); Index Foreign Leg. Per. (19??-); Index Leg. Period. (19??-); Leg. Resour. Index (1980-); LegalTrac (1980-); PAIS Int. Print (19??-).

US/0278-4939
VIEWS AND ESTIMATES OF THE COMMITTEE ON FOREIGN AFFAIRS ON THE BUDGET. (VIEWS AND ESTIMATES OF THE COMMITTEE ON FOREIGN AFFAIRS ON THE BUDGET FOR FISCAL YEAR.). [Views estim. Comm. Foreign Aff. budg.]. **Main/Corp** United States. Congress. House. Committee on Foreign Affairs. Began with issue for 1979/80. English. an. Congressional Budget Office, 2nd and D Streets SW, Washington DC 20515. **Tel** (202)226-2115. **LC** JX1706.A2; C66A. **DD** 353.0072. ***Continues*** *Views and Estimates of the Committee on International Relations on the Budget.*

US/0042-6571
VIRGINIA JOURNAL OF INTERNATIONAL LAW. [VA. j. int. law]. Vol. 3 (1963)-. Periodical. English. qt. $32.00. Virginia Journal of International Law, University of Virginia School of Law, Charlottesville VA 22901. **Tel** (804)924-3415. **ED** Peter Curley. **LC** JX1; .J57. **DD** 341/.05. Index available (Free). **Bk Rev. Ad Acc. Pr Rev. Circ:** 900 (ctrl). Documents available from The Genuine Article. ***Continues*** *Journal of the John Bassett Moore Society of International Law.*
Desc: Devoted to all fields to public and private international law-arbitration, litigation, act of state doctrine, human rights, law of the sea, and others.
Ind/Abst ABC POL SCI (19??-1984); Account. Art. (19??-); Am. Bibliogr. Slavic East Europ. Stud. (19??-); Bowne Dig. Corp. Sec. Lawyers (19??-); Curr. Law Index (1981-); Fed. Tax Artic. (19??-); Index Foreign Leg. Per. (19??-); Index Leg. Period. (19??-); Leg. Resour. Index (1981-); LegalTrac (1980-); Middle East Abstr. Index (19??-); Res. Alert (19??-) [Full Cov.].

US
VOLUNTARY FUNDS ADMINISTERED BY THE UNITED NATIONS HIGH COMMISSIONER FOR REFUGEES ACCOUNTS, AND REPORT OF THE BOARD OF AUDITORS. Main/Corp United Nations. Office of the United Nations High Commissioner for Refugees. **Added/Corp** United Nations. Board of Auditors. (19??)-. Government Publication. English. ir. United Nations Publications, 2 United Nations Plaza, Room DC2 0853, Department 007C, New York NY 10017. **Tel** (212)963-8303, (800)253-9646. **LC** TX1977; .A41 subser. **DD** 341.23/2 S; 341.48/6.

JA/0285-9211
WASEDA BULLETIN OF COMPARATIVE LAW. Added/Corp Waseda Daigaku. Hikakuho Kenkyujo. Vol. 1 (1981)-. Bulletin. English. ir. Institute of Comparative Law, Waseda

University, 6-1-1-chome Nishi Waseda Shinjuku, Tokyo 160 Japan. **(Subscription address:** Maruzen Company Ltd., PO Box 5050, Import & Export Department, Tokyo 100 31 Japan.**)** **LC** K27; .A74. **DD** 340/.2/05.

US/0743-7951
WISCONSIN INTERNATIONAL LAW JOURNAL. [Wis. int. law j.]. **Added/Corp** University of Wisconsin--Madison. Law School. Wisconsin International Law Society. Symposium. Vol. 1 (1982)-. Academic Scholarly Publication. English. Twice a year. $22.00. University of Wisconsin Law School, 975 Bascom Mall, Madison WI 53706-1399. **Tel** (608)262-3877, FAX (608)262-5485. **ED** Russ Klingaman. **LC** K27; .I79. **DD** 341/.05. **Circ:** 375.
Desc: Scholarly review of international law issues prepared by student and professional writers in the field.
Ind/Abst Curr. Law Index; Index Leg. Period.; Leg. Resour. Index; LegalTrac (1980-).

UK/0960-0949
WORLD ARBITRATION & MEDIATION REPORT. [World arbitr. mediat. rep.]. **Added/Corp** BNA International Inc. **VFOAT** World Arbitration and Mediation Report. Vol. 1, No. 1 (May 1990)-. Periodical. English. Twelve times a year. $455.00 North America; Fl890.40 Netherlands; Fl840.00 other. Transnational Juris Publishers, 1 Bridge Street/ Candy Dubenski, Irvington NY 10533. **Tel** (914)591-4288, FAX (914)591-2688. **ED** Joel Kolko. **[CCC].** Index available. cum. index. **Circ:** 2,000. ***Absorbed*** *BNA's Alternative Dispute Resolution Report, 0893-1704.*
Desc: Provides a US and global perspective on arbitration, mediation and other dispute resolution techniques.

US/0748-9692
WORLDLAW. VFOAT World Law. July-Aug. 1984-. Periodical. English. bm. $115.00. Worldlaw, 12021 Wilshire Boulevard/Suite 428, Los Angeles CA 90025. **LC** K27; .O73. **DD** 343/.087/05.

US/0889-7743
YALE JOURNAL OF INTERNATIONAL LAW, THE. [Yale j. int. law]. **Added/Corp** Yale Law School. Vol. 10, No. 1 (Fall 1984)-. Periodical. English. Twice a year. $25.00 US; $35.00 other. Yale Law School, PO Box 208215, New Haven CT 06520. **Tel** (203)432-7652, FAX (203)432-2592. **ED** Laura Chalk (editor's phone: (203)432-4884). **LC** JX1; .Y34. **DD** 341/.05. Index available. **Bk Rev**, (Qty: 8-20 per year). **Ad Acc, Adv Mgr:** Aaron Fellmeth. **Circ:** 550. ***Continues*** *Yale Journal of World Public Order, 0734-0494.*
Desc: Publishes articles on topics of current interest relating to international law and policy.
Ind/Abst Am. Bibliogr. Slavic East Europ. Stud.; Bowne Dig. Corp. Sec. Lawyers; Curr. Law Index (1984-); Index Leg. Period.; Leg. Resour. Index (1984-); LegalTrac (1984-).

NE/0074-445X
YEARBOOK / INTERNATIONAL COURT OF JUSTICE. [Yearb. - Int. Court Justice]. **Main/Corp** International Court of Justice. (1946/47)-. Government Publication. English. an. Price varies per volume. United Nations Publications, 2 United Nations Plaza, Room DC2 0853, Department 007C, New York NY 10017. **Tel** (212)963-8303, (800)253-9646. **LC** JX1971.6; .A25. **DD** 341.63.
Desc: Discusses the cases before the court pertaining to subjects such as territorial rights, law of the sea and treaty interpretation.

US/0082-8289
YEARBOOK OF THE INTERNATIONAL LAW COMMISSION. Main/Corp United Nations. International Law Commission. (1949)-. Government Publication. English. an. price varies per volume. United Nations Publications, 2 United Nations Plaza, Room DC2 0853, Department 007C, New York NY 10017. **Tel** (212)963-8303, (800)253-9646. **LC** JX1261; .U386. **DD** 341.0611. available on microfiche (from Unifo).
Desc: Contains summary records of International Law Commission sessions and documents relating to the subjects discussed, including the report to the General Assembly.

US/0082-8521
YEARBOOK OF THE UNITED NATIONS. [Yearb. U.N.]. **Main/Corp** United Nations. **Added/Corp** United Nations. Dept. of Public Information. United Nations. Office of Public Information. (1946/1947)-. Government Publication. English. ir. price varies per volume. United Nations Publications, 2 United Nations Plaza, Room DC2 0853, Department 007C, New York NY 10017. **Tel** (212)963-8303, (800)253-9646. **(Subscription address:** Kluwer Academic Publishing, PO Box 253, Accord Station, Hingham, MA 02018; phone (617)871-6600**)** **LC** JX1977.A37; Y4. **NLM** W1 UN258. **[CCC].**
Desc: Principle reference work of the United Nations, including details of UN activities on trade, industrial development, natural resources, food, science and technology, social development, populations, environment, etc.

US/0887-9117
YEARBOOK ON SOCIALIST LEGAL SYSTEMS. ***Ceased.*** [Yearb. Social. legal syst.]. **VFOAT** Year Book on Socialist Legal Systmes. (1986)-?. Periodical. English. an. Transnational Publishers Inc, PO Box 7282, Ardsley-on-Hudson NY 10503. **LC** K29; .E23. **DD** 340/.09171/7.

US/0251-4265
YEARBOOK / UNITED NATIONS COMMISSION ON INTERNATIONAL TRADE LAW. [Yearb. - U. N. Comm. Int. Trade Law]. **Main/Corp** United Nations Commission on International Trade Law. **VFOAT** International Trade Law Yearbook. Vol. 1 (1968/70)-. Government Publication. English. an. Price varies per volume. United Nations Publications, 2 United Nations Plaza, Room DC2 0853, Department 007C, New York NY 10017. **Tel** (212)963-8303, (800)253-9646. **LC** K1004.5; .U55. **DD** 341.7/54/05. available on microfilm.

GW/0044-2348
ZEITSCHRIFT FUER AUSLAENDISCHES OEFFENTLICHES RECHT UND VOELKERRECHT. [Z. ausl. off. Recht Volkerr.]. **Added/Corp** Institut fuer Auslaendisches Oeffentliches Recht und Voelkerrecht. (1929)-. Periodical. German (English). Four times a year. DM289.00. W Kohlhammer Verlag GmbH, Postfach 800430, D 70549 Stuttgart Germany. **Tel** 011 49 711 78631, FAX 011 49 711 7863263, telex 7-255820. **ED** Karl Doehring, Rudolf Bernhardt and Jochen Frowein. **LC** K30; .E27. **DD** 341.05. **[CCC].** cum. index. **Bk Rev. Ad Acc.** ctrl circ.
Desc: Contains discussions of foreign civil law and international law as well as opinions and reviews.
Ind/Abst ABC POL SCI; Energy Res. Abstr. (Feb. 1975-); Index Foreign Leg. Per.; Int. Bibliogr. Sociol.; Int. Polit. Sci. Abstr.

GW/0044-3638
ZEITSCHRIFT FUER VERGLEICHENDE RECHTSWISSENSCHAFT. (ZEITSCHRIFT FUER VERGLEICHENDE RECHTSWISSENSCHAFT, EINSCHLIESSLICH DER ETHNOLOGISCHEN RECHTSFORSCHUNG.). [Z. vgl. Rechtswiss.]. (1878)-. German. qt. Ferdinand Enke Verlag, Ruedigerstrasse 14, D-70469 Stuttgart Germany. **Tel** 011 49 711 8931124, 011 49 711 893123. **LC** K30; .E75. **[CCC].** cum. index. available on microfilm from University Microfilms International (UMI).
Ind/Abst Anthropol. Index; Index Foreign Leg. Per.

AU
ZRV : ZEITSCHRIFT FUER RECHTSVERGLEICHUNG, INTERNAT. PRIVATRECHT UND EUROPARECHT. VFOAT Zeitschrift fur Rechtsvergleichung, Internat. Privatrecht und Europarecht. (1991)-. Periodical. German. bm. 1470.00S. ***Continues*** *Zeitschrift fur Rechtsvergleichung, 0514-275X.*

JUDICIAL SYSTEMS

US
ADAMS COUNTY LEGAL JOURNAL. Added/Corp Adams County (Pa.) Bar Association. Vol. 1 (1959/1960)-. English. ir. William W. Gaunt and Sons Inc, 3011 Gulf Drive, Gaunt Building, Holmes Beach FL 34217. **Tel** (800)942-8683, (813)778-5211. Each issue contains an index to its own contents (no volume index)--loose. cum. index.
Desc: Containing opinions handed down in the 51st judicial district of Pennsylvania, comprised of Adams and Fulton counties, plus selected opinions from other districts.

US/1064-394X
ADMINISTRATIVE JUDICIARY NEWS AND JOURNAL, THE. [Adm. judic. news j.]. **Added/Corp** National Conference of Administrative Law Judges (U.S.). (19??)-. Periodical. English. qt (4 issues). $11.00. American Bar Association, 750 North Lake Shore Drive, Chicago IL 60611. **Tel** (312)988-5522, (312)988-5241, FAX (312)988-5528, telex 270593. **DD** 342.

FR
AGENDA DES PROFESSIONS JUDICIAIRES ET JURIDIQUES. (1975)-. French. 6 rue de Mezieres, Paris 75006 France. **LC** JN2303; .A4. **DD** 347/.44/013. ***Supersedes*** *Agenda et Annuaire de la Magistrature, du Barreau, du Notariat, des Officiers Ministeriels et de l'Enregistrement.*

US/0098-9738
'AHA' ILONO. Added/Corp Hawaii. Judiciary Dept. (19??)-. English. bm. Free. Hawaii Judiciary Branch, Public Information Office, PO Box 2560, Honolulu HI 96804. **Tel** (808)548-4634, FAX (808)548-6002. **LC** KFH510.A73; A35. **DD** 347/.969/01. **Circ:** 4,500.

US/0198-0319
ALABAMA RULES OF COURTS. Main/Corp Alabama. Courts. English. West Publishing Company, 610 Opperman Drive, PO Box 64526, Eagan MN 55123-1308. **Tel** (612)687-5618, (800)328-9352, FAX (612)687-5388, (800)562-2329. **(Subscription telephone:** FAX (612)688-3570**)** **LC** KFA529; .A192. **DD** 347.761/051.
Desc: Also includes some Federal rules.

US
ALASKA COURT SYSTEM NEWSLETTER. Newsletter. English. 303 K Street, Anchorage AK 99501. **LC** KFA1710.A15; A37. **DD** 347.798/01/05; 347.9807105. ***Formed by the union of*** *Magistrate Newsletter* ***and*** *Court Reporter.*

CN/0226-4196
ALBERTA COURT CALENDAR. [Alta. court cal.]. **Added/Corp** Alberta Court Services. (July/Dec. 1978)-. Periodical. English. sa. Free. Alberta Attorney General, 9833 109th Street / Erica Keller, Edmonton Alberta T5K 2E8 Canada. **Tel** (403)427-4992. **LC** KEA533; .A78. **DD** 347.7123/013; 347.123/0713; 347.7123/01.

CN/0823-2350
ALBERTA LEGAL TELEPHONE DIRECTORY. [Alta. leg. teleph. dir.]. **Added/Corp** Canada Law Book Limited. (1980)-. Directory. English. an. 15.00Can$. Canada Law Book Inc., 240 Edward Street, Aurora Ontario L4G 3S9 Canada. **Tel** (800)263-3269, (905)841-6472, FAX (905)841-5085. **DD** 340/.025/7123. **Bk Rev. Ad Acc.**
Desc: Contains a cumulative alphabetical listing of all lawyers and an alphabetical listing of judges. Arranged by name, each listing includes firm association, address, telephone number.

US
ALMANAC OF THE FEDERAL JUDICIARY. (19??)-. Directory. English. ir (includes semiannual updates). $295.00. Prentice-Hall Law and Business, 270 Sylvan Avenue, Englewood Cliffs NJ 07632. **Tel** (800)223-0231, (201)894-8538, FAX (201)894-8666. **ED** Steve Nelson.
Desc: Divided into two volumes with information on district judges, bankruptcy judges, and magistrate judges in Volume I; circuit judges and Supreme Court justices in Volume II.

US/0160-2578
AMERICAN BENCH, THE. (THE AMERICAN BENCH; JUDGES OF THE NATION.). **Added/Corp** Reginald Bishop Forster & Associates. 1st Edition (1977)-. English. an (Oct.). $275.00. Forster Long Inc, 3280 Ramos Circle, Sacramento CA 95827. **Tel** (916)362-3276, FAX 916362-5643. **ED** Marie T. Finn. **LC** KF8700.A19; A47. **DD** 347/.73/14025 [B]. Each issue contains an index to its own contents (no volume index)--loose.
Desc: Listing current judicial information including the Bill of Rights of the United States and each of the fifty states.

US/0145-8574
AMICUS CURIARUM. Main/Corp Maryland. Administrative Office of the Courts. Began with No. 98 (April 1976). English. mo. Administrative Office of the Courts / Maryland, Court of Appeals Building, PO Box 431, Baltimore MD 21401. **LC** KFM1708.A73; A33. **DD** 347/.752/05. ***Continues*** *Maryland. Administrative Office of the Courts. Newsletter.*

FR
ANNUAIRE DE LA COUR DE CASSATION. Main/Corp France. Cour de Cassation. French. an. Documentation Francaise, 29 Quai Voltaire, 75344 Paris Cedex 7 France. **Tel** 011 33 1 40157000, FAX 011 33 1 40157230, telex 204 826 DOCFRAN. **LC** KJV3792.A15; F7.

FR
ANNUAIRE DES PROFESSIONS JUDICIAIRES ET JURIDIQUES. French. an. $70.51. Journal des Notaires et des Notaires et Avocats, 6 rue Meziers, 75006 Paris France. **DD** 340/.025/44. ***Supersedes*** *Agenda et Annuaire de la Magistrature, du Barreau, du Notariat, des Officiers Ministeriels et de l'Enregistrement.*

US
ANNUAL REPORT, ALABAMA JUDICIAL SYSTEM. Main/Corp Alabama. Administrative Office of Courts. English. an. Administrative Office of Courts, 817 South Court Street, Montgomery AL 36104. **LC** KFA510; .A832. **DD** 347.761/01; 347.61071.

AT/0811-4498
ANNUAL REPORT BY THE INSPECTOR-GENERAL IN BANKRUPTCY ON THE OPERATION OF THE BANKRUPTCY ACT 1966. Main/Corp Australia. Inspector-General in Bankruptcy. **VFOAT** Annual Report on the Operation of the Bankruptcy Act 1966. (1991)-. English. Australian Government Publishing Service, GPO Box 84, Canberra

ACT 2601 Australia. **Tel** 011 61 6 2954411, FAX 011 61 6 2954455. **LC** HG3769.A84; A97. ***Continues*** *Australia. Attorney-General's Dept. Annual Report by the Attorney General on the Operation of the Bankruptcy Act 1966.*

CN/0711-2807
ANNUAL REPORT. JUDGES OF THE PROVINCIAL COURT SUPERANNUATION FUND. [Annu. rep., Judges Prov. Court Superann. Fund]. **Main/Corp** Saskatchewan. **VFOAT** Judges of the Provincial Court Superannuation Fund; Annual Report, Judges of the Provincial Court Superannuation Fund. 1978/79-. English. an. Saskatchewan Government Services, Regina Saskatchewan Canada. **LC** KES539.A72; S37. **DD** 354.7124/014; 347.1240714.

CN/0382-1803
ANNUAL REPORT - MINISTRY OF THE ATTORNEY GENERAL (TORONTO). (ANNUAL REPORT - MINISTRY OF THE ATTORNEY GENERAL (ONTARIO).). [Annu. rep. - Minist. Atty. Gen. (Tor.)]. **Main/Corp** Ontario. Ministry of the Attorney General. 1974/75-. English (French). an. Ministry of the Attorney General, 18 King Street East, Toronto Ontario M5C 1C5 Canada. **Tel** (416)965-9111. **LC** KEO855.A72; A8. **DD** 354/.713/065. ***Absorbed*** *Ontario. Provincial Court. Family Division. Annual Report for the Period of April 1.*

US
ANNUAL REPORT, MINNESOTA BOARD ON JUDICIAL STANDARDS FOR THE CALENDAR YEAR ... / MINNESOTA BOARD ON JUDICIAL STANDARDS. **Main/Corp** Minnesota Board on Judicial Standards. (1975)-. English. an. 202 Minnesota State Bank Building, 200 South Robert Street, St Paul MN 55107. **LC** KFM5925.5.D5; A852. **DD** 347.776/014; 347.760714.

US/0196-5433
ANNUAL REPORT - NATIONAL CENTER FOR STATE COURTS. (ANNUAL REPORT.). **Main/Corp** National Center for State Courts. (1973)-. English. an (Apr.). Free. National Center for State Courts, 300 Newport Avenue, PO Box 8798, Williamsburg VA 23185. **Tel** (804)253-2000, FAX (804)220-0449. **LC** KF8736.A16; N37. **DD** 347.73/3/06; 347.307106. **Circ:** 2,000.
Desc: An overview of the national center's work.

US
ANNUAL REPORT / NEW JERSEY JUDICIARY. **Main/Corp** New Jersey. Administrative Office of the Courts. **VFOAT** New Jersey Judiciary Annual Report; Annual Report of the New Jersey Judiciary. (Sept. 1, 1979/Aug 31, 1980)-. English. an. Free on request. Media Services, 25 Market Street CN037, Trenton NJ 08625. **Tel** (609)292-9580. **LC** KFN1871; .A37. **DD** 347.749/013; 347.490713. ***Continues*** *New Jersey. Administrative Office of the Courts. Annual Report of the Administrative Director of the Courts.*

US/0148-5229
ANNUAL REPORT OF THE ATTORNEY GENERAL OF THE UNITED STATES. **Main/Corp** United States. Dept. of Justice. (June 30, 1873)-. English. an. US Department of Justice, 10th Street & Constitution Avenue NW, Washington DC 20530. **Tel** (202)514-2000, FAX (202)633-4371. **LC** KF5107; .A632. **DD** 353.5. available on microfiche (Vols. for (1985-) distributed to depository libraries). ***Continues*** *United States. Dept. of Justice. Operations of the Department of Justice for the Fiscal Year June 30 ... .*

US
ANNUAL REPORT OF THE CHIEF ADMINISTRATOR OF THE COURTS - NEW YORK. **VFOAT** Report of the Chief Administrator of the Courts. Jan. 1, 1978-Dec. 31, 1978-. English. an. Office of Court Administration, 270 Broadway, New York NY 10007. **LC** KFN5950.A73; J8. **DD** 347.747/013; 347.470713. ***Continues*** *Report of the Administrative Board of the Judicial Conference, and the Office of Court Administration.*

US/0731-3195
ANNUAL REPORT OF THE COLORADO JUDICIARY. (ANNUAL REPORT OF THE COLORADO JUDICIARY / OFFICE OF THE STATE COURT ADMINISTRATOR.). **Main/Corp** Colorado. Office of the State Court Administrator. **VFOAT** Annual Report, Colorado Judiciary; Colorado Judiciary. (1980)-. English. an (Oct.). Free. Colorado State Judicial Department, 1301 Pennsylvania Street, Suite 300, Denver CO 80203-2416. **Tel** (303)837-3613, FAX (303)831-1814. **ED** Virginia Leavitt (phone:(303)861-1111). **LC** KFC1871; .S727. **DD** 347.788/013; 347.880713. ctrl circ. ***Continues*** *Colorado. Office of the State Court Administrator. Annual Statistical Report of the Colorado Judiciary.*

US
ANNUAL REPORT OF THE COMMISSION ON JUDICIAL DISCIPLINE, STATE OF HAWAII (FOR PERIOD JUNE 1, ... TO JUNE 30, ...). **Main/Corp** Hawaii. Commission on Judicial Discipline. 1st (June 1, 1979-June 30, 1980)-. English. an. PO Box 2560, Honolulu HI 96804. **LC** KFH525.5.D5; A832. **DD** 347.969/014; 349.690714.

US
ANNUAL REPORT OF THE JUDICIAL COUNCIL OF THE STATE OF WASHINGTON. **Main/Corp** Washington (State). Judicial Council. (1977)-. English. an. Seattle Judicial Council, 508 Condon Hall, 1100 NE Campus Parkway, Seattle WA 98195. **LC** KFW508.A73; J793. **DD** 347.797/01. ***Supersedes*** *Judicial Council of the State of Washington. Report.*

US
ANNUAL REPORT OF THE MASSACHUSETTS COMMISSION ON JUDICIAL CONDUCT. **Main/Corp** Massachusetts. Commission on Judicial Conduct. English. an. Commission on Judicial Conduct, 14 Beacon Street/Suite 102, Boston MA 02108. **LC** KFM2925.5.D5; A832. **DD** 347.744/014; 347.440714. ***Continues*** *Massachusetts. Commission on Judicial Conduct. Annual Report of the Commission on Judicial Conduct.*

US
ANNUAL REPORT / OFFICE OF THE ATTORNEY GENERAL, DEPARTMENT OF JUSTICE, STATE OF NEW MEXICO. **Main/Corp** New Mexico. Attorney General's Office. English. an. Office of the Attorney General / New Mexico, PO Drawer 1508, Santa Fe NM 87504. **LC** KFN4040; .A552. **DD** 353.9789008/8. ***Continues*** *Report of the Attorney General of New Mexico, 0749-2065.*

US
ANNUAL REPORT / STATE OF ALASKA, COMMISSION ON JUDICIAL CONDUCT. **Main/Corp** Alaska. Commission on Judicial Conduct. (19??)-. Periodical. English. an. Free. Commission on Judicial Conduct Judicial Conduct, 310 K Street/Suite 301, Anchorage AK 99501. **Tel** (907)272-1033. **ED** Marla N. Greenstein. **LC** KFA1725.5.D5; A853. **DD** 347.798/014; 347.980714. Index available. **Circ:** 150.
Desc: A report published each year to inform the public of the Commission's activities in a calendar year, including yearly statistics.

US/0191-8524
APPELLATE COURT ADMINISTRATION REVIEW. [Appell. court adm. rev.]. **Added/Corp** National Conference of Appellate Court Clerks. No. 1 (1978)-. Periodical. English. **LC** KF8750.A15; A66. **DD** 347/.73/243.
Ind/Abst Leg. Resour. Index (1980-?); LegalTrac (1980-1985).

CN/0826-2896
ATLANTIC LEGAL TELEPHONE DIRECTORY. [Atl. leg. teleph. dir.]. (1984/1985)-. Directory. English. an. 15.00Can$. Canada Law Book Inc., 240 Edward Street, Aurora Ontario L4G 3S9 Canada. **Tel** (800)263-3269, (905)841-6472, FAX (905)841-5085. **DD** 340/.025/715.
Desc: Provides information on law-related offices in the four Atlantic provinces. Lawyers, law firms, law societies, courts, legal aid offices, and more are covered.

SZ
ATTACKS ON JUSTICE : THE HARASSMENT AND PERSECUTION OF JUDGES AND LAWYERS. **Added/Corp** Centre for the Independence of Judges and Lawyers. **VFOAT** Harassment and Persecution of Judges and Lawyers. (July 1989/June 1990)-. English. Centre for the Independence of Judges and Lawyers, PO Box 120, CH-1224 Chene-Bougeries, Geneva, Switzerland. **LC** K2146.A13; H37. **DD** 347/.014/05; 342.71405. ***Continues*** *Harassment and Persecution of Judges and Lawyers.*

US/0455-0315
ATTORNEY GENERAL'S OPINIONS. **Main/Corp** Kentucky. Attorney General's Office. English. Kentucky Department of Education, Capitol Plaza Tower, 1st Floor, Frankfort KY 40601. **Tel** (502)564-4770, FAX (502)564-6771. **LC** KFK1590; .A552. **DD** 344/.769/07.

US
ATTORNEYS GENERAL OF THE STATES AND OTHER JURISDICTIONS, THE. **Added/Corp** National Association of Attorneys General. Council of State Governments. (19??)-. English. an. $10.00. Council of State Governments, PO Box 11910, Iron Works Pike, Lexington KY 40578-1910. **Tel** (800)800-1910, (606)231-1850.

US
BENCHMARK. ***Title Change.*** **Main/Corp** South Dakota. Supreme Court. Office of the Court Administrator. (1976/77)-(19??). English. an. South Dakota Unified Judicial System, State Court Administrator's Office, State Capitol, 500 East Capitol, Pierre SD 57501. **LC** KFS3570; .A86. **DD** 347.783/01. ***Continued by*** *South Dakota Courts.*
Ind/Abst Curr. Law Index (1984-); Leg. Resour. Index (1984-).

US
BENDER'S FEDERAL PRACTICE MANUAL. **Main/Corp** United States. Courts. (1953)-. English. ir. Matthew Bender & Company Inc., 1275 Broadway, Albany NY 12204. **Tel** (800)833-9844, (518)487-3000.

US
BIENNIAL REPORT / ATTORNEY GENERAL. **Main/Corp** Kentucky. Attorney General's Office. (19??)-. English. be. **LC** KFK1627.5.A8; A847. **DD** 353.9769008/8. ***Continues*** *Kentucky. Dept. of Law. Biennial Report of the Department of Law to ... Governor, Commonwealth of Kentucky for the Biennial Period ... as Required by KRS 15.080.*

US
BIENNIAL REPORT OF THE CONNECTICUT JUDICIAL DEPARTMENT. **Main/Corp** Connecticut. Judicial Dept. **Added/Corp** Connecticut. Office of the Chief Court Administrator. **VFOAT** Report of the Judicial Department, State of Connecticut. (1976/78)-. English. be. Connecticut Chief Court Administrator, Judicial Department, Hartford CT 06115. **LC** KFC4108; .A834. **DD** 353.9/746/5. ***Continues*** *Report of the Judicial Department, State of Connecticut.* ***Continued in part by*** *Biennial Report of the Connecticut Judicial Department. Statistics.*

US
BIENNIAL REPORT OF THE DEPARTMENT OF LAW TO ... GOVERNOR, COMMONWEALTH OF KENTUCKY FOR THE BIENNIAL PERIOD ... AS REQUIRED BY KRS 15.080. ***Title Change.*** **Main/Corp** Kentucky. Dept. of Law. (19??)-(19??). English. be. **LC** KFK1627.5.A8; A847. **DD** 353.9769008/8. ***Continues*** *Biennial Report of the Attorney General to the General of the Commonwealth of Kentucky for the Biennial Period ... as Required by KR 15.080.* ***Continued by*** *Kentucky. Attorney General's Office. Biennial Report.*

AG
BOLETIN DEL MINISTERIO DE JUSTICIA. Vol. 1, No. 1 (Jan./Mar. 1980)-. Periodical. Spanish. qt. Direccion General do Coordinacion, Gral Gelly y Obes 2289 - 4O Picso, 1425 Buenos Aires Argentina. **DD** 349.82/05.

CN/0521-0585
BRITISH COLUMBIA LEGAL TELEPHONE DIRECTORY, THE. **Added/Corp** Canada Law Book Limited. (1954)-. Directory. English. an. 15.00Can$. Canada Law Book Inc., 240 Edward Street, Aurora Ontario L4G 3S9 Canada. **Tel** (800)263-3269, (905)841-6472, FAX (905)841-5085. **DD** 340/.025/711.
Desc: Contains a cumulative alphabetical listing of all lawyers and an alphabetical listing of judges. Arranged by name, each listing includes firm association, address, telephone number.

US/0527-2173
CALIFORNIA COURTS COMMENTARY. **Added/Corp** California Judges Association. (19??)-. Periodical. English. bm. $25.00. California Judges Association, 301 Houward Street, Suite 1040, San Francisco CA 94105. **Tel** (415)495-1999, FAX (415)974-1209.

US/1044-1115
CALIFORNIA RULES OF COURT. FEDERAL. [Calif. rules court, Fed.]. **Main/Corp** California. 1987 Rev., Updated Ed.-. English. an. West Publishing Company, 610 Opperman Drive, PO Box 64526, Eagan MN 55123-1308. **Tel** (612)687-5618, (800)328-9352, FAX (612)687-5388, (800)562-2329. **(Subscription telephone:** FAX (612)688-3570) **LC** KF8816; .A192. **DD** 347.73/051/0979405. ***Continues in part*** *West's California Rules of Court: State and Federal, 0147-1317.*

US/0164-3339
CALIFORNIA SUPREME COURT SERVICE. V. 1- Sept. 29, 1978-. Periodical. English. sm. $150.00. American Institute of Continuing Legal Education, PO Box 71526, 350 South Figueroa Street, Los Angeles CA 90071. **LC** KFC45.1; .C34. **DD** 348/.794/043.

CN/0315-8322
CANADA LEGAL DIRECTORY. (1911)-. Directory. English. an. Carswell / Canada, 2075 Kennedy Road, Scarborough Ontario M1T 3V4 Canada. **Tel** (416)609-3800, (800)387-5164. **ED** R A Wharton. **DD** 340/.025/71. **Ad Acc.** ctrl circ.
Desc: Lists practicing lawyers and court officials plus synopsis and comparisons of law.

CN/0084-8573
CANADIAN LAW LIST (1951). (THE CANADIAN LAW LIST.). (1883)-. Directory. English. an (Apr.). 95.00Can$. Canada Law Book Inc., 240 Edward Street, Aurora Ontario L4G 3S9 Canada. **Tel**

Law—Judicial Systems

(800)263-3269, (905)841-6472, FAX (905)841-5085. **ED** Pat Egan. **DD** 340/.025/71. available on CD-ROM. *Absorbed* Carswell's Directory of Canadian Lawyers, 0411-1508.
Desc: Gives complete listings for all Canadian courts, judges, lawyers, cabinets, departments, ministries, boards, Crown corporations, legal aid offices and more, on a province-by-province basis across Canada.

CN/0843-7084
CANADIAN LEGAL FAX DIRECTORY.
[Can. leg. fax dir.]. **Added/Corp** Canada Law Book Limited. (1989)-. English. an. 36.00Can$. Canada Law Book Inc., 240 Edward Street, Aurora Ontario L4G 3S9 Canada. **Tel** (800)263-3269, (905)841-6472, FAX (905)841-5085. **DD** 340/.025/71.
Desc: Complete alphabetical listing of law firms along with their fax numbers.

US/0886-2435
CHANGE EXCHANGE. [Change exch.].
Added/Corp American Bar Association. Lawyers Conference Task Force on Reduction of Litigation Cost and Delay. (Nov. 1985)-. Periodical. English. qt (4 issues). $14.00. American Bar Association, 750 North Lake Shore Drive, Chicago IL 60611. **Tel** (312)988-5522, (312)988-5241, FAX (312)988-5528, telex 270593. **ED** Douglas K. Somerlot. **LC** KF8727.A15; C48. **DD** 347.73/31; 347.30713. **Circ:** 2,700.
Desc: Newsletter describing activities in the field of court cost and delay reduction.

US/0148-3188
CHARITABLE TRUST DIRECTORY, OFFICE OF ATTORNEY GENERAL.
(CHARITABLE TRUST DIRECTORY, OFFICE OF ATTORNEY GENERAL.). **Main/Corp** Washington (State). Office of the Attorney General. (19??)-. Directory. English. an. $20.00. Secretary of State / Washington, PO Box 40234, 505 East Union, Olympia WA 98504. **Tel** (206)753-7120. **ED** Jeanette Dieckman. **LC** HV98.W3; W37a. **DD** 361.7/6/025797. **Circ:** 500. *Continues* Directory of Charitable Organizations and Trusts Registered with the Office of Attorney General (Olympia), 0093-6693.
Desc: Brief description of registered organizations and sample grants.

US
CONDEMNATION PROCEDURES AND TECHNIQUES, FORMS. (19??)-. English. ir.
Matthew Bender & Company Inc., 1275 Broadway, Albany NY 12204. **Tel** (800)833-9844, (518)487-3000.

US
CONDOMINIUM LAW AND PRACTICE, FORMS. (19??)-. English. be. Matthew Bender &
Company Inc., 1275 Broadway, Albany NY 12204. **Tel** (800)833-9844, (518)487-3000.

US/0589-3577
CONNECTICUT CIRCUIT COURT REPORTS. CASES ARGUED AND DETERMINED IN THE APPELLATE DIVISION OF THE CIRCUIT COURT, AND MEMORANDA FILED IN THE CIRCUIT COURT OF THE STATE OF CONNECTICUT. Main/Corp Connecticut. Circuit
Court. Appellate Division. Vol. 1, (1961/63)-. Periodical. English. Circuit Court of the State of Connecticut, Hartford CT 06115. **DD** 345.

US/0731-7972
COURT COMMENTARIES. Added/Corp
Virginia. Supreme Court. Office of the Executive Secretary. (19??)-. Periodical. English. qt. Free. Court Commentaries, Supreme Court of Virginia, 100 North Ninth Street/3rd Floor, Richmond VA 23219. **Tel** (804)745-0014. **ED** Linda G. Robinson. **LC** KFV2910.A15; C68. **DD** 347.755/01; 347.55071. **Circ:** 1,600 (ctrl).

US/1046-249X
COURT MANAGER, THE. [Court manager].
Vol. 1, No. 1 (March 1986)-. Periodical. English. qt. $10.00. National Association for Court Management, National Center for State Courts, 300 Newport Avenue, Williamsburg VA 23185. **Tel** (804)253-2000. **LC** KF8732.A15; C685. **DD** 347.73/13. **Ad Acc. Circ:** 1,400 (ctrl). *Continues* Column/Court Crier.
Desc: Articles of interest to court managers, clerks and administrators.

US
COURT NEWS. Periodical. English. qt.
Administrative Office of the State Courts, 250 Benefit Street/Room 705, Providence RI 02903. **LC** KFR510; .A833. **DD** 347.745/01/05; 347.4507105.

US/0011-0647
COURT REVIEW. Added/Corp North American
Judges Association. Vol. 9, No. 2 (Sept./Oct. 1969)-. Periodical. English. Four times a year (Jan., April, July, Oct.). $25.00. American Judges Association, 300 Newport Avenue, Williamsburg VA 23187. **Tel** (804)253-2000 ext. 319. **ED** Leslie G. Johnson, (editor's address: PO Box 8850, University MS 38677, phone:

(601)232-5955). **LC** K3; .O9. **DD** 340/.0973. Index available. **Bk Rev**, (Qty: 1-2). **Ad Acc, Adv Mgr:** Anne Kelly, **Tel** (801)259-1841. **Circ:** 3,600 (ctrl). *Continues* Municipal Court Review (Denver, Colo.).
Desc: Issues of current interest to judges, judicial salary tables, book reviews and schedules of judicial education courses.
Ind/Abst Crim. Justice Abstr.

US
CRIMINAL JUSTICE EXPENDITURE AND EMPLOYMENT / OFFICE OF THE ATTORNEY GENERAL, KANSAS BUREAU OF INVESTIGATION, STATISTICAL ANALYSIS CENTER.
Added/Corp Kansas Bureau of Investigation. Statistical Analysis Center. **VFOAT** Criminal Justice Information System : Expenditure and Employment. (1980)-. Statistical Publication. English. an. Kansas Bureau of Investigation, Statistical Analysis Center, 3420 Van Buren, Topeka KS 66611. **LC** HV9475.K3; C74. **DD** 350.74/09781. *Continues* Employment and Expenditures for Criminal Justical Activities by Kansas Local Governments.

US
DETERMINATIONS OF THE NEW YORK STATE COMMISSION ON JUDICIAL CONDUCT. Main/Corp New York State Commission
on Judicial Conduct. Vol. 1 (1978-1979)-. English. ir. Free. State of New York Commission on Judicial Conduct, c/o Jack Corwin, 801 2nd Avenue, New York NY 10017. **Tel** (212)949-8860. **LC** KFN5984.5.D57; A4963. **DD** 347.747/014; 347.470714.

US/0364-0817
DIGEST OF OFFICIAL OPINIONS - ATTORNEY GENERAL (LITTLE ROCK).
(DIGEST OF OFFICIAL OPINIONS.). **Main/Corp** Arkansas. Attorney General's Office. English. Office of the Attorney General / Arkansas, Little Rock AR 72201. **LC** KFA4040; .A553. **DD** 348/.767/05.

US/0092-0843
DIGEST OF OFFICIAL OPINIONS - ATTORNEY GENERAL (TALLAHASSEE). (DIGEST OF OFFICIAL
OPINIONS.). [Dig. off. opin. - Atty. Gen.]. **Main/Corp** Florida. Dept. of Legal Affairs. (19??)-. English. Free. Florida Attorney General, The Capitol, Tallahassee FL 32301. **Tel** (904)488-4374. **LC** KFF440; .A552. **DD** 348/.759/05. **Circ:** 1,200 (ctrl).
Desc: Digest of official opinions of Florida's attorney general.

US/0012-2777
DIGEST OF OPINIONS OF THE ATTORNEY GENERAL. Main/Corp Oklahoma.
Attorney General's Office. Vol. 1 (Jan. 15/March 15, 1963)-. Periodical. English. mo. $5.00. Office of Attorney General / Oklahoma, 112 Capitol, Oklahoma City OK 73105. **Tel** (405)521-3921. **LC** UNC. **Circ:** 780.

US/0747-6949
DISTRICT OF COLUMBIA COURT RULES ANNOTATED. (DISTRICT OF
COLUMBIA COURT RULES ANNOTATED / PREPARED BY THE EDITORIAL STAFF OF THE PUBLISHERS.). **Added/Corp** Michie Company. **VFOAT** DC Court Rules Annotated; D.C. Court Rules Annotated. (1981)-. English. an. $65.00. Michie Company, PO Box 7587, Charlottesville VA 22906-7587. **Tel** (804)972-7600, (800)542-0957, FAX (800)643-1280. **LC** KFD1729; .A193. **DD** 347.753/051; 347.530751.

US
DISTRICT OF COLUMBIA COURT RULES SERVICE. (19??)-. English. $89.00. Rules
Service Company, 7615 Standish Place, Rockville MD 20855. **Tel** (301)424-9402, FAX (301)762-7853.

US/1056-2230
DOJ ALERT, THE. [DOJ alert]. VAT Department of
Justice Alert. Vol. 1, No. 1 (July 1991)-. Periodical. English. Twelve times a year. $244.13. Prentice-Hall Law and Business, 270 Sylvan Avenue, Englewood Cliffs NJ 07632. **Tel** (800)223-0231, (201)894-8538, FAX (201)894-8666. **DD** 340.
Desc: Covers the inner workings of all divisions of the Department of Justice. Gives up-to-the-minute reports of the latest policies, procedures and positions adopted by the Justice Department.

US
EXAMINING COURT DECISIONS AND OPINIONS OF THE ATTORNEY GENERAL CONSTRUING ALASKA STATUTES. 1980-81-. English. an. Legislative
Affairs Agency, Pouch Y, State Capitol, Juneau AK 99811. **LC** KFA1607; .A247. **DD** 347.798/014; 347.980714. *Continues* Report of Examination of Court Decisions Construing Alaska Statutes Rendered by the Supreme Court of Alaska.

US
EXECUTIVE SUMMARY OF THE KANSAS JUDICIAL BRANCH / OFFICE OF JUDICIAL ADMINISTRATION, AN.
Main/Corp Kansas. Office of Judicial Administration. English. an. Office of Judicial Administration, 301 West 10th, Topeka KS 66612. **LC** KFK510; .A854. **DD** 347.781/01; 347.81071.

US
FEDERAL CIRCUIT COURT RULES.
(19??)-. English. $39.00. Rules Service Company, 7615 Standish Place, Rockville MD 20855. **Tel** (301)424-9402, FAX (301)762-7853.

US/0164-4564
FEDERAL RULES SERVICE. [Fed. rules
serv.]. **VFOAT** Federal Rules Service with the Federal Index. Vol. 1 (1939)-. Periodical. English. mo. Lawyers Cooperative Publishing Company, Aqueduct Building, Rochester NY 14694. **Tel** (800)527-0430, (716)546-5530. **LC** KF8830; .F43. **DD** 347. **[CCC]**.

US/1055-5277
FJC DIRECTIONS. (FJC DIRECTIONS : A
PUBLICATION OF THE FEDERAL JUDICIAL CENTER.). [FJC dir.]. **Added/Corp** Federal Judicial Center. **VFOAT** Federal Judicial Center Directions. No. 1 (Apr. 1991)-. English. ir. Free. Federal Judicial Center, Dolly Madison House, 1520 H Street NW, Washington DC 20005. **Tel** (202)633-6347.
Ind/Abst Leg. Resour. Index; LegalTrac (1991-).

US/1047-1782
FLORIDA RULES OF COURT. STATE.
[Fla. rules court, State]. **Main/Corp** Florida. Supreme Court. **Added/Corp** West Publishing Company. (1987)-. English. West Publishing Company, 610 Opperman Drive, PO Box 64526, Eagan MN 55123-1308. **Tel** (612)687-5618, (800)328-9352, FAX (612)687-5388, (800)562-2329. **LC** KFF529; .A1925. **DD** 347.759/051; 347.590751. *Continues in part* Florida Rules of Court, 0735-6838.

US/0896-1913
FOR THE RECORD. [For the record].
Added/Corp Ohio Judicial Conference. Vol. 1, Issue 1 (Nov. 1987)-. Periodical. English. mo. Ohio Judicial Conference, State Office Tower, 30 East Broad, Columbus OH 43215. **Tel** (800)282-1510, IN OHIO (614)466-4150. **LC** KFO508; .A835. **DD** 347.771/01/05; 347.7107105. *Continues* Judicial Notice (Columbus, Ohio), 0279-859X.

CN/0709-2180
FORUM (VICTORIA). (FORUM.). Issue No. 1
(Jan./Feb. 1979)-. Periodical. English. bm. The Forum / Canada, Court Services Headquarters/6th Floor, 850 Burdett Avenue, Victoria British Columbia V8W 1B4 Canada. **LC** KEB533.A13; F67. **DD** 347.711/01/05. *Supersedes* Court's Reporter, 0382-1706.

US
FRIENDS OF THE COURT / LITTLE ROCK. (1993)-. Government Publication. English. qt.
Free. Arkansas Judicial Department, 625 Marshall Street, Justice Building, Little Rock AR 72201. **Tel** (501)371-2295. *Continues* Friends of the Court : Newsletter of the Arkansas Judicial Department.

US
FRIENDS OF THE COURT : NEWSLETTER OF THE ARKANSAS JUDICIAL DEPARTMENT. Title Change.
Added/Corp Arkansas. Judicial Dept. Arkansas. Administrative Office of the Courts. Vol. 1, No. 1 (Jan. 1982)-(1993). Periodical. English. qt. Arkansas Judicial Department, 625 Marshall Street, Justice Building, Little Rock AR 72201. **Tel** (501)371-2295. **LC** KFA4108.A15; A45. **DD** 347.767/01/05; 347.6707105. *Continues* Amicus Curiae, 0360-7739. *Continued by* Friends of the Court (Little Rock, Ark. : 1993).

MX
GACETA OFICIAL - PROCURADURIA GENERAL DE JUSTICIA DEL DISTRITO FEDERAL. Main/Corp Mexico (Federal District).
Procuraduria General de Justicia. Vol. 1 No. 1 (July 1977)-. Spanish. bm. **DD** 348.72/5305.

US/1055-7245
GEORGIA COURT RULES AND PROCEDURE. FEDERAL. [Ga. court rules
proced., Fed.]. **Added/Corp** West Publishing Company. (1988)-. English. West Publishing Company, 610 Opperman Drive, PO Box 64526, Eagan MN 55123-1308. **Tel** (612)687-5618, (800)328-9352, FAX (612)687-5388, (800)562-2329. **DD** 347. *Continues in part* Georgia Court Rules and Procedure, 0749-2669.

US
GEORGIA COURTS DIRECTORY.
Added/Corp Georgia. Administrative Office of the Courts. (19??)-. Directory. English. an (Aug.). $10.00. Judicial Council of Georgia, Administrative Office of the Courts,

244 Washington Street Southwest, Suite 550, Atlanta GA 30334. **Tel** (404)656-5171. **LC** KFG508.A19; G4. **DD** 347/.758/01025.

US/0147-7161
GEORGIA COURTS JOURNAL. **Added/Corp** Georgia. Administrative Office of the Courts. (19??)-. Periodical. English. Twelve times a year. Free. Judicial Council of Georgia, Administrative Office of the Courts, 244 Washington Street Southwest, Suite 550, Atlanta GA 30334. **Tel** (404)656-5171. **LC** KFG508.A15; G46. **DD** 347/.758/0105.

US/0145-2991
GEORGIA LEGAL DIRECTORY, THE. Directory. English. an. $6.00. Legal Directories Publishing Company, 9111 Garland Road, PO Box 189000, Dallas TX 75218. **Tel** (214)321-3238, 800 447-5375. **LC** KF192.G46; G46. **DD** 340/.025/758.

AG
GUIA DE TRIBUNALES NACIONALES Y DE LA PROVINCIA DE BUENOS AIRES. (19??)-. Spanish. La Diligencia Judicial, Avenida Juan B. Justo 225 - 7, Piso 14, Buenos Aires Argentina. **DD** 347/.82/014025.

SP
GUIA PROFESIONAL Y JUDICIAL. **Main/Corp** Ilustre Colegio Provincial de Abogados (Salamanca, Spain (Province)). Spanish. Ilustre Colegio Provinciae de Abogados, Palacio de Justicia Gran Via 7, Apdo de Correos 117, Salamanca Spain. **DD** 340/.025/4625.

UK/0266-3597
HAZELL'S GUIDE TO THE JUDICIARY AND THE COURTS. **Added/Corp** R. Hazell & Co. Holborn Law Society. **VFOAT** Hazell's Guide; Guide to the Judiciary and the Courts; Hazell's Guide to the Judiciary and the Courts with the Holborn Society's Bar List; Judiciary + Courts + Barristers + &c. (19??)-. English. an. £19.00. R Hazell & Company, PO Box 39, Henley Thames, RG9 5UA England. **Tel** 11 44 491 641018. **ED** Charles G Parker. Index available. **Ad Acc.**
Desc: Complete United Kingdom guide to the judiciary, courts of law, barristers and advocates.

US/0742-9967
IOWA RULES OF COURT. [Iowa rules court]. 1978-. English. an. West Publishing Company, 610 Opperman Drive, PO Box 64526, Eagan MN 55123-1308. **Tel** (612)687-5618, (800)328-9352, FAX (612)687-5388, (800)562-2329. **(Subscription telephone:** FAX (612)688-3570) **LC** KFI4729; .A194. **DD** 347.777/051; 347.770751.

US/0270-9805
JOURNAL / SUPREME COURT OF THE UNITED STATES. [J. - Supreme Court U.S.]. **Main/Corp** United States. Supreme Court. (1889)-. Government Publication. English. da (312 per year). Supreme Court of the United States, Washington DC 20543. **DD** 347/.73/2605.

US
JUDGE, THE. Periodical. English. mo (Sept. through May). $12.00. The Judge, E I White Hall, Syracuse University, College of Law, Syracuse NY 13210. **Tel** (315)423-2229. **ED** Paul Grenga and Joseph Redd. **Ad Acc. Circ:** 1,000. available on microfilm from University Microfilms International (UMI).

US/0047-2972
JUDGES' JOURNAL, THE. [Judges j.]. Vol. 10, No. 2 (April 1971)-. Periodical. English. qt (4 issues). $25.00. American Bar Association, 750 North Lake Shore Drive, Chicago IL 60611. **Tel** (312)988-5522, (312)988-5241, FAX (312)988-5528, telex 270593. **LC** K10; .U27. **DD** 347/.73/105. ***Continues*** *Trial Judges' Journal, 0564-2116.*
Ind/Abst Crim. Justice Abstr.; Curr. Law Index (1980-); Index Leg. Period.; Leg. Resour. Index (1980-); LegalTrac (1980-).

US
JUDGES' RETIREMENT SYSTEM : ANNUAL FINANCIAL REPORT AND REPORT OF OPERATIONS FOR THE FISCAL YEAR ENDED JUNE 30 ... / ADMINISTERED BY THE BOARD OF ADMINISTRATION, PUBLIC EMPLOYEES' RETIREMENT SYSTEM. **Main/Corp** California. Public Employees' Retirement System. Board of Administration. 1st (1980)-. English. an. Public Employees' Retirement System, PO Box 942705, Sacramento CA 94229-2705. **Tel** (916)326-3039. **LC** KFC980; .A864. **DD** 347.794/014; 347.940714. ctrl circ.

MY
JUDICIAL & LEGAL DIRECTORY. **VFOAT** Judicial and Legal Directory. Directory. English. Malaysian Law Publishers, Room 201/2nd Floor, Lee Yan Lian Building, Jalan Tun Perak, Kuala Lumpur Malaysia.

US/0193-7367
JUDICIAL CONDUCT REPORTER. **Added/Corp** Center for Judicial Conduct Organizations. American Judicature Society. Vol. 1, (Spring 1979)-. Periodical. English. Four times a year (Feb., May., Aug., Nov.). $20.00. American Judicature Society, 25 East Washington Street, Suite 1600, Chicago IL 60602. **Tel** (312)558-6900, FAX (312)558-9175. **ED** Lisa L. Milord. **LC** KF8779.A15; J8. **DD** 347.73/13. Index available. **Bk Rev.** ctrl circ. available on an online database.
Desc: Analyzes developments in judicial and disability, reports current decisions, reviews books and journal articles, and presents an annual survey of commission complaint disposition.

US/0270-0654
JUDICIAL FELLOWS PROGRAM, THE. **Main/Corp** United States. Supreme Court. English. an. The Supreme Court of the United States, Washington DC 20543. **LC** KF277.C65; U55. **DD** 347.73/13/0711; 347.307130711.

US
JUDICIAL STAFF DIRECTORY. **Added/Corp** Congressional Staff Directory (Firm). Vol. 1 (1986)-. English. an. $69.00 other. Staff Directories Ltd., PO Box 62, Mount Vernon VA 22121. **Tel** (703)739-0900, FAX (703)739-0234. **ED** Anna L. Brownson. **LC** KF8700.A19; J83. **DD** 347.73/1/025; 347.3071025. Index available. **Bk Rev.** available on CD-ROM.
Desc: Courts of national jurisdiction, including Supreme Court and Claims and Tax Court. Detailed information, alphabetical court locator, and bibliographies of judges and staff.

US/0098-261X
JUSTICE SYSTEM JOURNAL, THE. [Justice syst. j.]. **Added/Corp** Institute for Court Management. Institute for Court Management. Academy of Fellows. Vol. 1, (Winter 1974)-. Periodical. English. Three times a year. $30.00 (institution), $15.00 (individual). National Center for State Courts, 300 Newport Avenue, PO Box 8798, Williamsburg VA 23185. **Tel** (804)253-2000, FAX (804)220-0449. **ED** Keith O. Boyum. **LC** K10; .U794. **DD** 347/.73/13. Index available. cum. index. **Bk Rev. Pr Rev. Circ:** 900 (ctrl). available in microform. Documents available from The Genuine Article.
Desc: Addresses issues that have implications for justice system policy and addresses problems faces by those with responsibility for court administration.
Ind/Abst Crim. Justice Abstr.; Crim. Justice Period. Index (1980-); Curr. Contents Soc. Behav. Sci.; Curr. Law Index (1980-); Index Leg. Period.; Leg. Resour. Index (1980-); LegalTrac (1980-); Res. Alert [Full Cov.]; Soc. Sci. Cit. Index [Full Cov.].

US
JUSTITIA. Periodical. English (English). qt. Capitol Complex, Carson City NV 89710. **LC** KFN1110.A15; J87. **DD** 347.793/01.

US/0748-5255
KANSAS COURT RULES AND PROCEDURE. (KANSAS COURT RULES AND PROCEDURE : WITH AMENDMENTS RECEIVED TO ...). [Kans. court rules proced.]. English. $18.50. West Publishing Company, 610 Opperman Drive, PO Box 64526, Eagan MN 55123-1308. **Tel** (612)687-5618, (800)328-9352, FAX (612)687-5388, (800)562-2329. **(Subscription telephone:** FAX (612)688-3570) **LC** KFK529; .A194. **DD** 347.781/051; 347.810751.

US/0450-089X
KENTUCKY AND TENNESSEE LEGAL DIRECTORY, THE. Directory. English. an. Legal Directories Publishing Company, 9111 Garland Road, PO Box 189000, Dallas TX 75218. **Tel** (214)321-3238, 800 447-5375. **LC** KF192.K4; K45. **DD** 347.069.

US
LAW DIGEST (RICHMOND, VA.). (THE LAW DIGEST.). Vol. 1, No. 1 (May 1987)-. Periodical. English. mo. Office of the Attorney General / Virginia, Supreme Court Building, 1101 East Broad Street, Richmond VA 23219. **LC** KFV2840.A59; L39. **DD** 348.755/05/05. ***Formed by the union of*** *Virginia. Office of the Attorney General. Civil Digest, 0097-790X* ***and*** *Attorney General's Criminal Law Digest, 0884-7797.*

US/0740-0519
LAWYERS LETTER / JUDICIAL ADMINISTRATION DIVISION, AMERICAN BAR ASSOCIATION, LAWYERS CONFERENCE. **Added/Corp** JAD Lawyers Conference. **VFOAT** L.L.; LL. Vol. 1 No. 1 (July 1983)-. Periodical. English. Three times a year. $13.00. American Bar Association, 750 North Lake Shore Drive, Chicago IL 60611. **Tel** (312)988-5522, (312)988-5241, FAX (312)988-5528, telex 270593. **LC** KF8700.A15; L38. **DD** 347.73/1; 347.3071.

US
LEGISLATIVE MANUAL (NORTH CAROLINA. GENERAL ASSEMBLY. LEGISLATIVE SERVICES OFFICE). (LEGISLATIVE MANUAL.). **Added/Corp** North Carolina. General Assembly. Legislative Services Office. (19??)-. English. be. Legislative Services Office, 2129 State Legislative Building, Raleigh NC 27611. **LC** JK4130; .L37a. **DD** 328.756/0025.

SP
LISTA DE LOS SENORES QUE FORMAN LOS EXPRESADOS COLEGIOS. **Main/Corp** Colegio de Abagados de Zaragoza. **VFOAT** Guia Judicial de Aragon. Spanish. **DD** 340/.025/4655.

US/0734-0524
LONG RANGE JUDICIAL FACILITY PLAN. **Added/Corp** Colorado. Office of the State Court Administrator. **VFOAT** Colorado Judicial Facilities. (19??)-. English. an. Colorado State Judicial Department, 1301 Pennsylvania Street, Suite 300, Denver CO 80203-2416. **Tel** (303)837-3613, FAX (303)831-1814. **LC** NA4472.C6; L66. **DD** 725/.15.

US
MAINE RULES OF COURT, WITH AMENDMENTS. **Main/Corp** Maine. Courts. English. an. West Publishing Company, 610 Opperman Drive, PO Box 64526, Eagan MN 55123-1308. **Tel** (612)687-5618, (800)328-9352, FAX (612)687-5388, (800)562-2329. **(Subscription telephone:** FAX (612)688-3570) **LC** KFM529; .A195. **DD** 347.741/051.
Desc: Also includes some Federal rules.

US/0747-7872
MCKINNEY'S NEW YORK RULES OF COURT. (MCKINNEY'S NEW YORK RULES OF COURT : STATE AND FEDERAL.). **VFOAT** New York Rules of Court. 1982-. English. an. $16.00. West Publishing Company, 610 Opperman Drive, PO Box 64526, Eagan MN 55123-1308. **Tel** (612)687-5618, (800)328-9352, FAX (612)687-5388, (800)562-2329. **(Subscription telephone:** FAX (612)688-3570) **LC** KFN5992; .A195. **DD** 347.747/051; 347.470751. ***Continues*** *New York Court Rules, 0747-8429.*

US/0026-5543
MINNESOTA LEGAL REGISTER. **Added/Corp** Minnesota. Attorney General. Vol. 1 (Jan. 17, 1968)-. Periodical. English. Twelve times a year. $33.00 (two years). Register Mirror, 1414 Soo Line Building, Minneapolis MN 55402. **Tel** (612)332-0726.
Desc: Containing all opinions of the Minnesota Attorney General.

US/0732-6556
MISSOURI RULES OF COURT, STATE AND FEDERAL. [Mo. rules court, state fed.]. **VFOAT** Missouri Rules of Court. 1st. Ed. (1968)-. English. an. West Publishing Company, 610 Opperman Drive, PO Box 64526, Eagan MN 55123-1308. **Tel** (612)687-5618, (800)328-9352, FAX (612)687-5388, (800)562-2329. **(Subscription telephone:** FAX (612)688-3570) **LC** KFM8329; .A194. **DD** 347.778/051; 347.780751.

US
NATIONAL INSTITUTE OF JUSTICE CATALOG. **Added/Corp** National Institute of Justice (U.S.). No. 1 (Nov./Dec. 1991)-. Catalog. English. bm. Free US; $5.00 Canada; $10.00 others. National Criminal Justice Reference Services / NCJRS, Box 6000, 1600 Research Boulevard, Rockville MD 20850. **Tel** (301)251-5500. **LC** Z5703.4.C73; N37b. ***Continues in part*** *National Institute of Justice Reports, 1067-8573.*
Desc: Research findings to individuals who use them to improve criminal justice and the criminal justice system.

US
NCSC SUBSCRIPTION PACKAGE PLAN. (19??)-. English. Twelve times a year. $100.00. National Center for State Courts, 300 Newport Avenue, PO Box 8798, Williamsburg VA 23185. **Tel** (804)253-2000, FAX (804)220-0449.

US/0899-5052
NCSL CONFERENCE REPORT. [NCSL conf. rep.]. **Added/Corp** National Conference of State Legislatures. **VAT** National Conference of State Legislatures Conference Report. Vol. 1, No. 1 (June 1985)-. Periodical. English. qt. $20.00 US; $25.00 Canada. National Conference of State Legislatures, 1560 Broadway, Suite 700, Denver CO 80202. **Tel** (303)830-2054, FAX (303)863-8003. **ED** Julie Lays. **DD** 342.
Desc: Describes the services and activities of the National Conference of State Legislatures for legislators, staff and others. Feature articles highlight new programs, services, research activities, publications, NCSL policy positions, and upcoming meetings and seminars.

US/0364-233X
NEBRASKA JUDICIAL NEWSLETTER. Newsletter. English. State Court Administrator, Room 2412 State Capital, Lincoln NE 68509. **LC** KFN525.A15; N4. **DD** 347/.782/01405.

CN/0849-2271
NEOLEX (FREDERICTON). (NEOLEX / OFFICE OF THE ATTORNEY GENERAL, NEW BRUNSWICK.). [Neolex]. **Main/Corp** New Brunswick. Office of the Attorney General. **Added/Corp** New

Law —Judicial Systems

Brunswick. Law Reform Branch. **VFOAT** Neolex. Vol. 1, No. 1 (June 1990)-. Periodical. English (French). qt. **DD** 340.3/097151/05.

US/8750-2658
NEW JERSEY REPORTS AND NEW JERSEY SUPERIOR COURT REPORTS. [N.J. rep. N.J. Super. Court rep.]. Periodical. English. wk. $70.00. West Publishing Company, 610 Opperman Drive, PO Box 64526, Eagan MN 55123-1308. **Tel** (612)687-5618, (800)328-9352, FAX (612)687-5388, (800)562-2329. **(Subscription telephone:** FAX (612)688-3570) **DD** 348.

US
NEWS RELEASE - CALIFORNAIA. ADMINISTRATIVE OFFICE OF THE COURTS. **Main/Corp** California. Administrative Office of the Courts. (19??)-. Periodical. English.

US/0094-226X
NEWSLETTER & DIGEST OF SELECTED OPINIONS OF STATE ATTORNEYS GENERAL. Began with April/May 1969 issue. Newsletter. English. qt. PO Box 11910, Lexington KY 40578. **LC** KF294.N28; A4. **DD** 348/.73/5.

US/0098-9843
NEWSLETTER - COURT PRACTICE INSTITUTE. **Main/Corp** Court Practice Institute. Newsletter. English. Court Practice Institute, 127 North Dearborn Street, Chicago IL 60602. **LC** KF8911.A3; C68. **DD** 347/.73/7.

US/0364-362X
NORTH CAROLINA ATTORNEY GENERAL REPORTS. **Main/Corp** North Carolina. Dept. of Justice. Periodical. English. sa. PO Box 629, Raleigh NC 27602. **LC** KFN7840; .A555. **DD** 348/.756/05. **Continues** Biennial Report of the Attorney General of the State of North Carolina.

US/0732-281X
NORTH CAROLINA RULES OF COURT, WITH AMENDMENTS RECEIVED TO ... . **Title Change. Added/Corp** North Carolina. Supreme Court. United States. District Court (North Carolina) United States. District Court (North Carolina : Eastern District) United States. Court of Appeals (4th Circuit). **VFOAT** North Carolina Rules of Court, Desk Copy. (1973)-(19??). English. West Publishing Company, 610 Opperman Drive, PO Box 64526, Eagan MN 55123-1308. **Tel** (612)687-5618, (800)328-9352, FAX (612)687-5388, (800)562-2329. **(Subscription telephone:** FAX (612)688-3570) **LC** KFN7929; .A195. **DD** 347.756/051; 347.560751. **Split into** North Carolina Rules of Court. Federal **and** North Carolina Rules of Court. State.
Desc: Includes local rules for the U.S. District Courts for North Carolina, District Court for the Eastern District, rules of the U.S. court of Appeals for the Fourth Circuit, the Federal rules.

US/0148-9445
NORTH DAKOTA JUDICIAL MASTER PROGRAM, THE. **Main/Corp** North Dakota. Judicial Planning Committee. 1977/79-. Periodical. English. be. Judicial Planning Committee, State Capitol, Bismarck ND 58505. **LC** KFN9108; .A85. **DD** 347/.784/01.

US
NORTHERN CALIFORNIA COURT RULES. (19??)-. English. mo (12 issues). $119.00. Daily Journal Corporation, 915 East First Street, Los Angeles CA 90012. **Tel** (213)229-5300, FAX (213)680-3682. **Continues** Court Rules for Northern California.

FR
NOUVEAU POUVOIR JUDICIAIRE, LE. **Added/Corp** Union Syndicale des Magistrats. No. 271 (May 1975)-. Periodical. French. Four times a year. 166.50F. Union Sydicale des Magiotrats, 33 rue du Four, Paris 75006 France. **Tel** 011 33 1 43542126. **DD** 347/.44/014. **Continues** Pouvoir Judiciaire.

US/0147-3573
NUDIS VERBIS. Vol. 1 (Winter 1976)-. Periodical. English (English). qt. PO Box 2448, Raleigh NC 27602. **LC** KFN7908.A15; N8. **DD** 347/.756/0105.

CN/0318-3556
ONTARIO ANNUAL PRACTICE (1973). (THE ONTARIO ANNUAL PRACTICE.). (1973)-. Periodical. English. an. 67.00Can$. Canada Law Book Inc., 240 Edward Street, Aurora Ontario L4G 3S9 Canada. **Tel** (800)263-3269, (905)841-6472, FAX (905)841-5085. **ED** James J. Carthy. **DD** 347/.713/05. **Bk Rev. Ad Acc. Continues** Chitty, R. M. Willes, 1893-1970. Chitty's Ontario Annual Practice., 0084-8751.
Desc: Includes changes in the rules of practice and all significant cases for the past 30 years. Updated with supplements covering amendments to the current rules, forms and tariffs made within the year.

US
OPINION / STATE OF NEW MEXICO, OFFICE OF THE ATTORNEY GENERAL, DEPARTMENT OF JUSTICE. **Main/Corp** New Mexico. Attorney General's Office. English. Office of the Attorney General / New Mexico, PO Drawer 1508, Santa Fe NM 87504. **LC** KFN4040; .A5565. **DD** 348.73/5; 347.3085.

US
OPINIONS OF THE ATTORNEY GENERAL OF CALIFORNIA. **Main/Corp** California. Attorney General's Office. Vol. 1 (1943)-. Periodical. English. an. Matthew Bender & Company Inc., 1275 Broadway, Albany NY 12204. **Tel** (800)833-9844, (518)487-3000.

US/0748-9080
OPINIONS OF THE ATTORNEY GENERAL OF KENTUCKY. **Main/Corp** Kentucky. Attorney General's Office. (1960)-. English. qt (Mar., June, Sept., Dec.). must order direct. Banks-Baldwin Law Publishing Company, PO Box 1974, University Center, Cleveland OH 44106. **Tel** (216)721-7373. cum. index.
Desc: Published in cooperation with the office of the Kentucky Attorney General, this series provides the official opinions from 1968 to date, and on a continuing basis.

US
OPINIONS OF THE ATTORNEY GENERAL OF KENTUCKY FOR THE PERIOD JANUARY 1, 1968- JOHN B. BRECKINRIDGE, ATTORNEY GENERAL, 1968-1972. **Main/Corp** Kentucky. Attorney General's Office. Periodical. English. qt. $57.50, $595.00 (full set of opinions, 1968-87). Banks-Baldwin Law Publishing Company, PO Box 1974, University Center, Cleveland OH 44106. **Tel** (216)721-7373.

US/0748-6170
OPINIONS OF THE ATTORNEY GENERAL OF OHIO. **Main/Corp** Ohio. Attorney General's Office. **VFOAT** Ohio Attorney General Opinions. 1915/16-. English. qt $65.00. Banks-Baldwin Law Publishing Company, PO Box 1974, University Center, Cleveland OH 44106. **Tel** (216)721-7373. **(Subscription address:** Banks-Baldwin Law Publishing Company, University Center, PO Box 1974, Cleveland, OH 44106-9990) cum. index. **Continues in part** Annual Report of the Attorney General to the Governor of the State of Ohio.
Desc: Published in cooperation with the office of the attorney general, the issues comprise all official opinions released during the period.

US
OPINIONS OF THE ATTORNEY GENERAL OF THE STATE OF OREGON. **Main/Corp** Oregon. Dept. of Justice. Vol. 34, No. 1 (July 1/Sept. 30, 1968)-. English. mo. Oregon Department of Justice, 16 Justice Building, Salem OR 97310. **Tel** (503)378-4400. **LC** KFO2840; .A5566. **DD** 348.795/05; 347.95085. Index available. cum. index. **Circ:** 400. **Continues** Oregon. Dept. of Justice. Biennial Report and Opinions of the Attorney General of the State of Oregon.
Desc: Formal opinions issued by the Attorney General for the state of Oregon.

US
OPINIONS OF THE ATTORNEY GENERAL OF THE STATE OF WISCONSIN. **Main/Corp** Wisconsin. Attorney General's Office. Vol. 1 (1912/1913)-. Monographic series. English. ir. Price varies per volume. Wisconsin Department of Administration / Document Sales, PO Box 7840, 202 South Thornton Avenue, Madison WI 53707. **Tel** (608)266-3358. cum. index. **Continues** Biennial Report of the Attorney General of the State of Wisconsin.

US/0738-1247
PARASCOPE. (PARASCOPE : THE QUARTERLY PUBLICATION OF THE NATIONAL COMMITTEE OF APPELLATE COURT STAFF COUNSEL.). **Added/Corp** American Bar Association. National Committee of Appellate Court Staff Counsel. Vol. 1 (1979)-. Periodical. English. qt (4 issues). $19.00. American Bar Association, 750 North Lake Shore Drive, Chicago IL 60611. **Tel** (312)988-5522, (312)988-5241, FAX (312)988-5528, telex 270593. **LC** KF8750.A15; P37. **DD** 347.73/24/05; 347.307305.

US/1047-5087
PENNSYLVANIA RULES OF COURT. FEDERAL. [Pa. rules court, Fed.]. **Added/Corp** George T. Bisel Company. West Publishing Company. (1988)-. English. George T Bisel Company, 710 South Washington Square, Philadelphia PA 19106. **LC** KF8816; .A1973. **DD** 347.748/051; 347.480751. **Continues in part** Pennsylvania Rules of Court.

PH/0115-2483
PHILIPPINE LAW GAZETTE. Vol. 1 (Jan. 1972)-. Periodical. English. qt (March, June, Sept., Dec.). $75.00. Philippine Law Gazette, 13 Mapayapa Street, UP Village, Diliman Quezon City, 3004 Philippines. **Tel** 921-6356. **ED** Vicente B. Foz. **DD** 016.34/009599. Index available (Bound in Dec. issue). **Bk Rev. Ad Acc, Adv Mgr:** Arlene Dabu-Foz. **Circ:** 3,000 (ctrl).
Desc: Publishes original articles on law and legal issues, current decision of the Philippine Supreme Court, regulations and opinions of quasi-judicial offices and agencies.
Ind/Abst Index Philip. Period.

CN/0709-5139
PROVINCIAL JUDGES JOURNAL. [Prov. judges j.]. **VFOAT** Journal des Juges Provinciaux. V. 3, No. 1- Mar. 1979-. Periodical. English. qt. Free. Canadian Association of Provincial Court Judges, PO Box 246, Saint Stephen New Brunswick E3L 2X2 Canada. **DD** 347/.71/01405. ctrl circ. **Continues** Canadian Provincial Judges Journal, 0701-1806.
Ind/Abst Can. Legal Lit.; Index Can. Leg. Period. Lit.

US
QUARTERLY REPORT OF THE ATTORNEY GENERAL OF ALABAMA. **Main/Corp** Alabama. Attorney General's Office. Vol. 1 (Oct./Dec. 1935)-. Periodical. English. qt (Jan., Apr., July, Oct.). $5.00. Skinner Printing Company, PO Box 1787, Montgomery AL 36108. **Tel** (205)263-2537.

●US/1059-9134
REFERENCE GUIDES TO NATIONAL LEGAL SYSTEMS. **VFOAT** Mexican Legal System. (1992)-. Periodical. English. Greenwood Press Inc., PO Box 5007, Westport CT 06881-5007. **Tel** (203)226-3571, FAX (203)222-1502.

US/0148-9925
REPORT - ADMINISTRATIVE OFFICE OF PENNSYLVANIA COURTS. **Main/Corp** Administrative Office of Pennsylvania Courts. English. an. Administrative Office of Pennsylvania Courts, Room 1414/Three Pennsylvania Center Plaza, Philadelphia PA 19102. **LC** KFP71; .P46. **DD** 347/.748/013.

US
REPORT / CONNECTICUT, JUDICIAL REVIEW COUNCIL. **Main/Corp** Connecticut. Judicial Review Council. 1st (1978/80)-. English. te. Free. Judicial Review Council, PO Box 308, Manchester CT 06040. **Tel** (203)647-7000. **LC** KFC4125.5.D5; A847. **DD** 347.746/014; 347.460714. **Circ:** 600 (ctrl).
Desc: Periodic report of the doings of the Connecticut Judicial Review Council.

US/0195-5241
REPORT - NATIONAL CENTER FOR STATE COURTS. **Main/Corp** National Center for State Courts. Vol. 1, (1974)-. English. Twelve times a year. $12.00 Comes with National Center for State Courts Associates Program Membership or National Center for State Courts Periodical Plan, includes Master Calendar from National Center for State Courts. National Center for State Courts, 300 Newport Avenue, PO Box 8798, Williamsburg VA 23185. **Tel** (804)253-2000, FAX (804)220-0449. **LC** KF8736.A15; N37. **DD** 347.73/33; 347.3013.

US
REPORT OF ATTORNEY GENERAL TO THE GOVERNOR AND THE LEGISLATURE. **Main/Corp** Florida. Dept. of Legal Affairs. English. Department of Legal Affairs / Florida, The Capitol Building, Tallahassee FL 32399. **LC** KFF427.5.A8; A84. **DD** 340/.09759. **Continues** Florida. Attorney-General. Report.

US
REPORT OF THE ATTORNEY GENERAL. **Main/Corp** Michigan. Attorney General's Department. (1842)-. English. be (Spring/Summer). $34.00 (latest edition). Department of the Attorney General / Michigan, Opinions Librarian, PO Box 30212, Lansing MI 48909. **Tel** (517)373-1135.

US
REPORT OF THE ATTORNEY GENERAL TO THE CONGRESS OF THE UNITED STATES ON THE ADMINISTRATION OF THE FOREIGN AGENTS REGISTRATION ACT, AS AMENDED, FOR THE CALENDAR YEAR ... . June 28, 1942 - Dec. 1944-. English. an. US Department of Justice, 10th Street & Constitution Avenue NW, Washington DC 20530. **Tel** (202)514-2000, FAX (202)633-4371. **LC** JX1896; .U5. **DD** 351.74. available on microfiche (Vols. for (1981-) distributed to depository libraries).

US
REPORT OF THE MUNICIPAL COURT (SAN FRANCISCO). **Main/Corp** San Francisco. Municipal Court. 1978-. English. an. Municipal Court, San Francisco CA 94102. **LC** KFX2353.3.M8; A1452. **DD** 347.794/6102; 347.9461072. **Continues** Annual Report of the Municipal Court.

US
REPORT OF THE UNITED STATES ATTORNEY FOR THE DISTRICT OF CONNECTICUT FOR ... TO THE ATTORNEY GENERAL. **Main/Corp** United States. Attorney (Connecticut). (19??)-. English. US Attorney for the District of Connecticut, New Haven CT 06508. **LC** KF8700; .A8157. **DD** 353.9746008/8.

US
REPORT / SUPREME COURT, STATE OF ILLINOIS. **Main/Corp** Illinois. Supreme Court. English. an. 111 East Jefferson Street, Ottawa IL 61350. **LC** KFI1708; .A877. **DD** 347.773; 347.7307.

BL
REVISTA DA PROCURADORIA-GERAL DO ESTADO (RIO GRANDE DO SUL (BRAZIL)). (REVISTA DA PROCURADORIA-GERAL DO ESTADO.). **VFOAT** R.P.G.E. Began in 1979 with No. 24. Periodical. Portuguese. Three times a year. Instituto de Informatica Juridica da Procuradoria, Geral do Estado, Avenida Borges de Medeiros No 417, 110 Andar Porto Algere Brazil. **LC** K22; .I43. **DD** 342.81/06/05; 348.102605. ***Continues*** *Revista (Rio Grando do Sul (Brazil). Consultoria-Geral).*

US/0193-967X
RULES GOVERNING THE COURTS OF THE STATE OF NEW JERSEY, 1969 REVISION, AS AMENDED. ***Title Change.*** **Main/Corp** New Jersey. **Added/Corp** United States. District Court (New Jersey) New Jersey. Supreme Court. N.J. Court Rules, 1969. United States. Court of Appeals (3rd Circuit). (19??)-(1992). English. West Publishing Company, 610 Opperman Drive, PO Box 64526, Eagan MN 55123-1308. **Tel** (612)687-5618, (800)328-9352, FAX (612)687-5388, (800)562-2329. **(Subscription telephone:** FAX (612)688-3570) **LC** KFN2329; .A196. **DD** 347/.749/05. ***Continued by*** *New Jersey Rules of Court, 1070-6364.*
Desc: Rules governing the courts of the State of New Jersey, 1969 revision, as amended, including New Jersey evidence rules and rules for United States District Court and rules for United States Court of Appeals.

US
RULES OF THE SUPREME COURT OF LOUISIANA, ADOPTED AUGUST 31, 1973, EFFECTIVE JANUARY 1, 1974 AS AMENDED ... . **Main/Corp** Louisiana. Supreme Court. Periodical. English.

US/0146-163X
SECOND CIRCUIT REDBOOK. **Main/Corp** Federal Bar Council. 1975/76-. English. ir. Free to members of Federal Bar Council as part of dues, $35.00 nonmembers. Little Brown & Company, 34 Beacon Street, Boston MA 02108. **Tel** (617)227-0730, (800)759-0190. **LC** KF8840; .F38. **DD** 347/.73/22.

US/0145-2436
SELECTED STATISTICS ON THE OFFICE OF ATTORNEY GENERAL. **See** Law-Abstracting, Bibliographies and Statistics.

US
SHEPARD'S FEDERAL RULES CITATIONS : A COMPILATION OF CITATIONS TO THE FEDERAL RULES OF CIVIL PROCEDURE ... . **Added/Corp** Shepard's / McGraw-Hill. **VFOAT** Federal Rules Citations. 1st Ed. (1987)-. English. $480.00 (3 bound volumes), $206.00 (cumulative supplements). Shepards McGraw-Hill Inc, 555 Middle Creek Parkway, PO Box 35300, Colorado Springs CO 80935-3530. **Tel** (719)488-3000, FAX (800)525-0053.

US/0730-6229
SHEPARD'S PROFESSIONAL AND JUDICIAL CONDUCT CITATIONS. **Added/Corp** Shepard's/McGraw-Hill. **VFOAT** Professional and Judicial Conduct Citations. Vol. 1, No. 1 (Nov. 1980)-. English. Four times a year. $105.00 (bound volume), $242.00 (cumulative supplements). Shepards McGraw-Hill Inc, 555 Middle Creek Parkway, PO Box 35300, Colorado Springs CO 80935-3530. **Tel** (719)488-3000, FAX (800)525-0053. **LC** KF308.A535; S46. **DD** 174/.3/0973.
Desc: Attention is given to how lawyers and judges police their own professions.

US/0146-3241
SOUTH DAKOTA UNIFIED COURTS. English. State Capitol / South Dakota, 500 East Capitol, Pierre SD 57501. **LC** KFS3510.A15; S69. **DD** 347/.783/01.

US
SOUTH DAKOTA UNIFIED JUDICIAL SYSTEM. English. South Dakota Supreme Court, Office of Court Administration, 500 East Capitol, Pierre SD 57501. **LC** KFS3510.A15; S69. **DD** 347/.783/0105. ***Continues*** *South Dakota Unified Courts, 0146-3241.*

US/0275-2913
SPECIAL COURT NEWS. (SPECIAL COURT NEWS / BY THE ABA'S NATIONAL CONFERENCE OF SPECIAL COURT JUDGES.). **Added/Corp** National Conference of Special Court Judges (U.S.). (April 1980)-. Periodical. English. qt (4 issues). $11.00. American Bar Association, 750 North Lake Shore Drive, Chicago IL 60611. **Tel** (312)988-5522, (312)988-5241, FAX (312)988-5528, telex 270593. **LC** KF8759.A15; S66. **DD** 347.73/28/05; 347.307405.

US/0193-7081
STATE OF THE COLORADO JUDICIARY, THE. **Main/Corp** Colorado. Supreme Court. 1969-. English. an. Supreme Court of the State of Colorado, 323 State Capital, Denver CO 80203. **LC** KFC2310; .A874. **DD** 347.78803.

US
STATE OF THE JUDICIARY REPORT. **Main/Corp** Virginia. Supreme Court. English. an. Supreme Court of Virginia, Office of the Executive Secretary, 100 North 9th Street/3rd Floor, Richmond VA 23219. **Tel** (804)786-6455. **LC** KFV2471; .V57. **DD** 347.755/01/021; 347.55071021. ***Continues*** *Virginia. Supreme Court. Office of the Executive Secretary. State of the Judiciary Report.*

US/0276-5616
SUMMARY OF PROCEEDINGS. MANAGEMENT INSTITUTE. (SUMMARY OF PROCEEDINGS ... MANAGEMENT INSTITUTE / NATIONAL ASSOCIATION OF ATTORNEYS GENERAL, COMMITTEE ON THE OFFICE OF ATTORNEY GENERAL.). **Main/Conf** Management Institute. Began with 1971. Proceedings. English. ir. Committee on the Office of Attorney General, 3901 Barrett Drive, Raleigh NC 27609. **ED** Patton G Wheeler. **LC** KF5107.Z9; M35. **DD** 353.9/388.

UK/0039-5978
SUPREME COURT PRACTICE, THE. **Main/Corp** Great Britain. Supreme Court of Judicature. **Added/Corp** Great Britain. Supreme Court of Judicature. 1st Ed. (1967)-. English. Ten times a year. £95.00 Europe; £100.00 other. Sweet & Maxwell Ltd., South Quay Plaza, 183 Marsh Wall, London E14 9FT England. **Tel** 011 44 264 342899, FAX 011 44 264 342723, telex 929089 ITPINF G. **DD** 347.99/42. ***Continues*** *Annual Practice.*

US/0276-2463
SURVEY OF JUDICIAL SALARIES. [Surv. judic. salaries]. **Main/Corp** National Center for State Courts. **Added/Corp** National Center for State Courts. Vol. 4, No. 1 (Jan. 1978)-. English. Twice a year. $12.00 (one year); $50.00 Comes with National Center for State Courts Periodical Plan or National Centers for State Courts Associates Program Membership. National Center for State Courts, 300 Newport Avenue, PO Box 8798, Williamsburg VA 23185. **Tel** (804)253-2000, FAX (804)220-0449. **LC** KF8777.Z95; N38. **DD** 331.2/8134773/14; 331.2/8134730714. ***Continues*** *Survey of Judicial Salaries in State Court Systems, 0196-7304.*
Desc: Update of salary information for state court judges and state court administrators.

US/0040-6120
THIRD BRANCH, THE. **Added/Corp** Federal Judicial Center. United States. Administrative Office of the United States Courts. United States. Administrative Office of the United States Courts. Office of Legislative and Public Affairs. Vol. 1, No. 1 (Dec. 1968)-. Periodical. English. Twelve times a year. Free on request. Administrative Office of the United States Courts, 811 Vermont Avenue NW, Room 655, Washington DC 20544. **LC** KF8700.A16; T45. **DD** 347.99/73.

FI/0357-9190
TOIMINTAKERTOMUS / KORKEIN HALLINTO-OIKEUS. **Main/Corp** Finland. Korkein Hallinto-Oikeus. **VFOAT** Verksamhetsberattelse. Finnish (Swedish). an. Korkein Hallinto-Oikeus, Unioninkatu 16, 00130 Helsinki Finland. **Tel** 90-1853206. **LC** KJT2770.A13; F56. **Circ:** 900 (ctrl).

US
TRIAL JUDGES NEWS / NATIONAL CONFERENCE OF STATE TRIAL JUDGES. **Added/Corp** National Conference of State Trial Judges (U.S.). Vol. 1, No. 1 (Oct. 1981)-. English. qt (4 issues). $13.00. American Bar Association, 750 North Lake Shore Drive, Chicago IL 60611. **Tel** (312)988-5522, (312)988-5241, FAX (312)988-5528, telex 270593. **LC** KF8785.A15; T75. **DD** 347.73/14/05; 347.3071405. ***Continued in part by*** *Trial Judges Notes.*

BL
TRIBUNA DA JUSTICA. Periodical. Portuguese. wk. Cr$18,000. Hemeron Editora SA, Avenida Aclimacao No 226, CEP 01531, Sao Paulo Brazil. **LC** KHD2501.A15; T74.

US/0162-8674
UNITED STATES COURT DIRECTORY (UNITED STATES. ADMINISTRATIVE OFFICE OF THE UNITED STATES COURTS). (UNITED STATES COURT DIRECTORY.). **Added/Corp** United States. Administrative Office of the United States Courts. (19??)-. English. sa. Superintendent of Documents, US Government Printing Office, Washington DC 20402. **Tel** (202)275-3328, FAX (202)786-2377. **LC** KF8700.A19; U55. **DD** 347/.73/1025.

US/0732-7900
UNITED STATES COURTS (PICTORIAL SUMMARY), THE. (THE UNITED STATES COURTS.). **Added/Corp** United States. Administrative Office of the United States Courts. **VFOAT** Report of the Director of the Administrative Office of the United States Courts Workload for the Year Ended June 30. (19??)-. English. an. Administrative Office of the United States Courts, 811 Vermont Avenue NW, Room 655, Washington DC 20544. **LC** KF180; .U56. **DD** 347.73/13; 347.30713.

US
US SUPREME COURT PETITIONS & BRIEFS. TAX LAW SERIES. **See** Law.

US
VIRGINIA MAGISTRATE, THE. **Main/Corp** Virginia. Attorney General's Office. (19??)-. English. ir. Office of Attorney General / Criminal Division, 900 Fidelity Building, 830 E. Main Street, Richmond VA 23219. **LC** KFV2975.A59; A8. **DD** 345/.755/05.

US/0742-1095
WANT'S FEDERAL-STATE COURT DIRECTORY. [Want's Fed.-state court dir.]. **Added/Corp** Want Publishing Company. **VFOAT** Want's Federal State Court Directory; Federal-State Court Directory; Federal State Court Directory. (1984)-. Directory. English. an. $39.50 US (Except Washington DC), Canada and Mexico; $41.60 Washington DC (incls 6% sales tax); $52.50 others. Want Publishing Company, 1511 K Street Northwest, Suite 635, Washington DC 20005. **Tel** (202)783-1887, FAX (202)393-5106. **LC** KF8700.A19; F42. **DD** 347.73/025; 347.307025. **[CCC].** ***Continues*** *Federal Court Directory (Want Publishing Company), 0277-0199.*
Desc: Federal-State Court Directory is the nation's most widely-used court reference source. It is an essential reference for librarians, paralegals, business executives, and students. It has comprehensive directory listings, and a basic explanation of the federal and state court systems... plus a simplified organization chart for each state judiciary. A glossary of terms is also included.

AU
WIENER RICHTER, DER. **Added/Corp** Vereinigung der Osterreichischer Richter. No. 1 (Oct. 1981)-. Periodical. German. qt. Vereinigung der Osterreichischer Richter, Sektion Vienna Justizpalast, 1016 Vienna Austria. **DD** 349.436/13/05; 344.3613005.

US
WYOMING COURTS; NEWSLETTER OF THE WYOMING COURT SYSTEM. **Main/Corp** Wyoming. Judicial Planning Committee. Newsletter. English. bm. Judicial Planning Committee of Wyoming, Supreme Court Building, Cheyenne WY 82002. **LC** KFW4710; .A848. **DD** 347.787/01/05.

LABOR LAW

US/0362-8493
ACROSS THE TABLE. **VFOAT** Labor Relations in Local Government. (19??)-. Periodical. English. mo. $60.00, $15.00 (library). New York Conference of Mayors & Municipal Officials, 119 Washington Avenue, Albany NY 12210. **Tel** (518)463-1185, FAX (518) 463-1190. **ED** John Galligan. **LC** KFN5562.P8; A132. **DD** 344/.747/01890413539. cum. index. **Circ:** 1,600.
Desc: Labor relations publication for local government.

US/0742-616X
ADMINISTRATION LAW JUDGE DECISIONS REPORT. (ADMINISTRATIVE LAW JUDGE DECISIONS REPORT / FEDERAL LABOR RELATIONS AUTHORITY.). **Main/Corp** United States. Federal Labor Relations Authority. No. 1 (Nov. 27, 1981)-. English. bm. Iowa Department of Corrections, 523 East 12th Street, Capitol Annex, Des Moines IA 50319. **Tel** (515)281-4811, FAX (515)281-7345. **LC** KF5365; .A554 SUPPL. **DD** 344.73/018/0264; 347.304180264.

US/1049-9369
ALABAMA EMPLOYMENT LAW LETTER. [Ala. employ. law lett.]. (June 1990)-. Periodical. English. mo. $87.00. M. Lee Smith Publishers and Printers, 162 4th Avenue North, PO Box 198867, Nashville TN 37219. **Tel** (615)242-7395, (800)274-6774, FAX (615)256-6601. **ED** Richard Lehr, David Middlebrooks, and David Proctor, (address) Sirote and Permutt, 2222 Arlington Avenue South, PO Box 55904, Birmingham, Al 35255, (phone) 205-933-7111. **DD** 344.
Desc: Newsletter reporting the latest state specific employment law developments that affect companies in that state.

US/0272-9393
ALI-ABA COURSE OF STUDY. LABOR RELATIONS AND EMPLOYMENT LAW FOR THE CORPORATE COUNSEL AND THE GENERAL PRACTITIONER: MATERIALS. ***Title Change.*** **Main/Conf** I-ABA Course of Study: Labor Relations and Employment Law for the Corporate Counsel and the General Practitioner. **Added/Corp** American Law Institute-American Bar Association Committee on Continuing Professional Education. **VAT** American Law Institute-American Bar Association Course of Study. Labor Relations and Employment Law for the Corporate Counsel and the General Practitioner. Materials. (19??)-(19??). English. an. American Law Institute, 4025 Chestnut Street, Philadelphia PA 19104-3099. **Tel** (215)243-1661, (800)253-6397, FAX (215)243-1664. **LC** KF3319.3; .A16. **DD** 344.73/01; 347.3041. ***Continued by*** *Employment and Labor Relations for the Corporate Counsel and the General Practitioner.*

GW/0340-1790
AMTSBLATT DES BAYERISCHEN STAATSMINISTERIUMS FUER ARBEIT UND SOZIALORDNUNG. **Main/Corp** Bavaria (Germany). Staatsministerium fur Arbeit und Sozialordnung. (1971)-. German. sm. DM89.00 Germany; $47.50 US. Staatsministerium fur Arbeit und Sozialordnung, Winzererstrasse 9, W-8000 Munchen 40 Germany. **DD** 344/.433. ***Continues*** *Amtsblatt des Bayerischen Staatsministeriums fur Arbeit und Soziale Fursorge, 0005-7193.*

US/0191-118X
ANALYSIS OF WORKMEN'S COMPENSATION LAWS. **Main/Corp** Chamber of Commerce of the United States of America. **Added/Corp** Chamber of Commerce of the United States of America. (1976)-. English. an (Published in April). $15.00 members; $25.00 nonmembers. US Chamber of Commerce, 1615 H Street NW, Washington DC 20062. **Tel** (800)638-6582, (800)352-1450, FAX (202)887-3430. **LC** KF3612.5; .A15. **DD** 344.73/021/05; 347.3042105. ctrl circ. ***Continues*** *Analysis of Workmen's Compensation Laws, 0577-5183.*
Ind/Abst Stat. Ref. Index.

US/0743-4146
ANNUAL INSTITUTE OF EMPLOYMENT LAW. [Annu. Inst. Employ. Law]. **Main/Conf** Institute on Employment Law. **Added/Corp** Practising Law Institute. (1983)-. Periodical. English. an. $80.00 US; $94.00 other. Practising Law Institute, 810 Seventh Avenue, New York NY 10019-5818. **Tel** (212)765-5700, FAX (212)581-4670 general correspondence, (212)265-4742 orders and billing inquiries. **LC** KF3464.Z9; I54. **DD** 344.73/01133; 347.3041133. Index available. **Bk Rev.** available on videocassette. ***Continues*** *Annual Institute on Equal Employment Opportunity Compliance, 0198-9022.*
Desc: New developments in employment law.

US
ANNUAL LABOR & EMPLOYMENT LAW INSTITUTE. English. an. $57.50. Fred B. Rothman & Company, 10368 West Centennial Road, Littleton CO 80127. **Tel** (800)457-1986, (303)979-5657, FAX (303)978-1457, telex 87669.
Ind/Abst Leg. Resour. Index; LegalTrac (1980-).

IE
ANNUAL REPORT FOR THE YEAR ENDED ... / EMPLOYMENT APPEALS TRIBUNAL. **Main/Corp** Ireland. Employment Appeals Tribunal. 12th (31st Dec. 1979)-. English. an. 0.45p. Government Publications, 4 5 Harcourt Road, Dublin 2 Ireland. **Tel** 011 353 1 6613111 Ext.4005. **LC** KDK804; A874. **DD** 354.415001/8. **Bk Rev.** **Ad Acc.** **Circ:** 1,000 (ctrl). ***Continues*** *Ireland. Redundancy Appeals Tribunal. Annual Report.*

US/0147-6475
ANNUAL REPORT - MASSACHUSETTS LABOR RELATIONS COMMISSION. **Main/Corp** Massachusetts. Labor Relations Commission. (19??)-. English. an. 1604 Leverett Saltonstall Building, 100 Cambridge Street, Boston MA 02202. **LC** KFM2732; .A835. **DD** 344/.744/01. ***Continues*** *Massachusetts Labor Relations Commission. Report of the Activities of the Massachusetts Labor Relations Commission for the Fiscal Year ... .*

CN/0711-849X
ANNUAL REPORT / ONTARIO LABOUR RELATIONS BOARD. [Annu. rep. - Ont. Labour Relat. Board]. **Main/Corp** Ontario Labour Relations Board. (1981)-. English. an. 250.00Can$ Comes with Ontario Labour Relations Board Report. Ontario Labour Relations Board, 400 University Avenue, Toronto Ontario M7A 1VA Canada. **Tel** (416)326-7500. **LC** KEO641.A72; O57. **DD** 354.7130083.

US
ANNUAL REPORT ... OPINIONS / VERMONT LABOR RELATIONS BOARD. **Main/Corp** Vermont Labor Relations Board. **VFOAT** Vermont Labor Relations Board Opinions. English. an. **LC** KFV332.8.P77; A4983. **DD** 344.743/01890413539; 347.43041890413539. ***Continues*** *Vermont. State Labor Relations Board. Opinions.*

US
ANNUAL REPORT / STANDING COMMITTEE ON LABOR, NEW YORK STATE ASSEMBLY. **Main/Corp** New York (State). Legislature. Assembly. Standing Committee on Labor. **VFOAT** Annual Report of the Assembly Standing Committee on Labor. (1979)-. English. an. Assembly - New York Labor, State of New York Standing Committee on Labor, Albany NY 12248. **LC** KFN5556; .A245. **DD** 353.97470083. ***Continues*** *New York (State). Legislature. Assembly. Standing Committee on Labor. Annual Report of the Standing Committee on Labor.*
Desc: Information on labor laws, legislation and policy.

ZA
ANNUAL REPORTS FOR THE YEARS ... / REPUBLIC OF ZAMBIA, MINISTRY OF LABOUR AND SOCIAL SERVICES, INDUSTRIAL RELATIONS COURT. **Main/Corp** Zambia. Industrial Relations Court. English. an. K90.00. Industrial Relations Court, Government Printer, POB 30136, Lusaka Zambia. **Tel** 01-215401, telex 2A 40290. **DD** 344.6894/01/0269; 346.8940410269. **Bk Rev.** **Ad Acc.** **Circ:** 710.
Desc: Covers court activities; the approval of recognition agreements concluded between employee's organizations and employers; the hearing of applications complaints; and appeals and collective disputes.

UY
ANUARIO DE JURISPRUDENCIA LABORAL. (1976)-. Spanish. Derecho Laboral, Cerrito 420 Esc 404, Montevideo Uruguay. **DD** 344/.895/01.

GW/0003-7648
ARBEIT UND RECHT. [Arb. Recht]. **Added/Corp** Deutscher Gewerkschaftsbund. (1953)-. Periodical. German. mo. DM148.00 Germany; DM182.20 other. Bund Verlag GmbH, Postfach 900840, D 51118 Cologne Germany. **Tel** 011 49 2203 934758. **[CCC].**
Ind/Abst Foreign Lang. Index.

AU/0172-4576
ARBEITS- UND SOZIALRECHTLICHE SCHRIFTENREIHE. ***Ceased.*** (1965)-Series complete. Monographic series. German. ir. Springer-Verlag Wien, Sachsenplatz 4 6, PO Box 89, A-1201 Vienna Austria. **Tel** 011 43 1 3302415. **(Subscription address:** Springer Verlag New York Inc. / for North America, 44 Hartz Way, Secaucus NJ 07096.**)**

GW/0066-586X
ARBEITSRECHT DER GEGENWART, DAS. Vol. 1 (1963)-. German. an. DM190.00. Erich Schmidt Verlag GmbH, Postfach 304240, D 10724 Berlin Germany. **Tel** 011 49 30 25008525. **ED** G. Muller. **Bk Rev.** **Ad Acc.** ***Supersedes*** *Jahrbuch des Arbeitsrechts und der Damit ZusammenhAngenden Teile der Sozialpolitik.*
Desc: Yearbook covering labor law.

DK
ARBEJDSRETLIGE KENDELSER. Danish. an. Juristforbundets Forlag, Gothersgade 133, 1123 Kobenhavn K Denmark.

US/1075-9611
ARIZONA EMPLOYMENT LAW LETTER. English. mo. $95.00. M. Lee Smith Publishers and Printers, 162 4th Avenue North, PO Box 198867, Nashville TN 37219. **Tel** (615)242-7395, (800)274-6774, FAX (615)256-6601.

SW
ARSREDOVISNING / NOBELSTIFTELSEN. **Main/Corp** Nobelstiftelsen. **VFOAT** Annual Report. (19??)-. English (Swedish). Nine times a year. Stiftelsen Arbetsrattslig Tidskrift, Nybrogatan 28, Box 5191, S-10244 Stockholm Sweden. **Tel** 46 8 667 9685, FAX 46 8 660 4865. **LC** AS911; .N713. Index available. cum. index. **Bk Rev.** **Ad Acc.** **Circ:** 9,500 (ctrl). available on audiocassette.
Desc: Covers labor law and industrial relations.

AT/1030-7222
AUSTRALIAN JOURNAL OF LABOUR LAW. Vol. 1, No. 1 (May 1988)-. Periodical. English. Three times a year. 145.00Aus$. Butterworths Pty Ltd, 271-273 Lane Cove Road, PO Box 345, North Ryde NSW 2113 Australia. **Tel** 011 61 2 3354444, FAX 011 61 2 3354655. **ED** Richard Mitchell. Index available. **Bk Rev.**
Desc: Covers labor law and related issues, such as enterprise agreements, collective bargaining and equal opportunity.
Ind/Abst Index Leg. Period.; Leg. Resour. Index; LegalTrac (1988-).

BG
BANGLADESH LABOUR CASES. V. 1 (Dec. 1974)-. English. mo. $10.04. Srama Upadesta Kendra, 9 Motijheel Circular Road/3rd Floor, Dacca Bangladesh. **DD** 344/.5492/010264.

US/0897-7992
BENEFITS LAW JOURNAL. [Benefits law j.]. Vol. 1, No. 1 (Spring 1988)-. Periodical. English. qt. $184.00 US & Canada; $234.00 other. John Wiley & Sons, Inc., 605 Third Avenue, New York NY 10158-0012. **Tel** (212)850-6000, (212)850-6645, FAX (212)850-6088, telex 12-7063. **(Subscription address:** John Wiley & Sons Inc / New Jersey, PO Box 2575, Secaucus NJ 07096-2575.**)** **ED** Jane G Bensahel. **LC** K2; .E4. **DD** 344.73/01255; 347.3041255. **[CCC].** Index available. **Ad Acc.** available on microfilm from University Microfilms International (UMI).
Desc: Contains information on new types of benefits, new methods of benefit delivery and new legal requirements. Covers welfare benefits, changes in federal tax and labor laws, structuring and restructuring plans, judicial developments, and pending legislative proposals.
Ind/Abst Account. Tax Datab. (1988-) [Full Txt.]; Hum. Resour. Abstr.; Index Leg. Period. (1992-); Leg. Resour. Index; LegalTrac (1988-); PAIS Int. Print (1991-); Person. Manage. Abstr.; Work Relat. Abstr.

●US/1067-7666
BERKELEY JOURNAL OF EMPLOYMENT AND LABOR LAW. [Berkeley j. employ. labor law]. **Added/Corp** University of California, Berkeley. School of Law. (1993)-. Periodical. English. sa (Apr. and Oct.). $32.00 (individuals), $38.00 (institutions). University of California Press, 2120 Berkeley Way, Berkeley CA 94720. **Tel** (510)642-4191, (510)642-3907, FAX (510)642-9917. **ED** Rachel Nosowsky (Editor-in-Chief). **LC** K9; .N393. **DD** 344/.73/018905. **Bk Rev.** **Ad Acc.** ***Continues*** *Industrial Relations Law Journal, 0145-188X.*
Desc: Presents current developments in the labor and employment law field to scholars, practitioners and students.

PO
BOLETIM DO TRABALHO E EMPREGO. 2A I.E. SEGUNDA SERIE. **Main/Corp** Portugal. Ministerio do Trabalho. Servico de Informacao Cientifica e Tecnica. Bulletin. English. 600.00. Ministerio do Trabalho, Praca de Londres 2 10 Sala 1, Lisbon Portugal. **DD** 344/.469/01.

SP/0214-2406
BOLETIN DEL MINISTERIO DE TRABAJO Y SEGURIDAD SOCIAL. [Bol. - Minist. Trab. Segur. Soc.]. **Main/Corp** Spain. Ministerio de Trabajo y Seguridad Social. Began in (1988). Spanish. mo. Centro de Publicaciones Min Trabajo, Augustin de Bethencourt 11, 28071 Madrid Spain. **Tel** 011 34 1 5543400, 5330106. **LC** PAR. ***Continues*** *Boletinoficial del Ministerio de Trabajo, Sanidad y Seguridad Social. Spain. Ministerio de Trabajo, Sanidad, y Seguridad Social;* ***Absorbed*** *Jurisprudencia Laboral y de Seguridad Social, 0210-8836.*

IT/0394-6592
BOLLETTINO DEL LAVORO E DEI TRIBUTI. (1987)-. Periodical. Italian. wk (48 issues per year). L524000 Itlay; L596000 other. EDIS, Via S Franco 60, 29100 Piacenza Italy. **Tel** 011 39 523 25684, FAX 011 39 523 336782. **UDC** 331. **Bk Rev.** (Qty: 2-3). **Pr Rev.** ***Continues*** *Bollettino del Lavoro, 0391-822X.*
Desc: Information on legislation, jurisprudence and labor contracts.

CN/0715-5808
BRITISH COLUMBIA LABOUR RELATIONS BOARD DECISIONS. [B.C. Labour Relat. Board decis.]. **Added/Corp** Labour Relations Board of British Columbia. Western Legal Publications Ltd. (1979)-. Periodical. English. Twelve times a year. 199.50Can$. Western Legal Publications Ltd., 301 One Alexander Street, Vancouver BC V6A 1B2 Canada. **Tel** (800)663-0422, (604)687-5671. **DD** 331.89/09711.
Desc: Digests of all written and letter decision indexed by subject, labour code section, by parties, Labour Relations Board decisions, number and keyword index.

FR/0753-2601
BULLETIN DE DROIT COMPARE DU TRAVAIL ET DE LA SECURITE SOCIALE. [Bull. droit comp. trav. secur. soc.]. **Added/Corp** Universite de Bordeaux I. Faculte de Droit, des Sciences Sociales et Politiques. COMPTRASEC (Center). (1981)-. Periodical. French. an. 75.89F France; 90.00F Europe; 150.00F others. Comptrasec Faculte de Droit, Bourdeaux 1 Avenue Leon Duguit, 33604 Pessac Cedex France. **Tel** 011 33 16 56 80 61 50.

US/0363-8502
BULLETIN INDEX-DIGEST SYSTEM. SERVICE THREE. EMPLOYMENT TAXES. (BULLETIN INDEX-DIGEST SYSTEM. SERVICE 3, EMPLOYMENT TAXES / DEPARTMENT OF THE TREASURY, INTERNAL REVENUE SERVICE.).

Added/Corp United States. Internal Revenue Service. **VFOAT** Employment Taxes; Service 3 Employment Taxes. (19??)-. Bulletin. English. an (cumulative supplements). $19.00. Claitors Law Books, 3165 South Acadian, Baton Rouge LA 70808. **Tel** (504)344-0476, (800)274-1403. **(Subscription address:** Claitors Law Books, PO Box 3333, Baton Rouge, LA 70821**) LC** KF6362.3; .I53. **DD** 343/.73/052.
Desc: Contains the Finding List and Digest for all permanent tax matters published in the Internal Revenue Bulletin-Employment Taxes.

NE/0770-3724
BULLETIN OF COMPARATIVE LABOUR RELATIONS. [Bull. comp. labour relat.]. (1975)-. Monographic series. Dutch (English, French and German). ir. Price varies per volume. Kluwer Law and Taxation Publishers, Staverenstraat 32015, PO Box 23, 7400 GA Deventer Netherlands. **Tel** 011 31 5700 47261. **(Subscription address:** Kluwer Law & Taxation, 675 Massachusetts Avenue, Cambridge MA 02139.**) LC** K2; .U446. **DD** 344/.01/05; 342.4105. ***Continues** Bulletin (Katholieke Universiteit te Leuven (1970-). Instituut voor Arbeidsrecht).*
Ind/Abst Int. Labour Doc.; LABORDOC; PAIS Int. Print.

US/1049-9334
CALIFORNIA EMPLOYMENT LAW LETTER. [Calif. employ. law lett.]. Vol. 1, No. 1 (June 1990)-. Periodical. English. mo. $95.00. M. Lee Smith Publishers and Printers, 162 4th Avenue North, PO Box 198867, Nashville TN 37219. **Tel** (615)242-7395, (800)274-6774, FAX (615)256-6601. **ED** Stephen Pepe, Catherine Hagen, and Kathleen Hayward, (address) O'Melveny and Myers, 537 Newport Center Drive, Suite 610, Newport Beach, CA 92660, (phone)714-760-9600. **DD** 344.
Desc: Newsletter reporting the latest state specific employment law developments that affect companies in that state.

US
CALIFORNIA-FEDERAL PERSONNEL LAW UPDATE. **VFOAT** Federal Personnel Law Update; Personnel Law Update. **VAT** California Federal Personnel Law Update. Vol. 1, No. 1 (Dec. 1985)-. Periodical. English. Twelve times a year. $119.00 one year; $199.00 two years. Borgman Associates, 321 Lennon Lane, Walnut Creek CA 94598. **Tel** (510)944-5544, FAX (510)988-1888. **ED** Denise Daigle. **LC** KFC570.A15; C35. **DD** 344.794/01/05; 347.9404105. **Circ:** 1,800.
Desc: Carries practical information on the latest state-specific developments in personnel policies. Benefits, legal compliance, wage and hour law, worker's compensation and H. R. management are also included.

US/0363-129X
CALIFORNIA WORKERS' COMPENSATION REPORTER. Vol. 3 No. 7 (Aug. 1975)-. Periodical. English. mo. $280.00. California Workers' Compensation Reporter, PO Box 975, Berkeley CA 94701. **Tel** (510)444-2454. **ED** Melvin S. Witt. **LC** KFC592.A15; C34. **DD** 344/.794/021005. Index available. cum. index (($175.00 plus sales tax for cumulative index)). **Circ:** 1,350 (ctrl). ***Continues** California Workmen's Compensation Reporter, 0091-5211.*
Desc: Key developments in workers' compensation in California including reports and comments on appellate cases and WCAB decisions, legislative changes, and news of interest.

CN/0824-2607
CANADIAN CASES ON EMPLOYMENT LAW. [Can. cases employ. law]. Vol. 1, Pt. 1 (Oct./Nov. 1983)-. Periodical. English. mo. 102.00Can$ Canada; 88.75Can$ other. Carswell / Canada, 2075 Kennedy Road, Scarborough Ontario M1T 3V4 Canada. **Tel** (416)609-3800, (800)387-5164. **ED** David Harris. **DD** 344.71/01/02642. Index available. cum. index. **Ad Acc.**
Desc: Features all important decisions in employment law, outside the collective bargaining process from all Canadian jurisdictions selected by experts in the field.
Ind/Abst Can. Legal Lit.; Index Can. Leg. Period. Lit.

●US/1073-5720
CANADIAN EMPLOYMENT LAW FOR U.S. COMPANIES. (CANADIAN EMPLOYMENT LAW FOR U.S. COMPANIES / MCCARTHY, TETRAULT, CANADIAN BARRISTERS & SOLICITORS.). [Can. employ. law U.S. co.]. **Added/Corp** McCarthy, Tetrault (Firm). **VFOAT** Canadian Employment Law for US Companies; Canadian Employment Law. **VAT** Canadian Employment Law for United States Companies. (1994)-. Periodical. English. mo. $177.00. M. Lee Smith Publishers and Printers, 162 4th Avenue North, PO Box 198867, Nashville TN 37219. **Tel** (615)242-7395, (800)274-6774, FAX (615)256-6601. **DD** 344.

CN/0843-090X
CANADIAN EMPLOYMENT LAW TODAY. [Can. employ. law today]. Issue No. 1 (Nov. 23, 1987)-. Periodical. English. bw. 97.00Can$. MPL Communications, 133 Richard Street West, Suite 700, Toronto Ontario M5H 3M8 Canada. **Tel** (416)869-1177, FAX (416)869-0456. **DD** 344.71/01/05. ***Absorbed** Vector Union Report.*

Desc: Newsletter edited by a lawyer. Focuses on the new and changing field of Canadian employment law and how it affects management and employee relations.

CN/0831-7348
CANADIAN LABOUR ARBITRATION SUMMARiES. [Can. labour arbitr. summ.]. **Added/Corp** Canada Law Book Inc. Issue 1 (July 2, 1986)-. Periodical. English. wk. 397.00Can$. Canada Law Book Inc., 240 Edward Street, Aurora Ontario L4G 3S9 Canada. **Tel** (800)263-3269, (905)841-6472, FAX (905)841-5085. **ED** E.B. Willis. **DD** 344.71/0189143/02648.
Desc: Provides comprehensive coverage of labour arbitration in Canada covering approximately 3,500 awards each year.

CN/0317-0535
CANADIAN LABOUR RELATIONS BOARDS REPORTS. Vol. 1-3 Part 4 (1974)-. Periodical. English (French). ir. Butterworth Heinemann / Woburn, MA, 225 Wildwood Avenue, Unit B, Woburn MA 01801. **Tel** (800)366-2665, FAX (617)928-2620, telex 880052. **LC** KE3146.4; .C36. **DD** 344/.71/018/02646.

US/0740-1043
CANADIAN LEGAL & LEGISLATIVE BENEFITS REPORTER. (CANADIAN LEGAL & LEGISLATIVE BENEFITS REPORTER / INTERNATIONAL FOUNDATION OF EMPLOYEE BENEFIT PLANS.). [Can. leg. legis. benefits report.]. **Added/Corp** International Foundation of Employee Benefits Plans. **VFOAT** Canadian Legal and Legislative Benefits Reporter; L & L; L and L. Vol. 1, No. 1 (Oct. 1983)-. Periodical. English. International Foundation of Employee Benefit Plans, PO Box 69, 18700 West Bluemound Road, Brookfield WI 53008-0069. **Tel** (414)786-6700. **ED** Raymond Koskie and Mark Zigler. **LC** KE3298.A13; C36. **DD** 344.71/01255/05; 347.104125505. **Circ:** 3,000.
Desc: Review of recent Canadian law and cases in the area of employee benefits.

US
CASEHANDLING MANUAL - NATIONAL LABOR RELATIONS BOARD. **Main/Corp** United States. National Labor Relations Board. (1975)-. Government Publication. English. ir. $14.00. Superintendent of Documents, US Government Printing Office, Washington DC 20402. **Tel** (202)275-3328, FAX (202)786-2377. ***Continues** Field Manual - National Labor Relations Board.*
Desc: Relates to unfair labor practice proceedings, representation proceedings, and compliance proceedings.

US
CIS LAW REPRINTS. LABOR LAW SERIES : THE SUPREME COURT OF THE UNITED STATES PETITIONS AND BRIEFS. **VFOAT** Labor Law Series; Supreme Court of the United States Petitions and Briefs. Vol. 18, No. 1 (1984/85)-. English. ir. Congressional Information Service Inc, 4520 East-West Highway, Suite 800, Bethesda MD 20814-3389. **Tel** (800)638-8380, (301)654-1550, FAX (301)654-4033, telex 292386 CIS UR. ***Continues** BNA's Law Reprints. Labor Law Series.*

SP
CIVITAS (MADRID, SPAIN). (CIVITAS.). (19??)-. Periodical. Spanish. bm (6 issues). 11830ptas. Editorial Civitas SA, Igancio Ellacuria 3, 28017 Madrid Spain. **Tel** 011 34 1 7253156.
Ind/Abst LABORDOC.

US/0190-4310
CLASSIFIED INDEX OF DECISIONS OF THE REGIONAL DIRECTORS OF THE NATIONAL LABOR RELATIONS BOARD IN REPRESENTATION PROCEEDINGS. **Added/Corp** United States. National Labor Relations Board. (1976)-. Government Publication. English. qt. Superintendent of Documents, US Government Printing Office, Washington DC 20402. **Tel** (202)275-3328, FAX (202)786-2377. **LC** KF3386.28; .N37. **DD** 344/.73/0102648.

US/0092-4962
CLASSIFIED INDEX OF NATIONAL LABOR RELATIONS BOARD DECISIONS AND RELATED COURT DECISIONS. ***Suspended.*** **Added/Corp** United States. National Labor Relations Board. United States. National Labor Relations Board. Legal Research and Policy Planning Branch. United States. National Labor Relations Board. Decisions and Orders. United States. National Labor Relations Board. Court Decisions Relating to the National Labor Relations Act. **VFOAT** Classified Index of N.L.R.B. and Related Court Decisions. (19??)-Suspended (Dec. 1989). English. ir (4 cumulative issues). $18.00 US; $22.50 other. Superintendent of Documents, US Government Printing Office, Washington DC 20402. **Tel** (202)275-3328, FAX (202)786-2377. **LC** KF3362.7; .C55. **DD** 344/.73/0102648. available on microfilm from University Microfilms International (UMI).

CN/0836-3935
CODE DU TRAVAIL DU QUEBEC ET REGLEMENTS. **See** Economics-Labor.

US
CODE OF FEDERAL REGULATIONS. 20, EMPLOYEES BENEFITS. **Added/Corp** United States. Office of the Federal Register. **VFOAT** Employees' Benefits; CFR. 20, Employees' Benefits. (19??)-. English. an. Superintendent of Documents, US Government Printing Office, Washington DC 20402. **Tel** (202)275-3328, FAX (202)786-2377. available on microfiche.
Desc: Special edition of the Federal Register, containing a codification of documents.

US
CODE OF FEDERAL REGULATIONS. 29, LABOR. **Added/Corp** United States. Office of the Federal Register. **VFOAT** Labor; CFR. 29, Labor. (19??)-. English. an. $389.00 (parts 1900-1910). Regulations Management Corporation, 1505 Arlington Road, Bloomington IN 47404. **Tel** (812)333-7347. available on microfiche.
Desc: Special edition of the Federal Register, containing a codification of documents.

US/0010-079X
COLLECTIVE BARGAINING NEGOTIATIONS AND CONTRACTS. **Added/Corp** Bureau of National Affairs (Washington, D.C.). No. 1 (Oct. 8 1945)-. Periodical. English. bw. $828.00. Bureau of National Affairs Inc., 9435 Key West Avenue, Rockville MD 20850. **Tel** (800)372-1033, (301)258-1033, FAX (301)948-5823. **(Subscription address:** 9435 Key West Avenue Rockville MD 20850; telephone: FAX (301)948-5823**) ED** Mary P Dunn. **LC** HD6500; .B8. **DD** 331.116. **[CCC].**
Desc: A notification and reference service containing information designed to help unions and management prepare, negotiate, and administer contracts.

●US/1059-504X
COLORADO EMPLOYMENT LAW LETTER. [Colo. employ. law lett.]. **Added/Corp** Holland & Hart (Firm). Vol. 1, No. 1 (Jan. 1992)-. Periodical. English. mo. $87.00. M. Lee Smith Publishers and Printers, 162 4th Avenue North, PO Box 198867, Nashville TN 37219. **Tel** (615)242-7395, (800)274-6774, FAX (615)256-6601. **ED** John Husband, Sandra Goldman, and Jude Biggs, (address) 555 17th Street, Suite 2900, PO Box 8749 Denver, CO 80201, (phone)303-295-8000. **DD** 344.
Desc: Newsletter reporting the latest state specific employment law developments that affect companies in that state.

US/1043-5255
COMPARATIVE LABOR LAW JOURNAL. [Comp. labor law j.]. **Added/Corp** International Society for Labour Law and Social Security. U.S. National Branch. Wharton School. University of Pennsylvania. Law School. Vol. 8, No. 1 (Fall 1986)-. Periodical. English. qt. $30.00 US; $40.00 other. Comparative Labor Law, University of Pennsylvania, 2203 Steinberg Dietrich Hall, Philadelphia PA 19104. **Tel** (215)898-6851, FAX (215)898-2400. **ED** Janice R Bellace and Clyde W Summers. **LC** K3; .O43. **DD** 344/.01/05; 342.4105. Index available. cum. index. **Bk Rev. Ad Acc. Pr Rev. Circ:** 700. ***Continues** Comparative Labor Law, 0147-9202.*
Desc: Publishes articles dealing comparatively with an aspect of labor or employment law in two or more countries.
Ind/Abst Index Leg. Period.; Int. Labour Doc.; LABORDOC; Leg. Inf. Manage. Index; Leg. Resour. Index; LegalTrac (1988-); PAIS Int. Print (1991-).

●US/1064-4903
CONNECTICUT EMPLOYMENT LAW LETTER. (CONNECTICUT EMPLOYMENT LAW LETTER / PEPE & HAZARD.). [Conn. employ. law lett.]. **Added/Corp** Pepe & Hazard (Firm). Vol. 1, No. 1 (Jan. 1993)-. Periodical. English. mo. $95.00. M. Lee Smith Publishers and Printers, 162 4th Avenue North, PO Box 198867, Nashville TN 37219. **Tel** (615)242-7395, (800)274-6774, FAX (615)256-6601. **DD** 346.

US/0732-0833
CONNECTICUT WORKER'S COMPENSATION REVIEW OPINIONS. (CONNECTICUT WORKERS' COMPENSATION REVIEW OPINIONS : OPINIONS OF THE COMPENSATION REVIEW DIVISION OF THE WORKER'S COMPENSATION COMMISSION OF THE STATE OF CONNECTICUT.). [Conn. work. compens. rev. opin.]. **Main/Corp** Connecticut. Workers' Compensation Commission. Compensation Review Division. Vol. 1, No. 1-. English. qt. Butterworth Heinemann / Woburn, MA, 225 Wildwood Avenue, Unit B, Woburn MA 01801. **Tel** (800)366-2665, FAX (617)928-2620, telex 880052. **LC** KFC3942; .A553. **DD** 344.746/021; 347.460421.

CN/0827-4614
CONSTRUCTION INDUSTRY EMPLOYMENT LAW. ***Title Change.*** [Constr. ind. employ. law.]. **Added/Corp** Lancaster House (Firm). Vol.

1, No. 1 (Jan. 1985)-Vol. 8, No. 7/8 (July/Aug. 1992). Periodical. English. mo. Lancaster House Publishing, PO Box 133, 20 Dundas Street West, Toronto Ontario M5G 2G8 Canada. **Tel** (416)977-6618, FAX (416)977-5873. **DD** 344.71/01769/00264. ***Continued by*** *Lancaster's Construction Industry Employment Law News, 1194-4552.*

US/0195-9247
CONTRACTING FOR SERVICES; COURSE MANUAL. **Added/Corp** Federal Publications Inc. **VFOAT** Course Manual. (19??)-. English. an. Federal Publications Inc, 1120 20th Street Northwest, Washington DC 20036. **Tel** (202)337-7000, (800)922-4330, FAX (202)659-2233. **LC** KF849; .C64. **DD** 346.73/023.

US/0083-2219
COURT DECISIONS RELATING TO THE NATIONAL LABOR RELATIONS ACT. [Court decis. relat. Natl. Labor Relat. Act]. **Main/Corp** United States. National Labor Relations Board. **Added/Corp** United States. National Labor Relations Board. **VFOAT** Court Decisions--NLRA; Court Decisions--N.L.R.A. Vol. 1 (Dec. 31, 1939)-. Government Publication. English. ir. Superintendent of Documents, US Government Printing Office, Washington DC 20402. **Tel** (202)275-3328, FAX (202)786-2377. **LC** KF3360.A2; C68. **DD** 344.73/01/0264305; 347.30410264305. cum. index.

CM
CRADAT INFORMATIONS : BULLETIN DU CENTRE REGIONAL AFRICAIN D'ADMINISTRATION DU TRAVAIL. **Added/Corp** Centre Regional Africain d'Administration du Travail. **VFOAT** C.R.A.D.A.T. Informations. No. 15 (Oct. 1982)-. Bulletin. French. **DD** 344.6/01/05; 346.04105. ***Continues*** *Bulletin du Centre Regional Africain d'Administration du Travail.*
Ind/Abst LABORDOC.

UK
CRONER'S EMPLOYMENT LAW. (19??)-. Periodical. English. bm. £251.50. Croner Publ Ltd, Croner House, London Road, Kingston upon Thames, Surrey KT2 6SR England. **Tel** 011 44 81 5473333, FAX 081 547-2637.

CR
DEBATE LABORAL : REVISTA AMERICANA E ITALIANA DE DERECHO DEL TRABAJO. **Added/Corp** Universidad de Costa Rica. Italy. Ministero Degli Affari Esteri. Istituto Sindacale per la Cooperazione con i Paesi in via di Sviluppo. **VFOAT** DL. (1988)-. Periodical. Spanish. sa. $30.00. Revista Debate Laboral, Apartado 1119, 1002 San Jose, Costa Rica. **Tel** 011 506 550816. **LC** K4; .E3.
Ind/Abst Int. Labour Doc.; LABORDOC.

CN/0822-367X
DECISION OF THE UMPIRE. **Main/Corp** Canada. Office of the Umpire. **Added/Corp** Canada. Unemployment Insurance Commission. Canada. Employment and Immigration Canada (Commission). **VFOAT** Decision de l'Arbitre. **VAT** Decision de l'Arbitre (Ed. Anglaise et Francaise). (194?)-. Periodical. English (French). ir. Labour Canada / Employment & Immigration, Ottawa Ontario K1A 0J9 Canada. **Tel** (819)994-6111. **DD** 344.71/024/02643. ***Absorbed in part by*** *Decision de l'Arbitre, 0822-3688.*

US
DECISIONS AND ORDERS OF THE NATIONAL LABOR RELATIONS BOARD. **Main/Corp** United States. National Labor Relations Board. Vol. 1 (Dec. 7, 1935-July 1, 1936)-. English. ir. Price varies per volume. Superintendent of Documents, US Government Printing Office, Washington DC 20402. **Tel** (202)275-3328, FAX (202)786-2377. **DD** 331.154. cum. index. ***Continues*** *United States. National Labor Relations Board. Decisions of the National Labor Relations Board.*

US
DECISIONS AND ORDERS OF THE NEW YORK STATE LABOR RELATIONS BOARD. **Main/Corp** New York (State). State Labor Relations Board. 1937/38-. English. Williams Press Inc, PO Box 4025, Albany NY 12204. **Tel** (518)434-1141. **LC** HD5503. **DD** 331.15409747.

US/0278-7695
DECISIONS OF THE FEDERAL LABOR RELATIONS AUTHORITY. **Main/Corp** United States. Federal Labor Relations Authority. Vol. 1, (Jan. 1, 1979-Sept. 30, 1979)-. English. Federal Labor Relations Authority, 500 C Street SW, Washington DC 20424. **Tel** (202)382-0711. **LC** KF5365; .A554. **DD** 344.73/0189041353/0002648; 347.3041890413530002648. available on microfiche (Vols. for (1985-) distributed to depository libraries). ***Continues*** *Decisions and Reports on Rulings of the Assistant Secretary of Labor for Labor-Management Relations, 0091-2646.*

AT
DECISIONS - WORKERS COMPENSATION BOARD (VICTORIA). **Main/Corp** Victoria, Australia. Workers Compensation Board. Vol. 1, (1945)-. English.

AG
DERECHO DEL TRABAJO; REVISTA CRITICA MENSUAL DE JURISPRUDENCIA, DOCTRINA Y LEGISLACION. (1941)-. Periodical. Spanish. Twelve times a year. $600.00. La Ley SA, Tucuman 1471, 1050 Buenos Aires Argentina. **Tel** 011 54 1 495481, 011 54 1 495489. cum. index.
Ind/Abst Int. Labour Doc.; LABORDOC.

UY
DERECHO LABORAL; REVISTA DE DOCTRINA, JURISPRUDENCIA E INFORMACIONES SOCIALES. Vol. 1, No. 1 (May 1948)-. Periodical. Spanish. qt. Cerrito 420-ESC, 404 Montevideo Uruguay.

PY
DERECHO SOCIAL. Yearly Vol. 1 (Sept. 1978)-. Periodical. Spanish. Gs250.00 per issue. Instituto Paraguayo de Derecho del Trabajo, Casilla de Correo No 853, Asuncion Paraguay. **DD** 344.892/01; 348.92041.

PE
DERECHOS SOCIALES. **Added/Corp** Asociacion Peruana de Derechos Sociales. No. 1 (Nov. 1973)-. Spanish. Asociacion Peruana de Derechos, Jiron de la Union No 1011, Of 3 3er Piso, Lima Peru.

US/0270-4196
DETERMINATIONS OF THE NATIONAL MEDIATION BOARD. **Main/Corp** United States. National Mediation Board. Vol. 6 (July 1, 1976-June 30, 1979)-. English. an. $8.00. National Mediation Board, 1425 K Street Northwest, Washington DC 20572. **Tel** (202)523-5335. **LC** KF3386.A2; N37. **DD** 344.73/0188/0264. ***Continues*** *United States. National Mediation Board. Determination of Craft or Class of the National Mediation Board, 0891-9410.*

US
DIGEST AND DECISIONS OF THE EMPLOYEES' COMPENSATION APPEALS BOARD. **Main/Corp** United States. Employees' Compensation Appeals Board. **VFOAT** Digest of Decisions of the Employees' Compensation Appeals Board; Decisions of the Employees' Compensation Appeals Board. Vol. 36 (Oct. 1, 1984/Sept. 30, 1985)-. Government Publication. English. an. Superintendent of Documents, US Government Printing Office, Washington DC 20402. **Tel** (202)275-3328, FAX (202)786-2377. **LC** KF3626; .A553. **DD** 344.73/021; 347.30421. ***Formed by the union of*** *Decisions of the Employees' Compensation Appeals Board* ***and*** *Decisions of the Employees' Compensation Appeals Board. Index Digest.*

IT/1120-7965
DIRITTO & PRATICA DEL LAVORO / IPSOA. **Added/Corp** IPSOA, S.p.a. **VFOAT** Diritto e Pratica del Lavoro. (19??)-. Periodical. Italian. wk. L420000 Italy; L840000 other. IPSOA Editore SRL, Casella Postale 12055, Mastrangelo, 20120 Milan Italy. **Tel** 011 39 2 82476248. **DD** 344.45/01/05; 344.504105.

IT/0012-3404
DIRITTO DEL LAVORO. (IL DIRITTO DEL LAVORO.). [Dir. lav.]. **Added/Corp** Italy. Ministero delle Corporazione. Vol. 1 (Jan./Feb. 1927)-. Periodical. Italian. bm. L210000 Italy; L320000 other. Fondazione Diritto del Lavoro, 14 Via Gramsci, 00197 Rome Italy. **Tel** 011 39 6 3226649. **Bk Rev. Circ:** 1,500.
Desc: Concerned with collective bargaining, regulation of strikes, trade unions, industrial relations, dismissment, and all the most important aspects of Italian labor law through articles and cases.
Ind/Abst PAIS Int. Print.

IT
DIRITTO DELLE RELAZIONI INDUSTRIALI : RIVISTA DELLA ASSOCIAZIONE LAVORO E RICERCHE, ALAR. **Added/Corp** Associazione Lavoro e Ricerche. (1991)-. Periodical. Italian. sa. L70000.00 Italy; L105000.00 other. Giuffre Editore SPA, Via Busto Arsizio 40, 20151 Milan Italy. **Tel** 011 398 2 38089200. **ED** Luciano Spagnuolo Vigorita. **LC** K4; .I695. **DD** 344.45/01/05; 344.504105.
Desc: Strives to further contact and collaboration among different fields of experience and of professional life in both the academic and business worlds.

CN/0831-2516
DISMISSAL AND EMPLOYMENT LAW DIGEST. [Dismiss. employ. law dig.]. **Added/Corp** Canada Law Book Inc. Issue 1 (May 20, 1986)-. Periodical. English. Nine times a year. 87.00Can$. Canada Law Book Inc., 240 Edward Street, Aurora Ontario L4G 3S9 Canada. **Tel** (800)263-3269, (905)841-6472, FAX (905)841-5085. **ED** Howard A. Levitt. **DD** 344.71/012596.
Desc: Keeps readers up-to-date on all of the latest case law and all of the changes in the rapidly evolving area of dismissal law.

DK/0108-3627
DJF HANDBOGEN. 1983-. Danish. Jurist Okonomforbundets Forlag, Gothersgade 133, 1123 Copenhagen Denmark. **Tel** 011 45 1 33142920.

FR
DROIT AFRICAIN DU TRAVAIL. (19??)-. French. Twenty-three times a year. 3330.07F France; 3400.00F other. Editions d'Iena, 17 rue Thiers, Box Postale 2, 78110 le Vesinet France. **Tel** 011 33 1 39763993. **DD** 344.6/01/02648; 346.04102648.

CN/0712-9300
DROIT DU TRAVAIL EXPRESS. [Droit trav. express]. **Added/Corp** Societe Quebecoise d'Information Juridique. No. 1 (Jan. 13, 1982)-. Periodical. French. Fifty times a year. 435.00Can$. SOQUIJ Societe Quebecoise Info Juridique, 276 rue Street, Jacques Suite 310, Montreal Quebec H2Y 1N3 Canada. **Tel** (514)842-8745. **DD** 344.714/018/02648.
Desc: Furnishes each year more than 1,000 resumes of judgements and decisions relating to labor law.

FR/0222-4194
DROIT OUVRIER, LE. [Droit ouvrier]. **Added/Corp** Confederation Generale du Travail. Confederation Generale du Travail. Conseil Juridique. (1948)-. Periodical. French. Twelve times a year. 538.65F France; 720.00F other. SAEPJS / Societe Anonyme d'Edition de Publications et Journaux Syndicaux, CP 432, 93514 Montreuil Cedex France. **Tel** 011 33 1 48518306.
Ind/Abst Int. Labour Doc.

FR/0012-6438
DROIT SOCIAL. [Droit soc.]. **Added/Corp** France. Laws, Statutes, etc. Vol. 1 (1938)-. Periodical. French. ir. 802.00F France; 928.00F other. Les Editions Techniques et Economiques, 3 rue Soufflot, 75005 Paris France. **Tel** 33 1 46341030, FAX 33 1 46345583, telex 260 717 F. **NLM** W1 DR39E. Index available. cum. index. **Ad Acc, Adv Mgr:** Epstrin. **Circ:** 5,000.
Ind/Abst Index Foreign Leg. Per.; Int. Bibliogr. Sociol.; Int. Labour Doc.; Int. Polit. Sci. Abstr.; LABORDOC; PAIS Int. Print (1991-).

PL
DZIENNIK URZEDOWY MINISTERSTWA PRACY, PAC I SPRAW SOCJALNYCH. **Main/Corp** Poland. Ministerstwo Pracy, Pac I Spraw Socjalnych. V. 1 (No. 1); 30. May 1972-. Polish. Z40.00. Ministertwo Pracy PAC I Spraw Socjalnych, Centrala Kolportazu Prasy I Wydawnictw Ruch, Warszawa Poland.

US/0748-6197
EMPLOYEE BENEFIT PLANS. English. Practising Law Institute, 810 Seventh Avenue, New York NY 10019-5818. **Tel** (212)765-5700, FAX (212)581-4670 general correspondence, (212)265-4742 orders and billing inquiries. **LC** KF3512.Z9; E47. **DD** 344.73/01252; 347.3041252.

US/0882-5580
EMPLOYEE BENEFIT PLANS UNDER ERISA. (EMPLOYEE BENEFIT PLANS UNDER ERISA : FEDERAL REGULATIONS.). [Employ. benefit plans under ERISA]. **Added/Corp** Prentice-Hall, Inc. (19??)-. Periodical. English. an. Prentice-Hall Law and Business, 270 Sylvan Avenue, Englewood Cliffs NJ 07632. **Tel** (800)223-0231, (201)894-8538, FAX (201)894-8666. **LC** KF3512.A329; E47. **DD** 344.73/01252; 347.3041252.

US/0273-236X
EMPLOYEE BENEFITS CASES. **Added/Corp** Bureau of National Affairs (Washington, D.C.). (19??)-. English. wk. $889.00. Bureau of National Affairs Inc., 9435 Key West Avenue, Rockville MD 20850. **Tel** (800)372-1033, (301)258-1033, FAX (301)948-5823. **(Subscription address:** 9435 Key West Avenue, Rockville MD 20850; telephone: FAX (301)948-5823**)** **ED** David A Sayre. **LC** KF3509; .A513. **DD** 344.73/01252/02648; 347.304125202648. **[CCC].**
Desc: A decisional service that reports the full text of federal and state court opinions and selected decisions of arbitrators and the NLRB on employee benefits issues.

US/0278-8039
EMPLOYEE EMPLOYER FEDERAL EMPLOYMENT TAX GUIDE. Aug. 1980 Ed.-. English. Agsten Foundation, PO Box 649, Bluefield WV 24701. **LC** KF6436.A15; E46. **DD** 343.7305/2044; 347.30352044.

US
EMPLOYEE PROBLEM SOLVER. (19??)-. Monographic series. English. ir (Published 2 or 3 times per year). $70.00 (latest edition). Alexander Hamilton Institute Inc, 70 Hilltop Road, Ramsey NJ 07446-1119. **Tel** (201)825-8161, FAX (201)825-8696.

US/0098-8898
EMPLOYEE RELATIONS LAW JOURNAL. [Empl. relat. law j.]. Vol. 1 (Summer 1975)-. Periodical. English. qt. $184.00 US & Canada; $234.00 other. John Wiley & Sons, Inc., 605 Third Avenue, New York NY 10158-0012. **Tel** (212)850-6000, (212)850-6645, FAX (212)850-6088, telex 12-7063. **(Subscription address:** John Wiley & Sons Inc / New Jersey, PO Box 2575, Secaucus NJ 07096-2575.**) ED** Jane G. Bensahely. **LC** K5; .M64. **DD** 344/.73/0105. **CODEN** ERLJDC. **[CCC].** Index available. **Bk Rev. Ad Acc. Pr Rev.** available on microfilm and microfiche from University Microfilms International (UMI); available on an online database (file 648/Full-Text) from DIALOG. Documents available from The Genuine Article, UMI Article Clearinghouse, UMI Article Clearinghouse.
Desc: An asset for the personnel executive and attorney seeking to avoid problems generated by employees, unions, or various government agencies. Designed to give analysis and insights into handling problems about equal employment opportunity, occupational health and safety, labor-management relations, employee benefits, and compensation.
Ind/Abst ABI/INFORM Glob. Ed.; ABI Inform Ondisc (Fall 1975-); Acad. Search (Jan. 1993-); Bus. ASAP (1990-) [Full Txt.]; Bus. Index (1985-); Bus. Period. Index; Bus. Source (Jan. 1993-); Curr. Contents Soc. Behav. Sci.; Curr. Law Index (1980-); Gen. BusinessFile (1985-); Gen. Period. Index (1985-); Health Plan. Adminis.; Hospit. Health Admin. Index; Hum. Resour. Abstr.; Index Leg. Period.; INFO-SOUTH Abstr.; Leg. Resour. Index (1980-); LegalTrac (1980-); Mag. Search; PAIS Int. Print; Person. Manage. Abstr.; Res. Alert [Full Cov.]; Sage Fam. Stud. Abstr.; Soc. Sci. Cit. Index [Full Cov.]; Trade Ind. Index (1981-?); UMI ABI/Inform--Bus. Period. Ondisc [Full Txt.]; Vocat. Search (Jan. 1993-); Wilson Bus. Abstr.; Work Relat. Abstr.

US/0892-7545
EMPLOYEE RESPONSIBILITIES AND RIGHTS JOURNAL. (EMPLOYEE RESPONSIBILITIES AND RIGHTS JOURNAL / PUBLISHED FOR THE COUNCIL ON EMPLOYEE RESPONSIBILITIES AND RIGHTS.). [Employ. responsib. rights j.]. **Added/Corp** Council on Employee Responsibilities and Rights (U.S.). **VFOAT** Employee Responsibilities & Rights Journal. Vol. 1, No. 1 (Mar. 1988)-. Periodical. English. Four times a year. $140.00 institutions, $44.00 individuals US; $165.00 institutions, $51.00 individuals other. Plenum Press, 233 Spring Street, New York NY 10013-1578. **Tel** (212)620-8000, (800)221-9369, FAX (212)463-0742, (212)807-1047, telex 23/421139. **ED** Chimezie A.B. Osigweh. **LC** HD6958.5; .E48. **DD** 331/.01/1097305. **CODEN** ERRJE9. **[CCC].** available on microfilm and microfiche from University Microfilms International (UMI).
Desc: Features research on employee responsibilities and rights. Specific areas include management, communication, corporate social reoponsibility, organzational behavior, psychology, education, leadership, training, administration, philosophy and ethics.
Ind/Abst Acad. Search (Jan. 1993-); Bus. Source (Jan. 1993-); INFO-SOUTH Abstr.; Int. Polit. Sci. Abstr.; Mag. Search; PAIS Int. Print (1991-); Person. Manage. Abstr.; Psychol. Abstr. (1988-); PsycINFO; PsycLit; Soc. Plann. Policy Dev. Abstr.; U.S. Polit. Sci. Doc.; Vocat. Search (Jan. 1993-).

US/0271-1567
EMPLOYEE RETIREMENT INCOME SECURITY ACT : REPORT TO CONGRESS. [Empl. retire. income secur. act, Rep. Congr.]. **Main/Corp** United States. Dept. of Labor. Began with 1977. English. an. US Department of Labor, 200 Constitution Avenue NW, Washington DC 20210. **Tel** (202)219-7316, FAX (202)219-7312. **LC** KF3512; .A825. **DD** 344.73/01252. available on microfiche (Vols. for (1980)- distributed to depository libraries). ***Continues** Administration of the Employee Retirement Income Security Act, 0146-7352.*

US/0889-5422
EMPLOYEE TESTING & THE LAW. VFOAT Employee Testing and the Law; Employee Testing. Vol. 1, No. 3 (Nov. 1986)-. Periodical. English. Six times a year. $295.00. Vanguard Information Publications, PO Box 667, Chapel Hill NC 27514. **Tel** (919)67-2420. **ED** Ted Shults, Merle Thorpe, Roger B. Bernholz and G. Nicholas Herman. **LC** KF3457.3.A15; E46. **DD** 344.73/012596. Index available. cum. index. **Bk Rev. Circ:** 2,000. available on microfilm and microfiche from University Microfilms International (UMI).
Desc: Covers the legal, technical, and business developments involving employee testing including drug testing, polygraph testing, AIDS testing, and personality testing.

US/0360-9456
EMPLOYERS' GUIDE TO WORKERS' COMPENSATION AND SAFE EMPLOYMENT LAWS OF OREGON. V. 1-1975-. English. Employee Benefits Industrial Service Company, PO Box 19542, Portland OR 97219. **LC** KFO2742; .E45. **DD** 344/.795/021.

US/0882-6250
EMPLOYMENT ALERT. [Employ. alert]. Vol. 1, No. 1 (Sept. 7, 1984)-. Periodical. English. bw. $84.00. Research Institute of America, 117 East Stevens Avenue, Valhalla NY 10595. **Tel** (800)431-9025. **ED** James E Cheeks. **DD** 658. **[CCC].**
Desc: Reports on new legislation in the employment field.

US/0510-6222
EMPLOYMENT AND WAGES COVERED BY WISCONSIN'S U. C. LAW. Main/Corp Wisconsin. Employment Security Division. **VAT** Employment and Wages Covered by Wisconsin's Unemployment Compensation Law. English. qt. Wisconsin Department of Industry Labor & Human Relations, 201 East Washington Avenue, PO Box 7946, Madison WI 53707. **Tel** (608)266-0851. **LC** HD8053.W6; E47A. **DD** 331.2/9775. ***Continues** Employment and Wages Covered by Wisconsin's U.C. Law, 0510-6222.*

US/0745-9653
EMPLOYMENT-AT-WILL REPORTER. [Employ.-at-will rep.]. **Added/Corp** New England Legal Publishers. **VFOAT** Employment at Will Reporter. Vol. 1, No. 1 (May 1983)-. Periodical. English. Twelve times a year. $510.00. New England Legal Publishers, PO Box 425, Weston MA 02193. **Tel** (617)891-6200. **ED** Joseph Ambash. Index available. cum. index. **Circ:** 420.

CN/1183-3076
EMPLOYMENT BULLETIN - CANADA LAW BOOK INC. (THE EMPLOYMENT BULLETIN.). [Employ. bull. - Can. Law Book Inc]. **Added/Corp** Canada Law Book Inc. (1991)-. Periodical. English. Eight times a year. 107.00Can$. Canada Law Book Inc., 240 Edward Street, Aurora Ontario L4G 3S9 Canada. **Tel** (800)263-3269, (905)841-6472, FAX (905)841-5085. **ED** Brian A. Grosman. **DD** 344.71/01/05. ***Continues** The Employment Letter., 0836-2394.*
Desc: Covers workplace and employment issues. Tool for lawyers, human resource professionals, union and management negotiators and corporate executives.

UK
EMPLOYMENT CASE LAW INDEX. (19??)-. Periodical. English. £150.50. Croner Publ Ltd, Croner House, London Road, Kingston upon Thames, Surrey KT2 6SR England. **Tel** 011 44 81 5473333, FAX 081 547-2637.

US/0148-107X
EMPLOYMENT DISCRIMINATION DIGEST. V. 1- Dec. 1977-. Periodical. English. qt. $18.00. Employment Discrimination Digest, Management Information Associates, PO Box 887, 641 Longview Street, Montgomery AL 36102. **LC** KF3464.A15; E6. **DD** 344/.73/0113305.

US/1050-1193
EMPLOYMENT HEALTH LAW & BENEFITS. [Employ. health law benefits]. **Added/Corp** Employment Law and Education Center (Chicago, Ill.). **VFOAT** Employment Health Law and Benefits. (198?)-. Periodical. English. mo. $184.00. Employment Research Institute Inc., 5009 West Windsor, Chicago IL 60630. **Tel** (312)545-0585, FAX (312)545-0586. **ED** Bernard J. Farber. **LC** KF3574.G68; A497. **DD** 344.73/0125; 347.304125. Index available (Bound in Dec. iss.). cum. index. **Circ:** 200. ***Continues** Public Employment Health Reporter, 0890-1988.*
Desc: This magazine features articles on disability discrimination, Aids, drugs testing, workers compensation , pregnancy, smoking issues, and other employment health legal issues.

US
EMPLOYMENT LAW CITATIONS. English. $272.00 (4 bound volumes), $150.00 (cumulative supplements). Shepards McGraw-Hill Inc, 555 Middle Creek Parkway, PO Box 35300, Colorado Springs CO 80935-3530. **Tel** (719)488-3000, FAX (800)525-0053.

US/1052-2964
EMPLOYMENT LAW COUNSELOR. [Employ. law couns.]. (1990)-. Periodical. English. mo. $245.00. Business Laws Inc., 11630 Chillicothe Road, Chesterland OH 44026. **Tel** (216)729-7996, (800)759-0929, FAX (216)729-0645. **LC** KF3302; .E468. **DD** 344.73/01; 347.3041.

●UK
EMPLOYMENT LAW NEWS. (1993)-. English. Ten times a year. £95.00 Europe; £100.00 other. Sweet & Maxwell Ltd., South Quay Plaza, 183 Marsh Wall, London E14 9FT England. **Tel** 011 44 264 342899, FAX 011 44 264 342723, telex 929089 ITPINF G.

CN/0228-5266
EMPLOYMENT LAW REPORT, THE. [Employ. law rep.]. Vol. 1, No. 1 (Oct. 1980)-. Periodical. English. Twelve times a year. 560.00Can$ one year; $990.00 other. Concord Publishing Ltd, 14 Prince Arthur Avenue, Suite 209, Toronto, Ontario M5R 2A9 Canada. **Tel** (416)964-2758, FAX (416)964-0659. **DD** 344.71/01. Index available.
Desc: This report is designed to provide accurate and authoritative information.

US/1058-1308
EMPLOYMENT LAW REPORT (ROSEMOUNT, MINN.). (EMPLOYMENT LAW REPORT.). [Employ. law rep.]. Vol. 1, No. 1 (Sept. 1991)-. Periodical. English. mo. Data Research Inc., PO Box 490, Rosemount MN 55068. **Tel** (612)452-8267, (800)365-4900. **DD** 344.

●US/1069-7829
EMPLOYMENT LAW STRATEGIST. [Employ. law strateg.]. Vol. 1, No. 1 (May 1993)-. Periodical. English. ir. $145.00. Leader Publications, 345 Park Avenue South, New York NY 10010. **Tel** (800)888-8300 ext. 6170, (212)545-6170, FAX (212)696-1848. **DD** 346.

US/0270-2479
EMPLOYMENT LAW UPDATE. [Employ. law update]. Periodical. English. mo. $60.00. C&A Publishing Company, PO Box 971, Tulsa OK 74101. **LC** KF3302; .M37. **DD** 344.73/01/05.
Desc: A pragmatic newsletter for human resources executives including critical legislation and legal decisions, current issues/trends, helpful policies and checklists, and authoritative legal analysis.

US/0890-9253
EMPLOYMENT LAW UPDATE (EVANSVILLE, IND.). (EMPLOYMENT LAW UPDATE.). **Added/Corp** Rutkowski and Associates. **VFOAT** ELU. Vol. 1, No. 1 (Sept. 1986)-. Periodical. English. mo. $97.50 (one year), $175.00 (two year). Employment Law Update, Box 15250, Evansville IN 47716-0250. **Tel** (812)476-4520. **ED** Arthur D and Barbara Lang Rutkowski. **LC** KF3302; .E47. **DD** 344.73/01; 347.3041. Index available. cum. index.
Desc: A pragmatic, timely newsletter for human resources executives including critical legislation and legal decisions, current issues and trends, helpful policies and checklists, and authoritative legal analysis.

US/1055-6249
EMPLOYMENT LITIGATION REPORTER. [Employ. litig. report.]. (1991)-. Periodical. English. sm (24 issues). $800.00. Andrews Publications Inc., 1646 West Chester Pike, PO Box 1000, Westtown PA 19395. **Tel** (610)399-6600, (800)345-1101, FAX (610)399-6610. **LC** KF3471.A59; W76. **DD** 344.73/012596; 347.30412596. ***Continues** Wrongful Termination Litigation Reporter, 1055-6745.*
Desc: Offers attorneys and legal professionals timely, probing coverage of the entire spectrum of employment-related legal issues.

US/0149-6255
EMPLOYMENT PRACTICES DECISIONS. ***Ceased.*** **Added/Corp** Commerce Clearing House. Commerce Clearing House. Labor Law Reports: Employment Practices. Vol. 1 (1971)-(1993). Periodical. English. sa. Commerce Clearing House Inc., 4025 West Peterson Avenue, Chicago IL 60646-6085. **Tel** (312)583-8500, FAX (708)940-4600. **ED** A. E. Schechter. **LC** KF3464; .A513. **DD** 344/.73/0113302643.
Desc: Bound volumes of federal and state court cases involving issues of employment discrimination on account of race, color, sex, religion, national origin, age, mental and physical handicap, and of veterans' job rights.

US/0746-9683
EMPLOYMENT RELATIONS BULLETIN. [Employ. relat. bull.]. No. 1 (August 1982)-. Bulletin. English. mo (except July and August). Florida State University College of Law, Tallahassee FL 32306. **Tel** (904)644-0961. **ED** William F McHugh and Tommy E Roberts Jr. **DD** 344. **Circ:** 2,200.
Desc: Newsletter covering important developments in employment relations and labor laws, including AIDS, drugs, discrimination, sexual harassment, collective bargaining and immigration laws.

GW/0433-7050
ENTSCHEIDUNGEN DES BUNDESARBEITSGERICHTS. Main/Corp Germany (Federal Republic, 1949-). Bundesarbeitsgericht. (1954)-. Monographic series. German. ir. Price varies per volume. Walter de Gruyter Inc., PO Box 303421, D 10728 Berlin Germany. **Tel** 011 49 30 260050, FAX 011 49 30 26005251. **(Subscription address:** Walter de Gruyter Inc., 200 Saw Mill River Road, Hawthorne NY 10532.**)** ***Supersedes** Germany. Reicharbeitsgericht. Entscheidungen.*

US/0160-435X
EQUAL EMPLOYMENT COMPLIANCE UPDATE. (Aug. 1977)-. Periodical. English. Clark Boardman Callaghan, 155 Pfingsten Road, Deerfield IL 60015. **Tel** (800)323-8067. **LC** KF3464.A15; E68. **DD** 344/.73/01133. ***Supersedes** Equal Employment Compliance Special Report, 0160-4368.*

US/0161-4541
EQUAL EMPLOYMENT OPPORTUNITY COMPLIANCE. 1972-. English. Practising Law Institute, 810 Seventh Avenue, New York NY 10019-5818. **Tel** (212)765-5700, FAX (212)581-4670 general correspondence, (212)265-4742 orders and billing inquiries. **LC** KF3464.Z9; E64. **DD** 344/.73/01133.

US/0735-9187
EQUAL EMPLOYMENT OPPORTUNITY IN THE FEDERAL COURTS. (EQUAL EMPLOYMENT OPPORTUNITY IN THE FEDERAL COURTS / ADMINISTRATIVE OFFICE OF THE UNITED STATES COURTS.). **VFOAT** Equal Employment Opportunity Report. 1981-. English. an. Administrative Office of the United States Courts, 811 Vermont Avenue NW, Room 655, Washington DC 20544. **LC** KF8770; .A83. **DD** 347.73/1; 347.3071. available on microfiche (Vols. for 1981- distributed to depository libraries).

UK/0957-882X
EQUAL OPPORTUNITIES REVIEW. DISCRIMINATION CASE LAW DIGEST. **Added/Corp** Industrial Relations Services. **VFOAT** Discrimination Case Law Digest; EOR Discrimination Case Law Digest. (19??)-. Periodical. English. qt. £50.00. Eclipse Publications Ltd, 18 20 Highbury Place, London N5 1QP England. **Tel** 011 44 71 354 5858. **LC** KD3102.A13; E682.

US/1055-5307
ERISA LITIGATION REPORTER. [ERISA litig. report.]. **VFOAT** ELR. **VAT** Employee Retirement Income Security Act Litigation Reporter. Vol. 1, No. 1 (Mar./Apr. 1991)-. Periodical. English. Six times a year. $265.83. Prentice-Hall Law and Business, 270 Sylvan Avenue, Englewood Cliffs NJ 07632. **Tel** (800)223-0231, (201)894-8538, FAX (201)894-8666. **LC** KF3512.A15; E75. **DD** 344.73/01252/05; 347.304125205.
Desc: Provides explanations of recent cases and developments in ERISA litigation. Every issue contains four to eight discussions on the most important cases the authors believe have been decided.

CN
ESTIMATES. PART III, CANADA LABOUR RELATIONS BOARD. **Main/Corp** Canada. **VFOAT** Budget des Depenses. Partie III, Conseil Canadien des Relations du Travail. (19??)-. English (French). $3.00 Canada; $3.60 other. Canada Communication Group Publishers, Order Processing, Ottawa Ontario K1A 0S9 Canada. **Tel** (819)956-4800, (819)956-4802. **LC** KE3153.A72; C364. **DD** 354.710083.

US/0161-3138
EVIDENTIA. ***Ceased.*** Ceased Vol. 11. Periodical. English (English). qt. Criterion Inc, 9425 North MacArthur Boulevard, Irving TX 75063-4706. **Tel** (214)401-2100. **LC** KF1600.A15; E88. **DD** 340/.0973.
Desc: Statistical, economic and demographic analyses for the labor lawyer and personnel professional.

US/0885-7172
FAIR EMPLOYMENT COMPLIANCE. [Fair employ. compliance]. (19??)-. Periodical. English. Twenty-two times a year. $245.00 (one year), $440.00 (two year), $580.00 (three year). Management Resources Inc, 861 LaFayette Road, Suite 5, Hampton NH 03842. **Tel** (603)929-1600. **ED** Kennir Suan. **DD** 658. **Bk Rev**, (Qty: 2-12).
Desc: Report on news, court decisions, trends, legislation, company practices in EEO law and personnel practices.

US/0525-552X
FAIR EMPLOYMENT PRACTICE CASES. [Fair employ. pract. cases]. **Added/Corp** Bureau of National Affairs (Washington, D.C.). **VFOAT** FEP Cases. Vol. 1 (1969)-. English. bm. $942.00. Bureau of National Affairs Inc., 9435 Key West Avenue, Rockville MD 20850. **Tel** (800)372-1033, (301)258-1033, FAX (301)948-5823. **LC** KF3464; .A514. **DD** 344.73/01133; 331.11. **[CCC].** cum. index. ***Absorbed in part*** *Labor Relations Reporter, 0148-7981.*

US
FAIR LABOR STANDARDS HANDBOOK FOR STATES, LOCAL GOVERNMENTS AND SCHOOLS / GILBERT J. GINSBURG, DANIEL B. ABRAHAMS. (1985)-. Periodical. English. mo. $279.00 (includes loose-leaf handbook). Thompson Publishing Group, 7711 Anderson Road, Tampa FL 33634. **Tel** (800)677-3789, (813)282-8607.

US
FEDERAL EQUAL OPPORTUNITY REPORTER. English. Twenty-four times a year. $855.00 (postage included). LRP Publications, 747 Dresher Road, PO Box 980, Horsham PA 19044-0980. **Tel** (800)341-7874, (215)784-0860, FAX (215)784-9639, (215)784-0870.
Desc: Reports on the decisions of both the ORA and the courts on federal employee EEO appeals. Includes advance sheets highlighting cases of particular importance in each issue. All reported cases fully indexed, summarized and headnoted.

US
FEDERAL LABOR LAWS. **Main/Corp** United States. Periodical. English. US Department of Labor, 200 Constitution Avenue NW, Washington DC 20210. **Tel** (202)219-7316, FAX (202)219-7312.

US/0746-5653
FEDERAL REGULATION OF EMPLOYMENT NEWSLETTER. Feb. 10, 1983-. Newsletter. English. bw. $66.00. Research Institute of America, 117 East Stevens Avenue, Valhalla NY 10595. **Tel** (800)431-9025. **LC** KF3315. **DD** 344.73/01/05; 347.304105. ***Continues*** *FRES Newsletter, 0192-0839.*

US/0093-7630
FEP GUIDELINES. ***Title Change.*** [F.E.P. guidel.]. **Added/Corp** Bureau of Business Practice. **VAT** Fair Employment Practice Guidelines. (19??)-(19??). Periodical. English. mo. Bureau of Business Practice, 24 Rope Ferry Road, Waterford CT 06386. **Tel** (800)243-0876, (203)442-4365, (800)876-9105, FAX (203)443-1123. **ED** James O'Shea. **LC** HD4903.5.U58; F2. **DD** 331.1/33/0973. ***Continued by*** *Fair Employment Practices Guidelines, 1069-921X.*
Desc: Provides accurate and authoritative information on fair employment for personnel specialists, managers, and supervisors. Covers legal developments in the field of anti-discrimination law.

US
FIRST PAYMENTS, WEEKS COMPENSATED AND BENEFITS PAID TO WOMEN, BY INDUSTRIAL GROUP UNDER OHIO UNEMPLOYMENT COMPENSATION LAW / OHIO BUREAU OF EMPLOYMENT SERVICES. English. Division of Research and Statistics, Ohio Bureau of Employment Services, Columbus OH 43216. **LC** HD7096.U6; O25. **DD** 368.4/4/0088042.

US/1041-3537
FLORIDA EMPLOYMENT LAW LETTER. [Fla. employ. law lett.]. Vol. 1, No. 1 (Mar. 1989)-. Periodical. English. mo. $117.00. M. Lee Smith Publishers and Printers, 162 4th Avenue North, PO Box 198867, Nashville TN 37219. **Tel** (615)242-7395, (800)274-6774, FAX (615)256-6601. **(Subscription address:** Florida Law Letter.**) ED** Tom Harper, Haynsworth, Baldwin, Johnson and Harper, Suite 330, 111 Riverside Avenue, PO Box 40593, Jacksonville, Fl 32202-0593, (phone)904-353-9000. **LC** KFF331.A15; F55. **DD** 344.759/012/05; 347.59041205.
Desc: Newsletter reporting the latest state specific employment law developments that affect companies in that state.

US/0734-1105
FROM THE STATE CAPITALS. LABOR RELATIONS. ***Title Change.*** [From state cap., Labor relat.]. **VFOAT** Labor Relations. (Feb. 1982)-(19??). Periodical. English. mo. Wakeman Walworth Inc., 300 North Washington Street #204, Alexandria VA 22314. **Tel** (703)549-8606. **DD** 331. **[CCC].** ***Continues*** *From the State Capitals. Labor Law Developments in the State Capitals.* ***Merged with*** *From the State Capitals. Public Employee Policy, 0741-3521* ***to form*** *From the State Capitals. Employee Policy for the Private & Public Sectors, 1061-9674.*

US/1040-4813
GEORGIA EMPLOYMENT LAW LETTER. [Ga. employ. law lett.]. **Added/Corp** Georgia Law Letter Publishers. Vol. 1, No. 1 (Aug. 1988)-. Periodical. English. mo. $117.00. M. Lee Smith Publishers and Printers, 162 4th Avenue North, PO Box 198867, Nashville TN 37219. **Tel** (615)242-7395, (800)274-6774, FAX (615)256-6601. **(Subscription address:** Georgia Law Letter.**) ED** David Hagaman, (address) Clark, Paul, Hoover and Mallard, One Midtown Plaza, Suite 900, 1360 Peachtree Street NE Atlanta, GA 30309-3214, (phone)404-874-7500. **LC** KFG331.A15; G46. **DD** 344.758/01/05; 347.5804105.
Desc: Newsletter reporting the latest state specific employment law developments that affect companies in that state.

IT
GOIRNALE DI DIRITTO DEL LAVORO E DI RELAZIONI INDUSTRIALI. Vol. 1, No. 1 (1979)-. Periodical. Italian. Three times a year. L116000 Italy; L150000 other. Franco Angeli Riviste SRL, Viale Monza 106, 20127 Milan Italy. **Tel** 011 39 2 2827651, 011 39 2 289562. **LC** K7; .I53. **DD** 344.45/01; 344.5041.
Ind/Abst PAIS Int. Print.

US/0270-2487
GOVERNMENT UNION REVIEW. [Gov. union rev.]. **Added/Corp** Public Service Research Foundation (Vienna, Va.). Vol. 1 (Winter 1980)-. Periodical. English. qt (Mar., June, Sept., Dec.). $20.00. Public Service Research Foundation, 1761 Business Center Drive, Suite 230, Reston VA 22090-5333. **Tel** (703)438-3966, FAX (703)438-3935. **ED** Peter W Katsirubas. **LC** HD8008.A1; G63. **DD** 331.88/1135/0000973. Index available. cum. index. **Circ:** 4,000 (ctrl). available on microfilm and microfiche from University Microfilms International (UMI). Documents available from UMI Article Clearinghouse.
Desc: An academic journal featuring articles on public policy regarding public sector employer-employee relations with emphasis on the influence of public sector unions.
Ind/Abst ABI/INFORM Glob. Ed.; ABI Inform Ondisc (Winter 1986-); Curr. Index J. Educ.; Curr. Law Index (1981-); Educ. Adm. Abstr. (?-?); Gen. BusinessFile (1992-); Hum. Resour. Abstr. (?-?); Index Period. Artic. Relat. Law; Int. Labour Doc.; LABORDOC; Leg. Resour. Index (1981-); LegalTrac (1980-); PAIS Int. Print (1991-?); Sage Public Adm. Abstr. (?-?); Soc. Plann. Policy Dev. Abstr.; Sociol. Abstr.; UMI ABI/Inform--Bus. Period. Ondisc (Fall 1987-) [Full Txt.]; Urban Aff. Abstr.; Work Relat. Abstr.

●UK
GREEN'S EMPLOYMENT LAW BULLETIN. (1994)-. Bulletin. English. Six times a year. £99.00 Europe; £104.00 other. Sweet & Maxwell Ltd., South Quay Plaza, 183 Marsh Wall, London E14 9FT England. **Tel** 011 44 264 342899, FAX 011 44 264 342723, telex 929089 ITPINF G.

CN/0826-8673
GUIA SOCIAL DEL TRABAJADOR. [Guia soc. trab.]. 1982-. Spanish. an. Quebec Federation of Labour, 4th Floor/2100 Papineau Avenue, Montreal Quebec H2K 4J4 Canada. **DD** 344.714/01.

CN/0826-8681
GUIDA SOCIAL DO TRABALHADOR. [Guia soc. trab.]. 1982-. Portuguese. an. Quebec Federation of Labour, 4th Floor/2100 Papineau Avenue, Montreal Quebec H2K 4J4 Canada. **DD** 344.714/01.

CN/0826-869X
GUIDA SOCIALE DEL LAVORATORE. 1982-. Italian. an. Quebec Federation of Labour, 4th Floor/2100 Papineau Avenue, Montreal Quebec H2K 4J4 Canada. **DD** 344.714/01.

US/0196-7975
GUIDEBOOK TO FAIR EMPLOYMENT PRACTICES. **Main/Corp** Commerce Clearing House. **Added/Corp** Commerce Clearing House. Fair Employment Practices. Commerce Clearing House. Labor Law Reports : Employment Practices. (1973)-. English. an. $21.00. Commerce Clearing House Inc., 4025 West Peterson Avenue, Chicago IL 60646-6085. **Tel** (312)583-8500, FAX (708)940-4600. **LC** KF3464.Z9; C62. **DD** 344.73/01133; 347.3041133.
Desc: Expert guidance on current equal rights law in the field of employment, especially Title VII of the Civil Rights Act of 1964, the Americans with Disabilities Act of 1990, and the Civil Rights Act of 1991. Reviews actual employment practices: recruitment, screening, hiring, compensation, advancement and managerial control.

US/0072-8853
GUIDEBOOK TO LABOR RELATIONS. **Added/Corp** Commerce Clearing House. **VFOAT** C.C.H. Current Law Handybook Edition; CCH Current Law Handybook Edition. 1st Ed. (1960)-. English. an. $10.50. Commerce Clearing House Inc., 4025 West Peterson Avenue, Chicago IL 60646-6085. **Tel** (312)583-8500, FAX (708)940-4600. **ED** A. E. Schechter. **DD** 331.1502673.
Desc: Gives a clear picture of the federal labor relations rules developed under the National Labor Relations Act, and the Taft-Hartley Law, the Labor-Management Reporting and Disclosure Act, and other pertinent statutes.

US
HANDBOOK ON ERISA LITIGATION. **VAT** Handbook on Employee Retirement Income Security Act Litigation. (19??)-. English. an. $119.35. Prentice-Hall Law and Business, 270 Sylvan Avenue, Englewood Cliffs NJ 07632. **Tel** (800)223-0231, (201)894-8538, FAX (201)894-8666.

AU
HANDBUCH FUER PERSONAL- UND LOHNBUROS. German. an. ARD-Zeitschriftenverlag und Sozial- und Abgabenrechtlicher Informationsdienst, Scherff OHG, Habsburgerstrasse 6-8, Vienna Austria. **LC** KJJ1261.3; .H36.

UK
HARVEY INDUSTRIAL RELATIONS EMPLOYMENT LAW SERVICE. (19??)-. English. Price varies per issue. Butterworth & Co. Ltd. / Kent, England, Borough Green, Sevenoaks Kent TN15 8PH England. **Tel** 011 44 732-884567, FAX 011 44 732-885996.

US/0890-9245
HEALTH EMPLOYMENT LAW UPDATE. [Health employ. law update]. **VFOAT** HELU. (1985)-. Periodical. English. mo. $97.50 (one year), $175.00 (two year). Health Employment Law Update, PO Box 15250, Evansville IN 47716-0250. **Tel** (812)476-4520. **ED** Arthur D. & Barbara Lang Rutkowski. **LC** KF3580.H4; A133. **DD** 344.73/01; 347.3041. Index available. cum. index.
Desc: A pragmatic, timely newsletter for human resources executives including critical legislation and legal decisions, current issues and trends, helpful policies and checklists, and authoritative legal analysis.

US/0886-246X
HIGHLIGHTS OF FEDERAL UNEMPLOYMENT COMPENSATION LAWS. [Highlights Fed. unempl. compens. laws]. **Added/Corp** National Foundation for Unemployment Compensation & Workers' Compensation (U.S.). (Jan. 1986)-. English. ir. $20.00 (per copy). National Foundation for Unemployment Compensation and Workers Compensation / NFUCWC, 1331 Penn Avenue Northwest, Suite 1500, Washington DC 20002. **Tel** (202)682-1515, (202)682-1517. **LC** KF3671.A3; H54. **DD** 344.73/024; 347.30424.

US/0730-7624
HIGHLIGHTS OF STATE UNEMPLOYMENT COMPENSATION LAWS. (HIGHLIGHTS OF STATE UNEMPLOYMENT COMPENSATION LAWS / UBA.). [Highlights state unemploy. compens. laws]. **Added/Corp** National Foundation for Unemployment Compensation & Workers' Compensation (U.S.). (Jan. 1982)-. English. an. $18.00. National Foundation for Unemployment Compensation and Workers Compensation / NFUCWC, 1331 Penn Avenue Northwest, Suite 1500, Washington DC 20002. **Tel** (202)682-1515, (202)682-1517. **LC** KF3675.Z95; H54. **DD** 344.73/024; 347.30424.

US/1052-3332
HOFSTRA LABOR LAW JOURNAL. [Hofstra labor law j.]. **Added/Corp** Hofstra University. School of Law. Vol. 2, No. 1 (Spring-Fall 1984)-. Periodical. English. Twice a year. $14.00. Hofstra University, 109 Hofstra University Cultural Center, Hempstead NY 11550. **Tel** (516)463-5669. **LC** K8; .O44. **DD** 344.73/01/05; 347.304105. ***Continues*** *Hofstra Labor Law Forum, 0739-8220.*
Ind/Abst Curr. Law Index (1984-); Index Leg. Period.; Int. Labour Doc.; LABORDOC; Leg. Resour. Index (1984-); LegalTrac (1984-).

US/1053-0363
HR MANAGERS LEGAL REPORTER. [HR manager's legal report.]. **VAT** Human Resources Manager's Legal Reporter. Issue 255 (Nov. 1990)-. Periodical. English. mo. $110.00. Business & Legal Reports, 39 Academy Street, Madison CT 06443. **Tel** (203)245-7448, (800)727-5257, FAX (203)245-2559. **LC** KF3302; .P475. **DD** 344. **[CCC].** ***Continues*** *Personnel Manager's Legal Reporter, 0274-6506.*

UK
IDS EMPLOYMENT LAW CASES. (19??)-. English. ir (10 volumes with updates). £194.00 (10 binders), £170.00 (6 updates). Incomes Data Services, 193 St John Street, London EC1V 4LS England. **Tel** 011 44 71 250 3434, FAX 011 44 71 608 0949. **ED** Robert Pullen.

UK/1353-1573
IDS PENSIONS SERVICE BULLETIN. (19??)-. Bulletin. English. Ten times a year. £108.00. Incomes Data Services, 193 St John Street, London EC1V 4LS England. **Tel** 011 44 71 250 3434, FAX 011 44 71 608 0949. **ED** Helen Suddell. ctrl circ.
Desc: Includes a loose-leaf manual and a concise bulletin that explain legislation on pensions and analyzes the options open to employers. Subscribers are notified of legislative changes and key court decisions, and changes to company practice and patterns of benefit provision are monitored.

US
IHRC ETHNIC BIBLIOGRAPHY. **See** Ethnic Interests-Abstracting, Bibliographies and Statistics.

US/1049-9385
ILLINOIS EMPLOYMENT LAW LETTER. [Ill. employ. law lett.]. (July 1990)-. Periodical. English. mo. $87.00. M. Lee Smith Publishers and Printers, 162 4th Avenue North, PO Box 198867, Nashville TN 37219. **Tel** (615)242-7395, (800)274-6774, FAX (615)256-6601. **ED** Allan Gunn, (address) Matkov, Salzman, Madoff and Gunn, Suite 1500, 100 West Monroe Street, Chicago,IL 60603-1906, (phone)312-332-0777. **DD** 344. Index available. ctrl circ.
Desc: Newsletter reporting the latest state specific employment law developments that affect companies in that state.

US
ILLINOIS FAIR EMPLOYMENT PRACTICE REPORTS. **Main/Corp** Illinois. Fair Employment Practices Commission. Vol. 1 1974-. English. Fair Employment Practices Commission, 179 West Washington, Chicago IL 60602. **LC** KFI1534.5.D5; A494. **DD** 344.43/01133/02642.

US
ILLINOIS PUBLIC EMPLOYEE REPORTER. **VFOAT** Public Employee Reporter; Public Employee Reporter (Illinois Edition); Public Employee Reporter, Illinois. Vol. 1 (1985)-. Periodical. English. Twenty-four times a year. $655.00. LRP Publications, 747 Dresher Road, PO Box 980, Horsham PA 19044-0980. **Tel** (800)341-7874, (215)784-0860, FAX (215)784-9639, (215)784-0870. **LC** PAR.
Desc: A full-text subscription service reporting all significant decisions of the Illinois State, Local and Educational Labor Relations Boards and related Court decisions...comprehensively indexed and headnoted. Full text of the acts, rules and regulations are also included. The indexing is compatible with NPER.

CN/0843-7114
IMPACT, LABOUR LAW & MANAGEMENT PRACTICES. [Impact labour law manag. pract.]. **VFOAT** Labour Law & Management Practices; Impact, Labour Law and Management Practices. No. 1 (Apr. 1989)-. Periodical. English. Ten times a year. 115.00Can$. Canada Law Book Inc., 240 Edward Street, Aurora Ontario L4G 3S9 Canada. **Tel** (800)263-3269, (905)841-6472, FAX (905)841-5085. **DD** 344.71/01/05.
Desc: Links managers at all levels to the law which relates to the labour force. Written from both a legal as well as a managerial perspective, this newsletter provides analyses on the impact that developments have on present management practices and makes recommendations for change.

CN/0712-340X
INDEX DE LA LEGISLATION OUVRIERE. [Index legis. ouvriere]. No. 1 (Jan. 31, 1979)-. Periodical. French (English). bm. Free. Travail Canada, Publications Distribution, Federal/Provincial Relations, Ottawa Ontario K1A 0J2 Canada. **Tel** (819)997-3920. **DD** 016.34471/01. **Circ:** 350.

CN/0712-3418
INDEX OF LABOUR LEGISLATION. [Index labour legis.]. No. 1 (Jan. 31, 1979)-. Periodical. English (French). bm. Free. Labour Canada / Federal-Provincial Relations, Ottawa Ontario K1A OJ2 Canada. **Tel** (819)997-3920. **DD** 016.34471/01. **Circ:** 350.

US/1053-6191
INDIANA EMPLOYMENT LAW LETTER. [Indiana employ. law lett.]. **Added/Corp** Baker & Daniels. (January 1991)-. Periodical. English. mo. $87.00. M. Lee Smith Publishers and Printers, 162 4th Avenue North, PO Box 198867, Nashville TN 37219. **Tel** (615)242-7395, (800)274-6774, FAX (615)256-6601. **ED** John Neighbours and Todd Nierman, (address) Baker and Daniels, 300 North Meridian Street, Suite 2700, Indianapolis, IN 46024, (phone) 317-237-0300. **DD** 344.
Desc: Newsletter reporting the latest state specific employment law developments that affect companies in that state.

US
INDIVIDUAL EMPLOYMENT RIGHTS. Vol. 1, No. 1 (Sept. 2, 1986)-. Periodical. English. $620.00. Bureau of National Affairs Inc., 9435 Key West Avenue, Rockville MD 20850. **Tel** (800)372-1033, (301)258-1033, FAX (301)948-5823. **(Subscription address:** 9435 Key West Avenue, Rockville MD 20850; telephone: FAX (301)948-5823**)** **ED** Nancy J Sedmak.
Desc: Case reference and notification on individual employment rights issues including employment at will, privacy, polygraph testing, and other employee rights issues outside the traditional labor-management relations context.

AT/0155-2589
INDUSTRIAL ARBITRATION REPORTS, NEW SOUTH WALES, THE. **Main/Corp** Industrial Commission of New South Wales. Vol. 25, Pt. 2; 1927-. English. qt. Industrial Registrar's Office, 50 Phillip Street, Sydney 2000 New South Wales Australia. **Tel** 02-266-8111. **LC** PAR. Index available. ***Continues*** *Industrial Arbitration Reports, New South Wales.*
Desc: Reports for the Industrial Arbitration Commission of New South Wales.

UK/0306-2163
INDUSTRIAL CASES REPORTS. **Added/Corp** Great Britain. Court of Appeal. Incorporated Council of Law Reporting for England and Wales. (1975)-. Periodical. English. mo. £175.00 England; £190.00 other. Incorporated Council of Law Reporting for England and Wales, 3 Stone Buildings, Lincoln's Inn, London WC2A 3XN England. **Tel** (071)242-6471, FAX (071)831-5247. **ED** Carol Ellis and Hilary Jellie. **LC** KD3040.A38; I48. **DD** 344/.41/0102646. **Ad Acc.** ***Continues*** *Industrial Court Reports, 0306-9311.*

UK/0305-9332
INDUSTRIAL LAW JOURNAL (LONDON). (THE INDUSTRIAL LAW JOURNAL.). [Ind. law j.]. **Added/Corp** Industrial Law Society. Vol. 1 (March 1972)-. Periodical. English. qt. £35.00 UK and Europe; $64.00 other. Oxford University Press, Walton Street, Oxford OX2 6DP England. **Tel** 011 44 865 56767, FAX 011 44 865 267773, telex 837330 OXPRES G. **(Subscription address:** Oxford University Press / USA, Journals Marketing Department, Oxford University Press, 2001 Evans Road, Cary NC 27513.**)** **LC** K9; .N379. **DD** 344/.42/0105. **[CCC].** available on microfilm and microfiche from University Microfilms International (UMI). ***Continues*** *Industrial Law Society (Great Britain). Bulletin of the Industrial Law Society.*
Ind/Abst Appl. Soc. Sci. Index Abstr.; Aust. Leg. Mon. Dig.; Contents Pages Manage.; Index Leg. Period.; Int. Bibliogr. Sociol.; Int. Labour Doc.; LABORDOC; Leg. Resour. Index; LegalTrac (1980-).

MY/0127-3051
INDUSTRIAL LAW REPORTS (KUALA LUMPUR, MALAYSIA). (INDUSTRIAL LAW REPORTS.). **VFOAT** I.L.R.; ILR. (Jan. 1983)-. Periodical. English. mo. 150.00Mal$. Industrial Law Reports, 20 Jalan 1 87E Brickfields, Kuala Lumpur Malaysia. **Tel** 03 449084 5. **ED** Hamid Bin Ibrahim. **Ad Acc. Circ:** 900.

SA
INDUSTRIAL LAWS OF SOUTH AFRICA. **Main/Corp** South Africa. Laws, Statutes, etc. English. ir. R130.00 South Africa; $64.74 US. Juta Subscription Services, PO Box 14373, Kenwyn 7790 South Africa. **Tel** 011 27 21 7975101, FAX (021)761-5010, telex 523072 SA. **ED** A DeKock. **Circ:** 2,790 (ctrl).
Desc: Leading textbook on the complex body of laws which regulate conditions of employment and the employer-employee relationship in South Africa kept up to date by regular revision services.

UK
INDUSTRIAL RELATIONS LAW. (19??)-. Periodical. English. ir. £153.00. Croner Publ Ltd, Croner House, London Road, Kingston upon Thames, Surrey KT2 6SR England. **Tel** 011 44 81 5473333, FAX 081 547-2637.

UK/0969-3637
INDUSTRIAL RELATIONS LAW BULLETIN. (19??)-. Periodical. English. bw. £190.00 UK; £220.00 other. Eclipse Publications Ltd, 18 20 Highbury Place, London N5 1QP England. **Tel** 011 44 71 354 5858. **(Subscription address:** Industrial Relations Services, 18 20 Highbury Place, London N5 1QP England.**)**

US/0145-188X
INDUSTRIAL RELATIONS LAW JOURNAL. ***Title Change.*** [Ind. relat. law j.]. **Added/Corp** University of California, Berkeley. School of Law. (Spring 1976)-(1993). Periodical. English. sa. University of California Press, 2120 Berkeley Way, Berkeley CA 94720. **Tel** (510)642-4191, (510)642-3907, FAX (510)642-9917. **ED** Students of Boalt Hall School of Law, Univ. of California, Berkeley. **LC** K9; .N393. **DD** 344/.73/018905. **[CCC]. Bk Rev. Ad Acc. Circ:** 900 (ctrl). available on microfilm and microfiche from University Microfilms International (UMI). Documents available from UMI Article Clearinghouse. ***Continued by*** *Berkeley Journal of Employment and Labor Law, 1067-7666.*
Desc: Articles concerning industrial and labor relations law.
Ind/Abst ABI/INFORM Glob. Ed. (?-?); ABI Inform Ondisc (Summer 1976-); Crim. Justice Abstr. (-199?); Curr. Law Index (?-?); Gen. BusinessFile (1992-?); Index Leg. Period. (?-?); Leg. Resour. Index (1980-?); LegalTrac (1980-?); Person. Manage. Abstr. (?-?); UMI ABI/Inform--Bus. Period. Ondisc (Jan. 1987-?) [Full Txt.]; Work Relat. Abstr. (?-?).

UK
INDUSTRIAL RELATIONS LAW REPORTS. (Sept. 1972)-. Periodical. English. mo. £320.00 UK; $360.00 other. Eclipse Publications Ltd, 18 20 Highbury Place, London N5 1QP England. **Tel** 011 44 71 354 5858. **(Subscription address:** Industrial Relations Services, 18 20 Highbury Place, London N5 1QP England.**)** **LC** KD3005.A2; I5. **DD** 344.41/01/02642. cum. index.

UK
INDUSTRIAL RELATIONS LEGAL INFORMATION BULLETIN. **Added/Corp** Industrial Relations Services. **VFOAT** Legal Information Bulletin. (19??)-. Periodical. English. sm. £155.00 UK; £175.00 other. Eclipse Publications Ltd, 18 20 Highbury Place, London N5 1QP England. **Tel** 011 44 71 354 5858. **(Subscription address:** Industrial Relations Services, 18 20 Highbury Place, London N5 1QP England.**)** **ED** Marian Bell. **LC** KD3002; .I63. **DD** 344.41/01/05. Index available. cum. index. **Bk Rev. Circ:** 1,500.
Ind/Abst Leg. Resour. Index; LegalTrac (1988-); World Ceram. Abstr.

CN/1192-7283
INDUSTRIAL RELATIONS LEGISLATION IN CANADA. [Ind. relat. legis. Can.]. **Added/Corp** Canada. Labour Canada. (1989)-. English. an. 15.00Can$ Canada; 19.50Can$ other. Canada Communication Group Publishers, Order Processing, Ottawa Ontario K1A 0S9 Canada. **Tel** (819)956-4800, (819)956-4802.

AT
INDUSTRIAL REPORTS. **Added/Corp** Law Book Company. (1992)-. English. Law Book Company Ltd, 44 50 Waterloo Road, North Ryde 2113 Australia. **Tel** 61 2 8870177. **DD** 344.94/0189143/02642; 349.40418914302642. ***Continues*** *Industrial Arbitration Service Industrial Reports, 0728-8417.*
Ind/Abst Aust. Leg. Mon. Dig.

UK/0952-617X
INTERNATIONAL JOURNAL OF COMPARATIVE LABOUR LAW AND INDUSTRIAL RELATIONS, THE. **VFOAT** Comparative Labour Law and Industrial Relations. (19??)-. Periodical. English. Four times a year. $105.00.

Kluwer Law and Taxation Publishers, Staverenstraat 32015, PO Box 23, 7400 GA Deventer Netherlands. **Tel** 011 31 5700 47261. **(Subscription address:** US/Kluwer Law and Taxation, 675 Massachusetts Avenue, Cambridge, MA 02139, telephone: (617-354-0140) **Ind/Abst** Int. Labour Doc.

PO
INTERVENCOES E DESINTERVENCOES DO ESTADO EM EMPRESAS / MINISTERIO DO TRABALHO. **Added/Corp** Portugal. Ministerio do Trabalho. Portugal. Direccao Geral do Trabalho. (1979)-. Periodical. Portuguese. Ministerio do Trabalho, Praca de Londres 2 10 Sala 1, Lisbon Portugal. **LC** HD3616.P8; I57. **DD** 338.9469/005.

●US/1068-4239
IOMA'S REPORT ON COMPENSATION & BENEFITS FOR LAW OFFICES. **See** Economics-Labor.

US/1075-962X
IOWA EMPLOYMENT LAW LETTER. English. mo. $95.00. M. Lee Smith Publishers and Printers, 162 4th Avenue North, PO Box 198867, Nashville TN 37219. **Tel** (615)242-7395, (800)274-6774, FAX (615)256-6601.

BE
IRE EMPLOYMENT LAW : THE INTERNATIONAL NEWSLETTER ON ENGAGEMENTS AND DISMISSALS. Newsletter. English. qt. $195.00. ECS Wyatt Company SA, 273 Ave de Tervuren Boite 4, 1150 Brussels Belgium. **Tel** 011 32 2 7719910. **ED** M. Groushro. **Bk Rev**.

BE
JOURNAL DES TRIBUNAUX DU TRAVAIL. (19??)-. Periodical. French (Dutch). tm (44 issues per year). 9500F. Maison F Larcier SA, 39 rue des Minimes, B-1000 Bruxelles Belgium. **Tel** 011 32 2 512-4712, 512-9679. **LC** KJK1266.3; .J68. **DD** 344.493/01; 344.93041. Index available. **Bk Rev**. **Ind/Abst** Index Foreign Leg. Per.

IE/0790-0473
JOURNAL OF THE IRISH SOCIETY FOR LABOUR LAW. [J. Ir Soc. Labour Law]. **Added/Corp** Irish Society for Labour Law. Vol. 2 (1983)-. English. an (Published in November). £10.00 UK; £10.60 Europe; £11.36 other. University College Faculty of Law, Irish Soc. Lab, Dublin Ireland. **Tel** 011 353 1 693244. **ED** Tony Kerr. **LC** K10; .O84. **DD** 344.415/01; 344.15041. **Bk Rev**. **Ad Acc**. **Pr Rev**. **Circ:** 500. ***Continues** Journal (Irish Society for Labour Law), 0790-0473.*
Ind/Abst Curr. Law Index (1984-); Leg. Resour. Index (1984-); LegalTrac (1984-).

SZ/0378-7362
JUDGMENTS OF THE ADMINISTRATIVE TRIBUNAL OF THE INTERNATIONAL LABOUR ORGANISATION: ORDINARY SESSION. (JUDGMENTS OF THE ADMINISTRATIVE TRIBUNAL OF THE INTERNATIONAL LABOUR ORGANISATION.). [Judgm. Adm. Trib. Int. Labour Organ.: ordin. sess.]. **Main/Corp** International Labour Organisation. Administrative Tribunal. **VFOAT** Judgements of the ILO Administrative Tribunal. (1978)-. English. ir. $52.00. International Labour Office - ILO, Publications Sales Service, CH-1211 Geneva 22 Switzerland. **Tel** 011 41 22 7996111. **(Subscription address:** International Labour Office / Washington, DC, 1828 L Street Northwest, Suite 801, Washington DC 20036.**)** **LC** K1704.23; .J83. **DD** 341.7/63/0268. ***Continues** International Labour Office. Official Bulletin. Series C, 0378-5874.*

CN/0707-2775
JURISPRUDENCE EN DROIT DU TRAVAIL. DECISIONS DES COMMISSAIRES DU TRAVAIL. (JURISPRUDENCE EN DROIT DU TRAVAIL : DECISIONS DES COMMISSAIRES DU TRAVAIL / TRAVAIL-QUEBEC, CENTRE DE RECHERCHE ET STATISTIQUES SUR LE MARCHE DU TRAVAIL.). [Jurisprud. droit trav., Decis. commiss. trav.]. **Main/Corp** Quebec (Province). Centre de Recherche et de Statistiques sur le Marche du Travail. **VAT** Decisions des Commissaires du Travail. V. 11, No. 3 (July/Aug./Sept. 1979)-. Periodical. French. qt. Gouvernement du Quebec, 600 St Amable 4E Etage, Quebec Quebec G1R 4Z1 Canada. **DD** 344.714/01/02646. ***Continues** Jurisprudence en Droit du Travail (Decisions des Commissaires du Travail), 0707-2775.*

●US/1074-0422
KANSAS EMPLOYMENT LAW LETTER. (KANSAS EMPLOYMENT LAW LETTER / FOULSTON & SIEFKIN.). [Kans. employ. law lett.]. **Added/Corp** Foulston & Siefkin. Vol. 1, No. 1 (Apr. 1994)-. English. mo. $95.00. M. Lee Smith Publishers and Printers, 162 4th Avenue North, PO Box 198867, Nashville TN 37219. **Tel** (615)242-7395, (800)274-6774, FAX (615)256-6601. **DD** 344.

US
KANSAS EMPLOYMENT SECURITY LAW, G.S. 1949 ..., THE. **Main/Corp** Kansas. 1949- Ed. English. Kansas Department of Labor, Employment Security Division, Topeka KS 66603. **DD** 331.25444; 368.44.

US/1052-4371
KENTUCKY EMPLOYMENT LAW LETTER. [Ky. employ. law lett.]. **Added/Corp** Greenebaum, Doll & McDonald. (October 1990)-. Periodical. English. mo. $87.00. M. Lee Smith Publishers and Printers, 162 4th Avenue North, PO Box 198867, Nashville TN 37219. **Tel** (615)242-7395, (800)274-6774, FAX (615)256-6601. **ED** Richard Cleary, (address) Greenebaum Doll and McDonald, 3300 First National Tower, Louisville, KY 40202, (phone) 502-589-4200. **DD** 344.
Desc: Newsletter reporting the latest state specific employment law developments that affect companies in that state.

JA
KIKAN RODOHO. **Added/Corp** Sogo Rodo Kenkyujo. **VFOAT** Rodoho. (1951)-. Periodical. Japanese. qt. $128.00. **(Subscription address:** Kyowa Book Company Inc., 1-38 Kanda Jinbo-Cho, Chiyoda-Ku, Tokyo 101, Japan**)** cum. index.

GR
KODIKAS EPITHEORESEOS ERGATIKOU DIKAIOU. Greek, Modern. sm. Aristeidou 9, Athens 105 59 Greece. **LC** KKE1266; .K63. ***Continues** Kodix Epitheoreseos Ergatikou Dikaiou.*

KO
KYONGYONG KWA NODONG. **VFOAT** Management & Labor. Periodical. Korean. W8.500. Hanguk Nosa Munje Yongu Hyophoe, 310-6 4-ka Ulchi-ro, Chung-ku, Seoul South Korea. **LC** HD8730.5.A5; K95.

US/0193-5739
LABOR & EMPLOYMENT LAW. [Labor employ. law]. **Added/Corp** American Bar Association. Section of Labor and Employment Law. **VAT** Labor and Employment Law. Vol. 9, No. 3 (Apr. 1979)-. Periodical. English. an. $6.00. American Bar Association, 750 North Lake Shore Drive, Chicago IL 60611. **Tel** (312)988-5522, (312)988-5241, FAX (312)988-5528, telex 270593. **LC** KF325.15; .A4. **DD** 344/.73/0105. ***Continues** Labor Relations & Employment, 0163-5077.*
Ind/Abst Leg. Resour. Index (1980-); LegalTrac (1982-).

US
LABOR AND EMPLOYMENT LAW ANTHOLOGY. ***Suspended.*** (19??)-Suspended (19??). Periodical. English. an. International Library Law Book Publishers, 101 Lakeforest Boulevard, Suite 270, Gaithersburg MD 20877. **Tel** (800)359-3349, (301)990-7755, FAX (301)990-7642. **ED** Donald J. Hoyes. Index available. **Bk Rev**. **Pr Rev**.
Desc: Contains the selected labor and employment law review articles from over 900 US law review journals. Articles are printed in their entirety.

US/8756-792X
LABOR AND EMPLOYMENT LAW NEWSLETTER. (LABOR AND EMPLOYMENT LAW NEWSLETTER / KAYE, SCHOLER, FIERMAN, HAYS & HANDLER.). [Labor employ. law newsl.]. **Added/Corp** Kaye, Scholer, Fierman, Hays & Handler (Firm) Matthew Bender (Firm). Vol. 1, No. 1 (May 1984)-. Newsletter. English. an. Matthew Bender & Company Inc., 1275 Broadway, Albany NY 12204. **Tel** (800)833-9844, (518)487-3000. **ED** A.S. Christensen. **LC** KF3302; .L3. **DD** 344.73/01/05; 347.304105.

US/0047-3839
LABOR ARBITRATION IN GOVERNMENT. **Added/Corp** American Arbitration Association. (Jan. 1971)-. Periodical. English. Twelve times a year. $120.00. American Arbitration Association, 140 West 51st Street, New York NY 10020. **Tel** (212)484-4011, (212)484-4014, FAX (212)765-4874, telex 12463. **(Subscription address:** LRP Publications, PO Box 980, Horsham PA 19044.**)** **ED** Margaret Gibbons. **LC** KF3409.P77; A494. **DD** 347.304189041353. **Bk Rev**. **Ad Acc**. **Circ:** 3,500.
Desc: Summarizes selected arbitration awards involving public employees. Each case shows the issues, arguments, and the arbitrator's reasoning.

US/1043-5964
LABOR ARBITRATION INDEX (ANNUAL SUMMARY). (LABOR ARBITRATION INDEX.). [Labor arbitr. index]. **Added/Corp** Labor Relations Press. Vol. 1 (1970/1972)-. Periodical. English. an. $145.00. LRP Publications, 747 Dresher Road, PO Box 980, Horsham PA 19044-0980. **Tel** (800)341-7874, (215)784-0860, FAX (215)784-9639, (215)784-0870. **LC** KF3416; .L3. **DD** 331.89/143/0973. cum. index.
Desc: Reference to all published arbitration awards reported in the private, public and federal sectors by LRP, BNA, CCH, and AAA for the previous year. Each award is completely summarized and comprehensively indexed.

US/0744-5253
LABOR ARBITRATION INFORMATION SYSTEM. [Labor arbitr. inf. syst.]. **Added/Corp** Labor Relations Press. **VFOAT** Perspective; LAIS. Vol. 9, No. 1 (Jan. 1982)-. English. mo. $490.00. LRP Publications, 747 Dresher Road, PO Box 980, Horsham PA 19044-0980. **Tel** (800)341-7874, (215)784-0860, FAX (215)784-9639, (215)784-0870. **(Subscription address:** LRP Publications, PO Box 980, Horsham PA 19044.**)** **ED** Cheryl L. Lockett. **LC** KF3416; .L3. **DD** 344.73/0189143; 347.304189143. Index available. cum. index. **Bk Rev**. **Circ:** 400 (ctrl). ***Continues** Labor Arbitration Index, 0195-0762.*
Desc: Abstracts and full-text of 20 arbitration awards monthly. Complete indexing of 17 arbitration reports. Newsletter-arbitration, interviews, bibliographies, statistics, articles, etc.

US/8755-7886
LABOR CONTRACT LAW BULLETIN. [Labor contract law bull.]. **VFOAT** LCB; L.C.B. (April 1984)-. Bulletin. English. Twelve times a year. $61.94. Quinlan Publishing Company, 23 Drydock Avenue, Boston MA 02210-2387. **Tel** (617)542-0048, (800)229-2084, FAX (617)345-9646. **LC** KF3407.A75; L33. **DD** 344.73/0189/05; 347.30418905. **[CCC]**. available on microfilm and microfiche from University Microfilms International (UMI). ***Continues** Collective Bargaining Law Bulletin.*

US
LABOR LAW. (1972)-. English. ir. Matthew Bender & Company Inc., 1275 Broadway, Albany NY 12204. **Tel** (800)833-9844, (518)487-3000.

US/0892-4449
LABOR LAW ANTHOLOGY. ***Suspended.*** (1990)- Suspended (19??). Periodical. English. an. $99.95. International Library Law Book Publishers, 101 Lakeforest Boulevard, Suite 270, Gaithersburg MD 20877. **Tel** (800)359-3349, (301)990-7755, FAX (301)990-7642.

US/0023-6586
LABOR LAW JOURNAL (CHICAGO). (LABOR LAW JOURNAL.). [Labor law j.]. **Added/Corp** Commerce Clearing House. Vol. 1 (Oct. 1949)-. Periodical. English. mo. $120.00. Commerce Clearing House Inc., 4025 West Peterson Avenue, Chicago IL 60646-6085. **Tel** (312)583-8500, FAX (708)940-4600. **ED** A E Schechter. **LC** K12; .A2. **Pr Rev**. available on microfilm and microfiche from University Microfilms International (UMI). Documents available from The Genuine Article.
Desc: Presents significant articles on unions, management, law and government.
Ind/Abst Acad. Search (July 1993-); Bowne Dig. Corp. Sec. Lawyers; Bus. Index (1985-); Bus. Period. Index; Bus. Source (Jul. 1993-); Curr. Contents Soc. Behav. Sci.; Curr. Law Index (1980-); Fed. Tax Artic.; Gen. BusinessFile (1985-); Gen. Period. Index (1985-); High. Educ. Abstr. (1981-); Hospit. Health Admin. Index (v29n1,1978-v40n12,1989); Index Leg. Period.; INFO-SOUTH Abstr.; Int. Bibliogr. Sociol.; Int. Labour Doc.; LABORDOC; Leg. Resour. Index (1980-); LegalTrac (1980-); Mag. Search; PAIS Int. Print (1991-); Res. Alert [Full Cov.]; Soc. Sci. Cit. Index [Full Cov.]; SportSearch; Trade Ind. Index (1981-?);; Wilson Bus. Abstr.; Women Stud. Abstr.; Work Relat. Abstr.

US/0193-1628
LABOR LAW REPORT. [Labor law rep.]. Periodical. English. mo. Matthew Bender & Company Inc., 1275 Broadway, Albany NY 12204. **Tel** (800)833-9844, (518)487-3000. **LC** KF3365; .K47 SUPPL. **DD** 344/.73/0105.

US
LABOR LAW REPORTER. **Added/Corp** Commerce Clearing House. (1965)-. Periodical. English. ir. 483.00Aus$. CCH Australia Ltd, PO Box 230, North Ryde New South Wales, 2113 Australia. **Tel** 011 61 02 888 2555, FAX 011 61 02 888 7324.

US
LABOR LAWS OF INDIANA. **Main/Corp** Indiana. **Added/Corp** Indiana. Dept. of Commerce and Industries. Division of Labor. Indiana. Dept. of Public Works and Commerce. Division of Labor. Indiana. Dept. of Labor. Division of Labor. Indiana. State Chamber of Commerce. (19??)-. English. ir. Indiana Chamber of Commerce, 1 North Capitol / Suite 200, Indianapolis IN 46204. **Tel** (317)264-3110.

US
LABOR LAWS OF MAINE. **Main/Corp** Maine. English. be. $5.00. Maine Labor Department, 20 Union Street, Augusta ME 04333. **Tel** (207)289-3788, FAX (202)289-5292. **LC** KFM331.A29; L3. **DD** 331. ctrl circ.
Desc: Compilation of laws regarding employment of persons in the state of Maine.

US/8756-2995
LABOR LAWYER, THE. [Labor lawyer]. **Added/Corp** American Bar Association. Section of Labor and Employment Law. Vol. 1, No. 1 (Winter 1985)-. Periodical. English. qt. $30.00. American Bar Association, 750 North Lake Shore Drive, Chicago IL 60611. **Tel** (312)988-5522, (312)988-5241, FAX (312)988-5528,

Law —Labor Law

telex 270593. **LC** K12; .A23. **DD** 344.73/01/05; 347.304105. ***Absorbed*** *Committee Reports - Section of Labor and Employment Law, American Bar Association.* **Ind/Abst** Index Leg. Period.; Leg. Resour. Index; LegalTrac (1990-).

US
LABOR RELATIONS MASTER TABLE OF CASES. Vol. 1-45 (Dec. 1935-April 1960)-. English. ir. $72.00. Bureau of National Affairs Inc., 9435 Key West Avenue, Rockville MD 20850. **Tel** (800)372-1033, (301)258-1033, FAX (301)948-5823. **(Subscription telephone:** FAX (301)948-5823**)**

US/1043-5506
LABOR RELATIONS REFERENCE MANUAL. (LABOR RELATIONS REFERENCE MANUAL : THE LAW OF LABOR RELATIONS INCLUDING STATUTES, OPINIONS OF THE COURTS AND DECISIONS OF THE NATIONAL LABOR RELATIONS BOARD.). [Labor relat. ref. man.]. **Added/Corp** United States. National Labor Relations Board. United States. National War Labor Board (1942-1945) Bureau of National Affairs (Washington, D.C.). Vol. 1 (1936/1937)-. English. ir. $80.00 (per copy). Bureau of National Affairs Inc., 9435 Key West Avenue, Rockville MD 20850. **Tel** (800)372-1033, (301)258-1033, FAX (301)948-5823. **ED** Nancy J. Sedmak. **DD** 331. **[CCC]**. cum. index. ***Absorbed in part*** *Labor Relations Reporter, 0148-7981.*
Desc: Contains a table of cases, digest-summaries of all published NLRB decisions, and full-text of opinions of the U.S. Supreme Court, U.S. Courts of Appeals, and other courts.

US/0148-7981
LABOR RELATIONS REPORTER. [Labor relat. rep.]. **VFOAT** BNA Labor Relations Reporter. (1938)-. Periodical. English. ir. $3251.00. Bureau of National Affairs Inc., 9435 Key West Avenue, Rockville MD 20850. **Tel** (800)372-1033, (301)258-1033, FAX (301)948-5823. **DD** 331. **[CCC]**. ***Continues*** *Labor Relations Reports;* ***Absorbed*** *Labor Arbitration Reports, 1043-5514; Wage and Hour Cases, 1043-5689; Occupational Safety & Health Cases, 0095-5515.*
Desc: News and background information on management relations, decisions of boards and courts, and labor arbitration.
Ind/Abst Int. Labour Doc.

CN/0023-690X
LABOUR ARBITRATION CASES.
Added/Corp Central Ontario Industrial Relations Institute. Ontario Labour-Management Arbitration Commission. Ontario. Office of Arbitration. (1948)-. Periodical. English. bw. 115.00Can$. Canada Law Book Inc., 240 Edward Street, Aurora Ontario L4G 3S9 Canada. **Tel** (800)263-3269, (905)841-6472, FAX (905)841-5085. **ED** C.G. Simmons. **Ad Acc.**
Desc: Series of labor reports devoted solely to the reporting of Grievance Awards from all Canadian Provinces and jurisdictions.

CN/0821-2635
LABOUR ARBITRATION (VANCOUVER, B.C.). (LABOUR ARBITRATION.). [Lab. arbitrat.]. (1981)-. English. an. 70.00Can$. Continuing Legal Education Society of British Columbia, 203-1148 Hornby Street, Vancouver British Columbia V6Z 2C3 Canada. **Tel** (604)669-3544, FAX (604)669-9260. **LC** KEB404.3; .L28. **DD** 344.711/0189143. ***Continues*** *Current Problems in Labour Arbitration, 0821-2627.*

SZ/1014-7071
LABOUR LAW DOCUMENTS. Added/Corp International Labour Office. Vol. 1 (1990)-. Periodical. English. Three times a year. $68.00. International Labour Office - ILO, Publications Sales Service, CH-1211 Geneva 22 Switzerland. **Tel** 011 41 22 7996111. **(Subscription address:** International Labour Office / Washington, DC, 1828 L Street Northwest, Suite 801, Washington DC 20036.**) LC** K1701.2; .L3. **DD** 341.7/63/05. ***Continues*** *Legislative Series (Geneva, Switzerland), 0020-7764.*
Desc: Includes the most important texts of international conventions, laws and regulations enacted throughout the world on labour and social security.

II/0023-6977
LABOUR LAW JOURNAL. Added/Corp India. Courts. (Apr. 1949)-. Periodical. English. ir. $12.00. Current Book House, Maruti La Raghunath Dadaju Street, Bombay 1 India.
Desc: Includes chiefly reports of the Supreme Court and High Courts of India.
Ind/Abst Bus. Period. Index; Hospit. Health Admin. Index; Wilson Bus. Abstr.

CN/0848-5917
LABOUR LAW UPDATE. [Labour law update]. **Added/Corp** Canada. Labour Canada. Vol. 1, No. 1 (1990)-. Periodical. English. qt. 30.00Can$ Canada; 39.00Can$ other. Receiver General for Canada / Ottawa, Canada Comm Group Publishing, Ottawa Ontario K1A 0S9 Canada. **Tel** (819)956-4802, (800)661-2868. **DD** 016.34471/01/05.

CN/0823-1494
LABOUR TIMES. [Labour times]. **Added/Corp** Richard De Boo Limited. (19??)-. Periodical. English. mo. Richard de Boo Ltd, 70 Richmond Street East, Toronto Ontario N5C 1M8 Canada. **Tel** (416)445-4940. **DD** 344.71/01.

SW
LAG & [I.E. OCH] AVTAL. Added/Corp Stiftelsen Arbetsrattslig Tidskrift (Stockholm, Sweden). **VFOAT** Arbetsrattslig Tidskrift Lag & Avtal. (19??)-. Periodical. Swedish. ir (9 issues). Kr406.00 Sweden; Kr325.00 other. Lag Och Avtal, Box 5191, 102-44 Stockholm Sweden. **Tel** 011 46 8 6679685. **ED** Kerstin Ahlberg. **LC** K12; .A3. Index available. **Bk Rev. Ad Acc. Circ:** 9,046 (ctrl). available on audiocassette (for the blind).
Desc: Reports on Labour Court judgements, working environment cases and how statutes are applied at workplaces; includes new statutes, ordinances and agreements, debate articles and a diary covering collective-bargaining agreements.

CN
LANCASTER LABOUR LAW REPORTS. 2, LABOUR LAW NEWS. VFOAT Labour Law News. Vol. 15, No. 1 (Jan. 1989)-. Periodical. English. mo. 195.00Can$. Lancaster House Publishing, PO Box 133, 20 Dundas Street West, Toronto Ontario M5G 2G8 Canada. **Tel** (416)977-6618, FAX (416)977-5873. **Circ:** 1300. ***Continues*** *Labour Law News, 0380-2787.*

●CN/1194-4552
LANCASTER'S CONSTRUCTION INDUSTRY EMPLOYMENT LAW NEWS. [Lancaster's const. ind. employ. law news]. **Added/Corp** Lancaster House (Firm). **VFOAT** Construction Industry Employment Law News. Vol. 8, No. 9 (Sept. 1992)-. Periodical. English. mo. 125.00Can$. Lancaster House Publishing, PO Box 133, 20 Dundas Street West, Toronto Ontario M5G 2G8 Canada. **Tel** (416)977-6618, FAX (416)977-5873. **DD** 344.71/01769/00264. ***Continues*** *Construction Industry Employment Law., 0827-4614.*

●CN/1194-398X
LANCASTER'S WRONGFUL DISMISSAL EMPLOYMENT LAW NEWS. [Lanc. wrongful dismiss. employ. law news]. **Added/Corp** Lancaster House (Firm). **VFOAT** Wrongful Dismissal Employment Law News. Vol. 8, No. 9 (Sept. 1992)-. Periodical. English. mo. $95.00. Lancaster House Publishing, PO Box 133, 20 Dundas Street West, Toronto Ontario M5G 2G8 Canada. **Tel** (416)977-6618, FAX (416)977-5873. **DD** 344.71/012596. ***Continues*** *Wrongful Dismissal Employment Law., 0827-4673.*

IT
LAVORO 80. QUADERNI. VFOAT Lavoro Ottanta; Quaderni di Lavoro 80; Quaderni di Lavoro Ottanta. (1982)-. Periodical. Italian. Edaco / Via Padino 23, 20124 Milan Italy. **LC** K12; .A83. **DD** 344.45/0105; 344.504105.

IT
LAVORO E DIRITTO. Vol. 1, No. 1 (Jan. 1987)-. Periodical. Italian. qt. L90000.00 Italy; L120000.00 (surface mail), L150000.00 (airmail) other. Editrice Turistica SRL, Via Rasella 155, 00187 Rome Italy. **Tel** 011 39 6 4821539. **LC** K12; .A84. **DD** 344/.01/05; 342.4105. cum. index.

IT/0390-251X
LAVORO E PREVIDENZA OGGI. [Lavoro previd. oggi]. (Jan. 1974)-. Italian. mo. L140000 (Italy); L195000 (other). Giuffre Editore SPA, Via Busto Arsizio 40, 20151 Milan Italy. **Tel** 011 398 2 38089200. **ED** Eldo Chericomi. Index available. **Bk Rev. Ad Acc. Circ:** 2,100.
Desc: This journal gives information on laws, collective workers' agreements, jurisprudential decision and circulars issued by the government and welfare organizations.
Ind/Abst Int. Labour Doc.

US/0747-6469
LAW AND THE WORKPLACE. Periodical. English. bm. Proskauer Rose Goetz & Mendelssohn, 300 Park Avenue, New York NY 10022. **LC** KF3314; .L38. **DD** 344.73/01; 347.3041.

US
LAW OF WORKMEN'S COMPENSATION. (19??)-. English. ir. Matthew Bender & Company Inc., 1275 Broadway, Albany NY 12204. **Tel** (800)833-9844, (518)487-3000.

US/0458-9599
LEGAL-LEGISLATIVE REPORTER NEWS BULLETIN. Added/Corp International Foundation of Employee Benefit Plans. National Foundation of Health, Welfare and Pension Plans. (Jan. 1967)-. Periodical. English. ir. $425.00 group membership; $225.00 individuals. International Foundation of Employee Benefit Plans, PO Box 69, 18700 West Bluemound Road, Brookfield WI 53008-0069. **Tel** (414)786-6700. **ED** William J. Curtin. **LC** KF3512.A16; L4. **DD** 340. **[CCC]**. cum. index. **Circ:** 27,500. available in microform.
Desc: Review of recent U.S. law and cases in the area of employee benefits.

FR/0223-4726
LEGI SOCIAL. (19??)-. Periodical. French. Eleven times a year. 440.74F France; 545.00F others. Revue Fiduciaire, 100 rue la Fayette, 75485 Paris Cedex 10 France. **Tel** 011 33 1 48408044. **DD** 344.44/005; 344.404005.

US
LEGISLATIVE DIGEST : BILLS OF LABOR INTEREST PASSED BY THE NEW YORK STATE LEGISLATURE.
Main/Corp New York (State). Dept. of Labor. English. wk. State Document Room or the Assembly Document Room, Capitol Building, Albany NY 12224. **LC** KFN5556; .A473. **DD** 344.747/01/0262; 347.470410262. ***Continues*** *Legislative Digest of Labor and Related Bills Introduced in the New York State Legislature.*

BL
LIVLEX TRABALHISTA. Portuguese. Editorial Dimensao, rua da Quitada 45, 30 Andar GB, Rio de Janeiro Brazil.

●US/1059-5058
LOUISIANA EMPLOYMENT LAW LETTER. [La. employ. law lett.]. Vol. 1, No. 1 (Apr. 1992)-. Periodical. English. mo. $95.00. M. Lee Smith Publishers and Printers, 162 4th Avenue North, PO Box 198867, Nashville TN 37219. **Tel** (615)242-7395, (800)274-6774, FAX (615)256-6601. **ED** H. Mark Adams and Mary Ellen Jordan, (address) Jones, Walker, Waecheter, Poitevaent, Carrere and Denegre, Place St. Charles Avenue, New Orleans, LA 70170, (phone)504-582-8000. **DD** 344.
Desc: Newsletter reporting the latest state specific employment law developments that affect companies in that state.

US/0748-3120
MAINE BUSINESS AND EMPLOYMENT LAW. See Law-Corporate Law.

●US
MANAGEMENT POLICIES AND PERSONNEL LAW. VFOAT MPPL. (Jan. 1992)-. Periodical. English. bw. $395.00. Business Research Publications, 1333 H Street Northwest, 2nd Floor West, Washington DC 20005. **Tel** (202)842-3022, (800)822-6338, FAX (202)842-3023. **LC** HF5549.A2; M363. ***Formed by the union of*** *White Collar Management, 1040-4244; Personnel Policy Briefs, 1040-4252; Your Business and the Law (Business Research Publications, Inc.), 1040-4260* ***and*** *Creative Management, 1040-421X.*
Ind/Abst Int. Aerosp. Abstr.

UK/0309-0558
MANAGERIAL LAW. [Manage. law]. Vol. 18 (1975)-. English. bm. $1499.00. MCB University Press, 60 62 Toller Lane, Bradford West Yorkshire BD8 9BX England. **Tel** 011 44 274 499821, FAX 011 44 274 547143, telex 51317 MCBUNI G. **(Subscription address:** MCB University Press / US and Canada Subscriptions, PO Box 10812, Birmingham AL 35201-0812.**) ED** Jo Carby-Hall and Barrie O Pettnan. **LC** KD3006.A2; K57. **DD** 344/.42/0102638; 344.204102638. available on an online database (file 15/Full-Text) from DIALOG. Documents available from UMI Article Clearinghouse. ***Continues*** *Knight's Industrial Law Reports.*
Desc: Helps managers become conversant with implications of business legislation, in areas such as labor relations, employment conditions, training, marketing, physical distribution, production and more.
Ind/Abst ABI/INFORM Glob. Ed.; ABI Inform Ondisc (1986-).

US/0889-4493
MANAGER'S LEGAL BULLETIN. (MANAGER'S LEGAL BULLETIN / ALEXANDER HAMILTON INSTITUTE INCORPORATED.). [Manager's leg. bull.]. **Added/Corp** Alexander Hamilton Institute (U.S.). Vol. 1, No. 1 (July 1, 1986)-. Periodical. English. Twenty-four times a year. Price varies. Alexander Hamilton Institute Inc, 70 Hilltop Road, Ramsey NJ 07446-1119. **Tel** (201)825-8161, FAX (201)825-8696. **LC** KF3455.A15; M36. **DD** 344.73/01/05; 347.304105. Index available. **Circ:** 30,000.

US/1049-9377
MARYLAND EMPLOYMENT LAW LETTER. [Md. employ. law lett.]. (August 1990)-. Periodical. English. mo. $95.00. M. Lee Smith Publishers and Printers, 162 4th Avenue North, PO Box 198867, Nashville TN 37219. **Tel** (615)242-7395, (800)274-6774, FAX (615)256-6601. **ED** George Johnston and Patrick Stewart, (address) Venable, Baetjer and Howard, 2 Hopkins Plaza, Baltimore, MD 21201, (phone) 301-244-7586. **LC** KFM1534.A15; M37. **DD** 344.752/0105; 347.5204105.
Desc: Newsletter reporting the latest state specific employment law developments that affect companies in that state.

IT
MASSIMARIO DI GIURISPRUDENZA DEL LAVORO. VFOAT Giurisprudenza del Lavoro. (1925)-. Periodical. Italian. Six times a year. L130000 Italy; L170000 other. Servizio Italiano Pubblicazioni International, Viale Pasteur 6, 00144 Rome Italy. **Tel** 011 39 6 5920509, telex 614567 SIPIRM I. **ED** Giorgio Gramiccia. Index available. cum. index. **Ad Acc. Circ:** 3,500.
Desc: Furnishes texts of most important legal decision, concerning Italian labor, with editorial notes of interest to business and labor management.

FR
MEMENTO PRATIQUE FRANCIS LEFEBVRE: SOCIAL. (19??)-. French. Editions Francis Lefebvre, 5 rue Jacques Bingen, F-75854 Paris Cedex 17 France. **Tel** (1)47 63 12 60, FAX 46 22 72 66, telex 649 470 F. **DD** 344.44/02. **NLM** W 32.5; GF7 M5.
Desc: Contains information on legislation.

US/1046-9109
MICHIGAN EMPLOYMENT LAW LETTER. [Mich. employ. law lett.]. Vol. 1, No. 1 (Mar. 1990)-. Periodical. English. mo. $95.00. M. Lee Smith Publishers and Printers, 162 4th Avenue North, PO Box 198867, Nashville TN 37219. **Tel** (615)242-7395, (800)274-6774, FAX (615)256-6601. **ED** David Mikesell and Frank Mamat, (address) Honigman Miller Schwartz and Cohn, 2290 First National Building, Detroit, MI 48226-3583, (phone)313-256-7321. **DD** 346.
Desc: Newsletter reporting the latest state specific employment law developments that affect companies in that state.

US/0746-1461
MICHIGAN WORKERS' COMP DIGEST. ***Ceased.*** Vol. 1, No. 1 (Dec. 1982)-Ceased Vol. 10, No. 6 (June 1992). Periodical. English. mo. Pathfinder Associates, PO Box 5240, North Muskegon MI 49445. **Tel** (616)744-8462. **ED** Ronald E Hauxwell. **LC** KFM4542.A59; M5. **DD** 344.774/021/05; 347.74042105.
Desc: A summary of key Michigan's workers' compensation news and cases.

US/0899-9090
MICHIGAN WORKERS' COMPENSATION LAW REPORTER. [Mich. work. compens. law report.]. **Added/Corp** LRP Publications (Firm). **VFOAT** Workers' Compensation Law Reporter. Vol. 1 (1988)-. Periodical. English. Seven times a year. $495.00. LRP Publications, 747 Dresher Road, PO Box 980, Horsham PA 19044-0980. **Tel** (800)341-7874, (215)784-0860, FAX (215)784-9639, (215)784-0870. **DD** 344.
Desc: A full-text subscription service reporting the decisions of the new Michigan Appellate Commission, the existing Appeal Board and State Court Appeals. Indexed, summarized and headnoted.

US/1054-6367
MINNESOTA EMPLOYMENT LAW LETTER. [Minn. employ. law lett.]. **Added/Corp** Felhaber, Larson, Fenlon & Vogt, P.A. (March 1991)-. Periodical. English. mo. $87.00. M. Lee Smith Publishers and Printers, 162 4th Avenue North, PO Box 198867, Nashville TN 37219. **Tel** (615)242-7395, (800)274-6774, FAX (615)256-6601. **ED** Edward Bohrer and Stephen Burton, (address) Felhaber, Larson, Fenlon and Vogt, P.A. 222 South 9th Street, Suite 1935 Minneapolis, MN 55402-9174, (phone)612-339-6321. **DD** 344.
Desc: Newsletter reporting the latest state specific employment law developments that affect companies in that state.

●US/1074-0430
MISSISSIPPI EMPLOYMENT LAW LETTER. (MISSISSIPPI EMPLOYMENT LAW LETTER / WATKINS, LUDLAM & STENNIS.). [Miss. employ. law lett.]. **Added/Corp** Watkins, Ludlam & Stennis. Vol. 1, No. 1 (Apr. 1994)-. English. mo. $95.00. M. Lee Smith Publishers and Printers, 162 4th Avenue North, PO Box 198867, Nashville TN 37219. **Tel** (615)242-7395, (800)274-6774, FAX (615)256-6601. **DD** 344.

US/1054-6375
MISSOURI EMPLOYMENT LAW LETTER. [Mo. employ. law lett.]. **Added/Corp** Lashly & Baer, P.C. (March 1991)-. Periodical. English. mo. $94.00. M. Lee Smith Publishers and Printers, 162 4th Avenue North, PO Box 198867, Nashville TN 37219. **Tel** (615)242-7395, (800)274-6774, FAX (615)256-6601. **ED** Vance Miller and Robert Kaiser, (address) Lashly and Baer, 714 Locust Street, St. Louis, MO 63101, (phone) 314-621-2939. **DD** 344.
Desc: Newsletter reporting the latest state specific employment law developments that affect companies in that state.

US/0749-4637
MSPB/FLRA CASE DECISIONS. (MSPB/FLRA CASE DECISIONS : MERIT SYSTEMS PROTECTION BOARD & FEDERAL LABOR RELATIONS AUTHORITY.). [MSPB/FLRA case decis.]. **VFOAT** Merit Systems Protection Board & Federal Labor Relations Authority; FLRA Case Decisions; M.S.P.B./F.L.R.A. Case Decisions. **VAT** Merit Systems Protection Board Federal Labor Relations Authority Case Decisions; Federal Labor Relations Authority Case Decisions. Periodical. English. mo. Information Handling Services, 15 Inverness Way East, Englewood CO 80150. **Tel** (800)525-7052, (303)790-0600, FAX (303)397-2599, telex 4322083. **DD** 342.

US/0893-8172
MUNICIPAL WORKER LAW BULLETIN. [Munic. work. law bull.]. **VFOAT** MWLB. Vol. 13, No. 5 (May 1987)-. Bulletin. English. mo. $59.89. Quinlan Publishing Company, 23 Drydock Avenue, Boston MA 02210-2387. **Tel** (617)542-0048, (800)229-2084, FAX (617)345-9646. **DD** 342. **[CCC]**. available on microfilm and microfiche from University Microfilms International (UMI). ***Continues*** *Public Employee Law Bulletin, 0739-9294.*

US/0160-2586
NATIONAL DIRECTORY OF PROGRESSIVE AND RANK & FILE LABOR LAWYERS. **VAT** National Directory of Progressive and Rank and File Labor Lawyers. 1977-. Directory. English. $2.50. 712 South Grand View Street, Los Angeles CA 90057. **LC** KF195.L3; N37. **DD** 344/.73/01025.

CN/0835-8087
NATIONAL LABOUR REVIEW. ***Ceased.*** [Natl. labour rev.]. Vol. 1, No. 1 (Oct./Dec. 1987)-(19??). Periodical. English. qt. Jewel Publications, 316 Dufferin Road, Montreal Quebec H3X 2Y5 Canada. **Tel** (514)486-9662. **DD** 344.71/01/05.
Ind/Abst Can. Legal Lit.

US/0194-889X
NATIONAL PUBLIC EMPLOYMENT REPORTER. [Natl. public employ. report.]. **Added/Corp** Labor Relations Press. Public Employment Relations Services (U.S.). Vol. 1, (1979)-. Periodical. English. qt. $480.00. LRP Publications, 747 Dresher Road, PO Box 980, Horsham PA 19044-0980. **Tel** (800)341-7874, (215)784-0860, FAX (215)784-9639, (215)784-0870. **(Subscription address:** LRP Publications, PO Box 980, Horsham PA 19044.**) ED** Joan Grossman. **LC** KF3580.G6; A496. **DD** 344.73/0189041353/0002648. Index available. cum. index. **Circ:** 300 (ctrl). available on microfiche.
Desc: Abstracts of nationwide state labor board decisions, complete indexing, many access points, table of cases, citation tracker, microfiche option, parallel database, off-line searches.

US/0278-7636
NEBRASKA WORKMEN'S COMPENSATION REHEARING DECISIONS. Vol. 1, No. 1 (Nov. 9, 1981)-. Periodical. English. qt. $19.50. Mason Publishing Company, 289 East 5th Street, St Paul MN 55101-1904. **LC** KFN342; .A555. **DD** 344.782/021/02648; 347 82042102648.

US/0197-5978
NEGOTIATIONS. English. an. New Jersey School Boards Association, 315 West State Street, PO Box 909, Trenton NJ 08605. **Tel** (609)695-7600. **LC** KFN2132.8.T4; A138. **DD** 344.749/01890413711; 347. 49041890413711. ***Continues*** *Negotiations, 0197-5978.*

GW
NEUE ZEITSCHRIFT FUER ARBEITS UND SOZIALRECHT. ***Ceased.*** **VFOAT** NZA. 1. Vol. 1/2 (5. July 1984)-(1992). Periodical. German. bw. CH Beck Verlagsbuchhandlung, D 80791 Munich Germany. **Tel** 011 49 89 381891. **LC** K14; .E67. **DD** 344.43/01/05; 344.304105.
Ind/Abst Index Foreign Leg. Per.

US/0893-7133
NEW DEVELOPMENTS IN EMPLOYMENT DISCRIMINATION. [New dev. employ. discrim.]. **VFOAT** Employment Discrimination. (1987)-. Periodical. English. qt. $65.00. Butterworth Legal Publishers / Salem, NH, 8 Industrial Way, Building C, Salem NH 03079. **Tel** (800)548-4001, (603)898-9664. **ED** Michael Weisberg. **DD** 344.
Ind/Abst Vocat. Search (July 1993-).

●US/1064-2390
NEW JERSEY EMPLOYMENT LAW LETTER. [N.J. employ. law lett.]. **VFOAT** Employment Law Letter. (October 1992)-. Periodical. English. mo. $94.00. M. Lee Smith Publishers and Printers, 162 4th Avenue North, PO Box 198867, Nashville TN 37219. **Tel** (615)242-7395, (800)274-6774, FAX (615)256-6601. **ED** Joseph Fortunato, Edward Lynch, Gregory Parliman, Patrick McCarthy and Theresa Donahue Egler, (address) Pitney, Hardin, Kipp and Szuch, 200 Campus Drive, Florham Park, NJ 07932, (phone) 201-966-6300. **DD** 344.
Desc: Newsletter reporting the latest state specific employment law developments that affect companies in that state.

AT/0028-677X
NEW SOUTH WALES INDUSTRIAL GAZETTE. **Main/Corp** New South Wales. Dept. of Industrial Relations. **Added/Corp** New South Wales. Dept. of Industrial Relations. Industrial Gazette. **VFOAT** NSW Industrial Gazette; N.S.W. Industrial Gazette. Vol. 217, Pt. 1 (Apr. 1980)-. English. Fifty-two times a year. 584.00Aus$. Department Industrial Relations, PO Box 847, Award Sales Section, Darlinhurst NSW 2010 Australia. **Tel** 011 61 2 266 8387, FAX 011 61 2 266 8321. **LC** HD8849.N48; N48a. **DD** 344.944/01/0264; 349.440410264. Index available (Bound in last iss.). ctrl circ. ***Continues*** *New South Wales Industrial Gazette.*
Desc: Details concerning awards, variations, and official notifications. Also has a trade union section.

●US/1072-9178
NEW YORK EMPLOYMENT LAW LETTER. (NEW YORK EMPLOYMENT LAW LETTER / C.O'MELVENY & MYERS.). [N.Y. employ. law lett.]. **Added/Corp** O'Melveny & Myers. (1994)-. Periodical. English. mo. $95.00. M. Lee Smith Publishers and Printers, 162 4th Avenue North, PO Box 198867, Nashville TN 37219. **Tel** (615)242-7395, (800)274-6774, FAX (615)256-6601. **DD** 344.

US/0194-7354
NEW YORK WORKER'S COMPENSATION COMMENTS. Vol. 1 (Oct. 1978)-. Periodical. English. mo. $25.00. Compensation Comments, 15 Broad Street, Hamilton NY 13346. **Tel** (315)824-1473. **ED** John S. Hogg. **LC** KFN5592.A59; N48. **DD** 344.747/021. **Circ:** 150.
Desc: Covers New York worker's compensation law.

US
NEW YORK WORKERS' COMPENSATION LAW REPORTER. **Added/Corp** LRP Publications (Firm). Vol. 1 (1987)-. Periodical. English. sm. $610.00. LRP Publications, 747 Dresher Road, PO Box 980, Horsham PA 19044-0980. **Tel** (800)341-7874, (215)784-0860, FAX (215)784-9639, (215)784-0870.
Desc: A full-text subscription service reporting all New York Workers' Compensation decisions issued by the Full Board (13-member panel), the Court of Appeals and the Appellate Division and selected 3-Member Panel decisions, indexed and fully headnoted.

US/0194-8784
NLRB ADVICE MEMORANDUM REPORTER. **Added/Corp** Labor Relations Press. United States. National Labor Relations Board. **VAT** National Labor Relations oard Board Advice Memorandum Reporter. (19??)-. Periodical. English. mo. $525.00. LRP Publications, 747 Dresher Road, PO Box 980, Horsham PA 19044-0980. **Tel** (800)341-7874, (215)784-0860, FAX (215)784-9639, (215)784-0870. **(Subscription address:** LRP Publications, PO Box 980, Horsham PA 19044.**)** **LC** KF3438; .A86. **DD** 343.73/072; 347.30372. **[CCC]. Circ:** 270 (ctrl).
Desc: Provides the full text of all available advice memoranda issued by the NLRB General Counsel, cross-referenced under the NLRB's classification numbering system. A special section summarizes the month's important rulings.

US/1054-6359
NORTH CAROLINA EMPLOYMENT LAW LETTER. [N. C. employ. law lett.]. **Added/Corp** Womble, Carlyle, Sandridge & Rice. Vol. 1, No. 1 (Feb. 1991)-. Periodical. English. mo. $95.00. M. Lee Smith Publishers and Printers, 162 4th Avenue North, PO Box 198867, Nashville TN 37219. **Tel** (615)242-7395, (800)274-6774, FAX (615)256-6601. **ED** David Irvin and Richard Rainey, Womble Carlyle Sandridge and Rice, 2400 Wachovia Building, Winston-Salem, NC 27101, (phone)919-721-3600. **DD** 344.
Desc: Newsletter reporting the latest state specific employment law developments that affect companies in that state.

KO
NOSA MUNJE SARYE YONGUJIP. V. 1-Series; 1972-. Korean. 2500. Hanguk Nosa Munje Yongu Hyophoe, 310-6 4-ka Ulchi-ro, Chung-ku, Seoul South Korea. **LC** K14; .O78.

UK/0967-8115
OCCUPATIONAL PENSIONS LAW REPORTS. (1992)-. Periodical. English. ir. £255.00 UK; £275.00 other. Eclipse Publications Ltd, 18 20 Highbury Place, London N5 1QP England. **Tel** 011 44 71 354 5858.

PH
OFFICE OF THE PRESIDENT DECISIONS ON LABOR ISSUES, WITH DOCTRINAL SUMMARIES AND NOTES. V. 1-. English. an. Philippine Law Gazette, 13 Mapayapa Street, UP Village, Diliman Quezon City, 3004 Philippines. **Tel** 921-6356.

SZ/0378-5882
OFFICIAL BULLETIN. SERIES A / INTERNATIONAL LABOUR OFFICE. [Off. bull. - Int. Labour Office, Ser. A]. **Main/Corp** International Labour Office. **Added/Corp** International Labour Office. Vol. 58, No. 1 (1975)-. Periodical. English. Three times a year. $112.00 (combined subscription with Series B). International Labour Office - ILO, Publications Sales Service, CH-1211 Geneva 22 Switzerland. **Tel** 011 41 22

Law —Labor Law

7996111. (**Subscription address:** International Labour Office / Washington, DC, 1828 L Street Northwest, Suite 801, Washington DC 20036.) Index available. *Continues in part* Official Bulletin (International Labour Office : 1921), 0020-7772.
Desc: Information on the activities of the ILO, texts adopted by the International Labour Conference and other official documents.
Ind/Abst Middle East Abstr. Index.

US/1046-9206
OHIO EMPLOYMENT LAW LETTER. [Ohio empl. law lett.]. Vol. 1, No. 1 (Jan. 1990)-. Periodical. English. mo. $95.00. M. Lee Smith Publishers and Printers, 162 4th Avenue North, PO Box 198867, Nashville TN 37219. **Tel** (615)242-7395, (800)274-6774, FAX (615)256-6601. **ED** Dean Denlinger and Gary Greenberg, (address) Denlinger, Rosenthal and Greenberg, 425 Walnut Street, Suite 2310, Cincinnati, OH 45202, (phone)513-621-3440. **LC** KFO331.A15; O38. **DD** 344.771/01/05; 347.7104105.
Desc: Newsletter reporting the latest state specific employment law developments that affect companies in that state.

US/1060-7781
OHIO EMPLOYMENT PRACTICES LAW MONTHLY. *Ceased.* [Ohio employ. pract. law mon.]. **VFOAT** Employment Practices Law Monthly; Monthly. (1992)-(Dec. 1993). Periodical. English. mo. Banks-Baldwin Law Publishing Company, PO Box 1974, University Center, Cleveland OH 44106. **Tel** (216)721-7373. **DD** 344.

●CN/1195-0196
ONTARIO LABOUR AND EMPLOYMENT LEGISLATION. (1993)-. English. an. 35.00Can$. Canada Law Book Inc., 240 Edward Street, Aurora Ontario L4G 3S9 Canada. **Tel** (800)263-3269, (905)841-6472, FAX (905)841-5085.
Desc: Acts as a single source for Ontario labour and employment statutes and regulations.

US
OPINIONS ON REVIEW FOR THE YEAR ... / STATE OF MICHIGAN, DEPARTMENT OF LABOR, WORKERS' COMPENSATION APPEAL BOARD AND APPELLATE COMMISSION. **Main/Corp** Michigan. Workers' Compensation Appeal Board. English. mo. $1222.00. Opinions Press, Box 1095, Big Rapids MI 49307-0995. **Tel** (616)796-3236. **LC** KFM4542; .A555. **DD** 344.774/021; 347.740421. Index available. cum. index. **Circ:** 200 (ctrl).
Desc: Judicial opinions, headnoted and indexed, also indexed by case names.

AU
OSTERREICHISCHE LANDESBERICHTE ZUM INTERNATIONALEN KONGRESS FUER DAS RECHT DER ARBEIT UND DER SOZIALEN SICHERHEIT. **Main/Conf** International Congress of Labour Law and Social Security. **Added/Corp** Osterreichische Gesellschaft fuer Arbeitsrecht und Sozialrecht. (19??)-. German. ir.

PK/0552-9069
PAKISTAN LABOUR GAZETTE. [Pak. labour gaz.]. Began with issue for Apr. 1953. English. qt. Rs16.00 Pakistan; $40.00 US. NGM Communication, PO Box 2627, Karachi 75900 Pakistan. **Tel** 011 92 21 428625. **Circ:** 250.
Ind/Abst Int. Labour Doc.

US/1052-4363
PENNSYLVANIA EMPLOYMENT LAW LETTER. [Pa. employ. law lett.]. **Added/Corp** Morgan, Lewis & Bockius. (Oct 1990)-. Periodical. English. mo. $95.00. M. Lee Smith Publishers and Printers, 162 4th Avenue North, PO Box 198867, Nashville TN 37219. **Tel** (615)242-7395, (800)274-6774, FAX (615)256-6601. **ED** Harry Reagan and John Krampf, (address) Morgan, Lewis and Bockius, 2000 One Logan Square, Philadelphia, PA 19103-6993, (phone) 215-963-5000. **DD** 344.
Desc: Newsletter reporting the latest state specific employment law developments that affect the companies in that state.

US/0899-9104
PENNSYLVANIA WORKERS' COMPENSATION LAW REPORTER. [Pa. work. compens. law report.]. **VFOAT** Workers' Compensation Law Reporter. (198?)-. Periodical. English. Twenty-four times a year. $610.00. LRP Publications, 747 Dresher Road, PO Box 980, Horsham PA 19044-0980. **Tel** (800)341-7874, (215)784-0860, FAX (215)784-9639, (215)784-0870. **DD** 344.
Desc: A full-text subscription service reporting significant Workmen's Compensation Appeal Board decisions, all Appeals of Board decisions, Selected Third-Party cases and Selected Appeal to the Supreme Court of related cases.

●US/1071-0477
PENSION, PROFIT-SHARING, WELFARE, AND OTHER COMPENSATION PLANS. (PENSION, PROFIT-SHARING, WELFARE, AND OTHER COMPENSATION PLANS : ALI-ABA COURSE OF STUDY MATERIALS.). [Pension profit-sharing welf. compens. plans]. **Added/Corp** American Law Institute-American Bar Association Committee on Continuing Professional Education. **VFOAT** ALI-ABA Course of Study Materials; Pension, Profit-Sharing. (Oct. 15-17, 1992)-. English. an. $150.00. American Law Institute, 4025 Chestnut Street, Philadelphia PA 19104-3099. **Tel** (215)243-1661, (800)253-6397, FAX (215)243-1664. **LC** KF3509.Z9; A14. **DD** 344.73/01252. *Continues* ALI-ABA Course of Study : Pension, Profit Sharing, and Other Deferred Compensation Plans., 0191-3743.

US/0191-0302
PERISCOPE (OXFORD). (PERISCOPE.). English. $175.00. Peris, Box 573, Oxford NY 13830. **LC** KFN5562.P8; A136. **DD** 344.747/01890413539.

US
PERSONNEL LAW UPDATE. Vol. 1, No. 1 (Sept. 1986)-. Periodical. English. mo. $119.00. Council on Education in Management, 325 Lennon Lane, Walnut Creek CA 94598. **Tel** (510)944-5544. **LC** KF3302; .P47. **DD** 344.73/01; 347.3041.
Desc: In each issue, four attorneys alert you to changes in legislation, regulations, and court decisions dealing with personnel management.

PH
PHILIPPINE LABOR REPORTS : DECISIONS AND RULINGS OF SUPREME COURT, NATIONAL LABOR RELATIONS COMMISSION, BUREAU OF LABOR RELATIONS, AND OTHER LABOR AGENCIES. **Added/Corp** Philippines. Supreme Court. Philippines. National Labor Relations Commission. Philippines. Bureau of Labor Relations. Vol. 1, No. 1 (Jan. 1981)-. Periodical. English. mo. Labor Assistance Group Inc, 125 Kamias Road, Quezon City Philippines. **DD** 344.599/01/02648; 345.9904102648.

US/0195-3656
PRACTICAL LABOR LAW: COURSE MANUAL. **Added/Corp** Federal Publications Inc. (19??)-. English. an. Federal Publications Inc, 1120 20th Street Northwest, Washington DC 20036. **Tel** (202)337-7000, (800)922-4330, FAX (202)659-2233. **LC** KF3319.3; .H52. **DD** 344.73/01.

UN
PROBLEMY SOTSIALISTICHESKOI ZAKONNOSTI. **Added/Corp** Kharkivskyi Iurydychnyi Instytut. Vol. 1 (1976)-. Russian. an. Vyshcha Shkola, Ulitsa Universitetskaia 16, Kharkov Ukraine.
Desc: Information on industrial laws and legislation.

US/0193-3418
PROCEEDINGS OF NEW YORK UNIVERSITY ANNUAL NATIONAL CONFERENCE ON LABOR. [Proc. N.Y. Univ. Annu. Natl. Conf. Labor]. **Main/Conf** New York University National Conference on Labor. **Added/Corp** New York University. Institute of Labor Relations. 30th, (1977?)-. Proceedings. English. an. $110.00. Little Brown & Company, 34 Beacon Street, Boston MA 02108. **Tel** (617)227-0730, (800)759-0190. **LC** KF3319.A2; C6. **DD** 344./73/01. available on microfilm from University Microfilms International (UMI). *Continues* Proceedings of New York University ... Annual Conference on Labor, 0069-8563.
Ind/Abst Index Leg. Period.; Int. Labour Doc.; Leg. Resour. Index (1980-?).

US/0197-0232
PUBLIC EMPLOYEE RELATIONS COUNSELLOR. V. 1-. Periodical. English. I P M A, 1617 Duke Street, Alexandria VA 22314. **LC** KF5365.A15; P8. **DD** 342.73/068/05.

US/0734-726X
PUBLIC SECTOR LABOR RELATIONS. [Public sect. labor relat.]. English. an. Practising Law Institute, 810 Seventh Avenue, New York NY 10019-5818. **Tel** (212)765-5700, FAX (212)581-4670 general correspondence, (212)265-4742 orders and billing inquiries. **LC** KF3409.P77; P8. **DD** 344.73/0189041353; 347.304189041353.

AT/0155-9362
QUEENSLAND GOVERNMENT INDUSTRIAL GAZETTE, THE. (19??)-. Periodical. English. Fifty-one times per year. 280.00Aus$. Goprint Publications, PO Box 364, Woolloongaba Queenslands 4102 Australia. **Tel** 011 61 7 2463659. **LC** HD8881; .A4. **DD** 331.89/09943. *Continues* Queensland. Industrial Gazette.
Ind/Abst Aust. Leg. Mon. Dig.

US/0899-0794
RECENT TITLES IN LAW FOR THE SUBJECT SPECIALIST. LABOR AND EMPLOYMENT. [Recent titles law subj. spec., Labor employ.]. **Added/Corp** Ward & Associates. **VFOAT** Labor and Employment. Vol. 5, No. 1 (Jan./Mar. 1988)-. English. qt. $85.00. Ward & Associates, 317 South Division, Suite 66, Ann Arbor MI 48104. **Tel** (313)665-3520, FAX (313)665-7880. **LC** K1701; .N37. **DD** 016.344/04/05; 016.3424405. *Continues* National Legal Bibliography. Subject Area List. Labor and Employment, 8755-8068.

AU
RECHT DER ARBEIT / [HERAUSGEBER OSTERREICHISCHER ARBEITERKAMMERTAG], DAS. **Added/Corp** Osterreichischer Arbeiterkammertag. **VFOAT** D.R.d.A.; DRdA. (19??)-. Periodical. German. bm (6 issues). DM220.00. CH Beck Verlagsbuchhandlung, D 80791 Munich Germany. **Tel** 011 49 89 381891. **LC** K18; .E225. **DD** 344.436/01/05; 344.3.604105.

SP
REGLAMENTACION DEL SECTOR LABORAL. **Main/Corp** Spain. Spanish. 250. Fernando No 30, Barcelona Spain.

SP
REGLAMENTACION LABORAL, INDUSTRIA Y COMERCIO. **Main/Corp** Spain. Laws, Statutes, etc. Spanish. 300. Ediciones Alvarez, Paseo de Gracia 23, Barcelona Spain.

PY
REPERTORIO LABORAL (ASUNCION, PARAGUAY). (REPERTORIO LABORAL.). Periodical. Spanish. 3.000. Calle Azara, 180 Casi Independencia Nacional, Oficina 110, Asuncion Paraguay. **DD** 344.892/01/05; 348.9204105.

US/0148-3633
REPORT AND RECOMMENDATIONS TO THE GOVERNOR AND THE GENERAL ASSEMBLY. **Main/Corp** Illinois. Commission on Labor Laws. 1971-. English. Commission on Labor Laws, Room 202/State Office Building, Springfield IL 62706. **LC** KFI1531; .A843. **DD** 344/.773/01.

US/0147-3611
REPORT OF CASE DECISIONS. (REPORT OF CASE DECISIONS / FEDERAL LABOR RELATIONS AUTHORITY.). [Rep. case decis.]. **Main/Corp** United States. Federal Labor Relations Authority. **VFOAT** FLRA Report of Case Decisions; FLRA Report of Case Decisions and FSIP Releases. **VAT** Federal Labor Relations Authority Report of Case Decisions. (Apr. 19, 1979)-. Government Publication. English. ir. Superintendent of Documents, US Government Printing Office, Washington DC 20402. **Tel** (202) 275-3328, FAX (202)786-2377. *Continues* Federal Labor Relations Council (U.S.). Report of Case Decisions, 0147-3611.

IE
REPORTS OF IMPORTANT DECISIONS BY THE EMPLOYMENT APPEALS TRIBUNAL UNDER THE UNFAIR DISMISSALS ACT, 1977. **Main/Corp** Ireland. Employment Appeals Tribunal. Years 1977 and 1978-. English. ir. $2.47 U.S. Government Publications, 4 5 Harcourt Road, Dublin 2 Ireland. **Tel** 011 353 1 6613111 Ext.4005. **LC** KDK820; .A5557. **DD** 344.415/012596; 344.150412596. **Circ:** 1,000.

BL/0102-8774
REVISTA DE DIREITO DO TRABALHO (SAO PAULO). (REVISTA DE DIREITO DO TRABALHO.). [Rev. direito trab.]. (Jan./March 1976)-. Periodical. Portuguese. Six times a year. $50.00. Editorial Saraiva, Avenue Marechal Rondon 2231, 20950 001 Rio Janerio Brazil. (**Subscription address:** Revista de Direito do Trabalho, Avenue Rio Branco 109 703, 20054 Rio de Janeiro Brazil.) **ED** Alvaro Malheiros. **LC** K19; .D599. **DD** 344/.81/01. **Bk Rev**. **Ad Acc**. **Circ:** 5,000.
Desc: Commentaries, leading articles and jurisprudence of labor law.
Ind/Abst Int. Labour Doc.

BL/0048-7813
REVISTA LTR. [Rev. LTR]. **VFOAT** LTR. Periodical. Portuguese. mo. Cr$19,840. LTR Editora Sao Paulo, rua Xavier de Toledo 114, 10 Andar CEP 01, Sao Paulo Brazil. **DD** 344.81/01/02648; 348.104102648. *Continues* Legislacao do Trabalho.
Ind/Abst Int. Labour Doc.

PO
REVISTA TECNICA DO TRABALHO. No. 1 (June/79)-. Periodical. Portuguese. ir. 180.00 single issue. Revista Tecnica do Trabalho, Rua Clemente Meneres 47, 10 Esq Porto Portugal. **LC** HD8591; .R48.

IT/0392-7229
RIVISTA GIURIDICA DEL LAVORO. See Economics-Labor.

IT
RIVISTA GIURIDICA DEL LAVORO E DELLA PREVIDENZA SOCIALE. DOTTRINA, GIURISPRUDENZA. ***Title Change.*** (19??)-(19??). Periodical. Italian. Via dei Giordani 22, 00199 Rome Italy. **LC** K22; .I788. **DD** 344.45/01/05; 344.504105. ***Formed by the union of*** *Rivista Giuridica del Lavoro e della Previdenza Sociale. Dottrina* ***and*** *Rivista Giuridica del Lavoro e della Previdenza Sociale. Giurisprudenza.* ***Continued by*** *Rivista Giuridica del Lavoro, 0392-7229.*

IT
RIVISTA GIURIDICA DEL LAVORO E DELLA PREVIDENZA SOCIALE: GIURISPRUDENZA. Yearly Vol. 26- (Jan./April 1975)-. Italian. Societa Edizioni Giuridiche del Lavoro, Via del Giordani 22, Rome Italy. **LC** K22; .I79. **DD** 344/.45/0105. Index available. cum. index. **Circ:** 2,000 (ctrl). ***Supersedes in part*** *Rivista Giuridica del Lavoro.*

IT
RIVISTA GIURIDICA DEL LAVORO E DELLA PREVIDENZA SOCIALE: PREVIDENZA. Anno 26- (Genn./Giugno 1975)-. Periodical. Italian. bm. Tecnindustria Srl, Dr Ragno Edi, Via Crescenzio 43, 00193 Rome Italy. **Tel** 011 39 6 6875657. **LC** K22; .I794. ***Supersedes in part*** *Rivista Giuridica del Lavoro e Della Previdenza Sociale.*

IT/0393-2494
RIVISTA ITALIANA DI DIRITTO DEL LAVORO. [Riv. ital. diritto lav.]. Vol. 1, No. 1 (Jan./Mar. 1982)-. Periodical. Italian (summaries and/or abstracts in English, French, German and Spanish). qt. L170000.00 Italy; L255000.00 other. Giuffre Editore SPA, Via Busto Arsizio 40, 20151 Milan Italy. **Tel** 011 398 2 38089200. **ED** Giuseppe Pera. **LC** K22; .I83. **DD** 344.45/01/05; 344.504105. Index available. **Bk Rev. Ad Acc. Circ:** 3,500. ***Continues*** *Rivista di Diritto del Lavoro, 0035-6107.*
Desc: Publishes articles by the most well-known students of labor law.
Ind/Abst Foreign Lang. Index; PAIS Int. Print.

JA
RODO KANKEI BUNKEN SAKUIN. 1972-. Japanese. Aichi-Ken Kinro Kaikan, 2-32 Tsurumai Showa-ku, Nagoya 466 Japan. **LC** Z7165.J3; R57; HD8726.5.

US
RULES AND REGULATIONS ... AND STATEMENTS OF PROCEDURE / NATIONAL LABOR RELATIONS BOARD. **Main/Corp** United States. National Labor Relations Board. (1947)-. Government Publication. English. ir. $27.00 US; $33.75 other. Superintendent of Documents, US Government Printing Office, Washington DC 20402. **Tel** (202)275-3328, FAX (202)786-2377. ***Continues*** *United States. National Labor Relations Board. Rules and Regulations ... and National Labor Relations Act.*

GW
SAE, SAMMLUNG ARBEITSRECHTLICHER ENTSCHEIDUNGEN. **Main/Corp** Bundesvereinigung der Deutschen Arbeitgeberverbande. **VFOAT** Sammlung Arbeitsrechtlicher Entscheidungen. (19??)-. German. Eight times a year. DM118.00. Sammlung Arbeitsrechtlicher Entscheidungen, Gustav Heinemann Ufer 72, D 50968 Koln Germany. **Tel** 0221-37 95 125. **ED** Ernst Gunther Mager, Christel Finke-Hollweg. **LC** K2; .U5. Index available. cum. index. **Bk Rev**, (Qty: 40-50). **Acid Free. Circ:** 2,000 (ctrl). ***Continues*** *Arbeitgeber-Ausschuss Nordrhein-Westfalen. Sammlung Arbeitsrechtlicher Entscheidungen.*
Desc: Collection of judgements rendered by the European Court concerning labor law.

JA
SHAKAI HOKEN ROMU ROPPO. **Main/Corp** Japan. **Added/Corp** Nihon Shakai Hoken Romushikai. Nihon Shakai Hoken Romushikai Rengokai. Zenkoku Shakai Hoken Romushikai. (19??)-. Periodical. Japanese. ¥4000. Chuo Keizaisha, 31-2 Kanda Jinbocho 1, Chiyoda-ku 101, Tokyo Japan.

US/1048-0579
SHEPARD'S FEDERAL LABOR LAW CASE NAMES CITATOR. [Shepard's fed. labor law case names cit.]. **Added/Corp** Shepard's/McGraw-Hill. **VFOAT** Federal Labor Law Case Names Citator. (1989)-. English. bm (6 cumulative supplements). $295.00 (5 bound volumes), $87.00 (cumulative supplements). Shepards McGraw-Hill Inc, 555 Middle Creek Parkway, PO Box 35300, Colorado Springs CO 80935-3530. **Tel** (719)488-3000, FAX (800)525-0053. **DD** 344.

US/0559-779X
SHEPARD'S FEDERAL LABOR LAW CITATIONS. [Shepard's fed. labor law cit.]. **Added/Corp** Shepard's/McGraw-Hill. **VFOAT** Federal Labor Law Citations. (1959)-. English. ir. $1080.00 (12 bound volumes), $422.00 (cumulative supplements). Shepards McGraw-Hill Inc, 555 Middle Creek Parkway, PO Box 35300, Colorado Springs CO 80935-3530. **Tel** (719)488-3000, FAX (800)525-0053. **DD** 348.
Desc: Devoted to decisions and orders of the National Labor Relations Board and decisions of the federal courts on labor matters.

US/1049-5096
SHEPARD'S LABOR ARBITRATION CITATIONS. [Shepard's labor arbitr. cit.]. **Added/Corp** Shepard's/McGraw-Hill. **VFOAT** Labor Arbitration Citations. Vol. 1, No. 1 (Feb. 1990)-. English. qt. $140.00 (bound volume), $177.00 (cumulative supplements). Shepards McGraw-Hill Inc, 555 Middle Creek Parkway, PO Box 35300, Colorado Springs CO 80935-3530. **Tel** (719)488-3000, FAX (800)525-0053. **DD** 344.
Desc: Includes the latest federal and state case and statutory law relating to arbitration. This coverage includes not only references to appealed arbitration decisions, but also references to decisions handed down by arbitrators. These decisions are reported in Bureau of National Affairs Labor Arbitration Reports and Commerce Clearing House's Labor Arbitration Awards.

US/1049-2062
SKOLER, ABBOTT, HAYES & PRESSER'S MASSACHUSETTS EMPLOYMENT LAW LETTER. [Skoler, Abbott, Hayes & Presser's Mass. employ. law lett.]. **Added/Corp** Skoler, Abbott, Hayes & Presser. **VFOAT** Massachusetts Employment Law Letter. (April 1990)-. Periodical. English. mo. $87.00. M. Lee Smith Publishers and Printers, 162 4th Avenue North, PO Box 198867, Nashville TN 37219. **Tel** (615)242-7395, (800)274-6774, FAX (615)256-6601. **ED** Ralph Abbott, Jr and Judith McDonald, (address) Skoler, Abbott and Presser, One Monarch Place, Suite 2000, Springfield, MA 01144, (phone) 413-737-4753. **LC** KFM2731.A15; S39. **DD** 344.744/01/05; 347.4404105.
Desc: Newsletter reporting the latest state specific employment law developments that affect companies in that state.

FR/0223-7164
SOMMAIRES DE DROIT DU TRAVAIL. (19??)-. French. Ten times a year. 675.81F France. Editions de l'Avenir, 18 Ave de la Marne, 92600 Asnieres France. **Tel** 011 33 1 47930588. **DD** 344.44/01/05; 344.404105.

●US/1064-461X
SOUTH CAROLINA EMPLOYMENT LAW LETTER. [S.C. employ. law lett.]. **Added/Corp** McNair & Sanford, P.A. (Oct 1992)-. Periodical. English. mo. $87.00. M. Lee Smith Publishers and Printers, 162 4th Avenue North, PO Box 198867, Nashville TN 37219. **Tel** (615)242-7395, (800)274-6774, FAX (615)256-6601. **ED** Don Ries, (address) McNair Law Firm, 1301 Gervais Street, Columbia, SC 29201, (phone) 803-799-9800. **DD** 344.
Desc: Newsletter reporting the latest state specific employment law developments that affect companies in that state.

AU
SOZIALPOLITIK UND ARBEITSRECHT. (19??)-. German. Signum Verlag Gmbh. & Company KB, Reisnerstasse 40, A 1030 Wein Austria. **Tel** 011 43 1 71195. **DD** 344.436/01.

US
STATE WORKERS' COMPENSATION LAWS / U.S. DEPARTMENT OF LABOR, EMPLOYMENT STANDARDS ADMINISTRATION, OFFICE OF STATE LIAISON AND LEGISLATIVE ANALYSIS, DIVISION OF STATE WORKERS' COMPENSATION PROGRAMS. **Added/Corp** United States. Employment Standards Administration. Division of State Workers' Compensation Programs. United States. Employment Standards Administration. Branch of Workers' Compensation Studies. (19??)-. English. sa. Free. US Department of Labor Office of Information, 200 Constitution Avenue Northwest, Washington DC 20010. **Tel** (202)219-7343. **LC** KF3615.Z9; L3. **DD** 344.73/021; 347.30421. ***Continues*** *State Workmen's Compensation Laws.*

CN/0380-8300
STEWARDS' LEGISLATIVE HANDBOOK. **Main/Corp** Ontario Federation of Labour. 10th- Ed.; 1971-. Periodical. English. Ontario Federation of Labour, 15 Gervais Drive, Suite 202, Don Mills Ontario M3C 1Y8 Canada. **Tel** (905)441-2731. **DD** 344/.713/01. ***Continues*** *Ontario Federation of Labour. Stewards' Handbook, 0381-6516.*

US/0272-6548
STRIKES, STOPPAGES, AND BOYCOTTS. English. an. Practising Law Institute, 810 Seventh Avenue, New York NY 10019-5818. **Tel** (212)765-5700, FAX (212)581-4670 general correspondence, (212)265-4742 orders and billing inquiries. **LC** KF3431.Z9; S87. **DD** 344.73/01892; 347.3041892.

US
STUDY TIME : A QUARTERLY LETTER OF NEWS AND COMMENT FOR THE AAA LABOR ARBITRATOR. **Added/Corp** American Arbitration Association. (19??)-. Periodical. English. qt. Free (to members only). American Arbitration Association, 140 West 51st Street, New York NY 10020. **Tel** (212)484-4011, (212)484-4014, FAX (212)765-4874, telex 12463.
Desc: Provides labor arbitrators with thoughtful commentary and opinion on substantive and procedural matters. Announcements of conferences, seminars, and new publications also appear.

II
SUMMARIES OF IMPORTANT LABOUR JUDGEMENTS. V. 1- 1964/70-. English. 15.00. Punjab Haryana & Delhi Chamber of Commerce and Industry, Phelps Building, 9-A Connaught Place, New Delhi 110001 India. **DD** 344/.54/0102646.

US/0163-139X
SUMMARY OF PUBLIC SECTOR LABOR RELATIONS POLICIES. **Added/Corp** United States. Labor-Management Services Administration. (1976)-. English. an. US Department of Labor, 200 Constitution Avenue NW, Washington DC 20210. **Tel** (202)219-7316, FAX (202)219-7312. **LC** KF5365; .A87. **DD** 344/.73/0189041353. ***Continues*** *Summary of State Policy Regulations for Public Sector Labor Relations.*

BL
SUMULA TRIBUTARIA TRABALHISTA (SEMIMONTHLY). (SUMULA TRIBUTARIA TRABALHISTA : STT.). **VFOAT** STT; S.T.T. Portuguese. sm. Sumula Tributaria Trabalhista R Santa Luzia, 799 19O Andar, GR 1902 CEP 20.030, Rio de Janeiro RJ Brazil. **DD** 349.81/05; 348.1005.

BL
SUPLEMENTO DE ATUALIZACAO : LIVLEX TRABALHISTA. **VFOAT** Suplemento de Atualizacao : Livlex Previdencia Social e Acidentes do Trabalho. 1- Jan./Feb. 1975-. Portuguese. Editorial Dimensao, rua da Quitada 45, 30 Andar GB, Rio de Janeiro Brazil.

BL
SUPLEMENTO TRABALHISTA LTR. (19??)-. Periodical. Portuguese. Ltr Editora Ltda, Rua Apa 165, CEP 01201 Sao Paulo SP Brazil. **LC** KHD1782; .S87. **DD** 344.81/01/02648; 348/104102648.

US/0886-8557
TENNESSEE EMPLOYMENT LAW UPDATE, THE. [Tenn. employ. law update]. **Added/Corp** John-Carroll Enterprises. **VFOAT** Employment Law Uupdate. Vol. 1, No. 1 (Mar. 1986)-. Periodical. English. mo. $92.00 plus tax. M. Lee Smith Publishers and Printers, 162 4th Avenue North, PO Box 198867, Nashville TN 37219. **Tel** (615)242-7395, (800)274-6774, FAX (615)256-6601. **ED** John B Phillips, (address) Miller and Martin, Suite 100 Volunteer Building, 832 Georgia Avenue, Chattanooga, TN 37402-2289, (phone)615-756-6600. **LC** KFT331.A59; T46. **DD** 344.768/01; 347.68041. ctrl circ.
Desc: This newsletter keeps Tennessee employers up-to-date on matters involving EEO, hiring, firing, drug testing, AIDS, employee privacy, worker's and unemployment compensation, Tennessee legislation and much more.

US/0749-8233
TERMINATION OF EMPLOYMENT. [Termin. employ.]. **Added/Corp** Prentice-Hall, Inc. (Oct. 19, 1984)-. Periodical. English. mo. $450.65. Warren Gorham & Lamont Inc., Park Square Building, 31 St. James Avenue, Boston MA 02116-4112. **Tel** (617)423-2020, (800)950-1207, FAX (617)423-2026. **DD** 344.

US/1046-9214
TEXAS EMPLOYMENT LAW LETTER. [Tex. empl. law lett.]. Vol. 1, No., 1 (Jan. 1990)-. Periodical. English. mo. $95.00 plus tax. M. Lee Smith Publishers and Printers, 162 4th Avenue North, PO Box 198867, Nashville TN 37219. **Tel** (615)242-7395, (800)274-6774, FAX (615)256-6601. **(Subscription address:** Texas Employment Law Letter, PO Box 50444, 4800 Renaissance, Dallas TX 75250.**) ED** David Ellis and Michael Maslanka, (address) Clark, West, Keller, Butler and Ellis, Texas Employment Law Letter, PO Box 50444, Dallas, TX 75250-0444, (phone) 214-741-1001. **LC** KFT1531.A15; T49. **DD** 344.764/01/05; 347.6404105.
Desc: Newsletter reporting the latest state specific employment law developments that affect companies in that state.

FR/0224-4365
TRAVAIL ET EMPLOI. [Trav. emp.]. **Added/Corp** France. Ministere des Affaires Sociales et de la Solidarite Nationale. Service des Etudes et de la Statistique. France. Ministere de l'Emploi. France. Ministere du Travail. Service des Etudes et de la Statistique. France. Ministere du Travail et de la Participation. Service des Etudes et de la Statistique. France. Ministere du Travail et de la Participation. No. 1 (June 1979)-. Periodical. French. qt. 262.00F France; $68.00 US; £57.00 UK. Ministere Travail Service Etudes, Statistique Place Fontenoy, 75007 Paris France. **(Subscription address:** Documentation Francaise, 124 rue Henri Barbusse, 93308 Aubervilliers Cedex France.**)** **LC** HD8421; .T73. **DD** 331.12/042/0944.
Ind/Abst Int. Bibliogr. Sociol.; Int. Labour Doc.; LABORDOC; PAIS Int. Print; Selec. Coop. Index Manage. Period.

US/0091-5459
UNION LABOR REPORT. **Added/Corp** Bureau of National Affairs (Washington, D.C.). (19??)-. English. bw. $668.00. Bureau of National Affairs Inc., 9435 Key West Avenue, Rockville MD 20850. **Tel** (800)372-1033, (301)258-1033, FAX (301)948-5823. **ED** Bill L. Manville. **LC** KF3365; .U5. **DD** 344/.73/01. **[CCC].**
Desc: A notification and reference service that provides practical guidance on day-to-day labor relations questions and current reports on employee relations and union developments.

US/0190-5260
UNION LABOR REPORT WEEKLY NEWSLETTER. **Added/Corp** Bureau of National Affairs (Washington, D.C.). (19??)-. Periodical. English. wk. $142.00. Bureau of National Affairs Inc., 9435 Key West Avenue, Rockville MD 20850. **Tel** (800)372-1033, (301)258-1033, FAX (301)948-5823. **ED** Bill L. Manville. **[CCC].**
Desc: Presents a roundup of the latest developments in the labor field, including summaries of significant arbitration awards, labor facts, and special reports.

US/1042-461X
VIRGINIA EMPLOYMENT LAW LETTER. [Va. employ. law lett.]. **VFOAT** Employment Law Letter. (March 1989)-. Periodical. English. mo. $87.00 plus tax. M. Lee Smith Publishers and Printers, 162 4th Avenue North, PO Box 198867, Nashville TN 37219. **Tel** (615)242-7395, (800)274-6774, FAX (615)256-6601. **ED** James Meath and Robert Musik, Jr, (address) Williams, Mullen, Christian and Dobbins, Two James Center, 1021 East Cary Street, Richmond, VA 23210-1320, (phone) 804-643-1991. **LC** KFV2731.A15; V57. **DD** 344.755/01/05; 347.5504105. Index available. cum. index. **Circ:** 300.
Desc: Newsletter reporting the latest state specific employment law developments that affect companies in that state.

BL
VOX JURIS TRABALHISTA. (19??)-. Periodical. Portuguese. mo. **LC** K26; .O93.

●US/1072-0588
WASHINGTON EMPLOYMENT LAW LETTER. (WASHINGTON EMPLOYMENT LAW LETTER / PERKINS, COIE.). [Wash. employ. law lett.]. **Added/Corp** Perkins, Coie (Firm). (1994)-. Periodical. English. mo. $95.00. M. Lee Smith Publishers and Printers, 162 4th Avenue North, PO Box 198867, Nashville TN 37219. **Tel** (615)242-7395, (800)274-6774, FAX (615)256-6601. **DD** 344.

US/0364-8109
WEEKLY SUMMARY OF NLRB CASES. (WEEKLY SUMMARY OF NLRB CASES / NATIONAL LABOR RELATIONS BOARD, DIVISION OF INFORMATION.). **Main/Corp** United States. National Labor Relations Board. Division of Information. **VFOAT** Weekly Summary of N.L.R.B. Cases. **VAT** Weekly Summary of National Labor Relations Board Cases. W-1685 (Dec. 31, 1979-Jan. 4, 1980)-. Government Publication. English. wk. $126.00 US; $157.00 other. Superintendent of Documents, US Government Printing Office, Washington DC 20402. **Tel** (202)275-3328, FAX (202)786-2377. **LC** KF3364; .U55. **DD** 344.73/01/02648; 347.304102648. ***Continues*** *United States. National Labor Relations Board. Weekly Summary of N.L.R.B. Cases, 0364-8109.*
Desc: Contains a synopsis of each published decision of the NLRB in unfair labor practices and representative election cases; lists decisions of the NLRB administrative law judges and directions of elections by NLRB regional directors; carries guideline memoranda of the NLRB general counsel to field offices on important case-handling subjects; and carries notices of publication of volumes of NLRB decisions and orders, the NLRB Annual Report, and other agency informational literature.

II
WEST BENGAL LABOUR GAZETTE. Began with July 1957. Periodical. English. mo. Government of West Bengal / Labour, Department of Labour, Calcutta India. **DD** 344.54/1401/05; 345. 41404105.

CN/0317-6924
WESTERN LABOUR ARBITRATION CASES. ***Ceased.*** ( )-Vol. 2 (April 1986). English. ir. The Continuing Legal Education Society of British Columbia, 200-1148 Hornby Street, Vancouver British Columbia V6Z 2C3 Canada. **Tel** (604)669-3544. **ED** M A Hickling. **LC** KE3206.A49; W47. **DD** 344/.711/01890264.
Desc: The only comprehensive collection of grievance arbitration decisions in Western Canada. Includes extensive subject index, tables of cases cited, and indexes by arbitrator and ministry number.

US/0190-5244
WHAT'S NEW IN COLLECTIVE BARGAINING NEGOTIATIONS & CONTRACTS. **Added/Corp** Bureau of National Affairs (Washington, D.C.). **VAT** What's New in Collective Bargaining Negotiations and Contracts. (19??)-. Periodical. English. bw. $148.00. Bureau of National Affairs Inc., 9435 Key West Avenue, Rockville MD 20850. **Tel** (800)372-1033, (301)258-1033, FAX (301)948-5823. **ED** Mary P. Dunn.
Desc: Presents the latest developments in collective bargaining, including contract settlements, bargaining techniques and trends, and contract interpretations by the courts, administrative agencies, and arbitrators. Each issue features an insert, Facts for Bargaining, which contains statistical information.

US/1054-402X
WILEY EMPLOYMENT LAW UPDATE. [Wiley employ. law update]. **VFOAT** Employment Law Update. (1991)-. English. John Wiley & Sons, Inc., 605 Third Avenue, New York NY 10158-0012. **Tel** (212)850-6000, (212)850-6645, FAX (212)850-6088, telex 12-7063. **(Subscription address:** John Wiley & Sons / England, Baffins Lane, Chichester, West Sussex PO19 1UD England.**)** **LC** KF3319; .W48. **DD** 344.73/01; 347.3041.

●US/1059-5066
WISCONSIN EMPLOYMENT LAW LETTER. [Wis. employ. law lett.]. **Added/Corp** Melli, Walker, Pease & Ruhly (Firm). Vol. 1, No. 1 (Jan. 1992)-. Periodical. English. mo. $95.00 plus tax. M. Lee Smith Publishers and Printers, 162 4th Avenue North, PO Box 198867, Nashville TN 37219. **Tel** (615)242-7395, (800)274-6774, FAX (615)256-6601. **ED** Jack Walker and Susan Sheeran, (address) Melli, Walker, Pease and Ruhly, Suite 600 Insurance Building, 119 Martin Luther King Jr, Boulevard, PO Box 1664 Madison WI 53701, (phone)608-257-4812. **DD** 344.
Desc: Newsletter reporting the latest state specific employment law developments that affect companies in that state.

CN
WOMEN/PAY EQUITY EMPLOYMENT LAW. **VFOAT** Women Pay Equity Employment Law. Vol. 5, No. 1 (Jan. 1989)-. Periodical. English. mo. $95.00. Lancaster House Publishing, PO Box 133, 20 Dundas Street West, Toronto Ontario M5G 2G8 Canada. **Tel** (416)977-6618, FAX (416)977-5873. ***Continues*** *Women's Employment Law, 0828-6981.*

US/0748-7878
WORKER'S COMPENSATION LAW BULLETIN. [Work. compens. law bull.]. **VFOAT** WCLB; W.C.L.B. (197?)-. English. Twelve times a year. $59.99. Quinlan Publishing Company, 23 Drydock Avenue, Boston MA 02210-2387. **Tel** (617)542-0048, (800)229-2084, FAX (617)345-9646. **LC** KF3613.36; .W67. **DD** 344.73/021; 347.30421. **[CCC].** available on microfilm and microfiche from University Microfilms International (UMI). ***Continues*** *Workmen's Compensation Law Bulletin.*

US
WORKERS' COMPENSATION LAW OF THE STATE OF ARKANSAS. **Main/Corp** Arkansas. English. American Insurance Association, 85 John Street, New York NY 10038. **LC** KFA3942.A29; W67. **DD** 344.767/021. ***Continues*** *Workmen's Compensation Law of the State of Arkansas.*

US
WORKERS' COMPENSATION LAW OF THE STATE OF CONNECTICUT. **Main/Corp** Connecticut. English. American Insurance Association, 85 John Street, New York NY 10038. **LC** KFC3942.A29; W65. **DD** 344.746/021/02632, 347. 46042102632. ***Continues*** *Workmen's Compensation Law of the State of Connecticut.*

US
WORKERS' COMPENSATION LAW OF THE STATE OF HAWAII. **Main/Corp** Hawaii. English. $39.00. American Insurance Association, 85 John Street, New York NY 10038. **LC** KFH342.A29; W67. **DD** 344.969/021/02632.
Desc: Individual books for each state and the District of Columbia. Includes digest, full text of law and extracts of supplementary laws.

US
WORKERS' COMPENSATION LAW OF THE STATE OF WISCONSIN. **Main/Corp** Wisconsin. English. American Insurance Association, 85 John Street, New York NY 10038. **LC** KFW2742.A29; W67. **DD** 344.775/021/02632, 347. 75042102632. ***Continues*** *Workmen's Compensation Law of the State of Wisconsin.*

US/0748-4135
WORKERS' COMPENSATION LAWS OF CALIFORNIA, THE. **Main/Corp** California. (1975)-. English. an. Matthew Bender & Company Inc., 1275 Broadway, Albany NY 12204. **Tel** (800)833-9844, (518)487-3000. **ED** W.L. Hanna. **LC** KFC592.A29; W64. ***Continues*** *Workmen's Compensation Laws of California.*

US/0195-671X
WORKERS' COMPENSATION MANUAL FOR UNION REPRESENTATIVES. **Main/Corp** Ohio AFL-CIO. 7th- Ed.; 1977-. English. $60.00. Ohio AFL-CIO, 271 East State Street, Columbus OH 43215. **LC** KFO342; .O36. **DD** 344.771/021. ***Continues*** *Workmen's Compensation Manual for Union Representatives, 0195-6973.*

US/1053-0274
WRONGFUL DISCHARGE REPORT. [Wrongful disch. rep.]. **VFOAT** WDR. Vol. 1, Issue 5 (Oct. 1987)-. English. mo. $350.00. Andrews Publications Inc., 1646 West Chester Pike, PO Box 1000, Westtown PA 19395. **Tel** (610)399-6600, (800)345-1101, FAX (610)399-6610. **ED** Ronald C. Bishop. **LC** KF3471.A59; W77. **DD** 344.73/012596. Index available. cum. index. ctrl circ. ***Continues*** *Wrongful Discharge Case Law Reporter, 0893-8458.*
Desc: Offers human resource executives, corporate officers and in-house attorneys easy-to-read summaries of the latest developments in lawsuits alleging tort and contract claims against employers. Offers a broad geographic coverage of suits alleging breach of contract, retaliatory discharge, constructive discharge and public policy violations. Provides coverage of Title VII and Section 1983 claims, as well as of AIDS discrimination and drug testing cases. Articles deal with the ramifications of the Supreme Court's recent decisions redefining the parameters of civil rights protection, and provide complete coverage of the changing state of exceptions to the employment-at-will doctrine.

CN/0827-4673
WRONGFUL DISMISSAL EMPLOYMENT LAW. ***Title Change.*** [Wrongful dismiss. employ. law]. **Added/Corp** Lancaster House (Firm). Vol. 1, No. 1 (Jan. 1985)-Vol. 8, No. 7/8 (July/Aug. 1992). Periodical. English. mo. Lancaster House Publishing, PO Box 133, 20 Dundas Street West, Toronto Ontario M5G 2G8 Canada. **Tel** (416)977-6618, FAX (416)977-5873. **DD** 344.71/012596. ***Continued by*** *Lancaster's Wrongful Dismissal Employment Law News.*

PL
Z PROBLEMATYKI PRAWA PRACY I POLITYKI SOCJALNEJ / UNIWERSYTET SLASKI. Vol. 1-. Periodical. Polish (summaries and/or abstracts in French and Russian). 43.00. Uniwersytet Slaski, Ul Bankowa 14, 40-007 Katowice Poland. **Tel** 59-69-15, FAX 48 32 599-506, telex 0315584 USKPL. **LC** K16; .R576.

ZA
ZAMBIA INDUSTRIAL CASES REPORTS / REPUBLIC OF ZAMBIA, MINISTRY OF LABOUR AND SOCIAL SERVICES, INDUSTRIAL RELATIONS COURT, THE. **Main/Corp** Zambia. Industrial Relations Court. English. an. K8.40. Zambia Government Printer, POB 30136, Lusaka Zambia. **DD** 344.6894/01/0264. **Bk Rev. Ad Acc. Circ:** 540.
Desc: Contains judgements of the Industrial Relations Court.

AU/0044-2321
ZEITSCHRIFT FUER ARBEITSRECHT UND SOZIALRECHT. **VFOAT** ZAS. Vol. 1- Jan./Feb. 1966-. Periodical. German. bm. S435.00. Manzsche Verlagsbuchhandlung, Kohlmarkt 16 Postfach 163, A 1014 Vienna Austria. **Tel** 011 43 222 5316171. **ED** Theodor Tomandl. **LC** K30. Index available. **Bk Rev. Ad Acc.**

GW/0930-861X
ZEITSCHRIFT FUER AUSLANDISCHES UND INTERNATIONALES ARBEITS UND SOZIALRECHT. [Z. ausl. int. Arb.- Soz.r.]. **Added/Corp** Institut fuer Arbeitsrecht and Arbeitsbeziehungen in der Europaischen Gemeinschaft. Max-Planck-Institut fuer Auslandisches und Internationales Sozialrecht. **VFOAT** ZIAS. Vol. 1, No. 1 (Jan./March 1987)-. Periodical. German (English; summaries and/or abstracts in English and German). qt. $194.00 North America. Dr. Alfred Huethig Verlag GmbH, Postfach 102869, D 69018 Heidelberg Germany. **Tel** 011

Law —Labor Law

49 6221 489281. **(Subscription address:** Huethig Publishing Inc., 29 Macintosh Drive, Oxford CT 06478.**)** **Ind/Abst** PAIS Int. Print.

GW
ZFA, ZEITSCHRIFT FUER ARBEITSRECHT. VFOAT Zeitschrift fur
Arbeitsrecht. (19??)-. German. Four times a year (Mar., June, Sept., Dec.). DM142.00. Carl Heymanns Verlag KG, Luxemburger Strasse 449, D 50939 Cologne Germany. **Tel** 011 49 221 460100, telex 8 881 888. **ED** Gerhardt Bold and Wolfgang Zollue. **LC** K30; .F13. **DD** 344/.73/01. Index available. **Bk Rev. Ad Acc. Circ:** 1,200 (ctrl).
Desc: Treatises, statements and sentences on the workers' right.
Ind/Abst LABORDOC.

LAW ENFORCEMENT AND CRIMINOLOGY

CN/1183-9201
ACTION PREVENTION (SAINTE-FOY).
(ACTION PREVENTION.). [Action prev.]. **Added/Corp** Association de Sante et Securite des Pates et Papiers du Quebec. Association de Sante et Securite des Industries de la Foret du Quebec. Vol. 1, No 1 (Sept. 1991)-. Periodical. French. qt. Limited free distribution. ASSPQ et ASSIFQ, Bureau 102, 1200 Avenue Germain-Des-Pres, Sainte-Foy Quebec G1V 3M7 Canada. **DD** 363.11.

FR/0339-7858
ACTUALITE POLICIERE 1975, L'. (1975)-.
Periodical. French. qt. $30.00. CFTC Police en Tenue, 11 rue des Ursins, 75004 Paris France. **Tel** 011 33 1 43259682 ext. 3590. **UDC** 331.88. **Continues** L'Actualite Policiere. Police de Paris, 0339-784X.

SA
ADAC NEWS : DETENTION ACTION COMMITTEE NEWSLETTER. Added/Corp
Detention Action Committee (South Africa). **VFOAT** Detention Action Committee Newsletter. No. 5 (Apr. 1983)-. Newsletter. English. **Continues** Newsletter (Ad Hoc Detention Action Committee (South Africa)).
Ind/Abst Hum. Rights Intern. Rep.

US
ADMISSIONS TO JUVENILE INSTITUTIONS. Added/Corp Wisconsin. Division
of Corrections. Bureau of Planning, Development, and Research. Wisconsin. Division of Corrections. Office of Systems and Evaluation. Wisconsin. Division of Corrections. Office of Information Management and Operations. (1970)-. English. an. Wisconsin Division of Corrections, 149 East Wilson Street, Room 1050, Madison WI 53702. **Tel** (608)266-2471, FAX (608)267-0923. **LC** HV9105.W6; A32. **DD** 365/.42/09775. **Continues** Juveniles Admitted to Division of Corrections' Juvenile Institutions.
Desc: Information on juvenile delinquency and detention homes.

CN/0715-2973
ADULT CORRECTIONAL SERVICES IN CANADA. See Law-Abstracting, Bibliographies and
Statistics.

US/0095-4004
ADULT PROBATION ADMISSIONS.
Main/Corp Wisconsin. Division of Corrections. Office of Systems and Evaluation. (1976)-. English. an. Wisconsin Division of Corrections, 149 East Wilson Street, Room 1050, Madison WI 53702. **Tel** (608)266-2471, FAX (608)267-0923. **LC** HV7299; .A28e. **DD** 364.6/3/09775. **Continues** Adult Probation Admissions, 0095-4004.

US
ADULT PROSECUTION: REFERENCE TABLES. VFOAT Reference Tables : Adult
Prosecution; Crime and Delinquency in California. Periodical. English. an. 3301 C Street, PO Box 13427, Sacramento CA 95813.

US/0894-2366
ADVANCES IN CRIMINOLOGICAL THEORY. [Adv. criminolog. theory]. Vol. 1 (1989)-.
English. an. $49.95. Transaction Publishers / Rutgers State University, New Brunswick NJ 08903. **Tel** (908)932-2280 Ext. 105, FAX (908)932-3138. **ED** W. S. Laufer and F. Adler. **LC** HV6001; .A37. **DD** 364.
Desc: Exclusively dedicated to the dissemination of original work on criminological theory. Encourages theory construction and validation in existing criminological publications and furthers the free exchange of ideas, propositions, and postulates.

BA
AFAQ AMNIYAH. Added/Corp Bahrain. Wizarat
al-Dakhiliyah. **VFOAT** Affaq Amniya. Vol. 1, No. 1, (August 1983)-. Periodical. Arabic. qt. Al-Alaqat Al-Ammah, Bi-Wizarat Al-Dakhiliyah S B 13, Bahrain. **LC** HV8242.52.A2; A37.

TS
AL-AMN. Periodical. Arabic. mo. Shurtat Dubayy, Far
Al-Alaqat Al-Ammah, SB 1493, Dubayy Al-Imarat Al-Arabiyah Al-Muttahidah, Dubayy Trucial States. **LC** HV7551; .A55.

SU
AL-AMN WA-AL-HAYAH. V. 1, No 1
(July/August 1982)-. Periodical. Arabic. mo. 5 riyals (per issue) Saudi Arabi; $15.00 (per year) US. Al-Markaz Al-Arabi Lil-Dirasat Al-Amniyah Wa-Al-Tadrib, PO Box 6830, Bi-Al-Riyad Saudi Arabia. **Tel** (01)2460045, telex 400949 AMNEIA SJ. **ED** Faruk A Mourad, Mourad Ez El Arab and Salah Abdulaziz Al-Sheaibi. **LC** HV8266.A2; A48. Index available. **Bk Rev Ad Acc. Circ:** 10,000.
Desc: Covers all issues of importance to the security, social and judicial agencies of all Arab countries.

US/0279-5175
ALABAMA PEACE OFFICERS' JOURNAL. (ALABAMA PEACE OFFICERS'
JOURNAL / ALABAMA PEACE OFFICERS' ASSOCIATION.). **Added/Corp** Alabama Peace Officers' Association. (19??)-. Periodical. English. Four times a year. $10.00 associate members; $15.00 active members (individuals) Comes with Alabama Peace Officer's Association membership. Alabama Peace Officer's Association, 940 Pelham, Montgomery AL 36104. **Tel** (205)269-4328. **Ad Acc. Circ:** 4,000 (ctrl).
Desc: News and information about the Alabama Peace Officers Association and their members.

US/0274-7448
ALABAMA POLICE JOURNAL. Periodical.
English. qt. Alabama Police Journal, PO Box 1206, Vernon AL 35592.

NE
ALGEMEEN POLITIEBLAD VAN HET KONINKRIJK DER NEDERLANDEN.
Added/Corp Netherlands. Ministerie van Justitie. (18??)-. Periodical. Dutch. bw (26 issues). Fl30.00. Algemeen Politieblad, Postbus 20301, 2500 Eh Den Haag Netherlands. **Tel** 011 31 70 3706507. **LC** HV7551; .A42.

CN/0834-230X
ALLO POLICE (1986). (ALLO POLICE.). [Allo
police]. Vol. 34E, No. 40 (19 Oct. 1986)-. Periodical. French. wk. 86.67Can$ Canada; 95.00Can$ other. Merlin Pub Society, 1800 Parthenais, Montreal Quebec H2K 3S4 Canada. **Tel** (514) 844-2529. **DD** 364/.9714. **Continues** Le Vrai Allo Police, 0833-952X.

IO
ALMANAK KEPOLISIAN REPUBLIK INDONESIA. VFOAT Almanak Kepolisian R.I.
Indonesian. an. P T Dutarindo Adv, JL Pramuka Kav 72 Indonesia. **LC** HV8254.A2; A6.

US/1056-0319
AMERICAN JAILS. (AMERICAN JAILS : THE
MAGAZINE OF THE AMERICAN JAIL ASSOCIATION.). [Am. jails]. **Added/Corp** American Jail Association (U.S.). Vol. 1, No. 1 (Spring 1987)-. Periodical. English. Six times a year (Jan., Mar., May, July, Sept., Nov.). $25.00 Comes with American Jail Association membership. American Jail Association, 2053 Day Road, Suite 100, Hagerstown MD 21740. **Tel** (301)790-3930, FAX (301)790-2940. **ED** Ken Kerle. **LC** HV8745; .A75. **DD** 365/.973. **Bk Rev. Ad Acc, Adv Mgr:** Pat Cain, **Tel** (301)790-3930. **Circ:** 7,000.
Ind/Abst Crim. Justice Abstr.

US/1066-2316
AMERICAN JOURNAL OF CRIMINAL JUSTICE : AJCJ. [Am. j. crim. justice].
Added/Corp Eastern Kentucky University. College of Law Enforcement. Southern Association of Criminal Justice Educators. Southern Association of Criminal Justice. **VFOAT** AJCJ. Vol. 9, No. 1 (Fall 1984)-. Periodical. English. Twice a year. $60.00. Anderson Publishing Company, 2035 Reading Road, Cincinnati OH 45202. **Tel** (513)421-4142, (800)582-7295. **(Subscription address:** Anderson Publishing Company, PO Box 1576, Cincinnati OH 45201.**)** **ED** Mike Blankenship (phone: (615)929-5346). **DD** 345. **CODEN** AJCJE4. **Bk Rev, (Qty: 6-10). Pr Rev. Circ:** 500.
Continues Southern Journal of Criminal Justice.
Ind/Abst Crim. Justice Abstr.

US/0735-8547
AMERICAN JOURNAL OF POLICE. [Am. j.
police]. Vol. 1, No. 1 (1981)-. Periodical. English. qt. $65.00. Anderson Publishing Company, 2035 Reading Road, Cincinnati OH 45202. **Tel** (513)421-4142, (800)582-7295. **(Subscription address:** Anderson Publishing Company, PO Box 1576, Cincinnati OH 45201.**)** **LC** HV7551; .A53. **DD** 363.2/05. available on microfilm and microfiche from University Microfilms International (UMI).
Ind/Abst Crim. Justice Abstr.; Crim. Justice Period. Index.

US
AMERICAN SERIES OF FOREIGN PENAL CODES. See Law-Criminal Law.

SU
AMN (SAUDI ARABIA. IDARAH AL-AMMAH LIL-THAQAFAH WA-AL-TAWJIH). (AL-AMN / TUSDIRUHA
AL-IDARAH AL-AMMAH LIL-THAQAFAH WA-AL-TAWJIH BI-WIZARAT AL-DAKHILIYAH BI-AL-MAMLAKAH AL-ARABIYAH AL-SAUDIYAH.). Periodical. Arabic. Wizarat Al-Dakhiliyah, Al-Idarah Al-Ammah Lil-Thaqafah Wa-Al-Tawjih, Saudi Arabia. **LC** HV8242.35.A2; A46.

US/0270-2991
AMS STUDIES IN CRIMINAL JUSTICE.
[AMS stud. crim. justice]. No. 3 (1980)-. Monographic series. English. ir. Price varies per volume. AMS Press Inc., 56 East 13th Street, New York NY 10003. **Tel** (212)777-4700, FAX (212)995-5413, telex 710 581 2302.

US/0402-4249
ANGOLITE. Added/Corp Louisiana State
Penitentiary. Vol. 1, (Dec. 1952)-. Periodical. English. Six times a year (Feb., Apr., June, Aug., Oct., Dec.). $18.00 US; $24.00 Canada; $40.00 others. Angolite, Louisiana State Penitentiary, Angola LA 70712. **Tel** (504)655-4411 Ext. 2028. **ED** Wilbert Rideau. **LC** HV9475.L22; L63. **DD** 365/.976317. **Bk Rev. Circ:** 4,000.
Desc: News coverage of life in the Louisiana State Penitentiary and coverage of issues and events affecting the criminal justice system.
Ind/Abst Index Period. Artic. Relat. Law.

FR/0003-4452
ANNALES INTERNATIONALES DE CRIMINOLOGIE. [Ann. int. criminol.]. Added/Corp
International Society of Criminology. Centre National de la Recherche Scientifique (France). **VFOAT** International Annals of Criminology; Anales Internationales de Criminologia. (1962)-. Periodical. French (Spanish and English). an. 550.00F. International Society of Criminology, 4-14 Rue Ferrus, 75014 Paris France. **Tel** 011 33 1 45880023. **ED** Melun. **Ad Acc. Circ:** 700.
Continues Bulletin de la Societe Internationale de Criminologie.
Desc: Scientific articles and reports on criminology particularly reflecting the activities of the International Society of Criminology.
Ind/Abst Crim. Justice Abstr. (199?-); Int. Bibliogr. Sociol.; PAIS Int. Print (1991-).

US
ANNUAL ACTION PROGRAMS - MONTANA. BOARD OF CRIME COUNCIL. Main/Corp Montana. Board of Crime
Council. English. an. Montana Board of Crime Control, 1336 Helena Avenue, Helena MT 59601. **LC** HV7276; .A3C. **DD** 364/.9786.

HK
ANNUAL DEPARTMENTAL REPORT BY THE COMMISSIONER OF PRISONS.
Main/Corp Hongkong. Prison Dept. **Added/Corp** Hongkong. Prison Dept. Report of the Superintendent of Prisons. (19??)-. English. Hong Kong Government Information Service, Beaconsfield House, 4 Queens Road, Hong Kong Hong Kong. **Tel** 011 852 8428801 4, telex 61190 HKGIS.

US/0272-0736
ANNUAL GAMING CONFERENCE.
(ANNUAL GAMING CONFERENCE; [PROCEEDINGS]). **Main/Corp** Gaming Conference. **Added/Corp** Nevada Certified Public Accountants' Foundation for Education and Research. 1st (1979)-. English. an. **LC** KFN985.A75; G35. **DD** 344.793/0542; 347.9304542.

US/0276-8151
ANNUAL JOURNAL / PETER W. RODINO INSTITUTE OF CRIMINAL JUSTICE. [Annu. j. - Peter W. Rodino Inst. Crim.
Justice]. Vol. 1, No. 1 (1979)-. Periodical. English. an. Peter W Rodino Institute of Criminal Justice, 2039 Kennedy Boulevard, Jersey City NJ 07305. **LC** HV8143; .A76. **DD** 364/.9749.

US
ANNUAL PERSONNEL AND BUDGET STUDY OF OREGON LAW ENFORCEMENT AGENCIES. Main/Corp
Oregon. Board on Police Standards and Training. Research and Management Services. English. an. Oregon Board on Police Standard and Training, Suite 404/Executive House, 325 13th Street NE, Salem OR 97310. **LC** HV7571.O7; B6A. **DD** 363.2/2/09795.

US
ANNUAL PRIVACY AND SECURITY AUDIT REPORT ON THE PROCEDURES, POLICIES, AND PRACTICES OF THE DEPARTMENT OF LAW ENFORCEMENT FOR MAINTAINING CRIMINAL HISTORY RECORD INFORMATION FOR THE PERIOD ENDING ... / ILLINOIS CRIMINAL JUSTICE INFORMATION COUNCIL.
English. an. Illinois Criminal Justice, Information Council, 120 South Riverside Place, Chicago IL 60606. **LC** HV9305.I3; A55. **DD** 353.97730074.

Law —Law Enforcement and Criminology

US
ANNUAL PROGRAM PLAN FOR FISCAL YEAR ... / U.S. DEPARTMENT OF JUSTICE, NATIONAL INSTITUTE OF CORRECTIONS. **Main/Corp** National Institute of Corrections (U.S.). **VFOAT** Annual Program Plan. (1991)-. English. *Continues in part* Annual Program Plan and Academy Training Schedule for Fiscal Year ... .

US
ANNUAL REPORT. **Main/Corp** Texas Commission on Jail Standards. **VFOAT** Annual Report to the Governor, Lieutenant Governor, and Speaker of the House of Representatives of Texas. English. Texas Commission on Jail Standards, 611 South Congress/Suite 200, PO Box 12985, Austin TX 78704. **Tel** (512)463-5505. *Continues* Annual Report to the Governor, Lieutenant Governor, and the Speaker of the House of Representatives of Texas.

AT
ANNUAL REPORT. **Main/Corp** Queensland. Comptroller-General of Prisons. (19??)-. English. **LC** HV8473; .A3.

UK
ANNUAL REPORT AND ACCOUNTS / THE RAINER FOUNDATION. **Main/Corp** Rainer Foundation. (1984)-. English. The Rainer Foundation, 89A Blackheath Hill, London SE10 8TJ England. *Continues* Annual Report - The Rainer Foundation.

CN/0710-7412
ANNUAL REPORT - BRITISH COLUMBIA BOARD OF PAROLE. (ANNUAL REPORT.). [Annu. rep. - B.C. Board Parole]. **Main/Corp** British Columbia Board of Parole. (1980/81)-. English. **DD** 354.7110084/93.

US
ANNUAL REPORT / COLORADO DEPARTMENT OF CORRECTIONS. **Main/Corp** Colorado. Dept. of Corrections. English. an. **LC** HV7255; .A23A. **DD** 353.97880084/9/06. available on microfiche (from Colorado State depositories).

US
ANNUAL REPORT - CONNECTICUT JUSTICE COMMISSION. **Main/Corp** Connecticut Justice Commission. English. an. Connecticut Justice Commission, 75 Elm Street, Hartford CT 06115. **LC** HV7256; .A37A. **DD** 364/.9746.

US
ANNUAL REPORT / CRIME VICTIMS BOARD. **Main/Corp** New York (State). Crime Victims Board. **VFOAT** Crime Victims Board Annual Report. (1981/82)-. English. an. New York Crime Victims Board, Executive Department, 875 Central Avenue, Albany NY 12206. *Continues* Annual Report / New York (State). Crime Victims Compensation Board.

US/0095-179X
ANNUAL REPORT - CRIMINAL JUSTICE TRAINING AND STANDARDS COUNCIL. (ANNUAL REPORT - NORTH CAROLINA, CRIMINAL TRAINING AND STANDARDS COUNCIL.). **Main/Corp** North Carolina. Criminal Justice Training and Standards Council. 1973-. English. an. Criminal Training and Standards Council, PO Box 149, Raleigh NC 27602. **LC** HV7283; .A25A. **DD** 364.

US/0740-3038
ANNUAL REPORT - FEDERAL ENFORCEMENT TRAINING CENTER. (ANNUAL REPORT / FEDERAL LAW ENFORCEMENT TRAINING CENTER, DEPARTMENT OF THE TREASURY.). **Main/Corp** Federal Law Enforcement Training Center. 1978-. English. an. Federal Law Enforcement Training Center, Glynco GA 31524. **Tel** (912)267-2447. **LC** HV8143; .F445A. **DD** 363.2/07/15. **Circ:** 5,000. available on microfiche (Vols. for 1981/1982- distributed to depository libraries).
Desc: Report of the activities of the Federal Law Enforcement Training Center.

US/0362-9996
ANNUAL REPORT - GEORGIA ORGANIZED CRIME PREVENTION COUNCIL. **Main/Corp** Georgia. Organized Crime Prevention Council. (19??)-. English. an. Georgia Organized Crime Prevention Council, 1430 West Peachtree Street/Suite 318, Atlanta GA 30309. **LC** HV7260; .A28. **DD** 353.9/758/00756.

US/0094-4238
ANNUAL REPORT - GOVERNOR'S COMMITTEE ON CRIME, DELINQUENCY AND CORRECTIONS (CHARLESTON). (ANNUAL REPORT - GOVERNOR'S COMMITTEE ON CRIME, DELINQUENCY AND CORRECTIONS (WEST VIRGINIA).). **Main/Corp** West Virginia. Governor's Committee on Crime, Delinquency, and Corrections. English. an. Boy Scouts of Canada, British Columbia and Yukon Provincial Council, 719 West 16th Avenue, Vancouver Canada V5Z 1S8. **LC** HV7298; .A33B. **DD** 353.9/754/0074.

US/0275-0872
ANNUAL REPORT / LOS ANGELES POLICE DEPARTMENT. **Main/Corp** Los Angeles (Calif.). Police Dept. (1950)-. English. an. Los Angeles Police Department, Los Angeles CA 90024. **LC** HV7595.L7; A4. **DD** 352.2/09794/94. *Continues* Los Angeles (Calif.). Police Dept. Annual Report of the Police Department, City of Los Angeles, California.

SA
ANNUAL REPORT - NATIONAL COUNCIL, NICRO. **Main/Corp** National Institute for Crime Prevention and Rehabilitation of Offenders. National Council. 1970/71-. English (Afrikaans). **LC** HV9421.S6. **DD** 354/.68/00849. *Continues* Social Services Association of South Africa. National Council. Report.

US/0360-0483
ANNUAL REPORT - NEBRASKA COMMISSION ON LAW ENFORCEMENT AND CRIMINAL JUSTICE. **Main/Corp** Nebraska Commission on Law Enforcement and Criminal Justice. English. an. Nebraska Commission on Law Enforcement and Criminal Justice, 301 Centennial Mall South, PO Box 94946, Lincoln NE 68509. **LC** HV7277; .A272A. **DD** 353.9/782/0075. *Absorbed* Annual Report for Nebraska Law Enforcement Training Center.

US
ANNUAL REPORT - NEW JERSEY CASINO CONTROL COMMISSION. **Main/Corp** New Jersey. Casino Control Commission. (1978/1979)-. English. an. $120.00. New Jersey Casino Control Commission, Tennessee Avenue & Boardwalk, Atlantic City NJ 08401. **Tel** (609)441-3749. **LC** HV6721.N48; N47a. **DD** 353.97490076.

CN/0383-4379
ANNUAL REPORT OF THE CORRECTIONAL INVESTIGATOR. **Main/Corp** Canada. Correctional Investigator. **Added/Corp** Canada. Office of the Correctional Investigator. Rapport Annuel de l'Enqu„eteur Correctionnel. **VFOAT** Rapport Annuel de l'Enqueteur Correctionnel. (1974/-. Periodical. Multiple languages (English and French). an. Ottawa Correctional Investigator, Supply and Services Canada, Ottowa, Ontario K1A 0S9 Canada. **Tel** (613)993-6425. **LC** HV7315; .A38a. **DD** 354/.71/00849. **Circ:** 2,500. available with illustrations.

US/0278-0526
ANNUAL REPORT OF THE JUSTICE SYSTEM IMPROVEMENT ACT AGENCIES / BUREAU OF JUSTICE STATISTICS, LAW ENFORCEMENT ASSISTANCE ADMINISTRATION, NATIONAL INSTITUTE OF JUSTICE, OFFICE OF JUSTICE ASSISTANCE, RESEARCH, AND STATISTICS. [Annu. rep. Justice Syst. Improv. Act agencies]. 1st (Fiscal Year 1980)-. English. an. US Department of Justice, 10th Street & Constitution Avenue NW, Washington DC 20530. **Tel** (202)514-2000, **FAX** (202)633-4371. **LC** HV7245; .A66. **DD** 353.008/8/06. available on microfiche (Vols. for (1984-) distributed to depository libraries). *Continues* United States. Law Enforcement Assistance Administration. Annual Report.

MF
ANNUAL REPORT OF THE MAURITIUS POLICE FORCE. **Main/Corp** Mauritius. Police Force. (19??)-. English. an. L C Achille, Government Printer, Place d'Armes, Port Louis Mauritius. **LC** HV7848.M3; A3. **DD** 354/.69/820074. *Continues* Mauritius. Police Dept. Annual Report on the Mauritius Police Force and on Crime.

UK/0950-9305
ANNUAL REPORT OF THE POLICE COMPLAINTS AUTHORITY. [Annu. rep. Police Complain. Auth.]. **VFOAT** Annual Report - Independent Police Complaints Authority. (1986)-. English. an. £7.30. Her Majesty's Stationery Office, 51 Nine Elms Lane, London SW8 5DR England. **Tel** 011 44 71 873 8459, 011 44 71 873 8499, **FAX** 011 44 71 873 8499, 011 44 71 873 8456, telex 297138. **(Subscription address:** Her Majesty's Stationery Office, PO Box 276, Publications Centre, London SW8 5DT England.) **DD** 354.410074.

US
ANNUAL REPORT OF THE STATE DEPARTMENT OF YOUTH SERVICES FOR THE PERIOD BEGINNING JULY 1 ... AND ENDING JUNE 30 ... (SOUTH CAROLINA). **Main/Corp** South Carolina. Dept. of Youth Services. 1981/1982-. English. an. **LC** HV9105.S6; S68A. **DD** 353.97570084/9/088055. *Continues* Report to the People about the South Carolina Department of Youth Services, 0145-1553.

US
ANNUAL REPORT OF THE UTAH LIQUOR CONTROL COMMISSION. **See** Public Administration.

US/0092-3079
ANNUAL REPORT OF THE VIOLENT CRIMES COMPENSATION BOARD (NEWARK). (ANNUAL REPORT.). **Main/Corp** New Jersey. Violent Crimes Compensation Board. (1973)-. English. an. Violent Crime Compensation Board, 1100 Raymond Boulevard, Newark NJ 07102. **LC** HV8691.U5; N48a. **DD** 353.9/749/008488.

US
ANNUAL REPORT / OKLAHOMA POLICE PENSION & RETIREMENT BOARD. **Main/Corp** Oklahoma Police Pension & Retirement Board. (19??)-. English. an. Oklahoma Police Pension and Retirement Board, 201 NW 63rd Street 135, Oklahoma City OK 73116-8221. **LC** HV8145.O5; O39a. **DD** 353.97660074.

II
ANNUAL REPORT - PRISONS DEPARTMENT (INDIA). **Main/Corp** Karnataka, India. Dept. of Prisons. 1975/76-. English. Prisons Department, Inspector General of Prisons, Bangalore India. **LC** HV7371.K373; K37A. **DD** 365/.954/87. *Continues* Karnataka, India. Dept. of Prisons. Administration Report of the Prisons Department.

CN/0576-4076
ANNUAL REPORT / SOLICITOR GENERAL CANADA. [Annu. rep. - Solicit. Gen. Can.]. **Main/Corp** Canada. Solicitor General Canada. **VFOAT** Rapport Annuel. **VAT** Rapport Annuel - Sollicituer General Canada; Rapport Annuel du Sollicituer General du Canada; Rapport Annuel - Solliciteur General du Canada; Annual Report of the Solicitor General of Canada; Annual Report - Solicitor General of Canada. 1976/1977-. English (French). an. Free. Solicitor General Canada, Communications Group, 340 Laurier Avenue West, Ottawa Ontario K1A 0P8 Canada. **Tel** (613)991-2810. **LC** HV7315; .A383A. **DD** 354.710674. **Circ:** 6,400. *Continues* Canada. Ministry of the Solicitor General. Annual Report, 0576-4076.
Desc: Secretariat, Royal Canadian Mounted Police, National Parole Board, the Correctional Service of Canada, Canadian security, intelligence service.

US/0092-6051
ANNUAL REPORT - STATE OF MARYLAND. CRIMINAL INJURIES COMPENSATION BOARD. (ANNUAL REPORT.). **Main/Corp** Maryland. Criminal Injuries Compensation Board. 1st- 1969/70-. English. an. Maryland Criminal Injuries Compensation Board, 1123 Eutaw Street, 601 Jackson Towers, Baltimore MD 21201. **LC** HV7270; .A29. **DD** 353.9/752/008488.

US
ANNUAL REPORT - STATE OF NEVADA, DEPARTMENT OF MOTOR VEHICLES, HIGHWAY PATROL DIVISION. **Main/Corp** Nevada. Dept. of Motor Vehicles. Highway Patrol Division. 1971-. Periodical. English. an. Department of Motor Vehicles / Nevada, 555 Wright Way, Carson City NV 89701. *Continues* Annual Report - State of Nevada, Department of Motor Vehicles, Law Enforcement Division.

US/0272-8974
ANNUAL REPORT TO CONGRESS - URBAN INITIATIVES ANTI-CRIME PROGRAM. **Main/Corp** Urban Initiatives Anti-Crime Program (U.S.). **Added/Corp** United States. Dept. of Housing and Urban Development. 1st (1980)-. Government Publication. English. an. US Department of Housing and Urban Development, 451 Seventh Street SW, Washington DC 20401. **Tel** (202)708-0980, **FAX** (202)708-0299. **LC** HV7245; .U7a. **DD** 353.0074/06.

US
ANNUAL REPORT TO THE CITIZENS' ADVISORY BOARD ON CORRECTIONS. **Main/Corp** Kansas. Office of the Ombudsman for Corrections. (1976)-. English. Office of the Ombudsman of Correctional Institutions, 717 South Kansas Avenue, Topeka KS 66603-3807. **LC** HV7266; .A44a.
Desc: Presents for both the public and their elected representatives the scope and variety of correctionsl problems that come before the Ombudsman.

US
ANNUAL REPORT TO THE LEGISLATURE - CORRECTIONAL ASSOCIATION OF NEW YORK. **Main/Corp** Correctional Association of New York. (197?)-. English.

an. Correctional Association of New York, 135 East 15th Street, New York NY 10003. ***Continues*** *Correctional Association of New York. Annual Report.*

US/0196-7746
ANNUAL RESEARCH REVIEW - CALIFORNIA DEPARTMENT OF CORRECTIONS. **Main/Corp** California. Dept. of Corrections. English. an. California Department Corrections, 1515 S Street, Sacramento CA 95814. **Tel** (916)323-3593, FAX (916)322-2877. **LC** HV8324; .A33. **DD** 365/.9794.

US
ANNUAL STATISTICAL REPORT OF PENNSYLVANIA COUNTY PRISONS AND JAILS / DIVISION OF PLANNING AND RESEARCH. ***Title Change.*** **See** Law-Abstracting, Bibliographies and Statistics.

SP
ANUARIO DE DERECHO PENAL. Spanish. ir. 4900.00ptas. Ministerio de Justicia Centro, Publicaciones, Gran Via 76 8, 28013 Madrid Spain. **Tel** 011 34 1 5475422.

GW/0003-9225
ARCHIV FUER KRIMINOLOGIE. [Arch. kriminol.]. Vol. 66, No. 1. 2. (June 6, 1916)-. Academic Scholarly Publication. German. bm. DM411.00 Germany; DM414.00 other. Schmidt Roemhild, Mengstrasse 16 PF 2051, D 23552 Luebeck, Germany. **Tel** 11 49 451 16050. **ED** Friedrich Geerds. **LC** HV6003; .A7. **DD** 364/.05. **NLM** W1 AR235. **CODEN** ARKRAI. Index available. **Bk Rev. Ad Acc. Circ:** 850. Documents available from BIOSIS Document Express, CASDDS. ***Continues*** *Archiv fur Kriminal-Anthropologie und Kriminalistik.*
Ind/Abst Biol. Abstr.; Chem. Abstr.; EMBASE; Health Plan. Adminis.; Index Med.

EC
ARCHIVOS DE CRIMINOLOGIA, NEUROPSIQUIATRIA Y DISCIPLINAS CONEXAS. Publication began in Jan. 1937. Spanish (English). an. Instituto de Criminologia, AP 3663, Universidad Central del Ecuador, Quito Ecuador. **Tel** 521 120 OR 542 971. **ED** Hernando Roseroc. **LC** HV6005; .A65. **DD** 364.3305. Index available. **Bk Rev. Pr Rev. Circ:** 1,000 (ctrl).

US/8755-8300
ARREST LAW BULLETIN. [Arrest law bull.]. **VFOAT** A.L.B. (1976)-. Bulletin. English. mo. $59.80. Quinlan Publishing Company, 23 Drydock Avenue, Boston MA 02210-2387. **Tel** (617)542-0048, (800)229-2084, FAX (617)345-9646. **LC** KF9625.A59; A77. **DD** 345.73/0527; 347.305527. **[CCC].** Index Available, published separately, free-automatically sent. available on microfilm and microfiche from University Microfilms International (UMI).
Ind/Abst Crim. Justice Period. Index.

US/0161-6307
ATTORNEY GENERAL'S REPORT ON FEDERAL LAW ENFORCEMENT AND CRIMINAL JUSTICE ASSISTANCE ACTIVITIES. ***Ceased.*** **Main/Corp** United States. Dept. of Justice. **Added/Corp** United States. Dept. of Justice. Report on Federal Law Enforcement and Criminal Justice Assistance Activities. **VFOAT** Report on Federal Law Enforcement and Criminal Justice Assistance Activities; Federal Law Enforcement and Criminal Justice Assistance Activities. (1972)-(199?). English. be. US Department of Justice, 10th Street & Constitution Avenue NW, Washington DC 20530. **Tel** (202)514-2000, FAX (202)633-4371. **LC** KF9223; .A8423. **DD** 364/.973. ***Continues*** *Attorney General's Annual Report: Federal Law Enforcement and Criminal Justice Assistance Activities.*

US/0148-3854
AUDIT REPORT, DEPARTMENT OF JUDICIAL, STATE PROSECUTIONS. **Main/Corp** Tennessee. Division of State Audit. English. Tennessee Comptroller of the Treasury, Nashville TN 37219. **LC** KFT562; .A87. **DD** 353.9/768/0088.

US/0149-225X
AUDIT REPORT, STATE OF NEVADA DEPARTMENT OF PAROLE AND PROBATION, PAROLEE'S REVOLVING LOAN FUND; PRISONER'S WORK RELEASE REVOLVING LOAN FUND. **Main/Corp** Nevada. Legislature. Legislative Auditor. (19??)-. English. Legislative Auditor, Legislative Building, Capitol Complex, Carson City NV 89710. **LC** HV9305.N3; N45b. **DD** 353.9/793/00849.

US/0067-0561
AUGUST VOLLMER CRIMINALISTIC SERIES. Monographic series. English. ir. Price varies per volume. Charles C Thomas Publisher, 301-327 East Lawrence Avenue, Springfield IL 62717.

AT/0004-8658
AUSTRALIAN & NEW ZEALAND JOURNAL OF CRIMINOLOGY, THE. [Aust. N. Z. j. criminol.]. **Added/Corp** Australian and New Zealand Society of Criminology. **VFOAT** Australian and New Zealand Journal of Criminology. Vol. 1 (March 1968)-. Periodical. English. 120.00Aus$ (per volume). Butterworths Pty Ltd, 271-273 Lane Cove Road, PO Box 345, North Ryde NSW 2113 Australia. **Tel** 011 61 2 3354444, FAX 011 61 2 3354655. **ED** Christine Alder. **LC** HV6001; .A9. **DD** 364/.05. **[CCC].** Index available. **Bk Rev. Pr Rev. Circ:** 1,167 (ctrl). Documents available from The Genuine Article.
Desc: Forum for the discussion of the nature, causes, prevention and correction of criminal behavior.
Ind/Abst APAIS, Aust. Public Aff. Inf. Ser. (1980-); Aust. Leg. Mon. Dig.; Crim. Justice Abstr.; Crim. Penol. Police Sci. Abstr. (1968-); Curr. Contents Soc. Behav. Sci.; Curr. Law Index; Highw. Res. Abstr.; Leg. Resour. Index (1980-); LegalTrac (1981-); Res. Alert [Full Cov.]; Soc. Sci. Cit. Index [Full Cov.].

AT/1034-6627
AUSTRALIAN CRIMINOLOGY INFORMATION BULLETIN. **Added/Corp** Australian Institute of Criminology. **VFOAT** Information Bulletin. Vol. 1, No. 1 (Mar. 1990)-. Bulletin. English. bm (6 issues). 20.00Aus$ Australia; 25.00Aus$ other. Australian Institute of Criminology, 4 Marcus Clarke Street, Canberra ACT 2601 Australia. **Tel** 011 61 6 2740200, FAX 011 61 6 2740260, telex 61340. **ED** John Myrtle. **LC** HV6022.A8; A87. **DD** 364.994/05.
Desc: Contains information about current sources of Australian criminal justice information , including the latest update of CINCH, the Australian Criminology Database.

AT/0005-0024
AUSTRALIAN POLICE JOURNAL. [Aust. police j.]. Vol. 1 (Oct. 1946)-. Periodical. English. qt. $14.00 (Australia & New Zealand); 22.00Aus$ (other). New South Wales Police Department, Box 45, Sydney New South Wales 2001 Australia. **Tel** 011 61 2 3390277 ext.55289. **ED** Phil Peters. **LC** HV7551; .A9. **Bk Rev. Ad Acc. Circ:** 23,000 (ctrl).
Desc: Publishes articles of general interest and educational value to police.
Ind/Abst Crim. Penol. Police Sci. Abstr.; EMBASE.

CN/0821-0594
BASIC FACTS ABOUT CORRECTIONS IN CANADA. [Basic facts correct. Can.]. **VFOAT** Recueil de Donnees Concernant les Services Correctionnels Canadiens. 1982-. English (French). an. Communications Branch, Correctional Service of Canada, 340 Laurier Avenue, West Ottawa OntarioK1A O9P Canada. **LC** HV8483; .B38. **DD** 365/.971.

IO/0216-2563
BHAYANGKARA. 1 (June 1982)-. Periodical. English (Indonesian). qt. Lembaga Perguruan Tinggi Ilmu Kepolisian, Jl Tirtayasa Raya 6, Jakarta Indonesia. **LC** HV7551; .B47.

US
BIENNIAL REPORT. ***Title Change.*** **Main/Corp** Illinois Local Governmental Law Enforcement Officers Training Board. (1979/1980)-(198?). English. be. Illinois Local Governmental Law Enforcement Officers Training Board, Lincoln Tower Plaza, Suite 400, 524 South Second Street, Springfield IL 62701-1773. **LC** HV8145.I3; I394a. **DD** 352.2/09773. **Circ:** 1,500 (ctrl). ***Continues*** *Illinois Local Governmental Law Enforcement Officers Training Board. Annual Report.* ***Continued by*** *Illinois Local Governmental Law Enforcement Officers Training Board. Statewide System of In-Service Training.*
Desc: Report of local governmental grants-in-aid by state of Illinois for law enforcement training.

US/0149-340X
BIENNIAL REPORT - KANSAS ADULT AUTHORITY. [Bienn. rep. - Kans. Adult Auth.]. **Main/Corp** Kansas. Adult Authority. 1974/76-. English. be. Kansas Adult Authority, Suite 600, 818 Kansas Avenue, Topeka KS 66612. **LC** HV7266; .A46A. **DD** 353.9/781/00849. ***Continues*** *Biennial Report - Kansas Board of Probation and Parole, 0149-3396.*

US
BIENNIAL REPORT / MINNESOTA DEPARTMENT OF CORRECTIONS. **Main/Corp** Minnesota. Dept. of Corrections. (1979/80)-. English. be. Minnesota Department of Correction, 450 North Syndicate Street, Bigelow Building, Suite 300, St Paul MN 55104. **Tel** (612)642-0282, FAX (612)642-0223. **LC** HV7273; .A29. **DD** 353.97760084/9/05. ***Continues*** *Minnesota. Dept. of Corrections. Update - Minnesota Department of Corrections, 0195-6507.*

US
BIENNIAL REPORT - MISSOURI DIVISION OF CORRECTIONS. **Main/Corp** Missouri. Division of Corrections. English. be. Missouri Division of Corrections, PO Box 236, Jefferson City MO 65102. **Tel** (314)751-2389, FAX (314)751-4099. **LC** HV7275; .A33. **DD** 353.97780084/9/06. ***Continues*** *Missouri. Dept. of Corrections. Report.*

US
BIENNIAL REPORT OF THE OFFICE OF CRIME VICTIMS OMBUDSMAN. **Main/Corp** Minnesota. Office of Crime Victims Ombudsman. (1990)-. English. be. **LC** WMLC 91/5108. ***Continues*** *Minnesota. Crime Victims Reparations Board. Annual Report of the Crime Victims Reparations Board of Minnesota.*

US
BIENNIAL REPORT / STATE OF NORTH CAROLINA, DEPARTMENT OF HUMAN RESOURCES, DIVISION OF YOUTH SERVICES. **Main/Corp** North Carolina. Division of Youth Services. English. be. State Department of Human Resources / North Carolina, 701 Barbour Street, Raleigh NC 27603. **Tel** (919)733-4283. **LC** HV9105.N9; N672A. **DD** 364.6/088055.

US/0731-2393
BLOOD ALCOHOL TESTING FOR MOTOR VEHICLE DEATHS, WISCONSIN. (BLOOD ALCOHOL TESTING FOR MOTOR VEHICLE DEATHS, WISCONSIN / DIVISION OF HEALTH, BUREAU OF HEALTH STATISTICS.). Began in 1968. English. an. Wisconsin Division of Health, Bureau of Health Statistics, PO Box 309, Madison WI 53701. **LC** HE5614.3.W5; A2. **DD** 363.1/251. **NLM** W2 AW6 D53B.

CN/0847-8538
BLUE LINE MAGAZINE. [Blue line mag.]. Vol. 1, No. 1 (Jan. 1989)-. Periodical. English. Ten times a year (except July and Aug.). 23.36Can$ Canada; 50.00Can$ other. Blue Line Magazine, 4981 Highway 7 East, Unit 12 A, Suite 254, Markham Ontario L3R 1N1 Canada. **Tel** (905)640-3048, FAX (905)640-7547. **ED** Morley S. Lymburner. **DD** 363.2/0971. **Bk Rev. Ad Acc. Circ:** 8,000.
Desc: Targeted toward people involved in Canadian law enforcement.

US/0360-3245
BOMB SUMMARY. (BOMB SUMMARY / U.S. DEPARTMENT OF JUSTICE, FEDERAL BUREAU OF INVESTIGATION.). Began with 1973. English. an. Federal Bureau of Investigation, 10th Street and Pennsylvania Avenue NW, Washington DC 20535. **Tel** (202)324-3000, FAX (202)324-4705. **LC** HV8059; .U58A. **DD** 364.1/64.

CN/0228-2321
BOOMERANG, THE. [Boomerang]. **VFOAT** Maritime Penitentiary News. V. 1- June 1979-. Periodical. English. mo. $5.00. The Boomerang, PO Box A, Dorchester New Brunswick E0A 1M0 Canada. **DD** 365/.9715/23.

CN/0706-2893
BRITISH COLUMBIA POLICE JOURNAL. **VFOAT** Police Journal. **VAT** Police Journal (Vancouver). Vol. 1, No. 1 (Autumn 1978)-. Periodical. English. qt. 8.00Can$. British Columbia Police Commission, 1550 409 Granville Street, Vancouver British Columbia V6C 1T2 Canada. **LC** HV8159.B7; B75. **DD** 363.2/09711.

UK/0007-0955
BRITISH JOURNAL OF CRIMINOLOGY, DELINQUENCY AND DEVIANT SOCIAL BEHAVIOR, THE. (THE BRITISH JOURNAL OF CRIMINOLOGY.). [Br. j. criminol. delin. deviant behav.]. **Added/Corp** Institute for the Study and Treatment of Delinquency (Great Britain). Vol. 1, No. 1 (July 1960)-. Periodical. English. qt. £60.00 UK and Europe; $113.00 other. Oxford University Press, Walton Street, Oxford OX2 6DP England. **Tel** 011 44 865 56767, FAX 011 44 865 267773, telex 837330 OXPRES G. **(Subscription address:** Oxford University Press / USA, Journals Marketing Department, Oxford University Press, 2001 Evans Road, Cary NC 27513.) **ED** David Downes. **LC** HV6001; .L632. **DD** 364/.05. **NLM** W1 BR521. **CODEN** BJCDAR. **[CCC].** Index available. cum. index. **Bk Rev. Ad Acc. Pr Rev.** available on microfilm and microfiche from University Microfilms International (UMI). Documents available from The Genuine Article, UMI Article Clearinghouse. ***Continues*** *British Journal of Delinquency.*
Desc: A British journal of criminology involving delinquency and deviant social behavior.
Ind/Abst Acad. Search (July 1993-); Appl. Soc. Sci. Index Abstr.; Aust. Leg. Mon. Dig.; Br. Educ. Index; Br. Humanit. Index; Commun. Abstr.; Crim. Justice Abstr.; Crim. Penol. Police Sci. Abstr.; Curr. Contents Soc. Behav. Sci.; Curr. Law Index (1980-); Expand. Acad. Index (1984-); INFO-SOUTH Abstr.; Int. Bibliogr. Sociol.; Leg. Resour. Index (1980-); LegalTrac (1980-); Linguist. Lang. Behav. Abstr.; Middle East Abstr. Index; Newsp. Period. Abstr. (1991-); Psychol. Abstr. (1960-); PsycINFO (1990-); PsycLit; Res. Alert [Full Cov.]; Soc. Plann. Policy Dev. Abstr.; Soc. Sci. Source (Jul. 1993-); Soc. Sci. Cit. Index [Full Cov.]; Soc. Sci. Index; Soc. Sci. Index Fulltext (Summer 1988-) [Full Txt.]; Sociol. Abstr. (?-?); Stud. Women Abstr.

CN/0821-0357
BULLDOZER. [Bulldozer]. (1980)-. Periodical. English. sa. Bulldozer, PO Box 5052 Station A, Toronto Ontario M5W 1W4 Canada. **DD** 365/.7/0971. **Ind/Abst** Altern. Press Index (-199?).

BE
BULLETIN DE L'ADMINISTRATION PENITENTIAIRE (BELGIUM. MINISTERE DE LA JUSTICE). (BULLETIN DE L'ADMINISTRATION PENITENTIAIRE.). (19??)-. French. sa. 200F. Ministere Justice Service Central, Travail rue Berkendael 44, 1060 Brussels, Belgium. **Tel** 011 32 2 3493237. *Continues* Bulletin de l'Administration des Prisons.

US/0194-0767
BULLETIN, NATIONAL EMPLOYMENT LISTING SERVICE FOR THE CRIMINAL JUSTICE SYSTEM. *Ceased.* **See** Occupations and Careers.

US
BULLETIN. (NEW YORK (STATE). OFFICE OF JUSTICE SYSTEMS ANALYSIS. BUREAU OF STATISTICAL SERVICES). **Added/Corp** New York (State). Office of Justice Systems Analysis. Bureau of Statistical Services. (198?)-. Statistical Publication. English. New York Division of Criminal Services, Office of Justice Systems, Executive Park Tower, Stuyvesant Plaza, Albany NY 12203. **Tel** (518)457-8381. *Continues* Bulletin New York (State). Bureau of Criminal Justice Statistical Services.

JA
BULLETIN OF THE CRIMINOLOGICAL RESEARCH DEPARTMENT. Main/Corp Homu Sogo Kenkyujo. (1972)-. Directory. English. an. Research & Training Institute, Ministry of Justice, Homu Sogo Kenkyujo, 1-1-1 Kasumigaseki Chiyoda-ku, Tokyo Japan. **LC** HV6024.5; .H65a. **DD** 364.3/0952.

US/0742-7271
BULLETIN (UNITED STATES. BUREAU OF JUSTICE STATISTICS). **See** Law-Abstracting, Bibliographies and Statistics.

US
BUREAU OF CORRECTION ANNUAL REPORT. Main/Corp Pennsylvania. Bureau of Correction. **VFOAT** Annual Report of the Bureau of Correction. (1981)-. English. an. Free. Pennsylvania Department of Corrections, PO Box 598, Camp Hill PA 17011. **Tel** (717)975-4860, FAX (717)787-1758. **Circ:** 7,000. *Continues* Pennsylvania. Dept. of Justice. Bureau of Correction Annual Report.
Desc: Narrative and statistics on the activities of the department and its facilities.

US
BUREAU OF JUSTICE STATISTICS ANNUAL REPORT / U.S. DEPARTMENT OF JUSTICE, BUREAU OF JUSTICE STATISTICS. **See** Law-Abstracting, Bibliographies and Statistics.

US
BUSINESS CRIMES BULLETIN. See Business.

UK
BUTTERWORTHS LEGAL SERVICES DIRECTORY. Directory. English. an. Reed Information Services Ltd., Windsor Court, East Grinstead House, East Grinstead RH19 1BR England. **Tel** 011 44 342 326972, FAX 011 44 342 327100, telex 95127 INFSER G. **ED** Carol Straston. Index available. cum. index. **Ad Acc.** ctrl circ.
Desc: Source of information on investigators, arbitrators, computer services, law costs, loss adjustment, parliamentary agents, patent trademark agents, photographers, shorthand writers and translation services.

US/0896-9922
C.J. THE AMERICAS. [C.J. Am.]. **Added/Corp** Office of International Criminal Justice. **VFOAT** CJ the Americas. Vol. 1, No. 1 (Feb./March 1988)-. Periodical. English. bm. $24.00 (1 year), $42.00 (2 year) North America; $42.00 (1 year), $66.00 (2 year) other. Office of International Criminal Justice, 1333 South Wabash, Box 53, Chicago IL 60656. **Tel** (312)996-2784, (312)996-9267, FAX (312)413-2713, telex 270362. **ED** Gordon E Misner. **DD** 363. Index available. **Bk Rev. Ad Acc. Circ:** 3,000.

FR
CAHIERS DE DEFENSE SOCIALE. **Added/Corp** Societe Internationale de Defense Sociale. (19??)-. French (English and Spanish). an. Centro Nazionale di Prevenzione e Difesa Sociale, 3 Piazza Castello, 20121 Milan Italy. **Tel** (2)870.816, FAX (2)87.59.42, telex CNPDS 315 896(1). **LC** HV6002; .C33.
DD 364/.05. Index available. cum. index. **Ad Acc. Circ:** 500. *Supersedes* Bulletin de la Societe Internationale de Defense Sociale.

FR
CAHIERS DE LA SECURITE INTERIEURE / INSTITUT DES HAUTES ETUDES DE LA SECURITE INTERIEURE, LES. Added/Corp Institut des Hautes Etudes de la Securite Interieure. No 1 (Avril-Juin 1990)-. Periodical. French. qt. Documentation Francaise, 29 Quai Voltaire, 75344 Paris Cedex 7 France. **Tel** 011 33 1 40157000, FAX 011 33 1 40157230, telex 204 826 DOCFRAN. **LC** HV8203; .C28.

FR
CAHIERS VASILE STANCIU. Added/Corp Association Internationale des Amis de Vasile Stanciu. No. 1 (1988)-. French. an.

US
CALIFORNIA CAREER CRIMINAL APPREHENSION PROGRAM. ANNUAL REPORT TO THE LEGISLATURE / STATE OF CALIFORNIA, OFFICE OF CRIMINAL JUSTICE PLANNING. *Title Change.* **Main/Corp** California. Office of Criminal Justice Planning. 1st (1981)-(19??). English. an. **LC** HV7254; .A46a. **DD** 353.97640074. *Continued by* Career Criminal Apprehension Program.

US/0194-1682
CALIFORNIA CORRECTIONAL NEWS. **Added/Corp** California Probation, Parole and Correctional Association. **VFOAT** Correctional News. Vol.1 (Jan. 1947)-. Periodical. English. Ten times a year. $18.00. California Probation Parole and Correctional Association, 211 Lathrop Way, Suite M, Sacramento CA 95815. **Tel** (916)927-4888, FAX (916)927-4888. **ED** Susan Cohen. Index available. cum. index. **Ad Acc. Circ:** 3,200.
Desc: Professional journal for criminal justice and corrections professionals and others interested in the field.

US
CALIFORNIA DIRECTORY OF JUSTICE AGENCIES FOR JUVENILE AND ADULT. **Added/Corp** California Youth Authority. Prevention and Community Corrections Branch. **VFOAT** Directory of Justice Agencies for Juvenile and Adult. (1989-90)-. Directory. English. California Documents Section, POB 1015, North Highlands CA 95660. **LC** HV9503.C2; D57. **DD** 364.6/025/794. *Continues* Directory of Justice Agencies Serving Juveniles and Adults in California.

US/0008-1140
CALIFORNIA HIGHWAY PATROLMAN, THE. Added/Corp California Association of Highway Patrolmen. (19??)-. Periodical. English. Twelve times a year. $15.00 (one year); $28.00 (two years); $38.00 (three years). California Association of Highway Patrolmen, 2030 V. Street, Sacramento CA 95816. **Tel** (916)732-2155, FAX (916)452-3398. **(Subscription address:** P.O. Box 161209, Sacramento, CA 95816) **ED** Carol Perri (phone: (916)452-6751). **Ad Acc. Circ:** 20,000 (ctrl).
Desc: General interest publication with an emphasis on traffic safety, early California history and consumer interest pieces.

US/0199-7025
CALIFORNIA PEACE OFFICER, THE. **Added/Corp** Peace Officers' Association of the State of California. (Jan./Feb. 1980)-. Periodical. English. qt. $20.00 US; $35.00 other. California Peace Officers Association, 1455 Response Road, Suite 190, Sacramento CA 95815-4501. **Tel** (916)923-1825, FAX (916)263-6090. **ED** Leslie McGill. Index available. **Bk Rev,** (Qty: 4-8). **Ad Acc. Pr Rev. Circ:** 11,600 (ctrl). *Continues* California Peace Officers' Association Newsletter.
Desc: Magazine for members of California Peace Officers Association providing information on association happenings, legislation and articles of interest in the field of professional law enforcement.

US/0884-0075
CALIFORNIA PRISONER, THE. [Calif. prison.]. **Added/Corp** Prisoners Union (Calif.). (197?)-. Periodical. English. Six times a year. $20.00 (individuals), $30.00 (institutions). Prisoners Rights' Union, 2308 J Street, PO Box 1019, Sacramento CA 95812-1019. **Tel** (916)441-4214, FAX (916)442-2073. **ED** Kimberly Grob. **DD** 365. **Bk Rev. Ad Acc. Pr Rev. Circ:** 9,000.
Desc: Contains hundreds of listings to direct prisoners and their families to the services they need both while doing time and while integrating back into the community. Lists addresses and numbers for the 25 state prisons, offices in the California Department of Corrections, California legislators, and federal and state courts. It also includes a section on public and private resources for prisoners and their families.
Ind/Abst Altern. Press Index.

UK
CAMBRIDGE STUDIES IN CRIMINOLOGY. (1940)-. English. ir. price varies per volume. Ashgate Publishing Company, Old Post Road, Brookfield VT 05036. **Tel** (800)535-9544, (802)276-3837, FAX (802)276-3837.

US/1054-3821
CAMPUS CRIME. (CAMPUS CRIME REPORT.). [Campus crime]. Vol. 1, No. 1 (Jan. 1991)-. Periodical. English. mo. $264.00. Business Publishers Inc., 951 Pershing Drive, Silver Spring MD 20910-4464. **Tel** (301)587-6300, (800)274-0122, FAX (301)585-9075. **LC** HV8291.U6; C36. **DD** 363.2/89. **[CCC]**.
Desc: The nation's fastest growing newsletter dealing with the complex issues of campus security, legislation and liability. Each issue gives you at least 10 pages of timely information on the ever changing political and social issues surrounding crime on America's campuses.

US/0739-0394
CAMPUS LAW ENFORCEMENT JOURNAL. [Campus law enforce. j.]. **Added/Corp** International Association of Campus Law Enforcement Administrators. International Association of College and University Security Directors. (1971)-. Periodical. English. bm. $30.00 US; $35.00 other. International Association of Campus Law Enforcement Administration, 638 Prospect Avenue, Hartford CT 06105. **Tel** (203)233-4531, FAX (203)232-0819. **ED** Buck Tilson. **LC** HV8290; .C27. **DD** 363.2. **Ad Acc. Circ:** 1,200. available on microfilm from University Microfilms International (UMI).
Ind/Abst Crim. Justice Period. Index.

●US/1066-0739
CAMPUS SAFETY JOURNAL. Added/Corp California Community Colleges. Police Chiefs Association. (1993)-. Periodical. English. qt. $95.00. California Community Police Chief's Association, 915 L Street, Suite C435, Sacramento CA 95814.

CN/0824-0337
CANADIAN CRIME STATISTICS. See Law-Abstracting, Bibliographies and Statistics.

CN/0704-9722
CANADIAN JOURNAL OF CRIMINOLOGY. (CANADIAN JOURNAL OF CRIMINOLOGY. REVUE CANADIENNE DE CRIMINOLOGIE.). [Can. j. criminol.]. **Added/Corp** Canadian Criminal Justice Association. **VFOAT** Revue Canadienne de Criminologie. **VAT** Revue Canadienne de Criminologie (1978). Vol. 20, No. 1 (Jan. 1978)-. Periodical. English (French; summaries and/or abstracts in French). qt (Jan., Apr., Jul., Oct.). 45.00Can$ Canada; 60.00Can$ other. Canadian Criminal Justice Association, 383 Parkdale #304, Ottawa Ontario K1Y 4R4 Canada. **Tel** (613)725-3715, FAX (613)725-3720. **ED** Eric Linden. **LC** HV6001; .C3. **DD** 364/.971/05. **[CCC]**. Index available. **Bk Rev. Ad Acc. Pr Rev. Circ:** 1,200 (ctrl). available on microfilm and microfiche from University Microfilms International (UMI). Documents available from The Genuine Article, UMI Article Clearinghouse. *Continues* Canadian Journal of Criminology and Corrections, 0315-5390.
Desc: Journal concerned with theoretical and scientific aspects of the study of crime and with practical problems of law enforcement, administration of justice and treatment of offenders.
Ind/Abst Acad. Abstr. Full Text Elite (Jan. 1992-); Acad. Abstr. (Jan. 1992-); Acad. Search (Jan. 1992-); Am. Hist. Life (1986-1989); Appl. Soc. Sci. Index Abstr.; Can. Index (?-?); Can. Legal Lit.; Can. Period. Index; Crim. Justice Abstr.; Crim. Justice Period. Index; Crim. Penol. Police Sci. Abstr.; Curr. Contents Soc. Behav. Sci.; Curr. Law Index (1981-); Expand. Acad. Index (1984-); Index Can. Leg. Period. Lit.; INFO-SOUTH Abstr.; Leg. Resour. Index (1981-); LegalTrac (1981-); Mag. Search; Newsp. Period. Abstr. (1991-); Psychol. Abstr. (1978-); PsycINFO; PsycLit; Res. Alert [Full Cov.]; Sage Urban Stud. Abstr; Soc. Sci. Source (Jan. 1992-); Soc. Sci. Cit. Index [Full Cov.]; Soc. Sci. Index; Soc. Sci. Index Fulltext (Oct. 1988-) [Full Txt.]; Soc. Work Abstr. (Spring, Summer 1987-) [Select. Cov.].

CN/0318-806X
CANADIAN PEACE OFFICER. V. 1- April 1975-. Periodical. English. qt. $2.00. Canadian Peace Officer, 8612 151 Avenue, Edmonton Alberta T5E 5Y2 Canada. **DD** 363.2/05.

CN/0713-4517
CANADIAN POLICE CHIEF NEWSLETTER. [Can. police chief, Newsl.]. **Added/Corp** Canadian Association of Chiefs of Police. Vol. 1, No. 1 (Jan. 1982)-. Newsletter. English. qt. 50.00Can$ Canada; 60.00Can$ US; 70.00Can$ other. Canadian Association Chiefs Police, 112 Kent Street/Suite 1908, Tower B, Ottawa Ontario K1P 5P2 Canada. **Tel** (613)233-1106. **ED** S.H. Schultz. **DD** 363.2/3/0971. **Bk Rev. Ad Acc. Circ:** 1,200 (ctrl). *Continues* Canadian Police Chief, 0315-2464.

CN/0705-8810
CANADIAN POLICE COLLEGE JOURNAL. *Ceased.* **Main/Corp** Canadian Police College. **VFOAT** Journal du College Canadien de Police.

Vol. 1 (Summer 1977)-(1993). Periodical. English (French). qt. Canadian Police College Journal, PO Box 8900, Ottawa Ontario K1G 3J2 Canada.
Ind/Abst Crim. Justice Abstr.; Crim. Penol. Police Sci. Abstr.; Psychol. Abstr. (1984-); PsycINFO (1990-); PsycLit.

US
CAPITAL PUNISHMENT (PLANO, TEX.). (CAPITAL PUNISHMENT.). 1978-. English. be. Information Aids Inc., 2812 Exchange Street, Wylie TX 75098. **Tel** (214)442-0167. Index available. **Bk Rev.**

US/0198-9693
CAPITAL UNIVERSITY LAW REVIEW. [Cap. Univ. law rev.]. **Added/Corp** Capital University. Vol. 1, No. 1 (1972)-. Periodical. English. qt. Capital University Law School, 665 South High Street, Columbus OH 43215. **Tel** (614)445-8836. **LC** K3; .O37. **DD** 345/.73/005. **CODEN** CULRDZ. Index available (Bound in Nov. issue).
Ind/Abst Index Leg. Period. (19??-); Leg. Resour. Index (19??-); LegalTrac (1980-).

US
CENSUS OF LOCAL LAW ENFORCEMENT PERSONNEL. (Jan. 1983)-. English. be. Illinois Local Governmental Law Enforcement Officers Training Board, Lincoln Tower Plaza, Suite 400, 524 South Second Street, Springfield IL 62701-1773. **LC** HV8145.I3; L62. **DD** 331.12/5136322/09773. ***Continues*** *Local Law Enforcement Officers Census, State of Illinois.*

US/0734-9114
CERTIFIED PROTECTION PROFESSIONAL DIRECTORY. Added/Corp American Society for Industrial Security. (19??)-. English. an. American Society for Industrial Security, 1655 North Fort Myer Drive, Suite 1200, Arlington VA 22209. **Tel** (703)522-5800, FAX (703)522-5226, telex 901892 ASIS AGTN. **LC** HV8290; .C4. **DD** 363.2/89/02573.

US
CHARACTERISTICS OF NEW COURT COMMITMENTS / STATE OF NEW YORK, DEPARTMENT OF CORRECTIONAL SERVICES, DIVISION OF PROGRAM PLANNING, RESEARCH AND EVALUATION. Added/Corp New York (State). Dept. of Correctional Services. Division of Program Planning, Research and Evaluation. (1988)-. English. Department of Correctional Services, State Office Building Campus, Albany NY 12226. ***Continues*** *New Commitments.*

US/0749-3347
CHARACTERISTICS OF PERSONS ENTERING PAROLE. (CHARACTERISTICS OF PERSONS ENTERING PAROLE DURING ... AND ... / U.S. DEPARTMENT OF JUSTICE, BUREAU OF JUSTICE STATISTICS.). 1978/79-. English. be. National Criminal Justice Reference Services / NCJRS, Box 6000, 1600 Research Boulevard, Rockville MD 20850. **Tel** (301)251-5500. **ED** Larry Greenfeld. **LC** HV9304; .C48. **DD** 364.3/0973. ctrl circ. available on microfiche. ***Continues*** *Characteristics of the Parole Population, 0749-3339.*
Desc: Presents sex, age, race/ethnicity, education for persons entering parole with a follow up during the first year after release; includes sentencing, time served, conviction offense, prior commitments, and maximum sentence.

KO
CHIAN MUNJE. Periodical. Korean. mo. Chian Munje, Yonguso 163-3 2-ka Ulchiro Chung-ku, Seoul Korea. **LC** HV8258.A2; C47.

CH
CHIAO TUNG HSUEH KAN. First published in June 1978-. Chinese. Chung Yang Ching Kuan Hsueh Hsiao, Chiao Tung Hsi Hsueh Hui, Taipei Taiwan. **LC** HV8079.5; .C45.

US/0147-9881
CHILDREN IN CUSTODY. Main/Corp United States. National Criminal Justice Information and Statistics Service. English. be. US Department of Justice, 10th Street & Constitution Avenue NW, Washington DC 20530. **Tel** (202)514-2000, FAX (202)633-4371. **LC** HV9103; .C46. **DD** 365/.42/0973.

US/0507-0619
CHILDREN'S CASES DISPOSED OF BY THE JUVENILE COURTS. Main/Corp Virginia. Dept. of Corrections. Bureau of Management Information. English. Virginia Department of Corrections, 6900 Atmore Drive, Richmond VA 23225. **Tel** (804)674-3119, FAX (804)674-3587. **LC** KFV2471.55; .M35. **DD** 345/.755/08.

CH
CHING CHENG HSUEH PAO / CHUNG YANG CHING KUAN HSUEH HSIAO. Added/Corp Chung Yang Ching Kuan Hsueh Hsiao (China). Ching Cheng Yen Chiu So. **VFOAT** Journal of Police Science. (1982)-. Periodical. Chinese. sa. $100.00. Chung Yang Ching Kuan Hsueh Hsiao, Chiao Tung Hsi Hsueh Hui, Taipei Taiwan. **LC** HV7551; .C5193. **DD** 363.2/05.

CH
CHING HSUEH TSUNG KAN. POLICE SCIENCE QUARTERLY. Added/Corp Chung Yang Ching Kuan Hsueh Hsiao (China). **VFOAT** Police Science Quarterly. (19??)-. Periodical. Chinese (Chinese). qt. **LC** HV7551; .C5195. ***Supersedes*** *Ching Cha Hsueh Shu Shi Kan.*

US/1059-2423
CJ EUROPE. (CJ EUROPE : A CRIMINAL JUSTICE NEWSLETTER.). [CJ Eur.]. **Added/Corp** Office of International Criminal Justice. European Division. **VFOAT** Europe; Criminal Justice Europe; CJ. **VAT** Criminal Justice Europe. Vol. 1, No. 1 (Sept./Oct. 1991)-. Periodical. English. bm (6 issues). $24.00 North America; $42.00 other. Office of International Criminal Justice, 1333 South Wabash, Box 53, Chicago IL 60656. **Tel** (312)996-2784, (312)996-9267, FAX (312)413-2713, telex 270362. **LC** HV9960.E85; C52. **DD** 364.94/05.

US/0882-0244
CJ INTERNATIONAL. [CJ intern.]. **Added/Corp** University of Illinois. Center for Research in Law and Justice. **VFOAT** C.J. International. (Winter 1985)-. Periodical. English. bm. $24.00 (one year), $42.00 (two year) North America; $42.00 (one year), $66.00 (two year) other. Office of International Criminal Justice, 1333 South Wabash, Box 53, Chicago IL 60656. **Tel** (312)996-2784, (312)996-9267, FAX (312)413-2713, telex 270362. **ED** Richard H Ward. **DD** 364. Index available. **Bk Rev. Ad Acc. Circ:** 3,000.
Desc: For those interested in comparative criminal justice, offering information on criminal justice happenings across the globe including feature articles, travel notes, conferences, people, and organizations.
Ind/Abst Crim. Justice Abstr.; Crim. Penol. Police Sci. Abstr.

●US
CJ MANAGEMENT & TRAINING DIGEST. (Jan. 1995)-. English. sm. $295.00 (one year), $500.00 (two year), $700.00 (three year). Washington Crime News Services, 3918 Prosperity Avenue, Suite 318, Fairfax VA 22031-3334. **Tel** (703)573-1600, (800)422-9267, FAX (703)573-1604. ***Absorbed*** *Criminal Justice Digest, 0889-5724* ***and*** *Training Aids Digest, 0889-5732.*

US/0164-4815
CLO NEWS. Main/Corp Citizens for Law and Order. **VAT** Citizens for Law and Order News. (19??)-. Periodical. English. bm (6 issues). $10.00. Citizens for Law & Order, Box 13089, Oakland CA 94661. **Tel** (510)531-4664.

UK/0957-9664
CMBH CRIMINAL BEHAVIOUR AND MENTAL HEALTH. [CBMH. Crim. behav. ment. health]. **VFOAT** Criminal Behaviour and Mental Health. (1990)-. Periodical. English. qt. £78.00 (institutions), £48.00 (individuals) other. Whurr Publishers Ltd, 19B Compton Terrace, London N1 2UN England. **Tel** 011 44 71 359 5979, FAX 011 44 71 226 5290. **(Subscription address:** Turpin Distribution Services Limited, Blackhorse Road, Letchworth, Hertfordshire SG6 1HN, United Kingdom.**) ED** John Gunn, Pamela J. Taylor and David Farrington. **DD** 364.3. **Ad Acc.** Full Page (B&W) £195.00. Half Page (B&W) £125.00.
Desc: Contains research papers on the causes of crime and delinquency, the treatment of mentally abnormal offenders, the police, the probation service, the courts, the legal process, and the social services. Primarily aimed at psychiatrists and psychologists who work with mentally abnormal offenders or violent patients, or who are engaged in research or teaching on crime or the criminal justice system. Also pertains to lawyers, criminologists, sociologists and other social scientists.
Ind/Abst Crim. Justice Abstr.

FR
COLLECTED STUDIES IN CRIMINOLOGICAL RESEARCH. Vol. 1 (1967)-. English. ir. Council of Europe / Group Pact ED, Pharmacopoeia BP 907, 67029 Strasbourg Cedex 01 France. **Tel** 011 33 88 412036, FAX 011 33 88 41277181, telex 880388. **(Subscription address:** Manhattan Publishing Company, PO Box 650, Croton-on-Hudson NY 10520**) LC** HV6024. **DD** 364/.9/4.
Desc: A Collection of papers on the particular topic.

CN/0225-0535
COLLINS BAY CON. T. A. C. T. [Collins Bay con. t.a.c.t.]. **VFOAT** Collins Bay CONTACT. **VAT** Collins Bay Convict Together Against Cruel Times. Oct./Nov. 1978-. Periodical. English. mo. $4.00. Contact / Kingston, PO Box 190, Kingston Ontario K7L 4V9 Canada. **DD** 365/.9713/72. ***Continues*** *Avatar, 0382-7240.*

US
COMBINED ANNUAL REPORTS FOR FISCAL YEAR ... . Main/Corp Massachusetts. Criminal History Systems Board. English. an. Criminal History Systems Board, 80 Boylston Street/Room 740, Boston MA 02116. **LC** HV7271; .A393B. ***Formed by the union of*** *Annual Report of the Criminal History Systems Board, 0098-5112* ***and*** *Annual Report-The Commonwealth of Massachusetts, Security and Privacy Council, 0098-5759.*

CN/0381-095X
COMMUNICATOR (SPRINGHILL). ***Ceased.*** (THE COMMUNICATOR.). (1973)-?. Periodical. English. ir. Communicator/Nova Scotia, PO Box 2140, Springhill Nova Scotia Canada. **Tel** (902)597-3755. **DD** 365/.9716/11. ***Supersedes*** *Simsoc.*

US/0889-5767
COMMUNITY CRIME PREVENTION DIGEST. ***Title Change.*** [Community crime prev. dig.]. **Added/Corp** Washington National News Reports. Washington Criminal Justice Reports, Inc. **VFOAT** Washington National News Reports' Community Crime Prevention Digest. Vol. 7, No. 6 (Feb. 1980)-(Jan. 1995). Periodical. English. mo. Washington Crime News Services, 3918 Prosperity Avenue, Suite 318, Fairfax VA 22031-3334. **Tel** (703)573-1600, (800)422-9267, FAX (703)573-1604. **DD** 364. ***Continues*** *Community Crime Prevention Letter.* ***Absorbed by*** *Community Policing Digest.*

●US
COMMUNITY POLICING DIGEST. (1995)-. English. sm. $295.00 (one year), $500.00 (two year), $700.00 (three year). Washington Crime News Services, 3918 Prosperity Avenue, Suite 318, Fairfax VA 22031-3334. **Tel** (703)573-1600, (800)422-9267, FAX (703)573-1604. ***Absorbed*** *Comminity Crime Prevention Digest, 0889-5767* ***and*** *Crime Victims Digest, 0884-5107.*

UK
COMMUNITY SERVICE ORDERS IN ENGLAND AND WALES. Main/Corp Great Britain. Probation and After-Care Dept. English. **LC** HV7343; .A23A. **DD** 364.6/8.

US
COMPARISON OF THE YOUTH AUTHORITY'S INSTITUTION AND PAROLE POPULATIONS. Added/Corp California Youth Authority. English. New Jersey Department of Community Affairs, Cn 805 Bureau Const. Code Enforcer, Trenton NJ 08625. **Tel** (609)530-8792. **LC** HV9105.C2; C34e. **DD** 336.3/6/09794021. ***Continues*** *Comparison of Characteristics of Youth Authority Wards in Institutions and on Parole.*

US/1059-6569
COMPILER, THE. Vol. 1, July/Aug. (1979)-. Periodical. English. qt. Free. Information Resource Center, Illinois Criminal Justice Information Authority, 120 South Riverside Plaza, Chicago IL 60606. **Tel** (312)793-8550. **ED** Kevin Morison. **Bk Rev. Circ:** 6,000.

US
COMPREHENSIVE ANNUAL FINANCIAL REPORT OF THE HIGHWAY PATROLMENS' RETIREMENT FUND FOR THE FISCAL YEAR ENDING JUNE 30 ... - (MINNESOTA). Main/Corp Minnesota State Retirement System. **VFOAT** Comprehensive Annual Financial Report of the Highway Patrolmens Retirement Fund; Comprehensive Annual Report, Highway Patrolmens' Retirement Fund. English. an. Minnesota State Retirement System, 529 Jackson at 10th Street, St Paul MN 55101. **LC** HQ1064.U6; M586A. **DD** 353.97760083/5.

US/0098-5740
COMPREHENSIVE CRIMINAL JUSTICE PLAN, CRIMINAL JUSTICE PROGRAMS. Main/Corp Massachusetts. Committee on Criminal Justice. English. Commonvest Trust, 77 Beacon Street, Boston MA 02108-3421. **LC** KFM2962; .A814. **DD** 364.

US
COMPREHENSIVE LAW ENFORCEMENT AND CRIMINAL JUSTICE PLAN AND ACTION GRANT APPLICATION. Main/Corp Hawaii. State Law Enforcement Planning Agency. English. an. State Law Enforcement Planning Agency / Hawaii, Room 412/Kamamaku Building, 1010 Richards Street, Honolulu HI 96813. **LC** HV8330.5; .A3A. **DD** 364/.9969.

US/0093-8912
COMPREHENSIVE PLAN FOR CRIMINAL JUSTICE. (COMPREHENSIVE PLAN FOR CRIMINAL JUSTICE - CALIFORNIA.). **Main/Corp** California. Office of Criminal Justice Planning. (1974)-. English. Office of Criminal Justice Plan, PO Box 61047, Sacramento CA 95860. **LC** KFC1102; .A83. **DD** 364. ***Continues*** *California. Council on Criminal Justice. Comprehensive Plan for Criminal Justice.*

FR
COMPTE GENERAL DE L'ADMINISTRATION DE LA JUSTICE PENALE / MINISTERE DE LA JUSTICE. **See** Law-Abstracting, Bibliographies and Statistics.

RE
COMPTE-RENDU D'ACTIVITES / COMITE DEPARTEMENTAL DE DEFENSE CONTRE L'ALCOOLISME DE LA REUNION. **Main/Corp** Comite Departemental de Defense Contre l'Alcoolisme de la Reunion. French. an. Boite Postale 1047, 9010 S I D R Camelias, 97481 Saint-Denis CE France. **LC** HV5670.6; .A2. **DD** 362.2/9256/096891.

PH/0414-6883
CONSTABLE. (THE CONSTABLE.). **Added/Corp** Philippine Constabulary. Philippines Constabulary. Troop Information & Education Office. Philippines Constabulary. Troop Information and Historical Office. Vol. 1 (March 1967)-. Periodical. English. mo. Philippine Constabulary, Camp Crame, Quezon City Philippine. **LC** HV8255.A2; C66. **DD** 363.2/09599.
Ind/Abst Index Philip. Period. (-199?).

CN/0822-2592
CONTACT / COMITE NATIONAL MIXTE DE L'ACCP & SCF. ***Ceased.*** [Contact - Com. natl. mixte ACCP SCF]. **Added/Corp** Comite National Mixte de l'ACCP & SCF. **VAT** Contact - Comite National Mixte de l'Association Canadienne des Chefs de Police et des Services Correctionnels Federeaus. Vol. 1, No. 1 (Ete 1982)-(198?). Periodical. French. qt. Comite National Mixte de l'ACCP & SCF, 2E Etage 340 Ouest Av Laurier, Ottawa Ontario K1A 0P9 Canada. **DD** 365/.06/071.

US/0732-4464
CONTRIBUTIONS IN CRIMINOLOGY AND PENOLOGY. [Contrib. criminol. penol.]. No. 1 (1982)-. Monographic series. English. ir. Price varies per volume. Greenwood Press Inc., PO Box 5007, Westport CT 06881-5007. **Tel** (203)226-3571, FAX (203)222-1502.
Desc: Examines the issues on criminology and penology throughout the world. Historical as well as contemporary concerns are analyzed.

US
CORRECTIONAL COMPASS; OFFICIAL NEWSLETTER. **Main/Corp** Florida. Division of Corrections. Vol. 1 (Sept. 1, 1961)-. Periodical. English. mo. Free on request. Florida Department of Corrections, 2601 Blairstone Road, Tallahassee FL 32399. **Tel** (904)488-7480, FAX (904)488-4534.

CN/0070-0509
CORRECTIONAL LITERATURE PUBLISHED IN CANADA. **VFOAT** Ouvrages de Criminologie Publies au Canada. 1968-. Periodical. French (English). an. Le Conseil Canadien de Developpement Social, 55 Parkdale CP 3505 Succursale C, Ottawa Ontario K1Y 4G1 Canada. **DD** 016.364.

US
CORRECTIONAL POPULATIONS IN THE UNITED STATES / U.S. DEPT. OF JUSTICE, BUREAU OF JUSTICE STATISTICS. See Law-Abstracting, Bibliographies and Statistics.

US/0196-2353
CORRECTIONAL SERVICES NEWS. V. 1- Jan. 1976-. Periodical. English. mo. New York State Department of Correctional Services, State Office Building, Campus Building 2, Albany NY 12206.

●US/1075-203X
CORRECTIONS ALERT. [Corrections alert]. (1994)-. Periodical. English. bw (26 issues). $245.00. Corrections 2000, 7 Chelsea House, 2411 Crofton Lane, Crofton MD 21114. **Tel** (800)571-6397. **DD** 364.

US
CORRECTIONS DIGEST. (1970)-. Periodical. English. wk. $345.00 (one year), $600.00 (two year), $900.00 (three year). Washington Crime News Services, 3918 Prosperity Avenue, Suite 318, Fairfax VA 22031-3334. **Tel** (703)573-1600, (800)422-9267, FAX (703)573-1604. **ED** Betty B. Bosarge. **DD** 364. **Bk Rev. Circ:** 1,000. available in microform from University Microfilms International (UMI).
Desc: An information exchange for the correction and rehabilitation professional. Emphasis on prison management, career development, rehabilitation and treatment concepts, parole and probation trends, new programs, and court decisions.
Ind/Abst Crim. Justice Period. Index.

US/0364-1716
CORRECTIONS, STATE OF RHODE ISLAND. **Main/Corp** Rhode Island. Dept. of Corrections. 1972/73-. English. Massachusettes Department of Corrections, 100 Cambridge Street, Boston MA 02202. **Tel** (617)727-3301, FAX (617)727-7403. **LC** HV7289; .A25. **DD** 364.6/09745.

US/0190-2563
CORRECTIONS TODAY. [Correct. today]. **Added/Corp** American Correctional Association. Vol. 41, (Jan./Feb. 1979)-. Periodical. English. Seven times a year. American Correctional Association, 8025 Laurel Lakes Court, Laurel MD 20707-5075. **Tel** (301)206-5100, (800)222-5646, FAX (301)206-5061. **ED** Heidi Murphy. **LC** HV7231; .P853. **DD** 364.6/05. Index available. cum. index. **Bk Rev**, (Qty: 30-40). **Ad Acc, Adv Mgr:** Jennifer Butz. **Circ:** 24,000. available on microfilm and microfiche from University Microfilms International (UMI). Documents available from UMI Article Clearinghouse. ***Continues*** *American Journal of Correction, 0002-9203.*
Desc: Each issue provides an in-depth examination of major issues in corrections. Serves as a forum for presenting and discussing important issues in corrections.
Ind/Abst Acad. Ind. [Computer File] (1992-); Acad. Search (Jan. 1994-); Crim. Justice Abstr.; Crim. Justice Period. Index; Expand. Acad. Index (1989-); Index Period. Artic. Relat. Law; INFO-SOUTH Abstr.; Mag. Search; Newsp. Period. Abstr. (1991-); Soc. Sci. Source (Jul. 1993-); Soc. Sci. Index; Soc. Sci. Index Fulltext (Oct. 1988-) [Full Txt.].

US/0273-4230
CORRECTIONS YEARBOOK, THE. [Correct. yearb.]. 1981-. English. an. $1.75. Criminal Justice Institute, Spring Hill West, South Salem NY 10509. **Tel** (914)533-2000. **ED** George and Camille Camp. **LC** HV8482; .A24. **DD** 365/.973. ***Continues*** *Instant Answers to Key Questions in Corrections.*
Desc: Four volumes containing the most current (as of 1/1/93) facts and figures on Adult Correctional Systems (90 pp.), Juvenile Corrections, Probations/Parole, and Jails (each 66 pp.). State-by-state answers to the most frequently asked questions in correction. Set $30.00; Adult $10.00; others $8.00 each. Prior years available.

AT
COURTS OF SUMMARY JURISDICTION, SOUTH AUSTRALIA. **Added/Corp** South Australia. Attorney General's Office. Office of Crime Statistics. (19??)-. English. sa. Office of the Attorney-General / South Australia Office of Crime Statistics, Adelaide SA Australia. **DD** 364.994/021.

UK/0961-0286
CPN. CRIME PREVENTION NEWS. [CPN, Crime prev. news]. **VFOAT** Crime Prevention News. (1978)-. Periodical. English. Four times a year (Jan., Apr., July, Oct.). Free. Crime Prevention News, Room 137 Home Office of, Queen Annes Gate, London SW1H 9AT England. **Tel** 011 44 1 273-2946, FAX 011 44 1 273-2568. **ED** Jean Pavey. **Circ:** 115,000 (ctrl).
Desc: Covers crime prevention measures, policies and neighborhood watches.

US
CPOA TRAINING BULLETIN. (19??)-. Bulletin. English. mo. $120.00 (members); $140.00 (others). California Peace Officers Association, 1455 Response Road, Suite 190, Sacramento CA 95815-4501. **Tel** (916)923-1825, FAX (916)263-6090. **ED** Leslie McGill. **Pr Rev. Circ:** 180 (ctrl).

US/0011-1287
CRIME AND DELINQUENCY. [Crime delinq.]. **Added/Corp** National Council on Crime and Delinquency. **VFOAT** Crime & Delinquency. Vol. 6, No. 3 (July 1960)-. Periodical. English. qt (Jan., Apr., July, Oct.). $169.00. SAGE Periodical Press, 2455 Teller Road, Thousand Oaks CA 91320. **Tel** (805)499-0721, FAX (805)499-0871, telex 100799. **ED** Don C. Gibbons (Portland State University). **LC** HV6001; .N2. **DD** 364/.05. **NLM** W1 CR194. **CODEN** CRDLAL. **[CCC]**. Index available. **Ad Acc. Pr Rev. Acid Free. Circ:** 2,313. available on microfilm and microfiche from University Microfilms International (UMI). Documents available from The Genuine Article, UMI Article Clearinghouse. ***Continues*** *NPPA Journal;* ***Absorbed*** *NCCD News, 0027-6235.*
Desc: Addresses specific policy or program implications or issues social, political, and economic of great topical interest to the professional with direct involvement in criminal justice.
Ind/Abst Acad. Abstr. Full Text Elite (July 1990-); Acad. Abstr. (July 1990-); Acad. Ind. [Computer File] (1992-); Acad. Search (July 1990-); Appl. Soc. Sci. Index Abstr.; Crim. Justice Abstr.; Crim. Justice Period. Index; Crim. Penol. Police Sci. Abstr.; Curr. Contents Soc. Behav. Sci.; Curr. Index J. Educ.; Curr. Law Index (1980-); EMBASE; Expand. Acad. Index (1984-); INFO-SOUTH Abstr.; Int. Bibliogr. Sociol.; J. Plan. Lit.; Leg. Resour. Index (1980-); LegalTrac (1980-); Linguist. Lang. Behav. Abstr.; Mag. Search; Newsp. Period. Abstr. (1986-); PAIS Int. Print (1991-); Psychol. Abstr. (1966-); PsycINFO; PsycLit; Res. Alert [Full Cov.]; Sage Urban Stud. Abstr; Soc. Plann. Policy Dev. Abstr.; Soc. Sci. Source (Jul. 1990-); Soc. Sci. Cit. Index [Full Cov.]; Soc. Sci. Index; Soc. Sci. Index Fulltext (Aug. 1988-) [Full Txt.]; Soc. Work Abstr. (?-?); Sociol. Abstr.; Urban Aff. Abstr.

HK
CRIME AND ITS VICTIMS IN HONG KONG : A REPORT ON THE CRIME VICTIMIZATION SURVEY CONDUCTED IN ... BY THE CENSUS & STATISTICS DEPARTMENT, HONG KONG GOVERNMENT. **Added/Corp** Hong Kong. Census and Statistics Dept. (1979)-. Government Publication. English. ir. HK$54.00. Hong Kong Government Information Service, Beaconsfield House, 4 Queens Road, Hong Kong Hong Kong. **Tel** 011 852 8428801 4, telex 61190 HKGIS. **LC** HV6250.3.H85; C74. **DD** 364/.042/095125021.

US
CRIME AND JUSTICE ANNUAL REPORT. See Law-Abstracting, Bibliographies and Statistics.

AT/1030-1046
CRIME AND JUSTICE BULLETIN. [Crime justice bull.]. (1987)-. Bulletin. English. ir. Free. New South Wales Bureau of Crime Statistics and Res., GPO Box 6, Sydney 2001 Australia. **Tel** 011 61 02 257 0888, FAX 011 61 02 241 1783. **DD** 364.9944.

US/0192-3234
CRIME AND JUSTICE (CHICAGO, ILL.). (CRIME AND JUSTICE.). [Crime justice]. Vol. 1 (1979)-. Monographic series. English. ir. Price varies per volume. University of Chicago Press / Book Department, 11030 South Langley Avenue, Chicago IL 60628. **Tel** (800)621-2736, (312)568-1550, FAX (312)753-0811, telex 23933. **ED** Michael Tonry and Norval Morris. **LC** HV6001; .C672. **DD** 364/.05. **Circ:** 1,500. available on microfilm from University Microfilms International (UMI). Documents available from The Genuine Article.
Desc: Assures you of the latest research and perspectives by carefully selecting topics and commissioning authors.
Ind/Abst Curr. Law Index (1980-); Int. Bibliogr. Sociol.; Leg. Resour. Index (1980-?); LegalTrac; Res. Alert [Full Cov.].

US/1058-529X
CRIME BEAT. [Crime beat]. **VFOAT** Crimebeat. Vol. 1, No. 1 (Oct. 1991)-. Periodical. English. mo. $19.95 US; $27.95 other. 54 Corporation, 359 East 62nd Street, New York NY 10021. **Tel** (212)683-1017. **LC** HV6001; .C675. **DD** 364.

●CN/1191-386X
CRIME BUSTER (VANCOUVER). (CRIME BUSTER.). [Crime buster]. Vol. 1, No. 1 (Spring 1992)-. Periodical. English. Three times a year. Limited free distribution. Crime Buster, PO Box 4820, Vancouver British Columbia V6B 4A4 Canada. **DD** 364.4.

US/0011-1295
CRIME CONTROL DIGEST. [Wash. Crime News Serv. crime control dig.]. **Added/Corp** Washington Crime News Services. **VFOAT** Washington Crime News Services' Crime Control Digest. Vol. 1 (April 1967)-. Periodical. English. wk. $345.00 (one year), $600.00 (two year), $900.00 (two year). Washington Crime News Services, 3918 Prosperity Avenue, Suite 318, Fairfax VA 22031-3334. **Tel** (703)573-1600, (800)422-9267, FAX (703)573-1604. **ED** Betty B. Bosarge. **DD** 364. **Bk Rev. Circ:** 2,000. available on microfilm and microfiche from University Microfilms International (UMI).
Desc: A news service for law enforcement and criminal justice agencies. Provides coverage on court decisions affecting law enforcement, events, training, literature, products, police procedures, crime prevention and enforcement, federal and state legislation, and federal government programs.
Ind/Abst Crim. Justice Period. Index.

US
CRIME IN ARKANSAS. See Law-Abstracting, Bibliographies and Statistics.

US
CRIME IN COLORADO / COLORADO BUREAU OF INVESTIGATION. See Law-Abstracting, Bibliographies and Statistics.

US
CRIME IN CONNECTICUT. See Law-Abstracting, Bibliographies and Statistics.

US
CRIME IN FLORIDA. See Law-Abstracting, Bibliographies and Statistics.

US/0146-9029
CRIME IN HAWAII. See Law-Abstracting, Bibliographies and Statistics.

US
CRIME IN LOUISIANA. See Law-Abstracting, Bibliographies and Statistics.

US/0148-6292
CRIME IN MAINE (ANNUAL). See Law-Abstracting, Bibliographies and Statistics.

US/0160-7103
CRIME IN MONTANA. See Law-Abstracting, Bibliographies and Statistics.

US
CRIME IN SOUTH CAROLINA. See Law-Abstracting, Bibliographies and Statistics.

US
CRIME IN TEXAS. See Law-Abstracting, Bibliographies and Statistics.

US/0743-1872
CRIME LABORATORY DIGEST. See Law-Abstracting, Bibliographies and Statistics.

NE/0925-4994
CRIME, LAW, AND SOCIAL CHANGE. [Crime law soc. change]. Vol. 15, No. 1 (Jan. 1991)-. Periodical. English. Eight times a year. $700.00. Kluwer Academic Publishers, Postbus 322, 3300 AH Dordrecht, The Netherlands. **Tel** 011 (31) 78 524400, FAX 011 31 78 183273, telex 20083. **ED** Alan A. Block. **LC** HV6001; .C65. **DD** 364/.05. **CODEN** CSCJEL. **[CCC]. Pr Rev. Acid Free.** available on microfilm and microfiche from University Microfilms International (UMI). Documents available from The Genuine Article. ***Continues*** *Contemporary Crises, 0378-1100.*
Desc: Covers diverse issues important for understanding the interplay between crime, development and legal change, between class structures and crime, policing and punishment, and on comparative crime control. Within these larger categories the journal publishes essays examining a variety of issues such as the forces at work undermining national democratic movements and environmental activism, the organization of crime, and gender, race and ethnic equality.
Ind/Abst ABC POL SCI (1991-); Acad. Search (July 1993-); Am. Hist. Life; Crim. Justice Abstr.; Curr. Contents Soc. Behav. Sci.; Int. Bibliogr. Sociol.; Int. Polit. Sci. Abstr.; Left Index (199?-); Mag. Search; PAIS Int. Print (1991-); Res. Alert [Full Cov.]; Soc. Plann. Policy Dev. Abstr.; Soc. Sci. Cit. Index [Full Cov.]; Sociol. Abstr.

AU
CRIME PREVENTION AND CRIMINAL JUSTICE NEWSLETTER, U.N. ir. United Nations Division of Narcotic Drugs, Vienna International Center, PO Box 500, A-1400 Vienna Austria. **Tel** 011 43 222 211310.
Ind/Abst Hum. Rights Intern. Rep.

●US/1069-1324
CRIME PREVENTION FUNDING NEWS. [Crime prev. funding news]. (1993)-. Periodical. English. sm. $249.00. CD Publications, 8204 Fenton Street, Silver Spring MD 20910. **Tel** (800)666-6380, (301)588-6380, FAX (301)588-6385. **DD** 364.

US/0093-044X
CRIME PREVENTION REVIEW. (Oct. 1973)-. Periodical. English. qt. Crime Prevention Unit, Attorney General, 3580 Wilshire Boulevard, Los Angeles CA 90010. **LC** HV7431; .C74. **DD** 364/.9794. available on microfilm and microfiche from University Microfilms International (UMI).
Ind/Abst Crim. Justice Period. Index (-1989).

●US/1065-7029
CRIME PREVENTION STUDIES. (1993)-. English. ir (published 1-2 times per year). $47.50. Willow Tree Press, PO Box 249, Monsey NY 10952. **Tel** (914)354-9139, FAX (914)362-8376. **(Subscription address:** Library Research Associates Inc., Dunderberg Road, RD5 Box 41, Monroe NY 10950.**)**
Desc: Exclusively devoted to international research and practice on situational crime prevention and other measures to limit opportunities for crime. Papers include preventive oriented analyses of specific crime problems, evaluations of crime prevention programs and theoretical discussions of the philosophy and methods of situational crime prevention.

UK/0269-4905
CRIME PREVENTION TECHNOLOGY. (CRIME PREVENTION TECHNOLOGY : HIGH TECHNOLOGY SECURITY.). [Crime prev. technol.]. Vol. 1, No. 1 (April 1986)-. Periodical. English. Six times a year. Group Publishing Company Ltd, Maritime House, 1 Linton Road, Barking Essex 1G11 8HG England. **Tel** 011 44 81 591 3000.

●US
CRIME STATE RANKINGS. See Law-Abstracting, Bibliographies and Statistics.

US
CRIME TO COURT. (1973)-. English. mo. $12.00. South Carolina Educational TV Network, Box 11000 Marketing Department, Columbia SC 29211. **Tel** (800)553-7752, FAX (803)737-3503. cum. index. **Circ:** 1,000.
Desc: Continuing education television program for law enforcement officers.

US/0192-706X
CRIMES AGAINST BUSINESS. [Crimes against bus.]. Jan. 1977/June 1978-. English. Arno Press, 3 Park Avenue, New York NY 10016. **Tel** (212)725-2050. **ED** JB Kroll. **LC** HV6768; .C74. **DD** 364.1/68/05.

US/0747-8542
CRIMINAL DIVISION. (CRIMINAL DIVISION : ANNUAL REPORT / U.S. DEPARTMENT OF JUSTICE, CRIMINAL DIVISION.). **Main/Corp** United States. Dept. of Justice. Criminal Division. 1983-84-. English. an. US Department of Justice, 10th Street & Constitution Avenue NW, Washington DC 20530. **Tel** (202)514-2000, FAX (202)633-4371. **LC** KF9223; .A8424. **DD** 353.008/8.

US/0146-9177
CRIMINAL JUSTICE ABSTRACTS. See Law-Abstracting, Bibliographies and Statistics.

US/0093-8548
CRIMINAL JUSTICE AND BEHAVIOR. See Psychology.

US/0160-9688
CRIMINAL JUSTICE AND THE PUBLIC. Periodical. English. mo. $32.00. Crafton Publications Inc, 51 East 42nd Street/Room 417, New York NY 10017. ***Continues*** *Delinquency and Rehabilitation Report, 0094-2340.*

US/0887-7785
CRIMINAL JUSTICE (CHICAGO, ILL. 1986). (CRIMINAL JUSTICE.). [Crim. justice]. **Added/Corp** American Bar Association. Section of Criminal Justice. Vol. 1, No. 1 (Spring 1986)-. Periodical. English. qt (4 issues). $38.00. American Bar Association, 750 North Lake Shore Drive, Chicago IL 60611. **Tel** (312)988-5522, (312)988-5241, FAX (312)988-5528, telex 270593. **LC** KF9602; .C75. **DD** 345.73/05/05; 347.305505. available on microfilm and microfiche from University Microfilms International (UMI). ***Continues*** *Criminal Justice, 0092-2498.*
Ind/Abst Leg. Resour. Index.

US/0091-9128
CRIMINAL JUSTICE COMPREHENSIVE PLAN. (CRIMINAL JUSTICE COMPREHENSIVE PLAN (NEBRASKA).). **Main/Corp** Nebraska Commission on Law Enforcement and Criminal Justice. English. Nebraska Commission on Law Enforcement and Criminal Justice, 301 Centennial Mall South, PO Box 94946, Lincoln NE 68509. **LC** HV7277; .A255. **DD** 364.

US/0731-129X
CRIMINAL JUSTICE ETHICS. See Ethics.

US/0272-3816
CRIMINAL JUSTICE (GUILFORD, CONN.). (CRIMINAL JUSTICE.). [Crim. justice]. **VFOAT** Annual Editions: Criminal Justice. (1981)-. Periodical. English. an. Dushkin Publishing Group Inc., Sluice Dock, Guilford CT 06437. **Tel** (203)453-4351, (800)243-6532, FAX (203)453-6000. **ED** John Sullivan and Joseph Victor. **LC** HV8138; .A67. **DD** 364/.973/05. ***Continues*** *Readings in Criminal Justice.*
Desc: Provides up-to-date commentaries, articles, reports, and statistics from the most recent literature in the criminal justice field.

US/0194-0953
CRIMINAL JUSTICE HISTORY. [Crim. justice hist.]. Vol. 1 (1980)-. English (French). an. $59.50. Greenwood Press Inc., PO Box 5007, Westport CT 06881-5007. **Tel** (203)226-3571, FAX (203)222-1502. **LC** HV7921; .C75. **DD** 364/.9. **Bk Rev. Circ:** 450.
Desc: Publishes papers and articles on the history of crime and criminal justice.
Ind/Abst Am. Hist. Life (1980-).

US/0361-7378
CRIMINAL JUSTICE IN SOUTH DAKOTA. Main/Corp South Dakota. Division of Law Enforcement Assistance. (19??)-. English. Division of Law Enforcement Assistance, 118 West Capitol, Pierre SD 57501. **LC** HV7291; .A27. **DD** 364.

US/0145-4226
CRIMINAL JUSTICE JOURNAL (SAN DIEGO, CALIF.). ***Title Change.*** (CRIMINAL JUSTICE JOURNAL.). [Crim. justice j.]. **Added/Corp** Western State University College of Law. Vol. 1 (Spring 1976)-(1992). Periodical. English. sa. Western State University / College of Law, 1111 North State College Boulevard, Fullerton CA 92631. **Tel** (714)871-1820. **ED** Thomas Burger. **LC** K3; .R47. **DD** 345/.73/0505. **Bk Rev. Ad Acc. Circ:** 600. available on microfilm and microfiche from University Microfilms International (UMI). ***Continued by*** *San Diego Justice Journal, 1073-676X.*
Desc: Features articles of current interest to those involved in criminal justice. A law review published by the students of Western State University, San Diego.
Ind/Abst Crim. Justice Abstr.; Crim. Justice Period. Index; Curr. Law Index (1980-); Index Leg. Period.; Leg. Resour. Index (1980-); LegalTrac (1980-).

US
CRIMINAL JUSTICE MONOGRAPH. Monographic series. English. Price varies per volume. Criminal Justice Monograph, Huntsville TX 77340.

US/0095-7496
CRIMINAL JUSTICE NEWSLETTER (BLOOMINGTON). (CRIMINAL JUSTICE NEWSLETTER.). Newsletter. English. mo. 400 East Seventh Street, Bloomington IN 47401. **LC** KFI3562.A73; C7. **DD** 364.

US/0098-7670
CRIMINAL JUSTICE NEWSLETTER (SPRINGFIELD). (CRIMINAL JUSTICE NEWSLETTER.). Newsletter. English. ir. Illinois State Bar Association, 424 South Second, Springfield IL 62701. **Tel** (217)525-1760, FAX (217)525-0712. **ED** James J Heyda. **LC** KFI1762.A15; I55. **DD** 345/.773/05. **Circ:** 3,000. ***Continues*** *Criminal Law Newsletter.*

UK
CRIMINAL JUSTICE PACKAGE. English. ir. £6.00 (members of NACRO), £12.00 (nonmembers). NACRO Information Department, 169 Clapham Road, London, SW9 OPU England. **Tel** 011 44 71 582 6500.

US/0145-5818
CRIMINAL JUSTICE PERIODICAL INDEX. See Law-Abstracting, Bibliographies and Statistics.

US
CRIMINAL JUSTICE PLAN FOR NEW JERSEY. APPLICANTS GUIDE. ***Ceased.*** **Main/Corp** New Jersey. State Law Enforcement Planning Agency. (1978)-(199?). English. an. 3535 Quaker Bridge Road, Trenton NJ 08619. **LC** HV7280; .A46b. **DD** 364/.9749. ***Formed by the union of*** *New Jersey Plan for Criminal Justice, 0092-4652* ***and*** *Applicants Guide.*

US/0887-4034
CRIMINAL JUSTICE POLICY REVIEW. [Crim. justice policy rev.]. **Added/Corp** Indiana University of Pennsylvania. Indiana University of Pennsylvania. Dept. of Criminology. **VFOAT** CJPR. Vol. 1, No. 1 (Jan. 1986)-. Periodical. English. qt. $60.00 (institutions), $24.00 (individuals) US; $70.00 (institutions), $34.00 (individuals) Canada; $80.00 (institutions), $44.00 (individuals) other. Criminal Justice Policy Review, 210 Walsh Hall, Indian University of Pennsylvania, Indiana PA 15705. **Tel** (412)357-2471. **ED** Robert J. Mutchnick. **LC** HV9950; .C748. **DD** 364.973. Index available. cum. index. **Bk Rev**, (Qty: 4-8). **Circ:** 600 (ctrl).
Desc: Articles written by scholars and professionals committed to the study of criminal justice policy.
Ind/Abst Crim. Justice Abstr.; Crim. Penol. Police Sci. Abstr.

US
CRIMINAL JUSTICE PROFILE. ALAMEDA COUNTY. VFOAT Alameda County. 1976-. English. an. Bureau of Criminal Statistics, 77 Cadillac Drive, PO Box 13427, Sacramento CA 95813.

US
CRIMINAL JUSTICE PROFILE. ALPINE COUNTY. VFOAT Alpine County. 1976-. English. an. Bureau of Criminal Statistics, 77 Cadillac Drive, PO Box 13427, Sacramento CA 95813.

US/0734-0168
CRIMINAL JUSTICE REVIEW (ATLANTA, GA.). (CRIMINAL JUSTICE REVIEW.). [Crim. justice rev.]. Vol. 1 (Spring 1976)-. Periodical. English. sa. $30.00 (US), $33.00 (other) institution; $25.00 (US), $33.00 (other) individual. Georgia State University Public and Urban Affairs, PO Box 4018, Atlanta GA 30302-4018. **Tel** (404)651-3515, FAX (404)651-2737. **ED** Richard J Terrill. **LC** K3; .R493. **DD** 364. Index available. cum. index. **Bk Rev. Ad Acc. Pr Rev. Circ:** 1,000 (ctrl). available on microfilm and microfiche from University Microfilms International (UMI).
Desc: International and system wide in scope and focuses on trends, problems and research in criminalization, criminology, administration, law enforcement, courts, juvenile services, and corrections.
Ind/Abst Crim. Justice Abstr.; Crim. Justice Period. Index; Sage Urban Stud. Abstr.

UK
CRIMINAL STATISTICS, ENGLAND AND WALES. SUPPLEMENTARY TABLES. VOL. 1, PROCEEDINGS IN MAGISTRATES' COURTS. See Law-Abstracting, Bibliographies and Statistics.

UK
CRIMINAL STATISTICS, ENGLAND AND WALES. SUPPLEMENTARY TABLES. VOL. 3, TABLES BY POLICE FORCE AREAS AND SOME COURT AREAS. See Law-Abstracting, Bibliographies and Statistics.

NE/0168-9029
CRIMINALITEIT EN STRAFRECHTSPELEGING. See Law-Abstracting, Bibliographies and Statistics.

CN/0316-0041
CRIMINOLOGIE (MONTREAL). (CRIMINOLOGIE.). [Criminologie]. Vol. 8 (1975)-. French (summaries and/or abstracts in French and English). Twice a year (Jan., & Sept.). 18.00Can$ (individuals), 33.00Can$ (institutions) Canada; $20.00 others. Presses de l'Universite de Montreal, PO Box 6128 Station A, Montreal Quebec H3C 3J7 Canada. **Tel** (514)343-6933. **(Subscription address:** Periodica Inc., PO Box 444, 1155 Ducharme, Outremont Quebec H2V 4R6 Canada.**)** **ED** Denis Szabo. **DD** 364/.05. **Ad Acc. Circ:** 700. Documents available. ***Continues*** *ACTA Criminologica, 0065-1168.*
Desc: Of interest to professionals. Articles include research data, commentaries on recent publications, proposed legislation, and actual experiences.

Ind/Abst Can. Legal Lit.; Crim. Justice Abstr.; Crim. Penol. Police Sci. Abstr.; Linguist. Lang. Behav. Abstr.; Point Repere (1983-); Soc. Plann. Policy Dev. Abstr.; Sociol. Abstr.

CN/0316-0041
CRIMINOLOGIE (MONTREAL). (CRIMINOLOGIE.). [Criminologie]. Vol. 8 (1975)-. Periodical. French (English; summaries and/or abstracts in French and English). Twice a year (Jan., Sept.,). 18.00Can$ (individuals), 33.00Can$ (institutions) Canada; $20.00 (others). Presses de l'Universite de Montreal, PO Box 6128 Station A, Montreal Quebec H3C 3J7 Canada. **Tel** (514)343-6933. **(Subscription address:** Periodica Inc., PO Box 444, 1155 Ducharme, Outrement Quebec H2V 4R6 Canada.**)** **LC** HV6002; .A35. **DD** 364'.05. **Ad Acc.** ctrl circ. ***Continues*** *Acta Criminologica, 0065-1168.*

UK/0011-1376
CRIMINOLOGIST, THE. Added/Corp International Academy of Criminology. (19??)-. Periodical. English. qt. £36.15 UK; 37.50 other. Barry Rose Law Periodicals Ltd., Little London, Chichester West Sussex PO19 1PG England. **Tel** 011 44 243 787841, 011 44 243 783637, FAX 011 44 243 779174, 011 44 243 779278. **ED** R. Stone. Index available. **Bk Rev. Ad Acc.** ***Continues*** *Crime & Detection.*
Desc: Deals with criminal behavior in all its facets and scientific aspects of crime detection, pathology and associated subjects.
Ind/Abst Crim. Justice Abstr. (19??-); Crim. Penol. Police Sci. Abstr. (19??-).

US/0164-0240
CRIMINOLOGIST (COLUMBUS), THE. (THE CRIMINOLOGIST.). **Added/Corp** American Society of Criminology. (197?)-. Periodical. English. bm (6 issues). $7.50. American Society of Criminology, 1314 Kinnear Road, Suite 212, Columbus OH 43212. **Tel** (614)292-9207. **ED** Hugh D. Barlow. **Ad Acc. Circ:** 2,000 (ctrl).

AT/1033-4777
CRIMINOLOGY AUSTRALIA : QUARTERLY JOURNAL OF THE AUSTRALIAN INSTITUTE OF CRIMINOLOGY. Added/Corp Australian Institute of Criminology. Vol. 1, No. 1 (June/July 1989)-. Periodical. English. qt (4 issues). 30.00Aus$ Australia; 35.00Aus$ other. Australian Institute of Criminology, 4 Marcus Clarke Street, Canberra ACT 2601 Australia. **Tel** 011 61 6 2740200, FAX 011 61 6 2740260, telex 61340.

US/0011-1384
CRIMINOLOGY (BEVERLY HILLS). (CRIMINOLOGY.). [Criminology]. **Added/Corp** American Society of Criminology. Vol. 8, No. 1 (May 1970)-. Periodical. English. qt (4 issues). $90.00 institution, $50.00 individual. American Society of Criminology, 1314 Kinnear Road, Suite 212, Columbus OH 43212. **Tel** (614)292-9207. **ED** Douglas A. Smith. **LC** HV6001; .C68. **DD** 364/.05. **NLM** W1 CR196K. **CODEN** CRINYA. Index available (free). **Bk Rev. Ad Acc. Pr Rev. Circ:** 3,000 (ctrl). available on microfilm and microfiche from University Microfilms International (UMI). Documents available from The Genuine Article, UMI Article Clearinghouse. ***Continues*** *Criminologica.*
Ind/Abst Acad. Abstr. Full Text Elite (Jan. 1992-); Acad. Abstr. (Jan. 1992-); Acad. Search (Jan. 1992-); Crim. Justice Abstr.; Crim. Justice Period. Index; Crim. Penol. Police Sci. Abstr.; Curr. Contents Soc. Behav. Sci.; Curr. Law Index (1980-); EMBASE; Expand. Acad. Index (1984-); INFO-SOUTH Abstr.; J. Plan. Lit.; Leg. Resour. Index (1980-); LegalTrac (1980-); Linguist. Lang. Behav. Abstr.; Mag. Search; Middle East Abstr. Index; Newsp. Period. Abstr. (1991-); Psychol. Abstr. (1972-); PsycLit; Res. Alert [Full Cov.]; Soc. Plann. Policy Dev. Abstr.; Soc. Sci. Source (Jan. 1992-); Soc. Sci. Cit. Index [Full Cov.]; Soc. Sci. Index; Soc. Sci. Index Fulltext (Oct. 1988-) [Full Txt.]; Soc. Work Abstr. (?-?); Sociol. Abstr.; Women Stud. Abstr.

●NE/0928-8759
CRIMINOLOGY, PENOLOGY AND POLICE SCIENCE ABSTRACTS. **See** Law-Abstracting, Bibliographies and Statistics.

AT/1034-5329
CURRENT ISSUES IN CRIMINAL JUSTICE. Added/Corp University of Sydney. Institute of Criminology. Vol. 1, No. 1 (Oct. 1989)-. Periodical. English. Three times a year (Mar., July, Nov.). 60.00Aus$ Australia; 75.00Aus$ other. Institute of Criminology, 173 175 Phillip Street, Law School, Sydney 2000 Australia. **Tel** 011 61 02 2259239, FAX 011 61 02 2215635. ***Continues*** *University of Sydney. Institute of Criminology. Proceedings of the Institute of Criminology, 0085-7033.*
Ind/Abst APAIS, Aust. Public Aff. Inf. Ser. (1989-); Crim. Justice Abstr. (199?-).

US
DEATH ROW U.S.A. (1975)-. English. $225.00. William S. Hein & Company Inc., 1285 Main Street, Buffalo NY 14209. **Tel** (716)882-2600, (800)828-7571, FAX (716)883-8100, telex 91-209 WM S HEIN BUF.
Desc: Contains valuable information to those concerned with the topic of capital punishment. Statistical information on the number of death row inmates as well as statistical data on their race and sex. Every issue includes a list of states with and without capital punishment statutes. Also a state-by-state list of defendants on death row are included in each issue.

US/0191-877X
DEFENSE MANUAL. **See** Law-Civil Law.

IT
DEI DELITTI E DELLE PENE. Yearly Vol. 1, No. 1, (Jan./April 1983)-. Periodical. Italian. Three times a year. L70000 Italy; L100000 others. Associazione Gruppo Abele, Via Giolitti 21, 10123 Turin Italy. **Tel** 011 39 11 8142745, FAX 011 39 8395577. **ED** Andrea Ponta. **LC** HV6004; .D44. **DD** 364/.05. **Ad Acc, Adv Mgr:** Lulena Ortauda, **Tel** 011 814 2748.

●AG
DELITO Y SOCIEDAD. Added/Corp Universidad de Buenos Aires. Centro de Informatica Aplicada. Vol. 1, No. 1 (1992)-. Periodical. Spanish. sa. Universidad de Buenos Aires, Facultad de Ciencia Sociales, Talcahuano 256, 1o Piso - First Floor, Buenos Aires Argentina. **Tel** (541)476-0570. **ED** Juan S. Pegoraro.

US
DELPHI, THE. **See** Sociology-Social Services and Welfare.

US/0742-552X
DETENTION REPORTER. (1983)-. Periodical. English. mo. $48.00 US; $56.00 Canada; $64.00 other. CRS Inc, P.O.Box 365, Topsham ME 04086. **Tel** (207)725-9090, FAX (207)725-2578. **ED** Rod Miller. **LC** KF9730.A15; D47. **DD** 349.73/05; 347.3005. **Bk Rev.**
Desc: Monthly resource for detention and corrections offering news, resources, court case summaries, calendar and in-depth analysis of selected topics.

GW/0012-057X
DEUTSCHE POLIZEI. Added/Corp Gewerkschaft der Polizei im Gebiet der Deutschen Bundes Republik Einschliesslich des Landes Berlin. (Jan. 1950)-. Periodical. German. mo. Verlagsanstalt Deutsche Polizeiliterat, Forststrasse 3A, D 40721 Hilden Germany. **Tel** 011 49 211 71040. **LC** HV7551; .D4712. **[CCC].**
Ind/Abst Crim. Penol. Police Sci. Abstr.

IO
DHARMA WARTA. Indonesian. Badan Koordinasi Pelaksana Instruksi Presiden, Jalan Senopati 1/No 51, Jakarta Indonesia. **LC** HV7102; .D48.

US
DIMENSIONS ... . Main/Corp Michigan. State Dept. of Corrections. 1976-. English. an. Michigan Department of Corrections, PO Box 30003, Lansing MI 48909. **Tel** (517)373-0720, FAX (517)373-2628. **LC** HV7272; .A475. **DD** 353.9/774/00849. ***Continues*** *MDC, Michigan Department of Corrections Annual Report, 0363-9630.*

●US/1071-3530
DIRECTORY, JUVENILE & ADULT CORRECTIONAL DEPARTMENTS, INSTITUTIONS, AGENCIES & PAROLING AUTHORITIES / AMERICAN CORRECTIONAL ASSOCIATION. [Dir. juv. adult correct. dep. inst. agencies parol. auth.]. **Added/Corp** American Correctional Association. **VFOAT** Directory, Juvenile and Adult Correctional Departments, Institutions, Agencies and Paroling Authorities. (1992)-. English. an. $81.10 US; $92.50 Alaska, Hawaii & Puerto Rico; $95.00 other. American Correctional Association, 8025 Laurel Lakes Court, Laurel MD 20707-5075. **Tel** (301)206-5100, (800)222-5646, FAX (301)206-5061. **ED** Glenda Beal. **DD** 365/.973/025. **Circ:** 4500. available on microfiche. ***Continues*** *Juvenile and Adult Correctional Departments, Institutions, Agencies, and Paroling Authorities, United States and Canada, 0190-2555.*

US
DIRECTORY : JUVENILE AND ADULT CORRECTIONAL DEPARTMENTS, INSTITUTIONS, AGENCIES AND PAROLING AUTHORITIES, UNITED STATES AND CANADA. ***Title Change.*** 1975/76-1978. Directory. English. an. American Correctional Association, 8025 Laurel Lakes Court, Laurel MD 20707-5075. **Tel** (301)206-5100, (800)222-5646, FAX (301)206-5061. **Bk Rev. Ad Acc. Circ:** 6,000. ***Continues*** *Directory. Juvenile and Adult Correctional Institutions and Agencies of the United States of America, Canada, and Great Britain.* ***Continued by*** *Juvenile and Adult Correctional Departments, Institutions, Agencies and Paroling Authorities. United States and Canada.*
Desc: Lists administrative personnel, state level institutions, federal military in US and Canada, statistics on inmate populations, etc.

US
DIRECTORY OF ARIZONA CRIMINAL AND CIVIL JUSTICE AGENCIES AND DIGEST OF RELATED INFORMATION. VFOAT Directory of Arizona Criminal Justice Agencies; Arizona Criminal and Civil Justice Agencies. (1991)-. Directory. English. Track Down, Inc., 115 West McDowell Road, Phoenix AZ 85003. **LC** HV8145.A7; D57. **DD** 350.74/025/791. ***Continues*** *Arizona Criminal Justice Agencies ... Directory.*

US
DIRECTORY OF CRIMINAL JUSTICE AGENCIES IN ARIZONA. 1978-. Directory. English. an. Professional Plaza, 4820 North Black Canyon Freeway, Phoenix AZ 85017. **LC** HV8145.A7; D57. **DD** 350.74/025/791.

US/0097-6083
DIRECTORY OF LAW ENFORCEMENT AND CRIMINAL JUSTICE EDUCATION. ***Ceased.*** **Added/Corp** International Association of Chiefs of Police. Professional Standards Division. (1966)-(19??). English. an. International Association of Chiefs of Police, 515 North Washington, Alexandria VA 22314. **Tel** (800)843-4227. **LC** HV8143; .D56. **DD** 363.2/07/1073.

US
DIRECTORY OF LAW ENFORCEMENT PROFESSORS. 1970-. Directory. English. Anderson Publishing, 2035 Reading Road, Cincinnati OH 45202. **Tel** (513)421-4142, (800)582-7295, FAX (513)562-8116. **LC** HV8143; .D57. **DD** 363.2/07.

CN
DIRECTORY, SERVICES FOR VICTIMS OF CRIME. Added/Corp Canadian Criminal Justice Association. **VFOAT** Services for Victims of Crime; Services Aux Victimes d'Actes Criminels; Repertoire Services Aux Victimes d'Actes Criminels. (Jan. 1989)-. Directory. English (French). Twice a year. 17.25Can$. Canadian Criminal Justice Association, 383 Parkdale #304, Ottawa Ontario K1Y 4R4 Canada. **Tel** (613)725-3715, FAX (613)725-3720. **LC** HV6250.3.C2; D57. **DD** 362.88/025/71. **Circ:** 600.
Desc: List of names, addresses, phone numbers and descriptions of services to victims of crime.

US
DISCUSSION PAPER - SPECIAL COMMITTEE ON CRIMINAL JUSTICE. Main/Corp Association of the Bar of the City of New York. Special Committee on Criminal Justice. No. 1- Jan. 1978-. Periodical. English. 42 West 44th Street, New York NY 10036.

US
DOCS TODAY. VFOAT D.O.C.S. Today. Vol. 1, No. 1; May 1987-. Periodical. English. mo. New York State Correctional Services Department, State Office, Campus Building 2, Albany NY 12226. **Tel** (518)457-8134, FAX (518)457-7252.

US/0364-5754
DOCUMENT RETRIEVAL INDEX. VFOAT National Criminal Justice Document Retrieval Index. Vol. 1 (July 1972)-. Periodical. English. ir (cumulative issue every four years with annual supplements). $94.00 cumulative edition, $27.00 supplements. United States National Criminal Justice, Reference Service, Washington DC 20531. **Tel** (800)851-3420 OR (301)251-5100. **ED** Denise Galarraga. **LC** Z7164.P76; D63. **DD** 016.364. **Circ:** 300.
Desc: Access tool to the NCJRS Document Collection of 86,000 articles, books, reports and other materials in the subject area of criminal justice. It contains full bibliographic information plus annotation and carries indexes by subject, personal author, corporate author, access number and title. Because of these attributes, the Index can stand alone as a reference resource in this subject area.

●US
DRUG DEMAND REDUCTION NETWORK: A SUPPLEMENT TO THE LECC/VICTIM-WITNESS NETWORK NEWS/ U.S. DEPARTMENT OF JUSTICE, EXECTUVE OFFICE FOR UNITED STATES ATTORNEYS. Added/Corp Executive Office for U.S. Attorneys. **VFOAT** Network. Vol. 1, No. 1 (Jan./Feb. 1992)-. Periodical. English. bm. The Office, Room 1612, EQUSA, Main Justice Bldg., 10th and Pennsylvania, Washington DC 20530.

US/1055-6281
DRUG DETECTION REPORT. [Drug detect. rep]. Vol. 1, No. 1 (Apr. 5, 1991)-. Periodical. English. Twenty-four times a year. $295.00. Pace Publications / New York, PO Box 2972, Grand Central Station, New York NY 10163. **Tel** (212)685-5450, FAX (212)679-4701. **DD** 344.

US
EAGLE, THE. English. qt. $5.00 (libraries), $10.00 (regular) North America; $15.00 other. Eagle Publishing Company / Texas, PO Box 6303, Corpus Christi TX 78466-6303. **Tel** (512)888-6164. **ED** H Roehm. **Bk Rev. Ad Acc. Circ:** 3,000 (ctrl).
Desc: Investigators news.

US/0362-0697
ECONOMIC CRIME DIGEST. Periodical. English. National District Attorneys Association / Virginia, 99 Canal Center Plaza, Suite 510, Alexandria VA 22314. **Tel** (703)549-9222. **LC** HV6693; .E33A. **DD** 364.1/63/0973. ***Continues*** *Economic Crime Project Newsletter.*

US
EDMANDS & HIER POLICE LAW SERVICE. **VFOAT** Police Law Service. **VAT** Edmands and Hier Police Law Service. (198?)-. Periodical. English. qt (Jan., Apr., July, Oct.). $60.00. Edmands and Hier Police Law, P.O.Box 204, Waban MA 02168. **Tel** (617)969-7535.

FR/1164-8589
ENFANCE MAJUSCULE PARIS. (ENFANCE MAJUSCULE.). (1991)-. Periodical. French. Six times a year. 165.00F France; 235.00F other. Enfance Majuscule, 5 rue Gassendi, 75014 Paris France. **Tel** 011 33 1 48256186, FAX 011 33 1 46041187. **ED** Chalon Patricia. **UDC** 364-053.3/.6. **Bk Rev**, (Qty: 6/year). **Ad Acc**. ctrl circ. ***Continues*** *La Tribune de l'Enfance, 0041-283X.*

UK/0951-2721
ENIGMA VARIATIONS NEWS. ***Suspended.*** **See** Military and Defense.

IT/0394-8625
ESSECOME. [Essecome]. (1981)-. Periodical. Multiple languages. Eleven times a year. L95000.00 one year; L180000.00 two years. Edis SRL, Via E Ponente 20 / 4, 40133 Bologna Italy. **Tel** 011 39 51 382606 or 312205, FAX 011 39 51 380605. **UDC** 614.8. **Bk Rev. Circ:** 12,000.

CK
ESTADISTICA DE CRIMINALIDAD. **See** Law-Abstracting, Bibliographies and Statistics.

CN
ESTIMATES. PART III, CORRECTIONAL SERVICE CANADA. **Main/Corp** Canada. **VFOAT** Budget des Depenses. Partie III, Service Correctionnel Canada. (19??)-. English (French). $9.00 Canada; $10.80 other. Canada Communication Group Publishers, Order Processing, Ottawa Ontario K1A 0S9 Canada. **Tel** (819)956-4800, (819)956-4802. **LC** HV9506; .C36a. **DD** 354.710084/9.

CN
ESTIMATES. PART III, NATIONAL PAROLE BOARD. **VFOAT** Budget des Depenses. Partie III, Commission Nationale i.e. Nationnale des Liberations Conditionnelles. (19??)-. English (French). $6.00 Canada; $7.20 other. Canada Communication Group Publishers, Order Processing, Ottawa Ontario K1A 0S9 Canada. **Tel** (819)956-4800, (819)956-4802. **LC** HV9278; .C24a. **DD** 354.710084/93.

CN
ESTIMATES. PART III, ROYAL CANADIAN MOUNTED POLICE. **Main/Corp** Canada. **VFOAT** Budget des Depenses. Partie III, Gendarmerie Royale du Canada. (19??)-. English (French). $9.00 Canada; $10.80 other. Canada Communication Group Publishers, Order Processing, Ottawa Ontario K1A 0S9 Canada. **Tel** (819)956-4800, (819)956-4802. **LC** HV7641; .A28a. **DD** 354.710074.

PL/0860-3723
EUROCRIMINOLOGY / INSTITUTE OF CRIME PROBLEMS. **Added/Corp** Institute of Crime Problems (Warsaw, Poland). Vol. 1 (1987)-. English. **LC** HV6001; .E97.
Ind/Abst Crim. Justice Abstr. (199?-).

●NE/0928-1371
EUROPEAN JOURNAL ON CRIMINAL POLICY AND RESEARCH. [Eur. j. crim. policy res.]. (1993)-. Periodical. English. qt. $100.00 US; Fl180.00 Netherlands. Kugler Publications BV / Amsterdam, PO Box 11188, 1001 GD Amsterdam Netherlands. **Tel** 011 31 20 6278070. **UDC** 343.2.

US
EXPLOSIVES INCIDENTS REPORT. **Added/Corp** United States. Bureau of Alcohol, Tobacco, and Firearms. **VFOAT** 1976-1985, a 10-year Retrospective; Explosive Incidents Report. (1985)-. English. Bureau of Alcohol Tobacco and Firearms, 650 Massachusetts Avenue Northwest, Room 5100, Washington DC 20226. **Tel** (202)927-8056. ***Continues*** *Explosives Incidents, 0273-5032.*

CN/0381-7423
EYE SPY. **Added/Corp** Calgary Correctional Institution. No. 1 Mar. (1976)-. Periodical. English. Eye Spy Publications, Box 3250 Station B, Calgary Alberta T2M 4L9 Canada. **DD** 365/.97123/3.

CN/0710-1090
FACE A LA JUSTICE. [Face justice]. **Added/Corp** Ligue des Droits de l'Homme (Montreal, Quebec). Office des Droits des Detenus. Vol. 1 No. 1 (Oct. 1977)-. Periodical. French. bm. 20.00Can$. Journal Face a la Justice, 1030 Cherrier/Suite 300, Montreal Quebec H2L 1H9 Canada. **Tel** (514)522-5965. **ED** Jean Claude Bernheim. **DD** 364/.971. **Ad Acc. Circ:** 1,000.
Desc: Publishes material concerning the penal and judicial systems.
Ind/Abst Hum. Rights Intern. Rep.

DK
FAENGSELSVASENET. **Main/Corp** Denmark. Direktoratet for Kriminalforsorgen. **VFOAT** Prison Department. Danish (summaries and/or abstracts in English). Justitsministeriet Direktoratet for Kriminalforsorgern, Klareboderne 1, 1115 K Kbenhavn Denmark. **Tel** 01-13 87 53. **LC** HV8485.D4; A2.

US/0014-5688
FBI LAW ENFORCEMENT BULLETIN. [FBI law enforc. bull.]. **Added/Corp** United States. Federal Bureau of Investigation. United States. Federal Bureau of Investigation. Public Affairs Office. United States. Federal Bureau of Investigation. Office of Congressional and Public Affairs. **VFOAT** Law Enforcement Bulletin. **VAT** Federal Bureau of Investigation Law Enforcement Bulletin. Vol. 4, No. 10 (Oct. 1935)-. Government Publication. English. mo. $14.00 US; $22.50 other. Superintendent of Documents, US Government Printing Office, Washington DC 20402. **Tel** (202)275-3328, FAX (202)786-2377. available on microfilm and microfiche from University Microfilms International (UMI). Documents available from UMI Article Clearinghouse. ***Continues*** *Fugitives Wanted by Police.*
Ind/Abst Acad. Ind. [Computer File] (1992-); Acad. Search (July 1993-); Crim. Justice Abstr.; Crim. Justice Period. Index (-1989); Crim. Penol. Police Sci. Abstr.; Expand. Acad. Index (1989-); INFO-SOUTH Abstr.; Newsp. Period. Abstr. (1991-); PAIS Int. Print (1991-); Soc. Sci. Source (Jul. 1993-); Soc. Sci. Index; Soc. Sci. Index Fulltext (Oct. 1988-) [Full Txt.].

US
FEDERAL PRISONS JOURNAL. **Added/Corp** United States. Bureau of Prisons. Vol. 1, No. 1 (Summer 1989)-. Periodical. English. Four times a year. Free upon request to qualified subscribers in the Criminal Justice field. Federal Bureau of Prisons, 320 First Street Northwest, Room 640, Washington DC 20534. **Tel** (202)724-3198. **LC** HV9471; .F44. **DD** 365/.32.
Ind/Abst Crim. Justice Abstr. (199?-).

US/0014-9128
FEDERAL PROBATION. [Fed. probat.]. **Added/Corp** United States. Administrative Office of the United States Courts. United States Probation System. United States. Bureau of Prisons. **VFOAT** Federal Probation Newsletter; Federal Probation News Letter; Federal Probation Quarterly. (May/June 1937)-. Government Publication. English. qt. $7.00 domestic; $8.75 other. Superintendent of Documents, US Government Printing Office, Washington DC 20402. **Tel** (202)275-3328, FAX (202)786-2377. **ED** Lorene Lake. **DD** 364. **NLM** W1 FE234. **CODEN** FDEPA. cum. index. **Bk Rev. Pr Rev. Circ:** 4,300. available on microfilm and microfiche from University Microfilms International (UMI). Documents available from The Genuine Article, UMI Article Clearinghouse. ***Continues*** *News Letter (United States Probation System).*
Desc: Articles, reviews (books and journals), and columns on topics concerning preventative and correctional activities in delinquency and crime.
Ind/Abst Acad. Abstr. Full Text Elite (Jan. 1992-); Acad. Abstr. (Jan. 1992-); Acad. Search (Jan. 1992-); Crim. Justice Abstr.; Crim. Justice Period. Index; Crim. Penol. Police Sci. Abstr.; Curr. Contents Soc. Behav. Sci.; Curr. Law Index (1980-); EMBASE; Expand. Acad. Index (1984-); INFO-SOUTH Abstr.; Leg. Resour. Index (1980-); LegalTrac (1980-); Mag. Search; Middle East Abstr. Index; Newsp. Period. Abstr. (1991-); PAIS Int. Print (1991-); Psychol. Abstr. (1983-); PsycINFO (1990-); PsycLit; Res. Alert [Full Cov.]; Soc. Sci. Source (Jan. 1992-); Soc. Sci. Cit. Index [Full Cov.]; Soc. Sci. Index Fulltext (Sept. 1988-) [Full Txt.]; Soc. Work Abstr. [Select. Cov.]; Vocat. Search (Jan. 1992-).

US/1053-9867
FEDERAL SENTENCING REPORTER : FSR. [Fed. sentencing report.]. **Added/Corp** Vera Institute of Justice. **VFOAT** FSR. (June 1988)-. Periodical. English. bm. $108.00, $70.00 (students) US; add $6.00 postage other. University of California Press, 2120 Berkeley Way, Berkeley CA 94720. **Tel** (510)642-4191, (510)642-3907, FAX (510)642-9917. **ED** Daniel Freed and Mare Miller. **LC** KF9685.A59; F43. **DD** 345.73/0772/02642; 347.30577202642. **[CCC]. Pr Rev. Circ:** 2,400. available on microfilm and microfiche from University Microfilms International (UMI).

UK/0951-1288
FINGERPRINT WHORLD. [Fingerpr. whorld]. (1975)-. Periodical. English. Four times a year (Jan. Apr., July, Oct.). $40.00. Fingerprint Society, 5 Slate Close, Glenfield Leicester, LE3 8QQ England. **Tel** 011 44 462 32287. **ED** Graham Hughes (phone: (051)777-6366). **DD** 612.79. **Ad Acc, Adv Mgr:** M. Crockett, **Tel** 0926-415833. **Circ:** 2,000 (ctrl).
Desc: The advance study of fingerprints. The application to facilitate the co-operation among persons who are interested in this field of personal identification.

US/1059-7298
FIRE AND ARSON INVESTIGATOR, THE. **See** Fire Prevention.

US/0362-7322
FISCAL YEAR SUMMARY REPORT OF POPULATION MOVEMENT. **Added/Corp** Wisconsin. Division of Corrections. Bureau of Planning, Development, and Research. Wisconsin. Division of Corrections. Office of Systems and Evaluation. Wisconsin. Division of Corrections. Office of Information Management. Wisconsin. Division of Corrections. Office of Information Management and Operations. (19??)-. English. an. Wisconsin Division of Corrections, 149 East Wilson Street, Room 1050, Madison WI 53702. **Tel** (608)266-2471, FAX (608)267-0923. **LC** HV7299; .A28h. **DD** 365/.6/09775.
Desc: Provides movements of adults and juveniles under the supervision of state institutions and probation and parole supervision.

US
FIVE YEAR PLAN / CONNECTICUT DEPARTMENT OF CORRECTION. **Main/Corp** Connecticut. Dept. of Correction. (1990)-. English. an. Connecticut Department of Corrections, 340 Capitol Avenue, Hartford CT 06106. **Tel** (203)566-4457, FAX (203)566-1741. **LC** PAR.

US/0733-804X
FLORIDA CRIME AND DELINQUENCY. (FLORIDA CRIME AND DELINQUENCY : OFFICIAL ORGAN OF THE FLORIDA COUNCIL ON CRIME AND DELINQUENCY.). **VFOAT** Crime and Delinquency. Vol. 1, No. 1 (Fall 1977)-. Periodical. English. qt. Florida Crime and Delinquency Editor, 3715 SW 5th Place, Gainesville FL 32607.

US/0015-4229
FLORIDA POLICE JOURNAL. **Added/Corp** Florida Peace Officers' Association. (19??)-. Periodical. English. Four times a year. Florida Peace Officers Association, PO Box 5077, Tallahassee FL 32314. **Tel** (904)222-7070. **DD** 351.74.

US/0747-3117
FLORIDA SECURITY & INVESTIGATORS JOURNAL. (FLORIDA SECURITY & INVESTIGATORS JOURNAL : OFFICIAL PUBLICATION OF THE FLORIDA SECURITY AND INVESTIGATORS ASSOCIATION, INC.). **VFOAT** Florida Security and Investigators Journal. Periodical. English. qt. Florida Security & Investigators Association, PO Box 40, Bryceville FL 32009.

CN/0703-4725
FLUTE, LA. V. 32, No. 1- Oct. 1976-. Periodical. French. mo. Free. Fraternite des Policiers de la Cum, 480 Gilford, Montreal Quebec H2J 1N3 Canada. **DD** 363.2/09714/28. ***Continues*** *Police, 0380-8548.*

IT/0394-5243
FORCE (ROME, ITALY). (FORCE.). [Force]. 1986-. Periodical. Italian (summaries and/or abstracts in English). Six times a year. $46.00 (surface mail), $60.00 (airmail). Publi & Consult Spa, Via Tagliamento 29 2, 00198 Rome Italy. **Tel** 011 39 6 8546754. **LC** HV8212; .F67. Index available. **Ad Acc. Circ:** 32,500.

US/8756-8888
FORENSIC ACCOUNTING REVIEW. **See** Law-Corporate Law.

US/0277-982X
FORENSIC BULLETIN. **Added/Corp** Virginia. Bureau of Forensic Science. (19??)-. Bulletin. English. Free. Division of Forensic Science, Department of General Service, 1 North 14th Street, Richmond VA 23219. **Tel** (804)786-4706, FAX (804)371-8328. **ED** Paul Ferrara.
Desc: Provides comprehensive laboratory services for all of the Commonwealth of Virginia's more than 350 Law enforcement agencies.

US/0015-8275
FORTUNE NEWS. [Fortune news]. **Added/Corp** Fortune Society (New York, N.Y.). (1967)-. Periodical. English. Four times a year. $15.00. Fortune Society, 39 West 19th Street, New York NY 10011. **Tel** (212)206-7070. **ED** Richard Stratton & Kren White. **DD** 361. **Circ:** 35,000 (ctrl).
Desc: Educates people about criminal justice issues. Gives prisoners an opportunity to be heard through their contributions to newspapers.

CN/0847-0464
FORUM ON CORRECTIONS RESEARCH. [Forum correct. res.]. **Added/Corp** Correctional Service Canada. Vol. 1, No. 1 (1989)-. Periodical. English. qt. (free upon request). Correctional Service Canada, CR Serv Div, 340 Laurier Ave W, Ottawa ONT K1A 0P9 Canada. **Tel** (613)992-8423. **DD** 365/.971.
Ind/Abst Crim. Justice Abstr. (199?-).

US/0734-0842
FROM THE STATE CAPITALS. ALCOHOLIC BEVERAGE CONTROL. [From state cap., Alcohol. beverage control]. **VFOAT**

Law —Law Enforcement and Criminology

Alcoholic Beverage Control. (April 5, 1982)-. Periodical. English. wk. $211.50 (one year); $235.00 (two year) public and institutional libraries; $378.00 (one year), $420.00 (two year) other. Wakeman Walworth Inc., 300 North Washington Street #204, Alexandria VA 22314. **Tel** (703)549-8606. **ED** Emily Novick. **DD** 363. **[CCC].**
Continues From the State Capitals. Liquor Control, 0016-1780.
Desc: Covers liquor advertising, dram shop liability, license regulation, drunken driving laws, legal drinking ages.

US/0749-2790
FROM THE STATE CAPITALS. JUSTICE POLICIES. *Title Change.* [From state cap., Justice policies]. **VFOAT** Justice Policies. (198?)-(19??). Periodical. English. wk. Wakeman Walworth Inc., 300 North Washington Street #204, Alexandria VA 22314. **Tel** (703)549-8606. **ED** Emily Novick. **DD** 344. *Formed by the union of* From the State Capitals. Prison Administration, 0734-0885 *and* From the State Capitals. Judicial Administration (New Haven, Conn.), 0734-1091. *Continued by* From the State Capitals. Public Safety & Justice Policies, 1061-9704.
Desc: Sentencing guidelines, parole programs, public defender systems, court financing and fees, family and juvenile justice, victim compensation laws, inmate living conditions, security and staffing.

US/1061-9704
FROM THE STATE CAPITALS. PUBLIC SAFETY & JUSTICE POLICIES. [From state cap., Public saf. justice policies]. **VFOAT** Public Safety & Justice Policies; Public Safety and Justice Policies. Vol. 45, No. 40 (Oct. 7, 1991)-. Periodical. English. wk. $211.50 (one year), $378.00 (two year) public and institutional libraries; $235.00 (one year), $420.00 (two year) other. Wakeman Walworth Inc., 300 North Washington Street #204, Alexandria VA 22314. **Tel** (703)549-8606. **DD** 344. *Continues* From the State Capitals. Justice Policies, 0749-2790; *Absorbed* From the State Capitals. Drug Abuse Control, 0734-0877.

US/0148-9291
FUNDING REPORT - CONNECTICUT JUSTICE COMMISSION. Main/Corp Connecticut Justice Commission. (1976)-. English. an. Connecticut Justice Commission, 75 Elm Street, Hartford CT 06115. **LC** HV7256; .A4. **DD** 364/.9746. *Continues* Funding Report - Connecticut Planning Committee on Criminal Administration, 0363-9649.

US/0095-196X
G.C.B. BULLETIN. *Title Change.* Main/Corp Nevada. State Gaming Control Board. Bulletin. English. 515 E Musser Street, Carson City NV 89701. **LC** HV6721.N45; N47B. **DD** 353.9/793/00762. *Continued by* SIIS Industrial Insurance News.

US
GAMBLING / INFORMATION AIDS. Added/Corp Information Aids, Inc. Instructional Aides (Firm) Information Plus (Firm : Wylie, Tex.). **VFOAT** Gambling, Crime or Recreation?. (1978)-. English. be. $22.63. Information Aids Inc., 2812 Exchange Street, Wylie TX 75098. **Tel** (214)442-0167. Index available. **Bk Rev.**
Desc: Complete overview of gambling in America.

●US/1061-5326
GANG JOURNAL, THE. (1992)-. Periodical. English. qt. $60.00 US; $72.00 other. Vande Ver Publishers, Ltd, PO Box 226, Berrien Springs MI 49103-0226. **ED** George Knox. **Bk Rev. Ad Acc, Adv Mgr:** John Fitzholm, **Tel** (616)695-3442. **Pr Rev. Acid Free. Circ:** 500.
Desc: Research form any discipline related to gangs. Also contains perspectives and book reviews.

UK
GATELODGE : THE PRISON OFFICERS' MAGAZINE. Added/Corp Prison Officers' Association (London, England). **VFOAT** Gate Lodge ; Prison Officers' Magazine; POA Magazine ; P.O.A. Magazine. Vol. 76, No. 1 (Jan. 1986)-. Periodical. English. Twelve times a year. £4.00 England; £8.00 other. Prison Officers' Association, 245 Church Street, Edmonton London N9 9HW England. **Tel** (01)803-0255, FAX (01)803-1761. **ED** J. Sutcliffe and A. Sinclair. **LC** HV7231; .P83. **DD** 365/.941/05. **Bk Rev. Ad Acc. Circ:** 17,500. *Continues* Prison Officers' Magazine.
Desc: For and about the English prison officers.

PL/0867-0390
GAZETA POLICYJNA. (1990)-. Periodical. Polish. bw. $22.00. **(Subscription address:** ARS Polona, PO Box 1001, 00068 Warsaw Poland.**) UDC** 438.

US/0883-3087
GDG REPORT, THE. [GDG rep.]. (Jan. 1985)-. Periodical. English. qt (4 issues). $40.00. Glenn D. Gawkowski, PO Box 632, Trumbull CT 06611. **Tel** (203)371-0136. **ED** Glenn D. Gawkowski. **DD** 623. **Bk Rev. Circ:** 1,000 (ctrl).
Desc: Detailed reports on unusual or covert weapons, reports on weapons based books to law enforcement or related agencies.

US
GENESIS (NEW ORLEANS, LA.). (GENESIS.). Added/Corp Work Training Facility (New Orleans, La.). Vol. 1, No. 1 (Summer 1980)-. Periodical. English. qt. $2.50. Genesis / Work Training Facility, PO Box 3467, New Orleans LA 70177. **ED** Q.A. Wakkil-ud-Din and R. Crawford.

NE
GEVANGENISSTATISTIEK. Main/Corp Netherlands (Kingdom, 1815-). Centraal Bureau voor de Statistiek. 1950/51-. Dutch. be. Staatsuit AFD Verkoop, Fluwelenburgwal 18, Den Haag The Netherlands. **LC** HV8434; .A336. *Continues in part* Criminele Statistiek, Gevangenisstatistiek en Statistiek van de Toepassing der Kinderwetten.

●NE/0928-9313
GLOBAL JOURNAL ON CRIME AND CRIMINAL LAW. Vol. 1 (1993)-. English (Spanish, French and German; summaries and/or abstracts in Multiple languages). Twice a year (Jan./Feb. & June/July). $50.00 US; $75.00 others. Wm. W. Gaunt & Sons Inc.,, Gaunt Buildings, 3011 Gulf Drive, Holmes Beach FL 34217-2199. **Tel** (800)942-8683, (813)778-5252, FAX (813)778-5211. **(Subscription address:** TFLR Institute, PO Box 308, 5280 AH Baxtel, The Netherlands.**) ED** W. van der Wolf, (editor's address: Global Law Association, PO Box 308, 5280 AH Baxtel, The Netherlands, phone: (04116)-74813). Index available (Once a year). cum. index. **Bk Rev. Ad Acc. Circ:** 1,000 (ctrl).
Desc: This journal gives information on criminal law, crime, criminology, and international criminology.

US
GRANT$ FOR CRIME, LAW ENFORCEMENT, & ABUSE PREVENTION. See Philanthropy.

●US
GUIDE TO FEDERAL FUNDING FOR ANTI-CRIME PROGRAMS. See Public Administration.

US/1056-9340
GUIDE TO FEDERAL FUNDING FOR ANTI-DRUG PROGRAMS. See Drug Abuse and Alcoholism.

US/1055-4688
GUIDE TO GRADUATE PROGRAMS IN CRIMINAL JUSTICE AND CRIMINOLOGY. (GUIDE TO GRADUATE PROGRAMS IN CRIMINAL JUSTICE AND CRIMINOLOGY / ACJS). [Guide grad. programs crim. justice criminol.]. Added/Corp Academy of Criminal Justice Sciences. **VFOAT** ACJS ... Guide to Graduate Programs. **VAT** Academy of Criminal Justice Sciences ... Guide to Graduate Programs. (1989/1990)-. English. be. $15.00. Academy of Criminal Justice Sciences, Northern Kentucky University, 402 Nunn Hall, Highland Heights KY 41099. **Tel** (606)572-5634. **DD** 364.

US/1058-2975
GUNS & WEAPONS FOR LAW ENFORCEMENT. [Guns weapons law enforc.]. **VFOAT** Guns and Weapons for Law Enforcement; Guns and Weapons; Guns & Weapons. (Winter 1990)-. Periodical. English. Four times a year. $14.97 (two year). Harris Publications, 1115 Broadway/8th Floor, New York NY 10010. **Tel** (212)807-7100. **ED** Harry Kane. **LC** WMLC 91/4692. **DD** 799. **Ad Acc, Adv Mgr:** Parker Gentry.

US
GUNS CONTROL. (1985)-. English. be. Information Aids Inc., 2812 Exchange Street, Wylie TX 75098. **Tel** (214)442-0167. Index available. **Bk Rev.**
Desc: Complete overview of gun control issue.

JA
HANZAI-SHINRIGAKU KENKYU. VFOAT Japanese Journal of Criminal Psychology. No. 1- 1963-. Japanese (summaries and/or abstracts in multiple). Nihon Hanzai-Shinrigakkai, 11-7 2-chome Hikwawadai Nerima-ku, Tokyo Japan. **LC** HV6080; .H33. **NLM** W1 HA542.
Ind/Abst Psychol. Abstr. (1969-).

CN/0226-1499
HARVEST (EDMONTON). (HARVEST.). [Harvest]. No. 1- Sept./Oct. 1979-. Periodical. English. bm. $12.00 Canada; $18.00 US. Headway Copy Company, PO Box 4490, Station South Edmonton, Edmonton Alta. T6E 4T7 Canada. **DD** 363.4/5.

CN/0229-6470
HEBDO POLICE. [Hebdo police]. (1980)-. Periodical. French. $0.75 each issue. Hebdo Police, 4270 rue Papineau, Montreal Quebec H2H 1S9 Canada. **DD** 364/.9714.

US/0364-3441
HELPING THE EXOFFENDER. (HELPING THE EXOFFENDER ... A TEXAS DIRECTORY.).

1975/76-. Directory. English. State Bar of Texas, PO Box 12487, Capitol Station, Austin TX 78711. **Tel** (512)463-1411. **LC** HV9305.T4; H44. **DD** 364.8/025/764.

US
HOMICIDE IN CALIFORNIA. Main/Corp California. Bureau of Criminal Statistics and Special Services. (1978)-. English. California Bureau of Criminal Statistics, PO Box 13427, Sacramento CA 95813-4427. **Tel** (916)322-3360. **LC** HV6533.C2; C34a. **DD** 312/.276/09794. *Continues* California. Bureau of Criminal Statistics. Homicide in California, 0098-8537.

US/0749-2286
HOMICIDE SURVEILLANCE. (CENTERS FOR DISEASE CONTROL HOMICIDE SURVEILLANCE.). 1970-1978-. English. US Department of Health and Human Services, 200 Independence Avenue Southwest, Washington DC 20201. **LC** HV6528; .C46. **DD** 364.1/523/0973.

JA/0386-0728
HOMU SOGO KENKYUJO KENKYUBU KIYO. [Homu Sogo Kenkyujo Kenkyubu kiyo]. Main/Corp Homu Sogo Kenkyujo (Japan). Added/Corp Homu Sogo Kenkyujo (Japan). Bulletin of the Criminological Research Department. **VFOAT** Bulletin of the Criminological Research Department. (1960)-. Japanese (summaries and/or abstracts in English). 1-1-1 Kasumigaseki Chiyoda-ku, Tokyo Japan. **LC** HV7111; .H65a.

US
HOTLINE THE OFFICIAL NEWSLETTER OF AMERICA'S MOST WANTED. Added/Corp America's Most Wanted. (1991)-. Newsletter. English. **LC** WMLC 91/2058.

US/1061-8627
HOW TO DEFEND AND UPHOLD YOUR RIGHTS VS. THE POLICE. (1992)-. English. $25.00. Derek MC, Inc., PO Box 1857, Atlanta GA 30301-1857.

UK/0265-5527
HOWARD JOURNAL OF CRIMINAL JUSTICE, THE. [Howard j. crim. just.]. Vol. 23, No. 1 (Feb. 1984)-. Academic Scholarly Publication. English. Four times a year. £88.00 UK and Europe; $166.00 North America; £107.00 other. Basil Blackwell Publishers Ltd, 108 Cowley Road, Oxford OX4 1JF England. **Tel** 011 44 865 791100, FAX 011 44 865 791347, telex 837022 OXBOOK G. **(Subscription address:** Blackwell Publishers / UK, Marston Book Services, PO Box 87, Oxford OX2 0DT England.**) LC** HV8995.A1; H782. **[CCC].** available on microfilm and microfiche from University Microfilms International (UMI). *Continues* Howard Journal of Penology and Crime Prevention, 0073-3741.
Ind/Abst Appl. Soc. Sci. Index Abstr.; Crim. Justice Abstr.; Crim. Justice Period. Index; Crim. Penol. Police Sci. Abstr.; Int. Bibliogr. Sociol.; J. Plan. Lit.; Leg. Resour. Index; LegalTrac (1980-); PAIS Int. Print (1991-); Sage Race Relat. Abstr.; Sage Urban Stud. Abstr; Soc. Plann. Policy Dev. Abstr.

UK/1012-2710
ICC COMMERCIAL CRIME INTERNATIONAL. See Economics-Industry and Production.

US/0445-4111
ILLINOIS LAW ENFORCEMENT OFFICERS LAW BULLETIN. VFOAT Officers Law Bulletin. Vol. 1 (Jan. 1965)-. Bulletin. English. mo. $24.00. Illinois Law Enforcement, PO Box A 3046, Chicago IL 60690. **Tel** (312)338-4141.

US
ILLINOIS LAW OF CRIMINAL INVESTIGATION, THE. English. $47.50. 421 Ridgewood Avenue, Glen Ellyn IL 60137. **Tel** (708)858-6392. **ED** James P Manak. Index available. cum. index. **Circ:** 300.
Desc: A comprehensive case and statutory guide to Illinois criminal law and procedure and civil liability. Intended for public and criminal justice audiences.

US
ILLINOIS POLICE & LAW ENFORCEMENT DIRECTORY. VFOAT Illinois Police and Law Enforcement Directory; I.P.D.; IPD. Began in 1977/1978. Directory. English. $22.50. Minnesota Police & Peace Officer, 525 Park Street, Capitol Office #207, St Paul MN 55103. **Tel** (800)652-9799, (612)291-1119, FAX (612)291-0227. **LC** HV9475.I3; I29. **DD** 363.2/025/773.

US/0732-9849
ILLINOIS UNIFORM CRIME REPORTS USER'S GUIDE UPDATE. See Law-Abstracting, Bibliographies and Statistics.

US/0091-6994
IN (IOWA CITY). See The Arts.

US
IN THE PUBLIC INTEREST / OFFICE OF THE ATTORNEY GENERAL (NEW MEXICO). **Main/Corp** New Mexico. Attorney General's Office. Sept. 1984-. Periodical. English. Three times a year. Office of the Attorney General / New Mexico, PO Drawer 1508, Santa Fe NM 87504. **LC** KFN4027.5.A8; A826. **DD** 349.789/05; 347.89005. ***Continues*** *New Mexico. Attorney General's Office. Quarterly Report.*

US
INDEX TO THE ABSTRACTS ON CRIME AND JUVENILE DELINQUENCY, AN. **See** Law-Abstracting, Bibliographies and Statistics.

II/0376-9844
INDIAN JOURNAL OF CRIMINOLOGY. [Indian j. criminol.]. **Added/Corp** Indian Society of Criminology. Vol. 1 (July 1973)-. Academic Scholarly Publication. English. Twice a year. University of Madras Department of Psychology, Madras 600 005 India. **Tel** 566988. **(Subscription address:** Prints India, 11 Darya Ganj, New Delhi 110002 India.**)** **ED** V. R. Lakshminarayanan and K. V. Kaliappan. **LC** HV6201; .I48. **DD** 364/.0954. **CODEN** IJOCDS. **Bk Rev. Circ:** 750. Documents available from CASDDS.
Desc: Covers all aspects of criminology, criminological sciences, criminal biology, psychology, sociology, penology and subsidiary sciences.
Ind/Abst Appl. Soc. Sci. Index Abstr.; Chem. Abstr.; Crim. Justice Abstr.

II/0970-4345
INDIAN JOURNAL OF CRIMINOLOGY & CRIMINALISTICS, THE. [Indian j. criminol. crim.]. **VFOAT** Indian Journal of Criminology and Criminalistics. Vol. 1, No. 1 (Mar. 1981)-. Academic Scholarly Publication. English (Hindi). qt. Rs50.00 India; $30.00 North America; £10.00 other. Institute of Criminology and Forensic Science, 4-E Jhandewalan Extension, Rani Jhansi Road, New Delhi 110055 India. **Tel** 521481. **(Subscription address:** The Controller, Department of Publications, Civil Lines, Delhi 110054 India**)** **ED** K K Puri. **LC** HV7093; .I54. **DD** 364/.954. **NLM** W1 IN207D. **Bk Rev. Circ:** 300.
Ind/Abst EMBASE; Psychol. Abstr.; Soc. Plann. Policy Dev. Abstr.; Sociol. Abstr. (?-?).

II/0537-2429
INDIAN POLICE JOURNAL, THE. Began publication with July 1954 Issue. Periodical. English. qt. Indian Police Journal, Curzon Road, Barrack 1688/Gandhi Marg. **LC** HV7551.

KO
INDOPOP NONCHONG. **VFOAT** Korean Journal of Humanitarian Law. V. 1- ; 1977-. Periodical. English (Korean). Taehan Choksipcha S A, 523-1 Majang-dong Songdong-ku, Seoul Korea. **LC** HV640; .I44.

CN/0702-875X
INFORMATION - A R C A D. **Main/Corp** Association des Rencontres Culturelles Avec Les Detenus. V. 1- May 1973-. Periodical. French. ir. Association des Rencontres Culturelles Avec les Detenus, Arcad 750, Croissant Frontenac 4N5 Canada. **DD** 365/.6/09714.

BL
INFORMATIVO. **Main/Corp** Brazil. Departamento de Policia Federal. Divisao de Communicacao Social. (19??)-. Periodical. Portuguese. mo. Departamento de Policia Federal, Ed Bnde 6 Andar, Brazil. **LC** HV7239; .B73a.

PR/0095-0483
INFORME ANUAL - ESTADO LIBRE ASOCIADO DE PUERTO RICO, POLICIA DE PUERTO RICO. (INFORME ANUAL - POLICIA DE PUERTO RICO.). **Main/Corp** Puerto Rico. Insular Police. (19??)-. Spanish. Superintendente, Apartado 938 Hato Rey, San Juan Puerto Rico. **LC** HV7680; .A28a. **DD** 363.2/097295.

FR
INFRACTIONS DE LA COMPETENCE DU TRIBUNAL D'INSTANCE STATUANT EN MATIERE PENALE. French. Roger Bouyeron, 42 rue Saint-Faron, 77100 Meaux France. **LC** KJV8410.A218; I54.

●US
INMATE POPULATION FORECAST UPDATE, STATE OF WASHINGTON. **Added/Corp** Washington (State). Office of Financial Management. Forecasting Division. 1993-. English. ***Continues*** *Prison and Inmate Population Forecast, State of Washington.*

US/0148-3714
INSIDE OUT (NEW YORK). (INSIDE OUT.). English. Hanuman Foundation, 276 Riverside Drive, New York NY 10025. **LC** BL624; .I55. **DD** 248/.86.

US/0739-8514
INSTITUTE OF CRIMINOLOGY & FORENSIC SCIENCES BULLETIN. [Inst. Criminol. Forensic Sci. bull.]. **VFOAT** Institute of Criminology Forensic Sciences Bulletin; ICFS Bulletin. (1984)-. Bulletin. English. mo. $12.00. Institute of Criminology and Forensic Sciences, Box 28421, San Jose CA 95159. **Tel** (408)448-6210. **ED** Michael M Zanoni. **DD** 364. **Bk Rev. Ad Acc. Circ:** 200 (ctrl).
Desc: Addressing issues of interest to those in areas of criminology, criminalistics, and forensic science.

FR/0367-729X
INTERNATIONAL CRIMINAL POLICE REVIEW. [Int. crim. police rev.]. No. 1 (Sept. 1946)-. Academic Scholarly Publication. English. bm. 150.00F France; 170.00F other. ICPO Interpol Secretariat General, BP 6041, F-69411 Lyon Cedex 06 France. **Tel** 011 33 72 447000, FAX 011 33 72 447162 or 63, telex 301987. **LC** HV7551; .I64. **DD** 351.7405.
Ind/Abst Crim. Justice Abstr.; EMBASE.

US/0148-4648
INTERNATIONAL DRUG REPORT. **Main/Corp** International Narcotic Enforcement Officers Association. Vol. 15 (Jan. 1974)-. Periodical. English. Six times a year. $35.00 US; $41.00 Canada & Mexico; $60.00 Other. International Narcotic Enforcement Officers Association, 112 State Street, Suite 1200, Albany NY 12207. **Tel** (518)463-6232. **ED** Celeste Morga. **LC** HV5800; .I524a. **DD** 362.2/93. **Bk Rev. Circ:** 10,000 (ctrl). ***Continues*** *International Narcotic Report, 0020-806X.*
Desc: Covers topics of drug abuse enforcement such as: law, research, education, training, statistics, and legal implications.

FR/0252-063X
INTERNATIONAL EXCHANGE OF INFORMATION ON CURRENT CRIMINOLOGICAL RESEARCH PROJECTS IN MEMBER STATES OF THE COUNCIL OF EUROPE / DIRECTORATE OF LEGAL AFFAIRS, COUNCIL OF EUROPE, DIVISION OF CRIME PROBLEMS, COUNCIL OF EUROPE. **Added/Corp** Council of Europe. Division of Crime Problems. European Committee on Crime Problems. **VFOAT** Echange International d'Information sur les Projets de Recherches Criminologiques en Cours dans les Etats Membres du Conseil de l'Europe. (1966)-. English (French, German and Italian). ir. Manhattan Publishing Company, PO Box 650, Croton-on-Hudson NY 10520. **Tel** (914)271-5194. **LC** WMLC L 83/1354. ***Continues*** *International Exchange of Information on Current Criminological Research Projects in Member States.*

US/0192-4036
INTERNATIONAL JOURNAL OF COMPARATIVE AND APPLIED CRIMINAL JUSTICE. [Int. j. comp. appl. crim. justice]. **Added/Corp** Wichita State University. Dept. of Administration of Justice. Vol. 1, No. 1/2 (Spring/Fall 1977)-. Periodical. English. Twice a year (June and December). $30.00 (institutions); $22.00 (individuals). International Journal of Comparative and Applied Criminal Justice, Wichita State University, Department of Administration of Justice, Witchita KS 67208. **Tel** (316)689-3710. **ED** Dae H. Chang. **LC** HV6001; .I57. Index available. **Bk Rev. Ad Acc. Circ:** 800. available on microfilm and microfiche from University Microfilms International (UMI).
Desc: Designed to provide a publishing opportunity for scholars and scientists who are interested in comparative theory and empirical research in criminal justice.
Ind/Abst Crim. Justice Abstr.; Crim. Justice Period. Index; Crim. Penol. Police Sci. Abstr.; Curr. Law Index (1980-); Leg. Resour. Index (1980-); LegalTrac (1980-); Soc. Plann. Policy Dev. Abstr.; Sociol. Abstr. (?-?).

US/0306-624X
INTERNATIONAL JOURNAL OF OFFENDER THERAPY AND COMPARATIVE CRIMINOLOGY. [Int. j. offender ther. comp. criminol.]. **Added/Corp** Association for Psychiatric Treatment of Offenders. Association for the Professional Treatment of Offenders. Canadian Association for the Treatment of Offenders. Oregon Health Sciences University. Dept. of Psychiatry. Vol. 16, No. 1 (1972)-. Periodical. English. Four times a year. $90.00 (institutions); $105.00 others. Guilford Publications Inc., 72 Spring Street, New York NY 10012. **Tel** (212)431-9800, (800)365-7006, FAX (212)966-6708. **(Subscription address:** Turpin Distribution Services Limited, Blackhorse Road, Letchworth, Hertfordshire SG6 1HN, United Kingdom.**)** **ED** Edward M. Scott. **LC** HV9261; .J6. **DD** 364.3/05. **NLM** W1 IN77T. **CODEN** IOTCAH. **[CCC].** Index available. **Bk Rev. Pr Rev. Circ:** 750. available on microfilm and microfiche from University Microfilms International (UMI). Documents available from The Genuine Article. ***Continues*** *International Journal of Offender Therapy, 0020-7497.*
Desc: Provides an international forum for research, discussion and treatment of the variables associated with crime and delinquency. Emphasizes theoretical and practical issues related to the treatment of offenders.
Ind/Abst Appl. Soc. Sci. Index Abstr.; Crim. Justice Abstr.; Crim. Justice Period. Index; Curr. Contents Soc. Behav. Sci.; Curr. Law Index (1980-); Index Period. Artic. Relat. Law (19??-19??); Int. Bibliogr. Sociol.; Leg. Resour. Index (1980-); LegalTrac (1980-); Middle East Abstr. Index (1980-); Psychol. Abstr. (1972-); PsycINFO; PsycLit; Res. Alert [Full Cov.]; Soc. Plann. Policy Dev. Abstr.; Soc. Sci. Cit. Index [Full Cov.]; Sociol. Abstr.

US/0074-7688
INTERNATIONAL REVIEW OF CRIMINAL POLICY. ***Title Change.*** [Int. rev. crim. policy]. **VFOAT** Revue Internationale de Politique Criminelle; Revista Internacional de Politica Criminal. No. 1 (Jan. 1952)-(19??). Government Publication. English (French and Spanish). sa. United Nations Publications, 2 United Nations Plaza, Room DC2 0853, Department 007C, New York NY 10017. **Tel** (212)963-8303, (800)253-9646. **LC** JX1977; .A2. **DD** 364/.05. available on microfilm and microfiche from University Microfilms International (UMI). ***Continued by*** *International Review of Criminal Policy. Bibliography.*
Ind/Abst Index Foreign Leg. Per.

US
INTERNATIONAL REVIEW OF CRIMINAL POLICY. **VFOAT** International Review of Criminal Policy: Bibliography; Revue Internationale de Politique Criminelle: Bibliographie; Revista Internacional de Politica Criminal: Bibliografia. (1963)-. Government Publication. English. an. price varies per volume. United Nations Publications, 2 United Nations Plaza, Room DC2 0853, Department 007C, New York NY 10017. **Tel** (212)963-8303, (800)253-9646.
Desc: International perspective on juvinile justice.

UK/0269-7580
INTERNATIONAL REVIEW OF VICTIMOLOGY. **Added/Corp** World Society of Victimology. Vol. 1, No. 1 (1989)-. Periodical. English. qt. £79.00. AB Academic Publishers, PO Box 42 Bicester, OXON OX6 7NW England. **Tel** 011 44 869 320949. **LC** HV6250; .I57. **CODEN** IRVIE2.
Ind/Abst Crim. Justice Abstr. (199?-); Leg. Resour. Index; LegalTrac (1991-); Soc. Plann. Policy Dev. Abstr.

UK/0074-7890
INTERNATIONAL SECURITY DIRECTORY. 1st- Ed.; 1963-. Directory. English. be. £19.50 UK; $35.00 US. International Security Directory, PO Box 39, Henley-On-Thames Oxfordshire RG9 5UA England. **Tel** (0491)641018. **LC** HV7900; .I63. **DD** 363.2/025. **Ad Acc.**
Desc: Recognised worldwide as the most comprehensive and authoritative reference book available that brings together required data on the United Kingdom's Security Companies, their products and services, on Security Societies and professional bodies, and on Security Associations and their Member Companies worldwide.

IS/0075-1391
ISRAEL STUDIES IN CRIMINOLOGY. (ISRAEL STUDIES IN CRIMINOLOGY / INSTITUTE OF CRIMINOLOGY AND CRIMINAL LAW, TEL-AVIV UNIVERSITY.). [Isr. stud. criminol.]. **Added/Corp** Universitat Tel-Aviv. Makhon li-Kriminologyah ule-Mishpat Pelili. Vol. 1, 1970-. Monographic series. English. ir. Price varies per volume. Science Reviews Ltd, 18 Oaklands Gate, Northwood Middlesex, HA6 3AA England. **Tel** 011 44 923 823586.
Ind/Abst Psychol. Abstr. (1970-).

NE
JAARVERSLAG BETREFFENDE HET EXPERIMENT VERTROUWENSARTSEN INZAKE KINDERMISHANDELING. **Main/Corp** Netherlands (Kingdom, 1815-). Interdepartementale Commissie Kindermishandeling. Dutch. Interdepartementale Commissie Kindermishandeling, Staatsuitgeverij, S-Gravenhage Netherlands. **LC** HV776; .A16.

US/0739-0998
JAIL & PRISONER LAW BULLETIN. (JAIL & PRISONER LAW BULLETIN / AMERICANS FOR EFFECTIVE LAW ENFORCEMENT, INC., LAW ENFORCEMENT LEGAL DEFENSE CENTER.). [Jail prison. law bull.]. **Added/Corp** Americans for Effective Law Enforcement. Law Enforcement Legal Defense Center (Evanston, Ill.). **VFOAT** Jail and Prisoner Law Bulletin. (1982)-. Bulletin. English. mo. $158.00. Americans Effective Law Enforcement, 5519 North Cumberland Avenue/Suite 1008, Chicago IL 60656-1471. **Tel** (312)763-2800. **LC** KF9730.A15; J34. Index available. cum. index. **Circ:** 1,025. ***Continues*** *Jail & Prison Law Bulletin, 0194-1372.*
Desc: Reviews pertinent cases and selects those considered to have effective impact upon jail and prison personnel and their attorneys.

US
JAIL COMMITMENTS AND CONFINEMENTS. **Main/Corp** Virginia. Dept. of Corrections. Research and Reporting Unit. English. an.

Virginia Department of Corrections, 6900 Atmore Drive, Richmond VA 23225. **Tel** (804)674-3119, FAX (804)674-3587. **LC** HV7296; .A24B. **DD** 365/.9755/0212. ***Continues*** *Commitments to Jails.*

US/0748-2655
JOURNAL - AMERICAN CIVIL LIBERTIES UNION FOUNDATION. NATIONAL PRISON PROJECT. ***Title Change.*** (JOURNAL : A PROJECT OF THE AMERICAN CIVIL LIBERTIES UNION FOUNDATION, INC. / NATIONAL PRISON PROJECT.). [J. - Am. Civ. Lib. Union Found., Natl. Prison Project]. **Added/Corp** American Civil Liberties Union Foundation. National Prison Project. **VFOAT** Journal of the National Prison Project. No. 1 (Fall 1984)-(19??). Periodical. English. qt. National Prison Project, 1785 Connecticut Avenue Northwest, Washington DC 20009. **Tel** (202)234-4830, FAX (202)234-4890. **ED** Jan Elvin. **DD** 365. Index available. **Bk Rev**, (Qty: 1). **Circ:** 3,000. available on microfilm and microfiche from University Microfilms International (UMI). ***Continued by*** *National Prison Project Journal, 1076-769X.*
Desc: Features articles, reports, legal analysis, legislative news and other developments in the field.

US/1055-3835
JOURNAL OF ADDICTIONS & OFFENDER COUNSELING. **See** Psychology.

US/0449-5063
JOURNAL OF CALIFORNIA LAW ENFORCEMENT. **Added/Corp** California Peace Officers Association. Vol. 1 (1966)-. Academic Scholarly Publication. English. qt. $35.00 (nonmembers); $20.00 (members of Peace Officers Association). California Peace Officers Association, 1455 Response Road, Suite 190, Sacramento CA 95815-4501. **Tel** (916)923-1825, FAX (916)263-6090. **ED** Leslie McGill. Index available. cum. index. **Pr Rev. Circ:** 1,300.
Desc: Containing scholarly articles on current issues in the law enforcement and criminal justice field.
Ind/Abst Crim. Justice Abstr.; Crim. Penol. Police Sci. Abstr.

US/1043-9862
JOURNAL OF CONTEMPORARY CRIMINAL JUSTICE. [J. contemp. crim. justice]. **VFOAT** Contemporary Criminal Justice. Vol. 1 (April 1978)-. Periodical. English. qt. $50.00 (institutions), $15.00 (individual). CSULB Foundation, Department of Criminal Justice, 1250 Bellflower Boulevard, Long Beach CA 90840. **Tel** (213)985-4738, FAX (213)985-5695. **LC** HV7231; .J59. **DD** 364.973/05. **Bk Rev. Pr Rev. Circ:** 450.
Ind/Abst Crim. Justice Abstr.; Crim. Penol. Police Sci. Abstr.; Sage Urban Stud. Abstr.

US/0740-2708
JOURNAL OF CORRECTIONAL EDUCATION (1974). (JOURNAL OF CORRECTIONAL EDUCATION : OFFICIAL PUBLICATION OF THE CORRECTIONAL EDUCATION ASSOCIATION.). [J. correct. educ.]. **Added/Corp** Correctional Education Association (U.S.). Vol. 26, No. 1 (Winter 1974)-. Periodical. English. qt. (Comes with Correctional Education Assn membership). Correctional Education Association, 8025 Laurel Lakes Court, Laurel MD 20707. **Tel** (301)490-1440, FAX (301)206-5061. available on microfilm and microfiche from University Microfilms International (UMI). ***Continues*** *Correctional Education.*
Ind/Abst Crim. Justice Abstr.; Crim. Justice Period. Index; Crim. Penol. Police Sci. Abstr.; Curr. Index J. Educ. (March 1990-).

US/0735-648X
JOURNAL OF CRIME & JUSTICE. [J. crime justice]. **Added/Corp** Society of Police and Criminal Psychology. Midwestern Criminal Justice Association (U.S.). **VFOAT** Crime & Justice; Journal of Crime and Justice; Crime and Justice. (197?)-. Periodical. English. Twice a year. $60.00. Anderson Publishing Company, 2035 Reading Road, Cincinnati OH 45202. **Tel** (513)421-4142, (800)582-7295. **(Subscription address:** Anderson Publishing Company, PO Box 1576, Cincinnati OH 45201.**) ED** Peter C. Kratcoski. **LC** HV6201; .J68. **DD** 364/.05. **Bk Rev**. ctrl circ. available on microfilm and microfiche from University Microfilms International (UMI).
Desc: An interdisciplinary journal that includes theoretical and empirical studies, media reviews and editorial comments for criminal justice academicians and professionals.
Ind/Abst Crim. Justice Abstr.; Crim. Justice Period. Index.

US/0047-2352
JOURNAL OF CRIMINAL JUSTICE. [J. crim. justice]. (Mar. 1973)-. Periodical. English. bm. $410.00 The Americas; £275.00 other. Pergamon Press, An Imprint of Elsevier Science Ltd., The Boulevard, Langford Lane, Kidlington, Oxford OX5 1GB United Kingdom. **Tel** 011 44 865 843000, 011 44 865 843699, FAX 011 44 865 843010. **(Subscription address:** Elsevier Science Ltd. Oxford Fulfillment Centre, PO Box 800, Kidlington, Oxford OX5 1DX United Kingdom.**) ED** Kent B. Joscelyn. **LC** HV7231; .J62. **DD** 364/.05. **CODEN** JCJUDJ. **[CCC]. Pr Rev.** available on microfilm and microfiche from University Microfilms International (UMI). Documents available from The Genuine Article, UMI Article Clearinghouse.
Ind/Abst Acad. Search (July 1993-); Appl. Soc. Sci. Index Abstr.; Commun. Abstr.; Crim. Justice Abstr.; Crim. Justice Period. Index; Crim. Penol. Police Sci. Abstr.; Curr. Contents Soc. Behav. Sci.; Curr. Law Index (1980-); Expand. Acad. Index (1984-); INFO-SOUTH Abstr.; Int. Pharm. Abstr.; Leg. Resour. Index (1980-); LegalTrac (1980-); Newsp. Period. Abstr. (1991-); PAIS Int. Print (1991-); Psychol. Abstr. (1973-); PsycINFO; PsycLit; Res. Alert [Full Cov.]; Soc. Sci. Source (Jul. 1993-); Soc. Sci. Cit. Index [Full Cov.]; Soc. Sci. Index; Soc. Sci. Index Fulltext (1988-) [Full Txt.]; Urban Aff. Abstr.

US/1051-1253
JOURNAL OF CRIMINAL JUSTICE EDUCATION. (JOURNAL OF CRIMINAL JUSTICE EDUCATION : JCJE.). [J. crim. justice educ.]. **Added/Corp** Academy of Criminal Justice Sciences. **VFOAT** JCJE. Vol. 1, No. 1 (Spring 1990)-. Periodical. English. sa (Mar. & Sept.). $45.00 (US); $50.00 (other). Academy of Criminal Justice Sciences, Northern Kentucky University, 402 Nunn Hall, Highland Heights KY 41099. **Tel** (606)572-5634. **ED** Dorothy Bracey. **LC** HV7419.5; .J68. **DD** 364/.071/173. Index available. **Bk Rev. Ad Acc. Circ:** 2,500 (ctrl).
Ind/Abst Crim. Justice Abstr. (199?-).

US/1043-500X
JOURNAL OF OFFENDER MONITORING. [J. offender monit.]. (198?)-. Periodical. English. Four times a year (Feb., May, Aug., Nov.). $45.00 (regular); $65.00 (library). Alpha Enterprises, PO Box 326, Richmond KY 40476-0326. **Tel** (606)623-0792, FAX (606)623-0792. **ED** Dr. Victor E. Kappeler. **DD** 346. **Bk Rev. Ad Acc. Pr Rev. Circ:** 300. ***Continues*** *Offender Monitoring, 0894-4644.*
Desc: Contains full length articles written by leading scholars and practitioners on issues relating to electronic monitoring, drug and alcohol testing, surveillance, wiretapping, DNA testing, ignition inter-lock systems.

US/1050-9674
JOURNAL OF OFFENDER REHABILITATION. [J. offender rehabil.]. Vol. 16, No. 1/2 (1990)-. Periodical. English. qt. $175.00 US; $245.00 other. The Haworth Press Inc, 10 Alice Street, Binghamton NY 13904-1580. **Tel** (607)722-5857, (800)3-HAWORTH, FAX (607)722-1424. **ED** Nathaniel J. Pallone (editor's address: Rutgers-The State University of New Jersey, Livingston College Campus, 133 A Lucy Stone Hall, New Brunswick, NJ 08903). **LC** HV9261; .O33. **DD** 365/.66. **NLM** W1; JO802U. **CODEN** JOFHEB. **Bk Rev. Ad Acc. Pr Rev. Acid Free. Circ:** 195. available on microfilm and microfiche from University Microfilms International (UMI). Documents available from Haworth Document Delivery Service. ***Continues*** *Journal of Offender Counseling, Services & Rehabilitation, 0195-6116.*
Desc: Vehicle for publication of research and concepts in the rehabilitation of criminal offenders, both in custodial and community settings. Interdisciplinary in character with its authors representing the full range of mental health and social service professionals and international in scope.
Ind/Abst Abstr. Res. Pastor. Care Couns. (19??-); Curr. Index J. Educ. (1990-); Psychol. Abstr. (1990-); PsycINFO; Sage Urban Stud. Abstr; Soc. Plann. Policy Dev. Abstr.; Soc. Work Abstr. [Select. Cov.]; Sociol. Abstr. (1990-).

US/0882-0783
JOURNAL OF POLICE AND CRIMINAL PSYCHOLOGY. [J. police crim. psychol.]. **Added/Corp** Society of Police and Criminal Psychology. Vol. 1, Issue 1 (March 1985)-. Periodical. English. Twice a year. $35.00 institutions; $25.00 individuals. Southwest Texas State University / Academic Center, Hines Academic Center/Room 120, Dr W Mullins, San Marcos TX 78666. **Tel** (512)245-3344. **ED** Wayman C Mullins (editor's phone: (512)245-2174). **DD** 363. **Bk Rev**, (Qty: 1-2). **Ad Acc, Adv Mgr:** same as editor. **Pr Rev. Circ:** 250. available on microfilm from University Microfilms International (UMI).
Ind/Abst Crim. Justice Abstr.; Crim. Justice Period. Index.

US/0893-4827
JOURNAL OF POLYGRAPH SCIENCE, THE. [J. polygr. sci.]. **Added/Corp** National Training Center of Lie Detection (U.S.) National Training Center of Polygraph Science (U.S.). **VFOAT** Journal. (19??)-. Periodical. English. Six times a year. $57.00 (one year); $95.00 (two years). National Training Center of Polygraph Science, 200 West 57th Street, Suite 1400, New York NY 10019. **Tel** (212)755-5241. **ED** Richard O. Arther. **DD** 658. **Bk Rev**. ctrl circ. ***Continues*** *Journal of Polygraph Studies.*

US/0731-8332
JOURNAL OF PRISON & JAIL HEALTH. ***Ceased.*** [J. prison jail health]. **VFOAT** Journal of Prison and Jail Health. Vol. 2, No. 1 (Spring/Summer 1982)-Vol. 12. Periodical. English. sa. Human Sciences Press, PO Box 735, 233 Spring Street, New York NY 10013. **Tel** (212)620-8000, FAX (212)807-1047, telex 23421139. **(Subscription address:** UK & European Subscriptions: Eurospan Group, Journals & Serials Division, 3 Henrietta Street, Covent Garden, London WC2E 8LU England; Telephone: 011 44 71 240-0856 FAX: 011 44 71 379-0609**) ED** Nancy Neveloff Dubler. **LC** HV8833; .J67. **DD** 365/.66. **NLM** W1 JO844. **CODEN** JPJHD3. **[CCC].** available on microfilm and microfiche from University Microfilms International (UMI). ***Continues*** *Journal of Prison Health, 0192-7051.*
Desc: As a field of interdisciplinary interest and activity, prison health is achieving clearer definition. Addressed to physicians, prison health professionals, lawyers, correctional managers and inmate advocates, this journal marks the first publication solely devoted to discussions of health maintenance and self-care among inmates.
Ind/Abst Crim. Justice Abstr.; Crim. Penol. Police Sci. Abstr.; EMBASE; PAIS Int. Print (1991-); Psychol. Abstr. (1982-); PsycINFO (1982-); PsycLit; Soc. Plann. Policy Dev. Abstr.

CN/0838-164X
JOURNAL OF PRISONERS ON PRISONS. [J. prison. prisons]. Vol. 1, No. 1 (Summer 1988)-. Periodical. English. Twice a year. 20.00Can$ (institutions), 10.00Can$ (individuals). Journal of Prisoners on Prison, Box 54 University Centre, University of Manitoba, Winnipeg Manitoba R3T 2N2 Canada. **Tel** (204)474-8024. **ED** Howard Davidson. **DD** 365/.971. **Bk Rev. Pr Rev. Circ:** 1,000.

US/0278-1042
JOURNAL OF PROBATION AND PAROLE : THE JOURNAL OF THE NEW YORK STATE PROBATION OFFICERS ASSOCIATION. **Added/Corp** New York State Probation and Parole Officers Association. **VFOAT** Probation and Parole Journal. (Fall 1978)-. English. an. $10.00. New York State Probation Officers Association Inc, PO Box 8172, William E. Bishop, White Plains NY 10602. **Tel** (914)285-3165, FAX (914)285-3294. **ED** William Bishop. **LC** HV9305.N7; J68. **DD** 364.6/3/09747. **Bk Rev**, (Qty: 2-5). **Ad Acc. Pr Rev. Circ:** 500. ***Continues*** *Probation and Parole.*
Desc: Current community corrections.
Ind/Abst Crim. Justice Abstr.

US/0748-4518
JOURNAL OF QUANTITATIVE CRIMINOLOGY. [J. quant. criminol.]. Vol. 1, No. 1 (March 1985)-. Periodical. English. Four times a year. $215.00 institutions, $45.00 individuals US; $250.00 institutions, $53.00 individuals other. Plenum Press, 233 Spring Street, New York NY 10013-1578. **Tel** (212)620-8000, (800)221-9369, FAX (212)463-0742, (212)807-1047, telex 23/421139. **ED** James Alan Fox. **DD** 364. **CODEN** JQCRE6. **[CCC].** available on microfilm and microfiche from University Microfilms International (UMI).
Ind/Abst Crim. Justice Abstr.; Crim. Justice Period. Index; Crim. Penol. Police Sci. Abstr.; Index Period. Artic. Relat. Law; Psychol. Abstr. (1985-); PsycINFO (1990-); PsycLit; Risk Abstr.; Soc. Plann. Policy Dev. Abstr.

●US/1061-3455
JOURNAL OF QUESTIONED DOCUMENT EXAMINATION. **Added/Corp** Independent Association of Questioned Document Examiners. (1992)-. Periodical. English. Twice a year (Mar. Sept.). $40.00. IAQDE, 7907 Laird Street, Panama City FL 32408. **Tel** (904)233-9222. **LC** HV8074; .I53. **DD** 362.2/565/05. **Bk Rev**, (Qty: 2 / year). **Pr Rev. Circ:** 70 (ctrl). ***Continues*** *Independent Association of Questioned Document Examiners, Inc. : [Journal], 1056-8972.*
Desc: Contains papers and other information on document and handwriting identification. Specifically the latest issue contains articles on line quality, and the chemistry of handwriting.

US/0022-4278
JOURNAL OF RESEARCH IN CRIME AND DELINQUENCY, THE. **Added/Corp** National Council on Crime and Delinquency. Howard University. Center for Youth and Community Studies. (Jan. 1964)-. Periodical. English. ir. University Microfilms International, 300 North Zeeb Road, Ann Arbor MI 48106-1346. **Tel** (313)761-4700, (800)521-0600 Exts. 2490, 2491, FAX (313)973-1540. **[CCC].**

US/0022-4278
JOURNAL OF RESEARCH IN CRIME AND DELINQUENCY, THE. [J. res. crime delinq.]. **Added/Corp** National Council on Crime and Delinquency. Howard University. Center for Youth and Community Studies. Vol. 1 (Jan. 1964)-. Academic Scholarly Publication. English. qt (Feb., May, Aug., Nov.). $160.00. SAGE Periodical Press, 2455 Teller Road, Thousand Oaks CA 91320. **Tel** (805)499-0721, FAX (805)499-0871, telex 100799. **ED** Jeffrey Fagan (Rutgers University). **LC** HV6001; .J74. **NLM** W1 JO869. **[CCC]. Pr Rev. Acid Free.** available on microfilm and microfiche from University Microfilms International (UMI). Documents available from The Genuine Article, UMI Article Clearinghouse.
Desc: Reports on original research in crime and delinquency, with new theories and critical analysis of theories and concepts especially pertinent to research development in this field.
Ind/Abst Acad. Search (Jan. 1994-); Appl. Soc. Sci. Index Abstr.; Crim. Justice Abstr.; Crim. Justice Period.

Index; Crim. Penol. Police Sci. Abstr.; Curr. Contents Soc. Behav. Sci.; EMBASE; Expand. Acad. Index (1989-); INFO-SOUTH Abstr.; Int. Bibliogr. Sociol.; J. Plan. Lit.; Mag. Search; Middle East Abstr. Index; Newsp. Period. Abstr. (1991-); Psychol. Abstr. (1978-); Res. Alert [Full Cov.]; Sage Urban Stud. Abstr; Soc. Plann. Policy Dev. Abstr.; Soc. Sci. Source (Jul. 1993-); Soc. Sci. Cit. Index [Full Cov.]; Soc. Sci. Index Fulltext (Aug. 1988-) [Full Txt.]; Soc. Work Abstr. [Select. Cov.]; Sociol. Abstr.; Stat. Theory Method Abstr. (1974-1975).

●US/1065-3341
JOURNAL OF SAFE MANAGEMENT OF DISRUPTIVE AND ASSAULTIVE BEHAVIOR, THE. (THE JOURNAL OF SAFE MANAGEMENT OF DISRUPTIVE AND ASSAULTIVE BEHAVIOR : JSM.). [J. safe manage. disrupt. assaultive behav.]. **Added/Corp** National Crisis Prevention Institute (U.S.). **VFOAT** JSM. Vol. 1, Issue 1 (1992)-. Periodical. English. qt. $45.00. National Crisis Prevention Institute, 3315-K North 124th Street, Brookfield WI 53005. **DD** 362. **NLM** W1; JO872E. ***Continues*** *CPI National Report, 0740-7947.*

US/0195-9425
JOURNAL OF SECURITY ADMINISTRATION. [J. secur. adm.]. **Added/Corp** Indiana University of Pennsylvania. Academy of Security Educators and Trainers. Vol. 1, No. 2 (Fall 1978)-. Periodical. English. sa. $40.00 institutions, $25.00 individuals US; add $10.00 postage to other. BLSS, 10501 SW 99 Street, Miami FL 33176. **Tel** (305)279-9437. **ED** Norman R Bottom Jr. **LC** HV8290; .J68. **DD** 363.2/89/05. **Bk Rev. Ad Acc. Pr Rev. Circ:** 5,000. available on microfilm and microfiche from University Microfilms International (UMI). ***Continues*** *Journal of Security Administration and Private Police, 0195-9433.*
Desc: Focus is on security and loss control.
Ind/Abst Crim. Justice Abstr.; Crim. Justice Period. Index.

US/8755-1020
JOURNAL OF THE NATIONAL ASSOCIATION OF DOCUMENT EXAMINERS. [J. Natl. Assoc. Doc. Exam.]. **Added/Corp** National Association of Document Examiners (U.S.). Vol. 1, No. 1 (May 1980)-. Periodical. English. Four times a year. $50.00. Shirl Solomon, 200 Tamoshanter Drive, Palm Springs FL 33461. **ED** Phyllis Cook. **LC** WMLC 93/421. **DD** 363. Index available. **Bk Rev. Ad Acc. Circ:** 100.
Desc: News, articles and information on cases for the forensic document examiner or for handwriting experts.

CN/0824-5347
JUBILEE (MISSISSAUGA). (JUBILEE : NEWS OF THE PRISON FELLOWSHIP OF CANADA.). [Jubilee]. Fall Issue 1983-. Periodical. English. ir. Free. Prison Fellowship of Canada, Suite #3, 2171 Dunwin Drive, Mississauga Ontario L5L 1X2 Canada. **DD** 365/.66. ***Continues*** *Canadian Jubilee, 0821-5820.*

CN/0715-271X
JURISTAT. **See** Law-Abstracting, Bibliographies and Statistics.

CN/0225-4115
JUSTICE. (JUSTICE : DIRECTORY OF SERVICES.). [Justice]. **Added/Corp** Canadian Association for the Prevention of Crime. Canadian Criminal Justice Association. (1980)-. Directory. English (French). an. 25.00Can$. Association Canadienne de Justice Penale, Canadian Criminal Justice Association, 55 Av Parkdale, Ottawa Ontario K1Y 1E5 Canada. **Tel** (613)725-3715. **ED** R Jubinuille. **LC** HV9308; .C37a. **DD** 365/.025/71. **Circ:** 600. ***Continues*** *Directory of Correctional Services in Canada, 0070-5381.*
Desc: Listing of names, addresses and telephone numbers of all criminal justice agencies in Canada.
Ind/Abst Point Repere (19??-19??).

US
JUSTICE EXPENDITURE AND EMPLOYMENT EXTRACTS : DATA FROM THE ANNUAL GENERAL FINANCE AND EMPLOYMENT SURVEYS. (1981)-. English. Free. National Criminal Justice Reference Services / NCJRS, Box 6000, 1600 Research Boulevard, Rockville MD 20850. **Tel** (301)251-5500. **LC** HV8138; .J89. **DD** 338.4/3364973. ***Continues*** *Justice Expenditure and Employment in the U.S.*
Ind/Abst Predicasts Forecasts.

US/0741-8825
JUSTICE QUARTERLY. (JUSTICE QUARTERLY : JQ.). [Justice q.]. **Added/Corp** Academy of Criminal Justice Sciences. **VFOAT** JQ; J.Q. Vol. 1, No. 1 (March 1984)-. Periodical. English. qt. $10.00 (one year), $160.00 (two year), $225.00 (three year) US; $105.00 (one year), $170.00 (two year), $240.00 (three year) other. Academy of Criminal Justice Sciences, Northern Kentucky University, 402 Nunn Hall, Highland Heights KY 41099. **Tel** (606)572-5634. **ED** Edna Frez. **LC** HV7231; .J87. **DD** 364/.973. Index available. **Bk Rev. Ad Acc, Adv Mgr:** Pat Delancey. **Circ:** 2,500 (ctrl). available on an online database, CD-ROM, magnetic tape, and microfilm from University Microfilms International (UMI).
Desc: Development of knowledge in criminal justice. Solicit scholarship and research in other justice related areas.
Ind/Abst Crim. Justice Abstr.; Crim. Justice Period. Index; Crim. Penol. Police Sci. Abstr.

CN/0823-9436
JUSTICE REPORT. (JUSTICE REPORT: A PUBLICATION OF THE CANADIAN CRIMINAL JUSTICE ASSOCIATION.). [Justice rep.]. **Added/Corp** Canadian Criminal Justice Association. **VFOAT** Actualites-Justice. Vol. 1, No. 1 (Sept. 1984)-. Periodical. English (French). qt. 35.00Can$ Canada; 42.00Can$ other. Canadian Criminal Justice Association, 383 Parkdale #304, Ottawa Ontario K1Y 4R4 Canada. **Tel** (613)725-3715, FAX (613)725-3720. **LC** HV9960.C2; J87. **DD** 364.971/05. ***Continues*** *Canadian Association for the Prevention of Crime. Bulletin of the Canadian Association for the Prevention of Crime, 0705-9094.*
Ind/Abst Index Can. Leg. Period. Lit.

CN/0823-9436
JUSTICE REPORT. (ACTUALITES-JUSTICE : UNE PUBLICATION DE L'ASSOCIATION CANADIENNE DE JUSTICE PENALE.). [Justice rep.]. **Added/Corp** Association Canadienne de Justice Penale. **VFOAT** Justice Report. Vol. 1 No. 1 (Sept. 1984)-. Periodical. French (English). ir. Free to members. Association Canadienne de Justice Penale, Canadian Criminal Justice Association, 55 Av Parkdale, Ottawa Ontario K1Y 1E5 Canada. **Tel** (613)725-3715. **DD** 364/.06/071. ***Continues*** *Canadian Association for the Prevention of Crime. Bulletin de la Societe Canadienne pour la Prevention du Crime., 0705-9094.*
Ind/Abst Index Can. Leg. Period. Lit. (1992-).

NE/0168-5783
JUSTICIELE KINDERBESCHERMING. **See** Law-Abstracting, Bibliographies and Statistics.

US
JUVENILE COURT STATISTICS. **See** Law-Abstracting, Bibliographies and Statistics.

US/0091-3278
JUVENILE COURT STATISTICS (WASHINGTON). **See** Law-Abstracting, Bibliographies and Statistics.

US
JUVENILE JUSTICE AND DELINQUENCY PREVENTION PLAN. **Main/Corp** Mississippi. Criminal Justice Planning Commission. (19??)-. English. **LC** HV9105.M7; M58a. **DD** 364.3/6/09762.

US/0094-2413
JUVENILE JUSTICE DIGEST. **Added/Corp** Washington Crime News Services (U.S.). (1972)-. Periodical. English. sm. $195.00 (one year), $340.00 (two year), $580.00 (three year). Washington Crime News Services, 3918 Prosperity Avenue, Suite 318, Fairfax VA 22031-3334. **Tel** (703)573-1600, (800)422-9267, FAX (703)573-1604. **ED** Susan Kernus. **Bk Rev. Circ:** 1,000. available on microfilm and microfiche from University Microfilms International (UMI).
Desc: The latest legislative and policy developments, trends, court decisions and resource materials for the administrator and policy maker.
Ind/Abst Crim. Justice Period. Index.

US
JUVENILE JUSTICE INFORMATION SYSTEM : (JJIS) / KANSAS BUREAU OF INVESTIGATION, STATISTICAL ANALYSIS CENTER. **VFOAT** JJIS; J.J.I.S.; Annual Report. (1982)-. Statistical Publication. English. an. Kansas Bureau of Investigation, Statistical Analysis Center, 3420 Van Buren, Topeka KS 66611. **LC** HV9105.K2; K26A. **DD** 364.3/6/09781021. ***Continues*** *Kansas Juvenile Justice Information System.*

US
JUVENILE SERVICES ADMINISTRATION ANNUAL REPORT. **Main/Corp** Maryland Juvenile Services Administration. **Added/Corp** Maryland. Dept. of Health and Mental Hygiene. **VFOAT** Annual Report. English. Juvenile Services Administration, 201 West Preston Street, Baltimore MD 21201. **LC** HV742.M3; M33a. **DD** 353.97520084/9/083. ***Continues*** *Annual Statistical Report / Maryland. Juvenile Services Administration.*

JA
KAGAKU KEISATSU KENKYUJO NEMPO. **Main/Corp** Kagaku Keisatsu Kenkyujo. (19??)-. Periodical. Japanese. an. Kagaku Keisatsu Kenkyujo, 6 Sanancho Khiyoda-ku, Tokyo 102 Japan. **LC** HV7826; .A32. **Circ:** 1,000.

US/0274-4872
KEEPER'S VOICE. **Added/Corp** American Association of Correctional Officers. Northern Michigan University. Criminal Justice Dept. Northern Michigan University. Criminal Justice Training Center. (1979)-. Periodical. English. qt (Jan., Apr., July, Oct.). $20.00. International Association of Correctional Officerso, 1333 South Wabash Avenue, Box 53, Chicago IL 60605. **Tel** (312)996-5401. **ED** Bob Barrington. **Bk Rev. Ad Acc.** ctrl circ.

GW
KRIMINALIST, DER. Periodical. German. DM92.00. Verlag Deutsche Kriminalpolizei, Muth Verlag 4 Dusseldorf II, Kaiser-Friedrich-Ring 9, Dusseldorf Germany. **LC** HV6003; .K73.
Ind/Abst Crim. Penol. Police Sci. Abstr.

GW/0023-4699
KRIMINALISTIK. [Kriminalistik]. (May 1947)-. Academic Scholarly Publication. German. Eleven times a year. $108.00 North America. Dr. Alfred Huethig Verlag GmbH, Postfach 102869, D 69018 Heidelberg Germany. **Tel** 011 49 6221 489281. **(Subscription address:** Huethig Publishing Inc., 29 Macintosh Drive, Oxford CT 06478.**) ED** Waldemar Burghard, Eugen Thomann, Wolfgang Steinke, Jacob Meier and Horst Clages. **[CCC].** Index available. **Bk Rev. Ad Acc. Pr Rev. Circ:** 4,945 (ctrl). Documents available from The Genuine Article.
Desc: The leading source for police education, basic and advanced. Keeps readers informed of the latest developments in the field. Natural science applications to criminology and relevant laws.
Ind/Abst Crim. Penol. Police Sci. Abstr.; EMBASE; Energy Res. Abstr. (April 1976-); PAIS Int. Print (1991-?); Res. Alert [Full Cov.]; Soc. Sci. Cit. Index [Full Cov.].

AU
KRIMINALSOZIOLOGISCHE BIBLIOGRAPHIE. Vol. 1 (1973)-. German. Four times a year. S240.00 (institutions), S340.00 (individuals). Kriminalsoziologische Bibliographie, Museumstr Postf 1, A-1016 Vienna Austria. Index available. cum. index.
Desc: Articles, book reviews and discussions in the field of law, deviance, social control, and the social world.

GW
KRIMINOLOGISCHE SCHRIFTENREIHE. **Added/Corp** Deutsche Kriminologische Gesellschaft. Vol. 1 (1961)-. Monographic series. German. ir. price varies per volume. Kriminalistik Verlag GmbH, IM Weiher 10, D-69121 Heidelberg Germany. **Tel** 011 49 6221 489259, FAX 011 49 6221 489279.
Desc: Covers books by scholars in legal, social science, and medical fields exploring criminal psychology, environment crimes, computer security problems, diminished responsibility and other current topics.

SZ
KRIMINOLOGISCHES BULLETIN. **Added/Corp** Schweizerisches Nationalkomitee fur Geistige Gesundheit. Arbeitsgruppe fur Kriminologie. Schweizerische Arbeitsgruppe fur Kriminologie. **VFOAT** Bulletin de Criminologie. (19??)-. Bulletin. French (German). sa. 20.00F. Schweizerisches Nationalkomitee fur Geistige Gesundheit/Lueget 29, CH-8053 Zurich Switzerland. **LC** HV7052; .K74. **DD** 364/.9494.

GW
KRIMINOLOGISCHES JOURNAL. **Added/Corp** Arbeitskreis Junger Kriminologen. (19??)-. Periodical. German. qt. DM65.00. Juventa Verlag GmbH, Ehretstrasse 3, D 69469 Weinheim Germany. **Tel** 011 49 6201 61035, FAX 011 49 6201 13135. **LC** HV6003; .K77.

US/0023-9194
LAW AND ORDER. [Law order]. (Jan. 1953)-. Periodical. English. mo. $20.00 (1 year), $31.00 (2 year), $41.00 (3 year) US; $40.00 (1 year), $71.00 (2 year), $101.00 (3 year) other. Law and Order, PO Box 1150, Skokie IL 60076. **Tel** (708)256-8555, (800)843-9764, FAX (708)256-8674. **LC** HV7551; .L3. **Bk Rev. Ad Acc. Circ:** 25,000 (ctrl). available on microfilm and microfiche from University Microfilms International (UMI).
Desc: Designed to reach the chief executives in policing agencies with the latest information relating to their profession.
Ind/Abst Crim. Justice Abstr.; Crim. Justice Period. Index.

US
LAW ENFORCEMENT BULLETIN. **Main/Corp** Wisconsin. Crime Information Bureau. Bulletin. English. bw. Crime Information Bureau, PO Box 2718, Madison WI 53701.

US/0895-3945
LAW ENFORCEMENT INTELLIGENCE ANALYSIS DIGEST. ***Title Change.*** [Law enforc. intell. anal. dig.]. **Added/Corp** International Association of Law Enforcement Intelligence Analysts (U.S.). (1985)-(199?). Periodical. English. sm. International Association of Law Enforcement Intelligence Analysts, PO Box 876, Washington DC 20044. **Tel** (609)530-3414. **ED** Marilyn B Peterson. **DD** 364. **Bk Rev. Pr Rev. Circ:** 700 (ctrl). ***Continued by*** *IALEIA Journal, 1068-9796.*

US/0195-0290
LAW ENFORCEMENT LEGAL REPORTER INCORPORATED, THE. (THE LAW ENFORCEMENT LEGAL REPORTER INCORPORATED : [NEWSLETTER].). (1979)-. Periodical. English. Twelve times a year. $27.50 (one year); $50.00 (two years). Law Enforcement Legal

Reporter, PO Box 1356, Torrance CA 90505. **Tel** (213)603-7491. **ED** Elliott E. Alhadeff. **LC** KF9625.A59; L39. **DD** 345.73/052; 347.30552. Index available. **Circ:** 3,000 (ctrl).
Desc: Review of recent case decisions affecting California law enforcement in criminal area and application analysis.

US
LAW ENFORCEMENT LEGAL SUMMARIES. English. California Department of Justice, PO Box 13427, 1515 K Street, Second Floor, Sacramento CA 95814. **Tel** (916)324-5080. **LC** KFC1155.A73; L3. **DD** 345/.794/05.

US
LAW ENFORCEMENT LEGISLATIVE BUY-FUND : BIENNIUM REPORT. English. be. Bureau of Criminal Apprehension, 1246 University Avenue, St Paul MN 55104. **LC** HV8073; .L33. **DD** 353.97760074.

US/0364-1724
LAW ENFORCEMENT NEWS. (1975)-. Periodical. English. sm. $18.00 (one year), $34.00 (two year), $50.00 (three year). John Jay College, 899 10th Avenue, New York NY 10019. **Tel** (212)237-8442, FAX (212)237-8901. **ED** Peter Dodenhoff. **LC** HV8138; .L326. **DD** 363.2/3/097305. **Bk Rev**, (Qty: 22). **Ad Acc. Circ:** 5,000. available on microfilm and microfiche from University Microfilms International (UMI).
Desc: Covers progressive forms and approaches to the criminal justice system geared to the police audience.
Ind/Abst Crim. Justice Period. Index; Urban Aff. Abstr.

US/0747-7961
LAW ENFORCEMENT OFFICERS KILLED AND ASSAULTED. (LAW ENFORCEMENT OFFICERS KILLED AND ASSAULTED / U.S. DEPARTMENT OF JUSTICE, FEDERAL BUREAU OF INVESTIGATION.). 1982-. English. an. Federal Bureau of Investigation, 10th Street and Pennsylvania Avenue NW, Washington DC 20535. **Tel** (202)324-3000, FAX (202)324-4705. **LC** HV8143; .L39. **DD** 363.2/32. *Formed by the union of Law Enforcement Officers Killed, 0191-2712 and Assaults on Federal Officers, 0148-4257.*

US/0094-8438
LAW ENFORCEMENT REPORT. (LAW ENFORCEMENT REPORT / POSTAL INSPECTION SERVICE.). **Added/Corp** United States Postal Service. Postal Inspection Service. (19??)-. Periodical. English. bm. Free on request. US Postal Service / Communications and Public Affairs, Washington DC 20260. **LC** HE6094; .U53a. **DD** 343/.73/099202643. *Continues Law Enforcement Report, 0094-8438.*

US/0747-3680
LAW ENFORCEMENT TECHNOLOGY. [Law enforc. technol.]. (Mar./Apr. 1984-). Periodical. English. Twelve times a year. $60.00 US & Canada; $90.00 other. PTN Publishing Company, 445 Broad Hollow Road, Melville NY 11747. **Tel** (516)845-2700, FAX (516)845-7109. **ED** Susan Parker. **DD** 363. **Ad Acc. Circ:** 23,000 (ctrl). available on microfilm and microfiche from University Microfilms International (UMI). *Continues Law Enforcement Communications, 0193-0540.*
Desc: Management and technology information for senior law enforcement personnel and administrators.

●UK/1355-3259
LEGAL AND CRIMINOLOGICAL PSYCHOLOGY. See Psychology.

US/0364-5649
LEGISLATIVE REPORT ON JUVENILE PROBATION SUBSIDY. **Main/Corp** Nevada. Division of Juvenile Community Services. English. Nevada Department of Human Resources, 308 North Curry Street, Carson City NV 89701. **LC** HV7278; .A3. **DD** 364.6.

IT
LEGISLAZIONE PENALE. Italian. tq. L185.00 Italy; L277.50 other. Unione Tipografico Ed Torinese, Corso Raffaello 28, 10125 Turin Italy. **Tel** 011 39 11 6529340.

US/0271-5481
LIABILITY REPORTER. [Liabil. rep.]. **Main/Corp** Americans for Effective Law Enforcement. No. 73 (Jan. 1979)-. English. mo. $158.00. Americans for Effective Law Enforcement Inc, 5519 North Cumberland Avenue, Suite 1008, Chicago IL 60656-1471. **Tel** (312)763-2800, FAX (312) 763-3225. **ED** Bernaed Farber. **LC** KF1307.A73; A4. **DD** 346.7303/3. Index available. cum. index. **Circ:** 1,285. available on microfilm and microfiche from University Microfilms International (UMI). *Continues A.E.L.E. Law Enforcement Legal Liability Reporter, 0092-0940.*
Desc: The editor reviews pertinent cases and selects those considered to have effective impact upon law enforcement personnel and their attorneys.

FR/0024-1717
LIAISONS PARIS. 1963. [Liaisons Paris, 1963]. (1963)-. Periodical. French. wk.
Ind/Abst Point Repere (1979-1983).

IT
LIBERA VOCE DI POLIZIA ITALIANA. Italian. Eleven times a year. L98000.00 (ordinary), L150000.00 (sustainer). Sind Naz 5 Corpi Polizia Cong, Via Crescenzio 2, 00193 Rome Italy. **Tel** 011 39 6 6878153.

US
LIBRARY BOOK CATALOG. See Library and Information Sciences.

US
LIFE LINES : NEWSLETTER OF THE NATIONAL COALITION AGAINST THE DEATH PENALTY. **Added/Corp** National Coalition Against the Death Penalty. National Coalition to Abolish the Death Penalty. **VFOAT** Lifelines. (Spring 1981)-. Newsletter. English. bm.
Ind/Abst Hum. Rights Intern. Rep.

UK/0963-1054
LOCAL AUTHORITY LAW. (1991)-. English. Ten times a year. £75.00 Europe; £79.00 other. Sweet & Maxwell Ltd, South Quay Plaza, 183 Marsh Wall, London E14 9FT England. **Tel** 011 44 264 342899, FAX 011 44 264 342723, telex 929089 ITPINF G.

●US
LOOKING TOWARD THE FUTURE: A FIVE YEAR PLAN FOR THE IOWA DEPARTMENT OF CORRECTIONS / PREPARED BY THE IOWA DEPARTMENT OF CORRECTIONS, BUREAU OF RESEARCH AND PLANNING. **Main/Corp** Iowa. Dept. of Corrections. Bureau of Research and Planning. **VFOAT** Five Year Plan for the Iowa Department of Corrections; Five Year Plan for the Corrections System in Iowa. (1993)-. English. Iowa Department of Corrections, 523 East 12th Street, Capitol Annex, Des Moines IA 50319. **Tel** (515)281-4811, FAX (515)281-7345. **LC** HV8335; .D46b. **DD** 353.97770084/9/05. available on microfiche.

US
LOUISIANA PEACE OFFICER. **Added/Corp** Louisiana. Dept. of State Police. Louisiana. Dept. of Public Safety. Division of State Police. Louisiana. Dept. of Public Safety. Louisiana Peace Officers Association. Louisiana Sheriffs Association. Municipal Police Officers Association of Louisiana. Vol. 1 (1943)-. Periodical. English. qt. LPO Enterprises, 1312 North 22nd Street, Baton Rouge LA 70802. **Tel** (504)387-2645. *Supersedes Louisiana Policeman.*

●UK/0966-2847
LOW INTENSITY CONFLICT AND LAW ENFORCEMENT. [Low intensity confl. law enforc.]. **VFOAT** Law Intensity Conflict & Law Enforcement. (1992)-. Periodical. English. Three times a year. $125.00. Frank Cass & Company Ltd, Newbury House, 890-900 Eastern Avenue, Newbury Park, Ilford, Essex IG2 7HH United Kingdom. **Tel** 011 44 81 599 8866, FAX 011 44 81 599 0984, telex 897719. **DD** 306.605. **Ad Acc, Adv Mgr:** Anne Kidson.

NE/0169-9385
MAANDSTATISTIEK RECHTSBESCHERMING EN VEILIGHEID. See Law-Abstracting, Bibliographies and Statistics.

UK
MAGISTRATE, THE. Began in 1921. Periodical. English. mo. $20.69. Magistrates Association, 28 Fitzroy Square, London W1P 6DD England. **Tel** 01 387 2302. **ED** E R Horsman. **LC** KD7302; .M3. **DD** 347/.41/016. **Bk Rev. Ad Acc. Circ:** 26,000 (ctrl).
Desc: Short articles relating to law and practice of British magistrates' courts.

US/0098-079X
MAINE PROSECUTOR, CRIMINAL LEGISLATION MANUAL, THE. **VFOAT** Criminal Legislation Manual. English. Law & Legislative Ref Library, State House Station 43, Augusta ME 04330. **Tel** (207)289-1110. **LC** KFM562.A29; M34. **DD** 345.741/05.

MR
MAJALLAT AL-SHURTAH. **VFOAT** Revue de Police. Periodical. Multiple languages (Arabic and French). bm. 1.50. PO Box 437, Al-Rabat Morocco. **LC** HV8276.M6; M34.

US/0148-2602
MARYLAND POLICE AND CORRECTIONAL TRAINING COMMISSIONS REPORT TO THE GOVERNOR, THE SECRETARY OF PUBLIC SAFETY AND CORRECTIONAL SERVICES, AND MEMBERS OF THE GENERAL ASSEMBLY. **Main/Corp** Maryland. Police Training Commission. Began with Vol. for 1974/75. English. an. Pikesville Professional Building/Suite 14, 7 Church Lane, Pikesville MD 21208. **LC** HV7270; .A46. **DD** 363.2/07/15. *Supersedes Annual Report to the Governor and Members of the General Assembly - Maryland Police Training Commission, 0148-2610; Annual Report to the Governor, the Secretary of Public Safety and Correctional Services and Members of the General Assembly, 0090-9963.*

MF
MAURITIUS POLICE MAGAZINE, THE. **Added/Corp** Mauritius. Police Force. (19??)-. English (French). an. Office of the Commissioner of Police, Police Headquarters, Line Barracks, Port Louis Mauritius. **ED** A. Feillafe. **LC** HV7861.A2; M38. **DD** 363.2/0969/82. Index available. **Ad Acc. Circ:** 10,000. available on microfilm.
Desc: Short stories on police life, poems, poetry, and sports.

US
MEMBERSHIP UPDATE / CORRECTIONAL EDUCATION ASSOCIATION. **Main/Corp** Correctional Education Association (U.S.). **VFOAT** CEA Membership Update. **VAT** Correctional Education Association Membership Update. (19??)-. English. qt. $75.00 (institution), $35.00 (individual). Correctional Education Association, 8025 Laurel Lakes Court, Laurel MD 20707. **Tel** (301)490-1440, FAX (301)206-5061. **LC** HV8883.3.U5; C68a. **DD** 365/.66.

US/0895-4208
MILITARY POLICE (1987). (MILITARY POLICE.). [Mil. police]. **Added/Corp** US Army Military Police School. (Spring 1987)-. Government Publication. English. sa. $5.00; US; $6.25 other. Superintendent of Documents, US Government Printing Office, Washington DC 20402. **Tel** (202)275-3328, FAX (202)786-2377. **ED** Lois C. Perry. **LC** UB825.U54; M52. **DD** 355. Index available. **Bk Rev. Circ:** 10,000 (ctrl). available on microfilm and microfiche from University Microfilms International (UMI). *Continues Military Police Journal (Fort McClellan, Ala.), 0884-0024.*
Desc: Contains information about military police functions in combat. Objectives are to inform, motivate and provide a forum for the exchange of ideas.
Ind/Abst Air Univ. Libr. Index Mil. Period.

US/0093-2558
MINNESOTA ALCOHOL PROGRAMS FOR HIGHWAY SAFETY. See Public Health and Safety.

US/0026-5624
MINNESOTA POLICE JOURNAL. **Added/Corp** Minnesota Police and Peace Officers Association. Minnesota Chiefs of Police Association. (195?)-. Periodical. English. bm (Feb., Apr., Jun., Aug., Oct., Dec.). $13.00. Minnesota Police & Peace Officer, 525 Park Street, Capitol Office #207, St Paul MN 55103. **Tel** (800)652-9799, (612)291-1119, FAX (612)291-0227. **ED** Dennis J Flaherty. **Ad Acc. Circ:** 6,500. *Continues Minnesota Police and Peace Officers Bulletin.*
Desc: News and technical information for law enforcement officers of all ranks.

CN
MINUTES OF PROCEEDINGS AND EVIDENCE OF THE SUB-COMMITTEE ON THE PENITENTIARY SYSTEM IN CANADA. **Main/Corp** Canada. Parliament. House of Commons. Sub-Committee on the Penitentiary System in Canada. **VFOAT** Proces-Verbaux et Temoignages du Sous-Comite sur le Regime d'Institutions Penitentiaires au Canada. Oct. 26, 1976-. Proceedings. English (French). Printing and Publishing, Supply and Services Canada, Ottawa Ontario K1A 0S9 Canada. **LC** HV7315; .A39A. **DD** 365/.971.

US/1072-1037
MIRROR (1984). (THE MIRROR.). **Added/Corp** Minnesota Correctional Facility--Stillwater. **VFOAT** Prison Mirror. Vol. 97, No. 6 (Jan. 13, 1984)-. Newspaper. English (Spanish). Twenty-six times a year. $15.00 (regular); $5.00 (inmates and students); $27.00 other. Mirror Publications, Minnesota Correctional Facility, PO Box 55, Stillwater MN 55082. **Tel** (612)779-2809, FAX (612)779-2788. **ED** James Reed (editor's phone: (612)779-2809 Ext. 2551). **Circ:** 2,500. available on microfilm; available on microfiche from University Microfilms International (UMI). *Continues Prison Mirror (Stillwater, Minn. : 1982).*

GW/0026-9301
MONATSSCHRIFT FUER KRIMINOLOGIE UND STRAFRECHTSREFORM. [Monatsschr. kriminol. strafrechtsreform]. (Oct. 1953)-. Periodical. German. bm. DM138.00. Carl Heymanns Verlag KG,

Luxemburger Strasse 449, D 50939 Cologne Germany. **Tel** 011 49 221 460100, telex 8 881 888. **ED** H Schuler-Springorium. Index available. **Bk Rev**. **Ad Acc**. **Circ:** 1,000 (ctrl). ***Continues*** *Monatsschrift fur Kriminalbiologie und Strafrechtsreform.*
Desc: Covers the science of criminology and penal law reform.
Ind/Abst Crim. Justice Abstr. (199?-); Crim. Penol. Police Sci. Abstr.

US
MONTANA COMPREHENSIVE PLAN FOR CRIMINAL JUSTICE IMPROVEMENT. **Main/Corp** Montana. Board of Crime Control. **VFOAT** Comprehensive Plan for Criminal Justice Improvement. English. an. Montana Board of Crime Control, 1336 Helena Avenue, Helena MT 59601. **LC** HV7276; .A3B. **DD** 364/.9786. ***Continues*** *Montana Plan for Criminal Justice Improvement.*

US/0027-1004
MORALITY IN MEDIA INC. NEWSLETTER. ***Title Change.*** [Moral. Media inc. newsl.]. **Main/Corp** Morality in Media, Inc. **Added/Corp** Morality in Media. Newsletter. **VFOAT** MM Newsletter; MIM B.. (19??)-(19??). Newsletter. English. mo (except Jan., July, Aug., and Sept.). Morality in Media Newsletter, 474 Riverside Drive, New York NY 10115. **Tel** (212)870-3222. **ED** Evelyn Dukovic. **DD** 363. **Bk Rev**. **Ad Acc**. **Circ:** 50,000. ***Continued by*** *Morality in Media Newsletter, 1058-3459.*
Desc: Reports on the traffic in pornography getting to children, on obscenity law and its enforcement, on cases, decisions, community anti-porn activity.

BL
MUNDO POLICIAL. Portuguese. 180.00. Editorial Policial, rua Santana 1256, Buenos Aires Argentina. **LC** HV7551; .M76.

US/0889-7794
NARC OFFICER, THE. (THE NARC OFFICER : OFFICIAL PUBLICATION OF THE INTERNATIONAL NARCOTICS ENFORCEMENT OFFICERS ASSOCIATION.). [Narc off.]. **Added/Corp** International Narcotic Enforcement Officers Association. (198?)-. Periodical. English. Six times a year. $35.00. International Narcotic Enforcement Officers Association, 112 State Street, Suite 1200, Albany NY 12207. **Tel** (518)463-6232. **ED** Celeste Morga. **LC** WMLC 93/1160. **DD** 364. **Bk Rev**. **Ad Acc**. ctrl circ.
Desc: Content contains laws, cases, trends, and statistics on drug abuse arrests, investigations and general information.

●IT
NARCOMAFIE. (1993)-. Italian. mo (10 issues per year). L25000 Italy; L55000 other (comes with Animazione Sociale). Associazione Gruppo Abele, Via Giolitti 21, 10123 Turin Italy. **Tel** 011 39 11 8142745, FAX 011 39 8395577. **ED** Luigi Ciotti.

US/1042-5810
NATIONAL BULLETIN ON POLICE MISCONDUCT. [Natl. bull. police misconduct]. **VFOAT** Police Misconduct; LEMB; L.E.M.B. (Oct. 1988)-. Bulletin. English. mo. $52.91. Quinlan Publishing Company, 23 Drydock Avenue, Boston MA 02210-2387. **Tel** (617)542-0048, (800)229-2084, FAX (617)345-9646. **LC** KF5399.A59; L39. **DD** 346.7303/1/02638; 347.3063102638. **[CCC]**. available on microfilm and microfiche from University Microfilms International (UMI). ***Continues*** *Law Enforcement Misconduct Bulletin, 8755-8238.*

US/0198-6546
NATIONAL CRIMINAL JUSTICE THESAURUS. (NATIONAL CRIMINAL JUSTICE THESAURUS / [PREPARED FOR THE NATIONAL INSTITUTE OF JUSTICE, U.S. DEPARTMENT OF JUSTICE, BY ASPEN SYSTEMS CORP.]). [Natl. crim. justice thesaurus]. **Added/Corp** National Institute of Justice (U.S.) Aspen Systems Corporation. National Criminal Justice Reference Service (U.S.) National Institute of Law Enforcement and Criminal Justice. (19??)-. English. an. $25.00. National Criminal Justice Reference Services / NCJRS, Box 6000, 1600 Research Boulevard, Rockville MD 20850. **Tel** (301)251-5500. **LC** Z695.1.C84; U54a. **DD** 025.4/9364.

US/1066-5595
NATIONAL DIRECTORY OF LAW ENFORCEMENT ADMINISTRATORS, CORRECTIONAL INSTITUTIONS, AND RELATED GOVERNMENTAL AGENCIES. [Natl. dir. law enforc. adm. correct. inst. relat. agencies]. **Added/Corp** National Police Chiefs and Sheriffs Information Bureau. **VFOAT** National Directory of Law Enforcement Administrators and Correctional agencies; National Directory of Law Enforcement Administrators, Correctional Institutions, and related agencies; National Directory, Law Enforcement Administrators, Correctional Institutions, Related agencies; National Directory, Law Enforcement Administrators, Correctional institutions; National directory, law enforcement administrators, correctional institutions, and related agencies. (198?)-. Directory. English. an (Aug.). $55.00. National Police Chief and Sheriffs, PO Box 365, Stevens Point WI 54481. **Tel** (715)345-2772. **LC** HV8130; . N37. **DD** 363.2/025/73. **Ad Acc, Adv Mgr:** Jennifer Bailey, **Tel** (715)345-2772. **Circ:** 10,000. available on an online database from Mead Data Central. ***Continues*** *National Directory, Law Enforcement Administrators, Prosecutors, Correctional Institutions, and Related Agencies, 0733-3811.*
Desc: List of all the law enforcement agencies nationwide, including Canada. Some of the international law enforcement are listed to.

US/1064-4814
NATIONAL FIRE & ARSON REPORT, THE. [Natl. fire arson rep.]. **Added/Corp** Investigative Research International. **VFOAT** National Fire and Arson Report. Vol. 1, No. 1 (May/June 1982)-. Periodical. English. Four times a year. $28.00 US; $36.00 Canada; $55.00 other. Investigative Research International, PO Box 411087, Charlotte NC 28241. **Tel** (800)488-6327, FAX (704)588-1248. **ED** Barbara P. Goodnight. **DD** 364. Index available (bound in first issue). cum. index. **Bk Rev**. **Ad Acc**. **Circ:** 10,000.
Desc: Comprehensive resource for professional investigators, particularly fire and arson. Includes, latest investigative techniques, current legal issues, seminar/conference/training listings, fire prevention, insurance, etc.

●US/1067-7453
NATIONAL INSTITUTE OF JUSTICE JOURNAL. [Natl. Inst. Justice j.]. **Added/Corp** National Institute of Justice (U.S.). (1992)-. Periodical. English. bm. Free on request, US; $5.00 Canada; $10.00 other. National Criminal Justice Reference Services / NCJRS, Box 6000, 1600 Research Boulevard, Rockville MD 20850. **Tel** (301)251-5500. **LC** Z5703.4.C73; N37a; HV7245. **DD** 364. ***Continues in part*** *National Institute of Justice Reports, 1067-8573.*

US/0192-8228
NATIONAL JAIL AND ADULT DETENTION DIRECTORY. **Added/Corp** American Correctional Association. (1978)-. Directory. English. ir. $75.00. American Correctional Association, 8025 Laurel Lakes Court, Laurel MD 20707-5075. **Tel** (301)206-5100, (800)222-5646, FAX (301)206-5061. **LC** HV9463; .N37. **DD** 365/.025/73. **Bk Rev**. **Ad Acc**. **Circ:** 3,000.
Desc: List county jails with names of administrators, addresses, phone, statistical information on capacities, level of security, personnel, etc.
Ind/Abst Stat. Ref. Index.

US/1076-769X
NATIONAL PRISON PROJECT JOURNAL, THE. (THE NATIONAL PRISON PROJECT JOURNAL : A PROJECT OF THE AMERICAN CIVIL LIBERTIES UNION FOUNDATION, INC.). [Natl. Prison Proj. j.]. **Added/Corp** American Civil Liberties Union Foundation. National Prison Project. **VFOAT** Journal; NPP Journal. (19??)-. Periodical. English. qt. National Prison Project, 1785 Connecticut Avenue Northwest, Washington DC 20009. **Tel** (202)234-4830, FAX (202)234-4890. **ED** Jan Elvin. **DD** 365. Index available. **Bk Rev**, (Qty: 1). **Circ:** 3,000. available on microfilm and microfiche from University Microfilms International (UMI). ***Continues*** *Journal (American Civil Liberties Union Foundation. National Prison Project), 0748-2655.*
Desc: Features articles, reports, legal analysis, legislative news and other developments in the field.

US
NCPI HOTLINE. **Main/Corp** University of Louisville. National Crime Prevention Institute. **VAT** National Crime Prevention Institute Hotline. (19??)-. Periodical. English. qt. $25.00. National Crime Prevention Institute, Shelby Campus, University of Louisville, Louisville KY 40292. **Tel** (502)588-6987. ***Absorbed*** *NCPI Associates Newsletter.*

US
NEBRASKA COMPREHENSIVE CRIMINAL JUSTICE PLAN. **Main/Corp** Nebraska Commission on Law Enforcement and Criminal Justice. **VFOAT** Nebraska Criminal Justice Plan. English. an. Nebraska Commission on Law Enforcement and Criminal Justice, 301 Centennial Mall South, PO Box 94946, Lincoln NE 68509. **LC** HV7277; .A274A. **DD** 364/.9782/05.

US/1070-8316
NEBRASKA JUVENILE COURT REPORT. **See** Sociology-Social Services and Welfare.

US
NEVADA COMPREHENSIVE CRIMINAL JUSTICE PLAN. **Main/Corp** Nevada. Commission on Crime, Delinquency, and Corrections. English. Nevada Commission of Crime Delinquency and Corrections, Carson City NV 89710. **LC** HV7278; .A27A. **DD** 364/.9793/05. ***Continues*** *State of Nevada Comprehensive Criminal Justice Plan.*

US/0740-8994
NEW ENGLAND JOURNAL ON CRIMINAL AND CIVIL CONFINEMENT. [N. Engl. j. crim. civ. confin.]. **Added/Corp** New England School of Law. Vol. 9, No. 1 (Winter 1983)-. Periodical. English. Twice a year (Winter, Summer). $20.00. New England School of Law, 46 Church Street, Attention NEJCCC, Boston MA 02116. **Tel** (617)422-7238, FAX (617)422-7451. **ED** Larry Elman, Liz Levy, and David Carton. **LC** K14; .E79. **DD** 344.73/035; 347.30435. **Bk Rev**, (Qty: 2-4). **Circ:** 500 (ctrl). ***Continues*** *New England Journal on Prison Law, 0095-7364.*
Desc: Articles by judges, professors, students and other authorities in the fields of criminal confinement law, civil confinement law and juvenile law.
Ind/Abst Crim. Justice Abstr.; Crim. Penol. Police Sci. Abstr.; Curr. Law Index (1983-); Index Leg. Period.; Leg. Resour. Index (1983-); LegalTrac (1983-).

US/0094-7628
NEW HAMPSHIRE COMPREHENSIVE LAW ENFORCEMENT PLAN. **Main/Corp** New Hampshire. Governor's Commission on Crime and Delinquency. (19??)-. English. Commission on Crime & Delinquency, 18 Centre Street, Concord NH 03301. **LC** KFN1762; .A825. **DD** 364.

US
NEW JERSEY POLICE MANUAL. (19??)-. Periodical. English. ir. $23.00. Gann Law Books, 1 Washington Park Suite 1500, Newark NJ 07102. **Tel** (201)268-1200.

AT
NEWSBREAK. (19??)-. English. Nine times a year. Free on request. Correctional Services Division, 20 Albert Road, South Melbourne VIC 3205 Australia. **Tel** 011 61 03 698 6666, FAX 011 61 699 9851. **ED** Malcolm Feiner. **Circ:** 2,000 (ctrl).
Desc: News and information from the Office of the Director of the Correctional Services Division of the Victoria Department of Justice.

US/0195-7252
NEWSLETTER - INTERNATIONAL PRISONERS AID ASSOCIATION. **Main/Corp** International Prisoners Aid Association. **Added/Corp** International Prisoners Aid Association. Newsletter. (19??)-. Newsletter. English. Three times a year. $5.00. International Prisoners Aid Association, Department of Sociology, University of Louisville, Louisville KY 40292.

US/0197-8519
NEXUS (WILMINGTON). (NEXUS.). Periodical. English. qt. Delaware Council on Crime and Justice Inc, 701 Shipley Street, Wilmington DE 19801. **LC** HV8145.D3; N49. **DD** 364/.9751.

JA
NIHON TANTEI MEIKAN. 1978-. Japanese. ¥5000. Esu Ai Esu, 16 Minatocho 4, Naka-ku, Yokohama Japan. **LC** HV8099.J3; A24.

●US
NIJ PROGRAM PLAN / NATIONAL INSTITUTE OF JUSTICE. **Main/Corp** National Institute of Justice (U.S.). **VFOAT** National Institute of Justice Program Plan. (1993)-. English. US Department of Justice, 10th Street & Constitution Avenue NW, Washington DC 20530. **Tel** (202)514-2000, FAX (202)633-4371. ***Continues*** *National Institute of Justice (U.S.). Research and Evaluation Plan.*

US
NIMLO RESEARCH REPORT / NATIONAL INSTITUTE OF MUNICIPAL LAW OFFICERS. **Added/Corp** National Institute of Municipal Law Officers (U.S.). No. 155 (1970)-. Monographic series. English. ir. Price varies per volume. National Institute of Municipal Law Officers, 1000 Connecticut Avenue NW/Suite 800, Washington DC 20036. **Tel** (202)466-5424. **LC** KF5305; .N3. **DD** 342'.73'09. ***Continues*** *Report (National Institute of Municipal Law Officers).*

IT
NOI POLIZIA. (19??)-. Italian. ir (10 issues). L165000.00 Italy. Penta Diffusione, Via Viotti 9, 20133 Milan Italy. **Tel** 011 39 2 26680755.

DK/0029-1528
NORDISK TIDSSKRIFT FOR KRIMINALVIDENSKAB. [Nord. tidsskr. kriminalvidensk.]. Academic Scholarly Publication. Danish. ***Continues*** *Nordisk Tidsskrift for Straefferet.*
Ind/Abst EMBASE; Index Foreign Leg. Per.

US/0098-0498
NORTH DAKOTA COMPREHENSIVE CRIMINAL JUSTICE PLAN. **Main/Corp** North Dakota. Combined Law Enforcement Council. **VFOAT** Crime and Delinquency in North Dakota. English. North Dakota Combined Law Enforcement Council, Box B, Bismarck ND 58501. **LC** HV7284; .A25A. **DD** 364. ***Continues*** *North Dakota Comprehensive Law Enforcement Plan.*

US/0744-5148
NORTH DAKOTA PEACE OFFICER.
Periodical. English. qt. Executive Secretary John H Keating, PO Box 517, Fargo ND 58105.

UK
NOTIFIABLE OFFENCES RECORDED BY THE POLICE. (19??)-. Periodical. English. Four times a year. Free on request. Planning and Management Unit, 40 Wellesley Road, #1834 Lunar HS, Croydon, Surrey CR0 9YD England. **Tel** 011 44 81 760-2850.

FR/0753-4000
NOUVEAU DETECTIVE, LE. [Nouv. Detect.]. (1982)-. Periodical. French. wk. 510.00F. Editions Nuit et Jour, 9 rue Christiani, 75018 Paris, France. **Tel** 011 31 1 49251818. **UDC** 087.2. ***Continues*** *Qui? Police, 0221-4709.*

US
OCJP NEWSLINE : OFFICE OF CRIMINAL JUSTICE PLANNING QUARTERLY NEWSLETTER. ***Suspended.*** **Added/Corp** California. Office of Criminal Justice Planning. **VFOAT** Office of Criminal Justice Planning Newsline; Office of Criminal Justice Planning Quarterly Newsletter. Vol. 6, No. 3 (Fall 1991)-(19??). Periodical. English. ir. Office of Criminal Justice Planning, 1130 K Street, Suite 300, Sacramento CA 95814. **LC** HV7254; .A355. ***Continues*** *Newsline (California. Office of Criminal Justice Planning).*

US/0093-321X
OFFENDERS ADMITTED TO ADULT CORRECTIONAL INSTITUTIONS (MADISON). (OFFENDERS ADMITTED TO ADULT CORRECTIONAL INSTITUTIONS.). **Added/Corp** Wisconsin. Division of Corrections. Bureau of Planning, Development, and Research. Wisconsin. Division of Corrections. Office of Systems and Evaluation. Wisconsin. Division of Corrections. Office of Information Management and Operations. (19??)-. English. an. Wisconsin Division of Corrections, 149 East Wilson Street, Room 1050, Madison WI 53702. **Tel** (608)266-2471, FAX (608)267-0923. **LC** HV7299; .A22. **DD** 365/.6/09775.
Desc: Provides demographic and sentencing profiles on adult inmates admitted for supervision in Wisconsin prisons.

US/0092-9956
OFFENDERS RELEASED FROM ADULT CORRECTIONAL INSTITUTIONS (MADISON). (OFFENDERS RELEASED FROM ADULT CORRECTIONAL INSTITUTIONS.). English. an. Department of Health & Social Services / Wisconsin, 1 West Wilson Street, PO Box 309, Madison WI 53701. **LC** HV9305.W6; O34. **DD** 365/.647./09775. ***Continues*** *Offenders Released from Division of Corrections Adult Institutions in ... .*

US/0148-7213
OFFICE OF RESEARCH PROGRAMS LIST OF SELECTED PUBLICATIONS & RESEARCH PROJECTS IN PROGRESS. **Main/Corp** National Institute of Law Enforcement and Criminal Justice. Office of Research Programs. **VAT** Office of Research Programs List of Selected Publications and Research Projects in Progress. English. US Department of Justice, 10th Street & Constitution Avenue NW, Washington DC 20530. **Tel** (202)514-2000, FAX (202)633-4371. **LC** Z5703.5.U5; N37A; HV8138. **DD** 016.364/973.

US
OFFICIAL DIRECTORY. **Main/Corp** International Narcotic Enforcement Officers Association. (19??)-. English. an. International Narcotic Enforcement Officers Association, 112 State Street, Suite 1200, Albany NY 12207. **Tel** (518)463-6232. **ED** Celeste Morga. **LC** HV5801; .I63a. **DD** 363.4/5. ctrl circ.

US/0019-2171
OFFICIAL JOURNAL - ILLINOIS POLICE ASSOCIATION. **Main/Corp** Illinois Police Association. **Added/Corp** Illinois Association of Chiefs of Police. (1947)-. Periodical. English. Six times a year (Feb., Apr., June, Aug., Oct., Dec.). $12.00. Illinois Police Association, 7508 West North Avenue, Elmwood Park IL 60635. **Tel** (708)452-8332. **ED** Michael R. Hoffman. **LC** HV7551; .I38a. **DD** 363.2/09773. **Bk Rev. Ad Acc. Circ:** 20,000.
Desc: News and technical information for law enforcement officers of all ranks.

US/0164-8357
OHIO POLICE CHIEF, THE. Periodical. English. qt. Ohio Association of Chiefs of Police, 2929 Kenny Road, Columbus OH 43221.

US/0190-2571
ON THE LINE (COLLEGE, PARK MD.). (ON THE LINE.). [On line]. **Added/Corp** American Correctional Association. Vol. 1 (Nov. 1977)-. Periodical. English. ir (5 issues). Free to members. American Correctional Association, 8025 Laurel Lakes Court, Laurel MD 20707-5075. **Tel** (301)206-5100, (800)222-5646, FAX (301)206-5061. **DD** 365.

IT
ORDINE PUBBLICO : ORGANO D'INFORMAZIONE PER LE FORZE DI POLIZIA. (1952)-. Periodical. Italian. mo. L100000 Italy; L200000 other. Editore Ordine Pubblico Srl, Via Delle Quattro Fontane 33, 00184 Rome, Italy. **Tel** 011 39 6 4817296. **LC** HV8212; .O75. **DD** 363.2/0945/05.

US/0361-7254
OREGON'S COMPREHENSIVE CRIMINAL JUSTICE PLAN. **Main/Corp** Oregon. Law Enforcement Council. **VFOAT** Application for Action Grant. English. Oregon Law Enforcement Council, 2001 Front Street NE, Salem OR 97310. **LC** HV7287; .A34. **DD** 364.

UK
ORIGINAL STATISTICS, ENGLAND AND WALES. SUPPLEMENTARY TABLES. VOL. 2, PROCEEDINGS IN THE CROWN COURT. **See** Law-Abstracting, Bibliographies and Statistics.

CN/0382-4780
OUTLOOK (LETHBRIDGE). (OUTLOOK.). Feb. 1, 1970-. Periodical. English. ir. Lethbridge Correctional Institution, PO Box 490, Lethbridge Alberta T1J 3Z3 Canada. **DD** 365/.97123/4.
Ind/Abst Bibliogr. Mission.

CN/0707-2228
P. A. L., PREVENT, AVOID LOSSES. **VFOAT** P.E.P., Prevenir, Eviter Pertes. Vol. 1 (June 1977)-. Periodical. English (French). qt. Free. Loss Prevention Committee, Room 339/Fauteux Hall, University of Ottawa, Ottawa Ontario K1N 6N5 Canada. **DD** 364.4/09713/84. ctrl circ.

BE
PANOPTICON. Vol. 1, No. 1 (Nov./Dec. 1980)-. Periodical. Dutch (summaries and/or abstracts in English and French). Six times a year. 2300F (institutions), 1785F (individuals). Kluwer Edn Juridiques Belgique, Blvd E Bockstael 230, 1020 Brussels Belguim. **Tel** 011 32 2 7232111. **LC** HV7003; .P36. **Bk Rev. Ad Acc.** ctrl circ.
Desc: Publishes articles dealing with law enforcement and criminology.
Ind/Abst Crim. Penol. Police Sci. Abstr.

US
PAROLE IN THE UNITED STATES. **Main/Corp** National Council on Crime and Delinquency. Research Center. 1976/77-. English. an. US Department of Justice, 10th Street & Constitution Avenue NW, Washington DC 20530. **Tel** (202)514-2000, FAX (202)633-4371. **LC** HV9304; .N342A. **DD** 364.6/2/0973.

US/0031-3556
PEACE OFFICER (WARREN, MICH.). ***Title Change.*** (PEACE OFFICER.). [Peace off.]. **Added/Corp** Fraternal Order of Police. State Lodge of Michigan. (19??)-(19??). Periodical. English. qt. Labor Council Michigan Fraternal Order of Police, 667 East Big Beaver, Suite 205, Troy MI 48083. **DD** 331. available on microfilm and microfiche from University Microfilms International (UMI). ***Continued by*** *Police Officers Journal, 1062-5216.*

CN/0705-3908
PEN-VISTA. BILINGUAL EDITION. (PEN-VISTA.). V. 1- May 1977-. Periodical. English (French). mo. Distributed free to inmates of Archambault Maximum Security Institution, $5.00 others. Pen-Vista, PO Box 1210, Ste Anne Des Plaines Quebec J0N 1H0 Canada. **DD** 365/.9714/24.

CN/0704-481X
PENDULUM (KINGSTON). (PENDULUM.). [Pendulum]. Mar. 1979-. Periodical. English. mo. $7.00. Inmate Committee, Joyceville Institution, PO Box 880, Kingston Ontario K7L 4X9 Canada. **DD** 365/.9713/72. ***Continues*** *Advance, 0709-1710.*

US/0031-4404
PENNSYLVANIA CHIEFS OF POLICE ASSOCIATION BULLETIN. **Main/Corp** Pennsylvania Chiefs of Police Association. **Added/Corp** Pennsylvania Chiefs of Police Association. Bulletin. (19??)-. Bulletin. English. Four times a year. $50.00. Pennsylvania Chiefs of Police Association, 2941 North Front Street, Harrisburg PA 17110. **Tel** (717)236-1059, 800-672-PCPA. **Bk Rev. Ad Acc. Circ:** 1,500 (ctrl).
Desc: Fraternal police and law enforcement bulletin.

US/0161-9136
PENNSYLVANIA LAW ENFORCEMENT JOURNAL. V. 1- Dec. 1975-. Periodical. English. bm. Police Law Enforcement Journal, 500 Barnett Place, Hohokus NJ 07423. **LC** HV8145.P4; P48. **DD** 363.2/09748.

US/0098-7174
PENNSYLVANIA POLICE CRIMINAL LAW BULLETIN, THE. (1972)-. Bulletin. English. Twelve times a year. $27.00. The Pennsylvania Police, 2579 Warren Road, Indiana PA 15701. **Tel** (412)465-5165. **ED** Stanley Cohen. **LC** KFP575.A59; P4. **DD** 345/.748/05. Index available. **Bk Rev**, (Qty: 13). **Pr Rev. Circ:** 1,600.
Desc: The major objective of the publication is to keep Pennsylvania police abreast of developments in criminal law that affect police practices in the state of Pennsylvania.

●FR/0254-5225
PENOLOGICAL INFORMATION BULLETIN / COUNCIL OF EUROPE. **Added/Corp** Council of Europe. No. 17 (Dec. 1992)-. Periodical. English (French). Twice a year. Free. Council of Europe / Group Pact ED, Pharmacopoeia BP 907, 67029 Strasbourg Cedex 01 France. **Tel** 011 33 88 412036, FAX 011 33 88 41277181, telex 880388. ***Continues*** *Prison Information Bulletin, 0254-5233.*

US
PERSPECTIVE (MINNESOTA. DEPT. OF CORRECTIONS). (PERSPECTIVE / MINNESOTA DEPARTMENT OF CORRECTIONS.). Vol. 5, Issue 2 (Mar./Apr. 1979)-. Periodical. English. Free. Minnesota Department of Correction, 450 North Syndicate Street, Bigelow Building, Suite 300, St Paul MN 55104. **Tel** (612)642-0282, FAX (612)642-0223. ***Continues*** *Corrections Perspective.*
Ind/Abst Crim. Justice Period. Index (-1989).

US/0821-1507
PERSPECTIVES - AMERICAN PROBATION AND PAROLE ASSOCIATION. (PERSPECTIVES / AMERICAN PROBATION AND PAROLE ASSOCIATION INC.). [Perspect. - Am. Probat. Parole Assoc.]. **Added/Corp** American Probation and Parole Association. (1976)-. Periodical. English. qt (4 issues). $35.00 US; $40.00 other. Council of State Governments, PO Box 11910, Iron Works Pike, Lexington KY 40578-1910. **Tel** (800)800-1910, (606)231-1850. **(Subscription address:** Council of State Governments, PO Box 2167, Lexington, KY 40595**)** **DD** 364.6/3/0971.
Ind/Abst Crim. Justice Abstr.

US
PILLAR, THE. Periodical. English. mo. The Pillar, Box B, St Cloud MN 56301. **Tel** (612)251-3510.

UK/0477-2008
POLICE AND CONSTABULARY ALMANAC. [Police constabul. alm.]. (1861)-. English. an. £22.00 (UK & Eire); £24.00 (US); £27.50 (other). R Hazell & Company, PO Box 39, Henley Thames, RG9 5UA England. **Tel** 11 44 491 641018.

US/0092-8933
POLICE AND LAW ENFORCEMENT. (1972)-. English. an. $57.50. AMS Press Inc., 56 East 13th Street, New York NY 10003. **Tel** (212)777-4700, FAX (212)995-5413, telex 710 581 2302. **ED** Daniel J Homant and Daniel B Kennedy. **Bk Rev.** ctrl circ.
Desc: Presents articles covering the major facets of police work in America, theoretical and applied, as part of the criminal justice system.

US/1070-8111
POLICE AND SECURITY NEWS. [Police secur. news]. (19??)-. Periodical. English. bm (Jan., Mar., May, July, Sept., Nov.). $14.00 (one year). Days Communication Incorporated, PO Box 330, Kulpsville PA 19443. **Tel** (215)362-2233, FAX (215)368-9955. **ED** James Dever and Al Menear. **DD** 363. **Ad Acc, Adv Mgr:** Al Menear, **Tel** (215)538-1240. **Circ:** 20,800 (ctrl).
Desc: Edited for middle and upper management covering topics of technology, law and training, serving public and private enforcement.

US/0147-8877
POLICE BADGE, THE. Periodical. English. bm. $8.50. The Police Badge, 746 Chapel Street, New Haven CT 06510.

US/8756-355X
POLICE CAREER DIGEST. (198?)-. Periodical. English. bm. $32.00. Police Career Digest, Department LEC, PO Box 1672, Eaton Park FL 33840. **Tel** (813)666-3184. **ED** Michael D'Alto and Carol D'Alto. **LC** HV8143; .P62. **DD** 363.2/023/73. Index available. **Ad Acc. Circ:** 1,700 (ctrl). ***Continues*** *Police Career Information Digest, 8756-355X.*
Desc: Includes a list of current criminal justice job openings, feature articles, classified advertisements, limited display ads, and newsbriefs.

US/0893-8989
POLICE (CARLSBAD, CALIF.). (POLICE.). **VFOAT** Police Product News. (198?)-. Periodical. English. mo. $21.95 (1 year), $39.95 (2 year), $49.95 (3 year). Hare Publications Inc, 6300 Yarrow Drive, Carlsbad CA 92009. **Tel** (619)438-2511, (800)854-2706, FAX (619)931-5809, telex 697127. **LC** HV7936.E7; P64. **DD** 363.2/3/028. available on microfilm from University Microfilms International (UMI). ***Continues*** *Police Product News, 0164-5196.*

US/0032-2571
POLICE CHIEF, THE. [Police chief]. **Added/Corp** International Association of Chiefs of Police. Vol. 20, No. 1 (Jan. 1953)-. Periodical. English. mo. $25.00 (one year), $42.00 (two year). International Association of Chiefs of Police, 515 North Washington, Alexandria VA 22314. **Tel** (800)843-4227. **(Subscription address:** IACP Police Chief Subscriptions, PO Box 90976, Washington, DC 20090) **ED** Charles E. Higginbotham. Index available. **Bk Rev. Ad Acc. Circ:** 22,000 (ctrl). available on microfilm and microfiche from University Microfilms International (UMI). Documents available from UMI Article Clearinghouse. ***Continues*** *Police Chiefs News;* ***Absorbed*** *Police Yearbook.*
Desc: The official publication of the International Association of Chiefs of Police. Reports the major advances in the administration of law enforcement agencies.
Ind/Abst Acad. Search (July 1993-); Crim. Justice Abstr.; Crim. Justice Period. Index; Expand. Acad. Index (1989-); Highw. Res. Abstr.; INFO-SOUTH Abstr.; Mag. Search; Newsp. Period. Abstr. (1989-); PAIS Int. Print (1991-); Soc. Sci. Source (Jul. 1993-); Soc. Sci. Index; Soc. Sci. Index Fulltext (Nov. 1988-) [Full Txt.]; SportSearch; Urban Aff. Abstr.

US/0747-2579
POLICE CHRONICLE, THE. [Police chron.]. **Added/Corp** International Brotherhood of Police Officers. (19??)-. Periodical. English. mo. $7.20. National Association of Government Employees, 159 Burgin Parkway, Quincy MA 02169. **Tel** (617)268-5002.

US/1071-1724
POLICE COLLECTORS NEWS. (POLICE COLLECTORS NEWS : PC NEWS.). [Police collect. news]. **VFOAT** PC News. (198?)-. Periodical. English. mo. $20.00. Police Collectors News, Rural Route 1 Box 14, Baldwin WI 54002. **Tel** (715)684-2216. **ED** Mike Bondarenico. **DD** 363. **Bk Rev**, (Qty: 12). **Ad Acc. Circ:** 4,500.

●US/1061-1509
POLICE COMPUTER REVIEW. See Computers-Software.

UK
POLICE FORCE STATISTICS. See Law-Abstracting, Bibliographies and Statistics.

CN/1185-0361
POLICE GOVERNOR. (THE POLICE GOVERNOR : AN OFFICIAL PUBLICATION OF THE MUNICIPAL POLICE AUTHORITIES.). [Police gov.]. **Added/Corp** Municipal Police Authorities (Association). (1990)-. English. Limited free distribution. Naylor Communications, 920 Yonge Street/6th Floor, Toronto Ontario M4W 5C7 Canada. **Tel** (416)961-1028. **DD** 363.2/09713/05.

UK/0032-258X
POLICE JOURNAL (CHICHESTER). (THE POLICE JOURNAL.). [Police j.]. Vol. 1 (Jan. 1928)-. Academic Scholarly Publication. English. qt. £57.00 UK; £58.60 other. Barry Rose Law Periodicals Ltd., Little London, Chichester West Sussex PO19 1PG England. **Tel** 011 44 243 787841, 011 44 243 783637, FAX 011 44 243 779174, 011 44 243 779278. **ED** R. W. Stone. **LC** HV7551; .P57. **DD** 363.2/09171/241. Index available. cum. index. **Bk Rev. Ad Acc, Adv Mgr:** Dora Curtis. **Pr Rev. Acid Free.**
Desc: Deals with modern day policing methods throughout the English speaking world.
Ind/Abst Appl. Soc. Sci. Index Abstr. (19??-); Crim. Justice Abstr. (19??-); Crim. Justice Period. Index (19??-); Crim. Penol. Police Sci. Abstr. (19??-); EMBASE (19??-).

US/0749-5595
POLICE LABOR MONTHLY. [Police labor mon.]. Vol. 1, No. 1 (June 1982)-. Periodical. English. mo. $89.00. Police Labor Monthly, PO Box 6224, Huntsville TX 77340. **Tel** (409)291-7981. **ED** Jerry L. Dowling. **DD** 363. Index available. cum. index. **Circ:** 1,000 (ctrl).
Desc: Labor relations issues pertaining to law enforcement including new court rulings, legislation, economic analysis, union development, settlements, and trends.

US/0892-6573
POLICE LAW JOURNAL. Periodical. English. mo. $18.50. Police Law Journal, Appalachian Regional Bureau of Government, Appalachian State University, Boone NC 28608. **LC** KF5399.A15; P65. Index available. cum. index. **Circ:** 800.

US/1046-6835
POLICE LIABILITY REVIEW. [Police liabil. rev.]. Vol. 1, (Fall 1989)-. Periodical. English. Four times a year (Mar., June, Sept., Dec.). $65.00 (regular); $80.00 (library). Alpha Enterprises, PO Box 326, Richmond KY 40476. **Tel** (606)623-0792, FAX (606)623-0792. **ED** Dr. Victor E. Kappeler, Ph. D. **DD** 344. Index available. cum. index. **Pr Rev. Circ:** 500. available on microfilm; available on diskette from the publisher.
Desc: Provides comprehensive coverage of officially reported court cases involving the police and features articles on police liability. This journal can be used as a reference tool for those persons interested in police training and legal developments as they effect law enforcement.
Ind/Abst Crim. Justice Abstr. (199?-).

AT
POLICE LIFE. English. Ten times a year (monthly with combined issues in Jan./Feb. and July/Aug.). Free. Police Life, Box 2763Y G P O, Melbourne 3001 Australia. **Tel** 2652397, FAX 2652398.

SI
POLICE LIFE (ANNUAL). (POLICE LIFE.). **Added/Corp** Singapore. Police Force. (19??)-. Periodical. English. an. 15.00Sing$. Singapore Police Academy, Pearls Hill, Terrace Publ Affrs, Singapore 0316 Singapore. **Tel** 011 65 5353344. **LC** HV8253.A2; P64. **DD** 363.2/09595/7. ***Continues*** *Police Life Annual.*

US/0164-8365
POLICE MARKSMAN, THE. Added/Corp Police Marksman Association. (19??)-. Periodical. English. bm. $14.95. Police Marksman Association, 6000 A E Shirley Lane, Montgomery AL 36117. **Tel** (205)271-2010. **ED** Connie Adams Dees. **Bk Rev. Ad Acc. Circ:** 18,000.
Desc: Police training magazine dedicated to police firearms training and officer survival.

US/0738-0623
POLICE MISCONDUCT AND CIVIL RIGHTS LAW REPORT. See Political Science-Civil Rights.

US/0887-8285
POLICE OFFICER GRIEVANCES BULLETIN. [Police off. griev. bull.]. **VFOAT** POGB. (April 1986)-. Bulletin. English. mo. $59.92. Quinlan Publishing Company, 23 Drydock Avenue, Boston MA 02210-2387. **Tel** (617)542-0048, (800)229-2084, FAX (617)345-9646. **LC** KF5398.P6; A496. **DD** 344.73/0522/05. **[CCC].** available on microfilm from University Microfilms International (UMI). ***Continues*** *Police Officer/Employee Rights Law Bulletin, 8755-8246.*

●US/1062-5216
POLICE OFFICERS JOURNAL, THE. See Economics-Labor.

UK
POLICE REQUIREMENT SUPPORT UNIT BULLETIN. Bulletin. English. qt. Free. Home Office, Queen Anne's Gate, Room 137 Edit, London SW1H 9AT England. **Tel** 011 44 71 273 3762, FAX 011 44 71 273 2568.

UK/0309-1414
POLICE REVIEW (LONDON). (POLICE REVIEW.). [Police rev.]. Vol. 42, No. 2165 (July 6, 1934)-. Periodical. English. Fifty-two times a year. £61.20 (surface mail); £78.50 Europe, £116.30 Pacific Islanda, Australasia & Far East, £108.00 others. Police Review Publishing Company, 183 Marsh Wall South Quay PL 2, London E14 9FZ England. **Tel** 011 44 71 5372575, FAX 011 44 71 8311573. **ED** Brian Hilliard. **LC** HV7551; .P59. **DD** 351.74. Index available. cum. index. **Bk Rev. Ad Acc. Circ:** 31,500. ***Continues*** *Police Review and Parade Gossip.*
Desc: Police related law, news and features.
Ind/Abst Crim. Penol. Police Sci. Abstr.; Sage Race Relat. Abstr.

UK
POLICE STATISTICS ACTUALS. See Law-Abstracting, Bibliographies and Statistics.

UK
POLICE STATISTICS (CHARTERED INSTITUTE OF PUBLIC FINANCE AND ACCOUNTANCY. STATISTICAL INFORMATION SERVICE). See Law-Abstracting, Bibliographies and Statistics.

US/0141-2949
POLICE STUDIES. [Police stud.]. **Added/Corp** Academy of Criminal Justice Sciences. Police Section. Vol. 1, No. 1 (Mar. 1978)-. Periodical. English. qt. $65.00. Anderson Publishing Company, 2035 Reading Road, Cincinnati OH 45202. **Tel** (513)421-4142, (800)582-7295. **(Subscription address:** Anderson Publishing Company, PO Box 1576, Cincinnati OH 45201.) **ED** Dorothy Bracey. **LC** HV7551; .P5914. **DD** 363.2/05. **Bk Rev. Ad Acc. Circ:** 451 (ctrl). available on microfilm and microfiche from University Microfilms International (UMI).
Desc: Comprehensive source of information for practitioners and scholars interested in learning about the latest international developments in police management, education, science, and technology.
Ind/Abst Crim. Justice Abstr.; Crim. Justice Period. Index; Crim. Penol. Police Sci. Abstr.; PAIS Int. Print (1991-); Sage Urban Stud. Abstr; Soc. Plann. Policy Dev. Abstr.; Sociol. Abstr.

UK
POLICE WORLD. Added/Corp International Police Association. (19??)-. English. qt. £6.00. Police World, 1 Fox Road West Bridgford, Nottingham NG2 6AJ United Kingdom. **LC** HV7551; .P592. **DD** 363.2/05.

UK/0267-0739
POLICING. (1985)-. English. Four times a year. Carswell / Canada, 2075 Kennedy Road, Scarborough Ontario M1T 3V4 Canada. **Tel** (416)609-3800, (800)387-5164.
Ind/Abst Crim. Justice Abstr.

SZ/1043-9463
POLICING AND SOCIETY. [Policing soc.]. Vol. 1, No. 1 (1990)-. Periodical. English. qt. $186.00 (academic institutions), $291.00 (corporate institutions). Harwood Academic Publishers, PO Box 90, Reading RG1 8JL England. **Tel** 011 44 734 560080. **(Subscription address:** International Publishers Distributor at one of the following addresses: 820 Town Center Drive, Langhorne, PA 19047; or PO Box 90, Reading Berkshire RG1 8JL UK; or Kent Ridge PO Box 1180, Singapore 9111, Republic of Singapore) **LC** HV7551; .P6126. **DD** 306.2/8/05. **CODEN** POSOER. **[CCC].**
Ind/Abst Crim. Justice Abstr. (199?-); Int. Bibliogr. Sociol.; Soc. Plann. Policy Dev. Abstr.

UK/0967-1773
POLICING POLICY. ***Ceased.*** (19??)-(Dec. 1994). English. qt. Carfax Publishing Company, PO Box 25 Abingdon, Oxfordshire OX14 3UE England. **Tel** 011 44 235 555335, FAX (0279)31067, telex 817484. **[CCC].**

FI
POLIISIN JA TULLIN TIETON TULLEET RIKOKSET, PAIHTYNEENA SAILOON OTETUT JA PYSAKOINTIVIRHEET. **Main/Corp** Finland. Tilastokeskus. **VFOAT** Brott som Kommit till Pulisens och Tulens Kanedom, Berusade som Tagits I Forvar och Parkeringsfel; Brott some Kommit till Pulisens och Tulens Konnedom Berusade som Tagits I forvar och Parkeringsfel. Finnish (Swedish). Tilastokeskus, PL 504, Annankatu 44, 00101 Helsinki Finland. **Tel** 358-0-17341, FAX 358-0-17342474, telex 1002111 TILASTO SF. **LC** HV7015.5; .A25A.

FI/0355-2160
POLIISIN TIETOON TULLUT RIKOLLISUUS. See Law-Abstracting, Bibliographies and Statistics.

NE
POLITIE-ALMANAK. Dutch. an. Fl54.90. Uitgeversmij de Tijdstroom, Postbus 14, 7240 Lochem Netherlands. **Tel** 05730-53651, FAX 05730-56724. **LC** HV8220; .P6. cum. index. **Ad Acc.**
Desc: Police yearbook.

NE/0925-0980
POLITIE MAGAZINE. [Politie mag.]. (1991)-. Periodical. Dutch. Eleven times a year. Fl49.06. Vuga Uitgeverij B.V., Postbus 16400, Zeestraat 65, 2500 BK Gravenhage Netherlands. **Tel** 011 31 70 3614011, FAX 011 31 70 3632338. **(Subscription address:** Infolio BV, Postbus 16500, 2500 BM Den Haag Netherlands.) **ED** B. Huizing. **UDC** 351.74. ***Continues*** *RP-Magazine (Dokkum), 0921-6200; Rijkspolitie Magazine.*
Desc: Contains information of interest to members of the Dutch police force.

GW
POLIZEI, VERKEHR + TECHNIK. VFOAT Polizei, Verkehr und Technik; P.V.T.; PVT. (19??)-. Periodical. German. mo. DM51.60 Germany; DM66.00 other. Schmidt-Romhild, Mengstrasse 16, Postfach 2051, D 23552 Luebeck Germany. **Tel** 011 49 451 16050. **ED** Scheiber. **LC** HV8079.5; .P66. **DD** 363.2/332/0943. Index available. cum. index. **Bk Rev. Ad Acc. Circ:** 5,000 (ctrl). ***Continues*** *Polizei, Technik, Verkehr.*
Desc: Manual for the German police. Main parts are: traffic, automobile and dallistic.

IT
POLIZIA MODERNA. Added/Corp Italy. Direzione Generale Della Pubblica Sicurezza. (Jan. 1949)-. Periodical. Italian. Twelve times a year. L32000 Italy; L70000 other. Polizia Moderna, V Vastro Pretorio 5, 00185 Rome Italy. **Tel** 011 39 6 46675518. **LC** HV7551; .P66.

US/0197-7024
POLYGRAPH (LINTHICUM HEIGHTS). (POLYGRAPH.). [Polygraph]. V. 1- Mar. 1972-. Periodical. English. qt. $40.00 US and Canada; $50.00 other. American Polygraph Association, PO Box 1061, Severna Park MD 21146. **Tel** (410)647-0936. **ED** Norman Ansley, Janet Pumphrey. **LC** HV8078.A1; A44. **DD** 364.12/8. cum. index. **Bk Rev. Ad Acc. Circ:** 3,500. available on microfilm and microfiche from University Microfilms International (UMI). ***Continues in part*** *Journal of the American Polygraph Association.*
Desc: A journal featuring articles on polygraph operations, research, history, psychology, physiology, instrumentation, law, and training. Abstracts, book reviews, and law notes included.
Ind/Abst Crim. Justice Period. Index; Crim. Penol. Police Sci. Abstr.; Print. Abstr.

US/0093-5603
POPULATION ANALYSIS OF THE ILLINOIS ADULT PRISON SYSTEM. **Main/Corp** Illinois. Dept. of Corrections. Division of Research and Long Range Planning. English. Illinois

Department of Corrections, PO Box 19277, Springfield IL 62794. **Tel** (217)522-2666, FAX (217)522-5089. **LC** HV7262; .A28A. **DD** 365/.6/09773.

US
POPULATION MOVEMENT. Main/Corp
Kentucky State Penitentiary. English. Kentucky State Penitentiary, PO Box 128, Eddyville KY 42038-0128. **LC** HV8482.K4; K47. **DD** 365.6/09769.
 Desc: Statement of: Crimes committed, sentences received, nativity of prisoners, counties from which prisoners were received, age of prisoners, educational status, marital status, and number of convictions.

US/0744-1983
PORAC LAW ENFORCEMENT NEWS. (PORAC LAW ENFORCEMENT NEWS : OFFICIAL PUBLICATION OF THE PEACE OFFICERS' RESEARCH AND EDUCATION FOUNDATION.). **VFOAT** PORAC News; P.O.R.A.C. Law Enforcement News. **VAT** Peace Officers Research Association of California News. Periodical. English. mo. Peace Officers Research Association of California, Porac Suite, Senator Hotel, 12th and L Street, Sacramento CA 95814.

US/0147-8060
POST ALLOCATION OF FUNDS AND TRAINING ACTIVITY SUMMARY.
Main/Corp California. Commission on Peace Officer Standards and Training. **VAT** Peace Officer Standards and Training Allocation of Funds and Training Activity Summary. English. Commission on Peace Oficer Standards adn Training, 7100 Bowling Drive, Suite 250, Sacramento CA. **LC** HV7254; .A353A.

US
POST SCRIPTS / COMMISSION ON PEACE OFFICER STANDARDS AND TRAINING. Vol. 15, No. 4 (Dec. 1981)-. Periodical. English. qt. Commission on Peace Officers Standards and Training, 7100 Bowling Drive/Suite 250, Sacramento CA 95823. **Continues** P.O.S.T. Scripts Newsletter.

PO
PP; POLICIA PORTUGUESA. No. 193- May/June 1969-. Portuguese. 4.50 single issue. Comando-Geral da PSP, Avenida Antonio Augusto de Aguiar 18, Lisbon Portugal. **LC** HV7551; .P67. **Continues** Policia Portuguesa.

●US/1060-3212
PRAEGER SERIES IN CRIMINOLOGY AND CRIME CONTROL POLICY. (1993)-. Monographic series. English. ir. Price varies per volume. Praeger, Publishing Division of Greenwood Press, PO Box 5007, Westport CT 06881. **Tel** (203)226-3571.

US/0193-4015
PRETRIAL REPORTER, THE. Added/Corp
Pretrial Services Resource Center. Vol. 1 (June 1977)-. Periodical. English. bm. $48.00. Pretrial Services Resource Center, 1325 G Street Northwest, Suite 620, Washington DC 20005. **Tel** (202)638-3080. **LC** KF9632.A15; P73. **DD** 345.73/072/05.
 Desc: Research and technical assistance in area of jail overcrowding - particularly P.T. detention and alternatives to incarceration.

US/0270-2703
PRISON DECISIONS. [Prison decis.]. V. 1- 1974-. Periodical. English. mo. University of Toledo Law School, 2801 West Bancroft Street, Toledo OH 43606. **Tel** (419)537-2882. **LC** KF9728.A59; P74. **DD** 344.73/035/02643.
 Desc: Includes all reported decisions of the U. S. courts on prisoners' rights and correctional law and significant decisions of state courts.

US/0032-8855
PRISON JOURNAL (PHILADELPHIA, PA.), THE. (THE PRISON JOURNAL.). [Prison j.]. **Added/Corp** Pennsylvania Prison Society. Vol. 1 (Jan. 1921)-. Periodical. English. qt (Mar., June, Sept., Dec.). $85.00. SAGE Periodical Press, 2455 Teller Road, Thousand Oaks CA 91320. **Tel** (805)499-0721, FAX (805)499-0871, telex 100799. **ED** Alan T. Harland (Temple University). **LC** HV7231; .P8. **DD** 365/.05. cum. index. **Pr Rev. Acid Free. Circ:** 653. available on microfilm and microfiche from University Microfilms International (UMI). Documents available from UMI Article Clearinghouse. **Supersedes** Journal of Prison Discipline and Philanthropy.
 Desc: Devoted to topics of special interest in the field of corrections and criminal justice, including the advancement of theory, research, policy and practice in the area of imprisonment, and all related aspects of the more broadly defined field of correctional alternatives and penal sanctions. It is the official publication of the Pennsylvania Prison Society.
 Ind/Abst Crim. Justice Abstr.; Crim. Justice Period. Index; Crim. Penol. Police Sci. Abstr.; Humanit. Index; Newsp. Period. Abstr. (1992-).

US/0739-7577
PRISON LAW & ADVOCACY. [Prison law advocacy]. **VFOAT** Prison Law and Advocacy. Vol. 1 (Jan./Feb. 1980)-. Periodical. English. bm. $5.00 institutionalized persons, $35.00 other. Prison Law &

Advocacy, 343 South Dearborn #706, Chicago IL 60604. **LC** KFI1788.A59; P74. **DD** 344.773/035/05; 347.73043505.

US/0161-9632
PRISON LAW MONITOR. Added/Corp
Institution Educational Services. Vol. 1 (June 1978)-. Periodical. English. mo. $20.00 non-profit public interest organizations, $25.00 other institutions and individuals, $6.00 state and federal prisoners. Prison Law Monitor, 1806 T Street NW, Washington DC 20009. **LC** KF9728.A15; P73. **DD** 344/.73/03505.

●US/1065-0709
PRISON LIFE. [Prison life]. **VFOAT** Prison Life Magazine. Vol. 1, No. 1 (Jan. 1993)-. Periodical. English. bm. $19.95. Prison Life, 505 8th Avenue, 14th Floor, New York NY 10018. **Tel** (212)967-9760. **LC** HV9471; .P748. **DD** 365/.973/05.

UK/0300-3558
PRISON SERVICE JOURNAL. Added/Corp
Great Britain. Prison Commission. Great Britain. Prison Dept. (1960)-. Periodical. English. Four times a year (Jan., Apr., July, Oct.). £4.00 UK; £5.00 other. Prison Service Journal, Wotton Under Edge, Leyhill Glos GL12 8HL England. **Tel** 011 44 454 260681. **ED** Richard Tilt. **LC** HV7231; .P84. **[CCC]. Bk Rev. Circ:** 2,500. available on microfilm and microfiche from University Microfilms International (UMI).
 Desc: Forum of discussion for penal policy and practice in UK and worldwide articles on all aspects of prison work and life.
 Ind/Abst Appl. Soc. Sci. Index Abstr.; Crim. Justice Period. Index; Crim. Penol. Police Sci. Abstr.

US
PRISONERS IN STATE AND FEDERAL INSTITUTION ON ... . English. US Department of Justice, 10th Street & Constitution Avenue NW, Washington DC 20530. **Tel** (202)514-2000, FAX (202)633-4371.

US
PROBATION ADMINISTRATIVE MANAGEMENT SYSTEM / JUVENILE PROBATION MANAGEMENT INFORMATION SYSTEM. Main/Corp New Jersey. Juvenile Probation Management Information System. English. an. Administrative Office of the Courts / New Jersey, Richard J. Hughes Justice Complex, Trenton NJ 08625. **LC** HV9305.N48; N45A. **DD** 364.3/6/0974991.

US/0732-0965
PROBATION AND PAROLE DIRECTORY (COLLEGE PARK, MD.). (PROBATION AND PAROLE DIRECTORY : ADULT AND JUVENILE PROBATION AND PAROLE SERVICES, UNITED STATES AND CANADA.). **Added/Corp** American Correctional Association. 1st Ed. (1981)-. English. te (Publishes every three years). $66.10 (three years). American Correctional Association, 8025 Laurel Lakes Court, Laurel MD 20707-5075. **Tel** (301)206-5100, (800)222-5646, FAX (301)206-5061. **ED** Glenda Beal. **LC** HV9304; .P76. **DD** 350.84/93/02573. **Bk Rev. Ad Acc. Circ:** 3,000.
 Desc: Lists more than 6,000 probation and parole departments, agencies, chief officers, and court systems in the United States and Canada.

US/0276-6965
PROBATION AND PAROLE LAW REPORTS. Added/Corp Knehans-Miller Publications, Vol. 2, No. 1 (Jan. 1988)-. Periodical. English. mo. $115.00 US and Canada; $135.00 other. Knehans Miller Publications, PO Box 88, Warrensburg MO 64093. **Tel** (816)429-1102. **ED** Dane C Miller. **LC** KF9750.A59; P76. **DD** 345.73/077; 347.30577. Index available. cum. index. **Bk Rev. Ad Acc. Circ:** 500 (ctrl). **Continues** Probation and Parole Law Summaries, 0194-1801.
 Desc: In-depth summaries, often with verbatim excerpts, and thorough subject/jurisdiction indexing of all federal and state appellate court decisions dealing with all aspects of probation and parole.

CN/0317-3828
PROBATION & PAROLE STATISTICS (REGINA). See Law-Abstracting, Bibliographies and Statistics.

UK
PROBATION JOURNAL. Added/Corp National Association of Probation Officers, London. Vol.21 (March 1974)-. Periodical. English. qt. £10.00. National Association of Probation Officers, 3-4 Chivlry Road, Battersea London SW11 1HT. **Tel** 071-223-4887, FAX 071-223-3503. **ED** Nigel Stone. **Bk Rev. Ad Acc. Circ:** 7,000 (ctrl). **Continues** Probation.
 Desc: Social work with offenders in the criminal justice system and divorce court welfare.
 Ind/Abst Appl. Soc. Sci. Index Abstr.; Crim. Justice Abstr.; Sage Race Relat. Abstr.

UK/0264-6544
PROBATION SERVICE STATISTICS ... ESTIMATES. Title Change. See Law-Abstracting, Bibliographies and Statistics.

●UK
PROBATION SERVICE STATISTICS ... ESTIMATES AND ... ACTUALS. See Law-Abstracting, Bibliographies and Statistics.

UK/0265-573X
PROBATION STATISTICS, ENGLAND AND WALES / HOME OFFICE. See Law-Abstracting, Bibliographies and Statistics.

US/0884-5409
PROCEEDINGS / CARNAHAN CONFERENCE ON SECURITY TECHNOLOGY. [Proc. - Carnahan Conf. Secur. Technol.]. **Main/Conf** Carnahan Conference on Security Technology. (1984)-. Proceedings. English. an. $22.50. OES Publications, University of Kentucky, 226 Anderson Hall, Lexington KY 40506-0046. **Tel** (606)257-3361, FAX (606)257-3342. **ED** R William DeVore. **LC** HV7936.E7; C37. **DD** 363.2/32. ctrl circ. **Continues** Proceedings / Conference on Crime Countermeasures and Security, 0737-1160.
 Desc: A collection of papers presented during the 21st annual conference. Topics include computer security, LLTV intrusion detection, security robots, and antiterrorism technology.

US/0430-7615
PROCEEDINGS - FLORIDA CORRECTIONAL EDUCATION ASSOCIATION. Main/Corp Florida Correctional Education Association. Proceedings. English. Florida State Prison, PO Box 747, Starke FL 32091. **DD** 364.

US
PROCEEDINGS OF THE INTERAGENCY WORKSHOP. Main/Corp Sam Houston State University. Criminal Justice Center. Interagency Workshop. 14th (1979)-. Proceedings. English. an. Sam Houston State University Criminal Justice Center, Huntsville TX 77341. **Tel** (409)294-1692. **Continues** Proceedings ... Annual Interagency Workshop of the Institute of Contemporary Corrections and the Behavioral Sciences.

US/0093-7878
PROCEEDINGS OF THE NATIONAL CONFERENCE ON PUBLIC GAMING. (PROCEEDINGS.). **Main/Conf** National Conference on Public Gaming. 1973-. Proceedings. English. PO Box 1544, 253 East Palmetto Park Road, Boca Raton FL 33432. **LC** HV6715; .N37A. **DD** 364.1/72/0973.

AT
PROCEEDINGS OF THE RESIDENTIAL CONFERENCE OF THE AUSTRALIAN INSTITUTE OF CRIMINOLOGY. Main/Corp
Australian Institute of Criminology. 1st (1973)-. Proceedings. English. Australian Institute of Criminology, 4 Marcus Clarke Street, Canberra ACT 2601 Australia. **Tel** 011 61 6 2740200, FAX 011 61 6 2740260, telex 61340. **LC** HV6024.5; .A97a. **DD** 364/.994.

CN/0707-9044
PROCEEDINGS OF THE SUBCOMMITTEE ON CHILDHOOD EXPERIENCES AS CAUSES OF CRIMINAL BEHAVIOUR. Main/Corp Canada. Parliament. Senate. Sub-Committee on Childhood Experiences as Causes of Criminal Behaviour. **VFOAT** Deliberations du Sous-Comite sur la Delinquance Inputable aux Experiences de l'Enfance. **VAT** Childhood Experiences as Causes of Criminal Behaviour; Delinquance Imputable aux Experiences de l'Enfance. No. 1- June 30, 1977-. Proceedings. English (French). Printing and Publishing, Supply and Services Canada, Ottawa Ontario K1A 0S9 Canada. **LC** HV6115; .C36A. **DD** 364.2/5.

NE/0165-0076
PROCES ARNHEM. [Proces Arnhem]. (1972)-. Periodical. Dutch. Ten times a year. Fl99.00. Barneveldse Drukkerij en Uitgeverij BV, Postbus 67, 37700 AB Barneveld Netherlands. **Tel** 011 31 342094911, FAX 011 31 342013141. **Continues** Maandblad voor Berechting en Reclassering.

US/0090-6107
PROGRESS REPORT - MAINE LAW ENFORCEMENT PLANNING AND ASSISTANCE AGENCY. (PROGRESS REPORT.). **Main/Corp** Maine. Law Enforcement Planning & Assistance Agency. 1972-. English. an. Main Law Enforcement Planning and Assistance Agency, 295 Water Street, Augusta ME 04330. **LC** HV7269; .A3. **DD** 353.9/741/0074.

Law —Law Enforcement and Criminology

US/1057-087X
PROTECTION OFFICER NEWS. [Prot. off. news]. **Added/Corp** International Foundation for Protection Officers. Vol. 5, No. 3 (Oct./Dec. 1989)-. Periodical. English. qt. $18.00. Protection Officers Publishing, International Federation of Protection Officers, 200 4200 Meridian, Bellingham WA 98226. **Tel** (206)733-1571, FAX (206)671-4329. **DD** 363.2/89/0971. **Continues** Protection Officer Magazine, 0823-9304.
Desc: Designed to keep protection professionals current on trends within the security industry. Published by the International Foundation for Protection Officers, an organization established to facilitate training/certification needs of officers.

SZ/0256-4319
PROTECTOR. [Protector]. (1973)-. Periodical. German. bm (Plus special issue in June). 155.00F. Verlag Protector, Moehrlistrasse 69, Postfach 205, CH-8033 Zuerich Switzerland. **Tel** 011 41 1 3615600, FAX 011 41 1 3617715, telex 816063. **UDC** 62.

US/0048-5632
PROUD. **VFOAT** Proud Magazine. (197?)-. Periodical. English. Four times a year. $6.50. Proud Inc, 625 Euclid, Suite 200, St Louis MO 63108. **Tel** (314)361-7877.

CN/0824-6521
QUAKER COMMITTEE ON JAILS & JUSTICE (1981). (A QUAKER COMMITTEE ON JAILS & JUSTICE : [NEWSLETTER].). [Quaker Comm. Jails Justice]. **Added/Corp** Quaker Committee on Jails and Justice. Vol. 6, No. 3 (Fall 1981)-. Periodical. English. Quaker Committee on Jails & Justice, 60 Lowther Avenue, Toronto Ontario M5R 1C7 Canada. **DD** 365/.9713/541. **Continues** QCJJ, 0824-331X.
Ind/Abst Hum. Rights Intern. Rep.

US/1055-4491
QUARTERLY / ALLIANCE AGAINST FRAUD IN TELEMARKETING, COORDINATED BY THE NATIONAL CONSUMERS' LEAGUE. **Added/Corp** Alliance Against Fraud in Telemarketing. National Consumers' League. **VFOAT** AAFT Quarterly. **VAT** Alliance Against Fraud in Telemarketing Quarterly. Vol. 1, No. 1 (Spring 1991)-. Periodical. English. qt. $5.00. Alliance Against Fraud in Telemarketing, National Consumers' League, 815 15th Street NW, Washington DC 20005. **DD** 364.

CN/0703-5675
QUARTERLY JOURNAL - JOHN HOWARD SOCIETY OF QUEBEC. **Main/Corp** John Howard Society of Quebec. **VFOAT** Journal Trimestriel. V. 1- 1977-. Periodical. English (French). qt. $1.50 students, $3.00 others. JHSQ Quarterly Journal, 1647 Suite/Catherine Street West, Montreal Quebec H3H 1L9 Canada. **DD** 364.6/0971.

US
QUARTERLY REPORT FOR THE QUARTER ENDED ... / GAMING CONTROL BOARD. **Main/Corp** Nevada. State Gaming Control Board. Periodical. English. qt. **LC** HV6721.N45; N47C. **DD** 363.4/2/09793. **Continues** Nevada. State Gaming Control Board. Quarterly & Fiscal Year Report for ... of ... and Year-to-Date Comparisons ... Comparative Fiscal Year Report ... .

CN/0824-9415
QUARTERLY / ROYAL CANADIAN MOUNTED POLICE, THE. [Q. - R. Can. Mounted Police.]. **Main/Corp** Royal Canadian Mounted Police. **VFOAT** RCMP Quarterly; R.C.M.P. Quarterly. Vol. 44, No. 2 (Spring 1979)-. Periodical. English. qt. $5.00. The Editor RCMP Quarterly, RCMP HQ Ottawa, Ottawa Ontario K1A 0R2 Canada. **LC** HV7551; .R65. **DD** 363.2/0971. **Continues** Royal Canadian Mounted Police. R C M P Quarterly, 0033-6858.

US
QUESTION-MARK. (197?)-. Periodical. English. mo. $8.50. Mass Correctional Institution, Box 43, Inmate Resident Council, Norfolk MA 02056.

IT
QUESTIONE CRIMINALE, LA. Year 1- Jan./Apr. 1975-. Periodical. Italian. 8.000. Societa Editrice il Mulino, Strada Maggiore 37, 40125 Bologna Italy. **Tel** 011 39 51 256011, FAX 011 39 51 256034. **LC** HV6004; .Q46. **DD** 364/.05.

CN/1188-1968
RAPPORT ANNUEL / INSTITUT DE POLICE DU QUEBEC. [Rapp. annu. - Inst. police Que.]. **Main/Corp** Institut de Police du Quebec. (1991)-. French. **DD** 351.74/06/0714.

CN/0831-6473
RAPPORT D'ACTIVITE - SURETE DU QUEBEC. (RAPPORT D'ACTIVITE / SURETE DU QUEBEC POLICE.). [Rapp. act. - Surete Que.]. **Main/Corp** Surete du Quebec. Began with V. for 1979. French. an. Surete du Quebec, Service des Communications, 1701 rue Parthenais/Bureau 730, Montreal Quebec H2L 4K7 Canada. **LC** HV7642.Q4; Q44A. **DD** 354.7140074/06. **Continues** Surete du Quebec. Rapport des Activites, 0225-3267.

IT
RASSEGNA ITALIANA DI CRIMINOLOGIA : ORGANO UFFICIALE DELLA SOCIETA ITALIANA DI CRIMINOLOGIA : BULLETIN DU CENTRE INTERNATIONAL DE CRIMINOLOGIE CLINIQUE. **Added/Corp** Societa Italiana di Criminologia. International Centre for Clinical Criminology. Vol. 1, No. 1 (1990)-. Bulletin. Italian (summaries and/or abstracts in English). Four times a year. L80000.00 Italy; L120000.00 other. Giuffre Editore SPA, Via Busto Arsizio 40, 20151 Milan Italy. **Tel** 011 398 2 38089200. **ED** Giacomo Canepa. **LC** HV6004; .R36. **DD** 365/.945/05.
Desc: Forms a steady and fundamental reference point for the development of laws regarding criminology and legal psychiatry in Italy and Europe.
Ind/Abst Crim. Justice Abstr. (199?-).

IT
RASSEGNA PENITENZIARIA E CRIMINOLOGICA. **Added/Corp** Italy. Direzione Generale per Gli Istituti di Prevenzione e di Pena. Vol. 1, No. 1-2 (Jan./June 1979)-. Periodical. Italian (summaries and/or abstracts in English, French, German and Spanish). qt. L50000 Italy; L78000 other. Istituto Poligrafico Zecca Stato, Piazza Verdi 10, 00198 Rome Italy. **Tel** 011 39 6 85082307, 011 39 6 85082221. **LC** HV6004; .R37. **DD** 364/.05. **NLM** W1 RA905. **Continues** Quaderni di Criminologia Clinica, 0033-4928.

US/0093-383X
REFERENCE TABLES. DRUG ARRESTS AND DISPOSITIONS (SACRAMENTO). (REFERENCE TABLES : DRUG ARRESTS AND DISPOSITIONS.). **Main/Corp** California. Bureau of Criminal Statistics. **VFOAT** Drug Arrests and Dispositions Reference Tables; Crime and Delinquency in California. English. an. 3301 C Street, PO Box 13427, Sacramento CA 95813. **LC** HV7254; .A345. **DD** 364.4/5/09794.

BL
RELATORIO ESTATISTICO (SALVADOR, BRAZIL). **See** Law-Abstracting, Bibliographies and Statistics.

BL
RELATORIO ESTATISTICO - SERVICO DE ESTATISTICA POLICIAL E CRIMINAL. **See** Law-Abstracting, Bibliographies and Statistics.

AT/0157-3470
RELEASE. [Release]. (1969)-. Periodical. English. qt. 10.00Aus$ (Australia); 11.00Aus$ (other). Offenders Aid & Rehabilitation, 222 Halifax Street, ADelaide SA, 5000 Australia. **Tel** 11 61 8 2231988, FAX 11 61 8 2234460. **ED** Geoff Glanville. **DD** 364.6099423. **Bk Rev**, (Qty: 1 /year). **Ad Acc**. **Circ:** 3,500.

US/0277-7282
RELEASES FROM JUVENILE INSTITUTIONS (1979). (RELEASES FROM JUVENILE INSTITUTIONS.). **Added/Corp** Wisconsin. Division of Corrections. Office of Information Management. Wisconsin. Division of Corrections. Office of Information Management and Operations. Wisconsin. Division of Corrections. Office of Policy, Planning, and Budget. (1979)-. English. Wisconsin Division of Corrections, 149 East Wilson Street, Room 1050, Madison WI 53702. **Tel** (608)266-2471, FAX (608)267-0923. **LC** HV7299; .A28g. **DD** 364.3/6/09775. **Continues** Offenders Released from Juvenile Correctional Institutions, 0362-7470.

CN/0712-7588
RENDEZVOUS (BRANTFORD). (RENDEZVOUS / LA FONDATION POUR LES ARTS DANS LES PRISONS.). [Rendezvous]. Periodical. English (French). ir. Free. Prison Arts Foundation, 143 5th Avenue, Brantford Ontario N3S 1A3 Canada. **DD** 365/.66/0971. ctrl circ.

AT
REPORT AND STATEMENT OF ACCOUNTS - LIQUOR CONTROL COMMISSION. **Main/Corp** Victoria. Liquor Control Commission. (1968/1969)-. Government Publication. English. 12.00Aus$. Australian Government Publishing Service, GPO Box 84, Canberra ACT 2601 Australia. **Tel** 011 61 6 2954411, FAX 011 61 6 2954455. **LC** HV5675.A3; V54a. **DD** 354.9450076/1/06. Index available. cum. index. **Bk Rev**. **Circ:** 5,000.

US/0362-9198
REPORT - MARYLAND DIVISION OF CORRECTION. **Main/Corp** Maryland. Division of Correction. English. an. Division of Correction, 920 Greenmount Avenue, Baltimore MD 21202. **LC** HV7270; .A3. **DD** 353.9/752/00849.

US/1049-6785
REPORT OF CRIMINAL OFFENSES AND ARRESTS. [Rep. crim. offenses arrests]. **Added/Corp** Oregon. Law Enforcement Data System. **VFOAT** Criminal Offenses and Arrests. (1983)-. English. **LC** HV6793.O7; R46. **Formed by the union of** Analysis of Crime in Oregon **and** Oregon Law Enforcement Agencies Report of Criminal Offenses and Arrests.

US/0364-6580
REPORT OF PERSONS DISCHARGED FROM PAROLE AND PERSONS VIOLATING PAROLE. **Main/Corp** Virginia. Dept. of Corrections. English. Virginia Department of Corrections, 6900 Atmore Drive, Richmond VA 23225. **Tel** (804)674-3119, FAX (804)674-3587. **LC** HV7296; .A227C. **DD** 364.6/2/09755.

US/0362-7489
REPORT OF PROBATION SUPERVISION WORKLOAD. Title Change. **Main/Corp** Virginia. Dept. of Corrections. Bureau of Management Information. (19??)-(1992). English. an. Virginia Department of Corrections, 6900 Atmore Drive, Richmond VA 23225. **Tel** (804)674-3119, FAX (804)674-3587. **LC** HV7296; .H227b. **DD** 364.6/3/09755. **Continues** Report of Probation Supervision Workload, 0362-7489. **Continued by** Report of Probation Supervision Workload.

●US/0362-7489
REPORT OF PROBATION SUPERVISION WORKLOAD. **Main/Corp** Virginia. Dept. of Corrections. Bureau of Research, Reporting, and Evaluation. (1992)-. English. an. Virginia Department of Corrections, 6900 Atmore Drive, Richmond VA 23225. **Tel** (804)674-3119, FAX (804)674-3587. **LC** HV7296; .A227b. **DD** 364.6/3/09755. **Continues** Report of Probation Supervision Workload, 0362-7489.

US/0363-0633
REPORT OF RECIDIVISTS COMMITTED TO THE VIRGINIA STATE PENAL SYSTEM. **Main/Corp** Virginia. Dept. of Corrections. Bureau of Management Information. (19??)-. English. an. Virginia Department of Corrections, 6900 Atmore Drive, Richmond VA 23225. **Tel** (804)674-3119, FAX (804)674-3587. **LC** HV7296; .A227c. **DD** 365/.6/09755.

UK
REPORT OF THE COMMISSIONER OF POLICE OF THE METROPOLIS FOR THE YEAR. **Main/Corp** London (England). Commissioner of Police. (19??)-. English. an. £15.00. Directorate Pub. Affairs, Metro Police, Room 1334, New Scotland Yard, London SW1H 0BG England. **Tel** 011 44 71 2301212. **DD** 352.2.

II
REPORT OF THE NATIONAL POLICE COMMISSION (INDIA). **Main/Corp** India. National Police Commission. 1st-. English. an. Rs4.00. Jain Book Agency, Connaught Place, New Delhi 1 India. **LC** HV7808; .A35A. **DD** 354.540074/06.

US
REPORT ON DRIVING UNDER THE INFLUENCE OF ALCOHOL, OPERATING AFTER LICENSE SUSPENSION, AND HABITUAL OFFENDER REVOCATION VIOLATIONS. **Added/Corp** University of Southern Maine. Human Services Development Institute. Maine. Dept. of Human Services. 5th (Jan. 1-Dec. 31, 1986)-. English. 221 State Street, Augusta ME 04333. **LC** HE5620.D7; R46. **DD** 364.1/47. **Continues** Report on An Act to Reform the Statutes Relating to Driving Under the Influence of Intoxicating Liquor or Drugs.

US/0147-5355
REPORT ON FRINGE BENEFITS AND RELATED PRACTICES AFFECTING POLICEMEN. **Main/Corp** New York (State). Public Employment Relations Board. (19??)-. English. Public Employment Relations Board, 80 Wolf Road, Albany NY 12205-2604. **Tel** (518)457-2676. **LC** HV8145.N7; N44a. **DD** 331.2/55.

UK
REPORT ON THE ESTABLISHMENT AND WORK OF THE STATES POLICE FORCE. **Main/Corp** Jersey. English. £0.25. **LC** HV7726.J4; A25. **DD** 352/.2/094234.

US/0091-4118
REPORT - PENNSYLVANIA CRIME COMMISSION. (REPORT.). **Main/Corp** Pennsylvania Crime Commission. English. Commonwealth of Pennsylvania Office of the Attorney General, 523 East Lancaster Avenue, Saint Davids PA 19087. **LC** HV7288; .A2. **DD** 364/.9748.

US/0892-9378
REPORT WRITING UPDATE. ***Ceased.*** [Rep. writ. update]. Vol. 1, No. 1 (Spring 1987)-(1989). Periodical. English. qt. Innovative Systems, 29 Nob Hill Road, Whitethorn CA 95489. **DD** 364.
Desc: For law enforcement report writing instructors. A national newsletter with articles, reviews and ideas submitted from across the nation.

US
REPORTS / DEPARTMENT OF CORRECTIONS AND PAROLE BOARD, COMMONWEALTH OF VIRGINIA, THE. **Main/Corp** Virginia. Dept. of Corrections. English. an. Virginia Department of Corrections, 6900 Atmore Drive, Richmond VA 23225. **Tel** (804)674-3119, FAX (804)674-3587. **LC** HV7296; .A24A. **DD** 353.97550084/9/06.

JA
REPORTS OF NATIONAL RESEARCH INSTITUTE OF POLICE SCIENCE. Twice a year. National Research Institute of Police Science, National Police Agency, Tokyo Japan.
Ind/Abst PsycINFO (1980-); PsycLit.

UK
REPORTS : TO. **Main/Conf** Inter-African Conference. Treatment of Offenders. **Added/Corp** Commission for Technical Co-operation in Africa South of the Sahara. **VFOAT** Rapports: TD; Rapports: Traitement des Delinquants; Reports: Treatment of Offenders. Periodical. Multiple languages (English and French). Europa Publications Ltd, 18 Bedford Square, London WC1B 3JN England. **Tel** 011 44 71 5808236, telex 21540 EUROPA G. **DD** 338.9.

US
RESEARCH AND EVALUATION PLAN / NATIONAL INSTITUTE OF JUSTICE. ***Title Change.*** **Main/Corp** National Institute of Justice (U.S.). **VFOAT** National Institute of Justice Research and Evaluation Plan. (1992)-(1992). English. National Criminal Justice Reference Services / NCJRS, Box 6000, 1600 Research Boulevard, Rockville MD 20850. **Tel** (301)251-5500. **LC** HV9950; .N37a. **DD** 364.973/05. ***Formed by the union of*** *National Institute of Justice (U.S.). Evaluation Plan* ***and*** *National Institute of Justice (U.S.). Research Plan.* ***Continued by*** *National Institute of Justice (U.S.). NIJ Program Plan.*

UK/0305-9871
RESEARCH BULLETIN (GREAT BRITAIN. HOME OFFICE. RESEARCH AND PLANNING UNIT). (RESEARCH BULLETIN / HOME OFFICE RESEARCH AND PLANNING UNIT.). No. 13-. Bulletin. English. sa. Free. Home Office Research and Planning Unit, 50 Queen Anne's Gate, London SW1H 9AT England. **Tel** 01-213-7278, telex 24986. **ED** Peter Southgate. **LC** HV6941; .H65A. **DD** 364/.941. **Circ:** 4,000. ***Continues*** *Research Bulletin (Great Britain. Home Office. Research Unit).*
Desc: The contents reflect the wide range of work covered by the RPV and the varied methodologies employed. Articles summarize longer reports appearing elsewhere.
Ind/Abst Crim. Justice Abstr.

US
RESIDENTS IN WISCONSIN ADULT CORRECTIONAL FACILITIES ON ... WITH FIVE-YEAR TRENDS FOR ... . **Added/Corp** Wisconsin. Division of Corrections. Office of Information Management and Operations. (June 30, 1982)-. English. sa. Wisconsin Division of Corrections, 149 East Wilson Street, Room 1050, Madison WI 53702. **Tel** (608)266-2471, FAX (608)267-0923. **LC** HV7299; .A28j. **DD** 364.3/09775. ***Continues*** *Residents in Wisconsin Adult Correctional Institutions and Community Correctional Residential Centers on ... with Five-Year Trends for ..., 0732-1066.*

US
RESIDENTS IN WISCONSIN ADULT CORRECTIONAL INSTITUTIONS. **Main/Corp** Wisconsin. Division of Corrections. Office of Systems and Evaluation. Periodical. English. Department of Health & Social Services / Wisconsin, 1 West Wilson Street, PO Box 309, Madison WI 53701. **LC** HV7299; .A28C. **DD** 364.3/09775. ***Supersedes*** *Residents in Wisconsin Adult Correctional Institutions, 0363-0641.*
Desc: Provides a profile of demographic and sentence related data on adult male and female inmates of Wisconsin state institutions.

US/0732-0787
RESIDENTS IN WISCONSIN JUVENILE CORRECTIONAL INSTITUTIONS (1979). (RESIDENTS IN WISCONSIN JUVENILE CORRECTIONAL INSTITUTIONS ON ... WITH FIVE-YEAR TRENDS FOR ... .). **Added/Corp** Wisconsin. Division of Corrections. Office of Systems and Evaluation. Wisconsin. Division of Corrections. Office of Information Management. (19??)-. English. sa. Wisconsin Division of Corrections, 149 East Wilson Street, Room 1050, Madison WI 53702. **Tel** (608)266-2471, FAX (608)267-0923. **LC** HV7299; .A28d. **DD** 364.3/6/09775. ***Continues*** *Offenders Resident in Wisconsin Juvenile Correctional Institutions on .. with Five-Year Trends for ... (Madison, Wis. : 1979), 0732-0795.*
Desc: Includes trends for current year and the preceding years juvenile delinquency and correctional institutions.

US/0095-3180
RESOLUTION OF CORRECTIONAL PROBLEMS AND ISSUES. **Added/Corp** South Carolina. Dept. of Corrections. **VFOAT** Resolution. Vol. 1 (Fall 1974)-. Periodical. English. qt. $10.00. South Carolina Department of Corrections, PO Box 766, Columbia SC 29202. **LC** HV9261; .R47. **DD** 364.6/0973.

JA/0256-5471
RESOURCE MATERIAL SERIES. [Resour. mater. ser. - UNAFEI]. **Added/Corp** United Nations Asia and Far East Institute for the Prevention of Crime and Treatment of Offenders. **VFOAT** Report for ... and Resource Material Series. (1971)-. English. sa. UNAFEI, 1-26 Harumicho, Fuchu Japan. **LC** HV7431; .R46. **DD** 364.4.
Ind/Abst Crim. Justice Abstr.

CN/0714-4288
RESSOURCES ET VOUS. (RESSOURCES ET VOUS : PERIODIQUE DE LA SOCIETE DE CRIMINOLOGIE DU QUEBEC.). [Ressour. vous]. **Added/Corp** Societe de Criminologie du Quebec. No. 1 (July 1981)-. Periodical. French. mo. 6.00Can$. Societe de Criminologie Quebec, 425 rue Viger Ouest CH 620, Montreal Quebec H2Z 1X2 Canada. **Tel** (514)873-4239. **ED** Samir Rizkalla. **DD** 364/.9714. **Circ:** 500 (ctrl).
Desc: General description of a resource active in crime prevention, law enforcement or social and community help to ex-convicts.

US/0883-2234
RETAIL SECURITY MANAGEMENT LETTER. [Retail secur. manage. lett.]. **VFOAT** Retail Security Management. (19??)-. Periodical. English. mo. $127.00 (one year), $227.00 (two year). Strafford Publications Inc., 590 Dutch Valley Road Northeast, Atlanta GA 30324. **Tel** (404)881-1141, (800)926-7926, FAX (404)881-0074. **ED** M. M. Sweet and Jennifer Fogleman. **DD** 381. **Bk Rev**.
Desc: A news and information monthly edited exclusively for the executive with security and loss prevention responsibility in the retail and shopping center environments.

CN/0317-9222
RETRAITE, LE. First issue in July 1973?. French. Association de Bienfaisance et de Retraite de la Police de Montreal, 480 rue Gilford, Montreal Quebec H2J 1N3 Canada. **DD** 301.43/5.

US/0160-1091
REVIEW OF CURRENT RESEARCH. **Main/Corp** Massachusetts. Dept. of Correction. English. Leverett Saltonstall Building, Government Center, 100 Cambridge Street, Boston MA 02202. **LC** HV9274; .M37A. **DD** 364.6/09744.

US
REVIEW / WASHINGTON STATE REFORMATORY. **Added/Corp** Washington State Reformatory. **VFOAT** WSR Review; W.S.R. Review. **VAT** Washington State Reformatory Review. Vol. 4, Issue 2 (Apr. 1990)-. Periodical. English. **LC** HV9475.W22; W35. ***Continues*** *WSR Review, 0738-2731.*

YU/0034-690X
REVIJA ZA KRIMINALISTIKO IN KRIMINOLOGIJO. [Rev. krim. kriminol.]. (1950)-. Periodical. Slovenian. qt. **UDC** 343.9.
Ind/Abst Crim. Justice Abstr.

BO
REVISTA BOLIVIANA DE CIENCIAS PENALES / SOCIEDAD BOLIVIANA DE CIENCIAS PENALES. Yearly V. 1, No. 1, (May/June/July 1978)-. Periodical. Spanish. qt. Sociedad Boloviana de Ciencias Penales Secretaria General, Jenaro Sanjines 423 6TO Piso Of 610 Casillas 4171, 4854 La Paz Bolivia. **LC** HV6886; .R48. **DD** 364/.984/05.

CL
REVISTA DE CIENCIAS PENALES. **Added/Corp** Chile. Direccion General de Prisiones. Chile. Universidad, Santiago. Instituto de Ciencias Penales. (March/April 1935)-. Periodical. Spanish. ir. Editorial Juridica de Chile / Santiago, Casilla Postal 4256, Santiago Chile. **Tel** 011 56 2 2049900.

SP/0210-6035
REVISTA DE ESTUDIOS PENITENCIARIOS (1961). ***Ceased.*** (REVISTA DE ESTUDIOS PENITENCIARIOS.). [Rev. estud. penit.]. **Added/Corp** Spain. Direccion General de Prisiones. Yearly Vol. 17, No. 154 (Sept./Oct. 1961)-Issue 245. Periodical. Spanish. sm. Ministerio de Justicia, Centro de Publicaciones, Gran via 76-8, 28013 Madrid Spain. **Tel** 011 34 1 5475422. ***Continues*** *Revista de la Escuela de Estudios Penitenciarios.*

CK
REVISTA POLICIA NACIONAL DE COLOMBIA. **Main/Corp** Colombia. Policia Nacional. Periodical. Spanish. bm. Carrera 7A No 13-58 Oficina 801, Apartado Aereo 21356, Bogota Colombia. **LC** HV7551; .C6. ***Continues*** *Colombia. Fuerzas de Policia. Revista.*

BE
REVUE DE DROIT PENAL ET DE CRIMINOLOGIE. Periodical. French. Ten times a year. 3.780F Belgium; 4.800F EEC Countries; 5.200F other. Editions la Charte Sa, Rue Guimard 19, B 1040 Brussels Belgium. **Tel** 011 32 50 331235, FAX 011 32 50 343768. Index available. cum. index. **Bk Rev**, (Qty: 50). **Circ:** 1,000 (ctrl). available on microfilm and CD-ROM.
Desc: Journal of criminal law and criminology.
Ind/Abst Crim. Penol. Police Sci. Abstr.; Index Foreign Leg. Per.

FR/0035-1237
REVUE DE LA POLICE NATIONALE. **Added/Corp** France. Secretariat General pour la Police. France. Direction Enerale de la Police Nationale. France. Inspection Generale de la Police Nationale. **VFOAT** Police Nationale. (196?)-. Periodical. French. sa. 50.00F. Revue de la Police, 11 rue des Saussaires, Paris 8E France. **LC** HV7551; .R445. ***Continues*** *Revue de la Surete Nationale.*

FR/0035-3329
REVUE INTERNATIONALE DE CRIMINOLOGIE ET DE POLICE TECHNIQUE. [Rev. int. criminol. police tech.]. Vol. 7 (1953)-. Periodical. French. qt. 90.00F. Editions Marcel Meichtry, 26 Chemin de la Caroline, CH1213 Petit Lancy Switzerland. **Tel** 011 41 22 7911027, FAX 011 41 22 7928834. **ED** Pierre-Henri Bolle. **NLM** W1 RE876H. **[CCC]**. Index available. **Bk Rev**. **Ad Acc**. **Circ:** 2,500 (ctrl). ***Continues*** *Revue de Criminologie et de Police Technique.*
Desc: Covers technical & scientific criminology, forensic scientific police research, and general police technology.
Ind/Abst Crim. Justice Abstr.; Crim. Penol. Police Sci. Abstr.; PAIS Int. Print (?-?); Point Repere (1979); Psychol. Abstr. (1983-); PsycINFO (1983-); PsycLit.

FR/0035-3396
REVUE INTERNATIONALE DE POLICE CRIMINELLE. [Rev. int. police crim.]. (1946)-. Periodical. French (English, Spanish and Arabic). bm. 150.00F France; 170.00F other. ICPO Interpol Secretariat General, BP 6041, F-69411 Lyon Cedex 06 France. **Tel** 011 33 72 447000, FAX 011 33 72 447162 or 63, telex 301987. **UDC** 351.74:061.1 (100).

FR
REVUE PENITENTIAIRE ET DE DROIT PENAL (1940). (REVUE PENITENTIAIRE ET DE DROIT PENAL : BULLETIN DE LA SOCIETE GENERALE DES PRISONS.). **Added/Corp** Societe Generale des Prisons et de Legislation Criminelle. **VFOAT** Bulletin de la Societe Generale des Prisons. (1940)-. Bulletin. French. qt. 250.00F. Societe General des Prisons & Legislation Criminelle, 5 Petite Place, 78000 Versailles France. **Bk Rev**. ***Continues*** *Revue Penitentiaire et de Droit Penal et Etudes Criminologiques.*
Desc: Journal for criminal law dealing with conditions in the prisons.
Ind/Abst PAIS Int. Print.

US
RICHMOND POLICE ACTIVITIES LEAGUE : REPORT TO THE LEGISLATURE / SUBMITTED BY DEPARTMENT OF THE YOUTH AUTHORITY, RESEARCH DIVISION. ***Ceased.*** **Added/Corp** California Youth Authority. Research Division. (Jan. 1992)-(1992). English. **LC** HV7431; .R53.

NE
RIJKSPOLITIE MAGAZINE. ***Title Change.*** (19??)-(1992). Schaafsma & Brouwer, Postbus 10, NL 9100 Dokkum Netherlands. **Tel** 31 51903322. ***Continued by*** *Politie Magazine, 0925-0980.*

US/0271-3144
ROLE OF BEHAVIORAL SCIENCE IN PHYSICAL SECURITY, THE. [Role behav. sci. phys. secur.]. 1st- 1976-. Government Publication. English. an. US Department of Commerce, 14th Street & Constitution Avenue NW, Washington DC 20230. **Tel** (202)482-2000, FAX (202)482-3772. **ED** J J Kramer. **LC** QC100; .U57 subser; HV7431. **DD** 602.18 S; 364.4. **CODEN** XNBSAV.

CN/0315-9701
ROLL OF THE ORDER - THE PRIORY OF CANADA. [Repertoire des membres - Prieure du Canada]. **Main/Corp** Order of St. John. Priory of Canada. **VFOAT** Repertoire des Membres - Le Prieure du Canada. 1974-. English (French). an. Priory Secretary, Order of St John, PO Box 388 Station A, Ottawa Ontario K1N 8V4 Canada. **DD** 361.7/7. ***Continues*** *Roll of the Order in Canada, 0315-9728.*

AQ
ROYAL POLICE FORCE OF ANTIGUA AND BARBUDA MAGAZINE ..., THE.
Added/Corp Royal Police Force of Antigua and Barbuda. Royal Police Force of Antigua and Barbuda. Editorial Committee. (19??)-. English. an.

AT
SA POLICE. (19??)-. Periodical. English. mo. 48.00Aus$. Police Association of South Australia, PO Box 6032 Halifax Street, Adelaide SA 5000 Australia. **Tel** 011 61 08 212 3055, FAX 011 61 08 212 2002. **ED** Sam Bass. **Ad Acc.** ctrl circ.

US/1059-6178
SAFE BULLETIN : SCAM AND FRAUD EXCHANGE, THE. [SAFE bull.]. Vol.1 No.1 (Oct./Nov. 1991)-. Bulletin. English. mo. $39.00. The Safe Group, 1415 Queen Anne Road, PO Box 16, Teaneck NJ 07666. **DD** 364.

US
SAGE CRIMINAL JUSTICE SYSTEM ANNUALS. (1972)-. Monographic series. English. sa. price varies per volume. SAGE Periodical Press, 2455 Teller Road, Thousand Oaks CA 91320. **Tel** (805)499-0721, FAX (805)499-0871, telex 100799.

CN/1185-9164
SASKATCHEWAN CRIMES COMPENSATION BOARD ANNUAL REPORT. (THE SASKATCHEWAN CRIMES COMPENSATION BOARD ANNUAL REPORT FOR THE PERIOD ..). [Sask. Crim. Compens. Board annu. rep.]. **Main/Corp** Saskatchewan Crimes Compensation Board. (Apr. 1, 1990/Mar. 31, 1991)-. English. **DD** 344.7124/03288. ***Continues** Fiscal Year End Report., 1186-0545.*

NO
SCANDINAVIAN STUDIES IN CRIMINOLOGY. **Added/Corp** Scandinavian Research Council for Criminology. Vol. 1 (1965)-. Monographic series. English. ir. Price varies per volume. Scandinavian University Press, PO Box 2959 Toeyen, N 0608 Oslo 6 Norway. **Tel** 011 47 2 2575400, FAX 011 47 2 2575353, telex 71896 UROR N. **(Subscription address:** Scandinavian University Press, 200 Meacham Ave., Elmont NY 11003.**)**

CN/0316-4209
SCARLET & GOLD. **Added/Corp** Royal Canadian Mounted Police Veterans' Association. Vancouver Division. (1919)-. Periodical. English. an. 10.00Can$. Royal Canadian Mounted Police Veterans' Association / Vancouver, 1215 Alder Bay Walk, Vancouver BC V6H 3T6 Canada. **Tel** (604)738-4423. **DD** 354/.71/0074. **Bk Rev. Ad Acc. Circ:** 2,000.
Desc: Features true stories written by veterans and articles relating to veteran activities.

US
SCHOOL CRIME IN CALIFORNIA FOR THE ... SCHOOL YEAR. **Added/Corp** California. State Dept. of Education. **VFOAT** Standard School Crime Reporting Program. (1990)-. English. $3.50. Bureau of Publications, Sales Unit, California Department of Education, PO Box 271, Sacramento CA 95802-0271. **LC** HV6166; .C355. ***Continues** California. State Dept. of Education. Report to the California State Legislature Regarding the Standard School Crime Reporting Program.*

SZ/0036-7893
SCHWEIZERISCHE ZEITSCHRIFT FUER STRAFRECHT. **VFOAT** Revue Penale Suisse. Vol. 1 (1888)-. Periodical. Multiple languages (German and French). qt. 96.00F Switzerland; 108.00F other. Staempfli & Cie SA, Postfach 8326, CH-3001 Bern Switzerland. **Tel** 011 41 31 3006666, telex 031 911 515 EDMZ CH. **[CCC].** Index Available in last issue of each volume--loose separately paged. cum. index.
Ind/Abst Crim. Penol. Police Sci. Abstr.; Index Foreign Leg. Per.

US/8750-3808
SCLEOA UPDATE. (SCLEOA UPDATE / SOUTH CAROLINA LAW ENFORCEMENT OFFICERS ASSOCIATION.). **Added/Corp** South Carolina Law Enforcement Officers Association. **VFOAT** S.C.L.E.O.A. Update. **VAT** South Carolina Law Enforcement Officers Association Update. (198?)-. Periodical. English. bm. SCLEOA, 421 Zimalcrest Drive, Columbia SC 29210.

US/0882-1909
SCROGGINS NATIONAL LAW ENFORCEMENT DIRECTORY. [Scroggins natl. law enforc. dir.]. (1984)-. English (French). an. $47.95. Scroggins National Law Enforcement Directory, PO Box 945, Montrose CA 91021-0945. **Tel** (818)957-5671. **ED** David E. Scroggins. **LC** HV8130; .S38. **DD** 363.2/3/02573. Index available. **Ad Acc. Circ:** 10,000 (ctrl). available on diskette.
Desc: The first complete and cross-referenced listing of law enforcement agencies throughout the United States and Canada.

US/0037-0193
SEARCH AND SEIZURE BULLETIN. [Search seiz. bull.]. (Apr. 1964)-. Bulletin. English. Twelve times a year. $61.97. Quinlan Publishing Company, 23 Drydock Avenue, Boston MA 02210-2387. **Tel** (617)542-0048, (800)229-2084, FAX (617)345-9646. **LC** KF9630.A59; S4. **DD** 345.73/0522/05; 347.30552205. **[CCC].** Index Available, published separately, free-automatically sent. available on microfilm and microfiche from University Microfilms International (UMI).
Ind/Abst Crim. Justice Period. Index.

US
SEARCHLIGHT. Began in 1973. English. bm. Chicago Crime Commission, 79 West Monroe Street, Chicago IL 60603.
Ind/Abst Bibliogr. Mission.

UK
SECURITY & PROTECTION EQUIPMENT. English. mo. £33.00 UK; £38.00 other. Batiste Publishing Ltd, Pembroke House, Campsbourne Road, Hornsey, London N8 7PE England. **Tel** 011 44 81 340 3291. ***Continues** Security & Protection.*

US/0741-482X
SECURITY AND SPECIAL POLICE LEGAL UPDATE. **VFOAT** Security Legal Update. (19??)-. Periodical. English. mo. $158.00. Americans for Effective Law Enforcement Inc, 5519 North Cumberland Avenue, Suite 1008, Chicago IL 60656-1471. **Tel** (312)763-2800, FAX (312) 763-3225. **ED** Bernard Farber. **LC** KF5399.5.P7; A496. **DD** 344.73/0522; 347.304522. Index available. cum. index. **Circ:** 400.
Desc: Digest of current security law with an effective impact upon those professionals in the private security field.

●US
SECURITY DIRECTOR'S DIGEST. (Jan. 1995)-. English. wk. $345.00 (one year), $600.00 (two year), $900.00 (three year). Washington Crime News Services, 3918 Prosperity Avenue, Suite 318, Fairfax VA 22031-3334. **Tel** (703)573-1600, (800)422-9267, FAX (703)573-1604. ***Continues** Corporate Secuirty Digest, 0894-3826.*

US/0955-1662
SECURITY JOURNAL. [Secur. j.]. **Added/Corp** ASIS Foundation. Vol. 1, No. 1 (1989)-. Periodical. English. qt. $130.00 (institution), $80.00 (individual) US and Canada; $145.00 (institution), $95.00 (individual) other. Butterworth Heinemann / Woburn, MA, 225 Wildwood Avenue, Unit B, Woburn MA 01801. **Tel** (800)366-2665, FAX (617)928-2620, telex 880052. **ED** Robert D McCrie. **LC** HV8290; .S3745. **DD** 363.2/89/05. **CODEN** SJOUEN. **[CCC].** available on microfilm and microfiche from University Microfilms International (UMI). Documents available from Ask*IEEE.
Desc: Addresses current issues and the future of security professionals with articles written by scholars, researchers and practitioners.
Ind/Abst Crim. Justice Abstr. (199?-); INSPEC (April 1991-); Soc. Plann. Policy Dev. Abstr.

US/0889-0625
SECURITY LAW NEWSLETTER. [Secur. law newsl.]. **Added/Corp** Security Law Institute (Washington, D.C.) Crime Control Research Corporation (Washington, D.C.). **VFOAT** SLN. Vol. 1, No. 1 (Dec. 1981)-. Newsletter. English. mo. $125.00 (one year), $250.00 (two year) school; $297.00 (one year), $445.00 (two year) other. Crime Control Research Corp, 1063 Thomas Jefferson Northwest, Washington DC 20007. **Tel** (202)337-2700, FAX (202)337-8324. **DD** 344. Index available.
Desc: Update of legal developments affecting private security.
Ind/Abst Crim. Justice Period. Index.

US/0736-0401
SECURITY LETTER SOURCE BOOK. See Security Systems and Alarms.

US/0890-8826
SECURITY (NEWTON, MASS.). ***Title Change.*** (SECURITY.). [Security]. Vol. 23, No. 9 (Sept. 1986)-Vol. 28, No. 12 (Dec. 1991). Periodical. English. mo. Cahners Publishing Company, 249 West 17th Street, New York NY 10011. **Tel** (212)645-0067, FAX (212)242-6987. **LC** HV8290; .S4. **DD** 363.2/89/05. **CODEN** SECUEU. **[CCC].** available on microfilm and microfiche from University Microfilms International (UMI). Documents available from Ask*IEEE. ***Continues** Security World, 0037-0703.* ***Continued by** Security for Buyers of Products, Systems and Services.*
Desc: Covers methods and equipment used to protect lives, property and assets from all types of risk, including internal theft, business interruption, fire, burglary, robbery, fraud, shoplifting, industrial espionage, computer crime and terrorism. Editorial focus includes in-depth features and broad interest problem solving.
Ind/Abst F&S Index Plus Text, Int. [Select. Cov.]; INSPEC (Dec. 1987-); PROMT.

US/0732-8907
SENTENCES. (SENTENCES / WORLD PRISON POETRY CENTER.). Vol. 1, No. 1 (Apr., 1982)-. Periodical. English (Spanish). bm. $25.00 US and South America; $35.00 Europe and Australia. World Prison Poetry Center, PO Box 8000, New Haven CT 06530-8000. Index available. cum. index. **Circ:** 250 (ctrl).
Desc: Publishes poetry written by individuals while incarcerated. Every issue covers only one prison's poet.

AT/0725-654X
SENTENCING STATISTICS, HIGHER CRIMINAL COURTS, VICTORIA. See Law-Abstracting, Bibliographies and Statistics.

SA
SERVAMUS. **Added/Corp** South Africa. Police. (19??)-. Periodical. Afrikaans (English). Twelve times a year. R47.88. Sarp Publishers, PO Box 828, Pretoria 0001 South Africa. **Tel** 011 27 12 3220557, telex ZARPS. **ED** L.J. Haasbroek. **LC** HV8271.A5; S674. **DD** 363.2/0968. **Bk Rev. Ad Acc. Circ:** 54,200 (ctrl). ***Continues** South Africa. Police. SAP.*
Desc: Caters to the educational and social needs of the South African police force.

US/0028-016X
SHERIFF : THE MAGAZINE OF THE NATIONAL SHERIFFS' ASSOCIATION. **Added/Corp** National Sheriffs' Association. Vol. 43, No. 1 (Jan./Feb. 1991)-. Periodical. English. bm. National Sheriffs' Association, 1450 Duke Street, Alexandria VA 22314. **LC** HV7551; .N35. **DD** 363.2/82/097305. ***Continues** National Sheriff.*

US/0488-6186
SHERIFF'S STAR (TALLAHASSEE, FLA.), THE. (SHERIFF'S STAR.). **Added/Corp** Florida Sheriffs Association. (Mar. 1957)-. Periodical. English. Nine times a year (monthly with Dec./Jan., Mar./Apr., and Oct./Nov. issues combined). $5.00. Florida Sheriff's Association, PO Box 12519, Tallahassee FL 32317. **Tel** (904)877-2165. **ED** Carl Stauffer. **Circ:** 80,000 (ctrl).

SJ
SHURTAH (SHURTAT JUMHURIYAT AL-SUDAN AL-DIMUQRATIYAH. QISM AL-ALAQAT AL-AMMAH). (AL-SHURTAH : MAJALLAT SHURTAT JUMHURIIYAT AL-SUDAN AL-DIMUQRATIYAH.). Periodical. Arabic. qt. 2.50 single issue. S B 288, Al-Khartoum Sudan. **LC** HV7551; .S472.

GW/0300-3337
SICHERHEITSBEAUFTRAGTER. (1966)-. Trade Publication. German. mo. DM58.80 Germany; DM82.80 other. Dr. Curt Haefner Verlag GmbH, Bachstrasse 14, Postfach 106060, D 69050 Heidelberg Germany. **Tel** 011 49 6221 49063. **ED** Curt Haefner. **[CCC].** Index available. cum. index. **Bk Rev. Ad Acc. Circ:** 34,000 (ctrl).
Desc: Trade journal for security services in private industry and public service.

GW
SICHERHEITSTECHNIK. (19??)-. Periodical. German. Eleven times a year. DM252.40 Germany; DM262.40 other. Kriminalistik Verlag GmbH, IM Weiher 10, D-69121 Heidelberg Germany. **Tel** 011 49 6221 489259, FAX 011 49 6221 489279. **LC** HV7431; .S56. **DD** 362.8/8.

IT/0392-9000
SICUREZZA E PREVENZIONE: ANTICRIMINE, ANTINCENDIO, ANTINFORTUNISTICA. (1978)-. Periodical. Italian. mo (11 issues (July/Aug. issue combined)). L120000 Italy. Masson S.P.A, Via Statuto 2/4, 20121 Milan Italy. **Tel** 011 39 2 63671, FAX 011 39 2 6367211. **ED** Bruno Carlucci. **UDC** 331.823. **Circ:** 7,100.
Desc: A technical-scientific publication for crime prevention, fire-fighting and building automation. It brings together manufacturers, installers, end-users and category associations, suggesting preventive measures and presenting products, systems and devices available on the market.

SI
SINGAPORE POLICE JOURNAL. Periodical. English. $1.00 each issue. Thomson Road, Singapore 11 Singapore. **LC** HV7551; .S55. **DD** 363.2/09595/2.

NE
SLACHTOFFERS VAN MISDRIJVEN / CENTRAAL BUREAU VOOR DE STATISTIEK, HOOFDAFDELING STATISTIEKEN VAN CRIMINALITEIT EN RECHTSPELGING. **VFOAT** Victims of Crime. Dutch (summaries and/or abstracts in English). Fl15.00. Centraal Bureau voor de Statistiek, AFD ALG Zaken, Postbus 959, 2270 AZ Voorburg Netherlands. **Tel** 011 31 70 3373800, FAX 011 31 038 7429, telex 32692 CBS NL. **LC** HV6250.3.N4; S55.

Law —Law Enforcement and Criminology

CN/0381-6699
SLAMMER. V. 1- Oct. 1974-. Periodical. English. ir. $5.00. Slammer, Box 3000, Drumheller Alberta T0J 0Y0 Canada. **DD** 365/.97123/3. *Supersedes Inside News, 0381-6680.*

II/0037-7716
SOCIAL DEFENCE. [Soc. def.]. **Added/Corp** India (Republic). Central Bureau of Correctional Services. Vol. 1 (July 1965)-. Periodical. English. qt. Price varies. Central Bureau of Correctional Services, New Delhi, India. **(Subscription address:** Prints India, 11 Darya Ganj, New Delhi 110002 India.**) LC** HV9397. **CODEN** SDEFDL.
Ind/Abst Crim. Justice Abstr.; Psychol. Abstr.

US/1043-1578
SOCIAL JUSTICE (SAN FRANCISCO, CALIF.). (SOCIAL JUSTICE : A JOURNAL OF CRIME, CONFLICT & WORLD ORDER.). [Soc. justice]. Vol. 15, No. 1 (Spring 1988)-. Periodical. English. Four times a year. $75.00 (institutions), $30.00 (individuals) US; $85.00 (institutions), $34.00 (individuals) other. Social Justice, PO Box 40601, San Francisco CA 94140. **Tel** (415)550-1703, (415)647-4472. **ED** Tony Platt, Paul Takagi and Gregory Shank. **LC** HV6001; .C673. **DD** 364/.05. Index available. cum. index. **Bk Rev. Ad Acc. Pr Rev. Circ:** 3,000. available on microfilm and microfiche from University Microfilms International (UMI); available in microform from University Microfilms International (UMI). Documents available from The Genuine Article, UMI Article Clearinghouse. *Continues Crime and Social Justice, 0094-7571; Absorbed Contemporary Marxism, 0193-8703.*
Desc: Combines authoritative analyses of global issues, (peaceful resolution of conflicts, state terrorism, and human rights) with domestic policy concerns such as reducing crime and race and gender discrimination.
Ind/Abst Am. Hist. Life (1985-); Appl. Soc. Sci. Index Abstr.; Crim. Justice Abstr.: Expand. Acad. Index (1992-); Hum. Rights Intern. Rep.; J. Plan. Lit.; Left Index; Newsp. Period. Abstr. (1989-); Res. Alert [Full Cov.]; Soc. Sci. Cit. Index [Full Cov.]; U.S. Polit. Sci. Doc. (199?-).

US/0360-3431
SOURCEBOOK OF CRIMINAL JUSTICE STATISTICS. See Law-Abstracting, Bibliographies and Statistics.

US
SOUTHERN COALITION REPORT ON JAILS AND PRISONS. Added/Corp Southern Coalition on Jails and Prisons (U.S.). **VFOAT** Southern Coalition Report; Southern Coalition Report on Jails & Prison. (1974)-. Periodical. English. qt (Jan., May, Sept., Dec.). $20.00. Southern Prison Ministry, PO Box 120044, Nashville TN 37212. **Tel** (615)383-9610, **FAX** (615)298-1254. **ED** Joseph B. Ingle. **Circ:** 12,000 (ctrl).

US/0098-3845
SPECIAL REPORT - DIVISION OF CORRECTION, A. Main/Corp Maryland. Division of Correction. (19??)-. English. an. Division of Correction, 920 Greenmount Avenue, Baltimore MD 21202. **LC** HV7270; .A32a. **DD** 365/.9752.

US
SPECIAL STUDY - TEXAS DEPARTMENT OF CORRECTIONS, RESEARCH, PLANNING, AND DEVELOPMENT DIVISION. Main/Corp Texas. Dept. of Corrections. Research, Planning, and Development Division. No. 42- Jan. 1978-. Monographic series. English. Price varies per volume. Texas Department of Corrections, Research Planning & Development Division, 1100 West 49th Street, Austin TX 78756. **LC** HV7293; .A36D. **DD** 364.6/09764. *Continues Special Study - Texas Department of Corrections, Research and Development Division.*

US
SPECTATOR, THE. Vol. 1, No. 1 (June 30, 1987)-. English. State Prison of Southern Michigan, 4000 Cooper Street, Jackson MI 49201.

CE
SRI LANKA POLICE JOURNAL. Periodical. English. qt. Rs2.00 single issue. The Editorial Board, PO Box 1517, 15 Longdon Place 7, Colombo Sri Lanka Ceylon. **LC** HV7804.8.A2; S67. **DD** 363.2/09549/3.

US
STATE OF CORRECTIONS, PROCEEDINGS, ACA ANNUAL CONFERENCES. Added/Corp American Correctional Association. American Correctional Association. Congress of Correction. **VFOAT** Proceedings, ACA Annual Conferences; American Correctional Association Proceedings. (1988)-. Proceedings. English. an. $25.00; $75.00 Comes with American Correctional Association Professional II Level memberships. American Correctional Association, 8025 Laurel Lakes Court, Laurel MD 20707-5075. **Tel** (301)206-5100, (800)222-5646, **FAX** (301)206-5061. **LC** HV8987; .A5. *Continues American Correctional Association. Congress of Correction. Proceedings of the Annual Congress of Correction of the American Correctional Association, 0065-7948.*

US
STATE OF NEVADA COMPREHENSIVE CRIMINAL JUSTICE PROGRESS REPORT. Main/Corp Nevada. Commission on Crime, Delinquency, and Corrections. **VFOAT** Nevada Comprehensive Criminal Justice Progress Report. English. an. Nevada Commission on Crime Delinquency & Corrections, Carson City NV 89701. **LC** HV7278; .A27B. **DD** 364/.9793.

US/0149-2012
STATE OF NEVADA, DEPARTMENT OF PAROLE AND PROBATION, AUDIT REPORT. [State Nev. Dep. Parole Probat. audit rep.]. **Main/Corp** Nevada. Legislative Auditor. English. Legislative Auditor, Legislative Building, Capitol Complex, Carson City NV 89710. **LC** HV9305.N3; N45A. **DD** 353.9/793/00849.

US/0149-2144
STATE OF NEVADA, DEPARTMENT OF PAROLE AND PROBATION, RESTITUTION TRUST FUND, AUDIT REPORT. (AUDIT REPORT, STATE OF NEVADA DEPARTMENT OF PAROLE AND PROBATION, RESTITUTION TRUST FUND.). **Main/Corp** Nevada. Legislative Auditor. English. Legislative Auditor, Legislative Building, Capitol Complex, Carson City NV 89710. **LC** HV9305.N3; N45C. **DD** 353.9/793/00849.

US
STATE OF NEVADA UNIFORM CRIME REPORTS ... ANNUAL REPORT. Main/Corp Nevada. Dept. of Law Enforcement Assistance. **VFOAT** Nevada Uniform Crime Reports ... Annual Report. English. an. **LC** HV7278; .A277B. **DD** 364.1/09793.

US/0360-0629
STATE OF NEW YORK COMPREHENSIVE CRIME CONTROL PLAN. Main/Corp New York (State). Division of Criminal Justice Services. English. Division of Criminal Justice Services, 80 Centre Street, New York NY 10013. **LC** HV7282; .A24B. **DD** 364.

US/0096-3208
STATE OF NORTH CAROLINA UNIFORM CRIME REPORT. See Law-Abstracting, Bibliographies and Statistics.

US/0147-0434
STATE OF THE STATES ON CRIME AND JUSTICE. Main/Conf National Conference of State Criminal Justice Planning Administrator. English. National Conference of State Criminal Justice Planning Administration, 444 North Capitol Street NW/Suite 305, Washington DC 20001. **LC** HV8183; .N29A. **DD** 364/.973.

US/0192-4222
STATE PEACE OFFICERS JOURNAL. VFOAT Journal. (19??)-. Periodical. English. qt. $10.00. North American Publishing Company / Texas, PO Box 130155, Houston TX 77219. **Tel** (713)526-6425.

US
STATEWIDE SYSTEM OF IN-SERVICE TRAINING : ANNUAL REPORT, A. Main/Corp Illinois Local Governmental Law Enforcement Officers Training Board. **VFOAT** ASSIST Annual Report. (1989)-. English. Illinois Local Governmental Law Enforcement Officers Training Board, Lincoln Tower Plaza, Suite 400, 524 South Second Street, Springfield IL 62701-1773. **LC** HV8145.I3; I394a. **DD** 352.2/09773. *Continues Illinois Local Governmental Law Enforcement Officers Training Board Biennial Report.*

US/0097-7667
STATISTICAL DATA ON PERSONS RELEASED FROM PAROLE BY DISCHARGE AND VIOLATION. See Law-Abstracting, Bibliographies and Statistics.

AT
STATISTICAL REVIEW OF CRIME. See Law-Abstracting, Bibliographies and Statistics.

II
STATISTIK PENGADILAN NEGERI PROPINSI IRIAN JAYA MICROFORM. Added/Corp Indonesia. Kantor Statistik Propinsi Irian Jaya. **VFOAT** Statistik Pengadilan Negeri Provinsi Irian Jaya. (1984)-. Indonesian. **LC** Microfiche 86/50518. *Continues tStatistik Pengadilan Negeri dan Lembaga Pemasyarakatan (Jayapura, Indonesia).*

CN/0714-4555
STATISTIQUES CORRECTIONNELLES QUEBECOISES. (1981)-. French. an. **LC** HV9309.Q8; S7. **DD** 364.3/09714/021. *Continues in part Rapport Annuel / Direction Generale de la Probation et des Etablissements de Detention, 0317-736X.*

FR
STATISTIQUES CRIMINELLES INTERNATIONALES. See Law-Abstracting, Bibliographies and Statistics.

SW/1102-3937
STUDIES ON CRIME AND CRIME PREVENTION. (1992)-. English. an. Kr320.00, $51.00. Scandinavian University Press, PO Box 2959 Toeyen, N 0608 Oslo 6 Norway. **Tel** 011 47 2 2575400, **FAX** 011 47 2 2575353, telex 71896 UROR N. **(Subscription address:** Scandinavian University Press, 200 Meacham Ave., Elmont NY 11003.**) ED** Artur Solarz and Viveka Engwall.
Desc: Deals with etiological and phenomenological aspects of both traditional and modern forms of crime as well as with new ideas on crime prevention. Also publishes new methods of evaluation. Published for the Swedish National Council for Crime Prevention.
Ind/Abst Crim. Justice Abstr.

NZ
STUDY SERIES (VICTORIA UNIVERSITY OF WELLINGTON. INSTITUTE OF CRIMINOLOGY). (STUDY SERIES.). (1987)-. Monographic series. English. Price varies per volume. Institute of Criminology NZ, PO Box 600, Victoria Univ, Wellington New Zealand.

UK
SUMMARY OF RESEARCH WITHIN THE UNIT AND OF RESEARCH SUPPORTED BY GRANT. Main/Corp Great Britain. Home Office. Research Unit. English. Research Unit, Horseferry House Dean Ryle Street, London SW1 P2AW England. **LC** HV6024.5; .G73A. **DD** 364.

US/0148-4273
SUMMARY OF THE SOUTH DAKOTA CRIMINAL JUSTICE PLAN FOR ACTION, A. [Summ. S. D. crim. justice plan action]. **Main/Corp** South Dakota. Criminal Justice Commission. **VFOAT** South Dakota Criminal Justice Plan for Action. (19??)-. English. Criminal Justice Commission, 222 West Pleasant Drive, Pierre SD 57501. **LC** HV7291; .A24a. **DD** 364/.9783.

US
TARGET ARSON / UPDATE. English. Four times a year. free on request. Insurance Committ Arson Control, 110 Willian Street, New York NY 10038.

FI
TAYDENNYSKOULUTUS VUONNA ... .
Main/Corp Finland. Vankeinhoidon Koulutuskeskus. Finnish. an. Vankeinhoidon Koulutuskesus, PL 16, 04261 Kerava Finland. **LC** HV8883.3.F5; F56A.

US/1059-5082
TENNESSEE LAW ENFORCEMENT BULLETIN. [Tenn. law enforc. bull.]. (1977)-. English. bw. $85.00. M. Lee Smith Publishers and Printers, 162 4th Avenue North, PO Box 198867, Nashville TN 37219. **Tel** (615)242-7395, (800)274-6774, **FAX** (615)256-6601. **DD** 344.

US/0040-327X
TENNESSEE LAW ENFORCEMENT JOURNAL. Added/Corp Tennessee Law Enforcement Officers Association. (19??)-. Periodical. English. qt. $3.00. Callan Publishing Inc, 3033 Excelsior Boulevard, Minneapolis MN 55416. **Tel** (612)920-4848. **Circ:** 3,700.
Desc: Association news, general law enforcement-related articles.

US/0278-663X
TERRORISM (MINNEAPOLIS, MINN.). (TERRORISM.). [Terrorism]. Vol. 1, (Feb. 1986)-. Periodical. English. Four times a year (Feb., May, July, Oct.). $45.00. J. L. Scherer, 4900 18th Avenue South, Minneapolis MN 55417. **Tel** (612)722-2947. **ED** J. L. Scherer. **LC** HV6431; .T4583. **DD** 303.6/25/05. Index available. cum. index. ctrl circ. *Continues Terrorism (Minneapolis, Minn.), 0278-663X.*
Desc: Contains statistics, news and chronologies on terrorism.

US
TEXAS CRIME POLL. Main/Corp Sam Houston State University. Criminal Justice Center. Survey Research Program. English. sa. Sam Houston State University Criminal Justice Center, Huntsville TX 77341. **Tel** (409)294-1692. **LC** HV6793.T4; S35A. **DD** 364/.9764.

US
TEXAS CRIMINAL JUSTICE HIGHLIGHTS. Added/Corp Texas. Criminal Justice Division. Vol. 11 (March 1980)-. Periodical. English. mo. Criminal Justice Division, Office of Governor William P Clements Jr, Box 12428, Austin TX 78711. *Continues Criminal Justice Highlights, 0884-0164.*

US
TEXAS JUVENILE PROBATION STATISTICAL REPORT : STATISTICAL AND OTHER DATA ON THE JUVENILE JUSTICE SYSTEM IN TEXAS FOR CALENDAR YEARS ... ABBREVIATED. **See** Law-Abstracting, Bibliographies and Statistics.

US/0040-442X
TEXAS LAWMAN, THE. **Added/Corp** Sheriffs' Association of Texas. (19??)-. Periodical. English. Four times a year (Mar., June, Sept., Dec.). $25.00. Sheriffs Association of Texas, Box 4488, Austin TX 78765. **Tel** (512)445-5888. **ED** Charlotte Richards. **Ad Acc. Circ:** 2,000.

US/0040-4594
TEXAS POLICE JOURNAL. **Added/Corp** Texas Police Association. Vol. 1 (1953)-. Periodical. English. Twelve times a year. 420.00. Texas Police Association, Box 4247, Austin TX 78751. **Tel** (512)458-3140. **ED** Jack L. Ryle. **Circ:** 5,500 (ctrl).
Desc: Articles on law enforcement with subjects of interest to officers from all jurisdictions: prosecutors, judges and persons engaged in law enforcement training.
Ind/Abst Crim. Penol. Police Sci. Abstr.; Index Period. Artic. Relat. Law.

CN/0702-9004
TIGHTWIRE. [Tightwire]. Vol. 5, No. 5/6 (May/June 1979)-. Periodical. English. bm. $4.00 per year. Tightwire Publications, PO Box 515, Kingston Ontario K7L 4W7 Canada. **DD** C810/.8/0920692. ***Continues** Tightwire Publications., 0832-5650.*

NE/0165-182X
TIJDSCHRIFT VOOR CRIMINOLOGIE. [Tijdschr. criminol.]. Vol. 19 (Feb. 1977)-. Academic Scholarly Publication. Dutch (summaries and/or abstracts in English). bm. Fl63.50, Fl44.00 (students), Netherlands; $25.43 US. Uit Gauda Ouinta, PO Box 1148, 6801 MK Arnhem Netherlands. **ED** Ed Leuw. **LC** HV6005; .N4. Index available. **Bk Rev. Ad Acc. Circ:** 550 (ctrl). ***Continues** Nederlands Tijdschrift voor Criminologie.*
Desc: Information for criminologists and law students.
Ind/Abst Crim. Penol. Police Sci. Abstr.; EMBASE.

US/0733-6551
TODAY'S DELINQUENT. ***Suspended.*** (TODAY'S DELINQUENT / NATIONAL CENTER FOR JUVENILE JUSTICE.). [Today's delinq.]. Vol. 1 (1982)-Suspended with Vol. 7 (1988). English. an. $12.00. National Center for Juvenile Justice, 701 Forbes Avenue, Pittsburgh PA 15219. **Tel** (412)227-6950. **ED** Hunter Hurst. **LC** HV9104; .T65. **DD** 364.3/6/0973. **Circ:** 10,000.
Desc: Contains articles on current issues in juvenile delinquency.
Ind/Abst Crim. Justice Abstr.

JA
TOKYO NO HIKO SHONEN. **Added/Corp** Japan. Katei Saibansho (Tokyo). (19??)-. Japanese. Tokyo Hatei Saibansho, 2-3 Kasumigaseki 1-chome Chiyoda-ku, Tokyo 110 Japan. **LC** HV9207.T6; T63a.

UK
TOP SECURITY. Periodical. English. sm. Tieto Ltd, Bank House, 8-A Hill Road, Clevedon Avon BS21 7HH England. **Tel** 0272-876519. **LC** HV7551; .T66. **DD** 364.12.

US/0564-0881
TRAINING KEY. **Added/Corp** International Association of Chiefs of Police. (1964)-. Periodical. English. ir. $5.00 (police officers), $10.00 (individual members), $12.50 (non-members) each issue. International Association of Chiefs of Police, 515 North Washington, Alexandria VA 22314. **Tel** (800)843-4227.

AT/0817-8542
TRENDS AND ISSUES IN CRIME AND CRIMINAL JUSTICE. [Trends issues crime crim. justice]. **Added/Corp** Australian Institute of Criminology. (1986)-. Periodical. English. bm (6 issues). 30.00Aus$ Australia; 35.00Aus$ other. Australian Institute of Criminology, 4 Marcus Clarke Street, Canberra ACT 2601 Australia. **Tel** 011 61 6 2740200, FAX 011 61 6 2740260, telex 61340. **DD** 364.994.

US
TRIBAL AND BUREAU LAW ENFORCEMENT SERVICES AUTOMATED DATA REPORT: BILLINGS AREA. **Main/Corp** U.S. Indian Police Training Center. (19??)-. English. an. **LC** E78.M9; U64a. **DD** 364.1/08997.

US/0198-8891
TRIBAL AND BUREAU LAW ENFORCEMENT SERVICES AUTOMATED DATA REPORT: NAVAJO AREA. **Main/Corp** U.S. Indian Police Training Center. (19??)-. English. an. US Department of Interior Bureau of Indian Affairs, Washington DC 20240. **LC** E99.N3; U58a. **DD** 364.1/08997.

US/0198-8905
TRIBAL AND BUREAU LAW ENFORCEMENT SERVICES AUTOMATED DATA REPORT: TOTAL ALL AREAS. **Main/Corp** U.S. Indian Police Training Center. (19??)-. English. an. US Department of Interior Bureau of Indian Affairs, Washington DC 20240. **LC** E98.C87; .U55a. **DD** 364.1/08997.

US/0732-6688
U.S. IDENTIFICATION MANUAL. (U.S. IDENTIFICATION MANUAL : USIM.). **VFOAT** US Identification Manual; USIM; U.S.I.M. **VAT** United States Identification Manual. (19??)-. Periodical. English. ir (Updates 4 times per year). $155.00. Drivers License Guide Company, 1492 Oddstad Drive, Redwood City CA 94063. **Tel** (415)369-4849, (800)227-8827. **LC** HV8074; .U2. **DD** 363.2/58. ctrl circ.
Desc: Fraud prevention reference book showing all valid driver's licenses issued in the United States and Canada; includes military and other federal identification cards.

US
UNIFORM CRIME REPORT ARREST INFORMATION RELATING TO SUBSTANCE ABUSE IN SOUTH CAROLINA. English. Division of Planning Evaluation and Grant Management, 3700 Forest Drive/Suite 300, Columbia SC 29204. **LC** HV4999.3.S6; U54. **DD** 364.1/77/0973021.

US/0360-9146
UNIFORM CRIME REPORT FOR THE STATE OF MICHIGAN. **See** Law-Abstracting, Bibliographies and Statistics.

US
UNIFORM CRIME REPORTING. **Main/Corp** New Mexico State Police. **VFOAT** New Mexico Crime Reports. Began with 1976. English. an. New Mexico State Police, PO Box 1628, Santa Fe NM 87501. **LC** HV7281; .A37A. **DD** 364/.9789. ***Continues** State of New Mexico Uniform Crime Report.*

US
UNIFORM CRIME REPORTS. Periodical. English. qt. Federal Bureau of Investigation, 10th Street and Pennsylvania Avenue NW, Washington DC 20535. **Tel** (202)324-3000, FAX (202)324-4705.

US/0095-5752
UNIFORM CRIME REPORTS, COMMONWEALTH OF PENNSYLVANIA. **See** Law-Abstracting, Bibliographies and Statistics.

US
UNIFORM CRIME REPORTS, STATE OF FLORIDA. LAW ENFORCEMENET OFFICERS KILLED AND ASSAULTED, ANNUAL REPORT. **Added/Corp** Florida. Dept. of Law Enforcement. **VFOAT** Law Enforcement Officers Killed and Assaulted, Annual Report. (1988)-. English. Florida Department of Law Enforcement, PO Box 1489, VCR Special Services Bureau, Tallahassee FL 32302. **Tel** (904)488-5221. **LC** HV8145.F6; U54. **DD** 364.1/0883632. ***Continues in part** Uniform Crime Reports, State of Florida.*

US
UNIFORM CRIME REPORTS, STATE OF FLORIDA. LAW ENFORCEMENT EMPLOYEE DATA ANNUAL REPORT / COMPILED BY THE FLORIDA DEPARTMENT OF LAW ENFORCEMENT. **Added/Corp** Florida. Dept. of Law Enforcement. **VFOAT** Law Enforcement Employee Data Annual Report; Law Enforcement Employee Data. (1988)-. English. Florida Department of Law Enforcement, PO Box 1489, VCR Special Services Bureau, Tallahassee FL 32302. **Tel** (904)488-5221. **LC** HV8145.F6; U52. **DD** 331.12/513632/09759021. ***Continues in part** Uniform Crime Reports, State of Florida.*

US/0548-5851
UNIFORM CRIME REPORTS, STATE OF NEW JERSEY. **See** Law-Abstracting, Bibliographies and Statistics.

FI
VANKITILASTO. **Main/Corp** Finland. Tilastokeskus. **VFOAT** Fangstatistik. Multiple languages (Finnish and Swedish). Tilastokeskus, PL 504, Annankatu 44, 00101 Helsinki Finland. **Tel** 358-0-17341, FAX 358-0-17342474, telex 1002111 TILASTO SF. **LC** HV8435.3; .A45.

US
VERMONT COMPREHENSIVE PLAN FOR CRIMINAL JUSTICE. **Main/Corp** Vermont. Governor's Commission on the Administration of Justice. English. an. 149 State Street, Montpelier VT 05602. **LC** HV7295; .A3. **DD** 364/.9743.

US/0361-5170
VICTIMOLOGY. [Victimology]. Vol. 1 (Spring 1976)-. Periodical. English. qt. $25.00. Victimology Inc, 2333 N Vernon Street, Arlington VA 22207. **Tel** (703)528-3387. **LC** HV6250; .V53. **DD** 364. **NLM** W1 VI17S. **[CCC].** Documents available from UMI Article Clearinghouse.
Ind/Abst Abstr. Res. Pastor. Care Couns. (19??-); Crim. Justice Abstr. (19??-); Crim. Justice Period. Index (-1989); Curr. Law Index (1980-); Expand. Acad. Index (1984-); Int. Polit. Sci. Abstr. (19??-); Leg. Resour. Index (1980-); LegalTrac (1980-); Middle East Abstr. Index (1980-); Multicult. Educ. Abstr. (19??-); Newsp. Period. Abstr. (1991-); Psychol. Abstr. (1976-); PsycINFO (?-?); PsycLit (19??-); Soc. Sci. Index (19??-); Soc. Work Abstr. (?-?).

CN
VICTIMS OF VIOLENCE REPORT. **See** Sociology-Social Services and Welfare.

IT
VIGILE URBANO, IL. (19??)-. Periodical. Italian. mo. L150000 institution. Maggioli Editore, Casella Postale 290, 47037 Rimini, Italy. **Tel** 011 39 541 628666, FAX 011 39 541 742217.

US/0886-6708
VIOLENCE AND VICTIMS. [Violence vict.]. **Added/Corp** University of New Hampshire. Family Research Laboratory. Vol. 1, No. 1 (Spring 1986)-. Periodical. English. qt. $40.00 (individual, 1 year), $72.00 (individual, 2 year), $77.00 (institutions, 1 year), $129.00 (institutions, 2 year) US; $45.00 $45.00 (individual, 1 year), $82.00 (individual, 2 year), $86.00 (institutions, 1 year), $149.00 (institutions, 2 year) other. Springer Publishing Company, 536 Broadway, New York NY 10012-3955. **Tel** (212)431-4370, FAX (212)941-7842. **ED** Roland Maiuro, PhD. **LC** HV6250; .V56. **DD** 364.1/5/05. **NLM** W1; VI762H. **[CCC].**
Ind/Abst Crim. Justice Abstr.; EMBASE; Health Plan. Adminis.; Index Med. (spring 1986-); Int. Nurs. Index; Linguist. Lang. Behav. Abstr.; Psychol. Abstr. (1986-); PsycINFO (1990-); PsycLit; Sage Fam. Stud. Abstr.; Sage Urban Stud. Abstr; Soc. Plann. Policy Dev. Abstr.; Sociol. Abstr.

US/1064-5071
VIOLENT KIN!. [Violent kin!]. (1989)-. Periodical. English. qt. $11.95 US; $13.75 other. Violent Kin!, c/o Paul Meredith, 5065 Westwood Lake Drive, Miami FL 33165. **Tel** (305)271-3429. **ED** Paul Meredith. **DD** 929. **Bk Rev**, (Qty: 12-15).

US
VITAL STATISTICS IN CORRECTIONS. **See** Law-Abstracting, Bibliographies and Statistics.

CN/0713-0333
VOICE (OTTAWA). (THE VOICE / ELIZABETH FRY SOCIETY OF OTTAWA.). [Voice]. **Added/Corp** Elizabeth Fry Society of Ottawa. (1975)-. Periodical. English. qt. Free to members. Elizabeth Fry Society - Ottawa, 195A Bank Street, Ottawa Ontario K2P 1W7 Canada. **Tel** (613)238-1171. **DD** 365/.7/06071384. ***Continues** Newsletter (Elizabeth Fry Society of Ottawa).*

US/0894-3826
WASHINGTON CRIME NEWS SERVICES' CORPORATE SECURITY DIGEST. ***Title Change.*** [Wash. Crime News Serv. corp. secur. dig.]. **VFOAT** Corporate Security Digest. Vol. 1, No. 1 (Sept. 7, 1987)-(Jan. 1995). Periodical. English. wk. Washington Crime News Services, 3918 Prosperity Avenue, Suite 318, Fairfax VA 22031-3334. **Tel** (703)573-1600, (800)422-9267, FAX (703)573-1604. **ED** Betty Bosarge. **LC** HV6769; .W37. **DD** 364.973/05. **Bk Rev.** available on microfilm and microfiche from University Microfilms International (UMI). ***Formed by the union of** Computer Crime Digest, 0889-5694 **and** Washington Crime News Services' Security Systems Digest, 0037-069X. **Continued by** Security Director's Digest.*
Desc: Report on national issues affecting the corporate, commercial, industrial, institutional, governmental and military security industries. Keeps security professionals informed about computer security, espionage, terrorism, white collar crime, intrusion systems and more.

US/0889-5708
WASHINGTON CRIME NEWS SERVICES' NARCOTICS CONTROL DIGEST. ***Title Change.*** [Wash. Crime News Serv. narc. control dig.]. **VFOAT** Narcotics Control Digest. Vol. 1 (Jan. 6. 1971)-(Jan. 1995). Periodical. English. bw. Washington Crime News Services, 3918 Prosperity Avenue, Suite 318, Fairfax VA 22031-3334. **Tel** (703)573-1600, (800)422-9267, FAX (703)573-1604. **ED** Betty B Bosarge. **DD** 364. **Bk Rev. Circ:** 1,000. available in microform from University Microfilms International (UMI). ***Continues** Bulletin du Groupement Europeen Pour la Recherche Scientifique en Stomatologie & Odontologie, 0303-7479. **Absorbed by** Narcotics Enforcement and Prevention Digest.*
Desc: Information for supervisors, investigators, legislators and policy makers. Includes the latest news of federal, state and local activities, court decisions, etc.
Ind/Abst Crim. Justice Period. Index.

US/0889-5716
WASHINGTON CRIME NEWS SERVICES' ORGANIZED CRIME DIGEST. [Wash. Crime News Serv. organ. crime dig.]. **Added/Corp** Washington Crime News Services (U.S.). **VFOAT** Organized Crime Digest. Vol. 1, No. 1 (Jan. 1980)-. Periodical. English. Twenty-four times a year. $295.00 (one year), $500.00 (two year), $700.00 (three year). Washington Crime News Services, 3918 Prosperity Avenue, Suite 318, Fairfax VA 22031-3334. **Tel** (703)573-1600, (800)422-9267, FAX (703)573-1604. **LC** HV6446; .W37. **DD** 364.1/06/073.
Desc: An independent news summary of combative efforts against organized crime activities. Professional literature, training and career development opportunities. Enforcement trends and in-depth analysis of legislative and judicial actions.

US/0889-5732
WASHINGTON CRIME NEWS SERVICES' TRAINING AIDS DIGEST. *Title Change.* [Wash. Crime News Serv. train. aids dig.]. **Added/Corp** Washington Crime News Services. **VFOAT** Training Aids Digest. (1976)-(Jan. 1995). Periodical. English. mo. Washington Crime News Services, 3918 Prosperity Avenue, Suite 318, Fairfax VA 22031-3334. **Tel** (703)573-1600, (800)422-9267, FAX (703)573-1604. **DD** 364. *Absorbed by CJ Management & Training Digest.*
Desc: A monthly wrap-up of training systems available to all components of the criminal justice systems. Coverage includes courses, workshops, seminars, conferences, films, literature, products, events and job opportunities for criminal justice educators.

US/0884-5107
WASHINGTON CRIMINAL JUSTICE REPORT'S CRIME VICTIMS DIGEST. *Title Change.* [Wash. Crim. Justice Rep. crime vict. dig.]. **VFOAT** Crime Victims Digest. Vol. 1, No. 1 (Oct. 1983)-(Jan. 1995). English. mo. Washington Crime News Services, 3918 Prosperity Avenue, Suite 318, Fairfax VA 22031-3334. **Tel** (703)573-1600, (800)422-9267, FAX (703)573-1604. **ED** Susan Kernus. **LC** KF9763.A15; W37. **DD** 344.73/03288; 347.3043288. **Bk Rev** available on microfilm from University Microfilms International (UMI). *Absorbed by Community Policing Digest.*

US
WASHINGTON JAILS : A REPORT TO THE LEGISLATURE. Main/Corp Washington (State). Adult Corrections Division. **VFOAT** Washington Jails: A Report to the Washington State Legislature. English. Department of Social and Health Services / Washington, Mail Stop OB-41K, Olympia WA 98504. **LC** HV7297; .A3. **DD** /65/.9797. *Continues Jail Inspection Report.*

US/1053-0932
WEBB REPORT : A NEWSLETTER ON SEXUAL HARASSMENT BY SUSAN L. WEBB, THE. [Webb rep.]. (19??)-. Newsletter. English. ir. $120.00 (1 year), $180.00 (2 year), $240.00 (3 year). Premiere Publishing Limited, 145 NW 85th Street, Suite 103, Seattle WA 98117. **Tel** (206)782-7015. **DD** 305.

US/0891-6721
WHITE-COLLAR CRIME REPORTER, THE. [White-collar crime report.]. Vol. 1, No. 1 (Apr. 1987)-. Periodical. English. Ten times a year. $425.00. Andrews Publications Inc., 1646 West Chester Pike, PO Box 1000, Westtown PA 19395. **Tel** (610)399-6600, (800)345-1101, FAX (610)399-6610. **ED** John Lichtenberger. **LC** KF9350.A15; W48. **DD** 344.
Desc: Provides timely analysis of current developments in a variety of subject areas within white-collar practice.
Ind/Abst Crim. Justice Abstr. (199?-).

GW/0173-3303
WIRTSCHAFTSSCHUTZ + SICHERHEITSTECHNIK. [Wirtsch.schutz Sicherheitstech.]. **VFOAT** Wirtschaftsschutz und Sicherheitstechnik; W und S; W + S. (1980)-. Periodical. German. Ten times a year. DM252.40 Germany; DM262.40 other. Kriminalistik Verlag GmbH, IM Weiher 10, D-69121 Heidelberg Germany. **Tel** 011 49 6221 489259, FAX 011 49 6221 489279. (**Subscription address:** Verlagsgrupps Dr. A Huethig, Postfach 102869, D 69018 Heidelberg Germany) **LC** HV8290; .W57. **DD** 658.4/73/05. Index available. **Bk Rev. Ad Acc. Circ:** 5,300 (ctrl).
Desc: Covers the entire spectrum of commercial security, from white-collar crime to industrial espionage. Reports on new technological developments and thus aids communication between manufacturer and user.

US/0897-4454
WOMEN & CRIMINAL JUSTICE. [Women crim. justice]. **VFOAT** Women and Criminal Justice. Vol. 1, No. 1 (1989)-. Periodical. English. sa. $75.00 US; $105.00 other. The Haworth Press Inc, 10 Alice Street, Binghamton NY 13904-1580. **Tel** (607)722-5857, (800)3-HAWORTH, FAX (607)722-1424. **ED** Clarice Feinman (editor's address: Department of Criminal Justice, CN 4700, Trenton State College, Trenton, NJ 08650). **LC** HV7231; .W65. **DD** 364. **CODEN** WCJUER. **Bk Rev. Ad Acc. Pr Rev. Acid Free. Circ:** 229. available on microfilm and microfiche from University Microfilms International (UMI). Documents available from Haworth Document Delivery Service.
Desc: Original articles, debates, and discussions on current issues and practices and critical reviews of new legislative and court decisions. From time-to-time, special issues will be published that will focus on highly important topics. Provides scholars and practitioners with a single forum devoted to this emerging and critical new specialty area in the fields of criminal, justice, women.
Ind/Abst Crim. Justice Abstr. (199?-); PAIS Int. Print; Sage Fam. Stud. Abstr.; Soc. Plann. Policy Dev. Abstr.; Soc. Work Abstr. [Select. Cov.]; Women Stud. Abstr.

US
WOMEN POLICE MAGAZINE. English. Four times a year. $25.00 US; $35.00 other. International Association of Women Police, 5800-A North Sharon Amity Road BX252, Charlotte NC 28215. **Tel** (704)599-1455, FAX (704)599-1455. **ED** Mona Moore Mitchell. **Bk Rev,** (Qty: 4/year). **Ad Acc. Pr Rev. Circ:** 4,000 (ctrl).
Desc: By and about women police officers and professionalization of law enforcement and police services.

US/0160-5240
WORK RELEASE FOR MISDEMEANANTS IN MINNESOTA. Main/Corp Minnesota. Dept. of Corrections. Division of Research and Planning. English. an. Minnesota Department of Correction, 450 North Syndicate Street, Bigelow Building, Suite 300, St Paul MN 55104. **Tel** (612)642-0282, FAX (612)642-0223. **LC** HV7273; .A314B. **DD** 365/.65.

US/1055-0305
WOUND BALLISTICS REVIEW. (WOUND BALLISTICS REVIEW : JOURNAL OF THE INTERNATIONAL WOUND BALLISTICS ASSOCIATION / INTERNATIONAL WOUND BALLISTICS ASSOCIATION.). [Wound ballist. rev.]. **Added/Corp** International Wound Ballistics Association. Vol. 1, No. 1 (Winter 1991)-. Periodical. English. qt (4 issues). $40.00 US; $66.00 other. International Wound Ballistics Association, PO Box 634, Pinole CA 94564. **Tel** (510)724-1003. **LC** RA1121; .W68. **DD** 617.1/45/005. **NLM** W1; WO935G.

CN/0830-9221
YOUTH UPDATE (REXDALE, ONT.). (YOUTH UPDATE.). [Youth update]. **Added/Corp** Thistletown Regional Centre. (Spring 1983)-. Periodical. English. Three times a year (Apr., Sep., Dec.). 10.00CAN$ one year, 18.00CAN$ two year, 26.00CAN$ three year. Youth Update, 51 Panorama Court, Rexdale Ontario M9V 4L8 Canada. **Tel** (416)326-0690, FAX (416)326-0644. **ED** Jalal Shamsie and Cathy Hluchy. **DD** 364.3/6/05. Index available. cum. index. **Bk Rev. Circ:** 500 (ctrl).
Desc: Provides abstracts of clinically relevant articles related to antisocial behaviour in youth.

●RU
ZAKONNOST. Added/Corp Russia (Federation). Prokuratura. Russia (Federation). Ministerstvo Pechati i Informatsii. (1992)-. Periodical. Russian. mo. $44.00. (**Subscription address:** Victor Kamkin, Inc. 4956 Boiling Brook Pkwy., Rockville, MD 20852) *Continues Sotsialisticheskaia Zakonnost.*

LEGAL AID

●AT/1037-969X
ALTERNATIVE LAW JOURNAL.
Added/Corp Monash University. Faculty of Law. Vol. 17, No. 1 (Feb. 1992)-. English. bm. 63.00Aus$ (institution), 48.00Aus$ (individual) Australia; 85.00Aus$ (other). Legal Service Bulletin Co-Operative Ltd, Faculty of Law, Monash University, Clayton Victoria 3168 Australia. **Tel** 011 61 3 5440974, FAX (03)563-7820. *Continues Legal Service Bulletin.*
Ind/Abst APAIS, Aust. Public Aff. Inf. Ser. (1992-).

US/0734-1822
BALANCING THE SCALES. (BALANCING THE SCALES / LEGAL SERVICES OF NORTHEASTERN WISCONSIN.). Began publication with: V. 1, No. 1 (July/Aug. 1979). Periodical. English. qt. Legal Services of Northeastern Wisconsin, 417 Pine Street, Green Bay WI 54301. **Circ:** 3,000 (ctrl).

US/0888-1537
BIFOCAL. [Bifocal]. **Added/Corp** ABA Commission on Legal Problems of the Elderly. American Bar Association. Committee on Delivery of Legal Services to the Elderly. **VFOAT** Bar Associations in Focus on Aging and the Law. (19??)-. Periodical. English. Four times a year. $15.00. Common Legal Problems of the Elderly, American Bar Association, 1800 M Street Northwest, Washington DC 20036. **ED** Norma B. Gregerman. **LC** KF390.A4; B54. **DD** 344.73/0326; 347.304326. **Bk Rev.** **Circ:** 1,200.
Desc: Covers areas of the law of concern to senior citizens.

CN/0701-1598
BULLETIN DE L'AIDE JURIDIQUE. [Bull. aide jurid.]. **Added/Corp** Commission des Services Juridiques. Vol. 1 (Jan 1974)-. Bulletin. French. mo.
Ind/Abst Point Repere (1983-1990).

US/0009-868X
CLEARINGHOUSE REVIEW. [Clgh. rev.]. **Added/Corp** National Clearinghouse for Legal Services (U.S.) National Institute for Education in Law and Poverty (U.S.). (Sept. 1967)-. Periodical. English. Twelve times a year. $75.00 US; $95.00 other. National Clearinghouse for Legal Services, 205 West Monroe Street 2nd Floor, Chicago IL 60606. **Tel** (312)263-3830. **ED** Lucy Moss. **LC** KF390.5.P6; A163. **DD** 349.73/05; 347.3005. Index available. cum. index. **Bk Rev. Ad Acc. Circ:** 8,700. available on microfilm and microfiche from University Microfilms International (UMI); available on an online database.
Desc: Articles on poverty law, including health, welfare, employment, youth and consumer law, developments of currently litigated cases, and reviews of related documents and manuals.
Ind/Abst Curr. Law Index (1980-); Index Leg. Period.; Law Office Inf. Serv.; Leg. Resour. Index (1980-); LegalTrac (1980-).

AT/0811-6407
DEFENDER NORTH MELBOURNE.
[DefenderNorth Melb.]. **Added/Corp** Australian Defence Association. (1983)-. Periodical. English. Four times a year (Mar., June, Sept., Dec.). 15.00Aus$ Australia; 20.00Aus$ other. Australia Defence Association, PO Box 1131, Doncaster East 3109 Australia. **Tel** 011 61 3 8426203, FAX 011 61 3 8418413. **ED** Malcolm Kennedy. **DD** 355.00994. **Bk Rev,** (Qty: approx. 20/year). **Ad Acc, Adv Mgr:** M. J. O'Connor, **Tel** 03 8426203. **Circ:** 900. *Continues A.D.A. Journal, 0157-4310.*
Desc: Comment and opinion on Australian national defence and security.

US/0276-5365
DIRECTORY OF LEGAL AID AND DEFENDER OFFICES IN THE UNITED STATES, THE. [Dir. leg. aid def. off. U. S.]. **Added/Corp** National Legal Aid and Defender Association. **VFOAT** Directory of Legal Aid and Defender Offices in the United States and Territories. (19??)-. English. an (Nov. in odd years). $15.00 (members); $30.00 (non-members) latest edition. National Legal Aid and Defender's Association, 1625 K Street Northwest, 8th Floor, Washington DC 20006. **Tel** (202)452-0620. **LC** KF336; .A332. **DD** 347.73/17/025; 347.30717025. *Continues Directory (National Legal Aid and Defender Association). Directory.*

US
DIRECTORY OF PRIVATE BAR INVOLVEMENT PROGRAMS, THE.
Added/Corp Private Bar Involvement Project (American Bar Association) American Bar Association. Consortium on Legal Services and the Public. (1985)-. Directory. English. an $7.95. American Bar Association, 750 North Lake Shore Drive, Chicago IL 60611. **Tel** (312)988-5522, (312)988-5241, FAX (312)988-5528, telex 270593. **LC** KF336; .A336. **DD** 347.73/17; 347.30717. *Continues Private Bar Involvement Directory, 0741-7616.*

CN/0832-9370
EQUITY (TORONTO. 1986). See Political Science-Civil Rights.

AT/0817-3532
FREEDOM OF INFORMATION REVIEW.
[Freedom inf. rev.]. (1986)-. Periodical. English. bm. 25.00Aus$ (combined with Alternative Law Journal); 35.00Aus$ Australia; 47.00Aus$ other. Legal Service Bulletin Co-Operative Ltd, Faculty of Law, Monash University, Clayton Victoria 3168 Australia. **Tel** 011 61 3 5440974, FAX (03)563-7820. **DD** 342.940853.

AT
HEARSAY : LEGAL AID PRACTICE NOTES AND INFORMATION BULLETIN OF THE LEGAL AID COMMISSION OF WESTERN AUSTRALIA. Main/Corp Legal Aid Commission of Western Australia. (19??)-. Bulletin. English. qt. Free. Director of Legal Aid, 105 Saint George's Terrace, GPO Box L916, Perth Western Australia 6001 Australia. **Tel** (09)261-6222, FAX (09)321-8785. **ED** Jeremy Armitage. **DD** 347.941/017/05; 349.41071705. **Circ:** 4,000 (ctrl).
Desc: News of developments within the Legal Aid Commission of Western Australia.

US/0271-2032
LAW OF THE LAND. Main/Corp Legal Assistance of North Dakota, Inc. **VAT** Law of the Legal Assistance of North Dakota. English. Free. Legal Assistance of North Dakota Inc, PO Box 2419, Bismarck ND 58502. **LC** KFN8684.5.P6; L43. **DD** 344.784/03258.

Law — Legal Aid

UK
LEGAL AID: ANNUAL REPORTS OF THE LAW SOCIETY AND OF THE LORD CHANCELLOR'S ADVISORY COMMITTEE. Main/Corp Law Society (Great Britain). **Added/Corp** Great Britain. Advisory Committee on Legal Aid. (1974/75)-. English. an. 49 High Holborn, London WC1V 6HB England. **LC** KD512.A13; L39. **DD** 362.5/8. *Continues Legal Aid and Advice.*

US/0147-9458
LEGAL AID NEWS (NEW YORK), THE. (LEGAL AID NEWS.). **Added/Corp** Legal Aid Society (New York, N.Y.). Vol. 1 (May 1975)-. Periodical. English. bm (6 issues). Free on request. Legal Aid Society, 15 Park Row, New York NY 10030. **LC** KF337.N45; L42. **DD** 347/.747/01.

US
LEGAL ASSISTANCES NOTEBOOK. (19??)-. English. $85.00. ASAP Publications / California, 1081 Camino del Rio South, Suite 222, San Diego CA 92108. **Tel** (619)297-2727, FAX (619)297-2770.

●CN/1187-8754
MANITOBA LEGAL SERVICES DIRECTORY. [Manit. leg. serv. dir.]. **Added/Corp** Community Legal Education Association (Winnipeg, Man.). (1992)-. Directory. English (summaries and/or abstracts in French). $15.00. Community Legal Education Association, 304-283 Bannatyne Avenue, Winnipeg Manitoba R3B 3B2 Canada. **DD** 340/.025/7127. *Continues Manitoba Directory of Legal Services., 0841-2537.*

CN/0715-4186
NEWSLETTER - NATIONAL LEGAL AID RESEARCH CENTRE. (NEWSLETTER / NATIONAL LEGAL AID RESEARCH CENTRE). [Newsl. - Natl. Leg. Aid Res. Cent.]. **Added/Corp** National Legal Aid Research Centre (Canada). **VFOAT** Letter-Communique. **VAT** Letter-Communique - Centre National d'Information et de Recherche sur l'Aide Juridique. No. 1 (1981)-. Newsletter. English (French). qt. National Legal Aid Research Centre, Tabaret Hall, University of Ottawa, Ottawa Ontario K1N 6N5 Canada. **DD** 362/.5/8/0971.

US/0739-9111
NLADA CORNERSTONE. (THE NLADA CORNERSTONE / NATIONAL LEGAL AID AND DEFENDER ASSOCIATION.). [NLADA cornerstone]. **Added/Corp** National Legal Aid and Defender Association. **VFOAT** Cornerstone. **VAT** National Legal Aid and Defender Association Cornerstone. (June 1980)-. Periodical. English. Four times a year. $20.00. National Legal Aid Defenders Association, 1625 K Street Northwest, 8th Floor, Washington DC 20006. **Tel** (202)452-0620. **ED** Melanie L. Herman. **LC** KF336.A3; N53. **DD** 347.73/17; 347.30717. **Bk Rev**. ctrl circ. *Supersedes National Legal Aid and Defender Association. NLADA Washington Memo, 0196-1624.*

US/0270-8884
NOLSLETTER. Main/Corp Northeast Ohio Legal Services. **VAT** Northeast Ohio Legal Services Letter; NOLS Letter. (19??)-. English. NOLSletter, 804 Metropolitan Tower, Youngstown OH 44503. **LC** KFO84.5.P6; A136. **DD** 344.771/03258; 347.71043258.

US
POVERTY LAW REPORT. V. 1- Mar. 1973-. Periodical. English. Five times a year. $15.00. Southern Poverty Law Center, 400 Washington Avenue, Montgomery AL 36104. **Tel** (205)264-0286. **ED** H Randall Williams. **Circ**: 90,000 (ctrl). **Desc**: To defend rights of poor and to educate public as to their rights.

UK
REPORT OF THE LAW SOCIETY OF SCOTLAND ON THE LEGAL AID SCHEME. Main/Corp Law Society of Scotland. **VFOAT** Annual Report on the Scottish Legal Aid Scheme. English. an. **LC** KDC260.A13; L38. **DD** 347.411/012. *Continues Law Society of Scotland. Report on the Legal Aid Scheme.*

AT
REPORT OF THE LEGAL AID REVIEW COMMITTEE. Main/Corp Australia. Parliament. Legal Aid Review Committee. 1974-. English. $2.00. **LC** J905; .L3 subser.

II/0571-2726
REPORT OF THE SESSION - ASIAN-AFRICAN LEGAL CONSULTATIVE COMMITTEE. Main/Conf Asian African Legal Consultative Committee. 1st (1957)-. English.
Ind/Abst Index Foreign Leg. Per.

MARITIME LAW

CN/0703-3109
ALBERTA REPORTS (FREDERICTON, N.B. : BOUND CUMULATION). (ALBERTA REPORTS.). [Alta. rep.]. **Added/Corp** Alberta. Court of Appeal. Law Society of Alberta. Vol. 1 (1977)-. English. ir. Price varies. Maritime Law Book Ltd, PO Box 302, Fredericton New Brunswick, E3B 4Y9 Canada. **Tel** (506)453-9921, (800)561-0220. **LC** KEA104; .A24. **DD** 347.1230843.

US/0160-6786
AMC. AMERICAN MARITIME CASES. (AMERICAN MARITIME CASES.). [AMC, Am. marit. cases]. **Added/Corp** Maritime Law Association of the United States. Association of Average Adjusters of the United States. **VFOAT** AMC. Vol. 1, No. 1 (Jan. 1923)-. Periodical. English. Eleven times a year (10 issues and 1 bound volume). Price varies. American Maritime Cases, 28 East 21st Street, Baltimore MD 21218. **Tel** (410)752-2939, FAX (410)625-1174. **ED** Cahrles E. Quandt and Elliott B. Nixon. Index available. cum. index. **Ad Acc. Circ**: 1,200.
Desc: News and information that covers all aspects of maritime law.

US
ANCHOR NEWS. Added/Corp Manitowoc Maritime Museum. Manitowoc Submarine Memorial Association. (Oct. 1971)-. Periodical. English. Six times a year. $1.50. Manitowoc Maritime Museum, 75 Maritime Avenue, Manitowoc WI 54220. **Tel** (414)684-0218.
Ind/Abst Am. Hist. Life.

FR
ANNUAIRE DE DROIT MARITIME ET AERO-SPATIAL. Vol. 9 (1987)-. French. an. Editions A Pedone, 13 rue Soufflot, 75005 Paris France. **Tel** 011 33 1 43540597. *Continues Annuaire de Droit Maritime et Aerien, 0395-0468.*
Ind/Abst Index Foreign Leg. Per.

US/0360-0750
ANNUAL REPORT - ADVISORY COMMITTEE ON THE LAW OF THE SEA. Main/Corp United States. Advisory Committee on the Law of the Sea. English. an. US Department of State, 2201 C Street NW, Room 5819, Washington DC 20520. **Tel** (202)647-9859. **LC** JX4422.U5; U53A. **DD** 353.008/232.

FR/0767-1288
BULLETIN OFFICIEL DU MINISTERE DELEGUE CHARGE DE LA MER. Main/Corp France. Ministere Delegue Charge de La Mer. Bulletin. French. bm. Service des Ventes de l'Imprimerie Nationale, 2 rue Paul-Hervieu, 75732 Paris Cedex 15 France. **LC** KJV2784.59; .F7.

FR
BULLETIN OFFICIEL DU MINISTERE DES TRANSPORTS MARINE MARCHANDE (FRANCE). Main/Corp France. Ministere des Transports. Bulletin. French. tm. Service des Ventes de l'Imprimerie Nationale, 2 rue Paul-Hervieu, 75732 Paris Cedex 15 France. **DD** 343.44/096/02636; 344. 4039602636.

UK/0265-427X
CARGO CLAIMS ANALYSIS. *Ceased.* Ceased Vol. 6, No. 8 (Sept. 1989). Periodical. English. mo. Chiltern Publishing, 18 Burgess Wood Road, Beaconsfield Bucks HP9 1EQ England. **Tel** 011 44 494 673062, FAX 011 44 494 678914. **LC** K1176.A13; C37. **DD** 343/.096/05. **Ad Acc**. available on microfilm from University Microfilms International (UMI).

BE
CMI NEWS LETTER. Added/Corp International Maritime Committee. **VFOAT** C.M.I. News Letter. (19??)-. Periodical. English. qt. Kr545.00, $87.00. Scandinavian University Press, PO Box 2959 Toeyen, N 0608 Oslo 6 Norway. **Tel** 011 47 2 2575400, FAX 011 47 2 2575353, telex 71896 UROR N. **(Subscription address:** Scandinavian University Press, 200 Meacham Ave., Elmont NY 11003.**) LC** K1150.A13; C55. **DD** 343/.096/05; 342.39605.

NO
CMI NEWSLETTER AND YEARBOOK. Newsletter. English. qt. Kr545.00, $87.00. Scandinavian University Press, PO Box 2959 Toeyen, N 0608 Oslo 6 Norway. **Tel** 011 47 2 2575400, FAX 011 47 2 2575353, telex 71896 UROR N. **(Subscription address:** Scandinavian University Press, 200 Meacham Ave., Elmont NY 11003.**) ED** Henry Voet-Genicot. **Pr Rev.**
Desc: The object of CMI is to contribute by all appropriate means and activities to the unification of maritime and commercial law, maritime customs, usages and practices. Forty-four National Maritime Law Associations are members of the Committee.

US
CODE OF FEDERAL REGULATIONS. 33, NAVIGATION AND NAVIGABLE WATERS. Added/Corp United States. Office of the Federal Register. **VFOAT** Navigation and Navigable Waters; CFR. 33, Navigation Navigable Waters. (19??)-. Government Publication. English. an. Price varies, also comes with Code of Federal Code of Regulations Complete Set. Superintendent of Documents, US Government Printing Office, Washington DC 20402. **Tel** (202)275-3328, FAX (202)786-2377. **(Subscription address:** US Government Bookstore / O'Neil Building, 2023 3rd Avenue North, Birmingham AL 35203.**)** available on microfiche (Vols. for (1984-) distributed to some depository libraries).
Desc: Special edition of the Federal Register, containing a codification of documents.

US
CODE OF FEDERAL REGULATIONS. 46, SHIPPING. Added/Corp United States. Office of the Federal Register. **VFOAT** Shipping; CRF. 46, Shipping. (19??)-. English. an. Superintendent of Documents, US Government Printing Office, Washington DC 20402. **Tel** (202)275-3328, FAX (202)786-2377. available on microfiche.
Desc: Special edition of the Federal Register, containing a codification of documents.

US
DECISIONS OF THE FEDERAL MARITIME COMMISSION. Main/Corp United States. Federal Maritime Commission. **VFOAT** Federal Maritime Commission Reports. Vol. 7 (Sept. 1961 to Feb. Vol. 7 (Sept. 1961 to Feb. 1964)-. English. Federal Maritime Commission, 1100 L Street NW, Washington DC 20573. **Tel** (202)523-5773. **(Subscription address:** Superintendent of Documents, Government Printing Office, Washington, DC 20402-9325) **LC** KF2606; .A553. **DD** 343/.73/096402646. *Continues Decisions of the Federal Maritime Board, and Maritime Administration, Department of Commerce.*

US
DECISIONS OF THE MARITIME SUBSIDY BOARD, MARITIME ADMINISTRATION, DEPARTMENT OF COMMERCE. Main/Corp United States. Maritime Subsidy Board. **VFOAT** Maritime Subsidy Board, Maritime Administration, Department of Commerce Reports. Vol. 1, (Aug. 1961 to Sept. 1964)-. Government Publication. English. ir. US Department of Commerce, 14th Street & Constitution Avenue NW, Washington DC 20230. **Tel** (202)482-2000, FAX (202)482-3772.

GR
DIARKES KODIX NAUTERGATIKES & NAUTILIAKES NOMOTHESIAS / EKDIDETAI KAI DIEUTHYNETAI HYPO TOU INSTITOUTOU ERGATIKON MELETON, SYNTASSETAI HYOP EPITROPES EIDIKON. VFOAT Diarkes Kodix Nautergatikes Kai Nautiliakes Nomothesias; Nautiliake & Nautergatike Nomothesia; Nautiliake Kai Nautergatike Nomothesia. Greek, Modern. mo. Tzortz 20-22, Athens Greece.

UK
DIGEST : LLOYD'S LAW REPORTS. (1966/1970)-. English. an. Price varies. Lloyd's of London Press Ltd, Sheepen Place, Colchester, Essex, CO3 3LP England. **Tel** 011 44 206 772113, US: (212)529-9500, US: (800)955-6937, FAX 011 44 206 772880, US: (212)529-9826, telex 987321 LLOYDS G. **(Subscription address:** Lloyd's of London Press Inc. / North America, 611 Broadway, Suite 308, New York NY 10012.**) LC** KD1815.3; .H3. **DD** 343/.41/096. *Continues Henley, Henry Patten, Ed. Digest No. [1]- of Lloyd's List Law Reports.*
Desc: Provides a concise summary of the cases reported in the appropriate volumes.

IT/0012-348X
DIRITTO MARITTIMO. [Dir. maritt.]. (1899)-. Periodical. Italian (English and French). qt. L200000 Italy; L230000 other. Dirmar SNC, Via Rome 10 2, 16121 Genoa Italy. **Tel** 011 39 10 586441, FAX 011 39 10 594805, telex 270687. **UDC** 347. Index available.
Desc: Italian and foreign doctrine on jurisprudence and maritime law.

FR/0012-642X
DROIT MARITIME FRANCAIS, LE. French. mo. 1355F (add 140.00F postage) France; 1470F (add 265.00F postage) other. Le Droit Maritime Francais, 190 Boulevard Haussmann, Paris 75008 France. **Tel** (1)-45-63-11-55, telex NAVIMAR 290131 F. **ED** S Marpaud. Index available.
Ind/Abst Index Foreign Leg. Per.

UK
ENCYCLOPEDIA OF ARBITRATION LAW. English. ir. $265.00. Lloyd's of London Press Inc., 611 Broadway/Suite 308, New York NY 10012. **Tel** (212)529-9500, FAX (212)529-9826, telex 7105812659.

Bk Rev.
Desc: 242 arbitration cases from 1838 to the present day, including all the leading English cases. Cases are evaluated and facts and summaries are edited.

GR
EPITHEORESIS NAUTILIAKOU DIKAIOU. Year 1- (No. 1-); Mar. 1973-. Greek, Modern. 500.00. **LC** K5; .P59.

US
FEDERAL MARITIME COMMISSION DIGEST SERVICE. (Sept. 1970)-. English. Ten times a year. $300.00 (Includes supplements). Hawkins Publishing Company, PO Box 480, Mayo MD 21106. **Tel** (410)798-1677. Index available (Free). available in Loose-leaf.
Desc: Analysis of reports of the Federal Maritime Commission, relating to the Shipping and Merchant Marine Acts.

US/0735-8679
INDEX OF CURRENT REGULATIONS OF THE MARITIME ADMINISTRATION, MARITIME SUBSIDY BOARD, NATIONAL SHIPPING AUTHORITY.
Main/Corp United States. Maritime Administration. Revised as of Mar. 1, 1962-. English. an. US Department of Transportation / Maritime Administration, Room 721, Washington DC 20590. **Tel** (202)366-5807. **LC** KF2602.278; .U54. **DD** 343.73/096/02638; 347. 3039602638. ***Continues*** *Index of Current Regulations of The Federal Maritime Board, Maritime Administration, National Shipping Authority.*

UK/0268-0106
INTERNATIONAL JOURNAL OF ESTUARINE AND COASTAL LAW. ***Title Change.*** **VFOAT** Journal of Estuarine and Coastal Law. Vol. 1, No. 1 (Feb. 1986)-(19??). Periodical. English. qt. Graham & Trotman Ltd, Sterling House, 66 Wilson Road, London SW1V 1DE England. **Tel** 44 71 8211123. **LC** K9; .N845. **DD** 346.04/6917; 342.646917. **CODEN** IJELE6. available on microfilm and microfiche from University Microfilms International (UMI). ***Continued by*** *The International Journal of Marine and Coastal Law, 0927-3522.*
Desc: Covers all aspects of the law and coastal management. It carries major articles and provides a vigorous current legal developments sections supplied by a worldwide network of regular correspondents.
Ind/Abst GeoRef (?-?); J. Plan. Lit. (?-?); Leg. Resour. Index (?-?); LegalTrac (1980-?).

●UK
INTERNATIONAL MARITIME LAW. (1994)-. English. Ten times a year. £185.00 Europe; £194.00 other. Sweet & Maxwell Ltd., South Quay Plaza, 183 Marsh Wall, London E14 9FT England. **Tel** 011 44 264 342899, FAX 011 44 264 342723, telex 929089 ITPINF G.

JA
JITSUYO KAIJI ROPPO. **Main/Corp** Japan. Japanese. 2500. Seizando Shoten, 4-51 Minami-Motocho, Shinjuku-ku 160 Tokyo Japan. **LC** LAW.

US/0022-2410
JOURNAL OF MARITIME LAW AND COMMERCE. [J. marit. law commer.]. (1969)-. Periodical. English. Four times a year. $95.00 US; $125.00 others. Anderson Publishing Company, 2035 Reading Road, Cincinnati OH 45202. **Tel** (513)421-4142, (800)582-7295. **(Subscription address:** Anderson Publishing Company, PO Box 1576, Cincinnati OH 45201.**) ED** John P. McMahon. **LC** K10; .O88. **DD** 347.7/5/05. Index available. **Bk Rev. Ad Acc. Pr Rev. Circ:** 1,300 (ctrl). available on microfilm and microfiche from University Microfilms International (UMI). Documents available from The Genuine Article.
Desc: A specialized journal devoted primarily to shipping law practices of particular interest to maritime administrators, academic researchers and educators, maritime organizations and commerce. The journal provides an objective forum for the discussion and analysis of current cases and litigation.
Ind/Abst Contents Recent Econ. J. (1974, 1975, 1981-1987-); Curr. Law Index (1980-); Index Foreign Leg. Per.; Index Leg. Period.; Leg. Resour. Index (1980-); LegalTrac (1980-); PAIS Int. Print (1991-); Res. Alert [Full Cov.]; Soc. Sci. Cit. Index [Full Cov.].

II/0377-0494
JOURNAL OF SHIPPING, CUSTOMS & TRANSPORT LAWS. Periodical. English. ir. 45.00. Milan Law Publishers, PO Box 4591, 15/2 Navjivan 8, Bombay India. **DD** 343/.54/09605.

BE
JURISPRUDENCE DU PORT D'ANVERS. **VFOAT** Recjtspraak der Haven Van Antwerpen. (19??)-. Dutch (French; summaries and/or abstracts in French). tm. 1850F. Lloyd Anversois SA, Eiermarkt 23, Antwerpen Belgium. **Tel** (3)234 05 50. Index available. **Bk Rev. Circ:** 1,000. ***Continues*** *Jurisprudence du Port d'Anvers et des Autres Villes Commerciales et Industrielles de la Belgique.*
Desc: Contains verbatim reports of important judicial decisions in transport suppliers.

US
KNAUTH'S BENEDICT ON ADMIRALTY. (19??)-. English. ir. Price varies. Matthew Bender & Company Inc., 1275 Broadway, Albany NY 12204. **Tel** (800)833-9844, (518)487-3000.

US
LAW OF THE SEA BULLETIN. **Added/Corp** Law of the Sea Library. Office of the Special Representative of the Secretary-General for the Law of the Sea. United Nations. Office for Ocean Affairs and the Law of the Sea. No. 1 (Sept. 1983)-. Government Publication. English. sa. United Nations Publications, 2 United Nations Plaza, Room DC2 0853, Department 007C, New York NY 10017. **Tel** (212)963-8303, (800)253-9646. **LC** JX4408; .L344. **DD** 341.4/5/05.
Ind/Abst Aquat. Sci. Fish. Abstr. (Computer File); Ocean. Abstr.

US
LAW OF THE SEA INSTITUTE: WORKSHOP BOOKS. (1971)-. English. ir. $51.00. Law of the Sea Institute, University of Hawaii-Manoa, Richardson School of Law/Room 208, 2515 Dole Street, Honolulu HI 96822. **Tel** (808)956-6750, (808)956-3300, FAX (808)956-6402, telex 7431895.

US/0092-6426
LIMITS IN THE SEAS. [Limits seas]. **Added/Corp** United States. Dept. of State. Office of the Geographer. United States. Dept. of State. Office of Ocean Law and Policy. No. 1 (19??)-. English. ir. Free. Office of Geographer, 21st and C Street SW/Room 8742, Washington DC 20520. **Tel** (202)632-1428. **LC** JX4131; .L54. **DD** 341.44/8.
Ind/Abst Geogr. Abstr. Human Geogr. (?-?); Life Sci. Collect.

US
LLOYD'S AVIATION LAW. **VFOAT** Aviation Law. (June 1982)-. Periodical. English. sm. $415.00. Lloyd's of London Press Inc., 611 Broadway/Suite 308, New York NY 10012. **Tel** (212)529-9500, FAX (212)529-9826, telex 7105812659. **(Subscription address:** UK/ Sheepen Place, Colchester, Essex CO3 3LP England**) ED** Editors: George N. Tompkins, Jr., Claudia Fucigna. **LC** KF2400.A15; L56. **DD** 343.73/097; 347.30397. **Bk Rev. Circ:** 250.
Desc: A newsletter for lawyers, insurers and aviation industry executives worldwide that reports and comments on major cases in civil aviation; analyzes US and international court decisions; interprets their implications for the outcome of future cases and for the application of national and international law. It also monitors cases relating to jurisdiction, insurance, the Warsaw Convention and other international agreements affecting aviation-related industries and covers trends in product liability, anti-trust actions, deregulation, and damage awards.

US
LLOYD'S INSURANCE INTERNATIONAL. **See** Insurance.

UK/0024-5488
LLOYD'S LAW REPORTS. **VFOAT** Law Reports. Vol. 1 (1968)-. English. mo. $650.00. Lloyd's of London Press Ltd, Sheepen Place, Colchester, Essex, CO3 3LP England. **Tel** 011 44 206 772113, US: (212)529-9500, US: (800)955-6937, FAX 011 44 206 772880, US: (212)529-9826, telex 987321 LLOYDS G. **(Subscription address:** Lloyd's of London Press Inc. / North America, 611 Broadway, Suite 308, New York NY 10012.**) ED** M. d'Souza. **LC** KD1815.A2; L57. **DD** 343.4109/6/0264; 344.103960264. Index available. cum. index. **Ad Acc. Circ:** 2000. available on microfiche (subject indexes, citators, digests). ***Continues*** *Lloyd's List Law Reports.*
Desc: Provides verbatim reports of maritime and commercial cases and judgments in English, Scottish, Commonwealth and United States courts.

UK/0306-2945
LLOYD'S MARITIME AND COMMERCIAL LAW QUARTERLY. [Lloyd marit. commer. law q.]. **Main/Corp** Lloyd's (Firm). (May 1974)-. Periodical. English. qt. £73.00. Lloyd's of London Press Ltd, Sheepen Place, Colchester, Essex, CO3 3LP England. **Tel** 011 44 206 772113, US: (212)529-9500, US: (800)955-6937, FAX 011 44 206 772880, US: (212)529-9826, telex 987321 LLOYDS G. **(Subscription address:** Lloyd's of London Press Inc. / North America, 611 Broadway, Suite 308, New York NY 10012.**) ED** F.D. Rose. **LC** K12; .L6. **DD** 343.09/6/05. Index available. cum. index. **Circ:** 1,500. available on microfilm and microfiche from University Microfilms International (UMI).
Desc: Covers commercial and shipping law on an international scale. The editorial board, backed up by an international team of correspondents, ensures that each issue covers cases, judgments and decisions from all areas of the globe. A genuinely international journal, subscribers benefit from book reviews and a general information section noting international developments in the law, notable meetings and seminars. Also covers judgments and decisions from all areas together with analysis and comment for the practicing lawyer or commercial legal executive.
Ind/Abst Contents Recent Econ. J.; Curr. Law Index (1980-); Index Leg. Period.; Leg. Resour. Index (1980-); LegalTrac (1980-).

US
LLOYD'S MARITIME LAW. (198?)-. Periodical. English. sm. $345.00. Lloyd's of London Press Inc., 611 Broadway/Suite 308, New York NY 10012. **Tel** (212)529-9500, FAX (212)529-9826, telex 7105812659. **(Subscription address:** UK/ Sheepen Place, Colchester, Essex CO3 3LP England**) ED** Joseph C Sweeney, Chester D Hooper, and Jeff Myhre. **LC** K1150.A13; L56. **DD** 343/.096/05; 342.39605.
Desc: Reports on judicial and arbitration decisions, legal precedents, legislative developments and major economic trends that affect international shipping. Provides commentary on the long-term legal implications of court decisions and covers such specific issues as international jurisdictions, trends in damage awards, and liability for damage and injury. Read by lawyers, insurers and maritime industry executives in all parts of the world.

UK/0268-0696
LLOYD'S MARITIME LAW NEWSLETTER. [Lloyd's marit. law newsl.]. **VFOAT** LMLN. No. 1 (Nov. 1979)-. Periodical. English. sm (24 issues). £257.00. Lloyd's of London Press Ltd, Sheepen Place, Colchester, Essex, CO3 3LP England. **Tel** 011 44 206 772113, US: (212)529-9500, US: (800)955-6937, FAX 011 44 206 772880, US: (212)529-9826, telex 987321 LLOYDS G. **(Subscription address:** Lloyd's of London Press Inc. / North America, 611 Broadway, Suite 308, New York NY 10012.**) ED** Michael Daiches, Andrew Cooney (inhouse editor). **DD** 344.10396. **Circ:** 750.
Desc: Provides details of recent court decisions, judgments and new regulations within two weeks of their being heard, a benefit for any maritime or commercial lawyer, legal advisor or businessman who needs such information fast. Subscribers also receive exclusive details of recent London arbitrations, reports on legal decisions heard in South African, Canadian, American and occasionally Scandinavian courts, summaries of new legislation and current news items, and details of notable legal or commercial appointments.

CN/0226-8361
MARINE AFFAIRS BIBLIOGRAPHY. (MARINE AFFAIRS BIBLIOGRAPHY : A COMPREHENSIVE INDEX TO MARINE LAW AND POLICY LITERATURE.). [Mar. aff. bibliogr.]. **Added/Corp** Dalhousie Ocean Studies Programme. Dalhousie University. Faculty of Law. Vol. 1, No. 1 (Spring 1980)-. Bibliography. English (French). Five times a year (Published quarterly with annual cummulation). $95.00. Marine Affairs Bibliography, University of Virginia Law Library, Charlottesville VA 22901. **Tel** (804)924-3384, FAX (804)982-2232. **ED** Larry Wenger. **LC** Z6464.M2; W54; JX4408. **DD** 016.3414/5. **Circ:** 250.
Desc: A comprehensive index to marine law and policy literature.

US/0735-5912
MARINE POLICY REPORTS. ***Title Change.*** [Mar. policy rep.]. (1989-19??). Periodical. English. qt. Taylor & Francis Ltd., Rankine Road, Basingstoke Hampshire, RG24 8PR United Kingdom. **Tel** 011 44 256 840366, FAX 011 44 256 479438, telex 858540. **(Subscription address:** Taylor & Francis Inc., 1900 Frost Road, Suite 101, Bristol PA 19007-1598.**) DD** 351. ***Continues*** *Marine Policy Reports, 0735-5912.* ***Absorbed by*** *The International Journal of Marine and Coastal Law, 0927-3522.*
Ind/Abst Environ. Period. Bibliogr.; Int. Dev. Abstr.

US/0894-668X
MARITIME ADVISOR. COURT CASE DIGEST, THE. [Marit. advis., Court case dig.]. **VFOAT** Court Case Digest. Periodical. English. mo. Maritime Advisory Services Inc. / Stamford, CT, 10 Signal Road, Stamford CT 06902-7909. **Tel** (203)975-7070. **LC** KF1101.3; .M37. **DD** 343.73/096/02648 3039602648. ***Continues*** *Maritime Advisor, 0731-1486.*

NE/0920-1610
MARITIME INFORMATION REVIEW. [Marit. inf. rev.]. **Added/Corp** Association of Finnish Shipbuilders. (1986)-. Periodical. English. Eleven times a year (July/Aug. iss. combined). F350.00. Netherlands Maritime Information Center, CMO PO Box 21873, 3000AW Rotterdam Netherlands. **Tel** 011 31 10 4130960, FAX 011 31 10 4112857, telex 26585. **UDC** 656.61(048.8). Index available (Bound in each iss.). **Bk Rev**, (Qty: 15). available on an online database from ESA-ISA. ***Formed by the union of*** *Marna-News, 0167-546X* ***and*** *Ship Abstracts, 0346-1025.*

US
MARITIME LAW REPORTER. Vol. 1, No. 1 (June 1987)-. Periodical. English. bm. $185.00. Butterworth Heinemann / Woburn, MA, 225 Wildwood Avenue, Unit B, Woburn MA 01801. **Tel** (800)366-2665, FAX (617)928-2620, telex 880052. **LC** KF1097; .M37. **DD** 343.73/096/05.

US/1054-383X
MARITIMEWEEK (ARLINGTON, VA.). (MARITIMEWEEK.). [Marit.Week]. **VFOAT** Maritime

Week. Vol. 1, No. 1 (Jan. 22, 1991)-. Periodical. English. wk. $320.00 US; $360.00 other. Maritime Week, 4665 34th Street South, Suite 2, Arlington VA 22206-1701. **DD** 343.

US/0742-762X
MLA REPORT, THE. (THE MLA REPORT / THE MARITIME LAW ASSOCIATION OF THE UNITED STATES.). [MLA rep.]. **Added/Corp** Maritime Law Association of the United States. **VFOAT** M.L.A. Report. **VAT** Maritime Law Association Report. (Feb. 25, 1983)-. Periodical. English. sa. Maritime Law Association of the US, 1 State Street Plaza, New York NY 10004. **LC** KF1097; .M55. **DD** 343.73/096/05; 347.3039605. cum. index.

US
OCEAN AND COASTAL LAW JOURNAL. (19??)-. English. sa. $35.00 individuals; $50.00 institutions. Marine Law Institute, University of So. Maine, 246 Deering Avenue, Portland ME 04102. **Tel** (207)780-4474, FAX (207)780-4913. **ED** Alison Rieser. **Bk Rev.** ctrl circ. ***Continues*** *Territorial Sea Jounral, 1046-9680.*

US/1052-6730
OCEAN AND COASTAL LAW MEMO. [Ocean coast. law memo]. Issue 33 (Oct. 1989)-. Periodical. English. ir. Free. University of Oregon School of Law, Eugene OR 97403-1221. **Tel** (503)686-3845, FAX (503)346-3985. **LC** JX4419; .O28. **DD** 346. cum. index. **Circ:** 1,800. ***Formed by the union of*** *Coastal Law Memo, 0730-6822* ***and*** *Ocean Law Memo, 0361-2473.*
Desc: Current issues and developments in ocean and coastal law.

US/0090-8320
OCEAN DEVELOPMENT AND INTERNATIONAL LAW. [Ocean dev. int. law]. Vol. 1, No. 3 (Fall 1973)-. Periodical. English. qt. £126.00 UK; $208.00 other. Taylor & Francis Ltd., Rankine Road, Basingstoke Hampshire, RG24 8PR United Kingdom. **Tel** 011 44 256 840366, FAX 011 44 256 479438, telex 858540. **(Subscription address:** Taylor & Francis Inc., 1900 Frost Road, Suite 101, Bristol PA 19007-1598.**) ED** Jon L. Jacobson (editor's address: Coastal Law Center, School of Law, University of Oregon, Eugene, OR 97403-1221). **LC** JX1; .O25. **DD** 341.4/5/05. **[CCC].** Index available. **Bk Rev. Ad Acc. Pr Rev. Circ:** 800. available on microfilm and microfiche from University Microfilms International (UMI). Documents available from The Genuine Article, UMI Article Clearinghouse, Documents on Demand. ***Continues*** *Ocean Development and International Law Journal, 0883-4873.*
Desc: Devoted to all aspects of international and comparative law and policy concerning the management of ocean uses and activities. Focuses on the international aspects of ocean regulation, ocean affairs, and all forms of ocean utilization.
Ind/Abst Am. Bibliogr. Slavic East Europ. Stud.; AQUAREF; Aquat. Sci. Fish. Abstr. (Computer File); Can. Environ.; Contents Curr. Leg. Period.; Curr. Contents Soc. Behav. Sci.; Curr. Geogr. Publ. (199?-); Curr. Law Index (1980-); Electron. Commun. Abstr. J.; Energy Inf. Abstr.; Environ. Abstr.; Environ. Period. Bibliogr.; Expand. Acad. Index (1992-); Fish Rev.; Geogr. Abstr. Human Geogr.; GeoRef; Index Foreign Leg. Per.; Index Leg. Period.; Int. Dev. Abstr.; Int. Polit. Sci. Abstr.; ISMEC Bull.; Leg. Resour. Index (1980-); LegalTrac (1980-); Newsp. Period. Abstr. (1992-); Ocean. Abstr.; Oceanic Abstr. Indexes; PAIS Int. Print (1991-); Pollut. Abstr. Indexes; Public Aff. Inf. Serv. Bull.; Res. Alert [Full Cov.]; Saf. Sci. Abstr. J.; Sel. Water Resour. Abstr.; Ship Abstr.; Soc. Sci. Cit. Index [Full Cov.]; U.S. Polit. Sci. Doc.

US/8755-0474
OCEANS POLICY STUDY SERIES. [Oceans policy study ser.]. 1-. Monographic series. English. ir. Price varies per volume. Oceana Publications, Inc., 75 Main Street, Dobbs Ferry NY 10522. **Tel** (914)693-1320, FAX (914)693-0402. **LC** JX4408; .O35. **DD** 341.4/5. ***Continues*** *Oceans Policy Study, 0275-3006.*

UK/0950-4044
P & I INTERNATIONAL. Added/Corp Lloyd's of London Press. **VFOAT** P and I International; P&I International. Vol. 1, No. 1 (Jan. 1987)-. Periodical. English. mo. £152.00. Lloyd's of London Press Ltd, Sheepen Place, Colchester, Essex, CO3 3LP England. **Tel** 011 44 206 772113, US: (212)529-9500, US: (800)955-6937, FAX 011 44 206 772880, US: (212)529-9826, telex 987321 LLOYDS G. **(Subscription address:** Lloyd's of London Press Inc. / North America, 611 Broadway, Suite 308, New York NY 10012.**) ED** W. Robertson and Stuart Ashworth. **Circ:** 600.
Desc: Information source for those concerned with mutual insurance. Uses information from around the world to deal in detail with legislation, case law, developments in the Clubs, and problem areas such as cargo, personal injury, pollution, collisions, salvage, general average, fines, arbitrations, fraud, commodities and ship safety.

PH/0115-9003
PHILIPPINE SEAS. 1 (1/1982)-. Periodical. English. sa. **LC** JX18; .P44. **DD** 341.4/5/09599.

US/0557-8620
PROCEEDINGS OF THE ANNUAL CONFERENCE OF THE LAW OF THE SEA INSTITUTE. (PROCEEDINGS OF THE ANNUAL CONFERENCE OF THE LAW OF THE SEA INSTITUTE, UNIVERSITY OF RHODE ISLAND.). [Proc. annu. conf. Law Sea Inst.]. **Main/Corp** Law of the Sea Institute. Conference. **VFOAT** Proceedings, Law of the Sea Institute. (1966)-. Proceedings. English. an (1 issue). $58.00. Law of the Sea Institute, University of Hawaii-Manoa, Richardson School of Law/Room 208, 2515 Dole Street, Honolulu HI 96822. **Tel** (808)956-6750, (808)956-3300, FAX (808)956-6402, telex 7431895. **ED** T. Kuribayashi and E. Miles. **LC** JX4408; .L373. Index available. **Circ:** 500 (ctrl).
Desc: Contains proceedings of the Law of the Sea Institute's annual conference, with experts from the field of ocean policy, fisheries management, marine science and law in a neutral forum designed to further international discussion of important, current maritime issues.
Ind/Abst GeoRef; Index Leg. Period. (1992-).

US/0899-0727
RECENT TITLES IN LAW FOR THE SUBJECT SPECIALIST. TRANSPORTATION AND MARITIME LAW. [Recent titles law subj. spec., Transp. marit. law]. **VFOAT** Transportation and Maritime Law. Vol. 5, No. 1 (Jan.-March 1988)-. English. qt. $85.00. Ward & Associates, 317 South Division, Suite 66, Ann Arbor MI 48104. **Tel** (313)665-3520, FAX (313)665-7880. **DD** 016. ***Continues*** *National Legal Bibliography. Subject Area List. Transportation and Maritime Law, 8755-8173.*

FR
REVUE DE DROIT FRANCAIS COMMERCIAL, MARITIME ET FISCAL. 1.- Year; 1924-. Periodical. French. qt. 300.00F. 28 Boulevard Paul-Peytral, 13006 Marseille France. **Tel** 91 33 38 29, FAX 91 55 61 41, telex 441413 F SCAPEL. **ED** Christian Scapel.

IT/0390-3842
RIVISTA DI INFORMAZIONI MARITTIME. [Riv. inf. marit.]. Vol. 1 (1974)-. Italian. mo. L75.000. **ED** G Legitimo and G Merli. **LC** HE839; .R48. **DD** 387/.0945. ***Supersedes*** *Bollettino di Informazioni Marittime.*

JA
SEMPAKU ROPPO. Main/Corp Japan. Japanese. 8000. Seizando Shoten, 4-51 Minami-Motocho, Shinjuku-ku 160 Tokyo Japan.

US/1046-9680
TERRITORIAL SEA JOURNAL. ***Title Change.*** (TERRITORIAL SEA JOURNAL : A LEGAL AND POLICY JOURNAL ON U.S. OCEAN AND COASTAL LAW.). [Territ. sea j.]. **Added/Corp** Marine Law Institute. Vol. 1, No. 1 (1990)-(19??). Periodical. English. sa. Marine Law Institute, University of So. Maine, 246 Deering Avenue, Portland ME 04102. **Tel** (207)780-4474, FAX (207)780-4913. **ED** Alison Rieser. **LC** K24; .E77. **DD** 343.73/07692/05; 347.303769205. ctrl circ. ***Continues*** *Territorial Sea, 0890-0647.* ***Continued by*** *Ocean and Coastal Law Journal.*
Desc: A legal and policy journal on US ocean and coastal law.
Ind/Abst Index Leg. Period.

US/1048-3748
TULANE MARITIME LAW JOURNAL. [Tulane marit. law j.]. Vol. 12, No. 1; Fall 1987-. Periodical. English. sa. Tulane University / School of Law, New Orleans LA 70118. **LC** K13; .A67. **DD** 343.7309/6/05. ***Continues*** *Maritime Lawyer, 0099-0620.*
Ind/Abst Index Leg. Period.; Leg. Resour. Index; LegalTrac (1987-).

US/1061-3331
UNIVERSITY OF SAN FRANCISCO MARITIME LAW JOURNAL. [Univ. San Franc. marit. law j.]. **Added/Corp** University of San Francisco. Admiralty and Maritime Law Society. **VFOAT** USF Maritime Law Journal; Maritime Law Journal; U.S.F. Maritime Law Journal. Vol. 1, No. 1 (Summer 1989)-. Periodical. English. an. $30.00. USF Admiralty & Maritime Law Society, Kendrick Hall, San Francisco CA 94117. **Tel** (415)666-6154. **DD** 343.
Ind/Abst Index Leg. Period. (1992-).

US
WATER AND WATER RIGHTS. Added/Corp Allen Smith Company. (19??)-. English. ir. $675.00 (7 volume set), $180.00 (supplement). Michie Company, PO Box 7587, Charlottesville VA 22906-7587. **Tel** (804)972-7600, (800)542-0957, FAX (800)643-1280.
Desc: The preeminent treatsie on this highly complex area of law.

US/0737-044X
WATER LAW NEWSLETTER (BOULDER, COLO. : 1976). (WATER LAW NEWSLETTER / ROCKY MOUNTAIN MINERAL LAW FOUNDATION.). [Water law newsl.]. **Added/Corp** Rocky Mountain Mineral Law Foundation. University of Wyoming. Land & Water Law Center. Vol. 9, No. 1 (Spring 1976)-. Newsletter. English. Three times a year. $10.00 law school members; $20.00 other. Rocky Mountain Mineral Law Foundation, Porter Administration Building, 7039 East 18th Avenue, Denver CO 80220. **Tel** (303)321-8100, FAX (303)321-7657. **ED** George A. Gould. **LC** KF5552; .R62. **DD** 346.7304/691; 347.3064691. **Pr Rev. Circ:** 400. available in hardback. ***Continues*** *Rocky Mountain Mineral Law Newsletter. Water Law, 0737-0431.*
Desc: Nineteen reporters in 18 states cover water law and water rights issues, including court decisions at federal, state, and local levels; state and federal regulatory agencies/ and state and local statutory developments. State coverage includes Alaska, Arizona, California, Colorado, Idaho, Kansas, Montana, Nebraska, Nevada, New Mexico, North Dakota, Oklahoma, Oregon, South Dakota, Texas, Utah, Washinton, Washington Wyoming.
Ind/Abst Energy Res. Abstr. (July 1980-); GeoRef.

MILITARY LAW

US/0094-8381
AIR FORCE LAW REVIEW, THE. [Air Force law rev.]. **Added/Corp** Judge Advocate General School (United States. Air Force). Vol. 16, No. 1 (Spring 1974)-. Government Publication. English. sa. $10.00 domestic; $12.50 other. Superintendent of Documents, US Government Printing Office, Washington DC 20402. **Tel** (202)275-3328, FAX (202)786-2377. **LC** K25; .N43. **DD** 343/.73/0184005. cum. index. available on microfilm and microfiche from University Microfilms International (UMI). ***Continues*** *United States Air Force JAG Law Review, 0021-3527.*
Desc: Published by the office of the Judge Advocate General of the Air Force; provides a means for the exchange of ideas, experiences and information. Contains a survey of important legislative, administrative judicial developments in military and related law fields.
Ind/Abst Air Univ. Libr. Index Mil. Period.; Curr. Law Index (1980-); Fed. Tax Artic.; Index Leg. Period.; Leg. Resour. Index (1980-); LegalTrac (1981-).

US/0364-1287
ARMY LAWYER, THE. [Army lawyer]. **Added/Corp** Judge Advocate General's School (U.S.) United States. Dept. of the Army. Vol. 1 (Aug. 1971)-. Government Publication. English. mo. $19.00 domestic; $23.75 other. Superintendent of Documents, US Government Printing Office, Washington DC 20402. **Tel** (202)275-3328, FAX (202)786-2377. **LC** KF7209.A1; A74. **DD** 343/73/01. available on microfilm and microfiche from University Microfilms International (UMI). ***Absorbed*** *Advocate (Falls Church, Va.), 0094-2197.*
Ind/Abst Curr. Law Index (1980-); Fed. Tax Artic.; Index Leg. Period.; Leg. Resour. Index (1980-); LegalTrac (1980-).

US/0498-3637
BOARD OF CONTRACT APPEALS DECISIONS. ***Ceased.*** **Main/Corp** United States. Armed Services Board of Contract Appeals. **Added/Corp** Commerce Clearing House. United States. Armed Services Board of Contract Appeals. Decisions. (1957)-(Apr. 1993). English. an. Commerce Clearing House Inc., 4025 West Peterson Avenue, Chicago IL 60646-6085. **Tel** (312)583-8500, FAX (708)940-4600. **ED** Daniel Newquist. **LC** KF853.3.A2; A7. **DD** 346/.73/023. Index available. cum. index. **Circ:** 300.
Desc: Bound volumes of ASBCA, other Appeals Board decisions.

IO
BULLETIN HUKUM. Day 1, No. 1-. Bulletin. English (Indonesian). qt. JL Tanah Abang Timur, No 7, Jakarta Pusat Indonesia.

II/0045-7043
CIVIL & MILITARY LAW JOURNAL. Vol. 1 (Jan./March 1965)-. Periodical. English. qt. $50.00. Civil & Military Law Journal, D-1-24 Rajouri Garden, New Delhi 110027 India. **Tel** 584498. **(Subscription address:** Prints India, 11 Darya Ganj, New Delhi 110002 India.**)**

US/0883-0843
GUARDMOUNT. ***Suspended.*** [Guardmount]. **VFOAT** Guardmount Newsletter. Vol. 1 (Jan./Feb. 1985)-?. Periodical. English. bm. $20.00. Guardmount Inc, PO Box 37891, Omaha NE 68137. **Tel** (402)895-5601. **ED** Patricia Ewing-Grimes. **DD** 363. **Bk Rev. Ad Acc. Circ:** 4,000 (ctrl).
Desc: Newsletter for the Armed Forces Police. Also contains security related information, and employment opportunities in the security industry.

US/1044-8756
LAMPLIGHTER (CHICAGO, ILL.). (THE LAMPLIGHTER / AMERICAN BAR ASSOCIATION, STANDING COMMITTEE ON LEGAL ASSISTANCE FOR MILITARY PERSONNEL.). [LAMPlighter]. **Added/Corp** American Bar Association. Standing Committee on Legal Assistance for Military Personnel. **VFOAT** LAMP Lighter. **VAT** Legal Assistance for Military Personnel Lighter. Vol. 1, No. 1 (Spring 1989)-.

Periodical. English. qt (4 issues). Free on request. American Bar Association, 750 North Lake Shore Drive, Chicago IL 60611. **Tel** (312)988-5522, (312)988-5241, FAX (312)988-5528, telex 270593. **(Subscription address:** American Bar Association, 541 North Fairbanks Court, 15th Floor, Chicago IL 60611.**) LC** KF337.5.A7; A136. **DD** 349.73/024355/05; 347.30024355/05. ***Continues*** *Legal Assistance Newsletter, 0736-7309.*

US/0193-3906
MILITARY LAW REPORTER. ***Ceased.*** (MILITARY LAW REPORTER : A PROJECT OF THE PUBLIC LAW EDUCATION INSTITUTE.). Vol. 1, No. 1 (Jan.-Feb. 1973)-(1992). Periodical. English. bm. Public Law Education Inst, 1601 Conn Avenue NW 450, Washington DC 20009. **Tel** (202)232-1400. **ED** Lawrence M Baskir. **Circ:** 550.
Desc: Covers Judicial and administrative developments relating to the Armed Forces, National Guard, Veteran benefits, civilian employees of military and all aspects of selective service law.

US/0026-4040
MILITARY LAW REVIEW. [Mil. law rev.]. **Added/Corp** United States. Dept. of the Army. Judge Advocate General's School (U.S.). (1958)-. Government Publication. English. qt. $12.00 domestic; $15.00 other. Superintendent of Documents, US Government Printing Office, Washington DC 20402. **Tel** (202)275-3328, FAX (202)786-2377. **LC** K13; .I4. **DD** 343/.73/01. cum. index. **Pr Rev.** available on microfilm and microfiche from University Microfilms International (UMI). Documents available from The Genuine Article.
Desc: Designed as a medium for the military lawyer, active and reserve, to share the product of his experience and research with fellow lawyers in the Department of the Army.
Ind/Abst ABC POL SCI; Curr. Contents Soc. Behav. Sci.; Curr. Law Index (1980-); Fed. Tax Artic.; Index Leg. Period.; Leg. Resour. Index (1980-); LegalTrac (1980-); Middle East Abstr. Index; PAIS Int. Print (1991-); Res. Alert [Full Cov.]; Soc. Sci. Cit. Index [Full Cov.].

US/1049-0272
NAVAL LAW REVIEW. [Naval law rev.]. **Added/Corp** United States. Navy. Office of the Judge Advocate General. Naval Justice School (U.S.). Vol. 34 (1985)-. Periodical. English. an. $15.00. Naval Law Review, 360 Elliot Street, Newport RI 02841. **Tel** (401)841-3155. **LC** K14; .A88. **DD** 343.73/019; 347.30319. Index available. cum. index. **Bk Rev. Circ:** 2,000 (ctrl). available on microfilm and microfiche from University Microfilms International (UMI). ***Continues*** *JAG Journal, 0021-3519.*
Ind/Abst Index Leg. Period.; Leg. Resour. Index; LegalTrac (1985-).

GW
NEUE ZEITSCHRIFT FUER WEHRRECHT. Vol. 1, No. 1 (Jan. 1959)-. Periodical. German. Six times a year. DM180.80. J. Schweitzer Verlag, Zeppelinallee 43, Postfach 97 01 48, D 60325 Frankfurt Germany. **Tel** 011 39 69 793009 0, FAX 011 39 69 793009 48. **(Subscription address:** Luchterhand Verlagsauslieferng, Postfach 2352, 56513 Neuwied Germany; telephone: 011 49 26318010**) LC** LAW.

US/0279-103X
OBJECTOR (SAN FRANCISCO, CALIF.). (THE OBJECTOR.). **Added/Corp** Central Committee for Conscientious Objectors. Western Regional Office. Central Committee for Conscientious Objectors. Western Region. Vol. 2, No. 2 (March 31, 1981)-. Periodical. English. Six times a year (Feb., Apr., June, Aug., Oct., Dec.). $17.00 US, High School, Libraries and individual; $22.00 other. CCCO Western Region, 655 Sutter, Suite 514, San Francisco CA 94102. **Tel** (415)474-3002, FAX (415)474-2311. **ED** Sam Diener. **LC** UB343; .O24. **DD** 355.2/24/0973. Index available (1st issues of next volume.). **Bk Rev. Circ:** 1,000 (ctrl). ***Formed by the union of*** *Draft Counselors Newsletter* ***and*** *Newsletter on Military Law and Counseling.*
Desc: A journal for draft and military counselors, with up-to-date information concerning military and selective service laws and regulations.

US/0149-6557
ON WATCH (WASHINGTON). (ON WATCH.). **Added/Corp** National Lawyers Guild. Military Law Task Force. (197?)-. Periodical. English. mo. $10.00 institutions, $6.00 guild members and students, $7.50 others. National Lawyers Guild / Washington, Military Law Task Force, Antioch School of Law, 1624 Crescent Place Northwest, Washington DC 20009. **LC** KF7202; .O5. **DD** 343/.73/0105.

US/0899-076X
RECENT TITLES IN LAW FOR THE SUBJECT SPECIALIST. MILITARY AND SECURITY LAW. [Recent titles law subj. spec. Mil. secur. law]. **VFOAT** Military and Security Law. Vol. 5, No. 1 (Jan.-Mar. 1988)-. English. qt. $85.00. William S. Hein & Company Inc., 1285 Main Street, Buffalo NY 14209. **Tel** (716)882-2600, (800)828-7571, FAX (716)883-8100, telex 91-209 WM S HEIN BUF. **DD** 016. ***Continues*** *National Legal Bibliography. Subject Area List. Military and Security Law, 8755-8092.*

US/0193-8134
REPORTER (WASHINGTON. 1977), THE. (THE REPORTER / OFFICE OF THE JUDGE ADVOCATE GENERAL OF THE AIR FORCE.). **Added/Corp** United States. Air Force. Judge Advocate General. (1977)-. Government Publication. English. qt. $6.00 domestic; $7.50 other. Superintendent of Documents, US Government Printing Office, Washington DC 20402. **Tel** (202)275-3328, FAX (202)786-2377. **DD** 343/.73/01.
Desc: Provides a forum for the exchange of information pertinent to the practice of law in the military as well as the civilian community.
Ind/Abst Index U.S. Gov. Period.

BE/0556-7394
REVUE DE DROIT MILITAIRE ET DE DROIT DE LA GUERRE. Added/Corp International Society of Military Law and Law of War. **VFOAT** Military Law and Law of War Review; Tijdschrift voor Militair Recht en Oorlogsrecht; Zeitschrift fur Wehrrecht und Kriegsvolkerrecht; Rivista di Diritto Militare e di Diritto Della Guerra; Revista de Derecho Militar y Derecho de la Guerra. XXVIII, 1-2 (1989)-. Periodical. English (French, Dutch, German, Italian and Spanish). qt. $14.00. Auditorat General, Palais de Justice, B-1000 Brussels Belgium. **Tel** 011/32/2/5086611, FAX 011/32/25086085. **LC** K21; .D39. **DD** 343/.015/05; 342.315005. ***Continues*** *Revue de Droit Penal Militaire et de Droit de la Guerre.*

UK
ROYAL MILITARY POLICE JOURNAL. English. Four times a year. £5.50. Royal Military Police Reg HQ, Roussillon Barracks, Chichester Sussex England. **Tel** 011 44 243 786311. **ED** Lt. Colonel Reto PHM Squier. Index available. **Bk Rev**, (Qty: varies). **Ad Acc.** ctrl circ.

US/0163-1101
SHEPARD'S MILITARY JUSTICE CITATIONS. [Shepard's mil. justice cit.]. **Added/Corp** Shepard's, Inc. of Colorado Springs. Shepard's/McGraw-Hill. **VFOAT** Military Justice Citations. Vol. 1 (Mar. 1978)-. Periodical. English. Six times a year. $235.00 (bound volume), $247.00 (cumulative supplements). Shepards McGraw-Hill Inc, 555 Middle Creek Parkway, PO Box 35300, Colorado Springs CO 80935-3530. **Tel** (719)488-3000, FAX (800)525-0053. **DD** 348.
Desc: A compilation of citations that gives you a comprehensive research tool to current decisions of military courts and official military codes, orders and more.

US/0148-0693
SUMMARY OF ACTIVITIES - COMMITTEE ON ARMED SERVICES, UNITED STATES SENATE. Main/Corp United States. Congress. Senate. Committee on Armed Services. English. be. US Government Printing Office, Washington DC 20402. **LC** KF4987.A7; A247. **DD** 343/.73/01.

US/0272-9334
WEST'S MILITARY JUSTICE DIGEST. [West's mil. justice dig.]. No. 1- July 1980-. English. West Publishing Company, 610 Opperman Drive, PO Box 64526, Eagan MN 55123-1308. **Tel** (612)687-5618, (800)328-9352, FAX (612)687-5388, (800)562-2329. **(Subscription telephone:** FAX (612)688-3570**) LC** KF7605.3; .W47. **DD** 343.73/0143; 347.303143.

US/0147-7315
WEST'S MILITARY JUSTICE REPORTER. Added/Corp United States. Court of Military Appeals. West Publishing Company. **VFOAT** Military Justice Reporter. V. 1- 1975/76-. Periodical. English. bw (with bound cumulations). $50.00. West Publishing Company, 610 Opperman Drive, PO Box 64526, Eagan MN 55123-1308. **Tel** (612)687-5618, (800)328-9352, FAX (612)687-5388, (800)562-2329. **(Subscription telephone:** FAX (612)688-3570**) LC** KF7605.A2; W4. **DD** 343/.73/0143. ***Formed by the union of*** *Court-Martial Reports* ***and*** *United States. Court of Military Appeals. Decisions of the United States Court of Military Appeals.*

LEATHER AND FUR INDUSTRY

US/0003-1038
AMERICAN SHOEMAKING. [Am. shoemak.]. (19??)-. Periodical. English. Twelve times a year. $45.00 US; $55.00 Canada; $70.00 other. Shoe Trades Publishing Company, 61 Massachusetts Avenue, Arlington MA 02174. **Tel** (617)648-8160, FAX (617)492-0126, telex 325736 SHOETRADE. **ED** James Sutton. **Bk Rev. Ad Acc. Circ:** 3,000.
Desc: Footwear manufacturing.

IT
ANNUARIO SEAT. VOL. F, ABBIGLIAMENTO ED ESTETICA. **See** Clothing Industry and Fashion.

IT
ARPEL. (19??)-. Periodical. English (Italian, French, German and Spanish). Four times a year. $222.00 (one year), $364.00 (two years). ARS Arpel, Via Ippolito Nievo 33, 20145 Milan Italy. **Tel** 011 39 2 315951.
Desc: International magazine on leathergoods, luggage and leather garments.

AT
AUSTRALASIAN ANGORA MOHAIR JOURNAL. ***Title Change.*** **Added/Corp** Angora Mohair Breeders of Australasia. Vol. 1, No. 2 (Dec. 1983)-(1992). Periodical. English. bm. Angora Mohair Breeders of Australasia, PO Box 1104, Fyshwick Act 2609 Australia. **Tel** (062)391.244, FAX (062)391.270. **Ad Acc.** ctrl circ. ***Continues*** *Australasian Angora Mohair Magazine.* ***Continued by*** *Mohair Australia.*

NE
BEDRIJFSGEGEVENS VOOR DE DETAILHANDEL IN KOFFERS EN LEDERWAREN. Main/Corp Economisch Instituut Voor Het Midden- en Kleinbedrijf. Dutch. Neuhuyskade 94, Postbus 2818, S'Gravenhage The Netherlands. **LC** HD9780.N2; E25.

US/0740-6258
BUSINESS OF FUR, THE. [Bus. fur]. Vol. 1, No. 1 (Sept. 1983)-. Periodical. English. mo. $80.00 US; $110.00 other. Fur Publishing Plus Inc, 19 W 21st Street/Suite 403, New York NY 10010. **Tel** (212)727-1210, FAX (212)727-1218. **DD** 338. **Ad Acc. Circ:** 8,000 (ctrl).
Desc: All business and fashion issues related to fur and leather industries.

FR
CUIR, LE. Forty-seven times a year. Societe des Publications le Cuir, 1 rue Garnier, 92200 Neuilly Seine France. **Tel** 011 33 1 47381107, FAX 011 33 1 46249924, telex 610-672.

IT/0011-3034
CUOIO, PELLI, MATERIE CONCIANTI. [Cuoio, pelli, mater. conci.]. (1942)-. Academic Scholarly Publication. Italian. bm (6 issues). L71400 Italy; L120000 other. Stazione Sperimentale Ind Pelli Mat Conc, Via Poggioreale No. 39, 80143 Naples, Italy. **Tel** 011 39 81 268322, FAX 011 39 81 265574, telex 721160. **ED** L. P. Arena, A. M. Scandurra. **CODEN** CPMAAJ. Index available (bound in last issue). **Bk Rev**, (Qty: 10). **Ad Acc, Adv Mgr:** A. M. Scandurra. **Circ:** 18,000 (ctrl). Documents available from CASDDS. ***Continues*** *Bollettino della Regia Stazione Sperimentale per l'Industria delle Pelli e delle Materie Concianti, Napoli, 0366-2209.*
Ind/Abst AGRICOLA; Chem. Abstr.; Curr. Biotechnol.; Saf. Health Work.

DK/0011-6424
DANSK PELSDYRAVL. [Dan. pelsdyravl]. Began in 1944. Periodical. Danish. mo. ***Continues*** *Dansk Pelsdyrblad.*
Ind/Abst Anim. Breed. Abstr.; Index Vet.; Nutr. Abstr. Rev., Ser. B, Live Feeds and Feed.; Rev. Med. Vet. Entomol.; Vet. Bull.; Wheat Barley Trit. Abstr.

US/0276-2803
DEALER'S AND TRAPPER'S LISTING BOOK. English. Stroudsburg Fur Dressing Corporation, 1031 King Street, Stroudsburg PA 18360. **LC** HD9944.U44; D4. **DD** 380.1/436753/02573.

IT
ECO CUOIO : DELLE INDUSTRIE E DEI COMMERCI DEL CUOIO E DELLE CALZATURE. Edimark / Milan, Via Anfossi 36, 20135 Milan Italy. **Tel** 39 2 546-3091.

US/0094-3282
EMPRESS CHINCHILLA BREEDER (1974). (EMPRESS CHINCHILLA BREEDER.). [Empress chinchilla breed.]. **Added/Corp** Empress Chinchilla Breeders Cooperative. (1974)-. Periodical. English. mo. $25.00 US; $30.00 other. Empress Chinchilla Breeders, PO Box 318, Sixes OR 97476. **Tel** (503)332-3222, FAX (503)332-4704. **ED** W. Bird. **Ad Acc. Circ:** 325-400. ***Continues*** *Empress Chinchilla, 0013-6905.*
Desc: Magazine published for those interested in the chinchilla ranching industry.
Ind/Abst AGRICOLA.

FI/0430-5817
FINSK PALSTIDSKRIFT. [Fin. palstidskr.]. (1967)-. Periodical. Swedish. mo. Finlands Palsdjuruppfodares Forbund, (Finnish Fur Breeders' Association), PO Box 5, FIN-01601,, Vanda 60 Finland. **Tel** FAX 011 358 90 8498217. **UDC** 636.93. ***Continues*** *Turkistalous B.*
Ind/Abst Index Vet.; Nutr. Abstr. Rev., Ser. B, Live Feeds and Feed.

IT
FOTO SHOE 15. $160.00, 800.00F, DM235.00 Europe; $165.00 Africa, North and South America; 225.00Aus$, $180.00 Australia; $165.00 Asia. Editoriale Di Foto Shoe, Via Leonardo Da Vinci 43, 20090 Trezzano Naviglio Italy.
Desc: A review of technical information dealing with the allied footwear industries. Includes information on materials, machines, technology, components and accessories.

US/0016-2884
FUR AGE WEEKLY. [Fur age wkly.]. (19??)-. Periodical. English. wk. $80.00 US; $87.00 Canada; $205.00 other. Fur Age Weekly, PO Box 868, Glenwood Landing NY 11547. **Tel** (516)484-0631. **ED** E.R. Harrowe, Marc L. Rubman and Lisa Marcinek. **Bk Rev. Ad Acc. Circ:** 5,000.
Desc: Vertical publication of the world fur trade.

GW/0016-2914
FUR BULLETIN. (1954)-. Bulletin. German. ir. Winckelmann Verlag GmbH, Nidda Strasse 58, D 60329 Frankfurt Germany. **Tel** 011 49 69 239991.

CN/0225-6452
FUR CHIC. [Fur chic]. Began publication in March 1978. Periodical. English. ir. 27.00Can$ Canada and US; 35.00Can$ other. Publicon Publishing, Fur Chic Fourrure, 4626 St Catherine Street West, Montreal Quebec H3Z 1S3 Canada. **DD** 685/.24/05.

US/0744-7701
FUR RANCHER. [Fur rancher]. Vol. 58, (Jan. 1978)-. Periodical. English. Ten times a year. $20.00 US; $22.00 Canada; $24.00 other. Communications Marketing Inc, 9995 West 69th Street, Suite 201, Eden Prairie MN 55344. **Tel** (612)941-5820. **DD** 636. ***Continues*** *U.S. Fur Rancher.*

US
FUR SEAL INVESTIGATIONS. English. National Technical Information Service - NTIS, Room 2027S, 5285 Port Royal Road, Springfield VA 22161. **Tel** (703)487-4630, (703)487-4660, (703)487-4650, FAX (703)321-8547, telex 89-9405.

US/0016-2965
FUR TAKER, THE. **Added/Corp** Fur Takers of America. **VFOAT** Fur Takers. (19??)-. Periodical. English. Twelve times a year. $15.00. Fur Taker, Rt 3 Box 175, Manchester IA 52057. **Tel** (319) 927-5958.

CN/0845-6798
FUR TRADE JOURNAL OF CANADA (1987). (FUR TRADE JOURNAL OF CANADA.). [Fur trade j. Can.]. Vol. 65, No. 8 (1987)-. Periodical. English. mo. $18.00 Canada; $24.00 other. 176 Woolwich Street, Guelph Ontario N1H 7A1 Canada. **DD** 338.1/7608844. ***Continues*** *Fur Trade Journal, 0381-8535.*

IT
GUIDA DELLA PELLICCERIA. (19??)-. Italian. an. Pagin Edizioni, Via Forze Armate 260 13, 20152 Milan Italy. **Tel** 011 39 2 4531139.

FR/0399-5461
HEBDOCUIR. **VFOAT** Hebdo Cuir. (1976)-. Periodical. French. wk. 445.64F France; 587.66F other. Promotion Presse International, 7 Ter Cour Des Petites Ecuries, 75010 Paris France. **Tel** 011 33 1 42471205, FAX 011 33 1 47703394. **UDC** 66. **CODEN** 68.

JA/0018-1811
HIKAKU KAGAKU. [Hikaku Kagaku]. **VFOAT** Leather Chemistry. (1965)-. Japanese. qt. $283.50. Nihon Hikaku Gijutsu Kyokai, c/o Scleroprotein and Leather Research Institute, Tokyo Noko University, 3-5-8 Saiwai-cho Fuchu-shi, Tokyo 183 Japan. **(Subscription address:** Japan Publications Trading Company, Ltd., PO Box 5030, Tokyo International, Tokyo 100-31 Japan.**) ED** Board. **CODEN** HIKAAF. Index available. **Ad Acc. Circ:** 900. Documents available from CASDDS. ***Continues*** *Nihon Hikaku Gijutsu Kyokaishi, 0369-4046.*
Ind/Abst Chem. Abstr.

II/0376-978X
INDIA LEATHER & LEATHER PRODUCTS DIRECTORY. **VAT** India Leather and Leather Products Directory. Directory. English. $13.60 India; $17.85 Canada; $24.65 other. Export India Journal Publications, 8 Peters Road, Madras 600014 India. **LC** HD9780.I62; I53. **DD** 338.4/7/685202554. Index available. **Bk Rev. Ad Acc.** ctrl circ.

II/0019-574X
INDIAN LEATHER. [Indian Leather]. (1967)-. Periodical. English. mo. $45.00. **(Subscription address:** Prints India, 11 Darya Ganj, New Delhi 110002 India.**) UDC** 675.

RM/1017-2270
INDUSTRIA USOARA (1974). (INDUSTRIA USOARA. PIELARIE, CONFECTII DIN PIELE, PRELUCRAREA CAUCIUCULUI SI A MASELOR PLASTICE, STICLA, CERAMICA FINA, ARTICOLE CASNICE SI JUCARII, UTILAJE PENTRU INDUSTRIA USOARA.). [Ind. usoara]. **Added/Corp** Institutul de Cercetari Textile (Romania) Romania. Ministerul Industriei Usoare. **VFOAT** Pielaire, Confectii Din Piele, Prelucrarea Cauciucului Si A Maselor Plastice, Sticla, Ceramica Fina, Articole Casnice Si Jucarii, Utilaje Pentru Industria Usoara; Industria Usoara. (1974)-. Periodical. Romanian (summaries and/or abstracts in English, French, German and Russian). bm (6 issues). DM172.00. B N R S R, Sectorul 3, Bucuresti Romania. **(Subscription address:** Kubon & Sagner, ABT Zeitschriftenimport, D 80328 Munich Germany.**) LC** T4; .I333. Documents available from CASDDS. ***Continues*** *Industria Usoara. Seria B. Pielarie, Confectii de Piele, Prelucrarea Cauciucului si a Maselor Plastice, Sticla, Ceramica Fina, Articole Casnice, Utilaje, Piese de Schimb, Jucarii.*
Desc: Studies and articles in the field of the light industry.
Ind/Abst Chem. Abstr.; Coal Abstr.

FR
INDUSTRIE DE LA CHAUSSURE ET DES CUIRS ET PEAUX BRUTS ET TANNES DANS LES PAYS DE L'OCDE; STATISTIQUES. THE FOOTWEAR, RAW HIDES AND SKINS AND LEATHER INDUSTRY IN OECD COUNTRIES; STATISTICS, L'. **Main/Corp** Organisation for Economic Co-Operation and Development. **Added/Corp** Organisation for Economic Co-operation and Development. Footwear, Raw Hides and Skins and Leather Industry in OECD Countries; Statistics. **VFOAT** Footwear, Raw Hides and Skins and Leather Industry in OECD Countries. (1973/74)-. French (English). an. $4.50. OECD Publications and Information Center, 2 rue Andre-Pascal, 75775 Paris Cedex 16 France. **Tel** 011 33 1 45248167, US:(202)785-6323, FAX 011 33 1 45248500 OR 45248176, telex 620 160 OCDE. **LC** HD9778.A2; O7. **DD** 338.4/7/675. ***Continues*** *Industrie des Cuirs et Peaux et de la Chaussure dans les Pays de l'OCDE.*

FR/0980-1367
INDUSTRIE DU CUIR (PARIS, FRANCE : 1987). (INDUSTRIE DU CUIR.). [Ind. cuir]. **Added/Corp** A.F.I.C.T.I.C. (Association) Centre Technique Cuir, Chaussure, Maroquinerie. (Jan. 1987)-. Academic Scholarly Publication. French (English). Ten times a year (June/July and Aug./Sept. issues combined). 675.81F France; 920.00F other. Societe des Publications le Cuir, 1 rue Garnier, 92200 Neuilly Seine France. **Tel** 011 33 1 47381107, FAX 011 33 1 46249924, telex 610-672. **ED** Frederic Lavigne-Taddei. **CODEN** INCUEH. **Ad Acc, Adv Mgr:** J. Verry. **Circ:** 2,000. Documents available from CASDDS. ***Continues*** *Revue Technique des Industries du Cuir, 0035-4236.*
Desc: International magazine covering leather goods and the leather industry.
Ind/Abst Art Archaeol. Tech. Abstr.; Chem. Abstr. (1987-); CIS Abstr.; EMBASE.

CN/0823-6976
INTERNATIONAL FUR FASHION REVIEW. ***Ceased.*** [Int. fur fash. rev.]. Ceased (Dec. 1988). Periodical. English. bm. Fashion Mode Communications, 4626 St Catherine Street West, Montreal Quebec H3Z 1S3 Canada. **ED** Marsha Ross. **DD** 391. **Ad Acc. Circ:** 10,000 (ctrl).
Desc: Complete world-wide coverage of fur industry news, fashion, feature articles, etc.

UK
INTERNATIONAL LEATHER GUIDE. **VFOAT** Leather Guide. (1970)-. English. an. £89.00. Benn Business Information Service Ltd, Riverbank House, Angel Lane, Tonbridge Kent TN9 1SE England. **Tel** 011 44 732 362666, FAX 011 44 732 770483, telex 95454 BBIS. **ED** Pat Bryant. **LC** TS945; .E87. **DD** 675/.0029/4. **Circ:** 1,850. ***Continues*** *Leather Guide, 0140-413X.*
Desc: Worldwide coverage of hide and skin suppliers, tanners, merchants and chemical and machinery supplies. Alphabetical and by country listings of 1,400 hide and skin suppliers with details of the nature of business and the varieties of skins in which a company trades.

UK
JOURNAL & REPORT - NATIONAL UNION OF THE FOOTWEAR, LEATHER & ALLIED TRADES. ***Suspended.*** **Main/Corp** National Union of the Footwear, Leather & Allied Trades. **VAT** Journal and Report. Aug./Sept. 1977-?. Periodical. English. bm. £4.00 UK; £5.00 other. National Union Footwear, Leather Trades/Grange Earl Barton, Northampton NN6 OJH England. **Tel** 0604/810326, FAX 0604/812496. **ED** G F Browett. **Circ:** 4,500 (ctrl). ***Continues*** *National Union of the Footwear, Leather, & Allied Trades. Monthly Journal and Report.*

NR/0189-5222
JOURNAL OF LEATHER RESEARCH. (JOURNAL OF LEATHER RESEARCH / LEATHER RESEARCH INSTITUTE OF NIGERIA.). [J. leather res.]. **Added/Corp** Leather Research Institute of Nigeria (Zaria). Vol. 1, No. 1 (1983)-. Periodical. English. qt. Leather Research Institute of Nigeria, P M B 1952, Zaria Nigeria. **CODEN** JLRSDE. Documents available from CASDDS.
Ind/Abst Chem. Abstr.

US/0002-9726
JOURNAL OF THE AMERICAN LEATHER CHEMISTS ASSOCIATION, THE. [J. Am. Leather Chem. Assoc.]. **Main/Corp** American Leather Chemists Association. Vol. 1 (1906)-. Periodical. English. Twelve times a year. $110.00 US & Canada; $115.00 other. American Leather Chemists Association, Tanners Building, University of Cincinnati, PO Box 210014, Cincinnati OH 45221-0014. **Tel** (513)556-1197. **ED** Dr. Stephen H. Feairheller (editor's address: 804 Preston Road, Erdenheim PA 19118; editor's phone: (215)233-6610). **LC** TS940; .A5. **DD** 675/.2/05. **CODEN** JALCAQ. Index available. **Ad Acc, Adv Mgr:** Velma Becker, **Tel** (513)556-1197. **Pr Rev. Circ:** 1,150. available on microfilm and microfiche from University Microfilms International (UMI). Documents available from Article Express International, The Genuine Article, BIOSIS Document Express, CASDDS.
Desc: Articles are original research reports in the field of leather chemistry and technology. Other research articles and relevant patents issued are covered in abstract form.
Ind/Abst AGRICOLA [Select. Cov.]; Bioeng. Abstr.; Biol. Abstr.; Chem. Abstr.; Curr. Contents Eng. Tech. Appl. Sci.; Ei Page One; Eng. Index Annu. [Select. Cov.]; Index Vet.; Res. Alert [Full Cov.]; SCISEARCH; Soils Fert.; Vet. Bull.

II/0019-5758
JOURNAL OF THE INDIAN LEATHER TECHNOLOGISTS' ASSOCIATION. **Added/Corp** Indian Leather Technologists' Association. (1952)-. Periodical. English. mo. $45.00. Indian Leather Technologists' Association, Calcutta, India. **(Subscription address:** Prints India, 11 Darya Ganj, New Delhi, 110002 India, (Phone: 011 91 11 3268645)**) CODEN** JILTAV.

UK/0144-0322
JOURNAL OF THE SOCIETY OF LEATHER TECHNOLOGISTS AND CHEMISTS. [J. Soc. Leather Technol. Chem.]. **Added/Corp** Society of Leather Technologists and Chemists (Great Britain). Vol. 57, No. 1 (Jan./Feb. 1973)-. Academic Scholarly Publication. English. Six times a year. £39.00 (surface mail); £46.00 (airmail). Society of Leather Technologists and Chemists, 1 Edges Court, Moulton Northampton NN3 1UJ England. **Tel** 11 44 0604 647318, FAX 11 44 0604 647318. **ED** M.K. Leafe. **CODEN** JSLTBY. Index Available in first issue of next volume--attached. **Bk Rev**, (Qty: 3-4). **Ad Acc, Adv Mgr:** Robert Blakey, **Tel** 11 44 0532 621005. **Pr Rev. Circ:** 900. Documents available from The Genuine Article, CASDDS. ***Continues*** *Journal of the Society of Leather Trades's Chemists, 0037-9921.*
Desc: Scientific and technical articles on subjects relating to the manufacturing of leather.
Ind/Abst Chem. Abstr.; Curr. Contents Eng. Tech. Appl. Sci.; Curr. Technol. Index; Res. Alert [Full Cov.]; SCISEARCH.

JA
KAWA TO HAKIMONO. **VFOAT** Leather & Footwears. Japanese (Japanese). Tokyo-to Sangyo Rodo Kaikan, 106 Hashiba 1, Taito-ku Tokyo Japan. **LC** HD9780.A1; K38.

XR/0023-4338
KOZARSTVI. [Kozarstvi]. Periodical. Czech (English and German; table of contents in Russian, English and German). mo. **(Subscription address:** Artia Pegas Press Ltd., Palac Metro Narodni Trida 25, 11210 Prague 1 Czech Republic.**) LC** TS940; .K58. **CODEN** KOZAAT. Documents available from CASDDS.
Ind/Abst AGRICOLA; Chem. Abstr.; Saf. Health Work.

RU/0023-4354
KOZHEVENNO-OBUVNAIA PROMYSHLENNOST. (1959)-. Academic Scholarly Publication. Russian. mo. $99.95. **(Subscription address:** East View Publications Inc., 3020 Harbor Lane North, Suite 110, Minneapolis MN 55447.**) CODEN** KOOPAJ. Index available in last issue of volume--attached. Documents available from CASDDS.
Ind/Abst Art Archaeol. Tech. Abstr.; Chem. Abstr.; Saf. Health Work.

RU/0023-4885
KROLIKOVODSTVO I ZVEROVODSTVO. (1958)-. Periodical. Russian. bm. ***Continues in part*** *Karakulevodstvo i Zverovodstvo.*
Desc: Information on rabbit breeding and the breeding of animals for fur.
Ind/Abst Index Vet.; Nutr. Abstr. Rev., Ser. A, Hum. Exp.; Protozoolog. Abstr.

CN/0828-9859
LEATHER AND ALLIED PRODUCTS INDUSTRIES. (LEATHER AND ALLIED PRODUCTS INDUSTRIES / STATISTICS CANADA, INDUSTRY DIVISION, CENSUS OF MANUFACTURES SECTION.). [Leather allied prod. ind.]. **Added/Corp** Statistics Canada. Census of Manufactures Section. Statistics Canada. Industry Division. Statistics Canada. Annual Survey of Manufactures Section. **VFOAT** Industrie de Cuir et des Produits Connexes; Industrie du Cuir et des Produits Connexes. (1984)-. English (French). an. 38.00Can$ Canada; $46.00 US; $54.00 other.

Statistics Canada, Publications Sales & Services, Main Building Room 1710, Ottawa Ontario K1A 0T6 Canada. **Tel** (613)951-5078, (800)267-6677, FAX (613)951-1584, telex 053-3585. **LC** HD9780.C2; L43. **DD** 338.4/7685/0971/021. ***Continues*** *Leather Industries, 0319-8898.*
Desc: Annual census of manufacturers.

UK
LEATHER AND FOOTWEAR IN ASIA. (1986)-. Periodical. English (Chinese). Six times a year. £60.00. Benn Electronics Publishing Ltd, Sovereign Way Tonbridge, Kent TN9 1RW England. **Tel** 011 44 732 364422, telex 27844. **Ad Acc, Adv Mgr:** Graham Bond. **Circ:** 6,000. ***Continues*** *Leather in Asia, 0269-1418.*

US/0075-8345
LEATHER BUYERS GUIDE. ***Ceased.*** **VFOAT** Leather Buyers Guide & Directory. (19??)-(19??). English. an. Rumpf Publishing Company, Nickerson and Collins Division, 850 Busse Highway, Park Ridge IL 60068. **LC** HD9780.U5; L2. **DD** 338.4/7/68502573. ***Continues*** *L & S Leather Buyers Guide and Leather Trade Marks for Shoe and Accessory Leathers.*

US/0898-0128
LEATHER CONSERVATION NEWS. [Leather conserv. news]. **Added/Corp** Texas Memorial Museum. Materials Conservation Laboratory. (198?)-. Periodical. English. sa (April and October). $15.00. Paul S.Storch, Minnesota Historical Society, 345 Kellog Blvd. West, St. Paul MN 55102-1906. **Tel** (612)297-5774, FAX (612)296-9961. **ED** Paul S. Storch. **DD** 675. Index available (In July). cum. index. **Bk Rev**, (Qty: Varies). **Circ:** 200.
Desc: Journal of contributions from the field describing theoretical issues, current research and treatments of leather and leather objects in the collections of museums and other cultural institutions.
Ind/Abst Art Archaeol. Tech. Abstr.

UK/0269-1418
LEATHER IN ASIA. [Leather Asia]. (1986)-. Periodical. English. qt. £60.00. Benn Publications Ltd., Sovereign Way, Tonbridge TNQ 1RW England. **Tel** 011 44 732 364422, FAX 011 44 732 361534, telex 0732 95132 BENTON G. **DD** 338.47675095.
Ind/Abst PROMT [Full Txt.].

UK/0023-9739
LEATHER (LONDON). (LEATHER.). [Leather]. Vol. 151 No. 4056 (Jan. 3, 1964)-. Periodical. English. mo. £61.00 UK; £81.00 other. Benn Publications Ltd., Sovereign Way, Tonbridge TNQ 1RW England. **Tel** 011 44 732 364422, FAX 011 44 732 361534, telex 0732 95132 BENTON G. **LC** TS940; .L5. **DD** 338.4/7/67520942. available on microfilm and microfiche from University Microfilms International (UMI). ***Formed by the union of*** *Leather Trades Review* ***and*** *Leather Goods Manufacturer.*
Ind/Abst Art Archaeol. Tech. Abstr.; PROMT [Full Txt.].

US/0023-9763
LEATHER MANUFACTURER, THE. [Leather manuf.]. (18??)-. Academic Scholarly Publication. English. mo. $43.00 US; $55.00 Canada; $70.00 other. Shoe Trades Publishing Company, 61 Massachusetts Avenue, Arlington MA 02174. **Tel** (617)648-8160, FAX (617)492-0126, telex 325736 SHOETRADE. **ED** James Sutton. **CODEN** LEMAA7. **Bk Rev. Ad Acc. Circ:** 2,000. Documents available from CASDDS.
Ind/Abst Chem. Abstr. (1883-1983).

II
LEATHER SCIENCE ABSTRACTS : LESA. Added/Corp National Information Centre for Leather and Allied Industries (India). **VFOAT** LESA. (Jan. 1988)-. English. mo. $100.00. National Information Centre for Leather & Allied Industries, Adyar, Madras, India. **(Subscription address:** Prints India, 11 Darya Ganj, New Delhi 110002 India.**) LC** TS940; .L48. **DD** 675. ***Continues*** *Current Leather Literature.*

II/0023-9771
LEATHER SCIENCE (MADRAS). ***Suspended.*** (LEATHER SCIENCE.). [Leather sci.]. Jan. 1963-Suspended with Vol. 34, Dec. 1987. Periodical. English. mo. $25.00. Central Leather Research Institute, Adyar, Madras 600 020 India. **Tel** 412616. **ED** R B Mitra. **LC** TS940; .L47. **CODEN** LESCA. **Bk Rev. Ad Acc. Circ:** 150. Documents available from CASDDS. ***Continues*** *Bulletin of the Central Leather Research Institute.*
Desc: Contains original research articles, short communications, process papers, notes and news items.
Ind/Abst Art Archaeol. Tech. Abstr.; Chem. Abstr.

US/0884-660X
LEATHER TODAY. (LEATHER TODAY : LT.). [Leather today]. **VFOAT** LT. Vol. 1, No. 1 (Sept. 1985)-. Periodical. English. bm. $80.00 US; $110.00 other. Fur Publishing Plus Inc, 19 W 21st Street/Suite 403, New York NY 10010. **Tel** (212)727-1210, FAX (212)727-1218. **DD** 685.

II
LEATHER WARE. VFOAT Leatherware. (1986)-. Periodical. English. mo. $30.00. **(Subscription address:** Prints India, 11 Darya Ganj, New Delhi 110002 India.**)** ***Absorbed*** *Tanner.*

GW/0024-0176
LEDER. (DAS LEDER; FACHZEITSCHRIFT FUER DIE CHEMIE UND TECHNOLOGIE DER LEDERHERSTELLUNG.). [Leder]. **Added/Corp** Verein fuer Gerberei-Chemie und -Technik. (1950)-. Academic Scholarly Publication. German (summaries and/or abstracts in English, French and Spanish). mo. DM173.00. Eduard Roether Verlag KG, PO Box 101205, D 64212 Darmstadt Germany. **Tel** 011 49 6151 300116. **LC** TS940; .L54. **CODEN** LEDEA8. Index available. **Bk Rev. Ad Acc. Circ:** 2,200 (ctrl). available on microfilm from University Microfilms International (UMI). Documents available from CASDDS.
Desc: Technical journal for leather chemistry and technology which attends to the whole area of technology and chemistry of the leather production including the auxiliary materials.
Ind/Abst Art Archaeol. Tech. Abstr.; Chem. Abstr.

GW/0342-7641
LEDER UND HAUTEMARKT. [Leder HËautemarkt]. (1949)-. Periodical. German. Twenty-six times a year. DM406.80 Germany; DM412.25 others. Umschau Verlag, Postfach 110262, D-60037 Frankfurt Germany. **Tel** 011 49 69 2600692, FAX 011 49 69 2600223, telex 411964. **CODEN** LHGPDC. **[CCC].** Documents available from CASDDS.
Ind/Abst Chem. Abstr.; Saf. Health Work.

NE/0168-471X
LEDERINDUSTRIE / CENTRAAL BUREAU VOOR DE STATISTIEK, HOOFDAFDELING STATISTIEKEN VAN INDUSTRIE EN BOUWNIJVERHEID. VFOAT Tanneries and Leather Finishing. Dutch (summaries and/or abstracts in English). an. Fl9.50. Centraal Bureau voor de Statistiek, AFD ALG Zaken, Postbus 959, 2270 AZ Voorburg Netherlands. **Tel** 011 31 70 3373800, FAX 011 31 038 7429, telex 32692 CBS NL. **LC** HD9780.N2; L43.

NE/0168-5139
LEDERWARENINDUSTRIE, EXCL. KLEDING / CENTRAAL BUREAU VOOR DE STATISTIEK, HOOFDAFDELING STATISTIEKEN VAN INDUSTRIE EN BOUWNIJVERHEID. VFOAT Lederwarenindustrie, Exclusief Kleding; Manufacture of Products of Leather, Except Clothing. 1982-. Dutch (summaries and/or abstracts in English). an. Fl9.50. Centraal Bureau voor de Statistiek, AFD ALG Zaken, Postbus 959, 2270 AZ Voorburg Netherlands. **Tel** 011 31 70 3373800, FAX 011 31 038 7429, telex 32692 CBS NL. **LC** HD9780.N2; N48A. **DD** 338.4/7685/09492. ***Continues*** *Netherlands. Centraal Bureau Voor de Statistiek. Produktiestatistieken: Lederwarenindustrie, Excl. Kleding.*

II
LEXPORT. Main/Corp Export Promotion Council for Finished Leather & Leather Manufactures. English (English). Export Promotion Council for Finished Leather & Leather Manufactures, 15/46 Civil Lines, PO Box No 198, Kanpur 208001 India. **LC** HD9780.I62; E95A.
Desc: Consists of the annual report of the council.

IT
LINEAPELLE. Italian (English). qt. L65000 Italy. Lineapelle Editoriale Pub Srl, Via Brisa 3, 20123 Milan Italy. **Tel** 011 39 2 801026, FAX 011 39 2 860032. **Bk Rev. Ad Acc, Adv Mgr:** F. Bacchi, **Tel** 02-801020. **Circ:** 30,000 (ctrl).

CN/0068-8762
LLOYD'S CANADIAN FOOTWEAR AND LEATHER DIRECTORY. VAT Canadian Footwear and Leather Directory (1965). 41st Ed. (1964/65)-. English. an. 30.00Can$. Sentinel Business Publications, 7575 Trans Canada Highway, Suite 500, St. Laurent Quebec H4T 1V6 Canada. **Tel** (514)333-1116, FAX (514)631-8858. **ED** Carola Clifford. **LC** WMLC L 83/9956. **DD** 338.4/7/68502571. **Ad Acc. Circ:** 4,800 (ctrl). ***Continues*** *Willson's Canadian Footwear and Leather Directory, 0510-498X.*
Desc: A directory of product listings and suppliers to the footwear and leather industries in Canada.

US/8750-8311
LOCAL 1-FLM TEMPO. Added/Corp United Food and Commercial Workers International Union. Local 1-FLM. **VFOAT** Local 1 FLM Tempo; Tempo. **VAT** Local One Fur, Leather and Machine Tempo. Vol. 18 No. 2 (June 1984)-. Periodical. English. bm. United Food & Commercial Workers International Union, 1775 K Street NW, Washington DC 20006. **Tel** (202)223-3111. ***Continues*** *FLM Joint Board Tempo, 0162-5969.*

SZ/0024-0192
LSL; LEDER, SCHUKE, LEDERWAREN. VFOAT Leder, Schuhe, Lederwaren. V. 1- ; Jan. 1966-. Academic Scholarly Publication. German. mo. Deutscher Judo Verband, Redaktion Ippon Segewaldweg 40, D 12557 Berlin Germany. **Tel** 011 49 711 210770, telex 051 678. **LC** TS940; .L2. **DD** 685/.05. **CODEN** LSLEBB. Documents available from CASDDS.
Ind/Abst Chem. Abstr.

IT
MONDO DELLA CALZATURA : DESIGN E PRODUZIONE. (19??)-. Italian. Nine times a year. L100000 Italy; L130000 other. Servizi Editoriali Riuniti, Via IV Novembre 54, 20010 Seguro Sett Mil Italy. **Tel** 011 39 2 33501346.

US/0740-9117
NORTH AMERICAN RETAIL FURRIERS DIRECTORY. (19??)-. Directory. English. an. $50.00. Directory Enterprises, 141 West 28th Street, New York NY 10001. **LC** HD9944.U44; N67. **DD** 685/.24/029473.

CN/0838-4967
NORTH WEST COURANT. [North West courant]. **Added/Corp** Volunteers of Old Fort William. (Summer 1988)-. Periodical. English. qt. 10.00Can$. Volunteers of Old Fort William, Thunder Bay Ontario P0T 2Z0 Canada. **Tel** (802)577-8461. **DD** 971.3/12.

FR
OFFICIEL DE LA FOURRURE 1960, L'. (1960)-. Periodical. French. Six times a year. $72.00. L'Officiel de la Fourrure, 11 rue Faubourg Poissonniere, F-75009 Paris France. ***Continues*** *Fourrures Magazine, l'Official de la Fourrure, 1162-5724.*

IT
PELLICCE MODA. (19??)-. Italian (English). Seven times a year. L95000 Italy; L200000 other. Editoriale Albero, Via Branda Castiglioni 2 A, 20156 Milan Italy. **Tel** 011 39 2 38002901.

SP
PIEL. Spanish. Ediciones Doyma SA, Travesera de Gracia 17 21, 08021 Barcelona Spain. **Tel** 011 34 3 2000711, 011 34 3 4145706, FAX 011 34 3 2091136, telex 51964 INK E.
Ind/Abst Indice Med. Esp.

CC/0253-3642
PIGE KEJI. (PI KE KO CHI.). [Pige keji]. **Added/Corp** Chung-kuo Pi Ke Kung Yeh ko Ching Pao Chan. **VFOAT** Pige Keji. (19??)-. Academic Scholarly Publication. Chinese. mo. $33.97. **(Subscription address:** China International Book Trading Corporation, PO Box 399, Library Service Department, Beijing 100044 People's Republic of China.**) CODEN** PKKCDO. Documents available from CASDDS.
Desc: Chinese leather magazine.
Ind/Abst Chem. Abstr.

PL/0370-1743
PRZEGLAD SKORZANY. Added/Corp Poland. Ministerstwo Przemysu Lekkiego. (1946)-. Academic Scholarly Publication. Polish. bm. Price on Request. **(Subscription address:** ARS Polona, PO Box 1001, 00068 Warsaw Poland.**) LC** TS940; .P86. **CODEN** PRZKAX. Documents available from CASDDS.
Ind/Abst Chem. Abstr.

US/0027-4135
QUARTERLY - THE MUSEUM OF THE FUR TRADE. [Q. - Mus. Fur Trade]. **Main/Corp** Museum of the Fur Trade. **VFOAT** Museum of the Fur Trade Quarterly. (1965)-. Periodical. English. Four times a year (Jan., Apr., July, Oct.). $6.00 US; $7.00 other. Museum Fur Trade, HC-74 Box 18, Chadron NE 69337. **Tel** (308)432-3843. **ED** Charles E. Hanson Jr. **LC** HD9944.U44; C45a. Index Available, published separately, free-automatically sent (Every 4 years at no charge.). cum. index. **Bk Rev**, (Qty: 25). **Circ:** 2,600 (ctrl).
Desc: Articles on the material aspects of the North American fur trade. Book reviews in each issue and generous illustrations.
Ind/Abst Am. Hist. Life (1986-).

US/0732-6742
RAVE REVIEW, THE. Vol. 1, No. 1 (April 1982)-. Periodical. English. qt. David Hume's Leather World, PO Box 11769, Milwaukee WI 53211-0769.

MX
REVISTA DE LA FEDERACION MEXICANA DE QUIMICOS Y TECNICOS DEL CUERO. Periodical. Spanish. bm. Free to Mexico. Tehuantepec 255 Primer Piso, Mexico 7 DF Mexico. **Tel** 564-6600. **ED** E Izaguirre Aguilar. **Ad Acc.**

US/1064-0029
SANDY PARKER REPORTS. [Sandy Parker rep.]. (1977)-. Periodical. English. Fifty times a year. $125.00. Sandford Advertising Inc., PO Box 506, Valley Stream NY 11582. **Tel** (212)971-9091, FAX (212)695-9431. **DD** 338.
Desc: Covers international fur news.

US/0747-3753
SANDY PARKER'S FUR WORLD. [Sandy Parker's fur world]. **VFOAT** Fur World. (1984)-. Periodical.

English. wk. $50.00 (one year), $85.00 (two years), $125.00 (three years) US and Canada; $100.00 (one year), $170.00 (two years), $250.00 (three years) other. Fur World, 363 7th Avenue, New York NY 10001. **Tel** (212)971-9091, FAX (212)695-9431. **ED** Bernard Groger. **DD** 338. **Ad Acc. Circ:** 3,000 (ctrl). ***Continues*** *Sandy Parker Reports.*
Desc: Features news of retail stores, auctions, fashion trends, trade shows, pelt prices, wholesale buying, financial news and all other information pertaining to the Fur trade.

DK/0105-2403
SCIENTIFUR. Added/Corp Nordiske Jordbruksforskeres Forening. Fur Animal Division. Vol. 1, No. 1 (Feb. 1977)-. Periodical. English. qt. Kr500.00 (individuals members of IFASA), Kr600.00 other. International Fur Animal Scientific Association, PO Box 145 Okern, N 0509 Oslo Norway. **Tel** 011 47 2 2644150, FAX 011 47 2 2643591. **ED** Gunnar Joergensen (editor's address: PO Box 13, DK-8830 Tjele Denmark; editor's phone: 45 89 991502). Index available. cum. index. **Bk Rev. Ad Acc. Circ:** 600.
Desc: Original scientific reports and abstracts regarding all aspects in production of farmed fur-bearing animals.
Ind/Abst Agric. Eng. Abstr. (1991-); Anim. Breed. Abstr.; Dairy Sci. Abstr.; Index Vet.; Nutr. Abstr. Rev., Ser. B, Live Feeds and Feed.; Potato Abstr.; Vet. Bull.

US/0361-3232
SHOWCASE (NEW YORK). (SHOWCASE.). **Added/Corp** Luggage and Leather Goods Manufacturers or America, Inc., New York. Vol. 1, (Fall 1975)-. Periodical. English. Six times a year. $35.00. Luggage & Leather Goods, 350 Fifth Avenue, New York NY 10118. **Tel** (212)695-2340, FAX (212)643-8021. **ED** Michele Pittenger. **LC** HD9999.L83; U56. **DD** 338.4/7/685510973. **Ad Acc. Circ:** 11,500 (ctrl).
Desc: Contains articles edited for retailers, dealers, manufacturers and suppliers, about luggage, business cases, personal leather goods, handbags and accessories.

BL
SISTEMA DE INFORMACAO ESTATISTICA PARA A INDUSTRIA NACIONAL DE COUROS : BOLETIM DE INFORMACOES. Main/Corp Instituto Brasileiro do Couro, Calcados e Afins. Bulletin. Portuguese. Instituto Brasileiro do Couro Calcados E Afins, Caixa Postal 48 93.600, Estancia Velha Brazil. **LC** HD9778.B7; I56A.

XR
STROJIMPORT. See Textiles.

FR
TECHNICUIR. V. 1- 1967-. Periodical. French. ir. SETIC, 54 rue Rene Boulanger, Paris 10E France.

FR/0985-5556
TECHNIQUE CHAUSSURE MAROQUINERIE MODE. (1986)-. Periodical. French. Ten times a year. 400.00F France; 500.00F other. Societe Charles Vincent, 7 Ter Cour Des Petites Ecuries, 75010 Paris France. **UDC** 685.31. ***Continues*** *Techniques Chaussure Maroquinerie, 0246-134X.*

US/8750-233X
TRAPPER AND PREDATOR CALLER, THE. VFOAT Trapper & Predator Caller. (Aug. 1984)-. Periodical. English. mo. $16.95 US; $27.25 other. Krause Publications, 700 East State Street, Iola WI 54990-0001. **Tel** (715)445-2214, FAX (715)445-4087, telex 55 6461. **LC** SK283; .T68. **DD** 639/.11. **Bk Rev. Ad Acc. Circ:** 50,000 (ctrl). ***Continues*** *Trapper, 0739-0599.*
Desc: Covers the rural fur trade; taking and marketing of animal skins to be manufactured into garments, harvesting a renewable resource when managed biologically by state agencies.

US/0747-475X
TRAVELWARE. See Economics-Industry and Production.

IT
ULTIMISSIME PELLICCERIA. Italian. mo. L80.000 Italy; L100.000 other. Editrice SAE Srl, Via Cagnola 3, 20154 Milan Italy. **Tel** 39 2 3311003, 3311149, FAX 39 2 3311320. **ED** Elena Salvaneschi. **Bk Rev. Ad Acc. Circ:** 6,000.
Desc: Technical information, news and fashion magazine for furriers.

IT/1120-7795
VOGUE PELLE. See Clothing Industry and Fashion.

US
WEEKLY BULLETIN - WEEKLY BULLETIN LEATHER SHOE NEWS CO. ***Ceased.*** **Main/Corp** Weekly Bulletin Leather Shoe News Co. ( )-( ). Bulletin. English. wk. Weekly Bulletin of Leather & Shoe News, 100 Shaker Road, Harvard MA 01451-1230. **Tel** (617)542-2436. **ED** Louis C Schwaab. **LC** TS940; .W4. **DD** 338.4/7/68505. **Bk Rev. Ad Acc. Circ:** 2,800. ***Continues*** *Weekly Bulletin of Leather & Shoe News.*
Desc: Weekly news, markets, trade information for tanning and footwear manufacturing leather garment fields.

US/0894-3087
WORLD LEATHER. [World leather]. Vol. 1, No. 1 (Sept. 1987)-. Periodical. English. bm. $55.00. Shoe Trades Publishing Company, 61 Massachusetts Avenue, Arlington MA 02174. **Tel** (617)648-8160, FAX (617)492-0126, telex 325736 SHOETRADE. **ED** Iain Howie. **Bk Rev. Ad Acc.** ctrl circ.
Desc: International journal for tanning industry.

CC/1001-6813
ZHONGGUO PIGE. VFOAT China Leather. (1990)-. Academic Scholarly Publication. Chinese. mo. **DD** 685.2. Documents available from CASDDS. ***Continues*** *Pige Keji, 0253-3642.*
Ind/Abst Chem. Abstr.

LIBRARY AND INFORMATION SCIENCES

AU
1001 & 1 BUCH. (19??)-. German. Six times a year. S240.00. 1001 & 1 Buch, Bundesministerium fuer Unterricht, Kunst und Sport, Minoritenplatz 5, A-1014 Vienna Austria. **ED** Peter Schneck. **Bk Rev**, (Qty: 60). **Acid Free. Circ:** 8,500.
Ind/Abst Child. Lit. Abstr. (19??-).

CN/0226-7195
A. C. C. L. UNION LIST OF SERIALS. [A.C.C.L. union list ser.]. **Main/Corp** Alberta Council of College Librarians. **VAT** Alberta Council of College Librarians Union List of Serials. (1973)-. English. 30.00Can$. Alberta Council of College Librarians, Buchanan Library, 3000 College Drive, Lethbridge ALT T1K 1L6 Canada. **Tel** (403)382-6944. **DD** 018/.134.

US/0883-7376
A.P.L.I.C. SPECIAL PUBLICATION. [APLIC spec. publ.]. **Main/Corp** Association for Population/Family Planning Libraries and Information Centers, International. No. 1-. Monographic series. English. ir. Price varies per volume. Association for Population/Family Planning Libraries and Information Centers, c/o Population Council Library, 1 Dag Hammarskjold Plaza, New York NY 10017. **Tel** (212)644-1620. **DD** 026.
Ind/Abst Popul. Index (?-?).

CN/0835-8672
A RAYONS OUVERTS. (A RAYONS OUVERTS : BULLETIN DE LA BIBLIOTHEQUE NATIONALE DU QUEBEC.). [A rayons ouverts]. **Added/Corp** Bibliotheque Nationale du Quebec. Vol. 1, No. 1 (1988)-. Periodical. French. Four times a year. Free. Bibliotheque Nationale du Quebec, 1700 rue Saint Denis, Montreal Quebec H2X 3K6 Canada. **Tel** (514)873-1100 ext. 160. **DD** 027.5714. **Bk Rev. Circ:** 1,000 (ctrl). ***Separated from*** *L'Incunable, 0825-1746.*
Desc: Contains news from the library, special events, collections, and services.

CN/0703-5276
AALT TECHNICIAN. (THE A A L T TECHNICIAN.). **Main/Corp** Alberta Association of Library Technicians. **VAT** Alberta Association of Library Technicians Technician. Vol. 1 (Sept. 1975)-. Periodical. English. Four times a year. Free. Alberta Association of Library Technicians, PO Box 700, Edmonton Alberta T5J 2L4 Canada. **Tel** (403)424-7764. **DD** 023/.5. **Circ:** 270. ***Continues*** *AALT Technician Bulletin, 0228-9490.*

NE/0303-5964
ABHA. ANNUAL BIBLIOGRAPHY OF THE HISTORY OF THE PRINTED BOOK AND LIBRARIES. See Library and Information Sciences-Abstracting, Bibliographies and Statistics.

GW/0720-6763
ABI-TECHNIK. [ABI-Tech.]. **VFOAT** A.B.I.-Technik. **VAT** ABI Technik. (1981)-. Periodical. German. qt (Mar., June, Sept., Dec.). DM153.50 Germany; DM162.00 other. Verlag Karlheinz Holz, Rheingaustr 85, Postfach 3329, D-65023 Wiesbaden Germany. **Tel** 011 49 611 9450751, FAX 011 49 611 261124. **ED** Karleienz Holz. **LC** Z678.9.A1; A22. **DD** 025.3/028/54. Index available. **Ad Acc. Circ:** 2,000. available on an online database from CAN/OLE; DIALOG; ORBIT; and DATA-STAR. Documents available from Ask*IEEE.
Desc: Articles on technological aspects of library and information science, including data processing, automation, conservation, and inter-library techniques.
Ind/Abst INSPEC (1983-); Libr. Inf. Sci. Abstr.

AT/0726-0644
ABN NEWS / NATIONAL LIBRARY OF AUSTRALIA, AUSTRALIAN BIBLIOGRAPHIC NETWORK. Main/Corp Australian Bibliographic Network. **VFOAT** Australian Bibliographic Network News. No. 1 (Jan./Feb. 1982)-. Periodical. English. Six times a year (Jan., Mar., May, July, Sept., Nov.). 40.00Aus$. ABN Marketing & Training Sect, National Library of Australia, Parkes Place, Parkes 2601 Australia. **Tel** 011 61 62 621690, 011 61 62 621111, FAX 011 61 62 733648, telex 62100. **ED** Margaret Davey, (editor's address: Network Services Marketing, National Library of Australia, Canberra Australian Capital Territories, 2600 Australia, phone: 011 61 06 2621239). **LC** Z674.83.A82; A92a. **DD** 021.6/5/0994. **Circ:** 2,500 (ctrl).
Desc: Describes features and recent developments of the information services, and other services provided by Network at the National Library.
Ind/Abst AESIS Q.; Aust. Educ. Index (199?-); Aust. Libr. Inf. Sci. Abstr. (1982-1984, 1991-).

US
ABSTRACTS, STRENGTHENING RESEARCH LIBRARY RESOURCES PROGRAM. VFOAT Strengthening Research Library Resources Program; Higher Education Act, Title II-C. Government Publication. English. an. US Department of Education, 400 Maryland Avenue SW, Room 4181, Washington DC 20202. **Tel** (202)401-1576, FAX (202)272-5447. **ED** Louise V Sutherland. **Circ:** 500.
Desc: Projects undertaken by major American research libraries with grants under the Higher Education Act Title II - C during the fiscal year covered.

US/1055-4769
ACADEMIC AND LIBRARY COMPUTING. ***Title Change.*** **See** Computers-Microcomputers, Personal Computers.

US/0894-993X
ACADEMIC LIBRARY BOOK REVIEW. See Publishing-Books and Bookmaking.

IT/0001-4451
ACCADEMIE E BIBLIOTECHE D'ITALIA. [Accad. bibl. Ital.]. **Added/Corp** Italy. Ufficio Centrale per i Beni Librari e Gli Istituti Culturali. Italy. Direzione Generale delle Accademie e Biblioteche. Italy. Direzione Generale delle Accademie e Biblioteche e per la Diffusione della Cultura. Vol. 1 (July/Aug 1927)-. Periodical. Italian. qt. L80000 Italy; L130000 other. Organizzazione RAB SRL, Via Crocifisso 51, 00165 Rome Italy. **Tel** 011 39 6 632595, 6381177. available on microfilm and microfiche from University Microfilms International (UMI). ***Continues*** *Rivista Delle Biblioteche E Degli Archivi.*
Ind/Abst BHA : Biblio. Hist. Art; Libr. Inf. Sci. Abstr.; MLA Int. Bibl. Books Artic. Mod. Lang. Lit.; Romant. Move.

US/1051-0818
ACCESS (LANSING, MICH.). (ACCESS / LIBRARY OF MICHIGAN.). [Access]. **Added/Corp** Library of Michigan. **VFOAT** Library of Michigan Access. Vol. 8, No. 1 (July-Aug. 1990)-. Periodical. English. Six times a year. Free. Library of Michigan, Public Information Specialist, PO Box 30007, Lansing MI 48909. **Tel** (517)373-5578. **DD** 027. ***Continues*** *Library of Michigan Newsletter, 0739-8379.*

CN/0710-0132
ACCESS (LONDON, ONT.). (ACCESS : A NEWSLETTER OF THE LONDON PUBLIC LIBRARIES, GALLERIES, MUSEUMS.). Newsletter. English. mo. Free. London Public Libraries, 305 Queens Avenue, London Ontario N6B 3L7 Canada. **DD** 027.4713/26. ***Continues*** *Calendar of Events (London, Ont.).*

CN/0317-039X
ACCESS (VANCOUVER). (ACCESS.). No. 1- July 1974-. Periodical. English. Free. Greater Vancouver Library Council, 3622 East 1st Avenue, Vancouver BC V5M 1C3. **DD** 027.4/06/271133.

AT/1030-0155
ACCESS (VICTORIA, AUSTRALIA). See Education-Early Childhood and Primary Education.

UK
ACCESSIONS BULLETIN / TROPICAL DEVELOPMENT AND RESEARCH INSTITUTE, LIBRARY. Main/Corp Tropical Development and Research Institute (Great Britain) Library. **VFOAT** Library Accessions Bulletin; Library, Grays Inn Road Accessions Bulletin. No. 3 (1983)-. Bulletin. English. Tropical Development and Research Institute, 127 Clerkenwell Road, London EC1R 5DB England. ***Continues*** *Accessions Bulletin - Tropical Products Institute, Library.*

CN/0848-4856
ACCESSIONS LIST - EXTERNAL AFFAIRS AND INTERNATIONAL TRADE CANADA. LIBRARY. (ACCESSIONS LIST / LISTE D'ACQUISITIONS / AFFAIRES EXTERIEURES ET COMMERCE EXTERIEUR CANADA, BIBLIOTHEQUE. EXTERNAL AFFAIRS AND INTERNATIONAL TRADE CANADA, LIBRARY). [Access. list - Extern. Aff. Int. Trade Can., Libr.]. **Main/Corp** Canada. External Affairs and International Trade Canada. Library. **VFOAT** Liste d'Acquisitions. (Feb. 1990)-. Periodical. English (French). mo. **DD** 017/.5.

Continues Canada. Dept. of External Affairs. Library. Accessions List - Department of External Affairs, Library Services., 0705-4548.

DK/0084-9715
ACCESSIONSKATALOG - DENMARK. RIGSBIBLIOTEKAREMBEDET. **Main/Corp** Denmark. Rigsbibliotekarembedet. **VFOAT** Flleskatalog Over Danske Videnskabelige Og Faglige Bibliotekers Erhvervelser AF Udenlandsk Litteratur. V. 1- 1953-. Danish. an. kr1205.37. Dansk Bibliotekscenter AS, Tempovej 7 11, DK-2750 Ballerup Denmark. **Tel** 011 45 42 974000. **LC** Z941. available on microfiche. ***Supersedes** Katalog Over Erhvervelser Af Nyere Udenlandsk Litteratur Ved Statens Offentlige Biblioteker.*
Desc: Union catalogue of the acquisitions of foreign literature in Danish academic libraries.

DK
ACCESSIONSKATALOG FOR DRAMATISK BIBLIOTEK. **Main/Corp** Copenhagen. Universitet. Dramatisk Bibliotek. Danish. an. kr40.16. Dansk Bibliotekscenter AS, Tempovej 7 11, DK-2750 Ballerup Denmark. **Tel** 011 45 42 974000. **Circ:** 400 (ctrl). available in microform.
Desc: Union catalogue of the acquisitions of foreign literature in Danish academic libraries.

AT/1032-0431
ACLIS NEWS. (ACLIS NEWS AUSTRALIAN COUNCIL OF LIBRARIES & INFORMATION SERVICE.). **VFOAT** Australian Council of Libraries and Information Services News. (1988)-. Periodical. English. qt. 100.00Aus$. Australian Council of Libraries & Information Service, PO Box E202, Queen Victoria Terrace, Canberra ACT 2600 Australia. **Tel** 61 062 262 1244, FAX 61 062 273 4493. **Ad Acc**, **Adv Mgr:** Gordon Bower, **Tel** 61 6 2621200. ***Formed by the union of** ALICommunications, 0814-7809 **and** AACOBS Newsletter, 0725-5500.*
Ind/Abst AESIS Q.; Aust. Educ. Index; Aust. Libr. Inf. Sci. Abstr. (1988-).

UK/0263-6824
ACOLAM NEWSLETTER / STANDING CONFERENCE OF NATIONAL AND UNIVERSITY LIBRARIES, ADVISORY COMMITTEE ON LATIN AMERICAN MATERIALS. **VAT** advisory Committee on Latin American Materials Newsletter. No. 1 (May 1980)-. Newsletter. English. an. Editor Acolam Newsletter, National Library of Scotland, George IV Bridge, Edinburgh EH1 1EW United Kingdom. **LC** Z688.L4; A34. **DD** 015.8/034.

US/1043-6251
ACP HEALTH LIBRARY. ***Ceased.*** **See** Medical Science and Technology.

AT/0725-0037
ACQUISITION, BIBLIOGRAPHY, CATALOGUING NEWS / NATIONAL LIBRARY OF AUSTRALIA. ***Title Change.*** **Added/Corp** National Library of Australia. National Library of Australia. Bibliographical Services Branch. No. 1 (June 1981)-(19??). English. qt. National Library of Australia, Parkes Place, Canberra ACT, 2600 Australia. **Tel** 011 61 6 2621374, FAX 011 61 6 2731084. **LC** Z870.A1; A28. **DD** 027.594. **Circ:** 60 (ctrl). ***Continues** ROD News. **Continued by** NLA Gateways.*
Desc: Carries news relevant to Australian acquisition officers and catalogues from the National Library of Australia.
Ind/Abst Aust. Educ. Index (1983-); Aust. Libr. Inf. Sci. Abstr. (1982-1987).

US/0896-3576
ACQUISITIONS LIBRARIAN, THE. [Acquis. libr.]. Vol. 1 (1989)-. Academic Scholarly Publication. English. sa. $95.00 US; $133.00 other. The Haworth Press Inc, 10 Alice Street, Binghamton NY 13904-1580. **Tel** (607)722-5857, (800)3-HAWORTH, FAX (607)722-1424. **ED** Bill Katz (editor's address: State University of New York at Albany, School of Library and Information Science, Draper Hall 113, 135 Western Avenue, Albany, NY 12222). **LC** Z689.A15; A28. **DD** 025.2/05. **CODEN** AQLIER. **Bk Rev. Ad Acc. Pr Rev. Acid Free. Circ:** 355. available on microfilm and microfiche from University Microfilms International (UMI). Documents available from Ask*IEEE, Haworth Document Delivery Service, CASDDS.
Desc: Each issue is devoted to a single, broad, but well-defined and practical issue or topic of immediate concern to everyone working in library/information center acquisitions and collection development. This journal helps acquisitions librarians define and extend their roles and responsibilities. All articles in this journal are peer reviewed or refereed.
Ind/Abst Chem. Abstr.; Index Period. Artic. Relat. Law (19??-19??); Inf. Sci. Abstr.; INSPEC (No. 1 1989-); Libr. Inf. Sci. Abstr.

CN/1180-3592
ACQUISITIONS LIST - CANADIAN MUSEUM OF NATURE. LIBRARY SERVICES. (ACQUISITIONS LIST / LIBRARY SERVICES). [Acquis. list - Can. Mus. Nat., Libr. Serv.]. **Main/Corp** Canadian Museum of Nature. Library Services. **VFOAT** Liste des Acquisitions. (Apr. 29, 1990)-. Periodical. English (French). mo. Canadian Museum of Nature, PO Box 3443, Station D, Ottawa Ont K1P 6P4 Canada. **Tel** (613)990-6595, FAX (613)990-8818. **DD** 017/.5. ***Continues** National Museum of Natural Sciences (Canada). Library Services. Acquisitions List., 0840-9587.*

CN/0226-2487
ACQUISITIONS / METROPOLITAN TORONTO LIBRARY, CANADIAN HISTORY DEPARTMENT. [Acquis. - Metrop. Toronto Libr., Can. Hist. Dep.]. **Main/Corp** Metropolitan Toronto Library. Canadian History Dept. Vol. 1, No. 1 (Sept. 1982)-V. 1, No. 4 (Dec. 1982). Periodical. English. mo. Free. Metropolitan Toronto Library Board, 789 Yonge Street, Toronto Ontario M4W 2G8 Canada. **Tel** (416)393-7134, telex 06-22232. **DD** 016.971.

CN/0226-2509
ACQUISITIONS / METROPOLITAN TORONTO LIBRARY, GENERAL REFERENCE DEPARTMENT. [Acquis. - Metrop. Toronto Libr., Gen. Ref. Dep.]. **Main/Corp** Metropolitan Toronto Library. General Reference Dept. **Added/Corp** Metropolitan Toronto Library Board. Vol. 1, No. 1 (Mar. 1980)-. Periodical. English. mo. Metropolitan Toronto Library Board, 789 Yonge Street, Toronto Ontario M4W 2G8 Canada. **Tel** (416)393-7134, telex 06-22232. **DD** 016.02. ***Continues** Metropolitan Toronto Library. General Reference Dept. Selected List of New Titles, 0227-7476.*

AT
ACQUISITIONS NEWSLETTER. ***Ceased.*** **Main/Corp** National Library of Australia. (Aug. 1970)-(19??). English. bm. National Library of Australia, Parkes Place, Canberra ACT, 2600 Australia. **Tel** 011 61 6 2621374, FAX 011 61 6 2731084. **LC** Z975.C3; A26. **DD** 027.5944.

AT/0815-0494
ACQUISITIONS ULTIMO. [AcquisitionsUltimo]. (1983)-. English. ir. CSIRO Publications, PO Box 89, 314 Albert Street, East Melborne Victoria 3002 Australia. **Tel** 011 61 3 4187333, 4187217, FAX 011 61 3 4190459, telex AA 30236. **DD** 025.2. ***Continues** Acquisitions S.I.G. Newsletter, 0159-6241.*
Ind/Abst Aust. Educ. Index; Aust. Libr. Inf. Sci. Abstr. (1983-1986), (1989).

US/0193-1784
ACRL PUBLICATIONS IN LIBRARIANSHIP. **Main/Corp** Association of College and Research Libraries. **Added/Corp** Association of College and Research Libraries. Publications in Librarianship. **VAT** Association of College and Research Libraries. Publications in Librarianship. No. 34, (1975)-. Monographic series. English. ir. Price varies per volume. American Library Association, 50 East Huron Street, Chicago IL 60611. **Tel** (312)944-6780, (800)545-2433, FAX (312)944-2641. **(Subscription address:** American Library Association, Subscription Department, 434 West Downer, Aurora IL 60506-9936.) **LC** Z674; .A75. **DD** 658.8/09/0705730941. ***Continues** ACRL Monograph.*

CN/0821-5049
ACSI-ON. (ACSI-ON / L'ASSOCIATION CANADIENNE DES SCIENCES DE L'INFORMATION, SECTION DE MONTREAL.). [ACSI-ON]. Vol. 1, No. 1 (Feb. 1983)-. Periodical. French. ir. Free. Association Canadienne des Sciences de l'Information Section de Montreal, C P 159 Succursale Cote-des-Neiges, Montreal Quebec H3S 2S5 Canada. **DD** 025/.00971. ctrl circ.

PL
ACTA UNIVERSITATIS WRATISLAVIENSIS. BIBLIOTEKOZNAWSTWO. **Added/Corp** Uniwersytet Wrocawski. Uniwerstyet Wrocawski im. Boeslawa Bieruta. **VFOAT** Bibliotekoznawstwo. (1966)-. Monographic series. Polish (summaries and/or abstracts in French). Price varies per volume. **(Subscription address:** ARS Polona, PO Box 1001, 00068 Warsaw Poland.) **LC** Z671; .B727. ***Continues** Bibliotekoznawstwo.*

US/0363-0250
ACTION FOR LIBRARIES. [Action libr.]. **Added/Corp** Bibliographical Center for Research, Rocky Mountain Region. Vol. 1 (Oct. 1975)-. Periodical. English. Twelve times a year. Free in US; $10.00 other. Bibliographical Center for Research, 14394 East Evans Avenue, Aurora CO 80014. **Tel** (303)751-6277. **ED** Joyce Hillshafer. **Circ:** 2,500.
Desc: Newsletter for members of library services network in the Rocky Mountain region.
Ind/Abst Libr. Inf. Sci. Abstr.

ZA
ACTIVITIES OF THE LUSAKA CITY LIBRARIES. **Main/Corp** Lusaka, Zambia. City Libraries Section. English. an. Lusaka City Libraries, Lusaka Zambia. **LC** Z858.L87; L87A. **DD** 027.46894. ***Continues** Lusaka, Zambia. Activities of City Library Section.*

CU/0138-7324
ACTUALIDADES DE LA INFORMACION CIENTIFICA Y TECNICA. ***Title Change.*** [Actual. inf. cient. tec.]. **Main/Corp** Instituto de Documentacion e Informacion Cientifica y Tecnica (Academia de Ciencias de Cuba). (19??)-(19??). Periodical. Spanish. bm. Ediciones Cubanas, Obispo 527, Altos ESQ Bernaza, CP 10100 Havana Cuba. **Tel** 011 632980, 631942, FAX 011 631011, telex 512337, 6540. **LC** Z1007; .A15a. **CODEN** AITEEX. Documents available from Ask*IEEE. ***Continued by** Ciencias de la Informacion, 0864-4659.*
Desc: A medium for the exchange of experiences in the field of information sciences.
Ind/Abst INSPEC (1985-).

UK/0001-8015
ADAM INTERNATIONAL REVIEW. [ADAM int. rev.]. (1932)-. Periodical. English (French). qt. ADAM International Review, 28 Emperors Gate, London SW7 England. **LC** AP1; .A4. **DD** 052.
Ind/Abst MLA Int. Bibl. Books Artic. Mod. Lang. Lit.

AT/0811-9392
ADDLIS NEWS. **See** Drug Abuse and Alcoholism.

US/0163-3805
ADDRESS LIST, REGIONAL AND SUBREGIONAL LIBRARIES FOR THE BLIND AND PHYSICALLY HANDICAPPED. (ADDRESS LIST, REGIONAL AND SUBREGIONAL LIBRARIES FOR THE BLIND AND PHYSICALLY HANDICAPPED / NATIONAL LIBRARY SERVICE FOR THE BLIND AND PHYSICALLY HANDICAPPED.). **VFOAT** Regional and Subregional Libraries for the Blind and Physically Handicapped. Began with April 1976. English. sa. National Library Service for the Blind and Physically Handicapped, Library of Congress, 1291 Taylor Street Northwest, Washington DC 20542. **Tel** (800)424-8567, (202)707-5100, (800)424-9100. **LC** Z675.B6; A25. **DD** 027.6/63/02573. **NLM** Z 675.B6 A227.

US/8755-9846
ADLIB UPDATE. [Adlib update]. **Added/Corp** Advanced Library Concepts. No. 1 (June 23, 1984)-. English. sa. Free. Advanced Library, PO Box 246, Andover MA 01810. **DD** 025.

NE
ADONIS NEWS. (1990)-. Academic Scholarly Publication. English. qt. ADONIS BV, PO Box 17005, 1001 JA Amsterdam Netherlands. **Tel** 011 31 20 6262629. **CODEN** ADNSEA. Documents available from CASDDS.
Desc: Information on document delivery.
Ind/Abst Chem. Abstr.

US/1060-6645
ADVANCE NOTICE (PRINCETON, N.J.). ***Suspended.*** (ADVANCE NOTICE.). [Adv. not.]. Vol. 1, No. 1 (June 1991)-(199?). Periodical. English. qt. $24.00. Advance Notice, PO Box 1223, Princeton NJ 08542-1223. **DD** 005.

UK/0960-3247
ADVANCED SEARCHER. [Adv. search]. (1990)-. English. Six times a year. £88.00 UK; £98.00 other. Effective Technical Marketing Ltd., Enterprise House / Wilton Road, Humberston, Grimsby DN36 4AS England. **Tel** 11 44 472 210707, FAX 11 44 472 210304. **ED** Frank Ryan. **DD** 005.75. **Circ:** 200.
Desc: An in-depth analysis and comparison of the world of information database. Written for information professionals, information vendors and users of information.

US/0044-636X
ADVANCED TECHNOLOGY LIBRARIES. [Adv. technol. libr.]. **VFOAT** AT/L. Vol. 1 (Jan. 1972)-. Newsletter. English. mo. $89.00 (one year), $104.00 (two year). Macmillan Publishing Company, 100 Front Street, Box 500, Riverside NJ 08075-7500. **Tel** (800)257-5755, (609)461-6500, FAX (609)461-7070. **ED** Judy Duke and Carol Chin. **LC** Z671; .A35. **DD** 020/.5. **NLM** Z699.A1 A244. **CODEN** ATLBA. Index available. **Ad Acc. Circ:** 2,000. available on microfilm and microfiche from University Microfilms International (UMI). ***Supersedes** Advanced Technology Libraries, 0044-636X.*
Desc: Technology news and issues affecting libraries.
Ind/Abst Trade Ind. Index.

US/0065-2830
ADVANCES IN LIBRARIANSHIP. Vol. 1 (1970)-. Academic Scholarly Publication. English. ir. $59.95 (Vol. 18). Academic Press, Inc., 6277 Sea Harbor Drive, Orlando FL 32887. **Tel** (800)543-9534, (407)345-4100, FAX (407)363-9661. **ED** Melvin J. Voigt. **LC** Z674; .A4. **DD** 020/.5. **NLM** Z 671 A244. **CODEN** AVLSA. **[CCC].**

US/0732-0671
ADVANCES IN LIBRARY ADMINISTRATION AND ORGANIZATION. [Adv. libr. adm. organ.]. Vol. 1 (1982)-. English. an. $73.25. JAI Press Inc., 55 Old Post Road, Suite 2, PO Box 1678, Greenwich CT 06836-1678.

Tel (203)661-7602, FAX (203)661-0792. **ED** Gerard McCabe and Bernard Kreissman. **LC** Z678; .A33. **DD** 025.1/05.

US/0899-1227
ADVANCES IN LIBRARY INFORMATION TECHNOLOGY. [Adv. libr. inf. technol.]. **Added/Corp** Library of Congress. Cataloging Distribution Service. Issue No. 1 (1988)-. Monographic series. English. ir. Price varies per volume. Library of Congress / Cataloging Distribution Service, Washington DC 20541-5017. **Tel** (800)255-3666, (202)707-6100, FAX (202)707-1334. **LC** UNC. **DD** 025.

US/1052-262X
ADVANCES IN LIBRARY RESOURCE SHARING. ***Ceased.*** [Adv. libr. resour. shar.]. Vol. 1 (1990)-(1993/94). English. an. Mecklermedia Corporation, 11 Ferry Lane West, Westport CT 06880. **Tel** (203)226-6967, (800)632-5537, FAX (203)454-5840. **ED** Jennifer Cargill and Diane Graves. **LC** Z731; .A38. **DD** 021.6/4. **[CCC].**

●US/1063-2263
ADVANCES IN PRESERVATION AND ACCESS. [Adv. preserv. access]. Vol. 1 (1992)-. Periodical. English. an. $55.00 US; $60.00 South America, Central America, Canada & Mexico. Learned Information Inc., 143 Old Marlton Pike, Medford NJ 08055-8750. **Tel** (609)654-6266, FAX (609)654-4309. **LC** IN PROCESS; Z700.9; .A38. **DD** 025.

US/1040-4384
ADVANCES IN SERIALS MANAGEMENT. [Adv. ser. manage.]. Vol. 1 (1986)-. Periodical. English. an. $73.25. JAI Press Inc., 55 Old Post Road, Suite 2, PO Box 1678, Greenwich CT 06836-1678. **Tel** (203)661-7602, FAX (203)661-0792. **ED** Marcia Tuttle and Jean Cook. **LC** Z692.S5; A32. **DD** 025.3/432.

US
ADVENTURES OF THE INCREDIBLE LIBRARIAN. (April 1990)-. Periodical. English. qt. $28.80 US; $32.80 Canada and Mexico; $36.80 other. Incredible Librarian Books Inc., Box 25544, Library Lane, Tempe AZ 85285. **Tel** (602)731-9357.

NR/0189-6709
AFRICAN JOURNAL OF ACADEMIC LIBRARIANSHIP. **Added/Corp** Standing Conference of African University Libraries. Western Area. **VFOAT** AJAL. Vol. 1, No. 1 (June 1983)-. Periodical. English (French). sa. $50.00 US; $55.00 other. African Journal of Academic Librarianship, PO Box 46, University of Lagos, Akoka Yaba Lagos State Nigeria.
Ind/Abst Libr. Inf. Sci. Abstr.

NR/0795-4778
AFRICAN JOURNAL OF LIBRARY, ARCHIVES & INFORMATION SCIENCE. Vol. 1, No. 1 April (1991)-. Periodical. English. Twice a year (Apr. & Oct.). Price varies. Archlib Information Service, Botswana University, UI PO Box 20492, Ibadan Nigeria. **(Subscription address:** African Journal Library Archives & Information, c/o Dr. L. O. Anina, Private Bag 0022, Gaborone Botswana.**)** **LC** Z665.2.A35; A33. **DD** 020/.96/005.

UK/0305-862X
AFRICAN RESEARCH & DOCUMENTATION. [Afr. res. doc.]. **Added/Corp** African Studies Association of the United Kingdom. Standing Conference on Library Materials on Africa. No. 1 (1973)-. Periodical. English (French). Three times a year. £13.00 (surface mail), £20.00 (airmail). University of Birmingham / England, Edgbaston, Center for Byzantine Ottoman, Greek Street, Birmingham B15 2TT England. **Tel** 011 44 21 414 5733, FAX 011 44 21 414 5726. **ED** M. Mahoney. **LC** DT19.8; .A35. **DD** 960/.07/2. **NLM** Z 3501 A259. Index available. cum. index. **Bk Rev. Ad Acc. Circ:** 400. ***Formed by the union of*** *Bulletin of the African Studies Association of the United Kingdom* ***and*** *Library Materials on Africa.*
Desc: Covers African studies. Areas include bibliography, documentation, and research in progress; archives, library studies, historical sources, news and reports of conferences, meetings and seminars are included as well.
Ind/Abst Am. Hist. Life (1977-); Anthropol. Index; Libr. Inf. Sci. Abstr.; Rural Dev. Abstr.

US
AFRICANA ANNUAL. English. an. $65.00. Holmes & Meier Publishers Inc, 30 Irving Place, New York NY 10003. **Tel** (212)254-4100, FAX (212)254-4104, telex 236845. **ED** David E Gardinier. **Ad Acc.** ***Continues*** *Africana Journal, 0095-1080.*
Desc: A forum for thoughtful discussion of the issues, ideas, research and criticism of current African scholarship.

US/0148-7868
AFRICANA LIBRARIES NEWSLETTER (URBANA, ILL.). (AFRICANA LIBRARIES NEWSLETTER.). **Added/Corp** University of Illinois at Urbana-Champaign. African Studies Program. Michigan State University. Libraries. Michigan State University. African Studies Program. No. 34 (July 1983)-. Newsletter. English. Four times a year. Africana Libraries Newsletter, Michigan State University Library, East Lansing MI 48824. **Tel** (517)355-2366. ***Continues*** *Boston University Africana Libraries Newsletter.*

US/1051-5925
AFVA EVALUATIONS. ***Ceased.*** **See** Motion Picture.

US/1043-2094
AGAINST THE GRAIN (CHARLESTON, S.C.). (AGAINST THE GRAIN.). [Against grain]. (March 1989)-. Periodical. English. Five times a year. $25.00 US; $35.00 other. Against the Grain / Katina Strauch coordinator, Citadel Stations, Charleston SC 29424. **Tel** (803)792-8020, FAX (803)792-8019. **ED** Katina Strauch. **DD** 025. **Bk Rev**, (Qty: 5-15). **Ad Acc, Adv Mgr:** Edna Laughrey. **Circ:** 1,089.
Desc: Aim is to link publishers, vendors and librarians.
Ind/Abst Int. Aerosp. Abstr. (1991-).

AT/0812-8383
AGORA NORWOOD. [AgoraNorwood]. (1981)-. English. ir. **DD** 027.63.
Ind/Abst Aust. Educ. Index; Aust. Libr. Inf. Sci. Abstr. (1983-).

US/0095-2699
AGRICULTURAL LIBRARIES INFORMATION NOTES. [Agric. libr. inf. notes]. **Added/Corp** Technical Information Systems (U.S.) National Agricultural Library (U.S.). **VFOAT** ALIN. Vol. 1, No. 1 (Jan. 1975)-. Periodical. English. Twelve times a year. Free. National Agriculture Library, 10301 Baltimore Boulevard, Beltsville MD 20705. **Tel** (301)344-3937. **ED** Maria G. Pisa. **LC** Z675.A8; A29. **DD** 026/.63/0973. **Bk Rev. Circ:** 3,000.
Desc: Channel of communication to libraries, technical information specialists, extension workers, and scientists on agricultural information activities.
Ind/Abst AGRICOLA [Select. Cov.]; Inf. Sci. Abstr.; Libr. Inf. Sci. Abstr.

US
AGRICULTURAL LIBRARIES INFORMATION NOTES. SUPPLEMENT. **Added/Corp** United States. Dept. of Agriculture. Science and Education Administration. Technical Information Systems. No. 1, (Feb. 1978)-. Periodical. English. National Agriculture Library, 10301 Baltimore Boulevard, Beltsville MD 20705. **Tel** (301)344-3937.

US/0895-5506
AGRICULTURE MATERIALS IN LIBRARIES. (AGRICULTURE MATERIALS IN LIBRARIES [COMPUTER FILE] : A SUBSET OF THE OCLC ONLINE UNION CATALOG.). [Agric. mater. libr.]. **Added/Corp** OCLC. (1987)-. Catalog. English. $300.00 (OCLC members), $350.00 (nonmembers). OCLC Asia Pacific Services, 6565 Frantz Road, Dublin OH 43017. **Tel** (800)848-5878, (614)764-6394 or 6000, FAX (614)764-6096. **DD** 630.

CR
AIBDA ACTUALIDADES. **Added/Corp** Asociacion Interamericana de Bibliotecarios y Documentalistas Agricolas. No. 1 (Nov. 1981)-. Periodical. Spanish. ir (Published 2 or 3 times per year). $20.00 (individuals), $50.00 (institutions) Comes with Asociacion Interamericana de Bibliotecarios y Documentalistas Agricolas membership. AIBDA / Asociacion Interamericana de Bibliotecarios y Documentalistas Argicolas, Apartado 55, 2200 Coronado, San Jose Costa Rica. **Tel** 011 506 2290222.

US
AIIM BUYING GUIDE : THE OFFICIAL REGISTRY OF INFORMATION AND IMAGE MANAGEMENT PRODUCTS AND SERVICES / ASSOCIATION FOR INFORMATION AND IMAGE MANAGEMENT. **Added/Corp** Association for Information and Image Management (U.S.). **VFOAT** Buying Guide. **VAT** Association for Information and Image Management Buying Guide. (1985)-. English. an. $42.90 members; $86.90 non-members. Association for Information & Image Management, Business Office, 1100 Wayne Avenue/Suite 1100, Silver Spring MD 20910. **Tel** (301)587-8202, FAX (301)587-2711. **LC** HD9999.M47; A39. **DD** 681. ***Continues*** *Association for Information and Image Management (U.S.). Buying Guide.*

CN/0824-6505
AISPLAYBACK. [AISPlayback]. **Added/Corp** Association of Information Systems Professionals. Ottawa Chapter. **VAT** Association of Information Systems Professionals Playback. (1983)-. Periodical. English. mo. Free to members. Association of Information Systems Professionals, 104 Wilmot Road, Suite 201, Deerfield IL 60015. **Tel** (708)940-8800. **DD** 020/.624/71384. ***Continues*** *IWPlayback.*

JA/0020-2827
AJIA KEIZAI SHIRYO GEPPO. **Added/Corp** Ajia Keizai Kenkyujo (Tokyo, Japan) Library Bulletin. **VFOAT** Library Bulletin. Vol. 9, No. 5, Apr. (1967)-. Periodical. Japanese (table of contents in English). mo. $130.00. **(Subscription address:** Japan Publications Trading Company, Ltd., PO Box 5030, Tokyo International, Tokyo 100-31 Japan.**)** ***Continues*** *Ajia Keizei Kenyujo Shiryo Geppo.*

US/0747-6175
AJL NEWSLETTER. (AJL NEWSLETTER / ASSOCIATION OF JEWISH LIBRARIES.). [AJL newsl.]. **Main/Corp** Association of Jewish Libraries. **VAT** Association of Jewish Libraries Newsletter. (196?)-. Newsletter. English. Four times a year. $25.00 members (Comes with Judaica Librarianship Membership). Association of Jewish Libraries, 19 Brookfield Road, New Hyde Park NY 11040. **Tel** (212)532-4949 ext. 297. **ED** Irene S. Levin. **LC** WMLC 93/1092. **DD** 027. **Bk Rev. Ad Acc. Circ:** 750.
Desc: News and book reviews for Synagogue School and Center, and Judaic studies programs.

RU/0203-4972
AKTUALNYE VOPROSY BIBLIOTECHNOI RABOTY / GOSUDARSTVENNAIA BIBLIOTEKA SSSR IMENI V.I. LENINA. **Added/Corp** Gosudarstvennaia Biblioteka SSSR Imeni V. I. Lenina. (1982)-. Periodical. Russian. an. 0.45rub. Izdatelstvo Kniga, 50 Gorky Ulitsa, 125047 Moscow Russia. **LC** Z819.A1; .A56. **DD** 027.047/05.

IQ
AL-TAWTHIQ AL-ILAMI / TASDURU AN MARKAZ AL-TAWTHIQ AL-ILAMI LI-DUWAL AL-KHALIJ AL-ARABI. **VFOAT** Informational Documentation; Tawthiq Al-Elami. Periodical. Arabic (English). be. 1.500ID individuals, 5.00ID institutions; $15.00 US. Arab Gulf States Information Documentation Center, POB 5063, Baghdad Iraq. **Tel** 5564171, telex 213267 GIDAC. **ED** Jasim M Jirjees. **LC** Z674.5.P47; T39. **Bk Rev. Ad Acc. Circ:** 2,500 (ctrl). available on microfilm.
Desc: Studies and articles and reports; documentation of major anniversaries and conferences and seminars. Book reviews, lists of new books published on the gulf.

US/0084-6406
ALA HANDBOOK OF ORGANIZATION. ***Title Change.*** [ALA handb. organ.]. **Main/Corp** American Library Association. **VAT** American Library Association Handbook of Organization. 1971/72-?. English. an. American Library Association, 50 East Huron Street, Chicago IL 60611. **Tel** (312)944-6780, (800)545-2433, FAX (312)944-2641. **LC** Z673.A5; O72. **DD** 020/.622/73. **NLM** Z 673.A5A3. ***Supersedes*** *ALA Organizational Information.* ***Continued by*** *ALA Membership Directory, 0278-9019; ALA Handbook of Organization and Membership Directory, 0273-4605.*

US/0273-4605
ALA HANDBOOK OF ORGANIZATION AND MEMBERSHIP DIRECTORY. [ALA handb. organ. membsh. dir.]. **Main/Corp** American Library Association. **VAT** American Library Association Handbook of Organization and Membership Directory. (1980/1981)-. Directory. English. an. $30.00. American Library Association, 50 East Huron Street, Chicago IL 60611. **Tel** (312)944-6780, (800)545-2433, FAX (312)944-2641. **(Subscription address:** American Library Association, Subscription Department, 434 West Downer, Aurora IL 60506-9936.**)** **LC** Z673.A5; H37. **DD** 020/.622/02573. available on CD-ROM. ***Continues*** *ALA Handbook of Organization, 0084-6406; A.L.A. Membership Directory.*

US/0747-7201
ALA SURVEY OF LIBRARIAN SALARIES. **See** Economics-Labor.

US/0001-1746
ALA WASHINGTON NEWSLETTER. [ALA Wash. newsl.]. **Added/Corp** American Library Association. Washington Office. **VFOAT** Washington Newsletter. **VAT** American Library Association Washington Newsletter. Vol. 1, No. 1 (Jan. 27, 1949)-. Newsletter. English. mo. $25.00 North America; $30.00 other. American Library Association Washington Newsletter, 110 Maryland Avenue NE, Washington DC 20002. **Tel** (202)547-4440, FAX (202)547-7363. **ED** Eileen D Cooke and Carol C Henderson. **LC** Z671; .W3. **DD** 027.073. **NLM** Z 671 W318. **Circ:** 1,900 (ctrl). available on an online database. ***Formed by the union of*** *Monthly Report of the International Relations Board of the American Library Association* ***and*** *Federal Relations News.*
Desc: Informs librarians and educators of the current status of all federal legislation that concerns libraries and librarians.
Ind/Abst Libr. Lit.

US/0002-4295
ALABAMA LIBRARIAN, THE. **Added/Corp** Alabama Library Association. Vol. 1, (Dec. 1949)-. Periodical. English. Five times a year (Published quarterly with one membership directory). $25.00 US & Canada & Mexico; $55.00 other Comes with Alabama Library Association membership. Alabama Library Association,

400 South Union Street, Suite 255, Montgomery AL 36104. **Tel** (205)262-5210, FAX (205)834-6398. **ED** Sheila Delacroix, (editor's address: RBD Library, Auburn University, Auburn, AL 36849-5606, phone: (205)844-1717). **LC** Z671; .A65. **DD** 020.623. **Ad Acc, Adv Mgr Tel** (205)262-5210. **Circ:** 975 (ctrl). available on microfilm and microfiche from University Microfilms International (UMI).
Desc: Information about libraries, librarians and support groups in Alabama, or of interest in the Alabama area.

US
ALABAMA PUBLIC LIBRARY SERVICE ANNUAL REPORT. **Main/Corp** Alabama Public Library Service. (1976/77)-?. English. an. Alabama Public Library Service, 6030 Monticello Drive, Montgomery AL 36130. **Tel** (205)277-7330. **ED** Anthony W Miele. **LC** Z678.4.A3; A42a. **DD** 027.4/761. **Circ:** 1,700. ***Formed by the union of*** *Alabama Public Libraries* ***and*** *Statistics of Public Libraries in Alabama.* ***Continued in part by*** *Library Directory and ... Statistical Report.*
Desc: A report of the programs and projects of the State Library for the fiscal year, includes a directory of public libraries and statistical information pertinent to Alabama's public libraries.

US/0146-1028
ALASKA LIBRARY DIRECTORY.
Added/Corp Alaska State Library. Alaska Library Association. (197?)-. English. ir. $15.00 Comes with Alaska Library Association membership. Alaska Library Association, PO Box 81084, Fairbanks AK 99708. **Tel** (907)479-4522.

CN/0707-0306
ALBERTA GOVERNMENT LIBRARIES' NEWSLETTER. **Added/Corp** Alberta. Legislature Library. Consulting & Bibliographic Services Section. Alberta. Cooperative Government Library Services Section. Vol. 1, No. 1 (Nov. 4, 1974)-. Newsletter. English. Twelve times a year. 15.25Can$. Legislative Library - Alberta Government, 9718 107 Street, 902 Legislative Annex, Edmonton Alberta T5K 1E4 Canada. **Tel** (403)427-3837. ***Continues*** *Alberta Government Librarians' Newsletter, 0707-0896.*

CN/0715-1640
ALBERTA LIBRARY BOARD REPORT. [Alta. Libr. Board rep.]. **Main/Corp** Alberta Library Board. **VAT** Annual Report - Alberta Library Board. (1978/79)-. English. an. Free. Alberta Library Board, 16214 114 Avenue, Edmonton Alberta T5M 2Z5 Canada. **Tel** (403)427-2556. **LC** Z883.A12; A43A. **DD** 021.8/2/097123. **Circ:** 500 (ctrl).

CN/0705-6087
ALBERTA LIBRARY NEWS. ***Ceased.*** [Alta. libr. news]. **Added/Corp** Alberta. Cultural Development Branch. Libraries Division. Alberta. Cultural Development Division. Libraries Branch. Alberta. Cultural Development Division. Library Services Branch. **VAT** Mus Se Na He Kun. Vol. 1 (May 1972)-Vol. 19, No. 3 (Spring 1992). Periodical. English. mo. Alberta Library Services, 16214 114th Avenue South, Edmonton, Alberta T5M 2Z5 Canada. **Tel** (403)427-2556.

US/1047-949X
ALCTS NEWSLETTER. [ALCTS newsl.]. **Added/Corp** Association for Library Collections & Technical Services. **VAT** Association for Library Collections & Technical Services Newsletter. Vol. 1, No. 1 (1990)-. Newsletter. English. Six times a year. $25.00 US; $35.00 other. American Library Association, 50 East Huron Street, Chicago IL 60611. **Tel** (312)944-6780, (800)545-2433, FAX (312)944-2641. **(Subscription address:** American Library Association, Subscription Department, 434 West Downer, Aurora IL 60506-9936.**)** **ED** Yvonne A McLean. **LC** Z688.5; .A43. **DD** 020/.5. **CODEN** ALNWEA. available on microfilm from University Microfilms International (UMI); available on microfiche. ***Continues*** *American Library Association. Resources and Technical Services Division. RTSD Newsletter, 0360-5906.*
Ind/Abst Libr. Lit.

UK/0955-7490
ALEXANDRIA (ALDERSHOT).
(ALEXANDRIA.). [Alexandria]. **Added/Corp** British Library. Vol. 1, No. 1 (May 1989)-. Periodical. English. tq (3 issues). £84.00 (surface mail). Gower Publishing Co. Ltd., Gower House, Croft Road, Aldershot, Hampshire GU11 3HR England. **Tel** 011 44 252 331551, FAX 011 44 252 344405, telex 858001. **(Subscription address:** Ashgate Distribution Services, Unite 2-4 Lower Farnham Road, Aldershot GU12 4DY England.**)** **CODEN** ALEXE2.
Ind/Abst Ei Page One.

●CN/1193-1426
ALGONQUIN PERIODICALS, UNION LISTING / ALGONQUIN RESOURCE CENTRE, STUDENT SERVICES DIVISION. [Algonquin period. union listing]. **Main/Corp** Algonquin College. Resource Centre. Student Services Division. (1992)-. English. Algonquin College Resource Centre / 1385 Woodroffe Avenue, Nepean Ontario K2C 3H2 Canada. **DD** 018/.134. ***Continues*** *Algonquin College. Resource Centre.; Periodicals., 0712-9084.*

AT/0810-9265
ALISA. AUSTRALIAN LIBRARY AND INFORMATION SCIENCE ABSTRACTS.
See Library and Information Sciences-Abstracting, Bibliographies and Statistics.

US/8756-4173
ALKI. (ALKI : THE WASHINGTON LIBRARY ASSOCIATION JOURNAL.). [Alki]. **Added/Corp** Washington Library Association. Vol. 1, No. 1 (March 1985)-. Periodical. English. Three times a year (Mar., July, Dec.). $14.00. Washington Library Association - Alki, 1232 143rd Avenue SE, Bellevue WA 98007. **Tel** (509)838-6757. **LC** Z673.W3; A45. **DD** 020/.6232/797. **Ad Acc. Circ:** 1,300 (ctrl).
Desc: Contains philosophical and substantive analyses of current and enduring issues for and about Washington libraries, personnel and advocates as well as exchanges of opinion and information.

US
ALL NEWSLETTER / ACADEMIC LAW LIBRARIES SPECIAL INTEREST SECTION, AMERICAN ASSOCIATION OF LAW LIBRARIES. **Added/Corp** American Association of Law Libraries. Academic Law Libraries Special Interest Section. **VAT** Academic Law Libraries Newsletter. (19??)-. Newsletter. English. ir. $12.00 (must be a member of the American Association of Law Libraries). American Association of Law Libraries, 53 West Jackson Boulevard, Suite 940, Chicago IL 60604. **Tel** (312)939-4764, FAX (312)431-1097, telex ABA7603.
Ind/Abst Leg. Inf. Manage. Index.

US/1056-621X
ALLIANCE PLUS. (ALLIANCE PLUS [COMPUTER FILE].). [Alliance plus]. (1989)-. Periodical. English. qt. $950.00 (new subscriptions), $450.00 (renewals). Follett, 809 North Front Street, McHenry IL 60050. **Tel** (800)323-3397, FAX (815)344-8774. **DD** 025. **Circ:** 850.
Desc: Contains more than 400,000 Library of Congress MARC records that have been enhanced with reading level, interest level, review sources and annotations.

UK/0964-3400
ALPHANUMERIC REPORTS PUBLICATIONS INDEX. [Alphanumeric rep. publ. index]. **VFOAT** ARPI (Boston Spa). (1991)-. English. be. £26.00 UK; £31.00 other. British Library / Document Supply Centre, Boston Spa, Wetherby West Yorkshire LS23 7BQ England. **Tel** 0937 546060, FAX 0937 546333, telex 557381. **(Subscription address:** Turpin Distribution Services Limited, Blackhorse Road, Letchworth, Hertfordshire SG6 1HN, United Kingdom.**)** **DD** 017.536.

US/0162-6612
ALSC NEWSLETTER. **Main/Corp** Association for Library Service to Children. **VAT** Association for Library Service to Children Newsletter. Vol. 1 (Sept. 1978)-. Newsletter. English. sa. $20.00. American Library Association, 50 East Huron Street, Chicago IL 60611. **Tel** (312)944-6780, (800)545-2433, FAX (312)944-2641. **(Subscription address:** American Library Association, Subscription Department, 434 West Downer, Aurora IL 60506-9936.**)** available on microfilm from University Microfilms International (UMI).

US/0734-8991
ALTA NEWSLETTER. **Main/Corp** American Library Trustee Association. **VFOAT** A.L.T.A. Newsletter. (1982)-. Newsletter. English. bm. $40.00 (members only). American Library Trustee Association, 50 East Huron Street, Chicago IL 60611. **Tel** (800)545-2433, (312)280-2161. ***Continues*** *American Library Trustee Association. ALTA President's Newsletter, 0734-8649.*

US/0749-6885
ALTERNATIVE LIBRARY LITERATURE. (ALTERNATIVE LIBRARY LITERATURE : A BIENNIAL ANTHOLOGY.). [Altern. libr. lit.]. (1983)-. Periodical. English. be. $37.00 (includes shipping and handling). McFarland & Company, PO Box 611, Jefferson NC 28640. **Tel** (919)246-4460, FAX (919)246-5018. **ED** Sanford Berman and James P Danky. **LC** Z716.4; .A47. **DD** 020/.5. **Circ:** 600.
Desc: Articles selected represent major out-of-the-mainstream concerns and viewpoints, with sources ranging from established periodicals to genuinely "alternative" publications.

US
ALUMNI DIRECTORY / THE UNIVERSITY OF MICHIGAN, SCHOOL OF INFORMATION AND LIBRARY STUDIES.
See College and School Publications-Alumni.

US/0572-4953
AMERICAN ASSOCIATION OF LAW LIBRARIES NEWSLETTER. **Added/Corp** American Association of Law Libraries. Vol. 20, No. 7 (Mar. 1989)-. Newsletter. English. mo. American Association of Law Libraries, 53 West Jackson Boulevard, Suite 940, Chicago IL 60604. **Tel** (312)939-4764, FAX (312)431-1097, telex ABA7603. ***Continues*** *American Association of Law Libraries. Newsletter - American Association of Law Libraries, 0572-4953.*

US/0193-8207
AMERICAN INDIAN LIBRARIES NEWSLETTER. **Added/Corp** ALA OLSD Committee on Library Service for American Indian People. Vol. 1, No. 1 (Fall 1976)-. Newsletter. English. qt (Aug., Nov., Feb. and May.). $25.00 (institutions), $10.00 (individuals), $5.00 (students). American Indian Library Association, School of Library and Information Studies, University of Oklahoma, 401 W. Brooks, Norman OK 73019. **Tel** (405)325-3921, FAX (405)325-7648. **ED** Dr. Lotsee Patterson. **LC** Z711.8; .A49. **DD** 025.5/276/308997. available on microfilm and microfiche from University Microfilms International (UMI).
Desc: The newsletter of the American Indian Library Association.

US/0002-9769
AMERICAN LIBRARIES (CHICAGO, ILL.). (AMERICAN LIBRARIES.). [Am. libr.]. **Added/Corp** American Library Association. Vol. 1 (Jan. 1970)-. Periodical. English. Eleven times a year. $60.00 US, Canada & Mexico; $70.00 other. American Library Association, 50 East Huron Street, Chicago IL 60611. **Tel** (312)944-6780, (800)545-2433, FAX (312)944-2641. **(Subscription address:** American Library Association, Subscription Department, 434 West Downer, Aurora IL 60506-9936.**)** **ED** Thomas M Gaughan. **LC** Z673.A5; B82. **DD** 020.973. **NLM** Z 673 A508. **[CCC]. Bk Rev. Ad Acc. Circ:** 45,000 (ctrl). available on microfilm and microfiche from University Microfilms International (UMI). Documents available from UMI Article Clearinghouse, Magazine Collection. ***Supersedes*** *American Library Association. ALA Bulletin, 0364-4006.*
Desc: Covers news, feature articles, commentary on issues, product information, practical advice, monthly calendar of events, and job listings in library and information science.
Ind/Abst Acad. Abstr. Full Text Elite (Jan. 1989-) [Full Txt.]; Acad. Abstr. (Jan. 1989-); Acad. Search (Jan. 1989-); Access (1980-); Annu. Bibliogr. Engl. Lang. Lit.; Biogr. Index; Book Rev. Index; Chicano Index; Curr. Index J. Educ.; Educ. Index; Gen. Period. Index (1985-); Health Plan. Adminis.; Hospit. Health Admin. Index; INFO-SOUTH Abstr.; Inf. Instruc. Technol.; Inf. Sci. Abstr.; Int. Aerosp. Abstr. (1991-); Leg. Inf. Manage. Index; Libr. Inf. Sci. Abstr.; Libr. Lit.; Mag. Artic. Summar. Elite (Jan. 1989-) [Full Txt.]; Mag. Artic. Summar. Select (Jan. 1989-) [Full Txt.]; Mag. Artic. Summar. CD-ROM (Jan. 1989-); Mag. ASAP Plus [Full Txt.]; Mag. Index Plus (1989-); Mag. Index. Sel. (1986-); Mag. Search; Med. Rev. Dig.; Newsp. Period. Abstr. (1988-); Read. Guide Period. Lit.; Mag. Index (1977-); Urban Aff. Abstr.; Vocat. Search (Jan. 1989-) [Full Txt.].

US
AMERICAN LIBRARY LAWS. ***Ceased.*** **Added/Corp** American Library Association. League of Library Commissions. 1st Ed. (1930)-5th Ed. (?). English. American Library Association, 50 East Huron Street, Chicago IL 60611. **Tel** (312)944-6780, (800)545-2433, FAX (312)944-2641.

US/8756-0860
AMERICAN NATIONAL STANDARDS FOR INFORMATION SCIENCES. [Am. natl. stand. inf. sci.]. **Main/Corp** American National Standards Institute. (1985)-. Monographic series. English. ir. Price varies per volume. American National Standards Institute, 11 West 42nd Street, New York NY 10036. **Tel** (212)642-4900. **DD** 025. **CODEN** ASISEM. available in microform (from International Handling Services, and Information Marketing International). ***Continues*** *American National Standards Institute. Z39, American National Standards on Library and Information Sciences and Related Publishing Practices, 0276-0762.*

UK/0265-3389
AMERICAN STUDIES LIBRARY NEWSLETTER. [Am. stud. libr. newsl.]. **Added/Corp** SCONUL Advisory Committee on American Studies. No. 15 (Apr. 1984)-. Newsletter. English. SCONUL Advisory Committee on American Studies, c/o S Roberts, Reference Center, USIS/American Embassy, 55 Upper Brook Street, London W1A 2LH England. ***Continues*** *ASLG Newsletter, 0141-6383.*
Ind/Abst Libr. Inf. Sci. Abstr.

US/1040-5631
AMS STUDIES IN LIBRARY AND INFORMATION SCIENCE. [AMS stud. libr. inf. sci.]. (1989)-. Monographic series. English. ir. Price varies per volume. AMS Press Inc., 56 East 13th Street, New York NY 10003. **Tel** (212)777-4700, FAX (212)995-5413, telex 710 581 2302. **ED** Mary E Jackson. **DD** 025.
Desc: Covers topics in library and information science such as accessing materials for research using new technologies.

US
ANALYSES OF NEW JERSEY PUBLIC LIBRARY STATISTICS FOR ... . **See** Library and Information Sciences-Abstracting, Bibliographies and Statistics.

US/0736-5616
ANALYSES OF THE ... ILLINOIS PUBLIC LIBRARY STATISTICS. See Library and Information Sciences-Abstracting, Bibliographies and Statistics.

II
ANDHRA PRADESH ORIYANTAL RISARC JARNAL. **Added/Corp** Andhra Pradesh Government Oriental Manuscripts Library and Research Institute. (19??)-. Periodical. Urdu. sa. Andhra Pradesh Government Oriental Research, Institute Tarnaka, Hyderabad 500007 India. **Tel** 236487. ***Continues in part*** *Vijnana Sarasvati.*

IT
ANNALI DELLA BIBLIOTECA STATALE E LIBRERIA CIVICA DI CREMONA. **Added/Corp** Biblioteca Statale di Cremona. Vol. 21 (1970)-. Monographic series. Italian. ir. Price varies per volume. Libreria del Convegno Editrice, Corso Campi 72, 26100 Cremona Italy. **Tel** 011 39 372 22633. **LC** Z933; .C73. ***Continues*** *Annali della Biblioteca Governativa e Libreria Civica di Cremona.*
Ind/Abst BHA : Biblio. Hist. Art.

II/0003-4835
ANNALS OF LIBRARY SCIENCE AND DOCUMENTATION. [Ann. libr. sci. doc.]. (1964)-. Periodical. English. qt. $75.00. INSDOC, 14 Satsang Vihar Marg, New Delhi 110067 India. **Tel** 011 91 11 6863617, FAX 665837, telex 031-73099. **(Subscription address:** Prints India, 11 Darya Ganj, New Delhi 110002 India.) **ED** J.K. Ahluwalia. **LC** Z671; .A78. **DD** 020.5. Index available. **Bk Rev. Ad Acc. Circ:** 450. ***Continues*** *Annals of Library Science.*
Ind/Abst Indian Libr. Sci. Abstr.; Libr. Inf. Sci. Abstr.

CN/0825-3927
ANNUAIRE DES BIBLIOTHECAIRES-CONSEILS DU QUEBEC. [Annu. bibl.-cons. Que.]. 1984-. French. an. 3.00Can$. Corporation Des Bibliothecaires Professionnels Du Quebec, 360, Rue Lemoyne, Montreal Quebec H2Y 1Y3. **DD** 023/.2/025714. **Ad Acc.**
Desc: List of consultant librarians of Quebec and how to choose a consultant.

FR
ANNUAIRE DES MEMBRES DE L'ASSOCIATION DES BIBLIOTHECAIRES FRANCAIS. **Main/Corp** Association des Bibliothecaires Francais. French. ir (every two or three years). 80.00F, free with subscription to Bulletin d'Informations. Association des Bibliothecaires Francais, 7 rue des Lions St Paul, 75004 Paris France. **Tel** 11 33 1 48879787. **LC** Z673.A1; A67A. **DD** 020/.622/44. **Ad Acc. Circ:** 2,500 (ctrl).

FR/0182-6557
ANNUAIRE - LES AMIS DE LA BIBLIOTHEQUE HUMANISTE DE SELESTAT. **Main/Corp** Selestat, Alsace. Bibliotheque Humaniste. Societe des Amis. **Added/Corp** Selestat, Alsace. Bibliotheque Humaniste. Societe des Amis. Annuaire de la Societe des Amis de la Bibliotheque Humaniste de Selestat 1976- . **VFOAT** Annuaire de la Societe des Amis de la Bibliotheque Humaniste de Selestat. Vol. 26 (1976)-. French. ***Continues*** *Selestat, Alsace. Bibliotheque Municipale. Societe des Amis. Annuaire de la Societe des Amis de la Bibliotheque de Selestat.*
Ind/Abst BHA : Biblio. Hist. Art.

US/0570-9326
ANNUAL CHECKLIST OF PUBLICATIONS OF THE STATE OF ARIZONA. (ANNUAL CHECKLIST OF PUBLICATIONS OF THE STATE OF ARIZONA RECEIVED BY THE LIBRARY, ARCHIVES, AND PUBLIC RECORDS DIVISION DURING THE FISCAL YEAR.). [Annu. checkl. publ. State Ariz.]. **Main/Corp** Arizona. Division of Library, Archives, and Public Records. **VFOAT** Checklist of Publications of the State of Arizona. 1972/73-. English. an. Library Archives and Public Records Division, Phoenix AZ 85007. **Tel** (602)255-4343. **LC** Z1223.5.A75; A25; J87.A6. **DD** 015/.791. ***Continues*** *Annual Checklist of Publications of the State of Arizona, 0570-9326.*

US/0364-7803
ANNUAL PROGRAM; LIBRARY SERVICES AND CONSTRUCTION ACT - SOUTH CAROLINA. STATE LIBRARY, COLUMBIA. [Annu. program libr. serv. constr. act]. **Main/Corp** South Carolina. State Library, Columbia. 1972/73-. English. an. Free. South Carolina State Library / Reference Department, 1500 Senate Street, PO Box 11469, Columbia SC 29211. **Tel** (803)734-8666, FAX (803)734-8676. **ED** James B Johnson Jr. **LC** Z732.S72; S56A. **DD** 021/.009757. ctrl circ. ***Continues*** *South Carolina State Plan for the Use of Library Services and Construction Funds.*
Desc: Covers projects funded by LSCA funds in South Carolina.

AT/1034-1854
ANNUAL REPORT - AUSTRALIAN COUNCIL OF LIBRARIES AND INFORMATION SERVICES. (ANNUAL REPORT.). [Annu. rep. - Aust. Counc. Libr. Inf. Serv.]. **Added/Corp** Australian Council of Libraries and Information Services. **VFOAT** ACLIS Annual Report. (1989)-. English. an. Australian Council of Library and Information Service, PO Box E202, Queen Victoria Terrace, Canberra ACT 2600 Australia. **Tel** 011 61 062 262 1244. **DD** 021.640994. ***Formed by the union of*** *Annual Report - Australian Libraries and Information Council, 0811-9945* ***and*** *AACOBS Annual Report, 0812-6267.*
Ind/Abst AESIS Q.

US/0191-4316
ANNUAL REPORT - BIBLIOGRAPHICAL CENTER FOR RESEARCH. **Main/Corp** Bibliographical Center for Research. Rocky Mountain Region, Denver. (19??)-. English. an. Free on request. Bibliographical Center for Research, 14394 East Evans Avenue, Aurora CO 80014. **Tel** (303)751-6277. **LC** Z674.82.B5; B5a. **DD** 020/.7/207883.

UK
ANNUAL REPORT / BINGHAM PUBLIC LIBRARY, CIRENCESTER. **Main/Corp** Bingham Public Library. 5th (1909/1910)-. Periodical. English. Bingham Public Library, Cerencester England. ***Continues*** *Bingham Public Library. Report.*

US
ANNUAL REPORT - BIOMEDICAL LIBRARY REVIEW COMMITTEE, NATIONAL LIBRARY OF MEDICINE, NATIONAL INSTITUTES OF HEALTH. **Main/Corp** United States. National Library of Medicine. Biomedical Library Review Committee. (19??)-. English. an. National Library of Medicine, 8600 Rockville Pike, Bethesda MD 20894. **Tel** (301)496-6308.

UK/0305-7887
ANNUAL REPORT - BRITISH LIBRARY. **Main/Corp** British Library. Board. (1973-1974)-. English. an. Free to libraries in UK; £7.50 others. British Library / Press and Publisher Relations, 96 Euston Road, London NW1 2DB England. **Tel** 011 44 71 3237054. **LC** Z792; .B8593a. **DD** 027.5421/42. **CODEN** ARBLDQ. **Circ:** 4,000 (ctrl).
Desc: Facts and figures, new services, chief events and policies of UK National Library.

US
ANNUAL REPORT / DIVISION OF LIBRARY DEVELOPMENT AND SERVICES. **Main/Corp** Maryland. Division of Library Development and Services. (198?)-. English. **LC** Z678.4.M3; M37a. **DD** 021/.09752. ***Continues*** *Maryland. Division of Library Development and Services.; Report - Division of Library Development and Services, 0147-5703.*

VI
ANNUAL REPORT FOR FISCAL YEAR ... / BUREAU OF LIBRARIES, MUSEUMS, AND ARCHAEOLOGICAL SERVICES. **Main/Corp** Virgin Islands Bureau of Libraries, Museums, and Archaeological Services. English. an. Bureau of Libraries Museums and Archaeological Services, PO Box 390, Charlotte Amalie St US Virgin Islands. **LC** Z753.V57; V57A. **DD** 027.07297/22.

AT
ANNUAL REPORT FOR THE YEAR ENDED 30 JUNE ... . **Main/Corp** Tasmania. State Library Service. **Added/Corp** State Library of Tasmania. Tasmania. Parliament. **VFOAT** State Librarian Annual Report ... . (1986)-. English. Tasmanian Government Printer, GPO Box 307C, Hobart Tasmania 7000 Australia. **LC** Z871; .H72. ***Continues*** *Report of the State Library of Tasmania.*

US/0272-9385
ANNUAL REPORT - GRADUATE DEPT. OF LIBRARY AND INFORMATION SCIENCE, THE CATHOLIC UNIVERSITY OF AMERICA. **Main/Corp** Catholic University of America. Graduate Dept. of Library and Information Science. English. an. Graduate Department of Library & Information Science, Catholic University of America, Washington DC 20064. **Tel** (202)635-5085. **ED** Jean Lobkovich. **LC** Z669.C37; C38A. **DD** 020/.7/11753. ***Continues*** *Annual Report - Graduate Department of Library Science, the Catholic University of America, 0270-5575.*

US/0363-3306
ANNUAL REPORT - HUNTINGTON LIBRARY, ART GALLERY, BOTANICAL GARDENS. **Main/Corp** Henry E. Huntington Library and Art Gallery. **Added/Corp** Henry E. Huntington Library and Art Gallery. Huntington Annual Report. **VFOAT** Huntington Annual Report. 46th (1972/73)-. English. an (Nov.). Free. Henry E. Huntington Library, 1151 Oxford Road, San Marino CA 91108. **Tel** (818)405-2172, FAX (818)405-0225. **ED** Catherine Babcock. **LC** Z733; .S24. **DD** 027.4794/93. **Bk Rev. Ad Acc. Circ:** 5,000 (ctrl). ***Continues*** *Annual Report - Henry E. Huntington Library and Art Gallery, 0363-3292.*
Desc: Reflects year's activity in Areas of acquisitions, exhibitions, research, finances, volunteers, public programs in three divisions: art, library and botanical.

II
ANNUAL REPORT - INDIAN NATIONAL SCIENTIFIC DOCUMENTATION CENTRE. **Main/Corp** Indian National Scientific Documentation Centre. English. an. Free. INSDOC, 14 Satsang Vihar Marg, New Delhi 110067 India. **Tel** 011 91 11 6863617, FAX 665837, telex 031-73099. **LC** Z846; .D34. **DD** 025/.00954.

AT
ANNUAL REPORT / LAW LIBRARY, SUPREME COURT OF WESTERN AUSTRALIA. **Main/Corp** Western Australia. Supreme Court. Law Library. (19??)-. English. an. **LC** Z871.W53; W47a. **DD** 026/.349941.

AT/0155-4204
ANNUAL REPORT / LIBRARY COUNCIL OF NEW SOUTH WALES. **Main/Corp** Library Council of New South Wales. (1985-86)-. English. an. State Library of New South Wales, Macquarie Street, Sydney NSW 2000 Australia. **LC** Z870.N43; N48a. **DD** 027/.0944. ***Continues*** *Report of the Library Council of New South Wales, 0155-4204.*

US
ANNUAL REPORT - MIDWEST REGION LIBRARY NETWORK. **Main/Corp** Midwest Region Library Network. **VFOAT** MIDLNET Annual Report; M.I.D.L.N.E.T. Annual Report. 1976/77-. English. an. Midwest Region Library Network, 2420 Nicolet Drive, Green Bay WI 54302. **Tel** (414)465-2750.

SA
ANNUAL REPORT - NATAL PROVINCIAL LIBRARY SERVICE AND MUSEUM SERVICES. **Main/Corp** Natal Provincial Library Service. **VFOAT** Jaarverslag - Natalse Provinciale Biblioteek en Museumdienste. Multiple languages (Afrikaans and English). Natal Provincial Library Services, Pietermaritzburg South Africa. **LC** Z857.N3; N37A. **DD** 021/.00968/4.

US/1045-4837
ANNUAL REPORT / NATIONAL COMMISSION ON LIBRARIES AND INFORMATION SCIENCE. [Annu. rep. - U. S., Natl. Comm. Libr. Inf. Sci.]. **Main/Corp** United States. National Commission on Libraries and Information Science. **VFOAT** NCLIS Annual Report. 1980-81-. English. an. One free copy. National Commission on Libraries and Information Science, 1111-18th Street NW, Washington DC 20405. **Tel** (202)382-0840, FAX (202)382-0878. **ED** Dorothy P Gray. available on microfiche (from ERIC Document Distribution Center). ***Continues*** *United States. National Commission on Libraries and Information Science. Annual Report to the President and the Congress.*
Desc: Report to the President and the Congress.

AT
ANNUAL REPORT - NATIONAL LIBRARY OF AUSTRALIA. **Main/Corp** National Library of Australia. 8th (1967/1968)-. English. an. National Library of Australia, Parkes Place, Canberra ACT, 2600 Australia. **Tel** 011 61 6 2621374, FAX 011 61 6 2731084. **LC** Z871; .C32a. **DD** 027.5944. ***Continues*** *National Library of Australia. Council. Annual Report of the Council.*
Desc: Overview of the range of the library's operations.
Ind/Abst AESIS Q.

CN/0830-0089
ANNUAL REPORT / NATIONAL LIBRARY OF CANADA / RAPPORT ANNUEL / BIBLIOTHEQUE NATIONALE DU CANADA. [Annu. rep. - Natl. Libr. Can.]. **Main/Corp** National Library of Canada. **VAT** Rapport Annuel - Bibliotheque Nationale du Canada. (1984/1985)-. English (French). an. Free on request. National Library of Canada, 395 Wellington Street, Ottawa Ontario K1A 0N4 Canada. **Tel** (613)995-7969, (613)995-7969, (819)994-6881, FAX (613)991-9871. **DD** 027.571; 027.571/05. available in braille; available on audiocassette; available in large print. ***Continues*** *National Library of Canada. Annual Report of the National Librarian., 0315-9949.*
Desc: Describes the year's activities at the National Library of Canada.

US/0270-0107
ANNUAL REPORT OF OHIONET. [Annu rep. OHIONET]. **Main/Corp** Ohionet. 1977/1979-. English. an. Free. Ohionet, 1500 West Lane Avenue, Columbus OH 43221. **Tel** (614)486-2966. **ED** Ronald E Diener. **LC**

Z674.82.O38; O36A. **DD** 021.6/5. **Circ:** 250 (ctrl).
Desc: Summary of the previous fiscal year of Ohionet. Includes annual audit, program statement, list of member libraries, advisory council members and copy of the articles of incorporation.

US
ANNUAL REPORT OF OKLAHOMA LIBRARIES / COMPILED BY THE OKLAHOMA DEPARTMENT OF LIBRARIES. **Main/Corp** Oklahoma. Dept. of Libraries. (1984)-. English. **LC** Z732.O57; O47c. ***Absorbed in part*** *Oklahoma. Dept. of Libraries. Annual Report & Sirectory of Oklahoma Libraries (1981).*

RH
ANNUAL REPORT OF THE CHAIRMAN OF THE COUNCIL OF THE NATIONAL LIBRARY AND DOCUMENTATION SERVICE FOR THE YEAR ENDED ... . **Main/Corp** National Library and Documentation Service (Zimbabwe). Council. (1989)-. Periodical. English. Dugald Niven Library, 12th Avenue, Bulawayo Zimbabwe. **LC** Z857.Z55; N38a. **DD** 027.56891. ***Continues*** *National Free Library of Zimbabwe. Board. Annual Report of the Board of the National Free Library of Zimbabwe for the Year Ended ... .*

US
ANNUAL REPORT OF THE CONNECTICUT STATE LIBRARY. **Main/Corp** Connecticut State Library. English. an. Connecticut State Library, 231 Capital Avenue, Hartford CT 06115. **LC** Z733.C755; C65A. **DD** 017.5746.

US/0194-116X
ANNUAL REPORT OF THE MALDEN PUBLIC LIBRARY. **Main/Corp** Malden, Mass. Public Library. **VFOAT** Annual Reports of the Trustees and Librarian. (19??)-. English. an. Malden Public Library, 36 Salem Street, Malden MA 02148. **Tel** (617)324-0218, FAX (617)324-4467. **ED** Dina G. Malgeri. **LC** Z733; .M24. **DD** 027.4744/61. **Circ:** 300.
Desc: Narrative and financial reports of librarian and trustees for preceding calendar year.

CN/0700-2254
ANNUAL REPORT OF THE PARLIAMENTARY LIBRARIAN. **Main/Corp** Canada. Library of Parliament. **VFOAT** Rapport Annuel du Bibliothecaire Parlementaire. 1972/73-. Periodical. English (French). an. Free. Library of Parliament / Information & Reference Branch, Ottawa Ontario K1A 0A9 Canada. **Tel** (613)992-3122. **LC** Z736.C26; C36A. **DD** 027.6/5. ***Supersedes*** *Annual Report - Library of Parliament, 0700-2262.*

AT
ANNUAL REPORT OF THE UNIVERSITY LIBRARIAN. **Main/Corp** University of Queensland. Libraries. (19??)-. English. an. University of Queensland / Libraries, St. Lucia Queensland 4072 Australia. **LC** Z871.Q44; U55a. **DD** 027.7943.

NZ
ANNUAL REPORT OF THE UNIVERSITY LIBRARIAN FOR ... VICTORIA UNIVERSITY OF WELLINGTON, THE LIBRARY. **Main/Corp** Victoria University of Wellington. Library. English. an. **LC** Z871.V53; V53A. **DD** 027.79312/7.

US
ANNUAL REPORT, OKLAHOMA PUBLIC LIBRARIES IN COMMUNITIES AND STATE LIBRARIES / PREPARED BY THE DEPT. OF LIBRARIES, PUBLIC INFORMATION OFFICE. **Main/Corp** Oklahoma. Dept. of Libraries. Public Information Office. **Added/Corp** Oklahoma. Dept. of Libraries. **VFOAT** Oklahoma Public Libraries in Communities and State Libraries; Public Library Statistics. (19??)-. English. ***Continues*** *Annual Report, Oklahoma Public Library Statistics in Communities and State Institutions.*

US/0883-3508
ANNUAL REPORT / ONONDAGA COUNTY PUBLIC LIBRARY. **Main/Corp** Onondaga County Public Library. English. an. Onondaga County Public Library, 335 Montgomery Street, Syracuse NY 13202.

UK
ANNUAL REPORT - SOUTH WESTERN REGIONAL LIBRARY SYSTEM (ENGLAND). **Main/Corp** South Western Regional Library System (England). 26th (1962-63)-. English. an. South Western Regional Library System, Central Library College, Green Bristol BS1 5TL England. **LC** Z791.S63; S65A. **DD** 020/.6232/423. ***Continues*** *South Western Regional Library System. Annual Report for the Year Ended 31st March ... .*

US/0099-085X
ANNUAL REPORT - SOUTHEASTERN LIBRARY NETWORK. **Main/Corp** Southeastern Library Network. (1974)-. English. an. Southeastern Library Network, 1438 West Peachtree Street Northwest, Suite 400, Atlanta GA 30309. **Tel** (404)892-0943. **LC** Z732.A13; S68a. **DD** 021.6/5/0975.

US
ANNUAL REPORT / STANFORD UNIVERSITY LIBRARIES. **Main/Corp** Stanford University. Libraries. Periodical. English. an. Stanford University Libraries, Publications, Green Library / Room 312D, Stanford CA 94305. **Tel** (415)723-0461. ***Continues*** *Annual Report of the University Libraries.*

NR/0302-4873
ANNUAL REPORT - WESTERN STATE LIBRARY. [Annu. rep. - West. State Libr.]. **Main/Corp** Western State Library. English. an. PMB 5082, Ibadan Nigeria. **LC** Z858.W47; A55. **DD** 027.5669/2.

US/0066-4200
ANNUAL REVIEW OF INFORMATION SCIENCE AND TECHNOLOGY. [Annu. rev. inf. sci. technol.]. **Added/Corp** American Society for Information Science. American Documentation Institute. Vol. 1 (1966)-. English. an (Sept.). $92.50; Also comes with American Society for Information Science membership. Learned Information Inc., 143 Old Marlton Pike, Medford NJ 08055-8750. **Tel** (609)654-6266, FAX (609)654-4309. **ED** Martha E. Williams. **LC** Z699.A1; A65. **DD** 029.708. **NLM** Z 699.A1 A625. **CODEN** ARISBC. **[CCC]. Pr Rev.** Documents available from The Genuine Article, BIOSIS Document Express, Ask*IEEE, CASDDS.
Desc: Reviews numerous topics within the field of information science and technology; provides an annual source of ideas, trends, and references to the literature.
Ind/Abst Biol. Abstr. (-1978); Br. Archaeol. Bibliogr.; Chem. Abstr. (1966-1984); Compumath Citation Index [Full Cov.]; Curr. Contents Soc. Behav. Sci.; Curr. Index J. Educ.; Ei Page One; Inf. Sci. Abstr. [Full Cov.]; INSPEC; Int. Bibliogr. Sociol.; Res. Alert [Full Cov.]; Soc. Sci. Cit. Index [Full Cov.].

US/0196-6448
ANNUAL STATISTICS OF MEDICAL SCHOOL LIBRARIES IN THE UNITED STATES AND CANADA. **See** Library and Information Sciences-Abstracting, Bibliographies and Statistics.

UK
ANNUAL SURVEY OF MUSIC LIBRARIES. **Added/Corp** International Association of Music Libraries, Archives, and Documentation Centres. United Kingdom Branch. (1984)-. English. an. International Association of Music Libraries, Archives and Documentation Centres, United Kingdom Branch. **LC** ML110; .A56. **DD** 026.8/0941.

AT/1035-4832
ANNUAL SURVEY OF VICTORIAN PUBLIC LIBRARIES / VICTORIAN MINISTRY FOR THE ARTS. **Added/Corp** Victoria. Victorian Ministry for the Arts. (1988/1989)-. English. Library Council of Victoria, Public Libraries Division, 328 Swanston Street, Melbourne Victoria 3000 Australia. **Tel** 03-6699840, FAX 03-6631480, telex AA38104. **LC** Z870.V5; L48. **DD** 027.4/945. ***Continues*** *Library Council of Victoria. Annual Statistical Bulletin of Public Libraries in Victoria.*

MX
ANUARIO DE BIBLIOTECOLOGIA, ARCHIVOLOGIA E INFORMATICA. Spanish. an. Universidad Nacional Autonoma de Mexico, Instituto de Investigaciones Filosoficas, Apartado Postal 70 447, 04510 Mexico DF Mexico. **Tel** 52 5 5505215, FAX 52 5 5507014.

CN/0001-2203
APLA BULLETIN. [APLA bull.]. **Main/Corp** Atlantic Provinces Library Association. Vol. 22 (Fall 1958)-. Bulletin. English (French). Six times a year (Jan., Mar., May, July, Sept., Nov.). 25.00Can$. Atlantic Province Library Association, Dalhousie University, School of Library Science, Halifax Nova Scotia B3H 4HB Canada. **Tel** (902)424-5264 Ext. 175. **ED** Bradd Burningham. cum. index. **Ad Acc. Circ:** 600. available on microfilm and microfiche from University Microfilms International (UMI). ***Continues*** *Maritime Library Association. MLA Bulletin., 0384-8264.*
Desc: Articles and news of interest to Atlantic region librarians, library workers and trustees.
Ind/Abst Can. Period. Index; Libr. Inf. Sci. Abstr.

CN/0825-186X
APLIC BULLETIN. (APLIC BULLETIN / THE ASSOCIATION OF PARLIAMENTARY LIBRARIANS IN CANADA BULLETIN.). [APLIC bull.]. **VFOAT** Bulletin ABPAC; Bulletin APLIC/ABPAC. **VAT** Association of Parliamentary Librarians in Canada Bulletin; Bulletin Association des Bibliothecaires Parlementaires au Canada. No. 1 (Sept. 1983)-. Bulletin. French (English). sa. Free to member and other libraries on request. Association of Parliamentary Librarians in Canada, Association des Bibliothecaires Parlementaires Au Canada, Library of Parliament, Parliament Buildings, Ottawa Ontario K1A 0A9 Canada. **ED** Richard Pare. **DD** 027.5/06/071. **Circ:** 125 (ctrl).
Desc: A newsletter aimed at improving communication among the members of the association.

●US/1062-0664
APT FOR LIBRARIES. (APT FOR LIBRARIES: ALTERNATIVE PRESS TITLES FOR THE GENERAL READER.). [APT libr.]. **VFOAT** Alternative Press Titles for the General Reader. **VAT** Alternative Press Titles for Libraries. (1992)-. English. an. $12.00 (one year), $20.00 (two year) US; $15.00 (one year), $25.00 (two year) other. Crises Press, 1716 Southwest Williston Road, Gainesville FL 32608. **Tel** (904)335-2200. **ED** Charles Willett. **LC** Z1033.U58; A66. **DD** 011.5/6/05. Index available. **Bk Rev**, (Qty: 200). **Circ:** 100.
Desc: Bibliography and selection tool of books, periodicals, and non-book materials displayed at The Crisis Alternative Press Exhibit at the two preceeding conferences each year.

GW
ARBEITSBERICHT - ARBEITSSTELLE FUR DAS BIBLIOTHEKSWESEN. **Main/Corp** Deutscher Bibliotheksverband (German : West). Arbeitsstelle fur das Bibliothekswesen. German. Deutscher Bibliotheksverband, Bundesallee 184-185, 1000 Berlin 31 Germany. **LC** Z674; .B6 subser; Z673.A1. **DD** 020/.5 S; 020/.5.

●SZ
ARBIDO. (1995)-. French (German and Italian). Eleven times a year. 100.00F. Arbido, Effingerstrasse 35, Ch 3008 Bern Switzerland. **Tel** 011 41 31 3824240. ***Continues*** *Arbido R, 0258-0772; Arbido B, 0258-0764.*

IT/0409-5448
ARCHIGINNASIO, L'. (L'ARCHIGINNASIO : BULLETTINO DELLA BIBLIOTECA COMUNALE DI BOLOGNA.). [Archiginnasio]. **Added/Corp** Biblioteca Comunale dell'Archiginnasio (Bologna, Italy). Vol. 1, No. 1 (1906)-. Periodical. Italian. an. L50000 Italy; L60000 others. Biblioteca Comunale Archiginnasio, Comune Piazza Galvani 1, 40124 Bologna Italy. **Tel** 011 39 51 236488. **LC** Z933; .B69B.
Ind/Abst Am. Hist. Life (1960-); BHA : Biblio. Hist. Art; MLA Int. Bibl. Books Artic. Mod. Lang. Lit.

BE/0003-9748
ARCHIVES ET BIBLIOTHEQUES DE BELGIQUE. **See** Genealogy and Heraldry-Archives.

GW
ARCHIVIUM. (19??)-. an. $130.00. K.G. Saur Verlag KG, A Reed Reference Publishing Company, Part of Reed International PLC, Ortlerstrasse 8, D 81373 Munich Germany. **Tel** 011 49 89 769020, FAX 011 49 89 76902150, telex 5212067-SAUR-D.

XR/0004-0398
ARCHIVNI CASOPIS. **See** Genealogy and Heraldry-Archives.

CN/0315-9930
ARGUS (MONTREAL). (ARGUS.). [Argus]. **Added/Corp** Corporation des Bibliothecaires Professionnels du Quebec. (1971)-. Periodical. French (English; summaries and/or abstracts in English). Three times a year (Mar., Sept., Dec.). $35.00. Corporation Bibliothecaires Professionels Quebec, 307 rue Ste Catherine W/Room 320, Montreal Quebec H2X 2A3 Canada. **Tel** (514)845-3327, FAX (514)845-1618. **ED** Paulette Bernhard. **LC** Z673.C9533; A74. **DD** 020/.971. Index available. cum. index. **Ad Acc. Circ:** 1,200 (ctrl). ***Continues*** *Corporation of Professional Librarians of Quebec. Bulletin de Nouvelles.*
Desc: Articles deal with training, role, status and working conditions of the librarian in society; professionalism, new technologies, new markets, the economic and socio-polical environment, customer needs, products and documentary services, new directions and research in library and information studies, and contributions from other fields.
Ind/Abst Libr. Inf. Sci. Abstr.; Libr. Lit.; Point Repere (1983-).

US/0004-184X
ARKANSAS LIBRARIES. [Ark. libr.]. Ser. 2, Vol. 1 (June 1944)-. Periodical. English. bm. $70.00. Arkansas Library Association, 1100 North University, Suite 109, Little Rock AR 72207. **Tel** (501)661-1127, FAX (501)663-1218. **ED** Judith Briden (editor's address: ASU-Ellis Library, PO Box 2040, Jonesboro, AR 72467), Carta Castleberry (editor's address: UALR, Ottenheimer Library/AIEA, 2801 South University, Little Rock AR 72204). **LC** Z732; .A715. **DD** 027.0767. Index available (Dec.). **Bk Rev. Ad Acc. Pr Rev. Circ:** 800 (ctrl). available on microfilm and microfiche from University Microfilms International (UMI). ***Supersedes*** *Arkansas. Free Library Service Bureau. Arkansas Libraries;* ***Absorbed*** *Arkansas Library Association. ALA Newsletter.*
Desc: Any aspect of libraries or librarianship in Arkansas and other articles and material of interest to Arkansas librarians.
Ind/Abst Libr. Lit.; Ozark Period. Index.

US/1050-6098
ARL. [ARL]. **Main/Corp** Association of Research Libraries. **VAT** Association of Research Libraries. No. 150 (4 May 1990)-. Periodical. English. bm. $40.00 (nonmembers), $20.00 (members). Association of Research Libraries, 21 Dupont Circle, Washington DC 20036. **Tel** (202)296-2296. **DD** 021. ***Continues*** *Newsletter / Association of Research Libraries, 0066-9652.*

US/0147-2135
ARL STATISTICS. See Library and Information Sciences-Abstracting, Bibliographies and Statistics.

US
ARLIS/NA MEMBERSHIP DIRECTORY. **Main/Corp** ARLIS/North America. Directory. English. H W Wilson Company, 950 University Avenue, Bronx NY 10452. **Tel** (800)367-6770, (718)588-8400, FAX (718)590-1617, telex 4990003 HWILSON. **LC** Z5937.A74; A13. **DD** 026/.7/06273.

US/0743-040X
ARLIS/NA UPDATE. [ARLIS/NA update]. **Added/Corp** Art Libraries Society of North America. **VFOAT** Update; A.R.L.I.S. N.A. Update. **VAT** Art Libraries Society of North America Update. (1984)-. Periodical. English (Spanish and French). ir. Art Libraries Society of North America / ARLIS/NA, 3900 East Timrod Street, Tucson AZ 85711. **Tel** (602)881-8479, FAX (602)322-6778. **ED** Pamela J. Parry and Kathryn Jaughn. **LC** Z675.A85; A777. **Ad Acc. Circ:** 1,300 (ctrl).
Desc: An newsletter containing society, art library and job listings news.

PO/0871-6102
ARQUIVO COIMBRAO (BOLETIM DA BIBLIOTECA MUNICIPAL). Main/Corp Coimbra. Biblioteca Municipal. **Added/Corp** Coimbra. Biblioteca Municipal. Boletim da Biblioteca Municipal. Vol. 1 (July 1923)-. Periodical. Portuguese. **LC** Z946; .C65. **DD** 027.44698.
Ind/Abst BHA : Biblio. Hist. Art.

US/0730-7187
ART DOCUMENTATION. (ART DOCUMENTATION : BULLETIN OF THE ART LIBRARIES SOCIETY OF NORTH AMERICA.). [Art doc.]. **Added/Corp** Art Libraries Society of North America. Vol. 1, No. 1 (Feb. 1982)-. Periodical. English (French and Spanish). qt. $75.00 (institution), $55.00 (individual) North America; $55.00 (individuals), $65.00 (institutions) other Comes with Art Libraries Society of North America membership. ARLIS/NA, 4101 Lake Boone Trail, Suite 201, Raleigh NC 27607. **Tel** (919)787-5181. **ED** Beryl K. Smith and Kathryn Vaugh. **LC** Z5937; .A19; Z674.2. **DD** 026/.7. Index available. cum. index. **Bk Rev. Ad Acc. Pr Rev. Circ:** 1,300. available on microfilm from University Microfilms International (UMI). ***Continues*** *ARLIS/North America. ARLIS/NA Newsletter, 0090-3515.*
Desc: Includes articles and information relevant to art librarianship and visual resources curatorship, and art libraries society news.
Ind/Abst ARTbibliogr. Mod.; BHA : Biblio. Hist. Art; Libr. Inf. Sci. Abstr.

UK/0307-4722
ART LIBRARIES JOURNAL. [Art libr. j.]. **Added/Corp** Art Libraries Society. Art Libraries Society/UK and Eire. Vol. 1 (Spring 1976)-. Periodical. English. Four times a year (May, Aug., Oct., Dec.). £38.00 (surface mail), £47.00 (airmail) UK & Ireland; £76.00 others. ARLIS UK & Ireland, The Art Libraries Society of the United Kingdom and Ireland, 18 College Road Bromsgrove, Worcs. B60 2NE England. **Tel** 011 44 527 579298. **ED** Philip Pacey. **LC** Z675.A85; A78. **DD** 026/.7. Index available. **Bk Rev. Ad Acc. Circ:** 600. available in microform. ***Supersedes in part*** *Newsletter (Art Libraries Society), 0306-2228.*
Desc: Concerned with the documentation, bibliography and librarianship of art and design worldwide.
Ind/Abst Archit. Period. Index; ARTbibliogr. Mod. (1985-); Avery Index Archit. Period. Suppl. Colum. Univ. (19??-199?); BHA : Biblio. Hist. Art; Br. Archaeol. Bibliogr.; Ethnoarts Index; Inf. Sci. Abstr.; Libr. Inf. Sci. Abstr.; Libr. Lit.

JA/0571-2378
ASAHI JANARU. *Ceased.* VFOAT Asahi Journal. (1959)-(1992). Periodical. Japanese. wk. **(Subscription address:** Japan Publications Trading Company, Ltd., PO Box 5030, Tokyo International, Tokyo 100-31 Japan.**) LC** AP95.J2; A72. cum. index.

TH/1017-6748
ASIAN LIBRARIES. Vol. 1, No. 1 (Mar. 1991)-. Periodical. English. qt. $116.00. Library Marketing Services Ltd. / Bangkok, GPO Box 701, Bangkok 10501 Thailand. **Tel** 11 66 2 2471032. **LC** Z665.2.A78; A73.

US
ASIS ... HANDBOOK AND DIRECTORY. Main/Corp American Society for Information Science. **VFOAT** ASIS Handbook and Directory; Handbook and Directory. (1985)-. English. an (Mar.). $26.25 (members), $105.00 (non-members) Comes with American Society for Information Science membership. American Society Information Science, 8720 Georgia Avenue, Suite 501, Silver Spring MD 20910. **Tel** (301)495-0900, FAX (301)495-0810. ***Continues*** *American Society for Information Science. Handbook & Directory.*

AT/1034-9154
ASL. Added/Corp Australian Library and Information Association. Special Libraries Section. **VFOAT** Australian Special Libraries. (19??)-. Periodical. English. Four times a year. 45.00Aus$ Australia; 60.00Aus$ (surface mail), 70.00Aus$ (airmail). Australian Library & Information Association, PO Box E441, Queen Victoria Terrace, ACT 2600 Australia. **Tel** 011 61 6 2851877, FAX 011 61 6 282 2249. **ED** John Thawley. **LC** Z675.A2; A94a. **DD** 026/.000994. Index available. **Bk Rev. Ad Acc. Circ:** 1,500. ***Continues*** *ASLN.*
Desc: Aims to communicate new ideas and development, as they relate to Australian special librarians.
Ind/Abst Aust. Educ. Index (199?-); Aust. Libr. Inf. Sci. Abstr. (1982-1984,1985-).

UK/0305-0033
ASLIB INFORMATION (LONDON, ENGLAND : 1973). *Title Change.* (ASLIB INFORMATION.). [Aslib inf.]. **Added/Corp** ASLIB. **VFOAT** Information. Vol. 1, No. 1 (Jan. 1973)-(1993). Periodical. English. Ten times a year. ASLIB, Information House, 20-24 Old Street, London EC1V 9AP England. **Tel** 011 44 71 253 4488, FAX 011 44 71 430 0514, telex 23667 AJLIB G. **Bk Rev. Ad Acc. Circ:** 2,500. ***Continues in part*** *ASLIB Proceedings.* ***Continued by*** *Managing Information, 1352-0229.*
Desc: For anyone involved in the library and information professions. Regular features include guest editorials on topical issues, reviews of information technology and database developments, and reports on current trends in the management of information.
Ind/Abst Abstr. Hum. Comput. Interact. (19??-19??); HILITES (19??-19??); Libr. Inf. Sci. Abstr. (19??-19??); World Ceram. Abstr. (19??-19??); World Publ. Monit. (19??-19??).

UK/0001-253X
ASLIB PROCEEDINGS. [Aslib proc.]. **Added/Corp** Aslib. **VFOAT** Proceedings. (Jan. 1949)-. Academic Scholarly Publication. English. Ten times a year. £99.00 (member), £124.00 (non-member) Europe; £109.00 (member), £136.00 (non-member) other. ASLIB, Information House, 20-24 Old Street, London EC1V 9AP England. **Tel** 011 44 71 253 4488, FAX 011 44 71 430 0514, telex 23667 AJLIB G. **(Subscription address:** North America/ 143 Old Marlton Pike, Medford, NJ 08055-8707**) LC** Z673; .A627136. **DD** 026.006242. **NLM** Z 673 A835P. **CODEN** ASLPAO. **Ad Acc. Circ:** 3,300. Documents available from The Genuine Article, Ask*IEEE, CASDDS. ***Formed by the union of*** *Proceedings of the British Society for International Bibliography* ***and*** *Report of Proceedings of the ... Conference ... / Association of Special Libraries and Information Bureaux (Great Britain). Conference;* ***Absorbed*** *A.S.L.I.B. Information (London, England : 1929).* ***Continued in part by*** *ASLIB Information (London, England : 1973).*
Desc: Contains papers given at ASLIB meetings and conferences, as well as contributed papers pertinent to the field.
Ind/Abst Abstr. Hum. Comput. Interact.; ACM Guide Comput. Lit.; AGRICOLA; Anbar Account. Finan. Abstr. [Full Txt.]; Anbar Mark. Distr. Abstr. [Full Txt.]; Anbar Top Manage. Abstr. [Full Txt.]; Chem. Abstr. (1949-1985); Coal Abstr.; Compumath Citation Index [Full Cov.]; Comput. Rev.; Curr. Contents Soc. Behav. Sci.; Dairy Sci. Abstr.; Ei Page One; EMBASE; HILITES; Inf. Instruc. Technol.; Inf. Sci. Abstr. [Full Cov.]; INSPEC (April 1970-); Int. Aerosp. Abstr. (1991-); Libr. Inf. Sci. Abstr.; Libr. Lit.; Manage. Bibliogr. Rev.; Oper. Prod. Manage. Abstr. [Full Txt.]; Person. Train. Abstr. [Full Txt.]; Res. Alert [Full Cov.]; Res. High. Educ. Abstr.; Soc. Sci. Cit. Index [Full Cov.]; Soc. Res. Methodol. Abstr. (1992-); Women Manage. Rev. [Full Txt.]; World Ceram. Abstr.; World Publ. Monit.; World Surf. Coat. Abstr.

CN/0827-2735
ASPLO NEWSLETTER. (ASPLO NEWSLETTER / ASSOCIATION OF SMALL PUBLIC LIBRARIES OF ONTARIO.). [ASPLO newsl.]. Vol. 1, No. 1 (Apr. 1982)-. Newsletter. English. free to members; $5.00 library schools. Association of Small Public Libraries of Ontario, c/o Tillsonburg Public Library, Tillsonburg Ontario N4G 3P9 Canada. **DD** 027.4713.

AT/1030-3812
ASSIG NEWSLETTER. [ASSIG newsl.]. **Added/Corp** Australian Serials Special Interest Group. **VFOAT** Australian Serials Special Interest Group Newsletter. (1987)-. Newsletter. English. Four times a year (Mar., June, Sept., Dec.). 5.00Aus$ (members of Australian Library Information Association); 35.00Aus$ (Australia & New Zealand), 45.00Aus$ (other) nonmembers. Deakin University c/o Burwood Serials, Sect C I McGregor, 221 Burwood HYW, Burwood 3125 Australia. **DD** 027.005. **Bk Rev. Ad Acc. Circ:** 280.
Ind/Abst Aust. Educ. Index (19??-); Aust. Libr. Inf. Sci. Abstr. (1987-).

US/1051-3299
ASSISTANT EDITOR. *Suspended.* [Assist. ed.]. Vol. 1, No. 1 (Fall 1990)-Suspended with Vol. 4, No. 4 (199?). Periodical. English. ir. Chris Olson & Associates, 857 Twin Harbor Drive, Arnold MD 21012-1027. **Tel** (410)647-6708, FAX (410)647-0415. **ED** Suzanne Peake. **DD** 810. **Circ:** 500. available on diskette.
Desc: Original short articles, fillers and clip art that can be used by librarians in their newsletters. Computer diskettes are available.

UK/0004-5152
ASSISTANT LIBRARIAN. (THE ASSISTANT LIBRARIAN : OFFICIAL JOURNAL OF THE A.A.L.). [Assist. libr.]. **Added/Corp** Association of Assistant Librarians. **VFOAT** AL; A.L. Vol. 46, No. 1 (Jan. 1953)-. Periodical. English. Twelve times a year. £90.00. Association of Assistant Librarians, West Glamorgan County Library, 32 York Street, Leeds LS9 8TD England. **Tel** 011 44 532 488071. **ED** Debbie Shorley. **LC** Z671; .L691. **Bk Rev. Ad Acc. Circ:** 1,300 (ctrl). available on microfilm and microfiche from University Microfilms International (UMI). ***Continues*** *Library Assistant.*
Desc: Concerned with librarianship, information science and literary subjects of interest to go-ahead professionals.
Ind/Abst Art Archaeol. Tech. Abstr.; Child. Lit. Abstr. (19??-); Libr. Inf. Sci. Abstr.

CN/0708-0263
AT A GLANCE. Added/Corp Canadian Association of Special Libraries and Information Services. Edmonton Chapter. Vol. 1 (Aug. 1978)-. Periodical. English. Six times a year. 15.00Can$. Canadian Association Special Libraries & Information Services, 9660 104 Avenue, Edmonton Alberta T5H 4B5 Canada. **Tel** (403)427-1600. **DD** 026/.00097123/3. ctrl circ.

CN/0702-7559
AT THE LIBRARY. [At. libr.]. V. 1- March 1977-. Periodical. English. mo. Free. Regina Public Library, 2311 Twelfth Avenue, Regina Saskatchewan S4P 0N3 Canada. **Tel** (306)569-7595. **ED** Anne Campbell. **DD** 027.4/7124/4. **Bk Rev. Circ:** 10,000. available on microfilm from Saskatchewan Archives Board. ***Absorbed*** *Annual Report. Dunlop Art Gallery, 0827-9500.*
Desc: Lists library programs and services available throughout a system of eight branch libraries and two booktrailers.

US/1042-6469
AT YOUR SERVICE (BIRMINGHAM, ALA.). (AT YOUR SERVICE : YOUR QUARTERLY NEWSLETTER FROM EBSCO SUBSCRIPTION SERVICES.). [At your serv.]. **Added/Corp** EBSCO Subscription Services. (Winter/Spring 1987)-. Newsletter. English. qt. Free (EBSCO Subscription Service customers). EBSCO Industries Inc., PO Box 1943, Birmingham AL 35201-1943. **Tel** (205)991-1465, FAX (205)991-1479. **ED** Laura Ralstin. **DD** 070. available via Internet.
Desc: Designed to continually inform the library community of pertinent services, programs and activities of EBSCO Subscription Services and its divisions. Each issue includes: interface development updates, new/enhanced service announcements, CD-ROM product developments, library conference calendar, library automation column, plus feature articles.

US
ATLA MONOGRAPH SERIES. Main/Corp American Theological Library Association. **Added/Corp** American Theological Library Association. **VAT** American Theological Library Association Monograph Series. (1972)-. Monographic series. English. ir. Price varies per volume. Scarecrow Press Inc., 52 Liberty Street, PO Box 4167, Metuchen NJ 08840. **Tel** (908)548-8600, (800)537-7107.

●US/1065-092X
ATRIUM GROUP ADVISORY, THE. [Atrium Group adv.]. **Added/Corp** Library of Congress. Atrium Group. Vol. 1, Issue 1 (July 1992)-. Periodical. English. qt. Library of Congress / Atrium Group, Washington DC 20540. **DD** 025.

CN/0226-3688
ATULU, L'. [Atulu]. V. 1- Feb. 1979-. Periodical. French. mo. Free. Bibliotheque de Quebec, 37 rue Ste-Angele, Quebec G1R 4G5 Canada. **DD** 028.1/05. ctrl circ.

CN/0823-7859
AUDIO-FILE. [Audio-file]. **Added/Corp** CIRPA/ADISQ Foundation. Canadian Independent Record Production Association. Association du Disque et de l'Industrie du Spectacle Quebecoise. **VFOAT** Fichier Central. Vol. 1, No. 1 (June 1983)-. Periodical. English (French). ir. Limited Free Distribution. Audio-File, Canadian Independent Record Production Association, 144 Front Street West/Suite 330, Toronto Ontario M5J 2L7 Canada. **DD** 025/.06789912/0971.

UK/0302-3451
AUDIOVISUAL LIBRARIAN, THE. [Audiov. libr.]. **Added/Corp** Aslib. Audio-Visual Group. Library Association. Audiovisual Group. (1973)-. English. qt. £47.00 UK; £51.00 other. Audiovisual Library Group Association, Frongog Llanbadarn Fawr, Aberystwyth SY23 3HN Wales. **(Subscription address:** World-Wide Subscription Services, Unit 4, Gibbs Reed Farm Pashley Road, Ticehurst TN5 7HE England.**) ED** Ann Aungle. **LC** Z717; .A84. **DD** 025.17/7/05. Index available. cum. index. **Bk Rev. Ad Acc. Circ:** 4,000. available on microfilm and

microfiche from University Microfilms International (UMI). **Desc:** Official journal of the ASLIB and (UK) Library Association. Covers news, issues and events in the AV world.
Ind/Abst Cumul. Index Nurs. Allied Health Lit.; Educ. Technol. Abstr.; Inf. Instruc. Technol.; Inf. Sci. Abstr.; Libr. Inf. Sci. Abstr.; Libr. Lit.

●US
AUGUSTANA COLLEGE LIBRARY PUBLICATIONS. Added/Corp Augustana College (Rock Island, Ill.). Library. No. 36 (1992)-. Monographic series. English. Price varies per volume. ***Continues*** *Augustana Library Publications.*

CN/0714-7058
AURORA (GRAND CENTRE). (THE AURORA : NORTHERN LIGHTS LIBRARY CO-OPERATIVE NEWSLETTER.). [Aurora]. Vol. 1, No. 1 (Aug. 1982)-. Newsletter. English. bm. Northern Lights Library Co-Operative, Box 2070, Grand Centre, Alta T0A 1T0, Canada. **DD** 027.47123/3.

GW/0720-7123
AUSKUNFT. [Auskunft]. (1981)-. Periodical. German. qt. **UDC** 026/027(430.1-43.2).
Ind/Abst Libr. Inf. Sci. Abstr.

AT/1030-5033
AUSTRALASIAN PUBLIC LIBRARIES AND INFORMATION SERVICES. VFOAT APLIS. Vol. 1, No. 1 (Apr. 1988)-. Periodical. English. qt. 42.00Aus$. Auslib Press, PO Box 622, Blackwood South Australia, 5051 Australia. **Tel** 11 61 8 2784363, FAX 11 61 8 2784000. **ED** Alan L. Bumdy. **LC** Z870.A1; A78. **DD** 027.494. Index available. **Bk Rev. Ad Acc. Pr Rev. Circ:** 1,000.
Desc: Contains articles, news, and reviews for public libraries in Australia, New Zealand, and the region.
Ind/Abst Aust. Educ. Index (199?-); Aust. Libr. Inf. Sci. Abstr. (1991-); Libr. Inf. Sci. Abstr.

AT/0004-8623
AUSTRALIAN ACADEMIC AND RESEARCH LIBRARIES. (AUSTRALIAN ACADEMIC AND RESEARCH LIBRARIES : AARL.). [Aust. acad. res. libr.]. **Added/Corp** Library Association of Australia. University and College Libraries Section. **VFOAT** AARL. Vol. 1, No. 1 (Autumn 1970)-. Academic Scholarly Publication. English. Four times a year (Mar., June, Sept., Dec.). 45.00Aus$ Australia; 60.00Aus$ (surface mail),70.00Aus$ (airmail). Australian Library & Information Association, PO Box E441, Queen Victoria Terrace, ACT 2600 Australia. **Tel** 011 61 6 2851877, FAX 011 61 6 282 2249. **ED** J. I. Horacek. **LC** Z675.U5; A9. **DD** 027.7/0994. Index available. cum. index. **Bk Rev. Ad Acc. Circ:** 1,050. available on microfiche.
Desc: Articles on academic librarianship (university, college and research libraries) in Australia. Comprehensive statistical information published in a supplement.
Ind/Abst Annu. Bibliogr. Engl. Lang. Lit.; APAIS, Aust. Public Aff. Inf. Ser. (1972-); Aust. Educ. Index (1978-); Aust. Libr. Inf. Sci. Abstr. (1984-); Inf. Sci. Abstr.; Libr. Inf. Sci. Abstr.; Libr. Lit.

US/0898-3283
AUSTRALIAN & NEW ZEALAND JOURNAL OF SERIALS LIBRARIANSHIP. *Ceased.* [Aust. N. Z. j. ser. librariansh.]. **VFOAT** Australian and New Zealand Journal of Serials Librarianship; Journal of Serials Librarianship; ANZJSL. (1990)-Vol. 4, No. 4. Periodical. English. qt. The Haworth Press Inc, 10 Alice Street, Binghamton NY 13904-1580. **Tel** (607)722-5857, (800)3-HAWORTH, FAX (607)722-1424. **ED** Toby Burrows (editor's address: The University of Western Australia, University Library, Nedlands Western Australia 6009 Australia). **LC** Z692.S5; A93. **DD** 025.3/432. **Bk Rev. Ad Acc. Pr Rev. Acid Free. Circ:** 117. available on microfilm and microfiche from University Microfilms International (UMI). Documents available from Ask*IEEE, Haworth Document Delivery Service.
Desc: Focuses on both reviews and news of serials in Australia, New Zealand, and the South Pacific, and the practice of serials librarianship in this area of the world. Provides collection development tools for librarians around the world interested in new developments in Australasian libraries where serials constitute a significant portion of the library collection.
Ind/Abst Aust. Educ. Index (199?-?); Aust. Libr. Inf. Sci. Abstr. (1990-?); Index Period. Artic. Relat. Law; Inf. Sci. Abstr.; INSPEC (1990-?); Libr. Inf. Sci. Abstr.; Libr. Lit.; Ref. Z.

AT
AUSTRALIAN BOOKS IN PRINT.
Added/Corp D.W. Thorpe Pty. (197?)-. English. an. $115.00. D. W. Thorpe, A Reed Reference Publishing Company, A Subsidiary of Reed International Books Australia, 18 Salmon Street, Port Melbourne, Victoria 3207 Australia. **Tel** 011 61 3 6451511, FAX 011 61 3 6453981, telex 39476. **(Subscription address:** R.R. Bowker, PO Box 31, New Providence NJ 07974.) **ED** Maria Baxter. **LC** Z4011; .A85. **DD** 015.94. **NLM** Z 4011 A935. **Ad Acc. Circ:** 5,000. ***Continues*** *Bookbuyers Reference Book, 0524-0603.*
Desc: Provides bibliographic information on in-print books published in or about Australia or written by Australian authors.

AT/1031-5187
AUSTRALIAN LIBRARIES : ALED. VFOAT ALED; Australian Libraries, The Essential Directory. 1st Ed. (July 1988)-. English. be. Auslib Press, PO Box 622, Blackwood South Australia, 5051 Australia. **Tel** 11 61 8 2784363, FAX 11 61 8 2784000. **LC** Z870.A1; A83. **DD** 027/.0025/94.

AT/0004-9670
AUSTRALIAN LIBRARY JOURNAL, THE. [Aust. libr. j.]. **Added/Corp** Library Association of Australia. Vol. 1 (1951)-. Periodical. English. qt. 45.00Aus$ Australia; 60.00Aus$ (surface mail),70.00Aus$ (airmail). Australian Library & Information Association, PO Box E441, Queen Victoria Terrace, ACT 2600 Australia. **Tel** 011 61 6 2851877, FAX 011 61 6 282 2249. **ED** John Levett. **LC** Z671; .A9. **DD** 020.5. Index available. cum. index. **Bk Rev. Ad Acc. Circ:** 3,000. available on microfilm and microfiche from University Microfilms International (UMI).
Desc: Articles and reviews of interest to librarians in all fields, and information professionals.
Ind/Abst AESIS Q.; Annu. Bibliogr. Engl. Lang. Lit.; APAIS, Aust. Public Aff. Inf. Ser. (1963-); Aust. Educ. Index (1978-); Aust. Libr. Inf. Sci. Abstr. (1984-); Curr. Index J. Educ.; Inf. Sci. Abstr.; Libr. Inf. Sci. Abstr.; Libr. Lit.

AT/1034-8042
AUSTRALIAN LIBRARY REVIEW. [Aust. libr. rev.]. **Added/Corp** Charles Sturt University. Centre for Information Studies. (1990)-. Periodical. English. qt. 33.00Aus$. Charles Sturt University CRSR, PO Box 588, Wagga Wagga NSW 2650 Australia. **Tel** 011 61 69 222763, FAX 011 61 69 222764. **(Subscription address:** Charles Sturt University Center for Information Studies, Locked Bag 660, Wagga Wagga, New South Wales 2678 Australia, Telephone: 011 61 69 222584) **Pr Rev.** Documents available from Ask*IEEE. ***Continues*** *Riverina Library Review.*
Ind/Abst Aust. Libr. Inf. Sci. Abstr. (1984-1988),(1991-); INSPEC (Feb. 1990-).

AT/1036-1820
AUSTRALIAN LIBRARY TECHNICIANS ASSOCIATION NEWS. (1976)-. Periodical. English. qt.
Ind/Abst Aust. Educ. Index.

AT/0314-3767
AUSTRALIAN SOCIETY OF INDEXERS NEWSLETTER. (1976)-. Newsletter. English. Eleven times a year. 30.00Aus$ Australia; 35.00Aus$ other. Australian Society of Indexers, Hon Treasurer GPO Box 1251, Melbourne VIC 3001 Australia. **Tel** 011 03 418 7275. **ED** Elizabeth Baratto, (phone: (03)270-6666). **Bk Rev**, (Qty: varies). **Ad Acc. Circ:** 250 (ctrl).
Desc: Reports of activities of the society and articles on indexing topics of interest to members and subscribers.
Ind/Abst Aust. Educ. Index (199?-); Aust. Libr. Inf. Sci. Abstr. (1990-).

US/0005-1055
AUTOMATIC DOCUMENTATION AND MATHEMATICAL LINGUISTICS. [Autom. doc. math. linguist.]. Vol. 1 (Spring 1967)-. Academic Scholarly Publication. English (Russian). Six times a year. $895.00. Allerton Press, Inc., 150 Fifth Avenue, New York NY 10011. **Tel** (212)924-3950, FAX (212)463-9684, telex 427441 ALPRES. **ED** R.S. Gylyarevski. **LC** Z699.A1; A88. **DD** 025. **NLM** Z 699.A1 A939. **CODEN** ADMLAE. **[CCC]**. Documents available from Ask*IEEE, CASDDS.
Ind/Abst Chem. Abstr. (-1976); INSPEC (1982-); Math. Rev.; MLA Int. Bibl. Books Artic. Mod. Lang. Lit.; Zentralbl. Math. Ihre Grenzgeb.

CN
AUTOMATION IN LIBRARIES. Main/Corp C.A.C.U.L Workshop On Library Automation. **Added/Corp** Canadian Association of College and University Libraries. Committee on Automation. Vol. 1 (1967)-. English. an. Canadian Library Association, 200 Elgin Street, Suite 602, Ottawa Ontario K2P 1L5 Canada. **Tel** (613)232-9625.

AT/0818-2507
AV UPDATE. (1983)-. English. ir. Department of Family Service & Aboriginal & Islander Affairs Library, GPO Box 806, Brisbane QLD 4001 Australia. **ED** Kathleen Thompson.
Ind/Abst Aust. Educ. Index; Aust. Libr. Inf. Sci. Abstr. (1983-).

US/0192-8007
AXIS (WASHINGTON). *Suspended.* (AXIS.). V. 1- Aug. 1976-Suspended. Periodical. English. ir. $15.00. Metropolitan Washington Council of Governments, 777 North Capitol Street Northeast, Washington DC 20002-4239. **Tel** (202)962-3256.

CN/0381-6796
AXIS (WATERLOO). (AXIS.). Mar. 1974-. Periodical. English. Waterloo Regional Library, Marsland Centre/7th Floor, 20 Erb Street West, Waterloo Ontario N2L 1T2 Canada. **DD** 027.4/713/44.

CN/0701-094X
B P L BEEP, THE. Main/Corp Barrie Public Library. V. 1, No. 3- June/July 1974-. Periodical. English. bm. Barrie Public Library, Barrie Ontario Canada. **DD** 027.4/713/17. ***Continues*** *Take One, 0701-0958.*

DK/0905-4650
B70. Added/Corp Bibliotekarforbundet. **VFOAT** B 70; B Halvfjerds. (1990)-. Periodical. Danish. Twenty-two times a year. kr285.00. Bibliotekarforbundet, Lindevangs Alle 2, DK 2000 Frederiksberg Denmark. **Tel** 011 45 38 881770. **ED** Joergen Nielsen, Per Nyeng. **LC** Z671; .B58037. Index available. **Bk Rev. Ad Acc. Circ:** 6,000 (ctrl). available with illustrations. ***Continues*** *Bibliotek 70, 0006-1824.*
Desc: Provides information on libraries and library science.

IO/0125-9008
BACA. [Baca]. **Added/Corp** Pusat Dokumentasi Ilmiah Nasional (Indonesia). **VFOAT** Read. Vol. 1 (1974)-. Periodical. Indonesian (English). bm. $5.00. Pusat Dokumentasi Ilmiah Nasl, PO Box 3065 JKT, Djakarta 10002 Indonesia. **Tel** (021)583465, telex 62875 IA. **ED** Kosam Rimbarawa. **LC** Z671; .B25. **Bk Rev. Ad Acc. Circ:** 1,000 (ctrl).
Desc: News items about the activities of network systems for library documentation and information centers, on national, regional and international news.
Ind/Abst Libr. Inf. Sci. Abstr.

SW/0037-6477
BARN OCH KULTUR. [Barn kult.]. **Added/Corp** Bibliotekstjaenst. Vol. 16 (1970)-. Periodical. Swedish. Six times a year. Kr275.00. Bibliotekstjanst AB, Box 200, S-221 00 Lund Sweden. **Tel** 011 46 46 180000. ***Continues*** *Skolbiblioteket.*
Ind/Abst Child. Lit. Abstr. (19??-); Libr. Inf. Sci. Abstr.

US/0095-361X
BASIC STATE PLAN AND ANNUAL PROGRAM. Main/Corp Alabama Public Library Service. (19??)-. English. an. Alabama Public Library Service, 6030 Monticello Drive, Montgomery AL 36130. **Tel** (205)277-7330. **LC** Z732.A2; A44a. **DD** 027.4/761.

US/0005-6944
BAY STATE LIBRARIAN. [Bay State libr.]. Vol. 46, No. 1 (Jan. 1956)-. Periodical. English. Nine times a year. $15.00. Massachusetts Library Association, PO Box 556, Wakefield MA 01880. **Tel** (617)438-0779. **LC** Z673.M4; A15. **DD** 020.623. **Ad Acc. Circ:** 1,100 (ctrl). available on microfiche from University Microfilms International (UMI). ***Continues*** *Massachusetts Library Association Bulletin, 0275-8784.*
Desc: Contains articles on local, state, and national interest.
Ind/Abst Libr. Lit.

US/1045-6724
BAYVIEWS (OAKLAND, CALIF.). (BAYVIEWS : A JOURNAL OF BOOK REVIEWS AND OPINIONS WITH A WESTERN PERSPECTIVE.). [BayViews]. **Added/Corp** Association of Children's Librarians of Northern California. **VFOAT** Bay Views. Vol. 1, No. 1 (Sept. 1989)-. Periodical. English. Thirteen times a year. $30.00 Comes with Association of Children's Librarians membership. Association of Children's Librarians, PO Box 12471, Berkeley CA 94701. **Tel** (510)339-1666. **ED** Linda Perkins. **DD** 028. Index available. cum. index. **Bk Rev**, (Qty: 2400). **Pr Rev. Circ:** 375. ***Continues*** *ACL Reviews.*
Desc: New and information related to children's books.

US/0067-2734
BBA LIBRARY. BIOCHIMICA ET BIOPHYSICA ACTA LIBRARY. [B.B.A. libr.]. **VFOAT** Biochimica et Biophysica Acta Library. V. 1- 1963-. Academic Scholarly Publication. English. ir. Elsevier Science Publishing Company Inc, Madison Square Station, PO Box 882, New York NY 10159-0882. **Tel** (212)633-3950, FAX (212)633-3990. **CODEN** BBALAJ. Documents available from BIOSIS Document Express, CASDDS.
Ind/Abst Biol. Abstr.; Chem. Abstr. (1963-1977).

SW/0006-1867
BBL. BIBLIOTEKSBLADET. (BIBLIOTEKSBLADET.). [BBL, Biblioteksbl.]. **VFOAT** BBL. Vol. 1, No. 1 (1916)-. Periodical. Swedish. Ten times a year. Kr300.00. Swedish Library Association, Box 200, 22100 Sweden. **Tel** 046-180000. **ED** Barbro Blomberg. **LC** Z671; .B582. Index available. cum. index. **Bk Rev. Ad Acc. Circ:** 5,400 (ctrl). available on microfilm and microfiche from University Microfilms International (UMI).
Desc: Reflects the Swedish library world.
Ind/Abst Libr. Inf. Sci. Abstr.; Libr. Lit.

CN/0005-2876
BCLA REPORTER. Main/Corp British Columbia Library Association. Vol. 1 (Dec. 1957)-. Periodical. English. Six times a year. 45.00Can$ Comes with British Columbia Library Association membership. British Columbia Library Association, 110 6545 Bonsor Avenue, Burnaby British Columbia V5H 1H3 Canada. **Tel** (604)430-9633.

Library and Information Sciences

US/0163-9269
BEHAVIORAL & SOCIAL SCIENCES LIBRARIAN. [Behav. soc. sci. librar.]. **VAT** Behavioral and Social Sciences Librarian. Vol. 1 (Fall 1979)-. Academic Scholarly Publication. English. sa. $90.00 US; $126.00 other. The Haworth Press Inc, 10 Alice Street, Binghamton NY 13904-1580. **Tel** (607)722-5857, (800)3-HAWORTH, **FAX** (607)722-1424. **ED** Michael F. Winter (editor's address: 2050 Imperial Avenue, Davis, CA 95616). **LC** Z675.S6; B43. **DD** 026/.3/005. **NLM** Z 675.S6 B419. **CODEN** BSSLDR. **Bk Rev. Ad Acc. Pr Rev. Acid Free. Circ:** 286. available on microfilm and microfiche from University Microfilms International (UMI). Documents available from The Genuine Article, Ask*IEEE, Haworth Document Delivery Service.
Desc: Keeps all behavioral and social librarians up-to-date on the current developments in this field of librarianship. Articles present results of significant studies in the field.
Ind/Abst Abstr. Soc. Gerontol. (?-?); Appl. Soc. Sci. Index Abstr.; Arts Humanit. Citation Index [Select. Cov.]; Cumul. Index Nurs. Allied Health Lit.; Curr. Contents Soc. Behav. Sci.; Curr. Index J. Educ.; EMBASE; Index Period. Artic. Relat. Law; Inf. Sci. Abstr.; INSPEC (1981-1982-); Int. Polit. Sci. Abstr.; Libr. Inf. Sci. Abstr.; Libr. Lit.; PAIS Int. Print (1991-); Ref. Z.; Res. Alert [Full Cov.]; Soc. Sci. Cit. Index [Full Cov.]; Soc. Work Abstr. [Select. Cov.]; Stud. Women Abstr.

NR/0331-555X
BENDEL LIBRARY JOURNAL. [Bendel libr. j.]. **Added/Corp** Bendel State Library Board. Vol. 1, No. 1 (June 1978)-. Periodical. English. sa. Bendel State Library, PMB 1127, Benin City Nigeria. **Tel** 011 234 52 20081071. **ED** W.O. Mokogwu, J.O.U. Odiase, F.O. Egor, C.J. Ugbo. **LC** Z857.N5; B46. **DD** 027.0669. **Bk Rev. Ad Acc.** ctrl circ.
Ind/Abst Libr. Inf. Sci. Abstr.

US/0362-6881
BENTLEY LIBRARY ANNUAL, THE.
Main/Corp Bentley Historical Library. **VFOAT** Annual Report of the Bentley Historical Library, Michigan Historical Collections. English. an. University of Michigan / Johnston Hall, 115 Johnston Hall, Ann Arbor MI 48109. **LC** Z733.B476; B46. **DD** 026/.774/35.

DK/0107-9700
BERETNING FOR UNDERVISNINGSARET ... / DANMARKS BIBLIOTEKSSKOLE. **Main/Corp** Danmarks Biblioteksskole. Danish. an. Danmarks Biblioteksskole, Birketinget 6, 2300 S Kobenhavn Denmark. **LC** Z669.5.D4; D36A.

IO
BERITA PUSTAKAWAN. Vol. 1 (Oct. 1973)-. Indonesian. $15.00. Ikatan Pustakawan Indonesia, Merdeka Selatan No 11, Jakarta Indonesia. **Tel** (021)34252G. **ED** J N B Tairas. **LC** Z673.I28; A15. **Ad Acc. Circ:** 1,000.
Desc: Consisting of various articles on social sciences, humanities science and technology in connection with librarianship.

GW/0170-1738
BERLINER SIGELVERZEICHNIS / BERLINER GESAMTKATALOG ; DEUTSCHE STAATSBIBLIOTHEK, INSTITUT FUER LEIHVERKEHR UND ZENTRALKATALOGE ; DEUTSCHES BIBLIOTHEKSINSTITUT. **Added/Corp** Berliner Gesamtkatalog (Agency) Institut fur Leihverkehr und Zentralkataloge (Deutsche Staatsbibliothek) Deutsches Bibliotheksinstitut. (19??)-. German. **LC** Z801.B4; B38.
Continues Berliner Sigelverzeichnis mit Systematischem Verzeichnis der Sammelgebiete Wissenschaftlicher Literatur in Berlin (West).
Desc: Library information

GW
BERLINER SIGELVERZEICHNIS MIT SYSTEMATISCHEM VERZEICHNIS DER SAMMELGEBIETE WISSENSCHAFTLICHER LITERATUR IN BERLIN (WEST). **Title Change. Added/Corp** Deutscher Bibliotheksverband (Germany : West). Arbeitsstelle fur das Bibliothekswesen. Berliner Gesamtkatalog (Agency). (19??)-(19??). German. Deutsches Bibliotheksinstitut, Bundesallee 184 185, D 10717 Berlin Germany. **Tel** 011 49 30 8505186, 011 49 30 8505187, **FAX** 011 49 30 8505100. **LC** Z801.B4; B38.
Continues Berliner Sigelverzeichnis. **Continued by** Berliner Sigelverzeichnis (1990).

BE/0776-068X
BIB-KRANT LEUVEN. [Bib-Krant Leuven]. **VFOAT** Bibliotheken-Krant (Leuven). (1981)-. Periodical. Dutch. sm. 600.00F Belgium; 750.00F Netherlands. Plob, Tiensevest 142, Leuven 2000 Belgium. **Tel** 016 228933. **Bk Rev. Ad Acc. Circ:** 1,200.
Desc: Professional journal for library workers.

JA
BIBLIA. Japanese. sa. Tenri University Press, Tenri Central Library, Tenri-Shi, Nara 632 Japan. **Tel** 07436-3-1515, **FAX** 07436-3-7723. **Circ:** 1,000.
Ind/Abst Bibliogr. Mission.

CN/1183-1219
BIBLIO-CLIP : BULLETIN D'INFORMATION DU SERVICE DES BBLIOTHEQUES DE L'UQAM. [Biblio-clip]. **Added/Corp** Universite du Quebec a Montreal. Service des Bibliotheques. No 1 (Jan/Feb 1991)-. Bulletin. French. Limited free distribution. Universite du Quebec a Montreal, Services des Bibliotheques, CP 8888, Succursale A, Montreal Quebec H3C 3P8 Canada. **DD** 027.7714/28.

CN/0836-0464
BIBLIO-EXPRESS. [Biblio-express]. (Oct. 1987)-. Periodical. French. bm. Free. B.C.P. Gaspesie, 31 rue des Ecoliers, Cap-Chat Quebec G0J 1E0 Canada. **DD** 027.4714/77.

SP/0211-8238
BIBLIOMATICA. (1981)-. Periodical. Spanish. bm. 11500ptas. Univ Politecnica Facultad Info, Cettico Fgupm Urb Monte Principe, 28660 Madrid Spain. **Tel** 011 34 1 336740211. **UDC** 016:007.

IT/0073-2516
BIBLIOTECA DEGLI "HISTORIAE MUSICAE CULTORES". (1952)-. Periodical. Italian. ir. L95000. Casa Editrice Leo S. Olschki, Viuzzo del Pozzetto, Casella Postale 66, 50126 Florence Italy. **Tel** 011 39 55 6530684, **FAX** 011 39 55 6530214. **DD** 780.

IT
BIBLIOTECA (DEPUTAZIONE DI STORIA PATRIA PER LE ANTICHE PROVINCIE MODENESI). (BIBLIOTECA.). Monographic series. Italian. Price varies per volume.

IT
BIBLIOTECA DI ANTICHITA CIPRIOTE. 1-. Monographic series. Multiple languages (French and Italian). ir. Price varies per volume. Edizioni dell'Ateno, Casella Postale 7216, 00100 Rome Italy. **Tel** 759-3456.

IT
BIBLIOTECA DI STORIA TOSCANA MODERNA E CONTEMPORANEA. STUDI E DOCUMENTI. 1-. Monographic series. Italian. ir. Price varies per volume. Casa Editrice Leo S. Olschki, Viuzzo del Pozzetto, Casella Postale 66, 50126 Florence Italy. **Tel** 011 39 55 6530684, **FAX** 011 39 55 6530214.

IT
BIBLIOTECA NAPOLETANA. Periodical. Italian. Libreria Scientifica, Corso Umberto I 38 40, 80138 Naples Italy.

BL
BIBLIOTECA PUBLICA INFORMATIVO. **VFOAT** BP Informativo. V. 1- (No. 1-); March 1979-. Periodical. Portuguese. Avenida Sao Luis 281, Sao Paulo SP Brazil.

IT
BIBLIOTECA STORICA TOSCANA. SEZIONE DI STORIA DEL RISORGIMENTO. **VFOAT** Sezione di Storia del Risorgimento. 1-. Monographic series. Italian. Price varies per volume. Casa Editrice Leo S. Olschki, Viuzzo del Pozzetto, Casella Postale 66, 50126 Florence Italy. **Tel** 011 39 55 6530684, **FAX** 011 39 55 6530214.

IT
BIBLIOTECARIO, IL. No. 1 (Sept. 1984)-. Periodical. Italian. qt. L90000 Italy; L73000 other. Bulzoni Editore Srl, Via dei Liburni 14, 00185 Rome Italy. **Tel** 011 39 6 445-5207, **FAX** 011 39 6 445-0355. **LC** Z671; .B580247. **DD** 020/.5.
Ind/Abst Libr. Inf. Sci. Abstr.

IT/0392-8586
BIBLIOTECHE OGGI. Vol. 1, No. 1 (Nov/Dec. 1983)-. Periodical. Italian (summaries and/or abstracts in English; table of contents in English). Eleven times a year. L112000.00 Italy; L170000.00 other. Editrice Bibliografica, Viale Vittoria Veneto 24, 20124 Milan Italy. **Tel** 011 39 2 29006965, **FAX** 011 39 2 654624. **LC** Z809.A1; B49. **DD** 027.045.

●RU
BIBLIOTECHNOE DELO I BIBLIOGRAFIIA. **Added/Corp** Rossiiskaia Natsionalnaia Biblioteka. (1992)-. Periodical. Russian. mo. Lenin State Library of the USSR, Information Department on Culture and Arts, PR Kalinina 3, 101000 Moscow Russia. **Tel** 411167 GBL SU, telex 411167 GBL SU. **Continues** Bibliotechnoe Delo i Bibliografiia v SSSR, 0208-1997.

AG/0325-6251
BIBLIOTECOLOGIA Y DOCUMENTACION. [Bibliotecol. doc.]. V. 1, No. 1; Jan./June 1979-. Periodical. Spanish. sa. Casilla de Correo 68, Sucursal 1, Buenos Aires Argentina. **LC** Z671; .B58032. **DD** 020/.5.
Ind/Abst Libr. Inf. Sci. Abstr.

●RU/0869-4915
BIBLIOTEKA. **Added/Corp** Soviet Union. Ministerstvo Kultury. Russian S.F.S.R. Ministerstvo Kultury. Vseobshchaia Konfederatsiia Profsoiuzov SSSR. (1992)-. Periodical. Russian. mo. **(Subscription address:** East View Publications Inc., 3020 Harbor Lane North, Suite 110, Minneapolis MN 55447.) **LC** Z819.A1; B535. **Continues** Bibliotekar (Moscow, R.S.F.S.R.), 0006-1808.

RU/0132-2133
BIBLIOTEKA "KOMSOMOLSKOI PRAVDY". (1957)-. Monographic series. Russian. mo. $18.00 domestic airmail; $20.00 international airmail. **(Subscription address:** Victor Kamkin, 4956 Boiling Brook Parkway, Rockville MD 20852.) **ED** T. Kurella. **LC** AP50; .B514.

YU/0006-1816
BIBLIOTEKAR (BEOGRAD).
(BIBLIOTEKAR.). [Bibliotekar]. **Added/Corp** Drustvo Bibliotekara N.R. Srbije. Vol. 1 (1948-1949)-. Periodical. Serbo-Croatian (Roman). Three times a year. $42.00. **(Subscription address:** Jugoslovenska Knjiga, PO Box 36, YU 11001 Belgrade Yugoslovia.) **LC** Z671; .B58038. cum. index.
Ind/Abst Libr. Inf. Sci. Abstr.

PL/0208-4333
BIBLIOTEKARZ. [Bibliotekarz]. **Added/Corp** Zwiazek Bibliot ekarzy Polskich. Biblioteka Publiczna m. st. Warszawy. ,1934)-. Periodical. Polish. mo $63.00. **(Subscription address:** ARS Polona, PO Box 1001, 00068 Warsaw Poland.) **LC** Z671; .B5805.
Ind/Abst Libr. Inf. Sci. Abstr.; Libr. Lit.

RU/0869-608X
BIBLIOTEKOVEDENIE. (19??)-. Russian. Izdatelstvo Kniga, 50 Gorky Ulitsa, 125047 Moscow Russia. **(Subscription address:** East View Publications Inc., 3020 Harbor Lane North, Suite 110, Minneapolis MN 55447.) **Continues** Sovetskoe Bibliotekovedenie, 0134-6695.

RU/0320-7838
BIBLIOTEKOVEDENIE I BIBLIOGRAFIJA ZA RUBEZOM.
(BIBLIOTEKOVEDENIE I BIBLIOGRAFIJA ZA RUBEZHOM.). [Bibliotekoved. bibliogr. rub.]. **Added/Corp** Gosudarstvennaia Biblioteka SSSR Imeni V. I. Lenina. Vol. 1, (1958)-. Periodical. Russian. $61.00 domestic airmail; $67.00 international airmail. **(Subscription address:** Victor Kamkin, 4956 Boiling Brook Parkway, Rockville MD 20852.) **LC** Z671; .B5813. **NLM** Z 671 B581. cum. index.
Ind/Abst Libr. Inf. Sci. Abstr.

RU
BIBLIOTEKOVEDENIE I BIBLIOGRAFOVEDENIE: INOSTRANNAIA LITERATURA.
Added/Corp Informtsentr po Problemam Kultury i Iskusstva (Soviet Union). **VFOAT** Inostrannaia Literatura; Bibliotekovedenie i Bibliografovedenie: Za Rubezhom. (1978)-. Periodical. Russian (Multiple languages). mo. 0.25rub per issue. Gosudarstvennaia Biblioteka, Informatsionnyi Tsentr, Imeni V. I. Lenina, Prospekt Kalinina 3, 121019 Moscow Russia. **LC** Z666; .N686.
Continues Novosti Nauchnoi Literatury: Bibliotekovedenie i Bibliografovedenie. Inostrannaia Literatura.

BU
BIBLIOTEKOZNANIE, BIBLIOGRAFIIA, KNIGOZNANIE / NARODNA BIBLIOTEKA "SV. SV. KIRIL I METODII".
Added/Corp Narodna Biblioteka "Sv. sv. Kiril i Metodii.". (1991)-. Bulgarian. an. $18.50. Narodna Biblioteka Sv.sv. Kiril i Metodij, 88 V. Levski Boulevard, 1504 Sofia Bulgaria. **Tel** 011 359 2 882811, **FAX** 011 359 2 881600, telex 22432. **ED** H. Hadjihristov. **LC** Z674.5.B85; B53. **Circ:** 350.

DK
BIBLIOTEKSVEJVISER. 1970-. Danish. an. kr6.90 Denmark; $42.00 US. Dansk Bibliotekscenter AS, Tempovej 7 11, DK-2750 Ballerup Denmark. **Tel** 011 45 42 974000. **ED** Hanne Wiberg and Peter Heise. **LC** Z823.A1; B53. Index available. **Circ:** 2,000 (ctrl).
Desc: A guide to Danish public libraries; research and special libraries; library associations and institutions; library periodicals and foundations; and Nordic associations and periodicals.

LV
BIBLIOTEKU ZINATNES ASPEKTI. ASPEKTY BIBLIOTEKOVEDENIIA.
Added/Corp Vila Laca Latvijas PSR Valsts Biblioteka. **VFOAT** Aspekty Bibliotekovedeniia; Aspects of Librarianship. Vol. 1 (1977)-. Periodical. Latvian (Russian; summaries and/or abstracts in English). 0.70rub per issue. Gorkija lela 105, Riga Latvia. **LC** Z821.5.A1; B52. ***Continues*** *Riga. Valsts Biblioteka. Raksti. Trud.*

US/0734-1865
BIBLIOTHECA AMERICANA (CORAL GABLES, FLA.). (BIBLIOTHECA AMERICANA.). [Bibl. Am.]. Vol. 1, No. 1 (Sept. 1982)-. Periodical. English (Spanish). Five times a year. $60.00. Bibliotheca Americana, PO Box 24 1948, Miami State University, Coral Gables FL 33134. **Tel** (305)442-0364. **LC** E11; .B52. **DD** 970/.005.

NE/0067-8023
BIBLIOTHECA INDONESIA. Added/Corp Koninklijk Instituut voor Taal-, Land- en Volkenkunde (Netherlands). (1968)-. Monographic series. Multiple languages (English and Indonesian). Price varies per volume. Kitlu Press, PO Box 9515, 2300 RA Lieden Netherlands.

CN/0707-3674
BIBLIOTHECA MEDICA CANADIANA. [Bibl. med. Can.]. **Added/Corp** Canadian Health Libraries Association. Vol. 1 (Jan. 1979)-. Periodical. English (French). qt (Jan., Apr., July, Oct.). 65.00Can$. Canadian Health Libraries Association / Toronto, 3332 Yonge Street, Toronto Ontario M4P 3R1 Canada. **Tel** (416)485-0377, FAX (416)485-0377. **ED** Claire J Callaghan. **DD** 026/.61. **NLM** Z 675.M4; B5823. Index available. **Circ:** 600 (ctrl). ***Supersedes*** *Canadian Health Libraries Association. C H L A/A B S C Newsletter., 0700-5474.*
Desc: A vehicle for providing increased communication among health science libraries (and librarians) in Canada. A special commitment is made to reach and assist the worker in the smaller isolated health library.
Ind/Abst Cumul. Index Nurs. Allied Health Lit.; Libr. Inf. Sci. Abstr.

US/0277-3597
BIBLIOTHECA PRESS UPDATE. Vol. 1 (Aug. 1981)-. Periodical. English. mo. $21.00. Bibliotheca Press Update, PO Box 98378, Atlanta GA 30359. **LC** Discard.

SZ
BIBLIOTHECA ROMANICA (BERNE), SERIES PRIMA : MANUALIA ET COMMENTATIONES. Monographic series. Multiple languages (French, German and Italian). ir. Price varies per volume. Francke Verlag, Neuengasse 43, Postfach 1445, CH-3001 Bern Switzerland. **Tel** 011/41/31/221715, FAX 011/41/31/221723, telex 911822.

BE/0772-7003
BIBLIOTHEEK- EN ARCHIEFGIDS - VLAAMSE VERENIGING VOOR BIBLIOTHEEK-, ARCHIEF- EN DOCUMENTATIEWEZEN. (BIBLIOTHEEK- & ARCHIEF GIDS.). [Bibl.- archiefgids - Vlaam. Ver. Bibl.- Arch.- Doc.wez.]. **VFOAT** Bibliotheek- & Archiefgids; Bibliotheek- en Archief Gids; Bibliotheek- en Archiefgids. Vol. 60, No. 1 (Jan./April 1984)-. Periodical. Dutch (summaries and/or abstracts in English). Three times a year. 900F Belgium; 1,250F other. Vvbad-Administratie Bibliotheek- en Archiefgids, Goudblomstraat 10-12, B-2008 Antwerpen Belgium. **Tel** 3-231.83.49, FAX 3-232.42.94. **LC** Z671; .B584. Index available. cum. index. **Bk Rev. Ad Acc.** ***Continues*** *Bibliotheekgids, 0006-1956.*
Ind/Abst Libr. Lit.

NE/0165-1048
BIBLIOTHEEK EN SAMENLEVING. [Bibl. samenlev.]. Vol. 1 (Feb. 1973)-. Periodical. Dutch. mo (except July). Fl50.35, Fl38.00 (for members of NBLC). Nederlands Bibliotheek en Lektuurcentrum, Postbus 93054, 2509 AB's Gravenhage The Netherlands. **Tel** 070 141500, FAX 070 141600, telex 32102 NBLC NL. **ED** Frans J Stein. **LC** Z671; .B583. Index available. cum. index. **Bk Rev. Ad Acc. Circ:** 3,500 (ctrl). ***Formed by the union of*** *Mens en Boek* ***and*** *Openbare Bibliotheek.*
Desc: Informative, speculative and critical articles on public library work and its role in society.
Ind/Abst ARTbibliogr. Mod.; Libr. Inf. Sci. Abstr.

GW/0341-4183
BIBLIOTHEK. (BIBLIOTHEK FORSCHUNG UND PRAXIS.). [Bibliothek]. (1977)-. Periodical. German. Three times a year. DM228.00. K.G. Saur Verlag KG, A Reed Reference Publishing Company, Part of Reed International PLC, Ortlerstrasse 8, D 81373 Munich Germany. **Tel** 011 49 89 769020, FAX 011 49 89 76902150, telex 5212067-SAUR-D. **(Subscription address:** Stuttgarter Verlagskontor, Postfach 106016, D 70049 Stuttgart Germany**)** **LC** Z671; .B586. **DD** 020/.5. **[CCC]. Bk Rev. Ad Acc.** ctrl circ.
Ind/Abst Libr. Inf. Sci. Abstr.; Libr. Lit.

GW
BIBLIOTHEK DES BUCHWESENS. Vol. 1 (1972)-. Bibliography. German. ir. Price varies per volume. Anton Hiersemann Verlag, Rosenbergstrasse 113, D 70193 Stuttgart Germany. **Tel** 011 49 711 638264 5. **ED** R. W. Fuchs. **DD** 655. Index available. **Circ:** 1,000.
Desc: Monographs on books and printing history.

GW/0006-1964
BIBLIOTHEKAR. ***Ceased.*** (DER BIBLIOTHEKAR.). [Bibliothekar]. Began with 4. Yearly Vol. 1 (Jan. 1950)-Ceased ?. Periodical. German. mo. VEB Bibliographisches Institut, PSF 130, Gerichtsweg 26, 7010 Leipzig, Germany. **LC** Z671; .B588. **Bk Rev. Ad Acc. Circ:** 12,000. available on microfilm from University Microfilms International (UMI). ***Continues*** *Volksbibliothekar;* ***Absorbed*** *Buchbesprechung.*
Desc: Deals with current questions and problems in theory and practice of library and information science. Also contains literary contributions, short biographies of authors, bibliography and events.
Ind/Abst Libr. Inf. Sci. Abstr.; Libr. Lit.

GW/0940-7944
BIBLIOTHEKS-INFO. [Bibl.-Info]. **VFOAT** Bibliotheksinfo. (1991)-. Periodical. German. mo. DM40.00. Deutsches Bibliotheksinstitut, Bundesallee 184 185, D 10717 Berlin Germany. **Tel** 011 49 30 8505186, 011 49 30 8505187, FAX 011 49 30 8505100. **ED** Jana Krotzsch. **UDC** 02.

GW/0006-1972
BIBLIOTHEKSDIENST. [Bibliotheksdienst]. **Added/Corp** Deutsches Biblitheksinstitut. Deutsche Bibliothekskonferenz. Deutscher Buechereiverband. Deutscher Bibliotheksverband. (April 1967)-. Periodical. German. mo. DM60.00. Deutsches Bibliotheksinstitut, Bundesallee 184 185, D 10717 Berlin Germany. **Tel** 011 49 30 8505186, 011 49 30 8505187, FAX 011 49 30 8505100. **ED** Helmut Rosner, Karin Pauleweit, Werner Beck. **LC** Z801.A1; B54. Index available. **Bk Rev. Ad Acc. Circ:** 3,200. ***Supersedes*** *Buechereidienst, 0340-2231.*
Desc: Articles and short information on German librarianship.
Ind/Abst Libr. Inf. Sci. Abstr.

GW/0340-000X
BIBLIOTHEKSFORUM BAYERN. [Bibl.-forum Bayern]. Vol. 1 (1973)-. German. Three times a year. DM60.00. K.G. Saur Verlag KG, A Reed Reference Publishing Company, Part of Reed International PLC, Ortlerstrasse 8, D 81373 Munich Germany. **Tel** 011 49 89 769020, FAX 011 49 89 76902150, telex 5212067-SAUR-D. **(Subscription address:** Stuttgarter Verlagskontor, Postfach 106016, D 70049 Stuttgart Germany**)** **LC** Z801.B3; B52. **DD** 021/.00943/3. **[CCC]. Bk Rev. Ad Acc.** ctrl circ.
Ind/Abst Libr. Inf. Sci. Abstr.

GW/0175-6524
BIBLIOTHEKSRECHTLICHE VORSCHRIFTEN. [Bibl.recht. Verschr.]. (19??)-. German. an. DM50.00. Vittorio Klostermann, Frauenlobstrasse 22, D 60487 Frankfurt Germany. **Tel** 011 49 69 9708160. **UDC** 02:34(430.1).

GW
BIBLIOTHEKSWESEN IN DER DEUTSCHEN DEMOKRATISCHEN REPUBLIK, JAHRESBERICHT, DAS. German. an. 10.00M Germany. Library Association of the German Democratic Republic, Hermann-Matern-Strasse 57 104, Berlin Germany. **Tel** 236 2845, telex 115 147 2113 00. **LC** Z803.A1; B53. **DD** 020/.943. Index available. **Circ:** 700.
Desc: Includes developments and events in the fields of academic and public libraries, statistics, list of publications, legislation and international relations.

FR
BIBLIOTHEQUE DE LA PLEIADE. No. 1-. Monographic series. French. Price varies per volume. Editions Gallimard, 5 rue Sebastien Bottin, 75328 Paris Cedex 7 France. **Tel** 011 33 1 49544200.

FR/0343-6237
BIBLIOTHEQUE DE L'ECOLE DES CHARTES. Added/Corp Societe de l'Ecole des Chartes. Vol. 1 (1840)-. Periodical. French. sa. 100.00F Switzerland; $45.00 US and Canada. Librairie Droz SA, 11 rue Massot BP 389, CH 1211 Geneva 12 Switzerland. **Tel** 011 41 22 3466666, FAX 011 41 22 472391. **LC** D111; .B5. **DD** 940.105. cum. index. **Bk Rev. Circ:** 1,000. Documents available from The Genuine Article.
Desc: Medieval studies.
Ind/Abst Arts Humanit. Citation Index [Full Cov.]; BHA : Biblio. Hist. Art; Curr. Contents Arts Humanit.; Numis. Lit.; Res. Alert [Full Cov.]; Romant. Move.

FR/0523-5057
BIBLIOTHEQUE DES ARCHIVES DE PHILOSOPHIE. **See** Philosophy.

FR
BIBLIOTHEQUE DES ECOLES FRANCAISES D'ATHENES ET DE ROME. Added/Corp Ecole Francaise d'Athenes. Ecole Francaise de Rome. Vol. 1 (1877)-. Monographic series. French. ir. Price varies per volume. Diffusion de Boccard, 11 rue de Medicis, 75006 Paris France. **Tel** 011 33 1 43260037.

SZ
BIBLIOTHEQUE DES LETTRES MODERNES. 1 (1959)-. Monographic series. French. ir. Librairie Droz SA, 11 rue Massot BP 389, CH 1211 Geneva 12 Switzerland. **Tel** 011 41 22 3466666, FAX 011 41 22 472391.

FR/0988-1999
BIBLIOTHEQUE JEAN GENET. Vol. 1; 1988-. Monographic series. French. Price varies per volume. SEVPO, 192 rue St Honore, 75056 Paris France.

CN/0848-7464
BIBLIOTHEQUE POSTALE (1989). (BIBLIOTHEQUE POSTALE.). [Bibl. post.]. **Main/Corp** Service des Bibliotheques de l'Ontario, Nord. (Fall/Winter 1989/1990)-. Periodical. French. sa. Service des Bibliotheques de l'Ontario Nord, Bureau 2100, 11 Sud Rue Station, Kirkland, Ontario P2N 3P4 Canada. **DD** 017/.5. ***Continues*** *Service des Bibliotheques de l'Ontario, Baie James. Bibliotheque Postale., 0848-7464.*

PO/0870-4112
BIBLOS. Vol. 1 (1925)-. Portuguese. an. 2500$00. Biblioteca de Faculdade, Universidade de Coimbra, 3049 Coimbra Portugal. **Tel** 25551/2. cum. index. **Bk Rev. Circ:** 750.
Desc: Archaeology, visual arts, classical studies, music, literature, numismatics, philosophy, sociology, religion and geography.
Ind/Abst BHA : Biblio. Hist. Art; Libr. Inf. Sci. Abstr.; Libr. Lit.; Romant. Move.

AU/0006-2022
BIBLOS; OSTERREICHISCHE ZEITSCHRIFT FUER BUCH- UND BIBLIOTEKSWESEN, DOKUMENTATION, BIBLIOGRAPHIE, UND BIBLIOPHILIE. Added/Corp Gesellschaft der Freunde der Osterreichischen Nationalbibliothek. Vereinigung Osterreichischer Bibliothekare. Osterreichisches Institut fur Bibliotheksforschung, Dokumentations- und Informationswesen. Vol. 1, (Apr. 1952)-. Periodical. German. Four times a year (Apr., July, Sept., Dec.). $49.20. Gerold & Company, Wiehburggasse 26, A 1010 Vienna Austria. **Tel** 011 43 222 5124731. **ED** J. Stummvoll. **LC** Z671; .B5802. **NLM** Z 671 B595.
Ind/Abst Am. Hist. Life (1977-1986); Libr. Inf. Sci. Abstr.; Libr. Lit.

JA
BIBURIO: RYUKYU DAGAKU FUZOKU TOSHOKAN HO. THE UNIVERSITY OF THE RYUKYUS LIBRARY BULLETIN.
Added/Corp Ryukyu Daigaku. Toshokan. Ryukyu Daigaku. Toshokan. University of the Ryukyus Library Bulletin. **VFOAT** Ryukyu Dagaku Fuzoku Toshokan Ho; The University of the Ryukyus Library Bulletin. (19??)-. Bulletin. Japanese (Japanese). 1 Tonokuracho 3-chome, Naha Japan. **LC** Z846; .R9412.

JA/0006-2030
BIBUROSU. Added/Corp Kokuritsu Kokkai Toshokan (Japan). Renrakubu. Kancho Toshokan Kenkyukai. Kokuritsu Kokkai Toshokan (Japan). Shibu Toshokanbu. **VFOAT** Biblos, Monthly Report of Special Libraries; Biblios; Biblios, Monthly Magazine for Branch Libraries, Executive and Judicial, and Other Special Libraries. Vol. 1 (April, 1950)-. Periodical. Japanese. mo. $90.00. Kokuritsu Kokkai Toshokan, (National Diet Library), 1-10-1 Nagatacho Chiyoda-ku, Tokyo 100 Japan. **Tel** 03 3581-2331, FAX 03 3597-9104. **(Subscription address:** Maruzen Company Ltd., PO Box 5050, Import & Export Department, Tokyo 100 31 Japan.**)** **LC** Z675.A2; B47. **NLM** Z 671 B599.

US/0146-5635
BIENNIAL REPORT OF THE TEXAS LIBRARY AND HISTORICAL COMMISSION. Main/Corp Texas. Library and Historical Commission. **Added/Corp** Texas State Library. Biennial Report. (1909/10)-. English. be. Free. Texas State Library Clearinghouse, PO Box 12927, Capitol Station, Austin TX 78711. **Tel** (512)463-5435, FAX (512)463-5436. **LC** Z732; .T25. **DD** 027.509764/31.
Desc: Contains the Biennial report of the State Library, 1909/10,-1914/16,1924/26-1934/36.

US
BIENNIAL REPORT OF THE TEXAS STATE LIBRARY AND ARCHIVES COMMISSION. Main/Corp Texas State Library and Archives Commission. 1978/79-79/80 -. English. be. Free. Texas State Library/Clearinghouse, Library Development Division, PO Box 12927 Capitol Station, Austin TX 78711. **Tel** (512)463-5435, FAX (512)463-5436. **ED** Susan Hildebrand. **LC** Z732; .T25. **DD** 027.5764. **Circ:** 300 (ctrl). ***Continues*** *Biennial Report of the Texas Library and Historical Commission.*
Desc: Report of commission; covers each division, such as local records, archives, genealogy, library development.

US/0363-3500
BIENNIAL REPORT OF THE VERMONT DEPARTMENT OF LIBRARIES. **Main/Corp** Vermont. Dept. of Libraries. (19??)-. English. be. Vermont Department of Libraries, State Office Building, 109 State Street, Montpelier VT 05602. **Tel** (802)828-3265. **ED** Marianne K. Cassell. **Circ:** 500 (ctrl).
Desc: Report of agency, statistics of local libraries, and Vermont Library Directory (includes public, academic, special, and selected school libraries).

FR/0154-0262
BIOLOGIE VEGETALE, SCIENCES AGRICOLES. LEXIQUE. **See** Agriculture.

•US/1064-699X
BIOMEDICAL LIBRARY ACQUISITIONS BULLETIN [COMPUTER FILE]. [Biomed. libr. acquis. bull.]. **VFOAT** BLAB. No. 1 (Apr. 15, 1992)-. Bulletin. English. Free. David Morse, Norris Medical Library, 2003 Zonal Avenue, Los Angeles CA 90033. **DD** 026.

US/0090-3337
BIOSCENE. (BIOSCENE / BIOSIS). [BioScene]. **VFOAT** Bio Scene; BIOSIS Newsletter. (1971)-. Periodical. English. bm. Free on request. BioSciences Information Service, Biological Abstracts / BIOSIS, 2100 Arch Street, Philadelphia PA 19103-1399. **Tel** (800)523-4806 US, (215)587-4800 Pennsylvania and worldwide, FAX (215)587-2016, telex 831739. **DD** 574. **Circ:** 5,000. ***Absorbed*** *ZooScene.*
Desc: A newsletter reporting items of interest to users of all BIOSIS products, including Biological Abstracts, Biological Abstracts/RRM, BIOSIS Previews, Zoological Record, and others.

IT/0394-3666
BIT FIRENZE. ***Ceased.*** (BIT). [BitFirenze]. **VFOAT** Biblioteche in Toscana. (1984)-(Dec. 1992). Periodical. Italian. qt. Biblioteche in Toscana, Casella Postale 176, 50100 Florence Italy. **Tel** 011 39 55 210602, FAX 55-471225. **ED** Roberto Maini. **UDC** 02. **Bk Rev. Ad Acc. Circ:** 2,000.
Desc: Quarterly of the Italian Libraries Association in Tuscany. Short essays on what is news on the world of librarianship in Italy and abroad; special columns on books, reviews, CD ROM, computers, information from the US and Great Britain.

US
BLACK CAUCUS OF ALA NEWSLETTER / ALA BLACK CAUCUS. **Added/Corp** ALA Black Caucus. **VFOAT** BCALA Newsletter; Black Caucus Newsletter. (19??)-. Periodical. English. bm (6 issues). $7.50. Black Caucus of ALA, Rollins College, Box 2654, Winter Park FL 32789. **Tel** (407)646-2676. ***Continues*** *ALA Black Caucus. Black Caucus Newsletter.*

GO
BLIBAD : BULLETIN DE LIAISON A L'INTENTION DES BIBLIOTHECAIRES, ARCHIVISTES ET DOCUMENTALISTES AFRICAINS. **VFOAT** Bulletin de Liaison a l'Intention des Bibliothecaires, Archivistes et Documentalistes Africains. No. 1 (Jan. 1976)-. Bulletin. French. Ecole des Bibliothecaires Archivistes et Documentalistes de l'Universite de Dakar, B P 3252, Dakar Senegal.

US/0897-5167
BNA'S REVIEW OF WHAT'S NEW. [BNA's rev. what's new]. **VAT** Bureau of National Affairs' Review of What's New. Vol. 1, No. 1 (Jan. 1988)-. Periodical. English. qt. Free on request. Bureau of National Affairs Inc., 9435 Key West Avenue, Rockville MD 20850. **Tel** (800)372-1033, (301)258-1033, FAX (301)948-5823. **(Subscription telephone:** FAX (301)948-5823**) ED** Sarita Cabrera. **DD** 011.
Desc: A newsletter for librarians featuring new BNA information resources: books, looseleafs, newsletters, conferences, reports, videos, software, info-paks and online products.

UK/0968-3097
BNB ON CD-ROM [COMPUTER FILE]. **Added/Corp** British Library. National Bibliographic Service. **VFOAT** British National Library on CD-ROM. (19??)-. English. mo. £950.00 UK; £1090.00 Other. Chadwyck-Healey Limited, The Quorum Barnwell Road, Cambridge CB5 8SW England. **Tel** 011 44 223 215512, telex 9312102281 CH G. **LC** Z2001. available in print (As: British National Bibliography).
Desc: Backfile (two discs) covers 1950-1985; current discs are cumulative and cover 1986 to present. System requirements: IBM PC, XT, AT, PS/2, 286 386 or compatible; 640K memory; MS-DOS 3.1 or higher; any drive supporting Microsoft Extensions.

UK/0067-9488
BODLEIAN LIBRARY RECORD, THE. [Bodleian libr. rec.]. **Added/Corp** Bodleian Library. Vol. 1 (Oct. 1938)-. Periodical. English. Twice a year (Apr., Oct.). Price varies. Bodleian Library, Broad Street, Publication Office, Oxford OX1 3BG England. **Tel** 011 44 865 277000, FAX 011 44 865 277182, telex 83656. **ED** D. S. Porter. **LC** Z792.O94; B6. **DD** 027.742. **NLM** Z 921 B668. Index Available, published separately, free-automatically sent (Free). **Pr Rev. Circ:** 2,500. available on microfilm and microfiche from University Microfilms International (UMI). ***Continues*** *Bodleian Quarterly Record.*
Desc: Articles based in whole or part on Bodleian Library holdings of books and manuscripts. Descriptions of notable accessions. Shorter notes and publication of documents.
Ind/Abst Abstr. Engl. Stud.; Am. Hist. Life (1954-); Annu. Bibliogr. Engl. Lang. Lit.; BHA : Biblio. Hist. Art; Br. Humanit. Index; Child. Lit. Abstr. (19??-); MLA Int. Bibl. Books Artic. Mod. Lang. Lit.; Romant. Move.

DK/0006-5692
BOGENS VERDEN. [Bogens verden]. **VFOAT** BV. Vol. 1, No. 1 (May 1918)-. Periodical. Danish. Eight times a year. kr425.00. Danmarks Biblioteksforening, Trekronergade 15, 2500 Valby Denmark. **Tel** (36)30 86 82, FAX (36)30 80 80. **ED** Flemming Ettrup and Erik Skyum-Nielsen. **LC** Z671; .B674. Index available. **Bk Rev. Ad Acc. Circ:** 3,600 (ctrl). available on microfilm from University Microfilms International (UMI).
Desc: Information on Danish and foreign libraries and literature.
Ind/Abst Libr. Inf. Sci. Abstr.; Libr. Lit.

NO/0006-5811
BOK OG BIBLIOTEK. **See** Library and Information Sciences-Abstracting, Bibliographies and Statistics.

BL/0101-7268
BOLETIM ABDF. **VFOAT** Boletim A.B.D.F. New Series, V. 1, No. 1 (March/May 1978)-. Bulletin. Portuguese. qt. Associacao dos Bibliotecarios do Distrito Federal, CRN 702/703 Bl G Sobreloja, 70.000 Brasilia DF Brazil. **LC** Z769.A1; B64. **DD** 027.081. ***Continues*** *Boletim da ABDF.*

PO
BOLETIM DE BIBLIOGRAFIA PORTUGUESA. MATERIAL NAO LIVRO. Bulletin. Portuguese. an. 100$00 Portugal; $4.00 other. Biblioteca Nacional de Lisboa, Campo Grande 83, 1751 Lisbon Codex Portugal. **Tel** 011 351 1 767786, FAX 7933607, telex 62803. Index available. **Circ:** 500. ***Continues*** *Boletim de Bibliografia Portuguesa. Documentos Nao Textuais.*

PO
BOLETIM INFORMATIVO - FUNDACAO CALOUSTE GULBENKIAN, SERVICOS DE BIBLIOTECAS. **Main/Corp** Fundacao Calouste Gulbenkian. Servicos de Bibliotecas. Bulletin. Portuguese. Fundacao Calouste Gulbenkian, Servicos de Bibliotecas, Avenida de Berna, Lisbon Portugal. **LC** Z946; .L744.

NQ
BOLETIN - ASOCIACION DE BIBLIOTECAS UNIVERSITARIAS Y ESPECIALIZADAS DE NICARAGUA. **Main/Corp** Asociacion de Bibliotecas Universitarias y Especializadas de Nicaragua. Periodical. Spanish. Apartado 68, Leon Nicaragua. **LC** Z675.U5; A597A.

SP
BOLETIN DE INFORMACION (MADRID, SPAIN). (BOLETIN DE INFORMACION / MINISTERIO DE TRANSPORTES, TURISMO Y COMUNICACIONES.). No. 1 (Sept./Oct. 1982)-. Periodical. Spanish. bm. Ministerio de Agricultura, Pesca y Alimentacion, Secretaria General Tecnica, Centro de Publicaciones, Paseo de la Infanta Isabel 1,, 28071 Madrid Spain. **Tel** 011 91 347 55 51. **LC** HE261.A15; B64. **DD** 380.5/068.

SP/0044-9288
BOLETIN DE LA A.N.A.B.A. (BOLETIN DE LA ASOCIACION NACIONAL DE BIBLIOTECARIOS, ARCHIVEROS Y ARQUEOLOGOS.). [Bol. A.N.A.B.A.]. **Main/Corp** Asociacion Nacional de Bibliotecarios, Archiveros y Arqueologos. **Added/Corp** Biblioteca Nacional (Spain). **VFOAT** Boletin de la ANABA; Boletin. Ano 1, No. 1 (Feb. de 1950)-. Spanish. qt. 500.00ptas. Anabad, AP 14281, Paseo Calvo Sotelo 22, Madrid 1 Spain. **LC** Z673.A72; A2. **DD** 020/.622/46.

VE/0528-0761
BOLETIN DE LA BIBLIOTECA DE LOS TRIBUNALES DEL DISTRITO FEDERAL FUNDACION ROJAS ASTUDILLO. **Main/Corp** Caracas. Biblioteca de los Tribunales del Distrito Federal Fundacion Rojas Astudillo. No. 1- ; 1951-. Periodical. Spanish. Biblioteca de los Tribunales del Distrito Federal Fundacion Rojas Astudillo, Edificio Gradillas B 40 Piso, Caracus Venezuela.
Desc: Includes: Doctrina, legislacion, jurisprudencia, bibliografia juridica venezolana, vida y actividades de la biblioteca, memoria y cuenta de la Fundacion.

PE/0031-6067
BOLETIN DE LA BIBLIOTECA NACIONAL (LIMA). (BOLETIN DE LA BIBLIOTECA NACIONAL.). [Bol. Bibl. nac.]. **Main/Corp** Biblioteca Nacional (Peru). (1919)-. Spanish. an. **LC** Z907; .L72. **DD** 027.785.
Ind/Abst Am. Hist. Life (1964-1965,1971-1972); Anthropol. Index.

MX/0188-4492
BOLETIN DEL SISTEMA ESTATAL DE DOCUMENTACION DEL ESTADO DE MEXICO. **See** Public Administration.

GT
BOLETIN - GUATEMALA (CITY) BIBLIOTECA NACIONAL. **Main/Corp** Guatemala (City). Biblioteca Nacional. Vol. 1 (May 1932)-. Periodical. Spanish. qt. **LC** Z887.G91; B. **DD** 027.57281.

AG
BOLETIN INFORMATIVO DE LA ASOCIACION DE BIBLIOTECARIOS GRADUADOS DE LA REPUBLICA ARGENTINA. **Main/Corp** Asociacion de Bibliotecarios Graduados de la Republica Argentina. Periodical. Spanish. Asociacion de la Republica Argentina, Cordoba 1558 C de Correo 68 Suc 1, Buenos Aires Argentina. **LC** Z765.A1; A86A.

IT/0392-8438
BOLLETINO DELL'ISTITUTO CENTRALE PER LA PATOLOGIA DEL LIBRO. QUADERNI. (QUADERNI : BOLLETINO DELL'ISTITUTO CENTRALE PER LA PATOLOGIA DEL LIBRO.). [Boll. Ist. cent. patol. libro, Quad.]. **Added/Corp** Istituto Centrale per la Patologia del Libro Alfonso Gallo. (1983)-. Periodical. Italian. an. Istituto Centrale Patologia Libro, Via Milano 76, 00184 Rome Itlay. **Tel** 011 39 6 483947, 011 39 6 482911. **LC** Z701; .Q34. **DD** 025.7. ***Continues*** *Bollettino dell'Istituto di Patologia del Libro Alfonso Gallo, 0391-5972.*
Ind/Abst Biodeter. Abstr. (1991-).

•IT/1121-1490
BOLLETTINO AIB. **Added/Corp** Associazione Italiana Biblioteche. **VFOAT** Bollettino Associazione Italiana Biblioteche. Vol. 32, No. 1 (Mar. 1992)-. Periodical. Italian (summaries and/or abstracts in English). qt. L10000 Italy; L150000. Associazone Italiana Biblioteche, Casella Postale 2461, 00100 Rome Italy. **Tel** 011 39 6 4463532. **LC** Z671; .A894a. ***Continues*** *Associazione Italiana Biblioteche. Bollettino d'Informazioni - Associazione Italiana Biblioteche, 0004-5934.*

US/0197-0437
BOOK MARKS. **Added/Corp** South Dakota Library Association. Vol. 27 (Jan./Feb. 1976)-. Periodical. English. Six times a year (Jan., Mar., May, July, Sept., Nov.). $15.00. South Dakota Library Association, Rapid City Public Library, 610 Quincy, Rapid City SD 57702. **Tel** (605)394-4171. ***Continues*** *Catalyst, 0197-0437.*

US/0731-4388
BOOK REPORT (COLUMBUS, OHIO). (THE BOOK REPORT.). [Book rep.]. Vol. 1, No. 1 (May/June 1982)-. Periodical. English. Five times a year. $39.00 (one year), $70.00 (two year), $102.00 (three year) US; $47.00 (one year), $86.00 (two year), $126.00 (three year) Canada; $59.00 (one year), $110.00 (two year), $162.00 (three year) other. Linworth Publishing Company, 480 East Wilson Bridge Road, Suite L, Worthington OH 43085. **Tel** (614)436-7107, FAX (614)436-9490. **ED** Carolyn Hamilton and Cheryl Abdullan. **LC** Z675.S3; B65. **DD** 027.8/223/0973. Index available. **Bk Rev. Ad Acc. Circ:** 11,000. available on microfilm and microfiche from University Microfilms International (UMI). Documents available from UMI Article Clearinghouse.
Desc: Provides book reviews for subscribers. Librarians working daily with adolescent learners evaluate the content and suitability for the intended group.
Ind/Abst Acad. Search (July 1989-); Book Rev. Index; Child. Mag. Guide; Curr. Index J. Educ.; INFO-SOUTH Abstr.; Libr. Lit. (1991-); Mag. Artic. Summar. Elite (July 1989-); Mag. Artic. Summar. Select (July 1989-); Mag. Artic. Summar. CD-ROM (July 1989-); Mag. Search; Mid. Search (Jul. 1989-); Newsp. Period. Abstr. (1989-); Prim. Search (Jul. 1989-); TOM Gen. Index (1989-); Vocat. Search (July 1989-).

US/0092-7686
BOOKLEGGER MAGAZINE. ***Suspended.*** Vol. 1 (Nov./Dec. 1973)-Suspended with Vol. 4, No. 17. Periodical. English. bm. $8.00. Booklegger Magazine, 72 Ord Street, San Francisco CA 94114. **LC** Z671; .B627. **DD** 020/.5.

US/0006-7385
BOOKLIST (CHICAGO, ILL. 1969). (THE BOOKLIST / AMERICAN LIBRARY ASSOCIATION.). [Booklist]. **Added/Corp** American Library Association. **VFOAT** Booklist Including Reference Books Bulletin. Vol. 66, No. 1 (Sept. 1, 1969)-. Periodical. English. Twenty-two times a year. $65.00 US; $80.00 other. American Library Association, 50 East Huron Street, Chicago IL 60611. **Tel** (312)944-6780, (800)545-2433, FAX (312)944-2641. **(Subscription address:** American Library Association, Subscription Department, 434 West Downer, Aurora IL 60506-9936.**) LC** Z1035.A1; B65. **DD**

028.1/05. **NLM** Z 1035.A1; B7246. **[CCC].** available on microfilm from University Microfilms International (UMI). Documents available from UMI Article Clearinghouse. ***Continues*** *Booklist and Subscription Books Bulletin, 0730-8957.*
Ind/Abst Acad. Abstr. (July 1993-); Acad. Search (July 1993-); Am. Bibliogr. Slavic East Europ. Stud.; Book Rev. Digest; Book Rev. Index; Child. Lit. Abstr. (19??-); Comput. Rev. Index (1986-); Garden Lit. (1992-); Gen. Period. Index (1992-); INFO-SOUTH Abstr.; Leg. Inf. Manage. Index; Libr. Lit.; Mag. Artic. Summar. Elite (July 1993-); Mag. Artic. Summar. CD-ROM (July 1993-); Mag. Index Plus (1992-); Med. Rev. Dig.; Microcomput. Index (Jan. 1983-); Middle East Abstr. Index; Mid. Search (Jul. 1993-); Newsp. Period. Abstr. (1991-); Prim. Search (Jul. 1993-); Sci. Fict. Fantasy Book Rev. Index.

US/0006-7407
BOOKMARK, THE. [Bookmark]. Began Publication Jan. 1940. Periodical. English. qt. $15.00 North America; $30.00 other. New York State Library, Documents Gift & Exchange Section, Empire State Plaza, Albany NY 12230. **Tel** (518)474-5953. **ED** Joseph Shubert. **CODEN** BOKMA. **Bk Rev. Ad Acc.** ctrl circ. available on microfilm and microfiche from University Microfilms International (UMI).
Ind/Abst Libr. Lit.

US/0735-0295
BOOKMARK (MOSCOW, IDAHO), THE. (THE BOOKMARK.). V. 1- Sept. 1948-. Periodical. English. Four times a year. $5.00. University of Idaho / Library, Moscow ID 83843. **Tel** (208)885-6584. **ED** Gail Z Eckwright and Ron Force. **Bk Rev. Circ:** 1,150 (ctrl). available on microfilm and microfiche from University Microfilms International (UMI).
Desc: A newsletter for the academic community of the University of Idaho. Contains articles, statistics and news items about the library and libraries in general.
Ind/Abst Libr. Inf. Sci. Abstr.; Libr. Lit.

CN/0381-6028
BOOKMARK (VANCOUVER). (THE BOOKMARK.). [Bookmark]. **Added/Corp** British Columbia School Librarians' Association. (19??)-. Periodical. English. Four times a year. British Columbia Teachers Federation, 100-550 West 6th Avenue, Vancouver British Columbia V5Z 4P2 Canada. **Tel** (604)871-2283, (800)663-9163, FAX (604)871-2294, (604)871-2290. Index available. **Bk Rev. Ad Acc. Circ:** 1,300. ***Absorbed*** *BCTLA Reviews, 0826-5054.*
Ind/Abst Can. Educ. Index.

US/0006-7474
BOOKS AT IOWA. [Books Iowa]. **Added/Corp** Friends of the University of Iowa Libraries. University of Iowa. Libraries. No. 1 (Oct. 1964)-. Periodical. English. Twice a year (Apr., Nov.). $25.00. Friends of University of Iowa Libraries, University of Iowa Libraries, Iowa City IA 52242. **Tel** (319)335-5921. **ED** Robert A. McCown. **LC** Z881 .I644; B6. **DD** 027.7777/655. Index available. cum. index. **Circ:** 500 (ctrl).
Desc: Brief description of special collections in the University of Iowa libraries, with special emphasis on literature and the arts.
Ind/Abst Abstr. Engl. Stud.; Annu. Bibliogr. Engl. Lang. Lit.; Child. Lit. Abstr. (19??-); MLA Int. Bibl. Books Artic. Mod. Lang. Lit.

US
BOOKS IN LIBRARY AND INFORMATION SCIENCE. Vol. 1 (1972)-. Monographic series. English. ir. Price varies per volume. Marcel Dekker Inc., 270 Madison Avenue, New York NY 10016. **Tel** (212)696-9000, (800)228-1160, FAX (212)685-4540, telex 421419. **(Subscription address:** Marcel Dekker Inc, PO Box 5017, Monticello NY 12701.**)**
Desc: A series of books presenting information on library and information science. Topics include cataloging and classification and library automation systems.
Ind/Abst Math. Rev.

US
BOOKS IN PRINT WITH BOOK REVIEWS PLUS [COMPUTER FILE]. **Added/Corp** Bowker Electronic Publishing. **VFOAT** Book Reviews Plus; Books in Print, Reviews Plus; Books in Print/Reviews Plus. (198?)-. English. bm. $1595.00. R R Bowker Electronic Publishing, A Reed Reference Publishing Company, Part of Reed International PLC, 121 Chanlon Drive, New Providence NJ 07974. **Tel** (800)323-3288. **LC** Z1215; .B65. **Bk Rev.**
Desc: Contains over 180,000 current, full text book reviews. Updated monthly.

US/0891-9615
BORGO CATALOGING GUIDES. [Borgo cat. guides]. (1988)-. Monographic series. English. ir. Price varies per volume. Borgo Press, PO Box 2845, San Bernardino CA 92406. **Tel** (714)884-5813, (714)885-1161. **ED** Michael Burgess. **DD** 025.
Desc: Written by catalogers for catalogers, these guides provide timely surveys of cataloging practice in the Library of Congress classification scheme. Each book surveys a particular subject area, with coverage of the actual headings and class numbers used in LC in the post-AACR2 period.

US/0270-3653
BORGO REFERENCE LIBRARY, THE. [Borgo ref. libr.]. (1980)-. Monographic series. English. ir. Price varies per volume. Borgo Press, PO Box 2845, San Bernardino CA 92406. **Tel** (714)884-5813, (714)885-1161.

DK/0006-7792
BORN & BOGER. [Brn & bger]. **VFOAT** Brn Og Bger. Periodical. Danish (English). Eight times a year. kr385.00. Danmarks Skolebiblioteksforenings, Norrebrogade 159, DK-2200 Copenhagen N Denmark. **ED** Arne Holst and Ove Frank. **LC** Z671; .B625. **DD** 027.8/09489. ***Continues*** *Brn Og Boger.*
Ind/Abst Libr. Inf. Sci. Abstr.

US/0888-045X
BOTTOM LINE (NEW YORK, N.Y.), THE. (THE BOTTOM LINE.). [Bottom line]. Vol. 1, No. 1 (1987)-. Periodical. English. qt. $49.95. Neal-Schuman Publishers Inc., 100 Varick Street, New York NY 10013. **Tel** (212)925-8650, FAX (212)219-8916. **ED** Betty J. Turock. **LC** Z683; .B69. **DD** 021.8/3. **CODEN** BOLIEO. Index available. cum. index. **Bk Rev. Ad Acc, Adv Mgr:** Sue Kurpeski, **Tel** (617)293-2194. Documents available from Ask*IEEE.
Desc: Designed to help managers in all types of libraries best use their every dollar. Provides information on planning, budgeting, cash management, purchasing, investment, alternate funding, cost analysis, new technology and other financial tools and techniques.
Ind/Abst Ei Page One; Inf. Instruc. Technol.; INSPEC (1988-); Leg. Inf. Manage. Index; Libr. Lit.

US
BOWKER ANNUAL LIBRARY AND BOOK TRADE ALMANAC, THE. English. an. $155.00. R R Bowker, A Reed Reference Publishing Company, Part of Reed International PLC, PO Box 31, 121 Chanlon Drive, New Providence NJ 07974. **Tel** (908)464-6800, (800)521-8110, FAX (908)665-6688, telex 138-755. available on CD-ROM.
Desc: Unique compendium of essays, reports, and statistics that explore developing issues and challenges facing the information community.
Ind/Abst Predicasts Forecasts.

US/0068-0540
BOWKER ANNUAL OF LIBRARY AND BOOK TRADE INFORMATION, THE. (THE BOWKER ANNUAL OF LIBRARY AND BOOK TRADE INFORMATION / SPONSORED BY THE COUNCIL OF NATIONAL LIBRARY ASSOCIATIONS.). [Bowker annu. libr. book trade inf.]. **Added/Corp** R.R. Bowker Company. Council of National Library Associations. Council of National Library and Information Associations (U.S.). **VFOAT** Bowker Annual of Library & Book Trade Information; Bowker Annual Library and Book Trade Almanac; Bowker Annual; Library and Book Trade Almanac. 7th Ed. (1962)-. English. an. $155.00. Bowker A&I Publishing, A Reed Reference Publishing Company, Part of Reed International PLC, PO Box 31, New Providence NJ 07974. **Tel** (800)521-8110, (212)337-8174. **ED** Margaret Spier. **LC** Z731; .A47. **DD** 020/.5. **NLM** Z 671 A512. **[CCC].** Index available. ***Continues*** *American Library & Book Trade Annual, 0271-7441.*
Desc: This standard in library and book trade information is more efficient and more useful than ever, with more business and statistical information.
Ind/Abst Stat. Ref. Index.

AT/0812-9126
BREAK THROUGH CAMPSIE. [Break throughCampsie]. (1983)-. Periodical. English. qt. Canterbury Municipal Library Services, 139 Beamish St, Campsie NSW 2194 Australia. **ED** J Morrison. **DD** 027.6305.
Ind/Abst Aust. Educ. Index; Aust. Libr. Inf. Sci. Abstr. (1985-).

CN/0700-3641
BREEZE. (THE BREEZE.). V. 1- March 1976-. Periodical. English. Three times a year. Free. Chinook Regional Library, 1240 Chaplin Street West, Swift Current Saskatchewan S9H 0G8 Canada. **Tel** (306)773-3186. **ED** Frances Myhr. **DD** 027.4/7124/3. **Circ:** 150 (ctrl).
Desc: A means of expression between branch librarians, library assistants and trustees of the member communities of the Chinook Regional Library.

UK/0007-0173
BRIO (UNITED KINGDOM BRANCH, INTERNATIONAL ASSOCIATION OF MUSIC LIBRARIES). **See** Music.

UK/0269-0497
BRITISH JOURNAL OF ACADEMIC LIBRARIANSHIP. [Br. j. acad. librariansh.]. Vol. 1, No. 1 (Spring 1986)-. Periodical. English. Three times a year. £60.00. Taylor Graham Publishing, 500 Chesham House, 150 Regent Street, London W1R 5FA United Kingdom. **ED** Colin Harris. **LC** Z675.U5; B83. **DD** 027.7/0941. **Bk Rev. Ad Acc. Pr Rev.**
Ind/Abst Libr. Lit.

UK
BRITISH LIBRARIANSHIP AND INFORMATION WORK. **Added/Corp** Library Association. (1988)-. Academic Scholarly Publication. English. ir (two volumes/every 4/5 years). $140.00 (volume one), $105.00 (volume two). Library Association, 7 Ridgmount Street, London WC1E 7AE England. **Tel** 011 44 71 636-7543, FAX 011 44 71 436-7218, telex 21897. **ED** L. J. Taylor. **LC** Z666; .F5. **DD** 020/.941. **Pr Rev.** ***Continues*** *British Librarianship and Information Science.*
Desc: Information on library and information science in Britain.

UK/0305-5167
BRITISH LIBRARY JOURNAL, THE. [Br. Libr. j.]. **Main/Corp** British Library. Vol. 1 (Spring 1975)-. English. sa (May and November). $60.00 US; £35.00 UK; £40.00 other. British Library / Publications Sale Unit, Boston Spa, Wetherby, West Yorkshire LS23 7BQ England. **Tel** 011 44 937 546546 546543, FAX 011 44 937 546333, telex 557381. **ED** C. Wright. **LC** Z921.B854; B73. **DD** 027.5/421/42. Index available. **Ad Acc. Circ:** 900. Documents available from The Genuine Article.
Desc: Articles deal with aspects of the British Library. Bibliography, lists of acquisitions, and often illustrated.
Ind/Abst Am. Hist. Life (1975-); Annu. Bibliogr. Engl. Lang. Lit.; Art Archaeol. Tech. Abstr.; Arts Humanit. Citation Index [Full Cov.]; BHA : Biblio. Hist. Art; Br. Humanit. Index; Child. Lit. Abstr. (19??-); Curr. Contents Arts Humanit.; MLA Int. Bibl. Books Artic. Mod. Lang. Lit.; Res. Alert [Full Cov.]; Romant. Move.

UK/0307-9481
BRITISH LIBRARY NEWS. **Main/Corp** British Library. (1976)-. Periodical. English. mo. Free on request. British Library / Press and Publisher Relations, 96 Euston Road, London NW1 2DB England. **Tel** 011 44 71 3237054.
Ind/Abst Museum Abstr.; World Ceram. Abstr.

UK/0144-9958
BRITISH LIBRARY REFERENCE DIVISION NEWSPAPER LIBRARY NEWSLETTER. (THE BRITISH LIBRARY NEWSPAPER LIBRARY NEWSLETTER.). [Br. Libr. Ref. Div. Newsp. Libr. newsl.]. **Added/Corp** British Library. Newspaper Library. No. 1 (Autumn 1980)-. Newsletter. English. Twelve times a year. Free on request. British Library Newspaper Library, Colindale Avenue, London NW9 5HE England. **Tel** 011 44 71 323 7357.
Ind/Abst Libr. Inf. Sci. Abstr.

UK/0007-1544
BRITISH NATIONAL BIBLIOGRAPHY. **See** Library and Information Sciences-Abstracting, Bibliographies and Statistics.

UK/0959-4922
BRITISH REPORTS, TRANSLATIONS AND THESES RECEIVED BY THE BRITISH LIBRARY DOCUMENT SUPPLY CENTRE. **Main/Corp** British Library. Document Supply Centre. **VFOAT** BRTT. (198?)-. English. mo. £89.00 UK; £94.00 other. British Library / Publications Sale Unit, Boston Spa, Wetherby, West Yorkshire LS23 7BQ England. **Tel** 011 44 937 546546 546543, FAX 011 44 937 546333, telex 557381. **(Subscription address:** Turpin Distribution Services Limited, Blackhorse Road, Letchworth, Hertfordshire SG6 1HN, United Kingdom.**)** **Ad Acc.** Documents available from UMI Article Clearinghouse. ***Continues*** *British Reports, Translations and Theses.*
Desc: One-stop shop for vital research information.
Ind/Abst ABI/INFORM Glob. Ed.

US/0196-7223
BRS BULLETIN. ***Title Change.*** **See** Computers.

US/1045-4489
BSI HISTORY PROJECT, THE. [BSI arch. ser.]. **VFOAT** BSI Archival Series. **VAT** Baker Street Irregulars History Project. 1989-. Periodical. English. an. $18.95. Fordham University Press, Box L, Fordham University, Bronx NY 10458. **Tel** (718)817-4780, FAX (718)817-4785. **DD** 823.

GW/0340-0301
BUCH UND BIBLIOTHEK. [Buch bibl.]. **VFOAT** BUB. Vol. 23 (1971)-. Periodical. German. mo. DM130.00 Germany; DM145.00 other. Bock & Herchen Verlag, Postfach 1145, D 53581 Bad Honnef Germany. **Tel** 011 49 2224 5443. **ED** Dietrich Segebrecht, Manfred Rothe. Index available. cum. index. **Bk Rev. Ad Acc. Circ:** 6,000 (ctrl). ***Continues*** *Bucherei und Bildung.*
Ind/Abst Child. Lit. Abstr. (19??-); Libr. Inf. Sci. Abstr.; Libr. Lit.

CN/0380-7150
BULLETIN A B Q. [Bull. ABQ]. **Main/Corp** Quebec Library Association. **VFOAT** Q L A Bulletin. V. 13, No. 2, Nov. 1971-. Bulletin. English (French). Three times a year. $10.00-$70.00 (according to salary), $70.00 institutions, $85.00 commercial firms. Quebec Library Association, PO Box 2216, Dorval Quebec H9S 5J4 Canada. **Tel** (514)634-6760. **ED** Wendy Patrick. **Ad Acc.**

Circ: 200 (ctrl). *Continues* *Bulletin de Nouvelles / Quebec Library Association, 0380-7134.*
Ind/Abst Libr. Inf. Sci. Abstr.

SZ/0258-0764
BULLETIN ARBIDO. ***Title Change.*** (ARBIDO-B / VEREINIGUNG SCHWEIZERISCHER ARCHIVARE, VEREINIGUNG SCHWEIZERISCHER BIBLIOTHEKARE, SCHWEIZERISCHE VEREINIGUNG FUER DOKUMENTATION.). [Bull. ARBIDO]. **Added/Corp** Vereinigung Schweizerischer Archivare. Vereinigung Schweizerischer Bibliothekare. Schweizerische Vereinigung fuer Dokumentation. **VFOAT** Bulletin Arbido; Arbido B; Arbido Bulletin. Vol. 1, No. 1 (1986)-(19??). Periodical. French (German). bm. Arbido, Effingerstrasse 35, Ch 3008 Bern Switzerland. **Tel** 011 41 31 3824240. **LC** Z673.V43; .A73. ***Formed by the union of*** *Vereinigung Schweizerischer Bibliothekare. Nachrichten VSB/SVD, 0042-3807* ***and*** *Vereinigung Schweizerischer Archivare. Mitteilungen der Vereinigung Schweizerischer Archivare.* ***Merged into*** *Arbido.*

AT/0084-7852
BULLETIN / BIBLIOGRAPHICAL SOCIETY OF AUSTRALIA AND NEW ZEALAND. [Bull. - Bibliogr. Soc. Aust. N. Z.]. **Added/Corp** Bibliographical Society of Australia and New Zealand. Vol. 1, No. 1 (Mar. 1970)-. Periodical. English. Four times a year (Mar., June, Sept., Dec.). 30.00Aus$ (individuals), 40.00Aus$ (institutions) Australia & New Zealand; 32.00Aus$ (individuals), 48.00Aus$ (institutions) others Comes with Bibliographical Society of Australia & New Zealand membership. Bibliographical Society of Australia & New Zealand, 328 Swanston, St. Library of Victoria, South Melbourne 3000 Australia. **Tel** 011 61 3 6699032, FAX 011 61 3 6699958. **(Subscription address:** Australia National University / Department of English, c/o Dr. R. Foxton, PO Box 4, Canberra ACT 2601 Australia.**)** **ED** Dr. Ross Harvey. Index available. **Bk Rev**, (Qty: 12). **Ad Acc**, **Adv Mgr:** Brian Hubber, **Tel** 61 3 6699032. **Pr Rev. Circ:** 300.
Ind/Abst Annu. Bibliogr. Engl. Lang. Lit.; APAIS, Aust. Public Aff. Inf. Ser. (1981-); Aust. Educ. Index (199?-).

CN/0319-664X
BULLETIN - CANADIAN TALENT LIBRARY. **Main/Corp** Canadian Talent Library. Began in 1962. Bulletin. English. ir. Canadian Talent Library, 38 Yorkville Avenue, Toronto Ontario M4W 1L5 Canada. **Tel** (416)924-1411.

FR
BULLETIN DE L'ASSOCIATION DES BIBLIOTHECAIRES FRANCAIS. **Main/Corp** Association des Bibliothecaires Francais. Vol. 1, No. 1 (Jan./Feb. 1907)-. Bulletin. French. ir. Association Des, 65 rue de Richelieu, 75002 Paris France. **LC** Z673; .A8.
Ind/Abst Libr. Lit.

FR/0006-2006
BULLETIN DES BIBLIOTHEQUES DE FRANCE. [Bull. bibl. Fr.]. Vol. 1 (Jan. 1956)-. Bulletin. French (English). Six times a year. 400.00F France; 450.00F other. Bulletin des Bibliotheque de France, 61-65 rue Dutot, 75732 Paris Cedex 15 France. **Tel** 011 33 1 72444343. **(Subscription address:** Ecole National Superieure Bibliotheque, 17 21 BD du 11 Novembre 1918, 62623 Villeurbanne Cedex France.**)** **LC** Z671; .B93. Index available. **Bk Rev. Ad Acc. Circ:** 2,200. available on microfiche. ***Formed by the union of*** *France. Direction des Bibliotheques de France. Bulletin d'Informations* ***and*** *Paris. Bibliotheque Nationale. Bulletin de Documentation Bibliographique.*
Desc: Deals with publishing, reading, databases, automation, technical and scientific information. Each number is a special issue on a current event: reading in rural regions, electronic publishing, sociological study on users, and cost of information.
Ind/Abst Inf. Sci. Abstr.; Libr. Inf. Sci. Abstr.; Libr. Lit.

FR/0004-5365
BULLETIN D'INFORMATIONS DE L'ASSOCIATION DES BIBLIOTHECAIRES FRANCAIS. [Bull. inf. - Assoc. bibl. fr.]. **Added/Corp** Association des Bibliothecaires Francais. **VFOAT** Bulletin d'Informations. (1946)-. Bulletin. French. qt. 400.00F (France); 420.00F (other). Association des Bibliothecaires Francais, 7 rue des Lions St Paul, 75004 Paris France. **Tel** 11 33 1 48879787. **Bk Rev. Ad Acc. Circ:** 2,200 (ctrl).
Ind/Abst Libr. Inf. Sci. Abstr.

CN/0380-8076
BULLETIN - GEORGIAN BAY REGIONAL LIBRARY SYSTEM. **Main/Corp** Georgian Bay Regional Library System. Began publication April 1967. Bulletin. English. qt. Georgian Bay Regional Library System, 30 Morrow Road, Barrie Ontario L4N 3V8 Canada. **DD** 027.4/713/15.

US/0161-7397
BULLETIN - INTERNATIONAL ASSOCIATION OF ORIENTALIST LIBRARIANS. [Bull.- Int. Assoc. Orient. Librar.]. **Main/Corp** International Association of Orientalist Librarians. (Spring 1976)-. Bulletin. English. an (October). $15.00 (individual); $20.00 institution). University Libraries / Hong Kong, Pokfulam Road, University of Hong Kong, Hong Kong Hong Kong. **Tel** 011 852 8592200, FAX 011 852 8589420. **ED** Michael Costin. **LC** Z688.A75; I57a. **DD** 026/.00095. **Bk Rev. Ad Acc.** ***Continues*** *Newsletter - International Association of Orientalist Librarians, 0146-6992.*
Ind/Abst Libr. Inf. Sci. Abstr.

●CN/1193-2325
BULLETIN LS. [Bull. LS]. **Added/Corp** Alliance de la Fonction Publique du Canada. Groupe de la Bibliotheconomie. Alliance de la Fonction Publique du Canada. Bureau Regional d'Ottawa. **VFOAT** Bulletin du Groupe LS. No 1 (1992)-. Bulletin. French. Free for members. Alliance de la Fonction Publique du Canada, 233 rue Gilmore, Ottawa Ontario K2P 0P1 Canada. **DD** 331.7.

MW
BULLETIN / MALAWI NATIONAL LIBRARY SERVICE BOARD. **Added/Corp** Malawi National Library Service Board. No. 29 (May 1981)-. Bulletin. English. **LC** Z857.M3; A3. **DD** 017/.5/096897. ***Continues*** *Bulletin (Malawi National Library Service).*

JA/0911-3622
BULLETIN OF CENTRE FOR INFORMATICS. Vol. 1; Spring 1985-. Bulletin. Japanese (English). sa. Centre for Informatics, Waseda University, Tokyo Japan. **Tel** 03-200-1681, FAX 03-200-1681. **ED** Keiji Sakagami. **Circ:** 1,000 (ctrl). Documents available from Article Express International.
Desc: Bulletin on informatics.
Ind/Abst Comput. Rev.; Eng. Index Annu.

CN/0383-2791
BULLETIN OF OUTSTANDING ACQUISITIONS OF THE METROPOLITAN TORONTO CENTRAL LIBRARY. **Main/Corp** Metropolitan Toronto Central Library. V. 1- June 1975-. Bulletin. English. Metropolitan Toronto Library Board, 789 Yonge Street, Toronto Ontario M4W 2G8 Canada. **Tel** (416)393-7134, telex 06-22232. **DD** 018/.1. ***Continues*** *Quarterly Bulletin of Outstanding Achievements of the Metropolitan Toronto Central Library, 0383-2783.*

US/0095-4403
BULLETIN OF THE AMERICAN SOCIETY FOR INFORMATION SCIENCE. (BULLETIN OF THE AMERICAN SOCIETY FOR INFORMATION SCIENCE / ASIS.). [Bull. Am. Soc. Inf. Sci.]. **Main/Corp** American Society for Information Science. **Added/Corp** American Society for Information Science. **VFOAT** Bulletin. Vol. 1 (June/July 1974)-. Bulletin. English. Six times a year (Feb., Apr., June, Aug., Oct., Dec.). $60.00 US, Canada & Mexico; $70.00 others; $350.00 (institutional), $550.00 (corporate patron) Comes with American Society for Information Science membership. American Society Information Science, 8720 Georgia Avenue, Suite 501, Silver Spring MD 20910. **Tel** (301)495-0900, FAX (301)495-0810. **ED** Richard B. Hill. **LC** Z699.A1; A624a. **DD** 020/.5. **CODEN** BASICR. **[CCC]. Bk Rev. Ad Acc. Circ:** 4,000. available on microfilm and microfiche from University Microfilms International (UMI). Documents available from The Genuine Article, UMI Article Clearinghouse, UMI Article Clearinghouse, Ask*IEEE, UMI Article Clearinghouse. ***Continues*** *ASIS Newsletter, 0001-2513.* ***Continued in part by*** *American Society for Information Science. ASIS News, 0275-9160.*
Ind/Abst ABI/INFORM Glob. Ed.; ABI Inform Ondisc (June 1974-); Acad. Search (Jan. 1994-); Bus. Source (Jul. 1993-); Coal Abstr.; Curr. Index J. Educ.; Ei Page One; Gen. Period. Index (1985); GeoRef; Health Plan. Adminis.; Hospit. Health Admin. Index; INFO-SOUTH Abstr.; Inf. Instruc. Technol.; Inf. Sci. Abstr. (Feb. 1981-) [Full Cov.]; INSPEC (Feb. 1981-); Libr. Inf. Sci. Abstr.; Libr. Lit.; Mag. Index Plus (1989-); Newsp. Period. Abstr. (1988-); PAIS Int. Print; Res. Alert [Select. Cov.]; SCISEARCH; Soc. Sci. Cit. Index [Select. Cov.]; Soc. Work Abstr. [Select. Cov.]; Mag. Index (1978-); UMI ABI/Inform--Bus. Period. Ondisc (Dec. 1987-) [Full Txt.].

UK/0305-781X
BULLETIN OF THE ASSOCIATION OF BRITISH THEOLOGICAL AND PHILOSOPHICAL LIBRARIES. [Bull. Assoc. Br. Theol. Philos. Libr.]. **Main/Corp** Association of British Theological and Philosophical Libraries. No. 1 (Nov. 1956)-. Periodical. English. Three times a year. $20.00. ABTAPL Honorary Treasurer, c/o M. Walsh, 11-13 Cavendish Square, London W1M 0AN England. **Tel** 011 44 71 5806941. **ED** Patrick J. Lambe. **LC** Z675.T4; A85a. **DD** 026/.2/00941. cum. index. **Bk Rev. Ad Acc. Circ:** 250.
Desc: Carries news and information on the bibliography of theology and philosophy in the United Kingdom.
Ind/Abst Libr. Inf. Sci. Abstr.

US/0010-5821
BULLETIN OF THE CONGREGATIONAL LIBRARY. **Main/Corp** Congregational Library (Boston, Mass.). **Added/Corp** American Congregational Association. Bulletin of the American Congregational Association. Vol. 1 (Oct. 1949)-. Bulletin. English. Three times a year (Feb., June, Oct.). $5.00. Congregational Library, 14 Beacon Street, Boston MA 02108. **Tel** (617)523-0470. **ED** Harold F. Worthley. **LC** Z881; .B7. **DD** 026.258. Index available. cum. index. **Bk Rev. Circ:** 1,000 (ctrl). available on microfilm from University Microfilms International (UMI). ***Supersedes*** *Quarterly Bulletin - Congregational Library, 0364-7250; American Congregational Association. Report of the Directors.*
Desc: One article per issue on Congregational Christian history, and reviews of Library book purchases.

US/0734-2012
BULLETIN OF THE FRIENDS OF THE OWEN D. YOUNG LIBRARY. **Added/Corp** Owen D. Young Library. Friends. (19??)-. Periodical. English. an. $15.00. Friends of the Owen D Young Library, St Lawrence University, Canton NY 13617. **Tel** (315)379-5476. **ED** Lynn Ekfelt. **LC** Z733.O943; B84. **DD** 021.7. **Circ:** 450.

US/0025-7338
BULLETIN OF THE MEDICAL LIBRARY ASSOCIATION. [Bull. Med. Libr. Assoc.]. **Main/Corp** Medical Library Association. Vol. 1 (July 1911)-. Academic Scholarly Publication. English. qt. $136.00 US, Canada, and Mexico; $174.00 other. Medical Library Association, Suite 300, Six North Michigan Avenue, Chicago IL 60602-4805. **Tel** (312)419-9094, FAX (312)419-8950. **ED** Susan Crawford. **DD** 026. **NLM** Z 675.M4 M489B. **CODEN** BMLAAG. Index available (bound in October issue). **Bk Rev. Ad Acc. Pr Rev. Acid Free. Circ:** 6,200. available on microfilm and microfiche from University Microfilms International (UMI). Documents available from The Genuine Article, BIOSIS Document Express, Ask*IEEE.
Desc: Covers developments on the technical, administrative and biomedical information, research issues of interest to health science librarians as well as articles on education of librarians.
Ind/Abst Biol. Abstr.; Cumul. Index Nurs. Allied Health Lit.; Curr. Contents Soc. Behav. Sci.; EMBASE; Health Plan. Adminis.; Index Med.; Inf. Sci. Abstr.; INSPEC (Jan. 1982-); Int. Nurs. Index; Libr. Inf. Sci. Abstr.; Libr. Lit.; Nutr. Abstr. Rev., Ser. B, Live Feeds and Feed.; Nutr. Abstr. Rev., Ser. A, Hum. Exp.; Life Sci. Collect.; Res. Alert [Full Cov.]; Soc. Sci. Cit. Index [Full Cov.]; Trop. Dis. Bull.

IO/0304-5773
BULLETIN PERPUSTAKAAN DAN DOKUMENTASI. **Added/Corp** Asosiasi Perpustakaan, Arsip dan Dokumentasi Indonesia. (19??)-. Bulletin. Indonesian. qt. Rp200 single issue. Asosiasi Perpustakaan, Perpustakaan SPS Jalan Merdeka Selatan II, Jakarta Indonesia. **LC** Z671; .B94.

CN/0700-5431
BULLETIN - SOCIETE DES DIPLOMES DE L'ECOLE DE BIBLIOTHECONOMIE DE L'UNIVERSITE DE MONTREAL. **Main/Corp** Universite de Montreal. Ecole de Bibliotheconomie. Societe des Diplomes. Discontinued in 196-?. Bulletin. French. Societe des Diplomes de l'Ecole de Bibliotheconomie, Universite de Montreal, CP 6128, Montreal Quebec H3C 3J7 Canada. **DD** 020/.6234/714.

CN/0824-7749
BULLETIN - SPECIAL LIBRARIES ASSOCIATION, EASTERN CANADA CHAPTER. **Main/Corp** Special Libraries Association. Eastern Canada Chapter. V. 44- Oct. 1978-. Bulletin. English (French). Special Libraries Association, Eastern Canada Chapter, Directory Committee, PO Box 1538 Station B, Montreal Quebec H3B 3K3 Canada. ***Continues*** *Bulletin / Special Libraries Association. Montreal Chapter, 0381-9833.*

US/1052-9454
BULLETIN - SPECIAL LIBRARIES ASSOCIATION. EDUCATION DIVISION. [Bull. - Spec. Libr. Assoc., Educ. Div.]. **Main/Corp** Special Libraries Association. Education Division. **VFOAT** Bulletin of the Education Division, Special Libraries Association. Vol. 1, No. 1 (Fall 1978)-. Bulletin. English. Three times a year. $20.00 US; $39.00 Canada; $25.00 other. Special Libraries Association / Education Division, 1700 18th Street Northwest, Washington DC 20009. **Tel** (202)234-4700, FAX (202)265-9317. **ED** Amme Galler. **DD** 027. **Bk Rev. Ad Acc.** ***Separated from*** *Education Libraries, 0148-1061.*
Ind/Abst Curr. Geogr. Publ. (199?-).

US/0740-9753
BULLETIN (SPECIAL LIBRARIES ASSOCIATION. FLORIDA CHAPTER). (BULLETIN / FLORIDA CHAPTER, SPECIAL LIBRARIES ASSOCIATION.). **Added/Corp** Special Libraries Association. Florida Chapter. **VFOAT** Bulletin of the Florida Chapter, SLA. (198?)-. Bulletin. English. qt. $15.00. Florida and Caribbean Chapter SLA, PO Box 248214, Otto Richter Library, Coral Gables FL 33124. **Tel** (305)284-3935. **LC** Z732.F6; B84. ***Continues*** *Bulletin of the Florida Chapter, SLA.*
Ind/Abst Libr. Inf. Sci. Abstr.

US/0195-9077
BULLETIN - SPECIAL LIBRARIES ASSOCIATION, NORTH CAROLINA CHAPTER. **Main/Corp** Special Libraries Association. North Carolina Chapter. **VFOAT** NC SLA Bulletin. Bulletin. English (Spanish). qt. $5.00. Waller, 2640 Bexley, Durham NC 27707-3906. **Tel** (919)836-6225. **ED** Celia Pratt Carolina Power and Light Co., 411 Fayetteville Street, Raleigh NC 27602). **Ad Acc. Circ:** 275.
Desc: Official publication of the North Carolina chapter of the Special Libraries Association.

US/0277-2124
BULLETIN - SPECIAL LIBRARIES ASSOCIATION. SAN FRANCISCO BAY REGION CHAPTER. (BULLETIN.). **Main/Corp** Special Libraries Association. San Francisco Bay Region Chapter. **VFOAT** Bulletin - San Francisco Bay Region Chapter, Special Libraries Association; SLA SF Chapter Bulletin. Bulletin. English. Five times a year. $15.00 (members), $20.00 (nonmembers). Special Libraries Association / San Francisco Bay Region, San Francisco Bay Region Chapter, 760 Market Street/Room 315, San Francisco CA 94102. **ED** Leigh Dowley. **Ad Acc. Circ:** 600.

US
BURWELL DIRECTORY OF INFORMATION BROKERS. **VFOAT** Directory of Information Brokers. (1991)-. Directory. English. $51.50 (one year). Information Alternatives, PO Box 657, Woodstock NY 12498. **LC** Z674.5.U5; D57. **DD** 021/.0025/73. ***Continues*** *Directory of Fee-Based Information Services, 0147-1678.*

UK/0007-6538
BUSINESS ARCHIVES. **Added/Corp** Business Archives Council (Great Britain). (19??)-. Periodical. English. sa (May & November). £35.00 (institution), £80.00 (corporate), £25.00 (individual). Business Archives Council, 185 Tower Bridge Road, London SE1 1UF England. **Tel** 011 44 71 4076110. **ED** Alison Turton. **LC** HF5736; .B74. Index available. cum. index. **Bk Rev**, (Qty: 5-10). **Ad Acc, Adv Mgr:** W. S. Quinn-Robinson. **Pr Rev. Acid Free. Circ:** 500.
Desc: Deals with the arrangement and preservation of business archives and the management of modern records and includes articles, book notes and bibliographies of recently published technical literature.

US/1042-0746
BUSINESS INFORMATION ALERT. [Bus. inf. alert]. (1989)-. Periodical. English. Ten times a year (Monthly with July/Aug. and Nov./Dec. issues combined). $142.00 US; $162.00 other. Alert Publications Inc, 399 West Fullerton Parkway, Chicago IL 60614. **Tel** (312)525-7594, FAX (312)525-7015. **ED** Donna Tuke Heroy. **DD** 025. **[CCC]**. Index available. **Bk Rev. Ad Acc.** available on an online database from NEWSNET.
Desc: What's new in business publications, databases and research techniques.
Ind/Abst Leg. Inf. Manage. Index (19??-199?).

US/0892-6034
BUSINESS INFORMATION FROM YOUR PUBLIC LIBRARY. **See** Business.

UK/0266-3821
BUSINESS INFORMATION REVIEW. [Bus.inf. rev.]. Vol. 1, No. 1 (July 1984)-. Periodical. English. qt. £149.00 UK; $299.00 other. Headland Business Information, 1 Henry Smiths Terrace, Headland Cleveland, TS24 0PD England. **Tel** 011 44 429 231902, FAX 011 44 429 861403. **ED** Gerry Smith. **CODEN** BIREEY. Index available. cum. index. **Bk Rev. Circ:** 600 (ctrl). Documents available from UMI Article Clearinghouse, Ask*IEEE.
Ind/Abst ABI/INFORM Glob. Ed.; INSPEC (1987-); Libr. Inf. Sci. Abstr.; Manage. Market. Abstr.; PAIS Int. Print (1991-).

US/0191-4006
BUSINESS LIBRARY NEWSLETTER. (1979)-. Newsletter. English. mo. $56.00 US and Canada; $64.00 other. Business Library Newsletter, 427-3 Amherst Street/Suite 305, Nashua NH 03063. **Tel** (603)672-0705. **ED** Raymond Hubbard. Index available. **Bk Rev. Circ:** 400 (ctrl).
Desc: A publication which reviews and recommends the 12-15 most significant recently published titles in business and related fields.

UK
BUYING FOR LIBRARIES. ***Ceased.*** (Autumn 1984)-Ceased ?. Periodical. English. qt. Alan Armstrong & Associates Ltd, 72 Park Road, London NW1 4SH England. **Tel** (01)258-3740, FAX 01 724 7229, telex 297635 AAALTD C. **ED** Nigel Oxbrow. **LC** Z689; .B975. **DD** 025.2. **Bk Rev. Ad Acc. Circ:** 15,000 (ctrl).
Desc: News and reviews of products and services for the library and information world.

UK/0957-4085
C & L APPLICATIONS. ***Title Change.*** [C&L appl.]. **VFOAT** C and L Applications. **VAT** Computers and Libraries, Applications; Computers & Libraries, Applications. Vol. 3, No. 2 (Sept. 1989)-(19??). Periodical. English. Ten times a year. Information Partnership, 140 Tabernacle Street, Suite 4 2, London EC2A 4SD England. **Tel** 011 44 71 2530575, FAX 011 44 01 3516300. **ED** Peter Gillman. **CODEN** CLAPEE. Index available. cum. index. **Bk Rev. Ad Acc. Circ:** 250. Documents available from Ask*IEEE. ***Continues*** *Computers & Libraries, 0950-8392.* ***Continued by*** *TIP Applications.*
Ind/Abst INSPEC (Sept. 1989-?).

CN/0700-5474
C H L A/A B S C NEWSLETTER. [CHLA, ABSC newsl.]. **Main/Corp** Association des Bibliotheques de la Sante du Canada. **VAT** Canadian Health Library Association. Association des Bibliotheques de la Sante du Canada. Newsletter; Canadian Health Library Association Newsletter; Association des Bibliotheques de la Sante du Canada. Newsletter. No. 1- Winter 1977-. Newsletter. French (English). Free to members. Memorial University of Newfoundland / Health Sciences Centre, c/o R. B. Fredericksen, St John's Newfoundland A1B 3W6 Canada. **DD** 020/.622/71. ***Supersedes*** *Can Group News, 0703-8615.*
Ind/Abst Libr. Inf. Sci. Abstr.

US/1052-4754
C-L-A-S-S FORUM. [C-L-A-S-S forum]. **Added/Corp** Cooperative Library Agency for Systems and Services (Calif.). **VFOAT** CLASS Forum. Vol. 11, No. 1 (Oct. 1988)-. Periodical. English. Four times a year. $135.00 (Comes with Cooperative Library Agency for Systems & Services Membership). CLASS, 1415 Koll Circle, Suite 101, San Jose CA 95112-4698. **Tel** (408)453-0444 or (800)488-4559. **DD** 021. ***Continues*** *CLASS Online, 0162-492X.*

US
C USERS GROUP LIBRARY DIRECTORY. **See** Computers-Software.

CN/0829-254X
CAAT TRACKS. (CAAT TRACKS : CAAT COMMITTEE ON LEARNING RESOURCES NEWSLETTER.). [CAAT tracks]. **Added/Corp** Association of Colleges of Applied Arts and Technology of Ontario. Committee on Learning Resources. **VAT** Colleges of Applied Arts and Technology Tracks. Vol. 1, No. 1 (March 1986)-. Newsletter. English. Four times a year (March, June, Sept., Dec.). 20.00Can$. CAAT Committee on Learning Resources, St. Lawrence College Library, King & Portsmouth Avenues, Kingston Ontario K7L 5A6 Canada. **Tel** (613)544-5400 Ext. 1505. **ED** Barbara Carr and Barbara Love. **DD** 027.7/06/0713. **Bk Rev. Circ:** 60.
Desc: Publishes articles of interest to Ontario's community college resource centres, media centres and archives.

CN/1191-1468
CAAT TRACKS : INTERLIBRARY LOANS MANUAL. [Caat tracks, Interlibr. loans man.]. **VFOAT** Colleges of Applied Art and Technology Tracks; Interlibrary Loans Manual. **VAT** Colleges of Applied Art and Technology Tracks. Interlibrary Loans Manual. (1991)-. English. CAAT Committee on Learning Resources, St. Lawrence College Library, King & Portsmouth Avenues, Kingston Ontario K7L 5A6 Canada. **Tel** (613)544-5400 Ext. 1505. **DD** 025.6/2/09713.

BE/0007-9804
CAHIERS DE LA DOCUMENTATION. (LES CAHIERS DE LA DOCUMENTATION. BLADEN VOOR DE DOCUMENTATIE.). [Cah. doc.]. **Added/Corp** Association Belge de Documentation. **VFOAT** Bladen voor de Documentatie. Vol. 1 (1947)-. Periodical. French (English and Dutch). Five times a year (four issues plus one special issue). 1000F Belgium; 1500F other. Association Belge de Documentation, Boulevard L. Schmidt 119, BTE 3, 1040 Brussels Belgium. **Tel** 011 32 2 672-9748. **ED** G. Delcol. **LC** Z1008; .C12. **DD** 025/.05. Index available (Bound in next issue.). cum. index. **Ad Acc. Circ:** 300 (ctrl).
Desc: Information on documentation.
Ind/Abst Libr. Inf. Sci. Abstr.

US/0198-8433
CALIFORNIA ACADEMIC LIBRARIES LIST OF SERIALS MICROFORM. [Calif. acad. libr. list ser.]. 1980 Ed.-. English. CLASS, 1415 Koll Circle, Suite 101, San Jose CA 95112-4698. **Tel** (408)453-0444 or (800)488-4559. **DD** 025. ***Continues*** *University of California Union List of Serials. University of California (System). Division of Library Automation., 0146-1923.*
Desc: Includes serial holdings for University of California, the California State University and college, and Stanford University.

US/1056-1528
CALIFORNIA LIBRARIES. [Calif. libr.]. **Added/Corp** California Library Association. Vol. 1, No. 1 (Jan. 1991)-. Newsletter. English. mo (10 issues). comes with membership. California Library Association, 717 K Street, Suite 300, Sacramento CA 95814. **Tel** (916)447-8541, FAX (916)447-8394. **ED** James Healey (editor's phone: (408)924-2467). **LC** Z673.C16; C33. **DD** 027. **Bk Rev. Ad Acc, Adv Mgr:** Christie Braziel. **Circ:** 2,500 (ctrl). ***Continues*** *Newsletter - California Library Association, 0199-1299.*

US/0740-7688
CALIFORNIA LIBRARY DIRECTORY. 1983-. Directory. English. an. California State Library, PO Box 942837, Sacramento CA 94237. **Tel** (916)445-4027. **LC** Z732.C2; C473. **DD** 027/.0025/794. ***Continues in part*** *California Library Statistics and Directory.*

US/0097-9902
CALIFORNIA LIBRARY LAWS. **See** Law.

US/0741-031X
CALIFORNIA LIBRARY STATISTICS. **See** Library and Information Sciences-Abstracting, Bibliographies and Statistics.

US/8755-7711
CALIFORNIA LIBRARY TRUSTEES DIRECTORY. 1984-. Directory. English. an. California State Library, PO Box 942837, Sacramento CA 94237. **Tel** (916)445-4027. **LC** Z681.5; .C36. **DD** 021.8/2/025794. ***Continues*** *California Public Library Trustees and Commissioners State Directory, 0885-7938.*

US/0741-0344
CALIFORNIA STATE LIBRARY FOUNDATION BULLETIN. [Calif. State Libr. Found. bull.]. **Main/Corp** California State Library Foundation. **Added/Corp** California State Library. Foundation. No. 2, (Jan. 1983)-. Bulletin. English. qt. $20.00 US; $25.00 Canada. California State Library Foundation, 1225 8th Street, Suite 345, Sacramento CA 95814. **Tel** (916)447-6331. **ED** Gary E Strong. **LC** Z733.C13; C34. **DD** 027.5794. Index available. **Circ:** 2,100. ***Continues*** *Bulletin of the California State Library Foundation.*
Desc: Library related news, information and topics relevant to California history.
Ind/Abst Libr. Lit.

US/0276-6973
CALIFORNIA STATE LIBRARY NEWSLETTER. **Main/Corp** California State Library. **VFOAT** Newsletter. No. 1 (Jan. 1981)-. Newsletter. English. mo. Free to libraries. California State Library, PO Box 942837, Sacramento CA 94237. **Tel** (916)445-4027. **ED** Gary E Strong, Patricia Morris. **Circ:** 2,800. ***Continues in part*** *Across the Board (California Library Services Board).*
Desc: Offers news on California State Library activities. Provides information from a statewide perspective on library related legislation and budget issues, workshops, conferences, library statistics and trends, library literacy programs. Contains articles on individual public libraries which have received awards, run outstanding programs or are experiencing problems of interest to other libraries.

US/0730-093X
CAMLS NEWS. **Main/Corp** Cleveland Area Metropolitan Library System. **VFOAT** C.A.M.L.S. News. **VAT** Cleveland Area Metropolitan Library System News. Vol. 3 (1977)-. Newsletter. English. bm. Cleveland Area Metropolitan Library System, 3645 Warrensville Center/116, Cleveland OH 44122-5210. **Tel** (216)921-3900. **ED** Mildred H. Fry. **LC** Discard. **Circ:** 900 (ctrl). ***Continues*** *Cleveland Area Metropolitan Library System. Newsletter, 0730-3548.*
Desc: News of interest to members of the consortium; primarily consortium activities.

CN/0227-8804
CANADIAN INFORMATION INDUSTRY ASSOCIATION. (CANADIAN INFORMATION INDUSTRY ASSOCIATION : NEWSLETTER.). [Can. Inf. Ind. Assoc.]. Vol. 1, No. 1 (Sept. 1980)-. Newsletter. English. Free. Canadian Information Industry Association, Suite 900A, 77 Metcalfe Street, Ottawa Ontario K1P 5L6 Canada. **DD** 338.4/7025. ctrl circ.

●CN/1195-096X
CANADIAN JOURNAL OF INFORMATION AND LIBRARY SCIENCE, THE. [Can. j. inf. libr. sci.]. **Added/Corp** Canadian Association for Information Science. **VFOAT** Revue Canadienne des Sciences de l'Information et de Bibliotheconomie. Vol. 18, No. 1 (Apr. 1993)-. Periodical. English (French). qt (Mar., June, Sep., Dec.). $95.00. University of Toronto Press, 5201 Dufferin Street, Downsview Ontario M3H 5T8 Canada. **Tel** (416)667-7781, (416)667-7782, FAX (416)667-7803. **ED** Joan M. Cherry. **LC** Z1007; .C28. **DD** 020/.971/05. **CODEN** CJISEF. **Ad Acc.** ***Formed by the union of*** *Canadian Library Journal, 0008-4352* ***and*** *Canadian Journal of Information Science, 0380-9218.*
Desc: Dedicated to contributing to the advancement of information and library science in both English and French Canada by serving as a forum for discussion of theory and research.
Ind/Abst Soc. Sci. Cit. Index [Full Cov.].

CN/0380-9218
CANADIAN JOURNAL OF INFORMATION SCIENCE. ***Title Change.*** (THE CANADIAN JOURNAL OF INFORMATION SCIENCE. REVUE CANADIENNE DES SCIENCES DE L'INFORMATION.). [Can. j. inf. sci.]. **Added/Corp**

Canadian Association for Information Science. **VFOAT** Revue Canadienne des Sciences de l'Information. Vol. 1 (May 1976)-Vol. 17, No. 4 (Dec. 1992). Periodical. English (French). qt. University of Toronto Press, 5201 Dufferin Street, Downsview Ontario M3H 5T8 Canada. **Tel** (416)667-7781, (416)667-7782, FAX (416)667-7803. **ED** J Cherry. **LC** Z1007; .C28. **DD** 020/.5. **CODEN** CJISDE. **[CCC]. Bk Rev. Ad Acc. Pr Rev. Circ:** 400 (ctrl). Documents available from The Genuine Article, Ask*IEEE. ***Merged with** Canadian Library Journal **to form** Canadian Journal of Information and Library Science.*
Desc: A respected source of the most up-to-date research on library and information science, it is recognized internationally for its authoritative bilingual contributions to the field of information science. The journal is dedicated to the publication of research findings, both in full-length and in brief format, reviews of books, software, and technology and letters to the editor. Such diverse topics as the nature, representation and transfer of information, fundamental studies of information and communication theory, management and economics of information systems and services and the measurement and evaluation of information systems are covered in the journal's scope.
Ind/Abst Can. Index (?-?); Can. Period. Index (19??-); Compumath Citation Index [Full Cov.]; Comput. Rev.; Curr. Contents Soc. Behav. Sci.; Inf. Sci. Abstr. [Full Cov.]; INSPEC (1976-); Libr. Inf. Sci. Abstr.; Libr. Lit.; PAIS Int. Print (1991-?); Life Sci. Collect.; Res. Alert [Full Cov.]; Soc. Sci. Cit. Index (19??-19??) [Full Cov.].

CN/1180-176X
CANADIAN LAW LIBRARIES. See Law.

CN/0008-4352
CANADIAN LIBRARY JOURNAL. ***Title Change.*** [Can. libr. j.]. **Added/Corp** Canadian Library Association. Vol. 26-49, No. 5; (Jan./Feb. 1969)-(Oct. 1992). Periodical. English. bm. Canadian Library Association, 200 Elgin Street, Suite 602, Ottawa Ontario K2P 1L5 Canada. **Tel** (613)232-9625. **ED** Shelia Nelson. **CODEN** CLIJBX. **[CCC]. Bk Rev. Ad Acc. Pr Rev. Circ:** 6,000 (ctrl). Documents available from The Genuine Article, Ask*IEEE. ***Continues** Canadian Library, 0316-604X. **Merged with** Canadian Journal of Information Science **to form** tCanadian Journal of Information and Library Science.*
Desc: A forum for discussion, analysis and evaluation of issues in librarianship.
Ind/Abst Am. Hist. Life (1969-1984); Can. Index (1969-?); Can. Period. Index; Child. Lit. Abstr. (19??-); Curr. Contents Soc. Behav. Sci.; Curr. Index J. Educ.; INFO-SOUTH Abstr.; Inf. Instruc. Technol.; Inf. Sci. Abstr. (?-?); INSPEC (Dec. 1981-); Leg. Inf. Manage. Index; Libr. Inf. Sci. Abstr.; Libr. Lit.; Mag. Search; Pollut. Abstr. Indexes; Res. Alert [Full Cov.]; Soc. Sci. Cit. Index [Full Cov.].

CN/0707-7629
CANADIAN LOCATIONS OF JOURNALS INDEXED FOR MEDLINE. (CANADIAN LOCATIONS OF JOURNALS INDEXED FOR MEDLINE / HEALTH SCIENCES RESOURCE CENTRE, CANADA INSTITUTE FOR SCIENTIFIC AND TECHNICAL INFORMATION.). **Added/Corp** Canada Institute for Scientific and Technical Information. Health Sciences Resource Centre. National Research Council Canada. **VFOAT** Depots Canadiens des Revues Indexees pour Medline. 9th Ed. (1979)-. English (French). an. 40.00Can$. National Research Council of Canada, Receiver General for Canada, Ottawa Ontario K1A 0R6 Canada. **Tel** (613)993-0362, FAX (613)952-7656. **LC** Z6660; .C345; R5. **DD** 016.61/05. **NLM** ZW 1 C212. **Circ:** 385. ***Continues** Canadian Locations of Journals Indexed in Index Medicus, 0316-3938.*
Desc: Health sciences journals and locations in Canadian libraries.

CN/0226-8760
CANADIAN NETWORK PAPERS. [Can. netw. pap.]. **Added/Corp** National Library of Canada. **VFOAT** Documents sur les Reseaux Canadiens. No. 1 (1980)-. Monographic series. English (French). ir. Price varies per volume. Canada Communication Group Publishers, Order Processing, Ottawa Ontario K1A 0S9 Canada. **Tel** (819)956-4800, (819)956-4802. **CODEN** CNPADN.
Ind/Abst Libr. Inf. Sci. Abstr.

CN/0000-0345
CANADIAN SERIALS DIRECTORY. (CANADIAN SERIALS DIRECTORY. REPERTOIRE DES PUBLICATIONS SERIEES CANADIENNES.). **Added/Corp** University of British Columbia. Library. National Library of Canada. Bibliotheque Nationale du Quebec. **VFOAT** Repertoire des Publications Seriees Canadiennes. (1972)-. Directory. English (French). be. 45.00Can$. Reference Press, PO Box 70, Teeswater Ontario N0G 2S0 Canada. **Tel** (519)392-6634. **LC** Z6954.C2; C23. **DD** 016.051.
Desc: A bibliographic listing of magazines, newsletters, daily newspapers, annuals, yearbooks, and journals currently published in Canada. Designed as a reference and aid for librarians, booksellers, teachers, and the general public.

CN/0822-2576
CANADIAN UNION CATALOGUE OF LIBRARY MATERIALS FOR THE HANDICAPPED [MICROFORM] / CATALOGUE COLLECTIF CANADIEN DES DOCUMENTS DE BIBLIOTHEQUE POUR LES PERSONNES HANDICAPEES. **Added/Corp** National Library of Canada. **VFOAT** Catalogue Collectif Canadien des Documents de Bibliotheque pour les Personnes Handicapees.; CANUC: H. (198?)-. Bibliography. English (French). sa. 163.70Can$ Canada; 196.44Can$ other. National Library of Canada, 395 Wellington Street, Ottawa Ontario K1A 0N4 Canada. **Tel** (613)995-7969, (613)995-7969, (819)994-6881, FAX (613)991-9871. available on audiocassette; available in braille; available in large print.
Desc: Includes approximately 80,000 records of alternative format materials held in Canadian libraries, including records of serials in alternative formats and their locations.

US/0277-9285
CANADIAN VIEWPOINT (WILLOW GROVE, PA.). (CANADIAN VIEWPOINT / THE INTERNATIONAL INFORMATION/WORD PROCESSING ASSOCIATION.). [Can. viewp.]. **Added/Corp** Association of Information Systems Professionals. International Information/Word Processing Association. (1981)-. Periodical. English. bm. $50.00 includes membership. International Information/Word Processing Association, 1015 North York Road, Willow Grove PA 19090. **DD** 020/.624/71.

CN/0225-1574
CANADIANA AUTHORITIES. (CANADIANA AUTHORITIES MICROFORM / CANADIANA, VEDETTES D'AUTORITE.). [Can. auth.]. **Added/Corp** National Library of Canada. **VFOAT** Canadiana, Vedettes d'Autorite. (1979)-. English (French). qt. 141.15Can$. National Library of Canada, 395 Wellington Street, Ottawa Ontario K1A 0N4 Canada. **Tel** (613)995-7969, (613)995-7969, (819)994-6881, FAX (613)991-9871. **LC** 90/6756. **DD** 025.3/222. available on audiocassette; available in braille; available in large print. ***Continues** National Library of Canada. C A N / M A R C: Authorities, 0701-810X.*
Desc: Current list of authoritative personal and corporate name headings of Canadian origin essential for maintaining bibliographic control of a library collection.

SA/0008-5790
CAPE LIBRARIAN, THE. [Cape libr.]. **VFOAT** Kaapse Bibliotekaris : Amptelike Maandblad van die Kaapse Provinsiale Biblioteckdiens; Kaapse Bibliotekaris. Began in Nov. 1957. Periodical. Afrikaans (English). mo (except July and Dec.). R30.00 South Africa; Free to others 370.00F (surface mail), 458.00F (airmail) other. The Administration, PO Box 2108, 8000 Cape Town South Africa. **Tel** (021)258-2288, FAX (021)419-7541. **ED** Zirkea Ellis. **LC** Z671; .C32. Index available. cum. index. **Bk Rev. Circ:** 1,200 (ctrl). available on microfilm and microfiche from University Microfilms International (UMI).
Desc: Journal of the Cape Provincial Library Service. General and practical articles on promoting culture, group activities, displays, news, reviews of new library materials, accessions lists.
Ind/Abst Libr. Inf. Sci. Abstr.

JM/0255-7118
CARIBBEAN JOURNAL OF LEGAL INFORMATION : BULLETIN OF THE CARIBBEAN ASSOCIATION OF LAW LIBRARIANS, THE. See Law.

XR/0862-9382
CASOPIS INFORMACNICH PRACOVNIKU, KNIHOVNIKU A UZIVATELU INFORMACI, I. **Added/Corp** Ustredi Vedeckych, Technickych a Ekonomickych Informaci. (1991)-. Periodical. Czech. mo. **LC** Z665; .I14. ***Formed by the union of** Ceskoslovenska Informatika **and** Technicka Knihovna.*

US
CATALOG MICROFORM / CENTER FOR RESEARCH LIBRARIES. **Main/Corp** Center for Research Libraries (U.S.). **VFOAT** Center for Research Libraries Catalog; CRL Microfiche Catalog. 1st Ed. (Sept. 1982)-. Catalog. English. $45.00 CRL members, $65.00 other. Center for Research Libraries, 6050 South Kenwood Avenue, Chicago IL 60637. **Tel** (312)955-4545. **DD** 019/.1. ***Formed by the union of** Center for Research Libraries Catalogue, Monographs. Supplement, 0098-7662; Center for Research Libraries Catalogue. Newspapers **and** Center for Research Libraries Catalogue, Serials. Supplement, 0273-0766.*

US/0163-9374
CATALOGING & CLASSIFICATION QUARTERLY. [Cat. classif. q.]. **VFOAT** Cataloging and Classification Quarterly. Vol. 1, No. 1 (Fall 1980)-. Periodical. English. qt. $125.00 US; $175.00 other. The Haworth Press Inc, 10 Alice Street, Binghamton NY 13904-1580. **Tel** (607)722-5857, (800)3-HAWORTH, FAX (607)722-1424. **ED** Ruth Carter (editor's address: University of Pittsburgh Libraries, 271 Hillman Library, Pittsburgh, PA 15260). **LC** Z693.A15; C35. **DD** 025.3/05. **CODEN** CCQUDB. **Bk Rev. Ad Acc. Pr Rev. Acid Free. Circ:** 863. available on microfilm and microfiche from University Microfilms International (UMI). Documents available from Ask*IEEE, Haworth Document Delivery Service.
Desc: Provides a wealth of material on the bibliographic control and the practical constructs of cataloging and classification systems. Reports on the latest advances in techniques and principles of all bibliographic functions.
Ind/Abst Curr. Index J. Educ.; Index Period. Artic. Relat. Law; Inf. Instruc. Technol.; Inf. Sci. Abstr.; INSPEC (1982-); Leg. Inf. Manage. Index; Libr. Inf. Sci. Abstr.; Libr. Lit.; Pollut. Abstr. Indexes; Ref. Z.

US/0160-8029
CATALOGING SERVICE BULLETIN. (CATALOGING SERVICE BULLETIN / PROCESSING SERVICES.). [Cat. serv. bull.]. **Main/Corp** Library of Congress. Processing Services. **Added/Corp** Library of Congress. Processing Services. Library of Congress. Collections Services. No. 1 (Summer 1978)-. Bulletin. English. qt. $24.00 North America; $26.00 other. Library of Congress / Cataloging Distribution Service, Washington DC 20541-5017. **Tel** (800)255-3666, (202)707-6100, FAX (202)707-1334. **LC** Z693.A15; C37. **DD** 025./02/05. **CODEN** CSBUDE. cum. index. **Bk Rev. Ad Acc.** ***Continues** Library of Congress. Processing Dept. Cataloging Service, 0041-7890.*
Desc: Contains information relating to the Library of Congress cataloging and classification practices.

US/0739-3393
CATALOGING SERVICE BULLETIN INDEX. [Cat. serv. bull. index]. **VFOAT** Index to Cataloging Service Bulletin. No. 1-16 (Summer 1978-Spring 1982)-. English. an (Jan.). $30.00. Soldier Creek Press Inc., PO Box 734, Lake Crystal MN 56055. **Tel** (612)783-6620. **ED** Nancy B. Olson. **LC** Z693.A15; C37 Suppl. **DD** 025.3/2. Index available.

MX
CATALOGO - CENTRO DE DOCUMENTACION Y BIBLIOTECA, CASA DE CHILE EN MEXICO. **Main/Corp** Casa de Chile en Mexico. Centro de Documentation y Biblioteca. Spanish. Casa de Chile en Mexico, Centro de Documentacion y Biblioteca, Av Universidad 1134, Colonia del Valle, Mexico 12 DF Mexico.

UK/0008-7629
CATALOGUE & INDEX. (CATALOGUE & INDEX : PERIODICAL OF THE LIBRARY ASSOCIATION CATALOGUING AND INDEXING GROUP.). [Cat. index]. **Added/Corp** Library Association. Cataloguing and Indexing Group. **VFOAT** Catalogue and Index. No. 1 (Jan. 1966)-. Periodical. English. qt. £10.00; $20.00 US. The Library Association, Cataloguing & Indexing Group, 18 Apple Grove, Enfield Middlesex EN1 3DD England. **Tel** 0232 245133. **ED** Rodney Brunt. **LC** Z695; .C35. **NLM** Z 695.7 C357. **Bk Rev. Circ:** 3,500 (ctrl). available on microfilm and microfiche from University Microfilms International (UMI).
Desc: Presents articles on cataloguing, indexing and other related matters, including the planning, production or maintenance of library catalogues.
Ind/Abst Inf. Sci. Abstr.; Libr. Inf. Sci. Abstr.; Libr. Lit.

CN/0384-9724
CATALOGUE DES MICROEDITIONS. **Main/Corp** Bibliotheque Nationale du Quebec. Service de Microphotographie. 1974-. French. Bibliotheque National du Quebec, Ministere des Affairs Culturelles, 1700 rue Saint-Denis, Montreal Quebec H2X 3K6 Canada. **Tel** (514)873-7604, FAX (514)873-4310. **DD** 015/.714.

AT
CATALOGUE OF BOOKS ADDED TO THE NEW SOUTH WALES PARLIAMENTARY LIBRARY FROM THE ... WITH SUBJECT-INDEX. **Main/Corp** New South Wales. Parliament. Library. English. an. **LC** WMLC L 83/4624.

US
CATALOGUE OF DEPARTMENTALLY-OWNED FILMS HOUSED WITH FILM LIBRARY / THE GENERAL LIBRARIES. **Main/Corp** University of Texas at Austin. Film Library. (19??)-. English. The University of Texas at Austin / UTA, PO Box W, Austin TX 78712.

AT/0312-4371
CATALOGUING AUSTRALIA. **Added/Corp** Library Association of Australia. Cataloguers' Section. (19??)-. Periodical. English. qt. 31.00Aus$ Australia; 41.00Aus$ (surface mail), 51.00Aus$ (airmail). Australian Library & Information Association, PO Box E441, Queen Victoria Terrace, ACT 2600 Australia. **Tel** 011 61 6 2851877, FAX 011 61 6 282 2249. **ED** Christine Richardson. **LC** Z693.5.A8; C38. **DD** 025.3/0994.
Desc: Dealing with the Australian Library & Information

Association Catologuers Section.
Ind/Abst Aust. Educ. Index (199?-); Aust. Libr. Inf. Sci. Abstr. (1990-).

US/0730-711X
CATALYST (DES MOINES, IOWA : 1971), THE. (THE CATALYST.). **Added/Corp** Iowa Library Association. Vol. 25, No. 2 (Mar. 1971)-. Periodical. English. bm. $25.00. Iowa Library Association, 823 Insurance Exchange Building, Des Moines IA 50309. **Tel** (515)243-2172. **ED** Naomi Stovall. **LC** Z673; .I6423. **DD** 020/.6234/777. **Ad Acc. Circ:** 1,800 (ctrl). ***Continues*** *ILA Catalyst.*
Desc: Serves as a professional communications source for libraries and librarians throughout the state.

US/0008-820X
CATHOLIC LIBRARY WORLD, THE. [Cathol. libr. world]. **Added/Corp** Catholic Library Association. **VFOAT** CLA Handbook and Membership Directory. Vol. 1 (Nov./Dec. 1929)-. Periodical. English. Four times a year. $60.00. Catholic Library Association, 700 Terrace Heights, St. Mary's #26, Winona MN 55987. **Tel** (507)457-6935, (507)457-1563. **ED** Anthony Prete. **LC** Z671; .C36. **DD** 020/.5. Index available. **Bk Rev. Ad Acc. Circ:** 1500. available on microfilm and microfiche from University Microfilms International (UMI). ***Absorbed*** *Catholic Library Association. CLA Booklist.*
Desc: Provides current information on library and information science topics, media reviews, new product news and advertising.
Ind/Abst Book Rev. Index; Child. Lit. Abstr. (19??-); Curr. Index J. Educ.; Inf. Instruc. Technol.; Libr. Inf. Sci. Abstr.; Libr. Lit.; Abr. Cathol. Period. Lit. Index; Cathol. Period. Lit. Index.

MX
CB (MEXICO CITY, MEXICO : 1980). ***Ceased.*** (CB.). Vol. 3, No. 4 (June 1980)-(1985). Spanish. ir. CB Ciencia Bibliotecaria, Apto Postal 76 065, Mexico City 21 DF Mexico. **Tel** 563 0712. **LC** Z671; .C37. **DD** 020/.5. ***Continues*** *Ciencia Bibliotecaria, 0185-0105.*

US/8755-5727
CD DATA REPORT. ***Suspended.*** **See** Computers-Optical Storage, CD-ROM Applications.

US/1059-5260
CD-ROM HANDBOOK. [CD-ROM handb.]. **Added/Corp** EBSCO Subscription Services. **VFOAT** CD ROM Handbook. (1989)-. English. an. $19.95. EBSCO Publishing / Boston, 83 Pine Street, Peabody MA 01960. **Tel** (800)653-2726 North America, (508)535-8500, FAX (508)535-8545. **DD** 621. available on CD-ROM from EBSCO Publishing - Peabody.
Desc: Lists various CD-ROM products that are available for purchase through EBSCO Subscription Services or EBSCO Publishing. Contains product name, pricing information, and a brief description of the product.

US/0893-9934
CD-ROM LIBRARIAN. ***Title Change.*** **See** Computers.

●US/1066-274X
CD-ROM WORLD. **See** Computers-Optical Storage, CD-ROM Applications.

US/1052-2638
CD-ROMS IN PRINT (CD-ROM VERSION). **See** Computers-Optical Storage, CD-ROM Applications.

●US/1063-8784
CDMARC SERIALS. (CDMARC SERIALS [COMPUTER FILE] : THE CONSER DATABASE.). [CDMARC ser.]. **Main/Corp** CONSER Program. **Added/Corp** Library of Congress. Cataloging Distribution Service. **VFOAT** CD MARC Serials. (1992)-. English. qt (4 issues). $405.00 North America; $440.00 other. Library of Congress / Cataloging Distribution Service, Washington DC 20541-5017. **Tel** (800)255-3666, (202)707-6100, FAX (202)707-1334. **LC** Z699.4.C25. **DD** 025.
Desc: Access to CONSER serial records.

US/1041-2956
CDMARC SUBJECTS. ***Title Change.*** (CDMARC SUBJECTS [COMPUTER FILE].). [CDMARC subj.]. **Main/Corp** Library of Congress. Subject Cataloging Division. **Added/Corp** Library of Congress. Cataloging Distribution Service. **VFOAT** CD MARC Subjects. Issue 1 (June 1988)-(19??). English. qt. Library of Congress / Cataloging Distribution Service, Washington DC 20541-5017. **Tel** (800)255-3666, (202)707-6100, FAX (202)707-1334. **DD** 025. ***Continued by*** *Library of Congress. Office for Subject Cataloging Policy. CDMARC Subjects.*

US/1041-2956
CDMARC SUBJECTS. (CDMARC SUBJECTS [COMPUTER FILE].). [CDMARC subj.]. **Main/Corp** Library of Congress. Office for Subject Cataloging Policy. **Added/Corp** Library of Congress. Cataloging Distribution Service. **VFOAT** CD MARC Subjects. (199?)-. English. qt (Jan., Mar., Jun., Sep.). $360.00 North America; $475.00 other. Library of Congress / Cataloging Distribution Service, Washington DC 20541-5017. **Tel** (800)255-3666, (202)707-6100, FAX (202)707-1334. **LC** Z695. **DD** 025. ***Continues*** *Library of Congress. Subject Cataloging Division. CDMARC Subjects, 1041-2956.*

US/0897-3296
CDROM DATABASES. **See** Computers.

US/0895-2485
CDS CONNECTION. [CDS connect.]. **Added/Corp** Library of Congress. Cataloging Distribution Service. **VAT** Cataloging Distribution Service Connection. (1988)-. Periodical. English. sa. Free. Library of Congress / Cataloging Distribution Service, Washington DC 20541-5017. **Tel** (800)255-3666, (202)707-6100, FAX (202)707-1334. **DD** 025.

NZ
CENSUS OF LIBRARIES. **Main/Corp** New Zealand. Dept. of Statistics. (19??)-. English. ir. Government Printing Office / New Zealand, 10 Mulgrave Street, Wellington New Zealand. **Tel** 011 64 4 4737211, FAX 011 64 4 734943, telex GOVPRINT NZ 31320. **(Subscription address:** Government Printing Office / New Zealand, PO Box 12052, Wellington New Zealand.**)** ***Continues*** *New Zealand. Census and Statistics Dept. Census of Libraries.*
Desc: Statistics on book stocks, circulations, staff, finances, etc. of national, public, departmental and specialist libraries. Also includes statistics on tertiary institutes, schools and larger book clubs.

US/0887-1116
CENTENNIAL STATE LIBRARIES. [Centen. state libr.]. **Added/Corp** Colorado State Library. Vol. 1, No. 11/12 (Nov./Dec. 1985)-. Periodical. English. mo (12 issues). free upon request. Centennial State Libraries, 201 East Colfax Avenue, Room 309, Denver CO 80203. **Tel** (303)866-6732, FAX (303)830-0793. **ED** Kim Luchau. **DD** 027. **Bk Rev. Circ:** 3,000. ***Continues*** *Newsletter (Colorado State Library).*
Desc: Library news, events and information that interests library professionals, paraprofessionals, trustees, board members, friends and state legislators.

SP
CENTRO NACIONAL DE RESTAURACION DE LIBROS Y DOCUMENTOS : ACTIVIDADES. **Main/Corp** Centro Nacional de Restauracion de Libros y Documentos (Spain). Spanish. **LC** Z701; .C456A. **DD** 025.7.

KE
CHAIRMAN'S REPORT - EAST AFRICAN LIBRARY ASSOCIATION. KENYA BRANCH. ***Title Change.*** **Main/Corp** East African Library Association. Kenya Branch. English. an. Kenya Library Association, PO Box 46031, Nairobi Kenya. **Tel** 72550/1. **LC** Z673; .E3. **DD** 020/.6234/6762. ***Continued by*** *Maktaba.*

US/0276-0525
CHALLENGE TO CHANGE : LIBRARY APPLICATIONS OF CONCEPTS. ***Ceased.*** [Chall. change, Libr. appl. concepts]. No. 1-( )-?. Monographic series. English. ir. Libraries Unlimited Inc., PO Box 6633, Department 920, Englewood CO 80155. **Tel** (800)237-6124.

CN/0848-1059
CHANGING FACES, CHANGING TIMES. (CHANGING FACES, CHANGING TIMES : NEWSLETTER OF THE CLA INTEREST GROUP ON LIBRARY AND INFORMATION SERVICES FOR THE AGING.). [Chang. faces chang. times]. **Added/Corp** CLA Interest Group on Library and Information Services for the Aging. Vol. 1, No. 1 (Winter 1988)-. Periodical. English. sa. Free. CLA Interest Group On Library and Information Services for the Aging, c/o Editor, Sylvia Crooks, UBC School of Library Archival & Information Studies Vancouver British Columbia V6T 1Y3 Canada. **DD** 027.6/22/0971.

CN/0829-1152
CHANNEL (ONTARIO LIBRARY SERVICE, TRENT). ***Suspended.*** (CHANNEL.). [Channel]. (Spring 1985)-Suspended with (1987). Periodical. English. qt. Ontario Library Service Trent, 129 Church Street South, Richmond Ontario L4C 1W4 Canada. **DD** 027.4713/5. ***Continues*** *Comment (Ontario Library Service, Trent), 0834-2091.*

US
CHAPTER ONE : A NEWSLETTER FOR FRIENDS OF THE UNIVERSITY OF FLORIDA LIBRARIES. **Added/Corp** University of Florida. Libraries. Vol. 1, No. 1 (Fall 1990)-. Newsletter. English. sa.

CN/1191-0887
CHECK IT OUT!. (CHECK IT OUT! / MISSISSAUGA LIBRARY SYSTEM.). [Check it out!]. **Added/Corp** Mississauga Library System. Vol. 1, Issue 1 (Sept./Oct. 1991)-. Periodical. English. bm. Limited free distribution. Mississauga Library System, 110 Dundas Street West, Mississauga Ontario L5B 1H3 Canada. **DD** 027.4713/535.

US
CHECKLIST OF OFFICIAL PUBLICATIONS OF THE STATE OF ARIZONA. **Main/Corp** Arizona. Dept. of Library, Archives & Public Records. **VFOAT** Checklist of Publications of the State of Arizona. (1987)-. English. mo. Library Archives and Public Records Division, Phoenix AZ 85007. **Tel** (602)255-4343. ***Continues*** *Arizona Department of Library, Archives & Public Records. Monthly Checklist of Publications (Excluding Periodicals) of the State of Arizona.*

US
CHICAGO LAW LIBRARY BULLETIN. **Main/Corp** Chicago Association of Law Libraries. (19??)-. Periodical. English. ir (5 issues). Comes with Chicago Association of Law Libraries membership. Chicago Association of Law Libraries, PO Box 1767, Chicago IL 60690. **Tel** (312)551-2093.

US/0890-5746
CHILDREN'S BOOK REVIEW (PROVO, UTAH). (CHILDREN'S BOOK REVIEW / BRIGHAM YOUNG UNIVERSITY.). [Child. book rev.]. **Added/Corp** Brigham Young University. **VFOAT** BYU Children's Book Review. (1980)-. English. Five times a year. $15.00 (one year), $28.00 (two years). Brigham Young University / Department of Elementary Education, 215 McKay Building, Provo UT 84602. **Tel** (801)378-4077. **ED** Marsha D. Broadway. **DD** 028. Index available. **Circ:** 250.

US
CHILDREN'S CATALOG. **Added/Corp** H.W. Wilson Company. 1st Ed. (1909)-. Catalog. English. 16th Edition: $90.00 US and Canada; $100.00 other. H W Wilson Company, 950 University Avenue, Bronx NY 10452. **Tel** (800)367-6770, (718)588-8400, FAX (718)590-1617, telex 4990003 HWILSON. **LC** Z1037; .W76. **DD** 028.5.
Desc: Provides a balanced list of the new and established fiction and non-fiction titles written for children from preschool through the sixth grade.

FR/0154-0327
CHIMIE PURE ET CHIMIE APPLIQUEE. LEXIQUE. French. an. Informascience, Centre de Documentation Scientifique et Technique Service des Abonnements, 26 rue Boyer, 75971 Paris Cedex 20 France. **LC** Z695.1.C5; C47. **DD** 025.4/966.

CC
CHING PAO HSUEH KAN. **VFOAT** Qingbao Xuekan; Journal of Information Science. Periodical. Chinese. qt. RMBY0.50. Post Office Chung-tu Shih, Cheng-tu Shih, People's Republic of China. **LC** Z671; .C48. **DD** 020.5.

CN/0705-2480
CHINOOK REGIONAL LIBRARY DIRECTORY. **Main/Corp** Chinook Regional Library. 1977-. Directory. English. ir. Chinook Regional Library, 1240 Chaplin Street West, Swift Current Saskatchewan S9H 0G8 Canada. **Tel** (306)773-3186. **DD** 027.4/025/71243. **Circ:** 175 (ctrl).
Desc: A listing of names and addresses of staff, board members and other persons and organizations pertinent to the operation of the Chinook Regional Library.

US/0009-4978
CHOICE. [Choice]. **VFOAT** Books for College Libraries. Vol. 1 (March 1964)-. Academic Scholarly Publication. English. mo (11 issues). $165.00 US; $187.00 (surface mail) other. Association of College and Research Libraries, 50 East Huron Street, Chicago IL 60611. **Tel** (312)944-6780. **ED** Patricia Sabosik. **LC** Z1035; .C5. **[CCC]**. Index available. cum. index. **Bk Rev. Ad Acc. Circ:** 4,800. available on microfilm and microfiche from University Microfilms International (UMI). Documents available from UMI Article Clearinghouse.
Desc: Choice book reviews are brief, critical reviews of scholarly books and quality nonfiction titles commonly in a college or university library or on a scholar's bookshelf. Choice publishes more than 6500 new reviews each year providing one of the most complete sources of critical information on new academic books. Published by the Association of College and Research Libraries.
Ind/Abst Acad. Ind. [Computer File] (1992-); Book Rev. Digest; Book Rev. Index; Expand. Acad. Index (1992-); Leg. Inf. Manage. Index; Libr. Lit.; Newsp. Period. Abstr. (1991-); Sci. Fict. Fantasy Book Rev. Index.

CN/0706-2249
CHOIX : DOCUMENTATION IMPRIMEE. [Choix, Doc. impr.]. No. 78/1 Jan. 1978-. Periodical. French. Ten times a year. 110.00Can$ Canada; 130.00Can$ US; 180.00Can$ other. Services Documentaires Multimedia Inc, 75 rue de Port-Royal, Suite 300, Montreal Quebec H3L 3T1 Canada. **Tel** (514)382-0895, FAX (514)384-9139. Index available. cum. index. **Bk Rev. Circ:** 800 (ctrl). available on microfiche. ***Continues in part*** *Choix: Documentation des Bibliotheques, 0380-9935.*
Desc: List and analyses of French-language printed materials for adults and young people. Approximately 12,000 new entries per year. Database contents 150,000 entries.

CN/0706-2265
CHOIX JEUNESSE : DOCUMENTATION IMPRINEE. [Choix jeun., Doc. impr.]. **Added/Corp** Services Documentaires Multimedia. Quebec (Province). Centrale des Bibliotheques. No. 78/1 (Mar. 1978)-. Periodical. French. Ten times a year. 32.00Can$ Canada, 40.00Can$ US, 47.00Can$ other (without annual cumulative); 41.00Can$ Canada, 51.00Can$ US, 58.00Can$ other (with annual cumulative). Services Documentaires Multimedia Inc, 75 rue de Port-Royal, Suite 300, Montreal Quebec H3L 3T1 Canada. **Tel** (514)382-0895, FAX (514)384-9139. Index available. cum. index. ctrl circ. available on microfiche. ***Supersedes in part*** *Choix Jeunesse: Documentation pour les Enfants de 4 A 12 Ans., 0706-2400.*

UK/0309-4170
CHRISTIAN LIBRARIAN. Added/Corp Librarians' Christian Fellowship. (19??)-. English.
Ind/Abst Child. Lit. Abstr. (19??-).

US/0412-3131
CHRISTIAN LIBRARIAN (CEDARVILLE, OHIO), THE. (THE CHRISTIAN LIBRARIAN.). [Christ. librarian:]. **Added/Corp** Association of Christian Librarians. (1957)-. Periodical. English. qt. $20.00 US, Canada and Mexico; $24.00 other. The Christian Librarian, PO Box 4, Cedarville OH 45314. **Tel** (513)766-2211, FAX (513)766-2337. **ED** Ron Jordahl. **DD** 026. **CODEN** CHLIDJ. **Bk Rev. Ad Acc. Circ:** 425. available on microfilm and microfiche from University Microfilms International (UMI). Documents available from Ask*IEEE.
Desc: Includes professional articles, book reviews of library science, reference and religious books, and a review of current library literature.
Ind/Abst Child. Lit. Abstr. (19??-); Christ. Period. Index (-19??); INSPEC (Nov. 1981-); Libr. Inf. Sci. Abstr.

US/0163-3732
CHRONOLOG (PALO ALTO, CALIF.). (CHRONOLOG : MONTHLY NEWSLETTER OF THE DIALOG INFORMATION RETRIEVAL SERVICE.). [Chronolog]. **Added/Corp** DIALOG Information Retrieval Service. Lockheed Palo Alto Research Laboratory. Information Systems Programs. DIALOG Information Services. **VFOAT** Chronolog. Vol. 4, Issue 6 (July 1976)-. Newsletter. English. mo. Dialog Information Services, 3460 Hillview Avenue, Palo Alto CA 94304. **Tel** (415)858-4240, (800)334-2564. available on an online database (file 410/Full-Text) from DIALOG. ***Continues*** *DIALOG Chronolog.*
Ind/Abst Cumul. Index Nurs. Allied Health Lit.; Int. Aerosp. Abstr.; World Publ. Monit.

CC/1001-8867
CHUNG-KUO TU SHU KUAN HSUEH PAO. Added/Corp Chung-Kuo Tu Shu Kuan Hsueh Hui (Peking, China). **VFOAT** Zhongguo Tushuguanxuebao; Bulletin of the Library Science in China. (1991)-. Periodical. Chinese (summaries and/or abstracts in English). qt. Shu Mu Wen Hsien Chu Pan She, Chung-Kuo Kuo Chi Tu Shu Mao I Tsung Kung Ssu, PO Box 399, Pei-Ching, People's Republic of China. **LC** Z673.C52; T8. **DD** 020/.5. **CODEN** ZTXUEB. ***Continues*** *Tu shu Kuan Hsueh Tung Hsun.*

US/0009-6342
CHURCH & SYNAGOGUE LIBRARIES. [Church synag. libr.]. **Added/Corp** Church and Synagogue Library Association. **VAT** Church and Synagogue Libraries. (1967)-. Periodical. English. bm. $18.00 US; $21.00 Canada; $22.00 other. Church & Synagogue Library Association, PO Box 19357, Portland OR 97280. **Tel** (503)244-6919. **ED** Sarah T. Moore (phone: (313)435-6948). **LC** Z675.C5; C518. **DD** 027.6/7/0973. Index available. cum. index. **Bk Rev**, (Qty: varies). **Ad Acc, Adv Mgr:** Judith Janzen. **Pr Rev. Circ:** 3,200 (ctrl). available on microfilm and microfiche from University Microfilms International (UMI).
Desc: Articles, news, book and media reviews for the church or synagogue librarian.
Ind/Abst Christ. Period. Index.

US/0884-6197
CHURCH MEDIA LIBRARY MAGAZINE. [Church media libr. mag.]. **Added/Corp** Southern Baptist Convention. Sunday School Board. (198?)-. Periodical. English. Four times a year (Jan., Apr., July, Oct.). $13.10. Southern Baptist Convention, 901 Commerce, Suite 750, Nashville TN 37203. **Tel** (615)244-2355, FAX (615)742-8919. **(Subscription address:** Sunday School Board - Customer Service, 127 Ninth Avenue North, Nashville, TN 37234 USA; telephone: (800)458-2772**) DD** 027. ***Continues*** *Media: Library Services Journal, 0009-6423.*
Ind/Abst South. Baptist Period. Index.

BL/0100-1965
CIENCIA DA INFORMACAO. [Cienc. inf.]. **Added/Corp** Conselho Nacional de Desenvolvimento Cientifico e Tecnologico. Instituto Brasileiro de Informacao em Ciencia e Tecnologia. Instituto Brasileiro de Bibliografia e Documentacao. Vol. 1 (1972)-. Periodical. Portuguese (English; summaries and/or abstracts in English). sa. $17.00. IBICT, SCN-Quadra 2 Bloco K, 70710 Brasilia DF Brazil. **Tel** 011 55 61 3214888, telex (061)2481. **LC** Z1007; .C65. **Bk Rev. Circ:** 1,000 (ctrl). available on an online database from IBICT via "RENPAC".
Desc: Original papers about specific problems on information science and technology in Brazil; translations of relevant papers, reviews, communications, news, letters to editor, editorials, etc.
Ind/Abst Inf. Sci. Abstr.; Libr. Inf. Sci. Abstr.; Libr. Lit.; PAIS Int. Print.

CU/0864-4659
CIENCIAS DE LA INFORMACION. ***Suspended.*** **Added/Corp** Instituto de Documentacion e Informacion Cientifica y Tecnica (Academia de Ciencias de Cuba) Sociedad Cubana de Informacion Cientifica y Tecnica. (19??)-(19??). Periodical. Spanish (table of contents in English). qt. Ediciones Cubanas, Obispo 527, Altos ESQ Bernaza, CP 10100 Havana Cuba. **Tel** 011 632980, 631942, FAX 011 631011, telex 512337, 6540. **LC** Z1007; .A15a. Documents available from Ask*IEEE. ***Continues*** *Instituto de Documentacion e Informacion Cientifica y Tecnica (Academia de Ciencias de Cuba). Actualidades de la Informacion Cientifica y Tecnica, 0138-7324.*
Ind/Abst INSPEC (1991-).

●CN
CINFOLINK DIRECTORY OF INFORMATION SERVICES IN CHINA. (1993/1994)-. Directory. English. $50.00. Espial Productions Ltd., 85 Roe Avenue, Toronto Ontario M5M 2H6 Canada. **Tel** (416)485-8063. **LC** Z674.5.C6; C55.

CN/0715-8661
CISTI NEWS. (CISTI NEWS / CANADA INSTITUTE FOR SCIENTIFIC AND TECHNICAL INFORMATION.). [CISTI news]. **Added/Corp** Canada Institute for Scientific and Technical Information. National Research Council Canada. **VFOAT** Actualites ICIST. **VAT** Canada Institute for Scientific and Technical Information News; Actualites Institut Canadien a l'Information Scientifique et Technique. Vol. 1, No. 1 (Feb. 1983)-. Periodical. English (French). qt. Free. National Research Council of Canada, Receiver General for Canada, Ottawa Ontario K1A 0R6 Canada. **Tel** (613)993-0362, FAX (613)952-7656. **ED** Elizabeth Katz. **DD** 026/.50971. Index available. cum. index. **Circ:** 3,000. ***Continues*** *Infoscope., 0382-2400.*

●US/1061-7434
CITATIONS FOR SERIAL LITERATURE. (CITATIONS FOR SERIAL LITERATURE [COMPUTER FILE].). [Cit. ser. lit.]. **VFOAT** CSL. Vol. 1, No. 1 (Feb. 20, 1992)-. Periodical. English. Free. Marilyn Geller, Serials & Acquisitions Services, Room 14E-210A, Massachusetts Institute of Technology, Cambridge MA 02139-4307. **DD** 051.
Desc: Available through BITNET.

US
CLA HANDBOOK AND MEMBERSHIP DIRECTORY / CATHOLIC LIBRARY ASSOCIATION. ***Title Change.*** **Main/Corp** Catholic Library Association. (1986)-(19??). Directory. English. an. Catholic Library Association, 700 Terrace Heights, St. Mary's #26, Winona MN 55987. **Tel** (507)457-6935, (507)457-1563. **ED** Michael W Rechel. **LC** Z673; .C364a. **DD** 020/.622/73. Index available. **Ad Acc. Circ:** 3,000 (ctrl). ***Separated from*** *The Catholic Library World.* ***Continued by*** *National Membership Directory.*
Desc: Provides the names of current CLA officers, chapter presidents, section chairs, committee chairs and representatives, as well as the historical list of conventions and past officers, plus an alphabetical listing of CLA members and subscribers with geographical index.

US/1056-0904
CLASS UPDATE. [CLASS update]. **Added/Corp** Cooperative Library Agency for Systems and Services (Calif.). **VAT** Cooperative Library Agency for Systems and Services Update. Issue No. 1 (Mar. 22, 1991)-. Periodical. English. Cooperative Library Agency for Systems & Services, 1415 Koll Circle, Suite 101, San Jose CA 91152-4698. **DD** 025.

UK
CLASSIFICATION: A CLASSIFICATION SCHEME FOR THE INSPEC DATABASE /INSPEC. Added/Corp INSPEC (Information Service) Institution of Electrical Engineers. **VFOAT** INSPEC Classification. (1991)-. English. ir. Institution of Electrical Engineers / IEE, Michael Faraday House, Six Hills Way, Stevenage Herts SG1 2AY UK. **Tel** 011 44 438 313311, FAX 011 44 438 742840, telex 825578 IEESTV G. **(Subscription address:** IEE / UK, Publications Sales Department, PO Box 96, Stevenage, Herts, SG1 2SD England.**) LC** IN PROCESS. ***Continues*** *INSPEC Classification.*

US
CLEAR PURPOSE, COMPLETE COMMITMENT. Vol. 1 (1973-1977)-. English. an. Louisiana State Library, PO Box 131, Baton Rouge LA 70821. **LC** Z732.L88; C552. **DD** 027.0763.

US
CLENEXCHANGE (MILFORD, OHIO : 1984). (CLENEXCHANGE.). Vol. 1, No. 1 (Sept. 1984)-. Periodical. English. qt. Clenexchange, c/o Marie E Bryan, 250 First Street, Woodland CA 95695. **(Subscription address:** Elaine Wingate, American Library Association, 50 East Huron Street, Chicago, IL 60611**) ED** Marie E Bryan. **LC** Z668; .C743A. **DD** 020/.7/150973. **Bk Rev.** ***Continues*** *Clenexchange, 0360-0688.*

US/0736-0045
CLIC QUARTERLY. ***Ceased.*** (CLIC QUARTERLY : A JOURNAL OF OPINION, RESEARCH AND ADVOCACY IN THE FIELD OF LIBRARY AND INFORMATION RESOURCES MANAGEMENT.). [CLiC q.]. **Added/Corp** Citizen's Library Council of New York State. **VAT** Citizens' Library Council of New York State Quarterly. Vol. 1, No. 1 (1982)-Vol. 4 (1984). Periodical. English. qt. Citizens Library Council of New York State, 135 West Avenue, Draper Hall 113, Albany NY 12222. **Tel** (518)455-6288. **ED** Richard S Halsey. **LC** Z678.4.N7; C57. **DD** 025.1/09747. **Ad Acc. Circ:** 400. ***Continues*** *CLIC Newsletter (Citizens' Library Council of New York State).*
Desc: Deals with advocacy, opinion, and research in library, cultural, and information fields. Different types of library allied institution highlighted in each issue.
Ind/Abst Libr. Inf. Sci. Abstr. (?-?); Libr. Lit. (?-?).

II/0970-0943
CLIS OBSERVER. Added/Corp Centre for Library and Information Studies (New Delhi, India). Vol. 1, No. 1 (Apr. 1984)-. Periodical. English. qt. $20.00. CLIS Observer, C/30 Lajpat Nagar III, New Delhi 110024 India. **Tel** 6836119. **(Subscription address:** Prints India, 11 Darya Ganj, New Delhi 110002 India.**) ED** D R Kalia. **LC** Z665.2.I4; C58. **DD** 020/.954. **Bk Rev. Ad Acc. Circ:** 1,000 (ctrl).
Ind/Abst Indian Libr. Sci. Abstr.; Libr. Inf. Sci. Abstr.

US/0892-0605
CLR REPORTS. [CLR rep.]. **Added/Corp** Council on Library Resources. **VAT** Council on Library Resources Reports. Vol. 1, No. 1 (Feb. 1987)-. Periodical. English. ir (two to three times per year). Free. Council on Library Resources, 1785 Massachusetts Avenue Northwest, #313, Washington DC 20036. **Tel** (202)483-7474, FAX (202)483-6410. **ED** Ellen Timmer. **LC** Z671; .C64. **DD** 025. **Circ:** 4,000. ***Continues*** *CLR Recent Developments, 0034-1169.*
Desc: Describes programs of CLR, a private operating foundation.

US/0196-3309
CMLEA JOURNAL. Main/Corp CMLEA. **VAT** California Media and Library Educators Association Journal. Vol. 1 (Fall 1977)-. Periodical. English. sa. $15.00. CMLEA, 1499 Old Bayshore Highway, Suite 142, Burlington CA 94010. **Tel** (415)692-2350. **ED** Robert Skapura. **LC** Z675.S3; C183a. **DD** 027.8/09794. **Ad Acc Circ:** 1,800. available on microfiche. ***Formed by the union of*** *California School Libraries* ***and*** *Journal of Media and Technology.*
Desc: Addresses current issues of concern to librarians and media specialists working in educational institutions.
Ind/Abst Calif. Period. Index; Libr. Lit. (1991-).

US/0738-4319
COGNOTES. (COGNOTES : THE OFFICIAL CONFERENCE NEWSLETTER OF THE AMERICAN LIBRARY ASSOCIATION.). [Cognotes]. **Main/Corp** American Library Association. 102nd Annual Conference, Los Angeles (June 25, 1983)-. Newsletter. English. ir. Junior Members Round Table, c/o Ohio State University, 030 Main Library, 1858 Neil Avenue Mall, Columbus OH 43210. **ED** Jana Lonberger. ***Continues*** *Cognotes Daily News.*

US/0160-4953
COLLECTION BUILDING. [Collect. build.]. Vol. 1 (1978)-. Periodical. English. qt. $60.50 US; $63.50 Canada; $65.50 other. Neal-Schuman Publishers Inc., 100 Varick Street, New York NY 10013. **Tel** (212)925-8650, FAX (212)219-8916. **ED** Arthur Curley. **LC** Z689; .C67. **DD** 025.2/1. cum. index. **Bk Rev. Ad Acc.**
Desc: Strives to aid librarians in all facets of collection development. Designed to help improve your service to users. Provides practical and authoritative articles that study new informational formats and how to evaluate them; explore various aspects of collection development; provide studies and analyses of resource development; and examine the special needs of particular libraries.
Ind/Abst Inf. Sci. Abstr.; Libr. Inf. Sci. Abstr.; Libr. Lit.

FR
COLLECTION DES MELANGES DE LA BIBLIOTHEQUE DE LA SORBONNE. **VFOAT** Collection Melanges de la Bibliotheque de la Sorbonne. Monographic series. French. Price varies per volume. Aux Amateurs de Livres International, 62 Avenue de Suffren, 75015 Paris France. **Tel** 011 33 1 45671838.

US/0146-2679
COLLECTION MANAGEMENT. [Collect. manage.]. (1977)-. Periodical. English. qt. $125.00 US; $175.00 other. The Haworth Press Inc, 10 Alice Street, Binghamton NY 13904-1580. **Tel** (607)722-5857, (800)3-HAWORTH, FAX (607)722-1424. **ED** Peter Gellatly (editor's address: PO Box 15680, Seattle, WA 98115). **LC** Z703.6; .D4. **DD** 020/.5. **CODEN** COMADF. **Bk Rev. Ad Acc. Pr Rev. Acid Free. Circ:** 529 (ctrl).

available on microfilm and microfiche from University Microfilms International (UMI). Documents available from Haworth Document Delivery Service. ***Continues*** *De-Acquisitions Librarian, 0098-2121.*
Desc: Highly practical journal focuses on the important tasks of collection management and development and continues to be an essential resource for all librarians involved in this field. Examines the latest developments and their implications for college, university and research libraries of all types. Presents many different kinds of articles on an extensive range of topics.
Ind/Abst Cumul. Index Nurs. Allied Health Lit.; Index Period. Artic. Relat. Law; Inf. Instruc. Technol.; Inf. Sci. Abstr.; Leg. Inf. Manage. Index (19??-199?); Libr. Inf. Sci. Abstr.; Libr. Lit.; Ref. Z.

CN/0226-3300
COLLECTION UPDATE. [Collect. update]. No. 1- 1979-. Periodical. English. an. $6.50. Collection Update Library, University of Guelph, Guelph Ontario N1G 2W1 Canada. **ED** Carol Goodger-Hill. **DD** 027.7713/43. Index available. cum. index. **Circ:** 100 (ctrl).
Desc: Articles from our university community to increase awareness of the resources of library, particularly the special collections.

US/8755-3473
COLLECTIONS (NEWARK, DEL.). (COLLECTIONS.). [Collections]. **Main/Corp** University of Delaware. Library. Vol. 1 (1984)-. Periodical. English. ir. $25.00. University of Delaware Library Associates, University of Delaware Library, Newark DE 19717-5267. **Tel** (302)451-2231. **ED** Alice Schreyer. **DD** 027. **Circ:** 500 (ctrl).
Desc: Articles about or based on the manuscript, book or other collections of the University of Delaware Library.

●US/1065-5859
COLLECTIONS SERVICES NEWS. **Main/Corp** Library of Congress. Collections Services. (1992)-. Periodical. English. mo.

US/0010-0870
COLLEGE & RESEARCH LIBRARIES. [Coll. res. libr.]. **Added/Corp** Association of College and Reference Libraries (U.S.) Association of College and Research Libraries. **VFOAT** College & Research Libraries; C & RL. **VAT** College and Research Libraries. Vol. 1 (Dec. 1939)-. Academic Scholarly Publication. English. Six times a year (Jan., Mar., May, July, Sept., Nov.). $50.00 US; $55.00 Canada & Mexico; $60.00 others. Association of College and Research Libraries, 50 East Huron Street, Chicago IL 60611. **Tel** (312)944-6780. **LC** Z671; .C6. **NLM** Z 671 C697. **[CCC]. Bk Rev. Ad Acc. Pr Rev. Circ:** 10,000. available on microfilm and microfiche from University Microfilms International (UMI). Documents available from The Genuine Article.
Desc: Articles in all fields of interest and concern to academic and research librarians-scholarly and research oriented. Major scholarly serial in field of academic librarianship.
Ind/Abst Acad. Search (July 1993-); Am. Hist. Life (1964-); Annu. Bibliogr. Engl. Lang. Lit.; ARTbibliogr. Mod.; Book Rev. Index; Contents Pages Educ.; Curr. Contents Soc. Behav. Sci.; Curr. Index J. Educ.; Educ. Index; High. Educ. Abstr. (1985-); INFO-SOUTH Abstr.; Inf. Instruc. Technol.; Inf. Sci. Abstr. [Full Cov.]; Int. Labour Doc.; Law Office Inf. Serv.; Leg. Inf. Manage. Index (19??-199?); Libr. Inf. Sci. Abstr.; Libr. Lit.; PAIS Int. Print (1991-?); Pollut. Abstr. Indexes; Res. Alert [Full Cov.]; Soc. Sci. Cit. Index [Full Cov.]; Stud. Women Abstr.

US/0099-0086
COLLEGE & RESEARCH LIBRARIES NEWS. [Coll. res. libr. news]. **Added/Corp** Association of College and Research Libraries. **VAT** College and Research Libraries News. (Jan. 1967)-. Periodical. English. Eleven times a year. $35.00 US; $40.00 Canada and Mexico; $45.00 other. Association of College and Research Libraries, 50 East Huron Street, Chicago IL 60611. **Tel** (312)944-6780. **ED** George M Eberhart and Cheryl Robinson-Smith. **LC** Z671; .C62. **DD** 020. **NLM** Z 671 C697A. **[CCC]. Ad Acc.** available on microfilm and microfiche from University Microfilms International (UMI). ***Continues*** *ACRL News.*
Desc: Contains timely articles on new library technology as well as a highly interesting "People" column, and a classified advertising section.
Ind/Abst Acad. Search (July 1993-); Curr. Contents Soc. Behav. Sci.; Curr. Index J. Educ.; Educ. Index; Inf. Instruc. Technol.; Inf. Sci. Abstr.; Libr. Inf. Sci. Abstr.; Libr. Lit.; Pollut. Abstr. Indexes.

●US/1069-1316
COLLEGE & UNDERGRADUATE LIBRARIES. **VFOAT** College and Undergraduate Libraries. Vol. 1 (1994)-. Periodical. English. sa. $38.00 US; $53.20 other. The Haworth Press Inc, 10 Alice Street, Binghamton NY 13904-1580. **Tel** (607)722-5857, (800)3-HAWORTH, FAX (607)722-1424. **ED** Alice Harrison Bahr. **Acid Free.** Documents available from Ask*IEEE, Haworth Document Delivery Service.
Desc: Dedicated to helping academic libraries with small staffs, large needs, minimal travel budgets, and high goals.
Ind/Abst High. Educ. Abstr.; Inf. Sci. Abstr.; INSPEC; Libr. Inf. Sci. Abstr.; Oper. Res./Manag. Sci.; Ref. Z.

CN/0833-0980
COLLNET. (COLLNET : A NEWSLETTER OF THE COLLECTIONS DEVELOPMENT INTEREST GROUP OF THE ATLANTIC PROVINCES LIBRARY ASSOCIATION.). [CollNet]. (Oct. 1986)-. Newsletter. English. qt. Free. CollNet, c/o School of Library Service, Dalhousei University, Halifax Nova Scotia B3H 4H8 Canada. **DD** 025.2/06/0715.

US
COLORADO EDUCATION & LIBRARY DIRECTORY. **See** Education.

US/0147-9733
COLORADO LIBRARIES. [Colo. libr.]. **Added/Corp** Colorado Library Association. (1974)-. Periodical. English. Four times a year (Mar. June, Sept., Oct.). $25.00 US; $35.00 other. Colorado Library Association, PO Box 489, Pinecliff CO 80471. **Tel** (303)642-0203, FAX (303)642-0201. **(Subscription address:** CLA Office, PO Box 4636, Englewood, CO 80155**) ED** Melinda Chesbro, University of Colorado, Campus Box 184, Boulder, CO 80309 (phone: (303)492-7469). **DD** 020. **Bk Rev**, (Qty: 25). **Ad Acc. Circ:** 1,200 (ctrl). ***Continues*** *CL, Colorado Libraries.*
Desc: Contains articles describing activities of libraries in Colorado, as well as current innovations in library science.
Ind/Abst Libr. Inf. Sci. Abstr.; Libr. Lit.

US/0069-6374
COLUMBIA UNIVERSITY STUDIES IN LIBRARY SERVICE. Vol. 1 1934-. Monographic series. English. ir. Price varies per volume. Columbia University Press, 136 South Broadway, Irvington NY 10533. **Tel** (914)591-9111.

JM/0378-1070
COMLA NEWSLETTER. [COMLA newsl.]. **Added/Corp** Commonwealth Library Association. **VFOAT** Commonwealth Library Association Newsletter. (19??)-. Periodical. English. qt. Free to members; $35.00 membership. Commonwealth Library Association, PO Box 144 Mona, Kingston 7 Jamaica. **Tel** (809)927-2123. **ED** Paul Xuereb. **LC** WMLC 93/1452. cum. index. **Bk Rev. Ad Acc. Circ:** 500 (ctrl).
Desc: Articles of special interest to librarians with emphasis on Commonwealth countries, including small island nations together with Australia, Britain, Canada, India and Nigeria; also news items culled from COMLA members.
Ind/Abst Libr. Inf. Sci. Abstr.

US/8755-4143
COMLINE. [Comline]. Vol. 1, No. 1 (Nov. 1984)-. Periodical. English. Three times a year. Free. Board of Trade of Kansas City, 4800 Main Street/Suite 303, Kansas City MO 64112. **Tel** (816)753-7367. **DD** 025.

●US
COMMERCIAL LIBRARY PUBLICATIONS LIST / UNITED STATES DEPARTMENT OF STATE LIBRARY. **See** Encyclopedias and General Reference Books.

US/0148-6225
COMMITTEE ON EAST ASIAN LIBRARIES BULLETIN. (BULLETIN - ASSOCIATION FOR ASIAN STUDIES, INC., COMMITTEE ON EAST ASIAN LIBRARIES.). **Main/Corp** Association for Asian Studies. Committee on East Asia Libraries. No. 53 (July 1977)-. Periodical. English. tq. Comes with membership. Association for Asian Studies Inc., University of Michigan, 1 Lane Hall, Ann Arbor MI 48109. **Tel** (313)665-2490, FAX (313)665-3801. **(Subscription address:** Association for Asian Studies, 1858 Neil Avenue, Mall Room 310, Columbus OH 43210.**) ED** Diane Perushek. **LC** Z688.E25; A76a. **DD** 026/.95. **Bk Rev. Ad Acc. Circ:** 350 (ctrl). ***Continues*** *Newsletter - Association for Asian Studies, Inc., Committee on East Asian Libraries, 0571-5520.*
Ind/Abst Libr. Lit.

●US/1041-7893
COMMUNICATION SERIALS. **See** Communication.

US/8755-9579
COMMUNICATIONS FOR BETTER LIVING. [Commun. better living]. Began in 1984?. Periodical. English. mo. Communications for Better Living, 1523 Jameson Drive, Virginia Beach VA 23464-6445. **DD** 028.

US/0277-8955
COMMUNICATOR (CHICAGO, ILL. : 1981), THE. (THE COMMUNICATOR / THE CHICAGO PUBLIC LIBRARY, THE CHICAGO LIBRARY SYSTEM.). Vol. 1, No. 1 (Oct. 1981)-. Periodical. English. mo. Free. Chicago Public Library, 425 North Michigan Avenue, Chicago IL 60611. ***Formed by the union of*** *Chicago Library System Communicator, 0147-4707* ***and*** *Chicago Public Library Newsletter.*

US/0276-3915
COMMUNITY & JUNIOR COLLEGE LIBRARIES. [Community jr. coll. libr.]. **VFOAT** Community and Junior College Libraries. Vol. 1, No. 1 (Fall 1982)-. English. sa. $60.00 US; $84.00 other. The Haworth Press Inc, 10 Alice Street, Binghamton NY 13904-1580. **Tel** (607)722-5857, (800)3-HAWORTH, FAX (607)722-1424. **ED** Peggy Holleman (editor's address: West Campus Learning Resource Center, Pima Community College, Tucson, AZ 85709), J F Borowski (editor's address: Learning Resource Center, Oakton Community College, 1600 East Golf Road, Des Plaines, IL 60016). **LC** Z675.J8; C65. **DD** 027.7/05. **CODEN** CJCLDV. **Bk Rev. Ad Acc. Pr Rev. Acid Free. Circ:** 427. available on microfilm and microfiche from University Microfilms International (UMI). Documents available from Ask*IEEE, Haworth Document Delivery Service.
Desc: For all community and junior college librarians. Presents news of special relevance and importance such as new legislation, systems and development that affect the field.
Ind/Abst Curr. Index J. Educ. (March 1990); High. Educ. Abstr.; Inf. Sci. Abstr.; INSPEC (Fall 1982-); Libr. Inf. Sci. Abstr.; Libr. Lit.; Ref. Z.

US
COMPACT CAMBRIDGE MEDLINE [COMPUTER FILE]. **See** Medical Science and Technology.

FR
COMPILATION DES REFERENCES UNIVERSITAIRES. French. JB Bailliere, 37 Avenue des Champs Elysees, 75008 Paris France. **Tel** 011 33 1 49536900.

US/1058-5257
COMPLETE CATALOG - LIBRARY OF CONGRESS. CATALOGING DISTRIBUTION SERVICE, THE. (THE COMPLETE CATALOG / CATALOGING DISTRIBUTION SERVICE.). [Complete cat. - Libr. Congr., Cat. Distrib. Serv.]. **Main/Corp** Library of Congress. Cataloging Distribution Service. **VFOAT** Library of Congress, the Complete Catalog; Bibliographic Products and Services ... Complete Catalog. (1991)-. Catalog. English. an. Free on request. Library of Congress / Cataloging Distribution Service, Washington DC 20541-5017. **Tel** (800)255-3666, (202)707-6100, FAX (202)707-1334. **LC** Z733.U58; L38a. **DD** 016.0253/13. ***Continues*** *Access CDS, 1058-5249.*

US/1040-4074
COMPREHENSIVE MEDLINE/EBSCO CD-ROM. **See** Medical Science and Technology.

US/0715-9048
COMPUTER PROCESSING OF CHINESE & ORIENTAL LANGUAGES. **See** Linguistics.

US/0095-0130
COMPUTERIZED SERIALS SYSTEMS SERIES. **Added/Corp** Larc Association. Vol. 1 (1973)-. Monographic series. English. bm. Price varies per volume. Larc Press Ltd, 105 117 W 4th Avenue, Peoria IL 61602. **DD** 025.

US/1041-7915
COMPUTERS IN LIBRARIES. [Comput. libr.]. Vol. 9, No. 1 (Jan. 1989)-. Periodical. English. Ten times a year. $87.00 US; $103.79 Canada, Central and South America. Mecklermedia Corporation, 11 Ferry Lane West, Westport CT 06880. **Tel** (203)226-6967, (800)632-5537, FAX (203)454-5840. **(Subscription address:** Fulco, 30 Broad Street, Denville NJ 07834.**) ED** Eric Flower. **LC** Z678.9.A1; S6. **DD** 025.30285/416. **CODEN** CPLIE8. **[CCC].** Index available. cum. index. **Bk Rev. Ad Acc. Circ:** 4,200. available on microfilm and microfiche from University Microfilms International (UMI); available on an online database (file 648/Full-Text) from DIALOG. Documents available from Ask*IEEE, UMI Article Clearinghouse. ***Continues*** *Small Computers in Libraries, 0275-6722;* ***Absorbed*** *Systems Librarian & Automation Review, 0890-8354; Small Computers in Libraries. Buyer's Guide & Consultant Directory, 0896-9485.*
Desc: Covers computer technology in libraries.
Ind/Abst Acad. Ind. [Computer File] (1992-); Acad. Search (July 1993-); ACM Guide Comput. Lit.; Comput. Lit. Index; Comput. Rev. Index; Comput. Rev.; Curr. Index J. Educ.; Expand. Acad. Index (1992-); Gen. Period. Index (1985-); INFO-SOUTH Abstr.; Inf. Instruc. Technol.; Inf. Sci. Abstr.; INSPEC (Feb. 1989-); Int. Aerosp. Abstr.; Leg. Inf. Manage. Index; Libr. Inf. Sci. Abstr.; Libr. Lit.; Mag. ASAP Plus [Full Txt.]; Mag. Index Plus (1992-); Mag. Search; Microcomput. Index (Jan. 1989-); Newsp. Period. Abstr. (1992-); Trade Ind. ASAP [Full Txt.]; Trade Ind. Index [Full Txt.].

CN/1188-6331
COMPUTERS IN SCHOOL LIBRARIES. [Comput. sch. libr.]. Vol. 1, No. 1 (Sept. 1990)-. Periodical. English. Four times a year (Feb., May, Sept., Dec.). 13.00Can$. Computers in School Libraries, 1075 Red Pine Crescent, Mississauga ONT L5H 4E4 Canada. **Tel** (416)278-7412. **ED** Bruce Winter, (phone: (416)278-7412). **DD** 027.8/028/5. **Ad Acc.**

US/0896-0666
CONNECT (SUISUN, CALIF.). ***Ceased.*** (CONNECT.). [Connect]. July 1987-Ceased July 1989. Periodical. English. mo. Connect Libraries and Telecommunications, 4415 Tilbury Drive, San Jose CA

95130. **Tel** (408)973-3258. **ED** Steve Cisten. **DD** 020. **Bk Rev. Circ:** 200.
Desc: Covers developments in telecommunication technology, legislation and its use in libraries and information center.
Ind/Abst Geogr. Abstr. Human Geogr. (?-?).

US
CONNECTICARD ANNUAL STATISTICAL REPORT. See Library and Information Sciences-Abstracting, Bibliographies and Statistics.

US/0010-616X
CONNECTICUT LIBRARIES (1954-).
(1954)-. Periodical. English. mo (except combined July/Aug.). $35.00. Connecticut Library Association, PO Box 1046, Norwich CT 06105. **Tel** (203)232-4825. **ED** David L. Kapp. **Ad Acc. Circ:** 1,000 (ctrl). available on microfilm and microfiche from University Microfilms International (UMI).
Desc: Short articles (2,500 words) and news items relating to library activities in Connecticut and to activities of the Connecticut Library Association.
Ind/Abst Libr. Lit.

CN/1180-2014
CONNECTIONS - ONTARIO. MINISTRY OF CULTURE AND COMMUNICATIONS.
(CONNECTIONS.). [Connect. - Ont., Minist. Cult. Commun.]. **Added/Corp** Ontario. Ministry of Culture and Communications. Ontario. Libraries and Community Information Branch. **VFOAT** Connexions. **VAT** Connexions - Ontario. Ministere de la Culture et des Communications. Vol. 1, No. 1 (Spring 1990)-. Periodical. English (French). sa. Culture and Communications, Government of the Northwest Territories, PO Box 1320, Yellowknife Northwest Territories X1A 2L9 Canada. **DD** 354.7130085/2/05.
Desc: Information for public libraries and community information services.

US/0163-8610
CONSER. ***Title Change.*** (CONSER : [NEWSLETTER].). [CONSER]. **Added/Corp** OCLC. CONSER Program. **VFOAT** Conversion of Serials; CONSER Newsletter. No. 1 (Oct. 1978)-(1993). Periodical. English. sa. OCLC Asia Pacific Services, 6565 Frantz Road, Dublin OH 43017. **Tel** (800)848-5878, (614)764-6394 or 6000, FAX (614)764-6096. **LC** Z699.4.C25; C66. **DD** 025.3/432/0285. **CODEN** CNSRDL. ***Continued by** CONSERline, 1072-611X.*

US/0707-3747
CONSER MICROFICHE. [CONSER microfiche]. **Added/Corp** National Library of Canada. Library of Congress. **VFOAT** NLC/BNC CONSER Microfiche. (1978)-. English. an (current year supplements published during following year). $182.00 US. Library of Congress / Cataloging Distribution Service, Washington DC 20541-5017. **Tel** (800)255-3666, (202)707-6100, FAX (202)707-1334. **DD** 018/.134. **NLM** Z 6945 C753. Index available. cum. index.
Desc: Includes all serial records in the CONSER (Conversion of Serials) data base.

US/0190-3608
CONSER TABLES. ***Ceased.*** **Added/Corp** Library of Congress. Serial Record Division. (1979)-(19??). English. an (published in Feb. with update in July). Library of Congress / Cataloging Distribution Service, Washington DC 20541-5017. **Tel** (800)255-3666, (202)707-6100, FAX (202)707-1334. **LC** Z699.4.C25; B77. **DD** 025.3/4/3. **Bk Rev. Ad Acc.**
Desc: Reference tool for records in the CONSER database.

●US/1072-611X
CONSERLINE (WASHINGTON, D.C.).
(CONSERLINE [COMPUTER FILE] : NEWSLETTER OF THE CONSER (COOPERATIVE ONLINE SERIALS) PROGRAM, LIBRARY OF CONGRESS, AND OCLC, INC.). [CONSERline]. **Main/Corp** CONSER Program. **Added/Corp** Library of Congress. Serial Record Division. OCLC. **VFOAT** CONSER Line. No. 1 (Jan. 1994)-. Newsletter. English. sa. Free. OCLC Asia Pacific Services, 6565 Frantz Road, Dublin OH 43017. **Tel** (800)848-5878, (614)764-6394 or 6000, FAX (614)764-6096. **ED** Jean Hirons (Library of Congress) and Liz Bishoff (OCLC). **DD** 025. ***Continues** CONSER : [Newsletter], 0163-8610.*
Desc: A cooperative effort of the CONSER program containing contributions from program members and providing news of the CONSER program and related serials cataloging issues.

US/0192-2912
CONSERVATION ADMINISTRATION NEWS. [Conserv. adm. news]. **VFOAT** CAN; C.A.N. No. 1 (June 1979)-. Periodical. English. qt. $30.00. University of Texas Press, PO Box 7819, Austin TX 78713. **Tel** (512)471-4531, FAX (512)320-0668, telex 776453 UTEXPRES AUS. **ED** Robert H. Patterson. **Bk Rev. Ad Acc. Circ:** 500.
Desc: Publication of library and archival preservation.
Ind/Abst Abstr. Bull. Inst. Pap. Sci. Tech.; Art Archaeol. Tech. Abstr.; Graph. Arts Bull. Inst. Pap. Sci. Technol. (March 1989-July 1989); Inf. Instruc. Technol.; Libr. Inf. Sci. Abstr.; Libr. Lit.

US/0084-9243
CONTRIBUTIONS IN LIBRARIANSHIP AND INFORMATION SCIENCE. No. 1 (1972)-. Monographic series. English. Five times a year. Price varies per volume. Greenwood Press Inc., PO Box 5007, Westport CT 06881-5007. **Tel** (203)226-3571, FAX (203)222-1502. **ED** Paul Wasserman. **LC** UNC.

US/0145-8485
CONTRIBUTIONS TO LIBRARIANSHIP.
Added/Corp University of Texas at Austin. General Libraries. (1977)-. Monographic series. English. ir. Price varies per volume. University of Texas at Austin Perry Castaneda Library, Castaneda Library, 3.200, Austin TX 78712. **Tel** (512)471-3811. **ED** Mary Pound.
Desc: Monographs based on work programs of the general libraries, University of Texas at Austin.

SA
CONTRIBUTIONS TO LIBRARY SCIENCE. BIBLIOTEEKUNDIGE HYDRAES. Main/Corp South Africa. State Library. **Added/Corp** Pretoria. State Library. Biblioteekkundige Hydraes. No. 1 (1961)-. Monographic series. English (Afrikaans). ir. Price varies per volume. The State Library / Pretoria, PO Box 397, Pretoria South Africa. **Tel** 011 27 12 3861661. **LC** Z674; .P72. **Bk Rev. Ad Acc. Circ:** 350.
Desc: Series that deals with library and information science theory and practice in South Africa and Southern Africa.

●US/1060-8621
COOPERATIVE CATALOGING NEWS.
(COOPERATIVE CATALOGING NEWS: A PUBLICATION OF THE LIBRARY OF CONGRESS DESCRIPTIVE CATALOGING DIVISION.). [Coop. cat. news]. **Added/Corp** Library of Congress. Descriptive Cataloging Division. Vol. 1, No. 1 (Jan. 1992)-. Periodical. English. qt. Library of Congress / Descriptive Cataloging Division, The Division, Washington DC 20540. **DD** 025.

US/1040-4066
CORE MEDLINE/EBSCO CD-ROM. See Medical Science and Technology.

US/0734-449X
CORMOSEA BULLETIN. [CORMOSEA bull.]. **Added/Corp** Association for Asian Studies. Committee on Research Materials on Southeast Asia. **VAT** Committee on Research Materials on Southeast Asia Bulletin. Vol. 9 (1976)-. Periodical. English. sa. $10.00. Association for Asian Studies Inc., University of Michigan, 1 Lane Hall, Ann Arbor MI 48109. **Tel** (313)665-2490, FAX (313)665-3801. **ED** Constance M. Wilson. **LC** Z688.A75; S68. **DD** 026.959. **Bk Rev. Circ:** 175. ***Continues** CORMOSEA Newsletter, 0898-1949.*
Desc: Information about research in Southeast Asia and research materials for the study of Southeast Asia.

●US/0000-1392
CORNERSTONE (NEW PROVIDENCE, N.J.), THE. (THE CORNERSTONE : A QUARTERLY NEWSLETTER FOR CUSTOMERS OF R.R. BOWKER.). [Cornerstone]. **Added/Corp** R.R. Bowker Company. Vol. 1, No. 1 (Oct. 1, 1992)-. Newsletter. English. qt. Free to qualified persons. R R Bowker, A Reed Reference Publishing Company, Part of Reed International PLC, PO Box 31, 121 Chanlon Drive, New Providence NJ 07974. **Tel** (908)464-6800, (800)521-8110, FAX (908)665-6688, telex 138-755. **DD** 070.
Desc: Keeps you apprised of any new products or product enhancements, report on special offers and programs, and provide creative ideas for using Bowker's resources more effectively.

CN/0843-140X
CORPO CLIP. [Corpo clip]. No. 84 (March/April 1988)-. Periodical. French. ir. Corporation des Bibliothecaires Professionnels du Quebec, 307 Rue STE Catherine West, Room 320, Montreal QUE H2X 2A3 Canada. **Tel** (514)845-3327, FAX (514)845-1618. **DD** 020/.6234/714. ***Continues** Bulletin Argus, 0831-7909.*

US/0741-3270
CORPORATE AUTHOR AUTHORITY LIST. [Corp. author auth. list]. English. an. National Technical Information Service - NTIS, Room 2027S, 5285 Port Royal Road, Springfield VA 22161. **Tel** (703)487-4630, (703)487-4660, (703)487-4650, FAX (703)321-8547, telex 89-9405. **LC** Z695.8; .C67. **DD** 025.4/9.

●US/1061-5288
CORPORATE LIBRARY UPDATE.
(CORPORATE LIBRARY UPDATE : NEWS FOR INFORMATION MANAGERS AND SPECIAL LIBRARIANS.). [Corp. libr. update]. (1992)-. Periodical. English. bw. $69.00 US; $76.00 other. Cahners Publishing Company, 249 West 17th Street, New York NY 10011. **Tel** (212)645-0067, FAX (212)242-6987. **(Subscription address:** Corporate Library Update, PO Box 1983, Danbury CT 06813.**)** **DD** 025. **[CCC].**
Desc: Professional newsletter for librarians and information managers in a corporate environment. Each issue contains management tips, marketing ideas, new product and technological developments, seminar and convention listings, news stories, and classifieds.

US
COUNTY LINE, THE. Main/Corp Toledo-Lucas County Public Library. (197?)-. Periodical. English. mo. Free on request. Toledo-Lucas County Public Library, 325 Michigan Street, Toledo OH 43624. **Tel** (419)255-7055. **ED** Gretchen Kincaid. **Circ:** 3,000 (ctrl).
Desc: A record of the activities and resources of the Toledo-Lucas County Public Library for its friends and users.

US/0011-0418
COURIER (SYRACUSE). (THE COURIER.). [Courier]. **Added/Corp** Syracuse University Library Associates. (Apr. 1958)-. English. ir. Syracuse University / Law, College of Law, Ernest I. White Hall, Syracuse NY 13244-1030. **Tel** (315)443-3680, FAX (315)443-9568. **LC** Z881; .N676653. **DD** 027.7/747/66.
Ind/Abst MLA Int. Bibl. Books Artic. Mod. Lang. Lit.

CN/0319-8383
COURIER (TORONTO). (COURIER.). **Added/Corp** Special Libraries Association. Toronto Chapter. Vol. 10 (Oct. 1972)-. Periodical. English. Eight times a year. 5.00Can$. Special Library Association Toronto Chapter, West Tower City Hall CAO, 5th Floor, Toronto Ontario M5H 2N1 Canada. **Tel** (416)392-5582. ***Continues** Newsletter / Special Libraries Association. Toronto Chapter, 0584-830X; **Absorbed** Review / Special Libraries Association. Toronto Chapter.*
Ind/Abst Manage. Market. Abstr.

CN/0316-9448
COUTTS LIBRARY SERVICES. CURRENT CANADIAN BOOKS. See Bibliographies.

US/1059-1362
COVER-TO-COVER WITH CASPR.
[Cover-to-cover Caspr]. **Added/Corp** Caspr, Inc. **VFOAT** Cover to Cover with Caspr. Issue 1 (Spring 1991)-. Periodical. English. Caspr, Inc., 20111 Stevens Creek Road, Suite 270, Cupertino CA 95014. **DD** 025.

US
CPL NEWSLETTER / COUNCIL OF PLANNING LIBRARIANS. Added/Corp Council of Planning Librarians. **VAT** Council of Planning Librarians Newsletter. Vol. 1 (1967)-. Newsletter. English. qt. comes with membership. Council of Planning Librarians, 114 North Aberdeen, Chicago IL 60607-2004. **Tel** (312)955-9100.

US/0300-7561
CRAB, THE. Added/Corp Maryland Library Association. Vol. 1 (Aug. 1971)-. Periodical. English. bm (6 issues). $15.00. Maryland Library Association, 400 Cathedral Street, 3rd Floor, Baltimore MD 21201. **Tel** (410)727-7422. **ED** Beverly Rubenstein (editor's address: Baltimore Bar Library, 618 Mitchell Court House, Baltimore, MD 21202) and Richard Treleven (editor's address: 6131 Seal Lion Place Waldorf, MD 20603). **LC** Z673.M393; C7. **DD** 027.0752. **Bk Rev. Ad Acc. Circ:** 1,100 (ctrl). available on microfilm from Xerox; available on microfilm and microfiche from University Microfilms International (UMI). ***Continues** Maryland Libraries (1955).*
Desc: Aimed at supplying information of interest to members of the Maryland Library Association- personnel, workshops, etc.

CN/0316-7372
CRANE LIBRARY NEWS. [Crane Libr. news]. Vol. 1, No. 1 (Oct. 30, 1970)-. Periodical. English. Charles Crane Memorial Library Columbia, 1874 East Mall, Vancouver British Columbia V6T 1W5 Canada. **DD** 027.6/63.

CN/0827-3766
CRANE LIBRARY NEWS SUBSTITUTE.
Periodical. English. Free. Charles Crane Memorial Library Columbia, 1874 East Mall, Vancouver British Columbia V6T 1W5 Canada. **DD** 027.6/63.

CN/0228-9571
CRANE LIBRARY UPDATE. [Crane Libr. update]. Periodical. English. Crane Library, 2075 Westbrook Mall, Vancouver British Columbia V6T 1W5 Canada. **DD** 018/.138. ***Continues** Crane Library Update Circular, 0228-9563.*

CN/0228-9555
CRANE LIBRARY W.I.P. (CRANE LIBRARY W.I.P. : WORKS IN PROGRESS AT CRANE LIBRARY U.B.C.). [Crane Libr. W.I.P.]. **Main/Corp** Crane Library. **VAT** Crane Library Works in Progress; Works in Progress at Crane Library U.B.C. Mar. 13, 1979-. Periodical. English. Crane Library, 2075 Westbrook Mall, Vancouver British Columbia V6T 1W5 Canada. **DD** 018/.138.

US/1046-8692
CRISP THESAURUS. [CRISP thesaurus]. **VAT** Computer Retrieval of Information on Scientific Projects Thesaurus. (1986)-. English. an. National Institutes of

Health, 9000 Rockville Pike, Bethesda MD 20014. **Tel** (301)496-6975. **DD** 025. **NLM** Z 695.1.M4; M48. ***Continues*** *Medical and Health Related Sciences Thesaurus, 0092-6590.*

UK/0954-7487
CRITIQUE (LONDON). ***Title Change.*** (CRITIQUE.). [Crit.]. **Added/Corp** Aslib. Vol. 1, No. 1 (July/Aug. 1988)-(19??). Periodical. English (English). ASLIB, Information House, 20-24 Old Street, London EC1V 9AP England. **Tel** 011 44 71 253 4488, FAX 011 44 71 430 0514, telex 23667 AJLIB G. **LC** Z678.9.A1; C73. **DD** 025.3/0285/572. **CODEN** CRTQEI. Documents available from Ask*IEEE. ***Merged into*** *IT Link.*
Ind/Abst INSPEC (July-Aug. 1988-).

US
CRIV SHEET, THE. **Added/Corp** American Association of Law Libraries. Committee on Relations with Information Vendors. **VFOAT** C.R.I.V. Sheet. **VAT** Committee on Relations with Information Vendors Sheet. Vol. 11, No. 1 (Sept. 1988)-. Periodical. English. tq. Available only to members of American Association of Law Libraries. American Association of Law Libraries, 53 West Jackson Boulevard, Suite 940, Chicago IL 60604. **Tel** (312)939-4764, FAX (312)431-1097, telex ABA7603. **LC** Z675.L2; C75. ***Continues*** *Publications Clearing House Bulletin.*

HU/0133-705X
CSONGRAD MEGYEI KONYVTAROS. (1976)-. Hungarian. Three times a year.
Ind/Abst Magyar Konyv. Szak. Biblio.; Hungar. Libr. Info. Sci. Abstr.

US/0740-0632
CUADERNOS DE ALDEEU. (CUADERNOS DE ALDEEU / ASOCIACION DE LICENCIADOS Y DOCTORES ESPANOLES EN E.E.U.U.). [Cuad. ALDEEU]. **Added/Corp** Asociacion de Licenciados y Doctores Espanoles en E.E.U.U. **VFOAT** Cuadernos de A.L.D.E.E.U. **VAT** Cuadernos de Asociacion de Licenciados y Doctores Espanoles en los Estados Unidos. Vol. 1 No. 1 (Jan. 1983)-. Periodical. English (Spanish). Twice a year (Apr., Nov.). $18.00 (individuals); $30.00 (institutions). Juan Fernandez Jiminez, Division of Humanities, Penn State Erie, Erie PA 16563. **LC** AS30; .C8. **DD** 027.7749.
Ind/Abst MLA Int. Bibl. Books Artic. Mod. Lang. Lit.

VE/0506-6131
CUADERNOS - VENEZUELA. UNIVERSIDAD CENTRAL, CARACAS. ESCUELA DE PERIODISMO. **Main/Corp** Venezuela. Universidad Central, Caracas. Escuela de Periodismo. Vol. 1 (1959)-. Spanish. Universidad Central Caracas / Escuela de Periodismo, Caracas Venezuela. **DD** 070.

UK
CURRENT AFRICAN DIRECTORIES. (1972)-. Monographic series. English. an. Price varies per volume. Taylor & Francis Ltd., Rankine Road, Basingstoke Hampshire, RG24 8PR United Kingdom. **Tel** 011 44 256 840366, FAX 011 44 256 479438, telex 858540. **(Subscription address:** Taylor & Francis Inc., 1900 Frost Road, Suite 101, Bristol PA 19007-1598.**)**

●UK
CURRENT AWARENESS ABSTRACTS. **Added/Corp** Aslib. **VFOAT** Current Awareness Bulletin. Vol. 9, No.1 (Feb.1992)-. English. Ten times a year. £99.00 (member), £124.00 (non-member) Europe; £109.00 (member), £136.00 (non-member) other. ASLIB, Information House, 20-24 Old Street, London EC1V 9AP England. **Tel** 011 44 71 253 4488, FAX 011 44 71 430 0514, telex 23667 AJLIB G. **LC** Z671; .C87. **CODEN** CAABEV. ***Continues*** *Current Awareness Bulletin (London, England), 0265-9271.*

US/0882-3677
CURRENT AWARENESS SERVICE (CAMBRIDGE, MASS.). (CURRENT AWARENESS SERVICE / MONROE C. GUTMAN LIBRARY, HARVARD GRADUATE SCHOOL OF EDUCATION.). **Added/Corp** Monroe C. Gutman Library. (Sept. 1981)-. Periodical. English. Ten times a year (not published in July or August). $35.00. Harvard University Gutman Library, 6 Appian Way, Administrative Office, Cambridge MA 02138. **Tel** (617)495-4225, FAX (617)495-0540.

US
CURRENT CATALOG PROOF SHEETS, SEMIWEEKLY PROOF. ***Ceased.*** **Main/Corp** National Library of Medicine (U.S.). (19??)-(December 1992). Catalog. English. wk. Medical Library Association, Suite 300, Six North Michigan Avenue, Chicago IL 60602-4805. **Tel** (312)419-9094, FAX (312)419-8950. **Circ:** 350.
Desc: Timely printed version of the National Library of Medicine cataloging; contains cataloging records of English language, materials, including CIP packets, with index every fourth issue.

JA
CURRENT JAPANESE PERIODICALS FOR ... . **See** Publishing-Abstracting, Bibliographies and Statistics.

US
CURRENT LC SUBJECT HEADINGS IN THE FIELD OF RELIGION / PUBLISHED BY THE BIBLIOGRAPHIC SYSTEMS COMMITTEE OF THE AMERICAN THEOLOGICAL LIBRARY ASSOCIATION. ***Ceased.*** **See** Religion and Theology.

UK/0268-7372
CURRENT RESEARCH FOR THE INFORMATION PROFESSION. ***Ceased.*** **Added/Corp** Library Association. **VFOAT** Current Research. (1985)-(19??). English. an. Library Association, 7 Ridgmount Street, London WC1E 7AE England. **Tel** 011 44 71 636-7543, FAX 011 44 71 436-7218, telex 21897. **LC** Z669.7; .C86.

UK/0263-9254
CURRENT RESEARCH IN LIBRARY & INFORMATION SCIENCE. [Curr. res. libr. inf. sci.]. **Added/Corp** Library Association. **VFOAT** Current Research in Library and Information Science. Vol. 1, No. 1 (March 1983)-. Periodical. English. qt. £180.00 EEC; £205.00 other. Bowker Saur Ltd., A Reed Reference Publishing Company, Part of Reed International PLC, 59-60 Grosvenor Street, London WIX 9DA England. **Tel** 011 44 71 4935841, FAX 011 44 71 4991590. **(Subscription address:** World-Wide Subscription Services, Unit 4, Gibbs Reed Farm Pashley Road, Ticehurst TN5 7HE England.**)** **LC** Z669.7; .C87. **DD** 020/.72. **Ad Acc. Circ:** 500. available on magnetic tape (including back files to Jan. 1981); available on an online database (file LISA) from BRS; and (file 61) DIALOG; available on CD-ROM (as LISA PLUS). ***Continues*** *Radials Bulletin, 0302-2706.*
Desc: Offers a unique current awareness service for those who need to keep abreast of research and development work in librarianship, information science, documentation and the information aspects of other fields.
Ind/Abst World Publ. Monit. (19??-).

UK/0959-4914
CURRENT SERIALS RECEIVED. **Main/Corp** British Library. Document Supply Centre. **Added/Corp** British Library. Science Reference and Information Service. (April 1986)-. English. an. £58.00 UK; £63.00 other. British Library / Publications Sale Unit, Boston Spa, Wetherby, West Yorkshire LS23 7BQ England. **Tel** 011 44 937 546546 546543, FAX 011 44 937 546333, telex 557381. **(Subscription address:** Turpin Distribution Services Limited, Blackhorse Road, Letchworth, Hertfordshire SG6 1HN, United Kingdom.**)** **LC** Z6945; .B857. **CODEN** CRBCEM. **Ad Acc.** ***Continues*** *Current Serials Received / British Library. Lending Division, 0309-0655.*
Desc: Contains about 73,000 titles in all subject fields. Provides extensive coverage of significant journals published in Britain and throughout the world.
Ind/Abst AESIS Q.

US/0742-8227
CURRENT STUDIES IN LIBRARIANSHIP. [Curr. stud. librariansh.]. **Added/Corp** University of Rhode Island. Graduate Library School. Clarion University of Pennsylvania. College of Library Science. Texas Woman's University. School of Library and Information Studies. **VFOAT** CSIL. Vol. 1 (Spring 1977)-. Periodical. English. an (Dec.). $10.00 (one year), $19.00 (two year), $29.00 (three year). Clarion University of Pennsylvania / Department of Library Science, Clarion PA 16214. **Tel** (814)226-2314. **(Subscription address:** Clarion University of Pennsylvania, College of Library Science, Clarion, PA 16214**)** **ED** Rashelle S. Karp (phone: (814)226-2314). **Circ:** 220.
Desc: Articles published of general interest to all types of librarians.
Ind/Abst Libr. Inf. Sci. Abstr.

UK/0011-4421
CYLCHGRAWN LLYFRGELL GENEDLAETHOL CYMRU. (CYLCHGRAWN LLYFRGELL GENEDLAETHOL CYMRU. THE NATIONAL LIBRARY OF WALES JOURNAL.). [Cylchgr. llyfrg. genedl. Cymru]. **Main/Corp** National Library of Wales. **Added/Corp** National Library of Wales. Journal. **VFOAT** National Library of Wales Journal. Vol. 1 (1939)-. Periodical. English (Welsh). sa (June and Dec.). £12.00. National Library of Wales, Aberystwyth, Dyfed SY23 3BU Wales. **Tel** 011 44 970 623816, FAX 011 44 970 615709, telex 35165. **ED** B. F. Roberts. **Circ:** 400 (ctrl).
Ind/Abst Abstr. Engl. Stud.; Am. Hist. Life (1955-); BHA : Biblio. Hist. Art; Br. Humanit. Index; MLA Int. Bibl. Books Artic. Mod. Lang. Lit.

CN/0703-1688
D O R L S TECHNICAL SERVICES COMMITTEE'S INFORMATION EXCHANGE. **Main/Corp** DORLS Technical Services Committee. **VFOAT** Information Exchange. **VAT** Directors of Ontario Regional Library Systems Technical Services Committee's Information Exchange. Vol. 1 (Oct. 1976)-. Periodical. English. mo. Free. Provincial Library Service, 14th Floor/Mowat Block, Queen's Park, Toronto Ontario M7A 2R9 Canada. **DD** 025/.02/05. ctrl circ.

US/0070-2536
DAEDALUS LIBRARY, THE. V. 1- 1965-. Monographic series. English. ir. Price varies per volume. Beacon Press, 25 Beacon Street, Boston MA 02108.
Desc: Consists of articles that appeared originally in issued of Daedalus, some times in slightly revised versions.

JA
DAIGAKU TOSHOKAN KANKYU. **Added/Corp** Kokuritsu Daigaku Toshokan Kyogikai. **VFOAT** Journal of College and University Libraries. (1972)-. Periodical. Japanese. sa. $72.00. **(Subscription address:** Maruzen Company Ltd., PO Box 5050, Import & Export Department, Tokyo 100 31 Japan.**)** **LC** Z675.U5; D25.

JA/0388-5623
DAIGAKU TOSHOKAN KYORYOKU NYUSU. Periodical. Japanese. ¥3000 institution. Gakujutsu Bunken Fukyukai, c/o Tokyo Kodai, Ookayama 2, Meguro-ku 152, Tokyo-to Japan. **LC** Z675.U5; D27.

US/1048-471X
DALHOUSIE UNIVERSITY, SCHOOL OF LIBRARY AND INFORMATION STUDIES SERIES. [Dalhousie Univ. Sch. Libr. Inf. Stud. ser.]. **Added/Corp** Dalhousie University. School of Library and Information Studies. (1987)-. Monographic series. English. ir. Price varies per volume. Scarecrow Press Inc., 52 Liberty Street, PO Box 4167, Metuchen NJ 08840. **Tel** (908)548-8600, (800)537-7107. **LC** UNC. **DD** 025. ***Continues*** *Dalhousie University, School of Library Service (Series).*

AT/0818-9056
DANDENONG VALLEY LIBRARIES REPORTER. (1987)-. Periodical. English. bm. Dandenong Valley Regional Library Service, 336 Springvale Road, Springvale VIC 3171 Australia. **ED** M Lotrean.
Ind/Abst Aust. Educ. Index; Aust. Libr. Inf. Sci. Abstr. (1987-).

US/0011-6750
DARTMOUTH COLLEGE LIBRARY BULLETIN. **Main/Corp** Dartmouth College. Library. **Added/Corp** Dartmouth College. Baker Library. Bulletin. Vol. 1-5. (Apr. 1931)-. Bulletin. English. Twice a year (April and November). Free. Dartmouth College, Baker Library, Room 115, Hanover NH 03755. **Tel** (603)646-2236. **ED** Lois A. Krieger and Phillip N. Cronenwett. **DD** 020. cum. index. **Bk Rev**, (Qty: 2). **Circ:** 925.
Desc: Articles describe features of special interest and research of value to the library's collections.

US
DATA INFORMER, THE. ***Title Change.*** Vol. 2, No. 9 (Sept. 1985)-?. Periodical. English. mo. Information USA, PO Box E, Kensington MD 20895. **Tel** (301)924-0556, (800)955-7693, FAX (301)946-3004. **ED** Matthew J Lesko. available on an online database from NEWSNET. ***Continues*** *Data Base Informer.* ***Continued by*** *Leskos Info Power.*
Desc: Unusual sources of information on markets, companies, demographics and technology. Identifies little known databases, free experts in both public and private sector.

US/0737-6235
DBPH NEWSLETTER. **VFOAT** D.B.P.H. Newsletter. **VAT** Division for the Blind and Physically Handicapped Newsletter. Spring 1976-. Newsletter. English. qt. Free. Texas State Library Clearinghouse, PO Box 12927, Capitol Station, Austin TX 78711. **Tel** (512)463-5435, FAX (512)463-5436. **ED** Patsy Castro. **Circ:** 18,000.
Desc: Library related information, new services available, services provided by other agencies, newly acquired large print and recorded cassette books for the blind and physically handicapped.

CN/0831-4640
DEFI. (DEFI : REVUE DE L'ASSOCIATION DES DIRECTEURS DE BIBLIOTHEQUES PUBLIQUES DU QUEBEC.). [Defi]. **VFOAT** Defi. (Oct./Nov./Dec. 1985)-. Periodical. French (English). qt. Free. Association des Directeurs de Bibliotheques Publiques du Quebec, 777 Laurentien Saint-Laurent, Quebec H4M 2M7 Canada. **DD** 025.1/974714.

USUS/1058-6644
DELAWARE DIVISION OF LIBRARIES NEWSLETTER, THE. [Del. Div. Libr. newsl.]. **Added/Corp** Delaware. Division of Libraries. Vol. 1, No. 1 (Fall 1990)-. Newsletter. English. qt. Delaware Division of Libraries, 43 South DuPont Highway, Dover DE 19901. **DD** 027. ***Continues*** *News & Views (Dover, Del.).*

US/0884-7819
DESCRIPTOR FREQUENCY LIST. ***Title Change.*** [Descr. freq. list]. **Added/Corp** University of

Tulsa. Information Services Division. (19??)-(199?). English. an. University of Tulsa / College of Law, 3120 East 4th Place, Tulsa OK 74104. **Tel** (918)631-2431, FAX (918)631-3556, telex 497543 INFOSVC TU TUL. **LC** Z695.1.P43; P47. **DD** 025.4/95532/82. ***Continues*** *Petroleum Abstracts Information System Descriptor Frequency List, 0270-8272.* ***Continued by*** *Term Frequency List, 1060-5304.*
Desc: An alphabetical list of terms from both thesauri and their supplemental descriptor lists. It enumerates how many times a descriptor has been used to index material for the TULSA database, with a separate count for each use as a primary term.

GW
DEUTSCHE BIBLIOTHEK. (19??)-. Monographic series. German. ir. Price varies per volume. Akademie-Verlag GmbH, Muehlenstrasse 33 34, D 13162 Berlin Germany. **Tel** 011 49 30 47889300, FAX 011 49 30 47889357.

GW
DEUTSCHES BIBLIOTHEKSADRESSBUCH. August 1, 1974-?. German. Verlag Dokumentation, Postfach 711009, W-8000 Muenchen 71 Germany. **Tel** 089/791040, telex 5212067. **LC** Z801.A1; D488.

US/0191-3646
DEWEY DECIMAL CLASSIFICATION ADDITIONS, NOTES, AND DECISIONS. (DEWEY DECIMAL CLASSIFICATION ADDITIONS, NOTES, AND DECISIONS / THE LIBRARY OF CONGRESS, PROCESSING DEPARTMENT, DECIMAL CLASSIFICATION DIVISION.). [Dewey decim. classif. addit. notes decis.]. **Added/Corp** Library of Congress. Decimal Classification Division. **VFOAT** D.C. AND; DDC; D.D.C.; DC&. Vol. 2, No. 2 (Spring 1971)-. English. ir. Comes with Abridged Dewey Decimal Classification & Relative Index. OCLC Asia Pacific Services, 6565 Frantz Road, Dublin OH 43017. **Tel** (800)848-5878, (614)764-6394 or 6000, FAX (614)764-6096. **LC** Z696.D5; U6. **DD** 025.4/31. ***Continues*** *Decimal Classification Additions, Notes, and Decisions, 0083-1573.*

GW/0373-8825
DFW, DOKUMENTATION, INFORMATION. ***Ceased.*** [DFW, Dok., Inf.]. **VFOAT** Dokumentation, Information. Vol. 20 (Oct./Nov. 1971)-?. Periodical. German. bm. Nordwest Verlagsgesellschaft, Goebelstrasse 2, W-3000 Hannover 26 Germany. **Tel** 511 66 89 88. **LC** Z699.A1; D65. ***Continues*** *Dokumentation, Fachbibliothek, Werksbucherei.*
Ind/Abst Libr. Inf. Sci. Abstr. (?-?).

US/1047-3424
DIAL IN. ***Title Change.*** (DIAL IN : A GUIDE TO LIBRARY OPAC'S IN THE U.S. AND CANADA.). [Dial in]. (1991)-(1992). English. an. Mecklermedia Corporation, 11 Ferry Lane West, Westport CT 06880. **Tel** (203)226-6967, (800)632-5537, FAX (203)454-5840. **LC** Z699.22; .D5. **DD** 025.3/132/0257. ***Continued by*** *OPAC Directory, 1066-1425.*
Desc: This new annual lists the dial-in numbers to online public access catalogs from hundreds of libraries in North America. Entries include library name, address, data on special collection strengths, network membership, loan policies, requirements and restrictions on access.

US/0098-7395
DICTIONARY CATALOG OF THE COLUMBIA UNIVERSITY LAW LIBRARY. SUPPLEMENT. **Main/Corp** Columbia University. Libraries. Law Library. 1st- 1973-. Catalog. Multiple languages. GK Hall & Co, 100 Front Street, Riverside NJ 08075. **Tel** (800)257-5755 ext. 2223. **ED** G K Hall. **LC** LAW. **DD** 016.34.
Desc: One of the largest, this library contains about 465,000 volumes, rich in legal literature of the U.S. and the British Commonwealth, and excellent coverage of Roman and medieval law.

US/1059-0080
DIGITAL INFORMATION GROUP'S INFORMATION INDUSTRY BULLETIN. [Digit. Inf. Group's inf. ind. bull.]. **Added/Corp** Digital Information Group. **VFOAT** Information Industry Bulletin. (19??)-. Bulletin. English. Forty-eight times a year. $415.00. Digital Information Group, 51 Bank Street, Stamford CT 06901. **Tel** (800)255-0942, FAX (203)977-8310. **LC** HD999.I49; D53. **DD** 338.4/7004. ***Continues*** *Information Industry Bulletin, 0885-7660.*

US/0363-5414
DIKTA. [Dikta]. **Added/Corp** Southern Conference of Librarians for the Blind and Physically Handicapped. (Spring 1976)-. Periodical. English. Twice a year. $8.00. Southern Conference of Librarians for the Blind & Physically Handicapped, 420 Platt Street, Daytona Beach FL 32114. **Tel** (904)239-6050, FAX (904)239-6069. **ED** Michael Gunde. **LC** Z711.92.P5; D53. **DD** 027.6/65/05. **Bk Rev**, (Qty: 2/year). **Circ:** 200.
Desc: News and information concerning library services to the blind and physically handicapped.
Ind/Abst Libr. Inf. Sci. Abstr.

US/0897-9499
DIRECTIONS : A NEWSLETTER FROM EBSCO PUBLISHING. ***Suspended.*** [Directions]. **Added/Corp** EBSCO Publishing (Firm). Vol. 1, No. 1 (Fall 1987)-Suspended. Newsletter. English. qt. Free with subscription to The Index and Abstract Directory, or The Serials Directory, print or CD-ROM versions. EBSCO Publishing / Birmingham, The Serials Directory, PO Box 1943, Birmingham AL 35201-1943. **Tel** editorial inquiries (205)980-2773, toll-free US (800)826-3024, FAX (205)995-1582. **ED** Angie Brumley. **DD** 070. ctrl circ.
Desc: Covers library and information science news, specifically in relation to EBSCO Publishing products.

US/0360-473X
DIRECTIONS (NEW YORK, N.Y. 1975). (DIRECTIONS.). [Dir.]. Vol. 1, (Aug. 1975)-. Periodical. English. Eleven times a year. Baker & Taylor Company, 652 East Main Street, PO Box 6920, Bridgewater NJ 08807-0920. **Tel** (201)218-0400. **ED** Hal J. Hager. **LC** Z671; .D52. **DD** 020/.5. **Ad Acc. Circ:** 7,800 (ctrl).
Desc: A journal of titles for Academic and Research Libraries.
Ind/Abst AESIS Q.; GeoRef.

FJ/1011-5846
DIRECTIONS SUVA. [DirectionsSuva]. (1978)-. Academic Scholarly Publication. English. Twice a year. $125.00. University of the South Pacific / Institute of Education, PO Box 1168, Suva Fiji. **Tel** 679-313900, FAX 679-302409, telex FJ2276. **ED** Narattam Bhindi & Cliff Benson. **UDC** 37. Index available. cum. index. **Bk Rev**, (Qty: 2). **Pr Rev. Acid Free. Circ:** 500.
Desc: News and information on various aspects of education.
Ind/Abst Aust. Educ. Index.

CK
DIRECTORIO COLOMBIANO DE UNIDADES DE INFORMACION. 1976-. Spanish. Impr Nacional / Colombia, Carrera 13 No 60-34 4 Piso, Apartado Aereo 051580, Bogota Colombia. **LC** Z773.A1; D57.

US/0543-2774
DIRECTORY. **Main/Corp** Medical Library Association. (1950)-. English. an. $35.00 (members), $43.75 (nonmembers). Medical Library Association, Suite 300, Six North Michigan Avenue, Chicago IL 60602-4805. **Tel** (312)419-9094, FAX (312)419-8950. **LC** Z675.M4; M43. **Bk Rev. Ad Acc. Circ:** 5,500 (ctrl).
Desc: Reference for general association information, including committee charges; section and chapter officers and alphabetical listing of current membership.

US/0162-0290
DIRECTORY AND STATISTICS OF OREGON LIBRARIES. **Added/Corp** Oregon State Library. Library Development Services. Oregon State Library. (1977)-. Directory. English. an. $14.00. Oregon State Library, State Library Building, Salem OR 97310-0640. **Tel** (503)378-2112, FAX (503)588-7119. **ED** Jim Scheppke. **LC** Z732.O8; O64. **DD** 027/.0795. **Circ:** 625 (ctrl). ***Continues*** *Oregon. State Library, Salem. Directory of Oregon Libraries.*
Desc: Directory and statistical information for public, academic, and special libraries in Oregon.

UK/0305-7380
DIRECTORY / ART LIBRARIES SOCIETY. **See** The Arts-Art.

CN/0821-4638
DIRECTORY / CANADIAN ASSOCIATION OF LAW LIBRARIES. [Dir. - Can. Assoc. Law Libr.]. **Main/Corp** Canadian Association of Law Libraries. **VFOAT** Annuaire. **VAT** Annuaire - Association Canadienne des Bibliotheques de Droit. (July 1982)-. Directory. English (French). an. 25.00Can$. Carswell / Canada, 2075 Kennedy Road, Scarborough Ontario M1T 3V4 Canada. **Tel** (416)609-3800, (800)387-5164. **LC** Z673.C178; C35a. **DD** 026/.34/0971. ***Continues*** *Canadian Association of Law Libraries. List of Members, 0707-5219.*

CN/0702-8350
DIRECTORY - CENTRAL ONTARIO REGIONAL LIBRARY SYSTEM. **Main/Corp** Central Ontario Regional Library System. 1975-. Directory. English. an. Central Ontario Regional Library System, 129 Church Street South, Richmond Hill Ontario L4C 1W4 Canada. **DD** 027.4/025/71354.

GW/0376-8430
DIRECTORY - INTERNATIONAL ASSOCIATION OF LAW LIBRARIES. **See** Law.

CN/0315-2774
DIRECTORY - LAKE ONTARIO REGIONAL LIBRARY SYSTEM. **Main/Corp** Lake Ontario Regional Library System. (1967)-. Directory. English. an. Lake Ontario Regional Library System, 88 Wright Crescent, Kingston Ontario K7L 4T9. **DD** 027.4/025/7135.

US
DIRECTORY / LIBRARY OF CONGRESS. **Main/Corp** Library of Congress. **VFOAT** Library of Congress Directory. Directory. English. Library of Congress / Publications and Media, Washington DC 20540.

CN/0380-8068
DIRECTORY, MEMBER LIBRARIES, GEORGIAN BAY REGIONAL LIBRARY SYSTEM. **Main/Corp** Georgian Bay Regional Library System. Began with 1968 issue. Directory. English. Georgian Bay Regional Library System, 30 Morrow Road, Barrie Ontario L4N 3V8 Canada. **DD** 027.4/025/71317.

CN/0712-9777
DIRECTORY, NON-OPERATING LIBRARY BOARDS / GEORGIAN BAY REGIONAL LIBRARY SYSTEMS. [Dir., non-oper. libr. boards - Georgian Bay Reg. Libr. Syst.]. **Main/Corp** Georgian Bay Regional Library System. Directory. English. an. Free. Georgian Bay Regional Library System, 30 Morrow Road, Barrie Ontario L4N 3V8 Canada. **DD** 021.8/2/02571315. ctrl circ.

US/0889-4671
DIRECTORY OF ALABAMA HEALTH SCIENCE LIBRARIES AND HANDBOOK OF THE ALABAMA HEALTH LIBRARIES ASSOCIATION. **Added/Corp** Alabama Health Libraries Association. (1986)-. Directory. English. Four times a year. $25.00. University of Alabama at Birmingham, Lister Hill Library / B.J. Schorre, University Station, Birmingham AL 35294. **Tel** (205)934-2461, FAX (205)934-3545. **ED** Cindy Fedders (editor's address: Washington University School of Medicine Library, Box 8132, 660 South Euclid, St. Louis, MO 63110; phone: (314)362-2784). **Circ:** 200. ***Continues*** *Directory of Alabama Health Science Libraries, 0884-190X.*

CN/0382-3482
DIRECTORY OF ALBERTA GOVERNMENT LIBRARIES. **Added/Corp** Alberta. Legislature Library. Consulting & Bibliographic Services Section. Alberta. Legislature Library. Library Services Section. Alberta. Legislature Library. Cooperative Government Library Services Section. (Sept. 1975)-. English. Twice a year (June & Dec.). Price varies. Legislature Library Alberta Government, 902 Legislature Annex, 9718 107th Street, Edmonton Alberta T5K 1E4 Canada. **Tel** (403)427-3837. **LC** Z735.A45; D57. **DD** 027.5/025/7123. **Circ:** 250 (ctrl). ***Continues*** *Directory of Alberta Government Libraries, Edmonton, 0317-8188.*
Desc: Listing of all government (provincial) libraries in the province of Alberta.

AT/0811-6253
DIRECTORY OF ARTS LIBRARIES AND RESOURCE COLLECTIONS IN AUSTRALIA. **Added/Corp** Australia Council. (Aug. 1983)-. English. ir. $10.00. James Bennett Pty Ltd, 4 Collaroy Street, Collaroy New South Wales 2097 Australia. **Tel** (02)663-9999. **LC** Z675.A85; D56. **DD** 026/.7/002594.

AT
DIRECTORY OF AUSTRALIAN ACADEMIC AND RESEARCH LIBRARIES. **VFOAT** DAARL. 4th Ed. (1989)-. Directory. English. te. 42.00Aus$. Auslib Press, PO Box 622, Blackwood South Australia, 5051 Australia. **Tel** 11 61 8 2784363, FAX 11 61 8 2784000. **ED** Alan and Judith Bundy. **Ad Acc. Circ:** 850. ***Continues*** *Directory of Australian Academic Libraries.*
Desc: Guide to the collections, services, operations and staffing of Australia's academic and general research libraries.

AT/0729-4271
DIRECTORY OF AUSTRALIAN PUBLIC LIBRARIES. **Added/Corp** Footscray Institute of Technology. 1st Edition (1982)-. Directory. English. ir. 34.00Aus$. Auslib Press, PO Box 622, Blackwood South Australia, 5051 Australia. **Tel** 11 61 8 2784363, FAX 11 61 8 2784000. **LC** Z870.A1; D58.
Desc: Provides information on those public libraries which have bookmobiles, local history collections, database searching, use volunteers, etc.

AT
DIRECTORY OF COLLECTION STRENGTHS IN VICTORIAN LIBRARIES. **Added/Corp** Library Association of Australia. Acquisitions Section. Victorian Group. (1986)-. Periodical. English. be. Library Association of Australia / Acquisitions Section, Victorian Group, Melbourne NSW Australia. **ED** John Thawley and Philip Kent.

US
DIRECTORY OF COLORADO LIBRARIES ... & LIBRARY STATISTICS / COLORADO DEPARTMENT OF EDUCATION. **VFOAT** Directory of Colorado Libraries ... and Library Statistics. 1980-. Directory.

English. an. $5.00. Centennial State Libraries, 201 East Colfax Avenue, Room 309, Denver CO 80203. **Tel** (303)866-6732, FAX (303)830-0793. **ED** Dan Petro. **LC** Z732.C6; D57. **DD** 027/.0025/788. **Ad Acc. Circ:** 2,000 (ctrl). ***Continues*** *Directory of Colorado Libraries.*
Desc: A comprehensive listing of all library agencies in Colorado.

US/0730-5222
DIRECTORY OF DELAWARE LIBRARIES, A. **Added/Corp** Delaware Library Association. College and Research Libraries Division. (19??)-. English. ir. $12.00. Directory of Delaware Libraries, Box 1843, Wilmington DE 19899. **LC** Z732.D34; D57. **DD** 027/.0025/751. **Ad Acc. Circ:** 200.

US/1044-8829
DIRECTORY OF ENGINEERING DOCUMENT SOURCES. [Dir. eng. doc. sources]. (1971)-. Directory. English. $145.00. Global Engineering Documents Services, 15 Inverness Way East, Englewood CO 80112. **Tel** (800)624-3974. **LC** T10.7; .D57. **DD** 025.4/96.
Desc: Provides identification and sources for document initialisms identifying government, military and industry specifications, standards, and related publications.

US/0731-3594
DIRECTORY OF FEDERAL STATISTICAL DATA FILES. **See** Library and Information Sciences-Abstracting, Bibliographies and Statistics.

US
DIRECTORY OF FILM LIBRARIES IN NORTH AMERICA. **See** Motion Picture.

US/0095-7925
DIRECTORY OF HEALTH SCIENCES LIBRARIES IN THE UNITED STATES. **Added/Corp** American Medical Association. National Library of Medicine (U.S.) Case Western Reserve University. School of Library Science. (1969)-. English. ir. Medical Library Association, Suite 300, Six North Michigan Avenue, Chicago IL 60602-4805. **Tel** (312)419-9094, FAX (312)419-8950. **ED** F.L. Schick and S. Crawford. **LC** Z675.M4; D568. **NLM** Z 675.M4 D598.

CN/0225-5472
DIRECTORY OF INDUSTRIAL RELATIONS LIBRARIES IN CANADA. [Dir. ind. relat. libr. Can.]. Began with 1979. Directory. English. Alberta Department of Labour, 10808-99th Avenue/8th Floor, Edmonton Alberta T5K 0G5 Canada. **Tel** (403)427-8260. **LC** Z675.I53; D57. **DD** 027.6/9/02571.

US
DIRECTORY OF INFORMATION MANAGEMENT SOFTWARE FOR LIBRARIES, INFORMATION CENTERS, RECORD CENTERS. ***Title Change.*** **Added/Corp** Cibbarelli Associates. **VFOAT** Information Management Software for Libraries, Information Centers, Records Centers. (1983)-(1992). Periodical. English. be. Learned Information Inc., 143 Old Marlton Pike, Medford NJ 08055-8750. **Tel** (609)654-6266, FAX (609)654-4309. **ED** Edward J. Kazlauskas. Index available. **Circ:** 5,000. ***Continued by*** *Directory of Library Automation Software, Systems, and Services.*
Desc: Describes software packages useful for creation of files, library catalogs, databases and for automating entire library systems.

US
DIRECTORY OF LAW LIBRARIES. Directory. English. an. $60.00. American Association of Law Libraries, 53 West Jackson Boulevard, Suite 940, Chicago IL 60604. **Tel** (312)939-4764, FAX (312)431-1097, telex ABA7603. ctrl circ.

CN/0715-1624
DIRECTORY OF LIBRARIES AND ARCHIVAL INSTITUTIONS IN PRINCE EDWARD ISLAND. [Dir. libr. arch. inst. P.E.I.]. Directory. English. Provincial Library, University Avenue R.R. 7, Charlottetown PEI CIA 7N9 Canada. **ED** Joan Ricketts. **LC** Z735.P73; D57. **DD** 027/.0025/717. ctrl circ.

US/0278-5684
DIRECTORY OF LIBRARIES AND INFORMATION SOURCES IN THE PHILADELPHIA AREA. **VFOAT** Directory of Libraries and Information Services in the Philadelphia Area. Directory. English. be. Philadelphia Chapter / Special Libraries Association, c/o Jean Denio, Normandy Farm Estates - D 307, 1801 Morris Road, Blue Bell PA 19422. **LC** Z732.P6; D57. **DD** 027/.0025/74811. **Ad Acc. Circ:** 900. ***Continues*** *Directory of Libraries and Information Sources.*
Desc: Bibliography of holdings and personnel of corporate and and academic libraries in Mid-Atlantic area.

●CN/1191-1603
DIRECTORY OF LIBRARIES IN CANADA. [Dir. libr. Can.]. **VFOAT** Repertoire des Bibliotheques du Canada. 6th ed. (1992)-. Directory. English (French). an (Nov.). 135.00Can$. Micromedia Limited, 20 Victoria Street, Toronto Ontario M5C 2N8 Canada. **Tel** (416)362-5211, (800)387-2689, FAX (416)362-6161, telex 06524668. **DD** 027/.0025/71. ***Continues*** *Canadian Library Yearbook, 0827-3715.*

CN/0317-8536
DIRECTORY OF LIBRARIES IN MANITOBA. **Added/Corp** Manitoba. Public Library Services. (1973)-. Directory. English. be. Department of Tourism Recreation & Cultural Affairs, Historic Resources Branch, 1981 Portage Avenue, Winnipeg Man. R3J 0J9 Canada. **LC** Z735.M3; D57. **DD** 021/.0025/7127.

CN/0317-2465
DIRECTORY OF LIBRARIES IN NEWFOUNDLAND AND LABRADOR. **Added/Corp** Newfoundland Library Association. (1975)-. Directory. English. an. 25.00Can$. Newfoundland Library Association, PO Box 23192, St. John's Newfoundland A1B 4J9 Canada. **Tel** (709)737-3214, FAX (709)737-3118. **DD** 021/.0025/718. **Ad Acc. Circ:** 200.
Desc: A directory of libraries in Newfoundland and Labrador.

US/0743-4995
DIRECTORY OF LIBRARY AND INFORMATION CONSULTANTS IN METROPOLITAN WASHINGTON. [Dir. libr. inf. consult. metrop. Wash.]. 1st Ed. (1983)-. Directory. English. be. Metropolitan Washington Council of Governments, 777 North Capitol Street Northeast, Washington DC 20002-4239. **Tel** (202)962-3256. **LC** Z682.4.C65; D57. **DD** 023/.2/025753.

US/0894-7031
DIRECTORY OF LIBRARY & INFORMATION PROFESSIONALS. [Dir. libr. inf. prof.]. **VFOAT** Directory of Library and Information Professionals; DLIP. (1990)-. English. ir. $365.00. Gale Research Inc., 835 Penobscot Building, Detroit MI 48226. **Tel** (800)877-GALE, (313)961-2242, FAX (313)961-6083, telex TWX 810-221-7086. **DD** 020. available on CD-ROM from ALA Information Technology Publishing; Knowledge Access International; and The Faxon Company.
Desc: Lists professional librarians and information specialists based in the United States and Canada. Also biographical sketches of individuals who work or participate in the information field at a professional level.

●US/1071-264X
DIRECTORY OF LIBRARY AUTOMATION SOFTWARE, SYSTEMS, AND SERVICES. [Dir. libr. autom. softw. syst. serv.]. **Added/Corp** Learned Information (Firm). **VFOAT** Directory of Library Automation. (1993)-. English. sa. $79.00 per copy. Learned Information Inc., 143 Old Marlton Pike, Medford NJ 08055-8750. **Tel** (609)654-6266, FAX (609)654-4309. **ED** Pamela Cibbarelli. **LC** Z678.9.A3; D6. **DD** 025.3/44/025. ***Continues*** *Directory of Information Management Software for Libraries, Information Centers, Record Centers.*
Desc: Contains information on software packages used in automated libraries. Provides detailed descriptions of about 250 currently available microcomputer, minicomputer and mainframe software packages and services.

US/0160-6077
DIRECTORY OF LIBRARY REPROGRAPHIC SERVICES. **Added/Corp** American Library Association. Reproduction of Library Materials Section. 5th Edition (1973)-. English. ir. American Library Association, 50 East Huron Street, Chicago IL 60611. **Tel** (312)944-6780, (800)545-2433, FAX (312)944-2641. **(Subscription address:** American Library Association, Subscription Department, 434 West Downer, Aurora IL 60506-9936.**)** **DD** 778.3. ***Continues*** *Directory of Institutional Photocopying Services.*

US
DIRECTORY OF LIBRARY SYSTEMS IN NEW YORK STATE, A. **Added/Corp** New York State Library. Division of Library Development. (Fall 1976)-. English. an. $8.00. The New York State Library, Albany NY 12230. **LC** Z732.N7; D532. ***Formed by the union of*** *Directory of New York State Public Library Systems, 0070-5950* ***and*** *Directory of Reference and Research Library Resources Systems in New York State.*

UK/0419-2915
DIRECTORY OF LONDON PUBLIC LIBRARIES. Directory. English. **LC** Z791; .D5.

UK
DIRECTORY OF MEDICAL AND HEALTH CARE LIBRARIES IN THE UNITED KINGDOM AND REPUBLIC OF IRELAND. 5th Ed. (1982)-. Directory. English. $33.00. Library Association Publishing Ltd, 7 Ridgmount Street, London WC1E 7AE England. **Tel** 44 71 636-7543, FAX 44 71 436-7218, telex 93121 34504 LAG. ***Continues*** *Directory of Medical Libraries in the British Isles.*

CN/0846-2038
DIRECTORY OF MEMBERS / CANADIAN LIBRARY ASSOCIATION. [Dir. memb. - Can. Libr. Assoc.]. **Main/Corp** Canadian Library Association. (1990/1991)-. Directory. English. Canadian Library Association, 200 Elgin Street, Suite 602, Ottawa Ontario K2P 1L5 Canada. **Tel** (613)232-9625. **LC** Z673; .C36. **DD** 020/.25/71. ***Continues*** *CLA Directory of Members, 0835-0728.*

US/0092-4067
DIRECTORY OF MISSOURI LIBRARIES. [Dir. Mo. libr.]. **Added/Corp** Missouri State Library. (1966)-. Directory. English. ir. $20.00 (individuals); $30.00 (institutions) Comes with the Missouri Library Association Membership. Missouri Library Association, 1306 Business 63 South, Suite B, Columbia MO 65201. **Tel** (314)449-4627. **LC** Z732.M82; D57. **DD** 027/.0025/778. **Circ:** 1,000 (ctrl).
Desc: Statistical report of public, academic, special and institutional libraries.
Ind/Abst Stat. Ref. Index.

CN/0713-6358
DIRECTORY OF NEW BRUNSWICK LIBRARIES. [Dir. N.B. libr.]. **Added/Corp** Council of Head Librarians of New Brunswick. **VFOAT** Repertoire des Bibliotheques du Nouveau-Brunswick. 1st Ed. (Jan. 1976)-. Directory. English (French). Directory of New Brunswick Libraries, c/o Bibliotheque Champlain, Universite de Moncton, Moncton New Brunswick E1A 3E9 Canada. **DD** 027/.0025/715.

CN/0822-935X
DIRECTORY OF O.C.U.L. LIBRARIES. [Dir. O.C.U.L. libr.]. **Main/Corp** Ontario Council of University Libraries. **VAT** Directory of Ontario Council of University Libraries. (1980)-. Directory. English. an. 20.00Can$. University of Waterloo Press Davis Center Library, Waterloo Ontario N2L 3G1 Canada. **Tel** (519)885-1211 Ext 2112, FAX (519)746-5151. **DD** 027.7/025/713. ctrl circ.
Desc: Directory listings for Academic University Libraries in Ontario, Canada.

US/0193-6840
DIRECTORY OF ONLINE DATABASES. ***Title Change.*** [Dir. online databases]. Vol. 1 No. 1 (Fall 1979)-Vol. 13 No. 2 (July 1992). Directory. English. qt (July and January). Gale Research Inc., 835 Penobscot Building, Detroit MI 48226. **Tel** (800)877-GALE, (313)961-2242, FAX (313)961-6083, telex TWX 810-221-7086. **ED** Orest Balaban. **LC** Z699.22; .D56. **DD** 025/.04/025. **CODEN** DODADF. **[CCC].** available in microform. ***Merged with*** *Computer-Readable Data Bases, 0271-4477* ***and*** *Directory of Portable Databases, 1045-8352* ***to form*** *Gale Directory of Databases, 1066-8934.*
Desc: The top-rated reference to over 4,900 online databases available through over 700 online services worldwide. It identifies and comprehensively describes all types of online databases with clearly detailed and alphabetical listings.
Ind/Abst Int. Aerosp. Abstr. (19??-1992).

CN/0712-9785
DIRECTORY OF OPERATING LIBRARIES / GEORGIAN BAY REGIONAL LIBRARY SYSTEM. [Dir. oper. libr. - Georgian Bay Reg. Libr. Syst.]. **Main/Corp** Georgian Bay Regional Library System. Directory. English. an. Free. Georgian Bay Regional Library System, 30 Morrow Road, Barrie Ontario L4N 3V8 Canada. **DD** 027.4/025/71315. ctrl circ.

US
DIRECTORY OF PERIODICALS ONLINE. **Added/Corp** Federal Document Retrieval, Inc. (1985)-. Directory. English. $199.00 (if prepaid), $249.00 ($9.75 domestic shipping), $12.95 Canadian and overseas shipping). Library Alliance, Inc., 264 Lexington Avenue, Suite 4-C North, New York NY 10016. **Tel** (212)685-5297, FAX (212)213-6055. **ED** Catherine Chung.
Desc: Vol. 1 News, Law & Business; Vol. 2 Medicine & Social Science; Vol. 3 Science & Technology.

US
DIRECTORY OF PERIODICALS ONLINE. VOL. 2, MEDICINE & SOCIAL SCIENCE. **See** Library and Information Sciences-Abstracting, Bibliographies and Statistics.

AT
DIRECTORY OF PUBLIC LIBRARY SERVICES IN VICTORIA. **Added/Corp** Library Council of Victoria. Public Libraries Division. (19??)-. Directory. English. an. Library Council of Victoria, Public Libraries Division, 328 Swanston Street, Melbourne Victoria 3000 Australia. **Tel** 03-6699840, FAX 03-6631480, telex AA38104. **ED** David Button. **LC** Z870.V5; D56. **DD** 027.4/945. **Circ:** 1,500.

Desc: List of public library services in Victoria. Includes addresses and telephone numbers of all branches and names of chief librarians.

AT
DIRECTORY OF PUBLIC LIBRARY SERVICES, WESTERN AUSTRALIA. **Added/Corp** Library Board of Western Australia. (19??)-. English. an. 10.00Aus$ (add 10.00Aus$ postage if not prepaid). Library and Information Service of Western Australia, Alexander Library Building, Perth Cultural Centre, Perth 6000 Australia. **Tel** (09)427-3111, FAX (09)427 3256, telex WAINF. **LC** Z870.W4; D57. **DD** 025.5/2774941. Index available. **Circ:** 600 (ctrl).
Desc: Alphabetical listing of public libraries with addresses, bookstocks and opening hours.

PH
DIRECTORY OF SCHOOLS OFFERING LIBRARY SCIENCE. Directory. English. Philippine Association of Teachers of Library Science, National Library Building/Room 301, T M Kalaw Street, Manila 2801 Philippines. **LC** Z669.5.P45; D55. **DD** 020/.711/599.

●TH
DIRECTORY OF SOUTHEAST ASIAN ACADEMIC & SPECIAL LIBRARIES. (1992)-. Directory. English. $150.00 one year. Library Marketing Services Ltd. / Bangkok, GPO Box 701, Bangkok 10501 Thailand. **Tel** 11 66 2 2471032. cum. index. **Bk Rev**. **Ad Acc**. ctrl circ.

US/0731-633X
DIRECTORY OF SPECIAL LIBRARIES AND INFORMATION CENTERS. [Dir. spec. libr. inf. cent.]. 1st Ed. (1963)-. Directory. English. ir. $435.00. Gale Research Inc., 835 Penobscot Building, Detroit MI 48226. **Tel** (800)877-GALE, (313)961-2242, FAX (313)961-6083, telex TWX 810-221-7086. **ED** Joanna Zakalik. **LC** Z731; .D56. **DD** 026/.00025/73.
Desc: Details the specialized collections of books, periodicals, databases, and other information sources maintained and used by business, nonprofit associations, educational institutions, libraries, governmental agencies, and other types of organizations.

US/0741-4536
DIRECTORY OF SPECIAL LIBRARIES AND INFORMATION CENTERS IN TEXAS. **Added/Corp** Texas State Library. Library Development Division. Special Libraries Association. Texas Chapter. (1981)-. Directory. English. Texas State Library Clearinghouse, PO Box 12927, Capitol Station, Austin TX 78711. **Tel** (512)463-5435, FAX (512)463-5436. **LC** Z732.T25; T475. **DD** 026/.00025/764. ***Continues*** *Texas Special Libraries Directory, 0082-3163.*

AT
DIRECTORY OF SPECIAL LIBRARIES IN AUSTRALIA. **Main/Corp** Library Association of Australia. Special Libraries Section. (1952)-. Monographic series. English. ir. Price varies per volume. Australian Library & Information Association, PO Box E441, Queen Victoria Terrace, ACT 2600 Australia. **Tel** 011 61 6 2851877, FAX 011 61 6 282 2249. **ED** Brenda Pittard and Jan Cree. Index available. **Bk Rev**. **Ad Acc**.

CN/0319-2563
DIRECTORY OF SPECIAL LIBRARIES IN THE MONTREAL AREA. **Added/Corp** Special Libraries Association. Montreal Chapter. **VFOAT** Repertoire des Bibliotheques Specialisees de la Region de Montreal. (1975)-. Periodical. Multiple languages (English and French). be. 25.00Can$ (pages and binder), 20.00Can$ (pages), 5.00Can$ (binder). Special Libraries Association, Eastern Canada Chapter, Directory Committee, PO Box 1538 Station B, Montreal Quebec H3B 3K3 Canada. **ED** Linda Ordogh. **DD** 026/.00025/71428. ***Continues*** *Directory of Special Libraries in Montreal, 0070-6396.*
Desc: A comprehensive listing of special library holdings including subject specialties in the Montreal area.

AT/0314-9307
DIRECTORY OF STATE AND PUBLIC LIBRARY SERVICES IN QUEENSLAND. **Main/Corp** Library Board of Queensland. **VFOAT** State and Public Library Services in Queensland; Directory of State & Public Library Services in Queensland. (1987)-. Directory. English. an. Free. The Administration Officer, State Library of Queensland, PO Box 3488, South Brisbane Queensland 4101 Australia. **LC** Z870.Q44; L53a. **DD** 027.4943. Index available. ctrl circ.
Ind/Abst Aust. Educ. Index (199?-).

PH
DIRECTORY OF TEACHERS OF LIBRARY SCIENCE IN THE PHILIPPINES. Directory. English. Philippine Association of Teachers of Library Science, National Library Building/Room 301, T M Kalaw Street, Manila 2801 Philippines. **LC** Z669.5.P58; D57. **DD** 020/.711/599.

US/0748-2566
DIRECTORY OF THE NEW YORK METROPOLITAN REFERENCE AND RESEARCH LIBRARY AGENCY, METRO AND METROPOLITAN NEW YORK REGIONAL INTERSYSTEM COOPERATIVE LIBRARY NETWORK, INTERSHARE. **VFOAT** Directory of Metro Libraries and Buyers Guide. 1983-. Directory. English. an. $23.95. LDA Publishers, 42-36 209th Street, Bayside NY 11361. **Tel** (718)224-9484, FAX (718)224-9487.

US/1011-2952
DIRECTORY OF UNITED NATIONS SERIAL PUBLICATIONS. **Added/Corp** United Nations. United Nations. Advisory Committee for the Co-ordination of Information Systems. **VFOAT** United Nations Serial Publications. (1988)-. Government Publication. English. ir. $30.00. United Nations Publications, 2 United Nations Plaza, Room DC2 0853, Department 007C, New York NY 10017. **Tel** (212)963-8303, (800)253-9646. **LC** Z6482; .R43; JX1977. ***Continues*** *Register of United Nations Serial Publications.*
Desc: Listing of keyword index of 1800 serials published by 34 UN affiliated bodies and specialized agencies.

CN/0831-3148
DIRECTORY / ONTARIO LIBRARY SERVICE, RIDEAU. [Dir. - Ont. Libr. Serv., Rideau]. **Main/Corp** Ontario Library Service, Rideau. **VFOAT** Annuaire. (1985)-. Directory. English (French). an. Ontario Library Service-Rideau, Ottawa Ontario K1G 0N1 Canada. **DD** 027.4/025/7137. ***Continues*** *Directory - Eastern Ontario Library System.*

US
DIRECTORY / TEXAS LIBRARY ASSOCIATION. **Main/Corp** Texas Library Association. 1984-. Directory. English. an. 3355 Bee Cave Road, Suite 603, Austin TX 78746. ***Continues*** *Texas Library Association. Directory for Members.*

AT/0728-6481
DIXSON LIBRARY REPORT. [Dixson Libr. rep.]. (1982)-. Periodical. English. qt. University of New England Publishing Unit, Armidale New South Wales 2351 Australia. **Tel** 06 773-2898. **ED** K Schmude. **DD** 027.094. ***Continues*** *Current Developments (Australia), 0811-2045.*
Ind/Abst Aust. Educ. Index; Aust. Libr. Inf. Sci. Abstr. (1982-).

IO
DJURNAL PERPUSTAKAAN. Periodical. Multiple languages (Indonesian and English). Perpustakaan Umum Makassar, JL Kajaolalidjo 16, PO Box 16, Ujung Pandang Indonesia. **LC** Z671; .D57.

US/0272-037X
DLA BULLETIN (OAKLAND, CALIF.). (DLA BULLETIN / UNIVERSITY OF CALIFORNIA, DIVISION OF LIBRARY AUTOMATION.). [DLA bull.]. **VFOAT** University of California Division of Library Automation Bulletin; D.L.A. Bulletin. Vol. 1, No. 1 (Feb. 1981)-. Bulletin. English. qt. Free. DLA Bulletin, University of California, Division of Library Automation, Office of the President, 300 Lakeside Drive/Floor 8, Oakland CA 94612-3550. **Tel** (510)987-0564. **ED** Mary Jean Moore. **Circ:** 2,000. available on an online database.
Desc: Articles on the development of the University of California's online library catalog (MELVYL). Covers the system's functions, user services and supporting telecommunications network.
Ind/Abst Libr. Inf. Sci. Abstr.

US/1054-9692
DOCUMENT IMAGE AUTOMATION. ***Title Change.*** **See** Computers-Optical Storage, CD-ROM Applications.

US/1054-9706
DOCUMENT IMAGE AUTOMATION UPDATE. ***Title Change.*** **See** Computers-Optical Storage, CD-ROM Applications.

UK/0952-892X
DOCUMENT SUPPLY NEWS. **Added/Corp** British Library. Document Supply Centre. No. 14 (Dec. 1987)-. Periodical. English. Four times a year. Free. British Library / Publications Sale Unit, Boston Spa, Wetherby, West Yorkshire LS23 7BQ England. **Tel** 011 44 937 546546 546543, FAX 011 44 937 546333, telex 557381. ***Continues*** *British Library Document Supply Centre Newsletter, 0269-1175.*
Ind/Abst Museum Abstr.

FR/0012-4508
DOCUMENTALISTE (PARIS). (DOCUMENTALISTE : SCIENCES DE L'INFORMATION.). [Documentaliste]. **Added/Corp** Association Francaise des Documentalistes et Bibliothecaires Specialises. (1964)-. Periodical. French. Five times a year. 520.00F (France); 580.00F (other). ADBS Redaction Documentaliste, 25 rue Claude Tillier, F 75012 Paris France. **Tel** 11 33 1 43722525. **ED** J M Rauzier. **LC** Z1007; .D615. **CODEN** DSINE6. **Bk Rev**. **Ad Acc**. **Pr Rev**. **Circ:** 5,000. Documents available from Ask*IEEE. ***Continues*** *ADBS Informations.*
Ind/Abst INSPEC (Mar./April 1988-); LABORDOC; Libr. Inf. Sci. Abstr.; Libr. Lit.

AG
DOCUMENTATION BIBLIOTECOLOGICA. **Added/Corp** Bahia Blanca, Argentine Republic. Universidad Nacional del Sur. Centro de Documentacion Bibliotecologica. No. 1 (1970)-. Periodical. Spanish. ir. Centro de Documentacion Bibliotecologica, Universidad Nacional del Sur, Bahia Blanca Argentina. **ED** Atilio Peralta. **LC** Z671; .D63. **DD** 010. **Circ:** 250 (ctrl).
Desc: Dedicated to librarian topics.

CN/0315-2340
DOCUMENTATION ET BIBLIOTHEQUES. [Doc. bibl.]. **Added/Corp** Association Canadienne des Bibliothecaires de Langue Francaise. Vol. 19 (March 1973)-. Periodical. French. qt. 45.00Can$ Canada; 52.50Can$ other. ASTED Inc, 1030 rue Cherrier, Bureau 505, Montreal Quebec H2L 1H9 Canada. **Tel** (514)522-7833, FAX (514)521-9561. **LC** Z735.A1; A85. **DD** 020/.5. **CODEN** DCBBBO. Index available. **Bk Rev**. **Ad Acc**. ctrl circ. Documents available from Ask*IEEE. ***Continues*** *Association Canadienne des Bibliothecaires de Langue Francaise. Bulletin, 0004-5314.*
Desc: Oldest French review devoted to library science in America. Each issue contains approximately four articles, chronicles and a bibliographical part.
Ind/Abst Can. Period. Index; INSPEC (March 1973-); Libr. Inf. Sci. Abstr.; Libr. Lit.; Point Repere (1983-).

BE
DOCUMENTATION ON BOOKS / INTERNATIONAL UNIVERSITY CONTACT FOR MANAGEMENT EDUCATION. LITERATURE SERVICE. **See** Business-General Management.

US/0270-5095
DOCUMENTS TO THE PEOPLE. (DTTP. DOCUMENTS TO THE PEOPLE.). [Doc. people]. **Added/Corp** American Library Association. Government Documents Round Table. **VFOAT** Documents to the People; DTTP. Vol. 3, (Sept. 1974)-. Periodical. English. Four times a year (Mar., June, Sept., Dec.). $20.00 North America; $25.00 others. Sinai Rocha Moody Memorial Library, PO Box 97148, Baylor University, Waco TX 76798. **Tel** (817)755-2111 or 755-4606, FAX (817)755-3116. **ED** Jim Walsh (phone: (617)552-2414). **DD** 025. **Ad Acc**, **Adv Mgr:** Jill Moriearty. **Circ:** 1,800. available on microfilm and microfiche from University Microfilms International (UMI). ***Continues*** *Documents to the People, 0270-5095.*
Desc: Provides current information on government publications, technical reports, and maps at local, state, national and international levels on related government activities and documents librarianship.
Ind/Abst Leg. Inf. Manage. Index (19??-199?); Libr. Inf. Sci. Abstr.

●US/1060-4367
DOMES (MILWAUKEE, WIS.). **See** History(General)-History of the Middle East.

US/8756-2294
DYNIX DATALINE. (DYNIX DATALINE / DYNIX AUTOMATED LIBRARY SYSTEMS.). **Added/Corp** Dynix, Inc. (1984)-. Periodical. English. qt. $12.00. Dynix Inc, 151 East 1700 South, Provo UT 84606. **Tel** (801)373-1889, (800)288-8020. **ED** Tim Anderson and Russ Clement. **DD** 025. **Circ:** 3,500 (ctrl).
Desc: Company magazine, with articles and features on DYNIX activities and employees.

●US/1064-3486
EASTERN EXPRESS (OMAHA, NEB.). (EASTERN EXPRESS : THE NEWSLETTER OF THE EASTERN LIBRARY SYSTEM.). **Added/Corp** Eastern Library System (Neb.). (Mar. 1992)-. Newsletter. English. mo. Free. ELS, Eastern Library System, 11902 Elm Street, Suite 6A, Omaha NE 68144. ***Continues*** *ELS Nibbles, 1064-3494.*

US
EBSCO CD-ROM HANDBOOK. CD-ROM. ***Ceased.*** (19??)-(Fall 1993). English. an. EBSCO Publishing / Boston, 83 Pine Street, Peabody MA 01960. **Tel** (800)653-2726 North America, (508)535-8500, FAX (508)535-8545. available in print (from EBSCO Publishing).
Desc: Contains information on over 850 CD-ROM products which can be purchased through EBSCO. Each entry includes title, frequency, product description, information source, producer, hardware and software requirements and other pertinent information. All information is key word searchable and searches can be restricted by specifying a subject category, publisher and/or hardware format (IBM or MAC).

CN/0706-5205
ECHANGE (NORANDA). (L'ECHANGE.). V. 1- Jan. 1978-. Periodical. French. ir. $15.00. Bibliotheque Centrale de Pret de l'Abitibi-Temiscamingue, C P 266, Noranda Quebec J9X 2A9 Canada. **DD** 027.4/714/13.

VE/0506-5992
EDICIONES. **Main/Corp** Universidad Central de Venezuela. Biblioteca Central. Vol. 1 (1961)-. Spanish. Universidad Central / Venezuela, Biblioteca, Caracas Venezuela. **DD** 060.

PN
EDICIONES BIBLIOTECA JOSE AGUSTIN ARANGO CH. BOLETIN CULTURAL. Monographic series. Spanish. Price varies per volume. Banco Nacional de Panama, Casilla Postal 5220, Panama 5 Panama.

●AT
EDUCATION FOR LIBRARY AND INFORMATION SERVICES, AUSTRALIA. **Added/Corp** Australian Library and Information Association. Education for Library and Information Services Section. Vol. 1, No. 1 (Autumn 1992)-. Periodical. English. Three times a year (May, Aug., Nov.). 35.00Aus$ Australia; 45.00Aus$ (surface mail), 55.00Aus$ (airmail). Australian Library & Information Association, PO Box E441, Queen Victoria Terrace, ACT 2600 Australia. **Tel** 011 61 6 2851877, FAX 011 61 6 282 2249. **ED** Kate Beattie (editor's address: 1 Elgin Place, Carlton, Victoria, Australia 3053, phone: (61) 3 347 9194). **LC** WMLC 93/1902. **Bk Rev**, (Qty: 6-10). **Ad Acc. Pr Rev. Circ:** 250 (ctrl). ***Continues*** *Education for Librarianship, Australia.*
Desc: Contains scholarly articles, news, professional reports and reviews of materials relating to education for library and information science in Australia.

US/0148-1061
EDUCATION LIBRARIES. [Educ. libr.]. **Added/Corp** Special Libraries Association. Education Division. (1975)-. Periodical. English. Three times a year. $20.00. Education Division / UCLA, Special Libraries Association, c/o Diane Childs, UCLA Education and Psychology Library, 390 Towell Library Building, Los Angeles CA 90024-1516. **Tel** (310)825-4081. **(Subscription address:** SLA / Special Libraries Association, 18313 Subido Street, c/o Catherine Brown, Rowland Heights CA 81748.**) ED** Anne Galler (editor's address: 5596 Castlewood, Cote St Luc, Quebec Canada H4W 1T9). **LC** Z675.P3; B84. **DD** 027.7. **Bk Rev. Ad Acc. Circ:** 400 (ctrl). available on microfilm and microfiche from University Microfilms International (UMI). ***Continues*** *Bulletin (Special Libraries Association. Education Division), 0360-098X.* ***Continued in part by*** *Special Libraries Association. Education Division. Bulletin, 1052-9454.*
Desc: Practical journal for librarians in the field of education and library science.
Ind/Abst Curr. Index J. Educ.; Libr. Inf. Sci. Abstr.

UK/0957-9575
EDUCATION LIBRARIES JOURNAL. **Added/Corp** University of London. Institute of Education. Library. Vol. 32 No. 1 (Spring 1989)-. Periodical. English. Three times a year (Mar., Jul., Oct.). £10.00. University of London / Institute of Education Library, 20 Bedford Way, London WC1H 0AL England. **Tel** 11 44 71 5801122, FAX 11 44 71 4362186. **ED** Claire Drinkwater, 07-1-6126060. (index published separately). **Bk Rev. Ad Acc. Circ:** 500 (ctrl). available on microfilm and microfiche from University Microfilms International (UMI). ***Continues*** *Education Libraries Bulletin, 0013-1407.*
Desc: All aspects of bibliography and librarianship in the field of education and its related social sciences.
Ind/Abst Br. Educ. Index; Child. Lit. Abstr. (19??-).

US/0895-5514
EDUCATION MATERIALS IN LIBRARIES. (EDUCATION MATERIALS IN LIBRARIES [COMPUTER FILE] : A SUBSET OF THE OCLC ONLINE UNION CATALOG.). [Educ. mater. libr.]. **Added/Corp** OCLC. EMIL (1987)-. Catalog. English. $300.00 (OCLC members), $350.00 (nonmembers). OCLC Asia Pacific Services, 6565 Frantz Road, Dublin OH 43017. **Tel** (800)848-5878, (614)764-6394 or 6000, FAX (614)764-6096. **DD** 370.

UK/0264-0473
ELECTRONIC LIBRARY. (THE ELECTRONIC LIBRARY : THE INTERNATIONAL JOURNAL FOR MINICOMPUTER, MICROCOMPUTER, AND SOFTWARE APPLICATIONS IN LIBRARIES.). [Electron. libr.]. Vol. 1, No. 1 (Jan. 1983)-. Periodical. English. bm. £90.00. Learned Information Ltd., Woodside Hinksey Hill, Oxford OX1 5AU England. **Tel** 44 865 730275, FAX 44 865 736354, telex 23667. **(Subscription address:** Learned Information, Inc. / North America Subscriptions, 143 Old Marlton Pike, Medford NJ 08055-8750.**) ED** David I. Raitt. **LC** Z678.9; .I57. **DD** 025/.02/02854. **[CCC]. Pr Rev.** available on microfilm and microfiche from University Microfilms International (UMI). Documents available from Article Express International, The Genuine Article, Ask*IEEE.
Desc: An international journal which focuses on the impact of computerized storage, cataloging and retrieval applications in libraries and information centers. Reports on current and upcoming information technologies, with coverage that includes circulation control systems, database searching, acquisition systems, cataloging, text processing, management systems and the growing field of optical media
Ind/Abst Cumul. Index Nurs. Allied Health Lit.; Curr. Contents Eng. Tech. Appl. Sci.; Curr. Index J. Educ.; Ei Page One; Eng. Index Annu. [Select. Cov.]; Index Period. Artic. Relat. Law; Inf. Instruc. Technol.; Inf. Manage. Technol.; Inf. Sci. Abstr. [Full Cov.]; INSPEC (Oct. 1983-); Libr. Inf. Sci. Abstr.; Libr. Lit.; Microcomput. Index (Feb. 1989-); Print. Abstr.; Res. Alert [Full Cov.]; Soc. Sci. Cit. Index [Full Cov.]; Trade Ind. Index.

US
ELEMENTARY SCHOOL LIBRARY COLLECTION, THE. 1st Ed. (1965)-. English. an (Every two years). $102.95. Brodart Inc., 500 Arch Street, Williamsport PA 17705. **Tel** (800)233-8467 Ext. 572, FAX (717)326-1479. **ED** Linda Homa, (phone: (717)326-2461 Ext. 631). Index available (Bound in issue). **Bk Rev. Pr Rev. Circ:** 4,000. available on CD-ROM (Brodart Company).
Desc: This selection and collection development guide functions effectively as a reading, listening, viewing, guidance tool and as a cataloging aid. Used by schools, public libraries, and academic libraries that maintain collections of current materials for children. The elementary school library collection has consistently proved to be a cost effective comprehensive, and versitile resource.

CN/0824-782X
EMC. EDUCATIONAL MEDIA SPECIAL INTEREST COUNCIL. (EMC : NEWSLETTER / EDUCATIONAL MEDIA SPECIAL INTEREST COUNCIL.). [EMC, Educ. Med. Spec. Interest Counc.]. **VFOAT** Educational Media Council. **VAT** Educational Media Special Interest Council. Vol. 10, No. 3 (April 1981)-. Newsletter. English. Four times a year. 3.00Can$. Newfoundland Teachers Association, Educational Media Council, 3 Kenmount Road, St John's Newfoundland A1B 1W1 Canada. **Tel** (709)229-6559. **ED** K Bruce Lane. **DD** 027.8/06/0718. **Bk Rev. Ad Acc. Circ:** 500 (ctrl). ***Continues*** *Media Newfoundland, 0824-183X.*
Desc: Forum for teachers interested in educational media and resourced-based teaching.

US/0315-8888
EMERGENCY LIBRARIAN. [Emerg. libr.]. Vol. 1 (1973)-. Periodical. English. bm. 49.00Can$ Canada; $49.00 other. Dyad Services, 284 810 West Broadway, Vancouver BC V5Z 4C9 Canada. **Tel** (604)925-0266, FAX (604)925-0566. **(Subscription address:** Dyad Services, PO Box C34069, Department 284, Seattle WA 98124.**) ED** Ken Haycock. **[CCC].** Index available. cum. index. **Bk Rev. Ad Acc. Circ:** 10,000 (ctrl). available on microfilm and microfiche from University Microfilms International (UMI).
Desc: Canada's only independent library journal and one of the largest in the world. Designed for schools and public librarians. Covers professional reading, paperbacks for children, paperbacks for young adults, microcomputers, and curriculum software.
Ind/Abst Book Rev. Index; Can. Index; Can. Period. Index; Child. Lit. Abstr. (19??-); Child. Mag. Guide; Curr. Index J. Educ. (March 1990); Inf. Sci. Abstr. (?-?); Libr. Inf. Sci. Abstr.; Libr. Lit.; Women Stud. Abstr.

US/0737-9021
EMIE BULLETIN. (EMIE BULLETIN / AMERICAN LIBRARY ASSOCIATION, ETHNIC MATERIALS INFORMATION EXCHANGE ROUND TABLE.). [EMIE bull.]. **Added/Corp** American Library Association. Ethnic Materials Information Exchange Round Table. American Library Association. Ethnic Materials and Information Exchange Round Table. Queens College (New York, N.Y.). Graduate School of Library and Information Studies. **VFOAT** E.M.I.E. Bulletin. **VAT** Ethnic Materials Information Exchange bulletin. Vol. 1, No. 1 (Sept. 1983)-. Bulletin. English. qt. $15.00 US; $16.00 other. EMIE, NSF 316 Queens College, Flushing NY 11367. **Tel** (718)997-3626, (718)997-3790, FAX (718)997-3753. **ED** David Cohen. **Bk Rev**, (Qty: 5). **Ad Acc. Circ:** 800 (ctrl).

US
ENCYCLOPEDIA OF LIBRARY AND INFORMATION SCIENCE. Vol. 1 (1968)-. Monographic series. English. Price varies per volume. Marcel Dekker Inc., 270 Madison Avenue, New York NY 10016. **Tel** (212)696-9000, (800)228-1160, FAX (212)685-4540, telex 421419. **(Subscription address:** Marcel Dekker Inc, PO Box 5017, Monticello NY 12701.**) LC** Z1006; .E57. **DD** 020/.3. **NLM** Z 1006 E56.

US
ENCYCLOPEDIA OF LIBRARY AND INFORMATION SCIENCE. SUPPLEMENT. Vol. 36 (1983)-. English. an. Marcel Dekker Inc., 270 Madison Avenue, New York NY 10016. **Tel** (212)696-9000, (800)228-1160, FAX (212)685-4540, telex 421419. **(Subscription address:** Marcel Dekker Inc, PO Box 5017, Monticello NY 12701.**) ED** A. Kent.

FR/0154-0335
ENERGIE. LEXIQUE. **See** Energy.

BE/0771-1034
ENGLISH PAGES. [Engl. pages]. (1936)-. Periodical. English. Five times a year. De Sikkel Media, Krijgslaan 281 512, 9000 Gent Belgium. **Tel** 011 32 3 3124761. **UDC** 20. ***Continues*** *Home Chat, 0772-1269.*
Ind/Abst Soc. Plann. Policy Dev. Abstr.

CN/1182-8935
ENVIRONMENT LIBRARY ACQUISITIONS LIST - NEW BRUNSWICK. DEPT. OF THE ENVIRONMENT. LIBRARY. (ENVIRONMENT LIBRARY ACQUISITIONS LIST.). [Environ. Libr. acquis. list - N.B., Dept. Environ., Libr.]. **Main/Corp** New Brunswick. Dept. of the Environment. Library. (Feb. 1990)-. Periodical. English. mo. **DD** 016.3337/05. ***Continues*** *New Brunswick. Dept. of the Environment. Library. Library Acquisitions List., 1182-8943.*

CN/0836-088X
EPILOGUE (HALIFAX, N.S.). (EPILOGUE : CANADIAN BULLETIN OF THE HISTORY OF BOOKS, LIBRARIES, AND ARCHIVES.). [Epilogue]. **Added/Corp** Dalhousie University. School of Library and Information Studies. **VFOAT** Epilogue. No. 4 (Fall 1987)-. Bulletin. English (French). Twice a year. 23.00Can$ Canada; 25.00Can$ other. Dalhousie University / School of Library & Information Studies, Halifax Nova Scotia B3H 4H8 Canada. **Tel** (902)494-3656, FAX (902)494-2451, telex 019-21863. **ED** Dr. Bertrum H. MacDonald. **DD** 027.071/05. Index available. cum. index. **Bk Rev**, (Qty: 20-30). **Pr Rev.** ***Continues*** *Newsletter (SLIS Library History Group), 0832-1175.*
Desc: Includes research papers, reviews, and news on the history of the book with a primary emphasis on Canadian topics.

US
ERIC DESCRIPTOR AND IDENTIFIER USAGE REPORT. English. an. ERIC Document Reproduction Service, 3900 Wheeler Avenue, Alexandria VA 22304. **Tel** (703)823-0500 AND (800)227-3742.

FR
ESEIGNEMENTS PROFESSIONNELS, LES. **Main/Corp** Ecole National Superieure des Bibliotheques (France). (19??)-. French. Ecole Nationale Superieures des Bibliotheques, 2 rue de Louvois, Paris 2E France. **LC** Z669.5.F7; E26a. **DD** 020/.711/44.

CN
ESTIMATES. PART III, NATIONAL LIBRARY OF CANADA. **Main/Corp** Canada. **VFOAT** udget des Depenses. Partie III, Bibliotheque Nationale du Canada. (19??)-. English (French). $6.00 Canada; $7.20 other. Canada Communication Group Publishers, Order Processing, Ottawa Ontario K1A 0S9 Canada. **Tel** (819)956-4800, (819)956-4802. **LC** Z736.N37; C36a. **DD** 027.571.

GR
ETHNIKE BIBLIOTHEKE. **Main/Corp** Hetaireia Makedonikon Spoudon. (1946)-. Greek, Modern. ir. Society for Macedonian Studies, 4 Ethnikis Amynis Avenue, GR 546 21 Thessaloniki Greece. **Tel** 011 30 31 271195. Index available.
Desc: Series of independent books.

US/1048-5287
EUROPEAN JOURNAL OF SERIALS LIBRARIANSHIP. ***Title Change.*** Vol. 1, (1993)-(199?). Periodical. English. qt. The Haworth Press Inc, 10 Alice Street, Binghamton NY 13904-1580. **Tel** (607)722-5857, (800)3-HAWORTH, FAX (607)722-1424. **ED** Kathryn Rutz. **Bk Rev. Ad Acc. Pr Rev. Acid Free.** available on microfiche. Documents available from Haworth Document Delivery Service. ***Continues*** *British Journal of Serials Librarianship.* ***Continued by*** *EuroSerials, 1069-4641.*
Desc: Deals specifically with emerging issues of serials acquisitions, collection management, bibliographic control and resource sharing in Europe, including both Western and Eastern Europe and the United Kingdom.
Ind/Abst Inf. Sci. Abstr. (?-?).

AU/1018-0826
EUROPEAN RESEARCH LIBRARIES COOPERATION : THE LIBER QUARTERLY. **Added/Corp** Ligue des Bibliotheques Europeennes de Recherche. **VFOAT** LIBER Quarterly; ERLC; ERLC-LIBER. Vol. 1, No. 1 (1991)-. Periodical. English. Four times a year. S240.00. Akademische Druck & Verlagsanstalt, Schoenaugasse 6, Postfach 598, A 8010 Graz Austria. **Tel** 011 43 316 813460. ***Formed by the union of*** *LIBER News Sheet, 0721-6858 and Bulletin (Ligue des Bibliotheques Europeennes de Recherche), 0304-0224.*

●US/1069-4641
EUROSERIALS (BINGHAMTON, N.Y.). (EUROSERIALS.). **VFOAT** Euro Serials. Vol. 1, No. 1 (Feb. 1995)-. Periodical. English. Twice a year. $50.00 US; $70.00 other. The Haworth Press Inc, 10 Alice Street, Binghamton NY 13904-1580. **Tel** (607)722-5857, (800)3-HAWORTH, FAX (607)722-1424. **ED** Jim E. Cole, MA. **Acid Free.** Documents available from Haworth Document Delivery Service.
Desc: Provides information on serials management in Europe.

UK
EVANGELICAL LIBRARY BULLETIN. Bulletin. English. sa. £25.00. Evangelical Library Bulletin,

78A Chiltern Street, London W1M 2HB England. **Tel** 011 44 1 935 6997. **ED** G. Brady. **Bk Rev**. **Circ:** 1,500 (ctrl).
Desc: Contains articles of historical or biographical interest, news about the library and its worldwide branches, book reviews, and details of new publications available on loan to members.

CN/0226-9791
EX LIBRIS (OTTAWA). (EX LIBRIS.). [Ex libris]. **Main/Corp** International Development Research Centre (Canada). Library. V. 10, No. 1 (Jan. 1981)-. Periodical. English. mo. International Development Research Centre, Box 8500, Ottawa Ontario K1G 3H9 Canada. **Tel** (613)236-6163, telex 053-3753. **DD** 016.3309172/4. ***Continues*** *Library I D R C Library Bulletin, 0380-1411.*
Ind/Abst Popul. Index (?-?).

US/0894-9204
EXPLORATION AND PRODUCTION THESAURUS. [Explor. prod. thesaurus]. **Added/Corp** University of Tulsa. Information Services Dept. University of Tulsa. Information Services Division. 1st Ed. (Jan. 1965)-. English. $150.00 (general subscribers), $175.00 (nonsubscribers). Petroleum Abstracts, University of Tulsa, Information Services Division, 600 South College Avenue, Harwell Hall 101, Tulsa OK 74104-3189. **Tel** (800)247-8678, (918)631-2297, FAX (918)599-9361, telex 49 7543. **LC** Z695.1.P43; E89. **DD** 025.
Desc: An essential guide to searching the Tulsa database efficiently and effectively. Using the controlled vocabulary with which the database has been constructed, online searches can be planned.

US
EXPLORATIONS IN MUSIC LIBRARIANSHIP. ***Ceased.*** **Added/Corp** Music Library Association. Midwest Chapter. (June 1966)-(19??). Monographic series. English. Music Library Association, PO Box 487, Canton MA 02021. **Tel** (617)828-8450, FAX (617)828-8915. **LC** ML111; .E9.

US/1065-6960
EXPLORING BOOKS. ***Ceased.*** [Explor. books]. (19??)-(1993). Periodical. English. qt. Warren Publishing House Inc., PO Box 2250, 11625-G Airport Road, Everett WA 98203. **Tel** (206)353-3100, FAX (206)355-7007. **DD** 028.

SZ
EXTENSIONS AND CORRECTIONS TO THE UDC. **VFOAT** Universal Decimal Classification. English. an. £90.00 Europe, $171.00 other. International Federation for Information and Documentation, PO Box 90402, 2509 LK Hague Netherlands. **Tel** 011 31 70 3140509, FAX 011 31 70 834827, telex 34402 KB GV NL. **(Subscription address:** Turpin Transactions Ltd., Blackhorse Road, Letchworth, Hertfordshire SG6 1HN United Kingdom; Telephone: (0462) 672555, FAX: (0462) 480947**)**
Desc: Numbered in triennial series. Each annual issue contains all proposals to extend or revise the UDC and contains all proposals accepted during the past year, and also cumulates previous issues in the same series.

NE/0014-5874
F.I.D. NEWS BULLETIN. Year 1- ; 15 March 1951-. Bulletin. English. mo. £44.00 Europe, $80.00 other. International Federation for Information and Documentation, PO Box 90402, 2509 LK Hague Netherlands. **Tel** 011 31 70 3140509, FAX 011 31 70 834827, telex 34402 KB GV NL. **(Subscription address:** Turpin Transactions Ltd., Blackhorse Road, Letchworth, Hertfordshire SG6 1HN United Kingdom; Telephone: (0462) 672555, FAX: (0462) 480947**) ED** S Keenan. **Bk Rev**. **Ad Acc**. **Circ:** 1,500. available on microfilm and microfiche from University Microfilms International (UMI).
Desc: A section featuring news from national members. Starting in this issue, news from national members will become a regular feature of the bulletin.

US
F.I.S.C.A.L. DIRECTORY, FEE-BASED INFORMATION SERVICE CENTERS IN ACADEMIC LIBRARIES. **VFOAT** FISCAL Directory, Fee Based Information Service Centers in Academic Libraries. (1988)-. Directory. English. an. $29.00. FYI/County of Los Angeles Public Library, 12350 Imperial Highway, Norwalk CA 90650. **Tel** (800)582-1093, (310)868-4003, FAX (310)868-4065. ***Continues*** *Directory of Fee-Based Service Centers in Academic Libraries.*
Desc: Provides you with everything you need to know to take advantage of hundreds of specialized information services in the US and Canada.

UK/0141-3635
FACTOTUM (LONDON, ENGLAND). (FACTOTUM.). [Factotum]. **Added/Corp** British Library. Reference Division. No. 1 (March 1978)-. Periodical. English. Three times a year. Free. 18th Century Short Title Catalouging ESTC, Great Russell Street, London WC1B 3DG England. **Tel** 011 44 1 323-7257. **(Subscription address:** US and Canada/ ESTC/NIA, University of California, Riverside CA 92521-0132**) ED** J.L. Wood and D.R.S. Pearson. **LC** Z699.4.E17; F33. **DD** 025.3/16. Index available. cum. index. **Circ:** 2,500. ***Absorbed*** *ESTC Facsimile.*
Desc: Newsletter of the Eighteenth Century Short Title Catalogue.
Ind/Abst Annu. Bibliogr. Engl. Lang. Lit.

UK
FACTS AND FIGURES. (19??)-. English. an (Apr.). Free. British Library / Publications Sale Unit, Boston Spa, Wetherby, West Yorkshire LS23 7BQ England. **Tel** 011 44 937 546546 546543, FAX 011 44 937 546333, telex 557381. **ED** Katy King. **Circ:** 15,000 (ctrl).
Desc: Statistics of the British Library Document Supply Centre.

US/1060-314X
FAIRCHILDE INTERNATIONAL LIBRARY INSTITUTE : [NEWSLETTER] / FILI. [Fairchilde Int. Libr. Inst.]. **Added/Corp** Fairchilde International Library Institute. Vol. 1, No. 1 (Nov. 1, 1991)-. Periodical. English. mo. Free (members). Fairchilde International Library Institute, 113-115 West Seventh Street, Plainfield NJ 07060-1609. **DD** 025.

CN/0709-6488
FAUT LIRE, IL. No. 1 (May 1978)-. Periodical. French. ir. Free to libraries, $50.00 others. Diffusion Du Mont Royal Inc, 317 Benjamin Hudon Ville, Saint Laurent Quebec Canada H4N 1J1. **Tel** (514)331-4540. **DD** 028.1/05.

●US/1059-6852
FAXON GUIDE TO SERIALS. (FAXON GUIDE TO SERIALS : INCLUDING PERIODICALS, ANNUALS, CONTINUATIONS, GPO PUBLICATIONS, MONOGRAPHIC SERIES, NEWSPAPERS, PROCEEDINGS, TRANSACTIONS, YEARBOOKS AND CD-ROM.). [Faxon guide ser.]. (1992)-. Proceedings. English. Free. Faxon Press, PO Box 9102, Boston MA 02132. **LC** Z6941; .F28. **DD** 011. ***Continues*** *Faxon ... Librarians' Guide to Serials.*

US/0272-4537
FAXON ... LIBRARIANS' GUIDE TO CONTINUATIONS. [Faxon libr. guide contin.]. **VFOAT** Librarians' Guide to Continuations. 1981-. English. ir. Free to Faxon customers, $5.00 others. FW Faxon Company Inc., 15 Southwest Drive, Westwood MA 02090. **Tel** (617)329-3350. **LC** Z692.S5; F38. **DD** 025.2/832.

US/1043-1187
FAXON PLANNING REPORT, THE. [Faxon plan. rep.]. (1990)-. English. an. $45.00 US; $49.00 Canada. FW Faxon Company Inc., 15 Southwest Drive, Westwood MA 02090. **Tel** (617)329-3350. **ED** Michael Ault. **DD** 070. **Ad Acc**. **Circ:** 7,000 (ctrl). ***Formed by the union of*** *Faxon Collection Development Series. Part A, Library Profiles, 0897-6562* ***and*** *Faxon Collection Development Series. Part B, Publisher Profiles, 0897-6570.*
Desc: Provides in - depth information on library budget preparation and trends in serials publishing, based on surveys which Faxon sends out annualy.

US/1048-3403
FAXON REPORT, THE. [Faxon rep.]. (1990)-. Periodical. English. qt. Free. 15 Southwest Park, Westwood MA 02090. **DD** 025.

SW
FBR AKTUELLT. **Main/Corp** Forskningsbiblioteksradet (Sweden). V. 1- May 1973-. Swedish (summaries and/or abstracts in English). Box 6404, 113 82 6 Stockholm Sweden. **LC** Z675.R45; F62A.

US
FEDERAL DOCUMENT DEPOSITORIES AND RESOURCE INFORMATION FOR FLORIDA AND THE CARIBBEAN : A DIRECTORY. **Added/Corp** University of Florida. Libraries. Documents Dept. **VFOAT** Federal Depository Directory. (1991)-. Directory. English. be. ***Continues*** *Federal Document Depositories and Resource Information for Florida and Puerto Rico.*

US/0737-4178
FEDLINK TECHNICAL NOTES. [FEDLINK tech. notes]. **VFOAT** F.E.D.L.I.N.K. Technical Notes; Technical Notes. **VAT** Federal Library and Information Network Technical Notes. Vol. 1, No. 1 (Feb. 1983)-. Periodical. English. mo. Federal Library and Information Center Committee, Library of Congress, c/o D. Dolan, Washington DC 20540-5100. **Tel** (202)287-5000.

HU/0139-2115
FEJER MEGYEI KONYVTAROS. (1976)-. Hungarian.
Ind/Abst Magyar Konyv. Szak. Biblio.; Hungar. Libr. Info. Sci. Abstr.

CN/0014-9802
FELICITER. [Feliciter]. **Added/Corp** Canadian Library Association. Vol. 1 (Jan. 1956)-. Periodical. English. mo. Free to members. Canadian Library Association, 200 Elgin Street, Suite 602, Ottawa Ontario K2P 1L5 Canada. **Tel** (613)232-9625.
Ind/Abst Can. Index (?-?); Can. Period. Index (19??-).

NE
FENIX. **Added/Corp** Friends of Ideas and Action Foundation. (1990)-. English. **LC** HC59.69; .F465.
Desc: Speaks of developing countries.

US
FICHE 'N REEL NEWS : MICROFORM COLLECTIONS AT THE NEW YORK STATE LIBRARY. **VFOAT** Fiche and Reel. No. 1 (Jan. 26, 1989)-. Periodical. English. ir. New York State Library, Documents Gift & Exchange Section, Empire State Plaza, Albany NY 12230. **Tel** (518)474-5953.

II
FID/CR NEWSLETTER. **Main/Corp** International Federation for Documentation. Committee on Classification Research. **VAT** Federacion Internacional de Documentacion/Classification Research Newsletter. Newsletter. English. ir. Documentation Research and Training Centre, Indian Statistical Institute, Bangalore India.

II/0074-5804
FID/CR REPORT. **Main/Corp** International Federation for Documentation. Committee on Classification Research. **Added/Corp** Dansk Central for Dokumentation. Bangalore, India (City). Documentation Research and Training Centre. **VFOAT** FID/CR Report Series. (1964)-. English. Documentation Research and Training Centre, Indian Statistical Institute, Bangalore India.

FJ
FIJI LIBRARY ASSOCIATION NEWSLETTER. **Main/Corp** Fiji Library Association. Began with Nov. 1973 issue. Newsletter. English. mo. Fiji Library Association, PO Box 2292, Government Buildings, Suva Fiji. **ED** Marieta Inta. **LC** Z845.F5; F48A. **DD** 027/.096/11. **Bk Rev**. **Ad Acc**. **Circ:** 120.
Desc: A newsletter containing news and activities of libraries and librarians in Fiji.

US/0015-1297
FILM INFORMATION. V. 1- 1970-. Periodical. English. mo. $7.00. Film Information, Box 500 Manhattanville Station, New York NY 10027. available on microfilm from Xerox; available on microfilm and microfiche from University Microfilms International (UMI).

CN/0713-6099
FILM LIBRARY CATALOGUE / NATIONAL HEALTH AND WELFARE. [Film libr. cat. - Natl. Health Welf.]. **Main/Corp** Canada. Health and Welfare Canada. **VFOAT** Catalogue de la Cinematheque. **VAT** Catalogue de la Cinematheque - Ministere de la Sante Nationale et du Bien-Etre Social. English (French). Health and Welfare of Canada Information Directorate, Ottawa Ontario K1A 0K9 Canada. **Tel** (613)954-8576. **DD** 018/.137.

●US
FINANCIAL ASSISTANCE FOR LIBRARY AND INFORMATION STUDIES. **Added/Corp** American Library Association. Standing Committee on Library Education. (1993/1994)-. English. an. $1.00. Scole American Library Association, 50 East Huron Street, Chicago IL 60611. **Tel** (312)944-6780, (312)280-4277. **LC** Z668; .A575. ***Continues*** *Financial Assistance for Library Education, 0569-6275.*

US/0569-6275
FINANCIAL ASSISTANCE FOR LIBRARY EDUCATION. ***Title Change.*** [Financ. assist. libr. educ.]. **Added/Corp** American Library Association. Library Education Division. American Library Association. Standing Committee on Library Education. (1969/1970)-(1992/1993). English. an. American Library Association, 50 East Huron Street, Chicago IL 60611. **Tel** (312)944-6780, (800)545-2433, FAX (312)944-2641. **LC** Z668; .A575. **DD** 020/.7/11. **Circ:** 3,000. ***Continues*** *Fellowships, Scholarships, Grants-in-Aid, Loan Funds, and other Financial Assistance for Library Education.* ***Continued by*** *Financial Assistance for Library and Information Studies.*
Desc: Directory of scholarships, assistantships for library education, primarily at masters level. Includes listings from a variety of sources such as schools, associations, etc.

TZ
FINANCIAL STATEMENT FOR THE PERIOD COVERING FROM 1ST JANUARY TO 31ST DECEMBER ... / TANZANIA LIBRARY ASSOCIATION. **Main/Corp** Tanzania Library Association. English. an. Tanzania Library Association, PO Box 2645, Dar es Salaam Tanzania. **LC** Z673.T22; T36B. **DD** 020/.6234/678.

US/0892-7367
FINDING. [Finding]. **VFOAT** Finding, A Buyer's Guide. (1987)-. English. an. $34.95. LDA Publishers, 42-36 209th Street, Bayside NY 11361. **Tel** (718)224-9484, FAX (718)224-9487. **ED** Paul Ippolito and Margaret Riconda. **LC** Z684; .F56. **DD** 022/.9/025. Index

available. **Ad Acc.** **Circ:** 40,000 (ctrl).
Desc: Buyers' guide listing products and services for libraries and information centers.

FR/0980-322X
FIT : FORMATION INFORMATIQUE TECHNOLOGIE. (19??)-. French. Four times a year. 195.89F. ADITE, 14 Rue Corvisart, F-75013 Paris France. **Tel** 011 33 1 45358662.

CN/0826-3671
FIVE LIBRARY REGIONS ..., PROVINCE OF NEW BRUNSWICK, THE. [Five libr. reg., Prov. N.B.]. **Main/Corp** New Brunswick Library Service. **VFOAT** Five Library Regions. English. an. **DD** 027.4715.

CN/0228-7137
FLAG : THE FOOTHILLS LIBRARY ASSOCIATION GAZETTE, THE. [Flag. Foothills Libr. Assoc. gaz.]. **VAT** Foothills Library Association Gazette. Vol. 1, No. 1 (Sept. 1979)-. Periodical. English. Free. J Paine, Department of Communications Media, University of Calgary, Calgary Alberta T2N 1N4 Canada. **DD** 020/.622/71233. ctrl circ.

US/0882-908X
FLICC NEWSLETTER. (FLICC NEWSLETTER / FEDERAL LIBRARY AND INFORMATION CENTER COMMITTEE.). [FLICC newsl.]. **Added/Corp** United States. Federal Library and Information Center Committee. **VAT** Federal Library and Information Center Committee Newsletter. No. 132 (Jan. 1985)-. Newsletter. English. Four times a year. Free on request. Federal Library and Information Center Committee, Library of Congress, c/o D. Dolan, Washington DC 20540-5100. **Tel** (202)287-5000. **ED** Darlene Dolan, Telephone: (202)707-4828. **LC** Z675.G7; F55. **DD** 027.5/0973. **NLM** Z 675.G7; F106. **Circ:** 3,000. ***Continues*** *FLC Newsletter, 0014-5939.*
Desc: Reports on the activities of the Federal Library and Information Center community, disseminating news about and of interest to the federal information community and information concerns of the nation at large.
Ind/Abst Libr. Inf. Sci. Abstr.

CN/0845-3020
FLIS NEWSLETTER. [FLIS newsl.]. **VAT** Faculty of Library and Information Science Newsletter. No. 29 (Fall 1988)-. Newsletter. English. University Toronto Library, Toronto Ontario Canada. **ED** Karen Melville (editor's address: Faculty of Library and Information Science, University of Toronto, 140 St George Street, Toronto Ontario M5S 1A1). **DD** 020/.7/11713541. ***Continues*** *Newsletter (University of Toronto. Faculty of Library and Information Science), 0824-7811.*

US
FLORIDA INTERCOM. **Added/Corp** Florida. Dept. of Commerce. Vol. 1 (Dec. 1969)-. Periodical. English. mo. Florida State Library, R A Gray Building, Tallahassee FL 32301. **Tel** (904)487-2651, FAX (904)488-2746.

US
FLORIDA LIBRARY DIRECTORY. (1953)-. Directory. English. an. Free. Florida State Library, R A Gray Building, Tallahassee FL 32301. **Tel** (904)487-2651, FAX (904)488-2746. **ED** Laura J Hodges and E Walter Terrie. Index available. **Circ:** 1,500 (ctrl).
Desc: Presents statistical data from the preceeding year, following the categories of the National Center for Education Statistics; includes address listings for public, private, academic, institutional and special libraries and school media centers.

US/1059-034X
FLORIDA SUNLINK NEWS : SCHOOL LIBRARY MEDIA NETWORK / UNIVERSITY OF CENTRAL FLORIDA, COLLEGE OF EDUCATION. [Fla. Sunlink news]. **Added/Corp** University of Central Florida. College of Education. **VFOAT** Sunlink News. Vol. 1, no. 1 (Fall 1991)-. Periodical. English. Three times a year. Free. University of Central Florida College of Education, Sunlink, College of Education, ED 220, Orlando FL 32816. **DD** 027.

US/0740-4956
FOCUS, LIBRARY SERVICE TO OLDER ADULTS, PEOPLE WITH DISABILITIES. **VFOAT** Focus; Library Service to Older Adults, People with Disabilities. (1983)-. Periodical. English. mo. $16.00 US; $18.00 Canada; $20.00 other. Michael G. Gunde, 216 N Frederick Ave, Daytona Beach FL 32114-3408. **Tel** (904)257-4259, FAX (904)239-6069. **ED** Michael G. Gunde. **Bk Rev**, (Qty: 8). **Circ:** 150 (ctrl).
Desc: Discusses library programs and resources for older adults and people with disabilities.

US/0015-5152
FOCUS ON INDIANA LIBRARIES. **Added/Corp** Indiana Library Association. (1947)-. Periodical. English. Eleven times a year (monthly with July/August issue combined). $15.00. Indiana Library Federation, 1500 North Delaware, Indianapolis IN 46202. **Tel** (317)636-6613, FAX (317)634-9503. **LC** Z732.I4; F6. **DD** 020.623. **Ad Acc**, **Adv Mgr:** Editor, **Tel** (317)257-2040. **Circ:** 3,500. available on microfilm and microfiche from University Microfilms International (UMI).
Desc: Newspaper with current Indiana news for libraries, job openings, calendar, features. Official publication of Association, State Library. Occasional special inserts on one topic.

UK/0305-8468
FOCUS ON INTERNATIONAL & COMPARATIVE LIBRARIANSHIP. [Focus int. comp. librariansh.]. **VFOAT** Focus on International and Comparative Librarianship. Began with Vol. 1 (1967). Periodical. English. Three times a year (April, August and December). £10.50 UK; $20.00 US. International & Comparative Librarianship, 25 Bromford Gardens, Westfield Road, Edgbaston Birmingham B15 3XD United Kingdom. **Tel** 0970 828351 (EDITORIAL). **(Subscription telephone:** 021-454 0935**)** **ED** Michael Wise. **DD** 020. Index available. cum. index. **Bk Rev.** **Ad Acc.**
Desc: International dimension of librarianship from a British standpoint. Explores library development in the third world and seeks to service professionals wishing to work overseas.
Ind/Abst Inf. Sci. Abstr.; Libr. Inf. Sci. Abstr.; Ref. Z.

●US/1071-9997
FOCUS ON SECURITY. (FOCUS ON SECURITY : THE NEWSLETTER OF LIBRARY, ARCHIVE, AND MUSEUM SECURITY.). [Focus secur.]. Vol. 1, No. 1 (Oct. 1993)-. Periodical. English. Four times a year. $70.00. Traid Company, PO Box 9930, Moscow ID 83843. **Tel** (208)883-0817, FAX (208)883-5353. **ED** Eileen Brady. **LC** Z679.6; .F63. **DD** 025.8/2. **Bk Rev**, (Qty: 1-4). **Ad Acc**, **Adv Mgr:** Jon Gustafson. **Circ:** 100.
Desc: Features articles on building, personnel, and personal security, employee awareness, reviews of security systems and devices, and news of materials theft. It emphasizes information which can be put to immediate and practical use.

US/0275-4924
FOCUS ON THE CENTER FOR RESEARCH LIBRARIES. [Focus Cent. Res. Libr.]. **Main/Corp** Center for Research Libraries (U.S.). **VFOAT** Focus. Vol. 1, Issue 1 (Jan./Feb. 1981)-. Periodical. English. bm (6 issues). Free on request. Center for Research Libraries, 6050 South Kenwood Avenue, Chicago IL 60637. **Tel** (312)955-4545. **ED** Linda Naru. **LC** Z675.R45; C46a. **DD** 027.7/0973. **Circ:** 4,000. ***Continues*** *Center for Research Libraries (U.S.). Newsletter, 0008-9087.*
Desc: News of programs, policies, collections and new acquisitions for CRL members and staff.

US
FOLGER FACSIMILES, THE. English. ir. Associated University Press, 440 Forsgate Drive, Cranbury NJ 08512. **Tel** (609)655-4770.

CN/0838-2026
FONTANUS FROM THE COLLECTIONS OF MCGILL UNIVERSITY. (FONTANUS.). [Fontanus collect. McGill Univ.]. **Added/Corp** McGill University. Libraries. McGill University. Vol. 1 (1988)-. Periodical. English (summaries and/or abstracts in French). $15.00 per issue (individuals), $25.00 (institutions). Canadian Association of Geography, McGill University, 805 Sherbrooke Street West, Montreal Quebec H3A 2K6 Canada. **Tel** (514)398-4946. **LC** Z736.M36; F65. **DD** 027.7714/28.
Ind/Abst Child. Lit. Abstr. (19??-).

US/0733-3196
FOOTLOOSE LIBRARIAN, THE. ***Ceased.*** **See** Travel and Tourism.

US
FOOTNOTES / STATE LIBRARY COMMISSION OF IOWA. **Added/Corp** State Library Commission of Iowa. **VFOAT** Foot Notes. Vol. 1, No. 1 (Nov. 1976)-. Periodical. English. Twelve times a year. Free. State Library of Iowa, Office of Library Development, East 12th and 6 Rand, Des Moines IA 50319. **Tel** (515)281-6788. **Circ:** 2,000 (ctrl). ***Continues*** *Aardvark.*
Desc: News of state library programs and other information of interest to Iowa librarians.

US
FOR REFERENCE FROM METRO. **Added/Corp** New York Metroplolitan Reference and Research Library Agency. No. 157 Sept. (1986)-. Periodical. English. mo. New York Metropolitan Reference Research Library, 57 East 11th Street, New York NY 11201. **Tel** (718)852-8700. ***Continues*** *For Reference.*

US/1064-1351
FOR YOUR INFORMATION (SAN DIEGO, CALIF.). (FOR YOUR INFORMATION : COUNCIL OF CALIFORNIA COUNTY LAW LIBRARIANS NEWSLETTER.). [For your inf.]. **Added/Corp** Council of California County Law Librarians. No. 1 (Nov. 1976)-. Periodical. English. bm. Free Comes with Council of California County Law Libraries membership. CCCLL / Council of California Counties Law Libraries, 1105 Front Street, San Diego CA 92101. **Tel** (619)531-3900.
Ind/Abst Leg. Inf. Manage. Index (19??-).

CN/1187-6301
FORTHCOMING BOOKS - NATIONAL LIBRARY OF CANADA. (FORTHCOMING BOOKS.). [Forthcom. books - Natl. Libr. Can.]. **Main/Corp** National Library of Canada. **VFOAT** Canadian Cataloguing in Publication Program; Livre a Paraitre. (June 1987)-. Periodical. English (French). Twelve times a year. Free on request to Canadian publishers. National Library of Canada, 395 Wellington Street, Ottawa Ontario K1A 0N4 Canada. **Tel** (613)995-7969, (613)995-7969, (819)994-6881, FAX (613)991-9871. **DD** 015.71.
Desc: Listing provided by the National Library of Canada which coordinates the National CIP (Cataloguing in Publication) Program. CIP attempts to provide advance information on the books of all Canadian publishers so that it can be used by libraries and booksellers in selecting, ordering and cataloging books.

GW/0173-5187
FORUM MUSIKBIBLIOTHEK. (FORUM MUSIKBIBLIOTHEK / DEUTSCHES BIBLIOTHEKSINSTITUT.). [Forum Musikbibl.]. **Added/Corp** Deutsches Bibliotheksinstitut. Vol. 1, No. 1 (1980)-. German. qt. DM38.00. Deutsches Bibliotheksinstitut, Bundesallee 184 185, D 10717 Berlin Germany. **Tel** 011 49 30 8505186, 011 49 30 8505187, FAX 011 49 30 8505100. **ED** Marion Sommerfeld. **LC** ML110; .F67. **DD** 026/.78/05. Index available. **Bk Rev.** **Circ:** 250.
Desc: Articles and information for music libraries.
Ind/Abst Libr. Inf. Sci. Abstr.

CN/0831-3016
FORUM (REGINA, SASK.). (FORUM / SASKATCHEWAN LIBRARY ASSOCIATION.). [Forum - Sask. Libr. Assoc.]. **Added/Corp** Saskatchewan Library Association. Vol. 7, No. 4 (April 1985)-. Periodical. English. Five times a year. 25.00Can$, Includes the Saskatchewan Library Association Membership. Saskatchewan Library Association, Box 3388, Regina Saskatchewan S4P 3H1 Canada. **Tel** (306)787-2976. **ED** Colleen Murphy. **DD** 027.07124. **Bk Rev.** **Ad Acc.** **Circ:** 200 (ctrl). ***Continues*** *Saskatchewan Library Forum, 0703-8321.*
Desc: Issues of concern to libraries and library employees; reviews of Canadian materials and library reference materials; information on conferences and workshops.

US
FOUNDATIONS IN LIBRARY AND INFORMATION SCIENCE. Vol. 1 (1978)-. Monographic series. English. ir. $73.25. JAI Press Inc., 55 Old Post Road, Suite 2, PO Box 1678, Greenwich CT 06836-1678. **Tel** (203)661-7602, FAX (203)661-0792. **ED** Thomas W. Leonhardt and Murray S. Martin.

US/0046-5038
FREEDOM TO READ FOUNDATION NEWS. (NEWS.). **Main/Corp** Freedom to Read Foundation (U.S.). **Added/Corp** American Library Association. Office for Intellectual Freedom. (19??)-. English. qt. $25.00. American Library Association, 50 East Huron Street, Chicago IL 60611. **Tel** (312)944-6780, (800)545-2433, FAX (312)944-2641. **(Subscription address:** American Library Association, Subscription Department, 434 West Downer, Aurora IL 60506-9936.**)** **LC** KF4774.A16; F7. **DD** 342/.73/085. **Circ:** 1,700 (ctrl).
Desc: Covers activities of the Freedom to Read Foundation in defending freedom of speech and of the press.

US/0749-4092
FRIENDS OF THE LILLY LIBRARY NEWSLETTER, THE. [Friends Lilly Libr. newsl.]. **Added/Corp** Lilly Library (Indiana University, Bloomington). Friends of the Lilly Library. **VFOAT** Friends of the Lilly Library Occasional Newsletter; Newsletter; Occasional Newsletter. No. 1 (Fall 1982)-. Newsletter. English. **DD** 026.
Ind/Abst Child. Lit. Abstr. (19??-).

US/0192-5539
FRIENDSCRIPT. V. 1- Spring 1979-. Periodical. English. qt. University of Illinois Library Friends, 230 University Library, Urbana IL 61801.

US/1040-8258
FULLTEXT SOURCES ONLINE. (FULLTEXT SOURCES ONLINE / BIBLIODATA.). **Added/Corp** BiblioData (Firm). **VFOAT** Full Text Sources Online; BiblioData Fulltext Sources Online. (Winter 1989)-. Academic Scholarly Publication. English. sa (Jan. and Jul.). $180.00. Bibliodata, PO Box 61, Needham Heights MA 02194. **Tel** (617)444-1154, FAX (617)449-4584. **ED** Ruth Orenstein. **LC** Z6941.; F85; PN4832. **DD** 025.04. **CODEN** FSONEO. **Bk Rev.** available on an online database from DATA-STAR. Documents available from CASDDS.
Desc: Features date coverage, subject guide, update frequency and lag time information for newswires and major newspapers.
Ind/Abst Chem. Abstr. (1990-).

DK/0069-9896
FUND OG FORSKNING I DET KONGELIGE BIBLIOTEKS SAMLINGER. [Fund forsk. K. Bibl. saml.]. **Main/Corp** Kongelige

Bibliotek (Denmark). Vol. 1 (1954)-. Monographic series. Danish (summaries and/or abstracts in English, Danish, French and German). ir. Price varies per volume. Det Kongelige Bibliotek, Postboks 2149, 1016 Kobenhavn K Denmark. **Tel** 011 45 33 930111, FAX 011 45 33 329846, telex 15009. **ED** Carl Erik Bay and Jesper During Jorgensen. **LC** Z941; .C68. **Circ:** 500 (ctrl).
Ind/Abst Annu. Bibliogr. Engl. Lang. Lit.; Art Archaeol. Tech. Abstr.; BHA : Biblio. Hist. Art.

IT
GAZZETTINO LIBRARIO. (19??)-. Italian. Five times a year. L50000 Italy; L65000 other. Gazzettino Librario, Via Jacopo Nardi 6, 50132 Florence Italy. **Tel** 011 39 55 243253.

US
GENERAL LEGAL PUBLICATIONS UNION LIST / COMPILED AND EDITED BY THE UNION LIST COMMITTEE; FRANCES G. DURAKO - CHAIRPERSON, SIMA DABIRASHTIANI, ELMO F. DATTALO, ROBERT E. DICKEY, AND BETH E. SMITH. **See** Law.

US/0161-1550
GEODEX SYSTEM/S. Main/Corp Geodex International. (19??)-. Periodical. English. Three times a year. $535.00. Geodex Retrieval Systems, 669 Broadway, PO Box 279, Sonoma CA 95476. **Tel** (707)939-8476. Index available (Bound in all issues). ***Continues*** *Geodex Structural Information Service.*

US/0016-8319
GEORGIA LIBRARIAN, THE. [Ga. libr.]. **Added/Corp** Georgia Library Association. Vol. 1, March (1964)- Vol. 30 (Mar. 1993)-. Periodical. English. Four times a year (Mar., June, Sept., Dec.). $12.50. Georgia Library Association, PO Box 39, Young Harris GA 30582. **Tel** (404)827-8725, FAX (404)669-2705. **ED** Joanne Lincoln (address: Professional Library, Atlanta Public Schools, 2930 Forrest Hill Drive, SW Atlanta GA 30315) (phone: (404)827-8725). **LC** Z732.G4; G42. **DD** 020/.9758. **Bk Rev**, (Qty: 30-40). **Ad Acc, Adv Mgr:** Dale Luchsinger. **Circ:** 1,200 (ctrl). available on microfilm and microfiche from University Microfilms International (UMI).
Desc: News of Georgia libraries. Articles on all aspects of librarianship.
Ind/Abst Libr. Lit.

US/0148-7566
GET READY SHEET, THE. Added/Corp Mid-York Library System. (1977)-. Periodical. English. bw. $28.00. Mid-York Library System, 1600 Lincoln Avenue, Utica NY 13502. **Tel** (315)735-8328, FAX (315)735-0943. **ED** Nancy Hotaling and Diana Norton. Index available (every 3 months & the end of the year). cum. index (end of the year). **Bk Rev**. **Ad Acc**. **Circ:** 1,000 (ctrl).
Desc: Provide advance information about: author interviews on TV and radio talk shows; movie and TV tie-ins; and interesting news on the world of books.

US/1041-2697
GIS FORUM, THE. *Ceased.* [GIS forum]. **VAT** Geographic Information Systems Forum. Vol. 1, No. 1 (Jan. 1989)-(1991). Periodical. English. mo. The Publishing Company, 16306 Sir William Drive, Spring TX 77379. **Tel** (713)251-0252, FAX (713)376-6333. **ED** Francis L Hanigan. **LC** G70.2; .G57. **DD** 910/.285. **[CCC].** Index available. cum. index. **Circ:** 500.
Desc: Reports and analyzes the application of desk top mapping and geographic information systems to management problems within the the public and private sectors of the economy.

CN/0821-5693
GLABC DIRECTORY. [GLABC dir.]. **Main/Corp** Government Libraries Association of British Columbia. **VAT** Government Libraries Association of British Columbia Directory. Directory. English. an. Free. Ministry of Human Resources Library, 800 Cassiar Street, Vancouver British Columbia V5K 4N6 Canada. **DD** 027.5/025/711.

US/0743-9008
GMRMLN UPDATE. [GMRMLN update]. **VFOAT** G.M.R.M.L.N. Update; Update. **VAT** Greater Midwest Regional Medical Library Network Update. No. 1 (Apr. 1984)-. Periodical. English. ir. $2.00 members, $2.50 nonmembers. GMRMLN Management Office, Library of Health Sciences, Health Sciences Center, University of Illinois at Chicago, PO Box 7509, Chicago IL 60680. **DD** 500. ***Continues*** *MHSLN Update, 0277-9994.*

YU
GODISNJAK - NARODNA BIBLIOTEKA SRBIJE. Main/Corp Narodna Biblioteka sr Srbije. Serbo-Croatian (Cyrillic) (summaries and/or abstracts in English, French and Russian). an. Narodna Biblioteka Srbije, Arheografsko Odeljenje, Skerliceva 1, 11 000 Belgrad Yugoslavia. **LC** Z841; .B48. ***Continues*** *Belgrad. Narodna Biblioteka. Godisnjak.*

US/0740-624X
GOVERNMENT INFORMATION QUARTERLY. [Gov. inf. q.]. Vol. 1, No. 1 (1984)-. Periodical. English. qt. $150.00 (institutions), $60.00 (individuals) US; $170.00 (institutions), $80.00 (individuals) (surface mail), $190.00 (institutions), $100.00 (individuals) (air mail), other. JAI Press Inc., 55 Old Post Road, Suite 2, PO Box 1678, Greenwich CT 06836-1678. **Tel** (203)661-7602, FAX (203)661-0792. **ED** Peter Hernon and Charles McClure. **LC** Z688.G6; G68. **DD** 011/.53. **NLM** Z 688.G6; G721. **CODEN** GIQUEU. **[CCC]. Pr Rev.** Documents available from The Genuine Article, Ask*IEEE.
Ind/Abst Curr. Contents Soc. Behav. Sci.; Curr. Index J. Educ. (March 1990); Ei Page One; Geogr. Abstr. Human Geogr.; Inf. Instruc. Technol.; Inf. Sci. Abstr. [Full Cov.]; INSPEC (1985-); Int. Aerosp. Abstr.; Leg. Inf. Manage. Index; Libr. Inf. Sci. Abstr.; Libr. Lit.; PAIS Int. Print (1991-); Res. Alert [Full Cov.]; Soc. Plann. Policy Dev. Abstr.; Soc. Sci. Cit. Index [Full Cov.].

US/0277-9390
GOVERNMENT PUBLICATIONS REVIEW (1982). *Title Change.* (GOVERNMENT PUBLICATIONS REVIEW.). [Gov. pub. rev.]. Vol. 9, No. 1 (Jan./Feb. 1982)-(1993). Academic Scholarly Publication. English. bm. Pergamon Press Inc., 660 White Plains Road, Tarrytown NY 10591-5153. **Tel** (914)524-9200, FAX (914)333-2444, telex 13-7328. **(Subscription address:** UK/ Headington Hill Hall, Oxford OX3 0BW; Can/ 150 Consumers Road/Suite 104, Willowdale Ontario M2J 1P9; Aus-NZ/ POB 544, Potts Point NSW 2011) **ED** Steven D Zink. **NLM** Z 7164.G7 G721. **CODEN** GPRVDI. **[CCC]. Bk Rev. Ad Acc. Pr Rev.** available on microfilm and microfiche from University Microfilms International (UMI). Documents available from The Genuine Article, Ask*IEEE, CASDDS. ***Formed by the union of*** *Government Publications Review. Part A, Research Articles, 0196-335X* ***and*** *Government Publications Review. Part B, Acquisitions Guide to Significant Government Publications at All Levels, 0196-3368.* ***Continued by*** *Journal of Government Information.*
Desc: A forum for reviews, analysis, and news of government information programs and policies important to all fields and disciplines. Covers the production, distribution, library handling, bibliographic control, accessibility and use of government information in all formats and at all levels of government - federal, state and province, municipal, national, United Nations and International agencies.
Ind/Abst Am. Hist. Life (1982-); Arts Humanit. Citation Index [Select. Cov.]; Book Rev. Index; Chem. Abstr.; Curr. Contents Soc. Behav. Sci.; Curr. Index J. Educ. (March 1990); Index Period. Artic. Relat. Law; Inf. Sci. Abstr.; INSPEC (Jan./Feb. 1988-); Int. Labour Doc.; Leg. Inf. Manage. Index; Libr. Inf. Sci. Abstr.; Libr. Lit.; Middle East Abstr. Index; PAIS Int. Print (1991-); Res. Alert [Full Cov.]; Soc. Sci. Cit. Index [Full Cov.].

US/1061-3072
GPLLA NEWSLETTER. (GPLLA NEWSLETTER / GREATER PHILADELPHIA LAW LIBRARY ASSOCIATION.). **Main/Corp** Greater Philadelphia Law Library Association. **VFOAT** Newsletter. **VAT** Greater Philadelphia Law Library Association Newsletter. (197?)-. Newsletter. English. qt. $20.00 (membership). **LC** Z675.L2; G74a. **DD** 026.34/00973.
Ind/Abst Leg. Inf. Manage. Index (19??-).

US
GRADUATE LIBRARY EDUCATION PROGRAMS. Added/Corp American Library Association. Committee on Accreditation. (19??)-. English. sa. American Library Association, 50 East Huron Street, Chicago IL 60611. **Tel** (312)944-6780, (800)545-2433, FAX (312)944-2641. **(Subscription address:** American Library Association, Subscription Department, 434 West Downer, Aurora IL 60506-9936.) **DD** 020/.7/1173.

US
GRANITE STATE LIBRARIES. Added/Corp New Hampshire State Library. (19??)-. Periodical. English. Four times a year. Free. New Hampshire State Library, 20 Park Street, Concord NH 03301. **Tel** (603)271-2394.
Desc: News about New Hampshire libraries, librarians and trustees. Articles on library issues such as library budget, confidentiality, library automation etc.

US
GRANT$ FOR LIBRARIES AND INFORMATION SERVICES. **See** Philanthropy.

BG
GRANTHAGARA PARIKRAMA.
Added/Corp Dhaka Laibreri Sarkela. **VFOAT** Granthagar Parikrama. (19??)-. Periodical. Bengali (English). sa. **LC** Z665.2.B3; G73.
Ind/Abst Indian Libr. Sci. Abstr. (19??-).

●II
GRANTHANA. INDIAN JOURNAL OF LIBRARY STUDIES. Added/Corp Raja Rammohun Roy Library Foundation. **VFOAT** Indian Journal of Library Studies. (1990)-. English. sa. $35.00. Vikas Publishing House Pvt Ltd, 576 Masjid Road, Jangpura New Delhi, 110 014 India. **Tel** 011 91 11 4624605, FAX 011 91 11 4629140, telex 3165900. **(Subscription address:** Prints India, 11 Darya Ganj, New Delhi 110002 India.) **LC** Z665.2.I4; G7. **DD** 020/.954.
Ind/Abst Indian Libr. Sci. Abstr.; Inf. Sci. Abstr.

US/0889-5198
GRASSROOTS FOR HIGH RISQUE LIBRARIANS. Added/Corp North Carolina Library Association. Young Adult Committee. **VFOAT** Grassroots. (19??)-. Periodical. English. tq (Feb., May, Oct.). $5.00 (1 year), $10.00 (2 year) U.S., $7.50 (1 year), $15.00 (2 year) other. Henderson County Public Library, Joyce Hamilton, 301 N.Washington Street, Courier 679, Hendersonville NC 28739. **Tel** (704)697-4725. **DD** 027. **Bk Rev**, (Qty: 5). **Circ:** 200 (ctrl).
Desc: Contains book lists, reviews, program ideas, and pathfinders to help busy librarians give young adults library experience.

CN/0712-8533
GUIDE DE LA BIBLIOTHEQUE DU CENTRE AUDIO-VISUEL - COLLEGE JEAN-DE-BREBEUF. (GUIDE DE LA BIBLIOTHEQUE DU CENTRE AUDIO-VISUEL / COLLEGE JEAN-DE BREBEUF.). **Main/Corp** College Jean-de-Brebeuf. Bibliotheque du Pavillon Lalemant. 81/82-. French. an. Free. Guide de la Bibliotheque du Centre Audio-Visuel, c/o College Jean-de-Brebeuf, Bibliotheque du Pavillon Lalemant, 5625 Avenue Decelles Canada. **DD** 025.5/67714281. ctrl circ. ***Continues*** *Guide de la Bibliotheque, Politiques du Centre Audio-Visuel, 0227-6542.*

CN/0823-5686
GUIDE DE L'USAGER / UNIVERSITE DU QUEBEC A TROIS-RIVIERES, SERVICE DE LA BIBLIOTHEQUE, LE. [Guide usager - Univ. Que. Trois-Rivieres, Serv. bibl.]. **Main/Corp** Universite du Quebec A Trois-Rivieres. Service de la Bibliotheque. No. 1-. French. an. Universite du Quebec A Trois-Rivieres, CP 500 Pierre Andre Julien, Trois Rivieres Quebec G9A 5H7 Canada. **Tel** (819)376-5151. **DD** 025.5/77771445. ***Continues*** *Universite du Quebec a Trois-Rivieres. Services de Communications. Guide de l'Usager, 0225-5200.*

CN/0824-8095
GUIDE DES USAGERS / UNIVERSITE DE SHERBROOKE-BIBLIOTHEQUE GENERALE. [Guide usagers - Univ. Sherbrooke, Bibl. gen.]. **Main/Corp** Universite de Sherbrooke. Bibliotheque Generale. French. an. Free. Universite de Sherbrooke / Bibliotheques, Services des Bibliotheques, Sherbrooke Quebec J1K 2R1 Canada. **DD** 025.5/6771466. ctrl circ. ***Continues*** *University de Sherbrooke. Bibliotheque Generale. Guide de la Bibliotheque Generale, 0824-8087.*

CN/0824-8613
GUIDE GENERAL DES COMITES - ASTED. (GUIDE GENERAL DES COMITES.). [Guide gen. com. - ASTED]. **Main/Corp** ASTED. 1983-. French. an. Free. Association Pour L'Avancement Des Sciences Et Des Techniques De La Documentation, 7243, Rue St-Denis, Montreal Quebec H2R 2E3. **DD** 020/.6234/714. ***Continues*** *Annuaire des Comites et Delegation, 0229-7418.*

UK
GUIDE TO LIBRARIES AND INFORMATION UNITS IN GOVERNMENT DEPARTMENTS AND OTHER ORGANISATIONS. Added/Corp British Library. Science Reference and Information Service. **VFOAT** Guide to Libraries and Information Units. 29th Ed. (1990)-. Periodical. English. an. £36.00. British Library Science Reference Information Service, 25 Southampton Building, London WC21 1AW England. **Tel** 011 44 1 6361544. ***Continues*** *Guide to Government Department and Other Libraries.*

GW/0163-8386
GUIDE TO MICROFORMS IN PRINT. SUBJECT. [Guide microforms print, Subj.]. **Added/Corp** Microform Review Inc. (1978)-. English. an (May). $325.00. K.G. Saur Verlag KG, A Reed Reference Publishing Company, Part of Reed International PLC, Ortlerstrasse 8, D 81373 Munich Germany. **Tel** 011 49 89 769020, FAX 011 49 89 76902150, telex 5212067-SAUR-D. **(Subscription address:** Reed Reference Publishing Company / New Jersey, 131 Chanlaon Road, PO Box 31, New Providence NJ 07974.) **LC** Z1033.M5; G83. **DD** 016.099. **NLM** Z 1033.M5 G946A. ***Continues*** *Subject Guide to Microforms in Print, 0090-290X.*

AT/0156-6717
GUIDELINES. **See** Library and Information Sciences-Abstracting, Bibliographies and Statistics.

US
GUIDES TO THE HARVARD LIBRARIES. Began in 1947. Monographic series. English. ir. Price varies per volume. Harvard University Library, 25 Mount Auburn Street, Cambridge MA 02138. **Tel** (617)495-8596, FAX (617)496-8344. **LC** Z733. **DD** 027.7744.

GY
GUYANA LIBRARY ASSOCIATION BULLETIN. Vol. 1, No. 1 (July 1970)-. Bulletin. English. Twice a year. $10.00. Guyana Library Association, PO Box 10240, Georgetown Guyana. **Tel** 011 592 2 0262690. **ED** Karen Sills. **DD** 020.62.881. **Bk Rev. Ad Acc. Circ:** 75.
Desc: Covers all aspects of librarianship, documentation and information science as it seeks to bring to the attention of its readers developments in the library field in and outside Guyana. Aims to provide a medium of expression on all library related topics.
Ind/Abst Libr. Inf. Sci. Abstr.

HU/0238-2512
HAJDU-BIHAR MEGYEI KONYVTARI TEKA. (1987)-. Hungarian.
Ind/Abst Magyar Konyv. Szak. Biblio.; Hungar. Libr. Info. Sci. Abstr.

GW/0301-9225
HANDBUCH DER OFFENTLICHEN BIBLIOTHEKEN. [Handb. offentl. Bibl.]. 1972-. German. sa. DM58.00 (two year). Deutsches Bibliotheksinstitut, Bundesallee 184 185, D 10717 Berlin Germany. **Tel** 011 49 30 8505186, 011 49 30 8505187, FAX 011 49 30 8505100. **LC** Z801; .H353. **Circ:** 1,300. ***Continues** Handbuch der Offentlichen Buchereien.*
Desc: Collection of data about the public libraries in West Germany and about institutions, authorities and organizations who are concerned with public librarianship.

KO/0250-9083
HANGUG NUIHAG DOSEGWAN. (HANGUK UIHAK TOSOGWAN.). [Hangug nuihag dosegwan]. **VFOAT** Bulletin of Korean Medical Library Association; Bulletin KMLA. Academic Scholarly Publication. Korean. ir. Free. Yonsei University International, College of Medicine, CPO Box 8044, Seoul Korea. **Tel** 392-0161. **NLM** Z 675.74 H239. Documents available from CASDDS.
Ind/Abst Chem. Abstr.

CN/0844-5753
HAPPENINGS. [Happenings]. **Main/Corp** Calgary Public Library. (1988)-. Periodical. English. Three times a year. Free. Calgary Public Library / Public Relations Department, c/o W. R. Castell Library, 616 Macleod Trail Southeast, Calgary Alberta T2G 2M2 Canada. **Tel** (403)260-2640, FAX (403)237-5393. **ED** Glenna Cross and Carol Morrison. **DD** 027.47123/3. Index available. **Circ:** 2,000 (ctrl). ***Continues** Libreeze, 0226-711X.*
Desc: A magazine that primarily promotes free public programs. Also contains general information for library users and news of changes and special events.

US/0073-0564
HARVARD LIBRARIAN, THE. [Harv. libr.]. **Added/Corp** Harvard University. Office of the Director of the University Library. Harvard University. Library. University Librarian. Vol. 1 (Dec. 1957)-. English. Four times a year. Free. Harvard University Library, 25 Mount Auburn Street, Cambridge MA 02138. **Tel** (617)495-8596, FAX (617)496-8344. **ED** Timothy Hanke. **LC** Z881; .H34a. **DD** 027.7744/4. **Circ:** 3,500 (ctrl).
Desc: News of Harvard libraries, major exhibits, publications, and personnel, with occasional essays on collections and librarianship.
Ind/Abst Libr. Inf. Sci. Abstr.

US/0017-8136
HARVARD LIBRARY BULLETIN. [Harv. Libr. bull.]. **Main/Corp** Harvard University. Library. **Added/Corp** Harvard University. Library. Bulletin. **VFOAT** HLB. Vol. 1 (Winter 1947)-Vol. 36 (Fall 1988); New Series, Vol. 1 (Spring 1990)-. Bulletin. English. qt. $35.00. Harvard University Library, 25 Mount Auburn Street, Cambridge MA 02138. **Tel** (617)495-8596, FAX (617)496-8344. **ED** Kenneth E Carpenter (editor's telephone number: (617)495-7746). **LC** Z881; .H3403. **DD** 027.7744. **NLM** Z 881 H339H. cum. index. **Pr Rev. Circ:** 1,700. available on microfilm and microfiche from University Microfilms International (UMI). Documents available from The Genuine Article. ***Continues** Harvard University Library Notes, 1052-3685.*
Desc: Diverse scholarly essays on bibliography and the history holdings and exhibitions of Harvard libraries.
Ind/Abst Abstr. Engl. Stud.; Am. Hist. Life (1967-); Am. Bibliogr. Slavic East Europ. Stud. (19??-19??); Annu. Bibliogr. Engl. Lang. Lit.; Arts Humanit. Citation Index [Full Cov.]; BHA : Biblio. Hist. Art; Child. Lit. Abstr. (19??-); Curr. Contents Arts Humanit.; Garden Lit. (1992-); Libr. Inf. Sci. Abstr.; Lit. Crit. Regist. (1967-); Middle East Abstr. Index; MLA Int. Bibl. Books Artic. Mod. Lang. Lit.; Recent. Publ. Artic.; Res. Alert [Full Cov.]; Romant. Move.; Soc. Sci. Cit. Index [Select. Cov.]; Writ. Am. Hist.

US/1050-253X
HAWORTH SERIES IN INTERNATIONAL LIBRARY ACQUISITIONS. (1991)-. Monographic series. English. ir. Price varies per volume. The Haworth Press Inc, 10 Alice Street, Binghamton NY 13904-1580. **Tel** (607)722-5857, (800)3-HAWORTH, FAX (607)722-1424. **ED** Sul Lee. **Acid Free.** Documents available from Haworth Document Delivery Service.
Desc: Major focus will be on library acquisitions and collection development as they are practiced in major geographic areas of the world.

US/0732-894X
HCL CATALOGING BULLETIN. (HCL CATALOGING BULLETIN / HENNEPIN COUNTY LIBRARY, TECHNICAL SERVICES.). **Main/Corp** Hennepin County Library. Technical Services Division. **Added/Corp** Hennepin County Library. Technical Services Division. Cataloging Bulletin. **VFOAT** H.C.L. Cataloging Bulletin; Cataloging Bulletin. **VAT** Hennepin County Library Cataloging Bulletin. (19??)-. Bulletin. English. Six times a year (Jan., Mar., May, July, Sept., Nov.). $12.00. Hennepin County Library, 12601 Ridgedale Drive, Minnetonka MN 55343. **Tel** (612)541-8562. **ED** Sanford Berman (phone: (612)541-8570). **LC** Z693.A15; H46a. **DD** 025.3/05. **Circ:** 200. ***Continues** Hennepin County Library. Cataloging Section. Cataloging Bulletin, 0093-528X.*
Desc: News or altered cross-reference, DDC numbers, and subject headings, citing authorities, precedents, and applications.

HU/0864-991X
HEALTH INFORMATION AND LIBRARIES. Periodical. English. qt. $45.00 (add $4.00 airmail), (add $2.00 surface mail). Omikk Technoinform, PO Box 12, H-1428 Budapest Hungary. **Tel** 011 36 1 137609, FAX 011 36 1 138-2414, telex 22-4944 OMIKK H. **ED** Maria Bendaq and Tibor Koltay. **LC** Z675.M4; H36. **DD** 026.61/05. **NLM** Z 765.M4; H385. Index available. **Bk Rev. Ad Acc. Pr Rev.** ctrl circ.
Desc: Medical librarianship, traditional and computerized information, information processing and access, library organization and management, education.

UK/0265-6647
HEALTH LIBRARIES REVIEW. [Health libr. rev.]. **Added/Corp** Library Association. Medical, Health and Welfare Libraries Group. **VFOAT** Libraries Review. Vol. 1, No. 1 (Mar. 1984)-. Academic Scholarly Publication. English. qt (4 issues). $144.00 US & Canada; £82.50 Europe; £92.50 other. Blackwell Scientific Publications Ltd, Marston Book Services, PO Box 87, Oxford OX2 ODT UK. **Tel** 011 44 865 791155, FAX 011 44 865 791927, telex 837 515 MARDIS G. **LC** Z675.M4; H37. **DD** 026/.61/0941. **NLM** Z 675.M4; H388. **[CCC].** Index available (bound in last issue). available on microfilm and microfiche from University Microfilms International (UMI). ***Continues** Newsletter - Medical, Health and Welfare Libraries Group, 0266-853X.*
Ind/Abst Cumul. Index Nurs. Allied Health Lit.; Health Plan. Adminis.; Health Serv. Abstr.; Libr. Inf. Sci. Abstr.

CN/0708-9465
HEALTH SCIENCES INFORMATION IN CANADA. LIBRARIES. ***Ceased.*** (HEALTH SCIENCES INFORMATION IN CANADA; LIBRARIES. INFORMATION EN SCIENCES DE LA SANTE AU CANADA; BIBLIOTHEQUES.). [Health sci. inf. Can., Libr.]. **Added/Corp** Canada Institute for Scientific and Technical Information. Health Sciences Resource Centre. **VFOAT** Information en Sciences de la Sante au Canada; Bibliotheques. (1979)-(199?). Periodical. English (French). ir. National Research Council of Canada, Receiver General for Canada, Ottawa Ontario K1A 0R6 Canada. **Tel** (613)993-0362, FAX (613)952-7656. **DD** 026/.61/0971. **NLM** Z 675.M4 H4305. **Circ:** 250.

US/0162-0843
HEALTH SCIENCES SERIALS. (HEALTH SCIENCES SERIALS MICROFORM.). [Health sci. ser.]. **Main/Corp** National Library of Medicine (U.S.). (Jan. 1979)-. Government Publication. English. Four times a year (Jan., Apr., July, Oct.). $17.00 US; $21.25 other. Superintendent of Documents, US Government Printing Office, Washington DC 20402. **Tel** (202)275-3328, FAX (202)786-2377. **DD** 610. **NLM** ZW 1 H435. **CODEN** HSSED4.
Desc: Designed to assist health science librarians identify serial titles and locate the nearest library which can fill an interlibrary loan request. Derived from SERLINE, the online database maintained by NLM. Includes some 38,000 records, location information for about 6,700 titles, and bibliographic and acquisitions information to assist librarians in the management of their own serials collections.

II/0254-2595
HELLIS NEWSLETTER. (HELLIS NEWSLETTER : HEALTH LITERATURE LIBRARY & INFORMATION SERVICES / WORLD HEALTH ORGANIZATION, REGIONAL OFFICE FOR SOUTH EAST ASIA.). [HELLIS newsl.]. **Added/Corp** World Health Organization. Regional Office for South-East Asia. **VFOAT** H.E.L.L.I.S. Newsletter. **VAT** Health Literature Library & Information Services Newsletter. Vol. 1, No. 1 (Mar. 1982)-. Periodical. English. sa. Library / India, World Health Organization Regional Office for South East Asia/World Health House, New Delhi-110002 India. **NLM** Z 675.M4 H477.

II/0018-0521
HERALD OF LIBRARY SCIENCE. [Her. libr. sci.]. **Added/Corp** Sarada Ranganathan Endowment for Library Science. Vol. 1, No. 1 (Jan. 1962)-. Periodical. English. Four times a year (Jan., Apr., July, Oct.). $72.00. Lucknow University, C 239, Indira Nagar, Lucknow 226 016 India. **Tel** 011 91 22 381497. **(Subscription address:** C-239 Indira Nagar, Lucknow 226016 India**) ED** Professor Paula N. Kaula. **LC** Z671; .H44. **CODEN** HLBSAB. Index available. cum. index. **Bk Rev**, (Qty: 22). **Ad Acc. Pr Rev.** available on microfilm and microfiche from University Microfilms International (UMI). Documents available from Ask*IEEE.
Desc: Special numbers have been brought out on specific aspects of library and information science. The features includes, book reviews and comprehensive "Notes and News" from several countries.
Ind/Abst Indian Libr. Sci. Abstr.; INSPEC (Jan. 1972-); Libr. Inf. Sci. Abstr.; Libr. Lit.

US/0897-6775
HERITAGE EDUCATION QUARTERLY.
See Genealogy and Heraldry-Archives.

UK/0440-7334
HERTIS OCCASIONAL PAPER. ***Ceased.*** **Main/Corp** Hertis. **Added/Corp** Hertis Occasional Papers. **VFOAT** Occasional Papers. (1967)-(19??). Monographic series. English. Hatfield Polytechnic, PO Box 110, Hatfield England.

US/0197-6044
HIGH ROLLER. **Added/Corp** Nevada Library Association. **VFOAT** Highroller. V. 14, No. 5 (May/June 1977)-. Periodical. English. qt. $20.00. Nevada Library Association, University of Nevada, 4505 Maryland Parkway, Las Vegas NV 89154. **Tel** (702)739-3252, FAX (702)739-3050. **ED** Laralee Nelson (editor's phone: (702)895-3061). **LC** Z732.N38; N39a. **DD** 027.0793. **Bk Rev. Ad Acc. Circ:** 300. ***Continues** Nevada Libraries High Roller, 0148-5946.*
Desc: Publication of state library organization with items and articles of interest to those working in libraries and pertaining to the state organization.

AT/1035-624X
HINTERALIA. (1990)-. English. ir. ***Continues** Riverina Regional Group Newsletter, 0159-2815.*

US
HITCHHIKER. **Added/Corp** New Mexico. State Library, Santa Fe. (19??)-. Periodical. English. wk. Free on request. New Mexico State Library, 325 Don Gaspar, Santa Fe NM 87503. **Tel** (505)827-3800, FAX (505)827-3888.

US
HLA JOURNAL / HAWAII LIBRARY ASSOCIATION. ***Suspended.*** English. an. Hawaii Library Association, 1514 Makalampa Drive, Honolulu HI 96818. **LC** Z673; .H3. **DD** 020/.6234/969. ***Continues** Hawaiian Library Association Journal.*

CN/0826-0125
HLABC FORUM. [HLABC forum]. **Main/Corp** Health Libraries Association of B.C. **VAT** Forum - Health Libraries Association of B.C. Vol. 6, No. 4 (Nov. 1983)-. Periodical. English. qt (4 issues). Free to members. Kinsmen Rehabilitation Foundation of British Columbia, 2256 West 12th Avenue, Vancouver BC V6K 4L2 Canada. **Tel** (604)736-8841 (VOICE), (604)738-0603 (TDD), FAX (604)738-0015. **DD** 026/.61/09711. **Bk Rev. Ad Acc. Circ:** 70. ***Continues** British Columbia Health Libraries Association. BCHLA News, 0225-6142.*
Desc: Newsletter sent to members of the Health Libraries Association of British Columbia.

JA
HOKUSHINETSU CHIKU KOKURITSU DAIGAKU TOSHOKAN KYOGIKAI NEMPO. **Main/Corp** Hokushinetsu Chiku Kokuritsu Daigaku Toshokan Kyogikai. No. 21 (1975)-. Periodical. Japanese. Fukio Daigaku Fazoku, Toshokan 9-1 Bunkyo 3-chome, Fukui Japan. **LC** Z675.U5; H67a. ***Continues** Hokushin Chiku Kokuritsu Daigaku Toshokan Kyogikai Nempo.*

HK
HONG KONG LIBRARY ASSOCIATION JOURNAL. **Main/Corp** Hong Kong Library Association. **VFOAT** Hsiang-Kang Tu Shu Kuan Hsieh Hui Hsueh Pao. No. 1 (1969)-. English. an. HK$150.00 Hong Kong; $30.00 other. Hong Kong Library Association, GPO, Box 10095, Hong Kong Hong Kong. **ED** Lad Izesky. **LC** Z845.H6. **Ad Acc. Pr Rev. Circ:** 600.
Desc: Articles on Asian libranianship and general information science.
Ind/Abst Libr. Inf. Sci. Abstr.

US/0737-8076
HOT OFF THE COMPUTER. **Added/Corp** Westchester Library System (N.Y.). Vol. 1, No. 1 (1983)-. Periodical. English. ir. price varies per volume. Westchester Library System, 8 Westchester Plaza, D. Courtney, Elmsford NY 10523. **Tel** (914)592-8214.

US/0730-2274
HOTLINE. Periodical. English. mo. Free to consortium members, cooperatives, and interested individuals. The Greater Cincinnati Library Consortium, 3333 Vine Street, Cincinnati OH 45220. **Tel** (513)751-4422.

HU/0046-8304
HUNGARIAN LIBRARY AND INFORMATION SCIENCE ABSTRACTS.
See Library and Information Sciences-Abstracting, Bibliographies and Statistics.

US
HUNTINGTON LIBRARY PUBLICATIONS. **Main/Corp** Henry E. Huntington Library and Art Gallery. (19??)-. Monographic series. English. ir (published 4-6 times a year). Price varies per volume. Henry E. Huntington Library, 1151 Oxford Road, San Marino CA 91108. **Tel** (818)405-2172, FAX (818)405-0225.

JA
HYOGO KENRITSU TOSHOKAN ZOSHO MOKUROKU. **Main/Corp** Hyogo Kenritsu Toshokan. (1973)-. Japanese. Hyogo Kenritsu Toshokan, 1-ban 27-go Akashi Koen, Akashi-shi 673 Japan. **LC** Z955.H9; H93.

CN/0319-4442
I P L O NEWS. **Main/Corp** Institute of Professional Librarians of Ontario. Dec. 1971-. Periodical. English. Free. Institute of Professional Librarians of Ontario, 36B Prince Arthur Avenue, Toronto Ontario M5R 1A9. **DD** 020/.6234/713. ctrl circ.

US
I U B LIBRARIES FACULTY NEWSLETTER. Newsletter. English. ir. Free. Indiana University Libraries, Jennifer Paustenbaugh, Library C-2, Bloomington IN 47405. **Tel** (812)855-3403, FAX (812)855-2576. **ED** Jennifer Paustenbaugh. **Circ:** 2,500 (ctrl).
Desc: News of the Indiana University, Bloomington (IUB) libraries for IUB faculty and administrators.

UK
IAALD NEWS. **Main/Corp** International Association of Agricultural Librarians and Documentalists. **VAT** International Association of Agricultural Librarians and Documentalists News. Vol. 1 (1980)-. English. Four times a year. Drs. J. van der Burg, Secretary/Treasurer IAALD, Cirad/Cidarc B.P. 5035, 34032 Montpellier Cedex 1 France. **Tel** FAX (33)67615820.

CN/0227-1338
IASC BULLETIN. (IASC BULLETIN / BULLETIN SCAD.). [IASC bull.]. **Added/Corp** Indexing and Abstracting Society of Canada. **VFOAT** Bulletin SCAD. **VAT** Indexing and Abstracting Society of Canada Bulletin; Bulletin. Societe Canadienne pour l'Analyse de Documents. Vol. 3, No. 1/2 (June 1980)-. Periodical. English (French). ir. 30.00Can$ (individuals); 45.00Can$ (institutions) Comes with Indexing & Abstracting Society of Canada membership. Indexing and Abstracting Society of Canada, PO Box 744 Station F, Toronto Ontario M4Y 2N6 Canada. **Tel** (416)486-0239. **DD** 025.4/028. ***Continues*** *Indexing and Abstracting Society of Canada. Newsletter, 0704-1721.*

II/0018-8441
IASLIC BULLETIN. [IASLIC bull.]. **Main/Corp** Indian Association of Special Libraries and Information Centres. **VAT** Indian Association of Special Libraries and Information Centres bulletin. Vol. 1 (April 1956)-. Bulletin. English. qt. Price varies. Indian Association of Special Libraries and Information Centres, P291 CIT Scheme No 6M, PO Kankurgachi, Calcutta 700 054 India. **Tel** (033) 349651. **(Subscription address:** Prints India, 11 Darya Ganj, New Delhi 110002 India.**)** **ED** S Kapoor. **LC** Z671; .I45. **CODEN** IASLA9. Index available. **Bk Rev. Ad Acc. Circ:** 1,500 (ctrl). Documents available from BIOSIS Document Express.
Ind/Abst Biol. Abstr. (?-1985); Indian Libr. Sci. Abstr.; Libr. Inf. Sci. Abstr.

II/0073-6279
IASLIC SPECIAL PUBLICATION. **Main/Corp** Indian Association of Special Libraries and Information Centres. **Added/Corp** Indian Association of Special Libraries and Information Centres. Special Publication. No.1 (1960)-. Monographic series. English. an. Price varies per volume. Indian Association of Special Libraries and Information Centres, P291 CIT Scheme No 6M, PO Kankurgachi, Calcutta 700 054 India. **Tel** (033) 349651. **(Subscription address:** Prints India, 11 Darya Ganj, New Delhi 110002 India.**)** **LC** Z674; .I56.

US/0739-1137
IASSIST QUARTERLY. **See** Library and Information Sciences-Abstracting, Bibliographies and Statistics.

DK/1102-6103
IATUL NEWS. **VFOAT** International Association of Technological University Library News. (19??)-. English. Four times a year. Comes with membership; Fl160.00 (membership). International Association of Technological University Libraries, IATUL, PO Box 217, Twente University, 7500 AE Enschede Netherlands. **Tel** 011 31 53 892750. ***Absorbed*** *IATUL Quarterly, 0940-4117.*
Desc: The quarterly newsletter for the International Association of Technological University Libraries. Aims to provide a timely flow of information to the members. The Association itself is a voluntary organization consisting of a group of libraries, represented by their directors and senior librarians. It is small enough for the individual members to be able to develop a close relationship, yet widespread enough to cover the interests of libraries operating in virtually all modern social, economic and political situations.

US/0360-8409
ICARBS. ***Suspended.*** [ICarbS]. Vol. 1 (Fall/Winter 1973)-(19??). English. ir. $5.00. Morris Library, c/o David Koch, Carbondale IL 62901. **Tel** (618)453-2516. **ED** David Koch and Alan Cohn. **LC** Z881.C25; I25. **DD** 051. Index available. **Bk Rev. Ad Acc. Circ:** 600.
Desc: Publishes research emanating from Morris Library's special research collections. Funded by friends of Morris Library Group (Southern Illinois University).
Ind/Abst Abstr. Engl. Stud.; Am. Humanit. Index (-19??); Annu. Bibliogr. Engl. Lang. Lit.; MLA Int. Bibl. Books Artic. Mod. Lang. Lit.

US/0019-1213
IDAHO LIBRARIAN, THE. [Ida. libr.]. **Added/Corp** Idaho Library Association. Idaho State Library. Idaho State Library Association.a40. Vol. 1 (Apr. 1945)-. Periodical. English. Four times a year (Jan., Apr., July, Oct.). $15.00. University of Idaho Library, Mary Bolin, Moscow ID 83843. **Tel** (208)885-7737. **ED** Mary K. Bolin. **DD** 021. Index available. **Bk Rev**, (Qty: 5-10). **Ad Acc, Adv Mgr:** Diane Prorak, **Tel** (208)885-6235. **Circ:** 600. available on microfilm and microfiche from University Microfilms International (UMI).
Desc: Includes news, association business, feature articles and book reviews of interest to ILA members.
Ind/Abst Libr. Lit.; Stat. Ref. Index.

GW
IFLA ANNUAL. **Main/Corp** International Federation of Library Associations and Institutions. (1976)-. English (French and German). an. $50.00. K.G. Saur Verlag KG, A Reed Reference Publishing Company, Part of Reed International PLC, Ortlerstrasse 8, D 81373 Munich Germany. **Tel** 011 49 89 769020, FAX 011 49 89 76902150, telex 5212067-SAUR-D. **(Subscription address:** Reed Reference Publishing Company / New Jersey, 131 Chanlaon Road, PO Box 31, New Providence NJ 07974.**)** **LC** Z673; .I5848. **DD** 030/.621. **NLM** Z 673 I12. ***Continues*** *IFLA Annual.*
Desc: Proceedings of annual International Federation of Library Associations (IFLA) conference and official annual reports on IFLA activities of the year.

NE/0074-6002
IFLA DIRECTORY. **Main/Corp** International Federation of Library Associations and Institutions. **Added/Corp** International Federation of Library Associations and Institutions. **VFOAT** IFLA Directory. (1977)-. Directory. English. an (April (in even numbered years)). F600.00 (institutions); F150.00 (individuals); F75.00 other. International Federation Library Association, IFLA POB 95312, 2509 CH The Hague Netherlands. **Tel** 011 31 70 140884, FAX 011 31 70 3834827, telex 34402 KB NL. **LC** Z673; .I58485. Index available. **Circ:** 2,000. ***Continues*** *IFLA Directory.*
Desc: Contains the names and addresses of all officers, the professional groups with their terms of reference and their advisory bodies, the members of IFLA, and some further essential data on IFLA and its activities.

GW/0340-0352
IFLA JOURNAL. (IFLA JOURNAL / INTERNATIONAL FEDERATION OF LIBRARY ASSOCIATIONS.). [IFLA j.]. **Added/Corp** International Federation of Library Associations. International Federation of Library Associations and Institutions. **VFOAT** I.F.L.A. Journal. **VAT** International Federation of Library Associations Journal. (1975)-. Periodical. English (summaries and/or abstracts in French and German). qt (Feb., May, Aug., Nov.). $100.00. K.G. Saur Verlag KG, A Reed Reference Publishing Company, Part of Reed International PLC, Ortlerstrasse 8, D 81373 Munich Germany. **Tel** 011 49 89 769020, FAX 011 49 89 76902150, telex 5212067-SAUR-D. **(Subscription address:** Stuttgerter Verlagskontor, Postfatch 106016, D-70049 Stuttgart, Germany.**)** **ED** Carol Henry. **LC** Z672; .I128. **DD** 020/.5. **[CCC].** Index available. cum. index. **Bk Rev. Ad Acc. Pr Rev. Circ:** 4,000. available on microfilm and microfiche from University Microfilms International (UMI). Documents available from The Genuine Article. ***Continues*** *IFLA News.*
Desc: Contains articles on activities in IFLA context, articles with international relevance only, IFLA News.
Ind/Abst Curr. Contents Soc. Behav. Sci.; Energy Res. Abstr. (Mar. 1982-); Inf. Instruc. Technol.; Inf. Sci. Abstr.; Int. Labour Doc.; LABORDOC; Libr. Inf. Sci. Abstr.; Libr. Lit.; Res. Alert [Full Cov.]; Soc. Sci. Cit. Index [Full Cov.].

NE
IFLA PROFESSIONAL REPORTS / INTERNATIONAL FEDERATION OF LIBRARY ASSOCIATIONS AND INSTITUTIONS. **Added/Corp** International Federation of Library Associations and Institutions. No. 1 (1983)-. Monographic series. English. ir. Price varies per volume. International Federation Library Association, IFLA POB 95312, 2509 CH The Hague Netherlands. **Tel** 011 31 70 140884, FAX 011 31 70 3834827, telex 34402 KB NL.

II/0970-4728
ILA BULLETIN. [ILA bull.]. **Added/Corp** Indian Library Association. **VFOAT** Bulletin; Indian Library Association Bulletin. Vol. 11, No. 1 & 2 (Jan./June 1975)-. Bulletin. English. qt. $40.00. Indian Library Assocaiation, Delhi, India. **(Subscription address:** Prints India, 11 Darya Ganj, New Delhi 110002 India.**)** **LC** Z671; .I48. ***Continues*** *Bulletin (Indian Library Association), 0019-5782.*

US/0019-2104
ILLINOIS LIBRARIES. [Ill. libr.]. Vol. 1- Jan. 1919-. Periodical. English. Eight times a year (Sept., Oct., Nov., Jan., Feb., March, April, May). Free. Illinois State Library, Centennial Building, Springfield IL 62756. **Tel** (217)782-2994. **ED** Irma R Bostian. **LC** Z732.I2; I3. **DD** 020/.6234/773. **Circ:** 9,000 (ctrl). available on microfilm and microfiche from University Microfilms International (UMI).
Desc: A reference magazine for librarians, library schools, trustees, etc. Information for all types of libraries.
Ind/Abst Curr. Index J. Educ. (March 1990); Inf. Sci. Abstr. (?-?); Libr. Inf. Sci. Abstr.; Libr. Lit.; Urban Aff. Abstr.

AT/0813-6939
IMPART. [Impart]. (1984)-. Periodical. English. Three times a year. Free (members); 10.00Aus$ (non-members). Association of Local Government Librarians, Hurtsville City Library, McMahon Street, Hurstville 2220, Australia. **Tel** 11 61 02 579-6222 ext 331, FAX 11 61 02 570-5118. **ED** L Urane. **DD** 027.4944. **Ad Acc.** ***Continues*** *Newsletter of the N.S.W. Association for Local Government Librarians, 0815-5518.*

US/0046-8746
IMPRINT (SYRACUSE, N.Y.), THE. (THE IMPRINT : NEWSLETTER OF THE ONONDAGA COUNTY PUBLIC LIBRARY.). Vol. 1- 1977-. Newsletter. English. mo. Onondaga County Public Library, 335 Montgomery Street, Syracuse NY 13202.

US/0737-5972
IN THE GROVE. (IN THE GROOVE / PROFESSIONAL MEDIA SERVICE CORP.). **Added/Corp** Professional Media Service Corp. (1982)-. English. Eleven times a year (June/July is a double issue). $20.00 US; $26.00 others. Professional Media Service Corporation, 19122 South Vermont Avneue, Gardena CA 90248. **Tel** (213)532-9024, FAX (213)532-0131. **ED** Mary Holcomb and Peter Brown.
Desc: A catalog of recordings for librarians dealing with audio and video from billboards.

AT/0158-0876
INCITE (SYDNEY). (INCITE.). [Incite]. **Added/Corp** Library Association of Australia. (Jan. 25, 1980)-. Periodical. English. mo. 85.00Aus$ Australia; 105.00Aus$ (surface mail),`115.00Aus$ (airmail). Australian Library & Information Association, PO Box E441, Queen Victoria Terrace, ACT 2600 Australia. **Tel** 011 61 6 2851877, FAX 011 61 6 282 2249. **ED** Tanya Vojsk. **LC** Z673; .L7534. **DD** 020/.622/94. Index available. **Bk Rev. Ad Acc. Circ:** 8,000 (ctrl).
Desc: Newsletter for those working or interested in the library and information world.
Ind/Abst AESIS Q.; Aust. Educ. Index; Aust. Libr. Inf. Sci. Abstr. (1990-); Libr. Inf. Sci. Abstr.

UK/0959-4906
INDEX OF CONFERENCE PROCEEDINGS. ANNUAL CUMULATION. **Main/Corp** British Library. Document Supply Centre. (1988)-. English. an. £67.00 UK; £72.00 other. British Library / Publications Sale Unit, Boston Spa, Wetherby, West Yorkshire LS23 7BQ England. **Tel** 011 44 937 546546 546543, FAX 011 44 937 546333, telex 557381. **(Subscription address:** Turpin Distribution Services Limited, Blackhorse Road, Letchworth, Hertfordshire SG6 1HN, United Kingdom.**)** **LC** Z7403; .B8; AS2.5. **DD** 060/.5. **Ad Acc.** ***Continues*** *Index of Conference Proceedings Received. Annual Cumulation, 0144-7556.*

UK
INDEX OF CONFERENCE PROCEEDINGS RECEIVED. **Main/Corp** British Library. Lending Division. (1974/78)-. Proceedings. English. mo. £75.00 UK; £79.00, $164.20 (surface mail) other; £94.00 UK; £87.00, $180.84 (airmail) other. British Library / Document Supply Centre, Boston Spa, Wetherby West Yorkshire LS23 7BQ England. **Tel** 0937 546060, FAX 0937 546333, telex 557381. **Ad Acc. Circ:** 800. ***Continues*** *BLL Conference Index.*
Desc: Valuable aid to identification by keyword of conferences in all subjects held worldwide. Division is by keywords in titles and organizers.

UK/0144-7556
INDEX OF CONFERENCE PROCEEDINGS / THE BRITISH LIBRARY, DOCUMENT SUPPLY CENTRE. **Main/Corp** British Library. Document Supply Centre. ICP 256 (Jan. 1989)-. Proceedings. English. mo. British Library / Document Supply Centre, Boston Spa, Wetherby West Yorkshire LS23 7BQ England. **Tel** 0937 546060, FAX 0937 546333, telex 557381. **NLM** Z 5051; B862i. ***Continues*** *British Library. Document Supply Centre. Index of Conference Proceedings Received.*

SA
INDEX TO SOUTH AFRICAN PERIODICALS. **VFOAT** Repertorium van Suid-Afrikaanse Tydskrifartikels. (1949)-. English (Afrikaans). an. R30.00. State Library, PO Box 397, Pretoria 0001, Republic of South Africa. **Tel** 011 27 12 386-1661, FAX 011 27 12 325-5984, telex 3-22171SA. **LC** AI3; .I65. **NLM** ZAI 19.S7 I38. cum. index. **Circ:** 320. available on microfiche.

Desc: Index to contents of approximately 450 journals published in Southern Africa, arranged alphabetically under author and Library of Congress subject headings.

US/0887-4158
INDEX TO THE CATALOGING SERVICE BULLETIN. [Index Cat. serv. bull.]. **Added/Corp** Library of Congress. Processing Services. Cataloging Service Bulletin. (Indexes). No. 1/4 (Summer 1978/Spring 1979)-. English. an. $20.00. Stanford University Libraries, Publications, Green Library / Room 312D, Stanford CA 94305. **Tel** (415)723-0461. **ED** Shake Keshkeskian. **DD** 025. **Circ:** 350.
Desc: Cumulative index to the Library of Congress's cataloging policies and methodologies.

UK/0019-4131
INDEXER. (THE INDEXER : JOURNAL OF THE SOCIETY OF INDEXERS.). [Indexer]. **Added/Corp** Society of Indexers. American Society of Indexers. Australian Society of Indexers. Vol. 1, No. 1 (Mar. 1958)-. Periodical. English. sa. £30.00. The Society of Indexers, Huntersquay 33 Marlow Bottom, Marlow BKM SL7 3LZ United Kingdom. **ED** Hazel K. Bell. **NLM** Z 1007 I38. **CODEN** IDXRA5. Index available. **Bk Rev. Ad Acc. Circ:** 2,300 (ctrl). Documents available from Ask*IEEE.
Desc: Professional journal devoted to indexing in all its aspects.
Ind/Abst Book Rev. Index; Comput. Rev.; Inf. Sci. Abstr. [Full Cov.]; INSPEC (Oct. 1973-); Libr. Inf. Sci. Abstr.; Libr. Lit.; Soc. Plann. Policy Dev. Abstr.; Soc. Work Abstr. [Select. Cov.]; World Ceram. Abstr.

US
INDEXING : THE STATE OF OUR KNOWLEDGE AND THE STATE OF OUR IGNORANCE. English. $30.00. Learned Information Inc., 143 Old Marlton Pike, Medford NJ 08055-8750. **Tel** (609)654-6266, FAX (609)654-4309. **ED** Bella Hass Weinberg.
Desc: Emphasizing practical applications, the papers offer a distillation of the key ideas on the art of indexing while examining both the knowledge gained and the ignorance that still exists within the indexing community.

II/0970-4302
INDIAN JOURNAL OF LIBRARY SCIENCE. [Indian j. libr. sci.]. **Added/Corp** Institute of Librarians (India). (Jan./June 1975)-. Periodical. English. qt. $15.00. **(Subscription address:** Prints India, 11 Darya Ganj, New Delhi 110002 India.**)** **LC** Z671; .I46. **DD** 020/.5.

II/0019-5790
INDIAN LIBRARY SCIENCE ABSTRACTS. **See** Library and Information Sciences-Abstracting, Bibliographies and Statistics.

US/0275-777X
INDIANA LIBRARIES. **Added/Corp** Indiana Library Association. Indiana Library Trustee Association. Indiana State Library. Vol. 1, No. 1 (Spring 1981)-. Periodical. English. sa. $10.00. Indiana Library Federation, 1500 North Delaware, Indianapolis IN 46202. **Tel** (317)636-6613, FAX (317)634-9503. **Ad Acc, Adv Mgr Tel** (317)257-2040. **Circ:** 3,500. ***Supersedes*** *Library Occurrent, 0024-2454.*
Desc: Contains articles on theme with occasional potpourri issue of general interest. Journal for librarians.
Ind/Abst Art Archaeol. Tech. Abstr.; Libr. Lit.

US/0164-7660
INDIANA MEDIA JOURNAL. [Indiana media j.]. **Added/Corp** Association for Indiana Media Educators. Vol. 1 (Fall 1978)-. Periodical. English. Four times a year (Jan., Mar., June, Sept.). $10.00. Indiana Media Journal, C/O K. Burch, 1908 East 64th Street, South Drive, Indiananpolis IN 46220. **Tel** (317)257-8558, FAX (317)259-4191. **ED** Dr. Dan Callison, (editor's address: Slis-11 Indiana University, Bloomington IN 47405 phone: (812)855-2018). **Ad Acc, Adv Mgr:** Callison, **Tel** (812)855-2018. **Circ:** 1,000. ***Supersedes*** *Hoosier School Libraries, 0018-4802.*
Desc: Contains library and media information and articles.
Ind/Abst Libr. Lit.

IT/0394-0810
INDICIZZAZIONE, L'. (1986)-. Periodical. Italian (summaries and/or abstracts in English). sa (June & Dec.). L73000.00 Italy; L95000.00 other. Proxima SRL, Via S Francesco 24, 34133 Trieste Italy. **Tel** 011 39 40 371158. **UDC** 002. Bound Index published separately, free upon request.
Ind/Abst Inf. Sci. Abstr.; Libr. Inf. Sci. Abstr.

AT/0310-6659
INDONESIAN ACQUISITIONS LIST. **Main/Corp** National Library of Australia. **VFOAT** Daftar Pengadaan Bahan Indonesia. (1977)-. Periodical. English. Four times a year. Free on request. National Library of Australia, Parkes Place, Canberra ACT, 2600 Australia. **Tel** 011 61 6 2621374, FAX 011 61 6 2731084.
Desc: Lists Indonesian materials recently acquired by the National Library and three Australian academic libraries.

FR/0754-1996
INDUSTRIE DE L'INFORMATION. [Ind. inf.]. (1982)-. Periodical. French. da. 7000.00F. A Jour, 11 rue du Marche St Honore, 75001 Paris France. **Tel** 011 33 1 44553849. **UDC** 681.3. **[CCC].**

CN
INFO. (19??)-. English (French). ir. Free on request. National Library of Canada, 395 Wellington Street, Ottawa Ontario K1A 0N4 Canada. **Tel** (613)995-7969, (613)995-7969, (819)994-6881, FAX (613)991-9871.
Desc: A "news service" intended to publicize library doings and developments.

CN/1183-5540
INFO DOCUMENTATION (DRUMMONDVILLE). (INFO DOCUMENTATION / ASSOCIATION PROFESSIONNELLE DES TECHNICIENNES ET TECHNICIENS EN DOCUMENTATION DU QUEBEC.). [Info doc.]. **Added/Corp** Association Professionnelle des Techniciennes et Techniciens en Documentation du Quebec. **VAT** Info Documentation - Association Professionnelle des Techniciennes et Techniciens en Documentation du Quebec. (Febr. 1991)-. Periodical. French. qt. Free for members. Association Professionnelle des Techniciennes et Techniciens en Documentation du Quebec, CP 115, Drummondville, Quebec J2B 6V6 Canada. **DD** 020. ***Continues*** *Bulletin de Nouvelles (Association Professionnelle des Techniciennes et Techniciens en Documentation du Quebec)., 1186-1282.*

CN
INFO / ISM LIBRARY INFORMATION SERVICES. (1993)-. Periodical. English (French). Three times a year. Free on request. ISM Library Information Services, 3300 Bloor Street West, West Tower 16th Floor, Etobicoke Ontario M8X 2X2, Canada. **Tel** (416)236-7171, FAX (416)236-7541. **ED** Margaret Andrewes. **Circ:** 2,000 (ctrl).

US
INFOCONNECTION / NEVADA STATE LIBRARY AND ARCHIVES. **Added/Corp** Nevada State Library and Archives. **VFOAT** Info Connection. Vol. 1, No. 1 (Jan./Mar. 1991)-. Periodical. English. qt. Nevada State Library and Archives, Capitol Complex, Carson City NV 89710. ***Continues*** *Dateline, State Library & Archives.*

US/1040-2179
INFOCUS (PORTLAND, OR.). **See** Business-General Management.

NE/0169-2763
INFOMEDIARY. ***Title Change.*** Vol. 1, No. 1 (June 1985)-(1993). Periodical. English. qt. IOS Press, Van Diemenstraat 94, 1013 CN Amsterdam Netherlands. **Tel** 011 31 20 6382189, FAX 011 31 20 620 3419. **(Subscription address:** US and Canada/ Postal Drawer 10558, Burke, VA 22009-0558; Japan/ Highway Development Company Ltd., 1st Golden Building, 8-2-9 Ginza, Tokyo-Chuoku 104 Japan**)** **ED** Susan Klement. **LC** Z674.2; .I54. **DD** 020/.5. **CODEN** IFMDES. **[CCC].** ***Merged into*** *Information Services and Use.*
Desc: Interprets entrepreneurship in its widest sense, thus embracing the concerns of information practitioners in both the commercial and not-for-profit sectors.
Ind/Abst Int. Aerosp. Abstr.; Libr. Inf. Sci. Abstr.

AT/0816-200X
INFORMAA QUARTERLY. [Informaa q.]. (1984)-. Periodical. English. qt. Informaa Quarterly, GPO Box 227OU, Melbourne VIC 3001 Australia. **DD** 651.505.
Ind/Abst Aust. Educ. Index; Aust. Libr. Inf. Sci. Abstr. (1990-).

AG/0326-2642
INFORMACIONES (UNIVERSIDAD NACIONAL DE LA PLATA. BIBLIOTECA PUBLICA). (INFORMACIONES / BIBLIOTECA PUBLICA DE LA UNIVERSIDAD NACIONAL DE LA PLATA.). **Added/Corp** Universidad Nacional de La Plata. Biblioteca Publica. Vol. 7, No. 50 (Dec. 1976)-. Periodical. Spanish. qt. Universidad Nacional de la Plata, Plaza Rocha 137, La Plata Argentina. ***Continues*** *Informaciones (Universidad Nacional de La Plata. Biblioteca).*

SA
INFORMAT. **Main/Corp** State Library (South Africa). Vol. 1, No. 1 (Jan. 1985)-. Periodical. Afrikaans (English). bm. Free. State Library, PO Box 397, Pretoria 0001, Republic of South Africa. **Tel** 011 27 12 386-1661, FAX 011 27 12 325-5984, telex 3-22171SA.
Desc: Information leaflet of the State Library of Pretoria.

RU/0203-3054
INFORMATICS ABSTRACTS. [Inform. abstr.]. **Added/Corp** Vsesoiuznyi Institut Nauchnoi i Tekhnicheskoi Informatsii (Soviet Union). **VFOAT** Referativnyi Zhurnal: Informatika. Vol. 15 (1977)-. Periodical. English. mo. **(Subscription address:** Victor Kamkin, 4956 Boiling Brook Parkway, Rockville MD 20852.**)** **LC** Z1007; .A13. **DD** 029. ***Continues*** *Abstract Journal: Informatics.*
Ind/Abst Math. Rev.

US/0738-1522
INFORMATION AMERICA. [Inf. Am.]. Vol. 6, No. 1 (1983)-. Periodical. English. Three times a year. $90.00. Neal-Schuman Publishers Inc., 100 Varick Street, New York NY 10013. **Tel** (212)925-8650, FAX (212)219-8916. **LC** Z674.5.U5; S66. **DD** 027/.0025/73. ***Continues*** *Sources (Syracuse, N.Y.), 0145-2355.*

US
INFORMATION & INSTRUCTION TECHNOLOGIES. **See** Library and Information Sciences-Abstracting, Bibliographies and Statistics.

UK/0260-6879
INFORMATION AND LIBRARY MANAGER. ***Title Change.*** [Inf. libr. manager]. Vol. 1, No. 1 (June 1981)-?. Periodical. English. Six times a year. MCB University Press, 60 62 Toller Lane, Bradford West Yorkshire BD8 9BX England. **Tel** 011 44 274 499821, FAX 011 44 274 547143, telex 51317 MCBUNI G. **ED** Ken Bakewell. **LC** Z678; .I514. **DD** 025.1. **Bk Rev. Circ:** 450. ***Absorbed by*** *Logistics Information Management.*
Desc: Presents a number of articles concerned with the changing face of the profession. Technology and systems are covered. The way in which information is used and its values are becoming increasingly important, so these areas are given particular emphasis. Aims to increase awareness and understanding of the information professional's role. Also seeks to keep ahead of rapid changes within field.
Ind/Abst Educ. Technol. Abstr.; Libr. Inf. Sci. Abstr.

US/0895-9927
INFORMATION BROKER (HOUSTON, TEX.). (INFORMATION BROKER.). [Inf. brok.]. Vol. 5, No. 1 (Jan./Feb. 1987)-. Periodical. English. bm. $35.00. Burwell Enterprises, 3724 FM 1960 West, Suite 214, Houston TX 77069. **Tel** (713)537-9051, FAX (713)537-8332. **LC** IN PROCESS. **DD** 021. ***Continues*** *Journal of Fee-Based Information Services, 0190-2261.*

US/0049-7282
INFORMATION BULLETIN / WESTERN ASSOCIATION OF MAP LIBRARIES. [Inf. bull. - West. Assoc. Map Libr.]. **Main/Corp** Western Association of Map Libraries. **Added/Corp** Western Association of Map Libraries. Vol. 1, No. 3 (June 1970)-. Periodical. English. Three times a year. $25.00 US; $28.00 Canada; $30.00 Canada. Western Association of Map Libraries, c/o Richard E. Soares, PO Box 1667, Provo UT 84603. **Tel** (801)377-1240, FAX (801)378-3221. **Bk Rev. Ad Acc.** available on microfiche. ***Continues*** *Western Association of Map Libraries. Newsletter.*
Desc: Articles and bibliographies; list of new maps; atlas and book reviews.
Ind/Abst Bibliogr. Carto.; Geogr. Abstr. Phys. Geogr.; Geogr. Abstr. Human Geogr.; Geol. Abstr.; GeoRef; Libr. Inf. Sci. Abstr.; Libr. Lit.

UK/0142-5471
INFORMATION DESIGN JOURNAL. [Inf. des. j.]. (1979)-. Periodical. English. Three times a year. £40.00 (individuals), £90.00 (institutions) surface mail; £55.00 (individuals), £105.00 (institutions) airmail. Information Design Journal, PO Box 1978, Gerrards Cross, Bucks SL9 9BT England. **Tel** 011 753 892278. **[CCC].**
Ind/Abst ARTbibliogr. Mod.; Ergon. Abstr.; HILITES; Libr. Inf. Sci. Abstr.; Print. Abstr.; World Publ. Monit.

UK/0266-6669
INFORMATION DEVELOPMENT. [Inf. dev.]. Vol. 1, No. 1 (Jan. 1985)-. Periodical. English. Four times a year (Jan., Apr., July, Oct.). $135.00. Bowker Saur Ltd., A Reed Reference Publishing Company, Part of Reed International PLC, 59-60 Grosvenor Street, London WIX 9DA England. **Tel** 011 44 71 4935841, FAX 011 44 71 4991590. **(Subscription address:** World-Wide Subscription Services, Unit 4, Gibbs Reed Farm Pashley Road, Ticehurst TN5 7HE England.**)** **ED** J. Stephen Parker. **LC** Z672; .I45. **DD** 021.6/4. **CODEN** INDEE8. **Bk Rev. Ad Acc. Circ:** 550. available on microfiche. Documents available from Ask*IEEE.
Desc: Provides authoritative coverage of developments in information work throughout the world, with particular emphasis on the information needs and problems of developing countries.
Ind/Abst Curr. Index J. Educ. (19??-); Inf. Instruc. Technol. (19??-); Inf. Manage. Technol. (19??-); Inf. Sci. Abstr. (19??-); INSPEC (April 1985-)985-); Int. Labour Doc. (19??-); Libr. Inf. Sci. Abstr. (19??-); Libr. Lit. (19??-); Rural Dev. Abstr. (19??-); World Agric. Econ. (19??-).

FR
INFORMATION ET DOCUMENTATION - ASSOCIATION NATIONALE DE LA RECHERCHE TECHNIQUE. **Main/Corp** Association Nationale de la Recherche Technique. (1967)-. French (English). bm. Association National de la Recherche Technique, 101 Av Raymond Poincare, F-75116 Paris France. **Tel** 011 33 1 45017227, FAX 011 33 1 47018529, telex 642632. **LC** Z1007; .A77. **DD** 029.

US
INFORMATION FOR DECISION-MAKING, ANNUAL PROGRAM FOR LIBRARY DEVELOPMENT IN ARKANSAS. **Main/Corp** Arkansas State Library. (19??)-. English. an. **LC** Z732.A7; A58a. **DD** 027/0767.

CN/0826-1946
INFORMATION FOR MEMBERS / NOVA SCOTIA LIBRARY ASSOCIATION. [Inf. memb. - N.S. Libr. Assoc.]. **Main/Corp** Nova Scotia Library Association. 1983/1984-. English. an. Free to members. Nova Scotia Library Association, Halifax City Regional Library, 5381 Spring Garden Road, Halifax Nova Scotia B3J 1E9 Canada. **DD** 020/.6234/716. ***Continues*** *Nova Scotia Library Association. Members Handbook.*

US/0360-5817
INFORMATION HOTLINE. [Inf. hotline]. **Added/Corp** Science Associates/International, Inc. Vol. 8 (Jan. 1976)-. Periodical. English. ir (10 issues). $150.00 US; $175.00 other. Science Associates International Inc., 465 West End Avenue, New York NY 10024. **Tel** (212)873-0656, FAX (212)873-5587. **ED** Ivan Lyons. **LC** Q223; .S25. **DD** 029/.9/505. **CODEN** INHODN. **Bk Rev.** available on microfilm and microfiche from University Microfilms International (UMI). ***Continues*** *Information News and Sources, 0360-3148.*
Desc: Unsurpassed as the most accurate, comprehensive and objective source for the latest news on databases, information networks, innovative information services and research projects.
Ind/Abst F&S Index Plus Text, Int. [Select. Cov.]; Int. Aerosp. Abstr.; Int. Packag. Abstr.; Libr. Inf. Sci. Abstr.; World Publ. Monit.

US/0885-7660
INFORMATION INDUSTRY BULLETIN. ***Title Change.*** [Inf. ind. bull.]. **Added/Corp** Digital Information Group. (198?)-(19??). Bulletin. English. wk. Digital Information Group, 51 Bank Street, Stamford CT 06901. **Tel** (800)255-0942, FAX (203)977-8310. **DD** 338. ***Continued by*** *Digital Information Group's Information Industry Bulletin, 1059-0080.*
Ind/Abst Health Devices Alerts.

US/1051-6239
INFORMATION INDUSTRY DIRECTORY. [Inf. ind. dir.]. **Added/Corp** Gale Research Inc. 11th Ed. (1991)-. Directory. English. an. $495.00. Gale Research Inc., 835 Penobscot Building, Detroit MI 48226. **Tel** (800)877-GALE, (313)961-2242, FAX (313)961-6083, telex TWX 810-221-7086. **ED** Annette Novallo. **LC** Z674.3; .E53. **DD** 025.04/029/4. **CODEN** IIDIEJ. available on magnetic tape; available on diskette. ***Continues*** *Encyclopedia of Information Systems and Services, 0734-9068.*

US/0737-7770
INFORMATION INTELLIGENCE, ONLINE LIBRARIES, AND MICROCOMPUTERS. [Inf. intell., online libr. microcomputers]. **VFOAT** Libraries and Microcomputers; Online Libraries and Microcomputers; Information Intelligence. Vol. 1, No. 1 (Sept. 1983)-. Periodical. English. Ten times a year (Except July and Aug.). $43.75 (individual), $50.00 (institution) US & Canada & Mexico; $75.00 (individual), $87.50 (institution) others. Information Intelligence Inc., PO Box 31098, Phoenix AZ 85046. **Tel** (602)996-2283, (800)228-9982. **ED** George S. Machovec. **LC** Z678.9.A1; I544. **DD** 025.3/0285. **CODEN** IIOMEI. **[CCC].** Index available. cum. index. **Bk Rev. Ad Acc.** available on CD-ROM from CARL; NEWSNET; DATA-STAR; and DIALOG; available on an online database. Documents available from Ask*IEEE.
Desc: Aimed at library and information center developments and applications throughout North America. Feature articles cover new library online and automation applications, reviews of library-oriented software and hardware for online and CD-ROM use (many of which we have tested), news and trends, editorials, people, library networks, new online and CD-ROM databases, forthcoming meetings, publications, etc.
Ind/Abst INSPEC (Oct. 1987-); Libr. Inf. Sci. Abstr.; PTS Newsl. Database [Full Txt.].

US/0197-2847
INFORMATION INTERCHANGE (ATLANTA, GA.). (INFORMATION INTERCHANGE.). **Added/Corp** Georgia State University. William Russell Pullen Library. Vol. 1 (Jan. 1974)-. Periodical. English. Three times a year. Georgia State University / William Pullen Library, 104 Decatur Street Southeast, Atlanta GA 30303.

US
INFORMATION MANAGEMENT POLICIES AND SERVICES. (19??)-. English. ir. Price varies. Ablex Publishing Corporation, 355 Chestnut Street, Norwood NJ 07648. **Tel** (201)767-8450, (201)767-8455 (Customer Service), FAX (201)767-6717. **ED** Charles R. McClure and Peter Hernon.
Desc: Series of monographs, edited volumes and texts.

US/0897-3199
INFORMATION MANAGEMENT SOURCEBOOK. ***Title Change.*** (INFORMATION MANAGEMENT SOURCEBOOK : THE AIIM BUYING GUIDE AND MEMBERSHIP DIRECTORY.). [Inf. manage. sourceb.]. **Added/Corp** Association for Information and Image Management (U.S.). **VFOAT** AIIM Buying Guide and Membership Directory. (1987)-(19??). Directory. English. an. Association for Information & Image Management, Business Office, 1100 Wayne Avenue/Suite 1100, Silver Spring MD 20910. **Tel** (301)587-8202, FAX (301)587-2711. **ED** Meg Buckley. **LC** HD9999.M47; A39. **DD** 338.7/68643. Index available. **Ad Acc. Circ:** 8,000. ***Continues*** *AIIM Buying Guide.* ***Continued by*** *AIIM Buying Guide.*
Desc: Identifies the manufacturers of the products and services of the information and image management industry. Includes company listings, company profiles, products and services, and membership directory of the Association for Information and Image Management.

UK/0306-4573
INFORMATION PROCESSING & MANAGEMENT. [Inf. process. manage.]. **VAT** Information Processing and Management. Vol. 11 (June 1975)-. Periodical. English. bm. $559.00 The Americas; £375.00 other. Pergamon Press, An Imprint of Elsevier Science Ltd., The Boulevard, Langford Lane, Kidlington, Oxford OX5 1GB United Kingdom. **Tel** 011 44 865 843000, 011 44 865 843699, FAX 011 44 865 843010. **(Subscription address:** Elsevier Science Ltd. Oxford Fulfillment Centre, PO Box 800, Kidlington, Oxford OX5 1DX United Kingdom.**) ED** T. Saracevic. **LC** Z699.A1; I6. **DD** 029/.05. **CODEN** IPMADK. **[CCC].** available on microfilm from Microfilms International Marketing Corp.; available on microfilm and microfiche from University Microfilms International (UMI). Documents available from Article Express International, The Genuine Article, BIOSIS Document Express, Ask*IEEE, UMI Article Clearinghouse, CASDDS. ***Continues*** *Information Storage and Retrieval, 0020-0271;* ***Absorbed*** *Information Technology.*
Ind/Abst ABI/INFORM Glob. Ed.; ABI Inform Ondisc (Feb 1976-)(Feb. 1976-); ACM Guide Comput. Lit.; Bioeng. Abstr.; Biol. Abstr.; Bus. Index (1979-?); Chem. Abstr. (1975-1985); Compumath Citation Index [Full Cov.]; Comput. Rev.; Curr. Contents Eng. Tech. Appl. Sci.; Curr. Contents Soc. Behav. Sci.; Curr. Index J. Educ.; Curr. Lit. Sci. Sci.; Curr. Technol. Index; Ei Page One; Eng. Index Annu.; Ergon. Abstr.; Gen. BusinessFile (1992-); Inf. Instruc. Technol.; Inf. Sci. Abstr. [Full Cov.]; INSPEC (June 1975-); Libr. Inf. Sci. Abstr.; Libr. Lit.; Res. Alert [Full Cov.]; SCISEARCH; Soc. Sci. Cit. Index [Full Cov.]; Stat. Theory Method Abstr. (1976-1981); World Publ. Monit.; Zentralbl. Math. Ihre Grenzgeb.

US/0360-0971
INFORMATION REPORTS AND BIBLIOGRAPHIES. [Inf. rep. bibliogr.]. **Added/Corp** Science Associates/International, Inc. Vol. 4 (1975)-. Periodical. English. bm. $95.00 US; $125.00 other. Science Associates International Inc., 465 West End Avenue, New York NY 10024. **Tel** (212)873-0656, FAX (212)873-5587. **LC** Z699.A1; I55. **DD** 020/.5. **CODEN** INRBDY. available on microfilm. ***Continues*** *Information. Part 2, Reports, Bibliographies, 0046-9378.*
Desc: Selected library and information science guides, bibliographies, and state-of-the art reports commissioned by key government academic, and learned society groups.
Ind/Abst Libr. Lit.

UK/0959-8928
INFORMATION RESEARCH NEWS. (June 1990)-. Academic Scholarly Publication. English. Three times a year. £85.00. SUBIS, Mansion House, 19 Kingfield Road, Sheffield S11 9AS England. **Tel** 011 44 114 255 4433, FAX 011 44 114 255 4626. **Bk Rev. Ad Acc.** ***Continues*** *C R U S News, 0140-4253.*
Desc: Issues to include reports on a number of information retrieval projects in progress.

US/1040-1628
INFORMATION RESOURCES MANAGEMENT JOURNAL. [Inf. resour. manage. j.]. **Added/Corp** Information Resources Management Association. Vol. 1, No. 1 (Fall 1988)-. Periodical. English. qt. $100.00 (institutions), $60.00 (individuals). Idea Group Publishing, 4811 Jonestown Road, Suite 230, Harrisburg PA 17109. **Tel** (800)345-4332, (717)541-9150, FAX (717)541-9159. **ED** Mehdi Khosrowpour. **LC** WMLC 93/1310. **DD** 658. **CODEN** IRMAEZ. Index available. cum. index. **Bk Rev**, (Qty: 4). **Ad Acc. Pr Rev. Circ:** 600 (ctrl). Documents available from Ask*IEEE.
Desc: Applied research journal providing coverage of challenges, opportunities, problems, trends and solutions encountered by both scholars and practitioners in the field of information technology management.
Ind/Abst Inf. Sci. Abstr.; INSPEC (Fall 1988).

US/0020-0239
INFORMATION SCIENCE ABSTRACTS. **See** Library and Information Sciences-Abstracting, Bibliographies and Statistics.

US/0020-0255
INFORMATION SCIENCES. [Inf. sci.]. Vol. 1 (1968)-. Academic Scholarly Publication. English. Thirty times a year (8 volumes). $1471.00 US; $1561.00 other. Elsevier Science Publishing Company Inc, Madison Square Station, PO Box 882, New York NY 10159-0882. **Tel** (212)633-3950, FAX (212)633-3990. **ED** Paul Wang. **LC** Z699.A1; I59. **DD** 029.7. **CODEN** ISIJBC. **[CCC]. Ad Acc. Pr Rev.** available on microfilm and microfiche from University Microfilms International (UMI). Documents available from Article Express International, The Genuine Article, Ask*IEEE. ***Continued in part by*** *Information Sciences, Applications, 1069-0115.*
Desc: Original papers dealing with topics from such fields as engineering, mathematics, statistics, computer science, library science, physics, and management science.
Ind/Abst Acad. Search (Jan. 1994-); ACM Guide Comput. Lit.; Bioeng. Abstr.; Bus. Source (Jul. 1993-); Compumath Citation Index [Full Cov.]; Comput. Rev.; Curr. Contents Eng. Tech. Appl. Sci.; Ei Page One; Eng. Index Annu.; Geogr. Abstr. Phys. Geogr.; INFO-SOUTH Abstr.; INSPEC (Dec. 1968-); Int. Aerosp. Abstr.; Mag. Search; Math. Rev.; MLA Int. Bibl. Books Artic. Mod. Lang. Lit.; Pollut. Abstr. Indexes; Res. Alert [Full Cov.]; Sci. Cit. Index; SCISEARCH; Soc. Plann. Policy Dev. Abstr.; Soc. Sci. Cit. Index [Select. Cov.]; Sociol. Abstr.; Zentralbl. Math. Ihre Grenzgeb.

●US/1069-0115
INFORMATION SCIENCES, APPLICATIONS. [Inf. sci. appl.]. **VFOAT** Information Sciences. Vol. 1, No. 1 (Jan. 1994)-. Academic Scholarly Publication. English. bm (2 volumes). $200.00 US; $240.00 other. Elsevier Science Publishing Company Inc, Madison Square Station, PO Box 882, New York NY 10159-0882. **Tel** (212)633-3950, FAX (212)633-3990. **DD** 025. **CODEN** ISAPER. **[CCC].** ***Continues in part*** *Information Sciences, 0020-0255.*
Desc: Original papers dealing with topics from such fields as engineering, mathematics, statistics, computer science, library science, physics, and management science.
Ind/Abst Acad. Search (Jan. 1994-).

NE/0167-5265
INFORMATION SERVICES & USE. [Inf. serv. use]. **VFOAT** Information Services and Use. Vol. 1, No. 1 (Mar. 1981)-. Periodical. English. Four times a year. Fl396.00. IOS Press, Van Diemenstraat 94, 1013 CN Amsterdam Netherlands. **Tel** 011 31 20 6382189, FAX 011 31 20 620 3419. **ED** Arthur W. Elias, Cor van de Weteringh and Tamiko Matsumura. **LC** Z699.A1; I613. **DD** 025/.04/05. **CODEN** ISUDX8. available on microfilm and microfiche from University Microfilms International (UMI). Documents available from Ask*IEEE, CASDDS.
Desc: The journal is aimed at leaders in information management and applications in an attempt to keep them fully informed of fastmoving developments in fields such as: online systems, offline systems, library automation, micrographics, education and training, videotex, word processing, and telecommunications.
Ind/Abst Acad. Search (July 1993-); ACM Guide Comput. Lit.; Bus. Index (1985-); Bus. Source (Jul. 1993-); Chem. Abstr.; Commun. Abstr. (?-?); Comput. Lit. Index; Comput. Rev.; Curr. Index J. Educ.; Ei Page One; Fluid Abstr., Civil Eng.; Fluid Abstr. Proc. Eng.; FLUIDEX (1981-); Gen. BusinessFile (1985-); Gen. Period. Index (1985-); GeoRef; INFO-SOUTH Abstr.; Inf. Sci. Abstr. [Full Cov.]; INSPEC (March 1981-); Int. Aerosp. Abstr.; Libr. Inf. Sci. Abstr.; Mag. Search; Pollut. Abstr. Indexes; Trade Ind. Index; World Publ. Monit.

US/1052-1658
INFORMATION SERVICES UPDATE. **Added/Corp** Nebraska Library Commission. (1991)-. English. Free. Nebraska Library Commission, 1420 P Street, Lincoln NE 68508-1683. **Tel** (402)471-2045, FAX (402)471-2045.

US/0197-2243
INFORMATION SOCIETY, THE. [Inf. soc.]. Vol. 1, No. 1 (1981)-. Periodical. English. qt (4 issues). £60.00 UK; $99.00 other. Taylor & Francis Ltd., Rankine Road, Basingstoke Hampshire, RG24 8PR United Kingdom. **Tel** 011 44 256 840366, FAX 011 44 256 479438, telex 858540. **(Subscription address:** Taylor & Francis Inc., 1900 Frost Road, Suite 101, Bristol PA 19007-1598.**) ED** Robert H. Anderson and Joseph Becker, editor emeritus. **LC** Z668; .I47. **DD** 020/.5. **CODEN** INSCD8. **[CCC]. Bk Rev. Ad Acc. Circ:** 600 (ctrl). available on microfilm and microfiche from University Microfilms International (UMI). Documents available from Ask*IEEE, UMI Article Clearinghouse.
Desc: Provides a forum for thoughtful commentary and discussion of significant topics in the world of information, such as transborder data flow, regulatory issues, the impact of the information industry, information as a determinant of public and private organizational performance, and information and the sovereignty of the public. Because of the journal's international perspective, it has worldwide appeal to scientists and policy makers in government, education and industry.
Ind/Abst ABI/INFORM Glob. Ed.; ABI Inform Ondisc (1983-); Abstr. Hum. Comput. Interact.; Commun. Abstr.; Comput. Contents; Comput. Rev.; Electron. Pub. Abstr.; Ergon. Abstr.; HILITES; Inf. Sci. Abstr. [Full Cov.]; INSPEC (1981-); Libr. Inf. Sci. Abstr.; PAIS Bull. (1985-); PAIS Int. Print (1991-); Ref. Z.; Soc. Plann. Policy Dev. Abstr.; Sociol. Abstr.; World Publ. Monit.

US/0734-9637
INFORMATION SOURCES. (INFORMATION SOURCES : THE ANNUAL DIRECTORY OF THE INFORMATION INDUSTRY ASSOCIATION.). [Inf. sources]. **Main/Corp** Information Industry Association. **Added/Corp** Information Industry Association. Annual Directory of the Information Industry Association. (1983)-. Directory. English. an. $67.00 (members); $128.00

(non-members). Information Industry Association, 555 New Jersey Avenue Northwest, Suite 800, Washington DC 20001-2082. **Tel** (202)639-8262. **ED** Barbara E. Van Gorder and Ann Ellis. **LC** HC102; .I53a. **DD** 020/.622/73. **Bk Rev.** ***Continues*** *Information Industry Association. Membership Directory of the Information Industry Association, 0148-1053.*
Desc: The comprehensive directory to the world's leading information companies, it lists their key executives and the products they offer. Organized as the information industry's "yellow pages," it profiles over 460 leading edge companies involved in the generation. distribution and use of information.

US/1041-0031
INFORMATION STANDARDS QUARTERLY. (INFORMATION STANDARDS QUARTERLY / A PUBLICATION OF THE NATIONAL INFORMATION STANDARDS ORGANIZATION.). [Inf. stand. q.]. **Added/Corp** National Information Standards Organization (U.S.). **VFOAT** ISQ. Vol. 1, No. 1 (Jan. 1989)-. Periodical. English. Four times a year. $60.00 US; $80.00 other. National Information Standards Organization, PO Box 1056, Bethesda MD 20827. **Tel** (301)975-2814, FAX (301)869-8071, telex 19764 NBSUT. **ED** Walt Crawford. **LC** Z678.85; .I54. **DD** 025. **CODEN** ISQUEK. **Bk Rev. Circ:** 500. ***Continues*** *Voice of Z 39, 0163-626X.*
Desc: Reports on standards development in the US and internationally affecting the library and information community.
Ind/Abst Inf. Sci. Abstr.

●US/0887-5561
INFORMATION SYSTEMS JOURNAL. (1992)-. Periodical. English. mo. $36.00. Feedbak Publications, PO Box 201404, Austin TX 78720.

US/0730-9295
INFORMATION TECHNOLOGY AND LIBRARIES. [Infor. technol. libr.]. **Added/Corp** Library and Information Technology Association (U.S.). Vol. 1, No. 1 (March 1982)-. Periodical. English. Four times a year (Mar., June, Sept., Dec.). $50.00 US; $55.00 Canada and Mexico; $60.00 other. American Library Association, 50 East Huron Street, Chicago IL 60611. **Tel** (312)944-6780, (800)545-2433, FAX (312)944-2641. **(Subscription address:** American Library Association, Subscription Department, 434 West Downer, Aurora IL 60506-9936.**) LC** Z678.9.A1; J68. **DD** 025.3/028/54. **NLM** Z 699.A1 J86. **CODEN** ITLBDC. **[CCC]. Pr Rev.** available on microfilm and microfiche from University Microfilms International (UMI). Documents available from The Genuine Article, Ask*IEEE, UMI Article Clearinghouse, Magazine Collection. ***Continues*** *Journal of Library Automation, 0022-2240.*
Ind/Abst ABI/INFORM Glob. Ed.; ABI Inform Ondisc (Sept. 1976-); Acad. Search (July 1993-); ACM Guide Comput. Lit.; Arts Humanit. Citation Index [Select. Cov.]; Bus. Index (1982-?); Compumath Citation Index [Full Cov.]; Comput. Inf. Syst. Abstr. J.; Comput. Lit. Index; Comput. Rev. Index (1988-); Comput. Rev.; Curr. Contents Soc. Behav. Sci.; Curr. Index J. Educ.; Gen. Period. Index (1985-); INFO-SOUTH Abstr.; Inf. Instruc. Technol.; Inf. Sci. Abstr. [Full Cov.]; INSPEC (March 1982-); Int. Aerosp. Abstr.; Leg. Inf. Manage. Index; Libr. Inf. Sci. Abstr.; Libr. Lit.; Mag. Index Plus (1989-); Mag. Search; Newsp. Period. Abstr. (1988-); PAIS Int. Print (1991-?); Res. Alert [Full Cov.]; Soc. Sci. Cit. Index [Full Cov.]; Mag. Index (1982-); Trade Ind. ASAP [Full Txt.]; Trade Ind. Index [Full Txt.]; UMI ABI/Inform--Bus. Period. Ondisc (Dec. 1987-) [Full Txt.].

UK/0261-1732
INFORMATION TECHNOLOGY AND PEOPLE. ***Ceased.*** [Inf. technol. people]. Vol. 1 (1981/82)-Vol. 3, No. 12 (April 1984). Academic Scholarly Publication. English. mo. Elsevier Science Publishers Ltd, Crown House, Linton Road, Barking Essex IG11 8JU England. **Tel** 011 44 81 5947272, FAX 081-594-5942, telex 896950.
Ind/Abst Libr. Inf. Sci. Abstr.; World Publ. Monit.

US/1057-7939
INFORMATION TECHNOLOGY NEWSLETTER (HARRISBURG, PA.). (INFORMATION TECHNOLOGY NEWSLETTER.). [Inf. technol. newsl.]. Vol. 1, No. 1 (Fall 1990)-. Newsletter. English. Twice a year (Feb., Aug.). $20.00 (individual), $35.00 (institutions). Idea Group Publishing, 4811 Jonestown Road, Suite 230, Harrisburg PA 17109. **Tel** (800)345-4332, (717)541-9150, FAX (717)541-9159. **ED** Karen Cullings. **DD** 025. **Bk Rev**, (Qty: 2). **Ad Acc. Circ:** 600 (ctrl).
Desc: Forum for librarians and library staff. Designed to ask questions and get answers and assist in planning all aspects of implementing information technology resources.

US/8755-6286
INFORMATION TODAY. [Inf. today]. Vol. 1, Iss. 1 (Jan. 1984)-. Periodical. English. Eleven times a year. $45.95 (one year), $87.00 (two year), $129.00 (three year) US; $56.95 (one year) Canada & Mexico; $62.00 (one year) other. Learned Information Inc., 143 Old Marlton Pike, Medford NJ 08055-8750. **Tel** (609)654-6266, FAX (609)654-4309. **ED** Patricia Lane. **DD** 001. **[CCC]. Bk Rev. Ad Acc, Adv Mgr:** Michael V. Zarrello. **Circ:** 20,000. available on microfilm and microfiche from University Microfilms International (UMI); available on an online database (file 648/Full-Text) from DIALOG. Documents available from UMI Article Clearinghouse, Ask*IEEE.
Desc: Designed to meet the needs of the information professional in the world of electronic services. Provides coverage of online services, new databases, electronic publishing, library automation and technology, hardware, software, CD-ROM, etc. Delivers coverage of news and trends in the information industry.
Ind/Abst ABI/INFORM Glob. Ed.; ABI Inform Ondisc (Oct. 1987-); Health Devices Alerts; Index Period. Artic. Relat. Law; INSPEC (May 1985-); Leg. Inf. Manage. Index; Libr. Inf. Sci. Abstr.; Microcomput. Index (May 1987-); Trade Ind. ASAP [Full Txt.]; Trade Ind. Index [Full Txt.]; UMI ABI/Inform--Bus. Period. Ondisc (Oct. 1987-) [Full Txt.].

GW
INFORMATION UND DOKUMENTATION : ANNOTIERTE TITELLISTE. Main/Corp Germany (Democratic Republic, 1949-). Zentralinstitut fuer Information und Dokumentation. Multiple languages. 3.00 single issue. Kopernicker Str 325, Berlin 117 Germany. **LC** Z699.2; .G47A. **DD** 016.029.

UK/0965-3821
INFORMATION WORLD EN ESPANOL. [Inf. world Esp.]. (1992)-. Spanish. Eleven times a year. £50.00. Learned Information Ltd., Woodside Hinksey Hill, Oxford OX1 5AU England. **Tel** 44 865 730275, FAX 44 865 736354, telex 23667. **(Subscription address:** Learned Information, Inc. / North America Subscriptions, 143 Old Marlton Pike, Medford NJ 08055-8750.**) DD** 027.0946.

GW/0044-1457
INFORMATIONSDIENST BIBLIOTHEKSWESEN. ***Ceased.*** (1971)-(1992). Periodical. German. bm (7 issues per year). Deutsche Buecherei Leipzig, Deutscher Platz 1, D-04103 Leipzig Germany. **Tel** 011 49 341 88120. **UDC** 016. **CODEN** 002.

FR
INFORMATSIINYI BIULETEN - UKRAINSKA BIBLIOTEKA IMENY S. PETLIURY V PARYZHI. Main/Corp Ukrainska Biblioteka Imeny S. Petliury V Paryzhi. V. 1- (No. 1-35); Jan. 1959-. Ukrainian. ir. 6 rue de Palestine, Paris 75019 France. **LC** Z927; .U4A.

PL/0208-7286
INFORMATYKA / POLITECHNIKA SLASKA. Added/Corp Politechnika Slaska im. W. Pstrowskiego. No. 1 (1980)-. Periodical. Polish (summaries and/or abstracts in English and Russian). mo. $78.00. **(Subscription address:** ARS Polona, PO Box 1001, 00068 Warsaw Poland.**) LC** Z699.A1; I63. **DD** 001.6/05. **CODEN** ZNPIET.

VE
INFORME BIENAL - BANCO DEL LIBRO. Main/Corp Banco Del Libro. Spanish. Banco Del Libro, Apartado 5893, Caracas 1010 A Venezuela. **Tel** 011 58 2 3323136. **LC** Z786; .B3514.

●US/1061-3609
INFORMED LIBRARIAN, THE. [Inf. libr.]. Vol. 1, No. 1 (Apr. 1992)-. Periodical. English. mo. $129.00. Infosources Publishing, 140 Norma Road, Teaneck NJ 07666. **Tel** (201)836-7072, FAX (201)836-7072. **DD** 025.

US/0195-4318
INFORMER (RALEIGH), THE. (THE INFORMER.). **Added/Corp** Information Exchange System for Minority Personnel. Vol. 1 (1975)-. Periodical. English. qt. IESMP Inc, PO Box 668, Fort Valley GA 31030. **Tel** (912)825-7645. **ED** Dorothy M. Haith. **Bk Rev. Ad Acc. Circ:** 3,000.
Desc: Subjects related to black librarianship.

CN/0706-151X
INPUT. ***Ceased.*** (Jan. 1977)-Ceased Vol. 10, No. 6 (Nov. 1989). English. bm. Input, c/o Editor, Documentation Centre, University of Guelph Library, Guelph Ontario N1G 2W1 Canada. **Tel** (519)824-4120, X2310. **ED** Jim Brett. **DD** 025.17/3. Index available. **Bk Rev. Circ:** 100.
Desc: A government publications newsletter providing current information on government publications, activities and programs, and issues of concern to documents librarians.

CN/0832-9605
INSIDE OLA. [Inside OLA]. **VFOAT** Inside Ontario Libraries. **VAT** Inside Ontario Library Association. (Oct. 1986)-. Periodical. English. ir. Free (members and to subscribers of Focus). Ontario Library Association, 100 Lombard Street, Suite 303 Toronto, Ontario M5C 1M3 Canada. **Tel** (416)363-3388. **DD** 020/.6234/713.

US
INSIGHT (AKRON, OHIO). (INSIGHT.). **Added/Corp** Akron-Summit County Public Library. Vol. 27, No. 1 (Jan./Feb. 1987)-. Periodical. English. bm. $2.00. Akron Summit County Public Library, 55 South Main Street, Akron OH 44326. **Tel** (216)762-7621, FAX (216)762-6623. **ED** Patricia H. Latshaw. **Bk Rev. Circ:** 2,000. available with illustrations. ***Continues Owlet,*** *0030-7602.*
Desc: A newsletter published for the friends of the Akron-Summit county public library, government officials and the general public. It tells about library activities, new staff, and gives a complete calendar of library events.

US/0898-1795
INSIGHTS. (INSIGHTS : THE LIBRARY OF CONGRESS PROFESSIONAL ASSOCIATION NEWSLETTER.). **Main/Corp** Library of Congress. Professional Association. Vol. 19, No. 6 (Nov./Dec. 1987)-. Newsletter. English. bm. Library of Congress / Professional Association, c/o Staff Relations Office, LJ G112 Library of Congress, Washington DC 20540. **LC** Z733; .W3114. **DD** 027./088092. ***Continues*** *LCPA Newsletter, 0098-1648.*

GW/0019-0217
INSPEL. [INSPEL]. Vol. 1 (April 1966)-. Periodical. English (French and Russian). qt. DM48.00. Europaisches Patentamt, Erhardtstrabe 27, W-8000 Munchen 2 Germany. **ED** Kruse Gerhard. **LC** Z675.A2. **NLM** Z 671 I107. **CODEN** INPLBI. **[CCC].** Documents available from Ask*IEEE.
Ind/Abst Inf. Instruc. Technol.; INSPEC (Jan. 1972-); Libr. Inf. Sci. Abstr.; Libr. Lit.

US
INSTANT ART. (19??)-. Monographic series. ir. Linworth Publishing Company, 480 East Wilson Bridge Road, Suite L, Worthington OH 43085. **Tel** (614)436-7107, FAX (614)436-9490.

DK
INTER-EXLIBRIS. Main/Corp Frederikshavn Kunstmuseum. 1978-. Danish (English and German). an. Frederikshavn Kunstmuseum, Kallsvej 2, DK 9900 Frederikshavn Denmark. **LC** Z995; .F84A. **DD** 769.5.

MX
INTER FOLIA. No. 1- Oct. 1953-. Periodical. Spanish. Apartado 1625, Monterrey N L Mexico. **LC** Z885.N83; I57.

US/0738-7784
INTERCHANGE - ERIC PROCESSING AND REFERENCE FACILITY. (INTERCHANGE.). [Interchange - ERIC Proc. Ref. Fac.]. **Main/Corp** ERIC Processing and Reference Facility. **Added/Corp** ERIC Processing and Reference Facility. **VFOAT** ERIC Data Base Users Interchange; ERIC Users Interchange. No. 1 (Nov. 1972)-. English. ir. Free on request. ERIC Processing and Reference Facility, 1301 Piccard Drive, Suite 300, Rockville MD 20850. **Tel** (301)258-5500, FAX (301)251-5212. **(Subscription address:** Access ERIC, 1600 Research Boulevard, Rockville MD 20850.**) ED** Ted Brandhorst. **Circ:** 1,800.
Desc: A serial communicating matters pertaining to the ERIC database to principal information service providers using the ERIC publications, microfiche, database, etc.

US/0047-0414
INTERCOM (DISTRICT OF COLUMBIA LIBRARY ASSOCIATION). (INTERCOM.). [Intercom]. **Added/Corp** District of Columbia Library Association. Vol. 1 (July 1971)-. Periodical. English. mo (11 issues). District of Columbia Library Association, Box 14177 Benjamin Franklin Square, Washington DC 20044. **Tel** (202)727-1101. **LC** Z732.D62; I56. **DD** 020/.5. ***Supersedes*** *D.C. Libraries.*

US/0270-6717
INTERFACE (CHICAGO). (INTERFACE. ASSOCIATION OF SPECIALIZED AND COOPERATIVE LIBRARY AGENCIES.). **Added/Corp** Association of Specialized and Cooperative Library Agencies. American Library Association. Vol. 1 (Fall 1978)-. Periodical. English. Four times a year (Jan., Apr., June, Nov.). $15.00 US, Canada & Mexico; $25.00 other. American Library Association, 50 East Huron Street, Chicago IL 60611. **Tel** (312)944-6780, (800)545-2433, FAX (312)944-2641. **(Subscription address:** American Library Association, Subscription Department, 434 West Downer, Aurora IL 60506-9936.**) ED** Jeannette Smithee. **LC** Z672; .I58. **Bk Rev. Ad Acc. Circ:** 1,500 (ctrl). available on microfilm and microfiche from University Microfilms International (UMI). ***Formed by the union of*** *ASLA President's Newsletter, 0044-9660* ***and*** *HRLSD Journal, 0196-7371.*
Desc: Covers latest developments and news about state libraries, library networks and cooperatives, and libraries serving special populations.

UK/0264-1615
INTERLENDING & DOCUMENT SUPPLY. (INTERLENDING & DOCUMENT SUPPLY : THE JOURNAL OF THE BRITISH LIBRARY LENDING DIVISION.). [Interlend. doc. supply]. **Added/Corp** British Library. Lending Division. **VFOAT** Interlending and Document Supply. Vol. 11, No. 1 (Jan. 1983)-. Periodical. English. qt. $139.00 (librarians), $389.00 (non-librarians). MCB University Press, 60 62 Toller Lane, Bradford West Yorkshire BD8 9BX England. **Tel** 011 44 274 499821, FAX 011 44 274 547143, telex 51317 MCBUNI G. **(Subscription address:** MCB University Press / US and Canada Subscriptions, PO Box 10812, Birmingham AL

35201-0812.) **ED** David N Wood. **LC** Z921.B854; B15. **DD** 027.542. **CODEN** IDSUDQ. Index available. **Pr Rev. Circ:** 1,300. Documents available from The Genuine Article, Ask*IEEE. ***Continues*** *Interlending Review, 0140-2773.*
Desc: International in scope, it covers developments in individual countries and transactions between countries, also new methods of document delivery.
Ind/Abst Curr. Contents Soc. Behav. Sci.; Inf. Instruc. Technol.; INSPEC (Jan. 1983-); Libr. Inf. Sci. Abstr.; Libr. Lit.; Res. Alert [Full Cov.]; Soc. Sci. Cit. Index [Full Cov.]; World Ceram. Abstr.

US/8755-6332
INTERNATIONAL ASSOCIATION OF MARINE SCIENCE LIBRARIES AND INFORMATION CENTERS CONFERENCE SERIES. (INTERNATIONAL ASSOCIATION OF MARINE SCIENCE LIBRARIES AND INFORMATION CENTERS CONFERENCE SERIES.). [Int. Assoc. Mar. Sci. Libr. Inf. Cent. conf. ser.]. **Main/Conf** International Association of Marine Science Libraries and Information Centers. **Main/Corp** International Association of Marine Science Libraries and Information Centers. Conference. (1985)-. Proceedings. English. an. $15.00 members; $20.00 nonmembers. University of Texas at Austin / International Association of Marine Science Liraries & Information Centers (IAMSLIC), Marine Science Center, Port Arkansas TX 78373. **Tel** (512)749-6711. **LC** UNC. **DD** 026. **Circ:** 300.

GW/0340-0050
INTERNATIONAL CLASSIFICATION. ***Title Change.*** [Int. classif.]. **Added/Corp** International Society for Knowledge Organization. **VFOAT** IC. Vol. 1-19, No 4; May (1974)-(1992). Periodical. English (German). sa. Indeks Verlag, Woogstrasse 36A, D 60431 Frankfurt Germany. **Tel** 011 49 69 523690, FAX 011 49 69 520566. **ED** Ingetraut Dahlberg, Jean Perreault, Robert Friymann. **LC** Z696; .I553. **DD** 025.4/05. **CODEN** INCLDN. Index available. cum. index. **Bk Rev. Ad Acc. Pr Rev. Circ:** 800 (ctrl). available in microform. Documents available from The Genuine Article, Ask*IEEE. ***Continued by*** *Knowledge Organization, 0943-7444.*
Desc: Covers classification, taxonomy, concept theory, indexing, terminology, organization of knowledge, theory of science-articles, reports, communications, bibliographies, news sections and letters.
Ind/Abst Curr. Contents Soc. Behav. Sci.; Energy Res. Abstr. (March 1982-); Inf. Sci. Abstr. (?-1991); INSPEC (1978-); Libr. Inf. Sci. Abstr.; Libr. Lit.; Res. Alert [Full Cov.]; Soc. Sci. Cit. Index (19??-19??) [Full Cov.].

NE/0304-9701
INTERNATIONAL FORUM ON INFORMATION AND DOCUMENTATION. [Int. forum inf. doc.]. V. 1-. Periodical. English. qt. £50.00 Europe, $92.00 other. International Federation for Information and Documentation, PO Box 90402, 2509 LK Hague Netherlands. **Tel** 011 31 70 3140509, FAX 011 31 70 834827, telex 34402 KB GV NL. **(Subscription address:** Turpin Transactions Ltd., Blackhorse Road, Letchworth, Hertfordshire SG6 1HN United Kingdom; Telephone: (0462) 672555, FAX: (0462) 480947**)** **ED** A Mikhailov. **LC** Z1007; .I545. **DD** 020/.5. **CODEN** IFIDD7. **[CCC]. Bk Rev. Ad Acc. Pr Rev. Circ:** 450. Documents available from The Genuine Article, Ask*IEEE.
Desc: The journal is intended to cover the most important problems of information theory and practical activities which are of interest to information specialists all over the world.
Ind/Abst Abstr. Hum. Comput. Interact.; Curr. Contents Soc. Behav. Sci.; HILITES; Inf. Sci. Abstr. (?-?); INSPEC (Jan. 1982-); Libr. Inf. Sci. Abstr.; Libr. Lit.; Res. Alert [Full Cov.]; Soc. Sci. Cit. Index [Full Cov.].

●UK/1057-2317
INTERNATIONAL INFORMATION & LIBRARY REVIEW, THE. [Int. inf. libr. rev.]. **VFOAT** International Information and Library Review. Vol. 24, No. 1 (Mar. 1992)-. Academic Scholarly Publication. English. qt (4 issues). $220.00. Academic Press Ltd., A Division of Harcourt Brace & Company Ltd., 24-28 Oval Road, London NW1 7DX England. **Tel** 071 267 4466, FAX 071 482 2293, 071 485 4752, telex 25775 ACPRES G. **(Subscription address:** Harcourt Brace & Company, Ltd., Foots Cray, High Street, Sidcup Kent DA14 5HP England.**)** **ED** N. Moore and T. Carbo Bearman. **LC** Z671; .I64. **DD** 020/.5. Documents available from The Genuine Article. ***Continues*** *International Library Review, 0020-7837.*
Desc: Welcomed by librarians all over the world for its timely articles on progress and research in international and comparative librarianship, documentation, and information retrieval.
Ind/Abst Am. Hist. Life (1972-); Curr. Contents Soc. Behav. Sci.; Curr. Index J. Educ.; Libr. Inf. Sci. Abstr.; Libr. Lit.; Res. Alert [Full Cov.]; Soc. Sci. Cit. Index [Full Cov.].

II/0970-1850
INTERNATIONAL INFORMATION, COMMUNICATION & EDUCATION. [Int. inf. commun. educ.]. **VFOAT** I.N.I.C.A.E.; International Information, Communication, and Education; INICAE. Vol. 1, No. 1 (March 1982)-. Periodical. English. sa. $64.00. Lucknow University, C 239, Indira Nagar, Lucknow 226 016 India. **Tel** 011 91 22 381497. **(Subscription address:** Prints India, 11 Darya Ganj, New Delhi 110002 India.**)** **ED** Professor Paula N. Kaula. **LC** Z671; .I598. **DD** 020/.5. Index available. cum. index. **Bk Rev**, (Qty: 25). **Ad Acc, Adv Mgr:** Anil, **Tel** 381497. **Pr Rev.** Documents available from Ask*IEEE.
Ind/Abst Indian Libr. Sci. Abstr.; INSPEC (March 1986-)(1986-); Libr. Inf. Sci. Abstr.

UK/0953-556X
INTERNATIONAL JOURNAL OF INFORMATION AND LIBRARY RESEARCH. Vol. 1, No. 1 (1989)-. Periodical. English. Three times a year. $65.00. Taylor Graham Publishing, 500 Chesham House, 150 Regent Street, London W1R 5FA United Kingdom. **ED** Stephen A. Roberts. **LC** Z671; .I599. **DD** 020/.5.
Desc: Designed specifically for information professionals around the world who need to know how contemporary information research is shaping present and future information and library services.

UK/0268-4012
INTERNATIONAL JOURNAL OF INFORMATION MANAGEMENT. [Int. j. inf. manage.]. Vol. 6, No. 1 (March 1986)-. Periodical. English. Six times a year. $328.00 The Americas; £220.00 other. Butterworth Heinemann Publishers, Linacre House, Jordan Hill, Oxford OX2 8DP England. **Tel** 011 44 865 310366. **(Subscription address:** Elsevier Science Ltd. Oxford Fulfillment Centre, PO Box 800, Kidlington, Oxford OX5 1DX United Kingdom.**)** **ED** P. Hills and R. E. Wiggins. **LC** H61.9; .S65. **DD** 025/.063. **[CCC].** Index available. **Ad Acc. Pr Rev.** available on microfilm and microfiche from University Microfilms International (UMI). Documents available from The Genuine Article, UMI Article Clearinghouse, Ask*IEEE. ***Continues*** *Social Science Information Studies, 0143-6236.*
Desc: Provides a focus for the developing field of information management, linking practitioners and contributors to developments in the field of disciplines such as computer science, economics, social psychology, management and public administration.
Ind/Abst ABI/INFORM Glob. Ed.; Abstr. Hum. Comput. Interact.; Commun. Abstr. (?-?); Contents Pages Manage.; Curr. Contents Soc. Behav. Sci.; HILITES; Inf. Sci. Abstr. [Full Cov.]; INSPEC (1986-); Int. Labour Doc.; Int. Polit. Sci. Abstr.; Libr. Inf. Sci. Abstr.; PAIS Int. Print (1991-); Res. Alert [Full Cov.]; Soc. Plann. Policy Dev. Abstr.; Soc. Sci. Cit. Index [Full Cov.]; Zentralbl. Math. Ihre Grenzgeb.

US/0731-1265
INTERNATIONAL JOURNAL OF LEGAL INFORMATION. (INTERNATIONAL JOURNAL OF LEGAL INFORMATION : IJLI : THE OFFICIAL PUBLICATION OF THE INTERNATIONAL ASSOCIATION OF LAW LIBRARIES.). [Int. j. leg. inf.]. **Added/Corp** International Association of Law Libraries. Institute for International Legal Information. **VFOAT** IJLI; I.J.L.I. Vol. 10, No. 1 (Feb. 1982)-. Periodical. English. Three times a year. $55.00 (individuals), $80.00 (institutions). International Association of Law Libraries / Nashville, PO Box 158927, Nashville TN 37215. **Tel** (615)322-2726. **ED** Ivan Sipkov. **LC** Z675.L2; I58. **DD** 026/.34/005. Index available (published separately). **Bk Rev**, (Qty: more than 100). **Ad Acc. Circ:** 700. ***Continues*** *International Journal of Law Libraries.*
Ind/Abst Curr. Law Index (1982-); Index Foreign Leg. Per.; LABORDOC; Leg. Inf. Manage. Index; Leg. Resour. Index (1982-); LegalTrac (1982-); Libr. Inf. Sci. Abstr.

US/0892-4546
INTERNATIONAL LEADS. (INTERNATIONAL LEADS / ISSUED BY THE INTERNATIONAL RELATIONS ROUND TABLE OF THE AMERICAN LIBRARY ASSOCIATION.). [Int. leads]. **Added/Corp** American Library Association. International Relations Round Table. Vol. 1, No. 1 (Spring 1987)-. Periodical. English. qt. $7.00 ALA member, $12.00 nonmember. American Library Association, 50 East Huron Street, Chicago IL 60611. **Tel** (312)944-6780, (800)545-2433, FAX (312)944-2641. **(Subscription address:** American Library Association, Subscription Department, 434 West Downer, Aurora IL 60506-9936.**)** **LC** Z672; .L4. **DD** 020/.621. ***Continues*** *Leads (New York, N.Y.), 0458-8983.*
Ind/Abst Libr. Lit.

II/0970-0048
INTERNATIONAL LIBRARY MOVEMENT. (INTERNATIONAL LIBRARY MOVEMENT : ILM.). [Int. libr. mov.]. **VFOAT** ILM; I.L.M. (1979)-. Periodical. English. qt (March, June, Sept. and Dec.). $140.00. International Library Movement, P B #1 Model Town, Ambala City 134 003 India. **Tel** 91 171 440214. **(Subscription address:** Prints India, 11 Darya Ganj, New Delhi 110002 India.**)** **ED** N K Bhagi. **LC** Z671; .I636. **DD** 020/.5. **Bk Rev. Ad Acc. Circ:** 1,000. ***Continues*** *Indian Library Movement, 0377-7367.*
Desc: Concerned with the theory and practice of librarianship and information science; the problems of providing services to educationists, librarians, archivists and information scientists and feminists in established libraries and library science institutions with particular emphasis on the needs and problems of developing countries.
Ind/Abst Indian Libr. Sci. Abstr.; Libr. Inf. Sci. Abstr.

UK
INTERNATIONAL ON-LINE INFORMATION MEETING : PAPERS. **VFOAT** On-Line Information Meeting; On-Line Information; On Line Information; On Line Information Meeting. 1st (1977)-. Monographic series. English. an. $135.00. Learned Information Ltd., Woodside Hinksey Hill, Oxford OX1 5AU England. **Tel** 44 865 730275, FAX 44 865 736354, telex 23667. **(Subscription address:** Learned Information, Inc. / North America Subscriptions, 143 Old Marlton Pike, Medford NJ 08055-8750.**)** **LC** Z699.A1; I685a. **DD** 025/.04.

US/0890-4960
INTERNATIONAL PRESERVATION NEWS. (INTERNATIONAL PRESERVATION NEWS : A NEWSLETTER OF THE IFLA PROGRAMME ON PRESERVATION AND CONSERVATION.). [Int. preserv. news]. **Added/Corp** IFLA Programme on Preservation and Conservation. Library of Congress. National Preservation Program Office. **VFOAT** Internationale Nachrichten der Konservierung; Nouvelles Internationales de Preservation; Les Nouvelles Internationales de Preservation; Mezhdunarodnye Novosti Konservatsii. No. 1 (Sept. 1987)-. Periodical. English. Four times a year. Free. Library of Congress / National Preservation Program Office, Washington DC 20540. **Tel** (202)707-1840. **DD** 025.

UK/0269-0500
INTERNATIONAL REVIEW OF CHILDREN'S LITERATURE AND LIBRARIANSHIP. **VFOAT** IRCLL; I.R.C.L.L. Vol. 1, No. 1 (Spring 1986)-. Periodical. English. Three times a year. £49.50 UK; $94.50 other. Taylor Graham Publishing, 500 Chesham House, 150 Regent Street, London W1R 5FA United Kingdom. **ED** Margaret Kinnell. **Pr Rev.**
Ind/Abst Br. Educ. Index; Child. Lit. Abstr. (19??-); Libr. Lit.

US/0363-7549
INTERNATIONAL SUBSCRIPTION AGENTS. 1st Ed. (1963)-. English. American Library Association, 50 East Huron Street, Chicago IL 60611. **Tel** (312)944-6780, (800)545-2433, FAX (312)944-2641. **(Subscription address:** American Library Association, Subscription Department, 434 West Downer, Aurora IL 60506-9936.**)**

IT/0075-0026
INVENTARI DEI MANOSCRITTI DELLE BIBLIOTECHE D'ITALIA. Vol. 1- 1890-. Italian. ir. Casa Editrice, Viale Europa, CP 66 1-50126, Florence Italy. **ED** G Mazzatinti. ***Supersedes*** *Inventari dei Manoscritte Delle Biblioteche d'Italia.*

MX/0187-358X
INVESTIGACION BIBLIOTECOLOGICA. **Added/Corp** Universidad Nacional Autonoma de Mexico. Centro Universitario de Investigaciones Bibliotecologicas. Vol. 1, No. 1 (Aug. 1986)-. Periodical. Spanish. sa.
Ind/Abst Libr. Inf. Sci. Abstr.

US
IOWA PUBLIC LIBRARY STATISTICS / STATE LIBRARY COMMISSION OF IOWA. **See** Library and Information Sciences-Abstracting, Bibliographies and Statistics.

US
IOWA STATE UNIVERSITY LIBRARY INSTRUCTION MANUAL. English. ir. Waveland Press Inc, PO Box 400, Prospect Heights IL 60070. **LC** Z670; .I6. **DD** 025.5/677. ***Continues*** *Iowa State University. Library Instruction Manual.*

CI/0351-0123
IRCIHE BULLETIN / INTERNATIONAL REFERRAL CENTRE FOR INFORMATION HANDLING EQUIPMENT. **Added/Corp** International Referral Centre for Information Handling Equipment. (1975)-. Periodical. English. qt. $24.00. International Referral Centre for Information Handling Equipment, c/o Referral Centre of the University of Zagreb, Trg Marsala Tita 3, POB 327, 41001 Zagreb Croatia. **Tel** 011 38 41 427 866, FAX 011 38 41 427 903. **ED** Board. **CODEN** IRBUD5. **Ad Acc. Circ:** 600.

IE
IRISH LIBRARY BULLETIN. **Added/Corp** Browne and Nolan, ltd. V. 1- Jan. 1940-. Bulletin. English. bm. **LC** Z1035; .I7.

GW/0342-4634
ISBN REVIEW. [ISBN rev.]. **Main/Corp** International ISBN Agency. **Added/Corp** International ISBN Agency. Review. **VAT** International Standard Book Number Review. Vol. 1 (1977)-. Periodical. English. an. DM39.00. International ISBN AG, Potsdamer Str 33, D 10785 Berlin Germany. **Tel** 011 49 30 2662338.

JA
ISHIDATAMI. **Main/Corp** Nagasaki Kenritsu Nagasaki Toshokan. No. 1 (May 1973)-. Periodical. Japanese. bm. Nagasaki Kenritsu Nagasaki Toshokan, 1 Kami Nishiyamacho, 850 Nagasaki Japan. **LC** Z845.J4; N33a.

US/0892-094X
ISI ONLINE NEWS. [ISI online news]. **Added/Corp** Institute for Scientific Information. **VFOAT** Online News. **VAT** Institute for Scientific Information Online News. Vol. 4, No. 1 (Jan. 1987)-. Academic Scholarly Publication. English. Three times a year. Free. Institute for Scientific Information, 3501 Market Street, Philadelphia PA 19104. **Tel** (215)386-0100, (800)523-1850, FAX (215)386-6362, telex 84-5305. **(Subscription address:** Institute for Scientific Information, PO Box 71416, Chicago IL 60694.**)** **DD** 025. ***Continues*** *ISI Online, 0748-9722.*

●FR/1018-4783
ISSN COMPACT. (ISSN COMPACT + LIST OF SERIAL TITLE WORD ABBREVIATIONS [COMPUTER FILE] / ISDS INTERNATIONAL CENTRE.). [ISSN compact]. **VFOAT** ISSN Compact Plus List of Serial Title Word Abbreviations; ISSN Compact; List of Serial Title Word Abbreviations; ISDS Register on CD-ROM. **VAT** International Standard Serial Number Compact; International Serials Data Systems Register on Compact Disc Read Only Memory. Disc 1 (1992)-. Periodical. English (French). qt. 7500.00F. ISSN International Centre, 20 rue Bachaumont, F-75002 Paris France. **Tel** 011 33 1 42367381, FAX 011 33 1 40263243, telex SERIALS 219847F. **(Subscription address:** Chadwyck Healey France, 3 rue de Marivaux, 75002 Paris France; Telephone: 011 33 142868020**)** **CODEN** ILSAEN.

FR/1021-500X
ISSN REGISTER. TAPE EDITION. French. ir. 27500.00F. ISSN International Centre, 20 rue Bachaumont, F-75002 Paris France. **Tel** 011 33 1 42367381, FAX 011 33 1 40263243, telex SERIALS 219847F. ***Continues*** *ISDS Register, 0256-8888.*

RU
ISTORIIA BIBLIOTECHNOGO DELA V SSSR. **Added/Corp** Gosudarstvennaia Biblioteka SSSR Imeni V.I. Lenina. Nauchno-Issledovatelskii Otdel Bibliotekovedeniia i Teorii Bibliografii. (1975)-. Periodical. Russian. 0.62rub. Gosudarstvennaia Biblioteka, Informatsionnyi Tsentr, Imeni V. I. Lenina, Prospekt Kalinina 3, 121019 Moscow Russia. **LC** Z819.A1; I782.

UK/0954-2612
IT LINK. [IT link]. **VFOAT** Information Technology Link. (1988)-. English. Ten times a year. £68.00 (member), £85.00 (non-member) Europe; £74.00 (member), £93.00 (non-member) other. ASLIB, Information House, 20-24 Old Street, London EC1V 9AP England. **Tel** 011 44 71 253 4488, FAX 011 44 71 430 0514, telex 23667 AJLIB G. **(Subscription address:** North America: 143 Old Marlton Pike, Medford, NJ 08055-8750**)** **ED** David Bawden. **Bk Rev. Ad Acc. Circ:** 600. ***Absorbed*** *Automation Notes, 0954-7460.*
Desc: News and articles on information technology which relate particularly to libraries and information services.
Ind/Abst Libr. Inf. Sci. Abstr.

US/0893-7109
ITC NEWS - UNITED STATES. DEPT. OF AGRICULTURE. INFORMATION TECHNOLOGY CENTER. (ITC NEWS / INFORMATION TECHNOLOGY CENTER.). [ITC news - U.S., Dep. Agric., Inf. Technol. Cent.]. **VFOAT** I.T.C. NEWS. **VAT** Information Technology Center News. Began in 1983. Periodical. English. USDA Information Technology Center, 600 Maryland Avenue Southwest/Room 13, Washington DC 20024. **DD** 001.

SP/0214-0349
ITEM. **Added/Corp** Collegi Oficial de Bibliotecaris-Documentalistes de Catalunya. Vol.1 (1987)-. Periodical. Catalan (summaries and/or abstracts in English). sa. 2000ptas. Collegi Oficial de Bibliotecaris-Documentalistes de Catalunya, Ribera 8 Principal, 08003 Barcelona Spain. **Tel** 011 34 3 310-1345, FAX 011 34 3 319-6510. **ED** Ernest Abadal. **LC** Z673.C62; I88. **DD** 020/.946/7. Index available. cum. index. **Bk Rev. Ad Acc. Circ:** 1,500.
Desc: Deals with all aspects of library and information work in Catalonia and Spain.

BU/0204-6091
IZVESTIA NA NARODNATA BIBLIOTEKA KIRIL I METODIJ. [Izv. Nar. bibl. Kiril Metod.]. (1953)-. Periodical. Bulgarian. ir. $45.00. Narodna Biblioteka Sv.sv. Kiril i Metodij, 88 V. Levski Boulevard, 1504 Sofia Bulgaria. **Tel** 011 359 2 882811, FAX 011 359 2 881600, telex 22432. **UDC** 002.19. ***Continues*** *Izvestiia na Narodnata Biblioteka Kiril i Metodii i na Bibliotekata na Sofiiskiia Universitet Kliment Okhridski.*

NE
JAARBOEK OPENBARE BIBLIOTHEKEN. **Added/Corp** Nederlands Bibliotheek- en Lektuurcentrum. (19??)-. Dutch. an. NBLC, Postbus 93054, 2509 AB Den Haag Netherlands. **Tel** 011 31 70 3141500. **LC** Z815.A1; J3.

GW/0075-2215
JAHRBUCH DER BIBLIOTHEKEN, ARCHIVE UND INFORMATIONSSTELLEN DER DEUTSCHEN DEMOKRATISCHEN REPUBLIK. ***Ceased.*** Vol. 1 (1959)-Ceased Dec. 1990. German. World Amateur Boxing Magazine Editor's Office, P.O.Box 0141, 10321 Berlin/GERMANY. **Tel** (049.30)423 5932, (049.30)423 6766, FAX (049.30)423 5943.

GW/0075-2223
JAHRBUCH DER DEUTSCHEN BIBLIOTHEKEN. (JAHRBUCH DER DEUTSCHEN BIBLIOTHEKEN / HERAUSGEGEBEN VOM VEREIN DEUTSCHER BIBLIOTHEKARE.). **Added/Corp** Verein Deutscher Bibliothekare. Vol. 1 (1902)-. German. ir. Otto Harrassowitz Verlag, Taunusstrasse 14, Postfach 2929, D-65019 Wiesbaden Germany. **Tel** 011 49 611 5300, FAX 530570, telex 4186 135 OH D. **LC** Z801; .J2. cum. index.

GW
JAHRESBERICHT ... DER UNIVERSITAETSBIBLIOTHEK MAINZ MIT VERZEICHNIS DER UNIVERSITAETSBIBLIOTHEK UEBERLASSENER SCHRIFTEN MAINZER HOCHSCHULLEHRER. **Main/Corp** Universitatsbibliothek Mainz. (1989)-. German. an. **LC** Z802; .M245. **DD** 027.743/4351. ***Continues*** *Jahresbericht.*

GW/0174-3287
JAHRESBERICHT / GESELLSCHAFT FUR INFORMATION UND DOKUMENTATION. **Main/Corp** Gesellschaft fur Information und Dokumentation. German. an. Gesellschaft fur Information und Dokumentation MBH, Lyoner Strasse 44-48 Araballa-Center, W-6000 Frankfurt 71 Germany. **LC** Z699.A1; G47A. **DD** 025/.04/05.

US/0893-8598
JAPANESE AMERICAN VERNACULAR NEWSPAPERS, ABSTRACT-INDEX. ***Suspended.*** [Jpn. Am. vernac. newsp. abst.-index]. **VFOAT** Abstract-Index; Abstract Index. (Jan./March 1986)-Suspended with Vol. 1, 1986. Periodical. English. qt. $200.00. Japanese American Library, PO Box 590598, San Francisco CA 94159-0598. **Tel** (415)567-5006. **ED** Karl K Matsushita. **LC** PN4885.J35; J36. **DD** 016.071/3/089956073. Index available. **Bk Rev. Circ:** 100.
Desc: Abstracting news articles in all Japanese American vernacular newspapers in North America.

SP
JAPANESE REPORT SERIES : INFORMATION TECHNOLOGY. Spanish. mo. $370.00 US; £215.00 UK. Newmedia International Japan, AV Infanta Carlota 123 5 A, 08029 Barcelona Spain. **Tel** 011 34 3 4195690, FAX 414 42 13. **UDC** 68.

CH/1013-090X
JIAOYU ZILIAO YU TUSHUGUAN XUE. (JOURNAL OF EDUCATIONAL MEDIA & LIBRARY SCIENCES.). [Jiaoyu ziliao yu tushuguan xue]. **Added/Corp** Tan-Chiang ta Hsueh. Dept. of Educational Media Science. Chueh-Sheng Chi Nien tu Shu Kuan. **VFOAT** Chiao Yu Tzu Liao Yu Tu Shu Kuan Hsueh; EMLS; Journal of Educational Media and Library Sciences. Vol. 20, No. 1 (Autumn 1982)-. Periodical. English (Chinese). qt. $25.00. Journal of Educational Media & Library Sciences, Tamkang University, Tamsui Taipei 251 Taiwan. **Tel** (02)6215656, FAX (02)6226149. **ED** Shih-hsion Huang, Hwa-wei Lee, Chang C. Lee, Syh-shi Kao. **CODEN** CYTHD5. Index available. cum. index. **Circ:** 700 (ctrl). ***Continues*** *Chiao Yu Tzu Liao Ko Hsueh.*
Ind/Abst Inf. Sci. Abstr.; Libr. Inf. Sci. Abstr.

JA/0021-7298
JOHO KANRI. [Joho kanri]. **Added/Corp** Nihon Kagaku Gijutsu Joho Senta. **VFOAT** Information & Documentation. (1966)-. Periodical. Japanese. mo. $122.00. Japan Information Center of Science and Technology, 5-2 Nagatacho 2 chome, Chiyodaku, Tokyo 100 Japan. **(Subscription address:** Kyowa Book Company Inc., 1 38 Kanda Jinbocho Chiyoda-ku, Tokyo 101 Japan.**)** **NLM** Z 671 J73. **CODEN** JOKAAB. Documents available from Ask*IEEE, CASDDS. ***Continues*** *JICST Joho Kanri.*
Ind/Abst Chem. Abstr.; Coal Abstr.; INSPEC (1986-); Int. Aerosp. Abstr.; Libr. Inf. Sci. Abstr.

US/0099-1333
JOURNAL OF ACADEMIC LIBRARIANSHIP. [J. acad. librariansh.]. Vol. 1 (March 1975)-. Academic Scholarly Publication. English. bm. $125.00 (institutions), $50.00 (individuals), US; $145.00 (institutions), $70.00 (individuals) (surface mail), $165.00 (institutions), $90.00 (individuals) (air mail) other. JAI Press Inc., 55 Old Post Road, Suite 2, PO Box 1678, Greenwich CT 06836-1678. **Tel** (203)661-7602, FAX (203)661-0792. **ED** Charles Martel. **LC** Z671; .J58. **DD** 020/.5. **[CCC]. Bk Rev. Ad Acc. Pr Rev. Circ:** 2,700 (ctrl). available on microfilm and microfiche from University Microfilms International (UMI). Documents available from The Genuine Article.
Desc: Publishes articles that focus on problems and issues germane to college and university libraries. Provides a forum for authors to present research findings and, where applicable, their practical applications and significance. Also brings attention to its readers information about new and recently published books in library and information science, management, scholarly communication and higher education. Covers management and discipline-based software and information policy developments.
Ind/Abst Acad. Search (July 1993-); Book Rev. Index; Curr. Contents Soc. Behav. Sci.; Curr. Index J. Educ.; Educ. Index; INFO-SOUTH Abstr.; Inf. Instruc. Technol.; Inf. Sci. Abstr. [Full Cov.]; Leg. Inf. Manage. Index; Libr. Inf. Sci. Abstr.; Libr. Lit.; Res. Alert [Full Cov.]; Soc. Plann. Policy Dev. Abstr.; Soc. Sci. Cit. Index [Full Cov.].

●UK/0965-4380
JOURNAL OF AGSI. [J. AGSI]. **Added/Corp** Association for Global Strategic Information. **VFOAT** Journal - Association for Global Strategic Information. (1992)-. Periodical. English. Three times a year. $175.00. Infonortics Ltd, 9A High Street Calne, Wiltshire SN11 0BS England. **Tel** 011 44 249 814584, FAX 011 44 249 813656. **DD** 658.403805.
Desc: Serves as a forum for the exchange of ideas and experiences in the analysis of information, with a strong general interest in the delivery of information. Articles from areas such as corporate information management, natural language processing, electronic networks, methodology, the desktop PC, and benchmarking have been included.

US/0896-3568
JOURNAL OF BUSINESS & FINANCE LIBRARIANSHIP. [J. bus. finance librariansh.]. **VFOAT** Journal of Business and Finance Librarianship; Business & Finance Librarianship; Business and Finance Librarianship. Vol. 1, No. 1 (1990)-. Periodical. English. qt. $75.00 US; $105.00 other. The Haworth Press Inc, 10 Alice Street, Binghamton NY 13904-1580. **Tel** (607)722-5857, (800)3-HAWORTH, FAX (607)722-1424. **ED** William Fisher (editor's address: Division of Library and Information Science, San Jose State University, One Washington Square, San Jose, CA 95192-0029). **LC** Z675.B8; J65. **DD** 027.6/905. **CODEN** JBFLEY. **Bk Rev. Ad Acc. Pr Rev. Acid Free.** available on microfilm and microfiche from University Microfilms International (UMI). Documents available from Ask*IEEE, Haworth Document Delivery Service.
Desc: Covers the business information needs of all types of libraries and information centers worldwide. Although the immediate focus is on practice-oriented articles, it also provides an outlet for new empirical studies on business librarianship and business information.
Ind/Abst Inf. Sci. Abstr.; INSPEC (1990-); Leg. Inf. Manage. Index (19??-); Libr. Inf. Sci. Abstr.; Ref. Z.

UK
JOURNAL OF DOCUMENT AND TEXT MANAGEMENT. **See** Computers.

UK/0022-0418
JOURNAL OF DOCUMENTATION. [J. doc.]. **Added/Corp** Association of Special Libraries and Information Bureaux (Great Britain) Aslib. Vol. 1 (June 1945)-. Academic Scholarly Publication. English. qt. £83.00 (members), £104.00 (non-members) Europe; £91.00 (members), £114.00 (non-members) other. ASLIB, Information House, 20-24 Old Street, London EC1V 9AP England. **Tel** 011 44 71 253 4488, FAX 011 44 71 430 0514, telex 23667 AJLIB G. **(Subscription address:** North America: 143 Old Marlton Pike, Medford, NJ 08055-8750**)** **ED** Richard Kimber. **LC** Z1007; .J9. **DD** 010.5. **NLM** Z 1007 J86. **CODEN** JDOCAS. Index available. cum. index. **Bk Rev. Ad Acc. Pr Rev. Circ:** 3,500. Documents available from Article Express International, The Genuine Article, BIOSIS Document Express, Ask*IEEE, CASDDS.
Desc: Articles on most aspects of documentation, librarianship and information science, both theoretical and practical.
Ind/Abst Abstr. Bull. Inst. Pap. Sci. Tech.; Abstr. Hum. Comput. Interact. (1973-); ACM Guide Comput. Lit.; Arts Humanit. Citation Index [Select. Cov.]; Bioeng. Abstr.; Biol. Abstr. (-1986); Chem. Abstr.; Compumath Citation Index [Full Cov.]; Comput. Rev.; Curr. Contents Soc. Behav. Sci.; Curr. Index J. Educ.; Dairy Sci. Abstr.; Ei Page One; EMBASE; Eng. Index Annu.; Fluid Abstr., Civil Eng.; Fluid Abstr. Proc. Eng.; FLUIDEX (1973-1986); HILITES; Index Vet.; Inf. Instruc. Technol.; Inf. Sci. Abstr. [Full Cov.]; INSPEC (June 1970-); Libr. Inf. Sci. Abstr.; Libr. Lit.; Middle East Abstr. Index; MLA Int. Bibl. Books Artic. Mod. Lang. Lit.; Res. Alert [Full Cov.]; Soc. Plann. Policy Dev. Abstr.; Soc. Sci. Cit. Index [Full Cov.]; Sociol.

Abstr.; Stat. Theory Method Abstr. (1968-1971); Vet. Bull.; World Ceram. Abstr.; World Publ. Monit.; World Surf. Coat. Abstr.

US/0748-5786
JOURNAL OF EDUCATION FOR LIBRARY AND INFORMATION SCIENCE. (JOURNAL OF EDUCATION FOR LIBRARY AND INFORMATION SCIENCE / ALISE, ASSOCIATION FOR LIBRARY AND INFORMATION SCIENCE EDUCATION.). [J. educ. libr. inf. sci.]. **Added/Corp** Association for Library and Information Science Education. Vol. 25, No. 1 (Summer 1984)-. Academic Scholarly Publication. English. Five times a year (published within the seasons plus a directory). $60.00 US; $70.00 others. Association for Library and Information Science Education- ALISE, 4101 Lake Boone Trail, Suite 201, Raleigh NC 27607-4916. **Tel** (919)787-5181. **ED** Rosemary DuMont. **LC** Z671; .J64. **DD** 020/.5. cum. index. **Bk Rev. Pr Rev. Circ:** 1,700 (ctrl). available on microfilm and microfiche from University Microfilms International (UMI). Documents available from The Genuine Article, Ask*IEEE. ***Continues** Journal of Education for Librarianship, 0022-0604.*
Desc: Scholarly journal in the field of library and information science education; presents research, teaching methods and issues; international scope; association news.
Ind/Abst Acad. Search (July 1993-); Arts Humanit. Citation Index [Select. Cov.]; Contents Pages Educ.; Curr. Contents Soc. Behav. Sci.; Curr. Index J. Educ. (-1992); Educ. Index; High. Educ. Abstr. (1987-); Inf. Instruc. Technol.; Inf. Sci. Abstr. [Full Cov.]; INSPEC (Summer 1984-); Libr. Inf. Sci. Abstr.; Libr. Lit.; Mag. Search; Res. Alert [Full Cov.]; Soc. Sci. Cit. Index [Full Cov.]; Soc. Sci. Index.

●US/1062-7375
JOURNAL OF GLOBAL INFORMATION MANAGEMENT. [J. glob. inf. manag.]. **Added/Corp** Information Resources Management Association. **VFOAT** Global Information Management. Vol. 1, No. 1 (Winter 1993)-. Periodical. English. qt. $125.00 (institutions), $65.00 (individuals). Idea Group Publishing, 4811 Jonestown Road, Suite 230, Harrisburg PA 17109. **Tel** (800)345-4332, (717)541-9150, FAX (717)541-9159. **ED** Prashant Palvia. **LC** IN PROCESS; T58.64; .J68. **DD** 658. **CODEN** JGLMEY. Index available (bound in 2nd issue). **Bk Rev**, (Qty: 4). **Ad Acc. Pr Rev. Circ:** 300 (ctrl).
Desc: Focuses on providing coverage of research findings and expert advice on the development, utilization and management of global information technology.
Ind/Abst Inf. Sci. Abstr. [Full Cov.].

●US/1061-9321
JOURNAL OF INFORMATION ETHICS. **See** Ethics.

UK/0966-9248
JOURNAL OF INFORMATION NETWORKING. **See** Computers-Computer Networks.

NE/0165-5515
JOURNAL OF INFORMATION SCIENCE. [J. inf. sci.]. **Added/Corp** Institute of Information Scientists. Vol. 1 (Apr. 1979)-. Academic Scholarly Publication. English. bm. £115.00. Bowker Saur Ltd., A Reed Reference Publishing Company, Part of Reed International PLC, 59-60 Grosvenor Street, London WIX 9DA England. **Tel** 011 44 71 4935841, FAX 011 44 71 4991590. **(Subscription address:** World-Wide Subscription Services, Unit 4, Gibbs Reed Farm Pashley Road, Ticehurst TN5 7HE England.**)** **ED** Alan Gilchrist, B. C. Brookes and A. J. Meadows. **LC** Z1007; .J95. **DD** 020.5. **CODEN** JISCDI. **[CCC]. Pr Rev.** available on microfilm and microfiche from University Microfilms International (UMI). Documents available from Article Express International, The Genuine Article, Ask*IEEE, UMI Article Clearinghouse. ***Supersedes** Information Scientist.*
Desc: The journal is critical of assumptions which are inadequately supported by test or experience. To achieve its aims; it is assisted by an International Editorial Board of leading members of the profession.
Ind/Abst ABI/INFORM Glob. Ed. (19??-); ABI Inform Ondisc (Feb. 1981-); Acad. Search (July 1993-); ACM Guide Comput. Lit. (19??-); Bioeng. Abstr. (19??-); Bus. Index (1979-?); Bus. Source (Jul. 1993-); Coal Abstr. (19??-); Compumath Citation Index (19??-) [Full Cov.]; Comput. Lit. Index (19??-); Comput. Rev. (19??-); Curr. Lit. Sci. Sci. (19??-); Ei Page One (19??-); EMBASE (19??-); Eng. Index Annu. (19??-); Fluid Abstr., Civil Eng. (19??-); Fluid Abstr. Proc. Eng. (19??-); FLUIDEX (1979-); Gen. Period. Index (1985-); INFO-SOUTH Abstr. (19??-); Inf. Sci. Abstr. (19??-) [Full Cov.]; INSPEC (April 1979-); Int. Dev. Abstr. (19??-); Libr. Inf. Sci. Abstr. (19??-); Libr. Lit. (19??-); Mag. Search (19??-); Res. Alert (19??-) [Full Cov.]; Soc. Sci. Cit. Index (19??-) [Full Cov.]; Trade Ind. Index (19??-); World Text. Abstr. (19??-).

●II/0971-1988
JOURNAL OF INFORMATION SCIENCE AND TECHNOLOGY. [J. Inf. Sci. Technol.]. (1991)-. Periodical. English. qt. $70.00. **(Subscription address:** Prints India, 11 Darya Ganj, New Delhi 110002 India.**)** **UDC** 002.

UK/0268-3962
JOURNAL OF INFORMATION TECHNOLOGY : JIT. **See** Computers.

US/1042-4458
JOURNAL OF INTERLIBRARY LOAN & INFORMATION SUPPLY. ***Title Change.***
VFOAT Journal of Interlibrary Loan and Information Supply. Vol. 1, No. 1 (1990)-Vol. 3, No. 4 (1993). Periodical. English. qt. The Haworth Press Inc, 10 Alice Street, Binghamton NY 13904-1580. **Tel** (607)722-5857, (800)3-HAWORTH, FAX (607)722-1424. **ED** Leslie R. Morris (editor's address: Niagara University Library, Niagara University, NY 14109). **LC** Z713; .J68. **DD** 025.6/2. **CODEN** JILSEW. **Bk Rev. Ad Acc. Pr Rev. Circ:** 303. available on microfilm and microfiche from University Microfilms International (UMI). Documents available from Ask*IEEE, Haworth Document Delivery Service. ***Continued by** Journal of Interlibrary Loan, Document Delivery & Information Supply.*
Desc: Devoted to interlibrary loan problems and the basic expanding roles of interlibrary loan librarians. In addition to practice and research-based articles on interlibrary loan, this exciting new journal will focus on the broad spectrum of all library and information center functions that rely heavily on interlibrary loan and information supply. All articles are peer reviewed or refereed.
Ind/Abst Inf. Sci. Abstr.; INSPEC (1990-); Libr. Lit. (1991-).

●US/1072-303X
JOURNAL OF INTERLIBRARY LOAN, DOCUMENT DELIVERY & INFORMATION SUPPLY. [J. interlibr. loan doc. deliv. inf. supply]. Vol. 4, No. 1 (Fall 1993)-. Periodical. English. qt (Published during the academic year). $45.00 US; $63.00 other. The Haworth Press Inc, 10 Alice Street, Binghamton NY 13904-1580. **Tel** (607)722-5857, (800)3-HAWORTH, FAX (607)722-1424. **ED** Leslie R. Morris. **LC** Z713; .J68. **DD** 025. **Acid Free.** Documents available from Haworth Document Delivery Service. ***Continues** Journal of Interlibrary Loan & Information Supply, 1042-4458.*
Desc: Devoted to interlibrary loan problems and the basic expanding roles of interlibrary loan librarians.

AT/0729-1485
JOURNAL OF LAW AND INFORMATION SCIENCE. **See** Law.

UK/0961-0006
JOURNAL OF LIBRARIANSHIP AND INFORMATION SCIENCE. VFOAT JOLIS. Vol. 23 No. 1 (March 1991)-. Periodical. English. qt. £75.00. Bowker Saur Ltd., A Reed Reference Publishing Company, Part of Reed International PLC, 59-60 Grosvenor Street, London WIX 9DA England. **Tel** 011 44 71 4935841, FAX 011 44 71 4991590. **(Subscription address:** World-Wide Subscription Services, Unit 4, Gibbs Reed Farm Pashley Road, Ticehurst TN5 7HE England.**)** **LC** Z671; .J66. **CODEN** JLSCE6. available on microfilm from University Microfilms International (UMI). Documents available from The Genuine Article, Ask*IEEE. ***Continues** Journal of Librarianship, 0022-2232.*
Ind/Abst Curr. Contents Soc. Behav. Sci. (19??-); INSPEC (Mar. 1991-); Libr. Inf. Sci. Abstr. (19??-); Res. Alert (19??-) [Full Cov.]; Soc. Sci. Cit. Index (19??-) [Full Cov.].

US/0193-0826
JOURNAL OF LIBRARY ADMINISTRATION. [J. libr. adm.]. Vol. 1 (Spring 1980)-. Academic Scholarly Publication. English. qt. $105.00 US; $147.00 other. The Haworth Press Inc, 10 Alice Street, Binghamton NY 13904-1580. **Tel** (607)722-5857, (800)3-HAWORTH, FAX (607)722-1424. **ED** Sul Lee (editor's address: University of Oklahoma Libraries, 401 West Brooks, Norman, OK 73019). **LC** Z678; .J68. **DD** 025.1/05. **Bk Rev. Ad Acc. Pr Rev. Acid Free. Circ:** 1,005. available on microfilm and microfiche from University Microfilms International (UMI). Documents available from Ask*IEEE, UMI Article Clearinghouse, Haworth Document Delivery Service.
Desc: Represents the viewpoints, concerns and perspectives of top administration and middle-management. Contains theoretical and practical information articles with an emphasis on the application of theory to everyday problems. Publishes articles on accomplishments in actual practice and operations, providing information the library administrator wants and needs to know.
Ind/Abst ABI/INFORM Glob. Ed.; ABI Inform Ondisc; Acad. Search (July 1993-); Anbar Mark. Distr. Abstr. [Full Txt.]; Anbar Top Manage. Abstr. [Full Txt.]; Bus. Index (?-?); Curr. Index J. Educ.; EMBASE; Gen. Period. Index (1985-); INFO-SOUTH Abstr.; Inf. Sci. Abstr.; INSPEC (1986-); Leg. Inf. Manage. Index; Libr. Inf. Sci. Abstr.; Libr. Lit.; Mag. Search; Manage. Bibliogr. Rev.; Oper. Prod. Manage. Abstr. [Full Txt.]; PAIS Int. Print; Person. Train. Abstr. [Full Txt.]; Ref. Z.; Women Manage. Rev. [Full Txt.].

II/0970-714X
JOURNAL OF LIBRARY AND INFORMATION SCIENCE (DELHI). (JOURNAL OF LIBRARY AND INFORMATION SCIENCE.). [J. libr. inf. sci.]. **Added/Corp** Delhi. University Dept. of Library Science. Vol. 1 (June 1976)-. Periodical. English. sa. $18.00. Central News Agency Private Limited, 23 90 Connaught Circus, New Delhi India. **Tel** 011 91 11 344448. **(Subscription address:** Prints India, 11 Darya Ganj, New Delhi 110002 India.**)** **ED** P B Mangla. **LC** Z671; .J664. **DD** 020/.5. Index available. **Bk Rev. Ad Acc. Circ:** 350.
Ind/Abst Indian Libr. Sci. Abstr.; Inf. Sci. Abstr. (?-?); Libr. Inf. Sci. Abstr.; Libr. Lit.

II
JOURNAL OF LIBRARY SERVICE. V. 1- Aug. 1971-. Periodical. English. Rs22.00. 1760 Gandhi Road, Ahmedabad 1 India. **LC** Z845.I4; J68. **DD** 020/.954.

US/0742-1222
JOURNAL OF MANAGEMENT INFORMATION SYSTEMS. (JOURNAL OF MANAGEMENT INFORMATION SYSTEMS : JMIS.). [J. manage inf. syst.]. **VFOAT** JMIS; J.M.I.S. Vol. 1, No. 1 (Summer 1984)-. Periodical. English. qt. $220.00 US; $249.00 other. M. E. Sharpe Inc., 80 Business Park Drive, Armonk NY 10504. **Tel** (914)273-1800, (800)541-6563, FAX (914)273-2106. **ED** Vladimir Zwass. **DD** 658. **CODEN** JMISEB. available on microfilm and microfiche from University Microfilms International (UMI); available on an online database (file 15/Full-Text) from DIALOG. Documents available from UMI Article Clearinghouse, Ask*IEEE.
Desc: Publishes current research, case studies, and analysis of new developments for researchers and practitioners in management information systems.
Ind/Abst ABI/INFORM Glob. Ed.; ACM Guide Comput. Lit.; Anbar Account. Finan. Abstr. [Full Txt.]; Anbar Mark. Distr. Abstr. [Full Txt.]; Anbar Top Manage. Abstr. [Full Txt.]; Comput. Lit. Index; Comput. Rev.; Inf. Instruc. Technol.; INSPEC (Summer 1984-); Int. Abstr. Oper. Res. [Select. Cov.]; Manage. Bibliogr. Rev.; Oper. Prod. Manage. Abstr. [Full Txt.]; Oper. Res./Manag. Sci.; Person. Train. Abstr. [Full Txt.]; Qual. Control Appl. Stat.; Women Manage. Rev. [Full Txt.].

PH/0022-359X
JOURNAL OF PHILIPPINE LIBRARIANSHIP. [J. Philipp. librariansh.]. **Added/Corp** University of the Philippines. Institute of Library Science. Vol. 1, No. 1 (Mar. 1968)-. Periodical. English. sa. P60.00 Philippines; $15.00 other. Institute of Library Science, University of the Philippines, 3rd Floor/Gonzalez Hall, Diliman Quezon City 1101 Philippines. **Tel** 98-24-71. **ED** Rosa M Vallejo. **Ad Acc. Circ:** 500 (ctrl).
Desc: Deals with all aspects of library and information work in the Philippines.
Ind/Abst Index Philip. Period. (-199?); Libr. Inf. Sci. Abstr.; Libr. Lit.

●US/1047-7845
JOURNAL OF RELIGIOUS & THEOLOGICAL INFORMATION. [J. relig. theol. inf.]. **VFOAT** Journal of Religious and Theological Information. Vol. 1, No. 1 (1992)-. Periodical. English. sa. $48.00 US; $67.20 other. The Haworth Press Inc, 10 Alice Street, Binghamton NY 13904-1580. **Tel** (607)722-5857, (800)3-HAWORTH, FAX (607)722-1424. **ED** William C. Miller (editor's address: Nazaren Theological Seminary, 1700 East Meyer Boulevard, Kansas City, MO 64131). **LC** IN PROCESS. **DD** 020. **CODEN** JRTIE3. **Bk Rev. Ad Acc. Pr Rev. Acid Free.** available on microfiche. Documents available from Haworth Document Delivery Service.
Desc: Aims to be the primary journal in the field of theological librarianship, bibliography and information studies. It is a vehicle for articles pertaining to the production, dissemination, preservation, and bibliography of religious and theological information.
Ind/Abst Inf. Sci. Abstr.

US/0002-8231
JOURNAL OF THE AMERICAN SOCIETY FOR INFORMATION SCIENCE. [J. Am. Soc. Inf. Sci.]. **Main/Corp** American Society for Information Science. **VFOAT** A.JASIS. Vol. 21, (Jan./Feb. 1970)-. Academic Scholarly Publication. English. Ten times a year. $550.00 US; $650.00 Canada and Mexico; $687.50 other. John Wiley & Sons, Inc., 605 Third Avenue, New York NY 10158-0012. **Tel** (212)850-6000, (212)850-6645, FAX (212)850-6088, telex 12-7063. **(Subscription address:** John Wiley & Sons / England, Baffins Lane, Chichester, West Sussex PO19 1UD England.**)** **ED** Donald H. Kraft (editor's address: Department of Computer Science, Louisiana State University, Baton Rouge, LA 70803, editor's telephone number: (504)388-1495). **LC** Z1007; .A477. **DD** 020/.5. **NLM** Z 1007 A51. **CODEN** AISJB6. **[CCC]. Bk Rev. Ad Acc. Pr Rev. Circ:** 6,183. available on microfilm and microfiche from University Microfilms International (UMI). Documents available from Article Express International, The Genuine Article, UMI Article Clearinghouse, Ask*IEEE, CASDDS. ***Continues** American Documentation, 0096-946X.*

Desc: Serves as a forum for discussion and experimentation concerning the theory and practice of communicating information.
Ind/Abst ABI/INFORM Glob. Ed.; ABI Inform Ondisc (July 1974-); Abstr. Bull. Inst. Pap. Sci. Tech.; Acad. Search (July 1993-); ACM Guide Comput. Lit.; Am. Hist. Life (1955-1982); Art Archaeol. Tech. Abstr.; Arts Humanit. Citation Index [Select. Cov.]; Bus. Index (1979-?); Bus. Source (July 1993-); Chem. Abstr. (1970, 1985-) (19??-); Coal Abstr.; Compumath Citation Index [Full Cov.]; Comput. Rev.; Cumul. Index Nurs. Allied Health Lit.; Curr. Contents Soc. Behav. Sci.; Curr. Index J. Educ.; Curr. Lit. Sci. Sci.; Ei Page One; EMBASE; Eng. Index Annu.; Gen. Period. Index (1985-); GeoRef; Hospit. Health Admin. Index; Index Period. Artic. Relat. Law; INFO-SOUTH Abstr.; Inf. Instruc. Technol.; Inf. Sci. Abstr. [Full Cov.]; INSPEC (1970-); Int. Aerosp. Abstr.; Libr. Inf. Sci. Abstr.; Libr. Lit.; Linguist. Lang. Behav. Abstr.; Mag. Search; Manage. Contents; PAIS Int. Print (1991-?); Res. Alert [Full Cov.]; Soc. Plann. Policy Dev. Abstr.; Soc. Sci. Cit. Index [Full Cov.]; Soc. Work Abstr. [Select. Cov.]; Sociol. Abstr.; Stat. Theory Method Abstr. (1977); Mag. Index (1982-Dec. 1984).

US/0036-0473
JOURNAL OF THE RUTGERS UNIVERSITY LIBRARY, THE. [J. Rutgers Univ. Libr.]. **Added/Corp** Rutgers University. Library. Associated Friends. Rutgers University. Library. Rutgers University. Libraries. **VFOAT** Journal of the Rutgers University Libraries. Vol. 1, No. 1 (Dec. 1937)-. Periodical. English. Twice a year (June, Dec.). Free (members), $25.00 (non-members) others of Associated Friends Library. Rutgers University Library, Associated Friends of Library, New Brunswick NJ 08903. **Tel** (201)932-7006. **ED** Pamela Spence Richards. **LC** Z733; .R955F. **DD** 027.774942. **Circ:** 500 (ctrl).
Desc: Articles on the history of libraries, New Jersey history and the history of publishing as well as on bibliographical topics.
Ind/Abst Am. Hist. Life (1976-); Annu. Bibliogr. Engl. Lang. Lit.; MLA Int. Bibl. Books Artic. Mod. Lang. Lit.

US/0889-0277
JOURNAL OF THE SHAW HISTORICAL LIBRARY, THE. [J. Shaw Hist. Libr.]. **Added/Corp** Oregon Tech Development Foundation. Shaw Historical Library. Vol. 1, No. 1 (Fall 1986)-. Periodical. English. an. $16.00. Journal of the Shaw Historical Library, Oregon Institute of Technology, J Shaw Library, Klamath Falls OR 97601. **Tel** (503)885-1772. **DD** 979.
Ind/Abst Am. Hist. Life (1986-).

●US/0734-1768
JOURNAL OF THE SOCIETY FOR INFORMATION DISPLAY. **Added/Corp** Society for Information Display. **VFOAT** Journal of the SID. Vol. 1, No. 1 (Jan. 1993)-. Periodical. English. qt. **LC** TK7882.I6; J68. **[CCC].** Documents available from Article Express International. ***Continues** Proceedings of the Society for Information Display, 0734-1768.*
Ind/Abst ACM Guide Comput. Lit.; Comput. Rev.; Ei Page One; Eng. Index Annu.

UG
JOURNAL OF UGANDAN LIBRARIES. **Added/Corp** East African School of Librarianship. (19??)-. Periodical. English. sa. Editor of Journal of Ugandan Libraries, East African School of Librarianship, Makerere University, PO Box 7062, Kampala Uganda. **Tel** 554342, 531530. **ED** S Abidi. **LC** Z857.U3; U34. **DD** 027.0676/1. **Ad Acc. Circ:** 200. ***Continues** Uganda Libraries, 1015-8561.*
Ind/Abst Libr. Inf. Sci. Abstr.

US/0894-2498
JOURNAL OF YOUTH SERVICES IN LIBRARIES. [J. youth serv. libr.]. **Added/Corp** Association for Library Service to Children. American Library Association. Young Adult Services Division. **VFOAT** JOYS. Vol. 1, No. 1 (Fall 1987)-. Periodical. English. Four times a year (Jan., Apr., June, Nov.). $40.00 US; $50.00 other. American Library Association, 50 East Huron Street, Chicago IL 60611. **Tel** (312)944-6780, (800)545-2433, FAX (312)944-2641. **(Subscription address:** American Library Association, Subscription Department, 434 West Downer, Aurora IL 60506-9936.**)** **LC** Z718.1.A1; T6. **DD** 027. **[CCC].** available on microfilm and microfiche from University Microfilms International (UMI). ***Continues** Top of the News, 0040-9286.*
Ind/Abst Book Rev. Index (1987-); Child. Lit. Abstr. (19??-); Curr. Index J. Educ.; Educ. Index (1992-); Inf. Sci. Abstr. (?-?); Libr. Inf. Sci. Abstr.; Libr. Lit.; Med. Rev. Dig.

ZA/0049-853X
JOURNAL - ZAMBIA LIBRARY ASSOCIATION. [J. - Zamb. Libr. Assoc.]. **Main/Corp** Zambia Library Association. **VFOAT** Zambia Library Association Journal. Vol. 1 (Mar. 1969)-. Periodical. English. sa. $27.40 (nonmembers) Zambia; $30.00 (nonmembers) other. Zambia Library Association, PO Box 2839, Lusaka Zambia. **LC** Z857.Z3; Z35.
Ind/Abst Libr. Inf. Sci. Abstr.

UK
JOURNALS IN TRANSLATION. **Added/Corp** British Library. Lending Division. International Translations Centre. (1976)-. English. an. £55.00 UK; FI175.00. International Translations Center, Schuttersveld 2, 2611 WE Delft, The Netherlands. **Tel** 011 31 15 142242, 142243, FAX 011 31 15 158535, telex 38104. ***Continues** Translations Journals.*
Desc: Lists journals which are translated cover-to-cover, or selectively, together with journals which consist of translations of articles collected from multiple sources; included are the multi-source translation serials published by the various government sources in the United States.

US/0739-5086
JUDAICA LIBRARIANSHIP. [Jud. librariansh.]. **Added/Corp** Association of Jewish Libraries. Vol. 1, No. 1 (Fall 1983)-. Periodical. English. Twice a year. $25.00. Association of Jewish Libraries, 19 Brookfield Road, New Hyde Park NY 11040. **Tel** (212)532-4949 ext. 297. **LC** Z675.J4; A57. available on microfilm from University Microfilms International (UMI). ***Continues** AJL Bulletin, 0734-0516.*
Ind/Abst Genealogical Period. Annu. Index; Index Jew. Period.; Libr. Inf. Sci. Abstr.; Libr. Lit.

NE/0167-8477
JURIDISCHE BIBLIOTHECARIS, DE. [Jurid. bibl.]. (April 1980)-. Periodical. Dutch. sa. Jurinfo, Postbus 127, 5056 ZJ Berkel Enschot Netherlands.
Ind/Abst Libr. Inf. Sci. Abstr.

US/0075-4587
JUST B'TWX US. ***Ceased.*** Vol. 1 (1970)-Vol. 6 ( ). Periodical. English. ir. University of Colorado Libraries, PO Box 184, Boulder CO 80309. **Tel** (303)492-6176. **ED** Virginia Boucher. **Bk Rev. Ad Acc. Circ:** 400.
Desc: Deals with interlibrary loan matters.

JA/0387-8783
KANE : HITOTSUBASHI DAIGAKU FUZOKU TOSHOKAN HO. **VFOAT** Hitotsubashi Daigaku Fuzoku Toshokan Ho; The Hitotsubashi University Library Bulletin. Periodical. Japanese. Three times a year. Hitotsubashi Daigaku Fuzoku Toshokan, 1 Naka 2, Kunitachi-shi Japan. **Tel** 0425-72-1101, FAX 0425-73-3016. **LC** Z955.K814; K36. Index available. cum. index. **Circ:** 2,000 (ctrl).

JA
KAZE DAYORI. **Added/Corp** Tokushima Daigaku. Toshokan. Tokushima Daigaku Fuzoku Toshokan hÂo. (19??)-. Periodical. Japanese. Tokushima Daigaku Fuzoku Toshokan Ho, 1 Minami Josanjimamachi 2-chome, Tokushima 770 Japan. **LC** Z955; .T572a.

US/1055-8977
KENNEDY LIBRARY QUARTERLY, EASTERN WASHINGTON UNIVERSITY. [Kennedy Libr. q. East. Wash. Univ.]. **Added/Corp** Eastern Washington University. Kennedy Library. No. 1 (Winter 1991)-. Periodical. English. qt. Kennedy Library, MS84 Washington University, Cheney WA 99004-2475. **DD** 027.

US/0732-5452
KENTUCKY LIBRARIES. [Ky. libr.]. Vol. 45, No. 1 (Winter 1980)-. Periodical. English. Four times a year. $18.00. Kentucky Library Association, 1501 Twilight Trail, Frankfort KY 40601. **Tel** (502)223-5322. **ED** Bob Smith. **LC** Z732.K37; K47. **DD** 027.0769. **Bk Rev. Ad Acc. Circ:** 1,200 (ctrl). available on microfilm and microfiche from University Microfilms International (UMI). ***Continues** Kentucky Library Association Bulletin, 0022-734X.*
Desc: Library articles.
Ind/Abst Libr. Lit.

●US/1064-1211
KEY WORDS. (KEY WORDS : THE NEWSLETTER OF THE AMERICAN SOCIETY OF INDEXERS.). **Added/Corp** American Society of Indexers. (1992)-. Newsletter. English. bm. American Society of Indexers / California, 990 Winery Canyon Road, Templeton CA 93465. ***Continues** Newsletter (American Society of Indexers), 0733-3048.*

CN/0836-298X
KIDS CAN READ (LONDON, ONT.). ***Ceased.*** (KIDS CAN READ.). [Kids can read]. Vol. 1, No. 1 (Oct. 1986)-Vol. 7, No. 3 (June 1993). Periodical. English. ir. Kids Can Read, 249 Neville Drive, London Ontario N6G 1B9 Canada. **DD** 028.1/625054/05.

CN/1193-9540
KINGSTON PUBLIC LIBRARY INQUIRER, THE. [Kingst. Public Libr. inq.]. **Added/Corp** Kingston Public Library (Ont.). **VFOAT** Newsletter; Inquirer. (199?)-. Periodical. English. Limited free distribution. Kingston Public Library, 130 Johnson Street, Kingston Ontario K7L 1X8 Canada. **DD** 027.4713/72. ***Continues** Focus., 0319-4566.*

FI/0023-1843
KIRJASTOLEHTI. **Added/Corp** Suomen Kirjastoseura. Vol. 1 (1908)-. Periodical. Finnish (summaries and/or abstracts in English). mo. Fmk170.00. Academic Bookstore Akateeminen, Postilokero 23, FIN-00371 Helsinki Finland. **Tel** 011 358 0 12141. **(Subscription address:** Bookstore Tiedekirja, Kirkkokatu 14, SF 00170 Helsinki Finland.**)** cum. index.
Ind/Abst Libr. Inf. Sci. Abstr.; Libr. Lit.

FI/0358-9803
KIRJASTOTIEDE JA INFORMATIIKKA. (1981)-. Periodical. Multiple languages. qt. **UDC** 02.
Ind/Abst Libr. Inf. Sci. Abstr.

HU/0209-7788
KISALFOLDI KONYVTAROS. (1966)-. Hungarian.
Ind/Abst Magyar Konyv. Szak. Biblio.; Hungar. Libr. Info. Sci. Abstr.

CN/1188-052X
KIT AB' AL -ILM'. **Added/Corp** University of Toronto. FLIS Student Journal Governing Committee. University of Toronto. Faculty of Library and Information Science. **VFOAT** Book of Knowledge; Kitab Al-Ilm. Vol. 1, No. 1 (Summer 1991)-. Periodical. English. sa. $1.00 per issue. Flis Student Journal Governing Committee, Faculty of Library and Information Science, University of Toronto, 140 St. George Street, Toronto Ontario M5S 1A1 Canada. **DD** 020.

US/0160-3582
KIT - ASSOCIATION OF RESEARCH LIBRARIES. SYSTEMS AND PROCEDURES EXCHANGE CENTER. (SPEC KIT / SYSTEMS AND PROCEDURES EXCHANGE CENTER.). [Kit - Assoc. Res. Libr., Syst. Proced. Exch. Cent.]. **Main/Corp** Association of Research Libraries. Systems and Procedures Exchange Center. **Added/Corp** Association of Research Libraries. Systems and Procedures Exchange Center. **VFOAT** Kit. (1973)-. Periodical. English. Ten times a year. $185.00 (members); $280.00 (non-members); $380.00 others. Association of Research Libraries, 21 Dupont Circle, Washington DC 20036. **Tel** (202)296-2296. **(Subscription address:** Association of Research Libraries, Department 0692, Washington DC 20073.**)** **ED** Maxine K. Sitts. **LC** UNC. **CODEN** SPKIE9. Index available. cum. index. **Circ:** 450. available on microfiche from ERIC. ***Absorbed** Association of Research Libraries. Systems and Procedures Exchange Center. Spec Flyer, 0160-3574.*
Desc: Collections of selected documents from major research libraries, with a two-page management overview. Each issue explores a specific topic. Includes results and surveys, trends and issues.

GW/0524-0379
KLEINE SCHRIFTEN. **Main/Corp** Bonn. Universitat. Forschungsstelle fur Buchwissenschaft. (1964)-. Periodical. German. ir. DM68.00. J. B. Metzlersche Verlagsbuchhandling, Kernerstrasse 10 32 41, D-70028 Stuttgart Germany. **Tel** 011 49 711 22902-14, FAX 011 49 711 22902-90. **ED** J. Metzler Stuttgart. **DD** 020.
Ind/Abst MLA Int. Bibl. Books Artic. Mod. Lang. Lit.

●US/1065-8602
KLIATT (WELLESLEY, MASS.). (KLIATT.). [Kliatt]. (199?)-. Periodical. English. bm. $36.00 (one year), $68.00 (two year). Kliatt Young Adult Paperback Book Guide, 33 Bay Street Road, Wellesley MA 02158. **Tel** (617)237-7577. **LC** Z1037; .K565. **DD** 011. ***Continues** Kliatt Young Adult Paperback Book Guide, 0199-2376.*
Desc: Critical reviews of selected paperbacks, audiobooks, and educational software programs for junior high, high school, and public libraries.

XO
KNIZNICE A INFORMACIE. **Added/Corp** Matica Slovenska. (1991)-. Periodical. Slovak. bm. Matica Slovenska, Slovenska Narodna Kniznica Bibliograficke Oddelenie, Novomeskeho 32, 036 52 Martin Slovakia. **Tel** (842)313-71, FAX (842)331-88, telex 75331. **LC** Z671; .K583. Documents available from Ask*IEEE. ***Formed by the union of** Kniznice a Vedecke Informacie, 0322-807X **and** Citatel.*
Ind/Abst INSPEC (1991-).

XV/0023-2424
KNJIZNICA. **Added/Corp** Drustvo Bibliotekarjev Slovenije. Zveza Bibliotekarskih Drustev Slovenije. (1957)-. Slovenian (summaries and/or abstracts in English). qt (4 issues). $20.00. Zveza Bibliotekarskih Drustev Slovenije, Turjaska 1, Ljubljana, Slovenia. **Tel** 061 150 131. **ED** J. Gazvoda. **LC** Z671; .K592. **Bk Rev. Ad Acc. Circ:** 1,350. available on CD-ROM.
Ind/Abst Libr. Inf. Sci. Abstr.

●GW/0943-7444
KNOWLEDGE ORGANIZATION : KO. **Added/Corp** International Society for Knowledge Organization. **VFOAT** KO. Vol. 20 No. 1 (1993)-. Periodical. English. qt. DM120.00. Indeks Verlag, Woogstrasse 36A, D 60431 Frankfurt Germany. **Tel** 011 49 69 523690, FAX 011 49 69 520566. **LC** Z696; .I553. **DD** 025.4/05. **CODEN** KNOREM. ***Continues** International Classification, 0340-0050.*
Desc: Information concerning indexing and information retrieval.
Ind/Abst Soc. Sci. Cit. Index [Full Cov.].

LI/0204-2061
KNYGOTYRA. [Knygotyra]. (1970)-. Lithuanian (summaries and/or abstracts in English and Russian). ***Continues*** *BibliotekininkystÁes ir Bibliografijos Klausimai.*
Ind/Abst MLA Int. Bibl. Books Artic. Mod. Lang. Lit.

KO
KODAE TOSOGWAN PO. Main/Corp Koryo Taehakkyo. Chungang Tosogwan. **VFOAT** The Korea University Library Bulletin. Periodical. Korean. 1 Anam-dong Songbuk-ku, Seoul South Korea. **LC** Z955.K6634; K67A.

JA/0027-9153
KOKURITSU KOKKAI TOSHOKAN GEPPO. Main/Corp Kokuritsu Kokkai Toshokan (Japan). **Added/Corp** Kokuritsu Kokkai Toshokan (Japan). National Diet Library Monthly Bulletin. **VFOAT** National Diet Library Monthly Bulletin. (April 1961)-. Periodical. English (Japanese). mo. $170.00. Yurindo Insatsu, 47 Shiba Nishikubo Tomecho Minato-ku, Tokyo 105 Japan. **LC** Z955.T585; K64a. **NLM** Z 955 K77G.

JA
KOKURITSU KOKKAI TOSHOKAN SHOKUIN MEIBO. Main/Corp Kokuritsu Kokkai Toshokan (Japan). (19??)-. Japanese. Kokuritsu Kokkai Toshokan, (National Diet Library), 1-10-1 Nagatacho Chiyoda-ku, Tokyo 100 Japan. **Tel** 03 3581-2331, FAX 03 3597-9104. **LC** Z846; .K616.

RU
KOMPLEKTOVANIE I ISPOLZOVANIE KNIZKNYKH FONDOV MASSOVYKH BIBLIOTEK. ***Title Change.*** Periodical. Russian. **LC** Z819.A1; K64. ***Continued by*** *Sbornik Materialov po Komplektovaniiu I Ispolzovaniiu Knizhnykh Fondov MAssovykh Bibliotek RSFSR.*

HU/0023-3773
KONYVTARI FIGYELO. Added/Corp Orszagos Szechenyi Konyvtar Konyvtartudomanyi es Modszertani Koezpont. Orszagos Konyvtarugyi es Dokumentacios Tanacs. Vol. 1 (1955-). Periodical. Hungarian. bm. $22.00. **(Subscription address:** Kultura, Hungarian Foreign Trading Company, PO Box 149, H-1389 Budapest Hungary**) ED** Gero Zsoltne. **Bk Rev. Ad Acc. Circ:** 1,000.
Desc: A multi-purpose journal which contains all aspects of the librarianship in Hungary and in foreign countries.
Ind/Abst Magyar Konyv. Szak. Biblio.; Hungar. Libr. Info. Sci. Abstr.; Libr. Inf. Sci. Abstr.

HU/0209-4894
KONYVTARI JEGYZESEK. (1966)-. Hungarian.
Ind/Abst Magyar Konyv. Szak. Biblio.; Hungar. Libr. Info. Sci. Abstr.

HU/0865-1329
KONYVTARI LEVELEZO/LAP. (1989)-. Hungarian.
Ind/Abst Magyar Konyv. Szak. Biblio.; Hungar. Libr. Info. Sci. Abstr.

HU/0450-7886
KONYVTAROS. Added/Corp Hungary. Nepmuvelesi Miniszterium. Hungary. Muvelodesugyi Miniszterium. Vol. 6 Jan. (1956)-. Periodical. Hungarian. mo. Lapkiado Vallalat, Lenin Korut 9-11, 1073 Budapest 7, Hungary. **Tel** 222-408. **LC** Z674; .K55. ***Supersedes in part*** *Konyv.*
Ind/Abst Magyar Konyv. Szak. Biblio.; Hungar. Libr. Info. Sci. Abstr.

DK/0902-7270
KORT SAGT !. [Kort sagt !]. (1987)-. Periodical. Danish. mo. kr420.00. Danish Library Association Publishing, Trekronergade 15, DK-2500 Valby Denmark. **Tel** 4536308682, FAX 4536308080. **ED** Carsten Frederiksen, Carsten Berthelsen, Flemming Ettrup and Leaf Kajborg. **DD** 020.948 9. **CODEN** 02. **Ad Acc. Circ:** 2,500.
Desc: Newsletter on public library matters in Denmark and abroad.

US
KRAUS CURRICULUM DEVELOPMENT LIBRARY. CUMULATIVE SUBJECT INDEX. 1983-. English. an. Kraus Reprint and Periodicals, 358 Saw Mill River Road, Millwood NY 10546. **Tel** (914)762-2200, (800)223-8323, FAX (914)762-1195, telex 6818112. **LC** Z5814.C9; K7; LB1570. **DD** 375/.001/0973. ***Continues*** *Curriculum Development Library. Key-Word and Abstract Index (KAI); Curriculum Development Library. Cumulative Subject Index (CSI).*

GW
KURZDARSTELLUNG DER DOKUMENTATIONS-LEITSTELLE MODERNER ORIENT UND TATIGKEITSBERICHT. Main/Corp Dokumentations-Leitstelle Moderner Orient (Deutsches Orient-Institut). (19??)-. German. an. Deutsches Orient-Institut Dokumentations-Leitstelle Moderner Orient, D-2000 Hamburg 36, Neuer Jungferstieg 21, Germany. **LC** Z802.H176; H35a.

JA
KYUSHU GEIJUTSU KOKA DAIGAKU ZOKA TOSHO NOKUROKU. Main/Corp Kyushu Geijutsu Koka Daigaku. Toshokan. Multiple languages (Japanese, English, French, German and Italian). 226 Siobara Minami-ku 815, Fukuoka Japan. **LC** Z955.F824; K9. **DD** 025.4/3.

AT/0047-3774
L.A.S.I.E. (LASIE : INFORMATION BULLETIN OF THE LIBRARY AUTOMATED SYSTEMS INFORMATION EXCHANGE.). [L.A.S.I.E.]. Vol. 1, No. 1 (June, 1970)-. Periodical. English. Six times a year. 75.00Aus$ (institutions), 40.00Aus$ (individuals) Australia; 75.00Aus$ New Zealand & Papua New Guinea; 85.00Aus$ other. LASIE Australia Company Ltd, PO Box 442, Roseville NSW 2069 Australia. **Tel** 011 61 2 4131799, FAX 011 61 2 4131710, telex AA26054. **ED** Carmel Maquire. **CODEN** IBLEAS. cum. index. **Bk Rev. Ad Acc. Circ:** 400. available on microfilm. Documents available from Ask*IEEE.
Ind/Abst AESIS Q.; APAIS, Aust. Public Aff. Inf. Ser. (1973-); Aust. Educ. Index; Aust. Libr. Inf. Sci. Abstr. (1984-); Comput. Rev. (1973-); INSPEC (July/Aug. 1987-); Libr. Inf. Sci. Abstr.; Libr. Lit.

US/0041-7912
L.C. CLASSIFICATION: ADDITIONS AND CHANGES. Main/Corp Library of Congress. Subject Cataloging Division. **Added/Corp** Library of Congress. Classification Division. **VAT** Library of Congress Classification. Additions and Changes. (March/May 1928)-. English. qt. $95.00 North America; $105.00 other. Library of Congress / Cataloging Distribution Service, Washington DC 20541-5017. **Tel** (800)255-3666, (202)707-6100, FAX (202)707-1334. **LC** Z696; .U51. **DD** 025.4. **Bk Rev. Ad Acc.**
Desc: Contains the additions and changes made in the course of daily application of the classification schedules at the Library of Congress.

US
L.C. SUBJECT HEADINGS WEEKLY LISTS. Main/Corp Library of Congress. Cataloging Policy and Support Office. **VFOAT** LC Subject Headings Weekly Lists. (1993)-. Directory. English. mo. $435.00 North America; $465.00 other. Library of Congress / Cataloging Distribution Service, Washington DC 20541-5017. **Tel** (800)255-3666, (202)707-6100, FAX (202)707-1334. ***Continues*** *Library of Congress. Office of Subject Cataloging Policy. L.C. Subject Headings Weekly Lists.*

US/8755-366X
L.C. SUBJECT HEADINGS WEEKLY LISTS (DETROIT, MICH.). (L.C. SUBJECT HEADINGS WEEKLY LISTS.). [L.C. subj. head. wkly. lists]. **Main/Corp** Library of Congress. Subject Cataloging Division. **Added/Corp** Gale Research Company. **VFOAT** LC Subject Headings Weekly Lists. **VAT** Library of Congress Subject Headings Weekly Lists. Lists 1-19 (Oct. 1984)-. Periodical. English. Three times a year. $442.00. Gale Research Inc., 835 Penobscot Building, Detroit MI 48226. **Tel** (800)877-GALE, (313)961-2242, FAX (313)961-6083, telex TWX 810-221-7086. **ED** Kathleen Droste. **DD** 025.
Desc: An alphabetized cumulation of the Weekly Lists which reflect the additions and changes to the Library of Congress Subject Headings.

●UK
LA RECORD. Added/Corp Library Association. **VFOAT** Record; Library Association Record. Vol. 94, No. 1 (Jan. 1992)-. Periodical. English. mo. £79.50 UK; £98.00 other. Library Association, 7 Ridgmount Street, London WC1E 7AE England. **Tel** 011 44 71 636-7543, FAX 011 44 71 436-7218, telex 21897. **(Subscription address:** World-Wide Subscription Services, Unit 4, Gibbs Reed Farm Pashley Road, Ticehurst TN5 7HE England.**) LC** Z671; .L693. **Bk Rev. Ad Acc, Adv Mgr:** Andrew Nelson-Cole, **Tel** 071 636 7543, ext 245; FAX 071 323 6675. **Circ:** 25,500 (ctrl). ***Continues*** *Library Association Record, 0024-2195.*
Desc: The official journal of the Library Association, which is the professional body for practitioners in librarianship and information science. Contains current news coverage and lively four-colour features, book reviews, conferences, calendar. Audience: English, Welsh and Scottish local authorities, library and education boards in Northern Ireland, central and local library service points plus mobile libraries throughout the UK, universities and institutes of technology, colleges, schools and institutes of the University of London, polytechnics, and selected government and national special libraries.
Ind/Abst Book Rev. Index; Curr. Index J. Educ.; Libr. Inf. Sci. Abstr.; Libr. Lit.

AT/0041-3151
LA TROBE LIBRARY JOURNAL. [LaTrobe libr. j.]. **Main/Corp** La Trobe Library. **Added/Corp** La Trobe Library. Friends. La Trobe Library. Journal. Vol. 1 (Apr. 1968)-. English. sa. 20.00Aus$. Friends of the State Library of Victoria, 328 Swanston Street, Melbourne Victoria 3000 Australia. **Tel** 011 61 3 6699045, FAX 663 1480, telex AA38104. **LC** Z975; .M53. **DD** 027.4/94/5. Index available. cum. index. **Circ:** 850.
Desc: Articles about, or based on research using the collections of the state library of Victoria.
Ind/Abst Annu. Bibliogr. Engl. Lang. Lit.; APAIS, Aust. Public Aff. Inf. Ser. (1974-); Aust. Educ. Index.

US/0047-4053
LANTERN'S CORE, THE. Added/Corp Northwestern University (Evanston, Ill.). Library. (1970)-. Newsletter. English. mo. Free. Northwestern University Library, Northwestern University, Evanston IL 60208. **Tel** (708)491-7684. **ED** Board. **Bk Rev. Circ:** 650 (ctrl).
Desc: A reference tool used to identify the placement of essential tools (such as pencil sharpeners, typewriters, etc.) in libraries.

US
LATIN AMERICAN SERIALS LIST / U.T. AUSTIN, GENERAL LIBRARIES, BENSON COLLECTION. VFOAT Benson Latin American Collection Serials List. Began with May 1982. Periodical. Spanish (English). an. $20.00. Publications of the General Libraries, University of Texas at Austin, PO Box P, Austin TX 78713-7330. **Tel** (512)471-3811. **ED** Mary Pound. available on microfiche.
Desc: Lists serial titles and their bound holdings in the Benson Collection with OCLC records as of May 29, 1982.

UK/0023-9275
LAW LIBRARIAN (LONDON). (THE LAW LIBRARIAN.). [Law libr.]. **Added/Corp** British and Irish Association of Law Librarians. Vol. 1 (April 1970)-. Periodical. English. Four times a year. £42.00 Europe; £44.00 other. Sweet & Maxwell Ltd., South Quay Plaza, 183 Marsh Wall, London E14 9FT England. **Tel** 011 44 264 342899, FAX 011 44 264 342723, telex 929089 ITPINF G. **ED** B. M. Wells. **LC** Z675.L2; L38. **DD** 026/.34/00942. **CODEN** LALIE2. **[CCC]. Bk Rev. Ad Acc. Circ:** 750. Documents available from Ask*IEEE.
Desc: Law librarianship, legal bibliography, legal databases, aspects of librarianship, publishing, computer-assisted information retrieval and information work as they affect law libraries.
Ind/Abst Curr. Law Index (1980-); Index Leg. Period.; Inf. Sci. Abstr. (Apr. 1989-); INSPEC (April 1989-); Leg. Inf. Manage. Index (1980-); Leg. Resour. Index (1980-); LegalTrac (1980-); Libr. Inf. Sci. Abstr.; Libr. Lit.

UK/0268-8336
LAW LIBRARY INFORMATION REPORTS. [Law libr. inf. rep.]. No. 1 (1981)-. Monographic series. English. ir. $100.00 per individual report. Glanville Publishers Inc, 75 Main Street, Dobbs Ferry NY 10522. **Tel** (914)693-1320, FAX (914)693-0402. **ED** Roy M Mersky. **LC** UNC. **DD** 026.

US/0023-9283
LAW LIBRARY JOURNAL. [Law libr. j.]. **Added/Corp** American Association of Law Libraries. National Association of State Libraries. Public Document Clearing House Committee. Check-list of Session Laws. Supplement. Vol. 1 (Jan. 1908)-. Academic Scholarly Publication. English. Four times a year. $50.00 US; $55.00 other. American Association of Law Libraries, 53 West Jackson Boulevard, Suite 940, Chicago IL 60604. **Tel** (312)939-4764, FAX (312)431-1097, telex ABA7603. **ED** Richard A. Danner. **LC** K12; .A9364. **DD** 026.34. cum. index. **Bk Rev. Ad Acc. Pr Rev. Circ:** 5,000. available on microfilm and microfiche from University Microfilms International (UMI). Documents available from The Genuine Article. ***Absorbed*** *Law Library News.*
Desc: Publishes scholarly articles and practical pieces on law, legal information, and law librarianship.
Ind/Abst Curr. Contents Soc. Behav. Sci.; Index Leg. Period.; Inf. Instruc. Technol.; Inf. Sci. Abstr.; Int. Aerosp. Abstr.; Law Office Inf. Serv.; Leg. Inf. Manage. Index; Leg. Resour. Index (1980-); LegalTrac (1980-); Libr. Inf. Sci. Abstr.; Libr. Lit.; Res. Alert [Full Cov.]; Saf. Health Work (1980-); Soc. Sci. Cit. Index [Full Cov.].

US/0457-2483
LAW LIBRARY LIGHTS. [Law libr. lights]. Periodical. English. bm. $35.00. Law Library Lights, 1717 Largo Road, Upper Marlboro MD 20772. **Tel** (202)429-4094. **ED** Michael Saint-Onge. **LC** LAW. **DD** 026. **Ad Acc. Circ:** 750.
Desc: Features articles, bibliographies and regular columns.
Ind/Abst Leg. Inf. Manage. Index.

US/0147-1376
LAW LIBRARY NEWSLETTER. Added/Corp Information Handling Services. Library and Education Division. (19??)-. Newsletter. English. mo. Ms Judith Goater, 15 Inverness Way East, Englewood CO 80110. **LC** Z675.L2; L39. **DD** 026/.34/05.

US/0148-0553
LAW LINES. Added/Corp Law Library Association of Greater New York. Began in (Sept. 1976)-. Periodical. English. bm. **LC** Z675.L2; L393. **DD** 026.34.
Ind/Abst Leg. Inf. Manage. Index (19??-).

US/0736-4903
LC FOLK ARCHIVE FINDING AID. **See** Sociology-Manners and Customs.

US
LCOMM NEWS / LIBRARY COUNCIL OF METROPOLITAN MILWAUKEE.
Added/Corp Library Council of Metropolitan Milwaukee. Library Council of Metropolitan Milwaukee. News. Vol. 1, No. 1 (Oct. 1973)-. Periodical. English. Eleven times a year. $12.00. Library Council of Metro Milwaukee, 814 West Wisconsin Avenue, Milwaukee WI 53233. **Tel** (414)271-8470, FAX (414)278-2137. **ED** Janis Trebby. **Bk Rev. Ad Acc. Circ:** 420 (ctrl).
Desc: Newsletter of council and member activities with news of the library community in the Milwaukee metropolitan area, Wisconsin, and beyond.

US/0736-296X
LCPA BROADSIDE. VFOAT L.C.P.A. Broadside. **VAT** Library of Congress Professional Association Broadside. Vol. 1, No. 1 (Jan. 3, 1983)-. Periodical. English. bm. Free to LCPA members only. Library of Congress / Professional Association, c/o Staff Relations Office, LJ G112 Library of Congress, Washington DC 20540. **ED** Louis Drummond and Joe Puccio. **LC** Z733.U6; L35. **DD** 027.573/088092. **Circ:** 1,800 (ctrl).
Desc: Supplement to Insights, the LCPA Newsletter.

US/0882-6374
LCPA'S INDEX TO LIBRARY OF CONGRESS INFORMATION BULLETIN.
VFOAT Index to Library of Congress Information Bulletin. **VAT** Library of Congress Professional Association's Index to Library of Congress Information Bulletin. Vol. 43 (1984)-. Bulletin. English. an. $10.00. Library of Congress / Professional Association, c/o Staff Relations Office, LJ G112 Library of Congress, Washington DC 20540. **LC** Z733.U57; I612.

IE/0023-9542
LEABHARLANN, AN. [Leabharlann]. **Added/Corp** Library Association of Ireland. Library Association. Northern Ireland Branch. **VFOAT** Journal of the Library Association of Ireland. Vol. 1, No. 3 (June 1930)-. Periodical. English. Four times a year. 15.00p. Library Association of Ireland, 53 Upper Mount Street, Dublin 2 Ireland. **Tel** 011 353 1 6761167, 011 353 1 6761963. **LC** Z671; .L46. **DD** 020.622. **Bk Rev. Ad Acc.** ***Continues*** *Leabharlann;* ***Absorbed*** *Northern Ireland Libraries, 0029-3113.*
Ind/Abst Annu. Bibliogr. Engl. Lang. Lit.; Libr. Inf. Sci. Abstr.; Libr. Lit.

GW/0170-8643
LECTURE NOTES IN CONTROL AND INFORMATION SCIENCES. [Lect. notes control inf. sci.]. **Added/Corp** International Federation for Information Processing. Vol. 1 (1978)-. Monographic series. English. ir. Price varies per volume. Springer-Verlag GmbH & Company KG, Heidelberger Platz 3, D 14197 Berlin Germany. **Tel** 011 49 30 8207223, FAX 011 49 30 8214091, telex 183 319 SPBLN D. **(Subscription address:** Springer Verlag New York Inc. / for North America, 44 Hartz Way, Secaucus NJ 07096.**) [CCC].** Documents available from Article Express International, The Genuine Article, Ask*IEEE.
Desc: Contains topics on analysis and optimization of systems, performance evaluation, methodology, and theory of networks and systems.
Ind/Abst Compumath Citation Index [Full Cov.]; Ei Page One; Eng. Index Annu.; INSPEC; Math. Rev.; Res. Alert [Full Cov.]; SCISEARCH; Soc. Sci. Cit. Index [Select. Cov.]; Zentralbl. Math. Ihre Grenzgeb.

GW/0172-7788
LECTURE NOTES IN MEDICAL INFORMATICS. See Medical Science and Technology.

US/0747-9298
LEGAL INFORMATION MANAGEMENT INDEX. See Law-Abstracting, Bibliographies and Statistics.

US/0270-319X
LEGAL REFERENCE SERVICES QUARTERLY. See Law.

US
LESKOS INFO POWER. (19??)-. Periodical. English. mo. $54.00. Information USA, PO Box E, Kensington MD 20895. **Tel** (301)924-0556, (800)955-7693, FAX (301)946-3004. ***Continues*** *Data Informer.*

CN/0705-4890
LETTER OF THE LAA, THE. Main/Corp Library Association of Alberta. Issue No. 1 (Nov. 1977)-. Periodical. English. Five times a year. Free to members of the Library Association of Alberta. Library Association of Alberta, Box 64197, 5512 4th Street Northwest, Calgary Alberta T2K 6J1 Canada. **Tel** (403)228-0898, FAX (403)228-0929. **DD** 020/.6234/7123. ***Supersedes*** *Library Association of Alberta. LAA-LAA-LAA., 0318-8566.*

US/1059-3195
LETTER TO LIBRARIES ONLINE [COMPUTER FILE] : A NEWSLETTER OF THE OREGON STATE LIBRARY. [Lett. libr. online]. **Added/Corp** Oregon State Library. **VFOAT** LTLO. Vol. 1, No. 1 (Nov. 1991)-. Newsletter. English. mo. Must order direct. Oregon State Library, State Library Building, Salem OR 97310-0640. **Tel** (503)378-2112, FAX (503)588-7119. **DD** 025.
Desc: Available on Oregon State Library's Oregon Public Access Catalog.

CN/0702-3839
LIAISON II. Began publication in summer 1977?. Periodical. English. Niagara Regional Library System, 15 Lloyd Street, St. Catharines Ontario L2S 2N7 Canada. **DD** 027.4/713/51. ***Continues*** *Liaison, 0700-3390.*

CN/0380-9579
LIAISON (OTTAWA). (LIAISON.). **Added/Corp** Council of Federal Libraries (Canada). (Oct. 19, 1976)-. Periodical. English (French). Six times a year. Free on request. Privy Council Office Library, 1000 85 Sparks Street, Ottawa Ontario K1A 0A3 Canada. **Tel** (613)957-5133.

AT/0814-5539
LIB TEC. [Lib tec]. (1983)-. Periodical. English. qt. **ED** J Bailey, Sutherland Shire Public Library, Eton Street, Sutherland NSW 2232 Australia. **DD** 023'.3'09944. ***Continues*** *N.S.W. Library Technician Newsletter, 0159-2556.*
Ind/Abst Aust. Educ. Index.

UK
LIBRARIAN CAREER DEVELOPMENT: AN INTERNATIONAL JOURNAL. (19??)-. English. qt. $299.00. MCB University Press, 60 62 Toller Lane, Bradford West Yorkshire BD8 9BX England. **Tel** 011 44 274 499821, FAX 011 44 274 547143, telex 51317 MCBUNI G. **(Subscription address:** MCB University Press / US and Canada Subscriptions, PO Box 10812, Birmingham AL 35201-0812.**)**

●US/1069-0832
LIBRARIANS AT LIBERTY. (LIBRARIANS AT LIBERTY : AN INTERACTIVE NEWSLETTER.). (1993)-. Newsletter. English. sa. $10.00 US; $15.00 other. Crises Press, 1716 Southwest Williston Road, Gainesville FL 32608. **Tel** (904)335-2200. **ED** Charles Willett.
Desc: Covers the professional concerns of those working in library sciences and related fields.

US/1063-5386
LIBRARIANS COLLECTION LETTER. [Libr. collect. lett.]. **VFOAT** LCL. (1991)-. Periodical. English. Eleven times a year. $47.00. Librarians Collection Letter, PO Box 722, Westerly RI 02891. **Tel** (401)596-2877. **ED** Regan Robinson. **DD** 025. **Bk Rev,** (Qty: 3-6). **Circ:** 250.
Desc: For collection development staff in public libraries.

US/0093-1888
LIBRARIANS' HANDBOOK (BIRMINGHAM). (LIBRARIANS' HANDBOOK.). [Libr. handb.]. **Added/Corp** EBSCO Subscription Services. (1968)-. English. an. Free to qualified customers; $20.00 microfiche. EBSCO Industries Inc., PO Box 1943, Birmingham AL 35201-1943. **Tel** (205)991-1465, FAX (205)991-1479. **ED** Kathy Kosie. Index available. **Ad Acc. Circ:** 20,000 (ctrl).
Desc: Contains title ordering information, nation of origin, frequency of publication, special publisher ordering requirements and current publisher prices for more than 60,000 listings of serials.

US/0194-0112
LIBRARIANS' NEWSLETTER. ***Title Change.*** [Libr. newsl.]. **Added/Corp** John Wiley & Sons. **VFOAT** John Wiley & Sons Librarians' Newsletter. (19??)-(19??). Newsletter. English. ir. John Wiley & Sons, Inc., 605 Third Avenue, New York NY 10158-0012. **Tel** (212)850-6000, (212)850-6645, FAX (212)850-6088, telex 12-7063. **(Subscription address:** John Wiley & Sons / England, Baffins Lane, Chichester, West Sussex PO19 1UD England.**) DD** 015. **CODEN** JWSNDD. ***Continued by*** *Wiley Librarians' Newsletter, 1063-0686.*
Desc: Reports on new and forthcoming publications of all Wiley imprints, divisions and subsidiaries.

US/0739-0297
LIBRARIAN'S WORLD. [Libr. world]. **Added/Corp** Evangelical Church Library Association. (19??)-. Periodical. English. qt (Mar., June., Sept., Dec.). $12.00 US and Canada; $15.00 other. Evangelical Church Library Association, PO Box 353, Glen Ellyn IL 60138. **Tel** (708)668-0519. **ED** Nancy Dick. **Bk Rev. Ad Acc. Circ:** 650 (ctrl).
Desc: Reviews of current Christian books and media promotional tips technical and other helps geared to church librarians.

AT/1032-1438
LIBRARIES ALONE. [Libr. alone]. (1988)-. Periodical. English. be. International Association of Rural Isolated Libraries, PO Box 38, Turvey Park NSW 2650 Australia. **Tel** 011 61 69 222417. **DD** 027.01734.
Ind/Abst Libr. Inf. Sci. Abstr.

US/0894-8631
LIBRARIES & CULTURE. See Publishing-Books and Bookmaking.

US/1055-3665
LIBRARIES AND INFORMATION SERVICES TODAY : THE YEARLY CHRONICLE. ***Ceased.*** **Added/Corp** American Library Association. (1991)-(199?). English. American Library Association, 50 East Huron Street, Chicago IL 60611. **Tel** (312)944-6780, (800)545-2433, FAX (312)944-2641. cum. index. ***Continues*** *The ALA Yearbook of Library and Information Services.*
Desc: A yearly chronicle of library and information services.

UK/0961-4575
LIBRARIES DIRECTORY. (1990)-. Directory. English. be. £50.00. James Clarke & Co. Ltd., PO Box 60, Cambridge CB1 2NT England. **Tel** 0223 350865, FAX 0223 66951. **ED** Richard S Burnell, 0223-350865. Index available. **Ad Acc, Adv Mgr:** Lucy Simcox, **Tel** 0223-350865. ***Continues*** *Libraries Year Book, 0955-4645.*
Desc: Directory of public libraries and special libraries, including record offices in the UK and the Republic of Ireland.

US/0149-547X
LIBRARIES FOR COLLEGE STUDENTS WITH HANDICAPS. [Libr. coll. stud. handicaps]. **Added/Corp** State Library of Ohio. (1976)-. English. ir. The State Library of Ohio, 65 South Front Street, Columbus OH 43266. **Tel** (614)644-7051. **LC** Z711.92P2; L47. **DD** 027.6.

US
LIBRARIES IN MAINE. ***Title Change.*** **Added/Corp** Maine State Library. (19??)-(19??). English. an. Department of Educational and Cultural Services, Maine State Library, State House/Station 64, Augusta ME 04333. **LC** Z732.M2; L5. **DD** 027/.0025/741. ***Continues*** *Libraries of Maine.* ***Continued by*** *Maine Public Libraries.*

US
LIBRARIES IN THE NEWS. V. 2, No. 9- Sept. 4, 1971-. Periodical. English. mo. Office of Public Libraries and Interlibrary Cooperation, 550 Cedar Street, St Paul MN 55101.

UK
LIBRARIES IN THE UNITED KINGDOM AND THE REPUBLIC OF IRELAND.
Added/Corp Library Association. (19??)-. English. an. $35.00. Library Association, 7 Ridgmount Street, London WC1E 7AE England. **Tel** 011 44 71 636-7543, FAX 011 44 71 436-7218, telex 21897. **(Subscription address:** UNIPUB, 4611 F Assembly Drive, Lanham, MD 20706; Phone: (800)274-4888**) ED** Ann Harrold. **LC** Z791.A1; L4. **DD** 027/.0025/41.
Desc: A unique directory of central libraries; polytechnic libraries; selected national, government, and special libraries; and schools of librarianship. Addresses and telephone numbers are provided.

JA
LIBRARIES TODAY. GENDAI NO TOSHOKAN. Japanese. qt. $75.00. **(Subscription address:** Kyowa Book Company Inc., 1-38 Kanda Jinbo-Cho, Chiyoda-Ku, Tokyo 101, Japan (Phone: 03-3293-0727)**)**

US/0748-2035
LIBRARIES (TULSA, OKLA.). (LIBRARIES / THE UNIVERSITY OF TULSA.). [Libraries]. **Added/Corp** University of Tulsa. Libraries. **VFOAT** Libraries Newsletter. No. 1 (Fall 1983)-. Periodical. English. ir. Libraries, Director of Libraries, PL203 McFarlin Library, The University of Tulsa, Tulsa OK 74119. **Tel** (918)592-6000. **ED** Don Smith. **DD** 027. **Circ:** 500.

US
LIBRARY ACCESS : SERVICES FOR PEOPLE WITH DISABILITIES. ***Ceased.***
Added/Corp Indiana University, Bloomington. Institute for the study of Developmental Disabilities. Vol. 1, No. 1 (Jan. 1991)-Vol. 4 (April 1994). Periodical. English. qt. ISDD, 2853 East Tenth Street, Bloomington IN 47405. **ED** Marilyn Irwin. **LC** Z711.92.H3; L52.

CN/0382-4284
LIBRARY ACCESSIONS - ARCTIC INSTITUTE OF NORTH AMERICA. ***Title Change.*** **Main/Corp** Arctic Institute of North America. Library. Periodical. English. Arctic Institute of North America, University of Calgary, 2500 University Drive Northwest, Calgary Alberta T2N 1N4 Canada. **Tel** (403)220-7515, FAX (403)282-4609. ***Continued by*** *A S T I S Current Awareness Bulletin, 0705-8454.*

TH
LIBRARY ACCESSIONS LIST / UNESCO PRINCIPAL REGIONAL OFFICE FOR ASIA AND THE PACIFIC. Main/Corp UNESCO. Principal Regional Office for Asia and the Pacific. Library. No. 69 (Jan.-June 1987)-. Periodical. English. sa. UNESCO Regional Office for Education in Asia and the Pacific, PO Box 1425, General Post Office, Bangkok 10500 Thailand. ***Continues*** *Library Accessions List.*

US/0364-6408
LIBRARY ACQUISITIONS : PRACTICE AND THEORY. [Libr. acquis., Pract. theory]. **VFOAT** Library Acquisitions; LAPT. Vol. 1 (Jan. 1977)-. Academic Scholarly Publication. English. qt. $149.00 The Americas; £100.00 other. Pergamon Press, An Imprint of Elsevier Science Ltd., The Boulevard, Langford Lane, Kidlington, Oxford OX5 1GB United Kingdom. **Tel** 011 44 865 843000, 011 44 865 843699, FAX 011 44 865 843010. **(Subscription address:** Elsevier Science Ltd. Oxford Fulfillment Centre, PO Box 800, Kidlington, Oxford OX5 1DX United Kingdom.**) ED** Carol Pitts Hawks. **LC** Z689; .L515. **DD** 025.2/1. **CODEN** LAPTDK. **[CCC]. Pr Rev.** available in microform from Microforms International; and Pergamon Press; available on microfilm and microfiche from University Microfilms International (UMI). Documents available from The Genuine Article, Ask*IEEE, CASDDS.
Ind/Abst Chem. Abstr.; Curr. Contents Soc. Behav. Sci.; Inf. Instruc. Technol.; Inf. Sci. Abstr.; INSPEC (1982-); Leg. Inf. Manage. Index; Libr. Inf. Sci. Abstr.; Libr. Lit.; Pollut. Abstr. Indexes; Res. Alert [Full Cov.]; Soc. Sci. Cit. Index [Full Cov.].

US/0888-4463
LIBRARY ADMINISTRATION & MANAGEMENT. [Libr. admin. manage.]. **Added/Corp** Library Administration and Management Association. **VFOAT** Library Administration and Management. Vol. 1, No. 1 (Jan. 1987)-. Periodical. English. Four times a year (Jan., Mar., June, Sept.). $50.00 US, Canada & Mexico; $60.00 other. American Library Association, 50 East Huron Street, Chicago IL 60611. **Tel** (312)944-6780, (800)545-2433, FAX (312)944-2641. **(Subscription address:** American Library Association, Subscription Department, 434 West Downer, Aurora IL 60506-9936.**) ED** Donald E Riggs and Charles B Lowry. **LC** Z678; .A67a. **DD** 025. **[CCC]. Ad Acc. Circ:** 4,700. available on microfilm and microfiche from University Microfilms International (UMI). ***Continues*** *LAMA Newsletter, 0193-0451.*
Desc: Reports on current issues of concern to library managers and executives. Articles, news items and reviews help these professionals analyze and act appropriately on recent developments in their field.
Ind/Abst Curr. Index J. Educ.; Inf. Sci. Abstr.; Libr. Inf. Sci. Abstr.; Libr. Lit.

US/0746-6129
LIBRARY ADMINISTRATOR'S DIGEST. [Libr. adm. dig.]. **VFOAT** Administrator's Digest. Vol. 18, No. 1 (Jan. 1983)-. Periodical. English. Ten times a year (except July and Aug.). $39.00 (one year), $73.00 (two years), $106.00 (three years). Administrators Digest Press, PO Box 933, South San Francisco CA 94080. **Tel** (415)573-5474. **ED** Robert S. Alvarez. **DD** 025. Index available. cum. index. ctrl circ. available on microfilm and microfiche from University Microfilms International (UMI). ***Continues*** *Administrator's Digest (Orinda, Calif.), 0001-8422.*
Desc: Designed to keep literary administrators abreast of new ideas in all fields that have applications and implications for their library.

US/0196-0075
LIBRARY & ARCHIVAL SECURITY. [Libr. arch. secur.]. **VFOAT** Library and Archival Security. Vol. 2, No. 3/4 (1978)-. Periodical. English. sa. $115.00 US; $161.00 other. The Haworth Press Inc, 10 Alice Street, Binghamton NY 13904-1580. **Tel** (607)722-5857, (800)3-HAWORTH, FAX (607)722-1424. **ED** Alan Jay Lincoln and Carol Zall Lincoln (editor's address: Lowell University, 1 University Avenue, Lowell, MA 01854). **LC** Z679.6; .L5. **DD** 025.8/2. **Bk Rev. Ad Acc. Pr Rev. Acid Free. Circ:** 440 (ctrl). available on microfilm and microfiche from University Microfilms International (UMI). Documents available from Haworth Document Delivery Service. ***Continues*** *Library Security Newsletter, 0094-0216.*
Desc: The vital areas of security planning, policies and procedures, and strategies for both libraries and archives are the focus of this highly praised and important journal. Provides research articles, program descriptions and news in areas such as book/periodical theft, electronic security systems, fire security, management of overdues/circulation control, guard services, insurance policies and more.
Ind/Abst Crim. Justice Abstr.; Inf. Sci. Abstr.; Leg. Inf. Manage. Index (19??-199?); Libr. Inf. Sci. Abstr.; Libr. Lit.

UK/0954-1829
LIBRARY & INFORMATION BRIEFINGS. [Libr. inf. brief.]. **VFOAT** Library and Information Briefings. (1988)-. Monographic series. English. Ten times a year. £60.00 UK; £70.00 other. Library and Information Technology Centre, 235 High Holborn Polytechnic, London WC1V 7DN England. **Tel** 011 44 71 430 1561. **ED** Mary Feeney and John Mafyn. **DD** 020.941 338.47020941. **Circ:** 400.
Desc: Provides information on the legal and political environment of information and significant new technologies.
Ind/Abst Inf. Manage. Technol.

UK/0269-8161
LIBRARY AND INFORMATION NEWS. [Libr. inf. news]. **VFOAT** Library & Information News. (1980)-. Periodical. English. mo. £50.00 UK; £55.00 other. Dawson UK Ltd, Cannon House, Folkestone Kent CT19 5EE England. **Tel** 011 44 303-850101, FAX 011 44 303-850440, telex 96392. **ED** Alan Armstrong. **Bk Rev. Ad Acc. Circ:** 1,000 (ctrl).
Desc: Concise paragraphs of news, services, people, computer technology, books, courses, conferences, etc., all geared towards the library and information professional.
Ind/Abst World Publ. Monit.

UK/0141-6561
LIBRARY AND INFORMATION RESEARCH NEWS. [Libr. inf. res. news]. **VFOAT** LIRN : Library and Information Research News. Periodical. English. Three times a year. £25.00 UK; £28.00 other. Library & Information Research Group, University of Southampton, Southampton SO9 5NH England. **Tel** 061-273-8228. **ED** M O Smith and Payne. **Bk Rev. Ad Acc. Circ:** 250.
Desc: Articles, news, reviews on the library and information science field in the United Kingdom and overseas.
Ind/Abst Libr. Inf. Sci. Abstr.

UK
LIBRARY AND INFORMATION RESEARCH REPORT. 1982-. Monographic series. English. Price varies per volume. British Library, Great Russell Street, London WC1B 3DG England.

JA/0373-4447
LIBRARY AND INFORMATION SCIENCE. [Libr. inf. sci.]. **Added/Corp** Mita Toshokan Joho Gakkai. No. 6 (1968)-. Periodical. English (Japanese). an. $20.00. Mita Society of Library and Information Science, Keio University, Mita Minato-ku, Tokyo 108 Japan. **Tel** 011 81 3 3453 3920. **ED** Kimio Hosono. **LC** Z671; .L7165. **CODEN** LIFSBL. Index available. cum. index. **Pr Rev. Circ:** 1,650. Documents available from The Genuine Article, Ask*IEEE. ***Continues*** *Library Science.*
Desc: Thoughts and findings in the fields of library and information science.
Ind/Abst Curr. Contents Soc. Behav. Sci.; INSPEC (1972-); Libr. Inf. Sci. Abstr.; Libr. Lit.; Res. Alert [Full Cov.]; Soc. Sci. Cit. Index [Full Cov.].

UK/0024-2179
LIBRARY & INFORMATION SCIENCE ABSTRACTS. **See** Library and Information Sciences-Abstracting, Bibliographies and Statistics.

US/0739-506X
LIBRARY AND INFORMATION SCIENCE EDUCATION STATISTICAL REPORT. **See** Library and Information Sciences-Abstracting, Bibliographies and Statistics.

US/0740-8188
LIBRARY & INFORMATION SCIENCE RESEARCH. [Libr. inf. sci. res.]. **VFOAT** Library and Information Science Research. Vol. 5, No. 1 (Spring 1983)-. Periodical. English. qt. $125.00 institution. Ablex Publishing Corporation, 355 Chestnut Street, Norwood NJ 07648. **Tel** (201)767-8450, (201)767-8455 (Customer Service), FAX (201)767-6717. **ED** Jane Robbins-Carter. **LC** Z671; .L7153. **DD** 020/.5. **CODEN** LISRDH. **[CCC].** Index available. **Bk Rev. Ad Acc. Pr Rev. Circ:** 500. Documents available from The Genuine Article, Ask*IEEE. ***Continues*** *Library Research, 0164-0763.*
Desc: Reports results of library research to practicing librarians emphasizing application of research in planning, management, and operation of libraries.
Ind/Abst Curr. Contents Soc. Behav. Sci.; Curr. Index J. Educ.; Inf. Instruc. Technol.; Inf. Sci. Abstr. [Full Cov.]; INSPEC (1985-); Libr. Inf. Sci. Abstr.; Libr. Lit.; Res. Alert [Full Cov.]; Soc. Plann. Policy Dev. Abstr.; Soc. Sci. Cit. Index [Full Cov.]; Sociol. Abstr.

CN/0820-0521
LIBRARY AND INFORMATION SCIENCE UPDATE. [Libr. inf. sci. update]. **Added/Corp** University of Toronto. Faculty of Library and Information Science. Library. No. 74 (May 1982)-. Periodical. English. Twelve times a year. 24.00Can$ Canada, 48.00Can$ US, 31.00Can$ (surface mail); 54.00Can$ (airmail). Library and Information Science Update, 140 St George Street, Toronto Ontario M5S 1A1 Canada. **Tel** (416)978-7060, FAX (416)978-5762. **ED** Ellen Jones. **DD** 016.02. **Circ:** 250. ***Continues*** *Library Science Update, 0383-9087.*
Desc: A current awareness bulletin designed to meet the needs of information professionals.

CC/0252-3116
LIBRARY AND INFORMATION SERVICE. (TU SHU CHING PAO KUNG TSO.). [Libr. inf. serv.]. **Added/Corp** Chung-kuo ko Hsueh Yuan. Tu Shu Kuan. **VFOAT** Library and Information Service. (Feb. 1980)-. Academic Scholarly Publication. Chinese. bm. $52.80. Science Press, 16 Donghuangchenggen North Street, Beijing 100707, People's Republic of China. **Tel** 011 86 1 4019821, 011 86 1 4010642, FAX 011 86 1 4012180, 011 86 1 4019810, telex 210147. **ED** X. Ximeng. **LC** Z671; .T77. **DD** 020/.5. **Ad Acc. Circ:** 32,000. ***Continues*** *Tu Shu Kuan Kung Tso.*
Desc: Covers the science of library information and services.
Ind/Abst Libr. Inf. Sci. Abstr.

II
LIBRARY & LIBRARIAN, THE. V. 1-. Periodical. English. Rs20.00. **LC** Z845.I4; L5. **DD** 020/.954.

IS
LIBRARY ARCHIVES AND INFORMATION STUDIES. English. $25.00. Magnes Press, Hebrew University of Jerusalem, PO Box 7695, Jerusalem 91076 Israel. **Tel** 011 972 2 660341, 011 972 2 635291, FAX 011 972 2 633370, telex 25391.
Desc: Includes research papers in librarianship, archive and information studies, representing a multi-disciplinary range of topics, such as history of printing, the book and libraries, the sociology of books and reading, archives organization and such new fields as bibliometrics and information systems.

CN/0075-904X
LIBRARY ASSOCIATION OF ALBERTA OCCASIONAL PAPER, THE. **VFOAT** Occasional Paper. No. 1-. English. ir. Southern Alberta Institute of Technology, 1301 16 Avenue NW, Calgary Alberta Canada. **Tel** (403)934-5334. **ED** Marg Gamble. **Ad Acc. Circ:** 530 (ctrl).
Desc: Covers president's message; executive reports; financial statement; news from libraries around the province; across Canada news; and forthcoming events.

US/0898-6118
LIBRARY AUTOMATION NEWS. [Libr. autom. news]. **VFOAT** Follett Library Automation News; Follett LAN. (1985)-. Periodical. English. Three times a year. Free. Follett, 809 North Front Street, McHenry IL 60050. **Tel** (800)323-3397, FAX (815)344-8774. **DD** 025. ***Continues*** *Book Trak News.*

CN/0228-541X
LIBRARY BINDINGS (WEYBURN). (LIBRARY BINDINGS.). [Libr. bindings]. Vol. 1, No. 1 (Dec. 1970)-. Periodical. English. qt. Free. Southeast Regional Library, Box 550, Weyburn Saskatchewan S4H 2K7 Canada. **Tel** (306)842-3432. **DD** 027.47124/4. **Bk Rev. Circ:** 250.
Desc: Describes branch activities in 56 rural Saskatchewan branches, provides brief book reviews of new arrivals, 'helpful hints' and editorials.

US
LIBRARY BOOK CATALOG. Vol. 1 (1972)-. Catalog. English. an. US Department of Justice, 10th Street & Constitution Avenue NW, Washington DC 20530. **Tel** (202)514-2000, FAX (202)633-4371.

US/0024-2217
LIBRARY BOOKSELLER, THE. [Libr. books.]. (1949)-. Periodical. English. Twenty-six times a year. $75.00 (institution), $100.00 (individual). Scott Saifer, PO Box 9544, Berkeley CA 94709-0544. **Tel** (510)540-6951. **ED** Gail Rusin and Scott Snifes. **DD** 025. **Ad Acc, Adv Mgr:** S. Snifes, **Tel** (510)540-6951. **Circ:** 150. ***Continues*** *American Antiquarian Bookman.*
Desc: The Library Bookseller lists out-of-date titles need by institutional librarians for competitive quotation by book dealers.

AT
LIBRARY BULLETIN. **Main/Corp** Australia Music Centre. (19??)-. Bulletin. English. Australia Music Centre, PO Box N690, Grosvenor Place, Sydney New South Wales 2000 Australia.

UK
LIBRARY BULLETIN. **Main/Corp** Great Britain. Dept. of the Environment. Library. (1972)-. Bulletin. English. mo. £12.00. Department of the Environment and Transport, Government Building Block, 3 1 Spur 2 RMI, Limegreen Eastcote HA4 8ISEE. **Tel** 011 44 81 4295170. Index available. **Circ:** 2,000. ***Formed by the union of*** *Index to Periodical Articles* ***and*** *Classified Accessions List.*
Desc: Abstracts of current literature on social and environmental planning, roads, traffic, transport, recreation, housing, local government, water supplies, waste disposal, pollution and conservation.

AT/0811-1359
LIBRARY BULLETIN - AUSTRALIAN BROADCASTING TRIBUNAL. [Libr. bull. - Aust. Broadcast. Trib.]. (1982)-. English. ir. Australian Broadcasting Tribunal, PO Box 1308, North Sydney 2059 Australia. **Tel** 02 959-7811. **DD** 027.594.
Ind/Abst Aust. Educ. Index; Aust. Libr. Inf. Sci. Abstr. (1982-1986).

CN/0225-4484
LIBRARY BULLETIN - BOREAL INSTITUTE FOR NORTHERN STUDIES. (LIBRARY BULLETIN - BOREAL INSTITUTE FOR NORTHERN STUDIES [LIBRARY]). [Libr. bull. - Boreal Inst. North. Stud.]. **Main/Corp** Boreal Institute for Northern Studies. Library. Vol. 1 (Jan. 1980)-. Bulletin. English. mo. 20.00Can$. Boreal Institute of Northern Studies, University of Alberta, CW 401-B10 Science Building, Edmonton Alberta T6G 2E9 Canada. **LC**

Z1392.N6; B67a; F1090.5. **DD** 016.9719. ***Supersedes*** *Boreal Institute for Northern Studies. Library Accessions List, 0315-601X.*
Desc: A list, arranged by country, of all publications (old and new) processed each month by the library. General geographic focus is the Arctic and cold regions.

US
LIBRARY BULLETIN - CENTER ON SOCIAL WELFARE POLICY AND LAW. **See** Sociology-Social Services and Welfare.

SI/0073-9723
LIBRARY BULLETIN (INSTITUTE OF SOUTHEAST ASIAN STUDIES). (LIBRARY BULLETIN.). Began in 1971. Bulletin. English. ir. Price varies per volume. Institute of Southeast Asian Studies / Singapore, Heng Mui Keng Terrace, Pasir Panjang Road, Singapore 0511 Republic of Singapore. **Tel** (11) 65 8702447, FAX 011 65 7781735, telex 37068. **Bk Rev. Ad Acc. Circ:** 1,000 (ctrl).
Desc: A series on Southeast Asian librarianship and bibliography, each number on a different topic.

US/0148-7876
LIBRARY BULLETIN - TEXAS DEPARTMENT OF WATER RESOURCES. **See** Water Resources.

US/1071-2593
LIBRARY CAT NEWSLETTER, THE. **See** Pets.

US/0730-3785
LIBRARY COMPENSATION REVIEW. [Libr. compens. rev.]. Vol. 1, No. 1 (Winter 1982)-. Periodical. English. qt. $25.00. Graduate Library School, University of Arizona, 1515 East First Street, Tucson AZ 85721. **LC** Z682.3; .L52. **DD** 331.2/8102/0922.
Ind/Abst Libr. Inf. Sci. Abstr.

US/0895-531X
LIBRARY COMPUTER SYSTEMS AND EQUIPMENT REVIEW. ***Ceased.*** [Libr. comput. syst. equip. rev.]. Vol. 10, No. 1 (Jan.-June 1988)-(Dec. 1993). Periodical. English. sa. Mecklermedia Corporation, 11 Ferry Lane West, Westport CT 06880. **Tel** (203)226-6967, (800)632-5537, FAX (203)454-5840. **LC** Z678.9.A1; L54. **DD** 022/.9. **CODEN** LCSREA. **[CCC].** Documents available from The Genuine Article, Ask*IEEE. ***Continues*** *Computer Equipment Review, 0278-260X.*
Ind/Abst Compumath Citation Index [Full Cov.]; Consum. Index Prod. Eval. Inf. Source; INSPEC (Jan./June 1988-); Leg. Inf. Manage. Index (19??-); Libr. Inf. Sci. Abstr.; Libr. Lit.; Res. Alert [Full Cov.]; SCISEARCH; Soc. Sci. Cit. Index [Select. Cov.].

UK/0265-041X
LIBRARY CONSERVATION NEWS. **Added/Corp** British Library. Preservation Service. (1983)-. Periodical. English. qt. £15.00 UK; £19.00 other. British Library / Publications Sale Unit, Boston Spa, Wetherby, West Yorkshire LS23 7BQ England. **Tel** 011 44 937 546546 546543, FAX 011 44 937 546333, telex 557381. **(Subscription address:** Turpin Distribution Services Limited, Blackhorse Road, Letchworth, Hertfordshire SG6 1HN, United Kingdom.**)**
Desc: Essential reading for all who play a part in preserving for the future our written and printed heritage.
Ind/Abst Art Archaeol. Tech. Abstr.; Libr. Inf. Sci. Abstr.

US/0741-4188
LIBRARY CURRENTS. [Libr. curr.]. Vol. 1, No. 1 (Jan. 1984)-. Periodical. English. Twelve times a year. $42.00 US; $48.00 Canada & Mexico; $57.00 others. Practical Perspectives Inc., PO Box 202108, Austin TX 78720-2108. **Tel** (512)218-8038. **ED** Edward Seidenberg. Index available. **Bk Rev. Circ:** 800.
Desc: Summaries of key books, articles and reports in the library, management, and technical literature.

US/0145-5397
LIBRARY DEVELOPMENTS (AUSTIN, TEX.). (LIBRARY DEVELOPMENTS.). **Added/Corp** Texas State Library. Library Development Division. Texas State Library. Dept. of Library Development. Vol. 1, No. 1 (Jan./Feb. 1974)-. Periodical. English. Six times a year. Free. Texas State Library Clearinghouse, PO Box 12927, Capitol Station, Austin TX 78711. **Tel** (512)463-5435, FAX (512)463-5436. **ED** Raymond Hitt. **LC** Z732.T25; L53. **DD** 027.0764. **Circ:** 700 (ctrl).
Desc: A publication of the Library Development Division, this publication announces workshops and seminars, use of state and federal funds, reports of boards and commissions, and new materials in the library.

CN/1183-8701
LIBRARY DIRECTIONS : A NEWSLETTER OF UNIVERSITY OF MANITOBA LIBRARIES. [Libr. dir.]. **Main/Corp** University of Manitoba. Libraries. No. 1 (Fall 1991)-. Newsletter. English. sa. Free. University of Manitoba Libraries, University of Manitoba, Winnipeg Manitoba R3T 2N2 Canada. **DD** 027.77127.

US
LIBRARY DIRECTORY AND ... STATISTICAL REPORT. **Main/Corp** Alabama Public Library Service. (1986)-. Statistical Publication. English. an. Alabama Public Library Service, 6030 Monticello Drive, Montgomery AL 36130. **Tel** (205)277-7330. **LC** Z732.A25; A55A. ***Continues in part*** *Alabama Public Library Service Annual Report.*

UK/0269-963X
LIBRARY EQUIPMENT REPORT. ***Ceased.*** [Libr. equip. rep.]. (1986)-(Dec. 1994). Periodical. English. bm. Headland Business Information, 1 Henry Smiths Terrace, Headland Cleveland, TS24 0PD England. **Tel** 011 44 429 231902, FAX 011 44 429 861403. **(Subscription address:** Subscription Office, PO Box 1831, Birmingham, AL 35201-1831, USA, Telephone 800-633-9431**) DD** 022.9.
Desc: Presents objective, authoritative and jargon-free advice on all categories of library equipment, from microcomputers to rubber stamps.

CN/0838-360X
LIBRARY FOOTNOTES. (LIBRARY FOOTNOTES / NEWFOUNDLAND PUBLIC LIBRARY SERVICES.). [Libr. footnotes]. **Added/Corp** Newfoundland Public Library Services. Vol. 1 No. 1 (Spring 1988)-. Periodical. English. Four times a year. Free. Newfoundland Public Library Board, Arts & Culture Center, St. John's Newfoundland A1B 3A3 Canada. **Tel** (709)737-3953. **DD** 027.4718. ***Continues*** *Newfoundland Public Library Services. Newsletter; Newfoundland and Labrador Provincial Libraries., 0381-2022.*

US
LIBRARY HERALD. **Added/Corp** Delhi Library Association. Vol. 1 (April 1958)-. Periodical. English. qt. $25.00. Delhi Library Association, PO Box 1270 Queens Garden, Delhi 6 India. **Tel** 7112721. **ED** C P Vashishth.
Desc: Includes original contributions, reviews in library information science, documentation and computer application in library operations.
Ind/Abst Indian Libr. Sci. Abstr.; Libr. Inf. Sci. Abstr.

II/0024-2292
LIBRARY HERALD. [Libr. her.]. **Added/Corp** Delhi Library Association. Vol. 1 (Apr. 1958)-. Periodical. English. qt. $60.00. Delhi Library Association, PO Box 1270 Queens Garden, Delhi 6 India. **Tel** 7112721. **(Subscription address:** Prints India, 11 Darya Ganj, New Delhi 110002 India.**) LC** Z671; .L698. **DD** 020/.5. available on microfilm.

US/0737-8831
LIBRARY HI TECH. [Libr. hi tech]. **VFOAT** Library HiTech. Vol. 1, No. 1 (Summer 1983)-. Periodical. English. qt. $75.00 (institutions), $45.00 (individuals) regular subscription; $149.50 combined subscription with Library Hi Tech News. Pierian Press, PO Box 1808, Ann Arbor MI 48106. **Tel** (313)434-5530, (800)678-2435, FAX (313)434-6409. **ED** C. Edward Wall. **LC** Z671; .L699. **DD** 020/.5. **Bk Rev**, (Qty: 25). **Ad Acc, Adv Mgr:** Annette Wall, **Tel** 313-434-5530. **Circ:** 10,200 (ctrl). available on an online database, CD-ROM, magnetic tape, and microfilm from University Microfilms International (UMI). Documents available from Ask*IEEE.
Desc: Dedicated to providing information about current and emerging technologies in library and information science, and the publication of practical articles on the application of existing and developing systems. Provides a continuing education on the issues and options facing libraries that are planning to automate or upgrade their information systems.
Ind/Abst Acad. Abstr. (July 1993-); Acad. Search (July 1993-); ACM Guide Comput. Lit.; Book Rev. Index (1984-); Bus. Educ. Index; Comput. Lit. Index; Comput. Rev.; Consum. Index Prod. Eval. Inf. Source; Curr. Index J. Educ.; Inf. Instruc. Technol.; Inf. Sci. Abstr.; INSPEC (1984-); Int. Aerosp. Abstr.; Leg. Inf. Manage. Index; Libr. Inf. Sci. Abstr.; Libr. Lit.; Mag. Artic. Summar. Elite (July 1993-); Mag. Artic. Summar. CD-ROM (July 1993-); Microcomput. Index (Jan. 1985-); Ref. Z.; Trade Ind. Index.

US/0741-9058
LIBRARY HI TECH NEWS. [Libr. hi tech news]. **VFOAT** Library High Tech News; Library Hi/Tech News; L.H.T.N.; L.H.T. News; LHT News; LHTN. Vol. 1, No. 1 (Jan. 1984)-. Periodical. English. Ten times a year. $95.00 (institutions), $70.00 (individuals) regular subscription; $149.50 combined subscription with Library Hi Tech Journal. Pierian Press, PO Box 1808, Ann Arbor MI 48106. **Tel** (313)434-5530, (800)678-2435, FAX (313)434-6409. **ED** C. Edward Wall. **LC** Z678.9.A1; L55. **DD** 025/.02/02854. **Bk Rev. Ad Acc. Circ:** 10,200 (ctrl). available on microfilm and microfiche from University Microfilms International (UMI).
Desc: Supplements Library Hi Tech Journal by offering current awareness of new developments in library hi tech, vendor products, network news, new software and hardware, and people in technology.
Ind/Abst ACM Guide Comput. Lit.; Book Rev. Index (1984-); Comput. Lit. Index; Comput. Rev.; Index Period. Artic. Relat. Law; Inf. Instruc. Technol.; Inf. Sci. Abstr.; Int. Aerosp. Abstr.; Leg. Inf. Manage. Index; Libr. Inf. Sci. Abstr.; Microcomput. Index (Jan. 1989-).

UK/0024-2306
LIBRARY HISTORY. [Libr. hist.]. **Added/Corp** Library Association. Library History Group. Vol. 1 (Spring 1967)-. Periodical. English. Twice a year (July, Dec.). £11.00. British Library, Great Russell Street, London WC1B 3DG England. **ED** P. H. Morrish. **LC** Z721; .L634. Index available (Free). **Bk Rev. Ad Acc. Circ:** 1,500 (ctrl). ***Supersedes*** *Library Association. Library History Group. Newsletter; Newsletter - Library History Group.*
Desc: History of various types of libraries. Libraries and book collections
Ind/Abst Acad. Search (July 1993-); Am. Hist. Life (1967-1970, 1976-); Annu. Bibliogr. Engl. Lang. Lit.; Br. Humanit. Index; Hist. Source (July 1993-); INFO-SOUTH Abstr.; Libr. Inf. Sci. Abstr.; Libr. Lit.; Mag. Search.

●US
LIBRARY HISTORY ROUND TABLE NEWSLETTER. **Added/Corp** American Library Association. Library History Round Table. Vol. 1, No. 1 (Fall 1992)-. Newsletter. English. sa. American Library Association, 50 East Huron Street, Chicago IL 60611. **Tel** (312)944-6780, (800)545-2433, FAX (312)944-2641. **(Subscription address:** American Library Association, Subscription Department, 434 West Downer, Aurora IL 60506-9936.**)** ***Continues*** *LHRT Newsletter.*

US/0740-736X
LIBRARY HOTLINE. [Libr. hotline]. Vol. 12, No. 27 (Sept. 5, 1983)-. Periodical. English. wk (50 issues). $74.00 US; $91.00 other. Cahners Publishing Company, 249 West 17th Street, New York NY 10011. **Tel** (212)645-0067, FAX (212)242-6987. **(Subscription address:** Library Hotline, PO Box 1980, Danbury CT 06813.**) ED** Karl Nyren. **LC** Z671; .L2. **DD** 020/.5. **[CCC]. Ad Acc. Circ:** 2,600. ***Continues*** *LJ/SLJ Hotline, 0000-0078.*
Desc: Each issue covers news of personnel changes, trends, programs, funding, new library technology, and much more. In addition, each issue contains the most timely and comprehensive classifieds in the field.

US/0197-5587
LIBRARY IMAGINATION PAPER, THE. (Winter 1979)-. Periodical. English. Four times a year. $32.00 (one year), $64.00 (two year), $96.00 (three year) US; $36.00 (one year), $72.00 (two year), $108.00 (three year) other. Library Imagination Paper, 1000 Byus Drive, Charleston WV 25311. **Tel** (304)345-2378. **ED** Carol Bryan. **Circ:** 2,000.
Desc: Library clip art and ideas for use on library promotional materials. Articles on library public relations topics.

US/0270-6792
LIBRARY INSTRUCTION ROUND TABLE NEWS. [Libr. Instruct. Round Table news]. **VFOAT** LIRT News. (Oct. 1978)-. Periodical. English. qt. $30.00. American Library Association, 50 East Huron Street, Chicago IL 60611. **Tel** (312)944-6780, (800)545-2433, FAX (312)944-2641. **(Subscription address:** American Library Association, Subscription Department, 434 West Downer, Aurora IL 60506-9936.**)**

US/0734-3035
LIBRARY ISSUES. [Libr. issues]. Vol. 1, No. 1 (Sept. 1980)-. Periodical. English. bm. $40.00 (one year), $68.00 (two year). Mountainside Publishing Company, PO Box 8330, Ann Arbor MI 48107. **Tel** (313)662-3925. **ED** Richard M. Dougherty. **LC** Z675.U5; L5235. **DD** 027.7/0973. **[CCC]. Circ:** 700 (ctrl). available on microfilm.
Desc: Briefings for faculty and administrators addressing topics most crucial to academic libraries.

US/0363-0277
LIBRARY JOURNAL (1976). (LIBRARY JOURNAL.). [Libr. j.]. Vol. 101, No. 9 (May 1, 1976)-. Periodical. English. Twenty-one times a year. $87.50 US; $109.00 (includes GST) Canada; $149.00 other. Cahners Publishing Company, 249 West 17th Street, New York NY 10011. **Tel** (212)645-0067, FAX (212)242-6987. **(Subscription address:** Library Journal, PO Box 2606, Boulder CO 80322-2606.**) ED** John Berry. **LC** Z671; .L7. **DD** 020/.5. **NLM** Z 671 L6963. **[CCC]. Bk Rev. Ad Acc. Pr Rev. Circ:** 26,000 (ctrl). available on microfilm and microfiche from University Microfilms International (UMI). Documents available from The Genuine Article, UMI Article Clearinghouse. ***Continues*** *LJ, Library Journal, 0360-3113.*
Desc: Full-service magazine/working tool tailored to the information needs of librarians and managers in public, academic and corporate libraries.
Ind/Abst ABI/INFORM Glob. Ed.; ABI Inform Ondisc (1976-Oct. 1977); Acad. Abstr. Full Text Elite (Jan. 1989-) [Full Txt.]; Acad. Abstr. (Jan. 1989-); Acad. Ind. [Computer File] (1984-); Acad. Search (Jan. 1989-); Access (1980-); ACM Guide Comput. Lit.; Am. Bibliogr. Slavic East Europ. Stud.; Annu. Bibliogr. Engl. Lang. Lit.; Art Archaeol. Tech. Abstr.; Arts Humanit. Citation Index [Select. Cov.]; Book Rev. Digest; Book Rev. Index; Bus. Index (1979-?); Chicano Index; Child. Lit. Abstr. (19??-); Comput. Rev.; Cumul. Index Nurs. Allied Health Lit.; Curr. Contents Soc. Behav. Sci.; Curr. Index J. Educ.; Educ. Index; Expand. Acad. Index (1984-); Garden Lit. (1992-); Gen. Period. Index (1985-); Graph. Arts Bull. Inst. Pap. Sci. Technol. (July 1989-); Hospit. Health Admin. Index;

Humanit. Source (Jul. 1993-) [Full Txt.]; Index Period. Artic. Relat. Law; INFO-SOUTH Abstr.; Inf. Instruc. Technol.; Inf. Sci. Abstr.; Int. Labour Doc.; LABORDOC; Leg. Inf. Manage. Index; Leis. Recreat. Tour. Abstr.; Libr. Inf. Sci. Abstr.; Libr. Lit.; Mag. Artic. Summar. Elite (Jan. 1989-) [Full Txt.]; Mag. Artic. Summar. Select (Jan. 1989-) [Full Txt.]; Mag. Artic. Summar. CD-ROM (Jan. 1989-); Mag. Index Plus (1989-); Mag. Index Sel. Microfiche (1986-) [Full Txt.]; Mag. Index. Sel. (1986-); Mag. Search; Med. Rev. Dig.; Middle East Abstr. Index; Newsp. Period. Abstr. (1989-); Peace Res. Abstr. J. (1979-); Res. Alert [Full Cov.]; Romant. Move.; Sci. Fict. Fantasy Book Rev. Index; Soc. Sci. Cit. Index [Full Cov.]; Stat. Ref. Index; Mag. Index (1977-); TOM Gen. Index (1985-) [Full Txt.]; Trade Ind. Index; Urban Aff. Abstr.; Vocat. Search (Jan. 1989-) [Full Txt.].

US/0270-059X
LIBRARY LECTURES (KNOXVILLE). (LIBRARY LECTURES, THE UNIVERSITY OF TENNESSEE, KNOXVILLE.). [Libr. lect.]. **Main/Corp** University of Tennessee, Knoxville. Library. No. 28/30-1976/78-. English. te. University of Tennessee Main Library, Knoxville TN 37916. **Tel** (615)974-4306. **LC** Z674; .T45. **DD** 016.02. ***Continues*** *University of Tennessee Library Lectures.*

NZ/0110-4373
LIBRARY LIFE : NEW ZEALAND LIBRARY ASSOCIATION NEWSLETTER. **Added/Corp** New Zealand Library Association. No. 1 (Feb. 1978)-. Newsletter. English. mo. 45.00NZ$ New Zealand; 55.00NZ$ other. New Zealand Library Association Inc, PO Box 12-212, Brandon Street, Wellington 1 New Zealand. **Tel** 011 64 4 4735834, FAX 011 64 4 4723967. **ED** A. Bruorton. **LC** Z673.N683; L5. **DD** 020/.6234/931. **[CCC]. Ad Acc. Circ:** 2,000 (ctrl). ***Continues*** *New Zealand Library Association Newsletter.*
Desc: Newsletter sent to every library and librarian in New Zealand.
Ind/Abst Aust. Educ. Index; Aust. Libr. Inf. Sci. Abstr. (1983-1989, 1990-).

US
LIBRARY LIST. **Main/Corp** National Agricultural Library (U.S.). No. 1- 1942-. English. National Agricultural Library, 10301 Baltimore Boulevard, Beltsville MD 20705. **LC** Z881.U4; L5. **DD** 016.63.

US/0024-2373
LIBRARY LITERATURE. **See** Library and Information Sciences-Abstracting, Bibliographies and Statistics.

UK/0143-5124
LIBRARY MANAGEMENT (MCB PUBLICATIONS (FIRM)). (LIBRARY MANAGEMENT.). [Libr. manage.]. (1979)-. Monographic series. English. Eight times a year. $3199.00. MCB University Press, 60 62 Toller Lane, Bradford West Yorkshire BD8 9BX England. **Tel** 011 44 274 499821, FAX 011 44 274 547143, telex 51317 MCBUNI G. **(Subscription address:** MCB University Press / US and Canada Subscriptions, PO Box 10812, Birmingham AL 35201-0812.) **ED** Ken Bakewell. **LC** Z678; .L475. **DD** 025.1/05. **[CCC]. Circ:** 300. available on an online database (file 15/Full-Text) from DIALOG. Documents available from UMI Article Clearinghouse.
Desc: Focuses attention on a subject of immediate interest to the information professional. These recent studies typify the width of coverage and depth of analysis of the journal.
Ind/Abst ABI/INFORM Glob. Ed.; ABI Inform Ondisc (1986-); Libr. Inf. Sci. Abstr.

US
LIBRARY MANAGEMENT QUARTERLY. Vol. 9, No. 2 (Fall 1985)-. Periodical. English. qt. $25.00 US and Puerto Rico; $30.00 Western Hemisphere; $35.00 other (non-members). Library Management Division, PO Box 840, Valley Forge PA 19482. **Tel** (215)293-7255. **ED** Sarah Warner. **Bk Rev. Ad Acc. Circ:** 2,000. ***Continues*** *Library Management Bulletin, 0271-3306.*
Ind/Abst Libr. Inf. Sci. Abstr.

UK
LIBRARY MANAGER. (19??)-. English. mo. £36.00. Learned Information Ltd., Woodside Hinksey Hill, Oxford OX1 5AU England. **Tel** 44 865 730275, FAX 44 865 736354, telex 23667. **(Subscription address:** Learned Information, Inc. / North America Subscriptions, 143 Old Marlton Pike, Medford NJ 08055-8750.)

UK/0957-2791
LIBRARY MONITOR. ***Ceased.*** [Libr. monit.]. (1988)-No. 48 (Dec. 1992). English. mo. Infonortics Ltd, 9A High Street Calne, Wiltshire SN11 0BS England. **Tel** 011 44 249 814584, FAX 011 44 249 813656. **ED** Harry Collier. Index available. cum. index. **Bk Rev. Circ:** 300.
Desc: Analysis of current events and announcements in the field of electronic information of interest to libraries.

US/1054-9676
LIBRARY MOSAICS. [Libr. mosaics]. Vol. 1, No. 1 (Sept./Oct. 1989)-. Periodical. English. bm (Jan., Mar., May, Jul., Sep., Nov.). $20.00. Yenor Inc, PO Box 5171, Culver City CA 90231. **Tel** (310)410-1573. **LC** Z671; .L537. **DD** 331.
Desc: Focuses on library, media, and information center support staff issues, trends and developments. Features include interviews of, and articles by and about, support staff throughout the nation.
Ind/Abst Libr. Lit. (1991-).

US/0145-9627
LIBRARY NETWORKS. 1975-. English. be. $25.50. Knowledge Industry Publications Inc, 701 Westchester Avenue, White Plains NY 10604. **Tel** (914)328-9157, (800)800-5474, FAX (914)328-9093.

SZ/1017-6241
LIBRARY NEWS. **Main/Corp** United Nations Library (Geneva, Switzerland). **VFOAT** Nouvelles de la Bibliotheque. Vol. 1, No. 1 Jan. (1991)-. Periodical. English (French). **LC** Z729; .U558.

CN/0847-9488
LIBRARY NEWS - GEAC LIBRARY INFORMATION SYSTEM. (LIBRARY NEWS.). [Libr. news - GEAC Libr. Inf. Syst.]. **Added/Corp** GEAC Library Information System. (1989)-. Periodical. English. qt. Free. GEAC Computer Corporation, 11 Allstate Parkway, Markham Ontario L3R 9T8 Canada. **Tel** (416)475-0525, FAX (416)475-3847. **ED** Harrison Cheung. **DD** 025/.04/05. ***Continues*** *Library Newsletter (GEAC Library Information System), 0847-9496.*

AT/0155-8471
LIBRARY NEWS - LA TRABE UNIVERSITY LIBRARY. (1976)-. English. ir. La Trobe University, Borchardt Library, Bundoora VIC 3083 Australia.
Ind/Abst Aust. Educ. Index; Aust. Libr. Inf. Sci. Abstr. (1982-).

US/0468-5725
LIBRARY NOTES (CHAPEL HILL). (LIBRARY NOTES.). **Added/Corp** University of North Carolina. Library. (19??)-. Periodical. English. Twelve times a year. Free. Medical University of South Carolina, 171 Ashley Avenue, Charleston SC 29425. **Tel** (803)792-4435.

US/0275-9616
LIBRARY OF CONGRESS ACQUISITIONS. MANUSCRIPT DIVISION. [Libr. Congr. acquis., Manuscr. Div.]. **Main/Corp** Library of Congress. Manuscript Division. 1979-. English. an. Free. Library of Congress / Publications and Media, Washington DC 20540. **LC** Z733.L735. **DD** 027.573. **NLM** Z 733.L735; L697L. **Circ:** 2,000.
Desc: Covers recent manuscript acquisitions of the Library of Congress.

US/0739-7526
LIBRARY OF CONGRESS ACQUISITIONS. RARE BOOK AND SPECIAL COLLECTIONS DIVISION. [Libr. Congr. acquis., Rare Book Spec. Coll. Div.]. **Main/Corp** Library of Congress. Rare Book and Special Collections Division. 1980-. English. ir. Free. Library of Congress / Information Office, 101 Independence Avenue SE, Washington DC 20540. **Tel** (202)707-5108, FAX (202)707-9199. **LC** Z733.U6; L45B. **DD** 027.573. **NLM** Z 733.U4; L697L.
Desc: Listing of rare books and special collections acquired by the Library of Congress.

US
LIBRARY OF CONGRESS CLASSIFICATION SCHEDULES COMBINED WITH ADDITIONS AND CHANGES. **Added/Corp** Gale Research Company. (1986)-. Periodical. English. $5480.00. Gale Research Inc., 835 Penobscot Building, Detroit MI 48226. **Tel** (800)877-GALE, (313)961-2242, FAX (313)961-6083, telex TWX 810-221-7086. **ED** Rita Runchock and Kathy Droste. available on microfiche.
Desc: Each volume combines the current edition of every Library of Congress classification schedule together with all additions, changes and deletions.

US/0041-7904
LIBRARY OF CONGRESS INFORMATION BULLETIN. [Libr. Congr. inf. bull.]. **Added/Corp** Library of Congress. Library of Congress. Public Affairs Office. **VFOAT** L.C. Information Bulletin; LC Information Bulletin. Vol. 31, No. 1 (Jan. 6, 1972)-. Bulletin. English. ir. Library of Congress / Cataloging Distribution Service, Washington DC 20541-5017. **Tel** (800)255-3666, (202)707-6100, FAX (202)707-1334. **ED** Guy Lamolinara. **LC** Z733.U57; I6. **DD** 027.573. **NLM** Z 733 L697. Index available. **Bk Rev. Circ:** 10,000. available on microfilm and microfiche from University Microfilms International (UMI). ***Continues*** *Information Bulletin (Library of Congress), 0364-3980.*
Desc: Covers exhibitions, literary/music events, symposia, cataloging/online networking publications, copyright office, federal libraries, and library conference reports.
Ind/Abst Art Archaeol. Tech. Abstr.; Libr. Lit.

US/1048-9711
LIBRARY OF CONGRESS SUBJECT HEADINGS. ***Title Change.*** (LIBRARY OF CONGRESS SUBJECT HEADINGS.). [Libr. Congr. subj. head.]. **Main/Corp** Library of Congress. Office for Subject Cataloging Policy. **VFOAT** Subject Headings; LCSH. 13th Ed. (1990)-(1992). English. an. Library of Congress / Cataloging Distribution Service, Washington DC 20541-5017. **Tel** (800)255-3666, (202)707-6100, FAX (202)707-1334. **LC** Z695.Z8; L524a. **DD** 025.4/9. ***Continues*** *Library of Congress Subject Headings, 1048-9711.* ***Continued by*** *Library of Congress. Cataloging Policy and Support Office. Library of Congress Subject Headings.*

●US
LIBRARY OF CONGRESS SUBJECT HEADINGS IN MICROFORM. **Main/Corp** Library of Congress. **VFOAT** Library of Congress Subject Headings. (1992)-. Periodical. English. qt. $190.00 North America; $230.00 other. Library of Congress / Cataloging Distribution Service, Washington DC 20541-5017. **Tel** (800)255-3666, (202)707-6100, FAX (202)707-1334. ***Continues*** *Library of Congress. Subject Headings in Microform, 0361-5243.*

US
LIBRARY OF CONGRESS SUBJECT HEADINGS / PREPARED BY THE CATALOGING POLICY AND SUPPORT OFFICE, COLLECTIONS SERVICES. **Main/Corp** Library of Congress. Cataloging Policy and Support Office. **VFOAT** Subject Headings; Red Book; LCSH. 16th Edition (1993)-. Bibliography. English. an. $190.00 North America; $230.00 other. Library of Congress / Cataloging Distribution Service, Washington DC 20541-5017. **Tel** (800)255-3666, (202)707-6100, FAX (202)707-1334. **LC** Z695.Z8; L524a. ***Continues*** *Library of Congress. Office for Subject Cataloging Policy. Library of Congress Subject Headings.*

US/0895-1179
LIBRARY OUTREACH REPORTER. [Libr. outreach report.]. **VFOAT** LOR. Vol. 1, No. 1 (Sept./Oct. 1987)-. Periodical. English. Six times a year. $21.00 US; $27.00 other. Library Outreach Reporter, 1671 East 16th Street/Suite 226, Brooklyn NY 11229. **ED** Allan M. Kleiman. **LC** Z711.92.A32; L52. **DD** 025. **Bk Rev. Ad Acc. Circ:** 1,100.
Desc: Report on library services to the aging, disabled persons, ethnic services, jail/prison library service, literacy programs and bookmobile service.
Ind/Abst Libr. Lit. (1991-).

CN/0225-8307
LIBRARY OWNER'S MANUAL (1980). (LIBRARY OWNER'S MANUAL.). [Libr. own. man.]. **Main/Corp** Concordia University. Libraries. 1980-. English (French). an. Free. Library Owner's Manual, Concordia University Libraries, 1455 de Maisonneuve Boulevard West, Montreal Quebec H3G 1M8 Canada. **Tel** (514)848-7699. **ED** Lee Harris. **DD** 027.7714/281. Index available. **Circ:** 12,000. ***Continues*** *Concordia University. Libraries. Owner's Manual, 0709-6712.*
Desc: Description of services in Concordia University Libraries.

CN/0713-5386
LIBRARY POCKETFUL, A. [Libr. pocketful]. English. an. A Library Pocketful, c/o D Pilkey, Learning Resources Libraries, Roywood Public School, 11 Roywood Drive, Don Mills Ontario M3A 2C7 Canada. **DD** 027.8/222.

US/0164-9566
LIBRARY PR NEWS. **Added/Corp** Library Educational Institute. **VAT** Library Public Relations News. (Jan./Feb. 1978)-. Periodical. English. bm (6 issues). $29.95 US, $31.95 Canada, $37.95 others. Library Educational Institute Inc., RD 1, Box 219, New Albany PA 18833. **Tel** (717)746-1842, FAX (717)746-1114. **ED** Phil Bradbury. **Bk Rev. Ad Acc. Circ:** 3,000. ***Formed by the union of*** *Tips from Clip* ***and*** *Evil John's Almanac.*
Desc: Devoted to library public relations, display and promotion. Contains publicity and programming ideas, book and product reviews, exhibit and display techniques.
Ind/Abst Libr. Inf. Sci. Abstr.

II/0970-1052
LIBRARY PROGRESS (INTERNATIONAL). [Lib. prog. int.]. **VFOAT** Library Progress. Periodical. English (Hindi). sa. Rs80.00 India; $10.00 US; £10.00. A K Sharma Library Progress, PO Box 38, Modinagar GZB-201204, Delhi India. **ED** Ajay Kumar Sharma microfilm. **LC** Z730; .L53. **DD** 027.0172/4. **Bk Rev. Ad Acc. Circ:** 500 (ctrl). available on microfiche; available on microfilm.
Desc: Devoted to the advancement of library sciences; editorial board consists of learned professors of library science and leading working librarians at the national and international levels.
Ind/Abst Indian Libr. Sci. Abstr.; Libr. Inf. Sci. Abstr.

US/0024-2519
LIBRARY QUARTERLY (CHICAGO), THE. (THE LIBRARY QUARTERLY.). [Libr. q.]. **Added/Corp** University of Chicago. Graduate Library

School. Vol. 1 (Jan. 1931)-. Periodical. English. qt. $51.00 institution, $30.00 individual, $24.00 student. University of Chicago Press / Journals Division, PO Box 37005, 5720 South Woodlawn, Chicago IL 60637. **Tel** (312)753-3347, FAX (312)753-0811. **(Subscription telephone:** (312)753-8083**) ED** Howard Winger. **LC** Z671; .L713. **DD** 020.5. **NLM** Z 671 L6964I. **CODEN** LIBQAS. **[CCC].** cum. index. **Ad Acc. Pr Rev. Acid Free. Circ:** 2,600. available on microfilm and microfiche from University Microfilms International (UMI). Documents available from The Genuine Article, Ask*IEEE, UMI Article Clearinghouse.
Desc: Maintains informed research in all areas of librarianship historical, sociological, statistical, bibliographic, managerial, and educational. Combining traditional patterns of investigation with newer interdisciplinary approaches.
Ind/Abst Acad. Search (July 1993-); ACM Guide Comput. Lit.; Am. Hist. Life (1963-); Am. Bibliogr. Slavic East Europ. Stud.; Annu. Bibliogr. Engl. Lang. Lit.; Arts Humanit. Citation Index [Select. Cov.]; Book Rev. Index; Child. Lit. Abstr. (19??-); Comput. Rev.; Curr. Contents Soc. Behav. Sci.; Curr. Index J. Educ.; Gen. Period. Index (1985-); Index Period. Artic. Relat. Law; INFO-SOUTH Abstr.; Inf. Sci. Abstr.; INSPEC (Jan. 1972-); Leg. Inf. Manage. Index (19??-199?); Libr. Inf. Sci. Abstr.; Libr. Lit.; Mag. Index Plus (1989-); Mag. Search; Middle East Abstr. Index; Newsp. Period. Abstr. (1988-); Res. Alert [Full Cov.]; Res. High. Educ. Abstr.; Romant. Move.; Soc. Sci. Cit. Index [Full Cov.]; Mag. Index (1978-).

CN/0024-9270
LIBRARY RESEARCH NEWS / MCMASTER UNIVERSITY. [McMaster Univ. Libr. res. news]. **Added/Corp** McMaster University. Library. **VAT** Library Research News (Hamilton). Vol. 1, No. 1 (Winter 1968/69)-Vol. 13, No. 2 (Fall 1989); New Ser. 1, No. 1 (Spring 1991)-. Monographic series. English. sa (May/June and Sept./Oct.). Free on request. McMaster University Library Press, 1280 Main Street West, Hamilton Ontario L8S 4L6 Canada. **Tel** (905)525-9140 ext.24737, FAX (905)546-0625. **LC** UNC. **Circ:** 800.
Desc: Description of archives and collections held at McMaster University.
Ind/Abst Annu. Bibliogr. Engl. Lang. Lit.

US/0024-2527
LIBRARY RESOURCES & TECHNICAL SERVICES. [Libr. resour. tech. serv.]. **Added/Corp** American Library Association. Resources and Technical Services Division. **VFOAT** Library Resouces and Technical Services. **VAT** Library Resources and Technical Services. Vol. 1 (Winter 1957)-. Periodical. English. Four times a year (Jan., Apr., July, Oct.). $55.00 North America; $65.00 other. American Library Association, 50 East Huron Street, Chicago IL 60611. **Tel** (312)944-6780, (800)545-2433, FAX (312)944-2641. **(Subscription address:** American Library Association, Subscription Department, 434 West Downer, Aurora IL 60506-9936.**) LC** Z671; .L7154. **DD** 025.06273. **NLM** Z 695.7 L697. **CODEN** LRTSAH. **[CCC]. Pr Rev.** available on microfilm and microfiche from University Microfilms International (UMI); available on an online database (file 648/Full-Text) from DIALOG. Documents available from The Genuine Article, Ask*IEEE. ***Formed by the union of*** *Serial Slants, 0559-5258* ***and*** *Journal of Cataloging and Classification.*
Ind/Abst Art Archaeol. Tech. Abstr.; Arts Humanit. Citation Index [Select. Cov.]; Book Rev. Digest; Book Rev. Index; Curr. Contents Soc. Behav. Sci.; Curr. Index J. Educ.; Health Plan. Adminis.; Hospit. Health Admin. Index; Inf. Instruc. Technol.; Inf. Sci. Abstr.; INSPEC (Winter 1972-); Leg. Inf. Manage. Index; Libr. Inf. Sci. Abstr.; Libr. Lit.; Res. Alert [Full Cov.]; Sci. Cit. Index (19??-19??); SCISEARCH; Soc. Sci. Cit. Index [Full Cov.]; West. Hist. Q.

US/0364-1236
LIBRARY RESOURCES FOR THE BLIND & PHYSICALLY HANDICAPPED. (LIBRARY RESOURCES FOR THE BLIND & PHYSICALLY HANDICAPPED / NATIONAL LIBRARY SERVICE FOR THE BLIND AND PHYSICALLY HANDICAPPED.). **Added/Corp** Library of Congress. National Library Service for the Blind and Physically Handicapped. Library of Congress. Division for the Blind and Physically Handicapped. **VAT** Library Resources for the Blind and Physically Handicapped. (197?)-. English. an. Free. National Library Service for the Blind and Physically Handicapped, Library of Congress, 1291 Taylor Street Northwest, Washington DC 20542. **Tel** (800)424-8567, (202)707-5100, (800)424-9100. **LC** Z675.B6; L52. **DD** 027.6/63/02573. **Circ:** 5,000. ***Continues*** *Directory of Library Resources for the Blind and Physically Handicapped, 0278-7857.*
Desc: A directory of cooperating libraries for the blind and physically handicapped in the United States. Other library resources for the handicapped at the national level are listed in part II.

UK/0024-2535
LIBRARY REVIEW (GLASGOW). (LIBRARY REVIEW.). [Libr. rev.]. Vol. 1 (Spring 1927)-. Academic Scholarly Publication. English. Eight times a year. $1489.00. MCB University Press, 60 62 Toller Lane, Bradford West Yorkshire BD8 9BX England. **Tel** 011 44 274 499821, FAX 011 44 274 547143, telex 51317 MCBUNI G. **(Subscription address:** MCB University Press / US and Canada Subscriptions, PO Box 10812, Birmingham AL 35201-0812.**) ED** Stuart James. **LC** Z671; .L716. **DD** 020.5. **Bk Rev. Circ:** 1,000.
Desc: The only independent journal to provide in-depth coverage of all facets of the library and information science world. The library and information profession is in danger of fragmenting into small, specialist groups. Aims to reverse this movement and restore unity. Represents all viewpoints, combining scholarly and technical analysis with discussions of current and future trends.
Ind/Abst Abstr. Engl. Stud.; Am. Hist. Life (1973-); Am. Humanit. Index; Annu. Bibliogr. Engl. Lang. Lit.; Book Rev. Index; Inf. Instruc. Technol.; Libr. Inf. Sci. Abstr.; Libr. Lit.

US/0041-9788
LIBRARY REVIEW (LOUISVILLE, KY.). (LIBRARY REVIEW / THE UNIVERSITY OF LOUISVILLE.). **Added/Corp** University of Louisville. (1961)-. English. an. $10.00. University of Louisville, Belknap Campus, Louisville KY 40292. **Tel** (502)451-4074. **ED** W.F. Axton (editor's phone: (502)852-6762). **LC** Z881 .L898; L53. **DD** 027.7769/44. **Circ:** 700.
Desc: Articles researched in the special collections of the University of Louisville libraries and news of the library associates, a friends of the library group.

II/0024-2543
LIBRARY SCIENCE WITH A SLANT TO DOCUMENTATION. [Libr. sci. with slant doc.]. **Added/Corp** Documentation Research and Training Centre (Bangalore, India) Sarada Ranganathan Endowment for Library Science. **VFOAT** Library Science with a Slant to Documentation and Information Studies. Vol. 1, No. 1 (Mar. 1964)-. Academic Scholarly Publication. English. Four times a year. $75.00. Sarada Ranganathan Endowment for Library Science, 432 10th Cross/18th Main Road, J P Nagar II Phase, Bangalore 560 078 India. **Tel** 646330. **(Subscription address:** Prints India, 11 Darya Ganj, New Delhi 110002 India.**) ED** Professor A. Neelameghan. **LC** Z671; .L717. **NLM** Z 671 L697H. **CODEN** LSSDA8. Index Available, published separately, free-automatically sent. **Pr Rev.** available on microfilm and microfiche from University Microfilms International (UMI).
Desc: Publishes papers and scholarly review articles on classification, cataloging, computer-based info services, standards and other materials.
Ind/Abst Indian Libr. Sci. Abstr.; Libr. Inf. Sci. Abstr.; Libr. Lit.

NR/0331-0132
LIBRARY SCIENTIST, THE. [Libr. sci.]. **Added/Corp** Ahmadu Bello University. Dept. of Library Science. Ahmadu Bello University. Society of Library Science Students. (1974)-. Periodical. English.
Ind/Abst Libr. Inf. Sci. Abstr.

US/0075-5001
LIBRARY SERIES / UNIVERSITY OF KANSAS LIBRARIES. Added/Corp University of Kansas. Libraries. **VFOAT** University of Kansas Publications. No. 1 (1935)-. Monographic series. English. ir. Price varies per volume. University of Kansas / Lars Leon, Exchange Gift Unit, Acquisition Department, Lawrence KS 66045. **Tel** (913)864-4334. **ED** James Helyar.

US
LIBRARY SERVICE TO THE PEOPLE OF NEW YORK STATE. (Oct. 1, 1978-Sept. 30, 1983)-. English. an. The New York State Library, Albany NY 12230. **LC** Z678.5.N7; L66. **DD** 027.0747. ***Continues*** *Long-Range Plan for Library Service to the People of New York State, Utilizing Local, State, and Federal Resources.*

US
LIBRARY SERVICES AND CONSTRUCTION ACT. Main/Corp Alaska State Library. (19??)-. Periodical. English. an. Alaska Library Association, PO Box 81084, Fairbanks AK 99708. **Tel** (907)479-4522. **LC** Z733.A324; A4a. **DD** 027.5798.

US
LIBRARY SERVICES AND CONSTRUCTION ACT ANNUAL PROGRAM. Main/Corp Connecticut State Library. Dept. of Planning and Research. **VFOAT** L.S.C.A. Connecticut; LSCA Connecticut. English. Connecticut State Library, 231 Capital Avenue, Hartford CT 06115. **LC** Z732.C8; C65A. **DD** 027.0746.

US/0742-5759
LIBRARY SOFTWARE REVIEW. See Computers-Software.

US/8755-4267
LIBRARY STATISTICS OF COLLEGES AND UNIVERSITIES IN THE PACIFIC NORTHWEST. See Library and Information Sciences-Abstracting, Bibliographies and Statistics.

US/0094-2626
LIBRARY STATISTICS OF ILLINOIS COLLEGES AND UNIVERSITIES. See Library and Information Sciences-Abstracting, Bibliographies and Statistics.

US/0277-0288
LIBRARY SYSTEMS. [Libr. syst.]. **Added/Corp** American Library Association. **VFOAT** Library Systems Newsletter. Vol. 1, No. 1 (July 1981)-. Periodical. English. Twelve times a year. $45.00 US; $55.00 other. American Library Association, 50 East Huron Street, Chicago IL 60611. **Tel** (312)944-6780, (800)545-2433, FAX (312)944-2641. **(Subscription address:** American Library Association, Subscription Department, 434 West Downer, Aurora IL 60506-9936.**) ED** Richard W Boss and Judy McQueen. **[CCC].**
Ind/Abst Int. Aerosp. Abstr.; Leg. Inf. Manage. Index (19??-); Libr. Inf. Sci. Abstr.

US/1043-237X
LIBRARY TALK. [Libr. talk]. Vol. 1, No. 1 (Jan./Feb. 1988)-. Periodical. English. Five times a year. $39.00 (one year), $70.00 (two year), $102.00 (three year). Linworth Publishing Company, 480 East Wilson Bridge Road, Suite L, Worthington OH 43085. **Tel** (614)436-7107, FAX (614)436-9490. **DD** 027. **Bk Rev. Ad Acc. Circ:** 6,000.
Desc: Written by school librarians to provide information and ideas about such topics as storytelling, library aides and volunteers, reading motivation and the teaching of library skills.
Ind/Abst Book Rev. Index; Mid. Search (Jan. 1994-); Prim. Search (Jan. 1994-).

●UK/0964-7627
LIBRARY TECHNOLOGY NEWS LTN. VFOAT LTN. Issue No. 1 (Feb. 1992)-. Periodical. English. Five times a year. £40.00 UK; £45.00 other. Library Information Technology Centre, South Bank Technopark, 90 London Road, London SE1 6LN England. **Tel** 44 71 8157872, FAX 44 71 8156699. **LC** Z678.9.A1; .L52. **Ad Acc, Adv Mgr:** Lynda Agili, **Tel** 44 71 8157870. **Circ:** 450. ***Continues*** *Library Micromation News, 0262-7841.*

US/0024-2586
LIBRARY TECHNOLOGY REPORTS. [Libr. technol. rep.]. **Added/Corp** American Library Association. Vol. 12 (Jan. 1976)-. Periodical. English. bm (6 issues). $215.00 US; $240.00 Canada & Mexico; $290.00 other. American Library Association, 50 East Huron Street, Chicago IL 60611. **Tel** (312)944-6780, (800)545-2433, FAX (312)944-2641. **(Subscription address:** American Library Association, Subscription Department, 434 West Downer, Aurora IL 60506-9936.**) LC** Z684; .L75. **DD** 022/.9. **NLM** Z 671 L697M. **[CCC].** Documents available from UMI Article Clearinghouse, Magazine Collection.
Ind/Abst Acad. Search (Jan. 1994-); Comput. Rev. Index (1988-); Consum. Index Prod. Eval. Inf. Source; Gen. Period. Index (1985-); Index Period. Artic. Relat. Law (1976-); INFO-SOUTH Abstr.; Inf. Instruc. Technol.; Inf. Manage. Technol. (19??-); Inf. Sci. Abstr. (?-?); Leg. Inf. Manage. Index; Libr. Inf. Sci. Abstr.; Libr. Lit.; Mag. Index Plus (1989-); Mag. Search; Microcomput. Index (1984-?); Newsp. Period. Abstr. (1992-); Mag. Index (1978-).

US/0743-4839
LIBRARY TIMES INTERNATIONAL. (LIBRARY TIMES INTERNATIONAL : WORLD NEWS DIGEST OF LIBRARY AND INFORMATION SCIENCE.). [Libr. times int.]. Vol. 1, No. 1 (July 1984)-. Periodical. English. Four times a year. $28.00 (institutions), $20.00 (individuals) regular mail; $42.00 (institutions), $34.00 (individuals) airmail. Library Times International, PO Box 15661, Evansville IN 47716. **Tel** (812)473-2420. **ED** R. N. Sharma. **DD** 320.
Desc: World news digest of library and information science.
Ind/Abst Libr. Inf. Sci. Abstr.

US/0024-2594
LIBRARY TRENDS. [Libr. trends]. **Added/Corp** University of Illinois (Urbana-Champaign Campus). Library School. University of Illinois (Urbana-Champaign Campus). Graduate School of Library Science. University of Illinois at Urbana-Champaign. Graduate School of Library Science. University of Illinois at Urbana-Champaign. Graduate School of Library and Information Science. Vol. 1, No. 1 (July 1952)-. Periodical. English. Four times a year. $75.00 (one year), $135.00 (two year), institutions; $50.00 (one year), $90.00 (two year), individuals. University of Illinois Press, 1325 South Oak Street, Champaign IL 61820. **Tel** (217)333-0950, FAX (217)244-8082. **ED** Charles H. Davis. **LC** Z671; .L6173. **DD** 020.5. **NLM** Z 671 L698. **CODEN** LIBTA3. **[CCC]. Pr Rev. Circ:** 3,900. available on microfilm and microfiche from University Microfilms International (UMI). Documents available from The Genuine Article, Ask*IEEE, Magazine Collection.
Desc: Focuses on library and information science topics of interest to practicing librarians and information scientists and also to educators and students.
Ind/Abst Acad. Search (July 1993-); Annu. Bibliogr. Engl. Lang. Lit.; Chicano Index; Curr. Contents Soc. Behav. Sci.; Curr. Index J. Educ.; Gen. Period. Index (1985-); INFO-SOUTH Abstr.; Inf. Instruc. Technol.; Inf. Sci. Abstr.; INSPEC (Spring 1981-); Libr. Inf. Sci. Abstr.;

Libr. Lit.; Mag. Index Plus (1989-); Mag. Search; Middle East Abstr. Index; PAIS Int. Print; Res. Alert [Full Cov.]; Soc. Sci. Cit. Index [Full Cov.]; Mag. Index (1978-).

US/0895-2248
LIBRARY VIDEO MAGAZINE. VIDEORECORDING. ***Ceased.*** [Libr. video mag.]. -Ceased Vol. 4, No. 3 1990. Periodical. English. qt. American Library Association, 50 East Huron Street, Chicago IL 60611. **Tel** (312)944-6780, (800)545-2433, FAX (312)944-2641. **DD** 020.

UK/0953-9638
LIBRARY WORK. ***Ceased.*** [Libr. work]. (1988)-(19??). Periodical. English. qt. Information Audit, 113 High Street, Bembridge, Isle of Wight PO35 55F England. **Tel** 0983-874514. **ED** Janet Shuter and Jennifer Brice. **DD** 023.30941. **Bk Rev. Ad Acc. Circ:** 1,000.
Desc: Directed at library technicians, paraprofessionals, and assistants intended to promote professional awareness and development.
Ind/Abst Libr. Inf. Sci. Abstr.

CN/0714-2862
LIBRARY WORKER. See Economics-Labor.

US/1058-6768
LIBRES (KENT, OHIO). (LIBRES [COMPUTER FILE] : LIBRARY AND INFORMATION SCIENCE RESEARCH ELECTRONIC CONFERENCE.). [LIBRES]. **Added/Corp** Kent State University. Libraries. (Apr. 3, 1991)-. Periodical. English. wk. Kent State University / Library Science, School of Library Science, Kent OH 44242. **Tel** (216)672-2782, FAX (216)672-7965. **DD** 025.
Desc: Mode of access: Email on BITNET.

DK/0024-2667
LIBRI (KBENHAVN). (LIBRI.). [Libri]. **Added/Corp** International Federation of Library Associations. Communications. Vol. 1 (1950)-. Periodical. English. qt. kr1280.00 US, Canada and Japan; kr1250.00 other. Munksgaard International Publishers Ltd, PO Box 2148, DK-1016 Copenhagen K Denmark. **Tel** 011 45 33 12 70 30, FAX 011 45 33 12 93 87, telex 19431 MUNKS DK. **ED** Russell Bowden, Torkil Olsen and Irene Wormell. **LC** Z671; .L74. **DD** 020.5. **NLM** Z 671 L699. **[CCC].** Index available. **Bk Rev. Ad Acc. Pr Rev. Circ:** 1,400 (ctrl). Documents available from The Genuine Article.
Desc: Original papers on all aspects of librarianship including the history of books and publishing.
Ind/Abst Curr. Contents Soc. Behav. Sci.; Inf. Sci. Abstr.; Libr. Inf. Sci. Abstr.; Libr. Lit.; MLA Int. Bibl. Books Artic. Mod. Lang. Lit.; PAIS Int. Print (1991-); Res. Alert [Full Cov.]; Soc. Sci. Cit. Index [Full Cov.].

CN/0712-6115
LIBSAT. [Libsat]. **Added/Corp** Gananoque Public Library. Vol. 1, No. 1 (Apr. 1982)-. Periodical. English. Libsat, c/o Gananoque ublic Library, 100 Park Street, Gananoque Ontario K7G 2Y5 Canada. **DD** 027.4/02/07.

AT/0815-8428
LIBTECH NEWS. [Libtech news]. (1984)-. Periodical. English. bm. **ED** Ms J Fullerton, PO Box 298, North Quay QLD 4000 Australia. **DD** 023.309943.
Ind/Abst Aust. Educ. Index.

US/0739-8638
LIFLINE. ***Title Change.*** (LIFLINE / LIBRARY INSTRUCTION FORUM OF THE VLA.). **Added/Corp** Virginia Library Association. Library Instruction Forum. **VFOAT** LIF Line. **VAT** Library Instruction Forum Line. News Sheet 7 (Oct. 1978)-(19??). Periodical. English. Three times a year. Sweet Briar College, Sweet Briar College Alumnae Association, Sweet Briar VA 24595. **Tel** (804)381-6131, FAX (804)381-6132. ***Continues*** *News Sheet (Virginia Library Association. Library Instruction Forum).* ***Continued by*** *Alumnae Magazine.*

NE
LIJST VAN AANWINSTEN / UNIVERSITEITSBIBLIOTHEEK VAN AMSTERDAM. Main/Corp Universiteit van Amsterdam. Bibliotheek. **VFOAT** Lijst van Aanwinsten der Universiteitsbibliotheek van Amsterdam. Dutch. mo. Bibliotheek Technische Hogesch, Netherlands. ***Continues*** *Universiteit van Amsterdam. Bibliotheek. Aanwinsten.*

US/0887-3739
LILRC NEWSLETTER AND CALENDAR. [LILRC newsl. cal.]. **VAT** Long Island Library Resources Council Newsletter and Calendar. Newsletter. English. Long Island Library Resources Council, Melville Library Building/5th Floor, Stony Brook NY 11794. **DD** 027.

US/0735-0813
LINCOLN LIBRARY OF ESSENTIAL INFORMATION (COLUMBUS, OHIO : 1982), THE. (THE LINCOLN LIBRARY OF ESSENTIAL INFORMATION.). [Linc. libr. essent. inf.]. 42nd Ed. (1982)-. English. an. Frontier Publishing, PO Box FF, Sun City CA 92381. **Tel** (619)488-4168. **LC** AG105; .L55. **DD** 031. ***Continues*** *New Lincoln Library Encyclopedia, 0192-1177.*

US/0273-0227
LINDA HALL LIBRARY MISCELLANY. Main/Corp Linda Hall Library. **VFOAT** Miscellany. No. 1-Autumn 1980-. Periodical. English. Free. Paul Peterson Editor, Miscellany, Linda Hall Library City MO 64110. **Tel** (816)363-5020. **ED** Paul Peterson. **Bk Rev. Circ:** 3,500.
Desc: Information on activities, services and collections of Linda Hall Library of Science and Technology, for its friends and users.

CN/0703-7007
LINK (MISSISSAUGA. 1977). (LINK.). V. 5, No. 1- Jan. 1977-. Periodical. English. mo. Free. Mississauga Library System, 110 Dundas Street West, Mississauga Ontario L5B 1H3 Canada. **DD** 027.4/713/535. ***Continues*** *Mississauga Library Link, 0380-4704.*

AT/0158-5460
LINK-UP. [Link-up]. (1980)-. Periodical. English. bm (6 issues). Free on request. National Library of Australia, Parkes Place, Canberra ACT, 2600 Australia. **Tel** 011 61 6 2621374, FAX 011 61 6 2731084. **DD** 027.66305.
Ind/Abst Aust. Educ. Index.

CN/0383-0535
LINK (VICTORIA). (LINK.). V. 1- Dec. 1975-. Periodical. English. Greater Victoria Library, 794 Yates Street, Victoria BC V8W 1L4. **DD** 027.4/711/34.

US/0196-1977
LIPP. LIBRARY INSIGHTS, PROMOTION & PROGRAMS. ***Ceased.*** (LIBRARY INSIGHTS, PROMOTION & PROGRAMS.). **VAT** LIPP. Library Insights, Promotion and Programs. Vol. 1 (Aug. 1976)-(Dec. 1993). Periodical. English. mo. Library Insights, Promotion & Programs, PO Box 431, LaGrange IL 60525. **Tel** (708)579-0903.
Ind/Abst Libr. Inf. Sci. Abstr.

UK/0966-8799
LISA PLUS [COMPUTER FILE]. See Library and Information Sciences-Abstracting, Bibliographies and Statistics.

US
LISP NEWS. See Law.

AT/1039-3013
LIST. LIBRARY AND INFORMATION SCIENCE TRENDS. VFOAT Library and Information Sience Trends. (1990)-. Periodical. English. Six times a year. 70.00Aus$. Warringah Shire Council, Dee Why Library, Civil Drive, Dee Why NSW 2099 Australia. **Tel** 011 61 02 9820449, FAX 011 61 02 9715603. **Circ:** 150.
Desc: Contains current contents from key journals in library and information science trends.

UK
LIST OF SERIALS AVAILABLE IN CAMBRIDGE UNIVERSITY LIBRARY AND IN OTHER LIBRARIES CONNECTED WITH THE UNIVERSITY [MICROFORM]. Main/Corp Cambridge University Library. **VFOAT** List of Serials; Cambridge University Library List of Serials. (Oct. 1985)-. English. sa. £28.00 (initial purchase), £10.00 (thereafter). Cambridge University Library, West Road, Cambridge CB3 9DR England. **Tel** 0223 337733, FAX 0223 333160, telex 81395. **LC** Microfiche (w) 89/2543. available on microfiche. ***Formed by the union of*** *Current Serials Available in the University Library and in other Libraries Connected with the University, 0306-4174* ***and*** *List of Serials Available in the University Library and in other Libraries Connected with the University. Supplement.*
Desc: A union list of periodicals taken by the libraries of Cambridge University.

FR/0259-000X
LISTE D'ABREVIATIONS DE MOTS DES TITRES DE PUBLICATIONS EN SERIE. Added/Corp ISDS International Centre. International Organization for Standardization. **VFOAT** List of Serial Title Word Abbreviations. (1985)-. French (English). an. 980.00F France (one year); 230.00 other (one year). ISSN International Centre, 20 rue Bachaumont, F-75002 Paris France. **Tel** 011 33 1 42367381, FAX 011 33 1 40263243, telex SERIALS 219847F. **Ad Acc.** available on diskette. ***Continues*** *Liste d'Abreviations de Mots des Titres de Periodiques. Supplement.*
Desc: Contains the words of the titles of serials processed by the ISDS network and their abbreviations. Includes words of about 50 languages.

FR/0259-0018
LISTE D'ABREVIATIONS DE MOTS DES TITRES DE PUBLICATIONS EN SERIE. SUPPLEMENT. Added/Corp ISDS International Centre. **VFOAT** List of Serial Title Word Abbreviations. Supplement. (1985)-. French (English). an. 230.00F supplement. ISSN International Centre, 20 rue Bachaumont, F-75002 Paris France. **Tel** 011 33 1 42367381, FAX 011 33 1 40263243, telex SERIALS 219847F. **CODEN** LATSE4. available on diskette.
Desc: Information on abbreviations used in periodicals and library science.

CN/0826-1334
LISTE DES NOUVEAUTES - COLLEGE DE L'ASSOMPTION. BIBLIOTHEQUE DU COLLEGIAL. (BIBLIOTHEQUE DU COLLEGIAL, LISTE DES NOUVEAUTES / COLLEGE DE L'ASSOMPTION.). [Liste nouv. - Coll. L'Assomption, Bibl. coll.]. **Main/Corp** College de l'Assomption. Bibliotheque. Periodical. French. College de l'Assomption Bibliotheque, 270 Boulevard l'Ange-Gardien, l'Assomption Quebec J0K 1G0 Canada. **DD** 017/.1.

CN/1184-6038
LISTE DES NOUVELLES ACQUISITIONS - HOPITAL SAINT-VINCENT, OTTAWA, ONT. BIBLIOTHEQUE. See Medical Science and Technology.

●CN/1187-7154
LISTE DES RAPPORTS ANNUELS, BIBLIOTHEQUE PRINCIPALE JE, LIST OF ANNUAL REPORTS, MAIN LIBRARY (JE). See Public Administration.

CN/0228-5134
LISTING OF SUPPLEMENTARY DOCUMENTS / STATISTICS CANADA, LIBRARY. See Library and Information Sciences-Abstracting, Bibliographies and Statistics.

CN/0835-085X
LISTING OF SUPPLEMENTARY DOCUMENTS, SUPPLEMENT / STATISTICS CANADA, LIBRARY. See Library and Information Sciences-Abstracting, Bibliographies and Statistics.

AT/1035-4816
LISWA NEWSLETTER. (1990)-. Newsletter. English. bm. 20.00Aus$. Library and Information Service of W A, Alexander Library Building, Perth Cultural Center, Perth Western Australia 6000 Australia. **Tel** 09 427 3345, FAX 09 427 3336. **ED** Doug George. Index available. **Circ:** 630 (ctrl). ***Continues*** *News Letter - Library Service of Western Australia, 0159-7477.*
Ind/Abst Aust. Educ. Index.

US/1047-6989
LIT PAGE, THE. (THE LIT PAGE : THE MAGAZINE FOR LIBRARY LITERACY.). [Lit page]. (1990)-. Periodical. English. qt. $15.00. Library Outreach Reporter, 1671 East 16th Street/Suite 226, Brooklyn NY 11229. **DD** 021.

US/0196-1799
LITA NEWSLETTER. [LITA newsl.]. **Main/Corp** Library and Information Technology Association (U.S.). **Added/Corp** Library and Information Technology Association (U.S.) Newsletter. **VFOAT** L.I.T.A. Newsletter; Newsletter. **VAT** Library and Information Technology Association Newsletter. No. 1 (Winter 1980)-. Newsletter. English. Four times a year. $25.00 US; $30.00 Canada and Mexico; $40.00 other. American Library Association, 50 East Huron Street, Chicago IL 60611. **Tel** (312)944-6780, (800)545-2433, FAX (312)944-2641. **(Subscription address:** American Library Association, Subscription Department, 434 West Downer, Aurora IL 60506-9936.**) ED** Walt Crawford. **LC** Z678.9.A1; L518a. **DD** 020/.2854. **Circ:** 5,000.
Desc: News and activities, short articles on areas of interest to LITA members.
Ind/Abst Inf. Instruc. Technol.; Int. Aerosp. Abstr.

US/0196-3023
LLA BULLETIN. [LLA bull.]. **Main/Corp** Louisiana Library Association. **VAT** Louisiana Library Association Bulletin. Vol. 28, No. 4 (Winter 1965)-. Bulletin. English. Four times a year. $15.00. Louisiana Library Association, PO Box 3058, Baton Rouge LA 70821-3058. **Tel** (504)342-4928, FAX (504)342-3547. **ED** Florence Jumonville, The Historic New Orleans Collection, 533 Royal Street, New Orleans, LA 70130; Telephone:(504)523-4662. **LC** Z673; .L872. **DD** 020/.6234/763. Index available. **Bk Rev. Ad Acc. Circ:** 1,800. available on microfilm from University Microfilms International (UMI). ***Continues*** *Louisiana Library Association. Bulletin - Louisiana Library Association, 0024-6867.*
Desc: Reports of Louisiana activities, articles of interest to Louisiana readers, annual conference report, membership directory, financial and budgetary statements, book reviews.
Ind/Abst Libr. Lit.

UK
LOCAL STUDIES LIBRARIAN, THE. Added/Corp Library Association. Local Studies Group. Vol. 1, No. 1 (Spring 1982)-. Periodical. English. Twice a year. £3.00 England; £4.00 other. Library Association Local Studies Group, 33 Charnock Drive, Sheffield, S12 3HD England. **Tel** 011 44 904 644335.

US/0739-0386
LOEX NEWS. [LOEX news]. **Added/Corp** Eastern Michigan University. Center of Educational Resources. **VAT** Library Orientation-Instruction Exchange News. Vol. 1 (Mar. 16, 1973)-. Periodical. English. qt. $60.00. LOEX

News, Clearinghouse Library, Eastern Michigan University, Ypsilanti MI 48197. **Tel** (313)487-0168, FAX (313)487-8861. **ED** Linda Shirato. **Bk Rev. Circ:** 800.
Desc: Written for instruction libraries, primarily in academic libraries. Provides news and communication on areas of interest to libraries that have instruction programs, plus borrowing opportunities for members.

UK/0957-6053
LOGISTICS INFORMATION MANAGEMENT. [Logist. inf. manag.]. Vol. 2, No. 4 (Dec. 1989)-. Periodical. English. bm. $1249.00. MCB University Press, 60 62 Toller Lane, Bradford West Yorkshire BD8 9BX England. **Tel** 011 44 274 499821, FAX 011 44 274 547143, telex 51317 MCBUNI G. **(Subscription address:** MCB University Press / US and Canada Subscriptions, PO Box 10812, Birmingham AL 35201-0812.**) ED** A. Day. **LC** HF5415.6; .L634. **DD** 658.7/2/05. **CODEN** LINMEC. **[CCC].** Documents available from UMI Article Clearinghouse, Ask*IEEE. ***Continues** Logistics World, 0953-2137;* ***Absorbed** Information and Library Manager, 0260-6879.*
Ind/Abst ABI/INFORM Glob. Ed.; INSPEC (June 1990-).

US
LONG RANGE PROGRAM FOR LIBRARY DEVELOPMENT IN ALASKA. English. Alaska Department of Education, 801 West 10th Street, Room 200, Juneau AK 99811. **Tel** (907)465-2800, FAX (907)465-5279. **LC** Z732.A3; A55A. **DD** 027.0798. ***Continues** Long Range Program. Library Development in Alaska, 0094-8829.*

US
LONG-RANGE PROGRAM FOR LIBRARY DEVELOPMENT IN MISSISSIPPI. SUPPLEMENT. Main/Corp Mississippi. State Library Commission. English. PO Box 10700, Jackson MS 39209-0700. **Tel** (601)359-1036. **ED** Ann S Parkman. **LC** Z678.4.M7; M57A. **DD** 027.0762.

US
LONG-RANGE PROGRAM ... UPDATE & EXTENSION AND ANNUAL PROGRAM / OKLAHOMA DEPARTMENT OF LIBRARIES. Main/Corp Oklahoma. Dept. of Libraries. **VFOAT** Long-Range Program ... Update and Extension and Annual Program; Long-Range Program, Update & Extension; Annual Program; Library Services and Construction Act Long-Range Program, Update & Extension. FY 1983-1987-. Periodical. English. an. **LC** Z678.4.O5; O44A. **DD** 021.8/3/09766. ***Continues** Oklahoma. Dept. of Libraries. LSCA Annual Program.*

IE/0024-631X
LONG ROOM. Added/Corp Dublin. University. Friends of the Library. **VFOAT** Longroom. No. 1 (Spring 1970)-. Periodical. English. an. Trinity College / Ireland, Library Long Room, Dublin 2 Ireland. **Tel** 011 353 1 772941. **LC** Z921.D86; L65. **DD** 021.7/09418/3.
Ind/Abst Annu. Bibliogr. Engl. Lang. Lit.; Br. Humanit. Index.

CN/0709-4590
LRIS NEWSLETTER. See Forestry.

●CN/1193-2333
LS NEWSLETTER. [LS newsl.]. **Added/Corp** Public Service Alliance of Canada. Library Science Group. Public Service Alliance of Canada. Ottawa Regional Office. **VFOAT** Library Science Newsletter. No. 1 (1992)-. Newsletter. English. Free to members. Public Service Alliance of Canada, 233 Gilmour Street, Ottawa Ontario K2P 0P1 Canada. **Tel** (613)560-4211. **DD** 331.7.

CN/0715-7533
LTBC : LIBRARY TECHNICIANS ASSOCIATION OF BRITISH COLUMBIA. [LTBC, Libr. Tech, Assoc. B.C.]. **VAT** Library Technicians Association of British Columbia. Vol. 8, No. 5 (July 1982)-. Periodical. English. Library Technicians Association of British Columbia, PO Box 67515, Vancouver BC V5W 3T9. **DD** 020/.6234/711. ***Continues** BCALT, 0822-6725.*

AT/0725-7015
LU REES ARCHIVES. [Lu Rees arch.]. (1???)-. English. ir. University of Canberra, PO Box 1, Belconnen ACT 2616 Australia. **Tel** 011/61/6/2015111, FAX 011/61/6/2015999. **ED** P Clayton. **DD** 820.809282.
Ind/Abst Aust. Educ. Index; Aust. Libr. Inf. Sci. Abstr. (1983-).

II/0024-7219
LUCKNOW LIBRARIAN. [Lucknow libr.]. **Added/Corp** Uttar Pradesh Library Association. Lucknow Branch. (May 1962)-. Periodical. English. qt (4 issues). $40.00. Uttar Pradesh Library Association, Lucknow Branch, UP Library Association, PO Box 446, Lucknow 226 001 India. **(Subscription address:** Prints India, 11 Darya Ganj, New Delhi 110002 India.**) LC** Z671; .L8. available on CD-ROM.
Ind/Abst Indian Libr. Sci. Abstr.; Libr. Inf. Sci. Abstr.

CN/0226-0115
LUSOLT TALK. [LUSOLT talk]. **Main/Corp** Lakehead University. School of Library Technology. **VFOAT** L U S O L T Talk. **VAT** Lakehead University School of Library Technology Talk. V. 1- Dec. 1979-. Periodical. English. ir. Free. Department of Library and Information Studies, Lakehead University, Thunder Bay Ontario P7B 5E1 Canada. **Tel** (807)343-8420. **ED** LaRea Moody. **DD** 020/.7/1171312. ctrl circ.

US/0024-7472
LUTHERAN LIBRARIES. Added/Corp Lutheran Church Library Association. Vol. 1, (1958)-. Periodical. English. Four times a year (Mar., June, Sept., Dec.). $15.00 (one year), $25.00 (two year), $40.00 (three year). Lutheran Church Library Association, 122 West Franklin Avenue, Minneapolis MN 55404. **Tel** (612)870-3623. **ED** Felicity Hanson. Index available (Book titles.). cum. index. **Bk Rev. Circ:** 6,000.
Desc: Articles of interest to church librarians including library techniques and promotion. Reviews of current books for church libraries and news of LCLA Chapter activities.

CN/0315-9124
M.S.L.A.V.A. JOURNAL. ***Title Change.*** [M.S.L.A.V.A. j.]. **Main/Corp** Manitoba School Library Audio Visual Association. **VAT** Manitoba School Library Audio Visual Association journal. Vol. 3 (Sept. 1973)-(1993). Periodical. English. Six times a year. Manitoba Teachers Society, 191 Harcourt Street, Winnipeg Manitoba R3J 3H2 Canada. **Tel** (204)888-7961 ext.254, FAX (204)831-0877. ***Continues** Newsletter / Manitoba School Library Audio Visual Association, 0047-5777.* ***Continued by** MSLA journal, 1189-7163.*
Ind/Abst Can. Educ. Index.

DK/0905-5533
MAGASIN FRA DET KONGELIGE BIBLIOTEK. Added/Corp Kongelige Bibliotek (Denmark). (1990)-. Periodical. Danish. qt. Det Kongelige Bibliotek, Postboks 2149, 1016 Kobenhavn K Denmark. **Tel** 011 45 33 930111, FAX 011 45 33 329846, telex 15009. **ED** A. L. Philipson. ***Continues** Magasin Fra Det Kongelige Bibliotek Og Universitetsbiblioteket I, 0901-7496.*
Desc: Pertains to library science.

DK/0901-7496
MAGASIN FRA DET KONGELIGE BIBLIOTEK OG UNIVERSITETSBIBLIOTEKET I. ***Title Change.*** (1986)-?. Periodical. Danish. qt. Det Kongelige Bibliotek, Postboks 2149, 1016 Kobenhavn K Denmark. **Tel** 011 45 33 930111, FAX 011 45 33 329846, telex 15009. **ED** Jesper During Jorgensen. **LC** Z824.K65; M33. **Circ:** 3,500. ***Continued by** Magasin Fra Det Kongelige Bibliotek.*
Desc: Offers illustrated articles on books currently in the Danish Royal Library, with special attention to rare and historically significant volumes. Also contains articles on humanistic and linguistic subjects.

US
MAGAZINE RACK [COMPUTER FILE]. Added/Corp Information Access Company. (1990)-. English. Information Access Company, 362 Lakeside Drive, Foster City CA 94404. **Tel** (800)227-8431. **LC** AP2; .M33.
Desc: Features over 100,000 current articles from more than 300 publications. System requirements: IBM PC, XT, AT, Compaq 386 or compatible computer; 640K RAM; CD-ROM drive; PC-DOS or MS-DOS 3.1 or higher; MS-DOS CD-ROM extensions 2.1 or higher. Uses Folio Corporation's PreViews Software.

US/0000-0914
MAGAZINES FOR LIBRARIES. [Mag. libr.]. 1st Ed. (1969)-. English. ir (every three years). $139.95. R R Bowker, A Reed Reference Publishing Company, Part of Reed International PLC, PO Box 31, 121 Chanlon Drive, New Providence NJ 07974. **Tel** (908)464-6800, (800)521-8110, FAX (908)665-6688, telex 138-755. **ED** Bill Katz and Linda Sternberg Katz. **LC** Z6941; .M23; PN4832. **DD** 050/.25.
Desc: For the general reader and school, junior college, college, university, and public libraries. Lists over 6,500 outstanding periodicals, 2,000 of them for the first time under more than 130 subject classifications.
Ind/Abst Book Rev. Index.

HU/0025-0171
MAGYAR KONYVSZEMLE. See Library and Information Sciences-Abstracting, Bibliographies and Statistics.

HU/0133-736X
MAGYAR KONYVTARI SZAKIRODALOM BIBLIOGRAFIAJA, A. See Library and Information Sciences-Abstracting, Bibliographies and Statistics.

US/1064-5608
MAHD BULLETIN. (MAHD BULLETIN. MUSEUMS, ARTS AND HUMANITIES DIVISION, SPECIAL LIBRARIES ASSOCIATION.). [MAHD bull.]. **Added/Corp** Special Libraries Association. Museums, Arts and Humanities Division. **VFOAT** Special Libraries Association MAHD Bulletin; MAHD. **VAT** Museums, Arts, and Humanities Division Bulletin. Vol. 6, No. 2 (Spring, 1976)-. Bulletin. English. Four times a year (Fall, Winter, and Spring). $15.00. Hayden Plantarium, 81st Central Park West, C/O Sandra Kitt, New york NY 10024. **Tel** (212)572-3418. **ED** Andrew Berner. **DD** 026. **Bk Rev,** (Qty: 1 or 2). **Ad Acc. Circ:** 1,500 (ctrl). ***Continues** Bulletin (Special Libraries Association. Museums, Arts and Humanities Division).*

CN/0848-7456
MAILBOX LIBRARY SERVICE. [Mailb. libr. serv.]. **Main/Corp** Ontario Library Service, North. (Fall/Winter 1989/1990)-. Periodical. English. sa. Ontario Library Service, North, Bag Service 2100, 11 Station Road South, Kirkland Lake, Ontario P2N 3P4 Canada. **DD** 017/.5. ***Continues** Ontario Library Service, James Bay. Mailbox. English., 0714-4970.*

●US
MAINE ENTRY, THE. Added/Corp Maine Library Association. Maine Educational Media Association. Maine State Library. (1992)-. Periodical. English. qt. Comes with membership. Maine Library Association, Local Government Center, Community Drive, Augusta ME 04330. **Tel** (207)623-8428. ***Continues** Maine-ly Libraries.*

IO/0216-7506
MAJALAH ILMU PERPUSTAKAAN DAN INFORMATIKA. V. 1, No. 1 (Jan./Apr. 1981)-. Periodical. Indonesian. Three times a year. Rp2250. Jurusan Ilmu Perpustakaan FSUI, Kompleks UI Rawamangun, Jakarta Timur Indonesia. **LC** Z669.5.I6; M34.

IO
MAJALAH IPI. Main/Corp Ikatan Pustakawan Indonesia. **VAT** Majalah Ikatan Pustakawan Indonesia. Periodical. Indonesian (English). $7.00. Ikatan Pustakawan Indonesia, Merdeka Selatan No 11, Jakarta Indonesia. **Tel** (021)34252G. **LC** Z671; .I38A. **DD** 020/.5.

IO
MAJALAH PERPUSTAKAAN. Dec. 1978-. Periodical. Indonesian. Badan Pengembangan Perpustakaan Daerah Tk I Sum. Utara, Jalan Iskandar Muda No 270, Lantai II-Atlas, Medan Indonesia. **LC** Z845.S85; M34.

MY/0126-7809
MAJALAH PERPUSTAKAAN MALAYSIA. [Majallah perpustakaan Malays.]. **Added/Corp** Persatuan Perpustakaan Malaysia. (1978)-. Malay (English). an. 12.00Mal$ Malaysia; 13.30Mal$ other. University Malaya, Co-Op Bookshop, Kuala Lumpur 22-11, Lembah Pantai Malaysia. **LC** Z845.M3; M34. **DD** 027/.0595. ***Continues** Majalah Perpustakaan Malaysia.*
Ind/Abst Libr. Inf. Sci. Abstr.

KE/0253-5971
MAKTABA. [Maktaba]. **Added/Corp** Kenya Library Association. Vol. 1, (1974)-. Periodical. English. sa. $25.00. Kenya Library Association, PO Box 46031, Nairobi Kenya. **Tel** 72550/1. **LC** Z857.K4; M34. **DD** 021/.009676/2. **Bk Rev. Ad Acc. Circ:** 300-500. ***Continues** Chairman's Report - East African Library Association.*
Ind/Abst Libr. Inf. Sci. Abstr.

SU
MAKTABAT AL-IDARAH. VFOAT I.P.A. Library Bulletin. V. 1- March 1970-. Periodical. Arabic. Three times a year. 15 riyals Saudi Arabia; $8.00 US. PO Box 205, Al-Rujad Saudi Arabia. **Tel** 47661600, telex 201160 SJ. **ED** Mostafa Sadhan. **LC** JA26; .M33. Index available. cum. index. **Bk Rev. Circ:** 2,000 (ctrl). available on microfilm.
Desc: Serves as an outlet for papers and research on library and information science, reviews of books and articles. A current awareness section dealing with Saudi Arabian government documents.

CN/0710-3417
MALT NEWSLETTER. [MALT newsl.]. **Added/Corp** Manitoba Association of Library Technicians. Vol. 3, No. 1 (Jan. 1979)-. Periodical. English. qt. $20.00 institutions; $18.00 individuals. Manitoba Association of Library Technicians, Box 1872, Winnipeg Manitoba R3C 141 Canada. **Tel** (204)986-3250. **ED** Candace Bannister. **DD** 020/.6234/7127. **Bk Rev. Ad Acc. Circ:** 150. ***Continues** Newsletter (Manitoba Association of Library Technicians), 0826-6816.*
Desc: A clearinghouse of information pertaining to library technicians and the library field in general.

SW/0349-4225
MANADSJOURNALEN. VFOAT Manads Journalen. (July 1980)-. Periodical. Swedish. mo. Pressdata, Box 3263, 103 65 Stockholm Sweden. **Tel** 011 46 8 7996200. **LC** AP48; .M35. ***Continues** Veckojournalen.*

US
MANAGING INFORMATION. V. 1-. Monographic series. English. Price varies per volume. SAGE Periodical Press, 2455 Teller Road, Thousand Oaks CA 91320. **Tel** (805)499-0721, FAX (805)499-0871, telex 100799. **Acid Free.** Documents available from Ask*IEEE.
Ind/Abst INSPEC (Aug. 1981-).

CN/0319-406X
MANUAL & DIRECTORY - ONTARIO JOINT FICTION RESERVE. **Main/Corp** Ontario Joint Fiction Reserve. 1972-. Directory. English. be. Ontario Joint Fiction Reserve, Box 100, Wyoming Ontario N0N 1T0 Canada. **DD** 025.2/6.

US
MARC : TAPE, CD-ROM FOR RETROSPECTIVE CONVERSION. **Added/Corp** Library of Congress. Cataloging Distribution Service. **VFOAT** MARC Services from the Library of Congress. **VAT** Machine-Readable; Machine Readable Cataloging; Machine-Readable Cataloging Services from the Library of Congress; Machine Readable Cataloging Services from the Library of Congress. (1990)-. English. an. Library of Congress / Cataloging Distribution Service, Washington DC 20541-5017. **Tel** (800)255-3666, (202)707-6100, FAX (202)707-1334. **LC** Z699.4.M2; M18. **DD** 025.3/16. ***Continues*** *MARC Distribution Services.*

US/0731-2741
MARCHEMOS (EL PASO, TEX.). (MARCHEMOS.). Spanish. mo. $100.00. Southern Baptist Convention, 901 Commerce, Suite 750, Nashville TN 37203. **Tel** (615)244-2355, FAX (615)742-8919. **(Subscription address:** Sunday School Board - Customer Service, 127 Ninth Avenue North, Nashville, TN 37234 USA; telephone: (800)458-2772**)**

CN/0714-895X
MARIGOLD LIBRARY SYSTEM DIRECTORY. [Marigold Libr. Syst. dir.]. **Main/Corp** Marigold Library System. **VFOAT** Directory. **VAT** Directory - Marigold Library System. Jan. 1982-. Directory. English. sa. Free. Marigold Library System Directory, PO Box 1830, Strathmore Alberta T0J 3H0 Canada. **Tel** (403)934-5334. **DD** 027.4/025/71233. ctrl circ.

CN/0226-5737
MARIGOLD REPORT. [Marigold rep.]. **Added/Corp** Marigold Library System. Steering Committee. No. 1 (Nov. 1979)-. Periodical. English. Ten times a year. Free. Marigold Library System, Bag 1830, c/o South Alberta Library Services Calgary Alberta T2G 2M2 Canada, Strathmore Alberta T0J 3H0 Canada. **Tel** (403)934-5334. **DD** 027.47123/3.

US/0896-3908
MARKETING LIBRARY SERVICES. (MARKETING LIBRARY SERVICES : MLS.). [Mark. libr. serv.]. **VFOAT** MLS. Vol. 1, No. 1 (1988)-. Periodical. English. Eight times a year. $65.00 (one year), $122.00 (two year), US; $71.00 (one year) Canada and Mexico; $79.00 (one year) other. Learned Information Inc., 143 Old Marlton Pike, Medford NJ 08055-8750. **Tel** (609)654-6266, FAX (609)654-4309. **ED** Marydee Ojala. **DD** 658. Index available. **Bk Rev**.
Desc: Published for librarians. Provides information about designing and presenting plans for new services or acquiring new products. Informs readers of how to identify tactics in making speeches, get publicity, build a reputation for innovation and responsiveness, and keep careers on a competitive track.
Ind/Abst Int. Aerosp. Abstr.

US
MASSACHUSETTS STATE PUBLICATIONS, CHECKLIST. **Main/Corp** State Library of Massachusetts. Vol. 1 (1989)-. Periodical. English. qt. Documents Department, State Library of Massachusetts, 442 State House, Boston MA 02133. **Tel** (617)727-6279. **ED** Bette L Siegel. cum. index. ***Continues*** *Commonwealth of Massachusetts Publications Received by the Massachusetts State Library, 0465-1898.*
Desc: Listing of Massachusetts state agency publications received by the State Library of Massachusetts.

UK/0309-7471
MATERIAL MATTERS. **See** Children and Youth Interests.

JA
MAUL : MIYAGI-KEN DAIGAKU TOSHOKAN KYOKAI KAIHO. **Main/Corp** Miyagi-Ken Daigaku Toshokan Kyokai. Japanese. Miyagi-ken Daigaku Toshokan Kyokai Maul Henshu Iinkai, c/o Tohoku Daigaku Fuzoku, Toshokan Sendai Japan. **LC** Z845.M59; M59A.

US/0731-3675
MEDIA SPECTRUM. (MEDIA SPECTRUM / MICHIGAN ASSOCIATION FOR MEDIA IN EDUCATION.). [Media spectr.]. **Added/Corp** Michigan Association for Media in Education. Vol. 1, No. 1 (Spring 1974)-. Periodical. English. Four times a year (Feb., May, Aug., Dec.). $25.00. Michigan Association for Media in Education, 6810 South Cedar,, Suite 8, Lansing MI 48911. **Tel** (517)699-1717, FAX (616)842-9195. **ED** Freda Richards, (313)647-0586 and Marian West (313)663-5907. **Bk Rev**, (Qty: 10-12). **Ad Acc**, **Adv Mgr:** B.H Brooks, **Tel** (517)699-1717. **Circ:** 1,400 (ctrl).
Desc: Information about trends, materials, programs, and research in education, technology, and library science relevant to the school library media profession.

US/0276-3869
MEDICAL REFERENCE SERVICES QUARTERLY. [Med. ref. serv. q.]. Vol. 1, No. 1 (Spring 1982)-. Academic Scholarly Publication. English. qt. $95.00 US; $133.00 other. The Haworth Press Inc, 10 Alice Street, Binghamton NY 13904-1580. **Tel** (607)722-5857, (800)3-HAWORTH, FAX (607)722-1424. **ED** M. Sandra Wood (editor's address: George T Harrel Library, Milton S Hershey Medical Center, Pennsylvania State University, Box 850, Hershey, PA 17033),. **LC** R118.2; .M4. **DD** 025.5/27661/05. **NLM** Z 699.5 M39 M489. **CODEN** MRSQDK. **Bk Rev**. **Ad Acc**. **Pr Rev**. **Acid Free**. **Circ:** 1,072. available on microfilm and microfiche from University Microfilms International (UMI). Documents available from BIOSIS Document Express, Ask*IEEE, Haworth Document Delivery Service.
Desc: The working tool journal for medical and health sciences librarians. Regularly publishes practice-oriented articles relating to medical reference services with an emphasis on online search services.
Ind/Abst Biol. Abstr.; Cumul. Index Nurs. Allied Health Lit.; EMBASE; Health Plan. Adminis.; Hospit. Health Admin. Index; Inf. Instruc. Technol.; Inf. Sci. Abstr.; INSPEC (Spring 1983-); Leg. Inf. Manage. Index; Libr. Inf. Sci. Abstr.; Libr. Lit.

US/0565-811X
MEDICAL SUBJECT HEADINGS. **Main/Corp** National Library of Medicine (U.S.). (1960)-. English. an. $42.00 US; $52.50 other. National Library of Medicine, 8600 Rockville Pike, Bethesda MD 20894. **Tel** (301)496-6308. **LC** Z695.1.M48; U5. **DD** 025.3/361. **NLM** Z 695.1 M4 M489.
Desc: An alphabetical and categorized list of all of the subject descriptors used to analyze the biomedical literature in the National Library of Medicine.

US/0147-5711
MEDICAL SUBJECT HEADINGS. ANNOTATED ALPHABETIC LIST. [Med. subj. head., Annot. alph. list]. **Added/Corp** National Library of Medicine (U.S.). Medical Subject Headings Section. National Library of Medicine (U.S.). (19??)-. English. an. $47.00 US, Canada & Mexico; $89.00 other. National Library of Medicine, 8600 Rockville Pike, Bethesda MD 20894. **Tel** (301)496-6308. **(Subscription address:** National Technical Information Service, 5285 Port Royal Road, Springfield, VA 22161**)** **LC** Z695.1.M48; U52c. **DD** 025.4/961. **NLM** Z 695.1 M4 M4894.

US/0891-3994
MEDICAL SUBJECT HEADINGS. SUPPLEMENTARY CHEMICAL RECORDS. (MEDICAL SUBJECT HEADINGS. SUPPLEMENTARY CHEMICAL RECORDS / (U.S.) NATIONAL LIBRARY OF MEDICINE.). [Med. subj. head., Suppl. chem. rec.]. **Added/Corp** National Library of Medicine (U.S.) National Library of Medicine (U.S.). Medical Subject Headings Section. **VFOAT** Supplementary Chemical Records. (1983)-. English. an. $54.00 US, Canada & Mexico; $101.00 other. National Library of Medicine, 8600 Rockville Pike, Bethesda MD 20894. **Tel** (301)496-6308. **(Subscription address:** National Technical Information Service, 5285 Port Royal Road, Springfield, VA 22161**)** **DD** 025.

US/0147-099X
MEDICAL SUBJECT HEADINGS. TREE STRUCTURES. [Med. subj. head., Tree struct.]. **Added/Corp** National Library of Medicine (U.S.). Medical Subject Headings Section. National Library of Medicine (U.S.). (1972)-. English. an. $44.00 North America; $83.00 other. National Library of Medicine, 8600 Rockville Pike, Bethesda MD 20894. **Tel** (301)496-6308. **(Subscription address:** National Technical Information Service, 5285 Port Royal Road, Springfield, VA 22161**)** **LC** Z695.1.M48; U52b. **DD** 025.3/361. **NLM** Z 695.1 M4 M492.

US/0889-0773
MEDIUM (BOTHELL, WASH.). (THE MEDIUM.). **Added/Corp** Washington Library Media Association. Washington State Association of School Librarians. Washington Association for Educational Communication and Technology. Washington Educational Media Coordinating Council. Vol. 1 (Sept. 1976)-. Periodical. English. Three times a year. $20.00 US; $35.00 Canada. Washington Library Media Association, Box 1413, Bothell WA 98041. **Tel** (206)489-6258. **ED** Sue Weiss (editor's address: 23708-107th Place West, Edmonds WA 98020-5238). **DD** 027. **Ad Acc**, **Adv Mgr:** Marilyn Camp, **Tel** (509)534-8776. **Circ:** 1,300. ***Formed by the union of*** *Library Leads* ***and*** *Resources, The Official WAECT Journal.*
Desc: Journal for and by school library media professionals in Washington state.

US
MEDLINE KNOWLEDGE FINDER. / MODEL UM-11. **See** Medical Science and Technology.

US
MEDLINE KNOWLEDGE FINDER. UM-5. **See** Medical Science and Technology.

US
MEDLINE [COMPUTER FILE]. **See** Medical Science and Technology.

US/8755-1810
MEETINGS (NEW YORK, N.Y. 1980). (MEETINGS / LIBRARY JOURNAL.). [Meetings]. (1980)-. English. an. Library Journal / New York, 1180 Avenue of the Americas, New York NY 10036. **Tel** (212)916-1921. **ED** John N Berry III. **DD** 020. **Bk Rev**. **Ad Acc**. **Circ:** 26,000.
Desc: Full service publication addressed to the needs and interests of those who buy book and non-book materials and equipment in public, academic, special and business libraries.

RU
MEKHANIZATSIIA I AVTOMATIZATSIIA BIBLIOTECHNO-BIBLIOGRAFICHESKIKH PROTSESSOV. **Added/Corp** Akademiia Nauk SSSR. Biblioteka. (19??)-. Multiple languages (Russian and Multiple languages). 0.23rub. Biblioteka Akademii Nauk, Library of the Russian Academy of Sciences, Birzhevaia Liniia 1, 199034 St. Petersburg Russia. **Tel** 011 95 218-35-92, FAX 011 95 218-74-36. **LC** Z678.9.A2; M44.

US/0364-2410
MELA NOTES. (MELA NOTES / MIDDLE EAST LIBRARIANS ASSOCIATION.). [MELA notes]. **Main/Corp** Middle East Librarians Association. **Added/Corp** Middle East Librarians' Association. **VAT** Middle East Librarians Association Notes. No. 1 (Fall 1973)-. Periodical. English. Three times a year. $10.00. Middle East Librarians Association, c/o Michael Hopper, University of California Main Library, Santa Barbara CA 93106. **Tel** (805)893-8022, (805)893-8048. **ED** Brenda Bickett. **LC** PAR. **Bk Rev**. **Ad Acc**. **Circ:** 200 (ctrl).
Desc: Articles and reviews on Middle East librarianship and area studies.
Ind/Abst Libr. Inf. Sci. Abstr.

●US
MEMBERSHIP DIRECTORY. **Main/Corp** Association of Jewish Libraries. (1992)-. Directory. English. Association of Jewish Libraries, 19 Brookfield Road, New Hyde Park NY 11040. **Tel** (212)532-4949 ext. 297.

CN/0840-819X
MEMBERSHIP DIRECTORY AND HANDBOOK. [Memb. dir. handb. - Atl. Prov. Libr. Assoc.]. **Main/Corp** Atlantic Provinces Library Association. (1988/1989)-. Directory. English. an. Free to members. Atlantic Provinces Library Association, School of Library and Information Studies, Dalhousie University, Halifax Nova Scotia B3H 4HB Canada. **Tel** (902)424-3656 Ext. 175. **DD** 020/.6232/715. ***Continues*** *Membership Directory - Atlantic Provinces Library Association, 0707-3895.*

US
MEMBERSHIP DIRECTORY AND HANDBOOK / INDIANA LIBRARY DERATION. **Main/Corp** Indiana Library Federation. **VFOAT** Membership Directory. (1991)-. Directory. English. Indiana Library Federation, 1500 North Delaware, Indianapolis IN 46202. **Tel** (317)636-6613, FAX (317)634-9503. **LC** Z673; .I382. ***Continues*** *Membership Directory/Handbook.*

CN/0705-6834
MEMBERSHIP DIRECTORY - CANADIAN ASSOCIATION FOR INFORMATION SCIENCE. (MEMBERSHIP DIRECTORY - CANADIAN ASSOCIATION FOR INFORMATION SCIENCE. ANNUAIRE DES MEMBRES - ASSOCIATION CANADIENNE DES SCIENCES DE L'INFORMATION.). **Main/Corp** Canadian Association for Information Science. **VFOAT** Annuaire des Membres - Association Canadienne des Sciences de l'Information. (1977)-. Periodical. English (French). Free to members (membership $15.). Canadian Association for Information Science, PO Box 158 Station A, Ottawa Ontario K1N 8V2 Canada. **DD** 020/.622/71.

US/0270-4595
MEMBERSHIP DIRECTORY - FLORIDA LIBRARY ASSOCIATION. **Main/Corp** Florida Library Association. (1959)-. Directory. English. Segal/Crow, 1133 West Morse Boulevard 201, Winter Park FL 32789-3743. **LC** Z720.A45; F54A. **DD** 020/.92/2; B.

CN/0255-8114
MEMBERSHIP DIRECTORY / INTERNATIONAL ASSOCIATION OF MARINE SCIENCE LIBRARIES AND INFORMATION CENTERS. ***Title Change.*** [Membsh. dir. - Int. Assoc. Mar. Sci. Libr. Inf. Cent.]. **Main/Corp** International Association of Marine Science Libraries and Information Centers. (1983/1984)-(19??).

Directory. English. an. International Association of Marine Science Libraries and Information Centers, c/o Library, Harbor Branch Oceanographic Institution, 5600 Old Dixie Highway, Fort Pierce FL 34946. **Tel** (902)426-3675. **ED** J Elizabeth Sutherland. **LC** V13.A1; I57a. **DD** 026/.55146/0025. **Circ:** 200 (ctrl). ***Continued by*** *International Association of Aquatic and Marine Science Libraries and Information Centers. Membership Directory, 1021-495X.*
Desc: A list of members of the International Association of Marine Science Libraries and Information Centers.

CN/0828-7007
MEMBERSHIP LIST - CANADIAN ASSOCIATION OF MUSIC LIBRARIES (1984). (MEMBERSHIP LIST / CANADIAN ASSOCIATION OF MUSIC LIBRARIES). [Membsh. list - Can. Assoc. Music Libr.]. **Main/Corp** Canadian Association of Music Libraries. **VFOAT** Liste des Membres. (1984)-. English (French). an. 65.00Can$ (individuals); 80.00Can$ (institutions) Comes with Fontes Artis Musicae & Newsletter. Canadian Association of Music Libraries, 2500 University Drive Northwest, Music Library, Calgary Alberta T2N 1N4 Canada. **Tel** (403)220-3611, FAX (403)282-6837. **DD** 026/.78/02571. **Bk Rev**. **Ad Acc**. ctrl circ. ***Continues*** *Canadian Association of Music Libraries. Official Membership List, 0820-7631.*

FR/0987-3090
MEMOIRE DE TRAME. (1986)-. Periodical. French. sm. 1100.00F France; 1292.85F other. Tekhne / Libraire Communication, 7 rue des Carmes, 75005 Paris France. **Tel** 011 33 1 43547084. **ED** Caroline de Peyster. **UDC** 007. **Bk Rev**. **Circ:** 300 (ctrl).

SP
MEMORIA-INFORME / UNIVERSIDAD DE ZARAGOZA, BIBLIOTECA UNIVERSITARIA. **Main/Corp** Universidad de Zaragoza. Biblioteca Universitaria. **VFOAT** Informe. **VAT** Memoria informe. (19??)-. Spanish. an. Universidad de Zaragoza, Biblioteca Universitaria, Zaragoza Spain. **LC** Z832.U55; U54a. **DD** 027.746/553.

US/0889-5600
MENNONITE LIBRARIAN AND ARCHIVIST, THE. ***Ceased.*** [Mennon. libr. arch.]. **Added/Corp** Mennonite Historical Committee (Goshen, Ind.) North American Mennonite Archivists and Librarians. (19??)-(19??). Periodical. English. Mennonite Historical Committee, 1700 South Main Street, Goshen IN 46526. **DD** 027.

US/1040-7421
MERIDIAN - MAP & GEOGRAPHY ROUND TABLE (AMERICAN LIBRARY ASSOCIATION). **See** Geography-Cartography.

FR/0154-036X
METALLURGIE. LEXIQUE. **See** Metals and Metallurgy.

US/0887-1973
METRO HANDBOOK AND DIRECTORY OF MEMBERS. [METRO handb. dir. memb.]. **Added/Corp** New York Metropolitan Reference and Research Library Agency. (1986)-. Directory. English. an. $65.95 nonmembers; $23.95 members. New York Metropolitan Reference Research Library, 57 East 11th Street, New York NY 11201. **Tel** (718)852-8700. **ED** Paul B. Ippolito. **DD** 021. Index available. cum. index. **Ad Acc. Circ:** 1,100 (ctrl). ***Continues*** *Directory of the New York Metropolitan Reference and Research Library Agency, Metro.*
Desc: Includes membership information, programs, and services, access to Library Collections and exchange privileges. Includes other information in information retrieval systems and data bases, automated circulation systems, equipment for public use, special collections, personnel, meeting rooms, and buyers' guide. All information heavily indexed.

US/0732-801X
METRO MISCELLANEOUS PUBLICATION. [METRO misc. publ.]. Monographic series. English. Price varies per volume. New York Metropolitan Reference and Research Library Agency, 57 Willoughby Street, Brooklyn NY 11201. **Tel** (718)852-8700. **ED** Christine Stenstrom. **DD** 011. **Circ:** 1,600. ***Continues*** *Metro Miscellaneous Publications Series.*
Desc: Carries news about metro-sponsored services, programs and policies of interest to metro members and the library community in general.

CN/0226-255X
METROPOLITAN TORONTO LIBRARY. SCIENCE & TECHNOLOGY DEPT. ACQUISITIONS. (ACQUISITIONS - METROPOLITAN TORONTO LIBRARY. SCIENCE & TECHNOLOGY DEPT.). [Metrop. Toronto Libr., Sci. Technol. Dep., Acquis]. **Main/Corp** Metropolitan Toronto Library. Science & Technology Dept. Vol. 1 (March 1980)-. Periodical. English. mo. Metropolitan Toronto Library Board, 789 Yonge Street, Toronto Ontario M4W 2G8 Canada. **Tel** (416)393-7134, telex 06-22232. **DD** 016.5. ***Supersedes*** *Metropolitan Toronto Library Board. Science and Technology Library. Selected List of Acquisitions, 0384-0212.*

RU
MEZHDUNARODNYI FORUM PO INFORMATSII I DOKUMENTATSII. **Added/Corp** International Federation for Documentation. (197?)-. Periodical. Russian. Four times a year. $23.00. VINITI - Vsesoyuznyi Institut Nauchno-Tekhnicheskoi Informatsii, All-Union Scientific and Technical Information Institute, Baltiiskaia Ulitsa 14, 125219 Moscow Russia. **Tel** 238-46-00, FAX 9430060, telex 411160. **(Subscription address:** Victor Kamkin, 4956 Boiling Brook Parkway, Rockville MD 20852.**)**

HU/0133-4875
MEZOGAZDASAGI ES ELELMISZERIPARI KONYVTAROSOK TAJEKOZTATOJA. (1971)-. Hungarian. **Ind/Abst** Magyar Konyv. Szak. Biblio.

CN/0831-2249
MHLA BULLETIN. (MHLA/ABSM BULLETIN / MARITIME HEALTH LIBRARIES ASSOCIATION.). [MHLA bull.]. **VAT** Maritime Health Libraries Association Bulletin; ABSM Bulletin; Association des Bibliotheques Sante Maritimes, Bulletin. No. 7 (May 1986)-. Bulletin. English. qt. Free (members of the Maritime Health Libraries Association). Maritime Health Libraries Association, Suite 314 Lord Nelson Building, 5675 Spring Garden Road, Halifax Nova Scotia B3J 1H1 Canada. **DD** 026/.61/060715. ***Continues*** *NSHLA News, 0831-246X.*

CN/0848-9009
MHLA NEWS. [MHLA news]. **Added/Corp** Manitoba Health Libraries Association. **VAT** Manitoba Health Libraries Association News. Vol. 12, No. 1 (Fall 1989)-. Periodical. English. tq. Free to members (Membership, $15.00, individual; $50.00, institutions; $20.00, associates). Manitoba Health Libraries Association, PO Box 232, Winnipeg Manitoba R3M 3S7 Canada. **DD** 026/.61/.0607127. ***Continues*** *News (Manitoba Health Libraries Association)., 0821-1310.*

●US
MICHIGAN DOCUMENTS / COMPILED BY DENISE K. GERMAIN-PETERS. **Added/Corp** Library of Michigan. Vol. 1, No. 1 & 2 (Oct. 1991/Mar. 1992)-. Periodical. English. qt. Library of Michigan, Public Information Specialist, PO Box 30007, Lansing MI 48909. **Tel** (517)373-5578. ***Continues*** *Michigan Documents (Microfiche).*

US/0884-9919
MICHIGAN LIBRARIAN (1985). (MICHIGAN LIBRARIAN.). [Mich. libr.]. **Added/Corp** Michigan Library Association. Vol. 51, No. 1 (Jan./Feb. 1985)-. Periodical. English. Ten times a year. $40.00 US; $50.00 other. Michigan Librarian Association, 1000 Long Boulevard, Suite 1, Lansing MI 48911. **Tel** (517)694-6615, FAX (517)694-4430. **ED** Marianne Hartzell. **LC** Z673; .M6. **DD** 020. available on microfilm from University Microfilms International (UMI). ***Continues*** *Michigan Librarian Newsletter, 0149-435X.*

US/8755-5786
MICRO SOFTWARE REPORT. ***Suspended.*** [Micro softw. rep.]. Vol. 1 (July 1981-July 1982)-Suspended (19??). English. an. $97.50. Mecklermedia Corporation, 11 Ferry Lane West, Westport CT 06880. **Tel** (203)226-6967, (800)632-5537, FAX (203)454-5840. **ED** Jeanne Nolan. **DD** 001. **Ad Acc. Circ:** 450.
Desc: Describes microcomputer software programs for library functions including order information and type of equipment needed.

US/0742-2342
MICROCOMPUTERS FOR INFORMATION MANAGEMENT. **See** Computers-Microcomputers, Personal Computers.

US/0080-8857
MICROFILMING PROJECTS NEWSLETTER. No. 1 (Apr. 1964)-. Periodical. English. an. $8.50. Salalm, University of New Mexico, General Library, Albequerque NM 87131. **Tel** (505)277-5102. cum. index.

US/0002-6530
MICROFORM REVIEW. [Microform rev.]. Vol. 1 (Jan. 1972)-. Academic Scholarly Publication. English. qt. $140.00 US; $145.00 Canada. K.G. Saur Verlag KG, A Reed Reference Publishing Company, Part of Reed International PLC, Ortlerstrasse 8, D 81373 Munich Germany. **Tel** 011 49 89 769020, FAX 011 49 89 76902150, telex 5212067-SAUR-D. **ED** Susan Szasz. **LC** Z265; .M565. **DD** 025.17/9. **CODEN** MFRVA. **[CCC]. Ad Acc. Circ:** 1,400. available on microfilm from University Microfilms International (UMI). Documents available from Ask*IEEE.
Desc: Devoted to reviewing scholarly micropublications for libraries and educational institutions.
Ind/Abst ARTbibliogr. Mod.; Curr. Index J. Educ.; Index Period. Artic. Relat. Law (19??-19??); Inf. Instruc. Technol.; Inf. Sci. Abstr. (?-?); INSPEC (Jan. 1973-); Leg. Inf. Manage. Index; Libr. Inf. Sci. Abstr. (Jan. 1973-); Libr. Lit.

US
MICROFORM REVIEW SERIES IN LIBRARY MICROGRAPHICS MANAGEMENT. **VFOAT** Library Micrographics Management Series. (1975)-. Monographic series. English. ir. $140.00. KG Saur Inc., PO Box 31, New Providence NJ 07974. **Tel** (800)521-8110, (908)665-3576, FAX (908)771-7792.

HU/0134-0352
MIKROFILMEK CIMJEGYZEKE. MODERN NYOMTATVANYOK / ORSZAGOS SZECHENYI KONYVTAR. **Main/Corp** Orszagos Szechenyi Konyvtar. 1-. Hungarian. ir. Orszagos Szechenyi Konyvtar, Budavari Palota F Epulet, 1827 Budapest Hungary. **Tel** 757-533/475, FAX (361)156-8731, telex 224226.

JA
MINNA NO TOSHOKAN. **Added/Corp** Toshokan Mondai Kenkyukai. No. 1 (1977)-. Periodical. Japanese. mo. Toshokan Mondai Kenkyukai, c/o Nerima Kuritsu Shakujii, Toshokan 16-31, Shakujiidai 1, Nerima-ku 177, Tokyo Japan. **LC** Z845.J4; M54.

US/1056-0033
MINNESOTA AACR 2 TRAINERS SERIES. [Minn. AACR 2 Train. ser.]. **Added/Corp** Minnesota AACR 2 Trainers. No. 1 (1991)-. Monographic series. English. Actual Media Srl, L Go Antonelli 27, 00145 Rome Italy. **Tel** 011 39 6 5417100. **ED** Editor: No. 1- Edward Swanson. **DD** 025.

US/0044-9652
MINUTES OF THE MEETING - ASSOCIATION OF RESEARCH LIBRARIES. ***Title Change.*** [Minutes meet. - Assoc. Res. Libr.]. **Main/Corp** Association of Research Libraries. (Dec. 1932)-(1993). Proceedings. English. Twice a year. Association of Research Libraries, 21 Dupont Circle, Washington DC 20036. **Tel** (202)296-2296. **LC** Z673; .A84. **DD** 020.6. **NLM** Z 673 A849M. **Circ:** 500. ***Continued by*** *Association of Research Libraries. Meeting. Proceedings of the Meeting, 1075-0886.*
Desc: Edited proceedings of the semiannual membership meetings of the association, including both program and business sessions.
Ind/Abst Libr. Lit.

US/0194-388X
MISSISSIPPI LIBRARIES. [Miss. libr.]. **Added/Corp** Mississippi Library Commission. Mississippi Library Association. Vol. 43, (Spring 1979)-. Periodical. English. qt (Mar., June, Sept., Dec.). $16.00 US; $24.00 other. Mississippi Libraries Association, PO Box 20448, Jackson MS 39209-1448. **Tel** (601)352-3917. **ED** Sarah Price Armstrong (phone:(601)266-4652). **LC** Z671; .M5. **DD** 021/.009762. Index available. **Bk Rev**, (Qty: 12). **Ad Acc. Circ:** 1,200 (ctrl). available on microfilm and microfiche from University Microfilms International (UMI). ***Continues*** *Mississippi Library News, 0026-6302.*
Desc: Publishes significant articles, news and other data of interest to Mississippi librarians and library users.
Ind/Abst Libr. Lit. (-1987).

US/0899-6458
MISSOURI LIBRARIES. [Mo. libr.]. Vol. 1, No. 1 (June 1988)-. Periodical. English. bm. Free. Missouri State Library, Box 387, Jefferson City MO 65102-0387. **Tel** (314)751-3615, FAX (314)751-3612. **ED** Madeline Matson. **DD** 027. **Bk Rev. Circ:** 4,100 (ctrl).
Desc: Newsletter on Missouri state library activities and news about libraries and librarians in Missouri.

US/0164-0496
MISSOURI UNION LIST OF SERIAL PUBLICATIONS. Began with Vol. for 1978. English. an. $50.00 (microfiche). St Louis Public Library, 1301 Olive Street, St Louis MO 63103. **Tel** (314)241-2288. **ED** Dorothy Knipmeyer. **LC** Z6945; .M677; PN4832. **DD** 011/.34. available on microfiche. ***Continues*** *St. Louis Union List of Periodicals.*

GW
MITTEILUNGEN. **Main/Corp** Staatsbibliothek zu Berlin--Preussischer Kulturbesitz. (1992)-. Academic Scholarly Publication. German. tq. Preussischer Kulturbesitz, 10772 Berlin Germany. **Tel** 011 49 30 2662338, FAX 011 49 30 2662378. **LC** Z929.B625; S72a. ***Continues*** *Staatsbibliothek Preussischer Kulturbesitz. Mitteilungen - Staatsbibliothek Preussischer Kulturbesitz, 0038-8866.*
Ind/Abst BHA : Biblio. Hist. Art.

GW/0177-8358
MITTEILUNGSBLATT DER ARBEITSGEMEINSCHAFT KATHOLISCH-THEOLOGISCHER BIBLIOTHEKEN, AKTHB. [Mitt.bl. Arb.gem. Kathol.-Theol. Bibl. AKThB]. **VFOAT** Mitteilungsblatt der Arbeitsgemeinschaft Kath.-Theol. Bibliotheken. (1952)-. Periodical. German. an. DM20.00. Bibliothek d

Priesterseminars, Postfach 1330, Jesuitenstr 13, 5500 Trier Germany. **Tel** 49 651 719142. **ED** Dr. Michael Embach (editor's phone: 49 651 9484140). **UDC** 026.282. **Bk Rev**, (Qty: 10). **Ad Acc.**
Desc: Articles on the developement, history and organization of Catholic theological libraries.

GW/0042-3629
MITTEILUNGSBLATT - VERBAND DER BIBLIOTHEKEN DES LANDES NORDRHEIN WESTFALEN. [Mitteilungsbl. - Verb. Bibl. Landes Nordrh. - Westf.]. **Main/Corp** Verband der Bibliotheken des Landes Nordrhein-Westfalen. Vol. 1 (Aug. 1950)-. Periodical. German. Four times a year. DM42.00. Bock & Herchen Verlag, Postfach 1145, D 53581 Bad Honnef Germany. **Tel** 011 49 2224 5443. **LC** Z671; .V45. **DD** 020. **[CCC].** cum. index. **Bk Rev. Ad Acc.** ctrl circ. available on microfilm and microfiche from University Microfilms International (UMI).
Ind/Abst Libr. Inf. Sci. Abstr.; Libr. Lit.

US/0541-5489
MLA NEWS. Added/Corp Medical Library Association. **VFOAT** M.L.A. News. **VAT** Medical Library Association News. No. 1 (Nov. 1961)-. Periodical. English. Ten times a year (combined in June/July and November/December). $48.50 US, Canada, and Mexico; $61.50 other. Medical Library Association, Suite 300, Six North Michigan Avenue, Chicago IL 60602-4805. **Tel** (312)419-9094, FAX (312)419-8950. **ED** Julie Kesti (editor's address: 8225 Countrywood Road NE, Albuquerque, NM 87109). **LC** Z675.M4; M12. **DD** 026/.61/06073. **NLM** Z 675.M4 M489M.

US/0748-9285
MLA NEWS LETTER - MINNESOTA LIBRARY ASSOCIATION. (MLA NEWSLETTER.). **Added/Corp** Minnesota Library Association. **VFOAT** M.L.A. Newsletter. **VAT** Minnesota Library Association Newsletter. Vol. 1, No. 1 (July 5, 1974)-. Newsletter. English. Ten times a year (With July/Aug. and Nov/Dec. issues combined). $20.00. Minnesota Library Association, 1315 Lowry Avenue North, c/o Regional Library, Minneapolis MN 55411-1398. **Tel** (612)521-1735. **Ad Acc. Circ:** 1,000 (ctrl). ***Continues*** *North Country Librarian.*
Desc: News and announcements of Minnesota library issues, continuing education events and job listings.

II/0970-1435
MLBD NEWSLETTER. [MLBD Newl.]. **VFOAT** Motilal Banarsidass Newsletter. (1979)-. Periodical. Multiple languages. mo. $10.00. **(Subscription address:** Prints India, 11 Darya Ganj, New Delhi 110002 India.**)** **UDC** 908(54)(016).

US/0275-7583
MLC UPDATE. (MLC UPDATE : THE NEWSLETTER OF THE MICHIGAN LIBRARY CONSORTIUM.). **VAT** Michigan Library Consortium Update. Vol. 1, No. 1 (Sept./Oct. 1980)-. Newsletter. English. bm. Free (members), $12.00 (non-members). Michigan Library Consortium, 6810 South Cedar Street/Suite 8, Lansing MI 48911. **Tel** (517)694-4242, (800)292-1359, FAX (517)694-9303. **ED** Kevin C Flaherty. **Circ:** 750.
Desc: News of interest to libraries holding membership in Consortium.

US/0884-2205
MO INFO. (MO INFO: THE NEWSLETTER OF THE MISSOURI LIBRARY ASSOCIATION.). [Mo info]. **Added/Corp** Missouri Library Association. **VFOAT** Newsletter. (198?)-. Newsletter. English. bm. $20.00 US; $30.00 other; $30.00 (institutions), $20.00 (individuals) membership. Missouri Library Association, 1306 Business 63 South, Suite B, Columbia MO 65201. **Tel** (314)449-4627. **ED** Jean Ann McCartney. **LC** Z673; .M6916. **DD** 020/.6234/778. **Ad Acc. Circ:** 1,400. available in microform. ***Continues*** *Newsletter - Missouri Library Association, 0581-0205.*
Desc: News and information about activities and members of Missouri Library Association; other items of state or national interest related to libraries.

UN/0203-5650
MODELI I SISTEMY OBRABOTKI INFORMATSII. Vol. 1 (1982)-. Periodical. Russian. Vydavnyche Obiednannia Vyshcha Shkola Tarasovskaia, Kiev Ukraine.
Ind/Abst Zentralbl. Math. Ihre Grenzgeb.

US/0196-1527
MODERN AVIATION LIBRARY. See Aeronautics, Astronautics.

JA
MOMBUSHO TOSHOKAN YORAN. **Main/Corp** Japan. Mombusho. Toshokan. (19??)-. Japanese. Mombusho Toshokan, 2-2 Kasumigaseki 3 Chiyoda-ku, Tokyo Japan. **LC** Z846; .J3615.

US/0094-873X
MONTANA LIBRARY DIRECTORY, WITH STATISTICS OF MONTANA PUBLIC LIBRARIES. See Library and Information Sciences-Abstracting, Bibliographies and Statistics.

US
MONTHLY MEMO - MAINE LIBRARY ASSOCIATION AND MAINE STATE LIBRARY. Main/Corp Maine Library Association. Vol. 1 (May 1979)-. Periodical. English. mo. Free. Local Government Center, 45 University Drive, PO Box 2268, Augusta MA 04338. **Tel** (207)623-8428, FAX (207)626-5947. ***Continues in part*** *Downeast Libraries, 0738-5684.*

US/0899-4560
MORGAN DIRECTORY REVIEWS / MDR. [Morgan dir. rev.]. **VFOAT** MDR. (1988)-. Periodical. English. qt. $29.95 US; $39.95 other. Morgan-Rand Publications Inc., 1800 Byberry Road 800, Huntingdon Valley PA 19006. **Tel** (215)938-5511, FAX (215)988-0402. **ED** Mary Weakley. **LC** Z5771; .M67. **DD** 011. **[CCC].**
Desc: Targets library buyers of directories in print, floppy disk and CD-ROM formats.

SA/0027-2639
MOUSAION (PRETORIA, SOUTH AFRICA: 1983). (MOUSAION.). **Added/Corp** University of South Africa. Dept. of Library and Information Science. University of South Africa. Dept. of Library Services. Ser. 3, No. 1 (1983)-. English (Afrikaans). be. $16.50. University of South Africa, PO Box 392, Pretoria 0001 South Africa. **Tel** 011 27 12 4298468, FAX 011 (27)12 429 3321, telex (59)350068+. **LC** Z857.S7; M68. ***Continues*** *Mousaion II, 0027-2639.*
Desc: General and research articles on library and information science. Bibliographical information concerning relevant post-graduate research in South Africa.
Ind/Abst Libr. Lit.

US/0145-6180
MPLA NEWSLETTER (1975). (MPLA NEWSLETTER.). **Main/Corp** Mountain Plains Library Association. **Added/Corp** Mountain Plains Library Association. Newsletter. **VAT** Mountain Plains Library Association Newsletter. Vol. 20 (1976)-. Newsletter. English. Six times a year. $21.00 (one year), $38.00 (two years), $55.00 (three years) US; $26.00 (one year), $46.00 (two years), $63.00 (three years) other. Mountain Plains Library Association, University of South Dakota, ID Weeks Library, Vermillion SD 57069-2390. **Tel** (605)677-6082, FAX (605)677-5488. **ED** Jim Dertien. **LC** Z671; .M76. **DD** 021/.00978. **Bk Rev. Ad Acc. Circ:** 1,500 (ctrl). available on microfilm and microfiche from University Microfilms International (UMI). ***Continues*** *Mountain/Plains Library Association Quarterly.*
Desc: Happenings in and of interest to librarians in the Mountain Plains Library Association 11-state region.

US/0415-505X
MRL BULLETIN. Main/Corp Detroit. Public Library. Municipal Reference Library. **VAT** Municipal Reference Library Bulletin. Bulletin. English. bm. Free. Detroit Public Library, Municipal Reference Library, 1004 City-County Building, 2 Woodward, Detroit MI 48226. **Tel** (313)224-3885, FAX (313)964-6958. **Circ:** 580 (ctrl).
Ind/Abst Corros. Abstr.

●CN/1189-7163
MSLA JOURNAL. [MSLA j.]. **Added/Corp** Manitoba School Library Association. **VFOAT** Manitoba School Library Association Journal. Vol. 20, No. 4 (June 1993)-. Periodical. English. ir. Free. Manitoba Teachers Society, 191 Harcourt Street, Winnipeg Manitoba R3J 3H2 Canada. **Tel** (204)888-7961 ext.254, FAX (204)831-0877. **DD** 027.8. ***Continues*** *Manitoba School Library Audio Visual Association. M.S.L.A.V.A. Journal., 0315-9124.*

US
MSRRT NEWSLETTER. VAT Minnesota Social Responsibilities Round Table Newsletter. (19??)-. Newsletter. English. Ten times a year. $15.00. Minnesota Library Association, 1315 Lowry Avenue North, c/o Regional Library, Minneapolis MN 55411-1398. **Tel** (612)521-1735. **ED** Christopher Dodge. Index available. **Bk Rev. Circ:** 250 (ctrl).
Desc: Peace and justice news and commentary for the library community with special emphasis on annotations of alternative periodicals.

AT/0158-9431
MULTICULTURAL LIBRARIES NEWSLETTER. [Multicult. libr. newsl.]. (1981)-. Newsletter. English. sa. 15.00Aus$ (individuals) Australia; 25.00Aus$ other. Working Group Multicultural Library, Coburg City Library, PO Box 113, Coburg VIC 3058 Australia. **Tel** 011 61 03 3500256. **ED** Anne Holmes. **DD** 027.63. ***Continues*** *Newsletter - Working Group on Multicultural Library Services (Victoria).*
Ind/Abst Aust. Educ. Index; Aust. Libr. Inf. Sci. Abstr. (1984-).

KO
MUNHON CHONGBOHAK PO. VFOAT Journal of the Library and Information Science Society Journal of the Library & Information Science Society. V. 1- (1984)-. Periodical. Korean. Chonnam Taehakkyo Munhon Chongbohak Yonguhoe, 300 Yongbong-Dong Puk-ku, Kwangju-Si Korea. **Tel** 55-0011. **ED** Sang Wan Han. **LC** Z671; .M85. **Circ:** 1,000 (ctrl).
Desc: To study the trends in the library and information science field.

CN/0226-2533
MUNICIPAL REFERENCE LIBRARY ACQUISITIONS. [Munic. Ref. Libr. acquis.]. **Main/Corp** Metropolitan Toronto Library Board. Municipal Reference Library. V. 1- Mar. 1980-. Periodical. English. Free. Municipal Reference Library, 121 North La Salle, City Hall 1004, Chicago IL 60602. **Tel** (312)744-4992. **DD** 016.3077. ctrl circ. ***Supersedes*** *Metropolitan Toronto Library Board. Municipal Reference Library. Selected List of New Titles, 0381-033X.*

US/0027-4283
MUSIC CATALOGING BULLETIN. See Music.

US/0364-7501
MUSICAL MAINSTREAM, THE. See Music.

DK
MUSIKALIER I DANSKE BIBLIOTEKER. See Music.

HU
MUSZAKI EGYETEMI KONYVTAROS. Periodical. Hungarian. sa. XI Budafoki UT 4-6, Budapest Hungary. **LC** Z675.U5; M88.

HU/0027-3015
MUSZAKI EGYETEMI KONYVTAROS. (1964)-. Hungarian.
Ind/Abst Magyar Konyv. Szak. Biblio.

●US/1075-9719
N-COMPASS (LINCOLN, NEB.). (N-COMPASS.). [N-compass]. **Added/Corp** Nebraska Library Commission. **VFOAT** N Compass. Vol. 1, No. 1 (Winter 1994)-. Periodical. English. qt. Nebraska Library Commission, 1420 P Street, Lincoln NE 68508-1683. **Tel** (402)471-2045, FAX (402)471-2045. **DD** 021. ***Continues*** *Overtones (Lincoln, Neb.), 0884-920X.*

GW/0027-7436
NACHRICHTEN FUER DOKUMENTATION. [Nachr. Dok.]. **Added/Corp** Deutsche Gesellschaft fuer Dokumentation. Deutscher Normenausschuss. Fachnormenausschuss fuer Bibliotheks-, Buch-, und Zeitschriftenwesen. Vol. 1 (June 1950)-. Academic Scholarly Publication. German (summaries and/or abstracts in English). bm (Feb., Apr., June, Aug., Oct., Dec.). DM234.00. Verlag Hoppenstedt & Company, Postfach 100139, D 64201 Darmstadt Germany. **Tel** 011 49 6151 380436. **ED** Hanjoacbin Samulowitz. **LC** Z1007; .N3. **DD** 025. **NLM** Z 1007 N123. **CODEN** NADOAW. **[CCC]. Bk Rev. Ad Acc. Pr Rev. Circ:** 2,400 (ctrl). Documents available from The Genuine Article, Ask*IEEE, CASDDS. ***Supersedes*** *Dokumentation und Arbeitstechnik.*
Desc: Leading Germany journal for all areas of information science and documentation including parts of telecommunications and linguistics as well as online information.
Ind/Abst Arts Humanit. Citation Index [Select. Cov.]; Chem. Abstr.; Curr. Contents Soc. Behav. Sci.; Energy Res. Abstr. (March 1982-); Inf. Sci. Abstr.; INSPEC (April 1970-); Libr. Inf. Sci. Abstr.; Libr. Lit.; Res. Alert [Full Cov.]; Soc. Sci. Cit. Index [Full Cov.].

JA
NAGOYA KOGYO DAIGAKU FUZOKU TOSHOKAN GAIYO. Main/Corp Nagoya Kogyo Daigaku. Toshokan. Japanese. Nagoya Kogyo Daigaku Fuzoku Toshokan, Gokishocho Showaku, Nagoya 466 Japan. **LC** Z846.N334; N33A.

US/0195-9093
NAME AUTHORITIES. CUMULATIVE MICROFORM EDITION. (NAME AUTHORITIES MICROFORM.). **Main/Corp** Library of Congress. Catalog Publication Division. (1977/Sept. 1979)-. Directory. English (Multiple languages). qt. $250.00 US; $300.00 other. Library of Congress / Cataloging Distribution Service, Washington DC 20541-5017. **Tel** (800)255-3666, (202)707-6100, FAX (202)707-1334. **LC** Microfiche Z695.1; .P4. cum. index. ***Absorbed*** *Library of Congress Name Headings with References, 0093-0563.*
Desc: Includes personal and corporate names, conference headings, uniform titles, and series; also lists geographic names of political and civil jurisdictions established by the Library of Congress.

XR/0862-7487
NARODNI KNIHOVNA. Added/Corp Narodni Knihovna v Praze. (1990)-. Periodical. Czech. bm. **LC** Z795.A1; N37.

US/0892-1733
NASIG NEWSLETTER, THE. (THE NASIG NEWSLETTER : THE NEWSLETTER OF THE NORTH AMERICAN SERIALS INTEREST GROUP.). [NASIG newsl.]. **Added/Corp** North American Serials Interest Group. **VAT** North American Serials Interest Group Newsletter. Vol. 1 No. 1 (Jan. 1986)-. Newsletter. English. bm. $20.00 (membership) US and Canada; $30.00 other. North American Serials Interest Group, One Veterans

Square, Apt D-2, Media PA 19063. **(Subscription address:** Ann Vidor, 1981 Innwood Road, Atlanta, GA 30329) **ED** Lenore R Wilkas. **DD** 051. **CODEN** NASNE6. **Circ:** 800.

CH/0034-5016
NATIONAL CENTRAL LIBRARY NEWSLETTER. Main/Corp Kuo Li Chung Yang Tu Shu Kuan (China). **VFOAT** Kuo Li Chung Yang Tu Shu Kuan Tung Hsun. (Apr. 1969)-. Periodical. English (Chinese). qt. Free. National Central Library, Bureau of International Exchange of Publications, 20 Chung Shan South Road, Taipei Taiwan 10040. **Tel** FAX 02-311-0155. **ED** Teresa Wang Chang. **LC** Z846.K864; K86b. **DD** 027.551/249. **Circ:** 2,000 (ctrl).
Desc: The current status of the development of library and information science in the National Central Library.

US/1041-5653
NATIONAL INFORMATION STANDARDS SERIES. [Natl. inf. stand. ser.]. **Added/Corp** National Information Standards Organization (U.S.). (1989)-. Monographic series. English. ir. Price varies per volume. Transaction Publishers / Rutgers State University, New Brunswick NJ 08903. **Tel** (908)932-2280 Ext. 105, FAX (908)932-3138. **DD** 025.
Desc: Develops and promotes voluntary standards for information science, libraries, and related publishing practices. Its procedures for developing and approving standards ensure that all interested stakeholders have an opportunity to participate in the standards making process. NISO is accredited by the American National Standards Institute.

US/0191-359X
NATIONAL LIBRARIAN : THE NLA NEWSLETTER. [Natl. libr.]. **Added/Corp** National Librarians Association (U.S.). **VFOAT** NLA Newsletter. **VAT** National Librarians Association Newsletter. Vol. 2, No. 4 (Nov. 1977)-. Newsletter. English. qt. $15.00 (one year), $28.00 (two year), $39.00 (three year) US;"$18.00 (one year), $34.00 (two year), $48.00 (three year) other. National Librarians Association, PO Box 486, Alma MI 48801. **Tel** (517)463-7227, FAX (517)463-8694. **ED** Peter Dollard. **[CCC].** Index available. **Bk Rev. Ad Acc. Circ:** 500. ***Continues*** *NLA Newsletter.*
Desc: Professional concerns of librarians: certification, standards of performance, quality of education, ethics, and professional welfare.
Ind/Abst Libr. Inf. Sci. Abstr.

CN/0027-9633
NATIONAL LIBRARY NEWS. (NATIONAL LIBRARY NEWS / NOUVELLES DE LA BIBLIOTHEQUE NATIONALE.). [Natl. Libr. news]. **Main/Corp** National Library of Canada. **VFOAT** Nouvelles de la Bibliotheque Nationale. Vol. 1 (Jan./March 1969)-. Periodical. English (French). mo. Free on request. National Library of Canada, 395 Wellington Street, Ottawa Ontario K1A 0N4 Canada. **Tel** (613)995-7969, (613)995-7969, (819)994-6881, FAX (613)991-9871. **ED** Wendy Newmann. **LC** Z883.O76; N37a. **DD** 027.5/713/84. **Circ:** 5,000 (ctrl). available on audiocassette; available in braille; available in large print. ***Absorbed*** *Accessible, 0315-0003.* ***Continued in part by*** *National Library of Canada. National Library Technical News., 0820-8093.*
Desc: Information on programs and services of the National Library of Canada of interest to the library community.
Ind/Abst Can. Index (?-?); Can. Period. Index (19??-); Libr. Inf. Sci. Abstr.

AT/1032-1829
NATIONAL LIBRARY OF AUSTRALIA NEWS. Added/Corp National Library of Australia. **VFOAT** Library of Australia News; National. Vol. 1, No. 1 (Oct. 1990)-. Periodical. English. mo. Free on request. National Library of Australia, Parkes Place, Canberra ACT, 2600 Australia. **Tel** 011 61 6 2621374, FAX 011 61 6 2731084. **ED** Menna Thomas. **LC** IN PROCESS; Z871.N38; N38.
Ind/Abst Aust. Educ. Index.

US/0149-9939
NATIONAL LIBRARY OF MEDICINE AUDIOVISUALS CATALOG. ***Ceased.*** **Main/Corp** National Library of Medicine (U.S.). **VFOAT** Audiovisuals Catalog; NLM Audiovisuals Catalog. (1977)-(Dec. 1993). Catalog. English. qt (January-December cumulative annual). Superintendent of Documents, US Government Printing Office, Washington DC 20402. **Tel** (202)275-3328, FAX (202)786-2377. **LC** R835; .U49B. **DD** 016.61. **NLM** W 18 N28015. ***Absorbed*** *Index to Audiovisual Serials in the Health Sciences.*
Desc: Lists audiovisuals cataloged by NLM from new additions to AVLINE (Audiovisuals Online), the Library's computerized database of information on audiovisual items used in health sciences education.

US/0163-4569
NATIONAL LIBRARY OF MEDICINE PROGRAMS AND SERVICES. [Natl. Libr. Med. programs serv.]. **Main/Corp** National Library of Medicine (U.S). **Added/Corp** National Institutes of Health (U.S.). **VFOAT** Programs and Services. (Fiscal Year 1977)-. English. an. National Library of Medicine, 8600 Rockville Pike, Bethesda MD 20894. **Tel** (301)496-6308. **ED** Robert B. Mehnert. **NLM** Z 675.M4 U56AN. available in microform. ***Continues*** *National Library of Medicine (U.S.). Programs and Services, 0093-0393.*
Desc: Provides statistical and narrative information regarding the National Library of Medicine's activities during a given fiscal year. Includes information on policy and direction, library services and operations, computer and communications systems and specialized information services.

UK/0950-7086
NATIONAL LIBRARY OF SCOTLAND NEWS. [Natl. Libr. Scotl. news]. **VFOAT** NLS News; News - National Library of Scotland. (1986)-. Periodical. English. sa. National Library of Scotland, George IV Bridge, Edinburgh EH1 1EW Scotland. **Tel** 031 226 4531, telex 72638 NLSEDI G. **DD** 027.5411.
Ind/Abst Museum Abstr.

US/0882-4339
NATIONAL PRESERVATION NEWS. (NATIONAL PRESERVATION NEWS : A NEWSLETTER OF THE NATIONAL PRESERVATION PROGRAM OFFICE, THE LIBRARY OF CONGRESS.). [Natl. preserv. news]. **Added/Corp** Library of Congress. National Preservation Program Office. No. 1 (July 1985)-. Newsletter. English. ir. Free. Library of Congress, 101 Independence Avenue SE, Washington DC 20540. **Tel** (202)287-5000. **(Subscription address:** Library of Congress National Preservation Program, Room G07, Washington DC 20540.) **ED** Carolyn Morrow Mann. **LC** Z701; .N29. **DD** 025.7. **Circ:** 3,000. ***Continues*** *National Preservation Report, 0190-9819.*
Desc: Presents updates on preservation techniques printed materials.

US
NATIONAL UNION CATALOG. LC CARD NUMBER INDEX, THE. (19??)-. Catalog. English. mo. Humanities Press, 165 1st Avenue, Atlantic Highlands NJ 07716. **Tel** (908)872-1441, (800)221-3845, FAX (908)872-0717, telex 752233. **LC** Z881.A1; U3723. **DD** 018/.1.

US/0090-0044
NATIONAL UNION CATALOG OF MANUSCRIPT COLLECTIONS. ***Ceased.*** **Added/Corp** Library of Congress. Library of Congress. Descriptive Cataloging Division. Library of Congress. Manuscripts Section. **VFOAT** Library of Congress National Union Catalog of Manuscript Collections. (1959/1961)-Vol. 29 (1993). Catalog. English. an. Library of Congress / Cataloging Distribution Service, Washington DC 20541-5017. **Tel** (800)255-3666, (202)707-6100, FAX (202)707-1334. **LC** Z6620.U5; N3. **NLM** Z 6620.U5 N277. cum. index.
Desc: Some 2,000 collections housed permanently in American repositories are included in each volume including letters, transcripts of oral recordings, and other materials of historical importance or research potential.

RU/0548-0019
NAUCNO-TEHNICESKAA INFORMACIA. SERIA 1, ORGANIZACIA I METODIKA INFORMACIONNOJ RABOTY. (NAUCHNO-TEKHNICHESKAIA INFORMATSIIA. SERIIA I. ORGANIZATSIIA I METODIKA INFORMATSIONNOI RABOTY.). [Naucno-teh. inf., Ser. 1 Organ. metod. inf. rab.]. **Added/Corp** Vsesoiuznyi Institut Nauchnoi i Tekhnicheskoi Informatsii (Soviet Union). **VFOAT** Organizatsiia i Metodika Informatsionnoi Raboty. (1967)-. Academic Scholarly Publication. Russian. Twelve times a year. $79.95. VINITI - Vsesoyuznyi Institut Nauchno-Tekhnicheskoi Informatsii, All-Union Scientific and Technical Information Institute, Baltiiskaia Ulitsa 14, 125219 Moscow Russia. **Tel** 238-46-00, FAX 9430060, telex 411160. **(Subscription address:** East View Publications Inc., 3020 Harbor Lane North, Suite 110, Minneapolis MN 55447.) **LC** Z699.A1; N35. **CODEN** NTOMAA. Documents available from The Genuine Article, Ask*IEEE, CASDDS. ***Supersedes in part*** *Nauchno-Tekhnicheskaia Informatsiia.*
Ind/Abst Chem. Abstr.; Compumath Citation Index [Full Cov.]; INSPEC (1969-); Res. Alert [Full Cov.]; Soc. Sci. Cit. Index [Full Cov.].

US
NCIP NEWS. Added/Corp Association of Research Libraries. Office of Management Studies. **VAT** North American Collections Inventory Project News. No. 1 (Jan. 1986)-. Periodical. English. Five times a year. $75.00. Association of Research Libraries, 21 Dupont Circle, Washington DC 20036. **Tel** (202)296-2296.

US
NCLIS NEWS / U.S. NATIONAL COMMISSION ON LIBRARIES AND INFORMATION SCIENCE. Added/Corp United States. National Commission on Libraries and Information Science. Vol. 1, Issue 1 (Feb. 1990)-. Periodical. English.

US/1043-8807
NEBRASKA LIBRARIES. ***Title Change.*** [Neb. libr.]. **Added/Corp** Nebraska Library Commission. **VFOAT** Directory of Nebraska Libraries. (198?)-(19??). English. an. Nebraska Library Commission, 1420 P Street, Lincoln NE 68508-1683. **Tel** (402)471-2045, FAX (402)471-2045. **LC** Z732.N37; N38. **DD** 027/.0025/782. **Circ:** 750 (ctrl). ***Continues*** *Nebraska Library Directory, 1043-8815.* ***Continued by*** *Nebraska Library Directory (1991).*

US/0028-1883
NEBRASKA LIBRARY ASSOCIATION QUARTERLY. Added/Corp Nebraska Library Association. **VFOAT** NLAQ. Vol. 1, No. 1 (Spring 1970)-. Periodical. English. Four times a year (Mar., June, Sept., Dec.). $20.00. Bergen Mercy Hospital Library, 7500 Mercy Road, Omaha NE 68124. **Tel** (402)398-6092. **ED** Ron Norman. **LC** WMLC 93/1362. **Bk Rev. Ad Acc. Pr Rev. Circ:** 960 (ctrl).
Desc: News and events about Nebraska, official organization of the Nebraska Library Association and library information in general.
Ind/Abst Libr. Lit.

US
NEBRASKA LIBRARY DIRECTORY / COMPILED AND PUBLISHED BY NEBRASKA LIBRARY COMMISSION. Added/Corp Nebraska Library Commission. (1991)-. Directory. English. **LC** Z732.N37; N38. **DD** 027/.0025/782. ***Continues*** *Nebraska Libraries, 1043-8807.*

US/0362-1618
NELB LINK. Main/Corp New England Library Board. **VAT** New England Library Board Link. V. 1- Mar. 1976-. Periodical. English. bm. Free to US; $3.00 other. NELB, 231 Capitol Avenue, Hartford CT 06115.

JA
NENPO. Main/Corp Hyogo Kenritsu Toshokan. **VFOAT** Hyogo Kenritsu Toshokan Nenpo. (19??)-. Japanese. an. Hyogo Kenritsu Toshokan, 1-ban 27-go Akashi Koen, Akashi-shi 673 Japan. **LC** Z846.H9; H94a.

US
NET-LINK : NEWSLETTER OF THE NATIONAL NETWORK OF LIBRARIES OF MEDICINE, MIDCONTINENTAL REGION. Added/Corp National Network of Libraries of Medicine (U.S.). Midcontinental Region. Midcontinental Regional Medical Library Program. Vol. 19, Issue 1 (July 1991)-. Newsletter. English. bm. **NLM** Z 675.M4; O21. ***Continues*** *Octasphere.*

US/0160-9742
NETWORK PLANNING PAPER. (NETWORK PLANNING PAPER / NETWORK DEVELOPMENT OFFICE.). **Added/Corp** Library of Congress. Network Development Office. Library of Congress. Network Development and MARC Standards Office. No. 1 (1978)-. Monographic series. English. ir. Price varies per volume. Library of Congress / Cataloging Distribution Service, Washington DC 20541-5017. **Tel** (800)255-3666, (202)707-6100, FAX (202)707-1334. **LC** UNC. **DD** 025/.04/05. **NLM** Z 674.7 N476. **CODEN** NPPADM.
Desc: Provides information on topics concerning the networking community of libraries and library networks in the United States.

US/0093-3341
NETWORK (TEMPE). (NETWORK.). V. 1 (Jan. 1974)-. Periodical. English. qt. $24.00. Association for Library Automation, Research Communications, PO Box 27235, Tempe AZ 85282. **LC** Z678.9.A1; N47. **DD** 025/.02/02854. ***Continues*** *LARC Newsletter.*
Ind/Abst Comput. Rev.

US
NETWORKING IN KENTUCKY. Added/Corp Kentucky. Dept. for Library and Archives. (1984)-. Periodical. English. ir. Free on request. Kentucky Department for Librairies and Archives, 300 Coffee Tree Road, PO Box 537, Frankfort KY 40602. **Tel** (502)875-7000.

GW/0028-3126
NEUE BUECHEREI, DIE. (1964)-. Periodical. German. Five times a year. DM37.60. Die Neue Bucherei, Ludwigstrasse 16, D 80539 Munich Germany. **Tel** 011 49 89 2198247. **LC** Z801; .N48.

US
NEVADA LIBRARY DIRECTORY AND STATISTICS. **See** Library and Information Sciences-Abstracting, Bibliographies and Statistics.

US/0887-3844
NEW DIRECTIONS IN INFORMATION MANAGEMENT. [New dir. inf. manage.]. (1986)-. Monographic series. English. ir. Price varies per volume. Greenwood Press Inc., PO Box 5007, Westport CT 06881-5007. **Tel** (203)226-3571, FAX (203)222-1502. **LC** UNC. **DD** 025. ***Continues*** *New Directions in Librarianship, 0147-1090.*

US/1063-5408
NEW ENGLAND LIBRARIES. [New Engl. libr.]. **Added/Corp** New England Library Association. Vol. 23, No. 3 (June 1991)-. Periodical. English. ir (6 issues). Comes with New England Library Association

membership ($35.00 membership). New England Library Association, Countryside Offices, 707 Turnpike Street, North Andover MA 01845. **Tel** (508)685-5966. **LC** Z673; .N434. **DD** 020/.6232/74. ***Continues*** *New England Library Association. NELA Newsletter, 0027-6448.*

US/0749-0313
NEW HAMPSHIRE LIBRARY STATISTICS. See Library and Information Sciences-Abstracting, Bibliographies and Statistics.

US/0362-2967
NEW JERSEY AREA LIBRARY DIRECTORY. Directory. English. New Jersey State Department of Education / New Jersey, 225 West State Street, Cn 500, Trenton NJ 08625. **Tel** (609)984-0905. **LC** Z732.N6; N62. **DD** 021/.0025/749.

US/0028-5811
NEW JERSEY LIBRARIES. [N. J. libr.]. **Added/Corp** New Jersey Library Association. (1967); New Series Vol. 1 (Summer 1968)-. Periodical. English. Four times a year (Mar., June, Sept., Dec.). $12.00. New Jersey Library Association, PO Box 1534, Trenton NJ 08608. **Tel** (609)394-8032, FAX (609)394-8164. **ED** January Adams (editor's address: Ortho Diagnostic Library, 1001 Route 202, Raritan, NJ 08869 (phone: (908)218-8165). **LC** Z732.N6; N64. **DD** 021/.009749. **Ad Acc.** available on microfilm and microfiche from University Microfilms International (UMI).
Ind/Abst Libr. Lit.

US/0735-8571
NEW LIBRARY SCENE, THE. [New libr. scene]. **Added/Corp** Library Binding Institute. Vol. 1, No. 1 (Sept./Oct. 1982)-. Periodical. English. bm (6 issues). $18.00 US; $20.00 Canada; $21.00 other. Library Binding Institute / Edina, MN, 7401 Metro Boulevard, Suite 325, Edina MN 55439. **Tel** (612)835-4707, FAX (612)835-4780. **ED** Sally Grauer. **LC** Z671; .N433. **DD** 025.7/05. Index available. cum. index. **Bk Rev. Ad Acc. Circ:** 3,000. available on microfilm and microfiche from University Microfilms International (UMI). ***Continues*** *Library Scene, 0090-8746.*
Desc: Semi-specialized publication for librarians. Focus on conservation preservation, collection management, user services, and binding operations.
Ind/Abst Art Archaeol. Tech. Abstr.; Graph. Arts Bull. Inst. Pap. Sci. Technol. (Jan. 1989, Mar. 1989, Aug. 1989, Dec. 1989); Inf. Instruc. Technol.; Inf. Sci. Abstr.; Libr. Lit.

UK/0307-4803
NEW LIBRARY WORLD. [New libr. world]. Vol. 73 (July 1971)-. Periodical. English. Thirteen times a year. $1429.00. MCB University Press, 60 62 Toller Lane, Bradford West Yorkshire BD8 9BX England. **Tel** 011 44 274 499821, FAX 011 44 274 547143, telex 51317 MCBUNI G. **(Subscription address:** MCB University Press / US and Canada Subscriptions, PO Box 10812, Birmingham AL 35201-0812.**) ED** Ian Pettman. **LC** Z671; .L72. Index Available, published separately, free-automatically sent. **Bk Rev. Circ:** 1,100 (ctrl). available on microfilm and microfiche from University Microfilms International (UMI). ***Absorbed*** *Librarian's World.*
Desc: One of Britain's leading journals for librarians and information managers. In fact, a recent survey showed it to be one of the most valued publications in the field and its bright, lively approach makes the journal compulsive reading.
Ind/Abst Educ. Technol. Abstr.; Libr. Inf. Sci. Abstr.; Libr. Lit.; Sage Race Relat. Abstr.

US
NEW MEXICO LIBRARY DIRECTORY. Directory. English. an. New Mexico State Library, 325 Don Gaspar, Santa Fe NM 87503. **Tel** (505)827-3800, FAX (505)827-3888. **ED** Daryl Black. **LC** Z732.N65; N48. **DD** 027/.0025/789. ctrl circ.
Desc: Listing of names, addresses, telephone numbers and key personnel for all libraries - public, community, academic, special, school and church - in New Mexico.

US/0278-9329
NEW MEXICO LIBRARY STATISTICS. See Library and Information Sciences-Abstracting, Bibliographies and Statistics.

US/0028-6680
NEW SERIAL TITLES. Added/Corp Joint Committee on the Union List of Serials. Library of Congress. Library of Congress. Serial Record Division. Library of Congress. Cataloging Distribution Service. (Jan. 1953)-. Bibliography. English. ir (eight monthly issues, four quarterly issues and annual cumulations which are self-cumulative through periods of five or ten years). $440.00 North America; $490.00 other. Library of Congress / Cataloging Distribution Service, Washington DC 20541-5017. **Tel** (800)255-3666, (202)707-6100, FAX (202)707-1334. **LC** Z6945.U5; S42; PN4832. **DD** 016.05. **NLM** Z 6945; N532. **[CCC].** cum. index. ***Continues*** *Serial Titles Newly Received, 0090-0060.*
Desc: List of serial bibliographic records for titles cataloged by CONSER members.

AT
NEW SOUTH WALES GOVERNMENT DEPARTMENT LIBRARIES. English. Government Departments Unit, State Library of New South Wales, Level 8 CAGA Centre, 8-18 Bent Street, Sydney New South Wales 2000 Australia. **LC** Z870.N43; N49. **DD** 027.5/09944.

US/0897-1137
NEW TECH NEWS. [New tech news]. **Added/Corp** Council of Wisconsin Libraries. Vol. 1, No. 1 (April 1987)-. Periodical. English. Ten times a year (Jan., Feb., Mar., Apr., May, June/July, Aug./Sept., Oct., Nov., Dec.). $60.00. Council of Wisconsin Libraries, 728 State Street/Room 464, Madison WI 53706. **Tel** (608)263-4962, FAX (608)263-3684. **ED** Cheryl Bradley. **DD** 025. **Circ:** 350.
Desc: Written for busy professionals who need concise, practical information. This monthly publication reports on how librarians are using technology, and describes new products and trends and abstracts technical articles.

US
NEW YORK AND NEW JERSEY REGIONAL MEDICAL LIBRARY NEWS. V. 1- ; Oct. 1976-. Periodical. English. bm. New York Academy of Medicine, 2 East 103rd Street, New York NY 10029. **Tel** (212)876-8200.

AT/0157-7662
NEW ZEALAND BOOKS IN PRINT / NEW ZEALAND BOOK PUBLISHERS ASSOCIATION. See Publishing-Abstracting, Bibliographies and Statistics.

NZ/0028-8381
NEW ZEALAND LIBRARIES. [N.Z. libr.]. **Added/Corp** New Zealand Library Association. Vol. 1 (Aug. 1937)-. Periodical. English. qt (Mar., June, Sep., Dec.). 45.00NZ$ New Zealand; 55.00NZ$ other. New Zealand Library Association Inc, PO Box 12-212, Brandon Street, Wellington 1 New Zealand. **Tel** 011 64 4 4735834, FAX 011 64 4 4723967. **ED** K Porter. **LC** Z671; .N45. **DD** 020/.5. **[CCC].** Index available. cum. index. **Bk Rev. Ad Acc. Circ:** 2,000 (ctrl). available on microfilm and microfiche from University Microfilms International (UMI).
Desc: Aims to record significant developments in New Zealand librarianship, promote discussion on matters of library interest, contribute to continuing education and publish results of library research.
Ind/Abst Annu. Bibliogr. Engl. Lang. Lit.; Inf. Sci. Abstr.; Libr. Inf. Sci. Abstr.; Libr. Lit.

US/1074-3596
NEWBERRY NEWSLETTER, A. [Newberry newsl.]. **Added/Corp** Newberry Library. No. 1 (Sept. 1973)-. Periodical. English. ir. only available through Newberry Library Association membership. Newberry Library, 60 West Walton Street, Chicago IL 60610. **Tel** (312)943-9090 ext. 472. **ED** Terry Sullivan. **Circ:** 5,500 (ctrl).
Desc: Matters pertaining to the Newberry Library and its various activities: acquisitions, development, research and education, and library services, conservation, etc.

CN/0832-9249
NEWFOUNDLAND LIBRARY ASSOCIATION BULLETIN. [Nfld. Libr. Assoc. bull.]. (Fall 1985)-. Bulletin. English. sa. Free. Newfoundland Library Association, PO Box 23192, St. John's Newfoundland A1B 4J9 Canada. **Tel** (709)737-3214, FAX (709)737-3118. **DD** 020/.6234/718.

US
NEWS & VIEWS OF THE SOUTH CAROLINA LIBRARY ASSOCIATION. Main/Corp South Carolina Library Association. **VFOAT** News and Views of the South Carolina Library Association; News & Views; News and Views. Vol. 1, No. 1 (Feb. 1979)-. Periodical. English. Three times a year. $10.00 (institutions) South Carolina; $20.00 (institutions) other. South Carolina Library Association / Goose Creek, PO Box 219, Goose Creek SC 29445. **Tel** (803)792-8020. ***Absorbed*** *South Carolina Librarian.*

AT
NEWS BULLETIN - SCHOOL LIBRARY ASSOCIATION OF VICTORIA. [News bull. - Sch. Libr. Assoc. Vic.]. (1971)-. English. bm. (Comes with School Library Assn of Victoria membership). School Library Association of Victoria, PO Box 22, Ashburton VIC 3147 Australia. **Tel** (03)807 0464. **ED** Judy Buckley.
Ind/Abst Aust. Educ. Index; Aust. Libr. Inf. Sci. Abstr. (1990-).

US
NEWS BULLETIN - SPECIAL LIBRARIES ASSOCIATION, BOSTON CHAPTER. *Title Change.* Main/Corp Special Libraries Association. Boston Chapter. **VFOAT** News Bulletin of the Boston Chapter, SLA; Boston Chapter News Bulletin. (Sept. 1934). Bulletin. English. bm. Arthur D Little Inc, 15 Acorn Park, Cambridge MA 02140. **LC** Z671; .S75. ***Continued by*** *Boston Chapter News Bulletin, Including Maine, Massachussetts, New Hampshire, and Vermont.*

US/0146-1842
NEWS FOR SOUTH CAROLINA LIBRARIES. Main/Corp South Carolina. State Library, Columbia. (19??)-. Periodical. English. mo. South Carolina State Library, Box 11469, Columbia SC 29211. **LC** Z732.S72; S56b. **DD** 021/.009757. ctrl circ. ***Continues*** *News for South Carolina Libraries, 0146-1842.*

US/0747-6035
NEWS FROM C.U.N.Y. LIBRARIES. (NEWS FROM C.U.N.Y. LIBRARIES : A PUBLICATION OF THE LIBRARY ASSOCIATION OF THE CITY UNIVERSITY OF NEW YORK.). **VFOAT** News from CUNY Libraries. Periodical. English. bm. News from C U N Y Libraries, c/o Hunter College Libraries, 695 Park Avenue, New York NY 10021. **DD** 027.

FR/0257-0009
NEWS FROM ISDS. (NEWS FROM ISDS / INTERNATIONAL SERIALS DATA SYSTEM.). **Added/Corp** International Serials Data System. **VFOAT** News from I.S.D.S. No. 1 (1984)-. Periodical. English. Free on request. ISSN International Centre, 20 rue Bachaumont, F-75002 Paris France. **Tel** 011 33 1 42367381, FAX 011 33 1 40263243, telex SERIALS 219847F.

US/0731-3527
NEWS FROM THE LIBRARY OF CONGRESS. (NEWS FROM THE LIBRARY OF CONGRESS / INFORMATION OFFICE.). **Added/Corp** Library of Congress. Information Office. **VFOAT** News. (1939)-. Periodical. English. Four times a year. Free on request. National Library Service for the Blind and Physically Handicapped, Library of Congress, 1291 Taylor Street Northwest, Washington DC 20542. **Tel** (800)424-8567, (202)707-5100, (800)424-9100. **LC** Z733.U6; N44. **DD** 027.573.

AT/0810-042X
NEWS LETTER - LIBRARIANS' CHRISTIAN FELLOWSHIP OF AUSTRALIA. [News lett. - Libr. Christ. Fellowsh. Aust.]. (1982)-. English. ir. **ED** E Reid-Smith, PO Box 74, Wagga Wagga NSW 2650 Australia. **DD** 020.5.
Ind/Abst Aust. Educ. Index.

US/1047-417X
NEWS LIBRARY NEWS. (NEWS LIBRARY NEWS : BULLETIN OF THE NEWSPAPER DIVISION OF SPECIAL LIBRARIES ASSOCIATION.). [News libr. news]. **Added/Corp** Special Libraries Association. Newspaper Division. Special Libraries Association. News Division. Vol. 2 No. 3 (Jan. 1980)- Vol. 15 (1992-93)-. Bulletin. English. Four times a year (Published Quarterly). $30.00. Advocate Library, PO Box 588, Baton Rouge LA 70821. **Tel** (504)388-0327. **ED** Linda Henderson. **DD** 026. **Ad Acc, Adv Mgr:** Gay Nemeti, **Tel** (305)376-3403. Full Page (B&W) $400.00. Half Page (B&W) $200.00. **Circ:** 780. available on an online database from VU-TEXT. ***Continues*** *Short Takes.*

CN/0842-9707
NEWS / METROPOLITAN TORONTO REFERENCE LIBRARY. [News - Metrop. Tor. Ref. Libr.]. Vol. 14, No. 5 (June/July 1988)-. Periodical. English. bm. Free. Metropolitan Toronto Library Board, 789 Yonge Street, Toronto Ontario M4W 2G8 Canada. **Tel** (416)393-7134, telex 06-22232. **DD** 027.4713/541. ***Continues*** *News-Metropolitan Toronto Library Board, 0318-9244.*

US
NEWS / MONTANA STATE LIBRARY. Vol. 13, No. 1 (Jan. 1984)-. Periodical. English. mo. Montana State Library, 1515 East 6th Avenue, Helena MT 59620. **Tel** 444-5349, FAX 444-5612. **Pr Rev. Circ:** 1,400. ***Continues*** *Montana Newsletter.*

US/0027-965X
NEWS (NATIONAL LIBRARY OF MEDICINE (US)). (NEWS / NATIONAL LIBRARY OF MEDICINE.). [News - Natl. Libr. Med.]. **Added/Corp** National Library of Medicine (U.S.). Vol. 11, No. 10 (Oct. 1956)-. Periodical. English. ir (10 to 12 per year). Free on request. National Library of Medicine, 8600 Rockville Pike, Bethesda MD 20894. **Tel** (301)496-6308. **ED** Roger L. Gilkeson. **Circ:** 6,000 (ctrl). available on microfilm from University Microfilms International (UMI). ***Continues*** *News of the U.S. Armed Forces Medical Library.*
Desc: Provides information about the National Library of Medicine people, programs, projects and publications. Programs range from traditional library services to advanced computer information services.
Ind/Abst Cumul. Index Nurs. Allied Health Lit.

CN/0829-4321
NEWSLETTER / ALBERTA ASSOCIATION OF COLLEGE LIBRARIANS. [Newsl. - Alta. Assoc. Coll. Libr.]. **Added/Corp** Alberta Association of College Librarians. Vol. 7, No. 1 (Fall 1984)-. Newsletter. English. sa. 20.00Can$. Alberta Council of College Librarians, Buchanan Library, 3000 College Drive, Lethbridge ALT T1K 1L6 Canada. **Tel** (403)382-6944. **DD** 027.7/097123. ***Continues*** *Alberta Council of College Librarians. Newsletter - Alberta Council of College Librarians., 0707-7327.*

US/0733-3048
NEWSLETTER / AMERICAN SOCIETY OF INDEXERS. ***Title Change.*** [Newsl. - Am. Soc. Index.]. **Main/Corp** American Society of Indexers. **Added/Corp** American Society of Indexers. **VFOAT** ASI Newsletter. (29??)-(1992). Newsletter. English. qt. American Society of Indexers Inc, Box 386, Port Arnasas TX 78373. **Tel** (512)749-4052. **CODEN** NEAIEV. **Ad Acc. Circ:** 700 (ctrl). ***Continued by** Key Words, 1064-1211.*

US/0003-1399
NEWSLETTER - AMERICAN THEOLOGICAL LIBRARY ASSOCIATION. **Main/Corp** American Theological Library Association. **VFOAT** ATLA Newsletter. **VAT** American Theological Library Association Newsletter. (Nov. 1953)-. Newsletter. English. Four times a year. $15.00. American Theological Library Association, 820 Church Street, 3rd Floor, Evanston IL 60201. **Tel** (708)869-7788, FAX (708)869-8513. **LC** Z675.T4; A6.

US/1040-8517
NEWSLETTER / ASIAN/PACIFIC AMERICAN LIBRARIANS ASSOCIATION. [Newsl. - Asian/Pac. Am. Libr. Assoc.]. **Added/Corp** Asian/Pacific American Librarians Association. **VFOAT** APALA Newsletter. (198?)-. Periodical. English. Four times a year. $25.00 institutions; $10.00 individuals. Ball State University / Asian/Pacific American Librarians Association, c/o Jack Tsukammota, 4000 University Avenue, Muncie IN 47306. **Tel** (317)285-5722. **ED** Sharad Karkhanis. **DD** 020. ***Continues** Asian/Pacific American Librarians Association.*

US/0197-4815
NEWSLETTER - ASSOCIATION OF LAW LIBRARIES OF UPSTATE NEW YORK. **Main/Corp** Association of Law Libraries of Upstate New York. Vol. 1 (1974)-. Newsletter. English.
Ind/Abst Leg. Inf. Manage. Index (19??-).

AT/0728-3717
NEWSLETTER - AUSTRALIAN ASSOCIATION OF FILM AND VIDEO LIBRARIES. [Newsl. - Aust. Assoc. Film Video Libr.]. (1981)-. Periodical. English. qt. 20.00Aus$ (institutions); 15.00Aus$ (individuals). Australian Association of Film & Video Libraries, PO Box 142, Parkville VIC 3052 Australia. **Tel** 03 3472772, FAX (03)651-1502. **DD** 026.7914066094. Index available.
Ind/Abst Aust. Educ. Index.

AT/0311-5984
NEWSLETTER / AUSTRALIAN LAW LIBRARIANS' GROUP. ***Title Change.*** **Added/Corp** Australian Law Librarians' Group. **VFOAT** Australian Law Librarians' Group Newsletter; ALLG Newsletter. No. 1 (Dec. 1973)-No. 113 (Dec. 1992). Newsletter. English. bm. Australian Law Librarian's Group, PO Box E40, Queen Victoria Terrace, Canberra ACT 2600 Australia. **Tel** 011 61 6 2506577, FAX 011 61 6 2505941. **ED** Mrs. J. Elliott. **Bk Rev. Ad Acc. Circ:** 400. ***Continued by** Australian Law Librarian, 1039-6616.*
Ind/Abst Aust. Educ. Index (199?-); Aust. Libr. Inf. Sci. Abstr. (1981-); Leg. Inf. Manage. Index.

CN/0845-5376
NEWSLETTER / CANADIAN ASSOCIATION FOR GRADUATE EDUCATION IN LIBRARY, ARCHIVAL, AND INFORMATION STUDIES. See Education-Higher Education.

CN/0383-1299
NEWSLETTER / CANADIAN ASSOCIATION OF MUSIC LIBRARIES. [Newsl. - Can. Assoc. Music Libr.]. **Added/Corp** Canadian Association of Music Libraries. **VFOAT** Nouvelles; CAML Newsletter. **VAT** CAML Newsletter (1978); ACBM Nouvelles (1978). Vol. 7, No. 1 (Feb. 1978)-. Newsletter. English (French). Three times a year. $25.00 US; 80.00Can$ (institution), 65.00Can$ (individual) membership to Canadian Association of Music Libraries. Canadian Association of Music Libraries, 2500 University Drive Northwest, Music Library, Calgary Alberta T2N 1N4 Canada. **Tel** (403)220-3611, FAX (403)282-6837. **ED** Kathleen McMorrow. **DD** 026/.78/06071. **Bk Rev. Ad Acc. Circ:** 150 (ctrl). ***Continues** Canadian Association of Music Libraries. C A M L Newsletter, 0825-3730.*
Desc: Articles regarding Canadian music, cataloging practices, bibliographic projects, and information of interest to music libraries.

CN/0821-6657
NEWSLETTER - CHANGE. (NEWSLETTER / CHANGE, UTLAS USERS' GROUP). [Newsl. - Change]. **Added/Corp** CHANGE (Organization). (July 1982)-. Newsletter. English. an. Free. ISM Library Information Services, 3300 Bloor Street West, West Tower 16th Floor, Etobicoke Ontario M8X 2X2, Canada. **Tel** (416)236-7171, FAX (416)236-7541. **ED** Jim Oxman. **DD** 025/.04/09713541. **Circ:** 5,000 (ctrl).
Desc: Contains information of interest to libraries, particularly in Saskatchewan.

US/0736-8887
NEWSLETTER (CHINESE AMERICAN LIBRARIANS ASSOCIATION). (NEWSLETTER / CHINESE-AMERICAN LIBRARIANS ASSOCIATION.). [Newsl. - Chin. Am. Libr. Assoc.]. **Added/Corp** Chinese-American Librarians Association. No. 13 (Aug. 1978)-. Periodical. English. Three times a year (Feb., June, Oct.). $15.00 (individuals); $45.00 (institutions) Comes with Chinese American Librarians Association membership. Columbia College Univesity / Illinois, 600 South Michigan Avenue, c/o C Hsieh, Chicage IL 60605. **Tel** (312)663-1600 ext. 122. **ED** Diana Shih and Gladys Chaw. **Bk Rev. Ad Acc. Circ:** 500 (ctrl). ***Continues** Chinese American Librarians Association. Newsletter to Members and Friends.*
Desc: Contain news items promoting the Chinese-American librarianship, activities, member's and issues of the Asian-Americans.

US/0882-6846
NEWSLETTER - CONSORTIUM OF RHODE ISLAND ACADEMIC AND RESEARCH LIBRARIES. (NEWSLETTER / CONSORTIUM OF RHODE ISLAND ACADEMIC AND RESEARCH LIBRARIES, CRIARL.). **Main/Corp** Consortium of Rhode Island Academic and Research Libraries. Vol. 1, No. 1 (March 1982)-. Newsletter. English. Three times a year.

US
NEWSLETTER / CORNELL UNIVERSITY LIBRARIES, FLOWER VETERINARY LIBRARY. **Main/Corp** Flower Veterinary Library. **Added/Corp** New York State College of Veterinary Medicine. Vol. 24, No. 4 (July/Sept. 1982)-. Newsletter. English. qt. ***Continues** Cornell University Libraries Veterinary Library Newsletter.*

CN/0840-3902
NEWSLETTER - DALHOUSIE UNIVERSITY. SCHOOL OF LIBRARY AND INFORMATION STUDIES. (NEWSLETTER.). [Newsl. - Dalhous. Univ., Sch. Libr. Inf. Serv.]. **Main/Corp** Dalhousie University. School of Library and Information Studies. Vol. 16 (1986/87)-. Newsletter. English. Dalhousie University / School of Library & Information Studies, Halifax Nova Scotia B3H 4H8 Canada. **Tel** (902)494-3656, FAX (902)494-2451, telex 019-21863. **DD** 020/.7/1171622. ***Continues** Newsletter - Dalhousie University. School of Library Service, 0315-0054.*

US/0195-4016
NEWSLETTER - FINGER LAKES LIBRARY SYSTEM. **Main/Corp** Finger Lakes Library System. V. 1- Sept. 1979-. Newsletter. English. Finger Lakes Library System, PO Box 219, 314 North Cayuga Street, Ithaca NY 14850.

CN/0822-658X
NEWSLETTER (FRIENDS OF THE OTTAWA PUBLIC LIBRARY). (NEWSLETTER / THE FRIENDS OF THE OTTAWA PUBLIC LIBRARY.). [Newsl. - Friends Ottawa Public Libr.]. **VFOAT** Bulletin. **VAT** Bulletin - Amis de la Bibliotheque Publique d'Ottawa. Vol. 1, No. 2 (Nov. 1983)-. Newsletter. English (French). Free to members. Friends of the Ottawa Public Library, 120 Metcalfe Street, Ottawa Ontario K1P 5M2 Canada. **DD** 027.4/06/071384. ***Continues** Friends (Ottawa, Ont.), 0820-9901.*

CN/1189-9999
NEWSLETTER - HALIFAX DISTRICT SCHOOL BOARD. LIBRARY DEPT. (1989). (NEWSLETTER / DEPARTMENT OF SCHOOL LIBRARIES.). [Newsl. - Halifax Dist. Sch. Board, Libr. Dep.]. **Main/Corp** Halifax District School Board. Library Dept. (June 1989)-. Newsletter. English. Board of School Commissioners, Department of School Libraries, 2790 Oxford Street, Halifax NS B3L 2V5. **DD** 027.8/09716/225. ***Continues** Halifax District School Board. Library Dept. Library News., 0229-0162.*

US/0250-4294
NEWSLETTER - IFLA. SECTION OF BIOLOGICAL AND MEDICAL SCIENCES LIBRARIES. **Main/Corp** International Federation of Library Associations and Institutions. Section of Biological and Medical Sciences Libraries. **VAT** Newsletter - International Federation of Library Associations and Institutions. Section of Biological and Medical Libraries. (1980)-. English. qt. $10.00. IFLA Section of Biological & Medical Science, 146 Elmore Road, Rochester NY 14618. **Tel** (716)244-8703. **ED** Lucretia McClure. **Circ:** 150.

CN/0827-2743
NEWSLETTER / INSTITUTE OF VICTORIA LIBRARIANS. ***Title Change.*** [Newsl. - Inst. Vic. Libr.]. **Added/Corp** Institute of Victoria Librarians. **VFOAT** IVL Newsletter. **VAT** Institute of Victoria Librarians newsletter. (Spring 1980)-(1993). Newsletter. English. ir. Institute of Victoria Librarians, PO Box 634, Victoria British Columbia V8W 2X7 Canada. **DD** 020/.624/71134; 020/.6/2471128. ***Continued by** Newsletter (Victoria Librarians Association), 1198-5941.*

US
NEWSLETTER / INTERNATIONAL ASSOCIATION OF SCHOOL LIBRARIANSHIP. **Added/Corp** International Association of School Librarianship. Vol. 1, No. 1 (1971)-. Newsletter. English. qt. $20.00 US, Canada, Japan, Australia, Europe; $15.00 other. International Association of School Librarianship, Box 19586, Kalamazoo MI 49019. **Tel** (616)343-5728.

AT/0157-2229
NEWSLETTER - LIBRARY ASSOCIATION OF AUSTRALIA. NORTHERN TERRITORY BRANCH. (1978)-. English. ir.
Ind/Abst Aust. Educ. Index; Aust. Libr. Inf. Sci. Abstr.

CN/0823-1184
NEWSLETTER / MANITOBA LIBRARY TRUSTEES ASSOCIATION. [Newsl. - Manit. Libr. Trustees Assoc.]. **Added/Corp** Manitoba Library Trustees Association. (Winter 1979)-. Newsletter. English. ir. Free. Manitoba Library Trustees Association, Coulter Manitoba R0M 0G0 Canada. **Tel** (204)649-2390. **ED** Pat Downey. **DD** 027.47127. **Circ:** 40 (ctrl). ***Continues** Manitoba Library Trustees Association (Newsletter), 0823-1176.*
Desc: Information and/or announcements concerning public library concerns in Manitoba for Manitoba library trustees.

US/0749-338X
NEWSLETTER / MAP ONLINE USERS GROUP. ***Suspended.*** **Main/Corp** Map Online Users Group. No. 5 (Oct. 1980)-(19??). Newsletter. English. ir. $10.00. University of South Carolina Map Library, Columbia SC 29208. **Tel** (803)777-2802. **ED** Linda D Cottrell. **DD** 025. **Circ:** 100. ***Continues** OCLC Map Users Group. Newsletter, 0749-3398.*
Desc: News and information for map catalogers and reference librarians using map online data bases.

UK/0144-7599
NEWSLETTER MARC. USERS GROUP. [Newsl. Marc Users Group]. **VFOAT** Newsletter Machine Readable Cataloguing Users Group. (1976)-. English. qt.
Ind/Abst Libr. Inf. Sci. Abstr.

CN/0713-2727
NEWSLETTER (MARIGOLD LIBRARY SYSTEM). (NEWSLETTER.). [Newsl. - Marigold Libr. Syst.]. **Added/Corp** Marigold Library System. Vol. 1, No. 1 (Apr. 1982)-. Periodical. English. Four times a year (Mar., July, Sept., Dec.). 5.60Can$. Marigold Library System Newsletter, PO Box 1830, Strathmore Alberta T0J 3H0 Canada. **Tel** (403)934-5334. **DD** 027.47123/3. ctrl circ.

CN/0843-0217
NEWSLETTER / MCGILL UNIVERSITY GRADUATE SCHOOL OF LIBRARY AND INFORMATION STUDIES. See Education-Higher Education.

US
NEWSLETTER - MID-AMERICA ASSOCIATION OF LAW LIBRARIES. **Main/Corp** Mid-America Association of Law Libraries. (197?)-. Newsletter. English.
Ind/Abst Leg. Inf. Manage. Index (19??-).

US/0893-2956
NEWSLETTER - NEW MEXICO LIBRARY ASSOCIATION. (NEWSLETTER.). [Newsl. - N.M. Libr. Assoc.]. **Main/Corp** New Mexico Library Association. **VFOAT** New Mexico Library Association Newsletter; NMLA Newsletter. Vol.3, No.5 (Nov. 1975)-. Newsletter. English. Four times a year. $10.00. New Mexico Library Association, 11200 Montgomery Northeast Street 8, Albuquerque NM 87111. **Tel** (505)768-5174. **ED** Peter Ives and Heidi Miller. **DD** 027. **Ad Acc, Adv Mgr:** Carol Myers. **Circ:** 600. ***Continues** New Mexico Libraries Newsletter; New Mexico Library Bulletin; New Mexico Libraries Newsletter.*
Desc: Presents articles on libraries and librarians in New Mexico, with New Mexico Library Association news.

CN/1182-0209
NEWSLETTER / NOVA SCOTIA LIBRARY ASSOCIATION. [Newsl. - N.S. Libr. Assoc.]. **Added/Corp** Nova Scotia Library Association. **VFOAT** NSLA Newsletter. Vol. 17, No. 1 (Dec. 1989)-. Periodical. English. qt. Free to members, membership $5.00 (per year). Nova Scotia Library Association, Halifax City Regional Library, 5381 Spring Garden Road, Halifax Nova Scotia B3J 1E9 Canada. **DD** 020/.6/234716. ***Continues** NSLA News., 0319-8545.*

CN/0708-1979
NEWSLETTER OF THE YELLOWHEAD REGIONAL LIBRARY. **Main/Corp** Yellowhead Regional Library. V. 4, No. 4- Oct. 1978-. Newsletter. English. mo. Yellowhead Regional Library, PO Box 400, Spruce Grove Alberta T7X 2Y1 Canada. **Tel** (403)962-2003. **ED** Edith Parsons. **DD** 027.4/7123/3. **Bk Rev. Circ:** 300 (ctrl). ***Continues*** *Nexus, 0383-0748.*
Desc: Newsletter for library personnel in the region. Contains reviews and other news relevant to the region.

NE
NEWSLETTER ON EDUCATION AND TRAINING PROGRAMMES FOR INFORMATION PERSONNEL. ***Title Change.*** **Added/Corp** International Federation for Documentation. International Federation for Information and Documentation. International Federation for Documentation. General Secretariat. FID News Bulletin. International Federation for Information and Documentation. FID News Bulletin. Vol. 3, issue 1 (Spring 1981)-Vol. 14, issue 3 (Autumn 1992). Newsletter. English. qt. International Federation for Information and Documentation, PO Box 90402, 2509 LK Hague Netherlands. **Tel** 011 31 70 3140509, FAX 011 31 70 834827, telex 34402 KB GV NL. **ED** Marta Dosa. **LC** Z668; .N48. **CODEN** NETPDA. **Bk Rev. Circ:** 2,000. ***Continues*** *Newsletter on Education and Training Programmes for Specialized Information Personnel.* ***Continued by*** *ET Newsletter.*
Desc: Serves to support information, library and archives education worldwide.

US/0028-9485
NEWSLETTER ON INTELLECTUAL FREEDOM. [Newsl. intellect. freedom]. **Added/Corp** American Library Association. Committee on Intellectual Freedom. **VFOAT** Intellectual Freedom. (June 1952)-. Newsletter. English. Six times a year (Jan., Mar., May, July, Sept., Nov.). $40.00 US & Canada & Mexico; $50.00 other. American Library Association, 50 East Huron Street, Chicago IL 60611. **Tel** (312)944-6780, (800)545-2433, FAX (312)944-2641. **(Subscription address:** American Library Association, Subscription Department, 434 West Downer, Aurora IL 60506-9936.**)** **ED** Judith F. Krug. **LC** Z671; .N47. **[CCC]. Bk Rev. Circ:** 3,000. available on microfilm and microfiche from University Microfilms International (UMI).
Desc: Coverage of censorship incidents affecting libraries, schools and the press. Reports in court decisions and legislation affecting 1st Amendment rights and includes review and bibliography.
Ind/Abst Annu. Bibliogr. Engl. Lang. Lit.; Curr. Lit. Fam. Plan.; Libr. Lit.

US/1046-3410
NEWSLETTER ON SERIALS PRICING ISSUES. [Newsl. ser. pricing issues]. **Added/Corp** American Library Association. Resources and Technical Services Division. Association for Library Collections & Technical Services. **VFOAT** Newsletter on Serials Pricing. No. 2 (March 30, 1989)-. Newsletter. English. ir. Free on request. Marcia Tuttle, CB #3938 Davis Library, University of North Carolina at Chapel Hill, Chapel Hill NC 27599. **Tel** (919)962-1067. **LC** Z692.S5; N48. **DD** 025. **CODEN** NSPIEY. available on an online database from DATALINX; BITNET; and ALANET. ***Continues*** *ALA/RTSD Newsletter on Serials Pricing Issues, 1046-3402.*
Desc: Reports on committee meetings, discussion groups, court actions, and publishers' responses, and acts as a forum for letters and queries from librarians, authors, and publishers.

CN/0229-2645
NEWSLETTER / ONTARIO ASSOCIATION OF LIBRARY TECHNICIANS. [Newsl. - Ont. Assoc. Libr. Tech]. **Added/Corp** Ontario Association of Library Technicians. **VFOAT** Nouvelles. Vol. 1, No. 1 (Apr. 10, 1976)-. Newsletter. English (French). Three times a year. comes with membership. Ontario Association of Library Technicians- ABO Publications, PO Box 76010, Oakville Ontario L6M 3H5 Canada. **Tel** (905)890-1099. **ED** Pat Kitely. **DD** 023/.3. **Bk Rev. Circ:** 500 (ctrl).
Desc: Contains material relevant to library technicians, i.e. pertaining to library science, job placement, continuing education, regional information, conference information, etc.

US/0196-6707
NEWSLETTER - PITTSBURGH REGIONAL LIBRARY CENTER, INC. **Main/Corp** Pittsburgh Regional Library Center. (196?)-. Newsletter. English. ir (ten issues per year). $25.00. Pittsburgh Regional Library Center, Beatty Hall & Chatham Hall, Pittsburgh PA 15232. **Tel** (412)441-6409, FAX (412)441-6509. **ED** H E Broadbent III. **Circ:** 700.
Desc: Library resource sharing with particular emphasis on Western Pennsylvania, West Virginia and Western Maryland including OCLC applications, microcomputer, and continuing education.

NE
NEWSLETTER (ROUND TABLE OF NATIONAL CENTRES FOR LIBRARY SERVICES). (NEWSLETTER / ROUND TABLE OF NATIONAL CENTERS FOR LIBRARY SERVICES.). Newsletter. English. sa. Fl10.00. NBLC, Postbus 93054, 2509 AB Den Haag Netherlands. **Tel** 011 31 70 3141500. **LC** Z678.2; .N48. **DD** 025.1.

AT/0810-0926
NEWSLETTER - SOUTH AUSTRALIAN ADVISORY COMMITTEE ON LIBRARY SERVICES TO THE DISABLED. [Newsl. - S. aust. Advis. Comm. Libr. Serv. Disabl.]. (1982)-. Newsletter. English. ir. Free. State Library of South Australia, GPO Box 419, Adelaide South 5001 Australia. **Tel** 011 61 8 2077625, FAX 011 61 8 2077207. **ED** M. Bell. **DD** 027.663099423. **Bk Rev. Circ:** 200.
Desc: Strives to raise awareness among librarians about disability issues. Strives to raise awareness in the community of library services for people with disabilities.
Ind/Abst Aust. Educ. Index; Aust. Libr. Inf. Sci. Abstr. (1986-).

UK/0308-4035
NEWSLETTER - SOUTH-EAST ASIA LIBRARY GROUP. **Main/Corp** South-East Asia Library Group. (19??)-. Newsletter. English. an. £7.50. British Library Oriental & India Office of Collections, 197 Blackfriars Road, London SE1 8NG England. **Tel** 011 44 71 412 7655, FAX 011 44 71 412 7858.

US/0197-2707
NEWSLETTER-STATE, COURT, AND COUNTY LAW LIBRARIES SECTION. **Main/Corp** American Association of Law Libraries. State, Court, and County Law Libraries Section. Vol. 5 (Nov. 1977)-. Newsletter. English. mo. comes with membership. American Association of Law Libraries, 53 West Jackson Boulevard, Suite 940, Chicago IL 60604. **Tel** (312)939-4764, FAX (312)431-1097, telex ABA7603. **LC** Z675.L2; S75a. **DD** 026/.340/05. ***Continues*** *S.C.L.L. Newsletter, 0094-9817.*

AT/0819-1816
NEWSLETTER - STATE LIBRARY OF TASMANIA 1986. [Newsl. - State Libr. Tasman.1986]. (1986)-. Newsletter. English. State Library of Tasmania, 91 Murray St, Hobart TAS 7000 Australia. **Tel** 002 33 7511, FAX 002 31 0927. **ED** Kim Newman. **DD** 027.5946. **Circ:** 270. ***Continues*** *Weekly Newsletter - State Library of Tasmania, 0819-1840.*
Desc: Provides information on State Library policies, operations, and strategic tasks and on developments of interest. Articles and items of interest are provided by all staff from library work places across Tasmania.
Ind/Abst Aust. Educ. Index; Aust. Libr. Inf. Sci. Abstr. (1988-).

CN/0840-769X
NEWSLETTER / THIRD WORLD LIBRARIES INTEREST GROUP. [Newsl. - Third World Libr. Interest Group]. Vol. 1, Issue 1 (May 1988)-. Newsletter. English. Three times a year. Free. Third World Libraries Interest Group, c/o F Wakil, University of Saskatchewan Library, Saskatoon Saskatchewan S7N 0W0 Canada. **DD** 027.0172/4/06071.

US/0277-528X
NEWSLETTER - UNIVERSITY OF ILLINOIS AT URBANA-CHAMPAIGN, GRADUATE SCHOOL OF LIBRARY SCIENCE. **Main/Corp** University of Illinois at Urbana-Champaign. Graduate School of Library Science. No. 1 (Spring 1980)-. Newsletter. English. sa. Free. Graduate School of Library Science, 410 David Kinley Hall, University of Illinois, Urbana IL 61801. **ED** Rita Bartholomew.

CN/0380-1691
NEWSLETTER - VANCOUVER ISLAND REGIONAL LIBRARY. [Newsl. - Vanc. Isl. Reg. Libr.]. **Main/Corp** Vancouver Island Regional Library. Newsletter. English. Vancouver Island Regional Library, 10 Strickland Street, Nanaimo British Columbia Canada. **DD** 027.4/711/34.
Ind/Abst Int. Aerosp. Abstr.

US/0146-6348
NEWSLETTER - WAYNE STATE UNIVERSITY LIBRARIES. **Main/Corp** Wayne State University. Libraries. No. 1 (April 1977)-. Newsletter. English. ir. Free on request. Wayne University Library, 5265 Cass Avenue, Detroit MI 48202. **Tel** (313)577-4025. **ED** Bruce A. Shuman. ***Continues*** *Newsletter--Archives of Labor History and Urban Affairs.*

AT/0312-5270
NEWSLIB BRISBANE. [NewslibBris.]. (1975)-. Periodical. English. ir. State Library of Queensland, Public Libraries Service, 24 Macquarie St, Teneriffe QLD 4005 Australia. **ED** Joanna Reid. **DD** _a027.4943.
Ind/Abst Aust. Educ. Index; Aust. Libr. Inf. Sci. Abstr. (1983-).

CN/0227-6569
NEWSLINE - MANITOBA LIBRARY ASSOCIATION. (NEWSLINE : NEWSLETTER OF THE MANITOBA LIBRARY ASSOCIATION.). [Newsline - Man. Libr. Assoc.]. **Main/Corp** Manitoba Library Association. (1976)-. Periodical. English. bm. Free to members. Manitoba Library Association, 208 100 Arthur Street, Winnipeg Manitoba R3B 1H3 Canada. **Tel** (204)943-4567. **ED** S. Norma Godavari. **DD** 027.07127. **Bk Rev. Ad Acc. Circ:** 350 (ctrl). ***Continues*** *Manitoba Library Association. MLA Newsline., 0700-3684.*

US/0888-8698
NEWSNET ACTION LETTER. [NewsNet act. lett.]. **Added/Corp** Newsnet, Inc. **VFOAT** Action Letter. Vol. 1, No. 1 (May 1983)-. Periodical. English. mo (10 issues). Free. NewsNet Inc, 945 Haverford Road, Bryn Mawr PA 19010. **Tel** (800)345-1301, (215)527-8030. **ED** Ellen S. Keech. **DD** 025. ctrl circ. available on an online database from NEWSNET.
Desc: Provides information on system updates, enhancements and new services for NewsNet subscribers.

US
NEXUS (AURORA, COLO.). (NEXUS / CCPLS.). **Added/Corp** CCPLS (System) CCLS (System). Vol. 1, No. 1 (Nov. 1974)-. Periodical. English. Five times a year. Central Colorado Library System, 3805 Marshall Street, Wheat Ridge CO 80033. **Tel** (303)422-1150.

US/0090-0893
NFAIS NEWSLETTER. [NFAIS newsl.]. **Added/Corp** National Federation of Abstracting and Indexing Services. National Federation of Abstracting and Information Services (U.S.). **VFOAT** N.F.A.I.S. Newsletter. **VAT** National Federation of Abstracting and Indexing Services Newsletter. Vol. 15, No. 1 Feb. (1973)-. Newsletter. English. mo (January - December). $110.00 (one year); $198.00 (two year). National Federation of Abstracting & Information Services, 1429 Walnut Street, 13th Floor, Philadelphia PA 19102. **Tel** (215)563-2406, FAX (215)563-2848. **ED** Wendy Wicks. **NLM** Z 1007 N558. **CODEN** NFNLA6. Index available (published in March). **Bk Rev**, (Qty: (varies)). **Ad Acc.** ***Continues*** *National Federation of Science Abstracting and Indexing Services. News From Science Abstracting and Indexing Services, 0028-9124.*
Desc: A monthly current awareness publication containing feature articles on information industry hot topics and news columns reporting the latest in: industry products, services, publications, people news, international news, major meetings, joint ventures, copyright, legal issues, and mergers and acquisitions. Special features include a calendar of events, conferences and seminars in the industry; an update covering the government scene; and company profiles of the industry's leaders. Special editions of the newsletter include an annual index, member statistics, the Miles Conrad Memorial Lecture, and a special NFAIS Annual Conference write-up.
Ind/Abst Int. Aerosp. Abstr.; Text. Technol. Dig.

●US/1062-7952
NFAIS YEARBOOK OF THE INFORMATION INDUSTRY, THE. [NFAIS yearb. inf. ind.]. **Added/Corp** National Federation of Abstracting and Information Services (U.S.). **VFOAT** Yearbook of the Information Industry; NFAIS Yearbook. **VAT** National Federation of Abstracting and Information Services Yearbook of the Information Industry. (1992)-. Periodical. English. an. $40.00 members of NFAIS; $50.00 nonmembers. Learned Information Inc., 143 Old Marlton Pike, Medford NJ 08055-8750. **Tel** (609)654-6266, FAX (609)654-4309. **LC** IN PROCESS; Z674.2; .N3. **DD** 025. Index available (bound in each issue). **Circ:** 2 million.
Desc: Provides information professionals with insights into events that impacted the information industry over the past year and provides perspectives that examine how these events will affect the direction of the industry in the future.

NR/0331-0000
NIGERBIBLIOS. [Nigerbiblios]. **Added/Corp** National Library of Nigeria. (1976)-. Periodical. English. ir. Free on request. National Library of Nigeria, 4 Wesley Street, P M B 12626, Lagos Nigeria. **Tel** 011 234 1 630053, 011 234 1 634704. **LC** Z965.L24; N53. **DD** 027.5669.
Ind/Abst Libr. Inf. Sci. Abstr.

NR/0029-0122
NIGERIAN LIBRARIES. [Niger. libr.]. **Added/Corp** Nigerian Library Association. Vol. 1 (Feb. 1964)-. Periodical. English. Three times a year. $15.00. Ibadan University Libraries, Department of Library Studies, Ibadan Nigeria. **LC** Z673.N698; N5. ***Supersedes*** *Wala News.*
Ind/Abst Libr. Inf. Sci. Abstr.

NR/0189-4412
NIGERIAN LIBRARY AND INFORMATION SCIENCE REVIEW. [Niger. libr. inf. sci. rev.]. **Added/Corp** Nigerian Library Association. Oyo State Division. Vol. 1, No. 1 (May 1983)-. Periodical. English. sa. $35.00 Nigeria; $37.00

other. Ibadan University Libraries, Department of Library Studies, Ibadan Nigeria. **(Subscription address:** Ibadan University Library, PO Box 20672, UI Post Office, Ibadan Oyo State Nigeria.**)** **ED** B.C. Nzotta. **LC** Z857.N5; N53. **DD** 020/.9669. **Bk Rev. Ad Acc. Pr Rev. Circ:** 1000 (ctrl).
Desc: Devoted mainly to the publication of results of empirical research in the field of library and information science with particular reference to Nigeria and Africa.
Ind/Abst Libr. Inf. Sci. Abstr.; Libr. Lit.

JA
NIHON NOGAKU TOSHOKAN KYOGIKAI KAIHO. See Agriculture.

CN/0319-2792
NILITE NEWS. Began in Dec. 1971. Periodical. English. Niagara College of Applied Arts and Technology, Woodlawn Road, Welland Ontario L3B 5S2 Canada. **Tel** (416)735-2211. **ED** Robert J Bowman. **DD** 023/.5. **Circ:** 1,000.
Desc: Includes brief items on the program's students, staff, and activities.

AT
NLA GATEWAYS. (19??)-. English. Six times a year. $40.00. National Library of Australia, Parkes Place, Canberra ACT, 2600 Australia. **Tel** 011 61 6 2621374, FAX 011 61 6 2731084. ***Continues** Acquistion Bibliograhpy Cataloguing News.*

US/0146-3055
NLM TECHNICAL BULLETIN, THE. [NLM tech. bull.]. **VAT** National Library of Medicine Technical Bulletin. No. 96; April 1977-. Bulletin. English. mo. National Library of Medicine, 8600 Rockville Pike, Bethesda MD 20894. **Tel** (301)496-6308. **NLM** Z 699.5 M39 N107. ***Formed by the union of** Library Network/Medlars Technical Bulletin, 0090-1350 **and** Toxline Technical Bulletin, 0093-8793.*
Ind/Abst Cumul. Index Nurs. Allied Health Lit.

US/0095-053X
NLR: NATIONAL LIBRARY REPORTER. **VFOAT** National Library Reporter. Vol. 1 (Oct. 7 1974)-. Periodical. English. sm. $35.00. 9482 Kilimanjaro Road, Columbia MD 21045. **LC** Z731; .N2. **DD** 021/.00973.

US
NOCALL NEWSLETTER / NORTHERN CALIFORNIA ASSOCIATION OF LAW LIBRARIES. Added/Corp Northern California Association of Law Libraries. Vol. 1, No. 1 (Nov.-Dec. 1980)-. Newsletter. English. bm. Comes with NCALL membership. Northern California Association of Law Libraries, Santa Clara University, Santa Clara CA 95053. **Tel** (916)440-6011.
Ind/Abst Leg. Inf. Manage. Index (19??-).

NR
NOMINAL LIST OF PRACTISING LIBRARIANS IN NIGERIA. 1974-. English. an. National Library of Nigeria, 4 Wesley Street, P M B 12626, Lagos Nigeria. **Tel** 011 234 1 630053, 011 234 1 634704. **LC** Z965; .N38 subser; Z720.A46N5. **DD** 016.9669; 020/.92/2.

SW/0029-148X
NORDISK TIDSKRIFT FOR BOK-OCH BIBLIOTEKSVASEN. [Nord. tidskr. bok-biblioteksvas.]. Vol. 1 (1914)-. Periodical. Swedish. qt. Kr385.00, $62.00. Scandinavian University Press, PO Box 2959 Toeyen, N 0608 Oslo 6 Norway. **Tel** 011 47 2 2575400, FAX 011 47 2 2575353, telex 71896 UROR N. **(Subscription address:** Scandinavian University Press, 200 Meacham Ave., Elmont NY 11003.**)** **ED** I Collijn. **LC** Z671; .N55. Index available in last issue of volume--attached. cum. index.
Ind/Abst Libr. Inf. Sci. Abstr.; Libr. Lit.; MLA Int. Bibl. Books Artic. Mod. Lang. Lit.

US/0090-0605
NORTH AMERICAN LIBRARY EDUCATION DIRECTORY AND STATISTICS. See Library and Information Sciences-Abstracting, Bibliographies and Statistics.

US/0029-2540
NORTH CAROLINA LIBRARIES. [N. Carol. libr.]. **Added/Corp** North Carolina Library Association. Vol. 1 (1942)-. Periodical. English. qt. $32.00. North Carolina Library Association, 109 East Jones Street, Raleigh NC 27601. **Tel** (919)757-6222. **ED** Frances Bryant Bradburn. **LC** Z671; .N6. **DD** 020.623. **Bk Rev. Ad Acc. Circ:** 2,200. available on microfilm and microfiche from University Microfilms International (UMI).
Desc: All aspects of librarianship, especially in North Carolina.
Ind/Abst Libr. Lit.

US/0094-5455
NORTH DAKOTA ACADEMIC LIBRARY STATISTICS. See Library and Information Sciences-Abstracting, Bibliographies and Statistics.

US/0160-0095
NORTH DAKOTA STATE PLAN FOR LIBRARY DEVELOPMENT. Main/Corp North Dakota. State Library Commission. English. North Dakota State Library Commission, Bismarck ND 58505. **Tel** 224-2492. **LC** Z678.4.N9; N67A. **DD** 021/.009784. ctrl circ.

NE/0924-6509
NORTH-HOLLAND MATHEMATICAL LIBRARY. [N.-Holl. math. libr.]. **VFOAT** North Holland Mathematical Library. Vol. 1 (1971)-. Monographic series. English. ir. Price varies per volume. Elsevier Science Publishers BV, PO Box 211, 1000 AE Amsterdam Netherlands. **Tel** 011 31 20 5803642, FAX 011 31 20 5862696, telex 15682. Documents available from Ask*IEEE.
Ind/Abst INSPEC (1983-); Zentralbl. Math. Ihre Grenzgeb.

CN/1181-1358
NORTHERN ONTARIO CATALOG. (NORTHERN ONTARIO CATALOG [MICROFORM].). **Main/Corp** Ontario Library Service, North. (Mar. 1990)-. Catalog. English. **DD** 019/.1. ***Continues** Ontario Library Service--Voyageur. Tri-Regional Catalogue,, 0844-5133.*

CN/0715-2612
NOTABLE CANADIAN CHILDREN'S BOOKS. SUPPLEMENT. [Notable Can. child. books, Suppl.]. **Added/Corp** National Library of Canada. **VFOAT** Choix de Livres Canadiens pour la Jeunesse. Supplement. **VAT** Choix de Livres Canadiens Pour la Jeunesse. Supplement (1978) Canadian. (1975)-. Bibliography. English. Free on request. National Library of Canada, 395 Wellington Street, Ottawa Ontario K1A 0N4 Canada. **Tel** (613)995-7969, (613)995-7969, (819)994-6881, FAX (613)991-9871. **LC** Z1037; .N79; PN1009.A1. **DD** 011/.6254. available on audiocassette; available in braille; available in large print. ***Absorbed** Choix de Livres Canadiens pour la Jeunesse. Supplement, 1978 (Published 1980), 0715-2604.*
Desc: Describes recommended Canadian children's books as well as age-group suitability.

FR/0180-4278
NOTE D'INFORMATION / ASSOCIATION DES BIBLIOTHECAIRES FRANCAIS. French. ir. Free. Association des Bibliothecaires Francais, 7 rue des Lions St Paul, 75004 Paris France. **Tel** 11 33 1 48879787. **DD** 020. **Circ:** 2,000 (ctrl).

US/0572-8312
NOTES ON SELECTED ACQUISITIONS. Main/Corp Columbia University. Libraries. Periodical. English. Columbia University Libraries, 345 East 47th Street, Engineering Society Library, New York NY 10017.

US/0027-4380
NOTES (PHILADELPHIA, PA.). See Music.

US
NOTES. SUPPLEMENT FOR MEMBERS. See Music.

MX
NOTICIERO DE LA AMBAC. Main/Corp Asociacion Mexicana de Bibliotecarios. (196?)-. Periodical. Spanish. Four times a year (Jan., Apr., July, Oct.). $20.00. Asociacion Mex Bibliotecarios, Apartado Postal 27-651, 06760 Mexico DF Mexico. **Tel** 011 52 5 5751135, FAX 011 52 5 6525627. **Bk Rev. Ad Acc, Adv Mgr:** Lec. Jose Antonio Yanez, **Tel** 011 52 5 2279012. **Circ:** 1,000 (ctrl).
Desc: The serial contains information about conferences, scholarships, courses and others in Mexico and foreign.

US/1057-1019
NOTISES (EVANSTON, ILL.). (NOTISES.). [NOTISes]. **Added/Corp** Northwestern University (Evanston, Ill.). NOTIS Office. NOTIS Systems. NOTIS Systems. Documentation Services Dept. No. 1 (Mar. 8, 1985)-. Periodical. English. mo. $65.00. Notis Systems, Inc., 1007 Church Street, 2nd Floor, Evanston IL 30201-3622. **LC** Z699.4.N68; N66. **DD** 025. ***Continues** NOTIS Newsletter.*
Ind/Abst Int. Aerosp. Abstr.

CN/0833-0050
NOUVEAUTES DE LA BIBLIOTHEQUE ADMINISTRATIVE. *Ceased.* See Public Administration.

CN/0705-6370
NOUVELLES ACQUISITIONS - UNIVERSITE DE MONTREAL, BIBLIOTHEQUE DE MEDECINE VETERINAIRE. Main/Corp Universite de Montreal. Bibliotheque de Medecine Veterinaire. New Series, V. 10-23 June 1977-. Periodical. French. Bibliotheque de Medecine Veterinaire, Universite de Montreal, CP 5000, St-Hyacinthe Quebec J2S 7C6 Canada. **DD** 016.636089. ***Continues** Universite de Montreal. Faculte de Medecine Veterinaire. Bibliotheque. Nouvelles Acquisitions, 0318-4528.*

CN/0822-7527
NOUVELLES - ASSOCIATION DES BIBLIOTHEQUES DE L'ONTARIO. GUILDE DES SERVICES EN FRANCAIS. (NOUVELLES : BULLETIN D'INFORMATION SUR LES BIBLIOTHEQUES PUBLIQUES.). [Nouv. - Assoc. bibl. Ont., Guilde serv. fr.]. **VFOAT** Bulletin d'Information sur les Bibliotheques Publiques de l'Ontario. Oct. 1980-. Bulletin. French. Association des Bibliotheques de l'Ontario, Guilde des Services en Francais, c/o Federation des Bibliotheques du Centre-Nord, 334 Sud rue Regent, Sudbury Ontario P3C 4E2 Canada. **DD** 020/.6234/713.

CN/0316-0963
NOUVELLES - ASTED. (NOUVELLES - ASSOCIATION POUR L'AVANCEMENT DES SCIENCES ET DES TECHNIQUES DE LA DOCUMENTATION.). [Nouv. - ASTED]. **Main/Corp** Asted. **VFOAT** Nouvelles de l'ASTED Nouvelles Asted. **VAT** Nouvelles - Association pour l'Avancement des Sciences et des Techniques de la Documentation. No. 84/85-131, Jan./Feb. 1974-Nov./Dec. 1981; V. 1- (Jan./Feb./March 1982)-. Periodical. French. Asted, 3414 Avenue du Pars Bureau 202, Montreal Que H2X 2H5 Canada. **Tel** (514)281-5012. available on microfilm from Bibliotheque National du Quebec. ***Continues** Assocition Canadienne des Bibliothecaires de Langue Francaise. Nouvelles., 0044-9407.*

CN/0316-0432
NOUVELLES DE LA BIBLIOTHEQUE CENTRALE DE PRET. REGION DU SAGUENAY-LAC-SAINT-JEAN. (LES NOUVELLES DE LA BIBLIOTHEQUE CENTRALE DE PRET.). **Main/Corp** Bibliotheque Centrale de Pret du Saguenay-Lac-Saint-Jean. V. 1, No. 2- May 1974-. French. Bibliotheque Centrale de Pret du Saguenay-Lac-Saint-Jean, 100 Ouest rue Price, Alma Quebec G8B 4S1 Canada. **DD** 027.4/714/16. ***Continues** Bibliotheque Centrale de Pret du Saguenay-Lac-Saint-Jean. Bulletin de Nouvelles, 0318-1448.*

RU
NOVAIA SOVETSKAIA I INOSTRANNAIA LITERATURA PO BIBLIOTEKOVEDENIIU I BIBLIOGRAFII. Added/Corp Informtsentr po Problemam Kultury i Iskusstva (Soviet Union). (19??)-. Russian (Multiple languages). mo. 0.16rub (single issue). Gosudarstvennaia Biblioteka, Informatsionnyi Tsentr, Imeni V. I. Lenina, Prospekt Kalinina 3, 121019 Moscow Russia. **LC** Z666; .N68.

CN/0707-2457
NSSLA BULLETIN. (N S S L A BULLETIN.). **Main/Corp** Nova Scotia School Library Association. **Added/Corp** Nova Scotia Teachers Union. **VAT** Nova Scotia School Library Association Bulletin. (Vol. 5, No. 1, 1977)-. Bulletin. English. Three times a year. 10.00Can$ (includes membership). Nova Scotia Teachers Union, 3106 Dutch Village Road, Halifax Nova Scotia B3L 4L7 Canada. **Tel** (902)477-5621. **DD** 027.8/09716. ***Continues** S L A Bulletin, 0380-2035.*

NR/0331-1481
NSUKKA LIBRARY NOTES. Vol. 1, No. 1 (Dec. 1979)-. Periodical. English. ir. N15.00 Nigeria; $10.00 US; £5.00 UK. University of Nigeria Library, Nsukka Nigeria. **Tel** 771939/145, FAX 042-771939-145. **ED** M W Anyakoha. **LC** Z858.U465; N88. **DD** 027.7669. **Bk Rev. Ad Acc. Circ:** 500 (ctrl).
Desc: Articles in library and information science. News about staff and development in library services.

US
NTIS ALERT. LIBRARY & INFORMATION SCIENCES. Added/Corp United States. National Technical Information Service. (19??)-. Periodical. English. Twenty-four times a year. $145.00 US; $210.00 other. National Technical Information Service - NTIS, Room 2027S, 5285 Port Royal Road, Springfield VA 22161. **Tel** (703)487-4630, (703)487-4660, (703)487-4650, FAX (703)321-8547, telex 89-9405. Index available. ***Continues** Library & Information Services / NTIS, 0364-6467.*
Desc: Provides information on information systems, new technologies, marketing and user services, operations and planning, personnel, etc.

US/0734-7650
NUC. BOOKS. (NUC. BOOKS [MICROFORM] / LIBRARY OF CONGRESS.). [NUC, Books]. **Added/Corp** Library of Congress. **VFOAT** Books; National Union Catalog. Books. (1983)-. Bibliography. English. mo. $660.00 North America; $765.00 other. Library of Congress / Cataloging Distribution Service, Washington DC 20541-5017. **Tel** (800)255-3666, (202)707-6100, FAX (202)707-1334. **LC** Microfiche (w) 83/301. ***Formed by the union of** National Union Catalog, 0028-0348; Chinese Cooperative Catalog (Washington, D.C. : 1978), 0095-1072; Library of Congress. Monographic Series, 0093-0571 **and** Library of Congress. Subject Catalog, 0096-8803.*
Desc: Bibliographic records for books, pamphlets, manuscripts, map atlases, microform masters, and monographic government publications.

AT/0812-9258
NUCOS [MICROFORM] : NATIONAL UNION CATALOGUE OF SERIALS HELD IN AUSTRALIAN LIBRARIES. **Added/Corp** National Library of Australia. **VFOAT** National Union Catalogue of Serials Held in Australian Libraries. (Mar. 1984)-. Periodical. English. Twice a year (Mar. & Sept.). 80.00Aus$. National Library of Australia, Parkes Place, Canberra ACT, 2600 Australia. **Tel** 011 61 6 2621374, FAX 011 61 6 2731084. **LC** Microfiche (o) 93/6000.
Ind/Abst AESIS Q.

US/0888-0530
NURSING & ALLIED HEALTH (CINAHL) ... SUBJECT HEADING LIST. **See** Medical Science and Technology-Nursing.

US
NURSING SUBJECT HEADINGS. Periodical. English. Seventh Day Adventist Hospital Association, PO Box 871, Glendale CA 91209. **LC** Z695.1.N8. **DD** 610.73014.

US/0027-7134
NYLA BULLETIN. [NYLA bull.]. **Main/Corp** New York Library Association. **VAT** New York Library Association Bulletin. Vol. 1 (Feb. 15, 1953)-. Bulletin. English. Ten times a year. $50.00 Library; $100.00 Commercial/Business $75.00 Affiliate Organization. New York Library Association, 15 Park Row/Suite 434, New York NY 10038. **Tel** (212)227-8032. **LC** Z671; .N2. **DD** 020.5. **Bk Rev. Ad Acc, Adv Mgr:** C. Raphael, **Tel** (518)432-6952. **Circ:** 4000 (ctrl). available on microfilm and microfiche from University Microfilms International (UMI).
Desc: Reports news, concerns and issues involving librarians and librarianship in New York State and beyond.

US
NYSLAA NETWORK CONNECTION / NEW YORK STATE LIBRARY ASSISTANTS' ASSOCIATION. **Added/Corp** New York State Library Assistants' Association. **VFOAT** Network Connection. **VAT** New York State Library Assistants' Association Network Connection. Vol. 3, No. 3 (Winter 1991)-. Periodical. English. ***Continues*** *Newsletter (New York State Library Assistants' Association).*

RU
OBZORNAIA INFORMATSIIA: BIBLIOTEKOVEDENIE I BIBLIOGRAFOVEDENIE. **Added/Corp** Moscow. Publichnaia Biblioteka. Informatsionnyi Tsentr po Problemam Kultury i Iskusstva. Hussia (1923-U.S.S.R.). Ministerstvo Kultury. **VFOAT** Bibliotekovedenie I Bibliografovedenie. (19??)-. Periodical. Russian. sa. $4.80. **(Subscription address:** Victor Kamkin, 4956 Boiling Brook Parkway, Rockville MD 20852.**)**

US/0734-3698
OCCASIONAL MISCELLANY OF THE LIBRARY COMPANY OF PHILADELPHIA. [Occas. misc. Libr. Co. Philadelphia]. **Added/Corp** Library Company of Philadelphia. (1977)-. Periodical. English. Four times a year. $20.00 regular membership. Library Company of Philadelphia, 1314 Locust Street, Philadelphia PA 19107. **Tel** (215)546-3181. **ED** John Van Horne. **LC** Z733.L734; O26. **DD** 206.973/09748/11. **Circ:** 1,439 (ctrl).
Desc: Describes activities, exhibitions, and recent acquisitions of the library community.

US/0730-7160
OCCASIONAL PAPERS - ART LIBRARIES SOCIETY OF NORTH AMERICA. (OCCASIONAL PAPERS / ARLIS/NA.). [Occas. pap. - Art Libr. Soc. North Am.]. **Added/Corp** Art Libraries Society of North America. **VFOAT** Occasional Papers of the Art Libraries Society of North America. (1982)-. Monographic series. English. ir. Price varies per volume. Art Libraries Society of North America / ARLIS/NA, 3900 East Timrod Street, Tucson AZ 85711. **Tel** (602)881-8479, FAX (602)322-6778. **Circ:** 500 (ctrl).
Desc: Monograph series on topics of interest to art librarianship and visual resources.

US/0276-1769
OCCASIONAL PAPERS - UNIVERSITY OF ILLINOIS (URBANA-CHAMPAIGN CAMPUS). GRADUATE SCHOOL OF LIBRARY AND INFORMATION SCIENCE. (OCCASIONAL PAPERS / UNIVERSITY OF ILLINOIS AT URBANA-CHAMPAIGN, GRADUATE SCHOOL OF LIBRARY AND INFORMATION SCIENCE.). [Occas. pap. - Univ. Ill. (Urbana-Champaign Campus), Grad. Sch. Libr. Inf. Sci.]. **Added/Corp** University of Illinois at Urbana-Champaign. Graduate School of Library and Information Science. No. 148 (June 1981)-. Monographic series. English. ir. Price varies per volume. University of Illinois Graduate School of Library and Information Science, Lis Building, 501 East Daniel Street, Champaign IL 61820. **Tel** (217)333-1359. **ED** James S. Dowling. **LC** UNC. **[CCC]. Circ:** 500. available on microfilm from University Microfilms International (UMI). ***Continues*** *Occasional Papers - University of Illinois Graduate School of Library Science, 0073-5310.*
Desc: Deals with some aspect of librarianship and consist of manuscripts which, because of length, detail, specialization or temporary interest would not be published in a library periodical.

US/0195-6329
OCCASIONAL PAPERS - VIRGINIA LIBRARY ASSOCIATION. **Main/Corp** Virginia Library Association. (1979)-. Periodical. English. William Prince, Virginia Library Association, Virginia Polytechnic Institute, Blacksburg VA 24061.

US
OCCASIONAL PUBLICATION. **Main/Corp** Tennessee. University. Libraries. (1970)-. Monographic series. English. ir. Price varies per volume. University of Tennessee Main Library, Knoxville TN 37916. **Tel** (615)974-4306.

US/0148-2068
OCCASIONAL RESEARCH PAPER (BRIGHAM YOUNG UNIVERSITY. SCHOOL OF LIBRARY AND INFORMATION SCIENCES). ***Ceased.*** (OCCASIONAL RESEARCH PAPER - SCHOOL OF LIBRARY AND INFORMATION SCIENCES, BRIGHAM YOUNG UNIVERSITY.). **Added/Corp** Brigham Young University. School of Library and Information Sciences. No. 1 (1977)-(19??). Monographic series. English. ir. Brigham Young University / 5042 HBLL, c/o Dr. Nathan Smith, Provo UT 84602. **Tel** (801)378-2976. **ED** M.P. Marchant. **LC** UNC.

CN/0842-4136
OCLA-LINK. (OCLA-LINK : NEWSLETTER OF THE ONTARIO COURTHOUSE LIBRARIANS' ASSOCIATION.). [OCLA-link]. **VFOAT** Newsletter of the Ontario Courthouse Librarians' Association. **VAT** Ontario Courthouse Librarians' Association-Link. (1987)-. Newsletter. English. qt. Free to members. Ontario Courthouse Librarians' Association, c/o Hamilton Law Association, 50 Main Street East, Hamilton Ontario L8N 1E1 Canada. **DD** 026/.34.

US/1044-4858
OCLC/AMIGOS COLLECTION ANALYSIS CD. (OCLC/AMIGOS COLLECTION ANALYSIS CD [COMPUTER FILE] / OCLC/AMIGOS COLLECTION ANALYSIS SYSTEMS.). **Added/Corp** OCLC/AMIGOS Collection Analysis Systems. OCLC. AMIGOS Bibliographic Council. **VFOAT** OCLC AMIGOS Collection Analysis CD; Collection Analysis. **VAT** Online Computer Library Center AMIGOS Collection Analysis Compact Disk. (1989)-. English. OCLC Asia Pacific Services, 6565 Frantz Road, Dublin OH 43017. **Tel** (800)848-5878, (614)764-6394 or 6000, FAX (614)764-6096.

US/1044-3800
OCLC ANNUAL REPORT. [OCLC annu. rep.]. **Main/Corp** OCLC. (1985/86)-. English. an. Free. OCLC Asia Pacific Services, 6565 Frantz Road, Dublin OH 43017. **Tel** (800)848-5878, (614)764-6394 or 6000, FAX (614)764-6096. **LC** Z732.O5; O58a. **DD** 021. ***Continues*** *Annual Report / OCLC, 0730-5125.*

●US/1054-268X
OCLC CJK350 NEWSLETTER. **VFOAT** OCLC CJK Three Hundred Fifty Newsletter. **VAT** OCLC Chinese Japanese Korean 350 Newsletter. (1992)-. Newsletter. English. qt. Free. OCLC Asia Pacific Services, 6565 Frantz Road, Dublin OH 43017. **Tel** (800)848-5878, (614)764-6394 or 6000, FAX (614)764-6096.

US/8756-5196
OCLC MICRO. ***Title Change.*** [OCLC micro]. **Added/Corp** OCLC. Meckler Corporation. **VFOAT** Micro. **VAT** Online Computer Library Center Micro. Vol. 1 No. 1 (Mar. 1985)-Vol. 8 No. 6 (Dec. 1992). Periodical. English. bm. OCLC Asia Pacific Services, 6565 Frantz Road, Dublin OH 43017. **Tel** (800)848-5878, (614)764-6394 or 6000, FAX (614)764-6096. **ED** Ginni Voedisch. **LC** Z678.93.M53; O26. **DD** 025/.0028/5. **CODEN** OCMIEK. **[CCC].** Index available. **Bk Rev. Ad Acc. Circ:** 2,300. available on microfilm and microfiche from University Microfilms International (UMI). Documents available from Ask*IEEE. ***Continued by*** *OCLC Systems & Services, 1065-075X.*
Desc: Information to help IBM/PC and other microcomputer users make the most of the micros in their libraries. Presented in concise form and or on ready-to-run diskettes.
Ind/Abst Comput. Rev. Index (June 1986-); Inf. Sci. Abstr.; INSPEC (1986-); Libr. Inf. Sci. Abstr.; Libr. Lit. (1986-); Microcomput. Index (Jan. 1986-).

US/0163-898X
OCLC NEWSLETTER. [OCLC newsl.]. **Added/Corp** Ohio College Library Center. OCLC. No. 63 (1973)-. Periodical. English. bm (Feb., Apr., June, Aug., Oct., Dec.). Free. OCLC Asia Pacific Services, 6565 Frantz Road, Dublin OH 43017. **Tel** (800)848-5878, (614)764-6394 or 6000, FAX (614)764-6096. **ED** Philip Schieber, Nita Dean. **LC** Z674.82.O15; O215. **DD** 025. **Circ:** 20,000. ***Continues*** *Newsletter / Ohio College Library Center.*
Desc: Information about OCLC- related products, services, programs, people, and research.
Ind/Abst Inf. Sci. Abstr.; Int. Aerosp. Abstr.; Libr. Inf. Sci. Abstr.

●US/1060-6033
OCLC SELECTED TITLES. **Added/Corp** OCLC. **VFOAT** Online Computer Library Center Selected Titles; Selected titles. (1992)-. Periodical. English. qt. $250.00. OCLC Asia Pacific Services, 6565 Frantz Road, Dublin OH 43017. **Tel** (800)848-5878, (614)764-6394 or 6000, FAX (614)764-6096.

●US/1065-075X
OCLC SYSTEMS AND SERVICES. [OCLC syst. serv.]. **Added/Corp** OCLC. Meckler Corporation. Mecklermedia Corporation. **VFOAT** OCLC Systems and Services. (1993)-. Periodical. English. qt. $89.00 US & Canada; Aus$139.00 Australia; £59.00 other. MCB University Press, 60 62 Toller Lane, Bradford West Yorkshire BD8 9BX England. **Tel** 011 44 274 499821, FAX 011 44 274 547143, telex 51317 MCBUNI G. **ED** Dan Marmion. **LC** Z678.93.M53; O26. **DD** 025/.0028/5. **CODEN** OSSEEE. Documents available from Ask*IEEE. ***Continues*** *OCLC Micro, 8756-5196.*
Desc: Devoted to analysis and utilization of the Online Company Library Centre cataloging systems used by over 15,000 libraries worldwide. Includes articles on systems and service developments from OCLC, information on product compatability and availability, programs and solutions.
Ind/Abst Comput. Lit. Index; Comput. Rev. Index; Inf. Instruc. Technol.; Inf. Sci. Abstr.; INSPEC; Libr. Inf. Sci. Abstr.; Libr. Lit.

US/0193-3086
ODL SOURCE. **Main/Corp** Oklahoma. Dept. of Libraries. **VAT** Oklahoma Department of Libraries Source. Vol. 1, (Nov. 1976)-. Periodical. English. Twelve times a year. Free. Oklahoma Department of Libraries, 200 Northeast 18th Street, Oklahoma City OK 73105. **Tel** (405)521-2502, FAX (405)525-7804. **ED** Marilyn L. Vesely. **Circ:** 4,000. ***Supersedes*** *Oklahoma. Dept. of Libraries. ODL Newsletter.*
Desc: Information of interest to librarians concentrating on Oklahoma topics.

GW
OEFFENTLICHE BIBLIOTHEKEN IN BADEN-WUERTTEMBERG / HERAUSGEGEBEN VON DEN STAATLICHEN BUECHEREISTELLEN FREIBURG ... [ET AL.]. **Added/Corp** Staatliche Buechereistelle fuer den Regierungsbezirk Freiburg. Staatliche Fachstelle fuer das Oeffentliche Bibliothekswesen Freiburg. (19??)-. German. be. Staatliche Fachstelle fur das Offentliche Bibliothekswesen Freiburg, Lorracher Strasse 5A, 7800 Freiburg Germany. **Tel** 0761/441515. **LC** Z801.B25; O33. **DD** 027.443/46. **Circ:** 3,000.

CN/1184-8367
OFF THE SHELF (TORONTO). (OFF THE SHELF / THE CANADIAN NATIONAL INSTITUTE FOR THE BLIND, NATIONAL LIBRARY DIVISION.). [Off shelf]. **Added/Corp** Canadian National Institute for the Blind. Canadian National Institute for the Blind. National Library Division. Issue 1 (Spring 1990)-. Periodical. English. qt. Free to libraries. Canadian National Institute for the Blind, 1929 Bayview Avenue, Toronto Ontario M4G 3E8 Canada. **Tel** (416)480-7584. **DD** 026/.3624/10971. ***Continues*** *Library News (Canadian National Institute for the Blind)., 0842-6384.*

US/0748-2469
OFFICIAL DIRECTORY OF NEW JERSEY LIBRARIES AND MEDIA CENTERS. [Off. dir. N.J. libr. media cent.]. **Added/Corp** New Jersey Library Association. **VFOAT** Official Directory of New Jersey Libraries and Media Centers, and Buyers Guide. (1984)-. Directory. English. an. $74.10. LDA Publishers, 42-36 209th Street, Bayside NY 11361. **Tel** (718)224-9484, FAX (718)224-9487. **ED** Paul V Ippolito. **LC** Z732.N6; D57. **DD** 027/.0025/749. **Ad Acc. Circ:** 900. ***Continues*** *Directory of New Jersey Libraries and Media Centers, and Buyers Guide, 0749-3525.*
Desc: Over 1,500 libraries, public, academic, special, public and private schools are listed. A single source of information including: special collection, computers, software, etc. All heavily indexed.

●UK/0961-8163
OFFSHORE ENGINEERING INFORMATION BULLETIN. [Offshore eng. inf. bull.]. (1992)-. Periodical. English. mo. £38.00 (surface), £48.00 (airmail). Offshore Engineering Info Service, Heriot-Watt Univ, Riccarton Edinburgh, EH14 4AS Scotland. **Tel** 011 31 449 5111, FAX 011 31 451 3164. **ED** Arnold Myers. **DD** 016.6277. available via electronic mail. ***Continues*** *IOE Library Bulletin, 0142-4793.*
Desc: The first section is a list, with bibliographic details of the books, conference papers, standards, directories, reports, ect. acquired by the library in the previous month

dealing with the technology directly associated with the rational exploitation of the natural resources of the sea and seabed. Material on oil and gas exploration and production, offshore structures, underwater operations and instrumentation, diving, marine environmental protection and economics is included. The second is a list of publications, both recently published and forthcoming, of interest but not yet acquired by the acquired by the library. The third section is a diary of forthcoming meetings.

US/1047-5400
OHIO ARCHIVIST (1987), THE. (THE OHIO ARCHIVIST / THE SOCIETY OF OHIO ARCHIVISTS.). [Ohio arch.]. **Added/Corp** Society of Ohio Archivists. Vol. 18, No. 1 (Spring 1987)-. Periodical. English. Twice a year (Mar., Sept.). $10.00 (individuals), $15.00 (institutions). Society of Ohio Archivists, 2121 Tuttle Park Place, 209 Converse, Columbus OH 43210. **Tel** (614)292-2409, FAX (614)292-8916. **ED** Fred Lautzenheiser, (editor's address: Cleveland Clinic Archives, P-22, 9500 Euclid Avenue, Cleveland, OH 44195, phone: (216)444-2929). **DD** 025. **Bk Rev. Circ:** 220 (ctrl). ***Continues*** *Ohio Archivists Newsletter.*
Desc: Its goal is to share information concerning the archival profession and related professions. Contents includes articles about archives, council proceedings, president's column, meeting information, news notes and related information.

US/0360-8069
OHIO LIBRARIES. ***Ceased.*** **Main/Corp** Ohio. Auditor of State. (1972)-(19??). English. an. Ohio Libraries, c/o Thomas E Furguson, Suite 409/40 South 3rd Street, Columbus OH 43215. **LC** Z732.O5; O38A. **DD** 025.1/1/09771. ***Continues*** *Ohio Public Libraries.*
Ind/Abst Libr. Lit.

US/1046-4336
OHIO LIBRARIES (COLUMBUS, OHIO. 1988). (OHIO LIBRARIES.). [Ohio libr.]. **Added/Corp** Ohio Library Association. Ohio Library Trustee Association. Ohio Friends of the Library. Vol. 1, No. 1 (Jan./Feb. 1988)-. Periodical. English. Four times a year (Jan., Apr., July, Oct.). $35.00 US; $50.00 other. Ohio Library Council, 35 East Gay Street, Suite 305, Columbus OH 43215. **Tel** (614)221-9057, FAX (614)221-6234. **ED** Lynda Murray. **LC** Z671; .O373. **DD** 027. **CODEN** OHLIEG. **Bk Rev**, (Qty: varies). **Ad Acc. Circ:** 5,000 (ctrl). ***Formed by the union of*** *Ohio Libraries Newsletter; OLA Bulletin (Ohio Library Association : 1985); Ohio Library Trustee* ***and*** *Ohio Friends of the Library Newsletter.*
Desc: A monthly newsletter plus a quarterly journal concerning libraries.
Ind/Abst Libr. Lit.

US/0192-6942
OHIO MEDIA SPECTRUM. [Ohio media spectr.]. **Added/Corp** Ohio Educational Library Media Association. Vol. 29 (Jan. 1977)-. Periodical. English. Three times a year. $40.00. Ohio Educational Library Media Association, 1631 Northwest Professional Plaza, Columbus OH 43220. **Tel** (614)326-1460. **ED** Edward F. Newren. **LC** Z675.S3; O516. **DD** 027.8. Index available. **Bk Rev. Ad Acc. Circ:** 2,000 (ctrl). available on microfilm and microfiche from University Microfilms International (UMI). ***Formed by the union of*** *Bulletin - Ohio Association of School Librarians, 0030-0799* ***and*** *Educational Media in Ohio.*
Desc: A publication of the Ohio Educational Library Media Association. Provides information applicable to the daily jobs of library and media specialists.
Ind/Abst Libr. Inf. Sci. Abstr.; Libr. Lit.

CN/0843-5901
OHLA NEWSLINE. (OHLA NEWSLINE : THE OFFICIAL NEWSLETTER OF THE ONTARIO HOSPITAL LIBRARIES ASSOCIATION.). [OHLA newsline]. **Added/Corp** Ontario Hospital Libraries' Association. Ontario Hospital Association. **VAT** Ontario Hospital Library Association Newsline. Vol. 1 (1986)-. Newsletter. English. qt. Free to members. Ontario Hospital Libraries Association, c/o M Conchelos, Hospital Library, St Joseph's General Hospital, 384 Rogers Street, Peterborough Ontario K9H 7B6 Canada. **DD** 027.6/62/060713.

JA
OKINAWA TOSHOKAN KYOKAI SHI. **Main/Corp** Okinawa Toshokan Kyokai. (19??)-. Periodical. Japanese. Okinawa Library Association, Okinawa Prefectrual Library, 2-16 Yorimiya 1-chome, Naha Okinawa Japan. **LC** Z671; .O48a.

US/0030-1760
OKLAHOMA LIBRARIAN. [Okla. libr.]. **Added/Corp** Oklahoma Library Association. (Spring 1950)-. Periodical. English. Six times a year. $15.00. Oklahoma Librarian, 300 Hardy Drive, Edmond OK 73013. **Tel** (405)348-0506. **ED** Patti Gallad. **LC** Z732; .O572. **DD** 020/.6234/766. **Ad Acc. Circ:** 1,200. available on microfilm and microfiche from University Microfilms International (UMI).
Desc: Official publication of the Oklahoma Library Association, a professional organization for librarians of all types of libraries in Oklahoma.
Ind/Abst Libr. Inf. Sci. Abstr.; Libr. Lit.

US
OLAC NEWSLETTER. ***Title Change.*** Vol. 5, No. 1 (Mar. 1985)-. Newsletter. English. qt. ***Continued by*** *Newsletter (On-Line Audiovisual Catalogers), 0739-1153.*

HU/0230-6514
OMIKK HIRADO. (1982)-. Hungarian.
Ind/Abst Magyar Konyv. Szak. Biblio.

US/0895-187X
OMNI ONLINE DATABASE DIRECTORY. [Omni online database dir.]. **VFOAT** Online Database Directory. 1983-. Directory. English. Macmillan Publishing Company, 866 3rd Avenue, New York NY 10022. **Tel** (212)702-2000, (800)257-5755. **DD** 005.

US/1042-2706
ON CARL. (ON CARL : THE NEWSLETTER OF THE COLORADO ALLIANCE OF RESEARCH LIBRARIES.). [On CARL]. **VAT** On Colorado Alliance of Research Libraries. (July/Aug. 1988)-. Newsletter. English. bm. Free. 777 Grant, Suite 304, Denver CO 80203. **DD** 021.

US/1044-4327
ON THE ROAD (BROOKLYN, NEW YORK, N.Y.). (ON THE ROAD.). [On road]. **Added/Corp** Library Outreach Reporter Co. **VFOAT** Mobile Ideas for Libraries; OTR. Vol. 1 No. 1 (Fall 1989)-. Periodical. English. Four times a year. $12.00 US; $15.00 Canada. Library Outreach Reporter, 148 Liberty Street, Fords NJ 08863. **ED** Cathi Alloway. **DD** 027.

US/0748-8831
ONE-PERSON LIBRARY, THE. [One-pers. libr.]. **VFOAT** One Person Library; One Person Library. Vol. 1, No. 1 (May 1984)-. Periodical. English. mo. $75.00 US; $80.00 Canada; $85.00 other. OPL Resources, LTD, PO Box 948, Murray Hill Station, New York NY 10156. **Tel** (212)683-6285. **ED** Andrew Berner. **[CCC].** Index available. **Bk Rev. Ad Acc.** available on audiocassette from University Microfilms International (UMI).
Desc: Newsletter for librarians and managers who supervise single-staff libraries.

UK/0144-025X
ONLINE & CD NOTES. (19??)-. English. Ten times a year. £68.00 (member), £85.00 (non-member) Europe; £74.00 (member), £93.00 (non-member) other. ASLIB, Information House, 20-24 Old Street, London EC1V 9AP England. **Tel** 011 44 71 253 4488, FAX 011 44 71 430 0514, telex 23667 AJLIB G. **(Subscription address:** North America: 143 Old Marlton Pike, Medford, NJ 08055-8750**)**

UK
ONLINE BIBLIOGRAPHIC DATABASES. ***Suspended.*** **Added/Corp** Aslib. 2nd Edition (1981)-(19??). English. ir. Gale Research Inc., 835 Penobscot Building, Detroit MI 48226. **Tel** (800)877-GALE, (313)961-2242, FAX (313)961-6083, telex TWX 810-221-7086. **ED** J. L. Hall and M. J. Brown. **LC** Z699.22; .O58. **DD** 025.3/13. **NLM** Z 699.22 O58. ***Continues*** *On-Line Bibliographic Data Bases Directory, 0144-7890.*

AT/0816-956X
ONLINE CURRENTS. [Online curr.]. (1986)-. Periodical. English. Ten times a year (monthly with Jan./Feb. and July/Aug. issues combined). 138.00Can$ Australia; 156.00Can$ other. Enterprise Information Management, 6/217 Eastern Valley Way, Willoughby 2068, New South Wales, Australia. **Tel** 011 61 2 9587099, FAX 011 61 2 9580699. **DD** 025.040994.
Ind/Abst AESIS Q.; Aust. Educ. Index; Aust. Libr. Inf. Sci. Abstr. (1986-).

US/0741-0077
ONLINE DATABASE SEARCH SERVICES DIRECTORY. ***Ceased.*** [Online database search serv. dir.]. 1st Ed., Part 1 of 2 parts (Dec. 1983)-2nd Ed. ( ). Directory. English. ir. Gale Research Inc., 835 Penobscot Building, Detroit MI 48226. **Tel** (800)877-GALE, (313)961-2242, FAX (313)961-6083, telex TWX 810-221-7086. **ED** Doris Maxfield. **LC** QA76.55; .O55. **DD** 026.5/24.
Desc: Detailed information on over 1,700 libraries, information firms, and other organizations that provide computerized information retrieval and associated services. Entries are arranged geographically and furnish such information as online systems accessed, subject and database specializations, amount of search activity, staff size and searchers' names, how to arrange a search, fee structure, and other information for each organization or service listed.

US/0891-4672
ONLINE TODAY. ***Title Change.*** [Online today]. Periodical. English. mo. 5000 Arlington Centre Boulevard, PO Box 20212, Columbus OH 43220. **Tel** (614)457-8600, (800)848-8990, FAX (614)457-0438. **ED** Douglas G Branstetter. **DD** 004. **CODEN** ONTOEE. **Bk Rev. Ad Acc.** ctrl circ. Documents available from Ask*IEEE. ***Continues*** *Today, 0746-9810.* ***Continued by*** *CompuServe Magazine.*
Desc: An online information utility that provides at-home information retrieval, communication, news, shopping, banking, stock transactions, travel reservation systems, etc. for personal computer users in the US and Canada and Japan. The journal maintains a computer product review section, a new computer product announcement section, information industry news and computer book reviews.
Ind/Abst INSPEC (1985-1986).

CN/0820-537X
ONTARIO LIBRARY SERVICE ESCARPMENT : DIRECTORY. [Ont. Libr. Serv. Escarp.]. **Main/Corp** Ontario Library Service Escarpment. (1985/86)-. Directory. English. an. Ontario Library Service Escarpment, 1133 Central Avenue, Hamilton Ontario L8K 1N7 Canada. **DD** 027.4/025/713. ***Continues*** *Directory - South Central Regional Library System, 0319-0293.*

NE/0030-3372
OPEN. [Open]. (1969)-. Periodical. Dutch. mo (11 issues). Fl95.00. Stichting Vaktijdschrift, POB 572, 2600 AN Delft, The Netherlands. **Tel** 011 31 15 562073. **CODEN** OPNNBQ. Documents available from Ask*IEEE, CASDDS. ***Formed by the union of*** *Bibliotheekleven* ***and*** *Tijdschrift voor Efficientie en Documentatie.*
Ind/Abst Chem. Abstr.; INSPEC (June 1972-); Libr. Inf. Sci. Abstr.; Libr. Lit.; Soc. Res. Methodol. Abstr. (1992-).

CN/0709-8634
OPEN DOOR (BRITISH COLUMBIA LIBRARY TRUSTEES ASSOCIATION). (THE OPEN DOOR.). [Open door]. **Added/Corp** British Columbia Library Trustees Association. (1977)-. Periodical. English. Free to members. Vancouver Island Regional Library, 10 Strickland Street, Nanaimo British Columbia Canada. **DD** 027.4711.

US/0097-823X
OPERATING PLAN - STATE LIBRARY OF OHIO. (OPERATING PLAN.). **Main/Corp** State Library of Ohio. (19??)-. Periodical. English. Columbus State Library, 65 South Front Street, Columbus OH 43215. **LC** Z733.S83; S86a. **DD** 027.5771/57.

US
OPTICAL DISC IN LIBRARIES : USES & TRENDS. (1990)-. English. $79.50. Learned Information Inc., 143 Old Marlton Pike, Medford NJ 08055-8750. **Tel** (609)654-6266, FAX (609)654-4309.
Desc: For library and information professional interested in using optical discs in their libraries and information centers. For publishers, teachers, and students of library schools. Source of information on the use of optical discs in libraries.

FI/0358-5581
OPUSCULUM. Vol. 1, No. 1-. Periodical. Finnish (Swedish; summaries and/or abstracts in English). qt. Fmk120.00. Helsingin Yliopiston Kirjasto, PL312, SF-00171 Helsinki Finland. **Tel** 1912721, telex 122785 TSK SF. **LC** Z829.A1; O68.
Ind/Abst Am. Hist. Life (1984-).

US/1048-2199
ORALL NEWSLETTER. (ORALL NEWSLETTER / OHIO REGIONAL ASSOCIATION OF LAW LIBRARIES.). [ORALL newsl.]. **Added/Corp** Ohio Regional Association of Law Libraries. Cleveland-Marshall College of Law. Library. University of Akron. School of Law. Library. **VAT** Ohio Regional Association of Law Libraries Newsletter. Began with: Vol. 1978, No. 2 (July 1978)-. Newsletter. English. qt (Mar., Jun., Sep., Dec.). $10.00. Baker Hostetler Law Firm, 3200 National City Center, Cleveland OH 44114. **Tel** (513)887-3456, FAX (513)868-2609. **ED** Susan Miljenovic. **LC** Z675.L2; O65. **DD** 026.34/09771. ***Continues*** *Ohio Regional Association of Law Libraries. Newsletter - Ohio Regional Association of Law Libraries.*
Ind/Abst Leg. Inf. Manage. Index (19??-).

AT/0045-6705
ORANA. [Orana]. **Added/Corp** Library Association of Australia. Children's Libraries Section. (1977)-. Periodical. English. qt (4 issues). 30.00Aus$ Australia; 40.00Aus$ (surface mail), 50.00Aus$ (airmail). Australian Library & Information Association, PO Box E441, Queen Victoria Terrace, ACT 2600 Australia. **Tel** 011 61 6 2851877, FAX 011 61 6 282 2249. **LC** Z675.S3; O577. **DD** 027.62/6/0994. Index available. cum. index. **Bk Rev. Ad Acc. Circ:** 1,000. ***Continues*** *Children's Libraries Newsletter.*
Desc: Contains information about school and children's libraries.
Ind/Abst Annu. Bibliogr. Engl. Lang. Lit.; APAIS, Aust. Public Aff. Inf. Ser. (1980-); Aust. Educ. Index; Aust. Libr. Inf. Sci. Abstr. (1990-); Child. Lit. Abstr. (19??-).

GW/0474-330X
ORBIS ACADEMICUS. (ORBIS ACADEMICUS; PROBLEMGESCHICHTEN DER WISSENSCHAFT IN DOKUMENTEN UND DARSTELLUNGEN.). **VFOAT** Problemgeschichten der Wissenschaft in Dokumenten und Darstellungen. (1951)-. Monographic series. German. ir. Price varies per volume. Verlag Karl Alber GmbH, Hermann Herder Strasse 4, D 79104 Freiburg Germany. **Tel** 011 49 761 273495.

US
OREGON COUNTRY LIBRARY. Vol. 1-. Monographic series. English. Price varies per volume. Rainy Day Press, PO Box 3035, Eugene OR 97403.

US/0030-4735
OREGON LIBRARY NEWS. **VFOAT** OLA Oregon Library News. Vol. 1 (Dec. 1952)-. Periodical. English. mo. $30.00. Oregon Library Association, 1270 Clemeketa Street NE, Salem OR 97301. **Tel** (503)370-7019, FAX (503)370-7019. **ED** Carole Dickerson and Dennis Moler. ***Continues*** *Newsletter (Oregon Library Association).*

RU
ORGANIZATSIIA SISTEMATICHESKIKH I PREDMETNYKH KATALOGOV NAUCHNYKH BIBLIOTEK. **Added/Corp** Gosudarstvennaia Biblioteka SSSR Imeni V. I. Lenina. Otdel Sistematicheskikh i Predmetnykh Katalogov. Vol. 1 (1975)-. Periodical. Russian. 0.74rub. Gosudarstvennaia Biblioteka, Informatsionnyi Tsentr, Imeni V. I. Lenina, Prospekt Kalinina 3, 121019 Moscow Russia. **LC** Z693.A15; O74.

HU/0030-6010
ORVOSI KONYVTAROS, AZ. [Orv. kvt.]. **Added/Corp** Orszagos Orvostudomanyi Konyvtar es Dokumentacios Kozpont (Hungary). (1961)-. Hungarian. qt. $16.00. **(Subscription address:** Kultura, PO Box 149, H 1389 Budapest 62 Hungary**)** **LC** Z675.M4; O78. **NLM** Z 675.M4 O79.
Ind/Abst Libr. Inf. Sci. Abstr.

JA
OSAKA FURITSU NAKANOSHIMA TOSHOKAN KIYO. **Main/Corp** Osaka Furitsu Nakanoshima Toshokan. **Added/Corp** Osaka Furitsu Nakanoshima Toshokan. Kiyo. No. 11 (1975)-. Periodical. Japanese. Osaka Furitsu Nakanoshima Toshokan, 27 Nakanoshima 1-chome Kita-ku, Osaka Japan. **Tel** 06-203-4914, FAX 06-203-0474. **LC** Z955; .O764a. ***Continues*** *Osaka Furitsu Toshokan Kiyo.*

JA
OSAKA FURITSU NAKANOSHIMA TOSHOKAN ZOKA TOSHO MOKUROKU. **Main/Corp** Osaka Furitsu Nakanoshima Toshokan. 1973-. Multiple languages. an. Free. Osaka Furitsu Nakanoshima Toshokan, 27 Nakanoshima 1-chome Kita-ku, Osaka Japan. **Tel** 06-203-4914, FAX 06-203-0474. **LC** Z955; .O764B. **Circ:** 330 (ctrl). ***Supersedes in part*** *Osaka Furitsu Toshokan Zoka Tosho Mokuro.*

JA
OSAKA FURITSU YUHIGAOKA TOSHOKAN ZOKA TOSHO MOKUROKU. **Main/Corp** Osaka Furitsu Yuhigaoka Toshokan. 1973-. Japanese. an. Free (limited distribution to the public libraries, university libraries). Osaka Furitsu Yuhigaoka Toshokan, 2-7 Reijincho Tennoji-ku, Osaka 543 Japan. **Tel** 06-772-4660, FAX 06-772-9196. **LC** Z955; .O764C. Index available. ctrl circ. ***Supersedes in part*** *Osaka Furitsu Toshokan Zoka Tosho Mokuro.*

SA
OSAR/OSALL. English (English). R5.00. Organisasie van Suid-Afrikaanse Regsbiblioteke, Johannesburg 2000 South Africa. **LC** Z675.L2; O73A. **DD** 026/.34/000968.

HU/0324-2064
OSZK HIRADO. (1959)-. Hungarian.
Ind/Abst Magyar Konyv. Szak. Biblio.

US
OUR LIBRARY PRESENTS ... . **Main/Corp** United States International Trade Commission. Library. English. mo. Free. The Library / Washington, United States International Trade Commission, Washington DC 20436. **Tel** (202)252-1630. **ED** Janet R Damon. **Bk Rev. Circ:** 150 (ctrl). ***Continues*** *Library News & Acquisitions.*
Desc: Publishes monthly acquisitions, sample reference questions, guest list, review of one reference publication and a table of contents from current economic journals.

US/0030-7319
OUTRIDER / WYOMING STATE LIBRARY, THE. Periodical. English. mo. Wyoming State Library, Supreme Court & State Library Building, Cheyenne WY 82002. **Tel** (307)777-5915, FAX (307)777-6289. **ED** Linn Rounds. **Circ:** 1,550 (ctrl).
Desc: News about the state library, other Wyoming libraries and the field in general.

US/0884-920X
OVERTONES (LINCOLN, NEB.). ***Title Change.*** (OVERTONES.). [Overtones]. **Added/Corp** Nebraska Library Commission. Vol. 10, No. 1 (Jan. 1983)-(1993). Periodical. English. mo. Nebraska Library Commission, 1420 P Street, Lincoln NE 68508-1683. **Tel** (402)471-2045, FAX (402)471-2045. **ED** Mary Jo Ryan. **DD** 021. **Bk Rev. Circ:** 2,000 (ctrl). available on microfiche. ***Continues*** *Nebraska Library Commission. NLC Overtones, 0149-5011.* ***Continued by*** *N-Compass, 1075-9719.*
Desc: Newsletter of Nebraska library activities with selected items on national and regional events and information about activities of the NE library commission.

NE/0378-7656
P-NOTES / FID, FEDERATION INTERNATIONALE DE DOCUMENTATION. English (English). ir (approximately 20-30 issues). £27.00 Europe, $46.00 other. International Federation for Information and Documentation, PO Box 90402, 2509 LK Hague Netherlands. **Tel** 011 31 70 3140509, FAX 011 31 70 834827, telex 34402 KB GV NL. **(Subscription address:** Turpin Transactions Ltd., Blackhorse Road, Letchworth, Hertfordshire SG6 1HN United Kingdom; Telephone: (0462) 672555, FAX: (0462) 480947**)** **LC** Z696; .U8662. **DD** 025.4/32. ***Continues*** *PE.*
Desc: Proposals for revision and extension of the Universal Decimal System.

US/0743-1430
PAC-NEWS. ***Ceased.*** (PAC-NEWS / OCLC.). Issue 19 (Nov. 1983)-(1993). Periodical. English. ir. Free. OCLC Pacific Network, 250 West First Street/Suite 330, Claremont CA 91711. **Tel** (909)621-9998. **ED** Diann S Iverson. **Circ:** 3,000. ***Continues*** *Western Roundup.*
Desc: News of OCLC products and services in and about the OCLC Pacific Network.

US
PACKET (JACKSON, MISS. : 1985). (THE PACKET / MISSISSIPPI LIBRARY COMMISSION.). **Added/Corp** Mississippi Library Commission. (1985)-. Periodical. English. Six times a year. Free. Mississippi Library Commission, PO Box 10700, Jackson MS 39209-0700. **Tel** (601)359-1036. ***Continues*** *MLC Packet.*

CR
PAGINAS DE CONTENIDO: CIENCIAS DE LA INFORMACION. **Added/Corp** Asociacion Interamericana de Bibliotecarios y Documentalistas Agricolas. **VFOAT** Ciencias de la Informacion. (19??)-. Periodical. Spanish (English, French and Portuguese). ir. $20.00 (individuals), $50.00 (institutions) Comes with Asociacion Interamericana de Bibliotecarios y Documentalistas Agricolas membership. Asociacion Interamericana de Bibliotecarios y Documentalistas Agricolas / AIBDA, Apartado 55 2200 Coronado, San Jose Costa Rica. **Tel** 011 506 2290222, telex 8005 CATIE CR. **Circ:** 800.
Desc: It reproduces Tables of Contents of journals in the field of Library and Information Science held in the libraries cooperating with the service.

PK/0030-9966
PAKISTAN LIBRARY BULLETIN. [Pak. libr. bull.]. **Added/Corp** University of Karachi. Library Promotion Bureau. **VFOAT** PLB. Vol. 1 (Sept. 1968)-. Bulletin. English (Urdu). Four times a year (Mar., June, Sep., Dec.). $80.00. Library Promotion Bureau, University Karachi, PO Box 8421, Karachi 75270 Pakistan. **Tel** 011 92 29 671759. **ED** M. Adil Usmani, G. A. Sabzwari, Nasim Fatima, Akhtar Hanif and Rais A. Samdani. Index available ($10.00). cum. index. **Bk Rev**, (Qty: 10). **Ad Acc. Circ:** 2,000. ***Continues*** *Pakistan Library Bulletin, 0030-9966.*
Desc: Pakistan library bulletin, university library number school and childrens library number.
Ind/Abst Am. Hist. Life (1973-1986); Libr. Inf. Sci. Abstr.; Libr. Lit.

US/0278-9469
PALINET NEWS. **Added/Corp** Union Library Catalogue of Pennsylvania. PALINET and Union Library Catalogue of Pennsylvania. No. 1- (Aug. 23, 1974)-. Periodical. English. bm. free (to members), $15.00 (nonmembers). PALINET, 3420 Walnut Street, Philadelphia PA 19104.

CN/0824-152X
PALLISER PAGES. [Palliser pages]. Vol. 1 No. 1 (1973)-. Periodical. English. Free. Palliser Regional Library, PO Box 2500, Moose Jaw Saskatchewan S6H 6Y2 Canada. **DD** 027.47124/4. ctrl circ.

UK
PAMPHLETS. **Main/Corp** Library Association. No. 1 (1950)-. Monographic series. English. Price varies per volume.

US/0092-5497
PAPER CONSERVATION NEWS. **VFOAT** PC News. V. 1- May 1973-. Periodical. English. bm. $5.00. H Wayne Eley Associates, 15 Broadway, New Haven CT 06511. **LC** Z701; .P36. **DD** 025.8/4.
Ind/Abst Abstr. Bull. Inst. Pap. Sci. Tech.

US
PAPERS OF THE ... ANNUAL MEETING OF THE SEMINAR ON THE ACQUISITION OF LATIN AMERICAN LIBRARY MATERIALS. 26th (1981)-. English. an. ***Continues*** *Seminar on the Acquisition of Latin American Library Materials. Final Report and Working Papers of the ... Seminar on the Acquisition of Latin American Library Materials.*
Ind/Abst HAPI Hisp. Am. Period. Index (-199?).

US/0536-4604
PAPERS PRESENTED AT THE ALLERTON PARK INSTITUTE. (PAPERS.). [Pap. presented Allerton Park Inst.]. **Main/Corp** Allerton Park Institute. 1- 1956-. English. an. $20.00. University of Illinois Graduate School of Library and Information Sciences, LIS Building, 501 East Daniel Street, Champaign IL 61820. **Tel** (217)333-1359. **[CCC].** Index available. **Circ:** 300. available on microfilm from University Microfilms International (UMI).
Desc: Includes the collected papers presented at the annual Allerton Park Institute on various aspects of librarianship. Each volume is indexed.

CN/0820-2931
PARKLAND REGIONAL LIBRARY NEWSLETTER. [Parkland Reg. Libr. newsl.]. **VAT** Newsletter - Parkland Regional Library. Newsletter. English. mo. Free. Parkland Regional Library, PO Box 1000, Lacombe Alberta T0C 1S0 Canada. **DD** 027.47123/3.

FR
PASCAL. 205, SCIENCES DE L'INFORMATION, DOCUMENTATION. **Added/Corp** Institut de l'Information Scientifique et Technique (France). **VFOAT** Sciences de l'Information, Documentation; Information Science, Documentation; PASCAL. 205, Information Science, Documentation. (1991)-. Periodical. French (English). Eleven times a year. 1020.00F France; 1075.00F other. CNRS / Institut d'Information Scientifique et Technique, (Centre National de la Recherche Scientifique), 15 Quai Anatole France, Paris 75700 France. **Tel** 011 33 1 47531515, telex 299 356 F. **LC** Z699.2; .P233. ***Continues*** *PASCAL. T205, Sciences de l'Information, Documentation, 0761-1641.*
Desc: Information science and documentation.

IO
PEMBIMBING PEMBACA. Periodical. Indonesian. mo. Rp12000 Indonesia; $8.00 other. Klub Perpustakaan Indonesia, Jl Dr Wahidin #1, Jakarta-Pusat Indonesia. **Tel** 362981, telex 45905 PN BP JKT. **(Subscription address:** Sekretariat KPI, Jl Dr Wahidin No 1, Jakarta Pusat Indonesia**)** **ED** A Subagio, H Suhardjono, and Djoko Dwinanto. **LC** Z460.7; .P45. **Bk Rev. Ad Acc. Circ:** 7,500 (ctrl). ***Continues*** *Pembimbing Pembatja.*
Desc: Covers education, reading habits, librarianship and popular science, with book reviews and newsletter for the members of the Library Club (Klub Perpustakaan Indonesia).

US/0737-7843
PERIODICAL TITLE ABBREVIATIONS. [Period. title abbrev.]. **Added/Corp** Gale Research Company. (1969)-. English. ir. $200.00 (each volume). Gale Research Inc., 835 Penobscot Building, Detroit MI 48226. **Tel** (800)877-GALE, (313)961-2242, FAX (313)961-6083, telex TWX 810-221-7086. **ED** Leland G. Alkire Jr. **LC** Z6945.A2; P47; PN4832. **DD** 050/.148.
Desc: International coverage is provided for periodicals in all fields, including language and literature, linguistics, social science, medicine, science, and technology.

CN/1187-225X
PERIODICALS / OTTAWA PUBLIC LIBRARY. [Period. - Ott. Public Libr.]. **Main/Corp** Bibliotheque Publique d'Ottawa. **VFOAT** Periodiques; List of Periodicals and Newspapers in the Ottawa Public Library; Repertoire des Periodiques et Journaux de la Bibliotheque Publique d'Ottawa. **VAT** Periodiques - Bibliotheque Publique d'Ottawa (1991). (1991)-. English (French and English). Limited Free Distribution. Bibliotheque Publique D'Ottawa, 120 Rue Metcalfe, Ottawa Ontario K1P 5M2 Canada. **DD** 018/.134. ***Continues*** *Guide to Periodicals and Newspapers Available in the Ottawa Public Library System., 0831-3210.*

CN/1187-225X
PERIODICALS - OTTAWA PUBLIC LIBRARY (1991). (PERIODICALS / OTTAWA PUBLIC LIBRARY). [Period. - Ott. Public Libr.]. **Main/Corp** Ottawa Public Library. **VFOAT** Periodiques; List of Periodicals and Newspapers in the Ottawa Public Library; Repertoire des Periodiques et Journaux de la Bibliotheque Publique d'Ottawa. **VAT** Periodiques - Bibliotheque Publique d'Ottawa (1991). (1990/1991)-. English (French). Limited free distribution. Ottawa Public Library, 120 Metcalfe Street, Ottawa Ontario K1P 5M2 Canada. **DD** 018/.134. ***Continues*** *Guide to Periodicals and Newspapers Available in the Ottawa Public Library System., 0831-3210.*

US/1045-2338
PERMUTED MEDICAL SUBJECT HEADINGS. (PERMUTED MEDICAL SUBJECT HEADINGS / (U.S.) NATIONAL LIBRARY OF MEDICINE.). [Permut. med. subj. head.]. **Added/Corp** National Library of Medicine (U.S.). Medical Subject Headings Section. National Library of Medicine (U.S.). (19??)-. English. an. $40.00 US, Canada & Mexico; $75.00 other. National Library of Medicine, 8600 Rockville Pike, Bethesda MD 20894. **Tel** (301)496-6308. **(Subscription address:** National Technical Information

Service, 5285 Port Royal Road, Springfield, VA 22161) **LC** Z695.1.M48; U52d. **DD** 025.4/961. **NLM** Z 695.1 M4 M12.

UK/0960-1619
PERSONNEL TRAINING AND EDUCATION. [Pers. train. educ.]. **Added/Corp** Library Association. Personnel Training and Education Group. **VFOAT** Personnel Training and Education. Vol. 7, No. 1 (1990)-. Periodical. English. Three times a year (March, July, November). £40.00 UK; £45.00 other. Library Association Personnel Training Education Group, Staffordshire Poly, College Road, Stoke on Trent ST4 2DE England. **Tel** 011 44 782 744531, , FAX 011 44 782 744035. **(Subscription address:** L A - Personnel Training and Education Group, c/o Patrick Noon, Coventry University, Lanchester Library, Much Park Street, Coventry CV1 2HF England) ***Continues*** *Training and Education, 0264-8466.*
Desc: Publishes articles, information and updating on all aspects of human resourcing of libraries and information centres.

UK/0960-6513
PERSPECTIVES IN INFORMATION MANAGEMENT. ***Ceased.*** [Perpect. inf. manag.]. (1989)-Vol. 3, No. 2 (1993). English. Twice a year. Bowker Saur Ltd., A Reed Reference Publishing Company, Part of Reed International PLC, 59-60 Grosvenor Street, London WIX 9DA England. **Tel** 011 44 71 4935841, FAX 011 44 71 4991590. **LC** T58.64; .P48. **DD** 658.4/038.
Desc: Reviews of information management and technology by experts in the field.

HU/0209-6145
PEST MEGYEI KONYVTAROS. (1955)-. Hungarian.
Ind/Abst Magyar Konyv. Szak. Biblio.; Hungar. Libr. Info. Sci. Abstr.

US
PHILSOM/S : PERIODICAL HOLDINGS IN THE LIBRARY OF THE SCHOOL OF MEDICINE BY SUBJECT. **Main/Corp** Washington University, St. Louis, Mo. Libraries. Library of the School of Medicine. **VFOAT** Philsom/Philsoms. **VAT** Periodical Holdings in the Library of the School of Medicine by Subject. English. $6.00 per copy. Washington University School of Medicine, Box 8132, 4580 Scott Avenue, St Louis MO 63110. **Tel** (314)362-4226. **LC** Z6660; .W34A; R129. **DD** 016.61/05. **NLM** ZW 1 P573. ***Formed by the union of*** *Library Publication Number One: PHILSOM, Periodical Holdings in the Library of the School of Medicine. Washington University (St. Louis, Mo.). School of Medicine. Library* ***and*** *Library Publication Number Two: PHILSOMS, Periodical Holdings in the Library of the School of Medicine by Subject. Washington University (St. Louis, Mo.). School of Medicine. Library.*

●US/1065-6545
PHYSICIAN'S MEDLINE PLUS. **See** Medical Science and Technology-Abstracting, Bibliographies and Statistics.

FR/0154-0300
PHYSIQUE, CHIMIE. LEXIQUE. **Added/Corp** France. Centre National de la Recherche Scientifique. Centre de Documentation Scientifique et Technique. (19??)-. French. an. Informascience, Centre de Documentation Scientifique et Technique Service des Abonnements, 26 rue Boyer, 75971 Paris Cedex 20 France. **LC** Z695.1.C5; P47. **DD** 025.4/966.

FJ
PIC NEWSLETTER. **Added/Corp** University of the South Pacific. Pacific Information Centre. No. 5 (Apr. 1983)-. Periodical. English. Four times a year. Free. University of the South Pacific Library, Pacific Information Centre, PO Box 1168, Suva Fiji. **Tel** 313900, FAX 300830, telex 2276 USP FJ. **ED** Jayshree Manitora. **Circ:** 300. Documents available from FAXON Xpress. ***Continues*** *RBC Newsletter.*
Desc: News relating to the Pacific information Centre in the South Pacific.

US/0197-9299
PLA BULLETIN. [PLA bull.]. **Main/Corp** Pennsylvania Library Association. **VAT** Pennsylvania Library Association Bulletin. Vol. 24 (Jan. 1969)-. Bulletin. English. Eight times a year. $40.00. Pennsylvania Library Association, 1919 North Front Street, Harrisburg PA 17102. **Tel** (717)233-3113, (800)622-3308, FAX (717)233-3121. **ED** Phyllis Hurley. **LC** Z673.P395; A15. **DD** 020/.6/234748. **Bk Rev. Ad Acc. Circ:** 2,000 (ctrl). available on microfilm and microfiche from University Microfilms International (UMI). ***Continues*** *Pennsylvania Library Association. Bulletin.*
Desc: Association news, current happenings in library and information science and events in libraries in Pennsylvania.
Ind/Abst Index Philip. Period. (-199?); Libr. Lit.

US/0149-6417
PLAFSEP. PROCESSING (LIBRARIES)--ANECDOTES, FACETIAE, SATIRE, ETC.--PERIODICALS. **VFOAT** Processing (Libraries)--Anecdotes, Facetiae, Satire, etc.--Periodicals. **VAT** Processing, Libraries, Anecdotes, Facetiae, Satire, Et Cetera. Periodicals. V. 1- Nov. 1977-. Periodical. English. qt. $30.00. Massachusetts Library Association, PO Box 556, Wakefield MA 01880. **Tel** (617)438-0779. **ED** E Glenn Musser and Ron Bettencourt. **Circ:** 100 (ctrl).
Desc: Provides the members of the technical services section of the Massachusetts Library Association with current information, ideas, concepts, etc. within technical services, locally and nationally.

US/0148-4141
PLAIN TALK. **Main/Corp** Piedmont Libraries Acquisitions Information Network. **VAT** Piedmont Libraries Acquisitions Information Network Talk. V. 1-. Periodical. English. qt. Free. Duke University Library, PLAIN Talk, Acquisitions Department, Durham NC 27706.

US/0148-0413
PLANNING GUIDE ESEA IV, PART B: LIBRARIES AND LEARNING RESOURCES. **See** Education-School Organization and Administration.

CN/0835-4014
PLAY AND PARENTING CONNECTIONS. [Play parent. connect.]. **Added/Corp** Canadian Association of Toy Libraries. **VFOAT** Connections. **VAT** Canadian Association of Toy Libraries (1987). Vol. 10, No. 1 (Spring 1987)-. Periodical. English. qt. 25.00Can$. Canadian Association of Toy Libraries and Parent Resource Centres, 120 Holland Avenue / Suite 205, Ottawa Ontario K1Y 0X6 Canada. **Tel** (613)563-0438 or, (613)728-3307. **ED** C. Moher and V. Taylor. **DD** 027.62/5. **Bk Rev. Ad Acc. Circ:** 500 (ctrl). ***Continues*** *Newsletter - Canadian Association of Toy Libraries, 0709-5619.*

UK/0952-2360
PLAYBACK LONDON. [Playback Lond.]. (1992)-. Periodical. English. tq. Free. British Library National Sound Archive, 29 Exhibition Road, London SW7 2A5 England. **Tel** 0937 546060, FAX 0937 546333, telex 557381. **ED** Alan Ward. **Circ:** 12,000.
Ind/Abst Museum Abstr.

AT/0815-841X
PLD NEWSLETTER. [PLD newsl.]. **VFOAT** Public Libraries Department Newsletter. (1985)-. English. ir. State Library of New South Wales, Macquarie Street, Sydney New South Wales 2000 Australia. **Tel** (02)230-1629, FAX (02)232-4816, telex 12 1150. **DD** 027.494405. ***Continues*** *Newsletter - Public Libraries Division, State Library of N.S.W., 0314-6405.*
Ind/Abst Aust. Educ. Index.

US
PLL NEWSLETTER. **Added/Corp** American Association of Law Libraries. **VFOAT** Private Law Libraries Newsletter. Vol. 1, No. 1 (Fall 1985)-. Newsletter. English. qt. $25.00. American Association of Law Libraries, 53 West Jackson Boulevard, Suite 940, Chicago IL 60604. **Tel** (312)939-4764, FAX (312)431-1097, telex ABA7603. ***Continues*** *PLL Newsletter.*
Ind/Abst Leg. Inf. Manage. Index (19??-).

CN/0704-0628
PLUG IN. V. 1- Oct. 13, 1977-. English. Free. Midwestern Regional Library System, 637 Victoria Street North, Kitchener Ontario N2H 5G4 Canada. **DD** 025/.02/0971344. ctrl circ.

US/0030-8188
PNLA QUARTERLY. [PNLA q.]. **Main/Corp** Pacific Northwest Library Association. **Added/Corp** Pacific Northwest Library Association. Quarterly. **VAT** Pacific Northwest Library Association Quarterly. Vol. 1 (Oct. 1936)-. Periodical. English. qt. $20.00 US; $25.00 other. Pacific Northwest Library Association, 1631 E 24th Avenue, Eugene OR 97403. **Tel** (503)344-2027, FAX (503)341-5898. **ED** Katherine G Eaton. **LC** Z673.P11; Q3. **DD** 020.623. Index available. cum. index. **Bk Rev. Ad Acc. Circ:** 1,200. available on microfilm and microfiche from University Microfilms International (UMI). ***Absorbed*** *Pacific Northwest Library Association. Proceedings.*
Desc: Library trends, association information, library end information science papers.
Ind/Abst Libr. Inf. Sci. Abstr.; Libr. Lit.

US/1049-7765
POLAR LIBRARIES BULLETIN. [Polar libr. bull.]. Issue No. 37 (Winter 1990)-. Bulletin. English. sa. Free on request. Alaska Library Association, PO Box 81084, Fairbanks AK 99708. **Tel** (907)479-4522. **DD** 021. ***Continues*** *Northern Libraries Bulletin, 0048-0789.*

●US/1053-8747
POPULAR CULTURE IN LIBRARIES. [Pop. cult. libr.]. Vol. 1 (1993)-. Periodical. English. qt. $50.00 US; $70.00 other. The Haworth Press Inc, 10 Alice Street, Binghamton NY 13904-1580. **Tel** (607)722-5857, (800)3-HAWORTH, FAX (607)722-1424. **ED** Frank Hoffman (editor's address: School of Library Science, Sam Houston State University, Huntsville, TX 77341). **LC** Z688.P64; P68. **DD** 025.2/73064. **CODEN** PCLIEQ. **Bk Rev. Ad Acc. Pr Rev. Acid Free.** available on microfiche. Documents available from Haworth Document Delivery Service.
Desc: Provides information on the evaluation, acquisition, organization, preservation, and utilization of popular culture concepts and materials. Librarians, archivists, educators, and other professionals dealing with these collections will find this journal an excellent forum for the discussion of a variety of topics including the traditional biases against popular culture held by many academics. Includes peer reviewed academic papers along with invited editor reviewed feature papers as well as occasional and regular columns.
Ind/Abst Abstr. Anthropol. (19??-).

PL/0032-4752
PORADNIK BIBLIOTEKARZA. [Poradnik Bibl.]. **Added/Corp** Stowarzyszenie Bibliotekarzy Polskich. (Oct. 1949)-. Periodical. Polish. mo. $66.00. **(Subscription address:** ARS Polona, PO Box 1001, 00068 Warsaw Poland.) **LC** Z671; .P6.
Ind/Abst Libr. Inf. Sci. Abstr.

CN/0229-9712
POSITIVE (LONDON, ONT.). (POSITIVE). [Posit.]. Vol. 1, No. 1 (Feb. 1977)-. Periodical. English. Four times a year. 6.00Can$. University of Western Ontario, Visual Arts Department, Department B Maceachren, London Ontario N6A 5B7 Canada. **Tel** (519)679-2111 ext. 6185. **ED** Brenda MacEachern. **DD** 025.17/73. Index available. **Ad Acc. Circ:** 100.
Desc: Contains articles of interest to slide and photograph curators in the visual arts with particular emphasis on issues relative to Canadian visual resources collections.

US/0892-9343
PR ACTIVITY REPORT. (PR ACTIVITY REPORT. AMERICAN LIBRARY ASSOCIATION, PUBLIC INFORMATION OFFICE.). [PR act. rep.]. **Added/Corp** American Library Association. Public Information Office. **VAT** Public Relations Activity Report. (1987)-. Periodical. English. Five times a year. $25.00 US; $30.00 Canada & Mexico; $35.00 other. American Library Association, 50 East Huron Street, Chicago IL 60611. **Tel** (312)944-6780, (800)545-2433, FAX (312)944-2641. **(Subscription address:** American Library Association, Subscription Department, 434 West Downer, Aurora IL 60506-9936.) **DD** 021. **Circ:** 1,000.
Desc: Newsletter about ALA promotions and other PR opportunities for libraries.

CN/0712-9726
PRAPFALLS. (PRAPFALLS : NEWSLETTER OF THE PROVINCIAL/REGIONAL LIBRARY ASSOCIATION PRESIDENTS.). [Prapfalls]. **Added/Corp** Provincial/Regional Library Association Presidents. Issue No. 1 (Jan. 1982)-. Newsletter. English. ir. $10.00. Prapfalls, c/o Frances Morrison Library, 311 23rd Street, Saskatoon Saskatchewan S7K 0J6 Canada. **DD** 020/.623/0971.

CN/1184-1125
PREFACE (SASKATOON. 1990). (PREFACE.). [Preface]. **Added/Corp** Saskatoon Public Library. Vol. 2, No. 5 (Sept./Oct. 1990)-. Periodical. English. bm. Saskatoon Public Library, 311-23rd Street East, Saskatoon Saskatchewan S7K 0J6 Canada. **DD** 027.47124/25/05. ***Continues*** *Your Library Preface., 0830-5307.*

US/0899-9821
PREVIEW. ***Ceased.*** [Preview]. **VFOAT** Preview, Professional & Reference Literature Review. (Nov. 1988)-Ceased (Jan. 1992). Periodical. English. mo (July/Aug. issue combined). Mountainside Publishing Company, PO Box 8330, Ann Arbor MI 48107. **Tel** (313)662-3925. **ED** Christy J Havens. **LC** Z666; .P889. **DD** 020/.5. **[CCC].** Index available. cum. index. **Bk Rev. Ad Acc. Circ:** 2,000.
Desc: A compilation of reviews and review summaries covering library science and related fields and general reference materials.

US/1042-8216
PRIMARY SOURCES AND ORIGINAL WORKS. [Prim. sources orig. works]. **VFOAT** Primary Sources and Original Works. Vol. 1, No. 1/2 (1991)-. Monographic series. English. ir. $35.00 US; $49.00 other (Current Volume). The Haworth Press Inc, 10 Alice Street, Binghamton NY 13904-1580. **Tel** (607)722-5857, (800)3-HAWORTH, FAX (607)722-1424. **ED** Larry McCrank Dean (editor's address: Library and Instructional Services, Ferris State University, Big Rapids, MI 49307). **LC** Z688.A2; P75. **DD** 026/.944. **Bk Rev. Ad Acc. Pr Rev. Acid Free.** available on microfilm and microfiche from University Microfilms International (UMI). Documents available from Ask*IEEE, Haworth Document Delivery Service. ***Continues*** *Special Collections, 0270-3157.*
Desc: Devoted entirely to research, documentation and curatorship of primary sources and original works in archives, museums, and special library collections. Will publish feature articles, reports, reviews, columns, mini forums, collector and collection profiles, plus special issues that discuss current issues and challenges of the handling of primary sources in any kind of institutions.
Ind/Abst Inf. Sci. Abstr.; INSPEC; Libr. Inf. Sci. Abstr.

UK/0032-8898
PRIVATE LIBRARY. (THE PRIVATE LIBRARY.). [Priv. Libr.]. **Added/Corp** Private Libraries Association. (1958)-. Periodical. English. Four times a year. $40.00. Private Libraries Association, Ravelston South View

Road, Pinner Middlesex HA5 3YD England. **(Subscription address:** Private Libraries Association, Great Russell Street, London WC1B 3DG England**) ED** David Chambers. **LC** Z990; .P7. Index available. cum. index. **Bk Rev. Ad Acc. Circ:** 1,150. ***Continues*** *PLA Quarterly.*
Desc: Publishes essays concerned with private book collecting.
Ind/Abst Abstr. Engl. Stud.; ARTbibliogr. Mod.; BHA : Biblio. Hist. Art; Libr. Lit.

US/1044-3886
PRO-ACTION. ***Title Change.*** (EMPOWERMENT : NEWSLETTER OF THE AMERICAN LIBRARY ASSOCIATION, OFFICE FOR LIBRARY OUTREACH SERVICES.). [Empowerment]. **Added/Corp** American Library Association. Office for Library Outreach Services. Vol. 1, No. 1 (Summer 1989)-(19??). Newsletter. English. sa. American Library Association, 50 East Huron Street, Chicago IL 60611. **Tel** (312)944-6780, (800)545-2433, FAX (312)944-2641. **ED** Sibyl Moses. **DD** 027. ***Continued by*** *Empowerment (Chicago, Ill. : 1991), 1044-3886.*
Desc: Newsletter of the American Library Association, Office for Library Outreach Services covering many fields of library services.

RM/0032-924X
PROBLEME DE INFORMARE SI DOCUMENTARE. [Prob. inf. & doc.]. **Added/Corp** Institutul Central de Documentare Tehnica (Romania) Institutul National de Informare si Documentare. **VFOAT** Information and Documentation Problems. (1967)-. Periodical. Multiple languages (English, Romanian and French; summaries and/or abstracts in Russian). qt. $111.00. Institutul National de Informare si Documentare, Str. George Enescu 27-29, 70141 Bucharest Romania. **Tel** 6134010. **(Subscription address:** Ilexim Press Department, PO Box 1, 136-1-137, Bucharest, Romania.**) LC** Z1007; .P96. **DD** 029.7. **CODEN** PIDCA6. **Bk Rev. Circ:** 1,500. available with charts; available with illustrations. Documents available from Ask*IEEE.
Desc: Contains original articles of theory and practice in the fields of information and documentation.
Ind/Abst INSPEC (March 1972-); Libr. Inf. Sci. Abstr.

US
PROCEEDINGS - CONFERENCE ON FEDERAL INFORMATION RESOURCES. **Main/Conf** Conference on Federal Information Resources. **VFOAT** Federal Information Resources: Conference Proceedings. 1st- 1970-. Proceedings. English. an. Federal City College Press, Media Services Division, Washington DC 20001. **LC** Z675.G7; C65A. **DD** 027.5/0973.

UK/0582-303X
PROCEEDINGS OF THE ANNUAL CONFERENCE. **Main/Corp** Scottish Library Association. **Added/Corp** Scottish Library Association. Report of Proceedings. (19??)-. Monographic series. English. an. Price varies per volume. Scottish Library Association, Motherwell Business Centre, 124/6 Coursington Road, Motherwell ML1 1PW Scotland. **Tel** 011 44 698 252526, 011 44 698 252057, FAX 011 44 698 252057. **ED** Colin Dakers. **LC** Z673; .S422. **Ad Acc. Circ:** 500 (ctrl).
Desc: Contains the papers given at the annual conference of the Annual Conference of the Scottish Library Association.

US/0044-7870
PROCEEDINGS OF THE ASIS ANNUAL MEETING. [Proc. ASIS annu. meet.]. **Main/Corp** American Society for Information Science. **VAT** Proceedings of the American Society for Information Science Annual Meeting. Vol. 11 (1974)-. Proceedings. English. an (Nov.). Price varies, Comes with American Society Information Science membership. American Society Information Science, 8720 Georgia Avenue, Suite 501, Silver Spring MD 20910. **Tel** (301)495-0900, FAX (301)495-0810. **(Subscription address:** Learned Information, Inc., 143 Old Marlton Pike, Medford, NJ 08055, telephone: (609)654-6266**) ED** Carol Parkhurst. **NLM** Z 699.A1 A508P. **CODEN** PAISDQ. **[CCC]. Pr Rev.** Documents available from Article Express International, The Genuine Article, Ask*IEEE, CASDDS. ***Continues*** *American Society for Information Science. Meeting. Proceedings of the American Society for Information Science, 0160-0044.*
Desc: Papers and abstracts from the annual meeting of the American Society for Information Science.
Ind/Abst Bioeng. Abstr.; Chem. Abstr. (1974-1984); Compumath Citation Index [Full Cov.]; Curr. Contents Soc. Behav. Sci.; Curr. Index J. Educ.; Ei Page One; Eng. Index Annu.; INSPEC; Res. Alert [Full Cov.]; Soc. Sci. Cit. Index [Full Cov.].

US
PROCEEDINGS OF THE ASIS MID-YEAR MEETING. **Main/Corp** American Society for Information Science. (1972)-. Proceedings. English. an. Price varies, Comes with American Society Information Science membership. American Society Information Science, 8720 Georgia Avenue, Suite 501, Silver Spring MD 20910. **Tel** (301)495-0900, FAX (301)495-0810.
Ind/Abst Curr. Index J. Educ.

UK
PROCEEDINGS OF THE ... FID CONGRESS. **Main/Conf** FID Congress. 39th (1978)-. Proceedings. English. be. Price varies per volume. ***Continues*** *International Federation for Documentation World Congress : Proceedings.*

●US/1075-0886
PROCEEDINGS OF THE ... MEETING / ASSOCIATION OF RESEARCH LIBRARIES. [Proc. meet. - Assoc. Res. Libr.]. **Main/Corp** Association of Research Libraries. Meeting. **Added/Corp** Association of Research Libraries. 123rd (Oct. 20-22, 1993)-. Proceedings. English. Twice a year. $45.00 members; $70.00 nonmembers. Association of Research Libraries, 21 Dupont Circle, Washington DC 20036. **Tel** (202)296-2296. **DD** 020. ***Continues*** *Minutes of the Meeting - Association of Research Libraries, 0044-9652.*
Desc: Edited proceedings of the semiannual membership meetings of the association, including both program and business sessions.

CN/0702-0147
PROCEEDINGS OF THE NORTHERN LIBRARIES COLLOQUY. **Main/Conf** Northern Libraries Colloquy. **Added/Corp** Arctic Institute of North America. (19??)-. Proceedings. English. The Arctic Institute of North America, University of Calgary, 2500 University Drive Northwest, Calgary Alberta T2N 1N4 Canada. **Tel** (403)220-7515, FAX (403)282-4609. **LC** Z6005.P7; N67a; G606. **DD** 016.9198.

UG
PROCEEDINGS OF THE PUBLIC LIBRARIES BOARD STAFF CONFERENCE AND SEMINAR. **Main/Corp** Uganda. Public Libraries. Board. Proceedings. English. Public Libraries Board, PO Box 7117, 38 William Street, Kampala Uganda. **LC** Z857; .U3A. **DD** 027.4/676/1.

UK
PROCEEDINGS, PAPERS AND SUMMARIES OF DISCUSSIONS AT THE ... CONFERENCE. **Main/Corp** Library Association. **VFOAT** Proceedings of the Annual Conference. Proceedings. English. an. Library Association, 7 Ridgmount Street, London WC1E 7AE England. **Tel** 011 44 71 636-7543, FAX 011 44 71 436-7218, telex 21897. **LC** Z673.L7; P207. **DD** 020.622.

UK/0953-7279
PROFESSIONAL CALENDAR. [Prof. cal.]. (1988)-. English. Six times a year. £20.00 UK; £25.00 Europe, £28.00 other. ILS Library, University College of Wales Aberystwyth, Llanbadarn Fawr, Aberystwyth, Dyfed SY23 3AS Wales United Kingdom. **Tel** 44 970 622417, FAX 44 970 622190, telex 34391. **ED** R C Williams. **DD** 020. **Ad Acc.**
Desc: Listing of forthcoming courses, and conferences in librarianship and information science.

US/8755-0253
PROFESSIONAL DOCUMENT RETRIEVAL. ***Suspended.*** [Prof. doc. retr.]. Vol. 1, No. 1 (Fall 1984)-(1991). Periodical. English. qt. $15.00. The Information Store Inc., PO Box 3691, 550 Sansome Street, Suite 400, San Francisco CA 94105. **Tel** (415)433-5500. **ED** Michael R. Kennedy. **DD** 025. **[CCC]. Ad Acc. Circ:** 250.
Desc: Newsletter reporting on the state of the art of document retrieval, including sources and services, technology, management, and legal issues.

RU
PROGNOZIROVANIE RAZVITIIA BIBLIOTECHNOGO DELA V SSSR. **Main/Corp** Moscow. Publichnaia Biblioteka. Nauchno-Issledovatelskii Otdel Bibliotekovedeniia i Teorii Bibliografii. Vol. 1 (1972)-. Russian. 0.53rub each issue. **LC** Z819.A1; M66a.

UK/0033-0337
PROGRAM (ASLIB). (PROGRAM.). [Program]. **Added/Corp** Queen's University of Belfast. School of Library Studies. ASLIB. No. 1 (Mar. 1966)-. Periodical. English. Four times a year (Jan., Apr., July, Oct.). £83.00 (members), £104.00 (non-members) Europe; £91.00 (members), £114.00 (non-members) other. ASLIB, Information House, 20-24 Old Street, London EC1V 9AP England. **Tel** 011 44 71 253 4488, FAX 011 44 71 430 0514, telex 23667 AJLIB G. **ED** Lucy Tedd. **LC** Z678.9.A1; P76. **DD** 025.3/028/5. **CODEN** PRGRDU. Index available. cum. index. **Bk Rev. Ad Acc. Pr Rev. Circ:** 1,600. Documents available from Ask*IEEE.
Desc: Devoted to all aspects of the use of computers in libraries, including networks information systems, databases, data structures, file compaction, hardware and software developments.
Ind/Abst ACM Guide Comput. Lit.; Anbar Account. Finan. Abstr. [Full Txt.]; Anbar Mark. Distr. Abstr. (1973-) [Full Txt.]; Anbar Top Manage. Abstr. [Full Txt.]; Comput. Abstr.; Comput. Rev. (April 1969-); Educ. Technol. Abstr. (April 1969-); Fluid Abstr., Civil Eng.; Fluid Abstr. Proc. Eng.; FLUIDEX (1973-); Inf. Instruc. Technol.; INSPEC (April 1969-); Libr. Inf. Sci. Abstr.; Libr. Lit.; Manage. Bibliogr. Rev.; Microcomput. Index (1985-?); Oper. Prod. Manage. Abstr. (1985-) [Full Txt.]; Person. Train. Abstr. [Full Txt.]; Women Manage. Rev. [Full Txt.]; World Publ. Monit.

CN/0381-1476
PROGRAM - CANADIAN LIBRARY ASSOCIATION, CONFERENCE. **Main/Corp** Canadian Library Association. (1946)-. English. an. Free. Canadian Library Association, 200 Elgin Street, Suite 602, Ottawa Ontario K2P 1L5 Canada. **Tel** (613)232-9625. **DD** 020/.622/71.

UK/0033-0337
PROGRAM; NEWS OF COMPUTERS IN LIBRARIES. **Added/Corp** Belfast. Queen's University. School of Library Studies. Vol. 1 (March 1966)-. Periodical. English. qt. $200.00 US; $204.00 Canada & Mexico. ASLIB, Information House, 20-24 Old Street, London EC1V 9AP England. **Tel** 011 44 71 253 4488, FAX 011 44 71 430 0514, telex 23667 AJLIB G. **(Subscription address:** North America: 143 Old Marlton Pike, Medford, NJ 08055-8750**)**
Ind/Abst Soc. Sci. Cit. Index [Full Cov.].

NE/0377-7693
PROGRESS REPORT - F.I.A.B. (PROGRESS REPORT.). **Main/Corp** International Federation of Library Associations. **VAT** Progress Report - Federation Internationale de Associations de Bibliothecaires. English. Netherlands Congress Building Tower, 3rd Floor, POB 82128, Hague The Netherlands. **LC** Z672; .I57A. **DD** 020/.621.

US/1052-5726
PROGRESSIVE LIBRARIAN. [Progress. libr.]. **Added/Corp** Progressive Librarians Guild. (Summer 1990)-. Periodical. English. Three times a year. $15.00 (individuals), $30.00 (institutions). Progressive Librarians Guild, 330 West 42nd Street, 4th Floor, Empire State College, New York NY 10036. **Tel** (212)279-7380. **ED** Elaine Harger. **LC** Z716.4; .P77. **DD** 021. Index available. cum. index. **Bk Rev. Ad Acc. Circ:** 400.
Desc: Analysis of trends in librarianship from socially responsible/left perspective.
Ind/Abst Altern. Press Index (199?-).

CN/0702-8032
PROJECT: PROGRESS NEWSLETTER. **Added/Corp** Canadian Association of Public Libraries. (1976)-. Newsletter. English. Free. Canadian Library Association, 200 Elgin Street, Suite 602, Ottawa Ontario K2P 1L5 Canada. **Tel** (613)232-9625. **DD** 027.4/71.

AT/0810-9028
PROMETHEUS. **Added/Corp** University of Queensland. Dept. of Economics. Information Research Unit. Vol. 1, No. 1 (June 1983)-. Periodical. English. Twice a year (June & December). 35.00Aus$ Australia; 50.00Aus$ other. Prometheus, GPO Box 4, ANU Professor Lamberton, Canberra 2601 Australia. **Tel** 011 61-6-2493884, FAX 011 61 6 249 0312. **ED** D. M. Lamberton. **Bk Rev**, (Qty: 40-50 /year). **Ad Acc. Pr Rev. Circ:** 400 (ctrl). Documents available from Ask*IEEE.
Desc: Journal of issues in technological change, innovation, information economics, communication and science policy.
Ind/Abst APAIS, Aust. Public Aff. Inf. Ser.; INSPEC (June 1984-); PAIS Int. Print (1991-); Soc. Plann. Policy Dev. Abstr.

CN/0823-3306
PROVINCIAL FILM LIBRARY RESOURCE CATALOGUE. (RESOURCE CATALOGUE / PROVINCIAL FILM LIBRARY.). [Prov. Film Libr. resourc. cat.]. **Main/Corp** Alberta. Provincial Film Library. 1983-. English. Public Affairs Bureau, Provincial Film Library, 11510 Kingsway Avenue, Edmonton Alberta T5G 2Y5 Canada. **LC** Z883.E35; A43A. **DD** 011/.37.

PL/0033-202X
PRZEGLAD BIBLIOTECZNY. [Prz. bibl.]. **Added/Corp** Zwiazek Bibliotekarzy Polskich. Stowarzyszenie Bibliotekarzy Polskich. Vol. 1 (1927)-. Polish. qt. Price on Request. **(Subscription address:** ARS Polona, PO Box 1001, 00068 Warsaw Poland.**) ED** Barbara Sordylowa. **LC** Z671; .P97. available on microfilm from University Microfilms International (UMI). ***Supersedes*** *Przeglad Biblioteczny.*
Ind/Abst Libr. Inf. Sci. Abstr.

PL
PRZEGLAD PISMIENNICTWA ZAGADNIEN INFORMACJI. **Added/Corp** Instytut Informacji Naukowej, Techniczneji Ekonomicznej. (19??)-. Polish. Six times a year. $42.00 (latest volume). **(Subscription address:** ARS Polona, PO Box 1001, 00068 Warsaw Poland.**)**

US
PTS ONLINE NEWS. **Added/Corp** Predicasts, Inc. **VFOAT** P.T.S. Online News. (198?)-. Periodical. English. Four times a year. Free. Predicasts Inc., A Ziff Communications Company, 11001 Cedar Avenue, Cleveland OH 44106. **Tel** (800)321-6388, (216)795-3000, FAX (216)229-9944, telex 985 604. **(Subscription**

address: Information Access Company, PO Box 61000, Department 1851, San Francisco, CA 94161; Phone: (800)321-6388) **CODEN** PONED5.

US/1063-164X
PUBLIC-ACCESS COMPUTER SYSTEMS REVIEW, THE. **Added/Corp** Library and Information Technology Association. **VFOAT** Public Access Computer Systems Review. (1992)-. English. $20.00 (nonmember), $17.00 (ALA member). American Library Association, 50 East Huron Street, Chicago IL 60611. **Tel** (312)944-6780, (800)545-2433, FAX (312)944-2641. **(Subscription address:** American Library Association, Subscription Department, 434 West Downer, Aurora IL 60506-9936.)

●US/1056-4942
PUBLIC AND ACCESS SERVICES QUARTERLY. **VFOAT** Public Services Quarterly. (1994)-. Periodical. English. qt. $60.00 US; $84.00 other. The Haworth Press Inc, 10 Alice Street, Binghamton NY 13904-1580. **Tel** (607)722-5857, (800)3-HAWORTH, FAX (607)722-1424. **ED** Dr. Virgil Blake. **Acid Free.** Documents available from Haworth Document Delivery Service.
Desc: Focuses on the activities and operations of Library/Information Centers that involve direct interaction with the library's public. Will embrace both internal and external activities designed to enhance the relationship of the Library/Information Center and its clientele.

US/0163-5506
PUBLIC LIBRARIES. [Public libr.]. **Added/Corp** Public Library Association. Vol. 17 (Spring 1978)-. Periodical. English. Six times a year (Jan., Mar., May, July, Sept., Nov.). $50.00 US; $60.00 other. American Library Association, 50 East Huron Street, Chicago IL 60611. **Tel** (312)944-6780, (800)545-2433, FAX (312)944-2641. **(Subscription address:** American Library Association, Subscription Department, 434 West Downer, Aurora IL 60506-9936.) **ED** Sandra Garrison. **LC** Z731; .P932. **DD** 027.4/73. **[CCC].** Index available. **Bk Rev. Ad Acc. Pr Rev. Circ:** 7,000. available on microfilm and microfiche from University Microfilms International (UMI). ***Continues*** *PLA Newsletter, 0022-6998.*
Desc: Articles and regular features on public library services. Includes book review column.
Ind/Abst Curr. Index J. Educ.; Inf. Instruc. Technol.; Inf. Sci. Abstr.; Libr. Inf. Sci. Abstr.; Libr. Lit.

AT
PUBLIC LIBRARIES IN QUEENSLAND, STATISTICAL BULLETIN. **See** Library and Information Sciences-Abstracting, Bibliographies and Statistics.

US
PUBLIC LIBRARY CATALOG. **Added/Corp** H.W. Wilson Company. 5th Ed. (1968)-. Catalog. English. an (plus four annual paperbound supplements). 9th Edition: $180.00 US and Canada; $200.00 other. H W Wilson Company, 950 University Avenue, Bronx NY 10452. **Tel** (800)367-6770, (718)588-8400, FAX (718)590-1617, telex 4990003 HWILSON. ***Continues*** *Standard Catalog for Public Libraries.*
Desc: Chosen by a panel of public librarians, the books listed encompass a wide range of subjects including such contemporary topics as AIDS, problems of the aging, health and physical fitness and environmental concerns.

UK
PUBLIC LIBRARY EXPENDITURE IN SCOTLAND. English. an. £10.00. Scottish Library Association, Motherwell Business Centre, 124/6 Coursington Road, Motherwell ML1 1PW Scotland. **Tel** 011 44 698 252526, 011 44 698 252057, FAX 011 44 698 252057. **ED** GN Drummond. **LC** Z791.S35; P83. **DD** 025.1/1/09411. **Circ:** 80 (ctrl).
Desc: A summary and analysis of forthcoming expenditure by the 41 local authorities in Scotland with responsibility for library services.

UK/0268-893X
PUBLIC LIBRARY JOURNAL. [Public libr. j.]. **Added/Corp** Library Association. Public Libraries Group. Vol. 1, No. 1 (March/April 1986)-. Periodical. English. bm. $104.00. GRP Library Association, Somerset Library Admin Mt St, Somerset TA6 3ES England. **Tel** 011 44 278 451201. **(Subscription address:** Public Libraries GRP Harry Galloway, Woodspring Library Central Blvd., Avon BS23 1PL England (011 44 275 855164)) **ED** Rob Froud. **CODEN** PLJOET. Index available. **Bk Rev. Ad Acc. Circ:** 6,500. Documents available from Ask*IEEE. ***Continues*** *PLG News, 0261-4383.*
Ind/Abst INSPEC (March/April 1986-); Libr. Lit.

US/0195-6922
PUBLIC LIBRARY PROGRAM GUIDELINES. **Main/Corp** National Endowment for the Humanities. Division of Public Programs. (1979)-. English. an. National Endowment for the Humanities, 1100 Pennsylvania Avenue NW, Washington DC 20506. **Tel** (202)786-0438. **LC** Z731; .N37a. **DD** 021.8/3.

US/0161-6846
PUBLIC LIBRARY QUARTERLY (NEW YORK, N.Y.). (PUBLIC LIBRARY QUARTERLY.). [Public libr. q.]. (Spring 1979)-. Academic Scholarly Publication. English. qt. $90.00 US; $126.00 other. The Haworth Press Inc, 10 Alice Street, Binghamton NY 13904-1580. **Tel** (607)722-5857, (800)3-HAWORTH, FAX (607)722-1424. **ED** Richard L. Waters (editor's address: 2903 Pennsylvania Drive, Denton, TX 76205). **LC** Z671; .P9854. **DD** 027.4/05. **Bk Rev. Ad Acc. Pr Rev. Acid Free. Circ:** 604. available on microfilm and microfiche from University Microfilms International (UMI). Documents available from Haworth Document Delivery Service.
Desc: Addresses the major challenges and opportunities that face the nation's public libraries. Striking a meaningful balance between articles written by practitioners and those prepared by scholars. Provides new and stimulating ideas for the profession.
Ind/Abst Child. Lit. Abstr. (19??-); EMBASE; Index Period. Artic. Relat. Law; Inf. Instruc. Technol.; Inf. Sci. Abstr.; Libr. Inf. Sci. Abstr.; Libr. Lit.

CN/0706-7798
PUBLIC LIBRARY SERVICES NEWSLETTER. **Main/Corp** Manitoba. Public Library Services. (May/June 1978)-. Newsletter. English. Public Library Services, 139 Hamelin Street, Winnipeg Manitoba R3T 4H4 Canada.

UK/0307-0522
PUBLIC LIBRARY STATISTICS ... ESTIMATES. **See** Library and Information Sciences-Abstracting, Bibliographies and Statistics.

US/1051-0931
PUBLIC LIBRARY WATCH. (PUBLIC LIBRARY WATCH : REPORTING ON RESEARCH AND ISSUES OF INTEREST TO PUBLIC LIBRARIES.). [Public libr. watch]. **Added/Corp** University of Illinois at Urbana-Champaign. Library Research Center. Coalition for Public Library Research. **VFOAT** Watch. Vol. 1, No. 1 (June 1990)-. Periodical. English. Four times a year. Free (members); $50.00 (non-members). University of Illinois, 410 David Kinley Hall, 1407 West Gregory Street, Urbana IL 61801. **Tel** (217)333-1980. **ED** Diane Rothenberg. **DD** 027.
Desc: Newsletter's goal is to provide libraries with research-based commentary.

UK/0549-0782
PUBLICATIONS. **Main/Corp** Newcastle-upon-Tyne. University. Library. **VFOAT** University Library Publications. Began with 1, (1960)-. Monographic series. English. Price varies per volume. **DD** 027. ***Supersedes*** *Durham, Eng. University. King's College, Newcastle-Upon-Tyne. Library. King's College Library Publication.*

US/0094-2987
PUBLICATIONS RESOURCE MANUAL (SPRINGFIELD). (PUBLICATIONS RESOURCE MANUAL.). **Main/Corp** Illinois. Office of the Superintendent of Public Instruction. Publications and Library Resources Section. English. Springfield Publications Section, 325 South Fifth Street 62706. **LC** Z5819; .I44A. **DD** 016.37.
Ind/Abst Peace Res. Abstr. J. (1979-1982).

CC/1000-8489
QINGBAO KEXUE. (CHING PAO KO HSUEH.). [Qingbao kexue]. **VFOAT** Information Science; Qingbao Kexue. No. 1 (Jan. 1980)-. Periodical. Chinese (summaries and/or abstracts in English; table of contents in English). bm. Qingbao Kexue, 30 Yinhang Jie, Nangang qu, Harbin, Heilongjiang, 150001 People's Republic of China. **(Subscription address:** China International Book Trading Corporation, PO Box 399, Library Service Department, Beijing 100044 People's Republic of China.) **LC** Z671; .C49. **DD** 020/.5. **CODEN** QKJIEF. **Bk Rev. Ad Acc. Circ:** 5,000. Documents available from BLDSC, Ask*IEEE.
Ind/Abst INSPEC (1985-).

IT
QUADERNI / CENTRO DI RICERCHE INFORMATICHE PER I BENI CULTURALI. **Added/Corp** Scuola Normale Superiore (Italy). Centro di Ricerche Informatiche per i Beni Culturali. (1991)-. Italian. **LC** IN PROCESS; Z699.5.A75; Q37.
Ind/Abst BHA : Biblio. Hist. Art.

NE
QUARTERLY BULLETIN OF THE INTERNATIONAL ASSOCIATION OF AGRICULTURAL INFORMATION SPECIALISTS. **See** Agriculture.

SA/0038-2418
QUARTERLY BULLETIN OF THE SOUTH AFRICAN LIBRARY. [Q. bull. S. Afr. Libr.]. **Main/Corp** South African Library. **Added/Corp** South African Library. **VFOAT** Kwartaalblad van die Suid-Afrikaanse Biblioteek. Vol. 1, No. 1 (Sept. 1946)-. Bulletin. English (Afrikaans). Four times a year (Mar., June, Sept., Dec.). R50.00 South Africa; R57.00 others. South African Public Library, PO Box 496, Cape Town 8000 South Africa. **Tel** 011 44 21 244848, FAX 011 44 21 244848, telex CP 522604. **ED** P. E. Westra. **LC** Z965; .S767. **DD** 027.468. Index available. cum. index. **Bk Rev. Ad Acc. Circ:** 800. available on microfilm and microfiche from University Microfilms International (UMI).
Desc: History and bibliography of the Southern Africa collections of the South African library.
Ind/Abst Am. Hist. Life (1962-); Annu. Bibliogr. Engl. Lang. Lit.; Libr. Inf. Sci. Abstr.

II
QUARTERLY JOURNAL OF RLA. **Main/Corp** Rejasthan Library Association. **VFOAT** Rajasthana Pustakalaya Sangha Patrika. **VAT** Quarterly Journal of Rajasthan Library Association. V. 1- Mar. 1974-. Periodical. Multiple languages (English and Hindi). 191 Motimarg Bupunagar, Jaipur 302004 India. **LC** Z845.R34; R34A.

US/0146-8677
QUEENS COLLEGE STUDIES IN LIBRARIANSHIP. Began with No. 1, in 1977. Monographic series. English. Price varies per volume. Queens College, Political Science Department, 65-30 Kissena Boulevard, Flushing NY 11367. **Tel** (718)520-7000.

AT
QUILL, QUEENSLAND INTER-LIBRARY LIAISON. **Added/Corp** Library Association of Australia. Queensland Branch. **VFOAT** Queensland Inter-Library Liaison; QUILL. Vol. 1 (June 1960)-. Periodical. English. qt. $0.15 single issue. Queensland Branch of the Library Association of Australia, PO Box 212, West End Queensland 4101 Australia. **Tel** 253-5354. **ED** Geoff Chapman. **LC** Z870.Q44; Q55. **DD** 021/.009943. **Ad Acc. Circ:** 600 (ctrl).
Desc: Job listing, feature articles, news from meetings forthcoming events, comings and goings, promotional activities, letters to the editor and ideas exchange.
Ind/Abst Aust. Educ. Index; Aust. Libr. Inf. Sci. Abstr. (1989-).

JA/0289-5420
RAIBURARIANZU FORAMU. [Raiburarianzu foramu]. **VFOAT** Librarians Forum. Vol. 1, No. 1 (Spring 1984)-. Periodical. Japanese (Japanese). qt. ¥2520. Nihon Fakuson Kabushiki Kaisha 7-chome, Tokyo-to 106 Japan. **LC** Z671; .R25.

CN/0226-8019
RAPPORT ANNUEL - CORPORATION DES BIBLIOTHECAIRES PROFESSIONNELS DU QUEBEC. (RAPPORT ANNUEL : RAPPORTS PRESENTES AUX MEMBRES LORS DE LA ... ASSEMBLEE GENERALE ANNUELLE.). [Rapp. annu. - Corp. bibl. prof. Que.]. **Main/Corp** Corporation des Bibliothecaires Professionnels du Quebec. **VFOAT** Annual Report; Annual Reports. (1977)-. French (English). an. **DD** 020/.6234/714. ***Continues*** *Corporation des Bibliothecaires Professionnels du Quebec. Rapports Annuels, 0228-6505.*

CN/0710-6394
RAPPORT ANNUEL / SOCIETE QUEBECOISE D'INFORMATION JURIDIQUE. [Rapp. annu. - Soc. que. inf. jurid.]. **Main/Corp** Societe Quebecoise d'Information Juridique. **VAT** SOQUIJ Rapport Annuel; Rapport Annuel - SOQUIJ. 1976/77-. French. an. Societe Quebecoise d'Information Juridique, 10 rue St Jacques Bureau 101, Montreal Quebec H2Y 1L3 Canada. **Tel** (514)842-8745, FAX (514)844-8984. **DD** 026/.349714.

FR
RAPPORT D'ACTIVITE - CENTRE D'ETUDES DES SYSTEMES D'INFORMACION DES ADMINISTRATIONS (FRANCE). **Main/Corp** Centre d'Etudes des Systemes d'Information des Administrations (France). French. Centre d'Etudes des Systemes d'Information des Administrations, Zac de Bonneveine, 122 Av de Hambourg, 13008 Marsielle France. **LC** JN2738.E4; C46A. **DD** 354.44/00028/5.

CN
RAPPORT D'ACTIVITES - LA BIBLIOTHEQUE ADMINISTRATIVE. **Main/Corp** Quebec (Province). Direction Generale de l'Edition Gouvernementale. Bibliotheque Administrative. (19??)-. French. **LC** Z736; .Q395a. **DD** 027.5714.

CN/0822-4986
RAPPORT DU SERVICE DE LA BIBLIOTHEQUE DE L'UNIVERSITE DU QUEBEC A CHICOUTIMI. (RAPPORT DU SERVICE DE LA BIBLIOTHEQUE DE L'UNIVERSITE DU QUEBEC A CHICOUTIMI POUR L'ANNEE ...). [Rapp. Serv. bibl. Univ. Que. Chicoutimi]. **Main/Corp** Universite du Quebec a Chicoutimi. Bibliotheque. (1980/81)-. French. an. Bibliotheque de l'Universite du Quebec a Chicoutimi, 555 Boul de l'Universite, Chicoutimi Quebec

G7H 2B1 Canada. **DD** 027.7714/16. ***Continues*** *Rapport du Service de la Bibliotheque de l'Universite du Quebec a Chicoutimi pour les Annees ... .*

CN/0715-5867
RAPPORT - NORTH CENTRAL REGIONAL LIBRARY SYSTEM (NEWSLETTER). (RAPPORT.). [Rapp. - North Cent. Reg. Libr. Syst.]. **Main/Corp** North Central Regional Library System (Ont.). (197?)-. Periodical. English. bw. Free. North Central Regional Library System, 334 Regent Street South, Sudbury Ontario P3C 4E2 Canada. **DD** 027.4713. ctrl circ.

SW/0280-719X
RAPPORT (SVENSKA BIBLIOTEKARIESAMFUNDET). (RAPPORT / REPORT / SWEDISH ASSOCIATION OF UNIVERSITY AND RESEARCH LIBRARIES. SVENSKA BIBLIOTEKARIESAMFUNDET.). **Added/Corp** Svenska Bibliotekariesamfundet. Swedish Association of University and Research Libraries. Report. (19??)-. Periodical. English (German).

US/0884-450X
RARE BOOKS AND MANUSCRIPTS LIBRARIANSHIP. [Rare books manuscr. libr.]. **Added/Corp** Association of College and Research Libraries. **VFOAT** RBML. Vol. 1, No. 1 (April 1986)-. Academic Scholarly Publication. English. Twice a year (Spring & Fall). $30.00 US; $35.00 Canada & Mexico & Spain & other PUAS countries; $45.00 others. Association of College and Research Libraries, 50 East Huron Street, Chicago IL 60611. **Tel** (312)944-6780. **(Subscription address:** Choice, 100 Riverview Center, Middletown, CT 06457, telephone: (203)347-6933) **LC** Z688.R3; R39. **DD** 026/.09. **Bk Rev. Ad Acc.**
Desc: Features scholarly articles on the theory and practice of special collections librarianship, including the acquisition and collection development of rare books and manuscripts.
Ind/Abst Libr. Inf. Sci. Abstr.; MLA Int. Bibl. Books Artic. Mod. Lang. Lit.

US/0198-8344
RASD UPDATE. [RASD update]. **Main/Corp** American Library Association. Reference and Adult Services Division. **VAT** Reference and Adult Services Division Update. Vol. 1 (May/June 1980)-. Periodical. English. Four times a year (Jan., Apr., July, Oct.). $15.00 US, Canada & Mexico; $25.00 other. American Library Association, 50 East Huron Street, Chicago IL 60611. **Tel** (312)944-6780, (800)545-2433, FAX (312)944-2641. **(Subscription address:** American Library Association, Subscription Department, 434 West Downer, Aurora IL 60506-9936.) **ED** Steven Atkinson. **Circ:** 4,800. available on microfilm and microfiche from University Microfilms International (UMI). ***Absorbed*** *American Library Association. Reference and Adult Services Division., 0163-0237.*
Desc: Official newsletter of the American Library Association Reference and Adult Services Division. News of the division and about related activities.

CN/0715-8912
RAYON (SAINTE-AGATHE-DES-MONTS). (LE RAYON / B.C.P. LAURENTIDES.). [Rayon]. V. 1, No. 2, (Dec. 1981)-. Periodical. French. ir. Free to residents. Bibliotheque Centrale de Pret des Laurentides, C P 239, Ste Agathe des Monts Quebec J8C 3A3 Canada. **DD** 027.4714/22. ***Continues*** *Qui Suis-Je? (Sainte-Agathe-des-Monts, Quebec), 0822-0565.*

US
READER SERVICES LAW LIBRARIAN. **Added/Corp** American Association of Law Libraries. Reader Services Special Interest Section. (198?)-. Periodical. English. ir. American Association of Law Libraries, 53 West Jackson Boulevard, Suite 940, Chicago IL 60604. **Tel** (312)939-4764, FAX (312)431-1097, telex ABA7603. ***Continues*** *American Association of Law Libraries. Reader Services Special Interest Section. [Newsletter].*
Ind/Abst Leg. Inf. Manage. Index (19??-).

US/1058-1219
READERS' GUIDE ABSTRACTS (SCHOOL AND PUBLIC LIBRARY ED.). ***Title Change.*** **See** Library and Information Sciences-Abstracting, Bibliographies and Statistics.

US/1040-3558
READING EDGE (CROWNSVILLE, MD.), THE. (THE READING EDGE.). [Read. edge]. Vol. 1, No. 1 (May/June 1988)-. Periodical. English. bm. $16.95. The Reading Edge Inc, PO Box 682, Annapolis MD 21404. **DD** 028.
Desc: This publication presents concise, insightful reviews of the latest children's literature. Columns for special interest topics and educational software help develop and nurture a lifelong love of reading. An essential for every library, library professional, educator, and parent.

●US/1060-5673
READMORE REPORTER, THE. **See** Medical Science and Technology.

UK
RECAL CURRENT AWARENESS. English. Twenty-six times a year. £30.00 (individuals), £55.00 (institutions) UK; £55.00 (individuals), £69.00 (institutions) other. University of Strathclyde / Curran Building, 131 Saint James Road, Glasgow G4 0LS Scotland. **Tel** 011 44 41 5224400 ext. 3814, FAX 011 41 552 1283. **Circ:** 300. ***Continues*** *Recal.*
Desc: Current awareness list is produced by scanning and selecting relevant articles from over one hundred and fifty journals taken at the National Centre. These are listed overleaf and new titles are added as appropriate. These papers are entered under broad subject headings for ease of finding.

US/0300-7081
RECENT ADDITIONS / MUNICIPAL REFERENCE LIBRARY, CITY OF CHICAGO. **Main/Corp** Chicago (Ill.). Municipal Reference Library. Began with April 1958 issue. English. mo. Free. Municipal Reference Library, 121 North La Salle, City Hall 1004, Chicago IL 60602. **Tel** (312)744-4992. **LC** Z881.C53; C55A. **DD** 011/.34. ***Continues*** *Selected List of New Books in the Municipal Reference Library.*

US/0735-2336
RECENT ADDITIONS TO BAKER LIBRARY. [Recent addit. Baker Libr.]. **Main/Corp** Baker Library. **VFOAT** Recent Additions. Vol. 20 (Sept. 1979)-. Periodical. English. mo. $45.00 (one year), $80.00 (two year) US; $60.00 (one year), $100.00 (two year) other. Harvard Business School Publishing Division, Operations Department, Boston MA 02163. **Tel** (617)495-6192, (617)495-8948, FAX (617)495-6891, telex 6817229. **Circ:** 800 (ctrl). ***Continues*** *Baker Library. New Books in Business and Economics, Recent Additions to Baker Library, 0028-4319.*
Desc: Contains new titles, listed by broad subject areas. These include books, working papers, and reports of business, international, and US government organizations.

MX/0486-1205
RECENT BOOKS IN MEXICO. **Added/Corp** Centro Mexicano de Escritores. (Nov. 1954)-. Periodical. English (Spanish). Six times a year. Centro Mexicano de Escritores, LG Inclan 2709, VLA Cortes, Deleg B Juarez 03530 Mexico 13 DF Mexico. **Tel** 579 78 10. **LC** Z1411; .R4. **Circ:** 1,000.
Desc: Bibliographical reviews of books written originally in Spanish and printed in Mexico.

UK
RECORDS MANAGEMENT JOURNAL (LONDON, ENGLAND). (RECORDS MANAGEMENT JOURNAL.). **Added/Corp** Aslib. Vol. 1, No. 1 (Spring 1989)-. Periodical. English. Three times a year. £34.00 (member), £42.00 (non-member) Europe; £37.00 (member), £46.00 (non-member) other. ASLIB, Information House, 20-24 Old Street, London EC1V 9AP England. **Tel** 011 44 71 253 4488, FAX 011 44 71 430 0514, telex 23667 AJLIB G.

US/0735-7427
RED TAPE (DETROIT, MICH.). (RED TAPE.). **Added/Corp** Government Documents Round Table of Michigan. **VFOAT** Redtape. No. 1 (Jan.-Feb. 1979)-. Periodical. English. Four times a year. Michigan Library Association / Godort, 1000 Long Boulevard Suite 1, Lansing MI 48911. **Tel** (517)694-6615. **ED** Barbara R. Hulyk. **LC** Z688.G6; R43. **DD** 015.774/53. **Bk Rev.**
Desc: Covers current issues and information for documents users.

UK/0144-2384
REFER. (REFER : JOURNAL OF THE RSIS.). [Refer]. **Added/Corp** Library Association. Reference, Special, and Information Section. Vol. 1, No. 1 (Spring 1980)-. Periodical. English. Three times a year (Jan., May, Sept.). Free (members), £14.00 (non-members) UK; £16.00 other. Information Service Group Sales Off, 32 Beachcroft Road Wall Heath, Kingswinford DY6 OHX England. **Tel** 011 44 384 274025, FAX 011 44 384 400053. **(Subscription address:** 1SG Sales Agent, 32 Beachroft Road, Wall Heath, Kingswinford West Midlands DY6 0HX England) **ED** David Butcher. **LC** Z711; .R43. **DD** 025.5/2/0941. Index available. cum. index. **Bk Rev. Ad Acc. Circ:** 5,300.
Desc: Covers all aspects of reference and information work, with reviews of new references works, listing of official British and European communities.
Ind/Abst Libr. Inf. Sci. Abstr.

US/0887-3763
REFERENCE AND RESEARCH BOOK NEWS. [Ref. res. book news]. **VFOAT** Reference & Research Book News. Vol. 1, No. 1 (Spring 1986)-. English. Eight times a year. $58.00 institutional, $40.00 individual US and Canada; $70.00 institutional, $52.00 individual other. Book News Inc, 5600 NE Hassalo Street, Portland OR 97213. **Tel** (503)281-9230. **ED** Jane Erskine. **LC** Z1035.1; .R439. **DD** 028.1/2/05. **Bk Rev. Ad Acc. Circ:** 2,200 (ctrl).

Desc: Reviews of new reference books on all topics of interest to librarians in academic and public libraries. Contains over 600 reviews in each issue.
Ind/Abst Book Rev. Index (1987-).

US/8755-0962
REFERENCE BOOKS BULLETIN. (REFERENCE BOOKS BULLETIN / PREPARED BY THE AMERICAN LIBRARY ASSOCIATION REFERENCE BOOKS BULLETIN EDITORIAL BOARD.). [Ref. books bull.]. **Added/Corp** American Library Association. Reference Books Bulletin Editorial Board. (1984)-. English. an. $26.00 nonmember, $23.40 ALA member. American Library Association, 50 East Huron Street, Chicago IL 60611. **Tel** (312)944-6780, (800)545-2433, FAX (312)944-2641. **(Subscription address:** American Library Association, Subscription Department, 434 West Downer, Aurora IL 60506-9936.) **LC** Z1035.1; .S922. **DD** 028.1/2. ***Continues*** *Reference and Subscription Books Reviews, 0080-0430.*

US/0276-3877
REFERENCE LIBRARIAN, THE. [Ref. libr.]. No. 1/2 (Fall/Winter 1981)-. Periodical. English. sa. $115.00 US; $161.00 other. The Haworth Press Inc, 10 Alice Street, Binghamton NY 13904-1580. **Tel** (607)722-5857, (800)3-HAWORTH, FAX (607)722-1424. **ED** Bill Katz (editor's address: Suny Albany School of Library and Information Science, Draper Hall 113, 135 Western Avenue, Albany, NY 12222). **LC** Z711; .R444. **DD** 025.5/2. **CODEN** RELBD6. **Bk Rev. Ad Acc. Pr Rev. Acid Free. Circ:** 581. available on microfilm and microfiche from University Microfilms International (UMI). Documents available from Ask*IEEE, Haworth Document Delivery Service.
Desc: Each issue deals with a particular topic that is of current concern, interest, and of practical value for the practical reference librarian. Serves as the central resource for the professional librarian in this area. Provides contributions from experts in the field who review, synthesize and condense our current knowledge and the state of the art.
Ind/Abst Index Period. Artic. Relat. Law; Inf. Instruc. Technol.; Inf. Sci. Abstr.; INSPEC (Summer 1982-); Leg. Inf. Manage. Index (19??-); Libr. Inf. Sci. Abstr.; Libr. Lit.; Pollut. Abstr. Indexes.

US/1048-5384
REFERENCE POINTS. ***Ceased.*** [Ref. points]. **Added/Corp** Library of Congress. Loan Division. Vol. 1, No. 1 (1990)-(19??). Periodical. English. ir (2 or 3 per year). Library of Congress, 101 Independence Avenue SE, Washington DC 20540. **Tel** (202)287-5000. **DD** 025. **CODEN** REFPEJ.

CN
REFERENCE SERIES. **Main/Corp** University of Toronto. Library. Reference Dept. (19??)-. Monographic series. English. ir. Price varies per volume. St. George Campus Calendar, 315 Bloor Street West, Toronto ONT M5S 1A3 Canada. **Tel** (416)978-2011.

CN/0384-0697
REFLECTIONS (NORTH BATTLEFORD. 1976). (REFLECTIONS.). **Added/Corp** Lakeland Library Region. Vol. 4, No. 1 (1976)-. Periodical. English. Three times a year. Lakeland Library Region, 10023 Thatcher Drive, PO Box 813, North Battleford Saskatchewan S9A 2Z3 Canada. **Tel** (306)445-6108. **ED** Jim Kelly. **DD** 027.4/7124/2. **Bk Rev. Circ:** 200 (ctrl). ***Continues*** *Reflections from Lakeland, 0384-0689.*
Desc: Newsletter of the Lakeland Library Region, North Battleford, Saskatchewan.

US/0891-8880
REFORMA NEWSLETTER. [REFORMA newsl.]. **Main/Corp** REFORMA. **VFOAT** National Reforma Newsletter. (19??)-. Periodical. English. Four times a year. $35.00 (institutional libraries or library schools); $100.00 (corporate); $20.00 (individuals) Comes with Reforma membership. Reforma, PO Box 832, Anaheim CA 92815. **ED** Edward Erazo. **DD** 027. **Bk Rev. Ad Acc. Circ:** 600 (ctrl).
Desc: Promotes library service to Spanish speakers.

CN/0822-2983
REGARD SUR LA BIBLIOTHEQUE DU COLLEGE DE L'ASSOMPTION. [Regard bibl. Coll. Assomption]. **Main/Corp** College de l'Assomption. Bibliotheque. No. 1 (Sept. 1983)-. Periodical. French. mo. Free. Bibliotheque College de l'Assomption, 270 Boulevard, l'Ange-Gardien l'Assomption Quebec J0K 1G0 Canada. **Tel** (514)589-5621. **DD** 027.7714/416.

US/0149-4694
REGISTER OF INDEXERS. [Reg. index.]. **Added/Corp** American Society of Indexers. (197?)-. English. an. $15.00 (nonmembers), $10.00 (members). American Society of Indexers Inc, Box 386, Port Arnasas TX 78373. **Tel** (512)749-4052. **LC** Z695.94.U5; R43. **DD** 029.5/092/2.

SW
REGISTER OVER GALLANDE SFS-FORFATTNINGAR. Swedish. Kr225.00. Allmanna Forlaget Kundtjanst, S-162 89 Stockholm Sweden. **Tel** 8-7399630. **LC** LAW. **DD** 016.34/009485.

Library and Information Sciences

FR/0256-8888
REGISTRE DE L'ISDS ED. SUR BANDE MAGNETIQUE. *Title Change.* [Regist. ISDS Ed. bande magn.]. **VFOAT** Registre du Systeme International de Donnees sur Les Publications en s–erie (Ed. sur bande magn–etique); ISDS Register (Tape ed.); International Serials Data System Register (Tape ed.). (1977)-(1993). Periodical. Multiple languages. qt. ISSN International Centre, 20 rue Bachaumont, F-75002 Paris France. **Tel** 011 33 1 42367381, FAX 011 33 1 40263243, telex SERIALS 219847F. *Continued by* ISSN Register, 1021-500X.

CN/0384-5095
REGLEMENTS - A S T E D. *Title Change.* **Main/Corp** Asted. (1973)-. French. ASTED Inc, 1030 rue Cherrier, Bureau 505, Montreal Quebec H2L 1H9 Canada. **Tel** (514)522-7833, FAX (514)521-9561. **DD** 020/.6234/714. ctrl circ. *Continues* Reglements et Reglements Administratifs de l'Association Canadienne des Bibliothecaires de Langue Francaise, 0228-6424. *Continued by* Annuaire des Comites, 0226-3149.

CN/0318-8000
REGLES DE CATALOGAGE ANGLO-AMERICAINE. VERSION FRANCAISE. BULLETIN. (REGLES DE CATALOGAGE ANGLO-AMERICAINE, VERSION FRANCAISE.). No. 1- June 1974-. Periodical. French. De La Documentation, 360, Rue Le Moyne, Montreal Quebec H2Y 1Y3. **DD** 025.3/2/05.

US/0730-6350
RELIGION INDEXES. THESAURUS. **Added/Corp** American Theological Library Association. (1981)-. English. ir. $65.00. American Theological Library Association, 820 Church Street, 3rd Floor, Evanston IL 60201. **Tel** (708)869-7788, FAX (708)869-8513. **LC** Z695.1.T3; R44. **DD** 025.4/92.

FR/0758-816X
REPERTOIRE DES BANQUES DE DONNEES EN CONVERSATIONNEL. (1977)-. French. an. Association National de la Recherche Technique, 101 Av Raymond Poincare, F-75116 Paris France. **Tel** 011 33 1 45017227, FAX 011 33 1 47018529, telex 642632.

CN/1187-0419
REPERTOIRE DES BIBLIOTHEQUES UNIVERSITAIRES QUEBECOISES. (REPERTOIRE DES BIBLIOTHEQUES UNIVERSITAIRES QUEBECOISES /CONFERENCE DES RECTEURS ET DES PRINCIPAUX DES UNIVERSITES DU QUEBEC, SOUS-COMITE DES BIBLIOTHEQUES.). [Repert. bibl. univ. que.]. **Added/Corp** Conference des Recteurs et des Principaux des Universites du Quebec. Sous-Comite des Bibliotheques. (1990/1991)-. French (summaries and/or abstracts in English). be. 15.00Can$ per volume. Conference des Recteurs et des Principaux des Universites du Quebec (CREPUQ), Bureau 1200, 300 Rue Leo-Pariseau, CP 952, Succursale Place du Parc, Montreal Quebec H2W 2N1 Canada. **Tel** (514)288-8524. **DD** 027.7/025/714.

CN/1186-8511
REPERTOIRE TLRC. [Repert. TLRC]. **Added/Corp** Association Canadienne des Ludotheques et des Centre de Ressources pour la Famille. **VFOAT** Repertoire Toy Library Resource Centres. 3rd Edition (1991)-. French. Ressources pour la Famille, 205-120 Avenue Holland, Ottawa Ontario K1Y 0X6 Canada. **DD** 027.62/5.

UK
REPORT / BRITISH LIBRARY, RESEARCH AND DEVELOPMENT DEPARTMENT. **Main/Corp** British Library. Research and Development Dept. **Added/Corp** British Library. Board. **VFOAT** R&DD Report; British Library Research and Development Department Report. (1989/1990)-. English. *Continues* British Library. Research and Development Dept. Annual Report.

II/0418-5749
REPORT - DELHI. PUBLIC LIBRARY. **Main/Corp** Delhi. Public Library. (1952)-. English. New Delhi Public Library, Delhi Library Board, New Delhi India. **DD** 027.

IE
REPORT - DUBLIN. NATIONAL LIBRARY OF IRELAND. COUNCIL OF TRUSTEES. **Main/Corp** Dublin. National Library of Ireland. Council of Trustees. English. an. 7.50p. Government Publications, 4 5 Harcourt Road, Dublin 2 Ireland. **Tel** 011 353 1 6613111 Ext.4005. **LC** Z792; .D7955. **DD** 027.5415. **Circ:** 1,000.

NR
REPORT FROM THE LIBRARIES - NIGERIA. UNIVERSITY, NSUKKA. **Main/Corp** University of Nigeria, Nsukka. English. University of Nigeria, Nsukka Nigeria. **LC** Z858.N67; N53A. **DD** 027.7669.

AT
REPORT - MELBOURNE. UNIVERSITY. LIBRARY. **Main/Corp** Melbourne. University. Library. English. Melbourne University Press, PO Box 278, Carlton South Victoria 3053 Australia. **Tel** 011 61 3 347 3455, FAX 011 61 3 344 6214. **LC** Z871; .M36. **DD** 027.794.

US
REPORT OF THE DIRECTOR. **Main/Corp** Gregg-Graniteville Library. **VFOAT** USC Aiken Library Report; U.S.C. Aiken Library Report. 1984/85 -. English. an. University of South Carolina at Aiken, Gregg-Graniteville Library, Aiken SC 29801. **Tel** (803)648-6851, FAX (803)642-3302. **ED** F H Cubbedge. **LC** Z733.G84; G73A. ctrl circ. *Continues* Report of the Librarian.
Desc: An annual report of the library director.

US/8756-2782
REPORT OF THE DIRECTOR OF UNIVERSITY LIBRARIES TO THE VICE PRESIDENT OF UNIVERSITY SERVICES. (REPORT OF THE DIRECTOR OF UNIVERSITY LIBRARIES TO THE VICE PRESIDENT OF UNIVERSITY SERVICES FOR THE PERIOD ... / STATE UNIVERSITY OF NEW YORK AT BUFFALO.). **Main/Corp** State University of New York at Buffalo. University Libraries. English. an. University of New York at Buffalo, University Libraries, Buffalo NY. **LC** Z733.S837; S7B. **DD** 027.7747/97.

US
REPORT OF THE LIBRARIAN. **Main/Corp** Louisville Presbyterian Theological Seminary (1901-) Library. (19??)-. English. an. Louisville Presbyterian Theological Seminary, 1044 Alta Vista Road, Louisville KY 40205. **LC** Z733; .L892. **DD** 026.2.

US
REPORT OF THE LIBRARIAN TO THE PRESIDENT - ALLEGHENY COLLEGE, MEADVILLE, PA. **Main/Corp** Allegheny College, Meadville, Pa. Library. English. an. Allegheny College, Library, Meadville PA 16335. **LC** Z733; .M468. **DD** 027.7748.

US
REPORT OF THE LIBRARY COMMISSION OF MAINE. **Main/Corp** Maine. Library Commission. 1st (1900)-. English.

PK
REPORT OF THE LIBRARY SCIENCE DEPARTMENT. **Main/Corp** Karachi. University. Dept. of Library Science. English. Univ of Karachi, Department of Library Science, Karachi 32 Pakistan. **LC** Z669.5.P3; K35A. **DD** 027.7549/183.

NZ
REPORT OF THE TRUSTEES OF THE NATIONAL LIBRARY OF NEW ZEALAND AND OF THE NATIONAL LIBRARIAN. **Main/Corp** National Library of New Zealand. (19??)-. English. an. National Library of New Zealand, PO Box 1467, Wellington 1 New Zealand. **Tel** 011 64 4 474-3067, FAX (04)743042, telex NL30076. **LC** Z871.N36; N36a. **DD** 027.59312/7. **Circ:** 400.
Desc: Presented to the New Zealand Parliament, the report details the activities of the Trustees of the National Library, a statutory board, and the National Library.

BS
REPORT ON THE NATIONAL LIBRARY SERVICE. **Main/Corp** Botswana National Library Service. (19??)-. English. an. Botswana National Library Service, Private Bag 36, Gaborone Botswana. **Tel** 011 352288 352397. **LC** Z857.B68; B68a. **DD** 021/.00968/1.
Desc: Concerned with administrative matters such as finance, staffing, and staff training and development. Reviews the work and activities of the service.

UK
REPORT ON THE WORK OF THE LIBRARY / UNIVERSITY COLLEGE OF SOUTH WALES AND MONMOUTHSHIRE. **Main/Corp** University College of South Wales and Monmouthshire. Library. English. **LC** WMLC L 83/6450.

US
REPORT - SWARTHMORE COLLEGE, SWARTHMORE, PENNSYLVANIA. **Main/Corp** Swarthmore College, Swarthmore, Pennsylvania Library. English. an. Swarthmore College, Swarthmore PA 19081. **LC** Z733; .S984. **DD** 027.7748.

MW
REPORT TO SENATE / UNIVERSITY OF MALAWI LIBRARIES. **Main/Corp** University of Malawi. Libraries. English. University of Malawi Libraries, PO Box 280, Zomba Malawi. **LC** Z858.U46; R45. **DD** 027.76897. *Continues* University of Malawi. University Library Committee. Report to the Senate on the University Libraries.

US
REPORT - WASHINGTON UNIVERSITY (ST. LOUIS, MO.). **Main/Corp** Washington University (St. Louis, Mo.). Libraries. English. an. Journal of the History of Philosophy, Department of Philosophy, Washington University, Campus Box 1073, St Louis MO 63130-4899. **Tel** (314)432-8089. **LC** Z733. **DD** 027.7778.

CN/1184-9703
REPORTER - BRITISH COLUMBIA LIBRARY ASSOCIATION. (THE REPORTER : THE NEWSLETTER OF THE BRITISH COLUMBIA LIBRARY ASSOCIATION.). [Report. - B.C. Libr. Assoc.]. **Added/Corp** British Columbia Library Association. Vol. 35, No. 1 (Jan. 1991)-. Newsletter. English. bm. Free to members. British Columbia Library Association, 110 6545 Bonsor Avenue, Burnaby British Columbia V5H 1H3 Canada. **Tel** (604)430-9633. **DD** 020/.6/234711. *Continues* BCLA Reporter., 0005-2876.

US/0277-6537
REPORTER (UTICA, N.Y.). (REPORTER.). Periodical. English. ir. Mid-York Library System, 1600 Lincoln Avenue, Utica NY 13502. **Tel** (315)735-8328, FAX (315)735-0943.

US
RESEARCH ALERT. *See* Library and Information Sciences-Abstracting, Bibliographies and Statistics.

UK/0952-2832
RESEARCH BULLETIN / BRITISH LIBRARY RESEARCH AND DEVELOPMENT DEPARTMENT. **Added/Corp** British Library. Research and Development Dept. **VFOAT** BL R&DD Research Bulletin. No. 1 (Winter 1987)-. Bulletin. English. ir. Free. British Library Research and Development Department, 2 Sheraton Street, London W1V 4BH England. **Tel** 011 44 71 323 7054, FAX 011 44 71 323 7251, telex 21462. **ED** A.P. Warshaw. **LC** Z921.B854; R47. **CODEN** RBBDEA. **Circ:** 1,200.
Ind/Abst Museum Abstr.

US/0196-173X
RESEARCH LIBRARIES GROUP NEWS, THE. **Main/Corp** Research Libraries Group. **VFOAT** News. Issue No. 1 (July 1980)-. Periodical. English. Three times a year. Free. The Research Libraries Group Inc, 1200 Villa Street, Mountain View CA 94041. **Tel** (415)962-9951, telex 3719199. **ED** Hilary Hannon. **LC** Z674.82.R47; R49. **Circ:** 3,000. *Continues* Research Libraries Information Network. RLIN Newsletter, 0163-2388.
Desc: Contains articles of general interest on RLG's activities.

US/0145-0301
RESEARCH LIBRARY, RECENT ACQUISITIONS. **Main/Corp** Board of Governors of the Federal Reserve System (U.S.). No. 1 (June 1980)-. Periodical. English. mo. Free upon request. Board of Governors of the Federal Reserve System, Mail Stop 127, Washington DC 20551. **Tel** (202)452-3244 or 3245. *Continues* Research Library, Recent Acquisitions, 0145-0301.

US/0734-3310
RESEARCH STRATEGIES. (RESEARCH STRATEGIES : RS.). [Res. strategies]. **VFOAT** RS; R.S. Vol. 1, No. 1 (Winter 1983)-. Periodical. English. qt. $42.00 (one year), $76.00 (two year). Mountainside Publishing Company, PO Box 8330, Ann Arbor MI 48107. **Tel** (313)662-3925. **ED** Sharon Hogan. **LC** Z675.U5; R45. **DD** 025.5/677. **[CCC].** Bk Rev. Ad Acc. **Circ:** 1,000 (ctrl). available on microfilm and microfiche from University Microfilms International (UMI).
Desc: A journal of library concepts and bibliographic instruction.
Ind/Abst Curr. Index J. Educ.; Libr. Inf. Sci. Abstr.; Libr. Lit.

US
RESEARCH UPDATE. English. Three times a year (Jan., Mar., Aug.). Free to library professionals, $12.00 other. University Microfilms International, 300 North Zeeb Road, Ann Arbor MI 48106-1346. **Tel** (313)761-4700, (800)521-0600 Exts. 2490, 2491, FAX (313)973-1540. **ED** Tina L. Creguer.
Desc: Contains over 2,000 citations to dissertations recently published in 10 major areas.

FR/1142-2815
RESEAUX PARIS. 1989. *Ceased.* (RESEAUX.). [Reseaux Paris, 1989]. (1989)-(March 1993). Periodical. French. bm (6 issues). Association des Amis de la Bibliotheque en France, 1 Place Valhubert, 75013 Paris France. **Tel** 011 33 1 44060100. **UDC** 027(44).

US/0737-7797
RESOURCE SHARING & INFORMATION NETWORKS. [Resour. shar. inf. netw.]. **VFOAT** Resource Sharing and Information Networks. Vol. 1, No. 1/2 (Fall/Winter 1983)-. Academic Scholarly Publication. English. sa. $115.00 US; $161.00 other. The Haworth

Press Inc, 10 Alice Street, Binghamton NY 13904-1580. **Tel** (607)722-5857, (800)3-HAWORTH, FAX (607)722-1424. **ED** Robert P. Holley (editor's address: Wayne State University, 134 Purdy Library, Detroit, MI 48202). **LC** Z672; .R47. **DD** 021.6/5/05. **Bk Rev. Ad Acc. Pr Rev. Acid Free. Circ:** 300. available on microfilm and microfiche from University Microfilms International (UMI). Documents available from Ask*IEEE, Haworth Document Delivery Service. ***Continues*** *Resource Sharing & Library Networks, 0270-3173.*
Desc: Provides practical information addressing the current issues of library networking. A forum for ideas on the basic theoretical and practical problems faced by planners, practitioners and users of network services.
Ind/Abst ACM Guide Comput. Lit.; Comput. Rev.; EMBASE; Inf. Instruc. Technol.; Inf. Sci. Abstr.; INSPEC (Fall/Winter 1983-); Libr. Inf. Sci. Abstr.; PAIS Int. Print; Pollut. Abstr. Indexes.

US/0197-4742
RESOURCES IN LIBRARY AND INFORMATION SCIENCE. No. 1- Mar. 1978-. Periodical. English. mo. Free to Minnesota libraries. Office of Library Development and Services, 550 Cedar Street, St. Paul MN 55101. **Tel** (612)296-2821. **ED** Darlene M Arnold. **Circ:** 800 (ctrl). ***Supersedes*** *Professional Resources for Librarians, 0193-7731.*
Desc: Annotated acquisitions listing of library and information science titles received by Minnesota's state library agency.

CN/0823-9592
RETRIEVAL CODE INDEX - DATA RESOURCES OF CANADA. (RETRIEVAL CODE INDEX / DATA RESOURCES OF CANADA, CANADIAN ENERGY SERVICE.). [Retr. code index - Data Resour. Can.]. **VFOAT** Canadian Energy Service Retrieval Code Index. April 1982-. English. an. Free. Data Resources of Canada, 80 Bloor Street West/Suite 505, Toronto Ontario M5S 2V1 Canada. **DD** 025/.0633379/0971. ctrl circ.

US/0078-639x
REUNIONES BIBLIOTECOLOGICAS. **Added/Corp** Organization of American States. Library Development Program. Columbus Memorial Library. Pan American Union. (1964)-. Monographic series. English. ir. Price varies per volume. Organization of American States, 19th Street & Constitution Avenue NW, Suite 300, Washington DC 20006. **Tel** (202)458-6256. **LC** Z673.A1; P3. **DD** 020.

AT/0812-1567
REVIEW BULLETIN. (1974)-. English. ir. Statewide School Library Support Centre, Ground Floor, Rear Building, 67 High Street, Prahran VIC 3181 Australia. **ED** L Rolfe.
Ind/Abst Aust. Educ. Index; Aust. Libr. Inf. Sci. Abstr. (1982-).

AT
REVIEWPOINT. ***Ceased.*** (19??)-No. 71 (1992). English. Four times a year. Accountant Queensland Dept Ed, PO Box 33, Assistant Administrative Officer, North Quary Q 4002 Australia. **Tel** 61 7 2242804.
Ind/Abst Aust. Educ. Index; Aust. Libr. Inf. Sci. Abstr.

US
REVIEWS ON CARDS. (19??)-. English. ir (32 issues). $530.00 US; $650.00 other. Cahners Publishing Company, 249 West 17th Street, New York NY 10011. **Tel** (212)645-0067, FAX (212)242-6987. **(Subscription address:** Reviews on Cards, PO Box 1969, Danbury CT 06813.) **Bk Rev.**
Desc: Book reviews reprinted from Library Journal and School Library Journal magazines.

US
REVIEWS-ON-CARDS. **Main/Corp** Library Journal. **VFOAT** LJ: Library Journal Reviews-on-Cards. Periodical. English. $325.00 (LJ ROC), $250.00 (SLJ ROC), $465.00 (LJ/SLJ combination ROC) US; $350.00 (LJ ROC), $270.00 (SLJ ROC), $515.00 (LJ/SLJ combination ROC) other. Reviews on Cards, PO Box 444, Mount Morris IL 61054-0444. **Tel** (800)431-0715. **Circ:** 392.

CR/0250-3190
REVISTA AIBDA. (REVISTA AIBDA : REVISTA DE LA ASOCIACION INTERAMERICANA DE BIBLIOTECARIOS Y DOCUMENTALISTAS AGRICOLAS.). [Rev. AIBDA]. **Added/Corp** Asociacion Interamericana de Bibliotecarios y Documentalistas Agricolas. **VFOAT** Revista A.I.B.D.A. **VAT** Revista Asociacion Interamericana de Bibliotecarios y Documentalistas Agricolas. Vol. 1, No. 1 (Jan./June 1980)-. Periodical. Spanish (English, French and Portuguese; summaries and/or abstracts in English and Spanish). Twice a year (Jan. & July). $34.00. Asociacion Interamericana Bibliotecarios, Apartado 55, 2200 Coronado, San Jose Costa Rica. **Tel** 011 506 22900222. **CODEN** REVADJ. Documents available from Ask*IEEE.
Ind/Abst INSPEC (Jan.-June 1981-); Libr. Inf. Sci. Abstr.

UY/0544-9189
REVISTA - BIBLIOTECA NACIONAL. ***Title Change.*** **Main/Corp** Uruguay Biblioteca Nacional. **Added/Corp** Uruguay. Biblioteca Nacional. Departamento de Investigaciones. **VFOAT** Revista. (1966)-(199?). Periodical. Spanish. **LC** Z907; .M72. **DD** 027.5/895/05. ***Continued by*** *Deslindes.*
Ind/Abst HAPI Hisp. Am. Period. Index (19??-).

CU
REVISTA CUBANA CIENCIAS DE LA INFORMACION. Spanish. $31.00 Cuba; $36.00 other. Instituto de Documentation e Informacion Ceintifica y Tecnica, Capitolio Nacional, Prado y San Jose, Apartado Postal 2035, La Habana Cuba. cum. index.
Desc: Original articles on prestigious Cuban specialities within the field of information sciences.

BL/0100-0829
REVISTA DA ESCOLA DE BIBLIOTECONOMIA DA UFMG. (REVISTA DA ESCOLA DE BIBLIOTECONOMIA DA UNIVERSIDADE FEDERAL DE MINAS GERAIS.). [Rev. esc. bibliotecon. UFMG]. **Main/Corp** Minas Gerais, Brazil. Universidade Federal. Escola de Biblioteconomia. Vol. 1 (March/Sept. 1972)-. Academic Scholarly Publication. Portuguese (summaries and/or abstracts in English). sa. $35.00 US. Revista da Escola de Biblioteconomia da UFMG, Caixa Postal 1606, 30161-970 Belo Horizonte MG Brasil. **Tel** 55 31 448-5227, FAX 55 31 448-5200. **ED** Eduardo Jose Wense Dias. **LC** Z671; .M48a. **DD** 020/.5. Index available. cum. index. **Bk Rev**, (Qty: 4). **Pr Rev. Circ:** 600 (ctrl).
Desc: Presents research reports, articles, literature reviews, book reviews, dissertations and thesis abstracts on library and information science, bibliography, documentation and related areas.
Ind/Abst Inf. Sci. Abstr. (?-1991); Libr. Inf. Sci. Abstr.; Libr. Lit.

SP/0034-771X
REVISTA DE ARCHIVOS BIBLIOTECAS Y MUSEOS (MADRID, SPAIN : 1897). ***Suspended.*** (REVISTA DE ARCHIVOS BIBLIOTECAS Y MUSEOS.). [Rev. Arch. Bibl. Mus.]. Series 3, Issue 1, (1897)-Suspended. Periodical. Spanish. qt. 1800ptas Spain; 2200ptas other. Ministerio de Cultura Libreria, C Abdon Terradas 7, 28015 Madrid Spain. **Tel** 011 34 1 5448569. **UDC** 02069930.25. ***Continues*** *Boletin de Archivos, Bibliotecas Y Museos.*
Ind/Abst Am. Hist. Life (1954-1979); BHA : Biblio. Hist. Art; MLA Int. Bibl. Books Artic. Mod. Lang. Lit.; Romant. Move.

CK/0121-0203
REVISTA DE ASCOLBI / ASOCIATION COLOMBIANA DE BIBLIOTECOLOGOS Y DOCUMENTALISTAS, ASCOLBI. **Added/Corp** Asociacion Colombiana de Bibliotecologos y Documentalistas. **VFOAT** Revista de la Association Colombiana de Bibliotecarios. Vol. 1 No. 1 (1988)-. Periodical. Spanish. qt. $40.00. Rojas Eberhard Editores Ltda, Carrera 6A 51-21, Apartado Aereo 34270, Bogota DE Colombia. **Tel** 011 57 1 34270, FAX 011 57 1 6161408. **ED** Isabel Forero de Moreno. **LC** Z673.A629; R48. **DD** 020/.861/05. **Ad Acc. Circ:** 3,000 (ctrl). ***Continues*** *Boletin de la Asociation Colombiana de Bibliotecarios.*

BL/0100-7157
REVISTA DE BIBLIOTECONOMIA DE BRASILIA. [Rev. bibliotecon. Bras.]. **Added/Corp** Associacao dos Bibliotecarios do Distrito Federal. Universidade de Brasilia. Departamento de Biblioteconomia. (1973)-. Periodical. Multiple languages (Portuguese and Spanish; summaries and/or abstracts in English). Twice a year (Jan. & July). $35.00. Associacao Bibliotecarios DF, Crn 702 3 Bloco, G S Loja Coenc, 70000 Brasilia DF Brazil. **Tel** 011 55 61 2243825, 011 55 61 2243499. **LC** Z769.A1; R48.
Ind/Abst Libr. Inf. Sci. Abstr.; Libr. Lit.

SP
REVISTA DE LA BIBLIOTECA, ARCHIVO Y MUSEO DEL AYUNTAMIENTO DE MADRID. **Main/Corp** Madrid (Spain). Ayuntamiento. No. 1/2- 1977-. Spanish. sa. Delegacion de Cultura del Ayuntamiento de Madrid, Plaza de la Villa 4, Madrid 12 Spain. **LC** Z671; .R43. ***Continues*** *Revista de la Biblioteca, Archivo y Museo de Madrid.*

CU
REVISTA DE LA BIBLIOTECA NACIONAL JOSE MARTI. **Main/Corp** Havana. Biblioteca Nacional "Jose Marti.". No. 1-4, Vol. 1-6 (Jan. 1909)-(Dec. 1912); 2. Ser., Vol. 1 (1949)-. Periodical. Spanish. qt. $13.00. Ediciones Cubanas, Obispo 527, Altos ESQ Bernaza, CP 10100 Havana Cuba. **Tel** 011 632980, 631942, FAX 011 631011, telex 512337, 6540. **LC** Z897; .H2. **DD** 015.7291. cum. index. **Circ:** 10,000 (ctrl).
Desc: Contains previously unpublished research papers on Cuban culture and bibliographic and library studies related to the National Library's activities. It includes works of literary creation of particular significance in Cuba's cultural context.
Ind/Abst Am. Hist. Life (1959-1974, 1976-).

SP
REVISTA DE LIBRERIA ANTIQUARIA. Periodical. Catalan (Spanish). sa. 450ptas. Revista de Llibreria Antiquaria, Paletes 4, Barcelona 34 Spain. **LC** Z990; .R49. **DD** 070.5/0946/72.

VE
REVISTA DEL SINASBI. **Main/Corp** Comision Coordinadora del Sistema Nacional de Servicios de Bibliotecas e Informacion Humanistica. **VAT** Revista del Sistema Nacional de Servicios de Bibliotecas e Informacion Humanistica, Cientifica y Tecnologica. No. 1- ; July/Dec. 1978-. Periodical. Spanish. Comision Coordinadora Sinasbi, Apartado Postal 68350, Altamira Caracas 106 Venezuela.

SP/0210-0614
REVISTA ESPANOLA DE DOCUMENTACION CIENTIFICA. [Rev. esp. doc. cient.]. **Added/Corp** Spain. Centro Nacional de Informacion y Documentacion. Sociedad Espanola de Documentacion e Informacion Cientifica. Vol. 1, No. 1 (1977)-. Academic Scholarly Publication. Spanish (English, French and Portuguese). qt. 4240ptas Spain; 5500ptas other. Instituto de Informacion y Documentacion, Cientifica (CINDOC), Joaquin Costa, 22, 28002 Madrid Spain. **Tel** 011 34 1 563-5482 87, FAX (91)564 26 44, telex 22628 CIDMD E. **ED** Rosa Sancho Lozano. **LC** Z695.1.S3; R48. **DD** 025/.65. Index available. cum. index. **Bk Rev. Pr Rev. Circ:** 1,100 (ctrl). Documents available from Ask*IEEE, CASDDS.
Desc: Covers research in most fields of science. Has more than 80 institutes specifically devoted to research in the different fields of science.
Ind/Abst Chem. Abstr.; GeoRef; Inf. Sci. Abstr. (?-1991); INSPEC (1977-); Libr. Inf. Sci. Abstr.; Ref. Z.; Soc. Plann. Policy Dev. Abstr.; Sociol. Abstr. (?-?).

CK/0120-0976
REVISTA INTERAMERICANA DE BIBLIOTECOLOGIA / UNIVERSIDAD DE ANTIOQUIA, ESCUELA INTERAMERICANA DE BIBLIOTECOLOGIA. ***Ceased.*** [Rev. interam. bibl.]. (Jan./April 1978)-Ceased ?. Periodical. Spanish. Three times a year. Escuela Interamericana de Bibliotecologia, Universidad de Antioquia, Medellin Colombia. **Tel** 051-330301. **ED** Martha Alicia Perez. **LC** Z738.A1; R48. **DD** 027.08. **Bk Rev. Ad Acc. Circ:** 12,000 (ctrl).
Desc: Covers contemporary topics of the secular life and its relationship to the life of the church, offering in each issue a definition of significant current problems.
Ind/Abst Libr. Inf. Sci. Abstr.; Libr. Lit.

BL/0101-3394
REVISTA LATINOAMERICANA DE DOCUMENTACION. [Rev. latinoam. doc.]. Periodical. Portuguese (Spanish; summaries and/or abstracts in English). sa. Avenida W 3 Norte Quadra, 511 Bloco A, 70 750 Brasilia Distrito Federal Brazil. **LC** Z738.A1; R49. **DD** 020/.5.
Ind/Abst Libr. Inf. Sci. Abstr.

UY/0304-4343
REVISTA / UNIVERSIDAD DE LA REPUBLICA, ESCUELA UNIVERSITARIA DE BIBLIOTECOLOGIA Y CIENCIAS AFINES "ING. FEDERICO E. CAPURRO," BIBLIOTECA. **Added/Corp** Escuela Universitaria de Bibliotecologia y Ciencias Afines Ing. Federico E. Capurro. Biblioteca. **VFOAT** Revista EUBCA. (1983)-. Periodical. Spanish. **LC** Z783.A1; M67a. **DD** 027.0895. ***Continues*** *Boletin - Universidad de la Republica, Escuela Universitaria de Bibliotecologia y Ciencias Afines Ing. Federico E. Capurro, Biblioteca.*

SP
REVISTAS ESPANOLAS CON ISSN / INSTITUTO BIBLIOGRAFICO HISPANICO, CENTRO NACIONAL ESPANOL ISDS. **See** Bibliographies.

SZ/0258-0772
REVUE ARBIDO. ***Title Change.*** (ARBIDO-R / VEREINIGUNG SCHWEIZERISCHER ARCHIVARE, VEREINIGUNG SCHWEIZERISCHER BIBLIOTHEKARE, SCHWEIZERISCHE VEREINIGUNG FUER DOKUMENTATION.). [Rev. ARBIDO]. **Added/Corp** Vereinigung Schweizerischer Archivare. Vereinigung Schweizerischer Bibliothekare. Schweizerische Vereinigung fuer Dokumentation. **VFOAT** Revue Arbido; Arbido R; Arbido Revue. Vol. 1, No. 1 (1986)-(19??). Periodical. French (German). qt. Arbido, Effingerstrasse 35, Ch 3008 Bern Switzerland. **Tel** 011 41 31 3824240. **ED** Michael Gorin. **LC** Z837.A1; A73. **DD** 020/.9494. Index available. **Bk Rev. Ad Acc. Pr Rev.** ***Formed by the union of*** *Vereinigung Schweizerischer Bibliothekare. Nachrichten VSB/SVD, 0042-3807* ***and*** *Vereinigung Schweizerischer Archivare. Mitteilungen der Vereinigung Schweizerischer Archivare.* ***Merged into*** *Arbido.*
Ind/Abst Libr. Lit.

FR/0249-7344
REVUE DE LA BIBLIOTHEQUE NATIONALE. [Rev. Bibl. Natl.]. **Main/Corp** Bibliotheque Nationale (France). (Sept. 1981)-. French. qt. $98.00. Librairie Armand Colin, BP 22, 41354 Vineuil Cedex France. **Tel** 011 33 54 438994. **LC** Z927.P22; R48. **DD** 027.544. ***Continues*** *Bulletin de la Bibliotheque Nationale, 0338-4446.*
Ind/Abst BHA : Biblio. Hist. Art; Libr. Inf. Sci. Abstr.

US/0146-8685
RILA BULLETIN. **Main/Corp** Rhode Island Library Association. **VAT** Rhode Island Library Association Bulletin. 1927. Bulletin. English. Ten times a year. $15.00 US; $20.00 other. Rhode Island Library Association, 300 Richmond Street, Providence RI 02903-4222. **Tel** (401)467-8898, (401)781-2494. **(Subscription address:** 1825 Broad Street, Cranston, RI 02905**)** **ED** Judith Paster and John Bucci. Index available. cum. index. **Ad Acc. Circ:** 600 (ctrl). ***Continues*** *Bulletin of the Rhode Island Library Association.*
Desc: Newsletter with major articles of interest to librarians with emphasis on Rhode Island libraries. Focuses on library interests.

II
RILISAR BULLETIN : QUARTERLY JOURNAL OF RANGANATHAN INSTITUTE OF LIBRARY AND INFORMATION SCIENCE FOR APPLIED RESEARCH. **Added/Corp** Ranganathan Institute of Library and Information Science for Applied Research (Madras, India). (198?)-. Bulletin. English. qt. Rs24.00 (India), $20.00 (overseas). **LC** Z845.I4; R54. **DD** 027.054.
Ind/Abst Indian Libr. Sci. Abstr. (19??-).

US/0272-9644
RIO GRANDE CHAPTER BULLETIN. **Main/Corp** Special Libraries Association. Rio Grande Chapter. Bulletin. English. qt. Rio Grande Chapter, 3312 Black Hills Road NE, Albuquerque NM 87111. **Tel** (505)299-3527.

JO
RISALAT AL-MAKTABAH. **VFOAT** Majallat Risalat Al-Maktabah; Library Journal; Rissalat Al-Maktaba. V. 1- Oct. 1965-. Arabic (English). qt. 20.00JD. Jamiyat Al-Maktabat Al-Urduniyah, SB 6289, Amman Jordan. **Tel** 629412. **ED** Faronk Moaz and Amal Zash. cum. index. **Bk Rev. Ad Acc. Circ:** 1,000 (ctrl).
Desc: Features articles on libraries, a bibliography of recently published books and library news.
Ind/Abst Libr. Inf. Sci. Abstr.

US/0270-9104
RIVER CITY LIBRARY TIMES. Vol. 1 (May 1977)-. Periodical. English. mo. $3.00. Evansville-Vanderburgh, County Public Library, 22 Southeast 5th Street, Evansville IN 47708. **Tel** (812)428-8204. **ED** Cheryl Soper. **Circ:** 1,100 (ctrl). ***Supersedes*** *Staff News Bulletin.*
Desc: A newsletter outlining recent happenings in the Evansville-Vanderburgh Library. Also has information on upcoming activities.

AT/0812-7352
RIVERINA LIBRARY REVIEW. ***Title Change.*** [Riverina libr. rev.]. **Added/Corp** Riverina-Murray Institute of Higher Education. Centre for Information Studies. (1984)-(19??). Periodical. English. qt. Charles Sturt University CRSR, PO Box 588, Wagga Wagga NSW 2650 Australia. **Tel** 011 61 69 222763, FAX 011 61 69 222764. **CODEN** RLREER. ***Continued by*** *Australian Library Review, 1034-8042.*
Ind/Abst Aust. Educ. Index (?-?); Aust. Libr. Inf. Sci. Abstr. (?-19??).

US
ROM NEWSLETTER; A NEWS REPORT ON COM APPLICATIONS FOR LIBRARIES. (1977)-. Periodical. English. Information Design Inc, 3291 Keller, Santa Clara CA 95054.

US
ROSTER AND STATISTICS OF OKLAHOMA PUBLIC AND INSTITUTIONAL LIBRARIES. (1984)-. Government Publication. English. an. Free. Oklahoma Department of Libraries, 200 Northeast 18th Street, Oklahoma City OK 73105. **Tel** (405)521-2502, FAX (405)525-7804. **Circ:** 400. available on microfiche from CIS / Congressional Information Service, Inc. ***Continues*** *Annual Directory of Oklahoma Libraries.*

CN/0384-0123
ROUND TABLE (BARRIE). (ROUND TABLE.). Began publication in 197-. Periodical. English. Georgian Bay Regional Library System, 30 Morrow Road, Barrie Ontario L4N 3V8 Canada. **DD** 027.4/713/15.
Ind/Abst World Agric. Econ.

US/0033-7072
RQ. [RQ]. **Added/Corp** American Library Association. Reference and Adult Services Division. American Library Association. Reference Services Division. Vol. 1 (Nov. 1960)-. Periodical. English. Four times a year. $42.00 US & Canada & Mexico; $52.00 other. American Library Association, 50 East Huron Street, Chicago IL 60611. **Tel** (312)944-6780, (800)545-2433, FAX (312)944-2641. **(Subscription address:** American Library Association, Subscription Department, 434 West Downer, Aurora IL 60506-9936.**)** **LC** Z671; .R23. **DD** 025.5/2/0973. **NLM** Z 671 R115. **[CCC]. Pr Rev.** available on microfilm and microfiche from University Microfilms International (UMI); available on an online database (files 647,648/Full-Text) from DIALOG. Documents available from The Genuine Article, UMI Article Clearinghouse. ***Absorbed*** *Adult Services.*
Ind/Abst Acad. Search (July 1993-); Am. Hist. Life (1975-); Arts Humanit. Citation Index [Select. Cov.]; Book Rev. Index; Chicano Index; Comput. Rev. Index (1988-); Curr. Contents Soc. Behav. Sci.; Curr. Index J. Educ.; Gen. Period. Index (1985-); High. Educ. Abstr. (1986-); Index Period. Artic. Relat. Law; INFO-SOUTH Abstr.; Inf. Instruc. Technol.; Inf. Sci. Abstr. [Full Cov.]; Libr. Inf. Sci. Abstr.; Libr. Lit.; Mag. ASAP Plus [Full Txt.]; Mag. Index Plus (1989-); Mag. Search; Newsp. Period. Abstr. (1989-); PAIS Int. Print; Res. Alert [Full Cov.]; Sci. Fict. Fantasy Book Rev. Index; Soc. Sci. Cit. Index [Full Cov.]; Mag. Index (1978-); Trade Ind. ASAP [Full Txt.]; Trade Ind. Index [Full Txt.].

US/1057-8188
RSAP NEWSLETTER. **See** Library and Information Sciences-Abstracting, Bibliographies and Statistics.

US
RURAL AND SMALL LIBRARY SERVICES NEWSLETTER. **Added/Corp** Clarion University of Pennsylvania. Center for the Study of Rural Librarianship. **VFOAT** Newsletter. Vol. 1, No. 1 (Jan. 1990)-. Newsletter. English. bm (6 issues). $20.00. Norweld, 251 North Main Street, Bowling Green OH 43402.

US/0276-2048
RURAL LIBRARIES. [Rural libr.]. **Added/Corp** Clarion State College. Center for the Study of Rural Librarianship. Vol. 1, No. 1 (Winter 1980)-. Periodical. English. sa (March., Oct.). $10.00 US; $11.00 other. Clarion University of Pennsylvania / Center for the Study of Rural Librarianship, Clarion PA 16214. **Tel** (814)226-2014, (816)226-2271, FAX (814)226-2150. **ED** Mary Lou Pratt (phone: (814)226-2383). **LC** Z675.V7; R87. **DD** 027.4/05. **Circ:** 350 (ctrl).
Desc: Serves as a forum for the reporting of investigation, activities, and research related to rural library service.
Ind/Abst AGRICOLA [Select. Cov.]; Libr. Inf. Sci. Abstr.; Libr. Lit.

CN/0702-7745
S. A. L. T. NEWSLETTER. [S.A.L.T. newsl.]. **Main/Corp** Saskatchewan Association of Library Technicians. Mar. 1973-. Newsletter. English. qt. Free to members. SALT, 2233 MacKinnon Avenue, Saskatoon Saskatchewan S7J 1N5 Canada. **DD** 023/.5.

AT/0818-3236
S.A. LAW LIBRARIANS BULLETIN. [S.A. law libr. bull.]. **VFOAT** South Australian Law Librarians Bulletin. (1986)-. Periodical. English. qt. Attorney Generals Department, 99 Gawler Place, Adelaide SA 5000 Australia. **ED** S Vidler. **DD** 026.3499423.
Ind/Abst Aust. Educ. Index; Aust. Libr. Inf. Sci. Abstr. (1987-).

CN/0227-2261
SABINE/MAGAZINE. [Sabine/mag.]. No. 1- Jan. 1980-. Periodical. French. Informatech France-Quebec, 20 Edison Place Bonaventure, Montreal Quebec H5A 1A7 Canada. **DD** 025/.04.

●US/1062-3418
SAGAMORE PUBLISHING'S BOOK LOOK. [Sagamore Publ. book look]. **Added/Corp** Sagamore Publishing. **VFOAT** Book Look. Vol. 1, No.1 (1992)-. Periodical. English. qt. ELAR, 203 Commack Road, Suite 1010, Commack NY 11725. **Tel** (516)433-6530. **DD** 028.

UA
SAHIFAT AL-MAKTABAH. **Added/Corp** Jamiyat al-Maktabat al-Madrasiyah. **VFOAT** Egyptian Library Journal. (March 1969)-. Periodical. Arabic (summaries and/or abstracts in English). qt. $9.00. Egyptian School Library Association, 35 al-Galaa Street, Al-Qahirah United Arab Republic Egypt. **Tel** 753 001. **ED** Medhat Kazem. **LC** Z671; .S28. **Bk Rev. Ad Acc.**

AT/0812-7301
SALAC SIGNAL. [SALAC signal]. **VFOAT** South Australian Library Advisory Committee Signal. (1983)-. English. ir. **DD** 021.64099423.
Ind/Abst AESIS Q.; Aust. Educ. Index.

US/0098-6275
SALALM NEWSLETTER. **Main/Corp** Seminar on the Acquisition of Latin American Library Materials. **VAT** Seminar on the Acquisition of Latin American Library Materials Newsletter. Vol. 1 (Jan. 1973)-. Newsletter. English (Spanish and Portuguese). bm (6 issues). $25.00. SALALM Inc., General Library, University of Mexico, Albuquerque NM 87131. **Tel** (505)277-5102, FAX (505)277-0646. **ED** Laurence Hallewll. **LC** Z689; .S42a. **DD** 025.2. Index available. cum. index. **Bk Rev. Ad Acc. Circ:** 565.
Desc: Organ of the Seminar on the Acquisition of Latin American Library Materials. Deals with all aspects of Latin American librarianship.
Ind/Abst HAPI Hisp. Am. Period. Index (19??-).

US
SALARY SURVEY, CONNECTICUT PUBLIC LIBRARIES. **VFOAT** Salary Survey. English. an. Free. Connecticut State Library, 231 Capital Avenue, Hartford CT 06115. **ED** Rose H Harrison. **LC** Z682.4.P82; S25. **DD** 331.2/8102/09746. **Circ:** 400.
Desc: A compilation of salary data for Connecticut public libraries.

UK
SALE CATALOGUES OF LIBRARIES OF EMINENT PERSONS. (1971)-. English. ir. H W Wilson Company, 950 University Avenue, Bronx NY 10452. **Tel** (800)367-6770, (718)588-8400, FAX (718)590-1617, telex 4990003 HWILSON.

UK/0307-1456
SALG NEWSLETTER. (SALG NEWSLETTER / SOUTH ASIA LIBRARY GROUP.). [SALG newsl.]. **Added/Corp** South Asia Library Group. **VFOAT** S.A.L.G. Newsletter. No. 1 (Jan. 1973)-. Newsletter. English. an. £4.00. British Library Oriental & India Office of Collections, 197 Blackfriars Road, London SE1 8NG England. **Tel** 011 44 71 412 7655, FAX 011 44 71 412 7858. **ED** John Sims. **Circ:** 70. Documents available from BLDSC.
Desc: The group is concerned with the acquisition and use of books and manuscripts in the field of South Asian studies.
Ind/Abst Libr. Inf. Sci. Abstr.

US/0271-7603
SAMP CATALOG : SUPPLEMENT. [SAMP cat., Suppl.]. **Main/Corp** Center for Research Libraries (U.S.). **Added/Corp** Center for Research Libraries (U.S.) SAMP Catalog. **VAT** South Asian Microform Project Catalog. Supplement. (1976)-. Catalog. English. Center for Research Libraries, 6050 South Kenwood Avenue, Chicago IL 60637. **Tel** (312)955-4545. **LC** Z3499; .C45a; DS335. **DD** 016.959.
Desc: Listings and membership list of the South Asian Microfilm Project.

US
SCALL NEWSLETTER / SOUTHERN CALIFORNIA ASSOCIATION OF LAW LIBRARIES. **Main/Corp** Southern California Association of Law Libraries. (19??)-. Periodical. English. Five times a year. $13.50. Southern California Association of Law Libraries, 8391 Beverly Boulevard, Suite 300, Los Angeles CA 90048. **Tel** (213)740-6482. ***Continues*** *Southern California Association of Law Libraries. Newsletter.*
Ind/Abst Leg. Inf. Manage. Index (19??-).

DK/0036-5602
SCANDINAVIAN PUBLIC LIBRARY QUARTERLY. [Scand. publ. libr. q.]. **Added/Corp** Scandinavian State Directors of Public Libraries. (1968)-. Periodical. English. Four times a year. Kr200.00 Sweden; Kr235.00 Scandinavia; Kr255.00 other. Progek Prospar, Box 31003, S 400-32 Goteborg Sweden. **Tel** 011 46 31 243425. **ED** Anneli Ayras, Jes Petersen, Lis Byberg, and Elisabeth Nilsson. **LC** Z822; .S35. **DD** 027.4/48. Index available. **Circ:** 1,000 (ctrl). ***Supersedes*** *Reol.*
Ind/Abst Libr. Inf. Sci. Abstr.; Libr. Lit.

UK/0036-6595
SCHOOL LIBRARIAN, THE. [Sch. libr.]. **Added/Corp** School Library Association. Vol. 17 (March 1969)-. Periodical. English. qt. £45.00 UK. School Library Association, Liden Library, Barrington Close, Liden Swindon SN3 6HF England. **Tel** 0793-617838. **(Subscription address:** World-Wide Subscription Services, Unit 4, Gibbs Reed Farm Pashley Road, Ticehurst TN5 7HE England.**)** **ED** Sheila Ray and Keith Barker. **LC** Z675.S3; S27. **DD** 027.8/0942. Index available. **Bk Rev. Ad Acc. Circ:** 4,500 (ctrl). available on microfiche. ***Continues*** *School Librarian and School Library Review.*
Desc: Articles on school library skills, library management, children's writers. Substantial review section covering books for all ages.
Ind/Abst Book Rev. Index; Br. Educ. Index; Child. Lit. Abstr. (19??-); Libr. Inf. Sci. Abstr.; Libr. Lit.

US/0271-3667
SCHOOL LIBRARIAN'S WORKSHOP, THE. [Sch. libr. workshop]. **Added/Corp** Library Learning Resources, Inc. Center for Applied Research in Education. Vol. 1 (Sept. 1980)-. Periodical. English. mo (except July and Aug.). $42.00 (one year), $80.00 (two year), $118.00 (three year). Library Learning Resources Inc., 61 Greenbriar Drive, PO Box 87, Berkeley Heights NJ 07922-0087. **Tel** (201)635-1833, FAX (201)635-2614. **ED** Ruth Toor and Hilda K. Weisburg. **DD** 027. Index available. cum. index. **Bk Rev. Circ:** 7,500 (ctrl).
Desc: Covers current trends, teaching library skills,

bibliographies, bulletin boards, pencil games and reference questions. For grades K-12.
Ind/Abst Libr. Lit.

CN/0227-3780
SCHOOL LIBRARIES IN CANADA. (SCHOOL LIBRARIES IN CANADA / CANADIAN SCHOOL OF LIBRARY ASSOCIATION.). [Sch. libr. Can.]. **Added/Corp** Canadian School Library Association. Vol. 1, No. 1 (Autumn 1980)-. Periodical. English (French). Three times a year. 35.00Can$. Canadian Library Association, 200 Elgin Street, Suite 602, Ottawa Ontario K2P 1L5 Canada. **Tel** (613)232-9625. **ED** Marilyn Ming. **DD** 027.8/0971. **Bk Rev. Ad Acc. Circ:** 900 (ctrl). ***Continues*** *Moccasin Telegraph (Canadian School Library Association), 0076-9878.*
Desc: Provides information about the activities of the Canadian School Library Association and of recent developments in the field of school librarianship.
Ind/Abst Can. Index; Can. Period. Index; Libr. Inf. Sci. Abstr.; Libr. Lit.

CN/1181-9979
SCHOOL LIBRARY ADVOCATE. (THE SCHOOL LIBRARY ADVOCATE : THE JOURNAL OF THE P.E.I. SCHOOL LIBRARY ASSOCIATION.). [Sch. libr. advocate]. **Added/Corp** Prince Edward Island School Library Association. Vol. 1, No. 1 (Autumn 1990)-. Periodical. English. Three times a year. Free. Prince Edward Island Library Association, School Library Advocate, PO box 6500, Charlottetown, Prince Edward Island, C1A 8B5 Canada. **DD** 027.8.

AT/0814-334X
SCHOOL LIBRARY FORUM. [Sch. libr. forum]. (1984)-. Periodical. English. tq. **DD** 027.809945.
Ind/Abst Aust. Educ. Index (1984-).

US/0362-8930
SCHOOL LIBRARY JOURNAL (NEW YORK, N.Y.). (SCHOOL LIBRARY JOURNAL : SLJ.). [Sch. libr. j.]. **VFOAT** SLJ. Vol. 8, No. 1 (Sept. 1961)-. Periodical. English. mo. $74.50 US; $99.00 (includes GST) Canada; $119.00 (airmail) other (includes Star Track, a semi-annual supplement). Cahners Publishing Company, 249 West 17th Street, New York NY 10011. **Tel** (212)645-0067, FAX (212)242-6987. **(Subscription address:** School Library Journal, PO Box 2606, Boulder CO 80322-2606.**) ED** Phyllis L. Mandell (Managing Editor). **LC** Z675.S3; S29115. **DD** 027.8/05. **[CCC].** (bound in Dec. issue). cum. index. **Bk Rev**, (Qty: 4,000 per year). **Ad Acc.** Full Page (B&W) $3810.00. Half Page (B&W) $2655.00. Full Page (Color) $5185.00 (4-color). **Circ:** 42,000 (paid). available on microfilm. Documents available from UMI Article Clearinghouse, Magazine Collection. ***Continues*** *Junior Libraries.*
Desc: Information and reviews for librarians and media specialists who serve children and young adults in school and public libraries.
Ind/Abst Acad. Abstr. Full Text Elite (Dec. 1988-) [Full Txt.]; Acad. Abstr. (Dec. 1988-); Acad. Search (Dec. 1988-); Access (1980-); Book Rev. Digest; Book Rev. Index; Chicano Index; Child. Lit. Abstr. (19??-); Child. Mag. Guide (1981-); Contents Pages Educ.; Curr. Index J. Educ.; Educ. Index; Gen. Period. Index (1985-); INFO-SOUTH Abstr.; Inf. Instruc. Technol.; Inf. Sci. Abstr.; Libr. Inf. Sci. Abstr.; Libr. Lit.; Mag. Artic. Summar. Elite (Dec. 1988-) [Full Txt.]; Mag. Artic. Summar. Select (Jan. 1989-) [Full Txt.]; Mag. Artic. Summar. CD-ROM (Dec. 1988-); Mag. Index Plus (1989-); Mag. Index Sel. Microfiche (1986-) [Full Txt.]; Mag. Index. Sel. (1986-); Mag. Search; Med. Rev. Dig.; Mid. Search (Jan. 1989-) [Full Txt.]; Newsp. Period. Abstr. (1988-); Prim. Search (Jan. 1989-) [Full Txt.]; Sci. Fict. Fantasy Book Rev. Index; Mag. Index (1977-); TOM Gen. Index (1985-) [Full Txt.].

US/0889-9371
SCHOOL LIBRARY MEDIA ACTIVITIES MONTHLY. [Sch. libr. media act. mon.]. **VFOAT** Media Activities Monthly. Vol. 1, No. 1 (Sept. 1984)-. Periodical. English. mo (10 issues). $49.00 US; $62.00 other. LMS Associates, 17 East Henrietta Street, Baltimore MD 21230. **Tel** (410)685-8621. **ED** H.Thomas Walker. **LC** Z675.S3; S36. **DD** 027. Index available.
Desc: Focuses on practical activities and information for elementary and middle/junior high school library media specialists who operate skills-oriented library media programs.
Ind/Abst Curr. Index J. Educ.; Educ. Index (1992-); Libr. Lit. (1991-).

US/0739-7712
SCHOOL LIBRARY MEDIA ANNUAL. [Sch. libr. media annu.]. **VFOAT** School Library Media. Vol. 1 (1983)-. English. an. $42.50. Libraries Unlimited Inc., PO Box 6633, Department 920, Englewood CO 80155. **Tel** (800)237-6124. **ED** Carol Collier Kuhlthau. **LC** Z675.S3; S291158. **DD** 027.8/05. **Bk Rev. Ad Acc.**
Desc: Guide for library media specialists and district-level professionals. Summarizes the research of the year, highlighting several studies of interest, and reveals trends and patterns across the country.
Ind/Abst Curr. Index J. Educ.

US/1042-4245
SCHOOL LIBRARY MEDIA FOLDERS OF IDEAS FOR LIBRARY EXCELLENCE. [Sch. libr. media folders ideas libr. excell.]. **VFOAT** School Library Media; Folders of Ideas for Library Excellence; School Library Media FILE; FILE. (1989)-. English. an. $27.50. Hi Willow Research and Publications, Box 6633, Englewood CO 80155-6633. **Tel** (800)237-6124. **ED** David V. Loertscher. **LC** Z675.S3; S357. **DD** 027.8/223/05.
Desc: Information on media programs, school libraries and audio-visual services.

US/0278-4823
SCHOOL LIBRARY MEDIA QUARTERLY. (SCHOOL LIBRARY MEDIA QUARTERLY : JOURNAL OF THE AMERICAN ASSOCIATION OF SCHOOL LIBRARIANS.). [Sch. libr. media q.]. **Added/Corp** American Association of School Librarians. Vol. 10, No. 1 (Fall 1981)-. Periodical. English. Four times a year (Mar., June, Sept., Dec.). $40.00 US & Canada & Mexico; $50.00 other. American Library Association, 50 East Huron Street, Chicago IL 60611. **Tel** (312)944-6780, (800)545-2433, FAX (312)944-2641. **(Subscription address:** American Library Association, Subscription Department, 434 West Downer, Aurora IL 60506-9936.**) ED** Marilyn W Greenberg. **LC** Z675.S3; S2912. **DD** 027.8/05. **[CCC]. Bk Rev. Ad Acc. Circ:** 7,500 (ctrl). available on microfilm and microfiche from University Microfilms International (UMI). ***Continues*** *School Media Quarterly, 0361-1647.*
Desc: Read by building-level library media specialists, district supervisors and library educators. Covers the selection of print and nonprint media and the development of programs and services for K-12 libraries.
Ind/Abst Acad. Search (July 1993-); Book Rev. Index; Child. Lit. Abstr.; Comput. Rev. Index (1986-); Curr. Contents Soc. Behav. Sci.; Curr. Index J. Educ.; Educ. Index; Except. Child Educ. Resour.; INFO-SOUTH Abstr.; Inf. Instruc. Technol.; Inf. Sci. Abstr. (?-?); Libr. Inf. Sci. Abstr.; Libr. Lit.; Mag. Search; Med. Rev. Dig.

AT/0814-8392
SCHOOL LIBRARY NEWS. [Sch. libr. news]. (1984)-. Periodical. English. mo. Statewide School Library Support Centre, Ground Floor, Rear Building, 67 High Street, Prahran VIC 3181 Australia. ***Continues*** *SLB Newsletter, 0729-8730.*
Ind/Abst Aust. Educ. Index; Aust. Libr. Inf. Sci. Abstr. (1984-).

CN/0706-2915
SCHOOL LIBRARY NEWSLETTER. Newsletter. English. Free. Provincial Library, University Avenue R.R. 7, Charlottetown PEI CIA 7N9 Canada. ***Continues*** *School Library Association, 0706-2907.*

GW/0341-471X
SCHULBIBLIOTHEK AKTUELL. (1975)-. Periodical. German. Four times a year. DM38.00. Deutsches Bibliotheksinstitut, Bundesallee 184 185, D 10717 Berlin Germany. **Tel** 011 49 30 8505186, 011 49 30 8505187, FAX 011 49 30 8505100. **UDC** 027.7.
Ind/Abst Libr. Inf. Sci. Abstr.

SZ
SCHWEIZERISCHE BIBLIOTHEKEN. **See** Library and Information Sciences-Abstracting, Bibliographies and Statistics.

US/0036-8059
SCI-TECH NEWS. [Sci-tech news]. **Added/Corp** Special Libraries Association. (1949)-. Periodical. English. Four times a year. $20.00. Sci-Tech News, 7701 Legacy Drive, Plano TX 75024. **Tel** (214)334-4732. **DD** 020. **NLM** Z 671 S416. **CODEN** STNWAM. **Bk Rev. Ad Acc, Adv Mgr:** Mary Lee Kennedy, **Tel** (403)992-5066. **Circ:** 3,750. available on microfilm and microfiche from University Microfilms International (UMI). Documents available from Ask*IEEE. ***Continues*** *Alchemical Libraries Almanack.*
Desc: By and for librarians and information specialists in the fields of science and technology.
Ind/Abst INSPEC (Spring 1973-); Libr. Inf. Sci. Abstr.

US/0194-262X
SCIENCE & TECHNOLOGY LIBRARIES (NEW YORK, N.Y.). (SCIENCE & TECHNOLOGY LIBRARIES.). [Sci. technol. libr.]. **VFOAT** Science and Technology Libraries. Vol. 1, No. 1 (Fall 1980)-. Periodical. English. qt. $135.00 US; $189.00 other. The Haworth Press Inc, 10 Alice Street, Binghamton NY 13904-1580. **Tel** (607)722-5857, (800)3-HAWORTH, FAX (607)722-1424. **ED** Cynthia Steinke (editor's address: University of Minnesota, 499 Wilson Library, 309 19th Avenue South, Minneapolis, MN 55455). **LC** Z675.T3; S39. **DD** 026/.0005. **CODEN** STELDF. **Bk Rev. Ad Acc. Pr Rev. Acid Free. Circ:** 771. available on microfilm and microfiche from University Microfilms International (UMI). Documents available from Article Express International, Ask*IEEE, Haworth Document Delivery Service.
Desc: Provides a wealth of exciting and instructive material prepared specifically for the science and technology librarian. Represents the viewpoints, concerns and librarianship community in a lively, professional style that makes every issue an item to be read and referred to on a continuous basis. Each issue centers on a specialized theme, around which the major articles are focused.
Ind/Abst AGRICOLA; Curr. Index J. Educ.; Ei Page One; Eng. Index Annu. [Select. Cov.]; GeoRef; Inf. Instruc. Technol.; Inf. Sci. Abstr.; INSPEC (Fall 1982-); Leg. Inf. Manage. Index; Libr. Inf. Sci. Abstr.; Libr. Lit.; PAIS Int. Print; Ref. Z.

US/0147-6882
SCIENTIFIC AND TECHNICAL INFORMATION PROCESSING. [Sci. tech. inf. process.]. (1974)-. Periodical. English (Russian). Six times a year. $800.00. Allerton Press, Inc., 150 Fifth Avenue, New York NY 10011. **Tel** (212)924-3950, FAX (212)463-9684, telex 427441 ALPRES. **LC** Z699.A1; S37. **DD** 029/.9/5. **CODEN** STIPDD. **[CCC].** Documents available from BIOSIS Document Express, Ask*IEEE, CASDDS.
Ind/Abst Biol. Abstr. (-1983); Chem. Abstr.; Ei Page One; EMBASE; INSPEC (1984-).

UK/0950-0189
SCOTTISH LIBRARIES (1987). (SCOTTISH LIBRARIES.). [Scott. libr.]. **Added/Corp** Scottish Library Association. No. 1 (Jan./Feb. 1987)-. Periodical. English. Six times a year (Feb., Apr., June, Aug., Oct., Dec.). £27.00 UK; £29.00 other. Scottish Library Association, Motherwell Business Centre, 124/6 Coursington Road, Motherwell ML1 1PW Scotland. **Tel** 011 44 698 252526, 011 44 698 252057, FAX 011 44 698 252057. **ED** Colin D. Dakers and G. Alistair Campbell. **Bk Rev. Ad Acc. Circ:** 2,500 (ctrl). available on microfilm from University Microfilms International (UMI). ***Continues*** *Scottish Library Association. SLA News, 0048-9786.*
Desc: Articles of interest to those engaged in library and information spheres, news of association work, membership and reviews.
Ind/Abst Libr. Inf. Sci. Abstr.; Libr. Lit.; Museum Abstr.

UK
SCOTTISH LIBRARY AND INFORMATION RESOURCES. Added/Corp Scottish Library Association. **VFOAT** Scottish Library & Information Resources. (19??)-. English. an. £25.00 (two years). Scottish Library Association, Motherwell Business Centre, 124/6 Coursington Road, Motherwell ML1 1PW Scotland. **Tel** 011 44 698 252526, 011 44 698 252057, FAX 011 44 698 252057. **LC** Z791.S35; S376. **DD** 027/.0025/411.

US/0886-1560
SEARCH (SANTA CLARA, CALIF.). (SEARCH / SOUTH BAY COOPERATIVE LIBRARY SYSTEM, SOUTH NET.). **Added/Corp** South Bay Cooperative Library System. SouthNet. (19??)-. Periodical. English. Six times a year. $50.00 membership. South Bay Cooperative Library System, 180 West San Carlos Street, San Jose CA 95113. **Tel** (408)294-2345. **ED** Mary Clare Sprott. **DD** 025. **Bk Rev. Circ:** 350. ***Continues*** *News : South Bay Cooperative Library System.*
Desc: Covers news of public, special academic and school libraries in the South Bay area with emphasis on reference resources and networking.

JA
SEIRI GIJUTSU ZENKOKU KAIGI GIJUROKU. Added/Corp Nihon Toshokan Kyokai. Seiri Gijutsu Iinkai. (1970)-. Periodical. Japanese. ¥600. Nihon Toshokan Kyokai, 1-1-10 Taishido, Setagaya-ku, Tokyo 154 Japan. **Tel** FAX 81 3 3421 7588. **LC** Z688.5; .S454a.

UK/0960-1570
SELECT : NATIONAL BIBLIOGRAPHIC SERVICE NEWSLETTER. Main/Corp British Library. National Bibliographic Service. **VFOAT** National Bibliographic Service Newsletter; Newsletter of the National Bibliographic Service. No. 1 (June/July 1990)-. Newsletter. English. **CODEN** SELEER. ***Continues*** *British Library. Bibliographic Services. Newsletter.*

US/0278-0518
SELECTED FEDERAL AND STATE BOOK PROGRAM INFORMATION. [Sel. fed. state book program inf.]. 1976 Ed.-. English. an. Association of American Publishers, 1 Park Avenue, New York NY 10016. **LC** Z731; .S44. **DD** 021.8/3/0973.

US/0145-9309
SELECTED LIBRARY ACQUISITIONS. Main/Corp United States. Dept. of Transportation. Library Services Division. English. mo. Department of Transportation Office of Administrative Operations, Office of the Secretary, Library Services Division, Washington DC 20590.

●US/1065-7703
SELECTED NEW ACQUISITIONS / CALIFORNIA ACADEMY OF SCIENCES, LIBRARY. [Sel. new acquis. - Calif. Acad. Sci., Libr.]. **Main/Corp** California Academy of Sciences. Library. (Jan.-Apr. 1992)-. Periodical. English. bm. California Academy of Sciences, Golden State Park, San Francisco CA 94181-9961. **Tel** (415)221-5100. **DD** 025. ***Continues*** *California Academy of Sciences.; Selected Acquisitions.*

CN/0846-9415
SELECTIVE ACQUISITIONS. [Sel. acquis.]. **Main/Corp** Canada. Library of Parliament. Information and Technical Services Branch. **VFOAT** Acquisitions

Selectives. (Apr. 1990)-. Periodical. English (French). **DD** 017/.1. ***Continues*** *Canada. Library of Parliament. Selected Additions List.*

JA
SEMMON TOSHOKAN. **VFOAT** Semmon Toshokan Kyogikai Kaiho; Bulletin of Special Libraries Association, Japan. No. 40 (1969)-. Periodical. Japanese (Japanese). qt. ¥2000. Kokuritsu Kokkai Toshokan, (National Diet Library), 1-10-1 Nagatacho Chiyoda-ku, Tokyo 100 Japan. **Tel** 03 3581-2331, FAX 03 3597-9104. **LC** Z671; .S38A. ***Continues*** *Semmon Toshokan Kyogikai Kaiho.*

US
SENIOR HIGH SCHOOL LIBRARY CATALOG. **Main/Corp** H.W. Wilson Company. **Added/Corp** H.W. Wilson Company Standard Catalog for High School Libraries. 1st Ed. (1928)-. Catalog. English. ir. 14th Edition: $115.00 US and Canada; $130.00 other. H W Wilson Company, 950 University Avenue, Bronx NY 10452. **Tel** (800)367-6770, (718)588-8400, FAX (718)590-1617, telex 4990003 HWILSON.
Desc: Represents a well-balanced collection of outstanding fiction and non-fiction titles essential to the senior high school library collection.

US
SERIAL HOLDINGS. **Main/Corp** South Carolina. University. Library. (1976)-. English. sm. South Carolina University, University Libraries, University of South Carolina, Columbia SC 29208.

CN/0709-0536
SERIAL HOLDINGS IN NEWFOUNDLAND LIBRARIES. **Main/Corp** Memorial University of Newfoundland. Library. (1979)-. English. ir. Price varies. Memorial University of Newfoundland Library, Periodicals Division, St John's Newfoundland, A1C 5S7 Canada. **Tel** (709)753-8425, FAX (709)737-4569, telex 016-4677. **ED** Suzanne Ellison. **DD** 016.05. **Circ:** 130 (ctrl). available on microfiche. ***Continues*** *Memorial University of Newfoundland. Library. Serial Holdings in the Libraries of Memorial University of Newfoundland, St. John's Public Library and College of Trades and Technology., 0316-6597.*

US
SERIAL PUBLICATIONS CURRENTLY RECEIVED AND ON ORDER - EASTERN VIRGINIA MEDICAL SCHOOL, NORFOLK, VA. MOORMAN MEMORIAL LIBRARY. **Main/Corp** Eastern Virginia Medical School, Norfolk, VA. Moorman Memorial Library. 19 -. English. Eastern Virginia Medical School, PO Box 1980, Norfolk VA 23501.

UK/0267-3347
SERIAL PUBLICATIONS IN THE BRITISH MUSEUM, NATURAL HISTORY LIBRARY ON MICROFICHE. **See** Natural History.

US/0886-4179
SERIALS DIRECTORY (BIRMINGHAM, ALA. PRINT ED.), THE. (THE SERIALS DIRECTORY : AN INTERNATIONAL REFERENCE BOOK.). [Ser. dir.]. 1st Ed. (1986)-. Directory. English. an. $339.00 US; $369.00 Canada and Mexico; $389.00 (airmail) other (includes cumulative updates); $525.00 (CD-ROM) US; $535.00 (CD-ROM) Canada and Mexico; $575.00 (CD-ROM) other (CD-ROM includes quarterly cumulative update discs). EBSCO Publishing / Birmingham, The Serials Directory, PO Box 1943, Birmingham AL 35201-1943. **Tel** editorial inquiries (205)980-2773, toll-free US (800)826-3024, FAX (205)995-1582. **(Subscription address:** EBSCO Publishing / Boston, 83 Pine Street, PO Box 2250, Peabody MA 01960-7250.) **ED** Leanne Wofford. **LC** Z6941; .S464; PN4731. **DD** 050/.25. Index available (with each issue). available on CD-ROM from EBSCO Publishing - Birmingham; available on magnetic tape from EBSCO Publishing - Birmingham.
Desc: Over 155,000 international serial titles listed with information such as LC, DDC, UDC and NLM classifications, CODEN designators, title statement, key title, varying titles, preceding/succeeding information, and publisher name and address. Editorial descriptions, additional format availabilities and advertising rates are also noted. Included in the 9th Edition are ten indexes, some of which are: an alphabetical title index, ISSN, Copyright Clearance Center, Peer Reviewed, Serials available on CD-ROM, Serials available Online, and a New Title Index arranged by subject. Extensive abstracting and indexing information is also included as well as current subscription rates. New to the 9th Edition are full and half page ad rates, wire service affiliations, document delivery services and a notation for those titles published on acid-free paper.

US
SERIALS DIRECTORY / EBSCO CD-ROM, THE. (Summer 1988)-. Directory. English. an (with quarterly cumulative update discs). $525.00 US; $535.00 Canada and Mexico; $575.00 (airmail) other. EBSCO Publishing / Birmingham, The Serials Directory, PO Box 1943, Birmingham AL 35201-1943. **Tel** editorial inquiries (205)980-2773, toll-free US (800)826-3024, FAX (205)995-1582. **ED** Leanne Wofford (editor's telephone: (205)980-2773). available in print from EBSCO Publishing - Birmingham; available on magnetic tape from EBSCO Publishing - Birmingham.
Desc: Provides over 181,000 international serial titles with information such as LC, DDC, UDC and NLM classifications, CODEN designators, title statement, key title, varying titles, preceding/succeeding information, and publisher name and address. Editorial descriptions and additional format availabilities are also noted. For specialized searching, elements such as Copyright Clearance Center, Peer Reviewed notations and advertising data is also available. Extensive abstracting and indexing information is also included as well as current subscription rates. Special search features include greater-than/less-than and range searching for circulation and price data, limiters for customized searching, and customized local titles feature.

●US/1069-6164
SERIALS IN MICROFORM (ANN ARBOR, MICH. 1993). (SERIALS IN MICROFORM.). [Ser. microform]. **Added/Corp** University Microfilms International. (1993/1994)-. English. an. Free. University Microfilms International, 300 North Zeeb Road, Ann Arbor MI 48106-1346. **Tel** (313)761-4700, (800)521-0600 Exts. 2490, 2491, FAX (313)973-1540. **LC** Z6946; .S47. **DD** 017. ***Continues*** *Serials & Newspapers in Microform, 1063-0546.*

US/0361-526X
SERIALS LIBRARIAN, THE. [Ser. libr.]. Vol. 1 (Fall 1976)-. Academic Scholarly Publication. English. qt. $38.00 (individuals), $105.00 (institutions). The Haworth Press Inc, 10 Alice Street, Binghamton NY 13904-1580. **Tel** (607)722-5857, (800)3-HAWORTH, FAX (607)722-1424. **ED** Peter Gellatly (Editor's address: 1202 Bridges Road, RR #1, Pender Island, British Columbia, Canada V0N 2M0. **LC** Z692.S5; S48. **DD** 025.17/3. **CODEN** SELID4. **Bk Rev. Ad Acc. Pr Rev. Acid Free. Circ:** 1,165. available on microfilm and microfiche from University Microfilms International (UMI). Documents available from The Genuine Article, Haworth Document Delivery Service, CASDDS.
Desc: Devoted to serials management for librarians, this journal provides information to aid all serials librarians in their tasks. Topics include serials selection, acquisition, collection development, bibliographic control, etc.
Ind/Abst Acad. Search (July 1993-); Am. Hist. Life; Chem. Abstr.; Cumul. Index Nurs. Allied Health Lit.; Curr. Contents Soc. Behav. Sci.; Curr. Index J. Educ.; EMBASE; Index Period. Artic. Relat. Law; INFO-SOUTH Abstr.; Inf. Instruc. Technol.; Inf. Sci. Abstr.; Leg. Inf. Manage. Index; Libr. Inf. Sci. Abstr.; Libr. Lit.; Mag. Search; Pollut. Abstr. Indexes; Ref. Z.; Res. Alert [Full Cov.]; Soc. Sci. Cit. Index [Full Cov.].

US/0542-9560
SERIALS M.I.T. LIBRARIES. ***Title Change.*** **Main/Corp** Massachusetts Institute of Technology. Libraries. **VAT** Serials And Journals In The Massachusetts Institute of Technology Libraries. (1970)-. English. Twice a year. Office of the Director, Room 14S-216, MIT Libraries, Cambridge MA 02139. **LC** Z6945; .M44. **DD** 016.05. available on microfiche. ***Continues*** *Current Serials And Journals In The M.I.T. Libraries.* ***Continued by*** *Serials In The M.I.T. Libraries.*
Desc: This microfiche listing contains approximately 24,000 titles including information on holdings, dates, call numbers, and title changes.

US
SERIALS MASTER LIST. **Main/Corp** New York State Library. **VFOAT** NYS Library Master Serials Information List. (197?)-. English. ir. $60.00. New York State Library / CEC, Cultural Education Center, Albany NY 12230. **Tel** (518)474-7646.

UK/0953-0460
SERIALS (OXFORD, ENGLAND). (SERIALS : THE JOURNAL OF THE UNITED KINGDOM SERIALS GROUP.). **Added/Corp** UK Serials Group. **VFOAT** Journal of the United Kingdom Serials Group. Vol. 1, No. 1 (March 1988)-. Periodical. English. Three times a year. £53.72. United Kingdom Serials Group, 114 Woodstock Road, Witney OX8 6DY England. **Tel** 011 44 993 703466, FAX 011 44 993 778879. **LC** Z692.S5; S475. **DD** 025.3/432. **CODEN** SERIEZ. ***Continues*** *NewsLetter (UK Serials Group), 0141-545X.*

US/0098-7913
SERIALS REVIEW. [Ser. rev.]. Vol. 1 (Jan./June 1975)-. Periodical. English. qt. $75.00 (institutions), $45.00 (individuals). Pierian Press, PO Box 1808, Ann Arbor MI 48106. **Tel** (313)434-5530, (800)678-2435, FAX (313)434-6409. **ED** Cindy Hepfer. **LC** PN4832; .S47. **DD** 016.05. **NLM** ZAI 3 S485. **Bk Rev. Ad Acc.** available on microfilm and microfiche from University Microfilms International (UMI).
Desc: Contains practical information on the management and administration of serial departments, including automation, cataloging, and union lists. An additional feature is the inclusion of a section which reviews periodicals published either in regions or states or in certain selected categories such as little magazines or feminist journals.
Ind/Abst Abstr. Engl. Stud.; Book Rev. Index; Index Period. Artic. Relat. Law; Inf. Instruc. Technol.; Inf. Sci. Abstr.; Leg. Inf. Manage. Index; Libr. Inf. Sci. Abstr.; Libr. Lit.

CN/0317-0322
SERTEK. **Main/Corp** Universite de Montreal. Service des Bibliotheques. Direction des Services Techniques. No. 1- March 1975-. French. ir. Free. Universite de Montreal Service des Bibliotheques, Direction des Services Techniques, PO Box 6128 Station A, Montreal Quebec H3C 3J7 Canada. **ED** Ginette Darbon. **DD** 027.7/714/281.

CC
SHAN-HSI CHIAO YU (TAI-YUAN SHIH, CHINA). (SHAN-HSI CHIAO YU / SHANXI JIAOYU.). **VFOAT** Shanxi Jiaoyu. (19??)-. Periodical. Chinese. mo. RMBY0.25. Shan-hsi Chiao Yu, Post Office, Tai-Yuan Shih, People's Republic of China. **LC** LA1134.S48; S48. **DD** 370/.95117.

US/0273-2343
SHARE (BERKELEY, CALIF.). (SHARE.). [SHARE]. **Added/Corp** Women Library Workers (U.S.). **VFOAT** Sisters Have Resources Everywhere. **VAT** Sisters Have Resources Everywhere (Berkeley, Calif.). (197?)-. English. ir. $4.00 pre-paid, $5.00 invoiced. Women Library Workers, 2027 Parker Street, Berkeley CA 94704. **Tel** (510)843-0533. **LC** Z720.A4; S5a. **DD** 020/.92/2.

JA
SHOSHI SAKUIN TEMBO. **Added/Corp** Nihon Sakuinka Kyokai. Nihon Sakuinka Kyokai. Journal of Japan Indexers Association. Vol. 1 (1977)-. Periodical. Japanese. qt. ¥5200. Nichigai Asoshietsu, c/o Dai 3 Shimokawa Building, 23-8 Omori Kita 1-chome, Ota-ku 143, Tokyo-to Japan. **Tel** 03-763-7581 OR 03-764-0845. **ED** Shinichi Toda. **LC** Z695.9; .S5. cum. index. **Bk Rev. Ad Acc. Circ:** 1,300.
Desc: Official journal of Japan Indexers Association. Articles in all fields of interest and concern to theory, practice and history of bibliographies and indexes.

US/0037-4326
SHOW-ME LIBRARIES. [Show me libr.]. **Added/Corp** Missouri State Library. **VFOAT** Show Me Libraries. Vol. 1 (Oct. 1949)-. Periodical. English. sa (2 issues). $10.00 US & Canada; $20.00 other. Missouri State Library / PBL Office, PO Box 387, 2002 Missouri Boulevard, Jefferson City MO 65102. **Tel** (314)751-2680. **ED** Madeline Matson (phone: (314)751-2680). **LC** Z671; .S48. **DD** 027.0778. Index available. **Circ:** 2,500 (ctrl). available on microfilm and microfiche from University Microfilms International (UMI).
Desc: News features and editorials about Missouri libraries and librarians.
Ind/Abst Libr. Inf. Sci. Abstr.; Libr. Lit.; Ozark Period. Index.

SL/0377-5275
SIERRA LEONE LIBRARY JOURNAL, THE. [Sierra Leone libr. j.]. V. 1- Jan. 1974-. Periodical. English. sa. Editor J S T Thompson, PO Box 94, Fourah Bay College, University of Sierra Leone, Freetown Sierra Leone. **LC** Z857.A2; S557. **DD** 021/.00966/4.
Ind/Abst Libr. Inf. Sci. Abstr.

US
SIG NEWSLETTER. **Main/Corp** American Society for Information Science. Special Interest Group on the Automated Office of the Future (SIG/AOF). **VFOAT** A.S.I.G. Newsletter. No. AOF-1 (Dec. 1980)-. Periodical. English. ir. $6.00 (members only), Comes with American Society Information Science membership. American Society Information Science, 8720 Georgia Avenue, Suite 501, Silver Spring MD 20910. **Tel** (301)495-0900, FAX (301)495-0810.

CN/1185-1759
SIGNAL (LONDON, ONT.). (SIGNAL / SOUTHERN ONTARIO LIBRARY SERVICE). [Signal]. **Added/Corp** Southern Ontario Library Service. (Spring 1990)-. Periodical. English (summaries and/or abstracts in French). qt. Limited free distribution. Southern Ontario Library Service, 366 Oxford Street East, London Ontario N6A 1V8 Canada. **DD** 027.4713.

FI/0355-0036
SIGNUM. [Signum]. **Added/Corp** Suomen Kirjallisuuspalvelun Seura. Suomen Tieteellinen Kirjastoseura. Tietopalveluseura (Finland). (1968)-. Periodical. Finnish (English and Swedish). Eight times a year. Fmk250.00. Finnish Research Library Association, PO Box 217, SF-00171 Helsinki Finland. Index available. **Bk Rev. Ad Acc.**

SI/0085-6118
SINGAPORE LIBRARIES. [Singap. libr.]. **Added/Corp** Library Association of Singapore. Vol. 1 (1971)-. English. an (Dec.). $15.00. Library Association of Singapore, Bukit Merah Central, Singapore 0315 Singapore. **LC** Z845.S5; S56. **DD** 020/.5.
Ind/Abst Libr. Inf. Sci. Abstr.; Libr. Lit.

US/0885-3959
SISAC NEWS. (SISAC NEWS : THE REPORT OF THE SERIALS INDUSTRY SYSTEMS ADVISORY COMMITTEE.). [SISAC news]. **Added/Corp** Book

Industry Study Group. Serials Industry Systems Advisory Committee. **VAT** Serials Industry Systems Advisory Committee News. Vol. 1, No. 1 (Oct. 1985)-. English. ir (Published 2 or 3 times a year & 5 issues of SISAC Minutes). $150.00 (non-profit); $300.00 (commerical). Book Industry Study Group, 160 5th Avenue, New York NY 10010. **Tel** (212)929-1393, FAX (212)989-7542. **LC** Z692.S5; S55. **DD** 025.3/432. **CODEN** SISNEF.

DK
SKOLEBIBLIOTEKSARBOG. Began with Vol. for 1967/68. Danish. Danmarks Skolebiblioteksforenings, Norrebrogade 159, DK-2200 Copenhagen N Denmark. **LC** Z675.S3; S63.

US
SLA BIENNIAL SALARY SURVEY / SPECIAL LIBRARIES ASSOCIATION. **Added/Corp** Special Libraries Association. **VFOAT** Biennial Salary Survey. **VAT** Special Libraries Association Biennial Salary Survey. (1991)-. English. be. $40.50 (includes updates). Special Libraries Association / Education Division, 1700 18th Street Northwest, Washington DC 20009. **Tel** (202)234-4700, FAX (202)265-9317. **LC** Z682.4.S65; S59. ***Continues*** *SLA Triennial Salary Survey.*

AT/0156-5281
SLACAD NEWSLETTER. **VFOAT** School Library Association of Canberra and District Newsletter. (197?)-. Periodical. English. tq. **ED** C Haigh, PO Box 559, Civic Square, Canberra ACT 2608 Australia.
Ind/Abst Aust. Educ. Index.

US/0732-7447
SMITHSONIAN INSTITUTION LIBRARIES RESEARCH GUIDE. [Smithson. Inst. Libr. res. guide]. **Added/Corp** Smithsonian Institution. (198?)-. Monographic series. English. Price varies per volume. GK Hall & Co, 100 Front Street, Riverside NJ 08075. **Tel** (800)257-5755 ext. 2223. **LC** UNC.

UK/0038-0903
SOLANUS. [Solanus]. **Added/Corp** SCONUL Slavonic and East European Group. Standing Conference of National and University Libraries. Sub-Committee on Slavonic and East European Materials. No. 1 (1966)-. Periodical. English (Russian, German and French). an. £10.00. Private Libraries Association, Ravelston South View Road, Pinner Middlesex HA5 3YD England. **(Subscription address:** Slavic East European Collection / British Library, GR Russell Street, Dr. C. Thomas, London WCIB 3DG England.**) ED** Christine Thomas. **LC** DJK36.G7; S65. Index available. cum. index. **Bk Rev. Ad Acc.**
Desc: Deals with all aspects of the printed word in the Soviet Union and Eastern Europe.
Ind/Abst Anthropol. Index; Libr. Inf. Sci. Abstr.

US/0193-273X
SOLINEWS. **Added/Corp** Southeastern Library Network. Vol. 2 (Sept. 1974)-. Periodical. English. bm (6 issues). Free to members. SOLINET - Southeastern Library Network, 1438 West Peachtree Street Northwest, Suite 400, Atlanta GA 30309. **Tel** (404)892-0943, FAX (404)892-7879. **ED** Liz Hornsby. **Circ:** 900. ***Continues*** *Southeastern Library Network. Newsletter - Southeastern Library Network.*
Desc: Membership newsletter for members of SOLINET.

US/0272-2100
SOLINEWS UPDATE. **Added/Corp** Southeastern Library Network. Vol. 1 (Sept. 1980)-. Periodical. English. SOLINET - Southeastern Library Network, 1438 West Peachtree Street Northwest, Suite 400, Atlanta GA 30309. **Tel** (404)892-0943, FAX (404)892-7879.
Desc: Newsletter for Solinet members.

TZ
SOMENI. **Added/Corp** Tanzania Library Association. Kenya Literature Bureau. Vol. 1, (Apr. 1971)-. Periodical. English. **LC** Z857.T3; S65. ***Continues*** *Someni.*

US/0038-1853
SOUNDINGS (SANTA BARBARA). (SOUNDINGS.). [Soundings]. **Added/Corp** University of California, Santa Barbara. Library. Vol. 1 (May 1969)-. English. an (May). $4.00. University of California at Santa Barbara, 129 Library, Santa Barbara CA 93106. **Tel** (805)893-3014. **ED** Donald E. Fitch. **LC** Z881.C1579; S63. **DD** 081. **Circ:** 850 (ctrl).
Desc: Articles on library collections and recent acquisitions, plus campus lectures on library related topics, occasional poems, and translations.
Ind/Abst Am. Hist. Life (1985-); Curr. Contents Arts Humanit.; Guide Soc. Sci. Relig.; MLA Int. Bibl. Books Artic. Mod. Lang. Lit.

US/0275-6811
SOURCEBOOK OF LIBRARY TECHNOLOGY, THE. [Sourceb. libr. technol.]. **Added/Corp** American Library Association. (1975)-. English. be. $90.00. American Library Association, 50 East Huron Street, Chicago IL 60611. **Tel** (312)944-6780, (800)545-2433, FAX (312)944-2641. **(Subscription address:** American Library Association, Subscription Department, 434 West Downer, Aurora IL 60506-9936.**) NLM** Z 671 S724.

US/0094-9981
SOURCES (ALBUQUERQUE). (SOURCES.). **Main/Corp** New Mexico. University. General Library. No. 1 (Apr. 1973)-. Monographic series. English. ir. Price varies per volume. University of New Mexico Bookstore, Albuquerque NM 87131.

CN/0229-4605
SOURCES & RESOURCES (BRITISH COLUMBIA SCHOOL LIBRARIANS' ASSOCIATION). (SOURCES & RESOURCES : ADDITIONS & DELETIONS / BCSLA.). [Sources resour., Addit. deletions]. **Added/Corp** British Columbia School Librarians' Association. Vol. 1, No. 1 (Nov. 1978)-. Periodical. English. British Columbia School Librarians' Association, c/o British Columbia Teachers Federation, 2235 Burrard Street, Vancouver British Columbia V6J 3H9 Canada. **DD** 027.8/09711.

SA/0256-8861
SOUTH AFRICAN JOURNAL OF LIBRARY AND INFORMATION SCIENCE. [S. Afr. j. libr. inf. sci.]. **Added/Corp** Foundation for Education, Science, and Technology (South Africa). Bureau for Scientific Publications. South African Institute for Librarianship and Information Science. **VFOAT** Suid-Afrikaanse Tydskrif vir Biblioteek- en Inligtingkunde; Library and Information Science; Biblioteek- en Inligtingkunde. Vol. 52, No. 1 (March 1984)-. Periodical. English (Afrikaans). qt. R120.00 South Africa; R121.00 other. Foundation for Education Science & Technology, PO Box 1758, Pretoria 0001 South Africa. **Tel** 011 27 12 3226404, FAX 011 27 12 3207803. **LC** Z671; .S69. **[CCC]. Bk Rev. Circ:** 2,700 (ctrl). available on microfilm and microfiche from University Microfilms International (UMI). Documents available from Ask*IEEE. ***Continues*** *Suid-Afrikaanse Tydskrif Vir Biblioteek- en Inligtingwese, 0256-887X.*
Desc: Descriptive and research articles in library and information science.
Ind/Abst Inf. Sci. Abstr.; INSPEC (Dec. 1985-); Libr. Inf. Sci. Abstr.; Libr. Lit.

US/0197-5366
SOUTH ASIA LIBRARY NOTES & QUERIES. [South Asia libr. notes queries]. **Added/Corp** Association for Asian Studies. Committee on South Asian Libraries and Documentation. **VAT** South Asia Library Notes and Queries. No. 1 (Mar. 1978)-. Periodical. English. Twice a year (Spring & Fall). $8.00. Association for Asian Studies / University of Minnesota, S 10 Wilson Library, Minneapolis MN 55455. **Tel** (612)624-5801. **ED** M. L. P. Patterson and M. Yanuck. **LC** Z3185; .S64; DS335. **DD** 026/.954. Index available ($6.00). **Ad Acc.**

US/1046-5553
SOUTH CAROLINA PROGRAM FOR LIBRARY DEVELOPMENT, THE. (THE SOUTH CAROLINA PROGRAM FOR LIBRARY DEVELOPMENT ... UNDER THE LIBRARY SERVICES AND CONSTRUCTION ACT.). [S.C. program libr. dev.]. **VFOAT** Library Services and Construction Act. (1985)-. English. an. Free. South Carolina State Library / Reference Department, 1500 Senate Street, PO Box 11469, Columbia SC 29211. **Tel** (803)734-8666, FAX (803)734-8676. **ED** James B Johnson. **DD** 027. ctrl circ. ***Continues*** *South Carolina Program for Library Development ... Under the Library Services and Construction Act.*
Desc: Long-range plan for use of LSCA funds in South Carolina.

US
SOUTH CAROLINA PUBLIC LIBRARY ANNUAL STATISTICAL SUMMARY. **See** Library and Information Sciences-Abstracting, Bibliographies and Statistics.

US
SOUTH DAKOTA LIBRARY DIRECTORY. **Added/Corp** South Dakota State Library & Archives. (198?)-. Directory. English. an. Free. South Dakota State Library, 800 Governors Drive, Pierre SD 57501. **Tel** (605)773-3131, FAX (605)773-4950. **ED** Dorothy M. Liegl, Donna Gilliland. **LC** Z732.S9; D57. **DD** 027/.0025/783. **Circ:** 800 (ctrl). ***Continues*** *Directory of South Dakota Libraries.*
Desc: Directory information including name of library, institution, address, name of director, and phone number for public, school, academic, and special libraries. Arranged by city.

US/0272-7560
SOUTHEASTERN LAW LIBRARIAN. **Added/Corp** American Association of Law Libraries. Southeastern Chapter. Vol. 1 (Spring 1975)-. Periodical. English. qt. $5.00. Southeastern Chapter of the American Association of Law Librarians, University of Virginia School of Law, Charlottesville VA 22901.
Ind/Abst Leg. Inf. Manage. Index (19??-).

US/0038-3686
SOUTHEASTERN LIBRARIAN, THE. [Southeast. librar.]. **Added/Corp** Southeastern Library Association. Vol. 1 (Spring 1951)-. Periodical. English. qt. $35.00 (1 year), $70.00 (2 year), $105.00 (3 year). The Southeastern Librarian, PO Box 987, Tucker GA 30085. **Tel** (404)939-5080, FAX (404)892-7879. **ED** Theresa Johnson. **LC** Z673; .S716. **DD** 020.623. Index available. cum. index. **Ad Acc. Circ:** 1,800 (ctrl). available on microfilm and microfiche from University Microfilms International (UMI).
Desc: Subjects and information of interest to professional librarians.
Ind/Abst Libr. Lit.

US/1056-1021
SOUTHWESTERN ARCHIVIST. [Southwest. arch.]. **Added/Corp** Society of Southwest Archivists. Vol. 15, No. 1 (May 1990)-. Periodical. English. Four times a year (Feb., May, Aug., Nov.). $10.00 (individual); $25.00 (institution), Membership. Society of Southwest Archivist, PO Box 4090, C/O Martin Tres, Lubbock TX 79409. **Tel** (806)742-3749, FAX (806)742-0496. **ED** Leon C. Miller, (phone: (504)865-5685). **DD** 025. **Bk Rev**, (Qty: 2). **Ad Acc, Adv Mgr:** Ed, **Tel** (504)865-5685. **Circ:** 700. ***Continues*** *SSA Newsletter (Oklahoma City, Okla.), 0894-5772.*

RU/0134-6695
SOVETSKOE BIBLIOTEKOVEDENIE. ***Title Change.*** (SOVETSKOE BIBLIOTEKOVEDENIE / GOSUDARSTVENNAIA ORDENA LENINA BIBLIOTEKA SSSR IMENI V.I. LENINA.). [Sov. bibl.]. **Added/Corp** Gosudarstvennaia Biblioteka SSSR Imeni V. I. Lenina. (1973)-(1993). Periodical. Russian. bm. Izdatelstvo Kniga, 50 Gorky Ulitsa, 125047 Moscow Russia. **LC** Z819.A1; S67. **NLM** Z 819 S729. ***Continues*** *Biblioteki SSSR.* ***Continued by*** *Bibliotekovedenie, 0869-608X.*
Ind/Abst Libr. Inf. Sci. Abstr. (?-?); Libr. Lit. (?-?).

CN/0831-1994
SPECIAL DELIVERY (WINNIPEG). (SPECIAL DELIVERY / CANADIAN ASSOCIATION OF SPECIAL LIBRARIES AND INFORMATION SERVICES, MANITOBA CHAPTER.). [Spec. deliv.]. **Added/Corp** Canadian Association of Special Libraries and Information Services. Manitoba Chapter. Vol. 1, No. 1 (Dec. 1985)-. Periodical. English. ir. Carleton University / Linguistics, Department of Linguistics, Ottawa Ontario K1S 5B6 Canada. **Tel** (613)788-2808, (613)788-2340. **DD** 026/.0006/07127. available on an online database (file 149/Full-Text) from DIALOG.

CN/0843-7289
SPECIAL ISSUES. (SPECIAL ISSUES : CANADIAN ASSOCIATION OF SPECIAL LIBRARIES AND INFORMATION SERVICES NEWSLETTER.). [Special issues]. **VFOAT** Canadian Association of Special Libraries and Information Services Newsletter. Vol. 1, No. 1 (May 1989)-. Newsletter. English. qt. Special Issues, 351 Engineering Building, University of Manitoba, Winnipeg Manitoba R3T 2N2 Canada. **DD** 026/.0006/071.

US/0038-6723
SPECIAL LIBRARIES. [Spec. libr.]. **Added/Corp** Special Libraries Association. Vol. 1 (Jan. 1910)-. Periodical. English. ir (16 issues). $65.00 US; $75.00 other (includes Specialist). Special Libraries Association / Education Division, 1700 18th Street Northwest, Washington DC 20009. **Tel** (202)234-4700, FAX (202)265-9317. **ED** Maria C. Barry. **LC** Z671; .S72. **DD** 026. **NLM** Z 671 S741. **CODEN** SPLBAN. Index available. cum. index. **Bk Rev. Ad Acc. Pr Rev. Circ:** 14,000 (ctrl). available on microfilm. Documents available from The Genuine Article, UMI Article Clearinghouse, Ask*IEEE.
Desc: This publication includes valuable articles for librarians and information specialists on the organization and operation of information centers, technological advancements, education and public relations.
Ind/Abst ABI/INFORM Glob. Ed.; ABI Inform Ondisc (Nov. 1975-Jan. 1978); Acad. Search (July 1993-); Am. Hist. Life (1963-); Art Archaeol. Tech. Abstr.; ARTbibliogr. Mod.; Bibliogr. Carto.; Book Rev. Index; Bus. ASAP (1990-) [Full Txt.]; Bus. Index (1985-); Comput. Lit. Index; Cumul. Index Nurs. Allied Health Lit.; Curr. Contents Soc. Behav. Sci.; Curr. Index J. Educ.; Gen. BusinessFile (1985-); Gen. Period. Index (1985-); Health Plan. Adminis.; Hospit. Health Admin. Index; INFO-SOUTH Abstr.; Inf. Instruc. Technol.; Inf. Sci. Abstr. [Full Cov.]; INSPEC (July/Aug. 1971-); Int. Aerosp. Abstr.; Leg. Inf. Manage. Index; Libr. Inf. Sci. Abstr.; Libr. Lit.; Mag. ASAP Plus [Full Txt.]; Mag. Index Plus (1989-); Mag. Search; Newsp. Period. Abstr. (1988-); PAIS Int. Print (?-?); Public Aff. Inf. Serv. Bull.; Res. Alert [Full Cov.]; Soc. Sci. Cit. Index [Full Cov.]; Mag. Index (1977-); Trade Ind. ASAP [Full Txt.]; Trade Ind. Index [Full Txt.].

AT
SPECIAL LIBRARIES IN QUEENSLAND. **Main/Corp** Library Association of Australia. Special Libraries Section. (19??)-. English. an. **LC** Z870.Q44; L52a. **DD** 026/.0025/943.
Ind/Abst Aust. Educ. Index.

Library and Information Sciences

CN/0711-1770
SPECIAL LIBRARIES IN THE EDMONTON AREA (1981). (SPECIAL LIBRARIES IN THE EDMONTON AREA / CASLIS, EDMONTON CHAPTER.). [Spec. libr. Edmont. area]. **Main/Corp** Canadian Association of Special Libraries and Information Services. Edmonton Chapte. (1980)-. Periodical. English. an. CASLIS / Edmonton Chapter, 10436 8th Avenue, Edmonton Alberta T6E 1X6 Canada. **DD** 026/.00025/71233. *Continues Special Libraries in the Edmonton Metropolitan Area, 0228-8214.*

US/0273-9399
SPECIALIST (NEW YORK, N.Y.). (SPECIALIST.). [SpeciaList]. **Added/Corp** Special Libraries Association. Vol. 3, No. 5 (July 1980)-. Periodical. English. mo. $65.00 US; $75.00 other (comes with Special Libraries). Special Libraries Association / Education Division, 1700 18th Street Northwest, Washington DC 20009. **Tel** (202)234-4700, FAX (202)265-9317. **ED** Maria C Barry. **DD** 026. Index available. cum. index. **Bk Rev**. **Ad Acc**. **Circ:** 14,000 (ctrl).
Ind/Abst Inf. Sci. Abstr.

CE
SRI LANKA (ISBN) PUBLISHERS DIRECTORY. **VFOAT** Sri Lanka ISBN Publishers Directory. 1987-. Directory. English. Sri Lanka National Library Service Board, PO Box 1764, Independence Avenue, Colombo 7 Sri Lanka. **Tel** 011 94 1 685198, FAX 011 94 1 685201. **LC** Z464.S72; S75. **DD** 025.3.

CE
SRI LANKA LIBRARY REVIEW. **Added/Corp** Sri Lanka Association. Vol. 4, No. 2 (1972/1973)-. Academic Scholarly Publication. Multiple languages (English and Sinhalese). an. $15.00. Sri Lanka Library Association, OPA Centre, 275/75 Bauddhaloka Mawatha, Colombo 7 Sri Lanka. **Tel** 509103. **ED** Lionel R. Amarakoon. **LC** Z845.C4; C48. **Acid Free. Circ:** 250. *Continues Ceylon Library Review, 0009-0867.*

US/0749-1670
SRRT NEWSLETTER (CHICAGO, ILL.). (SRRT NEWSLETTER : A PUBLICATION OF THE SOCIAL RESPONSIBILITIES ROUND TABLE OF THE AMERICAN LIBRARY ASSOCIATION.). **Added/Corp** American Library Association. Social Responsibilities Round Table. **VAT** Social Responsibilities Round Table Newsletter. No. 74 (Dec. 1984)-. Newsletter. English. qt. $20.00 institution, $10.00 individual (nonmember); Free to ALA members. American Library Association, 50 East Huron Street, Chicago IL 60611. **Tel** (312)944-6780, (800)545-2433, FAX (312)944-2641. **(Subscription address:** American Library Association, Subscription Department, 434 West Downer, Aurora IL 60506-9936.) **LC** Z716.4; .S64. **DD** 021. *Continues American Library Association. Social Responsibilities Round Table. Newsletter - Social Responsibilities Round Table, 0065-9096.*

CC
SSU-CHUAN TU SHU KUAN HSUEH PAO. **VFOAT** Sichuan Tushuguan Xuebao; Journal of the Sichuan Society for Library Science; Sicuantushuguanxuebao. Began with Mar. 1979 issue. Periodical. Chinese (English). qt. Ssu-Chuan Sheng Tu Shu Kuan Hsueh Hui, Cheng-tu, People's Republic of China. **LC** Z671; .S77. **DD** 020/.5.

AT/0817-5810
STAFF DEVELOPMENT IN AUSTRALIAN LIBRARIES. *Ceased.* [Staff dev. Aust. Libr.]. (1986)-(Dec. 1993). Periodical. English. sa. Library Publications / University of South Australia, Holbrook Road, Underdale SA 5032 Australia. **Tel** 011 61 8 3026258. **ED** J. Hiscock. **DD** 020.7150994.
Ind/Abst Aust. Educ. Index; Aust. Libr. Inf. Sci. Abstr. (1986-).

US/0013-8495
STAFF REPORTER. **Main/Corp** Enoch Pratt Free Library, Baltimore. (19??)-. Periodical. English. mo. $3.00 (US), $5.00 (Canada), $8.00 (other). Enoch Pratt Library Publications, 400 Cathedral Street, Baltimore MD 21201. **Tel** (410)396-5305. **ED** Averil J. Kadis. **Circ:** 500.
Desc: Newsletter with information on innovative and traditional library services; meeting, conference, and workshop reports; announcements of budgetary decisions and policy changes; discussions of personnel problems, etc.

US/0085-6630
STANDARD PERIODICAL DIRECTORY, THE. (1965)-. Directory. English. an. $445.00. Oxbridge Communications Inc., 150 5th Avenue, Room 302, New York NY 10011. **Tel** (212)741-0231, FAX (212)633-2938. **(Subscription address:** US and Canada: Gale Research Co., 835 Penobscot Building, Detroit, MI 48226**) ED** Matthew Manning. **LC** Z6951; .S78. **DD** 016.051. **NLM** Z 6941 S785. Index available. cum. index. **Ad Acc**. available on labels; available on magnetic tape; available on diskette; available on CD-ROM.
Desc: Provides data on more than 75,000 periodicals in the United States an Canada. Types of periodicals included are business and consumer magazines; journals; newsletters, newspapers; directories; government publications; yearbooks; indexes and abstracts, etc.

US/0361-0241
START OF MESSAGE. **Added/Corp** Cleveland Health Sciences Library. Catalog Dept. Health Science OCLC Users Group. (Aug. 1975)-. Periodical. English. Four times a year. $25.00 (includes active institution membership), $5.00 (includes individual membership). University of California Davis / Health Sciences Lab, Davis CA 95616. **Tel** (916)752-9866. **ED** Lois H. Culler. **NLM** W1 ST797. ctrl circ.
Desc: The newsletter of the Health Sciences OCLC Users Group, an independent group composed of health sciences libraries and individuals who either use or are interested in the use of the services of OCLC, Inc., in health sciences libraries.

CN/0823-7646
STARTER COLLECTION FOR JUNIOR HIGH SCHOOLS, A. [Starter collect. jr. high sch.]. Nov. 1982-. English. an. Calgary Board of Education Program Resources Group, 3610-9th Street SE, Calgary Alberta T2G 3C5 Canada. **DD** 011/.62.

UK/0305-9189
STATE LIBRARIAN. (STATE LIBRARIAN : JOURNAL OF THE CIRCLE OF STATE LIBRARIANS.). [State libr.]. Vol. 23. No. 1 (Mar. 1975)-. Periodical. English. Three times a year. £6.00, £5.00 (nonmembers) UK; $20.00 US. State Librarian, c/o J Driels, Lambeth Bridge House/Room 120, Albert Embankment, London SE1 7SB England. **Tel** 01 211 3563. **ED** Janer Driels. **LC** Z675.G7; S78. **DD** 027.541. Index available. cum. index. **Bk Rev**. **Ad Acc. Circ:** 700. *Continues Bulletin of the Circle of State Librarians.*
Desc: Journal of the circle of state librarians describes development within, or that affect, national and government libraries.
Ind/Abst Libr. Inf. Sci. Abstr.; Libr. Lit.

US
STATE LIBRARY AGENCIES, A SURVEY PROJECT REPORT, THE. **Added/Corp** Association of Specialized and Cooperative Library Agencies. 1st Ed. (1973)-. Periodical. English. be. $25.00 (nonmember), $22.50 (member). American Library Association, 50 East Huron Street, Chicago IL 60611. **Tel** (312)944-6780, (800)545-2433, FAX (312)944-2641. **(Subscription address:** American Library Association, Subscription Department, 434 West Downer, Aurora IL 60506-9936.)

AT/0729-199X
STATISTICAL BULLETIN FOR PUBLIC LIBRARIES IN WESTERN AUSTRALIA. **See** Library and Information Sciences-Abstracting, Bibliographies and Statistics.

US/0733-2041
STATISTICS OF PUBLIC SCHOOL LIBRARIES / MEDIA CENTERS. **See** Library and Information Sciences-Abstracting, Bibliographies and Statistics.

US
STATISTICS OF SOUTH DAKOTA LIBRARIES. **See** Library and Information Sciences-Abstracting, Bibliographies and Statistics.

US/0099-0655
STATISTICS OF SOUTH DAKOTA PUBLIC LIBRARIES. **See** Library and Information Sciences-Abstracting, Bibliographies and Statistics.

US
STATISTICS OF SOUTH DAKOTA SCHOOL LIBRARIES. South Dakota State Library, 800 Governors Drive, Pierre SD 57501. **Tel** (605)773-3131, FAX (605)773-4950.

US/0731-8464
STATISTICS OF VIRGINIA PUBLIC LIBRARIES AND INSTITUTIONAL LIBRARIES. **See** Library and Information Sciences-Abstracting, Bibliographies and Statistics.

NE/0168-3462
STATISTIEK VAN DE OPENBARE BIBLIOTHEKEN / CENTRAAL BUREAU VOOR DE STATISTIEK, HOOFDAFDELING SOCIAAL-CULTURELE STATISTIEKEN. **See** Library and Information Sciences-Abstracting, Bibliographies and Statistics.

GW
STATISTIK DER KOMMUNALEN OFFENTLICHEN BIBLIOTHEKEN DER BUNDESREPUBLIK, REGIONALSTATISTIK. **See** Library and Information Sciences-Abstracting, Bibliographies and Statistics.

GW
STATISTISCHE UBERSICHTEN FUER DAS JAHR (UNIVERSITAT KIEL. INSTITUTS FUR WELTWIRTSCHAFT. BIBLIOTHEK). **See** Library and Information Sciences-Abstracting, Bibliographies and Statistics.

US/0145-4684
STEP UP YOUR AWARENESS. **VFOAT** Research Library. Step Up Your Awareness. Periodical. English. mo. Free to qualified subscribers. G D Searle & Company, PO Box 5110, Chicago IL 60680.

XR/0081-5896
STRAHOVSKA KNIHOVNA. [Strahovska knih.]. (1966)-. Czech (summaries and/or abstracts in German, English and French). Pamatnik Narodniho Pisemnictvi, Czech Republic. **LC** Z674; .S83.
Ind/Abst Am. Hist. Life (1966-); BHA : Biblio. Hist. Art.

CN/0227-4760
STRATEGY (LIBRARIES & LEARNING, INC.). (STRATEGY.). [Strategy]. Vol. 2, No. 1-. Periodical. English. $36.00. Libraries & Learning Inc, 284 Avenue Road, Toronto Ontario M4V 2G7 Canada. **DD** 027.8/05. *Continues Strategy (Moore & Moore Design), 0227-4760.*

US
STUDENT CONTRIBUTION SERIES. **Main/Corp** University of Maryland. School of Library and Information Services. No. 1 (1967)-. Periodical. English. ir. Price varies per volume. University of Maryland School of Library and Information Science, c/o Mrs. Herman, College Park MD 20742. **Tel** (301)454-4147, (301)454-2590. **Bk Rev**. **Ad Acc**.
Desc: Various subjects relating to library and information sciences. services.

CN/1194-3963
STUDENT LIBRARY HANDBOOK. (1993)-. English. an.

US
STUDIES IN LIBRARIANSHIP. **Main/Corp** Denver. University. Graduate School of Librarianship. (196?)-. Monographic series. English. ir. University of Denver Libraries, University Park, Denver CO 80210. **Tel** (303)753-2557. *Continues Studies in Librarianship.*

US/0099-0922
SUBJECT CATALOG OF THE LIBRARY. SUPPLEMENT. **Main/Corp** New York Academy of Medicine. Library. 1st- 1974-. Catalog. Multiple languages. GK Hall & Co, 100 Front Street, Riverside NJ 08075. **Tel** (800)257-5755 ext. 2223. **LC** Z6676; .N54 1969A SUPPL; R129. **DD** 016.61.

US/0732-927X
SUBJECT DIRECTORY OF SPECIAL LIBRARIES AND INFORMATION CENTERS. [Subj. dir. spec. libr. inf. cent.]. **VFOAT** Subject Directory of Special Libraries. 1st Ed. (1975)-. Directory. English. ir. $725.00 set. Gale Research Inc., 835 Penobscot Building, Detroit MI 48226. **Tel** (800)877-GALE, (313)961-2242, FAX (313)961-6083, telex TWX 810-221-7086. **ED** Joanna M. Zakalik. **LC** Z675.A2; S83. **DD** 026/.00025/73. **NLM** Z 675.A2; Y74dab. available on magnetic tape; available on diskette.
Desc: More than 13,000 entries are arranged under 14 subject chapters.

US/8756-002X
SUBJECT GUIDE TO BOOK REVIEWS. [Subj. guide book rev.]. Began in 1985. Periodical. English. mo. $60.00. Popular Information Press, 3023 Honeysucker Way NE, Salem OR 97303. **Tel** (503)364-9210. **DD** 028.

US/0361-5243
SUBJECT HEADINGS IN MICROFORM. *Title Change.* (SUBJECT HEADINGS IN MICROFORM / SUBJECT CATALOGING DIVISION, PROCESSING SERVICES.). [Subj. head. microform]. **Main/Corp** Library of Congress. Subject Cataloging Division. **VFOAT** Library of Congress Subject Headings in Microform. (1976)-(1992). Periodical. English. qt. Library of Congress / Cataloging Distribution Service, Washington DC 20541-5017. **Tel** (800)255-3666, (202)707-6100, FAX (202)707-1334. **LC** Microfiche Z695; Z663.78. **DD** 025. available on microfilm. *Continued by Library of Congress. Library of Congress Subject Headings in Microform.*
Desc: Cumulates subject headings with a separate fiche for children's subject headings. Allows users to determine which headings and references are currently authorized.

US/0066-0868
SUMMARY OF PROCEEDINGS. ANNUAL CONFERENCE / AMERICAN THEOLOGICAL LIBRARY ASSOCIATION. [Summ. proc., Annu. conf. - Am. Theol. Libr. Assoc.]. **Main/Corp** American Theological Library Association. (1948)-. Proceedings. English. an. $20.00 US; $22.00 other. American Theological Library

Association, 820 Church Street, 3rd Floor, Evanston IL 60201. **Tel** (708)869-7788, FAX (708)869-8513. **ED** Betty O'Brien. **LC** Z673; .A624. **DD** 026. cum. index. **Circ:** 700. ***Continues*** *Summary of Proceedings / Conference of Theological Librarians.*
Desc: Papers presented at the annual conference and reports of committees. Also contains minutes of the ATLA board.
Ind/Abst Index Book Rev. Relig.; Relig. Index One Period. (1973-).

US/0360-2435
SURVEY OF LIBRARY MATERIAL EXPENDITURES AT STANFORD UNIVERSITY LIBRARIES. **Main/Corp** Stanford University. Libraries. English. an. Stanford University Libraries, Publications, Green Library / Room 312D, Stanford CA 94305. **Tel** (415)723-0461. **LC** Z733.S813; S94. **DD** 025.1/977794/73.

US
SWALL BULLETIN. **Main/Corp** Southwestern Association of Law Libraries. (19??)-. Bulletin. English.
Ind/Abst Leg. Inf. Manage. Index (19??-).

US/0095-0874
SYMBOLS OF AMERICAN LIBRARIES. (SYMBOLS OF AMERICAN LIBRARIES / LIBRARY OF CONGRESS, UNION CATALOG DIVISION, PROCESSING DEPARTMENT.). **Added/Corp** Library of Congress. Union Catalog Division. Library of Congress. Catalog Publication Division. Library of Congress. Catalog Management and Publication Division. 10th Ed. (1969)-. Catalog. English. ir. $28.00 North America; $30.00 other. Library of Congress / Cataloging Distribution Service, Washington DC 20541-5017. **Tel** (800)255-3666, (202)707-6100, FAX (202)707-1334. **LC** Z881.U49; U6. **DD** 018/.1. **NLM** Z 881.A1; S986. **Bk Rev. Ad Acc.** ***Continues*** *Symbols Used in the National Union Catalog of the Library of Congress.*
Desc: A directory of identification symbols for libraries in the United States and Canada.

US/0164-8993
SYNERGY (DALLAS). (SYNERGY.). **Added/Corp** American Physical Therapy Association (Founded 1921). Texas Chapter. Southeastern District. (19??)-. Periodical. English. Twelve times a year. Free. Talon Regional Medical Library Program, UT Southwestern Medical Library, 5323 Harry Hines Boulevard, Dallas TX 75235-9049. **Tel** (214)688-2085, FAX (214)688-3277. **ED** Barbara A. Radke. **Bk Rev. Circ:** 2,000 (ctrl).
Desc: Newsletter for Region Five of the National Library of Medicine's Regional Medical Library Program. Serves medical libraries and their supporters in the states of Texas, Arkansas, Louisiana, Oklahoma, and New Mexico.

NO/0332-656X
SYNOPSIS. (SYNOPSIS; INFORMASJON OM INFORMASJON.). [Synopsis]. Periodical. Norwegian (summaries and/or abstracts in English). Six times a year. Free. Riksbibliotektjenesten, Postboks 2439 Solli, N-0202 Oslo 2 Norway. **Tel** +47 2 43 08 80, FAX 47 2 56 09 81. **ED** Kjellaug Scheie. **LC** Z671; .S96. **DD** 020/.5. Index available. **Bk Rev. Circ:** 1,700 (ctrl).
Desc: News of interest to professional librarians, taken from various journals in Scandinavia, Europe and USA. Reports and articles by Norwegians.
Ind/Abst Libr. Inf. Sci. Abstr.; World Surf. Coat. Abstr.

NE/0082-111X
SYNTHESE HISTORICAL LIBRARY. [Synth. hist. libr.]. (1969)-. Monographic series. English. ir. Price varies per volume. Kluwer Academic Publishers, Postbus 322, 3300 AH Dordrecht, The Netherlands. **Tel** 011 (31) 78 524400, FAX 011 31 78 183273, telex 20083. **(Subscription address:** Kluwer Academic Publishers / US Subscriptions, PO Box 253, Accord Station, Hingham MA 02018.**) LC** UNC. **[CCC].**
Ind/Abst Math. Rev.

NE
SYNTHESE LANGUAGE LIBRARY. Vol. 1 (1978)-. Monographic series. English. ir. Price varies per volume. Kluwer Academic Publishers, Postbus 322, 3300 AH Dordrecht, The Netherlands. **Tel** 011 (31) 78 524400, FAX 011 31 78 183273, telex 20083. **(Subscription address:** Kluwer Academic Publishers / US Subscriptions, PO Box 253, Accord Station, Hingham MA 02018.**)**

US/0882-3014
SYSTEMS RESEARCH AND INFORMATION SCIENCE. [Syst. res. inf. sci.]. (1985)-. Periodical. English. qt. $339.00 (academic institutions), $529.00 (corporate institutions). Gordon & Breach Science Publishers, Inc., PO Box 786, Cooper Station, New York NY 10276. **Tel** (212)206-8900, FAX (212)645-2459. **(Subscription address:** International Publishers Distributor at one of the following addresses: 820 Town Center Drive, Langhorne, PA 19047; or PO Box 90, Reading Berkshire RG1 8JL UK; or Kent Ridge PO Box 1180, Singapore 9111, Republic of Singapore**) ED** Frank George. **LC** IN PROCESS. **DD** 003. **CODEN** ISISE8. **[CCC]. Bk Rev. Ad Acc.** Documents available from Ask*IEEE.
Ind/Abst Abstr. Hum. Comput. Interact.; HILITES; INSPEC (1987-).

HU/0139-3499
SZABOLCS-SZATMAR MEGYEI KONYVTARI HIRADO. (1974)-. Hungarian.
Ind/Abst Magyar Konyv. Szak. Biblio.; Hungar. Libr. Info. Sci. Abstr.

CN/0836-155X
T-L NETWORK. ***Ceased.*** [T-L netw.]. **VFOAT** Teacher-Librarian Network. Vol. 12, No. 1 (Oct. 1987)-(1992). Periodical. English. Five times a year. Program Publications, Vancouver School Board, Program Services, Curriculum Resources, 2530-43rd Avenue East, Vancouver British Columbia V5R 2Y7 Canada. **ED** Liz Austrom. **DD** 027.8/09711. ***Continues*** *Your Newsletter, 0229-7914.*

●UK/0966-6745
TAKING STOCK LONDON. 1992. [Tak. stockLond. 1992]. (1992)-. Periodical. English. sa. £20.00. National Acquisitions Group, Westfield House, North Road, Horsforth, Leeds, LS18 5HG England. **Tel** 0532 591447. **ED** Lindsay Thomas. **DD** 025.233.

CN/0841-8195
TALL NEWSLETTER (1984). (TALL NEWSLETTER / TORONTO ASSOCIATION OF LAW LIBRARIANS.). [TALL newsl.]. **Added/Corp** Toronto Association of Law Librarians. **VAT** Toronto Association of Law Librarians Newsletter (1984). Vol. 4, No. 1 (Nov. 1984)-. Newsletter. English. bm. Price per issue varies. Toronto Association of Law Librarians, c/o Tory Tory, DesLauriers & Binnington Centre, Toronto Ontario M5K 1N2 Canada. **DD** 026.34/0060713/541. ***Continues*** *Newsletter (Toronto Association of Law Librarians), 0841-8187.*
Ind/Abst Leg. Inf. Manage. Index (19??-).

US/0190-7565
TALON ANNUAL REPORT. SOUTH CENTRAL REGIONAL MEDICAL LIBRARY PROGRAM. (TALON ANNUAL REPORT.). **Main/Corp** Talon Regional Medical Library Program. **VFOAT** Annual Report - TALON Regional Medical Library Program. **VAT** Texas, Arkansas, Louisiana, Oklahoma, New Mexico Annual Report. South Central Regional Medical Library Program. 1970-. English. an. University of Texas Health Science Center / Dallas, Dallas TX. **NLM** Z 675.M4 T152T.

GW/0723-4074
TASCHENBUCH INFORMATION & DOKUMENTATION. **VFOAT** Taschenbuch Information und Dokumentation. (1983)-. German. be. DM24.80 Germany; $19.80 US. IDD Verlag fur Internationale Dokumentation, Werner Flach KG W-6000 Frankfurt 50 Germany. **Tel** 069/57 77 77. **LC** Z674.3; .T37. **DD** 020/.202. **Ad Acc. Circ:** 3,000.
Desc: Up-to-date descriptive directory of databases, online-hosts, information brokers, libraries, scientific societies, specialized publishers. List of periodicals, newsletters, reference books, and standards.

US/0736-6469
TAX FOUNDATION'S LIBRARY BULLETIN. **Main/Corp** Tax Foundation. **VFOAT** Library Bulletin. (Sept./Oct. 1978)-. Bulletin. English. qt. Tax Foundation Inc., 1250 H Street Northwest, Suite 750, Washington DC 20005. **Tel** (202)783-2760, FAX (202)942-7675. **ED** Marion Marshall. **LC** Z7164.T23; T37; HJ9. **DD** 016.3362/00973. ctrl circ. ***Continues*** *Tax Foundation. Library. Library Bulletin, 0362-8426.*
Desc: Available to tax foundation members only.

NZ/0114-1090
TE PUNA MATAURANGA: THE NATIONAL LIBRARY OF NEW ZEALAND NEWSLETTER. ***Ceased.*** (1988)-(1992). Newsletter. English. qt. National Library of New Zealand, PO Box 1467, Wellington 1 New Zealand. **Tel** 011 64 4 474-3067, FAX (04)743042, telex NL30076. **ED** Bill Davidson. **Circ:** 2,500 (ctrl).
Desc: News of the national library of New Zealand.

AT
TEACHER-LIBRARIAN, THE. [Teach. libr.]. **Added/Corp** School Library Association of New South Wales. School Librarian Association of New South Wales. **VFOAT** Teacher Librarian; Teacher & Librarian. No. 1 (1965)-. Periodical. English. qt. School Library Association of New South Wales, 179 Beechcroft Road, Cheltenham NSW 2119 Australia. **ED** Maureen McMahon.
Ind/Abst Aust. Educ. Index; Aust. Libr. Inf. Sci. Abstr. (1981-).

●CN/1188-679X
TEACHING LIBRARIAN. (THE TEACHING LIBRARIAN : THE OFFICIAL MAGAZINE OF THE ONTARIO SCHOOL LIBRARY ASSOCIATION.). [Teach. libr.]. **Added/Corp** Ontario School Library Association. Ontario Library Association. (1992)-. Periodical. English. Three times a year (Jan., April, Oct.). 36.00Can$. The Teaching Librarian, Suite 303 100 Lombard Street, Toronto Ontario M5C 1M3 Canada. **Tel** (416)363-3388, FAX (416)941-9581. **DD** 027.8/09713/05.

BE
TECH-EUROPE. **Added/Corp** Europe Information Service. **VAT** Tech Europe. (19??)-. Government Publication. English (French). mo. 19400.00F. Europe Information Service, rue de Geneve 6, 1140 Brussels Belgium. **Tel** 011 32 2 242 6020, FAX 011 32 2 242 9549. **ED** Eve Damiens. **Ad Acc, Adv Mgr:** Lucyna Grauer. **Circ:** 500. available on an online database (file 636/Full-Text) from DIALOG.

US
TECHNICAL BULLETIN. **Added/Corp** Pittsburgh Regional Library Center. **VFOAT** PRLC Technical Bulletin. (1990)-. Bulletin. English. bm. PRLC, 103 Yost Boulevard, Pittsburgh PA 15221. **LC** Z674.82.P68; T4. ***Continues*** *PRLC/OCLC Information Bulletin.*

US/0195-4857
TECHNICAL SERVICES LAW LIBRARIAN. **Added/Corp** American Association of Law Libraries. Technical Services Special Interest Section. American Association of Law Libraries. On-Line Bibliographic Services Special Interest Section. Vol. 5 (Sept. 1979)-. Periodical. English. Four times a year. $10.00. American Association of Law Libraries, 53 West Jackson Boulevard, Suite 940, Chicago IL 60604. **Tel** (312)939-4764, FAX (312)431-1097, telex ABA7603. **(Subscription address:** Creighton University Law Library, 2500 California Plaza, Omaha NE 68178.**) ED** Cynthia A. Larter. **Bk Rev. Ad Acc. Circ:** 315. ***Continues*** *Law Cataloger.*
Desc: Covers all aspects of law library technical services, including cataloging, acquisitions, preservation, online systems, and networking.
Ind/Abst Leg. Inf. Manage. Index.

US/0731-7131
TECHNICAL SERVICES QUARTERLY. [Tech. serv. q.]. Vol. 1, Nos. 1/2 (Fall/Winter 1983)-. Periodical. English. qt. $125.00 US; $175.00 other. The Haworth Press Inc, 10 Alice Street, Binghamton NY 13904-1580. **Tel** (607)722-5857, (800)3-HAWORTH, FAX (607)722-1424. **ED** Gary Pitkin (editor's address: University of Northern Colorado, James A. Michener Library, Greeley, CO 80639). **LC** Z688.5; .T42. **DD** 025/.02/02854. **Bk Rev. Ad Acc. Pr Rev. Acid Free. Circ:** 653. available on microfilm and microfiche from University Microfilms International (UMI). Documents available from Ask*IEEE, Haworth Document Delivery Service.
Desc: Devoted to new trends in computers automation and advanced technologies in the technical operation of libraries and information centers. Keeps track of the changes and comments on them in theme as well as general issues. Provides a forum for voicing opinions and sharing experiences that have to do with many aspects of this new librarianship.
Ind/Abst Curr. Index J. Educ.; Index Period. Artic. Relat. Law; Inf. Instruc. Technol.; Inf. Sci. Abstr.; INSPEC (Fall/winter 1983-); Leg. Inf. Manage. Index; Libr. Inf. Sci. Abstr.; Libr. Lit.

US/0272-0884
TECHNICALITIES. [Technicalities]. Vol. 1, No. 1 (Dec. 1980)-. Periodical. English. Twelve times a year. $50.00 US; $65.00 others. Westport Publishers Inc, Media Division, 1102 Grand, Suite 2300, Lincoln NE 68510-1125. **Tel** (800)347-2665, (816)842-8111. **ED** Jennifer Cargill and Brian Alley. **LC** Z671; .T37. **DD** 020/.5. **Bk Rev. Ad Acc. Circ:** 700. available on microfilm and microfiche from University Microfilms International (UMI).
Desc: News, feature articles, reviews, columns, letters and interviews provide readers a wide array of thought provoking material within a refreshing informal newsletter.
Ind/Abst Inf. Instruc. Technol.; Libr. Inf. Sci. Abstr.; Libr. Lit.

US/0162-1564
TENNESSEE LIBRARIAN. [Tenn. libr.]. **Added/Corp** Tennessee Library Association. **VFOAT** TL. Vol. 1, No. 1 (Summer 1948)-. Periodical. English. Four times a year (Feb., May, Aug., Nov.). $10.00. Tennessee Library Association, PO Box 158417, Nashville TN 37215-8417. **Tel** (615)297-8316, FAX (615)269-1807. **ED** Marie Garrett (editor's telephone: (615)974-0013). **LC** Z671; .T4. **DD** 020/.6234/768. **Bk Rev. Ad Acc, Adv Mgr:** B.P. Ponnappa, **Tel** (615)974-4240. **Circ:** 1,600 (ctrl). available on microfilm and microfiche from University Microfilms International (UMI). ***Continues*** *Tennessee Libraries.*
Desc: News and information about Tennessee libraries and articles which inform and foster the profession of librarianship and which promote adequate library service for the people of Tennessee.
Ind/Abst Libr. Lit.

AU/0251-5253
TERMNET NEWS : JOURNAL OF THE INTERNATIONAL NETWORK FOR TERMINOLOGY (TERMNET). **See** Linguistics.

US/0040-4438
TEXAS LIBRARIES. [Texas libr.]. **Added/Corp** Texas State Library. Texas. State Library, Austin. Extension Division. Texas Library and Historical Commission. Vol. 1, (Nov. 1909)-. Periodical. English.

Four times a year. $20.00. Texas Library Association, 3355 Bee Cave Road, Suite 401, Austin TX 78746. **Tel** (512)328-1518, FAX (512)328-8852. **ED** Susan Hildebrand. **LC** Z671; .T46. **DD** 027.0764. **Bk Rev. Circ:** 2,000 (ctrl). available on microfilm and microfiche from University Microfilms International (UMI).
Desc: Library technology; library techniques; general library news (statewide). Feature items on books, reading, history, genealogy, research, persons involved with literature research, libraries.
Ind/Abst Am. Hist. Life (1986-); Libr. Lit.; West. Hist. Q.

US/0040-4446
TEXAS LIBRARY JOURNAL. [Texas libr. j.]. Vol. 26, No. 1 (Mar. 1950)-. Periodical. English. qt (Mar., Jun., Sep., Dec.). $20.00 US; $25.00 other. Texas Library Association, 3355 Bee Cave Road, Suite 401, Austin TX 78746. **Tel** (512)328-1518, FAX (512)328-8852. **ED** Josette Lyders. **DD** 020. Index available. **Ad Acc. Circ:** 5,300. available on microfilm and microfiche from University Microfilms International (UMI). ***Continues*** *Texas Library Association. News Notes.*
Desc: Contains regular columns on reference, automation, user education, oral history, grants, intellectual freedom, etc.
Ind/Abst Index Period. Artic. Relat. Law; Libr. Lit.

US/0082-3120
TEXAS PUBLIC LIBRARY STATISTICS.
See Library and Information Sciences-Abstracting, Bibliographies and Statistics.

US/0883-4261
TEXT ON MICROFORM. (TEXT ON MICROFORM : TOM.). [Text microform]. **VFOAT** TOM. (1985)-. Periodical. English. Ten times a year (published monthly except June and July). price varies per customer. Information Access Company, 362 Lakeside Drive, Foster City CA 94404. **Tel** (800)227-8431. **DD** 011.

NE/0921-3376
THEORY AND DECISION LIBRARY. [Theor. decis. libr.]. (19??)-. Monographic series. English. ir. Price varies per volume. Kluwer Academic Publishers, Postbus 322, 3300 AH Dordrecht, The Netherlands. **Tel** 011 (31) 78 524400, FAX 011 31 78 183273, telex 20083. **(Subscription address:** Kluwer Academic Publishers / US Subscriptions, PO Box 253, Accord Station, Hingham MA 02018.**)**
Ind/Abst Psychol. Abstr. (1981-); Zentralbl. Math. Ihre Grenzgeb.

US/0193-5151
THESAURUS - AMERICAN PETROLEUM INSTITUTE. (THESAURUS.). **Main/Corp** American Petroleum Institute. Central Abstracting and Indexing Service. 1st- Ed.; 1964-. English. an. $165.00, reduced prices for online searchers and nonprofit organizations. American Petroleum Institute, 275 Seventh Avenue, New York NY 10001. **Tel** (212)366-4040, FAX (212)366-4298. **(Subscription address:** 1970 Chain Bridge Road, McLean, VA 22109-6000) **ED** Elliott Linder. **LC** Z695.1.P43; A44A. **DD** 025.3/3665/5. **Circ:** 400. ***Continues*** *Information Retrieval System, Subject Authority List.*
Desc: Comprises the complete set of controlled index terms used to create the API petroleum industry data bases. Each term is listed with scope notes, cross references, and other usage guidance.

US/0739-8778
THESAURUS, MANUFACTURING ENGINEERING TERMS. [Thesaurus, manuf. eng. terms]. **Added/Corp** Society of Manufacturing Engineers. **VFOAT** Thesaurus; S.M.E. Thesaurus, Manufacturing Engineering Terms; Thesaurus of Manufacturing Engineering Terms; SME Thesaurus, Manufacturing Engineering Terms. 1st Ed. (1984)-. English. an. $27.00 per book. Society of Manufacturing Engineers, One SME Drive, PO Box 930, Member's Records Dept., Dearborn MI 48121-0930. **Tel** (313)271-1500, FAX (313)271-2861, telex 297742 SME UR (VIA RCA). **ED** P. Groen. **LC** Z699.5.M26; T47. **DD** 025.4/967.
Desc: Over 3,000 terms compiled from the SME INTIME database. Ideal for use when indexing and for information retrieval.

US/1052-3049
THIRD WORLD LIBRARIES. (THI3D [I.E. THIRD] WORLD LIBRARIES / ROSARY COLLEGE GRADUATE SCHOOL OF LIBRARY AND INFORMATION SCIENCE.). [Third world libr.]. **Added/Corp** Rosary College (River Forest, Ill.). Graduate School of Library and Information Science. **VFOAT** Third World Libraries. Vol. 1, No. 1 (Summer 1990)-. Periodical. English. Twice a year. $35.00 North America, Europe, Japan, Australia & New Zealand; $15.00 others. Rosary College, Graduate School of Library and Information Science, 7900 West Division Street, River Forest IL 60305. **Tel** (708)366-2490 ext. 303, FAX (708)366-5360. **LC** Z730; .T48. **DD** 020/.9172/4. **Bk Rev.** ctrl circ.

US
THORPE ROM. (19??)-. Periodical. English. mo. £118.00 (single disc); £327.00 (monthly); £230.00 (bi-monthly). J. Whitaker & Sons Ltd, 12 Dyott Street, London WC1A 1DF England. **Tel** 011 44 71 8368911, FAX 011 44 71 836 2909.

SW/0040-6872
TIDSKRIFT FOR DOKUMENTATION. [Tidskr. dok.]. **Added/Corp** Tekniska Litteratursallskapet. **VFOAT** TD. (1949)-. Periodical. Swedish. Four times a year. Price varies. TLS Forlangverksamhet, Nysatrav 31, 131 33 Nacka Sweden. **Tel** 011 46 8 7163405. **CODEN** TDDKA5. Documents available from Ask*IEEE. ***Continues*** *Teknisk Dokumentation.*
Ind/Abst INSPEC (1972-); Libr. Inf. Sci. Abstr.; Libr. Lit.

FI/0782-825X
TIETOPALVELU. (1986)-. Periodical. Finnish. Six times a year. Fmk190.00 Finland and Scandinavian countries; Fmk210.00 other. Tietopalveluseura, Harakantie 2, SF-02600 Espoo, Finland. **Tel** 011 358 0 518138. **ED** Marja Talikka. **UDC** 002. Index available (bound in Feb. issue). **Bk Rev. Ad Acc. Circ:** 1000.

UK
TIP APPLICATIONS. (19??)-. Periodical. English. Ten times a year. £30.00 UK; £35.00 other. Information Partnership, 140 Tabernacle Street, Suite 4 2, London EC2A 4SD England. **Tel** 011 44 71 2530575, FAX 011 44 01 3516300. ***Continues*** *C&L Applications.*

US/0092-6108
TITLE VARIES. Vol. 1 (Dec. 1973)-. Periodical. English. bm. $3.00. Title Varies, PO Box 704, Chapel Hill NC 27514. **LC** Z692.S5; T57. **DD** 025.3/4/3. **CODEN** TIVRA. Index Available, published separately, free-automatically sent.

US/0082-4526
TITLES IN SERIES / A HANDBOOK FOR LIBRARIANS AND STUDENTS. Vol. 1 Jan. (1953)-. English. ir. Scarecrow Press Inc., 52 Liberty Street, PO Box 4167, Metuchen NJ 08840. **Tel** (908)548-8600, (800)537-7107. **ED** E. A. Baer. **LC** AI3; .T5. **DD** 011.

TZ/0378-3375
TLA NEWSLETTER (1983). (TLA NEWSLETTER.). Newsletter. English. Tanzania Library Association, PO Box 2645, Dar es Salaam Tanzania. **LC** Z857.T3; N48. **DD** 027.0678. ***Continues*** *Newsletter (Tanzania Library Association).*

JA
TOKYO CHIKU KOKURITSU DAIGAKU TOSHOKAN NETTOWAKU KENKYUKAI KENKYU HOKOKU. 1981-1986-. Japanese. ¥980. Gakujutsu Bunken Fukyukai, c/o Tokyo Kodai, Ookayama 2, Meguro-ku 152, Tokyo-to Japan. **LC** Z674.83.J3; T64A.

HU/0133-8358
TOLNA MEGYEI KONYVTAROS. (1970)-. Hungarian.
Ind/Abst Magyar Konyv. Szak. Biblio.; Hungar. Libr. Info. Sci. Abstr.

UK/0967-6368
TOP 100 BUSINESS LIBRARIES. English. an. $179.00. Headland Business Information, 1 Henry Smiths Terrace, Headland Cleveland, TS24 0PD England. **Tel** 011 44 429 231902, FAX 011 44 429 861403.

US
TOPICAL INDEX FOR THE ANNUAL EDITIONS BASIC REFERENCE LIBRARY. **VFOAT** Basic Reference Library Index; Annual Editions : The ... Basic Reference Library. (1978/79)-. English. an. $10.95. Dushkin Publishing Group Inc., Sluice Dock, Guilford CT 06437. **Tel** (203)453-4351, (800)243-6532, FAX (203)453-6000.

JA
TOSHO. **See** Publishing-Books and Bookmaking.

JA
TOSHOKAN JANARU. **Added/Corp** Tokyo Geijutsu Daigaku. Toshokan. Tokyo Geijutsu Daigaku Fuzoku Toshokan Koho. (19??)-. Periodical. Japanese. Tokyo Geijutsu Daigaku Fuzoku Toshokan, Ueno Koen Taito-ku, Tokyo Japan. **LC** Z955.T687; T66.

JA/0287-0010
TOSHOKAN JOHO DAIGAKU KENKYU HOKOKU. **VFOAT** Research Report of University of Library and Information Science. V. 1, No. 1 (1982)-. Periodical. English (Japanese). sa. Toshokan Joho Daigaku Kasuga 1-2 Yatabe-machi, Tsukuba-gun Ibaraki-ken 305 Japan. **ED** Satoru Takeuchi. **LC** Z671; .T66. cum. index. **Pr Rev. Circ:** 800.
Desc: Contributors are the faculty members of the University of Library and Information Science and the contents include not only the studies of library and information science but also various liberal-arts subjects.

JA/0913-8005
TOSHOKAN KYORYOKU TSUSHIN. **VFOAT** Library Cooperation News. Japanese. bm. Free to limited members. The National Diet Library, 10-1-1 Chome Nagatacho, Chiyoda ku Tokyo 100 Japan. cum. index. **Bk Rev. Circ:** 4,000 (ctrl).
Desc: Correspondence of communication and information between National Diet Library and other libraries.

JA
TOSHOKAN NENKAN / HENSHU, NIHON TOSHOKAN KYOKAI TOSHOKAN NENKAN HENSHU IINKAI. 1982-. Japanese. an. ¥9800. Nihon Toshokan Kyokai, 1-1-10 Taishido, Setagaya-ku, Tokyo 154 Japan. **Tel** FAX 81 3 3421 7588. **LC** Z845.J4; T665.

JA/0385-4000
TOSHOKAN ZASSHI. [Toshokan zasshi]. **Added/Corp** Nihon Toshokan Kyokai. **VFOAT** Library Journal. (1907)-. Periodical. Japanese. mo. $144.00. **(Subscription address:** Kyowa Book Company Inc., 1 38 Kanda Jinbocho Chiyoda-ku, Tokyo 101 Japan.**) LC** Z671; .T685. Index available in last issue of volume--attached. cum. index.
Ind/Abst Libr. Inf. Sci. Abstr.

JA
TOSHOKANGAKU NEMPO / DOSHISHA DAIGAKU. **VFOAT** Doshisha Daigaku Toshokangaku Nempo. Began in 1975. Japanese. an. Doshisha Daigaku Toshokan Shisho Katei, Higashi-Iru Imadegawadori Karasumaru Kamigyo-ku, Kyoto-shi Japan. **LC** Z671; .T686.

JA
TOSHOKANHO. **Main/Corp** Tottori Daigaku. Toshokan. **VFOAT** The Tottori University Library Information; Tottori Daigaku Fuzoku Toshokan Ho. Japanese (Japanese). 1-1 Koyamacho, 680 Tottori Japan. **LC** Z955.T822; T67A.

JA/0040-9669
TOSHOKANKAI. **Added/Corp** Nihon Toshokan Kenkyukai. **VFOAT** Library World. (May 1947)-. Periodical. Japanese. bm. $118.50. Japan Institute of Library Science, Toshokangaku Kenkyuwitsu, Tenri Nara 632 Japan. **(Subscription address:** Japan Publications Trading Company, Ltd., PO Box 5030, Tokyo International, Tokyo 100-31 Japan.**)**

KO
TOSOGWAN. **VFOAT** Bulletin of the Central National Library. Periodical. Korean. mo. Kungnip Chungang Tosogwan, 100-177 1-ka Hoehyon-dong Chung-ku, Seoul Korea. **Tel** 753-8536. **LC** Z671; .T69.

KO
TOSOGWAN HWICHONG. **Main/Corp** Kungnip Chungang Tosogwan (Seoul, Korea). **VFOAT** The Information Book of the Central National Library; Information Book of the Central National Library. English (Korean). an. Kungnip Chungang Tosogwan, 100-177 1-ka Hoehyon-dong Chung-ku, Seoul Korea. **Tel** 753-8536. **LC** Z846.K85; K86A. **Circ:** 500.
Desc: Guide book of the Central National Library for users and visitors.

KO
TOSOGWAN MUNHWA. **Added/Corp** Hanguk Tosogwan Hyophoe. **VFOAT** KLA Bulletin. (1988)-. Periodical. Korean. bm. Hanguk Tosogwan Hyophoe, 100 177 1 Ka Hoehyon-dong Chung ku, Seoul 100 Korea. **LC** Z673; .H2586. ***Continues*** *Tohyop Hoebo.*

US/0738-4130
TRACINGS. ***Ceased.*** [Tracings]. Began with No. 1, June (1977)-(1992). Periodical. English. qt. Illinois Library Association, 33 West Grand Avenue/#301, Chicago IL 60610. **Circ:** 325 (ctrl).
Desc: Official newsletter of the Illinois Library Association Resources and Technical Services Section. Provides information to members on ILA and RTSS activities, programs, and special topics of current interest.

CN/0822-0344
TRAIT D'UNION - BIBLIOTHEQUE CENTRALE DE PRET DE L'ESTRIE. (LE TRAIT D'UNION.). [Trait union - Bibl. cent. pret Estrie]. **Added/Corp** Bibliotheque Centrale de Pret de l'Estrie. Vol. 1 No. 2, (April 1983)-. Periodical. French. qt. Free. Bibliotheque Centrale de Pret de l'Estrie, 4155 rue Brodeur, Sherbrooke Quebec J1L 1K4 Canada. **DD** 027.4714/6/05. ctrl circ. ***Continues*** *Anonyme, 0715-7487.*

FR
TRAVAUX DU CENTRE DE DOCUMENTATION ET DE BIBLIOGRAPHIE PHILOSOPHIQUES DE BESANCON. **Main/Corp** Universite de Besancon Centre de Documentation et de Bibliographie Philosophiques. Vol. 1 1973-. French. 20.00Can$ (students), 40.00Can$ (individuals), 60.00Can$ (institutions), 20.00Can$ (single issues). Les Belles Lettres, 95 Boulevard Raspail, 75006 Paris France. **Tel** (1)45.48.70.55, FAX (1)45.44.92.88, telex 200577 F. **LC** AS161; .B39 subser. **DD** 084/.1 S; 016.1.

CN/0703-1297
TRAVAUX ET RECHERCHES GRIC / GROUPE DE RECHERCHE EN INFORMATION ET COMMUNICATION. [Trav. rech. GRIC]. **VFOAT** Travaux et Recherches du Gric. **VAT** Travaux et Recherches Groupe de Recherche en Information et Communication. 1-. Monographic series. French. Price varies per volume. Edi-Gric, Dep d'Information et de Communication Pavillon, Casault Universite Laval, Quebec Quebec G1K 7P4 Canada. **DD** 001.51/05.

US/0893-6773
TRENDS IN LAW LIBRARY MANAGEMENT AND TECHNOLOGY. [Trends law libr. manage. technol.]. **VFOAT** Trends. Vol. 1, No. 1 (July/Aug. 1987)-. Periodical. English. mo. $75.00. Fred B. Rothman & Company, 10368 West Centennial Road, Littleton CO 80127. **Tel** (800)457-1986, (303)979-5657, FAX (303)978-1457, telex 87669. **ED** Dennis Store. **LC** Z675.L2; T74. **DD** 026.34.
Desc: Contains information on important developments in management and technology for law libraries.
Ind/Abst Leg. Inf. Manage. Index.

CN/1181-9839
TSIG NEWSLETTER. (TSIG NEWSLETTER : NEWSLETTER OF THE CLA TECHNICAL SERVICES INTEREST GROUP.). [TSIG newsl.]. **Added/Corp** CLA Technical Services Interest Group. **VFOAT** Technical Services Interest Group Newsletter. Vol. 1, No. 1 (Spring 1990)-. Newsletter. English. sa. Douglas College Library, P Swanson - Editor, PO Box 2503, New Westminister, British Columbia V3L 5B2 Canada. **DD** 025/.02.

CH/0363-3640
TU SHU KUAN HSUEH YU TZU HSUN KO HSUEH. [Tu shu kuan hsueh yu tzu hsun ko hsueh]. **VFOAT** Journal of Library & Information Science. V. 1- April 1975-. Periodical. Chinese (English). sa. $20.00. JLIS Editorial Board, Department of Social Education University, 162 Section 1, East Hoping Road, Taipei 10610 Taiwan. **(Subscription address:** Student Book Company Ltd., 198 Section 1, East Hoping Road, Taipei Taiwan 10610 China**)** **ED** Chen-ku Wang, Liu-Li Wu, James Ho, Mong-Chen Lin, Mei-Ho Lin, Nelson Chou, Li-Ling Kuo, Margaret C Fung. **LC** Z671; .T79. **CODEN** TSKHE4. Index available. **Bk Rev. Circ:** 800.
Desc: Serves as a forum for discussion of problems common to librarians and information scientists.
Ind/Abst Libr. Inf. Sci. Abstr.

CC/1000-4254
TU SHU KUAN TSA CHIH. [Tushuguan zazhi]. **VFOAT** Tushuguan Zazhi; Library Journal. Began in 1982 with No. 1-. Periodical. Chinese. qt. RMBY0.46. Shang-hai Shih Pao Kan Fa Hsing Chu, Shanghai China. **LC** Z671; .T833. **DD** 020/.5.

HU/0041-3917
TUDOMANYOS ES MUSZAKI TAJEKOZTATAS. [Tud. mus. tajek.]. Periodical. Hungarian (summaries and/or abstracts in English, Russian and German; table of contents in English, Russian and German). mo. 840.00ft. **(Subscription address:** Kultura, PO Box 149, H 1389 Budapest 62 Hungary**)** **ED** Peter Szanto. **LC** Q4; .T83. **CODEN** TMTAAG. **Bk Rev. Circ:** 1,300. Documents available from Ask*IEEE. ***Continues*** *Muszaki Konyvtarosok Tajekoztatoja.*
Desc: Studies, reports, reviews, news, etc. on library and information science. Contributions from Hungarian and foreign authors.
Ind/Abst Magyar Konyv. Szak. Biblio.; Hungar. Libr. Info. Sci. Abstr.; INSPEC (Nov.-Dec. 1971-); Libr. Inf. Sci. Abstr.

TU
TURK KUTUPHANECILIGI. **VFOAT** Bulletin of the Turkish Librarianship. Periodical. Turkish (English). qt. Turk Kutuphaneciler Dernegi, PK 175, Yenisehir Ankara Turkey. **LC** Z673.T8; A23. ***Continues*** *Turk Kutuphaneciler Dernegi.*

NZ/0110-1625
TURNBULL LIBRARY RECORD, THE. **Added/Corp** Friends of the Turnbull Library. Alexander Turnbull Library. No. 1 (Jan. 1940)-. Periodical. English. sa. 20.00NZ$. Turnbull Library Endowment Trust, Box 12-349, Wellington New Zealand. **Tel** 011 64 4 743000, telex 30076. **ED** J.E. Traue. **[CCC].** Index available. cum. index. **Pr Rev. Circ:** 1,100 (ctrl).
Desc: Articles reflect the library's major collecting and research interests: New Zealand, Australia and Pacific; Milton and early modern English studies; rare books; and fine printing.
Ind/Abst Annu. Bibliogr. Engl. Lang. Lit.

US/0161-5645
U.S. ENVIRONMENTAL PROTECTION AGENCY LIBRARY SYSTEM BOOK CATALOG. **Main/Corp** United States. Environmental Protection Agency. Library Systems Branch. **VFOAT** EPA Book Catalog; Library System Book Catalog. **VAT** United States Environmental Protection Agency Library System Book Catalog; Environmental Protection Agency Book Catalog. 1973-. Catalog. English. an. Environmental Protection Agency / Library Systems, Office of Planning and Management, Office of Administration Management and Organization Division, Library Systems Branch, Springfield VA 22161. available on microfiche (from the National Technical Information Service).
Desc: Includes the monographic collection of the 28 libraries comprising the Library System of the Environmental Protection Agency.

CN/0713-8172
UBC DATA LIBRARY CATALOGUE. MICROFORM. [UBC Data Libr. cat.]. **Main/Corp** University of British Columbia. Data Library. **VFOAT** Catalogue. **VAT** Catalogue - University of British Columbia. Data Library (Microform). English. an. Free. UBC Data Library Catalogue, c/o University of British Columbia, Data Library/Room 206, 6356 Agricultural Road, Vancouver British Columbia V6T 1W5 Canada. **DD** 016.3033/8/0971. ctrl circ. ***Continues*** *University of British Columbia. Data Library. Catalogue, 0319-5201.*

CN/0229-5954
UBC LIBRARY BULLETIN. [UBC libr. bull.]. **Main/Corp** University of British Columbia. Library. **VAT** University of British Columbia Library Bulletin (1973). (1973)-. Bulletin. English. ir. University of British Columbia Main Library, 1956 Main Hall, Vancouver British Columbia V6T 1Z1 Canada. **Tel** (604)228-5370, (604)822-5404. **DD** 027.78711/33. ctrl circ. ***Continues*** *University of British Columbia Library Bulletin.*

US
UCLA LIBRARIAN. **Main/Corp** University of California, Los Angeles. Library. **Added/Corp** University of California, Los Angeles. Library. Librarian. **VAT** University of California at Los Angeles Librarian. Vol. 1 (Oct. 16, 1947)-. English. Twelve times a year. $35.00. Friends of UCLA Library, University of California, 405 Hilgard Avenue, Los Angeles CA 90024. **Tel** (310)825-1201. **LC** Z881; .L8823. **DD** 027.7794.

US/0276-7570
UCMP QUARTERLY. [UCMP q.]. **VFOAT** UCMP. **VAT** Union Catalog of Medical Periodicals Quarterly. (Apr. 1973)-. English. qt (Jan., Apr., July and Oct.). $210.00 (members), $240.00 (non-members). Medical Library Center of New York, 5 East 102nd Street, 7th Floor, New York NY 10029. **Tel** (212)427-1630, FAX (212)876-6697. **ED** Robert Dempsey. **NLM** ZW 1 U42A. **Circ:** 700.
Desc: Union List (microfiche) of serials for health science libraries.

CN/1010-9501
UDT NEWSLETTER. (UDT NEWSLETTER / UNIVERSAL DATAFLOW AND TELECOMMUNICATIONS.). [UDT newsl.]. **Main/Corp** International Federation of Library Associations and Institutions. Universal Dataflow and Telecommunications Core Program. **Added/Corp** National Library of Canada. **VAT** Universal Dataflow and Telecommunications Newsletter. No. 1 (July 1987)-. Newsletter. English (French). Three times a year. Free on request. National Library of Canada, 395 Wellington Street, Ottawa Ontario K1A 0N4 Canada. **Tel** (613)995-7969, (613)995-7969, (819)994-6881, FAX (613)991-9871. **DD** 025/.04/05. available on audiocassette; available in braille; available in large print.
Desc: Covers topics related to library technology.

UK
UKOLN. OFFICE FOR LIBRARY AND INFORMATION NETWORKING. (19??)-. Newsletter. English. Free on request. Centre for Bibliographic Management, The Library, University of Bath, Claverton Down, Bath BA2 7AY England.

CN/0840-5832
ULCN. UNION LIST OF CANADIAN NEWSPAPERS. (ULCN [MICROFORM] : LCJC.). [UCLN, Union list Can. newsp.]. **Added/Corp** National Library of Canada. **VFOAT** LCJC; Union List of Canadian Newspapers; Liste Collective des Journaux Canadiens. **VAT** LCJC. Liste Collective des Journaux Canadiens. (Oct. 1988)-. Bibliography. English (French). 25.50Can$ Canada; 30.60Can$ other. National Library of Canada, 395 Wellington Street, Ottawa Ontario K1A 0N4 Canada. **Tel** (613)995-7969, (613)995-7969, (819)994-6881, FAX (613)991-9871. **LC** Microfiche (o) 93/6018; Z6954.C2; U43. **DD** 016.071/1. available on audiocassette; available in braille; available in large print.
Desc: Complete listing of Canadian newspapers for lending and location purposes.

US/0000-0175
ULRICH'S INTERNATIONAL PERIODICALS DIRECTORY. [Ulrich's int. period. dir.]. 11 Ed. (1965)-. Directory. English. an (includes Ulrich's Updates). $415.00. R R Bowker, A Reed Reference Publishing Company, Part of Reed International PLC, PO Box 31, 121 Chanlon Drive, New Providence NJ 07974. **Tel** (908)464-6800, (800)521-8110, FAX (908)665-6688, telex 138-755. **ED** Judith Salk. **DD** 011. **NLM** Z 6941 U45. **[CCC].** available on CD-ROM (Ulrichs Plus) from R.R. Bowker; available on microfiche; available on an online database. ***Continues*** *Ulrich's Periodicals Directory;* ***Absorbed*** *Irregular Serials & Annuals, 0000-0043.*
Desc: Directory of international serials and periodicals.

US/0000-1163
ULRICH'S NEWS. ***Ceased.*** (ULRICH'S NEWS : MONTHLY UPDATES, REPORTS AND RESOURCES FROM R. R. BOWKER'S INTERNATIONAL SERIALS DATABASE.). [Ulrich's news]. **Added/Corp** R.R. Bowker Company. Vol. 1, No. 1 (Feb. 1988)-(1992). Periodical. English. bm. R R Bowker, A Reed Reference Publishing Company, Part of Reed International PLC, PO Box 31, 121 Chanlon Drive, New Providence NJ 07974. **Tel** (908)464-6800, (800)521-8110, FAX (908)665-6688, telex 138-755. **DD** 070.

US/0000-0981
ULRICH'S ON MICROFICHE. (ULRICH'S AND IRREGULAR SERIALS AND ANNUALS [MICROFORM].). (1989)-. Periodical. English. qt. $325.00. R R Bowker, A Reed Reference Publishing Company, Part of Reed International PLC, PO Box 31, 121 Chanlon Drive, New Providence NJ 07974. **Tel** (908)464-6800, (800)521-8110, FAX (908)665-6688, telex 138-755.
Desc: Contains complete bibliographic listings, arranged by subject and title, for all periodicals and annuals listed in Ulrich's.

US/1068-0500
ULRICH'S PLUS. (ULRICH'S PLUS [COMPUTER FILE].). [Ulrich's plus]. **Added/Corp** R.R. Bowker Company. (1986)-. English. qt. $495.00. R R Bowker Electronic Publishing, A Reed Reference Publishing Company, Part of Reed International PLC, 121 Chanlon Drive, New Providence NJ 07974. **Tel** (800)323-3288. **LC** Z6941. **DD** 011. available in print; available on an online database from R.R. Bowker; available in microform.
Desc: Contains information on serials published throughout the world.

US/0000-1074
ULRICH'S UPDATE. [Ulrich's update]. **Added/Corp** R.R. Bowker Company. Vol. 1, No. 1 (Sept. 1988)-. Periodical. English. tq. $132.88 US; $154.14 other. R R Bowker, A Reed Reference Publishing Company, Part of Reed International PLC, PO Box 31, 121 Chanlon Drive, New Providence NJ 07974. **Tel** (908)464-6800, (800)521-8110, FAX (908)665-6688, telex 138-755. **ED** Judith Salk, Edvika Popilskis, and Frank McDermott. **DD** 050. **NLM** Z 6941; U451. **CODEN** ULUPE6. **[CCC].** Index available. available on microfiche; available on an online database; available on CD-ROM. ***Continues*** *Bowker International Serials Database Update, 0000-0892.*
Desc: Contains entries for periodicals and other serials newly added to Bowker International Serials Database. Contains title changes and cessation indices as well.
Ind/Abst Int. Aerosp. Abstr.

AG
UMBRAL 2000 I.E. DOS MIL. Vol. 1- Jan./July 1972-. Spanish. Direccion de Ensenanza Superior, Avda 44 No 790, La Plata Argentina. **LC** Z765.A1; U55. **DD** 020/.5.

US/0049-514X
UNABASHED LIBRARIAN, THE. No. 1 (Nov. 1971)-. Periodical. English. qt (Feb., May, Aug., Nov.). $30.00. Unabashed Librarian, General PO Box 2631, New York NY 10116. **Tel** (212)255-2429. **ED** Marvin H. Scilken. **LC** Z671; .U45. **DD** 020/.5. **Bk Rev. Ad Acc.**
Desc: The 'How I Run My Library Good' letter. Contains practical ideas, forms, procedures, library life, library humor, library poetry, booklists, etc.
Ind/Abst Libr. Lit.

CN/0822-1685
UNION LIST OF PERIODICALS / CASLIS, CALGARY CHAPTER. [Union list period. - CASLIS, Calg. Chapter]. **Main/Corp** Canadian Association of Special Libraries and Information Services. Calgary Chapter. 1983-. English. an. $150.00. Union List of Periodicals, c/o Susan Tyrrell, Panarctic Oils Ltd, 11th Floor/815-8th Avenue SW, PO Box 190, Calgary Alberta T2P 2H6 Canada. **DD** 018/.134. ***Continues*** *Canadian Association of Special Libraries and Information Services. Calgary Chapter. Union List of Serials, 0712-6972.*

US/0098-7816
UNIVERSITY AND COLLEGE LIBRARIES. **See** Library and Information Sciences-Abstracting, Bibliographies and Statistics.

AT/0157-3314
UNIVERSITY OF ADELAIDE LIBRARY NEWS. (1979)-. Academic Scholarly Publication. English. an. Free. University of Adelaide / Library, Barr Smith Library, Adelaide SA 5005 Australia. **Tel** 011 61 8 303 5069, FAX 011 61 8 232 3689, telex Univad AA89141. **ED** Alan Keig. Index available (Volume

One-Ten, 1979-1988). cum. index. **Circ:** 325 (ctrl).
Desc: University libraries and librarianship.
Ind/Abst Aust. Educ. Index; Aust. Libr. Inf. Sci. Abstr. (1990-).

CN/0713-7591
UNIVERSITY OF ALBERTA DATA LIBRARY CATALOGUE. [Univ. Alta. Data Libr. cat.]. **Main/Corp** University of Alberta. Data Library. **VFOAT** Data Library Catalogue. English. $9.90 each volume. University of Alberta Bookstore, Students Union Building, Edmonton Alberta T6G 2J7 Canada. **DD** 018/.1.

US/0361-1272
UNIVERSITY OF ROCHESTER LIBRARY BULLETIN. **Main/Corp** University of Rochester. Library. Vol. 1 (Nov. 1945)-. Bulletin. English. ir. Free. University of Rochester Library, River Station, Rochester NY 14627. **LC** Z881; .R676.
Ind/Abst Annu. Bibliogr. Engl. Lang. Lit.

CN/0316-5949
UNIVERSITY OF WATERLOO LIBRARY SERIALS LIST. (SERIALS LIST.). **Main/Corp** University of Waterloo. Library. (1966)-. Periodical. English. an. University of Waterloo Library, Waterloo Ontario N26 EG1 Canada. **DD** 016.05. ***Supersedes*** *University of Waterloo. Library. Serial Holdings.*

US/1055-4173
UNIVERSITY PRESS BOOKS FOR PUBLIC AND SECONDARY SCHOOL LIBRARIES. [Univ. press books public second. sch. libr.]. **Added/Corp** Association of American University Presses. Public Library Association. American Association of School Librarians. 1st Ed. (1991)-. English. Association of American University Presses Inc, Publications Department, 584 Broadway, Suite 410, New York NY 10012. **Tel** (212)941-6610, FAX (212)941-6618. **LC** Z1033.U64; U55. **DD** 016.0252/187473. ***Formed by the union of*** *University Press Books for Public Libraries, 0731-2857* ***and*** *University Press Books for Secondary School Libraries, 0887-1345.*

US/0731-2857
UNIVERSITY PRESS BOOKS FOR PUBLIC LIBRARIES. ***Title Change.*** [Univ. Press books public libr.]. **Added/Corp** Public Library Association. **VFOAT** Books for Public Libraries. 1st Ed. (1979)-(19??). English. an. Association of American University Presses Inc, Publications Department, 584 Broadway, Suite 410, New York NY 10012. **Tel** (212)941-6610, FAX (212)941-6618. **LC** Z731; .U67. **DD** 025.2/187473. ***Merged with*** *University Press Books for Secondary School Libraries, 0887-1345* ***to form*** *University Press Books for Public and Secondary School Libraries, 1055-4173.*

CN/0828-7694
UPDATE - CHINOOK REGIONAL LIBRARY. (UPDATE.). [Update - Chinook Reg. Libr.]. Vol. 1, No. 1 (Fall 1984)-. Periodical. English. sa. Chinook Regional Library, 1240 Chaplin Street West, Swift Current Saskatchewan S9H 0G8 Canada. **Tel** (306)773-3186. **ED** Frances I Myhr. **DD** 027.47/24/3. **Circ:** 500 (ctrl).
Desc: Meant as an avenue of information between the Chinook Regional Library and the general public.

US/0743-9652
UPDATE, GCLC. **VFOAT** Update, G.C.L.C. **VAT** Update: Greater Cincinnati Library Consortium. Periodical. English. qt. Free. The Greater Cincinnati Library Consortium, 3333 Vine Street, Cincinnati OH 45220. **Tel** (513)751-4422. **ED** Pat Yannarella. **Circ:** 365.
Desc: Newsletter of the Greater Cincinnati Library Consortium.

US/0160-9203
UPDATE (LIBRARY OF CONGRESS. NATIONAL LIBRARY SERVICE FOR THE BLIND AND PHYSICALLY HANDICAPPED). (UPDATE / NATIONAL LIBRARY SERVICE FOR THE BLIND AND PHYSICALLY HANDICAPPED.). [Update]. Vol. 1, No. 6, (May-June 1978)-. Periodical. English. qt. $10.00. National Library Service for the Blind and Physically Handicapped, Library of Congress, 1291 Taylor Street Northwest, Washington DC 20542. **Tel** (800)424-8567, (202)707-5100, (800)424-9100. **LC** HV1783; .U59. **DD** 362.4/1/0973.

US/0276-9298
URBAN ACADEMIC LIBRARIAN. [Urban acad. libr.]. **Added/Corp** City University of New York. Library Association. Vol. 1, No. 1 (Spring 1981)-. Periodical. English. sa. $15.00. Hunter College Library, 695 Park Avenue, New York NY 10021. **Tel** (212)772-4168. **LC** Z668; .U7. **DD** 020/.7/15. **[CCC]. Bk Rev. Ad Acc.** ***Continues*** *Lacuny Journal, 0094-615X.*
Desc: Covers New York state/city libraries. The audience: librarians and administrators. The five to six articles move from censorship and budget to "Profiles of Success: Interviews with Female Chief Librarians in the City University of New York."
Ind/Abst Inf. Sci. Abstr. (?-?); Libr. Lit. (19??-).

US
URBAN LIBRARIES COUNCIL NEWSLETTER : ULC EXCHANGE. Newsletter. English. mo. $50.00 US; $60.00 other. Urban Libraries Council, 1800 Ridge Avenue, Suite 208, Evanston IL 60201. **Tel** (708)866-9999, FAX (708)866-9989. **ED** Kathleen Reif. ctrl circ.

US/0749-9531
URISA NEWS (1982). (URISA NEWS : COMMUNICATIONS OF THE URBAN & REGIONAL INFORMATION SYSTEMS ASSOCIATION.). [URISA news]. **Added/Corp** Urban and Regional Information Systems Association. **VFOAT** U.R.I.S.A. News; News. **VAT** Urban and Regional Information Systems Association News. Issue 65 (Fall 1982)-. Periodical. English. bm (6 issues). Free to members of the Urban and Regional Information Systems Association; $90.00 membership. Urban Regional Information Systems Association, 900 Second Street Northeast, Suite 304, Washington DC 20002. **Tel** (202)289-1685, FAX (202)842-1850. **LC** HT390; .U75. **DD** 025. ***Continues*** *URISA.*

US/0364-5215
USBE NEWS. **Main/Corp** Universal Serials and Book Exchange. **Added/Corp** USBE, Inc. Universal Serials and Book Exchange. **VFOAT** USBE/News. **VAT** Universal Serials and Book Exchange News. Vol. 28 (Jan. 1976)-. English. mo. $75.00. USBE/News, 2969 West 25th Street, Cleveland OH 44113. **Tel** (216)241-6960. **ED** H. Gerald Phillips. **LC** Z690; .U7352. **DD** 025.2/6. **Circ:** 1,100 (ctrl). ***Continues*** *Newsletter - United States Book Exchange, 0041-753X.*
Desc: A newsletter/catalog for non-profit library cooperatives, listing publications from all disciplines.

US
UTAH LIBRARIES/NEWS. English. bm. $10.00. Utah Library Association, 2150 South 300 West, Salt Lake City UT 84115. **Tel** (801)466-5888. **ED** Dale Swensen. **Bk Rev. Ad Acc. Circ:** 600 (ctrl).
Desc: Newsletter of the Utah libraries.

US
UTAH PUBLIC LIBRARY SERVICE / PREPARED BY THE STATE LIBRARY COMMISSION OF UTAH. **Main/Corp** Utah. State Library Commission. **Added/Corp** Utah State Library Commission. Utah State Library. (1967)-. English. an. Utah State Library Commission, 2150 South 2nd Street West, Suite 16, Salt Lake City UT 84115. **ED** Sandi Long. **LC** Z732.U8; U79a. **DD** 027.4/792. **Circ:** 800. ***Continues*** *Utah State Library. Annual Report for Utah Public Library Service.*
Desc: Public Library statistics for the state of Utah.

CN/0225-1760
UTLAS NEWSLETTER (1979). ***Title Change.*** (U T L A S NEWSLETTER.). [UTLAS newsl.]. **Main/Corp** University of Toronto. Library Automation Systems. **VFOAT** UTLAS Newsletter. Vol. 4, No. 10 (Oct. 1979)-. Newsletter. English. mo. ISM Library Information Services, 3300 Bloor Street West, West Tower 16th Floor, Etobicoke Ontario M8X 2X2, Canada. **Tel** (416)236-7171, FAX (416)236-7541. **DD** 025.5/4. ***Continues*** *University of Toronto. Library Automation Systems. Newsletter, 0700-4397.* ***Continued by*** *Info.*

RU
V POMOSHCH MASSOVYM BIBLIOTEKAM. **Added/Corp** Gosudarstvennaia Biblioteka SSSR Imeni V.I. Lenina. (1973)-. Russian. 0.11rub. Izdatelstvo Kniga, 50 Gorky Ulitsa, 125047 Moscow Russia. **LC** Z819.A1; V2.

HU/0133-7351
VAS MEGYEI KONYVTARAK ERTESITOJE, A. (1976)-. Hungarian.
Ind/Abst Magyar Konyv. Szak. Biblio.; Hungar. Libr. Info. Sci. Abstr.

US/0042-1723
VASLA. **Main/Corp** Special Libraries Association. Virginia Chapter. Periodical. English. qt. Free to members. Institute of Textile Technology, 2551 Ivy Road, Charlottesville VA 22903-4641. **Tel** (804)296-5511, FAX (804)977-5400. **LC** Z675.A2; S75A. **DD** 026/.0006/0755. **Ad Acc. Circ:** 120 (ctrl).
Desc: Newsletter of the Virginia Chapter of Special Libraries Association.

CN/0225-5480
VEHICLE (QUEBEC). (LE VEHICULE : BULLETIN D'INFORMATION DU SERVICE DES BIBLIOTHEQUES D'ENSEIGNEMENT A L'INTENTION DES BIBLIOTHEQUES DU RESEAU COLLEGIAL.). [Vehicule]. No. 1 (June 1979)-. Bulletin. French. Gouvernement du Quebec, 600 St Amable 4E Etage, Quebec Quebec G1R 4Z1 Canada. **DD** 027.7/09714.

US/0364-7382
VERMONT LIBRARY DIRECTORY. **Added/Corp** Vermont. Dept. of Libraries. (19??)-. English. Vermont Department of Libraries, State Office Building, 109 State Street, Montpelier VT 05602. **Tel** (802)828-3265. **LC** Z732.V5; V635. **DD** 021/.0025/743.

GW
VERZEICHNIS LEIFERBARER BUCHER. SCHLAGWORT-VERZEICHNIS. **VFOAT** Subject Guide to German Books in Print; VLB-Schlagwort-Verzeichnis. (1978/79)-. German (English; summaries and/or abstracts in English). ir. $250.00. K.G. Saur Verlag KG, A Reed Reference Publishing Company, Part of Reed International PLC, Ortlerstrasse 8, D 81373 Munich Germany. **Tel** 011 49 89 769020, FAX 011 49 89 76902150, telex 5212067-SAUR-D. **(Subscription address:** Reed Reference Publishing Company / New Jersey, 131 Chanlaon Road, PO Box 31, New Providence NJ 07974.**)**
Desc: Subject arrangement of all available German-language publications.

US/1055-0267
VIDEO ANNUAL, THE. [Video annu.]. (1991)-. English. an (Mar.). $55.00. ABC Clio Press, PO Box 1911, 130 Cremona, Santa Barbara CA 93117. **Tel** (805)968-1911, (800)422-2546, FAX (805)685-9685. **LC** PN1992.93; .V5; Z692.V52; V45. **DD** 384.55/8/05.

US/0887-6851
VIDEO LIBRARIAN, THE. **See** Photography and Video.

US/1045-3393
VIDEO RATING GUIDE FOR LIBRARIES. [Video rat. guide libr.]. (1990)-. Periodical. English. qt. $89.50 (elementary and high schools), $126.00 other, US; $98.45 (elementary and high schools), $138.60 other, Canada. ABC Clio Press, PO Box 1911, 130 Cremona, Santa Barbara CA 93117. **Tel** (805)968-1911, (800)422-2546, FAX (805)685-9685. **ED** Timothy O'Donnell. **LC** Z692.V52; V53. **DD** 025.2/873. Index available. cum. index. **Bk Rev. Ad Acc. Circ:** 1,200.
Desc: Guide to new special interest and children's videos. Introduces more than 450 new titles from hundreds of producers, all accessed by subject, title, audience, price and top-rated selections. Reviews are by specially trained librarians with expertise in particular subject areas.
Ind/Abst Med. Rev. Dig.

II
VIJNANA SARASVATI. **Added/Corp** Andhra Pradesh Government Oriental Manuscripts Library and Research Institute. **VFOAT** Vijnana Saraswati : A Quarterly Oriental Research Journal of the Andhra Pradesh Government Oriental Manuscripts Library & Research Institute; Vijnana Saraswati. Vol. 1, No. 1 (Jan. 1984)-?. Periodical. Telugu (English). qt. Rs10.00. Andhra Pradesh Government Oriental Research, Institute Tarnaka, Hyderabad 500007 India. **Tel** 236487. **(Subscription address:** No 5-8-599, Ratan Mahal Building, Abid Road, Hyderabad 500 001 AP India**)** **ED** V V Krishnasastry. **LC** Z6605.O7; V54. Index available. **Bk Rev.** ctrl circ. ***Continued in part by*** *Andhra Pradesh Oriyantal Risarc Jarnal.*

UK/0305-5728
VINE. VERY INFORMAL NEWSLETTER ON LIBRARY AUTOMATION. (VINE.). [VINE. Very inf. newsl. libr. autom.]. **Added/Corp** Southampton University Library. No. 1 (Oct. 1971)-. Periodical. English. Four times a year. £65.00 UK; £80.00 other. Library Information Technology Centre, South Bank Technopark, 90 London Road, London SE1 6LN England. **Tel** 44 71 8157872, FAX 44 71 8156699. **ED** Jo Wood. **LC** Z678.9.A1; V56. **CODEN** VINEDT. cum. index. **Circ:** 700. available on microfiche. Documents available from Ask*IEEE.
Desc: Very informal newsletter for libraries and librarians.
Ind/Abst INSPEC (March 1979-); Libr. Inf. Sci. Abstr.

US
VIRGINIA REPORT ON PLANNING FOR INFORMATION TECHNOLOGY RESOURCES. **Added/Corp** Virginia. Council on Information Management. **VFOAT** Annual Report on the Status of Information Technology Resources Planning. (July 1990)-. English.

GR
VIVLIOGRAPHIKA. Vol. 1, No. 1 (Jan. 1973)-. Greek, Modern. 3 Vamva Street, T T 138 Athens Greece. **LC** Z671; .V54.

US/0896-0720
VLA NEWSLETTER. (VLA NEWSLETTER : NEWS OF THE VIRGINIA LIBRARY ASSOCIATION.). [VLA newsl.]. **Added/Corp** Virginia Library Association. **VAT** Virginia Library Association Newsletter. Vol. 1, No. 1 (Feb., 1987)-. Newsletter. English. Ten times a year. $60.00 (Comes with the Virginia Library Association Membership). Virginia Library Association, 669 South Washington Street, Alexandria VA 22314. **Tel** (703)519-7853, FAX (703)519-7732. **ED** Dan Ream and Lucretta McCulley. **DD** 020. **Ad Acc.** ctrl circ. ***Continues*** *Virginia Librarian (Arlington, Va. : 1986).*

AT/1036-1561
VOICES : THE QUARTERLY JOURNAL OF THE NATIONAL LIBRARY OF AUSTRALIA. **Added/Corp** National Library of Australia. Vol. 1, No. 1 (Autumn 1991)-. Periodical. English. qt. 48.00Aus$ Australia; 56.00Aus$ other. National Library of Australia, Parkes Place, Canberra ACT, 2600 Australia. **Tel** 011 61 6 2621374, FAX 011 61 6 2731084. **LC** Z871.N35; V65. **DD** 027.594.
Ind/Abst APAIS, Aust. Public Aff. Inf. Ser. (1993-); Aust. Educ. Index; Aust. Libr. Inf. Sci. Abstr. (1991-).

AT/1036-3858
WAATL CIRCULAR. **VFOAT** Western Australian Association of Toy Libraries Circular. (1990)-. Periodical. English. tq. ***Continues*** *Newsletter - Western Australian Association of Toy Libraries, 0811-9651.*

CN/0713-0546
WAPITI. (THE WAPITI / WAPITI REGIONAL LIBRARY.). [Wapiti]. Vol. 1, No. 1 (Nov. 1981)-. Periodical. English. sa. The Wapiti, Wapiti Regional Library, 145-12th Street East, Prince Albert Saskatchewan S6V 1B7 Canada. **DD** 027.47124/2.

US
WASHINGTON LIBRARIES. DIRECTORY OF LIBRARIES IN WASHINGTON STATE. ***Title Change.*** **Added/Corp** Washington State Library. **VFOAT** Directory of Libraries in Washington State; Directory of Libraries; Washington Libraries. Directory of Libraries. (1986)-(1992). Directory. English. an. Washington State University / Library, Washington Library Network AJ-11W, Olympia WA 98504. **LC** Z732.W28; A56. **DD** 027/.0025/797. ***Continues*** *Annual Statistical Bulletin. Directory of Libraries in Washington State.* ***Continued by*** *Directory of Washington Libraries.*

US
WASHINGTON NEWSLETTER. **Added/Corp** American Library Association. Washington Office. **VFOAT** ALA Washington Newsletter. V. 1- Jan. 27, 1949-. Newsletter. English. American Library Association Washington Newsletter, 110 Maryland Avenue NE, Washington DC 20002. **Tel** (202)547-4440, FAX (202)547-7363. **LC** Z671; .W3. ***Formed by the union of*** *Monthly Report* ***and*** *Federal Relations News.*

US
WASHINGTON PUBLIC LIBRARY STATISTICS / WASHINGTON STATE LIBRARY. **See** Library and Information Sciences-Abstracting, Bibliographies and Statistics.

US/0508-1165
WASHINGTON UNIVERSITY LIBRARY STUDIES. **Main/Corp** Washington University, St. Louis. Libraries. **VFOAT** Library Studies. 1- 1950-. Monographic series. English. Price varies per volume. Journal of the History of Philosophy, Department of Philosophy, Washington University, Campus Box 1073, St Louis MO 63130-4899. **Tel** (314)432-8089.

US/0043-3276
WEST VIRGINIA LIBRARIES. [West Va. librar.]. **Added/Corp** West Virginia Library Association. Vol. 1, (1947)-. Periodical. English. Six times a year (Jan., Mar., May, July, Sept., Nov.). $15.00. West Virginia Library Association, PO Box 884, Morgantown WV 26507-0884. **Tel** (304)293-5395. **(Subscription address:** West Virginia University, Main Library, c/o Mildred Moyers, Morgantown, WV 26506-6069) **ED** Yvonne Farley. **LC** Z673; .W42. **DD** 027.0754. **Bk Rev. Ad Acc, Adv Mgr:** Judy Duncan, **Tel** (304)722-4244. **Circ:** 1,000 (ctrl). available on microfilm and microfiche from University Microfilms International (UMI).
Desc: Articles, news, events concerning libraries as well as the association.
Ind/Abst Libr. Inf. Sci. Abstr.; Libr. Lit.

US/0512-4743
WEST VIRGINIA UNION LIST. **Added/Corp** West Virginia University. Library. **VFOAT** Union List; West Virginia Union List of Serials. (1985)-. English. an. $62.00. Wise Library, West Virginia University, PO Box 6069, Morgantown WV 26506-6069. **Tel** (304)293-5395. **ED** Mildred Moyers. **LC** Z6945; .W474; PN4832. **DD** 011/.34. **Circ:** 75. ***Continues*** *West Virginia Union List of Serials, 0512-4743.*

US/1052-2212
WHAT DO I READ NEXT?. [What do I read next]. **Added/Corp** Gale Research Inc. (1990)-. English. an. $90.00. Gale Research Inc., 835 Penobscot Building, Detroit MI 48226. **Tel** (800)877-GALE, (313)961-2242, FAX (313)961-6083, telex TWX 810-221-7086. **ED** Neil Barron, Wayne Barton, Kristin Ramsdell & Steven A. Stilwell. **LC** PN3427; .W43. **DD** 809.3/005.
Desc: Each volume points out the similarities of various titles so that readers can independently identify other titles of interest. Volumes begin with an overview of the genres and then list appropriate authors and titles, arranged alphabetically by author.

US/0882-472X
WHAT'S LINE. **Added/Corp** Alabama Regional Library for the Blind and Physically Handicapped. Alabama Public Library Service. Vol. 1, No. 2 (Summer 1979)-. Periodical. English. qt (Mar., June, Sept., Dec.). Free on request. Alabama Public Library Service, 6030 Monticello Drive, Montgomery AL 36130. **Tel** (205)277-7330. **ED** Fara Zelsky. **Circ:** 6,500. available in braille; available on audiocassette. ***Continues*** *Newsletter.*

UK/0951-8711
WHITAKER'S BOOKBANK CD-ROM SERVICE. [Whitaker's bookbank CD-ROM serv.]. (1987)-. English. mo. £410.00 (single disc); £1220.00 (monthly); £840.00 (bimonthly). J. Whitaker & Sons Ltd, 12 Dyott Street, London WC1A 1DF England. **Tel** 011 44 71 8368911, FAX 011 44 71 836 2909. **DD** 011.221. **Circ:** 900. available on microfiche; available in print; available on magnetic tape.
Desc: Contains books in print from over 17,000 publishers and distributors in the UK and Western Europe. Covers books in print, recently out of print, and forthcoming books.

US/0278-842X
WHO'S WHO IN SPECIAL LIBRARIES. **See** Biographies.

CN/0712-9297
WHSTC LIBRARY CATALOG. [WHSTC libr. cat.]. **VAT** Western Hemisphere Short Title Catalog Project Library Catalog. No. 1-. Catalog. English. Price varies per volume. WHSTC Project, School of Library and Information Science, University of Western Ontario, London Ontario N6G 1H1 Canada. **DD** 010.

UK/0043-5333
WIENER LIBRARY BULLETIN, THE. ***Suspended.*** [Wiener Libr. bull.]. **Main/Corp** Wiener Library. Vol. 1 (1946)-?. Bulletin. English. an. $6.00. Wiener Library, 4 Devonshire Street, London W1N 2BH England. **Tel** 01 636 72479. **LC** Z921.W6; W5. **DD** 909.82.
Ind/Abst Am. Hist. Life (1972-).

US/0043-5651
WILSON LIBRARY BULLETIN. [Wilson libr. bull.]. **Added/Corp** H.W. Wilson Company. Vol. 14, No. 1 (Sept. 1939)-. Bulletin. English. mo (except July and Aug.). $52.00 US and Canada; $58.00 other. H W Wilson Company, 950 University Avenue, Bronx NY 10452. **Tel** (800)367-6770, (718)588-8400, FAX (718)590-1617, telex 4990003 HWILSON. **ED** GraceAnne A DeCandido. **LC** Z1217; .W75. **DD** 020/.5. **NLM** Z 671 W749. **[CCC].** cum. index. **Bk Rev. Ad Acc, Adv Mgr:** Raissa Fomerand (Advertising sales director), **Tel** (914)834-2400 or FAX (914)834-2562. **Pr Rev. Circ:** 23,000 (ctrl). available on microfilm from Micromedia Limited; available on microfilm and microfiche from University Microfilms International (UMI). Documents available from The Genuine Article, UMI Article Clearinghouse, Magazine Collection. ***Continues*** *Wilson Bulletin for Librarians, 1050-8333.*
Desc: Devoted to libraries and librarianship, information science, books and publishing, plus technological communications.
Ind/Abst Acad. Abstr. Full Text Elite (Jan. 1992-); Acad. Abstr. (Jan. 1992-); Acad. Ind. [Computer File] (1984-); Acad. Search (Jan. 1992-); Access (1980-); Am. Hist. Life (1967-); Annu. Bibliogr. Engl. Lang. Lit.; Arts Humanit. Citation Index [Select. Cov.]; Book Rev. Index; Child. Lit. Abstr. (19??-); Comput. Rev. Index (1986-); Cumul. Index Nurs. Allied Health Lit.; Curr. Contents Soc. Behav. Sci.; Curr. Index J. Educ.; Educ. Index; Expand. Acad. Index (1984-); Garden Lit. (1992-); Gen. Period. Index (1985-); INFO-SOUTH Abstr.; Inf. Instruc. Technol.; Inf. Sci. Abstr.; Leg. Inf. Manage. Index; Libr. Inf. Sci. Abstr.; Libr. Lit.; Mag. Artic. Summar. Elite (Jan. 1992-); Mag. Artic. Summar. Select (Jan. 1992-); Mag. Artic. Summar. CD-ROM (Jan. 1992-); Mag. Index Plus (1989-); Mag. Index Sel. Microfiche (1990-) [Full Txt.]; Mag. Index. Sel. (1986-); Mag. Search; Med. Rev. Dig.; Newsp. Period. Abstr. (1989-); Pop. Period. Index; Read. Guide Period. Lit.; Res. Alert [Full Cov.]; Sci. Fict. Fantasy Book Rev. Index; Soc. Sci. Cit. Index [Full Cov.]; Mag. Index (1977-); TOM Gen. Index (1985-) [Full Txt.].

IT
WIMBLEDON : LA GENTE CHE LEGGE. ***Ceased.*** Vol. 1, No. 1 (Mar. 1990)-Vol. 4, No. 34 (Feb. 1993). Periodical. Italian (Italian). mo. Vespina Edizioni, V S Quintino 18, 00185 Rome Italy. **Tel** 011 39 6 70452371. **LC** Z1035.4; .W55. **DD** 028.1/0945.

CN/0824-4782
WIP FUN. (WIP FUN : WORKS IN PROGRESS OF FUN-STUFF / CHARLES CRANE MEMORIAL LIBRARY, UNIVERSITY OF BRITISH COLUMBIA.). [WIP fun]. **Main/Corp** Crane Library. **VAT** Works in Progress Fun. Vol. 1, No. 1 (Nov. 1982)-. Periodical. English. Free. Crane Library, 2075 Westbrook Mall, Vancouver British Columbia V6T 1W5 Canada. **DD** 011/.38. ctrl circ.

US/0884-593X
WIRED LIBRARIAN'S NEWSLETTER. ***Suspended.*** [Wired libr. newsl.]. **VFOAT** WLN: Not the Bibliographic Utility. Suspended (June 1990). Newsletter. English. mo. $15.00. Mikro Libraries, 393 South Haron Street/Suite D21, Jackson OH 45640. **DD** 020.
Ind/Abst Comput. Rev. Index (1986-).

US/0361-2848
WISCONSIN LIBRARY SERVICE RECORD. **Main/Corp** Wisconsin. Division for Library Services. 1973-. English. an. Division of Library Services, Department of Public Instruction, PO Box 7841, Madison WI 53707. **LC** L216; .B36 subser; Z732.W8. **DD** 025.5/09775.
Ind/Abst Stat. Ref. Index.

US/0278-6303
WLN PARTICIPANT. [WLN particip.]. **Added/Corp** Washington State Library. Washington Library Network. **VFOAT** Participant. **VAT** Washington Library Network Participant. (19??)-. Periodical. English. Six times a year. Free on request. Western Library Network - WLN, PO Box 3888, Lacey WA 98503. **Tel** (206)923-4000, (800)342-5956, FAX (206)923-4009. **ED** David Wasser. **DD** 025. **Bk Rev. Circ:** 1,000 (ctrl).
Desc: Publication detailing activities of the Western Library Network, an agency of the state of Washington. Provided to WLN users only.

US/0272-1996
WLW JOURNAL. ***Ceased.*** [WLW j.]. **Main/Corp** Women Library Workers (U.S.). **Added/Corp** Women Library Workers (U.S.). **VAT** Women Library Workers Journal. Vol. 5 (Jan./Feb. 1980)-Vol. 16, No. 4. Periodical. English. qt. McFarland & Company, PO Box 611, Jefferson NC 28640. **Tel** (919)246-4460, FAX (919)246-5018. **ED** Nancy Humphreys. **LC** Z682.4.W65; W57. **DD** 020/.82. **Bk Rev. Ad Acc. Circ:** 300. ***Continues*** *Women Library Workers, 0738-629X.*
Desc: Works to end discrimination against women in libraries and librarianship.
Ind/Abst Libr. Inf. Sci. Abstr.; Libr. Lit.; Ref. Sources.

GW/0300-2012
WOLFENBUTTELER BEITRAEGE. [Wolfenb. Beitr.]. No. 1 (1972)-. German. ir. Vittorio Klostermann, Frauenlobstrasse 22, D 60487 Frankfurt Germany. **Tel** 011 49 69 9708160.
Ind/Abst BHA : Biblio. Hist. Art; MLA Int. Bibl. Books Artic. Mod. Lang. Lit.

SW
WORK OF THE STOCKHOLM PUBLIC LIBRARY IN ..., THE. **Main/Corp** Stockholms Stadsbibliotek. English. an.

GW/0000-0221
WORLD GUIDE TO LIBRARIES. **VFOAT** Internationales Bibliotheks-Handbuch. Vol. 1 (1966)-. English (German). ir. $175.00. Gale Research Inc., 835 Penobscot Building, Detroit MI 48226. **Tel** (800)877-GALE, (313)961-2242, FAX (313)961-6083, telex TWX 810-221-7086. **ED** H Lengenfelder. **DD** 020.
Desc: Provides details on 43,000 libraries worldwide, the new edition adds over 2,000 libraries while deleting 1,000 defunct libraries.

US/0146-8014
WORLDWIDE GUIDE TO MEDICAL ELECTRONICS MARKETING REPRESENTATION, THE. 1st Ed. (1977)-. Periodical. English. be. International Bio-Medical Information Service, PO Box 756, Miami FL 33156. **Tel** (305)271-7272. **ED** Adeline B Hale and Arthur B Hale. **NLM** QT 22.1 W927.

US/0149-0567
WVLC NEWSLETTER. **Main/Corp** West Virginia Library Commission. **VAT** West Virginia Library Commission Newsletter. V. 20-. Newsletter. English. ir. Free. West Virginia Library Commission, Science and Culture Center, Charleston WV 25305. **ED** Frederic J Glazer. **LC** Z732.W5; W482B. **DD** 021/.009754. **Circ:** 1,500 (ctrl). ***Continues*** *Library Commission Newsletter.*

CN/0225-5081
Y U L SERIALS LIST. [YUL ser. list]. **Main/Corp** York University, Toronto, Ont. Libraries. **VAT** York University Libraries Serials List. (1978)-. Periodical. English. qt. $24.00. Microcatalogues, Room 310/Scott Library, York University, 4700 Keele Street, Downsview Ontario M3J 2R2 Canada. **DD** 016.05.

IS
YAD LAKORE. Hebrew (English). qt. $30.00. Center for Public Libraries - Israel, PO Box 242, Jerusalem 91002 Israel. **Tel** 011 972 2 252949.
Ind/Abst Libr. Inf. Sci. Abstr.

JA/0386-2062
YAKUGAKU TOSHOKAN. PHARMACEUTICAL LIBRARY BULLETIN. **Added/Corp** Nihon Yakugaku Toshokan Kyogikai. **VFOAT** Pharmaceutical Library Bulletin. Vol. 1 (Jan. 1956)-. Academic Scholarly Publication. Japanese. qt. ¥4000. Japan Pharmaceutical Library Association, c/o Faculty of Pharmaceutical Sciences, 7-3-1 Hongo Bunkyo-ku, Tokyo Japan. **Tel** 03-812-2111. **ED** K Asahina. **LC** Z675.P48; Y34. **NLM** Z 675.P5 Y15. **CODEN** YATODW. cum. index. **Circ:** 1,100. Documents available from CASDDS.
Ind/Abst Chem. Abstr.; Libr. Inf. Sci. Abstr.

US/0044-0175
YALE UNIVERSITY LIBRARY GAZETTE, THE. [Yale Univ. libr. gaz.]. **Main/Corp** Yale University. Library. **Added/Corp** Yale University. Library. Gazette. Vol. 1 (June 1926)-. Periodical. English. Four times a year (Apr., Oct.). $20.00. Yale University Library-Publications Office, Box 1603A Yale Station, New Haven CT 06520. **Tel** (203)432-2969, FAX (203)432-4047. **ED** Stephen Parks. **LC** Z733; .Y17G. **DD** 027.7746/8. **Circ:** 1,200 (ctrl).
Desc: Articles based on collections in various divisions of Yale Library and news of recent acquisitions. Occasionally catalogues of current exhibitions.
Ind/Abst Abstr. Engl. Stud.; Am. Hist. Life (1965-); Annu. Bibliogr. Engl. Lang. Lit.; ARTbibliogr. Mod.; BHA : Biblio. Hist. Art; Child. Lit. Abstr. (19??-); Middle East Abstr. Index; MLA Int. Bibl. Books Artic. Mod. Lang. Lit.; Romant. Move.

CN/0824-1457
YAYA. [Yaya]. **Added/Corp** Dalhousie University. School of Library Service. Canadian Library Association. Young Adult Special Interest Group. Issue # 1 (July 1984)-. Periodical. English. Twice a year. 10.00Can$. Young Adult Services Interest Group / YAYA, 227 15th Street NW, c/o Kari Brawn, Calgary Alberta T2N 2A8 Canada. **Tel** (403)270-0744. **ED** Kari Brawn. **DD** 027.62/6/06071. **Bk Rev**, (Qty: 2). **Circ:** 65 (ctrl).
Desc: Provides information for librarians, teachers, institutions, writers and parents interested in young adult literature and library services to young adults.

UK
YEAR BOOK / THE LIBRARY ASSOCIATION. **Main/Corp** Library Association. English. an. Library Association, 7 Ridgmount Street, London WC1E 7AE England. **Tel** 011 44 71 636-7543, FAX 011 44 71 436-7218, telex 21897. **LC** Z673; .L7Y. **DD** 020/.622/41. ***Continues*** *Library Association Year Book.*

UK/0269-4859
YOUTH LIBRARY REVIEW. (1986)-. English. County Library, Tricia Kings, Angel Row, Nottingham NG1 6HP United Kingdom.
Ind/Abst Child. Lit. Abstr. (19??-).

CN/1188-0384
YRL NEWS & VIEWS. [YRL news views]. **Added/Corp** Yellowhead Regional Library. **VFOAT** Yellowhead Regional Library News & Views. Vol. 1, No. 1 (Sept. 1991)-. Periodical. English. Three times a year. Limited free distribution. Yellowhead Regional Library, PO Box 400, Spruce Grove Alberta T7X 2Y1 Canada. **Tel** (403)962-2003. **DD** 027.47123.

XR
Z KNIHOVNICKE PRAXE. Czech. Statni Vedecka Knohovna, Olomouc Bezrucova 2 Czech Republic. **LC** S795.S47; Z2.

GW/0044-2380
ZEITSCHRIFT FUER BIBLIOTHEKSWESEN UND BIBLIOGRAPHIE. [Z. Bibliothekswes. Bibliogr.]. **Added/Corp** Verein Deutscher Bibliothekare. Verein der Diplombibliothekare an Wissenschaftlichem Bibliotheken. (1954-1992). Periodical. German. bm. DM94.00. Vittorio Klostermann, Frauenlobstrasse 22, D 60487 Frankfurt Germany. **Tel** 011 49 69 9708160. **ED** G Pflug. **LC** Z671; .Z4. **NLM** Z 671 Z48. **[CCC].** Documents available from The Genuine Article. ***Continues*** *Nachrichten fur Wissenschaftliche Bibliotheken;* ***Absorbed*** *Zentralblatt fur Bibliothekswesen, 0044-4081.* ***Continued in part by*** *Bibliographische Berichte, 0006-1506.*
Ind/Abst Arts Humanit. Citation Index [Select. Cov.]; Curr. Contents Soc. Behav. Sci.; Energy Res. Abstr. (March 1982-); Libr. Inf. Sci. Abstr.; Libr. Lit.; Res. Alert [Full Cov.]; Soc. Sci. Cit. Index [Full Cov.].

GW/0514-6364
ZEITSCHRIFT FUER BIBLIOTHEKSWESEN UND BIBLIOGRAPHIE. SONDERHEFT. 1- 1963-. Periodical. German. ir. Price not set as yet. Vittorio Klostermann, Frauenlobstrasse 22, D 60487 Frankfurt Germany. **Tel** 011 49 69 9708160.

GW/0417-2957
ZEITSCHRIFTENDIENST. **Main/Corp** Deutscher Buchereiverband. Arbeitsstelle fur das Buchereiwesen. (19??)-. Periodical. German. mo. DM430.00. Deutsches Bibliotheksinstitut, Bundesallee 184 185, D 10717 Berlin Germany. **Tel** 011 49 30 8505186, 011 49 30 8505187, FAX 011 49 30 8505100. **ED** Dagmar Weber-Tamschick. **DD** 016. **Circ:** 400.

RH/1015-6828
ZIMBABWE LIBRARIAN, THE. (THE ZIMBABWE LIBRARIAN / ZLA.). [Zimb. libr.]. **Added/Corp** Zimbabwe Library Association. Vol. 11, No. 1 and 2 (Jan./June 1979)-. Periodical. English. Twice a year. $20.00. Zimbabwe Library Association, PO Box 3133, Harare Zimbabwe. **LC** Z857.R45; R45. **DD** 027.06891. **Bk Rev. Ad Acc. Circ:** 350 (ctrl). ***Continues*** *Rhodesian Librarian, 0035-4848.*
Desc: Journal of the Zimbabwe Library Association.
Ind/Abst Libr. Inf. Sci. Abstr.

ABSTRACTING, BIBLIOGRAPHIES AND STATISTICS

NE/0303-5964
ABHA. ANNUAL BIBLIOGRAPHY OF THE HISTORY OF THE PRINTED BOOK AND LIBRARIES. (ANNUAL BIBLIOGRAPHY OF THE HISTORY OF THE PRINTED BOOK AND LIBRARIES.). **Added/Corp** International Federation of Library Associations. Committee on Rare and Precious Books and Documents. **VFOAT** ABHB. Vol. 1 (1970)-. Monographic series. English. ir. Price varies per volume. Kluwer Academic Publishers, Postbus 322, 3300 AH Dordrecht, The Netherlands. **Tel** 011 (31) 78 524400, FAX 011 31 78 183273, telex 20083. **(Subscription address:** Kluwer Academic Publishers / US Subscriptions, PO Box 253, Accord Station, Hingham MA 02018.**) LC** Z117; .A55. **DD** 016.00155/2. **NLM** Z 4 A105.

AT/0810-9265
ALISA. AUSTRALIAN LIBRARY AND INFORMATION SCIENCE ABSTRACTS. (AUSTRALIAN LIBRARY AND INFORMATION SCIENCE ABSTRACTS.). [ALISA, Aust. libr. inf. sci. abstr.]. **Added/Corp** Australian Clearing House for Library and Information Science. **VFOAT** Australian Library and Information Science Abstracts. (1982)-. Abstracting/Indexing Service. English. an. 60.00Aus$. Library Publications / University of South Australia, Holbrook Road, Underdale SA 5032 Australia. **Tel** 011 61 8 3026258. **ED** Barbara Blacoe. **DD** 016.0205. available on CD-ROM from AUSTROM; available on an online database from AUSINET.
Desc: A subject index to Australian literature in the field of library and information science. Attempts to comprehensively cover all current Australian literature, published and unpublished, on library and information science.

US/0065-910X
AMERICAN LIBRARY DIRECTORY. (AMERICAN LIBRARY DIRECTORY; A CLASSIFIED LIST OF LIBRARIES IN THE UNITED STATES AND CANADA, WITH PERSONNEL AND STATISTICAL DATA.). [Am. libr. dir.]. **Added/Corp** R.R. Bowker Company. Jaques Cattell Press. (1923)-. Statistical Publication. English. an. $239.95. R R Bowker, A Reed Reference Publishing Company, Part of Reed International PLC, PO Box 31, 121 Chanlon Drive, New Providence NJ 07974. **Tel** (908)464-6800, (800)521-8110, FAX (908)665-6688, telex 138-755. **LC** Z731; .A53. **DD** 021/.0025/73. **NLM** Z 731 A512. **[CCC].** available on magnetic tape, an online database, and CD-ROM. ***Continues in part*** *American Library Annual.*
Desc: Contains the most authoritative information available on more than 38,000 public, academic, special, and government libraries and library-related organizations in the US and Canada.

US
ANALYSES OF NEW JERSEY PUBLIC LIBRARY STATISTICS FOR ... . **VFOAT** New Jersey Public Library Statistics. 1981-. English. an. Free single copy. New Jersey State Library, 185 West State Street, Trenton NJ 08625. **Tel** (609)292-7306. **ED** Robert K Fortenbaugh. **LC** Z732.N6; A73. **DD** 027.4749. **Circ:** 650.
Desc: Data from New Jersey Public Library Statistics, analyzed in various ways, with libraries grouped by population and expenditure categories, and with regional and statewide averages, etc., given.

US/0736-5616
ANALYSES OF THE ... ILLINOIS PUBLIC LIBRARY STATISTICS. **VFOAT** Illinois Public Library Statistics; Illinois Public Library Statistics Analyses. 1974-75-. English. an. Illinois State Library, Centennial Building, Springfield IL 62756. **Tel** (217)782-2994. **ED** Herbert Goldhor. **LC** Z732.I2; A5. **DD** 027.4773.

US/0196-6448
ANNUAL STATISTICS OF MEDICAL SCHOOL LIBRARIES IN THE UNITED STATES AND CANADA. (ANNUAL STATISTICS OF MEDICAL SCHOOL LIBRARIES IN THE UNITED STATES AND CANADA / COMPILED BY HOUSTON ACADEMY OF MEDICINE-TEXAS MEDICAL CENTER LIBRARY.). [Annu. stat. med. sch. libr. U.S. Can.]. **Added/Corp** Houston Academy of Medicine-Texas Medical Center Library. Association of Academic Health Sciences Library Directors (U.S.). (1977-1978)-. Periodical. English. an. $100.00 (nonmembers), $50.00 (members). Association of Academic Health Sciences Library Directors, 2033 Sixth Avenue, Suite 804, Seattle WA 98121. **Tel** (206)441-6020. **LC** Z675.M4; A6. **DD** 026/.61/0973. **NLM** Z 675.M4 M49034. ***Continues*** *Medical Library Statistics.*

US/0147-2135
ARL STATISTICS. **Main/Corp** Association of Research Libraries. **VAT** Association of Research Libraries Statistics. (1975)-. Statistical Publication. English. an. $25.00 (members), $65.00 (nonmembers). Association of Research Libraries, 21 Dupont Circle, Washington DC 20036. **Tel** (202)296-2296. **(Subscription address:** Association of Research Libraries, Department 0692, Washington DC 20073.**) ED** Sarah Pritchard. **LC** Z675.U5; A78. **DD** 027.773. **Circ:** 1,200. available on diskette. ***Continues*** *Academic Library Statistics, 0571-6519.*
Desc: Describes the collections, staffing levels, expenditures, and interlibrary loan volume of all Association of Research Libraries member libraries in the US and Canada.
Ind/Abst Libr. Lit.; Stat. Ref. Index.

AT/0314-3767
AUSTRALIAN SOCIETY OF INDEXERS NEWSLETTER. **See** Library and Information Sciences.

PL/0006-1093
BIBLIOGRAFIA ZAWARTOSCI CZASOPISM / BIBLIOTEKA NARODOWA, INSTYTUT BIBLIOGRAFICZNY. **Added/Corp** Biblioteka Narodowa (Poland). Instytut Bibliograficzny. Vol. 1 (1947)-. Periodical. Polish. mo. $132.00. **(Subscription address:** ARS Polona, PO Box 1001, 00068 Warsaw Poland.**) LC** AI15; .B45. **NLM** ZAI 15 B577.

FR
BIBLIOGRAPHIE SPECIALE ANALYTIQUE. **Main/Corp** Organization For Economic Cooperation and Development. Library. **VFOAT** Special Annotated Bibliography. 1-. Periodical. French. **LC** Z7164.E2; O68. **DD** 629.8. ***Supersedes*** *Organisation for Economic Co-Operation and Development. Library. Bibliographie Speciale.*

NO/0006-5811
BOK OG BIBLIOTEK. (BOK OG BIBLIOTEK : TIDSSKRIFT FOR BIBLIOTEKER OG BOGVENNER.). [Bok bibl.]. Vol. 1, No. 1 (Feb. 1934)-. Periodical. Norwegian. Eight times a year. Kr150.00. Statens Bibliotektilsyn, Postboks 8145, Dep N 0033, Oslo 1 Norway. **Tel** 011 47 2 832585, FAX 011 47 02 831552. **ED** Live Slang. **LC** Z671; .B677. **DD** 020.5. **[CCC].** Index available. **Bk Rev. Ad Acc. Circ:** 11,000. ***Continues*** *For Folkeoplysning.*
Desc: Library journal covering professional issues as well as questions referring to the library in society.
Ind/Abst Libr. Inf. Sci. Abstr.; Libr. Lit.; MLA Int. Bibl. Books Artic. Mod. Lang. Lit.

US/0951-838X
BOOKS AND PERIODICALS ONLINE. [Books period. online]. Vol. 1, Pt. 1 (1987)-. English. an. $215.42 New York; $199.00 other. Library Alliance, Inc., 264 Lexington Avenue, Suite 4-C North, New York NY 10016. **Tel** (212)685-5297, FAX (212)213-6055. **ED** Nuchine Nobari. **LC** Z7164.C81; B725; HF5351. **DD** 025/.0634. **NLM** Z 6941; B724. **CODEN** BPONER. Index available. cum. index. **Bk Rev. Ad Acc. Circ:** 1,400. available on CD-ROM. ***Formed by the union of*** *Directory of Periodicals Online, Law and Business, 0884-089X* ***and*** *Directory of Periodicals Online, Science and Technology, 0884-0911 Directory of Periodicals Online, Medical and Humanities.*
Desc: Alphabetical directory of over 43,000 periodicals, books, newspapers, and newswires contained in over 1,800 business and legal databases and CD-ROMs.

UK/0007-1544
BRITISH NATIONAL BIBLIOGRAPHY. [Br. natl. bibliogr.]. **Added/Corp** British Library. Bibliographic Services Division. Council of the British National Bibliography. (19??)-. Bibliography. English. an (Apr.). £540.00 UK; £650.00 others. British Library / Bibliographic Service, Boston Spa, Wetherby West Yorkshire LS23 7BQ England. **Tel** 011 44 937 546160, FAX 011 44 937 546586, telex 557381. **(Subscription address:** Turpin Distribution Services Limited, Blackhorse Road, Letchworth, Hertfordshire SG6 1HN, United Kingdom.**) CODEN** BRNBBV. **Circ:** 3,500. available on CD-ROM (As: BNB on CD-ROM).
Desc: Lists new books and first issues of serial titles received by the Copyright Receipt Office of the British Library.
Ind/Abst Annu. Bibliogr. Engl. Lang. Lit.; Math. Rev.

US/0741-031X
CALIFORNIA LIBRARY STATISTICS. 1983-. English. an. California State Library, PO Box 942837, Sacramento CA 94237. **Tel** (916)445-4027. **ED** Collin Clark. **LC** Z732.C2; C475. **DD** 027.0794. **Circ:** 2,000. ***Continues in part*** *California Library Statistics and Directory, 0148-4583.*
Desc: Statistical tables for California public, academic, special, and state agency libraries.

●US
CD-ROM FINDER : THE WORLD OF CD-ROM PRODUCTS FOR INFORMATION SEEKERS. 5th Ed. (1993)-. Periodical. English. ir. $69.50. Learned Information Inc.,

143 Old Marlton Pike, Medford NJ 08055-8750. **Tel** (609)654-6266, FAX (609)654-4309. **ED** James Shelton. ***Continues*** *Optical Publishing Directory, 0896-9841.*
Desc: Contains over 1,400 titles described fully according to publisher, type of contents, language(s) used, geographical and chronological coverage, search software, and descriptions of each product's most prominent contents.

US/0743-9873
CHILDREN'S MAGAZINE GUIDE. [Child. mag. guide]. Vol. 34, No. 1 (Sept. 1981)-. Abstracting/Indexing Service. English. Nine times a year. $45.00 US; $49.00 other. R R Bowker, A Reed Reference Publishing Company, Part of Reed International PLC, PO Box 31, 121 Chanlon Drive, New Providence NJ 07974. **Tel** (908)464-6800, (800)521-8110, FAX (908)665-6688, telex 138-755. **ED** Judith M. Balsamo and Marion Sader. **LC** AI3; .S83. **DD** 051. **[CCC]**. cum. index. **Circ:** 14,500. ***Continues*** *Subject Index to Children's Magazines, 0039-4351.*
Desc: Subject index to articles in over 45 children's magazines and magazines for the librarian and education professional.

US
CONNECTICARD ANNUAL STATISTICAL REPORT. Mar. 1982 through Feb. 1983-. Statistical Publication. English. an. Interlibrary Loan Center, Connecticut State Library, Hartford CT 06106. **Tel** (203)566-2300. **LC** Z713.5.U6; C6B. **DD** 025.6/2. **Circ:** 250 (ctrl). ***Continues*** *Connecticard Semi-Annual Statistical Report.*

UK
CURRENT BRITISH JOURNALS. **Added/Corp** British Library. Lending Division. UK Serials Group. 3rd Ed. (1982)-. English. ir. £70.00 UK; £75.00 other. British Library / Publications Sale Unit, Boston Spa, Wetherby, West Yorkshire LS23 7BQ England. **Tel** 011 44 937 546546 546543, FAX 011 44 937 546333, telex 557381. **LC** Z6956.G6; G84; PN5124.P4. **DD** 052/.025. **NLM** Z 6956.G7; G946. **Ad Acc. Circ:** 1,500. ***Continues*** *Guide to Current British Journals.*

US/0731-3594
DIRECTORY OF FEDERAL STATISTICAL DATA FILES. [Dir. fed. stat. data files]. March 1981-. Statistical Publication. English. an. National Technical Information Service - NTIS, Room 2027S, 5285 Port Royal Road, Springfield VA 22161. **Tel** (703)487-4630, (703)487-4660, (703)487-4650, FAX (703)321-8547, telex 89-9405. **LC** HA37; .U113. **DD** 025/.0631/02573.

US/0884-0911
DIRECTORY OF PERIODICALS ONLINE. SCIENCE & TECHNOLOGY : INDEXED, ABSTRACTED & FULL TEXT. ***Title Change.*** **VFOAT** Science & Technology; Science and Technology. (1989)-(1993). Directory. English. an. Globe & Mail, 444 Front Street West, Toronto Ontario M5V 2S9 Canada. **Tel** (416)585-5000, FAX (416)585-5249. ***Merged with*** *Directory of Periodicals Online, Law & Business, 0884-089X* ***and*** *Directory of Periodicals Online, Medical & Humanities* ***to form*** *Books and Periodicals Online, 0951-838X.*

US
DIRECTORY OF PERIODICALS ONLINE. VOL. 2, MEDICINE & SOCIAL SCIENCE. [Dir. period. online, Vol. 2, Med. soc. sci.]. **VFOAT** Medicine & Social Science; Medicine and Social Science. (1989)-. Directory. English. sa. Federal Document Retrieval Inc, Washington DC 20002. **Tel** (202)789-2233.

PE/0015-0002
FENIX (LIMA). (FENIX : REVISTA DE LA BIBLIOTECA NACIONAL.). [Fenix]. **Added/Corp** Biblioteca Nacional (Peru). (1944)-. Spanish. an. Biblioteca Nacional del Peru, Apartado 2335, Lima Peru. **Tel** 011 51 14 287690. **LC** Z671; .F35. **DD** 020.5. cum. index.
Ind/Abst Am. Hist. Life (1964-); Annu. Bibliogr. Engl. Lang. Lit.

AT/0156-6717
GUIDELINES. [Guidelines]. (1969)-. English. Nine times a year (Feb.-Nov.). 90.00Aus$ Australia; 97.50Aus$ other. Bibliographic Services Pty.Ltd., PO Box 2, Mt. Waverly Victoria 3149 Australia. **Tel** 011 61 03 8073442, FAX 011 61 03 8072073. **DD** 016.05. available on microfiche; available on CD-ROM (available for OASIS library automation system and also for IBM compatibles).
Desc: A subject guide for Australian libraries.

HU/0046-8304
HUNGARIAN LIBRARY AND INFORMATION SCIENCE ABSTRACTS. **Added/Corp** Konyvtartudomanyi es Modszertani Kozpont (Hungary). Vol. 1 (1972)-. Abstracting/Indexing Service. English. sa. Free on exchange basis only. Hungarian Library and Information Science Abstracts, Orszagos Szechenyi Konyvtar, Muzeum U3 Konyvtartudomanyies, H-1827 Budapest Hungary. **Tel** 335 590. **ED** Feimer Agnes and Javori Ferencne. **LC** Z671; .H85. **DD** 020/.5. Index available. cum. index. **Bk Rev. Ad Acc. Circ:** 350. available on diskette.
Desc: An abstracting journal of Hungarian literature on librarianship and information science.

US/0739-1137
IASSIST QUARTERLY. (IASSIST QUARTERLY / INTERNATIONAL ASSOCIATION FOR SOCIAL SCIENCE INFORMATION SERVICE AND TECHNOLOGY.). [IASSIST q.]. **Added/Corp** International Association for Social Science Information Service and Technology. **VFOAT** I.A.S.S.I.S.T. Quarterly; Quarterly; IASSIST Newsletter. **VAT** International Association for Social Science Information Service and Technology quarterly. (19??)-. Periodical. English. Four times a year. $70.00 (with membership). University of California at Los Angeles / IASSIST, 405 Hilgard Avenue, GSLIS Building 304, Los Angeles CA 90024. **Tel** (301)825-0716. ***Continues*** *Newsletter - International Association for Social Science Service and Technology, 0145-238X.*
Ind/Abst Libr. Inf. Sci. Abstr.

US/1041-1321
INDEX AND ABSTRACT DIRECTORY, THE. (THE INDEX AND ABSTRACT DIRECTORY : AN INTERNATIONAL GUIDE TO SERVICES AND SERIALS COVERAGE.). [Index abstr. dir.]. Premier Edition (1989)-. Directory. English. ir. $189.00. EBSCO Publishing / Birmingham, The Serials Directory, PO Box 1943, Birmingham AL 35201-1943. **Tel** editorial inquiries (205)980-2773, toll-free US (800)826-3024, FAX (205)995-1582. **ED** Leanne Wofford. **LC** Z695.93; .I52. **DD** 025.3/025. **NLM** Z 695.93; I38. Index available (Vol. 2).
Desc: Two-Volume reference book containing over 56,000 serial titles covered by over 1,300 abstracting or indexing publications. Volume One is arranged alphabetically, with complete bibliographic information for each journal. Section Two consists of over 900 "active" abstracting and indexing publications, each one listing serial titles covered, both past and present with dates of coverage, full text notations, fully/selectively covered indicators as well as bibliographic information on the title itself. A subject index of abstracting and indexing publications is also included.

II/0019-5790
INDIAN LIBRARY SCIENCE ABSTRACTS. **Added/Corp** Indian Association of Special Libraries and Information Centres. Vol. 1 (Jan./March 1967)-. Abstracting/Indexing Service. English. qt. $20.00. Indian Association of Special Libraries and Information Centres, P291 CIT Scheme No 6M, PO Kankurgachi, Calcutta 700 054 India. **Tel** (033) 349651. **(Subscription address:** Prints India, 11 Darya Ganj, New Delhi 110002 India.) **ED** Shri Amitava Chatterjes. **LC** Z671; .I55. **DD** 020/.5. cum. index. **Circ:** 500 (ctrl).

US
INFORMATION & INSTRUCTION TECHNOLOGIES. Abstracting/Indexing Service. English. Pierian Press, PO Box 1808, Ann Arbor MI 48106. **Tel** (313)434-5530, (800)678-2435, FAX (313)434-6409.
Desc: Covers library management, information science, and educational publications that contain articles and product reviews related to library automation and educational technologies.

●UK
INFORMATION MANAGEMENT & TECHNOLOGY. **Added/Corp** Cimtech (Organization). **VFOAT** Information Management and Technology. Vol. 25, No. 1 (Jan. 1992)-. Abstracting/Indexing Service. English. Six times a year. £73.00 UK; £77.00 Europe; £91.00 other. Cimtech Limited, University of Hertfordshire, College Lane, Hatfield, Hertfordshire AL10 9AD England. **Tel** 11 44 707 284691, FAX 11 44 707 272121. **ED** Anne Grimshaw; 11 44 707 284698. **CODEN** IMTHEM. Index Available in first issue of next volume--attached. **Bk Rev**, (Qty: 9-10). **Ad Acc, Adv Mgr:** Cathy Godfrey, **Tel** 11 44 707 284692. **Circ:** 1,500. Documents available from Ask*IEEE. ***Continues*** *Information Media & Technology.*
Desc: Records of document management, micrographics, DIP systems, facsimiles and multimedia.
Ind/Abst Inf. Sci. Abstr.; INSPEC (Jan. 1992-).

US/0020-0239
INFORMATION SCIENCE ABSTRACTS. Vol. 4 (March 1969)-. Abstracting/Indexing Service. English. Twelve times a year. $555.00 US; $650.00 other. Plenum Press, 233 Spring Street, New York NY 10013-1578. **Tel** (212)620-8000, (800)221-9369, FAX (212)463-0742, (212)807-1047, telex 23/421139. **ED** H. Allcock. **LC** Z699.A1; D6. **DD** 020/.5. **NLM** Z 699.A1 D637. **[CCC]**. available on CD-ROM; available on an online database from DIALOG; available on microfilm and microfiche from University Microfilms International (UMI). ***Continues*** *Documentation Abstracts and Information Science Abstracts.*
Desc: Contains all abstracts in documentation, information recognition, systems and applications information. Generation information user and usage studies, information storage and retrieval for libraries and information services.
Ind/Abst Comput. Rev.

US/8756-0941
INFORMATION TIMES (1983). ***Ceased.*** (INFORMATION TIMES : A PUBLICATION OF THE INFORMATION INDUSTRY ASSOCIATION.). [Information times]. **Added/Corp** Information Industry Association. **VFOAT** New Information Times. (Nov. 1983)-(19??). Periodical. English. mo. Information Industry Association, 555 New Jersey Avenue Northwest, Suite 800, Washington DC 20001-2082. **Tel** (202)639-8262. **LC** QA75.5; .I534. **DD** 001.64/05. ***Continues*** *Information World, 0163-0067.*

US
IOWA PUBLIC LIBRARY STATISTICS / STATE LIBRARY COMMISSION OF IOWA. English. an. Free. State Library of Iowa, Office of Library Development, East 12th and 6 Rand, Des Moines IA 50319. **Tel** (515)281-6788. **ED** Gerry Rowland. **LC** Z732.I6; I735. **DD** 024.4777. **Circ:** 750.
Desc: Public library program and financial activity generated from standard form.

GW/0176-7593
LIBRARIES, INFORMATION CENTERS AND DATABASES IN SCIENCE AND TECHNOLOGY : A WORLD GUIDE. **VFOAT** Bibliotheken, Informationszentren und Datenbasen fur Wissenschaft und Technik : EIN Internationales Verzeichnis. 1st Ed. (1984)-. English (German). ir. $213.75. K.G. Saur Verlag KG, A Reed Reference Publishing Company, Part of Reed International PLC, Ortlerstrasse 8, D 81373 Munich Germany. **Tel** 011 49 89 769020, FAX 011 49 89 76902150, telex 5212067-SAUR-D. **LC** Z675.T3; L56. **DD** 026.6/025.
Desc: Listing institutions by country, this international directory provides information on over 11,000 libraries, online databases, and documentation centers in all areas of pure and applied sciences.

UK/0024-2179
LIBRARY & INFORMATION SCIENCE ABSTRACTS. [Libr. inf. sci. abstr.]. **Added/Corp** Library Association. Aslib. **VAT** Library and Information Science Abstracts. Vol. 1 (Jan./Feb. 1969)-. Abstracting/Indexing Service. English (French, German, Russian, Spanish, Czech, Polish, Italian, Dutch, Afrikaans, Bulgarian, Serbo-Croatian (Roman) and Japanese). mo. £345.00 EEC countries; £380.00 other. Bowker Saur Ltd., A Reed Reference Publishing Company, Part of Reed International PLC, 59-60 Grosvenor Street, London WIX 9DA England. **Tel** 011 44 71 4935841, FAX 011 44 71 4991590. **(Subscription address:** World-Wide Subscription Services, Unit 4, Gibbs Reed Farm Pashley Road, Ticehurst TN5 7HE England.) **LC** Z671; .L6. **DD** 016.02. **NLM** Z 666 L695. cum. index. **Pr Rev. Circ:** 2,000. available on an online database from BRS; ORBIT; and (file 61) DIALOG; available on magnetic tape; available on CD-ROM from SilverPlatter (US); available in hardback; available on microfilm and microfiche from University Microfilms International (UMI). ***Supersedes*** *Library Science Abstracts, 0459-262X.*
Desc: Abstracting service covering librarianship, information science, publishing and online computerized information systems.
Ind/Abst World Publ. Monit. (19??-).

US/0739-506X
LIBRARY AND INFORMATION SCIENCE EDUCATION STATISTICAL REPORT. (LIBRARY AND INFORMATION SCIENCE EDUCATION STATISTICAL REPORT / ASSOCIATION FOR LIBRARY AND INFORMATION SCIENCE EDUCATION.). [Libr. inf. sci. educ. stat. rep.]. **Added/Corp** ALISE Library and Information Science Education Statistics Committee. Association for Library and Information Science Education. (1983)-. Statistical Publication. English. an (published in July). $32.00. Association for Library and Information Science Education- ALISE, 4101 Lake Boone Trail, Suite 201, Raleigh NC 27607-4916. **Tel** (919)787-5181. **ED** Timothy W. Sineath. **LC** Z668; .L495. **DD** 020/.7/10973. **CODEN** ALIEEX. **Circ:** 300. available on microfilm. ***Continues*** *Library Education Statistical Report, 0743-6602.*
Desc: In-depth statistical reports from ALISE member graduate library schools on faculty, students, curriculum, finance, and continuing education.

US/1040-4333
LIBRARY HI TECH BIBLIOGRAPHY. [Libr. hi tech bibliogr.]. **VFOAT** LHT Bibliography. Vol. 1 (1986)-. Bibliography. English. an. $48.00. Pierian Press, PO Box 1808, Ann Arbor MI 48106. **Tel** (313)434-5530, (800)678-2435, FAX (313)434-6409. **LC** Z666; .L43. **DD** 016.02.

US/0024-2373
LIBRARY LITERATURE. [Libr. lit.]. **Added/Corp** H.W. Wilson Company. American Library Association. Junior Members Round Table. (1932)-. Abstracting/Indexing Service. English. bm. Sold on the service basis. H W Wilson Company, 950 University Avenue, Bronx NY 10452. **Tel** (800)367-6770, (718)588-8400, FAX (718)590-1617, telex 4990003 HWILSON. **ED** Cathy Rentschler. **LC** Z666; .C211. **DD** 016.02. Index available. cum. index. ctrl circ. available on

an online database from WILSONLINE; available on CD-ROM from WILSONDISC; available on magnetic tape from WILSONTAPE; available on diskette from WILSONSEARCH.
Desc: Contains citations to articles and reviews of books, periodicals, and audiovisual materials in the library and information science area. Covers such topics as automation, censorship, national and international libraries, library associations, public relations, information brokers and appointments and obituaries within the library community.

US
LIBRARY LITERATURE [COMPUTER FILE]. **Added/Corp** H.W. Wilson Company. (1984)-. Periodical. English. Four times a year. $1095.00. H W Wilson Company, 950 University Avenue, Bronx NY 10452. **Tel** (800)367-6770, (718)588-8400, FAX (718)590-1617, telex 4990003 HWILSON. **ED** Cathy Rentschler. Index available. cum. index. ctrl circ. available on magnetic tape from WILSONTAPE; available on diskette from WILSONSEARCH; available in print.
Desc: Contains citations to articles and reviews of books, periodicals and audiovisual materials in the library and information science area. Covers such topics as automation, censorship, national and international libraries, library associations, public relations, information on brokers, and appointments and obituaries within the library community. Sources include library periodicals, general periodicals, books, conference proceedings, pamphlets, microforms, films and library school theses.

US/8755-4267
LIBRARY STATISTICS OF COLLEGES AND UNIVERSITIES IN THE PACIFIC NORTHWEST. **Added/Corp** Pacific Northwest Library Association. Academic Division. Oregon State System of Higher Education. Interinstitutional Library Council. Pacific Northwest Library Association. Academic Interest Group. **VFOAT** Library Statistics of Colleges & Universities in the Pacific Northwest. (19??)-. English. Pacific Northwest Library Association, 1631 E 24th Avenue, Eugene OR 97403. **Tel** (503)344-2027, FAX (503)341-5898. **LC** Z675.U5; L5236. **DD** 027.7/0979.

US/0094-2626
LIBRARY STATISTICS OF ILLINOIS COLLEGES AND UNIVERSITIES. (LIBRARY STATISTICS OF ILLINOIS COLLEGES AND UNIVERSITIES : INSTITUTIONAL DATA.). **Main/Corp** Illinois State Library. English. an. Illinois State Library, Centennial Building, Springfield IL 62756. **Tel** (217)782-2994. **LC** Z732.I2; I24A. **DD** 027.7/09773.
Desc: Printed every year in an issue of Illinois Libraries.

MX/0186-3738
LIBRO Y EL PUEBLO, EL. [Libro pueblo]. **Added/Corp** Mexico. Secretaria de Educacion Publica. (1922)-. Periodical. Spanish. mo.
Ind/Abst Am. Hist. Life (1966-1967).

UK/0966-8799
LISA PLUS [COMPUTER FILE]. Abstracting/Indexing Service. English. qt. £875.00. Bowker Saur Ltd., A Reed Reference Publishing Company, Part of Reed International PLC, 59-60 Grosvenor Street, London WIX 9DA England. **Tel** 011 44 71 4935841, FAX 011 44 71 4991590. available in print (Library and Information Science Abstracts; Current Research in Library and Information Science).
Desc: Incorporates Library and Information Science Abstracts and Current Research in Library and Information Science. Provides access to over 100,000 citations.

US
LIST OF ADDITIONS, A. **Main/Corp** James Ford Bell Library. (1969)-. English. University of Minnesota Press, 2037 University Avenue Southeast, Minneapolis MN 55414. **Tel** (612)642-2516, (612)624-0005. **LC** Z881; .M6794. **DD** 016.382/094. ***Continues*** *Minnesota. University. Library. James Ford Bell Collection. James Ford Bell Collection; A List of Additions.*

CN/0228-5134
LISTING OF SUPPLEMENTARY DOCUMENTS / STATISTICS CANADA, LIBRARY. [Listing suppl. doc. - Stat. Can., Libr.]. **Main/Corp** Statistics Canada. Library. **Added/Corp** Statistics Canada. Library Services Division. **VFOAT** Liste de Documents Supplementaires. (1980)-. English (French). an. 34.00Can$ Canada; $41.00 US; $48.00 other. Statistics Canada, Publications Sales & Services, Main Building Room 1710, Ottawa Ontario K1A 0T6 Canada. **Tel** (613)951-5078, (800)267-6677, FAX (613)951-1584, telex 053-3585. **LC** Z7554.C2; S7a; HA745. **DD** 016.3171.
Desc: A systematic inventory of supplementary Statistics Canada documents available to the public. Included are technical papers, memoranda, and discussion and working papers.

CN/0835-085X
LISTING OF SUPPLEMENTARY DOCUMENTS, SUPPLEMENT / STATISTICS CANADA, LIBRARY. [Listing suppl. doc. suppl. - Stat. Can., Libr.]. **Main/Corp** Statistics Canada. Library. **VFOAT** Liste de Documents Supplementaires, Supplement. **VAT** Liste de Documents Supplementaires, Supplement - Statistique Canada. Bibliotheque. (1983)-. English (French). an. 5.00Can$ Canada; $6.00 other. Statistics Canada, Publications Sales & Services, Main Building Room 1710, Ottawa Ontario K1A 0T6 Canada. **Tel** (613)951-5078, (800)267-6677, FAX (613)951-1584, telex 053-3585. **DD** 016.3171. cum. index.
Desc: Systematic inventory of supplementary documents available to the public, including technical papers, memoranda, and discussion and working papers.

HU/0025-0171
MAGYAR KONYVSZEMLE. [M. konyvszl.]. **Added/Corp** Orszagos Szechenyi Konyvtar Magyar Tudomanyos Akademia. Konyvtartudomanyi Fobizottsag. Magyar Tudomanyos Akademia. Nyelv-es Irodalomtudomanyok Osztalya. **VFOAT** Magyarorszagi Konyveszet; Hazai Idoszaki Sajto Baltozasai; Bulletin de la Revue Bibliographique Hongroise. (1876)-. Periodical. Hungarian (English, French and German; summaries and/or abstracts in Italian and Russian). qt (4 issues). $21.00 Austria, Croatia, Czech Republic, Slovakia, Romania, Yugoslavia, Slovenia and Ukraine; $26.50 other. **(Subscription address:** Kultura, PO Box 149, H 1389 Budapest 62 Hungary; telephone: 011 36 1 359370) **LC** Z1007; .M2. **NLM** Z 1007 M213.
Ind/Abst Magyar Konyv. Szak. Biblio.; Am. Hist. Life (1972-); BHA : Biblio. Hist. Art; Hungar. Libr. Info. Sci. Abstr.; MLA Int. Bibl. Books Artic. Mod. Lang. Lit.

HU/0133-736X
MAGYAR KONYVTARI SZAKIRODALOM BIBLIOGRAFIAJA, A. **VFOAT** Hungarian Library Literature. (1973)-. Abstracting/Indexing Service. Hungarian. qt. DM5.00 per issue, DM25.00 per year (includes a separate index issue). Hungarian Library and Information Science Abstracts, Orszagos Szechenyi Konyvtar, Muzeum U3 Konyvtartudomanyies, H-1827 Budapest Hungary. **Tel** 335 590. **ED** Feimer Agnes and Javori Ferencne. **UDC** 02. Index available. cum. index. **Ad Acc. Circ:** 350. available on diskette.
Desc: A quarterly bibliography of Hungarian literature on librarianship and information science, with 1,300 to 1,400 bibliographic entries annually.

US/0197-0380
MLA DIRECTORY OF PERIODICALS. (MLA DIRECTORY OF PERIODICALS: A GUIDE TO JOURNALS AND SERIES IN LANGUAGES AND LITERATURES.). [MLA dir. period.]. **Main/Corp** Modern Language Association of America. **Added/Corp** Modern Language Association of America. Directory of Periodicals. **VFOAT** Directory of Periodicals. **VAT** Modern Language Association Directory of Periodicals. (1978/1979)-. Periodical. English. be. $130.00. Modern Language Association of America, 10 Astor Place, New York NY 10003-6981. **Tel** (212)614-6382, FAX (212)477-9863. **ED** Eileen M. Mackesy and Janet G. Nottenburg. **LC** P1.A1; M62a. **DD** 016/.405. **Acid Free.**
Desc: Companion volume to MLA International Bibliography with data on 3,000 journal and series regularly searched for the bibliography.

US/0094-873X
MONTANA LIBRARY DIRECTORY, WITH STATISTICS OF MONTANA PUBLIC LIBRARIES. **VFOAT** Statistics of Montana Public Libraries. Directory. English. an. Montana State Library, 1515 East 6th Avenue, Helena MT 59620. **Tel** 444-5349, FAX 444-5612. **LC** Z732.M9; M63. **DD** 021/.0025/786. **Pr Rev. Circ:** 450. ***Continues*** *Statistics of Montana Public Libraries, 0735-7818.*
Desc: Vols. for 1974 include statistical data for the preceding fiscal year.

US/0093-9676
NATIONAL UNION CATALOG. MOTION PICTURES AND FILMSTRIPS. ***Title Change.*** (THE NATIONAL UNION CATALOG; A CUMULATIVE AUTHOR LIST REPRESENTING LIBRARY OF CONGRESS PRINTED CARDS AND TITLES REPORTED BY OTHER AMERICAN LIBRARIES. MOTION PICTURES AND FILMSTRIPS.). **Added/Corp** American Library Association. Resources and Technical Services Division. Resources Committee. Library of Congress. **VFOAT** Library of Congress Catalog. Motion Pictures and Filmstrips; Motion Pictures and Filmstrips. (1953)-(19??). Periodical. English. ir. Library of Congress / Cataloging Distribution Service, Washington DC 20541-5017. **Tel** (800)255-3666, (202)707-6100, FAX (202)707-1334. **NLM** Z 881 U579c. ***Continues*** *Library of Congress Author Catalog. Films.* ***Continued by*** *Library of Congress Catalog. Motion Pictures and Filmstrips.*
Desc: Constitutes the quinquennial cumulation of the national union catalog ... Motion pictures and filmstrips.

US
NEVADA LIBRARY DIRECTORY AND STATISTICS. Directory. English. an. free. Nevada State Library, Library Development Division, Capitol Complex, Carson City NV 89710. **Tel** (702)887-2616, FAX (702)887-2630. **LC** Z732.N38; N4. **DD** 027/.0025/793. Index available. ctrl circ. ***Continues*** *Statistics with Directory of Nevada Libraries and Library Personnel.*
Desc: Lists of all libraries library personnelin Nevada giving addresses and telephone numbers. Gives latest fiscal year data from libraries.

US/0749-0313
NEW HAMPSHIRE LIBRARY STATISTICS. 1965-. English. an. New Hampshire State Library, 20 Park Street, Concord NH 03301. **Tel** (603)271-2394. **LC** Z733; .N49124. **DD** 027.0742. ***Continues*** *Library Statistics.*

US/0278-9329
NEW MEXICO LIBRARY STATISTICS. English. an. New Mexico State Library, 325 Don Gaspar, Santa Fe NM 87503. **Tel** (505)827-3800, FAX (505)827-3888. **LC** Z675.S7; N485. **DD** 027.5789.

US/0090-0605
NORTH AMERICAN LIBRARY EDUCATION DIRECTORY AND STATISTICS. **Main/Corp** Indiana. University. Graduate Library School. 1971/73-. Directory. English. Indiana Unviersity, Graduate Library School, Bloomington IN. **LC** Z668; .A584A. **DD** 020/.711/73. **NLM** Z 668 N864. ***Continues*** *North American Library Education Directory and Statistics, 0090-0605.*

US/0094-5455
NORTH DAKOTA ACADEMIC LIBRARY STATISTICS. **Main/Corp** North Dakota. State Library Commission. English. an. **LC** Z732.N9; N925 subser. **DD** 021/.009784 S; 027.7/09784.

CN/0702-0260
PERIODICALS AND NEWSPAPERS IN THE COLLECTIONS OF THE LIBRARY OF PARLIAMENT. **Main/Corp** Canada. Library of Parliament. **VFOAT** Revues et Journaux dans les Collections de la Bibliotheque du Parlement. 1977-. English (French). an. Library of Parliament / Information & Technical Services Branch, Ottawa Ontario K1A 0A9 Canada. **Tel** (613)996-3121. **ED** C Sutherland. **LC** Z6945; .C17915A; PN4731. **DD** 016.05. **Circ:** 400 (ctrl). ***Continues*** *Periodicals and Newspapers in the Library of Parliament, 0319-5945.*
Desc: Internal union list of library's periodical and newspaper holdings.

AT
PUBLIC LIBRARIES IN QUEENSLAND, STATISTICAL BULLETIN. Began with issue for 1968/72. Statistical Publication. English. an. $2.95. Library Board of Queensland, William Street, Brisbane Queensland 4000 Australia. **LC** Z870.Q44; P8. **DD** 027.4/943.

UK/0307-0522
PUBLIC LIBRARY STATISTICS ... ESTIMATES. English. an. £6.00. Chartered Institute of Public Finance and Accountancy, 2 3 Robert Street, London WC2N 6BH England. **Tel** 011 44 1 895 8823. **LC** Z791.A1; P82. **DD** 027.441.

GW
PUBLISHING BIBLIOGRAPHY LIBRARIES AND ARCHIVES IN RUSSIA AND EASTERN EUROPE. (19??)-. Bibliography. English. ir. Otto Harrassowitz Verlag, Taunusstrasse 14, Postfach 2929, D-65019 Wiesbaden Germany. **Tel** 011 49 611 5300, FAX 530570, telex 4186 135 OH D.

US/1058-1219
READERS' GUIDE ABSTRACTS (SCHOOL AND PUBLIC LIBRARY ED.). ***Title Change.*** (READERS' GUIDE ABSTRACTS.). [Read. guide abstr.]. Pt. 1 (Aug. 1991/Jan. 1992)-(199?). Abstracting/Indexing Service. English. sa. H W Wilson Company, 950 University Avenue, Bronx NY 10452. **Tel** (800)367-6770, (718)588-8400, FAX (718)590-1617, telex 4990003 HWILSON. **DD** 051. cum. index. ***Continues*** *Reader's Guide Abstracts (Print Ed. : Semiannual), 0899-1553.* ***Continued by*** *Readers' Guide Abstracts Select Edition.*

AT
REFERENCE SERVICES BIBLIOGRAPHIES. **Main/Corp** South Australia. State Library. Reference Services Branch. English. **LC** Z1009; .S74A; Z7964.A8; HQ1822. **DD** 011. ***Supersedes*** *State Library of South Australia. Research Services Branch. Research Service Bibliographie.*

US
RESEARCH ALERT. (19??)-. Abstracting/Indexing Service. English. wk. $330.00 other. Institute for Scientific Information, 3501 Market Street, Philadelphia PA 19104. **Tel** (215)386-0100, (800)523-1850, FAX (215)386-6362, telex 84-5305. **(Subscription address:** Institute for Scientific Information, PO Box 71416, Chicago IL 60694.) available on magnetic tape from Institute for Scientific Information. ***Continues*** *Ascatopics, 0730-8574.*
Desc: A weekly customized journal article alerting service that reports the most recent articles on a wide range of subjects, including: agriculture, food & veterinary

sciences, biotechnology, chemistry, economics, engineering & technology, environmental sciences, life sciences, medicine, pharmacology & medicinal chemistry, physics, and social & behavioral sciences.

PO/0251-1711
REVISTA DA BIBLIOTECA NACIONAL (LISBOA). (REVISTA DA BIBLIOTECA NACIONAL.). [Rev. Bibl. Nac.]. **Added/Corp** Biblioteca Nacional (Portugal). Vol. 1, No. 1 (Jan./June 1981)-. Periodical. Portuguese. Twice a year. $18.00. Biblioteca Nacional de Lisboa, Campo Grande 83, 1751 Lisbon Codex Portugal. **Tel** 011 351 1 767786, FAX 7933607, telex 62803. **LC** Z946.L72; R48. **DD** 011/.34. **Ad Acc.**
Desc: Portuguese culture, bibliographies and librarianship.
Ind/Abst Libr. Inf. Sci. Abstr.

US/1057-8188
RSAP NEWSLETTER. [RSAP newsl.]. **Added/Corp** Research Society for American Periodicals. **VFOAT** Research Society for American Periodicals Newsletter. (1990)-. Newsletter. English. sa. $5.00. Research Society for American Periodicals (RSAP), Box 5096, University of North Texas, Denton TX 76203. **Tel** (817)565-2134. **ED** James T. F. Tanner. **DD** 051. **Circ:** 300. available in Loose-leaf.
Desc: Includes society information and recent publications dealing with periodicals research.

SZ
SCHWEIZERISCHE BIBLIOTHEKEN. **Main/Corp** Switzerland. Bundesamt fur Statistik. **VFOAT** Bibliotheques Suisses. French (German). 4.00F. Bundesamt fuer Statistik, Schwarztorstrasse 96, CH 3003 Bern Switzerland. **Tel** 031 3236011, FAX 031 3236061. **LC** Z837.A1; S35.

US
SOUTH CAROLINA PUBLIC LIBRARY ANNUAL STATISTICAL SUMMARY. **Added/Corp** South Carolina State Library. University of South Carolina. College of Librarianship. **VFOAT** Public Library Annual Statistical Summary. (1980)-. Statistical Publication. English. an. South Carolina State Library / Reference Department, 1500 Senate Street, PO Box 11469, Columbia SC 29211. **Tel** (803)734-8666, FAX (803)734-8676. **LC** Z732.S72; S587. **DD** 027.0757. ctrl circ.

AT/0729-199X
STATISTICAL BULLETIN FOR PUBLIC LIBRARIES IN WESTERN AUSTRALIA. **Added/Corp** Library Board of Western Australia. Issue No. 1 (1980/81)-. Statistical Publication. English. an. 10.00Aus$ prepaid (add 10.00Aus$ postage if not prepaid). Library and Information Service of Western Australia, Alexander Library Building, Perth Cultural Centre, Perth 6000 Australia. **Tel** (09)427-3111, FAX (09)427 3256, telex WAINF. **LC** Z870.W4; S82. **DD** 027.4941. **Circ:** 500 (ctrl).
Desc: Statistical information on public libraries in Western Australia.

US/0733-2041
STATISTICS OF PUBLIC SCHOOL LIBRARIES / MEDIA CENTERS. [Stat. public sch. libr./media cent.]. **Added/Corp** National Center for Education Statistics. (Fall 1974)-. English. ir. National Center for Education Statistics / US Department of Education, 555 New Jersey Avenue NW, Washington DC 20208-5651. **LC** Z675.S3; S747. **DD** 027.8/0973.

US
STATISTICS OF SOUTH DAKOTA LIBRARIES. **Main/Corp** South Dakota State Library. 1975-. English. ir. Free. South Dakota State Library, 800 Governors Drive, Pierre SD 57501. **Tel** (605)773-3131, FAX (605)773-4950. **ED** Dorothy M Liegl and Donna Gilliland. **LC** Z732.S9; S64A. **DD** 027/.0783. **Circ:** 800 (ctrl).
Desc: Includes statistics on circulation, holdings, and fiscal support/expenditures for public, school, and academic libraries in South Dakota.

US/0099-0655
STATISTICS OF SOUTH DAKOTA PUBLIC LIBRARIES. **Main/Corp** South Dakota State Library Commission. English. ir. Free. South Dakota State Library, 800 Governors Drive, Pierre SD 57501. **Tel** (605)773-3131, FAX (605)773-4950. **ED** Dorothy M Liegl and Jerome Wagner. **LC** Z732.S9; S58A. **DD** 027.4/783. ctrl circ.

US/0731-8464
STATISTICS OF VIRGINIA PUBLIC LIBRARIES AND INSTITUTIONAL LIBRARIES. 1975-76-. English. an. Virginia State Library, 11th and Capital Streets, Richmond VA 23219. **LC** Z732.V8; V83A. **DD** 027.4755. ***Continues*** *Statistics of Virginia Public Libraries, 0095-3490.*

NE/0168-3462
STATISTIEK VAN DE OPENBARE BIBLIOTHEKEN / CENTRAAL BUREAU VOOR DE STATISTIEK, HOOFDAFDELING SOCIAAL-CULTURELE STATISTIEKEN. **VFOAT** Statistics on Public Libraries. Dutch. an. Fl25.00. Centraal Bureau voor de Statistiek, AFD ALG Zaken, Postbus 959, 2270 AZ Voorburg Netherlands. **Tel** 011 31 70 3373800, FAX 011 31 038 7429, telex 32692 CBS NL. **LC** Z815.A1; S73.

GW
STATISTIK DER KOMMUNALEN OFFENTLICHEN BIBLIOTHEKEN DER BUNDESREPUBLIK, REGIONALSTATISTIK. **Main/Corp** Deutscher Bibliotheksverband (Germany : West). Arbeitsstelle fur das Bibliothekswesen. **Added/Corp** Deutscher Bibliotheksverband (Germany : West). Arbeitsstelle fur das Bibliothekswesen. Gesamtstatistik. **VFOAT** Gesamtstatistik. (19??)-. German. an. Fehrbelliner Platz 3, 1000 Berlin W-31 Germany. **LC** Z801.A1; D483b.

GW
STATISTISCHE UBERSICHTEN FUER DAS JAHR (UNIVERSITAT KIEL. INSTITUTS FUR WELTWIRTSCHAFT. BIBLIOTHEK). (STATISTISCHE UEBERSICHTEN FUER DAS JAHR / BIBLIOTHEK DES INSTITUTS FUER WELTWIRTSCHAFT AN DER UNIVERSITAET KIEL.). **Added/Corp** Universitat Kiel. Institut fuer Weltwirtschaft. Bibliothek. (19??)-. German. an. Bibliothek des Instituts fuer Weltwirtschaft an der Universitaet Kiel, Dusternbrooker WEG 120, Postfach 4309, W-2300 Kiel 1 Germany. **Tel** 0431 884-7, telex 292479. **LC** Z802.K54; K54a. **DD** 027.743/3. **Circ:** 300 (ctrl). ***Continues*** *Universitaet Kiel. Institut fuer Weltwirtschaft. Bibliothek. Statistische Uebersichten und Bericht.*

US/0000-0140
SUBJECT COLLECTIONS. [Subj. collect.]. **Added/Corp** R.R. Bowker Company. (1958)-. English. ir. $275.00. R R Bowker, A Reed Reference Publishing Company, Part of Reed International PLC, PO Box 31, 121 Chanlon Drive, New Providence NJ 07974. **Tel** (908)464-6800, (800)521-8110, FAX (908)665-6688, telex 138-755. **ED** Lee Ash and William G. Miller.
Desc: Entries for more than 18,000 collections in over 11,000 academic, public, and special libraries and museums are indexed and cross-referenced under 37,000 LC subject headings, and provide full contact and descriptive information.

US/0082-3120
TEXAS PUBLIC LIBRARY STATISTICS. (TEXAS PUBLIC LIBRARY STATISTICS FOR ...). **Added/Corp** Texas State Library. Field Services Division. Texas State Library. Dept. of Library Development. Texas State Library. Library Development Division. (1968)-. English. an. Free on request. Texas State Library Clearinghouse, PO Box 12927, Capitol Station, Austin TX 78711. **Tel** (512)463-5435, FAX (512)463-5436. **LC** Z732.T25; T38. **DD** 027.4764. ***Continues*** *Texas Public Library Statistics, 0082-3120.*
Ind/Abst Stat. Ref. Index.

US/0098-7816
UNIVERSITY AND COLLEGE LIBRARIES. (STATISTICS OF NORTH CAROLINA UNIVERSITY AND COLLEGE LIBRARIES / COMPILED BY DIVISION OF STATE LIBRARY, NORTH CAROLINA DEPARTMENT OF CULTURAL RESOURCES.). [Univ. coll. libr.]. **Added/Corp** North Carolina. Division of State Library. (1963/1964)-. English. an. NC Department of Cultural Resources, Division of State Library, 109 East Jones Street, Raleigh NC 27611. **LC** Z732.N8; U5. **DD** 027.7/09756. ***Continues in part*** *Statistics of North Carolina Public Libraries, University and College Libraries, Special Libraries.*

US
WASHINGTON PUBLIC LIBRARY STATISTICS / WASHINGTON STATE LIBRARY. **Added/Corp** Washington State Library. **VFOAT** Public Library Statistics. (1991)-. English. Washington State University / Library, Washington Library Network AJ-11W, Olympia WA 98504. **LC** Z732.W28; A57. ***Continues*** *Washington Libraries. Public Library Statistics.*

GW/0936-0085
WORLD GUIDE TO LIBRARIES. 9th Ed. (1989)-. English (German). ir. $350.00. K.G. Saur Verlag KG, A Reed Reference Publishing Company, Part of Reed International PLC, Ortlerstrasse 8, D 81373 Munich Germany. **Tel** 011 49 89 769020, FAX 011 49 89 76902150, telex 5212067-SAUR-D. **(Subscription address:** Reed Reference Publishing Company / New Jersey, 131 Chanlaon Road, PO Box 31, New Providence NJ 07974.**) ED** Helga Lengenfelder. **LC** Z721; .I63. **DD** 027/.0025. **NLM** Z 721; I64. ***Continues*** *Internationales Bibliotheks-Handbuch, 0000-0221.*
Desc: Lists more than 40,000 institutions in 167 countries. Included are national, federal, regional, university and other academic, school, and public libraries that possess over 30,000 volumes.

GW/0724-8717
WORLD GUIDE TO SPECIAL LIBRARIES. **VFOAT** Internationales Handbuch der Spezialbibliotheken. 1st Ed. (1983)-. English. ir. $325.00. K.G. Saur Verlag KG, A Reed Reference Publishing Company, Part of Reed International PLC, Ortlerstrasse 8, D 81373 Munich Germany. **Tel** 011 49 89 769020, FAX 011 49 89 76902150, telex 5212067-SAUR-D. **ED** Helga Lengenfelder. **NLM** Z 675.A2; W927.
Desc: Includes entries for more than 32,000 libraries in 160 countries that are divided into five major categories: general, humanities, social sciences, medicine and life sciences, and science and technology.

LINGUISTICS

AT/0001-2793
A.U.M.L.A. (A.U.M.L.A. : JOURNAL OF THE AUSTRALASIAN UNIVERSITIES MODERN LANGUAGE ASSOCIATION.). [A.U.M.L.A.]. **Added/Corp** Australasian Universities Modern Language Association. Australasian Universities Language and Literature Association. **VFOAT** AUMLA. No. 1 (Aug. 1953)-. Periodical. English (summaries and/or abstracts in French and German). Twice a year (May, Nov.). 34.00Aus$. AUMLA, University of Sydney, Department of French SEC, Sydney NSW 2006 Australia. **Tel** 011 61 2 6922397. **ED** J. Hay. **LC** PB1; .A2. **DD** 410/.5. **Bk Rev. Ad Acc. Pr Rev. Circ:** 1,300 (ctrl). Documents available from The Genuine Article.
Desc: A journal of literary criticism, philology and linguistics.
Ind/Abst Abstr. Engl. Stud.; Annu. Bibliogr. Engl. Lang. Lit.; APAIS, Aust. Public Aff. Inf. Ser. (1973-); Arts Humanit. Citation Index [Full Cov.]; Curr. Contents Arts Humanit.; MLA Int. Bibl. Books Artic. Mod. Lang. Lit.; Res. Alert [Full Cov.].

AU/0171-5410
AAA, ARBEITEN AUS ANGLISTIK UND AMERIKANISTIK. [AAA, Arb. Angl. Am.]. **Added/Corp** Universitat Graz. Institut fur Englische Philologie. Universitat Graz. Institut fur Amerikanistik. Universitat Graz. Institut fur Anglistik. **VFOAT** Arbeiten aus Anglistik und Amerikanistik. No. 1 (1976)-. German (English). sa. DM74.00. Gunter Narr Verlag, Dishingerweg 5, D 72070 Tuebingen Germany. **Tel** 011 49 7071 78091, FAX (07071)75288. **ED** Bernhard Kettemann. **LC** PE3; .A16. **[CCC]**. Index available. **Bk Rev. Ad Acc. Circ:** 750 (ctrl). Documents available from The Genuine Article.
Desc: Studies of English and American studies, including language, literature and civilization.
Ind/Abst Annu. Bibliogr. Engl. Lang. Lit.; Arts Humanit. Citation Index [Full Cov.]; MLA Int. Bibl. Books Artic. Mod. Lang. Lit.; Res. Alert [Full Cov.].

US/0883-6795
AATF NATIONAL BULLETIN. (AATF NATIONAL BULLETIN / AMERICAN ASSOCIATION OF TEACHERS OF FRENCH.). [AATF natl. bull.]. **Added/Corp** American Association of Teachers of French. **VAT** American Association of Teachers of French National Bulletin. (19??)-. Bulletin. English (French). ir. American Association of Teachers of French, National Office, 57 East Armory Avenue, Champaign IL 61820. **ED** Jane Black Goepper. **DD** 847. **Circ:** 12,000 (ctrl).
Desc: Offers news of the profession, announcements and short articles of cultural and pedagogical interest.

US
AATSEEL'S NEWSLETTER / AMERICAN ASSOCIATION OF TEACHERS OF SLAVIC AND EAST EUROPEAN LANGUAGES. **See** Education.

US
AATSP PORTUGUESE NATIONAL NEWSLETTER. **Main/Corp** American Association of Teachers of Spanish and Portuguese. **VFOAT** Portuguese National Newsletter. Newsletter. English. North Carolina State University / Foreign Language, Department of Foreign Languages and Literatures, Box 5156, Raleigh NC 27650.

LH/0567-4980
ABHANDLUNGEN FUER DIE KUNDE DES MORGENLANDES / HRSG. VON DER DEUTSCHEN MORGENLANDISCHEN GESELLSCHAFT. **Main/Corp** Deutsche Morgenlandische Gesellschaft. Vol. No. 1 (1859)-. Monographic series. German. ir. Price varies per volume. Franz Steiner Verlag GmbH, Postfach 101061, D 70009 Stuttgart Germany. **Tel** 011 49 0711 2582372, FAX 011 49 0711 2582290, telex 723636 daz d. **ED** Tilman Nagel.
Desc: Monographs dedicated to Oriental and African languages and literatures.

GW/0178-8515
ABHANDLUNGEN ZUR SPRACHE UND LITERATUR. **See** Literature.

NE/0065-0382
ABR-NAHRAIN. **See** Religion and Theology-Bible.

UK/0955-4270
ACIS : JOURNAL OF THE ASSOCIATION FOR CONTEMPORARY IBERIAN STUDIES. Added/Corp Association for Contemporary Iberian Studies. **VFOAT** Journal of the Association for Contemporary Iberian Studies. Vol. 1, No. 1 (Spring 1988)-. Periodical. English (Spanish and Portuguese). Twice a year. £20.00. Association for Contemporary Iberian Studies, East Road, Anglia Polytechnic University, Cambridge CB1 1PT England. **Tel** 011 44 223 63271. **(Subscription address:** P. Bangs Language Centre, South Bank University, 103 Borough Road, London SE1 0AA England**) ED** F. Ariza. **Bk Rev. Ad Acc. Pr Rev. Circ:** 300 (ctrl).
Desc: Covers geography, history of Europe, international economics, conservation, teaching, linguistics, sociology, etc.

II/0157-6283
ACLALS BULLETIN. ***Ceased.*** **See** Literature.

CK
ACOPEL. Main/Corp Asociacion Colombiana de Profesores de Espanol Y Literatura a Nivel Superior. No. 1- Nov. 1971-. Spanish. Calle 31 No 83B-150, Medellin Colombia. **LC** PC4018; .A6813. **DD** 460/.5.

US/0270-4404
ACRONYMS, INITIALISMS & ABBREVIATIONS DICTIONARY. [Acron. initial. abbrev. dict.]. **Added/Corp** Gale Research Company. **VFOAT** Acronyms, Initialisms, and Abbreviations Dictionary. 5th Ed. (1976)-. English. ir. $245.00 (Volume 1), $220.00 (Volume 2), $280.00 (Volume 3). Gale Research Inc., 835 Penobscot Building, Detroit MI 48226. **Tel** (800)877-GALE, (313)961-2242, FAX (313)961-6083, telex TWX 810-221-7086. **ED** Jennifer Mossman. **LC** P365; .A28. **DD** 423/.1. **NLM** PE 1693 A179. ***Continues*** *Acronyms and Initialisms Dictionary, 0065-0889.*
Desc: Contains definitions of a wide variety of acronyms, initialisms, abbreviations, and similar contractions.

HU/0044-5975
ACTA ANTIQUA ACADEMIAE SCIENTIARUM HUNGARICAE. [Acta ant. Acad. Sci. Hung.]. **Added/Corp** Magyar Tudomanyos Akademia. **VFOAT** Acta Antiqua. Vol. 1 (1951)-. Academic Scholarly Publication. English (Russian, French and German). Four times a year. $98.00. Akademiai Kiado, Publishing House of the Hungarian Academy of Sciences, Prielle Kornelia u. 19-35, H-1117 Budapest Hungary. **Tel** 011 36 1 1811991, FAX 011 36 1 1811991, telex 22-6228 AKNYO H. **ED** Janos Harmatta. **LC** CC1; .A19. **[CCC]. Bk Rev. Ad Acc. Circ:** 750.
Desc: Publishes original articles in the field of classical philology. Covers history, literature, philology and material culture of the Ancient East, the Classical Antiquity and Byzantium.
Ind/Abst MLA Int. Bibl. Books Artic. Mod. Lang. Lit.; Numis. Lit.

SZ/0065-1273
ACTA GERMANICA. [Acta Ger.]. **Added/Corp** Sudafrikanischer Germanistenverband. Germanistenverband im Sudlichen Afrika. (1966)-. Multiple languages (English). ir. Price varies per volume. Verlag Peter Lang AG, Jupiterstrasse 15, CH-3000 Bern 15 Switzerland. **Tel** 011 41 31 9411122, FAX 011 41 31 321131. **LC** PF3010; .A27.
Desc: German and Dutch philology.
Ind/Abst MLA Int. Bibl. Books Artic. Mod. Lang. Lit.

DK/0374-0463
ACTA LINGUISTICA HAFNIENSIA / PUBLISHED UNDER THE AUSPICES OF THE LINGUISTIC CIRCLE OF COPENHAGEN. [Acta linguist. Hafn.]. **Added/Corp** Lingvistkredsen (Copenhagen, Denmark). Vol. 9, No. 1 (1965)-. Periodical. English (German and French). an. kr400.00 Denmark; kr574.00 other. CA Reitzels Forlag AS, Norregade 20, DK-1165 Copenhagen K Denmark. **Tel** 011 45 3 3122400. **LC** P2; .A3. **DD** 410/.5. ***Continues*** *Acta Linguistica, 0105-001X.*
Ind/Abst Annu. Bibliogr. Engl. Lang. Lit.; Lang. Teach.; Linguist. Lang. Behav. Abstr. (1973-) [Full Cov.]; Middle East Abstr. Index; MLA Int. Bibl. Books Artic. Mod. Lang. Lit.; Soc. Plann. Policy Dev. Abstr.; Sociol. Abstr.

HU/1216-8076
ACTA LINGUISTICA HUNGARICA. Added/Corp Akademiai Kiado. Vol. 38, No. 1-4 (1988)-. Academic Scholarly Publication. English (French and German). qt. $92.00. Akademiai Kiado, Publishing House of the Hungarian Academy of Sciences, Prielle Kornelia u. 19-35, H-1117 Budapest Hungary. **Tel** 011 36 1 1811991, FAX 011 36 1 1811991, telex 22-6228 AKNYO H. **CODEN** ALHUE8. ***Continues*** *Acta Linguistica Academiae Scientiarum Hungaricae, 0001-5946.*

DK/0001-6438
ACTA ORIENTALIA (KBENHAVN). (ACTA ORIENTALIA.). [Acta orient.]. Vol. 1 (1922)-. English. an. kr450.00. Munksgaard International Publishers Ltd, PO Box 2148, DK-1016 Copenhagen K Denmark. **Tel** 011 45 33 12 70 30, FAX 011 45 33 12 93 87, telex 19431 MUNKS DK. **ED** Soren Egerod. **LC** PJ1; .A4. **UDC** 809.5-012. **[CCC].** Index available. **Bk Rev. Circ:** 500 (ctrl). ***Absorbed*** *Monde Oriental.*
Desc: Devoted to the studies of the languages, history, archaeology and religions of the Orient.
Ind/Abst Index Islam. Lit.; Index Book Rev. Relig.; Middle East Abstr. Index; MLA Int. Bibl. Books Artic. Mod. Lang. Lit.; Middle East J.

PL/0065-1524
ACTA PHILOLOGICA. Added/Corp Warsaw. Uniwersytet. Wydzi Filologiczny. Warsaw. Universytet. Wydzial Filologii Obcych. (1968)-. Polish (summaries and/or abstracts in English). **LC** P19; .A4.
Ind/Abst Annu. Bibliogr. Engl. Lang. Lit.

HU/0567-8099
ACTA ROMANICA (SZEGED). (ACTA UNIVERSITATIS SZEGEDIENSIS DE ATTILA JOZSEF NOMINATAE. ACTA ROMANICA.). [Acta Rom.]. **Added/Corp** Jozsef Attila Tudomanyegyetem. **VFOAT** Acta Romanica. (1972)-. Periodical. French (Italian). ***Continues in part*** *Acta Universitatis Szegediensis. ActaGermanica et Romanica.*
Ind/Abst MLA Int. Bibl. Books Artic. Mod. Lang. Lit.

BL/0102-4264
ACTA SEMIOTICA ET LINGUISTICA. [Acta semiot. linguist.]. **Added/Corp** Sociedade Brasileira para Professores de Linguistica. Vol. 1 (1977)-. Periodical. English (French, Portuguese and Spanish). sa. **LC** P1.A1; A27. **DD** 410/.5.
Ind/Abst MLA Int. Bibl. Books Artic. Mod. Lang. Lit.

JA/0387-8082
ACTA SUMEROLOGICA. Added/Corp Hiroshima Daigaku. Dept. of Linguistics. Japanese Sumerological Society. Chukinto Bunka Senta (Japan). **VFOAT** A.S.J.; ASJ. No. 1 (1979)-. Periodical. English (French and German). Twice a year. $80.00. **(Subscription address:** Maruzen Company Ltd., PO Box 5050, Import & Export Department, Tokyo 100 31 Japan.**) LC** PJ4001; .A28. **DD** 499/.95.

XR/0567-8269
ACTA UNIVERSITATIS CAROLINAE. PHILOLOGICA. Added/Corp Universita Karlova. (1958)-. English (German and English; summaries and/or abstracts in Czech and Russian). ir. Price varies. Carolinum Press, Ovochny TRH 5, 11636 Prague 1 Czech Republic. **Tel** 011 42 2 228441. **LC** P9; .A24. ***Supersedes in part*** *Acta Universitatis Carolinae.*
Ind/Abst Soc. Plann. Policy Dev. Abstr.; Sociol. Abstr. (?-?).

FI
ACTA UNIVERSITATIS TAMPERENSIS. SER. A. See Literature.

PL/0137-1169
ACTA UNIVERSITATIS WRATISLAVIENSIS. STUDIA LINGUISTICA. Added/Corp Uniwersytet Wrocawski im. Bolesawa Bieruta. Wydzia Filologiczny. **VFOAT** Studia Linguistica. (1974)-. Monographic series. Polish (summaries and/or abstracts in English, French and German). Z20.00 single issue. **(Subscription address:** ARS Polona, PO Box 1001, 00068 Warsaw Poland.**) LC** P25; .S66.
Ind/Abst Curr. Contents Arts Humanit.

CN
ACTES. / ASSOCIATION CANADIENNE DE LINGUISTIQUE APPLIQUEE. Main/Corp Canadian Association of Applied Linguistics. Meeting. **Added/Corp** Universite Laval. Centre International de Recherches sur le Bilinguisme. **VFOAT** Actes; Proceedings. (19??)-. English (French and German). an. 16.00Can$. Actes de Association, Universite of Montreal, Sec de Lacla CP 6128, Montreal Quebec H3C 357 Canada. **Tel** (418)656-3232. **LC** P51; .C338a. **DD** 418/.007. **Bk Rev. Ad Acc. Circ:** 600 (ctrl).
Desc: Text on applied linguistics, teaching of English and French as second languages and translations.

US/0147-1236
ACTFL FOREIGN LANGUAGE EDUCATION SERIES, THE. [ACTFL foreign lang. educ. ser.]. **Main/Corp** American Council on the Teaching of Foreign Languages. **Added/Corp** American Council on the Teaching of Foreign Languages. **VFOAT** Foreign Language Education Series. **VAT** American Council on the Teaching of Foreign Languages Foreign Language Education Series. Vol. 8 (1976)-. Monographic series. English. ir. Price varies per volume. National Textbook Company, 4255 West Touhy Avenue, Lincolnwood IL 60646. **Tel** (708)679-5500, (800)323-4900, FAX (708)679-2494, telex TWX 9102230736. **ED** Patricia A. Westphal, Alan Garfinkel, Maurice W. Conner, David P. Benseler, Reid E. Baker, Renate A. Schulz, Robert C. Lafayette, and Frank M. Grittner. **LC** P10; .B7. **DD** 410. ***Continues*** *ACTFL Review of Foreign Languages Education, 0091-2476.*

CN/0001-7779
ACTUALITE TERMINOLOGIQUE. Added/Corp Canada. Bureau des Traductions. Direction Generale de la Terminologie et de la Documentation. Canada. Bureau des Traductions. Centre de Terminologie. Vol. 1 (Jan. 1968)-. Periodical. French (English). Twelve times a year. Canada Communication Group Publishers, Order Processing, Ottawa Ontario K1A 0S9 Canada. **Tel** (819)956-4800, (819)956-4802.

SJ
ADAB (JAMIAT AL-KHARTUM. KULLIYAT AL-ADAB). (ADAB : MAJALLAT KULLIYAT AL-ADAB, JAMIAT AL-KHARTUM.). No. 4 (1981)-. Periodical. Arabic. an. Adab: Majallat Kulliyar Al-Adab, Jamiat Al-Khartum, Sudan. **LC** PJ6001; .K48A. ***Continues*** *Majallat Kulliyat Al-Adab.*

US
ADDRESSES AND DISCUSSIONS PRESENTED AT THE ... ANNUAL READING CONFERENCE / CONDUCTED BY THE SCHOOL OF EDUCATION, UNIVERSITY OF SOUTH CAROLINA. Main/Conf Reading Conference (University of South Carolina). (1960)-. Periodical. English. an. University of South Carolina / School of Education, Columbia SC 29208. **LC** LB1050; .R4. **DD** 428.4.

US/0001-0898
ADE BULLETIN. [ADE bull.]. **Main/Corp** Association of Departments of English. **VAT** Association of Departments of English Bulletin. (19??)-. Bulletin. English. Three times a year (Apr., Sept., Dec.). $21.00 (individuals); $30.00 (institutions). Association of the Departments of English, A Subsidiary of the Modern Language Association, 10 Astor Place, New York NY 10003. **Tel** (212)614-6321. **ED** David Laurence. **LC** PE68.U5; A86a. **Bk Rev**, (Qty: 9). **Ad Acc, Adv Mgr:** Stephen Olsen, **Tel** (212)614-6317. Full Page (Color) $160.00. Half Page (Color) $90.00. **Acid Free. Circ:** 2,000. available on microfilm and microfiche from University Microfilms International (UMI).
Desc: Publishes articles on developments in scholarship, curriculum, and teaching in English studies.
Ind/Abst Curr. Index J. Educ.; MLA Int. Bibl. Books Artic. Mod. Lang. Lit.

US/0148-7639
ADFL BULLETIN. [ADFL bull.]. **Main/Corp** Association of Departments of Foreign Languages (U.S.). **Added/Corp** Association of Departments of Foreign Languages (U.S.) Bulletin. **VAT** Association of Departments of Foreign Languages Bulletin. Vol. 8 (Sept. 1976)-. Periodical. English. Three times a year (Jan., Apr., Sept.). $30.00 (institution), $21.00 (individual); $100.00 (one year). Association of Departments of Foreign Languages, A Subsidiary of the Modern Language Association, 10 Astor Place, New York NY 10003. **Tel** (212)614-6321, FAX (212)477-9863. **ED** Elizabeth Welles. **LC** P57.U7; A77a. **DD** 405. Index available. cum. index. **Bk Rev**, (Qty: 6). **Ad Acc.** Full Page (Color) $150.00. Half Page (Color) $85.00. **Pr Rev. Acid Free. Circ:** 1,870. available on microfilm and microfiche from University Microfilms International (UMI). ***Continues*** *Bulletin of the Association of Departments of Foreign Languages, 0148-8066.*
Desc: Concerned with professional and pedagogical matters relating to language teaching in colleges and universities.
Ind/Abst Curr. Index J. Educ.; MLA Int. Bibl. Books Artic. Mod. Lang. Lit.

●NE
ADVANCES IN CONSCIOUSNESS RESEARCH. (1995)-. Monographic series. English. ir. Price varies per volume. John Benjamins BV, Amsteldijk 44, PO Box 75577, 1070 AN Amsterdam Netherlands. **Tel** 011 31 20 6738156, FAX 011 31 20 739773. **(Subscription address:** John Benjamins North America, PO Box 27519, Philadelphia PA 19118-0519.**) ED** Maxim I. Stamenov and Gordon G. Globus.
Desc: Interdisciplinary series of monographs that provides a forum for the study of consciousness. The series brings together insights from psychology, anthropology, linguistics, neuroscience, cognitive science and philosophy to develop integrative approaches for investigation of the phenomena of consciousness.

US/0896-470X
ADVANCES IN DISCOURSE PROCESSES. [Adv. discourse process.]. Vol. 2 (1979)-. Monographic series. English. ir. Price varies per volume. Ablex Publishing Corporation, 355 Chestnut Street, Norwood NJ 07648. **Tel** (201)767-8450, (201)767-8455 (Customer Service), FAX (201)767-6717. **ED** Roy Freedle. **LC** UNC. **DD** 400. ***Continues*** *Discourse Processes: Advances in Research and Theory, 0164-0224.*
Desc: Book series of monographs and edited volumes on all aspects of discourse analysis.

US/0963-5580
ADVANCES IN SPEECH, HEARING, AND LANGUAGE PROCESSING. [Adv. speech hear. lang. process.]. Vol. 1 (1990)-. Periodical. English. an. $73.25. JAI Press Inc., 55 Old Post Road, Suite 2, PO Box 1678, Greenwich CT 06836-1678. **Tel** (203)661-7602, FAX (203)661-0792. **LC** TK7882.S65; A285; TK7882.S65; .A37. **DD** 612.39/9. **NLM** W1; AD873HK.

TU
AEGEAN JOURNAL OF LANGUAGE AND LITERATURE. **VFOAT** Ege Bat Dilleri Ve Edebiyat Dergisi. Periodical. English. Ege Universitesi / Faculty of Letters, Faculty of Letters, Bornova Izmir Turkey. **LC** PB5; .A4. **DD** 809/.005.

IT/0001-9593
AEVUM. [Aevum]. **Added/Corp** Universita Cattolica del Sacro Cuore. Facolta di Lettere e Filosofia. Universita Cattolica del Sacro Cuore. Facolta di Lettere. (1927)-. Periodical. Italian. Three times a year. $128.00. Vita e Pensiero, Pubblic University, Largo Gemelli 1, 20123 Milan Italy. **Tel** 011 39 2 72342310, 011 39 2 72342370. **LC** AP37; .A25. Documents available from The Genuine Article.
Ind/Abst Am. Hist. Life (1954-); Arts Humanit. Citation Index [Full Cov.]; Curr. Contents Arts Humanit.; MLA Int. Bibl. Books Artic. Mod. Lang. Lit.; Old Testam. Abstr.; Res. Alert [Full Cov.]; Romant. Move.; Soc. Sci. Cit. Index [Select. Cov.].

UK/0001-9720
AFRICA (LONDON. 1928). (AFRICA.). [Africa]. **Added/Corp** International African Institute. International Institute of African Languages and Cultures. Vol. 1 (Jan. 1928)-. Periodical. English (French and German). Four times a year (Mar., June, Sept., Dec.). £120.00 EEC Countries; £128.00 others; $230.00 North America. Edinburgh University Press, 22 George Square, Edinburgh EH8 9LF Scotland. **Tel** 011 44 31 650 6207, FAX 011 44 31 662 0053. **LC** PL8000; .I6. **DD** 496.05. **[CCC].** available on microfilm and microfiche from University Microfilms International (UMI). Documents available from The Genuine Article, UMI Article Clearinghouse. ***Continued in part by*** *International African Bibliography (Quarterly), 0020-5877.*
Desc: News and information on the proceedings of the executive council, list of members and includes reviews on the books.
Ind/Abst Am. Hist. Life (1954-); Anthropol. Lit. (1954-); Expand. Acad. Index (1992-); Geogr. Abstr. Human Geogr.; Index Book Rev. Relig. (1954-); Int. Bibliogr. Sociol.; Int. Dev. Abstr.; MLA Int. Bibl. Books Artic. Mod. Lang. Lit.; Multicult. Educ. Abstr. (1954-); Newsp. Period. Abstr. (1992-); Res. Alert [Full Cov.]; Rural Dev. Abstr.; Soc. Sci. Index; Stud. Women Abstr.

UK/0954-416X
AFRICAN LANGUAGES AND CULTURES. **Added/Corp** University of London. School of Oriental and African Studies. University of London. Dept. of African Languages and Cultures. University of London. Centre for African Studies. **VFOAT** ALC. Vol. 1, No. 1 (1988)-. Periodical. English. sa. £20.00 UK and Europe; $32.00 other. Oxford University Press, Walton Street, Oxford OX2 6DP England. **Tel** 011 44 865 56767, FAX 011 44 865 267773, telex 837330 OXPRES G. **(Subscription address:** Oxford University Press / USA, Journals Marketing Department, Oxford University Press, 2001 Evans Road, Cary NC 27513.**) ED** D. L. Appleyard. **LC** PL8000; .A29. **DD** 496/.05. **CODEN** ALCUEH. **[CCC]. Ad Acc. Pr Rev.**
Desc: Academic journal on African languages and cultures.
Ind/Abst Int. Bibliogr. Sociol.; Linguist. Lang. Behav. Abstr.; MLA Int. Bibl. Books Artic. Mod. Lang. Lit.; Soc. Plann. Policy Dev. Abstr.; Sociol. Abstr.

UK
AFRICAN LANGUAGES / LANGUES AFRICAINES. **Added/Corp** International African Institute. **VFOAT** Langues Africaines. Vol. 1 (1975)-. English (French). $13.00. International African Institute, 210 High Holborn, London WC1V 7BW England. **LC** PL8000; .A28. **DD** 496. ***Formed by the union of*** *Journal of African Languages, 0021-8545* ***and*** *African Language Review.*

BE
AFRICANA LINGUISTICA. Vol. 1 (1962)-. Multiple languages (English, Finnish and French). Musee Royal de l'Afrique Centrale, Stenweg OP Leuven 13, 1980 Tervuren Belgium. **Tel** 011 32 2 7675401. **LC** PL8000; .A33.
Ind/Abst Anthropol. Lit.; MLA Int. Bibl. Books Artic. Mod. Lang. Lit.

SZ
AFRICANA-SAMMLUNG UND AFRICANA-KATALOG IN DER STADTBIBLIOTHEK WINTERTHUR. **Main/Corp** Stadtbibliothek Winterthur. **VFOAT** Africana Sammlung und Africana Katalog in der Stadtbibliothek Winterthur. English (German). ir. Basler Afrika Bibliographien, Postfach 2037, CH-4001 Basel Switzerland. **Tel** 061/22.33.45. **LC** Z7106; .S7A; PL8000. **DD** 016.496. **UDC** 016:809.6. **Circ:** 600. ***Continues*** *Africana-Sammlung in der Stadtbibliothek Winterthur.*

FR
AFRICASCOPE. **VFOAT** Africa Scope. (19??)-. French. an (June). 100.00F. Editions Mermon, 20 rue de Fonparabie, 75020 Paris France. **Tel** 011 33 1 47637080 or 43678700. **LC** HC970.A1; A36.

GW/0002-0427
AFRIKA UND UBERSEE. [Afr. Ubersee]. **Added/Corp** Universitat Hamburg. Seminar fuer Afrikanische Sprachen und Kulturen. Universitat Hamburg. Seminar fuer Afrikanische. Vol. 36 (March 1952)-. Periodical. German (English and French). Twice a year. DM148.00. Dietrich Reimer Verlag, Unter Den Eichen 57, D-12203 Berlin Germany. **Tel** 011 49 30 8314081, FAX 011 49 30 831623. **LC** PL8000; .Z4. **DD** 496/.05. **[CCC].** cum. index. **Bk Rev. Ad Acc.** ***Continues*** *Zeitschrift fuer Eingeborenen-Sprachen.*
Ind/Abst Anthropol. Index; MLA Int. Bibl. Books Artic. Mod. Lang. Lit.

GW/0178-725X
AFRIKANISTISCHE ARBEITSPAPIERE. **Added/Corp** Universitaet zu Koeln. Institut fuer Afrikanistik. **VFOAT** Schriftenreihe des Koelner Institut fuer Afrikanistik; AAP. (March 1985)-. Periodical. English (French and German). qt. Universitaet zu Koeln, Institut fuer Afrikanistik, D-5000 Koeln 41 Germany. **LC** IN PROCESS.
Ind/Abst Linguist. Lang. Behav. Abstr.; Soc. Plann. Policy Dev. Abstr.; Sociol. Abstr.

US/0278-8969
AFRO-HISPANIC REVIEW. (AFRO-HISPANIC REVIEW : PUBLICATION OF AFRO-HISPANIC INSTITUTE.). [Afro-Hisp. rev.]. **Added/Corp** Afro-Hispanic Institute (U.S.) University of Missouri--Columbia. Dept. of Romance Languages. University of Missouri--Columbia. Black Studies Program. **VFOAT** Afro Hispanic Review. Vol. 1, No. 1 (Jan. 1982)-. Periodical. English (Spanish). Twice a year. $15.00. Romance Languages / University of Missouri, 143 Arts and Science, Columbia MO 65211. **Tel** (314)882-2030. **ED** Marvin A Lewis and Edward J Mullen. **LC** PQ7081.A1; A36. **DD** 860/.8/0896073. Index available. **Bk Rev. Ad Acc. Pr Rev. Circ:** 500.
Desc: Publishes literary criticism, book reviews, translations, creative writing, and relevant developments in the field. The Afro-Hispanic Review, a bilingual journal of Afro-Hispanic literature and culture, is jointly published by the Department of Romance Languages and the Black Studies Program of the University of Missouri-Columbia.
Ind/Abst MLA Int. Bibl. Books Artic. Mod. Lang. Lit.

US/0732-6416
AFROASIATIC DIALECTS. [Afroasiat. dialects]. Vol. 1 (1973)-. Monographic series. English. ir. Price varies per volume. Undena Publications, PO Box 97, Malibu CA 90265. **Tel** (310)649-2612. **(Subscription address:** Crescent Academic Services, 29528 Madera Avenue, Shafter, CA 93263, telephone: (805-746-5870**) ED** T. Penchoen. **LC** UNC. **Circ:** 300.
Desc: Data-oriented descriptions of Afro-Asiatic languages.
Ind/Abst Linguist. Lang. Behav. Abstr.; MLA Int. Bibl. Books Artic. Mod. Lang. Lit.; Soc. Plann. Policy Dev. Abstr.; Sociol. Abstr.

US/0362-3637
AFROASIATIC LINGUISTICS. ***Suspended.*** (MONOGRAPHIC JOURNALS OF THE NEAR EAST. AFROASIATIC LINGUISTICS.). [Afroasiat. linguist.]. **VFOAT** Afroasiatic Linguistics; MJNE; AAL. (1974)-(1992). Monographic series. English. ir. Price varies per volume. Undena Publications, PO Box 97, Malibu CA 90265. **Tel** (310)649-2612. **ED** R. Schuh. **LC** PJ991; .M66. **DD** 492. **Circ:** 300.
Desc: Linguistic contributions from Afro-Asiatic language group.
Ind/Abst Linguist. Lang. Behav. Abstr.; MLA Int. Bibl. Books Artic. Mod. Lang. Lit.; Old Testam. Abstr.; Soc. Plann. Policy Dev. Abstr.; Sociol. Abstr.

SP
AGALIA : REVISTA DA ASSOCIACOM GALEGA DA LINGUA. Periodical. Portuguese (Gallegan). qt.

UK/0961-8481
AHORA. (1991)-. Periodical. Spanish. bm. $25.00. Mary Glasgow Publications, Brookhampton Lane, Kineton, Warwickshire CV35 0JB England. **Tel** 011 44 926 640606, FAX 011 44 926 641016. **(Subscription address:** Scholastic Inc, PO Box 3710, Jefferson City MO 65102.**)**

IT
AION : ANNALI DEL SEMINARIO DI STUDI DEL MONDO CLASSICO, SEZIONE LINGUISTICA. **Added/Corp** Istituto Universitario Orientale (Naples, Italy). Sezione Linguistica. (1979)-. Periodical. Italian (English, French and German). Eight times a year. Price varies. Herder Editrice e Libreria SRL, Piazza Montecitorio 117-120, 00186 Rome Italy. **Tel** 011 39 6 679 4628, FAX 011 39 6 678 4751. **LC** P9; .A38. **DD** 410.

●IT/1122-195X
AION. SLAVISTICA : ANNALI DELL'ISTITUTO UNIVERSITARIO ORIENTALE DI NAPOLI / DIPARTIMENTO DI STUDI DELL'EUROPA ORIENTALE, SEZIONE SLAVISTICA. **Added/Corp** Istituto Universitario Orientale (Naples, Italy). Sezione Slavistica. **VFOAT** Slavistica; AION-Anglistica; Annali dell'Istituto Universitario Orientale di Napoli. Slavistica. (1993)-. Periodical. Italian (Czech, Polish and Russian). Edizioni Cadmo, Casella Postale 27, 50014 Fiesole Fi Italy. **LC** PG1; .A37. ***Formed by the union of*** *Annali del Dipartimento di Studi dell'Europa Orientale. Sezione Storico-Politico-Sociale, 1120-8422; Annali del Dipartimento di Studi dell'Europa Orientale. Sezione Letterario-Artistica* ***and*** *Annali del Dipartimento di Studi dell'Europa Orientale. Sezione Linguistico-Filologica.*
Desc: Covers Slavic philology and antiquities.

CN/0824-3050
AKADEMIAJ STUDOJ. 1983-. Esperanto. an. 17.00Can$. Akademiaj Studoj, c/o Esperanto Press, Bailieboro Ontario K0L 1B0 Canada. **Tel** (705)939-6088. **ED** R Eichholz. **DD** 499/.992/05. **UDC** 800.89. **Bk Rev. Circ:** 200.
Desc: Linguistic discussion about details of Esperanto, the inter-ethnic language and Esperanto terminology.
Ind/Abst Linguist. Lang. Behav. Abstr.; Soc. Plann. Policy Dev. Abstr.; Sociol. Abstr.

TA/0235-0041
AKHBOROTI AKADEMIIAI FANHOI RSS TOJIKISTON. SERIIAI SHARQSHINOSI TARIKH FILOLOGIIA. ***Title Change.*** **Added/Corp** Akademiiai Fanhoi RSS Tojikiston. **VFOAT** Seriiai Sharqshinosi, Tarikh, Filologiia; Seriia: Vostokovedenie, Istoriia, Filologiia; Izvestiia Akademii Nauk Tadzhikskoi SSR. Seriia; Tokovedenie, Istoriia, Filologiia. (1986)-(199?). Periodical. Tajik (Russian). qt. **LC** DK921; .A474. ***Continues in part*** *Akhboroti Akademiiai Fanhoi RSS Tojikiston, Shubai Fanhoi Jamiiati, 0321-1738.* ***Continued by*** *Akhbori Akademiiai Ilmhoi Jumhurii Tojikiston. Silsilai Sharqshinosi, Tarikh, Filologiia.*

RU
AKTUALNYE PROBLEMY LEKSIKOLOGII I SLOVOOBRAZOVANIIA. **Added/Corp** Novosibirskii Gosudarstvennyi Universitet. Kafedra Obshchego Iazyka. Vol. 1 (1972)-. Russian. 0.70rub per issue. **LC** PG2025; .A48.
Ind/Abst Annu. Bibliogr. Engl. Lang. Lit.

UK/0959-5740
AKTUELL. (1991)-. Periodical. German. bm. Mary Glasgow Publications, Brookhampton Lane, Kineton, Warwickshire CV35 0JB England. **Tel** 011 44 926 640606, FAX 011 44 926 641016. ctrl circ.
Desc: Written for intermediate and higher level learners of German.

US/0889-8731
AL-ARABIYYA. (AL-ARABIYAH : JOURNAL OF THE AMERICAN ASSOCIATION OF TEACHERS OF ARABIC.). [Arabiyya]. **VFOAT** Al-Arabiyah : Majallat Rabitat Asatidhat Al-Lughah Al-Arabiyah; Arabiyah. (Spring/Autumn 1975)-. Academic Scholarly Publication. Arabic (English). an (Jan.). $25.00. David M. Kennedy Center, 280 HRCB, Brigham Young University, Provo UT 84602. **Tel** (801)378-6528, FAX (801)378-7075. **ED** Mushira Eid (editor's address: Middle East Center, Building 413, University of Utah, Salt Lake City, UT 84112). **LC** PJ6001; .A73. **DD** 492/.7/05. **UDC** 809.27; 892.7. **Ad Acc, Adv Mgr:** Pil Parkinson. **Circ:** 350. ***Continues*** *NASHRA.*
Desc: Publishes scholarly and pedagogical articles and reviews in the Arabic language, literature and linguistics.
Ind/Abst Curr. Index J. Educ.; Index Islam.; Linguist. Lang. Behav. Abstr.; MLA Int. Bibl. Books Artic. Mod. Lang. Lit.; Soc. Plann. Policy Dev. Abstr.; Sociol. Abstr.; Middle East J.

SJ
AL-MAJALLAH AL-ARABIYAH LIL-DIRASAT AL-LUGHAWIYAH. **VFOAT** Arab Journal of Language Studies. V. 1, No. 1, (August 1982)-. Periodical. Arabic (English, French and German). sa. $12.00, $24.00 (institutions) US. Eastern Deims, PO Box 26, Khartoum Sudan. **Tel** TEACHING 223111, telex 240 65 LUGHA SD. **ED** Awn Al-Sharif Qasim. **LC** PJ6001; .M334. **UDC** 809.27. **Bk Rev. Ad Acc. Circ:** 2,000.
Desc: Covers the linguistics and teaching of the Arabic language; accepts articles in all fields of language studies with special reference to Arabic.

UA
AL-QISSAH. V. 1 (Sept. 1974)-. Periodical. Arabic. qt. £E0.15 per copy. Nadi Al-Qissah, 68 Qasr el Inee Street, United Arab Republic Egypt. **LC** PJ7677; .Q52.

US/0883-8526
ALASKA NATIVE LANGUAGE CENTER RESEARCH PAPERS. [Alsk. Native Lang. Cent. res. pap.]. **Added/Corp** Alaska Native Language Center. **VFOAT** ALNC Research Papers. No. 1 (1979)-. Monographic series. English. **DD** 497. **CODEN** ANLPER.
Ind/Abst Linguist. Lang. Behav. Abstr. (1979-) [Full Cov.]; Soc. Plann. Policy Dev. Abstr.

SP/0214-7602
ALAZET : REVISTA DE FILOLOGIA. **Added/Corp** Instituto de Estudios Altoaragoneses. (1989)-. Spanish. ***Separated from*** *Argensola.*
Desc: Information on Spanish philology and language.

CN/0382-5191
ALBERTA ENGLISH. [Alta. Engl.]. **Added/Corp** Alberta Teachers' Association. English Council. Vol. 9 No. 2 (Fall 1969)-. Periodical. English. ir. 40.00Can$ Comes with English Language Arts Council membership. Alberta Teachers Association, 11010-142 Street, Barnett House, Edmonton Alberta T5N 2R1 Canada. **Tel** (403)453-2411. ctrl circ. ***Continues*** *English Teacher, 0382-5183.*

CN/0318-5176
ALBERTA MODERN LANGUAGE JOURNAL. [Alta. mod. lang. j.]. **Added/Corp** Alberta Teachers' Association. Modern Language Council. Vol. 13 No. 1 (Fall 1974)-. English (French and German). ir. 20.00Can$ Comes with Modern Language Council membership. Alberta Teachers Association, 11010-142 Street, Barnett House, Edmonton Alberta T5N 2R1 Canada. **Tel** (403)453-2411. **DD** 407. **Bk Rev. Circ:** 420 (ctrl). available on microfiche from University Microfilms International (UMI). ***Continues*** *Modern Language Journal, 0318-5168.*

BL/0002-5216
ALFA. **See** Literature.

IT
ALFABETISMO E CULTURA SCRITTA. ***Ceased.*** New Ser., No. 1 (1988)-(19??). Periodical. Italian (Spanish). Bagatto Libri, Via Monzambano 5, 00185 Rome Italy. **LC** Z41.A2; A38. ***Continues*** *Notizie (Universita di Perugia).*

CN/0711-382X
ALGONQUIAN AND IROQUOIAN LINGUISTICS. **Added/Corp** University of Western Ontario. Dept. of Anthropology. University of Manitoba. Dept. of Native Studies. (1981)-. Periodical. English (French). qt. $12.00 US; 12.00Can$ other. University of Manitoba Department of Native Studies, Winnipeg Manitoba R3T 2N2 Canada. **Tel** (204)474-9676. **ED** John D Nichols. **DD** 497/.3/05. **CODEN** AIRLEA. **Bk Rev. Circ:** 200 (ctrl). ***Continues*** *Algonquian Linguistics, 0703-4768.*
Desc: American Indian languages and literatures, especially Algonquian and Iroquoian: news, running bibliography by language, technical articles, and research notes.

FR/0154-5868
ALMA. **Added/Corp** Universite de Clermont-Ferrand. Groupe d'Etudes Latines. Universite de Clermont-Ferrand II. Groupe d'Etudes Latines. **VFOAT** Annales Latini Montium Arvernorum. No. 1 (Jan. 1974)-. Periodical. French. an (July). 70.00F. Universite de Clermont, 29 Boulevard Gergovia, 63037 Clermont Ferrand France. **Tel** 011 73 344400.

II/0569-1176
ALOCANA. Began publication in 1951. Periodical. Hindi (Hindi). **LC** PK1931.

HU/0569-1338
ALTALANOS NYELVESZETI TANULMANYOK. [Alt. nyelvesz. tanulm.]. **Added/Corp** Magyar Tudomanyos Akademia. Nyelvtudomanyi Intezet. (1963)-. Academic Scholarly Publication. Hungarian. Akademiai Kiado, Publishing House of the Hungarian Academy of Sciences, Prielle Kornelia u. 19-35, H-1117 Budapest Hungary. **Tel** 011 36 1 1811991, FAX 011 36 1 1811991, telex 22-6228 AKNYO H. **LC** P10; .A5.
Ind/Abst MLA Int. Bibl. Books Artic. Mod. Lang. Lit.

GW/0002-6670
ALTSPRACHLICHE UNTERRICHT, DER. Series 1 (1951)-. Periodical. German. Six times a year (5 issues and 1 special annual issue). Erhard Friedrich Verlag, Postfach 100150, D 30917 Seelze Germany. **Tel** 011 49 511 4000452. **(Subscription address:** North America/ Journal Fulfillment Services, 44 Hartz Way, Secaucus, NJ 07094) **[CCC].**

US/0044-5665
AMERICAN FOREIGN LANGUAGE TEACHER. ***Suspended.*** [Am. foreign lang. teach.]. **VFOAT** AFLT. Began with V. 1 in Oct. 1970-Suspended. Periodical. English. qt. Advancement Press of America, 5440 Cass Avenue, Detroit MI 48202. **LC** P57.U7; A6. **DD** 405. **UDC** 372.880.0; 800.7. available on microfilm from University Microfilms International (UMI).

US/1040-8207
AMERICAN JOURNAL OF GERMANIC LINGUISTICS AND LITERATURES. (AMERICAN JOURNAL OF GERMANIC LINGUISTICS AND LITERATURES / SOCIETY FOR GERMANIC PHILOLOGY.). [Am. j. ger. linguist. lit.]. **Added/Corp** Society for Germanic Philology (U.S.) University of Hawaii at Manoa. College of Languages, Linguistics, and Literature. **VFOAT** AJGLL. Vol. 1, No. 1 (Jan. 1989)-. Periodical. English. Twice a year (Jan., July). $25.00 (individuals); $40.00 (institutions). Society for Germanic Philology, PO Box 020225, C/O Professor E. Fichtner, Brooklyn NY 11202. **Tel** (808)948-8516. **ED** Richard K. Seymour. **DD** 430. **Bk Rev. Circ:** 200 (ctrl).
Ind/Abst MLA Int. Bibl. Books Artic. Mod. Lang. Lit.

US/0002-9475
AMERICAN JOURNAL OF PHILOLOGY. **See** Classical Studies.

US/0277-7126
AMERICAN JOURNAL OF SEMIOTICS. [Am. j. semiot.]. **Added/Corp** Semiotic Society of America. Vol. 1, No. 1 (1981)-. Periodical. English. Four times a year. $35.00 (individuals); $45.00 (institutions). Semiotic Society of America, University of West Florida, PO Box 32086, Pensacola FL 32514. **Tel** (904)474-2186, 474-2797. **ED** Dean and Juliet Flower MacCannell. **LC** P99; .A46. **DD** 001.51/05. **Bk Rev. Ad Acc. Circ:** 750 (ctrl). Documents available from The Genuine Article.
Desc: Features articles published as critical essays analyzing texts, events, and cultural and natural objects using a semiotic methodology.
Ind/Abst Arts Humanit. Citation Index [Full Cov.]; Curr. Contents Arts Humanit.; Linguist. Lang. Behav. Abstr.; MLA Int. Bibl. Books Artic. Mod. Lang. Lit.; Res. Alert [Full Cov.]; Soc. Plann. Policy Dev. Abstr.; Soc. Sci. Cit. Index [Select. Cov.]; Sociol. Abstr.

US/0734-7545
AMERICAN LANGUAGE JOURNAL, THE. ***Title Change.*** [Am. lang. j.]. Vol. 1, No. 1 (Fall 1982)-?. Periodical. English. an. Ken Stratton Managing Editor, CESL Building 100, University of Arizona, Tucson AZ 85721. **Tel** (303)388-7000. **ED** Collen Gray. **LC** PE1128.A2; A53. **DD** 428/.007. **UDC** 802.0. **Ad Acc. Circ:** 1,000. ***Continued by*** *Journal of Intensive English Studies, 0899-885X.*
Desc: Papers applicable to intensive English programs: curriculum, evaluation, administration, teacher-training, theory, and practice.

US/0003-1283
AMERICAN SPEECH. [Am. speech]. **Added/Corp** American Dialect Society. Vol. 1 (Oct. 1925)-. Periodical. English. qt. $25.00 (institutions); $20.00 (individuals) US; $25.00 other. University of Alabama / School of Law, PO Box 870380, Tuscaloosa AL 35487-0380. **Tel** (205)348-1175. **ED** Ronald R. Butters (editor's address: Department of English, Duke University, Box 90018, Durham, NC 27708-0018). **LC** PE2801; .A6. **DD** 420/.97. **[CCC].** Index available in last issue of volume--attached. **Bk Rev. Pr Rev. Circ:** 1,800. available on microfilm and microfiche from University Microfilms International (UMI). Documents available from The Genuine Article, UMI Article Clearinghouse.
Desc: Devoted to the English language in North America and deals with current usage, slang, new words, regional and social varieties, changes now taking place, international influences on and from English, "correct" English and how "correctness" is determined, and glossaries of new and unusual words.
Ind/Abst Abstr. Engl. Stud.; Acad. Ind. [Computer File] (1992-); Acad. Search (July 1993-); Am. Hist. Life (1963-); Annu. Bibliogr. Engl. Lang. Lit.; Arts Humanit. Citation Index [Full Cov.]; Curr. Contents Arts Humanit.; Curr. Index J. Educ. (March 1990); Expand. Acad. Index (1989-); Humanit. Index; Humanit. Source (Jan. 1993-); Index Book Rev. Humanit.; INFO-SOUTH Abstr.; Lang. Lang. Behav. Abstr.; Lang. Teach.; Linguist. Lang. Behav. Abstr. (1968-) [Full Cov.]; Mag. Search; MLA Int. Bibl. Books Artic. Mod. Lang. Lit.; Newsp. Period. Abstr. (1991-); Ref. Sources; Res. Alert [Full Cov.]; Soc. Plann. Policy Dev. Abstr.; Soc. Sci. Cit. Index [Select. Cov.]; Sociol. Abstr.; Vocat. Search (July 1993-).

US/0890-4111
AMERICAN TRANSLATORS ASSOCIATION SCHOLARLY MONOGRAPH SERIES. [Am. Transl. Assoc. sch. monogr. ser.]. **Added/Corp** American Translators Association. State University of New York at Binghamton. Translation Research and Instruction Program. **VFOAT** Scholarly Monograph Series; American Translators Association Series. Vol. 1 (1987)-. Monographic series. English. ir. Price varies per volume. John Benjamins BV, Amsteldijk 44, PO Box 75577, 1070 AN Amsterdam Netherlands. **Tel** 011 31 20 6738156, FAX 011 31 20 739773. **(Subscription address:** John Benjamins North America, PO Box 27519, Philadelphia PA 19118-0519.) **ED** Marilyn Gaddis Rose. **LC** P306.A1; A53. **DD** 418/.02/0973.
Ind/Abst MLA Int. Bibl. Books Artic. Mod. Lang. Lit.

US/0721-1392
AMERICAN UNIVERSITY STUDIES. SERIES I, GERMANIC LANGUAGES AND LITERATURES. [Am. univ. stud., Ser. I, Ger. lang. lit.]. **VFOAT** American University Studies. Series 1, Germanic Languages and Literatures; American University Studies. Series One, Germanic Languages and Literatures; American University Studies. Series I, Germanic Languages and Literature; Germanic Languages and Literatures; Germanic Languages and Literature. (1981)-. Monographic series. English (German). ir. Price varies per volume. Peter Lang Publishing, 62 West 45th Street, 4th Floor, New York NY 10036. **Tel** (212)764-1471, (800)770-5264, telex 6973364 PLNY. **LC** UNC.
Ind/Abst MLA Int. Bibl. Books Artic. Mod. Lang. Lit.

US/0740-9257
AMERICAN UNIVERSITY STUDIES. SERIES II, ROMANCE LANGUAGES AND LITERATURE. [Am. univ. stud., Ser. II, Roman. lang. lit.]. **VFOAT** American University Studies. Series 2, Romance Languages and Literature; American University Studies. Series Two, Romance Languages and Litrature; Romance Languages and Literature. Vol. 5 (1983)-. Monographic series. English (French). ir. Price varies per volume. Peter Lang Publishing, 62 West 45th Street, 4th Floor, New York NY 10036. **Tel** (212)764-1471, (800)770-5264, telex 6973364 PLNY. **LC** UNC. ***Continues*** *American University Studies. Series II, Romance Languages, 0724-1437.*
Ind/Abst MLA Int. Bibl. Books Artic. Mod. Lang. Lit.

US/0741-0700
AMERICAN UNIVERSITY STUDIES. SERIES IV, ENGLISH LANGUAGE AND LITERATURE. [Am. univ. stud., Ser. IV, Engl. lang. lit.]. **VFOAT** American University Studies. Series Four, English Language and Literature; American University Studies. Series Four, English Language; English Language and Literature. (1984)-. Monographic series. English. ir. Price varies per volume. Peter Lang Publishing, 62 West 45th Street, 4th Floor, New York NY 10036. **Tel** (212)764-1471, (800)770-5264, telex 6973364 PLNY. **LC** UNC. ***Continues*** *American University Studies. Series IV, Anglo-Saxon Language and Literature, 0724-1453.*
Ind/Abst MLA Int. Bibl. Books Artic. Mod. Lang. Lit.

US/0739-6406
AMERICAN UNIVERSITY STUDIES. SERIES VI, FOREIGN LANGUAGE INSTRUCTION. [Am. univ. stud., ser. 6, for. lang. instr.]. **VFOAT** Foreign Language Instruction; American University Studies. Series 6, Foreign Language Instruction. Vol. 1-. English. ir. Peter Lang Publishing, 62 West 45th Street, 4th Floor, New York NY 10036. **Tel** (212)764-1471, (800)770-5264, telex 6973364 PLNY. **UDC** 800-07.

US/0740-0497
AMERICAN UNIVERSITY STUDIES. SERIES XII, SLAVIC LANGUAGES AND LITERATURE. **See** Literature.

US/0740-4557
AMERICAN UNIVERSITY STUDIES. SERIES XIII, LINGUISTICS. [Am. univ. stud., Ser. XIII, Ling.]. **VFOAT** American University Studies. Series 13, Linguistics; American University Studies. Series Thirteen, Linguistics; Linguistics. Vol. 1 (1984)-. Periodical. English. tq. Peter Lang Publishing, 62 West 45th Street, 4th Floor, New York NY 10036. **Tel** (212)764-1471, (800)770-5264, telex 6973364 PLNY. **LC** UNC. **DD** 410.
Ind/Abst MLA Int. Bibl. Books Artic. Mod. Lang. Lit.

FR/0221-8852
AMERINDIA. [Amerindia]. **Added/Corp** Societe d'Etudes Linguistiques et Anthropologiques de France. Centre National de la Recherche Scientifique (France). Equipe de Recherche Associee 431. (1976)-. Periodical. French (Spanish, English and Portuguese; summaries and/or abstracts in English, German, Portuguese and Russian). an. 75.00F North America and Europe; 80.00F other. Association Ethnolinguistique Amerind, B P 431, 75233 Paris Cedex 05 France. **ED** Andre Cauty. **LC** PM101; .A54. **DD** 497. cum. index. **Bk Rev. Circ:** 200 (ctrl).
Desc: American Indian linguistics and ethnolinguistics.
Ind/Abst Anthropol. Index; Anthropol. Lit.; MLA Int. Bibl. Books Artic. Mod. Lang. Lit.

NE/0304-0712
AMSTERDAM STUDIES IN THE THEORY AND HISTORY OF LINGUISTIC SCIENCE. SERIES I, AMSTERDAM CLASSICS IN LINGUISTICS, 1800-1925. **VFOAT** Amsterdam Classics in Linguistics, 1800-1925. (19??)-. Monographic series. English. ir. Price varies per volume. John Benjamins BV, Amsteldijk 44, PO Box 75577, 1070 AN Amsterdam Netherlands. **Tel** 011 31 20 6738156, FAX 011 31 20 739773. **(Subscription address:** John Benjamins North America, PO Box 27519, Philadelphia PA 19118-0519.) **ED** E.F. Konrad Koerner. ***Continues*** *Amsterdam Studies in the Theory and History of the Linguistic Science. Series 3: Studies in the History of Linguistics, 0304-0720.*
Desc: New editions of important 19th and 20th century works with introductions by current specialists in linguistics. These "classic" studies are placed within their historical context and their significance for contemporary linguistic pursuits is shown.
Ind/Abst MLA Int. Bibl. Books Artic. Mod. Lang. Lit.

NE/0165-716X
AMSTERDAM STUDIES IN THE THEORY AND HISTORY OF LINGUISTIC SCIENCE. SERIES II. CLASSICS IN PSYCHOLINGUISTICS. [Amst. stud. theory hist. linguist. sci., Ser. 2, Class. psycholinguist.]. (1978)-. Monographic series. English. ir. Price varies per volume.

John Benjamins BV, Amsteldijk 44, PO Box 75577, 1070 AN Amsterdam Netherlands. **Tel** 011 31 20 6738156, FAX 011 31 20 739773. **(Subscription address:** John Benjamins North America, PO Box 27519, Philadelphia PA 19118-0519.**)**
Ind/Abst MLA Int. Bibl. Books Artic. Mod. Lang. Lit.

NE/0304-0720
AMSTERDAM STUDIES IN THE THEORY AND HISTORY OF LINGUISTIC SCIENCE. SERIES III, STUDIES IN THE HISTORY OF THE LANGUAGE SCIENCES. **VFOAT** Amsterdam Studies in the Theory and History of Linguistic Science. Studies in the History of the Language Sciences. (198?)-. Monographic series. English. ir. Price varies per volume. John Benjamins BV, Amsteldijk 44, PO Box 75577, 1070 AN Amsterdam Netherlands. **Tel** 011 31 20 6738156, FAX 011 31 20 739773. **(Subscription address:** John Benjamins North America, PO Box 27519, Philadelphia PA 19118-0519.**) ED** E.F. Konrad Koerner. ***Continues*** *Amsterdam Studies in the Theory and History of Linguistic Science. Series III, Studies in the History of Linguistics.*
Desc: Established to meet the revival of interest in the field of linguistics and to provide an organized reservoir of information concerning the heritage of linguistic ideas of more than two millennia.
Ind/Abst MLA Int. Bibl. Books Artic. Mod. Lang. Lit.

NE/0304-0763
AMSTERDAM STUDIES IN THE THEORY AND HISTORY OF LINGUISTIC SCIENCE. SERIES IV, CURRENT ISSUES IN LINGUISTIC THEORY. [Amst. stud. theory hist. linguist. sci., 4, Curr. issues linguist. theory]. **VFOAT** Current Issues in Linguistic Theory. Vol. 1 (1975)-. Monographic series. English. ir. Price varies per volume. John Benjamins BV, Amsteldijk 44, PO Box 75577, 1070 AN Amsterdam Netherlands. **Tel** 011 31 20 6738156, FAX 011 31 20 739773. **(Subscription address:** John Benjamins North America, PO Box 27519, Philadelphia PA 19118-0519.**) ED** E.F. Konrad Koerner. **LC** UNC. **Bk Rev.**
Desc: A theory-oriented series which offers an alternative outlet for meaningful contributions to current linguistics in order to foster a diversity of opinion in the discipline.
Ind/Abst MLA Int. Bibl. Books Artic. Mod. Lang. Lit.

NE/0165-7267
AMSTERDAM STUDIES IN THE THEORY AND HISTORY OF LINGUISTIC SCIENCE. SERIES V, LIBRARY AND INFORMATION SOURCES IN LINGUISTICS. [Amst. stud. theory hist. linguist. sci., Ser. 5, Libr. inf. sources linguist.]. **VFOAT** Library and Information Sources in Linguistics. Vol. 1 (1977)-. Monographic series. English. ir. Price varies per volume. John Benjamins BV, Amsteldijk 44, PO Box 75577, 1070 AN Amsterdam Netherlands. **Tel** 011 31 20 6738156, FAX 011 31 20 739773. **(Subscription address:** John Benjamins North America, PO Box 27519, Philadelphia PA 19118-0519.**) ED** E. F. Konrad Koerner.
Desc: Supplies both librarians and scholars working in the field of language study with useful reference works. Publishes bibliographical works devoted to a particular subject, important linguistic doctrine or school, or outstanding scholar.
Ind/Abst MLA Int. Bibl. Books Artic. Mod. Lang. Lit.

NE
AMSTERDAMER BEITRAEGE ZUR ALTEREN GERMANISTIK. [Amst. Beitr. alteren Ger.]. Vol. 1 (1972)-. English (German, Dutch, Swedish, Norwegian and Danish). Twice a year. F85.00. Editions Rodopi BV, Keizersgracht 302-304, 1016 Ex Amsterdam Netherlands. **Tel** 011 31 20 6227507, FAX 011 31 20 380948. **LC** PD3; .A47. **CODEN** ABAGEV. **Bk Rev. Ad Acc.**
Ind/Abst Linguist. Lang. Behav. Abstr.; MLA Int. Bibl. Books Artic. Mod. Lang. Lit.; Soc. Plann. Policy Dev. Abstr.; Sociol. Abstr.

SP/0211-9358
ANALECTA MALACITANA. (ANALECTA MALACITANA: REVISTA DE LA SECCION DE FILOLOGIA DE LA FACULTAD DE FILOSOFIA Y LETRAS.). [Analecta malacit.]. **Added/Corp** Universidad de Malaga. Seccion de Filologia. **VFOAT** Anmal. Vol. 1 No. 1 (1978)-. Periodical. Spanish. Twice a year. 3000ptas Spain; $12.00 US. Universidad de Malaga / Filosofia, Facultad de Filosofia y Letras, Campus Teatinos, 29071 Malaga Spain. **Tel** 011 34 5 221-8660. **LC** P9; .A64. **DD** 410/.5.

GW/0569-986X
ANALECTA ROMANICA. Vol. 1 (1955)-. Monographic series. German. ir. Price varies per volume. Vittorio Klostermann, Frauenlobstrasse 22, D 60487 Frankfurt Germany. **Tel** 011 49 69 970160.

RM/0379-7880
ANALELE STIINTIFICE ALE UNIVERSITATII "AL. I. CUZA" DIN IASI. SERIE NOUA. SECTIUNEA III E, LINGVISTICA. **Added/Corp** Universitatea "Al. I. Cuza" din Iasi. (197?)-. Romanian (English, French and Romanian). an. DM164.00. **(Subscription address:** Kubon & Sagner, ABT Zeitschriftenimport, D 80328 Munich Germany.**) LC** P1.A1; A5. ***Continues in part*** *Analele Stiintifice Ale Universitatii Al. I. Cuza Din Iasi. Serie Noua. Sectiunea III E, Lingvistica-Literatura.*
Ind/Abst Annu. Bibliogr. Engl. Lang. Lit.; MLA Int. Bibl. Books Artic. Mod. Lang. Lit.

RM
ANALELE UNIVERSITATII BUCURESTI : LIMBI SI LITERATURI STRAINE. **Added/Corp** Universitatea din Bucuresti. **VFOAT** Limbi Si Literaturi Straine. Vol. 26, (1977)-. English (French, German, Romanian, Russian and Serbo-Croatian (Roman)). an. DM164.00. **(Subscription address:** Kubon & Sagner, ABT Zeitschriftenimport, D 80328 Munich Germany.**) LC** P1.A1; U5a. **DD** 410/.5. ***Continues*** *Universitatea din Bucuresti. Analele Universitatii Bucurest i. Filologie.*
Ind/Abst Annu. Bibliogr. Engl. Lang. Lit.

RM
ANALELE UNIVERSITATII DIN CRAIOVA : STIINTE FILOLOGICE. **Main/Corp** Universitatea Din Craiova. **Added/Corp** Universitatea din Craiova. Analele Universitatii din Craiova: Seria: Stiinte Filologice. **VFOAT** Analele Universitatii Din Craiova. Seria: Stiinte Filologice. (19??)-. Periodical. Romanian (summaries and/or abstracts in English, French, German and Italian). an. Universitatii din Craiova, A1 I Cuza St No 31, Craiova The Socialist Republic of Romania. **LC** P9; .U54a.
Ind/Abst Annu. Bibliogr. Engl. Lang. Lit.

RM
ANALELE UNIVERSITATII DIN GALATI. FASCICULA XIII. **See** Literature.

RM
ANALELE UNIVERSITATII DIN TIMISOARA. STIINTE FILOLOGICE. **Added/Corp** Universitatea din Timisoara. Facultatea de Filologie. **VFOAT** Stiinte Filologice. (1978)-. Periodical. Romanian (summaries and/or abstracts in French, German and Russian). an. DM164.00. **(Subscription address:** Kubon & Sagner, ABT Zeitschriftenimport, D 80328 Munich Germany.**) LC** P25; .T5. ***Continues*** *Analele Universitatii din Timisoara. Seria Stiinte Filologice.*
Ind/Abst Annu. Bibliogr. Engl. Lang. Lit.; Linguist. Lang. Behav. Abstr.; Soc. Plann. Policy Dev. Abstr.; Sociol. Abstr.

SP/0213-4365
ANALES DE FILOLOGIA HISPANICA / UNIVERSIDAD DE MURCIA. ***Suspended.*** **Added/Corp** Universidad de Murcia. **VFOAT** AFH. (1985)-Vol. 5 (1990). Spanish. an. Univ Murcia, Sec de Publicacion, Plaza de la Merced S N, 3001 Murcia Spain. **Tel** 011 34 968239405. **LC** WMLC 93/1056.

SP/0213-1811
ANALES DE LA ASOCIACION DE PALINOLOGOS DE LENGUA ESPAƒNOLA. [An. Asoc. Palinol. Leng. Esp.]. **Added/Corp** Ociacion de Palinologos de Lengua Espaƒnola. Cordoba. (1984)-. Periodical. Multiple languages. an. 2000ptas Spain; 2500ptas other. Dept Biologia Vegetal Ecologia Cience, DV Botanica Univ. Cordoba Fac Cience, 14004 Cordoba Spain. **Tel** 011 34 57 411211. **UDC** 581.

RU/0202-2435
ANALIZ STILEI ZARUBEZHNOI KHUDOZHESTVENNOI I NAUCHNOI LITERATURY. **Added/Corp** Russian S.F.S.R. Ministerstvo Vysshego Srednogo Spetsianogo Obrazovaniia. Vol. 1 (1978)-. Russian. te. 1.5rub. St Petersburg State University / Izdatelstvo Leningradskogo Universiteta, Universitetskaia Nab 7/9, 199034 St Petersburg Russia. **Tel** 011 95 218-97-88, FAX 011 95 218-51-52, telex 121481. **ED** A M Sokolov, O V Bokiy. **LC** PE1001; .A56. **Ad Acc. Circ:** 1,500.
Desc: Devoted to problems of style and registers. The authors' contributions concentrate on individual styles, stylistic characteristics of various trends in literature, stylistic functions of grammar and lexis.

FR/0181-7205
ANALYSES, THEORIE. **Added/Corp** Universite de Paris VIII: Vincennes. Departement d'Arabe. (19??)-. Periodical. French. qt. Univ de Paris Puv, 2 rue de la Liberte, 93526 Saint-Denis Cedex 02 France. **Tel** 011 33 1 49406750.

NE/0066-1554
ANATOLICA. (ANATOLICA; ANNUAIRE INTERNATIONAL POUR LES CIVILISATIONS DE L'ASIE ANTERIEURE.). [Anatolica]. **Added/Corp** Nederlands Historisch-Archaeologisch Instituut te Istanbul. (1967)-. Multiple languages (German, French and English). ir. Netherlands Institute Nabije Oosten, PO Box 9515, 2300 RA Leiden Netherlands. **Tel** 011 31 71 272020. **ED** E. van Donzel, J. Roodenberg, B. Flemming, C. Nijland, K. A. Yener and J. De Roos. **LC** WMLC L 83/1770. **Circ:** 300 (ctrl).
Desc: Studies of history and linguistics of the Christian era during the period of Islam.
Ind/Abst MLA Int. Bibl. Books Artic. Mod. Lang. Lit.

US/0895-366X
ANCHOR POINT. Vol. 1, No. 1 (Oct. 1987)-. Periodical. English. mo. $39.00. Cahill Mountain Press Inc., PO Box 286, Franktown CO 80116. **Tel** (303)841-8701, FAX (303)969-9177. **DD** 158.

CL/0071-1721
ANEJOS DE ESTUDIOS FILOLOGICOS. (1968)-. Monographic series. Spanish. ir. Price varies per volume. Universidad Austral de Chile, Facultad Med Veterinar de Chile, Casilla 567, Valdivia Chile. **Tel** 011 56 213911, FAX 011 56 212953, telex 271035 UNAUS CL. **LC** P25; .E8 SUPPL.

DK
ANGLES ON THE ENGLISH SPEAKING WORLD. **Added/Corp** Kbenhavns Universitet. Engelsk Institut. **VFOAT** Angles. No. 1 (Autumn 1986)-. Periodical. English. **LC** PE9; .A55. **DD** 420/.5.
Ind/Abst Annu. Bibliogr. Engl. Lang. Lit.; MLA Int. Bibl. Books Artic. Mod. Lang. Lit.

GW
ANGLIA : ZEITSCHRIFT FUER ENGLISCHE PHILOLOGIE. Vol. 1 (1878)-. German. sa. DM186.00. Max Niemeyer Verlag, Postfach 2140, D 72011 Tuebingen Germany. **Tel** 011 49 7071 989494, FAX 011 49 7071 87419. **ED** Helmut Gneuss, Hans Kasman, Eswin Wolff, and Theodor Wolpers. cum. index. **Bk Rev. Ad Acc.** Documents available from The Genuine Article.
Desc: Contributions on English (especially old and middle English) and American languages and literatures.
Ind/Abst Arts Humanit. Citation Index (19??-19??) [Full Cov.]; Curr. Contents Arts Humanit.; Linguist. Lang. Behav. Abstr.; MLA Int. Bibl. Books Artic. Mod. Lang. Lit.; Res. Alert [Full Cov.]; Soc. Plann. Policy Dev. Abstr.; Soc. Sci. Cit. Index [Select. Cov.]; Sociol. Abstr.

DK/0105-9963
ANGLICA ET AMERICANA. [Angl. am.]. (1977)-. Monographic series. English. ir. **DD** 420 820.9. **CODEN** 81.39389.3.
Ind/Abst MLA Int. Bibl. Books Artic. Mod. Lang. Lit.

DK/0066-1805
ANGLISTICA. Vol. 1 (1953)-. Monographic series. English. ir. Price varies per volume. Rosenkilde and Bagger, 3 Kron-Prinsens-Gade, PO Box 2184, DK 1017 Copenhagen K Denmark. **Tel** 011 45 1 157044. **LC** unc. **DD** 820/.9.

GW/0344-8266
ANGLISTIK & ENGLISCHUNTERRICHT. [Angl. Engl.unterr.]. **VFOAT** Anglistik und Englischunterricht; A & E; A und E; A. & E.; A. und E. (197?)-. Monographic series. German (English). Three times a year. Universitatsverlag Carl Winter, POB 106140, D 69051 Heidelberg Germany. **Tel** 011 49 6221 770260. **LC** UNC. **DD** 420/.5.
Ind/Abst Annu. Bibliogr. Engl. Lang. Lit.; MLA Int. Bibl. Books Artic. Mod. Lang. Lit.; Soc. Plann. Policy Dev. Abstr.; Sociol. Abstr.

GW/0179-1389
ANGLISTISCHE FORSCHUNGEN. [Angl. Forsch.]. Vol. 1 (1901)-. Monographic series. German. ir. Price varies per volume. Universitatsverlag Carl Winter, POB 106140, D 69051 Heidelberg Germany. **Tel** 011 49 6221 770260. **LC** UNC.
Desc: English linguistics and literature.
Ind/Abst MLA Int. Bibl. Books Artic. Mod. Lang. Lit.

US/0195-3400
ANISHINAABE GIIGIDOWIN. V. 1-Jan. 1976-. Periodical. English (Algonquian languages). Free. John Nichols Native Teacher Education Program, Faculty of Education Lakehead University, Thunder Bay Ontario P7B 5E1 Canada. **ED** J Nichols and E Nyholm. **DD** 497'.3. **UDC** 809.7.

SZ
ANNALAS DALA SOCIETAD RHAETO-ROMANSCHA. NSS. **See** History(General)-History of Europe.

FR/0180-4200
ANNALES DE L'INSTITUT D'ETUDES OCCITANES. [Ann. Inst. etud. occ.]. **Main/Corp** Institut d'Estudis Occitans (France). **VFOAT** Annals de l'Institut d'Estudis Occitans. (1948)-. Multiple languages (French and Provencal, Old).
Ind/Abst MLA Int. Bibl. Books Artic. Mod. Lang. Lit.

HU
ANNALES UNIVERSITATIS SCIENTIARUM BUDAPENTINENSIS DE ROLANDO EOTVOS NOMINATAE. SECTIO PHILOLOGICA MODERNA. **Main/Corp** Eotvos Lorand Tudomanyegyetem. V. 1-

1969/70-. English (French, German, Italian, Romanian, Russian and Spanish). an. $40.00. Philologica Moderna, PO Box 149, HI 389 Budapest Hungary. **LC** P10. **UDC** 800. **Ad Acc. Circ:** 500 (ctrl). ***Supersedes in part*** *Annales Universitatis Scientiarum Budapestinensis de Rolando Eotvos Nominatae. Section Philologica.*

HU/0572-7251
ANNALES UNIVERSITATIS SCIENTIARUM BUDAPESTINENSIS DE ROLANDO EOTVOS NOMINATAE. SECTIO LINGUISTICA. **Main/Corp** Eotvos Lorand Tudomanyegyetem. **VFOAT** Sectio Linguistica. (1970)-. English (French, German and Russian). an. Eotvos Lorand Tudomanyegyetem, Bolcseszettudomanyi Kar, Pesti BUL, H-1052 Budapest Hungary. **Tel** 36 11 180 966.

IT
ANNALI DELL'ISTITUTO UNIVERSITARIO ORIENTALE DI NAPOLI, SEMINARIO DI STUDI DEL MONDO CLASSICO, SEZIONE FILOLOGICO-LETTERARIA. **VFOAT** A.I.O.N; AION. Vol. 1 (1979)-. Italian (Italian). an. Herder Editrice e Libreria SRL, Piazza Montecitorio 117-120, 000186 Rome Italy. **Tel** 011 39 6 6794628.

IT/0391-5956
ANNALI - INSTITUTO UNIVERSITARIO ORIENTALE, SEZIONE GERMANICA. ANGLISTICA. (ANNALI. ANGLISTICA / ISTITUTO UNIVERSITARIO ORIENTALE, SEZIONE GERMANICA.). [Ann. - Ist. univ. orient., Sez. ger., Angl.]. **Added/Corp** Istituto Universitario Orientale (Naples, Italy). Sezione Germanica. Istituto Universitario Orientale (Naples, Italy). **VFOAT** Anglistica; Aion Anglistica. Vol. 17, No. 1 (1974)-. Periodical. English (Italian). an. L60000 Italy; L80000 other. Herder Editrice e Libreria SRL, Piazza Montecitorio 117-120, 00186 Rome Italy. **Tel** 011 39 6 679 4628, FAX 011 39 6 678 4751. **ED** Fernando Ferrara. **LC** PE9; .A566. **DD** 420/.5. ***Continues in part*** *Annali (Istituto Universitario Orientale (Naples, Italy). Sezione Germanica).*
Ind/Abst MLA Int. Bibl. Books Artic. Mod. Lang. Lit.

IT
ANNALI (ISTITUTO UNIVERSITARIO ORIENTALE (NAPLES, ITALY)). (ANNALI / ISTITUTO ORIENTALE DI NAPOLI.). **Added/Corp** Istituto Universitario Orientale (Naples, Italy) Istituto Universitario Orientale (Naples, Italy). Seminario di Studi Africani. Istituto Universitario Orientale (Naples, Italy). Seminario di Studi Asiatici. Vol. 1-10, No. 1-2, (1929-Dec. 1937/Mar. 1938)-. Periodical. English (French and Italian). qt. Herder Editrice e Libreria SRL, Piazza Montecitorio 117-120, 00186 Rome Italy. **Tel** 011 39 6 679 4628, FAX 011 39 6 678 4751. **ED** R. Rubinacci and L. Cagni. **LC** PJ6; .N32. **DD** 490/.5. **Bk Rev.** ***Continues*** *Annali (Instituto Orientale di Napoli).*
Ind/Abst Art Archaeol. Tech. Abstr.; Old Testam. Abstr.; Romant. Move.

IT/0547-2121
ANNALI - SEZIONE ROMANZA. [Ann. - Sez. roman.]. **Main/Corp** Istituto Orientale di Napoli. Sezione Romanza. Vol. 1 (1959)-. Periodical. Italian (summaries and/or abstracts in English, French, German, Portuguese and Spanish). sa (2 issues). L60000 Italy; L80000 other. Herder Editrice e Libreria SRL, Piazza Montecitorio 117-120, 00186 Rome Italy. **Tel** 011 39 6 679 4628, FAX 011 39 6 678 4751. **LC** PC4; .N3. ***Supersedes in part*** *Annali - Istituto Orientale di Napoli.*
Desc: Romance philology.
Ind/Abst MLA Int. Bibl. Books Artic. Mod. Lang. Lit.

II/0378-1143
ANNALS OF THE BHANDARKAR ORIENTAL RESEARCH INSTITUTE. (ANNALS OF THE BHANDARKAR ORIENTAL RESEARCH INSTITUTE, POONA.). [Ann. Bhandarkar Orient. Res. Inst.]. **Added/Corp** Bhandarkar Oriental Research Institute. Vol. 1 (1918/20)-. English. an. $31.00. Indian Books and Periodicals, 2429 Tilak Street, Pahar Ganj, New Delhi 110005 India. **(Subscription address:** Prints India, 11 Darya Ganj, New Delhi, 110002 India, (Phone: 011 91 11 3268645)) **ED** R N Dandekar and G B Pabule. **LC** PK101; .B6. cum. index. **Bk Rev. Circ:** 1,250.
Desc: Research papers on various aspects of oriental studies in general and indology in particular.
Ind/Abst Anthropol. Index; MLA Int. Bibl. Books Artic. Mod. Lang. Lit.; Numis. Lit.

FR
ANNEE PHILOLOGIQUE; BIBLIOGRAPHIE CRITIQUE ET ANALYTIQUE DE L'ANTIQUITE GRECO-LATINE, L'. Vol. 1 (1926)-. Periodical. French. an. 800.00F. Societe Edition Belles Lettres, 95 Boulevard Raspail, 75006 Paris France. **Tel** 011 33 1 45487055, FAX 011 33 1 45449288, telex 200577. **LC** Z7016; .M35A. **NLM** Z 7016 A613.
Ind/Abst Br. Archaeol. Bibliogr. (?-?).

BE
ANNUAIRE DE L'INSTITUT DE PHILOLOGIE ET D'HISTOIRE ORIENTALES ET SLAVES. SUPPLEMENT. (1982)-. Monographic series. French. Price varies per volume. Editions de l Universite de Bruxelles, Avenue Paul Heger 26, B-1050 Bruxelles Belgium.

UK/0066-3786
ANNUAL BIBLIOGRAPHY OF ENGLISH LANGUAGE AND LITERATURE. **See** Literature-Abstracting, Bibliographies and Statistics.

US/0271-9800
ANNUAL OF ARMENIAN LINGUISTICS. [Annu. Armen. linguist.]. Vol. 1 (1980)-(19??). Academic Scholarly Publication. English (French, German and Italian). an. $35.00. Cleveland State University / c/o J. A. Greppin, Cleveland OH 44115. **Tel** (216)687-3967, FAX (216)687-9366, telex 810-421-8252 CSU CLV. **ED** J A C Greppin. **LC** PK8001; .A56. **DD** 491/.992/05. **UDC** 809.198.1. **Bk Rev. Ad Acc. Circ:** 200 (ctrl).
Desc: A scholarly journal dealing with Armenian linguistics.
Ind/Abst Am. Bibliogr. Slavic East Europ. Stud. (19??-19??); Linguist. Lang. Behav. Abstr. (1986-) [Full Cov.]; MLA Int. Bibl. Books Artic. Mod. Lang. Lit.; Soc. Plann. Policy Dev. Abstr.; Sociol. Abstr.

US/1073-6255
ANNUAL OF THE SOCIETY FOR THE STUDY OF CAUCASIA, THE. [Annu. Soc. Study Cauc.]. **Added/Corp** Society for the Study of Caucasia. No. 1 (1989)-. Periodical. English. an. $15.00. Society for the Study of Caucasia, Rowan College, Department of History, Glassboro NJ 08028. **Tel** (609)863-5000. **LC** DK509; .A56. **DD** 947.
Desc: Contains information from the study of Caucasian languages.

CN/0382-1161
ANNUAL REPORT - COMMISSIONER OF OFFICIAL LANGUAGES. **Main/Corp** Canada. Office of the Commissioner of Official Languages. **VFOAT** Rapport Annuel. 1st (1970/71)-. English (French). an (April). Free. Commissioner of Official Languages, 110 O'Connor Street, Room 1414, Ottawa ONT K1A OT8 Canada. **Tel** (613)995-0730. **LC** JL25; .A3. **DD** 409.71. Index available. **Circ:** 12,000 (ctrl).
Desc: Provides Senators and members of Parliament as well as the general public with a yearly assessment of developments in language reform across Canada.

GW
ANNUAL REPORT ON ENGLISH AND AMERICAN STUDIES : AREAS. **VFOAT** AREAS. (1991/1992)-. Periodical. English. sa.

UK/0267-1905
ANNUAL REVIEW OF APPLIED LINGUISTICS. [Annu. rev. appl. linguist.]. **VFOAT** ARAL. (1980)-. Academic Scholarly Publication. English. an. $65.00 US, Canada & Mexico; £39.00 other. Cambridge University Press, The Edinburgh Building, Shaftesbury Road, Cambridge CB2 2RU United Kingdom. **Tel** 011 44 223 312393, FAX 011 44 223 325959. **(Subscription address:** Cambridge University Press / North America, 110 Midland Avenue, Port Chester NY 10573.) **ED** William Grabe. **LC** P129; .A56. **DD** 410/.5. **[CCC].** available on microfilm from University Microfilms International (UMI).
Desc: Provides researchers, teachers and students with a comprehensive, up-to-date review of research in developing fields of study. Covers such topics as bilingualism, psycholinguistics, computer-assisted instruction, sociolinguistics and lexicography. Bibliographic information on contributors, an author index and a subject index is also included. Provides discussion and over 500 new citations a year.
Ind/Abst Curr. Index J. Educ. (March 1990); Linguist. Lang. Behav. Abstr. (1984-) [Full Cov.]; MLA Int. Bibl. Books Artic. Mod. Lang. Lit.; Soc. Plann. Policy Dev. Abstr.; Sociol. Abstr.

CN/0822-2525
ANNUAL REVIEW OF THE ROYAL INSCRIPTIONS OF MESOPOTAMIA PROJECT. ***Suspended.*** [Annu. rev. R. Inscr. Mesop. Proj.]. **Added/Corp** RIM Project. **VFOAT** Annual Review of the RIM Project. Vol. 1 (1983)-(1991). English (French and German). an. $20.00. RIM Project, University of Toronto, 4 Bancroft Avenue, Toronto Ontario M5S 1A1 Canada. **Tel** (416)978-4790, FAX (416)987-5294. **ED** A. Kirk Grayson and L. S. Wilding. **DD** 492/.1. **Circ:** 500 (ctrl).

CN/0701-1865
ANTENNE (MONTREAL). (L'ANTENNE.). V. 1-Dec. 1969-. Periodical. French (English). bm. Societe des Traducteurs du Quebec, 1010 rue St Catherine Ouest/Bureau 540, Montreal Quebec H3B 1G4 Canada. **Tel** (514)861-1783, FAX (514)861-8117. **DD** 418/.02/062714. **UDC** 800.73(714). **Circ:** 2,000 (ctrl).
Desc: Information bulletin for the members of the Societe des Traducteurs du Quebec.

US/0003-5483
ANTHROPOLOGICAL LINGUISTICS. **See** Anthropology.

SZ/0257-9774
ANTHROPOS FRIBOURG. **See** Anthropology.

AU
ANTHROPOS (SALZBURG, AUSTRIA). (ANTHROPOS / IM AUFTRAGE DER OESTERREICHISCHEN LEO-GESELLSCHAFT MIT UNTERSTUTZUNG DER DEUTSCHEN GORRES-GESELLSCHAFT.). Vol. 1 (1906)-. Periodical. English (French, German and Italian). ir. 170.00F. **LC** GN1; .A7. cum. index.
Ind/Abst Anthropol. Index; Index Book Rev. Relig.; MLA Int. Bibl. Books Artic. Mod. Lang. Lit.; PsycINFO (1990-); PsycLit; Relig. Index One Period.

BE
ANTWERP PAPERS IN LINGUISTICS. **Added/Corp** Universitaire Instelling Antwerpen. Department Germaanse Filologie. Afdeling Linguistiek. (1975)-. Monographic series. English.
Ind/Abst Annu. Bibliogr. Engl. Lang. Lit.

RM/0066-4987
ANUAR DE LINGVISTICA SI ISTORIE LITERARA. **Added/Corp** Academia Republicii Socialiste Romania. Filiala Iasi. Centrul de Lingvistica, Istorie Literara si Folclor. (1965)-. Periodical. Romanian (summaries and/or abstracts in French). an. Editura Academia Republicii Socialiste Romania, Calea Victoriei Nr 125, R-79717 Bucuresti Romania. **Tel** telex 10376 PRSFI R. **LC** PC601; .A58. **DD** 459/.05. ***Continues*** *Anuarul de Filologie.*
Ind/Abst MLA Int. Bibl. Books Artic. Mod. Lang. Lit.

SP
ANUARI DE FILOLOGIA. SECCIO B, ESTUDIS ARABS / UNIVERSITAT DE BARCELONA, FACULTAT DE FILOLOGIA. **Added/Corp** Universidad de Barcelona. Facultad de Filologia. **VFOAT** Estudis Arabs. Vol. 13 (1990)-. Catalan (Arabic, Italian and Spanish). Universidad de Barcelona / Filologia, Facultad de Filologia Anuario de Filologia, Gran Via Corts Catalanes 585, 08007 Barcelona Spain. **LC** PJ6001; .A58. ***Continues in part*** *Anuario de Filologia, 0210-1343.*

SP
ANUARI DE FILOLOGIA. SECCIO C, LLENGUA I LITERATURA CATALANES / UNIVERSITAT DE BARCELONA, FACULTAT DE FILOLOGIA. **Added/Corp** Universidad de Barcelona. Facultad de Filologia. **VFOAT** Llengua i Literatura Catalanes. Vol. 13 (1990)-. Catalan. Universidad de Barcelona / Filologia, Facultad de Filologia Anuario de Filologia, Gran Via Corts Catalanes 585, 08007 Barcelona Spain. **LC** PC3801; .A5. ***Continues in part*** *Anuario de Filologia, 0210-1343.*

SP
ANUARI DE FILOLOGIA. SECCIO D, STUDIA GRAECA ET LATINA / UNIVERSITAT DE BARCELONA, FACULTAT DE FILOLOGIA. **Added/Corp** Universidad de Barcelona. Facultad de Filologia. **VFOAT** Studia Graeca et Latina. Vol. 13 (1990)-. Catalan (French, Greek, Ancient and Latin, Spanish). ir. Universidad de Barcelona / Filologia, Facultad de Filologia Anuario de Filologia, Gran Via Corts Catalanes 585, 08007 Barcelona Spain. **LC** PA9; .A58. ***Continues in part*** *Anuario de Filologia, 0210-1343.*

SP
ANUARI DE FILOLOGIA. SECCIO E, ESTUDIS HEBREUS I ARAMEUS / UNIVERSITAT DE BARCELONA, FACULTAT DE FILOLOGIA. **Added/Corp** Universidad de Barcelona. Facultad de Filologia. **VFOAT** Estudis Hebreus i Arameus. Vol. 14 (1991)-. Catalan. be. Universidad de Barcelona / Filologia, Facultad de Filologia Anuario de Filologia, Gran Via Corts Catalanes 585, 08007 Barcelona Spain. **LC** PJ4504; .A5. ***Continues in part*** *Anuario de Filologia, 0210-1343.*

SP
ANUARI DE FILOLOGIA. SECCIO F, ESTUDIOS DE LENGUA Y LITERATURA ESPANOLAS / UNIVERSITAT DE BARCELONA, FACULTAT DE FILOLOGIA. **Added/Corp** Universidad de Barcelona. Facultad de Filologia. **VFOAT** Estudios de Lengua y Literatura Espanolas. Vol. 13 (1990)-. Catalan (Spanish). Universidad de Barcelona / Filologia, Facultad de Filologia Anuario de Filologia, Gran Via Corts Catalanes 585, 08007 Barcelona Spain. **LC** PC4009; .A58. ***Continues in part*** *Anuario de Filologia, 0210-1343.*

SP
ANUARI DE FILOLOGIA. SECCIO G, FILOLOGIA ROMANICA / UNIVERSITAT DE BARCELONA, FACULTAT DE FILOLOGIA. **Added/Corp** Universidad de Barcelona. Facultad de Filologia. **VFOAT** Filologia

Romanica. Vol. 13 (1990)-. Catalan (French, Italian and Spanish). Universidad de Barcelona / Filologia, Facultad de Filologia Anuario de Filologia, Gran Via Corts Catalanes 585, 08007 Barcelona Spain. **LC** PC5; .A58. ***Continues in part*** *Anuario de Filologia, 0210-1343.*

CK
ANUARIO BIBLIOGRAFICO COLOMBIANO "RUBEN PEREZ ORTIZ". **See** Literature.

SP
ANUARIO DE ESTUDIOS FILOLOGICOS. **Added/Corp** Universidad de Extremadura (Caceres, Spain). Facultad de Filosofia y Letras. (1978)-. Periodical. French (Spanish). an. 2000.00ptas. Universidad Extremadura, Service Publi. Fac. F Y Letras, Caceres Spain. **Tel** 011 34 27 247650. **LC** P1.A1; A57. **DD** 410. **CODEN** AEFIEF.
Ind/Abst MLA Int. Bibl. Books Artic. Mod. Lang. Lit.

VE/0066-507X
ANUARIO DE FILOLOGIA (CARACAS). (ANUARIO DE FILOLOGIA / FACULTAD DE HUMANIDADES Y EDUCACION, UNIVERSIDAD DEL ZULIA.). [Anu. filol.]. **Added/Corp** Universidad del Zulia. Escuela de Letras. Universidad del Zulia. Facultad de Humanidades y Educacion. No. 1 (1962)-. Spanish. ir. $24.00. Facultad Humanidades y Education, Universidad del Zulia, Maracaibo Venezuela. **LC** P10; .A6. **DD** 410/.5.
Ind/Abst MLA Int. Bibl. Books Artic. Mod. Lang. Lit.

SP/0213-053X
ANUARIO DE LINGUISTICA HISPANICA. [Anu. linguist. hisp.]. **Added/Corp** Universidad de Valladolid. **VFOAT** ALH; A.L.H. Vol. 1 (1985)-. Spanish. an. 3000ptas (surface mail); 4115ptas Europe, 4915ptas US (airmail). Universidad de Valladolid / Publicaciones, Secretariado de Publicaciones, Calle Juan Mambrilla 7, 47003 Valladolid Spain. **Tel** 011 34 83 294144, 011 34 83 294499, FAX 011 34 83 302095, telex 26357 EDUCI E. **ED** German de Granda, Cesar Hernandez, and Emilio Ridruejo. **LC** PC4008; .A58. **DD** 056/.1. Index available. cum. index. **Bk Rev. Ad Acc. Pr Rev. Circ:** 500.

VE
ANUARIO (UNIVERSIDAD CENTRAL DE VENEZUELA. ESCUELA DE LETRAS). (ANUARIO / ESCUELA DE LETRAS.). **Added/Corp** Universidad Central de Venezuela. Escuela de Letras. **VFOAT** Anuario Escuela de Letras U.C.V.; Anuario Escuela de Letras UCV. (1979)-. Spanish. Escuela de Letras, Facultad de Humanidades y Educacion UCV, Ciudad Universitaria, Caracas Venezuela. **LC** P9; .A67. **DD** 410/.5.

AU/0066 5282
ANZEIGER FUER SLAVISCHE PHILOLOGIE. Vol. 1 (1966)-. Monographic series. German. ir. Price varies per volume. Akademische Druck & Verlagsanstalt, Schoenaugasse 6, Postfach 598, A 8010 Graz Austria. **Tel** 011 43 316 813460. **ED** Rudolf Aitzetmuller, Stanilaus Hafner and Linda Sadnik. **LC** PG1; .A6. **DD** 491.8/05. **Bk Rev. Ad Acc.**
Desc: Critical reports, announcements, discussions, detailed reviews, essays, and scientific research on important publications.

US/1041-679X
APPLIED LANGUAGE LEARNING. [Appl. lang. learn.]. **Added/Corp** Defense Language Institute (U.S.). Foreign Language Center. Vol. 1, No. 1 (Spring 1989)-. Periodical. English. Twice a year (Feb. & Oct.). Free on request. Defense Language Institute, Foreign Language Center, Presidio of Monterey CA 93944-5006. **Tel** (408)647-5638. **ED** Lidia Woytak. **LC** WMLC 93/3113; P129; .A663. **DD** 407. **CODEN** ALLEEE. available on microfilm from ERIC.
Ind/Abst Curr. Index J. Educ.; Linguist. Lang. Behav. Abstr. (1989-) [Full Cov.]; Soc. Plann. Policy Dev. Abstr.; Sociol. Abstr.

UK/0142-6001
APPLIED LINGUISTICS. [Appl. linguist.]. **Added/Corp** American Association for Applied Linguistics. British Association for Applied Linguistics. International Association of Applied Linguistics. Vol. 1, No. 1 (Spring 1980)-. Periodical. English. qt. £70.00 UK and Europe; $128.00 other. Oxford University Press, Walton Street, Oxford OX2 6DP England. **Tel** 011 44 865 56767, FAX 011 44 865 267773, telex 837330 OXPRES G. **(Subscription address:** Oxford University Press / USA, Journals Marketing Department, Oxford University Press, 2001 Evans Road, Cary NC 27513.**) ED** Alan Davies and Elaine Tarone. **LC** P129; .A66. **DD** 418/.005. **[CCC].** Index available. **Bk Rev. Ad Acc. Pr Rev.** available on microfilm and microfiche from University Microfilms International (UMI). Documents available from The Genuine Article.
Desc: Concerned with the relationship between theory and practice, covers work applying theoretical studies to practical problems. Promotes a principled approach to language learning.
Ind/Abst Abstr. Anthropol. (19??-); Br. Educ. Index; Curr. Contents Soc. Behav. Sci.; Curr. Index J. Educ. (March 1990-); Lang. Teach.; Linguist. Lang. Behav. Abstr. (1980-) [Full Cov.]; MLA Int. Bibl. Books Artic. Mod. Lang. Lit.; Multicult. Educ. Abstr.; Res. Alert [Full Cov.]; Soc. Plann. Policy Dev. Abstr.; Soc. Sci. Cit. Index [Full Cov.]; Sociol. Abstr.; Sociol. Educ. Abstr.; Spec. Educ. Needs Abstr.

UK/0142-7164
APPLIED PSYCHOLINGUISTICS. [Appl. psycholinguist.]. Vol. 1 (Feb. 1980)-. Academic Scholarly Publication. English. qt. $104.00 US, Canada & Mexico; £77.00 other. Cambridge University Press, The Edinburgh Building, Shaftesbury Road, Cambridge CB2 2RU United Kingdom. **Tel** 011 44 223 312393, FAX 011 44 223 325959. **(Subscription address:** Cambridge University Press / North America, 110 Midland Avenue, Port Chester NY 10573.**) ED** Catherine E. Snow and John L. Locke. **LC** P37; .A75. **DD** 401/.9. **NLM** W1 AP528M. **CODEN** APPSDZ. **[CCC]. Bk Rev. Pr Rev.** available on microfilm and microfiche from University Microfilms International (UMI). Documents available from The Genuine Article, BIOSIS Document Express.
Desc: Publishes original research papers on the psychological processes involved in language. It examines language development and defects in normal and retarded adults and children. Articles address the nature, acquisition and impairments of language expression and comprehension, including writing and reading. The journal gathers together work from a variety of fields including linguistics, psychology, psychiatry, education, speech, language, learning, sociology, hearing and neurology.
Ind/Abst Abstr. Anthropol. (19??-); Arts Humanit. Citation Index [Select. Cov.]; Biol. Abstr.; Br. Educ. Index; Curr. Contents Soc. Behav. Sci.; Curr. Index J. Educ.; EMBASE; Except. Child Educ. Resour. (19??-19??); Lang. Teach.; Linguist. Lang. Behav. Abstr. (1980-) [Full Cov.]; MLA Int. Bibl. Books Artic. Mod. Lang. Lit.; Multicult. Educ. Abstr.; Psychol. Abstr. (1980-); PsycINFO; PsycLit; Res. Alert [Full Cov.]; Soc. Plann. Policy Dev. Abstr.; Soc. Sci. Cit. Index [Full Cov.]; Sociol. Abstr.; Spec. Educ. Needs Abstr.

GW/0066-5576
APPROACHES TO SEMIOTICS. (1969)-. Monographic series. English. ir. Price varies per volume. Walter de Gruyter Inc. / Hawthorne, 200 Saw Mill River Road, Hawthorne NY 10532. **Tel** (914)747-0110, GERMANY: 011/49/30/260050, FAX (914)747-1326, telex 646677. **NLM** W1 AP535.
Ind/Abst MLA Int. Bibl. Books Artic. Mod. Lang. Lit.

NE/0066-5576
APPROACHES TO SEMIOTICS. PAPERBACK SERIES. ***Ceased.*** Monographic series. English (French). ir. Walter de Gruyter Inc. / Hawthorne, 200 Saw Mill River Road, Hawthorne NY 10532. **Tel** (914)747-0110, GERMANY: 011/49/30/260050, FAX (914)747-1326, telex 646677. **(Subscription address:** Germany/ PO Box 110240, 1 Berlin 11**) UDC** 801.7.

CN/0834-1443
AQUILON (YELLOWKNIFE). (L'AQUILON.). [Aquilon]. **Added/Corp** Association Culturelle Franco-Tenoise. Vol. 1, No. 1 (Feb. 1986)-. Periodical. French. Forty-eight times a year (Except Aug.). 18.00Can$ (individual), 30.00Can$ (institutions) Canada; 35.00Can$ (individual) others. Aquilon Editions Franco, Box 1325, Yellowknife NT X1A 2N9 Canada. **Tel** (403)873-6603, FAX (403)873-2158. **ED** Flgnes Billa. **DD** 971.9/2004114/005. **Bk Rev**, (Qty: 2). **Ad Acc. Circ:** 1,000 (ctrl).
Desc: General information about the actuality of the North.

UK/0959-4213
ARAM PERIODICAL. **Added/Corp** ARAM Society for Syro-Mesopotamian Studies. **VFOAT** ARAM. Vol. 1, No. 1 (Winter 1989)-. Academic Scholarly Publication. English (Arabic, French and German). sa. Price varies. ARAM Periodical, Oriental Institute, Pusey Lane, Oxford OX1 2LE England. **Tel** 011 44 865 514041, FAX 011 44 865 516824. **ED** Dr. Shafiq Abouzayd. **Pr Rev.**

US
ARAPAHO LANGUAGE AND CULTURE INSTRUCTIONAL MATERIALS SERIES. No. 1-. Monographic series. English. Price varies per volume. Arapaho Language and Culture Commission, PO Box 771, Ethete WY 82520. **UDC** 809.7.

GW/0343-8694
ARBEITSPAPIERE ZUR LINGUISTIK. (ARBEITSPAPIERE ZUR LINGUISTIK / INSTITUT FUER KOMMUNIKATIONSWISSENSCHAFTEN DER TECHNISCHEN UNIVERSITAT BERLIN.). [Arb.pap. Linguist.]. **Added/Corp** Technische Universitat Berlin. Institut fur Kommunikationswissenschaften. **VFOAT** Working Papers in Linguistics. (1978)-. Monographic series. German (English).
Ind/Abst MLA Int. Bibl. Books Artic. Mod. Lang. Lit.

AU/0066-6440
ARCHIV FUER ORIENTFORSCHUNG. Vol. 3 (1926)-. English (French and German). ir (Published every 2 years). Inst Orientalistik Uni Wien, Universitatsstr 7 V, A 1010 Vienna Austria. **ED** Hans Hirsch. **LC** PJ5; .A72. **DD** 490/.5. **Bk Rev.** ***Continues*** *Archiv fuer Keilschriftforschung.*
Desc: Covers topics of Near Eastern research, such as ancient sculpture and writing systems, ancient history and economics and assyriology.

GW/0066-6459
ARCHIV FUER PAPYRUSFORSCHUNG UND VERWANDTE GEBIETE. **Added/Corp** Staatliche Museen zu Berlin (Germany : East). Vol. 1 (1900)-. Monographic series. German. ir. Price varies per volume. BSB BG Teubner Verlagsgesellsc, PO Box 930, D 70510 Leipzig Germany. **Tel** 011 49 341 293158. **(Subscription address:** BG Teubner Stuttgart, Postfach 801069, D 70510 Stuttgart Germany.**) ED** Ulrich Wilcken (1900-27). **LC** PA3339; .A6.

GW/0003-8970
ARCHIV FUER DAS STUDIUM DER NEUEREN SPRACHEN UND LITERATUREN (1961). (ARCHIV FUER DAS STUDIUM DER NEUEREN SPRACHEN UND LITERATUREN.). [Arch. Stud. neueren Sprachen Lit.]. (1961)-. Periodical. German (English and French). sa. DM120.00. Erich Schmidt Verlag GmbH, Postfach 304240, D 10724 Berlin Germany. **Tel** 011 49 30 25008525. **ED** Werner Besch, Hugo Moser, Hartnut Steinecke, and Bennovon Wiese. **[CCC]. Bk Rev. Ad Acc.** Documents available from The Genuine Article. ***Continues*** *Archiv fuer das Studium der Neueren Sprachen Mit Literaturblatt und Bibliographie.*
Desc: Philology, Americanism, and German philology.
Ind/Abst Abstr. Engl. Stud.; Annu. Bibliogr. Engl. Lang. Lit.; Arts Humanit. Citation Index [Full Cov.]; Curr. Contents Arts Humanit.; Linguist. Lang. Behav. Abstr.; MLA Int. Bibl. Books Artic. Mod. Lang. Lit.; Res. Alert [Full Cov.]; Romant. Move.; Soc. Plann. Policy Dev. Abstr.; Soc. Sci. Cit. Index [Select. Cov.]; Sociol. Abstr.

XR/0044-8699
ARCHIV ORIENTALNI. **Added/Corp** Orientalni Ustav, Prague. Ceskoslovenska Akademie Ved. Orientalni Ustav. (Mar. 1929)-. Periodical. English (French, German, Russian and Spanish). Four times a year. $176.00. John Benjamins BV, Amsteldijk 44, PO Box 75577, 1070 AN Amsterdam Netherlands. **Tel** 011 31 20 6738156, FAX 011 31 20 739773. **(Subscription address:** John Benjamins North America, PO Box 27519, Philadelphia PA 19118-0519.**) ED** Blahoslav Hruska and L'ubica Obuchova. **LC** DS1; .A47.
Desc: Journal of African, Asian and Latin-American studies.
Ind/Abst Anthropol. Index; MLA Int. Bibl. Books Artic. Mod. Lang. Lit.

IT/0004-0207
ARCHIVIO GLOTTOLOGICO ITALIANO. [Arch. glottol. ital.]. Vol. 1 (1873)-. Periodical. Italian. Twice a year (June & Dec.). L72000 Italy; L98000 others. Editoriale Finanz le Monnier, PO Box 202, Via Meucci 2, 50015 Grassina Florence Italy. **Tel** 011 39 55 64910. **LC** PC4; .A7. Index available (Bound in last issue). cum. index. **Bk Rev. Ad Acc. Circ:** 750.
Ind/Abst Linguist. Lang. Behav. Abstr. (1986-) [Full Cov.]; MLA Int. Bibl. Books Artic. Mod. Lang. Lit.; Soc. Plann. Policy Dev. Abstr.; Sociol. Abstr.

IT/0392-1050
ARCHIVIO PER L'ALTO ADIGE. **See** Ethnic Interests.

SP/0570-7218
ARCHIVUM (OVIEDO). (ARCHIVUM : REVISTA DE LA FACULTAD DE FILOSOFIA Y LETRAS, DIVISION DE FILOLOGIA.). [Archivum]. **Added/Corp** Universidad de Oviedo. Division de Filologia. Universidad de Oviedo. Facultad de Filosofia y Letras. Vol. 1 (1951)-. Periodical. Spanish. an. 4300ptas. Universidad de Oviedo, Arguelles 19, 33003 Oviedo Spain. **Tel** 011 34 8 5210160. **LC** P1; .A69. **DD** 410/.5.
Ind/Abst MLA Int. Bibl. Books Artic. Mod. Lang. Lit.

FI/0066-6998
ARCTOS. (ARCTOS; ACTA PHILOLOGICA FENNICA.). **Added/Corp** Klassillis-Filologinen Yhdistys (Finland). Vol. 1-2 (1930-31); New Series Vol. 1 (1954)-. Monographic series. Multiple languages (English, German and Italian). ir. Price varies per volume. Academic Bookstore Akateeminen, Postilokero 23, FIN-00371 Helsinki Finland. **Tel** 011 358 0 12141. **LC** WMLC L 83/1491.

AG
ARGOS. [Argos]. Yearly V. 1- 1977-. Periodical. Spanish. an. Asociacion Argentina de Estudios Clasicos, Cramer 228, 1876 Bernal, Pcia de Buenos Aires Argentina. **Tel** 54-1-826-2410. **(Subscription address:** Beiruti 3199 - 4 A, 1425 Buenos Aires Republic of Argentina**) ED** Rodolfo P Buzon. **LC** PA9; .A6. **Bk Rev. Ad Acc. Circ:** 400.

FR
ARGOS. French. Three times a year. CRDP, 20 rue Daniel Casanova, 94170 Le Perr S Marne France. **Tel** 011 31 1 48727070.

CN/0840-4798
ARGUS SECTORIEL. [Argus sect.]. **VFOAT** Sectoriel. Vol. 5, No 1 (1988)-. Periodical. French. Twice a year (Summer & Winter). 54.00Can$ Canada; 64.00Can$ US; 74.00Can$ other. Argus Communications

Inc, 1161 Lac Cache, CP 26, St Alexis, Quebec, J0K 1V0 Canada. **Tel** (819)265-2072, FAX (819)265-3135. **DD** 050/.25/714. ***Continues*** *Argus Redactionnel., 0829-1292.*

US/0895-8920
ARIEL (LEXINGTON, KY.). See Literature.

US/0004-1483
ARIZONA ENGLISH BULLETIN.
Added/Corp Arizona English Teachers Association. Vol. 1 (Oct. 1958)-. Bulletin. English. Three times a year. $20.00 (individuals); $25.00 (institutions) Comes with Arizona English Teachers Association Membership. Arizona English Teachers Association, 6023 East Vernon Drive, C/O M. Davis, Scottsdale AZ 85257. **Tel** (602)947-9618. **ED** Suzanne Bratcher. **Bk Rev. Circ:** 500.
Desc: Concerns the teaching of English language arts.
Ind/Abst Linguist. Lang. Behav. Abstr.; Soc. Plann. Policy Dev. Abstr.; Sociol. Abstr.

SW/0066-7668
ARKIV FOR NORDISK FILOLOGI. [Ark. nord. filol.]. Vol. 1 (1883)-. Monographic series. Norwegian (German, English, French and Scandinavian). an. Price varies per volume. Lund University Press, Box 141, S-22100 Lund Sweden. **Tel** 011 46 46 312000, FAX 011 46 46 305338, telex 33345 EDUCATE S. **ED** Bengt Pamp and Christer Platzack. **LC** PD1503; .A7. Index available (Free). cum. index. **Bk Rev. Circ:** 500.
Desc: Contains articles on the Nordic philology, Nordic medieval literature and Nordic religion.
Ind/Abst Annu. Bibliogr. Engl. Lang. Lit.; MLA Int. Bibl. Books Artic. Mod. Lang. Lit.

SW/0302-8348
ARSSKRIFT - SYDSVENSKA ORTNAMNSSALLSKAPETS. (ARSSKRIFT.). [Arsskr. Sydsven. ortnamnssallsk.]. **Main/Corp** Sdsvenska Ortnamnssallskapet. (19??)-. Swedish. **LC** DL606; .S93a.
Ind/Abst Annu. Bibliogr. Engl. Lang. Lit.; MLA Int. Bibl. Books Artic. Mod. Lang. Lit.; Numis. Lit.

CK
ARTICULOS EN LINGUISTICA Y CAMPOS AFINES. No. 1 (Oct. 1974)-. Spanish. Instituto Linguistica de Verano, Bogota Colombia. **LC** PM5001; .A77. **DD** 498.
Ind/Abst Anthropol. Lit.; Linguist. Lang. Behav. Abstr. (1974-) [Full Cov.]; Soc. Plann. Policy Dev. Abstr.; Sociol. Abstr.

XR
ASIAN AND AFRICAN LINGUISTIC STUDIES. **Added/Corp** Universita Karlova. Dept. of Asian and African Studies. Universita Karlova. Dept. of Asian and Oriental Studies. (1979)-. English (German and Russian; summaries and/or abstracts in Czech). ir. Charles University / Univerzita Karlova, Ovocnytrh 5, 116 36 Prague 1 Czech Republic. **Tel** 228441. **(Subscription address:** Artia Pegas Press Ltd., Palac Metro Narodni Trida 25, 11210 Prague 1 Czech Republic.) **Bk Rev. Circ:** 100-300.

US/0066-9903
ASSYRIOLOGICAL STUDIES.
(ASSYRIOLOGICAL STUDIES / ORIENTAL INSTITUTE OF THE UNIVERSITY OF CHICAGO.). **Added/Corp** University of Chicago. Oriental Institute. (1931)-. Monographic series. English. ir. Price varies per volume. University of Chicago Oriental Institute, 1155 East 58th Street, Chicago IL 60637. **Tel** (312)702-9537. **ED** Tom Holland and Tom Urban. **LC** UNC. **Circ:** 750 (ctrl).
Desc: Specialized studies dealing with ancient Near Eastern languages that include Amorite, Akkadian, Aramaic, Sumerian and Hittite.

IT
ATHANOR. (1990)-. Periodical. Italian (French, English and Greek, Modern). an. L30000 Italy; L40000 other. Angelo Longo Editore, Via Paolo Costa 33, PO Box 431, 48100 Ravenna Italy. **Tel** 011 39 544 217026, FAX 011 39 544 217026. **ED** Augusto Pontio and Claude Gandelman. **LC** P99; .A83. **DD** 302.23/05. **Pr Rev. Circ:** 2,000.
Desc: Studies on semiotics, linguistics, literature, and philosophy.

GR
ATHENIAN (ATHENS, GREECE). (THE ATHENIAN.). (April 12, 1974)-. Periodical. English. mo. $48.00 Europe; $50.00 other. The Athenian Press Ltd., Konstantinou Tsatsou St 4, 105 58 Athens Greece. **Tel** 011 30 1 3223052, FAX 011 30 1 3223052. **ED** Sloane Elliott. **LC** PAR. Index available (bound separately). **Bk Rev**, (Qty: 8-10). **Ad Acc, Adv Mgr:** Katia Stamatiadou. **Circ:** 10,000.
Desc: Greece's English language magazine.

II
ATIMARSA. Periodical. Hindi (Hindi). 5.00. Yugantara Presa, S-362 Greater Kailash-I, New Delhi 110048 India. **LC** PK2047; .A85.

US/0894-6728
ATJ NEWSLETTER. [ATJ newsl.]. **Added/Corp** Association of Teachers of Japanese (U.S.). **VAT** Association of Teachers of Japanese Newsletter. (April 1978)-. Newsletter. English. Three times a year. $28.00 (individuals), $35.00 (institutions) US & Canada; $31.00 (individuals), $38.00 (institutions) others Comes with Association of Teachers of Japanese Membership. Association of Teachers of Japanese, Hillcrest 9, Middlebury College, Middlebury VT 05753. **Tel** (802)388-3711, Ext. 5915 or 5784, FAX (802)388-4329. **ED** Naomi Hanaoka McGloin. **DD** 495. **Circ:** 600 (ctrl). ***Continues in part*** *Journal-Newsletter of the Association of Teachers of Japanese, 0004-5810.*

FR/0996-4703
AU SERVICE DE L'ENSEIGNEMENT. FRANCAIS. See Education-Teaching and Curriculum.

SZ/0171-6867
AUSTRALIAN AND NEW ZEALAND STUDIES IN GERMAN LANGUAGE AND LITERATURE. See Literature.

●AT/1038-1562
AUSTRALIAN JOURNAL OF LANGUAGE AND LITERACY / ARA, THE.
Added/Corp Australian Reading Association. Vol. 15, No. 1 (Feb. 1992)-. Periodical. English. qt (Feb., May, Aug., Nov.). (comes with Australian Reading Association membership). Australian Reading Association, PO Box 78, Carlton VIC 2053 Australia. **Tel** 61 3 3472555. **ED** Bruce Shortland-Jones. **LC** LB1049.9; .A97. **CODEN** AJLLEL. ***Continues*** *Australian Journal of Reading, 0156-0301.*
Ind/Abst Aust. Educ. Index (199?-).

AT/0726-8602
AUSTRALIAN JOURNAL OF LINGUISTICS. (AUSTRALIAN JOURNAL OF LINGUISTICS : JOURNAL OF THE AUSTRALIAN LINGUISTIC SOCIETY.). [Aust. j. linguist.]. **Added/Corp** Australian Linguistic Society. Vol. 1, No. 1 (June 1981)-. Periodical. English. sa (June and Dec.). $43.00. LaTrobe University Press, LaTrobe University C A Day, Bundoora Victoria 3083 Australia. **Tel** 011 61 3 4791460, FAX (03)470 2011, telex AA 33143. **ED** David Bradley and Roland Sussex. **LC** P1; .A9. **DD** 410/.5. Index available. **Bk Rev. Ad Acc. Pr Rev. Circ:** 600. available on microfilm from University Microfilms International (UMI).
Desc: Concerned with all branches of general linguistics.
Ind/Abst Annu. Bibliogr. Engl. Lang. Lit.; APAIS, Aust. Public Aff. Inf. Ser. (1984-); Aust. Educ. Index (1981-); Int. Bibliogr. Sociol.; Linguist. Lang. Behav. Abstr. (1981-) [Full Cov.]; MLA Int. Bibl. Books Artic. Mod. Lang. Lit.; Soc. Plann. Policy Dev. Abstr.; Sociol. Abstr.

AT/0155-0640
AUSTRALIAN REVIEW OF APPLIED LINGUISTICS. [Aust. rev. appl. linguist.].
Added/Corp Applied Linguistics Association of Australia. (1977)-. Periodical. English. Twice a year (May & Nov.). 35.00Aus$ (individuals), 50.00Aus$ (institutions) Comes with Applied Linguistics Association of Australia membership. Applied Linguistics Association of Australia / ALAA, Centre for Language Learning and Teaching, University of Southern Queensland, Toowoomba, Queensland 4350 Australia. **Tel** 011 61 06 281 3366, telex 062813096. **ED** Tony Liddicoat. **DD** 410.994. **Bk Rev**, (Qty: 8-10). **Ad Acc, Adv Mgr:** R. Baldauf. **Pr Rev. Circ:** 700. ***Absorbed*** *Newsletter of the Applied Linguistics Association of Australia, 0313-8054.*
Ind/Abst Annu. Bibliogr. Engl. Lang. Lit.; Linguist. Lang. Behav. Abstr. (1980-) [Full Cov.]; Soc. Plann. Policy Dev. Abstr.

AT/0818-8149
AUSTRALIAN SLAVONIC AND EAST EUROPEAN STUDIES : JOURNAL OF THE AUSTRALIAN AND NEW ZEALAND SLAVISTS' ASSOCIATION AND OF THE AUSTRALASIAN ASSOCIATION FOR STUDY OF THE SOCIALIST COUNTRIES. **Added/Corp** University of Melbourne. Dept. of Russian and Language Studies. Australian and New Zealand Slavists' Association. Australasian Association for Study of the Socialist Countries. Vol. 1, No. 1 (1987)-. Periodical. English (Russian). sa. 25.00Aus$. University of Melbourne / Department of Russian Language and Literature, Parkville Victoria 3052 Australia. **Tel** 011 61 3 3445193. **ED** P.V. Cubberley. ***Continues*** *Melbourne Slavonic Studies, 0076-6267.*
Desc: Covers any Slavonic area, especially language, literature, history and social science.
Ind/Abst Am. Hist. Life (1990-); Am. Bibliogr. Slavic East Europ. Stud.; Linguist. Lang. Behav. Abstr.; MLA Int. Bibl. Books Artic. Mod. Lang. Lit.; Soc. Plann. Policy Dev. Abstr.; Sociol. Abstr.

IE/0791-0797
AUTHENTIK AUTHENTIK IN ENGLISH. (AUTHENTIK). [AuthentikAuthent. Engl.]. **VFOAT** Authentik in English. (1989)-. Periodical. English (Spanish, German, English, French and Irish). ir (5 issues per year). £44.70 UK; £38.00 other. Authentik, 27 Westland Square, Dublin 2 Ireland. **Tel** 011 10 353 16771515, FAX 011 10 353 6798039, telex 771512. **DD** 428.6. **Bk Rev. Ad Acc. Circ:** 40,000 (ctrl). available on audiocassette.
Desc: News items from various publications of the country of origin, reproduced with exercises for language learners together with a cassette of radio broadcasts.

US/0005-1055
AUTOMATIC DOCUMENTATION AND MATHEMATICAL LINGUISTICS. See Library and Information Sciences.

FR/0767-5259
AUTREMENT DIRE. (1984)-. Periodical. French. an. Presses Universitaires de Nancy, 25 rue Baron Louis, B P 454, 54001 Nancy Cedex France. **UDC** 80.

AT/0005-3503
BABEL. [Babel]. **Added/Corp** Australian Federation of Modern Language Teacher's Associations. Modern Language Teacher's Association of Victoria. No. 1-27, (Apr. 1956)-(Oct. 1964); New Series 2, Vol. 1 (Apr. 1965)-. Periodical. English (French and German). Three times a year (Apr., July, Oct.). 50.00Aus$ (institution), 45.00Aus$ (individual) Australia; 55.00Aus$ (institution), 50.00Aus$ (individual), surface mail; 50.00Aus$ (individuals), 60.00Aus$ (institutions) airmail. Australian Federation of Modern Language Teachers, c/o Angela Scarino, 9 Stanley Street, North Adelaide, 5006 Australia. **ED** Angela Scarino (phone: (08)2671584 home & (08) 3022726 work). **[CCC].** cum. index. **Bk Rev. Ad Acc. Pr Rev. Circ:** 2,000 (ctrl). ***Supersedes*** *Modern Language Teacher's Association of Victoria. Newsletter.*
Desc: Articles of interest to teachers of all foreign and second languages, and to applied linguists. Also includes a section on classroom technology.
Ind/Abst APAIS, Aust. Public Aff. Inf. Ser. (1973-); Aust. Educ. Index (1977-); Curr. Index J. Educ.; Lang. Teach.; Linguist. Lang. Behav. Abstr.; Soc. Plann. Policy Dev. Abstr.; Sociol. Abstr.

GW/0521-9744
BABEL (FRANKFURT). (BABEL.). [Babel].
Added/Corp International Federation of Translators. Vol. 1 (Sept. 1955)-. Periodical. French (English, French, German, Italian and Russian). Four times a year (Feb., May, Aug., Nov.). $80.00. John Benjamins BV, Amsteldijk 44, PO Box 75577, 1070 AN Amsterdam Netherlands. **Tel** 011 31 20 6738156, FAX 011 31 20 739773. **(Subscription address:** John Benjamins North America, PO Box 27519, Philadelphia PA 19118-0519.) **ED** Rene Haeseryn. **LC** PN241.A1; B15.
Desc: Designed primarily for translators and interpreters, yet of interest also for the nonspecialist concerned with current issues and events in the field of translation. Discusses the legal, financial and social aspects of the translator's profession.
Ind/Abst Curr. Index J. Educ.; Lang. Teach.; Linguist. Lang. Behav. Abstr.; MLA Int. Bibl. Books Artic. Mod. Lang. Lit.; Soc. Plann. Policy Dev. Abstr.; Sociol. Abstr.

BX/0005-3988
BAHANA. [Bahana]. **Added/Corp** Dewan Bahasa dan Pustaka Brunei. (1966)-. Periodical. Malay. mo. Price varies. Dewan Bahasa & Pustaka, Marketing Section, Bandar Ser Begawan 2064 Brunei. **LC** PL5101; .B33.
Desc: Information on Malay philology.

IO
BAHASA DAN SASTRA. 1-. Indonesian. qt. Jalan Daksinapati Barat IV, PO Box 2625, Rawamangun Jakarta 13220 Indonesia. **Tel** (021)4896558. **ED** Anton M Moeliono, S Effendi, A Latief, Sri Sukesi Adiwimarta, and Anita K Rustapa. **LC** PL5071; .A235. Index available. **Bk Rev. Circ:** 500 (ctrl). ***Continues in part*** *Bahasa Dan Kesusastraan, 0522-0238;* ***Continues*** *Pengajaran Bahasa Dan Sastra, 0126-0642.*

GW/0170-8007
BALKAN-ARCHIV. 1. V. (1925)-4. V. (1928); N.F. Vol. 1 (1976)-. German (Italian and Romanian). an. Helmut Buske Verlag Hamburg, Postfach 760244, D 2000 Hamburg 76 F R Germany. **Tel** 011 49 40 5236739. **ED** Wolfgang Dahmen and Johannes Kramer. **LC** PC603; .L4. **DD** 409/.496. **UDC** 805.9. **Circ:** 400. ***Continues*** *Jahresbericht des Instituts fur Rumanische Sprache (Rumanisches Seminar) zu Leipzig.*

BU/0324-1653
BALKANSKO EZIKOZNANIE. (BALKANSKO EZIKOZNANIE / BULGARSKA AKADEMIIA NA NAUKITE, OTDELENIE ZA EZIKOZNANIE, LITERATUROZNANIE I ETNOGRAFIIA.). [Balk. ezikozn.]. **Added/Corp** Bulgarska Akademiia na Naukite. Otdelenie za Ezikoznanie, Literaturoznanie i Etnografiia. Bulgarska Akademiia na Naukite. Otdelenie za Ezikoznanie, Literaturoznanie i Izkustvoznanie. Bulgarska Akademiia na Naukite. Edinen Tsentur za Ezik i Literatura. **VFOAT** Linguistique Balkanique. Vol. 1 (1959)-. Periodical. French (German, English and Russian; summaries and/or abstracts in Bulgarian). Three times a year. DM166.00. **(Subscription address:** Kubon & Sagner, ABT Zeitschriftenimport, D 80328 Munich Germany.) **LC** P381.B3; B3.
Ind/Abst Annu. Bibliogr. Engl. Lang. Lit.; Linguist. Lang. Behav. Abstr. (1985-) [Full Cov.]; MLA Int. Bibl. Books Artic. Mod. Lang. Lit.; Soc. Plann. Policy Dev. Abstr.; Sociol. Abstr.

IS/0792-3252
BALSANWT 'IBRIYT. [Balsanwt 'ibriyt]. **VFOAT** Hebrew Linguistica. (1989)-. Academic Scholarly

Publication. Hebrew. qt. Bar-Ilan University Press, Department of Hebrew and Semitic Languages, Ramat-Gan 52900 Israel. **Tel** 972-3-5318401. **ED** Maya Fruchtman. **UDC** 801. ***Continues** Blsnwt Bryt Hpsyt, 0334-3472.*
Ind/Abst Linguist. Lang. Behav. Abstr.; Soc. Plann. Policy Dev. Abstr.

IS
BALSHANUT 'IVRIT. **Added/Corp** Universitat Bar-Ilan. Mahlakah le-Lashon Ivrit Veli-Leshonot Shemiyot. **VFOAT** Hebrew Linguistics. (1989)-. Periodical. Hebrew (summaries and/or abstracts in English). an. $28.00. Universitat Bar-Ilan, Department of Philosophy, Ramat Gan 52900 Israel. **Tel** 11 972 3 5318575, 11 972 3 5318401, telex 342290 BARIL IL. **ED** Maya Fruchman. **CODEN** HELIEK. Index available. cum. index. ctrl circ. ***Continues** Balshanut 'Ivrit Hofshit, 0334-3472.*
Desc: Bulletin for Hebrew formal, computational and applied linguistics and modern Hebrew.
Ind/Abst MLA Int. Bibl. Books Artic. Mod. Lang. Lit.

LI/0045-1371
BALTISTICA. [Baltistica]. **Added/Corp** Lithuania. Valstybinis Aukstojo ir Specialiojo Vidurinio Mokslo Komitetas. Lithuania. Aukstojo ir Specialiojo Vidurinio Mokslo Ministerija. (1965)-. Periodical. Lithuanian (Russian, German, Latvian, English and French). sa. **LC** PG8001; .B33.
Ind/Abst MLA Int. Bibl. Books Artic. Mod. Lang. Lit.

RU
BALTO-SLAVIANSKIE ISSLEDOVANIIA / AKADEMIIA NAUK SSSR, INSTITUT SLAVIANOVEDENIIA I BALKANISTIKI. **Added/Corp** Institut Slavianovedeniia i Balkanistiki (Akademiia Nauk SSSR). (1980)-. Russian. an. 4.20rub. Izdatelstvo Nauka / Akademiia Nauk, Publishing House of the Russian Academy of Sciences, Leninskii Porspekt 14, 117901 Moscow Russia. **Tel** 011 95 954-21-53, FAX 011 95 938-21-44, telex 411964. **LC** PG8001; .B34. **DD** 491/.9/05.

FR/0067-3951
BANQUE DES MOTS (PARIS). (LA BANQUE DES MOTS.). [Banq. mots]. **Added/Corp** Conseil International de la Langue Francaise. (1971)-. Periodical. French. Twice a year. 220.00 France; 260.00 other. Conseil Internationale de Langue Francaise, 11 rue de Navarin, 75009 Paris France. **Tel** 11 33 1 48787395. **(Subscription address:** Editons Cilf- 21 Bis rue Cardinal Lemoine, 75005 Paris, France (telephone: 11 33 1 43547174)**)** **LC** PC2689; .B35. **CODEN** BAMOEH. Index available. **Bk Rev. Ad Acc. Circ:** 2,000.
Desc: Goal is to maintain the integrity of the French language throughout the world. Devoted to terminology; collates and comments on vocabularies from scientific, professional and leisure fields where standard and regional French are used.
Ind/Abst GeoRef; Point Repere (1983-).

US/0191-3484
BARRON'S QUESTIONS AND ANSWERS. COMPREHENSIVE ENGLISH, 3 AND 4. ***Title Change.*** (BARRON'S QUESTIONS AND ANSWERS: COMPREHENSIVE ENGLISH, 3 AND 4 YEARS.). **Main/Corp** Barron's Educational Series, Inc. **Added/Corp** Barrons's Educational Series, Inc. Barron's Regents Exams and Answers: Comprehensive English, 3 and 4 Years. **VFOAT** Questions and Answers. Comprehensive English, 3 and 4 Years; Comprehensive English, 3 and 4 Years; Barron's Regents Exams and Answers. Comprehensive English (3 and 4 Years). **VAT** Barron's Questions and Answers. Comprehensive English, Three and Four. (19??)-(19??). English. Barrons Educational Series, 250 Wireless Boulevard, Hauppauge NY 11788. **Tel** (516)434-3311. **LC** PE1114; .R32. **DD** 420/.76. ***Continued by** Barron's Regents Exams and Answers. Comprehensive English, 1069-2924.*

US/0146-6895
BARRON'S REGENTS EXAMS AND ANSWERS : FRENCH LEVEL 3, COMPREHENSIVE FRENCH. **Main/Corp** Barron's Educational Series, Inc. **VAT** Barron's Regents Exams and Answers: French Level Three, Comprehensive French. English. $2.50. Barrons Educational Series, 250 Wireless Boulevard, Hauppauge NY 11788. **Tel** (516)434-3311. **LC** PC2119; .B34A. **DD** 440/.76. **UDC** 804.0.

US/0191-3409
BARRON'S REGENTS EXAMS AND ANSWERS : SPANISH LEVEL 3, COMPREHENSIVE SPANISH. **Main/Corp** Barron's Educational Series, Inc. **VFOAT** Regents Exams and Answers: Spanish Level 3, Comprehensive Spanish. **VAT** Barron's Regents Exams and Answers. Spanish Level Three, Comprehensive Spanish. English. $2.95. Barrons Educational Series, 250 Wireless Boulevard, Hauppauge NY 11788. **Tel** (516)434-3311. **LC** PC4119; .E9. **DD** 468/.2/421076. **UDC** 806.0. ***Continues** Exams and Answers: Spanish Three Years.*

SZ/0067-4508
BASLER STUDIEN ZUR DEUTSCHEN SPRACHE UND LITERATUR. No. 1 (1942)-. Monographic series. German. ir. Price varies per volume. A Francke Verlag GmbH, Postfach 2560, Dischingerweg 5, D 72070 Tuebingen Germany. **Tel** 011 49 7071 78091 or 92.
Ind/Abst MLA Int. Bibl. Books Artic. Mod. Lang. Lit.

UK/0263-550X
BBC ENGLISH. (19??)-. English. Twelve times a year. £22.00 UK; £27.00 Europe; £30.00 others. TG Scott Subscriber Services, 6 Bourne Enterprise Center, Wrotham Road, Borough Green, Kent TN15 8DG England. **Tel** 011 44 01 732 884023, FAX 011 44 01 732 884034. available on audiocassette.
Desc: Magazine for people learning/teaching English as a foreign language. Includes a forty-minute cassette with every issue, pull out radio guide to all BBC English radio programmes worldwide; language schools directory.

CN/0229-0235
BCATML NEWSLETTER, THE. [BCATML newsl.]. Newsletter. English (French). mo. British Columbia Teachers Federation, 100-550 West 6th Avenue, Vancouver British Columbia V5Z 4P2 Canada. **Tel** (604)871-2283, (800)663-9163, FAX (604)871-2294, (604)871-2290. **DD** 407. **UDC** 802.0. ctrl circ.

GW/0084-5396
BEIHEFTE ZUR ZEITSCHRIFT FUER ROMANISCHE PHILOLOGIE. Vol. 1 (1905)-. Monographic series. English (French, German and Spanish). ir. Price varies per volume. Max Niemeyer Verlag, Postfach 2140, D 72011 Tuebingen Germany. **Tel** 011 49 7071 989494, FAX 011 49 7071 87419. **ED** Max Pfister. **LC** UNC.
Desc: Studies on romantic languages and literature.
Ind/Abst Curr. Contents Arts Humanit.; MLA Int. Bibl. Books Artic. Mod. Lang. Lit.

GW/0522-6341
BEITRAEGE ZUR DEUTSCHEN PHILOLOGIE. [Beitr. dtsch. Philol.]. Vol. 1 (1954)-. Monographic series. German. ir. Price varies per volume. Wilhelm Schmitz Verlag, Postfach 21108, Pestalozzstr 3, W-6300 Giessen F R Germany. **Tel** 011 49 641 491919. ***Continues** Giessenr Beitrage zur Deutschen Philologie. Neue Folge.*
Ind/Abst MLA Int. Bibl. Books Artic. Mod. Lang. Lit.

GW/0171-4155
BEITRAEGE ZUR FREMDSPRACHENVERMITTLUNG AUS DEM KONSTANZER SLI. [Beitr. Fremdspr.vermittl. Konstanz. SLI]. (1979)-. Periodical. Multiple languages. ir. **UDC** 372.880. ***Continues** Mitteilungen des Konstanzer SLI, 0344-7162.*
Ind/Abst Soc. Plann. Policy Dev. Abstr.

GW/0005-8076
BEITRAEGE ZUR GESCHICHTE DER DEUTSCHEN SPRACHE UND LITERATUR (TUEBINGEN). (BEITRAEGE ZUR GESCHICHTE DER DEUTSCHEN SPRACHE UND LITERATUR.). [Beitr. Gesch. dtsch. Sprache Lit.]. Vol. 77 (1955)-. Periodical. German (English). Three times a year. DM178.00. Max Niemeyer Verlag, Postfach 2140, D 72011 Tuebingen Germany. **Tel** 011 49 7071 989494, FAX 011 49 7071 87419. **ED** Hans Fromm, Rudolf Grosse. **LC** PF3003; .B52. **DD** 430; 830. **Bk Rev. Ad Acc.** Documents available from The Genuine Article.
Desc: Contributions on Germanic languages and literatures (from the beginning to early new high German).
Ind/Abst Arts Humanit. Citation Index [Full Cov.]; BHA : Biblio. Hist. Art; Curr. Contents Arts Humanit.; MLA Int. Bibl. Books Artic. Mod. Lang. Lit.; Res. Alert [Full Cov.]; Romant. Move.; Soc. Sci. Cit. Index [Select. Cov.].

GW/0067-5024
BEITRAGE ZUR GESCHICHTE DER PHILOSOPHIE UND THEOLOGIE DES MITTELALTERS. [Beitr. Gesch. Philos. Theol. Mittelalt.]. Vol. 1 (1927)-. Monographic series. German. ir. Price varies per volume. Aschendorffsche Verlagsbuchhandlung, Postfach 1124, D-48135 Muenster Germany. **Tel** 011 49 251 690132, telex 08-92 830 WN MS D. ***Continues** Beitrage zur Geschichte der Philosophie des Mittelalters.*

BW/1010-3996
BELARUSKAIA MOVA. [Belarus. mova]. Vol. 5-. Periodical. Byelorussian. an. 1.50rub. VYD-VA BDU, Maskoukaia 15, Minsk Byelarus. **LC** PG2831; .B444. **UDC** 808.26. ***Continues** Belaruskaia Mova / Movaznaustva.*
Ind/Abst MLA Int. Bibl. Books Artic. Mod. Lang. Lit.

BW/0234-1360
BELARUSKAIA MOVA I LITERATURA U SHKOLE. ***Title Change.*** **Added/Corp** Byelorussian S.S.R. Ministerstva Asvety. **VFOAT** Belorusskii lazyk i Literatura V Shkole. Began in (1988)-(1992). Periodical. Byelorussian. mo. **(Subscription address:** Victor Kamkin, 4956 Boiling Brook Parkway, Rockville MD 20852.**)** **LC** PG2830; .B45. ***Continued by** tRodnae Slova.*

BW/0320-7552
BELARUSKAJA LINGVISTYKA. (BELARUSKAIA LINGVISTYKA.). [Belarus. lingvist.]. **Added/Corp** Instytut Movaznaustva Imia IAkuba Kolasa. (1972)-. Byelorussian (summaries and/or abstracts in English, French, German and Russian). 0.38rub (single issue). **LC** PG2831; .B44.
Ind/Abst MLA Int. Bibl. Books Artic. Mod. Lang. Lit.

FR/0774-5141
BELGIAN JOURNAL OF LINGUISTICS. **Added/Corp** Cercle Belge de Linguistique. (1986)-. French (summaries and/or abstracts in Dutch and French). an. $48.00. John Benjamins BV, Amsteldijk 44, PO Box 75577, 1070 AN Amsterdam Netherlands. **Tel** 011 31 20 6738156, FAX 011 31 20 739773. **(Subscription address:** John Benjamins North America, PO Box 27519, Philadelphia PA 19118-0519.**)** **ED** Marc Dominicy and Viviane Chase-Wiernik (Managing Editor). **LC** P1; .B45. **DD** 410/.5. **CODEN** BJLIEN.
Desc: Each volume is topical and includes selected papers from the International meetings organized by the Linguistic Society of Belgium.
Ind/Abst Annu. Bibliogr. Engl. Lang. Lit.; Linguist. Lang. Behav. Abstr. (1986-) [Full Cov.]; MLA Int. Bibl. Books Artic. Mod. Lang. Lit.; Soc. Plann. Policy Dev. Abstr.; Sociol. Abstr.

NE/0929-7316
BENJAMINS TRANSLATION LIBRARY. (19??)-. Monographic series. English. ir. Price varies per volume. John Benjamins BV, Amsteldijk 44, PO Box 75577, 1070 AN Amsterdam Netherlands. **Tel** 011 31 20 6738156, FAX 011 31 20 739773. **(Subscription address:** John Benjamins North America, PO Box 27519, Philadelphia PA 19118-0519.**)**
Desc: Aims to stimulate academic research and training in translation studies, interpreting, LSP, terminology and lexicography. It provides a forum for a variety of approaches in historical, theoretical, applied and pedagogical contexts.

GW/0930-5440
BERICHTE - INSTITUT FUER PHONETIK DER UNIVERSITAT ZU KOLN. [Ber. - Inst. Phon. Univ. Koln]. **VFOAT** IPKoln-Berichte. (1973)-. Periodical. German. ir. **UDC** 801.4.
Ind/Abst Linguist. Lang. Behav. Abstr. (1986-) [Full Cov.]; Soc. Plann. Policy Dev. Abstr.; Sociol. Abstr.

US/0893-6935
BERKELEY INSIGHTS IN LINGUISTICS AND SEMIOTICS. [Berkeley insights linguist. semiot.]. Monographic series. English. ir. Price varies per volume. Peter Lang Publishing, 62 West 45th Street, 4th Floor, New York NY 10036. **Tel** (212)764-1471, (800)770-5264, telex 6973364 PLNY. **ED** Irmengard Rauch. **DD** 410. **Pr Rev.**
Desc: Contains advanced studies in linguistics and semiotics.

●US/1061-6055
BERKELEY MODELS OF GRAMMAR. [Berkeley models gramm.]. Vol. 1 (1992)-. Monographic series. English. ir. Price varies per volume. Peter Lang Publishing, 62 West 45th Street, 4th Floor, New York NY 10036. **Tel** (212)764-1471, (800)770-5264, telex 6973364 PLNY. **DD** 429.

GE/0572-6263
BERLINER BEITRAEGE ZUR NAMENFORSCHUNG. Vol. 1 (1967)-. Monographic series. German. ir. Price varies per volume. Verlag Hermann Boehlaus Nachfolger, Postfach 260, D 99403 Weimar Germany. **Tel** 011 49 3643 2071, . **(Subscription address:** Verlag H. Boehlaus Nachfolger, Postfach 546, D-72488 Sigmaringen Germany; telephone: 011 49 7571 728120**)** **ED** H. H. Bielfeldt and T. Witkowski.
Desc: The names of settlements in the former province of Brandenburg are illustrated documentarily with regard to their history and explained linguistically with a view to make the knowledge obtained usable for the history of Germanic and Slav languages.
Ind/Abst MLA Int. Bibl. Books Artic. Mod. Lang. Lit.

II
BHARATIYA NEPALI VANMAYA. **VFOAT** Vanmaya. 1 (1980)-. Periodical. Nepali. an. Rs8.00. Nepali Sahitya Sancayika Prakasana, C-14 Super Market, Darjiling India. **Tel** DE 3237. **ED** Kumar Ghising. **LC** PK2598.Z9; I533. **UDC** 809.149.3. Index available. **Bk Rev. Ad Acc.**

II/0523-1418
BHASHA. (1962)-. Periodical. Hindi (Hindi). qt. Rs10.00 India; £1.17 UK; $3.80 other. Ministry of Education, Government of India, New Delhi India. **Tel** 605211. **ED** Jagdish Chatorvedi. **LC** PK2030. **UDC** 809.143. **Bk Rev. Circ:** 1,000.
Desc: Selected stories, poems, and articles of all modern Indian languages are published in Hindi in this journal.

II
BHASHA ANI JIVANA : MARATHI-ABHYASA-PARISHAD-PATRIKA. V. 1, No. 1 (July 1983)-. Periodical. Marathi (Marathi). qt. Rs40.00

India; $10.00 US. Marathi Abhyas Parishad, A/2 Parimal Apte Road, Pune 411004 India. **Tel** 52009. **ED** Ashok R Kelkar. **UDC** 809.146. Index available. **Bk Rev.** **Ad Acc.** **Circ:** 250 (ctrl).
Desc: Popular articles, stories, etc. bearing on language communication, media, education, literature, etc. with special reference to Marathi language India.

GW
BIBLIOGRAPHIE FREMDSPRACHIGER GERMANICA. Yearly V. 1-1972-. German. qt. Deutscher Judo Verband, Redaktion Ippon Segewaldweg 40, D 12557 Berlin Germany. **Tel** 011 49 711 210770, telex 051 678. **LC** Z2221. ***Continues** Bibliographie Fremdsprachiger Werke Uber Deutschland und Personlichkeiten des Deutschen Sprachgebietes.*

GW
BIBLIOGRAPHIE LINGUISTISCHER LITERATUR. **See** Linguistics-Abstracting, Bibliographies and Statistics.

NE
BIBLIOTECA HISPANOAMERICANA Y ESPANOLA DE AMSTERDAM. **VFOAT** BHEA. (1984)-. Monographic series. English. Editions Rodopi BV, Keizersgracht 302-304, 1016 Ex Amsterdam Netherlands. **Tel** 011 31 20 6227507, FAX 011 31 20 380948.
Ind/Abst MLA Int. Bibl. Books Artic. Mod. Lang. Lit.

SP/0519-721x
BIBLIOTECA ROMANICA HISPANICA. III. MANUALES. Vol. 1 (1950)-. Monographic series. Spanish. ir. Price varies per volume. Editorial Gredos SA, Calle Sanchez Pacheco 81, 28002 Madrid Spain. **Tel** 011 34 1 4157408, FAX 011 34 1 5192033. available on microfiche.

SP/0519-7236
BIBLIOTECA ROMANICA HISPANICA. V. DICCIONARIOS. Vol. 1 (1954)-. Monographic series. Spanish. ir. Price varies per volume. Editorial Gredos SA, Calle Sanchez Pacheco 81, 28002 Madrid Spain. **Tel** 011 34 1 4157408, FAX 011 34 1 5192033.

AU/0255-2795
BIBLIOTERM. **Added/Corp** Infoterm. International Network for Terminology. **VFOAT** BIT. Vol. 1 (Oct. 6, 1983)-. Periodical. English (French). qt. 360Aus$ Europe; 410Aus$ other. TermNet Secretariat, Gruengasse 9 17, A-1050 Vienna, Austria. **Tel** (011 43 222)567763, FAX (0222)2163272, telex 115960. **LC** IN PROCESS. **CODEN** BIBTEX. **Circ:** 300 (ctrl).
Desc: Bulletin covering bibliographic information on mono and multilingual specialized vocabularies, periodicals pertaining to terminology, etc.

GW/0067-7477
BIBLIOTHECA GERMANICA. (1951)-. Monographic series. German. ir. Price varies per volume. A Francke Verlag GmbH, Postfach 2560, Dischingerweg 5, D 72070 Tuebingen Germany. **Tel** 011 49 7071 78091 or 92.

NE/0006-1913
BIBLIOTHECA ORIENTALIS. **See** History(General)-History of Asia.

FR/0343-6237
BIBLIOTHEQUE DE L'ECOLE DES CHARTES. **See** Library and Information Sciences.

BE
BIBLIOTHEQUE DES CAHIERS DE L'INSTITUT DE LINGUISTIQUE DE LOUVAIN. **Main/Corp** Universite Catholique de Louvain, Louvain-la-Neuve, Belgium. Institut de Linguistique. **VFOAT** Bibliotheque des CILL. (1976)-. Monographic series. English (French and German). Editions Peeters SA, Bondgenotenlaan 153, BP 41, B-3000 Leuven Belgium. **Tel** 32 16 235170, FAX 32 16 228500, telex 65987 PUL B.
Ind/Abst MLA Int. Bibl. Books Artic. Mod. Lang. Lit.

FR
BIBLIOTHEQUE RUSSE. **Main/Corp** Paris. Universite. Institut d'Etudes Slaves. V. 1- 1912-. Monographic series. French (Russian). ir. Price varies per volume. Institut d'Etudes Slaves, 9 rue Michelet, 75006 Paris France. **Tel** 011 33 1 43265089. **UDC** 808.2; 882; 947. **Circ:** 500.
Desc: Series dedicated to Russian linguistics, literature, history of ideas and art.

FR/0078-9976
BIBLIOTHEQUE RUSSE DE L'INSTITUT D'ETUDES SLAVES. **See** Literature.

IS
BIKORET U-FARSHANUT. **See** Literary and Political Reviews.

UK/0952-4096
BILINGUAL FAMILY NEWSLETTER, THE. **See** Family and Marriage.

●US
BILINGUAL RESEARCH JOURNAL. **See** Education.

US/0094-5366
BILINGUAL REVIEW. (THE BILINGUAL REVIEW. LA REVISTA BILINGUE.). [Biling. rev.]. **Added/Corp** City University of New York. City College. Dept. of Romance Languages. York College. Dept. of Foreign Languages. **VFOAT** Revista Bilingue; La Revista Bilingue. Vol. 1 (Jan./Apr. 1974)-. Periodical. English (Spanish). tq. $30.00. Arizona State University / Hispanic Research Center, Tempe AZ 85287-2702. **Tel** (602)965-3867, FAX (602)964-8309. **ED** Gary D. Keller. **LC** P115; .B54. **DD** 401. **Bk Rev**, (Qty: 9). **Ad Acc**, **Adv Mgr:** Theresa Hammon. **Circ:** 2,000. available on microfilm and microfiche from University Microfilms International (UMI). Documents available from UMI Article Clearinghouse.
Desc: Devoted to the linguistics and literature of bilingualism and bilingual education in the United States.
Ind/Abst Acad. Abstr. Full Text Elite (July 1993-) [Full Txt.]; Acad. Abstr. (Jan. 1993-); Acad. Search (Jan. 1993-); Am. Humanit. Index (-199?); Annu. Bibliogr. Engl. Lang. Lit.; Curr. Index J. Educ.; Educ. Index; HAPI Hisp. Am. Period. Index; Index Am. Period. Verse; Linguist. Lang. Behav. Abstr.; Mag. Artic. Summar. Elite (Jan. 1993-) [Full Txt.]; Mag. Artic. Summar. CD-ROM (Jan. 1993-); Middle East Abstr. Index; MLA Int. Bibl. Books Artic. Mod. Lang. Lit.; Soc. Plann. Policy Dev. Abstr.; Sociol. Abstr.

●US/1045-4365
BILINGUALISM TODAY. (1994)-. Periodical. English. Peter Lang Publishing, 62 West 45th Street, 4th Floor, New York NY 10036. **Tel** (212)764-1471, (800)770-5264, telex 6973364 PLNY.

CN/1192-1145
BILL PALMER'S WORD WATCHING. [Bill Palmer's word watch.]. Vol. 9, No. 1 (Mar. 1986)-. Periodical. English. Four times a year (Mar., June, Sept., Dec.). 11.00Can$ US & Canada; 12.00Can$ others. Bill Palmer's Word Watching, 220 Olivier, Suite 302, Westmount Quebec H3Z 2C5 Canada. **Tel** (514)932-6370. **ED** Bill Palmer. **DD** 428.1. **Circ:** 400. ***Continues** Palmer, Bill (William) Word Watching., 1193-6657.*
Desc: Acts as a forum for its readers to attack or honor the English language for discussions about changes; recommendations about grammar misuse (serious and hilarious); reviews of articles/books on usage; as well as for themes from word origins to politically correctness, vanishing commas to newly created words.

GW/0933-5315
BIOS : ZEITSCHRIFT FUER BIOGRAPHIEFORSCHUNG UND ORAL HISTORY. (1988)-. Periodical. German. sa. DM48.00. Leske Verlag & Budrich GmbH, Postfach 300551, Gerhart Hauptmann Strasse 27, W-5090 Leverkusen 3 Opladen Germany. **Tel** 011 49 21712079. **LC** CT21; .B49. **DD** 809/.93592/0005.
Ind/Abst Am. Hist. Life (1990-).

UK/0141-3805
BIRMINGHAM SLAVONIC MONOGRAPHS. [Birm. slav. monogr.]. (1977)-. Monographic series. English. ir. Price varies per volume. University of Birmingham / England, Edgbaston, Center for Byzantine Ottoman, Greek Street, Birmingham B15 2TT England. **Tel** 011 44 21 414 5733, FAX 011 44 21 414 5726. **ED** James Mullen. Index available. cum. index. **Pr Rev.**
Desc: Scholarly monographs on aspects of slavonic humanities and linguistics.

PL/0032-3802
BIULETYN POLSKIEGO TOWARZYSTWA JEZYKOZNAWCZEGO. [Biul. Pol. Tow. Jezykozn.]. **Added/Corp** Polskie Towarzystwo Jezykoznawcze. **VFOAT** Bulletin de la Societe Polonaise de Linguistique. No. 1 (1927)-. Polish (French, English and German). ir. **(Subscription address:** ARS Polona, PO Box 1001, 00068 Warsaw Poland.) **LC** P19.P6; A23.
Ind/Abst MLA Int. Bibl. Books Artic. Mod. Lang. Lit.

CN/0821-3917
BIULETYN ZWIAAZKU NAUCZYCIELSTWA POLSKIEGO W KANADZIE. **Added/Corp** Zwiazek Nauczycielstwa Polskiego w Kanadzie. **VFOAT** Biuletyn. (1961)-. Periodical. Polish. qt. 15.00Can$ Canada; $12.00 US. Polish Teacher's Association in Canada, 288 Roncesvalles Avenue, Toronto Ontario M6R 2M4 Canada. **Tel** (416)532-2876. **ED** Janina Gladun, Wanda Bujalska, Maria Bieniasz, Weronika Perkowska. **DD** 491.8/5/07071. **Circ:** 1,200 (ctrl).
Desc: Covers methods of teaching in the Heritage Language Schools, articles about child psychology, Polish literature, Polish customs and traditions, news from different Heritage Language Schools, inside news from Polish teachers association, teaching aids: songs, games, puzzles, puppet theatre pictures, and maps.

NE/0169-6165
BOCHUMER ANGLISTISCHE STUDIEN. [Boch. angl. Stud.]. **VFOAT** Bochum Studies in English. (1975)-. Monographic series. German. BR Gruner BV, Nieuwe Herengracht 31, 1011 RM Amsterdam Netherlands. **Tel** 20-264371.
Ind/Abst MLA Int. Bibl. Books Artic. Mod. Lang. Lit.

PO/0870-4600
BOLETIM DE FILOLOGIA. (BOLETIM DE FILOLOGIA / JUNTA DE EDUCACAO NACIONAL, CENTRO DE ESTUDOS FILOLOGICOS.). [Bol. filol.]. **Added/Corp** Centro de Estudos Filologicos (Portugal). Universidade de Lisboa. Centro de Linguistica. No. 1 (1932)-. Bulletin. Portuguese. qt. **LC** PC5001; .B6.
Ind/Abst MLA Int. Bibl. Books Artic. Mod. Lang. Lit.

US/0884-0091
BOLETIN - ACADEMIA NORTEAMERICANA DE LA LENGUA ESPANOLA. [Bol. - Acad. Norteam. Leng. Esp.]. **Main/Corp** Academia Norteamericana de la Lengua Espanola. **VFOAT** Boletin de la Academia Norteamericana de la Lengua Espanola. No. 1 (1976)-. Spanish. an. Acad Norteamer Lengua Espanola, C/O Juan Aviles, PO Box 349, New York NY 10116. **LC** PC4826; .A2a. **DD** 460.
Ind/Abst MLA Int. Bibl. Books Artic. Mod. Lang. Lit.

CL/0067-9674
BOLETIN DE FILOLOGIA. [Bol. filol.]. **Added/Corp** Universidad de Chile. Instituto de Filologia. Universidad de Chile. Instituto de Investigaciones Historico-Culturales. Universidad de Chile. Departamento de Linguistica y Filologia. Universidad de Chile. Departamento de Espanol. Vol. 5 (1947/49)-. Spanish. an. Universidad de Chile Department Linguistica / Casilla 10136, Santiago Chile. **Tel** 011 56 2 2732665. **LC** P25; .B62. ***Continues** Boletin del Instituto de Filologia de la Universidad de Chile, 0716-0984.*
Ind/Abst Am. Hist. Life (1966-1971); MLA Int. Bibl. Books Artic. Mod. Lang. Lit.

AG/0001-3757
BOLETIN DE LA ACADEMIA ARGENTINA DE LETRAS. **See** Literature.

HO/0065-0471
BOLETIN DE LA ACADEMIE HONDURENA DE LA LENGUA. **Main/Corp** Academic Hondurena de la Lengua. Yearly Vol. 1, No. 1 (July 1955)-. Periodical. Spanish. ir (2-3 times per year). $5.00. Academia Hondurena de Lengua, Apartado Postal 38, Tegucigalpa Honduras. **Tel** 22-92-6222-08-66. **ED** Jorge Fidel Duron. **LC** AS64.A3; A12. **DD** 056/.1. **Bk Rev**. **Ad Acc**. **Circ:** 1,000.
Desc: To enhance and improve the Spanish language.
Ind/Abst HAPI Hisp. Am. Period. Index (19??-); Soc. Plann. Policy Dev. Abstr.

SP/0210-4822
BOLETIN DE LA REAL ACADEMIA ESPANOLA. [Bol. R. Acad. Esp.]. **Main/Corp** Real Academia Espanola. Vol. 1, Issue 1 (Feb. 1914)-. Periodical. Spanish. Three times a year. 6037ptas Spain, 6260ptas others (certified mail); 7500ptas (airmail). Real Academia Espanola, Felipe IV 4, 28071 Madrid Spain. **(Subscription address:** Editorial Gredos, 1406 Sanchez Pacheco 81, 28002 Madrid Spain, telephone: 011 34 1 4157408) **LC** AS302; .M52. **DD** 056/.1. **Circ:** 2,000. Documents available from The Genuine Article.
Desc: List of new words in Spanish dictionary and studies about Spanish language.
Ind/Abst Am. Hist. Life (1965-); Arts Humanit. Citation Index [Full Cov.]; Curr. Contents Arts Humanit.; MLA Int. Bibl. Books Artic. Mod. Lang. Lit.; Res. Alert [Full Cov.]; Romant. Move.

AG/0020-3637
BOLETIN DEL INSTITUTO AMERICANO DE ESTUDIOS VASCOS. [Bol. Inst. am. estud. vascos]. **Main/Corp** Instituto Americano de Estudios Vascos. Yearly Vol. 1, No. 1 (April/June 1950)-. Periodical. Spanish. qt. $10.00 Argentina; $20.00 other. Editorial Vasca Ekin SPL, 4V Belgrano 1144, 1092 Buenos Aires Argentina. **ED** Andres de Irujo. Index available (annual). **Bk Rev**. **Circ:** 700.
Desc: Covers topics in Basque language and ethnic issues on cultural and socio-political levels.
Ind/Abst Am. Hist. Life.

SP
BOLETIN INFORMATIVO. **Main/Corp** Instituto Miguel de Cervantes. (1979)-. Spanish. ir. Inst Miguel Cervantes Filo Hi, Duque de Medinaceli 4, Madrid 14 Spain. **(Subscription address:** Consejo Superior Investigacion, Cientificas CSIC, Vitruvio 8, 28006 Madrid, Spain, telephone: 011 34 1 5612833) **LC** PC4019; .I5713. **DD** 860/.9. ***Continues** Boletin de Filologia Espanola, 0006-6265.*

IT/0577-277X
BOLLETINO - CENTRO DI STUDI FILOLOGICI E LINGUISTICI SICILIANI. **Main/Corp** Centro di Studi Filologici e Linguistici Siciliani. Vol. 1 (1953)-. Periodical. Italian. ir. Licosa Spa, PO Box

552, 50125 Florence Italy. **Tel** 011 39 55 645415. **DD** 450.
Ind/Abst MLA Int. Bibl. Books Artic. Mod. Lang. Lit.

IT
BOLLETINO DELL'ATLANTE LINGUISTICO ITALIANO. **Added/Corp** Istituto dell'Atlante Linguistico Italiano. Societat Filologjche Furlane. (1933)-. Periodical. Italian.
Ind/Abst MLA Int. Bibl. Books Artic. Mod. Lang. Lit.

IT/0433-3837
BOLLETTINO DELL ISTITUTO DI LINGUE ESTERE / UNIVERSITA DEGLI STUDI DI GENOVA, FACOLTA DI ECONOMIA E COMMERCIO. (1951)-. Periodical. Italian. Universita Degli Studi di Genova, Facolta di Economia e Commercio, Genova Italy.
Ind/Abst MLA Int. Bibl. Books Artic. Mod. Lang. Lit.

IT/0067-9879
BOLLETTINO DELL'ATLANTE LINGUISTICO MEDITERRANEO. ***Ceased.*** [Boll. Atlante linguist. mediterr.]. **VFOAT** Bulletin de l'Atlas Linguistique Mediterraneen. Vol. 1 (1959)-Ceased ?. Italian. ir. Casa Editrice Leo S. Olschki, Viuzzo del Pozzetto, Casella Postale 66, 50126 Florence Italy. **Tel** 011 39 55 6530684, FAX 011 39 55 6530214. **UDC** 804.
Ind/Abst MLA Int. Bibl. Books Artic. Mod. Lang. Lit.

IT/0392-7628
BOLLETTINO DELL'ISTITUTO DI FILOLOGIA GRECA. **Main/Corp** Universita di Padova. Istituto di Filologia Greca. (19??)-. Italian (French). ir. L'Erma di Bretschneider SPA, Via Cassiodoro 19, 00193 Rome Italy. **Tel** 011 39 6 6874127, 011 39 6 6874129, FAX 011 39 6 6874129. **LC** PA9; .P34a.

IT
BOLLETTINO DELL'ISTITUTO DI FILOLOGIA GRECA. SUPPLEMENTO. (1977)-. Monographic series. Italian. Price varies per volume. L'Erma di Bretschneider SPA, Via Cassiodoro 19, 00193 Rome Italy. **Tel** 011 39 6 6874127, 011 39 6 6874129, FAX 011 39 6 6874129.

IT/0006-6583
BOLLETTINO DI STUDI LATINI. (1971)-. Periodical. Italian. Twice a year. L80000.00 Italy; L96000.00 other. Lofredo Editore Napoli Spa, Via Consalvo 99 H Parco San Luigi, 80126 Naples Italy. **Tel** 11 39 81 5937073, FAX 11 39 81 5936953. **Bk Rev**.

US/0006-7121
BONJOUR (NEW YORK). (BONJOUR.). (19??)-. Periodical. French. mo. $25.00. Mary Glasgow Publications, Brookhampton Lane, Kineton, Warwickshire CV35 0JB England. **Tel** 011 44 926 640606, FAX 011 44 926 641016. **(Subscription address:** Scholastic Inc, PO Box 3710, Jefferson City MO 65102.**)** available on microfilm from University Microfilms International (UMI).

US/0093-934X
BRAIN AND LANGUAGE. **See** Medical Science and Technology-Neurology.

GW
BRAUNSCHWEIGER ANGLISTISCHE ARBEITEN. **Added/Corp** Technische Universitat Carolo-Wilhlmina. Institut fur Anglistik und Amerikanistik. (19??)-. Monographic series. German.
Ind/Abst MLA Int. Bibl. Books Artic. Mod. Lang. Lit.

FR
BRETAGNE LINGUISTIQUE : CAHIERS DU GROUPE DE RECHERCHE SUR L'ECONOMIE LINGUISTIQUE DE LA BRETAGNE, LA. **Added/Corp** Groupe de Recherche sur l'Economie Linguistique de la Bretagne. Centre de Recherche Bretonne et Celtique. (198?)-. French. an. $15.00. CRBC, Faculte des Lettres, Brest France. **Tel** 98 03 06 87. **LC** P12; .B7.

FR
BREVES DE LA DELEGATION GENERALE A LA LANGUE FRANCAISE. French. Three times a year. Free on request. Delegation Generale a la Langue Francaise, 1 rue Manutention, 75116 Paris France. **Tel** 011 33 1 40691224. ***Continues*** *Qui-Vive International; Breves du Commissariat General de la Langue Francaise, 0991-272X.*

SZ/0171-6662
BRITISH AND IRISH STUDIES IN GERMAN LANGUAGE AND LITERATURE. [Br. Ir. stud. Ger. lang. lit.]. **VFOAT** Britische und Irische Studien zur Deutschen Sprache und Literatur; Etudes Parues en Grande Bretagne et en Irlande Concernant la Philologie et Litterature Allemandes. No. 1 (1974)-. Monographic series. Multiple languages (English and German). H Lang, Munzgraben 2, CH-3000 7 Bern Switzerland.
Ind/Abst MLA Int. Bibl. Books Artic. Mod. Lang. Lit.

XR/0524-6881
BRNO STUDIES IN ENGLISH. [Brno stud. Engl.]. VOL. 1 (1959)-. English. be. kcs30.00. Mabarykova Univerzita Filozoficka Fakulta, A Novaka 1, 66088 Brno Czech Republic. **Tel** 75 00 50. **(Subscription address:** Artia, PO Box 790, Ve-Smeckach 30, Praha 1 Czechoslavakia**)** **ED** Josef Hladky. **LC** AS142; .B85 subser. **DD** 420/.05. **UDC** 802. **Bk Rev**. **Circ:** 500 (ctrl).
Ind/Abst Abstr. Engl. Stud.; Annu. Bibliogr. Engl. Lang. Lit.; Lang. Teach.; Linguist. Lang. Behav. Abstr.; MLA Int. Bibl. Books Artic. Mod. Lang. Lit.; Soc. Plann. Policy Dev. Abstr.; Sociol. Abstr.

GW/0340-5435
BUCHREIHE DER ANGLIA. **See** Literature.

GW
BUCHREIHE DER ZEITSCHRIFT FUER CELTISCHE PHILOLOGIE. Vol. 1 (1959)-. Monographic series. English. ir. Price varies per volume. Max Niemeyer Verlag, Postfach 2140, D 72011 Tuebingen Germany. **Tel** 011 49 7071 989494, FAX 011 49 7071 87419. **ED** Karl Horst Schmidt, Heinrich Wagner.
Desc: Series covering Celtic philology and languages.
Ind/Abst MLA Int. Bibl. Books Artic. Mod. Lang. Lit.

CM
BUDGET D'EQUIPEMENT ET DE RECHERCHE. **Main/Corp** University of Yaounde. Departement des Langues Africaines et Linguistique. French. Universite de Yaounde / Linguistics, Dept des Langues Africaines et Linguistics, Yaounde Cameroon. **LC** P59.U545; U54A. **DD** 410/.72. **UDC** 809.6.

RM
BULETINUL UNIVERSITATII DIN GALATI. FASCICULA I, STIINTE SOCIALE SI UMANISTE. **Added/Corp** Universitatea din Galati. (19??)-. Periodical. English (French, German and Romanian). an. Redactia Buletinului, 6200 Galati Str, Republicii Nr 47 Romania. **LC** P1.A1; B835.

BU/0005-4283
BULGARSKI JAZIK. (BULGARSKI EZIK.). [BÊlg. jazik]. **Added/Corp** Institut za Bulgarski Ezik (Bulgarska Akademiia na Naukite). (1951)-. Academic Scholarly Publication. Bulgarian. ir. Bulgarska Akademiia na Naukite, 7 Noemvri 1, Sofia Bulgaria. **LC** PG801; .B833.
Ind/Abst MLA Int. Bibl. Books Artic. Mod. Lang. Lit.

RM
BULLETIN. **Main/Corp** Societe Roumaine de Linguistique Romane. **VFOAT** Bulletin de la Societe Roumaine de Linguistique Romane. (1964)-. Bulletin. Romanian. an. **(Subscription address:** Ilexim Press Department, PO Box 1, 136-1-137, Bucharest, Romania.**)**

FR/0007-408X
BULLETIN ANALYTIQUE DE LINGUISTIQUE FRANCAISE. **Added/Corp** Institut National de la Langue Francaise (France) Centre de Recherche pour un Tresor de la Langue Francaise (France) Institut de la Langue Francaise (France). Vol. 1 (1969)-. Bulletin. French. sa (2 issues per year). 246.45F France; 335.00F other. Editions Klincksieck, 8 rue de la Sorbonne, 75005 Paris France. **Tel** 11 33 1 43545953, FAX 11 33 1 432252553. available on microfilm and microfiche from University Microfilms International (UMI). ***Supersedes*** *Bulletin Analytique de Lexicologie.*

CN/0825-2823
BULLETIN / ASSOCIATION CANADIENNE DE LINGUISTIQUE. ***Title Change.*** [Bull. - Assoc. can. linguist.]. **Main/Corp** Canadian Linguistic Association. (Spring 1984)-(1993). Bulletin. English (French). an. University of Toronto Press, 5201 Dufferin Street, Downsview Ontario M3H 5T8 Canada. **Tel** (416)667-7781, (416)667-7782, FAX (416)667-7803. **LC** P11; .C322. **DD** 410/.6/071. ctrl circ. ***Merged into*** *Canadian Journal of Linguistics, 0008-4131.*

SZ/0251-7256
BULLETIN CILA. ***Title Change.*** [Bull. CILA]. **Main/Corp** Commission Interuniversitaire Suisse de Linguistique Appliquee. **Added/Corp** Universite de Neuchatel. Centre de Linguistique Appliquee. **VAT** Bulletin Commission Interuniversitaire Suisse de Linguistique Appliquee. (1969)-(1994). Periodical. French (English, German and Italian). Twice a year (Apr., Oct.). Universite de Neuchatel, Centre de Linguistique Appliquee, Espace Louis Agassiz 1, CH-2000 Neuchatel Switzerland. **Tel** 011 41 38 213181. **LC** P51; .C622a. **DD** 418/.007. cum. index. **Bk Rev**. **Ad Acc**. **Circ:** 500. ***Continues*** *Bulletin de la Commission Interuniversitaire Suisse de Linguistique Appliquee.* ***Continued by*** *Bulletin Suisse de Linguistique Appliquee.*
Ind/Abst Lang. Teach.; Linguist. Lang. Behav. Abstr. (1971-) [Full Cov.]; MLA Int. Bibl. Books Artic. Mod. Lang. Lit.; Soc. Plann. Policy Dev. Abstr.; Sociol. Abstr.

CN/0848-7316
BULLETIN DE FRANCAIS 30. ***Title Change.*** (BULLETIN DE FRANCAIS 30 : PROGRAMME DES EXAMENS EN VUE DU DIPLOME.). [Bull. fr. 30]. **Added/Corp** Alberta. Alberta Education. Alberta. Student Evaluation and Records. Alberta. Student Evaluation Branch. (1989/1990)-(199?). Bulletin. French. **DD** 440/.071/27123. ***Continued by*** *Bulletin du Programme des Examens en Vue du Diplome. Francais 30, 1191-677X.*

●FR
BULLETIN DE LA COMMUNICATION PARLEE. **Added/Corp** Institut de la Communication Parlee. No. 1 (1991)-. Bulletin. French. an. 100.00F. Institut Communication Parlee, BP 25X, 38040 Grenoble Cedex France. **Tel** 011 33 1 76448218. **LC** P215; .B85. **DD** 414/.05. **CODEN** BCPAE4.
Ind/Abst Linguist. Lang. Behav. Abstr. (1991-) [Full Cov.]; Soc. Plann. Policy Dev. Abstr.; Sociol. Abstr.

SZ
BULLETIN DE LA SECTION DE LINGUISTIQUE DE LA FACULTE DES LETTRES DE LAUSANNE. **Added/Corp** Universite de Lausanne. Faculte des Lettres. Section de Linguistique. **VFOAT** Bullll. No 1 (1977)-. Bulletin. French.
Ind/Abst Linguist. Lang. Behav. Abstr. (1981-) [Full Cov.]; Soc. Plann. Policy Dev. Abstr.; Sociol. Abstr.

FR/0037-9069
BULLETIN DE LA SOCIETE DE LINGUISTIQUE DE PARIS. [Bull. Soc. linguist. Paris]. **Main/Corp** Societe de Linguistique de Paris. Vol. 1 (1869)-. Bulletin. French. sa. 990.00F (France); 1035.00F (other). Editions Klincksieck, 8 rue de la Sorbonne, 75005 Paris France. **Tel** 11 33 1 43545953, FAX 11 33 1 432252553. **LC** P12; .S4. **UDC** 804.
Desc: List of members.
Ind/Abst Annu. Bibliogr. Engl. Lang. Lit.; MLA Int. Bibl. Books Artic. Mod. Lang. Lit.; Romant. Move.

BE/0378-0708
BULLETIN DE L'ACADEMIE ROYALE DE LANGUE ET DE LITTERATURE FRANCAISES. [Bull. Acad. r. lang. litt. fr.]. **Added/Corp** Academie Royale de Langue et de Litterature Francaises de Belgique. Vol. 1 (1922)-. Bulletin. French. Three times a year. 800.00 F. Academie Royale de Langue et de Litterature Francaises, 1 Rue Ducale, 1000 Brussels Belgium. **LC** PC2009; .B84. **DD** 440/.5. cum. index.
Ind/Abst MLA Int. Bibl. Books Artic. Mod. Lang. Lit.; Romant. Move.

CM/0258-1302
BULLETIN DE L'ALCAM. [Bull. - ALCAM]. **Main/Corp** Institut des Sciences Humaines, Yaounde, Cameroon. Unite de Recherche Linguistique et Phonetique. **VAT** Bulletin de l'Atlas Linguistique du Cameroun. 1-. Bulletin. French. Institut des Sciences Humaines, BP 73, Yaounde Cameroon. **LC** P381.C34; I57A. **UDC** 809.6(671.1).
Ind/Abst MLA Int. Bibl. Books Artic. Mod. Lang. Lit.

FR/0184-6957
BULLETIN DE L'ASSOCIATION GUILLAUME BUDE. [Bull. Assoc. Guillaume Bude]. **Main/Corp** Association Guillaume Bude. **Added/Corp** Societe "Les Belles-Lettres.". No. 1 (Oct. 1923)-. Bulletin. French. Four times a year. 146.91F (individuals), 122.43F (institutions) France; 125.00F (individuals), 150.00F (institutions) others. Societe Edition Belles Lettres, 95 Boulevard Raspail, 75006 Paris France. **Tel** 011 33 1 45487055, FAX 011 33 1 45449288, telex 200577. **LC** PA12; .A6.
Ind/Abst BHA : Biblio. Hist. Art; MLA Int. Bibl. Books Artic. Mod. Lang. Lit.; Romant. Move.

CG
BULLETIN DE LIAISON - CENTRE DE LINGUISTIQUE THEORIQUE ET APPLIQUEE, UNIVERSITE NATIONALE DU ZAIRE. **Main/Corp** Universite Nationale du Zaire. Campus de Lubumbashi. Centre de Linguistique Theorique et Appliquee. Bulletin. French (English and Swahili). ir. 100.00CFAF. Universite Nationale du Zaire / Faculte des Lettres, B P 1607, Lubumbashi Congo (Zaire). **Tel** 295483. **LC** PC3680.Z3; U54A. **DD** 440/.7. **UDC** 809.635.6(675). Index available. ctrl circ.
Desc: Articles of interest to language teachers covering methods of instruction, editing, phonetics and grammar in Swahili, French and other languages of Zaire.

FR/0240-8805
BULLETIN DES ANGLICISTES MEDIEVISTES. **VFOAT** B.A.M. (1972)-. Periodical. Multiple languages. Association des Medievistes Anglicistes de l'Enseignement Superieur, Amiens France. **UDC** 802.022.
Ind/Abst Annu. Bibliogr. Engl. Lang. Lit.

PO/0379-4954
BULLETIN DES ETUDES PORTUGAISES ET BRESILIENNES. [Bull. etud. port. bres.]. **Added/Corp** Institut Francais de Lisbonne. (1973)-. Bulletin. French (Portuguese). ir. Association Diffusion Pense Francaise, 9 rue Anatole de la Forge, 75017 Paris France. **Tel** 011 33 1 42273297. **LC** AS304; .B8. ***Continues*** *Bulletin des Etudes Portugaises, 0379-2579.*

Desc: Bulletin of Portuguese and Brazilian studies.
Ind/Abst Am. Hist. Life (1973-); MLA Int. Bibl. Books Artic. Mod. Lang. Lit.

BE
BULLETIN DU CANGE / UNION ACADEMIQUE INTERNATIONALE. **Added/Corp** Union Academique Internationale. **VFOAT** Archivum Latinatis Medii Aevi. (1924)-. Bulletin. French. ir. Price varies per volume. Union Academy International Sect Admin, Rue Ducale I, B 1000 Brussels Belgium. **(Subscription address:** Librairie Droz Sa, 11 Rue Massot, 1211 Geneva 12 Switzerland, Tel. 41 22 466666**)** **LC** PA2801; .B8.
Ind/Abst MLA Int. Bibl. Books Artic. Mod. Lang. Lit.

CN/0825-6926
BULLETIN DU CONSEIL DE LA LANGUE FRANCAISE. [Bull. Cons. langue fr.]. Vol. 1, No. 1 (Summer 1984)-. Bulletin. French. qt. Conseil de la Langue Francaise, 800 Place d Youville 13 Etage, Quebec Quebec G1R 3P4 Canada. **DD** 440/.9714. **UDC** 804.0(714).

LU
BULLETIN LINGUISTIQUE, ETHNOLOGIQUE ET TOPONYMIQUE. Bulletin. Multiple languages (French and German). Institut Grand-Ducal Section de Linguistic de Folklore et de Toponymie, 5 rue Large Compte Cheques Postaux, Luxembourg 8776 Luxembourg. **LC** P1.A1; B84. **DD** 410/.5. **UDC** 801.311(435.9); 800. ***Continues*** *Bulletin Linguistique et Ethnologique.*

UK/0007-490X
BULLETIN OF HISPANIC STUDIES. [Bull. Hisp. stud.]. **Added/Corp** Institute of Hispanic Studies (Liverpool, England) University of Liverpool. School of Hispanic Studies. (1949)-. Periodical. English (Catalan, French, Portuguese and Spanish). qt (4 issues). $155.00 (institution), $50.00 (individual), $24.00 (student) US. Liverpool University Press, PO Box 147, Liverpool L69 3BX England. **Tel** (051)794 2233, FAX (051)708 6502, telex 627095. **(Subscription address:** Turpin Distribution Services Limited, Blackhorse Road, Letchworth, Hertfordshire SG6 1HN, United Kingdom.**)** **ED** Dorothy Sherman Severin and Ann L. Mackenzie. **LC** PC4008; .B8. **DD** 860.5. **[CCC].** Index available. cum. index. **Bk Rev. Ad Acc.** Documents available from The Genuine Article. ***Continues*** *Bulletin of Spanish Studies.*
Desc: The only learned journal published in Britain devoted exclusively to the languages and literature of Spain, Portugal and Latin America.
Ind/Abst Annu. Bibliogr. Engl. Lang. Lit. (19??-); Arts Humanit. Citation Index (19??-) [Full Cov.]; Br. Humanit. Index (19??-); Curr. Contents Arts Humanit. (19??-); HAPI Hisp. Am. Period. Index (19??-); MLA Int. Bibl. Books Artic. Mod. Lang. Lit. (19??-); Res. Alert (19??-) [Full Cov.]; Romant. Move. (19??-).

UK/0041-977X
BULLETIN OF THE SCHOOL OF ORIENTAL AND AFRICAN STUDIES. (BULLETIN OF THE SCHOOL OF ORIENTAL AND AFRICAN STUDIES, UNIVERSITY OF LONDON.). [Bull. Sch. Orient. Afr. Stud.]. **Added/Corp** University of London. School of Oriental and African Studies. Vol. 10, Part 3 (1940)-. Periodical. English. tq. £62.00 UK and Europe; $114.00 other. Oxford University Press, Walton Street, Oxford OX2 6DP England. **Tel** 011 44 865 56767, FAX 011 44 865 267773, telex 837330 OXPRES G. **(Subscription address:** Oxford University Press / USA, Journals Marketing Department, Oxford University Press, 2001 Evans Road, Cary NC 27513.**)** **LC** PJ3; .L6. **[CCC]. Bk Rev. Ad Acc. Circ:** 1,200. Documents available from The Genuine Article. ***Continues*** *Bulletin of the School of Oriental Studies (University of London).*
Desc: Advanced research in Oriental and African studies.
Ind/Abst Am. Hist. Life (1954-); Anthropol. Index; Anthropol. Lit.; Arts Humanit. Citation Index [Full Cov.]; Curr. Contents Arts Humanit.; Ethnoarts Index; Index Islam. Lit.; Index Book Rev. Relig.; Middle East Abstr. Index; MLA Int. Bibl. Books Artic. Mod. Lang. Lit.; Numis. Lit.; Res. Alert [Full Cov.]; Soc. Sci. Cit. Index [Select. Cov.]; Middle East J.

UK/0264-2190
BULLETIN OF THE SOCIETY FOR ITALIAN STUDIES. ***Ceased.*** [Bull. Soc. Ital. Stud.]. **Added/Corp** Society for Italian Studies. (19??)-(19??). Bulletin. English (Italian). be.
Ind/Abst MLA Int. Bibl. Books Artic. Mod. Lang. Lit. (?-?).

ZA
BULLETIN OF THE ZAMBIA LANGUAGE GROUP, THE. **Main/Corp** Zambia Language Group. Bulletin. English. Zambia Language Group, PO Box 2379, Lusaka Zambia. **LC** PL8021.Z3; Z34A. **DD** 301.2/1. **UDC** 809.6(689.4).

SZ
BULLETIN SUISSE DE LINGUISTIQUE APPLIQUEE. (1994)-. Periodical. French (English, German and Italian). Twice a year (Apr. & Oct.). 50.00F (institutions), 30.00F (individuals) Switzerland; 55.00F (institutions), 35.00F (individuals) other. Universite de Neuchatel, Centre de Linguistique Appliquee, Espace Louis Agassiz 1, CH-2000 Neuchatel Switzerland. **Tel** 011 41 38 213181. ***Continues*** *Bulletin CILA, 0251-7256.*
Desc: Reports concerning the teaching of foreign languages.

UK/0142-3363
BWLETIN Y BWRDD GWYBODAU CELTAIDD. (THE BULLETIN OF THE BOARD OF CELTIC STUDIES.). [Bwletin y Bwrdd Gwybodau Celtaidd]. **Main/Corp** University Of Wales. Board of Celtic Studies. **VFOAT** Bweltin y Bwrdd Gwybodau Celtaidd. Vol. 1 (Oct. 1921)-. Bulletin. English. an. $40.00 North America. University of Wales Press, 6 Gwennyth Street, Cathays Cardiff CF2 4YD Wales United Kingdom. **Tel** 011 44 222 231919. **(Subscription address:** North America/ Books International, PO Box 605, Herndon, VA 22070; telephone: (703)435-7064**)** **ED** D. Ellis Evans, J. Beverley Smith and Robin G. Livens. **LC** PB2101; .W3. **DD** 491.6/6. **Ad Acc. Circ:** 300. available on microfiche from University Microfilms International (UMI). Documents available from The Genuine Article.
Desc: The senior journal of the Board of Celtic Studies has three sections: language and literature, archaeology and art, history and law.
Ind/Abst Abstr. Engl. Stud.; Am. Hist. Life (1977-); Art Archaeol. Tech. Abstr.; Arts Humanit. Citation Index (19??-19??) [Full Cov.]; Curr. Contents Arts Humanit.; MLA Int. Bibl. Books Artic. Mod. Lang. Lit.; Res. Alert [Full Cov.].

FR/0240-8864
C.A.R.A. CENTRE AIXOIS DE RECHERCHES ANGLAISES. [C.A.R.A. Cent. aixois rech. angl.]. **VFOAT** Centre Aixois de Recherches Anglaises. (1981)-. Monographic series. Multiple languages. **UDC** 820. ***Continues*** *Actes du Centre Aixois de Recherches Anglaises, 0248-3890.*
Ind/Abst MLA Int. Bibl. Books Artic. Mod. Lang. Lit.

CN/0384-5311
C. A. U. T. G. NEWSLETTER. ***Title Change.*** [C.A.U.T.G. newsl.]. **Main/Corp** Canadian Association of University Teachers of German. **VFOAT** CAUTG Newsletter. **VAT** Canadian Association of University Teachers of German Newsletter. Vol. 1 No. 2 (Mar. 1973)-. Newsletter. English (summaries and/or abstracts in German). sa. Canadian Association of University Teachers of German, % Department of German Languages and Literature, Queen's University, Kingston, Ontario, K7L 3N6 Canada. **DD** 438/.007. ***Supersedes*** *Canadian Association of University Teachers of German. Newsletter.* ***Continued by*** *Canadian Association of University Teachers of German. CAUTG Bulletin, 1193-817X.*

US/0197-6893
C-L/CLL. COUNSELING-LEARNING COMMUNITY LANGUAGE LEARNING NEWSLETTER. [C-L/CLL, Couns.-learn. commun. lang. learn. newsl.]. **Added/Corp** Counseling-Learning Institutes. **VFOAT** Counseling-Learning Community Language Learning Newsletter. (197?)-. Newsletter. English. qt. $6.00. C-L/CLL Newsletters, PO Box 285, East Dubuque IL 61025. **Tel** (815)747-3071.

US/0007-9243
CA VA. **See** Education-Teaching and Curriculum.

BL/0102-5767
CADERNOS DE ESTUDOS LINGUISTICOS / UNIVERSIDADE ESTADUAL DE CAMPINAS, INSTITUTO DE ESTUDOS DA LINGUAGEM, DEPARTAMENTO DE LINGUISTICA. **Added/Corp** Universidade Estadual de Campinas. Departamento de Linguistica. (19??)-. Periodical. English (Portuguese). **LC** P1.A1; C32. **DD** 410/.5.
Ind/Abst Linguist. Lang. Behav. Abstr. (1981-) [Full Cov.]; MLA Int. Bibl. Books Artic. Mod. Lang. Lit.; Soc. Plann. Policy Dev. Abstr.; Sociol. Abstr.

BL/0101-3548
CADERNOS DE LINGUISTICA E TEORIA DA LITERATURA. ***Ceased.*** **Added/Corp** Universidade Federal de Minas Gerais. Centro de Extensao. Universidade Federal de Minas Gerais. Departamento de Linguistica e Teoria da Literatura. **VFOAT** Ensaios de Linguistica; Ensaios de Semiotica. (1978)-(19??). Periodical. Portuguese. sa. Universidade Federal de Minas, Dept. de Semiotica, Sala 446, Pampulha Belo Horizonte Brazil. **LC** P9; .C33. **DD** 410/.5.
Ind/Abst MLA Int. Bibl. Books Artic. Mod. Lang. Lit.

FR/0571-5865
CAHIERS DE L'ASSOCIATION INTERNATIONALE DES ETUDES FRANCAISES. [Cah. Assoc. int. etud. fr.]. **Added/Corp** Association Internationale des Etudes Francaises. No. 1 (July 1951)-. Monographic series. French. ir. Price varies per volume. Societe Edition Belles Lettres, 95 Boulevard Raspail, 75006 Paris France. **Tel** 011 33 1 45487055, FAX 011 33 1 45449288, telex 200577. **LC** PC2012; .A8.
Ind/Abst BHA : Biblio. Hist. Art; MLA Int. Bibl. Books Artic. Mod. Lang. Lit.; Romant. Move.

FR/0007-9871
CAHIERS DE LEXICOLOGIE. [Cah. lexicol.]. **Added/Corp** Besancon, France. Universite. Centre d'Etude du Vocabulaire Francais. Centre National de la Recherche Scientifique (France). Vol. 1 (1959)-. French. qt. $50.00 North America. Societe Nouvelle Didier Erudition, 6 rue de la Sorbonne, 75005 Paris France. **Tel** 011 33 1 43544757, FAX 011 33 1 40517385. **(Subscription address:** PO Box 830350, Birmingham, AL 35283-0350; telephone: (800)633-4931, (205)995-1567; FAX: (205)995-1588**)** **ED** B Quemada. **Bk Rev. Ad Acc. Circ:** 2,000 (ctrl). available on microfiche.
Desc: This journal publishes the inquiries concerning lexicology of the National Institute of French Languages.
Ind/Abst Lang. Teach.; Linguist. Lang. Behav. Abstr. (1972-) [Full Cov.]; MLA Int. Bibl. Books Artic. Mod. Lang. Lit.; Soc. Plann. Policy Dev. Abstr.; Sociol. Abstr.

FR/1163-765X
CAHIERS DE L'ICP RAPPORT DE RECHERCHE, LES. [Cah. ICP, Rapp. rech]. **VFOAT** Cahiers de l'Institut de la Communication Parlee. Rapport de Recherche. (1991)-. Periodical. French. an. **UDC** 534.
Ind/Abst Linguist. Lang. Behav. Abstr. (1991-); Soc. Plann. Policy Dev. Abstr.

FR/0153-3320
CAHIERS DE LINGUISTIQUE. ASIE ORIENTALE. **Added/Corp** Ecole des Hautes Etudes en Sciences Sociales. Centre de Recherches Linguistiques sur l'Asie Orientale. **VFOAT** Asie Orientale. No. 1 (Mar 1977)-. Periodical. French (English and Chinese). sa. 180.00F. Association Francaise Etudes Chinoise, 54 Boulevard Raspail, 75270 Paris Cedex 06 France. **Tel** 011 33 1 42221548. **ED** V. Alleton, A. Lucas, A. Peyraube, L. Sagary, A. Rygalogy. cum. index. **Bk Rev. Ad Acc.**
Desc: Linguistics and languages of Eastern Asia.
Ind/Abst Int. Bibliogr. Sociol.; Linguist. Lang. Behav. Abstr. (1986-) [Full Cov.]; MLA Int. Bibl. Books Artic. Mod. Lang. Lit.; Soc. Plann. Policy Dev. Abstr.; Sociol. Abstr.

SZ/0259-6199
CAHIERS DE LINGUISTIQUE FRANCAISE. [Cah. linguist. fr.]. (1980)-. Periodical. French. ir. price varies per issue. Librairie Droz SA, 11 rue Massot BP 389, CH 1211 Geneva 12 Switzerland. **Tel** 011 41 22 3466666, FAX 011 41 22 472391. **ED** L.E. Roulet. **UDC** 804.0.
Desc: Contains information on French linguistics.

FR
CAHIERS DE LINGUISTIQUE HISPANIQUE MEDIEVALE. **Added/Corp** Seminaire d'Etudes Medievales Hispaniques de l'Universite Paris-XIII. No. 1 (1976)-. Multiple languages (French and Spanish). an. Editions Klincksieck, 8 rue de la Sorbonne, 75005 Paris France. **Tel** 11 33 1 43545953, FAX 11 33 1 432252553. **(Subscription address:** CDU-SEDES, 88 Bd St Germain, 75005 Paris France**)** **LC** PC4001; .C34. **DD** 460.

RM/0007-988X
CAHIERS DE LINGUISTIQUE THEORIQUE ET APPLIQUEE. [Cah. linguist. theor. appl.]. **Added/Corp** Academia Republicii Populare Romine. Universitatea din Bucuresti. Academia Republicii Socialiste Romania. (1962)-. Periodical. English (French, German, Italian, Russian and Spanish). sa. $94.00 US. **(Subscription address:** Rodipet SA, Societatea Romana de Difuzare a Presei si Tipariturilor, Bucuresti Piata Pressei Libere Nr. 1 Sector 1, PO Box 33-57, Bucharest Romania.**)** **LC** P1.A1; C328.
Ind/Abst Annu. Bibliogr. Engl. Lang. Lit.; MLA Int. Bibl. Books Artic. Mod. Lang. Lit.

BE/0771-6524
CAHIERS DE L'INSTITUT DE LINGUISTIQUE DE LOUVAIN. [Cah. Inst. linguist. Louvain]. **VFOAT** CILL. (1975)-. Periodical. French (Multiple languages). ir. 1600F. Editions Peeters SA, Bondgenotenlaan 153, BP 41, B-3000 Leuven Belgium. **Tel** 32 16 235170, FAX 32 16 228500, telex 65987 PUL B. **ED** G. Jucquois and Y. Duhoux. **UDC** 811. **Bk Rev.** ***Continues*** *Cahiers de l'Institut de Linguistique, 0303-3880.*

DK/0591-0358
CAHIERS DE L'INSTITUT DU MOYENAGE GREC ET LATIN / UNIVERSITE DE COPENHAGUE. **Main/Corp** Kbenhavns Universitet. Institut for Grsk og Latinsk Middelalderfilologi. **Added/Corp** Kbenhavns Universitet. Institut for Grsk og Latinsk Middelalderfilologi. (1969)-. Monographic series. English (French, German and Latin). ir. Price varies per volume. Erik Paludan/Intl Boghandel, Fiolstraede 10, DK 1171 Copenhagen K Denmark. **Tel** 01/15 06 75. **ED** Sten Ebbesen. **Circ:** 500.
Desc: Editions and discussions of medieval texts, particularly on music, logic, and linguistics.

FR/0759-1586
CAHIERS DU CENTRE INTERDISCIPLINAIRE DES SCIENCES DU LANGAGE. 1979-. Periodical. French. Universite de Toulouse le Mirail, Service des Publications, 56 rue du Taur, 31000 Toulouse France.

RE/0337-6176
CAHIERS DU CENTRE UNIVERSITAIRE DE LA REUNION. [Cah. Cent. univ. la Reunion]. **Main/Corp** Centre Universitaire de la Reunion. French. Universitaire de la Reunion, rue de la Victoire, Saint-Denis Reunion. **LC** P381.R46; C45A. **DD** 440/.969/81.

SW/0256-1565
CAHIERS DU DEPARTEMENT DES LANGUES ET DES SCIENCES DU LANGAGE. **Added/Corp** Universite de Lausanne. Departement des Langues et des Sciences du Langage. **VFOAT** Cahiers du DLSL. No. 1 (1985)-. Periodical. French (German). **LC** P1.A1; C333. **DD** 410/.5.
Ind/Abst MLA Int. Bibl. Books Artic. Mod. Lang. Lit.

FR/0994-7736
CAHIERS DU LACITO PARIS. (CAHIERS DU LACITO.). [Cah. LACITO Paris]. **VFOAT** Cahiers du Laboratoire de Langues et Civilisations a Traditions Orale (Paris). (1986)-. Periodical. French (English). an. 1200F. Editions Peeters SA, Bondgenotenlaan 153, BP 41, B-3000 Leuven Belgium. **Tel** 32 16 235170, FAX 32 16 228500, telex 65987 PUL B. **ED** J.M.C. Thomas, M. Fr. Rombi, J. P. Caprile and M. Lebarbier. **UDC** 800. **Bk Rev. Ad Acc.**
Ind/Abst Soc. Plann. Policy Dev. Abstr.

SZ/0068-516X
CAHIERS FERDINAND DE SAUSSURE. (CAHIERS FERDINAND DE SAUSSURE / PUBLIES PAR LA SOCIETE GENEVOISE DE LINGUISTIQUE.). [Cah. Ferdinand de Saussure]. **Added/Corp** Societe Genevoise de Linguistique. (1941)-. Monographic series. French (English, German and Italian). ir. Price varies per volume. Librairie Droz SA, 11 rue Massot BP 389, CH 1211 Geneva 12 Switzerland. **Tel** 011 41 22 3466666, FAX 011 41 22 472391. **LC** P25; .C23. **[CCC].**
Ind/Abst Lang. Teach.; MLA Int. Bibl. Books Artic. Mod. Lang. Lit.

CN/0843-9559
CAHIERS FRANCO-CANADIENS DE LOUEST. [Cahiers fr.-can Ouest]. **Added/Corp** Centre d'Etudes Franco-Canadiennes de l'Ouest. (1989)-. Periodical. French. sa. 26.00Can$ (institutions), 22.00Can$ (individuals) Canada; 32.00Can$ other. Centre d'Etudes Franco-Canadiennes de Lousot, College Universitaire de Saint-Boniface, 200 Avenue de la Cathedrale, Saint-Boniface Manitoba R2H 0H7 Canada. **Tel** (204)233-0210, FAX (204)237-3240. **ED** Andre Fauchon (Phone: (204)233-0210). **DD** 971.2/004114. **Bk Rev. Ad Acc, Adv Mgr:** Raymond Theberge, **Tel** (204)233-0210. **Pr Rev.** ***Continues** Cefco; Centre d'Etudes Franco-Canadiennes de l'Ouest., 0226-0670.*

IV/0252-9386
CAHIERS IVOIRIENS DE RECHERCHE LINGUISTIQUE / INSTITUT DE LINGUISTIQUE APPLIQUU.N.A.C.I-ABIDJAN. **Added/Corp** Universite Nationale de Cote d'Ivoire. Institut de Linguistique Appliquee. **VFOAT** CIRL. No. 1 (Apr. 1977)-. Periodical. French (English). Twice a year. 6000.00CFAF Ivory Coast; 11000.00CFAF Europe; 11500.00CFAF others. Institute Linguistique Appliquee, BP 887, Abidjan 08 Ivory Coast. **Tel** 011 225 439000 Ext. 3435. **LC** P381.I9; C34. **DD** 409/.666/8. **CODEN** CIRLEW. Index available. **Bk Rev. Ad Acc. Circ:** 250.
Ind/Abst Int. Bibliogr. Sociol.; Linguist. Lang. Behav. Abstr. (1984-) [Full Cov.]; Soc. Plann. Policy Dev. Abstr.; Sociol. Abstr.

CN/0315-3967
CAHIERS LINGUISTIQUES D'OTTAWA. [Cah. linguist. Ottawa]. **Added/Corp** University of Ottawa. Dept. of Linguistics. University of Ottawa. Dept. of Linguistics and Modern Languages. University of Ottawa. Centre for Second Language Learning. No. 1 (Sept. 1971)-. English (French). ir. 8.00Can$. University of Ottawa Department of Linguistics, 78 Laurier Avenue, Ottawa Ontario K1N 6N5 Canada. **Tel** (613)231-3346. **LC** P1.A1; C34. **DD** 410/.5. **Bk Rev. Circ:** 250.
Desc: Papers on applied and theoretical linguistics written in French or English representing original contributions to the field.
Ind/Abst Lang. Teach.; Linguist. Lang. Behav. Abstr. (1973-) [Full Cov.]; MLA Int. Bibl. Books Artic. Mod. Lang. Lit.; Soc. Plann. Policy Dev. Abstr.; Sociol. Abstr.

CI/0350-7831
CAKAVSKA RIC. [Cakav. ric]. **Added/Corp** Matica Hrvatska, Split. (1971)-. Periodical. Serbo-Croatian (Roman). sa. **LC** PG1394; .C35.
Ind/Abst MLA Int. Bibl. Books Artic. Mod. Lang. Lit.

CN/0823-0579
CALGARY WORKING PAPERS IN LINGUISTICS. [Calg. work. pap. linguist.]. **Added/Corp** University of Calgary. LOGOS. **VFOAT** CWP in Linguistics. (1975)-. English. an (Oct.). 7.00Can$. University of Calgary Department of Linguistics, 2500 University Drive Northwest, Calgary Alberta T2N 1N4 Canada. **Tel** (403)220-6135. **DD** 410/.5.
Ind/Abst Linguist. Lang. Behav. Abstr. (1991-) [Full Cov.]; Soc. Plann. Policy Dev. Abstr.; Sociol. Abstr.

US/0742-7778
CALICO JOURNAL. **See** Computers-Computer Assisted Instruction.

US/0892-6964
CALIFORNIA READER, THE. **Added/Corp** California Reading Association. (196?)-. Periodical. English. qt. $5.00. California Reading Association, Irvine Avenue, Suite 118, Newport Beach CA 92660.
Ind/Abst Calif. Period. Index (19??-); Calif. Period. Microfi. (19??-).

US/8755-7134
CALL NEWS AND REVIEWS. [CALL news rev.]. **VFOAT** Call News & Reviews. **VAT** Computer-Assisted Language Learning News and Reviews. Vol. 1, No. 1-. Periodical. English. bm. $20.00. Call Publications, PO Box 18708, Los Angeles CA 90007. **DD** 407. **UDC** 800:311; 681.3:800.7.

●UK
CAMBRIAN MEDIEVAL CELTIC STUDIES. **VFOAT** CMCS. No. 26 (Winter 1993)-. Academic Scholarly Publication. English. sa. £10.00 (individual), £14.00 (institution). CMCS Publications, Department of Welsh, Old College, King Street, Aberystwyth, Dyfed SY23 2AX England. **ED** Patrick Sims-Williams. **LC** DA140; .C34. **Bk Rev. Ad Acc.** ***Continues** Cambridge Medieval Celtic Studies, 0260-5600.*
Desc: Medieval Celtic languages, literature, history, archaeology, art, etc., of Ireland, Scotland, Wales, Cornwall and Brittany.

UK/0260-5600
CAMBRIDGE MEDIEVAL CELTIC STUDIES. ***Title Change.*** [Camb. mediev. Celt. stud.]. **Added/Corp** University of Cambridge. Dept. of Anglo-Saxon, Norse & Celtic. **VFOAT** CMCS. No. 1 (Summer 1981)-(1993). Periodical. English. sa (July and December). CMCS Publications, Department of Welsh, Old College, King Street, Aberystwyth, Dyfed SY23 2AX England. **ED** Patrick Sims-Williams. **LC** DA140; .C34. **Bk Rev. Ad Acc. Pr Rev.** Documents available from The Genuine Article. ***Continued by** Cambrian Medieval Celtic Studies.*
Desc: Medieval Celtic languages, literature, history, archaeology, art, etc., of Ireland, Scotland, Wales, Cornwall and Brittany.
Ind/Abst Arts Humanit. Citation Index (?-?) [Full Cov.]; BHA : Biblio. Hist. Art (?-?); Br. Archaeol. Bibliogr. (?-?); Curr. Contents Arts Humanit. (?-?); MLA Int. Bibl. Books Artic. Mod. Lang. Lit. (?-?); Res. Alert (?-?) [Full Cov.]; Soc. Sci. Cit. Index (?-?) [Select. Cov.].

UK/0068-676X
CAMBRIDGE STUDIES IN LINGUISTICS. [Camb. stud. linguist.]. Vol. 1 (1969)-. Monographic series. English. ir. Price varies per volume. Cambridge University Press, The Edinburgh Building, Shaftesbury Road, Cambridge CB2 2RU United Kingdom. **Tel** 011 44 223 312393, FAX 011 44 223 325959. **(Subscription address:** Cambridge University Press / North America, 110 Midland Avenue, Port Chester NY 10573.**) ED** Penny Carter. **LC** UNC.
Desc: Monographs on all aspects of theoretical linguistics. Includes volumes on syntax and pragmatics.
Ind/Abst MLA Int. Bibl. Books Artic. Mod. Lang. Lit.

CN/0008-4131
CANADIAN JOURNAL OF LINGUISTICS. (CANADIAN JOURNAL OF LINGUISTICS. LA REVUE CANADIENNE DE LINGUISTIQUE.). [Can. j. linguist.]. **Added/Corp** Canadian Linguistic Association. **VFOAT** Revue Canadienne de Linguistique. Vol. 6, No. 2 (I.E.V.7), No. 1 (Fall 1961)-. Periodical. English (French). qt. $40.00. University of Toronto Press, 5201 Dufferin Street, Downsview Ontario M3H 5T8 Canada. **Tel** (416)667-7781, (416)667-7782, FAX (416)667-7803. **ED** Anne Rochette. **LC** P1; .C3. Index available. **Bk Rev. Ad Acc. Pr Rev. Circ:** 700. available on microfilm and microfiche from University Microfilms International (UMI). Documents available from The Genuine Article. ***Continues** Canadian Linguistic Association. Journal of the Canadian Linguistic Association, 0319-5732.*
Desc: Publishes articles on technical and scientific linguistics in both English and French. The journal also publishes book reviews in both languages dealing with all aspects of language and language analysis.
Ind/Abst Abstr. Anthropol.; Annu. Bibliogr. Engl. Lang. Lit.; Arts Humanit. Citation Index [Full Cov.]; Curr. Contents Arts Humanit.; Lang. Teach.; Linguist. Lang. Behav. Abstr. (1972-) [Full Cov.]; MLA Int. Bibl. Books Artic. Mod. Lang. Lit.; Res. Alert [Full Cov.]; Soc. Plann. Policy Dev. Abstr.; Soc. Sci. Cit. Index [Full Cov.]; Sociol. Abstr.

CN/0008-4506
CANADIAN MODERN LANGUAGE REVIEW, THE. [Can. mod. lang. rev.]. **Added/Corp** Ontario Modern Language Teachers' Association. **VFOAT** Revue Canadienne des Langues Vivantes; La Revue Canadienne des Langues Vivantes. Vol. 1 (Sept. 1944)-. Periodical. English (German, Italian, Polish, Russian, Spanish, Ukrainian and French). qt. $35.00 (institution), $25.00 (individual) US; 35.00Can$ (institutions), 25.00Can$ (individuals) Canada; $45.00 other. Canadian Modern Language, 237 Hellems Avenue, Welland Ontario L3B 3B8 Canada. **Tel** (905)734-3640, FAX (905)734-3640. **ED** Sally Rehorick and Viviane Edwards. **LC** PB5; .C36. **DD** 410/.7. **[CCC].** Index available. **Bk Rev. Ad Acc. Pr Rev. Circ:** 2,400. available on microfilm and microfiche from University Microfilms International (UMI). Documents available from The Genuine Article, UMI Article Clearinghouse.
Desc: Contains articles on pedagogy, applied linguistics, methodology, sociolinguistic classroom techniques, core, basic and French immersion, and on English, German, Italian, and Spanish as second languages.
Ind/Abst Am. Bibliogr. Slavic East Europ. Stud.; Can. Index; Can. Period. Index (19??-); Curr. Contents Soc. Behav. Sci.; Curr. Index J. Educ.; Educ. Index; Lang. Teach.; Linguist. Lang. Behav. Abstr.; MLA Int. Bibl. Books Artic. Mod. Lang. Lit.; Multicult. Educ. Abstr.; Res. Alert [Full Cov.]; Romant. Move.; Soc. Plann. Policy Dev. Abstr.; Soc. Sci. Cit. Index [Full Cov.]; Sociol. Abstr.; Spec. Educ. Needs Abstr.

CN/0714-5721
CANADIAN QUILL. [Can. quill]. Vol. 11, No. 2 (Nov. 1981)-. Periodical. English. Canadian Quill, c/o New Brunswick Teachers Association Brunswick E3B 5R6 Canada. **DD** 420/.7/12715. **UDC** 802.0-07(715). ***Continues** Chautauqua, 0710-7757.*

CN/0008-5006
CANADIAN SLAVONIC PAPERS. [Can. Slav. pap.]. **VFOAT** Revue Canadienne des Slavistes. Vol. 1, (1956)-. Academic Scholarly Publication. English (French). Four times a year (Mar., June, Sept., Dec.). 40.00Can$ Canada; 45.00Can$ other. University of Alberta / Slavonic Papers, Canadian Slavonic Papers, 347 Arts Building, Edmonton Alberta T6G 2E6 Canada. **Tel** (403)492-2566. **ED** E. W. Dowler. **LC** PG6; .C3. Index available. cum. index. **Bk Rev. Ad Acc. Circ:** 1,000 (ctrl). Documents available from The Genuine Article, UMI Article Clearinghouse. ***Absorbed** Etudes Slaves et Est-Europeennes, 0014-2190.*
Desc: An interdisciplinary scholarly publication devoted to the Soviet Union and Eastern Europe.
Ind/Abst Am. Hist. Life (1968-); Am. Bibliogr. Slavic East Europ. Stud.; Arts Humanit. Citation Index [Full Cov.]; BHA : Biblio. Hist. Art; Curr. Contents Arts Humanit.; Linguist. Lang. Behav. Abstr.; MLA Int. Bibl. Books Artic. Mod. Lang. Lit.; Newsp. Period. Abstr. (1991-); Res. Alert [Full Cov.]; Soc. Plann. Policy Dev. Abstr.; Sociol. Abstr.

SZ/0171-6859
CANADIAN STUDIES IN GERMAN LANGUAGE AND LITERATURE. **See** Literature.

AT/0311-4627
CANBERRA LINGUIST. [Canb. linguist]. (1974)-. Periodical. English (French and German). sa (June & Nov.). 20.00Aus$. Modern Language Teachers Association of the ACT, GPO Box 989, Canberra ACT 2601 Australia. **ED** Louise Jansen. **DD** _a407.129471.
Ind/Abst Aust. Educ. Index (199?-).

SP/0213-9715
CARABELA. [Carabela]. (1987)-. Periodical. Spanish. bm. $28.00. SGEL, Apdo de Correos 85, 28100 Madrid Spain. **Tel** 011 34 1 661-7000. **UDC** 806. Index available. **Ad Acc. Circ:** 4,000 (ctrl).
Desc: Articles from the Spanish and Latin American newspapers for the teaching of spanish as a foreign language.

JM
CARIB. **See** Literature.

CN/0824-7714
CARLETON PAPERS IN APPLIED LANGUAGE STUDIES. [Carleton pap. appl. lang. stud.]. **Added/Corp** Carleton University. Centre for Applied Language Studies. Vol. 1 (1984)-. Periodical. English (French and German). an. Carleton University Center for Applied Language Studies, Ottawa Ontario K1S 5B6 Canada. **Tel** (613)788-6612, telex 053-4232. **ED** Ian Pringle. **LC** PB35; .C28. **DD** 418/.007. **Circ:** 200. available on microfilm from University Microfilms International (UMI).
Desc: Working papers examining the underlying theoretical principles of language teaching, learning and research. Of particular interest are approaches to communicative language teaching, syllabus design, pedagogical implications of research on writing, discourse, analysis, and computer-assisted language learning.

Ind/Abst Linguist. Lang. Behav. Abstr.; MLA Int. Bibl. Books Artic. Mod. Lang. Lit.; Soc. Plann. Policy Dev. Abstr.; Sociol. Abstr.

US/0739-3474
CARRIER PIDGIN, THE. **Added/Corp** Stanford University. Dept. of Linguistics. University of Hawaii (Honolulu). Social Sciences and Linguistics Institute. (Feb. 1973)-. English. tq. $7.50 (individuals), $15.00 (institutions). University of Hawaii Foundation, University of Hawaii Monnoa Bachman 101, Honolulu HI 96822. **Tel** (809)956-2786. **LC** PM7801; .C37. **DD** 417/.2/05.
Ind/Abst Soc. Plann. Policy Dev. Abstr.

US/0737-9412
CARTE ITALIANE. **See** Literature.

IT
CARTE SEMIOTICHE : RIVISTA DELL'ASSOCIAZIONE ITALIANA DI STUDI SEMIOTICI. ***Ceased.*** No. 1 (Sept. 1985)-(19??). Periodical. Italian. an. Ses SRL, Via Degli Artisti 8C, 50132 Firenze Italy. **LC** P99; .C334. **DD** 001.51.

NE/0862-8459
CASOPIS PRO MODERNI FILOLOGII / CESKOSLOVENSKA AKADEMIE VED. **Added/Corp** Ustav Pro Jazyk Cesky CSAV. (1991)-. Academic Scholarly Publication. Czech (summaries and/or abstracts in English, French, German and Russian). sa. $58.00. John Benjamins BV, Amsteldijk 44, PO Box 75577, 1070 AN Amsterdam Netherlands. **Tel** 011 31 20 6738156, FAX 011 31 20 739773. **(Subscription address:** John Benjamins North America, PO Box 27519, Philadelphia PA 19118-0519.**)** **ED** Jaromir Povejsil. **LC** PB5; C38. Index available. **Bk Rev. Circ:** 1,350.

FR
CASSETTE NEWS. AUDIO CASSETTE. English. mo (except July, Aug., and Dec.). 1500.00F France; 1820.00F other. Telelingua, 13 BD Thiers, 78250 Meulan France. **Tel** 011 33 1 34747094.
Desc: Monthly English language program for foreign executives and professionals studying English.

IT
CE FASTU? : RIVISTA DELLA SOCIETA FILOLOGICA FRIULANA "GRAZIADO I. ASCOLI.". **Added/Corp** Societat Filologjche Furlane. (1939)-. Periodical. Italian (Raeto-Romance). sa. (Comes with Societa Filologica Friulana membership). Societa Filologica Friulana, Via Manin 18, 33100 Udine Italy. **Tel** 39 432 501598. **LC** PC947; .C38. **DD** 459/.9. ***Continues*** *Societat Filologjche Furlane. Bolletino della Societa Filologica Friulana "G. I. Ascoli" ("Ce Fastu?").*
Ind/Abst BHA : Biblio. Hist. Art.

US/0007-8069
CEA CRITIC. [CEA crit.]. **Added/Corp** College English Association. Texas A & M University. Dept. of English. College English Association. **VAT** College English Association Critic. Vol. 10 (1948)-. Periodical. English. Three times a year (Spring & Fall & Winter). $25.00 (individuals); $30.00 (institutions) Comes with College English Association Membership. College English Association, Nazareth College, 4525 East Avenue, Rochester NY 14618-3790. **Tel** (716)586-2525, Ext. 535, FAX (716)586-2452. **ED** Barbara Brothers and Bege Bowers. **LC** PE1011; .C69. **Bk Rev. Circ:** 2,000. available on microfilm and microfiche from University Microfilms International (UMI). Documents available from The Genuine Article. ***Continues*** *College English Association. Newsletter.*
Desc: Features articles by college English teachers and other professional writers, with particular emphasis on the teaching of language and literature at the college level. Some literary criticism also.
Ind/Abst Abstr. Engl. Stud.; Annu. Bibliogr. Engl. Lang. Lit.; Arts Humanit. Citation Index [Full Cov.]; Curr. Contents Arts Humanit.; Index Am. Period. Verse; MLA Int. Bibl. Books Artic. Mod. Lang. Lit.; Res. Alert [Full Cov.]; Soc. Sci. Cit. Index [Select. Cov.].

US/0007-8034
CEA FORUM. [CEA forum]. **Main/Corp** College English Association. **Added/Corp** Texas A & M University. Dept. of English. College English Association. Forum. **VAT** College English Association Forum. Vol. 1 (Oct. 1970)-. Periodical. English. qt. $30.00. College English Association, Nazareth College, 4525 East Avenue, Rochester NY 14618-3790. **Tel** (716)586-2525, Ext. 535, FAX (716)586-2452. **ED** Bege K Bowers and Barbara Brothers. **LC** PE11; .C6513. **DD** 820/.7/1173; 420. cum. index. **Bk Rev. Ad Acc. Circ:** 1,500. available on microfilm and microfiche from University Microfilms International (UMI). ***Continues in part*** *CEA Critic, 0007-8069.*
Desc: Publishes information and opinions on problems facing the college English discipline and possible solutions to these problems, and discuss innovations, changes, and advancements in the teaching of English in the college classroom.

Ind/Abst Am. Humanit. Index; Annu. Bibliogr. Engl. Lang. Lit.; Curr. Index J. Educ.; Index Am. Period. Verse; Lit. Crit. Regist.

CN/0710-197X
CELAT-INFORMATION. **See** Folklore.

IE/0069-1399
CELTICA (DUBLIN). (CELTICA.). [Celtica]. **Added/Corp** Dublin Institute for Advanced Studies. Vol. 1 (1946/50)-. English. ir. 20p Ireland; 25p other. Dublin Institute for Advanced Studies, 10 Burlington Road, Dublin 4 Ireland. **Tel** 011 353 1 680748. **LC** PB1001; .C63.
Ind/Abst MLA Int. Bibl. Books Artic. Mod. Lang. Lit.

GW/0008-9192
CENTRAL ASIATIC JOURNAL. **See** History(General)-History of Asia.

RM/0373-1545
CERCETARI DE LINGVISTICA. [Cercet. linguist.]. **Added/Corp** Academia Republicii Socialiste Romania. Institutul de Lingvistica din Cluj. Institutul de Lingvistica din Bucuresti. Vol. 1 (1956)-. Periodical. Romanian (summaries and/or abstracts in French, German and Russian). sa. DM203.00. **(Subscription address:** Kubon & Sagner, ABT Zeitschriftenimport, D 80328 Munich Germany.**)** ***Continues in part*** *Studii Si Cercetari Stiintifice.*
Ind/Abst MLA Int. Bibl. Books Artic. Mod. Lang. Lit.

CN/0577-4179
C'EST-A-DIRE (MONTREAL). (C'EST-A-DIRE...). **Added/Corp** Societe Radio-Canada. Comite de Linguistique. Vol. 1 No. 1 (Nov. 1960)-. Periodical. French. ir (Publishes 1 issues every 2 or 3 months). 17.30Can$. Canadian Broadcasting Corporation, CP 6000, Montreal Quebec H3C 3A8 Canada. **Tel** (514)597-7666. **DD** 448.1/05.

US/0886-005X
CHAMPS-ELYSEES (NASHVILLE, TENN.). (CHAMPS-ELYSEES [SOUND RECORDING].). [Champs-Elysees]. **Added/Corp** Champs-Elysees, Inc. No. 1 (1984)-. Periodical. French. Eleven times a year (June/July combined). $118.00 (US); $122.00 (Canada & Mexico); $138.00 (other). Champs-Elysees Inc, Box 158067, Nashville TN 37215-8067. **Tel** (800)824-0829, (615)383-8534, FAX (615) 297-3138. **ED** Dominique Laurent. **DD** 054.

FR/0757-9314
CHANTIERS AMERINDIA. (1982)-. Monographic series. French (Spanish and Portuguese). ir. Price varies per volume. Association Ethnolinguistique Amerind, B P 431, 75233 Paris Cedex 05 France. **UDC** 39 : 82 (72 + 8).
Desc: Articles about specific linguistics and issues. Texts in Native American languages.

US/0009-3424
CHEZ NOUS (NEW YORK). (CHEZ NOUS.). (19??)-. Periodical. French. wk. $25.00. Mary Glasgow Publications, Brookhampton Lane, Kineton, Warwickshire CV35 0JB England. **Tel** 011 44 926 640606, FAX 011 44 926 641016. **(Subscription address:** Scholastic Inc, PO Box 3710, Jefferson City MO 65102.**)** available on microfilm from University Microfilms International (UMI).

US/0163-2809
CHILDREN'S LANGUAGE. Vol. 1 (1978)-. English. Lawrence Erlbaum Associates, 365 Broadway, Suite 102, Hillsdale NJ 07642. **Tel** (201)666-4110, (800)926-6579, FAX (201)666-2394. **LC** P118; .C47. **DD** 401/.9. **NLM** W1 CH696H.
Desc: Information on language development in children.

FR/0766-4257
CHRONIQUES ITALIENNES. **Added/Corp** Universite de Paris III. U.E.R. d'Italien et de Roumain. Universite de Paris III. U.F.R. d'Italien et de Roumain. No. 1 (1985)-. Monographic series. French. ir. Price varies per volume. Chroniques Italiennes, 13 rue de Santeuil, 75005 Paris France. **Tel** 011 33 1 45874178. **Bk Rev. Ad Acc.** ctrl circ.

US
CHUNG-KUO WEN TZU (CHUNG-KUO WEN TZU PIEN CHI WEI YUAN HUI). (CHUNG-KUO WEN TZU / CHUNG-KUO WEN TZU PIEN CHI WEI YUAN HUI PIEN.). Periodical. Chinese. ir. $9.60. Yee Wen Publishing Company, 21 Vista Court, San Francisco CA 94080. **Tel** (415)873-7167. **LC** PL1004; .C577. **DD** 495.1/09. **UDC** 809.51(09).
Desc: Academic studies of the Chinese language, its origin and history.

CC/0578-1949
CHUNG-KUO YU EN (JEN MIN CHIAO YU CHU PAN SHE). (CHUNG KUO YU WEN.). **VFOAT** Zhongguo Yuwen. (July, 1952)-. Periodical. Chinese. Six times a year. $15.48 (surface mail); $24.92 (airmail). Chinese Academy of Social Sciences / Language Institute, (Zhongguo Shehui Kexueyuan), Shehui Kexue Zazhishe, A-158 Gulou Xidajie, Beijing 100720, People's Republic of China. **(Subscription address:** China International Book Trading Corporation, PO Box 399, Library Service Department, Beijing 100044 People's Republic of China.**)** **DD** 495.1.
Desc: Contains information on the Chinese language.
Ind/Abst Am. Hist. Life (1956-1957).

CH/0578-1930
CHUNG-KYO YU WEN (TAIPEI, TAIWAN). (CHUNG-KUO YU WEN.). Began in 1952. Periodical. Chinese. mo. $230.00. Chung-Kuo Yu Wen Yueh Kan She, PO Box 7-89, Taipei Taiwan. **LC** PL1004; .C585. **DD** 495.1/05. **UDC** 809.51.

HK
CHUNG WEN HSUEH HSI. **See** Literature.

RU
CHUVASHSKII IAZYK, LITERATURA I FOLKLOR. **Added/Corp** Nauchno-Issledovatelskii Institut pri Sovete Ministrov Chuvashskoi ASSR. (1972)-. Multiple languages (Russian and Chuvash). 1.31rub (single issue). Nauchno-Issl, Moskovskii Prospekt 29, Korpus 1, Cheboksary, Russia. **LC** PL381; .C47.

II/0970-8340
CIEFL BULLETIN NEW SERIES. (CIEFL BULLETIN.). [CIEFL bull.]. **Main/Corp** Central Institute of English and Foreign Languages. Vol. 9 (1973)-. Bulletin. English. Twice a year (June, Dec.). $12.00. Central Institute of English & Foreign Languages, Hyderadad, 500 007 India. ***Continues*** *Central Institute of English. Bulletin of the Central Institute of English.*
Ind/Abst Lang. Teach.; MLA Int. Bibl. Books Artic. Mod. Lang. Lit.; Soc. Plann. Policy Dev. Abstr.; Sociol. Abstr.

CN/0821-1876
CIRCUIT (MONTREAL). (CIRCUIT.). [Circuit]. **Added/Corp** Societe des Traducteurs du Quebec. No. 1 (June 1983)-. Periodical. French (English). qt. 25.00Can$ (non-members) Canada; 35.00Can$ (non-members) other. Corporation Professionnelle des Traducteurs et Interpretes Agrees du Quebec, 1140 Bouleverd, de Maisonneuve Ouest, Bureau 1060, Montreal Quebec H3A 1M8, Canada. **Tel** (514)845-4411, FAX (514)845-9903. **DD** 418/.02/05. **Bk Rev. Ad Acc, Adv Mgr:** Malboeuf, **Tel** (514)334-6742. **Circ:** 2,500 (ctrl).
Desc: Informative magazine dealing with language and communication.

IT/0392-8632
CIVILTA CLASSICA E CRISTIANA. ***Ceased.*** [Civilta class. crist.]. Vol. 1, No. 1 (Apr. 1980)-(Dec. 1993). Periodical. Italian. Three times a year (May, Sept., Dec.). Civilta Classica Christiana, C SO Firenze 33, 16136 Genoa Italy. **Tel** 39 10 221235. **LC** PA9; .C45. **DD** 880/.09. **UDC** 87. **Bk Rev. Pr Rev.** ***Continues*** *Rivista di Studi Classici.*
Ind/Abst MLA Int. Bibl. Books Artic. Mod. Lang. Lit.

US/0007-8549
CLA JOURNAL. [CLA j.]. **Main/Corp** College Language Association (U.S.). **VAT** College Language Association Journal. Vol. 1 (Nov. 1957)-. Periodical. English (French and Spanish). qt (Mar., June, Sept., Dec.). $35.00 (US); $36.50 (Canada); $40.50 (other). College Language Association, Morehouse College, PO Box 13, Atlanta GA 30314. **Tel** (404)681-2800, FAX (404) 681-2650. **ED** Cason L Hill. **LC** P1.A1; C22. **UDC** 800.6. Index available. **Bk Rev. Ad Acc. Circ:** 1,500. Documents available from The Genuine Article, UMI Article Clearinghouse.
Desc: Literary criticism and book reviews.
Ind/Abst Abstr. Engl. Stud.; Acad. Search (July 1993-); Annu. Bibliogr. Engl. Lang. Lit.; Arts Humanit. Citation Index [Full Cov.]; Curr. Contents Arts Humanit.; Expand. Acad. Index (1989-); Humanit. Index; Humanit. Source (Jul. 1993-); INFO-SOUTH Abstr.; Lit. Crit. Regist.; Mag. Search; MLA Int. Bibl. Books Artic. Mod. Lang. Lit.; Newsp. Period. Abstr. (1991-); Res. Alert [Full Cov.]; Women Stud. Abstr.

US/0550-5755
CLASSROOM PRACTICES IN TEACHING ENGLISH. (CLASSROOM PRACTICES IN TEACHING ENGLISH : A REPORT OF THE NCTE COMMITTEE TO REPORT PROMISING PRACTICES IN THE TEACHING OF ENGLISH.). [Classr. pract. teach. Engl.]. **Added/Corp** National Council of Teachers of English. Committee on Classroom Practices. NCTE Committee to Report Promising Practices in the Teaching of English. 3rd (1965-66)-. Monographic series. English. ir. Price varies per volume. National Council of Teachers of English, 1111 Kenyon Road, Urbana IL 61801. **Tel** (217)328-3870, FAX (217)328-9645. **LC** LB1580.U5; C57. **DD** 428/.007. ***Continues*** *Patterns and Models for Teaching English, 0885-7350.*

UK/0142-1042
CLICK LONDON. 1973. (1973)-. Periodical. English. bm. £13.99. Mary Glasgow Publications, Brookhampton Lane, Kineton, Warwickshire CV35 0JB England. **Tel** 011 44 926 640606, FAX 011 44 926 641016.

UK/0269-9206
CLINICAL LINGUISTICS & PHONETICS. [Clin. linguist. phon.]. **VFOAT** Clinical Linguistics and Phonetics; CL&P. Vol. 1, No. 1 (July-Sept. 1987)-. Periodical. English. qt. £108.00 UK; $167.00 other. Taylor & Francis Ltd., Rankine Road, Basingstoke Hampshire, RG24 8PR United Kingdom. **Tel** 011 44 256 840366, FAX 011 44 256 479438, telex 858540. **(Subscription address:** Taylor & Francis Inc., 1900 Frost Road, Suite 101, Bristol PA 19007-1598.**) ED** Martin J. Ball and Thomas W. Powell, associate editor. **LC** RC423.A1; C57. **DD** 616.85/5/005. **NLM** W1; CL726E. **[CCC]. Pr Rev.** available on microfilm from University Microfilms International (UMI). Documents available from The Genuine Article.
Desc: Concerned with disorders of speech and language and the interaction between them and the study of linguistics and phonetics. Work is also encouraged in other areas of clinical linguistics such as clinical dialectology/sociolinguistics, sign language and lip reading, childhood dysphasia and dyspraxia, and disordered communication in bilingual and multicultural settings.
Ind/Abst Curr. Contents Soc. Behav. Sci.; EMBASE; Linguist. Lang. Behav. Abstr. (1987-) [Full Cov.]; Res. Alert [Full Cov.]; Soc. Plann. Policy Dev. Abstr.; Soc. Sci. Cit. Index [Full Cov.]; Sociol. Abstr.

US/1049-9059
CLL JOURNAL : COMPUTER-ASSISTED ENGLISH LANGUAGE LEARNING JOURNAL. [CLL j.]. **Added/Corp** CALICO (Group) International Society for Technology in Education. Teachers of English to Speakers of Other Languages. CALL Interest Section. **VFOAT** Computer-Assisted English Language Learning Journal; CAELL Journal. Vol. 1, No. 1 (Feb. 1990)-. Periodical. English. qt. $35.00 (one year), $67.00 (two year) US; $45.00 (one year), $87.00 (two year) other. International Society for Technology in Education ISTE, University of Oregon, 1787 Agate Street, Eugene OR 97403-1923. **Tel** (503)346-4414, , FAX (503)346-5890. **DD** 407. **CODEN** CLJOEM. **[CCC]. *Continues*** *C.A.L.L. Digest, 0887-7742.*
Desc: Focuses on issues facing computer using language teachers. Covers trends, products, applications, research, and program evaluations.
Ind/Abst Linguist. Lang. Behav. Abstr.; Soc. Plann. Policy Dev. Abstr.; Sociol. Abstr.

GW/0936-5907
COGNITIVE LINGUISTICS. [Cogn. linguist.]. (1990)-. Periodical. English. qt. $112.80. Walter de Gruyter Inc., PO Box 303421, D 10728 Berlin Germany. **Tel** 011 49 30 260050, FAX 011 49 30 26005251. **LC** IN PROCESS; P37; .C57. **CODEN** COGLEJ. **[CCC].** Documents available from Ask*IEEE.
Desc: Presents a forum for linguistic research of all kinds on the interaction between language and cognition. It focuses on language as an instrument for organizing, processing and conveying information.
Ind/Abst ACM Guide Comput. Lit.; Comput. Rev.; INSPEC (1990-); Int. Bibliogr. Sociol.; Linguist. Lang. Behav. Abstr. (1990-) [Full Cov.]; MLA Int. Bibl. Books Artic. Mod. Lang. Lit.; Soc. Plann. Policy Dev. Abstr.; Sociol. Abstr.

SP/0436-2888
COLECCION FILOLOGICA. Vol. 1 1952-. Spanish. Universidad de Granada / Facultad de Farmacia, Campus Cartuja, Ser Publicaciones, 18071 Granada Spain. **Tel** 011 34 281356.

FR
COLLECTION DE GRAMMAIRES. **Main/Corp** Paris. Universite. Institut d'Etudes Slaves. Vol. 1, (1921)-. Monographic series. French. ir. Price varies per volume. Institut d'Etudes Slaves, 9 rue Michelet, 75006 Paris France. **Tel** 011 33 1 43265089.
Desc: Russian, Polish, Slovak and Bulgarian grammars.

BE
COLLECTION LATOMUS. See Classical Studies.

US/0010-096X
COLLEGE COMPOSITION AND COMMUNICATION. See Education-Higher Education.

US/0010-0994
COLLEGE ENGLISH. [Coll. Engl.]. **Added/Corp** National Council of Teachers of English. Vol. 1 (Oct. 1939)-. Periodical. English. Eight times a year. $50.00. National Council of Teachers of English, 1111 Kenyon Road, Urbana IL 61801. **Tel** (217)328-3870, FAX (217)328-9645. **ED** Louise Z. Smith. **LC** PE1; .C6. **DD** 820/.7/1173. Index available at issue of volume--attached. **Bk Rev. Ad Acc. Circ:** 16,000 (ctrl). available on microfilm and microfiche from University Microfilms International (UMI). Documents available from The Genuine Article, UMI Article Clearinghouse. ***Continues*** *English Journal.*
Desc: Articles on teaching college English, literary studies, literary and educational opinion. Book reviews, summaries or articles in other periodicals. Official publication of the National Council of Teachers of English.
Ind/Abst Acad. Abstr. Full Text Elite (July 1990-); Acad. Abstr. (July 1990-); Acad. Ind. [Computer File] (1987-); Acad. Search (July 1990-); Annu. Bibliogr. Engl. Lang. Lit.; Arts Humanit. Citation Index [Full Cov.]; Contents Pages Educ.; Curr. Contents Arts Humanit.; Curr. Index J. Educ.; Educ. Index; Expand. Acad. Index (1987-); Humanit. Source (Jul. 1990-); Index Am. Period. Verse; INFO-SOUTH Abstr.; Lang. Teach.; Linguist. Lang. Behav. Abstr.; Mag. Artic. Summar. Elite (July 1990-); Mag. Artic. Summar. Select (July 1990-); Mag. Artic. Summar. CD-ROM (July 1990-); MLA Int. Bibl. Books Artic. Mod. Lang. Lit.; Newsp. Period. Abstr. (1988-); Res. Alert [Full Cov.]; Romant. Move.; Sci. Fict. Fantasy Book Rev. Index; Soc. Plann. Policy Dev. Abstr.; Soc. Sci. Cit. Index [Select. Cov.]; Sociol. Abstr.; Vocat. Search (July 1990-); Women Stud. Abstr.

SZ/0010-1338
COLLOQUIA GERMANICA. [Colloq. Ger.]. **Added/Corp** University of Kentucky. Dept. of Germanic and Classical Languages and Literatures. University of Kentucky. Vol. 1 (1967)-. Periodical. English (German). Four times a year. A Francke Verlag GmbH, Postfach 2560, Dischingerweg 5, D 72070 Tuebingen Germany. **Tel** 011 49 7071 78091 or 92. **LC** PF3001; .C714. **DD** 430; 830. **[CCC].** Documents available from The Genuine Article.
Ind/Abst Arts Humanit. Citation Index [Full Cov.]; Curr. Contents Arts Humanit.; MLA Int. Bibl. Books Artic. Mod. Lang. Lit.; Res. Alert [Full Cov.]; Romant. Move.

FI/0069-6587
COMMENTATIONES HUMANARUM LITTERARUM. (COMMENTATIONES HUMANARUM LITTERARUM / SUOMEN TIEDESEURA.). [Commentat. hum. litt.]. **Main/Corp** Suomen Tiedeseura. **Added/Corp** Suomen Tiedeseura. (1922)-. Monographic series. English (French, German and Swedish). ir. Price varies per volume. Academic Bookstore Akateeminen, Postilokero 23, FIN-00371 Helsinki Finland. **Tel** 011 358 0 12141. **LC** P9; .F5. ***Continues*** *Suomen Tiedeseura. Ofversigt af Finska Vetenskaps-Societetens Forhandlingar.*
Ind/Abst Linguist. Lang. Behav. Abstr.; MLA Int. Bibl. Books Artic. Mod. Lang. Lit.; Soc. Plann. Policy Dev. Abstr.; Sociol. Abstr.

US/0740-0330
COMMENTS ON ETYMOLOGY. [Comments etymol.]. **Added/Corp** University of Missouri at Rolla. Vol. 1, (Oct. 1971)-. Periodical. English. Eight times a year (Oct. thru May). $10.00 (individuals); $16.00 (institutions). University of Missouri Department of Foreign Languages, C/O G. Cohen, Rolla MO 65401. **Tel** (314)341-4629. **ED** Gerald Cohen, (phone: (314)341-4869). **LC** P321; .C63. **DD** 412/.05. **Circ:** 70.
Desc: Etymology and Indo-European morphology.

FR/0336-1500
COMMUNICATION ET LANGAGES PARIS. [Commun. lang. Paris]. **VFOAT** Communication et Langages (Montrouge). (1969)-. Periodical. French. qt. 225.27F France; 241.00F other. Editions Retz, 1 3 rue du Depart, F 75014 Paris France. **UDC** 028.6 : 8.

SI
COMMUNICATIONS OF CHINESE AND ORIENTAL LANGUAGES INFORMATION PROCESSING SOCIETY. English (Chinese). qt. 40.00Sing$ Singapore & Malaysia; 100.00Sing$ other. Colips C/O Discs, National University of Singapore Kent Ridge, Singapore 0511 Singapore. **Tel** 011 65 7722782.

US/1061-4710
COMMUNICATIONS OF THE WORKSHOP FOR SCIENTIFIC LINGUISTICS. [Commun. Workshop Sci. Linguist.]. **Added/Corp** Workshop for Scientific Linguistics. University of Chicago. **VFOAT** CWSL. No. 1, (Oct. 17, 1990)-. Periodical. English. Three times a year. $15.00 US, $16.00 Canada, $19.00 others (individuals); $20.00 US, $21.00 Canada, $24.00 others (institutions). University of Chicago / CWSL, 1010 East 59th Street, Chicago IL 60637. **LC** P1; .C666. **DD** 410. **CODEN** CWSLEX.
Desc: Devoted to improving the scientific status of linguistics.

US/0010-4167
COMPARATIVE ROMANCE LINGUISTICS NEWSLETTER. [Comp. roman. linguist. newsl.]. **Added/Corp** University of Oklahoma. Dept. of Modern Languages. Modern Language Association's Discussion Group on Comparative Romance Linguistics. **VFOAT** CRLN. No. 1 (June 1951)-. English. sa (April & Oct.). $10.00 institutions, $8.00 individuals. Modern Language Association, University of Virginia, 402 Cabell Hall, Charlottesville VA 22903. **Tel** (804)924-7159. **ED** David Pharies. **LC** PC1; .C65. **DD** 440/.05. **Bk Rev. Circ:** 120.
Desc: Romance linguistics: personalia and bibliography.
Ind/Abst MLA Int. Bibl. Books Artic. Mod. Lang. Lit.

UK/0950-6756
COMPENDIA. (COMPENDIA; COMPUTER-GENERATED AIDS TO LITERATURE AND LINGUISTIC RESEARCH.). [Compend.]. Vol. 1 (1968)-. Monographic series. English. ir. Price varies per volume. W. S. Maney and Son Ltd., Hudson Road, Leeds LS9 7DL England. **Tel** 011 44 532 497481, FAX 011 44 532 486983.
Ind/Abst MLA Int. Bibl. Books Artic. Mod. Lang. Lit.

●US
COMPOSITION STUDIES : FRESHMAN ENGLISH NEWS. **Added/Corp** Texas Christian University. **VFOAT** Freshman English News. Vol. 20, No. 1 (Spring 1992)-. Periodical. English. Twice a year. $8.00 (individuals, U.S.), $12.00 (individuals, foreign); $20.00 (institutions, U.S.), $25.00 (institutions, foreign). Texas Christian University / English, PO Box 32875, Fort Worth TX 76129. **Tel** (817)921-7221, FAX (817)921-7333. **ED** Christina Murphy. **LC** PE1; .F74. **Bk Rev**, (Qty: 20-40 per year). **Ad Acc. Pr Rev. Circ:** 1,000. ***Continues*** *Freshman English News, 0739-4713.*
Ind/Abst Curr. Index J. Educ.

US/0891-2017
COMPUTATIONAL LINGUISTICS (ASSOCIATION FOR COMPUTATIONAL LINGUISTICS). See Computers.

UK/0958-8221
COMPUTER ASSISTED LANGUAGE LEARNING. **VFOAT** CALL. Vol. 1 (1990)-. Periodical. English. Four times a year. Fl286.00 (institutions). Swets & Zeitlinger BV, Heereweg 347B PO Box 825, 2160 SZ Lisse Holland. **Tel** 011 31 2521 35111, FAX 02521-15888, telex 41325. **(Subscription address:** Swets Publishing Service, PO Box 825, 2160 SZ Lisse The Netherlands**) ED** Keith Cameron. **CODEN** CALLEE.
Desc: This journal corresponds to an expressed need for a forum to discuss the latest discoveries in computer assisted language learning and to exchange experience and information about existing techniques. Articles cover the following topics, among others: pedagogical principles and their application to CALL; observations on, and evaluation of, CALL software; intelligent tutoring systems; the application of AI to language teaching; and the use of CALL with other forms of educational technology.
Ind/Abst Linguist. Lang. Behav. Abstr.; Soc. Plann. Policy Dev. Abstr.; Sociol. Abstr.

US/0715-9048
COMPUTER PROCESSING OF CHINESE & ORIENTAL LANGUAGES. (COMPUTER PROCESSING OF CHINESE & ORIENTAL LANGUAGES : AN INTERNATIONAL JOURNAL OF THE CHINESE LANGUAGE COMPUTER SOCIETY.). [Comput. process. Chin. orient. lang.]. **Added/Corp** Chinese Language Computer Society. **VFOAT** Computer Processing of Chinese and Oriental Languages. Vol. 1, No. 1 (July 1983)-. Periodical. English (Chinese). sa. $90.00. World Scientific Publishing Company, PO Box 128, Farrer Road, Singapore 9128 Singapore. **Tel** 011 65 3825663, FAX 011 65 3825919, telex RS 28561 WSPC. **(Subscription address:** US: World Scientific Publishing Co., Inc., 1060 Main Street, River Edge, NJ 07661 Telephone: (201)487-9655, Fax: (201)487-9656; Europe: World Scientific Publishing Co Ltd, 73 Lynton Mead, Totteridge, London N20 8DH United Kingdom Telephone: 011 44 81 4462461, Fax: 011 44 81 4463356; India: World Scientific Publishing Co Pte Ltd, 4911 9th Floor, High Point IV, 45 Palace Road, Bangalore 560 001 India Telephone: (80) 2205972, Fax: (80) 3344593, Telex: 0845-2900 PCO IN; Hong Kong: World Scientific Publishing (HK) Co, PO Box 72482, Kowloon Central Post Office, Hong Kong Telephone: 852-7718791, Fax: 852-7718155**) ED** Ching Y. Suen. **LC** PL1074.5; .C66. **DD** 495.1/0285. **CODEN** CPCLE6. **Ad Acc. Circ:** 300. Documents available from Ask*IEEE.
Ind/Abst INSPEC (Dec. 1987-).

UK/0885-2308
COMPUTER SPEECH & LANGUAGE. [Comput. speech lang.]. **VFOAT** Computer Speech and Language. Vol. 1, No. 1 (March 1986)-. Academic Scholarly Publication. English. qt. $200.00. Academic Press Ltd., A Division of Harcourt Brace & Company Ltd., 24-28 Oval Road, London NW1 7DX England. **Tel** 071 267 4466, FAX 071 482 2293, 071 485 4752, telex 25775 ACPRES G. **(Subscription address:** Harcourt Brace & Company, Ltd., Foots Cray, High Street, Sidcup Kent DA14 5HP England.**) ED** Frank Fallside and Stephen E Levinson. **LC** PAR. **DD** 006. **NLM** W1; CO457KE. **CODEN** CSPLEO. **[CCC].** Index available. cum. index. **Bk Rev.** Documents available from Article Express International, Ask*IEEE.
Desc: Publishes reports of original research related to quantitative descriptions of the recognition, understanding, production, and coding of speech by humans and/or machines.
Ind/Abst Abstr. Hum. Comput. Interact.; Comput. Rev.; Ei Page One; Eng. Index Annu.; Ergon. Abstr.; HILITES; INSPEC (1986-); Linguist. Lang. Behav. Abstr. (1987-) [Full Cov.]; Soc. Plann. Policy Dev. Abstr.; Sociol. Abstr.

CN/0227-2938
CONTACT (ASSOCIATION OF TEACHERS OF ENGLISH AS A SECOND LANGUAGE OF ONTARIO). (CONTACT.). [Contact]. V. 2 I.E. 3- Jan. 1976-. Periodical. English. qt. Free to members. Teachers of English as a Second Language Association of Ontario, PO Box 7014 Station A Canada. **DD** 420/.7. **UDC** 802.0. ***Continues*** *TESL Association of Ontario, 0227-292X.*

CN/0714-3192
CONTACT - UNIVERSITE SIMON FRASER. FACULTE D'EDUCATION. ***Ceased.*** (CONTACT : REVUE DESTINEE AUX PROFESSEURS DE FRANCAIS DE LA COLOMBIE BRITANNIQUE ET DU YUKON.). [Contact - Univ. Simon Fraser, Fac. educ.]. **Added/Corp** Simon Fraser University. Faculty of Education. Vol. 1, No 1 (Feb. 1982)-(1993). Periodical. French (English). qt. Simon Fraser University / Education, Faculty of Education, Burnaby British Columbia, V5A 1F6 Canada. **Tel** (604)291-4115, FAX (604)291-3143. **ED** Andre A. Obadia. **DD** 440/.7/0711. Index available. cum. index. **Bk Rev. Ad Acc. Circ:** 1,500.
Desc: Practical tips, teaching techniques directly applicable to the classroom, reviews on book and software, articles on the latest research, on teaching, and on teacher training.
Ind/Abst Linguist. Lang. Behav. Abstr.; Point Repere (1988-); Soc. Plann. Policy Dev. Abstr.; Sociol. Abstr.

FR/0247-915X
CONTRASTES (PARIS). (CONTRASTES : REVUE DE L'ASSOCIATION POUR LE DEVELOPPEMENT DES ETUDES CONTRASTIVES.). [Contrastes]. **Added/Corp** Association pour le Developpement des Etudes Contrastives (Paris, France). (Mar. 1981)-. Periodical. French. sa.
Ind/Abst Linguist. Lang. Behav. Abstr.; MLA Int. Bibl. Books Artic. Mod. Lang. Lit.; Soc. Plann. Policy Dev. Abstr.; Sociol. Abstr.

IT
CONTRIBUTI DELL'ISTITUTO DI FILOLOGIA MODERNA. SERIE ITALIANA. **See** Literature.

SZ/0069-9780
COOPER MONOGRAPHS ON ENGLISH AND AMERICAN LANGUAGE AND LITERATURE, THE. **See** Literature.

DK
COPENHAGEN STUDIES IN LANGUAGE. **Added/Corp** Handelshjskolen i Kbenhavn. Sproglige Afdeling. **VFOAT** CEBAL Series. No. 10 (1987)-. Periodical. English (French, Italian and Spanish). ***Continues*** *CEBAL Series.*
Ind/Abst MLA Int. Bibl. Books Artic. Mod. Lang. Lit.

DK/0906-7639
COPENHAGEN WORKING PAPERS IN LINGUISTICS. **Added/Corp** Kbenhavns Universitet. Institut for Allmen og Anvendt Sprogvidenskab. Vol. 1 (1991)-. English. IAAS Publications, IAAS, University of Copenhagen, Njalsgade 80, DK-2300 Copenhagen S, Denmark. **LC** IN PROCESS. ***Continues in part*** *Kbenhavns Universitet. Institut for Anvendt og Matematisk Lingvistik. Skrifter om Anvendt og Matematisk Lingvistik; Kbenhavns Universitet. Institut for Fonetik. Annual Report of the Institute of Phonetics of the University of Copenhagen, 0589-6681; Arbejdspapirer Udsendt af Institut for Lingvistik, Kbenhavns Universitet, 0109-2537.*

NE
COPTIC STUDIES. **See** History(General)-History of the Middle East.

US
CORNELL STUDIES IN CLASSICAL PHILOLOGY. **Added/Corp** Cornell University. Vol. 1 (1887)-. Monographic series. English. ir. Price varies per volume. Cornell University Press, 124 Roberts Place, Ithaca NY 14853. **Tel** (607)277-2338. **(Subscription address:** Cup Service, PO Box 3525, Ithaca, NY 6525**)**

US/0888-3122
CORNELL WORKING PAPERS IN LINGUISTICS. [Cornell work. pap. linguist.]. **Added/Corp** Cornell University. Dept. of Modern Languages and Linguistics. **VFOAT** Working Papers in Linguistics. No. 1 (Spring 1980)-. Monographic series. English. ir. Price varies per volume. DMLL Publications, Morrill Hall, Cornell University, Ithaca NY 14853. **Tel** (607)257-2775. **DD** 410.
Ind/Abst MLA Int. Bibl. Books Artic. Mod. Lang. Lit.

NE
COROLLA LONDINIENSIS. Vol. 1 (1981)-. English (Italian). an. J C Gieben Uitgeverij, Nieuwe Herengracht 35, 1011 Rm Amsterdam The Netherlands. **Tel** 011 33 20 6275170. **LC** PA1; .C84. **DD** 880/.9/001.

US/0193-3892
CORONICA, LA. [Coronica]. **Added/Corp** Modern Language Association of America. Spanish I Section. Modern Language Association of America. Spanish I. Bibliography and Research Committee. Modern Language Association of America. Division of Spanish Medieval Language and Literature. (Fall 1972)-. Periodical. English (Spanish). sa. $10.00 (one year), $18.00 (two year) individuals; $25.00 (one year) institutitions. Old Dominion University Foreign Language & Literature Department, Professor Barbara Weissberger, Norfolk VA 23529. **Tel** (804)683-3973. **ED** Dr. Spurgeon Baldwin. **LC** PC4001; .C67. **DD** 860/.5. Index available. **Bk Rev. Ad Acc. Pr Rev. Circ:** 500.
Desc: Journal and newsletter of the division on Spanish medieval language and literature of the modern language association of America.
Ind/Abst MLA Int. Bibl. Books Artic. Mod. Lang. Lit.

SZ
COSMOGLOTTA (SAINT GALL, SWITZERLAND). (COSMOGLOTTA.). Periodical. Multiple languages. qt. **LC** WMLC L 83/6616. ***Formed by the union of*** *Cosmoglotta. Serie A* ***and*** *Cosmoglotta. Serie B.*

NE/0165-9618
COSTERUS. [Costerus]. Vol. 1 (1972)-. Monographic series. English. ir. Editions Rodopi BV, Keizersgracht 302-304, 1016 Ex Amsterdam Netherlands. **Tel** 011 31 20 6227507, FAX 011 31 20 380948. **LC** PE1; .C66. **DD** 420/.5. Index available.
Desc: Monographs on all literary genres and periods; also linguistics.
Ind/Abst Abstr. Engl. Stud.; Linguist. Lang. Behav. Abstr.; MLA Int. Bibl. Books Artic. Mod. Lang. Lit.; Romant. Move.; Soc. Plann. Policy Dev. Abstr.; Sociol. Abstr.

US/1057-4190
COUNCIL CHRONICLE (URBANA, ILL.), THE. **See** Education-Early Childhood and Primary Education.

CN/0318-0220
COURIER (EDMONTON). (THE COURIER.). V. 10- Jan. 1972-. Periodical. English (French). ir (10 times a year). Alberta Teachers Association, 11010-142 Street, Barnett House, Edmonton Alberta T5N 2R1 Canada. **Tel** (403)453-2411. **UDC** 800.7. ctrl circ. ***Continues*** *Alberta Teachers' Association. Modern and Classical Language Council. Newsletter, 0318-0212.*

CN/0380-9757
COURRIER DE L'ENSEIGNEMENT INDIVIDUALISE A TOUTES LES ANIMATRICES ET A TOUS LES ANIMATEURS DU 2E CYCLE DE L'ELEMENTAIRE, LE. Vol. 1 (Sept. 1970)-. Periodical. French. Le Courrier du Francais-Cadre, 2673 Avenue de Ronde, Quebec Quebec G1J 4G5 Canada. **DD** 448/.3/421.

CN/1184-8677
COURRIER FRANCAIS (1991). (LE COURRIER FRANCAIS.). [Courr. fr.]. **Added/Corp** Union Nationale Francaise. No 430 (Jan. 1991)-. Periodical. French. mo. 2.80Can$ per number. Le Courrier Francais de Montreal, 429 Av Viger, Montreal Quebec H2L 2N9 Canada. **DD** 440/.9714/05. ***Continues*** *Courrier Francais de Montreal (1984)., 0836-3536.*

SP
COURSES FOR FOREIGNERS IN SPAIN. **Main/Corp** Spain. Ministerio de Educacion Y Ciencia. Secretaria General Tecnica. **VFOAT** Courses for Foreign Students in Spain. (19??)-. English. Ministerio de Educacion Y Ciencia, Madrid Spain. **LC** PC4068.S8; S62a. **DD** 460/.7/046.

CN/0829-1020
CPF IMMERSION REGISTRY, THE. ***Title Change.*** [CPF immers. regist.]. **Added/Corp** Canadian Parents for French. **VAT** Canadian Parents for French Immersion Registry. (198?)-(19??). English. an. Canadian Parents for French, 309 Cooper Street, Suite 210, Ottawa Ontario K2P 0G5 Canada. **Tel** (613)235-1481. **DD** 440/.7/1071. ***Continued by*** *The Immersion Registry.*

CN/0832-1310
CPF ONTARIO. ***Title Change.*** (CPF ONTARIO : [NEWSLETTER].). [CPF Ont.]. **Added/Corp** Canadian Parents for French. Ontario Chapter. **VAT** Canadian Parents for French Ontario. Issue No. 22 (Fall 1985)-Issue No. 49 (Fall 1992). Newsletter. English. qt. Canadian Parents for French, 309 Cooper Street, Suite 210, Ottawa Ontario K2P 0G5 Canada. **Tel** (613)235-1481. **DD** 440/.7/0713. ***Continues*** *Ontario Newsletter (Canadian Parents for French. Ontario Chapter), 0826-1857.* ***Continued by*** *Newsletter (Canadian Parents for French. Ontario Chapter), 1200-2178.*

NE/0920-9026
CREOLE LANGUAGE LIBRARY. [Creole lang. libr.]. (1986)-. Monographic series. English. te. Price varies per volume. John Benjamins BV, Amsteldijk 44, PO Box 75577, 1070 AN Amsterdam Netherlands. **Tel** 011 31 20 6738156, FAX 011 31 20 739773. **(Subscription address:** John Benjamins North America, PO Box 27519, Philadelphia PA 19118-0519.**)** **ED** Pieter Muysken and John Victor Singler. **UDC** 800.88.
Desc: Presents descriptive and theoretical studies designed to add significantly to the data available on pidgin and creole languages.
Ind/Abst MLA Int. Bibl. Books Artic. Mod. Lang. Lit.

AG
CRITICA & UTOPIA. **VAT** Critica e Utopia. No. 1 (1979)-. Periodical. Spanish. Three times a year. $25.00. Fucade, Avenia Cordoba 1261, 1055 Buenos Aires Argentina. **ED** Francisco Delich.

US/0278-7261
CRITICA HISPANICA. [Crit. hisp.]. Vol. 1 No. 1 (1979)-. Academic Scholarly Publication. English (Spanish). sa. $27.00 (1 year), $54.00 (2 year), $81.00 (3 year) US; $38.00 (1 year), $76.00 (2 year), $114.00 (3 year) surface mail, $42.00 (1 year), $84.00 (2 year), $126.00 (3 year) air mail other. Duquesne University Department of Modern Languages, Pittsburgh PA 15282. **Tel** (412)434-6416. **ED** Gregorio Cervantes Martin. **LC** PQ6001; .C68. **DD** 860/.9. **Bk Rev. Ad Acc. Circ:** 812 (ctrl). Documents available from The Genuine Article.
Desc: A journal devoted to scholarly articles and notes dealing with Hispanic literature and linguistics.
Ind/Abst Arts Humanit. Citation Index [Full Cov.]; Curr. Contents Arts Humanit.; Index Book Rev. Humanit. (1985-); MLA Int. Bibl. Books Artic. Mod. Lang. Lit.; Res. Alert [Full Cov.].

NE/0920-3060
CRITICAL THEORY. Vol.1 (1985)-. Monographic series. English. ir. $118.00. John Benjamins BV, Amsteldijk 44, PO Box 75577, 1070 AN Amsterdam Netherlands. **Tel** 011 31 20 6738156, FAX 011 31 20 739773. **(Subscription address:** John Benjamins North America, PO Box 27519, Philadelphia PA 19118-0519.**)** **ED** Dr. Iris Zavala and Myriam Diaz-Diocaretz. **Pr Rev.**
Desc: Offers the reader the opportunity to participate in a fruitful dialogue with the latest ideas from around the world on major critical theories.
Ind/Abst MLA Int. Bibl. Books Artic. Mod. Lang. Lit.

IT/0391-1535
CRONACHE ERCOLANESI. **Added/Corp** Centro Internazionale per lo Studio dei Papiri Ercolanesi. Vol. 1 (1971)-. Italian. an (Dec.). L150000 Italy; L170000 others. Gaetano Macchiaroli Editore, Via Michetti 11, 80127 Naples Italy. **Tel** 11 39 81 5783129, FAX 11 39 81 5780568. **DD** 480.

JA/0289-1239
CROSS CURRENTS. ***Suspended.*** **Added/Corp** Nihon Gaigo Kyoiku Kenkyujo. Vol. 1, No. 1 (Summer 1972)-Vol. 19 No. 2. Periodical. English (summaries and/or abstracts in Japanese). sa. Language Institute of Japan, 4-14-1 Shiroyama, Odawara Kanagawa 250 Japan. **Tel** 011 81 465 23 1677. **LC** P51; .C68. **DD** 418/.007. Documents available.
Ind/Abst Lang. Teach.; Linguist. Lang. Behav. Abstr.; Soc. Plann. Policy Dev. Abstr.; Sociol. Abstr.

US/0748-0164
CROSS CURRENTS (ANN ARBOR, MICH.). ***Ceased.*** (CROSS CURRENTS.). [Cross curr.]. **Added/Corp** University of Michigan. Dept. of Slavic Languages and Literatures. University of Michigan. Center for Russian and East European Studies. (1982)-Vol. 12. English. an. Yale University Press, PO Box 209040, New Haven CT 06520. **Tel** (203)432-0940, (800)987-7323, FAX (203)432-0948. **ED** Ladislav Matejka. **LC** PG13; .M46 subser; D1055. **DD** 491.8; 001.1/0943.
Desc: A yearbook of Central European Culture.
Ind/Abst Am. Bibliogr. Slavic East Europ. Stud.; Middle East Abstr. Index.

UK/0045-9127
CROWN LONDON. [Crown Lond.]. (1966)-. Periodical. English. ir. £13.99. Mary Glasgow Publications, Brookhampton Lane, Kineton, Warwickshire CV35 0JB England. **Tel** 011 44 926 640606, FAX 011 44 926 641016.

SA/0250-0035
CRUX (PRETORIA). (CRUX.). [Crux]. **Added/Corp** Foundation for Education, Science and Technology (South Africa). Vol. 1 (1967)-. Periodical. English. qt. R17.55 South Africa; R20.00 other. Foundation for Education Science & Technology, PO Box 1758, Pretoria 0001 South Africa. **Tel** 011 27 12 3226404, FAX 011 27 12 3207803. **ED** M.M. Hacksley. **DD** 371.3; 420; 800. Index available. cum. index. **Bk Rev. Ad Acc. Circ:** 3,117.
Desc: Journal for the teaching of English as a first, second or foreign language. It is intended for practicing teachers in schools.
Ind/Abst Annu. Bibliogr. Engl. Lang. Lit.; Lang. Teach.; MLA Int. Bibl. Books Artic. Mod. Lang. Lit.

SP
CUADERNOS DE FILOLOGIA CLASICA. ***Title Change.*** **Added/Corp** Universidad de Madrid. Facultad de Filosofia y Letras. Vol. 1-(1971)-(19??). Periodical. Spanish. sa. Editorial Complutense, Donoso Cortes 65 1RA Planta, 28003 Madrid Spain. **Tel** 011 34 1 3946372. **LC** PA9; .C8. ***Split into*** *Cuadernos de Filologia*

Clasica. Estudios Latinos; Cuadernos de Filologia Clasica. Estudios Griegos e Indoeuropeas.
Ind/Abst MLA Int. Bibl. Books Artic. Mod. Lang. Lit. (?-?).

SP
CUADERNOS DE FILOLOGIA CLASICA. ESTUDIOS LATINOS / FACULTAD DE FILOLGIA, DEPARTAMENTO DE FILOLOGIA LATINA, UNIVERSIDAD COMPLUTENSE DE MADRID. **See** Classical Studies.

SP/0214-6746
CUADERNOS DE FILOLOGIA. II, STUDIA LINGUISTICA HISPANICA. [Cuad. filol., II Stud. linguist. hisp.]. **VFOAT** Studia Linguistica Hispanica. 1-. Periodical. Catalan (German and Spanish). Universidad de Valencia / Moderna, Dept Moderna, 46080 Valencia Spain. **Tel** 011 34 3 3864100. **LC** PC4008; .C83. **DD** 460/.05. **UDC** 806.0. ***Continues in part*** *Cuadernos de Filologia (Universidad de Valencia. Seccion de Filologia Moderna).*
Ind/Abst MLA Int. Bibl. Books Artic. Mod. Lang. Lit.

SP/0211-0547
CUADERNOS DE INVESTIGACION FILOLOGICA. [Cuad. invest. filol.]. **Added/Corp** Colegio Universitario de Logrono. **VFOAT** C.I.F.; CIF. Vol. 1 (May 1975)-. Periodical. French (Spanish). sa. 1500ptas Spain; 1800ptas other. Servicio de Publicaciones / Rioja, Colegio Universitario de la Rioja, Obispo Bustamante 3, 26001 Logrono La Rioja Spain. **Tel** 011 34 41 23-16-99. **ED** Pilar Martinez Latre. **LC** P1.A1; C83. Index available. cum. index (every six numbers). **Bk Rev. Ad Acc. Pr Rev. Circ:** 500. available in microform.
Desc: Includes articles about classical, French, English and Spanish literature and linguistics.
Ind/Abst Annu. Bibliogr. Engl. Lang. Lit.; Linguist. Lang. Behav. Abstr.; MLA Int. Bibl. Books Artic. Mod. Lang. Lit.; Soc. Plann. Policy Dev. Abstr.; Sociol. Abstr.

SP/0212-0550
CUADERNOS DE TRADUCCION E INTERPRETACION. [Cuad. trad. interpret.]. **Added/Corp** Universidad Autonoma de Barcelona. Escuela Universitaria de Traductores e Interpretes. **VFOAT** Quaderns de Traduccio I Interpretacio. (1982)-. Periodical. Catalan (English and Spanish). an. 3000ptas. L'Estaquirot, Nuestra se Ora de Coll53, 08023 Barcelona Spain. **Tel** 011 34 3 2850327, telex 52040. **ED** Fernando Valls. **LC** P306.A1; C8. **Bk Rev. Circ:** 1,500 (ctrl).

XO
CUDZIE JAZYKY. **Main/Corp** Pedagogicka Fakulta V Banskej Bystrici. **VFOAT** Seria Spolocenskovedna. Cudzie Jazyky. 1- 1972-. Multiple languages (German and Slovak). 6.00. **LC** P25; .B25A.

US/1041-6226
CUED SPEECH ANNUAL. ***Title Change.*** (CUED SPEECH ANNUAL : JOURNAL OF THE NATIONAL CUED SPEECH ASSOCIATION.). [Cued speech annu.]. **Added/Corp** National Cued Speech Association. **VFOAT** Journal of the National Cued Speech Association. Vol. 1 (Summer 1985)-(19??). English. an. National Cued Speech Association, PO Box 31345, Raleigh NC 27622. **Tel** (919)828-1218. **ED** Carol J Boggs. **DD** 419. **Bk Rev.** ctrl circ. ***Continued by*** *Cued Speech Journal, 1059-8243.*

IT/0391-5654
CULTURA NEOLATINA. [Cult. neolat.]. **Added/Corp** Universita di Roma. Istituto di Filologia Romanza. Vol. 1 (1941)-. Periodical. Italian. qt. L120000 (Italy); L140000 (other). Enrico Mucchi Editore SRL, Via Emilia Est 1527, 41100 Modena Italy. **Tel** 011 39 59 374094, FAX 059/374096.
Ind/Abst MLA Int. Bibl. Books Artic. Mod. Lang. Lit.

NE
CURRENT APPROACHES TO AFRICAN LINGUISTICS. Vol. 1 (1983)-. English. ir. Price varies, Comes with Publications of African Languages and Linguistics. Walter de Gruyter Inc., PO Box 303421, D 10728 Berlin Germany. **Tel** 011 49 30 260050, FAX 011 49 30 26005251. **LC** PL8000; .C87. **DD** 496/.05.

CN
CURRENT INQUIRY INTO LANGUAGE AND LINGUISTICS. ***Title Change.*** (1971)-(19??). Monographic series. English. ir. Price varies per volume. Boreal Scholarly Publ Ltd, Box 20055 Beverly Postal Outlet, Edmonton Alta T5W 5E6 Canada. available on microfilm from University Microfilms International (UMI). ***Continued by*** Current Inquiry into Language, Linguistics, and Human Communications.
Ind/Abst MLA Int. Bibl. Books Artic. Mod. Lang. Lit.

CN
CURRENT INQUIRY INTO LANGUAGE, LINGUISTICS, AND HUMAN COMMUNICATIONS. **Added/Corp** Linguistic Research, Inc. (19??)-. Monographic series. English. Price varies per volume. Boreal Scholarly Publ Ltd, Box 20055 Beverly Postal Outlet, Edmonton Alta T5W 5E6 Canada. ***Continues*** *Current Inquiry into Language and Linguistics.*
Ind/Abst Soc. Plann. Policy Dev. Abstr.

UK/0957-4751
CURRENT RESEARCH IN FRENCH STUDIES AT UNIVERSITIES & POLYTECHNICS IN THE UNITED KINGDOM & IRELAND. ***Title Change.*** **Added/Corp** Society for French Studies (Great Britain). **VFOAT** Current Research in French Studies at Universities and Polytechnics in the United Kingdom and Ireland. Vol. 19 (1987-1988)-Vol. 21 (1991-1992). English. be. Society of French Studies / University of Bath, Secretary & Registrar's Department, Dr. John Harris, Bath BA2 7AY United Kingdom. **Tel** 011 44 225 826826 ext. 5045. **ED** John Harris. **LC** Z2175.A2; C87. **Circ:** 350. ***Continues*** *Current Research in French Studies at Universities and Polytechnics in the United Kingdom.* ***Continued by*** *Current Research in French Studies at Universities in the United Kingdom and Ireland.*
Desc: Catalogue of postgraduate research in French studies (languages, literature, social studies, history and civilization) at United Kingdom universities and polytechnics.

●UK/1350-9209
CURRENT RESEARCH IN FRENCH STUDIES AT UNIVERSITIES IN THE UNITED KINGDOM & IRELAND. **Added/Corp** Society for French Studies (Great Britain). **VFOAT** Current Research in French Studies at Universities in the United Kingdom and Ireland. Vol. 22 (1993-1994)-. English. be. Society of French Studies / University of Bath, Secretary & Registrar's Department, Dr. John Harris, Bath BA2 7AY United Kingdom. **Tel** 011 44 225 826826 ext. 5045. **LC** Z2175.A2; C87. ***Continues*** *Current Research in French Studies at Universities & Polytechnics in the United Kingdom & Ireland.*

US
CURRENT STUDIES IN LINGUISTICS SERIES. (1972)-. Monographic series. English. ir. Massachusetts Institute of Technology (MIT) Press, 55 Hayward Street, Cambridge MA 02142-1399. **Tel** (617)253-2889, (617)625-8481, FAX (617)258-6779. **(Subscription address:** MIT Press Books, 55 Hayward Street, Cambridge MA 02142.**)**
Ind/Abst MLA Int. Bibl. Books Artic. Mod. Lang. Lit.

US
DACTYLUS / DEPT. OF SPANISH AND PORTUGUESE & THE CENTER FOR MEXICAN AMERICAN STUDIES. **Added/Corp** University of Texas at Austin. Dept. of Spanish and Portuguese. University of Texas at Austin. Center for Mexican American Studies. Vol. 1, No. 1 (Jan. 1984)-. Periodical. English (Portuguese and Spanish). an. University of Texas Department of Spanish and Portuguese, Batts Hall 110, Austin TX 78712. **Tel** (512)471-4936. **LC** PC4008; .D33. **DD** 860.9/0005.
Ind/Abst MLA Int. Bibl. Books Artic. Mod. Lang. Lit.

JA/0303-0512
DAIYAMONDO GENDAI EIGO NO KISO CHISHIKI. [Daiyamondo gendai Eigo no kiso chishiki]. **Added/Corp** Daiyamondosha. **VFOAT** Essentials of Present-Day English; Gendai Eigo No Kiso Chishiki. (19??)-. Periodical. English (Japanese). ¥750. Daiyamondo Sha, (Diamond Inc.), 4-2 1-chome Kasumigaseki, Chiyoda-ku Tokyoto 100 Japan. **LC** PE1130.J3; D34.

YU
DALJE. V. 1, No. 1 (Spring 1982)-. Periodical. Serbo-Croatian (Roman). qt. 600.00. Nisro Osloboenje, 71000 Sarajevo Pavla, Goranina 13 Yugoslavia. **LC** PB5; .D34. **UDC** 808.6.

PP
DATA PAPERS ON PAPUA NEW GUINEA LANGUAGES. No. 32; 1987-. Monographic series. English. sa. Price varies per volume. Summer Institute of Linguistics / New Guinea, Box 233, Ukarumpa Via Lae, Papua New Guinea. **Tel** 011 675 773544 Ext 494, FAX 011 675 773507. **ED** John M Clifton. **Ad Acc. Circ:** 250. ***Continues*** *Workpapers in Papua New Guinea Languages.*
Desc: Linguistics research.
Ind/Abst MLA Int. Bibl. Books Artic. Mod. Lang. Lit.

US
DAVIS WORKING PAPERS IN LINGUISTICS. ***Suspended.*** **Added/Corp** University of California, Davis. Linguistics Program. No. 1 (1986)-. English. an. $11.50 (institutions), $8.50 (individuals) North America; $12.50 (institutions), $9.50 (individuals) other. University of California Press, 2120 Berkeley Way, Berkeley CA 94720. **Tel** (510)642-4191, (510)642-3907, FAX (510)642-9917. **ED** R D Van Valin.

BE/0376-8163
DEGRES. [Degres]. (Jan. 1973)-. Periodical. Multiple languages (English, French, German, Italian and Spanish). qt. 1400.00F Europe; 1550.00F other. Degres, PL C Meunier 2, Bte 13, 1180 Brussels Belgium. **Tel** 011 32 2 3450083. **LC** P99; .D43. **DD** 405. **Bk Rev. Ad Acc.** ctrl circ. Documents available from The Genuine Article.
Ind/Abst Annu. Bibliogr. Engl. Lang. Lit.; Arts Humanit. Citation Index [Full Cov.]; BHA : Biblio. Hist. Art; Curr. Contents Arts Humanit.; Linguist. Lang. Behav. Abstr.; MLA Int. Bibl. Books Artic. Mod. Lang. Lit.; Res. Alert [Full Cov.]; Soc. Plann. Policy Dev. Abstr.; Sociol. Abstr.

NE/0070-3826
DESCRIPTION AND ANALYSIS OF CONTEMPORARY STANDARD RUSSIAN. (1959)-. English. ir. Walter de Gruyter Inc. / Hawthorne, 200 Saw Mill River Road, Hawthorne NY 10532. **Tel** (914)747-0110, GERMANY: 011/49/30/260050, FAX (914)747-1326, telex 646677. **(Subscription address:** Germany/ PO Box 110240, 1 Berlin 11**)** **DD** 491.7.

GW/0011-9741
DEUTSCH ALS FREMDSPRACHE. [Dtsch Fremdspr.]. **Added/Corp** Johann Gottfried Herder-Institut. Vol. 1 (1964)-. Periodical. German. Four times a year. DM43.20 Germany; DM46.00 others. Langenscheidt KG, Crellestra 28-30, D 10827 Berlin Germany. **Tel** 011 49 30 7800020, telex 183175 LUGBL. **(Subscription address:** Postfach 401120, D 80711 Munich Germany, telephone 011 49 89 360960**)** **DD** 430. Index available. cum. index. Documents available.
Ind/Abst Lang. Teach.; Linguist. Lang. Behav. Abstr.; MLA Int. Bibl. Books Artic. Mod. Lang. Lit.; Soc. Plann. Policy Dev. Abstr.; Sociol. Abstr.

GW/0070-3893
DEUTSCH-SLAWISCHE FORSCHUNGEN ZUR NAMENKUNDE UND SIEDLUNGSGESCHICHTE. [Dtsch.-Slaw. Forsch. Namenkd. Siedl.gesch.]. **Added/Corp** Sachsische Akademie der Wissenschaften zu Leipzig. Historische Kommission. Sachsische Akademie der Wissenschaften zu Leipzig. Sprachwissenschaftliche Kommission. No. 1 (1956)-. Periodical. German. ir. DM75.00 (latest volume). Akademie-Verlag GmbH, Muehlenstrasse 33 34, D 13162 Berlin Germany. **Tel** 011 49 30 47889300, FAX 011 49 30 47889357. **(Subscription address:** VCH Publishers Inc., 303 Northwest 12th Avenue, Journals Department, Deerfield FL 33442.**)** **DD** 412; 943.
Ind/Abst MLA Int. Bibl. Books Artic. Mod. Lang. Lit.

GW/0418-8802
DEUTSCHE LEHRER IM AUSLAND. **Added/Corp** Verband Deutscher Lehrer im Ausland. (1954)-. Periodical. German. Four times a year. DM60.00 Germany; DM69.00 others. Schroedel Schulbuchverlag, Postfach 810555, Hildesheimer Str 202, 3000 Hannover 81 Germany. **Tel** 011 49 511 83880. **(Subscription address:** Hans Oeding Druckerei & Verlag, Postfach 3311, D 38023 Braunschweig Germany.**)** **DD** 378.3.

GW/0418-8993
DEUTSCHE REIHE FUER AUSLANDER. REIHE C : ERGANZUNGSHEFTE ZU GRAMMATISCHEN FRAGEN. **VFOAT** Erganzungshefte zu Grammatischen Fragen. 1- 1961-. Monographic series. German. Price varies per volume. Huber, Max-Hueber-Strasse 4, W-8045 Ismaning Bei Munich Germany. **Tel** (054)27 11 11. **UDC** 803.0-5.

GW
DEUTSCHE SCHRIFT, DIE. **Added/Corp** Bund fur Deutsche Schrift. (19??)-. German. qt. DM18.00. Bund fur Deutsche Schrift, Postfach 1110, W-2907 Ahlhorn Germany. **Tel** 04435/1313. **LC** PF3153; .D47. Index available. **Bk Rev. Ad Acc. Circ:** 1,100 (ctrl).
Desc: Promotes German lettering.

GW/0340-9341
DEUTSCHE SPRACHE. [Dtsch. Sprache]. **Added/Corp** Institut fuer Deutsche Sprache. (1973)-. Periodical. German. qt (4 issues). DM119.60. Erich Schmidt Verlag GmbH, Postfach 304240, D 10724 Berlin Germany. **Tel** 011 49 30 25008525. **ED** Siegfried Grosse, Odo Leys, Gerhard Stickel and Johannes Schwitalla. **LC** PF3003; .D48. **[CCC].** Index available. **Bk Rev. Ad Acc.** Documents available from The Genuine Article.
Desc: Deals with the German language.
Ind/Abst Arts Humanit. Citation Index [Full Cov.]; Curr. Contents Arts Humanit.; Lang. Teach.; Linguist. Lang. Behav. Abstr.; MLA Int. Bibl. Books Artic. Mod. Lang. Lit.; Res. Alert [Full Cov.]; Soc. Plann. Policy Dev. Abstr.; Sociol. Abstr.

GW/0170-3153
DEUTSCHE SPRACHE IN EUROPA UND UBERSEE. [Dtsch. Sprache Eur. Ubersee]. **Added/Corp** Institut fuer Deutsche Sprache. Vol. 1 (1977)-. Monographic series. German. ir. Price varies per volume. Franz Steiner Verlag GmbH, Postfach 101061, D 70009 Stuttgart Germany. **Tel** 011 49 0711 2582372, FAX 011 49 0711 2582290, telex 723636 daz d. **(Subscription address:** Brockhaus Commission, Kreidlerstrasse 9, D 70803 Kornwestheim Germany.**)** **ED** Sylvia Dickgieser, Hubert Eichheim, Bernd Kast, Gottfried Kolde.
Desc: Monographs dedicated to the German language as spoken by minorities all over the world.

GW/0012-1460
DEUTSCHUNTERRICHT. **See** Literature.

GW/0340-2258
DEUTSCHUNTERRICHT (STUTTGART). (DER DEUTSCHUNTERRICHT; BEITRAEGE ZU SEINER PRAXIS UND WISSENSCHAFTLICHEN GRUNDLEGUNG.). [Deutschunterricht]. (1948)-. Periodical. German. Six times a year. DM82.50 Germany; DM99.60 others. Erhard Friedrich Verlag, Postfach 100150, D 30917 Seelze Germany. **Tel** 011 49 511 4000452. **[CCC].**
Ind/Abst Linguist. Lang. Behav. Abstr.; MLA Int. Bibl. Books Artic. Mod. Lang. Lit.; Soc. Plann. Policy Dev. Abstr.; Sociol. Abstr.

GW/0176-4225
DIACHRONICA. [Diachronica]. Vol. 1, No. 1 (Spring 1984)-. Periodical. English (French and German). sa (Spring and Fall). $101.00. John Benjamins BV, Amsteldijk 44, PO Box 75577, 1070 AN Amsterdam Netherlands. **Tel** 011 31 20 6738156, FAX 011 31 20 739773. **(Subscription address:** John Benjamins North America, PO Box 27519, Philadelphia PA 19118-0519.**) ED** E.F. Konrad Koerner, Sheila Embleton. **LC** P140; .D5. **DD** 410/.5. **Bk Rev**, (Qty: 8). **Ad Acc.**
Desc: Forum for the exchange and synthesis of information concerning all aspects of Historical Linguistics and pertaining to all language families.
Ind/Abst Int. Bibliogr. Sociol.; Linguist. Lang. Behav. Abstr. (1984-) [Full Cov.]; MLA Int. Bibl. Books Artic. Mod. Lang. Lit.; Soc. Plann. Policy Dev. Abstr.; Sociol. Abstr.

BE/0773-7688
DIALECTES DE WALLONIE, LES. [Dialectes Wallonie]. **Added/Corp** Societe de Langue et de Litterature Wallonnes. **VFOAT** DW. (1972)-. French. **LC** PC3041; .D52. **DD** 447/.9/4934.
Ind/Abst MLA Int. Bibl. Books Artic. Mod. Lang. Lit.

UK
DIALOGOS. (19??)-. English. an. $55.00. Frank Cass & Company Ltd, Newbury House, 890-900 Eastern Avenue, Newbury Park, Ilford, Essex IG2 7HH United Kingdom. **Tel** 011 44 81 599 8866, FAX 011 44 81 599 0984, telex 897719. **Ad Acc, Adv Mgr:** Anne Kidson.
Desc: The purview of this journal is Greek language and literature, Greek history and archaeology and Greek culture and thought, present and past. It seeks to foster critical awareness and informed debate about the ideas, events, and achievements that make up this territory, by redefining their qualities, by exploring their interconnections and by reinterpreting their significance within Western culture and beyond.

NE/0167-8744
DIALOGOS HISPANICOS DE AMSTERDAM. [Dialog. hisp. Amst.]. (1980)-. Monographic series. Spanish (French). an. Price varies per volume. Editions Rodopi BV, Keizersgracht 302-304, 1016 Ex Amsterdam Netherlands. **Tel** 011 31 20 6227507, FAX 011 31 20 380948.
Ind/Abst MLA Int. Bibl. Books Artic. Mod. Lang. Lit.

CN/0715-7037
DIALOGUE - COUNCIL OF MINISTERS OF EDUCATION. (DIALOGUE.). [Dialogue - Counc. Minist. Educ.]. **Added/Corp** Council of Ministers of Education (Canada). **VFOAT** Dialogue. Vol. 1, No. 1 (June 1982)-. Periodical. Multiple languages (English and French). ir. Free. Council of Ministers of Education Canada, Suite 5-200, 252 Bloor Street West, Toronto Ontario M5S 1V5 Canada. **Tel** (416)964-2551, FAX (416)964-2296. **DD** 407/.0971. **Circ:** 4,500.
Desc: A newsletter on the teaching of English and French as second languages.

CN/0824-4189
DIALOGUE IMMERSION. **VFOAT** Revue Dialogue Immersion. V. 3. No. 2 (Feb. 1984)-. Periodical. French. sa. Free. Dialogue d'Immersion, c/o Conseil d'Immersion Association des Instituteurs du Nouveau-Brunswick, C P 752, Fredericton New Brunswick E3B 5R6 Canada. **Tel** 506-622-1406. **ED** Nicole Rousay. **DD** 440/.7. **UDC** 804.0-07(715). **Bk Rev. Circ:** 350 (ctrl). ***Continues*** *Je Porte, Tu Portes, 0712-9653.*
Desc: Provides new ideas in immersion, information on professional development and new challenges

CN/0226-6881
DIALOGUES ET CULTURES. [Dialogues cult.]. **Added/Corp** Federation Internationale des Professeurs de Francais. No. 21 (Mar. 1981)-. Periodical. French. an. 18.00F France; 35.00F other. Federation Internationale des Professeurs de Francais, 1 Avenue Leon Journault, 92311 Sevres France. **Tel** 011 33 1 46265316, FAX 011 33 1 46268169. **ED** J.P. Beland. **DD** 440/.7. cum. index. **Ad Acc. Circ:** 1,000 (ctrl). ***Continues*** *Dialogues (Quebec, Quebec), 0253-0007.*

SP
DICCIONARIO HISTORICO DE LA LENGUA ESPANOLA. **Main/Corp** Real Academia Espanola. Vol. 1 (1960)-. Monographic series. Spanish. ir. Price varies per volume. Real Academia Espanola, Felipe IV 4, 28071 Madrid Spain. **(Subscription address:** Editorial Gredos, 1406 Sanchez Pacheco 81, 28002 Madrid Spain.**)**

US/0197-6745
DICTIONARIES. [Dictionaries]. **Added/Corp** Dictionary Society of North America. No. 1 (1979)-. English (French). an. $20.00 US; $25.00 other; includes the DSNA Newsletter three times a year. Dictionary Society of North America, English Department, Indiana State University, Terre Haute IN 47809. **Tel** (812)237-3163. **ED** Richard W Bailey. **LC** P327; .D53. **DD** 413/.028. **CODEN** DICTEQ. **Bk Rev. Circ:** 500.
Desc: The making, use, history and collecting of dictionaries: monolingual, bilingual, general and special.
Ind/Abst Annu. Bibliogr. Engl. Lang. Lit.; Linguist. Lang. Behav. Abstr.; MLA Int. Bibl. Books Artic. Mod. Lang. Lit.; Soc. Plann. Policy Dev. Abstr.; Sociol. Abstr.

SW/0345-2360
DIDAKOMETRY AND SOCIOMETRY. [Didakom. sociom.]. (1969)-. Periodical. English. sa. **UDC** 37.
Ind/Abst Linguist. Lang. Behav. Abstr.; Soc. Plann. Policy Dev. Abstr.; Sociol. Abstr.

XR
DIDAKTIKA RUSTINY A JINYCH CIZICH JAZYKU. (THE DIDACTICS OF RUSSIAN AND OTHER FOREIGN LANGUAGES.). (1982)-. English. an. Charles University / Univerzita Karlova, Ovocnytrh 5, 116 36 Prague 1 Czech Republic. **Tel** 228441. **LC** Z5818.L35; D5; PB35. **DD** 016.418/007.
Desc: Information on modern languages.

US/0094-5870
DINE BIZAAD NANILIIH. [Dine bizaad naniliih]. **VFOAT** Navajo Language Review. V. 1- Winter 1974-. Periodical. Multiple languages (English and Navajo). qt. $8.00. Center for Applied Linguistics Department of Lingustics/Room 20E, 225 Massachusetts Institute of Technology, Cambridge MA 02139. **LC** PM2006; .D55. **DD** 497/.2. **UDC** 809.7.
Ind/Abst MLA Int. Bibl. Books Artic. Mod. Lang. Lit.

AT
DIRECTORY OF ACCREDITED AND RECOGNIZED PRACTITIONERS OF INTERPRETING & TRANSLATING. Directory. English. an (Aug.). 35.00Aus$. NAATI Executive Secretary, PO Box 349, Jamison Act, 2614 Australia. **Tel** 11 61 62 514044, FAX 11 61 62 531575. **ED** S. Bell. **Circ:** 200 (ctrl).

US/0743-5096
DIRECTORY OF BILINGUAL SPEECH-LANGUAGE PATHOLOGISTS AND AUDIOLOGISTS. **See** Physically Impaired.

US/0044-779X
DIRECTORY OF MEMBERS - AMERICAN PHILOLOGICAL ASSOCIATION. [Dir. memb. - Am. Philol. Assoc.]. **Main/Corp** American Philological Association. **VFOAT** APA Directory of Members, (1984)-. (1970)-. Directory. English. ir (Directory published in odd years & updates published in even years). $10.00 Comes with American Philological Association Membership. Scholars Press Customer Service, PO Box 6996, Alpharetta GA 30239. **Tel** (800)437-6692. **LC** P11; .A49. **DD** 480/.062/73. **Circ:** 2,750.

●CN/1188-102X
DIRECTORY OF MEMBERS OF THE ASSOCIATION OF TRANSLATORS AND INTERPRETERS OF ONTARIO. [Dir. memb. Assoc. Transl. Interpret. Ont.]. **Main/Corp** Association of Translators and Interpreters of Ontario. **VFOAT** Repertoire des Membres de l'Association des Traducteurs et Inerpretes de l'Ontario. (1992)-. Directory. English (French). ir. Free (members). Association Translators and Interpreter, 1 Nicholas Street, Suite 1402, Ottawa Ontario K1N 7B7 Canada. **Tel** (613)233-6395. **DD** 418/.02/025713. ***Continues*** *Association of Translators and Interpreters of Ontario. Repertoire., 0226-8868.*

●CN/1188-102X
DIRECTORY OF MEMBERS OF THE ASSOCIATION OF TRANSLATORS AND INTERPRETERS OF ONTARIO. (REPERTOIRE DES MEMBRES DE L'ASSOCIATION DES TRADUCTEURS ET INTERPRETES DE L'ONTARIO.). [Dir. memb. Assoc. Transl. Interpret. Ont.]. **Main/Corp** Association des Traducteurs et Interpretes de l'Ontario. **VFOAT** Repertoire des Membres de l'Association des Traducteurs et Interpretes de l'Ontario. (1992)-. French (English). ir. Free. Association Translators and Interpreter, 1 Nicholas Street, Suite 1402, Ottawa Ontario K1N 7B7 Canada. **Tel** (613)233-6395. **DD** 418/.02/025713. ***Continues*** *Association des Traducteurs et Interpretes de l'Ontario. Repertoire., 0226-8868.*

US/0426-5688
DIRECTORY OF MEMBERSHIP - FLORIDA COUNCIL OF TEACHERS OF ENGLISH. **Main/Corp** Florida Council of Teachers of English. (May 1959)-. Directory. English. Florida Council, Teachers of English, University of Florida 33620. **DD** 420.

US
DIRECTORY OF PROFESSIONAL PREPARATION PROGRAMS IN TESOL IN THE UNITED STATES. **Added/Corp** Teachers of English to Speakers of Other Languages. (1988)-. Directory. English. be. $19.00 (member TESOL); $25.45 (other). TESOL, 1600 Cameron Street/Suite 300, Alexandria VA 22314-2751. **Tel** (703)836-0774, FAX (703)836-7864. **LC** PE1128.A2; T4543. **DD** 428/.007/1173. ***Continues*** *Directory of Teacher Preparation Programs in TESOL and Bilingual Education, 0191-7641.*

US/0898-8528
DIRECTORY OF PROGRAMS IN LINGUISTICS IN THE UNITED STATES & CANADA. [Dir. programs linguist. U. S. Can.]. **Added/Corp** Linguistic Society of America. No. 12 (Sept. 1984)-. Directory. English. te (every 3 years). $20.00. Linguistic Society of America, 1325 18th Street Northwest, Washington DC 20036. **Tel** (202)835-1714. **LC** P57.U7; D57. **DD** 410/.7/1173. **Circ:** 1,500. ***Continues in part*** *LSA Bulletin, 0023-6365.*

US/0163-853X
DISCOURSE PROCESSES. [Discourse process.]. Vol. 1 (Jan./Mar. 1978)-. Periodical. English. qt (4 issues). $160.00. Ablex Publishing Corporation, 355 Chestnut Street, Norwood NJ 07648. **Tel** (201)767-8450, (201)767-8455 (Customer Service), FAX (201)767-6717. **ED** Roy O. Freedle. **LC** P302; .D55. **DD** 410/.5. **CODEN** DIPRDG. **[CCC].** Index available. **Bk Rev. Ad Acc. Pr Rev. Circ:** 650. Documents available from The Genuine Article, Ask*IEEE.
Desc: Forum for articles exchanging ideas from diverse disciplines which share a common interest in discourse.
Ind/Abst Arts Humanit. Citation Index [Select. Cov.]; Commun. Abstr. (?-?); Curr. Contents Soc. Behav. Sci.; Curr. Index J. Educ.; INSPEC (April/June 1988-); Lang. Teach.; Linguist. Lang. Behav. Abstr. (1978-) [Full Cov.]; MLA Int. Bibl. Books Artic. Mod. Lang. Lit.; Psychol. Abstr. (1984-); PsycINFO; PsycLit; Res. Alert [Full Cov.]; Soc. Plann. Policy Dev. Abstr.; Soc. Sci. Cit. Index [Full Cov.]; Sociol. Abstr.

GW/0342-1589
DISKUSSION DEUTSCH. Volume 1, Issue 1 (Sept. 1970)-. Periodical. German. bm (Feb., Apr., June, Aug., Oct., Dec.). DM68.18. Moritz Diesterweg, Postfach 630180, D-60351 Frankfurt Germany. **Tel** 11 49 69 420810, FAX 11 49 69 42081100. **ED** Hubert Ivo, Valentin Merkelbach, Rosemarie Rigol, and Hansthiel. **DD** 371.3; 430. **[CCC].** cum. index. **Bk Rev. Ad Acc.**
Desc: Directed at all those teaching German. It includes articles on didactic and methodological questions regarding German language and literature.

NE/0083-4998
DISPUTATIONES RHENO-TRAJECTINAE. **Main/Corp** Utrecht. Rijksuniversiteit. Instituut Voor Oosterse en Slavische Talen. Vol. 1 (1957)-. Monographic series. Dutch. ir. Price varies per volume. Walter de Gruyter Inc. / Hawthorne, 200 Saw Mill River Road, Hawthorne NY 10532. **Tel** (914)747-0110, GERMANY: 011/49/30/260050, FAX (914)747-1326, telex 646677. **(Subscription address:** Germany/ PO Box 110240, 1 Berlin 11**) DD** 490.

FR/0085-4786
DOCUMENTS DE LINGUISTIQUE QUANTITATIVE. 1-. Monographic series. French. ir. Price varies per volume. Dunod Gauthier Villars, 15 rue Gossin, 92543 Montrouge cedex France. **Tel** 011 33 1 46 56 52 66, FAX 011 33 1 46 57 40 69. **UDC** 800:311.

FR
DOCUMENTS PEDAGOGIQUES. **Main/Corp** Paris. Universite. Institut d'Etudes Slaves. Monographic series. French. ir. Price varies per volume. Institut d'Etudes Slaves, 9 rue Michelet, 75006 Paris France. **Tel** 011 33 1 43265089. **UDC** 808-07. **Circ:** 800.
Desc: Language teaching handbooks (Russian and Slavic).

NE/0165-2621
DOCUMENTS SUR L'ESPERANTO. [Doc. Esperanto]. (1977)-. Periodical. French. ir.
Ind/Abst Linguist. Lang. Behav. Abstr.; Soc. Plann. Policy Dev. Abstr.; Sociol. Abstr.

NE
DOKUMENTAAL. Dutch. qt. Fl20.00. WA Hendricks, Pieter de Hooghlaan 67, 1213 BS Hilversum Netherlands. **Tel** 011 31 35215228.

JA/0286-1291
DOSHISHA DAIGAKU EIGO EIBUNGAKU KENKYU. (DOSHISHA STUDIES IN ENGLISH.). [Doshisha Daigaku Eigo Eibungaku

kenkyu]. **Added/Corp** Doshisha Daigaku. Jimbun Gakkai. (1971)-. Periodical. Japanese (English).
Ind/Abst Soc. Plann. Policy Dev. Abstr.

FR/0767-4775
DOSSIERS DE L'AUDIOVISUEL.
Added/Corp Institut National de la Communication Audiovisuelle (France). No. 1 (May/June 1985)-. Periodical. French. Six times a year. 68.56F Europe; 118.23F others. Documentation Francaise, 29 Quai Voltaire, 75344 Paris Cedex 7 France. **Tel** 011 33 1 40157000, FAX 011 33 1 40157230, telex 204 826 DOCFRAN. **(Subscription address:** Documentation Francaise, 124 rue Henri Barbusse, 93308 Aubervilliers CDX France, telephone: 011 33 1 48395600 MME Milhau**) LC** P93.5; .D67. **DD** 001.55/3/05.

NE
DRIEMAANDELIJKSE BLADEN. Year 1-1949-. Dutch (German). qt. Fl15.00. Stichting Sasland, Postbus 1127, Groningen Netherlands. **Tel** 050-635966. **ED** J van der Kooi. **UDC** 908.492; 803.93-087. Index available. cum. index. **Bk Rev. Circ:** 400. ***Supersedes*** *Driemaandelijksche Bladen.*
Desc: Covers dialectology; regional history, literature and folklore; and regional culture.

US
DUQUESNE STUDIES. LANGUAGE AND LITERATURE SERIES. **See** Literature.

US/0070-7694
DUQUESNE STUDIES. PHILOLOGICAL SERIES. Vol. 1 (1960)-. English. ir (one or two times a year). Duquesne Studies / Language and Literature Series, 600 Forbes Avenue, Pittsburgh PA 15282. **Tel** (412)396-6610. **ED** Albert C. Labriola. **DD** 400; 800.
Desc: Explores the contexts that lead to, clarify, and influence the works of Spenser and Milton. Accordingly, the Greek and Roman classics, Patristic commentary, medieval religious and secular literature and drama, literary genres and modes, philosophical and scientific movements, the visual arts, and the like provide the background from which the explication of texts may proceed more systematically.

UK/0955-6427
DURHAM MODERN LANGUAGE SERIES. [Durh. mod. lang. ser.]. (1980)-. Monographic series. Multiple languages.
Ind/Abst MLA Int. Bibl. Books Artic. Mod. Lang. Lit.

UK/0309-6564
DUTCH CROSSING. **See** Literature.

NE/0376-8686
DUTCH STUDIES. **See** History(General)-History of Europe.

AT
EA JOURNAL. (1989)-. English. Twice a year. 30.00Aus$ Australia; 35.00Aus$ other. Elicos Association Ltd., 3 Union Street, Pyrmont NSW 2009 Australia. **Tel** 011 61 02 6606459, FAX 011 61 02 5523384. ***Continues*** *Tea News, 1033-0801.*

TZ
EACROTANAL INFORMATION. ***Ceased.*** **See** Anthropology.

UK
EAST EUROPEAN LANGUAGES AND LITERATURES. 2-. English. te. **LC** Z7043; .T472.

CN/0831-5825
ECHANGE (EDMONTON). (ECHANGE : LA REVUE PEDAGOGIQUE DU CONSEIL FRANCAIS DE L'ALBERTA TEACHERS' ASSOCIATION.). [Echange]. **Added/Corp** Alberta Teachers' Association. Conseil Francais. Vol. 13, No. 2 (Spring 1986)-. Periodical. French (summaries and/or abstracts in English). ir. 20.00Can$ Comes with Le Conseil Francais Membership. Alberta Teachers Association, 11010-142 Street, Barnett House, Edmonton Alberta T5N 2R1 Canada. **Tel** (403)453-2411. **DD** 371.1/006/07123. available on microfilm and microfiche from Micromedia Limited. ***Continues*** *Notre Langue et Notre Culture., 0380-5352.*

FR/0268-109X
ECLAT. English and French. Expediters of the Printed Word, 515 Madison Avenue, New York NY 10022. **Tel** 01-686-2599.

UK/0959-2253
EDINBURGH WORKING PAPERS IN APPLIED LINGUISTICS. **Added/Corp** University of Edinburgh. Dept. of Applied Linguistics. University of Edinburgh. Institute for Applied Language Studies. No. 1 (1990)-. English. an. University of Edinburgh, Department of Linguistics, George Square, Edinburgh Scotland EH8 9LL. **Tel** 011 44 31 6671011 Ext 6513. **CODEN** EWPLE6.
Ind/Abst Linguist. Lang. Behav. Abstr. (1991-) [Full Cov.]; Soc. Plann. Policy Dev. Abstr.

US/0163-3848
EDWARD SAPIR MONOGRAPH SERIES IN LANGUAGE, CULTURE, AND COGNITION. [Edward Sapir monogr. ser. lang. cult. cogn.]. **VFOAT** Monograph Series in Language, Culture, and Cognition. (1977)-. Monographic series. English. ir (two to four issues per year). Price varies per volume. Jupiter Press, PO Box 101, Lake Bluff IL 60044. **Tel** (708)234-3997. **ED** Valerie Becker Makkai. **Pr Rev. Circ:** 1,000.
Ind/Abst MLA Int. Bibl. Books Artic. Mod. Lang. Lit.

UK/0732-5819
EFL GAZETTE, THE. [EFL gaz.]. **VFOAT** E.F.L. Gazette. **VAT** English as a Foreign Language Gazette. (19??)-. Periodical. English. Twelve times a year. £32.00. EFL Gazette, 106 Dunyeats Road Broadstone, Dorset BH18 8AN England. **Tel** 011 44 202 699462. **[CCC].** available on microfilm and microfiche from University Microfilms International (UMI).
Ind/Abst Lang. Teach.

JA
EIGAKUSHI KENKYU / NIHON EIGAKUSHI GAKKAI. **Added/Corp** Nihon Eigakushi Gakkai. (19??)-. Periodical. English (Japanese). Nihon Eigakushi Gakkai, c/o Keio Gijuku Daigaku Shin, Kenkyushitsu 1-1 Hiyoshi 4 Kohoku-ku, Yokohama-shi Japan. **LC** DA4; .E42.

JA/0288-2876
EIGO EIBUNGAKU KENKYU HIROSHIMA. 1954. [Eigo Eibungaku KenkyuHiroshima, 1954]. **VFOAT** Hiroshima Studies in English Language and Literature. (1954)-. Periodical. Multiple languages. an. **DD** 820.
Ind/Abst MLA Int. Bibl. Books Artic. Mod. Lang. Lit.

JA/0388-2519
EIGO EIBUNGAKU KENKYU (TOKYO. 1976). (STUDIES IN ENGLISH LANGUAGE AND LITERATURE.). [Eigo Eibungaku kenkyu]. **VFOAT** English Language and Literature. No. 25 (Mar. 1975)-. Multiple languages (Japanese and English). an. **UDC** 802.0; 820. ***Continues*** *Studies in English Literature and Language.*
Ind/Abst MLA Int. Bibl. Books Artic. Mod. Lang. Lit.

JA
EIGO EIBUNGAKU RONSO. First issue No. 4-; 1976-. Multiple languages (Japanese and English). Ryukoku Daigaku Eigo Eibungaku Kenkyukai, Shichijo Omiya Shimokyo-ku, Kyoto Japan. **LC** PE9; .R9. ***Continues*** *Ryukoku Daigaku Eigo Eibungaku Ronso.*

JA
EIGO KYOIKU. THE ENGLISH TEACHERS' MAGAZINE. **Added/Corp** Tokyo Kyoiku Daigaku Eigo Kyoiku Kenkyukai. **VFOAT** English Teachers' Magazine. (19??)-. Periodical. Japanese (English). mo. $166.00. **(Subscription address:** Kyowa Book Company, Inc., 1-38 Kanda Jinbo-Cho, Chiyoda-Ku Tokyo 101, Japan**)**

IE/0013-2608
EIGSE. [Eigse]. **Added/Corp** National University of Ireland. Vol. 1, Pt. 1 (1939)-. Periodical. English (Irish and Scots). an. 10p. National University of Ireland, 49 Merrion Square, Dublin 2 Ireland. **Tel** 011 353 1 767246. **ED** Padraig A. Breatnach. **Bk Rev. Circ:** 500. Documents available from The Genuine Article.
Desc: Presents Irish language and literary studies.
Ind/Abst Arts Humanit. Citation Index (19??-19??) [Full Cov.]; Curr. Contents Arts Humanit.; MLA Int. Bibl. Books Artic. Mod. Lang. Lit.; Res. Alert [Full Cov.].

●US/1064-6663
ELEMENTA (YVERDON, SWITZERLAND). (ELEMENTA : JOURNAL OF SLAVIC STUDIES & COMPARATIVE CULTURAL SEMIOTICS.). [Elementa]. Vol. 1, No. 1 (1992)-. Periodical. English. Four times a year. $95.00 (academic institutions), $150.00 (corporate institutions). Harwood Academic Publishers / New York, PO Box 786, Cooper Station, New York NY 10276. **Tel** (212)206-8900, (201)643-7500. **(Subscription address:** International Publishers Distributor at one of the following addresses: 820 Town Center Drive, Langhorne, PA 19047; or PO Box 90, Reading Berkshire RG1 8JL UK; or Kent Ridge PO Box 1180, Singapore 9111, Republic of Singapore**) DD** 302. **CODEN** ESSSEE. **[CCC].**
Desc: Concerned with problems of sign systems and results of the comparison of different semiotic systems and texts with particular application to Slavic traditions.

GR/0013-6336
ELLENIKA (THESSALONIKE). (HELLENIKA.). [Ellenika]. **Added/Corp** Syllogos Pros Diadosin Ophelimon Vivlion (Greece) Hetaireia Makedonikon Spoudon. Vol. 1 (1928)-. Periodical. Greek, Modern (English, French and German). sa. $30.00. Society for Macedonian Studies, 4 Ethnikis Amynis Avenue, GR 546 21 Thessaloniki Greece. **Tel** 011 30 31 271195. **LC** PA1005; .H43.
Ind/Abst Am. Hist. Life (1954-); BHA : Biblio. Hist. Art; MLA Int. Bibl. Books Artic. Mod. Lang. Lit.

BL
ELOS. No. 1-. Periodical. French (Portuguese). $70.00 single issue. Associacao Brasileira dos Professores Universitarios de Frances, Avenida Presidente Antonio Carlos 58 40, 20020 Rio de Janeiro Brazil. **LC** PC2068.B7; E46. **DD** 440/.7/081. **UDC** 804.0-07(066)(81).

II/0970-048X
ELT FORUM JOURNAL OF ENGLISH STUDIES. [ELT forum j. Engl. stud.]. V. 1- March 1978-. Periodical. English. qt. $6.00. Elt Forum India, c/o Department of English, University Centre Tellicherry, Kerala 670101 India. **LC** PE1128.A2; E17. **DD** 820/.5. **UDC** 802.0.
Ind/Abst Lang. Teach.

UK/0951-0893
ELT JOURNAL. (ELT JOURNAL / OXFORD UNIVERSITY PRESS IN ASSOCIATION WITH THE BRITISH COUNCIL.). [ELT j.]. **Added/Corp** Oxford University Press. British Council. **VFOAT** English Language Teaching Journal. Vol. 36/1 (Oct. 1981)-. Periodical. English. qt. £40.00 UK and Europe; $70.00 other. Oxford University Press, Walton Street, Oxford OX2 6DP England. **Tel** 011 44 865 56767, FAX 011 44 865 267773, telex 837330 OXPRES G. **(Subscription address:** Oxford University Press / USA, Journals Marketing Department, Oxford University Press, 2001 Evans Road, Cary NC 27513.**) ED** Norman Whitney. **LC** PE1128.A2; E5. **DD** 428/.007. **CODEN** EJOUE5. Index available. **Bk Rev. Ad Acc. Circ:** 5,000 (ctrl). available on microfilm and microfiche from University Microfilms International (UMI). ***Continues*** *English Language Teaching Journal.*
Desc: An international journal for teachers of English as a foreign language. Contains survey articles, reviews, correspondence and an announcement section.
Ind/Abst Acad. Search (July 1993-); Br. Educ. Index; Curr. Index J. Educ. (March 1990); Educ. Index; INFO-SOUTH Abstr.; Lang. Teach.; Mag. Search; Soc. Plann. Policy Dev. Abstr.

ER/0422-9967
EMAKEELE SELTSI AASTARAAMAT.
Main/Corp Emakeele Selts. (1955)-. Estonian (summaries and/or abstracts in Russian). **LC** PH601.E5; A2.
Ind/Abst MLA Int. Bibl. Books Artic. Mod. Lang. Lit.

GW/0340-627X
ENCHORIA. (1971)-. Periodical. Multiple languages (English, French, German and Italian). an. Otto Harrassowitz Verlag, Taunusstrasse 14, Postfach 2929, D-65019 Wiesbaden Germany. **Tel** 011 49 611 5300, FAX 530570, telex 4186 135 OH D.
Desc: Egyptian language; Coptic philology.
Ind/Abst BHA : Biblio. Hist. Art.

GW/0013-8185
ENGLISCH. [Englisch]. **VFOAT** Eine Zeitschrift fuer Englischlehrer und Englischlehrerinnen. Vol. 1 (1966)-. Periodical. German (English). Four times a year (Mar., June, Sept., Dec.). DM33.30 Germany; DM34.00 others. Cornelsen Velhagen und Klasing, Postfach 100271, D 33502 Bielefeld 1 Germany. **Tel** 011 49 521 97190, FAX 05217872 260, telex 175218149 CORBI. **[CCC].**
Ind/Abst Lang. Teach.

AT/0425-0435
ENGLISH. A NEW LANGUAGE. **Added/Corp** Australia. Commonwealth Office of Education. (19??)-. Periodical. English. ir. (free upon request). ACT Department of Education & Science, Language Teaching Branch, PO Box 826, Woden ACT 2606 Australia. **Tel** 062 89-1333.
Ind/Abst Aust. Educ. Index (199?-).

GW
ENGLISH AND AMERICAN STUDIES IN GERMAN; SUMMARIES OF THESES AND MONOGRAPHS. (1968)-. Monographic series. German (English). ir. Price varies per volume. Max Niemeyer Verlag, Postfach 2140, D 72011 Tuebingen Germany. **Tel** 011 49 7071 989494, FAX 011 49 7071 87419. **ED** Horst Weinstock. **LC** PE3; .A6 Suppl. **DD** 420/.5. **Bk Rev. Ad Acc.**
Desc: Summaries of theses and monographs on English and American languages and literatures.

UK
ENGLISH & MEDIA MAGAZINE, THE.
Periodical. English. Twice a year. £38.00 full membership (includes NATE News newsletter and English in Education journal). NATE / National Association for the Teaching of English, 50 Broadfield Road, Broadfield Business Centre, Sheffield S8 0XJ England. **Tel** 011 44 114 2555419, FAX 011 44 114 2555296. ***Supersedes*** *English Magazine.*
Ind/Abst Br. Educ. Index.

US/0007-8204
ENGLISH EDUCATION. **See** Education-Teaching and Curriculum.

US/0889-4906
ENGLISH FOR SPECIFIC PURPOSES (NEW YORK, N.Y.). (ENGLISH FOR SPECIFIC PURPOSES.). [Engl. specif. purp.]. Vol. 5, No. 1 (1986)-. Periodical. English. Three times a year. $187.00 The Americas; £125.00 other. Pergamon Press, An Imprint of Elsevier Science Ltd., The Boulevard, Langford Lane, Kidlington, Oxford OX5 1GB United Kingdom. **Tel** 011 44 865 843000, 011 44 865 843699, FAX 011 44 865 843010. **(Subscription address:** Elsevier Science Ltd. Oxford Fulfillment Centre, PO Box 800, Kidlington, Oxford

OX5 1DX United Kingdom.) **ED** Ann M. Johns. **LC** PE1128.A2; E76. **DD** 428/.007. **[CCC]. Bk Rev. Ad Acc.** available on microfilm and microfiche from University Microfilms International (UMI). ***Continues*** *ESP Journal, 0272-2380.*
Desc: Publishes articles and research notes reporting basic research in the linguistic description of specialized varieties of English and the application of such research to specific methodological concerns. Topics include: discourse analysis, second language acquisition in specialized contexts, needs assessment, curriculum development and evaluation, materials preparation, teaching and testing, etc.
Ind/Abst Br. Educ. Index; Contents Pages Educ.; Curr. Index J. Educ.; Lang. Teach.; Linguist. Lang. Behav. Abstr. (1980-) [Full Cov.]; Soc. Plann. Policy Dev. Abstr.

AT/0155-2147
ENGLISH IN AUSTRALIA. [Engl. Aust.]. **Added/Corp** Australian Association for the Teaching of English. **VFOAT** Journal of the Australian Association for the Teaching of English. No. 1 (Nov. 1965)-. Periodical. English. Four times a year (Mar., June, Sept., Dec.). 16.00Aus$ Australia; 24.00Aus$ other. Australian Association for the Teaching of English Inc, PO Box 3203, Norwood South Australia 5067 Australia. **Tel** 011 61 8 3322845, FAX 011 61 8 3330394. **ED** Bill Corcoran. Index available. **Bk Rev. Ad Acc. Circ:** 5,500 (ctrl).
Desc: Articles of language arts for teachers and students. One issue consists only of book reviews.
Ind/Abst Annu. Bibliogr. Engl. Lang. Lit.; Aust. Educ. Index (1978-); Curr. Index J. Educ.

UK/0425-0494
ENGLISH IN EDUCATION. [Engl. educ.]. **Added/Corp** National Association for the Teaching of English. Vol. 1 (Spring 1967)-. Periodical. English. Three times a year (spring, summer and autumn). £38.00 full membership (includes NATE News newsletter and The English & Media Magazine); £22.00 library membership (journal only). NATE / National Association for the Teaching of English, 50 Broadfield Road, Broadfield Business Centre, Sheffield S8 0XJ England. **Tel** 011 44 114 2555419, FAX 011 44 114 2555296. Index available. cum. index. **Ad Acc.** available on microfilm and microfiche from University Microfilms International (UMI). ***Supersedes*** *N.A.T.E. Bulletin.*
Ind/Abst Br. Educ. Index; Child. Lit. Abstr. (19??-); Lang. Teach.

US/0013-8274
ENGLISH JOURNAL. See Education-Teaching and Curriculum.

US/0071-0601
ENGLISH LANGUAGE AND ORIENTATION PROGRAMS IN THE UNITED STATES. [Eng. lang. orientat. programs U. S.]. **Added/Corp** Institute of International Education (New York, N.Y.). (1964)-. English. te. $42.95. Institute of International Education / New York, 809 United Nations Plaza, New York NY 10017. **Tel** (212)984-5412, FAX (212)984-5452. **LC** PE1068.U5; E53. **DD** 428.
Desc: Guide for foreign students, business executives, refugees, and all others studying English as a second language. Describes 1,100 intensive ESL programs and courses at accredited US higher educational institutions, language schools and private secondary schools nationwide.

UK/0265-847X
ENGLISH LANGUAGE RESEARCH JOURNAL. ***Ceased.*** [Engl. lang. res. j.]. No. 1 (1980)-Ceased Vol. 4 (1990). English. an. English Language Research, University of Birmingham, PO Box 363, Birmingham B15 2TT England.
Ind/Abst Lang. Teach.

US/0307-8337
ENGLISH LANGUAGE TEACHING JOURNAL. (ELT JOURNAL [MICROFORM] / OXFORD UNIVERSITY PRESS IN ASSOCIATION WITH THE BRITISH COUNCIL.). **Added/Corp** Oxford University Press. British Council. **VFOAT** English Language Teaching Journal. Vol. 36/1 (Oct. 1981)-. Periodical. English. Oxford University Press, Walton Street, Oxford OX2 6DP England. **Tel** 011 44 865 56767, FAX 011 44 865 267773, telex 837330 OXPRES G. **[CCC].** ***Continues*** *English Language Teaching Journal.*
Ind/Abst Curr. Index J. Educ.; Educ. Index; Lang. Lang. Behav. Abstr.; Lang. Teach.

US/1054-1578
ENGLISH LEADERSHIP QUARTERLY. See Education-School Organization and Administration.

JA
ENGLISH LINGUISTICS : JOURNAL OF THE ENGLISH LINGUISTIC SOCIETY OF JAPAN. Added/Corp English Linguistic Society of Japan. Vol. 1 (Nov. 1984)-. Periodical. English.
Ind/Abst MLA Int. Bibl. Books Artic. Mod. Lang. Lit.

UK/0955-8950
ENGLISH REVIEW OXFORD. (ENGLISH REVIEW). [Engl. rev.Oxf.]. (1989)-. Periodical. English. Four times a year (Feb., April, Sept., Nov.). £18.95 UK; £23.00 Europe; £28.50 other. Philip Allan Publishers Ltd, Market Place, Deddington Oxford, OX15 0SE England. **Tel** 011 44 869 38652, FAX 011 44 869 38803. **DD** 820.9.

CN/0317-0802
ENGLISH STUDIES IN CANADA. [Engl. stud. Can.]. **Added/Corp** Association of Canadian University Teachers of English. **VFOAT** ESC. Vol. 1, (Spring 1975)-. Periodical. English. qt (Mar., June, Sept., Dec.). 50.00Can$ (one year), 135.00Can$ (three year) Canada; 52.00Can$ (one year), 140.00Can$ (three yera) other. English Studies in Canada, Carleton University, Department of English, Ottawa Ont K1S 5B6 Canada. **Tel** (613)788-2361, FAX (613)788-3544. **[CCC]. Bk Rev. Pr Rev.** ctrl circ. Documents available from The Genuine Article.
Desc: A journal of scholarship and criticism concerned with all literature written in the English language.
Ind/Abst Abstr. Engl. Stud.; Annu. Bibliogr. Engl. Lang. Lit.; Arts Humanit. Citation Index [Full Cov.]; Curr. Contents Arts Humanit.; MLA Int. Bibl. Books Artic. Mod. Lang. Lit.; Res. Alert [Full Cov.]; Romant. Move.

UK
ENGLISH STUDIES SERIES. No. 1 (1964)-. Monographic series. English. ir. Price varies per volume. Oxford University Press, Walton Street, Oxford OX2 6DP England. **Tel** 011 44 865 56767, FAX 011 44 865 267773, telex 837330 OXPRES G.

NE
ENGLISH STUDIES. TRANSLATION SUPPLEMENT. (1925)-. Periodical. English.

IS/0333-533X
ENGLISH TEACHERS' JOURNAL (ISRAEL) / MINISTRY OF EDUCATION AND CULTURE, PEDAGOGICAL SECRETARIAT. Added/Corp Israel. Pikuah al Horaat ha-Anglit. **VFOAT** Alon le-Morim le-Anglit. (19??)-. Periodical. English (summaries and/or abstracts in Hebrew). Twice a year (Jan. & July). $40.00. Onda Publications Ltd, 7 Hasadna Street, PO Box 2325, Raanana 43650 Israel. **Tel** 011 972 52 441645, FAX 011 972 52 441497. **LC** PE1068.I8; E53. **DD** 428/.007/05694. ***Absorbed*** *English Teaching Guidance.*
Ind/Abst Soc. Plann. Policy Dev. Abstr.

UK/0266-0784
ENGLISH TODAY. [Engl. today]. (Jan. 1985)-. Academic Scholarly Publication. English. qt (January, April, July and October). $79.00 US, Canada & Mexico; £49.00 other. Cambridge University Press, The Edinburgh Building, Shaftesbury Road, Cambridge CB2 2RU United Kingdom. **Tel** 011 44 223 312393, FAX 011 44 223 325959. **(Subscription address:** Cambridge University Press / North America, 110 Midland Avenue, Port Chester NY 10573.) **ED** Tom McArthur and David Crystal. **LC** PE1001; .E37. **DD** 420/.5. **[CCC].** available on microfilm and microfiche from University Microfilms International (UMI).
Desc: Covers all aspects of the language, including its uses and abuses, international variations, history, literature and linguistics, and usages and neologisms. Special articles and regular features keep readers up to date with current opinion and recent developments.
Ind/Abst Curr. Index J. Educ.; MLA Int. Bibl. Books Artic. Mod. Lang. Lit.; Soc. Plann. Policy Dev. Abstr.

SA/0046-2098
ENGLISH USAGE IN SOUTHERN AFRICA. ***Title Change.*** [Engl. usage south. Afr.]. **Added/Corp** University of South Africa. Human Sciences Research Council. University of South Africa. Dept. of English. Vol. 1 (1970)-(1993). English. sa. University of South Africa, PO Box 392, Pretoria 0001 South Africa. **Tel** 011 27 12 4298468, FAX 011 (27)12 429 3321, telex (59)350068+. **LC** PE3452 .S64; E54. **DD** 427/.9/68. **CODEN** EUSAE8.
Ind/Abst Annu. Bibliogr. Engl. Lang. Lit.

NE/0172-8865
ENGLISH WORLD-WIDE. [Engl. world-w.]. **VFOAT** English World Wide. **VAT** English World Wide. (1980)-. Academic Scholarly Publication. English. sa. $148.00. John Benjamins BV, Amsteldijk 44, PO Box 75577, 1070 AN Amsterdam Netherlands. **Tel** 011 31 20 6738156, FAX 011 31 20 739773. **(Subscription address:** John Benjamins North America, PO Box 27519, Philadelphia PA 19118-0519.) **ED** Manfred Gorlach. Index available. **Bk Rev. Ad Acc. Circ:** 500.
Desc: Focuses on scholarly discussions of new findings in the dialectology and sociolinguistics of the English-speaking communities (native and second-language speakers), but general problems of sociolinguistics, creolistics, and language planning are included if they have a direct bearing on modern varieties of English.
Ind/Abst Int. Bibliogr. Sociol.; Lang. Teach.; Linguist. Lang. Behav. Abstr. (1980-) [Full Cov.]; MLA Int. Bibl. Books Artic. Mod. Lang. Lit.; Soc. Plann. Policy Dev. Abstr.

FR/0300-2608
ENSEIGNEMENT DU RUSSE, L'. Periodical. French (Russian). an. 60.00F. Institut d'Etudes Slaves, 9 rue Michelet, 75006 Paris France. **Tel** 011 33 1 43265089. **UDC** 808.2-07. **Bk Rev. Ad Acc. Circ:** 700.
Desc: Pedagogical journal devoted to the teaching of Russian.

PL/0012-7825
EOS. [Eos]. **Added/Corp** Polskie Towarzystwo Filologiczne. Vol. 1 (1894)-. Periodical. Latin (Polish). sa. $50.00. **(Subscription address:** ARS Polona, PO Box 1001, 00068 Warsaw Poland.) **LC** P1.A1; E6.
Ind/Abst Geogr. Abstr. Human Geogr. (?-?); MLA Int. Bibl. Books Artic. Mod. Lang. Lit.

US
EPIC EVENTS. Vol. 1, No. 1 (March/April 1988)-. Periodical. English. bm. $18.00. NIRCF, 220 I Street NE, Suite 220, Washington DC 20002. **Tel** (202)544-0004, FAX (202)544-1905. **Circ:** 800.
Desc: News on language policy regarding official English.

US/1061-5938
EPIGRAPHIC SOCIETY OCCASIONAL PAPERS, THE. See Archaeology.

GR
EPISTEMONIKE EPETERIS TES PHILOSOPHIKES SCHOLES. Main/Corp Aristoteleion Panepistemion Thessalonikes. Philosophike Schole. (1927)-. Greek, Modern.
Ind/Abst MLA Int. Bibl. Books Artic. Mod. Lang. Lit.

SP/0213-201X
EPOS / UNIVERSIDAD NACIONAL DE EDUCACION A DISTANCIA, FACULTAD DE FILOLOGIA. Added/Corp Universidad Nacional de Educacion a Distancia. Facultad de Filologia. (198?)-. Periodical. Spanish. an. 3213ptas Spain; 3653ptas others. Libreria Marcial Pons, Tamayo y Baus 7, 28004 Madrid Spain. **Tel** 011 34 1 3194254.
Ind/Abst MLA Int. Bibl. Books Artic. Mod. Lang. Lit.

DK/0902-5162
EPSILON. Added/Corp Kbenhavns Universitet. Institut for Nygrsk og Balkanistik. **VFOAT** Modern Greek and Balkan Studies. No. 1 (1987)-. Periodical. English (French, German and Greek, Modern). ir. kr30.00. Institute of East European Studies, University Copenhagen Njalseate 78 3, DK 2300 Copenhagen S Denmark. **Tel** 011 65 31542211. **LC** DF701; .E67. **DD** 949.5/005. ***Continues*** *Scandinavian Studies in Modern Greek.*

BE/0751-9532
EQUIVALENCES. [Equivalences]. **Added/Corp** Institut Superieur de l'Etat des Traducteurs et d'Interpretes a Bruxelles. Association pour la Promotion de l'Etude des Langues Modernes. (1970)-. Periodical. French (English, German, Dutch, Spanish and Russian). Twice a year. 500.00F. Institut Super Traducteurs Interpretes, Rue Hazard 34, 1180 Brussels Belgium. **Tel** 011 32 2 3440080.
Ind/Abst MLA Int. Bibl. Books Artic. Mod. Lang. Lit.

IE/0332-0758
ERIU. See Literature.

SP/0425-2772
ESPANOL ACTUAL. Added/Corp Oficina Internacional de Informacion y Observacion del Espanol. Instituto de Cooperacion Iberoamericana. No. 1 (Nov. 10, 1963)-. Periodical. Spanish. sa (2 issues). $40.00. Arco Libros S A, Juan Bautista de Toledo 25, 28002 Madrid Spain. **Tel** 011 34 1 415-3687, 011 34 1 416-1371. **LC** PC4008; .E67. **DD** 460/.5. cum. index.
Desc: Spanish language.
Ind/Abst Lang. Teach.; MLA Int. Bibl. Books Artic. Mod. Lang. Lit.

AT
ESPANOL EN AUSTRALIA. Spanish. wk (published Tuesdays). 90.00Aus$ Australia; 210.00Aus$ New Zealand, South Pacific and PNG; 235.00Aus$ other. Ficobi Pty Ltd, PO Box 277, Marrickville 2204 Australia. **Tel** 011 61 2 516 2111, FAX 011 61 2 5162610. **ED** Arkel A. Almada. **Bk Rev**, (Qty: 50). **Ad Acc. Circ:** 20,000 (ctrl).

NE/0014-0635
ESPERANTO. Added/Corp Universal Esperanto Association. (June 18, I905)-. Periodical. Esperanto. Eleven times a year (July/Aug. issues combined). Fl55.00. Universala Esperanto-Asocio, Nieuwe Binnenweg 176, 3015 BJ Rotterdam Netherlands. **Tel** 011 31 10 4361044, FAX 011 31 10 4361751, telex 23721. **ED** I. Ertl. Index available in last issue of volume--attached (Bound in last issue). **Bk Rev**, (Qty: 60/year). **Ad Acc, Adv Mgr:** O. Buller. **Circ:** 5,500.
Ind/Abst MLA Int. Bibl. Books Artic. Mod. Lang. Lit.

NE/0165-2575
ESPERANTO DOCUMENTS. [Esperanto doc.]. **Added/Corp** Universal Esperanto Association. No. 1 (1975)-. Monographic series. English. Universala Esperanto-Asocio, Nieuwe Binnenweg 176, 3015 BJ Rotterdam Netherlands. **Tel** 011 31 10 4361044, FAX 011 31 10 4361751, telex 23721.
Ind/Abst MLA Int. Bibl. Books Artic. Mod. Lang. Lit.; Soc. Plann. Policy Dev. Abstr.

NE/0165-2524
ESPERANTO - DOKUMENTOJ. [Esperanto - dok.]. (1975)-. Periodical. Esperanto. ir. Universala Esperanto-Asocio, Nieuwe Binnenweg 176, 3015 BJ Rotterdam Netherlands. **Tel** 011 31 10 4361044, FAX 011 31 10 4361751, telex 23721.
Ind/Abst MLA Int. Bibl. Books Artic. Mod. Lang. Lit.

US/1056-0297
ESPERANTOUSA. Added/Corp Esperanto League for North America. **VFOAT** Esperanto USA; Esperanto; ELNA Newsletter. Periodical. English (Esperanto). Seven times a year. $15.00 (libraries and institutions), $30.00 (individuals). Esperanto League North America, Box 1129, El Cerrito CA 94530. **Tel** (415)653-0998. **ED** Donald Harlow. **DD** 499. **Circ:** 1,300. ***Continues*** *ELNA Newsletter, 0030-5065.*
Desc: Articles and announcements about the language problem and Esperanto as its solution.

SU/1011-7997
ESPMENA BULLETIN. (ESPMENA BULLETIN : ENGLISH FOR SPECIAL PURPOSES IN THE MIDDLE EAST AND NORTH AFRICA.). [Espmena bull.]. **Added/Corp** University of Khartoum. Faculty of Arts. English Language Servicing Unit. **VFOAT** English for Special Purposes in the Middle East and North Africa. Bulletin 2 (Autumn 1975)-. Bulletin. English. sa. **LC** PE3502.N42; E53. **DD** 428/.007/1156. ***Continues*** *English for Special Purposes in the Middle East & North Africa.*
Ind/Abst Lang. Teach.; Soc. Plann. Policy Dev. Abstr.

UK/0071-1357
ESSAYS AND STUDIES (LONDON, ENGLAND : 1950). See Literature.

CN
ESTIMATES. PART III, OFFICE OF THE COMMISSIONER OF OFFICIAL LANGUAGES. Main/Corp Canada. **VFOAT** Budget des Depenses. Partie III, Bureau du Commissaire aux Langues Officielles. (19??)-. English (French). $3.00 Canada; $3.60 other. Canada Communication Group Publishers, Order Processing, Ottawa Ontario K1A 0S9 Canada. **Tel** (819)956-4800, (819)956-4802. **LC** P119.32.C3; C34a. **DD** 354.710085/4.

CN
ESTIMATES. PART III, SECRETARY OF STATE, OFFICIAL LANGUAGES PROGRAM. Main/Corp Canada. **VFOAT** Budget des Depenses. Partie III, Secretariat d'Etat Programme des Langues Officielles. (19??)-. English (French). $6.00 Canada; $7.20 other. Canada Communication Group Publishers, Order Processing, Ottawa Ontario K1A 0S9 Canada. **Tel** (819)956-4800, (819)956-4802. **LC** P119.32.C3; C34b. **DD** 354.710085.

ER
ESTONIAN PAPERS IN PHONETICS. PUBLIKATTSII ESTONSKIKH FONETISTOV. Added/Corp Keele ja Kirjanduse Instituut (Eesti NSV Teaduste Akadeemia). **VFOAT** Publikatsii Estonskikh Fonetistov. (1972)-. Periodical. English (summaries and/or abstracts in Russian). 0.88rub. **LC** PH612; .E8. **DD** 494/.545/15.
Ind/Abst MLA Int. Bibl. Books Artic. Mod. Lang. Lit.

SP/0212-7636
ESTUDIOS DE LINGUISTICA. [Estud. linguist.]. **Added/Corp** Universidad de Alicante. Departamento de Lengua Espanola. Universidad de Alicante. Departamento de Filologia Espanola, Linguistica General y Teoria de la Literatura. No. 1 (1983)-. Spanish (summaries and/or abstracts in English). an. 3000ptas, Spain except Canary Island; 2820ptas, Canary Island. SECR Publicaciones, FAC F Y Letras DEP FIL ESP, 03071 Alicante Spain. **Tel** 011 34 6 5903480. **(Subscription address:** L'Estaquirot S A, Nuestra Senora del Coll 53, 08023 Barcelona Spain.**) LC** P9; .E83. **DD** 410/.5.
Ind/Abst Linguist. Lang. Behav. Abstr. (1983-) [Full Cov.]; MLA Int. Bibl. Books Artic. Mod. Lang. Lit.; Soc. Plann. Policy Dev. Abstr.

MX/0185-2647
ESTUDIOS DE LINGUISTICA APLICADA. [Estud. linguist. apl.]. (1981)-. Periodical. Spanish. sa. **DD** 410.72.
Ind/Abst MLA Int. Bibl. Books Artic. Mod. Lang. Lit.

CL/0071-1713
ESTUDIOS FILOLOGICOS. [Estud. filol.]. **Added/Corp** Universidad Austral de Chile. Facultad de Filosofia y Letras. Universidad Austral de Chile. Instituto de Filologia. Universidad Austral de Chile. Facultad de Filosofia y Humanidades. No. 1 (1965)-. Spanish. an (Oct.). $23.60. Universidad Austral de Chile / Inst Filologia, Casilla 567, Valdivia Chile. **Tel** 011 56 63 221312. **ED** Claudio Wagner. **LC** P25; .E8. Index available (bound in issue). **Bk Rev. Ad Acc. Circ:** 700. Documents available from The Genuine Article.
Desc: Publishes studies specializing in linguistics and literature.
Ind/Abst Am. Hist. Life (1964-1966); Arts Humanit. Citation Index [Full Cov.]; Curr. Contents Arts Humanit.; MLA Int. Bibl. Books Artic. Mod. Lang. Lit.; Res. Alert [Full Cov.]; Soc. Plann. Policy Dev. Abstr.; Sociol. Abstr.

SP/0213-1382
ESTUDIOS HUMANISTICOS. FILOLOGIA. VFOAT Filologia. Vol. 6 (1984)-. Spanish. an. Universidad de Leon / Filologia, Campus Vegazana, Departamento de Filologia Moderna, 24071 Leon Spain. **Tel** 011 34 87 291085. ***Continues in part*** *Estudios Humanisticos.*

SP
ESTUDIOS ROMANICOS. V. 1-. Periodical. Spanish. Universidad de Murcia / Servicio de Publicaciones, Calle Santo Cristo 1, 30001 Murcia Spain. **Tel** 011 34 68 363013. **LC** PC13; .E69. **DD** 440/.05. **UDC** 804.

BL/0102-4906
ESTUDOS ANGLO-AMERICANOS. [Estud. anglo-am.]. **Added/Corp** Associacao Brasileira de Professores Universitarios de Literatura Americana, Lingua e Literatura Inglesa. No. 1 (1977)-. Multiple languages (English and Portuguese). **LC** PE9; .E84. **DD** 420/.5.
Ind/Abst MLA Int. Bibl. Books Artic. Mod. Lang. Lit.

US/0014-164X
ETC. (ETC.; A REVIEW OF GENERAL SEMANTICS.). [Etc.]. **Added/Corp** International Society for General Semantics. **VFOAT** Et cetera Mar. 1977-. **VAT** Etcetera. Vol. 1 (Aug. 1943)-. Periodical. English. qt. $30.00 (one year), $60.00 (two year), $90.00 (three year). International Society for General Semantics, PO Box 728, Concord CA 94522. **Tel** (510)798-0311. **ED** Russell Joyner. **LC** B840; .E85. **DD** 149.9. **NLM** W1 ET423. Index available. **Bk Rev. Ad Acc. Circ:** 2,500. available on microfilm and microfiche from University Microfilms International (UMI). Documents available from UMI Article Clearinghouse.
Desc: Explores the role of language and other symbols in human affairs; how habitual uses of language, signs, and symbols shape thinking, influence actions, determine success or failure in communication.
Ind/Abst Acad. Abstr. Full Text Elite (July 1990-); Acad. Abstr. (July 1990-); Acad. Ind. [Computer File] (1987-); Acad. Search (July 1990-); Annu. Bibliogr. Engl. Lang. Lit.; Commun. Abstr. (?-?); Expand. Acad. Index (1987-); Humanit. Index; INFO-SOUTH Abstr.; Mag. Search; MLA Int. Bibl. Books Artic. Mod. Lang. Lit.; Newsp. Period. Abstr. (1990-); Psychol. Abstr. (1943-); PsycINFO; PsycLit; Soc. Plann. Policy Dev. Abstr.

US/0364-9288
ETHNOLOGUE. Added/Corp Wycliffe Bible Translators. Summer Institute of Linguistics. (1951)-. English. ir. price varies per volume. International Academic Bookstore, Box MKS5 7500, West Camp Wisdom Road, Dallas TX 75236. **Tel** (214)709-2404. **LC** P371; .E83. **DD** 410.

GS
ETIMOLOGIURI ZIEBANI / SAKARTVELOS SSR MECNIEREBATA AKADEMIA, ENATMECNIEREBIS INITITUTI. Added/Corp Enatmecnierebis Instituti (Sakartvelos SSR Mecnierebata Akademia) Arn. Cikobavas Sax. Enatmecnierebis Instituti. **VFOAT** Etimologicheskie Razyskaniia; EZ. (1987)-. Georgian (German; summaries and/or abstracts in Russian; table of contents in Russian). Izdatelstvo Metsniereba / Science Publishers, Ulitsa Kutuzova 19, 380060 Tbilisi 60 Georgia (Republic). **LC** PK9052; .E8.
Desc: Information on Kartvelian languages.

FR/0373-1928
ETUDES CELTIQUES. See Linguistics-Abstracting, Bibliographies and Statistics.

CN/0708-2398
ETUDES CREOLES. (ETUDES CREOLES / COMITE INTERNATIONAL DES ETUDES CREOLES.). [Etud. creoles]. **Added/Corp** Comite International des Etudes Creoles. Association des Universites Partiellement ou Entierement de Langue Francaise. **VFOAT** Bulletin International des Etudes Creoles; Bulletin des Etudes Creoles. (July 1978)-. Academic Scholarly Publication. French. sa. $45.00 North America. Societe Nouvelle Didier Erudition, 6 rue de la Sorbonne, 75005 Paris France. **Tel** 011 33 1 43544757, FAX 011 33 1 40517385. **(Subscription address:** PO Box 830350, Birmingham, AL 35283-0350; telephone: (800)633-4931, (205)995-1567 (outside US and Canada); FAX: (205)995-1588**) LC** PM7851; .A25. **DD** 447/.9729.
Desc: Provides an accessible forum for interdisciplinary discussion among creolists. Its goal is to promote and serve creole culture, languages, and society through scholarly understanding.
Ind/Abst MLA Int. Bibl. Books Artic. Mod. Lang. Lit.; Soc. Plann. Policy Dev. Abstr.

FR/0071-190X
ETUDES DE LINGUISTIQUE APPLIQUEE. [Etud. linguist. appl.]. Vol. 1 (1962)-. Periodical. French. qt. $86.00 North America. Societe Nouvelle Didier Erudition, 6 rue de la Sorbonne, 75005 Paris France. **Tel** 011 33 1 43544757, FAX 011 33 1 40517385. **(Subscription address:** PO Box 830350, Birmingham, AL 35283-0350; telephone: (800)633-4931, (205)995-1567 (outside US and Canada); FAX: (205)995-1588**) ED** G Galisson. **LC** P1.A1; E85. **DD** 418/.005. **Bk Rev. Ad Acc. Circ:** 1,500 (ctrl). available on microfiche.
Desc: An international review of applied linguistics and language. Each informative issue is devoted to a specific subject of interest and edited by experts in that field.
Ind/Abst Lang. Teach.; Linguist. Lang. Behav. Abstr. (1972-) [Full Cov.]; MLA Int. Bibl. Books Artic. Mod. Lang. Lit.; Soc. Plann. Policy Dev. Abstr.; Sociol. Abstr.

FR
ETUDES FINNO-OUGRIENNES. Added/Corp Universite de Paris III. Centre d'Etudes Finno-Ougriennes. Institut National des Langues et Civilisations Orientales. Chaire des Langues Finno-Ougriennes. Vol. 1 (1964)-. English (French, German and Russian). ir. 150.00F. Editions Klincksieck, 8 rue de la Sorbonne, 75005 Paris France. **Tel** 11 33 1 43545953, FAX 11 33 1 432252553. **LC** PH1; .E85. **DD** 494/.5/05. **Bk Rev.**
Desc: Information on Finno-Ugrian philology.
Ind/Abst MLA Int. Bibl. Books Artic. Mod. Lang. Lit.

FR/0014-2115
ETUDES GERMANIQUES. [Etud. ger.]. **Added/Corp** Societe des Etudes Germaniques. Vol. 1, No. 1 (Jan./Mar. 1946)-. Periodical. French (German). qt. $92.00. Societe Nouvelle Didier Erudition, 6 rue de la Sorbonne, 75005 Paris France. **Tel** 011 33 1 43544757, FAX 011 33 1 40517385. **(Subscription address:** PO Box 830350, Birmingham, AL 35283-0350; telephone: (800)633-4931, (205)995-1567 (outside US and Canada); FAX: (205)995-1588**) LC** DD1; .E8. cum. index. **Bk Rev. Ad Acc. Circ:** 2,000 (ctrl). available on microfiche. Documents available from The Genuine Article.
Desc: A quarterly review published in cooperation with the Society for Germanic Studies. Aims to promote an understanding of the literature and languages of Germany, Austria, Switzerland, Scandinavia, and the Netherlands.
Ind/Abst Annu. Bibliogr. Engl. Lang. Lit.; Arts Humanit. Citation Index [Full Cov.]; Curr. Contents Arts Humanit.; MLA Int. Bibl. Books Artic. Mod. Lang. Lit.; Res. Alert [Full Cov.]; Romant. Move.; Soc. Plann. Policy Dev. Abstr.; Soc. Sci. Cit. Index [Select. Cov.].

NG/0255-0393
ETUDES LINGUISTIQUES. (ETUDES LINGUISTIQUES : REVUE DU DEPARTEMENT DE LINGUISTIQUE DE L'UNIVERSITE DE NIAMEY.). [Etud. linguist.]. **Added/Corp** Universite de Niamey. Departement de Linguistique. (1979)-. Periodical. French (English and French). sa. Universite de Niamey, Departement de Linguistique, B P 418, Niamey Niger. **LC** PL8000; .E85. **DD** 409/.6.
Ind/Abst MLA Int. Bibl. Books Artic. Mod. Lang. Lit.

FR/0071-2124
ETUDES LINGUISTIQUES (PARIS). (ETUDES LINGUISTIQUES.). [Etud. linguist.]. 1- 1962-. Monographic series. French. Price varies per volume. **UDC** 800.
Ind/Abst Linguist. Lang. Behav. Abstr. (1973-) [Full Cov.]; Soc. Plann. Policy Dev. Abstr.

SW
ETUDES ROMANES DE LUND. Added/Corp Lunds Universitet. Vol. 1 (1940)-. Monographic series. French (Italian and Spanish). ir. Price varies per volume. Liber International, S-205 10 Malmo Sweden. **Tel** 46-40-70650. **ED** Lars Lindvall.
Desc: Monographs on French linguistics and literature.

DK
ETUDES ROMANES (ODENSE). (ETUDES ROMANES.). **Main/Corp** Odense Universitet. Vol. 1 (1971)-. Monographic series. French. ir. Price varies per volume. Lund University Press, Box 141, S-22100 Lund Sweden. **Tel** 011 46 46 312000, FAX 011 46 46 305338, telex 33345 EDUCATE S. **ED** Suzanne Schlyter.
Desc: Doctoral dissertations and monographs in French and Spanish linguistics and literature.
Ind/Abst MLA Int. Bibl. Books Artic. Mod. Lang. Lit.

US/0898-0454
EURASIAN LANGUAGE ARCHIVES. [Eurasian lang. arch.]. Vol. 1 (1988)-. Monographic series. English (German). ir. Price varies per volume. Eurolingua, PO Box 101, Bloomington IN 47402. **Tel** (812)332-8918. **ED** Gyula Decsy. **DD** 400. **Ad Acc. Circ:** 1,000.
Desc: Contains information on linguistic materials on 250 languages of Northern Eurasia in the area between Germany and Japan

•US
EURASIAN STUDIES YEARBOOK. (1993)-. English (German). an (Jan.). $74.00. Eurolingua, PO Box 101, Bloomington IN 47402. **Tel** (812)332-8918. **ED** Gyuula Decsy. **LC** DB901; .U72. Index available. **Bk Rev**, (Qty: 40). ctrl circ. ***Continues*** *Ural-Altaische Jahrbucher.*
Desc: Languages and cultures of people in East Eurasia from the point of view of genetic and area comparative research.

●UK/0963-7273
EUROPEAN JOURNAL OF DISORDERS OF COMMUNICATION. **See** Communication.

US/0213-246X
EUTOPIAS. ***Ceased.*** [Eutopias]. Vol. 1, No. 1-2 (Winter/Spring 1985)-Ceased Vol. 3. Periodical. Spanish. Three times a year. University of New Mexico Department of Spanish and Portuguese, 30 Folwell Hall, Minneapolis MN 55455. **Tel** (612)625-9028. **LC** P99; .E87. **DD** 001.51/05. **UDC** 806.0; 806.90.
Ind/Abst MLA Int. Bibl. Books Artic. Mod. Lang. Lit.

UK/0309-4375
EXETER LINGUISTIC STUDIES. **Added/Corp** University of Exeter. Vol. 1 (1976)-. Monographic series. English. ir. Price varies per volume. University of Exeter, Exeter EX4 4QR England. **Tel** 011 44 392 263066, FAX 011 44 392 263064. **ED** R.R.K. Hartmann. **Pr Rev.**
Desc: Attempts to bridge the gap between linguistic theory and practice, between linguistics and neighboring disciplines, and between English and other languages.
Ind/Abst MLA Int. Bibl. Books Artic. Mod. Lang. Lit.

PK/0014-4975
EXPLORATIONS. **Added/Corp** Government College (Lahore, Pakistan). Dept. of English Language and Literature. (1969)-. Periodical. English. sa. **LC** P1; .E95. **DD** 405.
Ind/Abst Annu. Bibliogr. Engl. Lang. Lit.

BU/0324-1270
EZIK I LITERATURA. [Ezik lit.]. **Added/Corp** Druzhestvo na Bulgaristite. Druzhestvo na Filolozite-Slavisti v Bulgariia. Suiuz na Nauchnite Rabotnitsi v Bulgariia. (1946)-. Periodical. Bulgarian (table of contents in English). bm (6 issues). DM193.00. **(Subscription address:** Kubon & Sagner, ABT Zeitschriftenimport, D 80328 Munich Germany.**) LC** PG801; .E9.
Ind/Abst Annu. Bibliogr. Engl. Lang. Lit.; MLA Int. Bibl. Books Artic. Mod. Lang. Lit.

BL/0103-1562
FACE (SAO PAULO, BRAZIL). (FACE.). V. 1, N. 1 (Jan./June 1988)-. Periodical. Portuguese (summaries and/or abstracts in Portuguese). sa. Cr$25.00. Educ-Editora da Puc-Sp, rua Monte Alegre 984, Sao Paulo 05014 Brazil. **Tel** (011)62.0280. **ED** Lucia Santaella. **LC** P99; .F33. **DD** 302.2. **Bk Rev. Circ:** 1,000.

GW
FACHDIENST GERMANISTIK. (198?)-. Periodical. German. Twelve times a year. DM84.00. Iudicium Verlag, Postfach 701067, D-81310 Munich Germany. **Tel** 011 49 89 717868.

AU
FACHSPRACHE. Wilhelm Braumueller, Servitengasse 5, A 1092 Vienna, Austria. **Tel** 011 43 1 3191482, 3191159.
Desc: This journal deals with the research, didactics and terminology of different special languages from all various kinds of fields. Every journal finishes with the completion of a special language bibliography.

AU/0251-1207
FACHSPRACHE. (FACHSPRACHE : INTERNATIONALE ZEITSCHRIFT FUER FACHSPRACHENFORSCHUNG, -DIDAKTIK UND TERMINOLOGIE.). [Fachsprache]. **VFOAT** Special Language. (1979)-. Periodical. English (French and German). sa. S650.00 Austria; S700.00 other. Wilhelm Braumueller, Servitengasse 5, A 1092 Vienna, Austria. **Tel** 011 43 1 3191482, 3191159. **LC** P120.S9; F33. **DD** 418/.005. cum. index. **Bk Rev. Ad Acc. Pr Rev.** ctrl circ.
Desc: Contains articles, reports of meetings, announcements of meetings, reviews, bibliographies, research for teachers, translators and journalists.
Ind/Abst Lang. Teach.; MLA Int. Bibl. Books Artic. Mod. Lang. Lit.; Soc. Plann. Policy Dev. Abstr.; Sociol. Abstr. (?-?).

AU/1017-3285
FACHSPRACHE 1990. [Fachsprache 1990]. (1990)-. Periodical. Multiple languages. bm. ***Continues*** *Special Language, 0256-2510.*

CC
FAN I TUNG HSUN. **VFOAT** Translators' Notes. No. 1 (Feb. 1980)-. Periodical. Chinese. bm. RMBY0.33. Science Press, 16 Donghuangchenggen North Street, Beijing 100707, People's Republic of China. **Tel** 011 86 1 4019821, 011 86 1 4010642, FAX 011 86 1 4012180, 011 86 1 4019810, telex 210147. **LC** PN241.A1; F36. **DD** 418/.02/05. **UDC** 800.3; 800.73.

CC
FANG YEN. **VFOAT** Fangyan; Dialect. (19??)-. Periodical. Chinese (table of contents in English). qt. $10,80. Science Press, 16 Donghuangchenggen North Street, Beijing 100707, People's Republic of China. **Tel** 011 86 1 4019821, 011 86 1 4010642, FAX 011 86 1 4012180, 011 86 1 4019810, telex 210147. **ED** Li Rong. **LC** PL1501; .F35. **DD** 495.1/7. **Bk Rev. Circ:** 8,000.
Desc: All aspects of dialectology. Description, (phonology, lexicon and grammar), distribution, grouping and development of Chinese dialects.

NE/0167-9392
FAUX TITRE: ETUDES DE LANGUE ET LITTERATURE FRANCAISES PUBLIEES. French (English). Humanities Press, 165 1st Avenue, Atlantic Highlands NJ 07716. **Tel** (908)872-1441, (800)221-3845, FAX (908)872-0717, telex 752233. Index available.

SP
FAVENTIA. **See** Literature.

US
FENIX. V. 1- Winter 1978-. Periodical. Spanish. sa. $3.00. Department of Spanish and Portuguese, University of California at Irvine, Irvine CA 92717. **UDC** 82; 800.

PL/0554-8144
FILOLOGIA ANGIELSKA - UNIWERSYTET IM. ADAMA MICKIEWICZA W POZNANIU. **VFOAT** Prace Wydziau Filologicznego. Seria: Filologia Angielska. (1966)-. Monographic series. Multiple languages. tw. **UDC** 802.0.
Ind/Abst MLA Int. Bibl. Books Artic. Mod. Lang. Lit.

IT/0391-2493
FILOLOGIA E CRITICA (SALERNO EDITRICE). **See** Literature.

IT
FILOLOGIA MODERNA. **Added/Corp** Universita Degli Studi di Trieste. Facolta di Lingue e Letterature Straniere con Sede in Udine. (1976)-. Monographic series. Multiple languages (French and Italian). ir. Price varies per volume. Pacini Editore Srl, Via A Gherardesca 1, 56121 Ospedaletto Pisa Italy. **Tel** 011 39 50 982439. **LC** PB5; .F54. **DD** 410/.5.

SP/0046-3841
FILOLOGIA MODERNA. ***Suspended.*** [Filol. mod.]. **Added/Corp** Madrid. Consejo Superior de Investigaciones Cientificas. No. 1 (Oct. 1960)-Suspended. Periodical. Spanish (English, French, German and Italian). Seccion de Filologia Moderna, Faculdad Filologia Cuidad University, Madrid 3 Spain.
Desc: Modern philology.
Ind/Abst Annu. Bibliogr. Engl. Lang. Lit.; MLA Int. Bibl. Books Artic. Mod. Lang. Lit.; Romant. Move. (1985-).

SP
FILOLOGIA NEOTESTAMENTARIA. **Added/Corp** Universidad de Cordoba (Spain). Facultad de Filosofia y Letras. Vol. 1, No. 1 (May 1988)-. Periodical. Spanish (English, French, German and Italian). sa. 3250.00ptas Spain; $35.00 other. Filologia Neotestamentaria, Fac Filosofia Letras/Apdo 309, 14080 Cordoba Spain. **Tel** (011)34 957 274692.
Ind/Abst Index Book Rev. Relig.; Relig. Index One Period.; Relig. Theol. Abstr. (199?-).

PL
FILOLOGIA POLSKA. **See** Literature.

IT
FILOLOGIA VENETA. (1988)-. Periodical. Italian. an. L60000. Editoriale Programma, via San Eufemia 5, 35121 Padua Italy. **Tel** 011 39 49 8753110.

HU/0015-1785
FILOLOGIAI KOZLONY. [Filol. kozl.]. **Added/Corp** Magyar Tudomanyos Akademia. Vol. 1, (Mar. 1955)-. Academic Scholarly Publication. Hungarian (German and French; summaries and/or abstracts in Russian). Four times a year. $20.00 Austria, Croatia, Czech & Slovak Republics, Romania, Yugoslavia, Slovenia & Ukraine; $17.00 others. Akademiai Kiado, Publishing House of the Hungarian Academy of Sciences, Prielle Kornelia u. 19-35, H-1117 Budapest Hungary. **Tel** 011 36 1 1811991, FAX 011 36 1 1811991, telex 22-6228 AKNYO H. **(Subscription address:** Kultura, Hungarian Foreign Trading Company, PO Box 149, H-1389 Budapest Hungary**) ED** M. Horanyi. **Bk Rev. Circ:** 500. ***Continues*** *Egyetemes Philologiai Kozlony.*
Desc: Covers the whole of modern European philology. Research results in various national literatures, comparative studies, literary theory, poetics, literary translation and analytical reviews.
Ind/Abst Annu. Bibliogr. Engl. Lang. Lit.; MLA Int. Bibl. Books Artic. Mod. Lang. Lit.; Soc. Plann. Policy Dev. Abstr.

●RU
FILOLOGICHESKIE NAUKI. (1992)-. Periodical. Russian. Six times a year. $99.95. Izdatelstvo Vysshaia Shkola, Neglinnaya Ulitsa,, Dom 29-14, GSP-4, Moscow 101430 Russia. **(Subscription address:** East View Publications Inc., 3020 Harbor Lane North, Suite 110, Minneapolis MN 55447.**) LC** P19; .R8. ***Continues*** *Nauchnye Doklady Vysshei Shkoly. Filologicheskie Nauki, 0130-9730.*
Desc: Information on philology.
Ind/Abst Annu. Bibliogr. Engl. Lang. Lit.; MLA Int. Bibl. Books Artic. Mod. Lang. Lit.

RU
FILOLOGICHESKIE ZAPISKI. **Added/Corp** Voronezhskii Gosudarstvennyi Universitet. Russian S.F.S.R. Ministerstvo Vysshego i Srednego Spetsialnogo Obrazovaniia. No. 1 (1971)-. Russian. **LC** PG2025; .F52.

CI/0449-363X
FILOLOGIJA. [Filologija]. **Main/Corp** Jugoslavenska Akademija Znanosti i Umjetnosti. **Added/Corp** Hrvatsko Filolosko Drustvo. (1957)-. Serbo-Croatian (Roman) (English and French). **LC** P19.J8; A25.
Ind/Abst MLA Int. Bibl. Books Artic. Mod. Lang. Lit.; Soc. Plann. Policy Dev. Abstr.

GR/1105-1000
FILOLOGIKE PROTOHRONIA. (PHILOLOGIKE PROTOCHRONIA.). [Filol. Protohr.]. (1943)-. Greek, Modern. **LC** AP85; .P45.
Ind/Abst MLA Int. Bibl. Books Artic. Mod. Lang. Lit.

SW/0083-6745
FILOLOGISKT ARKIV. **Added/Corp** Kungl. Vitterhets, Historie och Antikvitets Akademien. (1955)-. Monographic series. Swedish. ir. Price varies per volume. Kungliga Vitterhets Historie och Antikvitets Akademien, PO Box 5622, S-114 86 Stockholm Sweden. **(Subscription address:** Almqvist & Wiksell International, PO Box 4627, S-116 91 Stockholm Sweden.**) LC** P17; .V564. **DD** 410/.5. Index available. ***Supersedes in part*** *Antikvariska; Historiska Studier.*

UN
FILOLOHIIA. **Main/Corp** Kharkov. Universytet. Ukrainian. 1.40rub single issue. **LC** AS262; .K417 subser. **UDC** 800; 82. ***Continues*** *Kharkov. Universytet. Seriia Filolohichna.*

FI/0355-1253
FINNISCH-UGRISCHE FORSCHUNGEN. [Finn.-ugr. Forsch.]. Vol. 1, No. 1 (1901)-. Periodical. German. ir. Fmk150.00. Bookstore Tiedekirja, Kirkkokatu 14, Helsinki 00170 Finland. **Tel** 011 358 0 635177. **LC** PH1; .F5.
Ind/Abst MLA Int. Bibl. Books Artic. Mod. Lang. Lit.

GW/0341-7816
FINNISCH-UGRISCHE MITTEILUNGEN. [Finn.-ugr. Mitt.]. (March 1977)-. Periodical. German. sa. Helmut Buske Verlag Hamburg, Postfach 760244, D 2000 Hamburg 76 F R Germany. **Tel** 011 49 40 5236739. **LC** PH1; .F513. **DD** 494.5/05.
Ind/Abst Soc. Plann. Policy Dev. Abstr.

RU/0135-6569
FINNO-UGRISTIKA / MINISTERSTVO VYSSHEGO I SREDNEGO SPETSIALNOGO OBRAZOVANIIA RSFSR, MORDOVSKII GOSUDARSTVENNYI UNIVERSITET IMENI N.P. OGAREVA. **Added/Corp** Mordovskii Gosudarstvennyi Universitet Imeni N.P. Ogareva. (1978)-. Russian. 1.20rub. Mordovskii Gosudarstvennyi Universitet Imeni NP Ogareva / Mordovian N.P. Ogarev State University, Ulitsa Bolshevistskaia 68, Saransk 430000, Mordovian Autonomous Republic. **Tel** 4-45-63. **LC** PH1; .F52.

UK/0142-7237
FIRST LANGUAGE. [First lang.]. Vol. 1, Pt. 1, No. 1 (Feb. 1980)-. Periodical. English. Three times a year. £46.00 (institutions), £25.00 (individuals) UK; $99.00 (institutions), $56.00 (individuals) North & South America & Japan; £49.00 (institutions), £28.00 (individuals) other. Alpha Academic, Mill Lane, Chalfont St Giles, Buckingham HP8 4NR England. **Tel** 44 494 872509. **ED** K Durkin. **[CCC].** Index available. cum. index. **Bk Rev. Ad Acc. Circ:** 450.
Desc: An international research periodical concerned with all aspects of native language acquisition. It publishes theoretical, empirical and review papers in the several disciplines concerned with child language study.
Ind/Abst Br. Educ. Index; Child Dev. Abstr. Bibliogr.; Lang. Teach.; Linguist. Lang. Behav. Abstr. (1983-) [Full Cov.]; MLA Int. Bibl. Books Artic. Mod. Lang. Lit.; Psychol. Abstr. (1982-); PsycINFO; PsycLit; Soc. Plann. Policy Dev. Abstr.; Sociol. Abstr.; Spec. Educ. Needs Abstr.

US
FLORIDA ENGLISH JOURNAL, THE. **Added/Corp** Florida Council of Teachers of English. (19??)-. Periodical. English. Twice a year. $15.00 Comes with Florida Council of Teachers of English Membership. Florida Council Teachers English, 9544 Pebble Glen Avenue, Tampa FL 33647. **Tel** (813)974-3511. **ED** Gloria T. Pipkin.
Desc: Articles on the teaching of English in the middle,junior and senior high school grades. Some issues contain a specific thematic focus, but well-written articles on any aspect of English will be considered at any time.

US/0163-5425
FOCUS: TEACHING ENGLISH LANGUAGE ARTS. **Added/Corp** Southeastern Ohio Council of Teachers of English. Ohio University, Athens. Dept. of English. **VFOAT** Teaching English Language Arts. (19??)-. Periodical. English. Twice a year (Winter & Spring). $12.00 (one year); $30.00 (three

years). SOCTE, 1425 Newark Road, C/O Micheal Nern, Zanesville OH 43701. **Tel** (614)593-2750. **ED** Ronald Salomone. **LC** LB1576; .F59. **DD** 420/.7. **Circ:** 350.

NE/0165-4004
FOLIA LINGUISTICA. [Folia linguist.]. **Added/Corp** Societas Linguistica Europaea. Vol. 1 (1967)-. Periodical. English (French, German and Spanish). qt (plus 2 supplements). $182.85. Walter de Gruyter Inc., PO Box 303421, D 10728 Berlin Germany. **Tel** 011 49 30 260050, FAX 011 49 30 26005251. **[CCC].** Documents available from The Genuine Article.
Ind/Abst Am. Hist. Life (1967-); Annu. Bibliogr. Engl. Lang. Lit.; Arts Humanit. Citation Index [Full Cov.]; Curr. Contents Arts Humanit.; Int. Bibliogr. Sociol.; Lang. Teach.; Linguist. Lang. Behav. Abstr. (1971-) [Full Cov.]; Middle East Abstr. Index; MLA Int. Bibl. Books Artic. Mod. Lang. Lit.; Res. Alert [Full Cov.]; Soc. Plann. Policy Dev. Abstr.

NE/0168-647X
FOLIA LINGUISTICA HISTORICA. (FOLIA LINGUISTICA HISTORICA : ACTA SOCIETATIS LINGUISTICAE EUROPAEAE.). [Folia linguist. hist.]. **Added/Corp** Societas Linguistica Europaea. (1980)-. Periodical. English (French and German). sa. $165.00 (add $12.00 postage) with Folia Linguistica. Walter de Gruyter Inc., PO Box 303421, D 10728 Berlin Germany. **Tel** 011 49 30 260050, FAX 011 49 30 26005251. **LC** P140; .F64. **DD** 410/.5. Documents available from The Genuine Article.
Ind/Abst Annu. Bibliogr. Engl. Lang. Lit.; Arts Humanit. Citation Index [Full Cov.]; Curr. Contents Arts Humanit.; Linguist. Lang. Behav. Abstr. (1980-) [Full Cov.]; Middle East Abstr. Index; Res. Alert [Full Cov.]; Soc. Plann. Policy Dev. Abstr.; Soc. Sci. Cit. Index [Select. Cov.].

US/0882-3030
FOLIO (BROCKPORT, N.Y.). ***Ceased.* See** Literature.

US/0015-718X
FOREIGN LANGUAGE ANNALS. [Foreign lang. ann.]. **Added/Corp** American Council on the Teaching of Foreign Languages. Modern Language Association of America. Vol. 1 (Oct. 1967)-. Periodical. English. qt. $60.00 US, Canada, and Mexico; $70.00 other. American Council on Foreign Languages, 6 Executive Plaza, PO Box 1077, Yonkers NY 10701. **Tel** (914)963-8830, FAX (914)963-1275. **ED** Vicki Galloway. **LC** PB1; .F57. **DD** 405. cum. index. **Ad Acc. Pr Rev. Circ:** 8,000 (ctrl). available on microfilm and microfiche from University Microfilms International (UMI). Documents available from The Genuine Article.
Supersedes *Foreign Language Annals (New York, N.Y. : 1966);* ***Absorbed*** *American Council on the Teaching of Foreing Languages. Accent on ACTFL, 0271-7492.*
Desc: Describes innovative and successful teaching methods. Reports educational research or experimentation relevant to the concern and problems of the profession.
Ind/Abst Acad. Search (July 1993-); Chicano Index; Contents Pages Educ.; Curr. Contents Soc. Behav. Sci.; Curr. Index J. Educ.; Educ. Index; INFO-SOUTH Abstr.; Lang. Teach.; Mag. Search; Middle East Abstr. Index; Multicult. Educ. Abstr.; Res. Alert [Full Cov.]; Soc. Plann. Policy Dev. Abstr.; Soc. Sci. Cit. Index [Full Cov.].

UK/1350-1771
FORENSIC LINGUISTICS: THE INTERNATIONAL JOURNAL OF LANGUAGE AND THE LAW. (19??)-. English. Twice a year. $110.00 (US & Canada); £75.00 (UK); £80.00 (other). Routledge, 11 New Fetter Lane, London EC4P 4EE England. **Tel** 071 583 9855, FAX 071 842 2298. **(Subscription address:** Kinokuniya Company Ltd., 38-1 Sakuragaoka 5, chome Setagaya-ku, Tokyo 156 Japan.**)**

CK/0120-338X
FORMA Y FUNCION. **Added/Corp** Universidad Nacional de Colombia. Departamento de Filologia e Idiomas. Seccion de Linguistica. Vol. 1 (June 1981)-. Periodical. Spanish. **LC** P9; .F67. **DD** 410/.5. **CODEN** FOFUE6.
Ind/Abst Linguist. Lang. Behav. Abstr. (1988-) [Full Cov.]; Soc. Plann. Policy Dev. Abstr.

CN/0713-0627
FORNERI, IL. [Forneri]. **Added/Corp** Canadian Society for Italian Linguistics and Language Teaching. Vol. 1, No. 1, (Jan. 1981)-. Periodical. English (French and Italian). sa. Free to members, $5.00 others. University of Toronto / NF 217 Victoria College, c/o M. Danesi, 73 Queen's Park Crescent, Toronto Ontario M5S 1K7 Canada. **Tel** (416)978-5530. **(Subscription address:** University of Waterloo, St Jerome's College, c/o G Niccoli, Waterloo Ontario N2L 3G3 Canada**) ED** M Danesi. **DD** 450/.7/071. cum. index. **Bk Rev. Circ:** 500 (ctrl).
Desc: Articles, reviews, news, etc. on the teaching of Italian in a North American context.
Ind/Abst Soc. Plann. Policy Dev. Abstr.

GW/0342-782X
FORSCHUNGSBERICHTE / INSTITUT FUER PHONETIK UND SPRACHLICHE KOMMUNIKATION DER UNIVERSITAT MUNCHEN. [Forschungsber. - Inst. Phon. Sprachl. Kommun. Univ. Munch.]. **Added/Corp** Universitat Munchen. Institut fur Phonetik und Sprachliche Kommunikation. **VFOAT** FIPKM; F.I.P.K.M. (1973)-. German (English).
Ind/Abst Linguist. Lang. Behav. Abstr. (1973-) [Full Cov.]; Soc. Plann. Policy Dev. Abstr.

GW
FORUM. **Main/Conf** Anglistentag. Vol. 1- 1986-. German (English). an. ***Continues in part*** *Tagungsbeitrage und Berichte.*

NE/0015-8496
FORUM DER LETTEREN. **See** Literature.

UK/0015-8518
FORUM FOR MODERN LANGUAGE STUDIES. [Forum mod. lang. stud.]. **Added/Corp** University of St. Andrews. Vol. 1 (Jan. 1965)-. Periodical. English. qt. £56.00 UK and Europe; $105.00 other. Oxford University Press, Walton Street, Oxford OX2 6DP England. **Tel** 011 44 865 56767, FAX 011 44 865 267773, telex 837330 OXPRES G. **(Subscription address:** Oxford University Press / USA, Journals Marketing Department, Oxford University Press, 2001 Evans Road, Cary NC 27513.**) ED** J.R. Ashcroft, I.R.W. Higgins and D.D.R. Owen. **LC** PB1; .F63. **CODEN** FMLSEG. **[CCC]. Bk Rev. Ad Acc. Circ:** 450 (ctrl). available on microfilm and microfiche from University Microfilms International (UMI). Documents available from The Genuine Article.
Desc: Studies in the field of European language and literature, including English and American, from the Middle Ages to the present.
Ind/Abst Abstr. Engl. Stud.; Annu. Bibliogr. Engl. Lang. Lit.; Arts Humanit. Citation Index [Full Cov.]; Curr. Contents Arts Humanit.; Middle East Abstr. Index; MLA Int. Bibl. Books Artic. Mod. Lang. Lit.; Res. Alert [Full Cov.]; Romant. Move.; Soc. Plann. Policy Dev. Abstr.; Soc. Sci. Cit. Index [Select. Cov.].

US/0163-0768
FORUM LINGUISTICUM. [Forum linguist.]. Vol. 1; Aug. 1976-. Periodical. English. Three times a year. $30.00. Jupiter Press, PO Box 101, Lake Bluff IL 60044. **Tel** (708)234-3997. **ED** Valerie Becker Makkai. **DD** 410. Index available. cum. index. **Bk Rev. Ad Acc. Pr Rev. Circ:** 1,000.
Ind/Abst Lang. Teach.; MLA Int. Bibl. Books Artic. Mod. Lang. Lit.

US/0883-5640
FORUM OF PHI SIGMA IOTA, THE. [Forum Phi Sigma Iota]. **VFOAT** Forum. Periodical. English. $2.00. Phi Sigma Iota, Portland State University, c/o Professor Frank Vecchio, Portland OR 97207. **Tel** (203)773-8550. **ED** Sharon Magnokelli. **DD** 406. **UDC** 708.5. **Ad Acc. Circ:** 20,000.

US
FOUNDATIONS OF LINGUISTICS. Academic Scholarly Publication. English. ir. Elsevier Science Publishing Company Inc, Madison Square Station, PO Box 882, New York NY 10159-0882. **Tel** (212)633-3950, FAX (212)633-3990. **UDC** 800; 800.1.

NE/0168-2555
FOUNDATIONS OF SEMIOTICS. Vol. 1 (1983)-. Monographic series. English. ir. Price varies per volume. John Benjamins BV, Amsteldijk 44, PO Box 75577, 1070 AN Amsterdam Netherlands. **Tel** 011 31 20 6738156, FAX 011 31 20 739773. **(Subscription address:** John Benjamins North America, PO Box 27519, Philadelphia PA 19118-0519.**) ED** Achim Eschbach. **LC** UNC.
Desc: This series has been established in order to provide a forum for fundamental research in the field of semiotics. Includes reprints as well as translations, collections of articles, relevant conference proceedings, and analyses and syntheses of current research in semiotics.
Ind/Abst MLA Int. Bibl. Books Artic. Mod. Lang. Lit.; Zentralbl. Math. Ihre Grenzgeb.

NR/0015-9387
FRANCAIS AU NIGERIA. (LE FRANCAIS AU NIGERIA.). [Fr. Niger.]. **Added/Corp** Nigerian Association of French Teachers. (1965)-. Periodical. French (English). tq. Nigerian Association of French Teachers, Box 4063, U I Post Office, Ibadan Nigeria.
Ind/Abst MLA Int. Bibl. Books Artic. Mod. Lang. Lit.

FR/0184-7732
FRANCAIS AUJOURD'HUI: REVUE DE L'ASSOCIATION FRANCAISE DES ENSEIGNANTS DE FRANCAIS, LE. **Added/Corp** Association de Professeurs de Francais. Association Francaise des Enseignants de Francais. (March 1968)-. Periodical. French. Four times a year (Mar., June, Sept., Dec.). 275.00F France, 312.50F others (surface mail); 350.00F (airmail). Assn Francaise Enseignants de Francais, 19 rue des Martyrs, 75009 Paris Cedex 6 France. **Tel** 011 33 1 45264141.

FR/0015-9395
FRANCAIS DANS LE MONDE, LE. [Fr. monde]. Vol. 1 (May 1961)-. Periodical. French. Eight times a year. 480.00F (institution); 375.00 (individual). **LC** PC2065; .F7. cum. index. available on microfilm and microfiche from University Microfilms International (UMI).
Desc: Some numbers include phonorecords.
Ind/Abst Curr. Index J. Educ.; Lang. Teach.; MLA Int. Bibl. Books Artic. Mod. Lang. Lit.; Romant. Move.; Soc. Plann. Policy Dev. Abstr.; Sociol. Abstr.

FR/0015-9409
FRANCAIS MODERNE, LE. [Fr. mod.]. Vol. 1 (June 1933)-. Periodical. French. Twice a year (Both issues in July). 200.00F France; 250.00F others. Conseil Internationale de Langue Francaise, 11 rue de Navarin, 75009 Paris France. **Tel** 11 33 1 48787395. **LC** PC2002; .F73. **DD** 440/.5. available on microfilm. Documents available from The Genuine Article.
Ind/Abst Arts Humanit. Citation Index [Full Cov.]; Curr. Contents Arts Humanit.; Lang. Teach.; MLA Int. Bibl. Books Artic. Mod. Lang. Lit.; Res. Alert [Full Cov.]; Romant. Move.

FR/0222-0334
FRANCE LATINE, LA. (1954)-. Periodical. Multiple languages. ir. 110.00F France; $23.21 US. Edite par I L L O, 16 rue de la Sorbonne, 75005 Paris France. **Tel** 011 33 1 40462744. **UDC** 840.
Ind/Abst MLA Int. Bibl. Books Artic. Mod. Lang. Lit.

FR/1157-3740
FRANCIS BULLETIN SIGNALETIQUE. 524, SCIENCES DU LANGAGE. **Added/Corp** Institut de l'Information Scientifique et Technique (France). **VFOAT** Sciences du Langage; Linguistics. Vol. 45, No. 1 (1991)-. Bulletin. French. qt (4 issues). 495.00F France; 525.00F other. CNRS / Institut d'Information Scientifique et Technique, (Centre National de la Recherche Scientifique), 15 Quai Anatole France, Paris 75700 France. **Tel** 011 33 1 47531515, telex 299 356 F. **(Subscription address:** Institut d'Information Scientifique et Technique Diffusion, 2 Allee du Parc de Brabois, 54514 Vandoeuvre Nancy France.**) LC** Z7003; .B84. Index available (free). available on CD-ROM.
Continues *Bulletin Signaletique. 524, Sciences du Langage, 0007-5590.*

UK/0952-8571
FRANCO-BRITISH STUDIES : JOURNAL OF THE BRITISH INSTITUTE IN PARIS. **Added/Corp** British Institute in Paris. **VFOAT** Franco British Studies. No. 1 (Spring 1986)-. Periodical. English (French). sa. Office of the British Institute in Paris, 15 Woburn Square, London WC1H 0NS England.
Ind/Abst MLA Int. Bibl. Books Artic. Mod. Lang. Lit.; Soc. Plann. Policy Dev. Abstr.

UK/0957-1744
FRANCOPHONIE RUGBY. [Francophonie Rugby]. **Added/Corp** Association for Language Learning. (1990)-. Periodical. Multiple languages (English and French). Twice a year (June & Dec.). £20.00 UK; $40.00, £21.00 other. Association for Language Learning, 16 Regent Place, Rugby Warwickshire CV21 2PN England. **Tel** 011 44 788 546443, FAX 011 44 788 544149. **ED** Alan Smalley (editor's address: 10 Holt Park Way, Leeds, LS16 7QR England). **DD** 448.005. **Bk Rev. Ad Acc. Pr Rev.**
Desc: Contains articles, reviews and information of specific interest to students and teachers of particular languages.

GW/0071-9226
FRANKFURTER BEITRAEGE ZUR GERMANISTIK. [Frankf. Beitr. Ger.]. Vol. 1 (1967)-. Monographic series. German (English). ir. Price varies per volume. Universitatsverlag Carl Winter, POB 106140, D 69051 Heidelberg Germany. **Tel** 011 49 6221 770260. **DD** 830. **Circ:** 400-800.
Ind/Abst MLA Int. Bibl. Books Artic. Mod. Lang. Lit.

GW/0016-0970
FREMDSPRACHEN. ***Ceased.*** [Fremdsprachen]. (Fall 1957)-(19??). Periodical. German. qt. Deutscher Judo Verband, Redaktion Ippon Segewaldweg 40, D 12557 Berlin Germany. **Tel** 011 49 711 210770, telex 051 678. **UDC** 800.73.
Ind/Abst MLA Int. Bibl. Books Artic. Mod. Lang. Lit.

GW/0932-6936
FREMDSPRACHEN LEHREN UND LERNEN. **VFOAT** FLuL. (1987)-. German (English, French and Spanish). Chapman & Hall, 2-6 Boundary Row, London SE1 8HN England. **Tel** 011 44 71 865 0066, FAX 011 44 71 522 9623, telex 290164 Chapmag.
Continues *Bielefelder Beitreage zur Sprachlehrforschung, 0172-3510.*

GW/0340-2207
FREMDSPRACHLICHE UNTERRICHT, DER. [Fremdsprachl. Unterr.]. Periodical. German. bm (with one annual supplement). DM79.00 Germany; DM81.40 other. Erhard Friedrich Verlag, Postfach 100150, D 30917 Seelze Germany. **Tel** 011 49 511 4000452. **LC** PB35; .F75. **UDC** 800.73.
Desc: Educators' journal focusing on the teaching of foreign languages.
Ind/Abst Lang. Teach.

US/0275-4436
FRENCH-ENGLISH TRANSLATORS EXCHANGE. (FRENCH-ENGLISH TRANSLATORS EXCHANGE : FETX.). [Fr.-Engl. transl. exch.]. **VFOAT**

FETX. **VAT** French English Translators Exchange. 1 (Jan. - Feb. 1981)- = Vol. 1, No. 1-. Periodical. English. bm. $20.00. Translation Research Institute, 5914 Pulaski Avenue, Philadelphia PA 19144. **UDC** 802.0-073; 804.0-073.

US
FRENCH FORUM MONOGRAPHS. See Literature.

AT
FRENCH MONOGRAPHS. English (French). ir (annually). 7.50Aus$. Macquarie University, School of Modern Languages, North Ryde New South Wales 2113 Sydney Australia. **Tel** (02)805-7000, FAX (02)805-7054. **ED** Angus Martin. **LC** DC1; .F695. **DD** 944. ***Supersedes*** *Monographs for Teachers of French.*
Ind/Abst Romant. Move.

US/0016-111X
FRENCH REVIEW, THE. [Fr. rev.]. **Added/Corp** American Association of Teachers of French. Vol. 1 (Nov. 1927)-. Periodical. English (French). Six times a year (Feb., Mar., Apr., May, Oct., Dec.). $35.00 (six issues), $70.00 (twelve issues) US; $38.00 (six issues), $76.00 (twelve issues), other. American Association of Teachers of French, National Office, 57 East Armory Avenue, Champaign IL 61820. **ED** Ronald Tobin. **LC** PC2001; .F75. **DD** 440/.5. cum. index. **Bk Rev. Ad Acc. Circ:** 10,000 (individuals), 1,200 (library) (ctrl). available on microfiche from University Microfilms International (UMI); available on microfilm from Johnson Associates. Documents available from The Genuine Article.
Desc: French language, literature, pedagogy at all levels of the profession. Reviews of French novels, poetry, textbooks, linguistics, civilization and films plus relevant advertisements and announcements.
Ind/Abst Arts Humanit. Citation Index [Full Cov.]; BHA : Biblio. Hist. Art; Book Rev. Index; Curr. Index J. Educ.; Educ. Index; Lang. Teach.; MLA Int. Bibl. Books Artic. Mod. Lang. Lit.; Res. Alert [Full Cov.]; Soc. Plann. Policy Dev. Abstr.; Soc. Sci. Cit. Index [Select. Cov.]; Sociol. Abstr.

UK/0262-2750
FRENCH STUDIES BULLETIN. See Literature.

FA/0367-1704
FRODSKAPARRIT. (FRODSKAPARRIT; ANNALES SOCIETATIS SCIENTIARUM FAEROENSIS.). [Frodskaparrit]. (1952)-. Faroese.
Ind/Abst MLA Int. Bibl. Books Artic. Mod. Lang. Lit.

CH/1015-0021
FU JEN STUDIES : LITERATURE & LINGUISTICS. [Fu jen stud. lit. linguist.]. **Added/Corp** Fu Jen ta Hsueh, Hsin-Chuang Chen, Taiwan. Fu Jen ta Hsueh, Hsin-Chuang Chen, Taiwan. Wai yu Hsueh Yuan. No. 6 (1973)-. Academic Scholarly Publication. English (German, Spanish and French). an. NT$200.00 Taiwan; $10.00 other. Fu Jen University, College of Foreign Languages, 24205 Hsinchuang Taipei Taiwan. **Tel** (02)903-1111, FAX (886)02-9014733. **ED** Heliena Krenn. **LC** P1; .F8. **DD** 410/.5. Index available. cum. index. **Bk Rev**, (Qty: 1). **Pr Rev. Circ:** 300. ***Supersedes in part*** *Fu Jen Studies: Natural Sciences & Foreign Languages.*
Desc: Publishes articles on literature and linguistics with emphasis on exchange between China and the West.
Ind/Abst MLA Int. Bibl. Books Artic. Mod. Lang. Lit.

NE/0929-9998
FUNCTIONS OF LANGUAGE. (19??)-. Periodical. English. sa. $86.00. John Benjamins BV, Amsteldijk 44, PO Box 75577, 1070 AN Amsterdam Netherlands. **Tel** 011 31 20 6738156, FAX 011 31 20 739773. **(Subscription address:** John Benjamins North America, PO Box 27519, Philadelphia PA 19118-0519.) **ED** Kristin Davidse, Dirk Noel, Anne-Marie Simon-Vandenbergen.
Desc: Explores the functional perspective to the study of language-as-system and of texts-in-context. Discusses theoretical issues and areas of linguistic description relevant to the linguistic community at large.

JA/0425-4929
FURANSUGO FURANSU BUNGAKU KENKYU. Added/Corp Nihon Furansugo Furansu Bungakkai. **VFOAT** Etudes de Langue et Litterature Francaises. (1962)-. Periodical. Japanese. **LC** PC2009; .F865.
Ind/Abst MLA Int. Bibl. Books Artic. Mod. Lang. Lit.

SP
GACETA LITERARIA. No. 1- May 1973-. Periodical. Spanish. Apartado 40.001, Madrid Spain. **LC** P9; .G32. **UDC** 860.

JA
GAIKOKUGO GAIKOKU BUNGAKU KENKYU. ***Title Change.*** **Added/Corp** HokkaidÂo Daigaku. Bungakubu. **VFOAT** Essays in Foreign Languages and Literatures. (19??)-(19??). Multiple languages (English, French, German and Japanese). Hokkaido Daigaku, Kita 12-jo Nishi 6-chome Kita-ku, Sapporo Japan. **LC** P9; .G343. ***Continued by*** *Gengo Bunkabu Kiyo.*
Ind/Abst MLA Int. Bibl. Books Artic. Mod. Lang. Lit.

JA
GAKUJUTSU KENKYU : GAIKOKUGO GAIKOKU BUNGAKU HEN. VFOAT Scientific Researches. 24- 1975-. Multiple languages (Japanese and English). an. Waseda Daigaku Kyoikugakubu, 1-6-1 Nishi Waseda Shinjuku-ku, Tokyo Japan. **LC** P9; .G345. **UDC** 809.56. ***Supersedes*** *Gakujutsu Kenkyu: Sogohen.*

II
GALPAGUCCHA. Periodical. Bengali. qt. Rs25.00. Hiralal Chakravarti, 64 Sitaram Ghosh Street, Calcutta 700009 India. **Tel** 528320. **LC** PK1712; .G293. **Bk Rev. Ad Acc. Circ:** 2,500.

US
GDR BULLETIN: NEWSLETTER FOR LITERATURE AND CULTURE IN THE GERMAN DEMOCRATIC REPUBLIC. Vol. 1 (Apr. 1975)-. Newsletter. English (German). sa (Apr., Oct.). $5.00 (individuals); $15.00 (institutions). GDR Bulletin, Box 1104, Department of Germanic Languages, St Louis MO 63130. **Tel** (314)933-5106. **ED** Brigitte Rossbacher. **Bk Rev**, (Qty: 25). **Circ:** 350 (ctrl).

UK
GEIRIADUR, Y. VFOAT Dictionary of the Welsh Language. English. ir. University of Wales Press, 6 Gwennyth Street, Cathays Cardiff CF2 4YD Wales United Kingdom. **Tel** 011 44 222 231919.

JA/0431-1213
GENDAI YOGO NO KISO CHISHIKI. Added/Corp Jiyu Kokuminsha. **VFOAT** Jiyu Kokumin: Jitenban; Jiyu Kokumin: Tokuhetsugo. (1948)-. Periodical. Japanese. Jiyu Kokumin Sha, c/o Daiichi Seimei Bunkan, 8 Kyobashi-2 Chuo-ku, Tokyo Japan. **LC** PL684; .G38.

US/0016-6553
GENERAL LINGUISTICS. [Gen. linguist.]. **Added/Corp** University of Kentucky. Dept. of Modern Foreign Languages. State University of New York at Binghamton. Medieval & Renaissance Texts & Studies. Vol. 1 (Winter 1955)-. Periodical. English. qt (Jan., Apr., July, Oct.). $38.00 (one year), $100.00 (three year) institutions US; $22.00 (one year), $60.00 (three year) individuals US; $45.00 (one year), $120.00 (three year) institutions other; $28.00 (one year), $80.00 (three year) individuals other. State University of New York / Binghamton, MRTS - LN G99, Binghamton NY 13902. **Tel** (607)777-6758, FAX (607)777-2408. **DD** 410. cum. index. available on microfilm from University Microfilms International (UMI).
Ind/Abst Abstr. Anthropol.; Am. Bibliogr. Slavic East Europ. Stud.; Annu. Bibliogr. Engl. Lang. Lit.; Arts Humanit. Citation Index (19??-19??) [Full Cov.]; Lang. Teach.; Linguist. Lang. Behav. Abstr. (1972-) [Full Cov.]; Middle East Abstr. Index; MLA Int. Bibl. Books Artic. Mod. Lang. Lit.; Soc. Plann. Policy Dev. Abstr.

US/0072-0771
GENERAL SEMANTICS BULLETIN. [Gen. semant. bull.]. **Added/Corp** Lakeville, Conn. Institute of General Semantics. No. 1/2, (Autumn/Winter 1950)-. Bulletin. English. an. $15.00. Institute of General Semantics, 163 Engle Street, Apartment B4, Englewood NJ 07631. **Tel** (201)568-0551, FAX (201)569-1793. **LC** B820; .G4. **DD** 149.9; 190*. cum. index.
Ind/Abst Annu. Bibliogr. Engl. Lang. Lit.; Soc. Plann. Policy Dev. Abstr.; Sociol. Abstr.

JA
GENGO BUNKA KENKYU. VFOAT Studies in Language and Culture. 1- 1975-. Japanese (English; summaries and/or abstracts in Japanese, English, German and Russian). Osaka Baigaku Gengo Bunkabu, 1-1 Machikaneyama 560, Toyonaka Japan. **LC** P9; .G452. **UDC** 800; 908; 008.

JA/0286-2093
GENGO BUNKA KENKYU (MATSUYAMA-SHI, JAPAN). (GENGO BUNKA KENKYU.). **VFOAT** Studies in Language and Literature. Periodical. English (Japanese). sa. Matsuyama Shoka Daigaku Shokei Kenkyukai, 4-Banch 2 Bunkyo-cho, Matsuyama-shi Japan. **LC** P9; .G4523. **UDC** 800; 82.

JA
GENGO BUNKA RONSHU. Added/Corp Tsukuba Daigaku. Gendaigo Gendai Bunka Gakukei. **VFOAT** Gengobunka Ronshu; Studies in Languages and Cultures. No. 1 (1977)-. English (German and Japanese). Tsukuba Daigaku, 1-1 Tennodai 1-Chome Sakuramura Niihari-gun, Ibaraki-Ken 305 Japan. **LC** PB5; .G43. **DD** 405.

JA/0286-3855
GENGO BUNKABU KIYO. VFOAT Language and Culture. Vol. 1-. Periodical. English (French, Japanese and Russian). Hokkaido Daigaku, Kita 12-jo Nishi 6-chome Kita-ku, Sapporo Japan. **LC** P9; .G343 . **DD** 410/.5. **UDC** 800; 908; 008. ***Continues*** *Gaikokugo Gaikoku Bungaku Kenkyu.*
Ind/Abst MLA Int. Bibl. Books Artic. Mod. Lang. Lit.

JA
GENGO KENKYU. Added/Corp Nihon Gengo Gakkai. **VFOAT** Journal of the Linguistic Society of Japan. (1939)-. Periodical. Japanese. sa. $121.00. **(Subscription address:** Japan Publications Trading Company, Ltd., PO Box 5030, Tokyo International, Tokyo 100-31 Japan.)
Ind/Abst MLA Int. Bibl. Books Artic. Mod. Lang. Lit.; Soc. Plann. Policy Dev. Abstr.; Sociol. Abstr.

JA
GENGO NO KAGAKU. VFOAT Sciences of Language: The Journal of the Tokyo Institute for Advanced Studies of Language. No. 1- ; 1970-. Multiple languages (Japanese and English). Tokyo Gengo Kenkyujo, c/o Rebo Senta Building 4-5, Nishi Shijuku 8, Shijuku-ku 160, Tokyo Japan. **LC** P9; .G45. **UDC** 800.

JA
GENJI MONOGATARI NO TANKYU. Added/Corp Genji Monogatari Tankyukai. Shigematsu Nobuhiro Hakushi Shojukai. No. 1 (1974)-. Periodical. Japanese. Kazama Shobo Showa, 1-34 Kanda Jimbocho Chiyoda-ku, Tokyo Japan. **LC** PL788.4.Z5; G43.

US/0190-4671
GEOLINGUISTICS. [Geolinguistics]. **Added/Corp** American Society of Geolinguistics. (1974)-. English. an. $25.00. Dr William C Wooflson, Bronx Community College, Bronx NY 10453. **LC** P130; .G46. **DD** 409.
Desc: Covers areal linguistics.
Ind/Abst Linguist. Lang. Behav. Abstr. (1977-) [Full Cov.]; MLA Int. Bibl. Books Artic. Mod. Lang. Lit.; Soc. Plann. Policy Dev. Abstr.

US/1048-4205
GEORGETOWN JOURNAL OF LANGUAGES & LINGUISTICS, THE. ***Ceased.*** [Georget. j. lang. linguist.]. **Added/Corp** Georgetown University. School of Languages and Linguistics. **VFOAT** Georgetown Journal of Languages and Linguistics; Languages & Linguistics; Languages and Linguistics. Vol. 1, No. 1 (Winter 1990)-Vol. 3. Periodical. English. qt. Georgetown University School of Languages and Linguistics, 37 & O Street, Room 303, Washington DC 20057. **Tel** (202)687-6063. **LC** P1; .G46. **DD** 410/.5. **CODEN** GJLLEJ.
Ind/Abst Curr. Index J. Educ.; Linguist. Lang. Behav. Abstr. (1990-) [Full Cov.]; Soc. Plann. Policy Dev. Abstr.

US/0196-7207
GEORGETOWN UNIVERSITY ROUND TABLE ON LANGUAGES AND LINGUISTICS. [Georget. Univ. Round Table Lang. Linguist.]. **Main/Conf** Georgetown University Round Table on Languages and Linguistics. **Added/Corp** Georgetown University. School of Languages and Linguistics. **VFOAT** G.U.R.T., Georgetown University Round Table on Languages and Linguistics; GURT, Georgetown University Round Table on Languages and Linguistics. (1973)-. English. an. $35.00. Georgetown University School of Languages and Linguistics, 37 & O Street, Room 303, Washington DC 20057. **Tel** (202)687-6063. **LC** P53; .G39a. **DD** 410/.5. ***Continues*** *Report of the Annual Round Table Meeting on Linguistics and Language Studies, 0072-1212.*
Ind/Abst Linguist. Lang. Behav. Abstr. (1972-) [Full Cov.]; MLA Int. Bibl. Books Artic. Mod. Lang. Lit.; Soc. Plann. Policy Dev. Abstr.

NE/0378-4150
GERMAN LANGUAGE AND LITERATURE MONOGRAPHS. ***Ceased.*** **See** Literature.

II
GERMAN STUDIES IN INDIA. Added/Corp University of Kerala. Dept. of German. Vol. 3, No. 1/2 (Mar./June 1979)-. Periodical. German (English). qt. $10.00. University of Kerala Department of German, Trivandrum, India. **(Subscription address:** Prints India, 11 Darya Ganj, New Delhi 110002 India.) ***Continues*** *Indo-German.*

UK/0953-4822
GERMAN TEACHING. [Ger. teach.]. **Added/Corp** Association of Teachers of German. (1988)-. Periodical. Multiple languages. Twice a year (June & Dec.). £20.00 UK; $40.00, £21.00 other (Comes with Association of Language Learning membership). Association for Language Learning, 16 Regent Place, Rugby Warwickshire CV21 2PN England. **Tel** 011 44 788 546443, FAX 011 44 788 544149. **ED** Alistair Brien. **DD** 430.71. **Bk Rev. Ad Acc. Pr Rev.** ***Continues*** *Treffpunkt (London), 0265-8097.*
Desc: Contains articles, reviews and information of specific interest to students and teachers of particular languages.
Ind/Abst Br. Educ. Index.

GW/0016-8904
GERMANISCH-ROMANISCHE MONATSSCHRIFT. [Ger.-Rom. Monatsschr.]. Vol. 1 (Jan. 1909)-. Periodical. German (English and French). qt (4 issues). DM165.20 Germany; DM170.00 other. Universitatsverlag Carl Winter, POB 106140, D 69051 Heidelberg Germany. **Tel** 011 49 6221 770260. **ED** Conrad Wiedemann. **LC** PB3; .G3. Index available (free). cum. index. **Bk Rev. Circ:** 1,000. Documents available from The Genuine Article.
Desc: Covers Germanic and Romance philology.

Ind/Abst Annu. Bibliogr. Engl. Lang. Lit.; Arts Humanit. Citation Index [Full Cov.]; BHA : Biblio. Hist. Art; Curr. Contents Arts Humanit.; MLA Int. Bibl. Books Artic. Mod. Lang. Lit.; Res. Alert [Full Cov.]; Romant. Move.; Soc. Plann. Policy Dev. Abstr.; Sociol. Abstr. (?-?).

GW/0524-8414
GERMANISTIK (BERLIN). (GERMANISTIK.). German (English). sa. DM13.30. Werbegemeinschaft Elwert und Meurer GmbH, Berlin 62 Germany. **Tel** 030 784001. **LC** Z7037; .G47; PF3071. **DD** 016.43. **UDC** 803(01); 830(01). **Ad Acc. Circ:** 5,000.
Desc: Bibliography of new or recent publications, corresponding the themes linguistics and literature.

GW/0016-8912
GERMANISTIK (TUEBINGEN). See Linguistics-Abstracting, Bibliographies and Statistics.

GW/0435-5903
GERMANISTISCHE ABHANDLUNGEN (STUTTGART). (GERMANISTISCHE ABHANDLUNGEN.). [Ger. Abh.]. (1962)-. Monographic series. German. ir. Price varies per volume. J. B. Metzlersche Verlagsbuchhandling, Kernerstrasse 10 32 41, D-70028 Stuttgart Germany. **Tel** 011 49 711 22902-14, FAX 011 49 711 22902-90. **UDC** 830. **Bk Rev. Ad Acc.** ctrl circ.
Desc: Topics from all periods of German literature. Style, biography, sociological influences and literary currents are considered.
Ind/Abst MLA Int. Bibl. Books Artic. Mod. Lang. Lit.

GW
GERMANISTISCHE ARBEITSHEFTE. Vol. 1 (1970)-. Monographic series. German. ir. Price varies per volume. Max Niemeyer Verlag, Postfach 2140, D 72011 Tuebingen Germany. **Tel** 011 49 7071 989494, FAX 011 49 7071 87419. **ED** Franz Hundsnurscher, Otmar Werner.
Desc: Textbooks in Germanic linguistics for students of German.

GW/0072-1492
GERMANISTISCHE LINGUISTIK. (GERMANISTISCHE LINGUISTIK : BERICHTE AUS DEM FORSCHUNGSINSTITUT FUER DEUTSCHE SPRACHE DEUTSCHER SPRACHATLAS.). [Germ. Linguist.]. **Added/Corp** Philipps-Universitat Marburg. Forschungsinstitut fuer Deutsche Sprache "Deutscher Sprachatlas.". Vol. 1, (1969)-. Monographic series. German. ir. Price varies per volume. Georg Olms Verlag AG Weidmann, Hagentorwall 6 7, D 31134 Hildesheim Germany. **Tel** 011 49 5121 15010, telex 927454 OLMS D. **(Subscription address:** VVA Bertelsmann Distributors GmbH, Postfach 7777, D-33310 Guetersloh Germany.**)** **LC** PF3025; .G37. **[CCC]. Ad Acc.**
Ind/Abst Lang. Teach.

BE/0771-3703
GERMANISTISCHE MITTEILUNGEN. [Ger. Mitt.]. **Added/Corp** Belgischer Germanisten- und Deutschlehrerverband. (1975)-. Periodical. German. sa. 49.00F. Ferdinand Dummler Verlag, Postfach 1480, D 53004 Bonn Germany. **Tel** 011 49 228 223031. **ED** P.H. Nelde. **LC** PF3068.B4; G47. **Bk Rev. Ad Acc. Circ:** 1,000.
Desc: German language and literature.
Ind/Abst MLA Int. Bibl. Books Artic. Mod. Lang. Lit.; Soc. Plann. Policy Dev. Abstr.

SW/0435-5911
GERMANISTISCHE SCHRIFTENREIHE DER NORWEGISCHEN UNIVERSITATEN UND HOCHSCHULEN. No. 1 (1963)-. Monographic series. German. ir. Price varies per volume. Scandinavian University Press, PO Box 2959 Toeyen, N 0608 Oslo 6 Norway. **Tel** 011 47 2 2575400, FAX 011 47 2 2575353, telex 71896 UROR N. **(Subscription address:** Scandinavian University Press, 200 Meacham Ave., Elmont NY 11003.**)**

GW/0175-9388
GERMANISTISCHE TEXTE UND STUDIEN. [Ger. Texte Stud.]. (1975)-. Monographic series. German.
Ind/Abst MLA Int. Bibl. Books Artic. Mod. Lang. Lit.

RU
GERTSENOVSKIE CHTENIIA: INOSTRANNYE IAZYKI. Main/Corp Leningrad. Gosudarstvennyi Pedagogicheskii Institut Imeni A.I. Gertsena. **VFOAT** Inostrannye Iazyki. (19??)-. Russian. **LC** P9; .L42.

BE/0776-4111
GEZELLIANA. Added/Corp Universitaire Faculteiten St.-Ignatius. (1989)-. Periodical. Dutch. sa. ***Formed by the union of** Gezelliana **and** Gezellekroniek.*
Ind/Abst MLA Int. Bibl. Books Artic. Mod. Lang. Lit.

IT/0017-0461
GIORNALE ITALIANO DI FILOLOGIA. Vol. 1 (Feb. 1948)-. Periodical. Italian (Latin and Greek, Modern). Twice a year (May, & Nov.). L63000. Herder Editrice e Libreria SRL, Piazza Montecitorio 117-120, 00186 Rome Italy. **Tel** 011 39 6 679 4628, FAX 011 39 6 678 4751. **ED** Nino Scivoletto. **LC** P9; .G55. Index available (Bound in last issue.). **Circ:** 1,000 (ctrl).
Desc: Serious contribution to scientific research in textual criticism, literary exegesis, historical reconstruction and cultural investigation.
Ind/Abst MLA Int. Bibl. Books Artic. Mod. Lang. Lit.; Romant. Move.

US
GLAS KANADSKIH SRBA. VFOAT Voice of Canadian Serbs. Began with Dec. 27, 1934 issue. Periodical. Serbo-Croatian (Cyrillic). wk. $23.21. Avala Printing Publishing Company, 1297 Drovillard Road, Windsor 15 Ontario N8Y 2R6 Canada. **LC** F1035.S47. **UDC** 808.6.

FR
GLOSSA / LES CAHIERS DE L'UNADRIO. French. Glossa, Svc Abonnement Admin, 76 rue Jean Jaures, 62330 Isbergues France.

US/0072-4750
GLOSSARIA INTERPRETUM. Vol. 1 (1957)-. English. ir. Elsevier Science Publishing Company Inc, Madison Square Station, PO Box 882, New York NY 10159-0882. **Tel** (212)633-3950, FAX (212)633-3990. **DD** 413.

NE/0166-5790
GLOT. ***Ceased.*** **VFOAT** G.L.O.T. (197?)-Vol. 12, No. 3. Periodical. Dutch. tq. Foris Publications, PO Box 509, 3300 AM Dordrecht Netherlands. **Tel** 011 31 78 510454. **[CCC].**
Ind/Abst Annu. Bibliogr. Engl. Lang. Lit.; Linguist. Lang. Behav. Abstr. (1983-); Soc. Plann. Policy Dev. Abstr.

CK/0120-6516
GLOTTA. Added/Corp Instituto Meyer (Bogota, Colombia). Vol. 1, No. 1 (1986)-. Periodical. Spanish. tq. Instituto Meyer, Glotta, Apartado Aereo 43789, Bogota D E Colombia. **LC** P9; .G58. **DD** 410/.5.
Ind/Abst MLA Int. Bibl. Books Artic. Mod. Lang. Lit.

GW/0017-1298
GLOTTA (GOTTINGEN). (GLOTTA; ZEITSCHRIFT FUER GREICHISCHE UND LATEINISCHE SPRACHE.). [Glotta]. Vol. 1 (1909)-. Periodical. Multiple languages. ir (2 doubles issues per volume). DM98.00. Vandenhoeck & Ruprecht, Robert Bosch Breite 6, D-37079 Goettingen Germany. **Tel** 011 49 551 695911, FAX 011 49 551 695917, telex 965226 VAN d. **ED** Paul Kretschmer and Wilhelm Kroll. **LC** PA3; .G5. **[CCC].** Documents available from The Genuine Article.
Ind/Abst Arts Humanit. Citation Index (19??-19??) [Full Cov.]; Curr. Contents Arts Humanit.; MLA Int. Bibl. Books Artic. Mod. Lang. Lit.; Res. Alert [Full Cov.].

PL/0072-4769
GLOTTODIDACTICA. [Glottodidactica]. **Added/Corp** Uniwersytet im. Adama Mickiewicza w Poznaniu. Instytut Jezykoznawstwa. Vol. 1 (1966)-. Multiple languages. ir. $8.00. **(Subscription address:** ARS Polona, PO Box 1001, 00068 Warsaw Poland.**)**
Ind/Abst Lang. Teach.; Linguist. Lang. Behav. Abstr. (1972-) [Full Cov.]; MLA Int. Bibl. Books Artic. Mod. Lang. Lit.; Soc. Plann. Policy Dev. Abstr.

GW/0932-7991
GLOTTOMETRIKA. (1978)-. Periodical. English (French and German). Studienverlag Dr N Brockmeyer, Querenburger Hohe 283, W-4630 Bochum Germany. **LC** P138; .G59. **DD** 410/.72.
Ind/Abst Linguist. Lang. Behav. Abstr. (1978-) [Full Cov.]; Soc. Plann. Policy Dev. Abstr.

GW/0017-1417
GNOMON (MUNCHEN). (GNOMON.). [Gnomon]. Vol. 1 (1925)-. Periodical. German (English and French). Eight times a year. CH Beck Verlagsbuchhandlung, D 80791 Munich Germany. **Tel** 011 49 89 381891. **LC** PA3; .G6. **[CCC].** Documents available from The Genuine Article.
Ind/Abst Arts Humanit. Citation Index [Full Cov.]; BHA : Biblio. Hist. Art; MLA Int. Bibl. Books Artic. Mod. Lang. Lit.; Res. Alert [Full Cov.]; Soc. Sci. Cit. Index [Select. Cov.].

GW/0179-1834
GOPPINGER ARBEITEN ZUR GERMANISTIK. [Gopp. Arb. Ger.]. No. 1 (1968)-. Monographic series. German. ir (20 issues). Price varies per volume. Verlag Alfred Kummerle, Staibengasse 1, W 7073 Lorch FR Germany. **Tel** 011 49 7172 4844.
Ind/Abst MLA Int. Bibl. Books Artic. Mod. Lang. Lit.

SW/0072-4793
GOTEBORGER GERMANISTISCHE FORSCHUNGEN. Vol. 1 (1955)-. Monographic series. German. Price varies per volume. Scandinavian University Press, PO Box 2959 Toeyen, N 0608 Oslo 6 Norway. **Tel** 011 47 2 2575400, FAX 011 47 2 2575353, telex 71896 UROR N. **(Subscription address:** Scandinavian University Press, 200 Meacham Ave., Elmont NY 11003.**)** **DD** 439.
Ind/Abst MLA Int. Bibl. Books Artic. Mod. Lang. Lit.

NE
GRAMMA / TTT. Dutch. Foris Publications, PO Box 509, 3300 AM Dordrecht Netherlands. **Tel** 011 31 78 510454. ***Continues** Interdisciplinair Tijdschrift voor Taal en Tekstwetenschap.*
Ind/Abst Soc. Plann. Policy Dev. Abstr.

FR
GRAMMATICA (TOULOUSE, FRANCE). (GRAMMATICA.). 1- 1972-. French. 38.00F. Universite de Toulouse-Le Miral, Services des Publications, 4 rue Albert-Lautman, 31070 Toulouse France. **LC** PC2002; .G7. **UDC** 804.0-5.

GW/0436-2829
GRAMMATICA UNIVERSALIS. Vol. 1 (1966)-. German. Friedrich Frommann Verlag, Koenig Karlstrasse 27, D 70372 Stuttgart 50 Germany. **Tel** 011 49 711 9559690. **DD** 400.

IT
GRANDE DIZIONARIO DELLA LINGUA ITALIANA. REDAZIONE, DIRETTORE: GIORGIO BARBERI SQUAROTTI. (1961)-. Monographic series. Italian. ir. Price varies per volume. Licosa Spa, PO Box 552, 50125 Florence Italy. **Tel** 011 39 55 645415. **LC** PC1625; .B3.

AU/0376-5253
GRAZER BEITRAEGE. [Grazer beitr.]. Vol. 1- 1973-. English (German, Italian and French). an. S890.00. Editions Rodopi BV, Keizersgracht 302-304, 1016 Ex Amsterdam Netherlands. **Tel** 011 31 20 6227507, FAX 011 31 20 380948. **LC** PA1.A1; G7. Index available. **Bk Rev.** ctrl circ.
Ind/Abst MLA Int. Bibl. Books Artic. Mod. Lang. Lit.

AU/1015-0498
GRAZER LINGUISTISCHE STUDIEN. [Grazer linguist. Stud.]. **Added/Corp** Universitaat Graz. Institut fuer Allgemeine und Angewandte Sprachwissenschaft. Universitaat Graz. Institut fuer Sprachwissenschaft. **VFOAT** GLS. (Feb. 1, 1975)-. Monographic series. German (English, French and German). ir. Price varies per volume. Institut f Sprachwissenschaft, Mozartgasse 8, A 8010 Graz Austria. **Tel** 011 43 316 2802415. **LC** P1.A1; G73. **DD** 410/.5. **CODEN** GLSTEO.
Ind/Abst Linguist. Lang. Behav. Abstr. (1983-) [Full Cov.]; MLA Int. Bibl. Books Artic. Mod. Lang. Lit.; Soc. Plann. Policy Dev. Abstr.

NE/0924-655X
GRONINGER ARBEITEN ZUR GERMANISTISCHEN LINGUISTIK. [Gron. Arb. ger. Linguist.]. (1972)-. Monographic series. German. ir. **UDC** 803.0.
Ind/Abst MLA Int. Bibl. Books Artic. Mod. Lang. Lit.

GW/0533-3350
GRUNDLAGEN DER GERMANISTIK. [Grundl. Ger.]. Vol. 1 (1966)-. Monographic series. German. ir. Price varies per volume. Erich Schmidt Verlag GmbH, Postfach 304240, D 10724 Berlin Germany. **Tel** 011 49 30 25008525. **Bk Rev. Ad Acc.**
Desc: Studies on the German philology.
Ind/Abst MLA Int. Bibl. Books Artic. Mod. Lang. Lit.

JA
GRUNDRISS DER SLAVISCHEN PHILOLOGIE UND KULTURGESCHICHTE. German. ir. Walter de Gruyter Inc. / Hawthorne, 200 Saw Mill River Road, Hawthorne NY 10532. **Tel** (914)747-0110, GERMANY: 011/49/30/260050, FAX (914)747-1326, telex 646677. **(Subscription address:** Germany/ PO Box 110240, 1 Berlin 11**)**

●CN/1187-922X
GUIDE DES MEMBRES DE LA STQ. [Guide memb. STQ]. **Main/Corp** Translators' Society of Quebec. **VFOAT** Guide des Membres de la Societe des Traducteurs du Quebec. (1991/1992)-. English (French). Free to members. Societe des Traducteurs du Quebec, 1010 rue St Catherine Ouest/Bureau 540, Montreal Quebec H3B 1G4 Canada. **Tel** (514)861-1783, FAX (514)861-8117. **DD** 418.

●CN/1187-922X
GUIDE DES MEMBRES DE LA STQ (FRENCH EDITION). [Guide memb. STQ]. **Main/Corp** Societe des Traducteurs du Quebec. **VFOAT** Guide des Membres de la Societe des Traducteurs du Quebec. (1991/1992)-. French (English). Free for members. Societe des Traducteurs du Quebec, 1010 rue St Catherine Ouest/Bureau 540, Montreal Quebec H3B 1G4 Canada. **Tel** (514)861-1783, FAX (514)861-8117. **DD** 418.

US/1041-5459
GUIDE TO GRANTS & FELLOWSHIPS IN LINGUISTICS. [Guide grants fellowsh. linguist.]. **Added/Corp** Linguistic Society of America. **VFOAT** Guide to Grants and Fellowships in Linguistics. (198?)-. English. ir (every 3 years). $6.50. Linguistic Society of America, 1325 18th Street Northwest, Washington DC 20036. **Tel** (202)835-1714. **LC** P53; .G78. **DD** 410.
***Continues** Guide to Grants & Fellowships in Languages & Linguistics.*

SI/0129-7767
GUIDELINES. **Added/Corp** Regional English Language Centre. No. 1 (June 1979)-. Periodical. English. Twice a year (June and Dec.). 14.00Sing$. Seameo Regional Language Center, 30 Orange Grove Road, Singapore 1025 Singapore. **Tel** 011 65 7379044, FAX 011 65 7342753. **CODEN** GUIDEN.
Ind/Abst Lang. Teach.

GW/0072-9582
HAMBURGER PHILOLOGISCHE STUDIEN. [Hambg. philol. Stud.]. (1962)-. Monographic series. German. ir. Price varies per volume. Helmut Buske Verlag Hamburg, Postfach 760244, D 2000 Hamburg 76 F R Germany. **Tel** 011 49 40 5236739. **Circ:** 400 (ctrl).
Desc: Linguistic and literary works on all languages in all modern languages.
Ind/Abst MLA Int. Bibl. Books Artic. Mod. Lang. Lit.

GW/0440-1727
HAMBURGER ROMANISTISCHE DISSERTATIONEN. [Hambg. rom. Diss.]. **Added/Corp** Universitat Hamburg. Romanisches Seminar. (1966)-. Monographic series. German.
Ind/Abst MLA Int. Bibl. Books Artic. Mod. Lang. Lit.

ZA
HANDBOOK / THE UNIVERSITY OF ZAMBIA, SCHOOL OF EDUCATION, DEPARTMENT OF LITERATURE & LANGUAGES. **Main/Corp** University of Zambia. Dept. of Literature & Languages. English. 0.50. University of Zambia Department of Literature and Languages, POB 32379, Lusaka Zambia. **LC** P59.U55; U54A. **DD** 407/.116894. **UDC** 800(073.8)(689.4).

GW
HANDBUCHER ZUR SPRACH- UND KOMMUNIKATIONSWISSENSCHAFT. (1982)-. Monographic series. German. Price varies per volume. Walter de Gruyter Inc., PO Box 303421, D 10728 Berlin Germany. **Tel** 011 49 30 260050, FAX 011 49 30 26005251. **(Subscription address:** US and Canada/ 200 Saw Mill River Road, Hawthorne, NY 10532**)**

BE/0774-3254
HANDELINGEN / KONINKLIJKE ZUIDNEDERLANDSE MAATSCHAPPIJ VOOR TAAL- EN LETTERKUNDE EN GESCHIEDENIS. [Handel. - K. Zuidned. Maatsch. taal- Lett.kd. geschied.]. **Added/Corp** Koninklijke Zuidnederlandse Maatschappij voor Taal- en Letterkunde en Geschiedenis (Belgium). (19??)-. Dutch (French). **LC** P9; .H2.
Ind/Abst MLA Int. Bibl. Books Artic. Mod. Lang. Lit.

AU
HANDES AMSORYA. (1887)-. Periodical. Armenian. ir. S1,065. Mechitharisten Congregation in Wein, Mechitharistengasse 4, 1070 Vienna VII Austria. **Tel** 011 43 1 936417, 011 43 1 9379092. **ED** Augustin Szekula.
Ind/Abst MLA Int. Bibl. Books Artic. Mod. Lang. Lit.; Numis. Lit.

US/1056-2680
HANDS-ON ENGLISH. [Hands-on Engl.]. **VFOAT** Hands on English. Vol. 1, No. 1 (May/June 1991)-. Periodical. English. Six times a year. $16.00 US; $20.00 Canada & Mexico; $26.00 others. Literacy Volunteers of America, 5795 Widewaters Parkway, Syracuse NY 13214. **Tel** (315)445-8000. **DD** 418.

US/0073-0688
HARVARD STUDIES IN CLASSICAL PHILOLOGY. See Classical Studies.

US/0363-5570
HARVARD UKRAINIAN STUDIES. See History(General)-History of Europe.

BG
HARVEST (DACCA, BANGLADESH). (HARVEST : AN ANNUAL OF THE DEPARTMENT OF ENGLISH, JAHANGIRNAGAR UNIVERSITY.). Vol. 3 (1978-79)-. English. an. **LC** PE9; .H37. **DD** 410/.5. **UDC** 802.0. ***Continues*** *Bulletin of the Department of English, Jahangirnagar University.*

FR
HAUT PARLEUR / JOURNAL DE VULGARISATION. (19??)-. Periodical. French. mo. 298.73F France; 415.00F other. Les Publ Georges Ventillard, 2 A 12 rue de Bellevue, 75019 Paris Cedex 19 France. **Tel** 011 33 1 44848484.

LE/0250-9970
HAWLIYAT FAR AL-ADAB AL-ARABIYAH. **Added/Corp** Universite Saint-Joseph (Beirut, Lebanon). Departement des Lettres Arabes. **VFOAT** Annales du Departement des Lettres Arabes. Journal 1, (1981)-. Periodical. Arabic. an. Jamiat Al-Qiddis Yusuf, SB 293, Beirut Lebanon. **LC** DS36; .H38

US/0193-7162
HEBREW ANNUAL REVIEW. ***Suspended.*** [Heb. annu. rev.]. **Added/Corp** Ohio State University. Division of Hebrew Language and Literature. Vol. 1 (1977)-(1991). English. an (Sept.). $38.00. Ohio State University / Hebrew Annual Review, 256 Cunz Hall, 1841 Milliken Road, Columbus OH 43210. **Tel** (614)292-5569 or 0967. **ED** Reuben Ahroni. **LC** PJ4501; .H43. **DD** 892.4/09. **Circ:** 750. available on microfilm from University Microfilms International (UMI).
Desc: Studies in the areas of Hebrew language, Hebrew literature, and methodology of teaching Hebrew.
Ind/Abst Index Book Rev. Relig.; Int. Bibliogr. Sociol.; MLA Int. Bibl. Books Artic. Mod. Lang. Lit.; Relig. Index One Period.; Relig. Theol. Abstr.; Soc. Plann. Policy Dev. Abstr.

GW/0170-8821
HEIDELBERGER BEITRAEGE ZUR ROMANISTIK. [Heidelb. Beitr. Rom.]. (1974)-. Monographic series. German. H Lang, Munzgraben 2, CH-3000 7 Bern Switzerland.
Ind/Abst MLA Int. Bibl. Books Artic. Mod. Lang. Lit.

GW/0440-6044
HEIDELBERGER FORSCHUNGEN. (1952)-. Monographic series. German. ir. Price varies per volume. Universitatsverlag Carl Winter, POB 106140, D 69051 Heidelberg Germany. **Tel** 011 49 6221 770260.
Ind/Abst MLA Int. Bibl. Books Artic. Mod. Lang. Lit.

IT/0017-9981
HELIKON (ROMA). (HELIKON; RIVISTA DI TRADIZIONE E CULTURA CLASSICA.). [Helikon]. **Added/Corp** Universita di Messina. Vol. 1 (1961)-. Italian. ir. Price varies. Herder Editrice e Libreria SRL, Piazza Montecitorio 117-120, 00186 Rome Italy. **Tel** 011 39 6 679 4628, FAX 011 39 6 678 4751.

US/0741-1286
HERMES AMERICANUS. [Hermes am.]. **Added/Corp** Academia Latina Danburiensis. Vol. 1, No. 1 (1983)-. Periodical. Latin. qt. $25.00 (individuals), $40.00 (libraries). Academia Latina Danburiensis, PO Box 322, Bethel CT 06801. **Tel** (203)744-1730, (203)731-2827. **ED** A P Dobsevose. **Bk Rev. Ad Acc. Pr Rev. Circ:** 400.

FR/0440-7237
HERNE, L'. See Philosophy.

US/0073-201X
HEUTIGES DEUTSCH. REIHE 1: LINGUISTISCHE GRUNDLAGEN. **VFOAT** Linguistische Grundlagen. V. 1- 1970-. Monographic series. German. ir. Price varies per volume. Adlers Foreign Books Inc, 915 Foster Street, Evanston IL 60201. **Tel** (312)866-6329, telex 256262 EURO PUB EVN. **UDC** 803.0-024.

NP
HIMALANGUE. Vol. 1 (Nov. 1973)-. English. Three times a year. $0.50 single issue. Basudev Sharma, 1/11 Bhotebahal, Kathmandu Nepal. **LC** P1; .H55. **DD** 410/.8.

II
HINDI PRAYOGA VARSHIKI KOSA. **Added/Corp** Uttara Pradesa Hindi Samsthana. (1978)-. Hindi. an. Rs25.00. Director of Uttar Pradesh Hindi Samsthan Rajarshi Purushottamdas, Tandon Hindi Bhavan Mahatma Gandhi Marg, Lucknow India. **LC** PK1939; .H52.

US/0018-2133
HISPANIA. [Hispania]. **Added/Corp** American Association of Teachers of Spanish and Portuguese. American Association of Teachers of Spanish. Vol. 1 (Feb. 1918)-. Academic Scholarly Publication. English (Portuguese and Spanish). qt (Mar., May, Sept., and Dec.). $30.00. American Association of Teachers of Spanish and Portuguese / University of Northern Colorado, 106 Gunter Hall, Greeley CO 80639. **Tel** (303)351-1090. **ED** Theodore Sackett. **LC** PC4001; .H7. **DD** 460/.5. (bound in Dec. issue). cum. index. **Bk Rev. Ad Acc. Circ:** 12,000 (ctrl). available on microfilm and microfiche from University Microfilms International (UMI). Documents available from The Genuine Article.
Desc: A scholarly journal devoted to the interests of the teaching of Spanish and Portuguese.
Ind/Abst Am. Hist. Life (1954-); Arts Humanit. Citation Index [Full Cov.]; Book Rev. Index; Curr. Contents Arts Humanit.; Curr. Index J. Educ.; Educ. Index; HAPI Hisp. Am. Period. Index; Lang. Teach.; MLA Int. Bibl. Books Artic. Mod. Lang. Lit.; Res. Alert [Full Cov.]; Soc. Plann. Policy Dev. Abstr.; Soc. Sci. Cit. Index [Select. Cov.].

UK
HISPANIC ARTICLES IN SCHOLARLY PERIODICALS : ANNUAL BIBLIOGRAPHY. (19??)-. Bibliography. English (Catalan, French, Portuguese and Spanish). £10.00 (institutions), £7.50 (individuals) subscribers UK; £15.00 non-subscribers UK; $22.00 (institutions), $15.00 (individuals) subscribers US; $30.00 non-subscribers US; Free to students. Liverpool University Press, PO Box 147, Liverpool L69 3BX England. **Tel** (051)794 2233, FAX (051)708 6502, telex 627095. **ED** Ann McKenzie. **LC** PC4001; .A23.
Desc: Includes articles of literary, linguistic or historical interest relating to cultures and civilizations of Spain, Portugal, and Latin America. Generally excluded are articles on current affairs, politics, education, the social sciences, economics, statistics, Amerindian languages, music and the visual arts.

US/0271-0986
HISPANIC JOURNAL. See Literature.

US/0742-5287
HISPANIC LINGUISTICS. [Hisp. linguist.]. **VFOAT** HL. Vol. 1, No. 1 (Spring 1984)-. Periodical. English (Spanish, Portuguese, Catalan and Gallegan). Twice a year (Spring and Fall). $18.00 (individuals), $30.00 (institutions). Prisma Institute, 3 Folwell, 9 Pleasant Street Southeast, Minneapolis MN 55455. **Tel** (612)625-9028, FAX (612)626-0532. **ED** Carol A. Klee. **LC** PC4001; .H74. **DD** 460/.5. **Bk Rev. Ad Acc. Pr Rev. Circ:** 300.
Ind/Abst Linguist. Lang. Behav. Abstr. (1984-) [Full Cov.]; MLA Int. Bibl. Books Artic. Mod. Lang. Lit.; Soc. Plann. Policy Dev. Abstr.

US/0018-2176
HISPANIC REVIEW. [Hisp. rev.]. **Added/Corp** Pennsylvania. University. Dept. of Romance Languages. Hispanic Society of America. Vol. 1 (Jan. 1933)-. Periodical. English (Spanish). Four times a year (Jan., Apr., July, Oct.). $25.00 (individuals); $35.00 (institutions). Hispanic Review, University of Pennsylvania, 152 Williams Hall, Philadelphia PA 19104-6305. **Tel** (215)898-7420. **ED** Russell P. Sebold. **LC** PQ6001; .H5. **DD** 460.5. Index available. cum. index. **Bk Rev. Ad Acc. Circ:** 1,500. available on microfilm and microfiche from University Microfilms International (UMI). Documents available from The Genuine Article, UMI Article Clearinghouse.
Desc: A journal devoted to research in the hispanic languages and literatures.
Ind/Abst Acad. Abstr. Full Text Elite (July 1990-); Acad. Abstr. (July 1990-); Acad. Search (July 1990-); Am. Hist. Life (1967-); ARTbibliogr. Mod.; Arts Humanit. Citation Index [Full Cov.]; Curr. Contents Arts Humanit.; Expand. Acad. Index (1989-); HAPI Hisp. Am. Period. Index; Humanit. Index; INFO-SOUTH Abstr.; Mag. Search; MLA Int. Bibl. Books Artic. Mod. Lang. Lit.; Newsp. Period. Abstr. (1989-); Res. Alert [Full Cov.]; Soc. Plann. Policy Dev. Abstr.; Soc. Sci. Cit. Index [Select. Cov.]; Sociol. Abstr. (?-?).

PL
HISPANICA POSNANIENSIA / UNIWERSYTET IM. ADAMA MICKIEWICZA W POZNANIU. **Added/Corp** Uniwersytet im. Adama Mickiewicza w Poznaniu. (1990)-. Periodical. Spanish. Uniwersytet im Adama Mickiewicza, Departmento de Filoologias Hispanicas, Sowackiego 20, Pl 60-822, Poznan, Poland.

SZ/0170-8570
HISPANISTISCHE STUDIEN. See Literature.

HU
HISTOIRE COMPAREE DES LITTERATURES DE LANGUES EUROPEENNES. See Literature.

FR
HISTOIRE EPISTEMOLOGIE LANGAGE : HEL. **VFOAT** HEL; H.E.L. (1979)-. Periodical. French (English). sa. SHESL, Dep Rech Linguistiques, Univ Paris 7, 2 Place Jussieu, 75251 Paris Cedex 05 France.
Ind/Abst Linguist. Lang. Behav. Abstr. (1985-) [Full Cov.]; Soc. Plann. Policy Dev. Abstr.

NE/0302-5160
HISTORIOGRAPHIA LINGUISTICA. [Historigr. linguist.]. Vol. 1 (1974)-. Academic Scholarly Publication. Multiple languages (English, French and German). Three times a year. $199.00. John Benjamins BV, Amsteldijk 44, PO Box 75577, 1070 AN Amsterdam Netherlands. **Tel** 011 31 20 6738156, FAX 011 31 20 739773. **(Subscription address:** John Benjamins North America, PO Box 27519, Philadelphia PA 19118-0519.**)** **ED** E. F. Konrad Koerner and Hans-Josef Niederehe. **LC** P61; .H57. **DD** 410/.9. Index available (free). Documents available from The Genuine Article.
Desc: Intended to serve the ever growing scholarly interest of linguists, psycholinguists, and philosophers of language of divergent persuasions in the history of linguistic thought.
Ind/Abst Am. Hist. Life (1983-); Annu. Bibliogr. Engl. Lang. Lit.; Arts Humanit. Citation Index [Full Cov.]; Curr. Contents Arts Humanit.; Lang. Teach.; Linguist. Lang. Behav. Abstr. (1974-) [Full Cov.]; MLA Int. Bibl. Books Artic. Mod. Lang. Lit.; Res. Alert [Full Cov.]; Soc. Plann. Policy Dev. Abstr.

GW/0935-3518
HISTORISCHE SPRACHFORSCHUNG. **VFOAT** Historiche Linguistics. Vol. 1, No. 1 (1988)-. Periodical. German (English). sa. DM104.00. Vandenhoeck & Ruprecht, Robert Bosch Breite 6, D-37079 Goettingen Germany. **Tel** 011 49 551 695911, FAX 011 49 551 695917, telex 965226 VAN d. **LC** P501; .Z5. **DD** 417/.7/05. **CODEN** HISPE2. ***Continues*** *Zeitschrift fuer Vergleichende Sprachforschung, 0044-3646.*

Ind/Abst Annu. Bibliogr. Engl. Lang. Lit.; Linguist. Lang. Behav. Abstr. (1988-) [Full Cov.]; MLA Int. Bibl. Books Artic. Mod. Lang. Lit.; Soc. Plann. Policy Dev. Abstr.

GW
HISTORISCHE SPRACHFORSCHUNG. ERGANZUNGSHEFT. **VFOAT** Historical Linguistics. Erganzungsheft. (1990)-. Monographic series. German (English). ***Continues*** *Erganzungshefte zur Zeitschrift fur Vergleichende Sprachforschung.*
Ind/Abst Annu. Bibliogr. Engl. Lang. Lit.

HK/1015-2059
HONGKONG PAPERS IN LINGUISTICS AND LANGUAGE TEACHING. [Hongkong pap. linguist. lang. teach.]. (1989)-. Periodical. English. ***Continues*** *Working Papers in Linguistics and Language Teaching, 0253-1895.*
Ind/Abst Linguist. Lang. Behav. Abstr. (1983-) [Full Cov.]; Soc. Plann. Policy Dev. Abstr.

JA
HONYAKU NO SEKAI. **Added/Corp** Nihon Honyakuka Yosei Senta. (19??)-. Periodical. Japanese. mo. ¥6480. Dai N, Dempa Building, 14-10 Soto Kanda 2, Chiyoda-ku Tokyo Japan. **LC** P306.A1; H66.

FR/0769-0088
HOR YEZH. (1954)-. Periodical. Breton. 80.00F. Hor Yezh, 1 Place Charles Peguy, 29260 Lesneven France. **LC** PB2801; .H67.
Ind/Abst MLA Int. Bibl. Books Artic. Mod. Lang. Lit.

US/0018-6856
HOY DIA. ***Ceased.*** (19??)-No. 6 (1993). Periodical. Spanish. Six times a year. Mary Glasgow Publications, Brookhampton Lane, Kineton, Warwickshire CV35 0JB England. **Tel** 011 44 926 640606, FAX 011 44 926 641016. **(Subscription address:** Delta Systems Co., Inc., 1400 Miller Parkway, McHenry, IL 60050, telephone: (800)323-8270 or (815)363-3582**)** available on microfilm from University Microfilms International (UMI).

CC
HSIU TZU HSUEH HSI. **VFOAT** Xiucixuexi. 1982/1-. Periodical. Chinese. qt. RMBY0.43. Post Office Nan-Chang, People's Republic of China. **LC** PL1271; .H814346. **DD** 808/.04951.

US/1046-7599
HUMAN COMMUNICATION AND ITS DISORDERS (NORWOOD, N.J.). **See** Communication.

BE/0774-2908
HUMANISTICA LOVANIENSIA. [Humanist. Lovan.]. **Added/Corp** Universite Catholique de Louvain (1835-1969). Vol. 1 (1928)-. Periodical. English (Dutch and Latin). an. 3200F. Editions Peeters SA, Bondgenotenlaan 153, BP 41, B-3000 Leuven Belgium. **Tel** 32 16 235170, FAX 32 16 228500, telex 65987 PUL B. **ED** J. Ysewijn, G. Tournoy, C. Matheeussen and D. Sacre. Index available. ctrl circ.
Desc: Journal of Neo-Latin studies.
Ind/Abst MLA Int. Bibl. Books Artic. Mod. Lang. Lit.

PO
HUMANITAS (COIMBRA). (HUMANITAS.). **Added/Corp** Coimbra. Universidade. Instituto de Estudos Classicos. Vol. 1 (1947)-. Portuguese (English, French and German). an. Instituto Estudos Classicos, Faculdade Letras, 3049 Coimbra Codex Portugal. **Tel** 25551/2. **LC** PA9; .H8.

KO
HWASUL. Periodical. Korean. bm. Hanguk Hwasul Kyoyukhoe, 462-2 Pyongchang-Dong Chongno-ku, Seoul 110 Korea. **LC** PN4003; .H9.

US/1050-0049
IALL JOURNAL OF LANGUAGE LEARNING TECHNOLOGIES, THE. [IALL j. lang. learn. technol.]. **Added/Corp** International Association of Learning Laboratories. **VAT** International Association of Learning Laboratories Journal of Language Learning Technologies. Vol. 23, No. 1 (Winter 1990)-. Periodical. English. Three times a year (Feb., May, Nov.). $40.00 North America, $55.00 others (educational individuals); $55.00 North America, $70.00 others (individuals). International Association for Learning Laboratories, 1600 Grand Avenue, McCalester College, St. Paul MN 55105. **Tel** (612)696-6336. **ED** Read Gilgen (editor's address: Learning Services, University of Wisconsin, Madison WI 53706; telephone: (608)262-1408). **LC** PB36; .N35. **DD** 418/.0078. **CODEN** IJLTEV. **Bk Rev**, (Qty: 3). **Ad Acc.** **Pr Rev. Circ:** 470. available on microfilm and microfiche from University Microfilms International (UMI). ***Continues*** *Journal of Educational Techniques and Technologies, 0891-2521.*
Ind/Abst Curr. Index J. Educ.; Soc. Plann. Policy Dev. Abstr.

RU
IAZYK I OBSHCHESTVO. Vol. 1 (1967)-. Periodical. Russian. 1.5rub. Saratov N.G. Chernyshevskii State University, Astrakhanskaya Ulitsa 83, 410071 Saratov Russia. **Tel** 24-16-96, FAX 24-04-46, telex 241125. **LC** P40; .I2.

RU
IAZYKI I TOPONIMIIA. **Added/Corp** Tomskii Gosudarstvennyi Pedagogicheskii Institut. Vol. 1, (1976)-. Periodical. Russian. Izdatelstvo Tomskogo Universiteta / Tomsk State University, Prospekt Lenina 36, 634050 Tomsk Russia. **Tel** 23-44-65, FAX 22-24-66, telex 128258. **LC** P25; .I2.

SP/0019-0993
IBEROROMANIA. [Ibero-rom.]. (1969)-. Periodical. German (Catalan, English, French, Portuguese and Spanish). sa (2 issues). DM86.00. Max Niemeyer Verlag, Postfach 2140, D 72011 Tuebingen Germany. **Tel** 011 49 7071 989494, FAX 011 49 7071 87419. **ED** H. Bihler, D. Briesemeister, R. Eberenz, H. Geckeler, H.J. Neuschaefer, K. Poertl, M. Roessner. **LC** PC4001; .A2. **CODEN** IBERE2. Documents available from The Genuine Article.
Desc: Covers Spanish, Portuguese and Catalan philology.
Ind/Abst Arts Humanit. Citation Index [Full Cov.]; Curr. Contents Arts Humanit.; MLA Int. Bibl. Books Artic. Mod. Lang. Lit.; Res. Alert [Full Cov.]; Romant. Move.

TI/0018-862X
IBLA. (INSTITUT DES BELLES LETTRES ARABES : IBLA.). [IBLA]. **Added/Corp** Institut des Belles Lettres Arabes. **VFOAT** IBLA. (April 1937)-. Periodical. French (Multiple languages). Twice a year (June, Dec.). $31.00. Institut des Belles Lettres Arabes, 12 rue Djamaa el Haoua, Tunis Tunisia. **Tel** 011 261 1 560133. **LC** AS653; .I5. **DD** 068.611.
Ind/Abst Am. Hist. Life (1990); Anthropol. Index; MLA Int. Bibl. Books Artic. Mod. Lang. Lit.; Rural Dev. Abstr.; Soc. Plann. Policy Dev. Abstr.; Sociol. Abstr. (?-?); Middle East J.; World Agric. Econ.

NO/0801-5775
ICAME JOURNAL / INTERNATIONAL COMPUTER ARCHIVE OF MODERN ENGLISH. **Added/Corp** International Computer Archive of Modern English. NAVFs EDB-senter for Humanistisk Forskning. No. 11 (April 1987)-. Periodical. English. an. Kr125.00 all except Norway. Norwegian Computer Centre of Humanities, Harald Harafagresgt 31, N 5007 Bergen Norway. **Tel** 011 47 5 212954. **ED** Stig Johansson and Anna-Brita Stenstrom. **Bk Rev. Circ:** 300. ***Continues*** *ICAME News.*
Desc: Articles, reviews, and reports on machine-readable texts in English language research.
Ind/Abst Annu. Bibliogr. Engl. Lang. Lit.

US/0891-3978
IDEA FACTORY, THE. **Added/Corp** National Council of Teachers of English. Junior High/Middle School Assembly. (1979)-. Periodical. English. Four times a year. $10.00. Junior High/Middle School Assembly, 715 South Cypress Avenue, Marshfield WI 54449. **Tel** (505)983-9714.

US/1042-5330
IDEAS PLUS. **See** Education-Teaching and Curriculum.

AT
IDIOM. **See** Education-Teaching and Curriculum.

GW
IDIOMATICA. **Added/Corp** Tuebinger Arbeitsstelle "Sprache in SÈudwestdeutschland". (1973)-. Monographic series. German. ir. Price varies per volume. Max Niemeyer Verlag, Postfach 2140, D 72011 Tuebingen Germany. **Tel** 011 49 7071 989494, FAX 011 49 7071 87419. **ED** Arno Ruoff, Hermann Bausinger, Werner Besch, Walter Haas, Otmar Werner.
Desc: Monographs on the German language as spoken in the southwestern area of Germany, in Austria (Vorarlberg), and Liechtenstein.
Ind/Abst MLA Int. Bibl. Books Artic. Mod. Lang. Lit.

II/0378-2484
IJDL. INTERNATIONAL JOURNAL OF DRAVIDIAN LINGUISTICS. (INTERNATIONAL JOURNAL OF DRAVIDIAN LINGUISTICS.). [IJDL, Int. j. Dravidian linguist.]. **Added/Corp** University of Kerala. Dept. of Linguistics. **VFOAT** IJDL. Vol. 1 (Jan. 1972)-. Periodical. English. sa. $40.00. Dravidian Linguistics Association Publication Division, Kerla Paanini Building, ISDL Campus, St Xaviers College PO, Trivandrum 695586 South India. **Tel** 82653. **(Subscription address:** Prints India, 11 Darya Ganj, New Delhi, 110002 India, (Phone: 011 91 11 3268645)**)** **ED** V I Subramoniam and D Litt. **LC** PL4601; .A3. **DD** 494/.8. Index available. cum. index. **Bk Rev. Circ:** 2,000.
Ind/Abst MLA Int. Bibl. Books Artic. Mod. Lang. Lit.

US/0073-5175
ILLINOIS STUDIES IN LANGUAGE AND LITERATURE / UNIVERSITY OF ILLINOIS. ***Ceased.*** Vol. 17. Nos. 1/2 (1934)-?. Monographic series. English. University of Illinois at Urbana-Champaign / Library, Graduate School of Library and Information Science, Urbana IL 61801. **UDC** 800; 82. ***Continues*** *University of Illinois Studies in Language and Literature.*

CN/1187-0850
IMMERSION REGISTRY. (THE IMMERSION REGISTRY / CPF, CANADIAN PARENTS FOR FRENCH.). [Immers. regist.]. **Added/Corp** Canadian Parents for French. **VFOAT** Canadian Parents for French Immersion Registry; CPF Immersion Registry. (1990/1991)-. English. 30.00Can$ (one year), 70.00Can$ (three year). Canadian Parents for French, 309 Cooper Street, Suite 210, Ottawa Ontario K2P 0G5 Canada. **Tel** (613)235-1481. **DD** 440/.71/071025. ***Continues*** *The CPF Immersion Registry., 0829-1020.*

CN/1184-6178
IMPRESSIONS/EXPRESSIONS (WINNIPEG). (IMPRESSIONS/EXPRESSIONS : LA PUBLICATION DE L'ASSOCIATION MANITOBAINS DES PROFESSEURS DE FRANCAIS.). [Impr./expr.]. **Added/Corp** Association Manitobaine des Professeurs de Francais. Vol. 11, No. 2, (Dec. 1989)-. Periodical. French (summaries and/or abstracts in English). Four times a year. 14.00Can$. Manitoba Teachers Society, 191 Harcourt Street, Winnipeg Manitoba R3J 3H2 Canada. **Tel** (204)888-7961 ext.254, FAX (204)831-0877. **DD** 440/.7/07127. ***Continues*** *Ampitoufe., 0709-387X.*

US
IN GEARDAGUM : ESSAYS ON OLD ENGLISH LANGUAGE AND LITERATURE. **Added/Corp** Society for New Language Study (U.S.). (June 1974)-. English (English, Old). an. Society for New Language Study, PO Box 10596, Denver CO 80210. **Tel** (303)777-6115. **ED** W. C. Johnson. cum. index. **Bk Rev. Circ:** 100 (ctrl).
Desc: Includes old and middle English literature and language, criticism and philosophy.
Ind/Abst Abstr. Engl. Stud.; MLA Int. Bibl. Books Artic. Mod. Lang. Lit.

AT/1036-1421
IN OTHER WORDS NUNAWADING. **Added/Corp** stralian Institute of Interpreters and Translators. **VFOAT** AUSIT Journal. (1990)-. Periodical. English. an. 30.00Aus$ (institutions), 20.00Aus$ (individuals). AUSITC/Australian Institute of Interpreters & Translators, 13 Peacedale Grove, Nunawading Victoria 3131 Australia. **Tel** 61 3 8774369, FAX 61 3 5628660. **ED** Luciano Ginori (editor's address: PO Box 1009, Burwood NSW 2134 Australia; editor's phone: 61 2 7454827). **DD** 418.02. **Bk Rev**, (Qty: Varies). **Ad Acc, Adv Mgr:** same as editor. **Circ:** 1,000.

IT/0390-2412
INCONTRI LINGUISTICI. [Incontri linguist.]. **Added/Corp** Universita degli Studi di Trieste Universita degli Studi di Trieste. Facolta di Lingue e Letterature Straniere con Sede in Udine Trieste. Universita. Istituto di Glottologia e Filologia Classica. Trieste. Universita. Istituto di Glottologia. Vol. 1 (1974)-. Periodical. Italian. an. L175000. Giardini Editori Stampatori, Via Santa Bibbiana 28, 56127 Pisa Italy. **Tel** 011 39 50 934242.
Ind/Abst MLA Int. Bibl. Books Artic. Mod. Lang. Lit.

FR/0073-6074
INDEX TRANSLATIONUM. (INDEX TRANSLATIONUM. REPERTOIRE INTERNATIONAL DES TRADUCTIONS. INTERNATIONAL BIBLIOGRAPHY OF TRANSLATIONS.). **Added/Corp** League of Nations. International Institute of Intellectual Co-operation. Unesco. **VFOAT** Repertoire International des Traductions; International Bibliography of Translations. No. 1-31 (July 1932-Jan. 1940)- New Series No. 1 (1948)-. Bibliography. Latin (Multiple languages, English, French and Spanish). ir (Nov.). Prices varies per volume. UNESCO / France, 31 rue Francois Bonvin, 75732 Paris Cedex 15 France. **Tel** 011 33 1 45684564, 011 33 1 45684565, FAX 011 33 1 42733007, telex 204461 Paris. **(Subscription address:** UNIPUB, 4611 F Assembly Drive, Lanham MD 20706.**)** **LC** Z6514.T7; I42. **DD** 011/.7. **NLM** Z 6514.T7 I38.

II/0379-0037
INDIAN JOURNAL OF APPLIED LINGUISTICS. [Indian j. appl. linguist.]. Vol. 1, (Jan./June 1975)-. Periodical. Multiple languages (English and Hindi). sa. $45.00. Bahri Publications, PO Box 4453, 997A Street No 9, Gobindpuri Kalkaji, New Delhi 110019 India. **Tel** 011-6445710, 011-6448606. **(Subscription address:** Prints India, 11 Darya Ganj, New Delhi 110002 India.**)** **LC** PK101; .I54. **Ad Acc.**
Ind/Abst Lang. Teach.; Linguist. Lang. Behav. Abstr. (1987-) [Full Cov.]; MLA Int. Bibl. Books Artic. Mod. Lang. Lit.; Soc. Plann. Policy Dev. Abstr.

II/0378-0759
INDIAN LINGUISTICS. [Indian linguist.]. **Added/Corp** Linguistic Society of India. Vol. 1 (1931)-. Monographic series. English. ir. Price varies per volume. Linguistics Socety of India, Deccan College Postgraduate, Pune 411 006 India. **LC** PK1501; .L52.
Ind/Abst Linguist. Lang. Behav. Abstr. (1972-) [Full Cov.]; MLA Int. Bibl. Books Artic. Mod. Lang. Lit.; Soc. Plann. Policy Dev. Abstr.

US/1070-9371
INDIANA ENGLISH. [Ind. Engl.]. **Added/Corp** Indiana Council of Teachers of English. **VFOAT** Indiana Folklore; IE. Vol. 1 (1977)-. Periodical. English. Three times a year. $8.00 US; $10.00 other. Indiana Council of

Teachers of English, Indiana State University, Department of English / Root Hall A-238, Terre Haute IN 47809. **Tel** (812)237-6311. **ED** Robert Perrin, (editor's phone: (812)237-3147). **LC** PE65; .I5. **DD** 420. **Bk Rev**, (Qty: 1-2/year). **Circ:** 450. ***Supersedes*** *Indiana English Journal, 0019-6584.*
Desc: Publication of the Indiana Council of Teachers of English.
Ind/Abst Annu. Bibliogr. Engl. Lang. Lit.

US/0893-2913
INDIANA UNIVERSITY URALIC AND ALTAIC SERIES.
[Indiana Univ. Ural. Altaic ser.]. **Added/Corp** Indiana University, Bloomington. Research Institute for Inner Asian Studies. **VFOAT** Indiana University Uralic and Altaic Series. (197?)-. Monographic series. English. ir. Price varies per volume. Research Institute for Inner Asian Studies / Indiana University, Goodbody Hall 344, Bloomington IN 47405. **Tel** (812)855-1605. **ED** Denis Sinor. **DD** 494. **Bk Rev.** ***Continues*** *Uralic and Altaic Series, 0445-8486.*
Desc: Scholarly monographs and textbooks on the history, culture and languages of inner Asia and on Uralic and Altaic linguistics.
Ind/Abst MLA Int. Bibl. Books Artic. Mod. Lang. Lit.

US
INDICES - MONOGRAPHS IN PHILOSOPHICAL LOGIC & FORMAL LINGUISTICS.
Humanities Press, 165 1st Avenue, Atlantic Highlands NJ 07716. **Tel** (908)872-1441, (800)221-3845, FAX (908)872-0717, telex 752233.

CN/0227-2547
INDIRECTIONS.
[Indirections]. **Added/Corp** Ontario Council of Teachers of English. Vol. 1 (Fall 1975)-. Periodical. English. Three times a year. 50.00Can$ Comes with Ontario Council Teachers of English membership. Indirections, 23 Deepglade Cres., Willowdale ONT M2J 1B3 Canada. **Tel** (905)494-7661. **DD** 420/.7/0713.

NE/0019-7246
INDO-IRANIAN JOURNAL.
See Philosophy.

GW/0341-1850
INDOGERMANISCHE FORSCHUNGEN.
[Indoger. Forsch.]. (1891)-. German. an. $163.25. Walter de Gruyter Inc., PO Box 303421, D 10728 Berlin Germany. **Tel** 011 49 30 260050, FAX 011 49 30 26005251. **LC** P501; .I4. cum. index. Documents available from The Genuine Article.
Ind/Abst Annu. Bibliogr. Engl. Lang. Lit.; Arts Humanit. Citation Index (19??-19??) [Full Cov.]; Curr. Contents Arts Humanit.; Int. Bibliogr. Sociol.; MLA Int. Bibl. Books Artic. Mod. Lang. Lit.; Res. Alert [Full Cov.]; Soc. Sci. Cit. Index [Select. Cov.].

GW
INDOLOGIA BEROLINENSIS.
Added/Corp Museum fuer Indische Kunst Berlin. Berlin. Staatliche Museen (West Berlin). Berlin. Freie Universitat. Seminar fuer Indische Philologie. Berlin. Freie Universitat. Seminar fuer Indische Philologie und Kunstgeshichte. (1969)-. Monographic series. German. ir. Price varies per volume. E. J. Brill, Postbus 9000, 2300 PA Leiden Netherlands. **Tel** 011 31 71 312624, FAX 011 31 71 317532, telex 39296 BRILL NL.

IT
INDOLOGICA TAURINENSIA.
Added/Corp Istituto di Indologia. International Association of Sanskrit Studies. (1971)-. Italian (French and English). ir. $40.00 US. Herder Editrice e Libreria SRL, Piazza Montecitorio 117-120, 00186 Rome Italy. **Tel** 011 39 6 679 4628, FAX 011 39 6 678 4751. **ED** O. Botto.
Desc: Official organ of the International Association of Sanskrit Studies.

GW/0724-9616
INFO DAF. INFORMATIONEN DEUTSCH ALS FREMDSPRACHE.
See Education-Higher Education.

CN
INFORMATION COMMUNICATION.
English. an. 3.56Can$ (Canada); 7.35Can$ (US); 8.45Can$ (other). Speech and Voice Society, 300 Huron St New Col Rm 54K, Toronto ONT M5S 2X6 Canada. **Tel** (416)978-3162.
Ind/Abst MLA Int. Bibl. Books Artic. Mod. Lang. Lit.

FR/0222-9838
INFORMATION GRAMMATICALE (PARIS), L'.
(L'INFORMATION GRAMMATICALE.). [Inf. gramm.]. No. 1 (Jan./Feb. 1979)-. Periodical. French. qt. 160.00F France; 200.00F other. Society pour l'Information Grammaticale, University of Paris, Sorbonne IV, 1 rue Victor Cousin, 75005 Paris France. **ED** Sylire Mellet. **Bk Rev**, (Qty: 4/yr). **Pr Rev. Circ:** 650 (ctrl).
Ind/Abst MLA Int. Bibl. Books Artic. Mod. Lang. Lit.

AU
INFORMATIONEN ZUR DEUTSCHDIDAKTIK.
(1976)-. Periodical. German. ir. DM41.20 Germany; DM48.00 Europe; DM52.00 others. Schroedel Schulbuchverlag, Postfach 810555, Hildesheimer Str 202, 3000 Hannover 81 Germany. **Tel** 011 49 511 83880. **(Subscription address:** Hans Oeding Druckerei & Verlag, Postfach 3311, D 38023 Braunschweig Germany.**) LC** PF3065; .I47.

AU
INFOTERM NEWSLETTER.
Newsletter. English (French). Four times a year. 360.00Can$ Europe; 410.00Can$ other. TermNet Secretariat, Gruengasse 9 17, A-1050 Vienna, Austria. **Tel** (011 43 222)567763, FAX (0222)2163272, telex 115960. **ED** Magdalena Krommer-Benz. **Circ:** 150 (ctrl).
Desc: Provides up-to-date information on new developments in terminology, terminology documentation and teaching as well as reports on projects, meetings, etc.

CN/0710-4278
INITIALES (HALIFAX).
(INITIALES : TRAVAUX DES ETUDIANTS, DEPARTEMENT DE FRANCAIS, UNIVERSITE DALHOUSIE.). [Initiales]. **VFOAT** Initials : Students' Writings, Department of French, Dalhousie University. Vol. 1 (1981)-. French (English). an. 5.00Can$ Canada; $4.00 US. Dalhousie University / French Department, Halifax Nova Scotia B3H 3J5 Canada. **Tel** (902)494-2430. **ED** R Kocourek. **DD** 440. **UDC** 804.0; 840. **Pr Rev. Circ:** 150 (ctrl).
Desc: Graduate students' writings in the areas of French literature and linguistics, including stylistics, poetics, terminology, translation, dialectology and semiotics.

UZ
INOSTRANNYE IAZYKI V VUZAKH UZBEKISTANA.
Russian. 1.60rub single issue. Tashkenskii Gos Ped IN-T, Ulitsa Pedagogicheskaia, Tashkent 103 Uzbekistan. **LC** PB38.R8; I48.

RU/0130-6073
INOSTRANNYE JAZYKI V SKOLE.
(INOSTRANNYE IAZYKI V SHKOLE / MINISTERSTVO PROSVESHCHENIIA RSFSR.). [Inostr. jazyki sk.]. **Added/Corp** Russian S.F.S.R. Ministerstvo Prosveshcheniia. Russian S.F.S.R. Ministerstvo Narodnogo Obrazovaniia. (1948)-. Periodical. Russian (English, French and German). bm. $75.95. **(Subscription address:** East View Publications Inc., 3020 Harbor Lane North, Suite 110, Minneapolis MN 55447.**) LC** PB5; .I5. ***Continues*** *Inostrannyi lazyk v Shkole.*
Ind/Abst MLA Int. Bibl. Books Artic. Mod. Lang. Lit.; Soc. Plann. Policy Dev. Abstr.; Sociol. Abstr.

UN/0320-2372
INOZEMNA FILOLOGIJA.
(INOZEMNA FILOLOHIIA / MINISTERSTVO VYSHCHOI I SEREDNNOI SPETSIALNOI OSVITY URSR, LVIVSKYI ORDENA LENINA DERZHAVNYI UNIVERSYTET IM. I. FRANKA.). [Inozemna filol.]. **Added/Corp** Lvivskyi Derzhavnyi Universytet im. Iv. Franka. Ukraine. Ministerstvo Vyshchoi i Serednoi Spetsialnoi Osvity. (1964)-. Periodical. Ukrainian (summaries and/or abstracts in English). qt. **LC** P9; .I5.
Ind/Abst MLA Int. Bibl. Books Artic. Mod. Lang. Lit.

CN/0700-9429
INTERCOM (MONTREAL. ENGLISH EDITION).
(INTERCOM.). Oct. 1974-. Periodical. English. ir. Business Linguistic Center, 110 Sherbrooke Street West/Suite 2403, Montreal Quebec H3A 1G8 Canada. **DD** 410/.6/2714.

•US/1058-9902
INTERGENERATIONAL ISSUES IN SPEECH, HEARING, AND LANGUAGE.
[Intergener. issues speech hear. lang.]. **VFOAT** IGI-SHL. (1992)-. Periodical. English. sa. Dr. Jesse Dancer, IGI-SHL, Audiology and Speech Pathology Speech Communication 105, University of Arkansas at Little Rock, 2801 South University, Little Rock AR 72204. **LC** P87; .I5437. **DD** 302.2/05. **NLM** W1; IN685U.

US/0020-7071
INTERNATIONAL JOURNAL OF AMERICAN LINGUISTICS.
[Int. j. Am. linguist.]. **Added/Corp** Linguistic Society of America. American Anthropological Association. American Council of Learned Societies. Committee on American Native Languages. Joint Committee on American Native Languages. Conference on American Indian Languages. Vol. 1, No. 1 (July 1917)-. Periodical. English. qt (4 issues). $95.00 institution, $40.00 individual, $29.00 student. University of Chicago Press / Journals Division, PO Box 37005, 5720 South Woodlawn, Chicago IL 60637. **Tel** (312)753-3347, FAX (312)753-0811. **(Subscription telephone:** (312)753-8083**) ED** David S. Rood. **LC** PM101; .I5. **DD** 497/.05. **NLM** W1 IN7653N. **[CCC].** cum. index. **Pr Rev. Acid Free.** available on microfilm and microfiche from University Microfilms International (UMI). Documents available from The Genuine Article, UMI Article Clearinghouse.
Desc: A world forum for the study of all the languages native to North, Central and South America. Concentrates on the investigation of linguistic data and on the presentation of grammatical fragments and other documents relevant to Amerindian languages.
Ind/Abst Abstr. Anthropol.; Acad. Search (July 1993-); Annu. Bibliogr. Engl. Lang. Lit.; Anthropol. Index; Anthropol. Lit.; Arts Humanit. Citation Index [Full Cov.]; Curr. Contents Arts Humanit.; Curr. Contents Soc. Behav. Sci.; Expand. Acad. Index (1989-); HAPI Hisp. Am. Period. Index; Humanit. Index; Humanit. Source (Jul. 1993-); INFO-SOUTH Abstr.; Lang. Teach.; Linguist. Lang. Behav. Abstr. (1972-) [Full Cov.]; MLA Int. Bibl. Books Artic. Mod. Lang. Lit.; Newsp. Period. Abstr. (1991-); Res. Alert [Full Cov.]; Soc. Plann. Policy Dev. Abstr.; Soc. Sci. Cit. Index [Full Cov.].

NO/0802-6106
INTERNATIONAL JOURNAL OF APPLIED LINGUISTICS.
Added/Corp International Association of Applied Linguistics. **VFOAT** INJAL. Vol. 1, No. 1 (1991)-. Periodical. English. Twice a year (June and December). $95.00 (institution); $57.00 (individual). Novus Press, PO Box 748 Sentrum, N-0106 Oslo Norway. **Tel** 011 47 22 717450, FAX 011 47 22 718107. **CODEN** IJLNED. **Ad Acc. Pr Rev. Acid Free.**
Desc: The journal encourages the development of new fields of applied language study. It publishes original articles and reviews of current books, as well as notes and comments on points arising out of recently published articles.
Ind/Abst Curr. Index J. Educ.; Linguist. Lang. Behav. Abstr. (1991-) [Full Cov.]; MLA Int. Bibl. Books Artic. Mod. Lang. Lit.; Soc. Plann. Policy Dev. Abstr.; Sociol. Abstr.

UK/0950-3846
INTERNATIONAL JOURNAL OF LEXICOGRAPHY.
[Int. j. lexicogr.]. **Added/Corp** European Association for Lexicography. **VFOAT** IJL. Vol. 1, No. 1 (Spring 1988)-. Periodical. English. qt. £57.00 UK and Europe; $102.00 other. Oxford University Press, Walton Street, Oxford OX2 6DP England. **Tel** 011 44 865 56767, FAX 011 44 865 267773, telex 837330 OXPRES G. **(Subscription address:** Oxford University Press / USA, Journals Marketing Department, Oxford University Press, 2001 Evans Road, Cary NC 27513.**) ED** Robert Ilson. **LC** P327; .I53. **DD** 413/.028/05. **[CCC]. Bk Rev. Ad Acc.** available on microfilm and microfiche from University Microfilms International (UMI).
Desc: Theoretical, practical, diachronic and synchronic aspects of lexicography. Dictionaries of all types, phrase books, usage guides, etc. Related disciplines such as lexicology, terminology, semantics, pragmatics, are also included.
Ind/Abst Linguist. Lang. Behav. Abstr. (1988-) [Full Cov.]; MLA Int. Bibl. Books Artic. Mod. Lang. Lit.; Soc. Plann. Policy Dev. Abstr.

JA/0165-4055
INTERNATIONAL JOURNAL OF PSYCHOLINGUISTICS.
[Int. j. psycholinguist.]. (1972)-. Periodical. English (summaries and/or abstracts in French and Russian). Three times a year (March, September, & December). ¥4,800 (individuals), ¥8,400 (institutions) Japan; $50.00 (individuals), $80.00 (institutions) other. Center for Acaemic Socities Japan, Senri Life Science Center Building, Fourteenth Floor, 4-2 Shinsenri-higashi-machi, 1 Chome Toyonaka-shi, Osaka 565 Japan. **(Subscription address:** Japan Publications Trading Company, Ltd., PO Box 5030, Tokyo International, Tokyo 100-31 Japan.**) ED** Prof. Tatiana Slama-Cazacu (Editor's address: University of Bucharest, Str. Moxa 10, Bucharest 78109 Romania). **NLM** W1 IN777I. **[CCC].**
Desc: Devoted to theoretical and experimental research articles and their application to practical fields concerning speech comprehension / production, language acquisition, bilingualism, nonverbal aspects of communication and semiotics in psycholinguistic perspective, language disorders, speech technologies and human communication models, translation, foreign language learning, literary text analysis, mass communication media, and other fields of human communication.

UK/0959-6402
INTERNATIONAL JOURNAL OF SIGN LINGUISTICS.
Added/Corp International Sign Linguistics Association. **VFOAT** ISLA Journal. Vol. 1, No. 1 (1990)-. Periodical. English. sa.
Ind/Abst Linguist. Lang. Behav. Abstr. (1990-) [Full Cov.]; Soc. Plann. Policy Dev. Abstr.

US/0538-8228
INTERNATIONAL JOURNAL OF SLAVIC LINGUISTICS AND POETICS.
[Int. j. slav. linguist. poet.]. **VFOAT** IJSLP. (1959)-. Periodical. English (French, German, Polish and Russian). Twice a year. $40.00 (institutions): $20.00 (individuals). Slavica Publishers Inc., PO Box 14388, Columbus OH 43214-0388. **Tel** (614)268-4002. **ED** Dean S. Worth. **LC** PG1; .I5. **Bk Rev. Pr Rev. Circ:** 400. available on microfilm from University Microfilms International (UMI).
Desc: Articles on slavic linguistics and poetics.
Ind/Abst MLA Int. Bibl. Books Artic. Mod. Lang. Lit.

NE/0165-2516
INTERNATIONAL JOURNAL OF THE SOCIOLOGY OF LANGUAGE.
[Int. j. sociol. lang.]. **VFOAT** I.J.S.L.; IJSL. (1974)-. Periodical. English. bm. $258.80. Walter de Gruyter Inc., PO Box 303421, D 10728 Berlin Germany. **Tel** 011 49 30 260050, FAX 011 49 30 26005251. **ED** J. A. Fishman. **LC** P40; .I57. **DD** 401/.9. **CODEN** ISLGAH. **[CCC]. Bk Rev. Ad Acc. Pr Rev. Circ:** 800 (ctrl). Documents available from The Genuine Article.
Desc: Dedicated to the development of the sociology of

language in its broadest sense, as a truly international and interdisciplinary field.
Ind/Abst Abstr. Anthropol.; Anthropol. Lit.; Arts Humanit. Citation Index [Select. Cov.]; Curr. Contents Soc. Behav. Sci.; Int. Bibliogr. Sociol.; Int. Polit. Sci. Abstr.; Lang. Teach.; Linguist. Lang. Behav. Abstr. (1974-) [Full Cov.]; Middle East Abstr. Index; MLA Int. Bibl. Books Artic. Mod. Lang. Lit.; Psychol. Abstr. (1974-); PsycINFO; PsycLit; Res. Alert [Full Cov.]; Soc. Plann. Policy Dev. Abstr.; Soc. Sci. Cit. Index [Full Cov.]; Sociol. Abstr. [Full Cov.].

II
INTERNATIONAL JOURNAL OF TRANSLATION. **VFOAT** IJT. Vol. 1, No. 1 (Jan. 1989)-. Periodical. English. Twice a year (Jan., July). $52.00. Bahri Publications, PO Box 4453, 997A Street No 9, Gobindpuri Kalkaji, New Delhi 110019 India. **Tel** 011-6445710, 011-6448606. **(Subscription address:** Prints India, 11 Darya Ganj, New Delhi 110002 India.**)** **ED** Ujjal Singh Bahri. **LC** PAR. **CODEN** IJOTEC. **Bk Rev. Ad Acc. Circ:** 450.
Desc: It publishes original research exploring the processes involved in literary and technical translation both from a theoretical and methodological point of view.
Ind/Abst MLA Int. Bibl. Books Artic. Mod. Lang. Lit.

GW/0579-3998
INTERNATIONALE BIBLIOTHEK FUER ALLGEMEINE LINGUISTIK. **VFOAT** International Library of General Linguistics. (1971)-. Monographic series. German (English and French). ir. Price varies per volume. Wilhelm Fink Verlag, Ohmstrasse 5, D 80802 Munich Germany. **Tel** 011 49 89 348017, 348018. **ED** Eugenio Coseriu.
Desc: Monographic series on linguistics.

IT
INTERPRETE, L'. (1976)-. Monographic series. Italian (English, French, Latin and Spanish). Angelo Longo Editore, Via Paolo Costa 33, PO Box 431, 48100 Ravenna Italy. **Tel** 011 39 544 217026, FAX 011 39 544 217026.
Ind/Abst MLA Int. Bibl. Books Artic. Mod. Lang. Lit.

SZ/0047-1291
INTERPRETE, L'. **Added/Corp** Association d'Interpretes et de Traducteurs. (19??)-. Periodical. Multiple languages (French and German). qt. 30.00F. Association de Intrepretes Traducteurs, Case 5550, CH 1211 Geneve 11 Switzerland. **Tel** 011 41 22 7824909. **ED** Marianne Wanstall-Sayty. **LC** P306.A1; I62. **DD** 418/.02. **Bk Rev. Ad Acc. Circ:** 1,000.
Desc: Professional magazine on linguistics and translations.

US/0444-4663
IOWA ENGLISH BULLETIN. [Iowa Engl. bull.]. **Added/Corp** Iowa Council of Teachers of English. **VFOAT** Iowa English Bulletin. Yearbook; Iowa English Bulletin. Yearbook and Newsletter; Iowa English Bulletin Newsletter. Vol. 1, No. 1 (Jan. 1951)-. Bulletin. English. an (Mar.). $5.00. University of Northern Iowa Department of Modern Languages, C/O Richard Fehlman, Cedar Falls IA 50614-0504. **Tel** (319)273-2729. **ED** Joanne Brown and Bruce Horner. **DD** 820. **Circ:** 1,000. ***Absorbed*** *Iowa English Yearbook, 0075-0352.*
Desc: Designed to impart new ideas in the fields of pedagogy and composition theory.
Ind/Abst Abstr. Engl. Stud.; Lit. Crit. Regist.; MLA Int. Bibl. Books Artic. Mod. Lang. Lit.

US
IOWA JOURNAL OF COMMUNICATION. **See** Communication.

GW/0019-042X
IRAL, INTERNATIONAL REVIEW OF APPLIED LINGUISTICS IN LANGUAGE TEACHING. [IRAL, Int. rev. appl. linguist. lang. teach.]. **VFOAT** International Review of Applied Linguistics in Language Teaching; Revue Internationale de Linguistique Appliquee Enseignement des Langues; Internationale Zeitschrift fur Angewandte Linguistik in der Spracherziehung. Vol. 1 (Feb. 1963)-. Periodical. English (French and German; summaries and/or abstracts in French and German). qt. £72.00 UK and Europe; $132.00 other. Oxford University Press, Walton Street, Oxford OX2 6DP England. **Tel** 011 44 865 56767, FAX 011 44 865 267773, telex 837330 OXPRES G. **(Subscription address:** Oxford University Press / USA, Journals Marketing Department, Oxford University Press, 2001 Evans Road, Cary NC 27513.**)** **ED** Bertil Malmberg and Germard Nickel. **LC** P1.A1; I2. **CODEN** IRALA4. **[CCC]. Bk Rev. Ad Acc. Pr Rev. Circ:** 750 (ctrl). available on microfilm and microfiche from University Microfilms International (UMI). Documents available from The Genuine Article.
Desc: Theoretical linguistic research and its practical application to language teaching. Includes synoptic articles on different aspects of applied lingusitics, and reports on completed or continuing research projects.
Ind/Abst Acad. Search (July 1993-); Annu. Bibliogr. Engl. Lang. Lit.; Br. Educ. Index; Curr. Contents Soc. Behav. Sci.; Curr. Index J. Educ.; Educ. Index; INFO-SOUTH Abstr.; Int. Bibliogr. Sociol.; Lang. Teach.; Linguist. Lang. Behav. Abstr. (1972-) [Full Cov.]; Mag. Search; Middle East Abstr. Index; MLA Int. Bibl. Books Artic. Mod. Lang. Lit.; Psychol. Abstr. (1963-); Res. Alert [Full Cov.]; Soc. Plann. Policy Dev. Abstr.; Soc. Sci. Cit. Index [Full Cov.].

RU
IRANSKOE IAZYKOZNANIE / AKADEMIIA NAUK SSSR, INSTITUT IAZYKOZNANIIA. **Added/Corp** Institut Iazykoznaniia (Akademiia Nauk SSSR). (1980)-. Academic Scholarly Publication. Russian. an. 2.60rub. Izdatelstvo Nauka / Akademiia Nauk, Publishing House of the Russian Academy of Sciences, Leninskii Porspekt 14, 117901 Moscow Russia. **Tel** 011 95 954-21-53, FAX 011 95 938-21-44, telex 411964. **LC** PK6001; .I7. **DD** 491/.5/05.

IO/0304-2189
IRIAN. **See** Anthropology.

RU
ISSLEDOVANIIA PO ROMANO-GERMANSKOMU IAZYKOZNANIIU. **Added/Corp** Volgograd, Russia (City). Gosudarstvennyi Pedagogicheskii Institut. (19??)-. Periodical. Russian.
Ind/Abst Annu. Bibliogr. Engl. Lang. Lit.

US/1050-4273
ISSUES IN APPLIED LINGUISTICS. (ISSUES IN APPLIED LINGUISTICS : IAL.). [Issues appl. linguist.]. **Added/Corp** University of California, Los Angeles. Dept. of TESL & Applied Linguistics. **VFOAT** IAL. Vol. 1, No. 1 (June 1990)-. Periodical. English. Twice a year (June & Dec.). $25.00 (individual), $35.00 (institution) surface mail: $40.00 (individual), $50.00 (institution) airmail. University of California at Los Angeles, 3300 Rolfe Hall, 405 Hilgard Avenue, Los Angeles CA 90024. **Tel** (310)825-4321, (310)206-1985. **LC** P129; .I85. **DD** 418/.005. **CODEN** IALIE3.
Ind/Abst Curr. Index J. Educ.; Linguist. Lang. Behav. Abstr. (1990-) [Full Cov.]; Soc. Plann. Policy Dev. Abstr.

II
ISURI : DO. HARISIMHA GAURA VISVAVIDYALAYA, SAGARA KE HINDI-VIBHAGA KE ANTARGATA KRIYASILA BUNDELI-PITHA KA AYOJANA. 1 (83-84)-. Periodical. Hindi (Indic). an. Rs50.00. Department of Hindi, Dr Hari Singh Gaur Univ, Sagar India. **Tel** 2475/20. **ED** Kantikumar Jain. **LC** PK1968; .I78. **UDC** 809.143-087. Index available. cum. index. **Bk Rev. Circ:** 1,500 (ctrl).
Desc: Concentrates on dialect, literature, and culture of Bundelkhard.

IT
ITALIA DIALETTALE, L'. (L'ITALIA DIALETTALE; RIVISTA DI DIALETTOLOGIA ITALIANA.). **Added/Corp** Scuola Normale Superiore (Italy). Vol. 1, (1924)-. Periodical. Italian. an (Mar.). L70000 Italy; L120000 other. Giardini Editori Stampatori, Via Santa Bibbiana 28, 56127 Pisa Italy. **Tel** 011 39 50 934242. **ED** Clemente Merlo. **LC** PC1701; .I8. **DD** 457.
Ind/Abst MLA Int. Bibl. Books Artic. Mod. Lang. Lit.

IT/0391-7509
ITALIA FRANCESCANA. [Ital. frances.]. (1924)-. Periodical. Italian. Four times a year. $125.00 (all but Italy). L'Italia Francescana, Segret Tecn V Aurelia 424, 00165 Rome Italy. **Tel** 011 39 6 6630831. **UDC** 271.3.
Ind/Abst MLA Int. Bibl. Books Artic. Mod. Lang. Lit.

IT/0391-7495
ITALIA MEDIOEVALE E UMANISTICA. [Ital. medioev. um.]. (1958)-. Italian. an. L3400000. Editrice Antenore, Via G Rusca 15, 35100 Padua Italy. **Tel** 011 39 49 686566. **LC** PA9; .I8. **UDC** 805.0-023.
Ind/Abst BHA : Biblio. Hist. Art; MLA Int. Bibl. Books Artic. Mod. Lang. Lit.

UK/0261-4340
ITALIANIST. **See** Literature.

IT
ITALIANO & OLTRE. **VFOAT** Italiano e Oltre. Vol. 1, No. 1 (1986)-. Periodical. Italian. Five times a year. L60000 Italy; L70000 others. La Nuova Italia Editrice Spa, Via Ernesto Codignola, 50018 Scandicci Florence Italy. **Tel** 011 39 55 75901, FAX 011 39 55 7590208. **LC** PC1001; .I8. **DD** 450/.5.

US/0021-3020
ITALICA (NEW YORK, N.Y.). (ITALICA : BULLETIN OF THE AMERICAN ASSOCIATION OF TEACHERS OF ITALIAN.). [Italica]. Vol. 3, No. 1 (Feb. 1926)-. Bulletin. English (Italian). qt. $40.00. American Association of Teachers of Italian, Department of Language, Arizona State University, Tempe AZ 85287. **Tel** (602)965-6281. **LC** PC1068.U6. **DD** 450/.7. **UDC** 805.0-07. (Bound in last issue). cum. index. available on microfilm and microfiche from University Microfilms International (UMI). Documents available from The Genuine Article. ***Continues*** *Bulletin of the American Association of Teachers of Italian.*
Ind/Abst Arts Humanit. Citation Index; Curr. Contents Arts Humanit.; Curr. Index J. Educ.; MLA Int. Bibl. Books Artic. Mod. Lang. Lit.; Res. Alert; Romant. Move.; Soc. Plann. Policy Dev. Abstr.; Soc. Sci. Cit. Index [Select. Cov.].

GW/0171-4996
ITALIENISCH. **Added/Corp** Fachverband Italienisch in Wissenschaft und Unterricht (Frankfurt am Main, Germany) Deutsch-Italienische Vereinigung. (May 1979)-. Periodical. German. sa. DM29.40. Moritz Diesterweg, Postfach 630180, D-60351 Frankfurt Germany. **Tel** 11 49 69 420810, FAX 11 49 69 42081100. **ED** Arno Euler and Salvatore A.A. Sanna. **[CCC]. Bk Rev. Ad Acc.**
Desc: Journal for the Italian language and literature in science and education. Directed at language teachers on all levels of education.
Ind/Abst MLA Int. Bibl. Books Artic. Mod. Lang. Lit.

BE/0019-0829
ITL. INSTITUUT VOOR TOEGEPASTE LINGUISTIK. (ITL.). [ITL. Inst. Toegep. linguist.]. **Main/Corp** Katholieke Universiteit te Leuven. Instituut voor Toegepaste LinguÂistik. Vol. 1, (1968)-. Periodical. Dutch (English, French and German). Twice a year (Mar., July). 1500.00F. Instituut voor Toegepaste Linguistiek, Blijde Inkomststr 21, B-3000 Leuven Belgium. **Tel** 011 32 16 285030. **ED** Nicole Delbecque. **LC** P123; .K264a. Index available. **Bk Rev. Circ:** 400 (ctrl). available on diskette.
Desc: Contains articles and book reviews in the field of applied linguistics, in a broad sense, among others language teaching and foreign teaching.
Ind/Abst Lang. Teach.; MLA Int. Bibl. Books Artic. Mod. Lang. Lit.

BE
ITL : REVIEW OF APPLIED LINGUISTICS. **Added/Corp** Katholieke Universiteit Leuven. Afdeling Toegepaste Linguistiek. **VFOAT** Review of Applied Linguistics. (19??)-. Periodical. French. qt.
Ind/Abst Annu. Bibliogr. Engl. Lang. Lit.; Linguist. Lang. Behav. Abstr. (1972-) [Full Cov.]; MLA Int. Bibl. Books Artic. Mod. Lang. Lit.; Soc. Plann. Policy Dev. Abstr.

BU
IZKUSTVOTO NA PREVODA. **Added/Corp** Suiuz na Prevodachite v Bulgariia. (1976)-. Bulgarian (summaries and/or abstracts in English, French, German and Russian). 1.38lv. Ul G Gensv 4, Sofia Bulgaria. **LC** PN241.A1; I94.

●RU
IZVESTIIA AKADEMII NAUK. SERIIA LITERATURY I IAZYKA / ROSSIISKAIA AKADEMIIA NAUK. **Added/Corp** Rossiiskaia Akademiia Nauk. **VFOAT** Seriia Literatury i Iazyka; Literatury i Iazyka; Izvestiia Rossiiskoi Akademii Nauk. Seriia Literatury i Iazyka. (Jan./Feb. 1992)-. Academic Scholarly Publication. Russian (summaries and/or abstracts in English; table of contents in English). Six times a year. $126.00. Izdatelstvo Nauka / Akademiia Nauk, Publishing House of the Russian Academy of Sciences, Leninskii Porspekt 14, 117901 Moscow Russia. **Tel** 011 95 954-21-53, FAX 011 95 938-21-44, telex 411964. **(Subscription address:** East View Publications Inc., 3020 Harbor Lane North, Suite 110, Minneapolis MN 55447.**)** **LC** PG6; .A553. **DD** 410/.5. **CODEN** IALYEH. ***Continues*** *Izvestiia Akademii nauk SSSR. Seriia Literatury i Iazyka, 0321-1711.*
Ind/Abst Annu. Bibliogr. Engl. Lang. Lit.; MLA Int. Bibl. Books Artic. Mod. Lang. Lit.; Soc. Plann. Policy Dev. Abstr.; Sociol. Abstr.

BU/0068-3787
IZVESTIIA NA INSTITUTA ZA BULGARSKI EZIK. **Main/Corp** Bulgarska Akademiia Na Naukite, Sofia. Institut Za Bulgarski Ezik. Vol. 1 (1952)-. Academic Scholarly Publication. Bulgarian. an. Bulgarska Akademiia na Naukite, 7 Noemvri 1, Sofia Bulgaria. **(Subscription address:** Hemus Foreign Trade Organization, 6 Tzar Osvoboditel Boulevard, 1000 Sofia Bulgaria.**)** **LC** PG801; .B8.
Ind/Abst MLA Int. Bibl. Books Artic. Mod. Lang. Lit.

NE
JAARBOEK. **Main/Corp** Koninklijke Academie voor Nederlandse Taal- en Letterkunde. (1972)-. Dutch. an. 400F. Koninklijke Academie voor Nederlandse Taalen Letterkunde, Koningstraat 18, B-9000 Gent Belgium. **Tel** (091)25.27.74. **LC** PF1001; .V6. **Circ:** 300. ***Continues*** *Koninklijke Vlaamse Academie voor Taal- en Letterkunde. Jaarboek van de Koninklijke Vlaamse Academie voor Taal- en Letterkunde.*

GW
JAHRBUCH ... DES INSTITUTS FUER DEUTSCHE SPRACHE. **Added/Corp** Institut fuer Deutsche Sprache. (1975)-. German. an. Price varies according to size. Walter de Gruyter Inc., PO Box 303421, D 10728 Berlin Germany. **Tel** 011 49 30 260050, FAX 011 49 30 26005251. **LC** PF3003; .S78. **DD** 430/.5. ***Continues*** *Jahrbuch (Institut fuer Deutsche Sprache).*

GW/0083-5617
JAHRBUCH DES VEREINS FUER NIEDERDEUTSCHE SPRACHFORSCHUNG. [Jahrb. Ver. Niederdtsch. Sprachforsch.]. **Main/Corp** Verein fur

Niederdeutsche Sprachforschung. **VFOAT** Niederdeutsches Jahrbuch. (1875)-. German. an. Karl Wachholtz Verlag, Postfach 2769, Gansemarkt 1-3, W-2350 Neumunster F R Germany. **Tel** 011 49 4321 5670, FAX 011 49 4321 56778, telex 299 618 CURIR. **LC** PF5601; .V5. cum. index.
Ind/Abst MLA Int. Bibl. Books Artic. Mod. Lang. Lit.

GW/0342-6300
JAHRBUCH DEUTSCH ALS FREMDSPRACHE. Vol. 1 (1975)-. German. an. Iudicium Verlag, Postfach 701067, D-81310 Munich Germany. **Tel** 011 49 89 717868. **LC** PF3066; .J34.

GW/0449-5233
JAHRBUCH FUER INTERNATIONALE GERMANISTIK. [Jahrb. int. Ger.]. **Added/Corp** Internationale Vereinigung fuer Germanische Sprach- und Literaturwissenschaft. Vol. 1, No. 1 (1969)-. German (English and French). Twice a year (July, & Oct.). 92.00F. Verlag Peter Lang AG, Jupiterstrasse 15, CH-3000 Bern 15 Switzerland. **Tel** 011 41 31 9411122, FAX 011 41 31 321131. **ED** Hans-Gert Roloff. **LC** PD3; .J35. **Bk Rev. Ad Acc. Circ:** 650. Documents available from The Genuine Article.
Desc: Yearbook of international German philology. Published in connection with the International Association for German Language and Literature.
Ind/Abst Arts Humanit. Citation Index [Full Cov.]; Curr. Contents Arts Humanit.; MLA Int. Bibl. Books Artic. Mod. Lang. Lit.; Res. Alert [Full Cov.]; Romant. Move.; Soc. Sci. Cit. Index [Select. Cov.].

NE/0075-3114
JANUA LINGUARUM. SERIES MAIOR. [Janua ling., Ser. maior]. (1959)-. Monographic series. English. ir. Price varies per volume. Walter de Gruyter Inc. / Hawthorne, 200 Saw Mill River Road, Hawthorne NY 10532. **Tel** (914)747-0110, GERMANY: 011/49/30/260050, FAX (914)747-1326, telex 646677. **LC** UNC.
Ind/Abst MLA Int. Bibl. Books Artic. Mod. Lang. Lit.

SZ/0721-3719
JAPANISCHE STUDIEN ZUR DEUTSCHEN SPRACHE UND LITERATUR. **VFOAT** Etudes Japonaises en Langue et Litterature Allemandes; Japanese Studies in German Language and Literature. (1971)-. Monographic series. German. tw. Verlag Peter Lang AG, Jupiterstrasse 15, CH-3000 Bern 15 Switzerland. **Tel** 011 41 31 9411122, FAX 011 41 31 321131. **UDC** 803.0.
Ind/Abst MLA Int. Bibl. Books Artic. Mod. Lang. Lit.

XR
JAZYKOVEDNE AKTUALITY / VYDAVA JAZYKOVEDNE SDRUZENI PRI CSAV ... ET AL. **Added/Corp** Jazykovedne Sdruzeni pri CSAV. (1966)-. Czech. qt. **LC** P9; .J29.
Ind/Abst Annu. Bibliogr. Engl. Lang. Lit.

XO/0448-9241
JAZYKOVEDNE STUDIE. **Added/Corp** Ustav Slovenskeho Jazyka (Slovenska Akademia Vied). Jazykovedny Ustav Ludovita Stura. Vol. 1 (1956)-. Monographic series. Slovak (Russian; summaries and/or abstracts in German and Russian). ir. Price varies per volume. Veda, Publishing House of the Slovak Academy of Sciences, Klemensova 19, 814 30 Bratislava Slovakia. **Tel** (7)583-15. **(Subscription address:** John Benjamins North America, PO Box 27519, Philadelphia PA 19118-0519.**)** **LC** PG5201; .J3.

XO/0021-5597
JAZYKOVEDNY CASOPIS. **Added/Corp** Slovenksa Akademia Vied a Umeni, Bratislava. Slovenska Akademia Vied. (1946)-. Periodical. Slovak (English, German and Russian). sa. DM42.00. Veda, Publishing House of the Slovak Academy of Sciences, Klemensova 19, 814 30 Bratislava Slovakia. **Tel** (7)583-15. **(Subscription address:** Kubon & Sagner, ABT Zeitschriftenimport, D 80328 Munich Germany.**)** **ED** Jan Horecky. **LC** P9; .J3. **Bk Rev. Ad Acc. Circ:** 1,000 (ctrl). ***Absorbed*** *Linguistica Slovaca.*
Desc: Strictly devoted to linguistics, the journal prints articles about the contemporary written and spoken Slovak with consideration of the various dialects.
Ind/Abst Linguist. Lang. Behav. Abstr. (1972-) [Full Cov.]; Soc. Plann. Policy Dev. Abstr.

IS/0333-8347
JEWISH LANGUAGE REVIEW. [Jew. lang. rev.]. **VFOAT** JLR. 1 (1981)-. Periodical. English. an. $24.00. Association for Study of Jewish Language, University of Haifa, 1610 Eshkol Twr, Haifa 31 999 Israel. **Tel** 011 972 4 240190. **LC** PJ5061; .J38. **DD** 408/.9924. **UDC** 809.24. **[CCC].**
Ind/Abst Arts Humanit. Citation Index (19??-19??) [Full Cov.]; Soc. Plann. Policy Dev. Abstr.; Sociol. Abstr. (?-?).

XV/0021-6933
JEZIK IN SLOVSTVO. [Jezik slovst.]. Began publication with Oct. 1955 issue. Periodical. Slovenian. ir. **LC** PG1801. **UDC** 808.63.
Ind/Abst MLA Int. Bibl. Books Artic. Mod. Lang. Lit.

PL/0021-6941
JEZYK POLSKI (KRAKOW 1919). (JEZYK POLSKI.). [Jez. pol.]. **Added/Corp** Towarzystwo Miosmolow Jezula Polskiego. Vol. 1 (1913)-. Periodical. Polish. bm (5 issues). $29.00. **(Subscription address:** ARS Polona, PO Box 1001, 00068 Warsaw Poland.**)** **LC** PG6001; .J48. **DD** 491.8/5/05. cum. index.
Ind/Abst MLA Int. Bibl. Books Artic. Mod. Lang. Lit.

JA
JIJI EIGO KENKYU. THE STUDY OF CURRENT ENGLISH. **VFOAT** The Study of Current English. (19??)-. Periodical. Japanese (summaries and/or abstracts in English). Twelve times a year. $144.00. **(Subscription address:** Kyowa Book Company Inc., 1 38 Kanda Jinbocho Chiyoda-ku, Tokyo 101 Japan.**)**

II
JISTA. **Main/Corp** Indian Scientific Translators Association. V. 1- March 1972-. Periodical. English. qt. $3.50. INSDOC, 14 Satsang Vihar Marg, New Delhi 110067 India. **Tel** 011 91 11 6863617, FAX 665837, telex 031-73099. **LC** P306.A1; I46. **DD** 418/.02. **UDC** 800.3.

JA/0388-6417
JOCHI EIGO BUNGAKU KENKYU. [Jochi Eigo bungaku kenkyu]. **VFOAT** Sophia English Studies. (1976)-. Periodical. Multiple languages. an. **DD** 820.
Ind/Abst MLA Int. Bibl. Books Artic. Mod. Lang. Lit.

FR/0021-762X
JOURNAL ASIATIQUE. [J. asiat.]. **Added/Corp** Societe Asiatique (Paris, France) Centre National de la Recherche Scientifique (France). Ser. 3, Vol. 1-14, (Jan. 1836)-. Periodical. French. Twice a year (July, & Dec.). 500.00F France; 550.00F others. Societe Asiatique, 3 rue Mazarine, 75006 Paris France. **Tel** 011 33 1 44414314. ***Continues*** *Nouveau Journal Asiatique, 0021-762X.*
Ind/Abst MLA Int. Bibl. Books Artic. Mod. Lang. Lit.

CN/0833-1812
JOURNAL DE L'IMMERSION, LE. [J. immers.]. **Added/Corp** Association Canadienne des Professeurs d'Immersion. **VFOAT** Immersion Journal. Vol. 10, No. 1 (Nov. 1986)-. Periodical. French (English; summaries and/or abstracts in English). Three times a year. 45.00Can$. Canadian Association of Immersion Teachers, 72 Robertson Road, Nepean Ontario K2H 5Y8 Canada. **Tel** (613)727-6933, FAX (613)596-9010. **ED** Francoise Kartha (editor's address: Ministere de l'Education, c/o Saskatoon Public School Board OMLO/BMLO, 405, 3rd Avenue Sud, Saskatoon, SK S7K 1M4 Canada). **DD** 372.6/5/210971. **Bk Rev. Ad Acc. Circ:** 2,500 (ctrl). ***Continues*** *Les Nouvelles de l'ACPI, 0822-9333.*
Desc: Articles dealing with elementary and secondary immersion programs for the teaching and learning of French and English as second languages. Covers research reports, teaching methods, and curriculum development.

SA/1013-8471
JOURNAL FOR SEMITICS. **Added/Corp** Southern African Society for Semitics. **VFOAT** Tydskrif vir Semitistiek; JSem. Vol. 1, No. 1 (1989)-. Periodical. English (Afrikaans, Dutch, German and French). Twice a year. $20.00 South Africa; $35.00 others. University of South Africa, PO Box 392, Pretoria 0001 South Africa. **Tel** 011 27 12 4298468, FAX 011 (27)12 429 3321, telex (59)350068+. **LC** PJ3001; .J58. **DD** 492/.05.
Ind/Abst MLA Int. Bibl. Books Artic. Mod. Lang. Lit.

US/0731-6755
JOURNAL OF ADVANCED COMPOSITION. (JOURNAL OF ADVANCED COMPOSITION : JAC.). [J. adv. compos.]. **Added/Corp** Association of Teachers of Advanced Composition (U.S.). **VFOAT** JAC; J.A.C. (1980)-. Periodical. English. Three times a year. $20.00 (US), $25.00 (other) institutions; $15.00 (US), $20.00 (other) individuals. Journal of Advanced Composition, Department of English, Iowa State University, Ames IA 50011. **Tel** (515)294-3577, FAX (515)294-6814. **ED** Thomas Kent. **Bk Rev**, (Qty: 30). **Ad Acc. Pr Rev. Circ:** 900 (ctrl).
Desc: Covers teaching advanced writing in college: expository, creative, business, technical and professional writing pedagogy; research, theory, and practice.
Ind/Abst Am. Humanit. Index; Curr. Index J. Educ. (March 1990); MLA Int. Bibl. Books Artic. Mod. Lang. Lit.; Soc. Plann. Policy Dev. Abstr.

NE/0167-6164
JOURNAL OF AFRICAN LANGUAGES AND LINGUISTICS. [J. Afr. lang. linguist.]. **Added/Corp** Rijksuniversiteit te Leiden. Vakgroep Afrikaanse Taalkunde en Bantoeistiek. Vol. 1 (April 1979)-. Periodical. English (French). sa. $103.50. Walter de Gruyter Inc., PO Box 303421, D 10728 Berlin Germany. **Tel** 011 49 30 260050, FAX 011 49 30 26005251. **LC** PL8000; .J63. **DD** 409/.6. **[CCC].** Index available. cum. index. **Bk Rev. Ad Acc. Circ:** 500 (ctrl). available on microfilm from University Microfilms International (UMI).
Desc: A broad-based, international journal of wide academic scope, which offers articles on all aspects of African language studies.
Ind/Abst Anthropol. Lit.; Linguist. Lang. Behav. Abstr.

(1979-) [Full Cov.]; Middle East Abstr. Index; MLA Int. Bibl. Books Artic. Mod. Lang. Lit.; Soc. Plann. Policy Dev. Abstr.

US/0147-1635
JOURNAL OF BASIC WRITING. [J. basic writ.]. **Added/Corp** City University of New York. Instructional Resource Center. City University of New York. City College. Dept. of English. **VFOAT** Basic Writing. Vol. 1 (Spring 1975)-. English. sa. $15.00 (one year), $29.00 (two year) US; $20.00 (one year), $39.00 (two year) other. Instructional Resource Center, City University of New York, 535 East 80th Street, New York NY 10021. **Tel** (212)794-5445, FAX (212)794-5706. **ED** Bill Bernhardt and Peter Miller. **LC** PE1404; .J68. **DD** 808/.042/0711. Index available (every 2 years). cum. index. **Ad Acc. Circ:** 2,000 (ctrl). available on microfilm and microfiche from University Microfilms International (UMI).
Desc: For college faculty who teach basic writing. Provides a forum for theoretical discussions and practical applications for improving the teaching of basic writing.
Ind/Abst Curr. Index J. Educ.; Educ. Index (1992-); Soc. Plann. Policy Dev. Abstr.

UK/0075-4161
JOURNAL OF BYELORUSSIAN STUDIES. [J. Byeloruss. stud.]. **Added/Corp** Anglo-Byelorussian Society. (1965)-. English. ir. Anglo Byelorussian Society, 39 Holden Road, London N12 8HS England. **LC** DK507.A2; J68.
Ind/Abst MLA Int. Bibl. Books Artic. Mod. Lang. Lit.

●UK/0962-1377
JOURNAL OF CELTIC LINGUISTICS. Vol. 1 (1992)-. English. University of Wales Press, 6 Gwennyth Street, Cathays Cardiff CF2 4YD Wales United Kingdom. **Tel** 011 44 222 231919.

UK/0305-0009
JOURNAL OF CHILD LANGUAGE. [J. child lang.]. Vol. 1 (May 1974)-. Academic Scholarly Publication. English. Three times a year. $145.00 US, Canada & Mexico; £83.00 other. Cambridge University Press, The Edinburgh Building, Shaftesbury Road, Cambridge CB2 2RU United Kingdom. **Tel** 011 44 223 312393, FAX 011 44 223 325959. **(Subscription address:** Cambridge University Press / North America, 110 Midland Avenue, Port Chester NY 10573.**)** **ED** Katharine Perera. **LC** P118; .J68. **DD** 401/.9. **NLM** W1 JO583L. **Pr Rev.** available on microfilm and microfiche from University Microfilms International (UMI). Documents available from The Genuine Article.
Desc: Publishes articles on all aspects of language development in children, including crying, babbling, and auditory-perceptual ability in prelinguistic babies, the development of phonology, intonation, grammar, semantics, pragmatics, and the social and cognitive aspects of language. Also covers the study of related topics like imitation and parental speech to children. Cross-linguistic comparisons showing language universals and language differences are also included. Studies of the development of sign language, of the language of disabled children and of the development of reading and writing are included where they relate to more general matters on language development.
Ind/Abst Abstr. Anthropol.; Acad. Search (Jan. 1994-); Appl. Soc. Sci. Index Abstr.; Br. Educ. Index; Chicano Index; Child. Lit. Abstr. (19??-); Commun. Abstr. (?-?); Curr. Contents Soc. Behav. Sci.; Curr. Index J. Educ.; Dev. Med. Child Neurol.; Educ. Index; Educ. Adm. Abstr.; INFO-SOUTH Abstr.; Lang. Teach.; Linguist. Lang. Behav. Abstr. (1974-) [Full Cov.]; Mag. Search; Middle East Abstr. Index; MLA Int. Bibl. Books Artic. Mod. Lang. Lit.; Multicult. Educ. Abstr.; Psychol. Abstr. (1974-); PsycINFO; PsycLit; PsycScan: Develop. Psych.; Res. Alert [Full Cov.]; Sage Fam. Stud. Abstr.; Soc. Plann. Policy Dev. Abstr.; Soc. Sci. Cit. Index [Full Cov.]; Sociol. Abstr.; Spec. Educ. Needs Abstr.; Stud. Women Abstr.

US/0091-3723
JOURNAL OF CHINESE LINGUISTICS. [J. Chin. linguist.]. **Added/Corp** University of California, Berkeley. Project on Linguistic Analysis. **VFOAT** Chung-Kuo Yu Yen Hsueh Pao. Vol. 1 (Jan. 1973)-. Periodical. English (Chinese). Twice a year (Jan. & June). $25.00 (individuals), $35.00 (institutions). Project on Linguistic Analysis, 2222 Piedmont, Berkeley CA 94720. **Tel** (510)642-5937, (510)642-5939. **ED** William S-Y Wang. **LC** PL1001; .J68. **DD** 495.1. cum. index. **Bk Rev. Ad Acc. Circ:** 500 (ctrl). Documents available from The Genuine Article.
Desc: The journal publishes works on all aspects of the Chinese language: historical and descriptive, theoretical and applied, social, psychological and literary.
Ind/Abst Abstr. Anthropol. (19??-); Arts Humanit. Citation Index [Full Cov.]; Curr. Contents Arts Humanit.; Curr. Index J. Educ.; Linguist. Lang. Behav. Abstr. (1973-) [Full Cov.]; MLA Int. Bibl. Books Artic. Mod. Lang. Lit.; Res. Alert [Full Cov.]; Soc. Plann. Policy Dev. Abstr.; Soc. Sci. Cit. Index [Select. Cov.].

US/0075-4218
JOURNAL OF CROATIAN STUDIES. [J. Croat. stud.]. **Added/Corp** Croatian Academy of America. Vol. 1 (1960)-. English. an. $15.00 (individuals), $30.00 (institutions). Croatian Academy of America Inc, PO Box 1767, Grand Central Station, New York NY 10017. **ED** Jerome Jareb and Karlo Mirth. **LC** DB361; .J6. **DD** 491.

Bk Rev. Circ: 1,000 (ctrl).
Desc: Covers Croatian history, sociology, literature, linguistics, fine arts, economics and philosophy.
Ind/Abst Am. Hist. Life (1960-); Am. Bibliogr. Slavic East Europ. Stud.; MLA Int. Bibl. Books Artic. Mod. Lang. Lit.

US/0022-0256
JOURNAL OF CUNEIFORM STUDIES. [J. cuneif. stud.]. **Added/Corp** American Schools of Oriental Research. Vol. 1 (1947)-. Academic Scholarly Publication. English. sa (April, October). $52.25 institutions; $42.75 individuals. Scholars Press / Georgia, PO Box 15399, Atlanta GA 30333-0399. **Tel** (404)636-4757, (404)727-2320, FAX (404)727-2348. **ED** Erle Leichty. **LC** PJ3102; .J67. **DD** 492.1905. **CODEN** JCUSAV. **Bk Rev. Circ:** 625 (ctrl). available on microfilm and microfiche from University Microfilms International (UMI).
Desc: A scholarly review devoted to the languages, literatures, and cultures of ancient Mesopotamia, Syria, Anatolia, and Iran.
Ind/Abst Anthropol. Lit.; Index Book Rev. Relig. (19??-19??); Math. Rev.; MLA Int. Bibl. Books Artic. Mod. Lang. Lit.; Old Testam. Abstr.; Relig. Index One Period. (1949-19??); Relig. Theol. Abstr.; Soc. Plann. Policy Dev. Abstr.

●NE/0925-8558
JOURNAL OF EAST ASIAN LINGUISTICS. Vol. 1, No. 1 Jan. (1992)-. Periodical. English. tq. $366.00. Kluwer Academic Publishers, Postbus 322, 3300 AH Dordrecht, The Netherlands. **Tel** 011 (31) 78 524400, FAX 011 31 78 183273, telex 20083. **ED** James Huang and Y. Kuroda. **LC** PJ2; .J68. **Pr Rev. Acid Free.** available on microfilm and microfiche from University Microfilms International (UMI).
Desc: The study of East Asian languages, especially of Chinese, Japanese and Korean, has existed for a long time as a field, as demonstrated by the existence of programs in most institutions of higher learning and research that include these languages as a major component Speakers of these three languages have shared a great deal of linguistic heritage during the development of their languages through cultural contact, in addition to possible genealogical linkage. These languages accordingly possess various common features. Another important factor that ties them together as a field is that they have shared a common tradition of linguistic scholarship, a tradition that distinguishes itself from the study of western languages.
Ind/Abst Arts Humanit. Citation Index [Full Cov.]; Curr. Contents Arts Humanit.; Soc. Plann. Policy Dev. Abstr.; Soc. Sci. Cit. Index [Select. Cov.]; Sociol. Abstr.

II/0970-8332
JOURNAL OF ENGLISH AND FOREIGN LANGUAGES. [J. Engl. Foreign Lang.]. **VFOAT** JEFL. Journal of English and Foreign Languages. (1988)-. Periodical. English. sa. **UDC** 420-07.
Ind/Abst MLA Int. Bibl. Books Artic. Mod. Lang. Lit.; Soc. Plann. Policy Dev. Abstr.

US/0363-6941
JOURNAL OF ENGLISH AND GERMANIC PHILOLOGY, THE. (JEGP. JOURNAL OF ENGLISH AND GERMANIC PHILOLOGY.). [J. Engl. Ger. philol.]. **VFOAT** Journal of English and Germanic Philology. Vol. 58 (Jan. 1959)-. Academic Scholarly Publication. English. qt. $52.00 (one year), $93.60 (two year), institutions; $30.00 (one year), $54.00 (two year), individuals. University of Illinois Press, 1325 South Oak Street, Champaign IL 61820. **Tel** (217)333-0950, FAX (217)244-8082. **ED** Dale Kramer. **DD** 410. **[CCC].** Index available (free). **Bk Rev. Ad Acc. Circ:** 1,600. available on microfilm and microfiche from University Microfilms International (UMI). Documents available from The Genuine Article, UMI Article Clearinghouse. ***Continues*** *Journal of English and Germanic Philology, 0363-6941.*
Desc: Scholarly articles in English literature and language, American literature, German and Scandinavian languages and literatures.
Ind/Abst Abstr. Engl. Stud.; Acad. Search (July 1993-); Annu. Bibliogr. Engl. Lang. Lit.; Arts Humanit. Citation Index [Full Cov.]; Book Rev. Index; Expand. Acad. Index (1989-); Humanit. Index; Humanit. Source (Jul. 1993-); INFO-SOUTH Abstr.; MLA Int. Bibl. Books Artic. Mod. Lang. Lit.; Newsp. Period. Abstr. (1991-); Res. Alert [Full Cov.]; Soc. Plann. Policy Dev. Abstr.; Soc. Sci. Cit. Index [Select. Cov.].

KO
JOURNAL OF ENGLISH LANGUAGE AND LITERATURE, THE. Vol. 27, No. 1 (Spring 1981)-. Periodical. English (Korean). qt. English Language and Literature Association of Korea, 89 2 Shinmoon-Ro 2-Ka, Chongro-ku, Seoul 110 Republic of Korea. ***Continues*** *English Language and Literature.*
Ind/Abst Annu. Bibliogr. Engl. Lang. Lit.; MLA Int. Bibl. Books Artic. Mod. Lang. Lit.

II/0022-0876
JOURNAL OF ENGLISH LANGUAGE TEACHING (INDIA), THE. [J. Engl. lang. teach., India]. **Added/Corp** Society for the Promotion of Education in India. Vol. 1 (June 1965)-. Periodical. English. Six times a year (Feb., Apr., June, Aug., Oct., Dec.). $10.00. English Language Teachers Association, 3 1 Trust Link St Mandavelipak, Madras 600 028 India. **LC** PE1068.I4; J68.
Ind/Abst Lang. Teach.

US/0075-4242
JOURNAL OF ENGLISH LINGUISTICS. [J. Eng. linguist.]. V. 1 (1967)-. English. sa. $15.00. Journal of English Linguistics / University of Georgia, Athens GA 30602. **Tel** (706)542-2246. **ED** William A Kretzchimar Jr. **LC** PE1001; .J65. **DD** 420/.05. **UDC** 802.0. **[CCC]. Bk Rev. Ad Acc. Circ:** 600 (ctrl). Documents available from The Genuine Article.
Desc: An international journal devoted to articles and reviews of books on the modern and historical periods of the English language.
Ind/Abst Annu. Bibliogr. Engl. Lang. Lit.; Arts Humanit. Citation Index (19??-19??) [Full Cov.]; Lang. Teach.; Linguist. Lang. Behav. Abstr. (1973-) [Full Cov.]; MLA Int. Bibl. Books Artic. Mod. Lang. Lit.; Res. Alert [Full Cov.]; Soc. Plann. Policy Dev. Abstr.

II/0970-6232
JOURNAL OF ENGLISH STUDIES (WARANGAL), THE. (THE JOURNAL OF ENGLISH STUDIES.). [J. Eng. stud.]. **Added/Corp** Regional Engineering College. Dept. of English. (19??)-. Periodical. English. ir. Journal of English Studies, Regional Engineering College, Warangal 506004 AP India. **(Subscription address:** Prints India, 11 Darya Ganj, New Delhi 110002 India.**) LC** PE1; .J723. **DD** 420/.5.
Ind/Abst Abstr. Engl. Stud.

UK/0959-2695
JOURNAL OF FRENCH LANGUAGE STUDIES. **Added/Corp** Association for French Language Studies. **VFOAT** French Language Studies. Vol. 1, No. 1 (March 1991)-. Academic Scholarly Publication. English (French). sa. $79.00 US, Canada & Mexico; £47.00 other. Cambridge University Press, The Edinburgh Building, Shaftesbury Road, Cambridge CB2 2RU United Kingdom. **Tel** 011 44 223 312393, FAX 011 44 223 325959. **(Subscription address:** Cambridge University Press / North America, 110 Midland Avenue, Port Chester NY 10573.**) ED** Jacques Durand, Anthony Lodge and Carol Sanders. **LC** PC2001; .J68. **DD** 440/.5. **CODEN** JFSLEP.
Desc: Aims to encourage and promote theoretical, descriptive and applied studies of all aspects of the French language. The journal brings together research from the English and French speaking traditions, publishing significant work on French phonology, morphology, syntax, lexis and sematics, sociolinguistics and variation studies.
Ind/Abst Linguist. Lang. Behav. Abstr. (1991-) [Full Cov.]; Soc. Plann. Policy Dev. Abstr.

US/0147-5460
JOURNAL OF HISPANIC PHILOLOGY. [J. Hisp. philol.]. **VFOAT** JHP. Vol. 1 (Autumn 1976)-. Periodical. English (Spanish). Three times a year. $60.00 US; $70.00 other. Journal of Hispanic Philology, Florida State University, Department of Modern Languages and Linguistics, Tallahassee FL 32306. **Tel** (904)644-8199, FAX (904)644-0524. **ED** Daniel Eisenberg. **LC** PC4001; .J68. **DD** 460/.5. Index available. cum. index. **Bk Rev. Ad Acc. Pr Rev. Circ:** 500. Documents available from The Genuine Article.
Desc: Literature and historical linguistics of the Iberian peninsula through 1700.
Ind/Abst Arts Humanit. Citation Index (19??-19??) [Full Cov.]; Curr. Contents Arts Humanit.; Int. Bibliogr. Zeitschriftenliteratur Allen Gebieten Wissens; MLA Int. Bibl. Books Artic. Mod. Lang. Lit.; Res. Alert [Full Cov.]; Soc. Plann. Policy Dev. Abstr.

US/0092-2323
JOURNAL OF INDO-EUROPEAN STUDIES, THE. [J. Indo-Eur. stud.]. V. 1 (Spring 1973)-. Periodical. English. sa (published in 2 double issues per year). $80.00 (1 year), $230.00 (3 year) institutions and libraries; $40.00 (1 year), $115.00 (3 year) individuals. Foreign surface mail postage free. Foreign Airmail postage add $20.00 extra per year. Journal of Indo-European Studies, 6861 Elm Street, Suite 4H, McLean DC 22101. **Tel** (703)442-8010, FAX (703)847-9524. **ED** Roger Pearson, Edgar Polome and Marija Gimbutas. **LC** CB201; .J68. **DD** 910/.03. Index available. **Bk Rev. Ad Acc. Circ:** 1,100 (ctrl). available on microfilm and microfiche from University Microfilms International (UMI). Documents available from The Genuine Article.
Desc: Covers the linguistics, archaeology and mythology of Indo-European peoples.
Ind/Abst Abstr. Anthropol.; Am. Bibliogr. Slavic East Europ. Stud.; Annu. Bibliogr. Engl. Lang. Lit.; Anthropol. Index; Anthropol. Lit.; Arts Humanit. Citation Index [Full Cov.]; Curr. Contents Arts Humanit.; Middle East Abstr. Index; MLA Int. Bibl. Books Artic. Mod. Lang. Lit.; Res. Alert [Full Cov.]; Soc. Plann. Policy Dev. Abstr.

US/0899-885X
JOURNAL OF INTENSIVE ENGLISH STUDIES. [J. intensive Engl. stud.]. **Added/Corp** University of Arizona. Center for English as a Second Language. **VFOAT** JIES. Vol. 1, No. 1 (June 1987)-. Periodical. English. sa. $15.00 North America; $20.00 other. Dean Jensen Business Manager, CESL Building 100, University of Arizona, Tucson AZ 85721. **Tel** (602)621-3637, FAX (602)621-9180. **ED** Frank Pialorsi. **LC** PE1128.A2; A53. **DD** 428/.007. **CODEN** JENGEC. Index available. **Bk Rev. Ad Acc. Circ:** 150. ***Continues*** *American Language Journal, 0734-7545.*
Desc: Papers applicable to intensive English programs: curriculum, evaluation, administration, teacher-training, theory, and practice.
Ind/Abst Curr. Index J. Educ.; Linguist. Lang. Behav. Abstr. (1990-) [Full Cov.]; Soc. Plann. Policy Dev. Abstr.

JA
JOURNAL OF JAPANESE LINGUISTICS. **Added/Corp** Nanzan Daigaku. Dept. of Japanese. **VFOAT** JJL. Vol. 12 (1990)-. English. an. $35.00. Nanzan University, 18 Yamazato-cho, Showa-ku Nagoya 466 Japan. **Tel** 011 81 52 8323111, FAX 011 81 52 8336157. **ED** Yasuaki Abe. **LC** PL501; .P3. **Bk Rev,** (Qty: 1). **Ad Acc. *Continues*** *Papers in Japanese Linguistics, 0197-3150.*

US/0261-927X
JOURNAL OF LANGUAGE AND SOCIAL PSYCHOLOGY. **VFOAT** JLSP. Vol. 1, No. 1 (1982)-. Periodical. English. qt (Mar., June, Sept., Dec.). $170.00. SAGE Periodical Press, 2455 Teller Road, Thousand Oaks CA 91320. **Tel** (805)499-0721, FAX (805)499-0871, telex 100799. **ED** James Bradac and Kathy Kellermann. **LC** P40; .J68. **DD** 306.4/4/05. **[CCC].** Index available. **Bk Rev. Ad Acc. Acid Free. Circ:** 500.
Desc: Explores the social dimensions of language and the linguistic implications of social life. Articles are drawn from a wide range of disciplines, including linguistics, cognitive science, sociology, communication, psychology, education and anthropology.
Ind/Abst Abstr. Res. Pastor. Care Couns. (19??-); Commun. Abstr.; Int. Bibliogr. Sociol.; Linguist. Lang. Behav. Abstr. (1985-) [Full Cov.]; MLA Int. Bibl. Books Artic. Mod. Lang. Lit.; Psychol. Abstr. (1983-); PsycINFO; PsycLit; Soc. Plann. Policy Dev. Abstr.

NR
JOURNAL OF LANGUAGE ARTS AND COMMUNICATION (J.L.A.C.). **VFOAT** J.L.A.C.; JLAC. Vol. 1, No. 1 (March 1980)-. Periodical. English. $12.00. The Business Manager of J L A C Department of Language Arts, University of Ibadan, Ibadan Nigeria. **UDC** 800.

US/8755-0504
JOURNAL OF LANGUAGE FOR INTERNATIONAL BUSINESS, THE. [J. lang. int. bus.]. **Added/Corp** American Graduate School of International Management. Dept. of Modern Languages. **VFOAT** JOLIB; J.O.L.I.B. Vol. 1, No. 1 (Spring 1984)-. Periodical. English (Multiple languages). Twice a year. $15.00 (individuals), $25.00 (institutions) US; $20.00 (individuals), $30.00 (institutions) Canada & Mexico; $25.00 (individuals), $35.00 (institutions) others. Journal of Language International Business, American Graduate School, Department of Modern Language, Glendale AZ 85306. **Tel** (602)978-7255, (602)978-7124, FAX (602)439-1435, telex 187123. **ED** Robert M. Ramsey. **LC** PB5; .J68. **DD** 418/.007. **Bk Rev. Ad Acc. Circ:** 300.
Desc: Devoted to the teaching and study of foreign languages, English for international business, and cross-cultural studies.

US/1055-1360
JOURNAL OF LINGUISTIC ANTHROPOLOGY. **See** Anthropology.

UK/0022-2267
JOURNAL OF LINGUISTICS. [J. linguist.]. **Added/Corp** Linguistics Association of Great Britain. Vol. 1 (Apr. 1965)-. Academic Scholarly Publication. English. sa. $97.00 US, Canada and Mexico; £53.00 other. Cambridge University Press, The Edinburgh Building, Shaftesbury Road, Cambridge CB2 2RU United Kingdom. **Tel** 011 44 223 312393, FAX 011 44 223 325959. **(Subscription address:** Cambridge University Press / North America, 110 Midland Avenue, Port Chester NY 10573.**) ED** Nigel Vincent. **LC** P1; .J65. **DD** 410/.5. **[CCC]. Bk Rev. Pr Rev.** available on microfilm and microfiche from University Microfilms International (UMI). Documents available from The Genuine Article, UMI Article Clearinghouse.
Desc: Concerned with all branches of theoretical linguistics, including syntax, morphology, phonology, phonetics, semantics, pragmatics and historical, sociological, computational and psychological aspects of language and linguistic theory. Provides a survey of recent publications in the field with review articles on major works marking important theoretical advances as well as about twenty reviews and shorter notices in each issue.
Ind/Abst Abstr. Anthropol.; Acad. Search (Jan. 1994-); Arts Humanit. Citation Index [Full Cov.]; Curr. Index J. Educ.; Expand. Acad. Index (1989-); Humanit. Index; Humanit. Source (Jul. 1993-); INFO-SOUTH Abstr.; Int. Bibliogr. Sociol.; Lang. Teach.; Linguist. Lang. Behav. Abstr. (1972-) [Full Cov.]; Mag. Search; Middle East Abstr. Index; MLA Int. Bibl. Books Artic. Mod. Lang. Lit.; Newsp. Period. Abstr. (1991-); Res. Alert [Full Cov.]; Soc. Plann. Policy Dev. Abstr.; Soc. Sci. Cit. Index [Full Cov.].

NE/0341-7638
JOURNAL OF LITERARY SEMANTICS. [J. lit. semant.]. Vol. 1 (April 1972)-. Periodical. English (French and German). DM98.00 (institutions), DM76.00 (individuals). Julius Groos Verlag, Postfach 102423 Hertzstrasse 6, D 69104 Heidelberg Germany. **Tel** 011 49 6221 303621, FAX 011 49 6221 301993. **ED** Trevor Eaton (editor's address: Honeywood Cottage, 35 Seaton Avenue, Hythe, Kent CT21 5HH Great Britain). **LC** PN54; .J68. **DD** 809. **[CCC].** Index available. **Bk Rev**, (Qty: 10). **Ad Acc, Adv Mgr:** R. Wiendl. **Circ:** 600. Documents available from The Genuine Article.
Desc: Covers theoretical linguistics, applied linguistics, and contains articles on all aspects of literary semantics of a philosophical nature attempting to relate the study of literature to other disciplines.
Ind/Abst Arts Humanit. Citation Index [Full Cov.]; Curr. Contents Arts Humanit.; Lang. Teach.; Linguist. Lang. Behav. Abstr. (1974-) [Full Cov.]; MLA Int. Bibl. Books Artic. Mod. Lang. Lit.; Res. Alert [Full Cov.]; Romant. Move.; Soc. Plann. Policy Dev. Abstr.

●NE/0925-8531
JOURNAL OF LOGIC, LANGUAGE, AND INFORMATION. See Philosophy.

MM/0075-4285
JOURNAL OF MALTESE STUDIES. See Literature.

US/0195-475X
JOURNAL OF MAYAN LINGUISTICS. [J. Mayan linguist.]. V. 1- Spring 1978-. Periodical. English. ir. $8.00 students; $12.00 faculty. Jill Brody, Geoscience Publications, Department of Geography & Anthropology, Louisiana State University, Baton Rouge LA 70803. **Tel** (504)388-6245. **ED** Jill Brody. **LC** PM3961; .A36. **DD** 497/.4. **UDC** 809.7. **Bk Rev. Ad Acc. Pr Rev. Circ:** 125 (ctrl).
Desc: Mayan linguistics, Mayan languages, and linguistic treatment of Mayan hieroglyphics and Mayan culture.
Ind/Abst Anthropol. Lit.; Ethnoarts Index; Linguist. Lang. Behav. Abstr. (1984-) [Full Cov.]; MLA Int. Bibl. Books Artic. Mod. Lang. Lit.; Soc. Plann. Policy Dev. Abstr.

●BE/0778-9750
JOURNAL OF MEDIEVAL LATIN : A PUBLICATION OF THE NORTH AMERICAN ASSOCIATION OF MEDIEVAL LATIN, THE. Added/Corp North American Association of Medieval Latin. Vol. 1 (1991)-. English (French). an (Autumn). 1650F. Brepols Publishers, Steenweg OP Tielen 68, B-2300 Turnhout Belgium. **Tel** 011 32 14 402500.

US/0749-596X
JOURNAL OF MEMORY AND LANGUAGE. See Psychology.

●UK/1354-571X
JOURNAL OF MODERN ITALIAN STUDIES. (Autumn 1995)-. English. Three times a year. $75.00 US and Canada; £50.00 UK; $60.00 Other. Routledge, 11 New Fetter Lane, London EC4P 4EE England. **Tel** 071 583 9855, FAX 071 842 2298. **(Subscription address:** Kinokuniya Company Ltd., 38-1 Sakuragaoka 5, chome Setagaya-ku, Tokyo 156 Japan.**)**

UK/0143-4632
JOURNAL OF MULTILINGUAL AND MULTICULTURAL DEVELOPMENT. [J. multiling. multicult. dev.]. Vol. 1, No. 1 (1980)-. Periodical. English. bm. £85.00 (one year), £165.00 (two year), £242.00 (three year) UK; $179.00 (one year), $355.00 (two year), $520.00 (three year) other. Multilingual Matters Ltd., Frankfurt Lodge, Clevedon Hall, Clevedon Avon, BS21 7SJ England. **Tel** 011 44 275 876519, FAX 011 44 275 343096. **ED** Derrick Sharp. **LC** P115; .J68. **DD** 404/.2/05. **[CCC].** Index available. **Bk Rev. Ad Acc. Pr Rev. Circ:** 600. Documents available from The Genuine Article.
Desc: Covers the opportunities, difficulties and challenges of bilingual, multilingual and multicultural communities.
Ind/Abst Abstr. Anthropol.; Br. Educ. Index; Curr. Contents Soc. Behav. Sci.; Curr. Index J. Educ.; Int. Bibliogr. Sociol.; Lang. Teach.; MLA Int. Bibl. Books Artic. Mod. Lang. Lit.; Multicult. Educ. Abstr.; Res. Alert [Full Cov.]; Soc. Plann. Policy Dev. Abstr.; Soc. Sci. Cit. Index [Full Cov.]; Sociol. Abstr.; Sociol. Educ. Abstr.; Spec. Educ. Needs Abstr.

US/0022-2968
JOURNAL OF NEAR EASTERN STUDIES. [J. Near East. stud.]. **Added/Corp** University of Chicago. Dept. of Near Eastern Languages and Civilizations. University of Chicago. Dept. of Oriental Languages and Literatures. University of Chicago. Dept. of Oriental Languages and Civilizations. Vol. 1 (Jan. 1942)-. Periodical. English. qt (4 issues). $80.00 institution, $37.00 individual, $43.00 student. University of Chicago Press / Journals Division, PO Box 37005, 5720 South Woodlawn, Chicago IL 60637. **Tel** (312)753-3347, FAX (312)753-0811. **(Subscription telephone:** (312)753-8083**) ED** Robert D. Biggs. **LC** DS41; .J6. **DD** 492.05. **CODEN** JNESBT. **[CCC]. Pr Rev. Acid Free.** available on microfilm and microfiche from University Microfilms International (UMI). Documents available from The Genuine Article, UMI Article Clearinghouse, CASDDS. ***Supersedes** American Journal of Semitic Languages and Literatures, 1062-0516.*
Desc: Devoted exclusively to an examination of the ancient and medieval civilizations of the Near East. Appearing in its pages are contributions from scholars of international reputation on archaeology, art, history, literature, linguistics, religion, law and science. Old Testament and Islamic studies are also featured.
Ind/Abst Abstr. Anthropol.; Acad. Search (July 1993-); Anthropol. Lit.; Art Archaeol. Tech. Abstr.; Arts Humanit. Citation Index [Full Cov.]; Chem. Abstr.; Curr. Contents Arts Humanit.; Curr. Contents Soc. Behav. Sci.; Expand. Acad. Index (1989-); Humanit. Index; Humanit. Source (Jul. 1993-); Index Islam. Lit.; Index Book Rev. Relig.; INFO-SOUTH Abstr.; Mag. Search; Middle East Abstr. Index; MLA Int. Bibl. Books Artic. Mod. Lang. Lit.; New Testam. Abstr.; Newsp. Period. Abstr. (1991-); Old Testam. Abstr.; Relig. Index One Period. (1949-); Relig. Theol. Abstr.; Res. Alert [Full Cov.]; Soc. Plann. Policy Dev. Abstr.; Soc. Sci. Cit. Index [Full Cov.]; Sociol. Abstr.

UK/0911-6044
JOURNAL OF NEUROLINGUISTICS. [J. neurolinguist.]. Vol. 1, No. 1 (July 1985)-. Periodical. English. qt. $261.00 The Americas; £175.00 other. Pergamon Press, An Imprint of Elsevier Science Ltd., The Boulevard, Langford Lane, Kidlington, Oxford OX5 1GB United Kingdom. **Tel** 011 44 865 843000, 011 44 865 843699, FAX 011 44 865 843010. **(Subscription address:** Elsevier Science Ltd. Oxford Fulfillment Centre, PO Box 800, Kidlington, Oxford OX5 1DX United Kingdom.**) DD** 612. **NLM** W1; JO787T. **[CCC].** available on microfilm and microfiche from University Microfilms International (UMI). Documents available from The Genuine Article.
Desc: An international journal for the study of brain function in language behavior and experience.
Ind/Abst Linguist. Lang. Behav. Abstr. (1985-) [Full Cov.]; Res. Alert [Full Cov.]; Soc. Plann. Policy Dev. Abstr.; Soc. Sci. Cit. Index [Select. Cov.].

NE/0085-2414
JOURNAL OF NORTHWEST SEMITIC LANGUAGES. [J. northwest sem. lang.]. **Added/Corp** Association for the Study of Northwest Semitic Languages in South Africa. Vol. 1 (1971)-. English (German). ir. $26.00 universities; $37.00 others. University of Stellenbosch / Department of Semitic Languages and Cultures, Stellenbosch 7600 South Africa. **Tel** 011 27 02231 773203. **ED** Walter T. Claassen. **LC** PJ3001; .J59. cum. index. **Circ:** 400 (ctrl).
Ind/Abst Middle East Abstr. Index; MLA Int. Bibl. Books Artic. Mod. Lang. Lit.; New Testam. Abstr.; Old Testam. Abstr.; Relig. Theol. Abstr.

II/0022-3301
JOURNAL OF ORIENTAL RESEARCH, MADRAS, THE. Added/Corp Kuppuswami Sastri Research Institute. (1927)-. Periodical. English (Sanskrit and Tamil). ir. $35.00. Kuppuswami Sastri Research Institute, 84 Royapettah High Road, Mylapore Madras 600 004 India. **Tel** 011 91 44 847320. **ED** S. S. Janaki. **LC** PK101; .J6. **DD** 491/.1/05. Index available. cum. index. **Bk Rev. Circ:** 300.

NE/0022-3611
JOURNAL OF PHILOSOPHICAL LOGIC. [J. philos. logic]. **Added/Corp** Association for Symbolic Logic. Vol. 1, (Feb. 1972)-. Periodical. English. Six times a year. $542.00. Kluwer Academic Publishers, Postbus 322, 3300 AH Dordrecht, The Netherlands. **Tel** 011 (31) 78 524400, FAX 011 31 78 183273, telex 20083. **ED** Michael Dunn. **LC** BC51; .J68. **DD** 160/.5. **CODEN** JPLGA7. **[CCC]. Ad Acc. Pr Rev. Acid Free. Circ:** 1,000. available on microfilm and microfiche from University Microfilms International (UMI). Documents available from The Genuine Article.
Desc: Papers that utilize formal methods or that deal with topics in logical theory. Some instances of recent work of this kind are the treatments of universal grammar, pragmatics, conceptions of possibility, theories and mathematical truth in the history of philosophy, formalization of scientific theories, or logical structure in quantum mechanics.
Ind/Abst Acad. Search (July 1993-); Arts Humanit. Citation Index [Full Cov.]; Curr. Contents Arts Humanit.; Humanit. Source (Jul. 1993-); INFO-SOUTH Abstr.; Linguist. Lang. Behav. Abstr.; Mag. Search; Math. Rev.; MLA Int. Bibl. Books Artic. Mod. Lang. Lit.; Philos. Index; Res. Alert [Full Cov.]; Soc. Plann. Policy Dev. Abstr.; Sociol. Abstr.; Zentralbl. Math. Ihre Grenzgeb.

UK/0095-4470
JOURNAL OF PHONETICS. [J. phon.]. Vol. 1 (Jan. 1973)-. Academic Scholarly Publication. English. qt (4 issues). $250.00. Academic Press Ltd., A Division of Harcourt Brace & Company Ltd., 24-28 Oval Road, London NW1 7DX England. **Tel** 071 267 4466, FAX 071 482 2293, 071 485 4752, telex 25775 ACPRES G. **(Subscription address:** Harcourt Brace & Company, Ltd., Foots Cray, High Street, Sidcup Kent DA14 5HP England.**) ED** M. E. Beckman. **LC** P221; .J69. **DD** 414/.05. **UDC** 801.4. **CODEN** JPHNB9. **[CCC]. Pr Rev.** Documents available from The Genuine Article.
Desc: Publishes papers in the field of phonetics of an experimental or theoretical nature that are concerned with phonetic aspects of language and linguistic communication processes.
Ind/Abst Abstr. Anthropol.; Annu. Bibliogr. Engl. Lang. Lit.; Arts Humanit. Citation Index [Select. Cov.]; Curr. Contents Soc. Behav. Sci.; Int. Bibliogr. Sociol.; Lang. Teach.; Linguist. Lang. Behav. Abstr. (1982-) [Full Cov.]; MLA Int. Bibl. Books Artic. Mod. Lang. Lit.; Psychol. Abstr. (1973-); PsycINFO; PsycLit; Res. Alert [Full Cov.]; Soc. Plann. Policy Dev. Abstr.; Soc. Sci. Cit. Index [Full Cov.].

NE/0920-9034
JOURNAL OF PIDGIN AND CREOLE LANGUAGES. [J. Pidgin Creole lang.]. Vol. 1, No. 1 (1986)-. Periodical. English. sa. $136.00. John Benjamins BV, Amsteldijk 44, PO Box 75577, 1070 AN Amsterdam Netherlands. **Tel** 011 31 20 6738156, FAX 011 31 20 739773. **(Subscription address:** John Benjamins North America, PO Box 27519, Philadelphia PA 19118-0519.**) ED** Glenn Gilbert. **LC** PM7831; .J68. **DD** 417/.2/05.
Desc: Special emphasis is laid on the presentation of the results of current research in theory and description of pidgin and creole languages, and application of this knowledge to language planning, education, and social reform in creole-speaking societies.
Ind/Abst Int. Bibliogr. Sociol.; Linguist. Lang. Behav. Abstr. (1986-) [Full Cov.]; MLA Int. Bibl. Books Artic. Mod. Lang. Lit.; Soc. Plann. Policy Dev. Abstr.

NE/0378-2166
JOURNAL OF PRAGMATICS. [J. pragmat.]. Vol. 1 (April 1977)-. Academic Scholarly Publication. English. Twelve times a year (2 vols.). Fl810.00. Elsevier Science Publishers BV, PO Box 211, 1000 AE Amsterdam Netherlands. **Tel** 011 31 20 5803642, FAX 011 31 20 5862696, telex 15682. **ED** J L Mey, H Haberland and J O Ostman. **LC** P99.4.P72; J68. **DD** 410/.5. **[CCC]. Pr Rev.** available on microfilm and microfiche from University Microfilms International (UMI). Documents available from The Genuine Article, Ask*IEEE.
Desc: Attempts to bridge the gap between the developing fields of sociolinguistics, psycholinguistics, computational linguistics, applied linguistics, and psychiatry.
Ind/Abst Abstr. Engl. Stud. (1982-); Annu. Bibliogr. Engl. Lang. Lit.; Arts Humanit. Citation Index [Full Cov.]; Curr. Contents Arts Humanit.; Curr. Contents Soc. Behav. Sci.; INSPEC (Feb. 1991-); Int. Bibliogr. Sociol.; Lang. Teach.; Linguist. Lang. Behav. Abstr. (1977-) [Full Cov.]; Middle East Abstr. Index; MLA Int. Bibl. Books Artic. Mod. Lang. Lit.; Philos. Index; Psychoanal. Abstr.; Psychol. Abstr. (1990-); PsycINFO; PsycLit; PsycScan: Appl. Exp. Eng. Psych.; PsycScan: LD/MR; PsycScan: Neuropsych.; Res. Alert [Full Cov.]; Soc. Plann. Policy Dev. Abstr.; Soc. Sci. Cit. Index [Full Cov.]; Sociol. Abstr.

US/0090-6905
JOURNAL OF PSYCHOLINGUISTIC RESEARCH. [J. psycholinguist. res.]. **VFOAT** Psycholinguistic Research. Vol. 1 (1971)-. Periodical. English. Six times a year. $410.00 institutions, $82.00 individuals US; $480.00 institutions, $96.00 individuals other. Plenum Press, 233 Spring Street, New York NY 10013-1578. **Tel** (212)620-8000, (800)221-9369, FAX (212)463-0742, (212)807-1047, telex 23/421139. **ED** R.W. Rieber. **LC** P106; .J68. **DD** 001.5/1. **NLM** W1 JO857J. **CODEN** JPLRB7. **[CCC].** Index available. **Pr Rev.** available on microfilm and microfiche from University Microfilms International (UMI). Documents available from The Genuine Article, BIOSIS Document Express.
Desc: This international journal publishes selected papers from the several disciplines engaged in psycholinguistic research.
Ind/Abst Abstr. Anthropol.; Annu. Bibliogr. Engl. Lang. Lit.; Biol. Abstr.; Commun. Abstr. (?-?); Index Med.; Lang. Teach.; Linguist. Lang. Behav. Abstr. (1973-) [Full Cov.]; Middle East Abstr. Index; MLA Int. Bibl. Books Artic. Mod. Lang. Lit.; Psychol. Abstr. (1971-); PsycINFO; PsycLit; Res. Alert [Full Cov.]; Soc. Plann. Policy Dev. Abstr.; Soc. Sci. Cit. Index [Full Cov.]; Sociol. Abstr.; Stud. Women Abstr.

NE/0929-6174
JOURNAL OF QUANTITATIVE LINGUISTICS. (19??)-. Periodical. English. Three times a year. Fl273.00 (institutions). Swets & Zeitlinger BV, Heereweg 347B PO Box 825, 2160 SZ Lisse Holland. **Tel** 011 31 2521 35111, FAX 02521-15888, telex 41325. **(Subscription address:** Swets & Zeitlinger BV, PO Box 825, 2160 SZ LISSE, Holland**)**

UK/0141-0423
JOURNAL OF RESEARCH IN READING. See Education-Teaching and Curriculum.

●US/1060-3743
JOURNAL OF SECOND LANGUAGE WRITING. [J. second lang. writ.]. **VFOAT** JSLW. Vol. 1, No. 1 (Jan. 1992)-. Periodical. English. tq (3 issues). $85.00 institution. Ablex Publishing Corporation, 355 Chestnut Street, Norwood NJ 07648. **Tel** (201)767-8450, (201)767-8455 (Customer Service), FAX (201)767-6717. **LC** PE1128; .J68. **DD** 428/.005. **CODEN** JSLWEC.
Ind/Abst Curr. Index J. Educ.; Linguist. Lang. Behav. Abstr. (1992-) [Full Cov.]; Soc. Plann. Policy Dev. Abstr.

NE/0167-5133
JOURNAL OF SEMANTICS (NIJMEGEN). (JOURNAL OF SEMANTICS.). [J. semant.]. **Added/Corp** N.I.S. Foundation. Vol. 1, No. 1 (March 1982)-. Periodical. English. qt. £66.00 UK and Europe; $120.00 other. Oxford University Press, Walton Street, Oxford OX2 6DP England. **Tel** 011 44 865 56767, FAX 011 44 865 267773, telex 837330 OXPRES G. **(Subscription address:** Oxford University Press / USA, Journals Marketing Department, Oxford University Press, 2001 Evans Road, Cary NC 27513.**)** **ED** Peter Bosch. **LC** P325; .J64. **DD** 401/.43/05. **CODEN** JOSEEX. **[CCC]. Bk Rev. Ad Acc.** available on microfilm and microfiche from University Microfilms International (UMI). Documents available from Ask*IEEE.
Desc: Publishes articles, notes, discussions, and book reviews in the area of natural language semantics. It is explicitly interdisciplinary, in that it aims at an integration of philosophical, psychological and linguistic semantics as well as semantic work done in artificial intelligence and anthropology.
Ind/Abst Annu. Bibliogr. Engl. Lang. Lit.; INSPEC (1990-); Int. Bibliogr. Sociol.; Linguist. Lang. Behav. Abstr. (1984-) [Full Cov.]; MLA Int. Bibl. Books Artic. Mod. Lang. Lit.; Philos. Index; Soc. Plann. Policy Dev. Abstr.

UK/0022-4480
JOURNAL OF SEMITIC STUDIES. **See** Ethnic Interests.

●US/1068-2090
JOURNAL OF SLAVIC LINGUISTICS. (JOURNAL OF SLAVIC LINGUISTICS : JSL.). [J. Slav. linguist.]. **Added/Corp** Indiana University Linguistics Club. **VFOAT** JSL. Vol. 1, No. 1 (Winter/Spring 1993)-. Periodical. English. sa. $30.00 (individuals), $40.00 (institutions). Indiana University Linguistics Club, 720 East Atwater, Bloomington IN 47405. **Tel** (812)855-8673. **ED** George Fowler (editor's phone: (812)855-2624). **LC** PG1; .J68. **DD** 491.8/05. **Bk Rev**, (Qty: 2-3). **Ad Acc. Pr Rev. Circ:** 200.
Desc: Scholarly journal containing articles on Slavic linguistics.

US/0735-1259
JOURNAL OF TEACHING WRITING. (JOURNAL OF TEACHING WRITING / SPONSORED BY INDIANA UNIVERSITY-PURDUE UNIVERSITY AT INDIANAPOLIS.). [J. teach. writ.]. **Added/Corp** Indiana University-Purdue University at Indianapolis. Indiana Teachers of Writing. Vol. 1, No. 1 (Spring 1982)-. Periodical. English. sa. $20.00 (institutions), $10.00 (individuals) US; $25.00 (institutions), $15.00 (individuals) other. Journal of Teaching Writing, 425 University Boulevard, Indianapolis IN 46202. **Tel** (317)274-4777, FAX (317)274-2347. **ED** Barbara Cambridge and Kim Brian Lovejoy. **LC** PE1404; .J69. **DD** 808/.042/070772. Index available. cum. index. **Bk Rev**, (Qty: 4). **Pr Rev. Circ:** 2,000.
Desc: Theoretical and practical articles that relate to teaching and understanding writing. Topics include composing theory, cognitive development, revision, evaluation, literature and composition, business writing, creative writing, curriculum development, and innovative teaching techniques.
Ind/Abst Curr. Index J. Educ.; Lit. Crit. Regist.

US/0003-0279
JOURNAL OF THE AMERICAN ORIENTAL SOCIETY. [J. Am. Orient. Soc.]. **Main/Corp** American Oriental Society. Vol. 1 (1843)-. Periodical. English (French and German). qt. $65.00 US; $75.00 other. American Oriental Society, 111 E Hatcher Graduate Library, University of Michigan, Ann Arbor MI 48109. **Tel** (313)747-4760. **ED** Edwin Gerow. **LC** PJ2; .A6. Index available. **Bk Rev. Ad Acc. Circ:** 2,300 (ctrl). available on microfilm and microfiche from University Microfilms International (UMI). Documents available from The Genuine Article, UMI Article Clearinghouse.
Desc: Proceedings or Select minutes of meetings are inclued in each volume (except vol. 3 & 12).
Ind/Abst Arts Humanit. Citation Index [Full Cov.]; Curr. Contents Arts Humanit.; Expand. Acad. Index (1989-); Humanit. Index; Index Islam. Lit. (1980-); Index Book Rev. Relig.; Middle East Abstr. Index; MLA Int. Bibl. Books Artic. Mod. Lang. Lit.; Mod. Med.; New Testam. Abstr.; Newsp. Period. Abstr. (1991-); Numis. Lit.; Old Testam. Abstr.; Relig. Index One Period. (1980-); Relig. Theol. Abstr.; Res. Alert [Full Cov.]; Soc. Plann. Policy Dev. Abstr.; Soc. Sci. Cit. Index [Select. Cov.].

US/0885-9884
JOURNAL OF THE ASSOCIATION OF TEACHERS OF JAPANESE, THE. [J. Assoc. Teach. Jpn.]. **Added/Corp** Association of Teachers of Japanese (U.S.). **VFOAT** JATJ; Journal of the ATJ; Journal of the A.T.J. Vol. 7, No. 1 (Nov. 1972)-. Periodical. English. Twice a year (Apr., Nov.). $28.00 (individuals), $35.00 (institutions) US & Canada & Mexcio; $31.00 (individuals), $38.00 (institutions) others Comes with Journal of Association of Teachers of Japanese Membership and includes ATJ Newsletter. Association of Teachers of Japanese, Hillcrest 9, Middlebury College, Middlebury VT 05753. **Tel** (802)388-3711, Ext. 5915 or 5784, FAX (802)388-4329. **ED** David O. Mills, Carol Hochestedler and Marian B. Ury. **LC** PL501; .J68. **DD** 495. **Pr Rev. Circ:** 600. available on microfilm. ***Continues in part*** *Journal-Newsletter of the Association of Teachers of Japanese, 0004-5810.*
Desc: Articles on Japanese language, linguistics, and literature, including teaching methods. Translations of poetry, fiction and drama.
Ind/Abst Curr. Index J. Educ.; MLA Int. Bibl. Books Artic. Mod. Lang. Lit.

US/0009-4595
JOURNAL OF THE CHINESE LANGUAGE TEACHERS ASSOCIATION. [J. Chin. Lang. Teach. Assoc.]. **Added/Corp** Chinese Language Teachers Association. **VFOAT** Chung-Kuo Yu Wen Chiao Shih Hsueh Hui Hsueh Pao. (Feb. 1966)-. Periodical. English (Chinese). Three times a year (Feb., May, Oct.). $40.00 US; $45.00 Canada & Mexico; $60.00 others Comes with Chinese Language Teachers Association Membership and CLTA Newsletter. Chinese Language Teachers Association, Kalamazoo College, 1200 Academy, Kalamazoo MI 49006. **Tel** (616)337-7001, FAX (616)337-7251. **ED** James H. Y. Tai. **LC** PL1065; .C64. **DD** 495.1. **Bk Rev. Ad Acc. Circ:** 900. available on microfilm and microfiche from University Microfilms International (UMI). ***Continues*** *Newsletter (Chinese Language Teachers Association).*
Desc: Study and research of Chinese language teaching, linguistics and literature in the west.
Ind/Abst Curr. Index J. Educ.; MLA Int. Bibl. Books Artic. Mod. Lang. Lit.; Soc. Plann. Policy Dev. Abstr.

US
JOURNAL OF THE CHINESE LANGUAGE TEACHERS ASSOCIATION / CHUNG WEN CHIAO SHIH HSUEH HUI HSUEH PAO. Added/Corp Chinese Language Teachers Association. **VFOAT** Chung Wen Chiao Shih Hsueh Hui Hsueh Pao. (198?)-. Periodical. English (Chinese). Three times a year (Feb., May, Oct.). $40.00 US, $45.00 Canada & Mexico, $60.00 other, non-members; $20.00 associate member; $30.00 regular member; $40.00 supporting member; $60.00 other. Chinese Language Teachers Association, Kalamazoo College, 1200 Academy, Kalamazoo MI 49006. **Tel** (616)337-7001, FAX (616)337-7251. **ED** James Tai (phone: (614)292-5783). **Ad Acc, Adv Mgr:** Nikki Bado, **Tel** (614)292-5816.
Desc: The professional organization devoted exclusively to the study of Chinese linguistics, literature, and pedagogy in the West. This has become an international organization for teachers and scholars of Chinese studies.

II/0377-0575
JOURNAL OF THE GANGANATHA JHA KENDRIYA SANSKRIT VIDYAPEETHA. [J. Ganganatha Jha Kendriya Sanskrit Vidyapeetha]. **Main/Corp** Ganganatha Jha Kendriya Sanskrit Vidyapeetha. Vol. 27 (Jan. 1971)-. English. qt. $15.00. **(Subscription address:** Prints India, 11 Darya Ganj, New Delhi, 110002 India, (Phone: 011 91 11 3268645)**)** **LC** PK1501.G32. **DD** 491/.1. ***Continues*** *Journal of the Ganganatha Jha Research Institute.*
Ind/Abst MLA Int. Bibl. Books Artic. Mod. Lang. Lit.

UK/0025-1003
JOURNAL OF THE INTERNATIONAL PHONETIC ASSOCIATION. [J. Int. Phon. Assoc.]. **Main/Corp** International Phonetic Association. **Added/Corp** International Phonetic Association. Vol. 1, No. 1 (June 1971)-. Periodical. English (French). sa. $45.00. International Phonetic Association, University of Leeds, Department of Linguistics and Phonetics, Leeds LS2 9JT England. **Tel** 011 44 532 333563, FAX 0532-333566. **ED** I. Maddieson. **LC** P215; .M32. **Bk Rev. Ad Acc. Pr Rev. Circ:** 800 (ctrl). available on microfilm and microfiche from University Microfilms International (UMI). ***Continues*** *Maitre Phonetique.*
Ind/Abst Int. Bibliogr. Sociol.; Lang. Teach.; Linguist. Lang. Behav. Abstr. (1972-) [Full Cov.]; Middle East Abstr. Index; MLA Int. Bibl. Books Artic. Mod. Lang. Lit.; Soc. Plann. Policy Dev. Abstr.

UK/0075-7799
JOURNAL OF THE LANCASHIRE DIALECT SOCIETY, THE. [J. Lancs. Dialect Soc.]. **Added/Corp** Lancashire Dialect Society. (19??)-. English. **LC** PE1946; .A26. **DD** 427/.76.
Ind/Abst MLA Int. Bibl. Books Artic. Mod. Lang. Lit.

KE/0251-0421
JOURNAL OF THE LANGUAGE ASSOCIATION OF EASTERN AFRICA. [J. Lang. Assoc. East. Afr.]. **Main/Corp** Language Association of Eastern Africa. V. 1- 1970-. Periodical. English. sa. East African Literature Bureau. **LC** PL8016; .L35. **DD** 496. **UDC** 800.
Ind/Abst MLA Int. Bibl. Books Artic. Mod. Lang. Lit.

NR/0189-5680
JOURNAL OF THE LINGUISTIC ASSOCIATION OF NIGERIA : JOLAN. Added/Corp Linguistic Association of Nigeria. University of Nigeria, Nsukka. Dept. of Linguistics and Nigerian Languages. **VFOAT** JOLAN. No. 1 (1982)-. English. an. $40.00. Boston University / African Studies Center, 270 Bay State Road, Boston MA 02215. **Tel** (617)353-7306, FAX (617)353-4975, telex 9103501947. **ED** P Akujuoobi Nwachukwu. **LC** PL8021.N5; J68. **DD** 409.669/05. **Bk Rev. Ad Acc. Circ:** 1,000.
Desc: Descriptive and theoretical studies in the syntax, phonology, literature, historical and applied linguistics of Nigerian languages.
Ind/Abst MLA Int. Bibl. Books Artic. Mod. Lang. Lit.; Soc. Plann. Policy Dev. Abstr.

US/0742-5562
JOURNAL OF THE MIDWEST MODERN LANGUAGE ASSOCIATION, THE. (THE JOURNAL OF THE MIDWEST MODERN LANGUAGE ASSOCIATION / MMLA.). [J. midwest mod. lang. assoc.]. **Added/Corp** Midwest Modern Language Association. **VFOAT** MMLA. Vol. 17, No. 1 (Spring 1984)-. Periodical. English. Twice a year (May & Sept.). $15.00 (one year), $28.00 (two years), $39.00 (three years). Midwest Modern Language Association, 302 English/Philosophy Building, The University of Iowa, Iowa City IA 52242-1408. **Tel** (319)335-0331. **ED** Rudolf Kuenzli. **LC** P1.A1; M53a. **DD** 405. cum. index. **Bk Rev. Ad Acc.** Documents available from The Genuine Article. ***Continues*** *Midwest Modern Language Association. Bulletin, 0026-3419.*
Ind/Abst Abstr. Engl. Stud.; Am. Humanit. Index (-199?); Annu. Bibliogr. Engl. Lang. Lit.; Arts Humanit. Citation Index [Full Cov.]; MLA Int. Bibl. Books Artic. Mod. Lang. Lit.; Res. Alert [Full Cov.]; Soc. Sci. Cit. Index [Select. Cov.].

NZ/0032-4000
JOURNAL OF THE POLYNESIAN SOCIETY. (THE JOURNAL OF THE POLYNESIAN SOCIETY.). [J. Polyn. Soc.]. **Main/Corp** Polynesian Society (N.Z.). **Added/Corp** Polynesian Society (N.Z.) Transactions. Polynesian Society (N.Z.) Proceedings. Vol. 1 (1892)-. Periodical. English. qt (4 issues). 36.00NZ$ (member of The Polynesian Society); 18.00NZ$ (student); 55.00NZ$ (other). Polynesian Society, University of Auckland, Anthropology Department, Auckland 1 New Zealand. **Tel** 011 64 9 737999, FAX 011 64 9 3737441. **ED** Richard Moyle (editor's telephone: 011 64 9 3737599). **LC** GN2; .P7. **DD** 996/.005. cum. index. **Bk Rev. Ad Acc. Pr Rev. Circ:** 1,000 (ctrl). available on microfilm from University Microfilms International (UMI). Documents available from The Genuine Article.
Desc: Anthropology, ethnology, philology, history and antiquities of the Polynesians and other related peoples.
Ind/Abst Am. Hist. Life (1955-1960, 1964-); Anthropol. Lit.; Arts Humanit. Citation Index [Select. Cov.]; Curr. Contents Soc. Behav. Sci.; Ethnoarts Index; Int. Bibliogr. Sociol.; MLA Int. Bibl. Books Artic. Mod. Lang. Lit.; Res. Alert [Full Cov.]; Soc. Plann. Policy Dev. Abstr.; Soc. Sci. Cit. Index [Full Cov.]; Sociol. Abstr. (?-?).

UK/0079-5321
JOURNAL OF THE PRINTING HISTORICAL SOCIETY. Main/Corp Printing Historical Society. No. 1 (1965)-. English. an (Dec.). £20.00 Comes with Printing Historical Society membership. Printing Historical Society, 3 Greenstead Sawbridgeworth, Herts CM21 9NY England. **Tel** 011 44 865 510628. **LC** Z119; .P95613.
Ind/Abst Annu. Bibliogr. Engl. Lang. Lit.

●US/1055-4513
JOURNAL OF TRANSLATION AND TEXTLINGUISTICS. [J. transl. textlinguist.]. **Added/Corp** Summer Institute of Linguistics. **VFOAT** JOTT. (1991)-. English. Four times a year (Jan., Apr., July, Oct.). $34.95 US; $45.95 others. Summer Institute of Linguistic, 7500 West Camp Wisdom Road, Dallas TX 75236. **Tel** (214)709-2404, FAX (214)709-2433, telex 9108614123. **ED** Bonnie Grindstaff (phone: (214)709-2403. **LC** WMLC 93/1453. **DD** 220. **Bk Rev.** ctrl circ. available on microfiche. ***Continues*** *Occasional Papers in Translation and Textlinguistics, 0890-7749.*
Ind/Abst Index Book Rev. Relig.; Relig. Index One Period.

US/1051-144X
JOURNAL OF VISUAL LITERACY. [J. vis. lit.]. **Added/Corp** International Visual Literacy Association. **VFOAT** JVL. Vol. 8, No. 2 (Fall 1988)-. Periodical. English. Twice a year (July & Dec.). $12.00 (individuals); $18.00 (institutions). Ohio State University / College of Education, 174 Arps Hall, 1945 North High Street, Columbus OH 43210-3407. **Tel** (614)292-3407, FAX (614)292-8052. **ED** Ann De Vaney. **LC** LB1068; .J68. **DD** 371.3/35. **Bk Rev. Circ:** 200 (ctrl). ***Continues*** *Journal of Visual, Verbal Languaging, 0748-7525.*
Desc: Journal for the study of languaging and literacies, especially the study of visual languaging, the interrelationships of visual and verbal languages, and their role in educational theory and practice.

UK/0022-5401
JOURNAL OF WEST AFRICAN LANGUAGES, THE. [J. West Afr. lang.]. **Added/Corp** University of Ibadan. Institute of African Studies. West Arican Languages Survey. West African Lingusitic Society. Vol. 1, No. 1 (Jan. 1964)-. Periodical. English (French). sa. $30.00. Summer Institute of Linguistic, 7500 West Camp Wisdom Road, Dallas TX 75236. **Tel** (214)709-2404, FAX (214)709-2433, telex 9108614123. **ED** John Bendor-Samuel. **LC** PL8017; .J65. **Bk Rev. Ad Acc. Circ:** 250 (ctrl).

Desc: Publishes articles on West African languages including descriptive, comparative, and sociolinguistic aspects.
Ind/Abst Int. Bibliogr. Sociol.; Linguist. Lang. Behav. Abstr. (1985-) [Full Cov.]; MLA Int. Bibl. Books Artic. Mod. Lang. Lit.; Soc. Plann. Policy Dev. Abstr.

II/0377-0648
JSL, JOURNAL OF THE SCHOOL OF LANGUAGES. ***Suspended.*** (JOURNAL OF THE SCHOOL OF LANGUAGES.). [JSL. J. Sch. Lang.]. **Main/Corp** Jawaharlal Nehru University. School of Languages. (19??)-Suspended (199?). Periodical. English. sa (2 issues). Jawaharlal Nehru University Campus, New Mehrauli Road, New Delhi 110067 India. **ED** Anil Bhatti. **LC** P1; .J35a. **DD** 405.
Desc: The journal adopts an interdisciplinary approach to problems concerning superstructure phenomena like literature in their social contexts. It encourages discussion on structural and curriculum reform in the teaching of literature, language and linguistics in universities.
Ind/Abst MLA Int. Bibl. Books Artic. Mod. Lang. Lit.

YU
JUGOSLOVENSKI SEMINAR ZA STRANE SLAVISTE : YUS. **Main/Conf** Jugoslovenski Seminar Za Strane Slaviste. **VFOAT** YUS. Serbo-Croatian (Cyrillic). ir. Filozofski Fakultet U Novom Sadu, Institut Za Juznoslovenske Jezike, Novi Sad, Stevana Nusica BB Yugoslavia. **LC** PG432; .J84A.

MY/0127-3957
JURNAL BAHASA MODEN : JURNAL PUSAT BAHASA, UNIVERSITI MALAYA. **Added/Corp** Universiti Malaya. Pusat Bahasa. Vol. 1 (July 1983)-. Periodical. Malay (English). sa. 20.00Mal$ Malaysia; $40.00 US. Pusat Bahasa Universiti Malaya, 22-11 Malaysia. **Tel** 7555344, telex MA 37453. **ED** Zairab Alsdul, Cecilia Tong, Nesamalar Citravelu, Marie Elaine, Sushila Morais. **LC** PB5; .J87.
Desc: Articles are contributed by staff of Pusat Bathasa and topics cover the study of local and foreign language taught in schools locally and neighboring countries.

YU/0350-185X
JUZNOSLOVENSKI FILOLOG. [Juznosl. filol.]. **Added/Corp** Institut za Srpski Jezik (Srpska Akademija Nauka) Institut za Srpskohrvatski Jezik (Belgrade, Serbia). (1913)-. Periodical. Serbo-Croatian (Cyrillic) (French and German). **LC** PG1; .J8.
Ind/Abst MLA Int. Bibl. Books Artic. Mod. Lang. Lit.

FI/0358-6464
JYVASKYLA CROSS-LANGUAGE STUDIES. (1979)-. Monographic series. English. tw. **UDC** 800.
Ind/Abst MLA Int. Bibl. Books Artic. Mod. Lang. Lit.; Soc. Plann. Policy Dev. Abstr.

DK
K & K. See Literature.

JA
KAIGAI GENGOGAKU JOHO. **VFOAT** Current Trends in Overseas Linguistics. No. 1- (1978-1980)-. Japanese. ¥2600. Taishukan Shoten, 3-24 Kanda Nishiki-cho, Chiyoda-ku, Tokyo-to Japan. **LC** P9; .K34. **UDC** 800.

●LI/0202-3296
KALBOTYRA / VILNIUSSKII UNIVERSITET. **Added/Corp** Vilniaus Valstybinis V. Kapsuko Vardo Universitetas. (1992)-. Periodical. Lithuanian (Russian; summaries and/or abstracts in English, French and German; table of contents in English, French and German). qt. Mintis / Idea, Z Sierakausko 15, Vilnius 2600 Lithuania. **Tel** 3702 632 943. **LC** P9; .L72. ***Continues*** *Lietuvos TSR Aukstuju Mokyklu Mokslo Darbai. Kalbotyra.*

JA
KANAZAWA DAIGAKU BUNGAKUBU RONSHU. BUNGAKUKA HEN. **VFOAT** Studies and Essays. Language and Literature. 1980 Ed.-. Periodical. Japanese. Kanazawa Daigaku Bungakubu, 1-1 Marunouchi, Kanazawa-shi 920 Japan. **LC** PB5; .K36.

US/0739-0157
KANSAS ENGLISH. (KANSAS ENGLISH : THE BULLETIN OF THE KANSAS ASSOCIATION OF TEACHERS OF ENGLISH.). [Kan. Engl.]. **Added/Corp** Kansas Association of Teachers of English. **VFOAT** Bulletin of the Kansas Association of Teachers of English. (19??)-. Bulletin. English. Five times a year (Mar., May, Nov., & 2 issues in June). $35.00 institutions, $17.50 individuals (1 year). Kansas Association of Teachers of English, 7130 Rowland, Kansas City KS 66109. **Tel** (913) 295-6441. **ED** Albert J Geritz. **LC** PE1001; .K36. **DD** 420.7/12781. **Bk Rev. Ad Acc. Circ:** 500 (ctrl).
Desc: Publishes articles having to do with the theory and practice of teaching the language arts, including literature, composition, and current issues facing the profession.

US/1043-3805
KANSAS WORKING PAPERS IN LINGUISTICS. [Kans. work. pap. linguist.]. **VFOAT** KWPL. (1976)-. English. an. $10.00. University of Kansas Linguistics, Graduate Student Association, 427 Blake Hall, Lawrence KS 66044. **Tel** (913)864-4606. **DD** 410. cum. index. **Pr Rev. Circ:** 100.

GW/0170-8805
KASSELER ARBEITEN ZUR SPRACHE UND LITERATUR. [Kassel. Arb. Sprache Lit.]. (1977)-. Monographic series. German. ir. **UDC** 80 + 82.
Ind/Abst MLA Int. Bibl. Books Artic. Mod. Lang. Lit.

ER/0022-9601
KEEL JA KIRJANDUS. **Added/Corp** Eesti NSV Teaduste Akadeemia. Eesti NSV Kirjanike Liit. (Feb. 1958)-. Periodical. Estonian. mo. **LC** PH601; .K4.
Ind/Abst MLA Int. Bibl. Books Artic. Mod. Lang. Lit.

JA
KENKYU HOKOKU SHU - KOKURITSU KOKUGO KENKYUJO. **Main/Corp** Kokuritsu Kokugo Kenkyujo. **VFOAT** Occasional Papers. 1 (1978)-. Japanese. an. Kokuritsu Kokugo Kenkyujo, 9-14 Nishigaoka 3, Kita-ku 115, Tokyo Japan. **LC** PL501; .K65A.

JA/0302-8801
KENKYU NENKAN. [Kenkyu nenkan]. **Main/Corp** Kokugo Kyoiky Kenkyujo. No. 1- 1971-. Japanese. Meiji Tosho Shuppan, 3-11 Irifune 3 Chuo-ku (104), Tokyo Japan. **LC** PL519; .K578A.

US/0023-0197
KENTUCKY ENGLISH BULLETIN. See Literature.

TZ/0856-048X
KISWAHILI. (KISWAHILI : JARIDA LA CHUO CHA UCHUNGUZI WA LUGHA YA KISWAHILI.). [Kiswahili]. **Added/Corp** Chuo Kikuu Cha Dar es Salaam. Chuo Cha Uchunguzi wa Lugha ya Kiswahili. **VFOAT** Journal of the Institute of Swahili Research. Vol. 40, No. 2 (Sept. 1970)-. Periodical. English (Swahili, French and German). an (Sept.). $15.00. University of Dar es Salaam / Tanzania, Institute of Kiswahili Research, PO Box 35110, Dar es Salaam Tanzania. **Tel** 011 255 51 49192, 011 255 51 49162, FAX 011 255 51 48274, telex 41327. **ED** D.P.B. Massamba and S.A.K. Mlacha. **LC** PL8701; .K58. **Bk Rev. Circ:** 1,500. ***Continues*** *Swahili.*
Desc: Articles on all aspects of Kiswahili language and literature for the university students and above.
Ind/Abst Int. Bibliogr. Sociol.; MLA Int. Bibl. Books Artic. Mod. Lang. Lit.

GW
KLAGE : KOLNER LINGUISTISCHE ARBEITEN, GERMANISTIK. **Added/Corp** L.A.U.T. (Organization). **VFOAT** Kolner Linguistische Arbeiten, Germanistik. Nr. 1 (1978)-. Monographic series. German. ir. Price varies per volume. Gabel Verlag, Juelichstr 7, D 50354 Hurth Germany. **Tel** 011 49 2233 63550, FAX 011 49 2233 65866.

AU
KLAGENFURTER BEITRAEGE ZUR SPRACHWISSENSCHAFT. **Added/Corp** Klagenfurter Sprachwissenschaftliche Gesellschaft. (1975)-. Periodical. German. ir. **LC** P3; .K56.
Ind/Abst Annu. Bibliogr. Engl. Lang. Lit.

SA/1010-3465
KLASGIDS. [Klasgids]. **Added/Corp** Foundation for Education, Science, and Technology (South Africa). (19??)-. Periodical. Afrikaans. qt. R17.55 South Africa; R20.00 other. Foundation for Education Science & Technology, PO Box 1758, Pretoria 0001 South Africa. **Tel** 011 27 12 3226404, FAX 011 27 12 3207803. **ED** N.J. Suyman. **LC** PF861; .K48. Index available. cum. index. **Bk Rev. Circ:** 4,000.
Ind/Abst MLA Int. Bibl. Books Artic. Mod. Lang. Lit.

GW
KLEINE TEXTE FUER VORLESUNGEN UND UBUNGEN. No. 1- 1903-. Periodical. German. ir. Walter de Gruyter Inc., PO Box 303421, D 10728 Berlin Germany. **Tel** 011 49 30 260050, FAX 011 49 30 26005251. **(Subscription address:** US and Canada/ 200 Saw Mill River Road, Hawthorne, NY 10532**)** **UDC** 803.0-8.
Desc: Small texts for recitals and language exercises

YU/0454-0689
KNJIZEVNOST I JEZIK. Periodical. Serbo-Croatian (Roman). qt. **LC** PG1201.
Ind/Abst MLA Int. Bibl. Books Artic. Mod. Lang. Lit.

JA
KODAI ROSHIA KENKYU. **VFOAT** Studia Philologica Palaeorussica; Studia Philologica Vetera Russica. Japanese (Russian and Polish). an. $25.00. Nihon Kodai Roshia Kenkyukai, Nagoya University, Language Center, Chikusa-ku Furo-cho, Nagoya-shi 464-01 Japan. **ED** Iwao Yamaguchi. **LC** PG2739; .K63. **UDC** 808.2. **Circ:** 250.

GW/0171-0834
KODIKAS. [Kodikas]. **VFOAT** Code. (Jan. 1979)-. Periodical. English (French, German, Greek and Modern, Russian). sa. DM56.00. Gunter Narr Verlag, Dishingerweg 5, D 72070 Tuebingen Germany. **Tel** 011 49 7071 78091, FAX (07071)75288. **LC** P99; .K58. **DD** 001.51/05. **[CCC]. Bk Rev. Ad Acc. Circ:** 1,100. Documents available from The Genuine Article. ***Absorbed*** *ARS Semeiotica, 0147-5045.*
Desc: Publishes articles, reviews, discussions, informations, and reports in semiotics.
Ind/Abst Arts Humanit. Citation Index [Full Cov.]; MLA Int. Bibl. Books Artic. Mod. Lang. Lit.; Philos. Index; Res. Alert [Full Cov.]; Soc. Plann. Policy Dev. Abstr.

GW/0938-7986
KOGNITIONSWISSENSCHAFT. See Psychology.

JA
KOKUBUNGAKU KENKYU SHIRYOKAN HO. **Main/Corp** Kokubungaku Kenkyu Shiryokan. No. 1 (Dec. 1977)-. Japanese. Free. Kokubungaku Kenkyu Shiryokan, 16-10 Yutakamachi 1-chome, Shinagawa-ku 142, Tokyo Japan. **Tel** (03)785-7131. **LC** Z7072; .K565A; PL523. **UDC** 895.6. **Circ:** 1,700.
Desc: Newsletter of National Institute of Japanese Literature.

JA/0387-3110
KOKUGO TO KOKUBUNGAKU. [Kokugo to kokubungaku]. **Added/Corp** Tokyo Daigaku. Kokugo Kokubun Gakkai. 1st Ed. (May 1924)-. Periodical. Japanese. mo. $14.40 (per copy). Overseas Courier Service Company Ltd., 9 Shibaura 2-Chome Minato-Ku, Tokyo 108 Japan. **Tel** 011 81 3 3453 8311. **(Subscription address:** Overseas Courier Service of America Inc., 5 East 44th Street, New York NY 10017.**)**
Desc: First line post-graduate research work and new research theses on Japanese literature and linguistics.
Ind/Abst MLA Int. Bibl. Books Artic. Mod. Lang. Lit.

JA
KOKUGOGAKU. **Added/Corp** Kokugogakkai. **VFOAT** Studies in the Japanese Language. (Oct. 1948)-. Periodical. Japanese (table of contents in English). Four times a year. $124.00. **(Subscription address:** Kyowa Book Company Inc., 1 38 Kanda Jinbocho Chiyoda-ku, Tokyo 101 Japan.**)**

IO/0126-2491
KOMUNIKA. Periodical. Indonesian. Rp1800, Rp1500 (Students). Biro Hubungan Masyarakat Lipi, Jl Teuku Tjik Di Tiro 43, Jakarta Indonesia. **LC** P87; .K56. **UDC** 809.922.

GW/0344-6735
KONZEPTE DER SPRACH- UND LITERATURWISSENSCHAFT. [Konzepte Sprach- Lit.wiss.]. (1970)-. Monographic series. German. ir. Price varies per volume. Max Niemeyer Verlag, Postfach 2140, D 72011 Tuebingen Germany. **Tel** 011 49 7071 989494, FAX 011 49 7071 87419. **ED** Klaus Baumgaertner.
Ind/Abst MLA Int. Bibl. Books Artic. Mod. Lang. Lit.

DK/0105-0257
KOPENHAGENER BEITRAEGE ZUR GERMANISTISCHEN LINGUISTIK. [Kopenh. Beitr. germ. Linguist.]. 1- 1972-. German. Akademisk Forlag, Finsensvej 82, DK 2000 Frederiksberg Denmark. **Tel** 011 45 38 334212. **LC** PD3; .K65. **UDC** 803.
Ind/Abst MLA Int. Bibl. Books Artic. Mod. Lang. Lit.

GW/0342-0752
KORRESPONDENZBLATT DES VEREINS FUER NIEDERDEUTSCHE SPRACHFORSCHUNG. [Korresp.bl. Ver. niederdtsch. Sprachforsch.]. **Added/Corp** Verein fur Niederdeutsche Sprachforschung. (1876)-. Periodical. German. qt. DM10.00. Karl Wachholtz Verlag, Postfach 2769, Gansemarkt 1-3, W-2350 Neumunster F R Germany. **Tel** 011 49 4321 5670, FAX 011 49 4321 56778, telex 299 618 CURIR. **LC** PF5601; .V53a. Index available (bound in last issue).
Ind/Abst MLA Int. Bibl. Books Artic. Mod. Lang. Lit.

GW/0023-4567
KRATYLOS. (1956)-. Periodical. Multiple languages (English, French and German). an. Otto Harrassowitz Verlag, Taunusstrasse 14, Postfach 2929, D-65019 Wiesbaden Germany. **Tel** 011 49 611 5300, FAX 530570, telex 4186 135 OH D. **LC** P501; .K7. **[CCC].**

GW
KRITIKON LITTERARUM. Vol. 1 (1972)-. Monographic series. Multiple languages (French, German, Russian and Spanish). ir. Price varies per volume. Thesen Verlag Vowinckel & Company, 3 Place de la Gare, L 6674 Mertert Luxembourg. **Tel** 011 352 748715. **LC** P1.A1; K7. Index available. cum. index. **Bk Rev. Ad Acc.**

KO
KUGO KUNGMUNHAK YONGAM / KUGO KUNGMUN HAKHOE YOKKUM. 1977- Year. Korean. W9.000. Iu Chulpansa, 19-8 5-ro Chungmu-ro, Chung-ku, Seoul South Korea. **LC** PL901; .K77.

XO/0023-5202
KULTURA SLOVA. [Kult. slova]. **Added/Corp** Jazykovedny Ustav Ludovita Stura. Vol. 1 (1967)-. Periodical. Slovak. mo (ten isues per year). Kcs30.00; $14.00 other. Veda, Publishing House of the Slovak Academy of Sciences, Klemensova 19, 814 30 Bratislava Slovakia. **Tel** (7)583-15. **(Subscription address:** Kubon & Sagner, ABT Zeitschriftenimport, D 80328 Munich Germany.**) ED** Jan Kacala. **LC** PG5201; .K84. **Bk Rev. Ad Acc. Circ:** 3,600 (ctrl). ***Supersedes*** *Ceskoslovensky Terminologicky Casopis.*
Desc: Contains studies of leading Slovak philologists. Marked attention is paid to the problem of special terminology, its normalization and application in practice.
Ind/Abst MLA Int. Bibl. Books Artic. Mod. Lang. Lit.

PL/0023-5911
KWARTALNIK NEOFILOLOGICZNY. [Kwart. neofilol.]. **Added/Corp** Polska Akademia Nauk. Komitet Neofilologiczny. Vol. 1 (1954)-. Periodical. Polish (summaries and/or abstracts in French and Russian; table of contents in French and Russian). qt. $52.00. **(Subscription address:** ARS Polona, PO Box 1001, 00068 Warsaw Poland.**) LC** PB5; .K9.
Ind/Abst Abstr. Engl. Stud.; Annu. Bibliogr. Engl. Lang. Lit.; MLA Int. Bibl. Books Artic. Mod. Lang. Lit.

KO
KYONGNAM MUNHAK. Began in 1982. Periodical. Korean. Kyongnam Munin Hyophoe, 24-4 2-ka Pupyong-dong Chung-ku Pusan Korea. **LC** PL997.K942; K95.

US
LA-MATHIL. VFOAT Lamatchil. Periodical. Hebrew. bw. $12.00. 515 Park Avenue, New York NY 10016. **Tel** (212)752-0600. **ED** Clair Jackson. **LC** PJ4569; .L26. **UDC** 809.24. **Circ:** 5,000.
Desc: News of the world in easy to read Hebrew.

US/0195-377X
LACUS FORUM. Main/Corp Linguistic Association of Canada and the United States. **VAT** Linguistic Association of Canada and the United States Forum. (1974)-. English. an. $35.00 Comes with Linguistic Association of Canada and United States membership. Lacus, PO Box 101, Lake Bluff IL 60044. **Tel** (708)234-3997. **LC** P21; .L48a. **DD** 410/.5.

US/0882-1828
LADDER (WASHINGTON, D.C.), THE. (THE LADDER / PLAN, PUSH LITERACY ACTION NOW.). **Added/Corp** Push Literacy Action Now. (19??)-. Periodical. English. bm (Feb., Apr., June, Aug., Oct., Dec.). $25.00 US; $26.60 Canada; $30.00 other. PLAN Inc., 1332 G Street SE, Washington DC 20003. **Tel** (202)547-8903. **ED** Anthony A. Kroll, Jr. **DD** 028. **Bk Rev**, (Qty: 2). **Circ:** 500 (ctrl).

FR
LALIES : ACTES DES SESSIONES DE LINGUISTIQUE ET DE LITTERATURE. VFOAT Actes des Sessions de Linguistique et de Litterature. 1 (3-7 Sept. 1979)-. Periodical. French. an. Presses de l'Ecole Normale Superieure, 45 rue d'Ulm, 75230 Paris France. **Tel** 011 33 1 43291225. **(Subscription address:** 48 Boulevard Jourdan, F-75690 Paris Cedex 14 France**) ED** Jean Perrot and Jean Lallot. **LC** P21; .L34. **DD** 405. **UDC** 807. **Circ:** 500. ***Continues in part*** *Actes des Sessions de Linguistique.*
Desc: Collection of essays by various scholars comprises articles in comparative philology and delineates an approach of classical languages based on recent linguistic and literary theory.

NE/0165-8204
LAMPAS. [Lampas]. Began with Vol. 1 (July 1968). Periodical. Dutch (summaries and/or abstracts in English). qt. Fl62.50. Coutinho BV, Postbus 10, 1399 ZG Muiderberg Netherlands. **Tel** 011 49 2942 1888, FAX 011 49 2942 2171. **ED** Daan den Hengst. **UDC** 807. cum. index. **Bk Rev. Ad Acc. Circ:** 1,100 (ctrl).
Desc: Magazine for Dutch classical linguistics.

BE/0458-7251
LANGAGE ET L'HOMME, LE. Added/Corp Centre de Documentation et d'Etude des Problemes du Langage. (May 1966)-. Periodical. French (German and Dutch). Three times a year. 1600F Belgium; 1650F other. Editions de Boeck Wesmael, 4 rue Fonds, 1348 Louvain la Neuve Belgium. **Tel** 011 32 2 6273509. **ED** De Galocsy. Index available. cum. index. **Bk Rev. Circ:** 500.
Desc: Psycholinguistics, neurolinguistics, socio-linguistics, translation, terminology, and literature.
Ind/Abst Lang. Teach.; MLA Int. Bibl. Books Artic. Mod. Lang. Lit.; Soc. Plann. Policy Dev. Abstr.; Sociol. Abstr.

FR/0181-4095
LANGAGE ET SOCIETE. Added/Corp Maison des Sciences de l'Homme (Paris, France). **VFOAT** LS, Langage et Societe; L et S, Langage et Societe. (1977)-. Periodical. French (summaries and/or abstracts in English). Four times a year. 215.48F (institutions), 176.30F (individuals) France; 290.00F (institutions), 250.00F (indiviudals) other. Maison des Sciences de l'Homme, Bureau 413 54 Boulevard Raspail, 75270 Paris Cedex 06 France. **Tel** 011 33 1 49542013, 49542236, FAX 011 33 1 45488353, telex MSM203104F. **ED** Pierre Achard. **LC** P40; .L285. **DD** 401/.9. Index available. cum. index. **Bk Rev. Ad Acc. Circ:** 400.
Desc: Sociolinguistics, ethnolinguistics, socio-semiotic communication, speech, psycholinguistics, history of languages, sociology of language, discourse analysis.
Ind/Abst MLA Int. Bibl. Books Artic. Mod. Lang. Lit.

FR/0458-726X
LANGAGES (PARIS). (LANGAGES.). [Langages]. (March 1966)-. Periodical. French. Four times a year (Mar., June, Sept., Dec.). 300.00F France; 350.00F others. Livres Dix Larousse, 15 rue Rigaud, 94855 Ivry Sur Seine France. **Tel** 011 33 1 49596091. **(Subscription address:** Centrale des Revues, 11 rue Gossin, 92543 Montrouge Cedex France.**)**
Desc: A review on the international linguistic by Larouse, and in each issue has specific topics.
Ind/Abst Int. Polit. Sci. Abstr.; Lang. Teach.; MLA Int. Bibl. Books Artic. Mod. Lang. Lit.; Romant. Move.; Soc. Plann. Policy Dev. Abstr.

GW/0023-8252
LANGENSCHEIDT'S SPRACH-ILLUSTRIERTE. (1955)-. Periodical. German (English, French and Spanish). Four times a year (Feb., May, Aug., Nov.). Langenscheidt KG, Crellestra 28-30, D 10827 Berlin Germany. **Tel** 011 49 30 7800020, telex 183175 LUGBL. **(Subscription address:** Langenscheidt KG, Postfach 401120, D 80711 Munich Germany.**) ED** Friedrich Schmoe. **Ad Acc. Circ:** 11,000 (ctrl).
Desc: Presents short German texts (with difficult words translated into English, French and Spanish) for the individual language student and for use in the classroom.

NP
LANGHALI (KATHMANDU, NEPAL). (LANGHALI.). V. 1, No. 1 (May/August/Sept. 1983)-. Periodical. Nepali. mo. Rs9.00. Suresh Ale Magar Capital Photo. **LC** PL3801.M15; L36. **UDC** 809.149.3.

SI
LANGUAGE. VFOAT Yu Wen Lun Chi. First published in 1972-. Multiple languages (Chinese and English). $3.12. Singapore Linguistic Society, 177-A Outram Park, 3 Singapore. **LC** P121; .L385. **UDC** 800.
Ind/Abst Am. Bibliogr. Slavic East Europ. Stud.; Anthropol. Lit.; Curr. Index J. Educ.

CN/1183-1316
LANGUAGE ABUSE FORUM. (THE LANGUAGE ABUSE FORUM.). [Lang. abuse forum]. **Added/Corp** Language Abuse Institute. (Jan 1991)-. Periodical. English. bm. Limited free distribution. Language Abuse Institute, 530 Crawford Street, Toronto Ontario M6G 3J8 Canada. **DD** 306.4/4/082.

US/1048-9223
LANGUAGE ACQUISITION. [Lang. acquis.]. Vol. 1, No. 1 (1990)-. Periodical. English. qt. $100.00. Lawrence Erlbaum Associates, 365 Broadway, Suite 102, Hillsdale NJ 07642. **Tel** (201)666-4110, (800)926-6579, FAX (201)666-2394. **ED** Robert Berwick, Thomas Roeper, and Kenneth Wexler. **LC** P118; .L249. **DD** 401/.93/05. **CODEN** LAACEV.
Desc: Publishes contributions that offer explanatory insights into and advance knowledge of how language is acquired.
Ind/Abst Linguist. Lang. Behav. Abstr. (1990-) [Full Cov.]; MLA Int. Bibl. Books Artic. Mod. Lang. Lit.; Soc. Plann. Policy Dev. Abstr.

UK/0169-0965
LANGUAGE AND COGNITIVE PROCESSES. [Lang. cogn. processes]. Vol. 1, No. 1 (1985)-. Periodical. English. Six times a year. $297.00 US; £170.00 Europe; £175.00 other. Lawrence Erlbaum Associates Ltd., 27 Palmeira Mansions, Church Road, Hove East Sussex BN3 2FA England. **Tel** 011 44 273 207411. **(Subscription address:** Turpin Distribution Services Limited, Blackhorse Road, Letchworth, Hertfordshire SG6 1HN, United Kingdom.**) NLM** W1; LA616M. **CODEN** LCPRET. Documents available from The Genuine Article, BIOSIS Document Express.
Ind/Abst Abstr. Anthropol. (19??-); Arts Humanit. Citation Index [Select. Cov.]; Biol. Abstr. (1988-); Curr. Contents Soc. Behav. Sci.; Curr. Index J. Educ.; Ei Page One; Ergon. Abstr.; Linguist. Lang. Behav. Abstr. (1985-) [Full Cov.]; MLA Int. Bibl. Books Artic. Mod. Lang. Lit.; Psychoanal. Abstr.; Psychol. Abstr. (1979-); PsycINFO; PsycScan: Appl. Exp. Eng. Psych.; PsycScan: LD/MR; PsycScan: Neuropsych.; Res. Alert [Full Cov.]; Soc. Plann. Policy Dev. Abstr.; Soc. Sci. Cit. Index [Full Cov.].

UK/0271-5309
LANGUAGE & COMMUNICATION. [Lang. commun.]. **VFOAT** Language and Communication. Vol. 1, No. 1 (1981)-. Periodical. English. qt. $246.00 The Americas; £165.00 other. Pergamon Press, An Imprint of Elsevier Science Ltd., The Boulevard, Langford Lane, Kidlington, Oxford OX5 1GB United Kingdom. **Tel** 011 44 865 843000, 011 44 865 843699, FAX 011 44 865 843010. **(Subscription address:** Elsevier Science Ltd. Oxford Fulfillment Centre, PO Box 800, Kidlington, Oxford OX5 1DX United Kingdom.**) ED** Roy Harris and Talbot Taylor. **LC** P87; .L36. **DD** 001.51/05. **CODEN** LACOD8. **[CCC]. Pr Rev.** available on microfilm and microfiche from University Microfilms International (UMI). Documents available from The Genuine Article, Ask*IEEE, UMI Article Clearinghouse.
Ind/Abst Abstr. Anthropol. (19??-); Arts Humanit. Citation Index [Select. Cov.]; Commun. Abstr.; Curr. Contents Soc. Behav. Sci.; Curr. Index J. Educ.; Expand. Acad. Index (1992-); Inf. Sci. Abstr.; INSPEC (1981-); Lang. Teach.; Linguist. Lang. Behav. Abstr. (1981-) [Full Cov.]; MLA Int. Bibl. Books Artic. Mod. Lang. Lit.; Newsp. Period. Abstr. (1992-); Psychol. Abstr. (1981-); PsycINFO (1990-); PsycLit; Res. Alert [Full Cov.]; Soc. Plann. Policy Dev. Abstr.; Soc. Sci. Cit. Index [Full Cov.]; Sociol. Abstr.; Trade Ind. ASAP [Full Txt.].

NE/0921-5034
LANGUAGE AND COMPUTERS. English. ir. Editions Rodopi BV, Keizersgracht 302-304, 1016 Ex Amsterdam Netherlands. **Tel** 011 31 20 6227507, FAX 011 31 20 380948. **ED** W J Meys and Jan Harts. **Ad Acc. Circ:** 700.
Desc: Studies in practical linguistics.
Ind/Abst MLA Int. Bibl. Books Artic. Mod. Lang. Lit.

NE
LANGUAGE AND COMPUTERS: STUDIES IN PRACTICAL LINGUISTICS. English. Humanities Press, 165 1st Avenue, Atlantic Highlands NJ 07716. **Tel** (908)872-1441, (800)221-3845, FAX (908)872-0717, telex 752233. Index available.

UK/0950-0782
LANGUAGE AND EDUCATION. Vol. 1, No. 1 (1987)-. Periodical. English. qt. £79.00 (one year), £154.00 (two year), £224.00 (three year) UK; $169.00 (one year), $329.00 (two year), $479.00 (three year) other. Multilingual Matters Ltd., Frankfurt Lodge, Clevedon Hall, Clevedon Avon, BS21 7SJ England. **Tel** 011 44 275 876519, FAX 011 44 275 343096. **ED** David Corson and Viv Edwards. Index available. cum. index. **Bk Rev. Ad Acc. Circ:** 400.
Desc: The purpose is to encourage language specialists and language in education researchers to organise, construe and present their material in such a way as to highlight its educational implications, thereby influencing educational theorists and practitioners and therefore educational outcomes for individual children.
Ind/Abst Br. Educ. Index; Curr. Index J. Educ.; Educ. Technol. Abstr.; Soc. Plann. Policy Dev. Abstr.; Sociol. Educ. Abstr.

AT/1036-6709
LANGUAGE AND LANGUAGE EDUCATION. English. an. 18.00Aus$. National Languages & Literacy Institution of Australia, L2 112 Wellington Parade, East Melbourne VIC 3002 Australia. **Tel** 011 61 3 4162422, FAX 011 61 3 4160231.
Desc: Articles on inter-cultural communication and rapid profiling and be of particular interest to those involved with language policy and practice in schools.
Ind/Abst Aust. Educ. Index.

UK/0458-7294
LANGUAGE AND LANGUAGE LEARNING. No. 1 (1964)-. Monographic series. English. ir. Price varies per volume. Oxford University Press / New York, 200 Madison Avenue, New York NY 10016. **Tel** (212)679-7300, (919)677-0977, (800)451-7556, (800)445-9714, FAX (919)677-1303.

UK
LANGUAGE AND LEARNING. See Education-Teaching and Curriculum.

PP
LANGUAGE AND LINGUISTICS IN MELANESIA : JOURNAL OF THE LINGUISTIC SOCIETY OF PAPUA NEW GUINEA. Added/Corp Linguistic Society of Papua and New Guinea. Vol. 13, No. 1-2 (1981/1982)-. Periodical. English. sa. $35.00 (institutions), $20.00 (individuals). Linguistic Society of Papua New Guinea, PO Box 418, Ukarumpa Via Lae, Papua New Guinea. **Tel** telex 77611. ***Continues*** *Kivung.*
Ind/Abst Anthropol. Lit.; Linguist. Lang. Behav. Abstr. (1972-) [Full Cov.]; MLA Int. Bibl. Books Artic. Mod. Lang. Lit.; Soc. Plann. Policy Dev. Abstr.; Sociol. Abstr.

UK/0958-8140
LANGUAGE AND LITERACY NEWS. See Education-Teaching and Curriculum.

●UK/0963-9470
LANGUAGE AND LITERATURE. Added/Corp Poetics and Linguistics Association. Vol. 1, No. 1 (1992)-. Periodical. English. Three times a year. £54.00 Europe; £57.00 Other (Institutions). Longman Group Ltd., Fourth Avenue, Longman House, Harlow Essex CM19 5SR England. **Tel** 011 44 279 429655, FAX 011 44 279 431059, telex 81259. **CODEN** LLITET.

US/1057-6037
LANGUAGE AND LITERATURE (SAN ANTONIO, TEX.). (LANGUAGE AND LITERATURE.). [Lang. lit.]. **VFOAT** LNL. Vol. 7, No. 1-3 (1982)-. English (Spanish and French). an (Aug.). $30.00. Trinity University / Texas, 47-715 Stadium Drive, San Antonio TX 78212. **Tel** (512)736-7369. **ED** Dr. Bates L. Hoffer. **LC** PB1; .L56. **DD** 410/.5. **Bk Rev. Ad Acc. Pr Rev. Circ:** 200. ***Continues*** *Linguistics in Literature, 0147-0906.*

Desc: Language-oriented analyses of major works of fiction, reviews of books in the field and experimental literary criticism.

CN/0709-7751
LANGUAGE AND SOCIETY. [Lang. soc.]. **VFOAT** Langue et Societe. No. 1 (Autumn 1979)-. Periodical. English (French). qt (Mar., June, Sept., Dec.). Free. Commission of Official Languages, 110 O'Connor Street / Room 1414, Ottawa Ontario K1A 0T8 Canada. **Tel** (613)995-0730, FAX 9935082. **ED** Pierre Simard. **LC** P40; .L293. **DD** 404/.2/05. **UDC** 800(71). **[CCC].** Index available. cum. index. **Bk Rev**, (Qty: 2 per year). **Circ:** 22,000 (ctrl).
Desc: A bilingual magazine for those interested in language issues in Canada and other countries.
Ind/Abst Soc. Plann. Policy Dev. Abstr.

UK/0023-8309
LANGUAGE AND SPEECH. [Lang. speech]. Vol. 1, (Jan./Mar. 1958)-. Periodical. English. qt. £110.00 UK; $220.00 US; £120.00 other. Kingston Press Services Ltd, 43 Derwent Road, Whitton, Twickenham, Middlesex TW2 7HQ England. **Tel** 011 44 81 8933015. **LC** P1; .L32. **DD** 414.05. **NLM** W1 LA615. **Bk Rev. Ad Acc. Pr Rev.** available on microfilm and microfiche from University Microfilms International (UMI). Documents available from The Genuine Article.
Ind/Abst Abstr. Anthropol.; Curr. Contents Soc. Behav. Sci.; Curr. Index J. Educ.; Index Med.; Int. Aerosp. Abstr.; Lang. Teach.; Linguist. Lang. Behav. Abstr. (1972-) [Full Cov.]; Middle East Abstr. Index; MLA Int. Bibl. Books Artic. Mod. Lang. Lit.; Psychol. Abstr. (1958-); PsycINFO; PsycLit; Res. Alert [Full Cov.]; Soc. Plann. Policy Dev. Abstr.; Soc. Sci. Cit. Index [Full Cov.]; Sociol. Abstr.

US/0023-8317
LANGUAGE AND STYLE. [Lang. style]. **Added/Corp** Southern Illinois University at Carbondale. Vol. 1 (Winter 1968)-. Periodical. English. qt. $16.00 (individuals), $22.00 (institutions). Queens College, Political Science Department, 65-30 Kissena Boulevard, Flushing NY 11367. **Tel** (718)520-7000. **ED** E L Epstein. **LC** PN203; .L35. **DD** 808/.005. **Bk Rev. Ad Acc. Circ:** 600.
Desc: Articles on style in all of its manifestations, in all of the arts, and in all of its social and cultural contexts.
Ind/Abst Abstr. Engl. Stud.; Am. Humanit. Index (-199?); Annu. Bibliogr. Engl. Lang. Lit.; Middle East Abstr. Index; MLA Int. Bibl. Books Artic. Mod. Lang. Lit.; Romant. Move.; Soc. Plann. Policy Dev. Abstr.

US/0360-9170
LANGUAGE ARTS. **See** Education-Early Childhood and Primary Education.

US/0889-6917
LANGUAGE ASSOCIATION BULLETIN. **See** Education-Teaching and Curriculum.

●UK/0965-8416
LANGUAGE AWARENESS. Vol. 1, No. 1 (1992)-. Periodical. English. qt (4 issues). £79.00 (one year), £154.00 (two year), £224.00 (three year), UK; $169.00 (one year), $329.00 (two year), $479.00 (three year), other. Multilingual Matters Ltd., Frankfurt Lodge, Clevedon Hall, Clevedon Avon, BS21 7SJ England. **Tel** 011 44 275 876519, FAX 011 44 275 343096. **LC** IN PROCESS. **[CCC].**
Ind/Abst Br. Educ. Index.

US/0097-8507
LANGUAGE (BALTIMORE). (LANGUAGE.). [Language]. **Added/Corp** Linguistic Society of America. Vol. 1 (March 1925)-. Periodical. English. qt. $45.00 individual membership, $75.00 institution membership, (add $10.00 for postage) other. Linguistic Society of America, 1325 18th Street Northwest, Washington DC 20036. **Tel** (202)835-1714. **ED** Sarah Thomason. **LC** P1; .L3. **DD** 405. Index available. cum. index. **Bk Rev. Ad Acc. Pr Rev. Circ:** 7,000. available on microfilm and microfiche from University Microfilms International (UMI). Documents available from The Genuine Article, UMI Article Clearinghouse.
Ind/Abst Acad. Search (July 1993-); Annu. Bibliogr. Engl. Lang. Lit.; Anthropol. Index; Arts Humanit. Citation Index [Full Cov.]; Comput. Rev.; Curr. Index J. Educ.; Humanit. Index; Humanit. Source (Jul. 1993-); INFO-SOUTH Abstr.; Int. Bibliogr. Sociol.; Lang. Teach.; Linguist. Lang. Behav. Abstr. (1972-) [Full Cov.]; Mag. Search; MLA Int. Bibl. Books Artic. Mod. Lang. Lit.; Newsp. Period. Abstr. (1990-); Res. Alert [Full Cov.]; Soc. Plann. Policy Dev. Abstr.; Soc. Sci. Cit. Index [Full Cov.]; Sociol. Abstr.

US
LANGUAGE CENSUS REPORT FOR CALIFORNIA PUBLIC SCHOOLS. **Added/Corp** California. Educational Demographics Unit. (1988)-. English. California State Department of Education, PO Box 944272, 721 Capitol Mall, Sacramento CA 94244. **Tel** (916)657-2451, (916)445-7608, FAX (916)657-3000. ***Continues*** *Language Census Report.*

UK/0790-8318
LANGUAGE, CULTURE, AND CURRICULUM. **Added/Corp** Linguistics Institute of Ireland. Vol. 1, No. 1 (Spring 1988)-. Periodical. English. Three times a year. £64.00 (one year), £125.00 (two year), £183.00 (three year) UK; $139.00 (one year), $269.00 (two year), $389.00 (three year) other. Multilingual Matters Ltd., Frankfurt Lodge, Clevedon Hall, Clevedon Avon, BS21 7SJ England. **Tel** 011 44 275 876519, FAX 011 44 275 343096. **ED** Eoghan MacAogain. Index available. **Bk Rev. Ad Acc. Circ:** 300.
Desc: Covers bilingualism, multiculturalism, language contact, less-used languages, cultural studies, language education and curriculum design for second languages.
Ind/Abst Br. Educ. Index; Curr. Index J. Educ.; Linguist. Lang. Behav. Abstr. (1988-) [Full Cov.]; MLA Int. Bibl. Books Artic. Mod. Lang. Lit.; Soc. Plann. Policy Dev. Abstr.

●UK/1351-024X
LANGUAGE FORUM. (1993)-. Academic Scholarly Publication. English. Twice a year. £12.00. University of East Anglia, Centre for Research in Linguistics, School of Modern Languages, Norwich NR4 7TJ England. **Tel** 011 44 603 592738, FAX 011 44 603 250599. **ED** John Hutchins. **Pr Rev. Circ:** 150. Documents available from BLDSC. ***Continues*** *UEA Papers in Linguistics, 0951-2292.*

II/0253-9071
LANGUAGE FORUM. [Lang. forum]. (1975)-. Periodical. Multiple languages (English and Hindi). qt. $40.00. **(Subscription address:** Prints India, 11 Darya Ganj, New Delhi 110002 India.**)** **LC** P1.A1; L346. **DD** 405. **UDC** 800.
Ind/Abst MLA Int. Bibl. Books Artic. Mod. Lang. Lit.; Soc. Plann. Policy Dev. Abstr.

US
LANGUAGE IN EDUCATION. **See** Education.

CN/0823-4159
LANGUAGE IN FOCUS (MISSISSAUGA, ONT.). (LANGUAGE IN FOCUS.). [Lang. focus]. **VAT** ECCO. Language in Focus; Association of English Co-Ordinators and Consultants of Ontario. Language in Focus. No. 1-. Periodical. English. ir. Free to members. Ecco Monographs, Peel Board of Education, 73 King Street West Canada. **DD** 420/.7. **UDC** 802.0.

UK/0047-4045
LANGUAGE IN SOCIETY. [Lang. soc.]. Vol. 1 (April 1972)-. Academic Scholarly Publication. English. qt. $108.00 US, Canada and Mexico; £78.00 other. Cambridge University Press, The Edinburgh Building, Shaftesbury Road, Cambridge CB2 2RU United Kingdom. **Tel** 011 44 223 312393, FAX 011 44 223 325959. **(Subscription address:** Cambridge University Press / North America, 110 Midland Avenue, Port Chester NY 10573.**)** **ED** Dell Hymes. **LC** P41; .L34. **DD** 301.2/1. **CODEN** LGSCBO. **[CCC]. Bk Rev. Pr Rev.** available on microfilm and microfiche from University Microfilms International (UMI). Documents available from The Genuine Article.
Desc: An international joumal of sociolinguistics, concerned with all branches of speech and language as aspects of social life. Publishes empirical articles of general theoretical, comparative or methodological interest. Content varies from predominantly linguistic to predominantly social. In addition to original articles, the journal publishes reviews of recent books, brief accounts of work in progress and notes or comments on points arising from recent publications. Each issue carries numerous reviews of the latest important books in the field.
Ind/Abst Abstr. Anthropol.; Abstr. Engl. Stud.; Anthropol. Lit.; Appl. Soc. Sci. Index Abstr.; Arts Humanit. Citation Index [Select. Cov.]; Book Rev. Index (1984-); Br. Educ. Index; Curr. Contents Soc. Behav. Sci.; Curr. Index J. Educ.; Int. Bibliogr. Sociol.; Lang. Teach.; Linguist. Lang. Behav. Abstr. (1972-) [Full Cov.]; Middle East Abstr. Index; MLA Int. Bibl. Books Artic. Mod. Lang. Lit.; Multicult. Educ. Abstr.; Psychol. Abstr. (1972-); PsycINFO; PsycLit; Res. Alert [Full Cov.]; Romant. Move.; Sage Race Relat. Abstr.; Soc. Plann. Policy Dev. Abstr.; Soc. Sci. Cit. Index [Full Cov.]; Sociol. Abstr.; Sociol. Educ. Abstr.; Spec. Educ. Needs Abstr.; Stud. Women Abstr.

NE/0923-182X
LANGUAGE INTERNATIONAL. Vol. 1, Issue 1 (Jan./Feb. 1989)-. Periodical. English (French, German and Spanish). Six times a year. $109.00. John Benjamins BV, Amsteldijk 44, PO Box 75577, 1070 AN Amsterdam Netherlands. **Tel** 011 31 20 6738156, FAX 011 31 20 739773. **(Subscription address:** John Benjamins North America, PO Box 27519, Philadelphia PA 19118-0519.**)** **ED** Geoffrey Kingscott. **LC** P106; .L3175. **DD** 405. **CODEN** LAINE2. Index available. **Bk Rev. Ad Acc. Circ:** 4,000.
Desc: Geared to the practical needs and interests of language teachers, translators, interpreters, lexicographers, terminologists and those, whatever their calling, who have a professional interest in languages. Reports on new developments in relevant computer hardware and software, language processing, and literary translation, among other things.
Ind/Abst Soc. Plann. Policy Dev. Abstr.

US/0190-0382
LANGUAGE INTERVENTION SERIES. v. 1-. Monographic series. English. Price varies per volume. University Park Press, PO Box 4034, New York NY 10163. **ED** R L Schiefelbusch. **UDC** 800. **NLM** W1 LA616S.

US/0023-8333
LANGUAGE LEARNING. [Lang. learn.]. **Added/Corp** Research Club in Language Learning (Ann Arbor, Mich.). Vol. 1 (Jan. 1948)-. Periodical. English. qt. $70.00 (institutions), $45.00 (individuals). Language Learning, 178 Henry S. Frieze Building, 105 South State Street, Ann Arbor MI 48109-1285. **Tel** (313)763-9216. **ED** Alexander Z. Guiora. **LC** P1; .L33. **DD** 407. **NLM** W1 LA617. Index available. **Bk Rev. Pr Rev. Circ:** 2,500. available on microfilm and microfiche from University Microfilms International (UMI). Documents available from The Genuine Article.
Desc: Publishes research articles in the application of linguistic method and philosophical perspective to problem areas viewed as lying outside the traditional concerns of linguistics proper.
Ind/Abst Abstr. Anthropol.; Acad. Search (Jan. 1994-); Annu. Bibliogr. Engl. Lang. Lit.; Contents Pages Educ.; Curr. Contents Soc. Behav. Sci.; Curr. Index J. Educ.; Educ. Index; Humanit. Source (Jul. 1993-); INFO-SOUTH Abstr.; Lang. Teach.; Linguist. Lang. Behav. Abstr. (1972-) [Full Cov.]; Mag. Search; Middle East Abstr. Index; MLA Int. Bibl. Books Artic. Mod. Lang. Lit.; Multicult. Educ. Abstr.; Res. Alert [Full Cov.]; Soc. Plann. Policy Dev. Abstr.; Soc. Sci. Cit. Index [Full Cov.].

UK/0957-1736
LANGUAGE LEARNING JOURNAL : THE JOURNAL OF THE ASSOCIATION OF LANGUAGE LEARNING. **Added/Corp** Association for Language Learning (Great Britain). Vol. No. 1 (Mar. 1990)-. Periodical. English. Twice a year (Mar. & Sept.). £30.00 UK, $60.00, £33.00 other (surface mail); £38.00 (airmail). Association for Language Learning, 16 Regent Place, Rugby Warwickshire CV21 2PN England. **Tel** 011 44 788 546443, FAX 011 44 788 544149. **ED** Colin Wringe (editor's address: University of Keele, Department of Education, Keele Staffordshire ST5 5BT United Kingdom). **LC** P51; .L353. **DD** 418/.007. **CODEN** LLEJED. Index available. **Bk Rev. Ad Acc. Pr Rev. Circ:** 5,500. ***Formed by the union of*** *British Journal of Language Teaching, 0144-0888* ***and*** *Modern Languages, 0026-7945.*
Desc: Contains articles on the teaching and learning of languages, applied linguistics, language policy, current and topical issues, and ideas on and experiences of practical classroom teaching.
Ind/Abst Br. Educ. Index; Soc. Plann. Policy Dev. Abstr.

●SA/0256-5986
LANGUAGE MATTERS. STUDIES IN THE LANGUAGES OF SOUTHERN AFRICA. (1993)-. English. sa. $9.50. University of South Africa, PO Box 392, Pretoria 0001 South Africa. **Tel** 011 27 12 4298468, FAX 011 (27)12 429 3321, telex (59)350068+. ***Continues*** *English Usage in Southern Africa, 0046-2098.*
Ind/Abst Child. Lit. Abstr. (19??-).

US/0272-2690
LANGUAGE PROBLEMS & LANGUAGE PLANNING. [Lang. probl. lang. plann.]. **Added/Corp** Center for Research and Documentation on World Language Problems. **VFOAT** Language Problems and Language Planning; L.P.L.P.; LPLP. Vol. 4 (Spring 1980)-. Periodical. English (Multiple languages). Three times a year. $89.00. John Benjamins BV, Amsteldijk 44, PO Box 75577, 1070 AN Amsterdam Netherlands. **Tel** 011 31 20 6738156, FAX 011 31 20 739773. **(Subscription address:** John Benjamins North America, PO Box 27519, Philadelphia PA 19118-0519.**)** **ED** Probal Dasgupta, Klaus Schubert, and Humphrey Tonkin. **LC** P40.5.L35; L32. **DD** 409. Index available. **Bk Rev. Ad Acc. Circ:** 700 (ctrl). available on microfilm and microfiche from University Microfilms International (UMI). ***Continues*** *Lingvaj Problemoj Kaj Lingvo-Planado, 0165-2672.*
Desc: Publishes articles primarily on political, sociological, and economic aspects of language and language use. Especially concerned with relationships between and among language communities, particularly in international contexts, and in the adaptation, manipulation, and standardization of language for international use.
Ind/Abst Abstr. Anthropol. (19??-); Am. Bibliogr. Slavic East Europ. Stud.; Curr. Index J. Educ.; Int. Bibliogr. Sociol.; Int. Polit. Sci. Abstr.; Lang. Teach.; Linguist. Lang. Behav. Abstr. (1977-) [Full Cov.]; MLA Int. Bibl. Books Artic. Mod. Lang. Lit.; Soc. Plann. Policy Dev. Abstr.

SA/1018-3442
LANGUAGE PROJECTS' REVIEW. [Lang. proj. rev.]. (1986)-. Periodical. English. Four times a year. R40.00 South Africa; R60.00 others. National Language Project, PO Box 378, 7925 Salt River South Africa. **Tel** 11 27 21 4727601, FAX 11 27 21 472994.

US
LANGUAGE QUARTERLY / PUBLISHED AT THE UNIVERSITY OF SOUTH FLORIDA UNDER THE AUSPICES OF THE DIVISION OF LANGUAGE. **Added/Corp** University of South Florida. Division of Language. **VFOAT** USF Language Quarterly. Vol. 28, No. 1-2 (Winter/Spring 1990)-. Periodical. English. sa. $9.00. USF Language Quarterly, University of South Florida, Division of Language, College of Arts and Letters, 4202 Fowler Avenue, Tampa FL 33620. **Tel** (813)974-2547. **LC** P1.A1; L35. **DD** 809. **CODEN** LAQUET. ***Continues*** *USF Language Quarterly, 0732-3042.*
Ind/Abst Annu. Bibliogr. Engl. Lang. Lit.; Curr. Index J. Educ.

KO/0254-4474
LANGUAGE RESEARCH. (OHAK YONGU.). [Lang. res.]. **Added/Corp** Soul Taehakkyo. Ohak Yonguso. **VFOAT** Language Research. (1965)-. Periodical. Korean (English). Four times a year (Mar., June, Sept., Dec.). $25.00 (institutions); $18.00 (individuals). Seoul National University / South Korea, Sinlim Dong, Kwanack Ku Seoul 151 South Korea. **Tel** 011 82 2 7408358. **(Subscription address:** Language Research Institute, Seoul National University, San 56 1 Sinlim Dong Awanak ku, Seoul 151 742 South Korea.**) LC** P9; .O4.
Ind/Abst MLA Int. Bibl. Books Artic. Mod. Lang. Lit.; Soc. Plann. Policy Dev. Abstr.

JA/0913-3615
LANGUAGE RESEARCH BULLETIN / ICU. **Added/Corp** Kokusai Kirisutokyo Daigaku. Gogakuka. **VFOAT** Gogaku Kenkyu. Vol. 1, No. 1 (1986)-. Bulletin. English (Japanese). an. **LC** P1.A1; L353. **DD** 410/.5. ***Continues*** *Annual Reports (Kokusai Kirisutokyo Daigaku. Gogakuka), 0385-8960.*
Ind/Abst Linguist. Lang. Behav. Abstr. (1986-) [Full Cov.]; Soc. Plann. Policy Dev. Abstr.

UK/0388-0001
LANGUAGE SCIENCES (OXFORD). (LANGUAGE SCIENCES.). [Lang. sci.]. **Added/Corp** Kokusai Kirisutokyo Daigaku. Language Sciences Summer Institute. Vol. 1 (March 1979)-. Periodical. English. Four times a year. $239.00 The Americas; £160.00 other. Pergamon Press, An Imprint of Elsevier Science Ltd., The Boulevard, Langford Lane, Kidlington, Oxford OX5 1GB United Kingdom. **Tel** 011 44 865 843000, 011 44 865 843699, FAX 011 44 865 843010. **(Subscription address:** Elsevier Science Ltd. Oxford Fulfillment Centre, PO Box 800, Kidlington, Oxford OX5 1DX United Kingdom.**) ED** Fred C. C. Peng. **LC** P1; .L314. **DD** 410/.5. **NLM** W1; LA617N. **[CCC]**. Index available. cum. index. **Bk Rev. Circ:** 550 (ctrl). available on microfilm and microfiche from University Microfilms International (UMI). ***Supersedes*** *Language Sciences, 0023-8341.*
Desc: Interdisciplinary forum for free exchange of scholastic ideas on the study of language. It includes social linguistics, psycholinguistics, neurolinguistics, child language and general linguistics.
Ind/Abst Abstr. Anthropol.; Anthropol. Index; Anthropol. Lit.; Curr. Index J. Educ.; Lang. Teach.; Linguist. Lang. Behav. Abstr. (1972-) [Full Cov.]; Middle East Abstr. Index; MLA Int. Bibl. Books Artic. Mod. Lang. Lit.; Soc. Plann. Policy Dev. Abstr.; Sociol. Abstr.

JA/0289-7938
LANGUAGE TEACHER / JAPAN ASSOCIATION OF LANGUAGE TEACHERS, THE. **Added/Corp** Japan Association of Language Teachers. Vol. 8, No. 4 (Apr. 1984)-. Periodical. English. Twelve times a year. $80.00 US & Australia; $80.00 Asia; $60.00 Japan; $80.00 other. Japan Association of Language Teachers, 1 3 17 Kaizuka Kawasaki ku, Kawasaki shi210 Japan. **Tel** 011 81 44 2459753, FAX 011 81 44 2459754. **ED** Greta Gorsuch, (phone: (048)688-2446). Index available (Bound in Jan. iss., ($7.50)). **Bk Rev**, (Qty: 60). **Ad Acc. Pr Rev. Circ:** 3,650 (ctrl). ***Continues*** *JALT Newsletter, 0287-2420.*
Desc: This professional organization dedicated to the improvement of language learning and teaching in Japan. A vehicle for the exchange of new ideas and techniques and a means of keeping abreast of new developments in a rapidly changing field.
Ind/Abst Soc. Plann. Policy Dev. Abstr.

UK/0261-4448
LANGUAGE TEACHING. **See** Linguistics-Abstracting, Bibliographies and Statistics.

UK/0265-5322
LANGUAGE TESTING. Vol. 1, No. 1 (June 1984)-. Periodical. English. Three times a year. $135.00 North America; £77.50 Europe; £85.00 Other. Edward Arnold, 338 Euston Road, London NW1 3BH England. **Tel** 011 44 71 873 6000, FAX 011 44 071 873 6325. **(Subscription address:** Edward Arnold, PO Box 386, Avenel NJ 07001-0386.**) ED** D. Porter and J. Upshur. **LC** P53.4; .L375. **DD** 418/.0076. **[CCC]**. **Bk Rev**. available on microfilm and microfiche from University Microfilms International (UMI).
Desc: Provides a forum for the exchange of ideas and information between researchers and practitioners in such fields as English as a foreign language testing, English as a second language testing, mother tongue testing, assessment on child language acquisition and language pathology. Each issue includes major articles, reviews of tests and books, correspondence and news of relevant meetings and conferences. Special attention is focused on testing theory, experimental investigations and the follow-up of practical implications.
Ind/Abst Br. Educ. Index; Contents Pages Educ.; Curr. Index J. Educ.; Int. Bibliogr. Book Rev.; Int. Bibliogr. Period. Lit.; Lang. Teach.; Linguist. Lang. Behav. Abstr. (1985-) [Full Cov.]; Soc. Plann. Policy Dev. Abstr.

US/0954-3945
LANGUAGE VARIATION AND CHANGE. Vol. 1, No. 1 (1989)-. Academic Scholarly Publication. English. Twice a year. $55.00 US, Canada and Mexico; £37.00 other. Cambridge University Press / New York, 40 West 20th Street, New York NY 10011-4211. **Tel** (212)924-3900, (800)221-4512. **(Subscription address:** Cambridge University Press / Outside of North America, Journal Fulfillment Department, The Edinburgh Building, Cambridge CB2 2RU United Kingdom.**) ED** David Sankoff, William Labov and Anthony Kroch. available on microfilm and microfiche from University Microfilms International (UMI).
Desc: Dedicated exclusively to the study of linguistic variation and the capacity to deal with systematic and diachronic linguistics. Concentrates on the details of linguistic structure in actual speech production and processing, or writing, including contemporary or historical sources. Of vital interest to sociologists, phonologists, linguists, sociolinguists, psychologists, anthropologists and dialectologists.
Ind/Abst Anthropol. Lit.; Curr. Index J. Educ.; Linguist. Lang. Behav. Abstr. (1989-) [Full Cov.]; MLA Int. Bibl. Books Artic. Mod. Lang. Lit.; Soc. Plann. Policy Dev. Abstr.

●UK/0965-240X
LANGUAGES IN EUROPE. **See** Education.

UK/0261-0116
LANGUAGES OF ASIA AND AFRICA. [Lang. Asia Afr.]. (1981)-. Monographic series. English. ir. Price varies per volume. Routledge, 11 New Fetter Lane, London EC4P 4EE England. **Tel** 071 583 9855, FAX 071 842 2298. **(Subscription address:** Kinokuniya Company Ltd., 38-1 Sakuragaoka 5, chome Setagaya-ku, Tokyo 156 Japan.**)**

●NE/0927-3034
LANGUAGES OF DESIGN. Vol. 1, No. 1 (Sept. 1992)-. Academic Scholarly Publication. English. Four times a year (1 volume). Fl385.00. Elsevier Science Publishers BV, PO Box 211, 1000 AE Amsterdam Netherlands. **Tel** 011 31 20 5803642, FAX 011 31 20 5862696, telex 15682. **ED** Ray Lauzzana. **LC** P98; .L36. **CODEN** LADEEI. **Bk Rev. Ad Acc. Pr Rev. Acid Free.**
Desc: Devoted to research in formal languages and their use for the synthesis of words, images and sounds. Welcomes articles employing linguistic techniques to generate literary and "nonliterary" texts, music and visual works, including fine art, dance, theatre, architecture and all types of design. Formal design theory, generative grammars, shape grammars, and computational musicology are the central domain.

CN/0316-7429
LANGUAGES OF SOUTH INDIA. **Main/Corp** Metropolitan Toronto Library Board. Languages Co-Ordinator. (1???)-. Periodical. English. Languages Co-Ordinator of the Metropolitan Toronto Library Board, 214 College Street, Toronto Ontario M5T 1R4 Canada. **DD** 018/.12948.

●GW/0940-0788
LANGUAGES OF THE WORLD. **VFOAT** Langues du Monde; Lenguas del Mundo; A.Sprachen der Welt; A.LW. No. 1 (1991)-. Periodical. English. Four times a year. Lincom Europa, PO Box 1316, D 85703 Unterschleissh Germany. **Tel** 011 49 89 3149593.

US
LANGUAGES OF THE WORLD. CD-ROM. English. $950.00 all (except Canada, Denmark, Finland, France, Italy, Japan, Netherlands, Spain, Sweden, South Korea, and UK); DM1559.10 Austria, Germany, and Switzerland. National Textbook Company, 4255 West Touhy Avenue, Lincolnwood IL 60646. **Tel** (708)679-5500, (800)323-4900, FAX (708)679-2494, telex TWX 9102230736. **(Subscription address:** Austria, Germany, Switzerland; Oscar Brandstetter Verlag, Postfach 1708 Stiftstr 30, W-6200 Wiesbaden Germany**)**
Desc: Contains 7 million words, 18 dictionaries and 12 languages all on one CD-ROM disc.

SZ
LANGUE ET CULTURES. French. ir. 90.00F. Librairie Droz AG, 11 rue Massot, CH-1211 Geneva 12 Switzerland. **Tel** 46 66 66, FAX 67 23 91.

CN/0384-5710
LANGUE ET LITTERATURE FRANCAISES AU CANADA (1970). (LANGUE ET LITTERATURE FRANCAISES AU CANADA.). **Added/Corp** Quebec (Province). Ministere des Affaires Culturelles. (1970)-. Periodical. French. ir. Presses de l'Universite Laval, CP 2447 Avenue de la Medicine, Saint Foy Quebec G1K 7P4 Canada. **Tel** (418)656-5106, (418)656-2590. ***Continues*** *Bibliotheque Francaise et Romane. Serie E: Langue et Litterature Francaises au Canada, 0067-8384.*

FR/0023-8368
LANGUE FRANCAISE. [Lang. fr.]. Vol. 1 (Feb. 1969)-. Periodical. French. Four times a year (Feb., May, Sept., Dec.). 300.00F France; 350.00F others. Livres Dix Larousse, 15 rue Rigaud, 94855 Ivry Sur Seine France. **Tel** 011 33 1 49596091. **(Subscription address:** Centrale des Revues, 11 rue Gossin, 92543 Montrouge Cedex France.**) LC** PC2002; .L34. **[CCC]**. Documents available from The Genuine Article.
Ind/Abst Arts Humanit. Citation Index; Curr. Contents Arts Humanit.; Lang. Teach.; MLA Int. Bibl. Books Artic. Mod. Lang. Lit.; Res. Alert; Soc. Sci. Cit. Index [Select. Cov.].

CN/0226-7144
LANGUES ET LINGUISTIQUE. [Lang. linguist.]. **Added/Corp** Universit,e Laval. Departement de Langues et de Linguistique. **VFOAT** Travaux du Departement de Langues et Linguistique. **VAT** Langues et Linguistiques. No 1 (1975)-. Periodical. French (English and Spanish). an. 12.00Can$. Departement de Langues et Linguistique, Faculte des Lettres, Universite Laval, Quebec G1K 7P4 Canada. **Tel** (418)656-3263, FAX (418)656-2019. **LC** P1.A1; L355. **DD** 410/.5. Index available. cum. index. **Bk Rev**, (Qty: 5). **Ad Acc. Pr Rev. Circ:** 250 (ctrl). available on diskette.
Desc: Publishes articles and reviews on linguistic theories and their application to various disciplines of linguistics, to specific languages to other fields.
Ind/Abst Linguist. Lang. Behav. Abstr. (1981-) [Full Cov.]; MLA Int. Bibl. Books Artic. Mod. Lang. Lit.; Soc. Plann. Policy Dev. Abstr.; Sociol. Abstr.

FR/0023-8376
LANGUES MODERNES, LES. [Lang. mod.]. **Added/Corp** Association des Professeurs de Langues Vivantes de l'Enseignement Public. (1903)-. Periodical. French. ir (4 magazines and 4 newsletters). 293.83F France, 300.00F other (institutions). Association des Professeurs de Langue, 19 rue de la Glaciere, 75013 Paris France. **Tel** 011 33 1 47079482. **ED** Monique Mombert. **LC** PB2; .L35. **Bk Rev. Ad Acc. Circ:** 5,000.
Desc: The main French journal devoted to foreign language learning and teaching.
Ind/Abst Annu. Bibliogr. Engl. Lang. Lit.; Lang. Teach.; MLA Int. Bibl. Books Artic. Mod. Lang. Lit.; Romant. Move.; Soc. Plann. Policy Dev. Abstr.

FR/0184-7570
LANGUES NEO-LATINES, LES. (LES LANGUES NEO-LATINES : BULLETIN TRIMESTRIEL DE LA SOCIETE DES LANGUES NEO-LATINES.). [Lang. neo-lat.]. **Added/Corp** Societe des Langues Neo-Latines. Vol. 1, No. 1 (1947)-. Bulletin. French (Spanish, Italian and Catalan). qt. 320.00F. Societe des Langues Neolatines, 11 Avenue Martelet, 94500 Champigny Sur Mar France. **Tel** 33 1 47061902. **LC** WMLC 90/0262.
Ind/Abst MLA Int. Bibl. Books Artic. Mod. Lang. Lit.; Soc. Plann. Policy Dev. Abstr.

BE/0987-7738
LANGUES ORIENTALES ANCIENNES PHILOLOGIE ET LINGUISTIQUE. **Added/Corp** Association pour l'Etude des Langues Orientales Anciennes. **VFOAT** LOAPL. No. 1 (1988)-. Periodical. Multiple languages. an. 1500F. Editions Peeters SA, Bondgenotenlaan 153, BP 41, B-3000 Leuven Belgium. **Tel** 32 16 235170, FAX 32 16 228500, telex 65987 PUL B. **ED** G. Bohas, and R. Roquet. **Bk Rev.**

IS
LASHON VE-IVRIT. ***Ceased.*** **VFOAT** Language and Hebrew; Language & Hebrew. (Jan. 1990)-(1993). Periodical. Hebrew (table of contents in English). bm. Reches Publishing House, PO Box 75, Even Yehuda 40550 Israel. **Tel** 011 972 3 691175. **LC** IN PROCESS.

VC/0023-883X
LATINITAS. [Latinitas]. (Jan. 1953)-. Periodical. Latin. Four times a year (Jan., Mar., June, Sept.). L40000 Italy; $40.00 other. Libreria Editrice Vaticana, Citta del Vaticano, 00120 Vatican City. **Tel** 011 39 6 6983529, FAX 011 39 6 6984716. **LC** PA2009; .L37. Index available. cum. index. **Bk Rev. Ad Acc. Circ:** 1,500.
Desc: Reviews on linguistics, literature, philology, history, sciences, and diarium Latinum (Latin diary).
Ind/Abst Bibliogr. Mission.; MLA Int. Bibl. Books Artic. Mod. Lang. Lit.

BE/0023-8856
LATOMUS. **See** Literature.

LV/0130-0059
LATVIESU VALODAS KULTURAS JAUTAJUMI. [Latv. valodas kult. jautajumi]. **Added/Corp** Latvijas PSR Zurnalistu Savieniba. A. Upisa Valodas un Literaturas Instituts. Valodas un Literaturas Instituts (Latvijas PSR Zinatnu Akademija). Valodas Kulturas Grupa. (1965)-. Latvian. an.
Ind/Abst MLA Int. Bibl. Books Artic. Mod. Lang. Lit.

●SP/1131-9151
LAZARILLO SALAMANCA. (1992)-. Periodical. Spanish. sa. 1800ptas. Asociacion Internacional de Traductores, Interpretes y Profesores de Espanol, Calle Compania 65, 37008 Salamanca Spain. **Tel** 923-21-47-88, FAX 923-21-87-91. **ED** Carmen Perez. **UDC** 860. **CODEN** 806.0.

IE
LEACHTAI CHOLM CILLE. **See** Literature.

US/0023-964X
LEAFLET, THE. **See** Education.

CN/0711-1509
LEARN ENGLISH IN CANADA. (APPRENEZ L'ANGLAIS AU CANADA, APPRENEZ LE FRANCAIS AU CANADA). [Learn Engl. Can.]. **Added/Corp** Council of Second Language Programmes in Canada. **VFOAT** Learn English in Canada, Learn French in Canada; Apprenez le Francais au Canada. (1984)-. English (French; summaries and/or abstracts in Spanish, German, Japanese and Arabic). an. Free. Council of Second Language Programs in Canada, c/o Canadian Bureau for International Education, 85 Albert Street/Suite 1400, Ottawa Ontario K1P 6A4 Canada. **DD** 428/.07/1171. ***Continues*** *Learn English in Canada, Apprenez le Francais au Canada, 0711-1509.*

UK
LEARNING ENGLISH IN BRITAIN. ***Title Change.*** (1988)-(1992). English. an. John Catt Ltd, Great Glemham Saxmundham, Suffolk IP17 2DH England. **Tel** 07 0728 78666, FAX 07 0728 78415. **ED** Derek Bingham. Index available. **Ad Acc. Circ:** 5,000. ***Continued by*** *Languages in Europe.*

US/0893-7443
LEBEN (CLAYTON, MO.), DAS. (DAS LEBEN.). (198?)-. Periodical. German (English). Six times a year (Oct.-May with Dec./Jan. and Apr./May combined). $12.00. The Alan Company, Box 16250, Clayton MO 63105. **Tel** (314)531-1668. **DD** 438.

GW/0023-9909
LEBENDE SPRACHEN. [Lebende Sprachen]. **Added/Corp** Bundesverband der Dolmetscher und Ubersetzer. Vol. 1 (1956)-. Periodical. German (English, French and Spanish). qt. DM91.20 Germany; DM94.00 other. Langenscheidt KG, Crellestra 28-30, D 10827 Berlin Germany. **Tel** 011 49 30 7800020, telex 183175 LUGBL. **ED** S. F. Krollmann and G. Haensch. **LC** PB5; .L4. Index available. **Bk Rev. Ad Acc. Circ:** 4,000.
Desc: Multilingual glossaries of specialized terminology from all areas; articles on the theory/practice of translation and the training of analyses of translations.
Ind/Abst Lang. Teach.; MLA Int. Bibl. Books Artic. Mod. Lang. Lit.; Soc. Plann. Policy Dev. Abstr.

UK/0075-8566
LEEDS STUDIES IN ENGLISH. [Leeds stud. Engl.]. **Added/Corp** University of Leeds. School of English. Vol. 1 (1967)-. Periodical. English. an. Price varies per volume. University of Leeds / School of English, Leeds LS2 9JT England. **Tel** (0532)334738, FAX (0532)336017, telex 556473 UNILIDS G. **ED** Joyce Hill. **LC** PE10; .L4. **DD** 805. **Bk Rev. Circ:** 450. ***Continues*** *Leeds Studies in English and Kindred Languages.*
Desc: Research articles on old and middle English literature, old Icelandic language literature, and the historical study of the English language.
Ind/Abst Abstr. Engl. Stud.; Annu. Bibliogr. Engl. Lang. Lit.; Br. Archaeol. Bibliogr.; MLA Int. Bibl. Books Artic. Mod. Lang. Lit.; Romant. Move.

UK/0075-8574
LEEDS TEXTS AND MONOGRAPHS. (LEEDS TEXTS AND MONOGRAPHS: NEW SERIES.). [Leeds texts monogr.]. **Main/Corp** University of Leeds. School of English. **Added/Corp** University of Leeds. School of English. Vol 1 (1966)-. Monographic series. English. ir. Price varies per volume. University of Leeds / School of English, Leeds LS2 9JT England. **Tel** (0532)334738, FAX (0532)336017, telex 556473 UNILIDS G. **ED** Peter Meredith. **Circ:** 350. ***Continues*** *Leeds Texts and Monographs, 0075-8574.*
Desc: Texts and monographs relating to Old and Middle English Literature, history of the English Language, Old Icelandic Language and Literature.
Ind/Abst Annu. Bibliogr. Engl. Lang. Lit.; MLA Int. Bibl. Books Artic. Mod. Lang. Lit.

NE/0458-9971
LEIDSE GERMANISTISCHE EN ANGLISTISCHE REEKS. **See** Literature.

NE/0075-8647
LEIDSE ROMANTISCHE REEKS. **See** Literature.

IO
LEMBAGA. Vol. 1- Oct. 1970-. Indonesian. ir. **LC** PL5071; .L45.

GW
LENDEMAINS. **See** Literature.

FR/0153-0313
LENGAS. **Added/Corp** Universite Paul Valery. Centre d'Etudes Occitanes. Vol. 1 (1977)-. Periodical. French (Langue d'oc). sa (Apr. & Nov.). 120.00F France; 130.00F other. Universite Paul Valery, BP 5043 Route de Mende, 34032 Montpellier, Cedex 1 France. **Tel** 11 33 67 142000, FAX 011 33 67 142052. **ED** Ph. Gardy. **LC** PC3371; .L36. **DD** 301.21. **Bk Rev**, (Qty: 2). **Pr Rev. Circ:** 300 (ctrl).
Desc: Information on sociolinguistic studies, bilingualism, French language, and the language d'Occitan.

CK
LENGUAJE. **Added/Corp** Universidad del Valle. Programa de Postgrado en Linguistia y Espanol. Universidad del Valle. Departamento de Idiomas. (Feb. 1972)-. Periodical. Spanish. **LC** P9; .L38. **DD** 410.
Ind/Abst MLA Int. Bibl. Books Artic. Mod. Lang. Lit.

CK/0120-3479
LENGUAJE CALI. [LenguajeCali]. **VFOAT** Revista Lenguaje. (1972)-. Periodical. Spanish. ir. **DD** _a410.
Ind/Abst Linguist. Lang. Behav. Abstr. (1973-) [Full Cov.]; Soc. Plann. Policy Dev. Abstr.

PE/0024-0796
LENGUAJE Y CIENCIAS. [Leng. cienc.]. **Added/Corp** Universidad Nacional de Trujillo. Departamento de Idiomas y Linguistica. (19??)-. Periodical. Spanish. sa. $15.00. Universidad Nacional de Trujillo, Departamento de Idiomas y Linguistica, Trujillo Peru. **LC** P1.A1; L4.
Ind/Abst HAPI Hisp. Am. Period. Index; Lang. Teach.; Linguist. Lang. Behav. Abstr. (1972-) [Full Cov.]; MLA Int. Bibl. Books Artic. Mod. Lang. Lit.; Soc. Plann. Policy Dev. Abstr.

AG
LENGUAJES. **Added/Corp** Asociacion Argentina de Semiotica. Yearly Vol. 1 (April 1974)-. Periodical. Spanish. tq. Ediciones Nueva Vision, Tucuman 3748, Buenos Aires Argentina. **ED** Juan Carlos Indart. **LC** P9; .L39. **Bk Rev.**

VE/0503-8448
LENGUAS MODERNAS. **Main/Corp** Venezuela. Universidad Central, Caracas. Instituto de Lenguas Modernas. Vol. 1 (1954)-. Spanish. Universidad Central de Venezuela / Instituto de Lenguas Modernas, Caracas Venezuela. **DD** 808.8; 400.

CL/0716-0542
LENGUAS MODERNAS (SANTIAGO). (LENGUAS MODERNAS.). [Leng. mod.]. **Added/Corp** Universidad de Chile. Departamento de Lenguas Modernas. Universidad de Chile. Departamento de Linguistica. No. 1 (1974)-. Spanish (English, French, German and Italian). an. $20.00. Universidad de Chile / Linguistica, Deptamento de Literatura, Casilla Postal 10136, Santiago Chile. **Tel** 011 52 2 2725978 Ext 42, FAX 011 52 2 2716823. **ED** Aura Bocaz and Patricio Novoa (Co-editor). **CODEN** LEMOEJ. **Bk Rev. Pr Rev. Circ:** 600 (ctrl).
Desc: Deals with the acquisition of new languages, native and other. General themes about languages.
Ind/Abst HAPI Hisp. Am. Period. Index; Lang. Teach.; MLA Int. Bibl. Books Artic. Mod. Lang. Lit.

IS/0024-1091
LESHONENU. **Added/Corp** Vaad Ha-Lashon Ha-Ivrit Be-Erets-Yisrael. Akademyah La-Lashon Ha-Ivrit (Jerusalem) Vaad Ha-Pirsumim Shel Ha-Akademyah La-Lashon Ha-Ivrit. **VFOAT** Lesonenu. No. 1, (April 1928)-. Periodical. Hebrew (English; summaries and/or abstracts in English). Four times a year. $35.00. Academy of Hebrew Language, PO Box 3449, Jerusalem 91034 Israel. **Tel** 011 972 2 632242, FAX 011 972 2 617065. **ED** J. Blau. **LC** PJ4503; .L45. Index available (Bound in last issue). cum. index (Vol. 1, 26 & 35 for $3.00). **Bk Rev. Circ:** 600 (ctrl).
Desc: A journal for the study of the Hebrew language and cognate subjects.
Ind/Abst MLA Int. Bibl. Books Artic. Mod. Lang. Lit.; Old Testam. Abstr.; Relig. Theol. Abstr.; Soc. Plann. Policy Dev. Abstr.

IS
LESHONENU LA-AM. **Added/Corp** Academy of the Hebrew Language, Jerusalem. Mazkirut Ha-Madit. (19??)-. Hebrew. Four times a year. $25.00 (surface mail); $35.00 (airmail). Academy of Hebrew Language, PO Box 3449, Jerusalem 91034 Israel. **Tel** 011 972 2 632242, FAX 011 972 2 617065. **ED** Professor J. Blau and Dr. D. Talshir. **LC** PJ4513; .V2. Index available (Bound in last issue). cum. index (Vol. 1, 26 & 35 for $3.00). **Bk Rev. Circ:** 600. ***Continues*** *Vaad ha-Lashon Ha-Ivrit Be-Erets Yisrael. Leshonenu La-am.*
Desc: A popular journal of the Hebrew language.
Ind/Abst MLA Int. Bibl. Books Artic. Mod. Lang. Lit.

BL
LETRA (RIO DE JANEIRO, BRAZIL). **See** Literature.

BL/0101-3335
LETRAS DE HOJE. [Let. hoje]. No. 1- Oct. 1967-. Periodical. Portuguese (Spanish and English). qt. $35.00. Pontificia Univ Catolica, AV Ipirange 6681 Porto Alegre, Rio Grande Do Sul Brazil. **Tel** (0512)369400, telex (051)3349. **ED** Elvo Clemente. **LC** P25; .L47. **UDC** 800. **Bk Rev. Circ:** 1,000 (ctrl).
Desc: Covers linguistics, literature, criticism, bilingualism, phrasalgrammar, language contact, phonetical literary theory, comparative literature, sociolinguistics, second language reading, poetry, and drama.
Ind/Abst Soc. Plann. Policy Dev. Abstr.

IT/0024-130X
LETTERATO. **See** Literature.

BE/0024-1482
LEUVENSE BIJDRAGEN. (1946)-. Dutch (English and German). qt. 1500.00F. Leuvense Bydragen, Blyde Inkomstraat 21, 3000 Leuven Belgium. **Tel** 11 32 16 285030, FAX 011 32 16 285025. Index available. cum. index. **Bk Rev**, (Qty: 50). **Circ:** 350. ***Continues*** *Leuvensche Bijdragen.*
Ind/Abst Annu. Bibliogr. Engl. Lang. Lit. (19??-19??); Lang. Lang. Behav. Abstr.; MLA Int. Bibl. Books Artic. Mod. Lang. Lit.; Soc. Plann. Policy Dev. Abstr.

NE/0024-1539
LEVENDE TALEN. [Levende talen]. **Added/Corp** Vereniging van Leraren in Levende Talen. (1930)-. Periodical. Dutch. mo (10 issues). Fl185.00. Ver Van Leraren Levende Talen, Postbus 5148, 1007 AC Amsterdam The Netherlands. **Tel** 011 31 20 739424. **LC** PB5; .L47. **DD** 405. Index available. **Bk Rev. Ad Acc.** ctrl circ. ***Continues*** *Berichten en Mededelingen.*
Ind/Abst Annu. Bibliogr. Engl. Lang. Lit.; Lang. Teach.; MLA Int. Bibl. Books Artic. Mod. Lang. Lit.; Soc. Plann. Policy Dev. Abstr.; Sociol. Abstr.

GW
LEXICOGRAPHICA. **Added/Corp** Dictionary Society of North America. European Association for Lexicography. Vol. 1 (1985)-. German (English). an. DM182.00. Max Niemeyer Verlag, Postfach 2140, D 72011 Tuebingen Germany. **Tel** 011 49 7071 989494, FAX 011 49 7071 87419. **ED** Fredric F.M. Dolezal, Antonin Kucera, Alain Rey, Herbert Ernst Wiegand, Werner Wolski, Ladislav Zgusta. **CODEN** LEXCE4.
Desc: Provides information on lexicography.
Ind/Abst MLA Int. Bibl. Books Artic. Mod. Lang. Lit.

GW/0175-9264
LEXICOGRAPHICA. SERIES MAIOR. **Added/Corp** Dictionary Society of North America. European Association for Lexicography. (19??)-. Monographic series. English. ir. Price varies per volume. Max Niemeyer Verlag, Postfach 2140, D 72011 Tuebingen Germany. **Tel** 011 49 7071 989494, FAX 011 49 7071 87419.
Desc: Supplementary volumes to the International Annual for Lexicography.
Ind/Abst MLA Int. Bibl. Books Artic. Mod. Lang. Lit.

FR/0756-7138
LEXIQUE (LILLE). (LEXIQUE.). [Lexique]. **Added/Corp** Presses Universitaires de Lille. (1982)-. French. ir (1 or 2 times per year). Presses Univ de Lille, Rue de Barreau BP 199, 59654 Villeneuve Cedex France. **Tel** 011 33 20 916824, or 916535. **LC** WMLC 93/190. **CODEN** LXIQE2.
Ind/Abst MLA Int. Bibl. Books Artic. Mod. Lang. Lit.; Soc. Plann. Policy Dev. Abstr.

PE/0254-9239
LEXIS. (LEXIS.). [Lexis]. **Added/Corp** Pontificia Universidad Catolica del Peru. Departamento de Humanidades. (1977)-. Periodical. Spanish. sa. $34.00 Americas; $35.00 Europe; $37.00 other. Pontificia Universidad Catolica Peru, Fondo Editorial, Apartado 1761, Lima 1 Peru. **Tel** 011 51 14 622540, 011 51 14 622220 ext. 220. **ED** Jose Luis Rivarola. **LC** P9; .L434. **DD** 405. Index available. cum. index. **Bk Rev. Ad Acc. Pr Rev.** ctrl circ.
Ind/Abst MLA Int. Bibl. Books Artic. Mod. Lang. Lit.

CN/0707-7726
LIAISONS (MONTREAL). ***Suspended.*** (LIAISONS.). [Liaisons]. Vol. 1 (Jan. 1977)-(19??)-. Periodical. French. qt. 16.00Can$. Liaisons, Universite de Montreal, Montreal Quebec H3C 3J7 Canada. **Tel** (514)343-6653. **DD** 370/.71/09714. **UDC** 372.880.0(71). Index available. **Bk Rev. Ad Acc. Circ:** 3,500 (ctrl).
Desc: First language teaching in primary school and high school.

UK
LIBRARY OF ARABIC LINGUISTICS. (19??)-. Monographic series. English.
Ind/Abst MLA Int. Bibl. Books Artic. Mod. Lang. Lit.

FR
LIDIL : REVUE DE DIDACTIQUE DES LANGUES. French. sa. 150.00F France; 210.00F other. Presses Univ de Grenoble, BP 47X, 38040 Grenoble Cedex France. **Tel** 011 33 76 825651.

LI/0130-0172
LIETUVIU KALBOTYROS KLAUSIMAI. [Liet. kalbotyros klaus.]. **Added/Corp** Lietuvos TSR Mokslu Akademija. (1957)-. Periodical. Lithuanian (summaries and/or abstracts in Russian). an. **LC** PG8501; .L5.
Ind/Abst MLA Int. Bibl. Books Artic. Mod. Lang. Lit.

US
LIFETIME ENCYCLOPEDIA OF LETTERS. (19??)-. English. ir. $32.95. Macmillan Publishing Company, 100 Front Street, Box 500, Riverside NJ 08075-7500. **Tel** (800)257-5755, (609)461-6500, FAX (609)461-7070. **ED** Harold E. Meyer. **LC** PE1483. **DD** 808.6.
Desc: Contains business and personal letters for every conceivable situation or occasion. Contains more that 800 sample letters and 300 model sentences in 547 separate categories.

GW/0049-8653
LILI, ZEITSCHRIFT FUER LITERATURWISSENSCHAFT UND LINGUISTIK. [LiLi, Z. Literaturwiss. Linguist.]. **Added/Corp** Universitat-Gesamthochschule-Siegen. Gesamthochschule Siegen. **VFOAT** Zeitschrift feur Literaturwissenschaft und Linguistik. **VAT** Literaturwissenschaft und Linguistik, Zeitschrift fuer Literaturwissenschaft und Linguistik. Vol. 3, No. 11 (Sept. 1973)-. Monographic series. German. qt. DM100.00. Vandenhoeck & Ruprecht, Robert Bosch Breite 6, D-37079 Goettingen Germany. **Tel** 011 49 551 695911, FAX 011 49 551 695917, telex 965226 VAN d. **LC** P3; .Z36. **[CCC].** Documents available from The Genuine Article. ***Continues*** *Zeitschrift fur Literaturwissenschaft und Linguistik.*
Ind/Abst Arts Humanit. Citation Index [Full Cov.]; Curr. Contents Arts Humanit.; Lang. Teach.; MLA Int. Bibl. Books Artic. Mod. Lang. Lit.; Res. Alert [Full Cov.]; Romant. Move.; Soc. Plann. Policy Dev. Abstr.; Soc. Sci. Cit. Index [Select. Cov.].

RM/0024-3523
LIMBA ROMANA. [Limba rom.]. **Added/Corp** Academia Republicii Socialiste Romania. Academia Republicii Populare Romine. Vol. 14, No. 1 (1965)-. Periodical. Romanian. Six times a year. DM206.00. **(Subscription address:** Kubon & Sagner, ABT Zeitschriftenimport, D 80328 Munich Germany.**)** ***Continues*** *Limba Romina, 0024-3523.*
Desc: Publishes studies and articles on general linguistics.
Ind/Abst Linguist. Lang. Behav. Abstr. (1973-) [Full Cov.]; MLA Int. Bibl. Books Artic. Mod. Lang. Lit.; Soc. Plann. Policy Dev. Abstr.

RM
LIMBA SI LITERATURA ROMANA / SOCIETATEA DE STIINTE FILOLOGICE. **Main/Corp** Societatea de Stiinte Filologice din Republica Socialista Romania. **Added/Corp** Societatea de Stiinte Filologice din Republica Socialista Romania. (19??)-. Periodical. Romanian. qt. DM169.00. **(Subscription address:** Kubon & Sagner, ABT Zeitschriftenimport, D 80328 Munich Germany.**)**
Desc: Contains articles on grammar, vocabulary, style, and composition for pupils.

RM
LIMBA SI LITERATURA / SOCIETATEA DE STIINTE ISTORICE SI FILOLOGICE. **Main/Corp** Societatea de Stiinte Filologice din Republica Socialista Romania. **Added/Corp** Societatea de Stiinte Istorice si Filologice din R. P. R. Societatea de Stiinte Filologice din Republica Socialista Romania. No. 1 (1955)-. Periodical. Romanian (summaries and/or abstracts in English, French and Russian). Four times a year. DM188.00. **(Subscription address:** Kubon & Sagner, ABT Zeitschriftenimport, D 80328 Munich Germany.**)** **LC** PC601; .S6. ***Continues*** *Limba si Literatura.*
Desc: Collection of articles and studies for the information of the Romanian language teachers.

NE/0024-3841
LINGUA (AMSTERDAM, NETHERLANDS). (LINGUA.). [Lingua]. Vol. 1 (1947)-. Academic Scholarly Publication. English (French). Twelve times a year (3 vols.). Fl1110.00. Elsevier Science Publishers BV, PO Box 211, 1000 AE Amsterdam Netherlands. **Tel** 011 31 20 5803642, FAX 011 31 20 5862696, telex 15682. **ED** J G Kooij, E C Garcia, N V Smith, T Hoekstra, and A J B N Reichling. **LC** P9; .L47. **DD** 405. **NLM** W1 LI633. **CODEN** LINGAO. **[CCC].** cum. index. **Pr Rev.** available on microfilm and microfiche from University Microfilms International (UMI). Documents available from The Genuine Article.
Desc: Devoted to the problems of general linguistics.
Ind/Abst Abstr. Anthropol. (19??-); Abstr. Engl. Stud.; Arts Humanit. Citation Index [Full Cov.]; Curr. Contents Arts Humanit.; Curr. Contents Soc. Behav. Sci.; Lang. Teach.; Linguist. Lang. Behav. Abstr. (1971-) [Full Cov.]; Middle East Abstr. Index; MLA Int. Bibl. Books Artic. Mod. Lang. Lit.; Res. Alert [Full Cov.]; Soc. Plann. Policy Dev. Abstr.; Soc. Sci. Cit. Index [Full Cov.]; Sociol. Abstr.

BL/0101-4862
LINGUA E LITERATURA. [Ling. lit.]. Vol. 1 (1972)-. French (Portuguese and Spanish). an. **LC** P1.A1; L47.
Ind/Abst HAPI Hisp. Am. Period. Index (19??-); MLA Int. Bibl. Books Artic. Mod. Lang. Lit.; Romant. Move.

IT/0394-2813
LINGUA E NUOVA DIDATTICA : LEND. **Added/Corp** Lend (Group) British Council (Rome, Italy) France. Ambassade (Italy). Bureau linguistique. Deutsche Bibliothek Rom--Goethe-Institut. **VFOAT** Lend; Rivista Lend. (19??)-. Periodical. Italian (English and French). Four times a year. L35000 Italy; L50000 other. Lingua et Nuova Didattica, Piazza Sonnino 13, 00153 Rome Italy. **Tel** 011 39 6 5800076. **LC** PB35; .L537. **DD** 428/.007.

IT/0024-385X
LINGUA E STILE. [Ling. stile]. **Added/Corp** Universita di Bologna. Istituto di Glottologia. Vol. 1 (Jan./April 1966)-. Periodical. Italian (summaries and/or abstracts in English and Russian). qt. L82000.00 Italy; L135000.00 (surface mail), L155000.00 (airmail) other. Societa Editrice il Mulino, Strada Maggiore 37, 40125 Bologna Italy. **Tel** 011 39 51 256011, FAX 011 39 51 256034. **LC** P9; .L48. Documents available from The Genuine Article. ***Continues in part*** *Universita di Bologna. Istituto di Glottologia. Quaderni.*
Ind/Abst Arts Humanit. Citation Index [Full Cov.]; Curr. Contents Arts Humanit.; Lang. Lang. Behav. Abstr.; Lang. Teach.; MLA Int. Bibl. Books Artic. Mod. Lang. Lit.; Res. Alert [Full Cov.]; Romant. Move.; Soc. Plann. Policy Dev. Abstr.; Soc. Sci. Cit. Index [Select. Cov.].

IT/0024-3868
LINGUA NOSTRA. [Ling. nostra]. (Feb. 1939)-. Periodical. Italian. qt (4 issues). L90000 Italy; L110000 other. Le Lettere, Costa San Giorgio 28, 50125 Florence Italy. **(Subscription address:** Licosa SPA, PO Box 552, 50125 Florence Italy; telephone: 011 39 55 645415**)** **ED** Gianfranco Folena and Ghino Ghinassi. **LC** PC1001; .L5. Documents available from The Genuine Article.
Desc: Dedicated to the study of the Italian language from both historical and descriptive perspectives. Publishes reports on dialects, neologisms, teaching linguistics, etc. Each number concludes with a discussion of the most significant contributions to the Italian language to appear recently.
Ind/Abst Arts Humanit. Citation Index [Full Cov.]; Curr. Contents Arts Humanit.; Lang. Teach.; MLA Int. Bibl. Books Artic. Mod. Lang. Lit.; Res. Alert [Full Cov.]; Soc. Plann. Policy Dev. Abstr.; Sociol. Abstr. (?-?).

PO/0079-4740
LINGUA POSNANIENSIS. [Ling. Posnan.]. **Added/Corp** Poznanskie Towarzystwo Przyjacio Nauk. Komisja Jezykoznawcza. Poznanskie Towarzystwo Przyjacio Nauk. Komisja Filologiczna. (1949)-. English (Polish and French). an. **(Subscription address:** ARS Polona, PO Box 1001, 00068 Warsaw Poland.**)** **LC** P25; .L55. **DD** 410/.5.
Desc: Contains information on philology and comparative and general grammar.
Ind/Abst Linguist. Lang. Behav. Abstr. (1972-) [Full Cov.]; MLA Int. Bibl. Books Artic. Mod. Lang. Lit.; Soc. Plann. Policy Dev. Abstr.

BL
LINGUAGEM (RIO DE JANEIRO, BRAZIL). (LINGUAGEM.). Yearly V. 1, No. 1-. Periodical. Portuguese. sa. $20.00. Presenca Edicoes, rua do Cadete 204, Grupo 302 22.220, Rio de Janeiro Brasil. **LC** P9; .L485. **DD** 410/.5. **UDC** 806.90.

IT
LINGUE DEL MONDO. ***Ceased.*** Yearly Vol. 1 (Jan. 1934)-Ceased Dec. 1990. Periodical. Italian (English). bm. Valmartina Editore, Vld L Dottesio 1, 35138 Padova Italy. **Tel** 049/8710195. **ED** Nicholas Brownlees. **UDC** 800. Index available. **Bk Rev. Ad Acc.** ctrl circ.
Desc: Concerns language teaching, translations, new books in general and current happenings in the language field.
Ind/Abst Linguist. Lang. Behav. Abstr. (1985-) [Full Cov.]; Soc. Plann. Policy Dev. Abstr.

UK/0268-5965
LINGUIST (LONDON, ENGLAND : 1986). (THE LINGUIST : JOURNAL OF THE INSTITUTE OF LINGUISTS.). **Added/Corp** Institute of Linguists (Great Britain). Vol. 25, No. 1 (Winter 1986)-. Periodical. English. bm (6 issues). £25.00 UK; £30.00 other. Institute of Linguists, 24A Highbury Grove, London N5 2EA England. **Tel** 011 44 71 359 7445, FAX 011 44 71 354 0202. **ED** J. L. Kettle-Williams. **LC** P1; .I5. **DD** 410/.5. **Bk Rev. Ad Acc. Circ:** 7,000. ***Continues*** *Incorporated Linguist, 0019-3534.*
Desc: Contains articles for a specialized readership, together with items of current and more popular interest.
Ind/Abst Lang. Teach. (Winter 1986-); MLA Int. Bibl. Books Artic. Mod. Lang. Lit.; Soc. Plann. Policy Dev. Abstr.; Sociol. Abstr. (Winter 1986-).

US/0098-9053
LINGUISTIC ANALYSIS. [Linguist. anal.]. Vol. 1 (1975)-. Periodical. English. Four times a year (Mar, June, Sept, Dec). $116.00 (institution); $58.00 (individual); $35.00 (student). Linguistic Analysis, PO Box 95679, Seattle WA 98145. **Tel** (206)567-4373. **ED** Michael K. Brame. **LC** P123; .L49. **DD** 410. **UDC** 800. **[CCC].** Index available (4th issue, December, no charge). **Bk Rev** (Qty: 3-5 per year). **Pr Rev. Circ:** 2,500.
Desc: A research journal devoted to the publication of high quality articles in formal phonology, morphology, syntax and semantics.
Ind/Abst Abstr. Anthropol.; Arts Humanit. Citation Index (19??-19??) [Full Cov.]; Comput. Rev.; Lang. Teach.; Middle East Abstr. Index; MLA Int. Bibl. Books Artic. Mod. Lang. Lit.

NE/0165-7712
LINGUISTIC & LITERARY STUDIES IN EASTERN EUROPE. [Linguist. lit. stud. East. Eur.]. **VFOAT** LLSEE; Linguistic and Literary Studies in Eastern Europe. Vol. 1 (1979)-. Monographic series. English. ir. Price varies per volume. John Benjamins BV, Amsteldijk 44, PO Box 75577, 1070 AN Amsterdam Netherlands. **Tel** 011 31 20 6738156, FAX 011 31 20 739773. **(Subscription address:** John Benjamins North America, PO Box 27519, Philadelphia PA 19118-0519.**)** **ED** Petr Sgall and Eva Hajicova.
Desc: Emphasis of this series is on recent developments in linguistic research in Central and Eastern European countries; it includes analyses, translations, and syntheses of current research as well as studies in the history of linguistic scholarship.
Ind/Abst Math. Rev.; MLA Int. Bibl. Books Artic. Mod. Lang. Lit.

NE
LINGUISTIC BIBLIOGRAPHY FOR THE YEAR ... AND SUPPLEMENT FOR THE YEARS ... . **Added/Corp** Permanent International Committee of Linguists. International Council for Philosophy and Humanistic Studies. **VFOAT** Bibliographie Linguistique de l'Annee ... et Complement des Annees ...; Linguistic Bibliography; Bibliographie Linguistique. (1948)-. Bibliography. Multiple languages. ir. Price varies per volume. Kluwer Academic Publishers, Postbus 322, 3300 AH Dordrecht, The Netherlands. **Tel** 011 (31) 78 524400, FAX 011 31 78 183273, telex 20083. **(Subscription address:** Kluwer Academic Publishers / US Subscriptions, PO Box 253, Accord Station, Hingham MA 02018.**)** **LC** Z7001; .P4; P121. **DD** 016.41. ***Continues*** *Linguistic Bibliography for the Years ... .*

NE
LINGUISTIC CALCULATION. ***Ceased.*** (1983)-?. Monographic series. English. Kluwer Academic Publishers, Postbus 322, 3300 AH Dordrecht, The Netherlands. **Tel** 011 (31) 78 524400, FAX 011 31 78 183273, telex 20083.

US/0024-3892
LINGUISTIC INQUIRY. [Linguist. inq.]. (Jan. 1970)-. Periodical. English. qt. $50.00 (individuals), $108.00 (institutions). Massachusetts Institute of Technology (MIT) Press, 55 Hayward Street, Cambridge MA 02142-1399. **Tel** (617)253-2889, (617)625-8481, FAX (617)258-6779. **ED** Samuel Jay Keyser. **LC** P1; .L48. **DD** 410/.5. **[CCC]. Ad Acc. Pr Rev. Circ:** 2,700. available on microfilm and microfiche from University Microfilms International (UMI). Documents available from The Genuine Article.
Desc: Leads the field in research on current topics in linguistics.
Ind/Abst Abstr. Anthropol.; Annu. Bibliogr. Engl. Lang. Lit.; Arts Humanit. Citation Index [Full Cov.]; Curr. Contents Arts Humanit.; Curr. Contents Soc. Behav. Sci.; Int. Bibliogr. Sociol.; Lang. Teach.; Linguist. Lang. Behav. Abstr. (1972-) [Full Cov.]; Middle East Abstr. Index; MLA Int. Bibl. Books Artic. Mod. Lang. Lit.; Res. Alert [Full Cov.]; Soc. Plann. Policy Dev. Abstr.; Soc. Sci. Cit. Index [Full Cov.].

NE
LINGUISTIC MODELS. (1981)-. Monographic series. English. ir. Price varies. Foris Publications, PO Box 509, 3300 AM Dordrecht Netherlands. **Tel** 011 31 78 510454.

US/0737-4720
LINGUISTIC NOTES FROM LA JOLLA. (LINGUISTIC NOTES FROM LA JOLLA : PUBLICATION OF THE DEPARTMENT OF LINGUISTICS, UNIVERSITY OF CALIFORNIA, SAN DIEGO.). [Linguist. notes La Jolla]. **Added/Corp** University of California, San Diego. Dept. of Linguistics. **VFOAT** LNLJ; L.N.L.J. No. 1 (1969)-. English. ir. $9.00 (institutions); $7.00 (individuals). Linguistics Notes La Jolla, University of California, Department of Linguistics, C 800, La Jolla CA 92093. **Tel** (619)534-3600. **DD** 410. **CODEN** LNLJES.
Ind/Abst Linguist. Lang. Behav. Abstr. (1988-) [Full Cov.]; Soc. Plann. Policy Dev. Abstr.

NE/0167-6318
LINGUISTIC REVIEW, THE. [Linguist. rev.]. Vol. 1, No. 1 (Jan. 1981)-. Periodical. English. qt. $164.80. Walter de Gruyter Inc., PO Box 303421, D 10728 Berlin Germany. **Tel** 011 49 30 260050, FAX 011 49 30 26005251. **ED** Riny Huybregts, Jan Koster and Henk van Riemsdyk. **[CCC]. Ad Acc. Circ:** 800. available on microfilm from University Microfilms International (UMI). Documents available from The Genuine Article.
Desc: Papers in syntax, semantics, phonology and morphology.
Ind/Abst Annu. Bibliogr. Engl. Lang. Lit.; Arts Humanit. Citation Index [Full Cov.]; Curr. Contents Arts Humanit.; Linguist. Lang. Behav. Abstr. (1981-) [Full Cov.]; MLA Int. Bibl. Books Artic. Mod. Lang. Lit.; Res. Alert [Full Cov.]; Soc. Plann. Policy Dev. Abstr.; Soc. Sci. Cit. Index [Select. Cov.].

XV/0024-3922
LINGUISTICA. [Linguistica]. **Added/Corp** Raziskovalna Skupnost Slovenije. (19??)-. Serbo-Croatian (Roman) (, English, French, German, Italian and Slovenian). **LC** P25; .L553. ***Supersedes*** *Linguistica.*
Ind/Abst Linguist. Lang. Behav. Abstr. (1972-) [Full Cov.]; MLA Int. Bibl. Books Artic. Mod. Lang. Lit.; Soc. Plann. Policy Dev. Abstr.

BE/0304-2294
LINGUISTICA ANTVERPIENSIA. [Linguist. Antverp.]. **Added/Corp** Antwerp. Rijksuniversitair Centrum. Hoger Instituut voor Vertalers en Tolken. (1967)-. Periodical. Dutch (English and French). ir. 600F. RUCA, Schildersstraat 41, 2000 Antwerp Belgium. **ED** M. Windross. Index available. **Bk Rev. Circ:** 250.
Desc: Linguistics, applied linguistics and translation theory.
Ind/Abst Lang. Teach.; MLA Int. Bibl. Books Artic. Mod. Lang. Lit.; Soc. Plann. Policy Dev. Abstr.

●CN
LINGUISTICA ATLANTICA : JOURNAL OF THE ATLANTIC PROVINCES LINGUISTIC ASSOCATION. **Added/Corp** Atlantic Provinces Linguistic Association. Memorial University of Newfoundland. Linguistics Dept. Vol. 14 (1992)-. English (French). an (Spring or Summer). $19.85 US; 15.00Can$. Memorial University / Linguistics Department, St John's Newfoundland A1B 3X9 Canada. **Tel** (709)737-8134, FAX (709)737-4000. **ED** Dr. James R. Black. **Bk Rev. Pr Rev. Circ:** 130. ***Continues*** *Journal of the Atlantic Provinces Linguistic Association, 0706-6910.*
Desc: Scholarly papers on theoretical and descriptive linguistics, especially focused on Atlantic Canadian languages.

PL/0342-0884
LINGUISTICA BIBLICA. **See** Religion and Theology.

IT/0392-6907
LINGUISTICA COMPUTAZIONALE. [Linguist. comput.]. **Added/Corp** Consiglio Nazionale Delle Ricerche (Italy). Istituto di Linguistica Computazionale. Vol. 1, (1981)-. Monographic series. English (French and Italian). ir. Price varies per volume. Giardini Editori Stampatori, Via Santa Bibbiana 28, 56127 Pisa Italy. **Tel** 011 39 50 934242. **LC** UNC.

IT
LINGUISTICA E LETTERATURA. Vol. 1 (1976)-. Periodical. Italian. Twice a year. L190000 Italy; L350000 other. Giardini Editori Stampatori, Via Santa Bibbiana 28, 56127 Pisa Italy. **Tel** 011 39 50 934242. **LC** P9; .L488.

SP
LINGUISTICA ESPANOLA ACTUAL. **Added/Corp** Instituto de Cooperacion Iberoamericana (Madrid, Spain) Centro Iberoamericano de Cooperacion. **VFOAT** LEA. (1979)-. Periodical. Spanish. sa. $45.00. Arco Libros S A, Juan Bautista de Toledo 28, 28002 Madrid Spain. **Tel** 011 34 1 415-3687, 011 34 1 416-1371. **LC** PC4008; .L56. **DD** 460/.5.
Ind/Abst MLA Int. Bibl. Books Artic. Mod. Lang. Lit.

US/0887-9958
LINGUISTICA EXTRANEA. STUDIA. **VFOAT** Studia. (1978)-. Monographic series. English. **DD** 410.
Ind/Abst MLA Int. Bibl. Books Artic. Mod. Lang. Lit.

●XR
LINGUISTICA PRAGENSIA. **Added/Corp** Ustav pro Jazyk Cesky CSAV. (1991)-. Periodical. English (French, German, Italian and Spanish). Twice a year. $60.00. John Benjamins BV, Amsteldijk 44, PO Box 75577, 1070 AN Amsterdam Netherlands. **Tel** 011 31 20 6738156, FAX 011 31 20 739773. **(Subscription address:** John Benjamins North America, PO Box 27519, Philadelphia PA 19118-0519.**)** **ED** Libuse Duskova, Eva Havlova. **LC** P1.A1; L49. **DD** 410/.5. ***Continues in part*** *Philologica Pragensia, 0048-3885.*

PL/0208-4228
LINGUISTICA SILESIANA. **Added/Corp** Uniwersytet Slaski w Katowicach. (1975)-. Periodical. Polish (English, French, German and Russian). z16.00. **LC** P9; .L49. **DD** 410/.5.
Ind/Abst MLA Int. Bibl. Books Artic. Mod. Lang. Lit.

ER/0132-0777
LINGUISTICA URALICA. **Added/Corp** Eesti Teaduste Akadeemia. (1990)-. Periodical. English (German and Russian). Four times a year. $139.95. Mezhdunarodnaya Kniga, Smolenskaya Sennaya 32/34, G-200 Moscow Russia. **(Subscription address:** East View Publications Inc., 3020 Harbor Lane North, Suite 110, Minneapolis MN 55447.**)** **LC** PH1; .S473. **DD** 494. ***Continues*** *Sovetskoe Finnougrovedenie, 0038-5182.*
Ind/Abst MLA Int. Bibl. Books Artic. Mod. Lang. Lit.

CK/0120-5587
LINGUISTICA Y LITERATURA : REVISTA DEL DEPARTAMENTO DE ESPANOL. [Linguist. lit.]. Periodical. Spanish. sa. 1,400Col$ Colombia; $20.00 other. Departamento de Espanol, Facultad de Ciencias y Humanidades, Universidad de Antioquia, Apartado Aereo 1226. **ED** Oscar Castro G. **LC** P9; .L492. **DD** 409/.8. **UDC** 806.0; 860. cum. index (issue 1-9). **Bk Rev. Circ:** 1,000.
Desc: Contains articles of linguistics, literary creation, poems, events, and gives reviews in order to promote knowledge in the fields of literature and linguistics.
Ind/Abst Soc. Plann. Policy Dev. Abstr.

NE/0024-3949
LINGUISTICS. [Linguistics]. (Oct. 1963)-. Periodical. English (French and German). bm. $425.70. Walter de Gruyter Inc., PO Box 303421, D 10728 Berlin Germany. **Tel** 011 49 30 260050, FAX 011 49 30 26005251. **ED** Wolfgang Klein. **LC** P1.A1; L5. **DD** 410/.5. **NLM** W1 LI634. **[CCC].** cum. index. **Bk Rev. Ad Acc. Pr Rev. Circ:** 1,200. available on microfilm and microfiche from University Microfilms International (UMI). Documents available from The Genuine Article.
Desc: Provides an international forum for research in the language sciences.
Ind/Abst Abstr. Anthropol.; Arts Humanit. Citation Index [Full Cov.]; Int. Bibliogr. Sociol.; Lang. Teach.; Linguist. Lang. Behav. Abstr. (1972-) [Full Cov.]; Middle East Abstr. Index; MLA Int. Bibl. Books Artic. Mod. Lang. Lit.; Res. Alert [Full Cov.]; Soc. Plann. Policy Dev. Abstr.; Soc. Sci. Cit. Index [Full Cov.].

UK/0267-5498
LINGUISTICS ABSTRACTS. [Linguist. abstr.]. Vol. 1, No. 1 (1985)-. Academic Scholarly Publication. English. Four times a year. £175.00 UK & Europe; $329.00 North America; £212.00 other. Basil Blackwell Publishers Ltd, 108 Cowley Road, Oxford 0X4 1JF England. **Tel** 011 44 865 791100, FAX 011 44 865 791347, telex 837022 OXBOOK G. **(Subscription address:** Blackwell Publishers / UK, Marston Book Services, PO Box 87, Oxford OX2 0DT England.**)** **LC** P1; .L56. **DD** 016.41/05. **[CCC]. Circ:** 700. available on microfilm from University Microfilms International (UMI).
Ind/Abst MLA Int. Bibl. Books Artic. Mod. Lang. Lit.

US/0898-5898
LINGUISTICS AND EDUCATION. [Linguist. educ.]. Vol. 1, No. 1 (Spring 1988)-. Periodical. English. qt (4 issues). $90.00 institution. Ablex Publishing Corporation, 355 Chestnut Street, Norwood NJ 07648. **Tel** (201)767-8450, (201)767-8455 (Customer Service), FAX (201)767-6717. **ED** David Bloome. **LC** P40.8; .L56. **DD** 410/.5. **[CCC].** Index available. cum. index. **Ad Acc. Circ:** 300.
Desc: Reports research or reviews of research focusing on issues in linguistics and education, including classroom interaction, language diversity in educational settings, language policy and curriculum, written language learning in educational settings, and more.
Ind/Abst Abstr. Anthropol. (19??-); Curr. Index J. Educ.; Linguist. Lang. Behav. Abstr. (1988-) [Full Cov.]; MLA Int. Bibl. Books Artic. Mod. Lang. Lit.; Soc. Plann. Policy Dev. Abstr.

US/0888-8027
LINGUISTICS AND LANGUAGE BEHAVIOR ABSTRACTS. **See** Linguistics-Abstracting, Bibliographies and Statistics.

NE/0165-0157
LINGUISTICS AND PHILOSOPHY. [Linguist. philos.]. **VFOAT** L&P. Vol. 1 (Jan. 1977)-. Periodical. English. bm. $488.00. Kluwer Academic Publishers, Postbus 322, 3300 AH Dordrecht, The Netherlands. **Tel** 011 (31) 78 524400, FAX 011 31 78 183273, telex 20083. **ED** David Dowty and Francis Pelletier. **LC** P1.A1; L513. **DD** 410/.1. **CODEN** LIPHD6. **[CCC].** Index available. **Bk Rev. Ad Acc. Pr Rev. Acid Free. Circ:** 1,300. available on microfilm and microfiche from University Microfilms International (UMI). Documents available from The Genuine Article.
Desc: Studies focused on natural language: philosophy of language, linguistics, artificial intelligence, logic, questions and problems raised by linguistics as a science.
Ind/Abst Abstr. Anthropol.; Arts Humanit. Citation Index [Full Cov.]; Curr. Contents Arts Humanit.; Int. Bibliogr. Sociol.; Lang. Teach.; Linguist. Lang. Behav. Abstr. (1977-) [Full Cov.]; MLA Int. Bibl. Books Artic. Mod. Lang. Lit.; Philos. Index; Ref. Z.; Res. Alert [Full Cov.]; Soc. Plann. Policy Dev. Abstr.; Soc. Sci. Cit. Index [Select. Cov.]; Sociol. Abstr.; Zentralbl. Math. Ihre Grenzgeb.

NE
LINGUISTICS IN THE NETHERLANDS. (19??)-. English (Dutch, French and German). an. **LC** P21; .L497. **DD** 410/.5.
Ind/Abst Annu. Bibliogr. Engl. Lang. Lit.

US/0731-3500
LINGUISTICS OF THE TIBETO-BURMAN AREA. [Linguist. Tibeto-Burman area]. **Added/Corp** University of California, Berkeley. Dept. of Linguistics. (Fall 1974)-. Periodical. English. sa. $28.00. Berkeley Linguistics Society, 2337 Dwinell Hall, University of California, Berkeley CA 94720. **Tel** (510)642-2757, (510)642-5808, FAX (510)643-5688. **LC** PL3551; .A35. **DD** 495.4/005.
Ind/Abst Int. Bibliogr. Sociol.; MLA Int. Bibl. Books Artic. Mod. Lang. Lit.

NE/0166-0829
LINGUISTIK AKTUELL. **VFOAT** LA; Amsterdamer Arbeiten Zur Theoretischen und Angewandten Linguistik; Amsterdamer Arbeiten Zur Theoretischen & Angewandten Linguistik. (1980)-. Monographic series. English. ir. Price varies per volume. John Benjamins BV, Amsteldijk 44, PO Box 75577, 1070 AN Amsterdam Netherlands. **Tel** 011 31 20 6738156, FAX 011 31 20 739773. **(Subscription address:** John Benjamins North America, PO Box 27519, Philadelphia PA 19118-0519.**)** **ED** Werner Abraham. **LC** UNC.
Desc: Provides a platform for interdisciplinary studies in Linguistics and Communication Sciences. The series concentrates on studies in Germanic languages with a solid theoretical background.
Ind/Abst MLA Int. Bibl. Books Artic. Mod. Lang. Lit.

FR/0994-7744
LINGUISTIQUE AFRICAINE (PARIS, FRANCE). (LINGUISTIQUE AFRICAINE.). (1988)-. Periodical. French (English). sa. **LC** PL8000; .L56.
Ind/Abst Linguist. Lang. Behav. Abstr. (1990-) [Full Cov.]; MLA Int. Bibl. Books Artic. Mod. Lang. Lit.; Soc. Plann. Policy Dev. Abstr.

CG/1010-7274
LINGUISTIQUE ET SCIENCES HUMAINES. (LINGUISTIQUE ET SCIENCES HUMAINES : REVUE DU CENTRE DE LINGUISTIQUE THEORIQUE ET APPLIQUEE.). [Linguist. sci. hum.]. **Added/Corp** Universite Nationale du Zaire, Campus de Lubumbashi. Centre de Linguistique Theorique et Appliquee. (19??)-. Periodical. French. sa. **LC** PL8000; .L56. **DD** 496/.05. ***Formed by the union of*** *Africanistique (Lubumbashi, Zaire), 1013-2171; Philologie et Linguistique Romanes* ***and*** *Linguistique et Sciences Humaines, 1010-7274.*
Ind/Abst Soc. Plann. Policy Dev. Abstr.

FR/0246-6341
LINGUISTIQUE ET SEMIOLOGIE. (1978)-. Monographic series. French. ir. Price varies per volume. Presses Univ de Lyon, 86 rue Pateur, 69365 Lyon Cedex 07 France. **Tel** 011 33 16 78692048, 78 697082, FAX 011 33 78 695601. **UDC** 4.

FR/0075-966X
LINGUISTIQUE (PARIS. 1965), LA. (LA LINGUISTIQUE.). [Linguistique]. (1965)-. Periodical. French (English and French). sa. 310.00F France; 380.00F other. Presses Universitaires de France, Department des Revues, 14 Avenue du Bois de l'Epine, BP 90, 91003 Evry Cedex France. **Tel** (1)60 77 82 05, FAX (1) 60 79 20 45, telex PUF 600 474 F. **ED** F. Bentolila. **LC** P2; .L5. Documents available from The Genuine Article.
Desc: Both pure and applied linguistics are considered in this publication, as instruments of communication and expression. Structure of language is examined as a function of its use.
Ind/Abst Arts Humanit. Citation Index [Full Cov.]; Curr. Contents Arts Humanit.; Lang. Teach.; MLA Int. Bibl. Books Artic. Mod. Lang. Lit.; Res. Alert [Full Cov.]; Soc. Plann. Policy Dev. Abstr.; Soc. Sci. Cit. Index [Select. Cov.]; Sociol. Abstr.

FR
LINGUISTIQUE SEMIOLOGIE. ir. 130.00F (add 17.00F postage). Presses Univ de Lyon, 86 rue Pateur, 69365 Lyon Cedex 07 France. **Tel** 011 33 16 78692048, 78 697082, FAX 011 33 78 695601.

GW/0179-2180
LINGUISTISCHE ARBEITEN UND BERICHTE. (LINGUISTISCHE ARBEITEN.). [Linguist. Arb. Ber.]. Periodical. German. Germanistik der Freien Universitat Berlin, Habelschwerdter Allee 45, 1000 Berlin 33 Germany. **LC** P3; .L5. **UDC** 803.0.
Ind/Abst MLA Int. Bibl. Books Artic. Mod. Lang. Lit.

GW/0024-3930
LINGUISTISCHE BERICHTE. [Linguist. Ber.]. (1969)-. Periodical. German (English and French). bm (Feb., Apr., June, Aug., Oct., Dec.). DM252.40 Germany; DM284.40 other. Westdeutscher Verlag GmbH, Postfach 5829, D 65048 Wiesbaden Germany. **Tel** 011 49 611 160220. **LC** P1.A1; L515. **[CCC]. Ad Acc. Circ:** 1,600.
Ind/Abst Lang. Teach.; Linguist. Lang. Behav. Abstr. (1972-) [Full Cov.]; MLA Int. Bibl. Books Artic. Mod. Lang. Lit.; Soc. Plann. Policy Dev. Abstr.

GW
LINGUISTISCHE REIHE. V. 1- 1970-. Periodical. German (summaries and/or abstracts in English and French). ir. Adlers Foreign Books Inc, 915 Foster Street, Evanston IL 60201. **Tel** (312)866-6329, telex 256262 EURO PUB EVN. **UDC** 803.0.

NE/0378-4169
LINGVISTICAE INVESTIGATIONES. [Linguist. invest.]. **Added/Corp** Universite de Paris VIII: Vincennes. Departement de Linguistique. Centre National de la Recherche Scientifique (France). Laboratoire d'Automatique Documentaire et Linguistique. Vol. 1, No. 1 (1977)-. Periodical. French (English). sa. $199.00. John Benjamins BV, Amsteldijk 44, PO Box 75577, 1070 AN Amsterdam Netherlands. **Tel** 011 31 20 6738156, FAX 011 31 20 739773. **(Subscription address:** John

Benjamins North America, PO Box 27519, Philadelphia PA 19118-0519.) **ED** Maurice Gross, Jean-Claude Chevalier and Christian Leclere. **LC** P1.A1; L518. **DD** 410/.5.
Desc: Devoted to general linguistics; publishes articles in and bearing on all languages. Intends to emphasize the study of French. Publishes original studies in phonology, morphology, syntax and semantics, as well as bibliographies, theses, reports and reviews.
Ind/Abst Lang. Teach.; Linguist. Lang. Behav. Abstr. (1979-) [Full Cov.]; MLA Int. Bibl. Books Artic. Mod. Lang. Lit.; Soc. Plann. Policy Dev. Abstr.

NE/0165-7569
LINGVISTICAE INVESTIGATIONES. SUPPLEMENTA. [Linguist. invest., Suppl.]. **Added/Corp** Universite de Paris VIII: Vincennes. Departement de Linguistique. Centre National de la Recherche Scientifique (France). Laboratoire d'Automatique Documentaire et Linguistique. **VFOAT** LIS; L.I.S. Vol. 1 (1979)-. Monographic series. English (French). ir. Price varies per volume. John Benjamins BV, Amsteldijk 44, PO Box 75577, 1070 AN Amsterdam Netherlands. **Tel** 011 31 20 6738156, FAX 011 31 20 739773. **(Subscription address:** John Benjamins North America, PO Box 27519, Philadelphia PA 19118-0519.) **ED** Jean-Claude Chevalier, Maurice Gross and Christian Leclerc. **LC** UNC. **Circ:** 700.
Desc: French and general linguistics, modern linguistic theory and fundamental descriptive studies.
Ind/Abst MLA Int. Bibl. Books Artic. Mod. Lang. Lit.

RU/0130-9277
LINGVISTICHESKIE PROBLEMY FUNKTSIONALNOGO MODELIROVANIIA RECHEVOI DEIATELNOSTI. [Lingvist. probl. funkc. model. recevoj dejat.]. **Added/Corp** Leningradskii Gosudarstvennyi Universitet, Imeni A.A. Zhdanova. (1973)-. Russian. St Petersburg State University / Izdatelstvo Leningradskogo Universiteta, Universitetskaia Nab 7/9, 199034 St Petersburg Russia. **Tel** 011 95 218-97-88, FAX 011 95 218-51-52, telex 121481. **LC** P151; .L52.
Ind/Abst MLA Int. Bibl. Books Artic. Mod. Lang. Lit.

RU
LINGVISTIKA I PROBLEMY STILIA. **Added/Corp** Leningradskii Gosudarstvennyi Pedagogicheskii Institut Imeni A.I. Gertsena. No. 1 (1977)-. Periodical. Russian. 0.85rub single issue. **LC** P9; .L494.

CN/0317-1981
LISTE DES ACQUISITIONS - INFORMATHEQUE DE LINGUISTIQUE. UNIVERSITE D'OTTAWA. (LISTE DES ACQUISITIONS - UNIVERSITE D'OTTAWA, INFORMATHEQUE DE LINGUISTIQUE.). **Main/Corp** Universite d'Ottawa. Informatheque de Linguistique. **VFOAT** List of Accessions - University of Ottawa, Linguistic Documentation Centre. June 1974-. English (French). Linguistics Documentation Centre, University of Ottawa, Ottawa Ontario K1N 6N5 Canada. **DD** 016.41. **UDC** 800(01).
Desc: Computer Printout

XR/0024-4457
LISTY FILOLOGICKE (PRAGUE, CZECHOSLOVAKIA : 1946). (LISTY FILOLOGICKE.). [Listy filol.]. **Added/Corp** Ceskoslovenska Akademie Ved. Kabinet Pro Studia Recka, Rimska a Latinska. No. 70 (1946)-. Periodical. Czech (Czech; summaries and/or abstracts in English, French, German and Russian). qt. $126.00. John Benjamins BV, Amsteldijk 44, PO Box 75577, 1070 AN Amsterdam Netherlands. **Tel** 011 31 20 6738156, FAX 011 31 20 739773. **(Subscription address:** John Benjamins North America, PO Box 27519, Philadelphia PA 19118-0519.) **ED** Helena Kurzova. **LC** PA9; .L5. cum. index. ***Continues in part*** *Cesky Casopis Filologicky.*
Desc: Covers classical philology, archaeology, medieval Latin and humanistic studies, Old Czech language and literature.
Ind/Abst Am. Hist. Life (1955-1972); BHA : Biblio. Hist. Art; MLA Int. Bibl. Books Artic. Mod. Lang. Lit.; Numis. Lit.; Soc. Plann. Policy Dev. Abstr.

TU/0459-5106
LITERA. **See** Literature.

UK/0268-1145
LITERARY AND LINGUISTIC COMPUTING. **See** Computers.

FR/0755-4796
LIVRET DE LA RECHERCHE / INSTITUT NATIONAL DES LANGUES ET CIVILISATIONS ORIENTALES. **See** History(General)-History of Asia.

CM
LIVRET DU DEPARTEMENT DES LANGUES AFRICAINES ET LINGUISTIQUE. **Main/Corp** University of Yaounde. Department des Langues Africaines et Linguistique. English (French). Universite de Yaounde, Faculte des Lettres et Sciences Humaines, Prof. Sondengam BP 812, Yaounde Cameroon. **LC** P59.U545; U54B. **DD** 410. **UDC** 809.6.

NO/0801-1834
LIVSTEGN. **Added/Corp** Norsk Forening for Semiotikk. No. 1 (Feb. 1986)-. Periodical. Norwegian (English, French and Russian). sa. Nkr. 200 (membership, Nkr. 100 (student membership), Nkr. 50 (single issue). Universitet I Bergen, Romansk Institutt, Sydnesplass 9, 5007 Bergen Norway.
Ind/Abst MLA Int. Bibl. Books Artic. Mod. Lang. Lit.

UK/0309-6270
LOGOPHILE. ***Ceased.*** [Logophile]. Vol. 1, No. 1 (1977)-(19??). Periodical. English. qt.
Ind/Abst MLA Int. Bibl. Books Artic. Mod. Lang. Lit.

UK/0307-7144
LORE AND LANGUAGE. **See** Folklore.

FR/0758-4938
LOU PROUVENCAU A L'ESCOLO. Periodical. Provencal, Old (French). qt. 100.00F. CCP 1394-90 Marseille, 84 rue des Trois-Freres Carasso, 13004 Marseille France. **Tel** 91 49 0974. **LC** PC3201; .P76. **DD** 449/.05. **UDC** 804.90. **Circ:** 560.
Desc: Articles on linguistics, literature and teaching the Provencial language.

US
LSA ANNUAL MEETING HANDBOOKS. English. an. Price varies per volume. Linguistic Society of America, 1325 18th Street Northwest, Washington DC 20036. **Tel** (202)835-1714.

US/0023-6365
LSA BULLETIN. [LSA bull.]. **Added/Corp** Linguistic Society of America. Center for Applied Linguistics. Guide to programs in linguistics. **VAT** Linguistic Society of America Bulletin. No. 43 (April 1970)-. Bulletin. English. qt. Linguistic Society of America, 1325 18th Street Northwest, Washington DC 20036. **Tel** (202)835-1714. **LC** P11; .L5. **DD** 410/.5. available on microfilm from University Microfilms International (UMI). ***Continues*** *Bulletin - Linguistic Society of America, 0095-6031;* ***Absorbed*** *Guide to Programs in Linguistics, 0363-2210.* ***Continued in part by*** *Directory of Programs in Linguistics in the United States & Canada, 0898-8528.*
Ind/Abst Comput. Rev.

CN/0707-2147
LTA CONFERENCE. (ANNUAL REPORT, LTA CONFERENCE ... / LANGUAGE TEACHERS ASSOCIATION, NOVA SCOTIA TEACHERS UNION.). **Main/Corp** Nova Scotia Teachers Union. Language Teachers Association. Conference. **VAT** Nova Scotia Teachers Union. Annual Report. LTA Conference. 1977-. English (French). an. Nova Scotia Teachers Union, 3106 Dutch Village Road, Halifax Nova Scotia B3L 4L7 Canada. **Tel** (902)477-5621. **DD** 406/.0716. **UDC** 800.7(716).

CN/0827-3154
LUMO. [Lumo]. **Added/Corp** Kanada Esperanto Asocio. (1???)-. Periodical. Esperanto. an. 3.00Can$. Kanada Esperanto-Association, Box 126 STN Beaubien, Montreal QUE H2G 3C8 Canada. **Tel** (514)495-8442. **ED** Olga Dutemple. **Circ:** 300.
Desc: Information on the activities of national and international Esperanto movement.

SW/0076-1451
LUND STUDIES IN ENGLISH. [Lund stud. Engl.]. **Added/Corp** Lunds Universitet. (1933)-. Monographic series. English. ir. Price varies per volume. Lund University Press, Box 141, S-22100 Lund Sweden. **Tel** 011 46 46 312000, FAX 011 46 46 305338, telex 33345 EDUCATE S. **ED** Sven Backman and Jan Svartvik. **CODEN** LSENE6. Index available. cum. index.
Desc: Monographs on the English language and literature.
Ind/Abst Abstr. Engl. Stud.; MLA Int. Bibl. Books Artic. Mod. Lang. Lit.; Soc. Plann. Policy Dev. Abstr.

SW
LUNDASTUDIER I NORDISK SPRAKVETENSKAP. SERIE A. No. 1 (1943)-. Monographic series. Swedish. ir. Price varies per volume. Lund University Press, Box 141, S-22100 Lund Sweden. **Tel** 011 46 46 312000, FAX 011 46 46 305338, telex 33345 EDUCATE S.
Desc: Series covering Scandinavian languages.

SW/0348-2146
LUNDER GERMANISTISCHE FORSCHUNGEN. [Lunder ger. Forsch.]. 1.- 1934-. Swedish. ir. Liber International, S-205 10 Malmo Sweden. **Tel** 46-40-70650.
Ind/Abst MLA Int. Bibl. Books Artic. Mod. Lang. Lit.

US/0886-179X
LUZ (CLAYTON, MO.), LA. (LA LUZ.). [Luz]. (19??)-. Periodical. Spanish. Six times a year (Oct.-Dec., Feb.-April). $12.00. The Alan Company, Box 16250, Clayton MO 63105. **Tel** (314)531-1668. **ED** N. V. Corvalan. **DD** 468.
Desc: Classroom magazine in Spanish for multi-level learning. Makes Spanish come alive for students.

US/0149-5712
MAARAV. Vol. 1 (Autumn 1978)-. Periodical. English. an. $20.00 US; $21.50 Canada; $23.00 other. Maarav, 12 Empty Saddle Road, Rolling Hills Estates CA 90274. **Tel** (310)541-4573, FAX (310)541-2361. **ED** Bruce Zuckerman and Robert J Ratner. **LC** PJ3001; .M32. **DD** 492. **Bk Rev. Pr Rev. Circ:** 500 (ctrl).
Desc: The journal deals with northwest semitic philology, biblical studies and archaeology.
Ind/Abst Index Book Rev. Relig.; Int. Zeitschriftenschau Bibelwissenschaft Grenzgeb.; New Testam. Abstr.; Old Testam. Abstr.; Relig. Index One Period.; Relig. Theol. Abstr.

NE/0024-8851
MAATSTAF. [Maatstaf]. (1952)-. Periodical. Dutch (English). mo. Fl150.20. Weekbladpers, Postbus 1050, 1000 BB Amsterdam, Netherlands. **Tel** 011 31 20 5518711. **LC** AP15; .M3. Documents available from The Genuine Article.
Ind/Abst Arts Humanit. Citation Index [Full Cov.]; Curr. Contents Arts Humanit.; MLA Int. Bibl. Books Artic. Mod. Lang. Lit.; Res. Alert [Full Cov.]; Soc. Sci. Cit. Index [Select. Cov.].

JA
MACHIKANEYAMA RONSO : BUNGAKUHEN. **VFOAT** Machikaneyama Ronso: Literature. No. 5- 1972-. Japanese (summaries and/or abstracts in English, French and German). Osaka Daigaku Bungakubu, 1-1 Machikaneyamacho, Toyonaka Osaka Japan. **Tel** (06)844-1151. **LC** P9; .M23. ***Continues in part*** *Machikaneyama Ronso.*

FR/0025-0201
MAGYAR MUHELY. [Magyar muhely]. **VFOAT** Atelier Hongrois. Vol. 1 (May/June 1962)-. Periodical. Hungarian. **LC** UNC.
Ind/Abst Soc. Plann. Policy Dev. Abstr.; Sociol. Abstr.

HU/0025-0228
MAGYAR NYELV. [M. nyelv]. **Added/Corp** Magyar Nyelvtudomanyi Tarsasag. Vol. 1 (Jan. 1905)-. Academic Scholarly Publication. Hungarian. qt. $28.00. Akademiai Kiado, Publishing House of the Hungarian Academy of Sciences, Prielle Kornelia u. 19-35, H-1117 Budapest Hungary. **Tel** 011 36 1 1811991, FAX 011 36 1 1811991, telex 22-6228 AKNYO H. **LC** PH2001; .M3. **DD** 494/.511/05. cum. index.
Ind/Abst MLA Int. Bibl. Books Artic. Mod. Lang. Lit.; Soc. Plann. Policy Dev. Abstr.; Sociol. Abstr.

HU/0025-0236
MAGYAR NYELVOR. [M. nyelvor]. **Added/Corp** Magyar Tudomanyos Akademia, Budapest. Nyelvmuvelo Bizottsaga. Magyar Tudomanyos Akademia, Budapest. Anyanyelvi Bizottsaga. Vol. 1 (1872)-. Academic Scholarly Publication. Hungarian. qt. $26.50. Akademiai Kiado, Publishing House of the Hungarian Academy of Sciences, Prielle Kornelia u. 19-35, H-1117 Budapest Hungary. **Tel** 011 36 1 1811991, FAX 011 36 1 1811991, telex 22-6228 AKNYO H. **(Subscription address:** Kultura, PO Box 149, H 1389 Budapest 62 Hungary.) **ED** L. Lorincze. cum. index. **Bk Rev. Circ:** 3,300.
Ind/Abst MLA Int. Bibl. Books Artic. Mod. Lang. Lit.; Soc. Plann. Policy Dev. Abstr.; Sociol. Abstr.

UA
MAHADIR AL-JALSAT. **Main/Corp** Majma Al-Lughah Al-Arabiyah (Cairo, Egypt). 1934-. Arabic. **LC** PJ6011.

GW/0170-9135
MAINZER STUDIEN ZUR AMERIKANISTIK. **See** Literature.

II
MAITHILI AKADAMI PATRIKA. **VFOAT** Methili Akadami Patrika. Periodical. Maithili. bm. Rs15.00. Maithili Academy Patna, Patna India. **LC** PK1828.A2; M34. **UDC** 809.14.

IO/0126-4737
MAJALAH PEMBINAAN BAHASA INDONESIA. V. 1, No. 1 (March 1980)-. Periodical. Indonesian. qt. Rp1,050 Indonesian; $15.00 US. P T Bhratara Karya Aksara, Kotak Pos 01/JAT, Jakarta Timur Indonesia. **Tel** 4890280, telex 49283 BHRAKA IA. **ED** Paruti Sujiman, Anton M Moeliono, Harimurti Kridalaksana, Jus Badudu, Muhadjir, Abdul Chaer, M Sumanti, Bistok Siahaan. **LC** PL5071; .A32. **Bk Rev. Ad Acc.** ctrl circ.
Desc: Published in cooperation between Bhratara publishers and HPBI (Indonesian Linguistic Development Society); containing writings of linguistics, theory and teachings for the development of Indonesian language.

SY
MAJALLAH. **Main/Corp** Majma Al-Lughah Al-Arabiyah Bi-Dimashq. **Added/Corp** Majma Al-Lughah Al-Arabiyah Bi-Dimashq. Revue. **VFOAT** Revue. Magazine 41 (Jan. 1966)-. Periodical. Arabic. qt (4 issues). $12.00. Arab Academy of Damascus, PO Box 327, Damascus Syria. **Tel** 011 713 45 8713103. **ED** Shaker Fahan. **LC** PJ6001; .M34. **Bk Rev. Circ:** 2,000

(ctrl). ***Continues*** *Majma Al-Ilmi Al-Arabi Bi-Dimashq. Majallah.*
Desc: Subjects relating to linguistics, literature, Islamic history, and scientific terminology.
Ind/Abst Am. Hist. Life (1958-1971); MLA Int. Bibl. Books Artic. Mod. Lang. Lit.

IR/0259-9082
MAJALLAH-I ZABANSHINASI. VFOAT Iranian Journal of Linguistics; Majalle-Ye Zabanshenasi. (19??)-. Academic Scholarly Publication. Persian. sa. £11.50 Middle East; £14.00 Europe & Asia; £17.50 America & Far East. Iran University Press, 85 Park Avenue, PO Box 15875/4748, Tehran Iran. **Tel** 623232, FAX (008921)4661749, telex 213636-8-D5300. **ED** A.A. Sadeghi. **LC** PK6201; .M35. **Bk Rev.**
Desc: Each issue contains articles as well as comparative studies dealing with linguistics in general and topics directly related to Iran and Persian language in particular.

KU/0575-1454
MAJALLAT MAHAD AL-MAKHTUTAT AL-ARABIYAH / JAMIAT. VFOAT Revue de l'Institut des Manuscrits Arabes. (May 1955)-. Periodical. Arabic. sa. Majallat Mahad Al-Makhtutat Al-Arabiyah, S B 26897, Al-Kuwayt United Arab Republic. **LC** Z6605.A6; C3. **DD** 492.7. **UDC** 809.57-4.

UA
MAJALLAT MAJMA AL-LUGHAH AL-ARABIYAH. Main/Corp Majma al-Lughah al-Arabiyah (Cairo, Egypt). (1952)-. Periodical. Arabic. sa. **LC** PJ6011; .M3. ***Continues*** *Majma Fuad al-Awwal lil-Lughah al-Arabiyah. Majallat Majma Fuad al-Awwal lil-Lughah al-Arabiyah.*
Ind/Abst MLA Int. Bibl. Books Artic. Mod. Lang. Lit.; Middle East J.

XN/0025-1089
MAKEDONSKI JAZIK. [Maked. jaz.]. **Added/Corp** Skopje, Yugoslavia. Univerzitet. Katedra za Juznoslovenski Jazici. Institut za Makedonski Jazik (Skopje, Macedonia). (1950)-. Serbo-Croatian (Cyrillic). an. **LC** PG1161; .M3. cum. index.
Ind/Abst MLA Int. Bibl. Books Artic. Mod. Lang. Lit.

UZ/0320-2887
MAKTABDA UZBEK, RUS TILLARI VA ADABIETI. ***Title Change.*** **Added/Corp** Uzbek S.S.R. Ministerstvo Narodnogo Obrazovaniia. **VFOAT** Uzbekskii, Russkii Iazyki i Literatura v Shkole. (1991)-(199?). Periodical. Uzbek (Russian). bm. ***Continues*** *RusskiÊi Iazyk i Literatura v Uzbekskoi Shkole.* ***Continued by*** *Til va Adabiet Talimi.*

KO
MAL SORI. VFOAT Journal of the Phonetic Society of Korea; Phonetics. Periodical. Korean (English and French). sa. W7,000 Korea; $10.00 US. Taehan Umsong Hakhoe, San 56-1 Sillim-dong, Kwanak-ku, Seoul South Korea. **Tel** 880-5240 / 599-1670. **LC** P215; .M34. **UDC** 809.57-4. Index available. cum. index. **Bk Rev. Ad Acc. Circ:** 1,000.
Desc: Publishes papers or articles on phonetics, pronunciation, phonology, language teaching, speech therapy, etc.

US/0363-3659
MALEDICTA. [Maledicta]. **Added/Corp** International Maledicta Society. Maledicta: the International Research Center for Verbal Aggression. Vol. 1, No. 1 (Summer 1977)-. English. ir. $26.00 US; $27.00 other. Maledicta Press, PO Box 14123, Santa Rosa CA 95402-4761. **Tel** (707523-4761. **ED** Reinhold A Aman. **LC** P409; .M34. **DD** 418. **Bk Rev**, (Qty: 40). **Circ:** 4,000.
Desc: Essays and glossaries of offensive language (insults, curses, slurs) in all languages.
Ind/Abst Lang. Lang. Behav. Abstr.; MLA Int. Bibl. Books Artic. Mod. Lang. Lit.; Soc. Plann. Policy Dev. Abstr.; Sociol. Abstr.

US/0363-9037
MALEDICTA PRESS PUBLICATIONS. 1-. Monographic series. English. ir. Price varies per volume. Maledicta Press, PO Box 14123, Santa Rosa CA 95402-4761. **Tel** (707523-4761. **ED** Reinhold A Aman. **UDC** 800.862. **Bk Rev. Circ:** 4,000.
Desc: Dictionaries of ethnic, racial, sexual slurs. Originals and reprints.

NO/0024-855X
MALL OG MINNE. [Maal minne]. **Added/Corp** Bymalslaget. (1909)-. Academic Scholarly Publication. Norwegian. sa. Kr200.00 (institutions), Kr150.00 (individuals) Scandinavia; Kr230.00 (institutions), Kr180.00 (individuals) other. Forlagsentralen Tidsskriftavd, PB 150 Furuset, 1001 Oslo 10 Norway. **Tel** 011 47 2 2320995. **ED** Einar Lundeby and Bjarne Fidjestol. **LC** PD2601; .M3. Index available. cum. index. **Bk Rev. Ad Acc. Circ:** 500. available on microfilm from Indiana University Libraries Preservation Department. ***Continues Norvegia.***
Desc: Scholarly articles and papers on Norwegian language past and present, medieval literature, place names and folklore.
Ind/Abst Annu. Bibliogr. Engl. Lang. Lit.; MLA Int. Bibl. Books Artic. Mod. Lang. Lit.

II
MANAOCAI. VFOAT Mana Osai. Periodical. Tamil (Tamil). mo. Rs12.00. R Palanisami, 159 Vanniyar Street Choolaimedu PO, Madras 600094 India. **LC** DS480.45; .M34. **UDC** 809.48.

UK
MANCHESTER MEMOIRS / MANCHESTER LITERARY AND PHILOSOPHICAL SOCIETY. Added/Corp Manchester Literary and Philosophical Society. **VFOAT** Memoirs & Proceedings of the Manchester Literary & Philosophical Society. (1981)-. English. an. ***Continues*** *Manchester Literary and Philosophical Society. Memoirs and Proceedings.*

CN/0820-6066
MANITOBA MODERN LANGUAGE JOURNAL. ***Ceased.*** [Manit. mod. lang. j.]. **Added/Corp** Manitoba Modern Language Association. Manitoba Teachers' Society. Vol. 16, No. 3 (Spring 1982)-Vol. 26 No. 4 (May 1992). Periodical. English (summaries and/or abstracts in Multiple languages). Four times a year. $12.00. Manitoba Modern Language Journal, c/o Manitoba Teachers Society, 191 Harcourt Street, Winnipeg Manitoba R3J 3B2 Canada. **DD** 407. ctrl circ. ***Continues*** *Manitoba Modern Language Bulletin, 0315-2111.*

NE/0306-0020
MANTATOPHOROS. Began with Nov. 1972 issue. Periodical. English (Greek, Modern). sa. 17.50. ABN-Bank, Adam No 54.95.19.122, Amsterdam Netherlands. **LC** DF701; .M34. **UDC** 800.

BE/0542-6669
MARCHE ROMANE. [Marche romane]. **Added/Corp** Universite de Liege. Association des Romanistes. Vol. 1 (June 1951)-. Periodical. French (English, Italian and Spanish). ir. 600.00F. Association des Romanistes, Universiti Place Cockeill 3, B-000 Liege Belgium. **Tel** 32.41.22.41.08. **ED** Jeanne Wathelet-Willem and Jacques De Caluwe. **LC** PC2; .M33. **Bk Rev. Circ:** 500.
Ind/Abst MLA Int. Bibl. Books Artic. Mod. Lang. Lit.; Romant. Move.

SP
MARGES, ELS. (May 1974)-. Periodical. Catalan. Three times a year. 3840ptas. Curial Ediciones Catalanes S A, Bruc 144 Baixos, 08037 Barcelona Spain. **Tel** 011 34 3 2588101, FAX 207 74 27. **ED** Joaquim Molas, Jordi Castellanos, Manuel Jorba, Josep Murgades, Josep M. Nadal, Enric Sulla and Oan A. Argente. **LC** PC3801; .M37. Index available. cum. index.
Desc: Review devoted to language and literature.
Ind/Abst MLA Int. Bibl. Books Artic. Mod. Lang. Lit.

IT
MATERIALI E CONTRIBUTI PER LA STORIA DELLA NARRATIVA GRECO-LATINA. Main/Corp Perugia. Universita. Istituto di Filologia Latina. 1-. Italian. Editrice Elia, Viale dell'Universita 21-23, 00185 Rome Perugia Italy. **LC** PA3040; .P44A. **UDC** 87.

US/0076-5252
MATERIAUX POUR L'ETUDE DE L'EXTREME-ORIENT MODERNE ET CONTEMPORAIN. ETUDES LINGUISTIQUES. Main/Corp Maison des Sciences de l'Homme (Paris, France). Vol. 1 (1966)-. Monographic series. French. ir. Price varies per volume. Walter de Gruyter Inc. / Hawthorne, 200 Saw Mill River Road, Hawthorne NY 10532. **Tel** (914)747-0110, GERMANY: 011/49/30/260050, FAX (914)747-1326, telex 646677. **(Subscription address:** Germany/ PO Box 110240, 1 Berlin 11**) UDC** 809.51; 809.56.

JA
MATHEMATICAL LINGUISTICS. KEIYRKO KOKUGOGAKU. Added/Corp Mathematical Linguistics Society of Japan. **VFOAT** Keiyrko Kokugogaku. No. 1 (196?)-. Periodical. English.
Ind/Abst Linguist. Lang. Behav. Abstr. (1972-) [Full Cov.]; Soc. Plann. Policy Dev. Abstr.

US
MAYAN LINGUISTICS. (19??)-. Newsletter. English (Spanish). qt (Mar., Jun., Sept., Dec.). $5.00 US; $13.00 other. Mayan Linguis Knowles-Berry, 12618 Northeast 5th Avenue, Vancouver WA 98685. **Tel** (206)574-9604. **ED** Susan Knowles-Berry. **Circ:** 110 (ctrl). ***Continues*** *Mayan Linguistics Newsletter, 1062-1288.*

US/1062-1288
MAYAN LINGUISTICS NEWSLETTER. ***Title Change.*** [Mayan Linguist. Newsl.]. **VFOAT** MLN. (19??)- Vol. 19 (1993)- Vol. 12 (1993)-(19??). Newsletter. English (Spanish). Four times a year (Mar., June, Sept., Dec.). Mayan Linguis Knowles-Berry, 12618 Northeast 5th Avenue, Vancouver WA 98685. **Tel** (206)574-9604. **ED** Susan Knowles-Berry. **DD** 497. **Circ:** 110. ***Continued by*** *Mayan Linguistics.*

II
MAYGAMV. VFOAT Maigaum; Mayagamva. Periodical. Konkani (Kannada). sm. 200. G D'Souza Kala Kuteer Mannagudda, Bangalore 3 India. **ED** Gabriel D'Souza. **LC** PK2231; .A33. **Bk Rev. Ad Acc. Circ:** 5,000.

CN/0824-5282
MCGILL WORKING PAPERS IN LINGUISTICS. (MCGILL WORKING PAPERS IN LINGUISTICS / CAHIERS LINGUISTIQUES DE MCGILL.). [McGill work. pap. linguist.]. **Added/Corp** McGill University. Dept. of Linguistics. **VFOAT** Cahiers Linguistiques de McGill. Vol. 1, No. 1 (Dec. 1983)-. Academic Scholarly Publication. English (French). sa. 20.00Can$ North America; 22.00Can$ other. McGill Working Papers of Linguistics, 1001 Sherbrooke Street West, Department of Linguistics, Montreal Quebec H3A 1G5 Canada. **Tel** (514)398-4222. **ED** B. Shaer. **DD** 410/.5. **Circ:** 200 (ctrl).
Desc: Theoretical and applied linguistics including syntax, phonology, morphology, semantics, first and second language acquisition, neurolinguistics, sociolinguistics, and text linguistics.
Ind/Abst Linguist. Lang. Behav. Abstr. (1987-) [Full Cov.]; MLA Int. Bibl. Books Artic. Mod. Lang. Lit.; Soc. Plann. Policy Dev. Abstr.

SW/0348-3568
MEDDELANDEN FRAN INSTITUTIONEN FOR NORDISKA SPRAK VID STOCKHOLMS UNIVERSITET: MINS. Added/Corp Stockholms Universitet. Institutionen for Nordiska Sprak. **VFOAT** MINS. No. 1 (1977)-. Monographic series. Swedish. ir. Price varies per volume. Inst for Nordiska Sprak, Stockholms Universitet, S-106 91 Stockholm Sweden. **Tel** (08)162530. **ED** Barbro Soderberg. **LC** UNC. **Ad Acc.**
Desc: Papers and monographs about language, mainly Swedish.

NO
MEDDELELSER / UNIVERSITET I OSLO, SLAVISK-BALTISK AVDELING. Added/Corp Universitet i Oslo. Slavisk-Baltisk Avdeling. No. 59 (1990)-. Monographic series. Norwegian (English and Russian). Price varies per volume. ***Continues*** *Meddelelser (Universitet i Oslo. Slavisk-Baltisk Institutt).*

NE
MEDEDELINGEN VAN HET P.J. MEERTENS-INSTITUUT. **See** Folklore.

UK/0264-2786
MEDIEVAL ENGLISH THEATRE MODERN SPELLING TEXTS. [Mediev. Engl. Theatre mod. spell. texts]. **VFOAT** Medieval English Theatre Modern-Spelling Texts. (1983)-. Monographic series. English. ir.
Ind/Abst MLA Int. Bibl. Books Artic. Mod. Lang. Lit.

IT/0390-0711
MEDIOEVO ROMANZO. [Medioev. romanzo]. Vol. 1 (1974)-. Periodical. Italian. tq. L90000.00 Italy; L140000.00 (surface mail), L160000.00 (airmail). Societa Editrice il Mulino, Strada Maggiore 37, 40125 Bologna Italy. **Tel** 011 39 51 256011, FAX 011 39 51 256034. **LC** PC4; .M4. cum. index. Documents available from The Genuine Article.
Ind/Abst Arts Humanit. Citation Index [Full Cov.]; Curr. Contents Arts Humanit.; MLA Int. Bibl. Books Artic. Mod. Lang. Lit.; Res. Alert [Full Cov.]; Soc. Sci. Cit. Index [Select. Cov.].

GW/0724-7567
MEDITERRANEAN LANGUAGE REVIEW. [Mediterr. lang. rev.]. Vol. 1 (1983)-. Periodical. French (French, German, Italian and Spanish). ir (1 or 2 times per year). DM80.00. Otto Harrassowitz Verlag, Taunusstrasse 14, Postfach 2929, D-65019 Wiesbaden Germany. **Tel** 011 49 611 5300, FAX 530570, telex 4186 135 OH D. **ED** Alexander Borg and Paul Wexler. **LC** P381.M4; M43. **DD** 409/.182/2. **Bk Rev. Ad Acc. Circ:** 350.
Desc: Linguistic and cultural history of the Mediterranean.
Ind/Abst Linguist. Lang. Behav. Abstr. (1983-) [Full Cov.]; MLA Int. Bibl. Books Artic. Mod. Lang. Lit.; Soc. Plann. Policy Dev. Abstr.

UK/0025-8385
MEDIUM AEVUM. [Medium aevum]. **Added/Corp** Society for the Study of Mediaeval Languages and Literature (Oxford, England). (May 1932)-. Periodical. English (French and German). Twice a year. £20.00 UK; £25.00 other. Medium Aevum Publications, Dr. Pattison, Magdalen College, Oxford OX1 4AU England. **Tel** 011 44 865 276087. **ED** H. Cooper, L. Seiffert and E. Kennedy. **LC** PB1; .M4. **DD** 405. Index Available, published separately, free-automatically sent. cum. index (vols. 1-50). **Bk Rev. Ad Acc. Pr Rev. Circ:** 1,000. available on microfilm and microfiche from University Microfilms International (UMI). Documents available from The Genuine Article, UMI Article Clearinghouse. ***Supersedes*** *Arthuriana.*
Desc: Medieval European languages, literature and related subjects (e.g. history, art).

Ind/Abst Abstr. Engl. Stud.; Acad. Search (July 1993-); Annu. Bibliogr. Engl. Lang. Lit.; Arts Humanit. Citation Index [Full Cov.]; BHA : Biblio. Hist. Art; Br. Humanit. Index; Curr. Contents Arts Humanit.; Expand. Acad. Index (1989-); Humanit. Index; Humanit. Source (Jul. 1993-); Index Book Rev. Humanit.; INFO-SOUTH Abstr.; Mag. Search; Middle East Abstr. Index; MLA Int. Bibl. Books Artic. Mod. Lang. Lit.; Newsp. Period. Abstr. (1991-); Ref. Sources; Res. Alert [Full Cov.].

SW/0348-7741
MEIJERBERGS ARKIV FOR SVENSK ORDFORSKNING. [Meijerb. ark. sven. ordforskn.]. **Added/Corp** Meijerbergs Institut for Svensk Etymologisk Forskning. No. 1 (1937)-. Swedish. **LC** PD5571; .M45.
Ind/Abst MLA Int. Bibl. Books Artic. Mod. Lang. Lit.

FR/0077-2712
MELANGES - CENTRE DE RECHERCHES ET D'APPLICATIONS PEDAGOGIQUES EN LANGUES. (MELANGES PEDAGOGIQUES.). [Mel. - Cent. rech. appl. pedagog. lang.]. **Added/Corp** Universite de Nancy II. Centre de Recherches et d'Applications Pedagogiques en Langues. **VFOAT** Melanges CRAPEL; Melanges. (1970)-. Periodical. French (English). an. 352.00F (institutions three years), 187.00F (individuals three years) France; 407.00F (institutions three years), 227.00F (individuals three years) other. Centre de Recherches et d'Applications Pedagogiques, University de Nancy, 2 BP 3397, 54015 Nancy Cedex France. **Tel** 33 16 83980499, FAX 33 16 83980499. **ED** F Carton and P Riley (editor's phone: 33 16 83983412).
Ind/Abst Lang. Teach.; Soc. Plann. Policy Dev. Abstr.; Sociol. Abstr.

UA/0575-1330
MELANGES - INSTITUT DOMINICAIN D'ETUDES ORIENTALES DU CAIRE. **Main/Corp** Institut Dominicain d'Etudes Orientales du Caire. **Added/Corp** Institut Dominicain d'Etudes Orientales du Caire. M.I.D.E.O. **VFOAT** M.I.D.E.O. Vol. 1 (1954)-. Periodical. French (Multiple languages). ir. 3000F. Editions Peeters SA, Bondgenotenlaan 153, BP 41, B-3000 Leuven Belgium. **Tel** 32 16 235170, FAX 32 16 228500, telex 65987 PUL B. **(Subscription address:** Georges Bookshop, PO Box 220, Cairo Egypt; telephone: 011 20 2 3551827 or 2590104**)** **ED** George Andrawes Rezk. **LC** PJ9; .C3. **DD** 492/.7/05. Index available. **Bk Rev.**

FI/0355-0192
MEMOIRES DE LA SOCIETE NEOPHILOLOGIQUE DE HELSINKI. [Mem. Soc. neophilol. Helsinki]. **Added/Corp** Uusfilologinen Yhdistys. **VFOAT** Memoires de la Societe Neophilologique de Helsingfors. Vol. 1 (1893)-. English (French and German). ir. Price varies per volume. Modern Language Society, Hallituskatu 11, SF-00100 Helsinki Finland. **Tel** 011 358 0 1912504. **(Subscription address:** Tiedekirja, Kirkkokatu 14, SF-00170 Helsinki Finland**)** **ED** Marjatta Wis, Olli Valikanjas, Matti Rissanen. **LC** PB10; .N413.
Desc: A monographic series publishing research on German, English and Romance philology and linguistics.
Ind/Abst Annu. Bibliogr. Engl. Lang. Lit.; MLA Int. Bibl. Books Artic. Mod. Lang. Lit.

IT
MEMORIE / ACCADEMIA NAZIONALE DEI LINCEI, CLASSE DI SCIENZE MORALI, STORICHE E FILOLOGICHE. Monographic series. Italian (French, English, German, Latin and Spanish). Five times a year. Price varies per volume. Atti della Accademia Nazionale dei Lincei, Via della Lungara 10, 00165 Rome Italy. **Tel** 06/650.831. **LC** AS222; .R645. **Circ:** 650. ***Continues*** *Memorie della Classe di Scienze Morali e Storiche.*
Desc: This series of monographs publishes only contributions of fellows of academy of Lincei or scholars presented by a fellow. It requires a 200 word abstract.

RM
MEMORIILE SECTIEI DE STIINTE FILOLOGICE, LITERATURA SI ARTE. **Added/Corp** Academia Republicii Socialiste Romania. Sectia de Stiinte Filologice, Literatura si Arte. **VFOAT** Memoirs of the Section of Philological Sciences, Literature and Arts of the Academy of the Socialist Republic of Romania. (19??)-. Periodical. Romanian (English, French and Russian). be. lei9.25. Editura Academia Republicii Socialiste Romania, Calea Victoriei Nr 125, R-79717 Bucuresti Romania. **Tel** telex 10376 PRSFI R. **LC** P1.A1; M45. **DD** 405.

US/0160-2764
MESTER (LOS ANGELES). See Literature.

CN/0026-0452
META (MONTREAL). (META.). [Meta]. **Added/Corp** Universite de Montreal. Departement de Linguistique et de Philologie. Vol. 11 (Mar. 1966)-. Periodical. French (English). qt. 50.00Can$ institutions; 24.50Can$ (individuals) Canada; 29.00Can$ (individuals) other. Presses de l'Universite de Montreal, PO Box 6128 Station A, Montreal Quebec H3C 3J7 Canada. **Tel** (514)343-6933. **ED** Andre Clas. **LC** P306.A1; M35. **Bk Rev. Ad Acc. Circ:** 3,400 (ctrl). available on microfilm and microfiche from University Microfilms International (UMI). Documents available from The Genuine Article. ***Continues*** *Journal des Traducteurs, 0316-3024.*
Desc: Features wide-ranging articles on linguistics applied to translating and interpreting: translation theory, stylistics, comparative terminological studies, automatized translating, documentation, etc.
Ind/Abst Arts Humanit. Citation Index [Full Cov.]; Curr. Contents Arts Humanit.; MLA Int. Bibl. Books Artic. Mod. Lang. Lit.; Point Repere (1983-); Res. Alert [Full Cov.]; Soc. Plann. Policy Dev. Abstr.; Sociol. Abstr.

CN/0026-0452
META (MONTREAL). (META.). [Meta]. Vol. 11, No 1 (March 1966)-. Periodical. French (English). qt. 55.00Can$ institutions; 25.00Can$ (individuals) Canada; 30.00Can$ (individuals) other. Presses de l'Universite de Montreal, PO Box 6128 Station A, Montreal Quebec H3C 3J7 Canada. **Tel** (514)343-6933. **(Subscription address:** Periodica Inc., PO Box 444, 1155 Ducharme, Outrement Quebec H2V 4R6 Canada.**)** ***Continues*** *Journal des Traducteurs., 0316-3024.*
Ind/Abst Lang. Lang. Behav. Abstr.; MLA Int. Bibl. Books Artic. Mod. Lang. Lit.; Point Repere (1983-); Soc. Sci. Cit. Index [Select. Cov.]; Sociol. Abstr.

FR/0995-3310
METIS (PARIS, FRANCE). (METIS.). **Added/Corp** Ecole des Hautes Etudes en Sciences Sociales. Centre de Recherches Compares sur les Societes Anciennes (France). **VFOAT** Revue Metis. Vol. 1 No. 1 (1986)-. Periodical. French (English and Greek, Modern). Twice a year. 280.00F France; 320.00F others. Centre Louis Gernet Recherches, 10 rue Monsieur le Prince, 75006 Paris France. **Tel** 011 33 1 46331752.

US/0098-8030
MICHIGAN GERMANIC STUDIES. [Mich. Ger. stud.]. **Added/Corp** University of Michigan. Dept. of Germanic Languages and Literatures. Vol. 1 (Spring 1975)-. Academic Scholarly Publication. English (German and French). sa. $30.00 US; $32.00 other. University of Michigan Department of Germanic Languages and Literatures, 3110 Modern Language Building, Ann Arbor MI 48109-1275. **Tel** (313)764-8018, (313)747-0249, FAX (313)764-3521. **ED** Roy C Cowen. **LC** PD1; .M5. **DD** 430/.05. **Bk Rev**, (Qty: 16). **Ad Acc**, **Adv Mgr:** Harold Scholler. **Pr Rev. Circ:** 250. available on microfilm from University Microfilms International (UMI). Documents available from The Genuine Article.
Desc: Scholarly publication of the University of Michigan, Department of Germanic Languages and Literatures. Publishes articles and book reviews on literary and linguistic topics related to our field. Contributions may be written in English, German, or French.
Ind/Abst Arts Humanit. Citation Index (19??-19??) [Full Cov.]; Curr. Contents Arts Humanit.; MLA Int. Bibl. Books Artic. Mod. Lang. Lit.; Recent. Publ. Artic.; Res. Alert [Full Cov.]; Romant. Move.; Soc. Plann. Policy Dev. Abstr.; Soc. Sci. Cit. Index [Select. Cov.]; Sociol. Abstr.

US/0270-3629
MICHIGAN ROMANCE STUDIES. [Mich. roman. stud.]. **Added/Corp** University of Michigan. Dept. of Romance Languages. Vol. 1 (1980)-. Monographic series. English (translations available in French, Spanish and Italian). ir. Price varies per volume. Michigan Romance Studies, Department of Romance Languages, University of Michigan, Ann Arbor MI 48109. **Tel** (313)764-5344. **ED** Floyd Gray. **LC** PC1; .M53. **DD** 840/.09. **Bk Rev. Ad Acc. Pr Rev. Circ:** 500 (ctrl).
Desc: Essays in English on language and literature in romance languages.
Ind/Abst MLA Int. Bibl. Books Artic. Mod. Lang. Lit.

US/0076-8103
MICHIGAN SLAVIC CONTRIBUTIONS. **Added/Corp** University of Michigan. Dept. of Slavic Languages and Literatures. No. 1 (1968)-. Monographic series. English. ir. Price varies per volume. University of Michigan / Michigan Slavic Publications, 3040 Modern Language Building, Ann Arbor MI 48108. **Tel** (313)763-4496.
Ind/Abst MLA Int. Bibl. Books Artic. Mod. Lang. Lit.

US/0543-9930
MICHIGAN SLAVIC MATERIALS. **Added/Corp** University of Michigan. Dept. of Slavic Languages and Literatures. No. 1 (1962)-. Monographic series. Russian (English). an. $18.00. University of Michigan / Michigan Slavic Publications, 3040 Modern Language Building, Ann Arbor MI 48108. **Tel** (313)763-4496. **ED** Judrich Toman. **LC** PG13; .M46. **Bk Rev. Ad Acc.**

US
MICHIGAN SLAVIC TRANSLATIONS. **Added/Corp** University of Michigan. Dept. of Slavic Languages and Literatures. No. 1 (1972)-. Monographic series. English. ir. Price varies per volume. University of Michigan / Michigan Slavic Publications, 3040 Modern Language Building, Ann Arbor MI 48108. **Tel** (313)763-4496.

US/0272-717X
MID-HUDSON LANGUAGE STUDIES. [Mid-Hudson lang. stud.]. **Added/Corp** Associated Colleges of the Mid-Hudson Area Modern Language Association. Mid-Hudson Modern Language Association. Vol. 1 (1978)-. English. **LC** PN2; .M53. **DD** 809.
Ind/Abst MLA Int. Bibl. Books Artic. Mod. Lang. Lit.

US/0888-8752
MIDDLEBURY STUDIES IN RUSSIAN LANGUAGE AND LITERATURE. Vol. 1 (1989)-. Monographic series. English. ir. Price varies per volume. Peter Lang Publishing, 62 West 45th Street, 4th Floor, New York NY 10036. **Tel** (212)764-1471, (800)770-5264, telex 6973364 PLNY. **DD** 891.

CC
MIN TSU YU WEN. **VFOAT** Minzu Yuwen. (Feb. 1979)-. Periodical. Chinese. Six times a year. $9.83. China National Publ Industry Trade, PO Box 782, Beijing, People's Republic of China. **Tel** 011 86 1 4215031. **ED** Fu Mao-Ji. **LC** PL1004; .M56. **DD** 495.1/05. **Circ:** 4,000 (ctrl).
Desc: Contains description of Chinese minority languages and general linguistics, and comparative studies of Sino-Tibetan, Kam-Tai and Miao-Yao languages.

UK/0268-1064
MIND & LANGUAGE. [Mind lang.]. **VFOAT** Mind and Language. Vol. 1, No. 1 (Spring 1986)-. Academic Scholarly Publication. English. Four times a year. £102.50 UK and Europe; $194.00 North America; £125.00 other. Basil Blackwell Publishers Ltd, 108 Cowley Road, Oxford 0X4 1JF England. **Tel** 011 44 865 791100, FAX 011 44 865 791347, telex 837022 OXBOOK G. **(Subscription address:** Blackwell Publishers / UK, Marston Book Services, PO Box 87, Oxford OX2 0DT England.**)** **ED** M Davies. **LC** P37; .M55. **CODEN** MILAEB. **[CCC]. Bk Rev. Ad Acc. Circ:** 750. available on microfilm and microfiche from University Microfilms International (UMI). Documents available from Ask*IEEE.
Desc: Deals with the study of the phenomena of mind and language.
Ind/Abst INSPEC (Spring 1988-); Int. Bibliogr. Sociol.; Philos. Index; Soc. Plann. Policy Dev. Abstr.

US
MINNESOTA ENGLISH JOURNAL. See Education-Teaching and Curriculum.

SP/0544-3733
MINOS. [Minos]. **Added/Corp** Universidad de Salamanca. Colegio Trilingue. Universidad de Salamanca. Seminario de Filologia Clasica. Vol. 1 (1951)-. Periodical. Spanish. an. 6000ptas. Ediciones Universidad de Salamanca, Apartado Postal 325, 37080 Salamanca Spain. **Tel** 011 34 23 294598, FAX 011 34 23 263046. **LC** P1035; .M5. **CODEN** MNOSED.
Desc: Greek inscriptions and classical philology.
Ind/Abst MLA Int. Bibl. Books Artic. Mod. Lang. Lit.

CN/1187-2896
MINUTES OF PROCEEDINGS AND EVIDENCE OF THE STANDING COMMITTEE ON OFFICIAL LANGUAGES. [Minutes proc. evid. Standing Comm. Off. Lang.]. **Main/Corp** Canada. Parlement. Chambre des Communes. Comite Permanent des Langues Officielles. **VFOAT** Proces-Verbaux et Temoignages du Comite Permanent des Langues Officielles. 34th Parliament, 3rd Session, Issue No. 1 (May 30/June 11, 1991)-. Proceedings. French (English). **DD** 344.71/09.

SP/0544-408X
MISCELANEA DE ESTUDIOS ARABES Y HERBAICOS. [Misc. estud. arabes heb.]. V. 1 (1952)-. Periodical. Spanish. sa. **LC** PJ3001; .M5. **DD** 492/.05. **UDC** 809.24; 809.27.
Ind/Abst Am. Hist. Life (1962-1972); BHA : Biblio. Hist. Art; MLA Int. Bibl. Books Artic. Mod. Lang. Lit.

US/1049-1058
MIT WORKING PAPERS IN LINGUISTICS. [MIT work. pap. linguist.]. **Added/Corp** Massachusetts Institute of Technology. Dept. of Linguistics and Philosophy. **VAT** Massachusetts Institute of Technology Working Papers in Linguistics. (1979)-. Monographic series. English. ir. Price varies per volume. Massachusetts Institute of Technology (MIT) / Department of Linguistics and Philosophy, Room 20D 219, Cambridge MA 02139. **Tel** (617)253-3221. **DD** 410. **CODEN** MPLIEG.

II
MITHILA-BHARATI. 1- 1969-. Periodical. Undetermined (Maithili). **LC** PK1811.

GW/0076-9762
MITTELLATEINISCHES JAHRBUCH. [Mittellat. Jahrb.]. (1964)-. German (English, Italian and Latin). an. Anton Hiersemann Verlag, Rosenbergstrasse 113, D 70193 Stuttgart Germany. **Tel** 011 49 711 638264 5. **ED** F. Wagner. **LC** PA2802; .M56. Index available. **Bk Rev. Ad Acc. Circ:** 1,000.
Desc: Editions of, and monographs about, late Latin texts.
Ind/Abst MLA Int. Bibl. Books Artic. Mod. Lang. Lit.

GW
MITTELNIEDERDEUTSCHES HANDWORTERBUCH. German. ir. Price varies per volume. Karl Wachholtz Verlag, Postfach 2769, Gansemarkt 1-3, W-2350 Neumunster F R Germany. **Tel** 011 49 4321 5670, FAX 011 49 4321 56778, telex 299 618 CURIR. **ED** Gerhard Cordes. **Circ:** 500 (ctrl).
Desc: Dictionary of the Mittelniederdeutschen dialect.

AT
ML NEWSLETTER. Newsletter. English. ir. 30.00Aus$ individuals; 60.00Aus$ schools and libraries; 100.00Aus$ other. Modern Language Teachers Association, 217 Church Street, Richmond 3121 Australia. **Tel** 011 61 3 8719209, FAX 011 61 3 8719267. **ED** Barbara Imberger. **Bk Rev. Ad Acc. Circ:** 700.
Desc: Information relating to the teaching of all languages other than English.

US/1063-3316
MLA INTERNATIONAL BIBLIOGRAPHY. (MLA INTERNATIONAL BIBLIOGRAPHY [COMPUTER FILE].). [MLA int. bibliogr.]. **Added/Corp** Modern Language Association of America. H.W. Wilson Company. **VFOAT** Wilsondisc MLA International Bibliography. **VAT** Modern Language Association International Bibliography. (1981)-. Bibliography. English. qt. $1495.00. H W Wilson Company, 950 University Avenue, Bronx NY 10452. **Tel** (800)367-6770, (718)588-8400, FAX (718)590-1617, telex 4990003 HWILSON. **LC** Z7006; Z7006; .M645. **DD** 405. available on an online database from H W Wilson; available in print; available on diskette from WILSONSEARCH.
Desc: Database of citations to critical documents on folklore, language, linguistics, and literature, including articles from journals, monographs, collections and reference works. corresponding to the MLA International Bibliography of Books and Articles on Modern Languages and Literatures.

US/0024-8215
MLA INTERNATIONAL BIBLIOGRAPHY OF BOOKS AND ARTICLES ON THE MODERN LANGUAGES AND LITERATURES (COMPLETE ED.). **See** Linguistics-Abstracting, Bibliographies and Statistics.

US/0740-8730
MLA INTERNATIONAL BIBLIOGRAPHY OF BOOKS AND ARTICLES ON THE MODERN LANGUAGES AND LITERATURES (OPTION B). ***Ceased.*** **See** Literature.

US/0740-8722
MLA INTERNATIONAL BIBLIOGRAPHY OF BOOKS AND ARTICLES ON THE MODERN LANGUAGES AND LITERATURES (OPTION C). (MLA INTERNATIONAL BIBLIOGRAPHY OF BOOKS AND ARTICLES ON THE MODERN LANGUAGES AND LITERATURES.). [MLA int. bibl. books artic. mod. lang. lit.]. **Added/Corp** Modern Language Association of America. **VFOAT** M.L.A. International Bibliography of Books and Articles on the Modern Languages and Literatures. **VAT** Modern Language Association International Bibliography of Books and Articles on the Modern Languages and Literatures. (1981)-. Bibliography. English. an (Nov.). $500.00. Modern Language Association of America, 10 Astor Place, New York NY 10003-6981. **Tel** (212)614-6382, FAX (212)477-9863. available on CD-ROM; available on an online database.

US
MLA JOB INFORMATION LIST. ENGLISH ED. **See** Occupations and Careers.

US/0160-5720
MLA NEWSLETTER (NEW YORK). (MLA NEWSLETTER.). **Main/Corp** Modern Language Association of America. **VAT** Modern Language Association Newsletter. Vol. 1 (Mar. 1969)-. Newsletter. English. qt. $6.00. Modern Language Association of America, 10 Astor Place, New York NY 10003-6981. **Tel** (212)614-6382, FAX (212)477-9863. **ED** Judy Goulding. **Ad Acc. Acid Free. Circ:** 28,000 (ctrl).
Desc: Publishes news on the activities of the Modern Language Association and on the profession in general.

II
MLBD SERIES IN LINGUISTICS. Vol. 1-. Monographic series. English. Price varies per volume. Motilal Banarsidass, 41 UA Bundalow Road, Jawahar Nagar, Delhi 110007 India. **Tel** 011 91 11 2911985, FAX 011 91 11 2930689. **UDC** 800.

US/0026-7910
MLN. [MLN]. **Added/Corp** Johns Hopkins University. **VAT** Modern Language Notes. Vol. 77 (Jan. 1962)-. Periodical. English (French, German, Italian and Spanish). Five times a year. $82.00 US; $87.00 Canada and Mexico; $95.50 other. Johns Hopkins University Press, 2715 North Charles Street, Baltimore MD 21218-4319. **Tel** (410)516-6987, FAX (410)516-6968. **LC** PB1; .M6. **DD** 809. **[CCC].** Documents available from The Genuine Article, UMI Article Clearinghouse. ***Continues*** *Modern Language Notes, 0149-6611.*
Desc: Publishes articles on the theory, interpretation and history of Romance and Germanic languages.
Ind/Abst Abstr. Engl. Stud.; Acad. Abstr. Full Text Elite (July 1990-); Acad. Abstr. (July 1990-); Acad. Ind. [Computer File] (1987-); Acad. Search (July 1990-); Am. Bibliogr. Slavic East Europ. Stud. (19??-19??); Annu. Bibliogr. Engl. Lang. Lit.; Arts Humanit. Citation Index (19??-19??) [Full Cov.]; Book Rev. Index; Curr. Contents Arts Humanit.; Expand. Acad. Index (1987-); Humanit. Index; INFO-SOUTH Abstr.; Linguist. Lang. Behav. Abstr.; Lit. Crit. Regist.; Mag. Search; Middle East Abstr. Index; MLA Int. Bibl. Books Artic. Mod. Lang. Lit.; Newsp. Period. Abstr. (1991-); Res. Alert [Full Cov.]; Romant. Move.; Soc. Plann. Policy Dev. Abstr.; Soc. Sci. Cit. Index [Select. Cov.]; Sociol. Abstr.

NE/0026-7074
MNEMOSYNE. (MNEMOSYNE. BIBLIOTHECA CLASSICA BATAVA.). [Mnemosyne]. **VFOAT** Bibliotheca Classica Batava. Vol. 1-11 (1852-62); New Series Vol. 1-60 (1873-1933); New Series 3 Vol. 1-13 (1933/34-1947); New Series 4 Vol. 1 (1948)-. Periodical. English (French, German and Latin). Five times a year. Fl220.00 (institutions) Netherlands; $125.75 (institutions) other. E. J. Brill, Postbus 9000, 2300 PA Leiden Netherlands. **Tel** 011 31 71 312624, FAX 011 31 71 317532, telex 39296 BRILL NL. **ED** C. J. Ruijgh. **LC** PA9; .M6. **[CCC]. Circ:** 550. Documents available from UMI Article Clearinghouse.
Desc: First appeared in 1852 as a journal of textual critism. It focuses on all aspects of the ancient world, including inscriptions, papyri, language, religion and philosophy.
Ind/Abst Acad. Search (July 1993-); Humanit. Index; Humanit. Source (Jul. 1993-); INFO-SOUTH Abstr.; Mag. Search; MLA Int. Bibl. Books Artic. Mod. Lang. Lit.; Newsp. Period. Abstr. (1991-).

FR/0249-6267
MODELES LINGUISTIQUES. [Modeles linguist.]. **Added/Corp** Universite de Lille III. Centre Interdisciplinaire de Recherches en Linguistique. (1979)-. Periodical. French. sa. 130.00F France; 160.00F other. Modeles Linguistiques, URA 1030, 8 BD Louis XIV, 59046 Lille Cedex France. **Tel** 011 33 20 531100.
Ind/Abst MLA Int. Bibl. Books Artic. Mod. Lang. Lit.

GW
MODERN GERMAN STUDIES. **See** Literature.

US/0026-7902
MODERN LANGUAGE JOURNAL (BOULDER, COLO.), THE. (THE MODERN LANGUAGE JOURNAL.). [Mod. lang. j.]. **Added/Corp** National Federation of Modern Language Teachers Associations. Federation of Modern Language Teachers Associations. Association of Modern Language Teachers of the Central West and South. National Federation of Modern Language Teachers. Vol. 1 (Oct. 1916)-. Periodical. English. qt. $45.00 (one year), $88.00 (two year), $130.00 (three year) institution; $25.00 (one year), $50.00 (two year), $75.00 (three year) individuals. University of Wisconsin Press, Journal Division, 114 North Murray Street, Madison WI 53715. **Tel** (608)262-4952, FAX (608)262-8909. **ED** David P. Benseler. **LC** PB1; .M47. **DD** 407. **CODEN** MOLJA8. **[CCC].** Index available. **Bk Rev. Ad Acc. Pr Rev.** available on microfilm and microfiche from University Microfilms International (UMI). Documents available from The Genuine Article, UMI Article Clearinghouse.
Desc: Devoted primarily to methods, pedagogical research, and topics of professional interest to all language teachers. The journal of The National Federation of Modern Language Teachers Associations.
Ind/Abst Acad. Abstr. Full Text Elite (Dec. 1989-); Acad. Abstr. (Dec. 1989-); Acad. Search (Dec. 1989-); Am. Bibliogr. Slavic East Europ. Stud.; Annu. Bibliogr. Engl. Lang. Lit.; Arts Humanit. Citation Index [Select. Cov.]; Book Rev. Index; Contents Pages Educ.; Curr. Contents Soc. Behav. Sci.; Curr. Index J. Educ.; Educ. Index; Humanit. Source (Jul. 1990-); INFO-SOUTH Abstr.; Lang. Teach.; Mag. Search; Med. Rev. Dig.; Middle East Abstr. Index; MLA Int. Bibl. Books Artic. Mod. Lang. Lit.; Newsp. Period. Abstr. (1986-); Psychol. Abstr. (1928-); PsycINFO (1990-); PsycLit; Res. Alert [Full Cov.]; Soc. Plann. Policy Dev. Abstr.; Soc. Sci. Cit. Index [Full Cov.]; Sociol. Abstr.

UK/0026-7937
MODERN LANGUAGE REVIEW, THE. [Mod. lang. rev.]. **Added/Corp** Modern Humanities Research Association. Modern Humanities Research Association. Bulletin. Vol. 1 (Oct. 1905)-. Periodical. English. qt. $156.00. W. S. Maney and Son Ltd., Hudson Road, Leeds LS9 7DL England. **Tel** 011 44 532 497481, FAX 011 44 532 486983. **(Subscription address:** W.S. Maney & Son Limited, PO Box YR7, Leeds, LS9 7UU England.**) LC** PB1; .M65. **DD** 405. Index available in last issue of volume--attached. cum. index. Documents available from The Genuine Article, UMI Article Clearinghouse. ***Supersedes in part*** *Modern Language Quarterly.*
Desc: Contains original articles and reviews on medieval and modern languages and literature, including English. The official organ of the Modern Humanities Research Association, a role for which it is fitted by its long history, its high reputation and its international coverage.
Ind/Abst Abstr. Engl. Stud.; Acad. Ind. [Computer File] (1992-); Acad. Search (July 1993-); Annu. Bibliogr. Engl. Lang. Lit.; Arts Humanit. Citation Index [Full Cov.]; Book Rev. Index; Br. Humanit. Index; Curr. Contents Arts Humanit.; Expand. Acad. Index (1989-); Humanit. Index; Humanit. Source (Jul. 1993-); INFO-SOUTH Abstr.; Mag. Search; Middle East Abstr. Index; MLA Int. Bibl. Books Artic. Mod. Lang. Lit.; Newsp. Period. Abstr. (1989-); Res. Alert [Full Cov.]; Soc. Sci. Cit. Index [Select. Cov.].

US/0047-7729
MODERN LANGUAGE STUDIES. [Mod. lang. stud.]. **Added/Corp** Northeast Modern Language Association (U.S.). (Feb. 1971)-. Periodical. English (French, Spanish, Italian and German). Four times a year (Feb., May, Aug., Nov.). $30.00. Modern Language Studies, Department of English, Box 1852, Brown University, Providence RI 02912. **Tel** (401)863-3756. **ED** David H. Hirsch. **LC** PB1; .M67. **DD** 410/.5. **Bk Rev. Ad Acc. Circ:** 2,500 (ctrl). available on microfilm and microfiche from University Microfilms International (UMI). Documents available from The Genuine Article. ***Supersedes*** *NEMLA Newsletter, 0550-7073.*
Desc: Publishes articles of interest to teachers and scholars in the area of English, American, and comparative literature and of the modern languages.
Ind/Abst Abstr. Engl. Stud.; Am. Bibliogr. Slavic East Europ. Stud.; Annu. Bibliogr. Engl. Lang. Lit.; Arts Humanit. Citation Index (19??-19??) [Full Cov.]; Curr. Contents Arts Humanit.; Lit. Crit. Regist.; Middle East Abstr. Index; MLA Int. Bibl. Books Artic. Mod. Lang. Lit.; Res. Alert [Full Cov.]; Romant. Move.; Soc. Plann. Policy Dev. Abstr.

US/0026-8232
MODERN PHILOLOGY. [Mod. philol.]. **Added/Corp** Modern Language Association of America. Victorian Literature Group. Vol. 1 (June 1903)-. Periodical. English. qt (4 issues). $59.00 institution, $29.00 individual, $19.00 MLA individual members and students. University of Chicago Press / Journals Division, PO Box 37005, 5720 South Woodlawn, Chicago IL 60637. **Tel** (312)753-3347, FAX (312)753-0811. **(Subscription telephone:** (312)753-8083**) ED** Janel Mueller. **LC** PB1; .M7. **DD** 405. **[CCC]. Acid Free.** available on microfilm and microfiche from University Microfilms International (UMI). Documents available from The Genuine Article, UMI Article Clearinghouse.
Desc: Devoted to the study of literature from the Middle Ages to the present. Publishes the results of original literary and linguistic investigations as well as essays in criticism and analysis.
Ind/Abst Abstr. Engl. Stud.; Acad. Abstr. Full Text Elite (July 1990-); Acad. Abstr. (July 1990-); Acad. Ind. [Computer File] (1987-); Acad. Search (July 1990-); Annu. Bibliogr. Engl. Lang. Lit.; Arts Humanit. Citation Index [Full Cov.]; Book Rev. Index; Curr. Contents Arts Humanit.; Expand. Acad. Index (1987-); Humanit. Index; Humanit. Source (Jul. 1990-); INFO-SOUTH Abstr.; Lit. Crit. Regist.; Mag. Search; MLA Int. Bibl. Books Artic. Mod. Lang. Lit.; Newsp. Period. Abstr. (1989-); Res. Alert [Full Cov.]; Soc. Plann. Policy Dev. Abstr.

SW/0026-8577
MODERNA SPRAK. [Mod. sprak]. **Added/Corp** Riksforeningen foer Laerarna i Moderna Sprak (Sweden). Vol. 1 (1907)-. Periodical. Swedish (English, German, French and Spanish). sa (2 issues). Kr210.00 Sweden; Kr220.00 other. Dr. Claus Ohrt, Angen, S 560-34 Visingso Sweden. **Tel** 011 46 390 40604. **ED** Ulf Dantanus, Olof Eriksson, Johan Falk, Lars Fant, Mats Mobarg, Helmut Mussener and Claus Ohrt. **LC** PB5; .M6. **DD** 410/.5. **Bk Rev. Ad Acc. Circ:** 1,700. Documents available from The Genuine Article.
Desc: Covers modern philology.
Ind/Abst Abstr. Engl. Stud.; Annu. Bibliogr. Engl. Lang. Lit.; Arts Humanit. Citation Index [Full Cov.]; Curr. Contents Arts Humanit.; Lang. Teach.; MLA Int. Bibl. Books Artic. Mod. Lang. Lit.; Res. Alert [Full Cov.]; Romant. Move.; Soc. Plann. Policy Dev. Abstr.; Soc. Sci. Cit. Index [Select. Cov.].

AU/0026-8666
MODERNE SPRACHEN. [Mod. Sprachen]. **Added/Corp** Verband der Osterreichischen Neuphilologen. Verband der Osterreichischen Neuphilologen fuer Moderne Sprachen, Literatur und Padagogik. Vol. 1 (1956)-. Periodical. German. sa.
Ind/Abst Lang. Teach.; MLA Int. Bibl. Books Artic. Mod. Lang. Lit.

US/0147-5207
MON-KHMER STUDIES. [Mon-Khmer stud.]. **Added/Corp** Summer Institute of Linguistics. (1964)-. English. an. $30.00. International Academic Bookstore, Box MKS5 7500, West Camp Wisdom Road, Dallas TX 75236. **Tel** (214)709-2404. **ED** Stephen D. O'Harrow. **LC** PL4301; .A3. **DD** 495.9/3. **CODEN** MKSTEF. **Circ:** 200.
Desc: Original contributions that advance knowledge of the structure and history of individual Mon-Khmer languages or contribute to the reconstruction of proto-Mon-Khmer and proto-Austroasiatic.
Ind/Abst Linguist. Lang. Behav. Abstr. (1987-) [Full Cov.]; MLA Int. Bibl. Books Artic. Mod. Lang. Lit.; Soc. Plann. Policy Dev. Abstr.

US/0026-9271
MONATSHEFTE (MADISON, 1946). (MONATSHEFTE.). [Monatshefte]. **Added/Corp**

University of Wisconsin. Dept. of German. South-Central Modern Language Association. German Section. Central States Modern Language Teachers Association. **VFOAT** Monatshefte fur Deutschen Unterricht, Deutsche Sprache und Literatur. Vol. 38, No. 1 (Jan. 1946)-. Periodical. English (German). qt. $65.00 (one year), $128.00 (two year), $190.00 (three year), institution; $27.00 (one year), $54.00 (two year), $81.00 (three year) individuals. University of Wisconsin Press, Journal Division, 114 North Murray Street, Madison WI 53715. **Tel** (608)262-4952, FAX (608)262-8909. **LC** PF3003; .M6. **DD** 430/.5. **[CCC].** cum. index. available on microfilm and microfiche from University Microfilms International (UMI). ***Continues*** *Monatshefte fur Deutschen Unterricht.*
Ind/Abst MLA Int. Bibl. Books Artic. Mod. Lang. Lit.; Romant. Move.; Soc. Plann. Policy Dev. Abstr.

IT
MONDO LADINO : BOLLETTINO DELL'ISTITUTO CULTURALE LADINO. **Added/Corp** Istituto Culturale Ladino (Vigo di Fassa, Italy). (19??)-. Periodical. Italian (German and Ladino). Twice a year. L30000 Italy; L40000 other. Istituto Culturale Ladino, Loc San Giovanni, 38039 Vigo di Fassa Italy. **Tel** 011 39 462 64267, FAX 011 39 462 64909. **Bk Rev.** ctrl circ.
Desc: Every argument about history, geography, folklore, ethnic, linguistics, literature, archaeology, architecture of the ladin minority of the Dolomite area.

●US/1056-5019
MONOGRAPHS IN LINGUISTICS. (1992)-. Monographic series. English. Price varies per volume. Peter Lang Publishing, 62 West 45th Street, 4th Floor, New York NY 10036. **Tel** (212)764-1471, (800)770-5264, telex 6973364 PLNY.

●US/1065-9528
MONOGRAPHS IN LINGUISTICS AND THE PHILOSOPHY OF LANGUAGE. (1993)-. Monographic series. English. Price varies per volume. Peter Lang Publishing, 62 West 45th Street, 4th Floor, New York NY 10036. **Tel** (212)764-1471, (800)770-5264, telex 6973364 PLNY.

UK
MONT FOLLICK SERIES. V. 1- 1969-. Monographic series. English. ir. Price varies per volume. Manchester University Press, Journals Dept, Oxford Road, Manchester M13 9PL England. **Tel** 011 44 061 2735539, FAX 011 44 061 2743346, telex 668932. **ED** W Haas. **UDC** 801.8.
Desc: Series of volumes based on lectures devoted to the study of written language.

GW
MONUMENTA GERMANIAE ACUSTICA. **Main/Corp** Deutsches Spracharchiv. **Added/Corp** Institut fur Phonometrie Braunschweig. 1965-. German.

MX
MORPHE / UNIVERSIDAD AUTONOMA DE PUEBLA, MAESTRIA EN CIENCIAS DEL LENGUAJE. **Added/Corp** Universidad Autonoma de Puebla. Maestria en Ciencias del Lenguaje. Vol. 1, No. 1 (Jan./June 1986)-. Periodical. Spanish. sa. $44.00. Escuela de Filosofia y Letras, Universidad Autonoma de Puebla Codigo Postal 72000, Puebla Mexico. **ED** Adrian S Gimate-Welsh. **Ad Acc.**
Ind/Abst MLA Int. Bibl. Books Artic. Mod. Lang. Lit.

YU/0350-6525
MOSTOVI (BELGRADE). (MOSTOVI.). [Mostovi]. **Added/Corp** Udruzenje Knjizevnih Prevodilaca Srbije. (Jan./Mar. 1970)-. Periodical. Serbo-Croatian (Cyrillic). qt.
Ind/Abst MLA Int. Bibl. Books Artic. Mod. Lang. Lit.

FR/0243-6450
MOTS. **See** Political Science.

RU/0027-2833
MOVOZNAVSTVO (KIEV). (MOVOZNAVSTVO.). [Movoznavstvo]. **Added/Corp** Akademiia Nauk Ukrainskoi RSR. Viddil Literatury, Movy i Mystetstvoznavstva. Akademiia Nauk Ukrainskoi RSR. Viddilennia Literatury, Movy i Mystetstvoznavstva. (1967)-. Periodical. Ukrainian (table of contents in English). bm. $69.95. Izdatelstvo Naukova Dumka / Ukrainian Academy of Sciences, Vladimirskaia Ulitsa 54, 252601 Kiev Ukraine. **Tel** 225-63-66, telex 131376. **(Subscription address:** East View Publications Inc., 3020 Harbor Lane North, Suite 110, Minneapolis MN 55447.) **Bk Rev.**
Ind/Abst MLA Int. Bibl. Books Artic. Mod. Lang. Lit.

UN/0027-2833
MOVOZNAVSTVO; NAUKOVI ZAPYSKY. **Added/Corp** Akademiia Nauk URSR, Kiev. Instytut Movoznavstva. (1941)-. Ukrainian. bm. $63.00. Ukrainska Knyha, 962 Bloor Street West, Toronto Ontario M6H 1L6 Canada. **Tel** (416)534-7551. **(Subscription address:** Victor Kamkin, 4956 Boiling Brook Parkway, Rockville MD 20852.) **LC** PG3801; .A415.
Desc: Information on Ukrainian philology.

Ind/Abst Linguist. Lang. Behav. Abstr. (1972-) [Full Cov.]; MLA Int. Bibl. Books Artic. Mod. Lang. Lit.; Soc. Plann. Policy Dev. Abstr.; Sociol. Abstr.

FR/0027-2841
MOYEN-AGE. (LE MOYEN AGE; REVUE D'HISTOIRE ET DE PHILOLOGIE.). [Moyen-age]. (1888)-. Periodical. French. qt. 2641F Belgium; 2991F other Europe; 3041F other. De Boeck Wesmael SA, Fond Jean Paques 4, 1348 Louvain La Neuve Belgium. **Tel** 011 32 10 482509, FAX 32 (0) 2 6273650. **ED** A. Marignan, G. Platon, M. Wilmotte. **LC** D111; .M9. cum. index. Documents available from The Genuine Article.
Desc: History and medieval philosophy.
Ind/Abst Am. Hist. Life (1989-1990); Annu. Bibliogr. Engl. Lang. Lit.; Arts Humanit. Citation Index [Full Cov.]; BHA : Biblio. Hist. Art; Curr. Contents Arts Humanit.; MLA Int. Bibl. Books Artic. Mod. Lang. Lit.; Res. Alert [Full Cov.]; Romant. Move.; Soc. Sci. Cit. Index [Select. Cov.].

PH/0047-5289
MST ENGLISH QUARTERLY, THE. [MST Engl. q.]. **Added/Corp** Manila Teachers of Secondary English. Vol. 1 (1951)-. Periodical. English. Four times a year. $5.00. Office of Supervisors of Secondary English, Manila Science High School, Taft Avenue, Manila Philippines. **ED** Fe M. Navarro. **Circ:** 700 (ctrl).
Desc: Articles on the teaching of language, reading, and literature at the secondary level.
Ind/Abst Index Philip. Period. (-199?); Lang. Teach.

NE/0167-8507
MULTILINGUA. [Multilingua]. **Added/Corp** Commission of the European Communities. Vol. 1, No. 1 (1982)-. Periodical. English (French, German and Italian). qt. $153.50. Walter de Gruyter Inc., PO Box 303421, D 10728 Berlin Germany. **Tel** 011 49 30 260050, FAX 011 49 30 26005251. **CODEN** MULTDF. **[CCC].** Documents available from Ask*IEEE.
Ind/Abst ACM Guide Comput. Lit.; Comput. Rev.; INSPEC (1982-); Int. Bibliogr. Sociol.; MLA Int. Bibl. Books Artic. Mod. Lang. Lit.; Soc. Plann. Policy Dev. Abstr.; Sociol. Abstr.

UK
MULTILINGUAL MATTERS. (1982)-. Monographic series. English. ir. Price varies per volume. Multilingual Matters Ltd., Frankfurt Lodge, Clevedon Hall, Clevedon Avon, BS21 7SJ England. **Tel** 011 44 275 876519, FAX 011 44 275 343096. **LC** UNC.
Ind/Abst MLA Int. Bibl. Books Artic. Mod. Lang. Lit.

GW/0930-1127
MUNCHENER BEITRAEGE ZUR MEDIAVISTIK UND RENAISSANCE-FORSCHUNG. [Munch. Beitr. Mediav. Renaiss.-Forsch.]. **Added/Corp** Arbeo-Gesellschaft. (1967)-. Monographic series. German. **LC** UNC.
Ind/Abst MLA Int. Bibl. Books Artic. Mod. Lang. Lit.

GW/0170-3668
MUNCHENER OSTASIATISCHE STUDIEN. **See** Literature.

GW/0077-1910
MUNCHENER STUDIEN ZUR SPRACHWISSENSCHAFT. [Munch. Stud. Sprachwiss.]. **Added/Corp** Munchener Sprachwissenschaftlicher Studienkreis. (1952)-. Periodical. German (English). ir. R Kitzinger, Schellingstrasse 25, D 80799 Munich, Germany. **Tel** 011 49 89 283537, FAX 011 49 89 281394. **ED** B Forssman and Joahanna Narten and Karl Hoffmann. **LC** P25; .M8. **Circ:** 400 (ctrl).
Desc: Linguistics for Indo-German, Indo-Arian and all the old languages in the Middle East area.
Ind/Abst Annu. Bibliogr. Engl. Lang. Lit.; Linguist. Lang. Behav. Abstr. (1973-) [Full Cov.]; MLA Int. Bibl. Books Artic. Mod. Lang. Lit.; Soc. Plann. Policy Dev. Abstr.

KO
MUNHWA OYON. Periodical. English (Korean). Chusik Hoesa Munhwa Oyon, PO Box Sodaemun Ucheguk Sodaemun-ku, Seoul 120 Korea. **LC** PE1131; .M86.

KO
MUNHWAO HAKSUP. Vol. 1 (June 1968)-. Periodical. Korean. qt. **LC** PL901; .M85.

GO/0768-9403
MUNTU. ***Suspended.*** (MUNTU : REVUE SCIENTIFIQUE ET CULTURELLE DU CICIBA.). [Muntu]. **Added/Corp** Centre International des Civilizations Bantu. **VFOAT** Revue Scientifique et Culturelle du CICIBA. No. 1 (1984)-No. 8. Periodical. French (English, Spanish and Portuguese). sa. 10.000CFAF. CICIBA, PO Box 770, Libreville, Gabon. **Tel** 241 723222.

NE
MUSEUM PHILOLOGUM LONDINIENSE. Vol. 1 (1975)-. Multiple languages (English, French and Italian). ir. D&D Publishing, 1 Mavrokordatou, Athens St 10678 Greece. **ED** R. Browning and G. Giangrande. **LC** PA1.A1; M87. **DD** 880/.05.

GW/0027-514X
MUTTERSPRACHE (WIESBADEN). (MUTTERSPRACHE.). [Muttersprache]. **Added/Corp** Gesellschaft fuer Deutsche Sprache (Wiesbaden, Germany). (1949)-. Periodical. German. Four times a year (Mar., June., Sep., Nov.). DM140.80. Gesellschaft fur Deutsche Sprache EV, Postfach 2669, W 6200 Wiesbaden Germany. **Tel** 011 49 611 520031, FAX 011 49 611 51313. **LC** PF3003; .M85. **DD** 430/.5. Index available (Bound in next issue). **Bk Rev. Ad Acc. Circ:** 1,000. Documents available from The Genuine Article. ***Supersedes*** *Muttersprache.*
Desc: Linguistic research, theoretical foundations of the cultivation, language, semantics, etymology, and research in languages for special purposes.
Ind/Abst Arts Humanit. Citation Index (19??-19??) [Full Cov.]; MLA Int. Bibl. Books Artic. Mod. Lang. Lit.; Res. Alert [Full Cov.]; Soc. Plann. Policy Dev. Abstr.; Soc. Sci. Cit. Index [Select. Cov.].

NE/0167-5257
NAAMKUNDE. [Naamkunde]. **Added/Corp** Instituut voor Naamkunde te Leuven. Commissie voor Naamkunde en Nederzettingsgeschiedenis. Vol. 1 (1969)-. Periodical. Dutch. Four times a year (4 issues per volume). 950F. Editions Peeters SA, Bondgenotenlaan 153, BP 41, B-3000 Leuven Belgium. **Tel** 32 16 235170, FAX 32 16 228500, telex 65987 PUL B. **(Subscription address:** P J Meertens-Instituut, Postbus 19888, 1000 GW Amsterdam The Netherlands) **LC** PF701; .N3. Index available. **Bk Rev.** ctrl circ. ***Supersedes*** *Instituut voor Naamkunde te Leuven. Mededelingen.*
Ind/Abst Lang. Lang. Behav. Abstr.; Linguist. Lang. Behav. Abstr. (1978-) [Full Cov.]; MLA Int. Bibl. Books Artic. Mod. Lang. Lit.; Soc. Plann. Policy Dev. Abstr.

AT/1031-5411
NAATI NEWS. [NAATI news]. **VFOAT** National Accreditation Authority for Translators and Interpreters News. (1988)-. English. Four times a year (Mar., June, Sept, Dec.). 15.00Aus$. NAATI Executive Secretary, PO Box 349, Jamison Act, 2614 Australia. **Tel** 11 61 62 514044, FAX 11 61 62 531575. **ED** S. Bell. **DD** 418.02394. **Bk Rev. Ad Acc. Circ:** 1,100 (ctrl). ***Continues*** *Newsletter - National Accreditation Authority for Translators and Interpreters, 0727-534X.*

GW/0065-5287
NACHRICHTEN DER AKADEMIE DER WISSENSCHAFTEN IN GOTTINGEN. PHILOLOGISCH-HISTORISCHE KLASSE. [Nachr. Akad. Wiss. Gott., 1]. **Added/Corp** Akademie der Wissenschaften in Gottingen. Philologisch-Historische Klasse. **VFOAT** Nachrichten der Akademie der Wissenschaften in Gottingen. I, Philologisch-Historische Klasse. No. 1 (1941)-. Monographic series. German. ir. $112.00. Vandenhoeck & Ruprecht, Robert Bosch Breite 6, D-37079 Goettingen Germany. **Tel** 011 49 551 695911, FAX 011 49 551 695917, telex 965226 VAN d. **LC** P3; .N33. **Ad Acc.** ctrl circ. ***Formed by the union of*** *Nachrichten von der Gesellschaft der Wissenschaften zu Gottingen. Philologisch-Historische Klasse. Fachgruppe I: Altertumswissenschaft; Nachrichten von der Gesellschaft der Wissenschaften zu Gottingen. Philologisch-Historische Klasse. Fachgruppe II: Mittlere und Neuere Geschichte; Nachrichten von der Gesellschaft der Wissenschaften zu Gottingen. Philologisch-Historische Klasse. Fachgruppe III: Allgemeine Sprachwissenschaft. Ostliche Kulturkreise; Nachrichten von der Gesellschaft der Wissenschaften zu Gottingen. Philologisch-Historische Klasse. Fachgruppe IV: Neuere Philologie und Literaturgeschichte* ***and*** *Nachrichten von der Gesellschaft der Wissenschaften zu Gottingen. Philologisch-Historische Klasse. Fachgruppe V: Religionswissenschaft.*
Ind/Abst Am. Hist. Life (1954-1955,1958-1978); BHA : Biblio. Hist. Art; Energy Res. Abstr. (1954-1955, 1958-).

US
NAFSA STUDIES AND PAPERS. ENGLISH LANGUAGE SERIES. **Main/Corp** National Association for Foreign Student Affairs. **VAT** National Association for Foreign Student Affairs Studies and Papers. English Language Series. No. 1/2 (19??)-. English. an. **LC** PE1128.A2; N35. ***Continues*** *National Association for Foreign Student Advisers. NAFSA Studies and Papers. English language series.*

CN/0700-9445
NAME GLEANER. (THE NAME GLEANER. GLANURE DES NOMS.). **Added/Corp** Institut des Sciences Onomastiques du Canada. **VFOAT** Glanure des Noms. (Sept. 1976)-. Periodical. French (English). ir (3 or 4 a year). 20.00Can$, 10.00Can$ students, 15.00Can$ retired members. Canadian Society for the Study of Names, York University Department of Literature and Linguistics, North York ONT M3J 1PC Canada. **Tel** (905)736-2100, (905)736-5016. **DD** 412/.05.
Desc: Newsletter for the Canadian Society for the Study of Names.

US/0889-342X
NAOS (ENGLISH ED.). (NAOS : NOTES AND MATERIALS FOR THE LINGUISTIC STUDY OF THE SACRED). [NAOS]. **VFOAT** Notes and Materials for the Linguistic Study of the Sacred; Bulletin of the Names of the Sacred Project. **VAT** Names of the Sacred. Vol. 1, No.

1 (Winter 1985)-. Periodical. English (translations available in Spanish). an (Fall). $10.00 (individuals), $20.00 (institutions). NAOS, 1309 CL/University of Pittsburgh, Pittsburgh PA 15260. **Tel** (412)624-5225. **ED** Juan Adolfo Vazquez. **DD** 205. Index available (Vols. 1-4 only.). **Bk Rev**, (Qty: 20). **Circ:** 250.
Desc: Notes and materials for the linguistic study of the sacred. Bulletin of the names of the sacred project.

YU/0027-8084
NAS JEZIK.
[Nas jez.]. **Added/Corp** Lingvisticko Drustvo u Beogradu. Institut za Srpski Jezik (Srpska Akademija Nauka) Institut za Srpskohrvatski Jezik (Belgrade, Serbia). (1933)-. Periodical. Serbo-Croatian (Cyrillic). qt. 50.00 Din. Lingvisticko Drustvo, Institut za Srpskohrvatski Jezik, Belgrad Knez-Mihailova 35 Yugoslavia. **LC** PG1201; .N3.
Ind/Abst MLA Int. Bibl. Books Artic. Mod. Lang. Lit.

XR/0027-8203
NASE REC.
Added/Corp Ustav pro Jazyk Cesky CSAV. Ceska Akademie Ved a Umeni. Trida 3. Vol. 1 (1917)-. Periodical. Czech. Five times a year. DM110.00 Germany; DM145.00 other. **(Subscription address:** Kubon & Sagner, ABT Zeitschriftenimport, D 80328 Munich Germany.**)** **LC** PG4004; .N3. Index available. **Bk Rev. Circ:** 2,500.
Desc: Deals with problems of Czech and of language culture in general. Contains articles on the structure of Czech, on its stylistic variants, and on the norm and codification of the standard literary language.
Ind/Abst MLA Int. Bibl. Books Artic. Mod. Lang. Lit.; Soc. Plann. Policy Dev. Abstr.

LE
NASHRAT MARKAZ AL-ABHATH WA-AL-DIRASAT AL-ARABIYAH.
VFOAT Bulletin du Centre de Recherches et d'Etudes Arabes. Al-Silsilah Al-Jadidah No. 1 (Nov. 1983)-. Periodical. Arabic (French). Markaz Al-Abhath Wa-Al-Dirasat Al-Arabiyah Jamiat Al-Qiddis Yusuf, S B 293, Beirut Lebanon. **LC** PJ6069.U55; N37.

UK/0143-4136
NATE NEWS HUDDERSFIELD.
[NATE news Huddersfield]. **VFOAT** National Association for the Teaching of English News. (1978)-. Newsletter. English. Three times a year. £38.00 full membership (includes English in Education journal and The English & Media Magazine). NATE / National Association for the Teaching of English, 50 Broadfield Road, Broadfield Business Centre, Sheffield S8 0XJ England. **Tel** 011 44 114 2555419, FAX 011 44 114 2555296. ***Continues*** *Newsletter - National Association for the Teaching of English.*

AT/0814-9879
NATIONAL DIRECTORY OF TRANSLATORS, INTERPRETERS AND LANGUAGE AIDES.
[Natl. dir. transl. interpret. lang. aides]. (1985)-. English. an (Aug.). 20.00Aus$. NAATI Executive Secretary, PO Box 349, Jamison Act, 2614 Australia. **Tel** 11 61 62 514044, FAX 11 61 62 531575. **ED** S. Bell. **DD** 418.0202594. **Circ:** 100 (ctrl). available on diskette.

US/0749-1042
NATIONAL FORENSIC JOURNAL.
See Medical Science and Technology-Forensic Medicine, Medical Jurisprudence.

CN/0715-8904
NATIONAL NEWSLETTER (CANADIAN PARENTS FOR FRENCH).
(NATIONAL NEWSLETTER / CPF, CANADIAN PARENTS FOR FRENCH.). [Natl. newsl. - Can. Parents Fr.]. **Added/Corp** Canadian Parents for French. **VAT** CPF National Newsletter; Canadian Parents for French National Newsletter. Issue No. 10 (June 1980)-. Newsletter. English. Four times a year (Mar., June, Sept., Dec.). 25.00Can$ (regular); 50.00Can$ (supporter); 75.00Can$ (patron); 125.00Can$ (organization) Comes with Canadian Parents for French membership and includes National Newsletter. Canadian Parents for French, 309 Cooper Street, Suite 210, Ottawa Ontario K2P 0G5 Canada. **Tel** (613)235-1481. **DD** 440/.7071. ***Continues*** *Newsletter (Canadian Parents for French), 0229-7671.*

NE/0167-806X
NATURAL LANGUAGE AND LINGUISTIC THEORY.
(NATURAL LANGUAGE & LINGUISTIC THEORY.). [Nat. lang. linguist. theory]. **VFOAT** Natural Language and Linguistic Theory. Vol. 1, No. 1 (1983)-. Periodical. English. qt. $440.00. Kluwer Academic Publishers, Postbus 322, 3300 AH Dordrecht, The Netherlands. **Tel** 011 (31) 78 524400, FAX 011 31 78 183273, telex 20083. **ED** Joan Maling. **LC** P1; .N38. **DD** 410/.5. **[CCC].** Index available. **Bk Rev. Ad Acc. Pr Rev. Acid Free. Circ:** 1,300. available on microfilm and microfiche from University Microfilms International (UMI). Documents available from The Genuine Article.
Desc: Discussion of theoretical research paying attention to natural language data, bridging descriptive work and highly theoretical, less empirical work. A primary goal of the journal is to encourage work which makes complex language data accessible to those unfamiliar with the language area being studied, and work which makes complex theoretical positions more accessible to those working outside the theoretical framework under review.
Ind/Abst Abstr. Anthropol.; Annu. Bibliogr. Engl. Lang. Lit.; Arts Humanit. Citation Index [Full Cov.]; Curr. Contents Arts Humanit.; Curr. Contents Soc. Behav. Sci.; Linguist. Lang. Behav. Abstr. (1983-) [Full Cov.]; MLA Int. Bibl. Books Artic. Mod. Lang. Lit.; Res. Alert [Full Cov.]; Soc. Plann. Policy Dev. Abstr.; Soc. Sci. Cit. Index [Full Cov.].

UK/1351-3249
NATURAL LANGUAGE ENGINEERING.
See Computers.

US/0925-854X
NATURAL LANGUAGE SEMANTICS.
English. Three times a year. $303.00. Kluwer Academic Publishers, Postbus 322, 3300 AH Dordrecht, The Netherlands. **Tel** 011 (31) 78 524400, FAX 011 31 78 183273, telex 20083. **ED** Irene Heim and Angelika Kratzer. **Pr Rev. Acid Free.** available on microfilm and microfiche from University Microfilms International (UMI).
Desc: The journal seeks to encourage the convergence of approaches employing the concepts of logic and philosophy with perspectives of generative grammar on the relations between meaning and structure. It is devoted to semantics and its interfaces in grammar, especially syntax.

BE/0771-5080
NEDERLANDS VAN NU.
[Ned. nu]. (1979)-. Periodical. Dutch. Five times a year. 35.38F (members of Onze Taal), 44.81F (non-members) Europe; 47.50F (non-members) other. Vereniging Algemeen Nederlands, Cardinaal Mercierplein 1, 2800 Mechelen Belgium. **Tel** 011 32 15 401876. **UDC** 8. **Bk Rev. Ad Acc.** ctrl circ. ***Continues*** *Nu Nog, 0771-5048.*

HU/0418-4580
NEMET FILOLOGIAI TANULMANYOK.
See Literature.

CN/0713-214X
NEOLOGIE EN MARCHE.
[Neol. marche]. **Added/Corp** Quebec (Province). Office de la Langue Francaise. No. 16 (1980)-. French. Editeur Officiel du Quebec, 1283 Boul Charest Ouest, Quebec Quebec G1N 2C9 Canada. ***Formed by the union of*** *Neologie en Marche. Serie A. Langue Generale, 0380-9366* ***and*** *Neologie en Marche. Serie B. Langue de Specialites.*

PL/0208-5550
NEOPHILOLOGICA.
Added/Corp Uniwersytet Slaski w Katowicach. Vol. 1 (1980)-. French (German; summaries and/or abstracts in Polish and Russian). ir. Z900.00 (latest volume). Uniwersytet Slaski, Ul Bankowa 14, 40-007 Katowice Poland. **Tel** 59-69-15, FAX 48 32 599-506, telex 0315584 USKPL. **(Subscription address:** ARS Polona, PO Box 1001, 00068 Warsaw Poland.**)** **LC** PB5; .N39. **DD** 410/.5.

NE/0028-2677
NEOPHILOLOGUS.
[Neophilologus]. Vol. 1 (1915)-. Periodical. English (French, German, Italian and Spanish). qt. $352.00. Kluwer Academic Publishers, Postbus 322, 3300 AH Dordrecht, The Netherlands. **Tel** 011 (31) 78 524400, FAX 011 31 78 183273, telex 20083. **LC** PB5; .N4. **DD** 410/.5. Index available. cum. index. **Bk Rev. Circ:** 800. Documents available from The Genuine Article.
Ind/Abst Abstr. Engl. Stud.; Annu. Bibliogr. Engl. Lang. Lit.; Arts Humanit. Citation Index [Full Cov.]; Curr. Contents Arts Humanit.; Lit. Crit. Regist.; Middle East Abstr. Index; MLA Int. Bibl. Books Artic. Mod. Lang. Lit.; Res. Alert [Full Cov.]; Romant. Move.

PL/0239-8028
NEOTERM : JOURNAL OF THE INTERNATIONAL ORGANIZATION FOR UNIFICATION OF TERMINOLOGICAL NEOLOGISMS, AND WORLD BANK OF INTERNATIONAL TERMS.
(1984)-. Periodical. English (French). qt. Price on Request. **(Subscription address:** ARS Polona, PO Box 1001, 00068 Warsaw Poland.**)**

NP
NEPALI AKADAMI PATRIKA.
VFOAT Akadami Patrika. Periodical. Nepali (Nepali). 2.00. **LC** PK2595; .N38. **UDC** 809.149.3.

RU
NEPOLNOZNACHNYE SLOVA.
Added/Corp Stavropolskii Gosudarstvennyi Pedagogicheskii Institut. (1974)-. Periodical. Russian. 0.60rub. Izdatelstvo Stavropolskaia Pravda, Stavropol Ulitsa Spartaka 10, Stavropol Russia. **LC** PG2380; .N46.

HU/0586-3716
NEPRAJZ ES NYELVTUDOMANY.
See Anthropology.

US/0730-1359
NEUE GERMANISTIK.
Ceased. **See** Literature.

SZ
NEUE STUDIEN ZUR ANGLISTIK UND AMERIKANISTIK.
(1974)-. Monographic series. German. Verlag Peter Lang AG, Jupiterstrasse 15, CH-3000 Bern 15 Switzerland. **Tel** 011 41 31 9411122, FAX 011 41 31 321131.
Ind/Abst MLA Int. Bibl. Books Artic. Mod. Lang. Lit.

GW/0342-3816
NEUEREN SPRACHEN, DIE.
(DIE NEUEREN SPRACHEN : ZEITSCHRIFT FUER DEN FORSCHUNG UND UNTERRICHT AUF DEM FACHGEBIET DER MODERNEN FREMDSPRACHEN.). [Neueren Sprachen]. (1952)-. Periodical. German (English and French). bm (6 issues). DM54.00. Moritz Diesterweg, Postfach 630180, D-60351 Frankfurt Germany. **Tel** 11 49 69 420810, FAX 11 49 69 42081100. **ED** Horst Arndt. **[CCC]. Bk Rev. Ad Acc.** available on microfilm and microfiche from University Microfilms International (UMI). ***Continues*** *Zeitschrift fur Neuere Sprachen;* ***Absorbed*** *Lebenden Fremdsprachen* ***and*** *Neuphilologische Zeitschrift.*
Desc: Modern philology.
Ind/Abst Abstr. Engl. Stud.; Annu. Bibliogr. Engl. Lang. Lit.; Lang. Teach.; MLA Int. Bibl. Books Artic. Mod. Lang. Lit.; Romant. Move.; Soc. Plann. Policy Dev. Abstr.

GW
NEUINDISCHE STUDIEN.
Vol. 1 (1970)-. Monographic series. Multiple languages (German and English). ir. Price varies per volume. Otto Harrassowitz Verlag, Taunusstrasse 14, Postfach 2929, D-65019 Wiesbaden Germany. **Tel** 011 49 611 5300, FAX 530570, telex 4186 135 OH D. **LC** PK1502; .N48.

FI/0028-3754
NEUPHILOLOGISCHE MITTEILUNGEN.
[Neuphilol. Mitt.]. **Added/Corp** Uusfilologinen Yhdistys. Vol. 1 (1899)-. Periodical. English (German and French). qt (4 issues). FI290.00. Modern Language Society, Hallituskatu 11, SF-00100 Helsinki Finland. **Tel** 011 358 0 1912504. **(Subscription address:** Akateeminen Kirjakauppa, PO Box 23, SF 00371 Helsinki Finland.**)** **LC** PB10; .N415. **DD** 410/.5. Index available. cum. index. **Bk Rev.** Documents available from The Genuine Article.
Desc: Bulletin receiving articles on English, German and Romance linguistics and philology (preferably historical).
Ind/Abst Abstr. Engl. Stud. (1985-); Annu. Bibliogr. Engl. Lang. Lit.; Arts Humanit. Citation Index [Full Cov.]; Curr. Contents Arts Humanit.; MLA Int. Bibl. Books Artic. Mod. Lang. Lit.; Res. Alert [Full Cov.]; Romant. Move.; Soc. Plann. Policy Dev. Abstr.; Soc. Sci. Cit. Index [Select. Cov.].

NE/0301-6412
NEUROLINGUISTICS (AMSTERDAM).
(NEUROLINGUISTICS.). [Neurolinguistics]. 1-. Monographic series. English. ir. Price varies per volume. Swets & Zeitlinger BV, Heereweg 347B PO Box 825, 2160 SZ Lisse Holland. **Tel** 011 31 2521 35111, FAX 02521-15888, telex 41325. **ED** R Hoops and Y Lebrun. **UDC** 800; 159. **NLM** W1 NE328K. **CODEN** NEURDL. Documents available from BIOSIS Document Express.
Ind/Abst Biol. Abstr.

GW/0933-2715
NEUROLINGUISTIK : ZEITSCHRIFT FUER APHASIEFORSCHUNG UND -THERAPIE.
See Physical Therapy.

GW/0028-3983
NEUSPRACHLICHE MITTEILUNGEN AUS WISSENSCHAFT UND PRAXIS : NM.
See Education.

US
NEW ACCENTS.
English. ir. Routledge Chapman & Hall Inc, 29 West 35th Street, New York NY 10001. **Tel** (212)244-3336, (212)244-6412.
Ind/Abst MLA Int. Bibl. Books Artic. Mod. Lang. Lit.

UK/0307-2770
NEW GERMAN STUDIES.
[New Ger. stud.]. **Added/Corp** University of Hull. German Dept. **VFOAT** N.G.S.; NGS. Vol. 1, No. 1 (Spring 1973)-. Periodical. English. Three times a year (Jan., May, Oct.). £6.00 UK; £7.50 others. University of Hull Department of German, Dr. Alan Best, Hull HU6 7RX England. **Tel** 011 44 482-46311. **ED** Alan Best. **LC** PF3001; .N49. **DD** 830/.8. **Bk Rev. Ad Acc. Circ:** 300.
Desc: Articles dealing with German language, literature and institutions.
Ind/Abst MLA Int. Bibl. Books Artic. Mod. Lang. Lit.; Romant. Move.

II
NEW LANGUAGE PLANNING NEWSLETTER.
Added/Corp Central Institute of Indian Languages. Vol. 1, No. 1 (Sept. 1986)-. Periodical. Indonesian. qt. $5.50. Central Institute Indian Langage,

Manasagangorti, Mysore 570006, Karnataka India. **Tel** 11 91 23558. **ED** E. Annamalai and Bjorn Jernudd. **Bk Rev**, (Qty: 4). ctrl circ.
Ind/Abst Soc. Plann. Policy Dev. Abstr.

US/0731-2466
NEW SPEAKERS AND LECTURERS. [New speak. lect.]. Issue No. 1 (Apr. 1982)-. English. ir. $130.00 (two softbound supplements). Gale Research Inc., 835 Penobscot Building, Detroit MI 48226. **Tel** (800)877-GALE, (313)961-2242, FAX (313)961-6083, telex TWX 810-221-7086. **ED** Jacqueline O'Brien and Paul Wasserman. **LC** PN4007; .N48. **DD** 808.5/1/02573.
Desc: Two supplements will update speakers and lecturers: how to find them by providing information on new speakers and lecture bureaus.

NZ
NEW ZEALAND SLAVONIC JOURNAL.
See Humanities.

CN/0704-5905
NEWSLETTER FOR TARGUMIC & COGNATE STUDIES. (NEWSLETTER FOR TARGUMIC & COGNATE STUDIES / DEPARTMENT OF NEAR EASTERN STUDIES, UNIVERSITY OF TORONTO.). [Newsl. Targumic cogn. stud.]. **Added/Corp** University of Toronto. Dept. of Near Eastern Studies. **VFOAT** Newsletter for Targumic and Cognate Studies. (Feb. 1976)-. Newsletter. English. Twice a year (June and Dec.). $5.00. Newsletter for Targumic and Cognate Studies, Department of Near Eastern Studies, University of Toronto, Toronto Ontario M5S 1A1 Canada. **Tel** (416)978-3184. **ED** E. G. Clarke. **LC** BS709.4; .N48. **Circ:** 200. ***Continues*** *Newsletter for Targum Studies, 0704-5913.*
Desc: Listing of current publications, both books and articles, in the field.
Ind/Abst Old Testam. Abstr.

UK/0257-6554
NEWSLETTER - IATEFL. [Newsl. - IATEFL]. **VFOAT** Newsletter - International Association of Teachers of English as a Foreign Language. (19??)-. Newsletter. English. ir. £60.00 (institutions), £23.00 (individuals) other. IATEFL, 3 Kingsdown Chambers, Tankerton, Whitsable Kent CT5 2SJ England. **Tel** 011 44 227 276528, FAX 011 44 227 274415. **UDC** 37.

US/0002-8193
NEWSLETTER OF THE AMERICAN DIALECT SOCIETY. **Main/Corp** American Dialect Society. Vol. 1 (Feb. 1969)-. Newsletter. English. Three times a year. $30.00 Comes with American Dialect Society membership. American Dialect Society, MacMurray College, English Department, Jacksonville IL 62650. **Tel** (217)479-7000, FAX (217)245-5214. **LC** PE2801; .A57. **DD** 427/.973. **Ad Acc. Circ:** 975.
Desc: News of American Dialect Society meetings, committees and publications.
Ind/Abst MLA Int. Bibl. Books Artic. Mod. Lang. Lit.

VM
NGON NG. **Added/Corp** Vien Ngon Ng Hoc. (19??)-. Periodical. Vietnamese (table of contents in English). qt. Xunhasaba Exports and Imports, 7 Nguyen Thi Minh Khai Str, Dit 1 Ho Chi Minh City Vietnam. **Tel** 011 84 8 294893, telex 278 XUNHASABA.

JA
NICHIJOGO SHINDAN / ASAHI SHINBUNSHA YOGO KANJI HEN. 1-. Japanese. ¥240 single issue. Asahi Shinbunsha, 3-2 Tsukiji 5 Chuo-ku, Tokyo-to 104 Japan. **LC** PL645; .N49.

GW/0078-0545
NIEDERDEUTSCHES WORT. [Niederdtsch. Wort]. **Added/Corp** Westfalisches Worterbuch - und Flurnamenarchiv in Munster (Westfalen) Universitat Munster. Germanistisches Institut. (1960)-. German. an. DM35.34 Germany; DM38.00 other. Aschendorffsche Verlagsbuchhandlung, Postfach 1124, D-48135 Muenster Germany. **Tel** 011 49 251 690132, telex 08-92 830 WN MS D. **LC** PF5601; .N55. **Bk Rev.**
Desc: Contributions to the philology of low-German.
Ind/Abst MLA Int. Bibl. Books Artic. Mod. Lang. Lit.

NE/0028-9922
NIEUWE TAALGIDS. (DE NIEUWE TAALGIDS.). [Nieuwe taalgids]. Vol. 1 (1907)-. Periodical. Dutch. bm (6 issues). Fl69.00 Netherlands; Fl72.00 other. Wolters Noordhoff BV, Postbus 567, 9700 AN Groningen Netherlands. **Tel** 011 31 50 226886, FAX 011 31 50 264866. **LC** PF4; .N5. **DD** 439.3105. Index available (free).
Desc: Dutch philology.
Ind/Abst MLA Int. Bibl. Books Artic. Mod. Lang. Lit.; Soc. Plann. Policy Dev. Abstr.

JA/0912-5361
NIHONGO JANARU. **VFOAT** Nihongo Journal. Vol 1, No. 1 (1986)-. Periodical. English (Japanese). mo. 177.60Aus$. OCS Australia Pty Limited, PO Box 539, Mascot NSW 2020 Australia. **Tel** 011 61 02 693-5122, FAX 011 61 02 693-5805, telex 177267. **(Subscription address:** Maruzen Company Ltd., PO Box 5050, Import & Export Department, Tokyo 100 31 Japan.**)**

JA/0389-4037
NIHONGO KYOIKU. **Added/Corp** Society for the Teaching of Japanese as a Foreign Language. **VFOAT** Journal of Japanese Language Teaching. (19??)-. English (Japanese). Three times a year. $142.00. Nihongo Kyoiku Gakkai, 4th Mori Bldg., 19-12, toranomon 1-Chome, Minato-Ku, Tokyo 105 Japan. **(Subscription address:** Kyowa Book Company Inc., 1-38 Kanda Jinbo-Cho, Chiyoda-Ku Tokyo 101, Japan**)** **LC** PL539.3; .N27 .

JA
NIHONGO TO NIHONGO KYÂOIKU.
Added/Corp Keio Gijuku Daigaku, Tokyo. Kokusai Senta. 3 (1974)-. Periodical. Japanese. Keito Gijuku Daigaku Kokusai Senta, 15-45 Mita 2-chome Minato-ku, Tokyo 108 Japan. **LC** PL501; .N54.

JA
NIHONGOGAKU. **VFOAT** Nihongo gaku. (Nov. 1982)-. Periodical. Japanese. mo. $180.00. **(Subscription address:** Maruzen Company Ltd., PO Box 5050, Import & Export Department, Tokyo 100 31 Japan.**)**

UK/0143-859X
NIMLA. (JOURNAL OF THE MODERN LANGUAGE ASSOCIATION OF NORTHERN IRELAND.). [J. Mod. Lang. Assoc. North. Irel.]. **Added/Corp** Modern Language Association of Northern Ireland. New University of Ulster. **VFOAT** N.I.M.L.A.; NIMLA. (Oct. 1978)-. Periodical. English (French, German and Irish). an. £10.00. Secretary of the Editorial Board, Department of Modern Languages, New University of Ulster, Coleraine BT52 1SA Northern Ireland. **Tel** 0265 4141, FAX 0265 40903. **ED** Roy Blair (editor's address: Larne Grammar School, Larne BT40 1PQ Northern Ireland). **LC** PB1; .J68. **DD** 405. **Bk Rev. Ad Acc. Pr Rev. Circ:** 300.
Desc: Strives to keep readers up to date on developments in the field.
Ind/Abst Lang. Teach.

UK/0141-6340
NOMINA. [Nomina]. **Added/Corp** English Name-Studies. Vol. 1 (1977)-. English. an (current year edition published in the following year). £10.00 British Inland Postal Area; £12.00 other. NOMINA, c/o Gordon Anderson, 13 Church Street, Chesterton, Cambridge CB4 1DT England. **Tel** (0223)357585. **ED** O. J. Padel. **LC** DA645; .N65. **DD** 914.1/00321. **Bk Rev. Ad Acc. Circ:** 250.
Desc: An journal of name studies relating to Great Britian and Ireland.
Ind/Abst Annu. Bibliogr. Engl. Lang. Lit.; Br. Archaeol. Bibliogr.; MLA Int. Bibl. Books Artic. Mod. Lang. Lit.

NO/0332-5865
NORDIC JOURNAL OF LINGUISTICS. [Nord. j. linguist.]. **Added/Corp** Nordic Association of Linguists. Vol. 1 (1978-). Periodical. English. sa. Kr360.00, $67.00. Scandinavian University Press, PO Box 2959 Toeyen, N 0608 Oslo 6 Norway. **Tel** 011 47 2 2575400, FAX 011 47 2 2575353, telex 71896 UROR N. **(Subscription address:** Scandinavian University Press, 200 Meacham Ave., Elmont NY 11003.**)** **ED** Thorstein Fretheim. **LC** P1.A1; N67. **DD** 410/.5. **[CCC]. Bk Rev. Ad Acc. Pr Rev. Circ:** 600. available on microfilm from University Microfilms International (UMI). ***Supersedes*** *Norwegian Journal of Linguistics. Norsk Tiddsskrift for Sproggvidenskap.*
Desc: Concerned with all branches of linguistics. Preference is given to contributions of general theoretical of methodological interest and to studies of Scandinavian languages including Finnish and Lappish.
Ind/Abst Annu. Bibliogr. Engl. Lang. Lit.; Int. Bibliogr. Sociol.; Linguist. Lang. Behav. Abstr. (1972-) [Full Cov.]; MLA Int. Bibl. Books Artic. Mod. Lang. Lit.; Psychol. Abstr. (1981-); Soc. Plann. Policy Dev. Abstr.

SW
NORDISKT NAMNFORSKARREGISTER.
1973-. Swedish. Nordiska Samarbetskommitten for Namnforskning, St Johannesgatan 11, S-7522 Uppsala Sweden. **LC** P321.9; .N65. **UDC** 803.96-31.

NO/0332-7531
NORDLYD. [Nordlyd]. No. 1-. Periodical. English (German and Norwegian). ir. Free. School of Languages and Literature, PO Box 1090, 9001 Tromso Norway. **Tel** 478381688. **ED** Ernst Hakon Jahr. **LC** P1.A1; N674. **DD** 410/.5. **UDC** 800.73. **Circ:** 500.
Desc: Presents articles by language researchers at the School of Languages and Literature at the University of Tromso, and from others who have some connection with the University.
Ind/Abst Annu. Bibliogr. Engl. Lang. Lit.; Linguist. Lang. Behav. Abstr. (1979-) [Full Cov.]; Soc. Plann. Policy Dev. Abstr.

SW/0346-6728
NORNA-RAPPORTER. Vol. 1 (1973)-. Periodical. Swedish (English and German). ir. NORNA-Forlaget, Sankt Johannesgatan 11, S-752 21 Uppsala Sweden. **Tel** (018)181289. **Circ:** 300 (ctrl).

NO/0800-3076
NORSK LINGVISTISK TIDSSKRIFT : NLT. **VFOAT** NLT. (1983)-. Periodical. Norwegian (English and German). Twice a year (June and December). $40.00 (institution); $28.00 (individual);. Novus Press, PO Box 748 Sentrum, N-0106 Oslo Norway. **Tel** 011 47 22 717450, FAX 011 47 22 718107. **ED** Ernst Hakon Jahr. **Bk Rev. Ad Acc. Circ:** 300.
Desc: Presents articles and book reviews on Norwegian/Nordic languages and general linguistics within all fields of linguistics and language study.

NO/0332-7264
NORSKLREREN. [Norsklreren]. **VFOAT** Norsklraren. (1977)-. Periodical. Norwegian. qt. **DD** 372.4.
Ind/Abst MLA Int. Bibl. Books Artic. Mod. Lang. Lit.

US/0885-6001
NORTH CAROLINA STUDIES IN THE ROMANCE LANGUAGES AND LITERATURES. [N. C. stud. Roman. lang. lit.]. **Added/Corp** University of North Carolina at Chapel Hill. University of North Carolina at Chapel Hill. Dept. of Romance Languages. No. 132 (1973)-. Monographic series. English (French, Italian and Spanish). ir. Price varies per volume. University of North Carolina Press, 116 South Boundary Street, PO Box 2288, Chapel Hill NC 27515-2288. **Tel** (919)966-3561, FAX (919)966-3829. **LC** UNC. **DD** 440. ***Continues*** *Studies in the Romance Languages and Literatures, 0081-8666.*
Ind/Abst MLA Int. Bibl. Books Artic. Mod. Lang. Lit.

US
NORTH-HOLLAND LINGUISTIC SERIES. **VFOAT** North-Holland Linguistic Series. (197?)-. Monographic series. English. ir. Elsevier Science Publishing Company Inc, Madison Square Station, PO Box 882, New York NY 10159-0882. **Tel** (212)633-3950, FAX (212)633-3990.
Ind/Abst MLA Int. Bibl. Books Artic. Mod. Lang. Lit.; Zentralbl. Math. Ihre Grenzgeb.

DK/0108-8416
NORTH-WESTERN EUROPEAN LANGUAGE EVOLUTION. **VFOAT** North Western European Language Evolution; NOWELE. Vol. 1 (Aug. 1983)-. Periodical. English (German). sa. Kr117.12. Odense University Press, 55 Campusvej, DK-5230 Odense M Denmark. **Tel** 66 15 79 99, FAX 66 15 81 26. **ED** Hans Frede Nielsen. **Ad Acc.**
Ind/Abst Annu. Bibliogr. Engl. Lang. Lit.; MLA Int. Bibl. Books Artic. Mod. Lang. Lit.; Soc. Plann. Policy Dev. Abstr.

DK/0900-8675
NORTH-WESTERN EUROPEAN LANGUAGE EVOLUTION. SUPPLEMENT. **VFOAT** North Western European Language Evolution. Supplement. (1985)-. English (Danish). an. Comes with North-Western European Language Evolution. Odense University Press, 55 Campusvej, DK-5230 Odense M Denmark. **Tel** 66 15 79 99, FAX 66 15 81 26.
Desc: Covers historical linguistics and linguistic change.

BO
NOTAS Y NOTICIAS LINGUISTICAS. **VFOAT** N Y N Ling; N & N Ling. Periodical. Spanish. qt. $b7.00 Bolivia; $5.00 other. Instituto Boliviano de Cultura / Bolivia. **Tel** 378299. **LC** P9; .N67. **DD** 410/.5. **Circ:** 200 (ctrl).
Desc: Devoted to linguistic studies and cultural manifestations of native communities in Bolivia.

UK/0029-3970
NOTES AND QUERIES. [Notes & queries]. Vol. 1 (Nov. 1849)-. Academic Scholarly Publication. English. qt. £56.00 UK and Europe; $103.00 other. Oxford University Press, Walton Street, Oxford OX2 6DP England. **Tel** 011 44 865 56767, FAX 011 44 865 267773, telex 837330 OXPRES G. **(Subscription address:** Oxford University Press / USA, Journals Marketing Department, Oxford University Press, 2001 Evans Road, Cary NC 27513.**)** **ED** E. G. Stanley, D. Hewitt and L. G. Black. **LC** AG305; .N7. **DD** 032. **NLM** AG 105 N911. **[CCC].** Index available. cum. index. **Bk Rev. Ad Acc. Circ:** 1,300 (ctrl). available on microfilm and microfiche from University Microfilms International (UMI). Documents available from The Genuine Article, UMI Article Clearinghouse.
Desc: Devoted principally to English language and literature, lexicography, history and scholarly antiquarianism. Emphasis is on the factual rather than the speculative.
Ind/Abst Abstr. Engl. Stud.; Acad. Search (July 1993-); Am. Hist. Life (1955-); Annu. Bibliogr. Engl. Lang. Lit.; Arts Humanit. Citation Index [Full Cov.]; BHA : Biblio. Hist. Art; Br. Humanit. Index; Curr. Contents Arts Humanit.; Expand. Acad. Index (1989-); Humanit. Index; Humanit. Source (Jul. 1993-); INFO-SOUTH Abstr.; Mag. Search; MLA Int. Bibl. Books Artic. Mod. Lang. Lit.; Newsp. Period. Abstr. (1991-); Res. Alert [Full Cov.]; RILM Abstr.; Romant. Move.; Soc. Sci. Cit. Index [Select. Cov.].

US/0736-0673
NOTES ON LINGUISTICS. [Notes linguist.].
Added/Corp Summer Institute of Linguistics. No. 1 (Jan. 1977)-. Periodical. English. Four times a year. $19.95 US; $23.95 others. Summer Institute of Linguistic, 7500 West Camp Wisdom Road, Dallas TX 75236. **Tel** (214)709-2404, FAX (214)709-2433, telex 9108614123. **ED** Eugene Loos. **LC** P1; .N68. **DD** 410/.5. **Bk Rev. Circ:** 850 (ctrl). available on microfiche.
Desc: Designed to provide linguistic fieldworkers with news, reviews, announcements and articles that will stimulate a current interest in linguistics.
Ind/Abst Linguist. Lang. Behav. Abstr. (1987-) [Full Cov.]; MLA Int. Bibl. Books Artic. Mod. Lang. Lit.; Soc. Plann. Policy Dev. Abstr.

US/0737-6707
NOTES ON LITERACY. [Notes lit.]. **Added/Corp**
Summer Institute of Linguistics. (19??)-. Periodical. English. Four times a year. $19.95 US; $23.95 others. Summer Institute of Linguistic, 7500 West Camp Wisdom Road, Dallas TX 75236. **Tel** (214)709-2404, FAX (214)709-2433, telex 9108614123. **ED** Olive A. Shell. **DD** 410. **Bk Rev. Ad Acc. Circ:** 700. available on microfiche.
Desc: Contains articles concerning orthography and applied practical topics pertaining to literacy projects world-wide, occasional paper.
Ind/Abst Soc. Plann. Policy Dev. Abstr.

US/0163-7088
NOTES ON TEACHING ENGLISH.
Added/Corp Georgia-South Carolina College English Association. Georgia Southern College. Dept. of English, Journalism, and Philosophy. (Dec. 1973)-. Periodical. English. Twice a year. $5.00. Valdosta State College, Department of English, Valdosta GA 31698. **Tel** (912)333-5946. **ED** Richard A. Keithley. **LC** PE68.U5; N67. **DD** 820/.7.

US/0738-8624
NOTES PLUS. See Education-Teaching and Curriculum.

JA
NOTORU DAMU SEISHIN JOSJI DAIGAKU KIYO : GAIKOKUGO GAIKOKU BUNGAKU HEN. **Main/Corp** Notoru
Damu Seishin Josji Daigaku. **VFOAT** Notre Dame Seishin University Kiyo: Foreign Language Studies, Foreign Literature. V. 1- 1977-. Multiple languages (English and Japanese). Notoru Damu Seishin Joshi Daigaku, 16-9 Ifukucho 2, Okayama 700 Japan. **LC** P9. N68A.
***Supersedes** Kiyo.*

CN/0821-4549
NOUVELLES - ASSOCIATION DES PROFESSEURS DE FRANCAIS DES UNIVERSITES ET COLLEGES CANADIENS. (NOUVELLES DE L'ASSOCIATION DES PROFESSEURS DE FRANCAIS DES UNIVERSITIES ET COLLEGES CANADIENS.). [Nouv. - Assoc. profr. fr. univ. coll. can.].
Added/Corp Association des Professeurs de Francais des Universites et Colleges Canadiens. Vol. 1, No 2 (1983)-. Periodical. French. sa. Distribution gratuite restreinte. Association des Professeurs de Francais des Universites et Colleges Canadiens, c/o D Thaler, Department of French, University of Victoria, PO Box 1700, Victoria British Columbia V8W 2Y2 Canada. **DD** 440/.7/1171. ***Continues** Nouvelles (Association des Professeurs de Francais des Universites et Colleges Canadiens)., 0821-4549.*

IT/0392-2332
NOUVELLES DE LA REPUBLIQUE DES LETTRES (NAPLES, ITALY). (NOUVELLES DE LA REPUBLIQUE DES LETTRES.). [Nouv. republ. lett.].
Added/Corp Istituto Italiano per Gli Studi Filosofici. (1981)-. Periodical. English (French, German, Italian and Spanish). sa. L75000 Italy; L110000 other. Prismi Editrice Politechnica Napoli, F Caracciolo 13, 80122 Naples Italy. **Tel** 011 39 81 7612884, FAX 081 668339. **ED** Paul Dibon and Tullio Gregory. **LC** AS222.N775; A28. **DD** 050. **Bk Rev. Ad Acc. Circ:** 500 (ctrl).
Ind/Abst MLA Int. Bibl. Books Artic. Mod. Lang. Lit.; Philos. Index.

FR
NOUVELLES INSTRUCTIONS POUR L'ENSEIGNEMENT DES LETTRES DANS LE SECOND CYCLE DU SECOND DEGRE / CENTRE REGIONAL DE DOCUMENTATION PEDAGOGIQUE DE PARIS, LES.
French. 37 rue Jacob, 75270 Paris Cedex 06 France. **LC** P57.F8; N68. **DD** 410/.7/12044.

RU
NOVAIA INOSTRANNAIA LITERATURA PO OBSHCHESTVENNYM NAUKAM: IAZYKOZNANIE.
Added/Corp Institut Nauchnoi Informatsii po Obshchestvennym Naukam (Akademiia Nauk SSSR). (1976)-. Multiple languages (Russian and Multiple languages). mo. 0.30rub (single issue). Izdatelstvo Nauka / Akademiia Nauk, Publishing House of the Russian Academy of Sciences, Leninskii Porspekt 14, 117901 Moscow Russia. **Tel** 011 95 954-21-53, FAX 011 95 938-21-44, telex 411964. **LC** Z7003; .N59; P9.
***Continues** Novaia Inostrannaia Literatura Po lazykoznaniiu.*

RU
NOVAIA OTECHESTVENNAIA LITERATURA PO OBSHCHESTVENNYM NAUKAM. IAZYKOZNANIE / ROSSIISKAIA AKADEMIIA NAUK, INSTITUT NAUCHNOI INFORMATSII PO OBSHCHESTVENNYM NAUKAM. *Title Change.*
Added/Corp Institut Nauchnoi Informatsii po Obshchestvennym Naukam (Rossiiskaia Akademiia Nauk). **VFOAT** IAzykoznanie. (1992)-(1992). Periodical. Russian. mo. Inion An SSSR, Ulitsa Krasikova D 28/45, Moscow Russia. **Tel** 128.89.71. **(Subscription address:** East View Publications Inc., 3020 Harbor Lane North, Suite 110, Minneapolis MN 55447.**)** **LC** P106; .N68.
***Continues** Novaia Sovetskaia Literatura po Obshchestvennym Naukam. lazykoznanie, 0134-2762.*
***Continued by** Novaia Literatura po Sotsialnym i Gumanitarnym Naukam. IAzykoznanie.*

RU
NOVOE V RUSSKOI LEKSIKE : SLOVARNYE MATERIALY / AKADEMIIA NAUK SSSR, INSTITUT RUSSKOGO IAZYKA.
Added/Corp Institut Russkogo lazyka (Akademiia Nauk SSSR). (1977)-. Russian. an. 1.40rub. Izdatelstvo Russkii lazyk, K-9 Pushkinskaia Ulitsa, 103009 Moscow Russia. **LC** PG2680; .N68.

RU
NOVOE V ZARUBEZHNOI LINGVISTIKE.
Ceased. Vol. 8 (1978)-?. Periodical. Russian. Zubovskii Bulvar 17, Moscow 119021 Russia. **LC** P25; .N65.
***Continues** Novoe V Lingvistike.*

MX/0185-0121
NUEVA REVISTA DE FILOLOGIA HISPANICA. [Nueva rev. filol. hisp.].
Added/Corp Colegio de Mexico. Vol. 1 (July/Sept. 1947)-. Periodical. Spanish. sa (2 issues). $90.00 (institution) US and Canada. Colegio de Mexico AC, Camino Al Ajusco No 20, 10740 Mexico DF Mexico. **Tel** 011 52 5 6455955 Ext. 3133, telex 1777585 COLME. **ED** Beatriz Garza Cuaron. **LC** PC4008; .N84. **DD** 460.5. Index available (free). **Bk Rev. Ad Acc. Pr Rev. Circ:** 1,500.
Desc: Principal themes are on Hispanic and Hispanic American literature and Hispanic linguistics, theory and methodology on literature and linguistics, reviews, articles and a classified bibliography.
Ind/Abst Am. Hist. Life (1957-1974); HAPI Hisp. Am. Period. Index; Indice Hist. Esp. (1957-1974); MLA Int. Bibl. Books Artic. Mod. Lang. Lit.; Romant. Move.; Soc. Plann. Policy Dev. Abstr.; Sociol. Abstr.

IO
NUSA, LINGUISTIC STUDIES IN INDONESIAN AND LANGUAGES IN INDONESIA.
VFOAT N.U.S.A. Vol. 1 (1975)-. Monographic series. English. Nusa Linguistic Studies, PO Box 2811 JKT, Jakarta Indonesia.
Ind/Abst Linguist. Lang. Behav. Abstr. (1978-); Soc. Plann. Policy Dev. Abstr.

US
NWSS NEWS. (19??)-. Newsletter. English. bm.
$35.00 individuals, $50.00 institutions. Network of Women in Slavic Studies, PO Box 75586, Washington DC 20013. **Tel** (703)482-0171. **ED** Sally Stoecker.
Desc: Provides information on job and grant opportunities, Internet news, and announcements of meetings and special events.

HU/0029-6791
NYELVTUDOMANYI KOEZLEMENYEK.
[Nyelvtud. koezl.]. **Added/Corp** Magyar Tudomanyos Akademia, Budapest. Nyelvtudomanyi Bizottsag. Magyar Tudomanyos Akademia. Nyelv- es Irodalomtudomanyi Osztalya. (1862)-. Periodical. Hungarian. sa. $19.50. Magyar Tudomanyos Akademia, Nyelvtudomanyi Intezet, Szinhaz u. 5-9, 1014 Budapest, Hungary. **ED** L. Honti, M. Bakro-Nagy. **LC** AS142; .M313. **Bk Rev. Circ:** 700.
Ind/Abst Linguist. Lang. Behav. Abstr. (1972-) [Full Cov.]; MLA Int. Bibl. Books Artic. Mod. Lang. Lit.; Soc. Plann. Policy Dev. Abstr.

DK/0106-8040
NYS. NYDANSKE STUDIER & ALMEN KOMMUNIKATIONSTEORI. (NYDANSKE STUDIER & ALMEN KOMMUNIKATIONSTEORI : NYS.). [NyS, Nydan. stud. & almen kommunikationsteor.].
VFOAT Nydanske Studier og Almen Kommunikationsteori; NyS. (1970)-. Monographic series. Danish. **LC** PD3025; .N9. **DD** 439.8/1.
Ind/Abst MLA Int. Bibl. Books Artic. Mod. Lang. Lit.

RU
OBRABOTKA SIMVOLNOI INFORMATSII.
Main/Corp Akademiia Nauk SSSR. Vychislitelnyi Tsentr. Vol. 1, (1973)-. Academic Scholarly Publication. Russian. Izdatelstvo Nauka / Akademiia Nauk, Publishing House of the Russian Academy of Sciences, Leninskii Porspekt 14, 117901 Moscow Russia. **Tel** 011 95 954-21-53, FAX 011 95 938-21-44, telex 411964. **LC** P98; .A43a.

RU
OBSHCHESTVENNYE NAUKI V ROSSII. SERIIA 6, I AZYKOZNANIE / ROSSIISKAIA AKADEMIIA NAUK, INSTITUT NAUCHNOI INFORMATSII PO OBSHCHESTVENNYM NAUKAM. *Title Change.*
Added/Corp Institut Nauchnoi Informatsii po Obshchestvennym Naukam (Rossiiskaia Akademiia Nauk). **VFOAT** IAzykoznanie. **VAT** Obshchestvennye Nauki v Rossii. Seriia Shest, I Azykoznanie. (1992)-(1992). Academic Scholarly Publication. Russian (table of contents in English). bm. Izdatelstvo Nauka / Akademiia Nauk, Publishing House of the Russian Academy of Sciences, Leninskii Porspekt 14, 117901 Moscow Russia. **Tel** 011 95 954-21-53, FAX 011 95 938-21-44, telex 411964. **LC** P9; .08.
***Continues** Obshchestvennye Nauki v SSSR. Seriia 6, I Azykoznanie, 0202-2087.* ***Continued by** Sotsialnye i Gumanitarnye Nauki. Seriia 6, I Azykoznanie. Otechestvennaia Literatura.*

RU
OBSHCHESTVENNYE NAUKI ZA RUBEZHOM. SERIIA 6: IAZYKOZNANIE.
Added/Corp Akademiia Nauk SSSR. Institut Nauchnoi Informatsii i Fundamentalnaia Biblioteka po Obshchestvennym Naukam. **VFOAT** lazykoznanie. **VAT** Obshchestvennye Nauki za Rubezhom. Seriia Shest: lazykoznanie. (1973)-. Academic Scholarly Publication. Russian. qt. 0.70rub. Izdatelstvo Nauka / Akademiia Nauk, Publishing House of the Russian Academy of Sciences, Leninskii Porspekt 14, 117901 Moscow Russia. **Tel** 011 95 954-21-53, FAX 011 95 938-21-44, telex 411964. **ED** F M Berezin. **LC** P9; .O25.

AT/0042-0093
OCCASIONAL PAPER - UNIVERSITY OF SYDNEY, AUSTRALIAN LANGUAGE RESEARCH CENTRE. [Occas. pap. - Univ. Syd., Aust. Lang. Res. Centr.].
Main/Corp Sydney. University. Australian Language Research Centre. No. 1-. English. University of Sydney, 116 Darlington Road / H42, Sydney NSW 2006 Australia. **Tel** 011 61 2 6922666. **LC** PE3601; .S9.

AT/0314-3937
OCCASIONAL PAPERS - APPLIED LINGUISTICS ASSOCIATION OF AUSTRALIA. [Occas. pap. - Appl. Linguist. Assoc. Aust.].
Main/Corp Applied Linguistics Association of Australia. No. 1 (1977)-. Monographic series. English. ir. Price varies per volume; Also comes with Applied Linguistics Association of Australia membership. Applied Linguistics Association of Australia / ALAA, Centre for Language Learning and Teaching, University of Southern Queensland, Toowoomba, Queensland 4350 Australia. **Tel** 011 61 06 281 3366, telex 062813096. **Pr Rev.**
Ind/Abst Linguist. Lang. Behav. Abstr. (1978-) [Full Cov.]; Soc. Plann. Policy Dev. Abstr.

US/0889-6356
OCCASIONAL PAPERS IN LANGUAGE, LITERATURE AND LINGUISTICS. SERIES A. [Occas. pap. lang. lit. linguist., Ser. A].
No. 1 (Nov. 1966)-. Monographic series. English. **DD** 400.
Ind/Abst MLA Int. Bibl. Books Artic. Mod. Lang. Lit.

US/0885-5773
OCCASIONAL PAPERS ON LINGUISTICS. [Occas. pap. linguist.].
Added/Corp Southern Illinois University at Carbondale. Dept. of Linguistics. No. 1 (1977)-. Monographic series. English. **LC** UNC. **DD** 410.
Ind/Abst MLA Int. Bibl. Books Artic. Mod. Lang. Lit.

UK
OCCASIONAL PAPERS / UNIVERSITY OF ESSEX, DEPARTMENT OF LANGUAGE AND LINGUISTICS.
Added/Corp University of Essex. Dept. of Language and Linguistics. (19??)-. Monographic series. English.
Ind/Abst Linguist. Lang. Behav. Abstr. (1974-) [Full Cov.]; Soc. Plann. Policy Dev. Abstr.

US/0029-8115
OCEANIC LINGUISTICS. [Ocean. linguist.].
Added/Corp Southern Illinois University at Carbondale. Dept. of Anthropology. University of Hawaii (Honolulu). Dept. of Linguistics. Vol. 1 (Summer 1962)-. Periodical. English. sa (Summer and Winter). $26.00 (one year), $47.00 (two year), institutions, US and Canada; $31.00 (one year), $56.00 (two year), institutions, other; $20.00 (one year), $36.00 (two year) individuals, US and Canada; $21.00 (one year), $38.00 (two year), individuals, other. University of Hawaii Press, 2840 Kolowalu Street, Honolulu HI 96822. **Tel** (808)956-8833, (808)948-8697, FAX (808)988-6052. **ED** Byron W. Bender. **LC** PL5001; .O25. **DD** 499/.2. **Bk Rev. Ad Acc. Circ:** 375. available on microfilm from University Microfilms International (UMI).
Desc: Devoted exclusively to the study of the indigenous

languages of the Oceanic area: the aboriginal languages of Australia, the Papuan languages spoken in New Guinea, and the languages of the Austronesian family. Covers issues of linguistic theory that pertain to languages of the area, report research on historical relations, or furnish new information about inadequately described languages.
Ind/Abst Anthropol. Lit.; Int. Bibliogr. Sociol.; Linguist. Lang. Behav. Abstr. (1971-) [Full Cov.]; MLA Int. Bibl. Books Artic. Mod. Lang. Lit.; Soc. Plann. Policy Dev. Abstr.

US/0078-3188
OCEANIC LINGUISTICS. SPECIAL PUBLICATION. [Ocean. linguist., Spec. publ.]. **Added/Corp** University of Hawaii (Honolulu). Pacific and Asian Linguistics Institute. (1966)-. Monographic series. English. ir. Price varies per volume. University of Hawaii Press, 2840 Kolowalu Street, Honolulu HI 96822. **Tel** (808)956-8833, (808)948-8697, FAX (808)988-6052. **LC** UNC. **DD** 499.
Ind/Abst MLA Int. Bibl. Books Artic. Mod. Lang. Lit.

DK/0078-3293
ODENSE UNIVERSITY STUDIES IN ENGLISH. [Odense Univ. stud. Engl.]. **Main/Corp** Odense Universitet. **Added/Corp** Odense Universitet. Vol. 1 (1969)-. Monographic series. English. ir. Price varies per volume. Odense University Press, 55 Campusvej, DK-5230 Odense M Denmark. **Tel** 66 15 79 99, FAX 66 15 81 26. **LC** UNC. **Bk Rev**. **Ad Acc**. ctrl circ.
Desc: Language studies of English and American literature.
Ind/Abst MLA Int. Bibl. Books Artic. Mod. Lang. Lit.

DK
ODENSE UNIVERSITY STUDIES IN SCANDINAVIAN LANGUAGES AND LITERATURES. **Added/Corp** Odense Universitet. Vol. 3 (1972)-. Monographic series. Danish (English). ir. Price varies per volume. Odense University Press, 55 Campusvej, DK-5230 Odense M Denmark. **Tel** 66 15 79 99, FAX 66 15 81 26. **LC** PD1513; .O3. ***Continues*** *Odense Universitet. Studies in Scandinavian Languages.*
Desc: Scandinavian literature and linguistics.

KO
OEGUK MUNHWA YONGU. **VFOAT** Foreign Cultural Research. Periodical. English (Korean). Choson Taehakkyo Oeguk Munhwa Yonguso, 17 Pullo-dong, Tong-ku Kwangju-si Korea. **LC** P9; .O34.

US/0030-1035
OHIO READING TEACHER. [Ohio read. teach.]. **Added/Corp** Ohio Council of the International Reading Association. Ohio. State University, Bowling Green. College of Education. Vol. 1 (1967)-. Periodical. English. qt. $12.00 US; $24.00 other. Miami University / 401 McGuffey Hall, Oxford OH 45056. **Tel** (513)529-6451. **ED** Carolyn Andrews-Beck. **Bk Rev**, (Qty: 16). **Ad Acc**. **Pr Rev**. **Circ:** 1,500. available on microfilm from University Microfilms International (UMI).
Desc: Publishes original manuscripts relating to reading and language instruction. Contains articles dealing with practical suggestions and current issues.
Ind/Abst Curr. Index J. Educ.; Lang. Lang. Behav. Abstr.; Soc. Plann. Policy Dev. Abstr.

JA
OKINAWA KOKUSAI DAIGAKU BUNGAKUBU KIYO: EIBUNGAKKA-HEN. **Main/Corp** Okinawa Kokusai Daigaku. Eibungakka. **VFOAT** Bulletin of Department of English, Okinawa Kokusai University. English (Japanese). Okinawa Kokusai Daigaku Bungakubu, 276-2 Aza Ginowan, Okinawa-ken, Ginowan Japan. **LC** PE9; .O37A. **DD** 425/.05. **UDC** 802.0.

US/0030-1833
OKLAHOMA READER, THE. **Added/Corp** Oklahoma Reading Council. Vol. 1 (1966)-. Periodical. English. Three times a year (Fall, Winter, Spring). $10.00. Oklahoma Reading Council, Sec./Treasurer D. Dillen, 1900 Rolling Ridge, Bethany OK 73008. **Tel** (405)329-8743. **ED** Tim Green. **Ad Acc**. **Circ:** 1,800 (ctrl).
Desc: The professional journal of the Oklahoma reading council accepts articles dealing with reading instruction-teacher, training-classroom management and educational philosophies.

US/0739-8549
OLD ENGLISH NEWSLETTER. SUBSIDIA. **See** Literature.

KO
OLLON HAKPO. **VFOAT** Hanyang Communication Review. V. 1- (1980)-. Periodical. Korean (summaries and/or abstracts in English). Hanyang Taehakkyo Sinmun Pangsong Yonguso, 17 Haengdang-dong, Seongdong-gu 133, Seoul South Korea. **LC** P92.K6; O45.

KO
OMUN YONGU. V. 1- Oct. 1973-. Periodical. Korean. 200 each issue. Ilchogak, 9 Kongpyong-dong Chongno-ku, Seoul Korea. **LC** PL901; .O47.

KO
ONO. **VFOAT** Linguistic Journal of Korea. Vol. 1 (1976)-. Periodical. English (German and Korean). $6.00 members, $4.00 students. Linguistics Society of Korea, Ewha Womans University, 11-1 Daehyun, Seoul 120 Korea. **LC** P9; .O55. **UDC** 800.

KO
ONO (CHUNGNAM TAEHAKKYO. PUSOL ONO HULLYONWON). (ONO.). **VFOAT** Language. Periodical. English (Korean). an. Chungnam Taehakkyo Pusol Ono Hullyonwon, 220 Kungdon-ri Yusong-Up, Chungnam Korea 300-31. **LC** P9; .O553.

KO
ONOHAK. **VFOAT** Eoneohag. V. 1- 1976-. Periodical. Korean (summaries and/or abstracts in English and French). Hanguk Ono Hakhoe, c/o Department of Linguistics, Seoul National University, Seoul 151 Korea. **LC** P9. **UDC** 809.57.

BE/0078-463X
ONOMA. [Onoma]. **Added/Corp** International Centre of Onomastics. International Committee of Onomastic Sciences. Vol. 1 (1950)-. Periodical. French (English). Three times a year. 3000F. Editions Peeters SA, Bondgenotenlaan 153, BP 41, B-3000 Leuven Belgium. **Tel** 32 16 235170, FAX 32 16 228500, telex 65987 PUL B. **ED** K. Roelandts and W. van Langendonck. **LC** P323; .O6. Index available. cum. index. **Bk Rev**. ctrl circ.
Desc: Information from the International Committee of Onomastic Sciences.
Ind/Abst Br. Archaeol. Bibliogr.; Middle East Abstr. Index; MLA Int. Bibl. Books Artic. Mod. Lang. Lit.; Soc. Plann. Policy Dev. Abstr.

CN/0078-4656
ONOMASTICA CANADIANA. [Onomast. Can.]. **Added/Corp** Canadian Institute of Onomastic Sciences. Ukrainska Vilna Akademiia Nauk. (1967)-. Periodical. English (French). sa. 20.00Can$. Canadian Society for the Study of Names, York University Department of Literature and Linguistics, North York ONT M3J 1PC Canada. **Tel** (905)736-2100, (905)736-5016. **ED** W. Ahrens. **LC** F1004; .O5. **DD** 917.1/003. **Bk Rev**, (Qty: 10-12). **Pr Rev**. **Circ:** 200.
Desc: Content covers any subject relating to names. Preference is given to geographical and personal names relating to Canada.
Ind/Abst Can. Period. Index (19??-); MLA Int. Bibl. Books Artic. Mod. Lang. Lit.

CI/0475-0934
ONOMASTICA JUGOSLAVICA. [Onomast. Jugosl.]. **Added/Corp** Meuakademijski Odbor za Onomastiku. Jugoslavenska Akademija Znanosti i Umjetnosti. Razred za Filologiju. (1969)-. Multiple languages (, Macedonian and Slovenian; summaries and/or abstracts in English, French, German and Russian). an. **LC** PG451; .O54.
Ind/Abst MLA Int. Bibl. Books Artic. Mod. Lang. Lit.

XR
ONOMASTICKY ZPRAVODAJ CSAV. **VFOAT** Onomasticheskii Biulleten Chekhoslovatskoi Akademii Nauk; Onomastic Bulletin of the Czechoslovak Academy of Sciences. V. 24, No. 1-2-. Periodical. Czech (Polish, German and Russian). an. Free. Onomasticky usek UJC CSAV, Krakovska 10, 110 000 Prague 1 Czech Republic. **Tel** 264 301. **ED** Miloslava Knappova. **LC** PAR. cum. index. **Bk Rev**. **Ad Acc**. **Circ:** 350 (ctrl). ***Continues*** *Zpravodaj Mistopisne Komise Csav.*
Desc: Publishes articles dealing with personal and place names studies.

GR
ONOMATA : REVUE ONOMASTIQUE. an. Dr25.00. Soc Onomast Grecque, Sebastopol St 107, 115 26 Athens Greece.

JA/0911-0402
ONSEIGAKKAI KAIHO. **Main/Corp** Nihon Onseigakkai. **VFOAT** The Bulletin; Bulletin. No. 1 (1926)-. English (Japanese). Three times a year. ¥6,000. Nihon Onseigakkai, 13-12 Daita Japan. **Tel** 03-414-5363. **ED** Masao Onishi. **LC** PL541; .N54A. **UDC** 801.4. **Circ:** 1,300.
Desc: Brief essays (about 2,000 words) on phonetics: speech theory, speech education, speech pathology and speech art.
Ind/Abst Linguist. Lang. Behav. Abstr. (1972-) [Full Cov.]; MLA Int. Bibl. Books Artic. Mod. Lang. Lit.; Soc. Plann. Policy Dev. Abstr.; Sociol. Abstr.

NE
ONZE TAAL (AMSTERDAM, NETHERLANDS). (ONZE TAAL : ORGAAN VAN HET GENOOTSCHAAP "ONZE TAAL".). **Added/Corp** Genootschaap Onze Taal (Netherlands). Vol. 1, No. 1 (March 1932)-. Periodical. Dutch. Ten times a year (Feb./Mar. and July/Aug. issues combined). F43.00. Genootschap Onze Taal, Laan van Meedervoort 14 A, 2517 AK The Hague Netherlands. **Tel** 011 33 70 3561220. **ED** Frank Jansen, Erik van der Spek and Peter Smulders. **Bk Rev**. **Circ:** 15,500.
Desc: Covers all aspects of the Dutch language including spelling, grammar, idioms, dialects, new words, etymology, new trends, etc. Helps the layman to use his own language as correctly as possible.

US/0147-9962
ORAL ENGLISH. (OE, ORAL ENGLISH.). **Added/Corp** Le Moyne College. Vol 1 (Winter 1972)-. Periodical. English. qt. $1.00. **LC** PN4145; .O17. **DD** 810/.9/0054.
Ind/Abst Annu. Bibliogr. Engl. Lang. Lit.

BE/0030-4379
ORBIS; BULLETIN INTERNATIONAL DE DOCUMENTATION LINGUISTIQUE. (ORBIS / CENTRE INTERNATIONAL DE DIALECTOLOGIE GENERALE, PRES L'UNIVERSITE CATHOLIQUE DE LOUVAIN.). [Orbis; bull. int. doc. linguist.]. **Added/Corp** Centre International de Dialectologie Generale. (1952)-. Periodical. French (Multiple languages). an. 2700F. Editions Peeters SA, Bondgenotenlaan 153, BP 41, B-3000 Leuven Belgium. **Tel** 32 16 235170, FAX 32 16 228500, telex 65987 PUL B. **ED** R. Bosteels and P. Swiggers. **LC** P2; .O7. **Bk Rev**, (Qty: 15).
Ind/Abst Am. Bibliogr. Slavic East Europ. Stud.; Annu. Bibliogr. Engl. Lang. Lit.; Index Book Rev. Humanit. (1985-); Lang. Teach.; MLA Int. Bibl. Books Artic. Mod. Lang. Lit.

US/0146-678X
ORIENTAL INSTITUTE COMMUNICATIONS. **Main/Corp** University of Chicago. Oriental Institute. **Added/Corp** University of Chicago. Oriental Institute. No. 1 (1922)-. Monographic series. English. ir. Price varies per volume. University of Chicago Oriental Institute, 1155 East 58th Street, Chicago IL 60637. **Tel** (312)702-9537. **LC** PJ2; .C5. **DD** 956/.005.

BE/0474-6627
ORIENTALIA GANDENSIA. **Added/Corp** Rijksuniversiteit te Gent. Hoger Instituut voor Oosterse, Oosteuropese en Afrikaanse Taalkunde en Geschiedenis. Rijksuniversiteit te Gent. Sektie Niet-Westerse Filologie. (1964)-. Monographic series. Dutch (English and Russian). **LC** P1; .074.
Ind/Abst MLA Int. Bibl. Books Artic. Mod. Lang. Lit.

SW/0085-4522
ORIENTALIA GOTHOBURGENSIA. (1969)-. Monographic series. Swedish.
Ind/Abst MLA Int. Bibl. Books Artic. Mod. Lang. Lit.

BE/0085-4522
ORIENTALIA LOVANIENSIA PERIODICA. **Added/Corp** Katholieke Universiteit te Leuven. Instituut voor Orientalistiek. (1970)-. Multiple languages (English, French and German). an. 1600F. Editions Peeters SA, Bondgenotenlaan 153, BP 41, B-3000 Leuven Belgium. **Tel** 32 16 235170, FAX 32 16 228500, telex 65987 PUL B. **ED** G. Pollet, J. Quaegebeur, U. Vermeulen, L. Van Rompay, A. Schoors, K. Van Lerberghe, H. Vanstiphout, U. Libbrecht, W. Vande Walle. **LC** DS1; .O63. Index available. **Bk Rev**. ctrl circ.
Ind/Abst Int. Bibliogr. Sociol.; MLA Int. Bibl. Books Artic. Mod. Lang. Lit.; Old Testam. Abstr.; Soc. Plann. Policy Dev. Abstr.; Middle East J.

GW
ORIENTALISTISCHE LITERATURZEITUNG. **VFOAT** OLZ. Vol. 12, No. 1 (1909)-. Periodical. German. bm. $260.00. Akademie-Verlag GmbH, Muehlenstrasse 33 34, D 13162 Berlin Germany. **Tel** 011 49 30 47889300, FAX 011 49 30 47889357. **(Subscription address:** VCH Publishers Inc., 303 Northwest 12th Avenue, Journals Department, Deerfield FL 33442.) ***Continues*** *Orientalistische Litteratur-Zeitung.*
Ind/Abst Index Book Rev. Relig.; Old Testam. Abstr.

US/0192-401X
ORTESOL JOURNAL, THE. **Main/Corp** Oregon Teachers of English to Speakers of Other Languages. **VAT** The Oregon Teachers of English to Speakers of Other Languages Journal. Vol. 1 (1979)-. Periodical. English. ir. $8.95. Oregon Teacher English Speaker Other Languages (ORTESOL), 15203 Southeast River, Forest Drive, Milwaukie OR 97222. **LC** PE1128.A2; O73a. **DD** 428.2/4/07. **CODEN** ORJOEQ.
Ind/Abst Soc. Plann. Policy Dev. Abstr.

SW/0473-4351
ORTNAMNSSALLSKAPETS I UPPSALA ARSSKRIFT. [Ortnamnssallsk. Upps. arsskr.]. **Main/Corp** Ortnamnssallskapet i Uppsala (Sweden). (1936)-. Swedish. an. **LC** WMLC L 83/84.
Ind/Abst Annu. Bibliogr. Engl. Lang. Lit.; MLA Int. Bibl. Books Artic. Mod. Lang. Lit.

US
OSAMAYOR : GRADUATE STUDENT MAGAZINE / DEPT. OF HISPANIC L & L, UNIVERSITY OF PITTSBURGH. **Added/Corp** University of Pittsburgh. Dept. of Hispanic Languages and Literatures. Vol. 1, No. 1 (Apr. 1989)-. Periodical. Spanish (English and Portuguese). sa.
Ind/Abst MLA Int. Bibl. Books Artic. Mod. Lang. Lit.

II/0970-0277
OSMANIA PAPERS IN LINGUISTICS. [Osmania pap. linguist.]. V. 1- Feb. 1975-. Periodical. English. an. Rs15.00 India; $3.00 other. Osmania University Department of Linguistics, Hyderabad 500007 India. **Tel** 868951/227. **LC** P1; .O84. **DD** 410/.5. **UDC** 800. **Circ:** 500 (ctrl).

RU
OSNOVY BALKANSKOGO IAZYKOZNANIIA. **Added/Corp** Institut Iazykoznaniia (Akademiia nauk SSSR). Leningradskoe Otdelenie. (1990)-. Monographic series. Russian. ir. Price varies per volume. Izdatelstvo Nauka St. Petersburg, Mendeleevskaia Liniia 1, 199034 St. Petersburg, B-34 Russia. **Tel** 218-26-12.

US/0737-8858
OUTLOOK FOR THE MEDIA. (OUTLOOK FOR THE MEDIA / PAINE WEBBER MITCHELL HUTCHINS, INC. ... ANNUAL CONFERENCE.). [Outlook media]. **Main/Corp** Paine, Webber, Mitchell, Hutchins. Conference. 10th (1983)-. English. an. $85.00. Knowledge Industry Publications Inc, 701 Westchester Avenue, White Plains NY 10604. **Tel** (914)328-9157, (800)800-5474, FAX (914)328-9093. **LC** P96.F672; .U626A. **DD** 001.51/0973. ***Continues*** *Annual Conference on the Outlook for the Media.*

UK
OXFORD MODERN LANGUAGES AND LITERATURE MONOGRAPHS. (19??)-. Monographic series. English. ir. Price varies per volume. Oxford University Press / New York, 200 Madison Avenue, New York NY 10016. **Tel** (212)679-7300, (919)677-0977, (800)451-7556, (800)445-9714, FAX (919)677-1303.
Ind/Abst MLA Int. Bibl. Books Artic. Mod. Lang. Lit.

UK/0078-7256
OXFORD SLAVONIC PAPERS. **See** Linguistics-Abstracting, Bibliographies and Statistics.

●US/1065-8491
P.S.I. GUIDE, PREFIX/SUFFIX IDENTIFICATION FOR BEARINGS. **Added/Corp** Interchange, Inc. **VFOAT** P.S.I. Guide, Prefix Suffix Identification for Bearings; Prefix Suffix Identification for Bearings; Prefix/Suffix Identification for Bearings. **VAT** Prefix Suffix Identification Guide. (1992)-. English. be. Interchange Inc, PO Box 16244, St Louis Park MN 55416. **Tel** (612)929-6669, (800)669-6208, FAX (612)929-0395.

CC
PA SHIH NIEN TAI SAN WEN HSUAN / PA SHIH NIEN TAI SAN WEN HSUAN PIEN CHI TSU HSUAN PIEN. **VFOAT** Bashi Niandai Sanwenxuan. Began in 1980. Periodical. Chinese. an. RMBY0.66. Hsin Hua Shu Tien / Shang-Hai Fa Hsing So, Shanghai, People's Republic of China. **LC** PL2623; .P28. **DD** 895.1/45/08. **UDC** 809.51.

AT
PACIFIC LINGUISTICS. SERIES A. **Added/Corp** Australian National University. Research School of Pacific Studies. Dept. of Linguistics. (19??)-. Monographic series. English. ir. Price varies per volume. National Center for Development Studies, Australian National University, Canberra ACT 0200 Australia. **Tel** 011 61 6 2492760, FAX 011 61 6 2495525. **ED** S. Wurm. **LC** P11; .P3. **DD** 410. Index available. ***Continues*** *Pacific Linguistics. Series A, Occasional Papers.*

AT/0078-754X
PACIFIC LINGUISTICS. SERIES B: MONOGRAPHS. **Added/Corp** Australian National University Linguistic Circle of Canberra. No. 7 (1968)-. Monographic series. English. ir. Price varies per volume. National Center for Development Studies, Australian National University, Canberra ACT 0200 Australia. **Tel** 011 61 6 2492760, FAX 011 61 6 2495525. ***Continues*** *Linguistic Circle of Canberra Publications Series B: Monographs.*

AT/0078-7558
PACIFIC LINGUISTICS. SERIES C: BOOKS. **Added/Corp** Linguistic Circle of Canberra. No. 1 (1965)-. Monographic series. English. ir. Price varies per volume. National Center for Development Studies, Australian National University, Canberra ACT 0200 Australia. **Tel** 011 61 6 2492760, FAX 011 61 6 2495525. **ED** S. A. Wurm. Index available. cum. index.

AT/0078-7566
PACIFIC LINGUISTICS. SERIES D: SPECIAL PUBLICATIONS. **Added/Corp** Linguistic Circle of Canberra. Australian National University. Research School of Pacific Studies. Dept. of Linguistics. No. 3 (1971)-. Monographic series. English. ir. Price varies per volume. National Center for Development Studies, Australian National University, Canberra ACT 0200 Australia. **Tel** 011 61 6 2492760, FAX 011 61 6 2495525. **ED** S. A. Wurm. **LC** UNC. available on audiocassette. ***Continues*** *Linguistic Circle of Canberra. Bulletin.*

GW
PALAESTRA ... UNTERSUCHUNGEN UND TEXTE AUS DER DEUTSCHEN UND ENGLISCHEN PHILOLOGIE. (1898)-. Monographic series. German. ir. Price varies per volume. Vandenhoeck & Ruprecht, Robert Bosch Breite 6, D-37079 Goettingen Germany. **Tel** 011 49 551 695911, FAX 011 49 551 695917, telex 965226 VAN d.

FR/0031-0387
PALLAS (TOULOUSE, FRANCE). (PALLAS.). **Added/Corp** Universite de Toulouse. Faculte des Lettres. Universite de Toulouse. Faculte des Lettres et Sciences Humaines. Universite de Toulouse-Le Mirail. (1953)-. French (summaries and/or abstracts in English). Twice a year. 200.00F. Universite de Toulouse--Le Mirail, 56 Rue du Taur, 31000 Toulouse France. **Tel** 011 33 61 225831, FAX 011 33 61 218420. **(Subscription address:** Regisseur SVC des Publications, 56 rue du Taur, U Toulouse Mira, 31000 Toulouse France.**)** **LC** PA2; .P34. **DD** 937/.005.

PL/0078-866X
PAMIETNIK SOWIANSKI. [Pam. sow.]. **Added/Corp** Uniwersytet Jagiellonski. Studium Sowianskie. Polska Akademia Nauk. Komitet Sowianoznawstwa. Vol. 1 (1949)-. Periodical. Polish. an. $25.00. **(Subscription address:** ARS Polona, PO Box 1001, 00068 Warsaw Poland.**)** **LC** D377; .P27.
Ind/Abst MLA Int. Bibl. Books Artic. Mod. Lang. Lit.

KO
PANGON. 1 (1979. 1.)-. Periodical. Korean. sa. W1,300. Hanguk Chongsin Munhwa Yonguwon, 50 Unjung-dong, Songnam-si Korea. **LC** PL941; .A26.

GW
PAPER. SERIES B. **Added/Corp** L.A.U.D. (Organization). No. 157 (Nov. 1986)-. Monographic series. English (German). Price varies per volume. ***Continues*** *Paper. Series C (L.A.U.D.T. (Organization)).*

GW
PAPER. SERIES C. **Added/Corp** L.A.U.D. (Organization). **VFOAT** Series C. Monographic series. German (English). Price varies per volume. ***Continues*** *Paper. Series C (L.A.U.D.T. (Organization)).*

PL/0137-2459
PAPERS AND STUDIES IN CONTRASTIVE LINGUISTICS. [Pap. stud. contrastive linguist.]. **Added/Corp** Uniwersytet im. Adama Mickiewicza w Poznaniu. Center for Applied Linguistics. **VFOAT** Polish-English Contrastive Project; Polish English Contrastive Project. (1973)-. English (German). ir. Price varies per volume. Adam Mickiewicz University Press, Nowowiejskiego 55, 61734 Poznan Poland. **Tel** 011 48 527-380, FAX 011 48 61-526425. **ED** Jacek Fisiak. **LC** P134; .P36. **DD** 410/.5. **Bk Rev. Ad Acc. Circ:** 1,200 (ctrl).
Desc: Devoted to contrastive and comparative linguistics; carries original contributions, both applied and theoretical, concerning English and other languages.
Ind/Abst Linguist. Lang. Behav. Abstr. (1973-) [Full Cov.]; MLA Int. Bibl. Books Artic. Mod. Lang. Lit.; Soc. Plann. Policy Dev. Abstr.

US/0895-7894
PAPERS IN APPLIED LINGUISTICS--MICHIGAN. (PAPERS IN APPLIED LINGUISTICS--MICHIGAN : PALM.). [Papers appl. linguist. Mich.]. **Added/Corp** University of Michigan. English Language Institute. **VFOAT** PALM; Papers in Applied Linguistics, Michigan. Vol. 1, No. 1 (Fall 1985)-. Periodical. English. sa. $12.50. English Language Institute PALM, 1 Ctr Intl Prog, Michigan State University, East Lansing MI 48824. **Tel** (313)764-2413. **DD** 418.
Ind/Abst Linguist. Lang. Behav. Abstr. (1985-); Soc. Plann. Policy Dev. Abstr.

AT/0078-9062
PAPERS IN AUSTRALIAN LINGUISTICS. [Pap. Aust. linguist.]. **Added/Corp** Linguistic Circle of Canberra. Australian National University. Research School of Pacific Studies. Dept. of Linguistics. No. 1 (1967)-. Monographic series. English. ir. Price varies per volume. Anutech Pty Limited, GPO Box 4, Canberra Act, 2601 Australia. **Tel** 011 61 6 2492479, FAX 011 61 6 2575088. **LC** P11; .P3 subser. **DD** 499/.15/05. Index available. cum. index. **Bk Rev. Pr Rev. Circ:** 80.
Ind/Abst MLA Int. Bibl. Books Artic. Mod. Lang. Lit.

AT
PAPERS IN AUSTRONESIAN LINGUISTICS. **Added/Corp** Australian National University. Research School of Pacific Studies. Dept. of Linguistics. Linguistic Circle of Canberra. No. 1 (1991)-. Monographic series. English. ir. Price varies per volume. Anutech Pty Limited, GPO Box 4, Canberra Act, 2601 Australia. **Tel** 011 61 6 2492479, FAX 011 61 6 2575088. **LC** PL5021; .P37. Index available. cum. index.

AT/0078-9127
PAPERS IN LINGUISTICS OF MELANESIA. ***Title Change.*** [Pap. linguist. Melanes.]. (1968)-(19??). English. ir. Anutech Pty Limited, GPO Box 4, Canberra Act, 2601 Australia. **Tel** 011 61 6 2492479, FAX 011 61 6 2575088. **LC** P11; .P3 subser; PL6201. **DD** 410/.5. ***Absorbed by*** *Papers in Austronesian Linguistics.*
Ind/Abst MLA Int. Bibl. Books Artic. Mod. Lang. Lit.

AT/0078-9143
PAPERS IN PHILIPPINE LINGUISTICS. ***Title Change.*** [Pap. Philipp. linguist.]. No. 1 (1966)-(19??). Monographic series. English. ir. Anutech Pty Limited, GPO Box 4, Canberra Act, 2601 Australia. **Tel** 011 61 6 2492479, FAX 011 61 6 2575088. **LC** P11; .P3 subser. **DD** 499/.21/05. ***Absorbed by*** *Papers in Austronesian Linguistics.*
Ind/Abst MLA Int. Bibl. Books Artic. Mod. Lang. Lit.

AT/0811-0026
PAPERS IN PIDGIN AND CREOLE LINGUISTICS. [Pap. Pidgin Creole linguist.]. **Added/Corp** Linguistic Circle of Canberra. Australian National University. Research School of Pacific Studies. Dept. of Linguistics. (1978)-. Monographic series. English. ir. Price varies per volume. Anutech Pty Limited, GPO Box 4, Canberra Act, 2601 Australia. **Tel** 011 61 6 2492479, FAX 011 61 6 2575088. **LC** P11; .P3 subser.; PM7801. **DD** 410/.5; 417/.22. Index available. cum. index. **Bk Rev. Circ:** 80.
Ind/Abst MLA Int. Bibl. Books Artic. Mod. Lang. Lit.

US/0195-7260
PAPERS IN ROMANCE. ***Suspended.*** [Pap. roman.]. Vol. 1- Spring 1979-?. Periodical. English. Three times a year. $28.00. Papers in Romance, Romance Languages, GN 60, University of Washington, Seattle WA 98198. **Tel** (206)545-2084, (206)543-2075. **LC** PC1; .P36. **DD** 440/.05. **UDC** 804.
Ind/Abst MLA Int. Bibl. Books Artic. Mod. Lang. Lit.

US/0161-8822
PAPERS IN SLAVIC PHILOLOGY. [Pap. Slav. philol.]. **Added/Corp** University of Michigan. Dept. of Slavic Languages and Literatures. (1977)-. Monographic series. English. ir. price varies per volume. University of Michigan / Michigan Slavic Publications, 3040 Modern Language Building, Ann Arbor MI 48108. **Tel** (313)763-4496. **LC** PG13; .P36. **DD** 491.8/05.
Ind/Abst MLA Int. Bibl. Books Artic. Mod. Lang. Lit.

AT/0078-9178
PAPERS IN SOUTH EAST ASIAN LINGUISTICS. [Pap. South-East Asian linguist.]. **Added/Corp** Linguistic Circle of Canberra. Australian National University. Research School of Pacific Studies. Dept. of Linguistics. No. 1 (1967)-. Periodical. English. ir. Price varies per volume. Research School of Pacific Studies, ANU East Asian History, Canberra ACT 0200 Australia. **Tel** 011 61 6 2493140, FAX 011 61 6 2495525. **LC** P11; .P3 subser. **DD** 410/.959.
Ind/Abst MLA Int. Bibl. Books Artic. Mod. Lang. Lit.

CN
PAPERS OF THE ... ALGONQUIAN CONFERENCE. **Main/Conf** Algonquian Conference. **Added/Corp** National Museums of Canada. Carleton University. **VFOAT** Actes du ... Congres des Algonquinistes. (1968)-. English (French). an. 30.00Can$ Canada. Carleton University / Linguistics, Department of Linguistics, Ottawa Ontario K1S 5B6 Canada. **Tel** (613)788-2808, (613)788-2340. **LC** E99.A35; A44a.
Ind/Abst Anthropol. Lit.; MLA Int. Bibl. Books Artic. Mod. Lang. Lit.

GW
PAPIERE ZUR LINGUISTIK. (1979)-. Periodical. German. sa. Gunter Narr Verlag, Dishingerweg 5, D 72070 Tuebingen Germany. **Tel** 011 49 7071 78091, FAX (07071)75288. **ED** Johannes Bechert and Willi Mayerthaler. **LC** P3; .P35. **Bk Rev. Ad Acc. Circ:** 800. ***Continues*** *Munchener Papiere zur Linguistik.*
Desc: Analyzes theoretical linguistics and its connection with the analytical philosophy of formal and normal language.
Ind/Abst Linguist. Lang. Behav. Abstr. (1982-) [Full Cov.]; MLA Int. Bibl. Books Artic. Mod. Lang. Lit.; Soc. Plann. Policy Dev. Abstr.

GW/0341-3195
PAPIERE ZUR TEXTLINGUISTIK. [Pap. Textlinguist.]. **VFOAT** Papers in Textlinguistics. Vol. 1 (1972)-. Monographic series. Multiple languages (English, French and German). ir. Price varies per volume. Helmut Buske Verlag Hamburg, Postfach 760244, D 2000 Hamburg 76 F R Germany. **Tel** 011 49 40 5236739. **(Subscription address:** John Benjamins North America, PO Box 27519, Philadelphia PA 19118-0519.**)**
Desc: Series of monographs on textlinguistics.
Ind/Abst MLA Int. Bibl. Books Artic. Mod. Lang. Lit.

UK/0264-8334
PARAGRAPH (MODERN CRITICAL THEORY GROUP). (PARAGRAPH : THE JOURNAL OF THE MODERN CRITICAL THEORY GROUP.). [Paragraph (Mod. Crit. Theory Group)]. **Added/Corp** Modern Critical Theory Group (Great Britain). Vol. 1 (March 1983)-. Periodical. English. Three times a year. £43.00 UK and Europe; $83.00 US; £47.00 other. Edinburgh University Press, 22 George Square,

Edinburgh EH8 9LF Scotland. **Tel** 011 44 31 650 6207, FAX 011 44 31 662 0053. **ED** Felicity Baker. **LC** PN80; .P37. **DD** 700/.1. **[CCC]. Bk Rev. Ad Acc.** available on microfilm and microfiche from University Microfilms International (UMI). Documents available from The Genuine Article.
Desc: Articles and reviews in English exploring both critical theory in general and its application to literature and the other arts. Primary aim is to further the understanding and use of French critical thought in English-speaking countries.
Ind/Abst Arts Humanit. Citation Index [Full Cov.]; MLA Int. Bibl. Books Artic. Mod. Lang. Lit.; Res. Alert [Full Cov.]; Soc. Plann. Policy Dev. Abstr.

SZ
PARALLELES (UNIVERSITE DE GENEVE. ECOLE DE TRADUCTION ET D'INTERPRETATION). (PARALLELES : CAHIERS DE L'ECOLE DE TRADUCTION ET D'INTERPRETATION DE L'UNIVERSITE DE GENEVE.). **Added/Corp** Universite de Geneve. Ecole de Traduction et d'Interpretation. No. 1 (Feb. 1978)-. French (English, French, German, Italian and Spanish). an. Free. Ecole de Traduction et d'Interpetation, University of Geneve, 19 Place des Augustin, CH 1211 Geneva 4 Switzerland. **Tel** 011 41 22 7209333. **ED** Americo Ferrari. Index available. **Bk Rev. Circ:** 1,000 (ctrl).
Desc: A publication exclusively devoted to studies, articles and reviews in the field of translation and interpretation.

GR/0048-301X
PARNASSOS. [Parnassos]. **Added/Corp** Philologikos Syllogos Parnassos. (1959)-. Periodical. Greek, Modern (French, Italian and English). an. $80.00. Parnassos Literary Society, 8 St. George Karytsis Square, 10561 Athens Greece. **Tel** 011 30 1 3221917, FAX 011 30 1 3243398. **ED** Professor N. Livadary. **LC** PA5201; .P36. Index available. cum. index. **Bk Rev**, (Qty: 10). ctrl circ.
Ind/Abst MLA Int. Bibl. Books Artic. Mod. Lang. Lit.

IT/0031-2355
PAROLA DEL PASSATO, LA. See Classical Studies.

TH/0125-2488
PASAA. Added/Corp Sathaban Sun Phasa Angkrit (Thailand. Thabuang Mahawitthayalai). **VFOAT** Phasa. Vol. 3, No. 2 (Oct. 1973)-. Periodical. English (Thai). sa. $15.00. Chulalongkorn University, Language Institute, Phyathai Road, Bangkok 10330 Thailand. **Tel** 011 66 02 250 0982. **ED** Supanee Tianchareon. **LC** PE1068.T5; E53a. **DD** 428/.007/0593. **Bk Rev. Circ:** 500 (ctrl). ***Continues*** *English Language Center (Bangkok, Thailand) Bulletin of the English Language Center, 0857-6939.*
Desc: Presents information and ideas concerning issues in language learning and teaching, curriculum design and development, testing and evaluation, teacher training, research, brief reports and summaries.
Ind/Abst Lang. Teach.; Linguist. Lang. Behav. Abstr. (1972-) [Full Cov.]; MLA Int. Bibl. Books Artic. Mod. Lang. Lit.; Soc. Plann. Policy Dev. Abstr.; Sociol. Abstr.

AI/0130-6812
PATMA-BANASIRAKAN HANDES. [Patma-banasirakan andes]. **Added/Corp** Haykakan SSR Gitutyunneri Akademia. Haykakan SSH Gitutyunneri Akademia. **VFOAT** Istoriko-Filologicheskii Zhurnal. (1958)-. Periodical. Armenian (Russian). sa. $79.95. **(Subscription address:** East View Publications Inc., 3020 Harbor Lane North, Suite 110, Minneapolis MN 55447.**) LC** PAR. cum. index.
Ind/Abst Am. Hist. Life (1968-); ARTbibliogr. Mod.; MLA Int. Bibl. Books Artic. Mod. Lang. Lit.; Numis. Lit.

AT/0815-6816
PELANGI TOOWOOMBA. See Social Sciences.

FR/0182-7634
PELERIN D'ARES, LE. Periodical. English (French). qt. **LC** BL875.F8; P45.

SP
PERFICIT. Added/Corp Centro de Perfeccionamiento Clasico. Centro Superior de Perfeccionamiento Clasico. (1942)-. Bibliography. Spanish. Twice a year. $12.00. Revista Perficit, Apartado 340, 11137080 Salamanca Spain. **Tel** 011 34 23 225800, FAX 923-254275. **ED** Mlejandro Barcenilla. **LC** PA9; .P47. Index available. **Bk Rev**, (Qty: 100). **Acid Free. Circ:** 600.
Desc: Information on classical philology.

US/1059-0536
PERSPECTIVA (SOUTH HADLEY, MASS.). (PERSPECTIVA.). **Added/Corp** Educational News Service. (198?)-. Periodical. Spanish. mo. $18.00 (1 year), $32.00 (2 year) US; $25.00 (1 year), Canada; $35.00 (1 year) other. Education News Service, PO Box 60478, Florence MA 01075. **Tel** (413)586-4490. **ED** Bonifacio Contreras. **DD** 051. **Bk Rev. Ad Acc, Adv Mgr:** Sarah Clay. **Pr Rev. Circ:** 15,000 (ctrl).
Desc: An educational magazine of news, current events, and human interest stories written in intermediate Spanish. A bilingual (Spanish/English) glossary defines key terms and idiomatic phrases in each issue.

US/0192-2017
PERSPECTIVES ON WRITING AND SPEECH : RESEARCH, INSTRUCTION, AND CURRICULUM DEVELOPMENT. Periodical. English. Community College Press, New York City Community College, Brooklyn NY 11201. **LC** PE1001; .P47. **DD** 001.54/07/1173. **UDC** 800.73; 372.45.

DK
PERSPECTIVES, STUDIES IN TRANSLATOLOGY. VFOAT Studies in Translatology. (1993)-. Periodical. English. sa. Kr140.00. Museum Tusculanum Press, University of Copenhagen, Njalsgade 94, DK-2300 Copenhagen D Denmark. **Tel** 011 45 31542211. **LC** P306.A1; P47. **DD** 418/.02/05. **CODEN** PSTTE7.
Ind/Abst Soc. Sci. Cit. Index [Select. Cov.].

BL
PHASIS. V. 1- Sept. 1973-. Portuguese. Rua Carangola 288 - 7 Andar, Caixa Postal 905, Belo Horizonte Brazil. **LC** P9; .P48. **UDC** 806.90.

PH/0048-3796
PHILIPPINE JOURNAL OF LINGUISTICS. [Philipp. j. linguist.]. **Added/Corp** Linguistic Society of the Philippines. (June 1970)-. Periodical. English. sa (2 issues). $22.00 Philippines; $27.00 other. PSSC Central Subscription Service, PO Box 205 UP Diliman, Quezon City 1101 Philippines. **Tel** 011 63 2 9229621. **ED** Andrew B. Gonzalez. **LC** P1; .P39. **DD** 410/.5. **Bk Rev. Ad Acc. Circ:** 1,000.
Desc: Presents original studies in descriptive, comparative, historical and area linguistics as well as papers on the application of theory to language teaching.
Ind/Abst Anthropol. Lit.; Index Philip. Period.; Linguist. Lang. Behav. Abstr. (1970-) [Full Cov.]; MLA Int. Bibl. Books Artic. Mod. Lang. Lit.; Soc. Plann. Policy Dev. Abstr.

US/0079-1628
PHILOLOGICAL MONOGRAPHS. [Philol. monogr.]. **Added/Corp** American Philological Association. **VFOAT** Philological Monographs of The American Philological Association. No. 1 (1931)-. Monographic series. English. ir. Price varies per volume. Scholars Press Customer Service, PO Box 6996, Alpharetta GA 30239. **Tel** (800)437-6692. **LC** UNC. **DD** 410/.5.

US/0363-3470
PHILOLOGICAL PAPERS (1947). (PHILOLOGICAL PAPERS.). [Philol. pap.]. **Added/Corp** West Virginia University. Vol. 5 (1947)-. Monographic series. English. an. $12.50. West Virginia University Foundation Department for Languages, Chitwood Hall, Morgantown WV 26506. **Tel** (304)293-5121. ***Continues*** *Philological Studies, 0363-4124.*
Ind/Abst Abstr. Engl. Stud.; Annu. Bibliogr. Engl. Lang. Lit.; MLA Int. Bibl. Books Artic. Mod. Lang. Lit.

US/0031-7977
PHILOLOGICAL QUARTERLY. [Philol. q.]. **Added/Corp** University of Iowa. **VFOAT** PQ. Vol. 1 (Jan. 1922)-. Periodical. English. Four times a year. $25.00 institution; $15.00 individual. University of Iowa / Publications Order Department, Oakdale Hall, Iowa City IA 52242. **Tel** (319)335-4645, FAX (319)335-4039. **ED** William Kupersmith. **LC** P1; .P55. **DD** 410/.5. Index available (bound in last issue). cum. index. **Bk Rev. Ad Acc. Pr Rev. Circ:** 2,200 (ctrl). available on microfilm and microfiche from University Microfilms International (UMI). Documents available from The Genuine Article, UMI Article Clearinghouse.
Desc: A journal of scholarship and criticism of classical and modern languages and literatures.
Ind/Abst Abstr. Engl. Stud.; Acad. Search (July 1993-); Annu. Bibliogr. Engl. Lang. Lit.; Arts Humanit. Citation Index [Full Cov.]; Book Rev. Index; Curr. Contents Arts Humanit.; Expand. Acad. Index (1989-); Humanit. Index; Humanit. Source (Jul. 1993-); INFO-SOUTH Abstr.; Mag. Search; MLA Int. Bibl. Books Artic. Mod. Lang. Lit.; Newsp. Period. Abstr. (1991-); Res. Alert [Full Cov.]; Romant. Move.; Soc. Plann. Policy Dev. Abstr.; Sociol. Abstr.

CY
PHILOLOGIKE KYPROS / TOU HELLENIKOU PNEUMATIKOU HOMILOU KYPROU. Added/Corp Hellenikos Pneumatikos Homilos Kyprou. (1960)-. Greek, Modern. an. **LC** DS54.A2; P5.
Ind/Abst MLA Int. Bibl. Books Artic. Mod. Lang. Lit.

GW/0554-0674
PHILOLOGISCHE STUDIEN UND QUELLEN. [Philol. Stud. Qu.]. (1956)-. Monographic series. German. ir. Price varies per volume. Erich Schmidt Verlag GmbH, Postfach 304240, D 10724 Berlin Germany. **Tel** 011 49 30 25008525. **ED** Wolfgang Binder, Hugo Moser, Hugo Steger, Hartmut Steinecke.
Desc: Philological studies and sources.
Ind/Abst MLA Int. Bibl. Books Artic. Mod. Lang. Lit.

GW/0031-7985
PHILOLOGUS. [Philologus]. **Added/Corp** Akademie der Wissenschaften der DDR. Zentralinstitut fuer Alte Geschichte und Archaologie. Vol. 1-46, (1846-1888), Vol. 47. (Neue Folge, 1.- Bd.), (1889)-. Periodical. German (English and German). sa. $185.00. Akademie-Verlag GmbH, Muehlenstrasse 33 34, D 13162 Berlin Germany. **Tel** 011 49 30 47889300, FAX 011 49 30 47889357. **(Subscription address:** VCH Publishers Inc., 303 Northwest 12th Avenue, Journals Department, Deerfield FL 33442.**) LC** PA3; .P5. Documents available from The Genuine Article.
Ind/Abst Arts Humanit. Citation Index (19??-19??) [Full Cov.]; Curr. Contents Arts Humanit.; Math. Rev.; MLA Int. Bibl. Books Artic. Mod. Lang. Lit.; Res. Alert [Full Cov.].

KO
PHOENIX. Korean (Korean). **LC** PR1; .P5.
Ind/Abst MLA Int. Bibl. Books Artic. Mod. Lang. Lit.

SZ/0554-0992
PHONAI. LAUTBIBLIOTHEK DER EUROPAEISCHEN SPRACHEN UND MUNDARTEN. DEUTSCHE REIHE. Added/Corp Internationale Vereinigung Sprachwissenschaftlicher Schallarchive. Institut fuer Deutsche Sprache. Deutscher Spracharchive. Vol. 1 (1965)-. Monographic series. German. ir. Price varies per volume. Max Niemeyer Verlag, Postfach 2140, D 72011 Tuebingen Germany. **Tel** 011 49 7071 989494, FAX 011 49 7071 87419. **ED** Edeltraud Knetschke and Margret Sperlbaum. **Circ:** 500.
Desc: Covers phonetic and normalized texts of tape recorded conversations in German dialects with linguistic analysis.

SZ/0031-8388
PHONETICA. [Phonetica]. **Added/Corp** International Society of Phonetic Sciences. Vol. 1 (1957)-. Academic Scholarly Publication. English (French and German). qt. $238.00. S. Karger AG, Allschwilerstrasse 10, PO Box - Postfach - Case Postale, CH-4009 Basel Switzerland. **Tel** 011 41 61 306-1111, FAX 011 41 61 306-1234, telex CH 962 652. **ED** K. Kohler and R. Diehl. **LC** P215; .P53. **DD** 414. **NLM** W1 PH624. **CODEN** PHNTAW. **[CCC].** Index available. cum. index. **Bk Rev. Ad Acc. Pr Rev. Circ:** 1,000. available on microfilm from University Microfilms International (UMI). Documents available from The Genuine Article, BIOSIS Document Express. ***Supersedes*** *Archiv fur Vergleichende Phonetik.*
Desc: Features expert original work covering all aspects of speech communication, including phonology, speech physiology, articulation, acoustics, and perception. Papers published in this journal report both theoretical issues and empirical data. Discussions cover methods of speech analysis and synthesis, technical applications in the areas of text-to-speech as well as speech and speaker recognition.
Ind/Abst Biol. Abstr.; Curr. Contents Soc. Behav. Sci.; EMBASE; Index Med.; Lang. Teach.; MLA Int. Bibl. Books Artic. Mod. Lang. Lit.; Ref. Upd. Deluxe Ed.; Res. Alert [Full Cov.]; Soc. Sci. Cit. Index [Full Cov.].

US/0741-6164
PHONETICIAN, THE. [Phonetician]. **Added/Corp** International Society of Phonetic Sciences. (19??)-. Periodical. English (French and German). Three times a year. $22.00. International Society of Phonetic Sciences, USC, Department of Speech Language Pathology and Audiology, Columbia SC 29208. **Tel** (803)777-4813. ***Continues*** *ISPHS Circular Letters.*

UK/0952-6757
PHONOLOGY. Vol. 5, No. 1 (1988)-. Academic Scholarly Publication. English. Three times a year. $105.00 US, Canada and Mexico; £63.00 other. Cambridge University Press, The Edinburgh Building, Shaftesbury Road, Cambridge CB2 2RU United Kingdom. **Tel** 011 44 223 312393, FAX 011 44 223 325959. **(Subscription address:** Cambridge University Press / North America, 110 Midland Avenue, Port Chester NY 10573.**) ED** Colin J. Ewen and Ellen M. Kaisse. **LC** P215; .P56. **DD** 414/.05. available on microfilm from University Microfilms International (UMI). ***Continues*** *Phonology Yearbook.*
Desc: Devoted exclusively to phonology. Combines theoretical and empirical interests to create a forum for the productive interchange of ideas among phonologists and those working in related disciplines. Each issue includes a section of "Squibs and Replies," shorter pieces on topics of current or controversial interest, as well as research articles.
Ind/Abst Curr. Index J. Educ.; Linguist. Lang. Behav. Abstr. (1984-) [Full Cov.]; MLA Int. Bibl. Books Artic. Mod. Lang. Lit.; Soc. Plann. Policy Dev. Abstr.

CC
PING CHU CHUAN TUNG CHU MU HSUAN / LIAO-NING SHENG WEN HUA CHU CHU MU KUNG TSO SHIH PIEN. V. 1-. Chinese. an. RMBY0.64. Chung Feng Wen I Chu Pan She, Hsin Hua Shu Tien, Shen-Yang Liaoning, People's Republic of China. **LC** PL2579.P56; P56.

BE
PLURILINGUA. English (German and French). ir. $38.00 Belgium; $43.00 other. Vrijheidslaan 17 Av, La Liberte B1080, Brussels Belgium. **Tel** 011 32 2 4279960.

ED P. H. Nelde. Index available. **Bk Rev. Pr Rev. Circ:** 1,000 (ctrl).
Desc: A series of publications on contact linguistics of the Brussels Research Center on Multilingualism (minorities, languages in contact and in conflict).

US
PMLA PAPER. (19??)-. Periodical. English. an. Modern Language Association of America, 10 Astor Place, New York NY 10003-6981. **Tel** (212)614-6382, FAX (212)477-9863.

NE/0303-4178
POETICA (MUNCHEN). **See** Literature.

PL
POLONICA. **Added/Corp** Instytut Jezyka Polskiego (Polska Akademia Nauk). (1975)-. Polish (summaries and/or abstracts in English). an. z63.00. **LC** PG6004; .P6.
Ind/Abst MLA Int. Bibl. Books Artic. Mod. Lang. Lit.

PL
POLONISTYKA. **Added/Corp** Poland. Ministerstwo Oswiaty. Poland. Ministerstwo Oswiaty i Szkolnictwa Wyzszego. Poland. Ministerstwo Oswiaty i Wychowania. (1948)-. Periodical. Polish. mo (10 times a year). $52.00. **(Subscription address:** ARS Polona, PO Box 1001, 00068 Warsaw Poland.) **LC** PG6001; .P6.

US/1045-6716
POLYLINGUA (HOUGHTON, MICH.). (POLYLINGUA : A COLLEGE JOURNAL OF FOREIGN LANGUAGES.). **Added/Corp** Michigan Technological University. Vol. 1, No. 1 (Spring 1990)-. Periodical. English. Three times a year. Michigan Technological University, Department of Humanities, Walker Building, 1400 Townsend Drive, Houghton MI 49931. **Tel** (906)487-2390, FAX (906)487-2468. **LC** P51; .P63; LB1578; .P65. **DD** 418/.0071/1. **CODEN** POLGE2.
Ind/Abst Curr. Index J. Educ.

US/0892-5941
POMPEIIANA NEWSLETTER. **Added/Corp** Pompeiiana, Inc. (19??)-. Newsletter. English (Latin). Nine times a year. $15.00 US; $17.00 Canada; $26.00 England & Europe; $35.00 other. Pompeiiana Inc, 6026 Indianola Avenue, Indianapolis IN 46220. **Tel** (317)255-0589. **ED** B F Barcio. **DD** 470. **Bk Rev. Ad Acc. Circ:** 13,000 (ctrl). ***Continues*** *Newsletter (Pompeiiana, Inc.), 0892-595X.*
Desc: Published especially for Latin students, this newspaper features current articles about the study of Latin, the classical world, archaeology, art, mythology, Latin authors, new discoveries and all those things that spice up Latin classrooms but for which there is never enough time. An entire page of brain-teaser games, puzzles, and current song, movie and TV titles challenges students to use their Latin knowledge in fun ways. An entire page of especially contracted cartoons helps keep the paper light and lively. The majority of the articles (most of which are submitted by student and teacher subscribers) are in English but some Latin articles are included to challenge the students. The lead story (always in Latin) features the "hottest" rock music and movie stars, sport heroes or public figures. Blends the humorous and the serious while bringing the ancient world of Rome to life for your students - right down to cooking with authentic Roman recipes and an advice column which teaches culture subliminally while responding to fictional letters from Roman youth.

PL/0551-5343
PORADNIK JEZYKOWY. [Porad. jezyk.]. **Added/Corp** Towarzystwo Krzewienia Poprawnosci i Kultury Jezyka (Poland) Towarzystwo Naukowe Warszawskie. Komisja Jezykowa. Towarzystwo Kultury Jezyka (Poland). Vol. 1, No. 1 (1901)-. Periodical. Polish. mo (except July and Aug.). $32.00. **(Subscription address:** ARS Polona, PO Box 1001, 00068 Warsaw Poland.) cum. index.
Ind/Abst MLA Int. Bibl. Books Artic. Mod. Lang. Lit.

UK/0267-5315
PORTUGUESE STUDIES. **See** History(General).

GW
POSTILLA BOHEMICA. **See** Literature.

PL
PRACE INSTYTUTU JEZYKA POLSKIEGO. (1975)-. Monographic series. Polish. Price varies per volume. Zakad Narodowy Im Ossolinskich Przedmiescie 7, 00 068 Warsaw Poland.

PL
PRACE JEZYKOZNAWCZE. **Main/Corp** Wyzsza Szkoa Pedagogiczna W Krakowie. **VFOAT** Travaux Linguistiques. (1970)-. Polish (summaries and/or abstracts in English and Russian). ir. Z28.00 each issue. **(Subscription address:** ARS Polona, PO Box 1001, 00068 Warsaw Poland.) **ED** Michal Blicharski. **LC** AS142.K66; A2 subser. **UDC** 808.4. **Circ:** 300 (ctrl).
Desc: Polish and Slavonic language studies: Results of synchronus and diachronus studies on the Polish language and for confrontation Slavonic languages studies.

PL/0079-4678
PRACE KOMISJI JEZYKOZNAWCZEJ. **Main/Corp** Poznanskie Towarzystwo Przyjacio Nauk. Komisja Jezykoznawcza. (1962)-. Monographic series. Multiple languages (English, German and Polish; summaries and/or abstracts in French). **LC** PG6014; .P6.
Ind/Abst Soc. Plann. Policy Dev. Abstr.

PL/0079-3310
PRACE KOMISJI JEZYKOZNAWSTWA / POLSKA AKADEMIA NAUK--ODDZIA W KRAKOWIE. **Added/Corp** Polska Akademia Nauk. Oddzia w Krakowie. Komisja Jezykoznawstwa. No. 1 (1964)-. Monographic series. Polish (French and Latin).
Ind/Abst MLA Int. Bibl. Books Artic. Mod. Lang. Lit.

II/0970-9940
PRACI BHASA-VIJNAN (CALCUTTA). (PRACI BHASAVIJNAN.). [Praci bhasa-vijnan]. **Added/Corp** Bhasa Vidya Parishad. **VFOAT** Indian Journal of Linguistics. Vol. 1 (Jan./June 1974)-. Periodical. English. an. $20.00. Bangiya Vijnan Parishad, P-23 Raja Rajkrishna Street, Calcutta 700006 India. **Tel** 55-0660. **(Subscription address:** Prints India, 11 Darya Ganj, New Delhi 110002 India.) **ED** Bhakti P Mallik. **LC** P1; .P7. **DD** 410/.5. **Bk Rev. Ad Acc. Circ:** 525 (ctrl).
Desc: Dedicated to the development of all branches of linguistics in general and Indian linguistics in particular. It invites papers on theoretical and experimental linguistics and interdisciplinary studies throughout the world.
Ind/Abst MLA Int. Bibl. Books Artic. Mod. Lang. Lit.

II
PRADHIKRTA : GURU NANAKA DEVA YUNIVARSITI KE HINDI VIBHAGA KI SODHA PATRIKA. **VFOAT** Pradhikrit. V. 1, No. 1 (Feb./July 1984)-. Periodical. Hindi (Hindi). sa. 25.00, $10.00 US. Hindi Department, Guru Nanak Dev University, Amritsar 143005 India. **LC** PK1931; .A415.

NE/0920-3079
PRAGMATICS & BEYOND COMPANION SERIES. **VFOAT** Pragmatics and Beyond Companion Series. (1985)-. Monographic series. English. ir. Price varies per volume. John Benjamins BV, Amsteldijk 44, PO Box 75577, 1070 AN Amsterdam Netherlands. **Tel** 011 31 20 6738156, FAX 011 31 20 739773. **(Subscription address:** John Benjamins North America, PO Box 27519, Philadelphia PA 19118-0519.)
Desc: A companion series to Pragmatics & Beyond, consisting of larger monographs and collective volumes.
Ind/Abst Math. Rev.

NE/0922-842X
PRAGMATICS & BEYOND NEW SERIES. [Pragmat. beyond, New ser.]. **VFOAT** Pragmatics and Beyond. (1988)-. Monographic series. English. ir. Price varies per volume. John Benjamins BV, Amsteldijk 44, PO Box 75577, 1070 AN Amsterdam Netherlands. **Tel** 011 31 20 6738156, FAX 011 31 20 739773. **(Subscription address:** John Benjamins North America, PO Box 27519, Philadelphia PA 19118-0519.) **ED** Jacob L. Mey, Herman Parret and Jef Verschueren. **Bk Rev. Pr Rev. Acid Free.**
Desc: A continuation of Pragmatics & Beyond and its Companion Series. The New Series offers a selection of work covering the full richness of linguistics as an interdisciplinary field.
Ind/Abst MLA Int. Bibl. Books Artic. Mod. Lang. Lit.

●NE/0929-0907
PRAGMATICS & COGNITION. **VFOAT** Pragmatics and Cognition. Vol. 1, No. 1 (1993)-. Periodical. English. sa. $129.00. John Benjamins BV, Amsteldijk 44, PO Box 75577, 1070 AN Amsterdam Netherlands. **Tel** 011 31 20 6738156, FAX 011 31 20 739773. **(Subscription address:** John Benjamins North America, PO Box 27519, Philadelphia PA 19118-0519.) **ED** Marcelo Dascal. **LC** P99.4.P72; P77. **CODEN** PCOGEZ.
Desc: Seeks to bring together such disciplines as philosophy, linguistics, semiotics, cognitive science, neuroscience, artificial intelligence, ethology, and cognitive anthropology, among others. Also seeks to explore relations of all sorts between semiotic systems as used by humans, animals and machines, in connection with mental activities.

UK/0309-8141
PRAGMATICS. MICROFICHE. [Pragmat. microfiche]. Vol. 1 (1975)-. Periodical. English. Three times a year. Oxford Microform Publications, 19A Paradise Street, Oxford OX1 1LD England.
Ind/Abst Philos. Index.

BE/1018-2101
PRAGMATICS : QUARTERLY PUBLICATION OF THE INTERNATIONAL PRAGMATICS ASSOCIATION. **Added/Corp** International Pragmatics Association. Vol. 1, No. 1 (Mar. 1991)-. Periodical. English. qt (4 issues). $130.00. IPRA Secretariat, PO Box 33, B 2018 Antwerp 11 Belgium. **Tel** 011 32 3 2305574, FAX 011 32 3 2305574. **ED** Alessandro Duranti and Bambi Schieffelin. **LC** P99.4.P72; P67. **Bk Rev**, (Qty: 30-40). **Ad Acc. Pr Rev. Circ:** 1,200. ***Formed by the union of*** *IPRA Papers in Pragmatics; IPRA Working Document; IPRA Bulletin* ***and*** *IPRA Survey of Research in Progress.*
Desc: Cognitive, social and cultural approaches to language and communication. Interests touching psychology, sociology, anthropology and philosophy.
Ind/Abst Linguist. Lang. Behav. Abstr. (1987-); Soc. Plann. Policy Dev. Abstr.

XR/0032-6585
PRAGUE BULLETIN OF MATHEMATICAL LINGUISTICS, THE. [Prague bull. math. linguist.]. No. 1 (1964)-. Bulletin. English (German and French). sa. kcs5.00 Czechoslovakia. Charles University / Univerzita Karlova, Ovocnytrh 5, 116 36 Prague 1 Czech Republic. **Tel** 228441. **ED** Eva Hajicova. **UDC** 519.76. **CODEN** PBMLAT. Index available. cum. index. **Bk Rev. Circ:** 800 (ctrl). Documents available from Ask*IEEE.
Desc: Attention focused on mathematical linguistics and its applications. Papers published in English, German, and French.
Ind/Abst INSPEC (1971-); Linguist. Lang. Behav. Abstr. (1972-) [Full Cov.]; Math. Rev.; MLA Int. Bibl. Books Artic. Mod. Lang. Lit.; Soc. Plann. Policy Dev. Abstr.; Zentralbl. Math. Ihre Grenzgeb.

FR/0338-2389
PRATIQUES. **Added/Corp** Collectif de Recherche et d'Experimentation sur l'Enseignement du Francais. (19??)-. Periodical. French. Four times a year. 260.00F Europe; 280.00F other. Cresef, 8 rue du Patural, F-57000 Metz France. **Tel** 33 87 622586. **ED** Petitjean. **Ad Acc. Circ:** 79 (ctrl).
Desc: Scientific review of teaching French and linguistics.

GW/0341-5279
PRAXIS DEUTSCH. [Prax. Dtsch.]. (1973)-. Periodical. German. Seven times a year. DM102.90. Erhard Friedrich Verlag, Postfach 100150, D 30917 Seelze Germany. **Tel** 011 49 511 4000452. **UDC** 372.880.30 :373.

US/0731-0714
PRE/TEXT. [Pre/Text]. **Added/Corp** Eastern Illinois University. Dept. of English. University of Texas at Arlington. Dept. of English. **VFOAT** Pretext. Vol. 1, No. 1/2 (Spring/Fall 1980)-. Periodical. English. qt. $50.00 (institution), $20.00 (individual) US; $53.00 (institution), $23.00 (individual) Canada. Pre-Text, c/o Victor J Vitanza, PO Box 14621, Arlington TX 76019-1621. **Tel** (817)460-4205. **ED** Victor J Vitanza, (817)273-2692. **LC** P301; .P68. **DD** 808/.005. **Ad Acc. Pr Rev. Circ:** 500 (ctrl).
Desc: Exploratory articles on the interdisciplinary nature of rhetorical theory and metatheory, including research on written communication.
Ind/Abst Curr. Index J. Educ.; MLA Int. Bibl. Books Artic. Mod. Lang. Lit.; Soc. Plann. Policy Dev. Abstr.

XO
PREDNASKY ... LETHNEHO SEMINARA SLOVENSKEHO JAZYKA A KULTURY. **Main/Conf** Letny Seminar Slovenskeho Jazyka a Kultury. Periodical. Slovak. an.

RU
PREPODAVANIE INOSTRANNYKH IAZYKOV. **Added/Corp** Vsesoiuznaia Gosudarstvennaia Biblioteka Inostrannoi Literatury (Soviet Union). Vol. 1 (1973)-. Periodical. Russian. qt. **LC** Z5818.L35; P73.

US
PRICE LIST AND ORDER FORM FOR ENGLISH INSTRUCTIONAL MATERIALS. **See** Education-Teaching and Curriculum.

CI/0449-5527
PRILOZI I GRAA. **Main/Corp** Yugoslav Serbo-Croatian--English Contrastive Project. **Added/Corp** Zagreb. Universitet. Institut za Lingvistiku. (1969)-. English. **LC** PG1229; .Y84.

YU/0555-1137
PRILOZI PROUCAVANJU JEZIKA. [Pril. prouc. jez.]. **Added/Corp** Univerzitet u Novom Sadu. Katedra za Juznoslovenske Jezike. (1965)-. Serbo-Croatian (Cyrillic). an. **LC** PG431; .P74. **DD** 491.8/1/005.
Ind/Abst MLA Int. Bibl. Books Artic. Mod. Lang. Lit.

YU/0350-6673
PRILOZI ZA KNJIZEVNOST, JEZIK, ISTORIJU I FOLKLOR. [Pril. knjizev. jez. istor. folk.]. **Added/Corp** Univerzitet u Beogradu. Filoloski Fakultet. Vol. 1, No. 1 (1921)-. Periodical. Serbo-Croatian (Cyrillic). ir. $0.50 (per copy). Prilozi za Knjizenost Jezik Istoriju, University of Belgrad, Filoloski Fakult, Belgrade Yugoslavia. **Tel** 011 635-543. **LC** PG560; .P7.
Ind/Abst Am. Hist. Life (1962); MLA Int. Bibl. Books Artic. Mod. Lang. Lit.

●US/1068-073X
PRIMARY VOICES K-6. **See** Education-Early Childhood and Primary Education.

CN/0380-8815
PRISMA (SASKATOON). (PRISMA.). **Added/Corp** Saskatchewan Association of Teachers of German. Vol. 4 (Summer 1975)-. English (summaries and/or abstracts in German). ir. 10.00Can$ Comes with Saskatchewan Association of Teachers of German membership. Saskatchewan Teachers Federation, PO Box 1108, Saskatoon Saskatchewan, S7K 3N3 Canada. **Tel** (306)373-1660. **DD** 438/.007. ***Continues*** *Jetzt Wird Deutsch Gesprochen, 0380-8807.*

BN/0353-6386
PRIZMA. **Added/Corp** Drustvo za Primijenjenu Lingvistiku BiH. Vol. 1, No. 1 (1990)-. Serbo-Croatian (Roman).

SP
PROBLEMATA SEMIOTICA. (1984)-. Monographic series. Spanish. Universidad de Deusto, Departamento de Publicaciones, Ave Universidades s/n, 48007 Bilbao Spain. **Tel** (94)445 31 00, FAX 445 68 17, telex 34221 UDD E.
Ind/Abst MLA Int. Bibl. Books Artic. Mod. Lang. Lit.

RM
PROBLEME DE LINGUISTICA GENERALA. **Added/Corp** Academia Republicii Populare Romine. Academia Republicii Socialiste Romania. Vol. 1 (1959)-. Periodical. Romanian (summaries and/or abstracts in French and Russian). Editura Academia Republicii Socialiste Romania, Calea Victoriei Nr 125, R-79717 Bucuresti Romania. **Tel** telex 10376 PRSFI R. **LC** P25; .P7. **DD** 400.
Ind/Abst MLA Int. Bibl. Books Artic. Mod. Lang. Lit.

RU
PROBLEMY IZUCHENIIA INOSTRANNYKH IAZYKOV V ZAOCHNOI I VECHERNEI VYSSHEI SHKOLE. **Added/Corp** Russian S.F.S.R. Ministerstvo Vysshego i Srednego Spetsialnogo Obrazovaniia. (1976)-. Periodical. Russian. 0.70rub. St Petersburg State University / Izdatelstvo Leningradskogo Universiteta, Universitetskaia Nab 7/9, 199034 St Petersburg Russia. **Tel** 011 95 218-97-88, FAX 011 95 218-51-52, telex 121481. **LC** PB38.R8; P772.

NE/0921-4771
PROBUS. Vol. 1, No. 1 (1989)-. Periodical. English (French, Italian, Portuguese and Spanish). Three times a year. $133.65. Walter de Gruyter Inc., PO Box 303421, D 10728 Berlin Germany. **Tel** 011 49 30 260050, FAX 011 49 30 26005251. **ED** W. Leo Wetzels and Rafael A. Nunez Cedeno. **LC** PC1; .P76. **CODEN** PRUSE2. **Bk Rev**. **Ad Acc. Circ:** 200.
Ind/Abst Linguist. Lang. Behav. Abstr. (1989-) [Full Cov.]; MLA Int. Bibl. Books Artic. Mod. Lang. Lit.; Soc. Plann. Policy Dev. Abstr.

II
PROCEEDINGS AND TRANSACTIONS OF THE ALL-INDIA ORIENTAL CONFERENCE. **Main/Conf** All-India Oriental Conference. 1st- 1919-. Proceedings. English. Rs150.00. Bhandarkar Oriential Research Institute, Poona 411004 India. **Tel** 56936. **ED** R N Dandekar. **LC** PJ21. **DD** 490.6354. **UDC** 809.14. cum. index. ctrl circ.

US/0883-5500
PROCEEDINGS OF NELS. [Proc. NELS]. **Main/Corp** North Eastern Linguistic Society. **VFOAT** NELS; Proceedings of ALNE; ALNE; Proceedings of the North East Linguistic Society. **VAT** Proceedings of North Eastern Linguistic Society. (1982)-. English. an (Aug.). Price varies. Graduate Linguistic Student Association / Department of Linguistics, South College University of Massachusetts, Amherst MA 01003. **Tel** (413)545-6838. **LC** P21; .N65a. **DD** 410. **Circ:** 500. ***Continues*** *North Eastern Linguistic Society. Meeting. Proceedings of the ... Annual Meeting of the North Eastern Linguistic Society, 0742-3209.*

US/0363-2946
PROCEEDINGS OF THE ANNUAL MEETING OF THE BERKELEY LINGUISTICS SOCIETY. **Main/Corp** Berkeley Linguistics Society. (1975)-. Proceedings. English. an. $22.50 (institution) US. Berkeley Linguistics Society, 2337 Dwinell Hall, University of California, Berkeley CA 94720. **Tel** (510)642-2757, (510)642-5808, FAX (510)643-5688. **LC** P21; .B47a. **DD** 410/.5. Index available. cum. index. **Circ:** 1,000 (ctrl).
Desc: Contains the proceedings of the yearly conference held in Berkeley, California. The conference attracts hundreds of linguists from across the country.

UK/0068-6735
PROCEEDINGS OF THE CAMBRIDGE PHILOLOGICAL SOCIETY. [Proc. Camb. Philol. Soc.]. **Main/Corp** Cambridge Philological Society. (1882)-. Proceedings. English. an (Dec.). $36.00 US; $15.00 other. Colin Austin Cambridge, Trinity Hall, Cambridge CB2 1TJ England. **ED** Dr. G. Horrocks. **LC** P11; .C2. **DD** 410/.5. **Circ:** 1,500. Documents available from The Genuine Article.
Ind/Abst Arts Humanit. Citation Index (19??-19??) [Full Cov.]; Numis. Lit.; Res. Alert [Full Cov.]; Soc. Sci. Cit. Index [Select. Cov.].

UK/0068-6743
PROCEEDINGS OF THE CAMBRIDGE PHILOLOGICAL SOCIETY. SUPPLEMENT. ***Title Change.*** **Main/Corp** Cambridge Philological Society. **Added/Corp** Cambridge Philological Society. No. 1 (1965)-(19??). Proceedings. English. Basil Blackwell Publishers Ltd, 108 Cowley Road, Oxford 0X4 1JF England. **Tel** 011 44 865 791100, FAX 011 44 865 791347, telex 837022 OXBOOK G. **DD** 400. ***Continued by*** *Supplementary Volume (Cambridge Philological Society).*

UK
PROCEEDINGS OF THE CLASSICAL ASSOCIATION. **Main/Corp** Classical Association. V.1- 1904-. Proceedings. English. an. **LC** PA11. **UDC** 807. available on microfilm and microfiche from University Microfilms International (UMI).
Desc: Rules and list of members included in each volume.

US/0736-587X
PROCEEDINGS OF THE CONFERENCE - ASSOCIATION FOR COMPUTATIONAL LINGUISTICS. MEETING. (PROCEEDINGS OF THE CONFERENCE.). [Proc. conf. - Assoc. Comput. Linguist., Meet.]. **Main/Corp** Association for Computational Linguistics. Meeting. **VFOAT** ACL Proceedings. (19??)-. Proceedings. English. $50.00 nonmembers; $25.00 members. Association Computation Linguistics, 445 South Street, Morristown NJ 07960. **Tel** (301)829-4312. **CODEN** AMLCDE. Documents available from Article Express International. ***Continues in part*** *Finite String.*
Ind/Abst Bioeng. Abstr.; Ei Page One; Eng. Index Annu.; GeoRef.

US/1048-1656
PROCEEDINGS OF THE ... EASTERN STATES CONFERENCE ON LINGUISTICS. [Proc. East. States Conf. Linguist.]. **Main/Corp** Eastern States Conference on Linguistics. **VFOAT** ESCOL. (Sept. 1984)-. Proceedings. English. an. **DD** 410.
Ind/Abst Linguist. Lang. Behav. Abstr. (1984-) [Full Cov.]; Soc. Plann. Policy Dev. Abstr.

CN/0075-9597
PROCEEDINGS OF THE LINGUISTIC CIRCLE OF MANITOBA AND NORTH DAKOTA. **Main/Corp** Linguistic Circle of Manitoba and North Dakota. Vol. 1 (May 1959)-. Proceedings. English. an. $2.50. University of North Dakota / The Linguistic Circle, Grand Forks ND 58202. **Tel** (701)777-2941. **(Subscription address:** University of North Dakota, English Department, Professor Ben Collins, Grand Forks, ND 58202, (Phone: (710)777-3321)) **DD** 410/.5.

US/0740-6959
PROFESSION. [Profession]. **Added/Corp** Modern Language Association of America. Association of Departments of English. ADE Bulletin. Association of Departments of Foreign Languages (U.S.) ADFL Bulletin. (19??)-. Academic Scholarly Publication. English. an. $7.50. Modern Language Association of America, 10 Astor Place, New York NY 10003-6981. **Tel** (212)614-6382, FAX (212)477-9863. **LC** P57.U7; P75. **DD** 405. **Acid Free. Circ:** 32,000.
Desc: Publishes articles of opinion for and about those who teach and study modern languages. Each volume discusses current intellectual, curricular, and professional trends and issues, including the pleasures of poetry, methods of evaluating teacher performance, political correctness, the experiences of teaching abroad, and more.
Ind/Abst MLA Int. Bibl. Books Artic. Mod. Lang. Lit.

UK/0995-616X
PROFESSIONAL TRANSLATOR & INTERPRETER. ***Ceased.*** (19??)-(19??). English. Three times a year. Inst Translation Interpreting, 377 City Road, London EC1V 1NA England. **Tel** 011 44 71 7137600. **ED** Mike Shields. **Bk Rev**. **Ad Acc. Circ:** 2,500.
Desc: Matters of interest to translators and interpreters.

IT
PROFILO DEI DIALETTI ITALIANI. (1974)-. Monographic series. Italian. ir. Price varies per volume. Arti Grafiche Pacini Mariotti, Via S Maria 36, 56100 Pisa Italy.

UK/0268-7364
PROGRESS IN THE PSYCHOLOGY OF LANGUAGE. ***Ceased.*** [Prog. psychol. lang.]. Vol. 1 (1985)-(19??). Periodical. English. an. Lawrence Erlbaum Associates Ltd., 27 Palmeira Mansions, Church Road, Hove East Sussex BN3 2FA England. **Tel** 011 44 273 207411. **(Subscription address:** Turpin Distribution Services Limited, Blackhorse Road, Letchworth, Hertfordshire SG6 1HN, United Kingdom.**)** **LC** P37; .P74. **DD** 401/.9/05. **NLM** W1; PR682J.

IO
PROHEMIO. V. 1- April 1970-. Periodical. Spanish. Three times a year. **LC** P9.

CN/0300-3523
PROTEE. [Protee]. **Added/Corp** Universite du Quebec a Chicoutimi. Dep. des Sciences Humaines. Vol. 1 (Dec. 1970)-. Periodical. French. Three times a year. 34.00Can$ (institutions), 29.00Can$ (individuals) Canada; 44.00Can$ (institutions), 34.00Can$ (individuals) US and Pan America; 49.00Can$ (institutions), 39.00Can$ (individuals) other. University of Quebec Chicoutimi, Department of Arts and Lettres, 555 University Boulevard, Chicoutimi Quebec G7H 2B1 Canada. **Tel** (418)545-5375, FAX (418)545-5012. **ED** Francine Belle-Isle. **Bk Rev**, (Qty: 6). **Pr Rev. Circ:** 650 (ctrl).
Desc: Multidisciplinary journal in the field of semiotics, theoretical and applied to literature, arts, language, culture, etc.
Ind/Abst Am. Hist. Life (1975-1980, 1985-1986); Point Repere (1983-).

PL
PRZEGLAD RUSYCYSTYCZNY. Vol. 1-. Periodical. Polish (Russian). qt. Rsw Prasa-Ksiazka-Ruch Centrala Kolportazu Prasy I Wydawnictw, Ul Towarowa 28, 00-958 Warszawa Poland. **LC** PG2068.P6; P78.

II/0377-3132
PSYCHO-LINGUA. [Psycho-lingua]. **Added/Corp** Psycholinguistic Association of India. Vol. 1 (Jan. 1971)-. Periodical. English (Hindi). Twice a year. $25.00. Psycholinguistic Association of India, c/o Ravishankar University MP, Raipur India. **(Subscription address:** Prints India, 11 Darya Ganj, New Delhi 110002 India.**)** **LC** P1.A1; P78. **DD** 410.
Ind/Abst Psychol. Abstr. (1975-); PsycINFO; PsycLit; Soc. Plann. Policy Dev. Abstr.

CK
PUBLICACIONES DEL INSTITUTO CARO Y CUERVO. SERIE BIBLIOGRAFICA. **See** Linguistics-Abstracting, Bibliographies and Statistics.

CK/0073-9928
PUBLICACIONES. SERIES MINOR. **Main/Corp** Colombia. Instituto Caro y Cuervo. Vol. 1 (1950)-. Monographic series. Spanish. ir. Price varies per volume. Instituto Caro y Cuervo, Apartado 51502, Bogota Colombia. **Tel** 011 57 1 2557753, FAX 011 57 1 2170243. **DD** 460; 860. **Circ:** 2,000 (ctrl).

CN/0704-7037
PUBLICATION B / CENTRE INTERNATIONAL DE RECERCHES SUR LE BILINGUISME. **Added/Corp** Universite Laval. Centre International de Recherches sur le Bilinguisme. Vol. 1 (1967)-. Monographic series. English (French). ir. Price varies per volume. International Center for Research on Bilingualism, Universite Laval, Pavillon Casault, Quebec Quebec G1K 7P4 Canada. **Tel** (418)656-3232. **DD** 404/.2/05. **Ad Acc. Circ:** 150 (ctrl).

CN/0704-7037
PUBLICATION B. CENTRE INTERNATIONAL DE RECHERCHES SUR LE BILINGUISME. **Added/Corp** Universite Laval. Centre International de Recherches sur le Bilinguisme. (1967)-. Monographic series. French (English). ir. Price varies per volume. International Center for Research on Bilingualism, Universite Laval, Pavillon Casault, Quebec Quebec G1K 7P4 Canada. **Tel** (418)656-3232. **DD** 404/.2/05.

US/0002-8207
PUBLICATION OF THE AMERICAN DIALECT SOCIETY. [Publ. Am. Dialect Soc.]. **Added/Corp** American Dialect Society. No. 1 (April 1944)-. Monographic series. English. ir. Price varies per volume. American Dialect Society, MacMurray College, English Department, Jacksonville IL 62650. **Tel** (217)479-7000, FAX (217)245-5214. **ED** Dennis Baron. **LC** PE1702; .A5. **DD** 427. **Pr Rev. Circ:** 1,500. ***Continues*** *Dialect Notes.*
Desc: Monographs on the English language in North America and other languages as they relate to it.
Ind/Abst MLA Int. Bibl. Books Artic. Mod. Lang. Lit.; Soc. Plann. Policy Dev. Abstr.

SG/0418-2960
PUBLICATIONS - DAKAR. UNIVERSITE. SECTION DE LANGUES ET LITTERATURES. **Main/Corp** Dakar. Universite. Section de Langues et Litteratures. **VFOAT** Dakar. Universite. Section de Langues et Litteratures. No. 1, (1957)-. Periodical. French. Dakar Universite / Section de Langues et Litteratur, Dakar Fann Senegal. **DD** 400; 800.

US/0160-3124
PUBLICATIONS OF THE ARKANSAS PHILOLOGICAL ASSOCIATION. [Publ. Ark. Philol. Assoc.]. **Main/Corp** Arkansas Philological

Association. (Fall 1974)-. Periodical. English (French, Spanish and German). sa. $25.00 US; $28.00 Canada; $39.00 other. University of Central Arkansas Press, UCA Box 4933, Conway AR 72035. **Tel** (501)450-5150, FAX (501)450-5208. **ED** Robert E Lowrey. **LC** PB1; .A58A. **DD** 410/.5. **UDC** 802.0; 800.83. Index available. **Bk Rev**, (Qty: 2). **Pr Rev. Circ:** 200. available on microfilm.
Desc: Literary criticism, scholarship, and book reviews in English and modern languages. Articles are selected by the board from the year's conference proceedings. However, PAPA accepts unsolicited book reviews (500-1000).
Ind/Abst MLA Int. Bibl. Books Artic. Mod. Lang. Lit.

US/0194-035X
PUBLICATIONS OF THE MISSOURI PHILOLOGICAL ASSOCIATION. [Publ. Mo. Philol. Assoc.]. **Main/Corp** Missouri Philological Association. Vol. 1 (1976)-. English. an. $5.00 (nonmembers), free to members. Missouri Philological Association, Central Missouri State, English Department, Warrensburg MO 64093. **Tel** (816)429-4425. **LC** PB1; .M43a. **DD** 809.
Ind/Abst MLA Int. Bibl. Books Artic. Mod. Lang. Lit.

US/0030-8129
PUBLICATIONS OF THE MODERN LANGUAGE ASSOCIATION OF AMERICA. [Publ. Mod. Lang. Assoc. Am.]. **Added/Corp** Modern Language Association of America. **VFOAT** PMLA. Vol. 4, No. 1 (1888)-. Academic Scholarly Publication. English. Six times a year. $108.00. Modern Language Association of America, 10 Astor Place, New York NY 10003-6981. **Tel** (212)614-6382, FAX (212)477-9863. **ED** John W. Kronik. **LC** PB6; .M6. **DD** 809. cum. index. **Ad Acc, Adv Mgr:** Cynthia Port. Full Page (Color) $1045.00. Half Page (Color) $675.00. **Acid Free. Circ:** 35,050. available on microfilm and microfiche from University Microfilms International (UMI). Documents available from The Genuine Article, UMI Article Clearinghouse. ***Continues*** *Transactions and Proceedings of the Modern Language Association of America.*
Desc: Publishes articles of interest to those concerned with the study of language and literature.
Ind/Abst Abstr. Engl. Stud.; Acad. Search (July 1993-); Am. Bibliogr. Slavic East Europ. Stud.; Annu. Bibliogr. Engl. Lang. Lit.; Arts Humanit. Citation Index (19??-19??) [Full Cov.]; Child. Lit. Abstr. (19??-); Curr. Contents Arts Humanit.; Expand. Acad. Index (1992-); Humanit. Index; Humanit. Source (Jul. 1993-); INFO-SOUTH Abstr.; Mag. Search; Middle East Abstr. Index; MLA Int. Bibl. Books Artic. Mod. Lang. Lit.; Newsp. Period. Abstr. (1986-); Res. Alert [Full Cov.]; Romant. Move.

UK
PUBLICATIONS OF THE PHILOLOGICAL SOCIETY. **Main/Corp** Philological Society, London. (1913)-. Monographic series. English. ir. Price varies per volume. Basil Blackwell Publishers Ltd, 108 Cowley Road, Oxford 0X4 1JF England. **Tel** 011 44 865 791100, FAX 011 44 865 791347, telex 837022 OXBOOK G.
Ind/Abst MLA Int. Bibl. Books Artic. Mod. Lang. Lit.

FR
PUBLICATIONS - SOCIETE DES TEXTES FRANCAIS MODERNES. **Main/Corp** Societe des Textes Francais Modernes (Paris, France). (1921)-. Monographic series. French. sa. 210.00F (includes membership). Societe des Textes Francais Modernes, University of Paris IV Gilbert 1 R V Cousin, 75005 Paris France. **Tel** 11 33 1 40462643, or -44. **(Subscription address:** Aux Amateurs de Livres, 62 Av de Suffren, 75015 Paris France, Tel. 33 1 45671838**)**
Ind/Abst MLA Int. Bibl. Books Artic. Mod. Lang. Lit.

NE/0555-6406
PUBLISISTIK. **Added/Corp** Universitas Indonesia. Lembaga Publisistik. **VFOAT** Madjalah Ilmiah Bidang Komunikasi Massa Publisistik. (June 1964)-. Periodical. Indonesian. **LC** P92.172; P8.

II
PUNJAB JOURNAL OF ENGLISH STUDIES : PJES. **Added/Corp** Guru Nanak Dev University. Dept. of English. **VFOAT** PJES. Vol. 1 (1986)-. English. an. **LC** IN PROCESS. ***Continues*** *Punjab Journal of English Studies.*
Ind/Abst Soc. Plann. Policy Dev. Abstr.

NE/0165-8743
PURDUE UNIVERSITY MONOGRAPHS IN ROMANCE LANGUAGES. [Purdue Univ. monogr. roman. lang.]. Vol. 1 (1980)-. Monographic series. French. ir. Price varies per volume. Purdue University, Lafayette IN 47907. **ED** Allan Pasco, Allen Wood, Howard Mancing, Enrique Caracciolo-Trejo, Djelal Kadir. **LC** UNC.
Ind/Abst MLA Int. Bibl. Books Artic. Mod. Lang. Lit.

IT
QUADERNI DEL DIPARTIMENTO DI LINGUE E LETTERATURE STRANIERE MODERNE. **See** Literature.

IT
QUADERNI DI FILOLOGIA GERMANICA DELLA FACOLTA DI LETTERE E FILOSOFIA DELL'UNIVERSITA DI BOLOGNA. Vol. 1 (1980)-. Periodical. Italian (German and English). ir. L30000 (add L10000 for postage) Italy; $20.00 (add $10.00 for postage) US. Angelo Longo Editore, Via Paolo Costa 33, PO Box 431, 48100 Ravenna Italy. **Tel** 011 39 544 217026, FAX 011 39 544 217026. **ED** Fortunati Vita. **LC** PD9; .Q3. **DD** 430/.05. **UDC** 803.0; 830. **Circ:** 1,000.
Desc: Studies in European literature and general linguistics.
Ind/Abst MLA Int. Bibl. Books Artic. Mod. Lang. Lit.

IT
QUADERNI DI LINGUE E LETTERATURE STRANIERE / UNIVERSITA DEGLI STUDI DI PALERMO, FACOLTA DI MAGISTERO, ISTITUTO DI LINGUE E LETTERATURE STRANIERE. Periodical. Italian. Via Notarbartolo 5, 90141 Palermo Italy. **LC** PB4; .Q33. **DD** 405. **UDC** 800.83.

IT
QUADERNI DI LINGUE E LETTERATURE / UNIVERSIT·A DEGLI STUDI DI PADOVA, FACOLTA DI ECONOMIA E COMMERCIO, ISTITUTO DI LINGUE E LETTERATURE STRANIERE DI VERONA. **See** Literature.

IT
QUADERNI DI SCHEDE UMANISTICHE. **See** Literature.

IT/0393-1226
QUADERNI DI SEMANTICA. [Quad. semant.]. 1st Yr, No. 1 (Jan./June 1980)-. Periodical. English (Italian and French). sa. L74000 Italy; L120000 (surface mail), L150000 (airmail) other. Societa Editrice il Mulino, Strada Maggiore 37, 40125 Bologna Italy. **Tel** 011 39 51 256011, FAX 011 39 51 256034. **LC** P325; .Q28. **DD** 412/.05. **UDC** 801.56.
Ind/Abst MLA Int. Bibl. Books Artic. Mod. Lang. Lit.

IT/0393-24865
QUADERNI PATAVINI DI LINGUISTICA. **Added/Corp** Universita di Padova. Istituto di glottologia e fonetica. Centro per gli studi di fonetica del C.N.R. 1 (1979-80)-. Periodical. English (Italian). an. $32.00. Unipress Padova, Via C Battisti 231, 35121 Padova Italy. **Tel** 11 39 49 8752542, FAX 11 39 49 8752542. **LC** P1.A1; Q3. **DD** 410/.5.
Ind/Abst Linguist. Lang. Behav. Abstr. (1985-) [Full Cov.]; Soc. Plann. Policy Dev. Abstr.

GW/0179-3616
QUANTITATIVE LINGUISTICS. [Quant. linguist.]. (1978)-. Monographic series. English (French and German). Studienverlag Dr N Brockmeyer, Querenburger Hohe 283, W-4630 Bochum Germany. **LC** UNC.
Ind/Abst MLA Int. Bibl. Books Artic. Mod. Lang. Lit.

US/0002-7499
QUARTERLY BULLETIN OF THE AMERICAN ASSOCIATION OF TEACHERS OF ESPERANTO. **Main/Corp** American Association of Teachers of Esperanto. **VFOAT** Kvaronjara Bulteno de la Amerika Asocio de Instruistoj de Esperanto. Bulletin. English (Esperanto). qt. $10.00. American Association Teachers Esperanto, 4710 Dexter Drive/#3, Santa Barbara CA 93110-1325. **Tel** (805)967-5241. **ED** Dorothy Holland-Kaupp. **UDC** 800.892. **Bk Rev. Circ:** 100 (ctrl).
Desc: News of Esperanto classes in the US and abroad. Foreign language teaching methods. Information on Esperanto teaching materials and meetings.

US/0735-5920
QUARTERLY REVIEW ON DOUBLESPEAK. **See** Communication.

US/0033-5940
QUE TAL? (NEW YORK, N.Y.). (QUE TAL?). (19??)-. Periodical. Spanish. mo. $25.00. Mary Glasgow Publications, Brookhampton Lane, Kineton, Warwickshire CV35 0JB England. **Tel** 011 44 926 640606, FAX 011 44 926 641016. **(Subscription address:** Scholastic Inc, PO Box 3710, Jefferson City MO 65102.**)** available on microfilm from University Microfilms International (UMI).
Desc: Contains articles in Spanish for students in first level Spanish classes.

AT/0818-3279
QUEENSLAND STUDIES IN GERMAN LANGUAGE AND LITERATURE. [Qld. Stud. Ger. lang. lit.]. **Added/Corp** Queensland. University, Brisbane. Department of German. (1970)-. English. ir. A Francke Verlag GmbH, Postfach 2560, Dischingerweg 5, D 72070 Tuebingen Germany. **Tel** 011 49 7071 78091 or 92.
Ind/Abst MLA Int. Bibl. Books Artic. Mod. Lang. Lit.

GW/0481-3596
QUELLEN UND FORSCHUNGEN ZUR SPRACH- UND KULTURGESCHICHTE DER GERMANISCHEN VOLKER. (QUELLEN UND FORSCHUNGEN ZUR SPRACH- UND KULTURGESCHICHTE DER GERMANISCHEN VOLKER. NEUE FOLGE.). [Quellen Forsch. Sprach-Kult.gesch. ger. Volker]. Vol. 1 (1958)-. Monographic series. German. ir. Price varies per volume. Walter de Gruyter Inc., PO Box 303421, D 10728 Berlin Germany. **Tel** 011 49 30 260050, FAX 011 49 30 26005251. **(Subscription address:** US and Canada/ 200 Saw Mill River Road, Hawthorne, NY 10532**) LC** PD25; .Q4. ***Continues*** *Quellen und Forschungen zur Sprach- und Culturgeschichte der Germanischen Volker.*
Ind/Abst MLA Int. Bibl. Books Artic. Mod. Lang. Lit.

FR/0297-2638
QUI-VIVE INTERNATIONAL. ***Title Change.*** [Qui-vive int.]. No 1 (Nov. 1985)-(19??). Periodical. French. qt. Delegation Generale a la Langue Francaise, 1 rue Manutention, 75116 Paris France. **Tel** 011 33 1 40691224. ***Continued by*** *Breves de la Delegation Generale a la Langue Francaise.*
Ind/Abst Point Repere (1986-1987).

GW
QUICKBORN. Periodical. German. qt. DM30.00, free to members. Quickborn, Vereinigung fur Niederdeutsche, Sprache und Literatur e V, Alexander 16, 2000 Hamburg 1 Germany. **Tel** 0049/40/240809. **ED** Friedrich W Michelsen. **UDC** 803.1; 831. Index available. **Bk Rev. Circ:** 1,000. ***Continues*** *Quickborn, Vereinigung von Freunden der Niederdeutschen Sprache und Literatur in Hamburg. Mitteilungen.*
Desc: Essays on Low-German language and literature. News of Low-German books, records and events. Low-German in theatre, radio, school, church.

UK/0140-3397
QUINQUEREME. ***Ceased.*** [Quinquereme]. Vol. 1 (Jan. 1978)-(19??). Periodical. English. sm. The Treasurer Quinquereme, Univ Bath Sch, Modern Languages, Bath BA2 7AY England. **Tel** 0225 826826. **[CCC].**
Ind/Abst Arts Humanit. Citation Index (19??-19??) [Full Cov.]; Soc. Plann. Policy Dev. Abstr.; Sociol. Abstr.

US/0033-6602
QUINTO LINGO. ***Suspended.*** (QUINTO LINGO: THE MULTILINGUAL MAGAZINE.). [Quinto lingo]. Vol. 1 (Aug. 1964)-Suspended. English (German, Italian, Portuguese, Russian, Spanish and French). bm. $27.00 US, (add $7.50 for postage) other. Quinto Lingo, PO Box 9340, Alexandria VA 22304-0340. **Tel** (703)370-3750. **ED** Endel Peedo. **DD** 418/.007. **UDC** 800.73; 800.7. **Bk Rev. Ad Acc. Circ:** 15,000. available on microfilm and microfiche from University Microfilms International (UMI).
Desc: Publishes original investigations and theoretical papers dealing with worthwhile innovations in learning, teaching and education. The journal is primarily concerned with teacher education in all of its many aspects.

CN/0079-9335
R L S, REGIONAL LANGUAGE STUDIES ... NEWFOUNDLAND. [R L S, Reg. lang. stud., Nfld.]. **Added/Corp** Memorial University of Newfoundland. Folklore and Language Archive. Memorial University of Newfoundland. Dept. of English Language and Literature. No. 1 (Oct. 1968)-. Periodical. English. an. Free on request. Memorial University / Department of English, St. John's Newfoundland, AIC 5S7 Canada. **Tel** (709)737-8983. **ED** Robert Hollett. **DD** 427/.9/718. Index available. **Bk Rev. Circ:** 350 (ctrl).
Desc: Designed to spread information related to linguistic research being conducted in Newfoundland or related to the languages spoken in Newfoundland and Labrador. Contains notes on research and questions about puzzling problems, bibliographies, brief articles on aspects of language in this province and other related notes.
Ind/Abst MLA Int. Bibl. Books Artic. Mod. Lang. Lit.; Soc. Plann. Policy Dev. Abstr.

US/0033-7455
RAD (NEW YORK), DAS. (DAS RAD.). (19??)-. Periodical. German. Six times a year. $25.00. Mary Glasgow Publications, Brookhampton Lane, Kineton, Warwickshire CV35 0JB England. **Tel** 011 44 926 640606, FAX 011 44 926 641016. **(Subscription address:** Scholastic Inc, PO Box 3710, Jefferson City MO 65102.**)**
Desc: Contains articles in German for students in first level German classes.

CI
RADOVI STAROSLAVENSKOG ZAVODA. **Added/Corp** Staroslavenski Zavod "Svetozar Ritig." Institut Za Filologiju i Folkloristiku. (1988)-. Serbo-Croatian (Roman). **(Subscription address:** Mladost Export Import, PO Box 1028, Ilica 30,

41000 Zagreb Croatia.) **LC** PG6; .Z3. **CODEN** RSZAE2. ***Continues*** *Radovi Staroslavenskog Instituta.*
Ind/Abst Soc. Plann. Policy Dev. Abstr.

CI/0514-5090
RADOVI ZAVODA ZA SLAVENSKU FILOLOGIJU. [Rad. Zavoda slav. filol.]. **Added/Corp** Sveuciliste u Zagrebu. Zavod za Slavensku Filologiju. **VFOAT** Zbornik Radova Zavoda za Slavensku Filologiju. (1961)-. Serbo-Croatian (Roman) (summaries and/or abstracts in German and Russian). **LC** PG1; .Z3. ***Continues*** *Radovi Slavenskog Instituta.*
Ind/Abst MLA Int. Bibl. Books Artic. Mod. Lang. Lit.

US/0891-0545
RAFT (CLEVELAND, OHIO). (RAFT.). [Raft]. Vol. 1 (1987)-. Academic Scholarly Publication. English (Armenian). an. $35.00. Cleveland State University / c/o J. A. Greppin, Cleveland OH 44115. **Tel** (216)687-3967, FAX (216)687-9366, telex 810-421-8252 CSU CLV. **ED** J A C Greppin. **LC** PK8517; .R34. **DD** 891. **Bk Rev. Ad Acc. Circ:** 200 (ctrl).
Desc: A scholarly journal dealing with Armenian linguistics.
Ind/Abst MLA Int. Bibl. Books Artic. Mod. Lang. Lit.

II/0377-3310
RAJASTHAN JOURNAL OF ENGLISH STUDIES, THE. V. 1- July/Dec. 1974-. Periodical. English. sa. $10.00. Km Manju Joshi Memorial Society, Mathur House, Behind Jain School, Sikar India. **LC** PE9; .R34. **DD** 820/.9/954. **UDC** 802.0.

II
RAJASTHANNI SABADA KOSA. 1962-. Rajasthani (Rajasthani). **LC** PK2707.
Desc: Vol. 1 includes a short history of Rajasthani language and literature, in Hindi.

US/0272-2747
RAM'S HORN (HANOVER, N.H.), THE. (THE RAM'S HORN.). [Ram's horn]. **Added/Corp** Dartmouth College. Language Outreach. Rassias Foundation. (19??)-. Periodical. English (French). an (Dec.). $10.00. The Ram's Horn, Rassias Foundation, Dartmouth College, Hanover NH 03755. **Tel** (603)646-3719 Ext. 2922. **ED** Raymond Cormier and Micheline Lyons. **LC** PB35; .R2. **DD** 418/.007/1. **CODEN** RAHOEW. **Bk Rev. Ad Acc. Circ:** 2,000.
Desc: This publication includes essays and reviews by and for Rassias method/Dartmouth model adopters and enthusiasts.

CN/0229-9259
RAPPORT ANNUEL - CONSEIL DE LA LANGUE FRANCAISE. **Main/Corp** Quebec (Province). Conseil de la Langue Francaise. 1977/78-. French. an. Editeur Officiel du Quebec, 1283 Boul Charest Ouest, Quebec Quebec G1N 2C9 Canada. **LC** PC3601; .Q39A. **DD** 440/.6/0714. **UDC** 804.0(714).

BE
RAPPORT D'ACTIVITES DE L'INSTITUT DE PHONETIQUE. **Main/Corp** Brussels. Universite Libre. Institut de Phonetique. (19??)-. Academic Scholarly Publication. French (English). an. Institut des Langues Vivantes et de Phonetique, Avenue Franklin D Roosevelt 50, B 1050 Bruxelles Belgium. **Tel** 02 6502010, FAX 02 6502007. ctrl circ.
Desc: Covers phonetics, applied linguistics, signal processing, and more.
Ind/Abst Linguist. Lang. Behav. Abstr. (1972-) [Full Cov.]; MLA Int. Bibl. Books Artic. Mod. Lang. Lit.; Soc. Plann. Policy Dev. Abstr.

NG
RAPPORT D'ACTIVITES DU ... / ORGANISATION DE L'UNITE AFRICAINE, CENTRE D'ETUDES LINGUISTIQUES ET HISTORIQUES PAR TRADITION ORALE. **Main/Corp** Centre for Linguistic and Historical Studies by Oral Tradition. **VFOAT** Report on the Activities. (19??)-. English (French). Oua-Celhto, BP 878, Niamey Nigeria Africa. **LC** DT1; .C46a.

II
RASHTRABHASHA SANDESA : HINDI SAHITYA SAMMELANA KA MUKHAPATRA. Periodical. Hindi (Hindi). sm. **LC** PK1931; .A42. **UDC** 809.143.

NP
RASMI (KATHMANDU, NEPAL). (RASMI.). V. 1, No. 1, 1983/1984-. Periodical. Nepali. qt. Rs40.00. Rashmi, Office Kandel Kutir Kuleshwar, Kathmandu Nepal. **LC** PK2595; .R37. **UDC** 809.149.3.

CI
RASPRAVE ZAVODA ZA HRVATSKI JEZIK. **Added/Corp** Hrvatski Filoloski Institut u Zagrebu. Zavod za Hrvatski Jezik. (1991)-. Serbo-Croatian (Roman) (summaries and/or abstracts in English, French and German). Republicki Zavod za Statistiku, Central Bureau of Statistics of the Republic of Croatia, Ilica 3, Zagreb Croatia. **Tel** 011 385 41 45 44 22, FAX 011 385 41 42 94 13, 011 385 41 42 37 11, telex 21130 DZSTAT RH. **LC** PG1201; .J83. ***Continues*** *Rasprave Zavoda za Jezik IFF, 0351-434X.*

IT/0033-9725
RASSEGNA ITALIANA DI LINGUISTICA APPLICATA. [Rass. ital. linguist. appl.]. **Added/Corp** Centro Italiano di Linguistica Applicata. (1969)-. Periodical. English (Italian). Three times a year. L60000 Italy; L75000 other. Bulzoni Editore Srl, Via dei Liburni 14, 00185 Rome Italy. **Tel** 011 39 6 445-5207, FAX 011 39 6 445-0355. **ED** Renzo Titone.
Ind/Abst Curr. Index J. Educ.; Lang. Teach.; Linguist. Lang. Behav. Abstr. (1972-) [Full Cov.]; MLA Int. Bibl. Books Artic. Mod. Lang. Lit.; Soc. Plann. Policy Dev. Abstr.

NE/0922-4777
READING & WRITING. (READING AND WRITING.). [Read. writ.]. Vol. 1, No. 1 (1989)-. Periodical. English. qt. $356.00. Kluwer Academic Publishers, Postbus 322, 3300 AH Dordrecht, The Netherlands. **Tel** 011 (31) 78 524400, FAX 011 31 78 183273, telex 20083. **ED** R. Malatesha Joshi. **LC** BF456.R2; R338. **DD** 418/.4/05. **NLM** W1; RE103E. **CODEN** REWRE8. **[CCC].** Index available. **Bk Rev. Ad Acc. Pr Rev. Acid Free.** ctrl circ. available on microfilm and microfiche from University Microfilms International (UMI). Documents available from The Genuine Article.
Desc: Purpose of the journal is to publish high quality scientific articles pertaining to the processes, acquisition, and the loss of reading and writing skills. Publishes research articles, critical reviews, theoretical papers, case studies, and book reviews. Some topics that are appropriate for publication are: models of reading and writing; diagnosis and remediation of reading, writing, and spelling, etc.
Ind/Abst Curr. Contents Soc. Behav. Sci.; Educ. Index (1992-); Psychoanal. Abstr.; Psychol. Abstr. (1989-); PsycINFO; PsycScan: Appl. Exp. Eng. Psych.; PsycScan: LD/MR; PsycScan: Neuropsych.; Res. Alert [Full Cov.]; Soc. Plann. Policy Dev. Abstr.; Soc. Sci. Cit. Index [Full Cov.].

US/0034-0502
READING HORIZONS. [Read. horiz.]. **Added/Corp** Western Michigan University. Reading Center and Clinic. Homer L. J. Carter Reading Council. Western Michigan University. Psycho-Educational Clinic. Western Michigan University. College of Education. (1960)-. Periodical. English. Five times a year (Feb., Apr., Jun., Oct., Dec.). $25.00 (institutions), $20.00 (individuals) US; $30.00 (institutions), $25.00 (individuals) Canada; $30.00 (individuals), $35.00 (institutions) others. Reading Horizons, Western Michigan University, Kalamazoo MI 49008. **Tel** (616)387-3470. **ED** Jeanne Jacobson, Reading Clinic, (phone: (616)387-3517). Index available (published in the 5th edition of each issue). cum. index (yearly). **Bk Rev**, (Qty: 20-25). **Circ:** 1,000 (ctrl). available on microfilm and microfiche from University Microfilms International (UMI).
Desc: Ten informative articles each quarter about teaching, measuring, and improving student reading at all levels; especially helpful to new professionals in the field.
Ind/Abst Contents Pages Educ.; Curr. Index J. Educ.; Educ. Index; Soc. Plann. Policy Dev. Abstr.

US/0034-0510
READING IMPROVEMENT. [Read. improv.]. **Added/Corp** Project Innovation (Organization). **VAT** Reading Improv. Vol. 2, No. 1 (Fall 1964)-. Periodical. English. Four times a year. $20.00 (institutions), $15.00 (individuals). Project Innovation of Mobile, PO Box 8508, Spring Hill Station, Mobile AL 36608. **Tel** (205)633-7802. **ED** Phil Feldman. **LC** LB1050.5; .R39. **DD** 428/.4/05. Index available. **Bk Rev. Circ:** 2,000 (ctrl). available on microfilm and microfiche from University Microfilms International (UMI). ***Continues*** *Reading in High School.*
Desc: Includes reports of investigations and theoretical papers dealing with every conceivable aspect of reading instruction and reading improvement. Designed to communicate new developments to reading teachers and educators interested in improving reading instruction.
Ind/Abst Contents Pages Educ.; Curr. Index J. Educ.; Educ. Index; Soc. Plann. Policy Dev. Abstr.; Women Stud. Abstr.

UK/0264-2425
READING IN A FOREIGN LANGUAGE. **Added/Corp** University of Aston in Birmingham. Language Studies Unit. Vol. 1, No. 1 (March 1983)-. Periodical. English. Twice a year. £13.00 surface mail; £15.00 airmail. College St Mark & St John, Overseas Education Center, Derriford Road, Plymouth Devon PL6 8BH England. **Tel** 011 44 752 777188, FAX 011 44 752 786622, telex 45189. **ED** Alexander Urquhart (phone: (0752)761121). **CODEN** RFLAEB. Index Bound in First Issue. cum. index. **Bk Rev. Ad Acc. Circ:** 300 (ctrl).
Desc: Practice and theory of learning to read and teaching reading in any foreign language.
Ind/Abst Br. Educ. Index; Curr. Index J. Educ.

CN/0228-9652
READING MANITOBA. **See** Education-Teaching and Curriculum.

US/0886-0246
READING RESEARCH AND INSTRUCTION. (READING RESEARCH AND INSTRUCTION : THE JOURNAL OF THE COLLEGE READING ASSOCIATION.). [Read. res. instr.]. **Added/Corp** College Reading Association. **VFOAT** Journal of the College Reading Association. Vol. 25, No. 1 (Fall 1985)-. Periodical. English. qt. $50.00 US; $55.00 Canada; $58.00 other. College Reading Association, Pittsburg State University, Pittsburg KS 66762. **Tel** (316)235-4494, FAX (316)231-7515. **ED** Robert Cooter, Texas Christian University, Fort Worth, Texas; Telephone: (817)921-7770. **LC** LB1050; .J63. **DD** 428.4/05. Index available. cum. index. **Bk Rev. Ad Acc. Pr Rev. Circ:** 1,300 (ctrl). available on microfilm and microfiche from University Microfilms International (UMI). ***Continues*** *Reading World, 0149-0117.*
Desc: Basic and applied research related to reading and the language; pedagogical issues related to reading instruction.
Ind/Abst Contents Pages Educ.; Curr. Index J. Educ.; Educ. Index; High. Educ. Abstr. (1976); Psychol. Abstr. (1985-); PsycINFO; PsycLit.

US/0034-0553
READING RESEARCH QUARTERLY. [Read. res. q.]. **Added/Corp** International Reading Association. Vol. 1 (Fall 1965)-. Periodical. English (summaries and/or abstracts in French and Spanish). qt. $41.00. International Reading Association, 800 Barksdale Road, PO Box 8139, Newark DE 19714-8139. **Tel** (302)731-1600, FAX (302)731-1057, telex 5106002813 READING. **ED** Philip Gough. **LC** LB1050; .R42. **DD** 428.4/072. **CODEN** RRQUA6. **[CCC].** Index available. **Pr Rev. Circ:** 12,000 (ctrl). available on microfilm and microfiche from University Microfilms International (UMI). Documents available from The Genuine Article.
Desc: Technically oriented for those interested in reading research.
Ind/Abst Acad. Search (Jan. 1994-); Child. Lit. Abstr. (19??-); Contents Pages Educ.; Curr. Contents Soc. Behav. Sci.; Curr. Index J. Educ.; Educ. Index; Except. Child Educ. Resour. (19??-19??); INFO-SOUTH Abstr.; Lang. Lang. Behav. Abstr.; Lang. Teach.; Mag. Search; Middle East Abstr. Index; MLA Int. Bibl. Books Artic. Mod. Lang. Lit.; Multicult. Educ. Abstr.; Psychol. Abstr. (1965-); PsycINFO; PsycLit; Res. Alert [Full Cov.]; Soc. Plann. Policy Dev. Abstr.; Soc. Sci. Cit. Index [Full Cov.]; Spec. Educ. Needs Abstr.

US
READING STYLES NEWSLETTER. **See** Education.

UK/0034-0472
READING (SUNDERLAND). **See** Education-Teaching and Curriculum.

US/0034-0561
READING TEACHER, THE. [Read. teach.]. **Added/Corp** International Reading Association. International Council for the Improvement of Reading Instruction. Vol. 5 (Sept. 15, 1951)-. Periodical. English. Eight times a year. $41.00. International Reading Association, 800 Barksdale Road, PO Box 8139, Newark DE 19714-8139. **Tel** (302)731-1600, FAX (302)731-1057, telex 5106002813 READING. **ED** Janet R. Binkley. **LC** LB1573; .R28. **DD** 372.405. **CODEN** REDTAH. **[CCC].** cum. index. **Bk Rev. Ad Acc. Pr Rev. Circ:** 42,000 (ctrl). available on microfilm and microfiche from University Microfilms International (UMI). Documents available from The Genuine Article, UMI Article Clearinghouse. ***Continues*** *International Council for the Improvement of Reading Instruction. Bulletin.*
Desc: Geared to reading educators at the elementary level. Articles concern applied research, instructional techniques, program descriptions, and professional issues and controversies.
Ind/Abst Acad. Abstr. Full Text Elite (Oct. 1989-); Acad. Abstr. (Oct. 1989-); Acad. Ind. [Computer File] (1987-); Acad. Search (Oct. 1989-); Arts Humanit. Citation Index [Select. Cov.]; Book Rev. Index; Chicano Index; Child. Lit. Abstr.; Contents Pages Educ.; Curr. Contents Soc. Behav. Sci.; Curr. Index J. Educ.; Educ. Index; Except. Child Educ. Resour. (19??-19??); Expand. Acad. Index (1987-); INFO-SOUTH Abstr.; Lang. Lang. Behav. Abstr.; Mag. Artic. Summar. Elite (Oct. 1989-); Mag. Artic. Summar. Select (July 1989-); Mag. Artic. Summar. CD-ROM (Oct. 1989-); Mag. Search; Med. Rev. Dig.; Middle East Abstr. Index; Mid. Search (Jul. 1989-); Multicult. Educ. Abstr.; Newsp. Period. Abstr. (1988-); Prim. Search (Jul. 1989-); Psychol. Abstr. (1965-); PsycINFO (?-?); PsycLit; Res. Alert [Full Cov.]; Soc. Plann. Policy Dev. Abstr.; Soc. Sci. Cit. Index [Full Cov.]; Spec. Educ. Needs Abstr.

PR
READINGS IN SPANISH-ENGLISH CONTRASTIVE LINGUISTICS. 1973-. English. $4.50. Inter American University Press, PO Box 3255, San Juan PR 00936. **ED** R Nash. **LC** PC4099; .R42. **DD** 418. **UDC** 800.52.

FR
RECHERCHES CROISEES ARAGON/ELSA TRIOLET / GROUPE DE RECHERCHES EN LINGUISTIQUE ET SEMIOTIQUE (GRELIS), BESANCON [ET] FONDS ELSA TRIOLET-ARAGON DU CNRS, PARIS. **Added/Corp** Groupe de Recherches en Linguistique et Semiotique (France) Fonds Elsa Triolet-Aragon du CNRS. **VFOAT**

Recherches Croisees Aragon Elsa Triolet; Recherches Croisees. (1988)-. French. Societe Edition Belles Lettres, 95 Boulevard Raspail, 75006 Paris France. **Tel** 011 33 1 45487055, FAX 011 33 1 45449288, telex 200577. **LC** PAR; PQ2601.R2; Z855.

FR
RECHERCHES EN LINGUISTIQUE ETRANGERE. **Added/Corp** Universite de Besancon. Faculte des Lettres et Sciences Humaines. Universite de Besancon. Centre Specialise de Recherches en Linguistique Etrangere. (1973)-. French. ir. 100.00F. Societe Edition Belles Lettres, 95 Boulevard Raspail, 75006 Paris France. **Tel** 011 33 1 45487055, FAX 011 33 1 45449288, telex 200577. **LC** AS161; .B39 subser; P2. **DD** 084/.1 S; 410.

XO
RECUEIL LINGUISTIQUE DE BRATISLAVA. **Added/Corp** Jazykovy Kruzok v Bratislave. Cercle Linguistique de Bratislava. Slovenska Akademia Vied. Vol. 1 (1948)-. Czech (English, French, German and Russian). ir. Veda, Publishing House of the Slovak Academy of Sciences, Klemensova 19, 814 30 Bratislava Slovakia. **Tel** (7)583-15. **(Subscription address:** John Benjamins North America, PO Box 27519, Philadelphia PA 19118-0519.) **LC** P25; .R42.

FR/0034-222X
REEDUCATION ORTHOPHONIQUE. [Reeduc. orthoph.]. **VFOAT** Revue de l'ARPLOE. (1963)-. Periodical. French. qt. 600.00F. Reeducation Orthophonique, 10 rue de l Arivee, 75015 Paris France. **Tel** 011 33 1 45444885. **UDC** 615.851.4.

YU
REFERATI I SAOPSTENJA - NAUCNI SASTANAK SLAVISTA U VUKOVE DANE. **Main/Conf** Naucni Sastanak Slavista u Vukove Dane. **Added/Corp** Meunarodni Slavisticki Centar SR Srbije. (1971)-. Serbo-Croatian (Roman). an. Meunarodni Slavisticki Centar, Studetski Trg 3/1, Belgrad Yugoslavia. **LC** PG1207; .N37a.

US/0739-7356
REFLECTOR (UNIVERSITY PARK, MD.), THE. (THE REFLECTOR.). [Reflector]. Vol. 1 (Fall 1981)-. Periodical. English. Three times a year. $10.00. The Reflectory, 4017 Tennyson Road, University Park MD 20782. **LC** HV2474; .R43. **DD** 419/.05. **UDC** 802.0. **NLM** W1 RE1698P.

GW
REIHE GERMANISTISCHE LINGUISTIK. **VFOAT** Germanistische Linguistik. (19??)-. Monographic series. German. ir. Price varies per volume. Max Niemeyer Verlag, Postfach 2140, D 72011 Tuebingen Germany. **Tel** 011 49 7071 989494, FAX 011 49 7071 87419. **ED** Helmut Henne, Horst Sitta, Herbert Ernst Wiegand.
Desc: Series covering the German language.
Ind/Abst MLA Int. Bibl. Books Artic. Mod. Lang. Lit.

SI/0033-6882
RELC JOURNAL. [RELC j.]. **Added/Corp** Regional English Language Centre. Regional Language Centre. **VFOAT** R.E.L.C. Journal. **VAT** Regional English Language Centre Journal. Vol. 1 (June 1970)-. Periodical. English. sa (2 issues). $20.00. Seameo Regional Language Center, 30 Orange Grove Road, Singapore 1025 Singapore. **Tel** 011 65 7379044, FAX 011 65 7342753. **LC** PE1068.A7; R45. **DD** 428/.007/059. Index available (extra for $3.00). **Bk Rev. Ad Acc.** available on microfilm and microfiche from University Microfilms International (UMI).
Ind/Abst Lang. Teach.; MLA Int. Bibl. Books Artic. Mod. Lang. Lit.; Soc. Plann. Policy Dev. Abstr.

CN/0711-1177
RENDEZVOUS (FREDERICTON). (RENDEZVOUS : FOR NEW BRUNSWICK'S FRENCH SECOND LANGUAGE TEACHERS.). [Rendezvous]. Periodical. English. Three times a year. Free. New Brunswick Teachers' Association, PO Box 752, Fredericton New Brunswick E3B 5R6 Canada. **Tel** (506)452-8921. **DD** 448/.007. **UDC** 804.0-07(715). ctrl circ. ***Continues*** *French III Times, 0711-4605.*

IT
RENDICONTI (ACCADEMIA NAZIONALE DEI LINCEI. CLASSE DI SCIENZE MORALI, STORICHE E FILOLOGICHE). **See** Ethics.

BE
REPERTOIRE ALPHABETIQUE ET PHONETIQUE DES MARQUES INTERNATIONALES. an. Compu Mark, St Petersbliet 7, B-2000 Antwerpen Belgium. **Tel** 3 2318850.

CN/0845-311X
REPERTOIRE / CORPORATION DES TRADUCTEURS ET INTERPRETES DU NOUVEAU-BRUNSWICK. [Repert. - Corp. trad. interpret. N.-B.]. **Main/Corp** Corporation of Translators and Interpreters of New Brunswick. **VFOAT** Directory. **VAT** Directory - Corporation of Translators and Interpreters of New Brunswick (1989). (Jan. 1989)-. French (English). an. Free to members. Corporation of Translators and Interpreters of New Brunswick, PO Box 427, Fredericton New Brunswick E3B 4Z9 Canada. **Tel** (506)453-2920. **ED** Jose Ouimet. **DD** 418/.02/025715. **Ad Acc. Circ:** 150 (ctrl). available on diskette ((WANG OIS)). ***Continues*** *Annuaire / Corporation des Traduceurs et Interprets du Nouveau Brunswick, 0227-5546.*
Desc: A directory of members of the CTINB, the professional organization of translators, interpreters and terminologists of the province of New Brunswick.

●CN/1187-8711
REPERTOIRE / CORPORATION DES TRADUCTEURS, TRADUCTRICES, TERMINOLOGUES ET INTERPRETES DU NOUVEAU-BRUNSWICK. [Repert. - Corp. trad. trad. terminol. interpret. N.-B.]. **Main/Corp** Corporation of Translators, Terminologists and Interpreters of New Brunswick. **VFOAT** Directory. (Jan. 1992)-. English (French). Corporation of Translators, Terminologists and Interpreters of New-Brunswick, PO Box 427, Fredericton New Brunswick E3B 4Z9 Canada. **DD** 418/.02/0257151. ***Continues*** *Corporation of Translators and Interpreters of New Brunswick.; Repertoire., 0845-311X.*

CN/1187-4104
REPERTOIRE INTERNATIONAL DES DEPARTMENTS ET DES CENTRES DETUDES FRANCAISES. [Repert. int. dep. cent. etud. fr.]. **Main/Corp** Association des Universites Partiellement ou Entierement de Langue Francaise. **Added/Corp** UREF. **VFOAT** Repertoire; Departements et Centres Universitaires d'Etudes Francaises; Repertoire International des Departements et Centres Universitaires d'Etudes Francaises. (1991)-. French. 30.00Can$ per volume. Association des Universites Partiellement du Entierement de Langue Francaise-UREF, Service des Banques de Donnees, CP 400, Succursale Cote-Des-Neiges, Montreal Quebec H3S 2S7 Canada. **DD** 440/.71/1.

US/0360-4063
RESEARCH IN READING AND THE LANGUAGE ARTS. V. 1- Fall 1974-. English. $1.75 single issue. William Patterson College, 300 Pompton Road, Alumni Association, Wayne JN 07470. **LC** LB1049.9; .R48. **DD** 372.6. **UDC** 372.41.

GW/0179-4167
RESEARCH IN TEXT THEORY. [Res. text theory]. **VFOAT** Untersuchungen zur Texttheorie. (1977)-. Monographic series. English. Walter de Gruyter Inc., PO Box 303421, D 10728 Berlin Germany. **Tel** 011 49 30 260050, FAX 011 49 30 26005251.
Ind/Abst MLA Int. Bibl. Books Artic. Mod. Lang. Lit.

US/0034-527X
RESEARCH IN THE TEACHING OF ENGLISH. **See** Education-Teaching and Curriculum.

CN/0835-1813
RESEARCH ON LANGUAGE AND SOCIAL INTERACTION. [Res. lang. soc. interact.]. Vol. 20 (1987)-. Periodical. English. qt. $140.00 US & Canada; $165.00 other. Lawrence Erlbaum Associates, 365 Broadway, Suite 102, Hillsdale NJ 07642. **Tel** (201)666-4110, (800)926-6579, FAX (201)666-2394. **LC** P1; .P35. **DD** 401/.9/05. **[CCC]. Ad Acc. Acid Free.** available on microfilm and microfiche from University Microfilms International (UMI). ***Continues*** *Papers in Linguistics, 0031-1251.*
Desc: Dedicated to the dissemination of work that adds to our knowledge about language and social interaction. It applies to social interactions between individuals - in face-to-face encounters and/or through new communication technologies. Also applies to social interactions between institutions and their publics that are carried out through print or electronic media.
Ind/Abst Am. Bibliogr. Slavic East Europ. Stud.; Annu. Bibliogr. Engl. Lang. Lit.; Linguist. Lang. Behav. Abstr. (1973-) [Full Cov.]; Soc. Plann. Policy Dev. Abstr.

II
RESEARCH PAPERS - DEPARTMENT OF TAMIL, UNIVERSITY OF KERALA. **Main/Corp** University of Kerala. Dept. of Tamil. V. 5- 1974-. Periodical. English. an. University of Kerala Kariavattom, Trivandrum India. **LC** PL4751; .A35. **DD** 494/.811/05. **UDC** 809.48. ***Continues*** *Journal of the Department of Tamil.*

US/0085-3739
RESEARCH REPORT - NATIONAL COUNCIL OF TEACHERS OF ENGLISH. **Main/Corp** National Council of Teachers of English. **Added/Corp** National Council of Teachers of English. Committee on Research. **VFOAT** NCTE Research Report. No. 1 (1963)-. Monographic series. English. ir. Price varies per volume. National Council of Teachers of English, 1111 Kenyon Road, Urbana IL 61801. **Tel** (217)328-3870, FAX (217)328-9645. **LC** PE1011; .N295. **DD** 428.007.

BE/0771-095X
RESTANT. [Restant]. (1971)-. Periodical. Dutch. bm. **UDC** 8.
Ind/Abst MLA Int. Bibl. Books Artic. Mod. Lang. Lit.

SP/0214-4808
REVISTA ALICANTINA DE ESTUDIOS INGLESES. (1988)-. Periodical. Multiple languages. an. **UDC** 802.0.
Ind/Abst MLA Int. Bibl. Books Artic. Mod. Lang. Lit.

AG/0326-6400
REVISTA ARGENTINA DE LINGUISTICA. Vol. 1, No. 1 (March 1985)-. Periodical. Spanish. sa (March & Sept.). $45.00 US. Revista Argentina de Linguistica, Casilla de Correo 45, 5511 Gutier Mendoza Argentina. **Tel** 011 54 61 973278. **ED** Victor Miguel Castel. **Ad Acc. Circ:** 250 (ctrl).
Desc: Spanish philology.
Ind/Abst Linguist. Lang. Behav. Abstr. (1985-) [Full Cov.]; MLA Int. Bibl. Books Artic. Mod. Lang. Lit.; Soc. Plann. Policy Dev. Abstr.

BL/0101-8248
REVISTA BRASILEIRA DE LINGUA E LITERATURA. [Rev. bras. ling. lit.]. 1- 1st Half 1979-. Periodical. Portuguese. Livraria Padrao, rua Miguel Couto 40, Rio de Janeiro Brazil. **LC** PC5001. **DD** 469/.05. **UDC** 806.90; 860.
Ind/Abst MLA Int. Bibl. Books Artic. Mod. Lang. Lit.

SP/0211-5913
REVISTA CANARIA DE ESTUDIOS INGLESES. **Added/Corp** Universidad de La Laguna. Departamento de Ingles. **VFOAT** R.C.E.I. (198?)-. Periodical. English (Spanish). sa (2 issues). $60.00 (institution) US. Secretariado de Publ Universidad of Laguna, Universidad of Laguna, Departmento de Ingles/Filo, 38201 La Laguna Tenerife Spain. **LC** PE9; .R48. **DD** 420/.5.
Ind/Abst Annu. Bibliogr. Engl. Lang. Lit.; MLA Int. Bibl. Books Artic. Mod. Lang. Lit.; Soc. Plann. Policy Dev. Abstr.

SP/0034-7981
REVISTA DE DIALECTOLOGIA Y TRADICIONES POPULARES. **See** Folklore.

BL/0102-4450
REVISTA DE DOCUMENTACAO DE ESTUDOS EM LINGUISTICA TEORICA E APLICADA. **Added/Corp** Pontificia Universidade Catolica de Sao Paulo. Departamento de Linguistica. **VFOAT** Documentacao de Estudos em Linguistica Teorica e Aplicada; DELTA; Revista DELTA; D.E.L.T.A. Vol. 1, No. 1/2 (Aug. 1985)-. Periodical. Portuguese (English). sa. Departamento de Linguistica, Rua Monte Allegre, 984 05014 Sao Paulo Brasil. **LC** P1.A1; R4299. **DD** 410/.5.
Ind/Abst Linguist. Lang. Behav. Abstr. (1985-); Soc. Plann. Policy Dev. Abstr.

PR/0378-7974
REVISTA DE ESTUDIOS HISPANICOS (RIO PIEDRAS, P.R.). (REVISTA DE ESTUDIOS HISPANICOS.). [Rev. estud. hisp.]. **Added/Corp** University of Puerto Rico. Seminario de Estudios Hispanicos. Vol. 1 (1971)-. Periodical. Spanish (English). an. $18.50 (one year), $44.00 (three year) institutions; $9.00 (one year), $21.00 (two year) individuals. University de Puerto Rico / Oficina de Publicaciones, Apartado 23322 Estacion UPR, San Juan Puerto Rica 00931-1787. **Tel** (809)250-0615, (809)250-0725, (809)250-0725, FAX (809)753-9116. **ED** Jose Luis Vega. **LC** PC4001; .R48. **DD** 460. **Bk Rev. Ad Acc. Circ:** 1,000. Documents available from The Genuine Article. ***Supersedes*** *Revista de Estudios Hispanicos.*
Desc: Articles and research studies on Hispanic literature, philology, linguistics, folklore and civilization.
Ind/Abst Arts Humanit. Citation Index [Full Cov.]; Curr. Contents Arts Humanit.; MLA Int. Bibl. Books Artic. Mod. Lang. Lit.; Res. Alert [Full Cov.]; Romant. Move.

US/0034-818X
REVISTA DE ESTUDIOS HISPANICOS (UNIVERSITY, AL.). (REVISTA DE ESTUDIOS HISPANICOS.). [Rev. estud. hisp.]. **Added/Corp** University of Alabama. Dept. of Romance Languages. Vol. 1 (May 1967)-. Periodical. Spanish (English). Three times a year (Jan., May, Oct.). $21.00 (individuals), $33.00 (institutions) US; $37.00 other. Washington University School of Law, Campus Box 1120, One Brookings Drive, St Louis MO 63130-4899. **Tel** (314)935-6436, (314)935-6422, FAX (314)935-6493. **ED** Andrew Bush. **DD** 460. **[CCC]. Bk Rev. Ad Acc. Circ:** 500 (ctrl). available on microfilm and microfiche from University Microfilms International (UMI).
Desc: Publishes articles, interviews and book reviews concerning the literature of Spain and Latin America.
Ind/Abst Curr. Contents Arts Humanit.; MLA Int. Bibl. Books Artic. Mod. Lang. Lit.

SP
REVISTA DE FILOLOGIA DE LA UNIVERSIDAD DE LA LAGUNA. **Added/Corp** Universidad de La Laguna. No. 1 (1982)-. Periodical. Arabic (Spanish). an. 1300ptas. Universidad

de la Laguna, C San Agustin 30, 38201 La Laguna Tenerife Spain. **Tel** 011 34 922 263211. **LC** P1.A1; R43. **DD** 410/.5.
Ind/Abst Annu. Bibliogr. Engl. Lang. Lit.; MLA Int. Bibl. Books Artic. Mod. Lang. Lit.

SP/0210-9174
REVISTA DE FILOLOGIA ESPANOLA. [Rev. filol. esp.]. **Added/Corp** Centro de Estudios Historicos (Spain) Instituto Antonio de Nebrija. Instituto "Miguel de Cervantes.". (Jan./March 1914)-. Periodical. Spanish. Four times a year. $55.00. Consejo Superior Investigacion Cientificas (CSIC), Vitruvio 8, 28006 Madrid Spain. **Tel** 011 34 1 5612833, FAX 011 34 1 4113077, telex 42182. **LC** PQ6001; .R45. Documents available from The Genuine Article.
Ind/Abst Am. Hist. Life (1964-1965); Arts Humanit. Citation Index [Full Cov.]; Curr. Contents Arts Humanit.; MLA Int. Bibl. Books Artic. Mod. Lang. Lit.; Res. Alert [Full Cov.].

SP
REVISTA DE FILOLOGIA ROMANICA / SECCION DE FILOLOGIA ROMANICA. **See** Classical Studies.

CR
REVISTA DE FILOLOGIA Y LINGUISTICA DE LA UNIVERSIDAD DE COSTA RICA. **Main/Corp** Universidad de Costa Rica. **VFOAT** Revista de Filologia y Linguistica. Spanish. $5.00. Universidad de Costa Rica / Editorial, Apartado 75, 2060 Ciudad Universitaria, San Jose Costa Rica. **Tel** 011 506 2247051, 2253133. **LC** P9; .C67A. **UDC** 806.0; 860.

SZ
REVISTA DE INTERLINGUA. Periodical. mo. 10. **LC** PM8400; .A4. **DD** 499/.993/05. **UDC** 800.897.

SP/1130-8508
REVISTA DE LENGUA Y LITERATURA CATALANA, GALLEGA Y VASCA. (1991)-. Periodical. Multiple languages. an. Universidad Autonoma de Madrid / Departamento de Filologia Espanola, Carretera de Colmenar, km 15,000 Canto Blanco, 28049 Madrid Spain. **UDC** 801.

AG
REVISTA DE LENGUAS EXTRANJERAS. **Added/Corp** Mendoza, Argentine Republic (City). Universidad Nacional de Cuyo. Instituto de Lenguas Extranjeras. (1970)-. Periodical. Spanish (English). **LC** P1.A1; R44.

BL/0101-3505
REVISTA DE LETRAS (MARILIA). (REVISTA DE LETRAS / UNIVERSIDADE ESTADUAL PAULISTA.). [Rev. let.]. **Added/Corp** Universidade Estadual Paulista. Faculdade de Filosofia, Ciencias e Letras de Assis. Instituto de Letras, Historia e Psicologia de Assis. (1960)-. English (French, German, Italian, Portuguese and Spanish). an (August). $30.00. Fundacao Desenvolvimento Unesp, Av Rio Branco 1210, 01206 Sao Paulo SP Brazil. **Tel** 011 55 11 2237088. **LC** P1.A1; R443. **DD** 809; 809. Index available (bound in issue).
Ind/Abst HAPI Hisp. Am. Period. Index; MLA Int. Bibl. Books Artic. Mod. Lang. Lit.; Soc. Plann. Policy Dev. Abstr.; Sociol. Abstr.

SP/0212-5056
REVISTA DE LLENGUA I DRET. **See** Classical Studies.

SP/0210-1874
REVISTA ESPANOLA DE LINGUISTICA. [Rev. esp. linguist.]. **Added/Corp** Sociedad Espanola de Linguistica. Vol. 1, No. 1 (Jan./June 1971)-. Periodical. Spanish (summaries and/or abstracts in English). Twice a year. 2225ptas Spain; 2772ptas other. Editorial Gredos SA, Calle Sanchez Pacheco 81, 28002 Madrid Spain. **Tel** 011 34 1 4157408, FAX 011 34 1 5192033. **LC** P9; .R39. **Bk Rev.**
Ind/Abst Lang. Teach.; MLA Int. Bibl. Books Artic. Mod. Lang. Lit.

PE
REVISTA LATINOAMERICANA DE ESTUDIOS ETNOLINGUISTICOS. V. 1, (Year 1981)-. Periodical. Spanish. an. Ignacio Prado Pastor, Jiron Cuzco 484 Lima Peru. **Tel** 272913-277181. **ED** I Prado Pastor. **LC** PM101; .R48. **DD** 498/.05. **UDC** 800. Index available. **Bk Rev.** **Ad Acc.** **Circ:** 1,000.
Desc: A complete and exact review which covers 72 languages.

BL/0100-0888
REVISTA LETRAS (CURITIBA). (REVISTA LETRAS.). [Rev. let.]. **Added/Corp** Universidade Federal do Parana. Setor de Ciencias Humanas, Letras e Artes. Universidade Federal do Parana. Departamento de Linguistica, Letras Classicas e Vernaculas. Universidade Federal do Parana. Curso de Letras. **VFOAT** Letras. No. 21/22 (1973/1974)-. Portuguese (English, German, Portuguese and Spanish). an. Curso de Letras do Setor e Ciencias Humanas, Universidade Federal do Parana, rua General Caneiro, 460 - 110 Andar, Caixa Portal 441, CEP 80000-970 Curitiba Parana Brasil. **Tel** 041 264 2243. **ED** Marta Moraes da Costa. **LC** PB5; .R48. **DD** 410/.5. Index available. cum. index. **Pr Rev.** **Circ:** 348 (ctrl). ***Continues** Letras.*
Ind/Abst MLA Int. Bibl. Books Artic. Mod. Lang. Lit.

PO/0870-4139
REVISTA PORTUGUESA DE FILOLOGIA. [Rev. port. filol.]. **Added/Corp** Coimbra. Universidade. Instituto de Estudos Romanicos. Vol. 1 (1947)-. Portuguese. ir (every 2-3 years). Price varies per volume. Casa do Castelo, rua da Sofia 47-49, Coimbra 3000 Portugal. **Tel** 011 351 39 24686. **LC** PC5001; .R55. **DD** 469.05. cum. index.
Desc: Portuguese philology.
Ind/Abst MLA Int. Bibl. Books Artic. Mod. Lang. Lit.

CL/0035-0451
REVISTA SIGNOS. (SIGNOS : ESTUDIOS DE LENGUA Y LITERATURA.). [Rev. signos]. **Added/Corp** Universidad Catolica de Valparaiso. Instituto de Literatura Ciencias del Lenguaje. **VFOAT** Revista Signos de Valparaiso; Revista Signos. (1967)-. Periodical. Spanish. sa. $33.00 (Americas); $35.00 (others). Ediciones Universitarias de Valparaiso, Casilla 1415, Valparaiso Chile. **Tel** 011 56 31 252900. **LC** P9; .S4.
Ind/Abst MLA Int. Bibl. Books Artic. Mod. Lang. Lit.

UY
REVISTA SINTAXIS. **VFOAT** Sintaxis. V. 1- Nov. 1975-. Spanish. Casilla 1093, Montevideo Uruguay. **Tel** 801.56. **LC** AS89.A1; R48.

SP/0556-705X
REVISTA VALENCIANA DE FILOLOGIA. **Added/Corp** Valencia (City) Institute de Literatura y Estudios Filologicos. Vol. 1 (Jan./April 1951)-. Spanish. ir. Consejo Superior Investigacion Cientificas (CSIC), Vitruvio 8, 28006 Madrid Spain. **Tel** 011 34 1 5612833, FAX 011 34 1 4113077, telex 42182. **LC** P9; .R42.

BE/0035-0818
REVUE BELGE DE PHILOLOGIE ET D'HISTOIRE. (REVUE BELGE DE PHILOLOGIE ET D'HISTOIRE. BELGISCH TIJDSCHRIFT VOOR PHILOLOGIE EN GESCHIEDENIS.). [Rev. belge philol. hist.]. **Added/Corp** Fondation Universitaire de Belgique. Societe pour le Progres des Etudes Philologiques et Historiques. Belgium. Ministere de l'Education Nationale. **VFOAT** Belgisch Tijdschrift voor Philologie en Geschiedenis; RBPH. Vol. I (Jan. 1922)-. Periodical. French (English, German, Dutch and Flemish; summaries and/or abstracts in Flemish, French and German). Four times a year (Mar., June, Sept., Dec.). 2320F Belgium; 2800F others. Revue Belge de Phil et d Hist, rue de l Etoile Polaire 37, B 1080 Brussels Belguim. **LC** P2; .R4. **DD** 410/.5. **Bk Rev.** **Ad Acc.** **Circ:** 1,000. Documents available from The Genuine Article.
Desc: Covers history from antiquity to contemporary Europe and modern and classical philology.
Ind/Abst Am. Hist. Life (1954-1961, 1965-); Annu. Bibliogr. Engl. Lang. Lit.; Arts Humanit. Citation Index [Full Cov.]; BHA : Biblio. Hist. Art; Curr. Contents Arts Humanit.; MLA Int. Bibl. Books Artic. Mod. Lang. Lit.; Numis. Lit.; Res. Alert [Full Cov.]; Romant. Move.; Soc. Sci. Cit. Index [Select. Cov.].

LH
REVUE D'ASSYRIOLOGIE ET D'ARCHEOLOGIE ORIENTALE. Vol. 1, No. 1 (1884)-. Periodical. French. Kraus Reprint, FL 9491, Nendeln Liechtenstein. cum. index.

FR/0982-6548
REVUE DE BIBLIOLOGIE. **See** Literature.

CN/1193-1493
REVUE DE L'ACLA. [Rev. ACLA]. **Added/Corp** Association Canadienne de Linguistique Appliquee. **VFOAT** Revue de l'Association Canadienne de Linguistique Appliquee; Journal of the Canadian Association of Applied Linguistics; Journal of the CAAL. (1991)-. Periodical. Multiple languages. sa. 40.00Can$ Canada; 45.00Can$ other. Canadian Association of Applied Linguistics Secretariat, Department de Linguistique, CP 8888 Succ. A, Montreal Quebec H3C 3P8 Canada. **Tel** (514)987-8541, FAX (514)987-4652. **ED** M.N. Legoux. **DD** 418.007. Index available. cum. index. **Bk Rev**, (Qty: 10-20). **Ad Acc.** **Pr Rev.** **Circ:** 300 (ctrl). ***Continues** Bulletin de l'ACLA, 0709-9207.*

FR/0035-1458
REVUE DE LINGUISTIQUE ROMANE. [Rev. linquist. rom.]. **Added/Corp** Societe de Linguistique Romane. Vol. 1 (Jan./June 1925)-. French (Spanish, Portuguese and Italian). Twice a year (June, Dec.). 454.90F France; 480.00F others. Societe de Linguistique Romane, 44 Avenue De La Liberation, 54014 Nancy Cedex France. **Tel** (011)33 83 962176. **ED** M. Straka. **LC** PC2; .R35. **DD** 440/.05. Index available. cum. index. **Circ:** 1,200 (ctrl). Documents available from The Genuine Article.
Desc: Articles about romance languages and literatures, dialectology, lexicology and romance philology.
Ind/Abst Arts Humanit. Citation Index [Full Cov.]; Curr. Contents Arts Humanit.; Lang. Teach.; MLA Int. Bibl. Books Artic. Mod. Lang. Lit.; Res. Alert [Full Cov.]; Soc. Sci. Cit. Index [Select. Cov.].

FR/0035-1652
REVUE DE PHILOLOGIE, DE LITTERATURE ET D'HISTOIRE ANCIENNES. [Rev. Philol. Litt. Hist. Anc.]. **VFOAT** Revue de Philologie. (1845)-. Periodical. French. sa (2 issues). 473.93F France. Editions Klincksieck, 8 rue de la Sorbonne, 75005 Paris France. **Tel** 11 33 1 43545953, FAX 11 33 1 432252553. **LC** PA2; .R4. **DD** 480/.05. cum. index. available on microfilm and microfiche from University Microfilms International (UMI). Documents available from The Genuine Article.
Desc: Classical philology.
Ind/Abst Arts Humanit. Citation Index (19??-19??) [Full Cov.]; Curr. Contents Arts Humanit.; MLA Int. Bibl. Books Artic. Mod. Lang. Lit.; Res. Alert [Full Cov.]; Soc. Sci. Cit. Index [Select. Cov.].

BE/0035-1660
REVUE DE PHONETIQUE APPLIQUEE. [Rev. phon. appl.]. **Added/Corp** Universite de Mons. Universite de Mons. Ecole d'Interpretes Internationaux. Centre Universitaire de l'Etat a Mons. **VFOAT** Phonetique Appliquee. (1965)-. Periodical. English (French and German). qt. $54.00 North America. Societe Nouvelle Didier Erudition, 6 rue de la Sorbonne, 75005 Paris France. **Tel** 011 33 1 43544757, FAX 011 33 1 40517385. **(Subscription address:** PO Box 830350, Birmingham, AL 35283-0350; telephone: (800)633-4931, (205)995-1567 (outside US and Canada); FAX: (205)995-1588**)** **ED** R. Renard. **LC** P1; .C63. **DD** 418/.005. **Circ:** 1,500. available on microfilm from University Microfilms International (UMI).
Desc: Publishes the works of phonetiticans in Belgium, France and the entire world.
Ind/Abst Annu. Bibliogr. Engl. Lang. Lit.; Lang. Teach.; Linguist. Lang. Behav. Abstr. (1976-) [Full Cov.]; MLA Int. Bibl. Books Artic. Mod. Lang. Lit.; Soc. Plann. Policy Dev. Abstr.

FR/0373-1537
REVUE DES ETUDES GEORGIENNES ET CAUCASIENNES. **Added/Corp** Association des Etudes Georgiennes et Caucasiennes. No. 1 (1985)-. Periodical. French (English and German). an. 1500F. Editions Peeters SA, Bondgenotenlaan 153, BP 41, B-3000 Leuven Belgium. **Tel** 32 16 235170, FAX 32 16 228500, telex 65987 PUL B. **ED** G. Charachidze. **LC** DK673.2; .R48. **DD** 947/.95/005. **Bk Rev.** **Ad Acc.** ***Continues** Bedi Kartlisa, 0373-1537.*
Ind/Abst BHA : Biblio. Hist. Art.

FR/0035-2039
REVUE DES ETUDES GRECQUES. [Rev. etud. grecques]. **Added/Corp** Association pour l'Encouragement des Etudes Grecques en France. (1888)-. Periodical. French. Twice a year. 630.00F. Societe Edition Belles Lettres, 95 Boulevard Raspail, 75006 Paris France. **Tel** 011 33 1 45487055, FAX 011 33 1 45449288, telex 200577. **LC** DF10; .R4. cum. index. available on microfilm. ***Continues in part** Annuaire de l'Association pour l'Encouragement des etudes Grecques; **Absorbed** Bulletin Epigraphique, 0184-7007; Bulletin Archeologique **and** Bulletin Papyrologique.*
Desc: Greek language and literature.
Ind/Abst BHA : Biblio. Hist. Art; MLA Int. Bibl. Books Artic. Mod. Lang. Lit.

FR/0373-5737
REVUE DES ETUDES LATINES. [Rev. etud. lat.]. **Added/Corp** Societe des Etudes Latines. Vol. 1 (Oct. 1923)-. French. an (Nov.). 365.00F. Societe Edition Belles Lettres, 95 Boulevard Raspail, 75006 Paris France. **Tel** 011 33 1 45487055, FAX 011 33 1 45449288, telex 200577. **LC** PA2002; .R4. **DD** 470/.5. Documents available from The Genuine Article.
Ind/Abst Arts Humanit. Citation Index (19??-19??) [Full Cov.]; BHA : Biblio. Hist. Art; Br. Archaeol. Bibliogr. (-?); Curr. Contents Arts Humanit.; MLA Int. Bibl. Books Artic. Mod. Lang. Lit.; Res. Alert [Full Cov.]; Soc. Sci. Cit. Index [Select. Cov.].

FR/0223-3711
REVUE DES LANGUES ROMANES. [Rev. Lang. Romanes]. **Added/Corp** Societe pour l'Etude des Langues Romanes, Montpellier. Vol. 1 (1870)-. Periodical. French. sa (2 issues). 180.00F France; 200.00F other. Revue des Langues Romanes, BP 5043, Universite Paul Valery, 34032 Montpellier Cedex France. **Tel** 011 33 67 142326. **ED** Gerard Gouiran, Jean-Marie Petit and Patrick Sauzet. cum. index. **Bk Rev.** **Ad Acc.** **Circ:** 500. Documents available from The Genuine Article.
Desc: Issues are thematic; topics selected mainly from the fields of romance linguistics, medieval studies, and literature.
Ind/Abst Arts Humanit. Citation Index [Full Cov.]; Curr. Contents Arts Humanit.; MLA Int. Bibl. Books Artic. Mod. Lang. Lit.; Res. Alert [Full Cov.]; Romant. Move.; Soc. Plann. Policy Dev. Abstr.

FR/0373-6075
REVUE D'HISTOIRE DES TEXTES. **Added/Corp** Centre National de la Recherche Scientifique (France). Vol. 1 (1971)-. Monographic series. French (English and Spanish). ir. Price varies per volume. Brepols Publishers, Steenweg OP Tielen 68, B-2300 Turnhout Belgium. **Tel** 011 32 14 402500. **Circ:** 1,500. ***Supersedes** Institut de Recherche et d'Histoire des*

Textes (France). Bulletin.
Desc: Articles on the history of various texts, their provenance, chronology and analysis.
Ind/Abst BHA : Biblio. Hist. Art.

FR
REVUE DU MOYEN AGE LATIN.
Added/Corp Universite de Strasbourg. Faculte de Theologie Catholique. Lyons. Facultes Catholiques. Vol. 1 (Jan./Mar. 1945)-. French (English, Latin and German). Twice a year. Revue du Moyen Age Latin, Palais Universitaire, F-67084 Strasbourg Cedex France. **LC** PA2801; .R4. Documents available from The Genuine Article.
Ind/Abst Arts Humanit. Citation Index (19??-19??) [Full Cov.]; Curr. Contents Arts Humanit.; Res. Alert [Full Cov.].

CN/0710-0167
REVUE QUEBECOISE DE LINGUISTIQUE. [Rev. que. linguist.]. Vol. 11, No. 1 (1981)-. Periodical. French. Twice a year (Apr., & Nov.). 30.00Can$ Canada; 54.00Can$ others. University Quebec at Montreal - Service des Publications, PO Box 8888 Succursale Centre-Ville, Montreal Quebec H3C 3P8 Canada. **Tel** (514)987-7747, FAX (514)987-3251. **ED** Henri Wittman. **DD** 410/.5. Index available. cum. index. **Bk Rev. Ad Acc, Adv Mgr:** Colette Dicaire, **Tel** (514)987-4227. **Pr Rev. Circ:** 600 (ctrl). ***Continues*** *Cahier de Linguistique, 0315-4025.*
Desc: Diffusion of original research on linguistics, french language in North-America, artificial intelligence systems based on french languages of Francophone countries.
Ind/Abst Linguist. Lang. Behav. Abstr. (1984-) [Full Cov.]; MLA Int. Bibl. Books Artic. Mod. Lang. Lit.; Point Repere (1983-); Soc. Plann. Policy Dev. Abstr.

CN/0835-3581
REVUE QUEBECOISE DE LINGUISTIQUE THEORIQUE ET APPLIQUEE. (REVUE QUEBECOISE DE LINGUISTIQUE THEORIQUE ET APPLIQUEE : REVUE DE L'ASSOCIATION QUEBECOISE DE LINGUISTIQUE.). [Rev. que. linguist. theor. appl.]. **Added/Corp** Association Quebecoise de Linguistique. Vol. 5, No. 4 (Dec. 1986)-. Periodical. French. Four times a year. Association Quebecoise de Linguistique, CP 95, Trois-Rivieres Quebec G9A 5E3 Canada. **Tel** (819)378-8157. **ED** Henri Wittmann. Index available. cum. index. **Bk Rev. Ad Acc. Pr Rev. Circ:** 600 (ctrl). ***Continues*** *Revue Quebecoise de Linguistique (Trois-Rivieres, Quebec), 0835-3603.*
Desc: Diffusion of original research on linguistics, French language in North America, artificial intelligence systems based on French and languages of Francophone countries.
Ind/Abst Linguist. Lang. Behav. Abstr. (1984-) [Full Cov.]; MLA Int. Bibl. Books Artic. Mod. Lang. Lit.; Soc. Plann. Policy Dev. Abstr.

DK/0035-3906
REVUE ROMANE. [Rev. rom.]. **Added/Corp** Kbenhavns Universitet. Romansk Institut. Statens Humanistiske Forskningsrad (Denmark). (1966)-. Periodical. French. sa. kr325.00. Munksgaard International Publishers Ltd, PO Box 2148, DK-1016 Copenhagen K Denmark. **Tel** 011 45 33 12 70 30, FAX 011 45 33 12 93 87, telex 19431 MUNKS DK. **ED** Nils Soelberg. **[CCC].** Index available. **Circ:** 550 (ctrl). Documents available from The Genuine Article.
Desc: A journal devoted to Romance language and literature.
Ind/Abst Annu. Bibliogr. Engl. Lang. Lit.; Arts Humanit. Citation Index [Full Cov.]; Curr. Contents Arts Humanit.; MLA Int. Bibl. Books Artic. Mod. Lang. Lit.; Res. Alert [Full Cov.]; Romant. Move.; Soc. Sci. Cit. Index [Select. Cov.].

RM/0035-3957
REVUE ROUMAINE DE LINGUISTIQUE. [Rev. roum. linguist.]. **Added/Corp** Academia Republicii Populare Romine. Academia Republicii Socialiste Romania. Vol. 9, No. 1 (1964)-. Periodical. English (French, German and Russian). Six times a year. DM329.00. **(Subscription address:** Kubon & Sagner, ABT Zeitschriftenimport, D 80328 Munich Germany.**) LC** P1.A1; R45. cum. index. ***Continues*** *Revue de Linguistique, 1012-0769.*
Desc: Contains articles on Romanian linguistics.
Ind/Abst Annu. Bibliogr. Engl. Lang. Lit.; Lang. Teach.; Linguist. Lang. Behav. Abstr. (1972-) [Full Cov.]; MLA Int. Bibl. Books Artic. Mod. Lang. Lit.; Soc. Plann. Policy Dev. Abstr.

GW/0035-449X
RHEINISCHES MUSEUM FUER PHILOLOGIE. [Rhein. Mus. Philol.]. **VFOAT** Museum fuer Philologie. (1833)-. Periodical. German (English, French, Greek and Modern, Latin). qt. DM198.50 Germany; DM200.00 other. J. D. Sauerlaender Verlag, Finkenhofstrasse 21, D 60322 Frankfurt Germany. **Tel** 011 49 69 555217. **ED** Carl Werner Mueller. **LC** PA3; .R4. **DD** 938/.005. Index available. ***Continues*** *Rheinisches Museum fuer Philologie, Geschichte und Griechische Philosophie.*
Desc: Greek/Latin literature, codicology, ancient philosophy, classical archeology, ancient cultural and political history, ancient history of science, history of classical scholarship and textual criticism enclosed.
Ind/Abst Annu. Bibliogr. Engl. Lang. Lit.; MLA Int. Bibl. Books Artic. Mod. Lang. Lit.

US/0735-0198
RHETORIC REVIEW. VFOAT R.R.; RR. Vol. 1, No. 1 (Sept. 1982)-. Periodical. English. Twice a year (Jan., Sept.). $15.00 (institutions), $12.00 (individual). Rhetoric Review, Department of English, University of Arizona, Tucson AZ 85721. **Tel** (602)621-3371. **ED** Theresa Enos (phone: (602)621-3371). **LC** PN171.4; .R44. **DD** 808/.005. Index available (Bound in once a yr.). **Bk Rev**, (Qty: 12). **Ad Acc, Adv Mgr:** Ed. **Pr Rev. Circ:** 750 (ctrl).
Desc: The latest on essays of rhetoric and compsotion studies, including historical studies.
Ind/Abst Curr. Index J. Educ.; MLA Int. Bibl. Books Artic. Mod. Lang. Lit.; Soc. Plann. Policy Dev. Abstr.

US/0277-3945
RHETORIC SOCIETY QUARTERLY. [Rhetor. Soc. q.]. **Added/Corp** Rhetoric Society of America. **VFOAT** RSQ; R.S.Q. (Winter 1976)-. Periodical. English. qt (published within the seasons). $30.00. Rhetoric Society of America, St. Cloud State University, Department of Philosophy, St. Cloud MN 56301. **Tel** (612)255-2234, FAX (612)654-5337. **ED** Rex Veeder (editor's telephone: (612)654-5108). **LC** PN171.4; .R46. **DD** 808/.005. **Bk Rev**, (Qty: 20). **Ad Acc, Adv Mgr:** same as editor. **Pr Rev. Circ:** 1,300 (ctrl). ***Continues*** *Newsletter (Rhetoric Society of America).*
Desc: Publishes articles, reviews and bibliographies in rhetoric theory, criticism, history, pedagogy and research.
Ind/Abst MLA Int. Bibl. Books Artic. Mod. Lang. Lit.

US/0734-8584
RHETORICA. [Rhetorica]. **Added/Corp** International Society for the History of Rhetoric. Vol. 1, No. 1 (Spring 1983)-. Periodical. English (German). qt (Feb., May, Aug., Nov). $40.00 (individuals), $63.00 (institutions), $16.00 (students). University of California Press, 2120 Berkeley Way, Berkeley CA 94720. **Tel** (510)642-4191, (510)642-3907, FAX (510)642-9917. **ED** Michael Leff. **LC** PN183; .R45. **DD** 808/.009. **[CCC]. Bk Rev. Ad Acc. Pr Rev. Circ:** 950 (ctrl). available on microfilm and microfiche from University Microfilms International (UMI). Documents available from The Genuine Article.
Desc: Articles on the theory and practice of rhetoric in all periods and in all languages.
Ind/Abst Am. Hist. Life (1983-); Arts Humanit. Citation Index [Full Cov.]; Child. Lit. Abstr. (19??-); Curr. Contents Arts Humanit.; Lit. Crit. Regist.; MLA Int. Bibl. Books Artic. Mod. Lang. Lit.; Res. Alert [Full Cov.]; Soc. Plann. Policy Dev. Abstr.

GW/0720-5775
RHETORIK. Vol. 1 (1980)-. Periodical. German (English and German). an. DM68.00. Max Niemeyer Verlag, Postfach 2140, D 72011 Tuebingen Germany. **Tel** 011 49 7071 989494, FAX 011 49 7071 87419. **ED** Joachim Dyck, Walter Jens, Gert Ueding. **LC** PN171.4; .R47. **DD** 808/.005. **Bk Rev. Ad Acc. Circ:** 800.
Ind/Abst Index Book Rev. Relig.

IT/0391-4127
RICERCHE SLAVISTICHE. [Ric. slav.]. **Added/Corp** Universita di Roma. Istituto di Filologia Slava. (1952)-. Italian. an. $98.00. La Fenice Edizioni, Via Antonio Pignatelli 32, 00152 Rome Italy. **Tel** 011 39 6 538589, FAX 011 39 6 538589. **ED** Sante Gracio Hi. **LC** DR25; .R5.
Desc: Research in Slavic linguistics.
Ind/Abst MLA Int. Bibl. Books Artic. Mod. Lang. Lit.

IT
RID, RIVISTA ITALIANA DI DIALETTOLOGIA, SCUOLA, SOCIETA, TERRITORIO. VFOAT Rivista Italiana di Dialettologia, Scuola, Societa, Territorio. Vol. 1 (1976)-. Periodical. Italian (summaries and/or abstracts in English). an. L43000 Italy; L70000 other. Clueb Coop Libraria Univ Edi, Bologna Via Marsala 24, 40126 Bologna Italy. **Tel** 011 39 51 220736, 224780, FAX 011 39 51 237758. **LC** PC1701; .R22.
Ind/Abst MLA Int. Bibl. Books Artic. Mod. Lang. Lit.; Soc. Plann. Policy Dev. Abstr.

SP
RILCE : REVISTA DE FILOLOGIA HISPANICA. See Literature.

IT/0392-4866
RIVISTA DEGLI STUDI ORIENTALI. [Riv. studi orient.]. **Added/Corp** Universita di Roma. Scuola Orientale. Vol. 1 (1907)-. Monographic series. Italian (English, French, German and Spanish). ir. Price varies per volume. Bardi Editore, Salita de Crescenzi 16, 00186 Rome Italy. **Tel** 011 39 6 4393111. **LC** PJ6; .R4.
Ind/Abst MLA Int. Bibl. Books Artic. Mod. Lang. Lit.; Middle East J.

IT/0035-6085
RIVISTA DI CULTURA CLASSICA E MEDIOEVALE. See Literature.

IT
RIVISTA DI FILOLOGIA E DI ISTRUZIONE CLASSICA. VFOAT Rivista di Filologia Classica. Vol. 78 (1950)-. Periodical. Italian. qt. L71000 Italy; L9100 other. Loescher Editore, Via Vittorio Amedeo 18, 10121 Turin Italy. **Tel** 011 39 11 5624622. **LC** PA9; .R56. **DD** 480/.05. ***Continues*** *Rivista di Filologia Classica.*

IT
RIVISTA DI GRAMMATICA GENERATIVA. Vol. 1, No. 1 (1976)-. Periodical. Italian (English, French and German). an. L30000. Unipress Padova, Via C Battisti 231, 35121 Padova Italy. **Tel** 11 39 49 8752542, FAX 11 39 49 8752542. **ED** Gugliemo Cinque and Luigi Rizzi. **Ad Acc. Pr Rev. Circ:** 150.
Desc: Generative grammar, syntax, morphology and phonology: only in depth studies in framework of Chomsky's theory.
Ind/Abst Soc. Plann. Policy Dev. Abstr.

IT
RIVISTA DI LINGUISTICA. Vol. 1, No. 1 (1989)-. Periodical. English (French and Italian). sa (2 issues). L75000 Italy; L85000 Europe; L110000 other. Rosenberg & Sellier, Via Andrea Doria 14, 10123 Turin Italy. **Tel** 011 39 11 8127808, telex 224202 ROSSELI. **LC** P1.A1; R58. **DD** 410/.5.
Ind/Abst MLA Int. Bibl. Books Artic. Mod. Lang. Lit.

CN/0821-3216
RIVISTA DI STUDI ITALIANI. See Literature.

CL/0033-698X
RLA, REVISTA DE LINGUISTICA TEORICA Y APLICADA. (RLA.). [RLA, Rev. linquist. teor. apl.]. **Added/Corp** Universidad de Concepcion. Instituto Central de Lenguas. Universidad de Concepcion. Circulo Linguistico. **VFOAT** Revista de Linguistica Aplicada; Revista de Linguistica Teorica y Aplicada. Vol. 1, (1963)-. Academic Scholarly Publication. Spanish (English and French). an (Dec.). $9.00 (basic); $6.00 (airmail); $4.00 (surface mail). Universidad de Concepcion / Humanidades, Facultad de Educacion, Humanidades y Arte, Administracion de RLA, Casilla 82-C, Correo 3,, Concepcion Chile. **Tel** 011 56 41 234985 Ext. 2313, telex 259108. **ED** Adalberto Salas (phone: 234985 Anexo 2313). **LC** P9; R14. Index available (Vol. 20, 1982.). cum. index. **Bk Rev**, (Qty: 2-6). **Ad Acc. Pr Rev. Acid Free. Circ:** 600 (ctrl).
Desc: Sinchronic studies in the area of linguistics.
Ind/Abst Lang. Teach.; Linguist. Lang. Behav. Abstr. (1970-) [Full Cov.]; MLA Int. Bibl. Books Artic. Mod. Lang. Lit.; Soc. Plann. Policy Dev. Abstr.; Sociol. Abstr.

XR
ROCENKA KATEDER RUSISTIKY NA FILOZOFICKE A PEDAGOGICKE FAKULTE UNIVERZITY PALECKEHO. 1973-. Periodical. Czech (Russian). an. Fakulte Univerzity Paleckeho, Vytisk Neprodejny, Olomouc Czech Republic. **LC** PG2010; .R62. **DD** 491.7/05. ***Continues*** *Rocenka Katedry i.e. Kateder Rusistiky na Filosoficke a Pedagogicke Fakulte University Palackeho.*

PL/0080-3588
ROCZNIK SLAWISTYCZNY. [Rocz. slawistyczny]. **Added/Corp** Polska Akademia Nauk. Komitet Sowianoznawstwa. Polska Akademia Nauk. Komitet Jezykoznawstwa. Uniwersytet Jagiellonski. Studium Sowianskie. **VFOAT** Revue Slavistique. Vol. 1 (1908)-. Periodical. Polish. sa (2 issues). Price varies. **(Subscription address:** ARS Polona, PO Box 1001, 00068 Warsaw Poland.**) LC** PG1; .R6.
Desc: Deals with the Slavic language.
Ind/Abst MLA Int. Bibl. Books Artic. Mod. Lang. Lit.

BU
RODNA RECH. (1928)-. Periodical. Bulgarian. Ten times a year. DM117.00. **(Subscription address:** Kubon & Sagner, ABT Zeitschriftenimport, D 80328 Munich Germany.**) LC** PG801; .R6.
Ind/Abst Annu. Bibliogr. Engl. Lang. Lit.

●BW
RODNAE SLOVA. Added/Corp Belarus. Ministerstva Adukatsii. (1992)-. Periodical. Byelorussian. mo. **(Subscription address:** Victor Kamkin, 4956 Boiling Brook Parkway, Rockville MD 20852.**) LC** PG2830; .B45. ***Continues*** *Belaruskaia Mova i Litaratura u Shkole, 0234-1360.*

DK/0106-0821
ROLIG-PAPIR. Added/Corp Roskilde Universitetscenter. (197?)-. Monographic series. Danish.
Ind/Abst MLA Int. Bibl. Books Artic. Mod. Lang. Lit.

US
ROMANCE LINGUISTICS & LITERATURE REVIEW. Added/Corp University of California, Los Angeles. Romance Linguistics & Literature Graduate Students Association. Romance Linguistics & Literature Review. **VFOAT** Romance Linguistics and Literature Review. Vol. 1 (Fall 1988)-. English. an. $10.00. University of California at Los Angeles, 3300 Rolfe Hall, 405 Hilgard Avenue, Los Angeles CA 90024. **Tel** (310)825-4321, (310)206-1985.
Ind/Abst MLA Int. Bibl. Books Artic. Mod. Lang. Lit.

US
ROMANCE MONOGRAPHS, INC. (SERIES). See Literary and Political Reviews.

US/0035-7995
ROMANCE NOTES. [Roman. notes]. **Added/Corp** University of North Carolina (1793-1962). Dept. of Romance Languages. Vol. 1, (Nov. 1959)-. Periodical. English (French, Spanish, Italian and Portuguese). Three times a year (Jan., May, Sept.). $15.00 (individuals), $18.00 (institutions). University of North Carolina Department of Romance Languages, CB 3170, 237 Dey Hall, Chapel Hill NC 27599-3170. **Tel** (919)962-1025. **ED** G. Mallary Masters. **LC** PC1; .R58. **Circ:** 600 (ctrl). available on microfilm and microfiche from University Microfilms International (UMI). Documents available from The Genuine Article.
Ind/Abst Annu. Bibliogr. Engl. Lang. Lit.; Arts Humanit. Citation Index [Full Cov.]; Curr. Contents Arts Humanit.; MLA Int. Bibl. Books Artic. Mod. Lang. Lit.; Res. Alert [Full Cov.]; Romant. Move.

US/0035-8002
ROMANCE PHILOLOGY. [Roman. philol.]. Vol. 1 (Aug. 1947)-. Periodical. English (Multiple languages). qt (Feb., May, Aug., Nov.). $41.00 (individuals), $91.00 (institutions). University of California Press, 2120 Berkeley Way, Berkeley CA 94720. **Tel** (510)642-4191, (510)642-3907, FAX (510)642-9917. **ED** Jerry Craddock. **LC** PC1; .R6. **DD** 479.05. **[CCC]**. Index available. cum. index. **Bk Rev. Ad Acc. Pr Rev. Circ:** 1,200 (ctrl). available on microfilm and microfiche from University Microfilms International (UMI). Documents available from The Genuine Article, UMI Article Clearinghouse.
Desc: Articles on areas of historical romance linguistics and medieval romance literatures.
Ind/Abst Acad. Search (July 1993-); Annu. Bibliogr. Engl. Lang. Lit.; Arts Humanit. Citation Index [Full Cov.]; Curr. Contents Arts Humanit.; Expand. Acad. Index (1989-); Humanit. Index; Humanit. Source (Jul. 1993-); INFO-SOUTH Abstr.; Mag. Search; MLA Int. Bibl. Books Artic. Mod. Lang. Lit.; Newsp. Period. Abstr. (1991-); Res. Alert [Full Cov.]; Romant. Move.; Soc. Plann. Policy Dev. Abstr.; Soc. Sci. Cit. Index [Select. Cov.].

US/0883-1157
ROMANCE QUARTERLY. [Roman. q.]. Vol. 33, No. 1 (Feb. 1986)-. Periodical. English (French, Spanish and Italian). qt. $65.00 (institution), $36.00 (individual). Heldref Publications, 1319 Eighteenth Street Northwest, Washington DC 20036-1802. **Tel** (202)296-6267, (800)365-9753, FAX (202)296-5149. **ED** Brian J. Dendle. **LC** P1; .K4. **DD** 840/.09. Index available. cum. index. **Bk Rev. Ad Acc. Pr Rev. Circ:** 500 (ctrl). available on microfilm and microfiche from University Microfilms International (UMI). Documents available from The Genuine Article. ***Continues** Kentucky Romance Quarterly, 0364-8664.*
Ind/Abst Arts Humanit. Citation Index [Full Cov.]; BHA : Biblio. Hist. Art; Curr. Contents Arts Humanit.; Linguist. Lang. Behav. Abstr. (1986-); MLA Int. Bibl. Books Artic. Mod. Lang. Lit.; Res. Alert [Full Cov.]; Romant. Move.; Soc. Plann. Policy Dev. Abstr.

FR/0035-8029
ROMANIA. [Romania]. **Added/Corp** Societe des amis de la Romania. Vol. 1 No. 1 (Jan. 1872)-. Periodical. French. Twice a year. 420.00F. Societe des Amis de la Romania, 284 BD Raspail MME Vielliard, 75005 Paris France. **Tel** 011 33 1 47236104. **LC** PC2; .R6. **DD** 440/.05. Index available. cum. index. **Bk Rev.**
Ind/Abst BHA : Biblio. Hist. Art; MLA Int. Bibl. Books Artic. Mod. Lang. Lit.; Romant. Move.

US/0035-8118
ROMANIC REVIEW. See Literature.

BE/0080-3855
ROMANICA GANDENSIA. [Romanica gandensia]. **Added/Corp** Rijksuniversiteit te Gent. Faculteit der Letteren en Wijsbegeerte. (1953)-. Monographic series. French. Rijksuniversiteit van Gent, Medisch Recht Apotheekstraat 5, B-9000 Geny Belgium. **Tel** 3291253116.
Ind/Abst MLA Int. Bibl. Books Artic. Mod. Lang. Lit.

SW/0080-3863
ROMANICA GOTHOBURGENSIA. (19??)-. Monographic series. Multiple languages (French, Italian and Spanish).
Ind/Abst MLA Int. Bibl. Books Artic. Mod. Lang. Lit.

SZ/0080-3871
ROMANICA HELVETICA. (1935)-. Periodical. English (French, German and Italian). ir. A Francke Verlag GmbH, Postfach 2560, Dischingerweg 5, D 72070 Tuebingen Germany. **Tel** 011 49 7071 78091 or 92.

GW/0035-8126
ROMANISCHE FORSCHUNGEN. (ROMANISCHE FORSCHUNGEN; ORGAN FUER ROMANISCHE SPRACHEN, VOLKS-UND LITERATUREN.). [Rom. Forsch.]. **Added/Corp** Notgemeinschaft der Deutschen Wissenschaft (1920-1945). (1883)-. Periodical. German. ir. Price varies. Vittorio Klostermann, Frauenlobstrasse 22, D 60487 Frankfurt Germany. **Tel** 011 49 69 9708160. **LC** PC3; .R5. **[CCC]**. cum. index. Documents available from The Genuine Article.
Ind/Abst Arts Humanit. Citation Index [Full Cov.]; Curr. Contents Arts Humanit.; MLA Int. Bibl. Books Artic. Mod. Lang. Lit.; Res. Alert [Full Cov.]; Romant. Move.; Soc. Sci. Cit. Index [Select. Cov.].

GW
ROMANISTISCHE ARBEITSHEFTE. See Literature.

GW/0343-379X
ROMANISTISCHE ZEITSCHRIFT FUER LITERATURGESCHICHTE. **VFOAT** Cahiers d'Histoire des Litteratures Romanes. Vol. 1- ; 1977-. Periodical. German. qt. DM100.00. Universitatsverlag Carl Winter, POB 106140, D 69051 Heidelberg Germany. **Tel** 011 49 6221 770260. **ED** Henning Krauss. **UDC** 804; 840. **Bk Rev. Ad Acc. Circ:** 660 (ctrl). Documents available from The Genuine Article.
Desc: Romanic linguistics and literature.
Ind/Abst Arts Humanit. Citation Index [Full Cov.]; Curr. Contents Arts Humanit.; Res. Alert [Full Cov.]; Romant. Move.

GW/0080-3898
ROMANISTISCHES JAHRBUCH. [Rom. Jahrb.]. **Added/Corp** Hamburg. Universitat. Romanisches Seminar. Vol. 1 (1948)-. German. ir. Price varies according to size. Walter de Gruyter Inc., PO Box 303421, D 10728 Berlin Germany. **Tel** 011 49 30 260050, FAX 011 49 30 26005251. **LC** PC3; .R73. **DD** 440/.05. cum. index.
Ind/Abst MLA Int. Bibl. Books Artic. Mod. Lang. Lit.; Romant. Move.

RM/0557-272X
ROMANOSLAVICA / ASOCIATIA SLAVISTILOR DIN REPUBLICA POPULARA ROMINA. **Added/Corp** Asociatia Slavistilor din Republica Populara Romina. Asociatia Slavistilor din Republica Socialista Romania. Asociatia Slavistilor din Romania. Universitatea din Bucuresti. Facultatea de Limbi Straine. Universitatea din Bucuresti. Catedra de Limbi Slave. No. 1 (1958)-. Periodical. Romanian (Russian; summaries and/or abstracts in English, French and Russian; table of contents in French, Romanian and Russian). an. $45.00. **(Subscription address:** Ilexim Press Department, PO Box 1, 136-1-137, Bucharest, Romania.**) LC** PC601; .R65.
Ind/Abst MLA Int. Bibl. Books Artic. Mod. Lang. Lit.

BW/0134-9619
ROMANSKOE I GERMANSKOE IAZYKOZNANIE. [Rom. ger. azykozn.]. **Added/Corp** Minski Pedahahichny Instytut Zamezhnykh Mou. No. 4 (1974)-. Russian. an. 1.00rub. Izdatelstvo Vysheishaia Shkola, Masherova 11, 220048 Minsk Byelarus. **Tel** 0172 23-54-15, FAX 0172 23-54-15. **LC** PC5; .V56. ***Continues** Voprosy Filologii.*
Ind/Abst Annu. Bibliogr. Engl. Lang. Lit.; MLA Int. Bibl. Books Artic. Mod. Lang. Lit.

JA
RON SSHU - KOMAZAWA DAIGAKU GAIKOKUGOBU. **Main/Corp** Komazawa Daigaku, Tokyo. Gaikokugobu. (1972)-. Periodical. Japanese. Komazawa Daigaku Gaikokugobu, 23-1 Komazawa 1-chome, Setagaya-ku, Tokyo Japan. **LC** P9; .K37b.

XR
ROSSICA OLOMUCENSIA. Monographic series. Czech (Russian). ir. Price varies per volume. Rocenka Kateder Rusistiky na Filozoficke a Pedagogicke, Fakulte Univerzity Palackeho, Olomouc 77180 Czech Republic. **Tel** 22441 OR 208381. **ED** Miroslav Zahradka and Aroslav Reska. **UDC** 808; 808.2. **Bk Rev. Circ:** 300 (ctrl).
Desc: Prints papers dealing with the Russian language and literature including reviews of important works in Slavic linguistics and literature.

PL/0076-0390
ROZPRAWY KOMISJI JEZYKOWEJ. ODZKIE TOWARZYSTWO NAUKOWE. (ROZPRAWY.). [Rozpr. Kom. Jezyk., odz. Tow. Nauk.]. **Main/Corp** Odzkie Towarzystwo Naukowe. Komisja Jezykowa. (1954)-. Polish. an. Zakad Narodowy Im Ossolinskich We Wrocawiu, Krakowskie Przedmiescie 7, 00 068 Warsaw Poland. **LC** P19.L6; A3.
Ind/Abst MLA Int. Bibl. Books Artic. Mod. Lang. Lit.

CN/0229-8651
RSSI. RECHERCHES SEMIOTIQUES. SEMIOTIC INQUIRY. (RSSI : RECHERCHES SEMIOTIQUES.). [RSSI, Rech. semiot., Semiot. inq.]. **Added/Corp** Canadian Semiotic Association. **VFOAT** R.S.S.I.; Recherches Semiotiques; Semiotic Inquiry; RSSI : Semiotic Inquiry. Vol. 1, No. 1 (1981)-. Periodical. French (English). Three times a year. 65.00Can$ (institutions), 45.00Can$ (individuals) Canada; 70.00Can$ (institutions), 50.00Can$ (individuals) other. Recherches Semiotiques / University of Quebec, CP 8888 Succursale A, Montreal Quebec H3C 3P8 Canada. **Tel** (514)987-8404, (514)987-3796. **(Subscription address:** Christian Vandendorpe Secy ACS, Lettres Francaises, University of Ottawa, Ottawa ONT K1N 6N5 Canada.**) ED** Pierre Outllet. **LC** P99; .C275. **DD** 001.51. Index available. **Bk Rev. Circ:** 500 (ctrl). available on microfilm from University Microfilms International (UMI). ***Continues** Canadian Journal of Research in Semiotics, 0316-7917.*
Desc: Research in semiotics in all humanistic fields including the arts, architecture, anthropology, biology and sociology.
Ind/Abst BHA : Biblio. Hist. Art; MLA Int. Bibl. Books Artic. Mod. Lang. Lit.; Romant. Move.

UK/0957-1760
RUSISTIKA : THE RUSSIAN JOURNAL OF THE ASSOCIATION FOR LANGUAGE LEARNING. **Added/Corp** Association for Language Learning (Great Britain). **VFOAT** Russian Journal of the Association for Language Learning. No. 1 (June 1990)-. Periodical. English (Russian). Twice a year (June & Dec.). £20.00 UK; $40.00, £21.00 other. Association for Language Learning, 16 Regent Place, Rugby Warwickshire CV21 2PN England. **Tel** 011 44 788 546443, FAX 011 44 788 544149. **ED** Margaret Tejerizo (editor's address: Department of Salvonic Languages, University of Glasgow, Hetherington Building, Bute Gardens, Glasgow, G12 8QQ England). **CODEN** RUSIE5. Index available. **Bk Rev**, (Qty: varies). **Ad Acc, Adv Mgr:** Glenda Simmonds, **Tel** 0788 546443. **Circ:** 650 (ctrl). ***Formed by the union of** Journal of Russian Studies, 0047-276X **and** Association of Teachers of Russian (Great Britain). Newsletter - Association of Teachers of Russian, 0306-7432.*
Desc: Contains articles, reviews and information of specific interest to students and teachers of Russian.
Ind/Abst Br. Educ. Index.

US/0036-0252
RUSSIAN LANGUAGE JOURNAL. [Russ. lang. j.]. **VFOAT** Russkii Iazyk; Etudes de Russe. Vol. 20, No. 75/76 (1966)-. Periodical. English (Russian). Three times a year. $28.00 (individual), $33.00 (institution) US; $32 (individual), $37.00 (institution) Canada; $34.00 (individual), $39.00 (institution) other. Michigan State University Department of Linguistics and Languages, A 601 Wells, East Lansing MI 48824. **Tel** (517)355-5079. **DD** 491. **UDC** 808.2. cum. index. available on microfilm and microfiche from University Microfilms International (UMI). ***Continues** V Pomoshch Prepodavateliu Russkogo Iazyka V Amerike.*
Ind/Abst Am. Bibliogr. Slavic East Europ. Stud.; Curr. Index J. Educ.; Lang. Teach.; MLA Int. Bibl. Books Artic. Mod. Lang. Lit.; Soc. Plann. Policy Dev. Abstr.; Sociol. Abstr.

NE/0304-3487
RUSSIAN LINGUISTICS. [Russ. linguist.]. Vol. 1 (July 1974)-. Periodical. Multiple languages (English and Russian). Three times a year. $426.00. Kluwer Academic Publishers, Postbus 322, 3300 AH Dordrecht, The Netherlands. **Tel** 011 (31) 78 524400, FAX 011 31 78 183273, telex 20083. **ED** L Durovic, A G F van Holk and W Lehfeldt. **LC** PG2001; .R85. **[CCC]**. **Bk Rev. Ad Acc. Pr Rev. Acid Free. Circ:** 400. available on microfilm and microfiche from University Microfilms International (UMI). Documents available from The Genuine Article.
Desc: Grammar, phonetics and phonology, morphology, syntax and semantics, philological problems, Russian grammar and discourse analysis.
Ind/Abst Arts Humanit. Citation Index [Full Cov.]; Curr. Contents Arts Humanit.; Lang. Teach.; Linguist. Lang. Behav. Abstr. (1975-) [Full Cov.]; MLA Int. Bibl. Books Artic. Mod. Lang. Lit.; Res. Alert [Full Cov.]; Soc. Plann. Policy Dev. Abstr.; Sociol. Abstr.

GW/0935-8072
RUSSISTIK. **VFOAT** Rusistika. Vol. 1 (1989)-. Periodical. German (Russian). sa. £20.00 UK; $40.00 US; £21.00 other. Association of Teachers of Russian, c/o Mr F Beardon, 94 Ormonde Str H Barne, Sunderland SR4 7PN England. **Tel** 011 44 788 546443. **ED** Stephen Dalziel. **Bk Rev. Ad Acc. Circ:** 600 (ctrl).
Desc: Russian journal of the Association for Language Learning.

RU/0036-0368
RUSSKAIA RECH. **Added/Corp** Institut Russkogo Iazyka (Akademiia Nauk SSSR). (Jan./Feb. 1967)-. Academic Scholarly Publication. Russian. bm. $79.95. Izdatelstvo Nauka / Akademiia Nauk, Publishing House of the Russian Academy of Sciences, Leninskii Porspekt 14, 117901 Moscow Russia. **Tel** 011 95 954-21-53, FAX 011 95 938-21-44, telex 411964. **(Subscription address:** East View Publications Inc., 3020 Harbor Lane North, Suite 110, Minneapolis MN 55447.**) LC** PG2003; .R85. Index available. **Bk Rev.** available in microform.
Ind/Abst MLA Int. Bibl. Books Artic. Mod. Lang. Lit.

●RU
RUSSKAIA SLOVESNOST. **Added/Corp** Russia (Federation). Ministerstvo Obrazovaniia. (1993)-. Periodical. Russian. mo. ***Continues** Russkii Iazyk v SNG.*

●UN/0205-471X
RUSSKII IAZYK I LITERATURA V SREDNYKH UCHEBNYKH ZAVEDENIIAKH UKRAINY. **Added/Corp** Ukraine. Ministerstvo Osvity. (1992)-. Periodical. Russian. bm. ***Continues** Russkii Iazyk i Literatura v Srednykh Uchebnykh Zavedeniiakh USSR.*

Linguistics

RU
RUSSKII IAZYK I LITERATURA V UZBEKSKOI SHKOLE. **Added/Corp** Uzbek S.S.R. Ministerstvo Prosveshcheniia. (1958)-. Periodical. Russian. mo. $7.50. **(Subscription address:** Victor Kamkin, 4956 Boiling Brook Parkway, Rockville MD 20852.**)** **LC** PG2068.U9; R87.

ER
RUSSKII IAZYK V ESTONSKOI SHKOLE. **Added/Corp** Tartu Riiklik Ulikool. (19??)-. Periodical. Russian. bm. Tartu Riiklik Ulikool, Ulitsa Uilikooli 18, 202400 Tartu Estonia. **Tel** 30851. **(Subscription address:** Victor Kamkin, 4956 Boiling Brook Parkway, Rockville MD 20852.**) LC** AS262.T22; A25 subser; PG2129.E8.

MV/0202-5418
RUSSKII IAZYK V MOLDAVSKOI SHKOLE : [UCHEBNO-METODICHESKII ZHURNAL MINISTERSTVA PROSVESHCHENIIA MOLDAVSKOI SSR]. **Added/Corp** Moldavian S.S.R. Ministerstvo Prosveshcheniia. (19??)-. Periodical. Russian. bm. $5.50. Ministerstvo, 277033 Kishinev, Pr Lenina 85, Ministerstvo Prosveshcheniia Mssr, Kishinev Moldova. **LC** PG2068.M6; R83. **DD** 491.78/007/04981.

RU
RUSSKII IAZYK V SNG. *Title Change.* **Added/Corp** Akademiia Pedagogicheskikh Nauk SSSR. (1992)-(1992). Periodical. Russian. mo. Izdatelstvo Pedagogika, G-34 Smolenskii Boulevard D. 4, 119034 Moscow Russia. **CODEN** RYSNEE. *Continues* Russkii Iazyk v SSSR, 0868-9539. *Continued by* Russkaia Slovesnost.

RU/0036-0384
RUSSKIJ JAZYK ZA RUBEZOM. (RUSSKII IAZYK ZA RUBEZHOM.). [Russ. jazyk rub.]. **Added/Corp** Nauchno-Metodicheskii Tsentr Russkogo Iazyka (Moskovskii Gosudarstvennyi Universitet Im. M.V. Lomonosova). (1967)-. Periodical. Russian. bm. $67.00 airmail. **(Subscription address:** Victor Kamkin, 4956 Boiling Brook Parkway, Rockville MD 20852.**)** available in microform.
Ind/Abst MLA Int. Bibl. Books Artic. Mod. Lang. Lit.; Soc. Plann. Policy Dev. Abstr.; Sociol. Abstr. (?-?).

CN/0225-3550
S P E A Q JOURNAL. [SPEAQ j.]. **Main/Corp** Societe pour la Promotion de l'Enseignement de l'Anglais (Langue Seconde) au Quebec. Began publication in 1977 or 1978. Periodical. English (French). qt. Limited to members- membership $15.00 per year. Speaq, 7400 Boul Street Laurent 5E Etage, Montreal QUE H2R 2Y1 Canada. **Tel** (514)271-3700, **FAX** (514)948-1231. **DD** 428/.007/0714. **UDC** 802.0-07(714). *Continues* S P E A Q Journal, 0225-3550.
Ind/Abst Lang. Teach.

SA
SA JOURNAL OF LINGUISTICS. **Added/Corp** Linguistic Society of Southern Africa. Foundation for Education, Science and Technology (South Africa). Bureau for Scientific Publications. **VFOAT** SA Tydskrif vir Taalkunde; South African Journal of Linguistics; Suid-Afrikaanse Tydskrif vir Taalkunde. **VAT** South Africa Journal of Linguistics. Vol. 1, No. 1 (Oct. 1983)-. Periodical. English (Afrikaans). qt (4 issues). R87.00 South Africa; R90.00 other. Foundation for Education Science & Technology, PO Box 1758, Pretoria 0001 South Africa. **Tel** 011 27 12 3226404, **FAX** 011 27 12 3207803. **LC** P1.A1; S2. **DD** 410/.5.
Desc: Contains information on Afrikaans language and linguistics.
Ind/Abst Annu. Bibliogr. Engl. Lang. Lit.

UK/0305-9219
SAGA-BOOK. See Literature.

JA
SAGAMI KOKUBUN. **Main/Corp** Sagami Joshi Daigaku Kokubun Kenkyukai. No. 1 Issue 49 (1974)-. Periodical. Japanese. Sagami Joshi Daigaku, Kokubunka Dai 1 Kenkyushitsu 1-1 Bunkyo 2-chome, Sagamihara 228 Japan. **LC** PL501; .S25a.

AU/0080-5718
SALZBURGER STUDIEN ZUR ANGLISTIK UND AMERIKANISTIK. [Salzbg. Stud. Angl. Am.]. **Added/Corp** Universitat Salzburg. Institut fur Englische Sprache und Literatur. (19??)-. Monographic series. English. **LC** UNC.
Ind/Abst MLA Int. Bibl. Books Artic. Mod. Lang. Lit.

II
SAMSKRTA SAHITYA PARISHAT. Began publication in 1918. Periodical. Sanskrit (Sanskrit). **LC** PK401; .S3. **UDC** 809.12.

II/0558-3764
SAMSKRTAPRATIBHA. **Added/Corp** Sahitya Akademi. **VFOAT** Samskrita Pratibha. (1959)-. Periodical. Sanskrit. an. $2.00 (latest volume). Sahitya Akademi, National Academy of Letters, Rabindra Bhavan, Ferozeshah Road, New Delhi 110001 India. **Tel** 011 91 11 388667. **LC** PK401; .S32.

II
SAMSKRTAVIMARSAH. V. 1- July 1973-. English (Sanskrit). 15.00. Rashtriya Sanskrit Sansthan, 60, New Delhi India. **LC** PK401; .S323. **UDC** 809.12. *Absorbed* Vimarsa.

FI/0558-4639
SANANJALKA. (SANANJALKA : SUOMEN KIELEN SEURAN VUOSIKIRJA.). [Sananjalka]. **Added/Corp** Suomen Kielen Seura. (1959)-. Periodical. Finnish (summaries and/or abstracts in English, French and German). an. **LC** PH103; .S32.
Ind/Abst MLA Int. Bibl. Books Artic. Mod. Lang. Lit.

II
SATARANGI CAMALA. **Added/Corp** Camala Sahitya Samiti. (19??)-. Periodical. Hindi. **LC** PK1921; .S26.

US/1070-7395
SAYING IT BETTER. [Saying it better]. **Added/Corp** Grammar for Smart People, Inc. (Jan./Feb. 1991)-. Periodical. English. bm. $30.00 US; $36.00 Canada and Mexico; $42.00 other. Grammar for Smart People Inc., 1 Turkey Hill Road South, Westport CT 06880. **Tel** (203)454-5889, **FAX** (203)454-8623. **DD** 415.

XR
SBORNIK PEDAGOGICKE FAKULTY V PLZNI. CIZI JAZYKY. **VFOAT** Cizi Jazyky. Czech (German and Russian; summaries and/or abstracts in German and Russian). 22.00 single issue. **LC** PB35; .S42.

XR
SBORNIK PEDAGOGICKE FAKULTY V USTI NAD LABEM. RADA CIZICH JAZYKU. **VFOAT** Rada Cizich Jazyku. Began with vol. for 1974. Czech (English, German and Russian). 24.00. **LC** PB5; .S26.

XR/0231-7567
SBORNIK PRACI FILOSOFICKE FAKULTY BRNENSKE UNIVERSITY. A, RADY JAZYKOVEDNE. [Sb. pr. Filoz. Fak. Brnen. univ. Rada jazykovedna]. **Added/Corp** Universita J.E. Purkyne v Brne. Filozoficka Fakulta. Masarykova Univerzita v Brne. Filozoficka Fakulta. **VFOAT** Rady Jazykovedne; Sbornik Praci Filosoficke Fakulty Brnenske University. A, Rada Jazykovedna; Rada Jazykovedna; Series Linguistica; Studia Minora Facultatis Philosophicae Universitatis Brunensis. Series Linguistica. (1952)-. Periodical. Czech (English, French, German, Russian and Spanish). an. **LC** P19; .B78. **DD** 400.
Ind/Abst Soc. Plann. Policy Dev. Abstr.

RU
SBORNIK STATEI PO FRANTSUZSKOI LINGVISTIKE I METODIKE PREPODAVANIIA INOSTRANNOGO IAZYKA V VUZE. **Added/Corp** Moscow. Moskovskii Gosudarstvennyi Institut Inostrannykh Iazykov. Fakultet Frantsuzskogo Iazyka. Vol. 3 (1971)-. Russian. 0.35rub single issue. Izdatelstvo Pedagogika, G-34 Smolenskii Boulevard D. 4, 119034 Moscow Russia. **LC** PC2073; .S33. *Continues* Doklady I Soobshcheniia.

BU/0205-2679
SBORNIK ZA NARODNI UMOTVORENIJA I NARODOPIS. (SBORNIK ZA NARODNI UMOTVORENIIA I NARODOPIS ...). [Sb. nar. umotvor. narodop.]. **Main/Corp** Bulgarska Akademiia na Naukite. Vol. 1 (1889)-. Periodical. Bulgarian. Izdatelstvo na Bulgarskata Akademiia Na Naukite, 6 Rouski Boulevard, Sofia Bulgaria. **Tel FAX** 80 13 41, telex 22267 HEMKIK.
Ind/Abst MLA Int. Bibl. Books Artic. Mod. Lang. Lit.

SW/0280-7750
SCANDINAVIAN WORKING PAPERS ON BILINGUALISM. **Added/Corp** Stockholms Universitet. Dept. of Research on Bilingualism. Vol. 1 (1982)-. Periodical. English. ir. Kr65.00 (latest volume). University of Stockholm Center for Research on Bilingualism, S-106 91 Stockholm Sweden. **Tel** 011 48 8 162000. **LC** P115; .S28. **DD** 404/.2/05.

DK/0080-6765
SCANDO-SLAVICA. [Scando-slavica]. **Added/Corp** Association of Scandinavian Slavicists. Association of Scandinavian Slavicists and Baltologists. (1954)-. English (French, German, Italian and Russian). an. kr460.00. Munksgaard International Publishers Ltd, PO Box 2148, DK-1016 Copenhagen K Denmark. **Tel** 011 45 33 12 70 30, **FAX** 011 45 33 12 93 87, telex 19431 MUNKS DK. **ED** Gunnar Jacobsson. **LC** PG1; .S4. **DD** 491.8/05. **[CCC].** Index available. cum. index. **Circ:** 700.
Desc: Slavic and Baltic philology, literature, history, and archaeology.
Ind/Abst MLA Int. Bibl. Books Artic. Mod. Lang. Lit.

DK
SCANDO-SLAVICA. SUPPLEMENTUM. **VFOAT** Scando Slavica Supplementum. 1-. Monographic series. English (French and German). ir. Price varies per volume. Munksgaard International Publishers Ltd, PO Box 2148, DK-1016 Copenhagen K Denmark. **Tel** 011 45 33 12 70 30, **FAX** 011 45 33 12 93 87, telex 19431 MUNKS DK. **LC** PG1.

US/0161-7729
SCHOLARS' FACSIMILES AND REPRINTS (SERIES). (SCHOLARS' FACSIMILES & REPRINTS.). [Sch. facsim. repr.]. **VAT** Scholars Facsimiles and Reprints. Monographic series. English (French and Armenian). Price varies per volume. Scholars Facsimiles and Reprints Inc, PO Box 344, Delmar NY 12054-0344. **Tel** (513)439-5978. **ED** Norman Mangouni. available on microfiche.
Desc: Facsimile reprints of rare books of scholarly interest, primarily in English and American literature, history, philosophy, and religion.
Ind/Abst MLA Int. Bibl. Books Artic. Mod. Lang. Lit.

US/0032-6380
SCHOLASTIC VOICE. *Ceased.* [Scholast. voice]. Vol. 48, No. 2 (1970)-Vol. 76, No. 16 (1992). Periodical. English. ir (18 issues a school year). Scholastic Inc., 2931 East McCarty Street, PO Box 3710, Jefferson City MO 65102-9957. **Tel** (314)636-5271, (800)631-1586. **ED** Brenda Ealy. **LC** PE1001; .P7. **DD** 420/.5. **UDC** 802.0-8. **Ad Acc. Circ:** 250,000. available on microfilm from University Microfilms International (UMI). *Continues* Practical English, A Scholastic Magazine.
Desc: Short stories, plays, poems, and language games for students in grades 7-10.

GW/0080-696X
SCHRIFTEN UND QUELLEN DER ALTEN WELT. See Classical Studies.

GW
SCHRIFTENREIHE LINGUISTIK. 1977-. Monographic series. German. Price varies per volume. Bouvier GmbH & Co. KG ABT Verlag, AM Hof 28, D 53113 Bonn Germany. **Tel** 011 49 228 7290141.

SZ
SCHWEIZERISCHES IDIOTIKON. WORTERBUCH DER SCHWEIZERDEUTSCHEN SPRACHE. V. 1-. German. ir. 32.00F. J Huber and Company, Promenadenstrasse 16, CH-8500 Frauenfeld Switzerland. **Tel** (054)271111. **LC** PF5146. **UDC** 800.87:803.0-087.4(494). **Bk Rev. Ad Acc. Circ:** 1,000 (ctrl).
Desc: Dictionary of the Swiss German dialects.

UK/0080-8024
SCOTTISH GAELIC STUDIES. (SCOTTISH GAELIC STUDIES / ISSUED FROM THE CELTIC DEPT. OF THE UNIVERSITY OF ABERDEEN.). [Scott. gael. stud.]. **Added/Corp** University of Aberdeen. Celtic Dept. Vol. 1, Pt. 1 (April 1926)-. Periodical. English. ir. £10.00. University of Aberdeen / Scotland, Aberdeen AB9 1FX Scotland. **Tel** 011 44 0224 272547. **LC** PB1501; .S3. **DD** 491.6/3. cum. index.
Desc: Gaelic literature and language and Celtic philology.
Ind/Abst MLA Int. Bibl. Books Artic. Mod. Lang. Lit.

UK/0264-0198
SCOTTISH LANGUAGE. [Scott. lang.]. **Added/Corp** Association for Scottish Literary Studies. No. 1 (Autumn 1982)-. Academic Scholarly Publication. English (Gaelic (Scots)). an (Winter). £50.00. Association for Scottish Literary Studies, Department of English, Taylor Buildings, Aberdeen AB9 2UB Scotland. **Tel** 011 44 224 272634. **LC** PR8514; .S3 Suppl. **DD** 427/.941/05. **Bk Rev. Ad Acc. Pr Rev. Circ:** 850 (ctrl).
Desc: A scholarly journal that publishes articles on all aspects of the languages of Scotland.
Ind/Abst Annu. Bibliogr. Engl. Lang. Lit.; MLA Int. Bibl. Books Artic. Mod. Lang. Lit.; Soc. Plann. Policy Dev. Abstr.

UK
SCOTTISH LITERARY JOURNAL. THE YEAR'S WORK IN SCOTTISH LITERARY AND LINGUISTIC STUDIES. **Added/Corp** Association for Scottish Literary Studies. **VFOAT** Year's Work in Scottish Literary and Linguistic Studies; Scottish Literary Journal. Year's Work. (1984)-. English (Gaelic (Scots)). Twice a year. £50.00 membership. Association for Scottish Literary Studies, University of Aberdeen, Department of English, Taylor Buildings, Aberdeen AB9 2UB Scotland. **Tel** 011 44 224 272634. **ED** Kenneth Buthlay. Index available. cum. index. **Bk Rev. Ad Acc. Pr Rev. Circ:** 800 (ctrl). *Continues in part* Scottish Literary Journal. Supplement, 0952-6439.
Desc: One of the only two academic journals in the world devoted to Scottish literature. Covers all periods and aspects. Its supplements review important Scottish books.

UK/0265-3273
SCOTTISH SLAVONIC REVIEW. [Scott. slav. rev.]. No. 1 (1983)-. English (Russian). sa. £38.00 institutions; £25.00 individuals. Scottish Slavonic Review, Department of Slavonic Language / Literature, Glasgow G12 800 Scotland. **Tel** 011 44 41 339 8855 ext. 5418, 4731, FAX 041 330 4808, telex 777/70 UNIGLA. **ED** Peter Henry. **LC** PG1; .S45. **DD** 947/.00049163/05. Index available. **Bk Rev**. **Ad Acc**. **Pr Rev. Circ:** 400.
Desc: Publication on literatures, languages, history, cultures and arts in Eastern Europe. East-West cultural contacts.
Ind/Abst MLA Int. Bibl. Books Artic. Mod. Lang. Lit.

IS/0334-4509
SCRIPTA CLASSICA ISRAELICA. [Scr. class. Isr.]. **Added/Corp** Israel Society for the Promotion of Classical Studies. Vol. 1 (1974)-. Multiple languages (English, German and Latin). an. Jerusalem Academic Press, PO Box 2390, Jerusalem Israel. **LC** PA1; .S3.

US
SCRIPTA HUMANISTICA. See Literature.

IT/0392-1697
SCRITTURA E CIVILTA. Vol. 1 (1977)-. Periodical. Italian (English and French). an. L95000 Italy; L115000 other. Casa Editrice Leo S. Olschki, Viuzzo del Pozzetto, Casella Postale 66, 50126 Florence Italy. **Tel** 011 39 55 6530684, FAX 011 39 55 6530214.

US/0730-6245
SECOL REVIEW, THE. (THE SECOL REVIEW / SOUTHEASTERN CONFERENCE ON LINGUISTICS.). [SECOL rev.]. **Added/Corp** Southeastern Conference on Linguistics. **VFOAT** S.E.C.O.L. Review. **VAT** Southeastern Conference on Linguistics Review. Vol. 6, No. 1 (Spring 1982)-. Periodical. English. Twice a year (June & Dec.). $30.00. SECOL Review, Linguistics Program, USC Columbia, Columbia SC 29208. **Tel** (803)777-2171, FAX (803)777-9064. **ED** Greta Little and Michael Montgomery. **LC** P1; .S43. **DD** 410/.5. Index available. cum. index. **Bk Rev. Circ:** 250. ***Continues*** *SECOL Bulletin, 0192-3277.*
Desc: Covers all areas in linguistics, including phonology, morphology, syntax, socio-linguistics, psycho-linguistics, etc.
Ind/Abst Linguist. Lang. Behav. Abstr. (1987-) [Full Cov.]; MLA Int. Bibl. Books Artic. Mod. Lang. Lit.; Soc. Plann. Policy Dev. Abstr.

US/1055-4750
SECOND LANGUAGE INSTRUCTION/ACQUISITION ABSTRACTS. [Second lang. instr./acquis. abstr.]. **Added/Corp** Sociological Abstracts, Inc. **VFOAT** Second Language Instruction Acquisition Abstracts; SLIA. Vol. 1, No. 1 (July 1991)-. Periodical. English. sa (published in Jul. and Dec.). $80.00. Sociological Abstracts, PO Box 22206, San Diego CA 92192-0206. **Tel** (619)695-8803, FAX (619)695-0416. **LC** P51; .S336. **DD** 418/.007.
Desc: A scholarly reference work, published twice a year, containing informative English abstracts of articles on bilingual education, foreign or native language instruction, TESOL, and translation. Presents complete bibliographic citations, and precise indexing of articles culled from among 1,900 discipline-related serials published worldwide. Enhanced citations of relevant dissertations are also included.

UK/0267-6583
SECOND LANGUAGE RESEARCH. Vol. 1, No. 1 (June 1985)-. Periodical. English. Three times a year (February, June and October). $115.00 North America; £65.00 Europe; £72.50 Other. Edward Arnold, 338 Euston Road, London NW1 3BH England. **Tel** 011 44 71 873 6000, FAX 011 44 071 873 6325. **(Subscription address:** Edward Arnold, PO Box 386, Avenel NJ 07001-0386.**) ED** J. N. Pankhurst and Roger Hawkins. **[CCC]. Bk Rev. Ad Acc. Pr Rev. Circ:** 400. available on microfilm and microfiche from University Microfilms International (UMI). ***Continues*** *Interlanguage Studies Bulletin - Utrecht, 0165-9960.*
Desc: Seeks to promote interdisciplinary research linking second language studies with neighboring disciplines which contribute to the understanding of the psychological mechanisms that guide learners' individual behavior and their interaction with other language users. Areas covered include: first language acquisition, neurolinguistics, theoretical linguistics, experimental psycholinguistics, artificial intelligence, cognitive psychology, bilingual studies, and sociolinguistics. An extended book review section is also featured. Each volume includes one special guest edited number designed to focus in depth on a particular theme of current importance.
Ind/Abst Br. Educ. Index; Contents Pages Educ.; Curr. Index J. Educ. (March 1990); Int. Bibliogr. Book Rev.; Int. Bibliogr. Period. Lit.; Linguist. Lang. Behav. Abstr. (1985-) [Full Cov.]; MLA Int. Bibl. Books Artic. Mod. Lang. Lit.; Soc. Plann. Policy Dev. Abstr.

SP/0037-0894
SEFARAD. See Religion and Theology-Judaism.

SZ/0582-3951
SEGES (FRIBOURG). (SEGES.). [Seges]. **Added/Corp** Universite de Fribourg. Faculte des Lettres. (1963)-. Monographic series. English (French, German, Italian and).
Ind/Abst MLA Int. Bibl. Books Artic. Mod. Lang. Lit.

JA
SEINAN GAKUIN DAIGAKU EIGO EIBUNGAKU RON SHU. Main/Corp Seinan Gakuin Daigaku. Gakujutsu Kenkyujo. **VFOAT** Studies in English Language and Literature. (June 1960)-. Multiple languages (Japanese and English). 2-92 Nishishin, 6-chome Nishi-ku 814, Fukuoka Japan. **LC** PE9; .S4A. **UDC** 802.0; 820.
Ind/Abst MLA Int. Bibl. Books Artic. Mod. Lang. Lit.

US/0277-0598
SELECTA (CORVALLIS, OR.). (SELECTA : JOURNAL OF THE PNCFL, PACIFIC NORTHWEST COUNCIL ON FOREIGN LANGUAGES.). [Selecta]. **Added/Corp** Pacific Northwest Council on Foreign Languages. Vol. 1 (1980)-. Periodical. English (French, German, Italian, Spanish, Portuguese and Russian). an. $12.00 US; $17.00 other. Oregon State University / Department of Foreign Language & Literature, Kidder Hall 210, Corvallis OR 97331. **Tel** (503)737-2146. **LC** PB11; .P2. **DD** 405. ***Continues*** *Pacific Northwest Council on Foreign Languages. Proceedings, 0363-8391.*
Ind/Abst Am. Bibliogr. Slavic East Europ. Stud.; MLA Int. Bibl. Books Artic. Mod. Lang. Lit.

US/0559-3468
SELECTED ARTICLES FROM LANGUAGE LEARNING. Added/Corp Research Club in Language Learning (Ann Arbor, Mich.). No. 1 (1963)-. English. ir. Language Learning, 178 Henry S. Frieze Building, 105 South State Street, Ann Arbor MI 48109-1285. **Tel** (313)763-9216.

FR/0395-3556
SEMANTIKOS. [Semantikos]. **Added/Corp** Semantikos Association. Vol. 1 No. 1 (1975)-. Periodical. English (French). Twice a year (May, & Nov.). 62.00F (individuals); 95.00F (institutions). Association Semantikos, 8 rue des Boulangers, 75005 Paris France. **Tel** 033-12-05. **ED** R. Zuber. **Bk Rev. Ad Acc**. ctrl circ.

CN/0037-1939
SEMINAR (TORONTO). (SEMINAR.). [Seminar]. **Added/Corp** Australasian Universities Language and Literature Association. Germanic Section. Canadian Association of University Teachers of German. Vol. 1 (Spring 1965)-. Academic Scholarly Publication. English (German and French). qt (Jan., Apr., July, Oct.). $35.00. University of Toronto Press, 5201 Dufferin Street, Downsview Ontario M3H 5T8 Canada. **Tel** (416)667-7781, (416)667-7782, FAX (416)667-7803. **ED** Rodney Symington. **LC** PF3001; .S4. **DD** 430/.5. **[CCC]. Bk Rev**. ctrl circ. available on microfilm from University Microfilms International (UMI). Documents available from The Genuine Article.
Desc: Publication of articles relating to the German arts and literature. Presents issues of scholarly interest to students and instructors in this field, as well as to the general public.
Ind/Abst Am. Bibliogr. Slavic East Europ. Stud.; Arts Humanit. Citation Index [Full Cov.]; MLA Int. Bibl. Books Artic. Mod. Lang. Lit.; Res. Alert [Full Cov.].

US/0734-0478
SEMINARS IN SPEECH AND LANGUAGE. [Semin. speech, lang.]. Vol. 4, No. 1 (Feb. 1983)-. Academic Scholarly Publication. English. qt (Feb., May, AUg., Nov.). $113.00 (institutions), $65.00 (individuals) US; $138.00 (institutions), $90.00 (individuals) other. Thieme Medical Publishers Inc., 381 Park Avenue South, Suite 1201, New York NY 10016. **Tel** (212)683-5088, (212)683-5089, FAX (212)779-9020, telex 220 862 TSINC UR. **ED** R F Curlee. **LC** RC423.A1; S43. **DD** 616.85/5/005. **NLM** W1; SE489M. **CODEN** SSLAEB. **[CCC]**. cum. index. **Bk Rev. Ad Acc. Circ:** 1,400 (ctrl). available on microfilm and microfiche from University Microfilms International (UMI). Documents available from BIOSIS Document Express. ***Continues in part*** *Seminars, Speech, Language, Hearing, 0196-108X.*
Desc: Topic-oriented journal for the practitioner specializing in speech therapy and communicative disorders.
Ind/Abst Biol. Abstr. (1985-); EMBASE.

MX
SEMIOSIS. Added/Corp Universidad Veracruzana. Centro de Investigaciones Linguistico-Literarias. No. 1 (Jul. 1978)-. Spanish. sa.
Ind/Abst MLA Int. Bibl. Books Artic. Mod. Lang. Lit.

GW/0170-219X
SEMIOSIS. [Semiosis]. **Added/Corp** Universite de Perpignan. Institut de Recherche en Sciences de la Communication et de l'Education. Universitat Stuttgart. Asthetisch-Semiotisches Colloquium. (1976)-. Periodical. German (English and French). qt. DM43.00 Germany; DM57.80 other. Agis Verlag, Postfach 220, D 76492 Baden Baden Germany. **ED** Max Bense and Elisabeth Walther. **Bk Rev. Ad Acc**.
Desc: Semiotics and its applications.
Ind/Abst MLA Int. Bibl. Books Artic. Mod. Lang. Lit.; Soc. Plann. Policy Dev. Abstr.

FR
SEMIOSIS (PARIS, FRANCE). See Literature.

US/0093-9579
SEMIOTEXTE (NEW YORK). See Sociology.

NE/0922-5072
SEMIOTIC CROSSROADS. Vol. 1 (1988)-. Monographic series. English. ir. Price varies per volume. John Benjamins BV, Amsteldijk 44, PO Box 75577, 1070 AN Amsterdam Netherlands. **Tel** 011 31 20 6738156, FAX 011 31 20 739773. **(Subscription address:** John Benjamins North America, PO Box 27519, Philadelphia PA 19118-0519.**) ED** Paolo Fabbri, Herman Parret, Paul Perron, and Eric Landowski.
Desc: Emphasizes current tendencies in semiotic research in France and abroad.
Ind/Abst MLA Int. Bibl. Books Artic. Mod. Lang. Lit.

GW
SEMIOTIC WEB, THE. (1986)-. English. an. Price varies according to size. Walter de Gruyter Inc., PO Box 303421, D 10728 Berlin Germany. **Tel** 011 49 30 260050, FAX 011 49 30 26005251. **ED** Thomas E Sebeok and Jean Uniker-Sebeok. **LC** P99; .S3822. **DD** 302.2. Index available.

NE/0037-1998
SEMIOTICA. [Semiotica]. **Added/Corp** International Association for Semiotic Studies. International Council for Philosophy and Humanistic Studies. International Social Science Council. Vol. 1 (1969)-. English (French). Five times a year. $613.65. Walter de Gruyter Inc., PO Box 303421, D 10728 Berlin Germany. **Tel** 011 49 30 260050, FAX 011 49 30 26005251. **ED** Thomas A. Sebeok. **LC** B820; .S45. **[CCC]. Bk Rev. Ad Acc. Circ:** 850. Documents available from The Genuine Article. ***Supersedes in part*** *Social Science Information.*
Desc: Devoted to the study of signs and symbols in different societies and their cultural relevance.
Ind/Abst Abstr. Anthropol.; Arts Humanit. Citation Index [Full Cov.]; BHA : Biblio. Hist. Art; Curr. Contents Arts Humanit.; Film Lit. Index; Int. Bibliogr. Sociol.; Lang. Teach.; MLA Int. Bibl. Books Artic. Mod. Lang. Lit.; Res. Alert [Full Cov.]; Soc. Plann. Policy Dev. Abstr.; Soc. Sci. Cit. Index [Select. Cov.]; Sociol. Abstr.

US/0742-7611
SEMIOTICS. [Semiotics]. **Main/Corp** Semiotic Society of America. Meeting. (1980)-. English. an. $65.00. University Press of America, 4720 A Boston Way, Lanham MD 20706. **Tel** (301)459-3366, (800)462-6420. **LC** P99; .S3818a. **DD** 001.51.

FR/1160-9907
SEMIOTIQUES / CENTRE NATIONAL DE LA RECHERCHE SCIENTIFIQUE, INSTITUT NATIONAL DE LA LANGUE FRANCAISE, URL7-ANALYSE DU DISCOURS. Added/Corp Ecole des Hautes Etudes en Sciences Sociales. Groupe de Recherches Semio-Linguistiques. Vol. 1, No. 1 (Juin 1991)-. Periodical. French (English). sa. $42.00. Societe Nouvelle Didier Erudition, 6 rue de la Sorbonne, 75005 Paris France. **Tel** 011 33 1 43544757, FAX 011 33 1 40517385. **(Subscription address:** PO Box 830350, Birmingham, AL 35283-0350, telephone: (800)633-4931, (205)995-1567 (outside US and Canada); FAX: (205)995-1588**) LC** P99; .S46.
Desc: Multidisciplinary in its approach, this journal promotes the international exchange of ideas on the study of speech.

FR/0373-630X
SEMITICA. [Semitica]. **Added/Corp** Universite de Paris. Institut d'Etudes Semitiques. (1948)-. Monographic series. French. ir. Price varies per volume. Librairie d'Amerique et Dorien, 11 rue Saint Sulpice, F 75006 Paris France. **Tel** 011 33 1 43268635. **LC** PJ3001; .S4.
Ind/Abst Old Testam. Abstr.

GW/0935-7556
SEMITICA VIVA-SERIES DIDACTICA. (19??)-. German (English). ir. Otto Harrassowitz Verlag, Taunusstrasse 14, Postfach 2929, D-65019 Wiesbaden Germany. **Tel** 011 49 611 5300, FAX 530570, telex 4186 135 OH D. **ED** Otto Zastron. **Circ:** 400.
Desc: The series intends to make accessible, by means of systematically arranged language textbooks, a number of orally transmitted Semitic languages and dialects.

SP/0211-464X
SENARA. [Senara]. (1979)-. Multiple languages. an. **UDC** 8.
Ind/Abst MLA Int. Bibl. Books Artic. Mod. Lang. Lit.

SP
SENDEBAR : BOLETIN DE LA E.U.T.I. DE GRANADA. Added/Corp E.U.T.I. de Granada. Universidad de Granada. No. 1 (1990)-. Periodical. Spanish. an. 1500ptas. Universidad de Granada / Campus de Cartuja, 18071 Granada Spain. **Tel** 011 34 58 243930, 243931. **LC** P306.A1; S46. **DD** 418/.02/05.

BL/0102-6526
SERIE LINGUISTICA. [Ser. linguist.]. **Added/Corp** Summer Institute of Linguistics. **VFOAT** Linguistica. No. 3 (1974)-. Monographic series. Portuguese (English). ir. Price varies per volume. Bookroom Summer Institute of Linguistics, SAI/NO, Lote D/Bloco 3, 70770-730 Brasilia DF Brazil. **Tel** 55 61 272

1200, FAX 55 61 349 4909. **LC** PM5151; .S45.
Desc: Publishes data-oriented linguistic papers on Brazilian indigenous languages.
Ind/Abst Linguist. Lang. Behav. Abstr. (1973-) [Full Cov.]; MLA Int. Bibl. Books Artic. Mod. Lang. Lit.; Soc. Plann. Policy Dev. Abstr.

PE/0885-8691
SERIE LINGUISTICA PERUANA. [Ser. linguist. peru.]. **Added/Corp** Summer Institute of Linguistics. (19??)-. Monographic series. Spanish. ir. Price varies per volume. Instituto Linguistico de Verano, Casukka 4640, Lima 100 Peru. **Tel** 28 7993. **ED** Mary Ruth Wise. **DD** 460. available on microfiche (from 7500 West Camp Wisdom Road, Dallas TX 75236).
Desc: Includes bilingual dictionaries, descriptive and theoretical works on indigenous languages of Peru, and comparative linguistic studies.
Ind/Abst Linguist. Lang. Behav. Abstr. (1986-) [Full Cov.]; MLA Int. Bibl. Books Artic. Mod. Lang. Lit.; Soc. Plann. Policy Dev. Abstr.

UK/0950-2025
SESAME BULLETIN. ***Title Change.*** **Added/Corp** Sesame Computer Projects (Organization). Vol. 1, Parts 1 & 2 (Autumn 1986/Winter 1987)-(19??). Bulletin. English. qt. Sesame Computer Projects, 8 Avenue Road Harrogate, North Yorkshire HG2 7PG England. **LC** P98; .S48. **DD** 410.285. ***Merged with*** *Worldwide Product Directory* ***to form*** *Multilingual Computing, 1065-7657.*
Ind/Abst Soc. Plann. Policy Dev. Abstr.

CN
SHASHKEVYCHIIANA. **Added/Corp** Zapovidnyka Markiiana Shaskevycha u Vinninpegu. **VFOAT** Shaskevychiana. Vol. 1 No. 1 (1963)-. Periodical. Ukrainian. **LC** PG3948.S448; Z83.
Ind/Abst Am. Bibliogr. Slavic East Europ. Stud. (19??-19??).

JA
SHINBUNGAKU HYORON. **Added/Corp** Nihon Shinbun Gakkai. **VFOAT** Japanese Journalism Review. (19??)-. Japanese. an. Nihon Shinbun Gakkai, 3-1 Hongo 7, Bunkyo-ku, Tokyo-To Japan. **LC** P87; .S49.
Ind/Abst Int. Bibliogr. Sociol.

US/0302-1475
SIGN LANGUAGE STUDIES. [Sign lang. stud.]. **Added/Corp** Indiana University. Research Center for the Language Sciences. Gallaudet College. Linguistics Research Laboratory. Vol. 1 (1972)-. Periodical. English. Four times a year (Mar., June, Sept., Dec.). $40.00 (individuals), $60.00 (institutions) US & Canada; $50.00 (individuals), $60.00 (institutions) other. Linstok Press, 4020 Blackburn Lane, Burtonsville MD 20866. **Tel** (301)421-0268, FAX (301)421-0270. **ED** William C. Stokoe. **LC** HV2350; .S58. **DD** 001.56. **NLM** W1 SI388. **[CCC].** Index available. cum. index. **Bk Rev. Ad Acc. Pr Rev. Circ:** 450 (ctrl). available on CD-ROM.
Desc: Serves as a forum for reporting research into nonvocal communication, facial expression, gesticulation, face-to-face communication, kinesics, proxemics, and language networks.
Ind/Abst Anthropol. Index; Curr. Index J. Educ.; Except. Child Educ. Resour. (19??-19??); Lang. Teach.; MLA Int. Bibl. Books Artic. Mod. Lang. Lit.; Psychol. Abstr. (1988-); PsycINFO; PsycLit; Soc. Plann. Policy Dev. Abstr.

BL
SIGNIFICACAO. No. 1- August 1974-. Multiple languages (French and Portuguese; summaries and/or abstracts in French, Portuguese and English). Centro de Estudos Semioticos A J Greimas, rua Ramos de Azevedo 423, Jardim Paulista 14.100, Ribeirao Preto Brazil. **LC** P99; .S49. **UDC** 806.90-7.

KO
SIJO MUNHAK. (19??)-. Periodical. Korean. qt. W1,300. Sijo Munhak, 48-4 Puam-dong, Congno-ku, Seoul South Korea. **LC** PL975.6; .S497. ***Supersedes*** *Sijo Munhak.*

AT/1036-1243
SIL - AAIB OCCASIONAL PAPERS. [SIL - AAIB occas. pap.]. **VFOAT** Occasional Papers - SIL AAIB. (1991)-. Monographic series. English. ir. Price varies per volume. Summer Institute of Linguistics / Australia, PO Berrimah, NT 0828 Australia. **Tel** 089 844-021, FAX 089 844 321. **ED** Susanne Hargrave. **DD** 499.15. ***Formed by the union of*** *Work Papers of SIL-AAIB. Series A, 1030-9853* ***and*** *Work Papers of SIL-AAIB. Series B., 1030-9861.*

IT
SILENO. **VFOAT** Rivista di Studi Classici e Cristiani. (1975)-. Periodical. Italian (French). Four times a year. L128000 Italy; L162000 others. L'Erma di Bretschneider SPA, Via Cassiodoro 19, 00193 Rome Italy. **Tel** 011 39 6 6874127, 011 39 6 6874129, FAX 011 39 6 6874129.

KO
SINMUN KWA PANGSONG. Periodical. Korean. 5,000. Hanguk Sinmun Yonguso, 31 1-ka Taepyong-no, Chung-ku, Seoul South Korea. **LC** P87; .S56. ***Continues*** *Sinmun Pyongnon (Hanguk Sinmun Yonguso).*

US
SINO-PLATONIC PAPERS. **Added/Corp** University of Pennsylvania. Dept. of Oriental Studies. (1986)-. Monographic series. English. ir. Price varies per volume. University of Pennsylvania / Department of Oriental Studies, Philadelphia PA 19104. **Tel** (215)898-5000.

KO
SISA ILBONO YONGU. **VFOAT** Jiji Nihongo Kenkyu. Periodical. Japanese (Korean). mo. W30,000. Sisa Ilbonosa, 12-19 Kwanchol-dong Chongno-ku, Seoul 110 Korea. **LC** PL539; .S57.

RU
SISTEMNOE OPISANIE LEKSIKI GERMANSKIKH IAZYKOV. **Added/Corp** Leningradskii Gosudarstvennyi Universitet Imeni A.A. Zhdanova. (1976)-. Periodical. Russian. 0.70rub. Izdatelstvo Moskovskogo Universiteta, K-9 Ulitsa Gertsena 5/7, Moscow Russia. **Tel** (301)881-5973. **ED** K. Ivanova, H. Chupilina, and N. Osetrova. **LC** PE1585; .S49. **Ad Acc. Circ:** 800.
Desc: Lexical elements are analyzed in paradigmatic and syntagmatic, diachronic and synchronic aspects.
Ind/Abst Annu. Bibliogr. Engl. Lang. Lit.

GW/0080-5300
SITZUNGSBERICHTE DER SAECHSISCHE AKADEMIE DER WISSENSCHAFTEN, LEIPZIG, PHILOLOGISCH-HISTORISCHE KLASSE. **Main/Corp** Saechsische Akademie der Wissenschaften, Leipzig. Philologisch-Historische Klasse. **Added/Corp** Saechsische Akademie der Wissenschaften, Leipzig. Philologisch-Historische Klasse. Berichte ueber die Verhandlungen. Vol. 1 (1849)-. Monographic series. German. ir. Price varies per volume. Akademie-Verlag GmbH, Muehlenstrasse 33 34, D 13162 Berlin Germany. **Tel** 011 49 30 47889300, FAX 011 49 30 47889357. **(Subscription address:** VCH Publishers Inc., 303 Northwest 12th Avenue, Journals Department, Deerfield FL 33442.**)** **LC** AS182; .S213. **DD** 410.5. ***Continues*** *Saechsische Akademie der Wissenschaften, Leipzig. Berichte ueber die Verhandlungen der Koeniglich Saechsischen Gesellschaft der Wissenschaften zu Leipzig.*

ER/0320-6432
SKANDINAVSKIJ SBORNIK. (SKANDINAVSKII SBORNIK.). [Skand. sb.]. **Added/Corp** Tartu Riiklik Ulikool. **VFOAT** Skandinaavia Kogumik; Skrifter om Skandinavien. (1956)-. Multiple languages (Russian; summaries and/or abstracts in Estonian and Swedish). an. **LC** DL1; .S5.
Ind/Abst Am. Hist. Life (1971-); BHA : Biblio. Hist. Art.

NO
SKRIFTER - NORSK SPRAKRAD. **Main/Corp** Norsk Sprakrad. (19??)-. Norwegian. **LC** PD2602.A3; N6. **DD** 439.8/2. ***Continues*** *Norsk Spraknemnd. Skrifter.*

SW/0083-4661
SKRIFTER UTGIVNA AV INSTITUTIONEN FOR NORDISKA SPRAK VID UPPSALA UNIVERSITET. [Skr. utg. Inst. nord. spr. Upps. univ.]. **Added/Corp** Uppsala Universitet. Institutionen for Nordiska Sprak. (1953)-. Monographic series. Swedish.
Ind/Abst MLA Int. Bibl. Books Artic. Mod. Lang. Lit.

SW/0346-7856
SKRIFTER UTGIVNA AV LITTERATURVETENSKAPLIGA INSTITUTIONEN VID UPPSALA UNIVERSITET. **See** Literature.

XR/0037-6736
SLAVIA. **Added/Corp** Czechoslovakia. Ministerstvo Skolstvi a Narodni Osvety. Slovansky Ustav v Praze. Slovansky Ustav CSAV. Vol. 1 (1922)-. Periodical. Czech. qt (4 issues). DM221.00 Germany; DM257.00 other. Czech Academy of Sciences, Branisovska 31, 37005 Ceske Budejovice, Czech Republic. **Tel** 011 42 38 817 ext. 213, 214. **(Subscription address:** Kubon & Sagner, ABT Zeitschriftenimport, D 80328 Munich Germany.**)** cum. index.
Desc: The oldest review in the field of Slavistics from the Czech Republic. Publishes articles, discussions, reviews, criticism, etc. all on comparative Slavonic linguistics and literature.
Ind/Abst MLA Int. Bibl. Books Artic. Mod. Lang. Lit.

PL/0081-0002
SLAVIA OCCIDENTALIS. **Added/Corp** Poznanskie Towarzystwo Przyjacio Nauk. Wydzia Filologiczno-Filozoficzny. Vol. 1 (1921)-. Polish (summaries and/or abstracts in English and French). ir. $23.45. **(Subscription address:** ARS Polona, PO Box 1001, 00068 Warsaw Poland.**)** **LC** D377.A1; S56. cum. index.
Ind/Abst Soc. Plann. Policy Dev. Abstr.; Sociol. Abstr.

PL/0037-6744
SLAVIA ORIENTALIS. [Slavia Orient.]. **Added/Corp** Polska Akademia Nauk. Komitet Sowianoznawstwa. Vol. 6 (Oct. 1957)-. Periodical. Polish (table of contents in Russian and English). qt. Price on Request. **(Subscription address:** ARS Polona, PO Box 1001, 00068 Warsaw Poland.**)** available on microfilm. ***Continues*** *Kwartalnik Instytutu Polsko-Radzieckiego.*
Ind/Abst Am. Hist. Life (1964-1972, 1979-); MLA Int. Bibl. Books Artic. Mod. Lang. Lit.

●RU
SLAVIANSKII MIR : VESTNIK PRAZDNIKA SLAVIANSKOI PISMENNOSTI I KULTURY I MEZHDUNARODNOGO KONGRESSA SLAVIANSKIKH KULTUR. **Added/Corp** Mezhdunarodnyi Kongress Slavianskikh Kultur. (Apr. 1992)-. Periodical. Russian. mo.

US/0037-6752
SLAVIC AND EAST EUROPEAN JOURNAL. [Slav. East Eur. j.]. **Added/Corp** American Association of Teachers of Slavic and East European Languages. **VFOAT** SEEJ; S.E.E.J. Vol. 2, No. 1 (Spring 1957)-. Academic Scholarly Publication. English. Four times a year. $50.00 US; $55.00 other. ATSEEL / Department of Russian and Slavic Languages, University of Arizona, Modern Languages 340, Tucson AZ 85721. **Tel** (602)621-9766, FAX (602)621-9765. **ED** Gary Jahn, Department of Slavic Languages, University of Minnesota, Minneapolis, MN, 55455-0397; Telephone: (612)626-0279. **LC** PG38.U6; A5. **DD** 407. Index available. **Bk Rev**, (Qty: 75-100). **Ad Acc. Pr Rev. Circ:** 2,400. available on microfilm and microfiche from University Microfilms International (UMI); available on CD-ROM. Documents available from The Genuine Article, UMI Article Clearinghouse. ***Continues*** *AATSEEL Journal.*
Desc: Articles of scholarly nature on Slavic and East European languages, literatures, cultures, and pedagogy to advance language teaching.
Ind/Abst Acad. Search (July 1993-); Am. Bibliogr. Slavic East Europ. Stud.; Annu. Bibliogr. Engl. Lang. Lit.; Arts Humanit. Citation Index [Full Cov.]; BHA : Biblio. Hist. Art; Curr. Contents Arts Humanit.; Curr. Index J. Educ.; Expand. Acad. Index (1989-); Humanit. Index; Humanit. Source (Jul. 1993-); INFO-SOUTH Abstr.; Lang. Teach.; Mag. Search; MLA Int. Bibl. Books Artic. Mod. Lang. Lit.; Newsp. Period. Abstr. (1991-); Res. Alert [Full Cov.]; Romant. Move.; Soc. Plann. Policy Dev. Abstr.; Sociol. Abstr.

US/1070-5775
SLAVIC SYNTAX NEWSLETTER, THE. [Slav. syntax newsl.]. **Added/Corp** Michigan Slavic Publications (Organization). Vol. 1, No. 1 (May 1991)-. Periodical. English. qt (Feb., May, Sept., Dec.). $10.00. University of Michigan / Michigan Slavic Publications, 3040 Modern Language Building, Ann Arbor MI 48108. **Tel** (313)763-4496. **ED** Judrich Toman. **LC** PG201; .S53. **DD** 491. **Ad Acc.**

FI/0780-3281
SLAVICA HELSINGIENSIA. **Added/Corp** Helsingin Yliopisto. Slaavilaisten Kielten Laitos. (1983)-. Monographic series. English (Bulgarian and Russian). ir. Price varies per volume. **(Subscription address:** Department of Slavonic Languages, P. O. Box 4, Vuorikatu 5 B Univhe, SF 00014 Helsinki, Finland, telephone: 011 358 01912486**)** **LC** UNC; PG13; .S5233.

SW
SLAVICA LUNDENSIA. **Added/Corp** Lunds Universitet. Slaviska Institutionen. (1973)-. German (Russian and Polish; summaries and/or abstracts in English). an. Price varies per volume. Lunds Universitet, Slaviska Institutionen, Finngatan 12 S-223, 62 Lund Sweden. **Tel** 46 108821, FAX 46 108825. **LC** PG13; .S524. ***Supersedes*** *Sprakliga Bidrag.*

DK/0106-1313
SLAVICA OTHINIENSIA. [Slav. othiniensia]. **Added/Corp** Odense Universitet. Slavisk Institut. (1978)-. Danish (English, German, French and Russian). an. **LC** PG1; .S624.
Ind/Abst MLA Int. Bibl. Books Artic. Mod. Lang. Lit.

XR/0583-5380
SLAVICA PRAGENSIA. 1- 1959-. Czech (English, German and Russian). ir. Charles University / Univerzita Karlova, Ovocnytrh 5, 116 36 Prague 1 Czech Republic. **Tel** 228441. **UDC** 808.

XO/0037-6787
SLAVICA SLOVACA. **Added/Corp** Slovenska Akademia Vied. Ustav Svetovej Literatury a Jazykov. Vol. 1 (1966)-. Periodical. Slovak (summaries and/or abstracts in German and Russian). qt. DM58.00. Veda, Publishing House of the Slovak Academy of Sciences, Klemensova 19, 814 30 Bratislava Slovakia. **Tel** (7)583-15. **(Subscription address:** Kubon & Sagner, ABT Zeitschriftenimport, D 80328 Munich Germany.**)** **ED** Jozef Ruricka. **LC** PG1; .S625. **Bk Rev. Ad Acc. Circ:** 550 (ctrl).
Desc: Linguistics and literary criticism are its subjects with special devotion to comparative linguistics of Slovak

and other Slavic languages.
Ind/Abst Soc. Plann. Policy Dev. Abstr.; Sociol. Abstr. (?-?).

●FI/0789-2764
SLAVICA TAMPERENSIA. Added/Corp Tampereen Yliopisto. Filologian Laitos II. Slaavilainen Filolgia. (1992)-. Periodical. English (Finnish and Russian). Tampereen Yliopisto, Filologian Laitos II, Slaavilainen Filologia,, Tampere Finland. **LC** IN PROCESS. ***Continues*** *Issledovaniia po Russkomu Iazyku i Literature.*

XV/0350-6894
SLAVISTICNA REVIJA. [Slav. rev.]. **Added/Corp** Slavisticno Drustvo v Ljubljani. Institut za Slovenski Jezik (Slovenska Akademija Znanosti in Umetnosti) Institut za Literaturo pri Slovenski Akademiji. Slavisticno Drustvo Slovenije. (1948)-. Periodical. Slovenian (summaries and/or abstracts in English; table of contents in English). qt.
Ind/Abst MLA Int. Bibl. Books Artic. Mod. Lang. Lit.; Soc. Plann. Policy Dev. Abstr.

US/0193-1075
SLOVENE STUDIES. See History(General)-History of Europe.

XO/0037-6981
SLOVENSKA REC. (SLOVENSKA REC; CASOPIS PRE VYSKUM A KULTURU SLOVENSKEHO JAZYKA.). [Slov. rec]. Vol. 1 (Sept. 1932)-. Periodical. Slovak. bm. DM167.43 Germany; DM207.43 other. Veda, Publishing House of the Slovak Academy of Sciences, Klemensova 19, 814 30 Bratislava Slovakia. **Tel** (7)583-15. **(Subscription address:** Kubon & Sagner, ABT Zeitschriftenimport, D 80328 Munich Germany.**) ED** Frantisek Kocis. **LC** PG5201; .S5. **Bk Rev. Ad Acc. Circ:** 2,250 (ctrl).
Desc: Prints studies on the problems of Slovak orthography, pronunciation, and grammar. Special attention is devoted to theory of style and culture of the language.
Ind/Abst MLA Int. Bibl. Books Artic. Mod. Lang. Lit.; Soc. Plann. Policy Dev. Abstr.; Sociol. Abstr. (?-?).

XR
SLOVNIK JAZYKA STAROSLOVENSK'EHO. VFOAT Lexicon Linguae Palaeoslovenicae. (1977)-. Czech. Academia, Publishing House of the Czechoslovak Academy of Sciences, Czech AC SCI, Vodickova 40, PO Box 896, 112 29 Prague 1, Czech Republic. **Tel** 011 42 2 245117. **LC** PG693 .C45.
Desc: Devoted to the lexicography of the oldest Slavic Literary language.

GW/0037-7031
SLOVO A SLOVESNOST. [Slovo slovesn.]. **Added/Corp** Prazsky Linguisticky Krouzek. Ceskoslovenska Akademie Ved. Vol. 1 (1935)-. Periodical. Czech (English, French, German and Russian). qt. DM143.00 Germany; DM173.00 other. **(Subscription address:** Kubon & Sagner, ABT Zeitschriftenimport, D 80328 Munich Germany.**)** Index available. cum. index. **Bk Rev. Circ:** 1,200 (ctrl).
Desc: Discussion of grammar, lexicology, phonemic, stylistics, semantics, text theory and communication theory. Information on mathematical linguistics, computational linguistics, psycholinguistics, sociolinguistics and applied linguistics is also included.
Ind/Abst Annu. Bibliogr. Engl. Lang. Lit.; MLA Int. Bibl. Books Artic. Mod. Lang. Lit.

RU
SLOVO V SISTEMNYKH OTNOSHENIIAKH. Added/Corp Sverdlovskii Gosudarstvennyi Pedagogicheskii Institut. (19??)-. Russian. 0.70rub (single issue). Ministerstvo Prosveshcheniia RSFSR / Sverdlovsk, Ulitsa K Libknekhta 9, Sverdlovsk Russia. **LC** AS262.S86; A2 subser; PG2175.

CI/0583-6255
SLOVO (ZAGREB). (SLOVO.). [Slovo]. **Added/Corp** Staroslavenski Institut u Zagrebu. Staroslavenski Zavod u Zagrebu. (1952)-. Periodical. Serbo-Croatian (Roman) (summaries and/or abstracts in French). an. $30.00. **(Subscription address:** Mladost Export Import, PO Box 1028, Ilica 30, 41000 Zagreb Croatia.**) LC** PG1; .S65.
Desc: Covers Slavic philology.
Ind/Abst BHA : Biblio. Hist. Art; MLA Int. Bibl. Books Artic. Mod. Lang. Lit.; Soc. Plann. Policy Dev. Abstr.

RU
SLOVOOBRAZOVANIE I EGO MESTO V KURSE OBUCHENIIA INOSTRANNOMU IAZYKU. Added/Corp Dalnevostochnyi Gosudarstvennyi Universitet (Vladivostok, R.S.F.S.R.). (1973)-. Russian. an.
Ind/Abst Annu. Bibliogr. Engl. Lang. Lit.

FR
SOCIETE DES ANCIENS TEXTES FRANCAIS PUBLICATIONS. French. ir. Editions A et J Picard, 82 rue Bonaparte, 75006 Paris France. **Tel** 011 33 1 43269778.

GW/0933-1883
SOCIOLINGUISTICA. Vol. 1 (1987)-. English (French and German). an. DM94.00. Max Niemeyer Verlag, Postfach 2140, D 72011 Tuebingen Germany. **Tel** 011 49 7071 989494, FAX 011 49 7071 87419. **ED** Ulrich Ammon, Klans J. Mattheier, and Peter H. Nelde. **LC** P40.45.E85; S63. **DD** 306.4/4/09405. Index available. **Bk Rev. Ad Acc. Circ:** 600.
Desc: Intends to examine the complex social problems arising from the difficult relationships between languages, language varieties and societies in Europe from a supranational perspective, and to coordinate European research in sociolinguistics.

CN/0257-7135
SOCIOLINGUISTICS. [Sociolinguistics]. (1983-). Periodical. English. **UDC** 301. ***Continues*** *Sociolinguistics Newsletter, 0049-1217.*
Ind/Abst Linguist. Lang. Behav. Abstr. (1972-) [Full Cov.]; Soc. Plann. Policy Dev. Abstr.

KO
SOGANG OMUN. Vol. 1-. Periodical. Korean. Toso Chulpan Taeram, 87-1 Kyonji-dong, Chongno-ku Seoul Korea. **LC** PL901; .S64.

UK/0038-0849
SOL (NEW YORK), EL. (EL SOL.). (19??)-. Periodical. Spanish. Six times a year. $25.00. Mary Glasgow Publications, Brookhampton Lane, Kineton, Warwickshire CV35 0JB England. **Tel** 011 44 926 640606, FAX 011 44 926 641016. available on microfilm from University Microfilms International (UMI).
Desc: Articles in Spanish for students in second level Spanish classes.

CI/0352-8715
SOL (ZAGREB). (SOL.). [Sol]. **Added/Corp** Sveuciliste u Zagrebu. Filozofski Fakultet. (1986)-. Periodical. Serbo-Croatian (Roman) (summaries and/or abstracts in English). sa.
Ind/Abst Linguist. Lang. Behav. Abstr. (1986-) [Full Cov.]; Soc. Plann. Policy Dev. Abstr.

JA/0287-5357
SOPHIA LINGUISTICA. Added/Corp Jochi Daigaku. Daigakuin. Gaikoku Gogaku Kenkyuka. Jochi Daigaku. Kokusai Gengo Joho Kenkyujo. (1975)-. Japanese (English). Sophia University / Languages & Linguistics, Graduate School of Languages and Linguistics, Linguistic Institute for International Communication, 7-1 Kioi-Cho, Chiyoda-Ku, Tokyo 102 Japan. **LC** P1.A1; S66. **DD** 410/.5.
Ind/Abst Linguist. Lang. Behav. Abstr. (1976-) [Full Cov.]; Soc. Plann. Policy Dev. Abstr.

IT
SOT LA NAPE. Added/Corp Societat Filologjche Furlane. Vol. 34, No. 1 (Mar. 1982)-. Periodical. Raeto-Romance (Italian). qt. (Comes with Societa Filoligica Friulana membership). Societa Filologica Friulana, Via Manin 18, 33100 Udine Italy. **Tel** 39 432 501598. ***Continues*** *Ce Fastu? Sot la Nape.*
Ind/Abst BHA : Biblio. Hist. Art.

RU
SOTSIALNYE I GUMANITARNYE NAUKI. SERIIA 6, I AZYKOZNANIE. OTECHESTVENNAIA LITERATURA / ROSSIISKAIA AKADEMIIA NAUK, INSTITUT NAUCHNOI INFORMATSII PO OBSHCHESTVENNYM NAUKAM. Added/Corp Institut Nauchnoi Informatsii po Obshchestvennym Naukam (Rossiiskaia Akademiia Nauk). **VFOAT** IAzykoznanie. Otechestvennaia Literatura. **VAT** Sotsialnye i Gumanitarnye Nauki. Seriia Shest, I Azykoznanie. Otechestvennaia Literatura. (1993)-. Academic Scholarly Publication. Russian (table of contents in English). qt. Izdatelstvo Nauka / Akademiia Nauk, Publishing House of the Russian Academy of Sciences, Leninskii Porspekt 14, 117901 Moscow Russia. **Tel** 011 95 954-21-53, FAX 011 95 938-21-44, telex 411964. **LC** P9; .08. ***Continues*** *Obshchestvennye Nauki v Rossii. Seriia 6, I Azykoznanie.*

US
SOURCES OF ORIENTAL LANGUAGES AND LITERATURES / DOGU DILLERI VE EDEBIYATLARNN KAYNAKLAR. See History(General)-History of Asia.

II
SOUTH ASIAN LANGUAGE REVIEW. Vol. 1, No. 1 (Jan. 1991)-. Periodical. English. sa. $32.00. Creative Publishers, CB-24, Ring Road, Naraina, New Delhi 110028 India. **(Subscription address:** Prints India, 11 Darya Ganj, New Delhi 110002 India.**) LC** IN PROCESS.

US/0277-335X
SOUTH ATLANTIC REVIEW. (SOUTH ATLANTIC REVIEW : THE PUBLICATION OF THE SOUTH ATLANTIC MODERN LANGUAGE ASSOCIATION.). [South Atl. rev.]. Vol. 46, No. 1 (Jan. 1981)-. Periodical. English. Four times a year (Jan., May, Sept., Nov.). $30.00. South Atlantic Modern Language Association, University Station, PO Box 6109, Tuscaloosa AL 35486. **Tel** (205)348-9067, FAX (205)348-5298. **ED** Robert F. Bell. **LC** PB1; .S6. **DD** 809. **UDC** 800.83. Index available. cum. index (bound in each Nov. issue). **Bk Rev**, (Qty: 100). **Ad Acc, Adv Mgr:** Christel Bell. **Pr Rev. Circ:** 4,200 (ctrl). available on microfilm and microfiche from University Microfilms International (UMI). ***Continues*** *SAB, South Atlantic Bulletin.*
Desc: Publishes articles dealing with research in language and literature in the fields of English, American and other languages.
Ind/Abst Abstr. Engl. Stud.; Am. Humanit. Index; Annu. Bibliogr. Engl. Lang. Lit.; Lit. Crit. Regist.; MLA Int. Bibl. Books Artic. Mod. Lang. Lit.; Romant. Move.

US/0743-6831
SOUTH CENTRAL REVIEW. (SOUTH CENTRAL REVIEW / SOUTH CENTRAL MODERN LANGUAGE ASSOCIATION.). [South Cent. rev.]. **Added/Corp** South-Central Modern Language Association. Vol. 1, No. 1 & 2 (Spring/Summer 1984)-. Periodical. English. qt. $25.00. South Central Modern Language Association, Texas A & M University, Department of English, College Station TX 77843. **Tel** (409)845-7041. **ED** Joe Golson. **LC** PB1; .S64. **DD** 809; 809. **Bk Rev. Ad Acc, Adv Mgr:** Jo Hebert. **Pr Rev. Circ:** 1,700 (ctrl). ***Continues in part*** *South Central Bulletin, 0038-321X.*
Desc: Articles on any aspect of literature, literacy, history and language.
Ind/Abst Abstr. Engl. Stud.; Annu. Bibliogr. Engl. Lang. Lit.; Child. Lit. Abstr. (19??-); Lit. Crit. Regist.; MLA Int. Bibl. Books Artic. Mod. Lang. Lit.; Romant. Move.

MY/0127-046X
SOUTHEAST ASIAN REVIEW OF ENGLISH. (SOUTHEAST ASIAN REVIEW OF ENGLISH / ASSOCIATION FOR COMMONWEALTH LITERATURE & LANGUAGE STUDIES IN MALAYSIA.). [Southeast Asian rev. Engl.]. **Added/Corp** Association for Commonwealth Literature & Language Studies in Malaysia. Vol. 1, No. 1 (Dec. 1980)-. Periodical. English. Twice a year. $6.50. University of Malaya Co-op Bookshop, PO Box 1127, Jalan Pantai Baru, 59700 Kuala Lumpur Malaysia. **Tel** 011 60 3 7573976 or 7565425. **LC** PE9; .S68. **DD** 820/.8.
Ind/Abst MLA Int. Bibl. Books Artic. Mod. Lang. Lit.

US
SOUTHERN CALIFORNIA OCCASIONAL PAPERS IN LINGUISTICS. VFOAT Occasional Papers in Linguistics. No. 1- July 1973-. Monographic series. English. Price varies per volume. S C O P I L, University of Southern California, Department of Linguistics, Los Angeles CA 90007. **UDC** 800.

US/0737-4143
SOUTHWEST JOURNAL OF LINGUISTICS. [Southwest j. linguist.]. **Added/Corp** Linguistic Association of the Southwest (U.S.). Vol. 6, No. 1 (Spring 1983)-. Periodical. English. Twice a year. $15.00 (individuals); $30.00 (institutions). Linguistic Association of the Southwest, University of New Mexico, Department of Linguistics, Albuquerque NM 87131-1196. **Tel** (505)277-7416, FAX (505)277-6355. **ED** Alan Hudson and Eduardo Hernandez Chavez. **LC** P1; .J67. **DD** 410/.5. **Bk Rev**, (Qty: 5). **Ad Acc, Adv Mgr:** E. Hernandez, **Tel** (505)277-3347. **Pr Rev. Circ:** 350. ***Continues*** *Journal of the Linguistic Association of the Southwest, 0732-2615.*
Desc: Publishes articles dealing with either language contact or any of the languages of the Southwestern United States.
Ind/Abst Linguist. Lang. Behav. Abstr. (1975-) [Full Cov.]; MLA Int. Bibl. Books Artic. Mod. Lang. Lit.; Soc. Plann. Policy Dev. Abstr.

AJ/0131-677X
SOVETSKAA TURKOLOGIA. ***Title Change.*** (SOVETSKAIA TIURKOLOGIIA.). [Sov. turkol.]. **Added/Corp** Akademiia Nauk SSSR. Azarbaijan SSR Elmlar Akademiiasy. (1970)-(199?). Periodical. Russian. bm. **(Subscription address:** Victor Kamkin, 4956 Boiling Brook Parkway, Rockville MD 20852.**) LC** PL21; .A45. ***Supersedes*** *Nizami Adyna Adabiiat va Dil Institutu. Voprosy Dialektologii Tiurkskikh Iazykov.* ***Continued by*** *Tiurkologiia.*
Ind/Abst MLA Int. Bibl. Books Artic. Mod. Lang. Lit.; Middle East J.

NZ/0313-1459
SPAN. See Literature.

IT/1120-4583
SPEAK UP MILANO. [Speak up Milano]. (1985)-. Periodical. Italian. ir. L76800.00 Italy. RCS Rizzoli Periodici, Via A Rizzoli 2, 20132 Milan Italy. **Tel** 011 39 2 27200720. **UDC** 372.880.

FR/0982-3425
SPEAK UP PARIS. (SPEAK UP.). (1987)-. Periodical. English. Eleven times a year. 282.08F. Editions Atlas, BP 983, 27009 Evreux Cedex France. **Tel** 011 33 32 240130. **UDC** 082.

US/0584-8164
SPEAKER AND GAVEL. Added/Corp Delta Sigma Rho--Tau Kappa Alpha. Vol. 1 (Nov. 1963)-. Periodical. English. Four times a year. $5.00. Speaker & Gavel, George Mason University, Department of

Communications, Fairfax VA 22030. **Tel** (703)993-1093, FAX (703)993-1096. **ED** Star Muir. **LC** PN4009; .D4317. **Pr Rev. Circ:** 1,000 (ctrl). available on microfilm and microfiche from University Microfilms International (UMI). ***Formed by the union of*** *Gavel of Delta Sigma Rho* ***and*** *Speaker.*

CN/0229-6535
SPEAQ-OUT. (SPEAQ-OUT : BULLETIN DE LA SOCIETE POUR LA PROMOTION DE L'ENSEIGNEMENT DE L'ANGLAIS, LANGUE SECONDE, AU QUEBEC.). [SPEAQ-out]. **Added/Corp** Societe pour la Promotion de l'Enseignement de l'Anglais (Langue Seconde) au Quebec. (1973)-. Bulletin. English (French). Three times a year (Jan., Apr., Oct.). 25.00Can$. Speaq, 7400 Boul Street Laurent 5E Etage, Montreal QUE H2R 2YI Canada. **Tel** (514)271-3700, FAX (514)948-1231. **ED** Melvin Shantz. **DD** 420/.7/0714. **Bk Rev**, (Qty: 10-20). **Ad Acc. Circ:** 1,200 (ctrl).
Desc: This is for the members who are predominantly English as an second language teachers in the Province of Quebec. Contains articles of pedagogical interest and book reviews.

US/0065-9703
SPECIAL PUBLICATIONS / AMERICAN PHILOLOGICAL ASSOCIATION. [Spec. publ. - Am. Philol. Assoc.]. **Added/Corp** American Philological Association. (19??)-. Monographic series. English. ir. Price varies per volume. Scholars Press / Georgia, PO Box 15399, Atlanta GA 30333-0399. **Tel** (404)636-4757, (404)727-2320, FAX (404)727-2348. **DD** 410.
Desc: Includes directories and other special publications of the APA.

UK/0265-6191
SPEECH, HEARING AND LANGUAGE. **Added/Corp** University College, London. Dept. of Phonetics and Linguistics. (198?)-. Periodical. English.
Ind/Abst Soc. Plann. Policy Dev. Abstr.

US
SPEECH INDEX. **See** Linguistics-Abstracting, Bibliographies and Statistics.

NE/0165-084X
SPEKTATOR. **See** Literature.

SA
SPIL, STELLENBOSCH PAPERS IN LINGUISTICS. **Added/Corp** University of Stellenbosch. Dept. of General Linguistics. **VFOAT** Stellenbosch Papers in Linguistics. No. 1 (1978)-. Periodical. English.
Ind/Abst MLA Int. Bibl. Books Artic. Mod. Lang. Lit.

XR/0531-1985
SPISY UNIVERZITY J. E. PURKYNE V BRNE, FILOZOFICKA FAKULTA. ETUDES ROMANES DE BRNO. (ETUDES ROMANES DE BRNO.). [Spisy Univ. J. E. Purkyne Brne Filoz. fak., Etud. romanes Brno]. Vol. 1 (1965)-. French (Italian and Spanish). **LC** PC13; .E88; AS142; .B85. **DD** 408 S; 440.
Ind/Abst MLA Int. Bibl. Books Artic. Mod. Lang. Lit.

UK/0038-772X
SPOKEN ENGLISH. [Spok. Engl.]. **Added/Corp** English Speaking Board. Vol. 1, (May 1968)-. Periodical. English. Twice a year (Mar., Sept.,). £10.00 UK; £13.00 other. English Speaking Board International Ltd, 26A Princes Street, Southport Merseyside, PR8 1EQ England. **Tel** 011 44 704 501730. **ED** Margaret Edwards. **LC** LB1576.A1; S5. **DD** 420/.7. **NLM** W1 SP488D. **CODEN** SPEGE7. cum. index. **Bk Rev. Ad Acc. Circ:** 1,600 (ctrl). available on microfilm and microfiche from University Microfilms International (UMI).
Desc: Covers oral education at all age levels, in both state and independent sectors, and in specialized areas of catering, hairdressing, beauty, therapy and the disabled.
Ind/Abst Br. Educ. Index; Lang. Teach.

GW/0038-8459
SPRACHDIENST, DER. (DER SPRACHDIENST / HERAUSGEGEBEN VON DER GESELLSCHAFT FUER DEUTSCHE SPRACHE.). [Sprachdienst]. **Added/Corp** Gesellschaft fuer Deutsche Sprache (Wiesbaden, Germany). (Oct. 1957)-. Periodical. German. Six times a year (Jan., Mar., May, July, Sep., Nov.). DM66.60. Gesellschaft fur Deutsche Sprache EV, Postfach 2669, W 6200 Wiesbaden Germany. **Tel** 011 49 611 520031, FAX 011 49 611 51313. Index Bound in First Issue. **Bk Rev. Ad Acc. Circ:** 3,000.
Ind/Abst MLA Int. Bibl. Books Artic. Mod. Lang. Lit.

AU/0376-401X
SPRACHE. (DIE SPRACHE.). [Sprache]. **Added/Corp** Wiener Sprachgesellschaft. (1949)-. Periodical. German (English, French, German and Italian). an. Otto Harrassowitz Verlag, Taunusstrasse 14, Postfach 2929, D-65019 Wiesbaden Germany. **Tel** 011 49 611 5300, FAX 530570, telex 4186 135 OH D. **LC** P3; .S6. **Ad Acc, Adv Mgr:** A. Weddigen.
Ind/Abst Linguist. Lang. Behav. Abstr. (1972-) [Full Cov.]; MLA Int. Bibl. Books Artic. Mod. Lang. Lit.; Soc. Plann. Policy Dev. Abstr.

SZ/0253-4533
SPRACHE & KOGNITION. [Sprache Kognit.]. **VFOAT** Sprache und Kognition. Vol. 1, No. 1 (July 1982)-. Periodical. German (summaries and/or abstracts in English). qt. 151.00F. Verlag Hans Huber Ag Bern, Laenggass Strasse 76, CH 3000 Bern 9 Switzerland. **Tel** 011 41 31 3004500. **ED** H. Grimm, W. Deutsch, D. Dorner, J. Engelkamp. **LC** P37; .S65. **DD** 401/.9. **NLM** W1 SP6744. **[CCC]. Circ:** 300.
Desc: Publishes empirical and theoretical papers and critical overviews of language and cognition and interaction.
Ind/Abst MLA Int. Bibl. Books Artic. Mod. Lang. Lit.; Psychol. Abstr. (1982-); PsycINFO (1982-); PsycLit; Soc. Plann. Policy Dev. Abstr.

GW
SPRACHE DER GEGENWART. **Added/Corp** Institut fuer Deutsche Sprache. Vol. 1 (1967)-. Monographic series. German. ir. Price varies per volume. VVA Bertelsmann Dist GmbH, Postfach 7600, D 33310 Gutersloh Germany. **Tel** 011 49 5241 803294.

GW/0343-5202
SPRACHE UND DATENVERARBEITUNG. [Sprache Datenverarb.]. Vol. 1 (1977)-. Periodical. German. Twice a year. DM68.00 Germany; DM69.00 other. Institute Angew Komm and Sprachforsch, Ev Poppelsdorfer Allee 47, D 53115 Bonn Germany. **Tel** 011 49 228 735645. **ED** Harald Zimmermann and Winfried Lenders. **LC** P98; .S65. **CODEN** SPDADH. **Bk Rev. Ad Acc. Circ:** 500. Documents available from Ask*IEEE.
Desc: Draws from all fields pertaining to mechanized work with language as a medium of communication and information.
Ind/Abst Energy Res. Abstr. (March 1982-); INSPEC (1977-); MLA Int. Bibl. Books Artic. Mod. Lang. Lit.; Soc. Plann. Policy Dev. Abstr.

GW
SPRACHE UND INFORMATION. **VFOAT** S + I; S und I. (1982)-. Monographic series. German. ir. Price varies per volume. Max Niemeyer Verlag, Postfach 2140, D 72011 Tuebingen Germany. **Tel** 011 49 7071 989494, FAX 011 49 7071 87419. **ED** Istvan Batori, Walther von Hahn, Rainer Kuhlen, Winfried Lenders, Wolfgang Putschke, Hans Jochen Schneider, Harald Zimmermann.
Ind/Abst MLA Int. Bibl. Books Artic. Mod. Lang. Lit.

GW/0724-9713
SPRACHE UND LITERATUR IN WISSENSCHAFT UND UNTERRICHT. [Sprache Lit. Wiss. Unterr.]. **VFOAT** Sprache und Literatur. (1983)-. Periodical. German. sa. DM53.00 Germany; DM56.00 other. Wilhelm Fink Verlag, Ohmstrasse 5, D 80802 Munich Germany. **Tel** 011 49 89 348017, 348018. **ED** Hans Jurgen Heringer, Gerhard Kurz, and Gerhard Stotzel. **[CCC]. Bk Rev. Ad Acc. Circ:** 3,000 (ctrl). ***Continues*** *Linguistik und Didaktik.*
Desc: Topical discussions and recent research findings in the fields of language and literature.
Ind/Abst MLA Int. Bibl. Books Artic. Mod. Lang. Lit.; Soc. Plann. Policy Dev. Abstr.

AU/0038-8483
SPRACHKUNST. [Sprachkunst]. **Added/Corp** Osterreichische Akademie der Wissenschaften. Vol. 1 (1970)-. Periodical. German (English, French and Russian). sa (2 issues). Oesterreichischen Akademie Wissenschaften, Dr. Ignaz Seipel Platz 2, A-1010 Vienna Austria. **Tel** 011 43 1 51581. **ED** V. Herbert Foltinek, Walter Weiss and Gunther Wytrzens. **LC** P3; .S66. **CODEN** SPRAEK. **Bk Rev. Ad Acc. Circ:** 500 (ctrl). Documents available from The Genuine Article.
Desc: Mainly deals with the art of language.
Ind/Abst Annu. Bibliogr. Engl. Lang. Lit.; Arts Humanit. Citation Index (19??-19??) [Full Cov.]; Curr. Contents Arts Humanit.; MLA Int. Bibl. Books Artic. Mod. Lang. Lit.; Res. Alert [Full Cov.]; Romant. Move.

GW/0038-8505
SPRACHMITTLER, DER. [Sprachmittler]. **Added/Corp** Germany (West). Bundesministerium der Verteidigung. (19??)-. Periodical. German (French and German). Bundesministerium der Verteidigung, 1 Postfach 1388, W-53 Bonn 1 Germany. **Tel** 0228/124782, FAX 0228/126759. **LC** PB38.G39; S68.
Ind/Abst MLA Int. Bibl. Books Artic. Mod. Lang. Lit.

GW
SPRACHREPORT / INSTITUT FUER DEUTSCHE SPRACHE. **Added/Corp** Institut fuer Deutsche Sprache. **VFOAT** Sprach Report. Vol. 1 (1986)-. Periodical. German. Four times a year (Jan., Apr., July, Oct.). DM16.00. Institut fur Deutsche Sprache, Postfach 101621, 68016 Mannheim Germany. **Tel** 011 49 621 1581105. Index available. **Bk Rev. Circ:** 2,000 (ctrl).

SZ/0038-8513
SPRACHSPIEGEL. [Sprachspiegel]. Vol. 1- ; Jan. 1945-. Periodical. German. ir. **LC** PF3003; .S7. **DD** 430/.5. **UDC** 800.
Ind/Abst MLA Int. Bibl. Books Artic. Mod. Lang. Lit.

GW
SPRACHSTRUKTUREN. REIHE A: HISTORISCHE SPRACHSTRUKTUREN. **See** History(General).

●GW/0942-2919
SPRACHTYPOLOGIE UND UNIVERSALIENFORSCHUNG. Vol. 46, No. 1 (1993)-. Periodical. German (English). qt. $215.00. Akademie-Verlag GmbH, Muehlenstrasse 33 34, D 13162 Berlin Germany. **Tel** 011 49 30 47889300, FAX 011 49 30 47889357. **(Subscription address:** VCH Publishers Inc., 303 Northwest 12th Avenue, Journals Department, Deerfield FL 33442.) **Bk Rev.** ***Continues*** *Zeitschrift fur Phonetik, Sprachwissenschaft und Kommunikationsforschung, 0044-331x.*

GW/0344-8169
SPRACHWISSENSCHAFT. [Sprachwissenschaft]. Vol. 1 (1976)-. Periodical. German (French and English). qt. Universitatsverlag Carl Winter, POB 106140, D 69051 Heidelberg Germany. **Tel** 011 49 6221 770260. **ED** Rudolf Schetzeichel. **LC** P1.A1; S68. **Bk Rev. Ad Acc. Circ:** 550 (ctrl). Documents available from The Genuine Article.
Ind/Abst Arts Humanit. Citation Index (19??-19??) [Full Cov.]; Curr. Contents Arts Humanit.; MLA Int. Bibl. Books Artic. Mod. Lang. Lit.; Res. Alert [Full Cov.]; Soc. Sci. Cit. Index [Select. Cov.].

NO
SPRAK NYTT. **VFOAT** Spraknytt. Vol. 1 (1973)-. Periodical. Norwegian. qt. Free. Norsk Sprakrad, Postboks 8107 Dep, N-0032 Oslo 1 Norway. **Tel** 47-2-505900. **ED** E Pettersen and K Venaas. **LC** PD2601; .S67. **UDC** 803.96. **Bk Rev. Circ:** 17,000.
Desc: Contains information from the Norwegian Language Council and articles on Norwegian linguistics for the general public.

●SW/1101-1165
SPRAK OCH STIL. **VFOAT** Sprak & Stil. (1991)-. Swedish (summaries and/or abstracts in English). an. Kr128.00. Swedish Science Press, PO Box 118, S 751 04 Uppsala Sweden. **Tel** 011 46 18 365566, FAX 011 48 18 365277. **LC** PD5004; .S67. ***Continues*** *Nysvenska Studier, 0345-8768.*

SW/0038-8440
SPRAKVARD. [Sprakvard]. **Added/Corp** Namnden for Svensk Sprakvard. Svensk Spraknamnd. Institutet for Svensk Sprakvard. (1965)-. Periodical. Swedish (Danish and Norwegian). qt. Kr60.00. Svenska Spraknamnden, Lundagatan 42 Uppg 5 5 TR, S117 27 Stockholm Sweden. **Tel** 011 46 8 680150. **ED** Margareta Westman. **LC** PD5004; .S68. Index available. **Bk Rev. Ad Acc. Circ:** 4,500.
Desc: Linguistics and language planning.
Ind/Abst MLA Int. Bibl. Books Artic. Mod. Lang. Lit.

GW/0172-620X
SPRINGER SERIES IN LANGUAGE AND COMMUNICATION. Vol. 1 (1978)-. Monographic series. English. ir. Price varies per volume. Springer-Verlag GmbH & Company KG, Heidelberger Platz 3, D 14197 Berlin Germany. **Tel** 011 49 30 8207223, FAX 011 49 30 8214091, telex 183 319 SPBLN D. **(Subscription address:** Springer Verlag New York Inc. / for North America, 44 Hartz Way, Secaucus NJ 07096.) **LC** UNC.
Desc: Contains articles on grammar development, language concepts, aspects and language processing and learning to read.

DK/0038-8645
SPROG OG KULTUR. ***Ceased.*** [Sprog kultur]. **Added/Corp** Aarhus Universitet. Institut for Jysk Sprog- og Kulturforskning. (1932)-(19??). Danish. ir. Aarhus University Press, Aarhus University, Building 170, DK-8000 Aarhus C Denmark. **Tel** 011 45 86 197033, FAX 011 45 86 198433, telex 16600. **LC** DL101; .S6.
Ind/Abst MLA Int. Bibl. Books Artic. Mod. Lang. Lit. (?-?).

GW/0584-9705
SPUDASMATA; STUDIEN ZUR KLASSISCHEN PHILOLOGIE UND IHREN GRENZGEBIETEN. Vol. 1 (1964)-. Monographic series. German. ir. Price varies per volume. George Olms Verlag, Hagentorwall 7, D-31134 Hildesheim Germany. **Tel** 011 51 21 150 10, FAX 011 51 21 150 150. **ED** Hildebrecht Hommel, Ernst Zinn.

AT/0816-5432
SPUNTI E RICERCHE. **See** Literature.

AU/0258-837X
STANDARDTERM. (1986)-. English. Four times a year (Mar., June, Sept., Nov.). S260.00 Austria; S360.00 Europe; S410.00 others. TermNet Secretariat, Gruengasse 9 17, A-1050 Vienna, Austria. **Tel** (011 43 222)567763, FAX (0222)2163272, telex 115960. **Circ:** 300 (ctrl).
Desc: Offers up-to-date and regular information on terminology standardization.

SZ/0171-7219
STANFORD GERMAN STUDIES. [Stanf. Ger. stud.]. **Added/Corp** Stanford University. Dept. of German Studies. Vol. 1 (1973)-. Monographic series. German. ir. Price varies per volume. Verlag Peter Lang AG, Jupiterstrasse 15, CH-3000 Bern 15 Switzerland. **Tel** 011 41 31 9411122, FAX 011 41 31 321131.
Desc: Investigates the application of Fritz Mauthner's theories of language to the work of leading scientists and humanists of his day in order to develop a model underlying literary and scientific reforms of the period.
Ind/Abst MLA Int. Bibl. Books Artic. Mod. Lang. Lit.

US/1048-4833
STANFORD SLAVIC STUDIES. [Stanford Slav. stud.]. **Added/Corp** Stanford University. Dept. of Slavic Languages and Literatures. Vol. 1 (1987)-. Monographic series. English (Russian). ir. Stanford University / Slavic Department, Stanford University, Bldg 260, Room 279A, Stanford CA 94305. **LC** PG1; .S697. **DD** 491.8/05.
Ind/Abst MLA Int. Bibl. Books Artic. Mod. Lang. Lit.

US
STATEMENT (FORT COLLINS, CO.). (STATEMENT : JOURNAL OF THE COLORADO LANGUAGE ARTS SOCIETY.). **Added/Corp** Colorado Language Arts Society. Colorado State University. Dept. of English. (19??)-. English. Three times a year (Feb., May, Oct.). $15.00. Colorado Language Arts Society, C/O Bill McBride, Colorado State University, English Department, Fort Collins CO 80523. **Tel** (303)484-5261. **ED** William G. McBride. **LC** Discard. **Bk Rev. Ad Acc. Circ:** 1,200 (ctrl).
Desc: Focus of journal is on all aspects of language, arts and education. Kindergarten through graduate level.

RU
STATISTIKA RECHI I AVTOMATICHESKII ANALIZ TEKSTA. **Added/Corp** Institut Iazykoznaniia (Akademiia Nauk SSR) Akademiia Nauk SSSR. Nauchnyi Sovet po Kompleksnoi Probleme "Kibernetika." Sektsiia Semiotitki. (19??)-. Russian. 1.84rub. Izdatelstvo Nauka St. Petersburg, Mendeleevskaia Liniia 1, 199034 St. Petersburg, B-34 Russia. **Tel** 218-26-12. **LC** P98; .S82.

US/0888-3971
STATUS REPORT ON SPEECH RESEARCH. [Status rep. speech res.]. **Added/Corp** Haskins Laboratories. National Institute of Child Health and Human Development (U.S.). **VFOAT** Speech Research; Haskins Laboratories Status Report on Speech Research. (Feb. 1965)-. Monographic series. English. ir. $26.00. National Technical Information Service - NTIS, Room 2027S, 5285 Port Royal Road, Springfield VA 22161. **Tel** (703)487-4630, (703)487-4660, (703)487-4650, FAX (703)321-8547, telex 89-9405. **DD** 001. available on microfiche (ERIC Version for July/Dec. 1981- distributed to depository libraries).
Ind/Abst Soc. Plann. Policy Dev. Abstr.

SW/0281-5478
STOCKHOLM STUDIES IN BALTIC LANGUAGES. [Stockh. stud. baltic lang.]. (1983)-. Monographic series. Multiple languages. ir. Almqvist & Wiksell International, PO Box 4627, S-11691 Stockholm Sweden. **Tel** 011-46-8-6408800. **UDC** 808.
Ind/Abst MLA Int. Bibl. Books Artic. Mod. Lang. Lit.

SW/0346-6272
STOCKHOLM STUDIES IN ENGLISH. [Stock. stud. Engl.]. **Added/Corp** Stockholms Universitet. (1937)-. Monographic series. English (German and French). ir. Price varies per volume. Almqvist & Wiksell International, PO Box 4627, S-11691 Stockholm Sweden. **Tel** 011-46-8-6408800. **(Subscription address:** US/ 200 Meacham Avenue, Elmont, NY 11003; telephone: (516)352-7300, FAX: (516)352-7377**)**
Ind/Abst MLA Int. Bibl. Books Artic. Mod. Lang. Lit.

RU
STRUKTURNAIA I PRIKLADNAIA LINGVISTIKA. **Added/Corp** Leningradskii Gosudarstvennyi Universitet Imeni A.A. Zhdanova. (1978)-. Periodical. Russian (English). ir (issued every four years). 1.07rub each issue. St Petersburg State University / Izdatelstvo Leningradskogo Universiteta, Universitetskaia Nab 7/9, 199034 St Petersburg Russia. **Tel** 011 95 218-97-88, FAX 011 95 218-51-52, telex 121481. **ED** A S Heard. **LC** P9; .S7. **Ad Acc.**
Desc: Contains data from different languages. Includes problems of the general linguistics, quantitative linguistics, the problems of the development of information retrieval systems, automatic translation, and application of computers in humanities.

IT
STUDI DELL'ISTITUTO LINGUISTICO. **Main/Corp** Universita di Firenze. Istituto Linguistico. (19??)-. Periodical. English (French, German and Italian). **LC** PB5; .F58a. **DD** 410/.5.
Ind/Abst MLA Int. Bibl. Books Artic. Mod. Lang. Lit.

IT/0392-5110
STUDI DI FILOLOGIA ITALIANA. (STUDI DI FILOLOGIA ITALIANA : BULLETINO DELL'ACCADEMIA DELLA CRUSCA.). [Studi filol. ital.]. **Added/Corp** Accademia della Crusca. Vol. 1 (1927)-. Italian. an. L100000. Le Lettere, Costa San Giorgio 28, 50125 Florence Italy. **(Subscription address:** Licosa Spa, P. O. Box 552, 50125 Florence, Italy, telephone: 011 39 55 645415**)** **LC** PC1001; .S8. **DD** 450.82.
Desc: Studies in Italian philology.
Ind/Abst MLA Int. Bibl. Books Artic. Mod. Lang. Lit.

IT
STUDI DI FILOLOGIA TEDESCA. Multiple languages (Italian and German). Bulzoni Editore Srl, Via dei Liburni 14, 00185 Rome Italy. **Tel** 011 39 6 445-5207, FAX 011 39 6 445-0355.
Ind/Abst MLA Int. Bibl. Books Artic. Mod. Lang. Lit.

IT
STUDI DI GRAMMATICA ITALIANA. **Added/Corp** Accademia della Crusca, Florence. Vol. 1 (1971)-. Italian. an. L100000. Le Lettere, Costa San Giorgio 28, 50125 Florence Italy. **LC** PC1105; .S8.
Desc: Studies in Italian grammar.
Ind/Abst Linguist. Lang. Behav. Abstr. (1977-) [Full Cov.]; MLA Int. Bibl. Books Artic. Mod. Lang. Lit.; Soc. Plann. Policy Dev. Abstr.

IT
STUDI DI LESSICOGRAFIA ITALIANA / A CURA DELL'ACCADEMIA DELLA CRUSCA. Vol. 1-. Periodical. Italian. an. L42000 Italy; L60000 other. IRSA Verlag GES MBH, Ruedengasse 6, A 1030 Vienna Austria. **Tel** 011-43-222-7130136, FAX 011-43-222-7130130, telex 5704661. **ED** D'Arco Silvio Avalle. **LC** PC1600; .S78. **DD** 452/.05. **UDC** 805.0-3.
Desc: Italian lexicography.
Ind/Abst Romant. Move.

IT/0049-2361
STUDI E PROBLEMI DI CRITICA TESTUALE. [Studi probl. crit. testuale]. **Added/Corp** Cassa di Risparmio in Bologna. Vol. 1, (Oct. 1970)-. Periodical. Italian. Twice a year (Apr., Oct.). L83000 Italy; L128000 other. Studi e Problemi Critica Test, Via Castiglione 8, 40124 Bologna Italy. **Tel** 011 39 51 583420. **LC** P47; .S7. Documents available from The Genuine Article.
Ind/Abst Arts Humanit. Citation Index [Full Cov.]; Curr. Contents Arts Humanit.; MLA Int. Bibl. Books Artic. Mod. Lang. Lit.; Res. Alert [Full Cov.]; Romant. Move.

IT/0085-6827
STUDI E SAGGI LINGUISTICI. [Studi saggi linguist.]. **Added/Corp** Pisa. Universita. Istituto di Glottologia. Vol. 1, (1961)-. Italian. an. L70000.00 Italy; L120000.00 others. Giardini Editori Stampatori, Via Santa Bibbiana 28, 56127 Pisa Italy. **Tel** 011 39 50 934242.
Ind/Abst MLA Int. Bibl. Books Artic. Mod. Lang. Lit.

IT/0039-2952
STUDI GERMANICI. **See** Literature.

IT/0039-2987
STUDI ITALIANI DI FILOLOGIA CLASSICA. **See** Classical Studies.

IT/0394-3569
STUDI LINGUISTICI ITALIANI. Vol. 1 (1960)-. Periodical. Italian. Twice a year. L90000 Italy; L80000 other. Salerno Editrice, Via di Donna Olimpia 20, 00152 Rome Italy. **Tel** 011 39 6 58205684 or 688, FAX 06-53-15-688. **ED** Enrico Castellani and Luca Serianni. **LC** PC1001; .S84. **DD** 450/.5. **Bk Rev. Circ:** 500.
Desc: Research on history of Italian language and romance philology.

IT
STUDI LINGUISTICI SALENTINI. Began in 1965. Periodical. Italian. Associazione Linguistica, Villa Sebaste Via Per Campi 73051, Novoli (Leese) Italy. **LC** PC1809.S24; S8. **UDC** 805.0.

IT
STUDI ORIENTALI E LINGUISTICI / ISTITUTO DI GLOTTOLOGIA, UNIVERSITA DEGLI STUDI DI BOLOGNA. **Added/Corp** Universita di Bologna. Istituto di Glottologia. (1983)-. Periodical. Italian. Cooperativa Libraria Universitaria Editrice Bologna Soc Coop, A R L Via Marsala 24, 40126 Bologna Italy. **LC** P9; .S74. **DD** 410/.5.
Ind/Abst Soc. Plann. Policy Dev. Abstr.

PL/0081-6272
STUDIA ANGLICA POSNANIENSIA. [Stud. Ang. Posn.]. **Added/Corp** Uniwersytet im. Adama Mickiewicza w Poznaniu. Vol. 1 (1968)-. English. ir. **(Subscription address:** ARS Polona, PO Box 1001, 00068 Warsaw Poland.**)** **LC** PE1; .S87.
Desc: English philology.
Ind/Abst Annu. Bibliogr. Engl. Lang. Lit.; Lang. Teach.; MLA Int. Bibl. Books Artic. Mod. Lang. Lit.; Soc. Plann. Policy Dev. Abstr.

SW/0562-2719
STUDIA ANGLISTICA UPSALIENSIA. (ACTA UNIVERSITATIS UPSALIENSIS. STUDIA ANGLISTICA UPSALIENSIA.). [Stud. Angl. Ups.]. **Added/Corp** Uppsala Universitet. **VFOAT** Studia Anglistica Upsaliensia. (1963)-. Monographic series. English. Almqvist & Wiksell International, PO Box 4627, S-11691 Stockholm Sweden. **Tel** 011-46-8-6408800. **LC** UNC.
Ind/Abst MLA Int. Bibl. Books Artic. Mod. Lang. Lit.

UK/0081-6353
STUDIA CELTICA. [Stud. Celt.]. **Added/Corp** University of Wales. Board of Celtic Studies. Vol. 1 (1966)-. English (Welsh, French and German). be. £20.00 UK; $32.57 US. University of Wales Press, 6 Gwennyth Street, Cathays Cardiff CF2 4YD Wales United Kingdom. **Tel** 011 44 222 231919. **(Subscription address:** Books International Inc., PO Box 6069, McLean VA 22106.**)** **ED** J.E. Caerwyn Williams. **LC** PB1001; .S73. **DD** 491.6/05. Index available. **Bk Rev. Ad Acc. Circ:** 400.
Desc: Publishes contributions of the highest distinction from scholars in Indo-European philology in Continental and Insular Celtic, and in both branches of the latter.
Ind/Abst Br. Archaeol. Bibliogr.; MLA Int. Bibl. Books Artic. Mod. Lang. Lit.

FI/1235-1938
STUDIA FENNICA. LINGUISTICA. **Added/Corp** Suomalaisen Kirjallisuuden Seura. **VFOAT** Linguistica. (1990)-. Monographic series. English. ir. Price varies per volume. Finnish Literature Society, Hallituskatu 1, PB 259, 00171 Helsinki Finland. **Tel** 011 358 0 131231. **LC** P1; .S78; PH124; .S78. ***Continues in part** Studia Fennica, 0085-6835.*

BE/0081-6442
STUDIA GERMANICA GANDENSIA. **See** Literature.

PL/0137-2467
STUDIA GERMANICA POSNANIENSIA. [Stud. Ger. Posnan.]. **Added/Corp** Uniwersytet Poznanski. (1971)-. Monographic series. German. **LC** PF3003; .S8.
Ind/Abst Soc. Plann. Policy Dev. Abstr.

SW/0585-5160
STUDIA GERMANISTICA UPSALIENSIA. (ACTA UNIVERSITATIS UPSALIENSIS. STUDIA GERMANISTICA UPSALIENSIA.). [Stud. Ger. Ups.]. **Added/Corp** Uppsala Universitet. No. 1 (1964)-. Monographic series. German. Almqvist & Wiksell International, PO Box 4627, S-11691 Stockholm Sweden. **Tel** 011-46-8-6408800.
Ind/Abst MLA Int. Bibl. Books Artic. Mod. Lang. Lit.

PL/0208-4074
STUDIA GRAMATYCZNE / POLSKA AKADEMIA NAUK, INSTYTUT JEZYKA POLSKIEGO. 1-. Periodical. English (Polish and Russian). an. 60.00. Zakad Narodowy Im Ossolinskich We Wrocawiu, Krakowskie Przedmiescie 7, 00 068 Warsaw Poland. **LC** P201; .S8. **DD** 415. **UDC** 808.4-5.

GW/0081-6469
STUDIA GRAMMATICA. Vol. 1 (1962)-. German. ir. Price varies per volume. Akademie-Verlag GmbH, Muehlenstrasse 33 34, D 13162 Berlin Germany. **Tel** 011 49 30 47889300, FAX 011 49 30 47889357. **(Subscription address:** VCH Publishers Inc., 303 Northwest 12th Avenue, Journals Department, Deerfield FL 33442.**)** **UDC** 801.5.
Ind/Abst MLA Int. Bibl. Books Artic. Mod. Lang. Lit.

IE/0081-6477
STUDIA HIBERNICA. [Stud. hibernica]. **Added/Corp** St. Patrick's College (Dublin, Dublin). No. 1 (1961)-. Multiple languages (English and Irish). ir. 10.00p. St. Patricks College, Drumcondra, Dublin 9 Ireland. **Tel** 011 353 1 376191. **ED** S.E. Hannrachain. **LC** PB1201; .S88. **Bk Rev. Circ:** 1,000.
Desc: A journal of Irish studies, language, literature, history, archaeology, and long review section.
Ind/Abst Am. Hist. Life (1961-); Br. Archaeol. Bibliogr.; MLA Int. Bibl. Books Artic. Mod. Lang. Lit.

SW/0039-3193
STUDIA LINGUISTICA. [Stud. linguist.]. Vol. 1 (1947)-. Academic Scholarly Publication. French (English, German and Swedish). sa (2 issues). £52.00 UK & Europe; $84.50 North America; £58.50 other. Basil Blackwell Publishers Ltd, 108 Cowley Road, Oxford 0X4 1JF England. **Tel** 011 44 865 791100, FAX 011 44 865 791347, telex 837022 OXBOOK G. **(Subscription address:** Blackwell Publishers / UK, Marston Book Services, PO Box 87, Oxford OX2 0DT England.**)** **LC** P9; .S75. **DD** 405. **[CCC]. Bk Rev. Circ:** 800 (ctrl). Documents available from The Genuine Article.
Desc: General linguistics.
Ind/Abst Arts Humanit. Citation Index [Full Cov.]; Curr. Contents Arts Humanit.; Lang. Teach.; Linguist. Lang. Behav. Abstr. (1972-) [Full Cov.]; MLA Int. Bibl. Books Artic. Mod. Lang. Lit.; Res. Alert [Full Cov.]; Soc. Plann. Policy Dev. Abstr.; Soc. Sci. Cit. Index [Select. Cov.].

US/0886-0432
STUDIA LINGUISTICA ET PHILOLOGICA. [Stud. linguist. philol.]. (1975)-. Monographic series. English. ir. Price varies per volume. Anma Libri, PO Box 876, Saratoga CA 95070. **Tel** (408)741-0522, 741-1522. **ED** A. Juilland. **LC** UNC. **DD**

410.
Desc: Scholarly monograph series in linguistics.
Ind/Abst MLA Int. Bibl. Books Artic. Mod. Lang. Lit.

SW/0039-3274
STUDIA NEOPHILOLOGICA. [Stud. neophilol.]. Began with Vol. 1 (1928)-. Periodical. English (French, German, Italian and Spanish). sa. Kr500.00, $81.00. Scandinavian University Press, PO Box 2959 Toeyen, N 0608 Oslo 6 Norway. **Tel** 011 47 2 2575400, FAX 011 47 2 2575353, telex 71896 UROR N. **(Subscription address:** Scandinavian University Press, 200 Meacham Ave., Elmont NY 11003.**) ED** Lars Hermodsson. **LC** PB5; .S7. **DD** 405. cum. index. **Bk Rev. Ad Acc. Circ:** 700 (ctrl). available on microfiche. Documents available from The Genuine Article.
Desc: Publishes articles on English, German and Romance languages and literatures, and reviews of books in these fields.
Ind/Abst Abstr. Engl. Stud.; Annu. Bibliogr. Engl. Lang. Lit.; Arts Humanit. Citation Index [Full Cov.]; Curr. Contents Arts Humanit.; MLA Int. Bibl. Books Artic. Mod. Lang. Lit.; Res. Alert [Full Cov.]; Romant. Move.; Soc. Plann. Policy Dev. Abstr.

FI/0039-3282
STUDIA ORIENTALIA. (STUDIA ORIENTALIA / EDITED BY THE FINNISH ORIENTAL SOCIETY.). **Added/Corp** Suomen Itamainen Seura. (1925)-. Monographic series. English (French and German). ir. Price varies per volume. Academic Bookstore Akateeminen, Postilokero 23, FIN-00371 Helsinki Finland. **Tel** 011 358 0 12141. **LC** PJ9; .S86. **DD** 490/.5. cum. index.

SW/0081-6809
STUDIA PHILOLOGIAE SCANDINAVICAE UPSALIENSIA. **Added/Corp** Uppsala Universitet. Vol. 1 (1961)-. Monographic series. Multiple languages (Swedish and English). ir. Price varies per volume. Almqvist & Wiksell International, PO Box 4627, S-11691 Stockholm Sweden. **Tel** 011-46-8-6408800. **(Subscription address:** US/ 200 Meacham Avenue, Elmont, NY 11003; telephone: (516)352-7300, FAX: (516)352-7377**)**

CN/0829-2167
STUDIA PHONETICA. [Stud. phon.]. (1969)-. Monographic series. French. ir. Societe Nouvelle Didier Erudition, 6 rue de la Sorbonne, 75005 Paris France. **Tel** 011 33 1 43544757, FAX 011 33 1 40517385. **LC** P215; .S78.
Ind/Abst MLA Int. Bibl. Books Artic. Mod. Lang. Lit.

PL/0861-2085
STUDIA PHONETICA POSNANIENSIA. English (Polish). an. Z1500 Poland; $8.00 other. Adam Mickiewicz University Press, Nowowiejskiego 55, 61734 Poznan Poland. **Tel** 011 48 527-380, FAX 011 48 61-526425. **(Subscription address:** Adam Mickiewicz University Press INowowiejskiego 55, 61-734 Poznan, Poland**) ED** Maria Steffen. **Bk Rev. Ad Acc. Pr Rev. Circ:** 500 (ctrl).
Desc: A review of linguistic phonetics with preference to theory-oriented contributions.
Ind/Abst Soc. Plann. Policy Dev. Abstr.

JA/0300-1067
STUDIA PHONOLOGICA. (ONSEI KAGAKU KENKYU.). [Stud. phonol.]. **Added/Corp** Kyoto Daigaku. Onsei Kagaku Sogo Kenkyu Bukai. **VFOAT** Studia Phonologica. (1961)-. Multiple languages (English, German and Japanese). be. Kyoto Daigaku Onsei Kagaku Sogo Kenkyu Bukai, (Inst. for Phonetic Sciences, Kyoto University), c/o Mr. Makoto Nakajima, Kyoto Daigaku Kyoyobu Shinri, Gakka, Yoshida Nihonmatsucho, Sakyoku, Kyotoshi, Kyotofu 606, Japan. **LC** P215; .O53. **NLM** W1 ON375K.
Ind/Abst Linguist. Lang. Behav. Abstr. (1971-) [Full Cov.]; Soc. Plann. Policy Dev. Abstr.

CI/0039-3339
STUDIA ROMANICA ET ANGLICA ZAGRABIENSIA. N. 1- 1956-. English (Italian, French and Spanish). sa. 7000 Din Yugoslavia; $20.00 US. Filozofski Fakultet, D Salaja 3, 41000 Zagreb Croatia. **Tel** 513-155-304. **ED** Ivo Vidan. **LC** PC13. **UDC** 802.0; 804. **Circ:** 500 (ctrl).
Desc: Romance linguistics and literatures, English linguistics and literature, articles published in all Romance languages and in English.
Ind/Abst Annu. Bibliogr. Engl. Lang. Lit.; Lang. Teach.; Soc. Plann. Policy Dev. Abstr.; Sociol. Abstr.

PL/0137-2475
STUDIA ROMANICA POSNANIENSIA. **See** Romance and Adventure.

HU/0418-4564
STUDIA ROMANICA. SERIES LINGUISTICA. **Main/Corp** Kossuth Lajos Tudomanyegyetem. No. 1.- 1964-. Periodical. Tankonyvkiado, Szalay u 10 14 Postfiok 20, H 1055 Budapest V Hungary. **UDC** 804.

PL/0081-6884
STUDIA ROSSICA POSNANIENSIA. (STUDIA ROSSICA POSNANIENSIA.). [Stud. Ross. Posnan.]. **Added/Corp** Uniwersytet im. Adama Mickiewicza w Poznaniu. (1970)-. Polish (Russian; summaries and/or abstracts in English and Russian). **LC** PG2025; .S78.
Ind/Abst Soc. Plann. Policy Dev. Abstr.

SW/1100-8091
STUDIA SEMINARII LATINI UPSALIENSIS. **Added/Corp** Uppsala Universitet. Institutionen for Klassiska Sprak. (1990)-. Monographic series. Latin. Price varies per volume.

HU/0039-3363
STUDIA SLAVICA ACADEMIAE SCIENTIARUM HUNGARICAE. (STUDIA SLAVICA.). [Stud. slav. Acad. Sci. Hung.]. **Added/Corp** Magyar Tudomanyos Akademia. Nyelv- es Irodalomtudomanyok Osztalya. Vol. 1 (1955)-. Academic Scholarly Publication. Multiple languages (English, French, German, Hungarian and Russian). Four times a year. $96.00. Akademiai Kiado, Publishing House of the Hungarian Academy of Sciences, Prielle Kornelia u. 19-35, H-1117 Budapest Hungary. **Tel** 011 36 1 1811991, FAX 011 36 1 1811991, telex 22-6228 AKNYO H. **ED** Ferenc Papp and Attila Hollos. **LC** PG1; .S8. **[CCC]**. Index available. **Bk Rev. Ad Acc.** available with charts; available with illustrations. ***Supersedes*** *Etudes Slaves et Roumaines.*
Desc: Information on Slavic philology.
Ind/Abst Am. Hist. Life (1963-1971); MLA Int. Bibl. Books Artic. Mod. Lang. Lit.; Soc. Plann. Policy Dev. Abstr.; Sociol. Abstr.

FI/0781-3333
STUDIA SLAVICA FINLANDENSIA. [Stud. slav. Finl.]. **Added/Corp** Neuvostoliittoinstituutti. (1984)-. English (German and Russian). an.
Ind/Abst MLA Int. Bibl. Books Artic. Mod. Lang. Lit.

RM
STUDIA UNIVERSITATIS BABES-BOLYAI. PHILOLOGIA. **Main/Corp** Universitatea Babes-Bolyai. (19??)-. Academic Scholarly Publication. English (French, Romanian and Russian). sa. Universitatis Babes-Bolyai, Biblioteca Centrala Universitara, Str. Clinicilor 2, Cluj Napoca 3400 Romania. **Tel** 95 117092, FAX 95 117633. **(Subscription address:** Ilexim Press Department, PO Box 1, 136-1-137, Bucharest, Romania.**) LC** P19; .C5. **DD** 405. ***Continues*** *Studia Universitatis Babes-Bolyai. Series Philologia.*
Ind/Abst Annu. Bibliogr. Engl. Lang. Lit.; Soc. Plann. Policy Dev. Abstr.

SP/0214-736X
STUDIA ZAMORENSIA. **Added/Corp** Colegio Universitario de Zamora. (1980)-. Periodical. Spanish. an. **LC** DP302.Z1; S78. **DD** 946/.24.
Ind/Abst BHA : Biblio. Hist. Art.

XR/0585-5675
STUDIE A PRACE LINGUISTICKE. **Added/Corp** Ceskoslovenska Akademie Ved. Sekce Jazyka a Literatury. 1 (1954)-. Monographic series. Czech (summaries and/or abstracts in English and Russian). Price varies per volume. **LC** P9; .S78.

GW/0585-5853
STUDIEN ZU DEN BOGAZKOY-TEXTEN. [Stud. Bogazkoy-Texten]. **Added/Corp** Akademie der Wissenschaften und der Literatur (Germany). Kommission fur den Alten Orient. (1965)-. Monographic series. German. ir. Otto Harrassowitz Verlag, Taunusstrasse 14, Postfach 2929, D-65019 Wiesbaden Germany. **Tel** 011 49 611 5300, FAX 530570, telex 4186 135 OH D. **LC** P945; .S65.
Ind/Abst MLA Int. Bibl. Books Artic. Mod. Lang. Lit.

GW
STUDIEN ZUM FRUHNEUHOCHDEUTSCHEN. (1977)-. Monographic series. German. ir. Price varies per volume. Universitatsverlag Carl Winter, POB 106140, D 69051 Heidelberg Germany. **Tel** 011 49 6221 770260.
Desc: Studies of early new high-German language research of German Bible translations.

GW
STUDIEN ZUM KLEINEN DEUTSCHEN SPRACHATLAS. (1982)-. Monographic series. German. ir. Price varies per volume. Max Niemeyer Verlag, Postfach 2140, D 72011 Tuebingen Germany. **Tel** 011 49 7071 989494, FAX 011 49 7071 87419. **ED** Wolfgang Putschke, Werner Veith.
Ind/Abst MLA Int. Bibl. Books Artic. Mod. Lang. Lit.

GW/0081-7244
STUDIEN ZUR ENGLISCHEN PHILOLOGIE. [Stud. engl. Philol.]. Vol. 1 (1897)-Vol. 96 (1939); New Series Vol. 1 (1963)-. Monographic series. German. ir. Price varies per volume. Max Niemeyer Verlag, Postfach 2140, D 72011 Tuebingen Germany. **Tel** 011 49 7071 989494, FAX 011 49 7071 87419. **ED** Joerg Fichte, Lothar Fietz, Gerhard Mueller-Schwefe.
Desc: Series covering English philology.
Ind/Abst MLA Int. Bibl. Books Artic. Mod. Lang. Lit.

GW/0340-594X
STUDIEN ZUR GERMANISTIK, ANGLISTIK UND KOMPARATISTIK. [Stud. Ger., Angl. Kompar.]. Vol. 1 (1970)-. Monographic series. German (English). ir. Price varies per volume. Bouvier GmbH & Co. KG ABT Verlag, AM Hof 28, D 53113 Bonn Germany. **Tel** 011 49 228 7290141. **(Subscription address:** VVA Bertelsmann Distributors GmbH, Postfach 7777, D-33310 Guetersloh Germany.**) ED** Armin Arnolk and Alois M Haas. **LC** UNC.
Ind/Abst MLA Int. Bibl. Books Artic. Mod. Lang. Lit.

SP
STUDIEN ZUR PALAEGRAPHIE UND PAPYRUSKUNDE. German. qt. Adolf M. Hakkert Editore, Calle Alfambra 26, Las Palmas Gran Canaria Spain. **Tel** 011 34 28 277350.

GW/0178-126X
STUDIEN ZUR THEORETISCHEN LINGUISTIK. [Stud. theor. Linguist.]. (1982)-. Monographic series. German. ir. Price varies per volume. Wilhelm Fink Verlag, Ohmstrasse 5, D 80802 Munich Germany. **Tel** 011 49 89 348017, 348018.
Ind/Abst MLA Int. Bibl. Books Artic. Mod. Lang. Lit.

DK/0107-9212
STUDIER FRA SPROG- OG OLDTIDSFORSKNING. (STUDIER FRA SPROG- OG OLDTIDSFORSKNING; UDGIVNE AF DET PHILOLOGISK-HISTORISKE SAMFUND.). [Stud. sprog-oldtidsforsk.]. **Added/Corp** Filologisk-Historiske Samfund (Denmark). (1891)-. Periodical. Danish.
Ind/Abst MLA Int. Bibl. Books Artic. Mod. Lang. Lit.

SW/0585-3583
STUDIER I MODERN SPRAKVETENSKAP. [Stud. mod. sprakvetensk.]. **Added/Corp** Stockholms Universitet Nyfilologiska Sallskapet, Stockholm. **VFOAT** Stockholm Studies in Modern Philology. (1898)-. Swedish (English, French, German and Spanish). ir. Almqvist & Wiksell International, PO Box 4627, S-11691 Stockholm Sweden. **Tel** 011-46-8-6408800. **LC** PB18; .N94.
Ind/Abst Annu. Bibliogr. Engl. Lang. Lit.; MLA Int. Bibl. Books Artic. Mod. Lang. Lit.

FI/0356-0376
STUDIER I NORDISK FILOLOGI. [Stud. nord. filol.]. **Added/Corp** Svenska Litteratursallskapet i Finland. Vol. 1 (1910)-. Monographic series. Swedish. Svenska Litteratursallskapet I Finland, Snellmansgaten 9 11, 00170 Helsingfors 17 Finland. **ED** Lars Hulden. **LC** PD1513; .S85. Index available. cum. index. ctrl circ.
Ind/Abst MLA Int. Bibl. Books Artic. Mod. Lang. Lit.

US/0039-3533
STUDIES IN AFRICAN LINGUISTICS. [Stud. Afr. linguist.]. V. 1- Mar. 1970-. Periodical. English (French). Three times a year. $21.65 (one year) institutions Los Angeles County; $21.45 (one year) institutions all other counties in California;$20.00 (one year) institutions other; $12.99 (one year), $23.82 (two year) individuals Los Angeles County in California; $12.87 (one year), $23.60 (two year) individuals all other counties in California; $12.00 (one year), $22.00 (two year) individuals other. UCLA African Studies Center, 405 Hilgard Avenue, 10244 Bunche Hall, Los Angeles CA 90024. **Tel** (310)825-1218. **ED** Russell G Schuh. **LC** PL8000; .S85. **DD** 496. **UDC** 809.6. Index available. **Ad Acc. Pr Rev. Circ:** 350.
Desc: Descriptive and theoretical linguistics using African languages as the primary data source.
Ind/Abst Abstr. Anthropol.; Linguist. Lang. Behav. Abstr. (1970-) [Full Cov.]; MLA Int. Bibl. Books Artic. Mod. Lang. Lit.; Soc. Plann. Policy Dev. Abstr.; Sociol. Abstr.

GW
STUDIES IN DESCRIPTIVE LINGUISTICS. Vol. 1 (1979)-. Periodical. English. ir. Julius Groos Verlag, Postfach 102423 Hertzstrasse 6, D 69104 Heidelberg Germany. **Tel** 011 49 6221 303621, FAX 011 49 6221 301993.
Ind/Abst MLA Int. Bibl. Books Artic. Mod. Lang. Lit.

HU/0134-1790
STUDIES IN ENGLISH AND AMERICAN. [Stud. Engl. Am.]. V. 2-. English. **LC** PE25; .S82. **DD** 420/.5. **UDC** 802.0; 802.0(73). ***Continues*** *Angol es Amerikai Filologiai Tanulmanyok; Studies in English and American Philology.*
Ind/Abst MLA Int. Bibl. Books Artic. Mod. Lang. Lit.

US
STUDIES IN ENGLISH AND AMERICAN LITERATURE, LINGUISTICS, AND CULTURE. **See** Literature.

CH
STUDIES IN ENGLISH LITERATURE & LINGUISTICS. **Main/Corp** Kuo Li Tai-Wan Shih Fan Ta Hsueh. Ying Yu Hsi. **VFOAT** Ying Yu Yen Chiu Chi Kan. **VAT** Studies in English Literature and Linguistics. Began with 1976 issue. English (English). Taiwan Normal University Department of English, Taipei Taiwan. **LC** PE9; .K86A. **DD** 420/.5. **UDC** 802.0; 820. ***Continues***

Concentric.
Ind/Abst Linguist. Lang. Behav. Abstr. (1982-) [Full Cov.]; Soc. Plann. Policy Dev. Abstr.

PL
STUDIES IN HAMITO-SEMITIC. **VFOAT** Studia Hamito-Semitica. 1-. English. 24.00 each issue. Krakow, Ul Smolensk 14, Warszawa Poland. **LC** PG6014; .K732 subser. **UDC** 809.2.

UK
STUDIES IN INTERACTIONAL SOCIOLINGUISTICS. (1982)-. Monographic series. English.
Ind/Abst MLA Int. Bibl. Books Artic. Mod. Lang. Lit.

NE/0378-4177
STUDIES IN LANGUAGE. [Stud. lang.]. **Added/Corp** Foundations of Language (Organization). Vol. 1, No. 1 (1977)-. Periodical. English. sa. $224.00. John Benjamins BV, Amsteldijk 44, PO Box 75577, 1070 AN Amsterdam Netherlands. **Tel** 011 31 20 6738156, FAX 011 31 20 739773. **(Subscription address:** John Benjamins North America, PO Box 27519, Philadelphia PA 19118-0519.**)** **ED** Bernard Comrie, Michael Noonan, and Werner Abraham. **LC** P1.A1; F6. **DD** 410/.5. Documents available from The Genuine Article. ***Continues** Foundations of Language, 0015-900X.*
Desc: Deals with subjects basic to contemporary linguistics and philosophy; focuses on the foundations of language.
Ind/Abst Annu. Bibliogr. Engl. Lang. Lit.; Arts Humanit. Citation Index [Full Cov.]; Curr. Contents Arts Humanit.; Lang. Teach.; Linguist. Lang. Behav. Abstr. (1977-) [Full Cov.]; Math. Rev.; MLA Int. Bibl. Books Artic. Mod. Lang. Lit.; Res. Alert [Full Cov.]; Soc. Plann. Policy Dev. Abstr.; Soc. Sci. Cit. Index [Select. Cov.].

US/0586-6928
STUDIES IN LANGUAGE AND LINGUISTICS. ***Ceased.*** (1969/70)-(19??). English. ir. Texas Western Press, University of Texas at El Paso. **Tel** (915)747-5688. **ED** Dale L Walker and Nancy Hamilton. **LC** P25; .S7. **DD** 410. **UDC** 800.87(72/73). **Circ:** 200.
Desc: Examines attitudes in the United States, Mexico border area.

CH
STUDIES IN LANGUAGE AND LITERATURE. **Added/Corp** Kuo li Tai-wan ta Hsueh. Dept. of Foreign Languages and Literature. No. 1 (Mar. 1985)-. Periodical. English. an. $12.50 (subscription). National Taiwan University - Foreign Languages, Department of Foreign Languages and Literature, Taipei 10764 Taiwan.
Ind/Abst MLA Int. Bibl. Books Artic. Mod. Lang. Lit.

NE/0165-7763
STUDIES IN LANGUAGE COMPANION SERIES : SLCS. [Stud. lang. companion ser.]. **VFOAT** SLCS; S.L.C.S. Vol. 1 (1978)-. Monographic series. English. ir. Price varies per volume. John Benjamins BV, Amsteldijk 44, PO Box 75577, 1070 AN Amsterdam Netherlands. **Tel** 011 31 20 6738156, FAX 011 31 20 739773. **(Subscription address:** John Benjamins North America, PO Box 27519, Philadelphia PA 19118-0519.**)** **ED** Werner Abraham and Michael Noonan. **LC** UNC.
Ind/Abst Math. Rev.; MLA Int. Bibl. Books Artic. Mod. Lang. Lit.

US/0736-9867
STUDIES IN LANGUAGE LEARNING. [Stud. lang. learn.]. Began in 1975. Periodical. English. ir. $13.00 US; $15.00 other. Language Learning Laboratory, University of Illinois at Urbana Champaign, G-70 Foreign Languages Building, 707 South Mathews, Urbana IL 61801. **Tel** (217)333-9776, FAX (217)244-0190. **ED** C C Cheng. **LC** P129; .S84. **DD** 418/.005. **UDC** 800.7. **Bk Rev. Circ:** 300.
Desc: Primarily concerned with applied linguistics, and specifically with language acquisition, language pedagogy, stylistics and language planning.
Ind/Abst Lang. Teach.; Linguist. Lang. Behav. Abstr. (1976-) [Full Cov.]; MLA Int. Bibl. Books Artic. Mod. Lang. Lit.; Soc. Plann. Policy Dev. Abstr.

NE/0378-4177
STUDIES IN LANGUAGE ORIGINS. Vol. 1 (1989)-. Periodical. English. sa. $224.00. John Benjamins BV, Amsteldijk 44, PO Box 75577, 1070 AN Amsterdam Netherlands. **Tel** 011 31 20 6738156, FAX 011 31 20 739773. **(Subscription address:** John Benjamins North America, PO Box 27519, Philadelphia PA 19118-0519.**)** **ED** Bernard Comrie, Michael Noonan and Werner Abraham. **CODEN** SLORES.
Desc: Areas of central concern are: discourse grammar; syntactic, morphological and semantic universals; pragmatics; grammaticalization and grammaticalization theory; and the description of problems in individual languages from a discourse-pragmatic, functional, and typological perspective.
Ind/Abst Anthropol. Lit.

DK/0078-3315
STUDIES IN LINGUISTICS. **Main/Corp** Odense Universitet. **VFOAT** Odense University Studies in Linguistics. Vol. 1 (1968)-. Monographic series. German (English). ir. Price varies per volume. Odense University Press, 55 Campusvej, DK-5230 Odense M Denmark. **Tel** 66 15 79 99, FAX 66 15 81 26.

NE/0924-4662
STUDIES IN LINGUISTICS AND PHILOSOPHY. [Stud. linguist. philos.]. (1989)-. Monographic series. English. ir. Price varies per volume. Kluwer Academic Publishers / Massachusetts, PO Box 358, Accord Station, Hingham MA 02018. **Tel** (617)871-6600.
Ind/Abst Zentralbl. Math. Ihre Grenzgeb.

JA/0913-1507
STUDIES IN MEDIEVAL ENGLISH LANGUAGE AND LITERATURE. [Stud. mediev. Engl. lang. lit.]. (1986)-. Periodical. Multiple languages. an. **DD** 820. ***Continues** Chusei Eibungaku Danwakai Kaiho, 0289-1670.*
Ind/Abst MLA Int. Bibl. Books Artic. Mod. Lang. Lit.

PH/0116-0516
STUDIES IN PHILIPPINE LINGUISTICS. [Stud. Philipp. linguist.]. **Added/Corp** Linguistic Society of the Philippines. Summer Institute of Linguistics. Vol. 1 (Spring 1977)-. Periodical. English. Twice a year. Academic Publications / Philippines, Summer Institute of Linguistics, Box 2270 CPO, 1099 Manila Philippines. **Tel** 011 63 2 780061, telex 17772. **ED** Fe T. Otanes, Hazel Wrigglesworth. **LC** PL5501; .S8. **DD** 499/.21. Index available. cum. index. **Circ:** 200. available on microfiche.
Ind/Abst Anthropol. Lit.; Index Philip. Period. (-199?); MLA Int. Bibl. Books Artic. Mod. Lang. Lit.

US/0039-3738
STUDIES IN PHILOLOGY. [Stud. philol.]. **Added/Corp** University of North Carolina (1793-1962). Philological Club. Vol. 1 (1906)-. Periodical. English. qt (Jan., Apr., July, Oct.). $18.00 (one year), $51.00 (three year), (individual), $24.00 (one year), $69.00 (three year) (institution) US; $24.00 (one year), $69.00 (three year), (individual), $30.00 (one year), $87.00 (three year), (institution) other. University of North Carolina Press, 116 South Boundary Street, PO Box 2288, Chapel Hill NC 27515-2288. **Tel** (919)966-3561, FAX (919)966-3829. **ED** Jerry L. Mills. **LC** P25; .S8. **DD** 405. **[CCC].** cum. index. **Ad Acc. Circ:** 1,700 (ctrl). available on microfilm and microfiche from University Microfilms International (UMI). Documents available from The Genuine Article, UMI Article Clearinghouse.
Desc: Articles on literary subjects before 1900, chiefly English, but including classical, Romance and Germanic literatures.
Ind/Abst Abstr. Engl. Stud.; Acad. Abstr. Full Text Elite (Jan. 1992-); Acad. Abstr. (Jan. 1992-); Acad. Search (Jan. 1992-); Annu. Bibliogr. Engl. Lang. Lit.; Arts Humanit. Citation Index [Full Cov.]; BHA : Biblio. Hist. Art; Curr. Contents Arts Humanit.; Expand. Acad. Index (1989-); Humanit. Index; Humanit. Source (Jan. 1992-); INFO-SOUTH Abstr.; Lit. Crit. Regist.; Mag. Search; MLA Int. Bibl. Books Artic. Mod. Lang. Lit.; Newsp. Period. Abstr. (1991-); Res. Alert [Full Cov.]; Romant. Move.

US/0272-2631
STUDIES IN SECOND LANGUAGE ACQUISITION. (STUDIES IN SECOND LANGUAGE ACQUISITION / INDIANA UNIVERSITY.). [Stud. second lang. acquis.]. **Added/Corp** Indiana University, Bloomington. Indiana University Linguistics Club. Vol. 1 (1977)-. Academic Scholarly Publication. English (French, German and Spanish). qt. $94.00 US, Canada & Mexico; £61.00 other. Cambridge University Press / New York, 40 West 20th Street, New York NY 10011-4211. **Tel** (212)924-3900, (800)221-4512. **(Subscription address:** Cambridge University Press / Outside of North America, Journal Fulfillment Department, The Edinburgh Building, Cambridge CB2 2RU United Kingdom.**)** **ED** Albert Valdman. **LC** P118; .S83. **DD** 401/.9. **[CCC]. Bk Rev. Ad Acc. Circ:** 500 (ctrl). available on microfilm and microfiche from University Microfilms International (UMI).
Desc: Deals with the acquisition of a second language or languages whether by formal learning or assimilation in countries where different cultures live and communicate side by side. Also investigates many implications of such language contact. While preference is given to theoretically oriented papers and reports of empirical research, discussions of pedagogical issues are considered if they refer to major theoretical issues in the field. Each part contains articles, research notes and review articles.
Ind/Abst Curr. Index J. Educ.; Educ. Index; Lang. Teach.; Linguist. Lang. Behav. Abstr. (1985-) [Full Cov.]; MLA Int. Bibl. Books Artic. Mod. Lang. Lit.; Soc. Plann. Policy Dev. Abstr.

NE/0169-0124
STUDIES IN SLAVIC AND GENERAL LINGUISTICS. [Stud. slav. gen. linguist.]. Vol. 1 (1980)-. Periodical. English (German). ir. Humanities Press, 165 1st Avenue, Atlantic Highlands NJ 07716. **Tel** (908)872-1441, (800)221-3845, FAX (908)872-0717, telex 752233. **LC** PG1; .S82. **DD** 491.8/05. Index available.
Desc: Monographs on all aspects of Slavic and general linguistics and on noted linguists in this field.
Ind/Abst MLA Int. Bibl. Books Artic. Mod. Lang. Lit.

US/0049-2388
STUDIES IN THE LINGUISTIC SCIENCES. [Stud. linguist. sci.]. **VFOAT** SLS. Vol. 1 (Spring 1971)-. Periodical. English. Twice a year. $10.00 (per issue). University of Illinois Department of Linguistics, 4088 Foreign Language Building, 707 S. Math, Urbana IL 61801. **Tel** (217)333-3563. **ED** H. H. Hoch and E. G. Bakambra. **LC** P1; .S785. **DD** 410/.5. **UDC** 800. **Bk Rev. Circ:** 225 (ctrl).
Desc: Latest original research articles by the faculty and students of the Department of Linguistics, University of Illinois.
Ind/Abst Lang. Teach.; Linguist. Lang. Behav. Abstr. (1971-) [Full Cov.]; Middle East Abstr. Index; MLA Int. Bibl. Books Artic. Mod. Lang. Lit.; Soc. Plann. Policy Dev. Abstr.

NE
STUDIES IN THE SCIENCES OF LANGUAGE SERIES. **VFOAT** SSLS. (1975)-. Monographic series. English. ir. Price varies per volume. John Benjamins BV, Amsteldijk 44, PO Box 75577, 1070 AN Amsterdam Netherlands. **Tel** 011 31 20 6738156, FAX 011 31 20 739773. **(Subscription address:** John Benjamins North America, PO Box 27519, Philadelphia PA 19118-0519.**)** **ED** D. L. Goyvaerts. ***Continues** Story-Scientia Linguistic Series.*
Ind/Abst MLA Int. Bibl. Books Artic. Mod. Lang. Lit.

RM/0515-1694
STUDII DE GRAMATICA. [Stud. gram.]. **Main/Corp** Institutul de Lingvistica din Bucuresti. Vol. 1 (1956)-. Romanian. **LC** PC631; .A32.
Ind/Abst MLA Int. Bibl. Books Artic. Mod. Lang. Lit.

RM/0039-405X
STUDII SI CERCETARI LINGVISTICE. [Stud. cercet. linguist.]. **Added/Corp** Academia Republicii Populare Romine. Academia Republicii Socialiste Romania. (1950)-. Romanian. bm (6 issues). DM280.00. **(Subscription address:** Kubon & Sagner, ABT Zeitschriftenimport, D 80328 Munich Germany.**)**
Desc: Publishes studies on linguistics with an emphasis on Romanian philology.
Ind/Abst Annu. Bibliogr. Engl. Lang. Lit.; Linguist. Lang. Behav. Abstr. (1972-) [Full Cov.]; MLA Int. Bibl. Books Artic. Mod. Lang. Lit.; Soc. Plann. Policy Dev. Abstr.

AA/0563-5780
STUDIME FILOLOGJIKE. [Stud. filol.]. **Added/Corp** Akademia e Shkencave. Instituti Gjuhesise dhe i Letersise. Universiteti Shteteror i Tiranes. Instituti i Historise dhe i Gjuhesise. Vol. 18, No. 1 (1964)-. Periodical. Albanian (English; summaries and/or abstracts in French). qt (4 issues). $10.91. Book Distribution Enterprise, Rruga Kavajes, Tirana, Albania. **Tel** 011 355 42 27246. **LC** PG9501; .S78. ***Continues in part** Universiteti Shteteror i Tiranes. Buletin. Seria Shkencat Shoqerore.*
Desc: Albanian philology.
Ind/Abst Am. Hist. Life (1970-); MLA Int. Bibl. Books Artic. Mod. Lang. Lit.

●FI/0788-5695
STUDY IN FINLAND: ENGLISH LANGUAGE PROGRAMMES AND STUDIES IN FINNISH UNIVERSITIES / MINISTRY OF EDUCATION. **Added/Corp** Finland. Opetusministerio. (1991/1992)-. English. **LC** WMLC 91/1558.

GW/0179-2482
STUTTGARTER ARBEITEN ZUR GERMANISTIK. **See** Literature.

US/0039-4238
STYLE (FAYETTEVILLE). **See** Literature.

GW/0138-4694
SUDASIATISCHE SPRACHWISSENSCHAFTLICHE STUDIEN / AKADEMIE DER WISSENSCHAFTEN DER DDR, ZENTRALINSTITUT FUR SPRACHWISSENSCHAFT. Vol. 1 (1981)-. German. Zentralinstitut fur Sprachwissenschaft, Otto-Muschke-Str 22/23, 108 Berlin Germany.

GW/0170-5946
SUGIA, SPRACHE UND GESCHICHTE IN AFRIKA. **VFOAT** Sprache und Geschichte in Afrika. Vol. 1- 1979-. German (English and French). an. varies. Helmut Buske Verlag Hamburg, Postfach 760244, D 2000 Hamburg 76 F R Germany. **Tel** 011 49 40 5236739. **ED** Bernd Heine, Wilhelm J G Mohlig, Franz Rottland, Rainer Voben, Jurgen Winter. **LC** PL8000; .S92. **DD** 409/.6. **UDC** 809.6; 960. **Circ:** 400.
Desc: Language and linguistics and history of Africa.
Ind/Abst Anthropol. Lit.

SA
SUID-AFRIKAANSE TYDSKRIF VIR AFRIKATALE. **Added/Corp** African Language Association of Southern Africa. **VFOAT** African Languages; South African Journal of African Languages.

(1981)-. Periodical. Afrikaans (English). qt. R87.00 South Africa; R90.00 other. Foundation for Education Science & Technology, PO Box 1758, Pretoria 0001 South Africa. **Tel** 011 27 12 3226404, FAX 011 27 12 3207803. **LC** PL8021.S6; S85. ***Absorbed*** *Studies in Bantoetale Limi (Pretoria, South Africa : 1973);* ***Continues*** *Limi (Pretoria, South Africa : 1973).*
Ind/Abst MLA Int. Bibl. Books Artic. Mod. Lang. Lit.; Spec. Educ. Needs Abstr.

SA
SUID-AFRIKAANSE TYDSKRIF VIR AFRIKATALE. BYBLAD. **See** Literature.

US/0197-5129
SUMMARY OF INVESTIGATIONS RELATING TO READING. [Summ. invest. relat. read.]. **Main/Corp** International Reading Association. **Added/Corp** International Reading Association. Annual Summary of Investigations Relating to Reading. **VFOAT** Annual Summary of Investigations Relating to Reading. (1979)-. English. an. $15.00 (members); $23.00 (non-members). International Reading Association, 800 Barksdale Road, PO Box 8139, Newark DE 19714-8139. **Tel** (302)731-1600, FAX (302)731-1057, telex 5106002813 READING. **ED** Sam Weintraub. **LC** LB1050; .I4883b. **DD** 428.4/05. ***Supersedes in part*** *Reading Research Quarterly, 0034-0553.*
Desc: Summarizes research published in periodicals, books, conference proceedings, and other publications related to the field of reading.

US/1040-0850
SUMMER INSTITUTE OF LINGUISTICS AND THE UNIVERSITY OF TEXAS AT ARLINGTON PUBLICATIONS IN LINGUISTICS. **Added/Corp** Summer Institute of Linguistics. University of Texas at Arlington. **VFOAT** Publications in Linguistics. No. 84 (1988)-. Monographic series. English. Price varies per volume. Summer Institute of Linguistic, 7500 West Camp Wisdom Road, Dallas TX 75236. **Tel** (214)709-2404, FAX (214)709-2433, telex 9108614123. ***Continues*** *Summer Institute of Linguistics Publications in Linguistics.*
Ind/Abst MLA Int. Bibl. Books Artic. Mod. Lang. Lit.

FI
SUOMALAIS-UGRILAISEN SEURAN TOIMITUKSIA / MEMOIRES DE LA SOCIETE FINNO-OUGRIENNE. **Added/Corp** Suomalais-Ugrilainen Seura. **VFOAT** Memoires de la Societe Finno-Ougrienne; SUST; MSFOu. (1890)-. Monographic series. Finnish (English, French and German). ir. Price varies per volume. Academic Bookstore Akateeminen, Postilokero 23, FIN-00371 Helsinki Finland. **Tel** 011 358 0 12141. **(Subscription address:** Bookstore Tiedekirja, Kirkkokatu 14, SF 00170 Helsinki Finland.**)** **LC** PH1; .S6.
Ind/Abst MLA Int. Bibl. Books Artic. Mod. Lang. Lit.

BU/0204-8701
SUPOSTAVITELNO EZIKOZNANIE. [Spostav. ezikozn.]. **Added/Corp** Sofiiski Universitet "Kliment Okhridski". Vol. 3 (1978)-. Academic Scholarly Publication. Bulgarian (Russian, English, German, French and Spanish). bm. 90.00lv Bulgaria; $24.00 US. Tsar Osvoboditel, 15 Boulevard Ruski, Kliment Ohridski University of Sofia, 1040 Sofia Bulgaria. **Tel** 85 81 ext. 304, 44-30-49. **ED** Zivko Bojadziev. **LC** PG831; .B58. **DD** 491.8/1505. Index available (No. 6 of each year). **Bk Rev**, (Qty: 30-60). **Circ:** 600. ***Continues*** *Biuletin za Supostavitelno Izsledvane na Bulgarskiia Ezik s Drugi Ezitsi.*
Desc: Publishes articles, review articles and news items in the fields of contrastive linguistics, general linguistics, the theory and practice of translation and history of linguistics.
Ind/Abst Linguist. Lang. Behav. Abstr. (1978-) [Full Cov.]; Soc. Plann. Policy Dev. Abstr.

UK
SUPPLEMENTARY VOLUME (CAMBRIDGE PHILOLOGICAL SOCIETY). (SUPPLEMENTARY VOLUME - CAMBRIDGE PHILOLOGICAL SOCIETY.). **Added/Corp** Cambridge Philological Society. No. 4 (1977)-. Monographic series. English. ir. Price varies per volume. Colin Austin Cambridge, Trinity Hall, Cambridge CB2 1TJ England. ***Continues*** *Proceedings of the Cambridge Philological Society. Supplement.*

NE/0920-8399
SUPPLEMENTUM EPIGRAPHICUM GRAECUM. **See** Classical Studies.

US/0738-1417
SUPPORT FOR THE LEARNING AND TEACHING OF ENGLISH. (SUPPORT FOR THE LEARNING AND TEACHING OF ENGLISH : SLATE.). [Support learn. teach. Engl.]. **Added/Corp** National Council of Teachers of English. **VFOAT** SLATE; S.L.A.T.E. (19??)-. Newsletter. English. Three times a year. $15.00. National Council of Teachers of English, 1111 Kenyon Road, Urbana IL 61801. **Tel** (217)328-3870, FAX (217)328-9645. ***Continues*** *SLATE Newsletter.*

IT
SURE : TOP LEVEL ENGLISH. (19??)-. Italian. mo. L17,800 Italy; L22,800, $18.95 other. European Language Institute, Casella Postale 6, 62019 Recanati Italy. **Tel** 011 39 71 976465. **(Subscription address:** Midwest European Publishing, 8220 Christiana Ave., Skokie IL 60076.**)**

CI/0350-221X
SUVREMENA METODIKA NASTAVE HRVATSKOGA JEZIKA. (1991)-. Periodical. Serbo-Croatian (Roman). qt. Skolska Knjiga, PO Box 1039, Masarykova 28, 41001 Zagreb Croatia. **Tel** 011 41 4207842 513 155, telex 21894 YU SKK ZG. **LC** PG1219; .S96. ***Continues*** *Suvremena Metodika Nastave Hrvatskog III Srpskog Jezika.*

DK/0106-5378
SVANTEVIT. [Svantevit]. **Added/Corp** Dansk Slavistforbund. (1975)-. Periodical. Danish (English, German and Russian). sa. **LC** PG2001; .A28. **DD** 491.7/05.
Ind/Abst MLA Int. Bibl. Books Artic. Mod. Lang. Lit.

SW/0347-1837
SVENSKA LANDSMAL OCH SVENSKT FOLKLIV. [Sven. landsmal sven. folkliv]. **Added/Corp** Dialekt- och Folkminnesarkivet i Uppsala. Landsmals- och Folkminnesarkivet i Uppsala. **VFOAT** Archives des Traditions Populaires Suedoises. (193?)-. Periodical. Swedish (summaries and/or abstracts in English). an. **LC** PD5004; .S9. ***Continues*** *Svenska Landsmal ock Svenskt Folkliv.*
Ind/Abst MLA Int. Bibl. Books Artic. Mod. Lang. Lit.

YU
SVESKE ZADUZBINE IVE ANDRICA. **Added/Corp** Zaduzbina Ive Andrica u Beogradu. Vol. 1, No. 1 (1982)-. Periodical. German (Serbo-Croatian (Cyrillic)). Zaduzbina Ive Andrica, Brankova 23, 11000 Belgrad Yugoslavia. **LC** PG1418.A6; Z883.

NO/0039-7679
SYMBOLAE OSLOENSES. (SYMBOLAE OSLOENSES / AUSPICIIS SOCIETATIS GRAECO-LATINAE.). [Symb. Oslo.]. **Added/Corp** Societas Graeco-Latina (Oslo, Norway). Issue 3 (1925)-. English (German, Italian, Latin and French). an. Kr290.00, $52.00. Scandinavian University Press, PO Box 2959 Toeyen, N 0608 Oslo 6 Norway. **Tel** 011 47 2 2575400, FAX 011 47 2 2575353, telex 71896 UROR N. **(Subscription address:** Scandinavian University Press, 200 Meacham Ave., Elmont NY 11003.**)** **ED** Egil A. Kraggerud. **LC** PA19; .S8. ***Continues*** *Symbolae Arctoae.*
Desc: Series in classical studies, covering all branches of classical research and including contributions from scholars from all over the world.
Ind/Abst MLA Int. Bibl. Books Artic. Mod. Lang. Lit.

US/0039-7709
SYMPOSIUM (SYRACUSE). (SYMPOSIUM.). [Symposium]. **Added/Corp** Syracuse University. Dept. of Romance Languages. Syracuse University. Centro de Estudios Hispanicos. Vol. 1 (Nov. 1946)-. Periodical. English. qt. $68.00 (institution), $34.00 (individual). Heldref Publications, 1319 Eighteenth Street Northwest, Washington DC 20036-1802. **Tel** (202)296-6267, (800)365-9753, FAX (202)296-5149. **ED** Paul J. Archambault. **LC** PB1; .S9. **DD** 405. **CODEN** SYMPEZ. **[CCC]**. **Bk Rev**. **Ad Acc**. **Circ:** 700. available on microfilm and microfiche from University Microfilms International (UMI). Documents available from The Genuine Article, UMI Article Clearinghouse.
Desc: A journal in modern foreign literatures, includes research on authors, themes, periods, genres, works, and theory, frequently through comparative studies. Works are cited, and often discussed, in the original language.
Ind/Abst Acad. Search (Jan. 1994-); Arts Humanit. Citation Index [Full Cov.]; Humanit. Index; Humanit. Source (Jul. 1993-); INFO-SOUTH Abstr.; Mag. Search; MLA Int. Bibl. Books Artic. Mod. Lang. Lit.; Newsp. Period. Abstr. (1990-); Res. Alert [Full Cov.]; Romant. Move.; Soc. Plann. Policy Dev. Abstr.

US/0092-4563
SYNTAX AND SEMANTICS. [Syntax semant.]. Vol. 1 (1972)-. Monographic series. English. ir. Price varies per volume. Academic Press, Inc., 6277 Sea Harbor Drive, Orlando FL 32887. **Tel** (800)543-9534, (407)345-4100, FAX (407)363-9661. **ED** John P. Kimball. **LC** P1; .S9. **DD** 410/.5. **[CCC]**. Documents available from The Genuine Article.
Ind/Abst Arts Humanit. Citation Index [Full Cov.]; MLA Int. Bibl. Books Artic. Mod. Lang. Lit.; Res. Alert [Full Cov.]; Soc. Sci. Cit. Index [Full Cov.].

UK/0346-251X
SYSTEM (LINKOPING). (SYSTEM.). [System]. **Added/Corp** Pergamon Institute of English (Oxford) Universitetet i Linkoping. Institutionen for Sprak Och Litteratur. Vol. 1 (1973)-. Periodical. English. Four times a year. $202.00 The Americas; £135.00 other. Pergamon Press, An Imprint of Elsevier Science Ltd., The Boulevard, Langford Lane, Kidlington, Oxford OX5 1GB United Kingdom. **Tel** 011 44 865 843000, 011 44 865 843699, FAX 011 44 865 843010. **(Subscription address:** Elsevier Science Ltd. Oxford Fulfillment Centre, PO Box 800, Kidlington, Oxford OX5 1DX United Kingdom.**)** **ED** Norman Davies. **LC** P51; .S95. **DD** 418/.007. **[CCC]**. **Bk Rev**. **Ad Acc**. available on microfilm and microfiche from University Microfilms International (UMI).
Ind/Abst Br. Educ. Index; Contents Pages Educ.; Curr. Contents Soc. Behav. Sci.; Curr. Index J. Educ.; Educ. Technol. Abstr.; Lang. Teach.; Soc. Plann. Policy Dev. Abstr.; Sociol. Abstr.; Tech. Educ. Train. Abstr.

CN/0706-9987
T A Q JOURNAL, A. **Main/Corp** Association des Traducteurs Anglophones du Quebec. **VAT** Association des Traducteurs Anglophones du Quebec Journal. V. 1-June 1978-. Periodical. English. bm. Free. Association Des Traducteurs Anglophones Du Quebec, Room 602, Victoria Square, Montreal Quebec H2Y 2J3. **DD** 448/.02. **UDC** 800.73. ctrl circ.

BE/0039-8691
TAAL EN TONGVAL. [Taal tongval]. Vol. 1 (Jan. 1949)-. Periodical. Dutch (English). sa. 500.00F. Taal en Tongval, Visitatiestraat 187, B 9110 Gent Belgium. **ED** J.B. Berns, A. Weijnen and V.F. Vanacker. **LC** PF701; .T2. **DD** 439.3/17/05. **Bk Rev**. **Circ:** 360 (ctrl). available on microfilm.
Desc: Studies on dialects, Netherlands and northern part of Belgium.
Ind/Abst MLA Int. Bibl. Books Artic. Mod. Lang. Lit.

BE
TAAL EN TONGVAL. THEMANUMMER. **VFOAT** Themanummer. Vol. 1 (1987)-. Monographic series. Dutch. ir. Price varies per volume. Taal en Tongval, Visitatiestraat 187, B 9110 Gent Belgium.

●FR
TAL TRAITMENT AUTOMATIQUE DES LANGUES. (19??)-. French. Twice a year. 330.00F. Editions Klincksieck, 8 rue de la Sorbonne, 75005 Paris France. **Tel** 11 33 1 43545953, FAX 11 33 1 432252553. ***Continues*** *TA Informations.*

NE/0922-1166
TALEN GRONINGEN. (DE TALEN). (1988)-. Periodical. Dutch (English, German, French and Spanish). Ten times a year. Fl95.00. Wolters Noordhoff BV, Postbus 567, 9700 AN Groningen Netherlands. **Tel** 011 31 50 226886, FAX 011 31 50 264866. **UDC** 803.0. **CODEN** 804.0. **Bk Rev**. **Ad Acc**.

CC
TAO HUA YUAN. **VFOAT** Taohuayuan. Periodical. Chinese. bm. RMBY0.32. Chung-Kuo Chu Pan Tui Wai Mao I Tsung Kung SSU, PO Box 614, Beijing, People's Republic of China. **LC** PL2303; .T37. **DD** 895.1/09/005. **UDC** 895.1.

IS
TARBIZ; RIVON LE-MADE HA-YAHADUT. **See** Religion and Theology-Judaism.

NE/0924-1884
TARGET. Vol. 1 (1989)-. Periodical. English (French and German; summaries and/or abstracts in English and French). sa (2 issues). $118.00 North America. John Benjamins BV, Amsteldijk 44, PO Box 75577, 1070 AN Amsterdam Netherlands. **Tel** 011 31 20 6738156, FAX 011 31 20 739773. **(Subscription address:** John Benjamins North America, PO Box 27519, Philadelphia PA 19118-0519.**)** **ED** Gideon Toury and Jose Lambert. **LC** P306.A1; T37; P306.A1; T37. **DD** 418/.02/05. **CODEN** TARGEC. Index available. **Bk Rev**.
Desc: Focuses on the interrelationships between the position and role of translations in culture, the norms governing them, and the modes of the translation process under various cultural circumstances. Publishes original studies of theoretical, methodological and descriptive nature into translation problems. Various reports on current publications and research activities.
Ind/Abst MLA Int. Bibl. Books Artic. Mod. Lang. Lit.

NZ/0494-8440
TE REO. [Te Reo]. **Added/Corp** Linguistic Society of New Zealand. Vol. 1 (1958)-. English (French). an. Comes with Linguistic Society of New Zealand membership. Linguistic Society of New Zealand, University of Auckland, Auckland New Zealand. **Tel** 011 64 9 737999, FAX 011 64 9 733429. **ED** R. Harlow. Index available. cum. index. **Bk Rev**. **Ad Acc**. **Pr Rev**. **Circ:** 350.
Desc: Scientific description and study of the evolution and structure of languages. With special attention to indigenous and European languages in the Pacific.
Ind/Abst Annu. Bibliogr. Engl. Lang. Lit.; Int. Bibliogr. Sociol.; Lang. Teach.; MLA Int. Bibl. Books Artic. Mod. Lang. Lit.

AT/1033-0801
TEA NEWS SYDNEY. ***Title Change.*** [TEA news Syd.]. (1982)-(1989). Periodical. English. Twice a year. Elicos Association Ltd., 3 Union Street, Pyrmont NSW 2009 Australia. **Tel** 011 61 02 6606459, FAX 011 61 02 5523384. **DD** 428.3407. ***Continued by*** *E A Journal.*

US/0098-6291
TEACHING ENGLISH IN THE TWO-YEAR COLLEGE. **See** Education-Higher Education.

US
TEACHING OF ENGLISH. **Main/Corp** Florida. State University, Tallahassee. School of Education. No. 1 (1956)-. English. Florida State University / Education, School of Education, Tallahassee FL 32203. **LC** LB1631; .F63. **DD** 808.

US
TEAM. (19??)-. Periodical. English. ir. £13.99. Mary Glasgow Publications, Brookhampton Lane, Kineton, Warwickshire CV35 0JB England. **Tel** 011 44 926 640606, FAX 011 44 926 641016.

IE/0332-205X
TEANGA - IRISH ASSOCIATION FOR APPLIED LINGUISTICS. (TEANGA.). [Teanga - Ir. Assoc. Appl. Linguist.]. **VFOAT** Teanga. (1979)-. Periodical. English. ir. **DD** 410 491.62.
Ind/Abst MLA Int. Bibl. Books Artic. Mod. Lang. Lit.

US/0887-5324
TECH WRITING TIPS. ***Suspended.*** [Tech writ. tips]. (1986)-Suspended. Periodical. English. mo. $100.00. J S Hanna House, 183 Gifford Way, Sacramento CA 95864. **Tel** (916)486-1670. **DD** 808. **UDC** 800.852.

US/0740-8021
TENNESSEE LINGUISTICS. [Tenn. linguist.]. **Added/Corp** Tennessee Conference on Linguistics. Vol. 1, No. 1 (Winter 1981)-. Periodical. English. Twice a year. $8.00. Tennessee Conference on Linguistics / Department of English, Tennessee Technological University, PO Box 5053, Cooksville TN 38505. **Tel** (615)372-3343. **LC** P1; .T44. **DD** 410/.5. **Bk Rev. Circ:** 65. ***Continues*** *Bulletin (Tennessee Conference on Linguistics).*
Desc: Articles and linguistics by and of interest to linguists and language teachers in Tennessee and the Southeast.

US/0735-0783
TENNESSEE PHILOLOGICAL BULLETIN. [Tenn. philol. bull.]. **Added/Corp** Tennessee Philological Association. Vol. 1, No. 1 (Apr. 1964)-. Bulletin. English. an (Oct.). $7.00. University of Tennessee at Chattanooga, English Department, Chattanooga TN 37403. **Tel** (615)755-4623. **LC** PB1; .T46. **DD** 410/.5.
Ind/Abst Annu. Bibliogr. Engl. Lang. Lit.; MLA Int. Bibl. Books Artic. Mod. Lang. Lit.

CN/0225-3194
TERMINOGRAMME. (TERMINOGRAMME : BULLETIN DE LA DIRECTION DE LA TERMINOLOGIE.). **Added/Corp** Quebec (Province). Office de la Langue Francaise. Direction de la Terminologie. No. 1 (Jan. 1980)-. Periodical. French. bm. 37.00Can$ (one year), 64.00Can$ (two year). Les Publications du Quebec, CP 1190, Outremont Quebec H2V 4S7 Canada. **Tel** (514)948-1222, (800)463-2100, FAX (514)278-3030. **DD** 440/.9714.

CN/0225-1981
TERMINOLOGIE. [Terminologie]. V. 9- (41E-); April 1979-. Periodical. French. Universite Laval, Quebec G1K 7P4 Canada. **DD** 448/.1/05. **UDC** 804.0-3. ***Continues*** *Universite Laval. Comite de Terminologie. Bulletin, 0225-1973.*

LU/0256-7873
TERMINOLOGIE ET TRADUCTION / COMMISSION DES COMMUNAUTES EUROPEENES, DIRECTION TRADUCTION, SERVICE TERMINOLOGIE ET APPLICATIONS INFORMATIQUES. **Added/Corp** Commission of the European Communities. Service Terminologie et Applications Informatiques. No. 1- (1985)-. Periodical. French (English and German). Staatsuitgeverij, Christoffel Plantijnstraat 1, 2515 TZ'S Gravenhage Netherlands. **Tel** 070/78-95-70. **LC** P306.A1; T45. **DD** 418/.02/05. ***Formed by the union of*** *Bulletin de la Traduction* ***and*** *Bulletin de Terminologie (Luxembourg, Luxembourg).*
Ind/Abst Int. Labour Doc.

AU/0251-5253
TERMNET NEWS : JOURNAL OF THE INTERNATIONAL NETWORK FOR TERMINOLOGY (TERMNET). **Added/Corp** International Network for Terminology. Infoterm. (1980)-. Periodical. English (French). Four times a year. S900.00 (Europe); S950.00 (other). Termnet Secretariat, Gruengasse9 17, A 1050 Vienna Austria. **Tel** 11 43 222567763. **ED** Magdalena Krommer-Benz, MA and Regina Thaller. **LC** P305; .T45. **DD** 418/.02/05. **Bk Rev. Ad Acc. Circ:** 1,200 (ctrl).
Desc: Contains information on recent developments concerning TermNet members in various countries and information on institutions/organizations, etc. Some TNN are special issues devoted to a specific country or region.
Ind/Abst AESIS Q.

CN/0826-435X
TESL CANADA JOURNAL. [TESL Can. j.]. **Added/Corp** McGill University. Faculty of Education. **VFOAT** Revue TESL du Canada; T.E.S.L. Canada Journal; Revue T.E.S.L. du Canada. **VAT** Teaching English as a Second Language Canada Journal; Revue Teaching English as a Second Language du Canada. Vol. 1, No. 1 (Jan. 1984)-. Periodical. English (summaries and/or abstracts in French). sa. $28.00 individual; $40.00 institutional; $125.00 commercial. Tesl Canada, PO Box 707 Station C, Toronto Ontario M6J 3S1 Canada. **Tel** (305)534-7939. **LC** PE1128.A2; T453. **DD** 420/.7. **CODEN** TCJOEA. **Bk Rev. Ad Acc. Circ:** 3,500.
Ind/Abst Curr. Index J. Educ.; Soc. Plann. Policy Dev. Abstr.

US/1051-8886
TESOL MATTERS. **See** Education-Teaching and Curriculum.

US/0730-9325
TESOL MEMBERSHIP DIRECTORY. **Main/Corp** Teachers of English to Speakers of Other Languages. **Added/Corp** Teachers of English to Speakers of Other Languages. Membership Directory. (1972)-. English. be. $39.50 (members TESOL), $158.00 (nonmembers). TESOL, 1600 Cameron Street/Suite 300, Alexandria VA 22314-2751. **Tel** (703)836-0774, FAX (703)836-7864. **ED** Juana Hopkins. **LC** PE1128.A2; T38a. **DD** 428.2/4/025. **Ad Acc.**
Desc: A comprehensive listing of who's who in TESOL, with alphabetical and geographic listings of more than 11,000 individual, institutional and commercial members.

AT/0810-6649
TESOL NEWS. **See** Education-Teaching and Curriculum.

US/0039-8322
TESOL QUARTERLY. (TESOL QUARTERLY / TEACHERS OF ENGLISH TO SPEAKERS OF OTHER LANGUAGES.). [TESOL q.]. **Added/Corp** Teachers of English to Speakers of Other Languages. **VAT** Teachers of English to Speakers of other Languages Quarterly. Vol. 1, No. 1 (March 1967)-. Periodical. English. Four times a year. $130.00 (surface mail); $83.00 (individuals); $142.00 (institutions) Comes with Tesol membership. Teachers of English to Speakers of other Languages, 1600 Cameron Street, Suite 300, Alexandria VA 22314. **Tel** (703)836-0774. **ED** Sandra Silberstein. **LC** PE1128.A2; T454. **DD** 428/.007. Index available. cum. index. **Bk Rev. Ad Acc. Pr Rev. Circ:** 11,500 (ctrl). available on microfilm and microfiche from University Microfilms International (UMI). Documents available from The Genuine Article.
Desc: A professional, refereed journal representing a variety of cross-disciplinary interests, both theoretical and practical. Subjects featured include testing and evaluation, professional preparation, bilingual education, and psychology and sociology of language learning and teaching.
Ind/Abst Acad. Search (July 1993-); Chicano Index; Contents Pages Educ.; Curr. Contents Soc. Behav. Sci.; Curr. Index J. Educ.; Educ. Index; INFO-SOUTH Abstr.; Lang. Teach.; Mag. Search; Middle East Abstr. Index; MLA Int. Bibl. Books Artic. Mod. Lang. Lit.; Multicult. Educ. Abstr.; Res. Alert [Full Cov.]; Res. High. Educ. Abstr.; School Organ. Manage. Abstr.; Soc. Plann. Policy Dev. Abstr.; Soc. Sci. Cit. Index [Full Cov.]; Sociol. Abstr.; Sociol. Educ. Abstr.; Spec. Educ. Needs Abstr.

IT
TESTI E DOCUMENTI DE LETTERATURA E DI LINGUA. **See** Literature.

GR
TEUCHE TOU E.L.I.A. : PERIODIKE EKOSE TES HETAIREIAS HELLENIKOU LOGOTECHNIKOU KAI HISTORIKOU ARCHEIOU. **VFOAT** Teuche Tou ELIA. **VAT** Teuche Tou Hetaireias Hellenikou Logotechnikou kai Historikou Archeiou. Greek, Modern. **LC** PA1005; .T48.

US/0741-2576
TEXAS LINGUISTIC FORUM. **Added/Corp** University of Texas at Austin. Dept. of Linguistics. (1975)-. Monographic series. English. ir. Price varies per volume. Texas Linguistics Forum, University of Texas, Department of Linguistics, Calhoun Hall 501, Austin TX 78712-1196. **Tel** (512)471-1701. **LC** P1; .T47. **DD** 410/.5. Index available. **Circ:** 200 (ctrl).
Desc: A collection of working papers in linguistics.

US/0040-4691
TEXAS STUDIES IN LITERATURE AND LANGUAGE. **See** Literature.

DK/0105-7014
TEXT & KONTEXT. (TEXT & [I.E., UND] KONTEXT.). [Text & Kontext]. **VFOAT** Text und Kontext. (1973)-. Periodical. German. sa. $40.00. Redaktion / Denmark, Kobenhavns Universitet, Institut for Germansk Filologi, Njalsgade 80, DK-2300 Kopenhagen S Denmark. **Tel** 31 54 22 11, FAX 31 54 63 65. **ED** Klaus Bohnen and Bjorn Ekmann. **LC** PD3; .T49.
Ind/Abst MLA Int. Bibl. Books Artic. Mod. Lang. Lit.; Soc. Plann. Policy Dev. Abstr.

NE/0165-4888
TEXT (THE HAGUE). (TEXT.). [Text]. Vol. 1 (1981)-. Periodical. English. qt. $215.85. Walter de Gruyter Inc., PO Box 303421, D 10728 Berlin Germany. **Tel** 011 49 30 260050, FAX 011 49 30 26005251. **LC** P302; .T36. **DD** 001.51. **[CCC].**
Desc: Interdisciplinary journal for the study of discourse.
Ind/Abst Int. Bibliogr. Sociol.; Linguist. Lang. Behav. Abstr. (1981-) [Full Cov.]; Soc. Plann. Policy Dev. Abstr.

US/0278-6400
TEXTBOOK SERIES / AMERICAN PHILOLOGICAL ASSOCIATION. [Textb. ser. - Am. Philol. Assoc.]. **Added/Corp** American Philological Association. (198?)-. Monographic series. English. ir. Price varies per volume. Scholars Press / Georgia, PO Box 15399, Atlanta GA 30333-0399. **Tel** (404)636-4757, (404)727-2320, FAX (404)727-2348.
Desc: Texts with commentary of Latin and Greek authors designed for classroom use.

GW/0179-6844
TEXTCONTEXT. **VFOAT** Text Context. (1986)-. Periodical. German (English and French). Four times a year. DM88.00. Julius Groos Verlag, Postfach 102423 Hertzstrasse 6, D 69104 Heidelberg Germany. **Tel** 011 49 6221 303621, FAX 011 49 6221 301993. **LC** WMLC 93/1771. **CODEN** TCNTEB.
Ind/Abst Soc. Plann. Policy Dev. Abstr.

FR/0248-4579
TEXTES ET LANGAGES. **See** Literature.

FR/0079-001X
TEXTES PUBLIES PAR L'INSTITUT D'ETUDES SLAVES. **Main/Corp** Institut d'Etudes Slaves. 1-. Monographic series. French. ir. Price varies per volume. Institut d'Etudes Slaves, 9 rue Michelet, 75006 Paris France. **Tel** 011 33 1 43265089. **LC** PG13; .T4. **UDC** 808-8. **Circ:** 300.
Desc: Old Slavic and old Russian texts.

GW/0301-4428
THEORETICAL LINGUISTICS. [Theor. linguist.]. Vol. 1 (1974)-. Periodical. English. Twice a year. $137.80. Walter de Gruyter Inc., PO Box 303421, D 10728 Berlin Germany. **Tel** 011 49 30 260050, FAX 011 49 30 26005251. **ED** Helmut Schnelle. **LC** P1; .T5. **DD** 410/.5. **[CCC]. Bk Rev. Ad Acc.** Documents available from The Genuine Article.
Desc: Publishes natural and constructed languages. Linguistic methodology is included as well as the theory of meaning, syntax, phonology and phonetics.
Ind/Abst Arts Humanit. Citation Index [Full Cov.]; Curr. Contents Arts Humanit.; Lang. Teach.; Linguist. Lang. Behav. Abstr. (1974-) [Full Cov.]; Math. Rev.; Middle East Abstr. Index; Res. Alert [Full Cov.]; Soc. Plann. Policy Dev. Abstr.; Zentralbl. Math. Ihre Grenzgeb.

US/1051-6670
THEORETICAL STUDIES IN SECOND LANGUAGE ACQUISITION. [Theor. stud. second lang. acquis.]. Vol. 1 (1991)-. Monographic series. English. Price varies per volume. Peter Lang Publishing, 62 West 45th Street, 4th Floor, New York NY 10036. **Tel** (212)764-1471, (800)770-5264, telex 6973364 PLNY. **DD** 401.

CK/0040-604X
THESAURUS - INSTITUTO CARO Y CUERVO. (THESAURUS.). [Thesaurus - Inst. Caro Cuervo]. **Added/Corp** Instituto Caro y Cuervo. Vol. 7 (1951)-. Periodical. Spanish. tq (3 issues). $40.00. Instituto Caro y Cuervo, Apartado 51502, Bogota Colombia. **Tel** 011 57 1 2557753, FAX 011 57 1 2170243. Index available (published in Dec.). cum. index. **Bk Rev,** (Qty: 10). **Ad Acc, Adv Mgr:** Ignacio Chaves Cevas. **Circ:** 3,000 (ctrl). available on microfilm from University Microfilms International (UMI). ***Continues*** *Boletin del Instituto Caro y Cuervo.*
Desc: Essays on Spanish philology, linguistics, and literature.
Ind/Abst Am. Hist. Life (1967-1978); HAPI Hisp. Am. Period. Index; Lang. Teach.; MLA Int. Bibl. Books Artic. Mod. Lang. Lit.; Soc. Plann. Policy Dev. Abstr.; Sociol. Abstr.

NE/0040-7550
TIJDSCHRIFT VOOR NEDERLANDSE TAAL-EN LETTERKUNDE. [Tijdschr. Ned. taal-letterkd.]. **Added/Corp** Maatschappij der Nederlandse Letterkunde te Leiden. (1948)-. Periodical. Dutch. qt. Fl145.00. Stichting Dimensie, Leliestraat 37 A, 2313 BE Leiden Netherlands. **Tel** 011 31 71 146703. **ED** G.C. Zieleman. **LC** PF4; .T5. **[CCC]. Circ:** 392. Documents available from The Genuine Article. ***Continues*** *Tijdschrift voor Nederlandsche Taaleen Letterkunde.*
Desc: Publishes papers on Dutch linguistics, history of literature and theory of literature and gives reviews of important publications in these fields from the Netherlands and from abroad. Focus is on the historical aspects within these fields.
Ind/Abst Arts Humanit. Citation Index [Full Cov.]; Curr. Contents Arts Humanit.; MLA Int. Bibl. Books Artic. Mod. Lang. Lit.; Res. Alert [Full Cov.].

NE/0168-2148
TIJDSCHRIFT VOOR SKANDINAVISTIEK. [Tijdschr. skand.]. **Added/Corp** Rijksuniversiteit te Groningen.

Scandinavisch Instituut. Vol. 1 No. 1 (1980)-. Periodical. Dutch (Danish, Norwegian and Swedish). sa.
Ind/Abst MLA Int. Bibl. Books Artic. Mod. Lang. Lit.

US/0739-7003
TINTA (SANTA BARBARA, CALIF.). See Literature.

AJ
TIURKOLOGIIA. Added/Corp Azarbaijan Elmlar Akademiiasy. (199?)-. Periodical. Russian. bm. **LC** PL21; .A45. ***Continues*** *Sovetskaia Tiurkologiia, 0131-677X.*

KO
TOGIL MUNHAK. VFOAT Koreanische Zeitschrift fur Germanistik. Periodical. Korean (German). Hanguk Togo Tongmun Hakhoe, c/o German Department, Seoul National University, Seoul Korea. **LC** PT9; .T63. **DD** 830/.9. **UDC** 803.0.

JA/0385-406X
TOHOKU GAKUIN DAIGAKU RONSHU. EIGO, EIBUNGAKU. See Literature.

JA/0389-3081
TOKAI DAIGAKU KIYO. GAIKOKUGO KYOIKU SENTA. VFOAT Bulletin of the Foreign Language Center, Tokai University; Gaikokugo Kyoiku Senta Kiyo. Periodical. English (Japanese). Tokai University Press, Tokai Building 9F, 3-27-4 Shinjuku, Shinjukuku Tokyo 160 Japan. **Tel** 03 3561541, FAX 03 3411833. **LC** PB5; .T64. **UDC** 800.83.

KO
TONAM HAKPO. Series 1- ; 1978-. Periodical. Korean. Not for sale. Tonham Hakhoe, 318-4 Tongson-dong 4-ka, Songbuk-ku, Seoul South Korea. **LC** PL901; .T65.

US/0271-8294
TOPICS IN LANGUAGE DISORDERS. [Top. lang. disord.]. **Added/Corp** Aspen Systems Corporation. **VFOAT** T.L.D.; TLD. Vol. 1, No. 1 (Dec. 1980)-. Periodical. English. qt. $66.00 US and Canada. Aspen Publishers Inc., 7201 McKinney Circle, Frederick MD 21701. **Tel** (800)234-1660, (301)698-7100, FAX (301)251-5784, telex 5106014543. **(Subscription address:** Aspen Publishers Inc., PO Box 990, Frederick MD 21701.**) ED** Katharine G. Butler. **LC** RC423.A1; T66. **DD** 616.85/5/005. **NLM** W1 TO539Q. **[CCC]. Bk Rev. Pr Rev. Circ:** 5,130. available on microfilm and microfiche from University Microfilms International (UMI). Documents available from The Genuine Article.
Desc: Brings together professionals who have a clinical interest in language disorders; clarifies the application of theory to practice in treatment. Provides relevant information to practicing professionals dealing with the language handicapped.
Ind/Abst Acad. Search (July 1993-); Curr. Contents Soc. Behav. Sci.; Curr. Index J. Educ.; Educ. Index; Except. Child Educ. Resour.; INFO-SOUTH Abstr.; Mag. Search; Psychol. Abstr. (1981-); PsycINFO; PsycLit; Res. Alert [Full Cov.]; Soc. Plann. Policy Dev. Abstr.; Soc. Sci. Cit. Index [Full Cov.]; Sociol. Abstr.

NE
TOPICS IN SOCIOLINGUISTICS. VFOAT TSL. (1982)-. Monographic series. English. Foris Publications, PO Box 509, 3300 AM Dordrecht Netherlands. **Tel** 011 31 78 510454.
Ind/Abst MLA Int. Bibl. Books Artic. Mod. Lang. Lit.

PR/0040-9588
TORRE (RIO PIEDRAS (SAN JUAN), P.R.), LA. See Literature.

BL/0103-1813
TRABALHOS EM LINGUISTICA APLICADA. [Trab. linguist. apl.]. (1983-). Periodical. Multiple languages. sa. **UDC** 80.
Ind/Abst Linguist. Lang. Behav. Abstr. (1983-) [Full Cov.]; MLA Int. Bibl. Books Artic. Mod. Lang. Lit.; Soc. Plann. Policy Dev. Abstr.

MR
TRACES; LINGUISTIQUE SEMIOTIQUE. VFOAT Revue Traces. Yearly V. 1- (1-); 1979-. Periodical. French. sa. 36.00MD. A Bounfour, Revue Traces, 18 rue Brihi, Rabat Morocco. **LC** P99; .T73. **DD** 405. **UDC** 801.7.

FR/0395-773X
TRADUIRE / SOCIETE FRANCAISE DES TRADUCTEURS. Added/Corp Societe Francaise des Traducteurs. (19??)-. Periodical. French (English, Spanish and German). qt. 205.00F France; 343.00F North America Near East middle East and central Asia. Societe Francaise Traducteurs, 22 rue des Martyrs, 75009 Paris France. **Tel** 33 1 48784332, FAX 33 1 44530114. **ED** Denise Baccara. **Bk Rev. Ad Acc. Circ:** 1,800.
Desc: General and specific information on translation and translating problems and news. Glossaries on specialised subject matters. Reviews of books on translation and dictionaries.
Ind/Abst Linguist. Lang. Behav. Abstr. (1979-) [Full Cov.]; Soc. Plann. Policy Dev. Abstr.

SZ
TRANEL. Added/Corp Universite de Neuchatel. Institut de Linguistique. **VFOAT** Travaux Neuchatelois de Linguistique. (Dec. 1980)-. Periodical. French (English and German). **LC** P1.A1; T69. **DD** 410/.5.
Ind/Abst Linguist. Lang. Behav. Abstr. (1980-) [Full Cov.]; Soc. Plann. Policy Dev. Abstr.

US/0360-5949
TRANSACTIONS OF THE AMERICAN PHILOLOGICAL ASSOCIATION (1974). (TRANSACTIONS OF THE AMERICAN PHILOLOGICAL ASSOCIATION.). [Trans. Am. Philol. Assoc.]. **Main/Corp** American Philological Association. (1974)-. English. an. $55.00. Scholars Press / Georgia, PO Box 15399, Atlanta GA 30333-0399. **Tel** (404)636-4757, (404)727-2320, FAX (404)727-2348. **LC** P11; .A565. **DD** 480/.05. **CODEN** TAPAEI. **[CCC]. Circ:** 2,750. Documents available from The Genuine Article. ***Continues in part*** *Transactions and Proceedings of the American Philological Association, 0065-9711.*
Desc: Although the major emphases are upon literary, textual, and linguistic topics, practically all aspects of classical antiquity are included with the purview of TAPA.
Ind/Abst Arts Humanit. Citation Index (19??-19??) [Full Cov.]; Res. Alert [Full Cov.]; Soc. Plann. Policy Dev. Abstr.

UK/0958-5451
TRANSACTIONS OF THE GAELIC SOCIETY OF INVERNESS. (TRANSACTIONS.). [Trans. Gaelic Soc. Inverness]. **Main/Corp** Gaelic Society of Inverness. **VFOAT** Transactions of the Gaelic Society of Inverness; Communn Gaidhlig Inbhir-nis. Vol. 1 (1871)-. English. cum. index.
Ind/Abst MLA Int. Bibl. Books Artic. Mod. Lang. Lit.

JA/0538-6012
TRANSACTIONS OF THE INTERNATIONAL CONFERENCE OF ORIENTALISTS IN JAPAN. [Trans. Int. Conf. Orient. Japan]. **Added/Corp** Toho Gakkai. **VFOAT** Kokusai Toho Gakusha Kaigi Kiyo. No. 1 (1956)-. English (Japanese). an. **LC** PJ21; .I55. **DD** 495/.05.
Ind/Abst MLA Int. Bibl. Books Artic. Mod. Lang. Lit.

UK/0079-1636
TRANSACTIONS OF THE PHILOLOGICAL SOCIETY. [Trans. Philol. Soc.]. **Main/Corp** Philological Society (Great Britain). (1854)-. Academic Scholarly Publication. English. sa (2 issues). £91.50 UK & Europe; $171.00 North America; £110.00 other. Basil Blackwell Publishers Ltd, 108 Cowley Road, Oxford 0X4 1JF England. **Tel** 011 44 865 791100, FAX 011 44 865 791347, telex 837022 OXBOOK G. **(Subscription address:** Blackwell Publishers / UK, Marston Book Services, PO Box 87, Oxford OX2 0DT England.**) ED** J.H.W. Penney. **LC** P11; .P6. **DD** 410/.5. **[CCC].** cum. index. **Ad Acc. Circ:** 1,000. available on microfilm and microfiche from University Microfilms International (UMI). Documents available from The Genuine Article. ***Supersedes*** *Philological Society (Great Britain). Proceedings of the Philological Society.*
Desc: The oldest scholarly periodical devoted to the general study of language that has an unbroken tradition.
Ind/Abst Arts Humanit. Citation Index [Full Cov.]; Curr. Contents Arts Humanit.; Int. Bibliogr. Sociol.; Lang. Teach.; MLA Int. Bibl. Books Artic. Mod. Lang. Lit.; Res. Alert [Full Cov.]; Soc. Plann. Policy Dev. Abstr.

UK/0954-6316
TRANSACTIONS OF THE YORKSHIRE DIALECT SOCIETY. [Trans. Yorks. Dialect Soc.]. **Main/Corp** Yorkshire Dialect Society. Vol. 1, Pt. 1 (July 1898)-. English. an (Dec.). $4.00. The Yorkshire Dialect Society, Mr. S. Ellis, School of English, The University of Leeds, Leeds England. **Bk Rev. Circ:** 800 (ctrl).
Desc: Yorkshire and other dialects of English folklife and language lore.
Ind/Abst MLA Int. Bibl. Books Artic. Mod. Lang. Lit.

US/0890-4758
TRANSLATION PERSPECTIVES. (TRANSLATION PERSPECTIVES: SELECTED PAPERS.). [Transl. perspect.]. **Added/Corp** State University of New York at Binghamton. Translation Research and Instruction Program. National Resource Center for Translation and Interpretation (U.S.). (1983)-. Periodical. English. an. **LC** P306.A1; T72. **DD** 418/.02/05.
Ind/Abst MLA Int. Bibl. Books Artic. Mod. Lang. Lit.

US/0737-4836
TRANSLATION REVIEW. [Transl. rev.]. **Added/Corp** American Literary Translators Association. No. 1 (Spring 1978)-. Periodical. English. Three times a year. $35.00 US; $45.00 other. American Literary Translators Association, University of Texas at Dallas, Box 830688, Richardson TX 75083-0688. **Tel** (214)690-2093, FAX (214)690-2989. **ED** Rainer Schulte; Telephone: (214)690-2092). **LC** PN241.A1; T7. **DD** 418/.02/05. cum. index. **Bk Rev**, (Qty: 12). **Ad Acc, Adv Mgr:** Kuenzer. **Circ:** 1,250 (ctrl). available on microfilm and microfiche from University Microfilms International (UMI). Documents available from The Genuine Article.
Desc: Provides a forum for the exchange of ideas on the art and craft of literary translation. Publishes essays, articles, and reviews.
Ind/Abst Am. Bibliogr. Slavic East Europ. Stud.; Arts Humanit. Citation Index [Full Cov.]; Curr. Contents Arts Humanit.; MLA Int. Bibl. Books Artic. Mod. Lang. Lit.; Res. Alert [Full Cov.].

US/0738-4750
TRANSLATION SERVICES DIRECTORY. [Transl. serv. dir.]. **Main/Corp** American Translators Association. **VFOAT** ATA Translation Services Directory. 5th Ed. (1983)-. Directory. English. an. $50.00 (nonmembers), $35.00 (members). American Translators Association / Virginia, 1735 Jeff Davis Highway, Suite 903, Arlington VA 22202. **Tel** (703)892-1500. **ED** David E. Sharpe. **LC** PN241.A1; A5. **DD** 418/.02/02573. **Ad Acc. Circ:** 1,000. ***Continues*** *Professional Services Directory of the American Translators Association, 1043-3112.*
Desc: Names, addresses, background and services available of 600-700 translators and interpreters.

US/0730-3327
TRANSLATOR REFERRAL, TRANSLATION SERVICES DIRECTORY. VAT Translator Referral/Translation Services Directory. Began in 1982. Directory. English. an. $12.50. Translation Research Institute, 5914 Pulaski Avenue, Philadelphia PA 19144. **LC** P306.A1; T74. **DD** 418/.02/02573. **UDC** 800.73(036). ***Continues*** *Translator Referral Directory, 0096-3259.*

CN/0824-510X
TRANSMISSION (MONTREAL). (TRANSMISSION : BULLETIN D'INFORMATION DE L'ASSOCIATION DES TRADUCTEURS LITTERAIRES.). [Transmission]. **VFOAT** Literary Translators' Association Newsletter. Vol. 1, No. 1 (July 1982)-. Bulletin. English (French). ir (three-four times a year). Free. David Homel, Literary Translators, 1030 Cherrier #510, Montreal Quebec H2L 1H9 Canada. **Tel** (514)288-6690. **ED** David Homel. **DD** 418/.02/06071. **UDC** 800.73; 800.3. **Bk Rev. Circ:** 150 (ctrl).
Desc: Members' news, announcements, translations, politics, copyrights, international contacts, local initiatives across Canada, reports on Association activities and discussion of metier, authors.

FR/0765-1635
TRAVAUX DE DIDACTIQUE DU FRANCAIS LANGUE ETRANGERE. [Trav. didact. fr. lang. etrang.]. (1979)-. Periodical. French. sa. 60.00F France; 70.00F other. Regisseur Recettes Publ., Univ. P. Valery BP 5043, 34032 Montpellier CDX 1 France. **Tel** 011 33 67 142326. **UDC** 804.0.
Desc: Includes French for foreigners, grammar and linguistics.

BE
TRAVAUX DE LINGUISTIQUE. No. 1 (1969)-. Periodical. French. sa (2 issues). 1840F Belgium; 2090F Europe; 2140F other. Editions Duculot SA, Avenue de Lauzelle 65, B-1348 Louvain La Neuve Belgium. **Tel** 32 10 471911, FAX 32 10 471925. **Bk Rev. Circ:** 600.
Desc: Information on language and languages.
Ind/Abst Linguist. Lang. Behav. Abstr. (1979-) [Full Cov.]; MLA Int. Bibl. Books Artic. Mod. Lang. Lit.; Soc. Plann. Policy Dev. Abstr.

FR
TRAVAUX DE LINGUISTIQUE QUANTITATIVE. (19??)-. Monographic series. French. Slatkine Editions, PO Box 765, 1211 Geneva 3 Switzerland. **Tel** 011 41 22 762551. **LC** UNC.
Ind/Abst MLA Int. Bibl. Books Artic. Mod. Lang. Lit.

CN/0710-2534
TRAVAUX DE LINGUISTIQUE QUEBECOISE. [Trav. linguist. que.]. (1975)-. Periodical. French. Presses de l'Universite Laval, CP 2447 Avenue de la Medicine, Saint Foy Quebec G1K 7P4 Canada. **Tel** (418)656-5106, (418)656-2590. **LC** PC3608; .T7. **DD** 447/.9714.
Ind/Abst MLA Int. Bibl. Books Artic. Mod. Lang. Lit.

FR/0750-6112
TRAVAUX DE L'INSTITUT DE PHONETIQUE D'AIX. [Trav. Inst. phon. Aix]. **Main/Corp** Institut de Phonetique d'Aix-en-Provence. (1972)-. Multiple languages (English and French). ir. Price varies. Inst de Phone, c/o Jaqueline Cilia, URA 261 CNRS, University of Provence, 13621 AIX EN Provence France. **Tel** 11 33 16 42641258. **LC** P215; .I44. **DD** 414. **Circ:** 250.
Desc: Phonetic studies in physiology, acoustics, prosody, perception, acoustico-phonetic decoding, socio-phonetics, language teaching, signal processing, instrumentation and singing voice.

FR/0039-2235
TRAVAUX DE L'INSTITUT DE PHONETIQUE DE STRASBOURG REVUE. [Trav. Inst. phon. Strasb.brev.]. (1970)-. Periodical. French. **UDC** 801.4.
Ind/Abst Linguist. Lang. Behav. Abstr. (1972-) [Full Cov.]; Soc. Plann. Policy Dev. Abstr.

FR
TRAVAUX / UNIVERSITE JEAN MONNET-SAINT-ETIENNE, CENTRE INTERDISCIPLINAIRE D'ETUDE ET DE RECHERCHE SUR L'EXPRESSION CONTEMPORAINE. **Added/Corp** Universite Jean Monnet-Saint-Etienne. Centre Interdisciplinaire d'Etudes et de Recherches sur l'Expression Contemporaine. **VFOAT** C.I.E.R.E.C./Travaux. (1989)-. Monographic series. French. ***Continues*** *Travaux (Universite de Saint-Etienne. Centre Interdisciplinaire d'Etude et de Recherche sur l'Expression Contemporaine).*
Ind/Abst MLA Int. Bibl. Books Artic. Mod. Lang. Lit.

NE
TRENDS IN LINGUISTICS. STATE-OF-THE-ART REPORT. (1976)-. Monographic series. English. Price varies per volume. Walter de Gruyter Inc. / Hawthorne, 200 Saw Mill River Road, Hawthorne NY 10532. **Tel** (914)747-0110, GERMANY: 011/49/30/260050, FAX (914)747-1326, telex 646677. **(Subscription address:** Germany/ PO Box 110240, 1 Berlin 11**)**

NE
TRENDS IN LINGUISTICS. STUDIES AND MONOGRAPHS. Vol. 1 (1976)-. Monographic series. English. ir. Price varies per volume. Walter de Gruyter Inc. / Hawthorne, 200 Saw Mill River Road, Hawthorne NY 10532. **Tel** (914)747-0110, GERMANY: 011/49/30/260050, FAX (914)747-1326, telex 646677. **(Subscription address:** Germany/ P. O. Box 110240, 1 Berlin 11**)**

GW
TRENDS IN LINGUSTICS. DOCUMENTATION. (1984)-. Monographic series. English. Price varies per volume. Walter de Gruyter Inc., PO Box 303421, D 10728 Berlin Germany. **Tel** 011 49 30 260050, FAX 011 49 30 26005251. **(Subscription address:** US and Canada/ 200 Saw Mill River Road, Hawthorne, NY 10532**)**

US
TRENDS IN ROMANCE LINGUISTICS AND PHILOLOGY. (1980)-. Monographic series. English. ir. Price varies per volume. Walter de Gruyter Inc. / Hawthorne, 200 Saw Mill River Road, Hawthorne NY 10532. **Tel** (914)747-0110, GERMANY: 011/49/30/260050, FAX (914)747-1326, telex 646677. **(Subscription address:** Germany/ PO Box 110240, 1 Berlin 11**)**

FR/1148-7666
TRIBUNE DES INDUSTRIES DE LA LANGUE, LA. **Added/Corp** OFIL (Observatory). **VFOAT** Language industry tribune. (19??)-. Periodical. French (English). qt. 892.00F France; 906.65F other. OFIL, 2 Rue Abel, 75012 Paris France. **Tel** 011 33 1 42221888, FAX 011 33 1 42221481. **ED** Andre Abbou. **LC** IN PROCESS. cum. index. **Bk Rev**.

US/1044-8209
TROPOS (EAST LANSING, MICH.). (TROPOS.). [Tropos]. **Added/Corp** Michigan State University. Dept. of Romance and Classical Languages and Literatures. (1971)-. English (French and Spanish). $7.50. **DD** 808.
Ind/Abst MLA Int. Bibl. Books Artic. Mod. Lang. Lit.

RU/0320-0892
TRUDY SAMARKANDSKOGO GOSUDARSTVENNOGO UNIVERSITETA. IM. ALISERA NAVOI. ISSLEDOVANIA PO RUSSKOMU I SLAVANSKOMU AZYKOZNANIU. [Tr. Samar. gos. univ. im. Alisera Navoi, Issled. russ. slav. azykozn.]. (1968)-. Russian.
Ind/Abst Annu. Bibliogr. Engl. Lang. Lit.

JA/0389-8008
TSURUMI DAIGAKU KIYO. DAI 1-BU, KOKUGO KOKUBUNGAKU HEN. **VFOAT** Bulletin of Tsurumi College. Part 1, Studies in Japanese Language and Literature. Japanese. Tsurumi Daigaku, 1-3 Tsurumi 2 Tsurumi-ku, Yokohama-shi 230 Japan. **LC** PL501; .T78. **UDC** 809.56; 895.6.

JA/0389-8016
TSURUMI DAIGAKU KIYO. DAI 2-BU, GAIKOKUGO GAIKOKU BUNGAKU HEN. **VFOAT** Bulletin of Tsurumi College. Part 2, Studies in Foreign Languages and Foreign Literatures. Periodical. Japanese. Tsurumi Daigaku, 1-3 Tsurumi 2 Tsurumi-ku, Yokohama-shi 230 Japan. **LC** P9; .T75. **UDC** 800; 82.

CN/0835-8443
TTR : TRADUCTION, TERMINOLOGIE, REDACTION. [TTR, Trad. terminol. red.]. **Added/Corp** Universite du Quebec a Trois-Rivieres. Departement des Langues Modernes. **VFOAT** Traduction, Terminologie, Redaction. Vol. 1, No. 1 (1988)-. Periodical. French (summaries and/or abstracts in English). sa (Jan. & June). 34.00Can$ (institutions), 23.00Can$ (individuals) Canada; 37.00Can$ (institutions), 26.00Can$ (individuals) other. Universite du Quebec A Trois-Rivieres, CP 500 Pierre Andre Julien, Trois Rivieres Quebec G9A 5H7 Canada. **Tel** (819)376-5151. **(Subscription address:** TTR Jean Marc Gouanvic Bur 403, Univ Concordia, 7141 Sherbrooke, Montreal Quebec H4B 1R6 Canada; telephone: (514)848-7512**)** **DD** 418/.02/05.
Desc: Translating, interpreting, terminology and communication.
Ind/Abst MLA Int. Bibl. Books Artic. Mod. Lang. Lit.; Soc. Plann. Policy Dev. Abstr.

NE/0167-4773
TTT, INTERDISCIPLINAIR TIJDSCHRIFT VOOR TAAL- & TEKSTWETENSCHAP. ***Title Change.*** **VFOAT** Interdisciplinair Tijdschrift Voor Taal- en Tekstwetenschap; Interdisciplinair Tijdschrift Voor Taal- & Tekstwetenschap. **VAT** TTT. Vol. 1, No. 1 (Sept. 1981)-(19??). Periodical. Dutch. qt. Foris Publications, PO Box 509, 3300 AM Dordrecht Netherlands. **Tel** 011 31 78 510454. **ED** M Bolkestein. **[CCC]. Bk Rev. Ad Acc. Circ:** 600 (ctrl). ***Merged into*** *Gramma.*
Desc: Interdisciplinary journal for the study of language and text.
Ind/Abst Soc. Plann. Policy Dev. Abstr.

GW/0564-7959
TUBINGER BEITRAGE ZUR LINGUISTIK. (1969)-. Monographic series. German (English, French and German). ir. Price varies per volume. Gunter Narr Verlag, Dishingerweg 5, D 72070 Tuebingen Germany. **Tel** 011 49 7071 78091, FAX (07071)75288. **ED** Gunter Narr. **LC** UNC.
Desc: Publications dedicated to linguistic topics.

CC
TUNG HAI / CHE-CHIANG SHENG WEN HSUEH I SHU CHIEH LIEN HO HUI CHU PAN. **VFOAT** Dong Hai Wen Xue Yue Kan. Periodical. Chinese. mo. RMBY0.30. Chung-kuo Chi Tu Shu Mao I Tsung Kung SSU, Hang-chou Shih, People's Republic of China. **LC** PL2513; .T86. **DD** 895.1/09/005. **UDC** 895.1.

BE/0082-6847
TURCICA (PARIS). (TURCICA.). [Turcica]. **Added/Corp** Universite de Strasbourg. Institut de Turcologie. Association pour le Developpement des Etudes Turques. Universite des Sciences Humaines de Strasbourg. Centre National de la Recherche Scientifique (France). Vol. 1 (1969)-. Periodical. English (French and Turkish). ir. 2000F. Editions Peeters SA, Bondgenotenlaan 153, BP 41, B-3000 Leuven Belgium. **Tel** 32 16 235170, FAX 32 16 228500, telex 65987 PUL B. **ED** I. Melikoff, H. Inalcik, L. Bazin, J.L. Bacque-Grammont, E. van Donzel, R. Mantran, K. Kreiser and P. Dumont. **LC** DR401; .T718. **DD** 956.1/005. Index available. **Bk Rev**. **Ad Acc**.
Ind/Abst Am. Hist. Life (1978);(1978-).

TU
TURK DILI VE EDEBIYAT DERGISI. **Main/Corp** Istanbul. Universite. Edebiyat Fakultesi. (1946)-. Periodical. Turkish. mo. $80.00. Turkish Linguistic Society TDK, Ataturk Bulvari 217, Ankara 06680 Turkey. **Tel** 011 90 4 4286100, FAX 011 90 4 4285288. **ED** Turk Dil Kurumu Baskanligi. Index available (published separately). ***Continues*** *Turk Dili / Aylik Dil Dergisi, 0041-4220.*

TU
TURK EDEBIYATI DERGISI. (19??)-. Periodical. Turkish. mo. $50.00. Turk Edebiyati Dergisi, Divan Yolu Cad 14 Sultanahmet, Istanbul Turkey. **Tel** 5261615.

CN/1185-6084
TUSAGATSAIT (YELLOWKNIFE). (TUSAGATSAIT.). [Tusagatsait]. **Added/Corp** Northwest Territories. Dept. of Culture & Communications. No. 1 (April, 1991)-. Periodical. English. Culture and Communications, Government of the Northwest Territories, PO Box 1320, Yellowknife Northwest Territories X1A 2L9 Canada. **DD** 497.

UK
TUTTITALIA. (June 1990)-. English. Twice a year (June & Dec.). £20.00 UK; $40.00, £21.00 other. Association for Language Learning, 16 Regent Place, Rugby Warwickshire CV21 2PN England. **Tel** 011 44 788 546443, FAX 011 44 788 544149. **ED** Andrew Wilkin (editor's address: Department of Modern Languages, University of Strathclyde, Glasgow, G1 1XH England). Index available. **Bk Rev**, (Qty: varies). **Ad Acc, Adv Mgr:** Glenda Simmonds, **Tel** 0788 546443. **Pr Rev. Circ:** 950 (ctrl).
Desc: Contains articles, reviews and information of specific interest to students and teachers of particular languages.

RU
TVORCHESTVO A. P. CHEKHOVA. **Added/Corp** Rostovskii-na-Donu Gosudarstvennyi Pedagogicheskii Institut. Vol. 1 (1976)-. Periodical. Russian. Ministerstvo Prosveshcheniia RSFSR / Rostov-na-Donu, Gosudarstvennyi, Pedagogicheskii Institut, Ulitsa Engelsa 33, Rostov-na-Donu Russia. **LC** PG3458.Z8; T86.

NE/0167-7373
TYPOLOGICAL STUDIES IN LANGUAGE. [Typol. stud. lang.]. **VFOAT** TSL; T.S.L. (1982)-. Monographic series. English. ir. Price varies per volume. John Benjamins BV, Amsteldijk 44, PO Box 75577, 1070 AN Amsterdam Netherlands. **Tel** 011 31 20 6738156, FAX 011 31 20 739773. **(Subscription address:** John Benjamins North America, PO Box 27519, Philadelphia PA 19118-0519.**)** **ED** T. Givon and Joseph H. Greenberg (Honorary Editor). **LC** UNC.
Desc: A companion series to the journal "Studies in Language."
Ind/Abst MLA Int. Bibl. Books Artic. Mod. Lang. Lit.

CH
TZU LIAO HUI PIEN. **VFOAT** Ziliaohuibian. Vol. 1-. Chinese. Shan-Hsi Shih Fan Hsueh Yuan, Tai-Yuan, People's Republic of China. **LC** PL1071; .T97 . **DD** 495.1. **UDC** 809.51.

CC
TZU SHU YEN CHIU. **VFOAT** Cishu Yanjiu; Lexicographical Studies; Etudes Lexicographique. Vol. 1 (April 1979)-. Chinese. bm. RMBY0.50. Hsin Hua Shu Tien / Shang-Hai Fa Hsing So, Shanghai, People's Republic of China. **LC** PL1401; .T98. **DD** 495.1/3/05. **UDC** 809.51-3.

CH
TZU TIEN YEN CHIU TSUNG KAN. **VFOAT** Cidian Yanjiu Congkan. 1 (Feb. 1980)-. Chinese. ir. NT$0.78. Ssu-Chuan Sheng Hsin Hua Shu Tien, Cheng-tu, People's Republic of China. **LC** PL1411; .T98. **DD** 495.1/3/028. **UDC** 809.51.

US
UCLA OCCASIONAL PAPERS IN LINGUISTICS. **Added/Corp** University of California, Los Angeles. Dept. of Linguistics. **VFOAT** Occasional Papers in Linguistics. (19??)-. Monographic series. English. **LC** P121; .U353.
Ind/Abst Linguist. Lang. Behav. Abstr. (1984-) [Full Cov.]; MLA Int. Bibl. Books Artic. Mod. Lang. Lit.; Soc. Plann. Policy Dev. Abstr.

US/1067-9030
UCLA WORKING PAPERS IN PHONETICS. [UCLA work. pap. phon.]. **Added/Corp** University of California, Los Angeles. Phonetics Laboratory. **VFOAT** Working Papers in Phonetics; WPP; UCLA WPP. (197?)-. Periodical. English. ir (one or three times per year). $10.00 (one issue); $25.00 (three issues). Phonetics Laboratory, 405 Hilgard UCLA Linguistics, Los Angeles CA 90024. **Tel** (310)825-1254, FAX (310)206-5743. **ED** Ian Maddleson. **DD** 414. **Pr Rev. Circ:** 200. available on microfilm from University Microfilms International (UMI). ***Continues*** *Working Papers in Phonetics, 0575-4836.*
Ind/Abst Soc. Plann. Policy Dev. Abstr.

UK/0951-2292
UEA PAPERS IN LINGUISTICS. ***Title Change.*** [UEA pap. linguist.]. **Main/Corp** University of East Anglia. **VFOAT** Papers in Linguistics. (Apr. 1976)-(1993). English. University of East Anglia, Centre for Research in Linguistics, School of Modern Languages, Norwich NR4 7TJ England. **Tel** 011 44 603 592738, FAX 011 44 603 250599. ***Continued by*** *Language Forum.*
Ind/Abst Linguist. Lang. Behav. Abstr. (1984-) [Full Cov.]; Soc. Plann. Policy Dev. Abstr.

GW/0342-2356
UGARIT-FORSCHUNGEN. [Ugarit-Forsch.]. Vol. 1 (1969)-. Monographic series. English (French, German and Italian). ir. Price varies per volume. Verlag Butzon Bercker GmbH, Postfach 215, D 47613 Kevelaer Germany. **Tel** 011 49 2832 9290. **LC** PJ4150; .U4.
Ind/Abst Old Testam. Abstr.

UN/0130-5263
UKRAINSKA MOVA I LITERATURA V SHKOLI. **See** Literature.

UN/0320-3077
UKRAINS'KE MOVOZNAVSTVO. [Ukr. movoznavstvo]. Vol. 1- 1973-. Ukrainian. an. Vydavnyche Obiednannia Vyshcha Shkola Tarasovskaia, Kiev Ukraine. **LC** PG3801; .U44. **UDC** 808.3.
Ind/Abst MLA Int. Bibl. Books Artic. Mod. Lang. Lit.

BL
UNILETRAS : REVISTA DO DEPARTAMENTO DE LETRAS DA UEPG. **See** Literature.

US/0068-6484
UNIVERSITY OF CALIFORNIA PUBLICATIONS IN LINGUISTICS. ***Ceased.*** [Univ. Calif. publ., Linguist.]. **Added/Corp** University of California, Berkeley. **VFOAT** University of California Publications. Linguistics. Vol. 1, No. 1 (1934)-(19??). Monographic series. English. University of California Press, 2120 Berkeley Way, Berkeley CA 94720. **Tel**

(510)642-4191, (510)642-3907, FAX (510)642-9917. **DD** 410.
Ind/Abst MLA Int. Bibl. Books Artic. Mod. Lang. Lit.

US/0068-6492
UNIVERSITY OF CALIFORNIA PUBLICATIONS IN MODERN PHILOLOGY. [Univ. Calif. publ. mod. philol.]. **Added/Corp** University of California, Berkeley. **VFOAT** Publications in Modern Philology. Vol. 1, No. 1 (May 8, 1909)-. Monographic series. English. ir. Price varies per volume. University of California Press, 2120 Berkeley Way, Berkeley CA 94720. **Tel** (510)642-4191, (510)642-3907, FAX (510)642-9917. **LC** PB13; .C3. **DD** 410. **Pr Rev. Circ:** 850 (ctrl). ***Absorbed in part*** *Publications of the University of California at Los Angeles in Languages and Literature, 1051-8274.*
Desc: The journal welcomes manuscripts that deal with both Western and non-Western languages and literatures, including stylistics, criticism, literary theory, and interdisciplinary studies relating literature to other intellectual and aesthetic endeavors.
Ind/Abst MLA Int. Bibl. Books Artic. Mod. Lang. Lit.

US/0081-8593
UNIVERSITY OF NORTH CAROLINA STUDIES IN GERMANIC LANGUAGES AND LITERATURES. STUDIES IN THE GERMANIC LANGUAGES AND LITERATURES (CHAPEL HILL, N.C.). (STUDIES IN THE GERMANIC LANGUAGES AND LITERATURES / UNIVERSITY OF NORTH CAROLINA.). [Univ. N. C. stud. Ger. lang. lit.]. **Main/Corp** University of North Carolina (Chapel Hill Campus). **Added/Corp** University of North Carolina (1793-1962) University of North Carolina at Chapel Hill. (1949)-. Monographic series. English. ir. Price varies per volume. University of North Carolina Press, 116 South Boundary Street, PO Box 2288, Chapel Hill NC 27515-2288. **Tel** (919)966-3561, FAX (919)966-3829. **LC** PD25; .N6. **DD** 430.82.
Ind/Abst MLA Int. Bibl. Books Artic. Mod. Lang. Lit.

CN/0082-5336
UNIVERSITY OF TORONTO ROMANCE SERIES. **See** Literature.

US/0085-7947
UNIVERSITY OF WASHINGTON PUBLICATIONS. LANGUAGE AND LITERATURE. [Univ. Wash. publ. lang. lit.]. **Added/Corp** University of Washington. **VFOAT** Language and Literature; University of Washington Publications in Language and Literature. Vol. 1 (Oct. 1920)-. Monographic series. English. ir. Prices varies per volume. University of Washington Press Business Department, PO Box 50096, Seattle WA 98145-0096. **Tel** (206)543-8870. **DD** 805. ***Absorbed*** *University of Washington Publications in English.*

US/0042-062X
UNTERRICHTSPRAXIS, DIE. [Unterrichtspraxis]. **Added/Corp** American Association of Teachers of German. Vol. 1 (Spring 1968)-. Periodical. English (German). Twice a year (Apr., & Nov.). $35.00 Comes with American Association of Teachers of German membership. American Association of Teachers of German, 112 Haddontowne Court, Suite 104, Cherry Hill NJ 08034. **Tel** (609)795-5553, FAX (609)795-9398. **ED** George Peters. **LC** PF3065; .U5. **DD** 430/.7. Index available. **Bk Rev. Ad Acc. Pr Rev. Circ:** 7,000 (ctrl). available on microfilm and microfiche from University Microfilms International (UMI).
Desc: This pedagogical publication aims to assist classroom teachers of German, from elementary schools to colleges and universities, in improving their teaching skills.
Ind/Abst Curr. Index J. Educ.; Educ. Index (-1992); Lang. Teach.; MLA Int. Bibl. Books Artic. Mod. Lang. Lit.; Soc. Plann. Policy Dev. Abstr.

GW/0566-2818
UNTERSUCHUNGEN ZUR ROMANISCHEN PHILOLOGIE. [Unters. rom. Philol.]. Vol. 1 (1967)-. Monographic series. German. ir. Price varies per volume. Verlag Anton Hain Athenaeum, Wormer Strasse 99, D 55294 Bodenheim Germany. **Tel** 011 49 6135 3057. **DD** 479.
Ind/Abst MLA Int. Bibl. Books Artic. Mod. Lang. Lit.

GW/0083-4580
UNTERSUCHUNGEN ZUR SPRACH- UND LITERATURGESCHICHTE DER ROMANISCHEN VOLKER. **See** Literature.

GW/0042-0786
URAL-ALTAISCHE JAHRBUCHER. ***Title Change.*** [Ural-altai. Jahrb.]. **VFOAT** Ural-Altaic Yearbook. (1952)-(1992). German (English, French and Russian). an. Eurolingua, PO Box 101, Bloomington IN 47402. **Tel** (812)332-8918. **ED** Gynn Decsy. **LC** DB901; .U35. **Bk Rev. Ad Acc. Circ:** 500 (ctrl). ***Continues*** *Ungarische Jahrbucher.* ***Continued by*** *Eurasian Studies Yearbook.*
Desc: Languages and cultures of people in East Eurasia from the point of view of genetic and area comparative research.
Ind/Abst MLA Int. Bibl. Books Artic. Mod. Lang. Lit.

GW/0174-0652
URAL-ALTAISCHE JAHRBUCHER NEUE FOLGE. (1981)-. Periodical. German (English and French). ir. Otto Harrassowitz Verlag, Taunusstrasse 14, Postfach 2929, D-65019 Wiesbaden Germany. **Tel** 011 49 611 5300, FAX 530570, telex 4186 135 OH D. **UDC** 809.4.

GW/0042-0786
URAL-ALTAISCHE JAHRBUCHER (WIESBADEN, GERMANY : 1981). ***Title Change.*** (URAL-ALTAISCHE JAHRBUCHER.). [Ural-altai. Jahrb.]. **Added/Corp** Societas Uralo-Altaica. New Series, No. 1 (1981)-(19??). German (English, French and Russian). an. Eurolingua, PO Box 101, Bloomington IN 47402. **Tel** (812)332-8918. **ED** Gyula Decsy. **LC** PL1; .A47. **DD** 494/.05. Index available. **Bk Rev**, (Qty: 30-40). **Ad Acc. Circ:** 500. ***Continued by*** *Eurasian Studies Yearbook.*
Desc: Languages and cultures of people in East Eurasia from the point of view of genetic and area comparative research.
Ind/Abst MLA Int. Bibl. Books Artic. Mod. Lang. Lit.

US/0566-8824
URBAN LANGUAGE SERIES. Monographic series. English. ir. Price varies per volume. Center for Applied Linguistics, 1118 22nd Street NW, Suite 205, Washington DC 20037. **Tel** (202)429-9292. **UDC** 800.7.

PK
URDU. **Added/Corp** Anjuman Taraqqi-Yi Urdu Pakistan. (19??)-. Periodical. Urdu. qt. Rs15.00 per copy. The Anjuman Taraqqi-E-Urdu Pakistan, D.159-Block 7. Gulshan-E-Iqbal, Karachi Pakistan. **LC** PK1971; .U697.
Desc: A journal devoted to Urdu language, literature, criticism, and research.

NE/0042-1235
US WURK. [Us wurk]. Vol. 1 (1952)-. Periodical. Friesian (English, German and Dutch). qt. Fl25.00. Fries Instituut der Rijksuniversiteit, Oude Kijk in 't Jatstraat 26, 9712 EK Groningen Netherlands. **Tel** (050)635944. **LC** PF1401; .U8. **UDC** 803.93. Index available. cum. index. **Circ:** 400 (ctrl).
Desc: Covers Frisian linguistics, language history and literature.
Ind/Abst MLA Int. Bibl. Books Artic. Mod. Lang. Lit.; Soc. Plann. Policy Dev. Abstr.; Sociol. Abstr. (?-?).

US/0171-726X
UTAH STUDIES IN LITERATURE AND LINGUISTICS. **See** Literature.

UZ
UZBEK TILI VA ADABIETI MASALALARI. VOPROSY UZBEKSKOGO IAZYKA I LITERATURY. ***Title Change.*** **Added/Corp** A.S. Pushkin Nomidagi til va Adabiet Instituti. **VFOAT** Voprosy Uzbekskogo Iazyka i Literatury. (1958)-(19??). Periodical. Uzbek. qt. **(Subscription address:** Victor Kamkin, 4956 Boiling Brook Parkway, Rockville MD 20852.**)** ***Continued by*** *Uzbek Tili va Adabieti.*
Ind/Abst MLA Int. Bibl. Books Artic. Mod. Lang. Lit. (?-?).

UZ/0134-2258
UZBEK TILI VA ADABIETI / UZBEKISTON SSR FANLAR AKADEMIIASI, A.S. PUSHKIN NOMIDAGI TIL VA ADABIET INSTITUTI. **Added/Corp** A.S. Pushkin Nomidagi til va Adabiet Instituti. **VFOAT** Uzbekskii Iazyk i Literatura. (1963)-. Periodical. Uzbek. bm. **(Subscription address:** Victor Kamkin, 4956 Boiling Brook Parkway, Rockville MD 20852.**)** **LC** WMLC L 83/9949. ***Continues*** *Uzbek Tili va Adabieti Masalalari.*

II
VAICARIKI. V. 1- July 1971-. Periodical. Hindi (Hindi). Bharativa Vidva Mandira Sodha Pratishthana, Bikaner, Bikaner India. **LC** DS401; .V27. **UDC** 809.143.

GW/0172-7362
VARIETIES OF ENGLISH AROUND THE WORLD : GENERAL SERIES. Vol. 1 (1979)-. Monographic series. English. ir. Price varies per volume. John Benjamins BV, Amsteldijk 44, PO Box 75577, 1070 AN Amsterdam Netherlands. **Tel** 011 31 20 6738156, FAX 011 31 20 739773. **(Subscription address:** John Benjamins North America, PO Box 27519, Philadelphia PA 19118-0519.**)** **ED** Manfred Gorlach.
Ind/Abst MLA Int. Bibl. Books Artic. Mod. Lang. Lit.

SP
VERBA. **Added/Corp** Universidad de Santiago de Compostela. Vol. 1 (1974)-. Spanish (Gallegan, English and German). an. 4368ptas. Universidad de Santiago, Servicio de Publicaciones, 15706 Santiago Spain. **Tel** 011 34 981 563100. **(Subscription address:** L'Estaquirot SA, Nuestra Senora Del Coll 53, 08023 Barcelona Spain; telephone:011 34 3 285-0327**)** **ED** Constantino Garcia (editor's address: Facultad de Filologia, Universidad de Santiago, E015071 Santiago Spain). **LC** PC5411; .A35a. Index available (free). cum. index. **Bk Rev. Pr Rev. Circ:** 700 (ctrl).
Desc: Covers general and applied linguistics, linguistics of modern languages, romance linguistics, linguistic geography, with special reference to Galicia and the Galician language.
Ind/Abst Linguist. Lang. Behav. Abstr. (1981-) [Full Cov.]; MLA Int. Bibl. Books Artic. Mod. Lang. Lit.; Soc. Plann. Policy Dev. Abstr.

US/0162-0932
VERBATIM. [Verbatim]. Vol. 1 (1974)-. Periodical. English. qt (Jan, Apr, June, Oct). £11.50 Europe & Middle East; $$16.50 US, Canada & Mexico; $20.00 other. Verbatim, PO Box 78008, Indianapolis IN 46278. **Tel** (203)434-2104. **ED** Laurence Urdang. **LC** PE1001; .V43. **DD** 420/.05. **Bk Rev. Ad Acc. Circ:** 10,000. Documents available from The Genuine Article.
Desc: An informative, amusing, entertaining periodical, the largest circulation magazine of its kind in the world. Articles, reviews, correspondence and puzzles.
Ind/Abst Abstr. Engl. Stud.; Arts Humanit. Citation Index [Full Cov.]; Curr. Contents Arts Humanit.; MLA Int. Bibl. Books Artic. Mod. Lang. Lit.; Res. Alert [Full Cov.]; Soc. Plann. Policy Dev. Abstr.; Soc. Sci. Cit. Index [Select. Cov.]; Sociol. Abstr. (?-?).

FR/0182-5887
VERBUM (NANCY, FRANCE). (VERBUM : REVUE DE LINGUISTIQUE PUBLIEE PAR L'UNIVERSITE DE NANCY II.). **Added/Corp** Universite de Nancy II. Vol. 1, Issue 1 (1978)-. Periodical. French (English). Three times a year. 190.99F France; 240.00F other. Presses Universitaires Nancy, 42 avenue de la Liberation, 54001 Nancy Cedex France. **Tel** 011 33 83 935830, FAX 011 33 83 935839. **ED** R. Hodot. **Bk Rev. Ad Acc. Circ:** 500.
Ind/Abst Linguist. Lang. Behav. Abstr. (1985-) [Full Cov.]; Soc. Plann. Policy Dev. Abstr.

AU
VEROFFENTLICHUNGEN DER KOMMISSION FUR LINGUISTIK UND KOMMUNIKATIONSFORSCHUNG. No. 1- 1973-. German. ir. Dr Ignaz-Seipel-Platz, A-1010 Vienna Austria. **Tel** 51 581, telex 01-12 628. **ED** Alexander Issatschenko and Manfred Mayrhofer. **LC** AS142; .V31 subser. **UDC** 803. **Circ:** 500.
Desc: Covers linguistics, philology, comparative philology and idioms.

SZ
VERSANTS. No. 1 (Autumn 1981)-. French (German, Italian, Spanish and Raeto-Romance). Twice a year (Apr., & Nov.). 21.00F. Editions de la Baconniere SA, 19 Avenue du College, Case Postale 185, CH-2017 Boudry Switzerland. **Tel** (038)42 10 04. **ED** Marc Eigelinger. Index available. **Circ:** 600.
Desc: The Swiss review of romance literatures. Publishes literary studies and documents related to the French, Spanish, Italian and Catalan languages.

BE
VERSLAGEN EN MEDEDELINGEN - KONINKLIJKE ACADEMIE VOOR NEDERLANDSE TAAL - EN LETTERKUNDE. **Main/Corp** Koninklijke Academie voor Nederlandse Taal- en Letterkunde. (1972)-. Academic Scholarly Publication. Dutch. Three times a year. 1500F. Koningstraat 18, B-9000 Gent Belgium. **Tel** 011 09 225 27 74, FAX 011 09 223 27 18. **LC** PF1001; .V62. **Circ:** 290. ***Continues*** *Verslagen en Mededelingen - Koninklijke Academie voor Nederlandse Taal- en Letterkunde.*
Desc: Articles on Dutch literature and dutch linguistics.
Ind/Abst Annu. Bibliogr. Engl. Lang. Lit.

IT/0393-8255
VERSUS (MILAN, ITALY). (VERSUS : VS.). [VS]. Vol. 1 (Sept. 1971)-. Periodical. Italian (English and French). Three times a year. L30000 Italy; L60000 other. RCS Libri & Grandi Opere Spa, Via Mecenate 91, 20138 Milan Italy. **Tel** 011 39 2 50951. **ED** Umberto Eco. **LC** P99; .V47. **DD** 001.51/05.
Ind/Abst MLA Int. Bibl. Books Artic. Mod. Lang. Lit.

UN/0135-1117
VESTNIK KIEVSKOGO UNIVERSITETA. ROMANO-GERMANSKAIA FILOLOGIIA. **Added/Corp** Kyivskyi Derzhavnyi Universytet im. T.H. Shevchenka. **VFOAT** Romano-Germanskaia Filologiia. (1978)-. Russian. an. **LC** PE1095; .V48. **DD** 410. ***Continues*** *Visnyk Kyivskoho Universytetu. Romano-Hermanska Filolohiia.*
Ind/Abst Annu. Bibliogr. Engl. Lang. Lit.

RU/0130-0075
VESTNIK MOSKOVSKOGO UNIVERSITETA. SERIA IX : FILOLOGIIA. [Vestn. Mosk. univ., Ser. 9 Filol.]. **Main/Corp** Moskovskii Gosudarstvennyi Universitet Im. M. V. Lomonosova.

VFOAT Filologiia. (May/June 1977)-. Periodical. Russian. Six times a year. $69.95. Izdatelstvo Moskovskogo Universiteta, K-9 Ulitsa Gertsena 5/7, Moscow Russia. **Tel** (301)881-5973. **(Subscription address:** East View Publications Inc., 3020 Harbor Lane North, Suite 110, Minneapolis MN 55447.**) LC** P19; .M623. **Pr Rev.** ***Continues** Vestnik. Seriia X: Filologiia.*
Ind/Abst Annu. Bibliogr. Engl. Lang. Lit.; MLA Int. Bibl. Books Artic. Mod. Lang. Lit.; Soc. Plann. Policy Dev. Abstr.; Sociol. Abstr. (?-?).

●RU
VESTNIK SANKT-PETERBURGSKOGO UNIVERSITETA. SERIIA 2, ISTORIIA, IAZYKOZNANIE, LITERATUROVEDENIE. **See** History(General).

UK/0308-4957
VIDA HISPANICA (1972). (VIDA HISPANICA : JOURNAL OF THE ASSOCIATION OF TEACHERS OF SPANISH AND PORTUGUESE.). [Vida hisp.]. **Added/Corp** Association of Teachers of Spanish and Portuguese (Great Britain). (1972)-. Periodical. Spanish (Portuguese and English). Twice a year (June & Dec.). £20.00 UK; $40.00, £21.00 other. Association for Language Learning, 16 Regent Place, Rugby Warwickshire CV21 2PN England. **Tel** 011 44 788 546443, FAX 011 44 788 544149. **ED** Phil Turk (editor's address: Cotswold End, 15 Northleigh, Bradford-on-Avon, Wilts, BA15 2RG England). **LC** PC4065; .V53. **CODEN** VIHIEC. **Bk Rev. Ad Acc. Pr Rev. Circ:** 1,500.
***Continues** New Vida Hispanica.*
Desc: Information update for teachers, others interested in Spanish, Portuguese, Latin American language and culture.
Ind/Abst Br. Educ. Index; Lang. Teach.

US/0886-1846
VIE (CLAYTON, MO.), LA. (LA VIE.). [Vie]. (19??)-. Periodical. French. Six times a year (Monthly Oct.-May with Dec./Jan. and April/May issues combined). $12.00. The Alan Company, Box 16250, Clayton MO 63105. **Tel** (314)531-1668. **DD** 448.

HU
VILAG ES NYELV. Periodical. Hungarian. bm. 66.00ft. Magyar Eszperanto Szovetseg, I Szenthatomsag ter 1-3, H-1368 Budapest pf 193 Hungary. **Tel** 564-093, 563-659. **ED** Szenes Imre. **LC** P9; .V48. **UDC** 800.892. cum. index. **Bk Rev. Ad Acc. Circ:** 10,000 (ctrl).
Desc: Reports on the communication problems of the world. The results of Esperanto education. Effective methods of learning languages. The news of cultural life and international tourism.

US/1054-7606
VINYAR TENGWAR. [Vinyar tengwar]. **Added/Corp** Elvish Linguistic Fellowship. **VFOAT** VT. (Sept. 1988)-. Periodical. English. bm. $12.00 (U.S.), $15.00 (foreign). Carl F. Hostetter, 2509 Ambling Circle, Crofton MD 21114. **LC** PR6039.O32; Z89. **DD** 828/.91209.

US/0504-426X
VIRGINIA ENGLISH BULLETIN. [Va. Engl. bull.]. **Added/Corp** Virginia Association of Teachers of English. Vol. 1 (May 1951)-. Bulletin. English. sa. $15.00. Virginia Association of Teachers of English, Curriculum and Instruction, Virginia Tech, Blacksburg VA 24061-0313. **Tel** (703)231-5537, FAX (703)231-9075. **ED** Patricia D. Kelly. **LC** PE65; .V5. **DD** 375. **Bk Rev**, (Qty: 6-10). **Ad Acc. Circ:** 2,000.
Desc: Presents information on the teaching of language arts and English at all school levels.

FI/0042-6806
VIRITTAJA. [Virittaja]. **Added/Corp** Kotikielen Seura. **VFOAT** Uusi Jakso. (1897)-. Periodical. Finnish (summaries and/or abstracts in English, French and German). ir. **LC** PH101; .V57. available on microfilm from University Microfilms International (UMI).
Ind/Abst MLA Int. Bibl. Books Artic. Mod. Lang. Lit.

II/0507-1410
VISHVESHVARANAND INDOLOGICAL JOURNAL. [Vishveshvaranand Indol. j.]. **Added/Corp** Vishveshvaranand Vedic Research Institute. Vishveshvaranand Vishva Bandhu Institute of Sanskrit and Indological Studies. Vol. 1, No. 1 (Mar. 1963)-. Periodical. English (Hindi and Sanskrit). sa. Panjab University, PO Sadhu Ashram, Hoshiarpur Panjab India. **LC** PK101; .V495. **DD** 491/.1/05. cum. index.
Ind/Abst MLA Int. Bibl. Books Artic. Mod. Lang. Lit.

UN/0460-0452
VISNYK. SERIIA FILOLOHICHNA. **Main/Corp** Lvivskyi Derzhavnyi Universytet Im. Iv. Franka. No. 1 (196?)-. Russian (Ukrainian). Vyshcha Shkola, Ulitsa Universitetskaia 16, Kharkov Ukraine. **LC** PG3801; .L9214.
Desc: Information on Ukrainian philology.

II
VISVA HINDI DARSANA. **Added/Corp** Visva Hindi Pratishthana (India). No. 1 (January 1979)-. Periodical. Hindi. mo. Rs48.00 India; $4.00 US. Visva Hindi Pratishthana, C-13 Press Enclave, New Delhi 110017 India. **Tel** 669776. **LC** PK1931; .A48. cum. index. **Bk Rev. Ad Acc. Circ:** 2,000.
Desc: Deals with world literature culture and spiritualism. Works as a thread among the Hindi people of the world.

FR/0042-7306
VITA LATINA. No. 1 (June 1957)-. Periodical. French (Latin). Four times a year. 140.00F France: 160.00F others. Vita Latina, University Paul Valery, PB 4053, 34032 Montpellier Cedex France. **Tel** 011 33 37142020.

CN/0832-8315
VOICES (EDMONTON). (VOICES : A PUBLICATION OF THE ENGLISH LANGUAGE ARTS COUNCIL OF THE ALBERTA TEACHERS' ASSOCIATION.). [Voices]. **Added/Corp** Alberta English Language Arts Council. Vol. 1, No. 1 (Sept. 1986)-. Periodical. English. ir. 40.00Can$ Comes with English Languages Arts Council membership. Alberta Teachers Association, 11010-142 Street, Barnett House, Edmonton Alberta T5N 2R1 Canada. **Tel** (403)453-2411. **DD** 428/.007. ***Formed by the union of** Alberta English Notes., 0382-5175 **and** Alberta English Language Arts Council. Newsletter., 0708-8302.*

●US/1074-4762
VOICES FROM THE MIDDLE. **See** Education-Teaching and Curriculum.

RU
VOPROSY ADYGEISKOGO IAZYKOZNANIIA / ADYGEISKII NAUCHNO-ISSLEDOVATELSKII INSTITUT, EKONOMIKI, IAZYKA, LITERATURY I ISTORII. **Added/Corp** Adygeiskii Nauchno-Issledovatelskii Institut Ekonomiki, Iazyka, Literatury i Istorii. No. 1 (1980)-. Periodical. Russian. 1.00rub. **LC** PK9201.A4; V66. **DD** 491/.99.

RU
VOPROSY FILOLOGII. **Main/Corp** Leningrad. Universitet. Filologicheskii Fakuktet. (1970)-. Russian. 1.13rub (single issue). St Petersburg State University / Izdatelstvo Leningradskogo Universiteta, Universitetskaia Nab 7/9, 199034 St Petersburg Russia. **Tel** 011 95 218-97-88, FAX 011 95 218-51-52, telex 121481. **LC** P19; .L442a.

RU
VOPROSY FINNO-UGORSKOI FILOLOGII / LENINGRADSKII GOSUDARSTVENNYI UNIVERSITET IMENI A.A. ZHDANOVA. **Added/Corp** Leningradskii Gosudarstvennyi Universitet Imeni A.A. Zhdanova. (1962)-. Periodical. Russian. ir. St Petersburg State University / Izdatelstvo Leningradskogo Universiteta, Universitetskaia Nab 7/9, 199034 St Petersburg Russia. **Tel** 011 95 218-97-88, FAX 011 95 218-51-52, telex 121481. **LC** PH1; .V65.

RU
VOPROSY FONETIKI I FONOLOGII. **Added/Corp** Golovnoi Irkutskii Gosudarstvennyi Pedagogicheskii Institut. Irkutskii Pedagogicheskii Institut Inostrannykh Iazykov Im. Kho Shi Mina (R.S.F.S.R.). **VFOAT** Problemy Fonetiki i Fonologii. (1972)-. Russian. an.

RU
VOPROSY GERMANSKOI FILOLOGII. **Added/Corp** Kalininskii Gosudarstvennyi Universitet. (19??)-. Periodical. Russian. 0.95rub single issue. Kaliningradskii Gosudarstvennyi Universitet / Kaliningrad State University, Ulitsa A Nevskogo 14, 236041 Kaliningrad Russia. **Tel** 46-59-17, FAX 46-58-13, telex 262116. **LC** PF3095; .V633.

RU
VOPROSY IAPONSKOI FILOLOGII. **Added/Corp** Moscow. Universitet. Kafedra IaponskoÊi Filologii. (1970)-. Russian. Izdatelstvo Moskovskogo Universiteta, K-9 Ulitsa Gertsena 5/7, Moscow Russia. **Tel** (301)881-5973. **LC** PL523; .V6.

RU/0373-658X
VOPROSY IAZYKOZNANIIA. [Vopr. „azykozn.]. **Added/Corp** Institut Iazykoznaniia (Akademiia Nauk SSSR). (Jan./Feb. 1952)-. Academic Scholarly Publication. Russian. bm. $99.95. Izdatelstvo Nauka / Akademiia Nauk, Publishing House of the Russian Academy of Sciences, Leninskii Porspekt 14, 117901 Moscow Russia. **Tel** 011 95 954-21-53, FAX 011 95 938-21-44, telex 411964. **(Subscription address:** East View Publications Inc., 3020 Harbor Lane North, Suite 110, Minneapolis MN 55447.**) LC** P9; .V6. **[CCC].** Index available. **Bk Rev.**
Ind/Abst Annu. Bibliogr. Engl. Lang. Lit.; Linguist. Lang. Behav. Abstr. (1972-) [Full Cov.]; MLA Int. Bibl. Books Artic. Mod. Lang. Lit.; Soc. Plann. Policy Dev. Abstr.

RU/0507-3529
VOPROSY KLASSICHESKOI FILOLOGII. **Added/Corp** Moscow. Universitet. Kafedra Klassicheskoi Filologii. (1965)-. Russian. Izdatelstvo Moskovskogo Universiteta, K-9 Ulitsa Gertsena 5/7, Moscow Russia. **Tel** (301)881-5973. **LC** PA9; .V65.

RU
VOPROSY RUSSKOGO IAZYKOZNANIIA. **Added/Corp** Moskovskii Gosudarstvennyi Universitet. Kafedra Russkogo Iazyka. Vol. 1 (1976)-. Periodical. Russian. 1.21rub single issue. Izdatelstvo Moskovskogo Universiteta, K-9 Ulitsa Gertsena 5/7, Moscow Russia. **Tel** (301)881-5973. **LC** PG2003; .V67.

RU
VOPROSY SLOVOOBRAZOVANIIA V INDOEVROPEISKIKH IAZYKAKH. Vol. 1 (1976)-. Russian. 1.50rub. Izdatelstvo Tomskogo Universiteta / Tomsk State University, Prospekt Lenina 36, 634050 Tomsk Russia. **Tel** 23-44-65, FAX 22-24-66, telex 128258. **LC** P615; .V66.

RU
VOPROSY STRUKTURY GERMANSKIKH IAZYKOV. **Added/Corp** Omskii Gosudarstvennyi Pedagogicheskii Institut Imeni A.M. Gorkogo. (19??)-. Periodical. Russian. 1.00rub single issue. **LC** PD95; .V664.

RU
VOPROSY TATRSKOGO IAZYKOZNANIIA. **Added/Corp** Kazanskii Gosudarstvennyi Universitet Im. V.I. Ulianova-Lenina. Kafedra Tatarskogo Iazyka. **VFOAT** Tatar Tel Beleme Masalalare. (19??)-. Russian.

AT/1032-0458
VOX CANBERRA. **See** Education.

GW/0172-5300
VOX LATINA. **Added/Corp** Universitat des Saarlandes. (19??)-. Periodical. Latin. Four times a year (Mar., July, Oct., Dec.). DM36.00. Vox Latina Societes Latina, Fachbereich 6 3 PF 1150, D-66041 Saarbrucken Germany. **Tel** 011 49 681 3022592. Index available. cum. index. **Bk Rev. Ad Acc. Circ:** 1,500.
Desc: Text on various topics in Latin.

SZ/0042-899X
VOX ROMANICA. [Vox rom.]. Vol. 1 (Jan./June 1936)-. German (French and Italian). an. A Francke Verlag GmbH, Postfach 2560, Dischingerweg 5, D 72070 Tuebingen Germany. **Tel** 011 49 7071 78091 or 92. **LC** PC1.A1; V6. **DD** 479.105. **[CCC].**
Ind/Abst MLA Int. Bibl. Books Artic. Mod. Lang. Lit.; Soc. Plann. Policy Dev. Abstr.

NE
VRIJE FRIES, DE. **See** Literature.

CC
WAI KUO YU. **Added/Corp** Shang-hai wai kuo yu Hsueh Yuan. **VFOAT** Waiguoyu; Foreign Languages. (19??)-. Periodical. Chinese (English). bm. NT$0.35. Shang-Hai Shih Pao Kan Fa Hsing Chu, Shanghai, People's Republic of China. **LC** P9; .W35.
Ind/Abst MLA Int. Bibl. Books Artic. Mod. Lang. Lit.

NQ
WANI : UNA REVISTA SOBRE LA COSTA ATLANTICA. No. 1 (Sept./Dec. 1984)-. Periodical. Spanish (Central American Indian). qt. Centro de Investigaciones y Documentacion de la Costa Atlantica, Managua Nicaragua.

US/0083-7210
WARD-PHILLIPS LECTURES IN ENGLISH LANGUAGE AND LITERATURE. Vol. 1 (1967)-. Monographic series. English. ir. Price varies per volume. University of Notre Dame Press, PO Box 635, South Bend IN 46624. **Tel** (219)239-6349, (800)677-3232, FAX (219)239-8148. **DD** 420; 820.

UK/0960-877X
WATCHWORDS GCSE ENGLISH REVIEW. ***Ceased.*** (1991)-(1992). English. Four times a year. Philip Allan Publishers Ltd, Market Place, Deddington Oxford, OX15 0SE England. **Tel** 011 44 869 38652, FAX 011 44 869 38803.

GW/0509-9609
WEGE DER FORSCHUNG. (1963)-. Monographic series. German. ir. Wissenschaftliche Buchgesellschaft, Hindenburgstr 40, D 64295 Darmstadt Germany.
Ind/Abst MLA Int. Bibl. Books Artic. Mod. Lang. Lit.

GW/0043-2520
WELT DER SLAVEN. (DIE WELT DER SLAVEN.). [Welt Slaven]. Vol. 1 (1956)-. Periodical. German. ir. DM120.00. Verlag Otto Sagner, Postfach 340108, 80328 Munich, Germany. **Tel** 089-54218-0, FAX 089-54218218. **(Subscription address:** Kubon & Sagner, ABT Zeitschriftenimport, D 80328 Munich Germany.**) ED** Peter Rehder. **LC** PG1; .W4. **[CCC].** Documents available from The Genuine Article.
Desc: Slavic philology.
Ind/Abst Arts Humanit. Citation Index (19??-19??) [Full Cov.]; Curr. Contents Arts Humanit.; MLA Int. Bibl. Books Artic. Mod. Lang. Lit.; Res. Alert [Full Cov.].

GW/0043-2547
WELT DES ORIENTS, DIE. Issue 1 (1947)-. German. an. DM91.00. Vandenhoeck & Ruprecht, Robert Bosch Breite 6, D-37079 Goettingen Germany. **Tel** 011 49 551 695911, FAX 011 49 551 695917, telex 965226 VAN d. **LC** PJ10; .W45. **DD** 495. **[CCC]. Bk Rev.** ctrl circ.
Ind/Abst MLA Int. Bibl. Books Artic. Mod. Lang. Lit.

CH
WEN TZU YU WEN HUA. VFOAT Character and Culture; Han Tzu Hsien Tai Hua Yen Chiu Hui Hui Kan. 1981, 1-. Chinese (Chinese). NT$0.45. **LC** PL1175; .W46. **DD** 495.1/05. **UDC** 809.51.

BE
WERKBLAD NEDERLANDSE DIDACTIEK. See Education.

NR/0331-0531
WEST AFRICAN JOURNAL OF MODERN LANGUAGES. [West Afr. j. mod. lang.]. **Added/Corp** West African Modern Languages Association. **VFOAT** Revue Ouest Africaine des Langues Vivantes; WAJML; ROALV. No. 1 (Jan. 1976)-. Periodical. English (French). an. $25.00. West African Modern Languages Association, University of Maiduguri, Department of Languages and Linguistics, Borno State Nigeria.
Ind/Abst Lang. Teach.; MLA Int. Bibl. Books Artic. Mod. Lang. Lit.

US/0734-4503
WESTERN EUROPEAN SPECIALISTS SECTION NEWSLETTER. [West. Eur. Spec. Sect. newsl.]. **VFOAT** WESS Newsletter; W.E.S.S. Newsletter. Newsletter. English. sa. Free to members. WESS Newsletter, University of California-Santa Cruz, Collection Planning Unit, Santa Cruz CA 95064. **UDC** 800.83. ctrl circ. ***Continues*** *Western European Language Specialists Newsletter.*

UK/0143-2214
WHERE TO LEARN ENGLISH IN GREAT BRITAIN. English. an. $4.29. Truman and Knightly Education Trust, 76-78 Notting Hill Gate, London W11 3LJ England. **Tel** (01)727-1242. **ED** Huw Spanner. **LC** PE1068.G5; W47. **DD** 420/.7/1041. **UDC** 802.0-07(410). **Ad Acc. Circ:** 1,500 (ctrl).
Desc: A reference book that includes complete lists of schools and colleges offering courses in English as a foreign language.

AU/0083-9914
WIENER BEITRAEGE ZUR ENGLISCHEN PHILOLOGIE. [Wien. Beitr. engl. Philol.]. **Added/Corp** Universitat Wien. Institut fur Anglistik und Amerikanistik. Vol. 1, (1895)-. Monographic series. German (English). an. Price varies per volume. Wilhelm Braumueller, Servitengasse 5, A 1092 Vienna, Austria. **Tel** 011 43 1 3191482, 3191159. **ED** Wilhelm Braumuller. **LC** PR13; .W5. **DD** 420/.5. Index available. **Bk Rev. Ad Acc. Circ:** 600 (ctrl).
Desc: Yearbooks of studies in English language and literature.
Ind/Abst Annu. Bibliogr. Engl. Lang. Lit.; MLA Int. Bibl. Books Artic. Mod. Lang. Lit.

AU/0083-9922
WIENER BEITRAGE ZUR KULTURGESCHICHTE UND LINGUISTIK. See Anthropology.

GW
WIENER LINGUISTISCHE GAZETTE. **Added/Corp** Universitat Wien. Institut fur Sprachwissenschaft. **VFOAT** WLG. (1972)-. German (English). ir. Institut fuer Sprachwissenschaf, Berggasse 11 Univ Wien, A 1090 Vienna Austria. **LC** PF3003; .W44.
Ind/Abst Lang. Teach.; MLA Int. Bibl. Books Artic. Mod. Lang. Lit.; Soc. Plann. Policy Dev. Abstr.

AU/0084-0041
WIENER SLAVISTISCHES JAHRBUCH. [Wien. Slav. Jahrb.]. **Added/Corp** Universitat Wien. Seminar fuer Slavische Philologie. Universitat Wien. Institut fuer Slavische Philologie. Vol. 1 (1950)-. German (Russian and Czech). ir. Oesterreichischen Akademie Wissenschaften, Dr. Ignaz Seipel Platz 2, A-1010 Vienna Austria. **Tel** 011 43 1 51581. **ED** J. Vintr. **LC** PG1; .W5. **DD** 491.8/05. **Bk Rev. Circ:** 500. Documents available from The Genuine Article.
Desc: Scientific treatises on Slavic philology (language, literature and folklore).
Ind/Abst Arts Humanit. Citation Index (19??-19??) [Full Cov.]; Curr. Contents Arts Humanit.; MLA Int. Bibl. Books Artic. Mod. Lang. Lit.; Res. Alert [Full Cov.]; Soc. Sci. Cit. Index [Select. Cov.].

GW/0258-6819
WIENER SLAWISTISCHER ALMANACH. [Wien. slaw. Alm.]. (1978)-. Periodical. Russian (English and German). ir (4 issues per year). Gesellschaft zur Foerderung Slawistischer Studien Wien, Teschnergasse 4-17, A-1180 Vienna, Austria. **(Subscription address:** Kubon & Sagner, ABT Zeitschriftenimport, D 80328 Munich Germany.) **ED** Board. **LC** PG1; .W53.
Ind/Abst MLA Int. Bibl. Books Artic. Mod. Lang. Lit.

AU/0084-005X
WIENER STUDIEN. (1879)-. English (German). an. Oesterreichischen Akademie Wissenschaften, Dr. Ignaz Seipel Platz 2, A-1010 Vienna Austria. **Tel** 011 43 1 51581. **ED** Board. **LC** PA3; .W5. **DD** 480/.05. **Bk Rev. Ad Acc. Circ:** 600 (ctrl). available with illustrations; available on microfiche; available in reprints.

AU/0084-0076
WIENER ZEITSCHRIFT FUER DIE KUNDE DES MORGENLANDES. See History(General).

GW/0043-6089
WIRKENDES WORT (ZEITSCHRIFT). (WIRKENDES WORT.). [Wirk. Wort]. Vol. 1 (Oct./Nov. 1950)-. Periodical. German. Four times a year. DM105.00. VVA Bertelsmann Dist GmbH, Postfach 7600, D 33310 Gutersloh Germany. **Tel** 011 49 5241 803294. **[CCC].**
Ind/Abst MLA Int. Bibl. Books Artic. Mod. Lang. Lit.

US
WISCONSIN ENGLISH JOURNAL. **Added/Corp** Wisconsin Council of Teachers of English. Vol. 1 (Mar. 1959)-. Periodical. English. Three times a year (Feb., Apr., Oct.). $10.00. Wisconsin Council Teachers English, C/O Mary Ellen Alea, UW-Eau Claire, Eau Claire WI 54702-4004. **Tel** (715)836-5848, FAX (715)836-2026. **ED** Mary Ellen Alea and Steve Fisher. **LC** PE1; .W56. **Bk Rev**, (Qty: 1-3). **Circ:** 700 (ctrl).
Desc: Professional articles: teaching of writing, literature, language arts. Discussion of both content materials, theories, principles, and techniques. Book reviews.

US
WISCONSIN SPANISH TEACHER. **Added/Corp** University of Wisconsin--Madison. Dept. of Spanish and Portuguese. (19??)-. Periodical. English. Twice a year. $1.50. University Wisconsin, Department Spanish & Portuguese, Professor Rose, 1018 Van Hise Hall, Madison WI 53706.

US/8755-4550
WOMEN AND LANGUAGE. (WOMEN AND LANGUAGE : WL.). [Women lang.]. **VFOAT** WL; Women & Language. Vol. 8, No. 1-2 (Winter 1984)-. Periodical. English. sa. $15.00 (institutions), $10.00 (individuals). George Mason University Communications Department, 4400 University Drive, Fairfax VA 22030. **Tel** (703)993-1099, (703)352-1192, FAX (703)993-1096. **ED** Anita Taylor. **LC** P120.W66; W65. **DD** 408.8/042. **Bk Rev**, (Qty: 6-8). **Pr Rev. Circ:** 450. Documents available from UMI Article Clearinghouse. ***Continues*** *Women and Language News, 8755-4569.*
Desc: An interdisciplinary research periodical affiliated with the Organization for the Study of Communication Language and Gender. The mission is to provide a feminist forum for those interested in communication, language and gender.
Ind/Abst Expand. Acad. Index (1992-); MLA Int. Bibl. Books Artic. Mod. Lang. Lit.; Newsp. Period. Abstr. (1992-); Women Stud. Abstr.

NE
WOORDENBOEK DER NEDERLANDSCHE TAAL. Vol. 1 (1882)-. Dutch. ir. Martinus Nijhoff Publishers, Subsidiary of Kluwer Academic Publishers, Koraalrood 50, 2718 SC Zoetermeer Netherlands. **Tel** 011 31 79 684400. **LC** PF625; .W6.

US/0043-7980
WORD WAYS. [Word ways]. **VFOAT** Journal of Recreational Linguistics. Vol. 1 (Feb. 1968-. Periodical. English. Four times a year (Feb., May, Aug., Nov.). $20.00. Dr. A. Ross Eckler, Spring Valley Road, Morristown NJ 07960. **Tel** (201)538-4584. **ED** A. Ross Eckler. **LC** GV1507.W8; W67. Index available. cum. index (1968-1992 $10.00 each). **Bk Rev**, (Qty: 10). **Ad Acc, Adv Mgr Tel** (201)538-4584. **Circ:** 400. available on microfilm and microfiche from University Microfilms International (UMI).
Desc: Serious and light-hearted articles on playing with words. Exploring the sight and sound of language.
Ind/Abst MLA Int. Bibl. Books Artic. Mod. Lang. Lit.; Soc. Plann. Policy Dev. Abstr.

US/0043-7956
WORD (WORCESTER). (WORD : JOURNAL OF THE LINGUISTIC CIRCLE OF NEW YORK.). [Word]. **Added/Corp** Linguistic Circle of New York. International Linguistic Association. Vol. 1, No. 1 (Apr. 1945)-. Periodical. English. ir. $55.00 (institutions), $35.00 (individuals). International Linguistic Association, 613 West 155th Street, Hispanic Society, New York NY 10032. **Tel** (212)926-2234. **LC** P1; .W65. cum. index. available on microfilm and microfiche from University Microfilms International (UMI). Documents available from The Genuine Article.
Ind/Abst Anthropol. Index; Arts Humanit. Citation Index [Full Cov.]; Lang. Teach.; Linguist. Lang. Behav. Abstr. (1970-) [Full Cov.]; Middle East Abstr. Index; MLA Int. Bibl. Books Artic. Mod. Lang. Lit.; Res. Alert [Full Cov.]; Soc. Plann. Policy Dev. Abstr.; Soc. Sci. Cit. Index [Select. Cov.]; Sociol. Abstr.

UK/0959-6569
WORK IN PROGRESS - UNIVERSITY OF EDINBURGH. DEPARTMDENT OF LINGUISTICS. (WORK IN PROGRESS / LINGUISTICS DEPARTMENT, EDINBURGH UNIVERSITY.). [Work prog. - Univ. Edinb., Dept. Linguist.]. **Added/Corp** University of Edinburgh. Dept. of Linguistics. No. 4 (1970)-. English. an (Oct., or Nov.). £4.00. University of Edinburgh, Department of Linguistics, George Square, Edinburgh Scotland EH8 9LL. **Tel** 011 44 31 6671011 Ext 6513. ***Continues*** *Work in Progress (University of Edinburgh. Dept. of Phonetics and Linguistics), 0959-5732.*
Ind/Abst Linguist. Lang. Behav. Abstr. (1989-) [Full Cov.]; Soc. Plann. Policy Dev. Abstr.

UK
WORKER ESPERANTIST, THE. **Added/Corp** Sennacieca Asocio Tutmonda en Britio. (1934)-. Periodical. English. bm.

US/0473-9604
WORKING PAPERS IN LINGUISTICS (COLUMBUS, OHIO). (WORKING PAPERS IN LINGUISTICS.). [Work. pap. linguist.]. **Main/Corp** Ohio State University. Dept. of Linguistics. **Added/Corp** Ohio State University. Computer and Information Science Research Center. (1967)-. Monographic series. English. ir. Price varies per volume. Ohio State University / Department of Linguistics, 222 Oxley Hall, 1712 Neil Avenue, Columbus OH 43210. **Tel** (614)292-4052. **DD** 410. **Circ:** 500.
Ind/Abst Linguist. Lang. Behav. Abstr. (1971-) [Full Cov.]; MLA Int. Bibl. Books Artic. Mod. Lang. Lit.; Soc. Plann. Policy Dev. Abstr.

US/0884-0458
WORKING PAPERS IN LINGUISTICS (HONOLULU, HAWAII). (WORKING PAPERS IN LINGUISTICS.). [Work. pap. linguist.]. **Added/Corp** University of Hawaii at Manoa. Dept. of Linguistics. University of Hawaii (Honolulu). Dept. of Linguistics. (Jan. 1969)-. Periodical. English. qt. Department of Linguistics, University of Hawaii at Manoa, Honolulu Hawaii 96822. **LC** P1; .W673. **DD** 410/.5.
Ind/Abst Anthropol. Lit.

US/0892-8886
WORKING PAPERS IN LINGUISTICS (SEATTLE, WASH.). (WORKING PAPERS IN LINGUISTICS / DEPARTMENT OF LINGUISTICS, UNIVERSITY OF WASHINGTON.). [Work. pap. linguist.]. **Added/Corp** University of Washington. Dept. of Linguistics. (197?)-. Periodical. English. ir. Price varies. Working Papers in Linguistics, University of Washington, Department of Linguistics, Seattle WA 98195. **Tel** (206)543-2046. **DD** 410. **Bk Rev. Ad Acc. Circ:** 300.
Desc: Research papers in linguistics.
Ind/Abst Linguist. Lang. Behav. Abstr. (1987-) [Full Cov.]; Soc. Plann. Policy Dev. Abstr.

NO/0802-3956
WORKING PAPERS IN LINGUISTICS / UNIVERSITY OF TRONDHEIM. **Added/Corp** Universitetet i Trondheim. Dept. of Linguistics. (198?)-. English. University of Trondheim, Department of Linguistics, N-7055 Dragvoll Norway.
Ind/Abst MLA Int. Bibl. Books Artic. Mod. Lang. Lit.

SW/0280-526X
WORKING PAPERS - LUND UNIVERSITY, DEPARTMENT OF LINGUISTICS, GENERAL LINGUISTICS, PHONETICS. (WORKING PAPERS.). [Work. pap. - Lund univ. Dep. linguist. Gen. linguist. Phon.]. (1981)-. Monographic series. English. ir. **UDC** 801. ***Continues*** *Working Papers - Phonetics Laboratory, Department of General Linguistics, Lund University, 0348-4831.*
Ind/Abst MLA Int. Bibl. Books Artic. Mod. Lang. Lit.

AT
WORKING PAPERS ON LANGUAGE, GENDER & SEXISM. [Work. pap. lang. gend. sexism]. **VFOAT** Working Papers on Language, Gender and Sexism. (1991)-. English. sa. 40.00Aus$ (institutions): 25.00Aus$ (individuals). Monash University, Linguistics Department, Clayton VIC 3168 Australia. **Tel** 011 61 3 5654000, FAX 011 61 3 5652294. **Ad Acc. Pr Rev. Circ:** 100.
Ind/Abst Linguist. Lang. Behav. Abstr. (1991-) [Full Cov.]; Soc. Plann. Policy Dev. Abstr.

AT/0313-7791
WORKING PAPERS / SHLRC. **Added/Corp** Macquarie University. Speech, Hearing, and Language Research Centre. **VFOAT** Working Papers of the Speech, Hearing and Language Research Centre, Maquarie University. (1985)-. English. an. **CODEN** WPMCEB. ***Continues*** *Working Papers (Macquarie University. Speech & Language Research Centre), 0313-7791.*
Ind/Abst Soc. Plann. Policy Dev. Abstr.

US/0361-4700
WORKPAPERS OF THE SUMMER INSTITUTE OF LINGUISTICS, UNIVERSITY OF NORTH DAKOTA. **Main/Corp** Summer Institute of Linguistics. **VFOAT** Work

Papers - Summer Institute of Linguistics, University of North Dakota Session. Vol. 1 (1957)-. English. an (Aug.). Price varies. Summer Institute of Linguistic, 7500 West Camp Wisdom Road, Dallas TX 75236. **Tel** (214)709-2404, FAX (214)709-2433, telex 9108614123. **LC** P1; .S85B. **DD** 410. **UDC** 800.
Desc: Collections of a wide variety of linguistic papers.
Ind/Abst Anthropol. Lit.; MLA Int. Bibl. Books Artic. Mod. Lang. Lit.

GW/0509-1632
WORLD AND PRESS. [World press]. (19??)-. Periodical. English. sm. DM49.20 (Germany); DM73.20 (other). Eilers & Schuenemann Verlag, Postfach 106067, D 2800 Bremen Germany. **Tel** 011 49 421 3690347, FAX 011 49 421 3690339, telex 841 244397. **UDC** 07. Index available. **Ad Acc.**
Desc: Articles from different English and American newspapers.

UK/0883-2919
WORLD ENGLISHES. (WORLD ENGLISHES : WE.). [World Engl.]. **VFOAT** WE. Vol. 4, No. 2 (Summer 1985)-. Academic Scholarly Publication. English. Three times a year. £134.50 UK & Europe, $ 219.00 North America; £141.00 other. Basil Blackwell Publishers Ltd, 108 Cowley Road, Oxford 0X4 1JF England. **Tel** 011 44 865 791100, FAX 011 44 865 791347, telex 837022 OXBOOK G. **(Subscription address:** Blackwell Publishers / UK, Marston Book Services, PO Box 87, Oxford OX2 0DT England.**)** **ED** Braj Kachru. **LC** PE1128.A2; W67. **DD** 420/.5. **[CCC]**. available on microfilm and microfiche from University Microfilms International (UMI). ***Continues*** *World Language English, 0278-4335.*
Ind/Abst Br. Educ. Index; Contents Pages Educ.; Curr. Index J. Educ. (March 1990); Lang. Teach. (1985-); Linguist. Lang. Behav. Abstr. (1986-) [Full Cov.]; Soc. Plann. Policy Dev. Abstr.; Sociol. Abstr.

GW
WORTERBUCH DER KLASSISCHEN ARABISCHEN SPRACHE. (19??)-. German (English). Otto Harrassowitz Verlag, Taunusstrasse 14, Postfach 2929, D-65019 Wiesbaden Germany. **Tel** 011 49 611 5300, FAX 530570, telex 4186 135 OH D. **Circ:** 800.
Desc: Dictionary of classic Arabic.

US/0277-7789
WRITING INSTRUCTOR, THE. [Writ. instr.]. **Added/Corp** University of Southern California. **VFOAT** T.W.I.; TWI. (Fall 1981)-. Periodical. English. Three times a year (April, Aug., Nov.). $18.00 (individuals), $35.00 (institutions) US; $20.00 (individuals), $37.00 (institutions) Canada; $22.00 (individuals), $39.00 (institutions) other. Writing Instructor, University of Southern California, THH 440 - MC 0354, Los Angeles CA 90089-0354. **Tel** (213)740-3744, FAX (213)740-4100. **ED** Jennifer Welsh. **LC** PE1001; .W74. **DD** 808/.042/05. **Bk Rev.** **Ad Acc.** **Circ:** 550.
Desc: For high school and college composition teachers looking for practical and tested methods of implementing rhetorical and educational theory in their classes.
Ind/Abst Curr. Index J. Educ.; Educ. Index (1992-); Lit. Crit. Regist.

US/1040-3779
WRITING LAB NEWSLETTER. [Writ. lab newsl.]. **Added/Corp** National Writing Centers Association (U.S.). (19??)-. Newsletter. English. Ten times a year. $15.00. National Writing Centers Association, Department of Humanities, Michigan Tech University, Houghton MI 49931. **Tel** (906)487-2066. **LC** PE1404; .W7263. **DD** 808.

●US/1065-2442
WRITTEN AND SPOKEN HINDI. (WRITTEN AND SPOKEN HINDI : ELEMENTARY I AND II.). (1992)-. English. be. $35.00. U & K Publishing Co., PO Box 10604, Rockville MD 20849.

GW/0342-5932
WURZBURGER JAHRBUCHER FUR DIE ALTERTUMSWISSENSCHAFT. **See** Classical Studies.

US/0084-3482
YALE STUDIES IN ENGLISH. [Yale stud. Engl.]. Vol. 1 (1898)-. Monographic series. English. ir. Price varies per volume. Yale University Press, PO Box 209040, New Haven CT 06520. **Tel** (203)432-0940, (800)987-7323, FAX (203)432-0948. **DD** 810.
Ind/Abst Annu. Bibliogr. Engl. Lang. Lit.; MLA Int. Bibl. Books Artic. Mod. Lang. Lit.

US/0886-6880
YEARBOOK / CLAREMONT READING CONFERENCE. **Main/Conf** Claremont Reading Conference. 25th-. English. an. $20.00. Claremont Graduate School, c/o Malcolm P Douglass, Harper Hall 203, Claremont CA 91711. **Tel** (909)621-8000. **(Subscription address:** Claremont Graduate School, Harper 200, 150 East 10th Street, Claremont CA 91711-6160**)** **ED** Malcolm P Douglass. **LC** LB1049.95; .C57A. **DD** 372.4. Index available. cum. index. **Circ:** 1,500. available on microfilm and microfiche from University Microfilms International (UMI). ***Continues*** *Yearbook - Claremont College Reading Conference.*
Desc: Reports of the annual Claremont Reading Conference. Focuses on the nature of the reading (and writing) process and its relationship to thinking, learning, and knowing.
Ind/Abst Educ. Index.

UK/0306-2473
YEARBOOK OF ENGLISH STUDIES, THE. [Yearb. Engl. stud.]. **Added/Corp** Modern Humanities Research Association. Vol. 1 (1971)-. English. an. $104.00 US. W. S. Maney and Son Ltd., Hudson Road, Leeds LS9 7DL England. **Tel** 011 44 532 497481, FAX 011 44 532 486983. **(Subscription address:** W.S. Maney & Son Limited, PO Box YR7, Leeds, LS9 7UU England.**)**
Ind/Abst Abstr. Engl. Stud.; Annu. Bibliogr. Engl. Lang. Lit.; Arts Humanit. Citation Index (19??-19??) [Full Cov.]; Child. Lit. Abstr. (19??-); MLA Int. Bibl. Books Artic. Mod. Lang. Lit.; Romant. Move.

GR
YEARBOOK OF ENGLISH STUDIES / ARISTOTLE UNIVERSITY OF THESSALONIKI, FACULTY OF PHILOSOPHY, SCHOOL OF ENGLISH. **Added/Corp** Aristoteleio Panepistemio Thessalonikes. School of English. Vol. 1 (1989)-. English (Greek, Modern). an. **LC** PE9; .Y4.
Ind/Abst Annu. Bibliogr. Engl. Lang. Lit.

NE/0922-3495
YEARBOOK OF MORPHOLOGY. **VFOAT** Year Book of Morphology. (1988)-. English. an. Foris Publications, PO Box 509, 3300 AM Dordrecht Netherlands. **Tel** 011 31 78 510454. **(Subscription address:** Kluwer Academic Publishing Group, PO Box 322, 3300 AH Dordrecht Netherlands, (phone: 011 31 78 524400)**)** **CODEN** YEMOEQ.

US/0895-3562
YEARBOOK OF THE AMERICAN READING FORUM. [Yearb. Am. Read. Forum]. **Main/Corp** American Reading Forum. Annual Conference. **Added/Corp** Ball State University. **VFOAT** ARF ... Yearbook. **VAT** American Reading Forum ... Yearbook. 1st (1981)-. English. an (Dec.). $20.00. American Reading Forum, Department of Elementary Education, Utah State University, Logan UT 84322. **Tel** (801)750-1421 or 4123 or 2501. **ED** Hayes Bernard (phone: (801)750-1423). **LC** LB1049.95; .A48a. **DD** 428.4. **Circ:** 300. available on microfilm and microfiche from ERIC.

UK/0084-4144
YEAR'S WORK IN ENGLISH STUDIES. **See** Literature.

UK/0084-4152
YEAR'S WORK IN MODERN LANGUAGE STUDIES. (THE YEAR'S WORK IN MODERN LANGUAGE STUDIES.). [Year's work mod. lang. stud.]. **Added/Corp** Modern Humanities Research Association. **VFOAT** Modern Language Studies, Year's Work in. Vol. 1 (1930)-. English. an. $252.00 US. W. S. Maney and Son Ltd., Hudson Road, Leeds LS9 7DL England. **Tel** 011 44 532 497481, FAX 011 44 532 486983. **(Subscription address:** W.S. Maney & Son Limited, PO Box YR7, Leeds, LS9 7UU England.**)** **ED** D. A. Wells and G. Price. **LC** PB1; .Y45. **DD** 405.8.
Ind/Abst Br. Humanit. Index; MLA Int. Bibl. Books Artic. Mod. Lang. Lit.; Romant. Move.

SP/0006-6966
YELMO. ***Suspended.*** [Yelmo]. No. 1 (Aug./Sept. 1971)-(1988). Periodical. Spanish. bm. $27.00. La Revista del Profesor de Espanol, Apartado 877, 28080 Madrid Spain. **LC** PC4065; .Y44. available on microfilm and microfiche from University Microfilms International (UMI).
Ind/Abst Curr. Index J. Educ.; Lang. Teach.

US/0044-0442
YIDISHE SHPRAKH. [Yid. shprakh]. **Added/Corp** Yivo Institute for Jewish Research. Yivo Institute for Jewish Research. Section of Linguistics. **VFOAT** Yiddish Language. Vol. 1 (Jan./Feb. 1941)-. Periodical. Yiddish. ir. $50.00. Yivo Institute for Jewish Research, 1048 Fifth Avenue, New York NY 10028. **Tel** (212)535-6700. **ED** Mordkhe Schaechter. **LC** PJ5111; .Y53. **DD** 437. cum. index. **Bk Rev.** **Ad Acc.** **Circ:** 1,000.
Desc: Devoted to the problems of standard Yiddish.
Ind/Abst MLA Int. Bibl. Books Artic. Mod. Lang. Lit.; Soc. Plann. Policy Dev. Abstr.; Sociol. Abstr. (?-?).

KO
YONGHAK NONJIP. **VFOAT** English Studies. Periodical. English (Korean). Soul Taehakkyo Yongo Yongmun Hakhoe, San 56 Sillim-dong, Kwanak-ku, Seoul South Korea. **Tel** 880-5193. **ED** Song Nak-Heon. **LC** PE9; .Y66. **UDC** 802.0; 820. ctrl circ.
Desc: The contents included are as follows: phonology, semantics, syntax and English history in linguistics and criticism, novels, poetry and plays in American and English literature.

KO
YONSE OMUNHAK. **VFOAT** Journal of the Yonsei Language and Literature. Periodical. Korean. Yonse Taehakkyo Kugo Kungman Hakkwa, 134 Sinchon-dong, Sodaemun-ku, Seoul South Korea. **LC** PL901; .Y66. **UDC** 809.57.

UK/0307-3238
YORK PAPERS IN LINGUISTICS. [York pap. linguist.]. **Added/Corp** University of York. Dept. of Language. (1971)-. Monographic series. English. ir. Price varies per volume. University of York / Department of Language, Heslington York, Y01 5DD Engalnd. **Tel** 011 44 904 432650, FAX 011 44 904 433433, telex 57933 YORKUL. **ED** S. J. Harlow and A. R. Warner. **Bk Rev.** **Pr Rev.** **Circ:** 250.
Desc: Papers of general interest in descriptive and theoretical linguistics, including sociolinguistics and psycholinguistics.
Ind/Abst Int. Bibliogr. Sociol.; Lang. Teach.; Linguist. Lang. Behav. Abstr. (1989-) [Full Cov.]; Soc. Plann. Policy Dev. Abstr.

CC
YU WEN CHIAO HSUEH TUNG HSUN / YUWEN JIAOXUE TONGXUN. **Added/Corp** Yu wen Chiao Hsueh Tung Hsun She. **VFOAT** Yuwen Jiaoxue Tongxun. (19??)-. Periodical. Chinese. ir. RMBY0.34. Science Press, 16 Donghuangchenggen North Street, Beijing 100707, People's Republic of China. **Tel** 011 86 1 4019821, 011 86 1 4010642, FAX 011 86 1 4012180, 011 86 1 4019810, telex 210147. **LC** PL1068.C6; Y85. **DD** 495.1/07.

CC
YU WEN CHIAO YEN / YUWEN JIAOYAN. **Added/Corp** Che-Chiang Shih Fan Hsueh Yuan. Chung Wen Hsi. **VFOAT** Yuwen Jiaoyan. (19??)-. Periodical. Chinese. Post Office, Hang-Chou Shih, People's Republic of China. **LC** PL2258; .Y83. **DD** 495.1/07.

CH
YU WEN CHIH SHIH TSUNG KAN / PEI-CHING SHIH YU YEN HSUEH HUI PIEN. Periodical. Chinese. NT$0.50. Ti Chen Chu Pan She, 63 Fu Hsing Road, Beijing, People's Republic of China. **LC** PL1071; .Y797. **DD** 495.1. **UDC** 809.51.

CH
YU WEN HSUEH HSI (JEN MIN CHIAO YU CHU PAN SHE). (YU WEN HSUEH HSI.). **VFOAT** Yuwen Xuexi. Periodical. Chinese. mo. $6.21. Science Press, 16 Donghuangchenggen North Street, Beijing 100707, People's Republic of China. **Tel** 011 86 1 4019821, 011 86 1 4010642, FAX 011 86 1 4012180, 011 86 1 4019810, telex 210147. **ED** Cao Yu Zhang. **UDC** 809.51. **Bk Rev.** **Ad Acc.** **Circ:** 180,000.
Desc: Mainly meant to introduce the basic knowledge on learning and writing Chinese language and literature, and at the same time unfold discussions and research.

CC
YU WEN LUN TSUNG / SHANG-HAI SHIH YU WEN HSUEH HUI PIEN. **VFOAT** Yuwen Luncong. Vol. 1- (June 1981)-. Periodical. Chinese. RMBY1.10. Hsin Hua Shu Tien / Shang-Hai Fa Hsing So, Shanghai, People's Republic of China. **LC** PL1071; .Y84. **DD** 495.1. **UDC** 809.51.

CH
YU WEN YUEH KAN. **VFOAT** Yuwenyuekan. Periodical. Chinese. mo. NT$4.80. Post Office, South China Normal University, Kuang-Chou Shih, People's Republic of China. **Tel** 774911. **ED** Tang Qi-Yun. **LC** PL1009; .Y8. **DD** 495.1/05. **UDC** 809.51. **Bk Rev.** **Circ:** 130,000.
Desc: Concerns the common knowledge of the past and present language and literature to meet the need of the youth.

CC
YU YEN CHIAO HSUEH YU YEN CHIU. **Added/Corp** Pei-Ching Yu Yen Hsueh Yuan. **VFOAT** Yuyan Jiaxoue Yu Yanjiu; Language Teaching and Studies. (Sept. 1979)-. Periodical. Chinese (table of contents in English). qt. RMBY9.20. Chung-Kuo Kuo Chi Tu Shu Mao I Tsung Kung SSU, PO Box 2820, Beijing, People's Republic of China. **Tel** 23724. **ED** Zhu Yizhi. **LC** PL1065; .Y893. **DD** 495.1/07. **Bk Rev.** **Ad Acc.** **Circ:** 10,000.
Desc: Publishes papers on teaching Chinese as a foreign language, linguistic research, language pedagogy, and contrastive analysis of Chinese and foreign languages.

CC
YU YEN YEN CHIU / HUA CHUNG KUNG HSUEH YUAN CHUNG-KUO YU YEN CHIU SO. **VFOAT** Yuyan Yanjiu. First published in (July 1981)-. Periodical. Chinese. RMBY1.00. Hua Chung Kung Hsueh Yuan Chu Pan She Fa Hsing Pu Wu-han Shih, Hu-pei, People's Republic of China. **LC** PL1004; .Y8. **DD** 495.1.

CC
YU YEN YEN CHIU LUN TSUNG / NAN KAI TA HSUEH CHUNG WEN HSI YU YEN HSUEH CHIAO YEN SHIH PIEN. **VFOAT** Yuyanyanjiuluncong; Linguistic Studies. TI Chi-.

Periodical. Chinese. RMBY1.31. Tien-Chin Shih Hsin Hua Shu Tien, Tianjin, People's Republic of China. **LC** PL1075; .Y8. **DD** 495.1/05.

YU/0514-6143
ZBORNIK MATICE SRPSKE ZA FILOLOGIJU I LINGVISTIKU / MATICA SRPSKA, ODELJENJE ZA KNJIZEVNOST I JEZIK. **Added/Corp** Matica Srpska (Novi Sad, Serbia) Matica Srpska (Novi Sad, Serbia). Odeljenje za Knjizevnost i Jezik. **VFOAT** Archivum Philologicum et Linguisticum. (1985)-. Serbo-Croatian (Cyrillic) (Multiple languages). an. **LC** P19.M3; A15. ***Continues*** *Zbornik za Filologiju i Lingvistiku.*

YU/0350-0470
ZBORNIK MATICE SRPSKE ZA SLAVISTIKU / MATICA SRPSKA, ODELJENJE ZA KNJIZEVNOST I JEZIK. **Added/Corp** Matica Srpska (Novi Sad, Serbia) Matica Srpska (Novi Sad, Serbia). Odeljenje za Knjizevnost i Jezik. **VFOAT** Review of Slavic Studies; Slavisticheskii Sbornik. (1984)-. Periodical. Serbo-Croatian (Cyrillic) (summaries and/or abstracts in English, German and Russian). sa. **LC** PG13; .Z36. ***Continues*** *Zbornik za Slavistiku.*

YU
ZBORNIK ZA JEZIK I KNJIZEVNOST. **Added/Corp** Drustvo za Srpskohrvatski Jezik i Knjizevnost SR Crne Gore. **VFOAT** Sbornik lazyka i Literatury. (1972)-. Serbo-Croatian (Cyrillic) (Serbian; summaries and/or abstracts in English, French, German and Russian). **LC** PG1201; .Z35.
Ind/Abst MLA Int. Bibl. Books Artic. Mod. Lang. Lit.

GW/0341-0137
ZEITSCHRIFT DER DEUTSCHEN MORGENLANDISCHEN GESELLSCHAFT. [Z. Dtsch. Morgenland. Ges.]. **Added/Corp** Deutsche Morgenlandische Gesellschaft. (1846)-. Periodical. German (English). sa. DM168.00. Franz Steiner Verlag GmbH, Postfach 101061, D 70009 Stuttgart Germany. **Tel** 011 49 0711 2582372, FAX 011 49 0711 2582290, telex 723636 daz d. **ED** Tilman Nagel. **LC** PJ5; .D4. **[CCC]**. cum. index. Documents available from The Genuine Article.
Ind/Abst Arts Humanit. Citation Index [Full Cov.]; BHA : Biblio. Hist. Art; Curr. Contents Arts Humanit.; MLA Int. Bibl. Books Artic. Mod. Lang. Lit.; New Testam. Abstr.; Numis. Lit.; Old Testam. Abstr.; Res. Alert [Full Cov.]; Soc. Sci. Cit. Index [Select. Cov.]; Middle East J.

GW/0721-9067
ZEITSCHRIFT FUER SPRACHWISSENSCHAFT : ORGAN DER DEUTSCHEN GESELLSCHAFT FEUR SPRACHWISSENSCHAFT. **Added/Corp** Deutsche Gesellschaft feur Sprachwissenschaft. **VFOAT** Z.S.; ZS. Vol. 1, No. 1 (1982)-. Periodical. German (table of contents in English and French). Twice a year. DM94.00. Vandenhoeck & Ruprecht, Robert Bosch Breite 6, D-37079 Goettingen Germany. **Tel** 011 49 551 695911, FAX 011 49 551 695917, telex 965226 VAN d. **LC** P3; .Z39. **DD** 410/.5. **[CCC]**.

GW/0932-4461
ZEITSCHRIFT FUER ALTHEBRAISTIK. **VFOAT** ZAH. Vol. 1, No. 1 (1988)-. Periodical. German (English and French). sa (2 issues). DM219.00. W Kohlhammer Verlag GmbH, Postfach 800430, D 70549 Stuttgart Germany. **Tel** 011 49 711 78631, FAX 011 49 711 7863263, telex 7-255820. **ED** H. P. Muller and E. Jenni. **LC** PJ4501; .Z45. **DD** 492.4/05. Index available. **Ad Acc.** ctrl circ.
Desc: Hebrew language.
Ind/Abst MLA Int. Bibl. Books Artic. Mod. Lang. Lit.

GW/0170-026X
ZEITSCHRIFT FUER ARABISCHE LINGUISTIK. [Z. arab. Linguist.]. **VFOAT** Journal of Arabic Linguistics; Journal de Linguistique Arabe; ZAL. No. 1 (1978)-. Periodical. German (English). ir (1 or 2 per year). Otto Harrassowitz Verlag, Taunusstrasse 14, Postfach 2929, D-65019 Wiesbaden Germany. **Tel** 011 49 611 5300, FAX 530570, telex 4186 135 OH D. **[CCC]**.
Ind/Abst Linguist. Lang. Behav. Abstr. (1985-) [Full Cov.]; MLA Int. Bibl. Books Artic. Mod. Lang. Lit.; Soc. Plann. Policy Dev. Abstr.; Middle East J.

GW/0084-5302
ZEITSCHRIFT FUER CELTISCHE PHILOLOGIE. [Z. celt. Philol.]. Vol. 24, No. 1/2 (1953)-. German (English and French). an. DM136.00. Max Niemeyer Verlag, Postfach 2140, D 72011 Tuebingen Germany. **Tel** 011 49 7071 989494, FAX 011 49 7071 87419. **ED** Rolf Koedderitzsch, Herbert Pilch, Karl Horst Schmidt. Index available (free). **Bk Rev. Ad Acc.** Documents available from The Genuine Article. ***Continues*** *Zeitschrift fuer Keltische Philologie und Volkforschung.*
Desc: Contributions on Celtic languages and literatures.
Ind/Abst Arts Humanit. Citation Index (19??-19??) [Full Cov.]; Curr. Contents Arts Humanit.; MLA Int. Bibl. Books Artic. Mod. Lang. Lit.; Res. Alert [Full Cov.].

GW/0044-2496
ZEITSCHRIFT FUER DEUTSCHE PHILOLOGIE. [Z. dtsch. Philol.]. (1969)-. Periodical. German. qt (4 issues). DM204.00 students; DM224.00 other. Erich Schmidt Verlag GmbH, Postfach 304240, D 10724 Berlin Germany. **Tel** 011 49 30 25008525. **ED** Werner Besch, Hugo Moser, Harmut Steinecke, and Benno van Wiese. **LC** PF3003; .Z35. **[CCC]**. **Bk Rev. Ad Acc.** ctrl circ. Documents available from The Genuine Article.
Desc: German philology.
Ind/Abst Arts Humanit. Citation Index [Full Cov.]; Curr. Contents Arts Humanit.; MLA Int. Bibl. Books Artic. Mod. Lang. Lit.; Res. Alert [Full Cov.]; Romant. Move.; Soc. Plann. Policy Dev. Abstr.; Soc. Sci. Cit. Index [Select. Cov.].

GW
ZEITSCHRIFT FUER DEUTSCHE PHILOLOGIE. BEIHEFT. No. 1 (1969)-. Monographic series. German. ir. Price varies per volume. Erich Schmidt Verlag GmbH, Postfach 304240, D 10724 Berlin Germany. **Tel** 011 49 30 25008525. **ED** Werner Besch, Hugo Moser, Hartmut Steinecke, and Benno von Wiese. **Bk Rev. Ad Acc.** ctrl circ.
Desc: German philology.

GW/0044-2518
ZEITSCHRIFT FUER DEUTSCHES ALTERTUM UND DEUTSCHE LITERATUR. [Z. dtsch. Altert. dtsch. Lit.]. **VFOAT** Zeitschrift fuer Deutsches Altertum und Deutsche Litteratur; Zeitschrift fuer Deutsches Altertum und Deutsche Literatur. (1876)-. Periodical. German. qt. DM198.00. Franz Steiner Verlag GmbH, Postfach 101061, D 70009 Stuttgart Germany. **Tel** 011 49 0711 2582372, FAX 011 49 0711 2582290, telex 723636 daz d. **ED** Franz Josef Worstbrock. **[CCC]**. **Bk Rev. Ad Acc. Circ:** 800. available on microfilm. Documents available from The Genuine Article. ***Continues*** *Zeitschrift fuer Deutschen Alterthum.*
Desc: Covers the German language in its earlier developments (structure, word roots) and German literature.
Ind/Abst Arts Humanit. Citation Index [Full Cov.]; BHA : Biblio. Hist. Art; Curr. Contents Arts Humanit.; MLA Int. Bibl. Books Artic. Mod. Lang. Lit.; Res. Alert [Full Cov.]; Romant. Move.; Soc. Sci. Cit. Index [Select. Cov.].

GW/0044-1449
ZEITSCHRIFT FUER DIALEKTOLOGIE UND LINGUISTIK. (ZEITSCHRIFT FUER DIALEKTOLOGIE UND LINGUISTIK : ZDL.). [Z. Dialektol. Linguist.]. **VFOAT** Z.D.L.; ZDL. Vol. 36 (1969)-. Periodical. German (English). Three times a year. DM140.00. Franz Steiner Verlag GmbH, Postfach 101061, D 70009 Stuttgart Germany. **Tel** 011 49 0711 2582372, FAX 011 49 0711 2582290, telex 723636 daz d. **ED** Joachim Goschel, Rudolf Freudenberg and Dieter Stellmacher. **LC** PF5001; .Z4. **DD** 437/.005. **[CCC]**. Index available. **Bk Rev. Ad Acc. Circ:** 500. Documents available from The Genuine Article. ***Continues*** *Zeitschrift fuer Mundartforschung.*
Desc: Dedicated to German dialectology, problems of general dialectology as well as historical German linguistics.
Ind/Abst Annu. Bibliogr. Engl. Lang. Lit.; Arts Humanit. Citation Index [Full Cov.]; Curr. Contents Arts Humanit.; Lang. Lang. Behav. Abstr.; MLA Int. Bibl. Books Artic. Mod. Lang. Lit.; Res. Alert [Full Cov.]; Soc. Plann. Policy Dev. Abstr.; Soc. Sci. Cit. Index [Select. Cov.]; Sociol. Abstr.

GW/0044-2747
ZEITSCHRIFT FUER FRANZOSISCHE SPRACHE UND LITERATUR. [Z. fr. Sprache Lit.]. Vol. 11, (1889)-. Periodical. German (French). Three times a year. DM128.00. Franz Steiner Verlag GmbH, Postfach 101061, D 70009 Stuttgart Germany. **Tel** 011 49 0711 2582372, FAX 011 49 0711 2582290, telex 723636 daz d. **ED** Klaus W Hempfer and Peter Blumenthal. **[CCC]**. cum. index. **Bk Rev. Ad Acc. Circ:** 450. Documents available from The Genuine Article. ***Continues*** *Zeitschrift fuer Neufranzosische Sprache und Literatur mit Besonderer Berucksichtigung des Unterrichts im Franzosischen auf den Deutschen Schulen.*
Desc: Publishes articles about French language and literature.
Ind/Abst Arts Humanit. Citation Index [Full Cov.]; Curr. Contents Arts Humanit.; MLA Int. Bibl. Books Artic. Mod. Lang. Lit.; Res. Alert [Full Cov.]; Romant. Move.; Soc. Sci. Cit. Index [Select. Cov.].

GW
ZEITSCHRIFT FUER FREMDSPRACHENFORSCHUNG : ZFF: ORGAN DER DEUTSCHEN GESELLSCHAFT FUER FREMDSPRACHENFORSCHUNG (DGFF). **Added/Corp** Deutsche Gesellschaft fuer Fremdsprachenforschung. **VFOAT** ZFF. Vol. 1 (1990)-. Periodical. German. sa.

GW/0932-2221
ZEITSCHRIFT FUER KATALANISTIK. **Added/Corp** Deutsch-Katalanische Gesellschaft. Universitat Frankfurt am Main. Institut fuer Romanische Sprachen und Literaturen. Centre Unesco de Catalunya. **VFOAT** Revista d'Estudis Catalans. Vol. 1 (1988)-. German (Catalan and French). an. DM35.00. Katalanisches Kulturbuero, Jordanstrasse 10, D-60486 Frankfurt Germany. **LC** PAR.
Ind/Abst MLA Int. Bibl. Books Artic. Mod. Lang. Lit.

GW/0044-331X
ZEITSCHRIFT FUER PHONETIK, SPRACHWISSENSCHAFT UND KOMMUNIKATIONSFORSCHUNG. ***Title Change.*** [Z. Phonet., Sprachwiss. Kommunikationsforsch.]. (1961)-(1992). Periodical. German (English, French and Russian). qt. Akademie-Verlag GmbH, Muehlenstrasse 33 34, D 13162 Berlin Germany. **Tel** 011 49 30 47889300, FAX 011 49 30 47889357. **(Subscription address:** VCH Publishers Inc., 303 Northwest 12th Avenue, Journals Department, Deerfield FL 33442.**)** ***Continues*** *Zeitschrift fur Phonetik und Allgemeine Sprachwissenschaft.* ***Continued by*** *Sprachtypologie und Universalienforschung, 0942-2919.*
Ind/Abst Annu. Bibliogr. Engl. Lang. Lit.; Index Book Rev. Humanit.; Lang. Teach.; MLA Int. Bibl. Books Artic. Mod. Lang. Lit.

GW/0049-8661
ZEITSCHRIFT FUER ROMANISCHE PHILOLOGIE. [Z. rom. Philol.]. (1877)-. Periodical. English (French, German, Italian and Spanish). Three times a year. DM338.00. Max Niemeyer Verlag, Postfach 2140, D 72011 Tuebingen Germany. **Tel** 011 49 7071 989494, FAX 011 49 7071 87419. **ED** Max Pfister (editor's address: University of Saarlandes, Postfach 1150, D 66041 Saarbruecken, Germany). **LC** PC3; .Z5. **[CCC]**. Documents available from The Genuine Article.
Desc: Series covering Romance philology.
Ind/Abst Arts Humanit. Citation Index [Full Cov.]; MLA Int. Bibl. Books Artic. Mod. Lang. Lit.; Res. Alert [Full Cov.]; Soc. Plann. Policy Dev. Abstr.; Soc. Sci. Cit. Index [Select. Cov.].

GW/0044-3492
ZEITSCHRIFT FUER SLAVISCHE PHILOLOGIE. [Z. slav. Philol.]. **Added/Corp** Akademie der Wissenschaften und der Literatur (Germany). Vol. 1 (1924)-. Periodical. German. sa (2 issues). DM222.00. Universitatsverlag Carl Winter, POB 106140, D 69051 Heidelberg Germany. **Tel** 011 49 6221 770260. **LC** PG1; .Z4. **DD** 491.805. Index available (Free). cum. index. **Bk Rev. Ad Acc. Circ:** 500 (ctrl). Documents available from The Genuine Article.
Desc: Slavic philology.
Ind/Abst Arts Humanit. Citation Index [Full Cov.]; Curr. Contents Arts Humanit.; MLA Int. Bibl. Books Artic. Mod. Lang. Lit.; Res. Alert [Full Cov.]; Soc. Plann. Policy Dev. Abstr.; Sociol. Abstr. (?-?).

GW/0044-3506
ZEITSCHRIFT FUER SLAWISTIK. (ZEITSCHRIFT FUER SLAWISTIK / HERAUSGEGEBEN IM AUFTRAGE DER DEUTSCHEN AKADEMIE DER WISSENSCHAFTEN ZU BERLIN.). [Z. Slaw.]. **Added/Corp** Deutsche Akademie der Wissenschaften zu Berlin. Deutsche Akademie der Wissenschaften zu Berlin. Institut fuer Slawistik. Vol. 1, No. 1 (1956)-. Periodical. German. Four times a year. $145.00. Akademie-Verlag GmbH, Muehlenstrasse 33 34, D 13162 Berlin Germany. **Tel** 011 49 30 47889300, FAX 011 49 30 47889357. **(Subscription address:** VCH Publishers Inc., 303 Northwest 12th Avenue, Journals Department, Deerfield FL 33442.**)** **LC** PG1; .Z43. cum. index. Documents available from The Genuine Article.
Ind/Abst Am. Hist. Life (1988-); Arts Humanit. Citation Index [Full Cov.]; Curr. Contents Arts Humanit.; MLA Int. Bibl. Books Artic. Mod. Lang. Lit.; Res. Alert [Full Cov.]; Romant. Move.; Soc. Plann. Policy Dev. Abstr.; Soc. Sci. Cit. Index [Select. Cov.].

GW
ZEITSCHRIFT FUER VERGLEICHENDE SPRACHFORSCHUNG. ERGANZUNGSHEFTE. Vol. 1 (1921)-. Monographic series. German. ir. Price varies per volume. Vandenhoeck & Ruprecht, Robert Bosch Breite 6, D-37079 Goettingen Germany. **Tel** 011 49 551 695911, FAX 011 49 551 695917, telex 965226 VAN d.

JA
ZENKOKU TANKI DAIGAKU KIYO RONBUN SAKUIN. GOGAKU BUNGAKU HEN / HENSHU, TOSHOKAN KAGAKKAI. **VFOAT** Bulletin of Junior Colleges SIC Cumulative Index in Japan. Language and Literature. 1950-1979-. Japanese. 29000. Saitama Fukushikai, 7-31 Horinouchi 3 Niiza-shi, Saitama-ken 352 Japan. **LC** Z7003; .Z46; P121.

GW/0301-3294
ZGL. ZEITSCHRIFT FUER GERMANISTISCHE LINGUISTIK. (ZEITSCHRIFT FUER GERMANISTISCHE LINGUISTIK.). [ZGL, Z. ger. Linguist.]. **VFOAT** ZGL.

(1973)-. Periodical. German. Three times a year. $150.00. Walter de Gruyter Inc., PO Box 303421, D 10728 Berlin Germany. **Tel** 011 49 30 260050, FAX 011 49 30 26005251. **LC** PF3003; .Z45. **[CCC].** Documents available from The Genuine Article. ***Supersedes*** *Zeitschrift fur Deutsche Sprache.*
Ind/Abst Arts Humanit. Citation Index [Full Cov.]; Curr. Contents Arts Humanit.; Lang. Teach.; Linguist. Lang. Behav. Abstr. (1989-) [Full Cov.]; MLA Int. Bibl. Books Artic. Mod. Lang. Lit.; Res. Alert [Full Cov.]; Soc. Plann. Policy Dev. Abstr.

CH/1017-2300
ZHONGGUO YUWEN (TAIPEI). VFOAT Chinese Language Monthly (Taipei). (1952)-. Periodical. Chinese. mo. $13.30. **(Subscription address:** China International Book Trading Corporation, PO Box 399, Library Service Department, Beijing 100044 People's Republic of China.**)** **UDC** 809.51.

CH/1012-4195
ZHONGYANG YANJIUYUAN LISHI YUYAN YANJIUSUO JIKAN. See General Interest-General Interest-Asia.

GW/0341-5864
ZIELSPRACHE DEUTSCH. [Zielspr. Dtsch.]. **Added/Corp** Goethe-Institut (Munich, Germany). Vol. 1, (March 1970)-. Periodical. German. Four times a year. $24.00. Max-Hueber-Verlag, Max-Hueber-Strasse 4, D 85737 Ismaning Germany. **Tel** 011 49 89 96020, FAX 011 49 89 9602 358, telex 523613. **ED** Luts Gotze Schriftleiter, Ulrich Engel, Walter Schmidt, and Friedrich Schmoe. **LC** PF3003; .Z54. **DD** 438/.005. **[CCC].** Index available. **Bk Rev. Ad Acc. Circ:** 3,000 (ctrl). ***Continues*** *Deutschunterricht fur Auslander.*
Desc: Journal for applied linguistics and teaching methodology.
Ind/Abst Lang. Teach.; MLA Int. Bibl. Books Artic. Mod. Lang. Lit.; Soc. Plann. Policy Dev. Abstr.

GW/0342-6173
ZIELSPRACHE ENGLISCH. [Zielspr. Engl.]. **Added/Corp** Deutscher Volkshochschulverband. Padagogische Arbeitsstelle. Verband Osterreichischer Volkshochschulen. Verband der Schweizerischen Volkshochschulen. (Jan. 1972)-. Academic Scholarly Publication. German (English). Four times a year. DM38.00. Max-Hueber-Verlag, Max-Hueber-Strasse 4, D 85737 Ismaning Germany. **Tel** 011 49 89 96020, FAX 011 49 89 9602 358, telex 523613. **ED** A. Schmitz. **LC** PE1001; .Z5. **DD** 420. Index available. cum. index. **Bk Rev**, (Qty: 30 per year). **Ad Acc, Adv Mgr:** A. Ruhland. Full Page (B&W) DM650.00. Half Page (B&W) DM330.00. **Acid Free. Circ:** 1,500 (ctrl). available on microfilm from University Microfilms International (UMI).
Desc: English language teaching for adults.
Ind/Abst Lang. Teach.; Soc. Plann. Policy Dev. Abstr.

GW/0173-9522
ZIELSPRACHE RUSSISCH. *Ceased.* [Zielspr. Russ.]. (1980)-No. 4 (1993). Periodical. German (Russian). qt. Max-Hueber-Verlag, Max-Hueber-Strasse 4, D 85737 Ismaning Germany. **Tel** 011 49 89 96020, FAX 011 49 89 9602 358, telex 523613. **(Subscription address:** International Book Import Service Inc., 2995 Wall-Triana Highway B4, Huntsville, AL 35824**)** **ED** Frieohelm Denninshaus, Dmitri Milinski, Barbara Subik. **[CCC]. *Continues*** *Russisch.*
Ind/Abst Lang. Teach.

ABSTRACTING, BIBLIOGRAPHIES AND STATISTICS

GW
BIBLIOGRAPHIE LINGUISTISCHER LITERATUR. Added/Corp Stadt- und Universitaetsbibliothek Frankfurt am Main. Sondersammelgebiet Linguistik. **VFOAT** BLL. No. 4 (1978)-. Monographic series. German. an (Dec.). DM496.00. Vittorio Klostermann, Frauenlobstrasse 22, D 60487 Frankfurt Germany. **Tel** 011 49 69 9708160. **ED** Lehmann. ***Continues*** *Bibliographie Unselbstandiger Literatur. Linguistik.*

FR
BIBLIOGRAPHIE OCCITANE. 1919/42-. Multiple languages (French). **LC** Z7033.P8; B5; PC3201. **DD** 016.849/08.

AT
BIBLIOGRAPHY OF THE SUMMER INSTITUTE OF LINGUISTICS, AUSTRALIAN ABORIGINES BRANCH UP TO ... / COMPILED BY SANDRA RAY. Added/Corp Summer Institute of Linguistics. Australian Aborigines Branch. (Aug. 1979)-. Bibliography. English. ir. Summer Institute of Linguistics / Australia, PO Berrimah, NT 0828 Australia. **Tel** 089 844-021, FAX 089 844 321. **LC** Z7111; .R39; PL7001. **DD** 016.499/15. **Circ:** 350.
Desc: Includes two sections. Section I is labeled Technical Works and consists of articles, monographs and book reviews on linguistics, anthropology, literacy and education. It is primarily a listing of works by current members of the Summer Institute of Linguistics. Section II consists of several categories of works in Aboriginal languages.

FR/0373-1928
ETUDES CELTIQUES. [Etud. celt.]. No. 1 (June 1936)-. Monographic series. French (Italian, English and German). ir. Price varies per volume. Editions du CNRS, 22 rue Saint Armand, F 75015 Paris France. **Tel** 011 33 1 45075050. **(Subscription address:** CNRS Editions, 22-24 rue Saint-Amand, 75015 Paris France, telephone: 011 33 1 45331600**)** **ED** V. Kruta and P. Y. Lambert. Index available. cum. index. **Bk Rev. Circ:** 1,500. ***Supersedes*** *Revue Celtique.*
Desc: Archaeological and linguistic studies (Celtic languages, ancient and modern); new research, original articles, bibliographies and comparative studies.
Ind/Abst Br. Archaeol. Bibliogr.; MLA Int. Bibl. Books Artic. Mod. Lang. Lit.

GW/0016-8912
GERMANISTIK (TUEBINGEN). (GERMANISTIK.). [Germanistik]. Vol. 1 (Jan. 1960)-. Periodical. German. Four times a year. DM136.00. Max Niemeyer Verlag, Postfach 2140, D 72011 Tuebingen Germany. **Tel** 011 49 7071 989494, FAX 011 49 7071 87419. **ED** Matthias Reifegerste, Wilfried Barner, Richard Brinkmann, Ulla Fix, Klaus Grubmueller, Helmut Henne, Johannes Janota, Wolfram Mauser, Wilhelm Vosskamp. **LC** Z2235.A2; G4. **[CCC]. Bk Rev. Ad Acc.**
Desc: Journal with reviews and bibliographical references of monographs and contributions on German literature and language.
Ind/Abst MLA Int. Bibl. Books Artic. Mod. Lang. Lit.

UK/0261-4448
LANGUAGE TEACHING. [Lang. teach.]. **Added/Corp** Centre for Information on Language Teaching and Research. British Council. English Language & Literature Division. Vol. 15, No. 1 (Jan. 1982)-. Abstracting/Indexing Service. English. qt. $99.00 US, Canada and Mexico; £56.00 other. Cambridge University Press, The Edinburgh Building, Shaftesbury Road, Cambridge CB2 2RU United Kingdom. **Tel** 011 44 223 312393, FAX 011 44 223 325959. **(Subscription address:** Cambridge University Press / North America, 110 Midland Avenue, Port Chester NY 10573.**)** **ED** Valerie Kinsella. **LC** PB35; .L32. **DD** 407. **[CCC].** available on microfilm and microfiche from University Microfilms International (UMI). ***Continues*** *Language Teaching & Linguistics. Abstracts, 0306-6304.*
Desc: A compact digest of current thinking on both the theoretical and practical aspects of using, learning and teaching languages. Relevant research in related disciplines is covered as well as the teaching of particular languages. Each issue also contains an original and authoritative state-of-the-art article which surveys an important aspect of the field. A review of research in applied linguistics relevant to language teaching is also included annually.
Ind/Abst Br. Educ. Index; MLA Int. Bibl. Books Artic. Mod. Lang. Lit.

US/0888-8027
LINGUISTICS AND LANGUAGE BEHAVIOR ABSTRACTS. (LINGUISTICS AND LANGUAGE BEHAVIOR ABSTRACTS : LLBA.). [Linguist. lang. behav. abstr.]. **VFOAT** LLBA. Vol. 19, No. 1 (April 1985)-. Abstracting/Indexing Service. English. Five times a year. $240.00 US, Canada, Europe and Asia except India, Sri Lanka, Pakistan, South Africa, Australia, New Zealand and Venezuela; $180.00 other. Sociological Abstracts, PO Box 22206, San Diego CA 92192-0206. **Tel** (619)695-8803, FAX (619)695-0416. **ED** Lynette Hunter. **DD** 016. **NLM** Z 7004.P4; L106. **CODEN** LLBAAZ. **[CCC].** Index available. cum. index. **Bk Rev. Ad Acc. Circ:** 900. available on CD-ROM (as LLBA Disc) from SilverPlatter (US); available on an online database (as file LITS2) from DIALOG; (as file label LLBA on Knowledge Index) BRS/Colleague; (as file 36) BRS; and (as file label LLBA) DIALOG; available on microfilm from University Microfilms International (UMI). Documents available. ***Continues*** *Language and Language Behavior Abstracts, 0023-8295;* ***Absorbed*** *Reading Abstracts.*
Desc: LLBA presents nonevaluative abstracts of articles from around the world, complemented with coverage of recent books, occasional papers, monographs, technical reports, enhanced dissertation listings from Dissertation Abstracts International, and bibliographic citations for book reviews that appear in the journals LLBA abstracts.

US/0024-8215
MLA INTERNATIONAL BIBLIOGRAPHY OF BOOKS AND ARTICLES ON THE MODERN LANGUAGES AND LITERATURES (COMPLETE ED.). (MLA INTERNATIONAL BIBLIOGRAPHY OF BOOKS AND ARTICLES ON THE MODERN LANGUAGES AND LITERATURES (COMPLETE EDITION).). [MLA int. bibl. books artic. mod. lang. lit.]. **Added/Corp** Modern Language Association of America. **VFOAT** International Bibliography of Books and Articles on the Modern Languages and Literatures; MLA Bibliography; MLA International Bibliography. **VAT** Modern Language Association of America International Bibliography of Books and Articles on the Modern Languages and Literatures. (1969)-. Abstracting/Indexing Service. English. an. $950.00. Modern Language Association of America, 10 Astor Place, New York NY 10003-6981. **Tel** (212)614-6382, FAX (212)477-9863. **LC** Z7006; .M64. **Acid Free. Circ:** 3,000 (ctrl). available on CD-ROM from SilverPlatter (US); and (updates online) H W Wilson; available on an online database from OCLC. ***Continues*** *MLA International Bibliography of Books and Articles on the Modern Languages and Literatures, 0024-8215.*
Desc: An index of scholarly and critical works. Also lists dissertation abstracts.

GW
NICHTKONVENTIONELLE LITERATUR LINGUISTIK : INHALTSVERZEICHNIS DER NEUERWERBUNGEN. German (English, French and Spanish). an. Stadt-Und Universitatsbibliothek Frankfurt Am Main, 6000 Frankfurt Am Main 1, Bockenheimer Landstrasse 134-138, Frankfurt Germany. **Tel** (069)7907235, telex 414024 STUB D. **LC** Z7003; .N53; P121. **DD** 016.41/05. **UDC** 800:159; 800:316. Index available. **Circ:** 400 (ctrl).
Desc: Covers speech, language, linguistics, neurolinguistics, psycholinguistics, sociolinguistics, syntax, semantics, phonology and language teaching.

UK/0078-7256
OXFORD SLAVONIC PAPERS. [Oxf. Slav. pap.]. Vol. 1 (1950)-Vol. 13 (1967); New Series, Vol. 1 (1968)-. English. an. £30.00 - £35.00 (depending on volume). Oxford University Press, Walton Street, Oxford OX2 6DP England. **Tel** 011 44 865 56767, FAX 011 44 865 267773, telex 837330 OXPRES G. **(Subscription address:** Oxford University Press / USA, Journals Marketing Department, Oxford University Press, 2001 Evans Road, Cary NC 27513.**)** **LC** PG2025; .O96. **DD** 491.704. **Bk Rev. Ad Acc. Circ:** 1,000 (ctrl). available on microfilm from University Microfilms International (UMI).
Desc: Devoted to publication of original contributions and documents relating to languages, culture and history of Russia and other Slavonic countries. Biographical and review articles are included.
Ind/Abst Am. Hist. Life (1955-); Br. Humanit. Index; MLA Int. Bibl. Books Artic. Mod. Lang. Lit.

US/0892-5941
POMPEIIANA NEWSLETTER. See Linguistics.

CK
PUBLICACIONES DEL INSTITUTO CARO Y CUERVO. SERIE BIBLIOGRAFICA. Added/Corp Instituto Caro y Cuervo. **VFOAT** Serie Bibliografica. (1960)-. Spanish. ir. $18.00 (latest volume). Institute Caro y Cuervo, Apartado Aereo 51502, Bogota Colombia. **Tel** 011 57 1 2557753. **Circ:** 2,000 (ctrl).

US/0092-4423
RESOURCE GUIDE TO READING & LANGUAGE ARTS PROGRAMS & MATERIALS. 1973/74-. English. $1.50. Macmillan Publishing Company, 866 3rd Avenue, New York NY 10022. **Tel** (212)702-2000, (800)257-5755. **(Subscription address:** Front and Brown Street, Riverside, NJ 08370**)** **LC** Z5814.R25; R47. **DD** 016.428/2/07. **UDC** 800.73(01).

GW
ROMANISCHE BIBLIOGRAPHIE / BIBLIOGRAPHIE ROMANE / ROMANCE BIBLIOGRAPHY. VFOAT Bibliographie Romane; Romance Bibliography. (1961/1962)-. Bibliography. German. ir. Price varies per volume. Max Niemeyer Verlag, Postfach 2140, D 72011 Tuebingen Germany. **Tel** 011 49 7071 989494, FAX 011 49 7071 87419. **ED** Gustav Ineichen. **LC** Z7032; .Z45. cum. index. ***Continues*** *Zeitschrift fuer Romanische Philologie. Bibliographie.*
Desc: Bibliography of romance studies, especially in the field of linguistics (French, Spanish, Italian, Romanian, etc.).

US
SELECTED BIBLIOGRAPHIES IN LANGUAGE AND LITERATURE. *Ceased.* **Added/Corp** Modern Language Association of America. (1980)-(19??). Monographic series. English. Modern Language Association of America, 10 Astor Place, New York NY 10003-6981. **Tel** (212)614-6382, FAX (212)477-9863.
Ind/Abst MLA Int. Bibl. Books Artic. Mod. Lang. Lit.

US
SPEECH INDEX. (1935)-. Abstracting/Indexing Service. English. ir. Price varies. Scarecrow Press Inc., 52 Liberty Street, PO Box 4167, Metuchen NJ 08840. **Tel** (908)548-8600, (800)537-7107. **ED** Compiler: 1935-66, Roberta Briggs Sutton; 1966/70, Roberta Briggs Sutton and Charity Mitchell, 1971/75- Charity Mitchell.
Desc: An index to collections of world famous orations and speeches for various occasions.

GW/0506-7944
VERZEICHNIS DER ORIENTALISCHEN HANDSCHRIFTEN IN DEUTSCHLAND. SUPPLEMENTBAND. (1965)-. Monographic series. German (English). ir. Price varies per volume.

Franz Steiner Verlag GmbH, Postfach 101061, D 70009 Stuttgart Germany. **Tel** 011 49 0711 2582372, FAX 011 49 0711 2582290, telex 723636 daz d. **ED** D. George.
Desc: Catalogs of manuscripts in oriental and African languages to be found in German libraries and museums.

LITERARY AND POLITICAL REVIEWS

AT/0001-2793
A.U.M.L.A. **See** Linguistics.

GW
ABHANDLUNGEN. **Main/Corp** Marburger Gelehrten Gesellschaft. (19??)-. Monographic series. German. ir. Price varies per volume. Wilhelm Fink Verlag, Ohmstrasse 5, D 80802 Munich Germany. **Tel** 011 49 89 348017, 348018.
Desc: Monographic series on medieval literature.

US/0361-1663
ABRAXAS (MADISON). **See** Literature-Poetry.

US/0001-3560
ABSTRACTS OF ENGLISH STUDIES. ***Suspended.*** **See** Literary and Political Reviews-Abstracting, Bibliographies and Statistics.

CL/0716-0909
ACTA LITERARIA. **Added/Corp** Universidad de Concepcion. Instituto de Lenguas. Universidad de Concepcion. Departamento de Espanol. No. 1 (1975)-. Periodical. Spanish (French and English). an. $9.00 Chile; $13.00 other. Universidad de Concepcion / Humanidades, Facultad de Educacion, Humanidades y Arte, Administracion de RLA, Casilla 82-C, Correo 3,, Concepcion Chile. **Tel** 011 56 41 234985 Ext. 2313, telex 259108. **ED** Luis Munoz. **LC** PN1; .A28. **DD** 809. Index available. cum. index. **Bk Rev.** **Circ:** 600 (ctrl).
Desc: Theoretical literary studies; critical, historical and bibliographic analyses, preferably related to Spanish literatures.
Ind/Abst MLA Int. Bibl. Books Artic. Mod. Lang. Lit.

UA
AFKAR. Periodical. Arabic. Al-Markaz Al-Arabi Lil-Funun Wa-Al-Lugnat, 7 B Shari Al-Diwan, Garden City, Cairo Egypt. **LC** AP95.A6; A383.

II
ALIVE. (19??)-. Periodical. English. Twenty-six times a year. $60.00. Delhi Press Patra Prakashan Pvt Ltd, 3E Jhandewala Estate, New Delhi 110 055 India. **Tel** 526222. **(Subscription address:** Prints India, 11 Darya Ganj, New Delhi 110002 India.**)** **LC** AP8; .C25. **DD** 954/.005. ***Continues** Caravan.*

US/0162-8208
ALTADENA REVIEW, THE. ***Ceased.*** [Altadena rev.]. Vol. 1 (Summer 1978)-?. Periodical. English. ir. The Altadena Review Inc, PO Box 212, Altadena CA 91001. **ED** Robin Shectman. **Bk Rev.** **Circ:** 200 (ctrl).
Desc: Poetry, reviews of books of poetry, interviews with poets and articles of interest to poetry writers and readers.
Ind/Abst Am. Humanit. Index.

GW
ALTDEUTSCHE TEXTE IN KRITISCHEN AUSGABEN. (1969)-. Monographic series. German. ir. Price varies per volume. Wilhelm Fink Verlag, Ohmstrasse 5, D 80802 Munich Germany. **Tel** 011 49 89 348017, 348018. **ED** Werner Schroder.

US/0149-9408
AMERICAN BOOK REVIEW, THE. [Am. book rev.]. Vol. 1 (Dec. 1977)-. English. bm. $24.00 (one year), $40.00 (two year) Individual; $30.00 (one year), $52.00 (two year) Institution. American Book Review, English Department Publications Center, Box 494, University of Colorado, Boulder CO 80309. **Tel** (303)492-8947. **ED** John Tytell, Rochelle Ratner, and Donald Laing. **DD** 015. Index available (June). cum. index. **Bk Rev.** **Ad Acc.** **Circ:** 15,000. Documents available from The Genuine Article.
Desc: The only nationally distributed review medium which treats with equal seriousness, the literary publications of the small, large, and university, regional, minority and feminist presses.
Ind/Abst Am. Humanit. Index; Arts Humanit. Citation Index [Full Cov.]; Book Rev. Digest; Book Rev. Index; Curr. Contents Arts Humanit.; Res. Alert [Full Cov.]; Soc. Sci. Cit. Index [Select. Cov.].

US/0002-9823
AMERICAN LITERARY REALISM, 1870-1910. [Am. lit. .ealism 1870-1910]. **Added/Corp** University of Texas at Arlington. Dept. of English. **VAT** American Literary Realism, Eighteen Hundred and Seventy, Nineteen Hundred and Ten. No. 1 (Fall 1967)-. Periodical. English. Three times a year (Jan,, May, Oct.). $25.00 US; $31.00 other. McFarland & Company, PO Box 611, Jefferson NC 28640. **Tel** (919)246-4460, FAX (919)246-5018. **ED** Robert E. Fleming and Gary Scharnhorst. **Bk Rev.** **Ad Acc.** **Circ:** 600. Documents available from The Genuine Article.
Desc: Bibliographic and critical material dealing with American Realism 1870-1910.
Ind/Abst Abstr. Engl. Stud.; Am. Hist. Life (1974-); Am. Humanit. Index (199?-); Annu. Bibliogr. Engl. Lang. Lit.; Arts Humanit. Citation Index [Full Cov.]; Child. Lit. Abstr. (19??-); Curr. Contents Arts Humanit.; Index Book Rev. Humanit.; MLA Int. Bibl. Books Artic. Mod. Lang. Lit.; Ref. Sources; Res. Alert [Full Cov.]; Soc. Sci. Cit. Index [Select. Cov.]; West. Hist. Q.

US/0360-3709
AMERICAN POETRY REVIEW, THE. **See** Literature-Poetry.

US/0148-8414
AMERICAN SPECTATOR (ARLINGTON, VA.), THE. (THE AMERICAN SPECTATOR.). [Am. spect.]. **Added/Corp** Saturday Evening Club. Vol. 11, (Nov. 1977)-. Periodical. English. mo. $35.00. The American Spectator, 2020 North 14th Street, PO Box 549, Arlington VA 22216. **Tel** (703)243-3733, (800)341-1522. **ED** R Emmett Tyrrell Jr. **LC** AP2; .A31058. **DD** 051. Index available. **Bk Rev.** **Ad Acc.** **Circ:** 42,000. available on microfilm and microfiche from University Microfilms International (UMI); available on CD-ROM. Documents available from UMI Article Clearinghouse. ***Continues** Alternative, 0044-7382.*
Desc: An influential journal of public opinion, features investigative reporting, comprehensive book reviews, and informed analysis of current political and cultural affairs.
Ind/Abst Acad. Abstr. Full Text Elite (July 1989-); Acad. Abstr. (July 1989-); Acad. Search (July 1989-); Access (1978-1988); Am. Bibliogr. Slavic East Europ. Stud.; Book Rev. Index; Chicano Index; Expand. Acad. Index (1992-); Gen. Period. Index; Index Period. Artic. Relat. Law; INFO-SOUTH Abstr.; Mag. Artic. Summar. Elite (July 1989-); Mag. Artic. Summar. Select (July 1989-); Mag. Artic. Summar. CD-ROM (July 1989-); Mag. Index Plus (1989-); Mag. Index. Sel. (1989-); Mag. Search; Middle East Abstr. Index; Newsp. Period. Abstr. (1988-); PAIS Int. Print (1991-); Pop. Period. Index; Read. Guide Abstr. Select Ed.; Read. Guide Period. Lit.; Mag. Index (1989-); Vocat. Search (July 1989-).

US/1049-815X
AMERICAN WRITING (PHILADELPHIA, PA.). **See** The Arts.

JA/0387-2815
AMERIKA KENKYU (TOKYO. 1967). (AMERIKA KENKYU.). [Amerika kenkyua]. **VFOAT** The American Review. Japanese (summaries and/or abstracts in English). Tokyo Daigaku Kyoyobu, c/o Center for American Studies, 8-1 Komaba 3 Meguro-ku (153), Tokyo Japan. **LC** E151; .A595.

●US/1058-5915
AMS HENRY JAMES STUDIES. **See** Literature.

US/0569-9924
ANALES GALDOSIANOS. **Added/Corp** University of Pittsburgh. Vol. 1 (1966)-. English (Spanish). an (Annual & Supplement). Queens University Department of Spanish and Italian, Kingston K7L 3N6 Canada. **Tel** (613)545-2113. **ED** John W. Kronik. **LC** PQ6555.Z5; A68. **DD** 863/.5. **Bk Rev.** **Ad Acc.** **Circ:** 1,000 (ctrl).
Desc: Articles and reviews on Benito Perez Galdos and 19th century Spanish literature.
Ind/Abst MLA Int. Bibl. Books Artic. Mod. Lang. Lit.

IT
ANCORA. (19??)-. Italian. wk. L55000.00. l'Ancora, Piazza Duomo 7, 15011 Acqui Terme Italy. **Tel** 011 39 144 323767.

SZ
ANGLO AMERICAN FORUM. English. ir. 58.00F. Verlag Peter Lang AG, Jupiterstrasse 15, CH-3000 Bern 15 Switzerland. **Tel** 011 41 31 9411122, FAX 011 41 31 321131.
Ind/Abst MLA Int. Bibl. Books Artic. Mod. Lang. Lit.

II/0378-1143
ANNALS OF THE BHANDARKAR ORIENTAL RESEARCH INSTITUTE. **See** Linguistics.

CN/0003-5661
ANTIGONISH REVIEW, THE. [Antigonish rev.]. **Added/Corp** St. Francis Xavier University. Dept. of English. St. Francis Xavier University. Vol. 1 (Spring 1970)-. Periodical. English (French). Four times a year (Seasonally). 20.00Can$. St. Francis Xavier University, PO Box 135, Antigonish Nova Scotia B2G 1C0 Canada. **Tel** (902)867-3962, FAX (902)867-5153. **ED** George S. Sanderson. **LC** PN2; .A65. Index available (bound every fourth issue). cum. index. **Bk Rev**, (Qty: 12). Half Page (Color) 50. **Circ:** 800 (ctrl). available on microfiche from Micromedia Limited. Documents available from The Genuine Article.
Desc: Features poetry, fiction, reviews and critical articles from all parts of Canada, the United States and overseas. Original graphics used extensively to enliven the format. Prefers to introduce and promote new and unknown authors rather than rely upon established writers. Each issue contains the work of 20 to 30 poets, 5 or 6 fiction writers, reviews of 10 to 15 books and two or three general interest articles.
Ind/Abst Abstr. Engl. Stud.; Arts Humanit. Citation Index [Full Cov.]; Can. Index; Can. Period. Index; Curr. Contents Arts Humanit.; Curr. Contents Soc. Behav. Sci.; Index Am. Period. Verse; MLA Int. Bibl. Books Artic. Mod. Lang. Lit.; Res. Alert [Full Cov.]; Soc. Sci. Cit. Index [Select. Cov.].

US/0003-5769
ANTIOCH REVIEW, THE. [Antioch rev.]. Vol. 1 (Spring 1941)-. Periodical. English. Four times a year (Feb., May, Aug., Nov.,). $42.00 (institutions); $30.00 (individual). Antioch Review, PO Box 148, Yellow Springs OH 45387. **Tel** (513)767-6389. **ED** Robert S. Fogarty. **LC** AP2; .A562. **DD** 051. Index available (bound in fall issue). cum. index. **Bk Rev.** **Ad Acc.** **Circ:** 4,500. available on microfilm and microfiche from University Microfilms International (UMI); available on CD-ROM and an online database from H W Wilson. Documents available from UMI Article Clearinghouse. ***Absorbed** Monocle.*
Desc: A distinguished, well-established literary journal. Prints lively and cogent essays and critical analyses on political and social issues, fiction, poetry, polemics and book reviews. Occasional special issues on a topic of contemporary interest and importance.
Ind/Abst Abstr. Engl. Stud.; Acad. Search (July 1993-); Am. Hist. Life (1963-); Am. Bibliogr. Slavic East Europ. Stud.; Am. Humanit. Index; Annu. Bibliogr. Engl. Lang. Lit.; Arts Humanit. Citation Index [Full Cov.]; Book Rev. Digest; Book Rev. Index; Curr. Contents Arts Humanit.; Expand. Acad. Index (1989-); Film Lit. Index; Humanit. Index; Humanit. Source (July 1993-); Index Am. Period. Verse; INFO-SOUTH Abstr.; Linguist. Lang. Behav. Abstr.; Lit. Crit. Regist.; Mag. Search; MLA Int. Bibl. Books Artic. Mod. Lang. Lit.; Newsp. Period. Abstr. (1991-); Philos. Index; Res. Alert [Full Cov.]; Romant. Move.; Sage Public Adm. Abstr.; Soc. Plann. Policy Dev. Abstr.; Soc. Sci. Cit. Index [Select. Cov.]; Sociol. Abstr.

IT
APPUNTI DEL CIRCOLO CULTURALE G GHISLANDI. ***Ceased.*** (19??)-(Dec. 1992). Italian. Four times a year. Circolo Culturale G Ghislandi, Piazza Sant Antonio 2, 25043 Breno BS Italy. **Tel** 011 39 364 535248. **Bk Rev**, (Qty: 4/y). **Ad Acc.**

GW
ARBITRIUM : ZEITSCHRIFT FUER REZENSIONEN ZUR GERMANISTISCHEN LITERATURWISSENSCHAFT. [Arbitrium]. Vol. 1, Jan. Issue 1 (19??)-. Academic Scholarly Publication. German (English). Three times a year. DM108.00. Max Niemeyer Verlag, Postfach 2140, D 72011 Tuebingen Germany. **Tel** 011 49 7071 989494, FAX 011 49 7071 87419. **ED** Wolfgang Fruehwald and Wolfgand Harms. **Bk Rev.** **Ad Acc.** **Circ:** 500 (ctrl).
Desc: Reviews of scholarly books on German literature. Criticism.
Ind/Abst Romant. Move.

UK
ASSOCIATION FOR SCOTTISH LITERARY STUDIES. **Main/Corp** Association for Scottish Literary Studies. (19??)-. Monographic series. English. ir. £50.00 one year (membership). Association for Scottish Literary Studies, University of Aberdeen, Department of English, Taylor Buildings, Aberdeen AB9 2UB Scotland. **Tel** 011 44 224 272634.

CN/0316-5981
ATLANTIC PROVINCES BOOK REVIEW, THE. ***Title Change.*** [Atl. prov. book rev.]. **Added/Corp** Saint Mary's University. (Nov. 1974)-(1992). Periodical. English. qt. Atlantic Provinces Book Review, PO Box 1132, Bedford Nova Scotia Canada. **Tel** (902)420-5716. **ED** David Pigot. **DD** 028.1/05. **Bk Rev.** **Ad Acc.** **Circ:** 55,000 (ctrl). ***Continued by** Atlantic Books Today, 1192-3652.*
Desc: Atlantic Canada's national publication devoted to the review of Atlantic-directed books. Each issue contains 50 to 75 reviews of books about the region, published in Atlantic Canada or written by Atlantic Canadians, although important Canadian books also receive consideration. Distributed to individual subscribers, schools, libraries and universities across Canada.
Ind/Abst Book Rev. Index; Can. Index (?-?); Can. Period. Index.

FR
AU JOUR LE SIECLE. 1-. Monographic series. French. Price varies per volume. 73 rue du Cardinal-Lemoine, 75005 Paris France.

GW/0171-6530
AURORA-BUCHREIHE. **See** Biographies.

AT/0155-2864
AUSTRALIAN BOOK REVIEW. No. 1 (June 1978)-. Periodical. English. mo. Australian Book Review, PO Box 89, Parkville 3052 Australia. ***Supersedes** Australian Book Review.*
Ind/Abst Aust. Educ. Index (1978-19??); Book Rev. Index; Child. Lit. Abstr. (19??-).

AT/1036-1669
AUSTRALIAN LITERARY AWARDS AND FELLOWSHIPS. [Aust. lit. award. fellowsh.]. **VFOAT** ALAF. (1991)-. English. an. 30.00Aus$. D. W. Thorpe, A Reed Reference Publishing Company, A Subsidiary of Reed International Books Australia, 18 Salmon Street, Port Melbourne, Victoria 3207 Australia. **Tel** 011 61 3 6451511, FAX 011 61 3 6453981, telex 39476. **DD** 807.99405.
Desc: Provides comprehensive information on Australia's numerous literary prizes, scholarships and grants. Full details are provided, including entry deadlines, award announcement dates, prize money, eligibility criteria and contacts for the awards and fellowships.

AT/0004-9697
AUSTRALIAN LITERARY STUDIES. [Aust. lit. stud.]. **Added/Corp** University of Tasmania. Vol. 1 (June 1963)-. Academic Scholarly Publication. English. sa. 27.50Aus$ (regular & school libraries), 38.50Aus$ (tertiary institutions / libraries) Australia; 33.00Aus$ (individuals), 45.00Aus$ (institutions) other. University of Queensland Press, PO Box 42, St Lucia Queensland 4067 Australia. **Tel** 011 61 7 3652127, FAX 011 61 7 3651988, telex UNIVQLD AA40315. **ED** Laurie Hergenhan. **LC** PR9400; .A86. **DD** 820/.9/994. Index available. **Bk Rev**. **Ad Acc. Circ:** 1,200. available on microfilm and microfiche from University Microfilms International (UMI). Documents available from The Genuine Article.
Desc: Historical scholarly and critical articles; bibliographies and biographical information; interviews, reviews, lists of current research.
Ind/Abst Abstr. Engl. Stud.; Annu. Bibliogr. Engl. Lang. Lit.; APAIS, Aust. Public Aff. Inf. Ser. (1963-); Arts Humanit. Citation Index [Full Cov.]; Curr. Contents Arts Humanit.; Lit. Crit. Regist.; MLA Int. Bibl. Books Artic. Mod. Lang. Lit.; Res. Alert [Full Cov.]; Soc. Sci. Cit. Index [Select. Cov.].

US/0278-551X
AXIOS (LOS ANGELES, CALIF.). (AXIOS.). [Axios]. **VFOAT** Axios Newsletter. (1981)-. Periodical. English. bm. Axios Inc, 800 South Euclid Street, Fullerton CA 92632. **Tel** (714)526-6257. **ED** Daniel John Gorham. **DD** 281. **Bk Rev. Circ:** 14,601.
Desc: To challenge, provoke and startle.

AJ/0365-8554
AZERBAJDZANSKOR NEFTJANOE HOZJAJSTVO. (AZERBAIDZHANSKOE NEFTIANOE KHOZIAISTVO.). [Azerb. neft. hoz.]. **VFOAT** Azarbaijan Neft Tasarrufaty. (Dec. 1921)-. Academic Scholarly Publication. Russian (Azerbaijani). Twelve times a year. $79.00. **(Subscription address:** East View Publications Inc., 3020 Harbor Lane North, Suite 110, Minneapolis MN 55447.) **CODEN** AZNKAY. **[CCC].** Index available in last issue of volume--attached. Documents available from CASDDS. ***Continues*** *Narodnoe Khoziaistvo.*
Ind/Abst Chem. Abstr.; GeoRef.

US/1052-3154
BAKUNIN (DAVIS, CALIF.). (BAKUNIN.). [Bakunin]. No. 1 (Spring 1990)-. Periodical. English. an (Mar.). $10.00 (individuals), $20.00 (institutions). Bakunin, PO Box 1853, Simi Valley CA 93062. **Tel** (805)526-8900. **ED** Jordan Jones. **DD** 810. **Bk Rev**, (Qty: 15). **Ad Acc. Circ:** 1,000.
Desc: A magazine of poetry, fiction, essays, art works, and reviews. Much of this work though not all has a leftist political slant.

US/0149-0354
BARATARIA. Periodical. English. Three times a year. $5.00. Barataria, PO Box 15060, New Orleans LA 70175. ***Supersedes*** *Barataria Review.*

GW/0067-5202
BEITRAEGE ZUR ROMANISCHEN PHILOLOGIE DES MITTELALTERS. (1968)-. Monographic series. German (French). ir. Price varies per volume. Wilhelm Fink Verlag, Ohmstrasse 5, D 80802 Munich Germany. **Tel** 011 49 89 348017, 348018. **ED** Hans-Wilhelm Klein and Ernstpeter Ruhe.
Desc: Publishes monographic studies and criticism of medieval Romanic philology.

IT/0005-8351
BELFAGOR. [Belfagor]. Vol. 1 (Jan. 1946)-. Periodical. Italian. Six times a year (Jan., Mar., May, July, Sept., Nov.). L63000 Italy; L98000 others. Casa Editrice Leo S. Olschki, Viuzzo del Pozzetto, Casella Postale 66, 50126 Florence Italy. **Tel** 011 39 55 6530684, FAX 011 39 55 6530214. **LC** AP37; .B45. **DD** 055.1. Index Available, published separately, free-automatically sent. Documents available from The Genuine Article.
Ind/Abst Am. Hist. Life (1978-); Arts Humanit. Citation Index [Full Cov.]; Curr. Contents Arts Humanit.; MLA Int. Bibl. Books Artic. Mod. Lang. Lit.; Res. Alert [Full Cov.]; Romant. Move. (1978-); Soc. Sci. Cit. Index [Select. Cov.].

US/0191-7080
BERKELEY MONTHLY, THE. (19??)-. Periodical. English. Twelve times a year. $10.00. Berkeley Monthly, 910 Parker Street, Berkeley CA 94710. **Tel** (510)848-7900. **ED** Tracy Johnston. **Bk Rev. Ad Acc. Circ:** 80,000 (ctrl).
Desc: Emphasis on good writing above all, and covers the arts, local personalities and politics. Of special concern is humor, fun, and off-beat personal stories.

US
BERKELEY POETRY REVIEW, THE. No. 1 (Fall 1974)-. Periodical. English. an. $12.00. Berkeley Poetry Review, 700 Eshleman Hall, UC Berkeley, Berkeley CA 94720. **Tel** (510)540-8913. **DD** 810.

IT/0519-6396
BIBLIOTECA DI STUDI AMERICANI. ***Suspended.*** (Began in 1954)-(Suspended). Monographic series. Italian. ir. Price varies per volume. Edizioni di Storia e Letteratura, Via Lancellotti 18, Rome 00186 Italy. **Tel** 011 39 6 68806556. **ED** Agostino Lombardo. **Circ:** 700.
Desc: Studies on American literature and poetry.

IS
BIKORET U-FARSHANUT. **VFOAT** Criticism and Interpretation. 1- Mar. 1970-. Periodical. Hebrew (summaries and/or abstracts in English). ir. Bar-Ilan University Press, Ramat-Gan 52900 Israel. **Tel** 011 972 3 5318355, FAX 011 972 3 3476 01. **ED** Avraham Shaanan, H Weiss. Index available. cum. index. **Bk Rev. Circ:** 500 (ctrl).
Desc: Jewish studies in literature, linguistics, history and aesthetics.
Ind/Abst MLA Int. Bibl. Books Artic. Mod. Lang. Lit.

US/0193-7782
BILL-DALE MARCINKO'S AFTA. **VFOAT** Afta. Periodical. English. qt. $8.00. Bill Dale Marcinko Editor, 153 George Street/Apartment 2, New Brunswick NJ 08901. **Tel** (201)828-5467. **ED** Bill Dale Marcinko. **Bk Rev. Ad Acc. Circ:** 25,000.
Desc: Reviews, books, comics, films, videotapes, record albums, new publications, and covers political and sexual issues, especially relating to homosexuality, lesbianism, and feminism.

US/0006-3932
BITZARON. ***Ceased.*** **See** Religion and Theology-Judaism.

US/0193-6301
BLACK WARRIOR REVIEW, THE. [Black warrior rev.]. **Added/Corp** University of Alabama. **VFOAT** BWR; B.W.R. Vol. 1, No. 1 (Fall 1974)-. Periodical. English. Twice a year (Mar. & Oct.). $11.00 (individual); $17.00 (institution). Black Warrior Review, Box 2936, University AL 35487. **Tel** (205)348-4518. **ED** Leigh Ann Sackrider. **LC** PS1; .B55. **DD** 810/.5. Index available. **Bk Rev**, (Qty: 4-8). **Ad Acc, Adv Mgr:** Mark Drew. **Circ:** 1,500 (ctrl).
Desc: It features poetry, fiction, essays, and reviews by both established and developing writers.
Ind/Abst Am. Humanit. Index; Book Rev. Index (-1982); Index Am. Period. Verse; Lit. Crit. Regist.; MLA Int. Bibl. Books Artic. Mod. Lang. Lit.

FR/0982-8648
BLAIREAU PARIS. (BLAIREAU.). **Added/Corp** Association Generale des Institutrices et Instituteurs des Ecoles et Classes Maternelles Publiques (France). (1987)-. Periodical. French. mo (11 issues per year). 352.00F France, French-speaking Africa & Dom Tom; 376.00F other. Fleurus Presse International, 21 rue Faubourg St Antoine, 75550 Paris Cedex 11 France. **Tel** 011 33 1 40026300. **(Subscription address:** Fleurus Presse Service Abbonnements, BP 72, 77932 Perthes Cedex France.) **UDC** 087.5.

US/0160-628X
BLAKE. **See** The Arts.

US/0276-1564
BLOOMSBURY REVIEW, THE. [Bloomsbury rev.]. (198?)-. Periodical. English. Eight times a year. $18.00 (one year), $30.00 (two years), $42.00 (three years). Owaissa Communications Company Inc, PO Box 8928, Denver CO 80201. **Tel** (303)892-0620, FAX (303)892-5620. **ED** Thomas Auer. **DD** 028. **Bk Rev. Ad Acc. Circ:** 50,000 (ctrl).
Desc: National and international books reviewed. Interviews with authors, essays about important writers, topical issues, and poetry and book notices.
Ind/Abst Am. Bibliogr. Slavic East Europ. Stud. (19??-19??); Am. Humanit. Index (-199?); Book Rev. Index (1988-); Lit. Crit. Regist.

US/0882-648X
BOGG (ARLINGTON, VA.). **See** Literature.

US/0094-9426
BOOK FORUM. [Book forum]. Vol. 1 (Summer 1974)-. Academic Scholarly Publication. English. qt. $24.00 institutions, $18.00 individuals. Book Forum, PO Box 585, C/O Clarence Driskill, Niantic CT 06357. **Tel** (212)861-8328, (203)739-9497. **ED** Marilyn Wood. **LC** AS30; .B65. **DD** 052. Index available. **Bk Rev. Ad Acc. Circ:** 5,000.
Desc: Discussion of current literary and social issues as reflected in current scholarly books.
Ind/Abst Abstr. Engl. Stud.; Am. Humanit. Index (-199?); Annu. Bibliogr. Engl. Lang. Lit.; Book Rev. Index (?-Nov. 1988); Middle East Abstr. Index; MLA Int. Bibl. Books Artic. Mod. Lang. Lit.; Romant. Move.

US/1043-352X
BOOK NEWSLETTER (MINNEAPOLIS, MINN.). (BOOK NEWSLETTER.). [Book newsl.]. Newsletter. English. qt. Free. Augsburg Fortress Publishers, 426 South Fifth Street, Box 1209, Minneapolis MN 55440. **Tel** (800)328-4648, (612)330-3300. **ED** Roderick D Olson. Index available. **Bk Rev. Circ:** 37,000 (ctrl). ***Continues*** *Book Newsletter of Augsburg Publishing House, 0006-7296.*
Desc: Reviews of current religious books.

US/0006-7326
BOOK REVIEW DIGEST. **See** Literary and Political Reviews-Abstracting, Bibliographies and Statistics.

US/0145-627X
BOOK TALK (ALBUQUERQUE). **See** Publishing-Books and Bookmaking.

UK/0006-7482
BOOKS FOR YOUR CHILDREN. [Books child.]. Vol. 1 (1966)-. English. Three times a year. £8.00 UK; £10.00 other. Ragdoll Productions UK Ltd., PO Box 507, Birmingham B4 6BR England. **Tel** 011 44 21 643-6411, FAX 011 44 21 643-3152. **ED** Anne Wood. **LC** Z1037.A1; B59. **DD** 028.1. **Bk Rev**, (Qty: 200). **Ad Acc, Adv Mgr Tel** same as publisher. **Circ:** 12,000 (ctrl). available on microfilm from University Microfilms International (UMI).
Desc: Review of children's books both newly published and those republished to enable parents to select suitable books for their children.
Ind/Abst Book Rev. Index; Child. Lit. Abstr. (19??-).

GW
BOTE, DER. Periodical. German. 15.-. Walterhstr 28, 8000 Munchen 2 Germany. **Tel** (089)533328. **ED** Heinz Jacobi. **LC** PT1141.A2; M38. **Bk Rev. Circ:** 1,000. ***Continues*** *Martin-Greif-Bote.*
Desc: Works of Heinz Jacobi.

US
BRAZIL. (BRAZIL; A JOURNAL OF BRAZILIAN LITERATURE.). **VFOAT** Brasil. English (Portuguese). sa. $40.00. Brown University / Department of Portugese & Brazilian Studies, PO Box O, Providence RI 02912. **Tel** (401)863-3042, FAX (401)863-7261. **ED** Nelson H Vieira and Regina Zilberman. **Bk Rev. Circ:** 120.

CN/0382-8565
BRICK. [Brick]. No. 1 (April 1977)-. Periodical. English. Three times a year (Winter, Spring and Fall). 14.00Can$ institution, 10.00Can$ individual (Canada); 19.00Can$ institution, 15.00Can$ individual (other). Brick, Box 537 Station Q, Toronto Ontario M4T 2M5 Canada. **Tel** (416)466-7010. **ED** Linda Spalding. **LC** Z1035.A1; B714. **DD** 028.1; 028.1/05. **Bk Rev**, (Qty: 10). **Circ:** 2,000 (ctrl). available on microfilm.
Desc: A journal of literary reviews and essays on art.
Ind/Abst Can. Index (?-?); Can. Period. Index (19??-); World Ceram. Abstr.

US
BROADSIDE CRITICS SERIES. Monographic series. English. ir. Price varies per volume. Broadside, PO Box 04257, Detroit MI 48204-0257.

US/0883-2846
BROOKLYN LITERARY REVIEW. **See** College and School Publications-Alumni.

US/0007-2869
BUCKNELL REVIEW. [Bucknell rev.]. **Added/Corp** Bucknell University. Vol. 5, No. 1 (Dec. 1954)-. Periodical. English. Twice a year (Jan., Sept.). Associated University Presses, 440 Forsgate Drive, Cranbury NJ 08512. **Tel** (609)655-4770, FAX (609)655-8366. **ED** Pauline Fletcher. **LC** AP2; .B887. available on microfilm and microfiche from University Microfilms International (UMI). ***Continues*** *Bucknell University Studies.*
Ind/Abst Am. Hist. Life (1966-1973); Annu. Bibliogr. Engl. Lang. Lit.; BHA : Biblio. Hist. Art; MLA Int. Bibl. Books Artic. Mod. Lang. Lit.; Soc. Plann. Policy Dev. Abstr.; Sociol. Abstr. (?-19??).

CN/0821-6886
BULLETIN BAKHTINE, LE. [Bull. Bakhtine]. **VFOAT** Bakhtin Newsletter. No. 1 (1983)-. English (French). te (every three years). 8.00Can$. Revue Frontenac, Queens University, Department of French Studiews, Kingston Ontario K7L 3N6 Canada. **Tel** (613)545-2094. **ED** Clive Thomson. **DD** 016.801/95/05. cum. index. **Bk Rev. Ad Acc. Circ:** 200 (ctrl).
Desc: Bibliographical and reviews on Mikhail Bakhtin and the Bakhtin circle.

FR/0007-4209
BULLETIN CRITIQUE DU LIVRE FRANCAIS. [Bull. crit. livre fr.]. Vol. 1 (July/Oct. I.E. Sept. 1945)-. Bulletin. French. mo. 260.00F. Association Pour la Diffusion de la Pensee Francaise, 9 rue Anatole de la Froge, 75017 Paris France. **Tel** 227-32-97. **ED** Claude Boulet. **LC** Z2165. **DD** 015.44. **Bk Rev. Ad Acc.**

Circ: 5,000.
Desc: Review of recently published French books (literature, science and technology, the humanities and social sciences).
Ind/Abst Romant. Move.

BE
BULLETIN DE LA CLASSE DES LETTRES ET DES SCIENCES MORALES ET POLITIQUES. **Main/Corp** Academie Royale des Sciences, des Lettres et des Beaux-Arts de Belgique, Brussels. Classe des Lettres et des Sciences Morales et Politiques. Began in 1919. Bulletin. French. mo. 1.200F. Academie Royale de Medecine de Belgique, Palais Academies, rue Decale 1, 1000 Bruxelles Belgium. **Tel** 11 32 2 5112471, FAX (02)502-0712. Index available in last issue of volume--attached. **Circ:** 500 (ctrl). ***Continues in part*** *Bulletins de la Classe des Lettres et des Sciences Morales.*
Desc: Literary and political reviews.
Ind/Abst Am. Hist. Life (1954-); BHA : Biblio. Hist. Art; Numis. Lit.

FR/0338-0548
BULLETIN D'INFORMATIONS PROUSTIENNES. **Added/Corp** Ecole Normale Superieure (France) Centre d'Histoire et d'Analyse des Manuscrits Modernes. (Spring 1975)-. Bulletin. French. an. 142.18F France; 161.23F other. Presses de l'Ecole Normale Superieure, 45 rue d'Ulm, 75230 Paris France. **Tel** 011 33 1 43291225. **LC** PQ2631.R63; Z54545. **DD** 843/.912. **Circ:** 500.
Desc: Analysis of Marcel Proust's manuscripts. Bibliography of Proustian studies.
Ind/Abst Romant. Move.

●US
BULLETIN / SCIENCE FICTION AND FANTASY WRITERS OF AMERICA. **See** Literature.

UK/0301-7257
BYRON JOURNAL. (THE BYRON JOURNAL.). [Byron j.]. **Added/Corp** Byron Society. No. 1 (1973)-. Academic Scholarly Publication. English. an (April). Comes with Byron Society Institutional membership; $12.00 (membership). Byron Society Journal Ltd., 259 New Jersey Avenue, Collingswood NJ 08108. **Tel** (212)854-4632. **ED** Bernard Beatly. **LC** PR4379; .B78. **DD** 821/.7. **Bk Rev. Ad Acc. Circ:** 3,000 (ctrl). Documents available from The Genuine Article.
Desc: Scholarly articles, essays, and book reviews concerning the English Romantic poet, Lord Byron, and his circle.
Ind/Abst Arts Humanit. Citation Index [Full Cov.]; Curr. Contents Arts Humanit.; MLA Int. Bibl. Books Artic. Mod. Lang. Lit.; Res. Alert [Full Cov.]; Romant. Move.

US/0091-3421
C.L.C. CONTEMPORARY LITERARY CRITICISM. (CONTEMPORARY LITERARY CRITICISM.). **VFOAT** C.L.C. No. 1 (1973)-. Monographic series. English. ir. $115.00. Gale Research Inc., 835 Penobscot Building, Detroit MI 48226. **Tel** (800)877-GALE, (313)961-2242, FAX (313)961-6083, telex TWX 810-221-7086. **ED** Roger Matuz. **LC** PN771; .C59. **DD** 809/.04.
Desc: Recent criticism and evaluations of both new and established contemporary authors who are living or have died since 1959. A strong emphasis is placed on criticisms of authors who frequently appear on syllabuses of high school and college literature courses. There are about 15 author entries and about 350 individual excerpts per volume. The primary focus is on novelists, dramatists, poets, and short story writers. Scriptwriters and other creative writers are also evaluated from a literary perspective.

FR
CAHIERS CRITIQUES DE LA LITTERATURE. No. 1-4 (Sept., 1976)-(Fall 1978); New Series, No. 1/2 (Sept. 1979)-. Periodical. French (German). qt. $15.00. Eurographic, 32 rue des Annelets, 75019 Paris France.

FR/0184-7678
CAHIERS ELISABETHAINES. [Cah. elisabeth.]. **VFOAT** Bulletin du Centre d'Etudes et de Recherches Elisabethaines de l'Universite Paul Valery, Montpellier. No. 1 (Jan. 1972)-. Periodical. English (French). sa. 140.00F France; 180.00F other. Universite Paul Valery, BP 5043 Route de Mende, 34032 Montpellier, Cedex 1 France. **Tel** 11 33 67 142000, FAX 011 33 67 142052. **ED** L J Bordt and J M Maguin. **LC** PR1; .C22. **DD** 820/.9/003. Index available. cum. index. **Bk Rev. Ad Acc. Circ:** 450. Documents available from The Genuine Article.
Desc: Intends to bridge the gap between English Renaissance studies carried out in France and those pursued everywhere else in the world.
Ind/Abst Annu. Bibliogr. Engl. Lang. Lit.; Arts Humanit. Citation Index (19??-19??) [Full Cov.]; Curr. Contents Arts Humanit.; MLA Int. Bibl. Books Artic. Mod. Lang. Lit.; Res. Alert [Full Cov.]; Soc. Sci. Cit. Index [Select. Cov.].

FR
CAHIERS HENRI BOSCO. **See** Biographies.

RM/0257-7526
CAHIERS ROUMAINS D'ETUDES LITTERAIRES. [Cah. roum. etud. litt.]. No. 1 (1973)-. Periodical. English (French and German). Four times a year. DM268.00. **(Subscription address:** Kubon & Sagner, ABT Zeitschriftenimport, D 80328 Munich Germany.**) LC** PN1; .C33. **DD** 805.
Desc: Studies on aesthetics, criticism and the history of literature.
Ind/Abst Annu. Bibliogr. Engl. Lang. Lit.; MLA Int. Bibl. Books Artic. Mod. Lang. Lit.; Romant. Move.

FR/0575-1276
CAHIERS STAELIENS. [Cah. Stael.]. **Added/Corp** Societe des Etudes Staeliennes. (March 1962)-. Periodical. French. an. 120.00F. Jean Touzot, 38 rue Saint-Sulpice, 75278 Paris Cedex 06 France. **Tel** 011 33 1 43260388. **ED** Norman King (editor's address: 25 St Vincent Crescent, Glasgow C3 8LQ Grando Bretagne). **DD** 840. Index available. **Bk Rev. Circ:** 500.
Desc: Articles, reviews and documents concerning Germaine de Stael, Benjamin Constant and the Coppet Group.
Ind/Abst MLA Int. Bibl. Books Artic. Mod. Lang. Lit.; Romant. Move.

CU
CAIMAN BARBUDO (MICROFICHE). (EL CAIMAN BARBUDO.). No. 1- Jan. 1966-. Periodical. Spanish. mo. $15.00. Ediciones Cubanas, Obispo 527, Altos ESQ Bernaza, CP 10100 Havana Cuba. **Tel** 011 632980, 631942, FAX 011 631011, telex 512337, 6540. **LC** MICROFILM (O) 86/104. **Circ:** 20,000 (ctrl).
Desc: A cultural tabloid that spreads the creative work of the most outstanding young writers and artists. Contains literary and art criticism, plus articles, features, interviews, chronicles, sketches and essays related to the cultural life of young Cuban creators.

UK/0008-199X
CAMBRIDGE QUARTERLY. (THE CAMBRIDGE QUARTERLY.). [Camb. q.]. Vol. 1 (Winter 1965)-. Periodical. English. qt. £54.00 UK and Europe; $99.00 other. Oxford University Press, Walton Street, Oxford OX2 6DP England. **Tel** 011 44 865 56767, FAX 011 44 865 267773, telex 837330 OXPRES G. **(Subscription address:** Oxford University Press / USA, Journals Marketing Department, Oxford University Press, 2001 Evans Road, Cary NC 27513.**) ED** D.C. Gervais, R.D. Gooder, H.A. Mason, A.P. Newton and F.M. Rosslyn. **[CCC].** Index available. cum. index. **Bk Rev. Ad Acc. Circ:** 650. available on microfilm and microfiche from University Microfilms International (UMI). Documents available from The Genuine Article.
Desc: Principally literary criticism, but also articles on painting, sculpture, music and cinema. Each issue contains reviews of important new books as well as major articles on classic and contemporary work.
Ind/Abst Abstr. Engl. Stud.; Annu. Bibliogr. Engl. Lang. Lit.; Arts Humanit. Citation Index [Full Cov.]; BHA : Biblio. Hist. Art; Br. Humanit. Index; Curr. Contents Arts Humanit.; Humanit. Index; Middle East Abstr. Index; MLA Int. Bibl. Books Artic. Mod. Lang. Lit.; Res. Alert [Full Cov.]; Romant. Move.

UK/0950-6322
CAMBRIDGE STUDIES IN FRENCH. **See** Philosophy.

IT/1121-2993
CAMMINANDO INSIEME. [Cammin. insieme]. (1991)-. Periodical. Italian. qt. L20000. Assn Studio Prevenz Dipendenze, Usl 6 V le Trento Trieste 2, 33038 S Daniele Friuli Italy. **Tel** 011 39 432 949345.

CN/0383-770X
CANADIAN BOOK REVIEW ANNUAL. (1975)-. English. an (Aug.). 99.95Can$. Joyce M. Wilson, 44 Charles Street West, Suite 3205, Toronto Ontario M4Y 1R8 Canada. **Tel** (416)961-8537. **ED** Joyce Wilson. **LC** F1001; .C224. **DD** 028.1. Index available in last issue of volume--attached. **Bk Rev. Circ:** 2,000.
Desc: Succinct interesting reviews of new Canadian books within five basic categories: reference materials, humanities and applied arts, literature, social sciences, science and technology.

CN/0008-3631
CANADIAN FORUM. (THE CANADIAN FORUM.). [Can. forum]. Vol. 1, No. 1 (Oct. 1920)-. Periodical. English. Ten times a year (Jan./Feb. and July/Aug. issues combined). 22.00Can$ (individuals), 33.00Can$ (institutions) Canada; 39.00Can$ US; 47.00Can$ other. Canadian Forum, 5502 Atlantic, Halifax Nova Scotia B3H 1G4 Canada. **Tel** (902)421-7022, FAX (902)425-0166. **ED** Duncan Cameron (phone: (613)230-3078). **LC** AP5; .C125. **Bk Rev**, (Qty: 40). **Ad Acc, Adv Mgr:** M. Wile. **Circ:** 5,200. available on microfilm and microfiche from University Microfilms International (UMI). Documents available from UMI Article Clearinghouse. ***Continues*** *Rebel;* ***Absorbed*** *Willison's Monthly.*
Desc: Publishes commentary on Canadian political, cultural and artistic life. Analyzes literature, theatre, film and visual art, with award-winning fiction and poetry. Articles on foreign affairs go beyond news and trends.
Ind/Abst Acad. Abstr. Full Text Elite (Jan. 1992-); Acad. Abstr. (Jan. 1992-); Acad. Search (Jan. 1992-); Book Rev. Digest; Book Rev. Index; Can. Index; Can. Period. Index; Expand. Acad. Index (1992-); Gen. Period. Index (1985-); Hum. Rights Intern. Rep.; INFO-SOUTH Abstr.; Mag. Artic. Summar. Elite (Jan. 1992-); Mag. Artic. Summar. Select (Jan. 1992-); Mag. Artic. Summar. CD-ROM (Jan. 1992-); Mag. Index Plus (1989-); Mag. Search; Middle East Abstr. Index; Newsp. Period. Abstr. (1990-); Peace Res. Abstr. J. (1962-1965, 1972-1975); Read. Guide Period. Lit.; Mag. Index (1983-); TOM Gen. Index (1989-).

CN/0704-5646
CANADIAN POETRY (LONDON, ONT.). **See** Literature-Poetry.

FR
CENIT. (19??)-. French. ir. 290.00F France; 390.00F France. Cenit CNT, 33 rue des Vignoles, F 75020 Paris France. **Tel** 331 370 4686.

US/0272-1082
CENTURY (ALBUQUERQUE). (CENTURY.). [Century]. Vol. No. 1 (Oct. 1, 1980)-. Periodical. English. sm. $32.00 US; $37.00 other. Century, PO Box 709, Albuquerque NM 87103. **LC** AP2; .C377. **DD** 051.

US/0277-6995
CERVANTES (GAINESVILLE, FLA.). **See** Biographies.

US/0894-6396
CHAMINADE LITERARY REVIEW. No. 1 (Fall 1987)-. Periodical. English. sa. $10.00. Chaminade University of Honolulu, 3140 Waialae Avenue, Honolulu HI 96816-1578. **DD** 810.
Ind/Abst Index Am. Period. Verse.

UK/0308-0951
CHARLES LAMB BULLETIN, THE. [Charles Lamb bull.]. **Added/Corp** Charles Lamb Society. No. 1 (Jan. 1973)-. Bulletin. English. Four times a year (Jan., Apr., July, Oct.). £8.00 (individuals), £12.00 (institutions) UK; $14.00 (individuals), $21.00 (institutions) US, Comes with Charles Lamb Society membership. Charles Lamb Society, 28 Grove Lane Powell, London SE5 8ST England. **Tel** 011 44 71 5865112. **ED** Mary Wedd and Bill Ruddick. **LC** PR4863; .C46. **DD** 824/.7. Index available. **Bk Rev. Circ:** 350 (ctrl). ***Continues*** *C.L.S. Bulletin.*
Desc: Devoted to the work of Charles Lamb and his contemporaries. Articles and book reviews.
Ind/Abst Abstr. Engl. Stud.; Annu. Bibliogr. Engl. Lang. Lit.; Lit. Crit. Regist.; MLA Int. Bibl. Books Artic. Mod. Lang. Lit.; Romant. Move.

US/0741-9155
CHATTAHOOCHEE REVIEW, THE. **Added/Corp** DeKalb Community College. Vol. 1, No. 1 (Spring 1981)-. Periodical. English. qt. $15.00 (one year), $25.00 (two year). Chattahoochee Review, 2101 Womack Road, Dunwoody GA 30338-4497. **Tel** (404)393-3177, (404)393-3166, FAX (404)551-3201. **ED** Lamar York. cum. index. **Bk Rev. Ad Acc.** available on microfilm and microfiche from University Microfilms International (UMI).
Ind/Abst Am. Humanit. Index; Index Am. Period. Verse.

US/0009-2002
CHAUCER REVIEW, THE. [Chaucer rev.]. **Added/Corp** Modern Language Association of America. Chaucer Group. Vol. 1 (Summer 1966)-. Periodical. English. qt. $40.00 (institutions), $27.50 (individuals) US; $48.00 (institutions), $35.00 (individuals) other. Pennsylvania State University Press, 820 North University Drive, Suite C, University Park PA 16802-1003. **Tel** (814)865-1327, (800)326-9180, FAX (814)863-1408. **ED** Robert W. Frank Jr. **LC** PR1901; .C48. **[CCC]. Circ:** 1,450. available on microfilm and microfiche from University Microfilms International (UMI). Documents available from The Genuine Article, UMI Article Clearinghouse.
Ind/Abst Abstr. Engl. Stud.; Acad. Search (July 1993-); Annu. Bibliogr. Engl. Lang. Lit.; Arts Humanit. Citation Index [Full Cov.]; Curr. Contents Arts Humanit.; Expand. Acad. Index (1989-); Humanit. Index; Humanit. Source (Jul. 1993-); INFO-SOUTH Abstr.; MLA Int. Bibl. Books Artic. Mod. Lang. Lit.; Newsp. Period. Abstr. (1991-); Res. Alert [Full Cov.].

CH
CHENG CHIH PING LUN. **VFOAT** Political Review; The Political Review. Began with Sept. 10, 1958 issue. Periodical. Chinese. mo. NT$480.00. Cheng Chih Ping Lun She, PO Box 1303, Taipei Taiwan. **LC** D839; .C56. **DD** 951/.24905/05.

US/0147-5681
CHILDREN'S BOOK REVIEW INDEX. [Child. book rev. index]. Vol. 1 (1975)-. English. an. $109.00. Gale Research Inc., 835 Penobscot Building, Detroit MI 48226. **Tel** (800)877-GALE, (313)961-2242, FAX (313)961-6083, telex TWX 810-221-7086. **ED** Neil E. Walker and Beverly Baer. **LC** Z1037.A1; C475. **DD** 028.52.
Desc: More than 21,000 review citations that give access to reviewers' comments and opinions on more than 9,000 books written and/or recommended for children through age ten. Makes it easy to find a review by author's name, book title, or illustrator.

US/0090-7987
CHILDREN'S BOOK REVIEW SERVICE. [Child. book rev. serv.]. **Main/Corp** Children's Book Review Service. Vol. 1 (Sept. 1972)-. English. mo (with

winter and spring supplements). $40.00 US & Canada; $45.00 other. Childrens Book Review Service, 220 Berkeley Place 1D, Brooklyn NY 11217. **Tel** (718)622-4036. **ED** Ann L Kalkhoff. **LC** Z1037.A1; C476. **DD** 028.1. Index available. **Bk Rev. Circ:** 350 (ctrl).
Desc: Reviews of children's trade books for ages pre-school through high school. Reviewers either work with children or young adults or have subject specialities.
Ind/Abst Book Rev. Index.

US/0885-0429
CHILDREN'S LITERATURE ASSOCIATION QUARTERLY. [Child. Lit. Assoc. q.]. **Added/Corp** Children's Literature Association (U.S.). (19??)-. Periodical. English. Four times a year. $85.00 (institutions), $60.00 (individuals) US; add $10.00 postage other. Children's Literature Association, PO Box 138, Battle Creek MI 49106. **Tel** (616)965-8180. **ED** Gillian Adams (address: 5906 Fairland Drive, Austin TX 78731-4417; phone: (512)454-1799). **LC** PN1008.2; .C48. **DD** 809/.89282. Index available. **Bk Rev. Ad Acc. Circ:** 700 (ctrl). ***Continues** Children's Literature Association (U.S.). ChLA Newsletter.*
Desc: Articles critique a wide variety of works from children's literature. Ideas for teaching children's literature using literary criticism are also presented.
Ind/Abst Book Rev. Index; Child. Lit. Abstr.; MLA Int. Bibl. Books Artic. Mod. Lang. Lit.; Sci. Fict. Fantasy Book Rev. Index.

US/0362-4145
CHILDREN'S LITERATURE REVIEW. (1976)-. Periodical. English. sa. $103.00. Gale Research Inc., 835 Penobscot Building, Detroit MI 48226. **Tel** (800)877-GALE, (313)961-2242, FAX (313)961-6083, telex TWX 810-221-7086. **ED** Gerard J. Senick. **LC** PN1009.A1; C5139. **DD** 028.52.
Desc: Covers authors and illustrators of books for children from preschool through high school. Provides access to the ongoing scholarship of children's and young adult literature. Makes information quickly accessible through the Cumulative Indexes to Authors, Nationalities, and Titles that appear in each volume. Each author entry furnishes basic biographical information and an introduction to the individual's themes and styles, followed by critical excerpts on specific works. Many entries include an author's commentary.

FR/0529-777X
CINQUIEME SAISON. 1- Spring 1958-. Periodical. French. 9 rue des Mesanges, 92 Sceaux France.

US/0197-2227
CLASSICAL AND MODERN LITERATURE. **See** Classical Studies.

US/1061-737X
CLUTCH (FRANKFORT, KY.). (CLUTCH.). [Clutch]. No. 1 (1991)-. Periodical. English. sa. $10.00. Drill Press, 109 Liberty St., No. 1, San Francisco CA 94110. **Tel** (415)695-9773. **ED** Dan Hodge & Lawrence Oberc. **DD** 811. **Circ:** 300.
Desc: A literary review of an alternative nature, features both known and unknown writers.

US
CNL/REVIEW OF BOOKS. (19??)-. ir (4 issues per year). Comes with Council on National Literatures membership. Council on National Literatures, PO Box 81, Whitestone NY 11357. **Tel** (718)767-8380, FAX (718)767-8380.

AG
CODO A CODO. Vol. 1, No. 1 (Nov. 1990)-. Periodical. Spanish.

US
COLLEGE POETRY REVIEW. ***Suspended.*** Vol. 39 (Spring 1976)-Suspended (1986). Periodical. English. sa. $14.00. National Poetry Association, Box 218, Agoura CA 91301. ***Continues** America Sings.*

US/1046-3348
COLORADO REVIEW (1985). (COLORADO REVIEW.). [Colo. rev.]. Vol. 12, No. 2 (Spring/Summer 1985)-. Periodical. English. sa. $25.00 (institutions), $15.00 (individuals). University Press of Colorado, PO Box 849, Niwot CO 80544. **Tel** (303)530-5337, FAX (303)530-5306. **ED** Bill Tremblay, David Milofsky and Mary Crow. **DD** 810. Index available. **Bk Rev. Ad Acc. Circ:** 1,000. ***Continues** Colorado State Review (Fort Collins, Colo. : 1977), 0277-6014.*
Desc: Journal of contemporary literature combining fiction, poetry, interviews, articles, reviews and translations.
Ind/Abst Am. Humanit. Index; Index Am. Period. Verse.

US/0010-1982
COLUMBIA REVIEW. ***Ceased.*** **Added/Corp** Columbia University. (19??)-(19??). Periodical. English. sa. Columbia Review, 304 Ferris Booth Hall, Columbia University, New York NY 10027. **LC** AP2; .C673. ***Continues** Varsity Review.*

UY/0301-6579
COMENTARIOS BIBLIOGRAFICOS AMERICANOS. [C.B.A. anu.]. **VFOAT** CBA Anuario; CBA Yearbook; Anuario de CBA; Anuario CBA. **VAT** Comentarios Bibliograficos Americanos. (1969)-. Spanish (English). qt. $65.00 US; $75.00 other. E Darino /CBA, 222 Park Avenue South 2A, New York NY 10003. **Tel** (212)228-4024. **ED** Elida Darino. **LC** Z1601; .C3. Index available. cum. index. **Bk Rev.**
Desc: Bibliographic service that reviews new books from the Spanish publishing market. Also includes essays on bibliographical works of specific areas, articles, etc.

US/0732-6734
COMMONWEALTH NOVEL IN ENGLISH. [Commonw. novel Eng.]. **Added/Corp** Bluefield State College. Center for International Understanding. **VFOAT** C.N.I.E.; CNIE. Vol. 1, No. 1 (Jan. 1982)-. Periodical. English. sa. $16.00 institutions; $14.00 individuals. Bluefield State College, Center International Understanding, Bluefield WV 24701. **ED** Sudhakar R. Jamkhandi (editor's address: 219 Rock Street, Bluefield, WV 24701, phone: (304)327-4036). **LC** PR9080; .A17. **DD** 823/.0099171241. Index available. cum. index. **Bk Rev**, (Qty: 1-2). **Circ:** 700.
Desc: Features broad-based analyses of narrative strategies and textual criticism of commonwealth English novels.
Ind/Abst Abstr. Engl. Stud.; MLA Int. Bibl. Books Artic. Mod. Lang. Lit.

UK/0144-7564
COMPARATIVE CRITICISM. [Comp. crit.]. (1979)-. Academic Scholarly Publication. English. an (June). $98.00 US, Canada & Mexico; £58.00 other. Cambridge University Press, The Edinburgh Building, Shaftesbury Road, Cambridge CB2 2RU United Kingdom. **Tel** 011 44 223 312393, FAX 011 44 223 325959. **(Subscription address:** Cambridge University Press / North America, 110 Midland Avenue, Port Chester NY 10573.**) ED** Elinor S. Shaffer. **LC** PN863; .C58. **DD** 809. **CODEN** CMCRE3. **[CCC].** available on microfilm from University Microfilms International (UMI).
Desc: Annual journal that addresses questions of literary theory and criticism. Covers comparative studies in terms of theme, genre, movement and influence and their current reformulations, and to interdisciplinary perspectives. Includes articles, new poetry, fiction, translations of literary, scholarly and critical works, substantial reviews of major works in the field, and bibliographies of comparative literature in Britain, together with special bibliographies on the journal's annual themes or on the work if individual authors.
Ind/Abst Annu. Bibliogr. Engl. Lang. Lit.; MLA Int. Bibl. Books Artic. Mod. Lang. Lit.; Romant. Move.

IT/0010-504X
COMUNITA. [Comunita]. (1953)-. Periodical. Italian. an. L27000 Italy; L33650 other. Arnoldo Mondadori Editore, UFF Cont Abbonamenti, 20090 Segrate MI Italy. **Tel** 011 39 2 75422015, telex 320457 MONDMI I. cum. index. ***Continues** Rivista.*
Ind/Abst Am. Hist. Life (1971-1985); MLA Int. Bibl. Books Artic. Mod. Lang. Lit.

US/0092-7708
CONCH REVIEW OF BOOKS, THE. ***Suspended.*** [Conch rev. books]. Vol. 1, No. 1 (March 1973)-Vol. 4 (1976). Periodical. English. qt. $15.00 US; $17.00 other. Conch Typesetting, PO Box 777, Buffalo NY 14213-0777. **Tel** (716)885-3686. **ED** S. O. Anozie. **LC** Z3501; .C66. **DD** 028.1/096. **Bk Rev. Ad Acc. Circ:** 1,000.
Desc: In-depth and timely reviews of books and audiovisual materials about Africa, and comprehensive coverage of African book publishing and libraries.
Ind/Abst MLA Int. Bibl. Books Artic. Mod. Lang. Lit.

US/1055-7334
CONFLUENCE (BELPRE, OHIO). (CONFLUENCE.). **Added/Corp** Ohio Valley Literary Group. Marietta College. Vol. 1 (1990)-. Periodical. English. $4.00. Confluence, Barbara McCullough, Box 336, Belpre OH 45714. **DD** 808.

IT
CONFRONTI. La Tipografica Varese, Via Tonale 49, 21100 Varese Italy. **Tel** 011 39 332 332160.

US/0278-2324
CONJUNCTIONS (NEW YORK, N.Y.). (CONJUNCTIONS.). [Conjunctions]. (Winter 1981/1982)-. Periodical. English. sa. $25.00 (institutions), $18.00 (individuals). Conjunctions, Bard College, PO Box 5000, Annadale on Hudson NY 12504. **Tel** (914)758-7412. **ED** Bradford Morrow (editor's phone (212)477-1136). **LC** PN6010.5; .C66. **DD** 805. **Bk Rev. Ad Acc. Circ:** 8,000 (ctrl).
Desc: Literary journal featuring contemporary poetry, fiction, essays, interviews, translations, reviews, artwork. Has featured the work of more than 300 writers from 2 dozen countries.
Ind/Abst Am. Humanit. Index; Index Am. Period. Verse.

US/0010-6356
CONRADIANA. **See** Biographies.

NO
CONTEMPORARY APPROACHES TO IBSEN : PROCEEDINGS OF THE INTERNATIONAL IBSEN SEMINARY. (1965)-. Academic Scholarly Publication. English (French, German, Norwegian and Swedish). sa. Price varies per volume. Scandinavian University Press, PO Box 2959 Toeyen, N 0608 Oslo 6 Norway. **Tel** 011 47 2 2575400, FAX 011 47 2 2575353, telex 71896 UROR N. **(Subscription address:** Oxford University Press, Distribution Services, Saxon Way West, Corby, Nothants NN 189ES England.**) ED** Bjoern Hemmer and Vigdis Ystad. **LC** PT8890.A1; C66; PT8890.A1; I2 subser. **Bk Rev.** ***Continues** Ibsenaarboken, 0073-4365.*
Ind/Abst MLA Int. Bibl. Books Artic. Mod. Lang. Lit.

RM
CONVORBIRI LITERARE. Vol. 1 (Mar. 1, 1867)-. Romanian. wk. DM217.00. **(Subscription address:** Kubon & Sagner, ABT Zeitschriftenimport, D 80328 Munich Germany.**) LC** AP86; .C72.
Desc: Review for literature and art issued in Iasi.
Ind/Abst Annu. Bibliogr. Engl. Lang. Lit.; MLA Int. Bibl. Books Artic. Mod. Lang. Lit.

FR
CRAPOUILLOT, LE. (1915)-. French. Six times a year. Dawson France SA, BP 40, 91121 Palaiseau Cedex France. **Tel** 011 33 1 69104700, telex 220064F.

US/0884-3457
CREAM CITY REVIEW. [Cream city rev.]. **Added/Corp** University of Wisconsin--Milwaukee. Dept. of English. **VFOAT** CreamCity Review; CCR; C.C.R. (1975)-. Periodical. English. sa. $12.00 (one year), $22.00 (two year). Cream City Review, Box 413, University of Wisconsin - Milwaukee, Milwaukee WI 53201. **Tel** (414)963-4511. **ED** Mark Drechsler. **LC** PN6010.5; .C73X. **DD** 810. **Bk Rev**, (Qty: 10). **Circ:** 1,500.
Ind/Abst Am. Humanit. Index; Index Am. Period. Verse.

US/0011-1198
CRESSET (VALPARAISO), THE. (THE CRESSET.). [Cresset]. **Added/Corp** International Walther League. Walther League. Valparaiso University. Vol. 1, No. 1 (Nov. 1937)-. Periodical. English. mo (Sept. to May). $8.50 (one year), $14.75 (two year) US; $10.50 (one year), $18.75 (two year) Canada; $12.50 (one year), $22.75 (two year) other. Cresset, Valparaiso University, Valparaiso IN 46383. **Tel** (219)464-5274, FAX (219)464-5496. **ED** Gail McGrew Eifrig. **LC** AP2; .C893. **Bk Rev**, (Qty: 25). **Circ:** 4,700 (ctrl).
Desc: A review of literature, the arts, and public affairs from a Lutheran Christian perspective.
Ind/Abst Am. Humanit. Index (-199?); Annu. Bibliogr. Engl. Lang. Lit.; Book Rev. Index.

IT/0011-1449
CRISTALLO / CENTRO DI CULTURA DELL'ALTO ADIGE, IL. 1st Year, No. 1 (May 1959)-. Periodical. Italian. Three times a year. L15000. Centro di Cultura dell'Alto Adige, Via Napoli 1, 39100 Bolzano Italy. **Tel** (0471)201354. **ED** Giuseppe Negri. Index available. cum. index. **Bk Rev. Circ:** 1,000.
Ind/Abst MLA Int. Bibl. Books Artic. Mod. Lang. Lit.

US/0011-149X
CRITIC, THE. 1957-. Periodical. English. qt. $17.00 (one year), $25.00 (two year). Thomas More Association, 205 West Monroe Street/6th Floor, Chicago IL 60606. **Tel** (312)609-8880, (800)835-8965, FAX (312)609-8891. **ED** John L Sprague. **Circ:** 3,000. available on microfilm and microfiche from University Microfilms International (UMI). ***Continues** Books on Trial.*
Desc: Interviews with major Catholic personalities, thought-provoking commentary and debate, profiles of important Catholic literary figures, reviews of new books, and original fiction, poetry, satire and humor.
Ind/Abst Abr. Cathol. Period. Lit. Index; Cathol. Period. Lit. Index.

US/0278-7261
CRITICA HISPANICA. **See** Linguistics.

US
CRITICAL ESSAYS ON WORLD LITERATURE. **See** Literature.

AT/0070-1548
CRITICAL REVIEW (MELBOURNE), THE. (THE CRITICAL REVIEW.). [Crit. rev.]. No. 8 (1965)-. English. an. 8.00Aus$ (includes postage). The Critical Review, Australian National University, English Department, GPO Box 4, Canberra ACT 2600 Australia. **(Subscription address:** Australian National University, Philosophy Division, Research School of Social Sciences, GPO Box 4, Canberra ACT 2601 Australia; telephone: 011 61 6 2822278**) ED** S. L. Goldberg. **DD** 899; 820. **Circ:** 600. ***Continues** Melbourne Critical Review.*
Desc: A journal of substantial and provocative criticism over a wide range of literature and literary topics.
Ind/Abst Abstr. Engl. Stud.; APAIS, Aust. Public Aff. Inf. Ser.; MLA Int. Bibl. Books Artic. Mod. Lang. Lit.

US/0894-8860
CRITICAL REVIEW OF BOOKS IN RELIGION. [Crit. rev. books relig.]. (1988)-. English. an. $20.00 (institutions), $25.00 (non-subscriber institution). Scholars Press / Georgia, PO Box 15399, Atlanta GA 30333-0399. **Tel** (404)636-4757, (404)727-2320, FAX (404)727-2348. **LC** BL1; .C75. **DD** 200.

NE
CRITICAL STUDIES (AMSTERDAM, THE NETHERLANDS). See Literature.

US/0730-2304
CRITICAL TEXTS. ***Suspended.*** [Crit. texts]. Vol. 1, Issue No. 1 (Summer 1982)-Suspended. Periodical. English. Three times a year. $9.00 (individuals), $15.00 (institutions) US; $20.00 other. Critical Texts, Columbia University, English Department, 602 Philosophy Hall, New York NY 10027. **Tel** (212)854-3215. **ED** Joseph Childers. **LC** PN2; .C72. **DD** 801/.95/05. **Bk Rev**. **Ad Acc**. **Circ:** 850 (ctrl).
Desc: A book review of recent works on literary, political, philosophical, art and feminist theories, containing essays and interviews with prominent scholars in these fields.
Ind/Abst Am. Humanit. Index; ARTbibliogr. Mod.; BHA : Biblio. Hist. Art; Linguist. Lang. Behav. Abstr.; Lit. Crit. Regist.; MLA Int. Bibl. Books Artic. Mod. Lang. Lit.; Philos. Index; Soc. Plann. Policy Dev. Abstr.; Sociol. Abstr.

FR/0011-1600
CRITIQUE. (CRITIQUE : REVUE GENERALE DES PUBLICATIONS FRANCAISES ET ETRANGERES.). [Critique]. Vol. 1, No. 1 (June 1946)-. Periodical. French. Twelve times a year. 475.02F France; 620.00F others. Les Editions de Minuit, 7 rue Bernard-Palissy, 75006 Paris France. **Tel** 011 33 1 44393920, FAX 011 33 1 45448236. **ED** Jean Piel. **LC** Z1007; .C8. **Ad Acc**.
Desc: General review of French and other language publications on literature and philosophy.
Ind/Abst Annu. Bibliogr. Engl. Lang. Lit.; BHA : Biblio. Hist. Art; Linguist. Lang. Behav. Abstr.; MLA Int. Bibl. Books Artic. Mod. Lang. Lit.; Soc. Plann. Policy Dev. Abstr.; Soc. Sci. Cit. Index [Select. Cov.]; Sociol. Abstr.

US/0011-1619
CRITIQUE - BOLINGBROKE SOCIETY. (CRITIQUE.). [Critique - Bolingbroke Soc.]. **Added/Corp** Bolingbroke Society. Vol. 1, No. 1 (Winter 1956)-. Periodical. English. qt. $54.00 (institution), $32.00 (individual). Heldref Publications, 1319 Eighteenth Street Northwest, Washington DC 20036-1802. **Tel** (202)296-6267, (800)365-9753, FAX (202)296-5149. **ED** Geoffrey Green, Donald J. Greiner, and Larry McCaffery. **LC** PN3503; .C7. **DD** 801. **[CCC]**. **Bk Rev**. **Ad Acc**. **Circ:** 1,361. available on microfilm and microfiche from University Microfilms International (UMI). Documents available from The Genuine Article, UMI Article Clearinghouse. ***Continues*** *Faulkner Studies.*
Desc: Closely focused, critical essays on contemporary fiction and serious detailed discussions on the fiction of our time are presented in this journal.
Ind/Abst Abstr. Engl. Stud.; Acad. Search (Jan. 1994-); Annu. Bibliogr. Engl. Lang. Lit.; Arts Humanit. Citation Index [Full Cov.]; Book Rev. Index; Curr. Contents Arts Humanit.; Humanit. Index; Humanit. Source (Jul. 1993-); INFO-SOUTH Abstr.; Mag. Search; MLA Int. Bibl. Books Artic. Mod. Lang. Lit.; Newsp. Period. Abstr. (1991-); Res. Alert [Full Cov.]; Soc. Sci. Index.

CN/0820-8247
CRSCL NEWSLETTER. (CRSCL NEWSLETTER : CANADIAN RESEARCH SOCIETY FOR CHILDREN'S LITERATURE NEWSLETTER.). [CRSCL newsl.]. **VAT** Canadian Research Society for Children's Literature Newsletter. No. 1 (Jan. 1983)-. Newsletter. English. ir. 2.00Can$. University of Western Ontario / School of Library and Information Science, London Ontario N6A 1H1 Canada. **Tel** (519)661-3542. **ED** Catherine Ross and Delilah Deane. **DD** 809/.89282/072. **Circ:** 125. ***Continues*** *Canadian Research Society for Children's Literature (Newsletter), 0710-1406.*
Desc: Lists addresses, publications, and current research of Canadian researchers on children's literature.

SP
CUADERNOS HISPANOAMERICANOS. LOS COMPLEMENTARIOS. Vol. 1 (Dec. 1987)-. Spanish. Inst Cooperacion Iberoamerican 4, 28040 Madrid Spain.

US
CULTURAL WATCHDOG NEWSLETTER, THE. (197?)-. Newsletter. English. mo. $15.00. Cultural Watchdog Newsletter, L. Ehrenkrantz, 6 Winslow Road, White Plains NY 10606. **Tel** (212)986-0223.

●US/1063-9012
CURRENT BOOKS MAGAZINE. [Curr. books mag.]. Vol. 1, No. 1 (Summer 1992)-. Periodical. English. bm (6 issues). $17.95. Washington Media Group, PO Box 34468, Bethesda MD 20827. **Tel** (301)530-8200, FAX (301)530-8201. **ED** Edwin S. Grosvener. **DD** 813. **Ad Acc, Adv Mgr:** Natalie op de Beeck. **Circ:** 29,000 (ctrl).
Desc: Each issue includes 25 major excerpts varying in length from 900 to 5,000 words plus short takes and quotes from dozens of additional books. Covers a broad range of subjects such as history, issues, biography, travel, business, health, arts, humor, fiction, and poetry.

LB
CUTTINGTON RESEARCH JOURNAL. Vol. 1 (Jan. 1982)-. Periodical. English. an. $5.00 Liberia; $7.00 North America; $10.00 other. Managing Editor Cuttington Research Journal, Box 10-0277, 1000 Monrovia 10 Liberia. **ED** Eric S Wongo. **LC** AS695.A1; C87. **DD** 378/.0072. **Bk Rev**. **Ad Acc**. **Circ:** 500.
Ind/Abst Math. Rev.

US/0011-4936
D.H. LAWRENCE REVIEW, THE. [D. H. Lawrence rev.]. **VAT** David Herbert Lawrence Review. (Spring 1968)-. Academic Scholarly PublicationAcademic Scholarly Publication. English. Three times a year (Mar., June, Sept.). $14.00 (individuals) US; $15.00 (individuals) other; $20.00 (institutions) all countries. D. H. Lawrence Review, University of Delaware, Department of English, Newark DE 19716. **Tel** (302)454-1480 or 831-8069. **ED** Dennis Jackson (phone: (302)831-8069). **LC** PR6023.A93; Z6234. **DD** 823/.9/12. Index available in last issue of volume--attached. **Bk Rev**, (Qty: 25). **Ad Acc**. **Pr Rev**. **Circ:** 800. available on microfilm and microfiche from University Microfilms International (UMI). Documents available from The Genuine Article.
Desc: Serves as a forum for criticism, scholarship, reviews and bibliography of the work of D.H. Lawrence and his circle.
Ind/Abst Abstr. Engl. Stud.; Am. Humanit. Index (-199?); Annu. Bibliogr. Engl. Lang. Lit.; Arts Humanit. Citation Index [Full Cov.]; Curr. Contents Arts Humanit.; MLA Int. Bibl. Books Artic. Mod. Lang. Lit.; Res. Alert [Full Cov.].

DK/0106-4525
DANSKE STUDIER. [Dan. stud.]. **Added/Corp** Universitets-Jubilets Danske Samfund. Vol. 1-12 (1904)-. Periodical. Danish. an (June). kr201.00. CA Reitzels Forlag AS, Norregade 20, DK-1165 Copenhagen K Denmark. **Tel** 011 45 3 3122400. **ED** Iver Kjaer and Flemming Nielsen. **LC** PD3004; .D3. **Bk Rev**. **Circ:** 700. ***Continues*** *Dania.*
Desc: Studies in Danish literature, linguistics and folklore, inclusive of book reviews regarding reference literature covering these fields.
Ind/Abst Annu. Bibliogr. Engl. Lang. Lit.; MLA Int. Bibl. Books Artic. Mod. Lang. Lit.

US/0148-561X
DEGRE SECOND. ***Ceased.*** [Degre second]. **Added/Corp** Virginia Polytechnic Institute and State University. Dept. of Foreign Languages and Literatures. No. 1 (July 1977)-No. 13, (1992). Periodical. Multiple languages (English and French). Virginia Polytechnic Institute Literatures, 119 Femoyer Hall, Blacksburg VA 24061-0225. **Tel** (703)231-5362, FAX (703)231-7826. **ED** W Pierre Jacoebee. **LC** PQ1; .D43. **Bk Rev**. **Ad Acc**. **Pr Rev**. **Circ:** 225.
Desc: Studies in French and, occasionally, francophone literatures.
Ind/Abst MLA Int. Bibl. Books Artic. Mod. Lang. Lit.

FR/0987-1209
DIABOLO TOULOUSE. (DIABOLO.). **VFOAT** Diabolo Magazine. (1987)-. Periodical. French. mo. 455.00F French overseas depts. and territories; 352.60F France; 425.00F other Europe; 495.00F other. Milan Presse/Serv Abonnement, 300 Rue Leon Joulin, 31101 Toulouse Cedex France. **Tel** 011 33 1 61766464, FAX 011 33 1 61766400. **UDC** 087.5.

US/0300-7162
DIACRITICS. [Diacritics]. **Added/Corp** Cornell University. Dept. of Romance Studies. Vol. 1 (Fall 1971)-. Academic Scholarly Publication. English. Four times a year (March, June, September, December). $59.00 US; $62.50 Canada and Mexico; $67.40 other. Johns Hopkins University Press, 2715 North Charles Street, Baltimore MD 21218-4319. **Tel** (410)516-6987, FAX (410)516-6968. **ED** Richard Klein. **LC** PN80; .D5. **DD** 805. **[CCC]**. Index available. **Bk Rev**. **Ad Acc**. **Circ:** 1,400. available on microfilm and microfiche from University Microfilms International (UMI). Documents available from UMI Article Clearinghouse, The Genuine Article.
Desc: A forum for exchange among literary theorists, literary critics, and philosophers discussing literary issues. Each issue features articles in which contributors compare and analyze books on particular theoretical works and develop their own positions on the thesis, methods, and theoretical implications of those works.
Ind/Abst Abstr. Engl. Stud.; Am. Humanit. Index; Annu. Bibliogr. Engl. Lang. Lit.; Arts Humanit. Citation Index [Full Cov.]; Curr. Contents Arts Humanit.; Film Lit. Index; Linguist. Lang. Behav. Abstr.; Lit. Crit. Regist.; MLA Int. Bibl. Books Artic. Mod. Lang. Lit.; Res. Alert [Full Cov.]; Soc. Plann. Policy Dev. Abstr.; Soc. Sci. Cit. Index [Select. Cov.]; Sociol. Abstr.

BE
DIDASCALIES : CAHIERS OCCASIONNELS DE L'ENSEMBLE THEATRAL MOBILE. See Theater.

IT
DOCUMENTI. (19??)-. Italian. Cntro Docu Ingen Civil Archt, Planif Ter / Via Manara 11, Milan Italy.

US/0012-5245
DOLLARS & SENSE (SOMERVILLE, MASS.). See Economics.

RU/0012-6756
DRUZBA NARODOV. (DRUZHBA NARODOV.). [Druz. nar.]. **Added/Corp** Soiuz Pisatelei SSSR. (1939)-. Periodical. Russian. mo. $137.95. **(Subscription address:** East View Publications Inc., 3020 Harbor Lane North, Suite 110, Minneapolis MN 55447.**)**
Ind/Abst MLA Int. Bibl. Books Artic. Mod. Lang. Lit.; Curr. Dig. Post Sov. Press.

US/0012-8163
EARLY AMERICAN LITERATURE. [Early Am. lit.]. **Added/Corp** Modern Language Association of America. Early American Literature Section. Modern Language Association of America. Early American Literature Group. Modern Language Association of America. American Literature Division I. Vol. 3 (Spring 1968)-. Periodical. English. Three times a year. $18.00 (one year), $51.00 (three years) (individuals) US; $24.00 (one year), $69.00 (three years) (institutions) US; $28.00 (one year), $81.00 (three year), (individuals), other. University of North Carolina Press, 116 South Boundary Street, PO Box 2288, Chapel Hill NC 27515-2288. **Tel** (919)966-3561, FAX (919)966-3829. **ED** Everett Emerson. **LC** PS501; .E2. cum. index. **Bk Rev**. **Ad Acc**. **Circ:** 700 (ctrl). available on microfilm and microfiche from University Microfilms International (UMI). Documents available from The Genuine Article, UMI Article Clearinghouse. ***Continues*** *Early American Literature Newsletter, 0739-8301.*
Desc: Publishes scholarship and criticism of the literature of the 17th and 18th centuries and the early national period to about 1820.
Ind/Abst Abstr. Engl. Stud.; Acad. Search (July 1993-); Am. Hist. Life (1971-); Am. Humanit. Index; Annu. Bibliogr. Engl. Lang. Lit.; Arts Humanit. Citation Index [Full Cov.]; Curr. Contents Arts Humanit.; Expand. Acad. Index (1989-); Humanit. Index; Humanit. Source (Jul. 1993-); Index Book Rev. Relig.; INFO-SOUTH Abstr.; Lit. Crit. Regist.; Mag. Search; MLA Int. Bibl. Books Artic. Mod. Lang. Lit.; Newsp. Period. Abstr. (1991-); Relig. Index One Period. (1980-); Res. Alert [Full Cov.].

US
EARLY DRAMA, ART, AND MUSIC MONOGRAPH SERIES. See The Arts.

●US/1061-1479
ECRITIQUE (IOWA CITY, IOWA). See Literature.

NO/0013-0818
EDDA. [Edda]. Vol. 1 (1914)-. Periodical. Norwegian (Danish, Swedish and English). qt. Kr525.00, $88.00. Scandinavian University Press, PO Box 2959 Toeyen, N 0608 Oslo 6 Norway. **Tel** 011 47 2 2575400, FAX 011 47 2 2575353, telex 71896 UROR N. **(Subscription address:** Scandinavian University Press, 200 Meacham Ave., Elmont NY 11003.**)** **ED** Jorunn Hareide. **LC** PN9; .E5. **[CCC]**. cum. index. **Bk Rev**. **Ad Acc**. **Pr Rev**. **Circ:** 1,000.
Desc: Publishes general literary research by Scandinavian scholars and research on Scandinavian literature by scholars from all countries.
Ind/Abst Annu. Bibliogr. Engl. Lang. Lit.; MLA Int. Bibl. Books Artic. Mod. Lang. Lit.; Romant. Move.

GW/0931-3079
EDITIO. **Added/Corp** Arbeitsgemeinschaft fuer Germanistische Edition. Allgemeine Gesellschaft fuer Philosophie in Deutschland. Arbeitsgemeinschaft Philosophischer Editionen. Vol. 1 (1987)-. Academic Scholarly Publication. German (English and French). an. DM96.00 Germany. Max Niemeyer Verlag, Postfach 2140, D 72011 Tuebingen Germany. **Tel** 011 49 7071 989494, FAX 011 49 7071 87419. **ED** Winfried Woesler. **LC** PN162; .E26. **DD** 808/.027/05. **Bk Rev**. **Ad Acc**. **Circ:** 600.
Desc: Goal is the establishment of continuing international and interdisciplinary exchange of ideas and experiences among the editors and collaborators of editorial projects.
Ind/Abst MLA Int. Bibl. Books Artic. Mod. Lang. Lit.

US/0013-2683
EIRE-IRELAND (ST. PAUL). (EIRE-IRELAND.). [Eire-Irel.]. **Added/Corp** Irish American Cultural Institute. Vol. 1 (Spring 1966)-. Periodical. English (Irish). qt. $28.00 US; $34.00 other. Irish American Cultural Institute, 2115 Summit Avenue, Box 5026, St Paul MN 55105. **Tel** (612)962-6040, FAX (612)962-6043. **ED** Thomas Dillon Redshaw. Index available. cum. index. **Bk Rev**. **Ad Acc**. **Circ:** 6,000. available on microfilm from University Microfilms International (UMI). Documents available from The Genuine Article.
Desc: Publishes essays on any aspect of Irish civilization, but chiefly literature and history. Widely indexed. Upper level readership.
Ind/Abst Abstr. Engl. Stud.; Am. Hist. Life (1975-); Am. Humanit. Index; Annu. Bibliogr. Engl. Lang. Lit.; ARTbibliogr. Mod.; Arts Humanit. Citation Index [Full Cov.]; Curr. Contents Arts Humanit.; Lit. Crit. Regist.; MLA Int. Bibl. Books Artic. Mod. Lang. Lit.; Res. Alert [Full Cov.]; Soc. Sci. Cit. Index [Select. Cov.].

US/1054-3376
ELF (TONAWANDA, N.Y.). (ELF : ECLECTIC LITERARY FORUM.). **VFOAT** Eclectic Literary Forum; ELF Magazine. Vol. 1, No. 1 (Spring 1991)-. Periodical. English. qt (During seasons). $16.00 (individuals); $32.00 (institutions). Elf Associates, Inc., PO Box 392, Tonawanda NY 14150. **Tel** (716)695-7669. **ED** C. K. Erbes. **DD** 808. Index available (Author index available).

Bk Rev, (Qty: 5-10). **Ad Acc**, **Adv Mgr Tel** (716)695-2669. **Circ:** 6,000.
Desc: Publishes works by both new and established writers with emphasis on the emerging writers.

US/0013-8304
ELH. [ELH]. **Added/Corp** Tudor and Stuart Club (Johns Hopkins University). **VFOAT** Journal of Literary History. Vol. 1 (Apr. 1934)-. Periodical. English. Four times a year (Mar., June, Sept., and Dec.). $73.00 US; $77.70 Canada and Mexico; $85.80 other. Johns Hopkins University Press, 2715 North Charles Street, Baltimore MD 21218-4319. **Tel** (410)516-6987, FAX (410)516-6968. **ED** Ronald Paulson. **LC** PR1; .E5. **DD** 820.9. **[CCC]**. **Bk Rev**. **Ad Acc**. **Circ:** 2,100. available on microfilm and microfiche from University Microfilms International (UMI). Documents available from The Genuine Article, UMI Article Clearinghouse.
Desc: Publishes critical and interpretive essays in every specialty of English and American literature.
Ind/Abst Abstr. Engl. Stud.; Acad. Abstr. Full Text Elite (Jan. 1990-); Acad. Abstr. (Jan. 1990-); Acad. Ind. [Computer File] (1987-); Acad. Search (Jan. 1990-); Am. Hist. Life (1987-); Annu. Bibliogr. Engl. Lang. Lit.; Arts Humanit. Citation Index [Full Cov.]; Child. Lit. Abstr. (19??-); Curr. Contents Arts Humanit.; Expand. Acad. Index (1987-); Humanit. Index; Humanit. Source (Jul. 1990-); INFO-SOUTH Abstr.; Lit. Crit. Regist.; Mag. Search; MLA Int. Bibl. Books Artic. Mod. Lang. Lit.; Newsp. Period. Abstr. (1991-); Res. Alert [Full Cov.].

CN/0829-7681
ELS MONOGRAPH SERIES. [ELS monogr. ser.]. **Added/Corp** English Literary Studies. **VFOAT** English Literary Studies. **VAT** English Literary Studies Monograph Series. No. 1 (1975)-. Monographic series. English. ir (2 to 5 volumes per year). Price varies per volume. University of Victoria Department of English, PO Box 3045, Victoria British Columbia V8W 3P4 Canada. **Tel** (604)721-7236. **ED** Samuel L. Macey. **DD** 820.9. **Circ:** 400.
Desc: Literary critical studies of major authors writing in English.
Ind/Abst MLA Int. Bibl. Books Artic. Mod. Lang. Lit.

US/0193-5798
ENCLITIC. [Enclitic]. **Added/Corp** University of Minnesota. Board of Student Publications. Vol. 1 (Spring 1977)-. Periodical. English. sa. $36.00 US & Canada; $40.00 other. Enclitic, PO Box 36098, Los Angeles CA 90036-0098. **Tel** (310)931-6623. **ED** John O'Kane. Index available. **Bk Rev**. **Ad Acc**. **Pr Rev**. **Circ:** 5,000. available on microfiche; available on microfilm; available in microform.
Desc: A magazine of politics, new writing and cultural life for the engaging and engaged reader.
Ind/Abst Am. Humanit. Index; Film Lit. Index; MLA Int. Bibl. Books Artic. Mod. Lang. Lit.; Soc. Plann. Policy Dev. Abstr.

US/0363-4841
ENCOMIA. [Encomia]. **Added/Corp** International Courtly Literature Society. Vol. 1 (Spring 1975)-. English. an (Summer or Fall). $15.00. Arizona State University / c/o Dhira Mahoney, Department of English, Tempe AZ 85287. **Tel** (602)965-3168. **ED** Maria Dobozy (editor's address: Department of German, University of Utah, Salt Lake City, UT 84112). **LC** PN661; .E5. **DD** 809/.02. Index Bound in First Issue. **Bk Rev**, (Qty: 6-8). **Ad Acc**. **Circ:** 900.
Desc: Exhaustive international inventory--frequently with annotations--of articles, editions, critical works, translations, book reviews, and dissertations relevant to the study of the medieval literature of the Courts of Western Europe (with the exception of Arthurian material and chansons de geste).
Ind/Abst MLA Int. Bibl. Books Artic. Mod. Lang. Lit.

US/0013-8282
ENGLISH LANGUAGE NOTES. [Engl. lang. notes]. **Added/Corp** University of Colorado, Boulder. University of Colorado (Boulder Campus). Vol. 1 (Sept. 1963)-. Academic Scholarly Publication. English. qt. $20.00 (individual), $40.00 (institutional) US and Canada; $27.00 (individual), $47.00 (institutional) other. University of Colorado Department of English, Campus Box 226/ Department of English, Boulder CO 80309. **Tel** (303)492-7176. **ED** J Wallace Donald, (303)492-8388. **LC** PE1; .E53. **DD** 420/.5. Index available (published separately in June). **Bk Rev**, (Qty: 16). **Ad Acc**. **Pr Rev**. **Circ:** 1,000. Documents available from The Genuine Article, UMI Article Clearinghouse.
Desc: Short scholarly articles on literature in the English language, all countries and all periods from medieval through modern.
Ind/Abst Abstr. Engl. Stud.; Acad. Search (July 1993-); Annu. Bibliogr. Engl. Lang. Lit.; Arts Humanit. Citation Index [Full Cov.]; Curr. Contents Arts Humanit.; Expand. Acad. Index (1989-); Humanit. Index; Humanit. Source (Jul. 1993-); INFO-SOUTH Abstr.; Lit. Crit. Regist.; Mag. Search; MLA Int. Bibl. Books Artic. Mod. Lang. Lit.; Newsp. Period. Abstr. (1991-); Res. Alert [Full Cov.]; Romant. Move.

US/0013-8312
ENGLISH LITERARY RENAISSANCE. [Engl. lit. renaiss.]. Vol. 1 (Winter 1971)-. Periodical. English. Three times a year. $25.00 (institutions), $20.00 (individuals) US; $33.00 (institutions), $28.00 (individuals) other. English Literary Renaissance, University of Massachusetts, Bartlett Hall, Amherst MA 01003. **Tel** (413)545-5465, FAX (413)545-3880. **ED** Arthur F Kinney. **LC** PR1; .E43. **DD** 820.9/002. Index available. cum. index. **Ad Acc**. **Circ:** 1,000. Documents available from The Genuine Article.
Desc: A publication of texts, studies, and bibliographies in the intellectual context and literary achievement of Tudor and Stuart England.
Ind/Abst Abstr. Engl. Stud.; Acad. Search (July 1993-); Am. Hist. Life (1973-); Am. Humanit. Index; Annu. Bibliogr. Engl. Lang. Lit.; Arts Humanit. Citation Index [Full Cov.]; Curr. Contents Arts Humanit.; Humanit. Source (Jul. 1993-); INFO-SOUTH Abstr.; Lit. Crit. Regist.; Mag. Search; MLA Int. Bibl. Books Artic. Mod. Lang. Lit.; Res. Alert [Full Cov.]; Romant. Move.

US/0013-8339
ENGLISH LITERATURE IN TRANSITION, 1880-1920. [Engl. lit. transit. 1880-1920]. **Added/Corp** Purdue University. Dept. of English. Arizona State University. Dept. of English. **VAT** English Literature in Transition, Eighteen Hundred and Eighty-Nineteen Hundred and Twenty. Vol. 6 (1963)-. Periodical. English. sa (2 double issues published in January and Sept.). $18.00 (one year), $33.00 (two year) US; $24.00 (one year), $45.00 (two year) other. English Literature in Translation, Department of English, University of North Carolina, Greensboro NC 27412-5001. **Tel** (910)334-5446, FAX (910)334-3281. **ED** Robert Langenfeld. Index available. cum. index ($13.00 US; $15.00 other). **Bk Rev**. **Ad Acc**. **Pr Rev**. **Circ:** 900. available on microfilm and microfiche from University Microfilms International (UMI). Documents available from The Genuine Article. ***Continues*** *English Fiction in Transition, 1880-1920, 0364-3549.*
Desc: A publication on British literature and culture (1880-1920). Publishes articles, bibliographies, and reviews.
Ind/Abst Abstr. Engl. Stud. (1980-); Annu. Bibliogr. Engl. Lang. Lit.; Arts Humanit. Citation Index [Full Cov.]; Book Rev. Index; Child. Lit. Abstr. (19??-); Curr. Contents Arts Humanit.; Humanit. Index; Lit. Crit. Regist.; MLA Int. Bibl. Books Artic. Mod. Lang. Lit.; Res. Alert [Full Cov.]; Soc. Sci. Cit. Index [Select. Cov.].

FR/0013-9483
EPHEMERE, L'. Periodical. French. **DD** 054.

VE/1011-7989
ESCRITURA (CARACAS). (ESCRITURA.). [Escritura]. **Added/Corp** Universidad Central de Venezuela. Consejo de Desarrollo Cientifico y Humanistico. Universidad Central de Venezuela. Facultad de Humanidades y Educacion. Departamento de Publicaciones. No. 1 (Jan./June 1976)-. Periodical. Spanish. sa. Escritura Teoria y Critica, Apartado 65603, Caracas 1066 A Venezuela. **ED** Rafael Di Prisco. **LC** PQ7081.A1; E79. **DD** 860.9/98/05. **Ad Acc**. **Circ:** 1,000.
Desc: Theory and literary criticism mainly in Latin American literature.
Ind/Abst HAPI Hisp. Am. Period. Index; MLA Int. Bibl. Books Artic. Mod. Lang. Lit.

IT
ESPERIA. (1986)-. English. an.

US/0014-0767
ESPRIT CREATEUR, L'. [Esprit creat.]. Vol. 1 (Spring 1961)-. Periodical. French (English and French). Four times a year (Apr., July, Oct., Dec.). $17.00 (individuals); $32.00 (institutions) US & Canada & Mexico; $21.00 (individuals) others. Louisiana State University / Departments of French & Italian, Box 25333, Baton Rouge LA 70803. **Tel** (504)388-6627. **ED** John D. Erickson. Index available. **Bk Rev**. **Ad Acc**. **Circ:** 1,100. available on microfilm from University Microfilms International (UMI); and Xerox. Documents available from The Genuine Article.
Desc: Topical journal of French literature and literary theory and criticism.
Ind/Abst Am. Humanit. Index; Arts Humanit. Citation Index [Full Cov.]; Book Rev. Index; MLA Int. Bibl. Books Artic. Mod. Lang. Lit.; Res. Alert [Full Cov.]; Romant. Move.; Soc. Sci. Cit. Index [Select. Cov.].

US/0094-5404
ESSAYS IN LITERATURE. [Essays lit.]. **Added/Corp** Western Illinois University. Dept. of English. Vol. 1, (Spring 1974)-. Academic Scholarly Publication. English. sa (April, Dec.). $10.00 (1 year), $18.00 (2 year) US institutions; $12.00 (1 year), $22.00 (2 year) other institutions; $10.00 (1 year), individuals. Western Illinois University, 114 Simpkins Hall, Macomb IL 61455. **Tel** (309) 298-2212, FAX (309) 298-2289. **ED** Thomas P Joswick. **LC** PN2; .E84. **DD** 805. cum. index. **Pr Rev**. **Circ:** 575. available on CD-ROM; available on microfilm and microfiche from University Microfilms International (UMI). Documents available from The Genuine Article, UMI Article Clearinghouse.
Desc: Scholarly critical essays on British, American, and foreign-language literature.
Ind/Abst Abstr. Engl. Stud.; Acad. Search (July 1993-); Am. Bibliogr. Slavic East Europ. Stud.; Annu. Bibliogr. Engl. Lang. Lit.; Arts Humanit. Citation Index [Full Cov.]; Child. Lit. Abstr. (19??-); Curr. Contents Arts Humanit.; Expand. Acad. Index (1989-); Humanit. Index; Humanit. Source (Jul. 1993-); INFO-SOUTH Abstr.; Lit. Crit. Regist.; Mag. Search; MLA Int. Bibl. Books Artic. Mod. Lang. Lit.; Newsp. Period. Abstr. (1991-); Res. Alert [Full Cov.]; Romant. Move.

FR/0014-195X
ETUDES ANGLAISES. (ETUDES ANGLAISES : GRANDE-BRETAGNE, ETATS-UNIS.). [Etud. angl.]. Vol. 1 (1937)-. Academic Scholarly Publication. French (English). qt. $92.00. Societe Nouvelle Didier Erudition, 6 rue de la Sorbonne, 75005 Paris France. **Tel** 011 33 1 43544757, FAX 011 33 1 40517385. **(Subscription address:** PO Box 830350, Birmingham, AL 35283-0350; telephone: (800)633-4931, (205)9951567 (outside US and Canada); FAX: (205)995-1588) **ED** M M Martinet. **LC** PR1; .E8. **DD** 820.9. **Bk Rev**. **Ad Acc**. **Circ:** 2,000 (ctrl). available on microfiche. Documents available from The Genuine Article.
Desc: A scholarly review of British and American literary tradition and linguistic culture, from analysis of the earliest manuscripts to modern criticism of contemporary works.
Ind/Abst Abstr. Engl. Stud.; Annu. Bibliogr. Engl. Lang. Lit.; Arts Humanit. Citation Index [Full Cov.]; BHA : Biblio. Hist. Art; Curr. Contents Arts Humanit.; MLA Int. Bibl. Books Artic. Mod. Lang. Lit.; Res. Alert [Full Cov.]; Romant. Move.; Soc. Plann. Policy Dev. Abstr.; Soc. Sci. Cit. Index [Select. Cov.].

SZ
ETUDES BAUDELAIREINNES. BIBLIOGRAPHIE. See Literature-Poetry.

US/0363-1850
EUREKA REVIEW. ***Ceased.*** (Winter 1975/1976)-(19??). English. an. Orion Press / California, PO Box 366, Willows CA 95988. **LC** PS1; .E93. **DD** 810/.8/005.

FR/0014-2751
EUROPE. (EUROPE; REVUE LITTERAIRE MENSUELLE.). [Europe]. Vol. 1 No. 1 (Feb. 1923)-. Periodical. French (French). Eight times a year. 440.74F France; 550.00F other. Europe / Revue Litteraire Mensuelle, 64 Boulevard Auguste-Blanqui, 75013 Paris France. **Tel** 011 33 1 44 08 73 80, FAX 011 33 1 45 35 92 04. **ED** Charles Dorfynski. **LC** AP20; .E85. Index available. **Bk Rev**, (Qty: 8). **Ad Acc**. **Circ:** 5,000 (ctrl). Documents available from The Genuine Article.
Desc: French literary reviews; contains studies on literature; also poems and short stories of contemporary writers.
Ind/Abst Annu. Bibliogr. Engl. Lang. Lit.; Arts Humanit. Citation Index [Full Cov.]; Child. Lit. Abstr. (19??-); Coal Abstr.; MLA Int. Bibl. Books Artic. Mod. Lang. Lit.; Res. Alert [Full Cov.]; Soc. Sci. Cit. Index [Select. Cov.].

US/1058-8272
EVELYN WAUGH NEWSLETTER AND STUDIES. See Biographies.

US/0014-5483
EXTRAPOLATION. [Extrapolation]. **Added/Corp** Modern Language Association of America. Seminar on Science Fiction. Modern Language Association of America. Conference on Science-Fiction. Science Fiction Research Association. Wooster, Ohio. College of Wooster. Dept. of English. Vol. 1 (Dec. 1959)-. Academic Scholarly Publication. English. qt. $28.00 (one year), $54.00 (two year) (institutions), $18.00 (one year), $34.00 (two year) (individuals) US; $34.00 (one year), $66.00 (two year) (institutions), $24.00 (one year), $46.00 (two year) other. Kent State University Press / Journals Manager, Kent OH 44242-0001. **Tel** (216)672-7913, FAX (216)672-3104. **ED** Donald M. Hassler. **LC** PN3448.S45; E9. **DD** 808.83/876/05. **[CCC]**. Index available. cum. index. **Bk Rev**. **Ad Acc**. **Pr Rev**. **Circ:** 1,000. available on microfilm and microfiche from University Microfilms International (UMI). Documents available from The Genuine Article, UMI Article Clearinghouse. ***Continues*** *The Year's Scholarship in Science Fiction, Fantasy, and Horror Literature, 0741-2231.*
Desc: Scholarly study of science fiction and fantasy that contains analytic articles and bibliographic studies for scholars, teachers and science fiction fans.
Ind/Abst Abstr. Engl. Stud.; Acad. Abstr. Full Text Elite (July 1990-); Acad. Abstr. (July 1990-); Acad. Ind. [Computer File] (1988-); Acad. Search (July 1990-); Annu. Bibliogr. Engl. Lang. Lit.; Arts Humanit. Citation Index [Full Cov.]; Book Rev. Index (1988-); Child. Lit. Abstr. (19??-); Curr. Contents Arts Humanit.; Expand. Acad. Index (1988-); Humanit. Index; Humanit. Source (Jul. 1990-); INFO-SOUTH Abstr.; Mag. Search; MLA Int. Bibl. Books Artic. Mod. Lang. Lit.; Newsp. Period. Abstr. (1989-); Res. Alert [Full Cov.]; Sci. Fict. Fantasy Book Rev. Index.

US/1051-5011
FANTASY COMMENTATOR. See Literature.

US/0733-6357
FAULKNER NEWSLETTER AND YOKNAPATAWPHA REVIEW, THE. See Biographies.

HU/0015-1785
FILOLOGIAI KOZLONY. See Linguistics.

IT
FILUGELLO. Camera Comm Ind Art Agr / Reggio, Reggio Piazza Vittoria, Palazzo Affari, 42100 Reggio Emilia Italy. **Tel** 011 39 522 7961.

FI
FINSK TIDSKRIFT. **VFOAT** Finsk Tidskrift foer Vitterhet, Vetenskap, Konst och Politik. (Jan. 1935)-. Periodical. Swedish. mo. Painotalo Gillot, Eskilsgatan 3,, Turku-Aabo, 20500 Finland. ***Continues*** *Finsk Tidskrift foer Vitterhet, Vetenskap, Konst och Politik;* ***Absorbed*** *Granskaren.*
Ind/Abst MLA Int. Bibl. Books Artic. Mod. Lang. Lit.

FR/0015-3486
FLAMMES VIVES. 3.- Yearly volume; June 1950-. Periodical. French. Six times a year. Editions du Carmel, Venasque, 84210 Pernes les Fontns France. **Tel** 011 33 90 660366. ***Continues*** *Flammes.*

US/0091-4924
FLANNERY O'CONNOR BULLETIN, THE. **See** Biographies.

US/0162-721X
FOLLIES. (197?)-. Periodical. English. mo. $5.00. Random House Inc., 400 Hahn Road, Westminster MD 21157. **Tel** (800)726-0600, (800)733-3000, FAX (800)659-2436.

CN/1187-6301
FORTHCOMING BOOKS - NATIONAL LIBRARY OF CANADA. **See** Library and Information Sciences.

IE/0046-4694
FORTNIGHT (BELFAST). (FORTNIGHT; AN INDEPENDENT REVIEW FOR NORTHERN IRELAND.). **VFOAT** Independent Review for Northern Ireland. (Sept. 25, 1970)-. Periodical. English (Irish). mo (11 issues). 45p (institutions); 37p (individuals). Fortnight Publications Ltd, 7 Lower Crescent, Belfast BT7 1NR Northern Ireland. **Tel** 011 44 232 232353. **ED** Robin Wilson. Index available. cum. index. **Bk Rev. Ad Acc. Pr Rev. Circ:** 6,000.
Desc: Northern Ireland independent review of current affairs, books and arts.

US
FORUM LITERARIO. (197?)-. Periodical. Spanish. mo. ***Supersedes*** *Cuervo International.*

FR/0738-9299
FRANK. [Frank]. **Added/Corp** Northeastern University (Boston, Mass.). Vol. 1, No. 1 (June 1983)-. Periodical. English. sa. 300.00F (institutions), 150.00F (individuals). Frank Books SARL, BP 29, 94301 Vincennes Cedex France. **Tel** 011 33 1 43656405, FAX 011 33 1 43282074. **ED** David Applefield. **LC** PN771; .F73. **DD** 808.8/0005. **Ad Acc. Pr Rev. Circ:** 5,000.
Desc: Includes poetry, fiction, translations, interviews, photography, paintings, sculpture, etc. Past contributors include Calvino, Breytenbach, Burroughs, Bowles, E M Cioran, John Berger, Robert Coover, Ray Carver, Selby, Bukowski, Stephen Dixon, and Turkish, Philippine, and Nordic writers.
Ind/Abst Am. Humanit. Index (-199?).

US/0098-9355
FRENCH FORUM. [Fr. forum]. Vol. 1 (Jan. 1976)-. Periodical. Multiple languages (English and French). tq (winter, spring and fall). $45.00. French Forum, PO Box 130, Nicholasville KY 40340. **Tel** (606)885-1446. **ED** Raymond C. and Virginia A. La Charite. **LC** PQ1; .F82. **DD** 840/.9. Index available. cum. index. **Bk Rev. Ad Acc. Pr Rev. Acid Free. Circ:** 600 (ctrl). Documents available from The Genuine Article.
Desc: French literary criticism; serves scholars, students, and teachers of French literature at the college, graduate, and professional levels. Authoritative and contributive essays (in English and French) on all periods of French literature.
Ind/Abst Arts Humanit. Citation Index [Full Cov.]; Curr. Contents Arts Humanit.; Index Book Rev. Humanit.; MLA Int. Bibl. Books Artic. Mod. Lang. Lit.; Res. Alert [Full Cov.]; Romant. Move.

US/0271-6607
FRENCH LITERATURE SERIES. [French lit. ser.]. **Added/Corp** University of South Carolina. Dept. of Foreign Languages and Literatures. Vol. 1 (1973)-. Monographic series. English (French). an. Price varies per volume. Editions Rodopi BV, Keizersgracht 302-304, 1016 Ex Amsterdam Netherlands. **Tel** 011 31 20 6227507, FAX 011 31 20 380948. **ED** Freeman G. Henry. **Ad Acc. Circ:** 300.
Desc: Topical studies of French literature.
Ind/Abst MLA Int. Bibl. Books Artic. Mod. Lang. Lit.

UK/0016-1128
FRENCH STUDIES. [Fr. stud.]. **Added/Corp** Society for French Studies (Great Britain). Vol. 1 (Jan. 1947)-. Academic Scholarly Publication. English (French). Four times a year (Jan., Apr., July, Oct.). £60.00 UK; $110.00 others, includes French Studies Bulletin. Society for French Studies, C/O J. M. Lewis, Queens University, Department of French, Belfast BT7 INN North Ireland. **(Subscription address:** Professor C B Radford, Department of French, Queen's University, Belfast BT7 INN United Kingdom**)** **ED** A. W. Raitt. **LC** PQ1; .F85. **DD** 840.5. **Bk Rev. Ad Acc. Circ:** 2,000 (ctrl). Documents available from The Genuine Article, UMI Article Clearinghouse.
Desc: Scholarly articles in the fields of French language and literature from the Middle Ages to the present day. Occasional articles on French history and painting.
Ind/Abst Acad. Search (July 1993-); Am. Hist. Life (1983-); ARTbibliogr. Mod.; Arts Humanit. Citation Index [Full Cov.]; BHA : Biblio. Hist. Art; Br. Humanit. Index; Child. Lit. Abstr. (19??-); Curr. Contents Arts Humanit.; Expand. Acad. Index (1989-); Humanit. Index; Humanit. Source (Jul. 1993-); INFO-SOUTH Abstr.; Middle East Abstr. Index; MLA Int. Bibl. Books Artic. Mod. Lang. Lit.; Newsp. Period. Abstr. (1991-); Res. Alert [Full Cov.]; Romant. Move.; Soc. Sci. Cit. Index [Select. Cov.].

UK/0016-3929
GAIRM. (1952)-. Periodical. Gaelic (Scots) (English). Four times a year. £10.00. Gairm Publications, 29 Waterloo Street, Glasgow G2 6BZ Scotland. **Tel** 11 44 41 2211971. **ED** Prof. D.S. Thomson. **LC** AP75; .G35. **Bk Rev. Ad Acc. Pr Rev. Circ:** 1,000.
Desc: Comments on current affairs and public issues. Contains short stories, poetry and articles on general topics along with reviews, songs, pictures and cartoons.

US/0016-4100
GALLEY SAIL REVIEW, THE. Vol. 1 (Winter 1958)-. Periodical. English. Three times a year. $8.00. Galley Sail Review, 1630 University Avenue, Suite 42, Berkeley CA 94703. **Tel** (415)486-0187. **DD** 811.
Ind/Abst Am. Humanit. Index.

US
GAMBIT MAGAZINE : A JOURNAL OF THE OHIO VALLEY. (1986)-. English. an. $3.00 (per issue). PO Box 1122, Rockville MD 20850. **ED** Jane Somerville. ***Continues*** *Gambit (Parkersburg, W. Va.).*
Ind/Abst Am. Humanit. Index (-199?); Index Am. Period. Verse.

US/0016-6928
GENRE (NORMAN, OKLA.). (GENRE.). [Genre]. **Added/Corp** University of Oklahoma. University of Illinois at Chicago Circle. Plattsburgh State University College. Vol. 1, No. 1 (Jan. 1968)-. Periodical. English. Four times a year (Seasonally). $14.00 (individuals), $27.00 (institutions) US; $30.00 (other). University of Oklahoma Department of English, 760 Van Fleet Oval, Norman OK 73019. **Tel** (405)325-2908, (405)325-4661. **ED** R. Schleifer. **LC** PN80; .G4. **DD** 801.95. Index available in last issue of volume--attached. cum. index. **Bk Rev. Ad Acc. Circ:** 800 (ctrl). Documents available from The Genuine Article.
Desc: Devoted to the criticism of genre. Presents questions of genre in relation to interpretation of major literary texts, historical development of specific genres and theoretical discussion.
Ind/Abst Abstr. Engl. Stud.; Am. Humanit. Index (-199?); Annu. Bibliogr. Engl. Lang. Lit.; Arts Humanit. Citation Index [Full Cov.]; Child. Lit. Abstr. (19??-); Curr. Contents Arts Humanit.; Lit. Crit. Regist.; Middle East Abstr. Index; MLA Int. Bibl. Books Artic. Mod. Lang. Lit.; Res. Alert [Full Cov.]; Romant. Move.

IT
GENTILE OPERE. (19??)-. Monographic series. Italian. Price varies per volume. Le Lettere, Costa San Giorgio 28, 50125 Florence Italy. **(Subscription address:** Licosa Spa, PO Box 552, 50125 Florence Italy**)**

US/0897-0483
GEORGE SAND STUDIES. [George Sand stud.]. **Added/Corp** Friends of George Sand. Vol. 7, No. 1 & 2 (1984/1985)-. Periodical. English (French). an. $18.00. Hofstra University / Cultural Center, Hofstra Cultural Center, Hofstra University, Hempstead NY 11550. **Tel** (516)463-5006, (516)277-5457. **ED** Natalie Datlof, David A. Powell (Editors in Chief). **LC** PQ2417; .N48. **DD** 843/.7. **Bk Rev. Ad Acc.** Full Page (B&W) $50.00. Half Page (B&W) $25.00. **Circ:** 500 (ctrl). ***Continues*** *Newsletter (Friends of George Sand), 0161-6544.*
Ind/Abst MLA Int. Bibl. Books Artic. Mod. Lang. Lit.; Romant. Move.

US/0016-8890
GERMANIC REVIEW, THE. [Ger. rev.]. **Added/Corp** Columbia University. Dept. of Germanic Languages. Columbia University. Dept. of Germanic Languages and Literatures. Vol. 1 (Jan. 1926)-. Periodical. English (German). Four times a year (Seasonally). $34.00 (individual), $69.00 (institution). Heldref Publications, 1319 Eighteenth Street Northwest, Washington DC 20036-1802. **Tel** (202)296-6267, (800)365-9753, FAX (202)296-5149. **ED** Shelley Frisch, Inge D. Halpert, and Frederick Lubich. **LC** PD1; .G4. **DD** 430/.05. **[CCC]. Bk Rev. Ad Acc. Circ:** 1,150. available on microfilm and microfiche from University Microfilms International (UMI). Documents available from The Genuine Article, UMI Article Clearinghouse.
Desc: Created primarily for college and university scholars worldwide. Each issue delivers to its readers thoroughly documented, clear, and concise analyses of prose and poetry from German literature and thoughtful reviews of the newest books in the field.
Ind/Abst Acad. Abstr. Full Text Elite (Jan. 1991-) [Full Txt.]; Acad. Abstr. (Jan. 1991-); Acad. Ind. [Computer File] (1987-); Acad. Search (Jan. 1991-); Am. Bibliogr. Slavic East Europ. Stud.; Annu. Bibliogr. Engl. Lang. Lit.; Arts Humanit. Citation Index [Full Cov.]; Curr. Contents Arts Humanit.; Expand. Acad. Index (1987-); Humanit. Source (Jul. 1990-) [Full Txt.]; INFO-SOUTH Abstr.; Mag. Artic. Summar. Elite (Jan. 1991-) [Full Txt.]; Mag. Artic. Summar. CD-ROM (Jan. 1991-); Mag. Search; MLA Int. Bibl. Books Artic. Mod. Lang. Lit.; Newsp. Period. Abstr. (1989-); Res. Alert [Full Cov.]; Romant. Move.; Soc. Plann. Policy Dev. Abstr.; Soc. Sci. Source (Jan. 1984-) [Full Txt.]; Sociol. Abstr.

NE/0016-9730
GIDS. (DE GIDS : NIEUWE VADERLANDSCHE LETTEROEFENINGEN.). [Gids]. Vol. 1 (1837)-. Periodical. Dutch. mo. Meulenhoff Nederland, Postbus 256, 2170 AG Sassenheim Netherlands. **LC** AP15; .G4. cum. index.
Ind/Abst MLA Int. Bibl. Books Artic. Mod. Lang. Lit.

IT/0017-0461
GIORNALE ITALIANO DI FILOLOGIA. **See** Linguistics.

US/0160-2373
GLEANINGS (CAMBRIDGE). **See** Religion and Theology.

●US/1068-0586
GLOBAL CITY REVIEW. (1993)-. Periodical. English. sa. $15.00. Global City Review, 105 East Rock Road, New Haven CT 06511. **Tel** (212)532-5114. **(Subscription address:** Global City Review, PO Box 1267, Peter Stuyvesant Station, New York, NY 1003**)** **ED** Lindsay Abrams. **Bk Rev.**
Desc: Articles include poetry, reviews, fiction, essays, and interviews dealing with gender issues, gay and lesbian issues, racial issues, war and peace, environmental issues, language and postmodernism.

IT
GLOBALITA. (19??)-. English. Studi Servizi Internazionale, Via Lesmi 7, 20123 Milan Italy. **Tel** 011 39 2 8358476.

US/0734-3329
GOETHE YEARBOOK. **See** Biographies.

US/0363-8057
GRADIVA. [Gradiva]. **Added/Corp** State University of New York at Stony Brook. Vol. 1 (Summer 1976)-. English (Italian). qt. $25.00. State University of New York / French & Italian, Department of French & Italian, c/o Dr. Luigi Fontanella, Stony Brook NY 11794. **Tel** (516)632-7448. **ED** L Fontanella. **LC** PN80; .G7. **DD** 809. **Bk Rev. Ad Acc. Circ:** 300. Documents available from The Genuine Article.
Desc: Literary criticism with focus on psychoanalysis, semiotics, structuralism, Marxism, historicism and methodologies.
Ind/Abst Annu. Bibliogr. Engl. Lang. Lit.; Arts Humanit. Citation Index [Full Cov.]; Curr. Contents Arts Humanit.; MLA Int. Bibl. Books Artic. Mod. Lang. Lit.; Res. Alert [Full Cov.]; Romant. Move.

UK/0017-3231
GRANTA. [Granta]. (1889)-. Periodical. English. qt (Mar., July, Sept., Dec.). £21.95 (UK); £29.95 (Europe); £36.95 (all except US, Canada, Europe); $29.95 (US). Granta Publications Ltd, 2/3 Hanover yard Noel Road, London N1 8BE England. **Tel** 11 44 1 704 0470, FAX 11 44 1 704 0474. **ED** Bill Buford. **LC** PN2; .G68. **DD** 813/.008. **Ad Acc. Circ:** 100,000. available on microfilm and microfiche from University Microfilms International (UMI).
Desc: Paperback magazine publishing fiction, cultural and political journalism: fiction (including novellas and works-in-progress), essays, political analysis, journalism, etc.

US/0162-0304
GREENHOUSE REVIEW. (1975)-. Periodical. English. Three times a year. Greenhouse Review, 126 Escalona Drive, Santa Cruz CA 95060. **LC** PS580; .G74. **DD** 811/.5/408.

CN/0017-453X
GRONK. Ser. 1, No. 1- Jan. 1967-). Periodical. English. ir. Ganglia Press, 239 Queen Street West, Toronto Ontario Canada.

US/0198-1099
HARD CRABS. **Added/Corp** Maryland Writers Council. (197?)-. Periodical. English. Ten times a year. $4.00. Maryland Writers Council, 1110 St Paul Street, Baltimore MD 21202. **Tel** (410)685-5239.

US/0017-789X
HARPER'S (NEW YORK, N.Y.). (HARPER'S.). [Harper's]. **Added/Corp** Harper's Magazine Foundation. **VFOAT** Harper's Magazine. Vol. 253, No. 1516 (Sept. 1976)-. Periodical. English. Twelve times a year. $18.00 (one year); $28.00 (two years); $42.00 (three years). Harpers Magazine Company, 666 Broadway, 11th Floor, New York NY 10012. **Tel** (212)614-6500. **(Subscription address:** CDS Agency Hard Copy, PO Box 4966, Des Moines IA 50340.**)** **LC** AP2; .H3. **DD** 051. **[CCC].** Index available. **Bk Rev. Ad Acc. Circ:** 186,092. available on microfilm and microfiche from University Microfilms International (UMI). Documents available from UMI Article Clearinghouse, Magazine

Collection. ***Continues*** *Harper's Magazine, 1045-7143.*
Desc: Social and political dialogue for today's busy reader. Regular features include annotation, readings, forum, and the popular Harper's index.
Ind/Abst Abr. Read. Guide Period. Lit.; Acad. Abstr. Full Text Elite (Jan. 1984-); Acad. Abstr. (Jan. 1984-); Acad. Ind. [Computer File] (1984-); Acad. Search (Jan. 1984-); Am. Bibliogr. Slavic East Europ. Stud.; Annu. Bibliogr. Engl. Lang. Lit.; Biogr. Index; Book Rev. Digest; Book Rev. Index; Can. Period. Index (19??-); Expand. Acad. Index (1984-); Film Lit. Index; Gen. Period. Index (1985-); Index Am. Period. Verse; Index Period. Artic. Relat. Law (199?-); Infobank (1976-); Mag. Artic. Summar. Elite (Jan. 1984-); Mag. Artic. Summar. Select (Jan. 1984-); Mag. Artic. Summar. CD-ROM (Jan. 1984-); Mag. Express (1986-) [Full Txt.]; Mag. Index Plus (1989-); Mag. Index. Sel. (1986-); Mag. Search; Med. Rev. Dig.; Middle East Abstr. Index; Newsp. Period. Abstr. (1986-); Peace Res. Abstr. J. (1964-1988); Read. Guide Abstr. Select Ed.; Read. Guide Period. Lit.; Resource/One Ondisc; Mag. Index (1977-); TOM Gen. Index (1985-) [Full Txt.]; Vocat. Search (Jan. 1984-).

US/0887-5170
HAYDEN'S FERRY REVIEW. [Hayden's Ferry rev.]. Issue No. 1 (Spring 1986)-. English. an. $4.00. Arizona State University / Student Publications, Matthews Center, Tempe AZ 85287. DD 810.
Ind/Abst Index Am. Period. Verse.

US/0276-3362
HEMINGWAY REVIEW, THE. [Hemingway rev.]. **Added/Corp** Ohio Northern University. Vol. 1, No. 1 (Fall 1981)-. Periodical. English. sa. $20.00 (institution), $15.00 (individual) US and Canada. The Hemingway Society, Department of English, University of North Carolina at Chapel Hill, Chapel Hill NC 27599. **Tel** (508)325-7157, FAX (508)325-7157. **ED** Charles M Oliver. **LC** PS3515.E37; Z6194. **DD** 813/.52. Index available. cum. index. **Bk Rev. Circ:** 700 (ctrl). available on microfilm and microfiche from University Microfilms International (UMI). Documents available from UMI Article Clearinghouse. ***Continues*** *Hemingway Notes, 0046-7243.*
Desc: Criticism of the works of Hemingway.
Ind/Abst Abstr. Engl. Stud.; Acad. Search (July 1993-); Am. Hist. Life (1988-); Annu. Bibliogr. Engl. Lang. Lit.; Expand. Acad. Index (1989-); Humanit. Index; Humanit. Source (Jul. 1993-); INFO-SOUTH Abstr.; MLA Int. Bibl. Books Artic. Mod. Lang. Lit.; Newsp. Period. Abstr. (1991-).

US/0273-0340
HENRY JAMES REVIEW, THE. [Henry James rev.]. **Added/Corp** Henry James Society. Vol. 1 (Nov. 1979)-. Academic Scholarly Publication. English. tq (February, May, Nov.). $23.50 (individuals), $43.00 (institutions). Johns Hopkins University Press, 2715 North Charles Street, Baltimore MD 21218-4319. **Tel** (410)516-6987, FAX (410)516-6968. **ED** Daniel Mark Fogel. **LC** PS2124; .H46. **DD** 813/.4. **[CCC]. Bk Rev. Ad Acc. Circ:** 500 (ctrl). available on microfilm and microfiche from University Microfilms International (UMI).
Desc: Deals with critical essays and reviews by noted critics of James, such as Leon Edel, Lyall Powers, and Dorothea Krook. Special features include a centennial essay series marking the one-hundredth anniversary of each of James' important works, analytical reviews of James' studies by Richard A. Hocks, and an annotated bibliography.
Ind/Abst Abstr. Engl. Stud.; Annu. Bibliogr. Engl. Lang. Lit.; Index Book Rev. Humanit.; Lit. Crit. Regist.; MLA Int. Bibl. Books Artic. Mod. Lang. Lit.

UK
HENTY SOCIETY LITERARY SUPPLEMENT. No. 1 (Jan. 1987)-. Periodical. English. qt. Free to members.

US/0888-4153
HIGH PLAINS LITERARY REVIEW. [High Plains lit. rev.]. Vol. 1, No. 1 (Winter 1986)-. Periodical. English. tq (Apr., Aug., and Dec.). $20.00 (one year), $38.00 (two year), $55.00 (three year). High Plains Literary Review, 180 Adams Street/Suite 250, Denver CO 80206. **Tel** (303)320-6827, or (303)320-6828. **ED** Robert O. Greer Jr. **DD** 810. Index available. **Bk Rev**, (Qty: 6). **Ad Acc.**
Ind/Abst Am. Humanit. Index; Index Am. Period. Verse; MLA Int. Bibl. Books Artic. Mod. Lang. Lit.

US/0018-2176
HISPANIC REVIEW. See Linguistics.

GW/0018-2605
HISTORISCH-POLITISCHE BUCH, DAS. See History(General).

●GW
HOFMANNSTHAL : JAHRBUCH ZUR EUROPAISCHEN MODERNE. Added/Corp Hugo von Hofmannsthal-Gesellschaft. **VFOAT** Hofmannsthal-Jahrbuch. (1993)-. German. an. DM60.00 (membership). Hugo Von Hofmannsthal, Gesselschaft AM Flossgraben 4, D 79102 Freiburg BR Germany. **Tel** 011 49 761 22482. **LC** PT2617.O47; Z635. ***Formed by the union of*** *Hofmannsthal Blatter, 0441-6813* ***and*** *Hofmannsthal-Forschungen.*

US/0018-3644
HOLLINS CRITIC, THE. [Hollins crit.]. **Added/Corp** Hollins College. Vol. 1 (Feb. 1964)-. Periodical. English. Five times a year (Feb., Apr., June, Oct., Dec.). $6.00 (one year); $10.00 (two years); $14.00 (three years). The Hollins Critic, Box 9538, Hollins College VA 24020. **Tel** (703)362-6317. **ED** John Rees Moore. **LC** PS1; .H65. Index available (Free). **Bk Rev. Ad Acc. Circ:** 550 (ctrl). available on microfilm and microfiche from University Microfilms International (UMI).
Desc: Single essay on contemporary author's entire work; brief sketch and checklist of author's work and artist's sketch of subject. Poems and brief book reviews.
Ind/Abst Abstr. Engl. Stud.; Am. Humanit. Index; Annu. Bibliogr. Engl. Lang. Lit.; Index Am. Period. Verse; Lit. Crit. Regist.; MLA Int. Bibl. Books Artic. Mod. Lang. Lit.

CN/0094-9086
HOPKINS QUARTERLY. *Suspended.* (THE HOPKINS QUARTERLY.). [Hopkins q.]. Vol. 1 (April 1974)-Suspended (199?). Academic Scholarly Publication. English (French). qt (4 issues). International Hopkins Association, 81 Mary Street, St. Michael College, Toronto Ontario M5S 1J4 Canada. **Tel** (416)926-1300. **ED** Richard F. Giles. **LC** PR4803.H44; Z649. **DD** 821/.8. Index available. **Bk Rev. Ad Acc. Circ:** 375 (ctrl). Documents available from The Genuine Article.
Desc: Articles, notes, reviews on G.M. Hopkins and his circle: Bridges, Dixon, and Patmore. Literary and biographical works-critical, appreciative, and scholarly-published.
Ind/Abst Abstr. Engl. Stud.; Am. Humanit. Index; Annu. Bibliogr. Engl. Lang. Lit.; Arts Humanit. Citation Index (19??-19??) [Full Cov.]; Curr. Contents Arts Humanit.; Lit. Crit. Regist.; MLA Int. Bibl. Books Artic. Mod. Lang. Lit.; Res. Alert [Full Cov.]; Romant. Move.

CL/0716-3460
HOY. Vol. 1 (June 1-7 1977)-. Periodical. Spanish. wk. $360.00. Editorial MRL SA, Maria Luisa Santander 0436, Santiago Chile. **Tel** 011 56 2 2743797. **LC** AP63; .H774. **DD** 056/.1.

US/0018-702X
HUDSON REVIEW, THE. See The Arts.

FR/0996-9942
HUMORESQUES. Added/Corp Association Francaise pour le Developpement des Recherches sur le Comique, le Rire et l'Humour. **VFOAT** CORHUM. No. 1 (Oct. 1990)-. Periodical. French. sa. 106.79F European Union; 109.79F other. Univ de Paris Puv, 2 rue de la Liberte, 93526 Saint-Denis Cedex 02 France. **Tel** 011 33 1 49406750.

US
HURON REVIEW. Periodical. English. sa. Huron Review, 423 South Franklin Avenue, Flint MI 48503.

US
IBSEN NEWS AND COMMENT : NEWSLETTER OF THE IBSEN SOCIETY OF AMERICA. Added/Corp Ibsen Society of America. No. 1 (Spring 1980)-. Newsletter. English. an (June). $7.00. Pratt Institute, Dekalb Hall 3, Brooklyn NY 11205. **Tel** (718)636-3794. **ED** Sandra Saari and Thomas van Laan. **Bk Rev. Circ:** 200 (ctrl).
Desc: Journal of Ibsen year in America, recording significant aspects of textual interpretation and theatrical production of Ibsen's dramas relevant to the U.S. and Canada.

●US/1067-4128
ILLINOIS REVIEW, THE. Added/Corp Illinois Writers, Inc. (1993)-. Periodical. English. sa. $10.00 (individuals), $15.00 (institutions). Illinois State University / English, Department of English, Normal IL 61761-6901. **Tel** (309)438-5776. **ED** Jim Elledge. **Bk Rev. Ad Acc. Circ:** 300.

US/0733-9526
ILLINOIS WRITERS REVIEW. *Ceased.* Vol. 1, No. 1 (Apr. 1981)-Vol. 11, Issues B. Periodical. English. sa. Illinois Writers Inc, PO Box 1087, Champaign IL 61820-1087. **Tel** (217)429-0117. **ED** Kevin Stein. **Bk Rev**, (Qty: (15-20)). **Ad Acc. Circ:** 300 (ctrl).
Desc: Reviews and essays concerning primarily Illinois writers and publishers. Includes information for writers. Focused on, but not limited to, Illinois concerns.
Ind/Abst Am. Humanit. Index.

IT
INDAGINI E QUADERNI. Italian. qt. L30000 Italy; L130000 other. Ctro Studi Ric Econom Sociali, Via Mancini 14, 05100 Terni Italy. **Tel** 011 39 744 44047. **Bk Rev. Ad Acc.**

SP
INDEPENDIENTE. Spanish. da. 22005ptas Spain except Madrid; 33684ptas Madrid; 59373ptas North Africa and Europe; 105224ptas Middle East and Africa; 92487ptas Western Hemisphere; 143432ptas other. Ediobser SA, Marques de Riscal 11-1, 28010 Madrid Spain. **Tel** 011 34 1 3082353, 011 34 1 3082354.

UK/0306-4220
INDEX ON CENSORSHIP. [Index censorsh.]. **Added/Corp** Writers & Scholars International. (Spring 1972)-. Periodical. English. Six times a year. £30.00 (1 year), £55.00 (2 year), £80.00 (3 year) UK; $36.00 (1 year), $66.00 (2 year), $99.00 (3 year) US; £36.00 (1 year), £66.00 (2 year), £99.00 (3 year) other. Writers and Scholars International, Queen Victoria Street, London EC4N 4SS England. **Tel** 011 44 71 3296434, FAX 011 44 71 3296461. **ED** Philip Spender. **LC** K9; .N3. **DD** 344.05/31/05. **Bk Rev. Ad Acc. Circ:** 5,000. available on an online database from PAIS Intl. Documents available from The Genuine Article, UMI Article Clearinghouse.
Desc: Primary source about contemporary writers, journalists worldwide who have been silenced for political reasons. Publishes examples of banned literature, factual reports and comment.
Ind/Abst Altern. Press Index; Arts Humanit. Citation Index [Full Cov.]; Br. Humanit. Index; Curr. Contents Arts Humanit.; Expand. Acad. Index (1992-); Hum. Rights Intern. Rep.; Index Period. Artic. Relat. Law; Int. Bibliogr. Sociol.; Middle East Abstr. Index; MLA Int. Bibl. Books Artic. Mod. Lang. Lit.; Newsp. Period. Abstr. (1992-); Res. Alert [Full Cov.]; Soc. Plann. Policy Dev. Abstr.; Soc. Sci. Cit. Index [Select. Cov.]; Sociol. Abstr.

II
INDIAN SCHOLAR. Vol. 1, No. 1 (Jan. 1979)-. English. sa. $10.00. Dr J Srihari Rao Editor, Indian Scholar 3 Vivekanand, Nagar Raipur 492001 Madhya Pradesh India. **ED** J Srihari Rao. **LC** PR9480; .I5. **DD** 809/.8954. **Bk Rev. Ad Acc. Circ:** 1,000.

US/0738-386X
INDIANA REVIEW. [Indiana rev.]. Vol. 5, No. 1 (Winter 1982)-. Periodical. English. sa. $15.00 (institutions), $12.00 (individuals). Indiana Review, 316 North Jordan Avenue, Bloomington IN 47405. **Tel** (812)855-3439. **ED** Cara Diaconoff. **LC** PS536.2; .I45. **DD** 810/.8/0054. **Bk Rev**, (Qty: 15-20). **Ad Acc, Adv Mgr:** Mikki Smith. **Circ:** 2,500. ***Continues*** *Indiana Writes, 0149-3361.*
Desc: Publishes poetry, fiction and essays by up-and-coming as well as established writers.
Ind/Abst Am. Humanit. Index; Index Am. Period. Verse.

US/0145-0786
INTERNATIONAL POETRY REVIEW (GREENSBORO). (INTERNATIONAL POETRY REVIEW.). [Int. poet. rev.]. Vol. 1- Spring 1975-. Periodical. English (French, German, Spanish and English). sa. $20.00 institutions; $13.33 others. Dept of Romance Languages, Univ of NC at Greensboro, Greensboro NC 27412. **Tel** (919)273-1711, (919)334-5655. **ED** Mark Smith-Soto. **LC** PN6099; .I57. **DD** 808.81. **Bk Rev. Circ:** 300 (ctrl).
Desc: Translation of contemporary poetry in bilingual format. Also poetry originally in English. Publishes contemporary poetry from all over the world with facing translation, and poetry originally in English (preferably an international or cross-cultural theme).
Ind/Abst Am. Bibliogr. Slavic East Europ. Stud.; Am. Humanit. Index; Index Am. Period. Verse; Middle East Abstr. Index.

GW/0020-918X
INTERNATIONALE BIBLIOGRAPHIE DER REZENSIONEN WISSENSCHAFTLICHER LITERATUR. See Literary and Political Reviews-Abstracting, Bibliographies and Statistics.

GW
INTERNATIONALE BIBLIOGRAPHIE DER ZEITSCHRIFTENLITERATUR AUS ALLEN GEBIETEN DES WISSENS. See Literary and Political Reviews-Abstracting, Bibliographies and Statistics.

US/0732-6750
INTI (PROVIDENCE, R.I.). See Literature.

IT
IPPOGRIFO (BOLOGNA, ITALY). (L'IPPOGRIFO.). Vol. 1, N. 1 (April 1988)-(Dec. 1990). Periodical. Italian. Three times a year. L80.000 surface mail; L110.000 airmail. Societa Editrice il Mulino, Strada Maggiore 37, 40125 Bologna Italy. **Tel** 011 39 51 256011, FAX 011 39 51 256034. **ED** Giuseppe Gherpelli. **LC** DG420.5; .I73. **DD** 945/.005. **Ad Acc.**

●US/1068-9494
IRIS (ATLANTA, GA.). (IRIS : A QUARTERLY REVIEW.). (1993)-. Periodical. English. qt. $12.00. Iris Publications, Box 57112, Atlanta GA 30309. **Tel** (404)875-6775. **ED** Shirlene Holmes & G. Crawford. **Circ:** 500.

IE/0021-1427
IRISH UNIVERSITY REVIEW. [Ir. univ. rev.]. Vol. 1, No. 1 (Autumn 1970)-. Periodical. English (Irish). Twice a year (June, and Nov.). $30.00 (individuals); $40.00 (institutions). University College Dublin, C/O Dr. C. Murray, Department of English, Room K203, Belfield Dublin 4 Ireland. **Tel** 011 353 1 7068260 or 7061661. **ED** Dr. Christopher Murray. **LC** PR8700; .I73. **DD** 820/.8/09415. Index available ($10.00). cum. index. **Bk Rev. Ad Acc. Circ:** 1,000 (ctrl). available on microfiche. Documents available from The Genuine Article. ***Continues*** *University Review (Dublin, Ireland),*

0566-2478.
Desc: Journal of Anglo-Irish literature and criticism.
Ind/Abst Abstr. Engl. Stud.; Annu. Bibliogr. Engl. Lang. Lit.; Arts Humanit. Citation Index [Full Cov.]; Curr. Contents Arts Humanit.; MLA Int. Bibl. Books Artic. Mod. Lang. Lit.; Res. Alert [Full Cov.]; Soc. Sci. Cit. Index [Select. Cov.].

US/0899-3114
JAMES JOYCE LITERARY SUPPLEMENT. [James Joyce lit. suppl.]. **Added/Corp** University of Miami. Dept. of English. Graduate Program. **VFOAT** JJLS. No. 1 (May 1987)-. Periodical. English. sa (May & Dec.). $8.00. James Joyce Literary, PO Box 248145, University of Miami, English Department, Coral Gables FL 33124. **Tel** (305)284-3140, FAX (305)284-6758. **ED** Bernard Benstock. **LC** PR6019.O9; J35. **DD** 823. **Bk Rev**. **Ad Acc**. **Pr Rev. Circ:** 650 (ctrl).
Ind/Abst Abstr. Engl. Stud.; Am. Humanit. Index (199?-); Lit. Crit. Regist.

US/0021-4183
JAMES JOYCE QUARTERLY. [James Joyce q.]. **Added/Corp** University of Tulsa. Vol. 1 (Fall 1963)-. Academic Scholarly Publication. English. qt. $18.00 (institutions), $17.00 (individuals) US; $20.00 (institutions), $19.00 (individuals) other. The University of Tulsa, c/o Linda Frazier, 600 South College Avenue, Tulsa OK 74104. **Tel** (918)631-2503, FAX (918)584-0623. **ED** Thomas F. Staley. **LC** PR6019.O9; Z637. **DD** 823/.9/12. Index available. cum. index. **Bk Rev**. **Ad Acc. Circ:** 1,400 (ctrl). available on microfilm and microfiche from University Microfilms International (UMI). Documents available from The Genuine Article, UMI Article Clearinghouse.
Desc: Critical studies on all aspects of James Joyce, including scholarly essays, notes, and book reviews.
Ind/Abst Abstr. Engl. Stud.; Acad. Search (July 1993-); Am. Humanit. Index; Annu. Bibliogr. Engl. Lang. Lit.; Arts Humanit. Citation Index [Full Cov.]; Curr. Contents Arts Humanit.; Expand. Acad. Index (1989-); Humanit. Index; Humanit. Source (Jul. 1993-); INFO-SOUTH Abstr.; Lit. Crit. Regist.; MLA Int. Bibl. Books Artic. Mod. Lang. Lit.; Newsp. Period. Abstr. (1991-); Res. Alert [Full Cov.]; Romant. Move.

US/0891-5393
JAMES WHITE REVIEW, THE. [James White rev.]. Vol. 1, No. 1 (Fall 1983)-. Periodical. English. qt. $12.00 (one year), $20.00 (two year) US; $26.00 (one year), $34.00 (two year) Canada; $29.00 (one year), $37.00 (two year) other. James White Review, A Gay Mens, PO Box 3356, Minneapolis MN 55403. **Tel** (612)291-2913. **ED** Paul Willks. **LC** PS536.2; .J36. **DD** 810.8/09206642/05. **Bk Rev**, (Qty: 25/yr). **Ad Acc. Circ:** 4000 (ctrl).
Ind/Abst Am. Humanit. Index; Index Am. Period. Verse.

US/0738-9655
JOHN DONNE JOURNAL. (JOHN DONNE JOURNAL : STUDIES IN THE AGE OF DONNE.). [John Donne j.]. **Added/Corp** North Carolina State University. English Dept. Vol. 1, No. 1-2- (1982)-. Periodical. English. Twice a year (June & Dec.). $30.00. John Donne Journal, Box 8105 NCSU, Raleigh NC 27695-8105. **Tel** (919)515-3870. **ED** M. Thomas Hester and R. V. Young. **LC** PR2248; .A2. **DD** 821/.3. **Bk Rev**. **Ad Acc. Circ:** 500.
Desc: Features critical and textual studies (essays and notes on the poetry and prose of Donne and other 17th century authors) on any subject or text, Donne's birth and the Restoration.
Ind/Abst Annu. Bibliogr. Engl. Lang. Lit.; Lit. Crit. Regist.; MLA Int. Bibl. Books Artic. Mod. Lang. Lit.

US/0162-413X
JOSEPH CONRAD TODAY. **See** Biographies.

CN/0705-1328
JOURNAL OF CANADIAN POETRY. **See** Literature-Poetry.

II
JOURNAL OF LITERARY CRITICISM. Vol. 1, No. 1 (June 1984)-. Periodical. English. Twice a year (June, Dec.). Rs30.00 (individuals); Rs40.00 (institutions). Doaba House, 1668 Nai Sarak, Delhi 110006 India. **Tel** 274669. **LC** PN80; .J68. **DD** 809.

SA/0256-4718
JOURNAL OF LITERARY STUDIES (PRETORIA, SOUTH AFRICA). (JOURNAL OF LITERARY STUDIES.). **Added/Corp** SAVAL (Organization). **VFOAT** Tydskrif vir Literatuurwetenskap; JLS; TLW; JLS/TLW. Vol. 1, No. 1 (Jan. 1985)-. Periodical. Afrikaans (English). Four times a year. $14.00 (individual); $20.00 (institution). University of South Africa Theory of Literature Department, PO Box 392, Pretoria 0001 South Africa. **Tel** 011 27 12 4298468.
Ind/Abst Annu. Bibliogr. Engl. Lang. Lit.; MLA Int. Bibl. Books Artic. Mod. Lang. Lit.

US/0022-281X
JOURNAL OF MODERN LITERATURE. [J. mod. lit.]. **Added/Corp** Temple University. **VFOAT** JML. Vol. 1 (1970)-. Academic Scholarly Publication. English. ir (2 or 3 issues are always combine). $25.00 US, $45.00 Asia, $35.00 other (institutions); $20.00 US, $40.00 Asia, $30.00 other (individuals). Temple University / Modern Literature, Journal of Modern Literature, c/o M Levitt, 921 Anderson Hall, Philadelphia PA 19122. **Tel** (215)204-8505. **ED** Morton P. Levitt. **LC** PN2; .J6. **DD** 809/.04. Index available. **Bk Rev**. **Ad Acc**. **Pr Rev. Circ:** 2,000 (ctrl). available on microfilm from University Microfilms International (UMI). Documents available from UMI Article Clearinghouse.
Desc: A scholarly journal devoted to modernist literature from a historical and research-based standpoint.
Ind/Abst Abstr. Engl. Stud.; Acad. Abstr. Full Text Elite (July 1990-); Acad. Abstr. (July 1990-); Acad. Ind. [Computer File] (1992-); Acad. Search (July 1990-); Am. Bibliogr. Slavic East Europ. Stud.; Annu. Bibliogr. Engl. Lang. Lit.; Arts Humanit. Citation Index [Full Cov.]; Curr. Contents Arts Humanit.; Expand. Acad. Index (1988-); Film Lit. Index; Humanit. Index; Humanit. Source (Jul. 1990-); INFO-SOUTH Abstr.; Lit. Crit. Regist.; Mag. Search; Middle East Abstr. Index; MLA Int. Bibl. Books Artic. Mod. Lang. Lit.; Newsp. Period. Abstr. (1986-); Res. Alert [Full Cov.]; Romant. Move.

US/0894-6388
JOURNAL OF THE KAFKA SOCIETY OF AMERICA. [J. Kafka Soc. Am.]. **Added/Corp** Kafka Society of America. No. 2 (Dec. 1983)-. Periodical. English (German). sa. $25.00 (individual), $30.00 (library) US; $30.00 (individual), $35.00 (library) other. Kafka Society of America, Temple University, German Department AB 335, Philadelphia PA 19122. **Tel** (215)787-8282, FAX (215)204-3731. **(Subscription address:** M Luise Caputo - Mayr, Kafka Society of America, 3rd Floor, Anderson Hall, Temple University, Philadelphia PA 19122**) ED** M Luise Caputo-Mayr. **DD** 830. Index available. cum. index. **Bk Rev**. **Ad Acc**. **Pr Rev. Circ:** 600. ***Continues*** *Newsletter of the Kafka Society of America, 0741-6202.*
Desc: Articles, bibliography and information on Kafka in English and German languages.
Ind/Abst MLA Int. Bibl. Books Artic. Mod. Lang. Lit.

US/0277-710X
KAIROS (OAKLAND, CALIF.). (KAIROS.). [Kairos]. Vol. 1, No. 1 (1981)-. Periodical. English. sa. $6.00 per issue. Hermes House Press, c/o mandell, 127 West 15th Street, New York NY 10011. **ED** Alan Mandell and William Rasch. **LC** PN2; .K34. **DD** 805. **Bk Rev**. **Ad Acc. Circ:** 350.
Desc: Social and cultural criticism, poetry, reviews, contemporary issues and the arts.

US/0022-7994
KALKI (ORADELL). ***Ceased.*** (KALKI.). [Kalki]. Vol. 1 (1965)-(1993). Academic Scholarly Publication. English (French). an. James Branch Cabell Society, HC 63 Box 70A, Alstead NH 03602. **Tel** (903)886-5264. **ED** Paul Spencer (editor's address: HC 63, Box 79, Alstead, NH 03602). cum. index. **Bk Rev**. **Pr Rev. Circ:** 350 (ctrl).
Desc: A scholarly journal which publishes critical essays on Cabell and his contemporaries, book reviews, and diverse information about the period from 1900 to 1950 or so.
Ind/Abst Am. Humanit. Index; Annu. Bibliogr. Engl. Lang. Lit.; Lit. Crit. Regist.; MLA Int. Bibl. Books Artic. Mod. Lang. Lit.

FI/0355-0303
KANAVA (HELSINKI. 1973). (KANAVA.). [Kanava]. Vol. 1, No. 2- ; 1973-. Periodical. Finnish. Yhtynut Kunalehdet Oy, Hietalahdenranta 13, 00180 Helsinki 18 Finland. **LC** AP80; .A333. ***Continues*** *Aika.*
Ind/Abst MLA Int. Bibl. Books Artic. Mod. Lang. Lit.

US/0889-647X
KENTUCKY POETRY REVIEW. ***Ceased.*** [Ky. poet. rev.]. **VFOAT** KPR. Vol. 12 (Winter 1976)-(Spring 1992). Periodical. English. sa. $8.00. Kentucky Poetry Review, 1568 Cherokee Road, Wade Hall, Louisville KY 40205. **Tel** (502)451-5516. **ED** Wade Hall. **DD** 811. Index available. **Bk Rev**. **Ad Acc**. **Pr Rev. Circ:** 400 (ctrl). ***Continues*** *Approaches, 0003-7133.*
Desc: Original poetry on any subject or form.

US/0163-075X
KENYON REVIEW, THE. [Kenyon rev.]. **Added/Corp** Kenyon College. Vol. 1-32 No. 1-128; (Winter 1939)-(1970); New Ser., Vol. 1 (Winter 1979)-. Periodical. English. qt (Jan., April, July, Oct.). $22.00 (1 year), $40.00 (2 year), $60.00 (3 year) individuals; $24.00 (1 year), $48.00 (2 year), $72.00 (3 year) libraries. Kenyon Review, Kenyon College, Gambier OH 43022. **Tel** (614)427-3339, FAX (614)427-3077. **ED** Marilyn Hacker. **LC** AP2; .K426. **DD** 051. Index available. **Bk Rev**. **Ad Acc. Circ:** 5,000 (ctrl). available on microfilm and microfiche from University Microfilms International (UMI). Documents available from The Genuine Article, UMI Article Clearinghouse.
Desc: Poetry, fiction, essays, book reviews.
Ind/Abst Abstr. Engl. Stud.; Acad. Abstr. Full Text Elite (July 1990-); Acad. Abstr. (July 1990-); Acad. Ind. [Computer File] (1987-); Acad. Search (July 1990-); Am. Humanit. Index; Annu. Bibliogr. Engl. Lang. Lit.; Arts Humanit. Citation Index [Full Cov.]; Book Rev. Digest; Book Rev. Index; Curr. Contents Arts Humanit.; Expand. Acad. Index (1987-); Gen. Period. Index (1987-); Humanit. Index; Index Am. Period. Verse; INFO-SOUTH Abstr.; Mag. Search; MLA Int. Bibl. Books Artic. Mod. Lang. Lit.; Newsp. Period. Abstr. (1991-); Res. Alert [Full Cov.].

US
KIRKUS CHILDRENS. (19??)-. Periodical. English. mo. Kirkus Associates LP, 200 Park Avenue South, Suite 1118, New York NY 10003. **Tel** (212)777-4554, FAX (212)979-1352.

US
KIRKUS REVIEWS. **Added/Corp** Kirkus Service. Vol. 59, No. 15 (Aug 1, 1991)-. Periodical. English. Twenty-four times a year. Price varies according to book budget for libraries; $340.00 other. Kirkus Associates LP, 200 Park Avenue South, Suite 1118, New York NY 10003. **Tel** (212)777-4554, FAX (212)979-1352. **ED** Peggy Kaganoff. **LC** Z477; .K5. **DD** 028.1/0973. ***Continues*** *Jim Kobak's Kirkus Reviews.*
Desc: Publishes pre-publication reviews of close to 5,000 hardcover and trade paperback titles each year, both fiction and non-fiction, from large, small, and university presses, as well as titles for young adults and children.

GW/0075-6318
KLEINE DEUTSCHE PROSADENKMALER DES MITTELALTERS. Vol. 1- 1965-. Monographic series. German. ir. Price varies per volume. Wilhelm Fink Verlag, Ohmstrasse 5, D 80802 Munich Germany. **Tel** 011 49 89 348017, 348018. **ED** Kurt Ruh.
Desc: Publishes first and/or new editions of medieval German prose.

US/0738-8640
KNOWLEDGE (FORT WORTH, TEX.). (KNOWLEDGE.). [Knowledge]. **Added/Corp** World Olympiads of Knowledge. Vol. 1, No. 1 (1976)-. Periodical. English. Four times a year (Mar., June, Sept., Dec.). $30.00 US; $35.00 other. Knowledge, 3863 Southwest Loop 820, Suite 100, Fort Worth TX 76133. **Tel** (817)292-4272, FAX (817)294-2893. **ED** O. A. Battista. **Bk Rev**. ctrl circ.

US/0271-1990
KOBRIN LETTER, THE. Vol. 1, (Sept. 1980)-. Periodical. English. Seven times a year. $12.00 (one year); $20.00 (two year). Dr Beverly Kobrin, 732 Greer Road, Palo Alto CA 94303. **Tel** (415)856-6658. **ED** Beverly Kobrin. **Bk Rev**, (Qty: varies).
Desc: Reviews children's nonfiction books for teachers and librarians; provides practical ideas for using nonfiction in the classroom.

JA
KOKUBUNGAKU KAISHAKU TO KANSHO. Vol. 1, No. 1 (June 1936)-. Periodical. Japanese. mo. $194.00. **(Subscription address:** Kyowa Book Company Inc., 1 38 Kanda Jinbocho Chiyoda-ku, Tokyo 101 Japan.**)**

RU/0130-2671
KROKODIL. [Krokodil]. (July 1, 1922)-. Periodical. Russian. ir. $109.95. Bumazhny, Pr. 14, 101455 Moscow Russia. **Tel** 095-250-1086. **(Subscription address:** East View Publications Inc., 3020 Harbor Lane North, Suite 110, Minneapolis MN 55447.**) Circ:** 2,200,000. available on microfilm and microfiche from University Microfilms International (UMI).
Desc: Humor magazine of Russia.

CC
KUO WAI WEN HSUEH. **VFOAT** Guowai Wenxue; Literature Abroad. Periodical. Chinese. qt. RMBY0.45. Pei-Ching Chu Pan She, Post Office, Pei-Ching Shih, People's Republic of China. **LC** PN80; .K86. **DD** 809.

US/1048-9487
LAMBDA BOOK REPORT. **See** Homosexuality.

US/0737-0555
LANGSTON HUGHES REVIEW, THE. (THE LANGSTON HUGHES REVIEW : OFFICIAL PUBLICATION OF THE LANGSTON HUGHES SOCIETY.). [Langston Hughes rev.]. **Added/Corp** Langston Hughes Society. Vol. 1, No. 1 (Spring 1982)-. Periodical. English. sa. $10.00. Institute of African-American Studies, Department of English, University of Georgia, Athens GA 30602. **Tel** (706)542-5197, FAX (706)542-3071. **ED** Dolan Hubbard. **LC** PS3515.U274; Z673. **DD** 818/.5209. Index available. **Bk Rev**. **Ad Acc. Circ:** 260 (ctrl).
Desc: Publishes articles and notes on the life and work of Langston Hughes, and his contemporaries and the Hughesian tradition.
Ind/Abst MLA Int. Bibl. Books Artic. Mod. Lang. Lit.

US/0047-4134
LATIN AMERICAN LITERARY REVIEW. [Lat. Am. lit. rev.]. **Added/Corp** Carnegie-Mellon University. Dept. of Modern Languages. Vol. 1, (Fall 1972)-. Periodical. English. Twice a year (June and December). $21.00 (individual), $37.00 (institution) US; $29.00 (individual), $39.00 (institution) other. Latin American Literary Review, 121 Edgewood Avenue, Pittsburgh PA 15218. **Tel** (412)371-9023, FAX (412)371-9025. **ED** Yvette E. Miller. **LC** PQ7081.A1; L35. **DD** 860/.9. **Bk Rev**. **Ad Acc**. **Pr Rev. Circ:** 1,000 (ctrl). available on microfilm and microfiche from University

Microfilms International (UMI). Documents available from UMI Article Clearinghouse.
Desc: Literatures of Latin America and Latin American minorities in the United States. Contains feature articles, reviews of recent literary works, translations of poetry plays and prose fiction, and arts.
Ind/Abst Acad. Search (July 1993-); Am. Humanit. Index; Chicano Index; Expand. Acad. Index (1989-); HAPI Hisp. Am. Period. Index; Humanit. Index; Humanit. Source (Jul. 1993-); INFO-SOUTH Abstr.; Mag. Search; MLA Int. Bibl. Books Artic. Mod. Lang. Lit.; Newsp. Period. Abstr. (1991-).

FR
LATIN AMERICAN YEARLY REVIEW, THE. V. 1- 1973-. Periodical. English. an. $4.00. American College in Paris, 65 Quai d'Orsay, 75007 Paris France. **LC** F1414.2; .L34. **DD** 320.9/8/003.

HU
LATOHATAR. Periodical. Hungarian. an. $19.00 US. Lapkiado Vallalat, Lenin Korut 9-11, 1073 Budapest 7, Hungary. **Tel** 222-408. **(Subscription address:** Kultura, PO Box 149, H-1389, Budapest 62 Hungary) **ED** Gabor Garai. **LC** DB30; .L27. Index available. cum. index. **Bk Rev. Circ:** 10,000 (ctrl).
Desc: A selection of poems, short stories, essays, criticism, etc., from the contemporary Hungarian literary reviews and other periodicals.
Ind/Abst Am. Hist. Life (1954-1970).

US/0732-8001
LECTOR (BERKELEY, CALIF.). (LECTOR / CALIFORNIA SPANISH LANGUAGE DATA BASE.). [Lector]. **Added/Corp** California Spanish Language Data Base (Firm) Hispanex (Firm). Vol. 1, No. 1 (June 1982)-. Periodical. English (Spanish). sa. $45.00 US and Canada; $50.00 other. California Spanish Language, 16161 Ventura Boulevard/Suite 830, Encino CA 91436-2504. **Tel** (818)990-1885. **ED** Roberto Cabello-Argandona. **LC** Z1039.M5; L43. **DD** 028.1/05. **Bk Rev. Ad Acc. Circ:** 3,000 (ctrl).
Desc: Hispanic cultural and book review journal.

BE/0251-7388
LECTURES LIEGE. [Lectures Liege]. (1981)-. Periodical. French. bm. 1000.00F. Centre de Lecture Publique de la Communaute Francaise, 46 B rue Louvrex, 4000 Liege Belgium. **Tel** 011 32 41 224312.

US/0075-8833
LESSING YEARBOOK. [Lessing yearb.]. **Added/Corp** American Lessing Society. Vol. 1 (1969)-. English (German). an (June). $42.50. Wayne State University Press, 4809 Woodward Avenue, The Leonard N. Simons Building, Detroit MI 48201-1309. **Tel** (313)577-6119, (313)577-6120, FAX (313)577-6131. **ED** Edward P. Harris and Richard E. Schade. **LC** PT2405.5; .L47. **DD** 838/.6/09. Index available. **Bk Rev. Circ:** 1,000 (ctrl).
Desc: Reviews research in 18th Century German life and letters and offers original articles of related interest.
Ind/Abst MLA Int. Bibl. Books Artic. Mod. Lang. Lit.; Romant. Move.

UK
LIBER. Vol. 1, No. 1 (Oct. 1989)-. English. bm. Free with subscription to "Times Literary Supplement". Priory House, St Johns Lane, London EC1M 4BX England.

CN/0024-2020
LIBERTE (MONTREAL). **See** Literature-Poetry.

US/1056-3113
LICTON SPRINGS REVIEW / A NORTH SEATTLE COMMUNITY COLLEGE LITERARY GUILD PUBLICATION. **Added/Corp** North Seattle Community College Literary Guild. Vol. 1, No. 1 (Spring 1991)-. Periodical. English. Three times a year. $3.00. North Seattle Community College, Associated Student Body, Literary Guild, 9600 College Way North, Seattle WA 98103-3599. **DD** 810.

UK/0459-4541
LINES REVIEW. (Jan. 1954)-. Periodical. English. qt. £9.50. M. McDonald, Edgefield Road Loanhead, Midlothian EH20 9SY England. **Tel** 011 44 31 4400246, FAX 011 44 31 4400315. **ED** Trevor Royle. **Bk Rev. Circ:** 600. ***Continues** Lines.*
Desc: Poetry reviews.

US/0147-2593
LION AND THE UNICORN (BROOKLYN), THE. (THE LION AND THE UNICORN.). [Lion unic.]. Vol. 1 (1977)-. Periodical. English. Twice a year (June, December). $38.00 US; $40.65 Canada and Mexico; $42.00 other. Johns Hopkins University Press, 2715 North Charles Street, Baltimore MD 21218-4319. **Tel** (410)516-6987, FAX (410)516-6968. **ED** Jack Zipes. **LC** PN1009.A1; L54. **DD** 809/.89282. **[CCC]. Bk Rev. Ad Acc. Circ:** 1,000. available on microfilm and microfiche from University Microfilms International (UMI).
Desc: Critical journal of books for children. Each issue explores one theme or genre, or one aspect of the field of children's literature. Includes critical pieces and interviews.
Ind/Abst Abstr. Engl. Stud.; Annu. Bibliogr. Engl. Lang. Lit.; Child. Lit. Abstr. (19??-); Curr. Contents Arts Humanit.; Lit. Crit. Regist.; MLA Int. Bibl. Books Artic. Mod. Lang. Lit.

US/0744-3722
LIP (LANCASTER, PA.). ***Ceased.*** (LIP.). **Added/Corp** Lancaster Independent Press, Inc. (Pa.). (19??)-(1992). Periodical. English. mo. Lancaster Independent Press, PO Box 275, Lancaster PA 17604. **Tel** (717)397-3472. **ED** Clark Bagel. **Bk Rev. Ad Acc. Circ:** 3,400. available on microfilm. ***Continues** Lancaster Independent Press.*
Desc: News on progressive politics, feminism, peace, alternative film, book and music reviews and anti-nuclear issues. Includes some local news along with calendar of events.

GW/0179-7417
LISTEN (FRANKFURT AM MAIN, GERMANY). (LISTEN.). Vol. 1 (Oct. 1985)-. German. qt. DM20.00 Germany; DM25.00 other. Chok-Institut, Hamburger Allee 45, W-6000 Frankfurt 90 Germany. **Tel** 069/775592. **ED** Karl P Berhofer. cum. index. **Bk Rev. Ad Acc.** ctrl circ.
Desc: Review of books (fiction and non-fiction, philosophy, politics, history, theory and the arts).

US/0733-2165
LITERARY CRITICISM REGISTER. **See** Literary and Political Reviews-Abstracting, Bibliographies and Statistics.

US/0732-6637
LITERARY MAGAZINE REVIEW. [Lit. mag. rev.]. **Added/Corp** Kansas State University. Writers Society. Vol. 1, No. 1 (Winter 1982)-. Periodical. English. qt. $12.50 US; $18.50 other. Kansas State University / English, 122 Denison Hall, English Department, Manhattan KS 66506. **Tel** (913)532-6011 ext 16, FAX (913)532-7004. **ED** G. W. Clift. **LC** PN4878.3; .L48. **DD** 810/.9. Index available. cum. index. **Bk Rev. Circ:** 500.
Desc: Devoted to reviews of the current issues of literary magazines, here and abroad, and to commentary concerning the contemporary writing scene.
Ind/Abst Am. Humanit. Index; Annu. Bibliogr. Engl. Lang. Lit.; Book Rev. Index (1986-).

UK/0144-4360
LITERARY REVIEW (EDINBURGH). (THE LITERARY REVIEW.). [Lit. rev.]. No. 1 (Oct. 1979)-. Periodical. English. mo. £32.00 US and Canada; £28.00 Europe; £22.00 UK; £44.00 other. Literary Review, 51 Beak Street, London W1R 3LF England. **Tel** 011 44 71 437 9392, telex 919034. **ED** Auberon Waugm. **LC** NX645; .L57. **DD** 082. **Bk Rev. Ad Acc.** ***Absorbed** Quarto (London, England : 1979), 0143-4985.*

II/0304-1123
LITERARY REVIEW (LUCKNOW). (THE LITERARY REVIEW.). Vol. 1 (Jan./Mar. 1974)-. English. qt. 20.00. Literary Review / India, A-3/6 Nurakabagar, Lucknow 226007 India. **LC** Z1035.A1; L488. **DD** 028.1.

US/1058-8353
LITERARY SCANNER. [Lit. scanner]. Vol. 1, Issue 1 (Oct./Nov. 1991)-. Periodical. English. bm. $15.00. Literary Scanner, PO Box 1074, South Sioux City NB 68776. **DD** 809.

US/0740-2880
LITERATURE CRITICISM FROM 1400 TO 1800. [Lit. crit. 1400 1800]. **Added/Corp** Gale Research Company. **VFOAT** Literature Criticism from Fourteen Hundred to Eighteen Hundred. Vol. 1 (1984)-. English. ir. $115.00. Gale Research Inc., 835 Penobscot Building, Detroit MI 48226. **Tel** (800)877-GALE, (313)961-2242, FAX (313)961-6083, telex TWX 810-221-7086. **ED** James E. Person Jr. **LC** PN86; .L56. **DD** 809.
Desc: Provides excerpts from criticism of the works of authors who died between 1400 and 1800. Novelists, poets, playwrights, philosophers, historians, and other authors have been selected from all the world's literatures of the time period. Designed to serve as an essential complement to literature courses, each volume focuses on about eight to ten writers. Author portraits and illustrations, facsimile title-pages, facsimile manuscript pages, biographies, and pictures related to the authors' lives and works bring life to the entire series of critical work. Annotations are provided at the head of each critical excerpt, generally supplying commentary on the critics background or shedding light on his or her critical position.

RU
LITERATURNAIA ROSSIIA : EZHENEDELNIK PRAVLENIIA SOIUZA PISATELEI RSFSR I PRAVLENIIA MOSKOVSKOGO OTDELENIIA SOIUZA PISATELEIA RSFSR. **Added/Corp** Soiuz Pisatelei RSFSR. Pravlenie. Soiuz Pisatelei RSFSR. Moskovskoe Otdelenie. Pravlenie. Moskovskaia Pisatelskaia Organizatsiia (R.S.F.S.R.). Pravlenie. (1963)-. Periodical. Russian. wk. $103.95. **(Subscription address:** East View Publications Inc., 3020 Harbor Lane North, Suite 110, Minneapolis MN 55447.) **LC** AP50; .L519. Index available. **Bk Rev.**

AI/0130-3597
LITERATURNAJA ARMENIJA. (LITERATURNAIA ARMENIIA.). [Lit. Arm.]. **Added/Corp** Soiuz Pisatelei Armianskoi SSR. Vol. 1 (1958)-. Periodical. Russian. mo. $169.95. **(Subscription address:** East View Publications Inc., 3020 Harbor Lane North, Suite 110, Minneapolis MN 55447.)
Ind/Abst MLA Int. Bibl. Books Artic. Mod. Lang. Lit.

KG/0459-5637
LITERATURNYI KIRGIZSTAN. **Added/Corp** Soiuz Pisstelei Kirgizii. Vol. 1 (1955)-. Periodical. Russian. mo. $109.95. **(Subscription address:** East View Publications Inc., 3020 Harbor Lane North, Suite 110, Minneapolis MN 55447.) ***Supersedes** Almanakh.*

GW
LITTERAE. (LITTERAE; GOPPINGER BEITRAEGE ZUR TEXTGESCHICHTE.). No. 1 1971-. Monographic series. German. Price varies per volume. Verlag Alfred Kummerle, Staibengasse 1, W 7073 Lorch FR Germany. **Tel** 011 49 7172 4844.

DK/0106-620X
LITTERATUR & SAMFUND. **See** Literature.

CN
LITTERATURES DE LANGUES EUROPEENNES AU TOURNANT DU SIECLE, LECTURES D'AUJOURD'HUI. SERIE D, PERSPECTIVE CRITIQUE. (LES LITTERATURES DE LANGUES EUROPEENNES AU TOURNANT DU SIECLE, LECTURES D'AUJOURD'HUI. SERIE D, LA PERSPECTIVE CRITIQUE SOVIETIQUE.). **VFOAT** Perspective Critique Sovietique; Soviet Critical Perspective. No. 1-. English (French and Russian). ir. 9.00Can$ per issue, (add 1.50Can$ postage, 4.00Can$ for airmail). Groupe de Recherches International 1900, Comparative Literature, Carleton University, Ottawa Ontario K1S 5B6 Canada. **Tel** (613)564-2894. **LC** PN99.S65; L57. cum. index. **Circ:** 300.
Desc: Recent reception of Tolstoi, Chekhov, Andreev, Kuprin, Bunin, Mandel'Shtam and reassessment of Russian painting.

UK/0076-0188
LLEN CYMRU. [Llen cymru]. **Added/Corp** University of Wales. Board of Celtic Studies. Vol. 1 No. 1 (1950)-. Periodical. Welsh. an. £3.50. University of Wales Press, 6 Gwennyth Street, Cathays Cardiff CF2 4YD Wales United Kingdom. **Tel** 011 44 222 231919. **ED** Ceri W. Lewis. **Bk Rev. Ad Acc. Circ:** 300. available on microfiche from University Microfilms International (UMI).
Desc: Serves the needs of researchers in the field of Welsh literary history. Embraces all periods and publishes articles of literary and historical criticism.
Ind/Abst MLA Int. Bibl. Books Artic. Mod. Lang. Lit.

UK/0260-9592
LONDON REVIEW OF BOOKS, THE. [Lond. rev. books]. **VFOAT** London Review. Vol. 1, No. 1 (Oct. 25, 1979)-. Periodical. English. sm. $70.00 institutions; $48.00 individuals. London Review of Books, Tavistock House South, Tavistock Square, London WC1H 9JZ England. **Tel** 011 44 71 388 7487, FAX 071 383 4792. **(Subscription address:** Kable Publishers Aide, 308 East Hitt Street, Mount Morris, IL 61054) **ED** Karl Miller and Mary-Kay Wilmers. Index available. **Bk Rev. Ad Acc. Circ:** 15,000. available on microfilm from University Microfilms International (UMI).
Desc: Covers anthropology, the arts, history, literary and political reviews, poetry, short stories, sociology, philosophy, biography, etc.
Ind/Abst Annu. Bibliogr. Engl. Lang. Lit.; BHA : Biblio. Hist. Art; Book Rev. Digest; Book Rev. Index; Index Book Rev. Relig.; MLA Int. Bibl. Books Artic. Mod. Lang. Lit.; Romant. Move.; Soc. Plann. Policy Dev. Abstr.

CN
LONERGAN REVIEW. (19??)-. Periodical. English. an. 11.00Can$. Lonergan University College, Concordia University, 7141 Sherbrooke Street West, Montreal Quebec Canada H4B 1R6. **ED** Prudence Allen.

ER/0134-4536
LOOMING. **See** Literature.

US/0734-0699
LOONFEATHER. [Loonfeather]. Vol. 1 (Fall 1979)-. Periodical. English. Twice a year (May and Nov.). $7.50. Loonfeather A Magazine of, 426 Bemidji Avenue, Bemidji MN 56601. **Tel** (218)751-4869. **ED** Betty Rossi and Marsha Muirhead. **Ad Acc. Circ:** 300.
Desc: This magazine is the work of both emerging and established writers. This includes poems, artwork and essays.

US
LUCEAFARUL. **Added/Corp** Uniunea Scriitorilor din Republica Socialista Romania. (19??)-. Periodical. Romanian. wk. 208lei. Uniuea Scriitorilor din Republica Socialista Romania, Calea Victoriei 115, Bucharest, Romania. **ED** Nicolae Dan Runtelata. **LC** Microfilm 03179 PC; PC800. **Bk Rev. Circ:** 7,000. available with illustrations; available with charts.
Desc: Review of literature, art and literary criticism.

CN/0821-1485
LYNN RIVER REVIEW. [Lynn River rev.]. Vol. 1-. Periodical. English. ir. Lynn River Review, 27 Ormond Crescent, Simcoe Ontario N3Y 1Y3 Canada. **DD** C810/.8/0054. ***Continues*** *Lynnwood Literary Review.*

US/0890-7722
MAGILL BOOK REVIEW. See Publishing-Books and Bookmaking.

CN/0828-5020
MALCOLM LOWRY REVIEW, THE. [Malcolm Lowry rev.]. **Added/Corp** Wilfrid Laurier University. Dept. of English. No. 15 (Fall 1984)-. Periodical. English. Twice a year (Fall/Spring). 40.00Can$ (indvidual); 80.00Can$ (institutions) 10 issues over five-year period from Fall 1992 to Spring 1997; Numbers 1-10 $20.00 per set, Numbers 11-20 $40.00 per set, Numbers 21-30 $60.00 per set (Back issues). Wilfrid Laurier University / English Department, Waterloo Ontario N2L 3L5 Canada. **Tel** (519)884-1970. **ED** Paul Tiessen. **LC** PR6023.O96; Z718. **DD** 813/.54. **Bk Rev**, (Qty: varies). **Ad Acc. Pr Rev. Circ:** 100 -150. ***Continues*** *Malcolm Lowry Newsletter, 0228-8427.*
Desc: Work related to the life and writing of Malcolm Lowry.
Ind/Abst MLA Int. Bibl. Books Artic. Mod. Lang. Lit.

US/1045-7909
MANOA. (MANOA : A PACIFIC JOURNAL OF INTERNATIONAL WRITING.). [Manoa]. Vol. 1, No. 1 & 2 (Fall 1989)-. Periodical. English. sa (Spring and Fall). $22.00 (one year), $40.00 (two year) institution, $18.00 (one year), $32.00 (two year) individual, $15.00 (single issue), US and Canada; $26.00 (one year), $47.00 (two year) institution, $21.00 (one year), $38.00 (two year) individual, $15.00 (single issue), other. University of Hawaii Press, 2840 Kolowalu Street, Honolulu HI 96822. **Tel** (808)956-8833, (808)948-8697, FAX (808)988-6052. **ED** Robert Shapard & Frank Stewart. **LC** PN771; .M28. **DD** 808.8/0005. **CODEN** MANOE7. **Bk Rev. Ad Acc. Pr Rev. Circ:** 700. available in microform.
Desc: A literary review presenting North American and international fiction and poetry, plus articles of current cultural or literary interest and translations of new works from Asia and Pacific nations.
Ind/Abst Soc. Plann. Policy Dev. Abstr.

US
MANY CORNERS. (1973)-. Newspaper. English. ir. $8.50. Many Corners, 1503 Washington Avenue South, Minneapolis MN 55454. **Tel** (612)333-0031. **ED** Barry Casselman. **Bk Rev. Ad Acc. Circ:** 20,000. available on microfilm.
Desc: Independent newspaper featuring political analysis, coverage of performing arts, restaurants travel, and book reviews.

IT
MARCO POLO. (19??)-. Italian. Ten times a year. L50000 Italy; L100000 other. Marsilio Editori, Marittima Fabbricato 205, 30135 Venice Italy. **Tel** 011 39 41 5227822.

US/0025-3499
MARK TWAIN JOURNAL (1954). See Biographies.

US/0047-6161
MASSACHUSETTS STUDIES IN ENGLISH. ***Ceased.*** (MASSACHUSETTS STUDIES IN ENGLISH : MSE : JOURNAL OF THE UNIVERSITY OF MASSACHUSETTS GRADUATE ENGLISH PROGRAM.). [Mass. stud. Engl.]. **Added/Corp** University of Massachusetts (Amherst Campus). Dept. of English. University of Massachusetts at Amherst. Dept. of English. **VFOAT** MSE. Vol. 1 No. 1 (Spring 1967)-(1992). Periodical. English. sa. English Literary Renaissance, University of Massachusetts, Bartlett Hall, Amherst MA 01003. **Tel** (413)545-5465, FAX (413)545-3880. **ED** James M Dutcher. **LC** PR1; .M25. **DD** 820. Index available. **Circ:** 200 (ctrl). available on microfilm and microfiche from University Microfilms International (UMI).
Desc: Critical essays on literature.
Ind/Abst Abstr. Engl. Stud.; Annu. Bibliogr. Engl. Lang. Lit.; Lit. Crit. Regist.; MLA Int. Bibl. Books Artic. Mod. Lang. Lit.; Romant. Move.; Soc. Plann. Policy Dev. Abstr.

●CI
MATICA : CASOPIS HRVATSKE MATICE ISELJENIKA. Added/Corp Matica Iseljenika Hrvatske. (1993)-. Periodical. Serbo-Croatian (Roman). mo. Hrvatska Matica Iseljenika, Trnjanska BB, Zagreb Croatia. **Tel** 011 38 41 530002, FAX 0038 (41)539 111. ***Continues*** *Nova Matica, 0353-8052.*

US/0885-467X
MCNEESE REVIEW, THE. [McNeese rev.]. **Added/Corp** John McNeese Junior College. Vol. 1 (Spring 1948)-. Academic Scholarly Publication. English. an. $5.00 North America; $7.00 other. McNeese State University, Box 92940, Lake Charles LA 70609-2940. **Tel** (318)475-5593. **ED** Dr. Maarten Reilingh (editor's phone: (318)475-5041). **LC** AS36; .L872. **DD** 051. Index available. **Pr Rev. Circ:** 200.
Desc: Original, previously unpublished manuscripts, documented research of scholarly nature, and basically areas of humanities.
Ind/Abst Abstr. Engl. Stud.; MLA Int. Bibl. Books Artic. Mod. Lang. Lit.; Romant. Move.

US/0731-3403
MEDIEVAL & RENAISSANCE DRAMA IN ENGLAND. See Theater.

GW/0543-3533
MEDIUM AEVUM (MUNICH). (MEDIUM AEVUM; PHILOLOGISCHE STUDIEN.). Vol. 1 (1963)-. Monographic series. German. ir. Price varies per volume. Wilhelm Fink Verlag, Ohmstrasse 5, D 80802 Munich Germany. **Tel** 011 49 89 348017, 348018. **ED** Friedrich Ohly, Kurt Ruh and Werner Schroder.
Desc: Publishes monographic studies and criticism on medieval German literature.
Ind/Abst Br. Humanit. Index; Humanit. Index.

PE
MEMORIA DEL CONGRESO INTERNACIONAL DE LITERATURA IBEROAMERICANA. Main/Corp Congreso Internacional de Literatura Iberoamericana. (1938)-. Monographic series. Spanish. ir. Price varies per volume. Instituto Internacional de CL, 1312 University of Pittsburgh, Pittsburgh PA 15260. **ED** Alfredo A. Roggiano. **Ad Acc. Circ:** 2,000.
Desc: Presents essays, notes, reviews and bibliographies on Ibero-American literature.

AT/0728-5914
MERIDIAN (BUNDOORA, VIC.). (MERIDIAN : THE LA TROBE UNIVERSITY ENGLISH REVIEW.). Vol. 1, No. 1 (May 1982)-. Periodical. English. Twice a year (May & Oct.). 30.00Aus$ (individuals); 40.00Aus$ (institutions). LaTrobe University Press, LaTrobe University C A Day, Bundoora Victoria 3083 Australia. **Tel** 011 61 3 4791460, FAX (03)470 2011, telex AA 33143. **(Subscription address:** La Trobe University Press, PO Box 3083, Bundora 3083 Australia.**)** **ED** John Barnes. **LC** PN2; .M47. **DD** 809. **Bk Rev. Ad Acc. Circ:** 500 (ctrl).
Ind/Abst APAIS, Aust. Public Aff. Inf. Ser. (1986-).

GW/0026-0096
MERKUR. [Merkur]. (1947)-. Periodical. German. Eleven times a year (Sept./Oct. issues combined). DM170.00, (add DM30.00 for postage). Klett-Cotta Verlagsgemeinschft, PO Box 106016, D 70049 Stuttgart Germany. **Tel** 011 49 711 66720. **(Subscription address:** Stuttgerter Verlagskontor, Postfatch 106016, D-70049 Stuttgart, Germany.**)** **ED** J. Moras and H. Paeschke. **LC** AP30; .M43. **DD** 053. **[CCC].** Documents available from The Genuine Article.
Ind/Abst Abstr. Engl. Stud.; Am. Hist. Life (1954-1958); Arts Humanit. Citation Index [Full Cov.]; Int. Polit. Sci. Abstr.; MLA Int. Bibl. Books Artic. Mod. Lang. Lit.; Philos. Index; Res. Alert [Full Cov.]; Romant. Move.; Soc. Sci. Cit. Index [Select. Cov.].

US/0026-2420
MICHIGAN QUARTERLY REVIEW. [Mich. q. rev.]. **Added/Corp** University of Michigan. Vol. 1 (Jan. 1962)-. Periodical. English. Four times a year (Jan., Apr., July, Sept.). $20.00 US; $25.00 other. University of Michigan / Rackham, 3032 Rackham Building, Ann Arbor MI 48109-1070. **Tel** (313)764-9265. **ED** Laurence Goldstein. **LC** AS30; .M48. **DD** 051. Index Available in first issue of next volume--attached. **Bk Rev**, (Qty: varies). **Ad Acc, Adv Mgr:** Doris Knight. **Circ:** 1,700. available on microfilm and microfiche from University Microfilms International (UMI). Documents available from The Genuine Article, UMI Article Clearinghouse.
Supersedes *Michigan Alumnus Quarterly Review.*
Desc: An interdisciplinary journal which includes fiction, poetry, essays, book reviews, interviews of people of distinction, and annual special issues which focus on a single theme.
Ind/Abst Abstr. Engl. Stud.; Acad. Search (July 1993-); Am. Hist. Life (1964-1971);(1965-); Am. Bibliogr. Slavic East Europ. Stud.; Am. Humanit. Index; Annu. Bibliogr. Engl. Lang. Lit.; Arts Humanit. Citation Index [Full Cov.]; BHA : Biblio. Hist. Art; Book Rev. Index; Curr. Contents Arts Humanit.; Expand. Acad. Index (1989-); Film Lit. Index; Humanit. Index; Humanit. Source (Jul. 1993-); Index Am. Period. Verse; Index Book Rev. Humanit.; INFO-SOUTH Abstr.; Int. Aerosp. Abstr.; Lit. Crit. Regist.; Mag. Search; Middle East Abstr. Index; MLA Int. Bibl. Books Artic. Mod. Lang. Lit.; Newsp. Period. Abstr. (1991-); PAIS Int. Print (1991-?); Public Aff. Inf. Serv. Bull.; Res. Alert [Full Cov.]; Romant. Move.; Soc. Sci. Cit. Index [Select. Cov.]; SportSearch.

US/0026-4326
MILTON QUARTERLY. [Milton q.]. **Added/Corp** Ohio University. Dept. of English. Vol. 4, March (1970)-. English. Four times a year (Mar., May, Oct., Dec.). $28.00 (institution) US & other; $18.00 (individual) US & other. Ohio University / Milton Quarterly, Roy C. Flannagan, 381 Ellis Hall, Athens OH 45701. **Tel** (614)593-2831. **ED** Roy Flannagan. **LC** PR3579; .M48. **DD** 821/.4. **[CCC]. Bk Rev**, (Qty: 10-15/yr). **Ad Acc, Adv Mgr:** Jason Holtman, **Tel** (614)593-2831. **Circ:** 1,000. available on microfilm and microfiche from University Microfilms International (UMI). Documents available from The Genuine Article.
Continues *Milton Newsletter, 0146-4922.*
Desc: Articles and news items relating to the writings and life of John Milton, seventeenth century English poet and prose writer.
Ind/Abst Abstr. Engl. Stud.; Am. Humanit. Index; Annu. Bibliogr. Engl. Lang. Lit.; Arts Humanit. Citation Index [Full Cov.]; Curr. Contents Arts Humanit.; Humanit. Index; Lit. Crit. Regist.; MLA Int. Bibl. Books Artic. Mod. Lang. Lit.; Res. Alert [Full Cov.]; Romant. Move.

US/0076-8820
MILTON STUDIES. [Milton stud.]. Vol. 1 (1969)-. English. an. $49.95. University of Pittsburgh Press, 127 North Bellefield Avenue, Pittsburgh PA 15260. **Tel** (412)624-4110. **ED** James D Simmonds. **LC** PR3579; .M5. **DD** 821/.4. Index available. cum. index. **Circ:** 900 (ctrl). Documents available from The Genuine Article.
Desc: Criticism and analysis of the works of John Milton.
Ind/Abst Abstr. Engl. Stud.; Annu. Bibliogr. Engl. Lang. Lit.; Arts Humanit. Citation Index (19??-19??) [Full Cov.]; MLA Int. Bibl. Books Artic. Mod. Lang. Lit.; Res. Alert [Full Cov.].

US/0026-5667
MINNESOTA REVIEW (NEW YORK, N.Y.). (THE MINNESOTA REVIEW.). [Minn. rev.]. (Fall 1971)-. Periodical. English. sa (Spring and Fall). $12.00 (individuals); $24.00 (institutions & others outside US); $5.00 (surface mail); $10.00 (airmail). Minnesota Review, East Carolina University, Department of English, Greenville NC 27858. **Tel** (919)328-6388, FAX (919)328-4889. **ED** Jeffrey Williams. **Bk Rev**, (Qty: 25). **Ad Acc. Circ:** 1,500 (ctrl). available on microfilm and microfiche from University Microfilms International (UMI). Documents available from The Genuine Article.
Continues *Minnesota Review, 0026-5667.*
Desc: Publishes fiction, poetry, essays and reviews of a political and social orientation. Encourages non-sectarian, Marxist and feminist writings.
Ind/Abst Abstr. Engl. Stud. (1979-); Am. Humanit. Index; Annu. Bibliogr. Engl. Lang. Lit.; Arts Humanit. Citation Index (19??-19??) [Full Cov.]; Book Rev. Index; Curr. Contents Arts Humanit.; Film Lit. Index; Index Am. Period. Verse; Lit. Crit. Regist.; MLA Int. Bibl. Books Artic. Mod. Lang. Lit.; Res. Alert [Full Cov.]; Romant. Move.; Soc. Sci. Cit. Index [Select. Cov.].

US/1055-0690
MINORITY LITERARY EXPO. (MINORITY LITERARY EXPO : [DIRECTORY].). **VFOAT** Minority Literary Expo Directory Publication; Minority Literary Expo Directory; Minority Literary Expo Directory-Publication. (1991)-. English. $40.00. Fondren Enterprises 2000, 216 Avenue T, Pratt City, Birmingham AL 35214.

●US/1061-2246
MINORITY LITERARY EXPO (BIRMINGHAM, ALA.). (MINORITY LITERARY EXPO.). (1992)-. Periodical. English. $12.50. Minority Literary Expo, PO Box 37017, Birmingham AL 35237.

US/0026-7724
MODERN FICTION STUDIES. [Mod. fict. stud.]. **Added/Corp** Purdue University. Dept. of English. Purdue University. Modern Fiction Club. **VFOAT** MFS. Vol. 1 (Feb. 1955)-. Periodical. English (French, German, Spanish, Russian and Italian). qt. $45.00 US; $49.50 Canada and Mexico; $54.00 other. Johns Hopkins University Press, 2715 North Charles Street, Baltimore MD 21218-4319. **Tel** (410)516-6987, FAX (410)516-6968. **(Subscription address:** Modern Fiction Studies, Johns Hopkins University Press, PO Box 19666, Baltimore MD 21211.**)** **ED** William T. Stafford. **LC** PS379; .M55. **DD** 809.3. Index available. cum. index. **Bk Rev. Circ:** 3,500. available on microfilm and microfiche from University Microfilms International (UMI). Documents available from The Genuine Article, UMI Article Clearinghouse.
Desc: Criticism of modern fiction, 1880 to present.
Ind/Abst Abstr. Engl. Stud.; Acad. Abstr. Full Text Elite (July 1990-); Acad. Abstr. (July 1990-); Acad. Ind. [Computer File] (1987-); Acad. Search (July 1990-); Am. Bibliogr. Slavic East Europ. Stud.; Annu. Bibliogr. Engl. Lang. Lit.; Arts Humanit. Citation Index [Full Cov.]; BHA : Biblio. Hist. Art; Book Rev. Index; Curr. Contents Arts Humanit.; Expand. Acad. Index (1987-); Humanit. Index; INFO-SOUTH Abstr.; Lit. Crit. Regist.; Mag. Search; Middle East Abstr. Index; MLA Int. Bibl. Books Artic. Mod. Lang. Lit.; Newsp. Period. Abstr. (1989-); Res. Alert [Full Cov.]; Romant. Move.; Soc. Sci. Cit. Index [Select. Cov.].

US/0026-7929
MODERN LANGUAGE QUARTERLY (SEATTLE). (MODERN LANGUAGE QUARTERLY.). [Mod. lang. q.]. **VFOAT** MLQ. Vol. 1 (Mar. 1940)-. Periodical. English. qt (4 issues). $40.00 (institutions), $20.00 (individuals). Duke University Press, PO Box 90660, Durham NC 27708-0660. **Tel** (919)687-3600, (919)688-5134 (orders), FAX (919)688-4574, telex 802829. **ED** Marshall Brown and John C. Coldewey. **LC** PB1; .M642. **DD** 405. Index available. **Bk Rev. Circ:** 1,985. available on microfilm and microfiche from University Microfilms International (UMI). Documents available from The Genuine Article, UMI Article Clearinghouse.
Desc: A journal of critical literary history and analysis.
Ind/Abst Abstr. Engl. Stud.; Acad. Abstr. Full Text Elite (July 1990-); Acad. Abstr. (July 1990-); Acad. Ind. [Computer File] (1987-); Acad. Search (July 1990-); Annu. Bibliogr. Engl. Lang. Lit.; Arts Humanit. Citation Index [Full Cov.]; Expand. Acad. Index (1987-); Humanit. Index; Humanit. Source (Jul. 1990-); INFO-SOUTH Abstr.; Lit. Crit. Regist.; Mag. Search; Middle East Abstr. Index; MLA

Int. Bibl. Books Artic. Mod. Lang. Lit.; Newsp. Period. Abstr. (1991-); Res. Alert [Full Cov.]; Romant. Move.; Soc. Sci. Cit. Index [Select. Cov.].

US/0047-7729
MODERN LANGUAGE STUDIES. **See** Linguistics.

RM
MOFTUL ROMAN. **Added/Corp** Romania. Ministerul Culturii. Vol 1, No. 1 (1990)-. Periodical. Romanian. Six times a year. DM133.00. **(Subscription address:** Kubon & Sagner, ABT Zeitschriftenimport, D 80328 Munich Germany.**)** **LC** IN PROCESS. ***Continues*** *Urzica.*

US/0885-761X
MONOGRAPH SERIES - UNIVERSITY OF TULSA. (MONOGRAPH SERIES.). [Monogr. ser. - Univ. Tulsa]. **Main/Corp** University of Tulsa. No. 9-1970-. Monographic series. English. ir. Price varies per volume. University of Tulsa Academic Publications, Tulsa OK 74104. **Tel** (918)592-6000. **ED** Mary O'Toole. **LC** PR13; .T83. **DD** 809. **Circ:** 500. ***Continues*** *University of Tulsa. Dept. of English. Monograph Series.*
Desc: Various aspects of literature and criticism.
Ind/Abst Annu. Bibliogr. Engl. Lang. Lit.; MLA Int. Bibl. Books Artic. Mod. Lang. Lit.

IT/0027-3120
MULINO, IL. Vol. 1, No. 1 (Nov. 1951)-. Periodical. Italian. bm. L80000.00 Italy; L120000.00 (surface mail), L150000.00 (airmail) other. Societa Editrice il Mulino, Strada Maggiore 37, 40125 Bologna Italy. **Tel** 011 39 51 256011, FAX 011 39 51 256034. **LC** AP37; .M78. **DD** 055/.1. cum. index.
Ind/Abst Int. Polit. Sci. Abstr.; Soc. Plann. Policy Dev. Abstr.; Sociol. Abstr. (?-?).

GW
MUNCHENER ROMANISTISCHE ARBEITEN. (1932)-. Monographic series. German. ir. Price varies per volume. Wilhelm Fink Verlag, Ohmstrasse 5, D 80802 Munich Germany. **Tel** 011 49 89 348017, 348018. **ED** Hans Sckommodau.
Desc: Publishes monographic studies and criticism of Romanic literature.

GW/0077-1872
MUNCHNER GERMANISTISCHE BEITRAEGE. [Munch. ger. beitr.]. (1968)-. Monographic series. German. ir. Price varies per volume. Wilhelm Fink Verlag, Ohmstrasse 5, D 80802 Munich Germany. **Tel** 011 49 89 348017, 348018. **ED** Wolfgang Harms, Renate von Heydebrand and Theo Vennemann.
Desc: Publishes monograph studies and/or criticism on German literature.
Ind/Abst MLA Int. Bibl. Books Artic. Mod. Lang. Lit.

US/0734-9076
MYSTERY NEWS. [Mystery News]. Vol. 1, No. 1 (Nov. 1981)-. Periodical. English. bm (Feb., April, June, Aug., Oct., Dec.). $15.00. Mystery News, PO Box 1201, Port Townsend WA 98368-0901. **Tel** (206)765-4432. **ED** Harriet Stay. **DD** 808. **Bk Rev**, (Qty: 420). **Circ:** 2,300.
Desc: Previews, and reviews recently and soon to be published mystery books in all categories of the genre. Includes author interviews and mystery events.

RU/0027-8238
NAS SOVREMENNIK. (NASH SOVREMENNIK.). [Nas sovrem.]. **Added/Corp** Soiuz Pisatelei SSSR. Soiuz Pisatelei RSFSR. (1956)-. Periodical. Russian. mo. $99.95. **(Subscription address:** East View Publications Inc., 3020 Harbor Lane North, Suite 110, Minneapolis MN 55447.**)** **LC** PG3227; .N314. ***Supersedes*** *God Shesnadtsatyi-Dvadtsat Vtoroi.*
Ind/Abst MLA Int. Bibl. Books Artic. Mod. Lang. Lit.; Curr. Dig. Post Sov. Press.

US/0890-4197
NATHANIEL HAWTHORNE REVIEW : THE OFFICIAL PUBLICATION OF THE NATHANIEL HAWTHORNE SOCIETY, THE. [Nathaniel Hawthorne rev.]. **Added/Corp** Nathaniel Hawthorne Society. Hawthorne-Longfellow Library. Vol. 12, No. 1 (Spring 1986)-. Periodical. English. sa (April and November). $10.00 US; $12.00 other. Nathaniel Hawthorne Society, Bowdoin College, Hawthorne Longfellow Library, Brunswick ME 04011. **Tel** (207)725-3281. **ED** Frederick Newberry. **LC** PS1879; .N38. **DD** 813/.3. **Bk Rev**, (Qty: 4). **Circ:** 400. ***Continues*** *Newsletter (Nathaniel Hawthorne Society), 0162-9824.*
Desc: Devoted to Hawthorne studies.
Ind/Abst Am. Humanit. Index; Annu. Bibliogr. Engl. Lang. Lit.; MLA Int. Bibl. Books Artic. Mod. Lang. Lit.

US/0027-8378
NATION (NEW YORK, N.Y.), THE. (THE NATION.). [Nation]. (July 6, 1985)-. Periodical. English. wk (except for 1st week of Jan. and biweekly in July and Aug.). $58.00. The Nation, 72 Fifth Avenue, New York NY 10011. **Tel** (212)242-8400. **(Subscription address:** CDS SIFD Agency Control, 1901 Bell Avenue, Des Moines, IA 50315; Phone: (515)246-6812**)** **ED** Victor Navasky. **LC** AP2; .N2. **DD** 051. Index available. **Bk Rev. Ad Acc. Pr Rev. Circ:** 85,000. available on microfilm from Xerox. Documents available from The Genuine Article, UMI Article Clearinghouse, Documents on Demand.
Desc: America's oldest weekly review of politics and the arts. Investigative reporting, and liberal analysis; strives to be impassioned and irreverent.
Ind/Abst Acad. Abstr. Full Text Elite (Jan. 1984-) [Full Txt.]; Acad. Abstr. (Jan. 1984)-; Acad. Ind. [Computer File] (1984-); Acad. Search (Jan. 1984-); Altern. Press Index; Am. Bibliogr. Slavic East Europ. Stud.; Annu. Bibliogr. Engl. Lang. Lit.; Arts Humanit. Citation Index [Select. Cov.]; Biogr. Index; Book Rev. Digest; Book Rev. Index; Chicano Index; Child. Lit. Abstr. (19??-); Curr. Lit. Fam. Plan. (19??-199?); Energy Inf. Abstr.; Environ. Abstr.; Expand. Acad. Index (1984-); Film Lit. Index; Gen. Period. Index (1985-); Hum. Rights Intern. Rep.; Index Am. Period. Verse; Index Period. Artic. Relat. Law; INFO-SOUTH Abstr.; Infobank (Jan. 1969-); Mag. Artic. Summar. Elite (Jan. 1984-) [Full Txt.]; Mag. Artic. Summar. Select (Jan. 1984-); Mag. Artic. Summar. CD-ROM (Jan. 1984-); Mag. ASAP Plus; Mag. ASAP Sel. [Full Txt.]; Mag. Index Plus (1989-); Mag. Index Sel. Microfiche (1986-) [Full Txt.]; Mag. Index. Sel. (1986-); Mag. Search; Med. Rev. Dig.; Middle East Abstr. Index; Newsp. Period. Abstr. (1986-); Peace Res. Abstr. J. (1963-1967, 1970-1976); Read. Guide Abstr. Select Ed.; Read. Guide Period. Lit.; Res. Alert [Full Cov.]; Sage Race Relat. Abstr.; Soc. Sci. Source (Jan. 1984-) [Full Txt.]; Soc. Sci. Cit. Index [Full Cov.]; Mag. Index (1977-); TOM Gen. Index (1985-) [Full Txt.]; Vocat. Search (Jan. 1984-) [Full Txt.].

NE/0166-0586
NEDERLANDSE BOEK. (HET NEDERLANDSE BOEK.). [Ned. boek]. (1962)-. Periodical. Dutch. Six times a year (Mar., May, July, Sept., Nov., Dec.). Fl15.00. Nederlandse Boek, Prinsengracht 1065, 1017 JG Amsterdam Netherlands. **Tel** 011 31 20 623-3187. **ED** Wim J. Simons and Carla Dura. **UDC** 013.839.1. **Bk Rev. Ad Acc. Circ:** 20,000.

BW/0028-2588
NEMAN. [Neman]. **Added/Corp** Soiuz Pisatelei BSSR. (1945)-. Periodical. Russian. mo. $109.95. **(Subscription address:** East View Publications Inc., 3020 Harbor Lane North, Suite 110, Minneapolis MN 55447.**)** ***Continues*** *Sovetskaia Otchizna.*
Ind/Abst MLA Int. Bibl. Books Artic. Mod. Lang. Lit.

HU/0324-4652
NEOHELICON (BUDAPEST). (NEOHELICON.). [Neohelicon]. **Added/Corp** Akademiai Kiado. Vol. 1, (1973)-. Periodical. English (French, German and Russian). Twice a year. $184.00. John Benjamins BV, Amsteldijk 44, PO Box 75577, 1070 AN Amsterdam Netherlands. **Tel** 011 31 20 6738156, FAX 011 31 20 739773. **(Subscription address:** John Benjamins North America, PO Box 27519, Philadelphia PA 19118-0519.**)** **ED** Miklos Szabolcsi and Gyorgy Mihaly Vajda. **LC** PN851; .N46. **DD** 809. **[CCC].** Documents available from The Genuine Article.
Desc: An organ for studies in comparative and world literature. Focuses on studies which further a synthetic presentation of literary epochs, periods, trends and movements from a comparative point of view.
Ind/Abst Annu. Bibliogr. Engl. Lang. Lit.; Arts Humanit. Citation Index [Full Cov.]; Curr. Contents Arts Humanit.; MLA Int. Bibl. Books Artic. Mod. Lang. Lit.; Res. Alert [Full Cov.]; Romant. Move.; Soc. Sci. Cit. Index [Select. Cov.].

RM
NEUE LITERATUR. **Added/Corp** Uniunea Scriitorilor din Republica Socialista Romania. (19??)-. Periodical. German. Four times a year. DM145.00. **(Subscription address:** Kubon & Sagner, ABT Zeitschriftenimport, D 80328 Munich Germany.**)** **LC** AP86; .N46. available on microfilm.
Desc: Literary review.

UK/0950-2378
NEW FORMATIONS. No. 1 (Spring 1987)-. Periodical. English. Three times a year. £55.00 (institutions), £35.00 (individuals) UK; £58.00 (institutions), £35.00 (individuals) other. Lawrence Wishart Limited, 144 A Old South Lambeth Road, London FW8 1XX United Kingdom. **Tel** 011 44 71 8209281, FAX 011 44 71 5870469. **LC** CB428; .N49. **[CCC]. Bk Rev. Ad Acc, Adv Mgr:** R. Borthwick. **Circ:** 500.
Ind/Abst Int. Bibliogr. Sociol.

US/0028-6087
NEW LITERARY HISTORY. [New lit. hist.]. **Added/Corp** University of Virginia. Vol. 1 (Oct. 1969)-. Periodical. English. Four times a year (Feb., May, Aug., & Nov.). $79.00 US; $83.50 Canada & Mexico; $90.30 other. Johns Hopkins University Press, 2715 North Charles Street, Baltimore MD 21218-4319. **Tel** (410)516-6987, FAX (410)516-6968. **(Subscription address:** John Hopkins University Press, Journals Publishing Division, PO Box 19966, Baltimore MD 21211.**)** **ED** Ralph Cohen. **LC** PR1; .N44. **DD** 820.1. **[CCC]. Bk Rev. Ad Acc. Circ:** 1,900. available on microfilm and microfiche from University Microfilms International (UMI). Documents available from The Genuine Article, UMI Article Clearinghouse.
Desc: Focuses on theory and interpretation - the reasons for literary change, the definitions of periods, and the evolution of styles, conventions, and genres. Provides literary exchange between American and European scholars and has brought into English theorists whose works had never before been translated.
Ind/Abst Abstr. Engl. Stud.; Acad. Search (July 1993-); Am. Hist. Life (1969-1990); Annu. Bibliogr. Engl. Lang. Lit.; Arts Humanit. Citation Index [Full Cov.]; BHA : Biblio. Hist. Art; Child. Lit. Abstr. (19??-); Curr. Contents Arts Humanit.; Expand. Acad. Index (1989-); Film Lit. Index; Hist. Source (July 1993-); Humanit. Index; Humanit. Source (Jul. 1993-); INFO-SOUTH Abstr.; Linguist. Lang. Behav. Abstr.; Lit. Crit. Regist.; Mag. Search; MLA Int. Bibl. Books Artic. Mod. Lang. Lit.; Newsp. Period. Abstr. (1991-); Res. Alert [Full Cov.]; Romant. Move.; Soc. Plann. Policy Dev. Abstr.; Soc. Sci. Cit. Index [Select. Cov.]; Sociol. Abstr.

AT/0314-7495
NEW LITERATURE REVIEW. [New lit. rev.]. **Added/Corp** Australian National University. Dept. of English. **VFOAT** New Literatures Review. (1975)-. Periodical. English. Twice a year (May & Nov.). 15.00Aus$ (one year); 38.00Aus$ (three years). New Literatures Review, Northfields Avenue, University of Wollongong, Wollongong NSW 2522 Australia. **Tel** 011 61 042 213677, FAX 011 61 42 214471. **ED** Dr. Paul Sharrad. **LC** PR9080; .A4. **DD** 820/.9/9171241. **Bk Rev. Ad Acc, Adv Mgr:** K. Brooks. **Pr Rev. Circ:** 400 (ctrl). ***Absorbed*** *Arna.*
Desc: Critical discussion on writing from post colonial cultures in the context of current literary theory.
Ind/Abst Annu. Bibliogr. Engl. Lang. Lit.; APAIS, Aust. Public Aff. Inf. Ser. (1980-); MLA Int. Bibl. Books Artic. Mod. Lang. Lit.

US/0028-6400
NEW ORLEANS REVIEW, THE. [New Orleans rev.]. **Added/Corp** Loyola University (New Orleans, La.) New Orleans Consortium. Vol. 1 (Fall 1968)-. Periodical. English. Four times a year (Feb., May, Aug., Nov.). New Orleans Review, 6363 Saint Charles Avenue, Loyola University, New Orleans LA 70118. **Tel** (504)865-2294. **ED** John Biguenet. **LC** AP2; .N6212. **DD** 051. **Circ:** 1,000. available on microfilm and microfiche from University Microfilms International (UMI). Documents available from The Genuine Article.
Desc: A literary and arts magazine publishing the finest in contemporary fiction, poetry, and literary and film criticism.
Ind/Abst Abstr. Engl. Stud.; Am. Humanit. Index; Annu. Bibliogr. Engl. Lang. Lit.; Arts Humanit. Citation Index [Full Cov.]; Curr. Contents Arts Humanit.; Film Lit. Index; Index Am. Period. Verse; Lit. Crit. Regist.; MLA Int. Bibl. Books Artic. Mod. Lang. Lit.; Res. Alert [Full Cov.]; Romant. Move.

US/0047-9829
NEW PATRIOT (CHICAGO, ILL. 1988). (NEW PATRIOT.). [New patriot]. **Added/Corp** Patriotic Majority (Chicago, Ill.). Vol. 1, No. 1 (Apr. 1988)-. Periodical. English. bm. $17.76 US; $30.00 other. Patriotic Majority, 202 South State, Suite 1420, Chicago IL 60604. **Tel** (312)663-3517, FAX (312)663-3867. **ED** John Rossen. **DD** 320. **Bk Rev**, (Qty: 10-20). ***Continues*** *New Patriot (Chicago, Ill. : 1978).*
Desc: A non-political magazine which promotes the restoration of the ideals of the founders of the United States to public life.

US/0163-2299
NEW VIRGINIA REVIEW. Vol. 1 (1979)-. Periodical. English. an. $13.50. New Virginia Review Inc., 1306 East Cary Street, Suite 2A, Richmond VA 23219. **Tel** (804)782-1043. **LC** PS558.V5; N48. **DD** 810/.809755.

US/0028-7504
NEW YORK REVIEW OF BOOKS. [New York rev. books]. **VFOAT** New York Review. Vol. 1, (Feb. 25, 1963)-. English. Twenty-one times a year. $49.50. New York Review of Books, 250 West 57th Street, New York NY 10107. **Tel** (212)757-8070. **(Subscription address:** Palm Coast Data, PO Box 420235, Agency Department, Palm Coast FL 32142.**)** **ED** Bob Silvers and Barbara Epstein. **LC** AP2; .N655. **DD** 028.1/05. **Bk Rev. Ad Acc. Circ:** 125,000 (ctrl). available on microfilm and microfiche from University Microfilms International (UMI). Documents available from The Genuine Article, UMI Article Clearinghouse.
Desc: Contains essays concerning historical, literary and current political affairs and issues. Most recent issues contain essays concerning Byron, Charlie Chaplin, Poland, and Picasso.
Ind/Abst Acad. Abstr. Full Text Elite (Jan. 1989-); Acad. Abstr. (Jan. 1989)-; Acad. Ind. [Computer File] (1984-); Acad. Search (Jan. 1989-); Am. Bibliogr. Slavic East Europ. Stud.; Annu. Bibliogr. Engl. Lang. Lit.; Arts Humanit. Citation Index [Full Cov.]; BHA : Biblio. Hist. Art; Book Rev. Digest; Book Rev. Index; Child. Lit. Abstr. (19??-); Curr. Contents Arts Humanit.; Expand. Acad. Index (1984-); Film Lit. Index; Gen. Period. Index (1985-); Index Am. Period. Verse; Index Book Rev. Relig.; Index Period. Artic. Relat. Law; INFO-SOUTH Abstr.; Infobank (Jan. 1969-); Mag. Artic. Summar. Elite (Jan. 1989-); Mag. Artic. Summar. Select (Jan. 1989-); Mag. Artic. Summar. CD-ROM (Jan. 1989-); Mag. Express (1986-) [Full Txt.]; Mag. Index Plus (1989-); Mag. Index. Sel. (1986-); Mag. Search; Middle East Abstr. Index; MLA Int. Bibl. Books Artic. Mod. Lang. Lit.; Newsp. Period. Abstr. (1986-); Peace Res. Abstr. J. (1970-1972, 1975-1977, 1981, 1987); Read. Guide Abstr. Select Ed.; Read. Guide Period. Lit.; Res. Alert [Full Cov.]; Resource/One Ondisc;

Romant. Move.; Soc. Plann. Policy Dev. Abstr.; Soc. Sci. Cit. Index [Select. Cov.]; Sociol. Abstr.; Mag. Index (1977-); Women Stud. Abstr.

US/0028-7806
NEW YORK TIMES BOOK REVIEW, THE. [N.Y. times book rev.]. **VFOAT** Book Review. (Sept. 9, 1923)-. Periodical. English. wk. $52.00 US; $65.00 other. The New York Times, 229 West 43rd Street, New York NY 10036. **Tel** (800)631-2580, (212)556-1234, FAX (212)556-4603. **ED** Rebecca Sinkler. **DD** 028. cum. index. **Bk Rev. Ad Acc. Circ:** 78,000. available on microfilm and microfiche from University Microfilms International (UMI). Documents available from The Genuine Article, UMI Article Clearinghouse. ***Continues*** *New York Times Book Review and Magazine.*
Desc: Discusses current literary trends in several features about books and authors: paperback talk, spring and fall review of new books, and children's and Christmas issues.
Ind/Abst Abr. Read. Guide Period. Lit.; Acad. Abstr. Full Text Elite (Jan. 1989-); Acad. Abstr. (Jan. 1989-); Acad. Ind. [Computer File] (1984-); Acad. Search (Jan. 1989-); Am. Bibliogr. Slavic East Europ. Stud.; Annu. Bibliogr. Engl. Lang. Lit.; Arts Humanit. Citation Index [Full Cov.]; Book Rev. Digest; Book Rev. Index; Child. Lit. Abstr. (19??-); Curr. Contents Arts Humanit.; Expand. Acad. Index (1984-); Garden Lit. (1992-); Gen. Period. Index (1985-); Index Book Rev. Relig.; Index Period. Artic. Relat. Law; INFO-SOUTH Abstr.; Mag. Artic. Summar. Elite (Jan. 1989-); Mag. Artic. Summar. Select (Jan. 1989-); Mag. Artic. Summar. CD-ROM (Jan. 1989-); Mag. Express (1986-) [Full Txt.]; Mag. Index Plus (1989-); Mag. Index. Sel. (1986-); Mag. Search; Middle East Abstr. Index; Newsp. Period. Abstr. (1986-); Newsp. Abstr.; Read. Guide Abstr. Select Ed.; Read. Guide Period. Lit.; Res. Alert [Full Cov.]; Resource/One Ondisc; Romant. Move.; Sage Race Relat. Abstr.; Sci. Fict. Fantasy Book Rev. Index; Soc. Plann. Policy Dev. Abstr.; Soc. Sci. Cit. Index [Select. Cov.]; Sociol. Abstr.; Mag. Index (1977-); TOM Gen. Index (1985-); Vocat. Search (Jan. 1989-).

CN
NEWEST REVIEW, THE. [Newest rev.]. Vol. 1 (June 1975)-. English. bm (Feb., Apr., June, Aug., Oct., Dec.). 15.00Can$ (individuals), 22.00Can$ (institutions), Canada; 18.00Can$ (individuals), 25.00Can$ (institutions), other. NeWest Review, PO Box 394 RPO University, Saskatoon Saskatchewan, S7N 9Z9 Canada. **Tel** (306)934-1444, FAX (306)242-5004. **ED** Gail Youngberg. Index available. **Bk Rev**, (Qty: 40). **Ad Acc. Circ:** 1,000.
Desc: Provides coverage and analysis of social, cultural and political issues and events of importance to western Canadians. The literary component, both original work and reviews, is the backbone of the editorial effort. Also, reports regularly on the regional theatre scene and, when possible, on visual art musical events. Its goal is to provide a vehicle both for the articulation of regional culture and its analysis.
Ind/Abst Can. Index (?-?); Can. Period. Index (19??-).

US/0894-7945
NEWSLETTER OF THE AMERICAN ASSOCIATION OF AUSTRALIAN LITERARY STUDIES. [Newsl. Am. Assoc. Aust. Lit. Stud.]. **Added/Corp** American Association of Australian Literary Studies. **VFOAT** AAALS Newsletter. (198?)-. Periodical. English. Twice a year (May & Nov.). $35.00 (individuals), $45.00 (joint), $55.00 (group) Comes with American Association of Australian Literacy Studies membership. American Association of Australian Literary Studies, 1453 East 8020 South, Sandy Utah 84093. **Tel** (801)566-1720. **ED** Carolyn Bliss. **DD** 820. **Ad Acc. Circ:** 200.
Desc: Contains news of the activities of the American Association of Australian Literary Studies and its members, conferences of interest, calls for papers, appearances of publications and writers, strategies for teaching Australian literature, and opportunities for North American scholars of Australian literature.

US/0146-7891
NINETEENTH-CENTURY FRENCH STUDIES. [Ninet.-century Fr. stud.]. **Added/Corp** New York (State). State University College, Fredonia. Dept. of Foreign Languages. Vol. 1 (Fall 1972)-. Periodical. English (French). sa. $34.00 (1 year), $61.00 (2 year), $88.00 (3 year). Nineteenth-Century French Studies, c/o Thomas H Goetz, 6 Pine Drive, Fredonia NY 14063. **Tel** (716)673-3380. **ED** Thomas H Goetz. **LC** PQ1; .N55. **DD** 840/.9. Index available. **Bk Rev**, (Qty: 60-80). **Ad Acc. Pr Rev. Circ:** 850. available on microfilm and microfiche from University Microfilms International (UMI). Documents available from The Genuine Article.
Desc: Studies on all aspects of the 19th century French literature and criticism and related fields.
Ind/Abst Am. Hist. Life (1989-); Arts Humanit. Citation Index [Full Cov.]; BHA : Biblio. Hist. Art; Curr. Contents Arts Humanit.; Index Book Rev. Humanit.; MLA Int. Bibl. Books Artic. Mod. Lang. Lit.; Res. Alert [Full Cov.].

US/0732-1864
NINETEENTH-CENTURY LITERATURE CRITICISM. [Ninet.-century lit. crit.]. **Added/Corp** Gale Research Company. Gale Research Inc. **VFOAT** 19th Century Literature Criticism; Nineteenth Century Literature Criticism; N.C.L.C.; NCLC. Vol. 1 (1981)-. English. ir. $115.00. Gale Research Inc., 835 Penobscot Building, Detroit MI 48226. **Tel** (800)877-GALE, (313)961-2242, FAX (313)961-6083, telex TWX 810-221-7086. **ED** Joann Cerrito. **LC** PN761; .N56. **DD** 809/.034.
Desc: Convenient source of wide-ranging critical comment on authors who died between 1800 and 1899. Furnishes extensive excerpts from published criticism on the great novelists, poets, and playwrights of the nineteenth century. All genres and nationalities are represented, including important political, social, and economic writers. Entries contain biographical sketches, bibliographies for each selected critical passage, and sources for additional reading on the author.
Ind/Abst Curr. Contents Arts Humanit.

US/0029-2397
NORTH AMERICAN REVIEW, THE. [North Am. rev.]. Vol. 13, No. 32 (July 1821)-. Periodical. English. bm (6 issues). $18.00 US; $22.00 Canada; $24.00 other. North American Review, University of Northern Iowa, Cedar Falls IA 50614. **Tel** (319)273-6455. **LC** AP2; .N7. cum. index. available on microfilm and microfiche from University Microfilms International (UMI). Documents available from The Genuine Article, UMI Article Clearinghouse. ***Continues*** *North American Review and Miscellaneous Journal.*
Ind/Abst Acad. Search (July 1993-); Am. Hist. Life (1968-1976); Am. Humanit. Index; Annu. Bibliogr. Engl. Lang. Lit.; Arts Humanit. Citation Index [Full Cov.]; Book Rev. Index; Curr. Contents Arts Humanit.; Expand. Acad. Index (1989-); Humanit. Index; Humanit. Source (Jul. 1993-); Index Am. Period. Verse; INFO-SOUTH Abstr.; Mag. Search; Newsp. Period. Abstr. (1991-); Read. Guide Period. Lit.; Res. Alert [Full Cov.].

●US/1062-3353
NORTHWEST LITERARY FORUM. (1992)-. Periodical. English. bm. $15.00. North Lake Press, 2012 South 314th Suite 158, Federal Way WA 98003.

US/0029-3423
NORTHWEST REVIEW (EUGENE, OR.). (NORTHWEST REVIEW.). [Northwest rev.]. **Added/Corp** University of Oregon. Student Publications Board. University of Oregon. Vol. 1 (Spring 1957)-. Periodical. English. Three times a year (Jan., May, Sept.). $14.00 (individuals); $20.00 (institutions & libraries). University of Oregon Department of English, 369 PLC, Eugene OR 97403. **Tel** (503)346-3957. **ED** John Witte. **LC** AP2; .N855. **Bk Rev. Ad Acc. Circ:** 1,500. available on microfilm and microfiche from University Microfilms International (UMI).
Desc: Features poetry, fiction, art and essays, writer abroad, translation supplements, and artist's books.
Ind/Abst Abstr. Engl. Stud.; Am. Humanit. Index; Index Am. Period. Verse; MLA Int. Bibl. Books Artic. Mod. Lang. Lit.

US/0029-4047
NOTES ON CONTEMPORARY LITERATURE. [Notes contemp. lit.]. **Added/Corp** West Georgia College. (Jan. 1971)-. Periodical. English. Five times a year (Jan., Mar., May, Sept. and Nov.). $20.00. Notes on Contemporary Literature, English Department, West Georgia College, Carrollton GA 30118. **Tel** (404)836-6512. **ED** W. S. Doxey. **DD** 817. **Bk Rev. Ad Acc. Circ:** 200.
Desc: Criticisms and explications of literature since 1940.
Ind/Abst Abstr. Engl. Stud.; Annu. Bibliogr. Engl. Lang. Lit.; MLA Int. Bibl. Books Artic. Mod. Lang. Lit.

FR/0153-9027
NOUS VOULONS LIRE PESSAC. (NOUS VOULONS LIRE.). (1972)-. Periodical. French. Five times a year. 250.00F France; 300.00F other. Nous Voulons Lire, 85 cours du Marechal Juin, 33075 Bordeaux Cedex France. **Tel** 011 33 56 325151 ext 1200. **UDC** 028. Index available. **Bk Rev. Ad Acc. Pr Rev.** ctrl circ.
Desc: Reviews of children's books. Articles on various themes concerning children's youth literature.

YU/0353-8052
NOVA MATICA. ***Title Change.*** **Added/Corp** Matica Iseljenika Hrvatske. (1990)-(1993). Periodical. Serbo-Croatian (Roman) (English and Spanish). Twelve times a year. Hrvatska Matica Iseljenika, Trnjanska BB, Zagreb Croatia. **Tel** 011 38 41 530002, FAX 0038 (41)539 111. **ED** Boris Maruna (phone: (41)530 002). **LC** DR301; .M33. **Bk Rev. Ad Acc, Adv Mgr:** Babic, **Tel** (41)539 212. **Circ:** 4,000 (ctrl). ***Continues*** *Matica (Zagreb, Croatia), 0025-5920.* ***Continued by*** *Matica (Zagreb, Croatia : 1993).*
Desc: Devoted to preserving Croatian culture for emigrants all over the world.

US/0029-5132
NOVEL. (NOVEL; A FORUM ON FICTION.). [Novel]. Vol. 1, (Fall 1967)-. Periodical. English. Three times a year (Feb., June, Nov.). $14.00 (individuals), $20.00 (institutions) US; $16.80 (individuals), $24.00 (institutions) others. Brown University / Novel, PO Box 1984, Providence RI 02912. **Tel** (401)863-3756. **ED** Mark Spilka. **LC** PN3311; .N65. Index available. cum. index. **Bk Rev. Ad Acc. Circ:** 1,500. available on microfilm and microfiche from University Microfilms International (UMI). Documents available from The Genuine Article, UMI Article Clearinghouse.
Desc: A publication of theory and criticism of fiction.
Ind/Abst Abstr. Engl. Stud.; Acad. Abstr. Full Text Elite (July 1990-); Acad. Abstr. (July 1990-); Acad. Ind. [Computer File] (1987-); Acad. Search (July 1990-); Am. Bibliogr. Slavic East Europ. Stud.; Annu. Bibliogr. Engl. Lang. Lit.; Arts Humanit. Citation Index [Full Cov.]; Expand. Acad. Index (1987-); Humanit. Index; Humanit. Source (July 1990-); INFO-SOUTH Abstr.; Lit. Crit. Regist.; Mag. Search; MLA Int. Bibl. Books Artic. Mod. Lang. Lit.; Newsp. Period. Abstr. (1991-); Res. Alert [Full Cov.]; Romant. Move.

RU/0130-7673
NOVYJ MIR. (NOVYI MIR.). [Nov. mir]. **Added/Corp** Soiuz Pisatelei SSSR. (1925)-. Periodical. Russian. mo. $189.95. **(Subscription address:** East View Publications Inc., 3020 Harbor Lane North, Suite 110, Minneapolis MN 55447.) Index available. **Bk Rev.** available on microfilm from University Microfilms International (UMI). Documents available from The Genuine Article.
Ind/Abst Annu. Bibliogr. Engl. Lang. Lit.; Arts Humanit. Citation Index (19??-19??) [Full Cov.]; Curr. Contents Arts Humanit.; Lang. Lang. Behav. Abstr.; MLA Int. Bibl. Books Artic. Mod. Lang. Lit.; Res. Alert [Full Cov.]; Soc. Plann. Policy Dev. Abstr.; Sociol. Abstr.; Curr. Dig. Post Sov. Press.

US/0885-5919
OCCASIONAL REVIEW (SAN JOSE, CALIF.), THE. **See** Literature-Poetry.

FR/0338-1900
OEUVRES ET CRITIQUES. [Oeuvres crit.]. Vol. 1 (1976)-. Periodical. Multiple languages (English and French). sa. DM72.80 Germany; DM75.20 other. Gunter Narr Verlag, Dishingerweg 5, D 72070 Tuebingen Germany. **Tel** 011 49 7071 78091, FAX (07071)75288. **ED** Wolfgang Leiner. **LC** PQ2; .O35. **DD** 840/.9. **[CCC].** cum. index. **Bk Rev. Ad Acc. Circ:** 1,100.
Desc: Each volume discusses a literary work, an author or a group of works belonging to a special epoch or genre.
Ind/Abst MLA Int. Bibl. Books Artic. Mod. Lang. Lit.; Romant. Move.

US/1055-5609
ONE MEADWAY. [One Meadway]. **Added/Corp** Sarah Lawrence College. Issue No. 1 (Spring 1991)-. Periodical. English. sa. $18.00. One Meadway, 211 West 92nd Street, Number 47, New York NY 10025. **LC** PS501; .O54. **DD** 810.8/0005.
Desc: Literary review produced by Sarah Lawrence College graduate students. Majority of contributors are experienced writers with numerous publications in little magazines and other literary reviews.

SW/0030-4492
ORD & BILD. (ORD OCH BILD.). [Ord & Bild]. **VAT** Ord och Bild. (1892)-. Periodical. Swedish. bm (6 issues). Kr265.00. Ord & Bild, Box 2390, 403 16 Goteborg Sweden. **Tel** 011 46 31 7741740. **LC** AP48; .O6. **DD** 058/.7. Index available (free).
Ind/Abst BHA : Biblio. Hist. Art; MLA Int. Bibl. Books Artic. Mod. Lang. Lit.

UK/0305-1498
OXFORD LITERARY REVIEW, THE. [Oxf. lit. rev.]. (1974)-. Periodical. English. sa. £17.50 UK; £20.00 other. Oxford Literary Review, Wadham College, Oxford OX1 3PN United Kingdom. **Tel** 011 44 865 277959, FAX 44-865-277937. **ED** Robert Young. **LC** AP4; .O934. **DD** 052. Index available. **Bk Rev. Ad Acc. Circ:** 1,000 (ctrl). Documents available from The Genuine Article.
Desc: Critical analyses of literary, philosophical, political, psychoanalytical and feminist theory.
Ind/Abst Arts Humanit. Citation Index (19??-19??) [Full Cov.]; Curr. Contents Arts Humanit.; Lit. Crit. Regist.; MLA Int. Bibl. Books Artic. Mod. Lang. Lit.; Res. Alert [Full Cov.]; Romant. Move.

US/1056-2613
OXYGEN (SAN FRANCISCO, CALIF.). (OXYGEN : POEMS, STORIES, INVECTIVE, COMMENTARY.). [Oxygen]. No. 1 (Spring 1991)-. Periodical. English. $1.00 (single issue). Richard Hack, 537 Jones Street, #999, San Francisco CA 94102. **DD** 051.

US/0090-5674
PAIDEUMA (ORONO). **See** Biographies.

IT/1121-5542
PARALLELI ROZZANO. ***Ceased.*** (PARALLELI.). [ParalleliRozzano]. (1991)-(1993). Periodical. Italian. bm. Editoriale Domus, Via Achille Grandi 5-7, 20089 Rozzano Milan Italy. **Tel** 011 39 2 82472276, FAX 011 39 2 8255033. **ED** Claudio Serra. **UDC** 05.

US/0048-3028
PARNASSUS : POETRY IN REVIEW. **See** Literature-Poetry.

US/0731-4663
PASSAIC REVIEW. [Passaic rev.]. **Added/Corp** Passaic City Poets. (19??)-. Periodical. English. Twice a

year. Forstmann Library, 195 Gregory Avenue, Passaic NJ 07055. **Tel** (201)471-8077. **ED** Richard P. Quatrone. **LC** Discard. cum. index. **Ad Acc. Circ:** 500 (ctrl).

US/0276-0851
PAWLEYS ISLAND PERSPECTIVE, THE. Periodical. English. bm. $6.00. Pawleys Island Perspective Inc, PO Box 1260, Pawleys Island SC 29585.

HK/0031-4110
PEKING INFORMERS, THE. Added/Corp Ta Lu Yen Chiu So, Hongkong. (Sept. 1, 1960)-. Periodical. English. sm. $100.00. Continental Research Institute, GPO Box 5699, Hong Kong Hong Kong. **ED** Chow Ching-Wen. **LC** DS707; .P38.

US/8756-5668
PENNSYLVANIA REVIEW (PITTSBURGH, PA.), THE. See Literature.

UN
PERETS. (June 1941)-. Periodical. Ukrainian (Ukrainian). Twenty-four times a year. $109.95. **(Subscription address:** East View Publications Inc., 3020 Harbor Lane North, Suite 110, Minneapolis MN 55447.**) LC** AP115; .P39.

US/0740-7890
PERMAFROST. [Permafrost]. **Added/Corp** University of Alaska, Fairbanks. College of Arts and Sciences. Alaska Association for the Arts. Vol. 1 (April 1977)-. Periodical. English. sa. $7.00. Permafrost, University of Alaska-Fairbanks, Fairbanks AK 99775. **Tel** (907)474-5237. **ED** Marcia Mason and Robin Lewis. **Circ:** 500.
Desc: Publishes poetry, short fiction, and essays by Alaskan and outside writers.

US/0883-6086
PERSPECTIVES (TOLEDO, OHIO). ***Suspended.*** (PERSPECTIVES : A REVIEW JOURNAL OF THE COOPERATIVE SERVICES FOR CHILDREN'S LITERATURE, UNIVERSITY OF TOLEDO.). **Added/Corp** University of Toledo. Cooperative Services for Children's Literature. (1984)-?. Periodical. English. Three times a year. $7.50 Ohio residents; $10.00 other. Christopher-Gordon Publishers Inc, 480 Washington Street, Saint Norwood MA 02062. **Tel** (617)762-5577, FAX (617)762-2110. **ED** Hughes Moir. **LC** Z1037.A1; P44. **DD** 028.1/62. **Bk Rev. Ad Acc. Circ:** 1,000 (ctrl).
Desc: Reviews of children's and young adult book with suggested activities for integrating literature in K-12 curricula.
Ind/Abst Child. Lit. Abstr. (19??-19??).

UK/0144-7076
PN REVIEW (MANCHESTER, GREATER MANCHESTER : 1979). (PN REVIEW.). [PN rev.]. **Added/Corp** University of Manchester. Dept. of English. **VFOAT** P.N. Review. **VAT** Poetry Nation Review. No. 10 (1979)-. Periodical. English. bm. £24.50 (individual), £30.00 (institutions). World Wide Subscription Services, Unit 4, Gibbs Reed Farm, East Sussex TN5 7HE England. **Tel** (0580)200657, FAX (0580)200616. **ED** Michael Schmidt, Michael Freeman. **LC** PN1010; .P47. **DD** 808.81. Index available. cum. index. **Bk Rev. Ad Acc. Circ:** 2,000. ***Continues** Poetry Nation Review.*
Desc: Includes editorial news and notes, reports, readers' letters and extensive reviews. Consists of poems, fiction, translations, interviews, and informal pieces.
Ind/Abst Abstr. Engl. Stud.; MLA Int. Bibl. Books Artic. Mod. Lang. Lit.

US/0090-5224
POE STUDIES. See Biographies.

US/0731-5236
POETICS JOURNAL. ***Suspended.*** [Poet. j.]. No. 1 (Jan. 1982)-Suspended with (1983). Periodical. English. an. $20.00 (3 years) U.S. and Canada; $24.00 (3 years) other. Poetics Journal, 2639 Russell Street, Berkeley CA 94705. **Tel** (510)548-1817. **ED** Lyn Hejinian and Barrett Watten. **LC** PN1042; .P57. **DD** 809. Index available. **Bk Rev. Circ:** 900.
Desc: A journal of contemporary poetics by poets and prose writers and by other artists, critics, linguists, and political theorists. It features articles and reviews.
Ind/Abst Am. Humanit. Index.

CN/0709-3373
POETRY CANADA REVIEW. [Poetry Can. rev.]. **VFOAT** Review & Chronicle. Vol. 1, No. 2 (Winter 1979/80)-. Periodical. English (summaries and/or abstracts in French). Four times a year. $35.25 (institutions), $17.85 (individuals). Quarry Press Inc., PO Box 1061, Kingston Ontario K7L 4Y5 Canada. **Tel** (613)548-8429, FAX (613)548-1556. **ED** Barry Dempster. **DD** C811/.5408. **Bk Rev**, (Qty: 14). **Ad Acc, Adv Mgr:** Melanie. **Circ:** 2,000 (ctrl). available on microfilm from Micromedia Limited. ***Continues** Poetry Canada, 0708-496X.*
Desc: Canada's authoritative poetry voice, with interviews, essays, columns, reviews and contemporary poetry. Essential.
Ind/Abst Can. Index.

UK/0032-2156
POETRY REVIEW (LONDON). (POETRY REVIEW.). [Poetry rev.]. **Added/Corp** Poetry Society. Vol. 1 (Jan. 1912)-. Periodical. English. qt (4 issues). £26.00 (institutions), £20.00 (individuals) UK; £30.00 (institutions), £23.00 (individuals) other. Poetry Society, 22 Betterton Street, London WC2H 9BU England. **Tel** 011 44 71 2404810. **ED** Peter Forbes. **LC** PN1010; .P7. **DD** 821/.008. **Bk Rev. Ad Acc. Circ:** 5,000. Documents available from The Genuine Article. ***Supersedes** Poetical Gazette.*
Desc: Covers new poems and reviews of books of and about contemporary and 20th Century poetry. Includes articles, memoirs and other prose by poets.
Ind/Abst Abstr. Engl. Stud.; Arts Humanit. Citation Index [Full Cov.]; Curr. Contents Arts Humanit.; MLA Int. Bibl. Books Artic. Mod. Lang. Lit.; Res. Alert [Full Cov.].

FR
POINT, LE. No. 1- Nov. 1965-. Periodical. French. wk. $360.00. Le Point / Bathurst, 140 rue de Rennes, CP 878, 75280 Paris Cedex 06 France. **Tel** 011 33 1 45443900.

US
POISONED PEN, THE. ***Ceased.*** Ceased Vol. 7, No. 1. Periodical. English. qt. Jeffrey Meyerson, 8801 Shore Road, 6A East, Brooklyn NY 11209. **Tel** (718)833-8248.

US
POLITICAL ACTION COMMENTARY. English. ir (published monthly until legislative session, then weekly). $15.00 (members of the Florida Nurses Association); $30.00 (non-members). Florida Nurses Association, 1235 East Concord Street, PO Box 6985, Orlando FL 32803. **Tel** (407)896-3261.

US
POMPA. English. PO Box 5037, Southern Station, Hattiesburg MS 39406-5037. **ED** Hilton Anderson.
Ind/Abst Lit. Crit. Regist.

IT/0032-423X
PONTE (FIRENZE), IL. (IL PONTE.). [Ponte]. Vol. 1 (Apr. 1945)-. Periodical. Italian. Twelve times a year. L130000 Italy; L180000 others. Vallecchi Editore Spa, Viale Milton 7, 50129 Florence Italy. **Tel** 011 39 55 473843. **ED** Enzo Enriques Agnoletti. **LC** AP37; .P6. **DD** 055/.1. Index available in last issue of volume--attached. Documents available from The Genuine Article.
Desc: Covers news and voices of the political and cultural debates of our time.
Ind/Abst Am. Hist. Life (1954-); Arts Humanit. Citation Index (19??-19??) [Full Cov.]; Curr. Contents Arts Humanit.; MLA Int. Bibl. Books Artic. Mod. Lang. Lit.; Res. Alert [Full Cov.]; Romant. Move.; Soc. Sci. Cit. Index [Select. Cov.].

US/0032-4655
POPULAR TALISMAN BULLETIN. VFOAT Talisman Bulletin; Talisman. Since 1960. Bulletin. English. bm. Talisman Company, Box 948, Chicago IL 60690.

FR
PORPHYRE. French. mo. 270.00F France; 308.00F other. Editions du Porphyre, 4 Place du 18 Juin 1940, 75006 Paris France. **Tel** 011 33 1 42221894.

US/1058-7691
POWYS NOTES. [Powys notes]. **Added/Corp** Powys Society of North America. Vol. 1, No. 1 (Spring 1985)-. Periodical. English. Twice a year (Spring and Fall). $15.00. Powy's Society, Colgate University, C/O Constance Harsh, Hamilton NY 13346. **Tel** (315)824-7294, FAX (315)824-7176. **ED** Richard Maxwell (phone: (219)464-5069). **LC** PR6031.O867; Z796. **DD** 819. **Bk Rev**, (Qty: 4-6). **Ad Acc. Circ:** 130.
Desc: Journal presents scholarship, reviews and bibliography that further the understanding and appreciation of the literary works of the Powy's Family.

UK/0309-1619
POWYS REVIEW, THE. [Powys rev.]. **Added/Corp** Powys Society. No. 1 (Spring 1977)-. Periodical. English. sa. £8.80. St. Davids University College, c/o The Editor, Lampeter SA48 7ED Wales England. **Tel** 0570 422351. **ED** Belinda Humfrey. **LC** PR6031.O867; Z8. **Bk Rev. Ad Acc. Circ:** 1,000 (ctrl). Documents available from The Genuine Article.
Desc: Critical study of the works of John Cowper Powys, T.F. Powys and Llewelyn Powys and related literature from 1880 to the present.
Ind/Abst Arts Humanit. Citation Index [Full Cov.]; Curr. Contents Arts Humanit.; MLA Int. Bibl. Books Artic. Mod. Lang. Lit.; Res. Alert [Full Cov.].

US/0161-0414
PRAXIS (ITHACA). (PRAXIS.). **Added/Corp** Cornell University. Vol. 1 (Spring 1976)-. Periodical. English. ir. $10.00. Praxis, Box 20/North Campus Union, Cornell University, Ithaca NY 14853. **LC** AS30; .P73. **DD** 051.
Ind/Abst Am. Humanit. Index (-199?).

SA/1015-549X
PRETEXTS. VFOAT Pre Texts. Vol. 1, No. 1 (winter 1989)-. Periodical. English. sa. R30.00 (institutions); R17.00 (individuals) Africa. University of Cape Town English Department, Private Bag, Rondebosch 7700 South Africa. **Tel** 011 27 21 6509111. **LC** PN99.S59; P7.
Ind/Abst MLA Int. Bibl. Books Artic. Mod. Lang. Lit.

UK/0032-888X
PRIVATE EYE. (Oct. 1961)-. Periodical. English. bw. £16.00 UK; £23.00 other Europe; £29.00 other. Pressdram Ltd, 230 236 Lavender Hill, London SW11 1LE England. **Tel** 011 44 71 2280588. **LC** AP4; .P86.

IT
PROGRESSIO. English. bm. World Feder Christian Life Com, Casella Postale 9048, 00100 Rome Italy. **Tel** 6568079.

KZ
PROSTOR. (Jan. 1960)-. Periodical. Russian. mo. $81.00 domestic airmail; $91.00 international airmail. **(Subscription address:** Victor Kamkin, 4956 Boiling Brook Parkway, Rockville MD 20852.**) *Continues*** *Sovetskii Kazakhstan.*

US/0048-5659
PROUST RESEARCH ASSOCIATION NEWSLETTER. [Proust Res. Assoc. newsl.]. **Main/Corp** Proust Research Association. **Added/Corp** Proust Research Association. Newsletter. No. 1 (Mar. 1969)-. Newsletter. English (French). ir (Published once every eighteen months). Free. University of Kansas Proust Research Association, Department of French and Italian, Lawrence KS 66045. **Tel** (913)864-3388. **ED** J. Theodore Johnson Jr. **LC** PQ2631.R63; Z32. **DD** 843/.912. Index available. cum. index. **Bk Rev. Circ:** 300 (ctrl).
Desc: Aims to provide a forum for the discussion of problems relating to current research on Marcel Proust.
Ind/Abst MLA Int. Bibl. Books Artic. Mod. Lang. Lit.; Romant. Move.

CN/0827-5556
PUBLIC WORKS (LONDON, ONT.). ***Ceased.*** (PUBLIC WORKS.). [Public works]. No. 1 (1985)-(19??). Periodical. English. an. University of Western Ontario Department of English, Room 173, London Ontario N6A 3K7 Canada. **Tel** (519)673-1164. **DD** C810/.8/0054. ***Formed by the union of** Pom Seed, 0833-9368 **and** Literary Review (London, (Ont.), 0820-9368.*

US/0030-8129
PUBLICATIONS OF THE MODERN LANGUAGE ASSOCIATION OF AMERICA. See Linguistics.

US/0890-3433
PUCKERBRUSH REVIEW. [Puckerbrush rev.]. **VFOAT** PR. Vol. 1, No. 1 (Spring 1978)-. Periodical. English. Twice a year. $8.00. Puckerbrush Review, 76 Main Street, Orono ME 04473. **Tel** (207)866-4868, (207)581-3832. **ED** Constance Hunting. **DD** 808. **Bk Rev**, (Qty: 10). **Ad Acc. Circ:** 500.

IT
QUADERNI CRITICI DE L'ALBERO. 1-. Monographic series. Italian. Price varies per volume.

IT
QUADERNI DELLA BASSA MODENESE / GRUPPO STUDI BASSA MODENESE. (1987)-. Periodical. Italian. sa. ***Continues** Bassa Modenese.*
Ind/Abst BHA : Biblio. Hist. Art.

IT
QUADERNI EUROPEI. (19??)-. Italian. mo. Free on request. Eurosportello CCIAA Mi, Via delle Orsole 4, 20123 Milan Italy. **Tel** 011 39 2 85155692.

IT/0392-1867
QUADERNI FIORENTINI. [Quad. fiorentini]. (1972)-. Periodical. Multiple languages. ir. Giuffre Editore SPA, Via Busto Arsizio 40, 20151 Milan Italy. **Tel** 011 398 2 38089200. **UDC** 094.

IT/0033-4960
QUADERNI IBERO-AMERICANI. [Quad. ibero-am.]. **Added/Corp** Associazione per i Rapporti Culturali con la Spagna, il Portogallo e l'America Latina. Universita di Torino. Istituto di Letteratura Spagnola e Ibero-Americana. Vol. 1 (Aug./Oct. 1946)-. Periodical. Italian (English, Italian, Spanish and Portuguese). Twice a year (June & Dec.). $50.00 others; L50000 Italy. Quaderni Ibero Americani, Via Montebello 21, 10124 Turin Italy. **Tel** 011 39 11 8127272, FAX (011)83.25.84. **ED** Giovanni Maria Bertini. **LC** F1401; .Q83. **DD** 940. Index available. **Bk Rev. Ad Acc. Circ:** 1,100 (ctrl).
Desc: Articles about Spanish, Portuguese, and Latin-American literature.
Ind/Abst HAPI Hisp. Am. Period. Index; MLA Int. Bibl. Books Artic. Mod. Lang. Lit.; Soc. Plann. Policy Dev. Abstr.

II/0018-7437
QUEST. Added/Corp Indian Committee for Cultural Freedom. No. 1 (Aug. 1955)-. Periodical. English. sa. $10.00. New Quest, 850/8A Shivajinagar, Pune 411004

India. **Tel** 011 91 212 345246. **(Subscription address:** Prints India, 11 Darya Ganj, New Delhi 110002 India.**) LC** AP8; .Q4. ***Absorbed*** *Humanist Review.*

SP/0211-3325
QUIMERA (BARCELONA, SPAIN). (QUIMERA.). [Quimera]. No. 1 (Nov. 1980)-. Periodical. Spanish. mo (11 issues). 6500ptas Spain; 7500ptas Europe, $70.00 US (surface mail); 11000ptas Europe, $110.00 US others (airmail). Montesinos Editor SA, Valencia 290 2DO, 08007 Barcelona Spain. **Tel** 011 34 3 4880591, FAX 011 34 3 4887438. **ED** Miguel Riera. **LC** PN778; .Q55. **DD** 809. **Bk Rev. Ad Acc. Circ:** 22,000 (ctrl).
Desc: Literature and reviews of books.
Ind/Abst HAPI Hisp. Am. Period. Index; MLA Int. Bibl. Books Artic. Mod. Lang. Lit.; Romant. Move.

US/8755-3627
QUONDAM ET FUTURUS (BIRMINGHAM, ALA.). (QUONDAM ET FUTURUS.). [Quondam futur.]. **Added/Corp** Memphis State University. Dept. of English. Vol. 1, No. 1 (Spring 1991)-. Periodical. English. Four times a year. $20.00 US; $25.00 Canada; $30.00 other. Memphis State University / Department of English, Memphis TN 38152. **Tel** (901)678-4591, FAX (901)276-2226. **ED** Henry Hall Peyton III. **DD** 809. **Bk Rev. Ad Acc. Pr Rev. Circ:** 1,000. ***Formed by the union of*** *Quondam et Futurus, 8755-3627* ***and*** *Arthurian Interpretations, 0890-4944.*
Desc: Articles and book reviews concerning Arthurian and Medieval subject matter. All articles and reviews are written by scholars in their respective fields of expertise.

US
RAJAH. English. 4024 Modern Language Building, University of Michigan, Ann Arbor MI 48109. **ED** Nash Mayfield.
Ind/Abst Lit. Crit. Regist.

GR
RAM. English. mo (11 issues). $43.00 Cyprus, $55.00 Europe and Turkey; $60.00 other. Lambrakis Press SA, 3 Christou Lada, 102 37 Athens Greece. **Tel** 011 30 1 3237283, 011 30 1 3230221.

AT/0048-671X
RAMUS. **See** Classical Studies.

US/0275-1607
RARITAN. [Raritan]. **Added/Corp** Rutgers University. Vol. 1, No. 1 (Summer 1981)-. Periodical. English. qt. $20.00 (one year), $30.00 (two years) institutions, $16.00 (one year), $26.00 (two years) individuals. Rutgers University / New Brunswick, 31 Mine Street, New Brunswick NJ 08903. **Tel** (908)932-7887, FAX (908)932-7855. **ED** Richard Poirier. **LC** AS30; .R37. **DD** 051. Index available (bound fourth issue). **Bk Rev. Ad Acc. Circ:** 3,500 (ctrl). available on microfilm and microfiche from University Microfilms International (UMI). Documents available from The Genuine Article, UMI Article Clearinghouse.
Desc: Focuses on workings of cultural power, how movements help determine critical attitudes toward ideas in literature, media, social sciences and arts. Essays, essay reviews, some poetry and fiction.
Ind/Abst Abstr. Engl. Stud.; Acad. Search (July 1993-); Am. Hist. Life (1987-); Am. Humanit. Index; Annu. Bibliogr. Engl. Lang. Lit.; Arts Humanit. Citation Index [Full Cov.]; Curr. Contents Arts Humanit.; Expand. Acad. Index (1989-); Film Lit. Index (19??-); Humanit. Index; Humanit. Source (Jul. 1993-); Index Am. Period. Verse; Index Book Rev. Humanit. (1985-); INFO-SOUTH Abstr.; Lit. Crit. Regist.; Mag. Search; MLA Int. Bibl. Books Artic. Mod. Lang. Lit.; Newsp. Period. Abstr. (1991-); Res. Alert [Full Cov.]; Soc. Sci. Cit. Index [Select. Cov.].

●US/1066-3630
READERLY/WRITERLY TEXTS. (READERLY/WRITERLY TEXTS : ESSAYS ON LITERATURE AND LITERARY/TEXTUAL CRITICISM AND PEDAGOGY.). **VFOAT** Readerly Writerly Texts. (1993)-. Periodical. English. sa. $12.00 (institutions). Ollie O Oviedo, Languages and Literature Department, Eastern New Mexico University, Portales NM 88130.

MX/0486-1205
RECENT BOOKS IN MEXICO. **See** Library and Information Sciences.

US/0300-6425
RECOVERING LITERATURE. [Recover. lit.]. Vol. 1, No. 1 (Spring 1972)-. Periodical. English (French). an. $6.00. Recovering Literature, PO Box 805, Alpine CA 92001. **Tel** (619)659-0291. **ED** Gerald & Evelyn Bulter. **LC** PN2; .R37. **Bk Rev. Circ:** 200 (ctrl).
Desc: Literary criticism.
Ind/Abst Abstr. Engl. Stud.; Lit. Crit. Regist.; MLA Int. Bibl. Books Artic. Mod. Lang. Lit.; Romant. Move.

AG
REDACCION. No. 1, (Mar. 1973)-. Periodical. Spanish. mo. Editorial Replica, Av Independencia 2744, Buenos Aires Argentina. **LC** F2801; .R36.

US/0048-7384
RESOURCES FOR AMERICAN LITERARY STUDY. [Resour. Am. lit. study]. **Added/Corp** Virginia Commonwealth University. Dept. of English. University of Maryland, College Park. Dept. of English. Vol. 1 (Spring 1971)-. English. sa. $40.00 (institutions), $27.50 (individuals) US; $48.00 (institutions), $35.00 (individuals) other. Pennsylvania State University Press, 820 North University Drive, Suite C, University Park PA 16802-1003. **Tel** (814)865-1327, (800)326-9180, FAX (814)863-1408. **ED** Jackson R. Bryer. **LC** Z1225; .R46. **DD** 016.81. **[CCC]. Bk Rev. Ad Acc. Circ:** 500. available on microfilm and microfiche from University Microfilms International (UMI). Documents available from The Genuine Article.
Desc: Evaluative bibliographical essays on major authors, works, genres, trends, and periods. Also informative accounts of significant collections of research materials of literary and cultural interest available in archives and libraries.
Ind/Abst Annu. Bibliogr. Engl. Lang. Lit.; Arts Humanit. Citation Index [Full Cov.]; Curr. Contents Arts Humanit.; MLA Int. Bibl. Books Artic. Mod. Lang. Lit.; Res. Alert [Full Cov.].

US/0190-3233
REVIEW (CHARLOTTESVILLE). (REVIEW.). [Review]. Vol. 1 (1979)-. Academic Scholarly Publication. English. an (Nov.). $30.00 (latest volume). University Press of Virginia, PO Box 3608, Charlottesville VA 22903. **Tel** (804)924-3469. **ED** J. O. Hoge and J. L. W. West III. **LC** PR1; .R32. **DD** 820.9. **Bk Rev. Ad Acc.** ctrl circ.
Desc: Publishes important review-essays and reviews of scholarly literature. Aiming to publish 'definitive' reviews of significant works of literary scholarship.
Ind/Abst Annu. Bibliogr. Engl. Lang. Lit.; MLA Int. Bibl. Books Artic. Mod. Lang. Lit.

US/0276-0045
REVIEW OF CONTEMPORARY FICTION. [Rev. contemp. fict.]. Vol. 1, No. 1 (Spring 1981)-. Periodical. English. Three times a year (Jan., June, Sept.). $17.00 (individuals); $24.00 (institutions). Review of Contemporary Fiction, Fairchild Hall/ ISU, Normal IL 61761. **Tel** (309)438-7555, FAX (309)438-7422. **ED** John O'Brien. **LC** PN3503; .R45. **DD** 809.3. **[CCC]. Bk Rev. Ad Acc. Circ:** 3,000. available on microfilm and microfiche from University Microfilms International (UMI). Documents available from UMI Article Clearinghouse.
Desc: Devoted to criticism of contemporary fiction. Includes essays, interviews, fiction and book reviews.
Ind/Abst Acad. Search (July 1993-); Am. Humanit. Index (1986-); Book Rev. Index; Expand. Acad. Index (1989-); Humanit. Index; Humanit. Source (Jul. 1993-); INFO-SOUTH Abstr.; Lit. Crit. Regist.; Mag. Search; Middle East Abstr. Index; MLA Int. Bibl. Books Artic. Mod. Lang. Lit.; Newsp. Period. Abstr. (1991-).

US/0034-6640
REVIEW OF NATIONAL LITERATURES. [Rev. natl. lit.]. **Added/Corp** St. John's University (New York, N.Y.) Council on National Literatures. Vol. 1, No. 1 (Spring 1970)-. Academic Scholarly Publication. English. ir. Comes with Council on National Literatures membership. Council on National Literatures, PO Box 81, Whitestone NY 11357. **Tel** (718)767-8380, FAX (718)767-8380. **ED** Anne Paolucci. **LC** PN2; .R44. **DD** 809. cum. index. **Bk Rev. Ad Acc. Pr Rev. Circ:** 1,000 (ctrl).
Desc: Critical overviews of emergent literature and thematic assessments of traditional, comparative literature.
Ind/Abst Abstr. Engl. Stud.; Annu. Bibliogr. Engl. Lang. Lit.; Middle East Abstr. Index; MLA Int. Bibl. Books Artic. Mod. Lang. Lit.; Romant. Move.

US/0892-6212
REVIEW OF TEXAS BOOKS. **See** Publishing-Books and Bookmaking.

US/0164-341X
REVIEWERS' CONSENSUS. (REVIEWERS' CONSENSUS : EVALUATIONS FROM REVIEWS OF BOOKS FOR CHILDREN AND ADOLESCENTS.). Vol. 1, (1976)-. Periodical. English. qt. $15.00. Willow Tree Press, PO Box 249, Monsey NY 10952. **Tel** (914)354-9139, FAX (914)362-8376. **ED** Ned Luzmoor.

AT/0157-3705
REVIEWS JOURNAL. (THE CRNLE REVIEWS JOURNAL.). [Rev. j.]. **Added/Corp** Flinders University of South Australia. Centre for Research in the New Literatures in English. **VFOAT** RJ; R.J.; Reviews Journal; C.R.N.L.E. Reviews Journal. **VAT** Centre for Research in the New Literatures in English Reviews Journal. No. 1 (1979)-. Periodical. English. sa. 20.00Aus$ (institutions), 15.00Aus$ (individuals). Flinders University, South Australia Crnle, Bedford Park South Australia 5042 Australia. **Tel** 2752459. **ED** Annie Greet. **Bk Rev. Ad Acc. Circ:** 250 (ctrl).
Desc: Critical survey of English language literary publishing from the Post-Colonial Societies of the Commonwealth and beyond.

PE/0252-8843
REVISTA DE CRITICA LITERARIA LATINOAMERICANA. [Rev. crit. lit. latinoam.]. Vol. 1, (1st Semester 1975)-. Spanish (Portuguese). sa. $41.00 (airmail), $35.00 (surface mail). Latinoamericana Editores, University of California, Department of Spanish & Portg, Berkeley CA 94720. **Tel** (510)642-6771, FAX (510)643-8245. **ED** Cristina S. de Cornejo. **LC** PQ7081.A1; R33. **DD** 860. **Bk Rev. Ad Acc. Circ:** 1,500 (ctrl). Documents available from The Genuine Article.
Desc: Criticism on Latin American literature, bibliographies, notes, studies (essays), book reviews, etc.
Ind/Abst Arts Humanit. Citation Index [Full Cov.]; Curr. Contents Arts Humanit.; HAPI Hisp. Am. Period. Index; MLA Int. Bibl. Books Artic. Mod. Lang. Lit.; Res. Alert [Full Cov.].

RM/0034-8392
REVISTA DE ISTORIE SI TEORIE LITERARA. [Rev. ist. teor. lit.]. **Added/Corp** Academia Republicii Populare Romine. Academia Republicii Socialiste Romania. Institutul de Istorie si Literatura "G. Calinescu.". Vol. 1 (1952)-. Periodical. Romanian (summaries and/or abstracts in English, French, German and Russian). qt. DM223.00. **(Subscription address:** Kubon & Sagner, ABT Zeitschriftenimport, D 80328 Munich Germany.**) LC** PN9; .R44.
Desc: Publishes studies on Romanian and foreign literature.
Ind/Abst Annu. Bibliogr. Engl. Lang. Lit.; MLA Int. Bibl. Books Artic. Mod. Lang. Lit.

BL/0101-8051
REVISTA DE LETRAS (FORTALEZA). (REVISTA DE LETRAS : RL / UFC, CENTRO DE HUMANIDADES.). [Rev. kt.]. **Added/Corp** Universidade Federal do Ceara. Centro de Humanidades. **VFOAT** RL; R.L. Vol. 1, No. 1 (1978)-. Periodical. Portuguese. an. $30.00. Universidade Estadual Paulista, Av. Vicente Ferreira 1278, Caixa Posta 603, 17515-901 Marilia SP Brazil. **Tel** 0144 33 1844, FAX 0144 22 2504, telex 111 9016 UJME BR. **LC** AS80.A1; R423. **DD** 070.5/94/098131. **Bk Rev. Circ:** 1,000.

CU
REVISTA DE LITERATURA CUBANA. ***Suspended.*** Vol. 1, No. 1, (July 1983)-?. Periodical. Spanish. sa. $12.00. Ediciones Cubanas, Obispo 527, Altos ESQ Bernaza, CP 10100 Havana Cuba. **Tel** 011 632980, 631942, FAX 011 631011, telex 512337, 6540. **Circ:** 20,000 (ctrl).
Desc: Research and critical studies on authors, works, topics, personages, trends, stages and characteristics of Cuban literature.

SP/0034-8635
REVISTA DE OCCIDENTE. [Rev. occidente]. No. 1 (April/June 1980)-. Periodical. Spanish. mo. $102.00. Revista de Occidente, Fortuny 53, 28010 Madrid Spain. **Tel** 011 34 1 4104412. **LC** AP60; .R443. **DD** 056/.1. **[CCC].** Documents available from The Genuine Article. ***Continues*** *Revista de Occidente, 0034-8635.*
Desc: Dedicated to social sciences and humanities. Includes also a literary section by Spanish and Spanish American authors. Most of the issues focus on monographic topics of permanent interest, written by national and international essayists.
Ind/Abst Abstr. Engl. Stud.; Am. Hist. Life (1980-); Arts Humanit. Citation Index [Full Cov.]; Curr. Contents Arts Humanit.; MLA Int. Bibl. Books Artic. Mod. Lang. Lit.; Res. Alert [Full Cov.]; Romant. Move.; Soc. Sci. Cit. Index [Select. Cov.].

CN/0839-458X
REVUE ANDRE MALRAUX. ***Suspended.*** (REVUE ANDRE MALRAUX / ANDRE MALRAUX REVIEW.). [Rev. Andre Malraux]. **Added/Corp** Malraux Society. **VFOAT** Andre Malraux Review; RAMR. Vol. 18, No. 2 (Fall 1986)-(19??). Periodical. English (French). Twice a year (May & Nov.). 20.00Can$ (individuals), 24.00Can$ (institutions) Canada; $18.00 (individuals), $22.00 (institutions) US; $20.00 (individuals), $30.00 (institutions) other. University of Alberta / Romance Languages, Department of Romance Languages, Edmonton Alberta T6G 2E6 Canada. **Tel** (403)492-2003, (403)439-9393. **ED** Robert S. Thornberry. **LC** PQ2625.A716; Z74. **DD** 843/.912. **Bk Rev. Pr Rev. Circ:** 350. available on microfiche; available on microfilm; available on CD-ROM; available on diskette; available on audiocassette; available on videocassette; available in microform. ***Continues*** *Melanges Malraux, 0025-892X.*
Desc: An international journal devoted to all aspects of the life, works and influence of Andre Malraux (1901-1976). Solicits manuscripts, both substantial essays and notes from any critical, historical or scholarly approach. Publishes comparative studies, research-oriented scholarship and biographical articles and bibliographies. Material on subjects broadly related to Malraux is also welcome.
Ind/Abst MLA Int. Bibl. Books Artic. Mod. Lang. Lit.

FR
REVUE DES LIVRES POUR ENFANTS, LA. **Added/Corp** Joie par les Livres (Association). No. 56 (Oct. 1977)-. Periodical. French. bm. 253.00F (airmail), 190.00F (surface mail) France; 215.00F (surface mail) other. Joie par les Livres, 8 rue Saint-Bon, 75004 Paris 4 France. **Tel** 011 33 1 48876195. **LC** PN1009.A1; B84. **DD** 028.52. **Bk Rev. Ad Acc. Circ:** 5,000. ***Continues*** *Bulletin d'Analyse de Livres pour Enfants.*
Desc: Critical survey of new books for children from eight months to 14 years of age, with general information and articles on children's literature and libraries.
Ind/Abst Child. Lit. Abstr. (19??-).

CN/0229-2297
REVUE LITTERAIRE DU C.E.G.E.P. DE GRANBY. [Rev. litt. C.E.G.E.P. Granby]. **Added/Corp** College de Sherbrooke. Campus de Granby. (May 1979)-. Periodical. French. C.E.G.E.P. de Granby, 50 rue St-Joseph, Granby Quebec J2G 6T6 Canada. **DD** C840/.8/092375. ***Continues** Liber ... , 0229-2289.*

CN
RIKKA. Vol. 1, (Autumn 1974)-. Periodical. English. qt. Rikka, PO Box 70 Station A, Toronto Ontario M5W 1A2 Canada.

FR
RIMBAUD VIVANT. **Added/Corp** Societe des Amis de Rimbaud. (1973)-. Periodical. French. Twice a year. 50.00F. Amis de Rimbaud, c/o Mme Zuzanne Briet, 24 rue Gutenberg, 92100 Boulogne France. ***Continues** Etudes Rimbaldiennes.*
Ind/Abst Romant. Move.

US/0035-7200
ROAD APPLE REVIEW. Vol. 1 (Winter 1968/69)-. Periodical. English. qt. $4.00. Road Runner Press, 3263 Shorewood Drive, Oshkosh WI 54901.

US/0300-7936
ROBINSON JEFFERS NEWSLETTER. **See** Biographies.

RU/0235-7089
RODINA. Vol. 1 (1989)-. Periodical. Russian. mo. $159.95. **(Subscription address:** East View Publications Inc., 3020 Harbor Lane North, Suite 110, Minneapolis MN 55447.**)** **LC** DK1; .R6.

RU/0131-6044
ROMAN-GAZETA. (19??)-. Periodical. Russian. Twenty-four times a year. $112.95. **(Subscription address:** East View Publications Inc., 3020 Harbor Lane North, Suite 110, Minneapolis MN 55447.**)** **LC** AP50; .R6.

US
ROMANCE MONOGRAPHS, INC. (SERIES). (ROMANCE MONOGRAPHS, INC.). No. 1 (1972)-. Monographic series. English (Multiple languages). ir. Price varies per volume. University of Mississippi / Department of Modern Language, University MS 38677. **Tel** (601)232-7298. **ED** Jack Davis Brown. **Pr Rev.**
Desc: Literary criticism in the area of romance languages.

AG
RONDA LITERARIA. Periodical. Spanish. ir. Distribuidora Torres, Charcas 3918, 1425 Buenos Aires Argentina.

XR
ROSSICA OLOMUCENSIA. **See** Linguistics.

FR/0035-970X
RUE, LA. No. 1 (March 1968)-. Periodical. French. qt. Association Culturelle Louise Michel, 24 rue Paul Albert, 75018 Paris France.

RM/0035-8088
RUMANIAN REVIEW. [Rom. rev.]. **VFOAT** Romanian Review. (May 1946)-. Periodical. English (French, Russian and German). mo. $46.00. Romanian Review, 1 Piata Scinteii, PO Box 33-28, Bucharest 71341 Romania. **Tel** 17 38 36, telex 11 272. **(Subscription address:** Orion Press SRL, SPL Independentei 202-A, Bucharest 6 Romania.**)** **LC** DR201; .R8. **Bk Rev. Ad Acc. Circ:** 7,000. ***Continues** Rumanian Review.*
Desc: Covers the most distinguished signatures of Romanian men of culture along with every significant contribution this country has made to the world in fields such as literature, music, fine arts, aesthetics, philosophy, history or those involving two or more such academic disciplines.
Ind/Abst MLA Int. Bibl. Books Artic. Mod. Lang. Lit.

JA
RYUKYU DAIGAKU KOKUBUNGAKU TETSUGAKU RON SHU. **Main/Corp** Ryukyu Daigaku. Ho-bungakubu. **VFOAT** Ryudai Review of Japanese Literature & Philosophy. Multiple languages (English and Japanese). Ryukyu Daigaku Ho-Bungakubu, 1 Shuri Tonokuracho 3-chome, Naha Okinawa 903 Japan. **LC** AS552.R8; A3.

SP/0213-6449
SABER LEER. **Added/Corp** Fundacion Juan March. (Jan. 1987)-. Periodical. Spanish. Ten times a year. $20.00. Fundacion Juan March, Castello 77, 28006 Madrid Spain. **Tel** 11 34 1 435 4240. Index available in last issue of volume--attached. **Bk Rev. Pr Rev. Circ:** 5,000 (ctrl).
Desc: Journal of critical book reviews.

UK/0265-4881
SALISBURY REVIEW, THE. Issue No. 1 (Autumn 1982)-. Periodical. English. Four times a year (Mar., June, Sept., Dec.). £16.00 UK; £18.00 other; $35.00 North America. Claridge Press, 33 Canonbury Park South, London N1 2JW England. **Tel** 011 44 71-226-7791, FAX 011 44 071-354-0383. Index available. **Bk Rev,** (Qty: 30). **Circ:** 2,000.
Desc: A journal of conservative thought embracing literature, social issues as well as politics.
Ind/Abst Appl. Soc. Sci. Index Abstr.

US/0226-840X
SAMISDAT. [Samisdat]. Vol. 4, No. 1 (1974)-. English. ir. $25.00. SAMISDAT, Merritt Clifton, 456 Monroe Turnpike, Monroe CT 06468. **Tel** (514)263-4439. **ED** Merritt Clifton. **LC** PS615; .S17. **DD** 811/.008. **Bk Rev. Ad Acc. Circ:** 300. ***Continues** Berkeley Samisdat Review, 0883-3702.*
Desc: Essays, reviews, poetry, fiction, and original art work, addressing the leading environmental, social, economic, and political issues of the times. International contributor base and readership.
Ind/Abst Index Am. Period. Verse.

US/0194-0724
SAN FRANCISCO REVIEW OF BOOKS. [San Franc. rev. books]. **VFOAT** San Francisco Review. Vol. 1 (Apr. 1975)-. Periodical. English. qt. $16.00 (six issues), $32.00 (twelve issues). San Francisco Review of Books, 555 De Haro Street, Suite 220, San Francisco CA 94107. **Tel** (415)252-7708 (Donald Paul), FAX (415)252-8908. **ED** Jennifer Martinez. **DD** 028. **Bk Rev,** (Qty: 200-300/yr). **Ad Acc, Adv Mgr:** Donald Paul. **Circ:** 10,000, 24,000 (readership). available on microfilm and microfiche from University Microfilms International (UMI). ***Absorbed** Western Publisher.*
Desc: Through a well designed format of eclectic reviews, mixed with provocative features, and colorful interviews, the Review keeps abreast of literary currents that reflect our national and international interests.
Ind/Abst Book Rev. Digest; Book Rev. Index.

US/1055-8446
SANTA FE LITERARY REVIEW. (SANTA FE LITERARY REVIEW : SFLR.). [Santa Fe lit. rev.]. **VFOAT** SFLR. Vol. 1, No. 1 (Summer 1991)-. Periodical. English. qt. $18.00. Haven Hill Press, PO Box 8018, Santa Fe NM 87504. **DD** 810.

US/0735-1550
SAUL BELLOW JOURNAL. **See** Biographies.

FR
SCOLIES. **Added/Corp** Paris. Ecole Normale Superieure. (1971)-. French.

US/0360-2672
SCREE. Began in 1974?. Periodical. English. ir. $8.50. Duck Down Press, PO Box 1047, Fallon NV 89406. **Tel** (702)423-6643.

RM/0037-0517
SECOLUL 20. **Added/Corp** Uniunea Scriitorilor din Republica Populara Romina. Uniunea Scriitorilor din Republica Socialista Romania. **VFOAT** Secolul Douazeci. **VAT** Secolul Twenty. Vol. 1 (Jan. 1961)-. Periodical. Romanian. mo. DM206.00. **(Subscription address:** Kubon & Sagner, ABT Zeitschriftenimport, D 80328 Munich Germany.**)** **LC** PN6065.R8; S4. **DD** 809/.04. cum. index.
Desc: Review of world literature.
Ind/Abst Annu. Bibliogr. Engl. Lang. Lit.; MLA Int. Bibl. Books Artic. Mod. Lang. Lit.

SP/0037-2501
SERRA D'OR. [Serra d'or]. (1959)-. Periodical. Catalan. mo. 4900ptas Spain; 6600ptas Europe; $75.00 other. Abadia de Montserrat, Ausias March 92 98 Interior, 08013 Barcelona Spain. **Tel** 34 3 2450303 or 2314001, FAX 34 3 4473594. **ED** Maur M Boix. **LC** DP302.C57; S47. **DD** 946/.7/005. Index available. **Bk Rev. Ad Acc. Circ:** 17,000.
Ind/Abst Am. Hist. Life (1960-1975)(1969-).

US/0037-3052
SEWANEE REVIEW, THE. [Sewanee rev.]. **Added/Corp** University of the South. Vol. 1 (Nov. 1892)-. Periodical. English. qt (Jan., Apr., Jul., Oct.). $20.00 (1 year), $38.00 (2 year), $55.00 (3 year) US institutions; $25.00 (1 year), $48.00 (2 year), $70.00 (3 year) other institutions; $16.00 (one year), $28.00 (two year), $40.00 (three year) other. Sewanee Review, University of the South, 735 University Avenue, Sewanee TN 37375. **Tel** (615)598-1245. **ED** George Core. **LC** AP2; .S5. **DD** 809. **[CCC].** Index available. cum. index. **Bk Rev. Ad Acc. Circ:** 3,560 (ctrl). available on microfilm from Kraus Microform. Documents available from The Genuine Article, UMI Article Clearinghouse.
Desc: Presents a selection of criticism, fiction, and poetry written in the U.S., Canada, and the British Isles.
Ind/Abst Abstr. Engl. Stud.; Acad. Abstr. Full Text Elite (July 1990-); Acad. Abstr. (July 1990-); Acad. Ind. [Computer File] (1987-); Acad. Search (July 1990-); Am. Humanit. Index; Annu. Bibliogr. Engl. Lang. Lit.; Arts Humanit. Citation Index [Full Cov.]; Book Rev. Digest; Book Rev. Index; Curr. Contents Arts Humanit.; Expand. Acad. Index (1987-); Humanit. Index; Humanit. Source (Jul. 1990-); Index Am. Period. Verse; INFO-SOUTH Abstr.; Lit. Crit. Regist.; Mag. Search; MLA Int. Bibl. Books Artic. Mod. Lang. Lit.; Newsp. Period. Abstr. (1991-); Peace Res. Abstr. J. (1971-1975); Res. Alert [Full Cov.]; Romant. Move.; Soc. Sci. Cit. Index [Select. Cov.].

US
SEWANEE REVIEW [MICROFORM]. English. $50.00 per reel. Kraus International Publishing, Route 100, Millwood NY 10546. **Tel** (914)761-9600, telex 6711564.

US/0037-3214
SHAKESPEARE NEWSLETTER, THE. [Shakespeare newsl.]. **Added/Corp** University of Illinois at Chicago Circle. Dept. of English. Vol. 1 No. 1 (Mar. 1951)-. Newsletter. English. Four times a year (Feb., May, Aug., Nov.). $12.00. Iona College, 715 North Avenue, New Rochelle NY 10801. **Tel** (914)633-2000. **ED** Louis Marder. **LC** PR2885; .S48. **DD** 822.33. **Circ:** 2,000.
Desc: A wide-ranging survey of all biographical critical interpretation. Theatrical Shakespeare studies in digest form, book reviews, authorship, news, scholarly trends, festivals, and meetings.
Ind/Abst Abstr. Engl. Stud.; Annu. Bibliogr. Engl. Lang. Lit.; Lit. Crit. Regist.; MLA Int. Bibl. Books Artic. Mod. Lang. Lit.

UK/0080-9152
SHAKESPEARE SURVEY (CAMBRIDGE). **See** Biographies.

US/0883-9123
SHAKESPEAREAN CRITICISM (DETROIT, MICH.). (SHAKESPEAREAN CRITICISM : EXCERPTS FROM THE CRITICISM OF WILLIAM SHAKESPEARE'S PLAYS AND POETRY, FROM THE FIRST PUBLISHED APPRAISALS TO CURRENT EVALUATIONS.). [Shakespear. crit.]. **VFOAT** Shakespearean Criticism Yearbook. Vol. 1 (1984)-. English. ir. $120.00. Gale Research Inc., 835 Penobscot Building, Detroit MI 48226. **Tel** (800)877-GALE, (313)961-2242, FAX (313)961-6083, telex TWX 810-221-7086. **ED** Joseph C. Tardiff. **LC** PR2965; .S44. **DD** 822.3/3.
Desc: Presents a selection of critical excerpts on Shakespeare's works and performances of his works and serves as an introduction to the most significant commentators.

US/0741-5842
SHAW. [Shaw]. Vol. 1 (1981)-. Periodical. English. an. $35.00 US; $41.00 other. Pennsylvania State University Press, 820 North University Drive, Suite C, University Park PA 16802-1003. **Tel** (814)865-1327, (800)326-9180, FAX (814)863-1408. **ED** Stanley Weintraub. **LC** PR5366; .A15. **DD** 822/.912. **[CCC]. Bk Rev.** ***Continues** Shaw Review, 0037-3354.*
Desc: Devoted to studying Shaw. Odd numbered volumes have a theme; even numbered volumes are general studies of Shaw.
Ind/Abst Abstr. Engl. Stud.; Annu. Bibliogr. Engl. Lang. Lit.; MLA Int. Bibl. Books Artic. Mod. Lang. Lit.

JA/0288-6154
SHOIN LITERARY REVIEW. [Shoin lit. rev.]. (1968)-. Periodical. Multiple languages. an. **DD** 820. ***Continues in part** Kenkyu Kiyo - Shoin Joshi Gakuin Daigaku, 0288-612X.*
Ind/Abst MLA Int. Bibl. Books Artic. Mod. Lang. Lit.

IS
SIMAN KERIAH. 1- September 1972-. Hebrew. qt. $21.00. Siman Kria, POB 39267, Tel Aviv 61392 Israel. **Tel** (03)420995. **ED** M Perry. **LC** PJ5001; .S56. **Bk Rev. Ad Acc. Circ:** 3,000.
Desc: Fiction, poetry, criticism, poetics of literature. criticism, essays, theory of literature, reviews, etc.

CN/0226-3424
SIMCOE REVIEW. [Simcoe rev.]. No. 1- Winter 1976-. Periodical. English. sa. $2.00. English Department, Governor SIMCOE Secondary School, 15 Glenview Avenue, St Catharines Ontario L2N 2Z7 Canada. **DD** C810/.08/092375.

US/0037-5837
SIPAPU. [Sipapu]. (Jan. 1970)-. Periodical. English. sa (Jan. and July). Free to library school students, prisoners, and exchange papers, $8.00 US and Canada. Noel Peattie, 23311 County Road 88, Winters CA 95694. **Tel** (916)662-3364. **ED** Noel Peattie. **LC** CURRENT ISSUES ONLY. cum. index. **Bk Rev,** (Qty: 10). **Circ:** 430. available on microfilm from University of Southern California.
Desc: A newsletter for librarians, collectors, editors and others interested in third world studies, the Counter-Culture, Little Magazines and The Alternative Press. Library and other conference news, book reviews, interviews with leading personalities in the Counter-Cultural publishing scene.
Ind/Abst Altern. Press Index.

FR/0530-9190
SITUATION. **VFOAT** Collection Situation. No. 1- 1955-. Monographic series. French. ir. Price varies per volume. Lettres Modernes Minard, 45 rue de Saint Andre, 14123 Fleury Surrey Orne France. **Tel** 011 33 31 844706.

US/0037-6779
SLAVIC REVIEW. [Slavic rev.]. **Added/Corp** American Association for the Advancement of Slavic Studies. Vol. 22, No. 3 (Oct. 1961)-. Academic Scholarly Publication. English. Four times a year (Mar., June, Sept., Dec.). $50.00 (surface mail); $77.00 Europe, $87.00 Asia (airmail). American Association for the Advancement of Slavic Studies, 125 Panama Street, Stanford University, Acacia Building, Stanford CA 94305-6029. **Tel** (415)723-9668, FAX (415)725-7737, telex 348402 STANFRD STNU. **ED** Sidney Monas. **LC** D377.A1; A5. **DD** 940. Index available. cum. index. **Bk Rev. Ad Acc. Circ:** 5,200 (ctrl). available on microfilm and microfiche from University Microfilms International (UMI). Documents available from The Genuine Article, UMI Article Clearinghouse. ***Continues*** *American Slavic and East European Review, 1049-7544.*
Desc: Interdisciplinary scholarly journal of Soviet/East European Studies.
Ind/Abst ABC POL SCI; Acad. Abstr. Full Text Elite (July 1990-); Acad. Abstr. (July 1990-); Acad. Ind. [Computer File] (1987-); Acad. Search (July 1990-); Am. Hist. Life (1961-); Am. Bibliogr. Slavic East Europ. Stud.; Annu. Bibliogr. Engl. Lang. Lit.; Arts Humanit. Citation Index [Full Cov.]; BHA : Biblio. Hist. Art; Book Rev. Index; Curr. Contents Arts Humanit.; Expand. Acad. Index (1987-); Humanit. Index; INFO-SOUTH Abstr.; Int. Bibliogr. Sociol.; Int. Polit. Sci. Abstr.; Mag. Search; MLA Int. Bibl. Books Artic. Mod. Lang. Lit.; Newsp. Period. Abstr. (1986-); Res. Alert [Full Cov.]; Romant. Move.; Soc. Sci. Source (Jul. 1990-); Soc. Sci. Cit. Index [Select. Cov.]; Soc. Sci. Index; U.S. Polit. Sci. Doc.; West. Hist. Q.

US/0037-6868
SLOBODA (CHICAGO, ILL.). (SLOBODA. LIBERTY.). [Sloboda]. **Added/Corp** Serbian National Defense Council of America. **VFOAT** Liberty. (19??)-. Periodical. Serbo-Croatian (Roman). sm (except once in July). $25.00. Sloboda Liberty, 5782 North Elston Avenue, Chicago IL 60646. **Tel** (312)775-7773. **LC** AP56; .S56.

US/0037-7228
SMALL PRESS REVIEW. [Small press rev.]. Vol. 1 No. 1 (Spring 1967)-. Periodical. English. mo. $29.00 (one year), $39.00 (two year), $47.00 (three year) institutions; $23.00 (one year), $30.00 (two year), $33.00 (three year) individuals. Dustbooks, PO Box 100, Paradise CA 95969. **Tel** (916)877-6110. **ED** Len Fulton. **LC** WMLC L 83/2090. **Bk Rev**, (Qty: 100). **Ad Acc. Circ:** 3,500.
Desc: A running document containing news, reviews, features and updates on the listings in the international directory.
Ind/Abst Book Rev. Index.

US/0275-5203
SONORA REVIEW. [Sonora rev.]. No. 1 (Fall 1980)-. English. sa. $10.00. University of Arizona / English, c/o Bruce Upbin, Tucson AZ 85721. **Tel** (602)626-8383. **ED** Tony Brown and Kathy Florence (editor's phone: (602)621-1836). **LC** PS1; .S654. **DD** 810/.8. **Bk Rev**, (Qty: 1-3). **Ad Acc, Adv Mgr:** J Barnet, **Tel** (602)791-2257. **Circ:** 1,000.
Desc: Literary fiction and poetry. Also book reviews, interviews, and special issues.
Ind/Abst Index Am. Period. Verse.

US/0275-9527
SOUTH ASIAN REVIEW - SOUTH ASIAN LITERARY ASSOCIATION. (SOUTH ASIAN REVIEW.). [South Asian rev. - South Asian Lit. Assoc.]. **Added/Corp** South Asian Literary Association (U.S.). **VFOAT** S.A.L.A. Journal; SALA Journal. (19??)-. Periodical. English. an. $10.00 US & Canada; $15.00 other. University of North Florida, Department of Language and Literature, Jacksonville FL 32216. **Tel** (904)646-2580. **ED** Satya S. Pachori. **LC** PK180; .S68. **DD** 891/.1. **Circ:** 150 (ctrl).
Desc: Covers South Asian literature, culture, linguistics and east-west literary relations.
Ind/Abst MLA Int. Bibl. Books Artic. Mod. Lang. Lit.

US/0038-2876
SOUTH ATLANTIC QUARTERLY, THE. **See** Humanities.

US/0038-3163
SOUTH CAROLINA REVIEW, THE. [S. C. rev.]. **Added/Corp** Clemson University. Furman University. Vol. 1 (Nov. 1968)-. Periodical. English. Twice a year (Spring and Fall). $8.75 US & Canada; $10.25 other. Clemson University / English, Department of English, Clemson SC 29634-1503. **Tel** (803)656-3229. **ED** Mark Winchell. **LC** PS558.S6; S67. **DD** 810/.8/0054. **Bk Rev. Ad Acc. Pr Rev. Circ:** 650 (ctrl).
Desc: Fiction, poetry, and criticism is topic for this magazine.
Ind/Abst Abstr. Engl. Stud.; Am. Hist. Life (1972-1973); Am. Humanit. Index; Annu. Bibliogr. Engl. Lang. Lit.; Book Rev. Index; Index Am. Period. Verse; Lit. Crit. Regist.; MLA Int. Bibl. Books Artic. Mod. Lang. Lit.; Romant. Move.

AT/0038-4526
SOUTHERN REVIEW (ADELAIDE). (SOUTHERN REVIEW.). [South. rev.]. **Added/Corp** University of Adelaide. Dept. of English. Macquarie University. School of English and Linguistics. Vol. 1 (1963)-. Periodical. English. Three times a year. 40.00Aus$ (institutions); 25.00Aus$ (individuals). University of Adelaide / English, Department of English, GPO Box 498, Adelaide 5001 S Australia. **Tel** 011 61 8 2285627, FAX 011 61 8 2323375. **ED** Cathy Greenfield and Barbara Milich. **LC** PR1; .S68. **DD** 820/.9. Index available. **Bk Rev. Ad Acc. Pr Rev. Circ:** 400.
Desc: Articles and reviews on literature/literary theory, particularly from exponents of new radical critical discourses.
Ind/Abst Abstr. Engl. Stud.; Annu. Bibliogr. Engl. Lang. Lit.; APAIS, Aust. Public Aff. Inf. Ser. (1963-); Expand. Acad. Index (1989-); MLA Int. Bibl. Books Artic. Mod. Lang. Lit.; Romant. Move.

US/0038-4712
SOUTHWEST REVIEW. [Southwest rev.]. Vol. 10 (Oct. 1924)-. Periodical. English. Four times a year (Jan., Apr., July, Oct.). $20.00 individual, $25.00 institution. Southwest Review, Southern Methodist University, 307 Fondren Library West, Dallas TX 75275. **Tel** (214)768-1036, (214)768-1037, FAX (214)768-1408. **ED** Elizabeth Mills (senior editor). **LC** AP2; .S883. **DD** 051. **[CCC].** Index available (published in Oct. issue). **Ad Acc, Adv Mgr:** same as editor. **Circ:** 1,500. available on CD-ROM from Information Access Company; available on an online database from Information Access Company; available on microfilm and microfiche from University Microfilms International (UMI). Documents available from UMI Article Clearinghouse. ***Absorbed*** *Reviewer of Richmond* ***and*** *Reviewer, 0275-245X;* ***Continues*** *Texas Review.*
Desc: Presents works of writers and scholars from the surrounding states and offers analyses of problems and themes that are distinctly southwestern and, at the same time, publishes works of good writers regardless of their locales.
Ind/Abst Abstr. Engl. Stud.; Acad. Search (July 1993-); Am. Hist. Life (1963-); Am. Humanit. Index; Annu. Bibliogr. Engl. Lang. Lit.; Book Rev. Index; Expand. Acad. Index (1989-); Humanit. Index; Humanit. Source (Jul. 1993-); Index Am. Period. Verse; INFO-SOUTH Abstr.; Mag. Search; MLA Int. Bibl. Books Artic. Mod. Lang. Lit.; Newsp. Period. Abstr. (1991-); Romant. Move.; West. Hist. Q.

US/0276-7155
SOUTHWESTERN REVIEW (LAFAYETTE, LA.), THE. (THE SOUTHWESTERN REVIEW / DEPARTMENT OF ENGLISH AT THE UNIVERSITY OF SOUTHWESTERN LOUISIANA.). Began with Vol. for Spring 1975. English. an. Southwestern Review, Department of English, The University of Southwestern Louisiana, Lafayette LA 70504. **LC** PS501; .S6. **DD** 810/.8.

RU
SOVIET LITERATURE. Vol. 1 (1931)-. Periodical. English (French, Spanish, German, Polish and Russian). mo. $28.00. **(Subscription address:** Victor Kamkin, 4956 Boiling Brook Parkway, Rockville MD 20852.) ***Continues*** *Literature of the World Revolution.*
Desc: Publishes works by Soviet writers, with literary criticism, literary studies and Soviet art reproductions.
Ind/Abst MLA Int. Bibl. Books Artic. Mod. Lang. Lit.; Romant. Move.

FR/0221-833X
SPEAKEASY. (1978)-. Periodical. English. Five times a year. 68.56F France; 90.00F EEU; 100.00F other. Edition Fernand Nathan, 9 rue Mechain, 75676 Paris Cedex 14 France. **Tel** 011 33 1 45875000. **UDC** 4.

FR/0038-6944
SPECTACLE DU MONDE, LE. [Spect. monde]. April 1962-. Periodical. French. wk. 842.00F France; 1,000.00F other. Compagnie Francaise Journaux, 14 rue d'Uzes, 75081 Paris Cedex 02 France. **Tel** (1)42.33.21.84, FAX (1)42.33.10.10. **LC** AP20; .S66. **DD** 054/.1. Index available. **Ad Acc. Circ:** 90,000 (ctrl). ***Absorbed*** *Realites.*

FR
SPECTACLE DU MONDE / PERSPECTIVES / REALITIES, LE. No. 282 (Sept. 1985)-. English. mo. 540.00F France; 629.00F US; 550.00F other. Compagnie Francaise Journaux, 14 rue d'Uzes, 75081 Paris Cedex 02 France. **Tel** (1)42.33.21.84, FAX (1)42.33.10.10. Index available. **Ad Acc. Circ:** 90,000 (ctrl). ***Continues*** *Le Spectacle du Monde / Realities.*

US/0038-7134
SPECULUM. **See** History(General)-History of Europe.

US/0738-8993
SPOON RIVER QUARTERLY, THE. ***Title Change.*** Vol. 1 (Winter 1976)-(19??). Periodical. English. qt. Illinois State University / English, Department of English, Normal IL 61761-6901. **Tel** (309)438-5776. **ED** Dr. Lucia Cordell Getsi. ***Continued by*** *Spoon River Poetry Review.*
Ind/Abst Index Am. Period. Verse.

GW/0038-8475
SPRACHE IM TECHNISCHEN ZEITALTER. [Sprache tech. Zeitalt.]. **Added/Corp** Literarisches Colloquium Berlin. Vol. 1 (1961)-. Periodical. German. Four times a year (Mar., June, Sept., Dec.). DM44.00 includes supplement in Literatur im Technischen Zeitalter. Aufbau Verlag Berlin & Weimar, Franzoesische Str. 32, D 10117 Berlin Germany. **Tel** 011 49 30 22350, FAX 011 49 30 2298637. **(Subscription address:** IA Inter ABO Betreuungs GmbH, Postfach 103245, D 20022 Hamburg Germany.) **ED** Walter Hollerer and Norbert Miller. **LC** P3; .S58. **DD** 410/.5. Index available. **Ad Acc. Circ:** 2,000 (ctrl).
Desc: Forum for discussion and presentation of contemporary and modern literature.
Ind/Abst BHA : Biblio. Hist. Art; MLA Int. Bibl. Books Artic. Mod. Lang. Lit.; Philos. Index; Romant. Move.

US/0163-657X
STANFORD FRENCH REVIEW. [Stanf. Fr. rev.]. **Added/Corp** Stanford University. Dept. of French & Italian. Vol. 1 (Spring 1977)-. Academic Scholarly Publication. English (French). Twice a year. $74.50. Anma Libri, PO Box 876, Saratoga CA 95070. **Tel** (408)741-0522, 741-1522. **ED** Jean-Marie Apostocides. **LC** PQ1; .S7. **DD** 840/.9. **Bk Rev. Ad Acc.** Documents available from The Genuine Article.
Desc: Scholarly journal in French literature, history and culture.
Ind/Abst Arts Humanit. Citation Index [Full Cov.]; BHA : Biblio. Hist. Art; Curr. Contents Arts Humanit.; MLA Int. Bibl. Books Artic. Mod. Lang. Lit.; Res. Alert [Full Cov.]; Romant. Move.; Soc. Sci. Cit. Index [Select. Cov.].

US/0730-6857
STANFORD ITALIAN REVIEW. [Stanford Ital. rev.]. **Added/Corp** Stanford University. Dept. of French & Italian. (Spring 1979)-. Academic Scholarly Publication. English (Italian). Twice a year (Mar., Nov.). $69.50. Anma Libri, PO Box 876, Saratoga CA 95070. **Tel** (408)741-0522, 741-1522. **ED** John Freccero. **LC** PQ4001; .S73. **Bk Rev. Ad Acc.** Documents available from The Genuine Article.
Desc: Scholarly journal in Italian literature, history and culture.
Ind/Abst Arts Humanit. Citation Index (19??-19??) [Full Cov.]; Curr. Contents Arts Humanit.; MLA Int. Bibl. Books Artic. Mod. Lang. Lit.; Res. Alert [Full Cov.]; Romant. Move.; Soc. Sci. Cit. Index [Select. Cov.].

US/0886-666X
STANFORD LITERATURE REVIEW. [Stanf. lit. rev.]. **Added/Corp** Stanford University. Dept. of French & Italian. Vol. 1, No. 1 (Spring 1984)-. Academic Scholarly Publication. English. Twice a year (Spring & Fall). $69.50. Anma Libri, PO Box 876, Saratoga CA 95070. **Tel** (408)741-0522, 741-1522. **ED** J. M. Apostolides. **DD** 805. **Bk Rev. Ad Acc.**
Desc: Scholarly journal in literary theory. literary theory.
Ind/Abst MLA Int. Bibl. Books Artic. Mod. Lang. Lit.

US/0272-7730
STARMONT READER'S GUIDES. ***Ceased.*** [Starmont read. guide]. **VFOAT** Starmont Reader's Guides to Contemporary Science Fiction and Fantasy Authors. (1979)-(March 1993). Monographic series. English. ir. Borgo Press, PO Box 2845, San Bernardino CA 92406. **Tel** (714)884-5813, (714)885-1161. **ED** Roger Schlobin. **Circ:** 500-1500.
Desc: Critical monographs on science fiction and fantasy authors, complete with chronologies, bibliographies, notes, and indexes.

US/0737-1306
STARMONT STUDIES IN LITERARY CRITICISM (MERCER ISLAND, WASH.). (STARMONT STUDIES IN LITERARY CRITICISM.). [Starmont stud. lit. crit.]. (1983)-. Monographic series. English. ir. Price varies per volume. Starmont House, PO Box 851, Mercer Island WA 98040. **Tel** (206)232-848, FAX (206)232-9274. **ED** Thaddeus Dikty. Index available.
Desc: Monographs and essays on genre literature, complete with bibliographies and indexes.

CI
START (ZAGREB, CROATIA). (START.). (Jan. 1969)-. Periodical. Serbo-Croatian (Roman). Six times a year. $32.00. Oour Ini, Avenija Bratstava Jedinstva 4, 41000 Zagreb Croatia.

PK/0039-0313
STATESMAN, THE. (19??)-. Periodical. English. wk. Rs150.00. The Statesman, 260-C Commercial Area Pechs, Karachi 29 Pakistan. **Tel** 435627. **ED** Mohammad Owais. **LC** AP8; .S75. **DD** 052. **Bk Rev. Ad Acc. Circ:** 5,000 (ctrl).
Desc: Contains information about international-affairs, economic-affairs, book reviews, sports and films.

RM
STEAUA. **Added/Corp** Uniunea Scriitorilor din Republica Populara Romana. (19??)-. Periodical. Romanian. mo. DM169.00. **(Subscription address:** Kubon & Sagner, ABT Zeitschriftenimport, D 80328 Munich Germany.) **LC** AP86; .S8.
Desc: Review for literature and art issues in Cluj-Napoca.
Ind/Abst Annu. Bibliogr. Engl. Lang. Lit.; MLA Int. Bibl. Books Artic. Mod. Lang. Lit.

US/0039-100X
STEINBECK QUARTERLY. ***Ceased.*** **See** Biographies.

US/1065-0865
STEVE WILSON REPORT, THE. [Steve Wilson rep.]. (1991)-. Periodical. English. qt. $29.00 (US); $36.45 (Canada). DPJ Enterprise Inc, 3400N High Street, Suite 120, Columbus OH 43202. **Tel** (614)268-1094, FAX (614)263-5233. **DD** 158. **Bk Rev**.
Desc: The application of humor to life and work.

US/0146-2067
STONY HILLS. ***Suspended.*** [Stony hills]. Vol. 1-Suspended (Nov. 1983). Periodical. English. Three times a year. $5.00. D Kruchkow, Weeks Mills, New Sharon NE 04955.

IT
STUDI E TESTI (BARI, ITALY). (STUDI E TESTI.). (1985)-. Monographic series. Italian. Price varies per volume.

IT
STUDI LUNIGIANESI. Periodical. Italian.

IT/0585-4997
STUDI SUL BOCCACCIO. See Biographies.

IT
STUDIA GRATIANA. Vol. 1 (1953)-. Monographic series. Latin (English, Italian and German). ir. Price varies per volume. Editrice Las, Piazza dell Ateneo Salesiano 1, 00139 Rome Italy. **Tel** 011 872 90 626, FAX 06 872 90 629.

SW/0039-3274
STUDIA NEOPHILOLOGICA. See Linguistics.

GW/0585-5810
STUDIEN UND QUELLEN ZUR VERSGESCHICHTE. (1966)-. Monographic series. German. ir. Price varies per volume. Wilhelm Fink Verlag, Ohmstrasse 5, D 80802 Munich Germany. **Tel** 011 49 89 348017, 348018. **ED** Karl Bertau and Werner Schroder.
Desc: Monographic studies of German literature.

US/0145-7888
STUDIES IN 20TH CENTURY LITERATURE. [Stud. 20th century lit.]. **VFOAT** Studies in Twentieth Century Literature; STCL. Vol. 1, No. 1 (Fall 1976)-. Periodical. English. Twice a year (Jan., June). $20.00. Studies in 20th Century Literature, Kansas State University, Department of Modern Languages, Eisenhower Hall 104, Manhattan KS 66506. **Tel** (913)532-6760. **ED** Michael Ossar and Marshall Olds. **LC** PN771; .S78. **DD** 809/.04. Index available. cum. index. **Bk Rev. Ad Acc. Pr Rev. Circ:** 550.
Desc: Articles on 20th Century literature and literary theory in any genre. Exclusive emphasis on French, German, Russian, Spanish and Latin American literature on literary theory.
Ind/Abst Am. Bibliogr. Slavic East Europ. Stud.; Am. Humanit. Index; Lit. Crit. Regist.; MLA Int. Bibl. Books Artic. Mod. Lang. Lit.

US/0091-8083
STUDIES IN AMERICAN FICTION. [Stud. Am. fict.]. Vol. 1 (Spring 1973)-. Periodical. English. sa (May and December). $7.00 (individual), $12.00 (institution) US; $10.00 (individual), $14.00 (institution) other. Northeastern University / English, Department of English, Boston MA 02115. **Tel** (617)437-3687. **ED** James Nagel. **LC** PS370; .S87. **DD** 813/.009. **Bk Rev. Ad Acc. Circ:** 1,300 (ctrl). Documents available from The Genuine Article, UMI Article Clearinghouse.
Desc: Articles, notes and reviews on American fiction.
Ind/Abst Abstr. Engl. Stud.; Acad. Search (July 1993-); Am. Humanit. Index; Annu. Bibliogr. Engl. Lang. Lit.; Arts Humanit. Citation Index [Full Cov.]; Child. Lit. Abstr. (19??-); Curr. Contents Arts Humanit.; Expand. Acad. Index (1989-); Humanit. Index; Humanit. Source (Jul. 1993-); INFO-SOUTH Abstr.; Lit. Crit. Regist.; Mag. Search; MLA Int. Bibl. Books Artic. Mod. Lang. Lit.; Newsp. Period. Abstr. (1991-); Res. Alert [Full Cov.].

US/0039-3770
STUDIES IN SCOTTISH LITERATURE. [Stud. Scott. lit.]. Vol. 1 (July 1963)-. English. an. $16.00 (add $3.00 for postage) other. University of South Carolina English Department, Columbia SC 29208. **Tel** (803)777-2239, (803)787-6601. **ED** G. Ross Roy. **LC** PR8500; .S8. **DD** 820/.9/411. Index available. **Bk Rev. Circ:** 450 (ctrl).
Desc: Devoted to all aspects of Scottish literary studies including bibliographies, checklists, unpublished documents and letters.
Ind/Abst Abstr. Engl. Stud.; Am. Humanit. Index; Annu. Bibliogr. Engl. Lang. Lit.; Lit. Crit. Regist.; MLA Int. Bibl. Books Artic. Mod. Lang. Lit.; Romant. Move.

US/0039-3789
STUDIES IN SHORT FICTION. [Stud. short fict.]. **Added/Corp** Newberry College. Vol. 1 (Fall 1963)-. Academic Scholarly Publication. English. qt (4 issues). $22.00 (institution), $19.00 (individual). Studies in Short Fiction, Newberry College, 2100 College Street, Newberry SC 29108. **Tel** (803)276-5010, (803)321-5195. **ED** Gayle R. Swanson. **LC** PN3311; .S8. Index available (bound in last issue). cum. index. **Bk Rev. Circ:** 1,725 (ctrl). available on microfilm and microfiche from University Microfilms International (UMI). Documents available from The Genuine Article, UMI Article Clearinghouse.
Desc: A scholarly international journal devoted exclusively to serious commentary on short fiction.
Ind/Abst Abstr. Engl. Stud.; Acad. Search (July 1993-); Am. Bibliogr. Slavic East Europ. Stud.; Annu. Bibliogr. Engl. Lang. Lit.; Arts Humanit. Citation Index [Full Cov.]; Book Rev. Index (1986-); Curr. Contents Arts Humanit.; Expand. Acad. Index (1989-); HAPI Hisp. Am. Period. Index; Humanit. Index; Humanit. Source (Jul. 1993-); Index Book Rev. Humanit.; INFO-SOUTH Abstr.; Lit. Crit. Regist.; Mag. Search; Middle East Abstr. Index; MLA Int. Bibl. Books Artic. Mod. Lang. Lit.; Newsp. Period. Abstr. (1990-); Res. Alert [Full Cov.]; Romant. Move.; Women Stud. Abstr.

US/0190-2407
STUDIES IN THE AGE OF CHAUCER. See Biographies.

US/0149-015X
STUDIES IN THE AMERICAN RENAISSANCE. [Stud. Am. renaiss.]. (1977)-. Academic Scholarly Publication. English. an (Dec.). $40.00. University Press of Virginia, PO Box 3608, Charlottesville VA 22903. **Tel** (804)924-3469. **LC** PS201; .S86. **DD** 810/.9/003. **Bk Rev. Ad Acc.** ctrl circ.
Desc: Presents a wide range of scholarly articles including an annotated list of the year's book publications.
Ind/Abst Acad. Search (Jan. 1994-); Am. Hist. Life (1977-); Am. Humanit. Index; Child. Lit. Abstr. (19??-); Hist. Source (July 1993-); Humanit. Source (Jul. 1993-); Index Book Rev. Relig.; INFO-SOUTH Abstr.; Lit. Crit. Regist.; Mag. Search; MLA Int. Bibl. Books Artic. Mod. Lang. Lit.; Relig. Index One Period. (1977-).

US/0039-3827
STUDIES IN THE NOVEL. [Stud. novel]. **Added/Corp** North Texas State University. Vol. 1 (Spring 1969)-. Periodical. English. qt. $25.00 (institutions), $15.00 (individuals) US; $35.00 other. Studies in the Novel, PO Box 13706, North Texas State University, Denton TX 76203. **Tel** (817)565-2025. **ED** Gerald A Kirk. **LC** PN3311; .S82. **DD** 809.3/3/05. **Bk Rev. Ad Acc. Circ:** 1,500. available on microfilm and microfiche from University Microfilms International (UMI). Documents available from The Genuine Article, UMI Article Clearinghouse.
Desc: Articles on novels and novelists.
Ind/Abst Abstr. Engl. Stud.; Acad. Search (July 1993-); Am. Bibliogr. Slavic East Europ. Stud.; Annu. Bibliogr. Engl. Lang. Lit.; Arts Humanit. Citation Index [Full Cov.]; Child. Lit. Abstr. (19??-); Curr. Contents Arts Humanit.; Expand. Acad. Index (1989-); Humanit. Index; Humanit. Source (Jul. 1993-); INFO-SOUTH Abstr.; Lit. Crit. Regist.; Mag. Search; Middle East Abstr. Index; MLA Int. Bibl. Books Artic. Mod. Lang. Lit.; Newsp. Period. Abstr. (1991-); Res. Alert [Full Cov.]; Romant. Move.

IT
STUDIUM. (19??)-. Italian. bm (6 issues). L55000 Italy; L90000 other. Edizioni Studium, Casella Post 30100, 00100 Rome Italy. **Tel** 011 39 6 6865846, 011 39 6 6875456. **LC** AS221; .S87. Index available (bound in last issue).
Ind/Abst Am. Hist. Life (1973-); BHA : Biblio. Hist. Art; MLA Int. Bibl. Books Artic. Mod. Lang. Lit.

FR/0180-3840
SUIVRE, A. VFOAT A Suivre (Paris). (1978)-. Periodical. French. mo. 90.00Can$ US & Canada. A Suivre, 39 rue Madame, 75006 Paris France. **(Subscription address:** US & Canada: Periodica Inc., PO Box 444, 1155 Avenue Ducharme, Outremont Quebec H2V 4R6 Canada) **UDC** 08.

●US/1062-6387
SUN DANCER REVIEW. See Literature.

IT
SUSSIDI PATRISTICI. Vol. 1 (1981)-. Monographic series. Latin. Price varies per volume.

SW/0039-677X
SVENSK TIDSKRIFT. [Sven. tidskr.]. Vol. 1, (1911)-. Periodical. Swedish. Six times a year. $48.20 US, $99.42 others (airmail); kr204.00 US, kr408.00 Sweden, kr612.00 others (surface mail). Svensk Tidskrift, Linnegatan 28-30 IV, 11447 Stockholm Sweden. **Tel** 011 46 8 6675955. **LC** AP48; .S76. **DD** 058/.7. Index available. cum. index. **Bk Rev. Ad Acc. Circ:** 3,500.
Desc: Independent debate and ideological review.
Ind/Abst Am. Hist. Life (1954-).

UK/0265-8119
SWEDISH BOOK REVIEW. Added/Corp Swedish-English Literary Translators' Association. (Oct. 1983)-. Periodical. English. sa. $14.00. St. David's University College, Lampeter Dyfed Swedish Unit, 5A48 7ED Wales England. **Tel** 011 44 570422351. **LC** PT9368; .S9. **DD** 839.7/09. cum. index. ***Continues*** *Swedish Books.*
Ind/Abst MLA Int. Bibl. Books Artic. Mod. Lang. Lit.

US/0039-7709
SYMPOSIUM (SYRACUSE). See Linguistics.

PL/0039-8152
SZPILKI. (1935)-. Periodical. Polish. Fifty-two times a year. $143.00 (latest edition). **(Subscription address:** ARS Polona, PO Box 1001, 00068 Warsaw Poland.)

US/1054-514X
T.E. NOTES. (T.E. NOTES : A T.E. LAWRENCE NEWSLETTER.). [T.E. notes]. **VFOAT** T E Notes. (1990)-. Periodical. English. Ten times a year (except July and Aug.). $25.00 US; $30.00 Europe; $32.50 others. T.E. Notes, 653 Park Street, Honesdale PA 18431-1421. **Tel** (717)253-6706, FAX (717)253-6786. **ED** Denis W. McDonnell, Mary E. McDonnell and Janet A. Riesman. **DD** 920. **Bk Rev**, (Qty: (20-30)).
Desc: A newsletter dedicated to the furthering of research into the life and legend of T.E. Lawrence (Lawrence of Arabia), including articles by leading Lawrencian biographers and scholars, reviews and other publications and news on Lawrencian events (past, present and future).

CH/0049-2949
TAMKANG REVIEW. [Tamkang rev.]. **Added/Corp** Tan-Chiang Wen li Hsueh Yuan. Hsi Yang Yu Wen Yen Chiu So. **VFOAT** Tan Chiang Ping Lun. Vol. 1 (April 1970)-. Periodical. English (Chinese and English). Four times a year (Mar., June, Sept., Dec.). $20.00 (individuals), $40.00 (institutions). Tamkang Review, Graduate School of Language and Literature, Tamkang University, Tamsui Taipei 25137 Taiwan. **Tel** 011 886 2 6215656 ext. 329. **ED** Chang-fang Chen. **LC** PL2250; .T34. **DD** 895.1/09. Index available. cum. index. **Bk Rev. Ad Acc. Circ:** 1,000.
Desc: Publishes comparative studies of Chinese and foreign literatures, including the classical and modern literatures of East Asia and the West.
Ind/Abst Annu. Bibliogr. Engl. Lang. Lit.; MLA Int. Bibl. Books Artic. Mod. Lang. Lit.

GW
TEATRO DEL SIGLO DE ORO. EDICIONES CRITICAS. VFOAT Ediciones Criticas. (1982)-. Monographic series. Spanish.
Ind/Abst MLA Int. Bibl. Books Artic. Mod. Lang. Lit.

IT
TEMI DI VITA ITALIANA. Italian. qt. L33000 Italy; L50000 other. Istituto Poligrafico Zecca Stato, Piazza Verdi 10, 00198 Rome Italy. **Tel** 011 39 6 85082307, 011 39 6 85082221.

FR/0040-3075
TEMPS MODERNES. (LES TEMPS MODERNES.). [Temps mod.]. Vol. 1, No. 1 (Oct. 1945)-. Periodical. French. mo. 586.07F France. Editions Gallimard, 5 rue Sebastien Bottin, 75328 Paris Cedex 7 France. **Tel** 011 33 1 49544200. **(Subscription address:** Sodis, 128 Avenue Mal Lattre Tass BP 149, 77403 Lagny France; telephone: 011 33 1 60078215) **LC** AP20; .T42. Index available. **Circ:** 5,000. Documents available from The Genuine Article.
Ind/Abst Am. Hist. Life (1955-1959); Annu. Bibliogr. Engl. Lang. Lit.; Arts Humanit. Citation Index [Full Cov.]; Curr. Contents Arts Humanit.; Int. Bibliogr. Sociol.; Int. Polit. Sci. Abstr.; MLA Int. Bibl. Books Artic. Mod. Lang. Lit.; Point Repere; Res. Alert [Full Cov.]; Romant. Move.; Soc. Sci. Cit. Index [Select. Cov.].

US/0885-2685
TEXAS REVIEW (HUNTSVILLE, TEX.), THE. (THE TEXAS REVIEW.). [Tex. rev.]. **Added/Corp** Sam Houston State University. English Dept. Sam Houston State University. Division of English, Foreign Language, and Journalism. Vol. 1 (Spring 1980)-. Periodical. English. ir. $10.00 (one year); $18.00 (two year); $26.00 (three year). Sam Houston State University / English Department, English Department, Huntsville TX 77341. **Tel** (713)294-1429. **ED** Paul Ruffin. **LC** IN PROCESS. **DD** 349. **Bk Rev. Ad Acc. Circ:** 750 (ctrl).
Supersedes *Sam Houston Literary Review.*
Desc: Poetry, fiction, essays, reviews, and interviews.
Ind/Abst Am. Humanit. Index; Index Am. Period. Verse; MLA Int. Bibl. Books Artic. Mod. Lang. Lit.

US/0736-3974
TEXT (NEW YORK, N.Y. : 1985). (TEXT : TRANSACTIONS OF THE SOCIETY FOR TEXTUAL SCHOLARSHIP.). **Added/Corp** Society of Textual Scholarship. (1985)-. English. an. $45.00. AMS Press Inc., 56 East 13th Street, New York NY 10003. **Tel** (212)777-4700, FAX (212)995-5413, telex 710 581 2302. **ED** D. C. Greetham, W. Speed Hill. **LC** P47; .T39. **DD** 801/.959/05. Index available. ctrl circ. ***Continues*** *Text for ... .*
Desc: Provides new information, new methodologies, even new inspiration, for the tasks of textual scholarship.
Ind/Abst MLA Int. Bibl. Books Artic. Mod. Lang. Lit.

CN/0715-8920
TEXTE (TORONTO). (TEXTE.). [Texte]. Vol. 1 (1982)-. French (English). an. 33.00Can$ (institutions), 17.00Can$ (individuals) Canada; $36.00 (institutions), $20.00 (individuals) other. University of Toronto Press, 5201 Dufferin Street, Downsview Ontario M3H 5T8 Canada. **Tel** (416)667-7781, (416)667-7782, FAX (416)667-7803. **ED** Andrew Oliver, Brian T. Fitch. **DD** 801. Documents available from The Genuine Article.
Desc: Seeks to provide a forum for dialogue between the different approaches to the study of the literary text by

bringing together innovative and authoritative work on a given textual topic. With its critical debates, its analytical bibliographies and indexes, it constitutes an indispensable source of documentation as well as a research tool for all those who work with "texte".
Ind/Abst Res. Alert [Full Cov.].

CN
TEXTUAL STUDIES IN CANADA. [Textual stud. Can.]. **VFOAT** TSC; Etudes Textuelles au Canada; TSC/ETC. (1991)-. Multiple languages (English and French). sa. 22.00Can$. Cariboo University College, Box 3010, English Department, Kamloops, British Columbia, V2C 5N3 Canada. **Tel** (604)828-5000, (604)828-5248, FAX (604)828-5086. **ED** W.F. Garrett-Petts, Henry Hubert, James A. Reither. Index available. cum. index. **Bk Rev**, (Qty: 8-10). **Ad Acc, Adv Mgr:** Ron Smith. **Pr Rev. Circ:** 300.
Desc: Covers cultural texts of Canada including literature, visual arts, and interdisciplinary studies.

IC
TIMARIT MALS OG MENNINGAR. (Sept. 1938)-. Periodical. Icelandic. qt. $55.00. Mal OG Menning, Laugavegier 18, 101 Reykjavik Iceland. **Tel** 354-1-15199, telex 2265. **ED** Gudmundur Andri Thorsson. Index available. cum. index. **Bk Rev. Circ:** 3,000 (ctrl). ***Continues*** *Mal og Menning.*
Ind/Abst Annu. Bibliogr. Engl. Lang. Lit.; BHA : Biblio. Hist. Art.

US/0736-928X
TRIVIA. [Trivia]. Vol. 1 (Fall 1982)-. Periodical. English. Twice a year. $16.00 (individuals), $20.00 (institutions) US; $18.00 (individuals) Canada & Mexico; $22.00 (institutions) others. Trivia, PO Box 9606, North Amherst MA 01059-9606. **Tel** (413)367-0263. **ED** Erin Rice and Kay Parkhurst. **LC** HQ1402; .T75. **DD** 305.4/2/0973. Index available. cum. index. **Bk Rev**, (Qty: 2-3). **Ad Acc. Circ:** 5,000. available on microfilm from University Microfilms International (UMI).
Desc: Feminist writing that is rigorous, creative, and consistently subversive. You will find critical essays, reviews, translations and experimental prose that challenge the status quo, including the feminist status quo; that extend radical questioning to all realms of thought; that demand the creation of new forms.
Ind/Abst Altern. Press Index; Left Index; Stud. Women Abstr.

US/0275-6048
TURKISH STUDIES ASSOCIATION BULLETIN. [Turk. Stud. Assoc. bull.]. **Main/Corp** Turkish Studies Association. **Added/Corp** Turkish Studies Association. Bulletin. No. 1 (Oct. 1976)-. Periodical. English (Turkish). sa (Mar. & Sept.). $20.00 (individuals), $30.00 (institutions). Turkish Studies Association / Department of History, University of Maryland, College Park MD 20742. **Tel** (301)405-4303. **(Subscription address:** Turkish Studies Association, NES, Princeton University, 110 Jones Hall, Princeton NJ 08544-1008.**)** **ED** Professor Madeline C. Zilfi and Professor Douglas Howard. cum. index. **Bk Rev. Ad Acc. Pr Rev. Circ:** 350 (ctrl). ***Absorbed*** *Newsletter (Turkish Studies Association), 0275-6056.*
Desc: Articles, news, and reviews of Turkish and Ottoman studies.
Ind/Abst Index Islam. Lit.; Middle East J.

US/0564-559X
TWAYNE'S ENGLISH AUTHOR SERIES. **See** Biographies.

US/0276-8178
TWENTIETH-CENTURY LITERARY CRITICISM. [Twent.-century lit. crit.]. **Main/Corp** Gale Research Company. Vol. 1 (1978)-. English. ir. $115.00. Gale Research Inc., 835 Penobscot Building, Detroit MI 48226. **Tel** (800)877-GALE, (313)961-2242, FAX (313)961-6083, telex TWX 810-221-7086. **ED** Laurie DiMauro. **LC** PN771; .G27. **DD** 809/.04.
Desc: Critical evaluations of the major novelists, poets, and playwrights of 1900-1959. Each volume presents overviews of 10 to 12 authors. Each entry begins with an introductory biographical and critical essay on the author and a list of principal works. Critical excerpts follow, arranged chronologically, and represent the entire range of response to each author.
Ind/Abst Am. Bibliogr. Slavic East Europ. Stud.

US/0041-462X
TWENTIETH CENTURY LITERATURE. [Twent. century lit.]. Vol. 1 (April 1955)-. Periodical. English. qt. $25.00 individuals, $30.00 institutions. Hofstra University / Twentieth Century Literature, Room 211 Calkins, Hempstead NY 11550. **Tel** (212)757-5530, FAX (518)436-7433. **(Subscription address:** Twentieth Century Literature, 49 Sheridan Avenue, Albany, NY 12210; telephone: (212)564-4296**)** **ED** William McBrien. **LC** PN2; .T8. **DD** 809.04. **Circ:** 2,000. available on microfilm and microfiche from University Microfilms International (UMI). Documents available from The Genuine Article, UMI Article Clearinghouse.
Desc: Concerns all aspects of modern and contemporary literature.
Ind/Abst Abstr. Engl. Stud.; Acad. Abstr. Full Text Elite (July 1990-); Acad. Abstr. (July 1990-); Acad. Ind. [Computer File] (1987-); Acad. Search (July 1990-); Annu. Bibliogr. Engl. Lang. Lit.; Arts Humanit. Citation Index [Full Cov.]; Curr. Contents Arts Humanit.; Expand. Acad. Index (1987-); Humanit. Index; Humanit. Source (Jul. 1990-); INFO-SOUTH Abstr.; Lit. Crit. Regist.; Mag. Search; Middle East Abstr. Index; MLA Int. Bibl. Books Artic. Mod. Lang. Lit.; Newsp. Period. Abstr. (1990-); Res. Alert [Full Cov.].

US/0041-9524
UNIVERSITY OF DAYTON REVIEW, THE. [Univ. Dayt. rev.]. **Main/Corp** University of Dayton. **Added/Corp** University of Dayton. Review. Vol. 1 (Spring 1964)-. Periodical. English. ir (3 issues per year). Free. University of Dayton Law Review, 300 College Park, Dayton OH 45469. **Tel** (513)229-3642. **ED** Robert Conard. **LC** AS30; .U53. Index available. **Circ:** 1,500.
Ind/Abst Abstr. Engl. Stud.; Am. Bibliogr. Slavic East Europ. Stud.; Annu. Bibliogr. Engl. Lang. Lit.; MLA Int. Bibl. Books Artic. Mod. Lang. Lit.

US/0081-7775
UNIVERSITY OF NORTH CAROLINA. STUDIES IN COMPARATIVE LITERATURE. (STUDIES IN COMPARATIVE LITERATURE / UNIVERSITY OF NORTH CAROLINA.). [Univ. N. C. stud. comp. lit.]. **Added/Corp** University of North Carolina (1793-1962) University of North Carolina at Chapel Hill. **VFOAT** Studies in Comparative Literature. No. 1 (1950)-. Monographic series. English. ir. Price varies per volume. University of North Carolina Press, 116 South Boundary Street, PO Box 2288, Chapel Hill NC 27515-2288. **Tel** (919)966-3561, FAX (919)966-3829. **DD** 809.
Ind/Abst MLA Int. Bibl. Books Artic. Mod. Lang. Lit.

GW
UNSERE STIMME. Periodical. German. bm. DM60.00 Germany; $40.00 US. Verband Juedischer Heimatvertriebener und Fluechtlinge in der Bundesrepublik Deutschland E V Gaussstrasse 18, Frankfurt Germany. **Tel** (069) 43 55 40. **LC** DS101; .U56. **DD** 909/.04/924. **Bk Rev. Ad Acc. Circ:** 3,000 (ctrl).
Desc: Journal of Jewish refugees from eastern countries in the Federal Republic of Germany.

RM
UTUNK : ROMANIA SZOCIALISTA KOZTARSASAG IROSZOVETSEGENEK LAPJA. **Added/Corp** Uniunea Scriitorilor din Republica Socialista Romania. (19??)-. Periodical. Hungarian. wk. Uniunea Scriitorilor din Republica Socialista Romania, Calea Victoriei 115, Bucharest Romania. **(Subscription address:** Ilexim Press Department, PO Box 1, 136-1-137, Bucharest, Romania.**)** **Bk Rev.** available with charts; available with illustrations.
Desc: Literary review.

US/1069-7144
VEERY (CHICAGO, ILL.). (VEERY.). [Veery]. (1991)-. Periodical. English. Three times a year. $16.00 US; $33.00 other. Foxglove Company, 333 North Michigan Avenue, Suite 2032, Chicago IL 60601. **Tel** (312)804-0777. **ED** RH Crane & Steven Vita. **DD** 814.
Desc: Highly focused content is given over entirely to interviews.

US/0731-938X
VERIDIAN. Vol. 1, No. 1 (July 1981)-. Periodical. English. mo. $10.00. Veridian, PO Box 2324, Bloomington IN 47402.

SZ
VERSANTS. **See** Linguistics.

PO/0042-4447
VERTICE (LISBOA). (VERTICE.). [Vertice]. (1943)-. Periodical. Portuguese. mo. 6000$ Europe; 8190$ other. Editorial Caminho SA, Alameda S Antonio DOS CAP 6 B, 1100 Lisbon Portugal. **Tel** 011 351 1 8153487, 011 351 1 8153511. **LC** AP66; .V4. **DD** 056/.9.
Ind/Abst MLA Int. Bibl. Books Artic. Mod. Lang. Lit.

RM
VIATA ROMANEASCA : REVISTA A UNIUNII SCRIITORILOR DIN R.P.R. **Added/Corp** Uniunea Scriitorilor din Republica Populara Romina. Uniunea Scriitorilor din Republica Socialista Romania. (Mar. 1906)-. Periodical. Romanian. mo. DM158.00. **(Subscription address:** Kubon & Sagner, ABT Zeitschriftenimport, D 80328 Munich Germany.**)** **LC** PC829; .V45.
Desc: Review of literature and literary criticism.
Ind/Abst Annu. Bibliogr. Engl. Lang. Lit.; MLA Int. Bibl. Books Artic. Mod. Lang. Lit.

US/0042-5192
VICTORIAN NEWSLETTER, THE. [Vic. newsl.]. **Added/Corp** Modern Language Association of America. Victorian Literature Group. No. 1 (Apr. 1952)-. Newsletter. English. Twice a year (Apr., Nov.). $5.00 US; $6.00 other. Western Kentucky University / English Department, CH 106, Bowling Green KY 42101. **Tel** (502)745-6338. **ED** Ward Hellstrom. **LC** PR1; .V48. Index available ($5.00). cum. index (1952-1988). **Circ:** 850. available on microfilm and microfiche from University Microfilms International (UMI). Documents available from The Genuine Article.
Desc: Victorian British literature criticism.
Ind/Abst Abstr. Engl. Stud.; Am. Humanit. Index; Annu. Bibliogr. Engl. Lang. Lit.; Arts Humanit. Citation Index (19??-19??) [Full Cov.]; Child. Lit. Abstr. (19??-); Curr. Contents Arts Humanit.; Lit. Crit. Regist.; MLA Int. Bibl. Books Artic. Mod. Lang. Lit.; Res. Alert [Full Cov.]; Romant. Move.

US/0709-4698
VICTORIAN PERIODICALS REVIEW. [Vic. per. rev.]. **Added/Corp** Research Society for Victorian Periodicals. **VFOAT** V.P.R.; VPR. Vol. 12, No. 1 (Spring 1979)-. Periodical. English. Four times a year (Mr., June, Sept., Dec.). $18.00 (individuals); $23.00 (institutions). Southern Illinois University / Edwardsville - English, English Department, Edwardsville IL 62026-1436. **Tel** (618)692-2060. **ED** Barbara Quinn Schmidt. **LC** PN5124.P4; V52. **DD** 052. Index available. cum. index. **Bk Rev. Ad Acc. Pr Rev. Circ:** 650. available on microfilm and microfiche from University Microfilms International (UMI). ***Continues*** *Victorian Periodicals Newsletter, 0049-6189.*
Desc: Articles, reviews, announcements and annual bibliography concerning journals and newspaper history of Victorian and Edwardian Great Britain and the English speaking world.
Ind/Abst Am. Hist. Life (1979-); Am. Humanit. Index; Annu. Bibliogr. Engl. Lang. Lit.; Child. Lit. Abstr. (19??-); Lit. Crit. Regist.; MLA Int. Bibl. Books Artic. Mod. Lang. Lit.; Romant. Move.

US/0042-675X
VIRGINIA QUARTERLY REVIEW, THE. [Va. q. rev.]. **Added/Corp** University of Virginia. **VFOAT** VQR. Vol. 1 (Apr. 1925)-. Periodical. English. qt (Jan., Apr., Jul., Oct.). $22.00 institution, $15.00 individual (one year); $30.00 institution, $22.00 individual (two year); $50.00 institution, $30.00 individual (three year). Virginia Quarterly Review, 1 West Range, Charlottesville VA 22903. **Tel** (804)924-3124, (804)924-7692. **ED** Staige D. Blackford. **LC** AP2; .V76. **DD** 051. **Bk Rev. Ad Acc. Circ:** 4,000. available on microfilm and microfiche from University Microfilms International (UMI). Documents available from The Genuine Article, UMI Article Clearinghouse.
Desc: A national magazine of literature and discussion, now in its 69th year. Its interests include literature, politics, foreign affairs, history, sports, art, and science.
Ind/Abst Abstr. Engl. Stud.; Acad. Abstr. Full Text Elite (July 1990-); Acad. Abstr. (July 1990-); Acad. Ind. [Computer File] (1987-); Acad. Search (July 1990-); Am. Hist. Life (1954-); Annu. Bibliogr. Engl. Lang. Lit.; Arts Humanit. Citation Index [Full Cov.]; BHA : Biblio. Hist. Art; Book Rev. Digest; Book Rev. Index; Curr. Contents Arts Humanit.; Expand. Acad. Index (1987-); Humanit. Index; Index Am. Period. Verse; INFO-SOUTH Abstr.; Mag. Search; MLA Int. Bibl. Books Artic. Mod. Lang. Lit.; Newsp. Period. Abstr. (1991-); Res. Alert [Full Cov.]; Romant. Move.; Soc. Sci. Cit. Index [Select. Cov.].

US/0736-251X
VIRGINIA WOOLF MISCELLANY. [Virginia Woolf misc.]. **Added/Corp** California State College, Sonoma. Dept. of English. Sonoma State University. Dept. of English. Virginia Woolf Society. **VFOAT** V.W.M.; VWM. Vol. 1, No. 1 (Fall 1973); No. 2 (Spring 1974)-. Newsletter. English. Twice a year (Spring & Fall). Free. California State College at Sonoma, 1801 East Cotati Avenue, Department of English, Rohnert Park CA 94928. **Tel** (707)664-2140. **ED** J. J. Wilson. **LC** PR6045.O72; Z8937. **DD** 823/.912. Index available. cum. index. **Bk Rev. Pr Rev. Circ:** 1,500.
Desc: A modest newsletter keeping the Virginia Woolf scholars and lay readers and fans in touch with one another.
Ind/Abst Abstr. Engl. Stud.; Am. Humanit. Index; Annu. Bibliogr. Engl. Lang. Lit.; Lit. Crit. Regist.; MLA Int. Bibl. Books Artic. Mod. Lang. Lit.

MX/0042-6911
VISION. V.1- Nov. 1950-. Periodical. Spanish. sm. $52.00. Vision Inc. / Mexico, Arquimedes 199 Pisos 6TO Piso, 11560 Mexico DF Mexico. **Tel** 011 52 5 2036734, 011 52 5 2543097. Index available. **Bk Rev. Circ:** 200,000.

UN/0042-7470
VITCHYZNA; LITERATURNO-KHUDOZHNII ZHURNAL. **Added/Corp** Spilka Radianskykh Pysmennykiv Ukrainy. (19??)-. Periodical. Ukrainian. mo. $139.95. **(Subscription address:** East View Publications Inc., 3020 Harbor Lane North, Suite 110, Minneapolis MN 55447.**)** **LC** AP58.U5; V56.

US
VOICE LITERARY SUPPLEMENT. (VOICE LITERARY SUPPLEMENT : VLS.). **VFOAT** VLS; Village Voice Literary Supplement. No. 1 (Oct. 1981)-. English. mo. Village Voice, 36 Cooper Square, New York NY 10003. **Tel** (212)475-3333 ext. 5105.
Ind/Abst Access (1982-?); Book Rev. Digest; Book Rev. Index.

UK/0042-9422
VYZVOLNYI SHLIAKH. [Vyzvoln. slah]. **VFOAT** Liberation Path. Periodical. Ukrainian. mo. £30.00 UK; $60.00 US. Ukrainian Publishers Ltd, 200 Liverpool Road, London N1 1LF Great Britain. **Tel** 01 607 6266, FAX 01 607 6737. **ED** Illia Dmytriw. **LC** AP58.U5. Index available. cum. index. **Bk Rev. Circ:** 2,500.

Desc: Ukrainian political, social scientific and literary magazine in Ukrainian language.
Ind/Abst MLA Int. Bibl. Books Artic. Mod. Lang. Lit.

US/0149-6077
WASHOUT REVIEW. [Washout rev.]. Vol. 1 (Oct. 1975)-. Periodical. English. ir. $6.00. Mildred Publishing, 961 Birchwood Lane, Schenectady NY 12309-3118. **ED** Ellen Biss, Kathryn Poppino. **LC** PS580; .W37. **DD** 811/.5/408. **Circ:** 500. available with illustrations.

US
WAVES (SEATTLE, WASH.). ***Ceased.*** (WAVES.). Vol. 1, No. 1 (Dec. 1986)-Ceased (Oct. 1987). Periodical. English. mo. Northwest Passage, 1017 East Pike, Seattle WA 98122. ***Continues*** *Northwest Passage, 0029-3415.*

US/0890-9024
WEST HILLS REVIEW. ***Suspended.*** **See** Literature.

US/0043-4299
WESTERN WORLD REVIEW. V. 1- Dec. 1965-. Periodical. English. qt. Western World Press, PO Box 366, Sun City CA 92381.

US
WESTIGAN REVIEW OF POETRY, THE. Vol. 1, No. 1 (1969)-. Periodical. English. ir.

US/0511-8832
WHITTIER NEWSLETTER. **See** Biographies.

US/0196-6286
WILLIAM CARLOS WILLIAMS REVIEW. [William Carlos Williams rev.]. Vol. 6 (Spring 1980)-. Periodical. English. Twice a year. $15.00 institutions; $10.00 individuals. University of Texas / Department of English Literature, c/o B. Bremen, Austin TX 78712. **Tel** (512)471-7842, FAX (512)471-4909. **ED** Brian A. Bremen. **LC** PS3545.I544; Z957. **DD** 811/.52. **Bk Rev**, (Qty: 4-6 per year). **Ad Acc. Pr Rev. Circ:** 375. ***Continues*** *William Carlos Williams Newsletter, 0099-216X.*
Desc: A journal devoted to publishing articles, reviews, unpublished writings, and other material relating to the life and work of William Carlos Williams (1883-1963).
Ind/Abst Abstr. Engl. Stud.; Am. Humanit. Index; Annu. Bibliogr. Engl. Lang. Lit.; Lit. Crit. Regist.; MLA Int. Bibl. Books Artic. Mod. Lang. Lit.; Romant. Move.

US/0739-1277
WILLOW SPRINGS. No. 9 (Fall 1981)-. Periodical. English. sa. $10.00 US; $22.00 other. Eastern Washington University, PO Box 1063, Cheney WA 99004. ***Continues*** *Willow Springs Magazine.*
Ind/Abst Am. Humanit. Index; Index Am. Period. Verse.

US/0147-3166
WINESBURG EAGLE, THE. **See** Biographies.

US/0147-0868
WITTENBERG REVIEW OF LITERATURE & ART. **VAT** Wittenberg Review of Literature and Art. V. 1-. English. an. Wittenberg Review of Literature & Art, Box 1 Recitation Hall, Whittenberg University, Springfield OH 45501. **ED** Warren M Hagler, David Linde. **LC** PS580; .W57. **DD** 811.5/408. **Circ:** 200.
Desc: A publication specializing in poetry, short fiction, and artwork.

US/0738-1433
WOMEN'S REVIEW OF BOOKS, THE. [Women's rev. books]. **Added/Corp** Wellesley College. Center for Research on Women. Vol. 1, No. 1 (Oct. 1983)-. Periodical. English. Twelve times a year (monthly except Aug. and double issue publishes in July). $30.00 (one year), $56.00 (two years), $84.00 (three years) institutions US; $18.00 (one year), $32.00 (two years) individuals US; $35.00 (one year), $66.00 (two years), $99.00 (three years) institutions other; $23.00 (one year), $42.00 (two years) individuals other. Wellesley College Center for Research on Women, Wellesley MA 02181. **Tel** (617)283-2500, (617)283-2087, FAX (617)283-3645. **ED** Linda Gardiner. **LC** HQ1101; .W768. **DD** 028.1/088042. **[CCC].** Index available (included in last issue). cum. index. **Bk Rev. Ad Acc. Circ:** 11,000. available on microfilm from University Microfilms International (UMI). Documents available from UMI Article Clearinghouse.
Desc: We publish in-depth book reviews of books in all areas of women's studies and feminist writing, academic and general-interest, including reviews of poetry and fiction by women.
Ind/Abst Altern. Press Index; Am. Humanit. Index; Book Rev. Digest; Book Rev. Index; Chicano Index; Expand. Acad. Index (1992-); Index Book Rev. Relig.; Left Index; Newsp. Period. Abstr. (1992-); Women Stud. Abstr.

US/0043-8006
WORDSWORTH CIRCLE. [Wordsworth circ.]. **Added/Corp** Temple University. Dept. of English. Vol. 1 (Winter 1970)-. Periodical. English. Four times a year (Feb., May, Aug., Nov.). $20.00. Temple University, Department of Eenglish, 12th & Berks, Philadelphia PA 19122. **Tel** (215)204-4716. **ED** Marilyn Gaull. **LC** PR1; .W67. **DD** 820/.9/14. **Bk Rev. Ad Acc. Circ:** 1,000 (ctrl). available on microfilm and microfiche from University Microfilms International (UMI). Documents available from The Genuine Article.
Desc: A learned journal devoted to the study of English romantic poets and prose writers especially Coleridge, Wordsworth, Hazlitt, de Quincey and others.
Ind/Abst Abstr. Engl. Stud.; Am. Humanit. Index; Annu. Bibliogr. Engl. Lang. Lit.; Arts Humanit. Citation Index [Full Cov.]; Curr. Contents Arts Humanit.; Lit. Crit. Regist.; MLA Int. Bibl. Books Artic. Mod. Lang. Lit.; Res. Alert [Full Cov.]; Romant. Move.; Soc. Sci. Cit. Index [Select. Cov.].

●US/1076-9285
WORLD INTELLIGENCE REVIEW. (1994)-. English. bm. $35.00 (individual), $50.00 (institution). Heldref Publications, 1319 Eighteenth Street Northwest, Washington DC 20036-1802. **Tel** (202)296-6267, (800)365-9753, FAX (202)296-5149. ***Continues*** *Foreign Intelligence Literary Scene, 0749-9132.*

CN/0093-1705
WORLD LITERATURE WRITTEN IN ENGLISH. [World lit. writ. Engl.]. **Added/Corp** Modern Language Association of America. English Group 12--World Literature Written in English. Modern Language Association of America. Division 33--English Literature Other than British and American. University of Texas at Arlington. University of Guelph. **VFOAT** WLWE. No. 20 (Nov. 1971)-. Periodical. English. Twice a year (Spring & Autumn). 30.00Can$ Canada; 35.00Can$ US. University of Toronto Press, 5201 Dufferin Street, Downsview Ontario M3H 5T8 Canada. **Tel** (416)667-7781, (416)667-7782, FAX (416)667-7803. **ED** D. Brydon. **LC** PR1; .W65. **DD** 820/.9. **[CCC]. Bk Rev. Ad Acc. Circ:** 400. Documents available from The Genuine Article. ***Continues*** *World Literature Written in English Newsletter, 0732-622X.*
Desc: Publishes articles and reviews by scholars concerned with English literary arts.
Ind/Abst Abstr. Engl. Stud.; Am. Humanit. Index; Annu. Bibliogr. Engl. Lang. Lit.; Arts Humanit. Citation Index (19??-19??) [Full Cov.]; Can. Index; MLA Int. Bibl. Books Artic. Mod. Lang. Lit.; Res. Alert [Full Cov.].

US/0887-6681
XAVIER REVIEW. [Xavier rev.]. **Added/Corp** Xavier University of Louisiana. Vol. 1, No. 1/2 (1980/81)-. Periodical. English. Twice a year (May & Sept.). $10.00 (individuals), $15.00 (institutions). Xavier University, Department of English, New Orleans LA 70125. **Tel** (504)488-9014, FAX (504)482-1561. **ED** Thomas Bonner Jr., & R. E. Skinner. **LC** WMLC L 83/6787. **DD** 810. **Bk Rev**, (Qty: 2 - 6). **Ad Acc. Circ:** 500 (ctrl).
Desc: A journal devoted to the creative writing of the American South, African American and the Gulf of Mexico / Caribbean Basin. Publishes short fiction, poetry, short drama, novels-in-progres, critical essays and reviews.
Ind/Abst Lit. Crit. Regist.; MLA Int. Bibl. Books Artic. Mod. Lang. Lit.

US/0893-5378
YALE JOURNAL OF CRITICISM, THE. [Yale j. crit.]. **Added/Corp** Whitney Humanities Center. (1987)-. Periodical. English. Twice a year. $57.00 US; $60.00 Canada & Mexico; $63.00 other. Johns Hopkins University Press, 2715 North Charles Street, Baltimore MD 21218-4319. **Tel** (410)516-6987, FAX (410)516-6968. **(Subscription address:** John Hopkins University Press, Journals Publishing Division, PO Box 19966, Baltimore MD 21211.) **ED** Celeste Brusati, Jonathan Freedman, Christopher Miller, Sheila Murnaghan, and Sara Suleri. **LC** PN2; .Y34. **DD** 809. **[CCC].** available on microfilm and microfiche from University Microfilms International (UMI). Documents available from UMI Article Clearinghouse.
Desc: Site of interdisciplinary exchange in the humanities.
Ind/Abst Acad. Abstr. Full Text Elite (July 1990-); Acad. Abstr. (July 1990-); Acad. Ind. [Computer File] (1989-); Acad. Search (July 1990-); BHA : Biblio. Hist. Art; Expand. Acad. Index (1989-); Humanit. Source (Jul. 1990-); INFO-SOUTH Abstr.; Mag. Search; MLA Int. Bibl. Books Artic. Mod. Lang. Lit.; Newsp. Period. Abstr. (1989-).

US/0084-3695
YEARBOOK OF COMPARATIVE AND GENERAL LITERATURE. [Yearb. comp. gen. lit.]. **Added/Corp** Indiana University. Indiana University, Bloomington. National Council of Teachers of English. Comparative Literature Committee. Modern Language Association of America. Comparative Literature Section. American Comparative Literature Association. University of North Carolina (1793-1962). (1952)-. Monographic series. English (French and German). ir. Price varies per volume. Indiana University / Comparative Literature Program, Ballantine Hall 402, Bloomington IN 47405. **Tel** (812)855-2140, FAX (812)855-7070, telex 272279 INDIANA U BLOM. **ED** G. Chaitin. **LC** PN851; .Y4. Index available. **Bk Rev. Ad Acc. Circ:** 1,400 (ctrl). available on microfilm.
Desc: Comparative literature, translation theory, East-West literary relations, and comparative arts, including film.
Ind/Abst Abstr. Engl. Stud.; Am. Bibliogr. Slavic East Europ. Stud. (19??-19??); Am. Humanit. Index (-199?); Annu. Bibliogr. Engl. Lang. Lit.; MLA Int. Bibl. Books Artic. Mod. Lang. Lit.; Romant. Move.

II
YEARLY REVIEW. **Added/Corp** University of Delhi. Dept. of English. No. 1 (Dec. 1987)-. English. an. $14.60. University of Delhi, Department of English, Delhi, India. **(Subscription address:** Prints India, 11 Darya Ganj, New Delhi 110002 India.) **LC** PR1; .Y4. **DD** 820.9/0005.

US/0360-0157
YOUNG SOCIALIST (NEW YORK. 1972). ***Suspended.*** (YOUNG SOCIALIST.). Vol. 16 (Oct. 1972)-?. Periodical. English. ir. $5.00 US; $7.00 other. Young Socialist, PO Box 211, New York NY 10011. **Tel** (212)334-1110. **ED** Aaron Ruby. **LC** HX1; .Y56. **DD** 335/.005. **Bk Rev. Ad Acc. Circ:** 4,500. ***Continues*** *Young Socialist--The Organizer.*
Desc: Coverage of issues and activities from opposition to US intervention in Central America, protests against apartheid, to defense of legal abortion, and union rights.

GW/0341-7166
ZEITWENDE. [Zeitwende]. **VFOAT** Zeitwende die Neue Furche. (Jan. 1968)-. Periodical. German. Four times a year. DM40.00. Zeitwende Verlagsgesellschaft, Klauprechtstr 2, D 76137 Karlsruhe Germany. **Tel** 011 49 721 812835. **ED** Wolfgang Bohme. **[CCC].** Index available. cum. index. **Bk Rev. Ad Acc. Circ:** 700 (ctrl).
Desc: Reviews with contributions of science, spirit and literature.
Ind/Abst Am. Hist. Life (1968-1971).

CH/0528-9688
ZHENGLUN ZHOUKAN. (CHENG LUN CHOU KAN.). [Zhenglun zhoukan]. **VFOAT** China Critic Weekly. (1956)-. Periodical. Chinese. wk. Chung-kuo Hsin wen chu pan Kung ssu 1956-, Taipei Taiwan. ***Continues*** *Chu i yu kuo tse.*
Ind/Abst Am. Hist. Life.

CH/1016-4162
ZHONGWAI ZAZHI. **VFOAT** Kaleidoscope. (1967)-. Periodical. Chinese. Twelve times a year. $70.00. Kaleidoscope Monthly, 108 Lung Kiang Road / 3rd Floor, Taipei Taiwan. **Tel** 011 886 2 865364206. **UDC** 070.448(529).

CN/0227-2423
ZINOTAJS. **See** History(General)-History of Europe.

RU/0130-1616
ZNAMJA (MOSKVA). (ZNAMIA.). [Znama]. **Added/Corp** Soiuz Pisatelei SSSR. (1931)-. Periodical. Russian. mo. $119.95. Izdatelstvo Pressa, Myasnitskaia 24, 101877 Moscow Russia. **Tel** 011 95 923 2122, FAX 011 95 200 2259. **(Subscription address:** East View Publications Inc., 3020 Harbor Lane North, Suite 110, Minneapolis MN 55447.) **LC** AP50; .Z5. Index available. **Bk Rev. Ad Acc.** available on microfilm from University Microfilms International (UMI).
Ind/Abst MLA Int. Bibl. Books Artic. Mod. Lang. Lit.; Curr. Dig. Post Sov. Press.

ABSTRACTING, BIBLIOGRAPHIES AND STATISTICS

US/0001-3560
ABSTRACTS OF ENGLISH STUDIES. ***Suspended.*** [Abstr. Engl. stud.]. **Added/Corp** National Council of Teachers of English. University of Calgary. English Dept. Vol. 1, No. 1 (Jan. 1958)-Vol. 34, No. 4. Abstracting/Indexing Service. English. Four times a year (Mar., June, Sept., Dec.). £88.50. Basil Blackwell Publishers Ltd, 108 Cowley Road, Oxford 0X4 1JF England. **Tel** 011 44 865 791100, FAX 011 44 865 791347, telex 837022 OXBOOK G. **ED** Janis Svilpis and William Blackburn. **LC** PE25; .A16. **DD** 820/.5. **[CCC].** Index available. cum. index. **Ad Acc. Circ:** 1,465. available on microfilm and microfiche from University Microfilms International (UMI).
Desc: Research tool abstracting articles concerning literature (including literary criticism); abstracts indicate the contents of an article as concisely as possible and without editorial bias. A quick guide to utility of an article.
Ind/Abst MLA Int. Bibl. Books Artic. Mod. Lang. Lit.

CN/0227-1400
ANNUAL BIBLIOGRAPHY OF VICTORIAN STUDIES. [Annu. bibliog. Victorian stud.]. 1976-. Bibliography. English. an. Litir Database, University of Alberta, Department of English, Edmonton Alberta T6G 2E5 Canada. **Tel** (403)492-5937. **ED** Brahma Chaudhuri. **LC** Z2019; .A64; DA533. **DD** 016.941.

US/0006-7326
BOOK REVIEW DIGEST. [Book rev. digest.]. **Added/Corp** H.W. Wilson Company. Vol. 1 (Jan. 1906)-. Abstracting/Indexing Service. English. mo (except Feb. and July, and annual cumulation). $1,095 CD-ROM; Print edition sold on the service basis. H W Wilson Company, 950 University Avenue, Bronx NY 10452. **Tel** (800)367-6770, (718)588-8400, FAX (718)590-1617, telex 4990003 HWILSON. **ED** Martha Mooney. **LC** Z1219; .C95. **NLM** Z 1219 B723. cum. index. **Pr Rev.** ctrl circ. available on an online database from WILSONLINE;

available on CD-ROM from WILSONDISC; available on magnetic tape from WILSONTAPE; available on diskette from WILSONSEARCH. ***Continues*** *Cumulative Book Review Digest.*
Desc: Provides access to reviews of English-language fiction and non-fiction titles featured in 95 leading American, British, and Canadian periodicals. Offers a balanced up-to-date selection of reviews of over 6,400 adult and juvenile titles each year.

GW/0020-918X
INTERNATIONALE BIBLIOGRAPHIE DER REZENSIONEN WISSENSCHAFTLICHER LITERATUR.
VFOAT I.B.R.; International Bibliography of Book Reviews of Scholarly Literature; Bibliographie Internationale des Recensions de la Litterature; ANTE; IBR. Vol. 14, Pars 1 (1984)-. Abstracting/Indexing Service. English (French and German). ir (six volumes per year). DM2700.00. Zeller Verlag GmbH & Co., Postfac 1949, Jahnstrasse 15, D 49009 Osnabrueck Germany. **Tel** 011 49 541 404590, FAX 011 49 541 41255. **ED** Otto and Wolfram Zeller. **LC** Z5051; .I64; AS9. **Bk Rev. Ad Acc.** ctrl circ. available on CD-ROM; available on an online database. Documents available. ***Continues*** *Internationale Bibliographie der Rezensionen.*
Desc: Worldwide bibliography of book-reviews concerning publications of literature in all scholarly fields of knowledge.

GW
INTERNATIONALE BIBLIOGRAPHIE DER ZEITSCHRIFTENLITERATUR AUS ALLEN GEBIETEN DES WISSENS. VFOAT Internationale Bibliographie der Zeitschriftenliteratur; International Bibliography of Periodical Literature Covering all Fields of Knowledge; IBZ. Vol. 20, Part 1 (1984)-. Abstracting/Indexing Service. German (English and French). Twice a year (two parts of six cloth-bound volumes). DM4900.00. Zeller Verlag GmbH & Co., Postfac 1949, Jahnstrasse 15, D 49009 Osnabrueck Germany. **Tel** 011 49 541 404590, FAX 011 49 541 41255. **ED** Otto and Wolfram Zeller. Index available. **Bk Rev. Ad Acc.** ctrl circ. available on CD-ROM; available on an online database from University Library. ***Continues*** *Internationale Bibliographie der Zeitschriftenliteratur.*
Desc: Bibliography of articles from the periodical literature in all fields of knowledge with special emphasis on the humanities.

US/0733-2165
LITERARY CRITICISM REGISTER.
(LITERARY CRITICISM REGISTER : LCR.). [Lit. crit. regist.]. **VFOAT** LCR; L.C.R. Vol. 1, No. 1 (Feb. 1983)-. Abstracting/Indexing Service. English. Twelve times a year. $59.00 (institutions), $34.00 (individuals) US; $69.00 (institutions), $44.00 (individuals) Canada; $83.00 (institutions), $58.00 (individuals) other. Literary Criticism Register, PO Box 2086, DeLand FL 32721. **Tel** (904)736-6029. **ED** Nancy and Sims Kline (editor's address: PO Box 207, DeLand FL 32721). **LC** Z2011; .L76; PR83. **DD** 016.82/09. Index available. cum. index. **Ad Acc, Adv Mgr:** same as editor. **Circ:** 600 (ctrl).
Desc: Provides a bibliographical access to scholarship in English and American literary studies and critical theory relating to literature.

LITERATURE

US/0094-3320
13TH MOON. [13th moon]. **Added/Corp** 13th Moon, Inc. **VAT** Thirteenth Moon. Vol. 1 (1973)-. Periodical. English. Twice a year (1 issue per year in a double issue). $10.00. 13th Moon, Department of English, Suny-Albany, 1400 Washington Avenue, Alabany NY 12222. **Tel** (518)442-4181. **ED** Judith Johnson. **LC** PS508.W7; T45. **DD** 810/.5/405. **Bk Rev**, (Qty: 3-5). **Ad Acc. Circ:** 1,500.
Desc: This scholary and literary magazine is specializing in literature by women. Listing articles such as, poetry, fiction, drama, criticism and translations by the women.
Ind/Abst Am. Humanit. Index; Index Am. Period. Verse; MLA Int. Bibl. Books Artic. Mod. Lang. Lit.

FR/0291-3798
17 - 18. (BULLETIN DE LA SOCIETE D'ETUDES ANGLO-AMERICAINES DES XVIIE ET XVIIIE SIECLES.). [17 - 18]. **Added/Corp** Societe d'Etudes Anglo-Americaines des XVIIe et XVIIIe Siecles (France). **VFOAT** XVII-XVIII; Dix-Sept-Dix-Huit. No. 1 (Nov. 1975)-. Bulletin. French. sa. cum. index.
Ind/Abst Annu. Bibliogr. Engl. Lang. Lit.; MLA Int. Bibl. Books Artic. Mod. Lang. Lit.

US/0730-7330
201. Added/Corp Los Angeles Latino Writers Workshop (Calif.). **VFOAT** Two Hundred One; Two Hundred and One; Homenaje a la Ciudad de Los Angeles. (1982)-. English (Spanish). $4.00. G Bejarano, PO Box 26394, Los Angeles CA 90026.

US/0732-4650
A (BROOKLYN, N.Y.). (A : A JOURNAL OF CONTEMPORARY LITERATURE.). [A]. Vol. 1, No. 1 (Fall 1976)-. Periodical. English. an. $5.00. A A Journal of Contemporary, Box 42A510, York Station CA 90042.

CN/0705-8586
A T E N S CONFERENCE REPORT.
Main/Corp Association of Teachers of English of Nova Scotia. **VAT** Association of Teachers of English of Nova Scotia Conference Report. (1977)-. English. an. Association of Teachers of English of Nova Scotia, c/o Nova Scotia Teachers Union, PO Box 1060, Armdale Nova Scotia B3L 4L7 Canada. **DD** 820/.7.

AU/0171-5410
AAA, ARBEITEN AUS ANGLISTIK UND AMERIKANISTIK. See Linguistics.

SP/0572-3000
ABACO (MADRID, SPAIN). (ABACO : ESTUDIOS SOBRE LITERATURA ESPANOLA.). Vol. 1 (1969)-. Periodical. Spanish. Editorial Castalia, Zurbano 39, 28010 Madrid Spain. **Tel** 419 8940, or 419 5857. **LC** WMLC L 83/6828.

US
ABBEY. V. 1, No. 1- Spring 1970-. Periodical. English. qt. $2.00. 5360 Fallriver Row, Columbia MD 21044. **Tel** (410)730-4272. **ED** David Greisman. **Ad Acc. Circ:** 200 (ctrl).
Desc: A journal that asks the question, "What do you really think?" but decides to order pizza and a beer instead.

UK/0957-1248
_AABBEY CHRONICLE. (ABBEY CHRONICLE.). (1989)-. Newsletter. English. Three times a year. Abbey Chronicle, 30 Sidford High Street, Sidford, Devon EX10 9SL United Kingdom. **ED** Monica Godfrey. Index available. **Bk Rev**, (Qty: 2 - 20). **Circ:** 300.
Ind/Abst Child. Lit. Abstr. (19??-).

US/8756-0267
ABBWA JOURNAL. [ABBWA j.]. **Added/Corp** American Black Book Writers Association. **VAT** American Black Book Writers Association Journal. Vol. 1, No. 1 (Summer 1986)-. Periodical. English. Four times a year. $30.00 US; $40.00 other. American Black Book Writers Association (ABBWA), PO Box 10548, Marina Del Ray CA 90295. **Tel** (310)822-5195. **LC** Z479; .A23. **DD** 070.5/2.

●US/1058-2509
ABERATIONS (WALNUT CREEK, CALIF.). (ABERATIONS.). [Aberations]. (1992)-. Periodical. English. mo. $24.95. Experiences Unlimited, 544 Ygnacio Valley Road, #A13 PO Box 8040, Walnut Creek CA 94596. **DD** 813.

GW/0002-2985
ABHANDLUNGEN DER KLASSE DER LITERATUR / AKADEMIE DER WISSENSCHAFTEN UND DER LITERATUR. Added/Corp Akademie der Wissenschaften und der Literatur (Germany). Klasse der Literatur. (1950)-. Monographic series. German. ir. Price varies per volume. Franz Steiner Verlag GmbH, Postfach 101061, D 70009 Stuttgart Germany. **Tel** 011 49 0711 2582372, FAX 011 49 0711 2582290, telex 723636 daz d. **(Subscription address:** Brockhaus Commission, Kreidlerstrasse 9, D 70803 Kornwestheim Germany.**) LC** PN504; .A24. **DD** 809/.005.

LH/0567-4980
ABHANDLUNGEN FUER DIE KUNDE DES MORGENLANDES / HRSG. VON DER DEUTSCHEN MORGENLANDISCHEN GESELLSCHAFT. See Linguistics.

GW/0567-4999
ABHANDLUNGEN ZUR KUNST-, MUSIK- UND LITERATURWISSENSCHAFT. See The Arts.

GW/0178-8515
ABHANDLUNGEN ZUR SPRACHE UND LITERATUR. (1986)-. Monographic series. German. ir. **UDC** 804.
Ind/Abst MLA Int. Bibl. Books Artic. Mod. Lang. Lit.

II
ABHINAYA. Periodical. Bengali. qt. Rs12.00 India; $15.00 US. Dilipa Bandyopadhyaya, 131 Harish Mukherjee Road, Calcutta 70002 India. **Tel** 47-5337. **LC** PK1712.5; .A24. **Bk Rev. Circ:** 5,200 (ctrl).
Desc: Is the recognized organ of non-professional drama groups of India performing mainly Bengali dramas. It also organises free open air theatrical performances in winter every year named as Ganamancha.

II
ABHIRUCI (NEW DELHI, INDIA).
(ABHIRUCI.). V. 1, No. 1 (Feb. 1981)-. Periodical. Hindi (Hindi). qt. Rs15.00. Radhakrishna Prakashan, 2 Ansari Road Dariyagunj, New Delhi 110002 India. **LC** PK2030; .A23.

US/0895-3198
ABORIGINAL SCIENCE FICTION. [Aborig. sci. fict.]. **VFOAT** Aboriginal Science Fiction Magazine. Vol. 1, No. 4 (May-June 1987)-. Periodical. English. Four times a year (Mar., June, Sept., Dec.). $18.00 one year; $32.00 two year. Aboriginal SF, PO Box 2449, Woburn MA 01888. **Tel** (617)935-9326, FAX (617)932-3321. **ED** Charles C. Ryan. **LC** PN3433; .A23. **DD** 808.83/8762/05. **Bk Rev**, (Qty: 60). **Ad Acc, Adv Mgr:** Mary Ryan, **Tel** (617)935-9326. **Circ:** 14,000. ***Continues*** *Aboriginal SF, 0888-3475.*
Desc: A science fiction magazine with full color illustrations and lively short stories.
Ind/Abst Sci. Fict. Fantasy Book Rev. Index (1987-).

SW/0280-2414
ABRAKADABRA. (1981)-. Swedish. bm. Var Skola Forlag, Riddargatan 17, S-114 57 Stockholm, Sweden. ***Continues*** *Var Skola. Barnkultur., 0349-683X.*
Ind/Abst Child. Lit. Abstr. (19??-).

BL
ABRATES. Main/Corp Associacao Brasileira de Tradutores. **VAT** Associacao Brasileira de Tradutores. Yearly V. 1- June 1976-. Periodical. Portuguese. Associacao Brasileira de Tradutores, Av Almirante Barroso 97 3 Andar, Rio de Janeiro Brazil. **LC** PN241.A1; A88.

US/1058-9538
ABSTRACT ME. (1991)-. Periodical. English. bm. $3.00 (single issue, includes issue of Malcontent). Theatre of the Oblique, PO Box 703, Navesink NJ 07752. **DD** 810.

IT/1120-849X
ACHAB ROMA. [Achab Roma]. (1990)-. Periodical. Italian. Nine times a year. L30000 Italy; L100000 others. Bariletti Editori SRL, via Frisi 9, 00197 Rome Italy. **Tel** 011 39 6 8079015, FAX 011 39 6 8070628. **UDC** 82. **Bk Rev. Ad Acc.**

●US
ACLA BULLETIN. Added/Corp American Comparative Literature Association. Brigham Young University. College of Humanities. David M. Kennedy Center for International Studies. **VFOAT** Bulletin. Vol. 24, No. 2 (Spring / Summer 1993)-. Bulletin. English. sa. Free (members). American Comparative Literature Association, 5242 University of Oregon, Eugene OR 97403. **Tel** (503)346-0737. **LC** PN855; .A44. ***Continues*** *American Comparative Literature Association. ACLA Newsletter, 0891-3277.*
Desc: Bulletin of the ACLA, including announcements, directories, and articles.

US/0891-3277
ACLA NEWSLETTER. ***Title Change.*** (ACLA NEWSLETTER / AMERICAN COMPARATIVE LITERATURE ASSOCIATION.). [ACLA newsl.]. **Main/Corp** American Comparative Literature Association. **VAT** American Comparative Literature Association Newsletter. Vol. 14, Nos. 1 and 2 (Spring and Fall 1982)-Vol. 24, No. 1 (Fall/Winter 1992). Newsletter. English. sa (June and Dec.). American Comparative Literature Association, 5242 University of Oregon, Eugene OR 97403. **Tel** (503)346-0737. **ED** Larry H. Peer. **LC** PN855; .A44. **DD** 800. **Circ:** 1,500. ***Continues*** *American Comparative Literature Association. Newsletter - American Comparative Literature Association;* ***Absorbed*** *Heliconian.* ***Continued by*** *ACLA Bulletin.*
Desc: Bulletin of the ACLA, including announcements, directories, and articles.

II/0157-6283
ACLALS BULLETIN. ***Ceased.*** [ACLALS bull.]. **VFOAT** A.C.L.A.L.S. Bulletin. **VAT** Association for Commonwealth Literature and Language Studies Bulletin. (1967)-(19??). Bulletin. English. an. University of Aarhus / Department of English, Building 326, 8000 Aarhus C Denmark. **Tel** 011 45 89422124, 89422116, FAX 011 45 86191699. **UDC** 802.0; 82.
Ind/Abst Abstr. Engl. Stud. (19??-19??); MLA Int. Bibl. Books Artic. Mod. Lang. Lit. (19??-19??).

US
ACORN : STORIES, POEMS, ESSAYS, REVIEWS / ENTIRELY WRITTEN AND EDITED BY YOUNG WRITERS. Vol. 1, No. 1 (Apr. 1938)-. Periodical. English.
Ind/Abst BHA : Biblio. Hist. Art.

XV/0567-784X
ACTA NEOPHILOLOGICA. [Acta neophilol.]. **Added/Corp** Univerza v Ljubljani. Filozofska Fakulteta. (1968)-. Multiple languages (English and French). an. **LC** PN1; .A33. **DD** 809.
Ind/Abst MLA Int. Bibl. Books Artic. Mod. Lang. Lit.

SW/0585-3575
ACTA UNIVERSITATIS STOCKHOLMIENSIS. STOCKHOLM SLAVIC STUDIES. Added/Corp Stockholms Universitet. **VFOAT** Stockholm Slavic Studies. (1967)-. Monographic series. Swedish (Swedish). ir. Price varies per volume. Scandinavian University Press, PO Box 2959 Toeyen, N 0608 Oslo 6 Norway. **Tel** 011 47 2 2575400, FAX 011 47 2 2575353, telex 71896 UROR N. **(Subscription address:** Scandinavian University Press, 200 Meacham Ave., Elmont NY 11003.**)**

Literature

HU/0324-6523
ACTA UNIVERSITATIS SZEGEDIENSIS.
See History(General).

FI
ACTA UNIVERSITATIS TAMPERENSIS. SER. A. Added/Corp Tampereen Yliopisto. (19??)-. Monographic series. English. ir. Price varies per volume. University of Tampere, PO Box 617, SF Sales Office, 33101 Tampere Finland.
Ind/Abst Annu. Bibliogr. Engl. Lang. Lit.

FR
ACTES (UNIVERSITE PAUL VALERY. CENTRE D'ETUDES ET DE RECHERCHES SOCIOCRITIQUES).
(ACTES.). Vol. 1- 1976-. Monographic series. French. Price varies per volume. Centre d'Etudes Sociocritiques, Univ Paul Valley, BP 5043, 34032 Montpellier Cedex France. **Tel** 011 33 67 142326.

VE/0252-905X
ACTUALIDADES - CENTRO DE ESTUDIOS LATINOAMERICANOS ROMULO GALLEGOS. (ACTUALIDADES.). [Actual. - Cent. estud. latinoam. "Romulo Gallegos"]. Vol. 1 (1976)-. Periodical. Spanish. Bs1.00. Quinta Centro De Estudios Latinoamericanos, Romulo Gallegos, Apartado 29076. **LC** F1401; .A29. **UDC** 980=6.
Ind/Abst HAPI Hisp. Am. Period. Index (19??-); MLA Int. Bibl. Books Artic. Mod. Lang. Lit.

UA
ADAB AL-GHAD. Periodical. Arabic. ir. Al-Dar Al-Arabiyah Al-Hadithah Lil-Tijarah Al-Kharijiyah, 11 Ahari Abd Al-Khaliq Tharwat Khalid Juwayli, Al-Qahirah Egypt. **LC** PJ7501; .A28.

UA
ADAB WA-NAQD. Periodical. Arabic. £E0.50 single issue. Hizb Al-Tajammu Al-Watani Al-Taqaddumi Al-Wahdawi, 1 Shari Karim Al-Dawlah, Al-Qahirah Egypt. **LC** PJ7501; .A3.

II
ADABI MUJALLAH. Added/Corp University of Rajasthan. Shubah-yi Urdu o Farsi. (19??)-. Periodical. Urdu. an. Rs10.00. Department of Urdu and Persian, Jaipur India. **LC** PK2151; .A27.

AJ
ADABI PROSES / AZARBAIJAN SSR ELMLAR AKADEMIIASY, NIZAMI ADYNA KHALGLAR DOSTLUGHU ORDENLI ADABIIIAT INSTITUTU.
Added/Corp Nizami Adyna Adabiiiat Institutu. **VFOAT** Literaturnyi Protsess. (19??)-. Azerbaijani.

AT/0815-5992
ADELAIDE REVIEW. See The Arts.

US/0736-4970
ADRIFT. [Adrift]. No. 1 (Spring 1983)-. Periodical. English. sa. $10.00. Adrift, 239 East 5th Street Apartment 4D, New York NY 10003. **ED** Thomas McGonigle. **UDC** 820(73); 891.62. **Bk Rev**. **Ad Acc**. **Circ**. 1,000.
Desc: Features writings by Irish and American writers, any format as long as it's good.

TU
AEGEAN JOURNAL OF LANGUAGE AND LITERATURE. See Linguistics.

US/0891-7213
AEGEAN REVIEW. Suspended. [Aegean rev.]. **VFOAT** Aegean. (Fall/Winter 19??)- (19??). Periodical. English. sa. $18.00 US; $20.00 Canada; $21.00 Europe. Wire Press, 220 West 19th Street/Suite 2A, New York NY 10011. **Tel** (212)995-9835, (613)230-1893. **ED** Dino Siotis. **DD** 880. **Bk Rev**. **Ad Acc**. ctrl circ. **Continues** Coffeehouse.
Desc: A literary magazine devoted to Greek subjects by Greeks, Greek Americans and any others who have been inspired by Greece.

CN/0381-6656
AESTHETE, THE. V. 1 March 1973-. Periodical. English. qt. $.75 per no. Aesthete, c/o #1 378 Lafontaine, Vanier Ontario K1L 6X8 Canada. **DD** C810/.8/0054.

US/1048-3756
AETHLON (SAN DIEGO, CALIF.). See Recreation, Leisure-Sports.

IT
AEVUM ANTIQUUM / ISTITUTO DI FILOLOGIA CLASSICA E DI PAPIROLOGIA. Added/Corp Universita Cattolica del Sacro Cuore. Istituto di Filologia Classica e di Papirologia. Vol. 1 (1988)-. Italian. an. Vita e Pensiero, Public University, Largo Gemelli 1, 20123 Milan Italy. **Tel** 011 39 2 72342310, 011 39 2 72342370. **LC** PA9; .A38. **DD** 480/.05.

PK/0515-5649
AFKAR. (19??)-. Periodical. Urdu. mo. Rs94.00 Pakistan; Rs520.00 other. Afkar Monthly, Robson Road, Karachi Pakistan. **LC** AP95.U7; A33.

PO
AFRICA. V. 1- (No. 1-); July 1978-. Periodical. Portuguese. qt. 140.00. Rua da Alcantara 53, Lisbon Portugal. **LC** PQ9900; .A2.

●US/1062-4783
AFRICAN AMERICAN REVIEW. [Afr. Am. rev.]. **Added/Corp** Indiana State University. Dept. of English. Modern Language Association of America. Division on Black American Literature and Culture. **VFOAT** AAR. Vol. 26, No. 1 (Spring 1992)-. Periodical. English. Four times a year (Mar., June, Sept., Dec.). $24.00 (individuals), $44.00 (institutions) US; $31.00 (individuals), $51.00 (institutions) other. African American Review, Indiana State University, Department of English, Terre Haute IN 47809. **Tel** (812)237-2968, FAX (812)237-3156. **ED** Joe Weixlmann. **LC** E185.5; .N35. **DD** 810/.9/896073. Index available (back issues). **Bk Rev**. **Ad Acc**. Documents available from The Genuine Article, UMI Article Clearinghouse. **Continues** Black American Literature Forum, 0148-6179.
Desc: An official MLA division publication, AAR prints essays on African American Literature, theatre, art and culture; interviews, poetry, fiction, bibliographies, book reviews.
Ind/Abst Abstr. Engl. Stud.; Am. Hist. Life (1987-); Am. Humanit. Index (1991-); Arts Humanit. Citation Index [Full Cov.]; Book Rev. Index; Curr. Contents Arts Humanit.; Expand. Acad. Index (1992-); Film Lit. Index; Humanit. Index (?-?); Index Am. Period. Verse; Index Black Period.; Lit. Crit. Regist.; MLA Int. Bibl. Books Artic. Mod. Lang. Lit.; Newsp. Period. Abstr. (1990-); Res. Alert [Full Cov.]

UK/0065-4000
AFRICAN LITERATURE TODAY. [Afr. lit. today]. No. 1 (1968)-. Monographic series. English. ir. Price varies per volume. Africa World Press Inc., 11 Princess Road, Suite D, Lawrenceville NJ 08648. **Tel** (609)844-9583. **(Subscription address:** Plymbridge Distributors Ltd., Estover Road, Plymouth PL6 7PZ England.) **ED** E. D. Jones. **LC** PL8010; .A4. **DD** 896. **Continues** Association for African Literature in English. Bulletin of the Association for African Literature in English.
Ind/Abst Abstr. Engl. Stud.; Humanit. Index (?-?); MLA Int. Bibl. Books Artic. Mod. Lang. Lit.

UK/0065-4108
AFRICAN WRITERS SERIES. [Afr. writ. ser.]. (1976)-. Monographic series. English. ir. Price varies per volume. Heinemann Educational Books, 361 Hanover Street, Portsmouth NH 03801. **Tel** (800)541-2086, (603)431-7894. **LC** UNC.
Ind/Abst MLA Int. Bibl. Books Artic. Mod. Lang. Lit.

FR/0245-8160
AFRIQUE LITTERAIRE, L'. Suspended. [Afr. litt.]. No. 54-55 (1980)-(1993). Periodical. French. qt. $19.96. L'Afrique Litteraire SA, 2 rue Cretet, 75009 Paris France. **LC** DT1; .A54. **Continues** Afrique Litteraire et Artistique.
Ind/Abst ARTbibliogr. Mod. (1985-); Arts Humanit. Citation Index (19??-19??) [Full Cov.]; MLA Int. Bibl. Books Artic. Mod. Lang. Lit.

US/0278-8969
AFRO-HISPANIC REVIEW. See Linguistics.

SP
AGALIA : REVISTA DA ASSOCIACOM GALEGA DA LINGUA. See Linguistics.

US/0884-5816
AGE OF JOHNSON, THE. [Age Johnson]. (1987)-. Periodical. an. $50.00. AMS Press Inc., 56 East 13th Street, New York NY 10003. **Tel** (212)777-4700, FAX (212)995-5413, telex 710 581 2302. **ED** Paul J Korshin. **LC** PR3532; .A15. **DD** 828/.609. Index available. **Bk Rev**.
Desc: Studies Samuel Johnson and his circle in all aspects of the age: literature, history, the arts, etc.
Ind/Abst MLA Int. Bibl. Books Artic. Mod. Lang. Lit.

US/1046-218X
AGNI (BOSTON, MASS.). (AGNI.). [Agni]. (1988)-. Periodical. English. Twice a year. $24.00. AGNI / Creative Writing Department, Boston University, 236 Bay State Road, Boston MA 02215. **Tel** (617)353-5389, FAX (617)353-3653. **ED** Askold Melnyczuk. **LC** PS501; .A33. **DD** 810/.8/0054/05. Index available. **Bk Rev**. (Qty: 10). **Ad Acc, Adv Mgr:** Erin, **Tel** (617)353-7135. **Circ:** 1,500. available on microfiche; available on microfilm. **Continues** AGNI Review, 0191-3352.
Desc: Published poetry, fiction, commissioned essays, and reviews from established and upcoming writers.

UY
AGON. No. 1- Apr. 1954-. Periodical. Spanish. Ediciones Agon, Charcas 3918, 1425 Capital Republica Argentina. **UDC** 860(82). **Bk Rev**. **Ad Acc**.
Desc: Offers a challenge to the imagination through original poetry and stories. Literary prizes are announced and books from all fields of creative writings are reviewed.

JA
AICHI KENRITSU DAIGAKU BUNGAKUBU RON SHU: IPPAN KYOIKU HEN. Main/Corp Aichi Kenritsu Daigaku. Bungakubu. **Added/Corp** Aichi Kenritsu Joshi Tanki Daigaku. Aichi Kenritsu Daigaku. Bungakubu. Bulletin. **VFOAT** Bulletin of the Faculty of Literature, Aichi Prefectural University. No. 21 (1970)-. Japanese. Aicha Kenritsu Daigaku, 3-28 Takadacho Mizuho-ku, Nagoya Japan. **LC** AS552.A34; A28.

JA
AICHI KENRITSU DAIGAKU BUNGAKUBU RON SHU : KOKUBUNGAKUKA HEN. Main/Corp Aichi Kenritsu Daigaku. Bungakubu. Kokubungakuka. **VFOAT** Bulletin of the Faculty of Literature, Aichi Prefectural University. No. 21 (1970)-. Japanese. 3-28 Takadacho Mizuho-ku, Nagoya Japan. **LC** PL700; .A37A. **UDC** 895.6. **Continues in part** Aichi Kenritsu Daigaku Bungakubu Ron Shu: Gogaku, Bungaku.

FR/0180-3468
AILLEURS PARIS. [Ailleurs Paris]. (1977)-. Monographic series. French. ir. Price varies per volume. RCS France, 115 rue du Temple, 75003 Paris France. **Tel** 011 33 1 42783068. **(Subscription address:** Development Info Presse Dip, 70 rue Compans, 75019 Paris France.) **UDC** 30.

GR/1010-4569
AIOLIKA GRAMMATA. [Aiol. grammata]. (1971)-. Periodical. Greek, Modern. bm $15.00. **LC** PA5279.L45; A35.
Ind/Abst MLA Int. Bibl. Books Artic. Mod. Lang. Lit.

CN/0229-463X
AJAR. [Ajar]. **Added/Corp** D'Arcy McGee High School. Vol. 1, No. 1 (Mar. 1977)-. Periodical. English. sa. **DD** C811/.5408/09283.

PK
AJKAL. VFOAT Aajkal. Vol. 1- July 31, 1970-. Periodical. Urdu (Urdu). RS20.00. Ministry of Information and Broadcasting, Government of India, Patiala House, New Delhi 110 001 India. **Tel** 387983. **LC** PK2151; .A43.

PL
AKTA TOWARZYSTWA HISTORYCZNO-LITERACKIEGO W PARYZU. Added/Corp Towarzystwo Historyczno-Literackie w Paryzu. (1991)-. Polish. **LC** DK4010; .A482x.

RU
AKTUALNYE PROBLEMY LEKSIKOLOGII I SLOVOOBRAZOVANIIA. See Linguistics.

GW/0002-3957
AKZENTE (MUNCHEN). (AKZENTE.). [Akzente]. Vol. 1 (1954)-. Periodical. German. bm (6 issues). DM61.80. Carl Hanser Verlag, Postfach 860420, D 81631 Munich Germany. **Tel** 011 49 89 998300, FAX 011 49 89 984809. **ED** W. Hollerer and H. Bender. **LC** PT1141.A2; A6. **DD** 830/.8. **[CCC]**. Documents available from The Genuine Article.
Ind/Abst Arts Humanit. Citation Index [Full Cov.]; MLA Int. Bibl. Books Artic. Mod. Lang. Lit.; Res. Alert [Full Cov.]; Romant. Move.; Soc. Sci. Cit. Index [Select. Cov.].

SY
AL-ADAB AL-AJNABIYAH. V. 1- July 1974-. Periodical. Arabic. Ittihad Al-Kuttab Al-Arab, Shari Murshid Al-Khatir, PO Box 323, Dimashq Syria. **LC** PN9; .A34.

IQ
AL-ADIB AL-MUASIR. Periodical. Arabic. 2. Ittihad Al-Udaba Fi Al-Iraq, Andalus Square, PO Box 217, Baghdad Iraq. **LC** PJ7501; .A35.

TI
AL-AKHILLA. Periodical. Arabic. mo. SB 135, Tunis 1015 Tunisia. **LC** PJ8252.5; .A39.

US/0889-8731
AL-ARABIYYA. See Linguistics.

YE
AL-HIKMAH. V. 1- (No. 1-). Periodical. Arabic. mo. 125 riyals. Ittihad Al-Udaba, PO Box 98, Adan Yemen. **LC** PJ8001.Y4; H53. **Continues** Hikmah Al-Yamaniyah.

IS
AL-KARMIL. Added/Corp Ittihad Al-Amm Lil-Kitab Wa-al-Sihafiyin Al-Filastiniyin. **VFOAT** Karmel. (1981)-. Periodical. Arabic. an. $25.00. Institute of Middle East Studies, University of Haifa, C/O Dick Bruggeman, Haifa 31999 Israel. **Tel** 011 972 4 240655, FAX 011 972 4 342104, telex 46660.
Ind/Abst Middle East J.

JO
AL-MAHD LIL-THQAFAH WA-AL-FUNUN. VFOAT Mahd. Periodical. Arabic. qt. 5JD individuals, 10JD institutions. Majallat Al-Mahd Lil-Thqafah Wa-Al-Funun, S B 926710, Amman Jordan. **LC** PJ7501; .M33.

SY
AL-MAWQIF AL-ADABI. **VFOAT** Maoukef Al Adabi. V. 1- ; May 1971-. Periodical. Arabic. £Syr250.00. Irrihad Al-Kuttab Al-Arab, Shari Murshid Khatir, Dimashq Syria. **Tel** 244329. **ED** Ali Oklaorsan and Abdalah Abo Hiif. **LC** PJ7501; .M37. Index available. **Bk Rev. Ad Acc.** ctrl circ.
Desc: Concerns literature of all kinds; poetry, drama, short stories, fiction. Includes criticism, culture news and writers symposium.

AE
AL-RUYA / YUSDIRUHA ITTIHAD AL-KUTTAB AL-JAZAIRIYIN. **Added/Corp** Ittihad al-Kuttab al-Jazairiyin. (19??)-. Periodical. Arabic. qt. 5.00 single issue. Ittihad Al-Kuttab Al-Jazairiyin, 88 Shari Daydush Murad, Al-Jazair Algeria. **LC** PJ8260; .R89.

IQ
AL-TALIAH AL-ADABIYAH. Arabic. Cinema Al-Khayyan Street, Baghdad Iraq. **LC** PJ7501; .T34.

SY
AL-THAQAFAH. V. 1- Jan. 1975-. Arabic. £Syr2.00 per copy. Midhat Akkash, PO Box 2570, Dimashq Syria. **LC** PJ7501; .T46.

IQ
AL-THAQAFAH AL-AJNABIYAH. **VFOAT** Ath-Thkafa Al-Ajnebiah; Foreign Culture. Began in 1980. Periodical. Arabic. qt. 5.00ID Iraq; $14.00 other. Al-Thagafah Al-Ajnabiya, Dar Al-Shuun Al-Thaqafiyah Al-Amma Baghdad Iraq. **Tel** 4436044, FAX 4448760, telex 214135. **ED** Yasseen Taha Hafidh. **LC** PN9; .T47. **Bk Rev. Ad Acc.** ctrl circ.

CN/0146-4965
ALA BULLETIN : A PUBLICATION OF THE AFRICAN LITERATURE ASSOCIATION. **Main/Corp** African Literature Association. **Added/Corp** African Literature Association. **VFOAT** A.L.A. Bulletin. Vol. 8, No. 1 (Winter 1982)-. Academic Scholarly Publication. English (French and Portuguese). qt. $50.00. African Literature Association, University of Iowa, 219 North Clinton Street, Iowa City IA 52242. **Tel** (319)335-1682. **ED** S. H. Arnold. **LC** PL8009.5; .A37a. **DD** 809/.889/6. **Bk Rev. Ad Acc. Circ:** 1,000 (ctrl). ***Continues*** *African Literature Association. ALA Newsletter.*
Desc: News about all aspects of African literature. Covers Diaspora literatures and liberation struggles; occasional scholarly articles.

KG/0320-7390
ALA TOO. **Added/Corp** Kyrgyzstan Zzhazuuchular Soiuzu. Kirghiz S.S.R. Madaniiat Ministerstvosunun. **VFOAT** Ala-Too. (19??)-. Periodical. Kirghiz. mo. $119.95. **(Subscription address:** East View Publications Inc., 3020 Harbor Lane North, Suite 110, Minneapolis MN 55447.**)** **ED** T. Kasymbekov. **LC** WMLC L 83/582.
Desc: Kyrgyzian literature.

US/0890-1554
ALABAMA LITERARY REVIEW. [Ala. lit. rev.]. **Added/Corp** Troy State University. English Dept. Vol. 1 (Spring 1987)-. Periodical. English. sa. $9.00. Troy State University English Department, 253 Smith Hall, Troy AL 36082. **Tel** (205)670-3000 ext 3286. **ED** Theron Montgomery (205)670-3307. **LC** PS558.A5; A4. **DD** 810.8/9761/05. Index available. **Bk Rev**, (Qty: 10 per year). **Ad Acc, Adv Mgr:** Editor. **Pr Rev. Circ:** 800.
Desc: A state literary medium publishing poetry, fiction, short drama, interviews, essays, book reviews, photographs and graphic art. Only the highest quality of writing is published in this review.

II
ALAKANANDA. August 1973-. Periodical. Hindi (Hindi). 12.00. **LC** PK2047; .A42.

US/0887-0209
ALALITCOM, THE. (THE ALALITCOM : ALABAMA LITERARY COMPETITIONS : WINNING AUTHORS / ALABAMA WRITERS' CONCLAVE.). [Alalitcom]. **Added/Corp** Alabama Writers' Conclave. **VFOAT** The Alabama Literary Competitions. (1975)-. Periodical. English. an. Alalitcom, 960 Mountain Branch Drive, Birmingham AL 35226. **ED** Margaret Broduax and Jane Hinds. **DD** 810.
Desc: A collection of prize-winning short stories, poems, essays, articles and plays from state-wide literary competition.

US/0044-7064
ALALUZ. **Added/Corp** University of California, Riverside. Dept. of Literatures and Languages. University of California, Riverside. Dept. of Spanish. University of California, Riverside. Dept. of Spanish and Portuguese. Vol. 1 (1969)-. Periodical. Spanish (English). Twice a year (June, Dec.). $40.00. Department of Spanish & Portuguese, University of California, Riverside CA 92521. **Tel** (909)787-3406 or 7332. **ED** Ana Maria Fagundo. **Bk Rev. Circ:** 1,000 (ctrl).
Desc: A journal of contemporary poetry and short stories (Spain and Spanish American countries) are included.
Ind/Abst MLA Int. Bibl. Books Artic. Mod. Lang. Lit.

UA
ALAM AL-QISSAH / YUSDIRUHA NADI AL-QISSAH BI-AL-ISKANDARIYAH. V. 1, No. 1 (Aug./Sept. 1979)-. Periodical. Arabic. qt. £E0.20 single issue. 8 Shari Talatharb, Al-Attarin Al-Iskandariyah Egypt. **LC** PJ7677; .A4. **DD** 892/.7301/08. **UDC** 892.7.

US/0882-2840
ALAN REVIEW, THE. [ALAN rev.]. **Added/Corp** Assembly on Literature for Adolescents (National Council of Teachers of English). **VFOAT** A.L.A.N. Review. **VAT** Assembly on Literature for Adolescents Review. Vol. 6, No. 2 (Winter 1979)-. Periodical. English. Three times a year. $15.00. National Council of Teachers of English, 1111 Kenyon Road, Urbana IL 61801. **Tel** (217)328-3870, FAX (217)328-9645. **DD** 028. ***Continues*** *ALAN Newsletter.*
Ind/Abst Child. Lit. Abstr. (19??-); Curr. Index J. Educ. (March 1990-).

US/0737-268X
ALASKA QUARTERLY REVIEW. [Alsk. q. rev.]. **Added/Corp** University of Alaska, Anchorage. College of Arts and Sciences. Vol. 1, No. 1 & 2 (Fall 1982)-. Periodical. English. sa. $8.00 individuals; $10.00 institutions. University of Alaska Anchorage, 3211 Providence Drive, Anchorage AK 99508. **Tel** (907)786-1750. **ED** Ronald Spatz. **LC** PN2; .A53. **DD** 809/.03. **Bk Rev. Circ:** 1,000.
Desc: This publication includes fiction, poetry, traditional and experimental and literary criticism and reviews with emphasis on the relation between contemporary philosophy and literature.
Ind/Abst Am. Humanit. Index.

US/0888-3181
ALBA DE AMERICA. (ALBA DE AMERICA / ILCH.). [Alba Am.]. **Added/Corp** Instituto Literario y Cultural Hispanico. Vol. 1 (May 1983)-. Periodical. Spanish. sa (July and Sept.). $48.00. Instituto Literario y Cultural Hispanico, 8452 Furman Avenue, Westminister CA 92683. **Tel** (714)892-8285. **ED** Juana Alcira Arancibia. **LC** WMLC 93/2106. **DD** 860. **Bk Rev. Ad Acc. Circ:** 1,000.
Desc: Publication includes poetry, short stories, plays, literary criticism, bibliographies and interviews. Works are selected by an editorial board consisting of university professors.

CN/0384-8523
ALCHEMIST (LASALLE). (THE ALCHEMIST.). (Jan. 1975)-. Periodical. English. ir. $16.00. The Alchemist, Box 123, Lasalle Quebec H8R 3T7 Canada. **ED** Marco Fraticelli. **DD** C810/.8/0054. **Circ:** 500 (ctrl).
Desc: A magazine of prose, poetry, haiku and graphics. We are looking for material which explores the possibilities.

IS
ALE SEFER. See Religion and Theology-Judaism.

IS
ALE-SIAH (TEL-AVIV, ISRAEL : 1974). (ALE SIAH.). **Added/Corp** Hugim Le-sifrut. **VFOAT** Alei-Siah; Literary Conversations; Literary Conversation. **VAT** Alei Siah; Ale-Ssiah. (June 1974)-. Periodical. Hebrew. Twice a year. $10.00. Literary Circles Kibbutzim & Moshavim, 10 Dubnov Street, Tel Aviv Israel. **LC** PJ5001; .A48. ***Continues*** *Ba-hugim Le-sifrut.*

CK/0120-0216
ALEPH (MANIZALES, COLOMBIA). (ALEPH.). **Added/Corp** Universidad Nacional de Colombia. Sede Manizales. **VFOAT** Revista Aleph. (1966)-. Periodical. Spanish. qt (Mar., June, Sept., Dec.). $30.00. Revista Aleph, Apartado Aereo No 1080, Manizales Colombia. **Tel** 68-852588, 68-867334, FAX 68-863220. **ED** Carlos-Enrique Ruiz & Adela Londono. **LC** AP63; .A517. **DD** 056/.1. Index available. cum. index. **Bk Rev. Ad Acc. Pr Rev. Circ:** 2,000.
Desc: Essays on literature and philosophy; covers poetry and music with a section on cultural news. Cover features a work of art.

US/0065-616X
ALEXANDER LECTURES, THE. **Main/Corp** Toronto. University. Alexander Foundation. (1929-). Monographic series. English. ir. Price varies per volume. University of Toronto Press Book Department, 5201 Dufferin Street, Downsview Ontario M3H 5T8 Canada. **Tel** (416)667-7791, FAX (416)667-7832.

BL/0002-5216
ALFA. [Alfa]. **Added/Corp** Faculdade de Filosofia, Ciencias e Letras de Marilia. Departamento de Letras. Universidade Estadual Paulista. No. 1 (Mar. 1962)-. Periodical. Portuguese (English, French and German). an. $30.00. Fundacao Desenvolvimento Unesp, Av Rio Branco 1210, 01206 Sao Paulo SP Brazil. **Tel** 011 55 11 2237088. **LC** PN9; .A4. **DD** 805. Index available. **Bk Rev. Ad Acc. Circ:** 1,000 (ctrl).
Ind/Abst Linguist. Lang. Behav. Abstr. (1980-) [Full Cov.]; MLA Int. Bibl. Books Artic. Mod. Lang. Lit.; Soc. Plann. Policy Dev. Abstr.; Sociol. Abstr.

HU/0401-3174
ALFOLD. [Alfold]. **Added/Corp** Magyar Irok Szoevetsege. Debreceni Csoport. Hajdu-Bihar Megye (Hungary). Megyei Tanacs. (1956)-. Academic Scholarly Publication. Hungarian. mo. $5.00. Csokonai Publishing House, Varga u. 17 er. 10, 4024 Debrecen, Hungary. **Tel** 52 12626. **ED** P. B. Eva. **LC** AP82; .A55. **Bk Rev. Circ:** 1,825. ***Continues*** *Epituenk, 0200-500X.*
Desc: Hungarian literary periodical.
Ind/Abst MLA Int. Bibl. Books Artic. Mod. Lang. Lit.

UA
ALIF (CAIRO, EGYPT). (ALIF : JOURNAL OF COMPARATIVE POETICS.). **VFOAT** Journal of Comparative Poetics. No. 1 (Spring 1981)-. Periodical. Arabic (English). an. $5.00 individuals, $10.00 institutions. ALIF Department of English and Comparative Literature, The American University in Cairo, PO Box 2511, Cairo Arab Republic of Egypt. **LC** PN1; .A45. **DD** 809. **UDC** 82-1.

II
ALIGARH CRITICAL MISCELLANY, THE. Vol. 1, No. 1 (May 1988)-. Periodical. English. sa. $10.00. **(Subscription address:** Prints India, 11 Darya Ganj, New Delhi 110002 India.**)** **LC** PR1; .A44. **DD** 820.9/0005.
Ind/Abst Annu. Bibliogr. Engl. Lang. Lit.; MLA Int. Bibl. Books Artic. Mod. Lang. Lit.

II/0258-0365
ALIGARH JOURNAL OF ENGLISH STUDIES, THE. [Aligarh j. Engl. stud.]. **Added/Corp** Aligarh Muslim University. Dept. of English. Vol. 1 (1976)-. Periodical. English. sa. $15.00. Aligarh Muslim University Department of English, Alegarh 202001 India. **(Subscription address:** Prints India, 11 Darya Ganj, New Delhi 110002 India.**)** **ED** S M Jafar Zaki. **LC** PR1; .A45. **DD** 820/.9. Index available. cum. index. **Bk Rev. Circ:** 300 (ctrl).
Ind/Abst Annu. Bibliogr. Engl. Lang. Lit.; MLA Int. Bibl. Books Artic. Mod. Lang. Lit.; Romant. Move.

IT/0516-6551
ALIGHIERI, L'. [Alighieri]. Vol. 1 (Jan./July 1960)-. Italian. sa. L20000 Italy; L30000 other. Alighieri, Piazza Sonnino 5, 00153 Rome Italy. **Tel** 011 39 6 582019. **LC** PQ4331; .A17.
Ind/Abst MLA Int. Bibl. Books Artic. Mod. Lang. Lit.

IT
ALLEGORIA. ***Ceased.*** Vol. 1, No. 1 (1989)-(Dec. 1992). Periodical. Italian. qt. Franco Angeli Riviste SRL, Viale Monza 106, 20127 Milan Italy. **Tel** 011 39 2 2827651, 011 39 2 289562. ***Continues*** *Ombra d'Argo.*

US/0363-2377
ALLEGORICA. [Allegorica]. **Added/Corp** University of Texas at Arlington. Dept. of English. Vol. 1 (Spring 1976)-. Periodical. English. an (May). $10.00 US; $12.00 other. Allegorica, Texas A & M University, English Department, College Station TX 77843. **Tel** (409)845-3452. **ED** Craig Kallendorf. **LC** PN661; .A43. **DD** 808.8/002. **Bk Rev. Ad Acc. Circ:** 250.
Desc: Literal translations of Medieval and Renaissance literary works and documents unavailable in English or only in outmoded or inadequate translations - also articles and reviews.
Ind/Abst Annu. Bibliogr. Engl. Lang. Lit.; Middle East Abstr. Index; MLA Int. Bibl. Books Artic. Mod. Lang. Lit.; Romant. Move.

GW/0720-3098
ALLMENDE. 1981/No. 1-. Periodical. German. Three times a year. DM19.80 single issue. Jan Thorbecke Verlag GmbH and Company, Karlstrasse 10, Postfach 546, D 72482 Sigmaringen Germany. **Tel** 011 49 7571 728100, FAX 011 07571-728-280, telex 732534. **LC** PT1141.A2; A446. **DD** 830/.8. **UDC** 830.

SW
ALLT OM BOCKER. See Publishing-Books and Bookmaking.

FR
ALMANACH JULES VERNE. ***Ceased.*** (19??)-(1993). French. an. Editions Ramsay, 9 rue du Cherche Midi, 75006 Paris France. **Tel** 011 33 1 45445505.

US
ALMANAKH (NIU - IORK. 1980). (ALMANAKH ... KLUBA RUSSKIKH PISATELEI.). 80-. Periodical. Russian. an. $7.95. 20-44 Crescent Street, Apt 2A, New York NY 11105. **LC** PG3516; .A44. **UDC** 882.

SP
ALOR NOVISIMO. ***Ceased.*** Vol. 1, No. 1 (Dec. 1984)-(19??). Periodical. Spanish. qt. Alor Novisimo, Excma Diputacion Provincial, 06071 Badajoz Spain. **Tel** 924-224140/224141. **ED** Bernardo Victor Carande. **Circ:** 1,000. ***Continues*** *Nuevo Alor.*
Desc: Literary creation and criticism.

CN/0838-391X
ALPHA BEAT SOUP. [Alpha beat soup]. Issue 1 (June 1987)-. Periodical. English. Twice a year. 17.00Can$. Alpha Beat Press, 31A Waterloo Street, New Hope PA 18938. **Tel** (215)862-0299. **ED** Dave Christy. **DD** 810/.8/0054. Index available. cum. index. **Bk Rev. Pr Rev. Circ:** 500.
Desc: Beat, post-beat independent and modern writing poetry, prose, art and reviews.
Ind/Abst Index Am. Period. Verse.

CN/0701-0656
ALPHA (WOLFEVILLE). (ALPHA.). [Alpha]. **VFOAT** Alpha Arts Magazine; Alpha Literary Journal. Vol. 1 (Oct. 1976)-. Periodical. English. mo. 25c. per no. Acadia University, Box 298, Editions du Grade Pre, Wolfville Nova Scotia B0P 1X0 Canada. **Tel** (902)542-9872, (902)542-2201. **DD** C810/.8/0054.

GW
ALTDEUTSCHE TEXTBIBLIOTHEK. (1882)-. Monographic series. German. ir. Price varies per volume. Max Niemeyer Verlag, Postfach 2140, D 72011 Tuebingen Germany. **Tel** 011 49 7071 989494, FAX 011 49 7071 87419.
Desc: Series covering German literature.
Ind/Abst MLA Int. Bibl. Books Artic. Mod. Lang. Lit.

II
ALTRI TERMINI. No. 1- May 1972-. Periodical. Italian. Three times a year. L4500. Via Edificio Soolastico 33, Marano Di Naples 33 Italy. **LC** PN5; .A74.

US/0044-7412
AMANUENSIS. V. 1- Spring 1971-. Periodical. English. sa. $2.00. American Notes and Queries, Department of English, University of Kentucky, Lexington KY 40506. **LC** PS501; .A42. **DD** 700/.973.

US/1058-0751
AMAZING STORIES (1986). (AMAZING STORIES.). [Amazing stories]. Vol. 60, No. 3 (Mar. 1986)-. Periodical. English. qt (Mar., June, Sept., Dec.). $10.00 US and Canada; $16.00 other. TSR Inc., PO Box 5695, Boston MA 02206. **Tel** (414)248-3625, FAX (414)248-0389. **DD** 808. ***Continues*** *Amazing, 0279-1706.*

US/0743-2755
AMELIA. [Amelia]. (April 1984)-. Periodical. English. qt. $25.00 US; $27.00 Canada & Mexico; $41.00 others. Amelia, 329 E Street, Bakersville CA 93304. **Tel** (805)323-4064.
Desc: Poetry, fiction, articles, criticism, humor, and art. Information on new writers in every issue.
Ind/Abst Am. Humanit. Index; Index Am. Period. Verse.

US/1049-7153
AMERICAN LETTERS & COMMENTARY. [Am. lett. comment.]. **VFOAT** American Letters and Commentary. No. 1 (Fall 1988)-. Periodical. English. ir. American Letters & Commentary, 236 Beaumont Street, Brooklyn NY 11235. **DD** 810.

US/0896-7148
AMERICAN LITERARY HISTORY. [Am. lit. hist.]. Vol. 1, No. 1 (Spring 1989)-. Periodical. English. Four times a year. $70.00 institutions, $30.00 individuals US; $84.00 institutions, $44.00 other. Oxford University Press / New York, 200 Madison Avenue, New York NY 10016. **Tel** (212)679-7300, (919)677-0977, (800)451-7556, (800)445-9714, FAX (919)677-1303. **(Subscription address:** Oxford University Press / USA, Journals Marketing Department, Oxford University Press, 2001 Evans Road, Cary NC 27513.**) ED** Gordon Hutner. **LC** PS1; .A58. **DD** 810.9/0005. **[CCC].** Index available. cum. index. **Bk Rev. Ad Acc. Pr Rev. Circ:** 1,000. available on microfilm and microfiche from University Microfilms International (UMI).
Ind/Abst Am. Hist. Life (1989-); MLA Int. Bibl. Books Artic. Mod. Lang. Lit.

US/1051-5062
AMERICAN LITERARY REVIEW. [Am. lit. rev.]. **Added/Corp** University of North Texas. Creative Writing Program. University of North Texas. Center for Texas Studies. Vol. 1, No. 1 (Spring 1990)-. Periodical. English. sa (Published in Spring & Fall). $15.00 (one year), $28.00 (two year), $40.00 (three year). American Literary Review, North Texas State University, PO Box 13827, Denton TX 76203. **Tel** (817)565-2000, FAX (817)369-8770. **ED** Barb Rodman & Bill Cobb. **LC** PS536.2; .A44. **DD** 810.8/0005. **Ad Acc, Adv Mgr:** Rebecca Stephens, **Tel** (817)565-2127. **Pr Rev. Circ:** 1,000.

US/0065-9142
AMERICAN LITERARY SCHOLARSHIP. [Am. lit. scholarsh.]. (1963)-. Monographic series. English. ir. $48.00. Duke University Press, PO Box 90660, Durham NC 27708-0660. **Tel** (919)687-3600, (919)688-5134 (orders), FAX (919)688-4574, telex 802829. **ED** J. Albert Robbins. **LC** PS3; .A47. **DD** 810.
Desc: Acts as a guide to current published studies of American literature.
Ind/Abst MLA Int. Bibl. Books Artic. Mod. Lang. Lit.

US/0002-9831
AMERICAN LITERATURE. [Am. lit.]. **Added/Corp** Modern Language Association of America. American Literature Group. Vol. 1 (March 1929)-. Periodical. English. qt. $64.00 (institutions), $32.00 (individuals) US; $76.00 (institutions), $44.00 (individuals) other. Duke University Press, PO Box 90660, Durham NC 27708-0660. **Tel** (919)687-3600, (919)688-5134 (orders), FAX (919)688-4574, telex 802829. **ED** Cathy N. Davidson and Michael Moon (associate editor). **LC** PS1; .A6. **DD** 810.5. **[CCC].** cum. index. **Bk Rev. Ad Acc. Circ:** 4,500 (ctrl). available on microfilm and microfiche from University Microfilms International (UMI). Documents available from The Genuine Article, UMI Article Clearinghouse.
Desc: A journal of literary history, criticism, and bibliography, covering the works of American authors, past and present.
Ind/Abst Abstr. Engl. Stud.; Acad. Abstr. Full Text Elite (July 1990-); Acad. Abstr. (July 1990-); Acad. Ind. [Computer File] (1987-); Acad. Search (July 1990-); Am. Hist. Life (1963-); Annu. Bibliogr. Engl. Lang. Lit.; ARTbibliogr. Mod. (1984-); Arts Humanit. Citation Index [Full Cov.]; Book Rev. Digest (1963-); Book Rev. Index; Expand. Acad. Index (1987-); Humanit. Index; Humanit. Source (Jul. 1990-); INFO-SOUTH Abstr.; Lit. Crit. Regist.; Mag. Search; MLA Int. Bibl. Books Artic. Mod. Lang. Lit.; Newsp. Period. Abstr. (1986-); Res. Alert [Full Cov.]; Romant. Move. (1984-); Shock Vibr. Dig.; Soc. Sci. Cit. Index [Select. Cov.]; West. Hist. Q.; Women Stud. Abstr.

US/0899-1448
AMERICAN LITERATURE REVIEW. [Am. lit. rev.]. **VFOAT** ALR. (1988)-. Periodical. English. Three times a year. Free. Todd Publications, 18 North Greenbush Road, West Nyack NY 10994. **Tel** (914)358-6213, FAX (914)358-6213. **DD** 382. ***Continues*** *International Literature Review, 0897-1048.*

US/0003-0376
AMERICAN PEN, THE. V. 1- Summer 1969-. Periodical. English. qt. **LC** PN22; .A3813. **DD** 806/01. **UDC** 820(73). available on microfilm from University Microfilms International (UMI).

US/0163-8211
AMERICAN RAG, THE. ***Suspended.*** V. 1- Fall 1978-Suspended 1981. Periodical. English. qt. $11.00. The American Rag, c/o Frederick Douglass, Creative Arts Center Inc, 276 W 43rd St, New York NY 10036. **Tel** (212)944-9870. **LC** PS501; .A44. **DD** 700/.5.

US/1051-4813
AMERICAN SHORT FICTION. [Am. short fict.]. **Added/Corp** University of Texas Press. Texas Center for Writers. (Spring 1991)-. Periodical. English. qt. $36.00 (institutions), $24.00 (individuals) US; add $6.00 postage other. University of Texas Press, PO Box 7819, Austin TX 78713. **Tel** (512)471-4531, FAX (512)320-0668, telex 776453 UTEXPRES AUS. **LC** PS648.S5; A46. **DD** 813/.0108/005.
Desc: An anthology of original stories from writers of today.

US/0883-105X
AMERICAN STUDIES INTERNATIONAL. **See** History(General)-History of North, South, and Central America.

US/0721-1392
AMERICAN UNIVERSITY STUDIES. SERIES I, GERMANIC LANGUAGES AND LITERATURES. **See** Linguistics.

US/0740-9257
AMERICAN UNIVERSITY STUDIES. SERIES II, ROMANCE LANGUAGES AND LITERATURE. **See** Linguistics.

US/0741-0700
AMERICAN UNIVERSITY STUDIES. SERIES IV, ENGLISH LANGUAGE AND LITERATURE. **See** Linguistics.

US/0740-0497
AMERICAN UNIVERSITY STUDIES. SERIES XII, SLAVIC LANGUAGES AND LITERATURE. [Am. univ. stud., XII Slav. lang. lit.]. **VFOAT** American University Studies. Series Twelve, Slavic Languages and literature; American University Studies, Slavic Languages and Literature; Slavic Languages and Literature. Vol. 1 (1983)-. Monographic series. English. Peter Lang Publishing, 62 West 45th Street, 4th Floor, New York NY 10036. **Tel** (212)764-1471, (800)770-5264, telex 6973364 PLNY.
Ind/Abst MLA Int. Bibl. Books Artic. Mod. Lang. Lit.

US/0743-6645
AMERICAN UNIVERSITY STUDIES. SERIES XIX, .GENERAL LITERATURE. [Am. univ. stud., Ser. XIX, Gen. lit.]. **VFOAT** American University Studies. Series 19, General Literature; American University Series. Series Nineteen, General Literature; General Literature. Vol. 1 (1984)-. Monographic series. English. ir. Price varies per volume. Peter Lang Publishing, 62 West 45th Street, 4th Floor, New York NY 10036. **Tel** (212)764-1471, (800)770-5264, telex 6973364 PLNY. **LC** UNC. **DD** 800.
Ind/Abst MLA Int. Bibl. Books Artic. Mod. Lang. Lit.

US/0742-1923
AMERICAN UNIVERSITY STUDIES. SERIES XVIII, AFRICAN LITERATURE. [Am. univ. stud., Ser. XVIII, Afr. lit.]. **VFOAT** African Literature; American University Studies. Series Eighteen, African Literature; African Literature. Vol. 1 (1984)-. Monographic series. English. ir. Price varies per volume. Peter Lang Publishing, 62 West 45th Street, 4th Floor, New York NY 10036. **Tel** (212)764-1471, (800)770-5264, telex 6973364 PLNY. **ED** Michael Flamini. **LC** UNC. **DD** 820.
Ind/Abst MLA Int. Bibl. Books Artic. Mod. Lang. Lit.

US/0895-0512
AMERICAN UNIVERSITY STUDIES. SERIES XXIV, AMERICAN LITERATURE. [Am. univ. stud., Ser. XXIV Am. lit.]. **VFOAT** American University Studies. Series 24, American Literature; American Literature. Vol. 1 (1988)-. Monographic series. English. Peter Lang Publishing, 62 West 45th Street, 4th Floor, New York NY 10036. **Tel** (212)764-1471, (800)770-5264, telex 6973364 PLNY. **DD** 810.
Ind/Abst MLA Int. Bibl. Books Artic. Mod. Lang. Lit.

US/0884-4356
AMERICAN VOICE (LOUISVILLE, KY.), THE. (THE AMERICAN VOICE.). **Added/Corp** Kentucky Foundation for Women. No. 1, (1985)-. Periodical. English. Three times a year (Mar., June, Sept.). $15.00. Kentucky Foundation for Women Inc, Heyburn Building/Suite 1215, Broadway at Fourth Avenue, Louisville KY 40202. **Tel** (502)562-0045. **ED** Frederick Smock and Sallie Bingham. **LC** PS501; .A45. **DD** 810/.8. **Bk Rev. Ad Acc. Circ:** 2,000 (ctrl).
Desc: A magazine of contemporary literature publishing fiction, poetry and essays by new and established writers from the US, Canada, and Central and South America. Writers include: Chaim Potok, Isabel Allende, Jorge Luis Borges, Joan Givner, Marge Piercy, Ernest Cardenal, Reynolds Price, Fae Myenne N and others.
Ind/Abst Abstr. Engl. Stud.; Am. Humanit. Index; Index Am. Period. Verse.

US/1042-6213
AMERICAS REVIEW (HOUSTON, TEX.). (THE AMERICAS REVIEW.). [Am. rev.]. **VFOAT** Americas. Vol. 14, No. 1 (Spring 1986)-. Periodical. English (Spanish). qt. $20.00 (institutions), $15.00 (individuals) US; $25.00 (institutions), $20.00 (individuals) Canada and Mexico; $30.00 (institutions), $25.00 (individuals) other. Americas Review, University of Houston, 4800 Calhoun Road, Houston TX 77204. **Tel** (800)663-2783, (713)743-2847. **ED** Julian Olivares, Arte Publico Press, University of Houston, Houston, TX 77204-2090. **LC** PS508.M4; R47. **DD** 810/.8/0868. **Bk Rev**, (Qty: 12). **Ad Acc, Adv Mgr:** M. Tristan, **Tel** (713)741-2841. **Pr Rev. Circ:** 1,000 (ctrl). ***Continues*** *Revista Chicano-Riquena, 0360-7860.*
Desc: Contemporary literature, poetry and art by U.S. Hispanics.
Ind/Abst Am. Humanit. Index; Book Rev. Index; Chicano Index; HAPI Hisp. Am. Period. Index; Index Am. Period. Verse; MLA Int. Bibl. Books Artic. Mod. Lang. Lit.

UK/0951-2500
AMMONITE. Issue 1 (March 1987)-. English. Twice a year. £3.50 UK; £6.00 others. Ammonite Publications, 12 Priory Mead Beuton, Somerset BA10 OD2 England. **Tel** 0749-813349. **ED** John Howard Greaves. **Bk Rev**, (Qty: 12). **Ad Acc, Adv Mgr:** John H. Greaves. **Circ:** 200.
Desc: Presents myth, image and word towards the secondary millennium.

UK
AMON HEN. **Added/Corp** Tolkien Society. (19??)-. Periodical. English. Six times a year. £15.00 UK; £17.00 Europe & Eire; £20.00 others. Tolkien Society, Flat 5 357 High Street, Cheltenham GL GL50 3HT England. **Tel** 0242 577232. **LC** PR6039.O32; Z55. **DD** 828/.9/1209. **Bk Rev. Ad Acc. Circ:** 600 (ctrl).
Desc: Dedicated to the interest in the life and works of the late J. R. R. Tolkien.
Ind/Abst Child. Lit. Abstr. (19??-).

II
AMRTAYANA. **VFOAT** Amrutayan. Periodical. Oriya (Oriya). qt. Rs3.00. QR No VII R-1 Unit-1, Bhubaneswar 751009 India. **LC** PK2574.5; .A45.

US/0734-7618
AMS ARS POETICA. [AMS ars poet.]. **VFOAT** A.M.S. Ars Poetica; Ars Poetica. No. 1 (1983)-. Monographic series. English. ir. Price varies per volume. AMS Press Inc., 56 East 13th Street, New York NY 10003. **Tel** (212)777-4700, FAX (212)995-5413, telex 710 581 2302.
Desc: Covers theories of literature, historical poetics, prosody, narrative theory, rhetoric, modes of reading and exegesis, the nature of metaphors and fictions and their relation to theology, philosophy, ideology and science.
Ind/Abst MLA Int. Bibl. Books Artic. Mod. Lang. Lit.

●US/1058-5915
AMS HENRY JAMES STUDIES. (1992)-. Monographic series. English. Price varies per volume. AMS Press Inc., 56 East 13th Street, New York NY 10003. **Tel** (212)777-4700, FAX (212)995-5413, telex 710 581 2302.

●US/1058-2371
AMS INTERNATIONAL STUDIES. (1992)-. Monographic series. English. Price varies per volume. AMS Press Inc., 56 East 13th Street, New York NY 10003. **Tel** (212)777-4700, FAX (212)995-5413, telex 710 581 2302.

●US/1059-5406
AMS STUDIES IN 19TH CENTURY LITERATURE AND CULTURE. **VFOAT** AMS Studies in Nineteenth Century Literature and Culture; Studies in 19th Century Literature and Culture; Studies in Nineteenth Century Literature and Culture. (1992)-. Monographic series. English. Price varies per volume. AMS Press Inc., 56 East 13th Street, New York NY 10003. **Tel** (212)777-4700, FAX (212)995-5413, telex 710 581 2302.

US/1045-6023
AMS STUDIES IN GERMAN LITERATURE AND CULTURE. [AMS stud. Ger. lit. cult.]. (1991)-. Monographic series. English. AMS Press Inc., 56 East 13th Street, New York NY 10003. **Tel** (212)777-4700, FAX (212)995-5413, telex 710 581 2302. **DD** 830.

US/0270-2983
AMS STUDIES IN MODERN LITERATURE. [AMS stud. mod. lit.]. **VFOAT** A.M.S. Studies in Modern Literature; Studies in Modern Literature. (19??)-. Monographic series. English. Price varies per volume. AMS Press Inc., 56 East 13th Street, New York NY 10003. **Tel** (212)777-4700, FAX (212)995-5413, telex 710 581 2302.
Desc: Contains volumes on subjects such as social criticism in the fiction of Bernard Malamud, Edward Albee, Ezra Pound, Thornton Wilder, and essays on the realistic imagination.
Ind/Abst MLA Int. Bibl. Books Artic. Mod. Lang. Lit.

US/0196-6561
AMS STUDIES IN THE EIGHTEENTH CENTURY. [AMS stud. eighteenth century]. **VFOAT** Studies in the Eighteenth Century. (1980)-. Monographic series. English. ir. Price varies per volume. AMS Press Inc., 56 East 13th Street, New York NY 10003. **Tel** (212)777-4700, FAX (212)995-5413, telex 710 581 2302.
Desc: Series covering literary works from the eighteenth century.
Ind/Abst MLA Int. Bibl. Books Artic. Mod. Lang. Lit.

US/0196-657X
AMS STUDIES IN THE NINETEENTH CENTURY. [AMS stud. ninet. century]. No. 1 (1980)-. Monographic series. English. ir. Price varies per volume. AMS Press Inc., 56 East 13th Street, New York NY 10003. **Tel** (212)777-4700, FAX (212)995-5413, telex 710 581 2302. **ED** C Harvington and M Barnett.
Desc: Contains volumes on Wilkie Collins, Matthew Arnold, and Charles Dickens as well as others.
Ind/Abst MLA Int. Bibl. Books Artic. Mod. Lang. Lit.

NE/0304-6257
AMSTERDAMER BEITRAEGE ZUR NEUEREN GERMANISTIK. [Amst. Beitr. neueren Ger.]. Vol. 1 (1972)-. Monographic series. German. ir (2 issues). Price varies per volume. Editions Rodopi BV, Keizersgracht 302-304, 1016 Ex Amsterdam Netherlands. **Tel** 011 31 20 6227507, FAX 011 31 20 380948. **LC** PT9; .A47.
Desc: German literature.
Ind/Abst MLA Int. Bibl. Books Artic. Mod. Lang. Lit.

NE/0169-0221
AMSTERDAMER PUBLIKATIONEN ZUR SPRACHE UND LITERATUR. [Amst. Publ. Sprache Lit.]. Vol. 1 (1973)-. Monographic series. German. ir. Price varies per volume. Editions Rodopi BV, Keizersgracht 302-304, 1016 Ex Amsterdam Netherlands. **Tel** 011 31 20 6227507, FAX 011 31 20 380948. **ED** Glenn R. Cuomo. **LC** UNC.
Desc: Monographs in literature, written mainly in German.
Ind/Abst MLA Int. Bibl. Books Artic. Mod. Lang. Lit.

CC
AN-HUI WEN HSUEH. **VFOAT** Anhui Wenxue. (198?)-. Periodical. Chinese. mo. **(Subscription address:** China International Book Trading Corporation, PO Box 399, Library Service Department, Beijing 100044 People's Republic of China.**)** ***Continues*** *Wen Hsueh (Ho-Fei Shih, China).*
Desc: Covers Chinese literature.

II
ANAHUTA. Periodical. Hindi (Hindi). Rs5.00. Anahuta Phorama, 100 Satya Niketana, Nayi Dilli 110021 India. **LC** PK2030; .A46.

US/8755-3910
ANAIS (LOS ANGELES, CALIF.). (ANAIS.). [Anais]. **Added/Corp** Anais Nin Foundation. Vol. 1 (1983)-. Periodical. English. an. $7.50 US; $8.50 other. Anais Nin Foundation, 2335 Hidalgo Avenue, Los Angeles CA 90039. **Tel** (213)665-5017. **(Subscription address:** Anais Nin Foundation, 2335 Hidalgo Avenue, Los Angeles, CA 90039**) ED** Gunther Stuhlmann. **DD** 818. cum. index. **Bk Rev. Circ:** 1,000.
Desc: A critical, literary-biographical journal devoted to Anais Nin and her circle, including Henry Miller, Otto Rank, etc. Covers the literary life in Paris in the 1920s, later in the U.S., psychoanalysis, film, and foreign literatures.
Ind/Abst Am. Humanit. Index; MLA Int. Bibl. Books Artic. Mod. Lang. Lit.

RM/0379-7899
ANALELE STIINTIFICE ALE UNIVERSITATII "AL. I. CUZA" DIN IASI. SERIE NOUA. SECTIUNEA III F, LITERATURA. **Added/Corp** Universitatea "Al. I. Cuza" din Iasi. (197?)-. Romanian (English, French, Romanian and Spanish). an. DM164.00. **(Subscription address:** Kubon & Sagner, ABT Zeitschriftenimport, D 80328 Munich Germany.**) LC** PN709.R8; A5. ***Continues in part*** *Analele Stiintifice Ale Universitatii Al. I. Cuza Din Iasi. Serie Noua. Sectiunea III E, Lingvistica-Literatura.*
Ind/Abst Annu. Bibliogr. Engl. Lang. Lit.; MLA Int. Bibl. Books Artic. Mod. Lang. Lit.

RM/0068-3256
ANALELE UNIVERSITATII BUCURESTI. LIMBA SI LITERATURA ROMANA. [An. Univ. Bucur., Limba lit. rom.]. **Main/Corp** Universitatea din Bucuresti. **VFOAT** Limba si Literatura Romana. (1969)-. Periodical. Romanian (summaries and/or abstracts in French and Russian). an. DM164.00. **(Subscription address:** Kubon & Sagner, ABT Zeitschriftenimport, D 80328 Munich Germany.**) LC** PC601; .B8.
Ind/Abst MLA Int. Bibl. Books Artic. Mod. Lang. Lit.; Soc. Plann. Policy Dev. Abstr.

RM/0068-3264
ANALELE UNIVERSITATII BUCURESTI : LITERATURA UNIVERSALA SI COMPARATA. [An. Univ. Bucur., Lit. univers. comp.]. **Main/Corp** Universitatea din Bucuresti. **Added/Corp** Universitatea din Bucuresti. **VFOAT** Literatura Universala Si Comparata. Vol. 18 (1969)-. Periodical. Romanian (French and German; summaries and/or abstracts in English, Italian, Russian and Spanish). sa. **LC** PN9; .B8. ***Continues in part*** *Analele Universitatii Bucurest. Seria Stiinte Sociale. Filologie.*
Ind/Abst Am. Hist. Life (1969-1974); MLA Int. Bibl. Books Artic. Mod. Lang. Lit.

RM
ANALELE UNIVERSITATII DIN GALATI. FASCICULA XIII. Bulletin. Romanian (English and French). an. Price varies. Redactia Analelor, 6200 Galati, Str Domneasca Nr. 47 Romania. **Tel** 40 93 413602, FAX 40 93 412328.

SP/0569-9878
ANALES CERVANTINOS. [An. cervant.]. **Added/Corp** Instituto "Miguel de Cervantes.". Vol. 1, (1951)-. Academic Scholarly Publication. Spanish. an (Dec.). $45.91. Puvill Libros SA, Boters 10 Y Paja 29, 08002 Barcelona Spain. **Tel** 011 34 3 3181848. **Bk Rev.**
Desc: A collection of scholarly monographs on Cervantes, his work and the totality of his physical, historical and spiritual world.
Ind/Abst MLA Int. Bibl. Books Artic. Mod. Lang. Lit.

US/0272-1635
ANALES DE LA LITERATURA ESPANOLA CONTEMPORANEA. [Anal. lit. esp. contemp.]. **Added/Corp** Society of Spanish and Spanish-American Studies. **VFOAT** ALEC. Vol. 6 (1981)-. Academic Scholarly Publication. English (Spanish). tq. $60.00 (one year), $114.00 (two years), institution; $23.00 (one yera), $32.00 (two year), individual. Society of Spanish and Spanish-American Studies, Department of Spanish and Portuguese, University of Colorado, Campus Box 278, Boulder CO 80309-0278. **Tel** (303)492-7308, FAX (303)492-3699. **ED** Luis Gonzalez-del-Valle. **LC** PQ6144; .A53. **DD** 860/.9. **Bk Rev. Pr Rev. Circ:** 1,000. available on microfilm and microfiche from University Microfilms International (UMI). Documents available from The Genuine Article. ***Formed by the union of*** *Anales de la Narrativa Espanola Contemporanea, 0270-6334* ***and*** *Journal of Spanish Studies: Twentieth Century, 0092-1807.*
Desc: Scholarly articles studying all aspects of twentieth century Spanish literature (from Modernismo and the Generation of 1898). Book reviews, bibliographies and panoramic studies are also standard features.
Ind/Abst Arts Humanit. Citation Index [Full Cov.]; Curr. Contents Arts Humanit.; MLA Int. Bibl. Books Artic. Mod. Lang. Lit.; Res. Alert [Full Cov.].

SP
ANALES DE LITERATURA HISPANOAMERICANA. **Added/Corp** Universidad Complutense de Madrid. Catedra de Literatura Hispanoamericana. (1972)-. Spanish. an. $22.00. Editorial Complutense, Donoso Cortes 65 1RA Planta, 28003 Madrid Spain. **Tel** 011 34 1 3946372. **ED** Luis Sainz de Medrano. **LC** PQ7081.A1; A5. **Bk Rev. Pr Rev.** ctrl circ.
Desc: Critical articles on Spanish American literature. Also includes book reviews, information on doctoral theses and bibliography of works published in Spain on this field.
Ind/Abst HAPI Hisp. Am. Period. Index; MLA Int. Bibl. Books Artic. Mod. Lang. Lit.

CU/1017-8937
ANALES DEL CARIBE. **See** Humanities.

RU/0202-2435
ANALIZ STILEI ZARUBEZHNOI KHUDOZHESTVENNOI I NAUCHNOI LITERATURY. **See** Linguistics.

US/0362-7403
ANALOG ANNUAL. 1975-. English. an. $1.50. Pyramid Books, 919 Third Avenue, New York NY 10022. **LC** PS648.S3; A52. **DD** 808.83/876/05. **UDC** 860(7/8).

US/1059-2113
ANALOG SCIENCE FICTION & FACT. [Analog sci. fict. fact]. **VFOAT** Analog; Analog Science Fiction Science Fact; Analog Science Fiction/Science Fact. Vol. 111, No. 13 (Nov. 1991)-. Periodical. English. Fifteen times a year. $39.97 (one year), $74.94 (two year), $119.91 (three year). Dell Publishing Company Inc., 1540 Broadway, 9th Floor, New York NY 10036-4021. **Tel** (212)782-8532, FAX (212)782-8338. **(Subscription address:** CDS Agency Hard Copy, PO Box 4966, Des Moines IA 50340.**) LC** PZ1.A1; A48; PN6120.95.S33. **DD** 823/.0876/05. Documents available from Magazine Collection. ***Continues*** *Analog Science Fiction/Science Fact, 0161-2328.*
Ind/Abst Acad. Search (Jan. 1994-); Book Rev. Index; Expand. Acad. Index (1991-); Gen. Period. Index (1991-); Gen. Sci. Source (Jul. 1993-); INFO-SOUTH Abstr.; Mag. Index Plus (1991-); Mag. Search; Mid. Search (Jul. 1993-); Sci. Fict. Fantasy Book Rev. Index; Mag. Index.

II
ANANDA PATRIKA. V. 1, No. 1 (May/June 84)-. Periodical. Marathi (Marathi). bm. Rs3.00. Shankarrao Hatole, Anand Book Depot Jaisinghpura, Aurangabad 431004 India. **LC** PK2412.5; .A53.

SP
ANDRADE : REVISTA TRIMESTRAL DE POESIA. **VFOAT** Andrade. Spanish (Portuguese). 3.000ptas Spain; 6.000ptas Europe; 5.000ptas other. Editorial El Paisaje, Entre los Rios 10, 24760 Castrocalbon Leon Spain. **Bk Rev. Ad Acc.** ctrl circ.

US/0743-2410
ANDREJ BELYJ SOCIETY NEWSLETTER, THE. **See** Literature-Abstracting, Bibliographies and Statistics.

IC
ANDVARI. 1.- Vol.; 1874-. Icelandic. **UDC** 839.59. cum. index.
Ind/Abst Annu. Bibliogr. Engl. Lang. Lit.

US/0899-5273
ANELLO CHE NON TIENE, L'. **Added/Corp** Istituto Italiano di Cultura (Chicago, Ill.). Vol. 1, No. 1 (Fall 1988)-. Periodical. Italian (English). Twice a year. $25.00 (institutions), $15.00 (individuals) US; $30.00 (institutions), $20.00 (individuals) other. Anello Che Non Tiene / Italian Department, PO Box 4067, Yale St, New Haven CT 06520. **Tel** (203)432-7227. **ED** Ernesto Livorni. **LC** PQ4001; .A59. **DD** 850.9/0005. **Bk Rev**, (Qty: 10). **Ad Acc. Circ:** 300 (ctrl).
Desc: Covers modern Italian literature.
Ind/Abst MLA Int. Bibl. Books Artic. Mod. Lang. Lit.

DK/0105-9963
ANGLICA ET AMERICANA. **See** Linguistics.

GW/0179-1389
ANGLISTISCHE FORSCHUNGEN. **See** Linguistics.

SZ/0263-7383
ANNALES BENJAMIN CONSTANT. No. 1-. French (English, German and Italian). an. 45.00F Switzerland; $25.00 US. Institut Benjamin Constant, Bibliotheque Universitaire, CH-1015 Lausanne-Dorigny Switzerland. **Tel** 021/692.32.20, FAX 021/692.32.30. **LC** PQ2211.C24; A88. **DD** 848/.609. **UDC** 840. **Bk Rev. Ad Acc.** available on diskette. ***Continues*** *Cahiers Benjamin Constant;* ***Absorbed*** *Association Benjamin Constant. Bulletin de l'Association Benjamin Constant.*
Desc: Features articles, unpublished correspondence and documents, book reviews and a bibliography of Constant scholarship.
Ind/Abst Romant. Move.

CM
ANNALES DE LA FACULTE DES LETTRES ET SCIENCES HUMAINES SERIE LETTRES / UNIVERSITE DE YAOUNDE. **VFOAT** Serie Lettres; Annals of the Faculty of Letters and Social Sciences. Vol. 1, No. 1 (1985)-. Periodical. English (French). sa. ***Continues in part*** *Annales de la Faculte des Lettres et Sciences Humaines de Yaounde.*

SZ/0259-6563
ANNALES DE LA SOCIETE JEAN-JACQUES ROUSSEAU. [Ann. Soc. Jean-Jacques Rousseau]. (1905)-. Periodical. French. ir. 120.00F. Mr. Thierry Kern Treasurer, 4 rue de Saussure Darier Hents, CH 1204 Geneva Switzerland. **Tel** (22) 310

36 70. **ED** Charles Wirz. **UDC** 84. **Bk Rev.**
Desc: Studies on various aspects of life and works of Jean-Jacques Rousseau.

FR/0399-0443
ANNALES DU CENTRE DE RECHERCHES SUR L'AMERIQUE ANGLOPHONE. **Main/Corp** Centre de Recherches Sur l'Amerique Anglophone. **Added/Corp** Universite de Bordeaux III. Centre de Recherches Sur l'Amerique Anglophone. Maison des Sciences de l'Homme d'Aquitaine. **VFOAT** Annales du CRAA; Annales du C.R.A.A. (1972)-. Academic Scholarly Publication. French (English). an. 120.00F. C.L.A.N., Center de Recherches Sur, l'Amerique Anglophone Maison des Science de, l'Homme d'Aquitaine Esplanade des Antilles Domaine Universitaire, 33405 Talence Cedex France. **Tel** 56846800, FAX 56846810. **ED** Y. C. Grandjeat and Christian Lerat. **LC** F1022; .A56. **DD** 971/.005. **Circ:** 300.
Desc: Emigration and immigration ethnic literature and civilization in the United States.

FR/0547-2016
ANNALES LITTERAIRES. **Main/Corp** Universite de Nantes. (1967)-. Monographic series. French. ir. Price varies per volume. Societe Edition Belles Lettres, 95 Boulevard Raspail, 75006 Paris France. **Tel** 011 33 1 45487055, FAX 011 33 1 45449288, telex 200577.

IT/0392-095X
ANNALI DELLA SCUOLA NORMALE SUPERIORE DI PISA, CLASSE DI LETTERE E FILOSOFIA. [Ann. Sc. norm. super. Pisa, Cl. lett. filos.]. **Added/Corp** Scuola Normale Superiore (Italy). Classe di Lettere e Filosofia. (1971)-. Periodical. French (Italian and German). qt. L8000.00 Italy; L150000 other. Scuola Normale Superiore, Piazza Dei Cavalieri 7, I 56126 Pisa Italy. **Tel** 011 39 50509111. **LC** AS222; .P45. **DD** 065/.55. ***Continues*** *Scuola Normale Superiore (Italy). Annali ... Lettere, Storia e Filosofia.*
Ind/Abst Am. Hist. Life (1955-); ARTbibliogr. Mod. (1984-); BHA : Biblio. Hist. Art; MLA Int. Bibl. Books Artic. Mod. Lang. Lit.

IT/0390-0576
ANNALI DELL'ISTITUTO DI LINGUE E LETTERATURE GERMANICHE. ***Suspended.*** **Main/Corp** Universita di Parma. Istituto di Lingue e Letterature Germaniche. **Added/Corp** Universita di Parma. Istituto di Lingue e Letterature Germaniche. Vol. 1 (1973)-(Sept. 1990). English (Italian and German). Bulzoni Editore Srl, Via dei Liburni 14, 00185 Rome Italy. **Tel** 011 39 6 445-5207, FAX 011 39 6 445-0355. **LC** PF3009; .A56.

IT
ANNALI DELL'ISTITUTO UNIVERSITARIO ORIENTALE DI NAPOLI, SEMINARIO DI STUDI DEL MONDO CLASSICO, SEZIONE FILOLOGICO-LETTERARIA. **See** Linguistics.

IT
ANNALI DI CA' FOSCARI. **VFOAT** Annali Della Facolta di Lingue e Letterature Straniere di Ca Foscari. Vol. 1, (1962)-. Periodical. Italian. Three times a year. L150000 Italy; L200000 other. Paideia Editrice, Via Corsica 130, 25125 Brescia Italy. **Tel** 11 39 30 22094, FAX 011 39 30 223269.
Ind/Abst MLA Int. Bibl. Books Artic. Mod. Lang. Lit.; Middle East J.

US/0741-7527
ANNALI D'ITALIANISTICA. [Ann. ital.]. **Added/Corp** University of Notre Dame. Dept. of Modern and Classical Languages. Italian Section. University of North Carolina at Chapel Hill. Dept of Romance Languages. **VFOAT** Adl. Vol. 1 (1983)-. Periodical. English (Italian). an (Dec.). $29.00 US & Canada; $33.00 others. Annali d'Italianistica, University of North Carolina, CB 3170 328 Del Hall Cervigni, Chapel Hill NC 27599-3170. **Tel** (919)962-2032. **ED** Dino S. Cervigni. **LC** PQ4001; .A6. **DD** 850/.9. **Bk Rev. Ad Acc. Circ:** 550.
Desc: Promotes the study of Italian literature in its cultural context. Monographic in nature, the journal is receptive to a variety of topics and critical approaches.
Ind/Abst MLA Int. Bibl. Books Artic. Mod. Lang. Lit.; Romant. Move.

IT
ANNALI. SEZIONE GERMANICA. **Added/Corp** Istituto Universitario Orientale (Naples, Italy). **VFOAT** Sezione Germanica; AION Sezione Germanica; A.I.O.N. Sezione Germanica. (1991)-. Periodical. Italian (German). ir. L60000 Italy; L80000 others. Herder Editrice e Libreria SRL, Piazza Montecitorio 117-120, 00186 Rome Italy. **Tel** 011 39 6 679 4628, FAX 011 39 6 678 4751. **LC** PD9; .A566. ***Formed by the union of*** *Annali. Studi Tedeschi, 0392-6532* ***and*** *Annali. Filologia Germanica, 0392-6540 Aion-n.*

FR/0084-6473
ANNEE BALZACIENNE, L'. [Annee balzac.]. **Added/Corp** Groupe d'Etudes Balzaciennes. (1960-79); New Series No 1 (1980)-. French. ir. 270.00F. Groupe d Etudes Balzaciennes, 47 rue Raynovard, F-75016 Paris France. **LC** PQ2177.A2; A5. ***Supersedes*** *Etudes Balzaciennes.*
Ind/Abst MLA Int. Bibl. Books Artic. Mod. Lang. Lit.; Romant. Move.

FR/0183-9950
ANNEE ... DE LA SCIENCE-FICTION ET DU FANTASTIQUE, L'. 1977-1978-. French. an. Julliard, 8 rue Garanciere, Paris France. **LC** P96.S34; A55. **DD** 808.83/876. **UDC** 82-311.9.

CN/0849-3928
ANNUAIRE - UNION DES ECRIVAINES ET ECRIVAINS QUEBECOIS. **See** Journalism.

UK/0066-3786
ANNUAL BIBLIOGRAPHY OF ENGLISH LANGUAGE AND LITERATURE. **See** Literature-Abstracting, Bibliographies and Statistics.

UK
ANNUAL FOLIO LITERARY DINNER & DEBATE. **VFOAT** Folio Literary Dinner & Debate; Annual Folio Literary Dinner and Debate; Folio Literary Dinner and Debate. 3rd-. Monographic series. English. an. Price varies per volume. Folio Society Ltd, 202 Great Suffolk Street, London SE1 1PR England. ***Continues*** *Folio Debate.*

US/1047-8981
ANNUAL WORLD'S BEST SF, THE. [Annu. world's best sci. fict.]. **VFOAT** Donald A. Wollheim Presents the Annual World's Best SF. **VAT** Annual World's Best Science Fiction. 1972 -. English. an. Daw Books INC, 1301 Avenue of the Americas, New York NY 10019. **ED** D A Wollheim. **DD** 808. **UDC** 82-311.9. ***Continues*** *World's Best Science Fiction.*

US/0272-4359
ANOTHER CHICAGO MAGAZINE. **VFOAT** ACM. (Spring 1977)-. Periodical. English. Twice a year (April and October). $20.00. Left Field Press, 3709 North Kenmore, Chicago IL 60613. **Tel** (312)248-7665. **ED** Barry Silesky. **LC** PS580; .A53. **DD** 811.008/005. **Bk Rev**, (Qty: 20). **Ad Acc, Adv Mgr:** Sara Skolnik, **Tel** (708)869-3235. **Circ:** 2,500.
Desc: Contemporary Poetry, fiction, essays, book reviews, and 8 page art folio.
Ind/Abst Am. Humanit. Index; Index Am. Period. Verse.

US/0895-769X
ANQ (LEXINGTON, KY.). (ANQ.). [ANQ]. **Added/Corp** University Press of Kentucky. University of Kentucky. Dept. of English. **VAT** American Notes Queries. Vol. 1, No. 1 (Jan. 1988)-. Periodical. English. Four times a year (Jan., Apr., July, Oct.). $67.00 (institutional); $38.00 (individual). Heldref Publications, 1319 Eighteenth Street Northwest, Washington DC 20036-1802. **Tel** (202)296-6267, (800)365-9753, FAX (202)296-5149. **LC** PE1; .A57. **DD** 820/.9. Index available. **Bk Rev**, (Qty: 29). **Ad Acc. Pr Rev. Circ:** 550. Documents available from The Genuine Article, UMI Article Clearinghouse. ***Continues*** *American Notes & Queries, 0003-0171.*
Desc: Notes and short articles based on new research in American and English language and literature, films and linguistics.
Ind/Abst Abstr. Engl. Stud.; Acad. Search (July 1993-); Am. Humanit. Index (1988-); Annu. Bibliogr. Engl. Lang. Lit.; Arts Humanit. Citation Index [Full Cov.]; Book Rev. Index; Expand. Acad. Index (1989-); Humanit. Index; Humanit. Source (Jul. 1993-); INFO-SOUTH Abstr.; MLA Int. Bibl. Books Artic. Mod. Lang. Lit.; Newsp. Period. Abstr. (1988-); Res. Alert [Full Cov.].

FR/0751-7580
ANTARES LA VALETTE. [Antares Valette]. (198?)-. Periodical. French. qt. 150.00F France; 120.00F other. Antares, La Magali Chemin Calabro, 83160 la Valette France. **Tel** 94 75 01 86. **UDC** 82-3. Index available. cum. index. **Bk Rev. Ad Acc. Circ:** 3,500.
Desc: Dedicated to international science fiction and fantasy; in each issue no language can be represented by more than one story. Features fiction and articles, and some art.

IT
ANTEREM. Periodical. Italian (French and English). sa. L36.000. Ed Anterem, c/o F Ermini, Via Cantarane 10, 37129 Verona Italy.

FR/0767-2055
ANTIGONE. **See** Photography and Video.

NZ/0113-2415
ANTIPODAS : JOURNAL OF HISPANIC STUDIES OF THE UNIVERSITY OF AUCKLAND. **Added/Corp** University of Auckland. No. 1 (Dec. 1988)-. Spanish (English). an. $30.00 (institutions), $25.00 (individuals), North America and Europe; 30.00NZ$ (institutions), 25.00NZ$ (individuals) Australia and New Zealand. Antipodas, Spanish Section, University of Auckland, Private Bag Auckland New Zealand. **Tel** 3 737-999, FAX 64 9 3737449. **ED** Dr. M.S. Harvey, Prof. R.C. Boland. **Bk Rev. Ad Acc. Pr Rev. Circ:** 500.
Ind/Abst MLA Int. Bibl. Books Artic. Mod. Lang. Lit.

US/0893-5580
ANTIPODES (BROOKLYN, NEW YORK, N.Y.). (ANTIPODES : A NORTH AMERICAN JOURNAL OF AUSTRALIAN LITERATURE : THE PUBLICATION OF THE AMERICAN ASSOCIATION OF AUSTRALIAN LITERARY STUDIES.). [Antipodes]. **Added/Corp** American Association of Australian Literary Studies. Edward A. Clark Center for Australian Studies. Vol. 1, No. 1 (Mar. 1987)-. Periodical. English. Twice a year (June & Dec.). $20.00 (individuals); $35.00 (institutions). American Association of Australian Literary Studies, 190 6th Avenue, Brooklyn NY 11217. **Tel** (718)789-5826, FAX (718)482-5599. **ED** Robert Ross. **LC** PR9600; .A57. **DD** 820.9/994. **Bk Rev**, (Qty: 50). **Ad Acc, Adv Mgr:** M. Arkin. **Circ:** 600 (ctrl).
Desc: Features creative writing in the form of poetry, stories and essays by Australian writers and essays about Australian literature.
Ind/Abst APAIS, Aust. Public Aff. Inf. Ser. (1993-); Film Lit. Index (19??-); MLA Int. Bibl. Books Artic. Mod. Lang. Lit.

AG
ANTOLOGIA. (Spring 1974)-. Periodical. Spanish. qt. Ediciones Figaro, Av Ceballos 274, Chivilcoy Argentina. **LC** PQ7083; .A68. **DD** 860.

US/0003-5319
ANTUS. ***Ceased.*** [Anteus]. **VAT** Anteaus. (Summer 1970)-(Sept. 1994). Periodical. English. sa. Ecco Press, 100 Broad Street, Hopewell NJ 08525. **Tel** (609)466-4748. **ED** Daniel Halpern. **LC** PR1098; .A5. **DD** 820/.8.
Desc: An international literary magazine which features an array of essays, fiction, poetry and other works from some of the world's most respected authors.
Ind/Abst Humanit. Index; Index Am. Period. Verse; INFO-SOUTH Abstr.; Mag. Search.

SP
ANUARI DE FILOLOGIA. SECCIO F, ESTUDIOS DE LENGUA Y LITERATURA ESPANOLAS / UNIVERSITAT DE BARCELONA, FACULTAT DE FILOLOGIA. **See** Linguistics.

CK
ANUARIO BIBLIOGRAFICO COLOMBIANO "RUBEN PEREZ ORTIZ". **Added/Corp** Instituto Caro y Cuervo. Departamento de Bibliografia. **VFOAT** Anuario Bibliografico Colombiano. (1963)-. Spanish. an. $20.00 (latest edition). Instituto Caro y Cuervo, Apartado 51502, Bogota Colombia. **Tel** 011 57 1 2557753, FAX 011 57 1 2170243. ***Continues*** *Anuario Bibliografico Colombiano, 0570-393X.*
Desc: Specializes in philological and linguistic themes.

US/1044-0623
ANUARIO BIBLIOGRAFICO DE HISTORIA DEL PENSAMIENTO IBERO E IBEROAMERICANO. ***Suspended.*** [Anu. bibliogr. hist. pensam. Ibero iberoam.]. **Added/Corp** University of Georgia. Center for Latin American Studies. **VFOAT** Anuario Bibliografico. (1986)-Suspended (Vol.5, 19??). Periodical. Spanish. an. Georgia Ser. Hispanic Thought, Moore College, Department of Romance Languages, Athens GA 30602. **Tel** (706)542-3123. **LC** Z7129.S8; A58; B4561. **DD** 016.196/1.

PE
ANUARIO BIBLIOGRAFICO PERUANO. **See** Literature-Abstracting, Bibliographies and Statistics.

MX/0185-1373
ANUARIO DE LETRAS (MEXICO). (ANUARIO DE LETRAS : REVISTA DE LA FACULTAD DE FILOSOFIA Y LETRAS.). [Anu. let.]. **Added/Corp** Universidad Nacional Autonoma de Mexico. Facultad de Filosofia y Letras. Vol. 1 (1961)-. Spanish. an. $7.00. Unam Instituto Investiga Filologicas, Ciudad Universitaria, 04510 Mexico DF Mexico. **Tel** 011 52 5 6227487, 011 52 5 6650411. **LC** PN508; .A65. **DD** 809.
Ind/Abst Am. Hist. Life (1965-); HAPI Hisp. Am. Period. Index.

US/0890-6408
APALACHEE QUARTERLY, THE. (19??)-. Periodical. English. Four times a year. $20.00 (latest issues). Apalachee Quarterly, PO Box 20106, Tallahassee FL 32304. **Tel** (904)877-7411. **ED** Barbara Hamby, Pamela Ball, Claudia Johnson, Bruce Boehrer and Paul McCall. **DD** 808. **Bk Rev. Ad Acc. Circ:** 500.
Desc: Publishes fiction, poetry and essays.
Ind/Abst Am. Humanit. Index.

US/0363-2318
APPALACHIAN HERITAGE. [Appalachian heritage]. Vol. 1 (Winter 1973)-. Periodical. English. qt. $18.00 (one year), $34.00 (two year), $50.00 (three year). Appalachian Heritage, Hutchins Library, Berea College, Berea KY 40404. **Tel** (606)986-9341 Ext. 5260, FAX (606)986-9494. **ED** Sidney Saylor Farr. **LC** PS553; .A66. **DD** 810/.8/0975. **Bk Rev. Circ:** 1,000. available on

microfilm and microfiche from University Microfilms International (UMI).
Desc: A publication containing fiction, poetry, essays, interviews, articles, and book reviews about the Southern Appalachian region and its people.

CN/1183-3785
APPLESEED QUARTERLY. (APPLESEED QUARTERLY : JOURNAL OF THE STORYTELLERS SCHOOL OF TORONTO.). [Appleseed q.]. **Added/Corp** Storytellers School of Toronto. **VFOAT** Apple Seed Quarterly. Vol. 1, No. 1 (Feb. 1991)-. Periodical. English. qt. 20.00Can$. Storytellers School of Toronto, 412A College Street, Toronto Ontario M5T 1T3 Canada. **Tel** (416)924-8625. **ED** Lorne Brown (Editor's address: 44 Wentworth Avenue, Willowdale Ontario, M2N 1T7 Canada, phone: (416)225-1547). **DD** 808.5/43/05. **Bk Rev**, (Qty: 4). **Ad Acc. Circ:** 500 (ctrl).
Desc: Formed to promote and teach the art of storytelling, and provide resources towards this aim.

US/1059-1133
APPROACHES TO TEACHING WORLD LITERATURE. [Approaches teach. world lit.]. **Added/Corp** Modern Language Association of America. (1986)-. Monographic series. English. ir. Price varies per volume. Modern Language Association of America, 10 Astor Place, New York NY 10003-6981. **Tel** (212)614-6382, FAX (212)477-9863. ***Continues*** *Approaches to Teaching Masterpieces of World Literature.*
Desc: Each volume surveys critical materials and brings together essays that apply a variety of perspectives to teaching and studying the text.

NE
APPROACHES TO TRANSLATION STUDIES. No. 1 (1970)-. Monographic series. English. ir. Price varies per volume. Humanities Press, 165 1st Avenue, Atlantic Highlands NJ 07716. **Tel** (908)872-1441, (800)221-3845, FAX (908)872-0717, telex 752233. Index available.
Desc: Scholarly monographs on translation theory and literary translation.
Ind/Abst MLA Int. Bibl. Books Artic. Mod. Lang. Lit.

NP
APUNGO. V. 1- Feb./March 2029- 1973-. Nepali (Nepali). 0.50 per issue. Loka Mana Maske, 12/76 Mills Area Koshi Anchal, Viratanagara India. **ED** Loka Mana Maske. **LC** PK2598.A2; A77.

CL
APUNTES. **Added/Corp** Universidad Catolica de Chile. Teatro de Ensayo. Departamento de Publicidad y Relaciones Publicas. Universidad Catolica de Chile. Escuela de Artes de la Comunicacion. Universidad Catolica de Chile. Escuela de Teatro. (19??)-. Periodical. Spanish. Twenty times a year. $120.00. Cieplan, Av C Colon 3494, Comuna Condes, Santiago Chile. **Tel** 56 2 2283262. **ED** Maria de la Luz Hurtado. **LC** PN508; .A7. **DD** 862/.009. Index available. cum. index. **Bk Rev. Ad Acc. Circ:** 1,000.
Desc: Dedicated to theater, it reviews the principal theatre stagings of the moment in Chile. Has permanent sections on theatre theory, research, actor's formation, book reviews. Includes many photographs on latest theatre productions.

FR/0755-883X
AR FALZ. (1933)-. French. qt. 140.00F. Editions Skol Vreizh, 20 rue de Kerscoff, 29600 Morlaix France. **Tel** 98 62 17 20, FAX 98 62 02 38. **Bk Rev.** ctrl circ. available on diskette.
Desc: Covers Breton-French language and culture.

VE
ARAISA. **Added/Corp** Centro de Estudios Latinoamericanos Romulo Gallegos. (1975)-. Spanish. an. **LC** F1401; .A73.
Ind/Abst HAPI Hisp. Am. Period. Index (19??-).

UK/0959-4213
ARAM PERIODICAL. See Linguistics.

US/0003-7583
ARARAT (NEW YORK). (ARARAT.). [Ararat]. **Added/Corp** Armenian General Benevolent Union. Vol. 1, No. 1 (Winter 1960)-. Periodical. English. Four times a year (Jan., Apr., June, Oct.). $24.00 US & Canada; $32.00 others. Armenian General Benevolent Union, 585 Saddle River Road, Saddle Brook NJ 07662. **Tel** (201)797-7600, FAX (201)797-4883. **ED** Kieran Clifford. **LC** AP2; .A5959. Index available. cum. index. **Bk Rev. Ad Acc. Circ:** 2,200 (ctrl). available on microfilm and microfiche from University Microfilms International (UMI).
Desc: A literary publication covering Armenian subject matter including fiction, history, poetry, art, film, theatre, religion, dance, cooking, costume, and past and present cultural traditions.
Ind/Abst Am. Bibliogr. Slavic East Europ. Stud.

US/0271-0730
ARBA SICULA. Vol. 1-. Periodical. Multiple languages (English and Sicilian). sa. $25.00. Saint Finbar, 138 Bay 20th Street, Brooklyn NY 11214. **Tel** (718)998-5990. **ED** Gaetano Cipolla. **LC** PQ5902.S5; A73. **DD** 850/.8/09458. **UDC** 850. Index available. **Bk Rev. Circ:** 1,500 (ctrl).
Desc: Proverbs, poetry, anecdotes, historical commentary; both contemporary and classical Sicilian; Pinguistics; Narrative; fiction, etc.

CN/0714-5926
ARCADE (MONTREAL). (ARCADE.). [Arcade]. No. 1 (1982)-. Periodical. French. Three times a year. 30.00Can$ (institutions), 24.00Can$ (individuals) Canada; 40.00Can$ other. SODEP, 815 rue Ontario Est, Bureau 202, Montreal Quebec H21 1P1 Canada. **Tel** (514)523-7724, (514)525-2606, FAX (514)523-9401. **DD** C840/.8/0054.
Ind/Abst Women Stud. Abstr.

GW/0003-7982
ARCADIA. [Arcadia]. Vol. 1 (1966)-. Periodical. English (French and German). Three times a year. $135.00. Walter de Gruyter Inc., PO Box 303421, D 10728 Berlin Germany. **Tel** 011 49 30 260050, FAX 011 49 30 26005251. **(Subscription address:** US and Canada/ 200 Saw Mill River Road, Hawthorne, NY 10532) **LC** PN851; .A7. **DD** 809. **[CCC]. Bk Rev. Ad Acc. Circ:** 800. Documents available from The Genuine Article.
Desc: Publishes papers on studies of comparative literature.
Ind/Abst Arts Humanit. Citation Index [Full Cov.]; BHA : Biblio. Hist. Art; MLA Int. Bibl. Books Artic. Mod. Lang. Lit.; Res. Alert [Full Cov.].

GW
ARCHIPELAG : A. See Political Science-Socialism, Communism, Anarchism, Utopianism.

AU
ARCHIV FUER LITERATUR UND VOLKSDICHTUNG. **Added/Corp** Verband Deutscher Vereine fuer Volksunde. (1949)-. Periodical. German. ir. **LC** PN504; .A73.

GW/0003-8970
ARCHIV FUER DAS STUDIUM DER NEUEREN SPRACHEN UND LITERATUREN (1961). See Linguistics.

FR/0003-9675
ARCHIVES DES LETTRES MODERNES. [Arch. lett. mod.]. No. 1 (March 1957)-. Monographic series. French. ir. Price varies per volume. Lettres Modernes Minard, 45 rue de Saint Andre, 14123 Fleury Surrey Orne France. **Tel** 011 33 31 844706. **LC** UNC.
Desc: Modern French literature.
Ind/Abst Annu. Bibliogr. Engl. Lang. Lit.; MLA Int. Bibl. Books Artic. Mod. Lang. Lit.; Romant. Move.

RU
ARENA (MOSCOW, R.S.F.S.R.). (ARENA.). (1987)-. Russian. an. **LC** PG3283; .A73.

FR/0995-2187
ARGOS LE PERREUX. (ARGOS). (1989)-. Periodical. French. Three times a year. 90.00F France; 150.00F other. CRDP, 20 rue Daniel Casanova, 94170 Le Perr S Marne France. **Tel** 011 31 1 48727070. **UDC** 027.8(443.61).

CN/0004-1327
ARIEL. [Ariel]. **Added/Corp** University of Calgary. Vol. 1 (Jan. 1970)-. Academic Scholarly Publication. English. Four times a year (Jan., Apr., July, Oct.). 18.00Can$ (individuals); 27.00Can$ (institutions). University of Calgary Press, 2500 University Drive Northwest, Calgary Alberta T2N 1N4 Canada. **Tel** (403)220-7578. **ED** Ian Adam. **LC** PR1; .R352. **DD** 820.9. **Bk Rev. Ad Acc. Circ:** 900. Documents available from The Genuine Article, UMI Article Clearinghouse. ***Supersedes*** *Review of English Literature.*
Desc: Gives global representation to literatures in the English language through critical and scholarly studies, original poems and poems in translation. Particular emphasis is placed on comparative studies.
Ind/Abst Abstr. Engl. Stud.; Acad. Search (July 1993-); Arts Humanit. Citation Index [Full Cov.]; Can. Period. Index (1985-19??); Expand. Acad. Index (1989-); Humanit. Index; Humanit. Source (Jul. 1993-); INFO-SOUTH Abstr.; Lit. Crit. Regist. (1985-1986); Mag. Search; MLA Int. Bibl. Books Artic. Mod. Lang. Lit.; Newsp. Period. Abstr. (1991-); Res. Alert [Full Cov.]; Soc. Sci. Cit. Index [Select. Cov.].

IS/0004-1343
ARIEL (ENGLISH EDITION). (ARIEL.). [Ariel]. **Added/Corp** Israel. Misrad Ha-Huts. Mahlakah le-Kishre Tarbut u-Mada. Israel. Misrad Ha-Huts. Mahlakah le-Kishre Tarbut. Israel. Misrad Ha-Huts. Lishkah le-Kishre Tarbut. **VFOAT** Ariel. No. 1 (Jan. 1962)-. Periodical. English (French, German and Spanish). Four times a year. Ariel, 211 E 43rd Street, New York NY 10017. **Tel** (914)878-4100. **(Subscription address:** PO Box 5920, Patterson, NY 12563, telephone: (212)599-3666) **ED** Asher Weil. **LC** AP8; .A68. **DD** 052. **Bk Rev. Ad Acc. Circ:** 20,000 (ctrl). ***Supersedes*** *Cultural Events in Israel.*
Desc: Leading journal in the field of arts and culture in Israel.
Ind/Abst Index Jew. Period.; Middle East Abstr. Index; MLA Int. Bibl. Books Artic. Mod. Lang. Lit.; Romant. Move.

US/0895-8920
ARIEL (LEXINGTON, KY.). (ARIEL.). [Ariel]. **Added/Corp** Spanish and Italian Graduate Student Association (University of Kentucky). (198?)-. Periodical. English (Italian and Spanish). an. **DD** 859.
Ind/Abst MLA Int. Bibl. Books Artic. Mod. Lang. Lit.

US
ARION / BOSTON UNIVERSITY. Third Series, Vol. 1, No. 1 (Winter 1990)-. Periodical. English. Three times a year. $19.00 (individual), $35.00 (institution), $12.00 (student). Boston University / Brookline, MA, 745 Commonwealth Avenue, Room 435, Boston MA 02215. **Tel** (617)353-6480. **(Subscription address:** Arion, Office of Scholarly Publications, Boston University, 985 Commonwealth Avenue, Boston, MA 02215) **ED** Herbert Golder. Index available (in last volume of series). cum. index. **Bk Rev**, (Qty: 18). **Ad Acc, Adv Mgr:** Julie Seeger. **Circ:** 750 controlled, 2500 printed (ctrl). available on microfilm and microfiche from University Microfilms International (UMI). Documents available from The Genuine Article. ***Continues*** *Arion, 0095-5809.*
Desc: Literary essays, translations and reviews of ancient Greek and Roman culture.
Ind/Abst Am. Humanit. Index; Arts Humanit. Citation Index (19??-19??); Curr. Contents Arts Humanit.; Index Am. Period. Verse; MLA Int. Bibl. Books Artic. Mod. Lang. Lit. [Select. Cov.]; Res. Alert [Full Cov.].

●US/1059-8553
ARISTOS (TACOMA, WASH.). (ARISTOS.). [Aristos]. Vol. 1, No. 1 (Winter 1991/1992)-. Periodical. English. qt. $12.00. Penny L. Dunn, PO Box 7272, Tacoma WA 98407-0272. **DD** 810.

US/0004-1610
ARIZONA QUARTERLY, THE. [Ariz. q.]. **Added/Corp** University of Arizona. Vol. 1, (Spring 1945)-. Academic Scholarly Publication. English. Four times a year (Mar., June, Sept., Dec.). $12.00 (individuals); $16.00 (institutions). University of Arizona/ Arizona Quarterly, 541 B Main Library, Tucson AZ 85721. **Tel** (602)621-6396. **ED** Edgar A. Dryden. **LC** AP2; .A7265. **DD** 051. **Bk Rev**, (Qty: 2). **Ad Acc. Pr Rev. Circ:** 1,000. available on microfilm and microfiche from University Microfilms International (UMI).
Desc: These are scholarly articles on American literature, culture and theory.
Ind/Abst Abstr. Engl. Stud.; Am. Hist. Life (1963-); Am. Humanit. Index; Annu. Bibliogr. Engl. Lang. Lit.; Index Am. Period. Verse; Index Book Rev. Humanit.; Lit. Crit. Regist.; MLA Int. Bibl. Books Artic. Mod. Lang. Lit.; Romant. Move.; West. Hist. Q.

US/0044-8885
ARK RIVER REVIEW, THE. [Ark River rev.]. Vol. 1, (Spring 1971)-. Periodical. English. Anthony Sobin, English Department, Wichita State University, Wichita KS 67208. **LC** PS501; .A76. **DD** 810/.8/0054. **UDC** 820(73).
Ind/Abst Index Am. Period. Verse.

US/0164-6273
ARKANSAS TIMES. Periodical. English. wk. $10.00. Arkansas Times, PO Box 34010, Little Rock AR 72203. **Tel** (501)375-2985. **ED** Mel White. **Circ:** 34,697. ***Continues*** *Union Station Times.*
Ind/Abst Access (1985-?).

US
ARMCHAIR DETECTIVE, THE. (1981)-. Periodical. English. $25.00. Borgo Press, PO Box 2845, San Bernardino CA 92406. **Tel** (714)884-5813, (714)885-1161. **ED** Allen J. Hubin. **LC** PR830.D4; A75. **DD** 823/.0872/09.
Desc: A critical mystery magazine for mystery fans and academic libraries.

US/0004-217X
ARMCHAIR DETECTIVE, THE. [Armchair detect.]. Vol. 1 (1967)-. Periodical. English. Four times a year (Jan., Apr., July, Oct.). $26.00 (one year); $48.00 (two years). Armchair Detective, 129 West 56th Street, New York NY 10019. **Tel** (212)765-0902, FAX (212)265-5478. **ED** Kate Stine. **LC** PS374.D4; A75. **[CCC].** cum. index. **Bk Rev. Ad Acc. Circ:** 3,500.
Desc: Devoted to detective and mystery fiction. Short fictions, interviews, reviews, and critical articles about mystery fiction.
Ind/Abst Book Rev. Index (1986-); Film Lit. Index; MLA Int. Bibl. Books Artic. Mod. Lang. Lit.

SW/0349-053X
ARSBOK - VETENSKAPSSOCIETETEN I LUND. See Classical Studies.

US/0196-691X
ARTFUL DODGE. Vol. 1 (1979)-. Periodical. English (Multiple languages). ir. $16.00. Artful Dodge, Department of English, College of Wooster, Wooster OH 44691. **Tel** (216)262-8353. **ED** Daniel Bourne. Index available. **Bk Rev. Ad Acc. Circ:** 1,000.
Desc: Publishes new American literature plus translations from all over, especially Eastern Europe. Interviews with Borges, Laughlin, Merwin, Milosz and Sarraute.
Ind/Abst Am. Humanit. Index; Index Am. Period. Verse.

FR
ARTHUR RIMBAUD. 1- 1972-. French. 30.00F. Lettres Modernes Minard, 45 rue de Saint Andre, 14123 Fleury Surrey Orne France. **Tel** 011 33 31 844706. **LC** PN3; .R4 subser. **DD** 841/.8. **UDC** 840-1.

UK
ARTHURIAN LITERATURE. Vol. 1 (1981)-. Monographic series. English. an. price varies per volume. Boydell and Brewer Limited, PO Box 9, Woodbridge Suffolk, 1P12 3DF England. **Tel** 011 44 394 411320, FAX 011 44 394 411477. **(Subscription address:** Boydell & Brewer, PO Box 41026, Rochester NY 14604.**) LC** PN685; .A68. **DD** 809/.93351.

UK
ARTHURIAN STUDIES. Vol. 1 (1981)-. Monographic series. English. ir. Price varies per volume. Boydell and Brewer Limited, PO Box 9, Woodbridge Suffolk, 1P12 3DF England. **Tel** 011 44 394 411320, FAX 011 44 394 411477.

US/1053-3877
ARTHURIAN YEARBOOK, THE. [Arthurian yearb.]. (1991)-. Monographic series. English. ir. Price varies per volume. Garland Publishing Inc, 1000A Sherman Avenue, Hamden CT 06514. **Tel** 800-627-6273, (203)281-4487. **LC** PN686.A7; A78. **DD** 809/.93351.

US/0098-9363
ASCENT (URBANA, ILL.). (ASCENT.). Vol. 1 (1975)-. Periodical. English. Three times a year. $6.00. Ascent, PO Box 967, Urbana IL 61801. **ED** Audrey Curley (editor's phone: (217)367-5576). **LC** PS501; .A8. **DD** 810/.8/005. ctrl circ.
Ind/Abst Am. Humanit. Index; Index Am. Period. Verse.

GH/0855-000X
ASEMKA. (ASEMKA : A LITERARY JOURNAL OF THE UNIVERSITY OF CAPE COAST.). **Added/Corp** University of Cape Coast. Vol. 1, No. 1 (Jan. 1974)-. Periodical. Multiple languages (English and French). **LC** PL8009.5; .A78. **DD** 820/.9.
Ind/Abst MLA Int. Bibl. Books Artic. Mod. Lang. Lit.

JA
ASHITA: GEKKAN HAISHI. Added/Corp Nashi no Shin no Kai. (19??)-. Periodical. Japanese. ¥1000. Nashi No Shin No Kai, 14-30-704 Kami Osaki 3 Shinagawa-ku 141, Tokyo Japan. **LC** PL759.A1; A8.

XO/0571-2742
ASIAN AND AFRICAN STUDIES (BRATISLAVA, CZECHOSLOVAKIA). See History(General)-History of Asia.

AT/1035-7823
ASIAN STUDIES REVIEW. See History(General)-History of Asia.

●US/1065-2698
ASIMOV'S SCIENCE FICTION. [Asimov's sci. fict.]. Vol. 16, No. 12 & 13 (Nov. 1992)-. Periodical. English. Fifteen times a year. $39.97. Dell Publishing Company Inc., 1540 Broadway, 9th Floor, New York NY 10036-4021. **Tel** (212)782-8532, FAX (212)782-8338. **(Subscription address:** CDS Agency Hard Copy, PO Box 4966, Des Moines IA 50340.**) LC** PN6120.95.S33; I84. **DD** 813/.0876/08. ***Continues*** *Isaac Asimov's Science Fiction Magazine (New York, N.Y. : 1990), 1055-2146.*
Ind/Abst Sci. Fict. Fantasy Book Rev. Index (1992-).

IT
ASINO D'ORO, L'. (19??)-. Periodical. Italian. sa. L42000.00 Italy; L56000.00 other. Loescher Editore, Via Vittorio Amedeo 18, 10121 Turin Italy. **Tel** 011 39 11 5624622.

PR/0004-4903
ASOMANTE. (ASOMANTE / ASOCIACION DE GRADUADAS DE LA UNIVERSIDAD DE PUERTO RICO.). [Asomante]. **Added/Corp** University of Puerto Rico (System). Asociacion de Graduadas. Ano 1, No. 1 (Enero-Marzo 1945)-. Periodical. Spanish. qt. **LC** AP63; .A727. **DD** 056. ***Continues*** *Revista (University of Puerto Rico (System). Asociacion de Graduadas).*
Ind/Abst Am. Hist. Life (1965-1967); HAPI Hisp. Am. Period. Index (19??-).

FR/0004-6116
ASTRADO, L'. [Astrado]. (1965)-. Periodical. French (Provencal, Old).
Ind/Abst MLA Int. Bibl. Books Artic. Mod. Lang. Lit.

GW
ATHENAUM : JAHRBUCH FUR ROMANTIK. Vol. 1 (1991)-. German. Verlag Ferdinand Schoningh Gmbh, Juhenplatz 1, D 4790, Paderborn, Germany. **LC** PT361; .A8.

US
ATQ. THE AMERICAN TRANSCENDENTAL QUARTERLY. Added/Corp University of Rhode Island. **VFOAT** American Transcendental Quarterly. No. 37 (Winter 1978)-No. 62 (Dec. 1986); New Series 1 (Mar. 1987)-. Periodical. English. Four times a year (Mar., June, Sept., Dec.). $25.00. American Transcendental, Department of English, The University of Rhode Island, Kingston RI 02881-0812. **Tel** (401)792-2576. **ED** Tom H. Towers. **Circ:** 470. available on microfilm and microfiche from University Microfilms International (UMI). Documents available from The Genuine Article, UMI Article Clearinghouse. ***Continues*** *American Transcendental Quarterly.*
Desc: Studies of 19th Century American authors, literature and related social and cultural topics.
Ind/Abst Abstr. Engl. Stud.; Acad. Search (July 1993-); Am. Hist. Life (1987-); Am. Humanit. Index; Annu. Bibliogr. Engl. Lang. Lit.; Arts Humanit. Citation Index [Full Cov.]; Child. Lit. Abstr. (19??-); Curr. Contents Arts Humanit.; Expand. Acad. Index (1989-); Humanit. Index; Humanit. Source (Jul. 1993-); Lit. Crit. Regist.; MLA Int. Bibl. Books Artic. Mod. Lang. Lit.; Newsp. Period. Abstr. (1991-); Res. Alert [Full Cov.]; Soc. Sci. Cit. Index [Select. Cov.].

CN/0708-5389
ATROPOS. V. 1 (Spring 1978)-. Periodical. English (French). sa. $5.00 Canada; $6.00 other. Atropos Publishing, 325 Prince Edward Avenue, Otterburn Heights Quebec J3H 1W Canada. **DD** C810/.8/0054. **UDC** 820(73).

IT/0392-1336
ATTI, ISTITUTO VENETO DI SCIENZE, LETTERE ED ARTI. CLASSE DI SCIENZE MORALI, LETTERE ED ARTI. (ATTI CLASSE DI SCIENZE MORALI; LETTERE ED ARTI.). [Atti, Ist. veneto sci., lett. arti, Cl. sci. morali, lett. arti]. **Main/Corp** Istituto Veneto di Scienze, Lettere ed Arti. Classe di Scienze Morali, Lettere ed Arti. (19??)-. Italian. an. Istituto Veneto Scienze Lett Arti, Campo S Stefano 2945, 30124 Venice Italy. **Tel** 011 39 41 5210177.
Ind/Abst Am. Hist. Life (1964-1976); BHA : Biblio. Hist. Art; MLA Int. Bibl. Books Artic. Mod. Lang. Lit.

●US
AUDIOCASSETTE & COMPACT DISC FINDER : A SUBJECT GUIDE TO EDUCATIONAL AND LITERARY MATERIALS ON AUDIOCASSETTES AND COMPACT DISCS. Added/Corp National Information Center for Educational Media. **VFOAT** Audiocassette and Compact Disc Finder. (1993)-. English. Plexus Publishing Inc., 143 Old Marlton Pike, Medford NJ 08055. **Tel** (609)654-6500, FAX (609)654-4309. **LC** LB1044.4.Z9; A93. ***Continues*** *Audiocassette Finder.*

US/0889-7433
AURA (BIRMINGHAM, ALA.). (AURA : LITERARY/ARTS REVIEW.). [Aura]. **Added/Corp** University of Alabama at Birmingham. **VFOAT** Aura Literary/Arts Review. (Fall 1974)-. Periodical. English. sa (April & Nov.). $6.00. Aura /UAB, PO Box 76 University Center, University Station, Birmingham AL 35294. **Tel** (205)934-3216, (205)934-3354, FAX (205)-34-8070. **ED** Steven Mullen. **DD** 810. **Pr Rev. Circ:** 250 (ctrl).
Desc: Publishes quality poetry, prose, and art by both published and unpublished writers and artists.

IT/0004-8062
AUREA PARMA. See Humanities.

AT/1035-1205
AUREALIS MT. WAVERLEY. (AUREALIS.). [Aurealis Mt. Waverley]. (1990)-. Periodical. English. sa (June, Dec.). 24.00Aus$ (Australia); 30.00Aus$ (New Zealand) 31.00Aus$ (other). Chimaera Publications, PO Box 538, Mt Waverley Victoria, 3149 Australia. **Tel** 11 61 3 5341569. **ED** Dirk Strasser and Stephen Higgins. **DD** 823.087620803. **Bk Rev**, (Qty: 2-3). **Ad Acc. Circ:** 2,000.
Desc: Includes science fiction and fantasy short stories, articles, and reviews.

GW
AURORA (WUERZBURG). (AURORA: EICHENDORFF ALMANACH.). **Added/Corp** Eichendorffstiftung. Eichendorff - Gesellschaft. **VFOAT** Eichendorff Almanach. (1929)-. Monographic series. German. ir. Price varies per volume. Jan Thorbecke Verlag GmbH and Company, Karlstrasse 10, Postfach 546, D 72482 Sigmaringen Germany. **Tel** 011 49 7571 728100, FAX 011 07571-728-280, telex 732534. **LC** PT1856.Z5; A9. cum. index.
Ind/Abst BHA : Biblio. Hist. Art.

GW
AUSLANDSDEUTSCHE LITERATUR DER GEGENWART. Vol. 1-. Monographic series. German. ir. Price varies per volume. Georg Olms Verlag AG Weidmann, Hagentorwall 6 7, D 31134 Hildesheim Germany. **Tel** 011 49 5121 15010, telex 927454 OLMS D. **ED** Alexander Ritter. **UDC** 830.
Desc: The development of German literature in foreign countries, such as US, Romania, Belgium and Israel.

CN/0843-5049
AUSTRALIAN & NEW ZEALAND STUDIES IN CANADA. [Aust. N.Z. stud. Can.]. **Added/Corp** University of Western Ontario. Dept. of English. **VFOAT** Australian and New Zealand Studies in Canada. **VAT** Australian and New Zealand Studies in Canada. No. 1 (Spring 1989)-. Periodical. English. sa (June and Dec.). 18.00Can$. University of Western Ontario Department of English, Room 173, London Ontario N6A 3K7 Canada. **Tel** (519)673-1164. **ED** Thomas Tausky. **LC** PR9600; .A87. **DD** 820.9/994/05. **Bk Rev. Ad Acc. Pr Rev. Circ:** 200.
Desc: Interviews with four Australian writers; semioethnographic study of "marker traits in Australian literature." For anyone interested in Australian/New Zealand literature.
Ind/Abst MLA Int. Bibl. Books Artic. Mod. Lang. Lit.

SZ/0171-6867
AUSTRALIAN AND NEW ZEALAND STUDIES IN GERMAN LANGUAGE AND LITERATURE. (AUSTRALISCH-NEUSEELANDISCHE STUDIEN ZUR DEUTSCHEN SPRACHE UND LITERATUR.). [Aust. N.Z. Stud. Ger. lang. lit.]. **VFOAT** Australian and New Zealand Studies in German Language and Literature; Etudes Parues en Australie et Nouvelle Zelande en Relation avec la Philologie Allemande. (1971)-. Monographic series. Multiple languages (English and German). ir. Price varies per volume. Verlag Peter Lang AG, Jupiterstrasse 15, CH-3000 Bern 15 Switzerland. **Tel** 011 41 31 9411122, FAX 011 41 31 321131.
Ind/Abst MLA Int. Bibl. Books Artic. Mod. Lang. Lit.

AT/0045-026X
AUSTRALIAN AUTHOR, THE. Added/Corp Australian Society of Authors. (Jan. 1969)-. Periodical. English. Four times a year (Mar., June, Sept., Dec.). 24.00Aus$ Australia; 28.00Aus$ other. Australian Society of Authors Limited, 98 Pitt Street, Redfern New South Wales 2016 Australia. **Tel** 011 61 02 3180877, FAX 011 61 02 3180530. **ED** Donnie O'Grady, (editor's address: PO Box 1566, Strawberry Hills, 2012 Australia, phone: 011 61 2 3276630). **LC** PN101; .A68. **DD** 808/.02/0994. **Bk Rev. Ad Acc, Adv Mgr:** Ray Koppe, **Tel** 02 3180877. **Circ:** 2,750 (ctrl).
Desc: Contents include professional and literary articles. Australian letters continue to provide a solid basis on which matters of importance to the literary professional can be debated at length.
Ind/Abst Annu. Bibliogr. Engl. Lang. Lit.; APAIS, Aust. Public Aff. Inf. Ser.

AT/0004-9468
AUSTRALIAN JOURNAL OF FRENCH STUDIES. [Aust. j. Fr. stud.]. Vol. 1 (Jan./April 1964)-. Periodical. English (French). tq (3 issues). 30.00Aus$ Australia; 40.00Aus$ other. Monash University, Department of Romance Languages, French Section, Clayton Victoria 3168 Australia. **Tel** 011 61 3 5652217, FAX 011 61 3 5652948, telex 32691. **ED** Wallace Kirsop. **LC** PQ1; .A8. **DD** 840/.9. **UDC** 840(09). Index available (bound in last issue). cum. index. **Bk Rev**, (Qty: 5-10). **Pr Rev. Circ:** 530. Documents available from The Genuine Article.
Desc: History and criticism of French literature, French history and bibliography.
Ind/Abst Am. Hist. Life (1976-); APAIS, Aust. Public Aff. Inf. Ser. (1965-); Arts Humanit. Citation Index [Full Cov.]; Curr. Contents Arts Humanit.; MLA Int. Bibl. Books Artic. Mod. Lang. Lit.; Res. Alert [Full Cov.]; Romant. Move.

NE/0921-2531
AUSTRALIAN PLAYWRIGHTS. See Theater.

AT/0810-4468
AUSTRALIAN SHORT STORIES (CARLTON, VIC.). (AUSTRALIAN SHORT STORIES.). (19??)-. Periodical. English. qt (Mar., June, Sept., Dec.). 30.00Aus$ Australia; 38.00Aus$ other. Pascoe Publishing Pty Ltd, PO Box 42, Apollo Bay 3233 Australia. **Tel** 011 61 52 379227, FAX 011 61 52 376559. **ED** Bruce Pascoe, Lyn Harwood. **[CCC]. Ad Acc. Circ:** 8,000.
Desc: Short stories of good quality previously unpublished.

AT/1033-9434
AUSTRALIAN WOMEN'S BOOK REVIEW. See Women's Interests.

UK/1350-7532
AUSTRIAN STUDIES. (19??)-. English. an. £35.00. Edinburgh University Press, 22 George Square, Edinburgh EH8 9LF Scotland. **Tel** 011 44 31 650 6207, FAX 011 44 31 662 0053. **ED** Edward Timms and Ritchie Robertson. Index available. **Bk Rev**, (Qty: 10/y). **Ad Acc, Adv Mgr:** Kathryn MacLean. **Circ:** 750.
Desc: Focuses on the distinctive culture of the Austrian republic from 1750 to the present, it relates literature to psychology, philosophy, political theory, music, theatre and the visual arts.

IT/0005-0601
AUT AUT. See Philosophy.

UK/0005-0628
AUTHOR (LONDON. 1949). (THE AUTHOR.). [Author]. **Added/Corp** Society of Authors (Great Britain). Vol. 59, No. 3 (Spring 1949)-. Periodical. English. qt (Mar., June, Sept., Dec.). £20.00 UK; £25.00 (surface mail), £30.00 (air mail) other. Society of Authors, 84

Drayton Gardens, London SW10 9SB England. **Tel** 011 44 71 373 6642, FAX 011 44 71 373 5768. **ED** Derek Parker. **LC** PN101; .A8. **DD** 808/.025/05. **Bk Rev**, (Qty: 6). **Ad Acc**, **Adv Mgr:** K. Pool. **Circ:** 7,000. available on microfilm and microfiche from University Microfilms International (UMI). ***Continues** Author, Playwright and Composer.*
Desc: Covers authorship and relative business.
Ind/Abst Br. Humanit. Index; Child. Lit. Abstr. (19??-); Libr. Inf. Sci. Abstr.

US/1058-8906
AUTHORLINE - SAS INSTITUTE. (AUTHORLINE : SAS INSTITUTE'S NEWSLETTER FOR AUTHORS.). [Authorline - SAS Inst.]. **Main/Corp** SAS Institute. **VFOAT** Author Line. Issue No. 1 (3rd Quarter 1991)-. Newsletter. English. qt. Free. SAS Institute Inc., Box 8000, SAS Circle, Cary NC 27512. **Tel** (919)677-8000, FAX (919)677-8123. **DD** 005.

US/1040-5682
AUTHORS & ARTISTS FOR YOUNG ADULTS. [Authors artists young adults]. **VFOAT** Authors and Artists for Young Adults; Authors and Artists; Authors & Artists. (1989)-. English. sa. $63.00. Gale Research Inc., 835 Penobscot Building, Detroit MI 48226. **Tel** (800)877-GALE, (313)961-2242, FAX (313)961-6083, telex TWX 810-221-7086. **ED** Kevin Hile. **LC** PS490; .A98. **DD** 011/.62/05.
Desc: Provides information for high school and junior high school students about their favorite creative artists, including the people who create the movies, television programs, books, stage productions, lyrics, cartoons, and animated features that young adults most enjoy. Each volume covers between 20 and 25 different authors and artists and provides personal data, career information, a bibliography of writings, plus a distinctive sidelights section covering a range of topics.

US/0404-3030
AUTHORS GUILD BULLETIN. Added/Corp Authors' Guild (U.S.). (May 1956)-. Bulletin. English. ir. **LC** PN121; .A882. ***Supersedes** Author's League Bulletin.*

IT
AUTOBUS. Periodical. Italian. qt. L6.000. Gesto Srl, Via C Battisti 21, 20122 Milan Italy. **Tel** 011 39 2 55187581, FAX 011 39 2 5465310. **LC** PQ4001; .A94. **DD** 808.8.

IT
AUTOGRAFO : QUADRIMESTRALE DEL CENTRO DI RICERCA SULLA TRADIZIONE MANOSCRITTA DI AUTORI CONTEMPORANEI, UNIVERSITA DI PAVIA. Added/Corp Universita di Pavia. Centro di Ricerca Sulla Tradizione Manoscritta di Autori Contemporanei. Vol. 1, No. 1 (Feb. 1984)-. Periodical. Italian. qt. L30000 Italy; L50000 other. Vallecchi Editore Spa, Viale Milton 7, 50129 Florence Italy. **Tel** 011 39 55 473843. **LC** IN PROCESS. **Ad Acc.**

US/0741-1790
AVALON TO CAMELOT. *Suspended.* Vol. 1, No. 1 (Fall 1983)-Suspended. Periodical. English. qt. $15.00 US; $16.00 Canada. Avalon to Camelot, PO Box 6236, Evanston IL 60204. **UDC** 82-39.
Ind/Abst MLA Int. Bibl. Books Artic. Mod. Lang. Lit.

FR
AVANT-SIECLE, L'. VFOAT Avant Siecle. (1975)-. Monographic series. French. ir. Price varies per volume. Lettres Modernes Minard, 45 rue de Saint Andre, 14123 Fleury-sur-Orne France. **Tel** 011 33 31 844706, FAX 011 33 31 844809.

US/0899-3750
AVEC (PENNGROVE, CALIF.). (AVEC.). Vol. 1, No. 1 (1988)-. Periodical. English. Twice a year (May, Nov.). $15.00. Avec, PO Box 1059, Penngrove CA 94951. **Tel** (707)762-2370, FAX (707)769-0880. **ED** Cydney Chadwick. **DD** 810. **Ad Acc. Circ:** 100.
Desc: Innovative poetry and fiction from international artists for an international audience.

RU/0320-6858
AVRORA. Added/Corp Vsesoiuznyi Leninskii Kommunisticheskii Soiuz Molodezhi. Tsentralnyi Komitet. Soiuz Pisatelei RSFSR. Leningradskaia Pisatelskaia Organizatsiia. (1???)-. Periodical. Russian. mo. $99.95. **(Subscription address:** East View Publications Inc., 3020 Harbor Lane North, Suite 110, Minneapolis MN 55447.**)**

US/1055-792X
AWARD-WINNING BOOKS FOR CHILDREN AND YOUNG ADULTS. (AWARD-WINNING BOOKS FOR CHILDREN AND YOUNG ADULTS : AN ANNUAL GUIDE ... / BY BETTY L. CRISCOE.). [Award win. books child. young adults]. **VAT** Award Winning Books for Children and Young Adults. (1989)-. English. an. $79.50 latest edition. Scarecrow Press Inc., 52 Liberty Street, PO Box 4167, Metuchen NJ 08840. **Tel** (908)548-8600, (800)537-7107. **LC** Z1037; .C925; PN1009.A1. **DD** 028.1/62/079.

US/0194-6498
AWP NEWSLETTER (NORFOLK). *Title Change.* (AWP NEWSLETTER.). **Main/Corp** Associated Writing Programs. **VAT** Associated Writing Programs Newsletter. (197?)-(19??). Newsletter. English. mo (eight no. a year). Associated Writing Programs, Old Dominion University, Norfolk VA 23529. **Tel** (804)683-3839. **ED** D Daniel. **LC** PN101; .A88. **Bk Rev. Ad Acc. Circ:** 10,000 (ctrl). ***Continued by** AWP Chronicle.*
Desc: Aspects of creative writing, teaching, and publishing as it relates to our membership.

UK
BACONIANA. See Biographies.

NP
BAGAINCA. Annual 1, No. 1 (May/June 1981)-. Periodical. Nepali. qt. Rs2.00. Bagainca Traimasika Karyalaya, 16/2 Thamela Tola, Kathmandu Nepal. **LC** PK2598.A2; B26.

PH/0115-9321
BAGONG PAMANA. Added/Corp Cultural Center of the Philippines. National Media Production Center. Vol. 1, No. 1 (March 1981)-. Periodical. English (Tagalog, Cebuano and Iloko). qt. Cultural Center of the Philippines, Roxas Boulevard, Manila Philippines. **Tel** 8323876. ***Formed by the union of** Pamana, 0115-1703 **and** Lahi.*

IO
BAHASA DAN SASTRA. See Linguistics.

JA
BAIKA REVIEW. Added/Corp Baika Joshi Daigaku Ei-Bei Bungakukai. (19??)-. Periodical. English (Japanese). an. Baika Joshi Daigaku Ei-Bei Bungakukai, 171 Shukunosho 567, Ibaraki Japan. **Tel** 0726-43-6221. **LC** PR1; .B34. **Circ:** 2,000.
Desc: Writings on English and American literature and language.

CN/0408-2206
BAJAVAJA USKALOS'. (BAIAVAIA USKALOS; MAGAZINE.). [Bajavaja uskalos]. **Main/Corp** Baiavaia Uskalos. **VFOAT** Bayavaya Uskalos. (1951)-. Periodical. Byelorussian. an. 6.00Can$. Bayavaya Uskalos/Byelo Russian, 24 Tarlton Road, Toronto Ontario M5P 2M4 Canada. **Tel** (416)488-0048. **ED** Sergei Khmara. **LC** AP58.W5; B34. **Circ:** 500.
Desc: Ethnic poems and Belorussian news.

US/0005-4070
BAKER STREET JOURNAL, THE. [Baker Str. j.]. Vol. 1-4, No. 1 (Jan. 1946)-(Jan. 1949); New Series, Vol. 1 (1951)-. Periodical. English. qt. $17.50 US; $20.00 other. Baker Street Journal, PO Box 465, Hanover PA 17331. **(Subscription address:** Sheridan Press, 450 Fame Avenue, Hanover, PA 17331; telephone: (717)632-3535; FAX: (717)633-8900**) ED** Philip Schreffler. **LC** PR4623; .A17. **DD** 823/.8. **UDC** 82-312.4. **[CCC].** cum. index. **Bk Rev. Ad Acc. Circ:** 1,700. available on microfilm and microfiche from University Microfilms International (UMI).
Desc: Contains articles on Sherlock Holmes and the Sherlockian Scene.
Ind/Abst Am. Humanit. Index; Annu. Bibliogr. Engl. Lang. Lit.; MLA Int. Bibl. Books Artic. Mod. Lang. Lit.

RU
BALTO-SLAVIANSKIE ISSLEDOVANIIA / AKADEMIIA NAUK SSSR, INSTITUT SLAVIANOVEDENIIA I BALKANISTIKI. See Linguistics.

US/0733-0308
BAMBOO RIDGE. (BAMBOO RIDGE : THE HAWAII WRITERS QUARTERLY.). No. 1 (Dec. 1978)-. Periodical. English. qt. $16.00. Bamboo Ridge Press, PO Box 61781, Honolulu HI 96822-8781. **Tel** (808)599-4823. **ED** Eric Chock and Darrell Lum. cum. index. **Bk Rev**, (Qty: 1). **Ad Acc. Circ:** 350 (ctrl).
Desc: Contains the appreciation, understanding, and creation of literary, visual, audiovisual and performing arts by and about Hawaii's people.
Ind/Abst Am. Humanit. Index; Index Am. Period. Verse.

II
BAMLA CHOTA GALPA. Periodical. Bengali (Bengali). Rs2.50. Svadesaranjana Datta, 18 Padmapukur Road, Calcutta-20, Kalakata India. **LC** PK1716; .B23.

UK
BANDER SNATCH : THE LEWIS CARROLL SOCIETY NEWSLETTER. Added/Corp Lewis Carroll Society. **VFOAT** Bander-Snatch; Bandersnatch. (197?)-. Newsletter. English. qt. Lewis Carroll Society, 146 Headstone Lane, Middlesex HA2 6JT England. **LC** PAR.

SP
BANG. Periodical. Spanish. $1.50. Apartado de Correos 9331, Barcelona Spain. **LC** PN6700; .B35.

US
BARAT REVIEW, THE. Added/Corp Barat College of the Sacred Heart, Lake Forest, Ill. Vol. 1 (Jan. 1966)-. English. sa. **LC** AS36.B3; A2. **DD** 040.
Ind/Abst Annu. Bibliogr. Engl. Lang. Lit.

US/0364-2194
BARBEQUE PLANET. (1975)-. English. $0.50 per copy. Barbeque Planet, 4414 Illinois Avenue, Nashville TN 37209. **LC** PS501; .B35. **DD** 810/.5.

SW/0347-772X
BARNBOKEN. (1978)-. Swedish. bm. Svenska Barnboksinstitutet, 61 Odengaten, S-113 22 Stockholm, Sweden.
Ind/Abst Child. Lit. Abstr. (19??-).

FR/0067-4222
BAROQUE (MONTAUBAN). (BAROQUE.). [Baroque]. **Added/Corp** Centre National de Recherches du Baroque. Centre International de Synthese du Baroque. (1965)-. Academic Scholarly Publication. French. an. 180.00F France; 210.00F other. Baroque Revue Internationale, 30 rue la Banque, 82000 Montauban France. **Tel** 011 33 63 630567. **ED** Felix Castan. ***Supersedes** Journees Internationales d'Etude du Baroque Actes.*
Desc: Explores the civilization which flourished from the end of the 16th century through the end of the 18th century in Europe and Latin America. Baroque history and culture and their diverse manifestations are examined and analyzed in scholarly articles.
Ind/Abst MLA Int. Bibl. Books Artic. Mod. Lang. Lit.

SZ/0067-4508
BASLER STUDIEN ZUR DEUTSCHEN SPRACHE UND LITERATUR. See Linguistics.

US/0005-6677
BAUM BUGLE, THE. [Baum bugle]. **Added/Corp** International Wizard of Oz Club. (19??)-. Periodical. English. Three times a year. $15.00. International Wizard of Oz Club Inc., 220 North 11th Street, Escanaba MI 49829. **Tel** (217)432-5517. **ED** Michael Gessel. **LC** PS3503.A923; B3. **DD** 812/.4. Index available. **Bk Rev. Circ:** 2,500 (ctrl).
Desc: Includes articles about "Oz" authors, illustrators, books, plays, films, tapes, toys, music, etc.
Ind/Abst Child. Lit. Abstr. (19??-); MLA Int. Bibl. Books Artic. Mod. Lang. Lit.

IS/0302-8178
BAY ZIK. (BAY ZIKH.). [Bay zik]. **Added/Corp** Komitet far Yidisher Kultur in Yisroel. **VFOAT** By Zich. (1972)-. Yiddish. Komitet Jar Yidisher Kultur in Yisroel, 228 Bnei Ephraim Street Maoz Aviv, Tel Aviv Israel. **LC** PJ5161.A1; B39.

US/0730-5184
BEACON REVIEW. (19??)-. Periodical. English. qt. Le Beacon Presse, 2511 1/2 Yeslar Way, Seattle WA 98122. **LC** Discard.

UK
BEATRIX POTTER STUDIES. Added/Corp Beatrix Potter Society. Vol. 1 (1984)-. Proceedings. English. be. £6.50 or $11.00. Beatrix Potter Society, High Banks 26 Stoneborough Lane, Budleigh Salterton, Devon EX9 6HL England. ctrl circ.
Desc: Proceedings of the conferences of the Beatrix Potter Society.

US/0067-4737
BEAU-COCOA. No. 1- Autumn 1968-. Periodical. English. sa. L Addison, PO Box 409, New York NY 10035. **LC** PS508.N3; B4. **DD** 810/.8/0896. available on microfilm from University Microfilms International (UMI).

US/0732-2224
BECKETT CIRCLE, THE. (THE BECKETT CIRCLE : NEWSLETTER OF THE SAMUEL BECKETT SOCIETY). [Beckett circ.]. **Added/Corp** Samuel Beckett Society. **VFOAT** Le Cercle de Beckett. Vol. 1, No. 1 (Spring 1978)-. Periodical. English. Twice a year (Apr., Nov.). $12.00 (one year); $22.00 (two years) Comes with Samuel Beckett Society membership. Beckett Circle, English Department, Florida State University, Tallahassee FL 32306. **Tel** (904)644-4869, FAX (904)644-8817. **ED** Lois Oppenheim, (phone: (201)893-7423) and Karen Laughlin, (phone: (904)644-4230). **LC** PR6003.E282; Z4582. **DD** 848/.91409. Index available. **Bk Rev**, (Qty: 4). **Ad Acc, Adv Mgr:** Frederick N. Smith, **Tel** (704)547-2996. ctrl circ.
Ind/Abst Lit. Crit. Regist.

CN/0832-9966
BEFFROI. (LE BEFFROI : REVUE PHILOSOPHIQUE ET LITTERAIRE.). [Beffroi]. No. 1 (Dec. 1986)-. Periodical. French. Three times a year. 50.00Can$ North America; $50.00 other. Les Editions du Beffroi, 3550 rue du Long-Sault, Beauport Quebec G1E 1H6 Canada. **Tel** (418)663-3656. **DD** 805. **Bk Rev. Ad Acc. Circ:** 800 (ctrl).

GW/0172-0910
BEIHEFT ZUM BULLETIN JUGEND + LITERATUR. (1981)-. Monographic series. German. mo. Price varies per volume. Eulenhof-Verlag Ehrhardt, Heinold Eulenhof, W-2351 Hardebek Germany. **Tel**

Literature

04324/501, FAX 04324/8146. **ED** Ehrhardt F. Heinold. Index available. cum. index. **Bk Rev**. **Ad Acc**. **Acid Free**. **Circ**: 1,500. *Continues Beihefte Zum Bulletin Jugend + Literatur.*
 Desc: News and reviews for educators, teachers, social workers, librarians, critics, students, publishers, and other illustrators, booksellers and editors.
 Ind/Abst Child. Lit. Abstr. (19??-).

GW/0084-5396
BEIHEFTE ZUR ZEITSCHRIFT FUER ROMANISCHE PHILOLOGIE. See Linguistics.

GW/0005-8076
BEITRAEGE ZUR GESCHICHTE DER DEUTSCHEN SPRACHE UND LITERATUR (TUEBINGEN). See Linguistics.

GW/0179-4027
BEITRAEGE ZUR NEUEREN LITERATURGESCHICHTE. (BEITRAEGE ZUR NEUREN LITERATURGESCHICHTE. DRITTE FOLGE.). [Beitr. neueren Lit.gesch.]. Vol. 1 (1967)-. Monographic series. German. ir. Price varies per volume. Universitatsverlag Carl Winter, POB 106140, D 69051 Heidelberg Germany. **Tel** 011 49 6221 770260. *Supersedes Beitrage zur Neueren Literaturgeschichte. Neue Folge.*
 Ind/Abst MLA Int. Bibl. Books Artic. Mod. Lang. Lit.

GW
BEITRAEGE ZUR UKRAINISCHEN LITERATURGESCHICHTE. Monographic series. German. Price varies per volume. Universitatsverlag Carl Winter, POB 106140, D 69051 Heidelberg Germany. **Tel** 011 49 6221 770260.

BW/1010-4011
BELARUSKAJA LITARATURA. (BELARUSKAIA LITARATURA.). [Belarus. lit.]. **Added/Corp** Homelski Dziarzhauny Universitetet. (1977)-. Byelorussian. an. **LC** PG2834.2; .B44. *Continues Belaruskaia Litaratura i Litaraturaznaustva.*
 Ind/Abst MLA Int. Bibl. Books Artic. Mod. Lang. Lit.

US/0884-2957
BELLES LETTRES (ARLINGTON, VA.). (BELLES LETTRES.). [Belles lett.]. Vol. 1, No. 1 (Sept./Oct. 1985)-. Periodical. English. Four times a year (Jan., Apr., July, Oct.). $40.00. Belles Lettres, 11151 Captains Walk Court, Gaithersburg MD 20878. **Tel** (301)294-0278, FAX (301)294-0023. (**Subscription address**: 785 Verbenia Drive, Satellite Beach, FL 32937) **ED** Janet P Mullaney, Darcie Johnston. **LC** PN471; .B44. **DD** 818. Index available. cum. index. **Bk Rev**, (Qty: 300). **Ad Acc**, **Adv Mgr**: J. Mullaney, **Tel** (301)294-0278. **Circ**: 5,000 (ctrl). available on microfilm from University Microfilms International (UMI). Documents available from UMI Article Clearinghouse.
 Desc: Devoted to literature by women featuring reviews, interviews, rediscoveries, retrospectives, multicultural sections, and international spotlights. Substantive columns on nonfiction titles (by theme), literary/critical biographies, book publishing, and reprints also appear. For general readers as well as the literary cognoscenti.
 Ind/Abst Book Rev. Index (1988-); Expand. Acad. Index (1992-); Newsp. Period. Abstr. (1989-); Women Stud. Abstr.

US/0734-2934
BELLINGHAM REVIEW, THE. Vol. 1, No. 1 (Jan. 1977)-. Periodical. English. sa. $6.00. The Signpost Press Inc, 1007 Queen Street, Bellingham WA 98226. **Tel** (206)734-9781. **ED** Randy Jay Landon. **LC** PS501; .B38. **DD** 810/.8. **Bk Rev**. **Circ**: 700 (ctrl).
 Desc: Publishes poetry, fiction, and drama; also reviews, drawings and photographs.
 Ind/Abst Index Am. Period. Verse.

SW/0405-3923
BELLMANSSTUDIER. (BELLMANSSTUDIER, UTG. AV BELLMANSSALLSKAPET.). [Bellmansstudier]. **Main/Corp** Bellmanssallskapet. (1924)-. Periodical. Swedish. **LC** PT9678; .P43.
 Ind/Abst MLA Int. Bibl. Books Artic. Mod. Lang. Lit.

US/0887-4115
BELLOWING ARK. **Added/Corp** Bellowing Ark Society (U.S.). Vol. 1, No. 1 (Sept. 1984)-. Periodical. English. bm. $12.00 (one year), $20.00 (two year). Bellowing Ark, PO Box 45637, Seattle WA 98145. **Tel** (206) 545-8302. **DD** 810.
 Ind/Abst Index Am. Period. Verse.

US/0883-9131
BELOIT FICTION JOURNAL. [Beloit fict. j.]. Vol. 1, No. 1 (Fall 1985)-. Periodical. English. sa. $9.00. Beloit Fiction Journal, Beloit College, c/o Clint McCown, Box 11, Beloit WI 53511. **Tel** (608)365-3391. **ED** Clint McCown. **DD** 813. **Circ**: 500.
 Desc: Publish new contemporary short fiction of all themes and subject matter except pornography, political propaganda and religious dogma. Manuscript length ranges from 1-40 pages.

IT
BERENICE. Yearly V. 1, 1 (Nov. 1980)-. French (Italian). Three times a year. Lucaarini, Viale Mazzini 146, 00195 Rome Italy. **LC** PQ2; .B47. **DD** 840/.9.
 Ind/Abst MLA Int. Bibl. Books Artic. Mod. Lang. Lit.

UN
BEREZIL : LITERATURNO-KHUDOZHNII TA HROMADSKO-POLITYCHNYI ZHURNAL SPILKY PYSMENNYKIV UKRAINY.
 Added/Corp Spilka Pysmennykiv Ukrainy. (1991)-. Periodical. Ukrainian. mo. $109.95. (**Subscription address**: East View Publications Inc., 3020 Harbor Lane North, Suite 110, Minneapolis MN 55447.) **LC** AP58.U5; P64. *Continues Prapor, 0130-1608.*

IO
BERITA PENDIDIKAN SASTRA DAN SENI. **Main/Corp** Institut Keguruan Dan Ilmu Pendidikan, Manado, Indonesia. Fakultas Keguruan Sastra Seni. Indonesian (English). Institut Keguruan Dan ILMU Pendidikan, Jalan Jusuf Hasiru, Manado Indonesia. **LC** PN9; .I57A.

US
BERKLEY SHOWCASE, THE. V. 1- 1980-. English. Berkley Publishing Company, 200 Madison Avenue, New York NY 10016. **ED** V Schochet and J Silbersack.

JA
BESSATSU BUNGEI SHUNJU. VFOAT Bungei Shunju Bessatsu. (Jan. 1946)-. Periodical. Japanese. qt. $61.50. Bungei Shunju, 23 Kioi-cho 3, Chiyoda-ku 102, Tokyo-to Japan. (**Subscription address**: Japan Publications Trading Company, Ltd., PO Box 5030, Tokyo International, Tokyo 100-31 Japan.) **LC** AP95.J2; B47.

US/0888-3742
BEST AMERICAN ESSAYS, THE. [Best Am. essays]. (1986)-. English. an. $21.95 (hardback), $11.95 (paper). Houghton Mifflin Company, Wayside Road, Burlington MA 01803. **Tel** (800)225-3362, (617)272-1500. **LC** PS688; .B47. **DD** 814/.008.

US/0067-6233
BEST AMERICAN SHORT STORIES (BOSTON, MASS. : 1978). (THE BEST AMERICAN SHORT STORIES.). [Best Am. short stories]. (1978)-. Periodical. English. an. $24.95. Houghton Mifflin Company, Wayside Road, Burlington MA 01803. **Tel** (800)225-3362, (617)272-1500. **ED** Robie Macauley. **LC** PZ1; .B446235. **Circ**: 38,000. *Continues Best American Short Stories ... and the Yearbook of the American Short Story (Boston, Mass. : 1975), 0067-6233.*
 Desc: American short stories of the year as chosen by a distinguished writer of fiction. Previous judges include Gail Godwin, John Updike, Anne Tyler and others.

CN/0703-9476
BEST CANADIAN STORIES. (1977)-. English. an (Sept.). $29.95 (cloth edition), $15.95 (paper edition). Oberon Press, 400 350 Sparks Street, Ottawa Ontario K1R 7S8 Canada. **Tel** (613)238-3275. **ED** David Helwig. **LC** PZ1; .B4464; PR9197.3. **DD** C813/.01. **Circ**: 2,000. *Continues New Canadian Stories, 0316-7518.*
 Desc: Short stories.

US
BEST OF SECRETS. (1936)-. English. qt. $8.00 (one year), $16.00 (two year). Sterling Macfadden, 233 Park Avenue South, New York NY 10003. **Tel** (212)979-4800. *Continues Secrets, 0037-0649.*

US/0091-9217
BEST SCIENCE FICTION. English. Ace Books, 1120 Avenue of the Americas, New York NY 10036. **LC** PZ1.A1; B39; PS648.S3. **DD** 813/.0876.

US/0095-7119
BEST SCIENCE FICTION OF THE YEAR, THE. No. 1- 1972-. English. an. $1.50 per issue. Ballantine Books, 201 East 50th Street, New York NY 10022. **ED** T Carr. **LC** PZ1.A1; B393; PS648.S3. **DD** 813/.0876.

US
BEST SF. 1967-. English. an. **ED** H Harrison and B W Aldiss. **LC** PZ1.A1; PS648.S3. **DD** 823/.9/108.

US/0737-8580
BEST WORLD SHORT STORIES. [Best world short stories]. (1947)-. English. an. Appleton Century Crofts, Prentice Hall, 200 Old Tappan Road, Old Tappan NJ 07675. **Tel** (201)767-5188, (800)922-0579. **ED** John Cournos and Sybil Norton. **LC** PZ1; .B46. **DD** 808.83/1.

US/1041-2212
BESTIA (KIRKSVILLE, MO.). (BESTIA.). [Bestia]. **Added/Corp** Beast Fable Society. VFOAT Yearbook of the Beast Fable Society of America. Vol. 1 (May 1989)-. Periodical. English. an. $58.00. Northeast Missouri State University, Division of Fine Arts, Kirksville MO 63501. **Tel** (816)785-4442. (**Subscription address**: John Benjamins North America, PO Box 27519, Philadelphia PA 19118-0519.) **ED** Ben Bennani. **LC** PN982; .B45. **DD** 398.24/5/05. **Circ**: 500.
 Desc: Presents articles dealing with the beast fable and its sister genre in all literatures, languages and periods. It yearly publishes a selection of the most distinguished papers read at the annual international congress of the Beast Fable Society.
 Ind/Abst MLA Int. Bibl. Books Artic. Mod. Lang. Lit.

US/1051-4732
BETE (MIAMI, FLA.), LA. (LA BETE.). [Bete]. Winter (1991)-. Periodical. English. qt $28.00. Miami Artwords, Inc., PO Box 24-8782, Coral Gables FL 33124. **DD** 810.

UK
BETE NOIRE. No. 1 (Autumn 1984)-. Periodical. English. sa (Autumn and Spring). £4.00. University of Hull / American Studies Department, c/o John Osborne, Humberside HU6 7RX England. **Tel** 011 44 482 46311.
 Ind/Abst MLA Int. Bibl. Books Artic. Mod. Lang. Lit.

II/0523-1418
BHASHA. See Linguistics.

FR
BIBLIO 17. VFOAT Biblio Dix-Sept; Biblio Seventeen. (1981)-. Monographic series. French (English). ir. Price varies per volume. Wolfgang Leiner Romanisches, Wilhelmstrasse 50, W-72074 Tubingen Germany. **Tel** 07071-29-5754, FAX 07071-29-7282. **ED** Wolfgang Leiner. **LC** UNC. Index available. **Pr Rev**: **Circ**: 300.
 Desc: Publishes monographics, critical editions, bibliographies and college proceedings in the field of 17th Century French literature.
 Ind/Abst MLA Int. Bibl. Books Artic. Mod. Lang. Lit.

CN/0821-7572
BIBLIOFANTASIAC, THE. [Bibliofantasiac]. Periodical. English. bm. $1.25 per no. 802 Pape Avenue, Toronto Ontario M4K 3S7 Canada. **DD** C813/.0876/08.

SP
BIBLIOGRAFIA DE GALICIA / DISPOSIA NO MUSEO DE PONTEVEDRA. Gallegan (Gallegan and Spanish). **LC** Z2704.G11; B5; DP302.G11. **DD** 016.946/1.

GW/0523-2767
BIBLIOGRAPHIEN ZUR DEUTSCHEN LITERATUR DES MITTELALTERS. See Literature-Abstracting, Bibliographies and Statistics.

US/0742-6801
BIBLIOGRAPHIES AND INDEXES IN WORLD LITERATURE. [Bibliogr. indexes world lit.]. No. 1-. Monographic series. English. ir. Price varies per volume. Greenwood Press Inc., PO Box 5007, Westport CT 06881-5007. **Tel** (203)226-3571, FAX (203)222-1502. **DD** 016.

US/0147-250X
BIBLIOGRAPHY. BOOKS FOR CHILDREN. *Ceased.* See Children and Youth Interests-Abstracting, Bibliographies and Statistics.

IS/0334-309X
BIBLIOGRAPHY OF MODERN HEBREW LITERATURE IN TRANSLATION. VFOAT Modern Hebrew Literature in Translation; Bibliyografyah Shel Ha-Sifrut Ha-Ivrit Ha-Hadashah Be-Tirgum. No. 1, (1972-1976)-. Periodical. Bibliography. English. Twice a year (Published an double issue in April). $20.00. Institute of Translat Hebrew Literature, PO Box 10051, Hamat-Gan 52001 Israel. **Tel** (03)5796830, FAX (03)5796832, telex 341118 BXTV IL. **ED** Isaac Goldberg. **LC** Z7070; .B52; PJ5059. **DD** 016.8924. **Circ**: 300 (ctrl).
 Desc: Bibliography listing translations from modern Hebrew literature to bio-critical material on Hebrew writers, literature and book reviews.

DK/0067-7213
BIBLIOGRAPHY OF OLD NORSE-ICELANDIC STUDIES. See Literature-Abstracting, Bibliographies and Statistics.

SP
BIBLIOTECA DE AUTORES ESPANOLES. (1983)-. Monographic series. Spanish. Price varies per volume.

MX/0188-476X
BIBLIOTECA DE MEXICO. **Added/Corp** Consejo Nacional para la Cultura y las Artes (Mexico). No. 1 (Jan/Feb 1991)-. Periodical. Spanish. bm.

IT
BIBLIOTECA DELLA RICERCA. TESTI STRANIERI. VFOAT Testi Stranieri. (1983)-. Monographic series. French.
 Ind/Abst MLA Int. Bibl. Books Artic. Mod. Lang. Lit.

NE
BIBLIOTECA HISPANOAMERICANA Y ESPANOLA DE AMSTERDAM. See Linguistics.

SP/0519-7198
BIBLIOTECA ROMANICA HISPANICA. I. TRATADOS Y MONOGRAFIAS. (1952)-.
Monographic series. Spanish. ir. Price varies per volume. Editorial Gredos SA, Calle Sanchez Pacheco 81, 28002 Madrid Spain. **Tel** 011 34 1 4157408, FAX 011 34 1 5192033.

SP/0519-7201
BIBLIOTECA ROMANICA HISPANICA. II. ESTUDIOS Y ENSAYOS. 1- 1950-.
Monographic series. Spanish. ir. Price varies per volume. Editorial Gredos SA, Calle Sanchez Pacheco 81, 28002 Madrid Spain. **Tel** 011 34 1 4157408, FAX 011 34 1 5192033.

SP/0519-7228
BIBLIOTECA ROMANICA HISPANICA. IV. TEXTOS. (1950)-. Monographic series. Spanish. ir. Price varies per volume. Editorial Gredos SA, Calle Sanchez Pacheco 81, 28002 Madrid Spain. **Tel** 011 34 1 4157408, FAX 011 34 1 5192033.

SP/0519-7244
BIBLIOTECA ROMANICA HISPANICA. VI. ANTOLOGIA HISPANICA. 1 (1956)-.
Monographic series. Spanish. ir. Price varies per volume. Editorial Gredos SA, Calle Sanchez Pacheco 81, 28002 Madrid Spain. **Tel** 011 34 1 4157408, FAX 011 34 1 5192033.

SP/0519-7252
BIBLIOTECA ROMANICA HISPANICA. VII. CAMPO ABIERTO. (1961)-. Monographic series. Spanish. ir. Price varies per volume. Editorial Gredos SA, Calle Sanchez Pacheco 81, 28002 Madrid Spain. **Tel** 011 34 1 4157408, FAX 011 34 1 5192033.

SP/0519-7260
BIBLIOTECA ROMANICA HISPANICA. VIII. DOCUMENTOS. 1- 1962-. Monographic series. Spanish. ir. Price varies per volume. Editorial Gredos SA, Calle Sanchez Pacheco 81, 28002 Madrid Spain. **Tel** 011 34 1 4157408, FAX 011 34 1 5192033.

PL/0519-7929
BIBLIOTEKA ANALIZ LITERACKICH.
(1959)-. Periodical. Polish.
Ind/Abst MLA Int. Bibl. Books Artic. Mod. Lang. Lit.

RU/0132-2095
BIBLIOTEKA "OGONEK.". *Ceased.* (19??)-. Monographic series. Russian. wk. **(Subscription address:** East View Publications Inc., 3020 Harbor Lane North, Suite 110, Minneapolis MN 55447.**)** **LC** PG3201; .B5.

US/0742-1117
BIBLIOTHECA AFROASIATICA. [Bibl. Afroasiat.]. Vol. 1 (1982)-. Monographic series. English. ir. Price varies per volume. Undena Publications, PO Box 97, Malibu CA 90265. **Tel** (310)649-2612. **(Subscription address:** Crescent Academic Services, 29528 Madera Ave., Shafter, CA 93623, Tel. (805)746-5870**)**
Ind/Abst MLA Int. Bibl. Books Artic. Mod. Lang. Lit.

IC/0067-7841
BIBLIOTHECA ARNAMAGNANA. [Bibl. Arnamagn.]. **Added/Corp** Arnamagnanske Stiftelse. Vol. 1 (1941)-. Monographic series. Multiple languages. Munksgaard International Publishers Ltd, PO Box 2148, DK-1016 Copenhagen K Denmark. **Tel** 011 45 33 12 70 30, FAX 011 45 33 12 93 87, telex 19431 MUNKS DK. **LC** PT7113; .B5.
Ind/Abst MLA Int. Bibl. Books Artic. Mod. Lang. Lit.

FR
BIBLIOTHEQUE RUSSE. See Linguistics.

FR/0078-9976
BIBLIOTHEQUE RUSSE DE L'INSTITUT D'ETUDES SLAVES. [Bibl. russe Inst. etud. slaves]. **Added/Corp** Universite de Paris IV: Paris-Sorbonne. Institut d'Etudes Slaves. (1946)-. Monographic series. French. *Continues Bibliotheque de l'Institut Francais de Leningrad.*
Ind/Abst MLA Int. Bibl. Books Artic. Mod. Lang. Lit.

US/0146-7042
BIG DEAL. No. 1- Spring 1973-. English. an. $21.00. Barbara Baracks Big Deal, PO Box 830 Peter Stuyvesant Station, New York NY 10009. **LC** PS501; .B45. **DD** 811/.5/405.

II
BIKHAMA. Vol. 1, No. 1 (1980)-. Periodical. Nepali (Nepali). qt. Rs2.00. Bikhama Parivara Rinchenpong, W Sikkim India. **ED** Hari Shrestha Bandhu and Rinchupong, and W Sikkim. **LC** PK2598.A2; B543. **Ad Acc. Circ:** 500.

US/0094-5366
BILINGUAL REVIEW. See Linguistics.

BB/0006-2766
BIM (CHRIST CHURCH). *Suspended.* (BIM.). [Bim]. **Added/Corp** Young Men's Progressive Club (Barbados). Vol. 1 No. 1 (Dec. 1942)-(1990). Periodical. English. Twice a year. $2.50. Forney-Atlantic Shores, Christ Church, Barbados. **LC** AP6; .B5.

II
BINDU. Periodical. Hindi (Hindi). 10.00. **LC** PK2047; .B55.
Ind/Abst Archit. Period. Index.

US/0742-695X
BIO-BIBLIOGRAPHIES IN AMERICAN LITERATURE. [Bio-bibliogr. Am. lit.]. **VFOAT** BioBibliographies in American Literature. 1989-. English. ir. Greenwood Press Inc., PO Box 5007, Westport CT 06881-5007. **Tel** (203)226-3571, FAX (203)222-1502.

US/0162-4962
BIOGRAPHY (HONOLULU). See Biographies.

II
BISVARUPA. **VFOAT** Biswarupa. Periodical. Oriya (Oriya). mo. 4.50. Jagadish Rath 73, Kharabela Nagar Unit 3, Bhubaneswar 751001 India. **LC** PK2574.5; .B57.

PL/0067-902X
BIULETYN POLONISTYCZNY. **Added/Corp** Instytut Badan Literackich (Polska Akademia Nauk). Vol. 1 No. 1 (April 1958)-. Periodical. Polish. Four times a year. **(Subscription address:** ARS Polona, PO Box 1001, 00068 Warsaw Poland.**)** **LC** PG7001; .B55.
Ind/Abst MLA Int. Bibl. Books Artic. Mod. Lang. Lit.

CL/0716-2138
BIZANTION NEA HELLAS. [Biz. Nea Hell.]. **Added/Corp** Universidad de Chile. Centro de Estudios Bizantinos y Neohelenicos. (1970)-. Spanish (summaries and/or abstracts in English). an. **LC** PA5225; .B59.
Ind/Abst MLA Int. Bibl. Books Artic. Mod. Lang. Lit.

US/8756-0666
BLACK BEAR. [Black bear]. **VFOAT** Black Bear Review. 1-. Periodical. English. sa. $10.00. Black Bear Publications, 1916 Lincoln Avenue, Croydon PA 19020-8026. **Tel** (215)788-3543. **ED** Ave Jeanne and Ron Zettlemoyer. **DD** 811. **Bk Rev**. **Ad Acc. Circ:** 500 (ctrl).
Desc: Literary magazine publishing well crafted contemporary poetry and artwork. Themes used are: war/peace, environmental, political and minorities.
Ind/Abst Am. Humanit. Index.

US
BLACK BOOKS BULLETIN. WORDS WORK. **Added/Corp** Institute of Positive Education (Chicago, Ill.). **VFOAT** Words Work. Vol. 1, No. 1 (July/Aug. 1991)-. Bulletin. English. bm. Institute of Positive Education, 7524 Cottage Grove, Chicago IL 60619. **LC** Z1229.N39; B2.

CN/0316-2753
BLACK I. (THE BLACK I.). [Black i]. (Mar. 1972)-. Periodical. English (French).
Ind/Abst MLA Int. Bibl. Books Artic. Mod. Lang. Lit.

US/0045-222X
BLACK MARIA. *Ceased.* Vol. 1 (1971)-(1984). Periodical. English. Four times a year. Black Maria, PO Box 25187, Chicago IL 60625. **ED** Laurie Fortman. **LC** PS508.W7; B5. **Bk Rev**. **Ad Acc. Circ:** 1,000 (ctrl).
Desc: Feminist arts publication that caters especially to women. Literature and artwork.

US/0737-5522
BLACK MESSIAH. Premiere Issue-. Periodical. English. Three times a year. $12.00. Vagabond Press, PO Box 879, Ellensburg Washington 98926. **LC** PS501; .B54. **DD** 810/.8.

NR/0067-9100
BLACK ORPHEUS. [Black Orpheus]. **Added/Corp** Western Nigeria (Region). Ministry of Education. General Publications Section. Western Nigeria (Nigeria). Ministry of Education. General Publications Section. Mbari Ibadan. Mbari Club. No. 1 (Sept. 1957)-. Periodical. English. Twice a year. $25.00. Lagos University Press, Publishing Division, PO Box 132, Akoka-Yaba University Lagos, Lagos Nigeria. **Tel** 011 234 1 825048. **ED** Theo Vincent. **LC** PL8000; .B6. **Bk Rev**. **Ad Acc. Circ:** 500.
Desc: University's main journal of creative arts and humanities. Features topics on African literature, music, painting, sculpture, and other art forms.
Ind/Abst MLA Int. Bibl. Books Artic. Mod. Lang. Lit.

US/0190-4906
BLACK REVIEW, THE. No. 1-. Periodical. English. sa. $5.00. Blackberry Press, PO Box 9405, Baltimore MD 21228.

US
BLACK WRITER MAGAZINE, THE. **VFOAT** Black Writer. Periodical. English. qt. $15.00. Black Writers Conference Inc, Box 1030, Chicago IL 60690-1030. **Tel** (312)995-5195. **ED** Mable Terrell. **Bk Rev**.
Desc: Covers poetry, essays and short stories.

GW
BLATTER + BILDER. See The Arts-Art.

GW
BLATTER DER CARL-ZUCKMAYER-GESELLSCHAFT.
Vol. 1, No. 1 (Nov. 1, 1975)-. Periodical. German. Three times a year (three or four issues yearly). DM36.00. Carl-Zuckmayer-Gesellschaft, POB 33, W-6506 Hadlenheim Germany. **LC** PT2653.U33; Z585. **DD** 832/.912.

SZ/1010-3597
BLATTER DER RILKE-GESELLSCHAFT. Main/Corp
Rilke-Gesellschaft. (1972)-. Monographic series. German. ir. Price varies per volume. Jan Thorbecke Verlag GmbH and Company, Karlstrasse 10, Postfach 546, D 72482 Sigmaringen Germany. **Tel** 011 49 7571 728100, FAX 011 07571-728-280, telex 732534. **LC** PT2635.I65; Z843.
Ind/Abst MLA Int. Bibl. Books Artic. Mod. Lang. Lit.

SZ/0082-4186
BLATTER DER THOMAS MANN-GESELLSCHAFT. [Bl. Thomas Mann Ges.]. **Main/Corp** Thomas Mann-Gesellschaft. (1958)-. Monographic series. English. **LC** PT2625.A44; Z897.
Ind/Abst MLA Int. Bibl. Books Artic. Mod. Lang. Lit.

NE
BLIND (AMSTERDAM, NETHERLANDS).
See The Arts-Art.

SW/0005-3198
BLM. BONNIERS LITTERARA MAGASIN. (BONNIERS LITTERARA MAGASIN.).
[BLM, Bonniers litt. mag.]. **Added/Corp** Albert Bonniers Forlag. **VFOAT** BLM; BLM Med AVB. Vol. 1 (1932)-. Periodical. Swedish. Six times a year. Kr266.00 Scandinavia; Kr278.00 others. Ahlen & Akerlunds Forlags AB, Box 3217, S 10364 Stockholm Sweden. **(Subscription address:** Pressdata / Sweden, PO Box 3263, 103 65 Stockholm Sweden.**)** **ED** Georg Svensson. **LC** AP48; .B6. **Bk Rev**. **Ad Acc.** ctrl circ. *Absorbed All Varldens Bebrattare.*
Desc: Essays and reviews concerning modern as well as classical literature.
Ind/Abst Annu. Bibliogr. Engl. Lang. Lit.; MLA Int. Bibl. Books Artic. Mod. Lang. Lit.; Romant. Move.

CN/1183-1499
BLOOD & APHORISMS. [Blood Aphorisms].
VFOAT Blood and Aphorisms. (1991)-. Periodical. English. qt. 18.00Can$ (one year), 32.00Can$ (two year). Blood and Aphorisms, PO Box 702, Station P, Toronto, Ontario M5S 2Y4 Canada. **Tel** (416)535-0710. **ED** Mark Hickmott (managing editor). **DD** C810.80054.

US/1047-174X
BLOOD REVIEW, THE. (THE BLOOD REVIEW : THE JOURNAL OF HORROR CRITICISM.). [Blood rev.].
Vol. 1, No. 1 (Oct. 1989)-. Periodical. English. qt. $15.00 (public and academic libraries), $25.00 (other). Blood Review, 1200 Galapago 221, Denver CO 80204. **Tel** (303)629-1873. **(Subscription address:** Blood Review, PO Box 4394, Denver, CO 80204**)** **LC** PN3435; .B58. **DD** 810.9/16.
Desc: Literary journal devoted to covering the horror genre through the presentation of reviews, news essays and interviews.

US/0161-2506
BLOODROOT. *Suspended.* No. 1 (Fall 1976)-Suspended with Iss. 10 (1988). Periodical. English. ir. Bloodroot, Box 891, Grand Forks ND 58201. **Tel** (701)746-5858. **ED** Linda L Ohlsen. **LC** PS508.W7; B56. **DD** 810/.8/09287. **Circ:** 800 (ctrl).
Desc: Contents include short fiction and poetry.

CN/0820-8352
BLUE BUFFALO. [Blue buffalo]. Vol. 1, No. 1 (Oct. 1982)-. Periodical. English. Twice a year (Spring and Fall). 8.00Can$ one year 15.00Can$ two year. Dandelion Magazine Society, 922-9th Avenue Southeast, Calgary Alberta T2G 0S4 Canada. **Tel** (403)265-0524. **ED** Peter Past. **DD** C810/.8/097123. **Ad Acc. Circ:** 350-500 (ctrl).
Desc: Publishes in Alberta writing and visual art.

IT
BLUE GUITAR, THE. *Ceased.* Vol. 1 (1975)-Ceased Vol. 7, No.8. Periodical. English (Italian). an. Herder Editrice e Libreria SRL, Piazza Montecitorio 117-120, 00186 Rome Italy. **Tel** 011 39 6 679 4628, FAX 011 39 6 678 4751. **ED** Angela Giannitrapani. **LC** PR1098; .B48. **DD** 820/.8/00914. **Bk Rev**.

US/0743-2917
BLUE MOON. [Blue moon]. 1984 Ed.-. Periodical. English. an. $5.00. Red Herring Press, 1209 West Oregon Street, Urbana IL 61801. **DD** 813.

US/0198-9901
BLUELINE (POTSDAM, N.Y.). (BLUELINE.).
VAT Blue Line. (Summer/Fall 1979)-. Periodical. English. sa. $6.00 US; $7.00 other. Blueline, Potsdam College, SUNY, Potsdam NY 13676. **Tel** (315)267-2008. **ED** Anthony Tyler. **Bk Rev**, (Qty: 5). **Circ:** 500.
Desc: Features quality prose, fiction and poetry about the Adirondacks and other areas similar in geography and spirit.
Ind/Abst Am. Humanit. Index; Index Am. Period. Verse.

US/0006-5188
BLUESTONE; THE LITERARY QUARTERLY. No. 1 (1964)-. Periodical. English. ir. Woodstock Creative Arts, Box 355, Woodstock NY 12498.

●US/1062-6409
BLUFFS READER, THE. (1992)-. Periodical. English. qt. $20.00 (institutions). Bluffs Press, PO Box 11883, Memphis TN 38111-0883.

GW/0523-7971
BOCHUMER ARBEITEN ZUR SPRACH- UND LITERATURWISSENSCHAFT. [Boch. Arb. Sprach- Lit.wiss.]. **Added/Corp** Ruhr-Universitat Bochum. Abteilung fuer Philologie. (1967)-. Monographic series. German. ir. Price varies per volume. Wilhelm Fink Verlag, Ohmstrasse 5, D 80802 Munich Germany. **Tel** 011 49 89 348017, 348018. **LC** UNC.
Ind/Abst MLA Int. Bibl. Books Artic. Mod. Lang. Lit.

DK/0006-5692
BOGENS VERDEN. **See** Library and Information Sciences.

US/0882-648X
BOGG (ARLINGTON, VA.). (BOGG.). [Bogg]. (196?)-. Periodical. English. ir (two or three issues per year). $15.00. Bogg Publications, 422 North Cleveland Street, Arlington VA 22201. **Tel** (703)243-6019. **(Subscription address:** UK/ 31 Belle Uue Street, Filey N Yorkshire Y014 9HU; Aus/ 48 Academy Avenue, Mulgrave Victoria 3170; Can/ 532 Pall Mall Street, London Ontario N5Y 2Z6**)** **ED** John Elsberg, George Cairncross, Robert Boyce and Sheila Martindale. **DD** 820. Index available (Covers US issues). cum. index (In 1995). **Bk Rev**, (Qty: 50-100). **Pr Rev. Circ:** 800 (ctrl).
Desc: A journal of North American and British writing: poetry, numerous short reviews of American, Canadian, British magazines and books, essays on small press experiences and history in the US and UK.
Ind/Abst Am. Humanit. Index; Index Am. Period. Verse.

US/8756-8500
BOGUS REVIEW. [Bogus rev.]. Periodical. English. an. Bogusbooks, 120 West 9th Street, #10A, New York NY 10025. **DD** 810.

GW
BOHLAU FORUM LITTERARUM. Vol. 1 (1976)-. Monographic series. German. ir. Price varies per volume.

IC
BOKAORMURINN. SKJOLDUR. **VFOAT** Skjoldur. (1986)-. Periodical. Icelandic. qt.
Ind/Abst Annu. Bibliogr. Engl. Lang. Lit.

SW/0006-5846
BOKVAENNEN. [Bokvaennen]. **Added/Corp** Saellskapet Bokvaennerna (Sweden). Vol. 1 (Sept. 1946)-. Periodical. Swedish. Six times a year (Jan., Mar., June, Sept., Nov., Dec.). $42.00. Saellskapet Bokvaennerna, PO Box 102 85, 100 55 Stockholm Sweden. **Tel** 011 46 8 6605364. **ED** Lars-Ove Pollack. **LC** Z1007; .B684. Index available. cum. index. **Bk Rev. Ad Acc. Circ:** 1,400 (ctrl).
Desc: Magazine for those interested in literature, books, fine bindings, book collections, the history of books and literature.
Ind/Abst MLA Int. Bibl. Books Artic. Mod. Lang. Lit.

MH
BOLETIM DO INSTITUTO "LUIS DE CAMOES.". **Main/Corp** Instituto "Luis de Camoes.". Vol. 1, No. 1 (Dec. 1965)-. Bulletin. Portuguese. qt.
Ind/Abst MLA Int. Bibl. Books Artic. Mod. Lang. Lit.

US/0884-0091
BOLETIN - ACADEMIA NORTEAMERICANA DE LA LENGUA ESPANOLA. **See** Linguistics.

VE/1012-960X
BOLETIN / ACADEMIA VENEZOLANA DE LA LENGUA CORRESPONDIENTE DE LA ESPANOLA. [Bol. - Acad. venez. leng. corresp. esp.]. **Added/Corp** Academia Venezolana de la Lengua. (1963)-. Periodical. Spanish. sa. **LC** AS90; .C35. **DD** 860/.5. cum. index. ***Continues** Boletin de la Academia Venezolana, correspondiente de la Espanola.*
Ind/Abst Am. Hist. Life (1966-1970).

CK/0404-7710
BOLETIN CULTURAL Y BIBLIOGRAFICO. **Main/Corp** Biblioteca Luis-Angel Arango. (Jan. 1958)-. Periodical. Spanish. Four times a year. $30.00. Banco de la Republica Departamento Editorial, Calle 13 35 51, Bogota de 1 Columbia. **Tel** 011 57 1 2010900, 011 57 1 2776872. **LC** AS82.B26; A23.
Ind/Abst Am. Hist. Life (1964-1969, 1979-); MLA Int. Bibl. Books Artic. Mod. Lang. Lit.

AG/0001-3757
BOLETIN DE LA ACADEMIA ARGENTINA DE LETRAS. [Bol. Acad. Argent. Let.]. **Main/Corp** Academia Argentina de Letras. Vol. 1, No. 1 (Jan./March 1933)-. Periodical. Spanish. qt. $30.00. Academia Argentina de Letras, Sanchez de Bustamente 2663, 1425 Buenos Aries 25A Argentina. **Tel** 802-7509. **ED** Jorge Vocos Lescano. **LC** AS78; .B55. **DD** 056/.1. cum. index. **Circ:** 1,000 (ctrl).
Desc: Dedicated to publish the account of the activities of the corporation, the original studies of the members on the subjects related to their function and bibliographic information.
Ind/Abst Am. Hist. Life (1965-1977, 1979-); Romant. Move.

CL/0716-5463
BOLETIN DE LA ACADEMIA CHILENA CORRESPONDIENTE DE LA REAL ACADEMIA ESPANOLA. [Bol. Acad. Chil. corresp. R. Acad. Esp.]. **Main/Corp** Academia Chilena, Santiago de Chile. Vol. 1 (1915)-. Periodical. Spanish. **LC** AS81; .S25.
Ind/Abst Am. Hist. Life (1970-).

SP
BOLETIN DE LITERATURA MEDIEVAL. Spanish. an. 1150.00ptas Spain; 1085.00ptas other. Editorial Gredos SA, Calle Sanchez Pacheco 81, 28002 Madrid Spain. **Tel** 011 34 1 4157408, FAX 011 34 1 5192033. **Bk Rev. Pr Rev. Circ:** 1,000.

IT
BOLLETTINO DELL ISTITUTO DI FILOGIA DELL UNIVERSITA DI PADOVA. L'Erma di Bretschneider SPA, Via Cassiodoro 19, 00193 Rome Italy. **Tel** 011 39 6 6874127, 011 39 6 6874129, FAX 011 39 6 6874129.

IT/0006-6583
BOLLETTINO DI STUDI LATINI. **See** Linguistics.

US/0160-4694
BOMBAY GIN. Periodical. English. The Naropa Institute, Journal of Psychology, 2130 Arapahoe Avenue, Boulder CO 80302. **Tel** (303)444-0202. **LC** PS501; .B64. **DD** 810.8/005/4.

GW/0068-001X
BONNER ARBEITEN ZUR DEUTSCHEN LITERATUR. [Bonn. Arb. dtsch. Lit.]. (1957)-. Monographic series. German. ir. DM63.23 Germany; DM68.00 other. Bouvier GmbH & Co. KG ABT Verlag, AM Hof 28, D 53113 Bonn Germany. **Tel** 011 49 228 7290141.
Ind/Abst MLA Int. Bibl. Books Artic. Mod. Lang. Lit.

CN/1183-0832
BONNET DE NUIT, LE. [Bonnet nuit]. Vol. 1, No 1 (Dec. 1990)-. Periodical. French. Three times a year. 4.50Can$. Les Editions du Bonnet de Nuit, 1800 Est Rue Sherbrooke, Montreal, Quebec H2K 1B3 Canada. **DD** C840.8/0054/05.

US/1045-2966
BOOK AUTHOR'S NEWSLETTER. [Book author's newsl.]. 1988-. Newsletter. English. ir. F&W Publications, 1507 Dana Avenue, Cincinnati OH 45207. **Tel** (513)531-2222, FAX (513)531-1843. **(Subscription address:** CDS Agency Hard Copy, PO Box 4966, Des Moines IA 50340.**)** **DD** 808.

US/0896-9523
BOOK PEDDLER, THE. **Added/Corp** National Yiddish Book Center (U.S.). **VFOAT** Pakn-Treger. (1980)-. Periodical. English (Yiddish). qt. **DD** 839.
Ind/Abst Index Jew. Period. (199?-).

DK/0006-7377
BOOKBIRD. [Book bird]. **Added/Corp** International Board on Books for Young People. International Institute for Children's Literature and Reading Research. International Institute for Children's, Juvenile, and Popular Literature. **VFOAT** Book Bird. (1962)-. Periodical. English. Four times a year (Mar., June, Sept., Dec.). Kr30.00 US, Kr35.00 Canada, Kr 38.00 others (individuals) Kr40.00 US, Kr45.00 Canada, Kr48.00 others (institutions). Bookbird, 138 Stanley Coulter Hall, Purdue University, West Layfayette IN 47907-1359. **Tel** (317)494-0400, FAX (317)496-1700. **(Subscription address:** Bookbird, PO Box 3156, West Lafayette IN 47906.**)** **LC** PN1009.A1; B6. **DD** 028.05. Index available. **Bk Rev. Ad Acc.** ctrl circ. available on microfilm and microfiche from University Microfilms International (UMI).
Ind/Abst Child. Lit. Abstr. (19??-); Libr. Lit.

US/1041-7834
BOOKLURE (PASADENA, CALIF.). ***Ceased.*** (BOOKLURE.). [Booklure]. Vol. 1, No. 1 (Summer 1988)-(June 1993). Periodical. English. qt. Booklure, PO Box 70374, Pasadena CA 91107. **Tel** (818)797-4382. **DD** 028.

US
BOOKPRESS, THE. **See** Publishing-Books and Bookmaking.

UK
BOOKS FOR KEEPS. (1989)-. Periodical. English. bm. £22.50 (airmail) Southeast Asia and Oceania; £21.30 (airmail) other; £11.40 (surface mail) UK; £16.50 (surface mail) other. School Bookshop Association Ltd, 6 Brightfield Road, Lee London SE12 8QF England. **Tel** 081 852 4953. **ED** Chris Powling. **Circ:** 8,500. ***Absorbed** Children's Books.*
Desc: Review journal on children's books.
Ind/Abst Book Rev. Index; Child. Lit. Abstr. (19??-).

FI/0006-7490
BOOKS FROM FINLAND. **See** Publishing-Abstracting, Bibliographies and Statistics.

BN/0352-1044
BOOKS IN BOSNIA AND HERZEGOVINA. **Added/Corp** Yugoslav Authors' Agency for Bosnia and Herzegovina. Udruzenje Knjizevnika BiH. Vol. 1, No. 1 (1982)-. Periodical. English.
Ind/Abst MLA Int. Bibl. Books Artic. Mod. Lang. Lit.

CN/0707-6924
BOOKS NOW. V. 1- July 31, 1978-. Periodical. English. wk. Free. Our Books Atlantic, PO Box 968 Canada. **DD** C810/.8/09715. ctrl circ.

US/1040-7405
BOOTBLACK (BOYNTON BEACH, FLA.). (BOOTBLACK.). [Bootblack]. Vol. 1, No. 1 (Jan./Feb. 1989)-. Periodical. English. Six times a year. $24.00. Bootblack, 1001 Southwest 5th Court, Boynton Beach FL 33426. **Tel** (407)736-2340. **ED** Gilbert K. Westgard II. **DD** 813. Index available. **Bk Rev.**

US/0891-9623
BORGO LITERARY GUIDES. [Borgo lit. guides]. No. 1 (1991)-. Monographic series. English. ir. Price varies per volume. Borgo Press, PO Box 2845, San Bernardino CA 92406. **Tel** (714)884-5813, (714)885-1161. **ED** Michael and Mary Burgess. **DD** 800. Index available.
Desc: A new series of reference guides on literary topics, including awards, bibliographies, directories, cyclopedias, catalogues, and indexes.

US/0734-2306
BOSTON REVIEW (CAMBRIDGE, MASS. : 1982). (BOSTON REVIEW.). [Boston rev.]. **VFOAT** New Boston Review. Vol. 7, No. 1 (Feb. 1982)-. Periodical. English. Six times a year (Feb., Apr., June, Aug., Oct., Dec.). $15.00 (individuals), $18.00 (institutions) US; $21.00 (individuals), $24.00 (institutions) Canada & Mexico; $27.00 (individuals), $30.00 (institutions) others. Boston Review, C/O Kim Cooper, 33 Harrison Avenue, Boston MA 02111. **Tel** (617)350-5353, FAX (617)350-6633. **ED** Joshua Cohen and Kim Cooper. **Bk Rev**, (Qty: 30). **Ad Acc, Adv Mgr:** Kim Cooper. **Pr Rev. Circ:** 20,000 (ctrl). available on microfilm and microfiche from University Microfilms International (UMI). ***Continues** New Boston Review, 0361-168X.*
Desc: This journal is about the politics, literature, and contemporary culture.
Ind/Abst Am. Humanit. Index; Book Rev. Index; Index Am. Period. Verse; MLA Int. Bibl. Books Artic. Mod. Lang. Lit.

US/1067-2834
BOSTONIA (BOSTON, MASS. 1986). (BOSTONIA.). [Bostonia]. **Added/Corp** Boston University. Vol. 60, No. 3 (Oct. 1986)-. Periodical. English. Four times a year (Seasonally). $14.00 US; $20.00 others. Bostonia Magazine of Culture, 10 Lenox, Brookline MA 02146. **Tel** (617)353-2055, (617)353-6488, FAX (617)353-6488. **ED** K. Batsford (phone: (617)353-3081). **LC** LH1.B5; B72. **DD** 378.744. cum. index. **Bk Rev**, (Qty: 6-10). **Ad Acc, Adv Mgr:** M. Mediate, **Tel** (617)353-5390. ***Continues** Bostonia Magazine, 0164-1441.*
Desc: Articles are distinguished by an uncommon thoroughness and depth, and written by internationally acclaimed authors, poets and playwrights.

US/0885-9337
BOULEVARD (NEW YORK, N.Y.). (BOULEVARD.). [Boulevard]. Vol. 1, No. 1 & 2 (Winter 1986)-. Periodical. English. Three times a year (Single issue in September and double issue in April). $12.00 (one year), $20.00 (two year), $25.00 (three year). OpoJaz Inc, PO Box 30386, Philadelphia PA 19103. **Tel** (215)568-7062. **ED** Richard Burgin and David Brezovec. **DD** 810. **Ad Acc. Circ:** 3,000.
Desc: Publishes short stories, poetry, and essays on on contemporary culture and the arts.
Ind/Abst Am. Humanit. Index; Index Am. Period. Verse.

US/0190-3659
BOUNDARY 2. [Bound. 2]. **Added/Corp** State University of New York at Binghamton. Dept. of English. **VAT** Boundary Two. Vol. 1 (Fall 1972)-. Periodical. English. tq (3 issues). $60.00 (institutions), $24.00 (individuals) US; $69.00 (institutions), $33.00 (individuals) other. Duke University Press, PO Box 90660, Durham NC 27708-0660. **Tel** (919)687-3600, (919)688-5134 (orders), FAX (919)688-4574, telex 802829. **ED** Paul A. Bove. **LC** PN2; .B68. **DD** 808.8/004. **Bk Rev. Ad Acc. Circ:** 1,500. available on microfilm and microfiche from University

Microfilms International (UMI). Documents available from The Genuine Article, UMI Article Clearinghouse.
Desc: An international journal of literature and culture.
Ind/Abst Abstr. Engl. Stud.; Acad. Search (July 1993-); Am. Humanit. Index (-199?); Annu. Bibliogr. Engl. Lang. Lit.; Arts Humanit. Citation Index [Full Cov.]; Curr. Contents Arts Humanit.; Expand. Acad. Index (1988-); Film Lit. Index (19??-); Humanit. Index; Humanit. Source (Jul. 1993-); Index Am. Period. Verse; INFO-SOUTH Abstr.; Mag. Search; MLA Int. Bibl. Books Artic. Mod. Lang. Lit.; Newsp. Period. Abstr. (1991-); Res. Alert [Full Cov.]; Soc. Sci. Cit. Index [Select. Cov.].

US/0364-3344
BOX 749. **Added/Corp** Printable Arts Society. Seven Square Press. **VAT** Box Seven Forty Nine. Vol. 1 (Fall 1972)-. Periodical. English. $7.00 (4 issues). Printable Arts Society, 411 West 22nd Street, New York NY 10011. **ED** David Ferguson. **LC** PS501; .B68. **DD** 810/.5. **Circ:** 5,000. available with illustrations.

●US/1064-0096
BOX N' CHEST. [Box chest]. **VFOAT** Box and Chest; Geniphur Rankin's Box & Chest; Box & Chest. (1992)-. Periodical. English. mo. $10.00. DRS Publishing, PO Box 8145, Austin TX 78713-8145. **DD** 808.

BL/0103-751X
BRASIL PORTO ALEGRE. (BRASIL BRAZIL. A JOURNAL OF BRAZILIAN LITERATURE.). [Brasil Porto Alegre]. **VFOAT** Brazil (Porto Alegre). (1988)-. Periodical. Multiple languages (English and Portuguese). Twice a year (July, Dec.). $15.00 (individuals); $40.00 (institutions). Brown University / Department of Portugese & Brazilian Studies, PO Box O, Providence RI 02912. **Tel** (401)863-3042, FAX (401)863-7261. **ED** Nelson H. Vieira and Regina Zilberman. **UDC** 860. **Bk Rev**, (Qty: 10). **Pr Rev. Circ:** 130.
Desc: Fiction and poetry by the Brazilian authors and works of Brazilian literature.

US/0734-8665
BRECHT YEARBOOK, THE. [Brecht yearb.]. **Added/Corp** International Brecht Society. **VFOAT** Brecht Jahrbuch. Vol. 11 (1982)-. English (French, German and Spanish). an. $20.00 (regular member annual) income less than $20,000; $25.00 (regular member annual) income $20,000 and over; $30.00 (sustaning & institutions) Comes with International Brecht Society Membership. International Brecht Society, University of Georgia, Department of German Slavic Language, Athens GA 30602. **Tel** (706)542-3663. **ED** John Fuegi, Gisela Bahr, and Carl Werber. **LC** PT2603.R397; Z57734. **DD** 832/.912. **Bk Rev. Circ:** 1,100 (ctrl). ***Continues*** *Brecht-Jahrbuch, 0341-9525.*
Desc: Each collection of essays explores a different facet of contemporary Brecht studies.
Ind/Abst MLA Int. Bibl. Books Artic. Mod. Lang. Lit.

AU
BRENNER-STUDIEN. (1969)-. Monographic series. German.
Ind/Abst MLA Int. Bibl. Books Artic. Mod. Lang. Lit.

US/1052-1569
BRIDGE (OAK PARK, MICH.), THE. (THE BRIDGE : A JOURNAL OF FICTION AND POETRY.). [Bridge]. Vol. 1, No. 1 (1990)-. Periodical. English. sa (Feb. and July). $15.00. Bridge / Michigan, 14050 Vernon Street, Oak Park MI 48237. **Tel** (313)547-6823. **ED** Jack & Helen Zucker. **LC** PS536.2; .B74. **DD** 810.8/0005. **Bk Rev**, (Qty: 3 - 4). **Ad Acc. Circ:** 700.

UK
BRITISH AND IRISH AUTHORS. Academic Scholarly Publication. English. ir. Cambridge University Press, The Edinburgh Building, Shaftesbury Road, Cambridge CB2 2RU United Kingdom. **Tel** 011 44 223 312393, FAX 011 44 223 325959.

UK/0141-867X
BRITISH JOURNAL FOR EIGHTEENTH-CENTURY STUDIES, THE. [Br. j. eight. century stud.]. **Added/Corp** British Society for Eighteenth-Century Studies. **VFOAT** British Journal for 18th-Century Studies. Vol. 1 (Spring 1978)-. Periodical. English (French). sa. $66.00. Voltaire Foundation, University of Oxford, 99 Banbury Road, Oxford OX2 7RB England. **Tel** 011 44 865 284600, FAX 011 44 865 270740. **ED** Brean Hammond. **LC** CB411; .B74. **DD** 940.2/53/05. **Bk Rev. Ad Acc. Circ:** 500. ***Continues*** *Newsletter - British Society for Eighteenth-Century Studies.*
Desc: Covers all aspects of 18th Century studies.
Ind/Abst Annu. Bibliogr. Engl. Lang. Lit.; BHA : Biblio. Hist. Art; Br. Humanit. Index; MLA Int. Bibl. Books Artic. Mod. Lang. Lit.; Romant. Move.

UK
BRITISH SCIENCE FICTION BOOK INDEX. **VFOAT** British S-F Book Index. English. British Science Fiction Association, C O 269 Wykeham Road, Reading RG6 1PL England. **Tel** 011 44 734 318022.

US/0737-6340
BRONTE NEWSLETTER. [Bronte newsl.]. **Added/Corp** Bronte Society Periodicals. No. 1 (1982)-. English. an. £12.00 UK & Europe; £17.00 others Comes with Bronte Society membership. Bronte Parsonage / Bronte Society Museum, Haworth Keighley, West Yorkshire BD22 8DR England. **Tel** 011 44 535 642323, FAX 011 44 535 647131. **LC** PR4168; .A14. **DD** 823/.8/09. **Bk Rev. Circ:** 500 (ctrl).
Desc: Contains essays, and other articles of the bronte interest; as well as reports of seminars, conferences, society news, etc.

UK
BRONTE SOCIETY GAZETTE. (1990)-. English. Twice a year. £12.00 UK & Europe; £17.00 others Comes with Bronte Society membership. Bronte Parsonage / Bronte Society Museum, Haworth Keighley, West Yorkshire BD22 8DR England. **Tel** 011 44 535 642323, FAX 011 44 535 647131.

UK/0309-7765
BRONTE SOCIETY PUBLICATIONS. TRANSACTIONS. (BRONTE SOCIETY TRANSACTIONS.). [Bronte Soc. publ., Trans.]. **Main/Corp** Bronte Society. Vol. 11, No. 5 (1950)-. English. Twice a year (Apr. & Nov.). £12.00 UK & Europe; £17.00 others; Also comes with Bronte Society membership. Bronte Parsonage / Bronte Society Museum, Haworth Keighley, West Yorkshire BD22 8DR England. **Tel** 011 44 535 642323, FAX 011 44 535 647131. **ED** Edward Chitham and Mark Seaward. **LC** PR4168; .A4. **DD** 823/.8/09. Index available (free on request). **Bk Rev. Pr Rev. Circ:** 3,500 (ctrl). available on microfilm. ***Continues*** *Bronte Society. Bronte Society Publications.*
Desc: The purpose of this society and publication is to create a better understanding and appreciation of the story, and to bring closer together all those who honour the sisters, and to acts as the guardian of such letters, writings and personal belongings that could be acquired for the museum.
Ind/Abst Abstr. Engl. Stud.; Annu. Bibliogr. Engl. Lang. Lit.

UK/0950-6349
BROWNING SOCIETY NOTES. ***Ceased.*** [Browning Soc. notes]. **Main/Corp** Browning Society (London, England). **VFOAT** BSN; Notes; Society Notes. Vol. 2, No. 1 (March 1972)-Vol. 22 (1994). Periodical. English. sa. The Browning Society, 10 Pembridge Square, London W2 4ED England. **ED** Michael Meredith and Mairi Calcraft. **Bk Rev. Ad Acc. Circ:** 250. ***Continues*** *Society Notes - Browning Society (London, England).*
Desc: Literary; concerned with the Brownings, their circle and contemporaries.
Ind/Abst Abstr. Engl. Stud. (1982-); Annu. Bibliogr. Engl. Lang. Lit.; MLA Int. Bibl. Books Artic. Mod. Lang. Lit.

US/1055-6869
BROWNSTONE MYSTERY GUIDES. (1991)-. Periodical. English. Price varies per volume. Borgo Press, PO Box 2845, San Bernardino CA 92406. **Tel** (714)884-5813, (714)885-1161. **ED** Guy M. Townsend.
Desc: A continuing series of essays and bibliographies on the major and minor mystery writers of our times.

UK
BRUNTON'S MISCELLANY. V. 1- Autumn 1977-. Periodical. English. Three times a year. £4.95. Brunton's Miscellany, 28 A Dundas Street, Edinburgh EH3 6JN Scotland. **LC** PR8629; .B78. **DD** 820/.5.

GW/0340-5435
BUCHREIHE DER ANGLIA. (BUCHREIHE DER ANGLIA : ZEITSCHRIFT FUER ENGLISCHE PHILOLOGIE.). [Buchr. Angl.]. (1952)-. Monographic series. German. ir. Price varies per volume. Max Niemeyer Verlag, Postfach 2140, D 72011 Tuebingen Germany. **Tel** 011 49 7071 989494, FAX 011 49 7071 87419. **ED** Helmut Gneuss, Hans Kasmann, Erwin Wolff, Theordor Wolpers. **LC** PE25; .A47.
Desc: Monographs on English literature and language.
Ind/Abst Annu. Bibliogr. Engl. Lang. Lit.; MLA Int. Bibl. Books Artic. Mod. Lang. Lit.; Soc. Plann. Policy Dev. Abstr.; Sociol. Abstr.

II
BUDDHIPRAKASA. **Added/Corp** Gujarat Vidya Sabha. (19??)-. Periodical. Gujarati. mo. **LC** AP95.G8; B8.

EC/0304-1417
BUFANDA DEL SOL, LA. Spanish. Editorial Universitaria / Quito, AP 11-32, Quito Ecuador. **LC** PQ7081.A1; B83.

US/0195-1580
BUILDING BLOCKS. (19??)-. Periodical. English. Ten times a year (Except July & Aug.). $20.00 (one year), $36.50 (two years), $50.00 (three years). Building Blocks, 38W 567 Brindlewood, Elgin IL 60123. **Tel** (800)233-2448, (708)742-1013, FAX (708)742-1054.

JA
BUKKU ENDO TSUSHIN. No. 2- ; 1979-. Periodical. Japanese. ir. ¥5,500. Aoyama Takeshi, 21-6 Hongyotoku, Ichikawa Japan. **Tel** 0473-58-0947. **ED** Takeshi Aoyama. **LC** PL700; .B78. Index available. **Bk Rev. Circ:** 500.
Desc: Research for obscure materials in Japanese modern literature.

JA
BUKKYO BUNGAKU KENKYU. No. 1 (1974)-. Periodical. Japanese. Hozokan, Karasumaru Higashi Shimokyo-ku, Kyota Japan. **LC** PL721.B8; B8.

SP
BULGARSKI GLAS. **See** Political Science.

FR/0571-5350
BULLETIN - ASSOCIATION DES AMIS DE RABELAIS ET DE LA DEVINIERE. [Bull. - Assoc. amis Rabelais Deviniere]. **Main/Corp** Association des Amis de Rabelais et de La Deviniere. No 1 (1951)-. Bulletin. French.
Ind/Abst MLA Int. Bibl. Books Artic. Mod. Lang. Lit.

FR/0583-8797
BULLETIN BIBLIOGRAPHIQUE DE LA SOCIETE RENCESVALS. **Main/Corp** Societe Rencesvals. (1958)-. Bibliography. French. ir. Price varies per volume. Universite Liege, 43 Boulevard Frere Orban, B-4000 Liege Belgium. **LC** PQ201; .S66a. **DD** 016.841/1.

FR/0037-9506
BULLETIN DE LA SOCIETE PAUL CLAUDEL. **Main/Corp** Societe Paul Claudel (France). (1958)-. Bulletin. French. qt (Jan., Apr., July, Oct.). 165.00F France; 200.00F other. Madame Renee Nantet, 13 rue du Pont Louis Philippe, F-75014 Paris France. **Tel** 011 33 1 42 77 96 36, FAX 011 33 1 42 77 65 39. **ED** Jacqueline Veinstein. **LC** PQ2605.L2; Z878. **DD** 848/.9/1209. Index available. cum. index. **Bk Rev. Ad Acc. Circ:** 130 (ctrl). available in microform.
Desc: Features articles by outstanding international scholars covering the entire range of Claudel studies. Literature, theater, music, plastic arts, cinemas and philosophy - and also includes reviews and comprehensive bibliographies.
Ind/Abst Romant. Move.

FR/0221-7945
BULLETIN DE LA SOCIETE THEOPHILE GAUTIER. [Bull. Soc. Theophile Gautier]. No. 1 (1979)-. Bulletin. French. an. 100.00F France; $25.00 US. Universite Paul Valery, BP 5043 Route de Mende, 34032 Montpellier, Cedex 1 France. **Tel** 11 33 67 142000, FAX 011 33 67 142052. **ED** Claudine Lacoste. **Bk Rev.**
Desc: Scholarly articles, reviews and notes related to French writer Theophile Gautier and his immediate circle. Bibliography and news notes.
Ind/Abst MLA Int. Bibl. Books Artic. Mod. Lang. Lit.

BE/0378-0708
BULLETIN DE L'ACADEMIE ROYALE DE LANGUE ET DE LITTERATURE FRANCAISES. **See** Linguistics.

FR/0044-8133
BULLETIN DES AMIS D'ANDRE GIDE. **Added/Corp** Association des Amis d'Andre Gide. Universite de Lyon II. Unite d'Etudes Francaises. Universite Paul Valery. Centre d'Etudes litteraires du XX. siecle. Section Andre Gide. No. 11 (April 1971)-. Bulletin. French. qt. 250.00F France; 300.00F other. Association des Amis d'Andre Gide, BP 3741, F 54098 Nancy Cedex France. **Tel** 33 22 266658, FAX 33 22 78 591605. **LC** PQ2613.I2; Z612478. **DD** 848/.91209. ***Continues*** *Bulletin d'Informations.*
Ind/Abst MLA Int. Bibl. Books Artic. Mod. Lang. Lit.; Romant. Move.

FR/0335-508X
BULLETIN DES ETUDES VALERYENNES. [Bull. etud. Valeryennes]. **Added/Corp** Universite Paul Valery. Centre d'Etudes Valeryennes. No. 1 (April 1974)-. Bulletin. French. ir (2-3 times per year). 110.00F France; 135.00F other. Universite Paul Valery, BP 5043 Route de Mende, 34032 Montpellier, Cedex 1 France. **Tel** 11 33 67 142000, FAX 011 33 67 142052. **ED** Sage Bourjea. **Bk Rev**, (Qty: 3). **Circ:** 500 (ctrl).
Desc: Contains all relevant information concerning research on Valery en France and abroad.
Ind/Abst MLA Int. Bibl. Books Artic. Mod. Lang. Lit.

FR/0180-8567
BULLETIN D'INFORMATIONS ET DE RECHERCHES. [Bull. inf. rech., Amitie Charles Peguy]. **Added/Corp** Amitie Charles Peguy. (Jan./Mar. 1978)-. Bulletin. French. qt. 140.00F France; 150.00F other. Amities Charles Peguy, 12 rue Notre Dame des Champs, 75006 Paris France. **Tel** 011 33 1 45448038. **LC** PQ2631.E25; Z53324. **DD** 848/.91209. ***Continues*** *Feuillets (Amitie Charles Peguy).*
Ind/Abst MLA Int. Bibl. Books Artic. Mod. Lang. Lit.

FR
BULLETIN DU XVII SIECLE. Bulletin. French. Four times a year. $64.86 EEC; $75.00 other. Societe d'Etude du XVII Siecle, 11 place Marcelin Berthelot, 75005 Paris France. **Tel** 011 33 1 44271211, FAX 011 33

Literature

1 44271109. Index available.
Desc: Covers varied issues about literature and history of the seventeenth century.

FR/0007-4640
BULLETIN HISPANIQUE. [Bull. hisp.]. Vol. 1 (Jan./March 1899)-. Bulletin. French (English, Italian and Spanish). sa. 333.05F France; 395.00F other. Editions Biere, 22 rue du Peugue, 33000 Bordeaux France. **Tel** 011 33 56 999999. **LC** PQ6001; .B8. **DD** 860/.9. Documents available from The Genuine Article.
Ind/Abst Am. Hist. Life (1955-1956, 1967-); Arts Humanit. Citation Index [Full Cov.]; BHA : Biblio. Hist. Art; Curr. Contents Arts Humanit.; HAPI Hisp. Am. Period. Index; MLA Int. Bibl. Books Artic. Mod. Lang. Lit.; Res. Alert [Full Cov.]; Romant. Move.

FR
BULLETIN MARCEL PROUST. **Added/Corp** Societe des Amis de Marcel Proust et des Amis de Combray. No 40 (1990)-. French. an (May). 200.00F. Societe des Amis de Marcel Proust et des Amis de Combray, 4 rue du Docteur Proust, F 28120 Illiers Combray France. **Tel** 011 33 16 37243097. **LC** PQ2631.R63; Z54544. **Continues** Bulletin de la Societe des Amis de Marcel Proust et des Amis de Combray, 0583-8452.
Ind/Abst MLA Int. Bibl. Books Artic. Mod. Lang. Lit.

US/0008-9036
BULLETIN OF THE CENTER FOR CHILDREN'S BOOKS. [Bull. Cent. Child. Books]. **Main/Corp** University of Chicago. Center for Children's Books. **Added/Corp** University of Chicago. Center for Children's Books. University of Illinois at Urbana-Champaign. Center for Children's Books. **VFOAT** BCCB; Bulletin. Vol. 12 (Sept. 1958)-. Periodical. English. mo (except Aug.). $35.00 institutions; $29.00 individuals. University of Illinois Press, 1325 South Oak Street, Champaign IL 61820. **Tel** (217)333-0950, FAX (217)244-8082. **LC** Z1037.A1; C4. [CCC]. Index available (bound in July issue). available on microform and microfiche from University Microfilms International (UMI). **Continues** Bulletin of the Children's Book Center.
Ind/Abst Book Rev. Digest; Book Rev. Index; Sci. Fict. Fantasy Book Rev. Index.

US/0007-5108
BULLETIN OF THE COMEDIANTES. [Bull. Comediantes]. **Main/Corp** Comediantes (Association). Vol. 1 (Mar. 1949)-. Bulletin. English (Spanish). Twice a year (July, Dec.). $15.00 (individuals) ; $45.00 (institutions). Auburn University / Languages, Department of Foreign Languages, Auburn AL 36849. **Tel** (205)844-4345. **LC** PQ6098.7; .C64a. **DD** 862/.3/09. Documents available from The Genuine Article.
Ind/Abst Arts Humanit. Citation Index [Full Cov.]; Curr. Contents Arts Humanit.; MLA Int. Bibl. Books Artic. Mod. Lang. Lit.; Res. Alert [Full Cov.].

US/0192-2424
BULLETIN OF THE SCIENCE FICTION WRITERS OF AMERICA. **Title Change.** [Bull. Sci. Fict. Writ. Am.]. **Added/Corp** Science Fiction Writers of America. **VFOAT** S.F.W.A. Bulletin. (19??)-(19??). Bulletin. English. qt. Pulphouse Publishing, PO Box 1227, Eugene OR 97440. **Tel** (503)935-6322. **LC** PS374.S35; S14. **DD** 813/.0876/09. **Bk Rev.** **Ad Acc.** **Circ:** 1,000. available on microfilm and microfiche from University Microfilms International (UMI). **Continues** SFWA Bulletin, 0036-1364. **Continued by** Bulletin (Science Fiction and Fantasy Writers of America).
Ind/Abst Sci. Fict. Fantasy Book Rev. Index.

US/0887-4409
BULLETIN OF THE WEST VIRGINIA ASSOCIATION OF COLLEGE ENGLISH TEACHERS, THE. [Bull. W. V. Assoc. Coll. Engl. Teach.]. **Added/Corp** West Virginia Association of College English Teachers. (Spring 1974)-. Bulletin. English. an. $4.00 (latest edition). West Virginia Association of English Teachers, Department of English, Marshall University, Huntington WV 25701. **Tel** (304)696-6619. **DD** 808.
Ind/Abst MLA Int. Bibl. Books Artic. Mod. Lang. Lit.

●XXU
BULLETIN / SCIENCE FICTION AND FANTASY WRITERS OF AMERICA. **Added/Corp** Science Fiction and Fantasy Writers of America. **VFOAT** SFWA Bulletin. Vol. 25, Issue 4 (Winter 1992)-. Bulletin. English. qt. **Continues** Bulletin of the Science Fiction Writers of America.

FR/0081-0754
BULLETIN - SOCIETE CHATEAUBRIAND. **Main/Corp** Societe Chateaubriand, Chatenay-Malabry, France. **Added/Corp** France. Centre National des Lettres. No. 1-6, (1930)-. Bulletin. French. an. 230.00F. Societe Chateaubriand, 122 Boulevard de Courcelles, 75017 Paris France. **Tel** 011 33 1 42273441. **LC** PQ2206.Z5; S65. **DD** 843.65. Index available. cum. index. **Bk Rev.** **Circ:** 600 (ctrl).
Desc: Unedited scholarly letters and documents from specialists of the French literature of Romanticism. Always contains current bibliography and whole page illustrations.
Ind/Abst Romant. Move.

FR/0987-7940
BULLETIN / SOCIETE INTERNATIONALE D'ETUDES YOURCENARIENNES. **Added/Corp** Societe Internationale d'Etudes Yourcenariennes. Universite de Tours. No. 1 (Nov. 1987)-. Bulletin. French. Twice a year (June & Oct.). 120.00F. Societe Internationale d'Etudes Yourcenariennes, 7 rue Couchot, 72200 La Fleche France. **Bk Rev**

NE/0167-6520
BUMPER. [Bumper]. (1981)-. Periodical. Dutch. qt. Fl31.75. Wolters Noordhoff BV, Postbus 567, 9700 AN Groningen Netherlands. **Tel** 011 31 50 226886, FAX 011 31 50 264866. **UDC** 087.5.
Desc: Magazine for youth literature.

IO
BUNGA RAMPAI ILMU SASTRA. No. 2-. Periodical. English (Indonesian). sa. Fakultas Sastra Universitas Padjadjaran, Dipati Ukur 35, Bandung Indonesia. **LC** PN9; .B87. **DD** 809. **Continues** Bunga Rampai Ilmu-Ilmu Sastra.

JA
BUNGAKU. **VFOAT** Kikan Bungaku. (1990)-. Periodical. Japanese. Twelve times a year. $108.00. Iwanami Shoten Publishers, 2-5-5 Hitotsubashi, Chiyoda-ku, Tokyo 101-02, Japan. **Tel** 03 3265 4111, FAX 03 3221 8998, telex 39495. **(Subscription address:** Kyowa Book Company Inc., 1 38 Kanda Jinbocho Chiyoda-ku, Tokyo 101 Japan.**) Continues** Bungaku (Tokyo, Japan : 1933), 0389-4029.

JA
BUNGAKU KUKAN. **Added/Corp** Nijisseiki Bungaku Kenkyukai. 1 (March 1979)-. Periodical. Japanese. sa. ¥980. Nijisseiki Bungaku Kenkyukai, Issued by Kenkyukai, c/o Hosei Daigaku 62-Nenkan, Ichigaya Tamachi 162, Tokyo Japan. **LC** PN9; .B914.

JA
BUNGAKUKAI. (1947)-. Periodical. Japanese. mo. $176.00. **(Subscription address:** Kyowa Book Company Inc., 1-38 Kanda Jinbo-Cho, Chiyoda-Ku Tokyo 101, Japan**) LC** PL726.65; .B84. **Continues** Bungakukai (Bunka Koronsha).

JA
BUNGEI GENGO KENKYU: BUNGEIHEN. **Added/Corp** Tsukuba Daigaku. Bungei Gengogakukei. **VFOAT** Studies in Language and Literature. 1 (1976)-. Periodical. Japanese. an. Ibaraki-Ken Niihari-Gun, Sakura-Mura Tsukuba Daigaku, Bungi Gengogukukei, Oaza Tsumaki 30031 Japan. **LC** PN9; .B92.

JA
BUNGEI KENKYU. No. 1-. Periodical. Japanese (English). sa. Free Japan; (add ¥700 for postage) other. Meiji Daigaku Bungei Kenkyukai Surugadai Chiyoda-ku, Tokyo Japan. **ED** Kazuko Nakayama. **LC** PN9; .B924. Index available. **Bk Rev.** **Pr Rev.** **Circ:** 750 (ctrl).
Desc: A learned magazine composed mainly of articles contributed by members of Faculty of Literature, Meiji University.

JA
BUNGEI YOKOHAMA. **Added/Corp** Yokohama. Kyoiku Iinkai. Shakai Kyoikuka. (April 1972)-. Periodical. Japanese. Yokohama-shi Kyoiku Iinkai, 1-1 Minatocho, Naka-ku, Yokohama Japan. **LC** PL887.Y64; B84.

JA
BUNRIN. Periodical. Japanese. an. Free. Shoin Joshi Gakuin Daigaku Gakujutsu Kenkyukai, Sinohara Obanoyama-cho 1-chome Nada-ku Kobe-shi 657 Japan. **Tel** 078-882-6125, FAX 078-882-5032. **LC** PL700; .B835. **Circ:** 1,800 (ctrl).

UK/0954-0970
BUNYAN STUDIES. Vol. 1, No. 1 (Autumn 1988)-. Periodical. English. sa. Bunyan Studies, Parsifal Col 527 Finchley Road, London NW3 7BG England. **Tel** 011 44 1 794 0575.
Ind/Abst Am. Hist. Life (1988-1991); BHA : Biblio. Hist. Art; MLA Int. Bibl. Books Artic. Mod. Lang. Lit.

UK
BURNS CHRONICLE. **See** Biographies.

US/0363-5236
BYE CADMOS. **Added/Corp** American Institute for Writing Research. (1975)-. Periodical. English. sa. American Institute for Writing Research, PO Box 2129, New York NY 10017.

GW
BYZANTINISCH-NEUGRIECHISCHE JAHRBUCHER; INTERNATIONALES WISSENSCHAFTLICHES ORGAN. (1920)-. German.
Ind/Abst MLA Int. Bibl. Books Artic. Mod. Lang. Lit.

GW/0007-7704
BYZANTINISCHE ZEITSCHRIFT. **See** History(General)-History of Europe.

BE/0378-2506
BYZANTION (BRUXELLES). (BYZANTION; REVUE INTERNATIONALE DES ETUDIES BYZANTINES.). [Byzantion]. **Added/Corp** Societe Belge d'Etudes Byzantines. Centre National de Recherches Byzantines. Byzantine Institute of America. Vol. 1 (1924)-. Periodical. English (French, German, Greek, Modern and Italian, Latin). Twice a year. 2000F Belgium; 2280F other. Universa, rue Hoender 24, 9200 Wetteren Belgium. **Tel** 011/32/91/691563. **LC** PA5000; .B9.
Desc: Includes section "Comptes Rendus."
Ind/Abst BHA : Biblio. Hist. Art; MLA Int. Bibl. Books Artic. Mod. Lang. Lit.; Numis. Lit.

US
C A L ANTHOLOGY. English. an. $12.00 (paper); $22.45 (cloth). Norwoods Press, Box 88, Thomaston ME 04861. **Tel** (207)354-6550. **ED** Harley Fetlzer. **Circ:** 1,000 (ctrl).
Desc: Anthology which includes poetry and fiction published in America.

FR/0240-8864
C.A.R.A. CENTRE AIXOIS DE RECHERCHES ANGLAISES. **See** Linguistics.

US/1064-2609
C.A.R.E. PACKAGE, THE. (THE C.A.R.E. PACKAGE : CHILDREN'S AUTHORS MAKE READING EXCITING! / THE APPLE PEDDLER, THE C.A.R.E. package). **VFOAT** CARE Package. Vol. 1, No. 1 (1990)-. Periodical. English. Six times a year. $19.95 (one year); $50.00 (three years). Apple Peddler Inc., 25112 Woodfield School Road, Gaithersburg MD 20882. **Tel** (301)253-0694, FAX (301)253-0694. **ED** Kathy Rogers. **DD** 028. **Bk Rev** (Qty: 50). **Ad Acc.** **Circ:** 3,000.
Desc: Selected children literature used to entice children to read and help them write. The works of different authors are featured each issue.

FR/0294-0078
C.F. RAMUZ. **VFOAT** Serie C.F. Ramuz; Ramuz. (1982)-. French. ir. Lettres Modernes Minard, 45 rue de Saint Andre, 14123 Fleury-sur-Orne France. **Tel** 011 33 31 844706, FAX 011 33 31 844809.

CN/1183-3440
CABARET VERT. [Cabaret vert]. Vol. 1, No. 1 (1991)-. Periodical. English. $20.00 Canada; $20.00 other. Learn/Yeats & Co., PO Box 165, Station J, Toronto Ontario M4Y 4Y1 Canada. **DD** C810/.5.

US/1043-383X
CABIRION AND GAY BOOKS BULLETIN, THE. **See** Homosexuality.

IT/0007-9553
CAFFE; SATIRICO DI LETTERATURA E ATTUALITA, IL. Began publication in 1953. Periodical. Italian. qt. Officina Edizione, Passeggiata di Ripette 25, 00186 Rome Italy.

TR
CAGRINDEX : ABSTRACTS OF THE AGRICULTURAL LITERATURE OF THE CARIBBEAN. **See** Agriculture.

TR/0255-8319
CAGRINDEX / CAGRIS, CARIBBEAN INFORMATION SYSTEM FOR THE AGRICULTURAL SCIENCES. **See** Agriculture.

FR
CAHIERS. **Main/Corp** Amitie Charles Peguy. Vol. 1 (1948)-. French. ir. Lettres Modernes Minard, 45 rue de Saint Andre, 14123 Fleury Surrey Orne France. **Tel** 011 33 31 844706.
Ind/Abst MLA Int. Bibl. Books Artic. Mod. Lang. Lit.

FR/0338-7208
CAHIERS BLEUS. **Added/Corp** Centre Culturel Thibaud de Champagne. Amis des Cahiers Bleus (Troyes, France). (1975)-(1989) ; New Ser. No 1 (Spring 1990)-. Periodical. French. qt. **LC** PQ1141; .C33. **DD** 840.8/0054/05. cum. index.
Ind/Abst BHA : Biblio. Hist. Art.

CN/1183-4110
CAHIERS - CEGEP DE LIMOILOU. DEPARTEMENT DE FRANCAIS. (LES CAHIERS.). [Cahiers - Cegep Limoilou, Dep. fr.]. **Added/Corp** Cegep de Limoilou. Departement de Francais. Vol. 1, No 1 (Spring 1991)-. Periodical. French. sa. Limited free distribution. Departement de Francais, Cegep de Limoilou, CP 1400, Terminus Quebec Quebec G1K 7H3 Canada. **DD** C840.8/0054/05.

CN/1183-4110
CAHIERS - CEGEP DE LIMOILOU. DEPARTEMENT DE FRANCAIS. (LES CAHIERS.). [Cahiers - Cegep Limoilou, Dep. fr.]. **Added/Corp** Cegep de Limoilou. Departement de Francais. Vol. 1, No 1 (Spring 1991)-. Periodical. French. sa. Limited free distribution. **DD** C840.8/0054/05.

FR/0398-6659
CAHIERS CELINE. [Cah. Celine]. (1976)-. Monographic series. French. ir. Editions Gallimard, 5 rue Sebastien Bottin, 75328 Paris Cedex 7 France. **Tel** 011 33 1 49544200. **UDC** 8.

FR
CAHIERS CHARLES V. **See** History(General)-History of Europe.

FR/0291-2120
CAHIERS COLETTE. **Added/Corp** Societe des Amis de Colette. (1977)-. Periodical. French. an. 140.00F. Societe des Amis de Colette, 89520 St. Sauveur Puisay France. **Tel** 011 33 86455670. **LC** PQ2605.O28; Z4583.

FR/0294-0442
CAHIERS DE LA NOUVELLE, LES. [Cah. nouv.]. **Added/Corp** Universite d'Angers. Centre d'Etudes et de Recherches sur la Nouvelle en Langue Anglaise. **VFOAT** Journal of the Short Story in English. No. 1 (March 1983)-. Periodical. French (English). sa. 132.70F France; 165.00F other. Presses de l'Universite D'Angers, 5 rue le Notre, 49045 Angers Cedex 1 France. **Tel** 011 33 41 352100. **ED** Ben Forkner, C. Pamela Valette, and Jeanne Devoize. **Bk Rev. Ad Acc. Circ:** 200 (ctrl).
Desc: Devoted to the study of the short stories in the English Language. Includes articles, interviews, notes and symposium papers.
Ind/Abst Annu. Bibliogr. Engl. Lang. Lit.; MLA Int. Bibl. Books Artic. Mod. Lang. Lit.

FR/0243-2226
CAHIERS DE L'IMAGINAIRE, LES. [Cah. imagin.]. **Added/Corp** Societe des Cahiers de l'Imaginaire. (1980)-. Periodical. French. Twice a year. 240.00F France; 290.00F other. Editions L'Harmattan, 5 rue de l Ecole Polytechnique, 75005 Paris France. **Tel** 33 1 43547910, FAX 33 1 43258203.

SZ/0409-8536
CAHIERS DES AMIS DE ROBERT BRASILLACH. **Added/Corp** Association des Amis de Robert Brasillach. (June 1950)-. Periodical. French. sa. **LC** PQ2603.R315; Z6.
Ind/Abst MLA Int. Bibl. Books Artic. Mod. Lang. Lit.

FR/0751-4239
CAHIERS D'ETUDES GERMANIQUES. No 3 (1979)-. Periodical. French. an. 55 single issue. Marie-Helene Varnier, Bibliotheque de l'Uer d'Etudes Germaniques Universite de Provence, 29 Avenue Robert Schuman, 13621 Aix-en-Provence France. **LC** PT2; .C33. **DD** 830/.9. ***Continues** Etudes Germaniques (Universite d'Aix-Marseille. Centre d'Etudes Germaniques).*
Ind/Abst MLA Int. Bibl. Books Artic. Mod. Lang. Lit.

FR/0762-6193
CAHIERS DU CRIC. [Cah. C.R.I.C.]. **Added/Corp** Centre de Recherche Imaginaire et Creation. **VFOAT** Cahiers du Centre de Recherche Imaginaire et Creation. No. 1 (1985)-. French. ir. 120.00F France; 140.00F other. Centre de Recherche Imaginaire et Creation, Universite de Savoie, BPO 1104, 73011 Chambery Cedex France. **Tel** 33 79 692718. **ED** Jean Burgos. Index available. **Bk Rev. Circ:** 300.

US/1040-3647
CAHIERS DU DIX-SEPTIEME. [Cah. dix-sept.]. **Added/Corp** Southeast American Society for French Seventeenth-Century Studies. **VFOAT** C 17. Vol. 1, No. 1 (Spring 1987)-. Periodical. English (French). Twice a year (Spring & Fall). $12.00 (individual), $15.00 (institution). Cahiers du Dix-Septieme, University of Georgia, Department of Romance Languages, Athens GA 30602. **Tel** (706)542-3164, FAX (706)542-3287. **DD** 840.
Ind/Abst MLA Int. Bibl. Books Artic. Mod. Lang. Lit.

FR/0008-0152
CAHIERS DU MONDE HISPANIQUE ET LUSO-BRESILIEN. **Added/Corp** Toulouse. Universite. Institut d'Etudes Hispaniques, Hispano-Americaines et Luso-Bresiliennes. No. 1 (1963)-. Periodical. French. sa. 180,000F France; 125,000F other. Universite de Toulouse--Le Mirail, 56 Rue du Taur, 31000 Toulouse France. **Tel** 011 33 61 225831, FAX 011 33 61 218420. ***Continues** Caravelle.*
Ind/Abst Am. Hist. Life (1973-); HAPI Hisp. Am. Period. Index (-199?); MLA Int. Bibl. Books Artic. Mod. Lang. Lit.

CN/0843-9559
CAHIERS FRANCO-CANADIENS DE LOUEST. **See** Linguistics.

FR
CAHIERS FRANCO POLONAIS. (19??)-. French. an. 25.00F. Institut d'Etudes Slaves, 9 rue Michelet, 75006 Paris France. **Tel** 011 33 1 43265089.

FR/0222-1578
CAHIERS GERARD DE NERVAL. [Cah. Gerard de Nerval]. **Added/Corp** Societe Gerard de Nerval. No. 1 (1978)-. French. an. 100.00F France; 110.00F other. Societe Gerard de Nerval, 29 bis rue Charles de Gaulle, 90300 Offemont, France.
Ind/Abst MLA Int. Bibl. Books Artic. Mod. Lang. Lit.

FR/0008-025X
CAHIERS HAUT-MARNAIS, LES. **See** History(General).

FR/0068-5178
CAHIERS JEAN-COCTEAU (PARIS). (CAHIERS JEAN COCTEAU.). [Cah. Jean-Cocteau]. **Added/Corp** Societe des Amis de Jean Cocteau. Vol. 1 (1969)-. Monographic series. French. ir. Price varies per volume. Sodis, 128 Ave Marechal Lattre Tassig, 77400 Lagny France. **Tel** 011 33 1 64305557. **LC** PQ2605.O15; Z657.
Ind/Abst MLA Int. Bibl. Books Artic. Mod. Lang. Lit.; Romant. Move.

FR/0150-6943
CAHIERS JEAN GIRAUDOUX. [Cah. Jean Giraudoux]. **Added/Corp** Societe des Amis de Jean Giraudoux. Association des Amis de Jean Giraudoux. (1972)-. French. ir. 190.00F France; 215.00F Europe; 240.00F other. Societe des Amis de Jean Giraudoux, 1 Bis rue Louis Jouvet, 87300 Bellac France. **Tel** 55 68 12 79. **LC** PQ2613.I74; Z5625. **DD** 848/.9/1209. Index available (free on request). **Bk Rev. Circ:** 2,000 (ctrl).
Desc: Unknown texts of Jean Giraudoux; specialized articles about Giraudoux's books, and international activities of the association.
Ind/Abst MLA Int. Bibl. Books Artic. Mod. Lang. Lit.; Romant. Move.

FR/0068-5186
CAHIERS MARCEL PROUST. (1927)-. Monographic series. French. ir. Price varies per volume. Sodis, 128 Ave Marechal Lattre Tassig, 77400 Lagny France. **Tel** 011 33 1 64305557.

FR/0008-0365
CAHIERS NATURALISTES, LES. [Cah. nat.]. **Added/Corp** Societe Litteraire des Amis d'Emile Zola. Vol. 1 No. 1 (1955)-. French. an (Oct.). 150.00F France and ECC Countries; 160.00F others. Societe Litteraire Amis E Zola, BP 12, 77580 Villiers Morin France. **Tel** 011 33 16 1 47038941. **ED** Alain Pager. Index available. cum. index. **Bk Rev**, (Qty: 1). **Ad Acc. Circ:** 950.
Ind/Abst MLA Int. Bibl. Books Artic. Mod. Lang. Lit.

FR/0575-1144
CAHIERS PAUL CLAUDEL. (1959)-. French. ir. 219.00F. Editions Gallimard, 5 rue Sebastien Bottin, 75328 Paris Cedex 7 France. **Tel** 011 33 1 49544200. **(Subscription address:** Sodis, 128 Avenue Mal Lattre Tass, BP 149, 77043 Lagny France.**)**

CN/0713-4258
CAHIERS PAUL LEAUTAUD. [Cah. Paul Leautaud]. No. 1-. Periodical. French. $4.00 per number. Editions Bergeron, CP 606, Succursale N, Montreal Qubec H2X 3M6 Canada. **DD** 848/.91209.

FR/0084-8239
CAHIERS PAUL-LOUIS COURIER. **Added/Corp** Societe des Amis de Paul-Louis Courier. No 1-20, (Nov. 1968)-(Nov. 1978); Vol. 2, No 1 (June 1979)-. French. Twice a year (July, Dec.). 86.00F. Ste des Amis de PL Courier, MME Quilici 18 rue d Arsonval, F44600 Saint Nazaire France. **Tel** 011 33 47 202266. **Bk Rev. Ad Acc. Circ:** 300 (ctrl).
Desc: Covers the life and work of Paul Louis Courier in honoring his memory.

FR/0246-2648
CAHIERS ROGER NIMIER. **Added/Corp** Association des Cahiers Roger Nimier. (Spring 1980)-. French. an. 120.00F. Association des Cahiers Roger Nimier, 6 rue de Varenne, 75007 Paris France. **Tel** (1)45 48 91 61. Index available. **Circ:** 1,500.

FR
CAHIERS SAINT-EXUPERY. **Added/Corp** Association des Amis D'Antoine de Saint-Exupery. Comite. (1980)-. French. an. Editions Gallimard, 5 rue Sebastien Bottin, 75007 Paris France. **LC** PQ2637.A274; Z635. **DD** 848/.91209. available with illustrations.

FR/0181-7779
CAHIERS SAINT-JOHN PERSE. **Added/Corp** Centre National des Lettres. (1978)-. Periodical. French. ir. Editions Gallimard, 5 rue Sebastien Bottin, 75328 Paris Cedex 7 France. **Tel** 011 33 1 49544200. **LC** PQ2623.E386; Z647. **DD** 848/.91209.
Ind/Abst MLA Int. Bibl. Books Artic. Mod. Lang. Lit.

FR/0409-8846
CAHIERS SAINT-SIMON. **See** History(General).

FR/0220-5610
CAHIERS VICTORIENS & EDOUARDIENS. [Cah. Vic. Edouard.]. **Added/Corp** Universite Paul Valery. Centre d'Etudes et de Recherches Victoriennes et Edouardiennes. **VFOAT** Cahiers Victoriens et Edouardiens. No. 6 (March 1978)-. Periodical. English (French). sa. 130.00F France; 150.00F other. Centre d'Etudes et de Recherches Victoriennes et Edouardiennes, Universite Paul Valery, BP 5043, 34032 Montpellier Cedex, France. **Tel** 33 67 142326, FAX 33 67 142332. **ED** J C Amalric. **LC** PR463; .C33. **DD** 820/.9/008. cum. index. **Bk Rev**, (Qty: 2). **Circ:** 300 (ctrl). available on microfilm from University Microfilms International (UMI). Documents available from The Genuine Article. ***Continues** Cahiers d'Etudes et de Recherches Victoriennes et Edouardiennes.*
Desc: Articles on all aspects of the literature and culture of Victorian or Edwardian England.
Ind/Abst Annu. Bibliogr. Engl. Lang. Lit.; Arts Humanit. Citation Index [Full Cov.]; Curr. Contents Arts Humanit.; Lit. Crit. Regist.; MLA Int. Bibl. Books Artic. Mod. Lang. Lit.; Res. Alert [Full Cov.].

CN/0381-856X
CALEDONIAN (PRINCE GEORGE). (CALEDONIAN.). Periodical. English. Free. Caledonian, 3330 22nd Avenue, Prince George British Columbia V2N 1P8 Canada. **DD** C810/.8/092379.

US
CALENDAR OF LITERARY FACTS, A. (Dec. 1990)-. English. $45.00. Gale Research Inc., 835 Penobscot Building, Detroit MI 48226. **Tel** (800)877-GALE, (313)961-2242, FAX (313)961-6083, telex TWX 810-221-7086. **ED** Samuel J Rogal.
Desc: Quickly identifies and dates major literary events from the mid-fifteenth century to the present. Its broad, international scope makes this datebook unusual. Birth and death dates of about 2,000 literary figures are given, together with dates of major publications and other literary events.

FR/0575-2124
CALIBAN (TOULOUSE, FRANCE). (CALIBAN.). [Caliban]. **Added/Corp** Universite de Toulouse. Institut d'Etudes Anglaises et Nord-Americaines. Universite de Toulouse-Le Mirail. Institut d'Etudes Anglaises et Nord-Americaines. (1964)-. Multiple languages (English and French). an. 90.00F. Universite de Toulouse--Le Mirail, 56 Rue du Taur, 31000 Toulouse France. **Tel** 011 33 61 225831, FAX 011 33 61 218420. **LC** PR1; .C27. **DD** 820/.9.
Ind/Abst Abstr. Engl. Stud.; Annu. Bibliogr. Engl. Lang. Lit.; Index Am. Period. Verse; MLA Int. Bibl. Books Artic. Mod. Lang. Lit.

US/0279-1161
CALIFORNIA ENGLISH. [Calif. Engl.]. **Added/Corp** California Association of Teachers of English. Vol. 10, No. 3 (Sept. 1974)-. Periodical. English. Five times a year (Jan., Mar., May, Sept., Nov.). $35.00 (one year); $85.00 (two years) Comes with California Association of Teachers of English Membership. California Association of Teachers of English, PO Box 4427, Whittier CA 90607. **Tel** (310)946-1422. **DD** 427. ***Formed by the union of** CommuniCATE **and** California English Journal, 0008-1035.*
Ind/Abst Abstr. Engl. Stud.; Annu. Bibliogr. Engl. Lang. Lit.; Calif. Period. Index; Calif. Period. Microfi.

US/0045-3978
CALIFORNIA QUARTERLY. ***Suspended.*** [Calif. q.]. **Added/Corp** University of California, Davis. No. 1 (Summer 1971)-(1992). Periodical. English. sa (two or three no. a year). $10.00. University of California / Davis / English, English Department, Davis CA 95616. **Tel** (916)752-2729. **ED** Elliot L Gilbert. **LC** NX1; .C34. **DD** 700/.5. **Ad Acc. Circ:** 350.
Desc: Publishes poetry and short fiction of the highest literary quality, with emphasis on stylistic distinction.
Ind/Abst Am. Humanit. Index (-1992); Annu. Bibliogr. Engl. Lang. Lit.; Index Am. Period. Verse.

US/0161-2492
CALLALOO. [Callaloo]. No. 1 (Dec. 1976)-. Periodical. English. Four times a year. $54.00 US; $61.00 Canada and Mexico; $71.00 other. Johns Hopkins University Press, 2715 North Charles Street, Baltimore MD 21218-4319. **Tel** (410)516-6987, FAX (410)516-6968. **ED** Charles H. Rowell. **LC** NX506; .C34. **DD** 700/.8996075. **[CCC]. Bk Rev. Ad Acc. Circ:** 1,000 (ctrl). available on CD-ROM; available on microfilm and microfiche from University Microfilms International (UMI). Documents available from UMI Article Clearinghouse.
Desc: Publishes original works by and critical studies of black writers in the Americas and Africa, including poetry, short stories, plays, folklore, critical essays, cultural studies, interviews, visual art, and annotated bibliographies.
Ind/Abst Abstr. Engl. Stud.; Am. Hist. Life (1986-); Am. Humanit. Index; Book Rev. Index; Child. Lit. Abstr. (19??-); Expand. Acad. Index (1992-); Index Am. Period. Verse; Lit. Crit. Regist.; Mag. Search; MLA Int. Bibl. Books Artic. Mod. Lang. Lit.; Newsp. Period. Abstr. (1990-).

US/0889-7158
CALLIOPE (BRISTOL, R.I.). (CALLIOPE.). [Calliope]. **Added/Corp** Roger Williams College. Creative Writing Program. (19??)-. Periodical. English. sa. $5.00. Roger Williams University, Creative Writing Program, Bristol RI 02809. **Tel** (401)253-1040 Ext 2217. **ED** M. Christina. **DD** 810. **Circ:** 450 (ctrl).
Ind/Abst Am. Humanit. Index.

US/0147-1627
CALYX (CORVALLIS). (CALYX.). Vol. 1, (June 1976)-. Periodical. English. Twice a year (1 volume is 3 issues per 18 months). $22.50 US; $30.00 Canada; $36.00 other. Calyx Inc, PO Box B, Corvallis OR 97339. **Tel** (503)753-9384, FAX (503)753-0515. **ED** Margarita Donnelly. **LC** PS508.W7; C35. **DD** 810/.8/09287. **Bk Rev**, (Qty: 30). **Ad Acc. Circ:** 6,000.
Desc: An innovative and provocative feminist literary

Literature

journal.
Ind/Abst Am. Humanit. Index; Index Am. Period. Verse; Middle East Abstr. Index.

UK
CAMBRIDGE EDITION OF THE WORKS OF D.H. LAWRENCE. Academic Scholarly Publication. English. ir. price varies per volume. Cambridge University Press, The Edinburgh Building, Shaftesbury Road, Cambridge CB2 2RU United Kingdom. **Tel** 011 44 223 312393, FAX 011 44 223 325959. **(Subscription address:** North America/ Cambridge University Press, 40 West 20th Street, New York, NY 10011-4211; telephone: (212)924-3900**)**

UK/0950-6292
CAMBRIDGE STUDIES IN RUSSIAN LITERATURE. [Camb. stud. Russ. lit.]. (19??)-. Monographic series. English. ir. Price varies per volume. Cambridge University Press, The Edinburgh Building, Shaftesbury Road, Cambridge CB2 2RU United Kingdom. **Tel** 011 44 223 312393, FAX 011 44 223 325959. **(Subscription address:** Cambridge University Press / North America, 110 Midland Avenue, Port Chester NY 10573.**)**
Desc: Series for the study of Russian literature. Editions have appeared on Nikolai Zabolotsky and other Russian authors.
Ind/Abst MLA Int. Bibl. Books Artic. Mod. Lang. Lit.

CN/0823-6712
CAMROSE REVIEW, THE. [Camrose rev.]. 1-. Periodical. English. Three times a year. $8.00. Camrose REview, 3908-65 Street, Camrose Alta T4V 3R9 Canada. **DD** C810/.8/0054.

●CN/1193-9974
CANADIAN AUTHOR (1992). (CANADIAN AUTHOR.). [Can. author]. **Added/Corp** Canadian Authors Association. Vol. 68, No. 1 (Fall 1992)-. Periodical. English. Four times a year. 25.00Can$ (institutions), 15.00Can$ (individuals) Canada. Canadian Authors Association, 275 Slater Street, Suite 500, Ottawa, Ontario K1P 5H9 Canada. **Tel** (613)233-2846, FAX (613)235-8237. **ED** Gordon E. Symons, (Editor's Phone: (519)293-3579. **DD** C810.8/0054. **Bk Rev**. **Ad Acc.** Full Page (B&W) 500.00Can$. Half Page (B&W) 350.00Can$. **Circ:** 1,900 paid, 700 sold in stores, 300 promotional copies. **Continues** *Canadian Author & Bookman, 0008-2937.*
Desc: A writer's magazine featuring profiles on established writers, how-to articles, interviews, contest and award information, marketing information, book reviews, poetry, drama and fiction sections.

CN/0008-2937
CANADIAN AUTHOR & BOOKMAN. *Title Change.* [Can. author bookm.]. Vol. 45 (Fall 1969)-(1992). English. qt. Canadian Authors Association, 275 Slater Street, Suite 500, Ottawa, Ontario K1P 5H9 Canada. **Tel** (613)233-2846, FAX (613)235-8237. **ED** Diane Kerner. Index available. **Bk Rev**. **Ad Acc**. **Circ:** 6,000 (ctrl). **Continues** *Canadian Author & Bookman and Canadian Poetry, 0829-7703;* **Absorbed** *Literary Markets, 0712-4384.* **Continued by** *Canadian Author, 1193-9974.*
Desc: Features profiles and interviews with influential writers in many fields and discussion of important literary concerns by professional writers. Up-to-date and comprehensive market news, with contests and prizes; indispensable to the developing writer.
Ind/Abst Can. Index (?-?); Can. Period. Index.

CN
CANADIAN BOOKS FOR YOUNG PEOPLE. **VFOAT** Livres Canadiens pour la Jeuneusse. (19??)-. English (French). ir. $14.95. University of Toronto Press, 5201 Dufferin Street, Downsview Ontario M3H 5T8 Canada. **Tel** (416)667-7781, (416)667-7782, FAX (416)667-7803. **LC** Z1037; .C216; PN1009.A1. **DD** 011/.62.

CN/0711-2173
CANADIAN C.S. LEWIS JOURNAL, THE. [Can. C.S. Lewis j.]. **VFOAT** Canadian CS Lewis Journal. No. 1 (Jan. 1979)-. Periodical. English (French). sa. $10.00. Canadian CS Lewis Journal, PO Box 1700, Abbotsford BC V2S 7E7 Canada. **Tel** (604)853-7491, FAX (604)853-8951. **ED** Roger Stronstad. **DD** 828/.91209. **Bk Rev**. **Ad Acc**. **Circ:** 200.
Desc: Articles and items concerning C.S. Lewis.

CN/0319-0080
CANADIAN CHILDREN'S LITERATURE. [Can. child. lit.]. **Added/Corp** Canadian Children's Literature Association. No. 1 (1975)-. Academic Scholarly Publication. English (French). qt. 28.00Can$ Canada; 38.00Can$ other. Canadian Children's Literature, Department of English, University of Guelph, Guelph Ontario N1G 2W1 Canada. **Tel** (519)824-4120 ext. 3189, FAX (519)837-1315. **ED** Mary Rubio and Daniel Chouinard. **LC** PN1009.A1; C317. **DD** C810/.9/928205. **Bk Rev**. (Qty: 120). **Ad Acc**. **Circ:** 1,000 (ctrl).
Desc: Offers in-depth criticism of English and French Canadian literature for young people. Scholarly articles and reviews are supplemented by illustrations and photographs, and interviews with authors of children's books. The main themes and genres of children's

literature are covered in special issues. Children's records and other non-print materials are also reviewed. Source for parents, teachers and librarians.
Ind/Abst Abstr. Engl. Stud.; Book Rev. Index; Can. Index (?-?); Can. Lit. Index (1985-1986); Can. Period. Index; Child. Lit. Abstr. (19??-).

CN/0045-477X
CANADIAN FICTION MAGAZINE. [Can. fict. mag.]. No. 1 (Winter 1971)-. Periodical. English. Four times a year. $46.00 (institutions), $34.00 (individuals). Quarry Press Inc., PO Box 1061, Kingston Ontario K7L 4Y5 Canada. **Tel** (613)548-8429, FAX (613)548-1556. **ED** Geoff Hancock (editor's address: 109 Brunswick Street, Stratford Ontario N5A 3L9 Canada; editor's phone:(519)271-4546). Index available. **Ad Acc**, **Adv Mgr:** Bob. **Circ:** 1,000 (ctrl). available on microfilm from Micromedia Limited.
Desc: Canada's finest contemporary short story periodical.
Ind/Abst Abstr. Engl. Stud.; Am. Humanit. Index; Can. Index; Can. Period. Index; MLA Int. Bibl. Books Artic. Mod. Lang. Lit.

CN/0703-1459
CANADIAN JOURNAL OF IRISH STUDIES, THE. [Can. j. Ir. stud.]. **Added/Corp** Canadian Association for Irish Studies. Vol. 1, No. 1 (June 1975)-. Periodical. English (French). sa (July and Dec.). $13.50 (US & Canada); $16.50 (other). Canadian Journal of Irish Studies, University of Saskatchewan, Saskatoon Saskatchewan S7N 0W0 Canada. **Tel** (306)966-5500, FAX (306)966-8839. **ED** Ron Marken. **LC** PR8700; .C35. **DD** 820/.9/9415. **Bk Rev**, (Qty: 20). **Ad Acc**, **Adv Mgr:** Ron Marken, **Tel** (306)966-5500. **Pr Rev. Circ:** 800 (ctrl).
Desc: Studies in Irish literature, culture and history.
Ind/Abst Annu. Bibliogr. Engl. Lang. Lit.; MLA Int. Bibl. Books Artic. Mod. Lang. Lit.

CN/0705-3002
CANADIAN JOURNAL OF ITALIAN STUDIES. [Can. j. Ital. stud.]. **Added/Corp** Canadian Society for Italian Linguistics and Language Teaching. (Fall 1977)-. Periodical. Italian (English and French). sa. $40.00 institutions, $20.00 individuals. Symposium Press Limited, PO Box 89061, Hamilton Ontario L8S 4R5 Canada. **Tel** (416)528-8005. **ED** Stelio Cro. **LC** PQ4001; .C35. **DD** 850/.9. Index available. cum. index. **Bk Rev**. **Ad Acc.**
Desc: Articles, interviews, original creative literary writings on Italian literature, history, philosophy, art, film and drama.
Ind/Abst Am. Hist. Life (1980-); MLA Int. Bibl. Books Artic. Mod. Lang. Lit.; Romant. Move.

CN
CANADIAN LITERARY PERIODICALS INDEX. **See** Publishing-Abstracting, Bibliographies and Statistics.

CN/0008-4360
CANADIAN LITERATURE. [Can. lit.]. **Added/Corp** University of British Columbia. **VFOAT** Literature Canadienne. No. 1, (Summer 1959)-. Periodical. English (French). Four times a year (Mar., June, Sept., Dec.). 55.00Can$ (institutions), 40.00Can$ (individuals) Canada, 65.00Can$ (institutions), 50.00Can$ (individuals) other (surface mail). University of British Columbia / Canadian Literature, 223-2029 West Mall, Vancouver BC V6T 1Z2 Canada. **Tel** (604)228-2780, FAX (604)822-9452. **ED** Laurie Ricou and E. M. Kroller. Index available. cum. index. **Bk Rev**. **Ad Acc. Acid Free. Circ:** 2,000. available on microfilm and microfiche from University Microfilms International (UMI). Documents available from The Genuine Article, UMI Article Clearinghouse.
Desc: Devoted to the study of all aspects of Canadian writing. A mixture of articles, reviews and new poems, with occasional interviews and special features. Looks at the nation's literary heritage and at the many faces of contemporary fiction, drama, nonfiction and poetry.
Ind/Abst Abstr. Engl. Stud.; Acad. Abstr. Full Text Elite (Jan. 1992-); Acad. Abstr. (Jan. 1992)-; Acad. Search (Jan. 1992-); Am. Humanit. Index; Annu. Bibliogr. Engl. Lang. Lit.; Arts Humanit. Citation Index [Full Cov.]; Book Rev. Digest; Book Rev. Index; Can. Index (?-?); Can. Period. Index; Child. Lit. Abstr. (19??-); Curr. Contents Arts Humanit.; Expand. Acad. Index (1989-); Humanit. Index; Humanit. Source (Jan. 1992-); Index Am. Period. Verse; INFO-SOUTH Abstr.; Mag. Search; MLA Int. Bibl. Books Artic. Mod. Lang. Lit.; Newsp. Period. Abstr. (1991-); Res. Alert [Full Cov.]; Soc. Sci. Cit. Index [Select. Cov.].

CN/0319-051X
CANADIAN REVIEW OF COMPARATIVE LITERATURE. (CANADIAN REVIEW OF COMPARATIVE LITERATURE. REVUE CANADIENNE DE LITTERATURE COMPAREE.). [Can. rev. comp. lit.]. **Added/Corp** Canadian Comparative Literature Association. **VFOAT** Revue Canadienne de Litterature Comparee. Vol. 1 (Winter 1974)-. Periodical. English (French). qt. $70.00. University of Toronto Press, 5201 Dufferin Street, Downsview Ontario M3H 5T8 Canada. **Tel** (416)667-7781, (416)667-7782, FAX (416)667-7803. **LC** PN851; .C35. Documents available from The Genuine Article.

Desc: Provides a forum for scholars engaged in the study of literature from both an international and an interdisciplinary point of view.
Ind/Abst Abstr. Engl. Stud.; Am. Bibliogr. Slavic East Europ. Stud.; Annu. Bibliogr. Engl. Lang. Lit.; Arts Humanit. Citation Index (19??-19??) [Full Cov.]; Curr. Contents Arts Humanit.; Lit. Crit. Regist.; Middle East Abstr. Index; MLA Int. Bibl. Books Artic. Mod. Lang. Lit.; Res. Alert [Full Cov.]; Romant. Move.; Soc. Sci. Cit. Index [Select. Cov.].

CN
CANADIAN SHORT STORY INDEX. See Literature-Abstracting, Bibliographies and Statistics.

SZ/0171-6859
CANADIAN STUDIES IN GERMAN LANGUAGE AND LITERATURE. (KANADISCHE STUDIEN ZUR DEUTSCHEN SPRACHE UND LITERATUR. ETUDES CANADIENNES DE LANGUE ET LITTERATURE ALLEMANDES. CANADIAN STUDIES IN GERMAN LANGUAGE AND LITERATURE.). [Can. stud. ger. lang. lit.]. **VFOAT** Etudes Canadiennes de Langue et Litterature Allemandes; Canadian Studies in German Language and Literature. No. 1 (1970)-. Monographic series. German (English). H Lang, Munzgraben 2, CH-3000 7 Bern Switzerland.
Ind/Abst MLA Int. Bibl. Books Artic. Mod. Lang. Lit.

CN/0827-293X
CANADIAN WRITER'S JOURNAL. [Can. writ. j.]. (June 1984)-. Periodical. English. qt (Mar., June, Sept., Dec.). 15.00Can$ (one year), 25.00Can$ (two year). Gordon M. Smart Publications, Box 6618 Depot 1, Victoria British Columbia V8P 5N7, Canada. **Tel** (604)477-8807. **ED** Gordin M. Smart. **DD** 808/.02/05. **Bk Rev**, (Qty: 8-10). **Ad Acc. Circ:** 300 (ctrl).
Desc: How-to articles for writers by writers. All based on personal experiences.

GW/0933-2421
CANADIANA ROMANICA. [Can. Rom.]. (1987)-. Monographic series. Multiple languages. ir. Price varies per volume. Max Niemeyer Verlag, Postfach 2140, D 72011 Tuebingen Germany. **Tel** 011 49 7071 989494, FAX 011 49 7071 87419. **ED** Hans-Josef Niederehe, Lothar Wolf. **UDC** 840.
Ind/Abst MLA Int. Bibl. Books Artic. Mod. Lang. Lit.

CN/0706-6899
CANCELLED LEAVES. V. 1- Nov. 1978-. Periodical. English. ir. University of Western Ontario School of Library and Information Sciences, London Ontario N6A 3K7 Canada. **DD** C811/.5/408.

SP/0213-7895
CANENTE. (198?)-. Periodical. Spanish. ir. Canente, Diego de Vergara 4, 29009 Malaga Spain.

CN/0708-594X
CANSCAIP NEWS. See Children and Youth Interests.

US/0898-8463
CANTIGUEIROS (LEXINGTON, KY.). (CANTIGUEIROS : BULLETIN OF THE CANTIGUEIROS DE SANTA MARIA.). **Added/Corp** Cantigueiros de Santa Maria (Society). **VFOAT** Bulletin of the Cantigueiros de Santa Maria. Vol. 1, No. 1 (Fall 1987)-. Bulletin. English (Spanish and Portuguese). an (Aug.). $20.00 (institutions); $10.00 (individuals). Society Cantigueiros de Santa Maria, University of Cincinnati, Department of Romance Languages, Cincinnati OH 45221. **Tel** (513)241-1194, (513)556-1835. **LC** PQ9189.A44; C333. **DD** 780. **Bk Rev. Ad Acc. Pr Rev.**
Ind/Abst MLA Int. Bibl. Books Artic. Mod. Lang. Lit.

UK
CAPE. See The Arts.

CN/0315-3754
CAPILANO REVIEW, THE. 1/1 (Spring 1972)-. Periodical. English. qt. $25.00 (individual), $30.00 (institution) Canada; $30.00 (individual), $35.00 (institution) other. The Capilano Review, 2055 Purcell Way, North Vancouver British Columbia V7J 3H5 Canada. **Tel** (604)986-1911. **ED** Pierre Coupey. **LC** PR9194.9; .C33. **DD** 810/.8. Index available. **Ad Acc. Circ:** 1,000. available on microfilm and microfiche from University Microfilms International (UMI).
Desc: Typical issue includes poetry, prose and visual materials by writers and artists considered to be working in fresh, innovative ways.
Ind/Abst Am. Humanit. Index; Can. Period. Index (19??-); Index Am. Period. Verse.

US/1043-1500
CARDOZO STUDIES IN LAW AND LITERATURE. See Law.

CN/0825-5326
CARFAX (HULL, QUEBEC). (CARFAX.). [Carfax]. No. 1 (March/April/May 1984)-. Periodical. French. qt. 10.00Can$. PD Lacroix, 56-B Rue Garneau, Hull, Quebec J8X 1R8 Canada. **DD** 808.83/876.

JM
CARIB. No. 1 (1979)-. English. an. 15.00Jam$ Jamaica, $5.00 other. Victor L Chang Secretary, Wiaclals

English Department, University of the West Indies, Kingston 7 Jamaica. **Tel** (809)927-2217. **ED** Edward Baugh. **LC** PE3301; .C28. **DD** 409/.729. **Bk Rev. Circ:** 500 (ctrl).
Desc: The official publication of the West Indian Association for commonwealth literature and language studies. Devoted to the study of commonwealth literature in English.

JM/1018-2926
CARIBBEAN REVIEW OF BOOKS.
Added/Corp University of the West Indies Publishers' Association. **VFOAT** CRB. No. 1 (1991)-. Periodical. English. qt. CRB, PO Box 42, Mona, Kingston, Jamaica, W.I.

VI/0893-1550
CARIBBEAN WRITER, THE. [Caribb. writ.]. **Added/Corp** Caribbean Research Institute. Vol. 1, No. 1 (Spring 1987)-. Periodical. English. an. $10.50 US and possessions; $11.40 other. University of the Virgin Islands / Caribbean Writer, RR 2 Box 10000 Kingshill, St. Croix 00850 Virgin Islands. **Tel** (809)778-0246, FAX (809)778-8191. **ED** Erika J. Waters. **DD** 809. **Bk Rev**, (Qty: 10). **Ad Acc, Adv Mgr:** Carlyna Allard. **Circ:** 1,200.
Desc: International literary magazine that focuses on poetry and prose relating to the Caribbean.

US/0148-9968
CARIBE. V. 1- Spring 1976-. Periodical. Spanish. sa. $10.00. Department of European Languages and Literature, 1890 East-West Road, University of Hawaii, Honolulu HI 96822. **LC** PQ7081.A1; C37. **DD** 860.

CN/0317-7254
CARLETON GERMANIC PAPERS.
[Carleton Ger. pap.]. **Added/Corp** Carleton University. Dept. of German. (1973)-. Periodical. English (French and German). an. 4.00Can$. Carleton University / Department of German, Ottawa Ontario K1S 5B6 Canada. **Tel** (613)788-2115. **ED** E.M. Oppenheimer, R. Gould, A. Bohm, J. Goheen, J.B. Dallett, and B. Mogridge. **LC** PT1; .C36. **DD** 830/.9. **Circ:** 150 (ctrl).
Desc: Covers aspects of German language and literature.
Ind/Abst MLA Int. Bibl. Books Artic. Mod. Lang. Lit.

US/1050-3099
CARLYLE ANNUAL. ***Title Change.*** [Carlyle annu.]. No. 10 (1989)-(Dec. 1994). English. an (Mar.). Illinois State University / English, Department of English, Normal IL 61761-6901. **Tel** (309)438-5776. **DD** 824. ***Continues*** *Carlyle Newsletter, 0269-8226.* ***Continued by*** *Carlyle Studies Annual.*
Ind/Abst MLA Int. Bibl. Books Artic. Mod. Lang. Lit.

●US/1074-2670
CARLYLE STUDIES ANNUAL. (1994)-. English. an. $10.00. Illinois State University / English, Department of English, Normal IL 61761-6901. **Tel** (309)438-5776. **ED** Rodger L. Tarr. **Bk Rev. Ad Acc. Pr Rev. Circ:** 250. ***Continues*** *Carlyle Annual, 1050-3099.*

US/0008-6797
CAROLINA QUARTERLY. [Carol. q.]. **Added/Corp** University of North Carolina (1793-1962). Vol. 1 (Fall 1948)-. Periodical. English. Three times a year (Feb., June, Oct.). $12.00 (institutions), $10.00 (individuals) US; $14.00 (institutions), $12.00 (individuals) other. Carolina Quarterly, Greenlaw Hall, University of North Carolina, Chapel Hill NC 27599. **Tel** (919)962-0244, FAX (919)962-3520. **ED** Amber Vogel. **Bk Rev**, (Qty: 9). **Ad Acc. Circ:** 1,300. available on microfilm from University Microfilms International (UMI).
Desc: Early and later work by poets, fiction writers, and essayists.
Ind/Abst Am. Humanit. Index; Book Rev. Index; Index Am. Period. Verse.

US
CAROLINA WRITER. English.
Ind/Abst Lit. Crit. Regist.

US/0008-6894
CARRELL, THE. [Carrell]. **Added/Corp** University of Miami. Library Friends. Vol. 1 (June 1960)-. English. an (Nov.). $5.00 (latest issue). Friends University of Miami Library, c/o Ronald Naylor, PO Box 248214, Coral Gables FL 33124. **Tel** (305)284-4585. **ED** Ronald P. Naylor and Lawrence Donovan. **LC** Z881; .M61. **Circ:** 500 (ctrl).
Desc: Original poetry, literary reviews and art by faculty and students at the University of Miami and other places.
Ind/Abst Annu. Bibliogr. Engl. Lang. Lit.; MLA Int. Bibl. Books Artic. Mod. Lang. Lit.; Numis. Lit.

US/0737-9412
CARTE ITALIANE. [Carte ital.]. **Added/Corp** University of California, Los Angeles. Dept. of Italian. Vol. 1 (1979-80)-. Academic Scholarly Publication. English (Italian). an. $6.00 (individuals); $8.00 (institutions). University of California Department of Italian, 340 Royce Hall, Los Angeles CA 90024. **Tel** (213)825-1940. **LC** PQ4001; .C37. **DD** 850/.9. **Bk Rev. Ad Acc. Circ:** 2,000 (ctrl).
Desc: Scholarly publication of graduate student articles in all areas of Italian culture, focusing on literature and language.
Ind/Abst MLA Int. Bibl. Books Artic. Mod. Lang. Lit.; Romant. Move.

CU/0008-7157
CASA DE LAS AMERICAS. ***Title Change.*** [Casa Am.]. **Main/Corp** Casa de las Americas. Vol. 1, No. 1 (June/July 1960)-(19??). Periodical. Spanish. bm. Ediciones Cubanas, Obispo 527, Altos ESQ Bernaza, CP 10100 Havana Cuba. **Tel** 011 632980, 631942, FAX 011 631011, telex 512337, 6540. **LC** PN6; .C3. **DD** 860/.80/98. ***Supersedes*** *America.* ***Continued by*** *Revista Casa de las Americas.*
Ind/Abst Am. Hist. Life (1961-); ARTbibliogr. Mod. (1961-); Arts Humanit. Citation Index [Full Cov.]; Chicano Index (1961-); HAPI Hisp. Am. Period. Index (1961-); MLA Int. Bibl. Books Artic. Mod. Lang. Lit.

NE/0862-8459
CASOPIS PRO MODERNI FILOLOGII / CESKOSLOVENSKA AKADEMIE VED.
See Linguistics.

CN/0227-6127
CASSIOPEIA (BRAMPTON). (CASSIOPEIA.). [Cassiopeia]. Issue 1 (Feb. 1980)-. Periodical. English. ir. Free. Brampton Writers' Workshop, 25 Mordon Court, Brampton Ontario L6V 2B5 Canada. **DD** C810/.8/0054.

SP/0378-200X
CASTILLA (VALLADOLID). (CASTILLA : BOLETIN DEL DEPARTAMENTO DE LITERATURA ESPANOLA, UNIVERSIDAD DE VALLADOLID.). [Castilla]. **Added/Corp** Universidad de Valladolid. Departamento de Literatura Espanola. No. 1 (1980)-. Periodical. Spanish. an. 2288ptas Spain; 2478ptas others. Universidad Valladolid Secretariado Publicaciones, Juan Mambrillia 14, 47003 Valladolid Spain. **Tel** 011 34 83 294144, 011 34 82 294499. **LC** PQ6001; .C37. **DD** 860/.9.
Ind/Abst MLA Int. Bibl. Books Artic. Mod. Lang. Lit.

NE/0008-7556
CASTRUM PEREGRINI. [Castrum Peregrini]. No. 1 (1951)-. Periodical. German. Five times a year. DM101.00 Germany; DM106.50 others. Castrum Peregrini, PO Box 645, 1000 AP Amsterdam Netherlands. **Tel** 011 31 20 6235287. **ED** M. R. Goldschmidt. **LC** AP64; .C3. Index available. cum. index. **Bk Rev. Ad Acc. Circ:** 1,000.
Desc: Essays on literature, history of arts and history.
Ind/Abst BHA : Biblio. Hist. Art; MLA Int. Bibl. Books Artic. Mod. Lang. Lit.; Romant. Move.

SP/0214-3089
CATALAN WRITING. [Catalan writ.]. **Added/Corp** Institucio de les Lletres Catalanes. No. 1 (1988)-. Periodical. English. Twice a year. Free. Institucio des Lletres Catalanes, C Paseo de Gracia 41 20 1A, 08037 Barcelona Spain. **Tel** 011 34 93 2160800, FAX 011 34 93 216 01 25. **LC** PC3975.E1; C37. **DD** 849/.9080054. **Circ:** 2,500.
Desc: Promotes the catalan writers and provides information on the catalan literature.

US/0896-7423
CATALYST (ATLANTA, GA.). (CATALYST.). [Catalyst]. Fall (1986)-. Periodical. English. sa (2 issues). $5.00. Fulton County Arts Council, 236 Forsyth Street, Suite 400, Atlanta GA 30303. **Tel** (404)730-5785. **ED** Pearl Cleage. **DD** 810. Index available. **Bk Rev. Ad Acc.**
Desc: Presents writers and nationally-known authors in a format designed to stimulate discussion, encourage the exchange of ideas and draw people into reading poems, short stories, essays and other literary.

CN/0381-5005
CATALYST (BRANTFORD). (CATALYST.). **Added/Corp** Prison Arts Foundation. Vol. 1 (March 1975)-. Periodical. English (French; summaries and/or abstracts in French). ir. $5.00 Canada; $6.00 other. Prison Arts Foundation, 143 5th Avenue, Brantford Ontario N3S 1A3 Canada. **DD** C810/.8/0920692.

MX
CATHEDRA. Spanish. Ciudad Universitaria / Monterrey, Facultad de Filosofia y Letras de la Universidad Autonome de Nuevo Leon, Monterrey Mexico. **LC** AS63.N77; A2.
Ind/Abst Am. Hist. Life (1988-).

US/1045-9871
CATHER STUDIES. [Cather stud.]. **Added/Corp** University of Nebraska--Lincoln. Willa Cather Pioneer Memorial and Educational Foundation. Vol. 1 (1990)-. Periodical. English. ir. University of Nebraska Press, PO Box 880484, Lincoln NE 68588-0520. **Tel** (402)472-3584, (800)755-1105, FAX (402)472-6214, (800)526-2617. **ED** Susan J. Rosowski. **LC** PS3505.A87; Z592. **DD** 813/.52.
Ind/Abst MLA Int. Bibl. Books Artic. Mod. Lang. Lit.

US
CBC FEATURES. **Added/Corp** Children's Book Council (New York, N.Y.). **VAT** Children's Book Council Features. Vol. 39, No. 3 (Oct. 1984/July 1985)-. Periodical. English. sa. Children's Book Council, 568 Broadway, New York NY 10012. **Tel** (212)489-1638. **(Subscription address:** 350 Scotland Road, Orange, NJ 07050**)** cum. index. **Circ:** 40,000 (ctrl). ***Continues*** *Calendar (Children's Book Council (New York, N.Y.)).*
Ind/Abst Child. Lit. Abstr. (19??-).

US/0273-3315
CCLM NEWSLETTER. ***Ceased.*** [CCLM newsl.]. **Main/Corp** Coordinating Council of Literary Magazines. **VAT** Coordinating Council of Literary Magazines Newsletter. (1967)-(Spring 1988). Newsletter. English. qt. CCLM News, 666 Broadway 11th Floor, New York NY 10012. **Tel** (212)614-6551. **ED** Andrew Mossin. **Bk Rev. Ad Acc. Circ:** 1,500 (ctrl). ***Continues*** *Newsletter - CCLM, 0192-9887.*
Desc: Publication of news, views and information for literary magazines, publishers, and writers.

US
CD COREWORKS. CD-ROM. English. $475.00. Roth Publishing Inc, PO Box 406, Great Neck NY 11022. **Tel** (516)466-3676, (800)899-7684, FAX (516)829-7746.

US/0007-8069
CEA CRITIC. **See** Linguistics.

US/0147-3085
CELESTINESCA. [Celestinesca]. Vol. 1 (May 1977)-. Periodical. English (French and Spanish). Twice a year (May, Nov.). $10.00 US & Canada & Mexico; $15.00 other. Michigan State University Department of Romance and Classical Languages, c/o Joseph Snow, East Lansing MI 48824. **Tel** (517)355-8350, FAX (517)336-3844. **ED** Joseph T. Snow. **LC** PQ6428; .C43. **DD** 862/.2. Index available. cum. index. **Bk Rev**, (Qty: 4-8). **Circ:** 370 (ctrl).
Desc: Covers Rojas' Celestina and its derivatives and analogs, translations and stage adaptions, editions and illustrations. Includes news and bibliography sections.
Ind/Abst MLA Int. Bibl. Books Artic. Mod. Lang. Lit.

IE/0069-1399
CELTICA (DUBLIN). **See** Linguistics.

FR/0768-1305
CENTRE INTERUNIVERSITAIRE DE RECHERCHE SUR LA RENAISSANCE ITALIENNE. **VFOAT** Centre de Recherche sur la Renaissance Italienne. (1972)-. Monographic series. French. **UDC** 850"14".
Ind/Abst MLA Int. Bibl. Books Artic. Mod. Lang. Lit.

XR/0009-0468
CESKA LITERATURA. [Ceska lit.]. **Added/Corp** Ustav pro Ceskou Literaturu (Ceskoslovenska Akademie Ved) Ustav pro Ceskou a Svetovou Literaturu (Ceskoslovenska Akademie Ved). Vol. 1 (March 1953)-. Periodical. Czech (summaries and/or abstracts in English, French, German and Russian; table of contents in English, French, German and Russian). bm. $142.00. John Benjamins BV, Amsteldijk 44, PO Box 75577, 1070 AN Amsterdam Netherlands. **Tel** 011 31 20 6738156, FAX 011 31 20 739773. **(Subscription address:** John Benjamins North America, PO Box 27519, Philadelphia PA 19118-0519.**) ED** Miroslav Cervenka. **LC** PG5000; .C54. Documents available from The Genuine Article.
Ind/Abst Am. Hist. Life (1955-); Arts Humanit. Citation Index [Full Cov.]; Curr. Contents Arts Humanit.; MLA Int. Bibl. Books Artic. Mod. Lang. Lit.; Res. Alert [Full Cov.].

XR/0009-0786
CESKY JAZYK A LITERATURA. (1951)-. Periodical. Czech. Ten times a year. $31.20. **(Subscription address:** Artia Pegas Press Ltd., Palac Metro Narodni Trida 25, 11210 Prague 1 Czech Republic.**) DD** 491.86. ***Continues*** *Literatura ve Skole.*

US
CHAKRA. English. ir (two or three times a year). $5.50 US; $6.50 North America; $7.50 other. Freelance Press, Box 8551 Dept 38, FDR Station, New York NY 10022-9998. **ED** Liz Camps and Richard Behrens. **Bk Rev. Ad Acc. Circ:** 400.
Desc: Cyberotic art for a magical world. Visual and verbal art dealing with eroticism, mysticism, postmodernism, neopolitics, psychophilosophy, psychedelia and creative speculation.Contains photos, short stories, essays, plays, drawings, and interviews.

US/1056-4241
CHALLENGING THE LITERARY CANON. [Chall. lit. canon]. (1988)-. Monographic series. English. Approx. $35.00 (single issue). University of Rochester Press, 200 Administration, University of Rochester, Rochester NY 14627. **DD** 810.
Ind/Abst MLA Int. Bibl. Books Artic. Mod. Lang. Lit.

CN/0847-1711
CHAMPAGNE HORROR. [Champagne horror]. No. 1 (1990)-. English. $54.95 per volume. Champagne Productions, #265-919C Albert Street, Regina Saskatchewan S4V 1M4 Canada. **DD** 808.83/873808.

CN/0317-3399
CHAMPS D'APPLICATION. Winter (1974)-. French. Champs d'Application, CP 771, Trois-Rivieres Quebec G9A 5J9 Canada. **DD** C840/.5.

II/0970-5147
CHANDRABHAGA. [Chandrabhaga]. No. 1- Summer 1979-. Periodical. English. sa. Chandrabhaga Society, Tinkonia Bagicha, Cuttack 753001 India. **LC** PN2; .C47. **DD** 805.
Ind/Abst MLA Int. Bibl. Books Artic. Mod. Lang. Lit.

CC
CHANG-CHIANG. **VFOAT** Changjiang Wenxue Congkan; Chiangjiang Wenxuecongkan; Chang-Chiang Wen Hsueh Tsung Kan; Chang Chiang Wen Hsueh Tsung Kan. (19??)-. Periodical. Chinese. bm (6 issues). $20.16 (surface mail). **(Subscription address:** China International Book Trading Corporation, PO Box 399, Library Service Department, Beijing 100044 People's Republic of China.**)** **LC** PL2250; .C518. **DD** 895.1/09.

US/0093-9064
CHANGES MAGAZINE (BISBEE). (CHANGES MAGAZINE.). **VFOAT** Changes. English. $2.50 single issue. Hanson, PO Box 375, Bisbee AZ 85603-0375. **LC** PS501; .C47. **DD** 810/.8/0054.

KO
CHANGJAK KWA PIPYONG. Periodical. Korean. W1,000 single issue. Changjak Kwa Pipyong, 4 Naengchon-dong, Sodaemun-ku, Seoul South Korea. **LC** PL950.2; .C47.

US
CHAPBOOK MISCELLANY. **Main/Corp** Justin G. Schiller, Ltd. Vol. 1 (Spring 1970)-. Periodical. English. J G Schiller, PO Box 1667 FDR Station, New York NY 10022.

US/1056-9227
CHAPTER ONE FOR THE UNPUBLISHED WRITER IN ALL OF US. **See** Journalism.

US/0745-5828
CHARIOT (CRAWFORDSVILLE, IND.). (CHARIOT.). **Added/Corp** Ben Hur Life Association. (19??)-. Periodical. English. qt. Ben Hur Life Association, PO Box 312, Crawfordsville IN 47933.

US/0577-5574
CHARIOTEER, THE. **Added/Corp** Parnassos, Greek Cultural Society of New York. No. 1 (Summer 1960)-. English. an. $15.00 (one year); $28.00 (two year); $40.00 (three year). Pella Publishing Company, 337 West 36th Street, New York NY 10018-6402. **Tel** (212)279-9586. **ED** Carmen Capri-Karka. **LC** PA5273; .C45. **DD** 889/.3/408. **Bk Rev. Ad Acc. Circ:** 300.
Desc: Review of modern Greek literature and poetry.
Ind/Abst Am. Bibliogr. Slavic East Europ. Stud.

US/0098-9452
CHARITON REVIEW, THE. [Chariton rev.]. **Added/Corp** Northeast Missouri State University. Vol. 1 (Spring 1975)-. English. sa (April and December). $9.00. Chariton Review, Northeast Missouri State University, Kirksville MO 63501. **Tel** (816)785-4499, FAX (816)785-7486. **ED** Jim Barnes. **LC** PS501; .C48. **DD** 810/.8/005. **Bk Rev. Ad Acc. Circ:** 350.
Desc: Contemporary fiction, poetry, translations, and essays.
Ind/Abst Am. Humanit. Index; Index Am. Period. Verse.

UK/0963-4770
CHARLESTON MAGAZINE, THE. (1990)-. Academic Scholarly Publication. English. be (2 issues). £5.95 UK; £7.95 other. Charleston Magazine, Charleston Trust, N Firle, E Sussex BN8 6LL England. **Tel** 011 44 32 811626, FAX 011 44 32 811628. **ED** Frances Spalding. **Bk Rev**, (Qty: 6). **Ad Acc, Adv Mgr:** Jane Grylls, **Tel** 011 44 71 278 1927. **Pr Rev. Circ:** 3,000 (ctrl). ***Continues** Charleston Newsletter.*
Desc: The magazine concerns itself mainly with promoting understanding the appreciation of Charleston and Bloomsbury in their literary and artistic context.

US/0145-8973
CHASQUI (WILLIAMSBURG, VA.). (CHASQUI.). [Chasqui]. (Jan./Feb. 1972)-. Periodical. English (Portuguese and Spanish). Twice a year (May, Nov.). $9.00 (individual), $12.00 (institution). College of William & Mary, Department of Modern Languages, c/o H. M. Fraser, Williamsburg VA 23185. **Tel** (804)221-3691, FAX (804)221-3637. **ED** Thomas E. Lyon. **LC** PQ7081.A1; C48. **DD** 860/.9/98. **Bk Rev**, (Qty: 40). **Ad Acc. Pr Rev. Circ:** 350. Documents available from The Genuine Article.
Desc: Criticism of literature from the Hispanic world, book reviews, critical articles, bibliographies, creative writing, cultural notes, graphic arts.
Ind/Abst Arts Humanit. Citation Index [Full Cov.]; Curr. Contents Arts Humanit.; For. Prod. Abstr. (1991-); For. Abstr.; HAPI Hisp. Am. Period. Index; MLA Int. Bibl. Books Artic. Mod. Lang. Lit.; Res. Alert [Full Cov.]; Soc. Sci. Cit. Index [Select. Cov.].

US
CHAUCER NEWSLETTER : A PUBLICATION OF THE NEW CHAUCER SOCIETY, THE. **Added/Corp** New Chaucer Society. Vol. 1, no. 1 (Winter 1979)-. Newsletter. English. sa.
Ind/Abst Annu. Bibliogr. Engl. Lang. Lit.

US/0009-2185
CHELSEA (NEW YORK, N.Y.). (CHELSEA.). [Chelsea]. **Added/Corp** Chelsea Foundation. No. 6, (Winter 1960)-. Periodical. English. Twice a year (Mar. and Oct.). $11.00 US; $14.00 other. Chelsea Associates Inc, Box 5880 Grand Central Station, New York NY 10163. **Tel** (212)988-2276. **ED** Sonia Raiziss. **LC** AP2; .C506. **DD** 808. Index available. **Circ:** 1,300. available on microfilm and microfiche from University Microfilms International (UMI). ***Continues** Chelsea Review.*
Desc: An eclectic mix of international poetry, fiction, and non-fiction prose by new and established writers.
Ind/Abst Annu. Bibliogr. Engl. Lang. Lit.; Index Am. Period. Verse.

CN/0317-0500
CHESTERTON REVIEW, THE. [Chesterton rev.]. **Added/Corp** G.K. Chesterton Society. (Fall/Winter 1974)-. Periodical. English. Four times a year. $35.00. St. Thomas More College, 1437 College Drive, Saskatoon Saskatchewan S7N 0W6 Canada. **Tel** (306)966-8962, FAX (306)966-8904. **ED** Ian Boyd. **LC** PR4453.C4; Z584. **DD** 828/.912/09; 828/.912/09. **Bk Rev. Ad Acc.**
Desc: Journal of the G. K. Chesterton Society, founded at Spode House in England on May 26, 1974. The main purpose of the Society is the promotion of a critical interest in all aspects of the life and work of Chesterton.
Ind/Abst Am. Hist. Life (1974-1979); Am. Humanit. Index; MLA Int. Bibl. Books Artic. Mod. Lang. Lit.

CC
CHIANG NAN. **VFOAT** Jiangnan Literature. First published in 1981. Periodical. Chinese. qt. RMBY1.00. Chiang Nan Wen Hsueh She, 1 Sui An Lu, Hang-Chou Che-Chiang, People's Republic of China. **LC** PL2250; .C532. **DD** 895.1/08.

JA/0388-2241
CHIBA REVIEW. [Chiba rev.]. (1979)-. Periodical. Multiple languages. an. **DD** 820.
Ind/Abst MLA Int. Bibl. Books Artic. Mod. Lang. Lit.

US/0009-3696
CHICAGO REVIEW. [Chic. rev.]. **Added/Corp** University of Chicago. Vol. 1 (Winter 1946)-. Periodical. English. qt. $18.00 (individuals), $35.00 (institutions) US; $22.00 (individuals), $40.00 (institutions) other. Chicago Review, University of Chicago, 5801 South Kenwood Avenue, Chicago IL 60637. **Tel** (312)702-0887. **ED** David Nicholls. **LC** AP2; .C5152. **DD** 051. **Bk Rev**, (Qty: 12). **Ad Acc. Circ:** 2,500. available on microfilm from University Microfilms International (UMI). Documents available from UMI Article Clearinghouse.
Desc: Provides a continuing forum for contemporary poetry, essays, fiction, plays, translations, reviews, and art.
Ind/Abst Acad. Abstr. Full Text Elite (Jan. 1991-); Acad. Abstr. (Jan. 1991-); Acad. Ind. [Computer File] (1987-); Acad. Search (Jan. 1991-); Annu. Bibliogr. Engl. Lang. Lit.; ARTbibliogr. Mod.; Arts Humanit. Citation Index [Full Cov.]; Curr. Contents Arts Humanit.; Expand. Acad. Index (1987-); Humanit. Index; Index Am. Period. Verse; INFO-SOUTH Abstr.; Lit. Crit. Regist.; MLA Int. Bibl. Books Artic. Mod. Lang. Lit.; Newsp. Period. Abstr. (1990-); Res. Alert [Full Cov.]; Romant. Move.

US/0149-4503
CHICOREL INDEX TO SHORT STORIES IN ANTHOLOGIES AND COLLECTIONS. (19??)-. English. ir. Price varies. American Library Publishing Company, PO Box 4272, Sedona AZ 86340-4272. **Tel** (602)284-1162. **ED** M. Chicorel. **LC** Z5917.S5; C44; PN3373. **DD** 808.83/1/016. Index available. **Bk Rev.** available on microfiche.
Desc: Short stories by author, title, editor, as well as full anthology description. Contains a subject index.

US/1064-0541
CHILDREN'S BOOK BAG, THE. [Child. book bag]. **Added/Corp** Foundation for Children's Books. Vol. 1 (Summer 1985)-. Periodical. English. qt. $25.00 (individual membership), $40.00 (institutional membership). Foundation for Children's Books, 30 Common Street, Watertown MA 02172. **Tel** (617)926-8190, FAX (617)965-8184. **DD** 011. **Bk Rev.**
Desc: Up-to-date bibliography of quality childrens literature within a theme war, multicultural folktales and china.

CN/0705-0038
CHILDREN'S BOOK NEWS (TORONTO). **See** Children and Youth Interests.

IE/0791-2641
CHILDREN'S BOOKS IN IRELAND. **See** Publishing-Books and Bookmaking.

UK/1350-4347
CHILDREN'S FICTION ON FICHE. **See** Children and Youth Interests.

US/0093-0431
CHILDREN'S LITERARY ALMANAC. 1973-. English. be. $6.95. Kurian Reference Books, Box 154, Pelham NY 10803. **LC** PN1009.A1; C513. **DD** 809/.89282.

UK/0306-2015
CHILDREN'S LITERATURE ABSTRACTS. **See** Literature-Abstracting, Bibliographies and Statistics.

US/0749-3096
CHILDREN'S LITERATURE AWARDS AND WINNERS. (CHILDREN'S LITERATURE AWARDS AND WINNERS / DOLORES BLYTHE JONES.). [Child. lit. awards win.]. **VFOAT** Children's Literature Awards & Winners. 1st Ed. (1983)-. English. ir. $94.00. Gale Research Inc., 835 Penobscot Building, Detroit MI 48226. **Tel** (800)877-GALE, (313)961-2242, FAX (313)961-6083, telex TWX 810-221-7086. **ED** Dolores Blythe Jones. **LC** Z1037.A2; C545. **DD** 028.5/079.
Desc: This new directory of prizes, authors, and illustrators is the only comprehensive reference to all awards granted in the United States, other English-speaking countries, and internationally, for children's literature. More than 5,000 book titles are identified, and nearly 7,000 authors and illustrators are listed. Title and author/illustrator indexes have been added to make this work even more useful for selecting award-winning titles.

US/0045-6713
CHILDREN'S LITERATURE IN EDUCATION. [Child. lit. educ.]. Vol. 1 (March 1970)-. Periodical. English. qt. £22.00 (individuals), £75.00 (institutions) UK & Europe; $110.00 US; $130.00 other (special price to schools, kindergarten to grade 12 - $29.00 US, $35.00 other). Human Sciences Press, PO Box 735, 233 Spring Street, New York NY 10013. **Tel** (212)620-8000, FAX (212)807-1047, telex 23421139. **(Subscription address:** Eurospan Ltd., Journals and Serials Division, 3 Henrietta Street, Covent Garden, London WC2E 8LU England.**)** **ED** Anita Moss. **LC** Z1037.A1; C5. **DD** 028.52. **CODEN** CLEDEW. **[CCC].** Index available in last issue of volume--attached. available on microfilm and microfiche from University Microfilms International (UMI). Documents available from The Genuine Article.
Desc: A valuable learning tool for librarians, teachers, and others interested in developing a professional awareness and understanding of this field of literature. Features interviews with noted children's authors, critiques of classic and contemporary writing for young people, and articles about successful classroom reading projects.
Ind/Abst Abstr. Engl. Stud.; Acad. Search (July 1993-); Annu. Bibliogr. Engl. Lang. Lit.; Arts Humanit. Citation Index [Full Cov.]; Book Rev. Index; Br. Educ. Index; Child. Lit. Abstr.; Contents Pages Educ.; Curr. Contents Arts Humanit.; Curr. Index J. Educ.; Educ. Index; Linguist. Lang. Behav. Abstr.; Mag. Search; Mid. Search (Jul. 1993-); Prim. Search (Jul. 1993-); Res. Alert [Full Cov.]; Soc. Plann. Policy Dev. Abstr.; Sociol. Abstr.

US/0092-8208
CHILDREN'S LITERATURE (STORRS). **See** Children and Youth Interests.

US/0743-9873
CHILDREN'S MAGAZINE GUIDE. **See** Library and Information Sciences-Abstracting, Bibliographies and Statistics.

US/1060-5274
CHILDREN'S WRITER. [Child. writ.]. **Added/Corp** Institute of Children's Literature. Vol. 1, No. 1 (May/June 1991)-. Periodical. English. mo. $15.00. Institute of Children's Literature, 95 Long Ridge Road, West Redding CT 06896. **Tel** (800)243-9645. **DD** 070.

US/0897-9790
CHILDREN'S WRITER'S & ILLUSTRATOR'S MARKET. [Child. writ. illus. mark.]. **Added/Corp** Writer's Digest Books (Firm). **VFOAT** Children's Writer's and Illustrator's Market. (1989)-. English. an (Spring). $22.95. Writer's Digest Books, 1507 Dana Avenue, Cincinnati OH 45207. **Tel** (513)531-2222, (800)289-0963, FAX (513)531-4744. **ED** Lisa Carpenter. **LC** PN147.5; .C48. **DD** 070.5/2; 808.
Desc: Contains helpful articles, as well as markets for writing by children, for both writer's and illustrators.

CN/1183-3211
CHIMERE (SHERBROOKE). (CHIMERE : JOURNAL D'ART ET LETTRES, COLLEGE DE SHERBROOKE.). [Chimere]. **Added/Corp** College de Sherbrooke. Lettres et Langues. College de Sherbrooke. Arts Plastiques et Graphisme. (Sept. 1990)-. Periodical. French. qt. 1.00Can$ per issue. College de Sherbrooke, 475 rue Parc, Sherbrooke Quebec J1H 5M7 Canada. **DD** C840.8/092379/05.

US/1041-3928
CHINESE COMPARATIST. [Chin. comp.]. **Added/Corp** Chung-Kuo Pi Chiao Wen Hsueh Hsueh Hui. Lu Mei Hsueh Che Fen Hui. American Association of Chinese Comparative Literature. **VFOAT** Chung-Kuo Pi Chiao Wen Hsueh Chia T'ung Hsun; Zhong Guo Bi Jiao Wen Xue Jia Tong Xun; Chung-Kuo Pi Chiao Wen Hsueh Chia. No. 1 (Fall 1987)-. Periodical. English (Chinese). Twice a year. Chinese Comparative Literature Association, 2010 Sheridan Road, Wu Beiling, Evanston IL 60201. **LC** PL2274; .C456. **DD** 895.109/0005.
Ind/Abst MLA Int. Bibl. Books Artic. Mod. Lang. Lit.

CH/0009-4544
CHINESE CULTURE. [Chin. cult.]. **Added/Corp** Chung-kuo Wen Hua Yen Chiu So. Chung-kuo Wen Hua Hsueh Yuan. Institute for Advanced Chinese Studies. **VFOAT** Chung-Kuo Wen Hua Chi Kan. Vol. 1, No. 1 (July 1957)-. Periodical. English (Chinese). Four times a year (Mar., June, Sept., Dec.). $45.00 (surface mail); $53.00 Hong Kong, $56.00 US & Europe (airmail). Chinese

Culture University Press, PO Box 12, Yang Ming Shan, Taipei Taiwan. **Tel** 011 886 2 8611861. **ED** Shee Sung and Mou-Pin Lo. **LC** DS701; .C647. Index available. cum. index. **Bk Rev. Ad Acc.** available on microfilm and microfiche from University Microfilms International (UMI). **Desc:** Provides materials and information in the fields of philosophy, literature, history, political science and art for readers.
Ind/Abst Am. Hist. Life (1992-); Int. Bibliogr. Sociol.; Int. Polit. Sci. Abstr.; MLA Int. Bibl. Books Artic. Mod. Lang. Lit.

CH/0009-4617
CHINESE LITERATURE (BEIJING). (CHINESE LITERATURE.). [Chin. lit.]. (Autumn 1951)-. Periodical. English. Four times a year. $16.50 surface mail. **(Subscription address:** China International Book Trading Corporation, PO Box 399, Library Service Department, Beijing 100044 People's Republic of China.**)** **LC** DS777.55; .C45. **DD** 951/.005; 895. Documents available from The Genuine Article.
Desc: Focuses on outstanding contemporary Chinese literature. Selections from modern and ancient works are also published.
Ind/Abst Arts Humanit. Citation Index [Full Cov.]; Curr. Contents Arts Humanit.; MLA Int. Bibl. Books Artic. Mod. Lang. Lit.; Res. Alert [Full Cov.].

US/0161-9705
CHINESE LITERATURE (MADISON). (CHINESE LITERATURE, ESSAYS, ARTICLES, REVIEWS.). [Chin. lit.]. **VFOAT** Chung-kuo Wen Hsueh; CLEAR. Vol. 1, No. 1 (Jan. 1979)-. Periodical. English. an. $25.00 (individuals), $50.00 (institutions) US; $30.00 (individuals), $60.00 (institutions) other. Indiana University / East Asian Languages, Ballantine 402, Bloomington IN 47405. **Tel** (812)855-7537. **ED** Eugene Eoyang, William Nienhauser and Robert Hegel. **LC** PL2250; .C533. **DD** 895.1/09. Index available. cum. index. **Bk Rev. Ad Acc. Circ:** 325 (ctrl). available on microfilm and microfiche from University Microfilms International (UMI).
Desc: Journal on Chinese literature, modern and traditional.
Ind/Abst MLA Int. Bibl. Books Artic. Mod. Lang. Lit.

CH
CHINESE PEN. Added/Corp Chung-Hua Min Kuo Pi Hui. (Autumn 1972)-. Periodical. English. qt. $20.00. International P E N, 33 Lane 180 Kwan Fu So Road, Floor 5, Taipei Taiwan. **Tel** 011 886 2 7219101, FAX 011 886 2 7219101. **ED** Pang-yuan Chi. **LC** PL2250; .C535. **DD** 895.1/08/005. Index available. cum. index.
Ind/Abst Bibliogr. Mission.

CC
CHING MING. VFOAT Ching Ming Wen Hsueh Chi Kan. Periodical. Chinese. bm. RMBY1.00. Science Press, 16 Donghuangchenggen North Street, Beijing 100707, People's Republic of China. **Tel** 011 86 1 4019821, 011 86 1 4010642, FAX 011 86 1 4012180, 011 86 1 4019810, telex 210147. **LC** PL2513; .C5457 . **DD** 895.1/09/005.

CC
CHING NIEN WEN HSUEH. VFOAT Qingnian Wenxue. Periodical. Chinese. bm. RMBY0.40. Post Office Beijing, Beijing, People's Republic of China. **LC** PL2303; .C4267. **DD** 895.1/09/005.

US/0193-7774
CHINOPERL PAPERS. [CHINOPERL pap.]. **Main/Conf** Conference on Chinese Oral and Performing Literature. **Added/Corp** Cornell University. China-Japan Program. **VFOAT** Chung-Kuo Yen Chang Wen I Yen Chiu Hui Lun Chi. **VAT** Chinese Oral and Performing Literature Papers. No. 6 (1976)-. Monographic series. English (Chinese). ir. price varies per volume. CHINOPERL Papers, 110 Music Building, University of Pittsburgh, Pittsburgh PA 15260. **ED** Harold Shadick, Samuel Cheung, and Lindy Li Mark. **LC** PL2253; .C65. **DD** 782.81/0951. **Pr Rev. Circ:** 300. ***Continues*** *CHINOPERL News.*
Desc: Contains articles dealing primarily with oral Chinese literature (popular story telling, opera, ceremonial chanting, folksong) and various genres of Chinese verse and prose.

US/1058-6326
CHIPS OFF THE WRITER'S BLOCK CATHARSIS. See Journalism.

NE/0168-9878
CHLOE AMSTERDAM. (CHLOE.). [ChloeAmst.]. (1984)-. Monographic series. German. ir. Editions Rodopi BV, Keizersgracht 302-304, 1016 Ex Amsterdam Netherlands. **Tel** 011 31 20 6227507, FAX 011 31 20 380948. **UDC** 82.07. ***Continues*** *Daphnis. Beihefte, 0927-7897.*
Ind/Abst MLA Int. Bibl. Books Artic. Mod. Lang. Lit.

KO
CHONSON MUNHAK. Added/Corp Yukkun Chonggun Chakkadan (Korea). (19??)-. Periodical. Korean. **LC** PL969.8; .C5.

JA
CHOSA KENKYU HOKOKU. No. 1-. Japanese. Kokubungaku Kenkyu Shiryokan, 16-10 Yutakamachi 1-chome, Shinagawa-ku 142, Tokyo Japan. **Tel** (03)785-7131. **LC** Z3308.L5; C48; PL716. ***Continues*** *Kokubungaku Bunken Shiryo Shozai Chosa Mokuroku.*

CN/0843-7602
CHRISTIAN VISION. (CHRISTIAN VISION : NEWSLETTER FOR WRITERS, POETS AND ARTISTS.). [Christ. vis.]. (Winter 1989)-. Newsletter. English. Four times a year. 5.00Can$. Skysong Press, RR 1, Washago Ontario L0K 2B0 Canada. **Tel** (705)329-4835, FAX (705)329-1770. **ED** Steve Stanton. **DD** 070.5/2. **Bk Rev. Ad Acc. Circ:** 400.
Desc: Newsletter for writers, poets, and artists. Contains market listings, reviews and interviews.

US/0148-3331
CHRISTIANITY & LITERATURE. [Christ. lit.]. **Added/Corp** Conference on Christianity and Literature. **VFOAT** Christianity and Literature. Vol. 22, No. 2 (Winter 1973)-. Periodical. English. Four times a year. $20.00 (institutions), $15.00 (individuals) US; add $5.00 postage other. Christianity and Literature / West Georgia College, English Department, Carrollton GA 30118-2200. **Tel** (404)836-6512. **ED** Robert Snyder. **LC** PN49; .C49. **DD** 810/.8/0054; 260; 800. **Bk Rev**, (Qty: 80). **Ad Acc. Pr Rev. Circ:** 1,500 (ctrl). ***Continues*** *Newsletter of the Conference on Christianity and Literature.*
Desc: Dedicated to a growing awareness and understanding of the relationships between Christianity and the creation, study and teaching of literature.
Ind/Abst Abstr. Engl. Stud.; Annu. Bibliogr. Engl. Lang. Lit.; Christ. Period. Index (19??-); Index Book Rev. Relig.; Lit. Crit. Regist.; MLA Int. Bibl. Books Artic. Mod. Lang. Lit.; Relig. Index One Period. (1980-); Relig. Theol. Abstr.; Romant. Move.

AT/0729-4042
CHRISTIANS WRITING. [Christ. writ.]. (1981)-. Periodical. English. qt. 24.00Aus$ Australia; 40.00Aus$ other. Studio, 727 Peel Street, Albury NSW 2640 Australia. **Tel** 011 61 60 211135. **ED** Paul Grover. **DD** 808.80382. **Bk Rev**, (Qty: 20). **Ad Acc. Circ:** 300 (ctrl).
Desc: Poetry and prose, offering a venue for previously published, new and aspiring writers, and seeking to create a sense of community among christians writing.

US/0009-5931
CHRONICA (DAVIS). (CHRONICA.). **Added/Corp** Medieval Association of the Pacific. No. 1 (Fall 1967)-. Periodical. English. an. $15.00. Medieval Association of the Pacific, California State University, Department 550, University Parkway, San Bernardino CA 92407. **Tel** (909)880-5528. **ED** Thomas Head. **Bk Rev. Circ:** 425 (ctrl).

FR
CHRONIQUE DES ECRITS EN COURS, LA. No. 1 (May 1981)-. Periodical. French. ir. 35.00F (per issue). Editions de l Equinoxe, 176 rue Froment, 75011 Paris France. **LC** PQ1141; .C46. **DD** 840/.8.

CH
CHU FENG / CHUNG-KUO MIN CHIEN WEN I YEN CHIU HUI HU-NAN FEN HUI. Periodical. Chinese. qt. 0.40. Science Press, 16 Donghuangchenggen North Street, Beijing 100707, People's Republic of China. **Tel** 011 86 1 4019821, 011 86 1 4010642, FAX 011 86 1 4012180, 011 86 1 4019810, telex 210147. **LC** PL2445; .C575. **DD** 398.2/0951.

CC
CHU JEN. Vol. 1-, 1981-. Periodical. Chinese. RMBY0.99. Hsin Hua Shu Tien / Shang-Hai Fa Hsing So, Shanghai, People's Republic of China. **LC** AP215.C5; C48. **DD** 895.1/089282.

CC
CHU PEN. VFOAT Juben. Began in Jan. 1952. Periodical. Chinese. mo. RMBY0.40. Science Press, 16 Donghuangchenggen North Street, Beijing 100707, People's Republic of China. **Tel** 011 86 1 4019821, 011 86 1 4010642, FAX 011 86 1 4012180, 011 86 1 4019810, telex 210147. **LC** PL2603; .C416. **DD** 895.1/25.

CH
CHU PEN YUAN TI. VFOAT Juben Yuandi. Periodical. Chinese. bm. NT$0.48. Science Press, 16 Donghuangchenggen North Street, Beijing 100707, People's Republic of China. **Tel** 011 86 1 4019821, 011 86 1 4010642, FAX 011 86 1 4012180, 011 86 1 4019810, telex 210147. **LC** PN1609.C6; C48. **DD** 809.2.

JA/0388-0176
CHU-SHIKOKU STUDIES IN AMERICAN LITERATURE. [Chu-Shikoku stud. Am. lit.]. **VFOAT** Chu-Shikoku Amerika Bungaku Kenkyu (Hiroshima. 1978); Studies in American Literature (Hiroshima. 1978). (1978)-. Periodical. English. an. **DD** 810. ***Continues*** *Studies in American Literature (Hiroshima. 1962), 0388-0907.*
Ind/Abst MLA Int. Bibl. Books Artic. Mod. Lang. Lit.

CH/0578-0705
CHUAN CHI WEN HSUEH. See Biographies.

JA/0578-0780
CHUBUN KENKYU. No. 1 (May 1961)-. Periodical. English. Tenri Daigaku Chugokugakka Kenkyushitsu, Tenri Nara 632 Japan. **DD** 895.1.

JA/0385-0919
CHUGOKU BUNGAKU KENKYU (WASEDA DAIGAKU. CHUGOKU BUNGAKKAI). (CHUGOKU BUNGAKU KENKYU.). **Added/Corp** Waseda Daigaku. Chugoku Bungakkai. (19??)-. Japanese. an. Waseda Daigaku Chugoku Bungakukai, c/o Waseda Daigaku Bungakubu Chugoku Bungaku Kenkyushitsu Nai 42 Toyamacho Shinjuku-ku, Tokyo Japan. **LC** PL2250; .C556.

JA/0578-0934
CHUGOKU BUNGAKUHO. VFOAT Journal of Chinese Literature. No. 1- Oct. 1954-. Japanese (summaries and/or abstracts in English). an. $74.00. **(Subscription address:** Japan Publications Trading Company, Ltd., PO Box 5030, Tokyo International, Tokyo 100-31 Japan.**)** **LC** PL2250; .C5612. **DD** 895. cum. index.
Ind/Abst MLA Int. Bibl. Books Artic. Mod. Lang. Lit.

CC
CHUN FENG (SHEN-YANG SHIH, CHINA). (CHUN FENG.). **VFOAT** Chun Feng Hsiao Shuo Yueh Kan. Periodical. Chinese. bm. RMBY0.80. Chung-Kuo Chu Pan Tui Wai Mao I Tsung Kung SSU, PO Box 614, Beijing, People's Republic of China. **LC** PL2513; .C56. **DD** 895.1/09/005. ***Continues*** *Chun Feng Wen I Tsung Kan.*

CH
CHUNG FU HSUAN CHI. Periodical. Chinese. $100.00. Chung Yang Jih Pao, 83 Chung Hsiao West Road, 1 Section, Taipei Taiwan. **LC** PL2513; .C5757. **DD** 895.1/08/951249.

CC/0412-4154
CHUNG-KUO ERH TUNG. See Children and Youth Interests.

CC
CHUNG KUO HSIAO SHUO NIEN CHIEN. Chinese. China National Publishing Import & Export Corporation, 16 Gongti E Rd., Chaoyang Dist., Beijing 100704, People's Republic of China. **Tel** 011 8601 50630169, 5066688, FAX 011 8601 5063101, 5063010, telex 22313.

CC
CHUNG-KUO HSIEN TAI WEN HSUEH YEN CHIU TSUNG KAN / KAO HSIAO CHUNG-KUO HSIEN TAI WEN HSUEH YEN CHIU HUI [HO] PEI-CHING CHU PAN SHE HO PIEN. Added/Corp Kao Hsiao Chung-kuo Hsien tai wen Hsueh yen Chiu hui. Pei-Ching chu pan she. **VFOAT** Zhongguo Xian Dai Wen Xue Yan Jiu Congkan. Vol. 1 (1979)-. Periodical. Chinese. qt. $14.00. China National Publishing Import & Export Corporation, 16 Gongti E Rd., Chaoyang Dist., Beijing 100704, People's Republic of China. **Tel** 011 8601 50630169, 5066688, FAX 011 8601 5063101, 5063010, telex 22313. **LC** PL2302; .C523.

CH/1017-6462
CHUNG-KUO WEN CHE YEN CHIU CHI KAN. Added/Corp Chung Yang Yen Chiu Yuan. Chung-Kuo Wen Che Yen Chiu So. Chou Pei Chu. **VFOAT** Bulletin of the Institute of Chinese Literature and Philosophy. (1991)-. Chinese (English; table of contents in English). **LC** AS451; .C46.

CH
CHUNG-KUO WEN HSUEH YEN CHIU. ***Ceased.*** **Added/Corp** Kuo li Tai-wan ta Hsueh. Chung-kuo wen Hsueh Yen Chiu So. (1987)-(19??). Periodical. Chinese. National Taiwan University / Taipei, Research Institute, Chinese Literature, Taipei Taiwan. **LC** PL2250; .C564. **DD** 895.1/09.

US
CHUNG-KUO WEN I NIEN CHIEN. 1932-. Periodical. Chinese. Center for Chinese Research Materials / Washington DC, Association of Research Libraries, 1527 New Hampshire Avenue, Washington DC 20036. **LC** PL2303; .C542.

CH
CHUNG PIEN HSIAO SHUO NIEN PIEN. 1980-. Chinese. an. NT$1.69. Chiang-Su Sheng, Hsin Hua Shu Tien, Nan-Ching, People's Republic of China. **LC** PL2653; .C6854. **DD** 895.1/35/08.

CH
CHUNG WAI WEN HSUEH. VFOAT Chung-Wai Literary Monthly. No. 1 (June 1, 1972)-. Academic Scholarly Publication. Chinese. mo. $66.00 (institutions), $58.00 (individuals) Hong Kong and Macau; $76.00 (institutions), $64.00 (individuals) other. Chung Wai, Department of Foreign Language, National Taiwan University, Taipei 106 Taiwan. **Tel** 011 886 2 3639395, FAX 011 886 2 3639395. **ED** Chuen-cheng Wu. **LC** PN9; .C48. Index available. cum. index. **Ad Acc, Adv Mgr:** Chun-yen Chen, **Tel** 886-2-363-9395. **Pr Rev. Circ:**

3,000 (ctrl).
Desc: Scholarly papers on literature.
Ind/Abst MLA Int. Bibl. Books Artic. Mod. Lang. Lit.

HK
CHUNG WEN HSUEH HSI. **VFOAT** Chinese Learning. First published in Sept. 1975-. Periodical. Chinese (Chinese). $2.00 single issue. Shih Tai Chu Pan She, Time Press, 17/F Flat B7, Canal Road, Hsiang-Kang Hong Kong. **LC** PL1068.H6; C47.

KO
CHUNGGUK MUNHAK. **VFOAT** Journal of Chinese Literature. Periodical. Chinese (Korean). Chungmunhakkwa Yongusil, Yonse University, Seoul Korea. **LC** PL2250; .C59.

NP
CHYANKUTI. V. 1- Vaisakha 2030- 1973-. Nepali (Nepali). 1.00 single issue. Rashtravadi Svatantra Vidyarthi Mandala, Sankhuwasabha, Khandavari Nepal. **LC** PK2598.A2; C49.

US/0883-9816
CINCINNATI ROMANCE REVIEW. [Cincinnati roman. rev.]. **Added/Corp** McMicken College of Arts and Sciences. Dept. of Romance Languages and Literatures. (198?)-. Periodical. English. an (May). $10.00. University of Cincinnati / Department of Romance Languages and Literature, c/o John C. Seigneuret, Cincinnati OH 45221. **Tel** (513)821-9328. **DD** 840.
Ind/Abst MLA Int. Bibl. Books Artic. Mod. Lang. Lit.

US/0009-7349
CIRCULO - CIRCULO DE CULTURA PANAMERICANO. (CIRCULO : PUBLICACION DEL CIRCULO DE CULTURA PANAMERICANO.). [Circ. - Circ. Cult. Panam.]. **Added/Corp** Circulo de Cultura Panamericano. (1970)-. Academic Scholarly Publication. Spanish (English). an (Nov.). $25.00 US; $40.00 other. Circulo de Cultura Panamericano, 16 Malvern Place, Verona NJ 07004. **Tel** (201)239-3125. **ED** Elio Alba Buffill. **LC** F1408.3; .C47. **DD** 860. **Bk Rev**, (Qty: 15). **Circ:** 800 (ctrl).
Desc: Scholarly works in Latin American and Spanish literature and culture.
Ind/Abst MLA Int. Bibl. Books Artic. Mod. Lang. Lit.

US/1045-1943
CITY LIGHTS REVIEW. [City lights rev.]. No. 1 (1987)-. English. an. $10.00. City Lights Books, 261 Columbus Avenue, San Francisco CA 94133. **Tel** (415)362-8193. **(Subscription address:** Subco, PO Box 10233, Eugene OR 97404.) **ED** Lawrence Ferlinghetti and Nancy J Peters. **LC** PN6010.5; .C58. **DD** 081. **Bk Rev. Circ:** 5,000.

US/0007-8549
CLA JOURNAL. **See** Linguistics.

PR/0279-313X
CLARIDAD (SANTURCE, P.R.). (CLARIDAD : BOLETIN DEL MOVIMIENTO PRO INDEPENDENCIA DE PUERTO RICO.). [Claridad]. **Added/Corp** Movimiento Pro Independencia de Puerto Rico. Partido Socialista Puertorriqueno. Vol. 1, No. 1 (Jan. 1959)-. Newspaper. Spanish. wk (Friday). $30.00 Puerto Rico; $40.00 US. Editorial Claridad, Av Ponce de Leon 1866, PD 26 1 2, Santurce Puerto Rico 00909. **Tel** (809)726-5221, (809)726-5988.
Ind/Abst Index Am. Period. Verse.

US/0896-0011
CLASSICAL AND MEDIEVAL LITERATURE CRITICISM. [Class. mediev. lit. crit.]. **Added/Corp** Gale Research Company. **VFOAT** CMLC. (1988)-. English. ir. $103.00. Gale Research Inc., 835 Penobscot Building, Detroit MI 48226. **Tel** (800)877-GALE, (313)961-2242, FAX (313)961-6083, telex TWX 810-221-7086. **ED** Jelena O. Krstovic. **LC** PN681.5; .C57. **DD** 809/.005.
Desc: A convenient source of wide-ranging critical commentary emcompassing early classical and medieval literature from pre-Biblical epics of ancient Sumeria through the end of the fourteenth century. Furnishes extensive excerpts from criticism on authors, poets, playwrights, and literary works that contributed to human culture in many ages and areas. Each volume covers four to six authors or works of classical and medieval literature. Each entry begins with an introduction containing biographical, historical, and other background information.

US/1070-7557
CLASSICS CHRONICLE. [Class. chron.]. (19??)-. Periodical. English. Three times a year. $6.00. Concerned Classicists, 8951 Southwest 10th Terrace, Miami FL 33174. **Tel** (305)223-4380. **DD** 880.

FR/0578-459X
CLASSIQUES AFRICAINS. (1963)-. Periodical. French. be. Librairie Armand Colin, BP 22, 41354 Vineuil Cedex France. **Tel** 011 33 54 438994. **DD** 960.

US/0090-1237
CLAUDEL STUDIES. [Claudel stud.]. Vol. 1, (1972)-. Multiple languages (English and French). Twice a year (Mar., Nov.). $25.00 (institutions), $20.00 (individuals) US; $25.00 other. University of Dallas, Department of Foreign Language, 1845 East Northgate Drive, PO Box 464, Irving TX 75062. **Tel** (214)721-5229. **ED** Moses M. Nagy. **LC** PQ2605.L2; Z6224. **DD** 848/.9/1209. **Bk Rev. Circ:** 400 (ctrl). Documents available from The Genuine Article. ***Supersedes** Claudel Newsletter, 0069-4568.*
Desc: Journal publishes research papers, articles, monographs, notes, and reviews on Claudel. It has also published translations and taped discussions. The journal endeavors to make Claudel's work known.
Ind/Abst Arts Humanit. Citation Index (19??-19??) [Full Cov.]; Curr. Contents Arts Humanit.; MLA Int. Bibl. Books Artic. Mod. Lang. Lit.; Res. Alert [Full Cov.]; Romant. Move.

CK
CLAVE DE SOL. V. 1- Oct. 1972-. Periodical. Spanish. $144.00. Luzal Publicidad, Palace 52-75 Oficina 205, Medellin Colombia. **LC** PN6; .C55.

SP/0214-4123
CLIJ. [CLIJ]. **VFOAT** Cuadernos de Literatura Infantil y Juvenil. (1988)-. Periodical. Spanish. Eleven times a year. $75.00. Editorial Fontalba SA, Valencia 359 6TO 1, 08009 Barcelona Spain. **Tel** 011 34 3 4585508. **UDC** 82.93.

US/0884-2043
CLIO (FORT WAYNE, IND.). (CLIO.). [Clio]. **Added/Corp** Indiana University-Purdue University at Fort Wayne. University of Wisconsin--Parkside. Vol. 1, (Oct. 1971)-. Periodical. English. Four times a year (Jan., Mar., June, Oct.). $15.00 (individuals), $40.00 (institutions). Indiana University-Purdue Fort Wayne, 2101 Coliseum Boulevard East, Fort Wayne IN 46805. **Tel** (219)489-6753, FAX (219)481-6985, telex 272279. **ED** Henry Kozicki, Clark Butler and Andrew McLean. **LC** AS30; .C53. **DD** 901. Index available. cum. index. **Bk Rev. Ad Acc. Pr Rev. Circ:** 600. available in microform. Documents available from The Genuine Article, UMI Article Clearinghouse.
Desc: Concerned with literature, history and the philosophy of history. Literature as informed by historical understanding and historical writings considered as literature, philosophy of history, speculative and analytic.
Ind/Abst Abstr. Engl. Stud.; Acad. Search (July 1993-); Am. Hist. Life (1971-); Annu. Bibliogr. Engl. Lang. Lit.; Arts Humanit. Citation Index [Full Cov.]; Book Rev. Index; Curr. Contents Arts Humanit.; Expand. Acad. Index (1989-); Humanit. Index; Humanit. Source (Jul. 1993-); INFO-SOUTH Abstr.; Linguist. Lang. Behav. Abstr.; Lit. Crit. Regist.; Mag. Search; MLA Int. Bibl. Books Artic. Mod. Lang. Lit.; Newsp. Period. Abstr. (1991-); Philos. Index; Res. Alert [Full Cov.]; Soc. Plann. Policy Dev. Abstr.; Soc. Sci. Cit. Index [Select. Cov.]; Sociol. Abstr.; West. Hist. Q.

CN/0821-1450
CM : CANADIAN MATERIALS FOR SCHOOLS AND LIBRARIES. [CM, Can. mater. sch. libr.]. **Added/Corp** Canadian Library Association. **VFOAT** Canadian Materials for Schools and Libraries. Vol. 8, No. 1 (Winter 1980)-. Periodical. English. bm. 42.00Can$. Canadian Library Association, 200 Elgin Street, Suite 602, Ottawa Ontario K2P 1L5 Canada. **Tel** (613)232-9625. **LC** Z1378; .C33. **DD** 808.8/99282. ***Continues** Canadian Materials, 0317-4654.*
Ind/Abst Book Rev. Digest; Book Rev. Index (1988-); Can. Period. Index (19??-).

US
CNL/WORLD REPORT 1985. English. ir. Council on National Literature, PO Box 81, Whitestone NY 11357. **Tel** (718)767-3830.

US/1062-5011
COAL CITY REVIEW. [Coal city rev.]. No. 1 (Aug. 1990)-. Periodical. English. sa. $6.00. Coal City Review, 3116 Wescoe Hall, Lawrence KS 66045. **DD** 810.

CN/1184-7581
COASTLINES (SURREY). (COASTLINES.). [Coastlines]. **Added/Corp** White Rock & Surrey Writers Club. **VFOAT** Coast Lines. (1990)-. English. be. White Rock and Surrey Writers Club, Number 12, 15137 24th Avenue, Surrey, British Columbia V4H 2H7 Canada. **DD** C810/.8/0971133. ***Continues** Gems of Poetry and Prose., 0834-1737.*

US/1050-5873
COLBY QUARTERLY. [Colby q.]. **Added/Corp** Colby College. Vol. 26, No. 1 (March 1990)-. Periodical. English. qt. $12.00 (one year), $20.00 (two year), $28.00 (three year) US; add foreign postage $1.00/year (surface), $4.00/year (airmail). Colby Library Quarterly, Colby College Library, Waterville ME 04901. **Tel** (207)872-3284. **ED** Douglas Archibald. **LC** Z881; .W336. **DD** 820. available on microfilm and microfiche from University Microfilms International (UMI). Documents available from The Genuine Article. ***Continues** Colby Library Quarterly, 0010-0552.*
Desc: Articles on literature in English, special interests: Maine and regional literature and history, Irish Literature, art and literature.
Ind/Abst Abstr. Engl. Stud.; Am. Hist. Life (1975-); Annu. Bibliogr. Engl. Lang. Lit.; Arts Humanit. Citation Index [Full Cov.]; BHA : Biblio. Hist. Art; Curr. Contents Arts Humanit.; MLA Int. Bibl. Books Artic. Mod. Lang. Lit.; Res. Alert [Full Cov.].

US/0890-0086
COLD-DRILL MAGAZINE. [Cold-drill mag.]. **Added/Corp** Boise State University. Dept. of English. **VFOAT** Cold-Drill Magazine. (198?)-. Periodical. English. an. $6.95 (regular edition); $9.95 (deluxe edition). Cold Drill, 1910 University Drive, Boise State University, Boise ID 83725. **Tel** (208)385-4031, FAX (208)385-4373. **ED** Tom Trusky. **DD** 810. **Circ:** 500 (ctrl).

BL
COLECAO DOS AUTORES CELEBRES DA LITERATURA BRASILEIRA. Portuguese. ir. Fundacao Casa de Rui Barbosa, rua Sao Clemente, 134 Botafogo Brazil. **Tel** 021 2861297, FAX 021 2860580, telex 2137232. Index available.

UK/0076-0773
COLLECTED SEMINAR PAPERS / UNIVERSITY OF LONDON, INSTITUTE OF COMMONWEALTH STUDIES. **See** Social Sciences.

CN/0228-0337
COLLECTION ENCRE. [Collect. encre]. **VFOAT** Encre. Published since Feb. 1978?. Periodical. French. Free. Revue Encre, Cegep de St-Laurent B-41, 625 Boulevard Ste Croix, St-Laurent Quebec H4L 3X7Canada. **DD** C840/.8/09283.

NE/0169-0078
COLLECTION MONOGRAPHIQUE RODOPI EN LITTERATURE FRANCAISE CONTEMPORAINE. [Collect. monogr. Rodopi litt. fr. contemp.]. (1984)-. Monographic series. French. ir. **UDC** 840.
Ind/Abst MLA Int. Bibl. Books Artic. Mod. Lang. Lit.

FR
COLLECTION RECHERCHES GERMANIQUES. **VFOAT** Recherches Germaniques. No. 1; 1988-. Monographic series. German (English and French). Price varies per volume. Universite des Sciences Humaines, 22 rue Descartes, 67084 Strasbourg Cedex France. **Tel** 011 33 88 417317.

SZ/0530-9220
COLLECTION STENDHALIENNE. 1-. Monographic series. French. Price varies per volume. Editions du Grand-Chene, Chemin de Montagny, CH-1603 Aran Switzerland.

UK
COLLECTIONS - MALONE SOCIETY, LONDON. **Main/Corp** Malone Society. V. 1-. Monographic series. English. Price varies per volume. **LC** PR621; .M4.

US/0093-3139
COLLEGE LITERATURE. [Coll. lit.]. Vol. 1 (Winter 1974)-. Academic Scholarly Publication. English. Three times a year (Feb., June, Oct.). $24.00 (individuals); $48.00 (institutions). College Literature, 544 New Main, West Chester University, West Chester PA 19383. **Tel** (215)436-2901, FAX (215)436-3540. **ED** Kostas Myrsiades. **LC** PR1; .C65. **DD** 809. **CODEN** COLTEY. Index available (bound in Iss. 3, pubd Oct.). cum. index. **Bk Rev**, (Qty: 30/yr). **Ad Acc. Pr Rev. Circ:** 1,000 (ctrl). available on microfilm and microfiche from University Microfilms International (UMI); available on CD-ROM from Information Access Company. Documents available from The Genuine Article, UMI Article Clearinghouse.
Desc: Scholarly articles on major works and authors regularly taught in American colleges and universities.
Ind/Abst Abstr. Engl. Stud.; Acad. Search (Jan. 1993-); Am. Bibliogr. Slavic East Europ. Stud.; Am. Humanit. Index; Annu. Bibliogr. Engl. Lang. Lit.; Arts Humanit. Citation Index [Full Cov.]; Book Rev. Index; Child. Lit. Abstr. (19??-); Curr. Contents Arts Humanit.; Expand. Acad. Index (1989-); Humanit. Index; Humanit. Source (Jan. 1993-); INFO-SOUTH Abstr.; Linguist. Lang. Behav. Abstr.; Lit. Crit. Regist.; MLA Int. Bibl. Books Artic. Mod. Lang. Lit.; Newsp. Period. Abstr. (1991-); Res. Alert [Full Cov.]; Romant. Move.; Soc. Plann. Policy Dev. Abstr.; Soc. Sci. Cit. Index [Select. Cov.]; Sociol. Abstr.; Vocat. Search (Jan. 1993-).

SZ/0179-3780
COLLOQUIUM HELVETICUM. **Added/Corp** Schweizerische Gesellschaft fuer Allgemeine und Vergleichende Literaturwissenschaft. (1985)-. Periodical. German (English and French; summaries and/or abstracts in German and English). sa. 30.00F. Verlag Peter Lang AG, Jupiterstrasse 15, CH-3000 Bern 15 Switzerland. **Tel** 011 41 31 9411122, FAX 011 41 31 321131.
Ind/Abst MLA Int. Bibl. Books Artic. Mod. Lang. Lit.

PO/0010-1451
COLOQUIO : LETRAS. [Coloq., Let.]. **Added/Corp** Fundacao Calouste Gulbenkian. No. 1, (March 1971)-. Periodical. Portuguese. Six times a year (Jan., Mar., May, July, Sept., Nov.). $65.00 Europe; $80.00 others. Nobar Grupo Editorial L DA, rua da Cruz da Carreira 4B, 1100 Lisbon Portugal. **Tel** 011 351 1 3522490. **ED** David Mourao-Ferreira. **LC** NX7; .C642. **DD** 700/.5. **Bk Rev. Circ:** 4,000 (ctrl). Documents available

from The Genuine Article. ***Continues in part*** *Coloquio (Lisbon, Portugal), 0010-1451.*
Desc: Literary essays on Portuguese language, theory of literature and general literature.
Ind/Abst Arts Humanit. Citation Index [Full Cov.]; Curr. Contents Arts Humanit.; MLA Int. Bibl. Books Artic. Mod. Lang. Lit.; Res. Alert [Full Cov.]; Soc. Sci. Cit. Index [Select. Cov.].

US/1053-1831
COLOR WHEEL. [Color wheel]. No. 1 (Spring/Summer 1991)-. Periodical. English. sa. $8.00. Color Wheel Press, 4 Washington Court, Concord NH 03301. **DD** 808.

US/0194-0589
COLORADO-NORTH REVIEW. ***Ceased.*** **Added/Corp** University of Northern Colorado. Associated Students. (19??)-(1992). Periodical. English. sa. Colorado North Review, University Center, Greeley CO 80639. **Tel** (303)351-4487. **ED** Robert Payne. **LC** PS1; .C63. **DD** 810/.8. **Ad Acc. Circ:** 1,500 (ctrl). ***Continues*** *Nova.*
Desc: Submissions of poetry, short fiction, photography and artwork compiled in a magazine.

US
COLUMBA / THE MIDWEST REVIEW OF BOOKS. English. mo. $13.00. Columba / The Midwest Review, 101 East Wilson Bridge, Worthington OH 43085. **Tel** (614) 885-1031.

US/0161-486X
COLUMBIA, A MAGAZINE OF POETRY AND PROSE. [Columbia mag. poetry prose]. **Added/Corp** Columbia University. School of the Arts. Columbia University. School of General Studies. (1977)-. Periodical. English. an (Sept.). $6.00. Columbia University / 404 Dodge Hall, New York NY 10027. **Tel** (212)280-4391. **LC** PN6010.5; .C64. **DD** 810/.8/0054. **Ad Acc. Circ:** 2,000 (ctrl).
Desc: Articles and fiction to poetry, pays in copies and annual awards.

US/0069-6315
COLUMBIA ESSAYS ON MODERN WRITERS. Vol. 1 (1964)-. English. ir. Columbia University Press, 136 South Broadway, Irvington NY 10533. **Tel** (914)591-9111. **DD** 800.

US/0272-7404
COMEDY. [Comedy]. **VFOAT** Comedy Magazine. Vol. 1 (Summer 1980)-. Periodical. English. qt. $12.00. Trite Expectations, Inc., Box 505, Canal Street Station, New York NY 10013. **LC** PN1920; .C65. **DD** 817/.008.

US/0069-6412
COMITATUS. [Comitatus]. **Added/Corp** University of California, Los Angeles. Center for Medieval and Renaissance Studies. University of California, Los Angeles. English Medieval Club. University of California, Los Angeles. Medieval Guild. Vol. 1 (Dec. 1970)-. English. an (Oct.). $12.50 (individuals); $17.50 (institutions). UCLA Center of Medieval and Renaissance Studies, 212 Royce Hall, 405 Hilgard Avenue, Los Angeles CA 90024. **Tel** (310)825-1880, (310)825-1950. **ED** Blair Sullivan. **LC** PR251; .C65. **DD** 820.9. Index available. cum. index. **Bk Rev. Circ:** 600. Documents available from The Genuine Article.
Desc: Contains articles in the field of medieval and renaissance studies by graduate students and new scholars across the country, under the auspices of the UCLA Center for Medieval and Renaissance Studies.
Ind/Abst Annu. Bibliogr. Engl. Lang. Lit.; Arts Humanit. Citation Index (19??-19??) [Full Cov.]; BHA : Biblio. Hist. Art; Curr. Contents Arts Humanit.; MLA Int. Bibl. Books Artic. Mod. Lang. Lit.; Res. Alert [Full Cov.]; Soc. Sci. Cit. Index [Select. Cov.].

FR/0180-8214
COMMENTAIRE (JULLIARD). (COMMENTAIRE.). [Commentaire]. (March 1978)-. Periodical. French. qt. 295.00F (1 year), 550.00F (2 year), 800.00F (3 year) France; 330.00F (1 year), 635.00F (2 year), 930.00F (3 year) other. Commentaire, 116 rue du Bac, F-75007 Paris France. **Tel** 011 33 1 45493782, FAX 011 33 1 45443218. **ED** Jean-Claude Casanova. **LC** AP20; .C55. Index available. cum. index. **Bk Rev**, (Qty: 4). **Ad Acc. Circ:** 5,000.
Ind/Abst Int. Polit. Sci. Abstr.

FR/0395-6989
COMMONWEALTH. [Commonwealth]. **Added/Corp** Societe d'etudes des pays du Commonwealth (France). Vol. 1 (1975)-. Periodical. English (French). be. 130.00F. Societe d'Etude des Pays du Commonwealth, Faculte de Langues, 2 Boulevard Gabriel, 21000 Dijon France. **Tel** FAX 80 39 56 19. **ED** J.P. Durix. **LC** PN849.C5; C65. **DD** 809. Index available. **Bk Rev. Ad Acc. Circ:** 600.
Desc: Covers literature, civilization, language of former advanced research.

FR
COMMONWEALTH ESSAYS & STUDIES. English (French). sa. 130.00F. Commonwealth / France, Faculte de Langues, 2 Boulevard Gabriel, F-21000 Dijon France. **Tel** 011 33 80 895650, FAX 011 33 80 395648. **ED** J. P. Durix. **Bk Rev. Ad Acc. Pr Rev. Circ:** 500.

Desc: Essays on the new literatures in English. Assessment of Anglophone post-colonial literature.
Ind/Abst MLA Int. Bibl. Books Artic. Mod. Lang. Lit.

II/1013-9877
COMMONWEALTH QUARTERLY. [Commonw. q.]. Vol. 1 (Dec. 1976)-. Periodical. English. sa. $10.00. Vikramraj Urs, V V Mohalla 2823, VIII Gross Mysore 2 Karnataka State India. **(Subscription address:** Prints India, 11 Darya Ganj, New Delhi 110002 India.**) LC** PK5461.A1; C65. **DD** 805.
Ind/Abst MLA Int. Bibl. Books Artic. Mod. Lang. Lit.

US/0740-8943
COMMUNICATIONS FROM THE INTERNATIONAL BRECHT SOCIETY. [Commun. Int. Brecht Soc.]. **Added/Corp** International Brecht Society. **VFOAT** Communications; Brecht Newsletter. Vol. 1, No. 1 (Dec. 1971)-. Periodical. English (German). Twice a year. $20.00 (regular member annual) income less than $20,000.00; $25.00 (regular member annual) income $20,000.00 and over; $30.00 (sustaining & institutions) Comes with International Brecht Society Membership. International Brecht Society, University of Georgia, Department of German Slavic Language, Athens GA 30602. **Tel** (706)542-3663. **ED** Michael Gilbert. **LC** PT2603.R397; Z5835. **DD** 832/.912. **Bk Rev. Ad Acc. Circ:** 250 (ctrl).
Ind/Abst MLA Int. Bibl. Books Artic. Mod. Lang. Lit.

IT/0942-8917
COMPARAISON. Italian (German, French and English). sa. 80.00F. Verlag Peter Lang AG, Jupiterstrasse 15, CH-3000 Bern 15 Switzerland. **Tel** 011 41 31 9411122, FAX 011 41 31 321131. ***Continues*** *Comparatio : Revue International de Litterature Comparee.*

US/0195-7678
COMPARATIST, THE. [Comparatist]. **Added/Corp** Southern Comparative Literature Association. Vol. 1 (1977)-. English. an (May). $12.00 (one year); $23.00 (two years); $35.00 (three years). Southern Comparative Literture Association, 701 McClung Tower, Knoxville TN 37996. **ED** Mechtild Cranston. **LC** PN855; .C66. **DD** 809. **Bk Rev. Pr Rev. Circ:** 500.
Desc: Articles on most aspects of comparative literary studies.
Ind/Abst Am. Bibliogr. Slavic East Europ. Stud.; Am. Humanit. Index; Humanit. Index; Lit. Crit. Regist.; MLA Int. Bibl. Books Artic. Mod. Lang. Lit.; Romant. Move.

IT
COMPARATISTICA. Vol. 1 (1989)-. Periodical. English (French and Italian). an. L45000 Italy; L55000 other. Casa Editrice Leo S. Olschki, Viuzzo del Pozzetto, Casella Postale 66, 50126 Florence Italy. **Tel** 011 39 55 6530684, FAX 011 39 55 6530214.

●US/1070-955X
COMPARATIVE CULTURES AND LITERATURE. (1994)-. Monographic series. English. Price varies per volume. Peter Lang Publishing, 62 West 45th Street, 4th Floor, New York NY 10036. **Tel** (212)764-1471, (800)770-5264, telex 6973364 PLNY.

US/0010-4124
COMPARATIVE LITERATURE. [Comp. lit.]. **Added/Corp** American Comparative Literature Association. Modern Language Association of America. Comparative Literature Section. University of Oregon. Vol. 1 (Winter 1949)-. Periodical. English (Spanish, French and German). qt (Feb., May, Aug., Nov.). $32.00 institution; $20.00 individual. University of Oregon/Comparative Literature, 223 Friendly Hall, Eugene OR 97403. **Tel** (503)346-4022. **ED** Thomas R. Hart and Steven Rendall. **LC** PN851; .C595. **DD** 805. **Bk Rev. Circ:** 2,500 (ctrl). available on microfilm and microfiche from University Microfilms International (UMI). Documents available from The Genuine Article, UMI Article Clearinghouse.
Desc: Explores important problems of literary theory and literary history not confined to a single national literature.
Ind/Abst Abstr. Engl. Stud.; Acad. Abstr. Full Text Elite (Jan. 1991-); Acad. Abstr. (Jan. 1991-); Acad. Ind. [Computer File] (1992-); Acad. Search (Jan. 1991-); Am. Bibliogr. Slavic East Europ. Stud. (19??-19??); Annu. Bibliogr. Engl. Lang. Lit.; Arts Humanit. Citation Index [Full Cov.]; BHA : Biblio. Hist. Art; Book Rev. Index; Curr. Contents Arts Humanit.; Expand. Acad. Index (1989-); Humanit. Index; Humanit. Source (Jul. 1990-); INFO-SOUTH Abstr.; Lit. Crit. Regist.; Mag. Search; Middle East Abstr. Index; MLA Int. Bibl. Books Artic. Mod. Lang. Lit.; Newsp. Period. Abstr. (1988-); Res. Alert [Full Cov.]; Romant. Move.; Soc. Sci. Cit. Index [Select. Cov.].

●US/0899-9902
COMPARATIVE LITERATURE AND FILM STUDIES. (1993)-. English. Peter Lang Publishing, 62 West 45th Street, 4th Floor, New York NY 10036. **Tel** (212)764-1471, (800)770-5264, telex 6973364 PLNY.

CN/0045-7795
COMPARATIVE LITERATURE IN CANADA. **Added/Corp** University of Alberta. Dept. of Comparative Literature. Canadian Comparative Literature Association. Canadian Comparative Literature Association. Newsletter. **VFOAT** Litterature Comparee au Canada. Vol. 1 (Spring 1969)-. Periodical. English (French). sa. $7.00. University of British Columbia Department of English, C/O Richard Cavell, Vancouver Canada V6T 1Z1. **Tel** (604)822-5046. **ED** P.A. Robberecht. **LC** PN855; .C3513. **DD** 809/.8971. **Ad Acc. Circ:** 500.
Desc: Includes association business, abstracts of learned papers, new publications by members, miscellaneous information about comparative literature.

US/0010-4132
COMPARATIVE LITERATURE STUDIES (URBANA). (COMPARATIVE LITERATURE STUDIES.). [Comp. lit. stud.]. **VFOAT** CLS. Comparative Literature Studies. Vol. 1 (1964)-. Periodical. English (French and Spanish). qt. $40.00 (institutions), $27.50 (individuals) US; $48.00 (institutions), $35.00 (individuals) other. Pennsylvania State University Press, 820 North University Drive, Suite C, University Park PA 16802-1003. **Tel** (814)865-1327, (800)326-9180, FAX (814)863-1408. **ED** Roberts Edwards. **LC** PN851; .C63. **DD** 809. **[CCC].** Index available. cum. index. **Bk Rev. Ad Acc. Circ:** 1,000 (ctrl). available on microfilm and microfiche from University Microfilms International (UMI). Documents available from The Genuine Article, UMI Article Clearinghouse.
Desc: Articles on literary history and criticism, history of ideas, literary relations between East, West, North, and South America.
Ind/Abst Abstr. Engl. Stud.; Acad. Search (July 1993-); Am. Bibliogr. Slavic East Europ. Stud.; Annu. Bibliogr. Engl. Lang. Lit.; Arts Humanit. Citation Index [Full Cov.]; BHA : Biblio. Hist. Art; Book Rev. Index; Curr. Contents Arts Humanit.; Expand. Acad. Index (1989-); Humanit. Index; Humanit. Source (Jul. 1993-); INFO-SOUTH Abstr.; Mag. Search; Middle East Abstr. Index; MLA Int. Bibl. Books Artic. Mod. Lang. Lit.; Newsp. Period. Abstr. (1991-); Res. Alert [Full Cov.]; Romant. Move.

UK/0950-6756
COMPENDIA. **See** Linguistics.

US/0897-263X
COMPOSITION CHRONICLE. [Compos. chron.]. **VFOAT** CC. Vol. 1, No. 1 (Feb. 1988)-. Periodical. English. Nine times a year (Sept. thru May). $25.00 one year; $47.00 two years. Viceroy Publications, 3217 Bronson Hill Road, Livonia NY 14487. **Tel** (716)346-6860. **ED** Bill McCleary. **LC** PE1404; .C65. **DD** 808. Index available (Sept. iss.). cum. index. **Bk Rev**, (Qty: 9 per year). **Circ:** 600.
Desc: News of composition programs, reviews of professional books, how-to articles for writing teachers, and articles about important issues and developments in the field.

●US
COMPOSITION STUDIES : FRESHMAN ENGLISH NEWS. **See** Linguistics.

US/0197-1441
COMUNIUNEA ROMANEASCA. (ROMANIAN COMMUNION.). **VFOAT** Comuniunea Romaneasca. Vol. 1, No. 1 (Jan./March 1973)-. Periodical. English (Romanian). ir. Comuniunea Romaneasca, 19959 Riopelle, Detroit MI 48203. **Tel** (313)893-9237. **ED** George Alexe. **LC** DR212; .R65. **DD** 909/.0459. **Bk Rev. Circ:** 500.
Desc: Literary magazine of Romanian theology, culture and art promoting the heritage of Romanian-American ethnicity, spirituality and national friendship.

US/1048-9568
CONCHO RIVER REVIEW. [Concho River rev.]. **Added/Corp** Fort Concho Museum. Vol. 1, No. 1 (Spring 1987)-. Periodical. English. sa (Spring and fall). $12.00 (one year), $22.00 (two years). Fort Concho Museum Press, 213 East Avenue D, San Angelo TX 76903. **Tel** (915)657-4441, FAX (915)657-4540. **ED** Terence A. Dalrymple. **DD** 810. **Bk Rev**, (Qty: 10). **Ad Acc. Circ:** 200.
Desc: Features fiction, nonfiction, poetry, essays and reviews about Texas or by Texas writers.

CN/0822-546X
CONCOURS LITTERAIRE. [Concours litt.]. 1980-. French. an. Concours Litteraire, 415, Rue Des Ecoles, Drummondville Quebec J2B 1 J3. **DD** C840/.8/092375.

BL
CONFLUENCIA. **Added/Corp** Instituto de Lingua Portuguesa. No. 1 (1991)-. Periodical. Portuguese. sa. Instituto de Lingua Portuguesa, Liceu Literario Portugues, Rua Senador Dantas 118, CEP 20032, Rio de Janeiro, RJ, Brazil.

US/0010-5716
CONFRONTATION (SOUTHAMPTON, N.Y.). (CONFRONTATION.). [Confrontation]. **Added/Corp** Long Island University. No. 1 (Spring 1968)-. Periodical. English. Twice a year. $10.00 US; $15.00 Canada; $20.00 other. Confrontation, CW Post of Liu, English Department, Brookville NY 11548. **Tel** (516)299-2391, FAX (516)299-2735. **ED** Martin Tucker. **LC** PS501; .C66. **DD** 810. Index available. cum. index.

Bk Rev, (Qty: 40). Circ: 2,000. available on microfilm and microfiche from University Microfilms International (UMI). Documents available from The Genuine Article.
Desc: Literate fiction, poems, and essays open to all forms and styles.
Ind/Abst Am. Humanit. Index; Annu. Bibliogr. Engl. Lang. Lit.; Arts Humanit. Citation Index [Full Cov.]; Curr. Contents Arts Humanit.; Index Am. Period. Verse; Res. Alert [Full Cov.].

UK
CONRADIAN : THE JOURNAL OF THE JOSEPH CONRAD SOCIETY (U.K.), THE. **Added/Corp** Joseph Conrad Society (U.K.). **VFOAT** Journal of the Joseph Conrad Society (U.K). Vol. 6, No. 1 (April 1980)-. Periodical. English. Twice a year. £20.00. Joseph Conrad Society UK, 238-246 King Street, London W6 0RF England. **ED** Robert Hampson. **Bk Rev**, (Qty: 4). **Ad Acc. Circ:** 300 (ctrl). ***Continues*** *Journal of the Joseph Conrad Society (U.K.).*
Desc: Covers the life and works of Joseph Conrad.
Ind/Abst MLA Int. Bibl. Books Artic. Mod. Lang. Lit.

US/0898-8609
CONSTRUCTIONS. [Constructions]. 1984-. English (French). an. Anma Libri, PO Box 876, Saratoga CA 95070. **Tel** (408)741-0522, 741-1522. **LC** PQ1; .C66. **DD** 840/.9.

US/0010-7204
CONSUMPTION. **VFOAT** Consumption Magazine. V. 1- Fall 1967-. Periodical. English. qt. **LC** PS501; .C664. available on microfilm from University Microfilms International (UMI).

US/0010-7468
CONTEMPORARY AUTHORS. See Biographies.

US/0748-0636
CONTEMPORARY AUTHORS AUTOBIOGRAPHY SERIES. See Biographies.

US
CONTEMPORARY LITERARY CRITICS. English. $80.00. St. James Press, PO Box 33477, Detroit MI 48232-5477. **Tel** (800)345-0392.
Desc: A descriptive reference guide to 124 of the most important and influential twentieth-century critics in the English language.

US/0010-7484
CONTEMPORARY LITERATURE. [Contemp. lit.]. Vol. 9 (Winter 1968)-. Periodical. English. qt. $25.00 (one year), $50.00 (two year), $75.00 (three year), individuals; $63.00 (one year), $124.00 (two year), $184.00 (three year) institutions. University of Wisconsin Press, Journal Division, 114 North Murray Street, Madison WI 53715. **Tel** (608)262-4952, FAX (608)262-8909. **LC** PN2; .W55. **DD** 809.04. **[CCC]**. available on microfilm and microfiche from University Microfilms International (UMI). Documents available from The Genuine Article, UMI Article Clearinghouse. ***Continues*** *Wisconsin Studies in Contemporary Literature, 0146-4949.*
Desc: Offers criticism, review and research in modern literature, without restriction as to country or genre.
Ind/Abst Abstr. Engl. Stud.; Acad. Ind. [Computer File] (1992-); Acad. Search (July 1993-); Am. Bibliogr. Slavic East Europ. Stud.; Am. Humanit. Index (-199?); Annu. Bibliogr. Engl. Lang. Lit.; Arts Humanit. Citation Index [Full Cov.]; Child. Lit. Abstr. (19??-); Curr. Contents Arts Humanit.; Expand. Acad. Index (1989-); Humanit. Index; Humanit. Source (Jul. 1993-); INFO-SOUTH Abstr.; Lit. Crit. Regist.; Mag. Search; Middle East Abstr. Index; MLA Int. Bibl. Books Artic. Mod. Lang. Lit.; Newsp. Period. Abstr. (1991-); Res. Alert [Full Cov.]; Romant. Move.

UK
CONTEMPORARY NOVELISTS. (1972)-. English. ir. $120.00. Gale Research Inc., 835 Penobscot Building, Detroit MI 48226. **Tel** (800)877-GALE, (313)961-2242, FAX (313)961-6083, telex TWX 810-221-7086. **ED** James Vinson and Daniel Kirkpatrick.
Desc: Guide to the most important living English-language novelists, with biography, bibliography and criticism of each author listed.

IT/0010-762X
CONTENUTI. Vol. 1 (Sept./Oct. 1969)-. Periodical. Italian. mo (most issues combined). Luigi Pellegrini Editore, Casella Postale 158, Cosenza Rome 74 Italy.

FR
CONTINENT. (1975)-. French (Russian). **LC** PG3214; .C66. available on microfilm from University Microfilms International (UMI).

SZ
CONTINENT CENDRARS. **Added/Corp** Universitat Bern. Centre d'Etudes Blaise Cendrars. No. 1 (1986)-. French. an. Centre Etudes Blaise Cendrars, Unitobler Langgaesstraesse 4G, CH 3009 Berne Switzerland. **Tel** 011 41 31 617971. **LC** PQ2605.E55; Z632. **DD** 841/.912. cum. index. **Bk Rev.**
Desc: Publishes the unknown texts of the writer Blaise Cendrars. Studies of these texts, articles about Cendrars, bibliographies, book reviews and a list of members.

US/0743-3107
CONTINENTAL DRIFTER. **Added/Corp** University of Colorado, Boulder. Dept. of English. Vol. 1, No. 1 (1984)-. Periodical. English. an. $3.00. Continental Drifter, Campus Box 226, Department of English, University of Colorado, Boulder CO 80309. **LC** PN2; .C65. **DD** 808.8. ***Continues*** *Continental Drift, 0743-3093.*

US/0899-4307
CONTINUUM (NEW YORK, N.Y.). (CONTINUUM.). [Continuum]. Vol. 1 (1989)-. Periodical. English (French). an. $57.50. AMS Press Inc., 56 East 13th Street, New York NY 10003. **Tel** (212)777-4700, FAX (212)995-5413, telex 710 581 2302. **ED** David Lee Rubin. **LC** PQ226; .C66. **DD** 840.9/0005.
Desc: Exclusively devoted to theoretical, historical, and interpretive issues in the study of early modern French literature. Focuses on broad, centrally important themes; actively fosters new perspectives and methods.
Ind/Abst MLA Int. Bibl. Books Artic. Mod. Lang. Lit.

IT
CONTRIBUTI DELL'ISTITUTO DI FILOLOGIA MODERNA : SERIE INGLESE. **Main/Corp** Universita Cattolica del Sacro Cuore. Istituto di Filologia Moderna. V. 1- 1974-. English (Italian). L15500. 110 Largo Gemelli, 1 Milan 20123 Italy. **LC** PR1; .M54A.

IT
CONTRIBUTI DELL'ISTITUTO DI FILOLOGIA MODERNA. SERIE ITALIANA. **Added/Corp** Universita Cattolica del Sacro Cuore. Istituto di Filologia Moderna. Vol. 1 (1961)-. Periodical. Italian. Vita e Pensiero, Pubblic University, Largo Gemelli 1, 20123 Milan Italy. **Tel** 011 39 2 72342310, 011 39 2 72342370.
Ind/Abst MLA Int. Bibl. Books Artic. Mod. Lang. Lit.

US/1051-2853
CONTRIBUTIONS TO AFRICAN AMERICAN LITERATURE AND AFRICAN STUDIES. [Contrib. Afr. Am. lit. Afr. stud.]. (1991)-. Monographic series. English. be. Price varies per volume. Bedford Publishers Inc, 779 Kirts, Troy MI 48084. **DD** 810.

US/0193-6875
CONTRIBUTIONS TO THE STUDY OF SCIENCE FICTION AND FANTASY. [Contrib. study sci. fict. fantasy]. No. 1 (1982)-. Monographic series. English. ir. Price varies per volume. Greenwood Press Inc., PO Box 5007, Westport CT 06881-5007. **Tel** (203)226-3571, FAX (203)222-1502. **ED** Marshall B. Tymn.

US/0738-9345
CONTRIBUTIONS TO THE STUDY OF WORLD LITERATURE. [Contrib. stud. world lit.]. **Added/Corp** Hofstra University. (Nov. 1983)-. Monographic series. English. ir. Price varies per volume. Greenwood Press Inc., PO Box 5007, Westport CT 06881-5007. **Tel** (203)226-3571, FAX (203)222-1502. **DD** 809.
Ind/Abst MLA Int. Bibl. Books Artic. Mod. Lang. Lit.

SZ/0069-9780
COOPER MONOGRAPHS ON ENGLISH AND AMERICAN LANGUAGE AND LITERATURE, THE. [Cooper monogr. Engl. Am. lang. lit.]. **VFOAT** Cooper Monographs. (1956)-. Monographic series. English.
Ind/Abst MLA Int. Bibl. Books Artic. Mod. Lang. Lit.

US/0270-6687
CORONA (BOZEMAN). (CORONA.). [Corona]. **Added/Corp** Montana State University (Bozeman). Vol. 1 (1980)-. Monographic series. English. ir. Price varies per volume. Montana State University / Departments of History and Philosophy, Bozeman MT 59717. **Tel** (406)994-5200. **ED** Lynda Sexson and Michael Sexson. **LC** PS536.2; .C64. **DD** 810/.8/0054. **Bk Rev. Ad Acc. Circ:** 1,500.
Desc: Includes speculative essays, criticism, musical scores, artwork, photography, short stories and poetry. Intended for those who see boundaries as entrances and ends as beginnings.
Ind/Abst Am. Humanit. Index (-199?); MLA Int. Bibl. Books Artic. Mod. Lang. Lit.

BE
CORPUS CHRISTIANORUM. CLAVIS PATRUM GRAECORUM. ***Ceased.*** See Religion and Theology.

GW
CORPUS INSCRIPTIONUM LATINARUM, CONSILIO ET AUCTORIATE ACADEMIAE LITTERARUM REGIAE BORUSSICAE EDITUM. **Added/Corp** Akademie der Wissenschaften (Berlin, Germany). Vol. 1 1862-. Academic Scholarly Publication. German. Walter de Gruyter Inc., PO Box 303421, D 10728 Berlin Germany. **Tel** 011 49 30 260050, FAX 011 49 30 26005251.

NE/0165-9618
COSTERUS. See Linguistics.

●US/1063-5084
COTTON QUARTERLY, THE. [Cotton q.]. **Added/Corp** Art Puppies Shoot Pool (Firm) Blithar (Firm). Vol. 1, No. 4 (1992)-. Periodical. English. ir (5 issues). Art Puppies Shoot Pool, 34 Walnut #3, Watertown MA 02172. **Tel** (617)923-8144. **ED** R. G. Schamess. **DD** 813. **Circ:** 300. ***Continues*** *Tee Shorts, 1061-2254.*
Desc: Publishes works of sudden fiction on top quality white T-shirts.

US/0147-149X
COTTONWOOD (LAWRENCE, KAN.). (COTTONWOOD.). (198?)-. Periodical. English. Three times a year (Jan., May, Sept.). $15.00 (individual & libraries); $18.00 other. Cottonwood Review Press, University of Kansas, Kansas Union Box J, Lawrence KS 66045. **Tel** (913)864-3777. **ED** George F. Wedge. **LC** PS501; .C67. **DD** 810/.8. **Bk Rev**, (Qty: 10). **Circ:** 500. ***Continues*** *Cottonwood Review, 0589-8986.*
Desc: Contains a wide variety of poetry and fiction styles but tends not to accept academic writing, workshop produce or rhymed couplets.
Ind/Abst Am. Humanit. Index.

CC
COWRIE. **Added/Corp** Kuang-Hsi ta Hsueh. Comparative Literature and Translation Center. **VFOAT** Wen Pei. Vol. 1, Iss. 1 (1983)-. Periodical. English.
Ind/Abst MLA Int. Bibl. Books Artic. Mod. Lang. Lit.

US/0270-5702
CQ. CONNECTICUT QUARTERLY. (CONNECTICUT QUARTERLY : CQ.). [CQ, Conn. q.]. **VFOAT** CQ; C.Q. Vol. 1, No. 1 (March 1979)-. Periodical. English. qt. $7.50 US; $9.00 other. Connecticut Quarterly, PO Box 68, Enfield CT 06082.

II
CREATIVE FORUM. Vol. 1, No. 1 (March 1988)-. Periodical. English. qt. $40.00. Bahri Publications, PO Box 4453, 997A Street No 9, Gobindpuri Kalkaji, New Delhi 110019 India. **Tel** 011-6445710, 011-6448606. **(Subscription address:** Prints India, 11 Darya Ganj, New Delhi 110002 India.**)** **ED** R. K. Sinzh, Ravinder K. Balvin, and U. S. Bahri. **Bk Rev. Ad Acc. Circ:** 450 (ctrl).
Ind/Abst MLA Int. Bibl. Books Artic. Mod. Lang. Lit.

US/1059-0676
CREATIVE READING. [Creat. read.]. **VFOAT** CreativeReading. Vol. 1, No. 1 (Sept./Oct. 1991)-. Periodical. English. bm. $15.00. Goodin Enterprises, PO Box 6003, Springfield MO 65801. **DD** 810.

US/0736-4733
CREATIVE WOMAN (PARK FOREST SOUTH, ILL.), THE. See Women's Interests.

IT/0390-0142
CRITICA LETTERARIA. (1973)-. Periodical. Italian. Four times a year. L58000.00 Italy; L78000.00 other. Lofredo Editore Napoli Spa, Via Consalvo 99 H Parco San Luigi, 80126 Naples Italy. **Tel** 11 39 81 5937073, FAX 11 39 81 5936953. **LC** PQ4001; .C75. **Bk Rev.** Documents available from The Genuine Article. ***Supersedes*** *Filologia E Letteratura.*
Ind/Abst Arts Humanit. Citation Index [Full Cov.]; Curr. Contents Arts Humanit.; MLA Int. Bibl. Books Artic. Mod. Lang. Lit.; Res. Alert [Full Cov.]; Romant. Move.

US
CRITICAL BIBLIOGRAPHY OF FRENCH LITERATURE, A. See Literature-Abstracting, Bibliographies and Statistics.

US
CRITICAL ESSAYS ON AMERICAN LITERATURE. (19??)-. Monographic series. English. ir. Price varies per volume. Macmillan Publishing Company, 100 Front Street, Box 500, Riverside NJ 08075-7500. **Tel** (800)257-5755, (609)461-6500, FAX (609)461-7070.
Ind/Abst MLA Int. Bibl. Books Artic. Mod. Lang. Lit.

US
CRITICAL ESSAYS ON BRITISH LITERATURE. English. ir. GK Hall & Co, 100 Front Street, Riverside NJ 08075. **Tel** (800)257-5755 ext. 2223.
Ind/Abst MLA Int. Bibl. Books Artic. Mod. Lang. Lit.

US
CRITICAL ESSAYS ON WORLD LITERATURE. English. ir. GK Hall & Co, 100 Front Street, Riverside NJ 08075. **Tel** (800)257-5755 ext. 2223.
Ind/Abst MLA Int. Bibl. Books Artic. Mod. Lang. Lit.

UK
CRITICAL GUIDES TO FRENCH TEXTS. (1980)-. Monographic series. French. ir. Price varies per volume. Grant & Cutler, 55-57 Great Marlborough Street, London W1V 2AY England. **Tel** 011 44 71 734 2012, FAX 011 44 71 734 9272. **ED** Roger Little, Wolfgang van Funder, David Williams.
Ind/Abst MLA Int. Bibl. Books Artic. Mod. Lang. Lit.

UK
CRITICAL GUIDES TO SPANISH TEXTS. (1971)-. Monographic series. English. ir. Price varies per volume. Longwood Publishing Group, 27 South Main Street, Attn R Corrigan, Wolfeboro NH 03894. **Tel** (603)569-4576.
Ind/Abst MLA Int. Bibl. Books Artic. Mod. Lang. Lit.

CN/1180-193X
CRITICAL MASS (HALIFAX). **See** Literature-Poetry.

UK/0011-1562
CRITICAL QUARTERLY, THE. [Crit. q.]. **VFOAT** CQ. Vol. 1, No. 1 (Spring 1959)-. Academic Scholarly Publication. English. Four times a year (Mar., June, Sept., Dec.). £49.00 UK & Europe; $85.00 North America; £55.00 others. Basil Blackwell Publishers Ltd, 108 Cowley Road, Oxford 0X4 1JF England. **Tel** 011 44 865 791100, FAX 011 44 865 791347, telex 837022 OXBOOK G. **(Subscription address:** Blackwell Publishers / UK, Marston Book Services, PO Box 87, Oxford OX2 0DT England.**) ED** J. R. Banks, C. B. Cox, W. Hutchings, D. J. Palmer, A. Young, and Maureen Duffy /PM87. **LC** AP4; .C887. **DD** 820/.5. **CODEN** CRQUEF. **[CCC]. Bk Rev. Ad Acc. Circ:** 12,100. available on microfilm and microfiche from University Microfilms International (UMI). Documents available from The Genuine Article, UMI Article Clearinghouse.
Desc: A forum for new writing on literature and the arts.
Ind/Abst Abstr. Engl. Stud.; Acad. Search (July 1993-); Annu. Bibliogr. Engl. Lang. Lit.; Arts Humanit. Citation Index [Full Cov.]; Book Rev. Index; Br. Humanit. Index; Curr. Contents Arts Humanit.; Expand. Acad. Index (1989-); Humanit. Index; Humanit. Source (Jul. 1993-); INFO-SOUTH Abstr.; Linguist. Lang. Behav. Abstr.; Lit. Crit. Regist.; Mag. Search; Middle East Abstr. Index; MLA Int. Bibl. Books Artic. Mod. Lang. Lit.; Newsp. Period. Abstr. (1991-); Res. Alert [Full Cov.]; Romant. Move.; Soc. Plann. Policy Dev. Abstr.; Soc. Sci. Cit. Index [Select. Cov.]; Sociol. Abstr.

NE
CRITICAL STUDIES (AMSTERDAM, THE NETHERLANDS). (CRITICAL STUDIES.). Vol. 1, No. 1 (1989)-. Periodical. English. sa. $37.50 (institutions), $12.50 (individuals). Editions Rodopi BV, Keizersgracht 302-304, 1016 Ex Amsterdam Netherlands. **Tel** 011 31 20 6227507, FAX 011 31 20 380948. **LC** B809.3.A1; C74. **CODEN** CRSDE8.
Ind/Abst Linguist. Lang. Behav. Abstr.; MLA Int. Bibl. Books Artic. Mod. Lang. Lit.; Soc. Plann. Policy Dev. Abstr.; Sociol. Abstr.

UK/0011-1570
CRITICAL SURVEY. **VFOAT** CS. Vol. 1, No. 1 (1989)-. Periodical. English. Three times a year. £36.00 UK and Europe; $60.00 other. Oxford University Press, Walton Street, Oxford OX2 6DP England. **Tel** 011 44 865 56767, FAX 011 44 865 267773, telex 837330 OXPRES G. **(Subscription address:** Oxford University Press / USA, Journals Marketing Department, Oxford University Press, 2001 Evans Road, Cary NC 27513.**) LC** PR1; .C74. **DD** 820.9/0005. **[CCC].** available on microfilm and microfiche from University Microfilms International (UMI). ***Continues** Critical Survey (Hull, England), 0011-1570.*
Ind/Abst MLA Int. Bibl. Books Artic. Mod. Lang. Lit.

FR
CRITICON. **Added/Corp** Universite de Toulouse-Le Mirail. Institut d'Etudes Hispaniques et Hispano-Americaines. Universite de Toulouse-Le Mirail. Vol. 1 (1978)-. Periodical. Spanish (French). qt. 200.00F. L'Universite de Toulouse- Le Mirail, 56 rue Taur, 31000 Toulouse France. **Tel** 33 61 225831, FAX 33 61 218420. **Bk Rev.**

CI
CROATICA. **Added/Corp** Sveuciliste u Zagrebu. Institut za Znanost o Knjizevnosti. Jugoslavenska Akademija Znanosti i Umjetnosti. Institut za Knjizevnost i Teatrologiju. (1970)-. Serbo-Croatian (Roman). **LC** PG1600; .C76.
Ind/Abst MLA Int. Bibl. Books Artic. Mod. Lang. Lit.

CN/0226-6083
CROC. [Croc]. **VFOAT** C R O C. No. 1 (Oct. 1979)-. Periodical. French. mo. 27.99Can$ (one year), 47.95Can$ (two year) Canada; 32.00Can$ US. Dissuasion Conseil, 404 Boul Decarie Bur 201, Saint Laurent Quebec, H4L 5G1 Canada. **Tel** (514)744-1848. **ED** Jacques Hurtubise. **DD** 741.5/9714. **Bk Rev. Ad Acc. Circ:** 76,168 (ctrl).
Desc: French humor magazine containing comedy writers and cartoonists of Eastern Canada. Includes satire, parody, caricature and comic art.

US/0748-0164
CROSS CURRENTS (ANN ARBOR, MICH.). ***Ceased.*** **See** Linguistics.

US/0739-2354
CROSSCURRENTS (WESTLAKE VILLAGE, CALIF.). (CROSSCURRENTS.). (1981)-. Periodical. English. Four times a year (Mar., June, Sept., Dec.). $18.00 North America; $28.00 others. Crosscurrents / California, 2200 Glastonbury Road, Westlake Village CA 91361. **Tel** (881)991-1694.
Ind/Abst Index Am. Period. Verse.

US/0741-6210
CROTON REVIEW. **Added/Corp** Croton Council on the Arts (Croton-on-Hudson, N.Y.). Vol. 1 (Summer 1978)-. Periodical. English. an. $10.00. Croton Review, PO Box 277, Croton-on-Hudson NY 10520. **Tel** (914)271-3144. **ED** Ruth Lisa Schechter. **Ad Acc. Circ:** 2,000.
Desc: Contains prose and poetry from known and unknown US writers as well as art, essay and interviews from distinguished writers (non-solicited). Criteria for acceptance: language, substance, craft, originality.
Ind/Abst Am. Humanit. Index (-199?).

US/0888-4730
CRUCIBLE (WILSON, N.C.). (CRUCIBLE.). **Added/Corp** Atlantic Christian College. (19??)-. English. an (Fall). $5.25. Atlantic Christian College, West Lee Street, Wilson NC 27893. **Tel** (919)399-6456. **ED** T. L. Grimes, (editor's address: English Department, Barton College, Wilson, NC 27893, phone: (919)399-6456). **DD** 810. **Circ:** 250.
Desc: Articles on quality fiction and poetry.

US/0883-9980
CSL (NEW YORK, N.Y.). (CSL.). [CSL]. **Added/Corp** New York C.S. Lewis Society. **VFOAT** Bulletin of the New York C.S. Lewis Society. Vol. 2, No. 5 (Mar. 1971)-. Periodical. English. mo. $10.00 US; $15.00 other. New York C S Lewis Society, 84-23 77th Avenue, c/o Clara Sarrocco, Glendale NY 11385. **Tel** (718)846-7858. **ED** James Como (Editor's address: York College (CUNY), Jamaica, NY 11451). **LC** PR6023.E926; Z8. **DD** 828/.91209. Index available. cum. index. **Circ:** 550. ***Continues** Bulletin of the New York C.S. Lewis Society, 0883-9972.*
Desc: Publishes papers given at or submitted to the society works of C.S. Lewis.
Ind/Abst Abstr. Engl. Stud.; MLA Int. Bibl. Books Artic. Mod. Lang. Lit.

US
CTHULHU CALLS. V. 1- July 1973-. Periodical. English. qt. Northwest Community College, Powell WY 82435. **LC** PS374.S35; C84. **DD** 810/.8/0054.

SP
CUADERNO LITERARIO AZOR. **VFOAT** Cuadernos Literarios Azor. Began in 1964. Spanish. 50. Ediciones Rondas, C Peligro 8, Barcelona 12 Spain. **LC** PQ6170; .C8.

SP/0214-6738
CUADERNOS DE FILOLOGIA. III, LITERATURAS, ANALISIS. [Cuad. filol., III Lit. anal.]. **VFOAT** Literaturas, Analisis. (1981)-. German (Spanish). ir. Universidad de Valencia / Moderna, Dept Moderna, 46080 Valencia Spain. **Tel** 011 34 3 3864100. **LC** PQ6001; .C79. **DD** 860/.9. ***Continues in part** Cuadernos de Filologia (Universidad de Valencia. Seccion de Filologia Moderna).*
Ind/Abst MLA Int. Bibl. Books Artic. Mod. Lang. Lit.

CK/0120-0992
CUADERNOS DE FILOSOFIA Y LETRAS. **See** Philosophy.

SP/0211-0547
CUADERNOS DE INVESTIGACION FILOLOGICA. **See** Linguistics.

DR/0257-6457
CUADERNOS DE POETICA. **Added/Corp** Colectivo de Estudios Poeticos (Santo Domingo, Dominican Republic). Vol. 1, No. 1 (Sept./Dec. 1983)-. Periodical. Spanish (English and French). tq (April, August, December). $30.00 (institutions), $25.00 (individuals) Americas and Europe; $40.00 (institutions), $30.00 (individuals) other. Cuadernos de Poetica, Apartado Postal 1736, Santo Domingo Dominican Republic. **Tel** (809)687-1828. **(Subscription address:** The Faxon Company, Inc., 15 Southwest Park, Westwood MA 02090.**) ED** Andres Blanco Diaz. **LC** PN6; .C82. **DD** 809.
Desc: Dedicated to the study of poetry, writing, and other forms of literature.
Ind/Abst Index Am. Period. Verse; MLA Int. Bibl. Books Artic. Mod. Lang. Lit.

SP/0210-0061
CUADERNOS PARA INVESTIGACION DE LA LITERATURA HISPANICA. **Added/Corp** Seminario Menendez Pelayo. No. 1 (1978)-. Periodical. Spanish. an. $20.00. Fundacion Universitaria ESP, Alcala 93, 28009 Madrid Spain. **Tel** 011 34 1 4311122. **Bk Rev.** Documents available from The Genuine Article.
Desc: Covers Spanish and Hispano-American literature.
Ind/Abst Arts Humanit. Citation Index (19??-19??) [Full Cov.]; Curr. Contents Arts Humanit.; Res. Alert [Full Cov.]; Romant. Move.

UY
CUENTOS PARA OIR. 1.- 1976-. Periodical. Spanish. Radio Sarandi Enriqueta, Compte Y Rique 1281, Montevideo Uruguay. **LC** PQ8517.5; .C844.

IT/0391-5654
CULTURA NEOLATINA. **See** Linguistics.

US/0163-1209
CUMBERLANDS (PIKEVILLE. 1977). (CUMBERLANDS.). V. 14- Fall 1977-. Periodical. English. sa. $5.00. **LC** PS501; .C85. **DD** 810/.8/0054. ***Formed by the union of** Cumberlands **and** Twigs.*

US/1049-0396
CURLEY. [Curley]. Winter (1991)-. Periodical. English. Three times a year. $5.00. Sheila K Smith, PO Box 23521, Providence RI 02903. **DD** 808.

US/0893-5963
CURRENTS IN COMPARATIVE ROMANCE LANGUAGES AND LITERATURES. [Curr. comp. Roman. lang. lit.]. Monographic series. English. an. Price varies per volume. Peter Lang Publishing, 62 West 45th Street, 4th Floor, New York NY 10036. **Tel** (212)764-1471, (800)770-5264, telex 6973364 PLNY. **ED** Tamara Alvarex-Detrell and Michael G Paulson. **DD** 840.
Desc: Comparative studies in the romance languages and literatures.

CN/0714-6124
CURRICULUM RESOURCES. [Curric. resour.]. **Added/Corp** Vancouver School Board. Education Services Group. (1977)-. Monographic series. English (French). ir. Price varies per volume. Vancouver School Board, Education Services Group, 1595 West 10th Avenue, Vancouver British Columbia V6J 1Z8 Canada. **DD** 011/.62.

US/0734-9963
CUTBANK. [CutBank]. **Added/Corp** University of Montana (Missoula). Associated Students. **VFOAT** Cut Bank. (Spring 1973)-. Periodical. English. sa. $12.00. Cutbank, University of Montana, English Department, Missoula MT 59801. **Tel** (406)243-5231. **ED** David Curran. **LC** PS501; .C87. **DD** 810/.8. **Bk Rev. Ad Acc. Circ:** 300. available on microfiche.
Desc: Poetry and fiction of high quality by known and unknown authors from across the US and abroad. Also contains black and white art and photos when space is available. Also essays, interviews, and one act plays.
Ind/Abst Index Am. Period. Verse.

US/0737-139X
CUYAHOGA REVIEW. ***Ceased.*** [Cuyahoga rev.]. **Added/Corp** Cuyahoga Community College. Vol. 1, No. 1 (Spring 1983)-(19??). Periodical. English (Latin). an. Cuyahoga Community College, 11000 Pleasant Valley Road, Parma OH 44130. **Tel** (216)987-5033, (216)987-5000.
Ind/Abst MLA Int. Bibl. Books Artic. Mod. Lang. Lit.

US/0011-4359
CYCLO-FLAME. V. 14 (Spring 1966)-. English. be. Cyclo Flame, 212 West 1st Street, San Angelo TX 76903-5705. ***Formed by the union of** Cyclotron **and** Flame.*

FR
CYCNOS. **Added/Corp** Faculte des Lettres et Sciences Humaines de Nice. Departement d'Etudes Anglophones. Centre de Recherche sur les Ecritures de Langue Anglaise (Nice, France). **VFOAT** Revue Cycnos. (19??)-. Periodical. French. qt. **LC** PR1; .C9. **DD** 809.
Ind/Abst MLA Int. Bibl. Books Artic. Mod. Lang. Lit.

II
CYGNUS. 1979-. Periodical. English. $15.00. Department of English & Modern European Language, Lucknow University, Lucknow-226 007 India. **LC** PR1; .C93.

BL
D.O. LEITURA. **Added/Corp** Sao Paulo (Brazil : State) Imprensa Oficial do Estado. **VFOAT** Leitura. **VAT** Diario Oficial Leitura. Vol. 1, No. 1 (June 1982)-. Periodical. Portuguese. mo. Imprensa Oficial do Estado S A Biblioteca, Rua de Mooca 1921, 03103 Sao Paulo Brazil.

US
DACTYLUS / DEPT. OF SPANISH AND PORTUGUESE & THE CENTER FOR MEXICAN AMERICAN STUDIES. **See** Linguistics.

US/0084-9537
DADA SURREALISM. **See** The Arts.

LV
DADZIS. (1957)-. Periodical. Latvian. sm. $28.00. Latvijas KP CK Izdevnieciba, Komunaru Bulvari 6 226098, Riga Latvia. **LC** PN6211.L3; D3.

BG
DAINIKA BAMLA (ANNUAL). (DAINIKA BAMLA.). **VFOAT** Dainika Bamla, Barshika Samkhya. (1981)-. Periodical. Bengali. an. **LC** PK1712.5; .D34.

CN/0711-8813
DALHOUSIE FRENCH STUDIES. [Dalhousie Fr. stud.]. **Added/Corp** Dalhousie University.

Dept. of French. Vol. 1 (Oct. 1979)-. English (French). sa (begins with Sept. issue). 20.00Can$ plus postage. Dalhousie University / French Department, Halifax Nova Scotia B3H 3J5 Canada. **Tel** (902)494-2430. **ED** Hans R Runte. **DD** 840/.9. **Ad Acc. Pr Rev. Circ:** 300.
Desc: Articles on French and Francophone literature.
Ind/Abst MLA Int. Bibl. Books Artic. Mod. Lang. Lit.

CN/0011-5827
DALHOUSIE REVIEW, THE. [Dalhous. rev.]. Vol. 1 (April 1921)-. Periodical. English. Four times a year (Jan., Apr., July, Oct.). 17.76Can$ Canada; 28.00Can$ others. Dalhousie University Dalhousie Review, Sir James Dunn Building, Room 314, Halifax Nova Scotia B3H 3J5 Canada. **Tel** (902)494-2541, FAX (902)494-2319. **ED** Alan Andrews and J.A. Wainwright. **LC** AP5; .D3. Index available (published in last issue of each volume). **Bk Rev**, (Qty: 40). **Ad Acc. Pr Rev. Circ:** 1,000 (ctrl). available on microfilm and microfiche from University Microfilms International (UMI). Documents available from The Genuine Article, UMI Article Clearinghouse.
Desc: Invites contributions of articles in such fields as history, literature, political science and philosophy as well as prose fiction and poetry from both new and established writers (at home and worldwide).
Ind/Abst Abstr. Engl. Stud.; Acad. Search (Jan. 1993-); Am. Hist. Life (1954-1958, 1963-); Annu. Bibliogr. Engl. Lang. Lit.; Arts Humanit. Citation Index [Full Cov.]; Book Rev. Index (1988-); Can. Index; Can. Period. Index; Child. Lit. Abstr. (19??-); Curr. Contents Arts Humanit.; Expand. Acad. Index (1989-); Humanit. Index (1954-1958); Humanit. Source (Jul. 1993-); INFO-SOUTH Abstr.; Lit. Crit. Regist.; Mag. Search; Middle East Abstr. Index (1954-1958, 1963-); MLA Int. Bibl. Books Artic. Mod. Lang. Lit.; Newsp. Period. Abstr. (1990-); PAIS Int. Print (1991-?); Res. Alert [Full Cov.]; Sage Race Relat. Abstr.; Soc. Sci. Cit. Index [Select. Cov.]; West. Hist. Q.

CN/0383-9575
DANDELION. Vol. 1, (Summer 1975)-. Periodical. English. Twice a year (Summer and Winter). $10.00 (individual); $12.00 (institution). Dandelion Magazine Society, 922-9th Avenue Southeast, Calgary Alberta T2G 0S4 Canada. **Tel** (403)265-0524. **ED** John McDowell. **DD** C810/.8/0054. **Bk Rev**, (Qty: 8). **Ad Acc. Circ:** 700 (ctrl).
Desc: Combines the traditional and innovative in poetry, fiction and visual arts. Both short and long pieces appear. Its only criterion is excellence. Started in 1975, it continues to expand; interviews and profiles of Canadian authors as well as quality travel pieces are encouraged.
Ind/Abst Index Am. Period. Verse.

DK/0903-7837
DANMARK I SPEJLET. Vol. 1, No. 1 (May 1988)-. Periodical. Danish. Three times a year.

DK
DANSKE MAGAZIN. **Added/Corp** Danske Selskab for Fdrelandets Historie. (1843)-. Danish. cum. index. ***Continues*** *Nye Danske Magazin.*
Ind/Abst Am. Hist. Life (1965-).

US/0070-2862
DANTE STUDIES, WITH THE ANNUAL REPORT OF THE DANTE SOCIETY. [Dante stud. annu. rep. Dante Soc.]. **Main/Corp** Dante Society of America. **Added/Corp** Dante Society of America. Annual Report of the Dante Society. 84th (1966)-. English (English and Italian). an. State University of New York Press, State University Plaza, Albany NY 12246. **Tel** (518)472-5000, FAX (518)472-5038. **ED** A. Pelligrini. **LC** PQ4331; .A35. **Ad Acc. Circ:** 750. available on microfilm from University Microfilms International (UMI). ***Continues*** *Dante Society of America. Annual Report of the Dante Society, with Accompanying Papers.*
Ind/Abst MLA Int. Bibl. Books Artic. Mod. Lang. Lit.

SI/0303-0954
DAOYU JIKAN. (TAO YU CHI KAN.). **VFOAT** Island Quarterly. V. 1- July; 1972 Year 9 Month-. Periodical. Chinese. $0.30 each issue. Tohoku University, Sendai 980 Japan. **Tel** 0222-27-6200. **LC** PL3097.S5; T3.

SZ/0300-693X
DAPHNIS. [Daphnis]. (1972)-. Periodical. German (English). Four times a year. Editions Rodopi BV, Keizersgracht 302-304, 1016 Ex Amsterdam Netherlands. **Tel** 011 31 20 6227507, FAX 011 31 20 380948. **LC** PT177; .D36. **DD** 830/.9. **Bk Rev. Ad Acc. Circ:** 500. Documents available from The Genuine Article. ***Continues*** *Zeitschrift fuer Mittlere Deutsche Literatur.*
Ind/Abst Am. Hist. Life (1986-); Arts Humanit. Citation Index [Full Cov.]; Curr. Contents Arts Humanit.; MLA Int. Bibl. Books Artic. Mod. Lang. Lit.; Res. Alert [Full Cov.]; Soc. Sci. Cit. Index [Select. Cov.].

US
DARK CRIMES. 1st Ed. (1991)-. English. **LC** PS648.C7; D37.

LV/0207-4001
DAUGAVA. [Daugava]. **Added/Corp** Latvijas Padomju Rakstnieku Savieniba. (July 1977)-. Periodical. Russian. Six times a year. $99.95. Preses Nams / Press House, Balasta Dambis 3, Riga Latvia 1081. **Tel** 3712 465 732. **(Subscription address:** East View Publications Inc., 3020 Harbor Lane North, Suite 110, Minneapolis MN 55447.**) LC** PG9145.R1; D38.
Ind/Abst MLA Int. Bibl. Books Artic. Mod. Lang. Lit.

GW/0233-1594
DDR-LITERATUR ... IM GESPRACH. 1983-. German. an. **LC** PT3706; .D37. **DD** 830.9/9431/05.

US/1045-2923
DEADLY IMPULSE. Vol. 1, Issue 1 (1989)-. Periodical. English. qt. $7.20. Serial City Publications, PO Box 1285, Battle Creek MI 49016-1285. **DD** 810.

US/0070-3141
DECEMBER. **VFOAT** December Magazine. Vol. 1 (Dec. 1957)-. English. ir. Price varies. December Press, Box 302, Highland Park IL 60035. **Tel** (708)940-4122. **LC** PS501; .D43. **DD** 810; 700. available on microfilm and microfiche from University Microfilms International (UMI).

BE
DEDALE. (1975)-. French. Marabout S A, 65 rue de Limbourg, Verviers B-4800 Belgium. **LC** PQ1276.S35; D42. **DD** 843/.0876.
Desc: French science fiction.

CN/0835-0337
DEFI-A.C.L. **See** The Arts.

US/0161-7931
DELAP'S F & SF REVIEW. **VFOAT** Delap's F and SF Review; F & SF Review. **VAT** Delap's Fantasy and Science Fiction Review. Periodical. English. mo. $20.00. PO Box 46572, West Hollywood CA 90046.

YU/0011-7935
DELO (BEOGRAD). ***Ceased.*** (DELO; MESECNI KNJIZEVNI CASOPIS.). [Delo]. (March 1955)-(19??). Periodical. Serbo-Croatian (Roman). mo. Nolit, Terazije 31 Fah 133, Belgrade Yugoslavia. **Tel** 332-398. **ED** Slobodan Blagojevic. **LC** AP56; .D4. **DD** 891.8. **Bk Rev. Circ:** 1,695,186.
Desc: Contains poetry and texts from Yugoslavia and abroad, essays and reviews of books.
Ind/Abst MLA Int. Bibl. Books Artic. Mod. Lang. Lit.

US/0011-8869
DENVER QUARTERLY. [Denver q.]. **Added/Corp** University of Denver. Vol. 11, No. 4, (Winter 1977)- l. Periodical. English. Four times a year (Mar., June, Sept., Dec.). $18.00 (institution), $15.00 (individual). University of Denver Department of English, Jennifer Ward, Denver CO 80208. **Tel** (303)871-2892, FAX (303)871-2853. **ED** Donald Revell. **LC** AP2; .U733. **DD** 051. **Bk Rev**, (Qty: 4). **Ad Acc, Adv Mgr:** J Ward. **Circ:** 1,000 (ctrl). available on microfilm and microfiche from University Microfilms International (UMI). ***Continues*** *University of Denver Quarterly, 0041-9540.*
Desc: A journal of modern culture, including poetry, fiction, and essays and reviews.
Ind/Abst Am. Humanit. Index; Annu. Bibliogr. Engl. Lang. Lit.; Index Am. Period. Verse; Lit. Crit. Regist.; Middle East Abstr. Index; MLA Int. Bibl. Books Artic. Mod. Lang. Lit.

CN/0706-795X
DES LIVRES ET DES JEUNES. (DES LIVRES ET DES JEUNES : REVUE DE L'ASSOCIATION CANADIENNE POUR L'AVANCEMENT DE LA LITTERATURE DE JEUNESSE.). [Des livres jeunes]. **Added/Corp** Association Canadienne pour l'Avancement de la Litterature de Jeunesse. Vol. 1, No. 1 (Nov. 1978)-. Periodical. French. Three times a year. 12.20Can$. Association Canadienne pour l'Avancement de la Litterature de Jeunesse / A C A L J, CP 36025, Sherbrooke Quebec J1L 2L3 Canada. **Tel** (819)821-7406. **LC** Z1037.2; .D43. **DD** 028.5/34/089114. Index available. cum. index. **Ad Acc. Circ:** 1,600.
Ind/Abst Can. Period. Index (19??-); Point Repere (1983-).

US/0011-9210
DESCANT (FORT WORTH, TEX.). **See** College and School Publications.

CN/0382-909X
DESCANT (TORONTO). (DESCANT.). [Descant]. **Added/Corp** University of Toronto. Graduate English Association. No. 1 (Nov. 1970)-. Periodical. English. qt (published within the seasons of the year). 31.03Can$ (institutions), 22.47Can$ (individual) (one year), Canada; 35.00Can$ (institutions), 27.00Can$ (individuals) (two year) other. Descant, PO Box 314 Station P, Toronto Ontario M5S 2S8 Canada. **Tel** (416)603-0223. **ED** Janice Zawerbny. **LC** PR9194; .D39. **DD** 810.8/0971/05. **Ad Acc, Adv Mgr:** Elizabeth Mitchell, **Tel** (416)603-0223. **Circ:** 1,200. available on an online database from Canadian Business and Public Affairs Database.
Desc: Publishes poetry, fiction, graphics, photography, drama, interviews and essays from Canadian and international sources that have not been previously published.
Ind/Abst Am. Humanit. Index; Can. Index (?-?); Can. Period. Index (19??-); Curr. Contents Arts Humanit.; Index Am. Period. Verse.

●UY/0797-6402
DESLINDES : REVISTA DE LA BIBLIOTECA NACIONAL. **Added/Corp** Uruguay. Biblioteca Nacional. No. 1 (March 1992)-. Spanish. bm. Biblioteca Nacional de Uruguay, Impresora Cordon, Uruguay 1573, Montevideo Uruguay. ***Continues*** *Revista de la Biblioteca Nacional.*

RU/0418-7946
DETSKAIA LITERATURA. **Added/Corp** Dom Detskoi Knigi (Moscow, R.S.F.S.R.). (1950)-. Russian. mo. $89.95. **(Subscription address:** East View Publications Inc., 3020 Harbor Lane North, Suite 110, Minneapolis MN 55447.**) DD** 028.5.

RU
DETSKAYA LITERATURA. Russian. Detskaya Literatura, 6 Dobroslobodskaya Ulitsa, Moscow B-66, 10766 Russia.
Desc: Covers children's literature.
Ind/Abst Child. Lit. Abstr. (19??-).

CN/0707-9141
DEUS LOCI. ***Suspended.*** (DEUS LOCI : THE LAWRENCE DURRELL NEWSLETTER.). [Deus loci]. **VFOAT** Lawrence Durrell Newsletter. Vol. 1, No. 1 (Sept. 1977)-(1991). Newsletter. English. qt. $3.50. James A. Brigham / Department of English, Okanagan College, 1000 Klo Road, Kelowna British Columbia V1Y 4X8 Canada. **Tel** (604)762-5445. **LC** PR6007.U76; Z6. **DD** 828/.91209.
Ind/Abst MLA Int. Bibl. Books Artic. Mod. Lang. Lit.

GE/0012-043X
DEUTSCHE LITERATURZEITUNG. ***Ceased.*** **Added/Corp** Verband der Deutschen Akademien der Wissenschaften. Akademie der Wissenschaften der DDR. Vol. 1 (2. Oct. 1880)-(1993). Periodical. German. bm. Akademie-Verlag GmbH, Muehlenstrasse 33 34, D 13162 Berlin Germany. **Tel** 011 49 30 47889300, FAX 011 49 30 47889357. **(Subscription address:** VCH Publishers Inc., 303 Northwest 12th Avenue, Journals Department, Deerfield FL 33442.**)**

GW/0418-8926
DEUTSCHE NEUDRUCKE. REIHE: BAROCK. (1966)-. Monographic series. English. ir. Price varies per volume. Max Niemeyer Verlag, Postfach 2140, D 72011 Tuebingen Germany. **Tel** 011 49 7071 989494, FAX 011 49 7071 87419. **ED** Conrad Wiedemann. **DD** 060.

GW/0418-8950
DEUTSCHE NEUDRUCKE. REIHE: TEXTE DES 19. JAHRHUNDERT. Periodical. German. J. B. Metzlersche Verlagsbuchhandling, Kernerstrasse 10 32 41, D-70028 Stuttgart Germany. **Tel** 011 49 711 22902-14, FAX 011 49 711 22902-90. **DD** 060.

GW/0070-4334
DEUTSCHE TEXTE DES MITTELALTERS. (DEUTSCHE TEXTE DES MITTELALTERS / HERAUGEGEBEN IM AUFTRAGE DER AKADEMIE DER WISSENSCHAFTEN DER DDR VOM ZENTRALINSTITUT FUER SPRACHWISSENSCHAFT.). [Dtsch. Texte Mittelalt.]. **Added/Corp** Akademie der Wissenschaften (Berlin, Germany) Akademie der Wissenschaften der DDR. Zentralinstitut fuer Sprachwissenschaft. (1904)-. Monographic series. German. ir. Price varies per volume. Akademie-Verlag GmbH, Muehlenstrasse 33 34, D 13162 Berlin Germany. **Tel** 011 49 30 47889300, FAX 011 49 30 47889357. **(Subscription address:** VCH Publishers Inc., 303 Northwest 12th Avenue, Journals Department, Deerfield FL 33442.**) LC** PT1375; .D4.
Desc: Series covering German literature.
Ind/Abst MLA Int. Bibl. Books Artic. Mod. Lang. Lit.

GW/0012-0936
DEUTSCHE VIERTELJAHRSSCHRIFT FUER LITERATURWISSENSCHAFT UND GEISTESGESCHICHTE. [Dtsch. Vierteljahrsschr. Literaturwiss. Geistesgesch.]. (1923)-. Periodical. German (English). qt (4 issues). DM188.20. J. B. Metzlersche Verlagsbuchhandling, Kernerstrasse 10 32 41, D-70028 Stuttgart Germany. **Tel** 011 49 711 22902-14, FAX 011 49 711 22902-90. **ED** Richard Brinkmann and Walter Haug. **LC** PN4; .D4. Index available. cum. index. Documents available from The Genuine Article.
Desc: German literature.
Ind/Abst Am. Hist. Life (1988-); Annu. Bibliogr. Engl. Lang. Lit.; Arts Humanit. Citation Index [Full Cov.]; BHA : Biblio. Hist. Art; Curr. Contents Arts Humanit.; MLA Int. Bibl. Books Artic. Mod. Lang. Lit.; Philos. Index; Res. Alert [Full Cov.]; Soc. Sci. Cit. Index [Select. Cov.].

GW/0070-444X
DEUTSCHES DANTE - JAHRBUCH. [Dtsch. Dante - Jahrb.]. **Added/Corp** Deutsche Dante-Gesellschaft. (1???)-. German. ir. DM68.00. Boehlau Verlag GmbH & Cie / Koeln, Theodor Heuss STR 76, D-51149 Cologne Germany. **Tel** 011 49 2203 307021, FAX 011 49 2203 307349. **(Subscription address:** BDK Buecherdienst GmbH, Postfach 900120,

D 51111 Cologne Germany.) **ED** Marcella Roddewig. **Ind/Abst** BHA : Biblio. Hist. Art; MLA Int. Bibl. Books Artic. Mod. Lang. Lit.

SZ
DEUTSCHES LITERATUR LEXIKON. German. ir. 95.00F. KG Saur Verlag Bern, Neuengasse 43, CH-3001 Bern Switzerland. **Tel** 011 41 31 447019.

GW/0012-1460
DEUTSCHUNTERRICHT. Added/Corp Germany (East). Ministerium fuer Volksbildung. Vol. 1 (July 1948)-. Periodical. German. Eleven times a year (July/Aug. issues combined). DM71.50. Paedagogischer Zeitschriftenverlag GmbH, Postfach 269, D 10107 Berlin, Germany. **Tel** 011 49 30 20343431. **(Subscription address:** Cornelsen Velhagen & Klasing, Postfach 100271 Zeitschriften, D-33502 Bielefeld Germany.) **Ind/Abst** Soc. Plann. Policy Dev. Abstr.; Sociol. Abstr. (?-?).

●US/1061-6039
DEVELOPING YOUR CREATIVE WRITING STYLE AND LEARNING THE CRAFT OF WRITING. (1992)-. Periodical. English. bm. $48.00. Clemmons Creative Literacy Service and Company, Inc, 2346 A Lorillard Place, Bronx NY 10458. **Tel** (212)733-4529.

MY/0126-5059
DEWAN SASTERA. Added/Corp Dewan Bahasa dan Pustaka. (May 15, 1977)-. Periodical. Malay. mo. 57.60Mal$. Dewan Bahasa Dan Pustaka, Peti Surat 803, 50926 Kuala Lumpur Malaysia. **Tel** 001 60 3 2484211. **LC** PL5060; .A25. Index available (Free). **Circ:** 5,000. ***Continues*** *Dewan Sastra.*

PL/0012-2041
DIALOG (WARSAW, POLAND). (DIALOG.). [Dialog]. **Added/Corp** Zwiazek Literatow Polskich. Vol. 1 (May 1956)-. Periodical. Polish. mo. $51.00. **(Subscription address:** ARS Polona, PO Box 1001, 00068 Warsaw Poland.) **LC** PN1607; .D5. cum. index. **Ind/Abst** MLA Int. Bibl. Books Artic. Mod. Lang. Lit.

UK
DIALOGOS. See Linguistics.

RU
DIAPAZON. Added/Corp Vsesoiuznaia Gosudarstvennaia Biblioteka Inostrannoi Literatury (Soviet Union). No. 1 (1991)-. Periodical. Russian. qt.

US
DIARIST'S JOURNAL. English. qt. $12.00 US; $20.00 Canada; $35.00 other. Gazette Publications Inc, 102 West Water Street, Lansford PA 18232. **Tel** (717)645-4692. **ED** Ed Gildea. **Bk Rev. Ad Acc. Pr Rev. Circ:** Literature.

●US/1062-6972
DIASPORA (MAGNOLIA, ARK.). (DIASPORA: JOURNAL OF THE AA-HLCC/ ANNUAL AFRO-HISPANIC LITERATURE & CULTURE CONFERENCE.). (1992)-. Periodical. English. $20.00. Southern Arkansas University, PO Box 1220, Magnolia AK 71350.

US/0742-5473
DICKENS QUARTERLY. [Dickens q.]. **Added/Corp** Dickens Society. Vol. 1, No. 1 (March 1984)-. Periodical. English. qt. $20.00 US and Canada; $25.00 other. Dickens Society / University of Louisville, Grawemeyer Hall, Louisville KY 40292. **Tel** (502)852-5417, FAX (502)852-5682. **LC** PR4579; .D495. **DD** 823/.8. **[CCC]. Bk Rev. Ad Acc. Circ:** 547. Documents available from The Genuine Article. ***Continues*** *Dickens Studies Newsletter, 0012-2432.* **Ind/Abst** Abstr. Engl. Stud.; Am. Humanit. Index; Arts Humanit. Citation Index [Full Cov.]; Child. Lit. Abstr. (19??-); Curr. Contents Arts Humanit.; Lit. Crit. Regist.; MLA Int. Bibl. Books Artic. Mod. Lang. Lit.; Res. Alert [Full Cov.].

US/0084-9812
DICKENS STUDIES ANNUAL. [Dickens stud. annu.]. Vol. 1 (1970)-. English. an. $45.00. AMS Press Inc., 56 East 13th Street, New York NY 10003. **Tel** (212)777-4700, FAX (212)995-5413, telex 710 581 2302. **ED** Michael Timko, Fred Kaplan, and Edward Guiliano. **LC** PR4579; .D49. **DD** 823.8. Index available. **Bk Rev.** ***Continues*** *Dickens Studies, 0419-1099.* **Desc:** Of value to both the Dickens scholar and the specialist in Victorian studies. Covers the novelists, history, and aesthetics of mid- and late-nineteenth-century fiction. **Ind/Abst** Am. Humanit. Index (?-199?); Annu. Bibliogr. Engl. Lang. Lit.; Child. Lit. Abstr. (19??-); MLA Int. Bibl. Books Artic. Mod. Lang. Lit.

US/1054-8777
DICKENS' UNIVERSE. (1991)-. Periodical. English. Peter Lang Publishing, 62 West 45th Street, 4th Floor, New York NY 10036. **Tel** (212)764-1471, (800)770-5264, telex 6973364 PLNY.

UK/0012-2440
DICKENSIAN, THE. [Dickensian]. **Added/Corp** Dickens Fellowship (London, England). Vol. 1 (Jan. 1905)-. Periodical. English. Three times a year. £9.00 (individuals), £11.00 (institutions) UK; £10.00 (individuals), £13.00 (institutions) other. Dickens Fellowship, Dickens House, 48 Doughty Street, London WC1N 2LF England. **Tel** 011 44 71 405 2127, FAX 71 831 5175. **ED** Malcolm Andrews. **LC** PR4579; .D5. Index available. **Bk Rev**, (Qty: 12-20). **Ad Acc, Adv Mgr:** Edward Preston. **Circ:** 1500. Documents available from The Genuine Article. **Ind/Abst** Abstr. Engl. Stud.; Annu. Bibliogr. Engl. Lang. Lit.; Arts Humanit. Citation Index [Full Cov.]; Child. Lit. Abstr. (19??-); Curr. Contents Arts Humanit.; Lit. Crit. Regist.; MLA Int. Bibl. Books Artic. Mod. Lang. Lit.; Res. Alert [Full Cov.].

US/0360-215X
DICTIONARY OF CONTEMPORARY QUOTATIONS. VFOAT DCQ. Vol. 1 (1976)-. Periodical. English. ir (every 3 years). $55.00. John Gordon Burke Publisher Inc., PO Box 1492, Evanston IL 60204. **Tel** (708)866-8625, FAX (708)866-8625. **ED** John Gordon Burke. **LC** PN6081; .D525. **DD** 818/.02/05. **Desc:** Records quotations which are historically, sociologically, and politically significant. Citations to quotations are provided as well as author and subject index.

US
DICTIONARY OF LITERARY BIOGRAPHY. Vol. 1 (1978)-. Monographic series. English. ir. Price varies per volume. Gale Research Inc., 835 Penobscot Building, Detroit MI 48226. **Tel** (800)877-GALE, (313)961-2242, FAX (313)961-6083, telex TWX 810-221-7086. **LC** PS21; .D5. **Desc:** Concentrates on the major figures of a particular literary period, movement, or genre. Individual author entries chronicle each writer's career through a selection of literary documents, including letters, notebook and diary entries, interviews and contemporary book reviews. **Ind/Abst** MLA Int. Bibl. Books Artic. Mod. Lang. Lit.

US/0731-7867
DICTIONARY OF LITERARY BIOGRAPHY YEARBOOK. See Biographies.

SZ/0070-4806
DIDEROT STUDIES. [Diderot stud.]. Vol. 1 (1949)-. Monographic series. Multiple languages (English and French). ir. Price varies per volume. Librairie Droz SA, 11 rue Massot BP 389, CH 1211 Geneva 12 Switzerland. **Tel** 011 41 22 3466666, FAX 011 41 22 472391. **ED** Guiragussian. **LC** PQ1979; .D495. **DD** 848/5/08. **[CCC]. Bk Rev. Circ:** 500. **Desc:** Studies on the french literature and Diderot. **Ind/Abst** MLA Int. Bibl. Books Artic. Mod. Lang. Lit.; Romant. Move.

US/0163-0415
DIECIOCHO. [Dieciocho]. Vol. 1 (Spring 1978)-. Periodical. Spanish (English and Portuguese). sa. $17.00. Dieciocho, c/o Dr. Eva Rudat, 53 King Charles Lane, Newtown PA 18940. **Tel** (215)579-2995. **ED** David Gies. **LC** PQ6069; .D53. **DD** 860/.05. **Bk Rev. Circ:** 160 (ctrl). Documents available from The Genuine Article. **Desc:** Dedicated to the studies of the Hispanic enlightenment in the fields of literature, history and philosophy in Spain and Latin America and to theoretical studies in aesthetics and literary theory applied to any period of the hispanic literatures. **Ind/Abst** Arts Humanit. Citation Index [Full Cov.]; Curr. Contents Arts Humanit.; MLA Int. Bibl. Books Artic. Mod. Lang. Lit.; Res. Alert [Full Cov.].

BE/0012-2645
DIETSCHE WARANDE EN BELFORT. ***Title Change.*** [Dietsche Warande Belfort]. Vol. 131 (1986)-(19??). Periodical. Dutch. Ten times a year. Editions Peeters SA, Bondgenotenlaan 153, BP 41, B-3000 Leuven Belgium. **Tel** 32 16 235170, FAX 32 16 228500, telex 65987 PUL B. **ED** M Janssens, H Brems, Ph Vermoortel. **LC** AP15; .D52. Index available. **Bk Rev. Ad Acc. Circ:** 3,000 (ctrl). ***Formed by the union of*** *Dietsche Warande* ***and*** *Belfort.* ***Continued by*** *DWB.* **Desc:** Publishes creative work: poetry, and prose of young and old. There is a very severe selection process. Reviews of books on literature and of novels. **Ind/Abst** Annu. Bibliogr. Engl. Lang. Lit. (19??-1992); MLA Int. Bibl. Books Artic. Mod. Lang. Lit.

US/0162-8739
DIFFERENT DRUMMER (TOMS RIVER, N.J.), A. (A DIFFERENT DRUMMER.). [Differ. drum.]. (1975)-. Periodical. English. Twelve times a year. $26.00. SEB Enterprises-Drummer Press, Box 487, Toms River NJ 08753.

US/0012-2874
DIME NOVEL ROUND-UP (1953). (DIME NOVEL ROUND-UP.). **VFOAT** Round-Up. Vol. 21 No. 11 (Nov. 1953)-. Periodical. English. Six times a year (Feb., Apr., June, Aug., Oct., Dec.). $10.00 (one year); $18.00 (two years); $25.00 (three years). Edward T. LeBlanc Publications, 87 School Street, Fall River MA 02720. **Tel** (617)672-2082. **ED** Edward T. LeBlanc. **LC** PS374.D5; D48. **DD** 813/.008. Index available. cum. index. **Bk Rev. Ad Acc. Circ:** 400. ***Continues*** *Reckless Ralph's Dime Novel Round-Up.* **Desc:** A magazine devoted to the collecting, preservation and literature of the old time dime and nickel novels, libraries and story papers. **Ind/Abst** MLA Int. Bibl. Books Artic. Mod. Lang. Lit.

●US/1072-7655
DIMENSIONP2S (KILGORE, TEX.). (DIMENSION : CONTEMPORARY GERMAN-LANGUAGE LITERATURE.). **VFOAT** Dimension 2; Dimension Two. (1994)-. Periodical. English. tq. $40.00 (institution), $30.00 individual. Dimension 2, PO Box 2038, Kilgore TX 75663. **Tel** (903)983-7655. ***Continues*** *Dimension.* **Desc:** Presents German-language literature to an American audience.

US/0012-2882
DIMENSION; CONTEMPORARY GERMAN ARTS AND LETTERS. ***Ceased.*** Vol. 1 (1968)-(Dec. 1993). Periodical. English (German). Three times a year. Dimension, PO Box 26673, Austin TX 78755. **Tel** (512)345-0622. **ED** A Leslie Willson. **LC** AP2; .D564. **DD** 830.8/009/14. Index available in last issue of volume--attached. cum. index. **Circ:** 1,000. available on microfilm and microfiche from University Microfilms International (UMI). **Desc:** Contemporary German writing in a bilingual form with many first-time publications of German poetry, prose, and drama. **Ind/Abst** Am. Humanit. Index (?-199?); MLA Int. Bibl. Books Artic. Mod. Lang. Lit.

CN/1184-2717
DIRECTIONS - ONTARIO COUNCIL OF TEACHERS OF ENGLISH. (DIRECTIONS.). [Dir. - Ont. Counc. Teach. Engl.]. **Added/Corp** Ontario Council of Teachers of English. **VFOAT** OCTE Newsletter. Periodical. English. Free to members. Ontario Council of Teachers of English, Indirections, 750 Kingston Road, Toronto Ontario M4E 1R7 Canada. **DD** 420/.7/0713. ***Continues*** *OCTE Newsletter., 0828-4636.*

US/0734-0605
DIRECTORY OF AMERICAN POETS AND FICTION WRITERS, A. [Dir. Am. poets fict. writ.]. 1980-81-. Directory. English. ir. $31.95 (two year) institutions; $26.95 (two year) individuals. Poets & Writers Inc., 72 Spring Street, New York NY 10012. **Tel** (212)226-3586. **LC** PS129; .D55. **DD** 810/.25/73. **Circ:** 5,000. ***Formed by the union of*** *Directory of American Poets* ***and*** *Directory of American Fiction Writers.* **Desc:** Names, addresses, telephone numbers and representative publications of 6,600 contemporary poets and fiction writers who publish in the United States.

US/0884-6006
DIRECTORY OF LITERARY MAGAZINES. [Dir. lit. mag.]. **Added/Corp** Coordinating Council of Literary Magazines (U.S.) Council of Literary Magazines and Presses (U.S.). (1984)-. English. an. $15.00. Council Literary Magazine, 154 Christopher Street, Suite 3C, New York NY 10014-2839. **Tel** (212)741-9110, FAX (212)741-9112. **LC** Z6513; .C37; PN2. ***Continues*** *CCLM Literary Magazine Directory.* **Desc:** A directory of literary magazines listing editors, addresses, telephone numbers, material published, a description, recent contributions and more.

●RU
DIRIZHABL. (1992)-. Russian.

CN/0842-1420
DISCOURS SOCIAL (MONTREAL). (DISCOURS SOCIAL.). [Discours soc.]. **Added/Corp** McGill University. Comparative Literature Program. **VFOAT** Social Discourse. Vol. 1, No. 1 (Winter 1988)-. Periodical. English (French; summaries and/or abstracts in Italian and German). Four times a year. 65.00Can$ (institutions), 40.00Can$ (individuals) Canada; 70.00Can$ (insitutiions), 45.00Can$ (individuals) other. University que Mont Svc Publications, CP 8888, Succursale A, Montreal Quebec H3C 3P8 Canada. **Tel** (514)987-7747, (514)987-4851. **DD** 800/.5. Index available (Bound in all issues). cum. index. **Ind/Abst** MLA Int. Bibl. Books Artic. Mod. Lang. Lit.

●US/1066-7792
DISCOVERING AUTHORS. (DISCOVERING AUTHORS [COMPUTER FILE].). **Added/Corp** Gale Research, Inc. (1992)-. English. $500.00 (single version). Gale Research Inc., 835 Penobscot Building, Detroit MI 48226. **Tel** (800)877-GALE, (313)961-2242, FAX (313)961-6083, telex TWX 810-221-7086. **Desc:** Presents thorough biographical information and a full range of critical opinion on 300 of the most-studied authors from all time periods.

PY/0737-8742
DISCURSO. VFOAT Discurso, Revista de Estudios Iberoamericanos. Vol. 7, No. 1 (1989)-. Periodical. Spanish. sa. $60.00 (institutions), $40.00 (individuals). Centro Estudios Economia Sociedad, RCA Francesca 728 J Restrepo, Asuncion Paraquay. **Tel** 011 595 21 449677, FAX 011 595 21 449677. **ED** Javier Restrepo. **Bk Rev. Pr Rev. Circ:** 200. ***Continues*** *Discurso Literario.* **Desc:** Studies various themes of the Latin American

reality through literature. Tries to promote new talents in creative writing.
Ind/Abst MLA Int. Bibl. Books Artic. Mod. Lang. Lit.

PY/0737-8742
DISCURSO LITERARIO. ***Title Change.*** [Disc. lit.]. **Added/Corp** Centro de Estudios de Economia y Sociedad (Asuncion, Paraguay). **VFOAT** Discurso. Vol. 1, No. 1 (Autumn 1983)-(1992). Periodical. English (Portuguese and Spanish). sa. Centro Estudios Economia Sociedad, RCA Francesca 728 J Restrepo, Asuncion Paraquay. **Tel** 011 595 21 449677, FAX 011 595 21 449677. **ED** Juan Manuel Marcos. **LC** PQ7081.A1; D57. **DD** 860/.0998. Index available. **Bk Rev. Ad Acc. Circ:** 1,000. available on microfilm. ***Continued by*** *Discurso (Asuncion, Paraguay).*
Desc: Literary criticism and creative writing on Hispanic and Luso-Brazilian topics.
Ind/Abst MLA Int. Bibl. Books Artic. Mod. Lang. Lit. (?-?).

●PY
DISCURSO : REVISTA DE ESTUDIOS IBEROAMERICANOS. Vol. 10, No. 2 (1993)-. Periodical. English (Portuguese and Spanish). sa. Centro Estudios Economia Sociedad, RCA Francesca 728 J Restrepo, Asuncion Paraquay. **Tel** 011 595 21 449677, FAX 011 595 21 449677. **LC** PQ7081.A1; D57. ***Continues*** *Discurso Literario, 0737-8742.*

US/0734-0591
DISPOSITIO. (DISPOSITIO.). [Dispositio]. **Added/Corp** University of Michigan. Dept. of Romance Languages. Vol. 1, No. 1 (Feb. 1976)-. Periodical. English (French, Portuguese and Spanish). Twice a year (Starts in the Fall.). $15.00 (individual); $25.00 (institution). University of Michigan Department of Romance Languages, MBL 4222, Ann Arbor MI 48109. **Tel** (313)764-5344 or 764-5383. **ED** Walter D. Mignolo. **LC** P99; .D58. **DD** 001.51/05; 879.9. **Bk Rev**, (Qty: 4-8). **Ad Acc, Adv Mgr:** Kathe Johnson. **Circ:** 800 (ctrl).
Desc: Presents theoretical and metatheoretical articles on literary semiotics (science of signs) and semiotics of Latin American culture.
Ind/Abst Film Lit. Index (1980); HAPI Hisp. Am. Period. Index; MLA Int. Bibl. Books Artic. Mod. Lang. Lit.; Romant. Move.

HU
DISSERTATIONES SLAVICAE. SECTIO HISTORIAE LITTERARUM. **VFOAT** Sectio Historiae Litterarum; Slavistische Mitteilungen Materialy i Soobshcheniia Po Slavianovedeniiu. (1982)-. Periodical. Russian. **LC** PG500; .D57. ***Continues in part*** *Dissertationes Slavicae, 0586-3732.*

US/0196-9684
DISTINGUISHED LECTURERS SERIES. [Disting. lect. ser.]. No. 1-. Monographic series. English. ir. Price varies per volume. Bureau of Business Research / Texas, University of Texas at Austin, Box 7459, Austin TX 78713. **Tel** (512)471-1616, FAX (512)471-1063.

FR
DIX-NEUVIEME SIECLE : BULLETIN DE LA SOCIETE DES ETUDES ROMANTIQUES. **Added/Corp** Societe des Etudes Romantiques. **VFOAT** 19eme siecle. No. 1 (April 1985)-. Bulletin. French. sa. comes with membership. Societe des Etudes Romantiques, Fac Letters 2 rue Trefilerie, 42023 Saint Etienn, France. **Bk Rev.**
Desc: XIX Century worldwide newsletter.

RU
DNEVNAIA ZVEZDA; VOSTOCHNYI ALMANAKH. (19??)-. Russian. 1.54rub (single issue). Khudozh Lit-ra, B-78 Novo-Basmannaia 19, Moscow Russia. **LC** PJ486; .D5.

UN/0130-321X
DNIPRO. (DNIPRO : SHCHOMISIACHNYI LITERATURNO-KHUDOZHNII TA HROMADSKO-POLITYCHNYI ZHURNAL TSENTRALNOHO KOMITETU LKSMU.). [Dnipro]. **Added/Corp** Leninska Kommunistychna Spilka Molodi Ukrainy. Tsentralnyi Komitet. (1927)-. Periodical. Ukrainian. mo. $99.95. **(Subscription address:** East View Publications Inc., 3020 Harbor Lane North, Suite 110, Minneapolis MN 55447.) **LC** AP58.U5; D6.
Ind/Abst MLA Int. Bibl. Books Artic. Mod. Lang. Lit.

US/0749-260X
DOG RIVER REVIEW. [Dog River rev.]. Vol. 1, No. 1 (Spring 1982)-. Periodical. English. sa. $6.00 US; $10.00 other. Dog River Review, 5976 Billings Road, Parkdale OR 97041. **Tel** (503)352-6494. **ED** Laurence F Hawkins Jr. **DD** 810. **Bk Rev. Circ:** 250.
Desc: Mature poetry - all forms; fiction to 2,500 words. Black and white art. Reviews, satire and short plays.

US/0094-3118
DOGSOLDIER (SPOKANE). (DOGSOLDIER.). English. $1.75. Dogsoldier/E, 323 Boone, Spokane WA 99202. **LC** PS507; .D64. **DD** 810/.8/0054.

NE
DOKUMENTAAL. **See** Linguistics.

DK/0106-4487
DOLPHIN (ARRHUS, DENMARK). (THE DOLPHIN : PUBLICATIONS OF THE ENGLISH DEPARTMENT UNIVERSITY OF AARHUS.). No. 1 (Feb. 1979)-. Periodical. English (Danish). sa. **DD** 820/.9.
Ind/Abst MLA Int. Bibl. Books Artic. Mod. Lang. Lit.

RU/0130-3562
DON. (DON.). [Don]. **Added/Corp** Soiuz Pisatelei SSSR. Rostovskoe Oblastnoe Otdelenie. (1957)-. Periodical. Russian. mo. $109.95. **(Subscription address:** East View Publications Inc., 3020 Harbor Lane North, Suite 110, Minneapolis MN 55447.) **DD** 057. ***Supersedes*** *Don, 0130-3562.*

●US/1062-1385
DON THE BEAR SERIES. **See** Children and Youth Interests.

US/0882-486X
DORIS LESSING NEWSLETTER. [Doris Lessing newsl.]. **Added/Corp** Doris Lessing Society. Vol. 1 (Winter 1976)-. Newsletter. English. sa. $12.00 (institutions), $10.00 (individuals) North America; $14.00 other. Doris Lessing Society, Michigan State University, 201 Morrill Hall, East lansing MI 48824-1036. **Tel** (517)351-8163. **ED** Ruth Saxton (editor's address: English Department, Mills College, 5000 MacArthur Blouvard, Oakland CA 94613; editor's phone: (510)451-0219). **LC** PR6023.E833; Z4584. **DD** 823/.914. **Bk Rev**, (Qty: Varies). **Pr Rev. Circ:** 200.
Desc: Devoted to short essays & reviews about Doris Lessing and her work.
Ind/Abst Abstr. Engl. Stud.; Am. Humanit. Index; MLA Int. Bibl. Books Artic. Mod. Lang. Lit.

JA
DOSHISHA GAIKOKU BUNGAKU KENKYU. **VFOAT** Doshisha Studies in Foreign Literature. Began in 1971. Japanese (English, French, German, Chinese and Russian). Three times a year. ¥3,000. Doshisha Daigaku Gaikoku Bungakukai, Tanabe-cho Tsuzuki-gun, Kyoto 610-03 Japan. **Tel** 07746-5-7071. **ED** Masaaki Yamamoto. **LC** PN9; .D67. **Circ:** 2,000 (ctrl).

JA
DOSHISHA KOKUBUNGAKU. Began in 1961. Japanese. Doshisha Daigaku Kokubun Gakkai, Higashi Iru, Imadegawadori Karasumaru, Kamigyo-Ku, Kyoto-Shi Japan. **LC** PL700; .D68.

JA/0046-063X
DOSHISHA LITERATURE. **Added/Corp** Doshisha Eibungakkai. No. 19 (May 1956)-. Periodical. English. **LC** PE9; .D68. **DD** 820/.9.
Ind/Abst Soc. Plann. Policy Dev. Abstr.

AU/1013-2309
DOSTOEVSKY STUDIES : JOURNAL OF THE INTERNATIONAL DOSTOEVSKY SOCIETY. [Dostoevsky stud.]. **Added/Corp** International Dostoevsky Society. University of Utah. College of Humanities. **VFOAT** Dostevskii: Stat'i i Materialy. Vol. 1 (1980)-. English (French, German and Russian). sa. $35.00. CMTS USC / C. Schlacks Junior Publishing, 734 West Adams Boulevard, Kerckhoff Hall, Los Angeles CA 90089. **Tel** (213)743-1621. **ED** Rudolf Neuhauser and Nadine Natov. **LC** PG3328.Z6; I53a. **DD** 891.73/3. **Bk Rev. Ad Acc.** ctrl circ. ***Continues*** *Bulletin (International Dostoevsky Society), 0047-0686.*
Desc: Articles on Dostoevsky and works connected with him.
Ind/Abst MLA Int. Bibl. Books Artic. Mod. Lang. Lit.

UK/0012-5806
DOWNSIDE REVIEW, THE. [Downside rev.]. **Added/Corp** College of St. Gregory (Downside, England). St. Gregory's Society. Downside Abbey (Bath, England). Vol. 1 (July 1880)-. Periodical. English. qt. $38.00. Downside Review-Downside Abbey, Stratton on the Fosse, Bath BA3 4RH England. **Tel** 011 44 761232205, FAX 011 44 761232973. **ED** Daniel Rees. **LC** BX801; .D7. Index available. cum. index. **Bk Rev. Ad Acc. Circ:** 800. available on microfiche (from Kraus Reprint).
Desc: Articles on philosophy, metaphysics, theology, modernism, mysticism, church and Monastic History.
Ind/Abst Index Book Rev. Relig.; Index Relig. Period. Lit.; MLA Int. Bibl. Books Artic. Mod. Lang. Lit.; New Testam. Abstr.; Old Testam. Abstr.; Recent. Publ. Artic.; Relig. Index One Period. (1949-); Relig. Theol. Abstr.; Abr. Cathol. Period. Lit. Index; Cathol. Period. Lit. Index.

NE/0921-2507
DQR STUDIES IN LITERATURE. **VFOAT** D.Q.R. Studies in Literature; Dutch Quarterly Review Studies in Literature. (1986)-. Monographic series. English. ir. Price varies per volume. Editions Rodopi BV, Keizersgracht 302-304, 1016 Ex Amsterdam Netherlands. **Tel** 011 31 20 6227507, FAX 011 31 20 380948. Index available.
Desc: Studies on all aspects of English and American Literature.

US
DRAGON LODE, THE. English. The Dragon Lode, Cheryl Christian - Editor, 12417 Wycliff Lane, Austin TX 78727.
Ind/Abst Child. Lit. Abstr. (19??-).

US/0364-359X
DRAGONFLY (PORTLAND). (DRAGONFLY.). V. 1- Jan. 1973-. Periodical. English (Japanese). qt. $12.00 US; $14.00 Canada; $16.00 other. Middlewood Press, PO Box 11236, Salt Lake City UT 84147. **Tel** (801)966-8034. **ED** Richard Tice and Jack Lyon. **LC** PS593.H3; D7. **DD** 811/.06. Index available. **Bk Rev. Circ:** 400. ***Supersedes*** *Haiku Highlights.*
Desc: Contemporary English and Japanese haiku, historical and critical articles on Haiku, quarterly contests, oriental calligraphy and artwork.

US
DRAGON'S TEETH. No. 1 (Summer 1983)-. Periodical. English. sa.
Ind/Abst Child. Lit. Abstr. (19??-).

CN/0843-445X
DREAMS & VISIONS. [Dreams vis.]. **VFOAT** Dreams and Visions. (1989)-. Periodical. English. Four times a year. 15.00Can$. Skysong Press, RR 1, Washago Ontario L0K 2B0 Canada. **Tel** (705)329-4835, FAX (705)329-1770. **ED** Steve Stanton and Wendy Stanton. **DD** 823/.0108382. Index available. **Circ:** 250.
Desc: Features anthology of short stories with religious, moral or spiritual themes.

US/0896-6362
DREISER STUDIES. [Dreiser stud.]. **Added/Corp** Indiana State University. Dept. of English. Vol. 18, No. 1 (Spring 1987)-. Periodical. English. sa (May and Dec.). $10.00 (institutions), $7.00 (individuals) North America; $15.00 other. Indiana State University, Department of English, Terre Haute IN 47809. **Tel** (812)237-3163, FAX (812)237-3156. **ED** Frederic Rusch; telephone: (812)237-2304 or 3163. **LC** PS3507.R55; Z5893. **DD** 813/.52. Index available. **Bk Rev. Pr Rev.** ***Continues*** *Dreiser Newsletter, 0012-6098.*
Desc: It is dedicated to stimulating, coordinating and reporting Dreiser scholarship. Critical articles are welcome but priority given to bibliographical materials. Annual checklist of Dreiser scholarship.
Ind/Abst Am. Humanit. Index; Annu. Bibliogr. Engl. Lang. Lit.

US/0899-5443
DRUM. [Drum]. Began with 1969 issue. Periodical. English. an. $3.00 (libraries and universities). Drum, 115 New Africa House, University of Massachusetts, Amherst MA 01003. **Tel** (413)545-3185. **ED** Martha Grier-Deen. **DD** 810. **Circ:** 5,000.
Desc: An Afro-American arts and literature magazine serving the Third World community.

RU/0135-7832
DRUZHBA (IOSHKAR-OLA, R.S.F.S.R.). (DRUZHBA.). No. 1 (1975)-. Periodical. Russian. an. **LC** PG3504.M28; D78.

II
DUDHERI. Periodical. Nepali (Nepali). Rs3.00. **LC** PK2598.A2; D8.

US/0882-2549
DUPLEX PLANET, THE. **Added/Corp** Duplex Nursing Home (Jamaica Plain, Boston, Mass.). (197?)-. Periodical. English. bm. $12.00. The Duplex Planet, PO Box 1230, Saratoga Springs NY 12866. **Tel** (518)692-7410, FAX (518)692-7410. **ED** David Greenberger. **Circ:** 1,000.

US
DUQUESNE STUDIES. LANGUAGE AND LITERATURE SERIES. **Added/Corp** Duquesne University. **VFOAT** Language and Literature Series. Vol. 1 (1978)-. Monographic series. English. Price varies per volume. Duquesne Studies / Language and Literature Series, 600 Forbes Avenue, Pittsburgh PA 15282. **Tel** (412)396-6610.
Ind/Abst MLA Int. Bibl. Books Artic. Mod. Lang. Lit.

UK/0955-0666
DURHAM MEDIEVAL TEXTS. [Durh. mediev. texts]. (1987)-. Monographic series. English. ir. ***Continues*** *Durham and St. Andrews Medieval Texts, 0140-4261.*
Ind/Abst MLA Int. Bibl. Books Artic. Mod. Lang. Lit.

UK/0309-6564
DUTCH CROSSING. [Dutch cross.]. **Added/Corp** Bedford College. Dutch Dept. No. 1 (March 1977)-. Periodical. Dutch (English). Three times a year. £18.00 (institutions), £11.00 (individuals) Europe; £15.00 (institutions), £10.00 (individuals) UK; £21.00 (institutions), £12.00 (individuals) other. University College London / Dutch, Gower Street, Department of Dutch, Center for Low Country Studies, London WC1E 6BT England. **Tel** 011 44 71 387 7050 ext. 3113. **ED** Stephen Dalziel (editor's address: Zelenogorsk, 6 Commercial Road, Machen Newport, Gwent NP1 8NA). **CODEN** DUCRE2. cum. index. **Circ:** 400.
Ind/Abst BHA : Biblio. Hist. Art; MLA Int. Bibl. Books Artic. Mod. Lang. Lit.; Soc. Plann. Policy Dev. Abstr.

IS
DVADTSAT DVA. (1978)-. Periodical. Russian. Six times a year (Jan., Mar., May, July, Sept., Nov.). $75.00 one year; $95.00 other. Publishing Association Moscow, PO Box 44050, 61440 Tel Aviv Israel. **Tel** 972-3-394525. **ED** Foundation, Moscow Jezusalem. **LC** AP93; .D85. **Bk Rev. Ad Acc, Adv Mgr:** M. Baz-Oz, **Tel** 972-3-394525. **Circ:** 1,500.
Desc: Information and news on Israeli, Russian, and Middle East problems. Ideas in the area of culture, history, literature, original prose and poetry.

BE/0012-2645
DWB. **VFOAT** Dietsche Warande & Belfort. **VAT** Dietsche Warande en Belfort. (198?)-. Periodical. Dutch. bm (6 issues). 1600F. Editions Peeters SA, Bondgenotenlaan 153, BP 41, B-3000 Leuven Belgium. **Tel** 32 16 235170, FAX 32 16 228500, telex 65987 PUL B. **ED** H. Bousset, H. Brems, E. Van de Perre. **LC** AP15; .D52. Index available. **Bk Rev. Ad Acc.** ***Continues*** *Dietsche Warande en Belfort.*
Ind/Abst MLA Int. Bibl. Books Artic. Mod. Lang. Lit.

UN/0868-4790
DZVIN : CHASOPYS SPILKY PYSMENNYKIV UKRAINY. **Added/Corp** Spilka Pysmennykiv Ukrainy. (1990)-. Periodical. Ukrainian. mo. $149.95. **(Subscription address:** East View Publications Inc., 3020 Harbor Lane North, Suite 110, Minneapolis MN 55447.**)** **LC** AP58.U5; Z45. ***Continues*** *Zhovten, 0131-0100.*

CN/0071-1071
E.R.B.IVORE. [E.R.B.ivore]. **VAT** Erbivore; Edgar Rice Burroughs-Ivore. #3 (July 1967)-. Periodical. English. **DD** 809.3/87. ***Continues*** *Fantastic Worlds of Burroughs & Kline, 0710-037X.*

UK/0070-7872
EARLY ENGLISH TEXT SOCIETY (PUBLICATION). ***Title Change.*** (EARLY ENGLISH TEXT SOCIETY. ORIGINAL SERIES.). [Early Engl. Text Soc.]. **Added/Corp** Early English Text Society. **VFOAT** Original Series. (1864)-(19??). Monographic series. English. ir. Early English Text Society, C/O Wendy Collier, The Vicarage Drive, Hope Sheffield S30 2RN England. **LC** PR1119; .A2. ***Absorbed*** *Early English Text Society (Series). Extra Series.* ***Continued by*** *Early English Text Society (Series).*
Ind/Abst MLA Int. Bibl. Books Artic. Mod. Lang. Lit.

UK
EARLY ENGLISH TEXT SOCIETY : PUBLICATIONS. **Added/Corp** Early English Text Society. (19??)-. Monographic series. English. ir. Price varies per volume. Early English Text Society, C/O Wendy Collier, The Vicarage Drive, Hope Sheffield S30 2RN England. **LC** PR1119; .A2. ***Continues*** *Early English Text Society (Series). Original Series.*

US/0163-0989
EARTH'S DAUGHTERS. Vol. 1, No. 1 (Feb. 1971)-. Periodical. English. tq (Apr., July, Oct.). $14.00 (individuals); $22.00 (institutions). Earth's Daughters, Box 41, Central Park Station, Buffalo NY 14215. **Tel** (716)837-7778. **ED** Robin Willoughby. **LC** PS508.W7; E32. **DD** 810/.8/09287. Index available. cum. index. **Pr Rev. Circ:** 1,000.
Desc: This publication is a feminist arts periodical specializing in well crafted work, supportive of women in all their diversity. Publishes poetry, short prose and art.
Ind/Abst Am. Humanit. Index.

UK
EAST EUROPEAN LANGUAGES AND LITERATURES. **See** Linguistics.

CN/1187-3531
EASTWORD (HALIFAX). (EASTWORD : THE NEWSLETTER OF THE WRITERS' FEDERATION OF NOVA SCOTIA.). [Eastword]. **Added/Corp** Writers' Federation of Nova Scotia. **VFOAT** WFNS Eastword. (Feb./Mar. 1991)-. Newsletter. English. bm. Writers Federation of Nova Scotia, Suite 203, 5516 Spring Garden Road, Halifax Nova Scotia B3J 1G6 Canada. **Tel** (902)423-8116. **DD** 808/.02/060716. ***Continues*** *Writer's News., 0705-0704.*

CN/1183-0786
EBAUCHES (SAINT-FELIX-DE-KINGSEY). (EBAUCHES.). [Ebauches]. (Winter 1990)-. Periodical. French. qt. 15.00Can$. Editions de la Derniere Minute, CP 6, Saint-Felix-de-Kingsey, Quebec J0B 2T0 Canada. **DD** C840.8/0054/05.

CK/0012-9410
ECO. [Eco]. (May 1960)-. Periodical. Spanish. mo. $22.00. Libreria Buchholz, Avenida Jimenez de Quesada 8-40, Bogota Colombia. **LC** AP63; .E24.
Ind/Abst HAPI Hisp. Am. Period. Index (19??-); MLA Int. Bibl. Books Artic. Mod. Lang. Lit.

CN/0711-5474
ECRIRE (MONTREAL). (ECRIRE : VADE-MECUM A L'USAGE DES ECRIVAINS, JOURNALISTES ET PIGISTES.). [Ecrire]. 1982-. French. an. $14.95 per volume. Marche De L'Ecriture, 148 Succursale Youville, Montreal Quebec H2P 2VA Canada. **DD** 808.025/09714.

●US/1061-1479
ECRITIQUE (IOWA CITY, IOWA). (ECRITIQUE : MOUTHPIECE OF THE SAVANT=GARDE.). No. 1 (1992)-. Periodical. English (Multiple languages). ir. $6.00. Canonymous Press, PO Box 1534, Iowa City IA 52244-1534. **Tel** (319)339-1692. **ED** Daniel Smith. **DD** 051. **Bk Rev. Circ:** 200.
Desc: Publishes critical essays (theory, law, politics), poetry, fiction, artwork, historical documents and other works which do not fit into traditionally defined genres or categories.

CN/0229-7043
ECRITOIRE (MONTREAL). (L'ECRITOIRE : REVUE ETUDIANTE DU MODULE ETUDES LITTERAIRES DE L'UQAM.). Vol. 2, No. 1 Sept. 1979-. Periodical. French. sa. $1.00 per no. Module Etudes Litteraires, Universite de Quebec A Montreal, CP 8888 Succursale A, Montreal Quebec H3C 3P8 Canada. **DD** C840/.8/092375. ***Continues*** *Read Building, 0711-1045.*

CN/0013-0729
ECRITS DU CANADA FRANCAIS. [Ecrits Can. fr.]. (1954)-. Periodical. French. Four times a year. 35.00Can$ (institutions), 25.00Can$ (individuals) Canada; 35.00Can$ other. Ecrits du Canada Francais, 5754 Cote H. Antoine, Montreal Quebec H4A 1R9 Canada. **Tel** (514)488-5883. **DD** C840/.8.
Ind/Abst Point Repere (1983-).

CN/0228-7951
ECRITURE FRANCAISE DANS LE MONDE. ***Ceased.*** (ECRITURE FRANCAISE DANS LE MONDE / LA TRIBUNE DES FRANCOPHONES.). [Ecriture fr. monde]. **Added/Corp** Tribune des francophones (Collective). Vol. 2, Nos. 1/2 (1980)-Vol. 7, Nos. 1/2 (1985). Periodical. French. ir. Editions Naaman, CP 697, Sherbrooke Quebec J1H 5K5 Canada. **Tel** (819)563-1117. **DD** 840/.9. **Bk Rev. Ad Acc. Circ:** 3,000. ***Continues*** *Ecriture Francaise, 0708-4838.*
Desc: Independent, international and cultural journal of creative writing. Mouthpiece for French language authors and authors born in France but living outside their native country.

FR
ECRITURES / UNIVERSITE DE PARIS X, UNIVERSITE DE YAOUNDE. **Added/Corp** Universite de Paris X: Nanterre. University of Yaounde. Universite de Paris X: Nanterre. Centre de Semiotique Textuelle. (1984)-. Periodical. French. tq. 40.00F France; 57.00F other. Malesherbes Publications, 163 Boulevard Malesherbes, 75859 Paris France. **Tel** 011 33 1 48884600, FAX 011 33 1 48884601. **(Subscription address:** Iris Diffusion Distributor, 5090 rue de Bellechasse, Montreal Que H1T 2A2 Canada.**)** **LC** PC2002; .E25. **DD** 840.9/005.

SP
EDAD DE ORO (MADRID, SPAIN). (EDAD DE ORO.). **Added/Corp** Universidad Autonoma de Madrid. Departamento de Literatura Espanola. Universidad Autonoma de Madrid. Departamento de Filologia Espanola. **VFOAT** EdO. Vol. 1 (1982)-. Spanish. an. 3815ptas. Libreria Cuatros Caminos, Centra Colmenar Viejo KM 15 500, 28049 Madrid Spain. **Tel** 011 34 1 3720978. **LC** PQ6065; .E3. **DD** 860/.9/003. **Ad Acc.** ctrl circ.
Desc: Spanish literature of the XVII and XVI centuries.
Ind/Abst MLA Int. Bibl. Books Artic. Mod. Lang. Lit.

US
EDEBIYAT: JOURNAL OF MIDDLE EASTERN LITERATURES. English. Gordon & Breach Science Publishers, Inc., PO Box 786, Cooper Station, New York NY 10276. **Tel** (212)206-8900, FAX (212)645-2459. **(Subscription address:** International Publishers Distributor at one of the following addresses: 820 Town Center Drive, Langhorne, PA 19047; or PO Box 90, Reading Berkshire RG1 8JL UK; or Kent Ridge PO Box 1180, Singapore 9111, Republic of Singapore**)**
Desc: Publishes scholarly articles, translations and brief communications on all periods of Middle Eastern literature.

SZ/0364-6505
EDEBIYAT (PHILADELPHIA, PA.). (EDEBIYAT.). [Edebiyat]. **Added/Corp** University of Pennsylvania. Middle East Center. (1976)-. Periodical. English. sa. $79.00 university libraries; $124.00 other. Harwood Academic Publishers, PO Box 90, Reading RG1 8JL England. **Tel** 011 44 734 560080. **(Subscription address:** International Publishers Distributor at one of the following addresses: 820 Town Center Drive, Langhorne, PA 19047; or PO Box 90, Reading Berkshire RG1 8JL UK; or Kent Ridge PO Box 1180, Singapore 9111, Republic of Singapore**)** **LC** PJ2; .E33. **DD** 809/.8956. **Bk Rev. Circ:** 300.
Desc: Contains comparative and Near Eastern literature drawn from different areas of the Middle East. Of interest to social scientists and historians as well as to those in the humanities.
Ind/Abst MLA Int. Bibl. Books Artic. Mod. Lang. Lit. (?-?).

CN/1183-7020
EDGE DETECTOR: A MAGAZINE OF SPECULATIVE FICTION. (1988)-. Edge Detector, #803 1850 Lincoln Ave., Montreal H3H 1H4 Quebec.

UK/0267-6672
EDINBURGH REVIEW (EDINBURGH : 1985). (EDINBURGH REVIEW.). [Edinb. rev.]. No. 67/68 (1984)-. Periodical. English. sa. £22.00 UK & Europe; £24.00 other. Edinburgh University Press, 22 George Square, Edinburgh EH8 9LF Scotland. **Tel** 011 44 31 650 6207, FAX 011 44 31 662 0053. ***Continues*** *New Edinburgh Review, 0028-4645.*
Desc: Covers English literature.

UK
EDINBURGH STUDIES IN THE ENGLISH LANGUAGE. **VFOAT** ESEL. Vol. 1- 1988-. English. ir. Humanities Press, 165 1st Avenue, Atlantic Highlands NJ 07716. **Tel** (908)872-1441, (800)221-3845, FAX (908)872-0717, telex 752233. **LC** PE1001; .E29. **DD** 420/.5. Index available.
Desc: Series of scholarly monographs devoted to studies of English language which aims to add to understanding of history and structure of the language.

JA
EDO JIDAI BUNGAKUSHI / RYUMONSHA HEN. **Added/Corp** Ryumonsha (Fukuoka-shi, Japan). No. 1, (1980)-. Periodical. Japanese. ir. Inoue Toshiyuki, Edo Jidai Bungakushi Kankokai, 30-24 Kasumigaoka 2-chome, Higashi-ku 813, Fukuoka-shi Japan. **LC** PL726.35; .E32. ctrl circ.
Desc: Japanese literary history of the Edo period.

US/1054-0636
EDWARD C. ARMSTRONG MONOGRAPHS ON MEDIEVAL LITERATURE, THE. [Edward C. Armstrong monogr. mediev. lit.]. **VFOAT** Armstrong Monographs on Medieval Literature. (1979)-. Monographic series. English. **DD** 809.
Ind/Abst MLA Int. Bibl. Books Artic. Mod. Lang. Lit.

JA/0910-500X
EIBUNGAKU SHICHO. [Eibungaku schicho]. **VFOAT** Thought Currents in English Literature; Current Ideas in English Literature. (1949)-. Periodical. Multiple languages. an. **DD** 820. ***Continues*** *Aoyama Bungaku.*
Ind/Abst MLA Int. Bibl. Books Artic. Mod. Lang. Lit.

JA
EIBUNGAKU TO EIGOGAKU. **Added/Corp** Jochi Daigaku. **VFOAT** English Literature and Language. (19??)-. Japanese (English).
Ind/Abst MLA Int. Bibl. Books Artic. Mod. Lang. Lit.

CN/0840-6286
EIGHTEENTH-CENTURY FICTION (DOWNSVIEW, ONT.). (EIGHTEENTH-CENTURY FICTION.). [Eighteenth-century fict.]. **Added/Corp** McMaster University. University of Toronto Press. **VFOAT** Eighteenth Century Fiction. Vol. 1, No. 1 (Oct. 1988)-. Periodical. English (French). qt (Jan., Apr., July, Oct.). $55.00. University of Toronto Press, 5201 Dufferin Street, Downsview Ontario M3H 5T8 Canada. **Tel** (416)667-7781, (416)667-7782, FAX (416)667-7803. **ED** David Blewett. **LC** PN3495; .E34. **DD** 809.3/033/05. **[CCC].** Index available. **Bk Rev. Ad Acc. Circ:** 500 (ctrl). available on microfiche.
Desc: Devoted to the historical and critical investigation of all aspects of imaginative prose written from 1660-1832. Comparative studies of the fiction of two or more countries are particularly encouraged. Reviews are international in scope and interest.
Ind/Abst Am. Hist. Life (1988-); Child. Lit. Abstr. (19??-); MLA Int. Bibl. Books Artic. Mod. Lang. Lit.

JA/0288-2876
EIGO EIBUNGAKU KENKYU HIROSHIMA. 1954. **See** Linguistics.

JA/0388-2519
EIGO EIBUNGAKU KENKYU (TOKYO. 1976). **See** Linguistics.

IE/0013-2608
EIGSE. **See** Linguistics.

FR
EKHO; LITERATURNYI ZHURNAL. 1-. Periodical. Russian. qt. 60.00F. RTL/Ardis Publishers, Carl R Proffer, 2901 Heatherway, Ann Arbor MI 48104. **LC** PG3516; .E38.

●US
EL-E-PHANT. (1993)-. English. bm. $20.00. Sun & Moon Press / California, 6026 Wilshire Bldv., Los Angeles CA 90026. **Tel** (213)857-1115. **ED** Douglas Messerli. **Bk Rev.**
Desc: Focuses on current innovative fiction, poetry, and theatre, but also includes over-looked American literary and theatrical works of the past.

AU
ELIZABETHAN & RENAISSANCE STUDIES. **Added/Corp** Universitat Salzburg. Institut fur Englische Sprache und Literatur. Universitat Salzburg. Institut fur Englische Sprache und Literatur. Elizabethan Studies. (1972)-. Monographic series. English.
Ind/Abst MLA Int. Bibl. Books Artic. Mod. Lang. Lit.

●US/1066-7059
ELIZABETHAN REVIEW, THE. [Elizab. rev.]. Vol. 1, No. 1 (spring 1993)-. Periodical. English. sa. $47.00 (one year), $85.00 (two year) US; $58.00 (one year), $93.00 (two year) Europe; $65.00 (one year), $105.00 (two year) other. Elizabethan Review, 123 60 83rd Avenue, Kew Gardens NY 11415. **Tel** (718)575-9656. **ED** Gary B. Goldstein. **DD** 822. **Bk Rev**, (Qty: 12). **Ad Acc.** **Pr Rev.**

US/1059-4876
ELK RIVER REVIEW. [Elk River rev.]. **Added/Corp** Limestone Literary League. Vol. 1, No. 1 (June 1991)-. Periodical. English. sa. $10.00 (libraries), $12.00 (other institutions). Limestone Literary League, 606 Coleman Avenue, Athens AL 35611-3216. **DD** 810.

US/0160-7545
ELLEN GLASGOW NEWSLETTER, THE. [Ellen Glasgow newsl.]. Vol. 1, No. 1 (Oct. 1974)-. Newsletter. English. sa. $2.00 membership. Edgar E MacDonald, Box 565, Ashland VA 23005. **LC** PS3513.L34; Z654. **DD** 813/.52.
Ind/Abst MLA Int. Bibl. Books Artic. Mod. Lang. Lit.

CN/0046-1830
ELLIPSE. **Added/Corp** Universite de Sherbrooke. Faculte des Arts. (1969)-. Periodical. French (English). Twice a year. 14.00Can$ (institution), 12.00Can$ (individual) North America; 16.00Can$ (institution), 14.00Can$ (individuals) other. University de Sherbrooke/ CP 10/FAC, Des Lettres et Sciences Humaines, Quebec Quebec J1K 2R1 Canada. **Tel** (819)821-7277, FAX (819)821-7238. **ED** Charly Bouchara (editor's phone: (819)821-7000 ext. 3268). **LC** PR9194; .E43. **DD** 808.8. **Circ:** 750 (ctrl). available on microfilm from Micromedia Limited; available on an online database from CB & CAD.
Desc: Devoted to the presentation of Canadian poetry in translation. Each issue pairs two poets, one French, one English, and offers a selection of their work in the other language. An assessment of the work of both writers is presented in an article that introduces their work to the reading public of the culture, thus promoting a better understanding of the two main cultural groups in Canada.
Ind/Abst Abstr. Engl. Stud.; Am. Humanit. Index; Can. Index; Point Repere (1983-).

US/1040-1644
ELLIPSIS (LOS GATOS, CALIF.). (ELLIPSIS ... LITERATURE WITH A CERTAIN TWIST.). [Ellipsis]. (1988)-. Periodical. English. sa. $24.00 North America; $28.00 other. Ellipsis Press, 105A North Santa Cruz Avenue, Los Gatos CA 95030. **Tel** (408)354-1481, FAX (408)354-1463. **(Subscription address:** 1176 E Campbell Avenue, Campbell, CA 95008**)** **ED** Jonathan Ther, Joy Oestreicher and Ruth McCue. **DD** 810. **Circ:** 500.

CN/0228-0124
ELOIZES. (ELOIZES :REVUE DE L'ASSOCIATION DES ECRIVAINS ACADIENS.). [Eloizes]. **Added/Corp** Association des Ecrivains Acadiens. (Spring 1980)-. Periodical. French. sa (May, and Oct.). 15.50Can$. Association des Ecrivains, 140 Bogsford, Moncton New Brunswick E1C 4X4 Canada. **Tel** (506)854-3491. **DD** C840/.8/09715. **Bk Rev.** **Circ:** 300.
Desc: Poetic and prosaic texts of varied lengths and authors, drama extracts, essays, chronicles, etc.

US/0885-968X
EMBLEMATICA. [Emblematica]. Vol. 1, No. 1 (Spring 1986)-. Periodical. English. sa. $55.00. AMS Press Inc., 56 East 13th Street, New York NY 10003. **Tel** (212)777-4700, FAX (212)995-5413, telex 710 581 2302. **ED** Peter M Daly, Daniel Russell, and Egon Verheyen. **LC** CR1; .E42. **DD** 929.8/2.
Desc: An art form and a mode of symbolic communication, which belongs to the study of the history of art and literature.
Ind/Abst BHA : Biblio. Hist. Art; MLA Int. Bibl. Books Artic. Mod. Lang. Lit.

US/1042-9166
EMERALD CITY COMIX AND STORIES. (1987?)-. Periodical. English. bm. $5.25. Wonder Comix, Box 95402, Seattle WA 98145-2402. **DD** 051. **Bk Rev.** **Ad Acc.** **Circ:** 10,000.

●US/1059-6879
EMILY DICKINSON JOURNAL, THE. (1992)-. Periodical. English. sa. $50.00 (institutions), $30.00 (members), $25.00 (non-members). University Press of Colorado, PO Box 849, Niwot CO 80544. **Tel** (303)530-5337, FAX (303)530-5306.

GW
EMPIRISCHE LITERATURWISSENSCHAFT. 1977-. Monographic series. German. Price varies per volume. Athenaum Verlag GmbH, Adelheidstrabe 2, 6240 Tonigstein TS Germany. **Tel** 06174/3021.

US/0145-5494
ENDANGERED FAECES. English. $2.00. Strage Faeces Press, 122 New Wickham Drive, Penfield NY 14625. **LC** PS501; .E53. **DD** 810/.8/0054.

AT
ENDEAVOUR. Vol. 1 (1973)-. Periodical. English. qt.
Ind/Abst AgBiotech News Inf.

GW/0172-1992
ENGLISCH AMERIKANISCHE STUDIEN. [Engl.-am. Stud.]. **VFOAT** EAST; E.A.S.T. 1.- Yearly volume; March 1979-. Periodical. German (English). qt. DM44.00. EAST, Postfach 2565, W-4400 Munster Germany. **Tel** (251)22795. **ED** Dieter M Keiner. **LC** PE3; .E58. **DD** 420/.5. **Bk Rev.** **Ad Acc.** **Circ:** 3,000 (ctrl).
Desc: Journal for English and American studies in the fields of literature, language, history, politics and culture.

UK
ENGLISH. **Added/Corp** English Association, London. Vol. 1, No. 1 (1936)-. Periodical. English. Three times a year. **ED** George Cookson. ***Supersedes*** *English Association. Bulletin* ***and*** *English Association, London. Pamphlet.*

SA
ENGLISH ACADEMY REVIEW, THE. **Added/Corp** English Academy of Southern Africa. **VFOAT** EAR. Vol. 1 (1983)-. Periodical. English. an. R31.50. The English Academy of Southern Africa, PO Box 124, 2050 Wits South Africa.
Ind/Abst Annu. Bibliogr. Engl. Lang. Lit.

GW
ENGLISH AND AMERICAN STUDIES IN GERMAN; SUMMARIES OF THESES AND MONOGRAPHS. **See** Linguistics.

SA/0376-8902
ENGLISH IN AFRICA. [Engl. Afr.]. **Added/Corp** Institute for the Study of English in Africa. Vol. 1 (March 1974)-. English. sa (May and October). $22.25 (institution), $16.70 (individual). Institute for Study English in Africa, Rhodes University, Box 94, Grahamstown 6140 South Africa. **Tel** 011 27 461 26093, FAX 011 27 461 25642, telex 244219. **ED** D. G. N. Cornwell. **LC** PR9340; .A3. **DD** 820/.8/096. **Bk Rev.** **Circ:** 575. Documents available from The Genuine Article.
Desc: Forum for study of African literature and English as a language of Africa; articles on all aspects of English writing, other literatures and oral traditions.
Ind/Abst Annu. Bibliogr. Engl. Lang. Lit.; Arts Humanit. Citation Index [Full Cov.]; Curr. Contents Arts Humanit.; MLA Int. Bibl. Books Artic. Mod. Lang. Lit.; Res. Alert [Full Cov.].

UK/0013-8215
ENGLISH (LONDON). (ENGLISH.). [English]. **Added/Corp** English Association. Vol. 1 No. 1 (1936)-. Academic Scholarly Publication. English. Three times a year (Summer, Spring, Autumn). $240.00 (full), $90.00 (ordinary) US & Canada, £110.00 (full), £40.00 (ordinary) others; Comes with English Association Full and Ordinary membership. English Association, University of Leicester, 128 Regent Road, Leicester LE1 7PA England. **Tel** 011 44 533525927, FAX 011 44 533525928. **ED** M. Dodsworth and H. Baron. **LC** PR5; .E5. **DD** 820/.9. Index Available, published separately, free-automatically sent. **Bk Rev.** **Ad Acc.** **Circ:** 652. available on microfilm and microfiche from University Microfilms International (UMI). Documents available from The Genuine Article. ***Supersedes*** *Bulletin (English Association); Pamphlet (English Association : 1913).*
Desc: A journal of literary criticism publishing essays and reviews aimed at readers in higher education covering creative and critical scholarly work.
Ind/Abst Abstr. Engl. Stud.; Annu. Bibliogr. Engl. Lang. Lit.; Arts Humanit. Citation Index [Full Cov.]; Br. Humanit. Index; Curr. Contents Arts Humanit.; MLA Int. Bibl. Books Artic. Mod. Lang. Lit.; Res. Alert [Full Cov.]; Soc. Plann. Policy Dev. Abstr.

US
ENGLISH MANUSCRIPT STUDIES, 1100-1700. Vol. 1 (1989)-. English. an. £65.00. Basil Blackwell Publishers Ltd, 108 Cowley Road, Oxford 0X4 1JF England. **Tel** 011 44 865 791100, FAX 011 44 865 791347, telex 837022 OXBOOK G. **(Subscription address:** Marston Book Services Ltd., PO Box 87, Oxford OX2 0DT England.**)** **ED** Peter Beal and Jeremy Griffiths. **LC** Z115.E5; E55. **DD** 091/.0942.
Ind/Abst BHA : Biblio. Hist. Art.

IT/0425-0575
ENGLISH MISCELLANY. ***Suspended.*** Vol. 1 (1950)-Vol. 30 (1984). Multiple languages (English, French, German, Italian and Spanish). ir. Edizioni di Storia e Letteratu, Via Lancellotti 18, 00186 Rome Italy. **Tel** 011 39 6 68806556. **LC** PR13.
Desc: Articles on various aspects of English studies in Italy, humanistic in nature, concerning problems of text, translation and interpretation.
Ind/Abst Abstr. Engl. Stud.; Annu. Bibliogr. Engl. Lang. Lit.; MLA Int. Bibl. Books Artic. Mod. Lang. Lit.; Romant. Move.

US
ENGLISH NOVEL EXPLICATION. SUPPLEMENT. Vol. 1 (1976)-. English. ir. Shoe String Press, PO Box 4327, 925 Sherman Avenue, Hamden CT 06514. **Tel** (203)248-6307.

NE/0013-838X
ENGLISH STUDIES. [Engl. stud.]. Vol. 1, No. 1 (Feb. 1919)-. Periodical. English. bm. Fl429.00 (institutions), Fl317.00 (individuals). Swets & Zeitlinger BV, Heereweg 347B PO Box 825, 2160 SZ Lisse Holland. **Tel** 011 31 2521 35111, FAX 02521-15888, telex 41325. **(Subscription address:** Swets Publishing Service, PO Box 825, 2160 SZ Lisse Holland**)** **ED** T A Birrell and J M Blom. **LC** PE1; .E55. **DD** 420.5. **[CCC].** Index available. cum. index. **Bk Rev.** **Ad Acc.** **Circ:** 2,000. Documents available from The Genuine Article, UMI Article Clearinghouse. ***Continues in part*** *Student's Monthly.*
Desc: The scope of English Studies ranges from diachronic and synchronic studies of the English language, to the literatures both past and present of the English speaking world.
Ind/Abst Abstr. Engl. Stud.; Acad. Abstr. Full Text Elite (July 1990-); Acad. Abstr. (July 1990-); Acad. Ind. [Computer File] (1987-); Acad. Search (July 1990-); Annu. Bibliogr. Engl. Lang. Lit.; Arts Humanit. Citation Index [Full Cov.]; Curr. Contents Arts Humanit.; Expand. Acad. Index (1987-); Humanit. Index; Humanit. Source (Jul. 1990-); INFO-SOUTH Abstr.; Lang. Teach.; Lit. Crit. Regist.; Mag. Search; MLA Int. Bibl. Books Artic. Mod. Lang. Lit.; Newsp. Period. Abstr. (1989-); Res. Alert [Full Cov.]; Romant. Move.; Soc. Plann. Policy Dev. Abstr.; Sociol. Abstr.; Women Stud. Abstr.

SA/0013-8398
ENGLISH STUDIES IN AFRICA. [Engl. stud. Afr.]. Vol. 1 (Mar. 1958)-. Periodical. English. Twice a year (Mar., Sept.). R27.88 (institutions), R13.94 (individuals) South Africa; R17.50 (institutions), R8.75 (individuals) other. University of Witwatersrand Department of English, PO Wits, Johannesburg 2050 South Africa. **Tel** 011 27 11 7162832. **ED** G. Hughes. **LC** PR1; .E6. Index available. **Ad Acc.** **Circ:** 500. available on microfilm and microfiche from University Microfilms International (UMI). Documents available from The Genuine Article.
Desc: A journal of the humanities, with articles mainly on general literature.
Ind/Abst Abstr. Engl. Stud.; Annu. Bibliogr. Engl. Lang. Lit.; Arts Humanit. Citation Index (19??-19??) [Full Cov.]; Curr. Contents Arts Humanit.; Lit. Crit. Regist.; MLA Int. Bibl. Books Artic. Mod. Lang. Lit.; Res. Alert [Full Cov.]; Romant. Move.; Soc. Plann. Policy Dev. Abstr.

UK
ENGLISH STUDIES SERIES. **See** Linguistics.

US/0091-522X
ENVIOS. (ENVIOS; CUADERNOS DE LITERATURA.). [Envios]. Began with Aug. 1971 issue. Periodical. Spanish. qt. $4.00. PO Box M-228, Hoboken NJ 07030. **LC** PQ7370; .E57.

US/0897-4888
ENVOI (NEW YORK, N.Y.). (ENVOI.). [Envoi]. **Added/Corp** Columbia University. Dept. of English and Comparative Literature. Vol. 1, No. 1 (Spring/Summer 1988)-. Periodical. English. sa. $55.00. AMS Press Inc., 56 East 13th Street, New York NY 10003. **Tel** (212)777-4700, FAX (212)995-5413, telex 710 581 2302. **ED** Paul Spillenger. **LC** PN661; .E58. **DD** 809.
Desc: Devoted to scholarship and criticism in the field of medieval literature. Aims to review books on or related to medieval literature within a year of publication and provide a 'forum for the open discussion of ideas related, closely or more tenuously, to this field'.
Ind/Abst MLA Int. Bibl. Books Artic. Mod. Lang. Lit.

US
EOTU. English. bm. $18.00 US; $24.00 other. 1810 West State Street, Suite 115, Boise ID 83702. **ED** Larry Dennis. **Circ:** 500.
Desc: Covers experimental fiction and artwork.

GW/0340-0603
EPITAPH. [Epitaph]. Began in 1943?. Periodical. German (English). ir. 8.20. F Weber, Kapuzinerstrasse 41, 8000 Munchen 5 Germany. **LC** PT1141.A2; E6.

US/0145-1391
EPOCH (ITHACA). (EPOCH.). [Epoch]. **Added/Corp** Cornell University. Vol. 1, (Fall 1947)-. Periodical. English. Three times a year (January, May, and October). $11.00 US; $15.00 other. Cornell University / Epoch, 251 Goldwin Smith Hall, Ithaca NY 14853. **Tel** (607)255-3385, FAX (607)255-1454. **ED** Michael Koch. **LC** AP2; .E68. **DD** 051. Index available (published separately). **Ad Acc.** Full Page (B&W) $170.00. Half Page (B&W) $90.00. **Circ:** 1,000. available on microfilm and microfiche from University Microfilms International (UMI).
Desc: Publishes fiction, poetry, non-fiction essays and occasional reviews by unknown and established writers.
Ind/Abst Am. Humanit. Index; Index Am. Period. Verse.

SP
EQUIVALENCIAS. **See** Literature-Poetry.

FR/0425-1687
ERASME. (ERASME; COLLECTION DE TEXTES LATINS COMMENTES.). **VFOAT** Collection "Erasme". (1959)-. Monographic series. French. Price varies per volume. Presses Universitaires de France, Department des Revues, 14 Avenue du Bois de l'Epine, BP 90, 91003 Evry Cedex France. **Tel** (1)60 77 82 05, FAX (1) 60 79 20 45, telex PUF 600 474 F.

IT
ERBA D'ARNO. **See** The Arts.

CH
ERH TUNG WEN HSUEH HSUAN KAN. **VFOAT** Er Tong Wen Xue Xuan Kan. 1981, 1-. Periodical. Chinese. NT$0.36. Hsin Hua Shu Tien / Shang-Hai Fa Hsing So, Shanghai, People's Republic of China. **LC** AP215.C5; E74. **DD** 895.1/09/9282.

CC
ERH TUNG WEN HSUEH YEN CHIU. **VFOAT** Ertong Wenxue Yanjiu. Began in 1959. Periodical. Chinese. RMBY0.40. Shanghai Academy of Agricultural Sciences, 2901 Bei Di Road, Shanghai, People's Republic of China. **LC** PL2449; .E74. **DD** 895.1/09/9282.

SP
ERIA, EL. Spanish. qt. 4000ptas Spain; 8000ptas North America; 7000ptas other. Editorial El Paisaje, Entre los Rios 10, 24760 Castrocalbon Leon Spain. **(Subscription address:** El Eria, Entre los Rios 10, 24760-CASTROCALBON**) ED** Agustin Garcia Alonso. Index available. cum. index. **Bk Rev. Ad Acc. Circ:** 4,500 (ctrl).
Desc: Contains literature, biographies, narrations and poetry.

CN/0828-7686
ERINDALE REVIEW. [Erindale rev.]. Vol. 1 (1982)-. English. an. $5.00. Erindale College Student Union, Erindale College, University of Toronto, Mississauga Ontario L5L 1C6 Canada. **DD** C810/.8/0054.

IE/0332-0758
ERIU. (ERIU : FOUNDED AS THE JOURNAL OF THE SCHOOL OF IRISH LEARNING DEVOTED TO IRISH PHILOLOGY AND LITERATURE.). [Eriu]. **Added/Corp** School of Irish Learning (Dublin, Ireland) Royal Irish Academy. Vol. 1 (1904)-. English. an (Dec.). 15.00p (individuals); 20.00p (institutions). Royal Irish Academy, 19 Dawson Street, Dublin 2 Ireland. **Tel** 011 353 1 762570. **LC** PB1201; .E6.
Ind/Abst MLA Int. Bibl. Books Artic. Mod. Lang. Lit.

●US/1065-4844
ESC! (DEKALB, ILL.). (ESC! : THE LITERARY MAGAZINE FOR NEW WRITERS AND ARTISTS.). [ESC!]. **VFOAT** ESC! Magazine. (Summer 1992)-. Periodical. English. qt. $8.00. ESC!, c/o M R Potter, PO Box 168, Dekalb IL 60115-0168. **DD** 810.

BL/0102-6615
ESCRITA. [Escrita]. Yearly V. 1 (1975)-. Periodical. Portuguese. mo. Vertente Editura Ltda, rua dr Homera de Melo 446, 05007 Sao Paulo SP Brazil. **LC** PQ9500; .E73.
Ind/Abst MLA Int. Bibl. Books Artic. Mod. Lang. Lit.

AU
ESELSOHR. (19??)-. Periodical. German. sa. G Pilz, Stifterstrasse 4A, 4320 Perg Austria. **LC** PT1141.A2; E8.
Ind/Abst Child. Lit. Abstr. (19??-).

FR
ESPACES DE SAINT-JOHN PERSE. 1/2-. French. Diffusion Librairie H Champion, Paris France. **LC** PQ2623.E386; Z683. **DD** 848/.91209.

SP/0214-1396
ESPANA CONTEMPORANEA : EC. **VFOAT** EC. Vol. 1, No. 1 (1988)-. Periodical. Spanish (English). sa. $38.00 (1 year), $69.00 (2 year) institutions; $25.00 (1 year), $46.00 (2 year) individuals. Espana Contemporanea, Ohio State University, Dept. of Spanish, Columbus OH 43210. **Tel** (614)292-2621, FAX (614)292-2682. **ED** Dr. Samuel Amell.

IT/0392-3495
ESPERIENZE LETTERARIE. [Esper. lett.]. **Added/Corp** Societa Editrice Napoletana. Vol. 1 (Jan./March 1976)-. Periodical. Italian. qt. L80000 Italy; L100000 other. Casa Editrice Federico and Ardia, Via Ventaglieri 85, 80135 Naples Italy. **Tel** 011 39 81 5496478. **LC** PQ4001; .E76. **Bk Rev. Pr Rev.** ctrl circ.
Ind/Abst MLA Int. Bibl. Books Artic. Mod. Lang. Lit.; Romant. Move.

US/0093-8297
ESQ. [ESQ]. **Added/Corp** Washington State University. Dept. of English. **VAT** Emerson Society Quarterly. No. 54 1st Quarter (1969)-. Periodical. English. qt (Jan., Apr., July, Oct.). $30.00 (institutions), $23.00 (individuals) North America; $35.00 (institutions), $27.00 (individuals) other. Washington State University Press, Cooper Publications, Room 40, Pullman WA 99164. **Tel** (509)335-3518. **ED** Robert C. McLean and Albert J. von Frank. **LC** PS1629; .E6. **DD** 810/.9/003. **Bk Rev. Ad Acc. Circ:** 721 (ctrl). available on microfilm and microfiche from University Microfilms International (UMI). Documents available from The Genuine Article. ***Continues*** *Emerson Society Quarterly, 0013-6670.*
Desc: A journal of the American Renaissance, devoted to the study of 19th Century American Literature.
Ind/Abst Abstr. Engl. Stud.; Am. Humanit. Index; Annu. Bibliogr. Engl. Lang. Lit.; Arts Humanit. Citation Index [Full Cov.]; Curr. Contents Arts Humanit.; Lit. Crit. Regist.; MLA Int. Bibl. Books Artic. Mod. Lang. Lit.; Res. Alert [Full Cov.].

UK
ESSAYS AND STUDIES (LONDON). (ESSAYS AND STUDIES.). **Main/Corp** English Association (Great Britain). Vol. 1-32 (1910-1946)-New Series Vol. 1 (1948)-. English. an (July). $30.00 Comes with English Association Full membership. English Association, University of Leicester, 128 Regent Road, Leicester LE1 7PA England. **Tel** 011 44 533525927 FAX 011 44 533525928. **LC** PR13; .E4. **DD** 820.4. **Circ:** 300 (ctrl).
Desc: Collections of essays on literary and cultural issues, each volume being devoted to one particular topic.
Ind/Abst Annu. Bibliogr. Engl. Lang. Lit.; Br. Humanit. Index; Romant. Move.

UK/0071-1357
ESSAYS AND STUDIES (LONDON, ENGLAND : 1950). (ESSAYS AND STUDIES.). [Essays stud.]. **Added/Corp** English Association. **VFOAT** Essays & Studies. Vol. 3 (1950)-. English. an. $60.00. Boydell and Brewer Limited, PO Box 9, Woodbridge Suffolk, 1P12 3DF England. **Tel** 011 44 394 411320, FAX 011 44 394 411477. **LC** PR13; .E4. **DD** 820.4. Index available. **Bk Rev.** Documents available from The Genuine Article. ***Continues*** *English Studies (London, England).*
Ind/Abst Abstr. Engl. Stud. (1980-); Arts Humanit. Citation Index (19??-19??) [Full Cov.]; MLA Int. Bibl. Books Artic. Mod. Lang. Lit.; Res. Alert [Full Cov.].

UK/0080-4584
ESSAYS BY DIVERS HANDS. (ESSAYS BY DIVERS HANDS, BEING THE TRANSACTIONS OF THE ROYAL SOCIETY OF LITERATURE.). **Main/Corp** Royal Society of Literature of the United Kingdom, London. **Added/Corp** Royal Society of Literature of the United Kingdom, London. Transactions of the Royal Society of Literature of the United Kingdom. (1829)-. Monographic series. English. Price varies per volume.
Ind/Abst Annu. Bibliogr. Engl. Lang. Lit.; MLA Int. Bibl. Books Artic. Mod. Lang. Lit.; Romant. Move.

UK/0014-0856
ESSAYS IN CRITICISM. [Essays crit.]. Vol. 1, No. 1 (Jan. 1951)-. Periodical. English. qt. £39.00 UK and Europe; $80.00 other. Oxford University Press, Walton Street, Oxford OX2 6DP England. **Tel** 011 44 865 56767, FAX 011 44 865 267773, telex 837330 OXPRES G. **(Subscription address:** Oxford University Press / USA, Journals Marketing Department, Oxford University Press, 2001 Evans Road, Cary NC 27513.**) ED** Stephen Wall. **LC** PR1; .E75. **[CCC].** Index available. cum. index. **Bk Rev. Ad Acc. Circ:** 2,500 (ctrl). available on microfilm and microfiche from University Microfilms International (UMI). Documents available from The Genuine Article, UMI Article Clearinghouse.
Desc: A journal in academic criticism and book reviews in English literature.
Ind/Abst Abstr. Engl. Stud.; Acad. Abstr. Full Text Elite (July 1990-); Acad. Abstr. (July 1990)-; Acad. Ind. [Computer File] (1987-); Acad. Search (July 1990-); Annu. Bibliogr. Engl. Lang. Lit.; Arts Humanit. Citation Index [Full Cov.]; Br. Humanit. Index; Child. Lit. Abstr. (19??-); Curr. Contents Arts Humanit.; Expand. Acad. Index (1987-); Humanit. Index; Humanit. Source (Jul. 1990-); INFO-SOUTH Abstr.; Lit. Crit. Regist.; Mag. Search; MLA Int. Bibl. Books Artic. Mod. Lang. Lit.; Newsp. Period. Abstr. (1991-); Res. Alert [Full Cov.]; Romant. Move.

AT/0071-139X
ESSAYS IN FRENCH LITERATURE. [Essays Fr. lit.]. **Added/Corp** University of Western Australia. Dept. of French Studies. No. 1 (Nov. 1964)-. English. an (1 issue). Price varies. University Bookshop, PO Box 656, Nedlands WA 6009 Australia. **Tel** 61 9 380 2069. **LC** PQ12; .E86. Documents available from The Genuine Article.
Ind/Abst Arts Humanit. Citation Index (19??-19??) [Full Cov.]; Curr. Contents Arts Humanit.; MLA Int. Bibl. Books Artic. Mod. Lang. Lit.; Res. Alert [Full Cov.]; Romant. Move.

US/0738-0763
ESSAYS IN GRAHAM GREENE. [Essays Graham Greene]. Vol. 1 (1987)-. English. an. $25.00. Lucas Hall Press, University of St. Louis, 8001 Natural Bridge Road, St. Louis MO 63121. **Tel** (314)553-5617. **ED** Peter Wolfe. **LC** PR6013.R44; Z6328. **DD** 823/.912. **Bk Rev. Circ:** 500 (ctrl).

UK/0308-888X
ESSAYS IN POETICS. [Essays poet.]. **Added/Corp** British Neo-Formalist Circle. University of Keele. Vol. 1 (April 1976)-. Periodical. English. sa. £22.00 (institutions), £15.50 (individuals) UK; £27.00 (institutions), £19.75 (individuals) other. Drake Marketing, 89 St. Fagans Road, Cardiff CF5 3AE England. **Tel** 011 44 222 560333, telex 36113 UNKLIB G. **ED** J.M. Andrew and C.R. Pike. **LC** PN2; .E86. **DD** 805. **Bk Rev. Ad Acc. Circ:** 300. Documents available from The Genuine Article.
Desc: Articles on European and American literature and theory. Principally concerned with Russian formalism, structuralism and modern poetics, both in theoretical discussion and in textual analysis.
Ind/Abst Arts Humanit. Citation Index [Full Cov.]; Curr. Contents Arts Humanit.; MLA Int. Bibl. Books Artic. Mod. Lang. Lit.; Res. Alert [Full Cov.].

CN/0316-0300
ESSAYS ON CANADIAN WRITING. [Essays Can. writ.]. **Added/Corp** York University (Toronto, Ont.). **VFOAT** ECW. No. 1 (Winter 1974)-. Periodical. English (French). Three times a year (spring, summer and fall). $40.00 (institutions), $20.00 (individual). Essays on Canadian Writing, 2120 Queen Street East / Suite 200, Toronto Ontario M4E 1E2 Canada. **Tel** (416)694-3348, FAX (416)698-9906. **ED** Jack David and Robert Lecker. **LC** PR9180; .E86. **DD** 810.9/971/05. **Bk Rev. Ad Acc. Circ:** 1,000. available on microfilm from University Microfilms International (UMI). Documents available from UMI Article Clearinghouse.
Desc: Devoted to criticism of Canadian writers and their works. Concentrates on essays dealing with contemporary authors and current critical approaches; frequently publishes bibliographies and interviews, and full-length book reviews of fiction, poetry and criticism.
Ind/Abst Abstr. Engl. Stud.; Acad. Abstr. Full Text Elite (Jan. 1992-); Acad. Abstr. (Jan. 1992-); Acad. Search (Jan. 1992-); Am. Humanit. Index; Annu. Bibliogr. Engl. Lang. Lit.; Arts Humanit. Citation Index [Full Cov.]; Book Rev. Index; Can. Index; Can. Period. Index; Curr. Contents Arts Humanit.; Expand. Acad. Index (1989-); Humanit. Index; Humanit. Source (Jan. 1992-); INFO-SOUTH Abstr.; MLA Int. Bibl. Books Artic. Mod. Lang. Lit.; Newsp. Period. Abstr. (1991-); Res. Alert [Full Cov.]; Soc. Sci. Cit. Index [Select. Cov.].

US/0891-9593
ESSAYS ON FANTASTIC LITERATURE. [Essays fantast. lit.]. No. 1 (1986)-. Monographic series. English. ir. Price varies per volume. Borgo Press, PO Box 2845, San Bernardino CA 92406. **Tel** (714)884-5813, (714)885-1161. **ED** Robert Reginald. **DD** 814.
Desc: Short studies and collections of essays on science fiction and fantasy by the major critics and professionals in the genre.

CL/0071-1713
ESTUDIOS FILOLOGICOS. **See** Linguistics.

SP/0210-0525
ESTUDIOS MADRID. [Estudios Madrid]. (1945)-. Periodical. Spanish. Four times a year. 55ptas. Revista Estudios, Belisana 2, 28043 Madrid Spain. **Tel** 011 34 1 3002972, FAX 011 34 1 3002994. **UDC** 008. **Bk Rev. Ad Acc. Pr Rev. Circ:** 500 (ctrl).

BL/0102-4906
ESTUDOS ANGLO-AMERICANOS. **See** Linguistics.

BL
ESTUDOS HISTORICOS. **See** History(General)-History of North, South, and Central America.

BL/0103-1821
ESTUDOS PORTUGUESES E AFRICANOS : EPA. **Added/Corp** Universidade Estadual de Campinas. Nucleo de Estudos de Cultura e Expressao Portuguesa. Universidade Estadual de Campinas. Instituto de Estudos da Linguagem. **VFOAT** EPA; E.P.A. No. 1 (Mar. 1983)-. Periodical. Portuguese. sm. **LC** PQ9000; .E87.
Ind/Abst MLA Int. Bibl. Books Artic. Mod. Lang. Lit.

FR
ETHOS. 1- 1973-. Romanian (Romanian). an. Virgil Ierunca, Boite Postale 255, 19 Paris SN France. **LC** PC800; .E73.
Ind/Abst Anthropol. Lit.

FR
ETUDES ANGLO-AMERICAINES. **Added/Corp** Klincksieck (Firm). Vol. 5 (1983)-. Monographic series. French. Price varies per volume. 2 rue Gay Lussac, 22 Saint-Brieuc, CCP 1027, 2 Rennes France. ***Continues*** *Etudes Anglo-Saxonnes.*

SZ/0014-2026
ETUDES DE LETTRES. [Etud. lett.]. **Added/Corp** Universite de Lausanne. Faculte des Lettres. Societe des Etudes de Lettres. Vol. 1-27, (1937)-. Periodical. French. Four times a year (Mar., June, Sept., Dec.). 60.00F. Faculte des Lettres / Switzerland, BFSH 2, CH 1015 Lausanne Switzerland. **Tel** 011 41 21 464552. **Bk Rev.** ***Continues*** *Societe des Etudes de Lettres. Bulletin de la Societe des Etudes de Lettres.*
Desc: Research of the members of the faculty, contributions by authors invited by the faculty, study results, proceedings and monographic issues. Each issue deals with one specific subject.
Ind/Abst Abstr. Engl. Stud.; Annu. Bibliogr. Engl. Lang. Lit.; BHA : Biblio. Hist. Art; MLA Int. Bibl. Books Artic. Mod. Lang. Lit.; Romant. Move.

CN/0014-2085
ETUDES FRANCAISES (MONTREAL). (ETUDES FRANCAISES.). [Etud. fr.]. Vol. 1 (Feb. 1965)-. Periodical. French. tq (3 issues). 38.50Can$ institution. Presses de l'Universite de Montreal, PO Box 6128 Station A, Montreal Quebec H3C 3J7 Canada. **Tel** (514)343-6933. **(Subscription address:** Periodica Inc., PO Box 444, 1155 Avenue Ducharme, Outremont Quebec H2V 4R6 Canada; telephone: (514)274-5468) **ED** Robert Melancon. cum. index (1965-1984). **Ad Acc. Circ:** 700. available on microfilm and microfiche from University Microfilms International (UMI). Documents available from The Genuine Article.
Desc: Mainly literary, this thematic periodical deals with various questions that relate arts to human sciences, language to writing.
Ind/Abst Am. Hist. Life (1966-1975, 1982-); ARTbibliogr. Mod.; Arts Humanit. Citation Index (19??-19??) [Full Cov.]; BHA : Biblio. Hist. Art; Curr. Contents Arts Humanit.; MLA Int. Bibl. Books Artic. Mod. Lang. Lit.; Point Repere (1983-); Res. Alert [Full Cov.]; Romant. Move.

FR/0994-5490
ETUDES LAWRENCIENNES NANTERRE. (ETUDES LAWRENCIENNES.). (1986)-. Periodical. French. be. **UDC** 82.
Ind/Abst MLA Int. Bibl. Books Artic. Mod. Lang. Lit.

GW
ETUDES LITTERAIRES FRANCAISES. (1978)-. Monographic series. French (English and German). Gunter Narr Verlag, Dishingerweg 5, D 72070 Tuebingen Germany. **Tel** 011 49 7071 78091, FAX (07071)75288.
Ind/Abst MLA Int. Bibl. Books Artic. Mod. Lang. Lit.

CN/0014-214X
ETUDES LITTERAIRES (UNIVERSITE LAVAL). (ETUDES LITTERAIRES.). [Etud. litt.]. (April 1968)-. Periodical. French (English). Three times a year (Summer, Fall, & Winter). 36.00Can$ (institutions), 22.00Can$ (individuals) Canada; 26.00Can$ (individuals) others. Presses de l'Universite Laval, CP 2447 Avenue de la Medicine, Saint Foy Quebec G1K 7P4 Canada. **Tel** (418)656-5106, (418)656-2590. **(Subscription address:** Periodica Inc., P. O. Box 444, 1155 Avenue Ducharme, Outremont, QUE H2V 4R6 Canada, telephone: (514)274-5468**) ED** Monique Moser-Verrey. **LC** PQ2; .E83. **DD** 840.9. Index available. **Bk Rev. Ad Acc. Circ:** 800 (ctrl). available on microfilm from Bibliotheque National du Quebec; available on microfilm and microfiche from University Microfilms International (UMI). Documents available from The Genuine Article.
Desc: Theoretical studies in literature, cinema, and theater.
Ind/Abst Arts Humanit. Citation Index [Full Cov.]; Curr. Contents Arts Humanit.; MLA Int. Bibl. Books Artic. Mod. Lang. Lit.; Point Repere (1983-); Res. Alert [Full Cov.]; Romant. Move.

FR
ETUDES PROUSTIENNES. Began in 1973-. French. Editions Gallimard, 5 rue Sebastien Bottin, 75007 Paris France. **LC** PQ2631.R63; Z492. **DD** 843/.9/12.

SZ/0531-1969
ETUDES REBELAISIENNES. [Etud. rabelais.]. (1956)-. Monographic series. French. ir. Price varies per volume. Librairie Droz SA, 11 rue Massot BP 389, CH 1211 Geneva 12 Switzerland. **Tel** 011 41 22 3466666, FAX 011 41 22 472391. **LC** PQ1692; .A25.
Ind/Abst MLA Int. Bibl. Books Artic. Mod. Lang. Lit.

SW
ETUDES ROMANES DE LUND. See Linguistics.

CN/0226-9635
ETUDES SUR LE FUTURISME ET LES AVANT-GARDES. (ETUDES SUR LE FUTURISME ET LES AVANT-GARDES / STUDIES ON FUTURISM AND THE AVENT-GARDE / STUDI SUL FUTURISMO E LE ANGUARDIE.). [Etud. futur. avant-gardes]. **Added/Corp** University of Windsor. Dept. of French Languages and Literature. **VFOAT** Studies on Futurism and the Avant-Garde; Studi sul Futurismo e le Avantguardie. Vol. 1, No 1 (Jan. 1990)-. English (French and Italian). an. $24.00. University of Windsor / Department of French Languages and Literature, 333 Dieppe Place, Windsor, Ontario N8S 3V3 Canada. **Tel** (519)253-4232 ext. 2068. **DD** 809/.91.

US/0146-7220
EUDORA WELTY NEWSLETTER. [Eudora Welty newsl.]. Vol. 1, No. 1, Winter (1977)-. Newsletter. English. sa (winter and summer). $2.00 (US & Canada); $3.00 other. Eudora Welty Newsletter, University of Toledo, W. McDonald, Department of English, Toledo OH 43603. **Tel** (419)537-2318. **ED** W. U. McDonald. **LC** PS3545.E6; Z673. **DD** 813/.52. cum. index. **Bk Rev. Ad Acc. Circ:** 210.
Desc: Primary and secondary bibliographies and bibliographic notes on Eudora Welty and her works, news about publications, conferences on her writing and library collections.
Ind/Abst Am. Humanit. Index; Annu. Bibliogr. Engl. Lang. Lit.; Lit. Crit. Regist.; MLA Int. Bibl. Books Artic. Mod. Lang. Lit.

US/1040-9483
EUGENE O'NEILL REVIEW, THE. [Eugene O'Neill rev.]. **Added/Corp** Eugene O'Neill Society. Suffolk University. Vol. 13, No. 1 (Spring 1989)-. Periodical. English. sa (Spring and Fall). $10.00 US and Canada; $15.00 other; $20.00 membership. Suffolk University / English, Department of English, c/o Frederick Wilkins, Boston MA 02114. **Tel** (617)573-8272. **ED** Frederick C Wilkins. **LC** PS3529.N5; Z4583. **DD** 812/.52. Index available. **Bk Rev. Ad Acc. Pr Rev. Circ:** 450 (ctrl). ***Continues** Eugene O'Neill Newsletter, 0733-0456.*
Desc: Essays on O'Neill's life, work and times plus book and performance reviews, photos, news, notes and queries and records of the Eugene O'Neill Society and activity around the world.
Ind/Abst MLA Int. Bibl. Books Artic. Mod. Lang. Lit.

GW/0014-2328
EUPHORION. (EUPHORION; ZEITSCHRIFT FUER LITERATURGESCHICHTE.). (1894)-. Periodical. German. Four times a year (Mar., June, Sept., Nov.). DM165.20 Germany; DM170.00 others. Universitatsverlag Carl Winter, POB 106140, D 69051 Heidelberg Germany. **Tel** 011 49 6221 770260. **LC** PN4; .D5. Index available (Free). ***Supersedes** Vierteljahrschrift fur Litteraturgeschichte.*
Ind/Abst Annu. Bibliogr. Engl. Lang. Lit.

GW/0531-2167
EUPHORION. BEIHEFTE. Vol. 1-. Monographic series. German. ir. Price varies per volume. Universitatsverlag Carl Winter, POB 106140, D 69051 Heidelberg Germany. **Tel** 011 49 6221 770260.
Desc: Supplement to Euphorion, history of literature.

GW/0014-2328
EUPHORION (HEIDELBERG, GERMANY). (EUPHORION.). [Euphorion]. 45. Vol., 1. No. Periodical. German (English). qt. DM126.00. Universitatsverlag Carl Winter, POB 106140, D 69051 Heidelberg Germany. **Tel** 011 49 6221 770260. **ED** Rainer Grunter. **LC** PN4; .D5. **DD** 809. **Ad Acc. Circ:** 1,200. Documents available from The Genuine Article. ***Continues** Dichtung und Volkstum.*
Desc: Germanic literature.
Ind/Abst Arts Humanit. Citation Index [Full Cov.]; Curr. Contents Arts Humanit.; MLA Int. Bibl. Books Artic. Mod. Lang. Lit.; Res. Alert [Full Cov.].

NE
EUROPEAN JOYCE STUDIES. (1989)-. Monographic series. English. an. Price varies per volume. Editions Rodopi BV, Keizersgracht 302-304, 1016 Ex Amsterdam Netherlands. **Tel** 011 31 20 6227507, FAX 011 31 20 380948.

US/1050-9585
EUROPEAN ROMANTIC REVIEW. [Eur. romant. rev.]. Vol. 1, No. 1 (Summer 1990)-. Periodical. English. sa. $22.00 (institutions), $14.00 (individual). European Romantic Review, PO Box 591402, San Francisco CA 94159. **Tel** (213)839-6732. **ED** Frederick Burwick. **LC** PN603; .E82. **DD** 809/.9145/05. Index available. **Bk Rev**, (Qty: 10). **Ad Acc. Circ:** 500.
Desc: Dedicated to interdisciplinary study of 19th century Europe.
Ind/Abst Am. Hist. Life (1990-).

SP
EUSKAL HERRIKO POETAK. VFOAT Poetas del Pais Vasco. Spanish. 4.500ptas Spain; 7.000ptas North America; 6.000ptas other. Editorial el Paisaje / Aranguren, La Penorra 8-2, 48850 Aranguren Spain. **Tel** (94) 639 07 74. **ED** A Garcia Alonso. **Bk Rev. Ad Acc.** ctrl circ.

CN/0315-3770
EVENT (NEW WESTMINSTER). (EVENT.). [Event]. **Added/Corp** Douglas College, New Westminster, B.C. Vol. 1, (Spring 1971)-. Periodical. English. Three times a year. 15.00Can$ (one year), 25.00Can$ (two year). Event / Douglas College, PO Box 2503, New Westminster British Columbia, V3L 5B2 Canada. **Tel** (604)527-5293, FAX (604)527-5095. **ED** David Zieroth. **Bk Rev**, (Qty: 3). **Ad Acc. Circ:** 1,000. available on microfilm from Micromedia Limited.
Desc: Devoted to those who are writing well but are not yet established. Includes new fiction, poetry, reviews.
Ind/Abst Am. Humanit. Index; Can. Index; Can. Period. Index; Index Am. Period. Verse.

US
EVERGREEN. VFOAT Evergreen Review. Began with Vol. 8, No. 32 (1964). Periodical. English. Grove Press Inc, 841 Broadway/4th Floor, New York NY 10003. **Tel** (212)529-3600, telex 6720753. available on microfilm from University Microfilms International (UMI). ***Continues** Evergreen Review.*
Ind/Abst Annu. Bibliogr. Engl. Lang. Lit.

US/1042-6647
EX LIBRIS (PORTSMOUTH, N.H.). (EX LIBRIS.). (Nov. 1988)-. Periodical. English. mo. $25.00. New Hampshire Writers and Publishers Project, 855 Islington Street/Suite 225 Box 150, Portsmouth NH 03801. **Tel** (603)436-6331. **ED** Jack Savage. **DD** 808. **Bk Rev. Ad Acc. Circ:** 500 (ctrl).
Desc: Articles on publishing and writing in New Hampshire.

US/1041-2573
EXEMPLARIA (BINGHAMTON, N.Y.). (EXEMPLARIA.). [Exemplaria]. **Added/Corp** State University of New York at Binghamton. Medieval & Renaissance Texts & Studies. State University of New York at Binghamton. Center for Medieval and Early Renaissance Studies. University of Florida. Dept. of English. Loyola University (New Orleans, La.). Dept. of English. Vol. 1, No. 1 (Spring 1989)-. Periodical. English. sa (March & Oct.). $20.00 (one year), $50.00 (three year) individuals US; $40.00 (one year), $100.00 (three year) institutions US; $15.00 (one year), $38.00 (three year) students US; $30.00 (one year), $75.00 (three year) individuals other; $60.00 (one year), $150.00 (three year) institutions other; $25.00 (one year), $60.00 (three year) other. State University of New York / Binghamton, MRTS - LN G99, Binghamton NY 13902. **Tel** (607)777-6758, FAX (607)777-2408. **LC** PN661; .E94. **DD** 809/.02/05.
Ind/Abst MLA Int. Bibl. Books Artic. Mod. Lang. Lit.

US/0163-7282
EXETASIS. Vol. 1, (197?)-. Academic Scholarly Publication. English. ir. California State University / Northridge, Dearby Annex 213, F. McMahon Ed., Northridge CA 91324. **Tel** (818)885-2853. **ED** Fred McMahon. **Circ:** 350.
Desc: Scholarly essays about rhetoric used in major communications and events such as speeches, campaigns, movies and music.

CN/0380-6596
EXILE (TORONTO). (EXILE.). [Exile]. Vol. 1 (1972)-. Periodical. English. qt. 25.00Can$ (one year), 44.00Can$ (two year), 65.00Can$ (three year). Exile, PO Box 67 Station B, Toronto Ont M5T 2CO Canada. **Tel** (416)736-5209. **(Subscription address:** Exile, 20 Dale Avenue, Toronto Ontario M4W 1K4 Canada.**) ED** Barry Callaghan. **Circ:** 1,000. available on microfiche from Micromedia Limited.
Desc: Devoted to the imagination, fiction, poetry, drama, painting and drawing. Rooted in the mutual cultures of English and French Canada; publishing works from Serbia to Soviet Latvia to South Africa, Israel to Ireland to Uruguay to the United States.
Ind/Abst Can. Index.

US/0195-3516
EXIT (GLENMONT). (EXIT.). V. 2- Fall 1979-. Periodical. English. Three times a year. $7.00. Routes/Creative Arts Projects, Rd#1 Box 339, Glenmont NY 12077. ***Continues** Entrance.*

US/1070-6844
EXPANSE (BALTIMORE, MD.). (EXPANSE.). [Expanse]. **VFOAT** Expanse Magazine. Vol. 1, No. 1 (1993)-. Periodical. English. qt. $16.00. Expanse Magazine, Box 43547, Baltimore MD 21236-0547. **ED** Steven E. Fick. **DD** 813.
Desc: Includes original science fiction stories, and interviews with authors.

UK
EXPENSIVE. Periodical. English. **ED** O Whiteoak.

US/0361-9621
EXPLICACION DE TEXTOS LITERARIOS. [Explic. textos lit.]. **Added/Corp** California State University, Sacramento. Dept. of Spanish and Portuguese. California State University, Sacramento. Dept. of Foreign Languages. (1972)-. Periodical. Spanish. Twice a year (May, Nov.). $12.00 (individuals); $20.00 (institutions). California State University / Department of Foreign Languages, 6000 J Street, Sacramento CA 95819. **Tel** (916)278-5862. **LC** PQ6001; .E96. **DD** 860. Documents available from The Genuine Article.
Desc: Serves the Hispanic literary scholar as well as the student of Spanish/Latin American literature; publishes succinct, incisive articles explicating important aspects of past and current Hispanic letters; also contains reviews of selected important recent publications in Hispanic literature; frequent special issues.
Ind/Abst Arts Humanit. Citation Index (19??-19??) [Full Cov.]; Curr. Contents Arts Humanit.; HAPI Hisp. Am. Period. Index; MLA Int. Bibl. Books Artic. Mod. Lang. Lit.; Res. Alert [Full Cov.].

US/0014-4940
EXPLICATOR, THE. [Explicator]. **Added/Corp** University of South Carolina. Virginia Commonwealth University. Vol. 1 (Oct. 1942)-. Periodical. English. Four times a year (Seasonally). $56.00 (institution), $31.00 (individual). Heldref Publications, 1319 Eighteenth Street Northwest, Washington DC 20036-1802. **Tel** (202)296-6267, (800)365-9753, FAX (202)296-5149. **ED** George Arms, John P. Kirby, Nancy C. Martinez, and J. Edwin Whitesell. **LC** PR1; .E9. **DD** 820.5. **[CCC]. Bk Rev. Ad Acc. Circ:** 2,300. available on microfilm and microfiche from University Microfilms International (UMI). Documents available from The Genuine Article, UMI Article Clearinghouse.
Desc: Each issue contains 35-40 short essays of literary explication. Students and teachers of literature find this journal a useful reference source as well as a vehicle for their own informed judgments and interpretations.

Ind/Abst Abstr. Engl. Stud.; Acad. Abstr. Full Text Elite (July 1990-) [Full Txt.]; Acad. Abstr. (July 1990-); Acad. Ind. [Computer File] (1987-); Acad. Search (July 1990-); Annu. Bibliogr. Engl. Lang. Lit.; Arts Humanit. Citation Index [Full Cov.]; Curr. Contents Arts Humanit.; Expand. Acad. Index (1987-); Humanit. Index; Humanit. Source (Jul. 1993-) [Full Txt.]; INFO-SOUTH Abstr.; Lit. Crit. Regist.; Mag. Artic. Summar. Elite (July 1990-) [Full Txt.]; Mag. Artic. Summar. Select (July 1990-); Mag. Artic. Summar. CD-ROM (July 1990-); Mag. Search; MLA Int. Bibl. Books Artic. Mod. Lang. Lit.; Newsp. Period. Abstr. (1986-); Res. Alert [Full Cov.]; Romant. Move.

US/0097-806X
EXPLORATION (NORMAL, ILL.). (EXPLORATION.). [Explor.]. **Added/Corp** MLA Seminar on the Literature of Exploration. (19??)-. English. an. $3.00. Illinois State University / English, Department of English, Normal IL 61761-6901. **Tel** (309)438-5776. **LC** PN56.T7; E9. **DD** 910/.4.
Ind/Abst Abstr. Engl. Stud.

●US/1063-9675
EYEBALL (ST. LOUIS, MO.). (EYEBALL.). [Eyeball]. **VFOAT** Eye Ball. No. 1 (1992)-. Periodical. English. sa. $7.00. Eyeball, PO Box 8135, St. Louis MO 63108. **DD** 818.

RU/0201-6354
EZHEGODNIK KNIGI SSSR. Added/Corp Vsesoiuznaia Knizhnaia Palata. (1935)-. Russian. an. **LC** Z2491; .E9. **NLM** Z 2491 E99. **CODEN** EKNSDY. ***Continues*** *Ezhegodnik Gosudarstvennoi Tsentralnoi Knizhnoi Palaty RSFSR.*

US/1041-8164
F.O.C. REVIEW. [F.O.C. rev.]. **VFOAT** FOC Review; Review. **VAT** Friends of Civilization Review. (1988)-. Periodical. English. qt. $10.00 North America; $20.00 other. FOC Forum Inc, Box 101, Worth IL 60482. **Tel** (708)423-8607, (708)596-4734. **ED** William L Roach and Michael Ogorzaly. **DD** 810. **Bk Rev. Ad Acc. Pr Rev. Circ:** 500.
Desc: Publishes original literature, drawings, and sketches.

US
F. SCOTT FITZGERALD SOCIETY NEWSLETTER. English. sa. $10.00 (membership F.Scott Fitzgerald Society). F. Scott Fitzgerald Society, Hofstra University, English Department, Hempstead NY 11550. **Tel** (516)463-5454. **ED** Ruth Prigozy. **Bk Rev,** (Qty: 3-4). **Circ:** 300.

FR/0755-0960
FABULA (LILLE, FRANCE). (FABULA.). (March 1983)-. Periodical. French (English). sa. 100.00F. Presses Universitaires de France, Department des Revues, 14 Avenue du Bois de l'Epine, BP 90, 91003 Evry Cedex France. **Tel** (1)60 77 82 05, FAX (1) 60 79 20 45, telex PUF 600 474 F. **ED** Jean-Claude Dupas. **LC** PR823; .F3. **DD** 823/.009.
Desc: Devoted mainly to fiction in the English language and open to other debates. Publishes papers in French and English centering on specific topics or problems.
Ind/Abst Curr. Contents Arts Humanit.; MLA Int. Bibl. Books Artic. Mod. Lang. Lit.

US/1057-7459
FAIRFAX (COLUMBIA, MD.). (FAIRFAX : THE MAGAZINE OF SHORT STORIES AND SHORT NOVELS BY BLACK AMERICANS AND OTHER VOICES.). [Fairfax]. **VFOAT** Fairfax Magazine. Vol. 1, No. 1 (Autumn 1991)-. Periodical. English. qt. $22.00 US; $31.00 other. Fairfax Magazine, PO Box 502, Columbia MD 21045. **DD** 813.

FR/1244-5460
FAITS DE LANGUES EVRY. (FAITS DE LANGUES.). (1993)-. French. sa. 300.00F France; 350.00F other. Presses Universitaires de France, Department des Revues, 14 Avenue du Bois de l'Epine, BP 90, 91003 Evry Cedex France. **Tel** (1)60 77 82 05, FAX (1) 60 79 20 45, telex PUF 600 474 F.

US/0014-7079
FALCON (MANSFIELD), THE. (THE FALCON.). No. 1- Summer 1970-. Periodical. English. sa. $2.00. Mansfield State College, Belknap Hall, Mansfield PA 16933. **LC** PS501; .F33. **DD** 810/.5. available on microfilm and microfiche from University Microfilms International (UMI).
Ind/Abst Index Am. Period. Verse.

US/0094-5862
FAMILY ALBUM, THE. English. an. $6.95. **LC** PN6014; .G56. **DD** 808.8. ***Continues*** *Gold Star Family Album.*

US/0363-0560
FAMOUS PULP CLASSICS. No. 1- 1975-. English. $25.00. Fax Collector's Editions, Inc., Box F, West Linn OR 97068. **LC** PS509.A3; F34. **DD** 813/.0876.

US/0014-7508
FANTASTIC. ***Title Change.*** (1952)-(19??). Periodical. English. qt. TSR Inc., PO Box 5695, Boston MA 02206. **Tel** (414)248-3625, FAX (414)248-0389. **LC** AP2; .F178. **DD** 808.83/876/05. ***Absorbed by*** *Amazing, 1058-0751.*

US/0014-7508
FANTASTIC (FLUSHING. 1958). ***Title Change.*** (FANTASTIC.). **VFOAT** Fantastic Stories. Began in (1958)-(19??). Periodical. English. qt. TSR Inc., PO Box 5695, Boston MA 02206. **Tel** (414)248-3625, FAX (414)248-0389. ***Continues*** *Fantastic Science Fiction (New York, N.Y.).* ***Merged with*** *Amazing Stories (Purchase, N.Y. : 1979), 1060-5401* ***to form*** *Amazing, 0279-1706.*

US/0024-984X
FANTASY & SCIENCE FICTION. VFOAT Fantasy and Science Fiction; Magazine of Fantasy & Science Fiction. Vol. 73, No. 4 (Oct. 1987)-. Periodical. English. Eleven times a year. $26.00 US; $31.00 other. Mercury Press / US, 143 West Creamhill Road, West Cornwall CT 06796. **Tel** (203)672-6376, FAX (203)672-2643. Index available (bound in June and Dec. issues). cum. index. **Bk Rev. Ad Acc. Circ:** 60,000. available on microfilm and microfiche from University Microfilms International (UMI). Documents available from UMI Article Clearinghouse. ***Continues*** *Magazine of Fantasy and Science Fiction.*
Ind/Abst Newsp. Period. Abstr. (1988-).

US/0898-5979
FANTASY AND SCIENCE FICTION CONVENTIONEER'S GUIDE, THE. [Fantasy sci. fict. conv. guide]. **VFOAT** Con Guide. Vol. 1, No. 1 (March/May 1988)-. Periodical. English. qt. Impossible Dreams, 6827 Cerro Bajo, San Antonio TX 78239-3606. **DD** 813.

US/0277-0717
FANTASY BOOK. V. 1, No. 1 (Oct. 1981)-. Periodical. English. qt. $12.00. Fantasy Book Publisher, Box 60126, Pasadena CA 91106. **ED** Nick Smith. **Bk Rev. Ad Acc. Circ:** 4,000 (ctrl).
Desc: Features illustrated short fiction with an emphasis on fantasy and science fiction.

US/1051-5011
FANTASY COMMENTATOR. [Fantasy comment.]. (19??)-. Periodical. English. sa. $10.00 North America; $11.00 other. A Langley Searles Ed and Publisher, 48 Highland Circle, Bronxville NY 10708-5909. **Tel** (914)961-6799. **ED** A Langley Searles. **DD** 813. Index available. cum. index. **Bk Rev. Pr Rev. Circ:** 500.
Desc: Devoted to articles, reviews and verse in the area of science fiction and fantasy.
Ind/Abst Sci. Fict. Fantasy Book Rev. Index.

US/0271-7808
FANTASY VOICES. Vol. 1 (1982)-. Periodical. English. ir. Borgo Press, PO Box 2845, San Bernardino CA 92406. **Tel** (714)884-5813, (714)885-1161. **LC** PS374.F27; F36. **DD** 813/.0876/09.

US/0094-0887
FAR-WESTERN FORUM. ***Suspended.*** [Far-west. forum]. Vol. 1 (Feb. 1974)-(1988). English. Three times a year. $10.00 (institutions); $8.00 (individuals). Far-Western Forum, 20 Poppy Lane, Berkeley CA 94708. **LC** PN2; .F36. **DD** 809.
Ind/Abst Abstr. Engl. Stud.; MLA Int. Bibl. Books Artic. Mod. Lang. Lit.

US/0748-6022
FARMER'S MARKET (GALESBURG, ILL.). (FARMER'S MARKET.). Vol. 1, No. 1 (Feb. 1982)-. Periodical. English. sa. $12.00 US; $14.00 other. Midwest Farmer's Market, PO Box 1272, Galesburg IL 61402. **Tel** (309)828-2373. **ED** Jean C Lee. **Circ:** 500.
Desc: A magazine dedicated to the tradition of midwestern regional literature.
Ind/Abst Am. Humanit. Index; Index Am. Period. Verse.

US/0884-2949
FAULKNER JOURNAL, THE. [Faulkner j.]. **Added/Corp** Ohio Northern University. **VFOAT** FJ. Vol. 1, No. 1 Fall (1985)-. Academic Scholarly Publication. English. sa (March and September). $12.00 (individual); $18.00 (institution) US, Canada and Mexico; $25.00 other. Faulkner Journal/English Department, Professor D. Trouard, University of Akron, Akron OH 44325. **Tel** (216)972-5194. **ED** Dawn Trouard (editor's address: Faulkner Journal, Leigh Hall Room 204 B, Akron, Ohio 44325-1913, (216)972-5194). **LC** PS3511.A86; Z4584. **DD** 813/.52. **Ad Acc, Adv Mgr:** Dawn Trouard. **Circ:** 300. available on microfilm and microfiche from University Microfilms International (UMI).
Desc: Publishes scholarly criticism of William Faulkner.
Ind/Abst MLA Int. Bibl. Books Artic. Mod. Lang. Lit.

NE/0167-9392
FAUX TITRE: ETUDES DE LANGUE ET LITTERATURE FRANCAISES PUBLIEES. **See** Linguistics.

SP
FAVENTIA. (1979)-. Catalan (French, English and Spanish). sa. Departament de Classiques, Facultat de Lettre, Publicacions de la Universitat Autonoma de Barcelona, Barcelona Spain.

US/0197-5137
FEASTS & SEASONS. VFOAT Feasts and Seasons. Vol. 1, No. 1 (Jan./Feb. 1980)-. Periodical. English. bm. $20.00 US; $25.00 other. Cahill and Company, 145 Palisade Street, Dobbs Ferry NY 10525. **Tel** (800)448-8311. **LC** PN6010.5; .F4. **DD** 808.8.

CN/0712-3566
FENAISON. [Fenaison]. 1-. Periodical. French. ir. Fenaison, c/o Petit Seminaire de Quebec, 6 rue de l'Universite, CP 6000 H-V, Quebec Quebec G1R 4V6 Canada. **Tel** (418)694-1020. **DD** C840/.8/092375. ctrl circ.

AU
FETTFLECK. (1976)-. German. ir. $12.00 single issue. Antonio Fian, Auenweg 6, 9800 Spittal/Drau Austria. **LC** PT3827.C3; F47.

SP/0214-3771
FGL : BOLETIN DE LA FUNDACION FEDERICO GARCIA LORCA. Added/Corp Fundacion Federico Garcia Lorca. **VFOAT** Boletin de la Fundacion Federico Garcia Lorca. Vol. 1, No. 1 (Jan. 1987)-. Periodical. Spanish. Twice a year. 1200ptas. Fundacion Federico Garcia, Residencia Estudiante Pinar 21, Madrid 28006 Spain. **Tel** 011 34 1 2615779.
Ind/Abst MLA Int. Bibl. Books Artic. Mod. Lang. Lit.

US/0046-3736
FICTION. Vol. 1, (1972)-. Periodical. English. sa. $10.00 US; $15.00 other. City College of New York Department of English, Convent Avenue and 138th Street, New York NY 10031. **Tel** (212)650-6319. **LC** PN6010.5; .F53. **DD** 808.83/1. available on microfilm and microfiche from University Microfilms International (UMI).

AT/0819-5358
FICTION FOCUS. Added/Corp Western Australia. Ministry of Education. Curriculum Services Branch. Vol. 1, No. 1 (1987)-. Periodical. English. Twice a year (May & Oct.). 24.00Aus$. Ministry of Education / CMIS, 151 Royal Street, East Perth WA 6004 Australia. **Tel** 011 61 9 4204594, 011 61 9 4204515, FAX 011 61 09 4205005. **LC** Z1037.A1; F53. **DD** 028.5/35. Index available. cum. index. **Bk Rev. Circ:** 300.
Desc: Primarily fiction reviews of resources suitable for teenagers. A feature article is included in each issue.

US/0092-1912
FICTION INTERNATIONAL. [Fict. int.]. No. 1 (Fall 1973)-. Periodical. English. Twice a year (May, Oct.). $28.00 US; $33.00 Canada and Mexico; $36.00 other (institutions); $14.00 US; $19.00 Canada and Mexico; $22.00 others (individuals). San Diego State University Press, San Diego State University, San Diego CA 92182. **Tel** (619)594-6220. **ED** Harold Jaffe. **LC** PN3311; .F53. **DD** 805. **Bk Rev,** (Qty: 1-2). **Ad Acc, Adv Mgr:** S. Dollente, **Tel** (619)357-5536. **Circ:** 750. available on microfilm and microfiche from University Microfilms International (UMI).
Desc: International, innovative and postmodern fiction.
Ind/Abst Abstr. Engl. Stud.; Am. Humanit. Index (?-199?); Book Rev. Index.

US/0883-7503
FICTION (NOVATO, CALIF.). (FICTION.). [Fiction]. (1983)-. English. an. $8.95. Exile Press, 241 South Temelec Circle, PO Box 1768, Sonoma CA 95475. **Tel** (415)883-2132. **ED** Guy Daniels and Leslie Woolf Hedley. **LC** PS648.S5; F53. **DD** 813/.01/08.

UK/1350-4339
FICTION ON FICHE. (19??)-. English. qt. £175.00. British Library / Bibliographic Service, Boston Spa, Wetherby West Yorkshire LS23 7BQ England. **Tel** 011 44 937 546160, FAX 011 44 937 546586, telex 557381. **(Subscription address:** Turpin Distribution Services Limited, Blackhorse Road, Letchworth, Hertfordshire SG6 1HN, United Kingdom.**)**
Desc: Microfiche listing by author of adult novels and short story collections published worldwide in English, gaelic, Welsh and Irish since 1950.

CN/0015-0630
FIDDLEHEAD, THE. [Fiddlehead]. **Added/Corp** Bliss Carman Society of Fredericton. University of New Brunswick. Dept. of English. No. 1 (Feb. 1945)-. Periodical. English. qt. $28.00 (one year), $48.00 (two years) institutions; $24.00 (one year), $40.00 (two years) individuals. University of New Brunswick, PO Box 4400, Fredericton New Brunswick, E3B 5A3 Canada. **Tel** (506)453-4506, FAX (506)453-3538, telex 014-46202. **ED** Don McKay. **LC** PR9291.N4; F5. **DD** C810/.80054. **Bk Rev. Ad Acc. Circ:** 1,000 (ctrl). available on microfilm from Micromedia Limited. Documents available from The Genuine Article.
Desc: From its beginnings in 1945 as a local little magazine devoted mainly to student writers, it retains an interest in poets and writers of the Atlantic region and in young writers. However, in printing fiction and poetry from everywhere on the sole criterion of excellence, it is open to good work of every kind, looking always for vitality, freshness and surprise.
Ind/Abst Am. Humanit. Index; Arts Humanit. Citation Index [Full Cov.]; Can. Index; Can. Lit. Index (1985-1986); Can. Period. Index; Curr. Contents Arts Humanit.; Index Book Rev. Humanit.; Res. Alert [Full Cov.].

IT/0391-2493
FILOLOGIA E CRITICA (SALERNO EDITRICE). (FILOLOGIA E CRITICA.). Vol. 1, Issue 1 (Jan./April 1976)-. Periodical. Italian. Three times a year. L65000 Italy; L78500 other. Salerno Editrice, Via di Donna Olimpia 20, 00152 Rome Italy. **Tel** 011 39 6 58205684 or 688, FAX 06-53-15-688. **ED** Enrico Malato. cum. index. **Bk Rev. Circ:** 600.
Desc: Research on history of Italian literature and Italian romance philology.
Ind/Abst Romant. Move. (19??-).

PL
FILOLOGIA POLSKA. Main/Corp Oppeln. Wyzsza Szkoa Pedagogiczna. Vol. 13 (1975)-. Periodical. Polish. ir. Z700.00-Z1,200 Poland; $9.00-$12.00 US. Adam Mickiewicz University Press, Nowowiejskiego 55, 61734 Poznan Poland. **Tel** 011 48 527-380, FAX 011 48 61-526425. Index available. **Ad Acc. Circ:** 500. ***Continues*** *Historia Literatury.*
Desc: Every volume of the series is the monography written by one author. Respective issues are devoted to the polish literature or linguistic problems.

US
FINDING THE RIGHT SPEAKER. English. $10.00 members; $20.00 nonmembers. American Society of Association Executives, 1575 Eye Street NW, Washington DC 20005. **Tel** (202)626-2735, (202)626-2722, FAX (202)371-8825. **LC** PN4007; .F56. **DD** 808.5/1/02573.

AT/0818-3473
FINE LINE. [Fine line]. (1987)-. Periodical. English. an. 10.00Aus$ (Australia); 12.60 (US, Canada, UK, & Europe); 13.00Aus$ (other). Burnt Circle Books, PO Box 212, Brooklyn Park SA, 5032 Australia. **ED** Scott McCaffrey. **DD** 808.04275. **Ad Acc. Circ:** 700 (ctrl).
Desc: Journal of new writing including poetry, fiction, reviews and interviews.

US/0737-4704
FINE MADNESS. Added/Corp Had We But, Inc. Vol. 1, No. 1 (Summer/Fall 1982)-. Periodical. English. ir. $10.00 US; $12.00 other. Fine Madness, PO Box 31138, Seattle WA 98115-0176. **Tel** (206)632-0573. **ED** Sean Bentley, Louis Bergsagel, John Marshall, John Malek and C. Christine Deavel. **LC** PS615; .F46. **DD** 811/.54/08. **Bk Rev. Circ:** 750.
Desc: Publishes poems and fiction being written. The writing shows that a mind is working, not just a tongue.
Ind/Abst Am. Humanit. Index.

UK/0267-9612
FINNEGANS WAKE CIRCULAR, A. Vol. 1, No. 1 (Autumn 1985)-. Periodical. English. qt. £6.00 (UK); £7.00 (Europe); £8.00 (other). Finnegans Wake Circular, 100 Congleton Road, Sandbach Cheshire CW11 0DQ England.
Ind/Abst MLA Int. Bibl. Books Artic. Mod. Lang. Lit.

UK
FIREBIRD (HARMONDSWORTH, MIDDLESEX). (FIREBIRD.). 1-. Periodical. English. an. **LC** PR1307; .F53. **DD** 823/.008.

US/0898-0233
FIVE FINGERS REVIEW. [Five fingers rev.]. No. 1 (1984)-. Periodical. English. sa. $15.00 (one year), $28.00 (two year). Five Fingers Review, PO Box 15426, San Francisco CA 94115. **Tel** (415)661-8052. **DD** 810.
Desc: Covers modern American literature and poetry.
Ind/Abst Am. Humanit. Index (?-199?); Index Am. Period. Verse.

SP/1131-8848
FLORENTIA ILIBERRITANA. (1990)-. Periodical. Multiple languages. an. 4854ptas. Universidad de Granada / Campus de Cartuja, 18071 Granada Spain. **Tel** 011 34 58 243930, 243931. **UDC** 87.09.
Ind/Abst BHA : Biblio. Hist. Art.

US/0742-2466
FLORIDA REVIEW (ORLANDO, FLA.), THE. See Literature-Poetry.

US/1040-3205
FOCUSES (BOONE, N.C.). See Journalism.

GW/0015-5322
FOGRA-LITERATURDIENST. [Fogra-Literaturd.]. (1963)-. German. mo. Fogra, Streitfeldstrasse 19, D 81673 Munich Germany. **Tel** 011 49 89 431623. **UDC** 655.2/.3(01).
Ind/Abst Abstr. Bull. Inst. Pap. Sci. Tech.

AG
FOLIA LITERARIA. Added/Corp Ateneo Escritores de Moreno. (September 1977)-. Spanish.

US/0882-3030
FOLIO (BROCKPORT, N.Y.). ***Ceased.*** (FOLIO.). [Folio]. Began in 1970-Ceased with 1990 Iss. 19. Monographic series. English (French and Spanish). Department of Foreign Languages, State University of New York, Brockport NY 14420. **Tel** (716)395-2269. **ED** Martha O'Nan. **DD** 809. **UDC** 800.7. **Bk Rev. Ad Acc. Circ:** 500 (ctrl).
Desc: Contains articles on foreign languages and literatures.
Ind/Abst MLA Int. Bibl. Books Artic. Mod. Lang. Lit.; Print. Abstr.

US
FOLK LITERATURE OF THE SEPHARDIC JEWS. Vol. 1 (1971)-. English. ir. University of California Press, 2120 Berkeley Way, Berkeley CA 94720. **Tel** (510)642-4191, (510)642-3907, FAX (510)642-9917. **ED** James Kubeck.
Desc: Folk literature of the Sephardic Jews.

GW/0015-6175
FONTANE BLATTER. [Fontane-Bl.]. **Added/Corp** Kreis der Freunde Theodor Fontanes. Deutsche Staatsbibiothek. Theodor-Fontane-Archiv. Vol. 1 (1965)-. Periodical. German. sa. 15.40M. Theodor Fontane Archiv, Dortustr. 30-34, Postfach 59, 1561 Potsdam, Germany. **Tel** 0331-22983. **LC** PT1863.Z7; F58. cum. index. **Bk Rev. Circ:** 1,000 (ctrl).
Desc: Unknown texts by Theodore Fontane. Secondary literature: interpretations, analyses, comparatives, literary-historicals. Personal bibliographies.
Ind/Abst MLA Int. Bibl. Books Artic. Mod. Lang. Lit.

AN
FONTES RERUM MEXICANARUM. V. 1/1-. Periodical. Spanish (French and German; summaries and/or abstracts in English, French and German). ir. Akademische Druck & Verlagsanstalt, Schoenaugasse 6, Postfach 598, A 8010 Graz Austria. **Tel** 011 43 316 813460.

US/0192-8090
FOOM. No. 1- Spring 1973-. Periodical. English. qt. $4.00. Marvel Entertainment Group Inc., 387 Park Avenue South, New York NY 10016. **Tel** (212)576-8595, FAX (212) 576-9289. **LC** PN6725; .F65. **DD** 741.5/973.

IT
FORME E LA STORIA, LE. Vol. 1, No. 1-2 (1980)-. Periodical. Italian (English and French). Twice a year (June & Dec.). L50000 Italy; L80000 others. Rubbettino Editore, Viale dei Pini 8, 88049 Soveria Mannelli Italy. **Tel** 011 39 0968-662034, FAX 011 39 968-662035. **ED** Professor Mieolo Mineo and Professor Sergio Romagnoli. Index available. **Bk Rev. Ad Acc. Pr Rev. Circ:** 1,000 (ctrl).

GW/0934-5337
FORSCHUNGEN ZU PAUL VALERY. Added/Corp Universitat Kiel. Forschungs- und Dokumentationszentrum Paul Valery. **VFOAT** Recherches Valeryennes; Valery-Forschungen. (1988)-. Periodical. German.
Ind/Abst MLA Int. Bibl. Books Artic. Mod. Lang. Lit.

GW/0177-9370
FORSCHUNGEN ZUR GESCHICHTE DER ALTEREN DEUTSCHEN LITERATUR. [Forsch. Gesch. alteren dtsch. Lit.]. (1980)-. Monographic series. German. Wilhelm Fink Verlag, Ohmstrasse 5, D 80802 Munich Germany. **Tel** 011 49 89 348017, 348018. **LC** UNC.
Ind/Abst MLA Int. Bibl. Books Artic. Mod. Lang. Lit.

US/0000-0965
FORTHCOMING BOOKS FOR CHILDREN. ***Ceased.*** [Bowker's forthcom. child. books]. Vol. 1, No. 1 (March-July 1987)-Ceased (Sept. 1989). Periodical. English. bm. R R Bowker, A Reed Reference Publishing Company, Part of Reed International PLC, PO Box 31, 121 Chanlon Drive, New Providence NJ 07974. **Tel** (908)464-6800, (800)521-8110, FAX (908)665-6688, telex 138-755. **DD** 028. **[CCC].**

CI/0015-8445
FORUM. Added/Corp Jugoslavenska Akademija Znanosti i Umjetnosti. Razred za Suvremenu Knjizevnost. Hrvatska Akademija Znanosti i Umjetnosti. Razred za Knjizevnost. Vol. 1 (1962)-. Periodical. Serbo-Croatian (Roman). ir. $60.00. Hrvatska Akademija Znanosti i Umjetnosti / Croatian Academy of Sciences & Arts, Zrinski TRG 11, 41000 Zagreb Croatia. **Tel** 011 38 41 433 661, FAX 011 38 41 433 383. **LC** AP56; .F6.
Desc: Information on Croatian literature.
Ind/Abst MLA Int. Bibl. Books Artic. Mod. Lang. Lit.

NE/0015-8496
FORUM DER LETTEREN. [Forum lett.]. Vol. 1 (Feb. 1960)-. Periodical. Dutch. Four times a year (Mar., June, Sept., Dec.). Price varies. Smits B V, Westeinde 135, 2512 GW Den Haag Netherlands. **Tel** 011 31 70 895390. **LC** PN9; .F65. Index available (Free). **Bk Rev. Ad Acc. Circ:** 800 (ctrl). ***Continues*** *Museum, 0169-5657.*
Desc: Literature and linguistic articles and reviews.
Ind/Abst Am. Hist. Life (1955-1956, 1962-1977); Annu. Bibliogr. Engl. Lang. Lit.; MLA Int. Bibl. Books Artic. Mod. Lang. Lit.

UK/0015-8518
FORUM FOR MODERN LANGUAGE STUDIES. See Linguistics.

GW/0931-4091
FORUM HOMOSEXUALITAT UND LITERATURE. Added/Corp Universitat-Gesamthochschule-Siegen. Forschungsschwerpunkt Homosexualitat und Literatur. **VFOAT** Forum; Homosexualitat und Literatur. (1987)-. Periodical. German. Three times a year. DM15.00. Forum Homosexualitot Und Literatur Universitaet-Gh Siegen, FB 3, Postfach 101240, 5900 Siegen Germany. **Tel** 0271 740 4597, FAX 0271 740 2330. **ED** Wolfgang Popp. **LC** PN56.H57; F68. **DD** 809/.93353/05. Index available. cum. index. **Bk Rev**, (Qty: 10). **Ad Acc, Adv Mgr:** Wolfgang Popp. Full Page (B&W) DM250. Half Page (B&W) DM150. **Acid Free.** ctrl circ.
Desc: Scientific discussion forum on questions of the connection between literature and homosexuality. Essays on homosexual writers and terms in literary works; forgotten primar texts of elder german authors; selecting bibliography on actual prints.
Ind/Abst MLA Int. Bibl. Books Artic. Mod. Lang. Lit.

US/0014-5858
FORUM ITALICUM. [Forum ital.]. **VFOAT** Fl. Vol. 1, No. 1 (Jan. 1967)-. Periodical. English (French, Italian, Portuguese and Spanish). sa. $30.00 institutions; $20.00 individuals. Center for Italian Studies, State University of New York at Stony Brook, Forum Italicum: A Journal of, Italian Studies, Stony Brook NY 11794-3359. **Tel** (516)632-7444. **ED** M Ricciardelli and Albert N Mancini. **LC** PQ4001; .F67. cum. index. **Bk Rev. Ad Acc. Circ:** 1200 (ctrl). Documents available from The Genuine Article.
Desc: Literature, language and culture of Italy and other countries in relation to Italy. Includes poetry, fiction and translations.
Ind/Abst Arts Humanit. Citation Index [Full Cov.]; Curr. Contents Arts Humanit.; MLA Int. Bibl. Books Artic. Mod. Lang. Lit.; Res. Alert [Full Cov.]; Romant. Move.; Soc. Plann. Policy Dev. Abstr.; Sociol. Abstr.

US/0306-4964
FOUNDATION. Added/Corp Science Fiction Foundation. No. 1 (Mar. 1972)-. Periodical. English. tq. £22.50 (surface mail); £25.00 (airmail). New Worlds, 71 73 Charing Cross Road, London WC2 England. **LC** PN3448.S45; F68. **DD** 823/.0876/09. Index Available Published separately--free--upon request.
Ind/Abst MLA Int. Bibl. Books Artic. Mod. Lang. Lit.

UK/0306-4964
FOUNDATION (DAGENHAM). (FOUNDATION.). [Foundation]. **Added/Corp** Science Fiction Foundation. North East London Polytechnic. (Mar. 1972)-. Periodical. English. Three times a year. £22.50. New Worlds, 71 73 Charing Cross Road, London WC2 England. **LC** PS374.S35; F68. **DD** 813/.0876/09. cum. index.
Ind/Abst Child. Lit. Abstr. (19??-); MLA Int. Bibl. Books Artic. Mod. Lang. Lit.; Sci. Fict. Fantasy Book Rev. Index.

UK
FOUNDATION: THE REVIEW OF SCIENCE FICTION. English. ir. £20.00 per vol. Science Fiction Foundation, Longbridge Road, Dagenham, Essex RM8 2AS England. **Tel** 011 44 1 590 7722 ext. 2179.

●US/1070-7549
FOUR DIRECTIONS (TELLICO PLAINS, TENN.), THE. (THE FOUR DIRECTIONS : AMERICAN INDIAN LITERARY QUARTERLY.). [Four dir.]. **VFOAT** American Indian Literary Quarterly. Vol. 1, No. 1 (Winter 1992)-. Periodical. English. qt. $21.00 (one year), $38.00 (two years), $56.00 (three years) US; $24.20 (one year), $44.40 (two years), $65.60 (three years) Canada; $24.60 (one year), $45.20 (two years), $66.80 (three years) other. Snowbird Publishing Co., PO Box 729, Tellico Plains TN 37385. **Tel** (615)982-7261, FAX (615)681-3418. **ED** Joanna and William Meyer. **LC** PS508.I5; F68. **DD** 810. Index available (bound in 4th issue). **Bk Rev**, (Qty: 4 or more). **Ad Acc, Adv Mgr:** William Meyer. **Circ:** 750.
Desc: All writing by American Indian poets, authors, scholars. Poetry, short stories, essays, articles, reviews, commentaries.

US/0015-9107
FOUR QUARTERS. [Four q.]. **Added/Corp** La Salle College. (1951)-. Periodical. English. Twice a year (Nov., May). $8.00 (one year); $13.00 (two year); $20.00 (three year). La Salle University, 1900 West Olney Avenue, Philadelphia PA 19141. **Tel** (215)951-1145, 951-1600, FAX (215)951-1488. **ED** John J. Keenan. **LC** AP2; .F853. **DD** 051. Index available. cum. index. **Bk Rev. Ad Acc, Adv Mgr:** J. Cawley. **Circ:** 1,000. available on microfilm and microfiche from University Microfilms International (UMI).
Desc: Fiction, poetry and essays for college-educated audience with literary interests. Emphasis is on technical mastery with genuine insight.
Ind/Abst Am. Humanit. Index (-199?); Annu. Bibliogr. Engl. Lang. Lit.; Index Am. Period. Verse.

US/0198-9928
FOUR ZOAS JOURNAL. Began publication with No. 1 in 1972. Periodical. English. $12.50 for 3 numbers. Four Zoas, 86 West Alverd, Springfield IL 01108.

Literature

US/0015-9220
FOXFIRE. [Foxfire]. Vol. 1 (Spring 1967)-. Periodical. English. sa. $12.95. Foxfire Fund Inc, c/o Ann Moore, PO Box 541, Mountain City GA 30562. **Tel** (706)746-5828, FAX (706)746-3185. **ED** Sabrina J. Ritchie. **LC** PS1; .F68. **DD** 917.5. **Circ:** 2,000 (ctrl). available on microfiche (Library of Congress) from University Microfilms International (UMI).
 Desc: The contents are drawn from the indigenous Appalachian culture from which the Rabun County High School students who edit it hail.
 Ind/Abst Access (1976-1987); MLA Int. Bibl. Books Artic. Mod. Lang. Lit.

●XO
FRAGMENT. Roc.6, 1 (1992)-. Periodical. Czech. **Continues** Fragment K.

US
FRAGMENTOS DE BARRO. VFOAT Pieces of Clay. 1st (Spring 1976)-. Periodical. English (Spanish). an. San Diego Mesa College, 7250 Mesa College Drive, San Diego CA 92111. **LC** PS508.M4; F72. **DD** 810/.8/086872.

FR/0222-0334
FRANCE LATINE, LA. See Linguistics.

FR/1157-3732
FRANCIS BULLETIN SIGNALETIQUE. 523, HISTOIRE ET SCIENCES DE LA LITTERATURE. Added/Corp Institut de l'Information Scientifique et Technique (France). Sciences Humaines et Sociales. VFOAT Histoire et Sciences de la Litterature; History and Sciences of Literature. Vol. 45, No. 1 (1991)-. Bulletin. French. qt (4 issues). 575.00F France; 605.00F other. CNRS / Institut d'Information Scientifique et Technique, (Centre National de la Recherche Scientifique), 15 Quai Anatole France, Paris 75700 France. **Tel** 011 33 1 47531515, telex 299 356 F. **(Subscription address:** Institut d'Information Scientifique et Technique Diffusion, 2 Allee du Parc de Brabois, 54514 Vandoeuvre Nancy France.) **LC** Z6513; .B82. Index available (free). available on CD-ROM. **Continues** Bulletin Signaletique. 523, Histoire et Sciences de la Litterature.

IT
FRANCOFONIA. Added/Corp Universita di Bologna. (Fall 1981)-. Periodical. French (French). sa. L50000 Italy; L65000 other. Casa Editrice Leo S. Olschki, Viuzzo del Pozzetto, Casella Postale 66, 50126 Florence Italy. **Tel** 011 39 55 6530684, FAX 011 39 55 6530214. **ED** Liano Petroni. Index available. **Bk Rev**, (Qty: 12/yr). **Ad Acc. Circ:** 184 (ctrl).
 Desc: Studies and research in French literature.
 Ind/Abst MLA Int. Bibl. Books Artic. Mod. Lang. Lit.

FR
FRANCOIS MAURIAC. 1- 1975-. French. Lettres Modernes Minard, 45 rue de Saint Andre, 14123 Fleury Surrey Orne France. **Tel** 011 33 31 844706. **LC** PN3; .R4 subser. **DD** 848/.9/1209.

US
FRANK NORRIS STUDIES. English. sa (May & Oct.). (Comes with Frank Norris Society membership). Frank Norris Society Inc, Florida State University, English Department, Tallahassee FL 32306. **Tel** (904)664-1522. **Pr Rev.**
 Ind/Abst MLA Int. Bibl. Books Artic. Mod. Lang. Lit.

UK
FREDERIC W. H. MYERS MEMORIAL LECTURES. Monographic series. English.

CN/0714-4172
FREE-FALL (BANFF, ALTA.). (FREE-FALL.). [Free-fall]. 1975-. Periodical. English. an. Free. Banff Centre, School of Fine Arts, Box 1020, Banff Alberta T0L 0C0 Canada. **Tel** (403)762-6159. **DD** C810/.8/0054. ctrl circ.

US/0016-0369
FREE LANCE, THE. (1953)-. Periodical. English. an. Free Lance, 6005 Grand Avenue, Cleveland OH 44104. **Tel** (216)431-7116. **LC** PS501; .F7.

UK
FREE-LANCE WRITING & PHOTOGRAPHY. See Photography and Video.

CN/0705-1379
FREELANCE (REGINA). (FREELANCE.). **Added/Corp** Saskatchewan Writers' Guild. (1969)-. Periodical. English. Ten times a year. 40.00Can$ Comes with Saskatchewan Writers Guild membership. Saskatchewan Writers Guild, PO Box 1154, Regina SASK S4P 3R9 Canada. **Tel** (306)757-6310. **ED** April Davies. **DD** C810/.9/0054. **Bk Rev**. **Ad Acc. Circ:** 600 (ctrl).
 Desc: News on the writing scene in Saskatchewan and Canada. Columns on writing, market information: also poetry and short fiction, reviews, comment.

AU
FREIBORD. (March 1976)-. Periodical. German. qt. S40.00 single issue. Freibord, Aegidig 6/19, 1060 Vienna Austria. **LC** PT1141.A2; F69. **DD** 830/.8/00914.

US
FRENCH FORUM MONOGRAPHS. (1976)-. Monographic series. English. ir. Price varies per volume. French Forum, PO Box 130, Nicholasville KY 40340. **Tel** (606)885-1446.
 Ind/Abst MLA Int. Bibl. Books Artic. Mod. Lang. Lit.

US/0271-6607
FRENCH LITERATURE SERIES. See Literary and Political Reviews.

AT
FRENCH MONOGRAPHS. See Linguistics.

UK/0262-2750
FRENCH STUDIES BULLETIN. [Fr. stud. bull.] **Added/Corp** Society for French Studies (Great Britain). No. 1 (1982)-. Bulletin. English. Four times a year. 60.00F Comes with French Studies membership. Society for French Studies, C/O J. M. Lewis, Queens University, Department of French, Belfast BT7 INN North Ireland.
 Ind/Abst MLA Int. Bibl. Books Artic. Mod. Lang. Lit.

SA/0259-0247
FRENCH STUDIES IN SOUTHERN AFRICA. [Fr. stud. South. Afr.]. **Added/Corp** Cahiers de l'AFSSA. No. 1- 1971/72-. French (English). ir (one to two issues per year). R12.00 South Africa; $4.60 US. University of Pretoria / Department of French, Pretoria 0002 South Africa. **Tel** 012 4202031. **(Subscription address:** University of Cape Town, Department of French, Rondebosh 7700 South Africa) **ED** Leopold Peeters, Jane Robertson, Edgar Sienaert. **LC** PQ2; .F73. **DD** 840/.9/968. Index available. cum. index. **Bk Rev**. **Ad Acc. Circ:** 320.
 Desc: Contains the discussion of topics in French language and literature problems of teaching French in third world countries and societies.
 Ind/Abst MLA Int. Bibl. Books Artic. Mod. Lang. Lit.; Romant. Move.

US/0085-0888
FRENCH XX BIBLIOGRAPHY. See Literature-Abstracting, Bibliographies and Statistics.

GW
FRIEDRICH GOTTLIEB KLOPSTOCK WERKE UND BRIEFE. (19??)-. German. ir. DM528.00 (latest issue). Walter de Gruyter Inc., PO Box 303421, D 10728 Berlin Germany. **Tel** 011 49 30 260050, FAX 011 49 30 26005251.

●US/1069-5656
FRINGE WARE REVIEW. See Computers-Computer Industry and Industry Directories.

CN/0709-2830
FRONT (KINGSTON. 1978). (THE FRONT.). [Front]. 3 (Aug. 1978)-. Periodical. English. The Front, PO Box 1355, Kingston Ontario K7L 5C6 Canada. **DD** C810/.8/0054. **Continues in part** It Needs to Be Said/The Front, 0383-6622.

FR/0760-7237
FRUITS. No. 1, (Dec. 1983)-. Periodical. French. IRFA Inst Rech Fruits Agrumes, BP 5035, 34032 Montpellier France. **Tel** 011 33 1 45531692, telex 610992. **LC** PN3; .F78. **DD** 805.
 Ind/Abst Hortic. Abstr.; Leis. Recreat. Tour. Abstr.; Protozoolog. Abstr.; Rev. Med. Vet. Mycology; Rev. Plant Pathol.; Rural Dev. Abstr.; World Agric. Econ.

CH
FU-CHIEN WEN HSUEH. VFOAT Fujian Wenxue. Periodical. Chinese. mo. $9.18. Science Press, 16 Donghuangchenggen North Street, Beijing 100707, People's Republic of China. **Tel** 011 86 1 4019821, 011 86 1 4010642, FAX 011 86 1 4012180, 011 86 1 4019810, telex 210147. **LC** PL3031.F82; F83.

CH/1015-0021
FU JEN STUDIES : LITERATURE & LINGUISTICS. See Linguistics.

NE/0929-9998
FUNCTIONS OF LANGUAGE. See Linguistics.

GW/0176-2753
FUNDEVOGEL. (1984)-. German. Dipa-Verlag, Nassauer Str. 1, 6000 Frankfurt 50, Germany.
 Ind/Abst Child. Lit. Abstr. (19??-).

●US/1065-7983
FURIOUS FICTIONS. [Furious fict.]. (1992)-. Periodical. English. Three times a year. $13.00. Furious Fictions, PO Box 423665, San Francisco CA 94142. **Tel** (415)431-0461. **ED** Joseph Lerner. **DD** 808. **Bk Rev**. **Ad Acc. Circ:** 1,600.
 Desc: Includes short works of fiction and poetry by new and emerging writers.

US/8756-8640
G. W. REVIEW, THE. [G.W. rev.]. VFOAT GW Review. Vol. 1, No. 1 (1980)-. Periodical. English. Twice a year. $4.00. G W Review, Box 20 Marvin Center, George Washington University, 800 21st Street NW. **ED** April Robbins. **LC** PS501; .G2. **DD** 810/.8.
 Desc: Publishes fiction, poetry and essays.

SP
GACETA LITERARIA. See Linguistics.

FR/0047-4916
GAI SABER (TOLOZA). (GAI SABER.). [Gai saber]. No. 1, (1919)-. Periodical. Langue d'oc. Four times a year. 78.36F France; 90.00F others. Gai Saber, les Dames, 31320 Aureville France. **Tel** 011 33 61730870.
 Ind/Abst MLA Int. Bibl. Books Artic. Mod. Lang. Lit.

JA
GAIKOKU BUNGAKU. Multiple languages (Japanese and English). Utsunomiya Daigaku Gaikoku Bungaku Kenkyushitsu, Minemachi 350, Utsunomiya 320 Japan. **LC** PN9; .G3.

US/0435-0464
GALAXY MAGAZINE. (GALAXY READER.). 1st-. Periodical. English. Doubleday & Company Inc, 501 Franklin Avenue, Garden City NY 11530. **ED** H L Gold. **LC** PZ1.G22; Gal.

●US/1066-7709
GALE'S LITERARY INDEX. (GALE'S LITERARY INDEX [COMPUTER FILE].). [Gale's lit. index]. **Added/Corp** Gale Research Inc. VFOAT Literary Index. (Feb. 1993)-. English. $149.00 (IBM single version), $225.00 (IBM network version). Gale Research Inc., 835 Penobscot Building, Detroit MI 48226. **Tel** (800)877-GALE, (313)961-2242, FAX (313)961-6083, telex TWX 810-221-7086. **DD** 016.
 Desc: Lets users access information by author, title, Gale series title, author birth and death years or nationality.

SP
GALIBO : REVISTA DE LITERATURA. Periodical. French (Spanish). Ediciones Norba 10004, Apartado de Correos 423, Caceres Spain. **LC** PN6; .G35. **DD** 840.8/0005.

IT/0016-4097
GALLERIA. [Galleria]. (1951)-. Periodical. Italian. Three times a year. L30000 Italy; L60000 others. Salvatore Sciascia Editore, Corso Unmerto 111, 93100 Caltanissetta Italy. **Tel** 011 39 934 551509.
 Ind/Abst Arts Humanit. Citation Index (19??-19??) [Full Cov.]; MLA Int. Bibl. Books Artic. Mod. Lang. Lit.

US/0161-2549
GALLIMAUFRY. Vol. 1, (Summer 1973)-. Periodical. English. Four times a year (Jan., Apr., July, Oct.). 24.00Aus$ (non-members), 20.00Aus$ (members). Project Adventure Australia, 332 Banyule Road, View Bank Victoria 3085 Australia. **Tel** 011 61 3 4576494. **ED** M. MacArthur. **LC** PS501; .G34. **DD** 810.8/005/4. **Bk Rev. Circ:** 200.

SW/0280-6487
GARDAR. [Gardar]. **Added/Corp** Samfundet Sverige-Island. Statens Humanistiska Forskningsrad. (1970)-. Periodical. Multiple languages (Swedish and Icelandic; summaries and/or abstracts available). an. **Ind/Abst** MLA Int. Bibl. Books Artic. Mod. Lang. Lit.

NP
GARIMA. Periodical. Nepali (Nepali). Rs5.00. **LC** PK2598.A2; G34.

US
GARLAND LIBRARY OF MEDIEVAL LITERATURE. Vol. 1 (1981)-. Monographic series. English. Garland Publishing, 1000A Sherman Avenue, Hamden CT 06514. **Tel** (800)627-6273, (203)281-4487, FAX (203)230-1186.
 Ind/Abst MLA Int. Bibl. Books Artic. Mod. Lang. Lit.

US
GARLAND MEDIEVAL TEXTS. No. 1 (1980)-. Monographic series. English. Garland Publishing Inc, 1000A Sherman Avenue, Hamden CT 06514. **Tel** 800-627-6273, (203)281-4487.
 Ind/Abst MLA Int. Bibl. Books Artic. Mod. Lang. Lit.

US/1045-2907
GARVIN'S LARGE PRINT READER. [Garvin's large print read.]. Vol. 1, No. 1 (July 1, 1989)-. Periodical. English. bm. $48.00. Catherine Garvin, PO Box 2092, Natchez MS 39121. **DD** 810.

UK/0951-7200
GASKELL SOCIETY JOURNAL, THE. Added/Corp Gaskell Society. Vol. 1 (Summer 1987)-. English. an. £18.00. Gaskell Society, Far Yew Tree House/ Over Tabley, Knutsford Cheshire England. **Tel** 011 44 61 2733333. **ED** Alan Shelston. **LC** PR4711; .G33. **DD** 823/.8. **Circ:** 3,507.
 Desc: Promotes and encourages the study and appreciation of the work and life of Elizabeth Cleghorn Gaskell.
 Ind/Abst Annu. Bibliogr. Engl. Lang. Lit.; MLA Int. Bibl. Books Artic. Mod. Lang. Lit.

●US/1062-015X
GASLIGHT (CLEVELAND, MINN.). (GASLIGHT: TALES OF THE UNSANE.). (1992)-. Periodical. English. Three times a year. $11.75 (U.S.), $14.00 (Can.). Strait-Jacket Publications, PO Box 21, Cleveland MN 56017. **ED** Melissa Gish. **Bk Rev**, (Qty: 6). **Ad Acc, Adv Mgr:** Melissa Gish. **Pr Rev. Acid Free. Circ:** 200.
Desc: Macabre horror, nothing extremely graphic. Science fiction, fantasy, dark fantasy, short fiction, essays, reviews, letters, with extensive artwork.

CN/0706-5280
GASOLINE RAINBOW. V. 1- 1977-. English. an. $1.00 per number. U of A Literary Society, University of Alberta, Department of English, Edmonton Alberta T6G 2E1 Canada. **DD** C813/.5/408.

US/1058-9112
GATHERING OF THE TRIBES, A. [Gather. tribes]. **VFOAT** Tribes. Vol. 1, No. 1 (Fall 1991)-. Periodical. English. qt. $30.00. Tribes Communications, Tompkins Square Station, PO Box 20693, New York NY 10009. **Tel** (212)674-8262. **(Subscription address:** Ubiquity Distributors, 607 DeGraw Street, Brooklyn NY 11217.**) ED** Steve Cannon. **DD** 810. **Bk Rev. Ad Acc, Adv Mgr:** Christian Howe. **Circ:** 2,000.

CN/1180-0666
GATHERINGS (PENTICTON). (GATHERINGS : THE EN'OWKIN JOURNAL OF FIRST NORTH AMERICAN PEOPLES.). [Gatherings]. **Added/Corp** En'Owkin International School of Writing. En'Owkin Centre. Vol. 1, Issue 1 (Fall 1990)-. English. an. 12.95Can$. Theytus Books Ltd., PO Box 20040, Penticton, British Columbia V2A 8K3 Canada. **Tel** (604)493-7181. **DD** C810.8/0897.

AG
GATO NEGRO, EL. Vol. 1, No. 1 (Oct. 1990)-. Periodical. Spanish.

US/8755-3651
GATO TUERTO, EL. [Gato tuerto]. 1 (Summer 1984)-. Periodical. Spanish (English, Italian and Portuguese). Four times a year. $12.00 US. Ediciones El Gato Tuerto, PO Box 210277, San Francisco CA 94121. **Tel** (415)752-0473. **ED** Carlota Caulfield and Servando Gonzalez. **DD** 705. **Bk Rev. Ad Acc. Circ:** 3,000 (ctrl).
Desc: Contains poetry, short stories, essays, art, criticism, book reviews, works dealing with Spanish, Latin America and Caribbean literatures.

US/0276-7910
GAVEA-BROWN. [Gavea-Brown]. **VAT** Gavea, Brown. Vol. 1, No. 1 (Jan./June, 1980)-. Periodical. English (Portuguese). sa. $15.00 (individuals), $20.00 (institutions). Brown University / Department of Portugese & Brazilian Studies, PO Box O, Providence RI 02912. **Tel** (401)863-3042, FAX (401)863-7261. **ED** Onesimo T Almeida. **LC** PQ9470; .A23. **DD** 810/.8/08691. **Bk Rev. Ad Acc. Circ:** 1,500.
Desc: A bilingual journal of Portuguese-American letters and studies.

US/0270-0085
GAYOSO STREET REVIEW, THE. Vol. 1, No. 1-. Periodical. English. Three times a year. $6.00. Gayoso Street Review, PO box 11736, Memphis TN 38111. **LC** PS501; .G38. **DD** 810/.8.

US/0193-533X
GAZETTE (NEW YORK. 1979), THE. (THE GAZETTE.). V. 1- Winter 1979-. Periodical. English. qt. $25.00 (membership). The Wolfe Pack, PO Box 822 Ansonia Station, New York NY 10023. **Tel** (212)874-5917. **ED** Joel Levy (editor's address: 5413 Marlin Street, Rockville MD 20853). **LC** PS3537.T733; Z68. **DD** 813/.52. Index available. cum. index. **Circ:** 250 (ctrl).

US
GDR BULLETIN: NEWSLETTER FOR LITERATURE AND CULTURE IN THE GERMAN DEMOCRATIC REPUBLIC. See Linguistics.

GW/0016-5921
GEIST UND LEBEN (WURZBURG). (GEIST UND LEBEN : ZEITSCHRIFT FEUR ASZESE UND MYSTIK.). [Geist Leben]. (June 1947)-. Periodical. German. Six times a year (Feb., Apr., June, Aug., Oct., Dec.). DM80.40. Echter Wuerzburg, Postfach 5560, Julius Promenade 64, D 97070 Wuerzburg Germany. **Tel** 011/49/931/3091153, FAX 011/49/931/16735. **ED** Echter Wurzburg. **LC** BV5015; .G4. cum. index. **Bk Rev. Ad Acc. Circ:** 4,000 (ctrl). ***Continues** Zeitschrift fur Aszese und Mystik.*
Desc: Articles of spirituality (asceticism, mysticism).
Ind/Abst New Testam. Abstr.

CN/1181-6554
GEIST (VANCOUVER). (GEIST.). [Geist]. **Added/Corp** Geist Foundation. (Oct. 1990)-. Periodical. English. Five times a year. Can$20.00. Geist Foundation, 1062 Homers Street, Suite 100, Vancouver, British Columbia, V6B 2W9 Canada. **Tel** (604)681-9161, FAX (604)681-8250. **ED** Stephen Osborne. **DD** 700/.971/05. **Bk Rev. Ad Acc, Adv Mgr:** Kevin Barefoot. **Circ:** 13,000 (ctrl). available on microfiche from University Microfilms International (UMI).

SP
GEMMA : REVISTA INTERNACIONAL DE LITERATURA. Spanish (English, Italian, French and Arabic). mo. 5.500ptas Spain and Portugal; 8.000ptas Europe; 10.000ptas Africa and Asia; 10.000ptas North America. Editorial el Paisaje / Aranguren, La Penorra 8-2, 48850 Aranguren Spain. **Tel** (94) 639 07 74. **ED** Agustin Garcia Alonso. **Bk Rev. Ad Acc. Circ:** 5,000.

CN/0834-1737
GEMS OF POETRY AND PROSE. [Gems poetry prose]. **Added/Corp** White Rock & Surrey Writers Club. (1986)-. English. be. $7.95, $4.00 per issue. Gems of Poetry & Prose, c/o K Magnusson, 14253 Vine Avenue, White Rock British Columbia V4B 2S9 Canada. **Tel** (604)531-7955. **ED** Lynda James and Kristiana Magnusson. **DD** C810/.8/0971133. **Bk Rev. Circ:** 1,000 (ctrl). ***Continues** Gems of Poetry, 0827-3138.*
Desc: Poetry and prose written by literary contestants and by members of White Rock and Surrey Writer's Club.

JA
GENDAI TANKA. (19??)-. Periodical. Japanese. be. ¥2300. Yoshida, 2-16 Minami Ikebukuro 1 Toshima-ku, Tokyo Japan. **LC** PL758.A1; G46.

US/1048-0870
GENERALIST PAPERS, THE. **Added/Corp** Generalist Association (U.S.). Vol. 1, No. 1 (1990)-. Periodical. English. bm. $12.00 US; $15.00 Canada and Mexico; $20.00 other. Smith / New York, 69 Joralemon Street, Brooklyn NY 11201. **Tel** (718)552-0623. **ED** Harry Smith. **LC** AP2; .G46. Index available. cum. index. **Circ:** 2,000. ***Continues** Pulpsmith, 0276-0436.*
Desc: Besides editor Harry Smith, contributors include Richard Nason (on Deconstruction) and Marshall Brooks, who explores the James Farrell Underground and looks backward to find a contemporary lesson in the first American newspaper, Publick Occurrences.

JA/0286-2093
GENGO BUNKA KENKYU (MATSUYAMA-SHI, JAPAN). See Linguistics.

DK
GEORG BRANDES ARBOG. 1975-. Danish. Georg Brandes Biblioteket, Smallegade 43, 2000 Kbenhavn F Denmark. **LC** PT8125.B8; Z645.

GW
GEORG BUECHNER JAHRBUCH. **Added/Corp** Forschungsstelle Georg Buechner. (1981)-. Monographic series. German. ir. Price varies per volume. Max Niemeyer Verlag, Postfach 2140, D 72011 Tuebingen Germany. **Tel** 011 49 7071 989494, FAX 011 49 7071 87419. **ED** Thomas Michael Mayer. **LC** PT1828.B6; G42. **DD** 832/.7.

US/0953-0754
GEORGE ELIOT, GEORGE HENRY LEWES NEWSLETTER, THE. No. 1 (Sept. 1982)-. Newsletter. English. ir (2 issues or 1 double issue per year). $10.00. Northern Illinois University English Department / Prof. William Baker, Dekalb IL 60115. **Tel** (815)753-1857.
Ind/Abst MLA Int. Bibl. Books Artic. Mod. Lang. Lit.

●UK
GEORGE ELIOT REVIEW : JOURNAL OF THE GEORGE ELIOT FELLOWSHIP, THE. **Added/Corp** George Eliot Fellowship. No. 23 (1992)-. English. **LC** PR4679; .G46. ***Continues** George Eliot Fellowship Review.*
Ind/Abst MLA Int. Bibl. Books Artic. Mod. Lang. Lit.

US/0161-7435
GEORGE HERBERT JOURNAL. [George Herbert j.]. Vol. 1 (Fall 1977)-. Periodical. English. sa (2 issues). $20.00. Sacred Heart University, 5151 Park Avenue, c/o Sidney Gottlieb, Fairfield CT 06432. **Tel** (203)371-7810. **ED** Sidney Gottlieb. **LC** PR3508; .G46. **DD** 821/.3. Index available (published irregularly in journal). cum. index. **Bk Rev**, (Qty: 8-12). **Ad Acc, Adv Mgr:** same as editor. **Pr Rev. Circ:** 450 (ctrl).
Desc: Publishes essays, notes, and reviews on materials relevant to George Herbert in particular and 17th Century literature and thought in general.
Ind/Abst Abstr. Engl. Stud.; Am. Humanit. Index; Annu. Bibliogr. Engl. Lang. Lit.; Lit. Crit. Regist.; MLA Int. Bibl. Books Artic. Mod. Lang. Lit.

●US/1066-1506
GEORGETOWN REVIEW (GEORGETOWN, KY.). (GEORGETOWN REVIEW.). (1993)-. Periodical. English. sa (2 issues). $10.00. Georgetown Review, 400 East College Street, Box 227, Georgetown KY 40324. **ED** Michael Campbell and Steven Carter.
Ind/Abst Am. Humanit. Index.

US/0016-8386
GEORGIA REVIEW, THE. [Georgia rev.]. Vol. 1 (Spring 1947)-. Periodical. English. qt. $18.00 (1 year), $30.00 (2 year), $42.00 (three year) US; $23.00 (one year), $40.00 (two year) other. Georgia Review, University of Georgia, Athens GA 30602. **Tel** (706)542-3481, FAX (706)542-0047. **ED** Stanley W Lindberg. **LC** AP2; .G375. **DD** 051. Index available. **Bk Rev. Ad Acc. Circ:** 5,300 (ctrl). available on microfilm and microfiche from University Microfilms International (UMI). Documents available from The Genuine Article, UMI Article Clearinghouse.
Desc: Covers American thought and literature. Including essays, poetry, fiction, graphics, book reviews for an interdisciplinary audience.
Ind/Abst Abstr. Engl. Stud.; Acad. Ind. [Computer File] (1992-); Acad. Search (July 1993-); Am. Hist. Life (1963-); Am. Humanit. Index; Annu. Bibliogr. Engl. Lang. Lit.; Arts Humanit. Citation Index [Full Cov.]; BHA : Biblio. Hist. Art; Book Rev. Index; Curr. Contents Arts Humanit.; Expand. Acad. Index (1989-); Film Lit. Index; Humanit. Index; Humanit. Source (Jul. 1993-); Index Am. Period. Verse; INFO-SOUTH Abstr.; Lit. Crit. Regist.; MLA Int. Bibl. Books Artic. Mod. Lang. Lit.; Newsp. Period. Abstr. (1991-); Res. Alert [Full Cov.]; Romant. Move.; Soc. Plann. Policy Dev. Abstr.; Sociol. Abstr.

US/0884-8696
GEORGIA STATE LITERARY STUDIES. [Ga. State lit. stud.]. **Added/Corp** Georgia State University. Dept. of English. **VFOAT** Literary Studies. Vol. 1 (1987)-. Monographic series. English. Price varies per volume. AMS Press Inc., 56 East 13th Street, New York NY 10003. **Tel** (212)777-4700, FAX (212)995-5413, telex 710 581 2302. **DD** 820.
Desc: Covers topics in literature. There have been volumes on subjects such as British novelists since 1900, the Harlem Renaissance, and the work of Conrad Aiken.
Ind/Abst MLA Int. Bibl. Books Artic. Mod. Lang. Lit.

NE/0378-4150
GERMAN LANGUAGE AND LITERATURE MONOGRAPHS. ***Ceased.*** [Ger. lang. lit. monogr.]. Vol. 1 (1976)-(19??). Monographic series. German (English). ir. John Benjamins BV, Amsteldijk 44, PO Box 75577, 1070 AN Amsterdam Netherlands. **Tel** 011 31 20 6738156, FAX 011 31 20 739773. **(Subscription address:** John Benjamins North America, PO Box 27519, Philadelphia PA 19118-0519.**)**
Ind/Abst MLA Int. Bibl. Books Artic. Mod. Lang. Lit. (?-?).

UK/0016-8777
GERMAN LIFE AND LETTERS. [Ger. life lett.]. Vol. 1-4, (Oct. 1936)-(Oct.1939); New Ser., Vol. 1 (Oct.1947)-. Academic Scholarly Publication. English. Four times a year. £94.00 UK & Europe; $183.00 North America; £118.00 other. Basil Blackwell Publishers Ltd, 108 Cowley Road, Oxford 0X4 1JF England. **Tel** 011 44 865 791100, FAX 011 44 865 791347, telex 837022 OXBOOK G. **(Subscription address:** Blackwell Publishers / UK, Marston Book Services, PO Box 87, Oxford OX2 0DT England.**) ED** L. A. Willoughby. **LC** AP4; .G43. **[CCC]**. Index available (Free). cum. index. **Ad Acc.** available on microfilm and microfiche from University Microfilms International (UMI). Documents available from The Genuine Article.
Desc: Articles on all aspects of German literature and culture.
Ind/Abst Am. Hist. Life (1989-); Arts Humanit. Citation Index [Full Cov.]; Br. Humanit. Index; Child. Lit. Abstr. (19??-); Curr. Contents Arts Humanit.; MLA Int. Bibl. Books Artic. Mod. Lang. Lit.; Res. Alert [Full Cov.]; Romant. Move.; Soc. Plann. Policy Dev. Abstr.

US/0016-8831
GERMAN QUARTERLY, THE. [Ger. q.]. **Added/Corp** American Association of Teachers of German. American Association of Teachers of German. AATG Membership Directory. Vol. 1 (Jan. 1928)-. Periodical. English (German). Four times a year (Jan., Mar., May, Nov.). $60.00 Comes with American Association of Teachers of German membership. American Association of Teachers of German, 112 Haddontowne Court, Suite 104, Cherry Hill NJ 08034. **Tel** (609)795-5553, FAX (609)795-9398. **ED** Paul Michael Lutzeler. **LC** PF3001; .G3. **DD** 430.7. Index available. **Bk Rev. Ad Acc. Pr Rev. Circ:** 7,700 (ctrl). available on microfilm and microfiche from University Microfilms International (UMI). Documents available from The Genuine Article. ***Continued in part by** Membership Directory - AATG.*
Desc: Literary and philological scholarship from the outstanding authorities in the German speaking world with book reviews, special reports and announcements.
Ind/Abst Am. Bibliogr. Slavic East Europ. Stud.; Arts Humanit. Citation Index [Full Cov.]; Book Rev. Index; Child. Lit. Abstr. (19??-); Curr. Contents Arts Humanit.; Educ. Index; Lang. Teach.; MLA Int. Bibl. Books Artic. Mod. Lang. Lit.; Res. Alert [Full Cov.]; Soc. Plann. Policy Dev. Abstr.; Soc. Sci. Cit. Index [Select. Cov.]; Sociol. Abstr.

US/0149-7952
GERMAN STUDIES REVIEW. See History(General)-History of Europe.

SZ/0721-3727
GERMANIC STUDIES IN AMERICA. [Ger. stud. Am.]. No. 30 (1979)-. Monographic series. English (German). ir. Price varies per volume. Verlag Peter Lang AG, Jupiterstrasse 15, CH-3000 Bern 15 Switzerland. **Tel** 011 41 31 9411122, FAX 011 41 31 321131. **Circ:** 450. ***Continues*** *German Studies in America.*
Desc: Reevaluates the Historia von D Johann Fausten as a work of formulaic fiction which inverts the structural pattern of the medieval saints' legends, subverting Catholic values in favor of Lutheran ones.
Ind/Abst MLA Int. Bibl. Books Artic. Mod. Lang. Lit.

FR/0072-1484
GERMANICA. 1- 1960-. Monographic series. Multiple languages (French and German). ir. Price varies per volume. Societe Nouvelle Didier Erudition, 6 rue de la Sorbonne, 75005 Paris France. **Tel** 011 33 1 43544757, FAX 011 33 1 40517385.
Desc: Collection of doctorate thesis in the French universities-13 titles published.

XR
GERMANICA OLOMUCENSIA. Added/Corp Univerzita Palackeho v Olomouci. Filozoficka Fakulta. (1978)-. Periodical. English (German; summaries and/or abstracts in Czech). **LC** P19; .O522 subser; PD9. **DD** 430/.5. ***Continues*** *Germanistica Olomucensia.*
Ind/Abst Annu. Bibliogr. Engl. Lang. Lit.

GW/0524-8414
GERMANISTIK (BERLIN). See Linguistics.

BE/0771-3703
GERMANISTISCHE MITTEILUNGEN. See Linguistics.

SW/0435-5911
GERMANISTISCHE SCHRIFTENREIHE DER NORWEGISCHEN UNIVERSITATEN UND HOCHSCHULEN. See Linguistics.

GW/0175-9388
GERMANISTISCHE TEXTE UND STUDIEN. See Linguistics.

CN/0317-4956
GERMANO-SLAVICA. [Ger.-Slav.]. **Added/Corp** University of Waterloo. Dept. of Germanic and Slavic Languages and Literature. No. 1 (Spring 1973)-. Periodical. English (German and Russian). an. 9.00Can$ (individuals), 12.00Can$ (institutions) Canada; 12.00Can$ (individuals), 15.00Can$ (institutions) others. University of Waterloo Department of Germanic and Slavic Language Literature, Waterloo ONT N2L 3G1 Canada. **Tel** (519)885-1211 ext 2138. **ED** S. Hoefert. **LC** PT123.S58; G47. **Bk Rev. Ad Acc. Circ:** 300. Documents available from The Genuine Article.
Desc: A Canadian journal of Germanic and Slavic comparative studies.
Ind/Abst Am. Bibliogr. Slavic East Europ. Stud.; Arts Humanit. Citation Index [Full Cov.]; Curr. Contents Arts Humanit.; MLA Int. Bibl. Books Artic. Mod. Lang. Lit.; Res. Alert [Full Cov.]; Romant. Move.

GW
GESAMMELTE WERKE IN EINZELAUSGABEN. ***Ceased.*** **VFOAT** Sholokhov Mikhail Ausgaben. (19??)-(19??). German. ir. Verlag Volk und Welt, Glinkastr 13-15, D 10117 Berlin Germany. **Tel** 011 49 30 2202851, telex BERLIN DDR.

GW
GESCHICHTE DER DEUTSCHEN LITERATUR VON DEN ANFAENGEN BIS ZUR GEGENWART. (19??)-. German. ir. Price varies per volume. CH Beck Verlagsbuchhandlung, D 80791 Munich Germany. **Tel** 011 49 89 381891.

US/0749-7644
GESTUS. ***Title Change.*** [Gestus]. Vol. 1 (Spring 1985)-Vol. 2 (Winter 1986). Periodical. English. qt. Gestus, 59 South New Street, Dover DE 19901. **LC** PT2603.R397; Z6217. **DD** 832/.912. ***Continued by*** *Gestus, 0749-7644.*
Desc: A quarterly journal of Brechtian studies.
Ind/Abst Am. Humanit. Index.

US/0898-4557
GETTYSBURG REVIEW (1988). (THE GETTYSBURG REVIEW.). [Gettysbg. rev.]. **Added/Corp** Gettysburg College. **VFOAT** Gettysburg. (Winter 1988)-. Periodical. English. qt (Jan., Apr., July, Oct.). $18.00 (one year), $32.00 (two year), $45.00 (three year). The Gettysburg Review, Gettysburg College, Gettysburg PA 17325. **Tel** (717)337-6770, FAX (717)337-6775. **ED** Peter Stitt. **LC** AS30; .G48. **DD** 814. Index available in last issue of volume--attached. **Bk Rev**, (Qty: 20). **Ad Acc, Adv Mgr:** E. Clarke, **Tel** (717)337-6771. **Circ:** 2,500 (ctrl). ***Continues*** *Gettysburg Review.*
Desc: A multidisciplinary journal of art and ideas featuring original poetry, fiction, essays, essay reviews and artwork by well-known and beginning professionals.
Ind/Abst Am. Hist. Life (1988-); Am. Humanit. Index; Index Am. Period. Verse; MLA Int. Bibl. Books Artic. Mod. Lang. Lit.

BE/0776-4111
GEZELLIANA. See Linguistics.

US/0016-9633
GHOST DANCE. Vol. 1. Periodical. English. qt. Ghostdance Press, 526 Forest, East Lansing MI 48823. **ED** H Fox. **LC** PS501; .G48. **DD** 810/.8/0054. available on microfilm and microfiche from University Microfilms International (UMI).

NE
GIDS (AMSTERDAM, NETHERLANDS). See Political Science.

IT/0017-0496
GIORNALE STORICO DELLA LETTERATURA ITALIANA. [G. stor. lett. ital.]. Vol. 1 (1883)-. Periodical. Italian. Four times a year. L99000 Italy; L128000 others Comes with Rivista di Filologia e di Instruzione Classica. Loescher Editore, Via Vittorio Amedeo 18, 10121 Turin Italy. **Tel** 011 39 11 5624622. **LC** PQ4001; .G5. Documents available from The Genuine Article.
Ind/Abst Arts Humanit. Citation Index [Full Cov.]; Curr. Contents Arts Humanit.; MLA Int. Bibl. Books Artic. Mod. Lang. Lit.; Res. Alert [Full Cov.]; Romant. Move.

UK
GISSING JOURNAL, THE. Added/Corp Gissing Trust. Vol. 27, No. 1 (Jan. 1991)-. Periodical. English. qt. £12.00 (institutions), £8.00 (individuals). Gissing Trust, 7 Town Lane, Idle Bradford BD10 8PR England. **ED** Pierre Coustillas (Editor's Address: 10 Rue Gay-Lussac, 59110 La Madeleine, France). **LC** PR4717; .G55. **DD** 823/.8. **Bk Rev. Circ:** 220. ***Continues*** *Gissing Newsletter, 0017-0615.*
Ind/Abst MLA Int. Bibl. Books Artic. Mod. Lang. Lit.

RU
GLAS. VFOAT New Russian Writing. (1991)-. Periodical. English (translations available in Russian). Four times a year (Jan., Apr., July, Oct.). £25.80 (individuals), £38.50 (institutions). Zephyr Press, 13 Robinson Street, Somerville MA 02145. **Tel** (617)628-9726, FAX (617)776-8246. **(Subscription address:** Glas, Department of Russian Literature, University of Birmingham, B15 2TT England.**) ED** Natasha Perova (Moscow), Arch Tait (U.K.), and Ed Hogan (U.S.A.). **LC** PG3199; .G53713. **Ad Acc, Adv Mgr:** Arch Tait. **Circ:** 2,500.
Desc: Thematic collections of the contemporary Russian short stories in English translation, with poetry, photographs, and works rescued from the archives.

RU/0869-3102
GLAS. (1991)-. Periodical. Russian (English). ir. $159.95. **(Subscription address:** East View Publications Inc., 3020 Harbor Lane North, Suite 110, Minneapolis MN 55447.**) LC** PG3227.5; .G537.

●US/1055-7520
GLIMMER TRAIN STORIES. [Glimmer train stories]. **VFOAT** Glimmer Train. Issue 1 (Winter 1992)-. Periodical. English. qt (Feb., May, Aug., Nov.). $29.00 one year; $49.00 two years. Glimmer Train Press Inc, 812 southwest Washington Street, Suite 1205, Portland OR 97205-3216. **Tel** (503)221-0836, FAX (503)221-0837. **ED** Linda Davies. **LC** PS642; .G57. **DD** 813/.0108/005. **Pr Rev. Acid Free. Circ:** 20,000.
Desc: Entrancing short-story magazine packed in a tall paperback format and printed on recycled, acid-free paper, fully illustrated, including glorious color covers. Recent authors: Richard Bausch, Joyce Thompson, Thompson Nunez, Joyce Carol Oated, oates Dixon.

US/0364-1708
GLYPH. No. 1-. Periodical. English. Three times a year. $5.00. c/o Richard Hoffman, 130 West 16th Street, New York NY 10011. **LC** PS501; .G57. **DD** 810/.8/005.
Ind/Abst Annu. Bibliogr. Engl. Lang. Lit.

GW
GOETHE DIE SCHRIFTEN ZUR NATURWISSENSCHAFT. (19??)-. German. ir. Price varies per volume. Verlag Hermann Boehlaus Nachfolger, Postfach 260, D 99403 Weimar Germany. **Tel** 011 49 3643 2071, . **(Subscription address:** Verlag H. Boehlaus Nachfolger, Postfach 546, W 7480 Sigmaringen Germany; telephone: 011 49 7571 728120**)**

JA
GOETHE-JAHRBUCH. Added/Corp Nihon GÂete KyÂokai. (19??)-. Periodical. German. Goeth-Gesellschaft, c/o Nippon-Universitat, 156 Sakurajosui 3-25-40, Setagaya-ku, Tokyo Japan. **LC** PT2046; .G74.
Ind/Abst Romant. Move.

GW/0323-4207
GOETHE-JAHRBUCH (WEIMAR). (GOETHE-JAHRBUCH.). [Goethe-Jahrb.]. **Added/Corp** Goethe-Gesellschaft (Weimar, Germany). **VFOAT** Goethe Jahrbuch. (1972)-. English. ir. Price varies. Verlag Hermann Boehlaus Nachfolger, Postfach 260, D 99403 Weimar Germany. **Tel** 011 49 3643 2071, . **LC** PT2045; .G695. **DD** 831. Documents available from The Genuine Article. ***Supersedes*** *Goethe.*

Ind/Abst Arts Humanit. Citation Index [Full Cov.]; BHA : Biblio. Hist. Art; Curr. Contents Arts Humanit.; MLA Int. Bibl. Books Artic. Mod. Lang. Lit.; Res. Alert [Full Cov.].

UK
GOETHE WORTEBUCH. German. ir. Erasmus Antiquariaat Boekhande, Postbus 19140, 100 GC Amsterdam Netherlands. **Tel** 011 31 20 6276952.

AT/0157-3950
GOING DOWN SWINGING. (1980)-. English. an. 16.00Aus$. Going Down Swinging, PO Box 64, Coburg Victoria 3058 Australia. **Tel** 03 4841552. **ED** Kevin Brophy and M. Lysenko (editors' phone: 03 3802528). **Bk Rev**, (Qty: 10-20/year). **Ad Acc. Pr Rev. Circ:** 1,000 (ctrl).
Desc: Prose, poetry, reviews - experimental, avant-garde; young writers, unknown writers.

IS
GOLDENE KEYT, DI. Added/Corp Histadrut Ha-Kelalit Shel Ha-Ovdim Be-Erets-Yisrael. No. 1 (Winter 1949)-. Periodical. Yiddish (Hebrew). Four times a year. $35.00. Di Goldene Keyt, Rechow Weizmann 30, Tel Aviv Israel. **Tel** (3)21-81-91. **ED** Abraham Sutzkewer. **LC** DS101; .G595. Index available ($10.00). cum. index. **Bk Rev.**
Desc: Periodical for literature and social problems.
Ind/Abst MLA Int. Bibl. Books Artic. Mod. Lang. Lit.

US/1056-1498
GOLIARD (WOOSTER, OHIO). (GOLIARD.). **Added/Corp** College of Wooster. (1990)-. Periodical. English. $2.00 (single issue). College of Wooster, Box C3190, Wooster OH 44691. **DD** 808.

US/0046-6158
GOOD OLD DAYS. (19??)-. Periodical. English. mo. $12.97. House of White Birches, 306 East Parr Road, Berne IN 46711. **Tel** (219)589-8741, FAX (219)589-8093. **(Subscription address:** Palm Coast Data, PO Box 420235, Agency Department, Palm Coast FL 32142.**) ED** Ken Tate. **Ad Acc. Circ:** 85,000.
Desc: A look into the nostalgic past through authentic photos, drawings, cartoons, comics, memories, features, songs, poems, letters, first-person narratives, and recipes.

US/1058-1871
GOOD OLD DAYS. SPECIAL ISSUES (1991). (GOOD OLD DAYS. SPECIAL ISSUES.). [Good old days, Spec. issues]. (1991)-. Periodical. English. bm (6 issues per year). $9.95. House of White Birches, 306 East Parr Road, Berne IN 46711. **Tel** (219)589-8741, FAX (219)589-8093. **(Subscription address:** Palm Coast Data, PO Box 420235, Agency Department, Palm Coast FL 32142.**) ED** Ken Tate. **DD** 920. **Circ:** 25,200. ***Continues*** *Fireside Companion (Berne, Ind.), 1050-480X.*
Desc: Contains recollections of yesterday with lighthearted anecdotes of days gone by.

GW
GRABBE-JAHRBUCH. Added/Corp Grabbe-Gesellschaft. **VFOAT** Grabbe Jahrbuch. Vol. 1 (1982)-. German. an. DM48.00. Aisthesis Verlag, Postfach 380, W 4800 Bielefeld 1 Germany. **LC** PT2253.G3; G7. **DD** 832/.7.

CN/0315-7423
GRAIN. Added/Corp Saskatchewan Writers' Guild. Saskatchewan Arts Board. Vol. 1 (June 1973)-. Periodical. English. qt. 19.95Can$ (one year), 34.95Can$ (two years). Saskatchewan Writers Guild, PO Box 1154, Regina SASK S4P 3R9 Canada. **Tel** (306)757-6310. **ED** Mick Burrs, Byrna Barclay, Mary Shepperd and Christa Donaldson. **LC** PR9194; .G7. **DD** 810/.8/0054. Index available. cum. index. **Circ:** 850.
Desc: Publishes excellence in literary and visual art. Includes work by well-known and up-and-coming writers that provides satisfying and stimulating reading. Widely acknowledged to be one of Canada's finest literary magazines.
Ind/Abst Am. Humanit. Index; Can. Lit. Index (1985-1986); Index Am. Period. Verse.

US/0194-4029
GRAMERCY REVIEW, THE. (GRAMERCY REVIEW; A JOURNAL OF CONTEMPORARY POETRY AND FICTION.). V. 1- 1977-. Periodical. English. qt. Gramercy Review, 5536 Bryant Street, Pittsburgh PA 15206. **Tel** (213)741-5872.

US/0734-5496
GRAND STREET. [Grand str.]. Vol. 1, No. 1 (Autumn 1981)-. Periodical. English. Four times a year (Jan., Apr., July, Oct.). $40.00 (one year); $74.00 (two years). Grand Street, 131 Varick Street, Room 90, New York NY 10013. **Tel** (212)807-6548. **(Subscription address:** Fulco, P. O. Box 3000, Dept. GRS, Denville, NJ 07834, telephone: (201)627-2427**) LC** PN6010.5; .G68. **DD** 808.8. **Bk Rev. Ad Acc. Circ:** 4,000. Documents available from UMI Article Clearinghouse.
Desc: Cutting-edge international fiction, essays, poetry, along with magnificent portfolios of art and photography.
Ind/Abst Acad. Search (July 1993-); Am. Bibliogr. Slavic East Europ. Stud.; Am. Humanit. Index (-199?); Expand. Acad. Index (1989-); Humanit. Index; Humanit. Source

Literature

(Jul. 1993-); Index Am. Period. Verse; INFO-SOUTH Abstr.; Mag. Search; MLA Int. Bibl. Books Artic. Mod. Lang. Lit.; Newsp. Period. Abstr. (1991-).

RU
GRANITSA; LENINGRADSKIE PISATELI O POGRANICHNIKAKH. Vol. 1, (1968)-. Russian. 0.87rub single issue. Lenizdat, Fontanka 59, St. Petersburg Russia. **LC** PG3228.A72; G7.

US/0092-5268
GRANTS AND AWARDS AVAILABLE TO AMERICAN WRITERS. Added/Corp American Center of P.E.N. **VFOAT** Grants and Awards. (197?)-. English. be. $15.00 institutions, $10.00 individuals. Pen American Center, 568 Broadway, New York NY 10012. **Tel** (212)334-1660, FAX (212)334-2181. **ED** John Morrone. **LC** PN171.P75; G73. **DD** 001.4/4. **Circ:** 5,000. **Continues** List of Grants and Awards Available to American Writers, 0075-983X.
 Desc: Awards for poets, reserach grants for journalists, production opportunities for dramatists, prizes for fiction and translation. An indexed volume of more than 500 American and international awards for writers.

US/0093-3163
GRANTS AND AWARDS AVAILABLE TO FOREIGN WRITERS. Added/Corp American Center of P.E.N. (1973)-. English. $2.00, series completed 1976. Pen American Center, 568 Broadway, New York NY 10012. **Tel** (212)334-1660, FAX (212)334-2181. **LC** PN171.P75; G74. **DD** 807/.9.

GW/0343-1258
GRATIA. [Gratia]. **Added/Corp** Universitat Gottingen. Seminar fur Deutsche Philologie. Arbeitsstelle fur Renaissanceforschung. (1977)-. Monographic series. German.
 Ind/Abst MLA Int. Bibl. Books Artic. Mod. Lang. Lit.

US/0743-7471
GRAYWOLF ANNUAL, THE. [Graywolf annu.]. 1-. English. an. Graywolf Press, PO Box 75006, St Paul MN 55175. **ED** Scott Walker. **LC** PS648.S5; G7. **DD** 813/.01/08.
 Desc: Anthology of literary short fiction or creative non-fiction.

US/0160-2144
GREAT RIVER REVIEW. Vol. 1 (1977)-. Periodical. English. sa. $10.00. Great River Review, 211 West 7th Street, Winona MN 55987. **Tel** (507)454-6564. **ED** Orval Lund, Jr. & Monica Drealan DeGrazia. **LC** PS273; .G74. **DD** 810/.8/0054. **Bk Rev**, (Qty: 12). **Circ:** 800 (ctrl).
 Desc: Dedicated to publishing fiction and creative poetry, paying particular attention to midwestern writers.
 Ind/Abst Am. Humanit. Index.

US/1042-8208
GREAT STREAM REVIEW. Ceased. [Gt. Stream rev.]. Vol. 1, No 1 (Spring 1989)-(1993). Periodical. English. sa. Lycoming College, Box 66, Williamsport PA 17701. **DD** 810.

US/0895-9307
GREEN MOUNTAINS REVIEW. [Green Mt. rev.]. **Added/Corp** Johnson State College. (1974)-. Periodical. English. sa. $12.00 (one year), $18.00 (two year). Johnson State College, Johnson VT 05656. **Tel** (802)635-2356. **LC** PS1; .G73. **DD** 810.
 Desc: Publishes poetry, fiction, essays, and interviews of promising newcomers and well-known writers.

CN/0824-2992
GREEN'S MAGAZINE. [Green's mag.]. Vol. 1, No. 1 (Fall 1972)-. Periodical. English. Four times a year (Jan., Apr., July, Oct.). $12.00. Green's Magazine, PO Box 3236, Regina Saskatchewan S4P 3H1 Canada. **ED** David Green. **DD** 810/.8/0054. Index Available Received separately--bound from publisher (October issue). **Bk Rev**, (Qty: 2-4). **Ad Acc. Circ:** 300 (ctrl).
 Desc: Short fiction and poetry for family reading. An a wide range of subjects, from juvenile to sci-fi, humor and adventure.

US/0017-4084
GREENSBORO REVIEW, THE. [Greensboro rev.]. **Added/Corp** University of North Carolina at Greensboro. No. 1 (May 1966)-. Periodical. English. Twice a year (March and September). $8.00 (one year); $20.00 (three year). Greensboro Review, University of North Carolina, Department of English, Greensboro NC 27412-5001. **Tel** (919)334-5459. **ED** Jim Clark, (919)334-5459. **Circ:** 500. available on microfilm and microfiche from University Microfilms International (UMI).
 Ind/Abst Am. Humanit. Index; Index Am. Period. Verse.

US/0533-2869
GREYFRIAR (LOUDONVILLE N.Y.). Suspended. (GREYFRIAR). [Greyfriar]. **Added/Corp** Siena College. Siena College. Dept. of English. **VFOAT** Siena Studies in Literature. (1960)-(1993). Periodical. English. an. Free. Siena College, Dept of English, Loudonville NY 12211. **Tel** (518)783-2362. **ED** Dr. A. F. Gulliver. **LC** PN2; .G7. **DD** 809. Index available. cum. index. **Circ:** 1,000. **Continues** Greyfriar Lectures.

Desc: Periodical of literary criticism.
 Ind/Abst Annu. Bibliogr. Engl. Lang. Lit.; MLA Int. Bibl. Books Artic. Mod. Lang. Lit.

NE
GRONIGEN COLLOQUIA ON THE NOVEL. Vol. 1- 1988-. Periodical. English (German and Italian). **LC** PA3040; .G76. **DD** 883.009.

UK/0046-6506
GROWING POINT. Ceased. See Children and Youth Interests.

US/0149-4228
GRUB STREET. (19??)-. Periodical. English. $1.50 single issue. Grub Street, 2839 Valentine Avenue, Bronx NY 10458. **LC** PS501; .G78. **DD** 810/.5.

CN/0700-9917
GUARD THE NORTH. Began with Dec. 1972 issue. Periodical. English. 0.50Can$ per no. Guard the North, PO Box 65583, Vancouver British Columbia V5N 5K5 Canada. **DD** 809.3/876/0%.

US/0160-6565
GUEST AUTHOR. 1978-. English. an. $7.45. Hermes Press, 51 Lenox Street, Brockton MA 02401. **LC** PN452; .G84. **DD** 802/.5.

SP
GUIA DE CONCURSOS : REVISTA DE INFORMACION CULTURAL Y LITERARIA. Spanish. mo. 5.500ptas Spain; 8.000ptas Europe; 10.000ptas Africa and Asia; 5.500ptas Portugal; 10.000ptas North America. Editorial el Paisaje / Aranguren, La Penorra 8-2, 48850 Aranguren Spain. **Tel** (94) 639 07 74. **ED** Agustin Garcia Alonso. **Bk Rev. Ad Acc. Circ:** 5,000.

UK
GUIDE TO LITERARY PRIZES, GRANTS AND AWARDS. Ceased. Added/Corp National Book League (Great Britain) Society of Authors (Great Britain) Book Trust (Great Britain). **VFOAT** Literary Prizes, Grants and Awards in Britain and Ireland; Literary Prizes, Grants & Awards in Britain and Ireland; Guide to Literary Prizes, Grants and Awards in Britain and Ireland. (1982)-Ceased (19??). English. be. **LC** PN171.P75; G83. **DD** 002/.079/41. **Continues** Guide to Literary Prizes.

AT/1035-5391
GUIDE TO NEW AUSTRALIAN BOOKS. [Guide new Aust. books]. **VFOAT** GNAB. (1990)-. Periodical. English. bm (6 issues). $70.00 (airmail). D. W. Thorpe, A Reed Reference Publishing Company, A Subsidiary of Reed International Books Australia, 18 Salmon Street, Port Melbourne, Victoria 3207 Australia. **Tel** 011 61 3 6451511, FAX 011 61 3 6453981, telex 39476. **(Subscription address:** R.R. Bowker, PO Box 31, New Providence NJ 07974.) **DD** 015.94005. available on CD-ROM.
 Desc: Australian periodical providing complete listings of new books, along with bibliographic details and descriptive annotations. Indexed by over 100 subject groups.

UK
GUIDE TO SELECTING PLAYS, THE. Main/Corp French, Samuel, Firm, Publishers. (19??)-. Monographic series. English. ir. Price varies per volume. Samuel French Ltd, 52 Fitzroy Street, London W1P 6JR England. **Tel** 011 44 1 3879373, FAX 011 44 1 3872161. **ED** Amanda Smith. **LC** PN6112.5; .F7. **DD** 016.80882. Index available. **Circ:** 20,000.
 Desc: Synopses of story, cast and characters of over 2,000 modern plays.

US/0897-4195
GUIDE TO WRITERS CONFERENCES, THE. [Guide writ. conf.]. 1st Ed. (1988)-. English. an. $18.95. Shaw Associates, 625 Biltmore Way, Suite 1406, Coral Gables FL 33134. **Tel** (305)446-8888, FAX (305)446-1837. **LC** PN133.U5; G85. **DD** 808.

US/1055-8985
GUILT & GARDENIAS / THE ARTS COUNCIL. Added/Corp Society for the Preservation of Vaudeville and Variety Arts. Arts Council of Fayetteville/Cumberland County (Fayetteville, N.C.). **VFOAT** Guilt and Gardenias. Vol. 1, No. 1 (1991)-. Periodical. English. qt. $7.00. Society for the Preservation of Vaudeville and Variety Arts, 301 Hay Street, PO Box 318, Fayetteville NC 28302-0318. **DD** 808.

ES/0017-5447
GUION LITERARIO. Vol. 1, No. 1 (Jan. 1956)-. Periodical. Spanish. ir. Departamento Editorial, Del Ministerio de Cultura, San Salvador El Salvador.

US/0896-2251
GULF COAST. [Gulf coast]. **Added/Corp** University of Houston. Dept. of English. (198?)-. Periodical. English. sa. $12.00. University of Houston Department of English, Creative Writing, 4800 Calhoun, Houston TX 77204. **Tel** (713)528-2329. **DD** 810. **Continues** Domestic Crude.

US
GULLIVERIANA. (1970)-. Periodical. English. ir. Scholars Facsimiles and Reprints Inc, PO Box 344, Delmar NY 12054-0344. **Tel** (513)439-5978. **LC** PZ1; .G974.

NP
GUNAKESARI. V. 1- Asvina/Marga 2029- Oct./Dec. 1972-. Nepali (Nepali). 1.00 single issue. **LC** PK2598.A2; G78.

JA
GUNZO. (1946)-. Periodical. Japanese. mo. $190.00 California; $196.00 other US; $223.00 Europe; $247.00 Asia; $199.00 other. **(Subscription address:** Kinokuniya Company Ltd., 38-1 Sakuragaoka 5, chome Setagaya-ku, Tokyo 156 Japan.) **ED** Kodan-Sha. **LC** PL755.55; .G86. **Bk Rev. Ad Acc.**
 Desc: Novels.

●US/1071-5126
GYPSY BLOOD REVIEW. [Gypsy blood rev.]. **VFOAT** GBR. (Fall 1992)-. Periodical. English. qt. $15.00. Gypsy Blood Review, 1717 South Quincy St., Tulsa OK 74120-7019. **Tel** (918)599-1028. **ED** J. Simpson. **DD** 811. **Ad Acc, Adv Mgr:** Stan Faulkner. **Circ:** 250.

UK/0306-5480
H. G. WELLS NEWSLETTER, THE. Added/Corp H.G. Wells Society. **VAT** Herbert George Wells Newsletter. Vol. 2, No. 1 (Summer 1981)-. Periodical. English. Twice a year (Apr. & Oct.). £12.00. HG Wells Society / Department of English, Nene Coll Moulton, Northampton NNZ 7AL United Kingdom. **Tel** 011 44 604 735500 ext. 2133. **ED** Christopher Rolfe. **Bk Rev. Ad Acc. Circ:** 500. **Continues** H.G. Wells Society. Newsletter.

CH
HAI HSIA. VFOAT Hai Xia. V. 1 Jan. 1981. Periodical. Chinese. qt. NT$1.00. Fu-Chien Sheng Hsin Hua Shu Tien, Fu-Chou, People's Republic of China. **LC** PL12513; .H35. **DD** 895.1/09/005.

HK
HAI YANG WEN I. Vol. 1 (1974)-. Periodical. Chinese. $2.50 single issue. The Ocean Literary Press, No 3 on Ning Lane, Sai Ying Pun Hong Kong. **LC** PL2250; .H34.

JA/0389-4274
HAIKU BUNGAKUKAN KIYO. VFOAT Haiku Bungakkan Kiyo. No. 1-. Japanese. ¥1500 single issue. Haijin Kyokai 28-10, Huakunin-cho 3 Shinjuku-ku, Tokyo Japan. **LC** PL729.A1; H34.

GW/0939-3781
HALBASIEN. (1991)-. Periodical. German. sa. **LC** PT3961; .H34. **DD** 830.9/9496/05.

US/0733-6616
HAMBONE (STANFORD, CALIF.). (HAMBONE.). [Hambone]. Vol. 1 (Spring 1974)-. Periodical. English. an. $12.00. Mr. Nathaniel Mackey, 134 Hunolt Street, Santa Cruz CA 95060-2809. **Tel** (408)426-3072. **ED** Nate Mackey.
 Ind/Abst Am. Humanit. Index.

GW/0072-9582
HAMBURGER PHILOLOGISCHE STUDIEN. See Linguistics.

II/0256-2480
HAMLET STUDIES. [Hamlet stud.]. Vol. 1 (Apr. 1979)-. Periodical. English. an (summer). $18.00. Hamlet Studies / Rangoon Villa, 1 10 West Patel Nagar, New Delhi 110 008 India. **Tel** 011 91 11 5747399. **(Subscription address:** Prints India, 11 Darya Ganj, New Delhi 110002 India.) **ED** R. W. Desai. **LC** PR2807; .H267. **DD** 822.3/3. **[CCC].** Index available. cum. index. **Bk Rev**, (Qty: 6). **Ad Acc. Circ:** 300.
 Desc: An international journal of research exclusively on Shakespeare's Hamlet.
 Ind/Abst Abstr. Engl. Stud.; MLA Int. Bibl. Books Artic. Mod. Lang. Lit.

ZA
HANDBOOK / THE UNIVERSITY OF ZAMBIA, SCHOOL OF EDUCATION, DEPARTMENT OF LITERATURE & LANGUAGES. See Linguistics.

SZ
HANDBUCH DER DEUTSCHEN LITERATURGESCHICHTE. (19??)-. Monographic series. German. ir. Price varies per volume. KG Saur Verlag Bern, Neuengasse 43, CH-3001 Bern Switzerland. **Tel** 011 41 31 447019.

US/0440-2316
HANGING LOOSE. See Literature-Poetry.

KO
HANGUK MUNHAK. V. 1- Nov. 1973-. Periodical. Korean. mo. W300 single issue. 269 Chongjin-dong Chongno-ku, Seoul Korea. **LC** PL950.2; .H35.

KO
HANGUK MUNHAK PIPYONG SONJIP / HANGUK MUNHAK PYONGNONGA HYOPHOE. V. 1-Series ('81)-. Periodical. Korean. W4,500. IU Chulp Ansa 19-8, 5-ka Chungmu-ro, Chung-ku Seoul Korea. **LC** PL951; .H36.

KO
HANGUK UI MUNHAK. V. 1-Series. Periodical. Korean. W1.500. Hanguk Munhak Hyophoe, Samuguk 32, Tangju-dong, Seoul Korea. **LC** PL950.2; .H355.

●US/1070-6569
HARSH MISTRESS. [Harsh mistress]. Issue 1 (Spring/Summer 1993)-. Periodical. English. qt. $12.00. Harsh Mistress Science Fiction Adventures, Box 13, Greenfield MA 01302. **LC** WMLC 93/1893. **DD** 808. **Circ:** 3,000.

US/0017-8004
HARVARD ADVOCATE (CAMBRIDGE, MASS.), THE. (THE HARVARD ADVOCATE.). [Harv. advocate]. **Added/Corp** Harvard University. (1869)-. Periodical. English. Four times a year (Jan., March, May and Nov.). $17.00 (institutions), $15.00 (individuals); $20.00 other. Harvard Advocate, Advocate House, 21 South Street, Cambridge MA 02138. **Tel** (617)495-0737. **ED** Alp T. Aker. **DD** 810. **Bk Rev. Ad Acc, Adv Mgr:** Thomas Cheung. **Circ:** 4000. available on microfilm and microfiche from University Microfilms International (UMI). ***Continues*** *Advocate (Cambridge, Mass.)*; ***Absorbed*** *Harvard Critic.*
Ind/Abst Index Am. Period. Verse.

US/0073-0513
HARVARD ENGLISH STUDIES. [Harv. eng. stud.]. **Added/Corp** Harvard University. Dept. of English. (1970)-. Monographic series. English. ir. Price varies per volume. Harvard University Press, 79 Garden Street, Cambridge MA 02138. **Tel** (617)496-1344, (800)448-2242. **DD** 810.
Ind/Abst MLA Int. Bibl. Books Artic. Mod. Lang. Lit.; Romant. Move.

US/0073-0548
HARVARD JOURNAL OF ASIATIC STUDIES. **See** History(General)-History of Asia.

US
HARVARD REVIEW. English. sa (April and October). $12.00. Harvard University / Poetry Room, Harvard College Library, Cambridge MA 02138. **Tel** (617)495-2454. **ED** Stratis Haviaras. **Bk Rev**, (Qty: 130). **Ad Acc, Adv Mgr:** Joyce Wilson. **Circ:** 2,000.
Desc: Publishes poetry, fiction and essays and articles by both promising and prominent writers from all over the country and the world.

US/0073-0696
HARVARD STUDIES IN COMPARATIVE LITERATURE. [Harv. stud. comp. lit.]. **Added/Corp** Harvard University. Vol. 1 (1910)-. Monographic series. English. ir. Price varies per volume. Harvard University Press, 79 Garden Street, Cambridge MA 02138. **Tel** (617)496-1344, (800)448-2242. **DD** 805.
Ind/Abst Annu. Bibliogr. Engl. Lang. Lit.; MLA Int. Bibl. Books Artic. Mod. Lang. Lit.

US/0073-0718
HARVARD STUDIES IN ROMANCE LANGUAGES. [Harv. stud. roman. lang.]. **Added/Corp** Harvard University. Dept. of Romance Languages and Literatures. Vol. 1 (1915)-. Monographic series. English (French and Spanish). ir. Price varies per volume. Harvard University, Department of Romanace Language, 201 Boylston Hall, Cambridge MA 02138. **Tel** (617)495-2546. **ED** Per Nykrog. **LC** UNC. **DD** 840.
Ind/Abst MLA Int. Bibl. Books Artic. Mod. Lang. Lit.

US/0362-7888
HARVEST (FARMINGTON). (HARVEST.). 1974-. Periodical. English. Connecticut Writers League, PO Box 78, Farmington CT 06032.
Ind/Abst Biocont. News Inf.; Biodeter. Abstr.

US/0093-9625
HAWAII REVIEW. **Added/Corp** University of Hawaii. Associated Students. Vol. 1, No. 2 (Spring 1973)-. Periodical. English (Portuguese, German, Spanish, French, Japanese and Hawaiian). Three times a year. $15.00. University of Hawaii Department of English, 1733 Donaghho Road, Honolulu HI 96822. **Tel** (808)956-8548. **ED** Teya Maman. **LC** PS571.H3; H38. **DD** 810/.8/0054. **Bk Rev. Ad Acc. Circ:** 4,000 (ctrl). ***Continues*** *Hawaii Literary Review, 0090-8274.*
Desc: Poetry, prose, reviews and translations written by both local and non-local writers. Topics may deal with Hawaii and the Pacific Basin.
Ind/Abst Am. Humanit. Index; Index Am. Period. Verse.

GR
HE LEXE. (Jan. 1981)-. Periodical. Greek, Modern. mo.
Desc: Covers modern Greek literature and the arts.

II
HE RAMA. Periodical. Hindi (Hindi). 10.00. Valmiki Asrama, Kingsway Camp, Delhi 110009 India. **LC** PK2030; .H4.

●US/1061-4567
HEARTHSIDE READER, THE. (1992)-. Periodical. English. bm. $10.00. KT Media Communications, PO Box 50131, Idaho Falls ID 83405.

US/0887-2597
HEARTLAND JOURNAL. ***Ceased.*** [Heartl. j.]. **VFOAT** Heart Land Journal. (Fall/Winter 1983)-Ceased (Feb. 1990). Periodical. English. Three times a year. Creative Arts of 60 Inc, Box 55115, Madison WI 53705. **Tel** (608)238-4781. **ED** Lenore Coberly and Jeri McCormick. **Ad Acc. Circ:** 3,000.
Desc: Contains the writing and visual art of persons over 60. Forty-eight pages of poetry, prose, photos, drawings.

US/1042-5381
HEAVEN BONE. [Heaven bone]. Vol. 1, No. 1 (1987)-. Periodical. English. Twice a year (Mar. & Nov.). $16.95 US; $25.00 Canada; $26.95 Europe; $29.95 others. Heaven Bone Press, PO Box 486, Chester NY 10918. **DD** 810.

US/0885-7822
HEAVY METAL. [Heavy met.]. **VFOAT** Heavy Metal Magazine. No. 1 (Apr. 1977)-. Periodical. English (translations available in French). Six times a year (Jan., Mar., May, July, Sept., Nov.). $12.95 US; $20.95 other. Heavy Metal, 584 Broadway, Suite 608, New York NY 10012. **Tel** (212)274-8462. **ED** Julie Simmons Lynch. **DD** 741. **Bk Rev. Ad Acc. Circ:** 135,000 (ctrl).
Desc: A science fiction and fantasy magazine. Editorial content is both contemporary and futuristic in theme.

GW/0073-1560
HEBBEL JAHRBUCH. [Hebbel Jahrb.]. **Added/Corp** Friedrich Hebbel-Gesellschaft Deutsche Hebbel-Gesellschaft. (1939)-. German. an. DM38.00. Westholsteinische Verlagsanst Boyens & Co., Postfach 1880, D 25738 Heidelberg Germany. **Tel** 011 49 481 68860. **ED** Gunter Hautzschel and Voeker Schulz. **LC** PT2296.A1; H43. **DD** 832.77. **Circ:** 600.
Desc: The yearbook contains findings from international Germanistic scientists about literature and the reception of Hebbel-Literature.
Ind/Abst MLA Int. Bibl. Books Artic. Mod. Lang. Lit.

IS/0792-0393
HEBREW UNIVERSITY STUDIES IN LITERATURE AND THE ARTS. ***Ceased.*** **Added/Corp** Universitah ha-Ivrit bi-Yerushalayim. Makhon le-Safot, Sifruyot ve-Omanuyot. **VFOAT** HSLA. Vol. 11, No. 1 (Spring 1983)-(1993). Periodical. English (French). Three times a year. Magnes Press, Hebrew University of Jerusalem, PO Box 7695, Jerusalem 91076 Israel. **Tel** 011 972 2 660341, 011 972 2 635291, FAX 011 972 2 633370, telex 25391. **LC** PN1; .J46a. **DD** 809. Documents available from The Genuine Article. ***Continues*** *Hebrew University Studies in Literature, 0333-5690.*
Ind/Abst Abstr. Engl. Stud.; Annu. Bibliogr. Engl. Lang. Lit.; Arts Humanit. Citation Index (19??-19??) [Full Cov.]; Curr. Contents Arts Humanit.; Middle East Abstr. Index; MLA Int. Bibl. Books Artic. Mod. Lang. Lit.; Res. Alert [Full Cov.].

GW/0170-8821
HEIDELBERGER BEITRAEGE ZUR ROMANISTIK. **See** Linguistics.

GW/0440-6044
HEIDELBERGER FORSCHUNGEN. **See** Linguistics.

GW/0073-1692
HEINE-JAHRBUCH. [Heine-Jahrb.]. **Added/Corp** Landes- und Stadtbibliothek Dusseldorf. Heine-Archiv. Heinrich-Heine-Institut. Heinrich-Heine-Gesellschaft. (1962)-. German. an (Sept.). DM25.00. Hoffmann und Campe Verlag, Harvestehuder Weg 45, W 2000 Hamburg 13 FR Germany. **Tel** 011 49 40 44188223. **ED** Joseph A. Kruse. **LC** PT2328; .H43.
Desc: These are collection of research and essays on the life, writings and influence of 19th century German writer Heinrich Heine, with commentary on his poetry, music and literary criticism and his memoirs.
Ind/Abst BHA : Biblio. Hist. Art; MLA Int. Bibl. Books Artic. Mod. Lang. Lit.; Romant. Move.

US/0017-9884
HEIRS. Vol. 1 (Mar. 1968)-. Multiple languages (English, Spanish and Chinese). an. Heirs, 3562 18th Street, San Francisco CA 94110. **Tel** (415)824-8604.

NE
HELICON; REVUE INTERNATIONALE DES PROBLEMES GENERAUX DE LA LITTERATURE. **Added/Corp** International Committee on Modern Literary History. Vol. 1 (1938)-. Periodical. English (German, Spanish, French and Italian). ir. E. J. Brill, Postbus 9000, 2300 PA Leiden Netherlands. **Tel** 011 31 71 312624, FAX 011 31 71 317532, telex 39296 BRILL NL. **LC** PN1; .H4.

HU/0017-999X
HELIKON. [Helikon]. **Added/Corp** Magyar Tudomanyos Akademia. Irodalomtorteneti Intezet. (1964)-. Academic Scholarly Publication. Hungarian (table of contents in French and Russian). qt. $23.50. Akademiai Kiado, Publishing House of the Hungarian Academy of Sciences, Prielle Kornelia u. 19-35, H-1117 Budapest Hungary. **Tel** 011 36 1 1811991, FAX 011 36 1 1811991, telex 22-6228 AKNYO H. **(Subscription address:** Kultura, Hungarian Foreign Trading Company, PO Box 149, H-1389 Budapest Hungary**) ED** B. Kopeczi. **LC** PN9; .V53. **DD** 809. Index available. cum. index. **Bk Rev. Circ:** 1,400 (ctrl). ***Continues*** *Vilagirodalmi Figyelo.*
Desc: Comparative literature.
Ind/Abst Am. Hist. Life (1971-); Annu. Bibliogr. Engl. Lang. Lit.; MLA Int. Bibl. Books Artic. Mod. Lang. Lit.

IT
HELLAS. Vol. 1, No. 1 (1980)-. Periodical. Italian (French, Polish and Spanish). sa.
Ind/Abst Am. Humanit. Index (199?-).

US/1044-5331
HELLAS. (HELLAS : A JOURNAL OF POETRY AND THE HUMANITIES.). (Spring 1990)-. Periodical. English. sm. $12.00 North America; $16.00 other. 304 South Tyson Avenue, Glenside PA 19038. **Tel** (215)884-1086. **ED** Gerald Harnett. **LC** PS615; .H39. **DD** 811.008/005. Index available. **Ad Acc. Circ:** 1,000.

II
HELO. No. 1- April/June 1974-. Periodical. Rajasthani. 10.00. **LC** PK2708.45; .H44.

GW/0440-7164
HERMAEA. [Hermaea]. **VFOAT** Hermaea, Germanistische Forschungen. (1905)-. Monographic series. German. ir. Price varies per volume. Max Niemeyer Verlag, Postfach 2140, D 72011 Tuebingen Germany. **Tel** 011 49 7071 989494, FAX 011 49 7071 87419. **ED** Hans Fromm, Hans-Joachim Mahl.
Desc: Monographs on German literature.
Ind/Abst MLA Int. Bibl. Books Artic. Mod. Lang. Lit.

GW/0018-0777
HERMES (WIESBADEN). (HERMES : ZEITSCHRIFT FUER CLASSISCHE PHILOLOGIE.). [Hermes]. Vol. 1 (1866)-. Periodical. English (French and German). qt. DM198.00. Franz Steiner Verlag GmbH, Postfach 101061, D 70009 Stuttgart Germany. **Tel** 011 49 0711 2582372, FAX 011 49 0711 2582290, telex 723636 daz d. **ED** Jochen Bleicken, Siegmar Dopp, and Hartmut Erbse. **LC** PA3; .H5. **[CCC].** Index available in last issue of volume--attached.
Ind/Abst MLA Int. Bibl. Books Artic. Mod. Lang. Lit.; Soc. Sci. Cit. Index [Select. Cov.].

FR/0440-7237
HERNE, L'. **See** Philosophy.

II
HESPERUS REVIEW. (19??)-. English. qt. Rs4.00 India; £8.00 UK; $10.00 US. Gautam Chandra Chunder, 23 Nirmal Chunder Street, Calcutta 700 012 India. **Tel** 26-8248. **Ad Acc. Circ:** 500 (ctrl).

JA/0440-8047
HIKAKU BUNGAKU. **Added/Corp** Nihon Hikaku Bungakukai. **VFOAT** Journal of Comparative Literature. 1st Vol. (1958)-. Periodical. Japanese (English, French and German; summaries and/or abstracts in English, French and German). an. Price varies. **(Subscription address:** Japan Publications Trading Company, Ltd., PO Box 5030, Tokyo International, Tokyo 100-31 Japan.**)** ***Supersedes*** *Hikaku Bungaku Kenkyu.*

NP/0377-9661
HIMALI SAUGATA. V. 1- 2028- 1971-. Nepali (Nepali). 2.00. Sunsasari Hilla Humali Pustakalaya Sunsari Dist, Himali Pustakalaya, Mehendra Nagara Nepal. **LC** PK2598.A2; H55.

II
HINDI SAHITYABDAKOSA. 1- 1967-. Hindi (Hindi). **LC** PK2030; .H554.

SZ/0258-235X
HINWEISE UND STUDIEN ZUM LEBENSWERK VON ALBERT STEFFEN. No. 1 (1986)-. Periodical. German. ir (two or three issues a year). 8.00F (each issue). Verlag fur Schone Wissenschaften, Unterer Zielweg 36, CH-4143 Donarch Switzerland. **Tel** 061 701 39 11. **ED** Heinz Matile. ***Continues*** *Therapeutische Dichtung.*

US/1050-6802
HIPPO MAGAZINE. (HIPPO.). [Hippo mag.]. (Autumn & Winter 1988)-. Periodical. English. sa. $4.50 North America; $5.00 other. Chautauqua Press, 38834 Boniface Drive, Malibu CA 90265. **ED** Karl Heiss. **DD** 808. **Ad Acc. Pr Rev. Circ:** 150.
Desc: Open to all writing of quality meaning and interest to the human spirit. Most of what is submitted and fits these criteria is fiction; however, Hippo is open to all writing.

MG
HIRATRA / SAMPANA TENY SY LAHABOLANA ARY RIBA MALAGASY.
VFOAT Revio Hiratra. Periodical. Malagasy (French). an. 2000FMG. Departement de Langue Litterature et Civilisation Malgaches, BP 907 Postes 611 et 612, Antananarivo Madagascar. **Tel** 24114. **Ad Acc. Circ:** 1,500 (ctrl).
Desc: Studies about Malagasy languages, literature, traditions and customs.

US/0363-048X
HISPAMERICA. 1- 1975-. Spanish. $15.00. 5 Pueblo Court, Gaithersburg MD 20878. **LC** PQ7081.A1; H572. **DD** 860/.9.

US/0363-0471
HISPAMERICA (COLLEGE PARK).
(HISPAMERICA.). [Hispamerica]. Vol. 1, No. 1 (July 1972)-. Periodical. Spanish. Three times a year (Apr., Aug., Dec.). $30.00. Hispamerica, 5 Pueblo Court, Gaithersburg MD 20878. **Tel** (301)948-3494, FAX (301)314-9752. **ED** Saul Sosnowski. **LC** PQ7081.A1; H57. **DD** 860/.9. **CODEN** HSPAEC. Index available. **Bk Rev. Ad Acc. Pr Rev. Circ:** 1,000 (ctrl). Documents available from The Genuine Article.
Desc: Spanish American literature: essays, fiction, poetry, interviews, reviews, drama by internationally known and by new authors.
Ind/Abst Arts Humanit. Citation Index [Full Cov.]; Curr. Contents Arts Humanit.; HAPI Hisp. Am. Period. Index; MLA Int. Bibl. Books Artic. Mod. Lang. Lit.; Res. Alert [Full Cov.]; Soc. Sci. Cit. Index [Select. Cov.].

UK
HISPANIC ARTICLES IN SCHOLARLY PERIODICALS : ANNUAL BIBLIOGRAPHY. See Linguistics.

US/0893-2395
HISPANIC ISSUES. [Hisp. issues]. **Added/Corp** Prisma Institute (Minneapolis, Minn.). (1987)-. Monographic series. English. ir. Price varies per volume. University of Minnesota Press, 2037 University Avenue Southeast, Minneapolis MN 55414. **Tel** (612)642-2516, (612)624-0005. **DD** 860. Index available.
Ind/Abst MLA Int. Bibl. Books Artic. Mod. Lang. Lit.

US/0271-0986
HISPANIC JOURNAL. [Hisp. j.]. **Added/Corp** Indiana University of Pennsylvania. Dept. of Foreign Languages. Vol. 1 (Fall 1979)-. Periodical. English (Spanish). sa (April, Oct.). $15.00 (individuals), $30.00 (institutions). Indiana University of Pennsylvania / Department of Spanish, 462 Sutton Hall, Indiana PA 15705. **Tel** (412)357-2100. **ED** Joseph B. Spieker. **LC** PC4001; .H723. Index available. cum. index. **Bk Rev. Pr Rev. Circ:** 600.
Desc: Articles of literary criticism of Spanish and Latin American literature, language and culture. Book reviews and summaries are included.
Ind/Abst HAPI Hisp. Am. Period. Index; MLA Int. Bibl. Books Artic. Mod. Lang. Lit.; Romant. Move.

SZ/0170-8570
HISPANISTISCHE STUDIEN. [Hisp. Stud.]. (1974)-. Monographic series. German.
Ind/Abst MLA Int. Bibl. Books Artic. Mod. Lang. Lit.

US/0018-2206
HISPANOFILA. [Hispanofila]. Vol. 1 No. 1 (Sept. 1957)-. Periodical. Multiple languages (English, Spanish and Portuguese). Three times a year (Jan., May, Sept.). $18.00 (individuals); $21.00 (institutions). University of North Carolina Department of Romance Languages, CB 3170, 237 Dey Hall, Chapel Hill NC 27599-3170. **Tel** (919)962-1025. **ED** Fred Clark. **LC** PQ6001; .H55. **DD** 860/.5. **Bk Rev. Circ:** 500 (ctrl). available on microfilm and microfiche from University Microfilms International (UMI). Documents available from The Genuine Article.
Ind/Abst Arts Humanit. Citation Index [Full Cov.]; Curr. Contents Arts Humanit.; MLA Int. Bibl. Books Artic. Mod. Lang. Lit.; Res. Alert [Full Cov.]; Romant. Move.

HU
HISTOIRE COMPAREE DES LITTERATURES DE LANGUES EUROPEENNES. **VFOAT** Comparative History of Literatures in European Languages. Monographic series. English (French). Price varies per volume. Humanities Press, 165 1st Avenue, Atlantic Highlands NJ 07716. **Tel** (908)872-1441, (800)221-3845, FAX (908)872-0717, telex 752233.

FR
HISTOIRE LITTERAIRE DE LA FRANCE.
(1733)-. French. Kraus Reprint and Periodicals, 358 Saw Mill River Road, Millwood NY 10546. **Tel** (914)762-2200, (800)223-8323, FAX (914)762-1195, telex 6818112.
Desc: Contains biographical and critical articles on individual authors in French literature.

FI/0073-2702
HISTORISKA OCH LITTERATURHISTORISKA STUDIER.
[Hist. litteraturhist. stud.]. 1 (1925)-. Swedish. an. Fmk100.00. Svenska Litteratursallskapet I Finland, Snellmansgaten 9 11, 00170 Helsingfors 17 Finland. **ED** Helena Solstrand-Pipping. **LC** PT9205; .S75. Index available. cum. index. ctrl circ. ***Continues in part*** *Forhandlingar och Uppsatser.*
Ind/Abst Am. Hist. Life (1956-); MLA Int. Bibl. Books Artic. Mod. Lang. Lit.

GW/0441-6813
HOFMANNSTHAL BLATTER. ***Title Change.*** [Hofmannsthalblatter]. **Added/Corp** Hugo von Hofmannsthal-Gesellschaft. (1968)-(1993). Periodical. German. sa. Hugo Von Hofmannsthal, Gesselschaft AM Flossgraben 4, D 79102 Freiburg BR Germany. **Tel** 011 49 761 22482. **ED** Leonhard Fiedler. **LC** PT2617.O47; Z73676. ***Absorbed by*** *Hofmannsthal Jahrbuch zur Europaischen Moderne.*
Desc: Publishes original research articles on early 20th century Austrian poet and playwright Hugo von Hofmannsthal, as well as document texts, sketches and correspondence. Includes bibliography of new literature on the subject.
Ind/Abst MLA Int. Bibl. Books Artic. Mod. Lang. Lit.

SZ
HOFMANNSTHAL-FORSCHUNGEN. ***Title Change.*** **Added/Corp** Arbeitsstelle Basel der Kritischen Hofmannsthal-Ausgabe. Hugo von Hofmannsthal-Gesellschaft. **VFOAT** Hofmannstahl Forschungen. Vol. 1 (1971)-(19??). Monographic series. German. ir. Hugo Von Hofmannsthal, Gesselschaft AM Flossgraben 4, D 79102 Freiburg BR Germany. **Tel** 011 49 761 22482. **ED** Wolfram Mauser. ***Absorbed by*** *Hofmannsthal Jahrbuch zur Europaischen Moderne.*
Desc: Publishes scholarly research on the work and life of Hugo von Hofmannsthal, early 20th century Austrian poet and playwright.

US/0195-802X
HOFSTRA UNIVERSITY CULTURAL & INTERCULTURAL STUDIES. [Hofstra Univ. cult. intercult. stud.]. **Added/Corp** Hofstra University. **VFOAT** Cultural & Intercultural Studies; Cultural and Intercultural Studies. **VAT** Hofstra University Cultural and Intercultural Studies. No. 1 (1980)-. Monographic series. English. ir. Price varies per volume. AMS Press Inc., 56 East 13th Street, New York NY 10003. **Tel** (212)777-4700, FAX (212)995-5413, telex 710 581 2302. **ED** C Harvington and M Barnett.
Desc: Presents volumes examining authors such as George Sands, Heinrich von Kleist, and William Cullen Bryant.

GW/0340-6849
HOLDERLIN-JAHRBUCH. [Hoelderlin-Jahrb.]. **Added/Corp** Holderlin-Gesellschaft. (1947)-. German. an. DM84.00. JCB Mohr / Paul Siebeck, Postfach 2040, D 72010 Tuebingen Germany. **Tel** 011 49 7071 9230, FAX 011 49 7071 51104, telex 7/262872 mohr d. **ED** Bernhard Boeschenstein, Gerhard Kurz. ***Continues*** *Iduna (Tubingen, Germany).*
Desc: Published under the auspices of the Holderlin Society. Contains reports and essays on this lyric poet, focusing on his debt to classical Greek poetry and philosophy in form and content, as well as stylistic analyses.
Ind/Abst BHA : Biblio. Hist. Art; MLA Int. Bibl. Books Artic. Mod. Lang. Lit.; Romant. Move.

CN/1180-1670
HOLE. [Hole]. Issue 1 (Spring 1990)-. Periodical. English. sa. 8.00Can$ North America; 16.00Can$ other. Hole Magazine, 147 Sweetland Avenue, Ottawa Ontario K1N 7V1 Canada. **Tel** (613)230-6981, FAX (613)234-0871. **ED** Louis Cabri and Robert Manery. **DD** C810.8/0054. **Bk Rev. Circ:** 300.
Desc: A magazine of contemporary writing and reading.

NE
HOLLANDS MAANDBLAD. ***Ceased.*** Vol. 4, No. 183 (Jan. 17, 1963)-(19??). Periodical. Dutch. mo. Trio Goemans BV, Postbus 256, 2170 AG Sassemheim Netherlands. ***Continues*** *Hollands Weekblad.*

US/0273-303X
HOME PLANET NEWS. [Home planet news]. (197?)-. Periodical. English. Three times a year. $8.00 (four issues); $15.00 (eight issues); $20.00 (twelve issues). Home Planet News, PO Box 415, Stuyvesant Station, New York NY 10009. **Tel** (718)769-2854. **ED** Donald Lev. Index available. cum. index. **Bk Rev**, (Qty: 15-20). **Ad Acc. Circ:** 1,000.
Desc: Presents quality poetry and fiction, together with book, theater and art reviews.
Ind/Abst Am. Humanit. Index (199?-).

UK/0018-4543
HONEST ULSTERMAN, THE. No. 1 (May 1968)-. Periodical. English. ir (3 or 4 times per year). Ulsterman Publications, 102 Elm Park Mansions PK Walk, London SW10 0AP England. **LC** AP4; .H85. **DD** 052.
Ind/Abst Annu. Bibliogr. Engl. Lang. Lit.

GW/0018-4942
HOREN : JUNGER LITERATURKREIS, DIE. Vol. 1 (1955)-. Periodical. German. Four times a year (Mar., June, Sept., Dec.). DM49.00. Wirtschaftsverlag NW, Verlag fur Neue Wissenschaft GmbH, Postfach 101110, D-27511 Bremerhaven Germany. **Tel** 011 49 471 46093, 011 49 471 46094, 011 49 471 46095, FAX 011 49 471 42765. **ED** Kurt Morawietz. **LC** PN4; .H67. **Bk Rev. Ad Acc. Circ:** 5,500.
Ind/Abst MLA Int. Bibl. Books Artic. Mod. Lang. Lit.

IO/0441-2168
HORISON. (1966)-. Periodical. English. Twelve times a year. $46.80. PT Gramedia/ Export Department, JL Gajah Mada 104/ PO Box 615, Jakarta 11140 Indonesia. **Tel** 011 62 21 6297809 Ext. 4610, FAX 011 62 21 6498475, telex 41216. **LC** PL5080; .A28.

FI/0018-4950
HORISONT (VASSA, FINLAND).
(HORISONT.). Began in 1954. Periodical. Swedish. bm. $22.00. Kerstin Troberg, Bollgatan 12 C, 65230 Vasa 23 Finland. **LC** PT9958; .H67. cum. index.
Ind/Abst Annu. Bibliogr. Engl. Lang. Lit.; MLA Int. Bibl. Books Artic. Mod. Lang. Lit.

CN/0229-1215
HORIZONS SF. [Horiz. SF]. Periodical. English. mo. 2.00Can$ (per issue) Canada; $2.50 (per issue) US. UBC Science Fiction Society, Box 75, Student Union Building, University of British Columbia, Vancouver British Columbia Canada. **ED** Tricia Schulte, Duncan Stewart, and John Wong. **DD** C813/.087608. **Bk Rev. Ad Acc. Circ:** 200 (ctrl). ***Continues*** *Horizons (Vancouver, B.C. : 1979), 0229-1207.*
Desc: Prints science fiction and fantasy, mainly for a university audience in Canada.

US/1044-405X
HORN BOOK GUIDE TO CHILDREN'S AND YOUNG ADULT BOOKS, THE. See Children and Youth Interests.

US/0896-9965
HORNS OF PLENTY, MALCOLM COWLEY AND HIS GENERATION. [Horns plenty Malcolm Cowley his gener.]. **VFOAT** Horns of Plenty. Vol. 1, No. 1 (Spring 1988)-. Periodical. English. qt. $15.00 (individuals), $20.00 (institutions) North America; $25.00 other. Horns of Plenty, 113 Wolpers Road, Park Forest IL 60466. **Tel** (312)728-4671. **ED** Yolanda Butts and William Butts. **DD** 811. **Bk Rev. Circ:** 400 (ctrl).
Desc: The latest in creative and critical thought on Malcolm Cowley (1898-1989) and that generation of writers born around the turn of the century.
Ind/Abst MLA Int. Bibl. Books Artic. Mod. Lang. Lit.

US/0748-2914
HORROR SHOW, THE. [Horror show]. Began Nov. 1982. Periodical. English. qt. $14.00. Phantasm Press Star, 14848 Misty Springs Lane, T Oak Run CA 96069. **Tel** (916)472-3540. **ED** David B Silva. **DD** 813. **Bk Rev. Ad Acc. Circ:** 4,000.
Desc: Slanted toward the horror fan, it includes an equal presentation of fiction and non-fiction.

UK/0305-926X
HOUSMAN SOCIETY JOURNAL. [Housman Soc. j.]. **Main/Corp** Housman Society. Vol. 1 (1974)-. English. an. £7.00 UK; £8.00 other. Housman Society, 1 Warwick Hall Gardens, Bromsgrove, B60 2AU England. **Tel** 0527 73604. **ED** Alan Holden. **LC** PR4809.H15; H64a. **DD** 821/.9/12. **Bk Rev. Ad Acc.**
Desc: Lives and works of A.E. Housman, Clementine Housman and Lawrence Housman.
Ind/Abst Annu. Bibliogr. Engl. Lang. Lit.; MLA Int. Bibl. Books Artic. Mod. Lang. Lit.

US/0888-3521
HOWLING DOG. Vol. 1, No. 1 (Spring 1985)-. Periodical. English. qt. $10.00. **DD** 811.
Ind/Abst Am. Humanit. Index (199?-).

CH
HSI CHU HSUEH HSI / CHUNG YANG HSI CHU HSUEH YUAN PIEN. **VFOAT** Xijuxuexi. Periodical. Chinese. NT$0.55. Science Press, 16 Donghuangchenggen North Street, Beijing 100707, People's Republic of China. **Tel** 011 86 1 4019821, 011 86 1 4010642, FAX 011 86 1 4012180, 011 86 1 4019810, telex 210147. **LC** PL2357; .H72. **DD** 895.1/2/005.

CC
HSIAO HSI TSUNG KAN. **VFOAT** Xiaoxi Congkan. Periodical. Chinese. RMBY0.25. Hsin Hua Shu Tien / Shang-Hai Fa Hsing So, Shanghai, People's Republic of China. **LC** PL2603; .H7333. **DD** 895.1/25/08.

CC
HSIAO PENG YU. ***Ceased.*** **VFOAT** Xiao Peng You. Periodical. Chinese. Sun Ya Publications Ltd, 1065 Kings Rd, Suite 1306, Cause Way Bay Hong Kong. **Tel** 5 647587.

CH
HSIAO SHUO LIN (HARBIN, CHINA).
(HSIAO SHUO LIN.). **VFOAT** Xiaoshuolin; Xiao Shuo Lin. Periodical. Chinese. mo. NT$0.35. Post Office, Harbin, People's Republic of China. **LC** PL2443; .H72. **DD** 895.1/35/08.

CC
HSIAO SHUO YUEH PAO. **VFOAT** Xiaoshuo Yuebao; Story Monthly. (Jan. 1980)-. Periodical. Chinese.

mo. $36.24. **(Subscription address:** China International Book Trading Corporation, PO Box 399, Library Service Department, Beijing 100044 People's Republic of China.) **LC** PL2653; .H76617.
Desc: Covers Chinese fiction and short stories.

CC
HSIN-CHIANG MIN CHIEN WEN HSUEH. Vol. 1, (Dec. 1981)-. Periodical. Chinese. Hsin-Chiang Hsin Hua Shu Tien, Wu-Lu-Mu-Chi, People's Republic of China. **LC** PL2446; .H7353. **DD** 398.2/0951/6.

CH
HSIN-CHIANG WEN HSUEH. VFOAT Xinjiang Wenxue. Periodical. Chinese. mo. NT$0.30. Chuan Kuo Ko Ti Yu Chu, Lan-Chou, People's Republic of China. **Tel** 66117, 66293. **LC** PL3031.S552; H84.

CH
HSIN HAI. (1982)-. Periodical. Chinese. mo. Hsin Hai Tsa Chih She, Taipei Taiwan. **LC** AP95.C4; H73134. **DD** 951/.24905/05.

CC
HSIN KANG. VFOAT Xingang; Xin Gang. Began with July 1956 issue. Periodical. Chinese. mo. RMBY0.35. Chung-Kuo Chu Pan Tui Wai Mao I Kung SSU, Shing-Hai Fen Kung SSU, 380 Pei Su-Chou Road, Shanghai, People's Republic of China. **LC** PL2513; .H663. **DD** 895.1/09/005.

CH
HSIN TSUN. VFOAT Xin Cun. Periodical. Chinese. bm. NT$0.35. Chi-Lin Sheng Hsin Hua Shu Tien, Chang-Chuan Shih, People's Republic of China. **LC** AP95.C4; H763.

CC
HSIN WEN HSUEH SHIH LIAO. VFOAT Xinwenxue Shiliao. V. 1, 1978-. Periodical. Chinese. qt. RMBY1.00. Science Press, 16 Donghuangchenggen North Street, Beijing 100707, People's Republic of China. **Tel** 011 86 1 4019821, 011 86 1 4010642, FAX 011 86 1 4012180, 011 86 1 4019810, telex 210147. **LC** PL2303; .H744. **DD** 895.1/09/005.

CC
HUA CHENG. VFOAT Huacheng. (April 1979)-. Periodical. Chinese. bm. $30.02. **(Subscription address:** China International Book Trading Corporation, PO Box 399, Library Service Department, Beijing 100044 People's Republic of China.) **LC** PL2303; .H79.
Desc: Covers Chinese literature.

CH
HUANG KUAN. VFOAT Crown. (Feb. 1953)-. Periodical. Chinese. ir. $77.00. Crown Magazine, No 50 Lane 120 Tun Hua Road, Taipei Taiwan. **Tel** 011 886 2 7168888.
Desc: Covers Chinese literature.

IO/0852-8225
HUMOR. No. 1 (Oct. 10-23, 1990)-. Periodical. Indonesian. bm. **LC** PN6222.I56; H85.

●HU
HUNGARIAN QUARTERLY, THE. Vol. 34, No. 129 (Spring 1993)-. Periodical. English. Four times a year (Mar., June, Sept., Dec.). $34.00 (individuals), $45.00 (institutions) US & Canada; $30.00 (individuals), $41.00 (institutions) Western Europe; $36.00 (individuals), $47.00 (institutions) others. MTI Hungarian News Agency, PO Box 3, H 1426 Budapest, Hungary. **Tel** 011 36 1 756722, FAX 011 36 1 188297, telex 224373 224374. **LC** DB901; .N476. ***Continues*** *NHQ; the New Hungarian Quarterly.*
Ind/Abst Arts Humanit. Citation Index [Full Cov.]; Soc. Sci. Cit. Index [Select. Cov.].

HU
HUNGARIAN STUDIES IN ENGLISH : HSE. Added/Corp Kossuth Lajos Tudomanyegyetem. Institute of English and American Studies. **VFOAT** HSE. Vol. 22 (1991)-. Periodical. English. an. Australian Government Publishing Service, GPO Box 84, Canberra ACT 2601 Australia. **Tel** 011 61 6 2954411, FAX 011 61 6 2954455. **LC** DB926; .A76. ***Continues*** *Angol Filologiai Tanulmanyok, 0570-0973.*
Ind/Abst Abstr. Engl. Stud.; Annu. Bibliogr. Engl. Lang. Lit.; MLA Int. Bibl. Books Artic. Mod. Lang. Lit.

US/0018-7895
HUNTINGTON LIBRARY QUARTERLY, THE. See The Arts-Art.

KO
HYONDAE MUNHAK. (19??)-. Periodical. Korean. Twelve times a year. $172.00. **(Subscription address:** Dong A Book Store, 9828 Garden Grove Boulevard #104, Garden Grove, CA 92644 USA) **LC** PL950.2; .H96.

US/0018-8328
HYPERION (BERKELEY). ***Suspended.*** (HYPERION.). [Hyperion]. Vol. 1 Winter 1970-Suspended with Vol. 8, 1980. Periodical. English. sa. $5.00. Paul and Foster Foreman, Thorp Springs Press, 803 Red River, Austin TX 78701. **Tel** (919)967-8666.

US/1058-3297
HYPHEN MAGAZINE. VFOAT Hyphen. Vol. 1, Issue 1 (1991)-. Periodical. English. Three times a year. $12.00. Shoestring Publications, PO Box 516, Somonauk IL 60552. **Tel** (815)498-3547. **DD** 818.

US
I & L / INSTITUTE FOR THE STUDY OF IDEOLOGIES AND LITERATURE. VFOAT I Y L. **VAT** Ideologies and Literature. Monographic series. Spanish (English and Portuguese). Price varies per volume. Institute for the Study of Ideologies and Literature, 4 Folwell Hall, 9 Pleasant Street SE, University of Minnesota, Minneapolis MN 55455. **Tel** (612)373-7998.

US/0271-9061
I.O. EVANS STUDIES IN THE PHILOSOPHY & CRITICISM OF LITERATURE. [I.O. Evans stud. philos. crit. lit.]. **VFOAT** Evans Studies in the Philosophy & Criticism of Literature; Studies in the Philosophy & Criticism of Literature. **VAT** I.O. Evans Studies in the Philosophy and Criticism of Literature. No. 1 (1982)-. Monographic series. English. ir. Price varies per volume. Borgo Press, PO Box 2845, San Bernardino CA 92406. **Tel** (714)884-5813, (714)885-1161. **ED** Boden Clark.
Desc: Include monographs on general literacy topics, histories and discussions of genre fiction, anthologies of essays on specific literary themes, philosophical discussions of literature, and books of related interest.

US/1056-5000
IBERICA. [Iberica]. (1991)-. Monographic series. English. Peter Lang Publishing, 62 West 45th Street, 4th Floor, New York NY 10036. **Tel** (212)764-1471, (800)770-5264, telex 6973364 PLNY. **DD** 860.

IE/0019-1027
ICARUS. No. 1- May 1950-). Periodical. English. ir. University of Dublin, Trinity College, Regent House, Dublin 2 Ireland.

US/1054-1381
ICARUS (NEW YORK, N.Y.). (ICARUS.). [Icarus]. Vol. 1 (Winter 1991)-. Periodical. English. qt (Jan., Apr., Aug., Oct.). $30.55 (US); $38.55 (other). Rosen Publishing Group, 29 East 21st Street, New York NY 10010. **Tel** (800) 237-9932, (212) 777-3017, FAX (212) 777-0277. **DD** 808.

US/1043-7010
ICE RIVER. [Ice river]. (Summer 1987)-. Periodical. English. Three times a year. $9.00 North America; $12.00 other. Ice River Inc, 953 North Gale, Union OR 97883. **Tel** (503)562-5638. **ED** David Memmott, Nico Vassilakis, Noemie Maxwell, and Michael Chocholak. **DD** 810. **Bk Rev. Ad Acc. Pr Rev. Circ:** 500.
Desc: Speculative writing (SF, surrealism, futurism, modern fantasy, magical realism), fantastic art and contemporary music.

CN/0229-1495
ICHOR. [Ichor]. **VFOAT** Ichor: a Magazine of Surreal Prose. 1 (Winter 1980)-. Periodical. English. qt. $8.50. Crescent Publications, PO Box 419 Station A, Ottawa Ontario K1N 8V4 Canada. **DD** C838/.540808.

BE/0772-3784
IDES ... ET AUTRES. [Ides autres]. **VFOAT** Collection "Ides ... et Autres.". (1974)-. Periodical. French. Eight times a year. 1500F. Bernard Goorden, BP33, Uccle 4, B 1180 Brussels Belgium. **ED** Bernard Goorden. Index available. ctrl circ. available on diskette.

AT/1032-1640
IDIOM 23. [Idiom 23]. (1988)-. English. Twice a year (May & Oct.). 10.00Aus$ (Australia); 14.00Aus$ (US & Canada); 14.50Aus$ (Germany, Greece, USSR, Yugoslavia, UK, Africa, Poland, Netherlands, & Jamaica; 13.25Aus$ (Hong Kong, India, Japan, Philippines, & Vietnam); 12.60Aus$ (Malaysia & Singapore); 12.10Aus$ (New Zealand & Guinea). Humanities & Social Sciences, University College of Central Queensland, Rockhampton Queensland 4700 Australia. **Tel** 011 61 79 369501, FAX 011 61 79 361361. **ED** Liz Huf and Stuart Glorer. **DD** 820.8003. **Bk Rev. Ad Acc. Pr Rev. Circ:** 600.
Desc: Australian short stories, poetry, book reviews, and critical writing.

RU
IDISHE GAS, DI. Russian. Twelve times a year. $95.95. **(Subscription address:** East View Publications Inc., 3020 Harbor Lane North, Suite 110, Minneapolis MN 55447.) ***Continues*** *Sovetish Heimland, 0134-4315.*

IT
IDRA. Italian. sa. L50000.00 Italy; L60000.00 other. Anabasi Edizioni, V S Giovanni Sul Muro 4, 20121 Milan Italy. **Tel** 011 39 2 86454193.

US/1061-9232
ILF CALENDAR NEWSLETTER. (ILF CALENDAR NEWSLETTER : INTERACTIVE LITERATURE FOUNDATION NEWSLETTER OF LIVE ACTION ROLE PLAYING GAMES AND RELATED EVENTS.). [ILF cal. newsl.]. **Added/Corp** Interactive Literature Foundation. **VAT** Interactive Literature Foundation Calendar Newsletter. (1991)-. Newsletter. English. qt. $3.00. Interactive Literature Foundation, PO Box 196, Merrifield VA 22116-0196. **DD** 794.

BL
ILHA DO DESTERRO / DEPTO. DE LINGUA E LITERATURA ANGLO-AMERICANAS, UNIVERSIDADE FEDERAL DE SANTA CATARINA. Added/Corp Universidade Federal de Santa Catarina. Depto. de Lingua e Literatura Anglo-Americanas. Universidade Federal de Santa Catarina. Programa de Pos-Graduacao em Ingles e Literatura Correspondente. **VFOAT** Exile's Island. No. 1 (Mar. 1979)-. English. sa. **LC** Discard; PN6010.5; .I442.
Ind/Abst MLA Int. Bibl. Books Artic. Mod. Lang. Lit.

US
ILLINOIS ENGLISH BULLETIN : OFFICIAL PUBLICATION OF THE ILLINOIS ASSOCIATION OF TEACHERS OF ENGLISH. Added/Corp Illinois Association of Teachers of English. Vol. 29, No. 1 (Oct. 1941)-. Periodical. English. Four times a year (Jan., Mar., May, Oct.). $20.00. Illinois Association of Teachers of English, 608 South Wright Street, Urbana IL 61801. **Tel** (217)333-1006, FAX (217)333-4321. **ED** James Stottlar. **Circ:** 1,600. ***Continues*** *Bulletin (Illinois Association of Teachers of English).*
Desc: News and teaching articles place emphasis on composition and literature.

US/0748-1780
IMAGE (ST. LOUIS, MO.). (IMAGE.). [Image]. **VFOAT** Image Magazine. (197?)-. Periodical. English. bm. $15.95 US; $23.00 other. Image Magazine, 3117 North 7th Street, West Monroe LA 71291. **Tel** (318)396-4366. **ED** Anthony J. Summers. **DD** 810. **Bk Rev. Circ:** 600 (ctrl).
Desc: A collection of poetry, fiction, artwork, reviews, photographs and creative works.

VE
IMAGEN : ARTES, LETRAS, ESPECTACULOS. ***Title Change.*** **Added/Corp** Instituto Nacional de Cultura y Bellas Artes. Consejo Nacional de la Cultura. No. 1 (June 1971)-(19??). Periodical. Spanish. wk. Semanario de Arte Literatura, Escriba Al Apartado 50995, Caravus Venezuela. **LC** PQ8530; .I45. ***Continues*** *Imagen.* ***Continued by*** *Imagen (Caracas, Venezuela : 1988).*

CN/0846-1015
IMAGINARY TALES. [Imagin. tales]. Issue No. 1 (May/June 1990)-. Periodical. English. qt. Imaginary Tales, PO Box 1559, Brockville, Ontario K6V 6E6 Canada. **DD** C810.8/0054.

CN/0709-8855
IMAGINE (MONTREAL). (IMAGINE ...). **VFOAT** Revue de Science-Fiction Quebecoise. Vol. 1 (Sept./Nov. 1979)-. Periodical. French. qt. 20.00Can$ (one year), 38.00Can$ (two years) Canada; 30.00Can$ (one year), 58.00Can$ (two years) other. Imagine, 3418 De La Paix, Sainte Foy Quebec G1X 3W6 Canada. **Tel** (418)658-9966, FAX (418)658-6100. **ED** Marc Lemaire. **DD** 808.83/876. Index available. cum. index. **Bk Rev,** (Qty: 50). **Ad Acc. Circ:** 600 (ctrl).
Desc: Mainly concerned with science fiction. Presents short stories, book reviews and essays on various topics.

IT
IMMAGINE RIFLESSA, L'. (Jan./April 1977)-. Periodical. Italian. Twice a year. L40000. Edizioni Orso, Via Piacenza 66, 15100 Alessandria Italy. **Tel** 011 39 131 252349. **ED** Nicolo Pasero. **LC** PN5; .I44. **DD** 805. **Bk Rev. Ad Acc. Circ:** 1,000.
Desc: A journal of sociology of literature which pays attention to the literary text in connection with the social context in which it appears.

FR/0242-5149
IMPREVUE (MONTPELLIER). (IMPREVUE.). [Imprevue]. **Added/Corp** Universite Paul Valery. Centre d'Etudes et Recherches Socio-critiques. Vol. 1 (1978)-. Periodical. French (Spanish). sa. 120.00F France; 150.00F other. Centre d'Etudes Sociocritiques, Univ Paul Vallery, BP 5043, 34032 Montpellier Cedex France. **Tel** 011 33 67 142326. **LC** AS161; .I465. **DD** 054/.1. **Bk Rev. Circ:** 600 (ctrl).
Desc: Studies in literary texts on films. Studies in theory and culture, criticism and socialism.
Ind/Abst MLA Int. Bibl. Books Artic. Mod. Lang. Lit.

AU/0304-1239
IMPULSE (WIEN). (IMPULSE.). [Impulse]. (19??)-. Periodical. German. qt. S80.00. **LC** PT1141.A2; I48.

IT
IN FORMA DI PAROLE. ***Ceased.*** Vol. 10 (Mar. 1980)-(19??). Czech (German and Italian). Three times a year. Coop Editoriale Elitropia, Via Benedetto Croce 19, 42100 Reggio Emilia Italy. **LC** PN5; .I45. **DD** 808.8.

US/1059-1230
IN YOUR FACE. See Ethnic Interests.

AG/0326-0941
INCIPIT. [Incipit]. **Added/Corp** Seminario de Edicion y Critica Textual (Buenos Aires, Argentina). Vol. 1 (1981)-. Periodical. Spanish. an (Aug.). $15.00. Seminario de Edicion de Critica, Textural Riobamba 950, 1116 Buenos Aires Argentina. **(Subscription address:** Incipit, Michigan State University, c/o J. Snow, Romance Classical Languages Department, East Lansing MI 48824.) **ED** German Orduna. **LC** PQ6001; .I5. Index available. **Bk Rev. Ad Acc. Circ:** 500 (ctrl).
Desc: Publishes original studies of textual criticism on Spanish and Hispanic American literature in all periods.
Ind/Abst MLA Int. Bibl. Books Artic. Mod. Lang. Lit.

US/0019-3763
INDEPENDENT SHAVIAN, THE. [Indep. Shavian]. **Added/Corp** New York Shavians. Bernard Shaw Society. Vol. 1, No. 1 (Oct. 1962)-. Periodical. English. Three times a year (varies). $20.00. Bernard Shaw Society Inc., PO Box 1159 Madison Square Station, New York NY 10159-1159. **Tel** (212)989-7833. **ED** Richard Nickson and Douglas Laurie (phone: (212)982-9885). **LC** PR5366; .A136. **DD** 822/.912. Index available (published separately). cum. index. **Bk Rev. Ad Acc. Circ:** 500. available on microfilm and microfiche from University Microfilms International (UMI). ***Continues*** *Regional.*
Desc: Features book and theatre reviews, illustrations, critical articles, rarely printed original pieces by G.B. Shaw, and other material relating to the life, work, and interests of Bernard Shaw, his circle, and his world.
Ind/Abst Abstr. Engl. Stud.; Annu. Bibliogr. Engl. Lang. Lit.; Lit. Crit. Regist.; MLA Int. Bibl. Books Artic. Mod. Lang. Lit.

US/0090-9130
INDEX OF AMERICAN PERIODICAL VERSE. **See** Literature-Abstracting, Bibliographies and Statistics.

UK
INDEX OF ENGLISH LITERARY MANUSCRIPTS. English. Mansell Publishing Ltd, Stanley House, #3 Fleets Lane, Poole Dorset BH15 3AJ England. **Tel** 011 44 71 8394900.

UK
INDEX OF ISLAMIC LITERATURE. **See** Literature-Abstracting, Bibliographies and Statistics.

UK/0267-2472
INDEX OF MIDDLE ENGLISH PROSE. [Index Middle Engl. Prose]. (1984)-. English. ir. £25.00, $45.00. Boydell and Brewer Limited, PO Box 9, Woodbridge Suffolk, 1P12 3DF England. **Tel** 011 44 394 411320, FAX 011 44 394 411477. **DD** 820.9001.

CH
INDEX TO CHINESE PERIODICAL LITERATURE / CHUNG-HUA MIN KUO CHI KAN LUN WEN SO YIN. **Added/Corp** Chung Yang T'u Shu Kuan, Taipei. **VFOAT** Index to Chinese Periodicals. (January 1972)-. Periodical. Chinese. Four times a year (Feb., May, Aug., Nov.). $69.00. Center Chinese Studies Taiwan, 20 Chungshan South Road, Taipei Taiwan. **Tel** 011 886 2 3147321. **(Subscription address:** NCL Subscription Service, 20 Chungshan South Road, Taipei Taiwan Republic of China) **LC** AI19.C5; C57. **NLM** Z 6958.C5 C5593. ***Supersedes*** *Chung-hua Min Kuo Chi Kan Lun Wen So Yin: Ko Hsueh Chi Shu Pu; Chung-hua Min Kuo Chi Kan Lun Wen So Yin: Jen Wen She Hui Ko Hsueh Pu.*

UK
INDEX TO DEVELOPMENT LITERATURE. (1988)-. English. Six times a year (Jan., Mar., May, July, Sept., Nov.). £22.00 UK; £26.00 others. ODI Publications, Regents College, Inner Circle Regents Park, London NW1 4N5 England. **Tel** 011 44 71 487 7413. **(Subscription address:** Oversead Development Institute, 10-11 Percy Street, London W1P 0JB England)

US/0882-5947
INDEX TO SCIENCE FICTION ORIGINAL ANTHOLOGIES. [Index sci. fict. orig. anthol.]. (1985)-. Periodical. English. an. TWAC Press, Box 87, MIT Branch Post Office, Cambridge MA 02139.

US/0732-0655
INDEX TO THE SCIENCE FICTION MAGAZINES (1979). (INDEX TO THE SCIENCE FICTION MAGAZINES / COMPILED BY JERRY BOYAJIAN AND KENNETH R. JOHNSON.). [Index sci. fict. mag.]. (1979)-. English. an. $4.50. New England Science Fiction Association, PO Box 809, Framingham MA 01701. **LC** Z5917.S36; I553; PS374.S35. **DD** 016.813/0876/08.

US/0743-4103
INDEX TO THE SEMI-PROFESSIONAL FANTASY MAGAZINES. [Index semi-prof. fantasy mag.]. 1982-. English. an. $3.00. TWACI Press, PO Box 87, M I T Branch/Post Office, Cambridge MA 02139. **LC** Z6514.F35; I5; PN56.F34. **DD** 016.80883/876.

II
INDIAN AUTHOR. V. 1-. Periodical. English. $3.00. Authors Guild of India, C 12 South Extension Park I, New Delhi 110049 India. **LC** PN109; .I54. **DD** 809/.8954.

II/0537-6554
INDIAN JOURNAL OF ENGLISH STUDIES. (THE INDIAN JOURNAL OF ENGLISH STUDIES : THE OFFICIAL ORGAN OF THE INDIAN ASSOCIATION FOR ENGLISH STUDIES.). [Indian j. Engl. stud.]. **Added/Corp** Indian Association for English Studies. (1960)-. English. an (Nov.). $12.00 (one year); $30.00 (three years). Indian Association of English Studies, C/O Dr. Rk. Dhawan J., 391 North Rajinder, Nagar New Delhi 110 060 India. **Tel** 011 91 11 5737849. **LC** PR1; .I55.
Ind/Abst Annu. Bibliogr. Engl. Lang. Lit.

II
INDIAN LITERARY REVIEW, THE. Vol. 1, No. 1 (May 1978)-. Periodical. English. mo. **LC** PR9480; .I49. **DD** 820.
Ind/Abst MLA Int. Bibl. Books Artic. Mod. Lang. Lit.

II/0019-5804
INDIAN LITERATURE (NEW DELHI). (INDIAN LITERATURE.). [Indian lit.]. **Added/Corp** Sahitya Akademi. Vol. 1 (Oct. 1957)-. Periodical. English. bm. $35.00. Sahitya Akademi, National Academy of Letters, Rabindra Bhavan, Ferozeshah Road, New Delhi 110001 India. **Tel** 011 91 11 388667. **(Subscription address:** Prints India, 11 Darya Ganj, New Delhi 110002 India.) **LC** AP8; .I395. Documents available from The Genuine Article.
Ind/Abst Abstr. Engl. Stud.; Annu. Bibliogr. Engl. Lang. Lit.; Arts Humanit. Citation Index [Full Cov.]; Curr. Contents Arts Humanit.; MLA Int. Bibl. Books Artic. Mod. Lang. Lit.; Res. Alert [Full Cov.].

●US/1065-0350
INDIANA JOURNAL OF HISPANIC LITERATURES. (INDIANA JOURNAL OF HISPANIC LITERATURES : IJHL.). **Added/Corp** Indiana University, Bloomington. Dept. of Spanish and Portuguese. **VFOAT** IJHL. (1992)-. Periodical. English. sa. $20.00 (one year), $35.00 (two year), $55.00 (three year). Indiana University / Department of Spanish and Portuguese, Ballantine Hall 875, Bloomington IN 47405.

II
INDO-IRANICA. **See** General Interest-General Interest-Asia.

US/1050-7280
INFINITY LIMITED. [Infin. ltd.]. (1988)-. Periodical. English. Four times a year (Mar., June, Sept., Dec.). $12.50. Infinity Limited, PO Box 2713, Castro Valley CA 94546. **ED** Genie Lester. **DD** 810. **Bk Rev**, (Qty: 1-2). **Ad Acc. Circ:** 1,000.
Desc: Contains fiction and poetry by talented yet lesser recognized writers.

BE/0774-4323
INFOR MARECHALERIE. [Infor Marechalerie]. (1986)-. Periodical. French. Six times a year (Feb., Apr., June, Aug., Oct., Dec.). 900F Belgium; 1200F Luxembourg & Northerlands; 1500F Switerland; 1600F other. Diasse Mr Falisse, 16 rue d'Opprebais, 5922 Maleves STE Marie Belguim. **Tel** 011 32 10 888898, FAX 011 32 10 88 9934. **ED** Falisse Dominique. **UDC** 682.1. Index available. **Bk Rev. Ad Acc, Adv Mgr:** F. Dominique. **Circ:** 5,000. available on diskette.

FR/0020-0123
INFORMATION LITTERAIRE, L'. [Inf. litt.]. Vol. 1, (Jan/Feb. 1949)-. Periodical. French. Five times a year (Feb., Apr., June, Oct., Dec.). 264.75F France; 280.00F other. Societe Edition Belles Lettres, 95 Boulevard Raspail, 75006 Paris France. **Tel** 011 33 1 45487055, FAX 011 33 1 45449288, telex 200577. **LC** PN3; .I5. available on microfilm.
Ind/Abst MLA Int. Bibl. Books Artic. Mod. Lang. Lit.

CN/0710-4278
INITIALES (HALIFAX). **See** Linguistics.

US/0190-0234
INKLINGS. 1-. Periodical. English. ir. Mudborn Press, 209 West de la Guerra, Santa Barbara CA 93101. **Tel** (805)962-9996.
Ind/Abst Abstr. Graphic Arts Tech. Found. (1979, 1984); Graph. Arts Bull. Inst. Pap. Sci. Technol. (Jan. 1989, May 1989).

GW/0176-3733
INKLINGS. **Added/Corp** Inklings-Gesellschaft fur Literatur und Asthetik. **VFOAT** Inklings-Jahrbuch; Inklings-Jahrbuch fur Literatur und Asthetik. (1983)-. German (English). an. **LC** PR478.I54; I54. **DD** 823/.0876/09.
Ind/Abst MLA Int. Bibl. Books Artic. Mod. Lang. Lit.

RU/0130-6073
INOSTRANNYE JAZYKI V SKOLE. **See** Linguistics.

NE/0167-3696
INS AND OUTS. Periodical. English. ir. $15.00 Europe and England, $20.00 others. Ins and Outs Press, PO Box 3759, Amsterdam Netherlands. **LC** PR9091; .I58. **DD** 820/.8.

US/0094-2715
INSCAPE (PASADENA). (INSCAPE.). **Added/Corp** Pasadena City College. Vol. 30 (1974)-. English. an. $1.50. Pasadena City College, English Department, 1570 East Colorado Boulevard, Pasadena CA 91106. **Tel** (310)578-7371. **LC** PS508.C6; P53. **DD** 810/.8/0054. ***Continues*** *Pipes of Pan.*
Ind/Abst ARTbibliogr. Mod.

CN/0380-2957
INSIDE (NELSON). (INSIDE.). No. 1- Feb. 1975-. Periodical. English. 0.25Can$ per no. E Kluge, #302/60 High Street, Nelson British Columbia V1K 3Z4 Canada. **DD** C810/.8/0054.

US/0275-021X
INSIDE/OUT (NEW YORK, N.Y. : 1980). ***Ceased.*** (INSIDE/OUT.). Vol. 1, No. 1 (Spring 1980)-Ceased ?. Periodical. English. ir. Time Capsule Inc, GPO Box 1185, NY NY 10116. **Tel** (212)675-7197. **ED** Matthew Hejna and Marc Crawford. **Ad Acc. Circ:** 3,000.
Desc: Fiction, poetry and artwork from America's prisons.

US/0742-5244
INSIGHT (BOSTON, MASS.). (INSIGHT / FRANKLIN RESEARCH & DEVELOPMENT CORPORATION.). [Insight]. **Added/Corp** Franklin Research and Development Corporation. (19??)-. Periodical. English. qt. $78.00 (includes: Insight's insight, Equity briefs, Vital industry reports and Annual Index). Franklin Research and Development Corp., 711 Atlantic Avenue, Boston MA 02111. **Tel** (617)423-6655. **ED** Patrick McVeigh. **Bk Rev**, (Qty: 4/yr). **Circ:** 2,500.
Desc: INSIGHT is an investment newsletter focused on the field of socially responsible investing. It supplies specific investment advice for those wishing to integrate their social and financial values.

US/0897-9804
INSPIRATIONAL WRITER'S MARKET. 1989-. English. an. $14.95. Writer's Digest Books, 1507 Dana Avenue, Cincinnati OH 45207. **Tel** (513)531-2222, (800)289-0963, FAX (513)531-4744.

CN/0715-4011
INTERIOR VOICE. [Inter. voice]. **VFOAT** Interior Voice Regional Arts Magazine. No. 1 (Winter 1981/82)-. Periodical. English. qt. $1.50 per no. Interior Voice, PO Box 117, Kelowna BC V1Y 7N2. **DD** C810/.8/0054.

IT
INTERMEDIAIRE DES CASANOVISTES, L'. Vol. 1 (1984)-. French (English and Italian). Bruno Buonomo La Rossa, Pallonetto S Chiara 8, 80134 Naples Italy. **Tel** 011 39 81 5520424. ***Continues*** *Casanova Gleanings.*
Ind/Abst MLA Int. Bibl. Books Artic. Mod. Lang. Lit.

CN/0315-4149
INTERNATIONAL FICTION REVIEW. (THE INTERNATIONAL FICTION REVIEW.). [Int. fict. rev.]. **Added/Corp** International Fiction Association. **VFOAT** I.F.R.; IFR. Vol. 1 (Jan. 1974)-. Academic Scholarly Publication. English. sa (Aug. and Dec.). $15.00 (institution), $12.00 (individual). University of New Brunswick International Fiction Association, Department of German and Russian, Fredericton New Brunswick E3B 5A3 Canada. **Tel** (506)453-4636. **ED** Saad Elkhadem. **LC** PN3311; .I57. **DD** 809.3/005. Index available (published in second issue). **Bk Rev. Circ:** 500. available on microfiche (from Toronto : Micromedia). Documents available from The Genuine Article.
Desc: Publishes scholarly articles.
Ind/Abst Am. Bibliogr. Slavic East Europ. Stud.; Am. Humanit. Index; Arts Humanit. Citation Index [Full Cov.]; Can. Index; Curr. Contents Arts Humanit.; Middle East Abstr. Index; MLA Int. Bibl. Books Artic. Mod. Lang. Lit.; Res. Alert [Full Cov.]; Romant. Move.

UK/0020-7950
INTERNATIONAL MEDIEVAL BIBLIOGRAPHY. **See** Literature-Abstracting, Bibliographies and Statistics.

●US/1060-6084
INTERNATIONAL QUARTERLY (TALLAHASS., FLA.). (INTERNATIONAL QUARTERLY: I/Q.). **VFOAT** I Q. (1992)-. Periodical. English. qt. $40.00. International Quarterly, PO Box 10521, Tallahassee FL 32302-0521. **Tel** (904)224-5078, FAX (904)224-5127. **ED** Van K. Brock. Index available in last issue of volume--attached. **Bk Rev**, (Qty: 2 per issue). **Ad Acc, Adv Mgr:** Van K. Brock. **Acid Free. Circ:** 2,000.
Desc: Publishes poetry, fiction, non-fiction and reviews,

as well as visual art. Serves as a venue for creative work, and as an active agent for freedom of literary and artistic expression around the world.

UK
INTERNATIONAL RARE BOOK PRICES. MODERN FIRST EDITIONS. ***Title Change.*** **See** Publishing-Books and Bookmaking.

GW/0340-4528
INTERNATIONALES ARCHIV FUER SOZIALGESCHICHTE DER DEUTSCHEN LITERATUR. [Int. Arch. Sozialgesch. dtsch. Lit.]. Vol. 1 (1976)-. Periodical. Multiple languages (English, French and German). Twice a year. DM136.00. Max Niemeyer Verlag, Postfach 2140, D 72011 Tuebingen Germany. **Tel** 011 49 7071 989494, FAX 011 49 7071 87419. **ED** Wolfgang Fruehwald, Goerg Jaeger, Dieter Langewiesche, Alberto Martino. **LC** PT3; .I58. cum. index. **Bk Rev. Ad Acc.** Documents available from The Genuine Article.
Desc: Contributions on the social history of German literature.
Ind/Abst Am. Hist. Life (1988-); Arts Humanit. Citation Index [Full Cov.]; Curr. Contents Arts Humanit.; MLA Int. Bibl. Books Artic. Mod. Lang. Lit.; Res. Alert [Full Cov.]; Romant. Move.; Soc. Sci. Cit. Index [Select. Cov.].

IT
INTERPRES. Vol. 1 (1978)-. Italian. an. L75000 Italy; L80000 other. Salerno Editrice, Via di Donna Olimpia 20, 00152 Rome Italy. **Tel** 011 39 6 58205684 or 688, FAX 06-53-15-688. **ED** Mario Martelli. **LC** DG445; .I57. **DD** 945/.05/05. **Bk Rev. Ad Acc. Circ:** 500.
Desc: Research on history of Italian renaissance literature.

US/0363-9991
INTERSTATE. ***Ceased.*** No. 1 (Spring 1974)-Ceased (1989). Periodical. English. qt. Interstate, PO Box 7068, Austin TX 78722. **Tel** (512)451-8874. **ED** Loris Essary. **Bk Rev. Circ:** 500 (ctrl).
Desc: Non-traditional writing and art; strong international emphasis.

UK/0264-3596
INTERZONE. Vol. 1, No. 1 (Spring 1982)-. Periodical. English. bm. £15.00 UK; £18.00 other. Popular Fictions, 217 Preston Drove, Brighton BN1 6FL England. **Tel** 011 44 273 504710. ***Absorbed Million, 0960-832X.***
Ind/Abst Child. Lit. Abstr. (19??-); Sci. Fict. Fantasy Book Rev. Index.

US/0732-6750
INTI (PROVIDENCE, R.I.). (INTI.). [INTI]. (1974)-. Periodical. Spanish (English). sa. $25.00 (individuals), $45.00 (institutions) US; $60.00 other. Providence College, c/o Roger Carmosino, Department of Modern Languages, Providence RI 02918. **Tel** (401)865-2111, FAX (401)865-2057. **ED** Roger B. Carmosino. **LC** PQ6001; .I57. **DD** 860/.05. Index available. cum. index. **Bk Rev**, (Qty: 10). **Ad Acc. Pr Rev. Circ:** 1,000 (ctrl).
Desc: Hispanic literature, literary criticism, poetry, short stories, interviews, review of books, special issues on reown contemporary authors and bibliographies.
Ind/Abst HAPI Hisp. Am. Period. Index; Index Am. Period. Verse; MLA Int. Bibl. Books Artic. Mod. Lang. Lit.

US/0020-9864
INTREPID. No. 1- Mar. 1964-. English. be. $6.00. Interpid, PO Box 110 Central Park Station, Buffalo NY 14215. **Tel** (716)884-1891. **ED** A de Loach. **LC** PN6014; .I495. **DD** 808.8/0005. cum. index.

US/0021-0331
IO. See Anthropology.

US/0021-065X
IOWA REVIEW, THE. [Iowa rev.]. **Added/Corp** University of Iowa. School of Letters. University of Iowa. Graduate College. Vol. 1 (Winter 1970)-. Periodical. English. Three times a year. $18.00 (individuals), $20.00 (institutions) US; $21.00 (individuals), $23.00 (institutions) other. University of Iowa / Publications Order Department, Oakdale Hall, Iowa City IA 52242. **Tel** (319)335-4645, FAX (319)335-4039. **ED** David Hamilton. **LC** PS501; .I68. **DD** 810/.8. Index available (bound in last issue). **Bk Rev. Ad Acc. Circ:** 1,000 (ctrl). available on microfilm and microfiche from University Microfilms International (UMI).
Desc: A literary journal devoted to publishing fiction, poetry, essays, and criticism.
Ind/Abst Abstr. Engl. Stud.; Am. Humanit. Index; Annu. Bibliogr. Engl. Lang. Lit.; Index Am. Period. Verse; Lit. Crit. Regist.; MLA Int. Bibl. Books Artic. Mod. Lang. Lit.

PK/0021-0773
IQBAL REVIEW. Added/Corp Iqbal Academy Pakistan. (19??)-. Periodical. English (Urdu and Persian). Four times a year (Jan., Apr., July, Oct.). $10.00 (individuals); $15.00 (institutions). Iqbal Academy Pakistan, 116-McLeod Road, Lahore Pakistan. **Tel** 011 92 42 856010. **ED** Muhammad Munawwar. **LC** BP80.I6; I65. Index available (Free). cum. index. **Bk Rev. Ad Acc. Circ:** 500.
Desc: Studies in Iqbal's life, poetry and thought, Islamic studies, philosophy, history, comparative religion, art and literature.
Ind/Abst Index Islam. Lit.; MLA Int. Bibl. Books Artic. Mod. Lang. Lit.

US/1051-5364
IRANSHINASI (BETHESDA, MD.). (MAJALLAH-I IRAN SHINASI.). **Added/Corp** Keyan Foundation (U.S.). **VFOAT** Iran Shinasi; Iranshinasi; Iranshenasi; Iran Shenasi. (Spring 1989)-. Periodical. Persian (English). qt. $65.00 (institutions), $35.00 (individuals). Iranshenasi, PO Box 1038, Rockville MD 20849-1038. **Tel** (301)279-2564. **ED** Jalal Matini. **DD** 891. **Bk Rev. Ad Acc. Circ:** 1,500.
Ind/Abst Middle East J.

GW/0724-5548
IRB-LITERATURAUSLESE. Added/Corp Fraunhofer-Gesellschaft. Informationszentrum Raum und Bau. **VFOAT** IRB Literaturauslese. Monographic series. German. Price varies per volume.

FR/0291-2066
IRIS (MONTPELLIER). (IRIS.). [Iris]. **Added/Corp** Universite Paul Valery. Centre de Recherches sur les Litteratures Iberiques et Ibero-Americaines Modernes. No. 1 (1981)-. French (Spanish). an (Published in Nov.). 100.00F France; 130.00F other. Universite Paul Valery, BP 5043 Route de Mende, 34032 Montpellier, Cedex 1 France. **Tel** 11 33 67 142000, FAX 011 33 67 142052. **ED** G. Cazottes & P. Jourdan. **Bk Rev**, (Qty: 1). **Circ:** 300 (ctrl).
Ind/Abst MLA Int. Bibl. Books Artic. Mod. Lang. Lit.

US/0140-895X
IRISH LITERARY STUDIES. (1977)-. Monographic series. English. ir. Price varies per volume. Rowman & Littlefield Publishing Inc., 8705 Bollman Place, Savage MD 20763. **Tel** (301)306-0400. **(Subscription address:** University Press of America Inc., 4720 Boston Way, Suite A, Lanham MD 20706.**) ED** Homer Dickens. ctrl circ.

US/0733-3390
IRISH LITERARY SUPPLEMENT. [Irish lit. suppl.]. Vol. 1, No. 1 (Spring 1982)-. Periodical. English. sa. $10.00. Irish Studies, 114 Paula Boulevard, Selden NY 11784. **Tel** (516)698-8243. **ED** Robert G. Lowery. **Bk Rev. Ad Acc. Circ:** 4,000 (ctrl). available on microfilm.
Desc: Reviews Irish interest books.
Ind/Abst Am. Humanit. Index; Book Rev. Index (1988-).

HU/0021-1478
IRODALOMTORTENET (BUDAPEST. 1912). (IRODALOMTORTENET : A MAGYAR IRODALOMTORTENETI TARSASAG HAVI FOLYOIRATA.). [Irodalomtortenet]. **Added/Corp** Magyar Irodalomtorteneti Tarsasag. (Jan/Feb 1912)-. Periodical. Hungarian. Four times a year. 20.00ft Austria, Croatia, Czech Republic, Slovakia, Romania, Yugoslavia, Slovenia & Ukraine; 23.00ft others. **(Subscription address:** Kultura, PO Box 149, H 1389 Budapest 62 Hungary.**)**
Ind/Abst Am. Hist. Life (1971-); MLA Int. Bibl. Books Artic. Mod. Lang. Lit.

UK
IRON. VFOAT Iron Magazine. Periodical. English. Three times a year. £7.00 UK; $20.00 US. Iron Press, 5 Marden Terrace, Tyne and Wear, Cullercoats North Shields 4PD NE30 England. **Tel** 091-2531901. **ED** Peter Mortimer, Ian McMillan. **LC** PN6010.5; .I76. **DD** 805. **Ad Acc. Circ:** 800.
Desc: Contemporary fiction and poetry. No more than five poems or two stories at one time.

US/1055-2146
ISAAC ASIMOV'S SCIENCE FICTION MAGAZINE (1990). ***Title Change.*** (ISAAC ASIMOV'S SCIENCE FICTION MAGAZINE.). [Isaac Asimov's sci. fict. mag.]. Vol. 14, No. 3 (Mar. 1990)-(1992). Periodical. English. mo. Davis Publications Inc., 274 Riverside Avenue, Westport CT 06880-4808. **DD** 813. available on microfilm and microfiche from University Microfilms International (UMI). ***Continues Isaac Asimov's Science Fiction, 1045-6414. Continued by Asimov's Science Fiction, 1065-2698.***
Desc: The best in all new science fiction.
Ind/Abst Sci. Fict. Fantasy Book Rev. Index (1990-1992).

RU/0130-6634
ISKATEL. (19??)-. Periodical. Russian. bm. $31.00 airmail. Izdatelstvo Molodaia Gvardiia, Novodmitrovskaya Ul., 5A, 125015 Moscow Russia. **Tel** 095-285-0830. **(Subscription address:** Victor Kamkin, 4956 Boiling Brook Parkway, Rockville MD 20852.**) LC** IN PROCESS.

RU
ISKUSSTVO LEKTORA. Vol. 1 (1973)-. Russian. 0.16rub (single issue). Izdatelstvo Znanie, Novaya Pl., 3-4,, 101835 Moscow Russia. **LC** PN4193.L4; I8.

AT/1035-3127
ISLAND. No. 43/44 (Winter 1990)-. Periodical. English. qt. 36.00Aus$ (Australia), 50.00Aus$ (other) institution; 26.00Aus$ (Australia), 40.00Aus$ (other) individual. Island / Australia, PO Box 207, Sandy Bay Tasmania, 7005 Australia. **Tel** 11 61 2 202325, FAX 11 61 2 202186. **Bk Rev. Ad Acc. Circ:** 2,000. ***Continues Island Magazine, 0156-8124.***
Ind/Abst APAIS, Aust. Public Aff. Inf. Ser. (1988-); Child. Lit. Abstr. (19??-).

AT/1035-3127
ISLAND. SANDY BAY. (ISLAND.). [Island Sandy Bay]. (1990)-. Periodical. English. qt. 30.00Aus$ (individuals), 40.00Aus$ (institutions), 25.00Aus$ (students, pensioners, and unemployed) Australia; 46.00Aus$ (individuals), 56.00Aus$ (institutions) other. Island / Australia, PO Box 207, Sandy Bay Tasmania, 7005 Australia. **Tel** 11 61 2 202325, FAX 11 61 2 202186. **DD** 820.5. **Bk Rev. Ad Acc, Adv Mgr:** Lynne Hardwick. Full Page (B&W) 300.00Aus$. Half Page (B&W) 180.00Aus$. **Circ:** 1,500. ***Continues** Island Magazine (Sandy Bay), 0725-2951.*

US
ISLANDICA. Added/Corp Cornell University. Libraries. Vol. 1 (1908)-. Monographic series. English. ir. Price varies per volume. Cornell University Press, 124 Roberts Place, Ithaca NY 14853. **Tel** (607)277-2338. **LC** PT7102; .I7.

NZ/0110-0858
ISLANDS. ***Ceased.*** [Islands]. (Spring 1972)-Ceased (1987). Periodical. English. qt. Robin Rudding, 4 Sealy Road, Torbay Auckland 10 New Zealand. **Tel** 0011 64940 39007. **LC** PZ1; .I83; PR9637.3. **DD** 823/.01. **[CCC].**
Ind/Abst Abstr. Engl. Stud.

US
ISLE / INTERDISCIPLINAREY STUDIES IN LITERATURE AND ENVIRONMENT. See Environmental Issues-Ecology.

II
ISTAHARA. VFOAT Istahar. Periodical. Oriya (Oriya). qt. 5.00. Nityananda Satpathy, C-30 Utkal University Campus, Bhubaneswar 7510 India. **LC** PK2574.5; .I78.

II
ISURI : DO. HARISIMHA GAURA VISVAVIDYALAYA, SAGARA KE HINDI-VIBHAGA KE ANTARGATA KRIYASILA BUNDELI-PITHA KA AYOJANA. See Linguistics.

IT/0021-2881
ITALIA CHE SCRIVE, L'. [Ital. scrive]. Vol. 1- April, 1918-. Periodical. Italian. mo. Italia Che Scrive, Via Angelo Secchi 3, Rome Italy. **LC** Z2345; .I88. cum. index.
Ind/Abst MLA Int. Bibl. Books Artic. Mod. Lang. Lit.

IT/0021-2881
ITALIAN BOOKS AND PERIODICALS. See Literature-Abstracting, Bibliographies and Statistics.

CN/0827-6129
ITALIAN CANADIANA. [Ital. Can.]. **Added/Corp** Centre for Italian Canadian Studies. Centro Canadese Scuola e Cultura Italiana. Vol. 1, No. 1 (Spring 1985)-. Periodical. English (Italian; summaries and/or abstracts in French). an. $10.00 (per copy) individuals; $13.00 (per copy) institutions. Erindale College, 3359 Mississauga Road, Mississauga Ont L5L 1C6, Canada. **DD** 971/.00451/05.
Ind/Abst Am. Hist. Life (1988-).

UK/0075-1634
ITALIAN STUDIES. [Ital. studies]. **Added/Corp** Society for Italian Studies. Vol. 1, (July 1937)-. English. an. $46.50. Dawson UK Ltd, Cannon House, Folkestone Kent CT19 5EE England. **Tel** 011 44 303-850101, FAX 011 44 303-850440, telex 96392. **LC** PQ4001; .I76.
Desc: Reviews and public letters of Italian Studies in England.
Ind/Abst Am. Hist. Life (1988-); Annu. Bibliogr. Engl. Lang. Lit.; BHA : Biblio. Hist. Art; Br. Humanit. Index; MLA Int. Bibl. Books Artic. Mod. Lang. Lit.; Romant. Move.

UK/0261-4340
ITALIANIST. (THE ITALIANIST : JOURNAL OF THE DEPARTMENT OF ITALIAN STUDIES, UNIVERSITY OF READING.). [Italianist]. **Added/Corp** University of Reading. Dept. of Italian Studies. University College, Dublin. Dept. of Italian Studies. No. 1 (1981)-. English (Italian). an. £10.00. University of Reading Department of Italian Studies, Whiteknights Reading RG6 2AA England. **Tel** 011 44 734 875123 ext. 348. **ED** Z.G. Baranski, S.W. Vinall. cum. index. **Ad Acc. Pr Rev. Circ:** 500 (ctrl).
Desc: Journal of Italian studies including articles on language, linguistics, literature, history, cinema, art and politics.
Ind/Abst MLA Int. Bibl. Books Artic. Mod. Lang. Lit.; Soc. Plann. Policy Dev. Abstr.

IT/0391-3368
ITALIANISTICA. [Italianistica]. Vol. 1 (Jan./Apr. 1972)-. Periodical. Italian. Three times a year (Apr., Sept., Dec.). L190000 Italy; L290000 other. Giardini Editori Stampatori, Via Santa Bibbiana 28, 56127 Pisa Italy. **Tel** 011 39 50 934242. **LC** PQ4001; .I78.
Ind/Abst MLA Int. Bibl. Books Artic. Mod. Lang. Lit.; Romant. Move.

Literature

FR/0751-2163
ITALIQUES / UNIVERSITE DE LA SORBONNE NOUVELLE (PARIS III), U.E.R. D'ITALIEN ET ROUMAIN, CENTRE DE RECHERCHES SUR L'ITALIE MODERNE ET CONTEMPORAINE. Added/Corp Universite de Paris III. Centre de Recherches sur l'Italie Moderne et Contemporaine. Universite de Paris III. Groupe d'Etudes et de Recherches sur la Traduction (Domaine Italien-Francais). No. 1 (Oct. 1981)-. French. an. 50.00F (latest volume). Universite Paris III CRIMC, 13 rue de Santeuil, 75005 Paris France. **Tel** 011 33 1 45874178. **ED** Mario Fusco. **LC** PQ4001; .I83. **DD** 850/.9. Index available. **Bk Rev**. **Ad Acc**. **Circ**: 300 (ctrl).

RU
IUG : IZDANIE NA DRUZHESTVOTO NA PISATELITE--KHASKOVO. Added/Corp Druzhestvo na Pisatelite--Khaskovo. (1980)-. Periodical. Bulgarian. an. 1.51rub. **LC** PG1000; .I93. **DD** 891.8/1/08.

RU
IUNOSTJ. Russian. mo. $99.95. **(Subscription address:** East View Publications Inc., 3020 Harbor Lane North, Suite 110, Minneapolis MN 55447.**)**

BN/0021-3381
IZRAZ. (IZRAZ : CASOPIS ZA KNJIZEVNU I UMJETNICKU KRITIKU.). [Izraz]. (1957)-. Periodical. Serbo-Croatian (Cyrillic). mo. **LC** PN9; .I9.
Ind/Abst Annu. Bibliogr. Engl. Lang. Lit.; MLA Int. Bibl. Books Artic. Mod. Lang. Lit.

UK/0305-8182
JABBERWOCKY. [Jabberwocky]. Added/Corp Lewis Carroll Society. Vol. 1 (1969)-. Periodical. English. qt. £10.00 (individuals), £12.00 (institutions) Europe; £13.00 (individuals), £15.00 (institutions) other. Lewis Carroll Society, 146 Headstone Lane, Middlesex HA2 6JT England. **ED** Selwyn Goodacre. **LC** PR4612; .J3. **DD** 828/.8/09. Index available. **Bk Rev**. **Circ**: 350 (ctrl).
Desc: Articles relating to the life and works of Lewis Carroll/Charles Dodgson.
Ind/Abst MLA Int. Bibl. Books Artic. Mod. Lang. Lit.

US/1042-7082
JACARANDA REVIEW, THE. *Ceased.* Vol. 1, No. 1 (Fall 1985)-(199?). Periodical. English. sa. Jacaranda Review, Department of English, UCLA, Los Angeles CA 90024. **Tel** (310)825-4945. **DD** 810.
Ind/Abst Index Am. Period. Verse.

AU
JACOBEAN STUDIES. English. ir. Longwood Publishing Group, 27 South Main Street, Attn R Corrigan, Wolfeboro NH 03894. **Tel** (603)569-4576.
Desc: Numbered series.

II/0970-0692
JADAVPUR JOURNAL OF COMPARATIVE LITERATURE. [Jadavpur j. comp. lit.]. Added/Corp Jadavpur University. Dept. of Comparative Literature. (1961)-. Bengali (English). an. $15.00. Jadavpur Journal of Comparative Literature, Jadavpur University, Department of Compaartive Literature, Calcutta 32 India. **(Subscription address:** Prints India, 11 Darya Ganj, New Delhi, 110002 India, (Phone: 011 91 11 3268645)**)** **LC** PN851; .J3. **UDC** 8.091.
Ind/Abst MLA Int. Bibl. Books Artic. Mod. Lang. Lit.

GW/0070-4318
JAHRBUCH DER DEUTSCHEN SCHILLERGESELLSCHAFT. (JAHRBUCH DER DEUTSCHEN SCHILLERGESELLSCHAFT / IM AUFTRAG DER DEUTSCHEN SCHILLERGESELLSCHAFT.). [Jahrb. dtsch. Schillerges.]. **Main/Corp** Deutsche Schillergesellschaft. Added/Corp Deutsche Schillergesellschaft. Vol. 1 (1957)-. Academic Scholarly Publication. German. an (Dec.). DM48.00 Germany; DM54.00 others. Alfred Kroener Verlag, Postfach 1109, Reinsburgstr 56, W-7000 Stuttgart 1 Germany. **(Subscription address:** Postfach 102862, D 70024 Stuttgart Germany, telephone: 011 49 711 620221**)** **LC** PT105; .D4. **DD** 830. Documents available from The Genuine Article.
Desc: Contains scholarly studies about German literature from the 16th century to present.
Ind/Abst Arts Humanit. Citation Index (19??-19??) [Full Cov.]; MLA Int. Bibl. Books Artic. Mod. Lang. Lit.; Res. Alert [Full Cov.]; Romant. Move.

AU
JAHRBUCH DER GRILLPARZER-GESELLSCHAFT. Added/Corp Grillparzer-Gesellschaft. (1890)-. German. an. $370.00. Bergland Verlag, Spengergasse 39, A-1051 Vienna Austria. **Tel** 011 43 1 555641.
Ind/Abst MLA Int. Bibl. Books Artic. Mod. Lang. Lit.

GW/0075-3580
JAHRBUCH DER JEAN-PAUL-GESELLSCHAFT. [Jahrb. Jean-Paul-Ges.]. **Main/Corp** Jean-Paul-Gesellschaft. Vol. 1 (1966)-. German. an. DM55.00. CH Beck Verlagsbuchhandlung, D 80791 Munich Germany. **Tel** 011 49 89 381891. **LC** PT2456; .A14. **DD** 838/.609.
Continues Hesperus (Bayreuth, Germany).
Ind/Abst MLA Int. Bibl. Books Artic. Mod. Lang. Lit.; Romant. Move.

GW/0300-1989
JAHRBUCH DER KARL-MAY-GESELLSCHAFT. (JAHRBUCH.). [Jahrb. Karl-May-Ges.]. **Main/Corp** Karl-May-Gesellschaft. 1970-. German. Hansa-Verlag, Hamburg 63 Germany. **LC** PT2625.A848; Z73.
Ind/Abst MLA Int. Bibl. Books Artic. Mod. Lang. Lit.

GW/0075-2371
JAHRBUCH DER RAABE-GESELLSCHAFT. [Jahrb. Raabe-Ges.]. Added/Corp Raabe-Gesellschaft. (1960)-. German. an. DM64.00. Max Niemeyer Verlag, Postfach 2140, D 72011 Tuebingen Germany. **Tel** 011 49 7071 989494, FAX 011 49 7071 87419. **ED** Josef Daum, Hans-Juergen Schrader. **LC** PT2451.Z5; A23. **DD** 833/.8.
Continues Raabe-Jahrbuch, 0483-7886.
Ind/Abst MLA Int. Bibl. Books Artic. Mod. Lang. Lit.

GW/0448-133X
JAHRBUCH DER SAMMLUNG KIPPENBERG. [Jahrb. samml. Kippenberg]. Vol. 1 (1921)- Vol. 10 (1935); New Series, Vol. 1 (1963)-. Monographic series. German. ir. Price varies per volume. Insel Verlag, Lindenstr 29-35, PF 101945, W 6000 Frankfurt 1 F R Germany. **Tel** 011 49 69 756010. **LC** PT2045; .J3.
Ind/Abst MLA Int. Bibl. Books Artic. Mod. Lang. Lit.

GW/0938-863X
JAHRBUCH DER VILLA VIGONI. [Jahrb. Villa Vigoni]. (1990)-. German. an. DM70.00. Max Niemeyer Verlag, Postfach 2140, D 72011 Tuebingen Germany. **Tel** 011 49 7071 989494, FAX 011 49 7071 87419. **UDC** 001.

GW/0071-9463
JAHRBUCH DES FREIEN DEUTSCHEN HOCHSTIFTS. [Jahrb. Freien Dtsch. Hochstifts]. **Main/Corp** Freien Deutsches Hochstift (Frankfurt Am Main, Germany). Added/Corp Freies Deutsches Hochstift (Frankfurt am Main, Germany). (1902)-. German. an (Nov.). DM94.00. Max Niemeyer Verlag, Postfach 2140, D 72011 Tuebingen Germany. **Tel** 011 49 7071 989494, FAX 011 49 7071 87419. **ED** Christoph Perels. **LC** AS182; .F622. **Bk Rev**. **Ad Acc**. *Continues* Freies Deutsches Hochstift (Frankfurt am Main, Germany). Berichte.
Desc: Yearbook with contributions on German literature of the 19th century (especially Goethe, Brentano and Von Arnim).
Ind/Abst BHA : Biblio. Hist. Art; MLA Int. Bibl. Books Artic. Mod. Lang. Lit.

GW/0083-5617
JAHRBUCH DES VEREINS FUER NIEDERDEUTSCHE SPRACHFORSCHUNG. See Linguistics.

AU
JAHRBUCH DES WIENER GOETHE-VEREINS. Added/Corp Wiener Goethe-Verein. Vol. 64 (1960)-. Academic Scholarly Publication. German (English). an. S250.00 Austria; $20.00 US. Wiener Goethe Verein, Stallburggasse 2, 1010 Vienna 1 Austria. **ED** Herbert Zeman. **LC** PT2045; .W6. **Bk Rev**, (Qty: 10-15). **Ad Acc**. Full Page (B&W) S500.00. **Circ**: 750 (ctrl). *Continues* Chronik des Wiener Goethe-Vereins.
Desc: Deals with German and Austrian literature, mainly in the age of Goethe (18th and 19th century), and with Austrian literature in general.
Ind/Abst MLA Int. Bibl. Books Artic. Mod. Lang. Lit.

GW/0070-3923
JAHRBUCH - DEUTSCHE AKADEMIE FUER SPRACHE UND DICHTUNG (DARMSTADT). (JAHRBUCH / DEUTSCHE AKADEMIE FUER SPRACHE UND DICHTUNG IN DARMSTADT.). [Jahrb. - Dtsch. Akad. Sprache Dicht. Darmst.]. **Main/Corp** Deutsche Akademie fuer Sprache und Dichtung. Added/Corp Deutsche Akademie fuer Sprache und Dichtung. (1954)-. Periodical. German. an. DM28.00. Deutsche Akademie Sprache & Dichtung, Alexandraweg 23, D-64287 Darmstadt Germany. **Tel** 011 49 6151 40920, FAX 011 649 6151 409299. **(Subscription address:** Luchterhand Literaturverlag, Muehlenkamp 6C, D 22303 Hamburg Germany.**)** **ED** Michael Assmann. **LC** PF3013; .D4. **DD** 430; 830. **Circ**: 400 (ctrl).
Desc: Yearbook of the German Academy of Language and Poetry. Contribution to language and literature, speeches of prize winning authors of the academy, commemorations of dead members, bibliography, list of members and notices.
Ind/Abst MLA Int. Bibl. Books Artic. Mod. Lang. Lit.

GW/0070-4326
JAHRBUCH - DEUTSCHE SHAKESPEARE-GESELLSCHAFT WEST. [Jahrb. - Dtsch. Shakespeare-Ges. West]. **Main/Corp** Deutsche Shakespeare-Gesellschaft West. (1965)-. German (English). an (Oct.). DM84.00. Verlag Ferdinand Kamp GmbH & Company, Postfach 101309, D-44713 Bochum Germany. **Tel** 011 49 234 91420, FAX 011 49 234 18492. **ED** Werner Habicht, Manfred Pfister and Kurt Tezeli V. Rosador. **LC** PR2889; .D42. **Bk Rev**. ctrl circ. *Continues* Shakespeare Jahrbuch (Heidelberg, Germany); *Absorbed* Shakespeare Jahrbuch.
Desc: Essays on Shakespeare research, critical book reviews, theatre discussions, interpretations, Shakespeare on film and TV, reports on Shakespeare institutions and events.
Ind/Abst Abstr. Engl. Stud.; Annu. Bibliogr. Engl. Lang. Lit.; BHA : Biblio. Hist. Art; MLA Int. Bibl. Books Artic. Mod. Lang. Lit.

FI/0781-3619
JAHRBUCH FUER FINNISCH-DEUTSCHE LITERATURBEZIEHUNGEN. [Jahrb. finn.-dtsch. Lit.bezieh.]. Added/Corp Deutsche Bibliothek (Helsinki, Finland). No. 13 (1979)-. German. an. Fmk100.00. Deutsche Bibliothek, Pohj Makasiinikatu 7, SF-00131 Helsinki 13 Finland. **Tel** 90/669363. **ED** Kurt Nyholm, In Schellbach-Kopra, Maria-Liisa Nevala. **LC** PH300; .J33. **DD** 894/.541/09. Index available. **Bk Rev**. **Ad Acc**. **Circ**: 1,300. *Continues* Mitteilungen aus der Deutschen Bibliothek, 0355-4546.
Desc: Deals with contacts between Finnish and German literature in a larger historical cultural context and publishes translations of Finnish and Finland-Swedish literature.

GW/0723-0516
JAHRBUCH / THOMAS-MORUS-GESELLSCHAFT. Added/Corp Thomas-Morus-Gesellschaft. VFOAT Thomas-Morus-Jahrbuch. (19??)-. Periodical. German. an. Konrad Triltsch Druck & Verlagsanstalt, PF 6660, D 97016 Wuerzburg Germany. **Tel** 011 49 931 308030. **LC** PR2322; .J34. **DD** 828/.209.

GW/0174-4720
JAHRBUCH ZUR LITERATUR IN DER DDR / HERAUSGEGEBEN IM AUFTRAG DES ARBEITSKREISES LITERATUR UND GERMANISTIK IN DER DDR VON PAUL GERHARD KLUSSMANN UND HEINRICH MOHR. Added/Corp Arbeitskreis Literatur und Germanistik in der DDR. Vol. 1 (1980)-. Monographic series. German. ir. Price varies per volume. Bouvier GmbH & Co. KG ABT Verlag, AM Hof 28, D 53113 Bonn Germany. **Tel** 011 49 228 7290141. **(Subscription address:** VVA Bertelsmann Distributors GmbH, Postfach 7777, D-33310 Guetersloh Germany.**)** **LC** PN4; .J34.

GW/0453-9842
JAHRESGABE - KLAUS-GROTH-GESELLSCHAFT. [Jahresgabe - Klaus-Groth-Ges.]. **Main/Corp** Klaus-Groth-Gesellschaft (Germany). Began in 1955. Periodical. German. Klaus-Groth-Gesellschaft, Luttenheid 48, 2240 Heide in Holstein Germany. **LC** PT4848.G7; Z74. **DD** 831/.7.
Ind/Abst MLA Int. Bibl. Books Artic. Mod. Lang. Lit.

US
JAMES FENIMORE COOPER SOCIETY NEWSLETTER, THE. Added/Corp James Fenimore Cooper Society. No. 1 (Spring 1989)-. Newsletter. English.
Ind/Abst Am. Humanit. Index (199?-).

UK/0143-6333
JAMES JOYCE BROADSHEET. No. 1 (Jan. 1980)-. Periodical. English. Three times a year (Feb., June, Oct.). £5.00 UK; £6.00 other. University of Leeds School of English, Leeds LS2 9JT England. **Tel** 011 44 532 334739, FAX 0532 334774, telex 556473 UNILDS 9.

JA
JAPANESE LITERATURE TODAY. Added/Corp Nihon PEN Kurabu. VFOAT Litterature Japonaise d'Aujourd'hui. No. 1 (March 1976)-. Periodical. English. an. $46.00. Japanese P E N Club, 265 Shuwa Residential Hotel, 9-1-7 Akasaka Minato-ku, Tokyo Japan. **(Subscription address:** Japan Publications Trading Company, Ltd., PO Box 5030, Tokyo International, Tokyo 100-31 Japan.**)** **LC** PL700; .J32. **DD** 895.6/09. *Supersedes* Japan P.E.N. News.

SZ/0721-3719
JAPANISCHE STUDIEN ZUR DEUTSCHEN SPRACHE UND LITERATUR. See Linguistics.

US/0892-8665
JASNA NEWS. [JASNA news]. Added/Corp Jane Austen Society of North America. **VAT** Jane Austen Society of North America News. (198?)-. Periodical.

English. Twice a year. $15.00. Jane Austen Society of North America, 860 North Lake Shore Drive, Chicago IL 60611. **Tel** FAX (312)266-0081. **(Subscription address:** Jane Austen Society of North America, 2650 D Matheson Way, Sacramento CA 95864.**) ED** Garnet L. Bass. **DD** 813. **Bk Rev. Ad Acc. Circ:** 2,300 (ctrl). ***Continues*** *Jane Austen Society of North America. News.*
Desc: Contains news of the society, book reviews, and other articles concerning publications, literature, history, and society relevant to the study of Jane Austen and her work.

II
JAYANTI. Vol. 1 Jan. 1973-. Periodical. Tamil (Tamil). 3.50. **LC** PL4758.5; J38.

CN/0820-6333
JE NE VEUX PAS MOURIR A L'ACADEMIE FRANCAISE. Vol. 1, No. 1-. Periodical. French. mo. $1.95 per no. Charlie Val, CP 363, Succursale Verdun, Verdun Quebec, H4G 3G1. **DD** C848/.5407.

US/0889-759X
JEAN RHYS REVIEW. [Jean Rhys rev.]. Vol. 1, No. 1 (Fall 1986)-. Periodical. English (French). sa. $28.00 (institutions), $19.00 (individuals). Nora Gaines, PO Box 811, Planitarium Station, New York NY 10024. **Tel** (212)884-5854. **ED** Nora Gaines. **LC** PR6035.H96; Z74. **DD** 823/.912. **Bk Rev. Pr Rev.**
Desc: Provides a forum for research and criticism concerning the work of Jean Rhys.
Ind/Abst MLA Int. Bibl. Books Artic. Mod. Lang. Lit.

US/0094-1360
JEFFERSONIAN REVIEW, THE. Periodical. English. bm. $5.00. F. Conneen III, PO Box 3864, Charlottesville VA 22903. **LC** PS559.C55; J43. **DD** 810/.8/0054.

HU/0447-6425
JELENKOR. (JELENKOR : IRODALMI ES MUVESZETI FOLYOIRAT.). [Jelenkor]. (1958)-. Periodical. Hungarian. mo. $20.00. Jelenkor Irodalmi es Muveszeti Kiado, Szechenyi ter 17, 7621 Pecs, Hungary. **ED** I. Csuhai. **Bk Rev. Circ:** 3,000. available with illustrations.
Desc: Deals mainly with the contemporary Hungarian literature: poems, prose pieces, and chapters of novels. Critical works are published regularly.
Ind/Abst MLA Int. Bibl. Books Artic. Mod. Lang. Lit.

CH
JEN MIN WEN HSUEH. VFOAT Renmin Wenxue. (1949)-. Periodical. Chinese. mo. RMBY23.40. Zuojia Chubanshe, 10 Nongzhanguan Nanli, Beijing 100026, People's Republic of China. **Tel** 500-3120. **(Subscription address:** China International Book Trading Corporation, PO Box 399, Library Service Department, Beijing 100044 People's Republic of China.**) ED** Liu Xinwu. **LC** PL2513; .J39. **DD** 895.1/08/005.
Desc: Includes short stories, essays, poetry and children's literature.

US/0021-5880
JEOPARDY (BELLINGHAM, WASH.). (JEOPARDY.). **Added/Corp** Western Washington State College. Western Washington University. (1966)-. Periodical. English. an (May). $4.00. Jeopardy, Western Washington University, Belingham WA 98225. **Tel** (206)676-3118. **ED** Susan E. Hilton. **DD** 810. **Circ:** 4,000.
Desc: Finest quality poetry, prose and artwork.

US/0075-3726
JEWISH BOOK ANNUAL. [Jew. book annu.]. (1944)-. English (Hebrew and Yiddish). an. $27.50. Jewish Book Council of America, 15 East 26th Street, New York NY 10016. **Tel** (212)532-4949. **ED** Jacob Kabakoff. **LC** PN6067. **DD** 296. Index available. **Circ:** 1,000. ***Continues*** *Jewish Book Week Annual.*
Desc: Record of American Jewish literary creativity and Jewish book production, as well as of Jewish literary contributions in Israel and other lands.
Ind/Abst Am. Bibliogr. Slavic East Europ. Stud. (19??-19??).

CN/0315-2685
JEWISH DIALOGUE. VFOAT Dialog. (Spring 1970)-. Periodical. English. qt. D J Publishing Company, 1498 Yonge Street/Suite 7, Toronto Ontario M4T 1Z6 Canada. **Tel** (416) 921-2074. **ED** Joe Roseblatt. **LC** AP92; .J44. **DD** 050.

US/0896-8152
JEWISH STORYTELLING NEWSLETTER. [Jew. storytell. newsl.]. **VFOAT** Jewish Story Telling Newsletter. (1985)-. Newsletter. English. qt. $10.00. Jewish Storytelling Center, 92nd Street YM-YMHA Library, 1395 Lexington Avenue, New York NY 10128. **DD** 808.

CI/0021-6925
JEZIK : CASOPIS ZA KULTURU HRVATSKOGA KNJIZEVNOG JEZIKA. [Jezik]. **Added/Corp** Hrvatsko Filolosko Drustvo. (1952)-. Periodical. Serbo-Croatian (Roman). Five times a year. $16.00. Hrvatsko Filolosko Drustvo, Djure Sallja 3, 41000 Zagreb Croatia. **Tel** 011 385 41 513155. **(Subscription address:** Mladost Export Import, PO Box 1028, Ilica 30, 41000 Zagreb Croatia.**) LC** PG1201; .J4.
Ind/Abst MLA Int. Bibl. Books Artic. Mod. Lang. Lit.

PL
JEZYK ROSYJSKI. Added/Corp Poland. Ministerstwo Oswiaty i Wychowania. Vol. 1, No. 1 (1948)-. Periodical. Polish (Russian; summaries and/or abstracts in Polish and Russian). ir (5 issues). $18.00. **(Subscription address:** ARS Polona, PO Box 1001, 00068 Warsaw Poland.**) LC** PG2068.P6; A35.

JA
JIDO BUNGAKU ANYUARU. VFOAT Yearbook of Children's Literature. Began with issue for 1982. Periodical. Japanese (Japanese). an. ¥7500. Kaiseisha 3-5, Ichigaya Sadohara-cho Shinjuku-ku, Tokyo-to 162 Japan. **LC** PN1008.2; .J53.

JA
JIDO BUNGAKU KENKYU. Japanese. ¥800 single issue. Nihon Jido Bungaku Gakkai, c/o Tokyo Kyoiku Kenkyujo 48-23 Sakae-cho Kita-ku, Tokyo-to 114 Japan. **LC** PL751.5; .J54.

II
JIVANA SAHITYA. Periodical. Hindi (Hindi). mo. 6.00. Sasta Sahitya Mandal, New Delhi India. **LC** PK2030; .J58.

JA
JOCHI DAIGAKU DOITSU BUNGAKU RONSHU. Added/Corp Jochi Daigaku. Jochi Daigaku Doitsu Bungakukai. **VFOAT** Beitrage zur Deutschen Literatur. 1 (1964)-. Periodical. Multiple languages (Japanese and German). an. Jochi Daigaku Bungakubu, Dokubungaku Ken-Kyushitsu, 7 Kioicho Chiyoda-ku, Tokyo Japan. **LC** PT9; .J6.

JA/0388-6417
JOCHI EIGO BUNGAKU KENKYU. See Linguistics.

US
JOHN COLET ARCHIVE OF AMERICAN LITERATURE, 1620-1920, THE. ***Ceased.*** **VFOAT** John Colet Archive. No. 1 (Spring 1974)-. Periodical. English. sa. John Colet Press, 31 St James Avenue/#925-26, Boston MA 02116. **Tel** (617)426-2303, FAX (617)426-9767.

US/0021-728X
JOHNSONIAN NEWS LETTER. [Johnsonian news lett.]. **Added/Corp** Modern Language Association of America. English VIII. Vol. 1, (Dec. 1940)-. Academic Scholarly Publication. English. Four times a year (Mar., June, Sept., Dec.). $6.00 US & Canada; $6.50 others. University of Chicago / English, Department of English, 1050 East 59th Street, Chicago IL 60637. **Tel** (312)702-7989, (312)702-8536. **ED** Stuart Sherman. **LC** PR1; .J64. **Bk Rev. Circ:** 1,800.
Desc: Provides news of interest to students, collectors, and scholars of 18th century english literature, particularly of Samuel Johnson (1709-1784), English author and lexicographer, and his circle. Recurring features include information on recent publications, news of scholarly meetings and exhibitions, and a column title Johnson and Boswell notes.
Ind/Abst Abstr. Engl. Stud.; Annu. Bibliogr. Engl. Lang. Lit.; Romant. Move.

US/1051-1865
JOURNAL OF AFRO-LATIN AMERICAN STUDIES AND LITERATURES, THE. (1991)-. English. Twice a year (Spring and Fall). $45.00. Department of Modern Languages and Literatures, Howard University, 2400 6th Street NW, Locke Hall, Washington DC 20059. **Tel** (202)806-6758. **ED** Rosangela Maria Vieira.
Desc: Strives to promote scientific investigation and awareness of issues that have been faced by African-Latin American citizens from colonial times to the present. Committed to underscoring the significance of the rich and diverse contribution of peoples with African ancestry to the life, culture, and the art of the continent.

NE/0085-2376
JOURNAL OF ARABIC LITERATURE. [J. Arab lit.]. Vol. 1 (1970)-. Periodical. English. Three times a year. Fl149.00 Netherlands; $85.25 other. E. J. Brill, Postbus 9000, 2300 PA Leiden Netherlands. **Tel** 011 31 71 312624, FAX 011 31 71 317532, telex 39296 BRILL NL. **ED** J.E. Montgomery. **LC** PJ7501; .J63. **DD** 892.7/05. **[CCC]. Circ:** 270. Documents available from The Genuine Article.
Desc: Deals with Arabic literature as literature in the narrow sense of imaginative writing in verse and prose. It provides a forum for the discussion of Arabic literature, both classical and modern, by Arabs and non-Arabs. The journal publishes essays in literary appreciation, assessments of trends and movements of individual authors and of single works, and bibliographies.
Ind/Abst Arts Humanit. Citation Index [Full Cov.]; Curr. Contents Arts Humanit.; Index Islam. Lit.; Index Book Rev. Relig.; MLA Int. Bibl. Books Artic. Mod. Lang. Lit.; Relig. Index One Period. (1980-); Res. Alert [Full Cov.]; Middle East J.

II/0970-5309
JOURNAL OF ARTS & IDEAS. See The Arts.

US
JOURNAL OF BECKETT STUDIES. [J. Beckett stud.]. **Added/Corp** Florida State University. Dept. of English. **VFOAT** JOBS. Vol. 1, No. 1 and 2 (Spring 1992)-. Academic Scholarly Publication. English. Twice a year (Fall and Spring). $15.00 (individual); $25.00 (institution). Florida State University / Department of English, Tallahassee FL 32306. **Tel** (904)644-6038, FAX (904)644-0811. **ED** Professor S. E. Gontarski. **LC** PR6003.E282; Z4585. **Bk Rev**, (Qty: 8-10). **Ad Acc. Pr Rev. Circ:** 500. ***Continues*** *Journal of Beckett Studies, 0309-5207.*
Desc: Scholarly analyses, reviews and articles on the work of Samuel Beckett and work related to drama and literature.
Ind/Abst Annu. Bibliogr. Engl. Lang. Lit.; MLA Int. Bibl. Books Artic. Mod. Lang. Lit.

CN/0047-2255
JOURNAL OF CANADIAN FICTION. [J. Can. fict.]. (Winter 1972)-. Periodical. English. ir. Bellrock Press Association, 2050 Mackay Street, Montreal 107 Quebec Canada. **LC** PR9195.7; .J68. **DD** 813/.54/080971. available on microfiche from University Microfilms International (UMI).
Ind/Abst Am. Humanit. Index (-199?); Annu. Bibliogr. Engl. Lang. Lit.; Can. Index (?-?); Can. Period. Index; MLA Int. Bibl. Books Artic. Mod. Lang. Lit.

UK/0021-9894
JOURNAL OF COMMONWEALTH LITERATURE. (THE JOURNAL OF COMMONWEALTH LITERATURE.). [J. commonw. lit.]. **Added/Corp** University of Leeds. (Sept. 1965)-. Periodical. English. tq (3 issues). £62.00. Bowker Saur Ltd., A Reed Reference Publishing Company, Part of Reed International PLC, 59-60 Grosvenor Street, London WIX 9DA England. **Tel** 011 44 71 4935841, FAX 011 44 71 4991590. **(Subscription address:** World-Wide Subscription Services, Unit 4, Gibbs Reed Farm Pashley Road, Ticehurst TN5 7HE England.**) ED** A. Niven and Caroline Bundy. **LC** PR1; .J67. **DD** 820.05. **[CCC]. Bk Rev. Ad Acc. Circ:** 1,200. available on microfilm and microfiche from University Microfilms International (UMI); available on CD-ROM. Documents available from The Genuine Article, UMI Article Clearinghouse.
Desc: Provides a focal-point for discussion of literature in English outside Britain and the United States of America. The first number of each volume consists of an issue of critical studies and essays; the second is the bibliography issue, providing an annual checklist of publications in each region of the Commonwealth.
Ind/Abst Abstr. Engl. Stud. (19??-); Acad. Search (Jan. 1993-); Annu. Bibliogr. Engl. Lang. Lit. (19??-); Arts Humanit. Citation Index (19??-19??) [Full Cov.]; Br. Humanit. Index (19??-); Curr. Contents Arts Humanit. (19??-); Expand. Acad. Index (1989-); Humanit. Index (19??-); Humanit. Source (Jul. 1993-); Mag. Search (19??-); MLA Int. Bibl. Books Artic. Mod. Lang. Lit. (19??-); Newsp. Period. Abstr. (1991-); Res. Alert (19??-) [Full Cov.]

●US/1064-752X
JOURNAL OF COMMUNICATION AND TRANSFORMATIONAL MYTH. See Folklore.

II/0252-8169
JOURNAL OF COMPARATIVE LITERATURE & AESTHETICS. See The Arts-Art.

●US/1065-755X
JOURNAL OF CREATIVE WRITING AND BIBLIOTHERAPY, THE. See Journalism.

US/1059-0196
JOURNAL OF DURASSIAN STUDIES. [J. Durassian stud.]. **Added/Corp** Duras Society. George Mason University. Foreign Languages & Literatures. Vol. 1 (Fall 1989)-. English (French). **DD** 840.
Ind/Abst Film Lit. Index (19??-).

KO
JOURNAL OF ENGLISH LANGUAGE AND LITERATURE, THE. See Linguistics.

US/0737-4828
JOURNAL OF EVOLUTIONARY PSYCHOLOGY. [J. evol. psychol.]. **Added/Corp** Institute for Evolutionary Psychology. (19??)-. Periodical. English. sa (Mar. and Aug.). $13.00 (one year), $25.00 (two year), $30.00 (three year). Institute of Evolutionary Psychology, 5117 Forbes Avenue, Pittsburgh PA 15213. **Tel** (412)621-7057. **ED** Paul Neumarkt. **LC** PN56.P93; J68. **DD** 801/.92. **Bk Rev. Circ:** 300 (ctrl). available on CD-ROM.
Desc: Articles on literature from a psychological aspect either Freudian or Jungian or any other psychological aspect; also poetry.
Ind/Abst MLA Int. Bibl. Books Artic. Mod. Lang. Lit.; Psychol. Abstr. (1982-); PsycINFO.

US/0147-5460
JOURNAL OF HISPANIC PHILOLOGY. **See** Linguistics.

II/0302-1319
JOURNAL OF INDIAN WRITING IN ENGLISH, THE. [J. Indian writ. Engl.]. Vol. 1 (Jan. 1973)-. English. sa (Jan. and July). $24.00. Gulbarga University, G. S. Balarma, Gupta Department of English, Gulbarga 585106 India. **ED** G. S. Balarama Gupta. **LC** PR9480; .J64. **DD** 820/.9/954. **Bk Rev. Ad Acc.** Full Page (B&W) Rs.2000. Half Page (B&W) RS.1000. **Circ:** 1,000.
Desc: Publishes creative writing in English by Indians and critical writing on Indians.
Ind/Abst Annu. Bibliogr. Engl. Lang. Lit.; MLA Int. Bibl. Books Artic. Mod. Lang. Lit.

NE/1044-8985
JOURNAL OF INTERDISCIPLINARY LITERARY STUDIES. [J. interdiscip. lit. stud.]. **Added/Corp** Universiteit van Amsterdam. Vakgroep Spaans-Portugees. University of Nebraska--Lincoln. Dept. of Modern Languages and Literatures. **VFOAT** Cuadernos Interdisciplinarios de Estudios Literarios; JILS/CIEL. Vol. 1, No. 1 (Spring 1989)-. Periodical. Spanish (English and Catalan). sa. $30.00 (1 year), $50.00 (2 year) institutions; $20.00 (1 year), $35.00 (2 year) individuals. Manuel L. Abellan, Spuistraat 134, Department of Hispanic Studies, 1012 VB Amsterdam Netherlands. **Tel** 011 31 20 5254267, FAX 011 31 20 5254429. **ED** Manuel L. Abellan. **DD** 860. Index available. cum. index. **Bk Rev**, (Qty: 6). **Circ:** 400.
Ind/Abst MLA Int. Bibl. Books Artic. Mod. Lang. Lit.

USUS/0047-2514
JOURNAL OF IRISH LITERATURE, THE. ***Ceased.*** [J. Ir. lit.]. Vol. 1, No. 1 Jan. (1972)-(Dec. 1993). Periodical. English. Three times a year (Jan., May, Sept.). Proscenium Press, PO Box 361, Newark DE 19711. **Tel** (302)764-8477. **LC** PR8830; .J68. **DD** 820/.8/09415. Documents available from The Genuine Article.
Ind/Abst Abstr. Engl. Stud.; Am. Humanit. Index; Arts Humanit. Citation Index [Full Cov.]; Curr. Contents Arts Humanit.; MLA Int. Bibl. Books Artic. Mod. Lang. Lit.; Res. Alert [Full Cov.].

US/8755-4208
JOURNAL OF KENTUCKY STUDIES, THE. Vol. 1, Issue 1 (July 1984)-. Periodical. English. an. $3.00. Office of the Bursar, Northern Kentucky University, Journal of Kentucky Studies, Highland Heights KY 41076. **LC** F451; .J78. **DD** 976.9/005.
Desc: Journal includes poetry, short stories, photography, and literary criticism.

NE/0341-7638
JOURNAL OF LITERARY SEMANTICS. **See** Linguistics.

II
JOURNAL OF LITERATURE AND AESTHETICS. **VFOAT** J.L.A.; JLA. Periodical. English. qt. $9.00 surface mail, $12.00 airmail. Dr S Sreenivasan, Department of English, T K M M College, Nangiarkulangara Haripad Keraka-690 513 India. **LC** PN2; .J585. **DD** 808.8.

MM/0075-4285
JOURNAL OF MALTESE STUDIES. **Added/Corp** Royal University of Malta. Chair of Maltese. Old University (Malta). Chair of Maltese. University of Malta. Faculty of Education. University of Malta. Dept. of Maltese. **VFOAT** JMS. No. 1 (1961)-. Periodical. English (Italian and French). ir. Price varies. University of Malta, Publications Office, Msida Malta. **Tel** 336451, FAX 356/336450, telex HIEDUC MW. **ED** Oliver Friggieri. **LC** DG987; .J68. **DD** 945.8/5/005. **Circ:** 500.

US/1053-6981
JOURNAL OF NARRATIVE AND LIFE HISTORY. [J. narrat. life hist.]. **VFOAT** Narrative and Life History. Vol. 1, No. 1 (1991)-. Periodical. English. qt. $135.00 US & Canada; $160.00 other. Lawrence Erlbaum Associates, 365 Broadway, Suite 102, Hillsdale NJ 07642. **Tel** (201)666-4110, (800)926-6579, FAX (201)666-2394. **LC** PN212; .J68. **DD** 808/.005. **CODEN** JNLHEY.
Ind/Abst Soc. Plann. Policy Dev. Abstr.

US/0022-2925
JOURNAL OF NARRATIVE TECHNIQUE, THE. [J. narrat. tech.]. **Added/Corp** Eastern Michigan University. Dept. of English. Vol. 1 (Jan. 1971)-. Periodical. English. tq. $20.00 (US), $30.00 (other) institution; $15.00 (US), $25.00 (other) individual. Eastern Michigan University / English Dept., Department of English, I Wojeik-Andrews, Ypsilanti MI 48197. **Tel** (313)487-0150. **ED** George Perkins and Barbara Perkins. **LC** PE1425; .J68. **DD** 820.9. **Bk Rev**, (Qty: 3). **Circ:** 600 (ctrl).
Desc: Narrative theory of literature in English and other languages.
Ind/Abst Abstr. Engl. Stud.; Am. Bibliogr. Slavic East Europ. Stud.; Am. Humanit. Index; Annu. Bibliogr. Engl. Lang. Lit.; Arts Humanit. Citation Index [Full Cov.]; Curr. Contents Arts Humanit.; Lit. Crit. Regist.; MLA Int. Bibl. Books Artic. Mod. Lang. Lit.; Res. Alert [Full Cov.]; Romant. Move.

NZ/0112-1227
JOURNAL OF NEW ZEALAND LITERATURE : JNZL. **Added/Corp** Victoria University of Wellington. Dept. of English. **VFOAT** JNZL; J.N.Z.L. No. 1 (1983)-. English. an. 15.00NZ$. Journal of New Zealand Literature, Univ. Otago English Dept., PO Box 56, Dunedin New Zealand. **Tel** 011 64 03 4798617, FAX 011 64 03 4741607. **ED** Lawrence Jones and Heather Murray. **Ad Acc. Circ:** 400.
Ind/Abst Annu. Bibliogr. Engl. Lang. Lit.

US/0897-3075
JOURNAL OF POPULAR LITERATURE. ***Ceased.*** [J. pop. lit.]. **VFOAT** JPL. Vol. 1, No. 1 (Spring/Summer 1985)-Vol. 5 No. 1 (1993). Periodical. English. sa. Popular Press Journals Area, Bowling Green State University, Bowling Green OH 43403. **Tel** (419)372-7866, (419)372-7865. **DD** 801. **Bk Rev. Ad Acc.**
Ind/Abst Romant. Move.

US/0927-7544
JOURNAL OF REAL ESTATE LITERATURE. English. sa. $234.00. Kluwer Academic Publishers / Massachusetts, PO Box 358, Accord Station, Hingham MA 02018. **Tel** (617)871-6600. **ED** James Kau and C.F. Simmons. **[CCC]. Acid Free.**
Desc: The scope of the journal includes that of the traditional literature journal listing published research, dissertations and works in progress, but also including information on software and databases for the researcher and publishing case studies and other teaching aids to support the classroom instruction of real estate.

US/0091-5637
JOURNAL OF SOUTH ASIAN LITERATURE. [J. South Asian lit.]. **Added/Corp** Michigan State University. Asian Studies Center. Vol. 9 (Spring 1973)-. Periodical. English. Twice a year (June, Dec.). $21.00 (individuals); $27.00 (institutions). Michigan State University / Department of English, 201 Morrill Hall, East Lansing MI 48824-1035. **Tel** (517)355-9571, (517)355-7570. **ED** Conni Zellar and Surjit Dulai. **LC** PK1501; .M34. **DD** 891/.1. **Bk Rev. Ad Acc. Pr Rev. Circ:** 450 (ctrl). available on microfilm and microfiche from University Microfilms International (UMI). Documents available from The Genuine Article. ***Continues** Mahfil, 0025-0503.*
Desc: Devoted to the study and dissemination of South Asian literature. Publishes literary criticism on and selections from the literatures of South Asia covering all periods--classical, medieval, modern, and contemporary--and major languages of the Subcontinent.
Ind/Abst Annu. Bibliogr. Engl. Lang. Lit.; Arts Humanit. Citation Index (19??-19??) [Full Cov.]; Curr. Contents Arts Humanit.; Int. Bibliogr. Sociol.; MLA Int. Bibl. Books Artic. Mod. Lang. Lit.; Res. Alert [Full Cov.].

II
JOURNAL OF TELUGU STUDIES : RESEARCH QUARTERLY OF TELUGU UNIVERSITY. (1988)-. Periodical. English (Telugu). qt. RS20.00. Sri TD Prasada Rao Registrar, Telugu University, Kala Bhavan Pradesh India. **LC** DS432.T4; J68.

US/0587-5064
JOURNAL OF THE AMERICAN STUDIES ASSOCIATION OF TEXAS. **See** History(General)-History of North, South, and Central America.

II
JOURNAL OF THE DEPARTMENT OF ENGLISH (UNIVERSITY OF CALCUTTA. DEPT. OF ENGLISH). (JOURNAL OF THE DEPARTMENT OF ENGLISH.). Vol. 14, No. 1 (1978-79)-. Periodical. English. an. Rs15.00. UCAC/Secretary, Calcutta University, Journal and Bulletin Section, Asutosh Building, Calcutta 700073 India. **Tel** 38-0071, FAX 31-1536, telex 31-5250. **ED** Arun Kumar Dasgupta. **LC** PR1; .C25. **DD** 820/.9. **Bk Rev. Circ:** 1,000 (ctrl). available on microfilm; available on microfiche. ***Continues** Bulletin of the Department of English.*
Ind/Abst MLA Int. Bibl. Books Artic. Mod. Lang. Lit.

UK/0144-008X
JOURNAL OF THE EIGHTEEN NINETIES SOCIETY. (JOURNAL.). [J. Eighteen Nineties Soc.]. **Main/Corp** Eighteen Nineties Society. No. 6/7 (1975)-. English. ***Continues** Francis Thompson Society. Journal.*
Ind/Abst MLA Int. Bibl. Books Artic. Mod. Lang. Lit.

PK
JOURNAL OF THE ENGLISH LITERARY CLUB, THE. **See** Literature-Poetry.

US/0897-0521
JOURNAL OF THE FANTASTIC IN THE ARTS. ***Ceased.*** [J. fantast. arts]. **Added/Corp** International Association for the Fantastic in the Arts. **VFOAT** JFA. Vol. 1, No. 1 (1988)-Vol. 3, No. 3, (1993). Periodical. English. qt. Orion Publications, 1807 Cold Springs Road, Liverpool NY 13090. **Tel** (315)451-0760. **DD** 700.
Ind/Abst Sci. Fict. Fantasy Book Rev. Index.

US/1055-1948
JOURNAL OF THE WRITERS GUILD OF AMERICA. WEST. [J. Writ. Guild Am. West]. **Added/Corp** Writers Guild of America, West. **VFOAT** Journal; WGAW Journal. Vol. 3, No. 1 (Dec./Jan. 1990)-. Periodical. English. mo. $40.00 US; $45.00 Canada; $50.00 other. Writers Guild of America, 8955 Beverly Boulevard, Los Angeles CA 90048. **Tel** (310)550-1000, FAX (310)550-8185. **ED** Bill Meis. **DD** 810. **Bk Rev. Ad Acc, Adv Mgr:** Dianna Hightower, **Tel** (310)455-4210. **Circ:** 10,000 (ctrl). ***Continues** Writers Guild of America, West Journal.*

CN/0701-1792
JOURNAL OF UKRAINIAN GRADUATE STUDIES. **See** History(General)-History of Europe.

BB/0258-8501
JOURNAL OF WEST INDIAN LITERATURE. **Added/Corp** University of the West Indies (Cave Hill, Barbados). Dept. of English. **VFOAT** J.W.I.L.; JWIL. Vol. 1, No. 1 (Oct. 1986)-. Periodical. English. Twice a year (Apr., & Oct.). $20.00. Journal of West Indian Literature, University of the West Indies, English Department, PO Box 64, Bridgetown Barbados. **Tel** (809)425-1310, FAX (809)425-1527, telex UNIVADOS WB 2257. **ED** Dr. Mark McWatt. **Bk Rev**, (Qty: 6-8). **Ad Acc. Circ:** 250.
Desc: Publishes research on West Indian literature, including some comparative Caribbean literature and reviews.

US/1045-084X
JOURNAL : THE LITERARY MAGAZINE OF THE OHIO STATE UNIVERSITY, THE. [J. - Ohio State Univ., Dep. Engl.]. **Added/Corp** Ohio State University. Dept. of English. Ohio Arts Council. Vol. 10, No. 1 (Fall/Winter 1986/87)-. Periodical. English. sa. $8.00. Ohio State University / Department of English, 164 West 17th Avenue, Columbus OH 43210. **Tel** (614)292-6555, (614)488-8634. **ED** Kathy Fagan and Michelle Herman. **DD** 810. Index available. **Bk Rev**, (Qty: 1-4). **Ad Acc. Circ:** 1,000. ***Continues** Ohio Journal, 0740-2139.*

FR/0982-6904
JOYCE. [Joyce]. (1987)-. Periodical. French. Eight times a year. 280.00F France; 510.00F Europe; 580.00F Algeria, Morocco & Tunisia; 650.00F French speaking Africa & Mideast; 810.00F North, South and Central America; 950.00F other. Alsojoy Diffusion, 9 11 13 Rue du Col Pierre Avia, 75015 Paris France. **Tel** 011 33 1 48244400. **UDC** 087.2-055.2.

US/1049-0809
JOYCE STUDIES ANNUAL. [Joyce stud. annu.]. **Added/Corp** Harry Ransom Humanities Research Center. (1990)-. English. an. $35.00 (institutions), $25.00 (individuals) US, add $4.00 postage other. University of Texas Press, PO Box 7819, Austin TX 78713. **Tel** (512)471-4531, FAX (512)320-0668, telex 776453 UTEXPRES AUS. **LC** PR6019.O9; Z669. **DD** 823/.912. **[CCC].**
Desc: Emphasizes the areas of historical, textual, and comparative criticism featuring previously unpublished material from the Harry Ransom Humanities Research Center's Joyce collection.
Ind/Abst MLA Int. Bibl. Books Artic. Mod. Lang. Lit.

IT
JOYCE STUDIES IN ITALY. **VFOAT** Joyce in Rome. Vol. 1 (1984)-. English.

CN/0711-7671
JSW. JOURNAL OF STUDENT WRITING. (THE JOURNAL OF STUDENT WRITING.). [JSW, J. stud. writ.]. **VAT** Journal of Student Writing. No. 6 (Aug. 1984)-. English. an. University of New Brunswick Studies in Canadian Literature, Fredericton New Brunswick E3B 5A3 Canada. **Tel** (506)453-4598, FAX (506)453-4599. **DD** 820/.9. ***Continues** JSW, 0711-7671.*

CN/0316-8417
JUBILEE (GORRIE). (JUBILEE.). No. 1- June 1974-. Periodical. English. ir. $3.00. Jubilee Press, R.R. No. 2, Gorrie Ontario N0G 1X0. **DD** C810/.8/0054. available on microfilm from University Microfilms International (UMI).

GW/0177-4247
JUGENDBUCHMAGAZIN. (1979)-. German. qt. Arbeitskreis das Gute Jugendbuch e.v., Spindelgang 9, 4300 Essen 16 Germany. ***Continues** Das Gute Jugendbuch, 0433-0196.*
Ind/Abst Child. Lit. Abstr. (19??-).

FR
JULES VERNE. 1-. French. 50.00F. Lettres Modernes Minard, 45 rue de Saint Andre, 14123 Fleury Surrey Orne France. **Tel** 011 33 31 844706. **LC** PN3; .R4 subser.

FR
JULIEN GRACQ. **VFOAT** Serie Julien Gracq; Gracq. (1991)-. French. Lettres Modernes Minard, 45 rue de Saint Andre, 14123 Fleury Surrey Orne France. **Tel** 011 33 31 844706.

GW/0938-202X
JULIT. **VFOAT** Jugendliteratur. (1990)-. German. Schweizerischer Bund fur Jugendliteratur, Gewerbestr 8, 6330 Cham, Switzerland. **Continues** Informationen des Arbeitskreises fur Jugendliteratur, 0175-6621.
Ind/Abst Child. Lit. Abstr. (19??-).

II
JUNELI. Periodical. Nepali. Rs0.75. Dayalakshmi Chapakhana, Bhojpur India. **LC** PK2598.A2; J86.

CC
JUNG SHU WEN HSUEH TSUNG KAN. No. 1 (Sept. 1979)-. Periodical. Chinese. qt. RMBY1.06. Fu-Chien Shen Hsin Hua Shu, Tien Fu-Chou, People's Republic of China. **LC** PL2513; .J86. **DD** 895.1/09/005.

AU
JUNGE LITERATUR AUS OSTERREICH. (1980)-. German. an. **LC** PT3823; .J79. **DD** 830/.8/09436.

MY
JURNAL DEWAN BAHASA. **Added/Corp** Dewan Bahasa dan Pustaka. **VFOAT** Jurnal Bahasa. (Sept. 1989)-. Periodical. Malay. mo. $27.00. Yayasan Persuratan Ilmu, Tingkat Tiga,Wisma Mirama, 50460 Kuala Lumpur Malaysia. **Tel** 03-2481011. **Continues** Dewan Bahasa.

II
JYOTSNA. (19??)-. Hindi (Hindi). mo. 15.00. Jyotsna Karylana, Bandhu Kuti Path 8, Rajendranagar Patna 800016 India. **LC** PK2030; .J95.

DK
K & K. **VFOAT** K Og K; Kultur Og Klasse; Kritik Og Kulturanalyse; Kultur & Klasse; Kritik & Kulturanalyse. (1989)-. Periodical. Danish (Swedish and Norwegian). Twice a year. Kr250.00 Denmark; Kr302.00 Europe; Kr338.00 other. Forlaget Medusa, Postboks 1, 2840 Holte Denmark. **Tel** 45 2 424000. **ED** Jorgen Holmagaard. cum. index. **Bk Rev** (Qty: 8-10). **Ad Acc. Circ:** 600 (ctrl). **Continues** Kultur Og Klasse, 0105-7367.
Desc: Covers literature, cultural studies, mass communications, and semiotics.

II
KADAMBINI. Periodical. Hindi. Twelve times a year. $6.50 (surface mail); $13.00 (airmail). Hindustan Times Ltd, 18-20 Kasturba Gandhi Marg, New Delhi 110001 India. **Tel** 011 91 11 3318201. **ED** Rajendra Awasthy. **Bk Rev. Ad Acc. Circ:** 150,000.
Desc: Covers all subjects possible in life and literature.

II
KAHANI. Periodical. Hindi (Hindi). Rs8.00. Sarasvati Presa, 5 Sardar Patel Marg, Allahabad India. **LC** PK2077; .K25.

II
KAKATIYA JOURNAL OF ENGLISH STUDIES. V. 1- Mar. 1976-. Periodical. English. $1.00. Kakatiya University, Department of English, Vidyaratmapur Warangal Andhra Pradesh, 506001 India. **LC** PR9480; .K34. **DD** 820/.9.

JA
KAKU. Fall Edition 1977-. Periodical. Japanese. ¥580. Kaiho Shuppansho, 1247 Kuboyoshicho, Naniwa-ku 556, Osaka Japan. **LC** PL755.8; .K34.

II
KALAMA. **Main/Corp** Kalama (Calcutta, India). Periodical. Hindi (Hindi). **LC** PK2030; .K33.

US/0748-8742
KALEIDOSCOPE (AKRON, OHIO), THE. (THE KALEIDOSCOPE.). **Added/Corp** United Cerebral Palsy of Akron and Summit County. (1979)-. Periodical. English. sa. $9.00 (individuals), $14.00 (institutions) US; $14.00 (individuals), $19.00 (institutions) Canada; $17.00 (individuals), $22.00 (institutions) other. Kaleidoscope Press United Disability Services, 326 Locust Street, Akron OH 44302-1876. **Tel** (216)762-9755, FAX (216)762-0912. **ED** Darshan Perusek. **LC** PS153.P48; K34. **DD** 810/.8/03520816. **Bk Rev** (Qty: 2). **Pr Rev. Circ:** 1,500. available on audiocassette from Braille Institute.
Desc: Unique disability magazine. Creatively explores the experiences of disability through fiction, essays, poetry, and artwork. Award-winning leader in disability studies. Not advocacy, medical, or rehabilitation journal. Challenges and overcomes stereotypical attitudes about disability. Promotes balanced portrayals of all people. Appeals to broad readership.
Ind/Abst Am. Humanit. Index; Index Am. Period. Verse.

FI/0355-0311
KALEVALASEURAN VUOSIKIRJA. **Added/Corp** Kalevalaseura. Suomalaisen Kirjallisuuden Seura. (1921)-. Finnish. **LC** PH325; .K34.
Ind/Abst MLA Int. Bibl. Books Artic. Mod. Lang. Lit.

PL
KAMENA. **Added/Corp** Zwiazek Literatow Polskich. Lubelski Oddzia. (1933)-. Polish. qt. Price on Request. **(Subscription address:** ARS Polona, PO Box 1001, 00068 Warsaw Poland.) **LC** AP54; .K35.

RU
KAMENNYI POIAS / KURGANSKAIA, ORENBURGSKAIA, CHELIABINSKAIA PISATELSKIE ORGANIZATSII. **Added/Corp** Kurganskaia Pisatelskaia Organizatsiia. Orenburgskaia Pisatelskaia Organizatsiia. Cheliabinskaia Pisatelskaia Organizatsiia. (19??)-. Russian. an. **LC** PG3505.K872; K36.

II
KANKAVATI. Periodical. Gujarati (Gujarati). 10.00. Dahyabhai Jivanaji Nayaka, Nani Chipwad Ambaji Road 1, Surata India. **ED** D J Nayaka. **LC** PK1855; .K36.

US/0146-3217
KANSAS WRITER'S MARKET. (1977)-. English. Bernard Zicks Real Estate, PO Box 630, Solana Beach CA 92075. **LC** PN101; .K35. **DD** 808/.005.

US/0022-8990
KARAMU (CHARLESTON, ILL.). (KARAMU.). [Karamu]. **Added/Corp** Eastern Illinois University. (196?)-. Periodical. English. an. $7.50. Eastern Illinois University, Karamu Association, English Department, Charleston IL 61920. **Tel** (217)581-5614. **ED** Peggy Brayfield. **Circ:** 400.
Desc: Publishes contemporary and experimental fiction and poetry for a college educated audience.
Ind/Abst Annu. Bibliogr. Engl. Lang. Lit.

SY
KARMEL (BEIRUT, LEBANON). (AL-KARMEL.). **Added/Corp** Ittihad Al-Amm Lil-Kuttab Wa-al-Sufiyin Al-Filastiniyin. **VFOAT** Al-Karmel. No. 1, (Winter 1981)-. Periodical. Arabic. ir. Union of Arab Writers, Murshid Khatir St, BP 3230 Damascus Syria. **LC** PN9; .K37.

GW/0170-8805
KASSELER ARBEITEN ZUR SPRACHE UND LITERATUR. See Linguistics.

US/1054-3015
KASUN RE'O BEDTIME STORIES. (1991)-. Monographic series. English. $18.60. Kasun Re'O, 3916 East 15th Avenue, Gary-Aetna IN 46403.

GR
KATATHESE. (19??)-. Periodical. Greek, Modern. Boukoumanis Editions, 1 Mauromikhali Str., 106 79 Athens Greece. **Tel** 01 3618502, FAX 01 3630669. **ED** Elias Boukoumanis. **LC** PA5271; .K37.

II
KATHA PRIZE STORIES. No. 1 (1991)-. English. Rs65.00. Katha, C II/27, Tilak Lane, New Delhi 110001 India. **LC** PK5461; .K37. **DD** 891/.1.

II
KATHALAKSHMI. Periodical. Marathi (Marathi). **LC** PK2416.

II
KATHANA. Pravesanka (July-August 1980)-. Periodical. Hindi (Hindi). bm. Rs15.00. Kathan Sampadakiya Karyalaya, B-3/4 Ranapratap Bagh, Delhi 110007 India. **LC** PK2046; .K37.

US/0453-4387
KEATS-SHELLEY JOURNAL. [Keats-Shelley j.]. **Added/Corp** Keats-Shelley Association of America. **VFOAT** Keats, Shelley Journal. Vol. 1 (1952)-. Academic Scholarly Publication. English. an. $20.00 (individuals); $28.00 (institutions) Comes with Keats-Shelley Association Membership and Keats-Shelley Review. Keats-Shelley Association, New York Public Library, 5th Avenue at 42nd Street, Room 226, New York NY 10018. **Tel** (212)764-0655. **ED** Stuart Curran. **LC** PR4836; .A145. **DD** 821.705. **[CCC]**. **Bk Rev. Circ:** 1,100. Documents available from The Genuine Article.
Desc: Scholarly journal devoted to Keats, Shelley and the younger romantics.
Ind/Abst Abstr. Engl. Stud.; Annu. Bibliogr. Engl. Lang. Lit.; Arts Humanit. Citation Index (19??-19??) [Full Cov.]; Curr. Contents Arts Humanit.; Humanit. Index; MLA Int. Bibl. Books Artic. Mod. Lang. Lit.; Res. Alert [Full Cov.]; Romant. Move.

UK
KEATS-SHELLEY REVIEW. **VFOAT** Keats Shelley Review. No. 1; Autumn 1986-. Periodical. English. an. Free with purchase of The Keats-Shelley Journal; £5.00 other. Keats-Shelley Memorial Association, Department of English, University of Bristol, 315 Woodland Road, Bristol BS8 1TB England. **Tel** 0272/303407. **(Subscription address:** Keats-Shelley Memorial Association, Flat 1, 33 Aberdeen Road, London N5 2UG England) **ED** Timothy Webb. **LC** PR4836; .A15. **DD** 821/.7/09. **Bk Rev. Ad Acc. Pr Rev. Circ:** 1,500. Documents available from The Genuine Article.
Continues Keats-Shelley Memorial Bulletin, Rome, 0453-4395.
Desc: Studies of the life and works of the younger romantics (especially Keats, Shelley and Byron) and of their circles; reviews of books concerning these subjects and romanticism in general.
Ind/Abst Annu. Bibliogr. Engl. Lang. Lit.; Arts Humanit. Citation Index (19??-19??) [Full Cov.]; Curr. Contents Arts Humanit.; MLA Int. Bibl. Books Artic. Mod. Lang. Lit.; Res. Alert [Full Cov.]; Romant. Move.

US
KEEPSAKE SERIES. **Main/Corp** Book Club of California. (1933/34)-. English. an. Book Club of California, 312 Sutter Street, Room 510, San Francisco CA 94108. **Tel** (415)781-7532, FAX (415)781-7537.

GW
KEILSCHRIFTURKUNDEN AUS BOGHAZKOEI. **Added/Corp** Staatliche Museen zu Berlin (Germany). Vorderasiatische Abteilung. Deutsche Orient-Gesellschaft. Deutsche Akademie der Wissenschaften zu Berlin. Institut fuer Orientforschung. (1921)-. German. an. DM48.00. Akademie-Verlag GmbH, Muehlenstrasse 33 34, D 13162 Berlin Germany. **Tel** 011 49 30 47889300, FAX 011 49 30 47889357. **LC** PJ3721.B6; K4.

CN/0541-623X
KEITH CALLARD LECTURES. **Main/Corp** McGill University. Centre for Developing-Area Studies. 1- 1965-. Monographic series. English. ir. Price varies per volume. McGill University / Centre for Developing Area Studies, 3715 Peel Street Room 219, Montreal H3A 1X1 Canada. **Tel** (514)398-3508.

US/0192-1207
KELTICA. See History(General)-History of Europe.

US/0023-0197
KENTUCKY ENGLISH BULLETIN. [Ky. Engl. bull.]. Vol. 1 (1951)-. Bulletin. English. Three times a year. $10.00. Western Kentucky University / English Department, CH 106, Bowling Green KY 42101. **Tel** (502)745-6338. **DD** 420.

US
KENTUCKY PHILOLOGICAL REVIEW. **Added/Corp** Kentucky Philological Association. Meeting. Kentucky Philological Association. Northern Kentucky University. English. Murray State University, Print Services, Murray KY 42071. **LC** PN31; .K46a. **Continues** KPA Bulletin, 0277-3384.
Ind/Abst MLA Int. Bibl. Books Artic. Mod. Lang. Lit.

US/0954-2965
KEROUAC CONNECTION. [Kerouac Connect.]. (1984)-. Periodical. English. qt. Kerouac Connection, PO Box 462004, Escondido CA 92046-2004. **ED** Mitchell Smith. **DD** 813.54.
Desc: Literary and poetry journal dedicated to the works of Jack Kerouac and other Beat Generation writers.

SI
KESENIAN MASYARAKAT. **VFOAT** Social Culture. V. 1- Sept. 1971-. Periodical. English (Malayalam). Commercial Malay Literary Service, PO Box 150, Geylang Singapore. **LC** PN2960.S5; K47.

PK
KHAVATIN DAIJIST. V. 1- May 1972-. Periodical. Urdu. mo. Hamidah Bano, Urdu Bazar, Karachi Pakistan. **LC** PK2151; .K45.

RU
KHUDOZHESTVENNOE TVORCHESTVO / AKADEMIIA NAUK SSSR, NAUCHNYI SOVET PO ISTORII MIROVOI KULTURY, KOMISSIIA KOMPLEKSNOGO IZUCHENIIA KHUDOZHESTVENNOGO TVORCHESTVA. (1982)-. Russian. an. 1.90rub. Izdatelstvo Nauka St. Petersburg, Mendeleevskaia Liniia 1, 199034 St. Petersburg, B-34 Russia. **Tel** 218-26-12. **LC** PN53; .K48.

GW/0453-8501
KIELER STUDIEN ZUR DEUTSCHEN LITERATURGESCHICHTE. [Kiel. Stud. dtsch. Lit.gesch.]. Vol. 1 (1963)-. Monographic series. German. ir. Price varies per volume. Karl Wachholtz Verlag, Postfach 2769, Gansemarkt 1-3, W-2350 Neumunster F R Germany. **Tel** 011 49 4321 5670, FAX 011 49 4321 56778, telex 299 618 CURIR. **ED** Erich Trunz. **Circ:** 600 (ctrl).
Desc: History of literature from Schleswig-Holstein.
Ind/Abst MLA Int. Bibl. Books Artic. Mod. Lang. Lit.

IR
KILK. **VFOAT** Kelk. (1990)-. Periodical. Persian. mo. **LC** PK6401; .K54.

US/0896-1336
KINDERBOOK NEWSLETTER, THE. [Kinderbook newsl.]. **VFOAT** Kinderbook. Began March 1987. Newsletter. English. Ten times a year. $36.00. JCV Publications, Inc., Box 24624, Edina MN 55424. **DD** 808.
Desc: Publication for writers and illustrators of children's literature.

Literature

CN/1184-7603
KINDRED SPIRITS OF P.E.I. [Kindred spirits P.E.I.]. **VFOAT** Kindred Spirits of Prince Edward Island. 1st Issue (Spring 1990)-. Periodical. English. qt. 16.00Can$ Canada; $18.00 US; $25.00 other. Kindred Spirits of P.E.I., Silver Bush, Park Corner, Rural Route 2, Kensington, Prince Edward Island C0B 1M0 Canada. **DD** C813/.52.
Ind/Abst Genealogical Period. Annu. Index.

US/1056-781X
KINESIS (WHITEFISH, MONT.). (KINESIS.). No. 1 (1991)-. Periodical. English. bm. $10.00. Kinesis, PO Box 4007, Whitefish MT 59937. **DD** 810.

US
KINGFISHER (BERKELEY, CALIF.). (KINGFISHER.). Vol. 1, No. 1 (1987)-. Periodical. English. sa. $10.00 North America. Kingfisher, Box 9783, North Berkeley CA 94709. **Tel** (510)893-2425. **ED** Ruthie Singer, Barbara Schultz, Andrea Beach, and Lorraine Hilton-Gray. **LC** PS501; .K56. **DD** 810/.8. **Ad Acc. Circ:** 2,000.
Desc: Primary focus is on publishing new authors.

RU
KINOSTSENARII; ALMANAKH. Added/Corp Soviet Union. Gosudarstvennyi Komitet po Kinematografii. (1973)-. Russian. Six times a year. $79.95. **(Subscription address:** East View Publications Inc., 3020 Harbor Lane North, Suite 110, Minneapolis MN 55447.) **LC** PG3273; .K55.
Desc: Contains Russian fiction.

UK/0023-1738
KIPLING JOURNAL. (THE KIPLING JOURNAL; THE ORGAN OF THE KIPLING SOCIETY.). [Kipling j.]. **Added/Corp** Kipling Society. No. 1 (March 1927)-. Academic Scholarly Publication. English. Four times a year (Mar., June, Sept., Dec.). $35.00 (institutions), $22.00 (individuals). Kipling Society, Department of English, Rockford College, Rockford IL 61108. **Tel** (815)226-4183, FAX (815)226-4119. **ED** George Webb. **LC** PR4856; .A14. **DD** 823.89. **Bk Rev** (Qty: 12-16). **Ad Acc, Adv Mgr:** Dr. Karim. **Pr Rev. Circ:** 1,500.
Desc: Publishes scholarly articles on the writings and life of Rudyard Kipling and his comtemporaries.
Ind/Abst Abstr. Engl. Stud.; Am. Humanit. Index; Annu. Bibliogr. Engl. Lang. Lit.; MLA Int. Bibl. Books Artic. Mod. Lang. Lit.

FI/0355-0176
KIRJALLISUUDENTUTKIJAIN SEURAN VUOSIKIRJA. [Kirjallisuudentutk. seuran vuosik.]. **Added/Corp** Suomalaisen Kirjallisuuden Seura. **VFOAT** Annuaire des Historiens de la Literature; Yearbook of the Literary Research Society. (1929)-. Finnish. **LC** PN509; .K5.
Ind/Abst MLA Int. Bibl. Books Artic. Mod. Lang. Lit.

CE
KIRUTAYUKAM. 1 (Jan./Feb. 1981)-. Periodical. Tamil (Tamil). **LC** PL4758.45; .K57.

TZ/0856-048X
KISWAHILI. See Linguistics.

BA
KITABAT. VFOAT Ketabat. (19??)-. Periodical. Arabic. Four times a year. BD4.50 Bahrain; BD20.00 other. Dar Al-Ghad, PO Box 5050, Manama Bahrain. **Tel** 716021/243844, FAX 716021. **ED** Ali A. Khalifa. **LC** AP95.A6; .K53. Index available. **Bk Rev**. **Ad Acc. Pr Rev. Circ:** 6,000 (ctrl).
Desc: Poetry, short novels, cultural reports, studies and research about literature and arts.

US/0747-9034
KITABNAMAH-I RAHAVARD. VFOAT Ketabnamen Rahavard; Rahavard. Began in 1983?. Periodical. Persian. mo. $50.00. Rahavard Publications, 8306 Wilshire Boulevard/Suite 105, Beverly Hills CA 90211. **DD** 808.

US
KITABU CHA JUA. English. $6.00. PO Box 771, San Francisco CA 94101. **LC** AP2; .K62. **DD** 810/.8/0896. **Continues** Journal of Black Poetry.

KO
KIWON. VFOAT Age. Periodical. Korean. W300 single issue. Kiwon, 129-15 Chung-dong, Chungnim-ku, Seoul South Korea. **LC** PL950.2; .K59.

JA/0388-3647
KIYO - KYORITSU JOSHI TANKI DAIGAKU. BUNKA. [Kiyo - Kyoritsu Joshi Tanki Daigaku. Bunka]. **VFOAT** Journal of Kyoritsu Women's College. Department of Language and Literature. Collected Essays - Kyoritsu Women's Junior College. Literature Department (1973); Kyoritsu Joshi Daigaku Bunka Kiyo. (1973)-. Periodical. Multiple languages. an. **DD** 800. **Continues in part** Kiyo - Kyoritsu Joshi Daigaku. Tanki Daigakubu. Bunka, 0388-3582.
Ind/Abst MLA Int. Bibl. Books Artic. Mod. Lang. Lit.

SA/1010-3465
KLASGIDS. See Linguistics.

GW
KLEINE TEXTE FUR VORLESUNGEN UND UBUNGEN. See Linguistics.

YU/0350-6428
KNJIZEVNA ISTORIJA. [Knj. ist.]. (1968)-. Periodical. Serbo-Croatian (Cyrillic) (summaries and/or abstracts in English and Russian). **LC** PG560; .K54.
Ind/Abst MLA Int. Bibl. Books Artic. Mod. Lang. Lit.

YU/0350-4123
KNJIZEVNA KRITIKA. [Knjiz. krit.]. Knjizevni Klub "Vuk Karadzic." Knjizevni Klub "Obelisk" (Belgrade, Serbia). Vol. 1, No. 1 (1970)-. Periodical. Serbo-Croatian (Roman). bm. **LC** PG560; .K55.
Ind/Abst MLA Int. Bibl. Books Artic. Mod. Lang. Lit.

CI/0455-0463
KNJIZEVNA SMOTRA. Added/Corp Hrvatsko Filolosko Drustvo. (1969)-. Periodical. Serbo-Croatian (Roman). qt. **LC** PN9; .K55.
Ind/Abst Annu. Bibliogr. Engl. Lang. Lit.

JA
KODAI CHUSEI KOKUBUNGAKU. Periodical. Japanese. Hiroshima Heian Bungaku Kenkyukai, Hiroshima Daigaku Bungakubu Kokubungaku Kenkyushitsu Nai Higashi Senda-cho Naka-ku, Hiroshima-shi Japan. **LC** PL726.115; .K63.

JA
KODOMO NO TOMO. (1977)-. Periodical. Japanese. mo. $93.00 California; $99.00 other US. **(Subscription address:** Kinokuniya Company Ltd., 38-1 Sakuragaoka 5, chome Setagaya-ku, Tokyo 156 Japan.) **LC** PZ49.2; .K62.

MV/0130-2337
KODRY. (KODRY : LITERATURNO-KHUDOZHESTVENNYI I OBSHCHESTVENNO-POLITICHESKII ZHURNAL SOIUZA PISATELEI MOLDAVII). [Kodry]. **Added/Corp** Uniunia Skriitorilor Din RSS Moldoveniaske. (1968)-. Periodical. Russian. mo. $109.95. **(Subscription address:** East View Publications Inc., 3020 Harbor Lane North, Suite 110, Minneapolis MN 55447.) **Continues** Dnestr.

JA
KOJO. Vol. 1 No. 1 (1979)-. Periodical. Japanese. bm. ¥300. Kojo Sha, c/o Kusakabe Kojo Sha, 143-9 Kita Akitsu, Tokorozawa 359 Japan. **LC** PL755.8; .K64.

JA
KOKOTSUGAKU. Added/Corp Nippon Kokotsu Gakkai. **VFOAT** Journal for Oracle Bone Studies. (19??)-. Periodical. Japanese. ¥2500. Toyo Bunka Kenkyujo, Tokyo Daigaku, Hongo 7-chome, Tokyo 113 Japan. **LC** PL2447; .K64.

JA
KOKUBUNGAKU KENKYU SHIRYOKAN HO. See Linguistics.

JA
KOKUBUNGAKU KENKYU SHIRYOKAN KIYO. Main/Corp Kokubungaku Kenkyu Shiryokan. **VFOAT** Bulletin of the National Institute of Japanese Literature. No. 1-. Japanese (Japanese). Kokubungaku Kenkyu Shiryokan, 16-10 Yutakamachi 1-chome, Shinagawa-ku 142, Tokyo Japan. **Tel** (03)785-7131. **LC** PL700; .K597A. **Ad Acc. Circ:** 500.
Desc: Collected papers, written by the scholars of the National Institute of Japanese Literature, on the classic Japanese literature and philological problems.

JA
KOKUBUNGAKU NENJIBETSU RONBUNSHU. CHUKO / HENSHU, GAKUJUTSU BUNKEN. 1980-. Japanese. an. ¥23900 (Set). Hobun Shuppan, 10-29 Sengen-cho 2 Higashikurume-shi, Tokyo-to Japan. **LC** PL726.2; .K63.

JA
KOKUBUNGAKU NENJIBETSU RONBUNSHU. CHUSEI / GAKUJUTSU BUNKEN FUKYUKAI. 1980-. Japanese. an. ¥9500 per volume in 2 parts. Hobun Shuppan, 10-29 Sengen-cho 2 Higashikurume-shi, Tokyo-to Japan. **LC** PL726.3; .K63.

JA
KOKUBUNGAKU NENJIBETSU RONBUNSHU. JODAI / GAKUJUTSU BUNKEN FUKYUKAI. 1981-. Japanese. an. ¥9800 per volume. Hobun Shuppan, 10-29 Sengen-cho 2 Higashikurume-shi, Tokyo-to Japan. **LC** PL726.12; .K643.

JA
KOKUBUNGAKU NENJIBETSU RONBUNSHU. KINDAI / GAKUJUTSU BUNKEN KANKOKAI. 1 (1981)-. Japanese. an. ¥7600. Hobun Shuppan, 10-29 Sengen-cho 2 Higashikurume-shi, Tokyo-to Japan. **LC** PL726.55; .K63.

JA
KOKUBUNGAKU NENJIBETSU RONBUNSHU. KINSEI / GAKUJUTSU BUNKEN FUJYUKAI. 1980-. Japanese. an. ¥9800 per volume in 2 parts. Hobun Shuppan, 10-29 Sengen-cho 2 Higashikurume-shi, Tokyo-to Japan. **LC** PL726.35; .K597.

JA
KOKUBUNGAKU NENJIBETSU RONBUNSHU. KOKUBUNGAKU IPPAN / GAKUJUTSU BUNKEN FUKYUKAI. 1980-. Japanese. an. ¥8800 per volume. Hobun Shuppan, 10-29 Sengen-cho 2 Higashikurume-shi, Tokyo-to Japan. **LC** PL700; .L598.

JA/0387-3110
KOKUGO TO KOKUBUNGAKU. See Linguistics.

JA/0387-7280
KOKUSAI NIHON BUNGAKU KENKYU SHUKAI KAIGIROKU. Main/Conf International Conference on Japanese Literature in Japan. **VFOAT** Proceedings of the International Conference on Japanese Literature in Japan. No. 1- 1977-. Japanese (summaries and/or abstracts in English). Kokubungaku Kenkyu Shiryokan, 16-10 Yutakamachi 1-chome, Shinagawa-ku 142, Tokyo Japan. **Tel** (03)785-7131. **LC** PL703; .I57A. **Circ:** 800 (ctrl).
Desc: Proceedings of the International Conference on Japanese Literature in Japan.

SZ/0075-6520
KOLNER ROMANISTISCHE ARBEITEN. [Kolner Rom. Arb.]. **Added/Corp** Universitat zu Koln. Romanisches Seminar. (19??)-. Monographic series. German. ir. Price varies per volume. Librairie Droz SA, 11 rue Massot BP 389, CH 1211 Geneva 12 Switzerland. **Tel** 011 41 22 3466666, FAX 011 41 22 472391. **[CCC]**.
Desc: Literature of romance languages.
Ind/Abst MLA Int. Bibl. Books Artic. Mod. Lang. Lit.

MV/0236-1485
KOLUMNA. Added/Corp LKSM Moldavii. TSK. Uniunia Skriitorilor din RSS Moldoveniaske. (1990)-. Periodical. Russian. mo. $109.95. **(Subscription address:** East View Publications Inc., 3020 Harbor Lane North, Suite 110, Minneapolis MN 55447.) **LC** DK509.74; .G67. **Continues** Gorizont (Kishinev, Moldavian S.S.R.), 0233-7053.

●**RU**
KOMMENTARII. (1992)-. Russian.

PL
KONIEC WIEKU. Added/Corp Krakowski Klub Artystyczno-Literacki. (1990)-. Periodical. Polish. qt. **Continues** Pismo Literacko-Artystyczne, 0239-5924.

RU/0259-4412
KONTEKST. [Kontekst]. **Added/Corp** Institut Mirovoi Literatury Imeni A.M. Gorkogo. (1972)-. Russian. an. 1.67rub. Izdatelstvo Nauka / Akademiia Nauk, Publishing House of the Russian Academy of Sciences, Leninskii Porspekt 14, 117901 Moscow Russia. **Tel** 011 95 954-21-53, FAX 011 95 938-21-44, telex 411964. **LC** PN9; .K65.
Ind/Abst MLA Int. Bibl. Books Artic. Mod. Lang. Lit.

GW/0344-6735
KONZEPTE DER SPRACH- UND LITERATURWISSENSCHAFT. See Linguistics.

XV
KORESPONDENCE POMEMBNIH SLOVENCEV / EPISTULAE SLOVENORUM ILLUSTRIUM / ACADEMIA SCIENTIARUM ET ARTIUM SLOVENICA, CLASSIS II: PHILOLOGIA ET LITTERAE. Added/Corp Slovenska Akademija Znanosti in Umetnosti. Razred za Filoloske in Literarne Vede. (19??)-. Monographic series. Slovenian.
Ind/Abst MLA Int. Bibl. Books Artic. Mod. Lang. Lit.

HU/0023-415X
KORTARS. [Kortars]. (1957)-. Periodical. Hungarian. Twelve times a year. $28.00. Pallas Lap es Konyvkiado Vallalat, Lenin korut 9-11, H-1906 Budapest, Hungary. **Tel** 36 1 2210285. **(Subscription address:** Kultura, PO Box 149, H-1389, Budapest 62 Hungary, (phone: 011 36 1 359370)) **ED** Szaraz Gyorgy and Thiery A'rpad. **LC** PH3144; .K56. Index available. cum. index. **Bk Rev**. **Ad Acc. Circ:** 10,000.
Desc: Covers literature, short stories, essays, poetry, drama and criticism.
Ind/Abst MLA Int. Bibl. Books Artic. Mod. Lang. Lit.

FR
KOVCHEG. No. 1 (1978)-. Periodical. Russian. mo. $109.96. Ludmila Bokov, 322 West 108th Street, New York NY 10025. **Tel** (212)865-1164.

Literature

RU
KRATKAIA LITERATURNAIA ENTSIKLOPEDIA. Russian. ir. **(Subscription address:** East View Publications Inc., 3020 Harbor Lane North, Suite 110, Minneapolis MN 55447.**)**

GW
KRAUS HEFTE. Ceased. Vol. 1 (Jan. 1977)-(1994). Periodical. German. qt. Text Kritik GmbH, Levelingstrasse 6A, 8000 Munchen 80 Germany. **Tel** 089/432929. **ED** S. Scheichl and C. Wagenknecht. **LC** PT2621.R27; K72.

GW/0935-9060
KRIEG UND LITERATUR. See History(General)-History of Europe.

DK/0454-5354
KRITIK (KBENHAVN). (KRITIK.). [Kritik]. Vol. 1 No. 1 (1967)-. Periodical. Danish. Four times a year. kr460.80. Munksgaard International Publishers Ltd, PO Box 2148, DK-1016 Copenhagen K Denmark. **Tel** 011 45 33 12 70 30, FAX 011 45 33 12 93 87, telex 19431 MUNKS DK. **LC** PN9; .K75.
Ind/Abst BHA : Biblio. Hist. Art; MLA Int. Bibl. Books Artic. Mod. Lang. Lit.

GR
KRITIKA PHYLLA. (1971)-. Periodical. Greek, Modern. bm. **LC** PA5201; .K7.
Ind/Abst MLA Int. Bibl. Books Artic. Mod. Lang. Lit.

LV
KRITIKAS GADAGRAMATA. (1972)-. Latvian. an. 1.30rub. Liesma / Flame Publishing House, Aspazijas Bulv 24, Riga Latvia 1455. **Tel** 3712 223 063. **LC** PG9000; .K74.
Ind/Abst MLA Int. Bibl. Books Artic. Mod. Lang. Lit.

NO
KRITIKK JOURNALEN. VFOAT Kritikkjournalen; Kritikk. (19??)-. Norwegian. Twice a year. Kr385.00, $81.00. Scandinavian University Press, PO Box 2959 Toeyen, N 0608 Oslo 6 Norway. **Tel** 011 47 2 2575400, FAX 011 47 2 2575335, telex 71896 UROR N. **(Subscription address:** Scandinavian University Press, 200 Meacham Ave., Elmont NY 11003.**) LC** PT8301; .K7.

BE
KRITISCH AKKOORD. (19??)-. Periodical. Dutch. an. Uitgeverij Manteau, Beeldhousersstraat 12, B-2000 Antwerpen Belgium. **LC** PT5001; .K73.
Desc: Covers Dutch and Flemish literature.

CC
KU FENG. VFOAT Gu Feng. Periodical. Chinese. Nan-Ching Ta Huseh, Nan-Ching, People's Republic of China. **LC** PAR.

CC
KU SHIH HUI. VFOAT Gushihui. (July 1963)-. Periodical. Chinese. bm. RMBY0.18. Science Press, 16 Donghuangchenggen North Street, Beijing 100707, People's Republic of China. **Tel** 011 86 1 4019821, 011 86 1 4010642, FAX 011 86 1 4012180, 011 86 1 4019810, telex 210147. **LC** PL2653; .K764. **DD** 895.1/301/08.

CC
KU TAI WEN HSUEH LI LUN YEN CHIU / CHUNG-KUO KU TAI WEN HSUEH LI LUN HSUEH HUI PIEN. V. 1-. Chinese. Shang-Hai Ku Chi Chu Pan She, Shang-Hai China. **LC** PL2254; .K8. **DD** 801/.95/0951.

CH
KU TIEN WEN HSUEH / CHUNG-KUO KU TIEN WEN HSUEH YEN CHIU HUI CHU PIEN. Added/Corp Chung-kuo Ku Tien Wen Hsueh Yen Chiu Hui. Vol. 1 (1979)-. Chinese. an. Taiwan Hsueh Sheng Shu Chu, 298 Lo SSU Fu Lu Third Section, Taipei Taiwan. **LC** PL2250; .K822. **DD** 895.1/09.

CC
KU TIEN WEN HSUEH LUN TSUNG. 1 (May 1980)-. Periodical. Chinese. Shen-Hsi Sheng Hsin Hua Shu Tien, Hsi-An, People's Republic of China. **LC** PL2254; .K83.

CC
KU TIEN WEN HSUEH LUN TSUNG (CHI LU SHU SHE). (KU TIEN WEN HSUEH LUN TSUNG / SHE HUI KO HSUEH CHAN HSIEN PIEN CHI PU PIEN.). Periodical. Chinese. RMBY1.90. Chi Lu Shu She, Shan Tung, People's Republic of China. **LC** PL2254; .K84. **DD** 895.1/09.

CC
KUANG-HSI WEN HSUEH. Vol. 7 (July 1980)-. Periodical. Chinese. mo. Post Office / China, People's Republic of China. **LC** PL3031.K883; K82. **DD** 895.1/08/005. **Continues** Kuang-Hsi Wen I.
Ind/Abst NAPRALERT.

NR/0331-4545
KUKA. See Literature-Poetry.

FR/0023-5148
KULTURA (PARIS). (KULTURA.). [Kultura]. **Added/Corp** Instytut Literacki (Paris, France). (1947)-. Periodical. Polish. ir (10 issues). 124.00F US, Canada, Mideast Europe, Morocco, Algeria and Tunisia; 125.00F Africa and Western Hemisphere; 133.60F other. Institut Litteraire, 91 Avenue de Poissy, Mesnil le Roi, 78600 Maisons Laffitte France. **Tel** 011 33 1 39621904, FAX 011 33 1 39625752. **LC** AP54; .K85. Index available (bound in Dec. issue). **Bk Rev. Ad Acc.** ctrl circ.
Ind/Abst MLA Int. Bibl. Books Artic. Mod. Lang. Lit.

XR
KULTURA (PRAGUE, CZECHOSLOVAKIA). See Newspapers.

DK/0106-5734
KUNAPIPI. (Kunapipi). (1979)-. Periodical. English. Three times a year. $68.50 institutions; $43.50 individuals. University of Aarhus / Department of English, Building 326, 8000 Aarhus C Denmark. **Tel** 011 45 89422124, 89422116, FAX 011 45 86191699. **ED** Anna Rutherford (editor's phone: 011 45 86241909). **Bk Rev**, (Qty: occasionally). **Ad Acc. Circ:** 1,000. **Continues** Commonwealth Newsletter.
Desc: Arts magazine with special emphasis on the new literatures written in English. Aims to introduce the work of new or little known writers of talent, to provide critical evaluation of the work of living authors both famous and unknown, and to be truly international.
Ind/Abst Annu. Bibliogr. Engl. Lang. Lit.; MLA Int. Bibl. Books Artic. Mod. Lang. Lit.

JA
KUNGMIN MUNHAK. 1942-. Periodical. Japanese (Korean). Kukhak Charyowon, 15-1 Inhyon-Dong, Chung, Ku, Seoul Korea. **LC** PL969.8; .K6.

HK
KUO CHI NAN SHE HSUEH HUI TSUNG KAN / KUO CHI NAN SHE HSUEH HUI PI SHU CHU PIEN. Added/Corp Kuo Chi Nan She Hsueh Hui. Nan She. (1990)-. English. **LC** PL2250; .K8.

CH
KUO WEN HSUEH PAO. Added/Corp Kuo li Tai-wan Shih fan ta Hsueh. Kuo wen hsi. **VFOAT** Bulletin of Chinese of National Taiwan Normal University. (June 1972)-. Chinese. an.
Ind/Abst Am. Hist. Life (1966-1986).

GW
KURSCHNERS DEUTSCHER LITERATUR-KALENDER. VAT Durschners Deutscher Literatur Kalender. Vol. 48 (1937/38)-. German. ir. Walter de Gruyter Inc. / Hawthorne, 200 Saw Mill River Road, Hawthorne NY 10532. **Tel** (914)747-0110, GERMANY: 011/49/30/260050, FAX (914)747-1326, telex 646677. **LC** Z2230; .K92. **DD** 830/.9; B. **Continues** Kurschners Deutscher Literatur-Kalender auf das Jahr ... .

US/1049-328X
KUUMBA (LOS ANGELES, CALIF.). (KUUMBA.). [Kuumba]. No. 1 (Spring 1991)-. Periodical. English. qt. $4.50. BLK Publishing Company, PO Box 83912, Los Angeles CA 90083-0912. **Tel** (310)410-0808, FAX (310)410-9250. **DD** 810.
Desc: Kuumba is a journal of poetry dedicated to the celebration of the lives and experiences of black lesbians and gay men.

PL/0239-6629
KWARTA. (1983)-. Periodical. Polish. qt. $19.00. **(Subscription address:** ARS Polona, PO Box 1001, 00068 Warsaw Poland.**) UDC** 884.

JA
KYESONG MUNHAK. V. 1- (1981)-. Periodical. Korean. 2.000. Kyesong Munhakhoe, 277 Taesin-dong Chung-ku, Taegu Korea. **LC** PL969.8; .K94.

●UN/0869-3595
KYIVSKA STAROVYNA. (1992)-. Periodical. Ukrainian. bm.

JA/0454-8132
KYUSHU AMERICAN LITERATURE. Added/Corp Kyushu Amerika Bungaku. No. 1 (June 1958)-. English. an.
Ind/Abst MLA Int. Bibl. Books Artic. Mod. Lang. Lit.

FR
L.-F. CELINE. 1- 1974-. French. Lettres Modernes Minard, 45 rue de Saint Andre, 14123 Fleury Surrey Orne France. **Tel** 011 33 31 844706. **LC** PN3; .R4 subser. **DD** 809.

RU
LABIRINT/EKSTSENTR. VFOAT Labirint Ekstsentr. No. 1 (1991)-. Russian.

US/0896-8705
LACTUCA (SUFFERN, N.Y.). (LACTUCA.). No. 1 (Jan. 1986)-. Periodical. English. ir. $10.00 US; $13.00 Canada; $14.00 others. Lactuca Publications, PO Box 621, Suffern NY 10901. **Tel** (914)356-9236. **DD** 810.
Ind/Abst Am. Humanit. Index; Index Am. Period. Verse.

US/0193-7588
LAGNIAPPE. Vol. 1 (Spring 1974)-. Periodical. English. qt. $1.00 single issue. Lagniappe Magazine, PO Box 1073, Oxford MS 38655. **LC** PS551; .L25. **DD** 810/.8.
Ind/Abst Account. Art.; Fed. Tax Artic.

US/0147-7196
(LAGUNA), A. (A.). (197?)-. Periodical. English. sa. $2.50 (general), $2.00 (students), $5.00 (libraries and institutions). A Press Ltd, Box 311, Laguna NM 87026. **Tel** (505)988-1183.

US/0887-4492
LAKE EFFECT. [Lake eff.]. **Added/Corp** Lake County Writers Group (Oswego, N.Y.). Vol. 1, No. 1 (Spring 1986)-. Periodical. English. qt. $5.00. Lake County Writers Group, Lake Effect, PO Box 315, Oswego NY 13126. **DD** 700.
Ind/Abst Am. Humanit. Index (199?-).

US/0889-6410
LAKE STREET REVIEW, THE. Ceased. [Lake Str. rev.]. **VFOAT** LSR; L.S.R. Vol. 1 (Spring 1976)-Ceased Vol. 25 (1991). Periodical. English. sa. Lake Street Review, PO Box 7188 Powerhorn Station, Minneapolis MN 55407. **DD** 810.
Ind/Abst Am. Humanit. Index; Index Am. Period. Verse.

NZ/0023-7930
LANDFALL. [Landfall]. Vol. 1 (Mar. 1947)-. Periodical. English. Twice a year (May, Nov.). $25.00 US. Oxford University Press / New Zealand, PO Box 11-149 Ellerslie, Auckland 5 New Zealand. **Tel** 011 64 9 5233134. **(Subscription address:** North America / William W. Gaunt & Sons, Inc., 3011 Gulf Drive, Gaunt Building, Holmes Beach, FL 34217; telephone: (813)778-5211**) ED** Mark Williams, Hugh Lauder, Iain Sharp, Anna Smith, Michele Leggatt and Judith Baker. **LC** AP7; .L35. **DD** 052. Index available. cum. index. **Bk Rev. Ad Acc. Circ:** 1,800. Documents available from The Genuine Article.
Desc: Contains short stories, poetry, reviews, interviews, commentary, criticism, art, etc.
Ind/Abst Abstr. Engl. Stud. (?-?); Am. Hist. Life (1956-1975); Annu. Bibliogr. Engl. Lang. Lit. (?-?); Arts Humanit. Citation Index (19??-19??) [Full Cov.]; Br. Humanit. Index (?-?); Curr. Contents Arts Humanit.; MLA Int. Bibl. Books Artic. Mod. Lang. Lit. (?-?); Res. Alert [Full Cov.].

●UK/0963-9470
LANGUAGE AND LITERATURE. See Linguistics.

US/1057-6037
LANGUAGE AND LITERATURE (SAN ANTONIO, TEX.). See Linguistics.

CN/0384-5710
LANGUE ET LITTERATURE FRANCAISES AU CANADA (1970). See Linguistics.

US/0363-8472
LARGE-PRINT SCORES AND BOOKS CATALOG. See Music.

US/1057-0055
LAST WORD (FRIENDSWOOD, TEX.), THE. See Journalism.

US/0888-5613
LATIN AMERICAN INDIAN LITERATURES JOURNAL. [Lat. Am. Indian lit. j.]. **Added/Corp** Geneva College (Beaver Falls, Pa.). Dept. of Foreign Languages. Vol. 1, No. 1 (Spring 1985)-. Periodical. English (Spanish). Twice a year (June, Dec.). $38.00 (one year); $74.00 (two years); $110.00 (three years). Penn State University / Pennsylvania, University Drive, McKeesport Camp, McKeesport PA 15132. **Tel** (412)675-9466, FAX (412)675-0943. **ED** Dr. Mary Preuss. **DD** 897. Index available. cum. index. **Bk Rev**, (Qty: 10-15). **Ad Acc. Pr Rev. Circ:** 400 (ctrl). Documents available from The Genuine Article. **Continues** Latin American Indian Literature, 0160-8045.
Desc: Studies and articles on Latin American Indian literatures, art and archaeology. Texts in Indian languages with commentaries translations. Central American Pictorial study, rock art report and bibliography of recent books related to Latin American Indian literatures, these by indigenous authors.
Ind/Abst Anthropol. Lit.; Arts Humanit. Citation Index [Full Cov.]; Curr. Contents Arts Humanit.; Ethnoarts Index; HAPI Hisp. Am. Period. Index; Index Book Rev. Relig.; MLA Int. Bibl. Books Artic. Mod. Lang. Lit.; Relig. Index One Period.; Relig. Theol. Abstr.; Res. Alert [Full Cov.]; Soc. Sci. Cit. Index [Select. Cov.].

RU
LATINSKAIA AMERIKA (KHUDOZHESTVENNAIA LITERATURA (FIRM)). (LATINSKAIA AMERIKA.). No.1 (1983)-. Russian. mo. $79.95. **(Subscription address:** East View Publications Inc., 3020 Harbor Lane North, Suite 110, Minneapolis MN 55447.**)**

BE/0023-8856
LATOMUS. Vol. 1 (Jan./March 1937)-. Periodical. French (English, German, Italian, Latin and Spanish). qt (4 issues). 3000F. J Dumortier Bibauw, Avenue Van Cutsem 18, 7500 Tournai Belgium. **Tel** 011 32 69214713, . **LC** PA2002; .L3. **DD** 870.5. Index available (bound in 4th issue). cum. index. **Bk Rev.** Documents available from The Genuine Article.
Desc: Covers Latin language and literature.
Ind/Abst Arts Humanit. Citation Index [Full Cov.]; BHA : Biblio. Hist. Art; Br. Archaeol. Bibliogr.; Curr. Contents Arts Humanit.; MLA Int. Bibl. Books Artic. Mod. Lang. Lit.; Numis. Lit.; Res. Alert [Full Cov.]; Soc. Sci. Cit. Index [Select. Cov.].

RU
LAUREATY LENINSKOGO KOMSOMOLA. (1967)-. Russian. 1.63rub. Izdatelstvo Molodaia Gvardiia, Novodmitrovskaya Ul., 5A, 125015 Moscow Russia. **Tel** 095-285-0830. **LC** PG3199; .L38.

US/0023-9003
LAUREL REVIEW / WEST VIRGINIA WESLEYAN COLLEGE, THE. [Laurel rev.]. **Added/Corp** West Virginia Wesleyan College. Northwest Missouri State University. Dept. of English. Vol. 1 (1961)-. Periodical. English. sa (Jan. and June). $8.00 (one year), $14.00 (two year), $22.00 (three year). Greentower Press, Department of English, Northwest Missouri State University, Maryville MO 64468. **Tel** (816)562-1265, FAX (816)562-1900. **ED** Beth Richards, William Trowbridge, David Slater. **LC** PS221; .L38; WMLC 93/4087. **[CCC].** Index available (bound in Feb. issue, $5). **Ad Acc, Adv Mgr:** Loren Gruber, **Tel** (816)562-1265. **Pr Rev. Circ:** 900. available on microfilm from University Microfilms International (UMI).
Desc: Seeks well-crafted poems and fiction with fresh imagery, precise use of language, and an awareness that poetry should be accessible to a range of serious readers.
Ind/Abst Am. Humanit. Index; Annu. Bibliogr. Engl. Lang. Lit.; Index Am. Period. Verse.

IT
LAVORO CRITICO. (Jan./Mar. 1975)-. Periodical. Italian. Three times a year. L40000 Italy; L60000 others. Lacaita Pietro Editore, via Cadorna 20, 74024 Manduria ta Italy. **Tel** 011 34 99 8711124. **LC** PQ4001; .L37.
Ind/Abst Romant. Move.

IE
LEACHTAI CHOLM CILLE. (19??)-. Monographic series. English (Irish).
Ind/Abst MLA Int. Bibl. Books Artic. Mod. Lang. Lit.

US/1049-5983
LEADING EDGE (PROVO, UTAH), THE. (THE LEADING EDGE.). [Lead. edge]. **Added/Corp** Brigham Young University. **VFOAT** Leading Edge Magazine; TLE. (April 1981)-. Periodical. English. Three times a year. $8.00 (one year), $15.00 (two years), $21.00 (three years) US; $9.00 (one year), $17.00 (two years), $24.00 (three years) Canada; $11.00 (one year), $21.00 (two years), $30.00 (three years) other. Leading Edge, 3163 JKHB, Provo UT 84602. **Tel** (801)378-4455. **ED** Michael Carr. **DD** 813. **Bk Rev**, (Qty: 15). **Ad Acc, Adv Mgr:** Lee Ann Setzer. **Circ:** 1,000.

US/0075-8396
LEBARON RUSSELL BRIGGS PRIZE HONORS ESSAYS IN ENGLISH. [LeBaron Russell Briggs prize honors essays Engl.]. Monographic series. English. ir. Price varies per volume. Harvard University Press, 79 Garden Street, Cambridge MA 02138. **Tel** (617)496-1344, (800)448-2242. **DD** 808.

US/0897-5280
LECTURA DANTIS (CHARLOTTESVILLE, VA.). (LECTURA DANTIS.). [Lectura Dantis]. **Added/Corp** University of Virginia. Italian Program. Vol. 1, No. 1 (Fall 1987)-. English (Italian). Twice a year. $10.00. Lectura Dantis, University of Virginia, 452 Cabell Hall, Charlottesville VA 22903. **Tel** (804)924-7159. **DD** 851.
Ind/Abst MLA Int. Bibl. Books Artic. Mod. Lang. Lit.

IT
LECTURES. (May 1979)-. Monographic series. Italian. sa. Price varies per volume. Edizioni Dal Sud, Via Gen Bellomo Fl, 70124 Bari Italy.

US/0578-2775
LECTURES IN MEMORY OF LOUISE TAFT SEMPLE. **Added/Corp** University of Cincinnati. (19??)-. Monographic series. English. ir. Price varies per volume. Princeton University Press, 41 William Street, Princeton NJ 08540. **Tel** (609)258-4900.

UK/0075-8574
LEEDS TEXTS AND MONOGRAPHS. See Linguistics.

SP
LEER. **VFOAT** Leer en ... . No. 1 (Jun. 1985)-. Periodical. Spanish. Eleven times a year (monthly with Aug./Sep. issues combined). L3770 Italy; L7100 Europe; L8600 other. Revista Leer, D Ramon de la Cruz 88 ESC 2-1B, 28006 Madrid Spain. **Tel** 011 34 1 4017117, FAX 011 34 1 4017530.

US/1056-7429
LEFT BANK. [Left bank]. No. 1 (Winter 1991)-. Periodical. English. Twice a year (June & Dec.). $16.00. Blue Heron Publishing, 24450 Northwest Hansen Road, Hillsboro OR 97124. **Tel** (503)621-3911, FAX (503)621-9826. **ED** Linny Stovall. **LC** PS570; .L44. **DD** 810. **Ad Acc. Circ:** 3,000.
Desc: Each issue is based on a theme. A large part non-fiction, but poetry, photos, black & white cartoons, and short fiction are included.

US/0748-4321
LEGACY (AMHERST, MASS.). (LEGACY.). [Legacy]. **Added/Corp** University of Massachusetts at Amherst. Dept. of English. Vol. 1, No. 1 (Spring 1984)-. Periodical. English. sa. $20.00 (individuals), $30.00 (institutions) US; $23.00 (individuals), $35.00 (institutions) other. Pennsylvania State University Press, 820 North University Drive, Suite C, University Park PA 16802-1003. **Tel** (814)865-1327, (800)326-9180, FAX (814)863-1408. **ED** Martha Ackmann, Karen Dandurand and Joanne Dobson. **LC** PS149; .L43. **DD** 810/.9/9287. **[CCC]. Bk Rev. Ad Acc. Circ:** 500 (ctrl). Documents available from The Genuine Article.
Desc: A journal of 18th, 19th and early 20th century American women writers, with literary, historical, cultural, biographical and bibliographical articles.
Ind/Abst Abstr. Engl. Stud.; Arts Humanit. Citation Index [Full Cov.]; Book Rev. Index; Lit. Crit. Regist.; MLA Int. Bibl. Books Artic. Mod. Lang. Lit.; Res. Alert [Full Cov.]; Soc. Sci. Cit. Index [Select. Cov.]; Stud. Women Abstr.; Women Stud. Abstr.

US/1058-1847
LEGEND (WASHINGTON, D.C.). (LEGEND : THE AFRICAN HERITAGE LITERATURE REVIEW.). [Legend]. **Added/Corp** African Heritage Literature Society. (1991)-. Periodical. English. bm. The African Heritage Literature Society, 1730 K Street NW, Suite 304, Washington DC 20006. **DD** 810.

IT
LEGGERE. Vol. 1 (May 1988)-. Periodical. Italian. mo (except Jan. & Aug.). L75000.00 Italy; L95000.00 Europe; L150000.00 other. Rosellina Archinto SAS, Via Magolfa 14, 20143 Milan Italy. **Tel** 011 39 2 89400404, FAX 011 39 2 89400376. **LC** IN PROCESS. **Bk Rev. Ad Acc.** ctrl circ.
Desc: Publication covering modern literature.

IT
LEGGERE DONNA. See Women's Interests.

NE/0458-9971
LEIDSE GERMANISTISCHE EN ANGLISTISCHE REEKS. **Added/Corp** Rijksuniversiteit te Leiden. (1962)-. Monographic series. Multiple languages (English, Dutch and German). ir. Price varies per volume. E. J. Brill, Postbus 9000, 2300 PA Leiden Netherlands. **Tel** 011 31 71 312624, FAX 011 31 71 317532, telex 39296 BRILL NL. **Bk Rev. Ad Acc.**
Desc: This series comprises publications by members of Leiden University in the field of English language and literature and Germanic languages and literatures in the widest sense.

NE/0075-8647
LEIDSE ROMANTISCHE REEKS. Monographic series. Dutch. ir. Price varies per volume. E. J. Brill, Postbus 9000, 2300 PA Leiden Netherlands. **Tel** 011 31 71 312624, FAX 011 31 71 317532, telex 39296 BRILL NL. **Bk Rev. Ad Acc.**
Desc: This series comprises publications by members of the Leiden University in the field of Romanistic languages and literatures.

AU/0024-0788
LENAU-FORUM. **Added/Corp** Internationale Lenau-Gesellschaft. Vol. 1 (1969)-. Monographic series. German. ir. Price varies per volume. Internationale Lenau-Gesellschaft, Postfach 144, A-1103 Vienna Austria. **ED** Dr. Nikolaus Britz. **LC** PT2393.Z4; L46. **Circ:** 1,500.
Ind/Abst MLA Int. Bibl. Books Artic. Mod. Lang. Lit.; Romant. Move.

GW
LENDEMAINS. (1975)-. Periodical. German (French). qt. DM53.40. VVA Bertelsmann Dist GmbH, Postfach 7600, D 33310 Gutersloh Germany. **Tel** 011 49 5241 803294.
Ind/Abst MLA Int. Bibl. Books Artic. Mod. Lang. Lit.

RU
LEPTA. **Added/Corp** Soiuz Pisatelei SSSR. (1991)-. Periodical. Russian. mo. $34.00. Lepta International, 1 7 Kutuzovsky Prospekt, Moscow 121248 Russia. **Tel** 011 7 95 2430366. **LC** PG3227.5; .S684. ***Continues*** *Sovetskaia Literatura (Moscow, R.S.F.S.R.), 0236-0934.*

RU
LETOPIS PERIODICHESKIKH I PRODOLZHAIUSHCHIKHSIA IZDANII / GOSUDARSTVENNYI KOMITET SOVETA MINISTROV SSSR PO DELAM IZDATELSTV, POLIGRAFII I KNIZHNOI TORGOVLI [I] VSESOIUZNAIA KNIZHNAIA PALATA. **Added/Corp** Gosudarstvennyi Komitet Soveta Ministrov SSSR po Delam Izdatelstv, Poligrafii i Knizhnoi Torgovli. Vsesoiuznaia Knizhnaia Palata. Gosudarstvennyi Komitet SSSR po Delam Izdatelstv, Poligrafii i Knizhnoi Torgovli. (1975)-. Russian. mo. $39.95. Izdatelstvo Kniga, 50 Gorky Ulitsa, 125047 Moscow Russia. **(Subscription address:** East View Publications Inc., 3020 Harbor Lane North, Suite 110, Minneapolis MN 55447.**) LC** Z6956.S65; L47; PN5355.S65. **DD** 016.057/1. ***Continues in part*** *Letopis Periodicheskikh Izdanii SSSR.*

BU
LETOPISI : IZDANIE NA SUIUZA NA BULGARSKITE PISATELI. **Added/Corp** Suiuz na Bulgarskite Pisateli. (1991)-. Periodical. Bulgarian. mo. DM151.00. **(Subscription address:** Kubon & Sagner, ABT Zeitschriftenimport, D 80328 Munich Germany.**) LC** PG1020.7; .L47. ***Continues*** *Septemvri, 0204-7349.*

BL
LETRA (RIO DE JANEIRO, BRAZIL). (LETRA.). **Added/Corp** Universidade Federal do Rio de Janeiro. Faculdade de Letras. No. 1 (Jan/July 1980)-. Periodical. Portuguese. Universidade Federal do Rio de Janeiro / Letras, Faculdade de Letras, Av Chile No 330, Rio de Janeiro Brazil. **LC** P9; .L42a. **DD** 410/.5.

AG/0326-2928
LETRAS DE BUENOS AIRES. Vol. 1, No. 1, (Oct./Dec. 1980)-. Periodical. Spanish. Three times a year. $48.00. Editorial Lumen, PO 1055 Via Monte 1674, Buenos Aires Argentina. **ED** Victoria Pueyrredou. **LC** PQ7600; .L47. **DD** 860/.8. cum. index. **Bk Rev. Ad Acc. Circ:** 2,000.
Desc: Critical and non-critical essays, short stories, and poetry.

BL/0101-3335
LETRAS DE HOJE. See Linguistics.

US/0277-4356
LETRAS FEMENINAS. [Let. fem.]. **Added/Corp** Asociacion de Literatura Femenina Hispanica. Vol. 1, No. 1 (Spring 1975)-. Academic Scholarly Publication. English (Spanish). Twice a year. $25.00 institution, $20.00 individual. University of Nebraska / Department of Modern Language, 1030 Oldfather Hall, Lincoln NE 68588. **Tel** (402)472-3710, FAX (402)472-1123. **ED** Adelaida Lopez de Martinez. **LC** PQ6055; .L48. **DD** 860/.8/09287. **Bk Rev**, (Qty: (12-16)). **Ad Acc. Pr Rev. Circ:** 400 (ctrl).
Desc: Includes scholarly articles, interviews, book reviews, and other items of interest concerning Hispanic women writers around the world, as well as original creative works by Hispanic women writers. Published by the Association Deliteratura Femenina Hispanica since 1975. All articles are refereed. Articles published in English or Spanish.
Ind/Abst HAPI Hisp. Am. Period. Index; Index Am. Period. Verse; MLA Int. Bibl. Books Artic. Mod. Lang. Lit.

US/0897-7542
LETRAS PENINSULARES. [Let. Penins.]. Vol. 1, No. 1 (Spring 1988)-. Periodical. English (Spanish). Three times a year. $36.00 (1 year), $68.00 (2 year), $102.00 (3 year) institutions, $45.00 (1 year), $85.00 (2 year), $135.00 (3 year) individuals, US; $40.00 (1 year), $76.00 (2 year), $114.00 (3 year) institutions, $49.00 (1 year), $93.00 (2 year) individuals, other. Letras Peninsulares, Department of Romance & Classic Languages, MSU, East Lansing MI 48824-1112. **Tel** (517)355-8350, (517)355-8364. **ED** Mary S. Vasquez. **LC** PQ7000; .L47. **DD** 860. **Bk Rev**, (Qty: 25-40). **Ad Acc. Pr Rev. Circ:** 300.
Desc: Literary criticism, interviews, and bibliographies on the literature of Spain from the 18th century to the present.
Ind/Abst MLA Int. Bibl. Books Artic. Mod. Lang. Lit.

US/0882-3804
LETTER EXCHANGE, THE. (198?)-. Periodical. English. Three times a year (Jan., June, Oct.). $20.00 (1 year); $36.00 (2 years). Letter Exchange, PO Box 6218, Albany CA 94706. **Tel** (510)526-7412. **ED** Stephen Sikora. Index available. cum. index. **Bk Rev. Ad Acc. Circ:** 3,000. ***Continues*** *Reader's League Catalogue of Correspondence.*
Desc: A magazine for letter-writers containing listings for correspondence on literature, movies, culture, daily life, etc. Devoted to the revival of personal correspondence.

IT
LETTERA INTERNAZIONALE. (198?)-. Periodical. Italian. qt. L50000. Lettera Internazionale, Via Dogana Vecchia 3, 00186 Rome Italy. **Tel** 011 39 6 68300644. **LC** PN5; .L55.

IT/0024-130X
LETTERATO. (IL LETTERATO.). [Letterato]. (1952)-. Periodical. Italian. Luigi Pellegrini Editore, Casella Postale 158, Cosenza Rome 74 Italy.
Ind/Abst MLA Int. Bibl. Books Artic. Mod. Lang. Lit.

IT
LETTERATURA ITALIANA. STUDI E TESTI, LA. **VFOAT** Studi e Testi. Vol. 1-. Monographic series. Italian. ir. Price varies per volume. Riccardo Ricciardi Editore, Via Manzoni 10, 20121 Milan Italy. **Tel** 011 39 2 804248, 011 39 2 875155.

IT
LETTERATURE D'AMERICA. V. 1, No. 1 (Winter 1980)-. Periodical. Italian (summaries and/or abstracts in English, Portuguese and Spanish). qt. L38000 Italy; L57000 other. Bulzoni Editore Srl, Via dei Liburni 14, 00185 Rome Italy. **Tel** 011 39 6 445-5207, FAX 011 39 6 445-0355. **ED** Dario Puccini. **LC** PN843; .L47. **DD** 809/.891812.
Ind/Abst MLA Int. Bibl. Books Artic. Mod. Lang. Lit.

IT
LETTERATURE D'OLTRALPE E D'OLTREOCEANO. SAGGI E STUDI. 1-1972-. Monographic series. Italian. ir. Price varies per volume. Casa Editrice Leo S. Olschki, Viuzzo del Pozzetto, Casella Postale 66, 50126 Florence Italy. **Tel** 011 39 55 6530684, FAX 011 39 55 6530214.

IT/0024-1334
LETTERE ITALIANE. [Lett. ital.]. Vol. 1 (Jan./Mar. 1949)-. Periodical. Italian. qt (4 issues). L75000 Italy; L95000 other. Casa Editrice Leo S. Olschki, Viuzzo del Pozzetto, Casella Postale 66, 50126 Florence Italy. **Tel** 011 39 55 6530684, FAX 011 39 55 6530214. **ED** G. Searpat. **LC** PQ4001; .L47. Index available (bound in all issues). Documents available from The Genuine Article.
Desc: Covers Italian literature.
Ind/Abst Arts Humanit. Citation Index [Full Cov.]; Curr. Contents Arts Humanit.; MLA Int. Bibl. Books Artic. Mod. Lang. Lit.; Res. Alert [Full Cov.]; Romant. Move.

US
LETTERS. Vol. 1 (Summer 1974)-. Periodical. English. an. $10.00. Letters, PO Box 614, Saratoga Springs NY 12866. **LC** PN6069.W65; L47. **DD** 810/.8/09287.

UK
LETTERS OF DH LAWRENCE. Academic Scholarly Publication. English. ir. $64.50 US and Canada. Cambridge University Press, The Edinburgh Building, Shaftesbury Road, Cambridge CB2 2RU United Kingdom. **Tel** 011 44 223 312393, FAX 011 44 223 325959.

IT/0024-1350
LETTORE DI PROVINCIA, IL. [Lett. prov.]. Vol. 1, (June 1970)-. Periodical. Italian (French and English). Three times a year. L30000 Italy; L65000 other. Angelo Longo Editore, Via Paolo Costa 33, PO Box 431, 48100 Ravenna Italy. **Tel** 011 39 544 217026, FAX 011 39 544 217026. **ED** Tino Dalla Valle. Index available. **Bk Rev. Ad Acc. Circ:** 1,500 (ctrl).
Desc: Essays on European literature and poetry.
Ind/Abst MLA Int. Bibl. Books Artic. Mod. Lang. Lit.

FR/0151-8801
LETTRE DE MICHEL DEBRE, LA. [Lett. Michel Debre]. (1977)-. Periodical. French. mo (10 issues). 146.91F France; 150.00F other. Lettre de Michel Debre, 20 rue Jacob, F-75006 Paris France. **UDC** 32.

FR/0762-3690
LETTRE INTERNATIONALE. ***Suspended.*** No. 1 (1984)-((19??). Periodical. French. Four times a year. Lettre Internationale SARL, 14 16 rue des Petits Hotels, 75010 Paris France. **Tel** 011 33 1 42463987. **LC** PN3; .L47. **DD** 809.

CN/0382-084X
LETTRES QUEBECOISES. [Lett. que.]. No. 1 (Mar. 1976)-. Periodical. French. Four times a year (Published within the seasons). 16.82Can$ (individuals), 23.36Can$ (institutions) Canada; 20.00Can$ (individuals), 27.00Can$ (institutions) others. Les Editions Valmont, CP 1840 Station B, Montreal Quebec H3B 3L4 Canada. **Tel** (514)525-9518, FAX (514)525-7537. **(Subscription address:** Lettres Quebecoises, 1781 St. Hubert, Montreal H2L 3Z1 Canada**) ED** Adrien Therio. **DD** C840/.9. **Bk Rev. Ad Acc, Adv Mgr:** Benoit Marion. **Circ:** 5,000 (ctrl).
Desc: This is a magazine of "l'actualite litteraire" for Quebec. Presents books published in the field of literature, (novels, poetry, theatre, essays).
Ind/Abst Can. Period. Index (19??-); MLA Int. Bibl. Books Artic. Mod. Lang. Lit.; Point Repere (1983-).

BE
LETTRES ROMANES / UNIVERSITE CATHOLIQUE DE LOUVAIN, LES. **Added/Corp** Universite Catholique de Louvain (1970-). Universite Catholique de Louvain (1835-1969). Vol. 1, No. 1 (Feb. 1947)-. Periodical. French. qt (4 issues). 850.00F Belgium; 950.00F other. Les Lettres Romanes, Place Blaise Pascal 1, 1348 Louvain la Neuve Belgium. **Tel** 011 32 10 474921, FAX 011 32 10 472579. **LC** PC2; .L4. Index available (bound in Nov. issue). **Bk Rev. Circ:** 600 (ctrl). Documents available from The Genuine Article.
Desc: Publishes articles, critical reviews and bibliographical notes about history of the Romance literatures and their authors.
Ind/Abst Arts Humanit. Citation Index [Full Cov.]; Curr. Contents Arts Humanit.; MLA Int. Bibl. Books Artic. Mod. Lang. Lit.; Res. Alert [Full Cov.].

IT/0459-1623
LETTURE CLASSENSI. **Added/Corp** Opera di Dante (Institution : Ravenna, Italy). (1966)-. Italian (English). an. Angelo Longo Editore, Via Paolo Costa 33, PO Box 431, 48100 Ravenna Italy. **Tel** 011 39 544 217026, FAX 011 39 544 217026. **LC** PQ4331; .A215. **DD** 851/.1. **Circ:** 1,500.
Desc: Studies in Dante Alighieri.
Ind/Abst MLA Int. Bibl. Books Artic. Mod. Lang. Lit.

GW
LEXIKON DES FRUHGRIECHISCHEN EPOS. (19??)-. German. ir. DM238.00 (latest issue). Vandenhoeck & Ruprecht, Robert Bosch Breite 6, D-37079 Goettingen Germany. **Tel** 011 49 551 695911, FAX 011 49 551 695917, telex 965226 VAN d.

FR/0760-5641
LEZ VALENCIENNES / UNIVERSITE DE VALENCIENNES. **Added/Corp** Universite de Valenciennes et du Hainaut-Cambresis. No. 6 (1981)-. Monographic series. English (French and German). an. Price varies per volume. Presses University Valenciennes, Le Mont Houy, 59326 Valenciennes Cedex France. **Tel** 011 33 27 141193. **LC** UNC. ***Continues*** *Cahiers de l'U.E.R. Froissart.*

IT/0026-5748
LG ARGOMENTI : RIVISTA CENTRO STUDI LETTERATURA GIOVANILE. **Added/Corp** Centro Studi Letteratura Giovanile (Genoa, Italy). **VFOAT** L.G. Argomenti. Vol. 13, No. 1/2 (1977)-. Periodical. Italian. Four times a year. L40000. Biblioteca Internazionale e de Amicis, Centro Studi Letteratura Giovanile, via Archimede 44, 16142 Genova Italy. **Tel** 010 509181. **LC** PN1009.A1; M53. **DD** 809/.89282. **Circ:** 1,600. ***Continues*** *Minuzzolo.*

CC
LI SHIH WEN HSUEH. V. 1-. Periodical. Chinese. RMBY1.20. Hsin Hua Shu Tien / Kuang-Tung Sheng China, People's Republic of China. **LC** PL2653; .L5322. **DD** 895.1/35/08.

FR
LIBERTITRES. ***Title Change.*** (1991)-(1993). Periodical. French. mo. L'Agence Periscoop Multimedia, 12 rue Gilodesque Agropolis, 34080 Montferrier France. **Tel** 011 33 67753229. **LC** DT1; .L63. ***Continues*** *Intertitres, 1157-2973.* ***Continued by*** *Titra.*

US/0899-8272
LIBIDO (CHICAGO, ILL.). (LIBIDO.). [Libido]. Vol. 1, No. 1 (Fall 1988)-. Periodical. English. qt. $26.00 (1 year), $50.00 (2 year) US; $36.00 (1 year), $70.00 (2 year) Canada; $46.00 (1 year), $90.00 (2 year) Europe; $56.00 (1 year), $110.00 (2 year) other. Libido Inc, PO Box 146721, Chicago IL 60614. **Tel** (312)728-5979. **LC** HQ450; .L53. **DD** 810.

IT/0024-2683
LIBRI E RIVISTE D'ITALIA. **Added/Corp** Italy. Servizio Spettacolo, Informazioni e Proprieta Intellettuale. Italy. Centro di Documentazione. Italy. Ufficio della Proprieta Letteraria, Artistica e Scientifica. Italy. Servizi delle Informazioni e della Proprieta Letteraria, Artistica e Scientifica. Italy. Ministerio per i Beni Culturali e Ambientali. Divisione Editoria. Vol. 1 No. 1 (March 1950)-. Periodical. Italian (English, French, German and Spanish). Three times a year. L36000 Italy; L55000 others. Istituto Poligrafico Zecca Stato, Piazza Verdi 10, 00198 Rome Italy. **Tel** 011 39 6 85082307, 011 39 6 85082221. **LC** Z2345; .L63. **NLM** Z 2345 L697.

GW/0936-4242
LICHTENBERG-JAHRBUCH. **Added/Corp** Lichtenberg-Gesellschaft. 1988-. German. Saarbruecker Druckerei und Verlag GmbH, Halberstrasse 3, Postfach 442, W-6000 Saarbruecken Germany. **Tel** (0681)64941, FAX 0681-635545, telex 4 421 SDV D. **LC** B2681.L44; A16. **DD** 838/.609. ***Continues*** *Photorin, 0172-0015.*

FR/0398-9992
LICORNE, LA. [Licorne]. **Added/Corp** Universite de Poitiers. Faculte des Lettres et des Langues. (1976)-. Periodical. French.
Ind/Abst MLA Int. Bibl. Books Artic. Mod. Lang. Lit.

CH
LIEN HO PAO ... TUAN PIEN HSIAO SHUO CHIANG TSO PIN CHI. Chinese. an. NT$100.00. Lin Ching Chu Pan Shih Yeh Kung Ssu, 555 Chung Hsiao East Road, 4 Section, Taipei Taiwan. **LC** PL2653; .L5373. **DD** 895.1/301/08.

CH
LIEN HO WEN HSUEH. **VFOAT** Unitas. (November 1984)-. Periodical. Chinese. mo. $73.00 US; $90.00 Canada. Evergreen Publishing and Stationery, 136 South Atlantic Boulevard, Monterey Park CA 91754. **Tel** (818)284-9066, FAX (818)284-1571. **LC** PL2303; .L484. **DD** 895.1/09/005.

LI/0459-3472
LIETUVOS TSR AUKSTUJU MOKYKLU MOKSLO DARBAI: LITERATURA. **VFOAT** Uchenye Zapiski Vysshikh Uchebnykh Zavedenii Litovskoi SSR:. (1958)-. Periodical. Lithuanian. tq. Mintis / Idea, Z Sierakausko 15, Vilnius 2600 Lithuania. **Tel** 3702 632 943.
Ind/Abst MLA Int. Bibl. Books Artic. Mod. Lang. Lit.

●US/1064-8186
LIGHT (CHICAGO, ILL.). (LIGHT.). [Light]. No. 1 (Spring 1992)-. Periodical. English. Four times a year. $12.00 one year; $22.00 two year. Light, Box 7500, Chicago IL 60680. **Tel** (312)271-2432. **ED** John Mella. **DD** 811. (bound in last issue publish in December). **Bk Rev**, (Qty: 4-8). **Ad Acc, Adv Mgr:** John Mella, **Tel** (708)853-1028. **Circ:** 1,000.

US
LIKHT SHTRALN. **VFOAT** Licht-Stralen. Periodical. Yiddish. 150 Hewes Street, Brooklyn NY 11211. **LC** PJ5120; .A33.

GW/0049-8653
LILI, ZEITSCHRIFT FUER LITERATURWISSENSCHAFT UND LINGUISTIK. **See** Linguistics.

US/1058-5656
LIMITED INFINITY. (1991)-. Periodical. English. qt. $15.00 US; $20.00 Canada. Limited Infinity, PO Box 16124, Encino CA 91416-6124. **DD** 810.

US/0736-1084
LINDEN LANE MAGAZINE. **See** The Arts.

IT
LINEA D'OMBRA. Vol. 1, No. 1 (March 1983)-. Periodical. Italian. bm (6 issues). L85000 Italy; L100000 other. Linea d'Ombra Edizioni Srl, Via Gaffurio 4, 20124 Milan Italy. **Tel** 011 39 2 6690931, FAX 011 39 2 6691299. Index available. **Bk Rev. Ad Acc, Adv Mgr:** Miriam Corradi.
Desc: Monthly of history, pictures and more. Pays close attention to the current and new literary news.

UK/0266-1500
LINEN HALL REVIEW. (THE LINEN HALL REVIEW.). [Linen Hall rev.]. **Added/Corp** Linen Hall Library (Belfast, Northern Ireland). (Spring 1984)-. Periodical. English. qt (4 issues). £3.50 British Isles; £5.00 other. Linen Hall Review, 17 Donegall Square North, Belfast BT1 5GD Northern Ireland. **Tel** (0232)221707. **ED** John Gray and Paul Campbell. **Circ:** 5,000. ***Absorbed*** *Irish Booklore, 0044-8346.*
Desc: A northern view of the world of Irish books and literature.
Ind/Abst Annu. Bibliogr. Engl. Lang. Lit.; Libr. Inf. Sci. Abstr.

CC
LING NAN WEN SHIH. Began in 1983. Periodical. Chinese. sa. RMBY1.00. Kuang-Chou Ku Chi Shu Tien, 338 Beijing Road, Kuang-chou, People's Republic of China. **LC** DS793.K7; L58. **DD** 951/.27/005.

IT
LINGUA, LETTERATURA, CIVILTA / UNIVERSITA DI PERUGIA. **Added/Corp** Universita di Perugia. (1979)-. Periodical. Italian (English and French).
Ind/Abst Am. Hist. Life (1979-).

CK/0120-5587
LINGUISTICA Y LITERATURA : REVISTA DEL DEPARTAMENTO DE ESPANOL. **See** Linguistics.

US/8756-5609
LININGTON LINEUP. Jan. 84-. Periodical. English. Six times a year. $12.00. Rinehart S Potts, 1223 Glen Terrace, Glassboro NJ 08028. **Tel** (609)589-1571. **ED** Rinehart S Potts. **LC** PS3562.I515; Z75. **DD** 813/.54. **Bk Rev. Ad Acc. Circ:** 400 (ctrl).
Desc: Study works of Elizabeth Linington (pseudonyms Anne Blaisdell, Lesley Egan, Egan O'Neill, Dell Shannon); historical fiction and mysteries.

AT
LINQ. **Added/Corp** James Cook University of North Queensland. Dept. of English. English Language Literature Association. **VFOAT** Literature in North Queensland. Vol.1 (Sept. 1971)-. Periodical. English (French and German). sa (May and October). 20.00Aus$ (individuals), 25.00Aus$ (institutions) Australia; 25.00Aus$ (individuals), 30.00Aus$ (institutions) other. Editorial Committee / James Cook University, Department of Engineering, Townsville Queensland 4811 Australia. **Tel** 011 61 77814336. **ED** Dr. Phillip A. Kelly. **Bk Rev**, (Qty: 10-12/yr). **Pr Rev. Circ:** 300.
Desc: A regional literary journal.
Ind/Abst Annu. Bibliogr. Engl. Lang. Lit.; APAIS, Aust. Public Aff. Inf. Ser.; MLA Int. Bibl. Books Artic. Mod. Lang. Lit.

FR/0338-5019
LIRE. [Lire]. No. 1 (1976)-. Periodical. French. mo (11 issues). 269.34F France; 373.00F other. L'Express, 61 Avenue Hoche, 75008 Paris Cedex France. **Tel** 011 33 1 44625430.

BW
LITARATURA I MASTATSTVA. Added/Corp Byelorussian S.S.R. Ministerstvo Kultury. Saiuz Pismennikau BSSR. (19??)-. Periodical. Byelorussian. wk. $149.95. **(Subscription address:** East View Publications Inc., 3020 Harbor Lane North, Suite 110, Minneapolis MN 55447.**) LC** UNC.
Ind/Abst MLA Int. Bibl. Books Artic. Mod. Lang. Lit.

TU/0459-5106
LITERA. V. 1- ; 1954-. Periodical. English. **LC** PN2. **DD** 405. ***Continues*** *Ingiliz Filolojisi Dergisi.*

XR/0231-5904
LITERARNI ARCHIV. (LITERARNI ARCHIV : SBORNIK PAMATNIKU NARODNIHO PISEMNICTVI.). [Lit. arch.]. **Added/Corp** Pamatnik Narodniho Pisemnictvi (Prague, Czechoslovakia). (1966)-. Czech (summaries and/or abstracts in English and German). an.
Ind/Abst Am. Hist. Life (1966-).

XO
LITERARNY TYZDENNIK : CASOPIS ZVAZU SLOVENSKYCH SPISOVATELOV. Vol. 1, 1 (Sept. 21 1988)-. Periodical. Slovak. wk. **(Subscription address:** Artia Pegas Press Ltd., Palac Metro Narodni Trida 25, 11210 Prague 1 Czech Republic.**) LC** PG5407; .L58.

CN
LITERARY CAVALCADE. See Education.

US/0024-4511
LITERARY CAVALCADE. [Lit. cavalc.]. Vol. 1 (Oct. 1948)-. Periodical. English. Eight times a year (published during school year). $25.00. Scholastic Inc., 2931 East McCarty Street, PO Box 3710, Jefferson City MO 65102-9957. **Tel** (314)636-5271, (800)631-1586. **LC** AP2; .L574. **DD** 805. available on microfilm and microfiche from University Microfilms International (UMI).

II/0024-452X
LITERARY CRITERION, THE. [Lit. criterion]. (1952)-. Periodical. English. Four times a year (Jan., Apr., July, Oct.). $30.00. Bangalore University, CN Srinath Department of English, Jnanabharathi Bangalore 560056 India. **Tel** 355 299. **(Subscription address:** Prints India, 11 Darya Ganj, New Delhi 110002 India.**) ED** C. D. Narasimhaiah and C. N. Srinath. **LC** PR1; .L5. **DD** 820/.9. cum. index (1952-1991, ($25.00)). **Bk Rev**, (Qty: 20). **Ad Acc. Circ:** 1,000.
Desc: Focus is on Indian literature in English, Commonwealth and American literature. Textual and analytical criticism of most important and relevant contemporary writing is encouraged.
Ind/Abst Abstr. Engl. Stud.; Annu. Bibliogr. Engl. Lang. Lit.; MLA Int. Bibl. Books Artic. Mod. Lang. Lit.

II/0255-2779
LITERARY ENDEAVOUR, THE. [Lit. endeavor]. (1979)-. Periodical. English. Four times a year. Dr. L. Asinarayana, F-3 Block 6, HIG, Opp., Water Tank,, Bagh, Lingampalli, Hyderanad 500 004 India. **(Subscription address:** Prints India, 11 Darya Ganj, New Delhi 110002 India.**) Bk Rev. Ad Acc.**
Ind/Abst MLA Int. Bibl. Books Artic. Mod. Lang. Lit.

II/0024-4554
LITERARY HALF-YEARLY, THE. [Lit. half-yrly.]. Vol. 1 (Jan 1960)-. English. sa. $20.00. Institute of Commonwealth Studies and English Language, Anjali 96, 7th Main Jayalakshmipuram, Mysore 570 012 India. **Tel** 23030. **(Subscription address:** Prints India, 11 Darya Ganj, New Delhi 110002 India.**) ED** Anniah Gowda. **LC** AP8; .L5. **DD** 820.5. Index available. cum. index. **Bk Rev. Ad Acc. Circ:** 1,000 (ctrl).
Desc: Contributions which should not exceed 3,000 words for prose articles, and stories or 30 lines for verse, with notes on contributors.
Ind/Abst Abstr. Engl. Stud.; Annu. Bibliogr. Engl. Lang. Lit.; MLA Int. Bibl. Books Artic. Mod. Lang. Lit.

●US/1064-8062
LITERARY IMAGE. (1992)-. English. $25.00. Brandon House, PO Box 240, Bronx NY 10471. **Tel** (914)423-9200.

US/0198-151X
LITERARY MARKET REVIEW. [Lit. mark. rev.]. No. 1 (Mar. 1980)-. Periodical. English. qt. $2.00. Kunnupapampil P Andrews, 73-47 255th Street, Glen Oaks NY 11004.

US/0160-8703
LITERARY ONOMASTICS STUDIES. ***Ceased.*** [Lit. onomast. stud.]. Vol. for 1974-. English. an. State University College, Department of Foreign Language and Literature, Brockport NY 14420. **Tel** (716)395-2269. **ED** Grace Alvarez-Altman. **LC** PN56.N16; L58. **DD** 809. **Bk Rev. Ad Acc. Circ:** 200.
Desc: Research in the use of names of authors, their significance and how they affect the interpretation of the work.
Ind/Abst Chicano Index; MLA Int. Bibl. Books Artic. Mod. Lang. Lit.

II
LITERARY READER. Main/Corp Writers Workshop, Calcutta. 1st- 1972-. English. an. $10.00. 169/92 Lake Gardens, Calcutta 45 India. **Tel** 46-8325. **ED** P Lal. **LC** PR9480; .A4. **DD** 828. **Bk Rev. Circ:** 1,000.
Desc: Indian creative writing in English.

US/0891-6365
LITERARY RESEARCH. ***Ceased.*** (LITERARY RESEARCH : LR.). [Lit. res.]. **Added/Corp** Literary Research Association. **VFOAT** LR. Vol. 11, No. 1 (Winter 1986)-Vol. 15 (1993). Periodical. English. qt (Jan., April, July, and Oct.). The University of Maryland, Department of English, c/o Aletha Hendrickson Managing Editor, College Park MD 20742. **Tel** (301)454-2511. **ED** Michael J Marcuse and Aletha Hendrickson (editor's telephone number: (301)795-1367). **LC** PN73; .L57. **DD** 809. Index available. cum. index. **Bk Rev. Ad Acc. Circ:** 400. ***Continues*** *Literary Research Newsletter, 0362-1294.*
Desc: Covers all aspects of literary research including enumerative and descriptive bibliography, textual criticism and pedagogy.
Ind/Abst Am. Humanit. Index; Arts Humanit. Citation Index (19??-19??) [Full Cov.]; Lit. Crit. Regist.; MLA Int. Bibl. Books Artic. Mod. Lang. Lit.

CN/1188-7494
LITERARY REVIEW OF CANADA, THE. [Lit. rev. Can.]. Vol. 1, No. 1 (Dec. 1991)-. Periodical. English. Eleven times a year. $26.00 (individual); $34.00 (institution). Literary Review of Canada Inc., 3266 Yonge Street, Suite 1830, Toronto ONT M4N 3P6 Canada. **Tel** FAX (416)322-4852. **ED** P. A. Dutil. **DD** C818/.54/009. **Bk Rev**, (Qty: 75). **Ad Acc. Circ:** 1,500.
Desc: Reviews of non-fiction books written by Canadians.

US/0024-4589
LITERARY REVIEW (TEANECK), THE. (THE LITERARY REVIEW.). [Lit. rev.]. **Added/Corp** Fairleigh Dickinson University. Vol. 1 (Autumn 1957)-. Periodical. English. Four times a year (Jan., Apr., July, Oct.). $18.00 (one year); $30.00 (two years). Farleigh Dickinson University, 285 Madison Avenue, Madison NJ 07940. **Tel** (201)593-8564. **ED** Walter Cummins. **LC** AP2; .L6377. **DD** 051. Index available. **Bk Rev. Circ:** 1,100. available on microfilm from University Microfilms International (UMI). Documents available from UMI Article Clearinghouse.
Desc: Fiction, poetry, and literary essays of high quality.
Ind/Abst Acad. Search (July 1993-); Am. Bibliogr. Slavic East Europ. Stud.; Am. Humanit. Index (199?-); Annu. Bibliogr. Engl. Lang. Lit.; Arts Humanit. Citation Index [Full Cov.]; Curr. Contents Arts Humanit.; Expand. Acad. Index (1989-); Humanit. Index; Humanit. Source (Jul. 1993-); Index Am. Period. Verse; INFO-SOUTH Abstr.; Lit. Crit. Regist.; Mag. Search; MLA Int. Bibl. Books Artic. Mod. Lang. Lit.; Newsp. Period. Abstr. (1991-); Res. Alert [Full Cov.].

US/0024-4597
LITERARY SKETCHES. [Lit. sketches]. (196?)-. Academic Scholarly Publication. English. Eleven times a year. $7.00 (one year), $12.50 (two years). Literary Sketches, PO Box 810571, Dallas TX 75381. **Tel** (214)243-8776. **ED** Olivia Murray Nichols. **DD** 800. Index available (published separately). cum. index. **Bk Rev**, (Qty: 4-6). **Ad Acc. Circ:** 500. ***Continues*** *Books (Williamsburg, Va.).*
Desc: Articles on topics related to books and authors. Non-scholarly, though for discriminating readers.
Ind/Abst Abstr. Engl. Stud.

GW/0024-4627
LITERAT, DER. Vol. 1 (1958)-. Periodical. German. Twelve times a year. DM55.00. Der Literat, Postfach 102235, W 6000 Frankfurt F R Germany. **Tel** 011 49 69 771632, telex 288892. **ED** Inka Bohl M. A. and Theodor Tauchel. **LC** PN4; .L46. Index available. cum. index. **Bk Rev. Ad Acc. Circ:** 3,000.
Desc: A special magazine for literature and art.

US/0895-9269
LITERATI CHICAGO. Vol. 1, No. 1 (Winter 1988)-. Periodical. English. Three times a year. $16.00. Literati Chicago, 5 North Wabash Avenue, Suite 1409, Chicago IL 60602. **LC** PS572.C5; L57. **DD** 810.8/0977311/05.

US/1054-9404
LITERATI INTERNAZIONALE. (1991)-. Periodical. English. sa. $20.00. Literati Internazionale, 213 West Institute Place, #207, Chicago IL 60610.

SA/0258-2279
LITERATOR. Added/Corp Literatorvereniging van Suid-Afrika. (19??)-. Periodical. Afrikaans (English and French; summaries and/or abstracts in English). tq. **LC** PN1; .L58.
Ind/Abst Annu. Bibliogr. Engl. Lang. Lit.

GW/0343-1657
LITERATUR FUER LESER. (1978)-. Periodical. German. Four times a year. DM63.20 Germany; DM64.00 others. Verlag Peter Lang AG, Jupiterstrasse 15, CH-3000 Bern 15 Switzerland. **Tel** 011 41 31 9411122, FAX 011 41 31 321131. **ED** Herbert Kaiser and Dieter Mayer. **LC** PT3; .L57. **DD** 830.9/0005. **Bk Rev. Ad Acc. Circ:** 1,500.
Desc: Addresses questions of didactic and historical literary interpretation in articles on textual, historical and genre analysis. Each issue centers around one theme.

GW/0024-4643
LITERATUR IN WISSENSCHAFT UND UNTERRICHT : LWU. [Lit. Wiss. Unterr.]. **Added/Corp** Universitat Kiel. Englisches Seminar. No. 1 (1968)-. Periodical. German (English). qt. DM39.80 Germany; DM44.00 other. Verlag Koenigshausen & Neumann, Postfach 6007, W 8700 Wuerzburg Germany. **Tel** 011 49 931 76401, FAX 011 49 931 83620. **ED** R Bohm, D Jager, H Kruse and P Nicolaisen. **LC** PN4; .L517. Index available. cum. index. **Bk Rev**, (Qty: 20/yr). **Ad Acc. Circ:** 1,800 (ctrl).
Desc: A journal of close reading in the English and German languages.
Ind/Abst Abstr. Engl. Stud.; Annu. Bibliogr. Engl. Lang. Lit.; MLA Int. Bibl. Books Artic. Mod. Lang. Lit.; Romant. Move.

GW/0075-9937
LITERATUR UND WIRKLICHKEIT. [Lit. Wirklichk.]. Vol. 1 (1967)-. Monographic series. German. ir. Price varies per volume. VVA Bertelsmann Dist GmbH, Postfach 7600, D 33310 Gutersloh Germany. **Tel** 011 49 5241 803294. **(Subscription address:** Postfach 7777, D 33310 Guetersloh Germany, telephone: 011 49 5241 803294**)**
Ind/Abst MLA Int. Bibl. Books Artic. Mod. Lang. Lit.

PL/0137-2548
LITERATURA. (Oct. 1972)-. Periodical. Polish. mo. $48.00. **(Subscription address:** ARS Polona, PO Box 1001, 00068 Warsaw Poland.**) LC** PG7001; .L58. available on microfilm. ***Continues*** *Wspoczesnosc.*

HU/0133-2368
LITERATURA (BUDAPEST). (LITERATURA.). [Literatura]. **Added/Corp** Magyar Tudomanyos Akademia. Irodalomtudomanyi Intezet. Vol. 1 (1974)-. Periodical. Hungarian. qt. $19.50. Literatura, Magyar Tudomanyos Akademia, Irodalomtudomanyi Intezet Menesi ut 11-13, 1118 Budapest, Hungary. **Tel** 36 1 166 5938, FAX 36 1 185 3876. **ED** B. Pomogats. **LC** PH3001; .L57. **Bk Rev. Ad Acc. Circ:** 950.
Desc: Covers Hungarian literature.
Ind/Abst MLA Int. Bibl. Books Artic. Mod. Lang. Lit.

UN
LITERATURA, DITY, CHAS. 1979-. Periodical. Ukrainian. an. 0.90rub. Veselka Publishers, 63 Melnikov Street, Kiev GSP, 252050 Ukraine. **Tel** 2139501, 2130512. **ED** Irina Boiko. **LC** PG3930; .L57. **Circ:** 12,000.
Desc: Contains an annual collection of materials concerning the problems of literature for children in the Soviet Union, and the world over.

IT
LITERATURA FOIRO. No. 1 (1970)-. Periodical. Esperanto. bm.
Ind/Abst MLA Int. Bibl. Books Artic. Mod. Lang. Lit.

RU/0459-5351
LITERATURA I ISKUSSTVO. Added/Corp Gosudarstvennaia Biblioteka SSSR Imeni V.I. Lenina. (1967)-. Russian. Gosudarstvennaia Biblioteka, Informatsionnyi Tsentr, Imeni V. I. Lenina, Prospekt Kalinina 3, 121019 Moscow Russia. **LC** Z6513; .L57. ***Continues*** *Khudozhestvennaia Literatura, Literaturovedenie, Iskusstvo.*

LI
LITERATURA IR MENAS. Added/Corp Lietuvos TSR Rasytoju Sajunga. Lietuvos Rasytoju Sajunga. **VFOAT** Literatura i Iskusstvo. (July 21, 1946)-. Periodical. Lithuanian. wk. $149.95. Mintis / Idea, Z Sierakausko 15, Vilnius 2600 Lithuania. **Tel** 3702 632 943. **(Subscription address:** East View Publications Inc., 3020 Harbor Lane North, Suite 110, Minneapolis MN 55447.**) LC** PG8501; .L57.
Ind/Abst MLA Int. Bibl. Books Artic. Mod. Lang. Lit.

MX/0188-2546
LITERATURA MEXICANA. Added/Corp Universidad Nacional Autonoma de Mexico. Centro de Estudios Literarios. Vol. 1, No. 1 (1990)-. Periodical. Spanish. sa. $40.00 (US, Canada & Europe); $24.00 (Caribbean, Central & South America). Unam Instituto Investiga Filologicas, Ciudad Universitaria, 04510 Mexico DF Mexico. **Tel** 011 52 5 6227487, 011 52 5 6650411.
Ind/Abst MLA Int. Bibl. Books Artic. Mod. Lang. Lit.

PL
LITERATURA NA SWIECIE. No. 1 (1971)-. Periodical. Polish. mo. $51.00. **(Subscription address:** ARS Polona, PO Box 1001, 00068 Warsaw Poland.**)**

RU/0024-4716
LITERATURA RADZIECKA. (19??)-. Periodical. Russian. mo. **(Subscription address:** Victor Kamkin, 4956 Boiling Brook Parkway, Rockville MD 20852.**)**

RU/0024-4724
LITERATURA V SHKOLE. **Added/Corp** Russian S.F.S.R. Narodnyi Komissariat Prosveshcheniia. Russian S.F.S.R. Ministerstvo Prosveshcheniia. (1936)-. Periodical. Russian. Six times a year. $69.95. **(Subscription address:** East View Publications Inc., 3020 Harbor Lane North, Suite 110, Minneapolis MN 55447.**)** **LC** PN59; .L5. ***Supersedes in part*** *Russkii lazyk I Literatura V Srednei Shkole.*

SP
LITERATURA Y SOCIEDAD. (19??)-. Monographic series. Spanish. ir. 2650.00ptas (Vol. 35), 6000.00ptas (Vol. 36), 1900.00ptas (Vol. 37). Editorial Castalia, Zurbano 39, 28010 Madrid Spain. **Tel** 419 8940, or 419 5857. **LC** UNC.

US/0732-1929
LITERATURE AND BELIEF. (LITERATURE AND BELIEF / CENTER FOR THE STUDY OF CHRISTIAN VALUES IN LITERATURE, BRIGHAM YOUNG UNIVERSITY.). [Lit. belief]. **Added/Corp** Brigham Young University. Center for the Study of Christian Values in Literature. Vol. 1 (1981)-. Academic Scholarly Publication. English. an. $5.00 (US); $7.00 (other). Literature and Belief, Brigham Young University, English Department, Provo UT 84602. **Tel** (801)378-2304. **ED** Jay Fox. **LC** PN49; .L4997. **DD** 809/.93382. **Bk Rev**. **Pr Rev. Circ:** 1,000 (ctrl). available on microfiche.
Desc: Publishes scholarly, interpretative articles that focus on moral/religious considerations, bibliographical articles, book reviews, short stories, interviews, personal essays or poems.
Ind/Abst Abstr. Engl. Stud.; Lit. Crit. Regist.; MLA Int. Bibl. Books Artic. Mod. Lang. Lit.

US/0885-3274
LITERATURE AND CONTEMPORARY REVOLUTIONARY CULTURE. (LITERATURE AND CONTEMPORARY REVOLUTIONARY CULTURE : JOURNAL OF THE SOCIETY FOR THE STUDY OF CONTEMPORARY HISPANIC AND LUSOPHONE REVOLUTIONARY LITERATURES.). [Lit. contemp. revolut. cult.]. **Added/Corp** Society for the Study of Contemporary Hispanic and Lusophone Revolutionary Literatures. (1985)-. English (Portuguese and Spanish). an. $20.00 (includes membership). **LC** PQ7081.A1; L557. **DD** 809/.93358.
Ind/Abst MLA Int. Bibl. Books Artic. Mod. Lang. Lit.

UK/0306-1973
LITERATURE & HISTORY. [Lit. hist.]. **Added/Corp** Thames Polytechnic. (March 1975)-. English. sa. $60.00 institutions; $40.00 individuals. Manchester University Press, Journals Dept, Oxford Road, Manchester M13 9PL England. **Tel** 011 44 061 2735539, FAX 011 44 061 2743346, telex 668932. **ED** John N. King, Philip Martin, Roger Richardson and Alan Armstrong. **LC** AS122.T45; A25. **DD** 052. **Bk Rev**. **Ad Acc. Circ:** 800 (ctrl). Documents available from The Genuine Article.
Desc: Interdisciplinary debate in literature and history. Key articles are combined with a reviews section, providing both research and commentary on developments in current publications.
Ind/Abst Am. Hist. Life (1975-); Arts Humanit. Citation Index [Full Cov.]; Book Rev. Index (19??-Feb. 1990); Br. Humanit. Index; Humanit. Index; MLA Int. Bibl. Books Artic. Mod. Lang. Lit.; Res. Alert [Full Cov.].

US/0024-4759
LITERATURE AND PSYCHOLOGY. [Lit. psychol.]. **Added/Corp** National Association for Psychoanalytic Criticism. Conference on Literature and Psychology. Modern Language Association of America. General Topics 10. (1951)-. Periodical. English (French and Spanish). Four times a year (Jan., Apr., July, Oct.). $24.00 (institutions), $15.00 (individuals). Literature and Psychology, Rhode Island College, Department of English, Providence RI 02908. **Tel** (401)456-8670. **ED** Richard Feldstein and Morton Kaplan. **LC** PN49; .L5. **CODEN** LIPSA. **Bk Rev**. **Ad Acc**. **Pr Rev. Circ:** 800. available on microfilm and microfiche from University Microfilms International (UMI). Documents available from The Genuine Article, UMI Article Clearinghouse.
Desc: Journal of literary criticism as informed by depth psychology. We particularly encourage the submission of essays on such subjects as psychoanalysis and other modes of critical theory.
Ind/Abst Abstr. Engl. Stud.; Acad. Search (Jan. 1994-); Annu. Bibliogr. Engl. Lang. Lit.; Arts Humanit. Citation Index [Full Cov.]; Curr. Contents Arts Humanit.; Expand. Acad. Index (1989-); Film Lit. Index (19??-); Humanit. Index; Humanit. Source (Jul. 1993-); INFO-SOUTH Abstr.; Mag. Search; Middle East Abstr. Index; MLA Int. Bibl. Books Artic. Mod. Lang. Lit.; Newsp. Period. Abstr. (1991-); Psychol. Abstr. (1967-); PsycINFO; PsycLit; Res. Alert [Full Cov.]; Romant. Move.; Soc. Plann. Policy Dev. Abstr.

US/1040-7928
LITERATURE AND THE SCIENCES OF MAN. [Lit. sci. man]. (1989)-. English. an. Peter Lang Publishing, 62 West 45th Street, 4th Floor, New York NY 10036. **Tel** (212)764-1471, (800)770-5264, telex 6973364 PLNY. **DD** 301.

UK/0269-1205
LITERATURE & THEOLOGY. [Lit. theol.]. **VFOAT** Journal of Literature and Theology; Literature and Theology; Journal of Literature & Theology. Vol. 1, No. 1 (March 1987)-. Periodical. English. qt. £56.00 UK and Europe; $105.00 other. Oxford University Press, Walton Street, Oxford OX2 6DP England. **Tel** 011 44 865 56767, FAX 011 44 865 267773, telex 837330 OXPRES G. **(Subscription address:** Oxford University Press / USA, Journals Marketing Department, Oxford University Press, 2001 Evans Road, Cary NC 27513.**)** **ED** David Jasper (editor's address: St. Chad's College, University of Durham, Durham DH1 3RH). **LC** PN49; .L49966. **DD** 809/.93382/05. **[CCC]**. **Bk Rev**. **Ad Acc**. available on microfilm and microfiche from University Microfilms International (UMI). ***Continues*** *National Conference on Literature and Religion Newsletter.*
Desc: Provides a forum for discussion of interdisciplinary issues and approaches which are central to contemporary critical debate. It is neither a journal of theology nor a journal of literary studies, but exists within the creative tension between the two disciplines. Matters of mutual interest include narrative, the intellectual and cultural context of literature, myth, etc.
Ind/Abst Br. Humanit. Index; Index Book Rev. Relig.; MLA Int. Bibl. Books Artic. Mod. Lang. Lit.; Relig. Index One Period.; Relig. Theol. Abstr.; Romant. Move.

AT/1034-6244
LITERATURE BASE. ***Suspended.*** (THE LITERATURE BASE.). [Litt. base]. (1990)-Vol. 5, No. 3. Periodical. English. qt. Magpies Magazine, 10 Armagh Street, Victoria Park Western Australia 6100 Australia. **Tel** 011 61 9 4721355, FAX 011 61 9 3618295. **ED** Alf Mappin. **DD** 028.53405.
Ind/Abst Aust. Educ. Index.

US/0024-4767
LITERATURE EAST & WEST. [Lit. east west]. **Added/Corp** Modern Language Association of America. Oriental-Western Literary Relations Group. Modern Language Association of America. Conference on Oriental-Western Literary Relations. **VAT** Literature East and West. Vol. 1 (Spring 1954)-. Periodical. English. an. Literature East & West, 2601 University Avenue, Austin TX 78712. **Tel** (512)471-1365. **LC** PN2; .L67. **DD** 805. available on microfilm and microfiche from University Microfilms International (UMI).
Ind/Abst Abstr. Engl. Stud.; Annu. Bibliogr. Engl. Lang. Lit.; MLA Int. Bibl. Books Artic. Mod. Lang. Lit.

US/1043-6928
LITERATURE, INTERPRETATION, THEORY. (LITERATURE, INTERPRETATION, THEORY : LIT.). [Lit. interpret. theory]. **VFOAT** Lit; Lit, Literature, Interpretation, Theory. Vol. 1, No. 1/2 (Dec. 1989)-. Periodical. English. ir. Gordon & Breach Science Publishers, PO Box 90, Reading RG1 8JL England. **Tel** 011 44 734 560080, FAX 011 44 734 568211. **(Subscription address:** International Publishers Distributor at one of the following addresses: 820 Town Center Drive, Langhorne, PA 19047; or PO Box 90, Reading Berkshire RG1 8JL UK; or Kent Ridge PO Box 1180, Singapore 9111, Republic of Singapore**)** **LC** PPN2; .L58. **DD** 809. **CODEN** LINTEX. **[CCC]**.
Ind/Abst MLA Int. Bibl. Books Artic. Mod. Lang. Lit.

UK/0141-335X
LITERATURE OF ART, THE. **VAT** Lit. Art. V. 1-. English. mo. $12.00. Art Book Company, 18 Endell St England.

US/0197-8829
LITERATURE (WASHINGTON). (LITERATURE / NATIONAL ENDOWMENT FOR THE ARTS.). [Literature]. **VFOAT** Literature Program. English. an. National Endowment for the Arts, 1100 Pennsylvania Avenue Northwest, Washington DC 20506. **Tel** (202)682-5400, (202)682-5435. **LC** PN51; .L5735. **DD** 810/.79.

US
LITERATURE [MICROFORM] / NEWSBANK, INC. **Added/Corp** NewsBank, Inc. Vol. 9, Card 65 (March 1983)-. Periodical. English. Six times a year. $350.00 libraries; $270.00 high schools and junior high schools; $530.00 institutions. Newsbank Inc, 58 Pine Street, New Canaan CT 06840. **Tel** (800)243-7694, (800)762-8182, FAX (203)966-6254. ***Continues*** *NewsBank. Literature, 0737-4011.*

BU/0459-5564
LITERATUREN ARKHIV / BULGARSKA AKADEMIIA NA NAUKITE, INSTITUT ZA BULGARSKA LITERATURA. **Added/Corp** Institut za Literatura (Bulgarska Akademiia na Naukite). (1959)-. Monographic series. Bulgarian. ir. Bulgarian Academy of Sciences / Publishing House, Ulitsa Akademiia G. Bonchev, 1113, Sofia Bulgaria. **LC** PG1000; .B8227.

XN/0024-4791
LITERATUREN ZBOR. [Lit. zbor]. Began publication in 1954. Periodical. Macedonian. bm. **LC** PG1161; .L5.
Ind/Abst MLA Int. Bibl. Books Artic. Mod. Lang. Lit.

GW/0934-6503
LITERATURMAGAZIN. **VFOAT** Literatur Magazin. 1 (1973)-. Monographic series. German. ir. Price varies per volume. Rowohlt Taschenbuch Verlag, Postfach 1349, D 21462 Reinbek Germany. **Tel** 011 49 40 72720. **(Subscription address:** Adlers Foreign Books Inc., 915 Foster Street, Evanston IL 60201.**)** **LC** PN4; .L57.

BU/0324-0495
LITERATURNA MISL. (LITERATURNA MISUL.). [Lit. misl]. **Added/Corp** Institut za Literatura (Bulgarska Akademiia na Naukite). (1957)-. Periodical. Bulgarian. Six times a year. DM283.00. Bulgarian Academy of Sciences, 1 rue 15 Noemvri, 1040 Sofia Bulgaria. **Tel** 011 359 2 803127. **(Subscription address:** Kubon & Sagner, ABT Zeitschriftenimport, D 80328 Munich Germany.**)** cum. index.
Desc: Covers Bulgarian literature.
Ind/Abst Annu. Bibliogr. Engl. Lang. Lit.; MLA Int. Bibl. Books Artic. Mod. Lang. Lit.

RU
LITERATURNAIA CHECHENO-INGUSHETIIA. (19??)-. Periodical. Russian. **LC** PG3505.G76; L57.

GS/0458-0311
LITERATURNAIA GRUZIIA. **Added/Corp** Sakartvelos Sabcota Mcerlebis Kavsiri. Vol. 1 (1957)-. Periodical. Russian. mo. $109.95. **(Subscription address:** East View Publications Inc., 3020 Harbor Lane North, Suite 110, Minneapolis MN 55447.**)**

RU
LITERATURNAIA UCHEBA. **Added/Corp** Soiuz Pisatelei SSSR. Vsesoiuznyi Leninskii Kommunisticheskii Soiuz Molodezhi. Tsentralnyi Komitet. (1978)-. Periodical. Russian. Six times a year. $69.95. **(Subscription address:** East View Publications Inc., 3020 Harbor Lane North, Suite 110, Minneapolis MN 55447.**)** **LC** PG3227; .L47.

RU
LITERATURNOE NASLEDSTVO. **Added/Corp** Akademiia Nauk SSSR. Institut Literatury. Kommunisticheskaia Akademiia, Moscow. Nauchno-Issledovatelskii Institut Literatury i Iskusstva. Rossiikaia Assotsiatsiia Proletarskikh Pisatelei. Vol. 1 (1931)-. Monographic series. Russian. ir. Price varies per volume. **(Subscription address:** East View Publications Inc., 3020 Harbor Lane North, Suite 110, Minneapolis MN 55447.**)** **LC** PN9; .L5.

RU/0321-2904
LITERATURNOE OBOZRENIE. [Lit. obozr.]. **Added/Corp** Soiuz Pisatelei SSSR. (Jan. 1973)-. Periodical. Russian. mo. $119.95. **(Subscription address:** East View Publications Inc., 3020 Harbor Lane North, Suite 110, Minneapolis MN 55447.**)** **LC** PG2900; .L54.
Ind/Abst MLA Int. Bibl. Books Artic. Mod. Lang. Lit.

AJ
LITERATURNYI AZERBAIDZHAN. **Added/Corp** Soiuz Pisatelei Azerbaidzhana. (1931)-. Periodical. Russian. Six times a year. $99.95. **(Subscription address:** East View Publications Inc., 3020 Harbor Lane North, Suite 110, Minneapolis MN 55447.**)**

US
LITERATURNYI KURER. **VFOAT** Literary Courier. No. 1-. Periodical. Russian (English). mo. Lambs Club, c/o Literary Courier, 130 West 44 Street, New York NY 10036.

GW/0075-997X
LITERATURWISSENSCHAFTLICHES JAHRBUCH. [Literaturwiss. Jahrb.]. **Added/Corp** Gorres-Gesellschaft. (1926)-. German. an. Price varies per volume. Duncker und Humblot Verlag, Postfach 410329, D-12113 Berlin Germany. **Tel** 011 49 30 79000612, 011 49 30 79000613. **LC** PT13; .L52.
Desc: German yearbook of literary sciences.
Ind/Abst MLA Int. Bibl. Books Artic. Mod. Lang. Lit.

GW
LITFASS. Vol. 1 (Jan. 1976)-. Periodical. German. qt. 16.00M. Postfach 420464, O-1000 Berlin 42 Germany. **LC** PT1141.A2; L57.

CN/0821-4077
LITIR NEWSLETTER OF VICTORIAN STUDIES. [Litir newsl. Vic. stud.]. **VFOAT** Litir Newsletter. No. 1 (Spring 1983)-. Newsletter. English. Three times a year. Free. Litir Database, University of Alberta, Department of English, Edmonton Alberta T6G 2E5 Canada. **Tel** (403)492-5937. **DD** 820/.9/008. ctrl circ.

US
LITMAG 500, THE. **VFOAT** Lit Mag Five Hundred; Lit Mag 500. English. Poeticorp, Publishing Company, PO Box 1152, Northampton MA 01061.

SP
LITORAL. No. 1 (May 1968)-. Periodical. Spanish (English, French and German). Twice a year (two double issues per year). 7210ptas Spain; $80.00 Europe; $85.00

the Americas. Litoral, Urbanizacion la Roca 107 C, Torremolinos Malaga Spain. **Tel** 11 34 52 384200, FAX 011 34 52 2380758. **ED** Jose Maria Amado. **LC** PN6054; .L57. cum. index. **Bk Rev. Ad Acc. Circ:** 3,500 (ctrl). ***Supersedes*** *Litoral.*

XR/0862-8424
LITTERARIA PRAGENSIA. Added/Corp Ustav pro Ceskou a Svetovou Literaturu (Ceskoslovenska Akademie Ved). (1991)-. Periodical. English (French, German, Italian, Portuguese and Spanish). sa. $60.00. John Benjamins BV, Amsteldijk 44, PO Box 75577, 1070 AN Amsterdam Netherlands. **Tel** 011 31 20 6738156, FAX 011 31 20 739773. **(Subscription address:** John Benjamins North America, PO Box 27519, Philadelphia PA 19118-0519.**) ED** Anna Houskova, Zdenek Hrbata. **LC** IN PROCESS. ***Continues in part*** *Philologica Pragensia, 0048-3885.*

DK/0106-620X
LITTERATUR & SAMFUND. [Litt. & samf.]. **VAT** Litteratur og Samfund. (1974)-. Periodical. Danish. **Ind/Abst** MLA Int. Bibl. Books Artic. Mod. Lang. Lit.

FR/0459-5815
LITTERATURE AFRICAINE. 1- 1964-. Monographic series. French. Price varies per volume.

FR/0336-5654
LITTERATURE ORALE ARABO-BERBERE. [Litt. orale arabo-berbere]. Periodical. French. **LC** PJ2301; .L57. **Ind/Abst** Anthropol. Lit.

FR/0047-4800
LITTERATURE (PARIS. 1971). (LITTERATURE.). [Litterature]. **Added/Corp** Universite de Paris VIII: Vincennes. Department de Litterature Francaise. No. 1 (Feb. 1971)-. Periodical. French. Four times a year (Feb., May, Oct., Dec.). 300.00F France; 350.00F others. Dunod Gauthier Villars, 15 rue Gossin, 92543 Montrouge cedex France. **Tel** 011 33 1 46 56 52 66, FAX 011 33 1 46 57 40 69. **(Subscription address:** Centrale des Revues, 11 rue Gossin, 92543 Montrouge Cedex France.**) [CCC].** Documents available from The Genuine Article.
Desc: Each issue is devoted to specific areas and topics. Publishes articles treating theoretical research as well as their pedagogical applications.
Ind/Abst Arts Humanit. Citation Index; Curr. Contents Arts Humanit.; MLA Int. Bibl. Books Artic. Mod. Lang. Lit.; Res. Alert.

FR/0992-5279
LITTERATURES CLASSIQUES. No. 11 (Jan. 1989)-. Periodical. French. sa. Aux Amateurs de Livres Intl, 62 Avenue de Suffren, 75015 Paris France. **LC** PN743; .L57. **DD** 809/.032/05. ***Continues*** *Cahiers de Litterature du XVIIe Siecle.*

CN/0838-1453
LITTERATURES (MONTREAL). (LITTERATURES DEPARTEMENT DE LANGUE ET LITTERATURE FRANCAISES.). [Litteratures]. **Added/Corp** McGill University. Departement de Langue et Litterature Francaises. (1988)-. Periodical. French. Twice a year (Apr. & Nov.). 20.00Can$ Canada; 24.00Can$ US. McGill University / Department of French and Litteratrues, Montreal Que H3A 1X9 Canada. **Tel** (514)398-6880, FAX (514)398-8557. **ED** J. Terrasse. **DD** 840/.8. **Pr Rev.**
Desc: A journal of literary theory and criticism.

FR
LITTERATURES POPULAIRES DE TOUTES LES NATIONS, LES. V. 1-47, 1881-1903; New Series, V. 1- 1931-. Monographic series. French. Price varies per volume.

FR/0563-9751
LITTERATURES (TOULOUSE). (LITTERATURES.). [Litteratures]. **Added/Corp** Universit,e de Toulouse-Le Mirail. No. 1 (Spring 1980)-. Periodical. French. sa. 160.00F. L'Universite de Toulouse- Le Mirail, 56 rue Taur, 31000 Toulouse France. **Tel** 33 61 225831, FAX 33 61 218420. **LC** PN3; .L57. **DD** 809. Documents available from The Genuine Article. ***Continues*** *Litteratures (Universite de Toulouse-Le Mirail : 1971).*
Ind/Abst Annu. Bibliogr. Engl. Lang. Lit.; Arts Humanit. Citation Index (19??-19??) [Full Cov.]; Curr. Contents Arts Humanit.; MLA Int. Bibl. Books Artic. Mod. Lang. Lit.; Res. Alert [Full Cov.]; Soc. Sci. Cit. Index [Select. Cov.].

CN/0843-4182
LITTEREALITE. (LITTEREALITE : UNE REVUE D'ECRITS ORIGINAUX ET DE CRITIQUE.). [LitteRealite]. Vol. 1, No 1 (Spring 1989)-. Periodical. French (English). sa. $30.00 (institutions), $25.00 (individuals). York University / Department of Geography, 4700 Keele Street, North York Ontario M3J 1P3 Canada. **Tel** (905)736-2100, FAX (905)736-5103. **ED** Sergio Villani. **DD** 840/.9. Index available. **Bk Rev. Pr Rev. Circ:** 300.

US/0024-5054
LITTLE REVIEW, THE. V. 1- Spring 1969-. Periodical. English. sa. Marshall University / English, Department of English, Huntington WV 25755-2646. **Tel** (304)696-3155. available on microfilm from University Microfilms International (UMI).
Ind/Abst Index Am. Period. Verse.

CC
LIU CHUAN. VFOAT Liuquan. Periodical. Chinese. qt. RMBY1.00. Shan-Tung Sheng Hsin Hua Shu Tien, Chi-Nan, People's Republic of China. **LC** PL2513; .L57. **DD** 895.1/08/005.

US/1062-0087
LIVE LETTERS. [Live lett.]. Vol. 1, Issue 1 (Summer 1991)-. Periodical. English. sa. $36.00 (institutions). Live Letters Press, 156 Hunter Street, Kinston NY 12401. **DD** 808.

UK/0309-3700
LIVERPOOL CLASSICAL MONTHLY : LCM. **See** Antiques.

UK/0261-1538
LIVERPOOL MONOGRAPHS IN HISPANIC STUDIES. [Liverp. monogr. Hisp. stud.]. (1982)-. Monographic series. English. Liverpool University Press, PO Box 147, Liverpool L69 3BX England. **Tel** (051)794 2233, FAX (051)708 6502, telex 627095.
Ind/Abst MLA Int. Bibl. Books Artic. Mod. Lang. Lit.

US
LIVING AUTHOR SERIES. Added/Corp Pan American University. School of Humanities. No. 1 (1978)-. Monographic series. English.
Ind/Abst MLA Int. Bibl. Books Artic. Mod. Lang. Lit.

FR
LIVING HAND. 1- Fall 1973-. English. sa. $2.50. Compton Press, c/o Paul Auster Paris France. **LC** PN6010.5; .L58. **DD** 808.8/004.

XV/0459-6242
LIVRE SLOVENE, LE. [Livre slov.]. **Added/Corp** Drustvo Slovenskih Knjizevnikov. Vol. 1 (May 1963)-. Periodical. French. **LC** PG1900; .A33.
Ind/Abst MLA Int. Bibl. Books Artic. Mod. Lang. Lit.

FR/0223-4289
LIVRES JEUNES AUJOURD'HUI. (1970)-. Periodical. French. Ten times a year (July/Aug. & Sept./Oct. issues combined). 250.00F France; 295.00F others. Union Natl Cult Bibl pour Tous Paris France, 22/26 Rue Jules Vanzuppe, 94200 Ivry sur Seine France. **Tel** 011 33 1 49607663. **ED** M. J. Poisson and M. Tiberghien. **UDC** 016. **Ad Acc, Adv Mgr:** M. J. Cartalel. **Circ:** 3,800.

SP
LLETRA DE CANVI. No. 1 (Nov. 1987)-. Periodical. Catalan. mo. 3100ptas (surface mail) Spain; 3290ptas (surface mail), 3655ptas (airmail) North America; 3290ptas (surface mail), 3475ptas (airmail) other. Montesinos Editor SA, Valencia 290 2DO, 08007 Barcelona Spain. **Tel** 011 34 3 4880591, FAX 011 34 3 4887438. **LC** PN9; .L58. **Bk Rev. Ad Acc.** ctrl circ.
Desc: Articles and reviews about literature, art, theater, etc.
Ind/Abst MLA Int. Bibl. Books Artic. Mod. Lang. Lit.

II
LOCANA (BANGALORE, INDIA). (LOCANA.). **VFOAT** Lochana. Vol. 1, No. 1 (June 1983)-. Periodical. Kannada (Kannada). sa. Rs6.00. B M SRI Memorial Foundation, 54-3rd Cross Gavipuram Extension, Bangalore 560019 India. **LC** PL4650; .L63.

US/0047-4959
LOCUS (CAMBRIDGE, MASS.). (LOCUS.). [Locus]. Issue 1-182, (1968-1975)- Vol. 9, (Jan. 16, 1976)-. Trade Publication. English. Twelve times a year. $41.00 (surface mail); $70.00 Europe & South America, $81.00 Australia & Asia & Africa (airmail); $53.00 others (first class mail). Locus Publications, PO Box 13305, Oakland CA 94661. **Tel** (510)339-9196, FAX (510)339-8144. **ED** Charles N. Brown. Index available. **Bk Rev. Ad Acc. Circ:** 9,000. available on microfilm and microfiche from University Microfilms International (UMI).
Desc: A trade journal for science fiction professionals and interested readers. It covers the publishing industry as well as the literary side.

US
LONDON COLLECTOR, THE. (19??)-. English. an. Wolf House Books, Box 6657, Grand Rapids MI 49506. **LC** PS3523.O46; Z76. **DD** 813/.52.

UK/0024-6085
LONDON MAGAZINE. [Lond. mag.]. Vol. 1-8, (Feb. 1954)-. Periodical. English. Six times a year. £38.00 UK; £43.00 other. World Wide Subscription Services, Unit 4, Gibbs Reed Farm, East Sussex TN5 7HE England. **Tel** (0580)200657, FAX (0580)200616. **ED** Alan Ross. **LC** PR1; .L65. **DD** 820/.8. **Bk Rev. Ad Acc. Circ:** 4,000.
Desc: Literary, arts magazine.
Ind/Abst Annu. Bibliogr. Engl. Lang. Lit.; BHA : Biblio. Hist. Art; Film Lit. Index.

●US/1062-7790
LONE STAR LITERARY QUARTERLY. [Lone Star lit. q.]. **VFOAT** LSLQ. Vol. 1, No. 1 (Winter 1992)-. Periodical. English. qt. $24.95. HL Newsom, PO Box 50270, Austin TX 78763. **DD** 813.

US/8756-5099
LONG POND REVIEW. Added/Corp Suffolk County Community College. English Dept. (19??)-. Periodical. English. be. $5.00. Russ Steinke, Sufford Community College, English Department, Selden Long Island NY 11784. **Tel** (516)451-4110. **ED** Russ Steinke. **LC** PS536.2; .L59. **DD** 810/.8/0054. **Bk Rev. Ad Acc. Circ:** 500.

US/0741-4242
LONG STORY, THE. No. 1 (Spring 1983)-. English. an. $5.00 (regular), $6.00 (library) US; $7.00 (regular), $8.00 (library) other. The Long Story, 11 Kingston Street, North Andover MA 01845. **Tel** (508)686-7638. **ED** R Peter Burnham. **LC** WMLC L 83/400. **Circ:** 450 (ctrl).
Desc: For serious literary people; publishes long stories (8-20,000 words) of various genres, and themes, with a preference for committed fiction.
Ind/Abst Am. Humanit. Index.

US/0893-3898
"LOOKING UP" TIMES, THE. (THE "LOOKING UP" TIMES / BY MAINE SURVIVORS OF INCEST.). [Look. up times]. (1985)-. Periodical. English. Twice a year (May, & Nov.). $25.00. Looking Up, RFD 1 Box 3360, Mt Vernon ME 04352. **Tel** (207)293-2750. **ED** Gayla M. Woodsum. **DD** 810. **Circ:** 3,000 (ctrl).
Desc: Contains miscellaneous literary writings by survivors of incest, on the subject of incest victimization.

ER/0134-4536
LOOMING. Added/Corp Eesti Noukogude Kirjanike Liit. Eesti Kirjanikkude Liit. Eesti Kirjanike Litt. **VFOAT** Tvorchestvo. (1923)-. Periodical. Estonian. mo. $29.50. **(Subscription address:** Victor Kamkin, 4956 Boiling Brook Parkway, Rockville MD 20852.**) LC** AP95.E4; L6.
Ind/Abst MLA Int. Bibl. Books Artic. Mod. Lang. Lit.

US
LOST AND FOUND TIMES. No. 1 (Aug. 1975)-. Periodical. English. Twice a year. $20.00. Luna Bisonte Productions, 137 Leland Avenue, Columbus OH 43214. **ED** John Bennett. **Ad Acc. Circ:** 350.
Desc: Covers avante-garde literature and art.

US/1048-2172
LOST CREEK LETTERS. [Lost Creek lett.]. Spring (1990)-. Periodical. English. qt. $16.00. Lost Creek Publications, RR2 Box 373A, Rushville MO 64484. **Tel** (816)688-7454. **ED** Pamela Montgomery. **DD** 810. **Ad Acc, Adv Mgr:** same as Editor. **Circ:** 150.
Desc: Literary magazine publishing fiction, poetry and cartoons.

US/0091-2948
LOST GENERATION JOURNAL. [Lost gener. j.]. Vol. 1 (May 1973)-. Periodical. English. an. $10.00. Lost Generation Journal Inc., C/O Dr. Wood, Route 5 Box 134, Salem MO 65559. **Tel** (314)729-2545. **ED** Tom Wood and Deloris Wood. **LC** NX504; .L67. **DD** 700/.973. **[CCC]. Bk Rev. Ad Acc.**
Desc: Deals with Americans who went to Paris to start careers between 1919-39. Writers and artists such as expatriates Ray, Hemingway, Pound, and Stein, and many more.
Ind/Abst Abstr. Engl. Stud.; Am. Humanit. Index; Annu. Bibliogr. Engl. Lang. Lit.; Lit. Crit. Regist.; MLA Int. Bibl. Books Artic. Mod. Lang. Lit.

UA/0002-0664
LOTUS (CAIRO). (LOTUS.). [Lotus]. **Added/Corp** Permanent Bureau of Afro-Asian Writers. **VFOAT** Lutus. No. 6 (Oct. 1970)-. Periodical. English (French and Arabic). qt. Permanent Bureau of Afro-Asian Writers, 104 Sharia Kasr El-Aini, Cairo Egypt. **LC** PN2; .A47. **DD** 808.8/004. ***Continues*** *Afro-Asian Writings, 0568-1928.*
Desc: Modern literature.
Ind/Abst Acad. Ind. [Computer File] (1992-); Expand. Acad. Index (1992-); MLA Int. Bibl. Books Artic. Mod. Lang. Lit.

US/0890-0477
LOUISIANA LITERATURE. (LOUISIANA LITERATURE : LA LIT / SOUTHEASTERN LOUISIANA UNIVERSITY.). [La. lit.]. **Added/Corp** Southeastern Louisiana University. Dept. of English. **VFOAT** La Lit. (1984)-. Periodical. English. Twice a year (May & Dec.). $10.00 (individuals), 12.50 (institutions). Southeastern Louisiana University / Louisiana Literature, PO Box 792, Hammond LA 70402. **Tel** (504)549-5022. **ED** Larry Gray. **DD** 810.
Ind/Abst Am. Humanit. Index (199?-); MLA Int. Bibl. Books Artic. Mod. Lang. Lit.

US/0148-3250
LOUISVILLE REVIEW, THE. Added/Corp University of Louisville. No. 1 (Fall 1976)-. Periodical. English. Twice a year. $8.00. University of Louisville Department of English, Louisville KY 40298. **Tel** (502)852-6801. **ED** Sena Naslund. **LC** PS501; .L68. **DD**

Literature

810/.8/0054. **Circ:** 500 (ctrl).
 Desc: A poetry and fiction magazine that includes new and previously published writers.

CN/0227-5449
LOVE MAKES THE WORLD GO AWRY. [Love makes world go awry]. No. 1- Periodical. English. qt. $2.00. Fran Skene, 207 West 21st Avenue, Vancouver BC V5Y 2E4 Canada. **DD** C813/.5403.

US/0899-8361
LOVECRAFT STUDIES. [Lovecraft stud.]. Vol. 1, (Fall 1979)-. Periodical. English. Twice a year (Apr., Oct.). $10.00. Necronomicon Press, 101 Lockwood Street, West Warwick RI 02893. **Tel** (401)828-5319. **ED** S. T. Joshi. **DD** 813. **Bk Rev**, (Qty: 5-10). **Circ:** 500.
 Desc: About the life, work and writings of H. P. Lovecraft.
 Ind/Abst MLA Int. Bibl. Books Artic. Mod. Lang. Lit.; Sci. Fict. Fantasy Book Rev. Index.

CC
LU HSUN YEN CHIU NIEN KAN / HSI PEI TA HSUEH LU HSUN YEN CHIU SHIH PIEN. VFOAT Annual of Lu Xun Study. 1979-. Chinese. an. RMBY3.00. Science Press, 16 Donghuangchenggen North Street, Beijing 100707, People's Republic of China. **Tel** 011 86 1 4019821, 011 86 1 4010642, FAX 011 86 1 4012180, 011 86 1 4019810, telex 210147. **LC** PL2754.S5; Z753764. **DD** 895.1/35.

CC
LU HSUN YEN CHIU TZU LIAO / PEI-CHING LU HSUN PO WU KUAN, LU HSUEN YEN CHIU SHIH PIEN. VFOAT Luxun Yanjiu Ziliao. Chinese. RMBY1.00. Hsin Hua Shu Tien / Tien-Chin, Tien-Chin Shih, People's Republic of China. **LC** PL2754.S5; Z753766. **DD** 895.1/35.

CC
LU HSUN YEN CHIU WEN TSUNG. VFOAT Luxun Yanjiu Wencong. 1 (March 1980)-. Periodical. Chinese. Four times a year. RMBY1.08. Hunan Renmin Chubanshe, Yin Pen Nan Lu, Changsha, People's Republic of China. **Tel** 83389, telex 3652. **ED** Huang Renpei. **LC** PL2754.S5; Z7539. **DD** 895.1/35.

US/0891-1444
LUA MI. (LUS MI.). [Lua mi]. (1986)-. Periodical. Vietnamese. bm. Lsua Msi Magazine, PO Box 1366, Orange CA 92668. **DD** 895.

RM/0458-435X
LUCEAFARUL. Added/Corp Uniunea Scriitorilor din Republica Populara Romina. Vol. 1 (1958)-. Periodical. Romanian. wk. DM217.00. **(Subscription address:** Kubon & Sagner, ABT Zeitschriftenimport, D 80328 Munich Germany.**)**
 Ind/Abst Annu. Bibliogr. Engl. Lang. Lit.; MLA Int. Bibl. Books Artic. Mod. Lang. Lit.

US/1051-5968
LULLWATER REVIEW. [Lullwater rev.]. **Added/Corp** Emory University. Vol. 1, No. 1 (Spring 1990)-. Periodical. English. sa. $10.00. Lullwater Review, Emory University, PO Box 22036, Atlanta GA 30322. **DD** 810.
 Ind/Abst Am. Humanit. Index (199?-).

CN/0709-8030
LULU REVU. [Lulu revu]. No. 1- July 1978-. Periodical. English. ir. $4.00 per 6 issues. Pubbug Press Publications, 11220 Bird Road, Richmond British Columbia V6X 1N8 Canada. **DD** 813/.0876.

CN
LUMEN. English. an. 28.95Can$ Canada; 32.95Can$ others. Academic Printing and Publishing, PO Box 4218, South Edmonton, Alberta T6E 4T2 Canada. **Tel** (403)435-5898.

CN/1184-8626
LUMIERE D'ENCRE. [Lumiere encre]. **Added/Corp** Regroupement des Ecrivains de l'Abitibi-Temiscamingue. Vol. 7, No. 1 (Feb. 1991)-. Periodical. French. ir. Free for members; 28.50Can$ per year other. Regroupement des Ecrivains de L'Abitibi-Temiscamingue, CP 53, Val D'OR Quebec J9P 4N9 Canada. **DD** C840.8/09714/13. **Continues** Bulletin du Regroupement des Ecrivains de l'Abitibi-Temiscamingue., 0838-1488.

SW/0076-1451
LUND STUDIES IN ENGLISH. See Linguistics.

FR
LUVAH. No. 1, (Dec. 1982)-. Periodical. French. qt. 100. **LC** PQ1141; .L88. **DD** 840/.8.

US/0897-9715
LYCEUM TIMES, THE. (THE LYCEUM TIMES : THE OFFICIAL JOURNAL OF THE PEDANTIC LYCEUM OF HERESY, ANARCHY, AND CROQUET.). [Lyceum times]. Vol. 1, No. 1 (Nov. 1987)-. Periodical. English. bm. $5.00. The Pedantic Lyceum for Heresy, Anarchy, and Croquet, 1112 McGee/Suite C, Norman OK 73069. **DD** 810.

US/0897-6716
LYRA (GUTTENBERG, N.J.). (LYRA.). (1987)-. Periodical. English. qt. $10.00 (individuals), $15.00 (institutions). Lyra Inc, PO Box 3188, Guttenberg NJ 07093. **DD** 810.
 Ind/Abst Index Am. Period. Verse.

SW/0460-0762
LYRIKVANNEN. [Lyrikvannen]. Began in 1954. Periodical. Swedish. bm. Lyrikvannen, Box 130, S 101 21 Stockholm Sweden. cum. index.
 Ind/Abst Annu. Bibliogr. Engl. Lang. Lit.; MLA Int. Bibl. Books Artic. Mod. Lang. Lit.

NE/0024-8851
MAATSTAF. See Linguistics.

US/1049-9776
MACHIAVELLI STUDIES. [Machiavelli stud.]. **Added/Corp** International Machiavelli Society. Vol 1 (1987)-. English (Italian). an. $15.00 (individuals), $25.00 (institutions). University of New Orleans / Foreign Language Dept., Foreign Language Department, New Orleans LA 70148. **Tel** (504)286-6657. **ED** Edmund Jacobitti and Victor A Santi. **LC** PQ4627.M2; Z4585. **DD** 320.1/092. **Bk Rev**, (Qty: 3). **Circ:** 250.
 Desc: Contains articles on any aspect of Machiavelli Scholarship, book reviews, debates, and bibliographies.

US/1054-2655
MAD RIVER. (MAD RIVER : A JOURNAL OF ESSAYS.). [Mad river]. **Added/Corp** Wright State University. No. 1 (Winter 1991)-. Periodical. English. Three times a year. $18.00. Mad River, Department of Philosophy, Wright State University, Dayton OH 45435. **DD** 814.

II
MADHUMATI. Periodical. Hindi. mo. Rs10.00. Rajasthan Sahitya Akademi Sangam, Udayapura India. **LC** PK2103.R3; M28.

US
MADISON REVIEW, THE. (1979)-. Periodical. English. Twice a year. $10.00. Madison Review / Department of English, 600 North Park Street / White Hall, Madison WI 53706. **Tel** (608)263-3800. **ED** Melissa Klein, Mark Emerson. **Ad Acc. Circ:** 1,500.

US/0890-6890
MAGAZINE (ABINGTON, PA.). (MAGAZINE.). [Magazine]. **Added/Corp** Pennsylvania College English Association. Vol. 1, Iss. 1/2 (1989)-. Periodical. English. sa. $5.00. Pennsylvania College English Association, Penn State Erie, The Behrend College, Division of Humanities and Social Sciences, Station Road, Erie PA 16563. **DD** 810.
 Ind/Abst MLA Int. Bibl. Books Artic. Mod. Lang. Lit.

FR/0024-9807
MAGAZINE LITTERAIRE. [Mag. litt.]. (Nov. 1966)-. Periodical. French. mo (except July). 305.00F France; 410.00F (surface mail), 530.00F (air mail) other. Magazine Litteraire, 40 rue des Saints-Peres, 75007 Paris France. **Tel** 011 33 1 45441451, FAX 011 33 1 45488636. **LC** PN3; .M33. **DD** 809. Index available. **Bk Rev. Ad Acc. Circ:** 75,000.
 Ind/Abst Point Repere (1983-); Sci. Fict. Fantasy Book Rev. Index.

IE
MAGILL ANNUAL. English. Magill, 14 Merrion Row, Dublin 2 Ireland. **Tel** 610133. **LC** AP4; .M215. **DD** 052.

CN/0702-6803
MAGOOK. No. 1- Oct. 29 1977-. Periodical. English. ir. $1.95 per no. Magook Publishers Ltd., 254 Bartley Drive, Toronto Ontario M4A 1G1 Canada. **DD** C810/.8/09282.

AT/0817-0088
MAGPIES. (198?)-. Periodical. English. Five times a year. 26.30Aus$ (metro), 26.75Aus$ (country) Western Australia; 27.80Aus$ (City Capitol metro), 28.45Aus$ (country) other states; 35.50Aus$ (New Zealand). Magpies Magazine, 10 Armagh Street, Victoria Park Western Australia 6100 Australia. **Tel** 011 61 9 4721355, FAX 011 61 9 3618295.
 Ind/Abst Aust. Educ. Index; Aust. Libr. Inf. Sci. Abstr.; Book Rev. Index; Child. Lit. Abstr. (19??-).

HU/0541-9298
MAGYAR NYELVJARASOK. [M. nyelvj.]. V. 1- 1951-. Hungarian (summaries and/or abstracts in English, French, German and Russian). an. **ED** G Barczi. **LC** PH2701; .M3. **Supersedes** Magyar Nepnyelv.
 Ind/Abst MLA Int. Bibl. Books Artic. Mod. Lang. Lit.

II
MAHANADI REVIEW, THE. Periodical. English. qt. Mahanadi Books, Mansingpatna Math Lane, Cuttack 753008 India. **LC** PR9494; .M33. **DD** 891/.1/05.

IS/0333-838X
MAHUT. Added/Corp Mekhon Haberman le-Mehkere Sifrut. **VFOAT** Journal of Jewish Literature & Art. (1989)-. Hebrew. Agudat Zehut, POB 1544, Ramat Gan 52-115 Israel. **LC** PJ5001; .Z44. **Continues** Zehut.

GW/0170-9135
MAINZER STUDIEN ZUR AMERIKANISTIK. [Mainz. Stud. Am.]. (1972)-. Monographic series. German. ir. **UDC** 802.0 + 820.
 Ind/Abst MLA Int. Bibl. Books Artic. Mod. Lang. Lit.

II
MAITHILI AKADAMI PATRIKA. See Linguistics.

CN/0025-1216
MALAHAT REVIEW, THE. [Malahat rev.]. **Added/Corp** University of Victoria (B.C.). No. 1 (Jan. 1967)-. Periodical. English. Four times a year (Mar., June, Sept., Dec.). 25.00Can$ US & Canada; 30.00Can$ others. The Malahat Review, University of Victoria, PO Box 3045, Victoria BC V8W 3P4 Canada. **Tel** (604)721-8524. **ED** Constance Rooke and Marlene Cookshaw. **DD** 808.8'004. **Bk Rev. Ad Acc. Circ:** 1,800 (ctrl).
 Desc: A "generalist" literary magazine, open to all schools of writing and not espousing any particular ideology or aesthetic; publishes mainly poetry and fiction with a mix of new and celebrated writers. Each issue includes a substantial review section. Meticulously edited and features the work of gifted visual artists.
 Ind/Abst Abstr. Engl. Stud.; Am. Humanit. Index (1985-1986); Annu. Bibliogr. Engl. Lang. Lit.; Can. Index; Can. Period. Index (19??-); Index Am. Period. Verse; MLA Int. Bibl. Books Artic. Mod. Lang. Lit.

MW
MALAWIAN WRITERS SERIES. Began publication in 1974. Monographic series. English. ir (three or four issues per year). Price varies per volume. Popular Publications / Malawi, PO Box 5592, Limbe Malawi. **ED** Allan E Ulanga. **Bk Rev. Ad Acc. Circ:** 2,000 (ctrl).
 Desc: Covers plays, shot stories, poems and novels in both English and Chichewa.

US/1062-9173
MALCONTENT, THE. [Malcontent]. (1991)-. Periodical. English. The Malcontent, Ed Hoyer, Jr., Periodicals Department, Hilton C Buley Library, Southern Connecticut State University, 501 Crescent Street, New Haven CT 06515. **DD** 810.

UY
MALDOROR. (1967)-. Periodical. Spanish. ir. **LC** PQ8510; .A29.
 Ind/Abst HAPI Hisp. Am. Period. Index.

US/0737-8688
MALINI. See Ethnic Interests.

UK/0308-6674
MALLORN. [Mallorn]. **Added/Corp** Tolkien Society (England). (1971)-. Periodical. English. an. £17.00 UK; £18.00 other. Tolkien Society, Flat 5 357 High Street, Cheltenham GL GL50 3HT England. **Tel** 0242 577232. **ED** Patrica Reynolds. **LC** WMLC 93/356. **Bk Rev. Ad Acc. Circ:** 700 (ctrl).
 Desc: Dedicated to prompt research and educating the public in the life and works of Professor J R R Tolkien.
 Ind/Abst Child. Lit. Abstr. (19??-); MLA Int. Bibl. Books Artic. Mod. Lang. Lit.

FJ
MANA. Added/Corp South Pacific Creative Arts Society. Vol. 2 (Oct. 1977)-. Periodical. English. sa. $8.00. South Pacific Creative Arts Society, Box 1168, Institute Pacific Studies / USP, Suva Fiji Islands. **Tel** 011 679 313900. **ED** Marjorie Crocombe. **Bk Rev. Continues** Mana Review.
 Desc: Poetry, short stories, reviews, literary criticism, and plays, etc.
 Ind/Abst MLA Int. Bibl. Books Artic. Mod. Lang. Lit.

PO/0377-1164
MANA ANNUAL OF CREATIVE WRITING, THE. Added/Corp South Pacific Creative Arts Society. (1973)-. English. an. Fiji South Pacific Creative Arts Society, Box 5083, Suva Fiji. **LC** DU1; .M35. **DD** 990.

II
MANASABHARATI : SRI RAMACARITAMANASA CATUSSATABDI SAMAROHA SAMITI, MADHYAPRADESA, BHOPALA KI MASIKA MUKHAPATRIKA. Periodical. Hindi (Hindi). mo. 30.-. Gandhi Bhavan Shamala Hills, Bhopal 462002 India. **Tel** 73837. **ED** Gorelal Shukla. **LC** PK1947.9.T83; R33525. **Bk Rev. Ad Acc. Circ:** 2,300. **Continues** Manasa Samacara.
 Desc: Devoted to study and appreciation of the legend of Ramchandra as sung in Sanskrit and other languages against the backdrop of Indian culture.

CC
MANG CHUNG. VFOAT Mang Zhong. Periodical. Chinese. mo. RMBY0.35. Science Press, 16 Donghuangchenggen North Street, Beijing 100707, People's Republic of China. **Tel** 011 86 1 4019821, 011 86 1 4010642, FAX 011 86 1 4012180, 011 86 1 4019810, telex 210147. **LC** PL2303; .M27. **DD** 895.1/09/005.

Literature

II/0304-1247
MANJARI. [Manjari]. English (English). an. 3.00. A Sen, B-42 Panchshila Enclave, New Delhi, 110017 India. **LC** PK2047; .M36. **DD** 891/.43/05.

FR/0025-2492
MANTEIA. No. 1 (1967)-. Periodical. French.

NP
MANTHANA (KATHMANDU, NEPAL). (MANTHANA.). (19??)-. Periodical. Nepali. bm. $6.00. Lajimpat, Post Box 1766, Kathmandu 711000 Nepal. **LC** PK2598.A2; M32.

RM/1010-5492
MANUSCRIPTUM. (MANUSCRIPTUM : REVISTA TRIMESTRIALA EDITATA DE MUZEUL LITERATURII ROMANE.). [Manuscriptum]. **Added/Corp** Muzeul Literaturii Romane (Romania). Vol. 1, No. 1 (1970)-. Periodical. Romanian. qt. DM169.00. **(Subscription address:** Kubon & Sagner, ABT Zeitschriftenimport, D 80328 Munich Germany.) **LC** PC800; .M35.
Ind/Abst Annu. Bibliogr. Engl. Lang. Lit.; MLA Int. Bibl. Books Artic. Mod. Lang. Lit.

AU/0025-2638
MANUSKRIPTE. (19??)-. Periodical. German. Four times a year. S315.00. Forum Stadtpark Graz, Stadtpark 1, Camera Austria, A-8010 Graz Austria. **Tel** 011 43 316 827734, 825369, FAX 011 43 316 8253696. **ED** Alfred Kolleritsch. **LC** PT1141.A2; M35. **Ad Acc. Circ:** 3,500 (ctrl).
Desc: Previously unpublished works in literature mostly of young authors.

MX
MARGENES (PUEBLA, MEXICO). (MARGENES.). Periodical. Spanish. qt. $6.00. Escuela de Filosofia Y Letras, 3 Ote 403, Puebla Mexico. **LC** PN6; .M37. **DD** 808.8.

US
MARGIN : A QUARTERLY MAGAZINE FOR IMAGINATIVE WRITING AND IDEAS. English. 46 Shepart Street #42, Cambridge MA 02138. **ED** Robin Magowan and James Magowan.
Ind/Abst Am. Humanit. Index (-199?); Index Am. Period. Verse.

US/0897-9286
MARION ZIMMER BRADLEY'S FANTASY MAGAZINE. [Marion Zimmer Bradley's fantasy mag.]. (Summer 1988)-. Periodical. English. Four times a year (Jan., Apr., July, Oct.). $21.25. Marion Zimmer Bradley Ltd., PO Box 249, Berkeley CA 94701. **Tel** (510)601-9000. **(Subscription address:** P.O. Box 11095, Piedmont, CA 94611) **ED** Marion Zimmer Bradley. **DD** 810. **Ad Acc, Adv Mgr:** Rachel Holman, **Tel** (510)644-9222. **Circ:** 3,000.
Desc: This is original fantasy short stories. Included are editoral's on the writings, and interviews with the fantasy writer's.

US/1060-3409
MARJORIE KINNAN RAWLINGS JOURNAL OF FLORIDA LITERATURE, THE. [Marjorie Kinnan Rawlings j. Fla. lit.]. **Added/Corp** Marjorie Kinnan Rawlings Society. **VFOAT** Journal of Florida Literature. Vol. 2 (1989/1990)-. English. an. $10.00 (institutions), $5.00 (individual). Illinois State University / English, Department of English, Normal IL 61761-6901. **Tel** (309)438-5776. **ED** Rodger L. Tarr. **LC** PS3535.A845; Z4587. **DD** 813/.52. **Bk Rev. Ad Acc. Pr Rev. Circ:** 450. **Continues** Rawlings Journal, 1052-7583.

US/1042-5357
MARK TWAIN CIRCULAR. [Mark Twain circ.]. **Added/Corp** Mark Twain Circle. Vol. 1, No. 1 (Jan. 1987)-. Periodical. English. Four times a year. comes with Mark Twain Journal. Mark Twain Journal, English Department, Charleston College, Charleston SC 29424. **Tel** (803)723-0487. **LC** PS1329; .M28. **DD** 818/.409.
Ind/Abst Am. Humanit. Index (199?-).

US/0272-6378
MARK TWAIN SOCIETY BULLETIN. [Mark Twain Soc. bull.]. **Added/Corp** Mark Twain Society (Elmira, N.Y.). Vol. 1, No. 1, Feb. (1978)-. Bulletin. English. Twice a year (January and July). $5.00. Mark Twain Society, PO Box 3225, Elmira NY 14905. **Tel** (607)734-6943. **ED** Herbert Wisbey and Robert Jerome. **LC** PS1329; .M34. **DD** 818/.409. Index available. cum. index. **Bk Rev,** (Qty: 1). **Circ:** 225 (ctrl)
Desc: Mark Twain material.

US/1045-4292
MARTHA'S KIDLIT NEWSLETTER. See Children and Youth Interests.

US/0892-807X
MARYLAND POETRY REVIEW (BROOKLANDVILLE, MD.). See Literature-Poetry.

GW
MARZBLATT. German. Literarisches Infozentrum, Bahnhofstrasse 24, 4250 Bottrop Germany. **LC** PT1141.A2; M32.

AU/0025-4606
MASKE UND KOTHURN. [Maske Kothurn]. **Added/Corp** Universitaet Wien. Institut fuer Theaterwissenschaft. Vol. 1 (1955)-. Periodical. English (German). ir. S980.00. Boehlau Verlag GmbH & Co KG, Sachsenplatz 4 6 PF 87, A 1201 Vienna Austria. **Tel** 011 43 222 3302427. **(Subscription telephone:** 011 43 1 3302433) **LC** PN2004; .M36.
Ind/Abst MLA Int. Bibl. Books Artic. Mod. Lang. Lit.; Romant. Move.

US
MASTERPLOTS II. (19??)-. English. an. $1295.00. EBSCO Publishing / Boston, 83 Pine Street, Peabody MA 01960. **Tel** (800)653-2726 North America, (508)535-8500, FAX (508)535-8545. Index available. **Pr Rev.**
Desc: Masterplots II, used together with its companion works, allows you to access a wealth of information about an individual book, a particular author or genre.

RU
MASTERSKAIA. Vol. 1 (1975)-. Russian. 0.28rub. Izdatelstvo Molodaia Gvardiia, Novodmitrovskaya Ul., 5A, 125015 Moscow Russia. **Tel** 095-285-0830. **LC** PN145; .M39.

NE/0932-9714
MATATU. (1987)-. Periodical. English (French, German and Portuguese). Twice a year. Fl80.00 (institutions); Fl45.00 (individuals). Éditions Rodopi BV, Keizersgracht 302-304, 1016 Ex Amsterdam Netherlands. **Tel** 011 31 20 6227507, FAX 011 31 20 380948. **ED** Holger E. Ghling, Geoffrey V. Davis, and Frank Schulze-Engler. **LC** DT1; .M35. **CODEN** MAATEP. **Bk Rev. Ad Acc. Pr Rev. Circ:** 700 (ctrl).
Ind/Abst MLA Int. Bibl. Books Artic. Mod. Lang. Lit.; Soc. Plann. Policy Dev. Abstr.

IT
MATERIALI E CONTRIBUTI PER LA STORIA DELLA NARRATIVA GRECO-LATINA. See Linguistics.

II
MATIPANI. VFOAT Mati Pani. Periodical. Maithili (Maithili). mo. 22.00. Bhavani Prakashan, Mudlidhar Press Musallapur, Patna 800006 India. **LC** PK1818.45; .M37.

CN/0318-3610
MATRIX (LENNOXVILLE). (MATRIX.). [Matrix (Lennoxv.)]. **Added/Corp** Champlain Regional College. Lennoxville Campus. Dept. of English. Vol. 1 (Spring 1975)-. Periodical. English. Three times a year. 22.00Can$ (institutions), 15.00Can$ (individuals) Canada; 27.00Can$ (institutions), 20.00Can$ (individuals) US; 30.00Can$ (institutions), 23.00Can$ (individuals) other. Linda Leith, CP 100St Anne de Bellevue, Quebec H9X 3L4 Canada. **Tel** (514)426-8654, FAX (514)426-8658. **ED** Linda Leith and Kenneth Radu. **DD** C810/.8/0054. **Bk Rev,** (Qty: 30-40). **Ad Acc, Adv Mgr:** Beryl Parker or Linda Leith. **Circ:** 2,000. available on microfilm from Micromedia Limited; available on microfiche from Micromedia Limited; available on an online database from Micromedia Limited.
Desc: Includes opinionated articles on film, theatre, photography, art, a substantial review section, plus translations, travel writing, interviews, original fiction and poetry.
Ind/Abst Can. Index; Can. Lit. Index (1985-1986); Can. Period. Index (1989-); Curr. Contents Life Sci.

US/0742-9738
MAWA REVIEW. (MAWA REVIEW : QUARTERLY PUBLICATION OF THE MIDDLE ATLANTIC WRITERS ASSOCIATION.). [MAWA rev.]. **Added/Corp** Middle Atlantic Writers' Association (U.S.). **VFOAT** M.A.W.A. Review. Vol. 1, No. 1 (Spring 1982)-. Periodical. English. sa. $10.00 (U.S.), $12.50 (Canada). MAWA Review, 2400 Montebello Terrace, Baltimore MD 21214. **LC** PS153.N5; M28.
Ind/Abst MLA Int. Bibl. Books Artic. Mod. Lang. Lit.

II/0303-3066
MAYA MARATHI. [Maya Marathi]. **VFOAT** Mai Marathi. Periodical. Marathi. mo. Rs20.00. Brhanmaharashtra Mandala, Pahad Ganj, Navi Dilli India. **LC** PK2400; .M34.

IE
MAYNOOTH REVIEW, THE. Added/Corp St. Patrick's College (Maynooth, Ireland). **VFOAT** Reiviu Mha Nuad. Vol. 1, No. 1 (June 1975)-. Periodical. English. sa. **Ind/Abst** MLA Int. Bibl. Books Artic. Mod. Lang. Lit.

PO
MEA VILLA : REVISTA DA BIBLIOTECA PUBLICA MUNICIPAL DE V.N. DE GAIA. No. 1 (July 1985)-. Periodical. Portuguese. **LC** PQ9000; .M4. **DD** 869.09/946915.

AT/0815-953X
MEANJIN (PARKVILLE, VIC.). (MEANJIN.). [Meanjin]. **Added/Corp** University of Melbourne. (1977)-. Periodical. English. qt. 30.00Aus$ Australia; 40.00Aus$ other. University of Melbourne / Meanjin, 99 Barry Street, Parkville 3052 VIC Australia. **Tel** 011 61 3 3446950, FAX (03)344-5104. **ED** Jenny Lee. **LC** AP7; .M4. Index available. cum. index. **Bk Rev. Ad Acc. Circ:** 3,000. available on microfiche. Documents available from The Genuine Article. **Continues** Meanjin Quarterly.
Desc: Australian writing: fiction, poetry, reviews, essays on culture, history, politics, literature and the arts. A journal of writing and discussion of a broad range of Australian cultural concerns.
Ind/Abst Abstr. Engl. Stud.; Annu. Bibliogr. Engl. Lang. Lit.; APAIS, Aust. Public Aff. Inf. Ser. (1977-); Arts Humanit. Citation Index [Full Cov.]; Book Rev. Index; Curr. Contents Arts Humanit.; MLA Int. Bibl. Books Artic. Mod. Lang. Lit.; Res. Alert [Full Cov.]; Soc. Plann. Policy Dev. Abstr.; Soc. Sci. Cit. Index [Select. Cov.].

CN/0076-5872
MEDIAEVAL STUDIES. See History(General)-History of Europe.

GW
MEDIEN IN FORSCHUNG + UNTERRICHT. SERIE A. VFOAT Medien in Forschung und Unterricht. Serie A. (1980)-. Monographic series. German. ir. Price varies per volume. Max Niemeyer Verlag, Postfach 2140, D 72011 Tuebingen Germany. **Tel** 011 49 7071 989494, FAX 011 49 7071 87419. **ED** Dieter Baacke, Wolfgang Gast, Erich Strassner.
Ind/Abst MLA Int. Bibl. Books Artic. Mod. Lang. Lit.

US
MEDIEVAL ACADEMY BOOKS.
Added/Corp Medieval Academy of America. No. 90 (1980)-. Monographic series. English. ir. Price varies per volume. Medieval Academy of America, 1430 Massachusetts Avenue, Cambridge MA 02138. **Tel** (617)491-1622. **Continues** Mediaeval Academy Books.

UK/0025-8385
MEDIUM AEVUM. See Linguistics.

SW
MEDLEMSFORTECKNING. Main/Corp Sveriges Forfattarforbund. Swedish. Box 5252, 102 45 5 Stockholm Sweden. **LC** PT9205.S85; A25.

AG
MEGAFON. Suspended. Added/Corp Centro de Estudios Latinoamericanos (Argentina). Vol. 1, No. 1 (July 1975)-?. Periodical. Spanish. sa. $25.00. Fernado Garcia Cambeiro, Cochabamba 244, 1150 Buenos Aires Argentina. **Tel** (541)361-0473. **LC** F1408.3; .M426. **DD** 980/.005. **Bk Rev. Ad Acc. Circ:** 500.
Desc: Literary criticism, poetry, fiction, philosophical essays, etc. from Argentina and Latin America.
Ind/Abst HAPI Hisp. Am. Period. Index (19??-).

IS/0333-7030
MEHKERE YERUSHALAYIM BE-FOLKLOR YEHUDI / HA-UNIVERSITAH HA-IVRIT BI-YERUSHALAYIM, HA-FAKULTAH LE-MADAE HA-RUAH, HA-MAKHON LE-MADAE HA-YAHADUT. See Folklore.

IS/0333-693X
MEHKERE YERUSHALAYIM BE-SIFRUT IVRIT / HA-UNIVERSITAH HA-IVRIT BI-YERUSHALAYIM, HA-FAKULTAH LE-MADAE HA-RUAH, HA-MAKHON LE-MADAE HA-YAHADUT. **Added/Corp** Universitah ha-Ivrit bi-Yerushalayim. Makhon le-Madae ha-Yahadut. **VFOAT** Jerusalem Studies in Hebrew Literature. (1981)-. Periodical. Hebrew. ir. price varies per volume. Magnes Press, Hebrew University of Jerusalem, PO Box 7695, Jerusalem 91076 Israel. **Tel** 011 972 2 660341, 011 972 2 635691, FAX 011 972 2 633370, telex 25391. **LC** PJ5001; .M43 Hebr.

AT
MELBURNER BLETER. Added/Corp Jewish National Library and Cultural Centre "Kadimah". **VFOAT** Melbourne Chronicle. No. 1- Dec. (1975)-. Periodical. Multiple languages (English and Yiddish). an. 12.00Aus$. Jewish Cultural Centre and National Library, "Kadimah", 7 Selwyn Street Elsternwick, Victoria 3185, Melbourne Australia. **Tel** 523-9817, FAX 523-6161. **ED** Dr. Serge Libermanan--English, Moishe Ajzenbud--Yiddish. **LC** DS101; .M42. **Bk Rev,** (Qty: 3). **Ad Acc. Circ:** 1,000.
Desc: Independent cultural social periodical, promoting various aspects of Jewish culture with special emphasis on Yiddish language. Creative writing in both Yiddish and English is included.

PE
MELIBEA. Yearly V. 1- Nov. 1975-. Spanish. Casimiro Ulloa 125, Lima Peru. **LC** F3401; .M45. **DD** 056/.1.

US/0163-755X
MELUS. (MELUS; SOCIETY FOR THE STUDY OF THE MULTI-ETHNIC LITERATURE OF THE UNITED STATES.). [Melus]. **Added/Corp** Society for the Study of the Multi-Ethnic Literature of the United States. **VAT** Multi-Ethnic Literature of the United States. (Sept. 1974)-. Academic Scholarly Publication. English. Four times a year (Mar., June, Sept., Dec.). $40.00 US & Canada; $48.00 other. MELUS, Department of English, 272 Bartlett Hall, University of Massachusetts, Amherst MA 01003. **Tel** (413)545-3166. **ED** Joseph T. Skerrett Jr. **LC** PN843; .M18. **DD** 808.8/9973. Index available. **Bk Rev. Ad Acc. Pr Rev. Circ:** 750. available on microfilm and microfiche from University Microfilms International (UMI). Documents available from UMI Article Clearinghouse.
Desc: Literature, folklore, poetry, fiction, autobiography, film by and about ethnic Americans, both races of immigrant groups is the focus of the scholarly and critical articles.
Ind/Abst Abstr. Anthropol.; Abstr. Engl. Stud.; Acad. Search (July 1993-); Am. Bibliogr. Slavic East Europ. Stud. (19??-19??); Am. Humanit. Index; Annu. Bibliogr. Engl. Lang. Lit.; Expand. Acad. Index (1988-); Humanit. Index; Humanit. Source (Jul. 1993-); INFO-SOUTH Abstr.; Mag. Search; MLA Int. Bibl. Books Artic. Mod. Lang. Lit.; Newsp. Period. Abstr. (1989-).

US/0193-8991
MELVILLE SOCIETY EXTRACTS. [Melville Soc. extr.]. **Main/Corp** Melville Society. **Added/Corp** Melville Society. **VFOAT** Extracts. No. 34 (May 1978)-. Periodical. English. Four times a year (Feb., May, Sept., Nov.). $7.00 (individuals); $10.00 (institutions). Melville Society Extracts, Salisbury State University, Treasurer John Wenke, Salisbury MD 21801. **Tel** (410)543-6445. **ED** John Bryant. **LC** PS2386; .A14. Index available (Every 6 years). cum. index. **Bk Rev**, (Qty: 4). **Pr Rev. Circ:** 800 (ctrl). ***Continues*** *Extracts - Melville Society, 0193-7626.*
Desc: Life, times and writings of the American author Herman Melville (1819-1891).
Ind/Abst Abstr. Engl. Stud.; Am. Humanit. Index; Lit. Crit. Regist.; MLA Int. Bibl. Books Artic. Mod. Lang. Lit.

BE
MEMOIRES DE LA CLASSE DES LETTRES. COLLECTION IN-8. Added/Corp Academie Royale des Sciences, des Lettres et des Beaux-Arts de Belgique. Classe des Beaux-Arts. Academie Royale des Sciences, des Lettres et des Beaux-Arts de Belgique. Classe des Lettres et des Sciences Morales et Politiques. **VFOAT** Memoires de la Classe des Lettres. Collection In-Octavo. (1906)-. Monographic series. French. Academie Royale des Sciences d'Outre-Mer, BP 3, 1 rue Defacqz, B-1050 Brussels, Belgium. cum. index.

RM
MEMORIILE SECTIEI DE STIINTE FILOLOGICE, LITERATURA SI ARTE. See Linguistics.

US/0025-9233
MENCKENIANA. [Menckeniana]. **Added/Corp** Enoch Pratt Free Library. No. 1 (Spring 1962)-. Periodical. English. qt. $12.00 US; $15.00 other. Enoch Pratt Library Publications, 400 Cathedral Street, Baltimore MD 21201. **Tel** (410)396-5305. **ED** Charles A. Fecher. **LC** PS3525.E43; Z69. available on microfilm and microfiche from University Microfilms International (UMI).
Ind/Abst Abstr. Engl. Stud.; Am. Humanit. Index; Annu. Bibliogr. Engl. Lang. Lit.; MLA Int. Bibl. Books Artic. Mod. Lang. Lit.

CC
MENG YA. Added/Corp Chung-Kuo Tso Chia Hsieh Hui. Shang-hai Fen Gui. **VFOAT** Mengya. (1956)-. Periodical. Chinese. Twelve times a year. $16.00. **(Subscription address:** China International Book Trading Corporation, PO Box 399, Library Service Department, Beijing 100044 People's Republic of China.**) LC** PL2250; .M44. ***Absorbed*** *Chun Chung Wen i (Shang-Hai, China); Chieh Tou Wen I* ***and*** *Kung Jen Hsi Tso.*
Desc: Covers Chinese literature.

US
MERIDIANO 70 I.E. SETENTA. No. 1- Autumn 1975-. Periodical. Spanish (English). sa. $3.00. Meridiano 70 Batts Hall 112, University of Texas, Austin TX 78712. **LC** PQ6001; .M48. **DD** 860/.8/0064.

US/0898-154X
MERVEILLES & CONTES. (MERVEILLES & CONTES / MARVELS & TALES / WUNDER & MAERCHEN / MARAVILLAS & CUENTOS / MERAVIGLIE & RACCONTI.). [Merveilles contes]. **Added/Corp** University of Colorodo, Boulder. College of Arts and Sciences. **VFOAT** Merveilles et Contes; Marvels and Tales; Wunder und Marchen; Maravillas y Cuentos; Meraviglie e Racconti; Marvels & Tales; Wunder & Marchen; Maravillas & Cuentos; Meraviglie & Racconti. Vol. 1, No. 1 (May 1987)-. Periodical. English (French, German, Italian and Spanish). sa. $20.00. University of Colorado / Merveilles et Contes, Campus Box 238, Boulder CO 80309. **Tel** (303)492-7226. **LC** WMLC 93/1524. **DD** 398.
Ind/Abst Child. Lit. Abstr. (19??-).

SZ/0309-1309
MERVYN PEAKE REVIEW, THE. [Mervyn Peake rev.]. **Added/Corp** Mervyn Peake Society. No. 3 (Autumn 1976)-. Periodical. English. sa. $22.00. Mervyn Peake Society, 46 Belmont Lane, Chislehurst KT BR7 6BJ England. **LC** PR6031.E183; Z77a. **DD** 741/.092/4. **[CCC].** ***Continues*** *Mervyn Peake Society. Newsletter - The Mervyn Peake Society.*
Ind/Abst Abstr. Engl. Stud.; MLA Int. Bibl. Books Artic. Mod. Lang. Lit.

US/0160-2764
MESTER (LOS ANGELES). (MESTER.). [Mester]. **Added/Corp** University of California, Los Angeles. Dept. of Spanish and Portuguese. Vol. 1 (April 1970)-. Periodical. Portuguese (Spanish and English). Twice a year (June, Nov.). $18.00 (individuals), $30.00 (institutions) US & Canada & Mexico; $24.00 (institutions) Latin America; $23.00 (individuals), $29.00 (institutions) others. UCLA Mester, Department of Spanish and Portuguese, 405 Hilgard Avenue, Los Angeles CA 90024. **Tel** (310)825-6014 Ext. 1430. **ED** Carmela Zanelli. **LC** PQ6170; .M47. **DD** 860. **CODEN** MEEREX. Index available. cum. index. **Bk Rev**, (Qty: 2). **Ad Acc, Adv Mgr Tel** (310)825-6014. **Pr Rev. Circ:** 500 (ctrl). Documents available from The Genuine Article.
Desc: Dedicated to the studies of Hispanic and Luso-Brazilian literatures and linguistics. Publishes articles by well-known scholars as well as by graduate students.
Ind/Abst Arts Humanit. Citation Index [Full Cov.]; Curr. Contents Arts Humanit.; HAPI Hisp. Am. Period. Index; Index Am. Period. Verse; MLA Int. Bibl. Books Artic. Mod. Lang. Lit.; Res. Alert [Full Cov.].

US/1061-3811
METAGAME (SOMERVILLE, MASS.). (METAGAME : THE JOURNAL OF THE SOCIETY FOR INTERACTIVE LITERATURE.). [Metagame]. **Added/Corp** Society for Interactive Literature. (1991)-. Periodical. English. qt. $10.00 (membership). Society for Interactive Literature, SIL, PO Box 44-1478, Somerville MA 02144. **DD** 793. ***Separated from*** *Metagame (Merrifield, Va.), 1062-306X.*

LI/0134-3211
METAI : LIETUVOS RASYTOJU SAJUNGOS MENRASTIS. Added/Corp Lietuvos Rasytoju Sajunga. (1991)-. Periodical. Lithuanian. mo. $119.95. Sajunga, Metai, Gedimino Pr. 37, MTP-11, 232600 Vilnius Lithuania. **(Subscription address:** East View Publications Inc., 3020 Harbor Lane North, Suite 110, Minneapolis MN 55447.**) LC** PG8701; .M48. ***Continues*** *Pergale.*

US/0885-7253
METAPHOR AND SYMBOLIC ACTIVITY. Vol. 1, No. 1 (1986)-. Periodical. English. qt. $180.00 US & Canada; $205.00 other. Lawrence Erlbaum Associates, 365 Broadway, Suite 102, Hillsdale NJ 07642. **Tel** (201)666-4110, (800)926-6579, FAX (201)666-2394. **LC** PN228.M4; M45. **DD** 302.2. **Pr Rev.** Documents available from The Genuine Article.
Ind/Abst Arts Humanit. Citation Index [Select. Cov.]; Curr. Contents Soc. Behav. Sci.; MLA Int. Bibl. Books Artic. Mod. Lang. Lit.; Psychol. Abstr. (1986-); PsycINFO (1990-); PsycLit; Res. Alert [Full Cov.]; Soc. Plann. Policy Dev. Abstr.; Soc. Sci. Cit. Index [Full Cov.].

AT/0814-8805
METAPHYSICAL REVIEW, THE. VFOAT TMR. No. 1 (July 1984)-. Periodical. English. ir (five issues per year). 25.00Aus$. Bruce Gillespie, GPO Box 5195 AA, Melbourne Victoria 3001 Australia. **Tel** (03)419-4797. **ED** Bruce Gillespie. **LC** PN3433; .M47. **Bk Rev. Ad Acc. Circ:** 200.
Desc: Reviews and general articles about science fiction fantasy, films, music, the science fiction, social world (fandom), and nostalgia.
Ind/Abst Sci. Fict. Fantasy Book Rev. Index.

US/0543-615X
METMENYS. [Metmenys]. No. 1, (1959)-. Periodical. Lithuanian. Twice a year (May, Nov.). $15.00 US; $18.00 Lithuania; $17.00 other. Metmenys, C. O. Aleksas Vaskelis, 306 55th Place, Downers Grove IL 60516. **ED** Vytautas Kavolis. **LC** AP95.L5; M4. **DD** 059. Index available. cum. index. **Bk Rev. Circ:** 850 (ctrl).
Desc: Publishes contemporary writings of Lithuanian writers and poets. Articles on philosophy, social sciences, linguistics, folklore literary essays and reviews and reproductions of contemporary Lithuanian artworks.
Ind/Abst MLA Int. Bibl. Books Artic. Mod. Lang. Lit.

IT
METRICA. (1978)-. Italian. an. L65000. Riccardo Ricciardi Editore, Via Manzoni 10, 20121 Milan Italy. **Tel** 011 39 2 804248, 011 39 2 875155. **LC** PN1045; .M47. **DD** 809.1.
Desc: Deals with versification.

US/1058-1715
METROPOLITAIN (ARLINGTON, VA.). (METROPOLITAIN.). [Metropolitain]. **VFOAT** Metropolitain Washington. Autumn (1991)-. Periodical. English. qt. $10.00. City of Light Publications, 6307 North 31st Street, Arlington VA 22207. **DD** 810.

●US/1073-3027
MFE COLLECTORS' BOOKLINE. VFOAT MFE Collectors' Book Line. (1992)-. English. mo. $135.00. Booked Up, Box 150119, San Rafael CA 94915. **ED** David M. Brown.

US/0098-8030
MICHIGAN GERMANIC STUDIES. See Linguistics.

US/0270-3629
MICHIGAN ROMANCE STUDIES. See Linguistics.

US/0194-1313
MICKLE STREET REVIEW, THE. ***Ceased.*** No. 1 (1979)-Ceased (1991). Periodical. English. an. Walt Whitman Association, 326 Mickle Street, Camden NJ 08103. **Tel** (609)757-6129. **(Subscription address:** Box 1493, Camden, NJ 08101**) ED** Geoffrey Sill. **LC** PS3224; .M53. **DD** 811/.3. **Bk Rev. Ad Acc. Circ:** 500.
Desc: Published by the Walt Whitman Association which maintains the Whitman house as a historic site. Includes poetry, essays, and reviews on Walt Whitman.
Ind/Abst Am. Humanit. Index; MLA Int. Bibl. Books Artic. Mod. Lang. Lit.

US/0747-8895
MID-AMERICAN REVIEW. [Mid-Am. rev.]. **Added/Corp** Bowling Green State University. Dept. of English. Bowling Green State University. Creative Writing Program. **VFOAT** Mid American Review. Vol. 1, No. 1 (Spring 1981)-. Periodical. English. Twice a year (May & Dec.). $12.00 (one year), $20.00 (two years), $28.00 (three years). Bowling Green State University / Department of English, 106 Hanna Hall, Bowling Green OH 43403. **Tel** (419)372-2725, (419)372-8370. **ED** Robert Early, George Looney and Wayne Barham. **LC** PS501; .M53. **DD** 810/.8. Index available. cum. index. **Bk Rev**, (Qty: 10-20). **Ad Acc, Adv Mgr:** Wayne Barham. **Circ:** 600 (ctrl). ***Continues*** *Itinerary.*
Desc: Small press literary review published fiction and poetry and translations and criticism by contemporary authors.
Ind/Abst Am. Humanit. Index; Index Am. Period. Verse; MLA Int. Bibl. Books Artic. Mod. Lang. Lit.

US/0190-2911
MIDAMERICA (EAST LANSING). (MIDAMERICA.). [Midamerica]. **Added/Corp** Society for the Study of Midwestern Literature (U.S.) Michigan State University. Center for the Study of Midwestern Literature. (1974)-. English. an.
Ind/Abst Abstr. Engl. Stud.; Annu. Bibliogr. Engl. Lang. Lit.; MLA Int. Bibl. Books Artic. Mod. Lang. Lit.

GW
MIDDLE ENGLISH TEXTS. VFOAT MET. (1975)-. Monographic series. English. ir. Price varies per volume. Universitatsverlag Carl Winter, POB 106140, D 69051 Heidelberg Germany. **Tel** 011 49 6221 770260. **ED** M. Goerlach and O. S. Pickering.
Desc: Designed to be complementary to the EETS programme. Verse and prose of all kinds are considered.
Ind/Abst MLA Int. Bibl. Books Artic. Mod. Lang. Lit.

US/0888-8752
MIDDLEBURY STUDIES IN RUSSIAN LANGUAGE AND LITERATURE. See Linguistics.

US/1058-2517
MIDNIGHT ZOO. [Midnight zoo]. Vol. #1, Issue #1 (Jan./Feb. 1991)-. Periodical. English. bm. $29.95. Midnight Zoo, 544 Ygnacio Valley Road, #A13, PO Box 8040, Walnut Creek CA 94596. **LC** PS648.H6; M54. **DD** 813/.087. ***Continues*** *Amazing Experiences, 1051-1725.*

US/0885-4742
MIDWESTERN MISCELLANY. [Midwest. misc.]. **Added/Corp** Society for the Study of Midwestern Literature (U.S.). Michigan State University. Center for the Study of Midwestern Literature. Vol. 1 (1974)-. English. ir. $20.00 (regular), $30.00 (full) membership, Comes with Society for the Study of Midwestern Literature Membership. Society for the Study of Midwestern Literature, 240 Ernst Bessey Hall, Michigan State University, East Lansing MI 48824. **Tel** (517)353-4370. **LC** PS273; .M63. **DD** 810.
Ind/Abst Abstr. Engl. Stud.; Annu. Bibliogr. Engl. Lang. Lit.; Lit. Crit. Regist.; MLA Int. Bibl. Books Artic. Mod. Lang. Lit.

PL/0026-3567
MIESIECZNIK LITERACKI. [Mies. lit.]. Vol 1, No. 1 (1966)-. Periodical. Polish. mo. $44.00. **(Subscription address:** ARS Polona, PO Box 1001, 00068 Warsaw Poland.**) LC** AP54; .M5.
Ind/Abst Annu. Bibliogr. Engl. Lang. Lit.; BHA : Biblio. Hist. Art; MLA Int. Bibl. Books Artic. Mod. Lang. Lit.

US/0163-2469
MILFORD SERIES, POPULAR WRITERS OF TODAY, THE. VFOAT Popular Writers of Today. (19??)-. Monographic series. English. ir. Price varies per volume. Borgo Press, PO Box 2845, San Bernardino CA 92406. **Tel** (714)884-5813, (714)885-1161. **ED** Dr. Dale Salwak. Index available. **Circ:** 500.

Desc: Monographic critiques of popular authors, or interviews with one or more authors. The focus is on the work of a writer rather than his life.

US
MILL, THE. No. 1- Aug. 1976-. Periodical. English. be. White Ewe Press, Box 939 North Calvert Street 1F, Baltimore MD 21202.

IT
MILLELIBRI. ***Ceased.*** **VFOAT** Mille Libri. No. 1 (Dec. 1987)-(Jan. 1994). Periodical. Italian. mo. Editoriale Giorgio Mondadori S.P.A., via Cadore 19, 20135 Milan Italy. **LC** PQ4001; .M49. **DD** 850.9/0005.

UK/0960-832X
MILLION BRIGHTON. ***Title Change.*** (1990)-(1993). Periodical. English. bm. Popular Fictions, 217 Preston Drove, Brighton BN1 6FL England. **Tel** 011 44 273 504710. ***Absorbed by*** *Interzone, 0264-3596.*
Ind/Abst Child. Lit. Abstr. (19??-).

NP
MIMALAH. Lyah 1- Kachala/Silla 1094- 1973-. Periodical. Newari (Newari). 3.00 each issue. Prema Ratna Tuladhar, 12/262 Nhyokha, PB 267, Kathmandu Yem India. **LC** PL3801.N5; M55.

II
MIMSELA. Periodical. Sino-Tibetan (Manipuri). bm. 3.00. Liberty Publishing Corporation, India. **LC** PL4001.M316; M55.

US
MINNESOTA ENGLISH JOURNAL. **See** Education-Teaching and Curriculum.

US/0890-0566
MINNESOTA LITERATURE NEWSLETTER. [Minn. lit. newsl.]. (1974)-. Newsletter. English. mo (10 issues). $10.00; $1.00 (single issue). Minnesota Literature, 1 Nord Circle, St. Paul MN 55127. **Tel** (612)483-3904. **ED** Mary Bround Smith. **DD** 808. **Ad Acc, Adv Mgr:** same as publisher. **Circ:** 700 (ctrl).
Desc: A newsletter by and for Minnesota writers and supporters of literature.

US/1061-6535
MINNESOTA WRITING PROJECT. [Minn. writ. project]. **Added/Corp** University of Minnesota. Center for Interdisciplinary Studies of Writing. (1991)-. Periodical. English. qt. $10.00. Center for Interdisciplinary Studies of Writing, University of Minnesota, 207 Church Street SE, Minneapolis MN 55455. **DD** 810.

US
MIR (PHILADELPHIA, PA.). (MIR.). **VFOAT** Peace. 1-. Periodical. Russian. qt. $24.00 individuals, $48.00 universities and libraries. Publishing House of Peace Inc, PO Box 6162, Philadelphia PA 19115. **Tel** (215)934-5512. **ED** Joset Vinoburov. **LC** PG3227; .M53. **Circ:** 2,000. ***Continues*** *Shalom.*
Desc: Devoted to literature, art, science, and sports.

CN/0713-6722
MIRIAD. [Miriad]. No. 1 (July 1980)-. Periodical. English. qt. $1.50 per no. Miriad, 61 Warren Avenue, Toronto Ontario M4A 1Z5 Canada. **DD** 809.3/876/05.

US/0047-7559
MISSISSIPPI REVIEW. [Miss. rev.]. **Added/Corp** University of Southern Mississippi. Center for Writers. **VFOAT** MR, Mississippi Review. (Jan. 1972)-. Periodical. English. sa. $15.00 US; $17.00 other. Mississippi Review, USM Box 5144, Hattiesburg MS 39406-5144. **Tel** (601)266-4321, FAX (601)266-5757. **ED** Frederick Barthelme. **LC** PS501; .M57. **DD** 810/.8/0054. Index available. **Ad Acc. Circ:** 2,000 (ctrl). available on microfilm and microfiche from University Microfilms International (UMI).
Desc: Contemporary, nonregional fiction and poetry, interviews and criticism.
Ind/Abst Am. Humanit. Index; Index Am. Period. Verse.

US/0191-1961
MISSOURI REVIEW, THE. [Miss. rev.]. **Added/Corp** University of Missouri-Columbia. Dept. of English. (Spring 1978)-. Periodical. English. Three times a year. $15.00 (1 year), $27.00 (2 year), $36.00 (3 year) US; $18.00 (1 year) other. University of Missouri - Columbia, 1507 Hillcrest Hall, Columbia MO 65211. **Tel** (314)882-4474, FAX (314)884-4671. **ED** Speer Morgan and Greg Michalson. **LC** PS1; .M57. **DD** 810/.8/0054. **Bk Rev. Ad Acc. Circ:** 2,000. available on an online database from Review Online (Source Network).
Desc: Fiction, poetry, interviews, reviews, essays, and other literary features.
Ind/Abst Am. Humanit. Index; Index Am. Period. Verse; MLA Int. Bibl. Books Artic. Mod. Lang. Lit.

IT/0392-6397
MISURE CRITICHE. Vol. 1, No. 1/2 (Oct. 1971/Jan. 1972)-. Periodical. Italian. qt. L78.000 Italy; L120.000 other. Conte, Via A D Isernia 59, 80122 Naples Italy.

GW/0941-7842
MITTEILUNGEN DER KARL-MAY-GESELLSCHAFT. [Mitt. Karl-May-Ges.]. (1969)-. Periodical. German. qt. free to members. Karl-May-Gesellschaft, Maximiliankorso 45, W-1000 Berlin 28 Germany. **UDC** 830. Index available. cum. index. **Bk Rev. Ad Acc. Circ:** 1,800 (ctrl).
Desc: Articles by KMG-members referring to all aspects of the works of Karl May.

NE/0076-9754
MITTELLATEINISCHE STUDIEN UND TEXTE. Vol. 1 (1965)-. Monographic series. Multiple languages (English and German). ir. Price varies per volume. E. J. Brill, Postbus 9000, 2300 PA Leiden Netherlands. **Tel** 011 31 71 312624, FAX 011 31 71 317532, telex 39296 BRILL NL.
Desc: Covers Latin literature and philology both Medieval and Modern.

UK
MIXED MOSS. (MIXED MOSS : THE JOURNAL OF THE ARTHUR RANSOME SOCIETY.). English. Mixed Moss, Abbot Hall, Kendal, Cumbria CA9 5AL, United Kingdom.
Ind/Abst Child. Lit. Abstr. (19??-).

●US/1057-2899
MLA DIRECTORY OF SCHOLARLY PRESSES IN LITERATURE AND LANGUAGE. [MLA dir. sch. presses lang. lit.]. **Added/Corp** Modern Language Association of America. **VFOAT** Directory of Scholarly Presses in Literature and Language. **VAT** Modern Language Association Directory of Scholarly Presses in Literature and Language. (1991)-. Directory. English. ir. $50.00 per copy. Modern Language Association of America, 10 Astor Place, New York NY 10003-6981. **Tel** (212)614-6382, FAX (212)477-9863. **ED** James L. Harner. **LC** Z286.P46; M4. **DD** 070.5/94. **Acid Free.**
Desc: Describes the fields of interest, submission requirements, contract provisions, and editorial procedures of publishers of book-length literary and linguistic studies.

US/0740-8730
MLA INTERNATIONAL BIBLIOGRAPHY OF BOOKS AND ARTICLES ON THE MODERN LANGUAGES AND LITERATURES (OPTION B). ***Ceased.*** (MLA INTERNATIONAL BIBLIOGRAPHY OF BOOKS AND ARTICLES ON THE MODERN LANGUAGES AND LITERATURES.). [MLA int. bibl. books artic. mod. lang. lit.]. **Added/Corp** Modern Language Association of America. **VFOAT** M.L.A. International Bibliography of Books and Articles on the Modern Languages and Literatures; International Bibliography of Books and Articles on the Modern Languages and Literatures. (1981)-No longer available. Bibliography. English. Modern Language Association of America, 10 Astor Place, New York NY 10003-6981. **Tel** (212)614-6382, FAX (212)477-9863. **DD** 016.

US/0740-8722
MLA INTERNATIONAL BIBLIOGRAPHY OF BOOKS AND ARTICLES ON THE MODERN LANGUAGES AND LITERATURES (OPTION C). **See** Linguistics.

YU
MLADA KULTURA. V. 1- Sept. 1972-. Serbo-Croatian (Roman). 100.00. **LC** PG560; .M55.

GW
MODELLANALYSEN LITERATUR. (198?)-. Monographic series. German. **LC** UNC.
Ind/Abst MLA Int. Bibl. Books Artic. Mod. Lang. Lit.

US/0026-7503
MODERN AUSTRIAN LITERATURE. [Mod. Austrian lit.]. **Added/Corp** International Arthur Schnitzler Research Association. Vol. 1 (Spring 1968)-. Periodical. English (German). Three times a year. $20.00 (individuals), $30.00 (institutions) US; $25.00 (individuals), 35.00 (insitutions) other. Modern Austrian Literature, California State University, Department of Foreign Languages, San Bernardino CA 92407. **Tel** (714)880-5851. **ED** Donald G Daviau. **LC** PT3810; .I52. **DD** 830.9/9436. Index available. cum. index. **Bk Rev. Ad Acc. Circ:** 700 (ctrl). available on microfilm and microfiche from University Microfilms International (UMI). Documents available from The Genuine Article. ***Supersedes*** *Journal of the International Arthur Schnitzler Research Association.*
Desc: A journal devoted to Austrian literature and culture of the 19th and 20th centuries.
Ind/Abst Am. Bibliogr. Slavic East Europ. Stud.; Arts Humanit. Citation Index [Full Cov.]; Curr. Contents Arts Humanit.; MLA Int. Bibl. Books Artic. Mod. Lang. Lit.; Ref. Sources; Res. Alert [Full Cov.]; Soc. Sci. Cit. Index [Select. Cov.].

US/8755-8963
MODERN CHINESE LITERATURE. [Mod. Chin. lit.]. **Added/Corp** San Francisco State University. Center for the Study of Modern Chinese Literature. **VFOAT** Chung-Kuo Hsien Tai wen Hsueh. Vol. 1, No. 1 (Sept. 1984)-. Periodical. English. sa. $25.00. Modern Chinese Literature, Department of Oriental Languages, University of Colorado, Campus Box 279, Boulder CO 80309. **Tel** (303)492-3486. **LC** PL2303; .M63. **DD** 895.1/09/005. ***Continues*** *Modern Chinese Literature Newsletter.*
Ind/Abst Arts Humanit. Citation Index (19??-19??) [Full Cov.]; MLA Int. Bibl. Books Artic. Mod. Lang. Lit.

CN/0026-7694
MODERN DRAMA. **See** Theater.

US/1055-999X
MODERN DRAMATISTS RESEARCH AND PRODUCTION SOURCEBOOKS. [Mod. dram. res. prod. sourceb.]. No. 1 (1991)-. Monographic series. English. Price varies per volume. Greenwood Press Inc., PO Box 5007, Westport CT 06881-5007. **Tel** (203)226-3571, FAX (203)222-1502. **DD** 809.

GW
MODERN GERMAN STUDIES. Vol. 1 (1978)-. Monographic series. English (German).
Ind/Abst MLA Int. Bibl. Books Artic. Mod. Lang. Lit.

IS/0334-4266
MODERN HEBREW LITERATURE. [Mod. Heb. lit.]. **Added/Corp** Makhon le-tirgum sifrut Ivrit (Israel). (Spring 1975)-. Periodical. English. Four times a year. $9.00. Institute of Translat Hebrew Literature, PO Box 10051, Hamat-Gan 52001 Israel. **Tel** (03)5796830, FAX (03)5796832, telex 341118 BXTV IL. **ED** Gershon Shaked. **LC** PJ5001; .M63. **DD** 892.4/09. **Bk Rev. Circ:** 2,000 (ctrl). available on microfilm and microfiche from University Microfilms International (UMI). Documents available from The Genuine Article. ***Continues*** *Hebrew Book Review.*
Desc: Helps the English-speaking reader keep abreast of Israel's literary scene. Includes a great variety of literary topics and reviews of recent works. Just revamped into a new magazine format.
Ind/Abst Arts Humanit. Citation Index [Full Cov.]; Curr. Contents Arts Humanit.; Middle East Abstr. Index; MLA Int. Bibl. Books Artic. Mod. Lang. Lit.; Res. Alert [Full Cov.].

II
MODERN INDIAN SHORT STORIES. **Added/Corp** Indian Council for Cultural Relations. Vol. 1 (1975)-. English (Undetermined).

US/0026-7856
MODERN INTERNATIONAL DRAMA. [Mod. int. drama]. (Sept. 1967)-. Periodical. English. sa (Apr., Oct.). $12.50 (institutions), $7.00 (individuals) US and Mexico; $13.50 (institutions), $10.00 (individuals) Canada; $12.50 (individuals) other. Modern International Drama, c/o Theatre Department, SUNY at Binghamton, Binghamton NY 13902. **Tel** (607)777-2704. **ED** G E Wellwarth, A M Pasquariello. **LC** PN6111; .M63. **DD** 808.82/04. **Ad Acc. Circ:** 500 (ctrl). available on microfilm and microfiche from University Microfilms International (UMI). Documents available from The Genuine Article.
Desc: Publication of previously untranslated plays.
Ind/Abst Am. Bibliogr. Slavic East Europ. Stud.; Arts Humanit. Citation Index (19??-19??) [Full Cov.]; Curr. Contents Arts Humanit.; Middle East Abstr. Index; Res. Alert [Full Cov.].

US/0270-9406
MODERN JEWISH STUDIES ANNUAL. [Mod. Jew. stud. annu.]. **VFOAT** MJS Annual. (1978)-. English (Yiddish). an. $3.50. Queens College, Political Science Department, 65-30 Kissena Boulevard, Flushing NY 11367. **Tel** (718)520-7000. **ED** Joseph C Landis. **LC** PS153.J4; C65. **DD** 810/.9/8924. Index available. **Bk Rev. Ad Acc. Circ:** 750 (ctrl). ***Continues*** *Conference on Modern Jewish Studies Annual, 0270-9392.*
Desc: Research and criticism in Jewish literature in any language and in the historical and cultural context. English translations of literature and criticism accepted.

US/1040-9068
MODERN SHORT STORIES. ***Suspended.*** Dec. 1988-?. Periodical. English. bm. $9.95 US; $12.95 Canada. Claggk Publications, PO Box 473, Mt Morris IL 61054-9932. **Tel** (212)661-3322. **(Subscription address:** PO Box 473, Mt Morris, IL 61054-8026) **ED** Glen Steckler. **DD** 813. **Ad Acc.**
Desc: Devoted to the publication of contemporary short fiction. Each published story is accompanied by original pictorials and illustrations.

●US/1071-6068
MODERNISM/MODERNITY (BALTIMORE, MD.). (MODERNISM & MODERNITY.). [Mod./mod.]. **VAT** Modernism modernity. (1993)-. Periodical. English. Three times a year. $52.00 US; $55.60 Canada & Mexico; $59.40 other. Johns Hopkins University Press, 2715 North Charles Street, Baltimore MD 21218-4319. **Tel** (410)516-6987, FAX (410)516-6968. **(Subscription address:** John Hopkins University Press, Journals Publishing Division, PO Box 19966, Baltimore MD 21211.) **DD** 301.

CN/0225-1582
MOEBIUS. [Moebius]. (1977)-. Periodical. French. qt. $35.00 (1 year), $60.00 (2 year) individuals, $55.00 (1 year), $95.00 (2 year) institutions, US; 35.00Can$ individuals, 55.00Can$ institutions, Canada. Les Editions Triptyque, CP 5670 Succursale C, Montreal Quebec H2L 2H0 Canada. **Tel** (514)524-5900. **ED** Robert Giroux. **LC** UNC. **DD** C841/.540809714. **Bk Rev. Ad Acc. Circ:** 750 (ctrl).
Desc: An interview with a writer; a general theme with poems, short stories and short essays.
Ind/Abst Can. Lit. Index (1985-1986); Point Repere (1992-).

CI/0544-7267
MOGUCNOSTI. Added/Corp Matica Hrvatska, Split. (1954)-. Periodical. Serbo-Croatian (Roman). mo. **LC** AP56; .M6.
Ind/Abst MLA Int. Bibl. Books Artic. Mod. Lang. Lit.

AG
MOLINO DE PIMIENTA, EL. No. 1 (Sept./Oct. 1983)-. Periodical. Spanish. Three times a year. **LC** PN778; .M58. **DD** 808.

US
MONARCH NOTES. CD-ROM. (19??)-. English. $79.95. Bureau of Electronic Publishing Inc., 141 New Road, Parsippany NJ 07054. **Tel** (201)808-2700, FAX (201)808-2676. Index available. cum. index.
Desc: Multimedia guide to understanding the literary classics.

US/0885-7512
MONOGRAPHIC REVIEW. (MONOGRAPHIC REVIEW / REVISTA MONOGRAFICA.). [Monogr. rev.]. **VFOAT** Revista Monografica. Vol. 1 (1985)-. English (Spanish, Portuguese, Catalan and French). an (Feb.). $35.00. Monographic Review Revista, PO Box 8401, UT Permian Basin, Odessa TX 79762-0001. **Tel** (915)367-2249, FAX (915)367-2115. **ED** Genaro J. and Janet Perez. **DD** 860. **Ad Acc. Pr Rev. Circ:** 500 (ctrl).
Desc: A professional journal of criticism in the Hispanic literatures. Devoted to a single theme, or major writer while offering a variety of critical viewpoints and methodologies.
Ind/Abst MLA Int. Bibl. Books Artic. Mod. Lang. Lit.; Romant. Move.

US/1049-2917
MONTAIGNE STUDIES. [Montaigne stud.]. **Added/Corp** University of Massachusetts at Amherst. Dept. of French and Italian. Vol. 1, No. 1 (Nov. 1989)-. Periodical. English (French, German, Italian and Spanish). Twice a year (Sept., Dec). $20.25 (individuals), $24.00 (institutions). University of Chicago Department of Humanities, 1050 East 59th Street, Chicago IL 60637. **Tel** (312)702-8026. **ED** Daniel Martin. **LC** PQ1643.A2; M66. **DD** 844/.3. **Pr Rev. Circ:** 200. available on diskette.
Desc: Studies by college professors of the Essays by Montaigne.
Ind/Abst MLA Int. Bibl. Books Artic. Mod. Lang. Lit.

US
MONTEMORA. 1- Fall 1975-. Periodical. English (English, French, Japanese and Spanish). $3.50 each issue. **LC** PN6010.5; .M66. **DD** 805.

II/0581-300X
MONTHLY NEWS BULLETIN. Main/Corp Sahitya Akademi. Began in 1964. Bulletin. English. Sahitya Akademi, National Academy of Letters, Rabindra Bhavan, Ferozeshah Road, New Delhi 110001 India. **Tel** 011 91 11 388667. **LC** PK101. **DD** 891.1.

CN/0707-5316
MONTREAL WRITERS' FORUM. V. 1- Oct. 1978-. Periodical. English. 5.50Can$. Montreal Writers' Forum, Box 333, Morin Heights, Quebec J0R 1H0 Canada. **DD** C810/.8/0054.

US/0196-2604
MOODY STREET IRREGULARS. [Moody Str. irregul.]. Vol. 1, No. 1 (Winter 1978)-. Periodical. English (French). Four times a year. $20.00 (regular); $30.00 (library). Moody Street Irregulars, PO Box 157, Clarence Center NY 14023. **Tel** (716)741-3393. **ED** Joy Walsh. **LC** PS3521.E735; Z783. **DD** 813/.54. Index available. **Bk Rev**, (Qty: 5-10). **Ad Acc. Pr Rev. Circ:** 700.
Desc: This periodical publishes work by or about Jack Kerouac, an American writer of the fifties. It also publishes work in the spirit of Kerouac.
Ind/Abst Am. Humanit. Index (-199?); Index Am. Period. Verse; Lit. Crit. Regist.; MLA Int. Bibl. Books Artic. Mod. Lang. Lit.

CN/0842-1765
MOOSEHEAD ANTHOLOGY. [Moosehead anthol.]. (1988)-. Periodical. English. ir. 13.45Can$ Canada; 14.95Can$ other. Moosehead Anthology, PO Box 169, Ayer's Cliff Quebec J0B 1C0 Canada. **Tel** (416)361-0618. **(Subscription address:** DC Books, Box 662, 1495 rue de l'Eglise, Montreal QUE H4L 4V9 Canada.**)** **LC** PR9194; .M66. **DD** 810.8/0005. ***Continues*** *Moosehead Review, 0228-7404.*

YU
MORAVSKA LIRA. Added/Corp Zajednica Kulture Velika Plana. (19??)-. Serbo-Croatian (Roman). **LC** PG1400; .M67.

FR/0047-8105
MOREANA. [Moreana]. **Added/Corp** Association Amici Thomae Mori. **VFOAT** Gazette Thomas More; Thomas More Gazette; Bulletin Thomas More; Moreana, Gazette. Vol. 1, No. 1 (Sept. 1963)-. Periodical. English (French). Three times a year (Mar., June, Dec.). $65.00 (institutions), $50.00 (individuals). Amicale Thomas More, 29 rue Volney, BP 808, 49008 Angers Cedex France. **Tel** 011 33 41 871932, 011 33 41 816697, FAX 011 33 41 887442. **ED** Clare M. Murphy. **LC** PR2322; .M66. **DD** 942.052. cum. index. **Bk Rev**, (Qty: 3). **Ad Acc, Adv Mgr:** Marc Hadour. **Circ:** 850. Documents available from The Genuine Article.
Desc: Provides news on the life, writings and world of Mori. Discusses lives, translations, theses, plays and other documents.
Ind/Abst Abstr. Engl. Stud.; Am. Hist. Life (1975-1978); Annu. Bibliogr. Engl. Lang. Lit.; Arts Humanit. Citation Index [Full Cov.]; Curr. Contents Arts Humanit.; MLA Int. Bibl. Books Artic. Mod. Lang. Lit.; Res. Alert [Full Cov.]; Soc. Sci. Cit. Index [Select. Cov.].

CN/0027-1276
MOSAIC (WINNIPEG). (MOSAIC.). [Mosaic]. Vol. 1 (Oct. 1967)-. Periodical. English (French; summaries and/or abstracts in French). Four times a year (Mar., June, Sept., Dec.). 35.00Can$ (includes GST) Canada; $35.00 US; $40.00 other. Mosaic, 208 Tier Building, University of Manitoba, Winnipeg Manitoba R3T 2N2 Canada. **Tel** (204)474-9763, FAX (204)261-9086. **ED** Evelyn J. Hinz. **LC** PN2; .M68. **DD** 809/.005. **[CCC]**. Index available in last issue of volume--attached. **Ad Acc, Adv Mgr:** M. McLean. **Circ:** 800. available on microfilm and microfiche from University Microfilms International (UMI). Documents available from The Genuine Article, UMI Article Clearinghouse.
Desc: A journal for the interdisciplinary study of literature, Mosaic serves as a medium of communication to and among individuals and groups directly affected by the Foundation as well as interested parties including other federal officials involved in scientific affairs, science writers, and others who share a concern for the progress of science.
Ind/Abst Abstr. Engl. Stud.; Am. Humanit. Index; Arts Humanit. Citation Index [Full Cov.]; BHA : Biblio. Hist. Art; Can. Index (?-?); Can. Period. Index; Expand. Acad. Index (1989-); Humanit. Index; Mag. Artic. Summar. Elite (Jan. 1992-Sept.1992); Mag. Artic. Summar. Select; MLA Int. Bibl. Books Artic. Mod. Lang. Lit.; Newsp. Period. Abstr. (1991-); Res. Alert [Full Cov.]; Soc. Sci. Cit. Index [Select. Cov.].

RU/0131-2332
MOSKVA. [Moskva]. **Added/Corp** Soiuz Pisatelei SSSR. Soiuz Pisatelei SSSR. Moskovskoe Otdelenie. Soiuz Pisatelei RSFSR. Orgkomitet. Soiuz Pisatelei RSFSR. Moskovskoe Otdelenie. Soiuz Pisatelei RSFSR. Moskovskaia Pisatelskaia Organizatsiia. (1957)-. Periodical. Russian. mo. $129.95. **(Subscription address:** East View Publications Inc., 3020 Harbor Lane North, Suite 110, Minneapolis MN 55447.**)** **LC** AP50; .M667. Index available. **Bk Rev**. available on microfilm from University Microfilms International (UMI).
Ind/Abst MLA Int. Bibl. Books Artic. Mod. Lang. Lit.; Curr. Dig. Post Sov. Press.

US/0027-1438
MOST (LAUSANNE). (MOST.). [Most]. **Added/Corp** Slovak Institute (Cleveland, Ohio.) Slovak Writers' and Artists' Association. Vol. 1, (1954)-. Periodical. Slovak. Twice a year (May, Oct.). $5.00. Slovak Institute, 2900 East Boulevard, Cleveland OH 44115. **LC** AP58.S53; M6.
Ind/Abst Annu. Bibliogr. Engl. Lang. Lit.

YU/0350-6525
MOSTOVI (BELGRADE). See Linguistics.

CN/1180-5781
(M)OTHER TNGUES. ((M)OTHER TNGUES [SIC].). [(M)other tngues]. **VFOAT** Mother Tongues. Premier Issue (Summer 1990)-. Periodical. English. sa. $6.00 per issue. Beach Grove Press, c/o R Fertig, Rural Route 2, Alders Unit C-14, Ganges, British Columbia V0S 1E0 Canada. **DD** 809/.049.

US/0278-2286
MOTIF (COLUMBUS, OHIO). ***Suspended.*** **See** Folklore.

US/0893-8288
MOUNT OLIVE REVIEW. [Mt. Olive rev.]. **Added/Corp** Mount Olive College. Vol. 1, No. 1 (Spring 1987)-. Periodical. English. an. Mount Olive Review, Mount Olive College, Mount Olive NC 28365. **DD** 810.
Ind/Abst MLA Int. Bibl. Books Artic. Mod. Lang. Lit.

US
MOVING OUT. Added/Corp Wayne State University. No. 1 (March 1971)-. Monographic series. English. ir. $9.00 (institutions), $6.00 (individuals). Moving Out, Box 21249, Detroit MI 48221. **Tel** (313)478-0529. **ED** Margaret Kaminksi, Joan Gartland, Jan Mordenski and Alinda Wasner. **Bk Rev. Ad Acc. Circ:** 750 (ctrl). available on microfilm from Bell & Howell.
Desc: Feminist literary and arts journal publishing quality poetry, fiction, articles, art, photos, interviews, criticism, reviews, parts-of-novels, long-poems, plays concerning women's lives and literature.

CN/0226-0174
MOYEN FRANCAIS. (LE MOYEN FRANCAIS.). [Moyen fr.]. (1977)-. Monographic series. French (English, Italian and German). Twice a year (June, Dec.). Price varies per volume. Ed Ceres, CP 1386, Place Bonaventure, Montreal Quebec H5A 1H3 Canada. **Tel** (514)937-7138. **ED** G. Di Stefano and Rose M. Bidler. **DD** 840/.9/022. cum. index. **Bk Rev**, (Qty: 10-12). **Circ:** 500 (ctrl).
Desc: Presents studies, unedited texts, bibliographies which illustrate the actual tendencies of research on the French language and literature of the 14th and 15th centuries.
Ind/Abst MLA Int. Bibl. Books Artic. Mod. Lang. Lit.

IS/0027-2892
MOZNAYIM. Added/Corp Agudat Ha-Sofrim Ha-Ivrim Be-Erets-Yisrael. (1955)-. Periodical. Hebrew. mo. $95.00. Ludwig Mayer Ltd, POB 1174, 91000 Jerusalem Israel. **Tel** 011/972/2/252628, FAX 011/972/2/290774. **ED** H Pessah. Index available. **Bk Rev. Ad Acc.**
Desc: Official organ of the Israeli Writers Association.

IS/0027-2892
MOZNAYIM. ***Title Change.*** **Added/Corp** Agudat Ha-Sofrim Ha-Ivrim Be-Yisrael. (1933)-. Periodical. Hebrew. mo. Ludwig Mayer Ltd, POB 1174, 91000 Jerusalem Israel. **Tel** 011/972/2/252628, FAX 011/972/2/290774. cum. index. ***Supersedes*** *Moznayim.* ***Superseded by*** *Moznayim.*
Ind/Abst MLA Int. Bibl. Books Artic. Mod. Lang. Lit.

GW/0580-1362
MUENCHENER TEXTE UND UNTERSUCHUNGEN ZUR DEUTSCHEN LITERATUR DES MITTELALTERS. (MUENCHENER TEXTE UND UNTERSUCHUNGEN ZUR DEUTSCHEN LITERATUR DES MITTELALTERS / HERAUSGEGEBEN VON DER KOMMISSION FUER DEUTSCHE LITERATUR DES MITTELALTERS DER BAYERISCHEN AKADEMIE DER WISSENSCHAFTEN.). [MĒunch. Texte Unters. dtsch. Lit. Mittelalt.]. **Added/Corp** Bayerische Akademie der Wissenschaften. Kommission fuer Deutsche Literatur des Mittelalters. (1961)-. Monographic series. German. ir. Price varies per volume. Max Niemeyer Verlag, Postfach 2140, D 72011 Tuebingen Germany. **Tel** 011 49 7071 989494, FAX 011 49 7071 87419. **LC** UNC.
Desc: Series covering German literature.
Ind/Abst MLA Int. Bibl. Books Artic. Mod. Lang. Lit.

US/0027-3112
MULCH. V. 1- Apr. 1971-. Periodical. English. qt. $10.00. Mulch Press, PO Box 598, Northampton MA 01060. **LC** PN6010.5; .M8. **DD** 808.8/004.

TZ
MULIKA. Added/Corp Chuo Kikuu Cha Dar es Salaam. Chuo Cha Uchunguzi Wa Lugha Yiswahili. No. 1 (1971)-. Periodical. Swahili. an (March). $15.00. University of Dar es Salaam / Tanzania, Institute of Kiswahili Research, PO Box 35110, Dar es Salaam Tanzania. **Tel** 011 255 51 49192, 011 255 51 49162, FAX 011 255 51 48274, telex 41327. **ED** Professor Chomi and Dr. Mwansoko. **LC** PL8701; .M8. cum. index. **Bk Rev. Ad Acc. Circ:** 3,000.
Desc: The Kiswahili language journal is for the secondary school pupils, colleges and teachers on various aspects of Kiswahili language and literature.

GW/0930-1127
MUNCHENER BEITRAEGE ZUR MEDIAVISTIK UND RENAISSANCE-FORSCHUNG. See Linguistics.

GW/0170-3668
MUNCHENER OSTASIATISCHE STUDIEN. Vol. 1 (1970)-. Monographic series. German. ir. Price varies per volume. Franz Steiner Verlag GmbH, Postfach 101061, D 70009 Stuttgart Germany. **Tel** 011 49 0711 2582372, FAX 011 49 0711 2582290, telex 723636 daz d. **ED** Wolfgang Bauer, Herbert Franke, Wolfram Naumann, Helwig Schmidt-Glintzer.
Desc: Monographs about Chinese, Japanese and Korean literature, history, philosophy, and language.

US/8755-4925
MUNDUS ARABICUS. [Mundus arab.]. **VFOAT** Alam Al-Arabi. Vol. 1 (1981)-. English (Arabic). an. Dar Mahijar, PO Box 56, Cambridge MA 02238. **LC** PJ7501; .M76. **DD** 892.

KO
MUNHAK KWA CHISONG. (19??)-. Periodical. Korean. qt. Munhak Kwa Chisong SA, 35-84 Tongui-dong Chongno-ku, Seoul South Korea. **LC** PL950.2; .M77.

KO
MUNHAK SASANG. (19??)-. Periodical. Korean. mo. $120.71 US, Canada, and India; $129.24 Europe,

Central and South America, Africa, and Middle East. Munhak Sasang SA, Jokson Hyundae BD 80 Jokson DG, Jongro ku Seoul 110 052 Korea. **Tel** 011 82 01 736-9467736-1861. **LC** PL950.2; .M78.

KO
MUNHAK UI SIDAE. V. 1- (1983)-. Periodical. Korean. W3,200. Pulpit Chulpansa, 2-39 Yokchon-dong Unpyong-ku, Seoul Korea. **LC** PL969.8; .M87.

II
MUNTAKHAB AFSANE. 1963-. Urdu (Urdu). **ED** Ahraz Naqvi. **LC** PK2190.

US/0898-2392
MUSE (GRAHAM, N.C.). (MUSE.). [Muse]. Vol. 1, No. 6 (May/June 1988)-. Periodical. English. bm. $18.00 US; $21.00 other. Muse Magazine Inc, PO Box 45, Burlington NC 27216-0045. **DD** 811. ***Continues*** *Muse Letter, 0898-2376.*

NR/0331-3468
MUSE (NSUKKA). (THE MUSE : LITERARY JOURNAL OF THE ENGLISH ASSOCIATION AT NSUKKA.). [Muse]. **Added/Corp** English Association at Nsukka. (1963)-. English. an. **LC** PR9387.5; .M87. **DD** 820/.8/09669.
Ind/Abst MLA Int. Bibl. Books Artic. Mod. Lang. Lit.

US
MUSE'S MILL. English. qt. $12.50. Muse's Mill, Box 2117, Ashland KY 41105-2117. **ED** Carol Hanshaw, Terry Clarke, Kay Evicks, and Mike McDonald. **Ad Acc. Circ:** 300.

GW
MUSIL-FORUM. 1. Vol., 1 (1. Halbjahresheft 1975)-. German (Italian, English and French). an. DM45.00. Internationale Robert-Musil-Gesellschaft Geschaftsstelle, Bau 35, Universitat des Saarlandes, W-6600 Saarbrucken 11 Germany. **Tel** (0681)302-3334. **ED** Jurgen Tkoming. **LC** PT2625.U8; Z815. **DD** 833/.912. **Bk Rev. Circ:** 700 (ctrl).
Desc: Devoted to Robert Musil and the Austrian literature. Regular features, where readers, authors, and editors debate each other.

US/0270-3521
MVR. Added/Corp Western Illinois University. College of Arts and Sciences. **VFOAT** Mississippi Valley Review of Creative Writing; Mississippi Valley Review. (197?)-. Periodical. English. Twice a year (Apr., Nov.). $12.00 (one year); $20.00 (two years); $30.00 (three years). Western Illinois University / English, Department of English, Macomb IL 61455. **Tel** (309)298-1588. **ED** Forrest Robinson. **Circ:** 400.
Desc: Covers stories and poems.

US/0146-3160
MYSTERY FANCIER, THE. ***Ceased.*** Vol. 1, No. 1 (Jan. 1977)-Vol. 13, No. 4 (Fall 1992). Periodical. English. bm. Mystery Fanicer, 1711 Clifty Drive, Madison IN 47250. **Tel** (812)273-6908. **LC** PN3448.D4; M97. **DD** 813/.0872/09.
Ind/Abst Annu. Bibliogr. Engl. Lang. Lit.

US
MYSTERY MAGAZINE. Periodical. English.

US/1043-3473
MYSTERY READERS JOURNAL. (MYSTERY READERS JOURNAL : THE JOURNAL OF MYSTERY READERS INTERNATIONAL.). **Added/Corp** Mystery Readers International. Vol. 5, No. 1 (Spring 1989)-. Periodical. English. qt. $22.50. Mystery Readers International, PO Box 8116, Berkeley CA 94707. **Tel** (415)540-1909. **ED** Janet A. Rudolph. **DD** 810. **Bk Rev. Ad Acc. Circ:** 1,000 (ctrl). ***Continues*** *MRA Journal.*

●CN/1192-8700
MYSTERY REVIEW, THE. [Mystery rev.]. Vol. 1, No. 1 (Fall 1992)-. Periodical. English. qt (Jan., Apr., July, Sept.). 21.50Can$ (includes GST) Canada; $20.00 US; $25.00 other. Mystery Review, PO Box 233, Colborne, Ontario, KOK 1SO Canada. **Tel** (613)475-4440, FAX (613)475-3400. **ED** Barbara J. Davey. **DD** 823/.087209/005. **Bk Rev,** (Qty: 12). **Ad Acc, Adv Mgr:** Chris von Hessert. **Circ:** 4,000.
Desc: Provides information about new mystery releases, interviews with authors and others related to the mystery genre, real life mysteries, word games and puzzles related to mystery.

US/0742-5503
MYSTICS QUARTERLY (IOWA CITY, IOWA). (MYSTICS QUARTERLY.). [Mystics q.]. Vol. 10, No. 1 (Mar. 1984)-. Periodical. English. Four times a year (Mar., June, Sept., Dec.). $15.00 (individuals); $20.00 (institutions). University of Cincinnati / Department of English, McMicken Hall 69, Cincinnati OH 45221. **Tel** (513)556-3937. **ED** Valerie Lagorio and Ritamary Bradley. **LC** BV5077.G7; A13. **DD** 248.2/2/05. **Bk Rev. Ad Acc. Pr Rev. Circ:** 472 (ctrl). ***Continues*** *14th Century English Mystics Newsletter, 0737-5840.*
Desc: International journal devoted to the study of the medieval English and continental mystics.
Ind/Abst Index Book Rev. Relig.; MLA Int. Bibl. Books Artic. Mod. Lang. Lit.; Relig. Index One Period.

FR
MYTHES, CROYANCES ET RELIGIONS DANS LE MONDE ANGLO-SAXON. **See** Religion and Theology.

US/0146-9339
MYTHLORE. [Mythlore]. **Added/Corp** Mythopoeic Society (U.S.). **VFOAT** Myth Lore. (Jan. 1969)-. Periodical. English. Four times a year (Mar., June, Sept., Dec.). $15.00 (members); $20.00 (non-members). Mythopoeic Society, 1008 North Monterey Street, Alhambra CA 91801. **Tel** (818)284-0848. **ED** Glen Goodknight and Sarah Beach. **LC** PR478.F35; M9. **DD** 809.3/876. Index available. cum. index. **Bk Rev. Ad Acc. Circ:** 600 (ctrl). ***Absorbed*** *Tolkien Journal.*
Desc: Studies relating to the works of J. R. R. Tolkien, C. S. Lewis and Charles Williams in particular, fantasy and mythology in general.
Ind/Abst Abstr. Engl. Stud.; Am. Humanit. Index (-199?); Annu. Bibliogr. Engl. Lang. Lit.; Child. Lit. Abstr. (19??-); MLA Int. Bibl. Books Artic. Mod. Lang. Lit.; Sci. Fict. Fantasy Book Rev. Index.

US/0146-9347
MYTHPRINT. [Mythprint]. **Added/Corp** Mythopoeic Society (U.S.). **VAT** Myth Print. (19??)-. Periodical. English. Twelve times a year. $7.50 (members), $12.50 (nonmembers). Mythopoeic Society, 1008 North Monterey Street, Alhambra CA 91801. **Tel** (818)284-0848. **ED** David S. Bratman. **Bk Rev. Ad Acc. Circ:** 300 (ctrl).
Desc: Newsletter of the Mythopoeic Society. Contains reviews and notices of current events in the field of fantasy, literature with a special emphasis on Tolkien, Lewis and Williams.
Ind/Abst Abstr. Engl. Stud.

US
N.E.S.F.A. INDEX TO SHORT SCIENCE FICTION. Added/Corp New England Science Fiction Association. **VFOAT** NESFA Index to Short Science Fiction; New England Science Fiction Association Index to Short Science Fiction; NESFA Index to Short SF. (1987)-. Periodical. English. ir. New England Science Fiction Association, PO Box 809, Framingham MA 01701. **LC** Z5917.S36; I55. ***Continues*** *N.E.S.F.A. Index to the Science Fiction Magazines and Original Anthologies, 0747-7546.*

US/0894-7120
NABOKOVIAN, THE. [Nabokovian]. **Added/Corp** Vladimir Nabokov Society. No. 13 (Fall 1984)-. Periodical. English. sa. $9.00 (individuals), $11.00 (institutions) US. Slavic Languages & Literatures, University of Kansas, Lawrence KS 66045. **Tel** (913)864-3313. **LC** PG3476.N3; Z94. **DD** 813/.54. cum. index. ***Continues*** *Vladimir Nabokov Research Newsletter, 0886-4993.*
Desc: Devoted wholly to the life and writings of Vladimir Nabokov. Publishes the annual Nabokov bibliography; news of Nabokov studies around the world; abstracts of articles, books, and dissertations; annotations to Nabokov's works; special features, including previously unpublished interviews and other writings; photographs and illustrations; special bibliographies; notes and queries.
Ind/Abst Am. Bibliogr. Slavic East Europ. Stud.; Annu. Bibliogr. Engl. Lang. Lit.; MLA Int. Bibl. Books Artic. Mod. Lang. Lit.

UA
NADI AL-QISSAH (ALEXANDRIA, EGYPT). (NADI AL-QISSAH.). **Added/Corp** Qasr Thaqafat al-Hurriyah (Alexandria, Egypt) Nadi al-Adab bi-Qasr al-Hurriyah (Alexandria, Egypt) Qasr Thaqafat al-Hurriyah (Alexandria, Egypt). Nadi al-Adab. (1980)-. Periodical. Arabic. mo. 1 Tariq Al-Zaim Jamal Abd Al-Nasir Qasr Thaqafat Al-Hurriyah, Al-Iskandariyah Egypt. **LC** PJ8216; .N3.

HU
NAGYVILAG. Added/Corp Magyar Irok Szovetsege. Vol. 1, (1956)-. Periodical. Hungarian. Twelve times a year. $40.00. **(Subscription address:** Kultura, PO Box 149, H 1389 Budapest 62 Hungary) **LC** PN6065.H8; N23.
Ind/Abst Annu. Bibliogr. Engl. Lang. Lit.

JA
NAMI. (1967)-. Periodical. Japanese. Shincho Sha, 71 Yaraicho Shinjuku-ku, Tokyo-To 162 Japan. **LC** PL700; .N33.

US
NANCY DREW MYSTERY STORIES. (1930)-. Monographic series. English. Price varies per volume. Grosset & Dunlap, 51 Madison Avenue, New York NY 10010. **LC** PZ7.K23; Nan.
Desc: Follows the adventures of a talented teenage sleuth as she unravels numerous intriguing mysteries.

II
NANDANA. Periodical. Bengali (Bengali). mo. Rs22.00. Communist Party of India, 5 Randi Jhansi Road, New Delhi 1 Road. **Tel** 3310762, telex 3165982 CNSIN. **LC** PK1700; .N36.

PK
NAQSH. Periodical. Urdu (Urdu). **LC** PK2151.

●US/1063-3685
NARRATIVE (COLUMBUS, OHIO). (NARRATIVE.). [Narrative]. **Added/Corp** Society for the Study of Narrative Literature. Vol. 1, No. 1 (Jan. 1993)-. Periodical. English. Three times a year. $40.00 institutions, $25.00 individuals US; $47.08 institutions, $31.03 individuals Canada; $44.00 institutions, $29.00 individuals other. Ohio State University Press, 1070 Carmack Road, 180 Pressey Hall, Columbus OH 43210. **Tel** (614)292-6930, (614)292-1407, FAX (614)292-2065. **ED** James P. Phelan. **LC** PE1425; .N37. **DD** 820.
Desc: Publishes work on the English, American, and European novel and its forebears; also on film and narrative theory.

II
NATUNA PRAWAHA. Periodical. Assamese (Assamese). 3.50. Renn Goswami, Jaya Press Gauhati - 3, Guwaha India. **LC** PK1560; .A28.

II
NATUNA PURUSHA. V. 1- October 1972-. Periodical. Assamese (Assamese). 1.00 single issue. Hema Cetiya, Amolapati Assam, Dibrugara India. **LC** PK1560; .A3.

II
NAULO MUKTI. Vol. 1, No. 1 (Feb./March 1981)-. Periodical. Nepali (Nepali). bm. Rs2.00. Janardan Thapa, 27/249 Kelgarh Colony, Varanasi 221002 India. **LC** PK2597.5; .N27.

II
NAVA-PATHA. Patha 1, Paila 1 July/August/September 2037 Oct./Nov. 1980-). Periodical. Nepali (Nepali). qt. Rs3.00. **LC** PK2598.A2; N34.

II/0028-1492
NAVALAKATHA. (19??)-. Gujarati (Gujarati). mo. Rs35.00 India; Rs350.00 other. Saha Sevantilala Cimanalala Evergreen Industrial State, Block No 47 Shakti Mill Lane Hans Road Mahalakshomi, Bombay 11 India. **Tel** 4923772/4943088/4945223. **ED** P S Shah. **LC** PK1858; .N35. **Bk Rev. Ad Acc. Circ:** 15,000.
Desc: A complete novel in each issue usually based on Indian culture.

II
NAVARAGA. VFOAT Nava-Raga. Periodical. Nepali (Nepali). qt. Rs12.00. Bikash Pustakalaya, Som Tea Garden, Darjeeling India. **LC** PK2597.5; .N33.

II/0376-6578
NAYA. (19??)-. Periodical. Hindi (Hindi). qt. Rs8.00. Naya Office, 38/276 Rajendranagar-16, Patsna India. **LC** PK2030; .N4.

II
NAYA PRATIKA. Vol. 1- Jan. 1974-. Periodical. Hindi (Hindi). mo. National Publishing House, 2125 Ansari Road, 23 Daryaganj Delhi 110 002 India. **LC** PK2039; .N38.

GR
NEA POREIA : LOGOTECHNIKO PERIODIKO. (1955)-. Periodical. Greek, Modern. ir. Nea Poreia, Venizelou 14, 54624 Thessaloniki Greece. **Tel** 011 30 31 273450. **LC** PA5201; . N43.
Ind/Abst Annu. Bibliogr. Engl. Lang. Lit.; MLA Int. Bibl. Books Artic. Mod. Lang. Lit.

US/1051-9823
NEBRASKA ENGLISH AND LANGUAGE ARTS JOURNAL. (NEBRASKA ENGLISH AND LANGUAGE ARTS JOURNAL : THE OFFICIAL PUBLICATION OF THE NEBRASKA ENGLISH AND LANGUAGE ARTS COUNCIL.). [Neb. Engl. lang. arts j.]. **Added/Corp** Nebraska English and Language Arts Council. Vol. 36, 1 & 2 (Fall/Winter 1990/91)-. Periodical. English. qt. $20.00. Kearney State College, Department of English, Kearney NE 68849. **LC** PS41; .N28. **DD** 810/.71/1. ***Continues*** *Nebraska English Journal.*

US/0741-5567
NEBULA AWARDS, THE. [Nebula awards]. **Added/Corp** Science Fiction Writers of America. No. 18 (1983)-. English. an. Harcourt Brace Jovanovich Professional Publishing, 465 South Lincoln Drive, Troy MO 63379. **LC** PS648.S3; N38. **DD** 813/.0876/08. ***Continues*** *Nebula Award Stories (New York, N.Y.: 1982), 0731-6690.*

CN/0317-2104
NEBULA (NORTH BAY). ***Suspended.*** (NEBULA.). No. 1, Feb. 1975-Suspended 1983. English. qt. $11.61. Nebula Press, 970 Copeland Street, North Bay Ontario P1A 2E3 Canada. **Tel** (705)472-5127. **DD** C810/.8/0054.

US/0277-5166
NEGATIVE CAPABILITY. Vol. 1, No. 1 (July 1981)-. Periodical. English. Three times a year. $18.00 (institutions), $15.00 (individuals). Negative Capability, 62 Ridgelawn Drive South, Mobile AL 36608. **Tel**

(205)460-6146. **ED** Sue Brannan Walker. **LC** Discard. Index available. cum. index. **Bk Rev. Ad Acc. Circ:** 1,000 (ctrl).
Desc: Presents essays, fiction, poetry, art that are touchstones for being in the world today.
Ind/Abst Am. Humanit. Index (-199?); Index Am. Period. Verse; MLA Int. Bibl. Books Artic. Mod. Lang. Lit.

CC
NEI MENG-KU TUAN PIEN HSIAO SHUO HSUAN / CHUNG-KUO TSO CHIA HSIEH HUI NEI MENG-KU FEN HUI PIEN.
Periodical. Chinese. RMBY1.25. Hsin Hua Shu Tien / Nei Meng-ku, Nei Meng-ku, People's Republic of China. **LC** PL3031.I52; N44. **DD** 895.1/35/08095177.

HU/0418-4580
NEMET FILOLOGIAI TANULMANYOK.
(ARBEITEN ZUR DEUTSCHEN PHILOLOGIE.). [Nem. filol. tanulm.]. **Added/Corp** Kossuth Lajos Tudomanyegyetem. Nemet Tanszek. Kossuth Lajos Tudomanyegyetem. Germanisztikai Intezet. **VFOAT** Nemet Filologiai Tanulmanyok. (1965)-. German. an. **LC** PT105; .N4. **DD** 430.
Ind/Abst MLA Int. Bibl. Books Artic. Mod. Lang. Lit.

CN/0228-913X
NEOLOGY / EDMONTON SCIENCE FICTION AND COMIC ARTS SOCIETY.
[Neology]. Periodical. English. qt. Neology, PO Box 4071, Edmonton Alberta T6A 4S8 Canada. **ED** T W Phinney. **DD** 823/.087609. **Bk Rev. Circ:** 150 (ctrl). ***Continues*** *Newsletter (Edmonton Science Fiction and Comic Arts Society), 0228-9121.*
Desc: A magazine/newsletter by and for science fiction fans. Despite its small print run, its circulation is virtually worldwide. Other major topics are: fantasy; comic books; games; science; and media portrayal of all the above.

CN/1186-8945
NEPENTHES (MONTREAL). (NEPENTHES : REVUE LITTERAIRE.). [Nepenthes]. **Added/Corp** Association Generale des Etudiants et Etudiantes du College de Rosemont. No 1 (1991)-. Periodical. French. ir. Limited free distribution for college students. Association Generale des Etudiants et Etudiantes du College de Rosemont, 6400 16E Avenue, Montreal Quebec H1X 2S9 Canada. **DD** C840.8/092379.

GW/0077-7668
NEUDRUCKE DEUTSCHER LITERATURWERKE. (1961)-. Monographic series. German. ir. Price varies per volume. Max Niemeyer Verlag, Postfach 2140, D 72011 Tuebingen Germany. **Tel** 011 49 7071 989494, FAX 011 49 7071 87419. **ED** Hans Heurik Krummacher. ***Formed by the union of*** *Neudrucke Deutscher Literaturwerke des 16. und 17. Jahrhunderts* ***and*** *Neudrucke Deutscher Literaturwerke des 18. und 19. Jahrhunderts.*
Desc: Critical editions of German literature, especially 16th-18th centuries.
Ind/Abst MLA Int. Bibl. Books Artic. Mod. Lang. Lit.

GW/0548-2712
NEUE BEITRAEGE ZUR LITERATURWISSENSCHAFT. Vol. 1 (1955)-. Monographic series. German. ir. Price varies per volume. Aufbau Verlag Berlin & Weimar, Franzoesische Str. 32, D 10117 Berlin Germany. **Tel** 011 49 30 22350, FAX 011 49 30 2298637.
Ind/Abst MLA Int. Bibl. Books Artic. Mod. Lang. Lit.

GW/0028-3150
NEUE DEUTSCHE LITERATUR.
Added/Corp Deutscher Schriftsteller-Verband. **VFOAT** NDL. Neue Deutsche Literatur. (Jan. 1953)-. Periodical. German. mo. $27.31. Aufbau Verlag Berlin & Weimar, Franzoesische Str. 32, D 10117 Berlin Germany. **Tel** 011 49 30 22350, FAX 011 49 30 2298637. **LC** PT3; .N4. **DD** 830/.9.
Ind/Abst Romant. Move.

US/0730-1359
NEUE GERMANISTIK. ***Ceased.*** [Neue Ger.]. Vol. 1, No. 1 (Fall 1980)-?. Periodical. English (German). sa. University of Minnesota Department of German, 9 Pleasant Street, Minneapolis MN 55455. **Tel** (612)625-9350. **LC** PF3001; .N48. **DD** 830/.9. **Bk Rev. Circ:** 200.
Desc: Promotes interest in German language graduate studies by providing a publication-forum for graduate students.
Ind/Abst MLA Int. Bibl. Books Artic. Mod. Lang. Lit. (?-?).

SZ
NEUE STUDIEN ZUR ANGLISTIK UND AMERIKANISTIK. See Linguistics.

RU/0028-4009
NEVA. (NEVA : ORGAN SOIUZA SOVETSKIKH PISATELEI SSSR.). [Neva]. **Added/Corp** Soiuz Pisatelei SSSR. Soiuz Pisatelei RSFSR. Soiuz Pisatelei RSFSR. Leningradskoe Otdelenie. Leningradskaia Pisatelskaia Organizatsiia. (Apr. 1955)-. Periodical. Russian. mo. $129.95. **(Subscription address:** East View Publications Inc., 3020 Harbor Lane North, Suite 110, Minneapolis MN 55447.) available on microfilm and microfiche from University Microfilms International (UMI).
Ind/Abst MLA Int. Bibl. Books Artic. Mod. Lang. Lit.; Curr. Dig. Post Sov. Press.

US
NEW ACCENTS. See Linguistics.

US/0895-1381
NEW ADVOCATE (BOSTON, MASS.), THE. (THE NEW ADVOCATE.). [New advocate]. (1988)-. Periodical. English. Four times a year (Mar., June, Sept., Dec.). $45.00. Christopher-Gordon Publishers Inc, 480 Washington Street, Saint Norwood MA 02062. **Tel** (617)762-5577, FAX (617)762-2110. **ED** Joel Taxel, University of Georgia, Athens GA. **DD** 028. Index Bound in First Issue. **Bk Rev. Ad Acc. Circ:** 5,000 (ctrl). ***Continues*** *Advocate (Athens, GA.), 0730-3114.*
Desc: Quarterly journal written by and for educators who teach with children's literature in the classroom.
Ind/Abst Book Rev. Index; Child. Lit. Abstr. (19??-); Curr. Index J. Educ. (March 1990-).

US
NEW AMERICAN FICTION SERIES, THE.
1- 1984-. Monographic series. English. Price varies per volume. Sun and Moon Press / Maryland, 4330 Hartwick Road, College Park MD 20740. **Tel** (301)523-0629.

US
NEW AMERICAN PLAYS. (1965)-. English. ir. Farrar Straus and Giroux Inc, 19 Union Square West, New York NY 10003. **Tel** (212)741-6900. **ED** Robert W. Corrigan. **LC** PS634; .N36.

US/0893-7842
NEW AMERICAN WRITING. [New Am. writ.]. 1st Issue (1987)-. English. sa (May, and Oct.). $16.00 (institutions), $12.00 (individuals) US; $18.00 other. Oink Press, 2920 West Pratt Boulevard, Chicago IL 60645. **Tel** (312)764-1048. **ED** Paul Hoover and Maxine Chernoff. **DD** 810. Index available. **Bk Rev. Ad Acc. Circ:** 2,000. ***Continues*** *Oink!, 0883-8518.*
Desc: Contemporary American poetry, non-fiction prose and fiction.
Ind/Abst Am. Humanit. Index; Index Am. Period. Verse.

UK/0269-2414
NEW BEACON REVIEW. [New beacon rev.]. No. 1 (July 1985)-. Periodical. English. ir. £3.50. New Beacon Books Ltd, 76 Stroud Green Road, London N4 3EN England. **Tel** 011 44 71 2724889. **LC** PN6068; .N48. **DD** 809.889/6.

CN/0832-932X
NEW CANADIAN REVIEW. ***Ceased.*** [New Can. rev.]. Vol. 1, No. 1 (Spring 1987)-Vol. 3, No. 1 (?). Periodical. English. qt. New Canadian Review, PO Box 717, Pointe-Claire-Dorval Quebec H9R 4S8 Canada. **Tel** (514)636-9845. **ED** Lino Leitao. **DD** C810/.8/0054. **Bk Rev. Ad Acc. Circ:** 1,000 (ctrl).
Desc: A multi-cultural literary journal that enhances a Canadian/world mosaic. Includes fiction, poetry, essays, and book reviews.

SA/1010-5565
NEW CLASSIC. ***Title Change.*** [New clas.]. No. 1 (1975)-(19??). Multiple languages (Afrikaans and English). **LC** PL8014.S62; N48. **DD** 820. ***Supersedes*** *Classic.* ***Continued by*** *Classic (Johannesburg, South Africa : 1982).*
Ind/Abst MLA Int. Bibl. Books Artic. Mod. Lang. Lit. (?-?).

UK/0950-5814
NEW COMPARISON. **Added/Corp** University of Warwick. Graduate School of Comparative Literature. No. 1 (Summer 1986)-. Periodical. English. sa. £49.00 institutions; £25.00 individuals. University of Essex Department of Literature, Wivenhoe Park, Colchester CO4 3SQ England. **LC** PN851; .C64. **DD** 809/.005. ***Continues*** *Comparison.*
Ind/Abst Annu. Bibliogr. Engl. Lang. Lit.; MLA Int. Bibl. Books Artic. Mod. Lang. Lit.

SA/1017-5415
NEW CONTRAST. Vol. 18, No. 1 (Autumn 1990)-. Periodical. English (Afrikaans). Four times a year. R72.00 South Africa & Southern Africa; £30.00 Europe Australia & Hong Kong; $52.00 other. South African Literary Journal Ltd, PO Box 3841, Cape Town 8000 South Africa. **Tel** 27 21 6856259, FAX 27 21 6857174. **LC** PR9364.9; .N49. **DD** 820.8/0968. **Bk Rev. Ad Acc. Circ:** 600. ***Formed by the union of*** *Contrast, 0589-574X* ***and*** *Upstream, 0258-7416.*
Desc: Publishes creative and critical work, short stories, poetry and reviews of particular interest to students of African and Southern African literature.

US/1050-415X
NEW DELTA REVIEW. [New delta rev.]. **Added/Corp** Louisiana State University (Baton Rouge, La.). Department of English. Creative Writing Program. Vol. 1, No. 1 (1984)-. Periodical. English. sa. $7.00. New Delta Review, Lousiana State University, English Department, Baton Rouge LA 70803. **Tel** (504)388-2236, (504)388-4079. **ED** Catherine Williamson and Nicola Mason. **DD** 810. **Bk Rev,** (Qty: 6). **Ad Acc. Circ:** 200. ***Continues*** *Manchac Magazine.*
Desc: A small literary magazine that publishes fiction, poetry, essays and reviews.

US
NEW DIMENSIONS. (1980)-. English. Harper & Row Publishers Inc, 10 East 53rd Street, New York NY 10022. **Tel** (717)343-4761. ***Continues*** *New Dimensions Science Fiction.*

US
NEW DIMENSIONS. EDITED BY ROBERT SILVERBERG. 1st Ed. (1971)-. Monographic series. English. ir. Price varies per volume. Harper & Row Publishers Inc, 10 East 53rd Street, New York NY 10022. **Tel** (717)343-4761. **(Subscription address:** Keyston Industrial Park, Scranton, PA 18512**)** **LC** PZ1; .N395. **DD** 823'.0876.

US/0099-0906
NEW DIMENSIONS SCIENCE FICTION.
Title Change. **VFOAT** New Dimensions. (19??)-(19??). English. an. Harper & Row Publishers Inc, 10 East 53rd Street, New York NY 10022. **Tel** (717)343-4761. **(Subscription address:** Keystone Industrial Park, Scranton, PA 18512**)** **LC** PZ1.A1; N39; PS648.S3. **DD** 813/.0876. ***Continues*** *New Dimensions.* ***Continued by*** *New Dimensions (1980).*

US/1053-1297
NEW ENGLAND REVIEW (1990). (NEW ENGLAND REVIEW.). [N. Engl. rev.]. **Added/Corp** Bread Loaf Writers' Conference of Middlebury College. Middlebury College. Vol. 13, No. 1 (Fall 1990)-. Periodical. English. Four times a year. $23.00 (individuals), $40.00 (institutions) US; $33.00 (individuals), $50.00 (institutions) others. University Press of New England, 23 South Main Street, Hanover NH 03755. **Tel** (800)421-1561, (603)643-7110, FAX (603)643-1540. **ED** Terry Hummer. **LC** PN2; .N48. **DD** 808.8. **Bk Rev.** available on microfilm and microfiche from University Microfilms International (UMI). Documents available from The Genuine Article, UMI Article Clearinghouse. ***Continues*** *New England Review and Bread Loaf Quarterly, 0736-2579.*
Ind/Abst Acad. Search (July 1993-); Annu. Bibliogr. Engl. Lang. Lit.; Arts Humanit. Citation Index [Full Cov.]; Expand. Acad. Index (1990-); Humanit. Index; Newsp. Period. Abstr. (1989-); Res. Alert [Full Cov.].

US/0094-033X
NEW GERMAN CRITIQUE. [New Ger. crit.]. Vol. 1 (Winter 1973)-. Periodical. English. Three times a year. $65.00 (institutions), $28.00 (individual) US; $74.75 (institutions), $32.20 (individuals). Telos Press LTD, 431 East 12th Street, New York NY 10009. **Tel** (212)228-6479, FAX (212)228-6379. **ED** David Bathrick, Helen Feherary, Andreas Huyssen, Miriam Hansen, Anson Rabinbach and Jack Zipes. **LC** PT1; .N46. **DD** 914.3/03. **Bk Rev. Ad Acc. Circ:** 3,000. Documents available from The Genuine Article.
Desc: Interdisciplinary journal of German studies.
Ind/Abst Acad. Search (July 1993-); Altern. Press Index (-199?); Am. Hist. Life (1983-); Am. Bibliogr. Slavic East Europ. Stud.; Arts Humanit. Citation Index [Full Cov.]; Curr. Contents Arts Humanit.; Film Lit. Index (19??-); INFO-SOUTH Abstr.; Left Index; Mag. Search; Middle East Abstr. Index; MLA Int. Bibl. Books Artic. Mod. Lang. Lit.; Res. Alert [Full Cov.]; Soc. Plann. Policy Dev. Abstr.; Soc. Sci. Cit. Index [Select. Cov.]; Sociol. Abstr.

US/0889-0145
NEW GERMAN REVIEW. [New Ger. rev.]. **Added/Corp** University of California, Los Angeles. Dept. of Germanic Languages. Vol. 1 (1985)-. Periodical. English (German). an. $5.00 (individuals), $8.00 (institutions). UCLA / Department of Germanic Languages, 302 Royce Hall, Los Angeles CA 90024. **Tel** (310)825-3955. **DD** 830.
Ind/Abst MLA Int. Bibl. Books Artic. Mod. Lang. Lit.

UK/0307-2770
NEW GERMAN STUDIES. See Linguistics.

US/1054-0873
NEW HISTORICISM, THE. [New hist.]. **Added/Corp** University of California Press. (1987)-. Monographic series. English. ir. varies per volume. University of California Press, 2120 Berkeley Way, Berkeley CA 94720. **Tel** (510)642-4191, (510)642-3907, FAX (510)642-9917. **DD** 820.
Ind/Abst MLA Int. Bibl. Books Artic. Mod. Lang. Lit.

●US/1073-8576
NEW JERSEY REVIEW OF LITERATURE, THE. [N.J. rev. lit.]. **VFOAT** New Jersey Review. Vol. 1, No. 1 (Winter 1994)-. Periodical. English. Four times a year (Jan., Apr., July, Oct.). $20.00 (individuals), $25.00 (institutions). New Jersey Review Literature, 62 Pemberton Drive, Matawan NJ 07747. **Tel** (908)583-2541. **ED** Brian Holmes. **LC DD** 810. **Bk Rev,** (Qty: 4). **Ad Acc. Circ:** 700.
Desc: A journal of poetry, short stories, essays, and reviews written by New Jersey authors as well as authors of other regions of the US and Canada. An emphasis is placed on readable artistic poetry.

US/0145-8388
NEW LAUREL REVIEW. [New laurel rev.]. **Added/Corp** New Orleans Poetry Forum. Vol. 1 (1972)-. Periodical. English. an. $9.00 (individuals); $11.00 (institutions). Lee Meitzen Grue, 828 Lesseps Street, New

Orleans LA 70117. **Tel** (504)947-6001. **ED** Lee Meitzen Grue. **LC** WMLC L 83/5729. **DD** 810. Index available. **Bk Rev. Circ:** 500 (ctrl).
Desc: Contains poetry, short fiction, translation and visual art. Also, essays by artists on art, interviews critical articles and detachable art.
Ind/Abst MLA Int. Bibl. Books Artic. Mod. Lang. Lit.

US/0146-4930
NEW LETTERS. [New lett.]. **Added/Corp** University of Missouri at Kansas City. Vol. 38 (Fall 1971)-. Periodical. English. Four times a year (Jan., Apr., July, Oct.). $17.00 (individuals); $20.00 (institutions) includes New Letters Book Reviewer. University of Missouri / Kansas, 5100 Rockhill Road, Kansas City MO 64110. **Tel** (816)235-1168, FAX (816)235-5191. **ED** James McKinley. **LC** PS501; .N47. **DD** 820/.8. Index available. **Ad Acc. Circ:** 2,000. ***Continues*** *University Review (Kansas City, MO 1963), 0042-0379.*
Desc: A literary publication featuring fiction, poetry, art, photography, scholarship, satire, and special issues.
Ind/Abst Abstr. Engl. Stud.; Am. Humanit. Index; Annu. Bibliogr. Engl. Lang. Lit.; Index Am. Period. Verse; MLA Int. Bibl. Books Artic. Mod. Lang. Lit.; Romant. Move.

US
NEW LETTERS REVIEW OF BOOKS. ***Suspended.*** **Added/Corp** University of Missouri at Kansas City. **VFOAT** Review of Books. Vol. 1, No. 1 (1987)-Vol. 5, No. 1. Periodical. English. qt. $4.00, free (with companion title). University of Missouri at Kansas City, 5100 Rockhill Road, Kansas City MO 64110. **Tel** (816)235-1168. **LC** Z1035.A1; N49.

CN/0702-7532
NEW LITERATURE & IDEOLOGY. [New lit. ideol.]. **Added/Corp** Norman Bethune Institute. **VFOAT** New Literature and Ideology; We Are the Heirs of Norman Bethune. No. 19 (Feb. 1976)-. Periodical. English. ir. National Publications Centre, PO Box 727 Adelaide Station, Toronto Ontario M5C 2J8 Canada. **Tel** (416)252-3658. ***Separated from*** *Alive Magazine: Literature & Ideology, 0318-6512.*
Ind/Abst Abstr. Engl. Stud.

II
NEW MISCELLANY, THE. Added/Corp Writers Workshop (Calcutta, India). No. 1 (Jan./Apr. 1990)-. Periodical. English. Rs40.00. Writers Workshop, 162/92 Lake Gardens, Calcutta-700 045 India. ***Continues*** *Miscellany.*

US/1048-8324
NEW MYSTERY. VFOAT New Mystery Magazine. No. 1 (1990)-. Periodical. English. qt. $37.77 (one year), $57.77 (two year). New Mystery Group, 175 Fifth Avenue, Room 2001, Flatiron Building, New York NY 10010. **Tel** (212)352-1582, (800)452-6054. **DD** 813.
Desc: Mystery, crime, and suspense stories from selected mystery writers.

US/1055-9868
NEW MYTHS. (NEW MYTHS : MSS.). [New myths]. **Added/Corp** SUNY-Binghamton Foundation. **VFOAT** New Myths/MSS. Vol. 1, No. 1 (1990)-. Periodical. English. sa. State University of New York Binghamton, Po Box 6000, Binghamton NY 13901. **Tel** (607)777-2404. **ED** Robert Mooney. **LC** PS501; .N476. **DD** 810. **Bk Rev. Ad Acc.** ctrl circ. ***Continues*** *MSS (Binghamton, N.Y.), 0738-9469.*
Desc: Introduces new writers to publishing.
Ind/Abst Am. Humanit. Index (199?-).

US/0737-5387
NEW OBSERVATIONS. (1981)-. Periodical. English (French, German, Italian and Spanish). Six times a year. $22.00 (one year); $38.00 (two years). New Observations, 611 Broadway, Suite 701, New York NY 10012. **Tel** (212)677-8561. **ED** Ciri Johnson. **LC** NX504; .N45. **DD** 700/.5. Index available (free). cum. index. **Bk Rev. Ad Acc. Circ:** 1,200.
Desc: A non-profit contemporary arts journal written, edited and published from within the arts community. Each issue has a guest editor and a different lively topic.

US/0894-6078
NEW PRESS (QUEENS, N.Y.), THE. (THE NEW PRESS.). [New press]. (198?)-. Periodical. English. qt. $15.00 (1 year), $29.00 (2 year), $43.00 (3 year) US; $19.00 (1 year), $37.00 (2 year), $55.00 (3 year) other. New Press, 53-35 Hollis Court Boulevard, Flushing NY 11365. **Tel** (718)229-6782. **DD** 810. **Ad Acc. Circ:** 1,200.
Desc: Short stories, essays, and poems.

CN/0227-0455
NEW QUARTERLY. (THE NEW QUARTERLY.). [New q.]. Vol. 1 No. 1 (Spring 1981)-. Periodical. English. qt (Jan., Apr., July, Oct.). 20.00Can$ (institutions), 18.00Can$ (individuals) Canada; 23.00Can$ (institutions), 20.00Can$ (individuals) other. English Language Proficiency Program, University of Waterloo, Waterloo Ontario N2L 3G1 Canada. **Tel** (519)885-1211 ext. 2837. **ED** M. Merikle. **DD** C810/.8/0054. **Pr Rev. Circ:** 400.
Desc: Covers new talent and directions in Canadian writing; publishes poetry, short fiction and excerpts from novels; also devotes an issue each year to a new genre, writer or group of writers.
Ind/Abst Can. Period. Index (1985-1986, Vol. 10, No. 4 Winter 1991-).

US/0899-3440
NEW RAIN. [New rain]. No. 1 (1991)-. Periodical. English. qt. $15.00. New Rain, PO Box 2087, Chapel Hill NC 27515-2087. **DD** 808.

UK/0028-6540
NEW RAMBLER. [New rambl.]. **Added/Corp** Johnson Society of London. (1941)-. Periodical. English. ir. £6.00. Johnson Society of London, 10 Beaumont Buildings, David Parker, Oxford 0X1 2LL England. **Tel** 011 44 0865 58795. **ED** David Parker. **LC** PR3532; .A16.
Ind/Abst Annu. Bibliogr. Engl. Lang. Lit.

US/0028-6575
NEW RENAISSANCE, THE. **See** The Arts.

US/0360-1455
NEW RIVER REVIEW. No. 1 (Fall 1975)-. Periodical. English. Twice a year. $4.00. Radford College, PO Box 5874, Radford VA 24142. **Tel** (703)731-5289, (703)639-2696. **LC** PS501; .N48. **DD** 810/.8/0054.

US
NEW SERIES. Added/Corp Rice University Studies (Press). **VFOAT** Rice University Studies. New Series. No. 1 (1983)-. Monographic series. English. Rice University, PO Box 1892, Houston TX 77251. ***Continues*** *Rice University Studies, 0035-4996.*
Ind/Abst Annu. Bibliogr. Engl. Lang. Lit.

US/0730-515X
NEW SOUTHERN LITERARY MESSENGER, THE. Periodical. English. qt. $6.00. Charles M Lohmann, 302 South Laurel Street, Richmond VA 23220. **Tel** (804)780-1244. **ED** Charles Lohmann. **Circ:** 500.
Desc: Stories and local poetry for lovers of fresh air, unfamiliar and unregulated, informed and formulated, anti-disfackulated and unfunktified, good stuff hot or cold.

TR/0387-4185
NEW VOICES (DIEGO MARTIN, TRINIDAD AND TOBAGO). (THE NEW VOICES.). [New voices]. Began with Feb. 1973 issue. Periodical. English. sa. $10.00 US. The New Voices, PO Box 3254, 1 Sapphire Drive, Diego Martin Trinidad and Tobago. **Tel** 637-4516. **ED** Anson Gonzalez. Index available. cum. index. **Bk Rev. Ad Acc. Circ:** 500.
Desc: Journal for the promotion or creative writing in the Caribbean. Publishes poetry, fiction and criticism by and about Caribbean people and the Caribbean. Prizes are awarded as available for articles. Contributors are also expected to be subscribers.

US/1054-9366
NEW VOICES IN POETRY AND PROSE. [New voices poet. prose]. **VFOAT** Poetry and Prose. Spring/Summer (1991)-. Periodical. English. sa. $8.00. New Voices, PO Box 52196, Shreveport LA 71135. **DD** 810.

US/0094-4645
NEW VOICES (NEW PALTZ). (NEW VOICES.). English. $2.50 single issue. D Fried, 102 Butterville Road, New Paltz NY 12561. **LC** PS536.2; .N38. **DD** 810/.8.

UK/0954-2116
NEW WELSH REVIEW, THE. Vol. 1, No. 1 (Summer 1988)-. Periodical. English. qt. £15.00 (1 year), £25.00 (2 year). New Welsh Review, 49 Park Place, University of Wales/Gym Building, Cardiff CF1 3AT England. **Tel** 011 44 222 665529, FAX 011 44 222 388367. **ED** Robin Reeves. **Bk Rev**, (Qty: 200). **Ad Acc. Circ:** 1,000.
Desc: Articles pertaining to criticism, poetry, reviews and stories.
Ind/Abst MLA Int. Bibl. Books Artic. Mod. Lang. Lit.

US/0092-6698
NEW WRITERS (NEW YORK). (NEW WRITERS.). V. 1- Fall 1973-. English. $1.95 per issue. Literary Workshop Publications, 507 5th Avenue, New York NY 10017. **LC** PZ1.A1; N43; PS648.S5. **DD** 813/.01.

UK
NEW WRITING SCOTLAND. Added/Corp Association for Scottish Literary Studies. **VFOAT** NWS. (1983)-. English (Gaelic (Scots)). an (Oct.). £50.00. Association for Scottish Literary Studies, University of Aberdeen, Department of English, Taylor Buildings, Aberdeen AB9 2UB Scotland. **Tel** 011 44 224 272634. **LC** PR8630; .N49. **DD** 820.8/09411/05.

US/0149-1040
NEW YORK LITERARY FORUM. ***Suspended.*** [N. Y. lit. forum]. Vol. 1 (Spring 1978)-(1993). Monographic series. English. ir. Price varies per volume. New York Literary Forum, 50 East 77th Street, New York NY 10021. **Tel** (212)535-4329. **ED** Jeanine P. Plottel. Index available. **Bk Rev. Ad Acc. Circ:** 3,000 (ctrl).
Desc: Each volume deals with a topic of current interest to scholars and students of literature and the arts. Example: comedy, fragments, melodrama, and women's autobiographical writings.
Ind/Abst Abstr. Engl. Stud.; MLA Int. Bibl. Books Artic. Mod. Lang. Lit.

US/1052-9438
NEW YORK REVIEW OF SCIENCE FICTION, THE. [N. Y. rev. sci. fict.]. No. 1 (Sept. 1988)-. Periodical. English. Twelve times a year. $30.00 (individuals), $34.00 (institutions) US & Canada; $43.00 other. Dragon Press, Box 78, Pleasantville NY 10570. **Tel** (914)769-5545. **ED** David G. Hartwell, Kathryn Cramer, and Gordon Van Gelder. **LC** PN3433; .N48. **DD** 823/.087609/005. cum. index. **Bk Rev**, (Qty: 100). **Ad Acc. Circ:** 1,000.
Desc: A critical journal devoted to the genres of speculative fiction: science fiction, fantasy, and horror.
Ind/Abst Sci. Fict. Fantasy Book Rev. Index.

US/0721-4030
NEW YORKER STUDIEN ZUR NEUEREN DEUTSCHEN LITERATURGESCHICHTE. (1982)-. Monographic series. German. Verlag Peter Lang AG, Jupiterstrasse 15, CH-3000 Bern 15 Switzerland. **Tel** 011 41 31 9411122, FAX 011 41 31 321131. **DD** 830.
Ind/Abst MLA Int. Bibl. Books Artic. Mod. Lang. Lit.

NZ/0077-9970
NEW ZEALAND FICTION. (1970)-. Monographic series. English. ir. Price varies per volume. Oxford University Press, Walton Street, Oxford OX2 6DP England. **Tel** 011 44 865 56767, FAX 011 44 865 267773, telex 837330 OXPRES G. **ED** Bill Pearson.

NZ/0110-7380
NEW ZEALAND JOURNAL OF FRENCH STUDIES. [N.Z. j. Fr. stud.]. **Added/Corp** Massey University. Dept. of Modern Languages. **VFOAT** NZ Journal of French Studies. Vol. 1, No. 1 (May 1980)-. Periodical. English. sa. 16.00NZ$ New Zealand; 20.00NZ$ other. Massey University / Department of European Languages, PB 11222, Palmerston North New Zealand. **Tel** 011 64 6 3569099 Ext. 7630. **LC** PQ9; .N48. **[CCC].**
Ind/Abst MLA Int. Bibl. Books Artic. Mod. Lang. Lit.

US/0163-6251
NEWCASTLE FORGOTTEN FANTASY LIBRARY, THE. (19??)-. Monographic series. English. qt. Price varies per volume. Newcastle Publishing, 13419 Saticoy, North Hollywood CA 91605.
Desc: Great classics of imaginative literature, with colorful covers, scholarly introductions, and illustrations, carefully selected by SF critics Robert Reginald and Douglas Menville for their readability, historical significance, and entertainment value.

US/0197-8071
NEWS-LETTER OF THE SOCIETY FOR THE STUDY OF SOUTHERN LITERATURE, THE. [Newsl. - Soc. Study South. Lit.]. **Main/Corp** Society for the Study of Southern Literature. Vol. 1 (May 1968)-. Academic Scholarly Publication. English. sa. Comes with Society for the Study of Southern Literature membership. Society for the Study of Southern Literature, c/o David C. Estes, Department of English, Loyola University, New Orleans LA 70125. **Tel** (504)865-2476. **ED** Stephen Flinn Young (editor's address: Box 5078, University of Southern Mississippi, Hattiesburg MS 39406). **LC** PS261; .S518a. **DD** 810/.9/975. **Circ:** 450.
Desc: Organized to promote the scholarly study of Southern literature, history and culture.

US/0028-9396
NEWSBOY. [Newsboy]. **Added/Corp** Horatio Alger Society. (196?)-. Periodical. English. Six times a year. $20.00 North America; $25.00 other. Horatio Alger Society, 4907 Allison Drive, Lansing MI 48910-5682. **Tel** (517)882-3203. **ED** William R Gowen (telephone: (708)566-9217). **LC** PS1029.A3; Z74. Index available. **Bk Rev**, (Qty: 5 / year). **Ad Acc. Circ:** 300 (ctrl).
Desc: The life and times of Horatio Alger, Jr. his works and contemporary authors.
Ind/Abst MLA Int. Bibl. Books Artic. Mod. Lang. Lit.

CN/0712-9955
NEWSLETTER / ACADEMY OF CANADIAN WRITERS. [Newsl. - Acad. Can. Writ.]. Vol. 1, No. 1 (Sept. 1979)-. Newsletter. English. qt. Free. Academy of Canadian Writers, 295 Fennell Avenue, Hamilton Ontario L9C 5R7 Canada. **DD** C810/.5.

US/0272-9911
NEWSLETTER - AUGUST DERLETH SOCIETY. [Newsl. - August Derleth Soc.]. **Main/Corp** August Derleth Society. **VFOAT** August Derleth Society Newsletter; ADS Newsletter. (1977)-. Newsletter. English. qt. comes with membership. August Derleth Society, 61 Tecomwas Drive, Uncasville CT 06382. **Tel** (203)848-0636, (608)273-0520. **LC** PS3507.E69; Z54a. **DD** 818/.5209.

UK/0260-3780
NEWSLETTER - BEATRIX POTTER SOCIETY. (THE BEATRIX POTTER SOCIETY.). [Newsl. - Beatrix Potter Soc.]. (1980)-. English. Four

times a year (Jan., Apr., July, Oct.). £7.00 (individual), £10.00 (institutions) UK; £14.00 (individual), £20.00 (institutions) others Comes with Beatrix Potter Society membership. Beatrix Potter Society, High Banks 26 Stoneborough Lane, Budleigh Salterton, Devon EX9 6HL England. **ED** Pam Lancaster (editor's address: 33 Mill Street, Hereford HR1 2NX England). **DD** 823.912. **Ad Acc. Circ:** 900.
Desc: Promotes the study and appreciation of the life and works of Beatrix Potter who was not only the author of "The Tale of Peter Rabbit" and other classics of children's literature but also a landscape and natural history artist, diarist, farmer and conservationist.

UK/0307-3335
NEWSLETTER - BRITISH SCIENCE FICTION ASSOCIATION. (MATRIX.). [BSFA newsl.]. **VFOAT** B.S.F.A. Newsletter. (1975)-. Periodical. English. bm. £12.00. British Science Fiction Association Ltd, 60 Bournemouth Road, Folkestone Kent CT19 5AZ England. **(Subscription address:** 33 Thornville Road, Hartlepool Cleveland TS28 8EW England) **ED** Jenny Glover. **Ad Acc. Circ:** 1,000.
Desc: Newsletter containing listings and information on science fiction.

CN/0713-3960
NEWSLETTER / CENTRE FOR EDITING EARLY CANADIAN TEXTS. [Newsl. - Cent. Ed. Early Can. Texts]. **Added/Corp** Centre for Editing Early Canadian Texts. No. 1 (1982)-. Newsletter. English. an. Free. Newsletter / Canada, c/o Centre for Editing Early Canadian Texts, Room 1901/Arts Tower, Carleton University, Ottawa Ontario K1S 5B6 Canada. **ED** Mary Jane Edwards. **DD** 808/.02. **Circ:** 300 (ctrl).
Desc: Newsletter of projects to edit major works of early English Canadian prose.

CN/0702-8245
NEWSLETTER FOR UGARITIC STUDIES. [Newsl. Ugaritic stud.]. **Added/Corp** Canadian Society of Biblical Studies. Section for Ugaritic Studies. Society of Biblical Literature. Section for Ugaritic Studies. **VFOAT** Ugaritic Studies. No. 9 (March 1976)-. Newsletter. English. sa. Free on request. University of Saskatchewan / Department of Religious Studies, Newsletter for Ugaritic, Saskatoon Saskatchewan S7N 0W0 Canada. **Tel** (306)966-6771. **ED** P.C. Craigie. **LC** Z7098; .N49; PJ4150. **DD** 016.492/6. ***Continues*** *Newsletter (Society of Biblical Literature. Section for Ugaritic Studies).*

US/0085-6304
NEWSLETTER - SOCIETY FOR THE STUDY OF MIDWESTERN LITERATURE (U.S.). (NEWSLETTER - SOCIETY FOR THE STUDY OF MIDWESTERN LITERATURE.). [Newsl. - Soc. Study Midwest. Lit. (U. S.)]. **Main/Corp** Society for the Study of Midwestern Literature (U.S.). Vol. 1 No. 1 (March 1971)-. Newsletter. English. Three times a year. $20.00 (regular), $30.00 (full) membership Comes with Society for the Study of Midwestern Literature Membership. Society for the Study of Midwestern Literature, 240 Ernst Bessey Hall, Michigan State University, East Lansing MI 48824. **Tel** (517)353-4370. **LC** PS501; .S63. **DD** 810.
Ind/Abst Abstr. Engl. Stud.; Annu. Bibliogr. Engl. Lang. Lit.; MLA Int. Bibl. Books Artic. Mod. Lang. Lit.

CN/0701-9890
NEWSLETTER / SOCIETY OF THE SEVEN SAGES. [Newsl. - Soc. Seven Sages]. **Added/Corp** Society of the Seven Sages. (Jan. 15, 1976)-. Newsletter. English (French). an. 5.00Can$. Society of the Seven Sages, c/o Hans R Runte, Department of French/Dalhousie University, Halifax Nova Scotia B3H 3J5 Canada. **Tel** (902)424-2430. **ED** Hans R Runte. **DD** 806. **Bk Rev. Ad Acc. Circ:** 150 (ctrl).
Desc: Disseminates research news and work in progress for all areas of seven sages studies, with emphasis on bibliographical information.

US/0043-9533
NEWSLETTER-WRITERS GUILD OF AMERICA, WEST. **Main/Corp** Writers Guild of America, West. (195?)-. Newsletter. English. mo (11 issues). $40.00 US; $45.00 Canada; $50.00 other. Writers Guild of America, 8955 Beverly Boulevard, Los Angeles CA 90048. **Tel** (310)550-1000, FAX (310)550-8185. **ED** Bill Meis. **Bk Rev. Ad Acc, Adv Mgr:** Dianna Hightower, **Tel** (310)455-4210. **Circ:** 10,000 (ctrl).

CN/0382-831X
NEWSLETTER - WRITERS' UNION OF CANADA. **Main/Corp** Writers' Union of Canada. No. 1 (June 1973)-. Newsletter. English. ir. comes with membership. Periodical Writers Association of Canada, 24 Ryerson Avenue, Toronto Ontario M5T 2P3 Canada. **Tel** (416)868-6914, (416)504-1645, FAX (416)860-0826. **DD** 806.

CN/0384-1642
NEWSPACKET (ORILLIA). (NEWSPACKET.). **Added/Corp** Stephen Leacock Associates. (Spring 1970)-. Periodical. English. Three times a year. 10.00Can$. Stephen Leacock Associates, PO Box 854, Orillia ONT L3V 6KB Canada. **Tel** (705)325-6546. **ED** Kathy Hunt. **Circ:** 3,000 (ctrl).
Desc: Informs supporters and the interested public of the work by the Stephen Leacock Associates, formed to encourage the use of humor in book writing.

US
NEXUS. (19??)-. Periodical. English. qt. Wright State University - Literary Magazine, E186G Student Union, Dayton OH 45435. **Tel** (513)873-5533, FAX (513)873-5536.

CM
NGAM : CAHIERS DU DEPARTEMENT DE LITTERATURE AFRICAINE COMPAREE, UNIVERSITE DE YAOUNDE. No. 1/2 (Jan./June 1977)-. Periodical. French. sa. B Fonlon, Department of Negro African Literature, University of Yaounde, PO Box 755, Yaounde Cameroun West Africa.

US/1054-0466
NGAN PHNG. [Ngan Phng]. (1991)-. Periodical. Vietnamese (English). qt. $8.00. Ngan Phng, PO Box 10202, McLean VA 22102-8202. **DD** 808.

US
NIGHT CRY. Periodical. English. qt. Gallery Magazine, PO Box 254, Mt. Morris IL 61054. **Tel** (212)779-8900, (800)435-0715. **LC** PS648.H6; N49. **DD** 813/.0872/08.

CN/0715-5549
NIGHTWINDS. [Nightwinds]. Vol. 1, No. 1 (Summer 1979)-. Periodical. English. $5.00. Nightwinds, PO Box 1442, Guelph Ontario N1H 6N9 Canada. **DD** C813/.087608.

US/1055-842X
NIHILISTIC REVIEW, THE. Vol. 1 No. 1 Spring (1991)-. Periodical. English. qt. $12.00. The Nihilistic Review, PO Box 1074 South, Sioux City NB 98776. **DD** 810.

JA
NIHON BUNGAKU. **Added/Corp** Nihon Bungaku Kyokai. **VFOAT** Japanese Literature. No. 1 (Nov. 1958)-. Academic Scholarly Publication. Japanese. mo (12 issues). ¥930.00. Nihon Bungaku Kyokai, 17-10 Minami Otsuka 2-chome Toshima-ku, Tokyo Japan. **Tel** 03-3941-2740, FAX 03-3941-2740. **ED** Senri Sugai. **LC** PL700; .N54. **Ad Acc. Circ:** 5000.
Desc: Mainly contains essays and dissertations.

JA
NIHON EIGA SHINARIO SENSHU. Japanese. ¥2200. Eijinsha 32-10 Higashi, Ikebukuro 5 Toshima-ku, Tokyo-To 170 Japan. **LC** PN1997.A1; N62.

JA
NIHON HADI KYOKAI KAIHO. BULLETIN OF THE THOMAS HARDY SOCIETY OF JAPAN. **Main/Conf** Nihon Hadi Kyokai. **VFOAT** Bulletin of the Thomas Hardy Society of Japan. Bulletin. Japanese. Nihon Hadi Kyokai, c/o Kanazawa Daigaku Hobungakubu Eibungaku, Kenkyushitsu Marunouchi, Kanazawa Japan 920. **LC** PR4752; .A26.

CN/0710-2658
NIMBUS TWO. [Nimbus two]. Vol. 2, No. 2 (Spring 1981)-. Periodical. English. qt. $6.00. Nimbus Press, 69 Chatworth Drive, Toronto Ontario M4R 1R8 Canada. **DD** C810/.8/0054. ***Continues*** *Nimbus, 0708-5656.*

US/0029-053X
NIMROD (TULSA). (NIMROD.). [Nimrod]. **Added/Corp** University of Tulsa. Arts and Humanities Council of Tulsa. (1956)-. Periodical. English. Twice a year (Apr. & Oct.). $11.50 one year; $21.00 two years; $30.50 three years. Arts/Humanities Council Tulsa, 2210 South Main, Tulsa OK 74114. **Tel** (918)584-3333. **ED** Francine Ringold. **LC** PS535.5; .N56. **DD** 810.8/0005. Index available. cum. index. **Ad Acc, Adv Mgr:** Elizabeth Thompson, **Tel** (918)584-3333. **Pr Rev. Circ:** 5,000. available on audiocassette.
Desc: International journal of fiction and poetry, publishes vigorous new writing.
Ind/Abst Am. Humanit. Index; Annu. Bibliogr. Engl. Lang. Lit.; Index Am. Period. Verse.

US/0890-5495
NINETEENTH CENTURY CONTEXTS. [Ninet.-century contexts]. **Added/Corp** Interdisciplinary Nineteenth-Century Studies (Association) Northeastern University (Boston, Mass.). College of Arts and Sciences. Northeastern University (Boston, Mass.). Dept. of English. **VFOAT** 19th-Century Contexts. Vol. 11, No. 1 (Spring 1987)-. Periodical. English. Four times a year. Includes Interdisciplinary Nineteenth Century Studies Membership. Gordon & Breach Science Publishers, PO Box 90, Reading RG1 8JL England. **Tel** 011 44 734 560080, FAX 011 44 734 568211. **(Subscription address:** International Publishers Distributor at one of the following addresses: 820 Town Center Drive, Langhorne, PA 19047; or PO Box 90, Reading Berkshire RG1 8JL UK; or Kent Ridge PO Box 1180, Singapore 9111, Republic of Singapore) **ED** Stuart Peterfreund and Chuck Dyke. **LC** PR3579; .M47. **DD** 820/.9/007. **Bk Rev. Ad Acc. Pr Rev. Circ:** 500 (ctrl). ***Continues*** *Romanticism Past and Present, 0733-6519.*
Desc: Explores the 19th century.
Ind/Abst Abstr. Engl. Stud. (1987-); Am. Hist. Life (1981-); ARTbibliogr. Mod. (1987-); BHA : Biblio. Hist. Art; Lit. Crit. Regist. (1987-); MLA Int. Bibl. Books Artic. Mod. Lang. Lit.; Romant. Move. (1987-).

US/0891-9356
NINETEENTH-CENTURY LITERATURE. [Ninet.-century lit.]. **VFOAT** Nineteenth Century Literature. Vol. 41, No. 1 (June 1986)-. Periodical. English. qt. $28.00 (individuals), $45.00 (institutions), $17.00 (students) US; add $6.00 postage other. University of California Press, 2120 Berkeley Way, Berkeley CA 94720. **Tel** (510)642-4191, (510)642-3907, FAX (510)642-9917. **ED** G. B. Tennyson, Thomas Wortham, & Ronald Lear. **LC** PR451; .N56. **DD** 820/.9/008. **[CCC].** cum. index. **Bk Rev. Ad Acc. Pr Rev. Circ:** 2,400 (ctrl). available on microfilm and microfiche from University Microfilms International (UMI); available via fax from University Microfilms International (UMI); available in reprints from AMS Reprint Company. Documents available from The Genuine Article, UMI Article Clearinghouse. ***Continues*** *Nineteenth-Century Fiction, 0029-0564.*
Desc: Includes articles on Austen, Scott, Dickens, Thackeray, The Brontes, Trollope, Meredith, James and others as well as literary history and theory.
Ind/Abst Abstr. Engl. Stud. (June 1986-); Acad. Abstr. Full Text Elite (July 1990-); Acad. Abstr. (July 1990-); Acad. Ind. [Computer File] (1987-); Acad. Search (July 1990-); Am. Hist. Life (1964-); Annu. Bibliogr. Engl. Lang. Lit. (June 1986-); Arts Humanit. Citation Index [Full Cov.]; Book Rev. Index; Child. Lit. Abstr. (19??-); Expand. Acad. Index (1987-); Humanit. Index (June 1986-); Humanit. Source (Jul. 1990-); INFO-SOUTH Abstr.; Lit. Crit. Regist.; Mag. Search; MLA Int. Bibl. Books Artic. Mod. Lang. Lit.; Newsp. Period. Abstr. (1991-); Res. Alert [Full Cov.]; Romant. Move.; Soc. Sci. Cit. Index [Select. Cov.]; Soc. Sci. Index; Women Stud. Abstr. (June 1986-).

US/1052-0406
NINETEENTH CENTURY PROSE. [Ninet. century prose]. **Added/Corp** United States Naval Academy. Dept. of English. Mesa State College. **VFOAT** 19th Century Prose. Vol. 16, No. 1 (Winter 1989)-. Periodical. English. Twice a year (Jan., July). $17.00 (individuals); $35.00 (institutions). University Press of Colorado, PO Box 849, Niwot CO 80544. **Tel** (303)530-5337, FAX (303)530-5306. **ED** Lawrence W. Mazzeno. **LC** PR4023; .A14. **DD** 828/.80809/05. **Bk Rev. Pr Rev. Circ:** 400. Documents available from The Genuine Article. ***Continues*** *Arnoldian, 0160-4848.*
Desc: Articles, notes and reviews about 19th century non-fiction prose writers.
Ind/Abst Am. Humanit. Index (19??-); Arts Humanit. Citation Index [Full Cov.]; Curr. Contents Arts Humanit.; Lit. Crit. Regist.; MLA Int. Bibl. Books Artic. Mod. Lang. Lit.; Res. Alert [Full Cov.]; Soc. Sci. Cit. Index [Select. Cov.].

II
NINETEENTH CENTURY STUDIES. **Added/Corp** Bibliographical Research Centre. No. 1 (Jan. 1973)-. Periodical. English. qt. $8.00. Biographical Research Centre, 1/3 Krishnaram Bose Street, Calcutta-4 India. **LC** PK101; .N55. **DD** 891/.4/09004.
Ind/Abst Am. Hist. Life (1987-).

US/1056-425X
NINETEENTH-CENTURY STUDIES (ANN ARBOR, MICH.). (NINETEENTH-CENTURY STUDIES.). [Ninet.-cent. stud.]. **VFOAT** Nineteenth Century Studies. (1986)-. Monographic series. English. University of Rochester Press, 200 Administration, University of Rochester, Rochester NY 14627. **DD** 081.
Ind/Abst MLA Int. Bibl. Books Artic. Mod. Lang. Lit.

US/0893-7931
NINETEENTH-CENTURY STUDIES (CHARLESTON, S.C.). (NINETEENTH-CENTURY STUDIES.). [Ninet.-century stud.]. **Added/Corp** Southeastern Nineteenth-Century Studies Association. **VFOAT** 19th Century Studies. **VAT** Nineteenth Century Studies. Vol. 1 (1987)-. English. an (May). $15.00 (individuals); $25.00 (institutions). Citadel Association, Department of English, Charleston SC 29409. **Tel** (803)953-5140. **ED** Suzanne Ozment. **LC** CB415; .N55. **DD** 940/.05. **Bk Rev,** (Qty: 8-12). **Ad Acc. Pr Rev. Circ:** 200.
Ind/Abst MLA Int. Bibl. Books Artic. Mod. Lang. Lit.

II
NIRANTARA. **VFOAT** Nirantar. July 1984-. Periodical. Bengali (Bengali). ir. 10.00 per issue. 2/4 C Sahajahan Road, Mohammadpur Dhaka 7 Bengal India. **LC** PK1712.5; .N58.

MV
NISTRU : [ORGAN AL UNIUNII SKRIITORILOR DIN RSS MOLDOVENIASKE]. **Added/Corp** Uniunia Skriitorilor din RSS Moldoveniaske. (19??)-. Periodical. Moldavian. mo. Str Kievului 98, 277612 Kishineu Moldova. **LC** PC794.M66; O47. **DD** 891.7/08. ***Continues*** *Nistrul.*

●US/1062-1423
NITE-WRITER'S LITERARY ARTS JOURNAL. **VFOAT** Nite Writer's Literary Arts Journal. (1992)-. Periodical. English. qt. $15.00. Nite Owl Press, 104 Fremont Street, Pittsburgh PA 15210-2106.

IS/0792-0318
NOAH. **Added/Corp** Asociacion Internacional de Escritores Judios en Lengua Hispana y Portuguesa. **VFOAT** Noaj. Vol. 1, No. 1 (Aug. 1987)-. Periodical. Spanish (Portuguese). an. $30.00 (institutions); $20.00 (individuals). Noaj, PO Box 4658, Jerusalem 91042 Israel. **Tel** 972 2 439468, FAX 972 2 633005.
Ind/Abst MLA Int. Bibl. Books Artic. Mod. Lang. Lit.

US/1062-4171
NOBODY QUARTERLY, THE. Vol. 1, No. 1 (Fall 1991)-. Periodical. English. qt. $2.00 (single issue). The Nobody Quarterly, 2843 North 47th Street, Milwaukee WI 53210. **DD** 810.

CN/0384-5176
NOCTILUCA. Vol. 1 (Feb. 1967)-. Periodical. English.
Ind/Abst Am. Humanit. Index (199?-).

DK/0109-3967
NORDICA. Vol. 1 (1984)-. Danish (summaries and/or abstracts in English and German). an. Kr97.60. Odense University Press, 55 Campusvej, DK-5230 Odense M Denmark. **Tel** 66 15 79 99, FAX 66 15 81 26.

NO/0029-1870
NORSK BOKFORTEGNELSE. [Nor. bokfort.]. **Added/Corp** Norske Bokhandlerforening. Universitetsbiblioteket i Oslo. Norske Avdeling. **VFOAT** Norwegian National Bibliography; Arskatalog Over Norsk Litteratur; Arskatalog. (1847)-. Newspaper. Norwegian. Eleven times a year. Kr380.00. Norwegian Booksellers Association, Ovre Vollgate 15, 0158 Oslo 1 Norway. **Tel** 011 47 2 410 760. **(Subscription address:** Wennergren Cappelen A S, Postboks 738 Sentrum, 0105 Oslo 1 Norway.) ***Continued in part by*** *Norsk Bokfortegnelse. Musikktrykk.*
Ind/Abst Annu. Bibliogr. Engl. Lang. Lit.

NO/0078-1266
NORSK LITTERR ARBOK. [Nor. litt. arb.]. **Added/Corp** Norske Samlaget. (1966)-. Norwegian. ir. Kr309.00 (includes postage). Forlagsentralen Tidsskriftavd, PB 150 Furuset, 1001 Oslo 10 Norway. **Tel** 011 47 2 2320995. **ED** Geir Mork and Leif Maehle. **LC** PT8301; .N66. Index available. **Bk Rev.**
Desc: Scandinavian and Norwegian literature.
Ind/Abst MLA Int. Bibl. Books Artic. Mod. Lang. Lit.

NO/0332-7264
NORSKLREREN. **See** Linguistics.

●US/1063-0724
NORTH CAROLINA LITERARY REVIEW. (NORTH CAROLINA LITERARY REVIEW : NCLR.). [N. C. lit. rev.]. **Added/Corp** East Carolina University. Dept. of English. North Carolina Literary and Historical Association. **VFOAT** NCLR. Vol. 1, No. 1 (Summer 1992)-. Periodical. English. sa (Apr. and Oct.). $17.00 (one year), $31.00 (two years). North Carolina Literary Review, East Carolina University, English Department, Greenville NC 27858. **Tel** (919)757-4876, (919)757-6041. **ED** Alex Albright. **DD** 818. **Bk Rev**, (Qty: 6-10). **Ad Acc. Pr Rev. Circ:** 1,200 (ctrl).
Desc: For general interest readers; contributors are professional writers and academics able to write for a general, literate audience. Includes interviews with North Carolina writers, art, photos, fiction and poetry.

US/1046-9389
NORTH STONE REVIEW, THE. [North stone rev.]. Vol. 1, No. 1 (Spring 1971)-. English. sa. $30.00. The North Stone Review, D Station, Box 14098, Minneapolis MN 55414. **Tel** (612)721-8011. **LC** PS1; .N65. **DD** 810.8/005/4.
Ind/Abst Am. Humanit. Index (199?-); Index Am. Period. Verse (-1978).

UK/0265-7295
NORTH WIND. **Added/Corp** George MacDonald Society (London, England). (19??)-. Periodical. English. an. comes with George MacDonald Society membership. George MacDonald Society, 61 Longdales Road, Lincoln LN2 2JS England. **Tel** 011 44 522 532967.
Ind/Abst MLA Int. Bibl. Books Artic. Mod. Lang. Lit.

US/0549-8880
NORTHEAST. (1963)-. English. Twice a year. $38.00 (institutions), $33.00 (individuals) US; $60.00 other. Juniper Press, 1310 Shorewood Drive, La Crosse WI 54601. **Tel** (608)788-0096. **ED** John Judson, Joanne Judson. **DD** 810. **Bk Rev**, (Qty: varies). ctrl circ.
Desc: Reviews of other poetry titles.
Ind/Abst Index Am. Period. Verse.

US/0190-3012
NORTHERN NEW ENGLAND REVIEW. [North. New Engl. rev.]. **Added/Corp** Franklin Pierce College. Editing and Publishing Course. Franklin Pierce College. Print Club. Vol. 1 (1973)-. Periodical. English. an. $5.00. Franklin Pierce College, PO Box 825, Rindge NH 03461. **Tel** (603)899-5111. **DD** 810. **Bk Rev. Ad Acc. Circ:** 600 (ctrl).
Desc: Literary journal which prints exclusively the works of Northern New England residents. Publishes poetry, fiction, and articles which reflect the attitudes of the region.

AT/0314-989X
NORTHERN PERSPECTIVE. (19??)-. English. sa (June & Dec.). 15.00Aus$ (Australia); 30.00Aus$ (other). Northern Territory University, PO Box 40146, Dripstone Road, Casuarina NT 0811 Australia. **Tel** 61 89 466666. **Bk Rev**, (Qty: 15-20). **Pr Rev. Acid Free. Circ:** 500 (ctrl).
Desc: Containing articles that relates to literary in some way to activities in Northern Australia, Southeast Asia, and Western Pacific regions, plus poetry and short stories.
Ind/Abst APAIS, Aust. Public Aff. Inf. Ser. (1988-).

US/0899-708X
NORTHLAND QUARTERLY, THE. [Northl. q.]. Vol. 1, No. 1 (1988)-. Periodical. English. qt. $20.00. Rio Salado Books, 1522 East Southm #2161, Tempe AZ 85282. **ED** Jody Namio Wallace. **DD** 810. **Bk Rev. Ad Acc. Circ:** 750 (ctrl).
Desc: Literary journal containing contemporary short fiction, poetry and progressive political commentary.

IT
NOSSIDE : QUADERNI DI SCRITTURA FEMMINILE. **Added/Corp** Nosside (Center). (1990)-. Periodical. Italian. Rubbettino Editore, Viale dei Pini 8, 88049 Soveria Mannelli Italy. **Tel** 011 39 0968-662034, FAX 011 39 968-662035. **LC** PQ4203; .N67. **DD** 850.8/09287/05.

FR/0249-6275
NOTA BENE (PARIS, FRANCE). (NOTA BENE.). No. 1 (Winter 1981)-. Periodical. French. qt. 140F. 9 rue Ampere, Paris 75017 France. **LC** PN6023; .N67. **DD** 809.

IT
NOTE, RECENSIONI, NOTIZIE. Periodical. Italian. qt. Documents available from Ask*IEEE. ***Continues*** *Piccole Note.*
Ind/Abst INSPEC (1968-); Zentralbl. Math. Ihre Grenzgeb.

AT
NOTES & FURPHIES. **Added/Corp** Association for the Study of Australian Literature (Australia). **VFOAT** Notes and Furphies. (Oct. 1978)-. Periodical. English. sa. 20.00Aus$ (one year), 50.00Aus$ (three year) institutions, 25.00Aus$ (one year), 60.00Aus$ (three year) individuals. Notes & Furphies, c/o Narelle Shaw, University of Tasmania, School of Humanities, PO Box 1214, Launceston Tas 7250 Australia. **Tel** 011-61-003-260225, FAX 011-61-003-263664. **ED** Dr. CA Cranston, (phone) 004-247011, (address) PO Box 215 Devonport, Tasmania 7310. **Circ:** 600 (ctrl).
Desc: Bulletin of Association for the Study of Australian Literature specialising in news research reports and notes about Australian literature.

FR/0468-8678
NOTES BIBLIOGRAPHIQUES. [Notes bibliogr.]. (1945)-. Periodical. French. mo (with July-Aug. and Sept.-Oct. issues combined). 420.00F France; 580.00F other. Union Natl Cult Bibl pour Tous Paris France, 22/26 Rue Jules Vanzuppe, 94200 Ivry sur Seine France. **Tel** 011 33 1 49607663. **ED** M.J. Poisson. cum. index. **Ad Acc, Adv Mgr:** J. Cartalas. **Circ:** 3,800 (ctrl).
Desc: Monthly material concerning literary production, including information on editorial events and literature.

US/0029-4071
NOTES ON MISSISSIPPI WRITERS. ***Ceased.*** [Notes Miss. writ.]. **Added/Corp** Mississippi. University of Southern Mississippi, Hattiesburg. English Dept. Vol. 1 (Spring 1968)-Vol. 25, No. 1 (Jan. 1993). Academic Scholarly Publication. English. sa (Jan., July). University of Southern Mississippi, C/O H. Anderson, Box 5037, Department of English, Hattiesburg MS 39406. **Tel** (601)266-4319, (601)266-4130. **ED** Hilton Anderson. **LC** PS266.M7; N67. **DD** 810/.99762. **Bk Rev. Circ:** 300.
Desc: Scholarly works about writers from Mississippi.
Ind/Abst Abstr. Engl. Stud. (?-?); Annu. Bibliogr. Engl. Lang. Lit. (?-?); Lit. Crit. Regist. (?-?); MLA Int. Bibl. Books Artic. Mod. Lang. Lit. (?-?).

US/1045-6619
NOTES ON MODERN IRISH LITERATURE. [Notes mod. Ir. lit.]. Vol. 1 (1989)-. Periodical. English. Twice a year. $12.00 US; $14.00 Canada; $18.00 Other. Notes on Modern Irish Literature, c/o E. Kopper Jr., 108 Farmington Drive, Butler PA 16001. **ED** E.A. Kopper (Editor's Telephone: (412)738-2371). **DD** 820. **Ad Acc.**
Ind/Abst MLA Int. Bibl. Books Artic. Mod. Lang. Lit.

●US/1059-566X
NOTIONS, POTIONS. (NOTIONS, POTIONS : A COLLECTION OF VIVID IMAGININGS.). Vol. 1, No. 1 (1992)-. Periodical. English. qt. $15.00 (U.S.), $22.00 (Can.). May Kimmer, PO Box 1916, Centreville VA 22020. **DD** 810.

UK/0029-4586
NOTTINGHAM FRENCH STUDIES. [Nott. Fr. stud.]. **Added/Corp** University of Nottingham. Vol. 1 (May 1962)-. Periodical. English (French). Twice a year (May & Oct.). £12.00. Nottingham French Studies, University of Nottingham, French Department, Nottingham NG72RD England. **Tel** 011 44 602 515872. **ED** Editor: 1962- L. Thorpe. **LC** PQ1; .N6. **DD** 840/.9. **Circ:** 300. Documents available from The Genuine Article.
Desc: Studies in the french literature.
Ind/Abst Arts Humanit. Citation Index [Full Cov.]; BHA : Biblio. Hist. Art; Br. Humanit. Index; Curr. Contents Arts Humanit.; MLA Int. Bibl. Books Artic. Mod. Lang. Lit.; Res. Alert [Full Cov.]; Romant. Move.

UK/0078-2122
NOTTINGHAM MEDIEVAL STUDIES. **See** History(General).

CN/0318-2835
NOUS JOURNAL. V. 1- Spring 1975-. English. ir. $1.50. All About US/NOUS Autres, PO Box 1985, Ottawa K1P 5R5. **DD** C810/.8/0928205.

NE
NOUVEAU RECUEIL COMPLET DES FABLIAUX. ir. Van Gorcum & Company BV, PO Box 43, NL 9400 AA Assen Netherlands. **Tel** 011 31 5920 46846, FAX 011 31 5920 72064. **ED** Willem Noomen and Nico van d en Boogaard. Index available. **Bk Rev. Ad Acc. Circ:** 800 (ctrl).
Desc: The NRCF will contain the complete edition of French Fabliaux, altogether 127 titles.

FR/0758-170X
NOUVEAUX CAHIERS D'ALLEMAND. **Added/Corp** Association des Nouveaux Cahiers d'Allemand. Association pour le Developpement de l'Allemand en France. Universite de Nancy II. Centre de Recherches Germaniques. **VFOAT** N.C.A.; NCA. (1983)-. Periodical. French (German). Four times a year. 166.50F. ANCA, 18 rue d Iena, Richardmenil, 54630 Flavigny Moselle France. **Tel** 011 33 16 83256594. Index available. cum. index. **Ad Acc. Pr Rev.** ***Continues*** *Cahiers d'Allemand.*

CN/0703-8011
NOUVELLE LITTERATURE ET IDEOLOGIE. No. 21- Aug. 1977-. Periodical. French. Institut Norman Bethune, Le Centre National de Publications, CP 727 Succursale Adelaide, Toronto Ontario M5C 2J8 Canada. **DD** 808.8/004.

MC
NOUVELLE REVUE DE PARIS (MONACO). (LA NOUVELLE REVUE DE PARIS.). **VFOAT** NRP. No. 1 (March 1985)-. Periodical. French. Twice a year. 250.00F France; 280.00F other. Societe Urania, 2 Place du 11 Novembre, 91330 Yerres France. **Tel** 011 33 93 303341.

FR/0294-1414
NOUVELLE REVUE DU XVIE SIECLE. [Nouv. rev. 16e siecle]. **Added/Corp** Societe Francaise des Seiziemistes. **VFOAT** Nouvelle Revue du 16e Siecle. Vol. 1 (1983)-. French. an. Societe Francaise Seiziemistes, 35 rue 11 Novembre A. Gaucher, 42023 St. Etienne Cedex 2 France. **Tel** 011 33 77 252202. Documents available from The Genuine Article.
Ind/Abst MLA Int. Bibl. Books Artic. Mod. Lang. Lit.; Res. Alert [Full Cov.].

FR/0029-4802
NOUVELLE REVUE FRANCAISE (PARIS, FRANCE : 1959). (LA NOUVELLE REVUE FRANCAISE.). [Nouv. rev. fr.]. (Feb. 1959)-. Periodical. French. Eleven times a year. 480.90F France; 501.00F other. Editions Gallimard, 5 rue Sebastien Bottin, 75328 Paris Cedex 7 France. **Tel** 011 33 1 49544200. **ED** 49 rue de la Vanne, 92126 Montrouge France; telephone: 011 31 1 49544200. Documents available from The Genuine Article. ***Continues*** *Nouvelle Nouvelle Revue Francaise.*
Ind/Abst Annu. Bibliogr. Engl. Lang. Lit.; Arts Humanit. Citation Index [Full Cov.]; MLA Int. Bibl. Books Artic. Mod. Lang. Lit.; Point Repere (1979); Res. Alert [Full Cov.]; Romant. Move.

CN/0821-4549
NOUVELLES - ASSOCIATION DES PROFESSEURS DE FRANCAIS DES UNIVERSITES ET COLLEGES CANADIENS. **See** Linguistics.

RU
NOVAIA INOSTRANNAIA LITERATURA PO OBSHCHESTVENNYM NAUKAM: LITERATUROVEDENIE. ***Title Change.*** **Added/Corp** Institut Nauchnoi Informatsii po Obshchestvennym Naukam (Akademiia Nauk SSSR). (1976)-(1992). Academic Scholarly Publication. Russian (Multiple languages). mo. Izdatelstvo Nauka / Akademiia Nauk, Publishing House of the Russian Academy of Sciences, Leninskii Porspekt 14, 117901 Moscow Russia. **Tel** 011 95 954-21-53, FAX 011 95 938-21-44, telex 411964. **LC** Z6513; .N65; PN583. ***Continues*** *Novaia*

Inostrannaia Literatura po Literaturovedeniiu. ***Merged with*** *Novaia Otechestvennaia Literatura po Obshchestvennym Naukam. Literaturovedenie* ***to form*** *Novaia Literatura po Sotsialnym i Gumanitarnym Naukam. Literaturovedenie.*

●RU
NOVAIA LITERATURA PO SOTSIALNYM I GUMANITARNYM NAUKAM. LITERATUROVEDENIE / ROSSIISKAIA AKADEMIIA NAUK, INSTITUT NAUCHNOI INFORMATSII PO OBSHCHESTVENNYM NAUKAM.
Added/Corp Institut Nauchnoi Informatsii po Obshchestvennym Naukam (Rossiiskaia Akademiia Nauk). **VFOAT** Literaturovedenie. (1993)-. Academic Scholarly Publication. Russian. mo. Izdatelstvo Nauka / Akademiia Nauk, Publishing House of the Russian Academy of Sciences, Leninskii Porspekt 14, 117901 Moscow Russia. **Tel** 011 95 954-21-53, FAX 011 95 938-21-44, telex 411964. **LC** PN583; .N68. ***Formed by the union of*** *Novaia Otechestvennaia Literatura po Obshchestvennym Naukam. Literaturovedenie* ***and*** *Novaia Inostrannnaia Literatura po Obshchestvennym Naukam. Literaturovedenie.*

●RU
NOVAIA OTECHESTVENNAIA I INOSTRANNAIA LITERATURA PO OBSHCHESTVENNYM NAUKAM. AFRIKA. BLIZHNII I SREDNII VOSTOK / ROSSIISKAIA AKADEMIIA NAUK, INSTITUT NAUCHNOI INFORMATSII PO OBSHCHESTVENNYM NAUKAM.
Added/Corp Institut Nauchnoi Informatsii po Obshchestvennym Naukam (Rossiiskaia Akademiia Nauk). **VFOAT** Afrika, Blizhnii i Srednii Vostok. (1992)-. Periodical. Russian. mo. Inion An SSSR, Ulitsa Krasikova D 28/45, Moscow Russia. **Tel** 128.89.71. ***Continues*** *Novaia Sovetskaia i Inostrannaia Literatura po Obshchestvennym Naukam. Blizhnii i Srednii Vostok, Afrika, 0134-2916.*

RU
NOVAIA SOVETSKAIA I INOSTRANNAIA LITERATURA PO KULTURE I ISKUSSTVU : OBSHCHIE PROBLEMY KULTURY I KULTURNOGO STROITELSTVA. **Added/Corp** Informtsentr po Problemam Kultury i Iskusstva (Soviet Union). (Nov./Dec. 1974)-. Russian (Multiple languages). mo. Gosudarstvennaia Biblioteka, Informatsionnyi Tsentr, Imeni V. I. Lenina, Prospekt Kalinina 3, 121019 Moscow Russia. **LC** Z2510.3; .N68. ***Continues*** *Novaia Sovetskaia Literatura Po Obshchim Problemam Kultury I Kulturnogo Stroitelstva.*
Desc: Covers literature and intellectual life.

RU
NOVAIA SOVETSKAIA LITERATURA PO OBSHCHESTVENNYM NAUKAM.
Added/Corp Institut Nauchnoi Informatsii po Obshchestvennym Naukam (Akademiia Nauk SSSR). (1990)-. Academic Scholarly Publication. Russian. mo. Izdatelstvo Nauka / Akademiia Nauk, Publishing House of the Russian Academy of Sciences, Leninskii Porspekt 14, 117901 Moscow Russia. **Tel** 011 95 954-21-53, FAX 011 95 938-21-44, telex 411964. **LC** Z2953; .N65; DR305. ***Continues*** *Novaia Sovetskaia i Inostrannaia Literatura po Obshchestvennym Naukam. Sotsialisticheskaia Federativnaia Respublika I Ugoslaviia, 0134-3009.*

RU
NOVAIA SOVETSKAIA LITERATURA PO OBSHCHESTVENNYM NAUKAM: EKONOMIKA. ***Title Change.*** **Added/Corp** Institut Nauchnoi Informatsii po Obshchestvennym Naukam (Akademiia Nauk SSSR). (1976)-(199?). Academic Scholarly Publication. Russian. mo. Izdatelstvo Nauka / Akademiia Nauk, Publishing House of the Russian Academy of Sciences, Leninskii Porspekt 14, 117901 Moscow Russia. **Tel** 011 95 954-21-53, FAX 011 95 938-21-44, telex 411964. **LC** Z7165.R9; N6; HC335. ***Continues*** *Novaia Sovetskaia Ekonomicheskaia Literatura.* ***Continued by*** *Novaia Otechestvennaia Literatura po Obshchestvennym Naukam. Ekonomika, 0134-272X.*

US/0897-9812
NOVEL & SHORT STORY WRITER'S MARKET. [Nov. short story writ. mark.]. **VFOAT** Novel and Short Story Writer's Market. (1989)-. English. an (published in Feb.). $19.95. Writer's Digest Books, 1507 Dana Avenue, Cincinnati OH 45207. **Tel** (513)531-2222, (800)289-0963, FAX (513)531-4744. **ED** Robin Gee. **LC** PN3355; .F47. **DD** 808. Index available (free). ***Continues*** *Fiction Writer's Market, 0275-2123.*
Desc: Provides marketing information on 1,900 fiction publishers. Also contains helpful articles and interviews with professional writers.

LV
NOVYI GORIZONT. (1991)-. Periodical. Russian. mo. ***Continues*** *Gorizont (Riga, Latvia), 0132-6252.*

IE
NUA-AOIS. **Added/Corp** Cumann Liteartha (University College, Dublin). **VFOAT** Nua Aois. (19??)-. Periodical. Irish.

US/0048-1084
NUEVA NARRATIVA HISPANOAMERICANA. Vol. 1 (Enero 1971)-. Periodical. Spanish. sa. **LC** PQ7081.A1; N85.
Ind/Abst HAPI Hisp. Am. Period. Index (19??-).

US/1048-6380
NUEVO TEXTO CRITICO. [Nuevo texto critico]. **Added/Corp** Stanford University. Dept. of Spanish and Portuguese. Vol. 1 (1988)-. Periodical. Spanish (Portuguese). Twice a year. $30.00 (individuals), $40.00 (institutions). Neuvo Texto Critico, Stanford University, Spanish and Portugese Department, Stanford CA 94305. **Tel** (415)725-0112, FAX (415)723-0482. **LC** PQ7081.A1; N858. **DD** 860/.9/98.
Ind/Abst HAPI Hisp. Am. Period. Index.

US/0898-1140
NUEZ (NEW YORK, N.Y.), LA. (LA NUEZ.). [Nuez]. Vol. 1, No. 1 (1988)-. Periodical. Spanish. Three times a year. $15.00 (institutions), $12.00 (individuals) US; $18.00 other. La Nuez, Box 023617, Brooklyn NY 11202. **Tel** (718)624-8936. **ED** Rafael Bordao and Celeste Ewers. **LC** PQ7074.5; .N84. **DD** 860.8/098/05. Index available. **Bk Rev. Ad Acc. Circ:** 1,000 (ctrl).
Desc: International magazine of literature and art in Spanish. Contributors are well-known.

CN/0823-2490
NUIT BLANCHE. [Nuit blanche]. **VFOAT** Bulletin. No. 6 (Spring/Summer 1982)-. Periodical. French. Four times a year. 18.00Can$ (one year), 32.00Can$ (two years) Canada; $22.00 (one year) US; 30.00Can$ (one year) other. Nuit Blanche, 1026 rue St-Jean/Bureau 403, Quebec Province of Quebec G1R 1R7 Canada. **Tel** (418)692-1354, FAX (418)692-1355. **DD** 809/.04/05. **Circ:** 8,000 (ctrl). ***Continues*** *Bulletin Pantoute.*
Desc: Presents book reviews, each issue a dossier about contemporary literature.
Ind/Abst Can. Period. Index (19??-); Point Repere.

US
NUMBER ONE. Vol. 1 (1973)-. English. an. Free. Volunteer State Community College, Humanities Division Nashville Pike, Gallatin TN 37066. **Tel** (615)451-8600. **ED** Jeanne Irelan. **Circ:** 1,000.

CC
NUNG MIN WEN HSUEH. Periodical. Chinese. bm. RMBY0.25. Post Office, Ho-Pei, People's Republic of China. **LC** PL2513; .N86. **DD** 895.1/09/005.

IT
NUOVA PROSA. Vol. 1, No. 1 (Oct. 1987)-. Periodical. Italian. Three times a year. L25000 Italy; L35000 other. Nuova Prosa, V Le San Michele Al Carso, 26 20144 Milan Italy. **Tel** 011 39 2 6684152.

US/1061-9771
NUTHING SACRED. [Nuthing sacred]. **VFOAT** Nothing Sacred. (1991)-. Periodical. English. bm. $10.00. Graalcolm Graphics, PO Box 3516, Hollywood CA 90078. **DD** 810.

US/0896-3053
O-BLEK (STOCKBRIDGE, MASS.). (O-BLEK.). [O-blek]. **VFOAT** O Blek; Oblek; Oblique. (1987)-. Periodical. English. sa. $15.00 (one year), $27.00 (two year), $39.00 (three year) institutions, $10.00 (one year), $18.00 (two year), $26.00 (three year) individuals. Garlic Press Foundation, Box 1242, Stockbridge MA 01262. **Tel** (413)528-0462. **ED** Connell McGrath. **DD** 810. Index available. **Circ:** 1,000.
Desc: Contains fiction, experimental & lyric poetry.

US/0894-7899
OAK SQUARE. [Oak sq.]. (Fall 1985)-. Periodical. English. qt. $8.00. Oak Square Publications, PO Box 1238, Allston MA 02134. **DD** 813.
Ind/Abst Am. Humanit. Index (199?-).

JA
OBERISUKU. **VFOAT** Obelisk. 1 (July 1973)-. Periodical. Japanese. qt. ¥1800. Kase Teiko, c/o Mr Kunihiro Soeda, 309 Owada Yachiyo-shi Chiba-ken 276, Tokyo Japan. **LC** PN9; .O23.

JA/0288-6065
OBERON. [Oberon]. (1953)-. Periodical. Japanese. an. **DD** 820.
Ind/Abst MLA Int. Bibl. Books Artic. Mod. Lang. Lit.

RU
OBSHCHESTVENNYE NAUKI V ROSSII. SERIIA 7, LITERATUROVEDENIE / ROSSIISKAIA AKADEMIIA NAUK, INSTITUT NAUCHNOI INFORMATSII PO OBSHCHESTVENNYM NAUKAM. ***Title Change.*** **Added/Corp** Institut Nauchnoi Informatsii po Obshchestvennym Naukam (Rossiiskaia Akademiia Nauk). **VFOAT** Literaturovedenie. (1991)-(1992). Periodical. Russian (table of contents in English). bm. **LC** PN9; .O24. ***Continues*** *Obshchestvennye Nauki v SSSR. Seriia 7, Literaturovedenie, 0202-2095.* ***Continued by*** *Sotsialnye i Gumanitarnye Nauki. Seriia 7, Literaturovedenie. Otechestvennaia Literatura.*

RU/0202-2117
OBSHCHESTVENNYE NAUKI ZA RUBEZHOM. SERIIA 7: LITERATUROVEDENIE. ***Title Change.*** **Added/Corp** Institut Nauchnoi Informatsii i Fundamentalnaia Biblioteka po Obshchestvennym Naukam (Akademiia Nauk SSSR). **VFOAT** Literaturovedenie. **VAT** Obshchestvennye Nauki za Rubezhom. Seriia Sem : Literaturovedenie. (1973)-(199?). Academic Scholarly Publication. Russian. qt. Izdatelstvo Nauka / Akademiia Nauk, Publishing House of the Russian Academy of Sciences, Leninskii Porspekt 14, 117901 Moscow Russia. **Tel** 011 95 954-21-53, FAX 011 95 938-21-44, telex 411964. **ED** E. F. Truschenko. **LC** PN9; .O25. ***Continued by*** *Sotsialnye i Gumanitarnye Nauki. Seriia 7, Literaturovedenie. Zarubezhnaia Literatura.*

US/0888-4412
OBSIDIAN II. [Obsidian II]. **Added/Corp** North Carolina State University. English Dept. **VFOAT** Obsidian Two; Obsidian 2. Vol. 1, No. 1 & 2 (Spring-Summer 1986)-. Academic Scholarly Publication. English. Twice a year (Spring, Fall). $12.00 (one year); $20.00 (two years). Obsidian II, North Carolina State University, Department of English, Box 8105, Raleigh NC 27695-8105. **Tel** (919)515-4153. **ED** Gerald Barrax. **LC** PR1110.B5; O3. **DD** 820/.8/0896. Index available. cum. index. **Bk Rev. Ad Acc. Circ:** 500 (ctrl). available on microfilm and microfiche from University Microfilms International (UMI). Documents available from UMI Article Clearinghouse. ***Continues*** *Obsidian, 0360-6724.*
Desc: Publishes creative works by black writers and scholarly, critical work by any writers on black literature.
Ind/Abst Abstr. Engl. Stud. (1986-); Am. Humanit. Index; Expand. Acad. Index (1992-); Index Am. Period. Verse; Lit. Crit. Regist.; MLA Int. Bibl. Books Artic. Mod. Lang. Lit.; Newsp. Period. Abstr. (1992-).

BU/0029-7852
OBZOR. **Added/Corp** Bulgaria. Komitet za Priiatelstvo i Kulturni Vruzki sus Chuzhbina. Suiuz na Bulgarskite Pisateli. Natsionalna Komisiia NR Bulgariia za IUNESKO. Bulgaria. Komitet za Izkustvo i Kultura. No. 1 (Winter 1967)-. Periodical. English (English). qt. $5.00. **(Subscription address:** Hemus Foreign Trade Organization, 6 Tzar Osvoboditel Boulevard, 1000 Sofia Bulgaria.) **ED** Liliana Stefanova. **LC** AP4; .O32. available on microfilm from University Microfilms International (UMI).

US/0889-6356
OCCASIONAL PAPERS IN LANGUAGE, LITERATURE AND LINGUISTICS. SERIES A. **See** Linguistics.

RU
OCHERK. (1979)-. Periodical. Russian. 0.80rub. Sovremennik, Iartsevskaia 4 Izdatelstvo Sovremennik, 121351 Moscow G-351 Russia. **LC** PG3263; .O25.

DK
ODENSE UNIVERSITY STUDIES IN SCANDINAVIAN LANGUAGES AND LITERATURES. **See** Linguistics.

UK/0954-190X
ODI INDEX TO DEVELOPMENT LITERATURE. (INDEX TO DEVELOPMENT LITERATURE.). [ODI index dev. lit.]. **VFOAT** ODI Periodicals Reference Bulletin. (1988)-. English. Six times a year (Jan., Mar., May, July, Sept., Nov.). £22.00 UK; £26.00 other. ODI Publications Regents College, Inner Circle Regents Park, London NW1 4NS England. **Tel** 011 44 71 487 7413. ***Continues*** *Periodicals Reference Bulletin - ODI Library, 0950-9186.*
Desc: This guide contains articles of over 300 journals, working papers, and research reports. Material is extensively cross referenced, by topic, country and region.

KO
OEGUK MUNHAK. **VFOAT** The Literature Today; Literature Today. V. 1- (1984-Summer)-. Periodical. Korean. qt. W3,500. Oeguk Munhak, 569 Socho-dong Kangnam-ku, Seoul Korea. **LC** PN9; .O34.

AU/1013-9966
OESTERREICH IN GESCHICHTE UND LITERATUR MIT GEOGRAPHIE. **See** History(General)-History of Europe.

FR
OEUVRES COMPLETES DE DIDEROT. (19??)-. Monographic series. French. ir. Price varies per volume. Hermann Editeurs Sciences Arts, 293 rue Lecourbe, F 75015 Paris France. **Tel** 011 33 1 45574540, telex 200595.

US/0000-1376
OF CABBAGES AND KINGS. See Children and Youth Interests.

US/1059-3993
OFF THE SHELF (HUMBLE, TEX.). *Ceased.* (OFF THE SHELF.). [Off shelf]. **Added/Corp** Progressive Educational Concepts. (1990)-(Spring 1994). Periodical. English. qt. Progressive Educational Concepts Inc, PO Box 2761, Humble TX 77347. **Tel** (713)358-8027, FAX (713)852-6560. **ED** Kenneth Kowen, 1502 Chestnut Ridge, Humble, TX. **DD** 028. **Bk Rev**, (Qty: 100). **Ad Acc.**

US
OHIO JOURNAL OF THE ENGLISH LANGUAGE ARTS. **Added/Corp** Ohio Council of Teachers of English Language Arts. **VFOAT** Journal of the English Language Arts. (1990)-. Periodical. English. sa (Mar., Oct.). $18.00. Youngstown State University, 1069 Edgewood Dr, c/o R. McClain, Chillicothe OH 44601. **Tel** (614)775-7494. **LC** LB1575.5.U5; O44. ***Continues*** *English Language Arts Bulletin.*

US/0360-1013
OHIO REVIEW (ATHENS), THE. (THE OHIO REVIEW.). [Ohio rev.]. **Added/Corp** Ohio University. **VFOAT** OR; O.R. Vol. 13, No. 1 (Fall 1971)-. Periodical. English. Three times a year. $15.00 (one year), $40.00 (three year). Ohio University / Ohio Review, 209C Ellis Hall, c/o Wayne Dodd, Athens OH 45701. **Tel** (614)593-1900. **ED** Wayne Dodd & Robert Kusley. **LC** AS30; .O43. **DD** 081. cum. index. **Bk Rev**, (Qty: 6). **Ad Acc. Circ:** 2,000. Documents available from UMI Article Clearinghouse. ***Continues*** *Ohio University Review, 0078-4257.*
Desc: Publishes contemporary American poetry, fiction, essays, and book reviews.
Ind/Abst Acad. Search (July 1993-); Am. Humanit. Index; Annu. Bibliogr. Engl. Lang. Lit.; Expand. Acad. Index (1989-); Humanit. Index; Humanit. Source (Jul. 1993-); Index Am. Period. Verse; INFO-SOUTH Abstr.; Lit. Crit. Regist.; Mag. Search; MLA Int. Bibl. Books Artic. Mod. Lang. Lit.; Newsp. Period. Abstr. (1990-); Romant. Move.

US/0030-1248
OHIOANA QUARTERLY. [Ohioana q.]. **Added/Corp** Martha Kinney Cooper Ohioana Library Association. **VFOAT** Ohioana, of Ohio and Ohioans. Vol. 9, No. 3 (Autumn 1966)-. Periodical. English. Four times a year (Mar., June, Sept., Dec.). $20.00 Comes with Ohioana Library Association Membership. Ohioana Library Association, 65 South Front Street, Room 1105, Columbus OH 43215. **Tel** (614)466-3831. **ED** Barbara Maslekoff. **Bk Rev. Ad Acc. Circ:** 2,000 (ctrl). ***Continues*** *Ohioana.*
Desc: Articles about Ohio writers, literature, arts. Articles by Ohioans on literature and the arts. Reviews of books by Ohioans or on Ohio Ohioans.
Ind/Abst Abstr. Engl. Stud.; Am. Humanit. Index (-199?); Annu. Bibliogr. Engl. Lang. Lit.

US/0899-983X
OJANCANO (CHAPEL HILL, N.C.). (OJANCANO.). [Oj,ancano]. **Added/Corp** University of North Carolina at Chapel Hill. Dept. of Romance Languages. (Oct. 1988)-. Periodical. Spanish (English). sa. $40.00 (institutions), $18.00 (individuals). Ojancano, Pablo Casaso CB 3170, University of North Carolina, Department of Romance Languages, Chapel Hill NC 27599. **Tel** (919)962-1025. **LC** PQ6001; .O5. **DD** 868.
Ind/Abst MLA Int. Bibl. Books Artic. Mod. Lang. Lit.

NR/0331-0566
OKIKE. [Okike]. No. 1 (April 1971)-. Periodical. English. Three times a year. $24.00. Okike - The Registry, PO Box 53, Nsukka Enugu State Nigeria. **ED** Ossie Enekwe. **LC** PR9898.N5; A4. **DD** 820. Index available. **Bk Rev. Ad Acc. Circ:** 1,000.
Desc: A journal of African writing.
Ind/Abst MLA Int. Bibl. Books Artic. Mod. Lang. Lit.

NR
OKIKE EDUCATIONAL SUPPLEMENT. English. Okike - The Registry, PO Box 53, Nsukka Enugu State Nigeria. **LC** PR9340; .A4. **DD** 820/.9.

PL/0239-6874
OKOLICE. (1974)-. Periodical. Polish. mo. $39.00. **(Subscription address:** ARS Polona, PO Box 1001, 00068 Warsaw Poland.**)** **UDC** 308. **CODEN** 338.

US/0030-1973
OLD ENGLISH NEWSLETTER. [Old Engl. newsl.]. **Added/Corp** Modern Language Association of America. Old English Division. State University of New York at Binghamton. Center for Medieval and Early Renaissance Studies. Modern Language Association of America. Old English Group. Ohio State University. Center for Medieval and Renaissance Studies. Vol. 1 (April 1967)-. Newsletter. English. Four times a year. Old English Newsletter, Cemers Suny-Binghamton, PO Box 6000, Binghamton NY 13901. **Tel** (607)777-2730. **ED** P. E. Szarmach. **LC** PE101; .O44. **Circ:** 900 (ctrl).
Desc: Bibliography, reviews, news and notes about research and teaching in Anglo-Saxon studies.
Ind/Abst Annu. Bibliogr. Engl. Lang. Lit.; Br. Archaeol. Bibliogr.; Lit. Crit. Regist.; MLA Int. Bibl. Books Artic. Mod. Lang. Lit.

US/0739-8549
OLD ENGLISH NEWSLETTER. SUBSIDIA. [Old Engl. newsl., Subsidia]. **Added/Corp** State University of New York at Binghamton. Center for Medieval and Early Renaissance Studies. Modern Language Association of America. Old English Division. **VFOAT** Subsidia. Vol. 1 (1978)-. Newsletter. English. an. Price varies per volume. Old English Newsletter, Cemers Suny-Binghamton, PO Box 6000, Binghamton NY 13901. **Tel** (607)777-2730. **ED** P. E. Szarmach. **LC** UNC. **DD** 829/.09. **Circ:** 100 (ctrl).
Desc: Research and teaching aids in Anglo-Saxon studies.

US/0890-0450
OLD HICKORY REVIEW. **Added/Corp** Jackson Writers Group (Jackson, Tenn.). Vol. 1 (May 1969)-. Periodical. English. sa. $12.00. Old Hickory Review, PO Box 1178, Jackson TN 38302. **Tel** (901)424-3277. **ED** Dorothy Stanfill, Bill Nance, Edna Lackie, Rubye Yopp. **DD** 810.
Desc: Presents poetry and short stories. Published by The Jackson Writers Group.

US/0381-9132
OLIFANT. [Olifant]. **Added/Corp** Societe Rencesvals. American-Canadian Branch. (Oct. 1973)-. Periodical. English (French, Spanish and German). Twice a year (Feb., Oct.). $12.00 (individuals), $18.00 (institutions), Canada; $15.00 (individuals), $24.00 (institutions) other. University of Virginia Department of French, C/O R. F. Cook, 350 Cabell Hall, Charlottesville VA 22903. **Tel** (804)296-2838. **(Subscription address:** Department of French, 301 Cabell Hall, University of Virginia, Charlottesville, VA 22903**)** **ED** Robert F. Cook. **LC** PN689; .O57. **DD** 809.1/3. **Bk Rev. Circ:** 400.
Desc: Publishes studies relative to medieval epic poetry in the romance languages.
Ind/Abst Am. Humanit. Index; MLA Int. Bibl. Books Artic. Mod. Lang. Lit.

XR
OLOMOUCKO-LUBLINSKY RUSISTICKY SBORNIK. **Added/Corp** Univerzita Palackeho v Olomouci. Filozoficka Fakulta. (1988)-. Czech (Polish and Russian; summaries and/or abstracts in German and Russian; table of contents in German and Russian). Slavisticka Knihovna Filozoficke Fakulty, Univerzity Palackeho, Krizkovskeho 10, 771 80 Olomouc, Prague Czech Republic. ***Continues*** *Rusisticky Sbornik Olomoucko-Lublinsky.*

CN/1180-5765
ON OUR WAY (PRINCE ALBERT). (ON OUR WAY.). [On our way]. **Added/Corp** Saskatchewan Literacy Network. Pine Grove Correctional Centre (Sask.). Vol. 1, No. 1 (June 1990)-. Periodical. English. mo (10 issues). 50.00Can$ institutions; 15.00Can$ individuals. Saskatchewan Literacy Network, PO Box 1520, Saskatoon, Saskatchewan S7K 3R5 Canada. **Tel** (306)653-7178, (306)653-7368. **DD** 428.6/2/05.

CN/0316-4055
ONTARIO REVIEW (WINDSOR, ONT.). (THE ONTARIO REVIEW.). [Ont. rev.]. No. 1 (Fall 1974)-. Periodical. English. Twice a year (Apr., Oct.). $12.00 (one year); $22.00 (two years); $30.00 (three years). Ontario Review Press, 9 Honey Brook Drive, Princeton NJ 08540. **Tel** (609)737-9542. **ED** Raymond J. Smith and Joyce Carol Oates. **LC** NX1; .O57. **DD** 700/.5. Index available. cum. index. **Ad Acc. Circ:** 1,000. available in microform from Micromedia Limited.
Desc: Publishes fiction, poetry, essays, photographs, graphics and interviews with contemporary authors.
Ind/Abst Am. Humanit. Index; Index Am. Period. Verse; Lit. Crit. Regist.; MLA Int. Bibl. Books Artic. Mod. Lang. Lit.

US/1043-884X
ONTHEBUS (LOS ANGELES, CALIF.). (ONTHEBUS.). **VFOAT** On the Bus. Vol. 1, No. 1 (Winter 1989)-. Periodical. English. Twice a year. $27.00 (three issues) US; $29.50 (three issues) Canada; $31.50 (three issues) other. Bombshelter Press, 6421 1/2 Orange Street, Los Angeles CA 90048. **Tel** (213)651-5488, FAX (310)376-9923. **ED** Jack Grapes. **DD** 810. **Bk Rev**, (Qty: 40). **Ad Acc. Circ:** 3,500.
Desc: Contains poetry, fiction, interviews, book reviews, art & photographs.

CN/0048-1939
OPEN LETTER (TORONTO). (OPEN LETTER.). [Open lett.]. (1966)-. Periodical. English. Three times a year. Open Letter / Toronto, 499 Dufferin Avenue, London Ontario N6B 2A1 Canada. **Tel** (519)673-5732.
Ind/Abst Annu. Bibliogr. Engl. Lang. Lit.; Can. Index; Can. Period. Index (1991-).

US
OPEN READING. Second Series No. 1- Mar. 1972-. Periodical. English. ir. Sonomas State College, c/o Division of Humanities, Rohnert Park CA 94928.

II
OPINION; LITERARY QUARTERLY. V. 1- Winter 1974-. Periodical. English. qt. A D Gorwala, 40 C Ridge Road, Bombay India. **LC** PR9494; .O63. **DD** 820/.8/0954.

SW/0283-653X
OPSIS KALOPSIS. (1986)-. Swedish. bm. Opsis Kalopsis, Box 7681, S-103 95 Stockholm Sweden.
Ind/Abst Child. Lit. Abstr. (19??-).

CN/1183-2703
OPUNTIA (CALGARY). (OPUNTIA.). [Opuntia]. #1 (Mar. 1991)-. Periodical. English. $1.00 per number. Dale Spiers, PO Box 6830, Calgary Alberta T2P 2E7. **ED** Editor, 1991 Dale Speirs. **DD** C810.8/015.

US/1056-5027
ORACLE STORY. [Oracle story]. **Added/Corp** Association of African Writers. (Summer 1993)-. Periodical. English. Four times a year. $25.00 (individuals); $30.00 (institutions). Rising Star Publications, 2105 Amherst Road, Hyattsville MD 20783. **Tel** (301)422-2665. **DD** 808.

DK/0105-7510
ORBIS LITTERARUM. [Orbis litt.]. (1943)-. Periodical. Danish (English, French and German). bm. kr1290.00 US, Canada and Japan; kr1270.00 other. Munksgaard International Publishers Ltd, PO Box 2148, DK-1016 Copenhagen K Denmark. **Tel** 011 45 33 12 70 30, FAX 011 45 33 12 93 87, telex 19431 MUNKS DK. **ED** Morten Nojgaard, Niels Jorgen Skydsgaard, and Bengt Algot Sorensen. **LC** PN1; .O7. **DD** 809. **[CCC].** Index available. **Bk Rev. Ad Acc. Circ:** 700 (ctrl). Documents available from The Genuine Article.
Desc: Study of European and American literature, concentrating on literary theory and the principles of literary history and criticism.
Ind/Abst Abstr. Engl. Stud.; Annu. Bibliogr. Engl. Lang. Lit.; Arts Humanit. Citation Index [Full Cov.]; Curr. Contents Arts Humanit.; Lit. Crit. Regist.; Middle East Abstr. Index; MLA Int. Bibl. Books Artic. Mod. Lang. Lit.; Res. Alert [Full Cov.]; Romant. Move.

II
ORBIT (GAYA, INDIA). (ORBIT.). No. 1 (1982)-. Periodical. English. ir. $6.00. Dr H M Prasad, 296 Anugrahpuri, Gaya 823001 India. **LC** PR1; .O73.

US/0474-3326
ORBIT (NEW YORK). ***Ceased.*** (ORBIT.). (1966)-Completed Series Vol. 21 (19??). English. ir. J.B. Lippincott Company, 227 East Washington Square, Philadelphia PA 19106-3780. **Tel** (215)238-4200 or 4454, FAX (215)238-4227. **LC** PZ1.A1; O7. **DD** 808.83/876/05.

US/0474-3369
ORCRIST. [Orcrist]. No. 1-. English. ir. $2.00. c/o R C West, 1918 Madison Street, Madison WI 53711. **Tel** (608)255-3067. **ED** Richard C West. **LC** PR6039.O32; O72. **DD** 828/.91209. **Bk Rev. Circ:** 500. available in microform from University Microfilms International (UMI).
Desc: Primarily essays on fantasy in literature and the other arts, emphasizing (but not limited to) the work of JRR Tolkien.
Ind/Abst MLA Int. Bibl. Books Artic. Mod. Lang. Lit.

CN/0703-1254
ORGAN (ABBOTSFORD). (THE ORGAN.). V. 1- Jan. 1977-. Periodical. English. an. The Organ / Abbotsford, Fraser Valley College, 33844 King Road RR 2, Abbotsford British Columbia V25 4N2 Canada. **Tel** (604)853-7441. **ED** Graham Dowden. **DD** C810/.8/092379. **Bk Rev. Circ:** 500.

CN/0703-1246
ORGAN (WINNIPEG). (THE ORGAN.). Vol. 1 (Fall 1976)-. Periodical. English. $3.00. The Organ / Winnipeg, 269 Church Avenue, Winnipeg Manitoba R2W 1B9 Canada. **DD** C810/.8/0054.

GW/0030-5197
ORIENS EXTREMUS. [Oriens extremus]. Vol. 1 (July 1954)-. Periodical. German (English). ir. Otto Harrassowitz Verlag, Taunusstrasse 14, Postfach 2929, D-65019 Wiesbaden Germany. **Tel** 011 49 611 5300, FAX 530570, telex 4186 135 OH D. **ED** Ronald Schneider, Hans Stumpfeldt, Klau Wenk and Klaus Antoni. **LC** DS501; .O67. **DD** 950/.05. **[CCC].** Index available. **Bk Rev. Circ:** 600.
Desc: Journal for language, art and culture of the far east.
Ind/Abst Am. Hist. Life (1973-); MLA Int. Bibl. Books Artic. Mod. Lang. Lit.

SW/0085-4522
ORIENTALIA GOTHOBURGENSIA. See Linguistics.

JA
ORIJIN SHOSETSU JIDAI. (1977)-. Periodical. Japanese. ¥1000. Orijin Shobo, c/o Tanimoto Building, 1-22 Shimo Meguro, 3-chome Meguro-ku, Tokyo Japan. **LC** PL770.A1; O75.

RM/0030-560X
ORIZONT. [Orizont]. **Added/Corp** Uniunea Scriitorilor din Republica Socialista Romania. Uniunea Scriitorilor din Republica Populara Romina. (Jan. 1964)-. Periodical.

Romanian. wk. DM188.00. **(Subscription address:** Kubon & Sagner, ABT Zeitschriftenimport, D 80328 Munich Germany.**) LC** PC601; .O75.
Desc: Socio-political and literary weekly.
Ind/Abst Annu. Bibliogr. Engl. Lang. Lit.; MLA Int. Bibl. Books Artic. Mod. Lang. Lit.

US/0730-3475
ORO MADRE. Began with issue for April 1981?. Periodical. English. qt. $5.00 (4 issues). Glazier Publications Inc, PO Box 7324, Fremont CA 94536.

SZ
ORTE. Periodical. German. qt. 35.00F Switzerland; 45.00F other. W Bucher, Postfach 2028, 8033 Zurich Switzerland. **Tel** (01)363 02 34. **ED** Werner Bucher. **LC** PN849.S9; 076. Index available. **Bk Rev. Ad Acc. Circ:** 2,000 (ctrl).
Desc: Modern, actual literature.

US/1053-0193
OSHKAABEWIS NATIVE JOURNAL. [Oshkaabewis native j.]. **VFOAT** Oshkaabewis Journal. Vol. 1, No. 1- (1990)-. Periodical. English. qt. $20.00 (individuals); $30.00 (institutions). American Indian Studies Center Sanford Hall #19, 1500 Birchmond Drive NE, Bemidji MN 56601-2699. **ED** Dave Gonzales. **LC** E75; .O83. **DD** 970.004/97. **Bk Rev.**

II/0474-8107
OSMANIA JOURNAL OF ENGLISH STUDIES. [Osmania j. Engl. stud.]. **Added/Corp** Osmania University, Hyderabad, India. Dept. of English. (1961)-. English. an. $15.00. Osmania University Department of English, Hyderabad 500 007 India. **(Subscription address:** Prints India, 11 Darya Ganj, New Delhi 110002 India.**) LC** PR1; .O75. **DD** 820/.9.
Ind/Abst MLA Int. Bibl. Books Artic. Mod. Lang. Lit.

US/0882-3006
OSTERREICH IN AMERIKANISCHE SICHT. (OSTERREICH IN AMERIKANISCHER SICHT : OSTERREICH-SEMINARE DES AMERICAN COUNCIL FOR THE STUDY OF AUSTRIAN LITERATURE (ACSAL) ANLASSLICH DER JAHRESTAGUNGEN DER AMERICAN ASSOCIATION OF TEACHERS OF GERMAN (AATG).). **Added/Corp** American Council for the Study of Austrian Literature. Austrian Association of Teachers of German. Austrian Institute (New York, N.Y.). (1981)-. English (German). $7.50 (ASCAL membership). **LC** PT3810; .O43. **DD** 830.
Ind/Abst MLA Int. Bibl. Books Artic. Mod. Lang. Lit.

US/8756-4696
OTHER VOICES (HIGHLAND PARK, ILL.). (OTHER VOICES.). [Other voices]. Vol. 1, No. 1 (Spring 1985)-. Periodical. English. Twice a year (May, Nov.). $20.00 (individuals) US; $30.00 others; $24.00 (institutions) US & Canada. Other Voices IL, Department of English, PO Box 4348, Chicago IL 60680. **Tel** (708)831-4684. **ED** Dolores Weinberg, Lois Hauselman and Sharon Sloan Fiffer. **LC** PS642; .O86. **DD** 813/.01/08. Index available. **Ad Acc. Pr Rev. Circ:** 1,500 (ctrl).
Desc: An independent market for quality fiction. Dedicated to original fresh, diverse stories and novel-experts, and to publishing new and established writers.
Ind/Abst Am. Humanit. Index.

IT
OTTO NOVECENTO. (19??)-. Italian. Five times a year. L70000.00 Italy; L110000.00 other. Otto Novecento, Pza Giovanni XXIII 2, 21022 Azzate Italy. **Tel** 011 39 332 458395. **Bk Rev. Ad Acc. Pr Rev. Circ:** 1000 (ctrl). Documents available from The Genuine Article.
Ind/Abst Arts Humanit. Citation Index [Full Cov.]; Curr. Contents Arts Humanit.; Res. Alert [Full Cov.].

US/1055-4130
OUR WRITE MIND. [Our write mind]. **VFOAT** Our Right Mind. Issue #1 (1991)-. English. $7.50. Julian Associates, 6831 Spencer Highway, #203, Pasadena TX 77505. **DD** 808.

US/0030-7181
OUTDOORS UNLIMITED. [Outdoors unltd.]. **Added/Corp** Outdoor Writers Association of America. (19??)-. Periodical. English. Twelve times a year. $300.00 + $100.00 initiation fee. Outdoor Writers Association of America Inc, 2017 Cato Avenue, Suite 101, State College PA 16801. **Tel** (814)234-1011. **ED** Carol J. Kersavage. **DD** 810. Index available. cum. index. **Bk Rev. Circ:** 2,600 (ctrl).

US/0739-4969
OUTERBRIDGE. [Outerbridge]. **Added/Corp** College of Staten Island. English Dept. Vol. 1, No. 1 (Spring 1975)-. Periodical. English. an. $5.00. College of Staten Island / English Department, Room A323, 2800 Victory Boulevard, Staten Island NY 10314. **Tel** (718)390-7779. **ED** Charlotte Alexander, Linda Principe (Associate Editor). Index available (free). cum. index. **Circ:** 700.
Desc: Presents crafted poems and fiction. Back issues are available.
Ind/Abst Am. Humanit. Index; Humanit. Index; Index Am. Period. Verse.

AT/0813-5886
OUTRIDER (INDOOROOPILLY, QLD.). (OUTRIDER.). **Added/Corp** Australia Council. Literature Board. (June 1984)-. Periodical. English. sa (1 double issue or 2 single issues). 25.00Aus$ Australia; 40.00Aus$ other. Outrider, PO Box 210 Indooroopilly, 4068 Queensland Australia. **Tel** 011 61 7 371-6166, FAX 011 61 07 371-3549. **LC** PR9614; .O9. **DD** 820.8/0994/05. **[CCC]. Circ:** 1,000.
Desc: Contemporary Australian literature.

AT/0030-7416
OVERLAND. **See** General Interest-General Interest-Australia and Oceania.

US/1044-6486
OWL CREEK JOURNAL, THE. [Owl Creek j.]. (Nov. 1988)-. Periodical. English. mo. $10.00 (individuals), $8.00 (non-profit organizations). Sacred Earth Alliance of Kenyon College, PO Box 545, Gambier OH 43022. **DD** 810.

UK/0078-7191
OXFORD GERMAN STUDIES. [Oxf. Ger. stud.]. (1966)-. English (German). ir. $36.00 (latest volume). WA Meeuws Thorntons Oxford Ltd., 11 Broad Street, Oxford OX1 3AR England. **Tel** (0865)242939. **ED** T. J. Reed and N. Palmer. **LC** PT1; .O94. **DD** 830/.9. **Ad Acc. Circ:** 1,500 (ctrl). Documents available from The Genuine Article.
Ind/Abst Arts Humanit. Citation Index (19??-19??) [Full Cov.]; Curr. Contents Arts Humanit.; MLA Int. Bibl. Books Artic. Mod. Lang. Lit.; Res. Alert [Full Cov.]; Romant. Move.

UK
OXFORD HISTORY OF ENGLISH LITERATURE, THE. (19??)-. Monographic series. English. ir. Price varies per volume. Oxford University Press, Walton Street, Oxford OX2 6DP England. **Tel** 011 44 865 56767, FAX 011 44 865 267773, telex 837330 OXPRES G. **(Subscription address:** Oxford University Press / USA, Journals Marketing Department, Oxford University Press, 2001 Evans Road, Cary NC 27513.**) ED** Bonamy Dobree, John Buxton, Norman Davis and F.P. Wilson.

UK
OXFORD MODERN LANGUAGES AND LITERATURE MONOGRAPHS. **See** Linguistics.

UK/0306-9222
OXYRHYNCHUS PAPYRI, THE. Vol. 1 (1898)-. English. ir. Price varies. Turpin Transactions Ltd, Blackhorse Road, Letchworth Hertfordshire SG6 1HN England. **Tel** 011 44 462 672555, FAX 011 44 462 480947. **LC** PA3315.

US/0886-8697
OZ COLLECTOR, THE. [Oz collect.]. **Added/Corp** Books of Wonder (Firm). Vol. 1, No. 1 (Summer 1985)-. Periodical. English. sa (April, Oct.). $5.00. Books of Wonder, 132 7th Avenue, 18th Street, New York NY 10011. **Tel** (212)989-3270, FAX (212)989-1203. **LC** WMLC 93/1510. **DD** 790.

US
OZIANA. **Added/Corp** International Wizard of Oz Club. (19??)-. Periodical. English. ir (published in different months each year). $2.00. International Wizard of Oz Club Inc., 220 North 11th Street, Escanaba MI 49829. **Tel** (217)432-5517.

UK
P.E.N. NEW POETRY. **Added/Corp** PEN. **VFOAT** PEN New Poetry; New Poetry ... P.E.N. **VAT** Poets, Essayist, Novelists New Poetry. No. 1 (1986)-. English. Quartet Books, 2729 Goodge Street, London W1P 1FD England. **ED** R Nye.

CC
PA SHIH NIEN TAI SAN WEN HSUAN / PA SHIH NIEN TAI SAN WEN HSUAN PIEN CHI TSU HSUAN PIEN. **See** Linguistics.

ER/0552-7155
PAAR SAMMUKEST EESTI KIRJANDUSE UURIMISE TEED. (PAAR SAMMUKEST EESTI KIRJANDUSE UURIMISE TEED / EESTI NSV TEADUSTE AKADEEMIA, FR. R. EREUTZWALDI NIMELINE KIRJANDUSMUUSEUM.). **Added/Corp** Fr. R. Kreutzwaldi Nimeline Kirjandusmuuseum. (1966)-. Estonian (summaries and/or abstracts in Russian and German). ***Continues*** *Paar Sammukest Eesti Kirjanduse ja Rahvaluule Uurimise Teed.*
Ind/Abst MLA Int. Bibl. Books Artic. Mod. Lang. Lit.

●US/1065-1594
PACIFIC COAST JOURNAL (CAMPBELL, CALIF.). (PACIFIC COAST JOURNAL.). [Pac. Coast j.]. Vol. 1, No. 1 (Summer 1992)-. Periodical. English. qt. $10.00. French Bread Publications, PO Box 355, Campbell CA 95009-0355. **DD** 810.

US/0078-7469
PACIFIC COAST PHILOLOGY. [Pac. Coast philol.]. **Added/Corp** Philological Association of the Pacific Coast. Vol. 1, (April 1966)-. Multiple languages (English, French, German and Spanish). an (November). $6.00. Pacific Coast Philology, Pepperdine University, c/o Cynthia Clegg, Humanities, Malibu CA 90263. **ED** Cynthia Clegg, (310)456-4435. **LC** P1.A1; P32. **Ad Acc. Circ:** 1,000.
Desc: Scholarship in languages and literatures.
Ind/Abst Annu. Bibliogr. Engl. Lang. Lit.; MLA Int. Bibl. Books Artic. Mod. Lang. Lit.

US/0739-8360
PACIFIC REVIEW (SAN DIEGO, CALIF.). (PACIFIC REVIEW.). [Pac. rev.]. **Added/Corp** San Diego State University. Dept. of English and Comparative Literature. (1982)-. English. Twice a year (May & Oct.). $6.00. Pacific Review, San Diego State University, Department of English & Literature, San Diego CA 92182. **Tel** (619)265-5443. **ED** Stephen Shapiro. **LC** PS536.2; .P27. **DD** 810/.8. **Bk Rev**, (Qty: 3/yr). **Circ:** 400. ***Continues*** *Pacific Poetry and Fiction Review, 0743-8648.*
Desc: A literary magazine that publishes poetry, fiction, essays, other non-fiction like book reviews and interviews, art and photography, and is bound at San Diego State University.
Ind/Abst Am. Hist. Life (1989-); Am. Humanit. Index (-199?); Geogr. Abstr. Human Geogr.; Int. Dev. Abstr.; Rice Abstr.; World Agric. Econ.

US
PACKAGE PLAN FOR FOTONOVELAS / CHILDRENS PACKAGE SPANISH LANGUAGE POPULAR FICTION. English. mo. $256.00. Hispanic Books Distributors Inc, 1665 West Grant Road, Tucson AZ 85745. **Tel** (602)882-9484, (800)634-2124, FAX (602)882-7696.

US/1053-9247
PAINTED HILLS REVIEW. [Paint. hills rev.]. No. 1 (Jan. 1991)-. Periodical. English. qt. $12.00 (institution), $10.00 (individual). Painted Hills Review, PO Box 494, Davis CA 95617-0494. **DD** 808.

PK
PAKISTANI ADAB. V. 1- November 1974-. Periodical. Urdu (Urdu). 20.00. 141-A Sindhi Muslim Housing Society, Saidah Gazdar Pakistan. **ED** Saidah Gazdar. **LC** PK2151; .P34.

US/0277-1535
PALABRA, LA. ***Suspended.*** [Palabra]. Vol. 1, No. 1 (Spring 1979)-Suspended with Vol. 5, No. 2, 1985. Periodical. Spanish. sa. $15.00. La Palabra, 1616 East Westchester Drive, Tempe AZ 85282. **Tel** (602)838-7237. **ED** Justo S Alarcon. **LC** PQ7070; .A27A. **DD** 860/.8. **Bk Rev.**
Desc: Chicano literature and criticism, Mexican-American, literary.
Ind/Abst MLA Int. Bibl. Books Artic. Mod. Lang. Lit.

CU/0552-9395
PALANTE. **VFOAT** Palante y Palante. 1- 1961?-. Periodical. Spanish. wk. $50.00. Ediciones Cubanas, Obispo 527, Altos ESQ Bernaza, CP 10100 Havana Cuba. **Tel** 011 632980, 631942, FAX 011 631011, telex 512337, 6540. **Circ:** 20,000 (ctrl).
Desc: A satirical humor magazine. This 16-page tabloid is printed in two colors in photogravure. Caricatures, photos and texts of a humorous nature on the current national and international political, economic, cultural and sports scenes.

PL/0031-0514
PAMIETNIK LITERACKI. [Pam. lit.]. **Added/Corp** Towarzystwo Literackie Imienia Adama Mickiewicza. Instytut Badan Literackich (Poland) Instytut Badan Literackich (Polska Akademia Nauk). Vol. 1 (1902)-. Periodical. Polish. qt. $120.00. **(Subscription address:** ARS Polona, PO Box 1001, 00068 Warsaw Poland.**) LC** PG7001; .P3. **DD** 891.8/5/09. Documents available from The Genuine Article. ***Continues*** *Pamietnik Towarzystwa Literackiego Imienia Adama Mickiewicza.*
Ind/Abst Am. Hist. Life (1954-1956); Arts Humanit. Citation Index [Full Cov.]; Curr. Contents Arts Humanit.; MLA Int. Bibl. Books Artic. Mod. Lang. Lit.; Res. Alert [Full Cov.]; Soc. Sci. Cit. Index [Select. Cov.].

UK
PAMIETNIK LITERACKI (ZWIAZEK PISARZY POLSKICH NA OBCZYZNIE). (PAMIETNIK LITERACKI.). V. 1-. Periodical. Polish. £5.00 single issue. Polska Fundacja Kulturalna, 9 Charleville Road, London W14 9JL England. **LC** PG7367; .P35.

PL/0031-0522
PAMIETNIK TEATRALNY. **Added/Corp** Panstwowy Instytut Sztuki (Poland) Instytut Sztuki (Polska Akademia Nauk). Vol. 1 (1952)-. Periodical. Polish (summaries and/or abstracts in French). qt. Price on Request. **(Subscription address:** ARS Polona, PO Box 1001, 00068 Warsaw Poland.**) LC** PN2859.P6; P3.
Ind/Abst Annu. Bibliogr. Engl. Lang. Lit.; BHA : Biblio. Hist. Art; MLA Int. Bibl. Books Artic. Mod. Lang. Lit.

CN/1183-8337
PAN DEL MUERTO. [Pan muerto]. **Added/Corp** University of Toronto. Graduate English Dept. Vol. 1 (1991)-. English. University of Toronto Graduate English Department, 7 King's College Circle, Toronto Ontario M5S 1A1 Canada. **DD** 820/.5.

US/0031-062X
PANACHE. [Panache (N.Y.)]. No. 1 (1965)-. English. Panache, Box 77, Sunderland MA 01375. **LC** PS501; .P3. **DD** 810/.8/0054.

US/0275-519X
PANDORA (DENVER, COLO.). (PANDORA.). [Pandora]. Vol. 1, No. 3 (1979)-. Periodical. English. qt. $10.00 (two year). Empire Books, Box 625, Murray KY 42071. **ED** Meg MacDonald Wickstrom. **Bk Rev. Ad Acc. Circ:** 500 (ctrl). ***Continues** Pandora, a Femzine, 0162-0142.*
Desc: Covers science fiction and fantasy, artwork, poetry, articles, and reviews.

TU
PANELLENION HEMEROLOGION TOU ETOUS. **VFOAT** Panellenion Hemerologion; Hemerologion. (1909)-. Greek, Modern. an. **LC** PA5271; .P26.

CC
PAO KAO WEN HSUEH HSUAN KAN. First published in 1984. Periodical. Chinese. bm. RMBY0.55. Hsin Hua Shu Tien / Cheng-Tu, Cheng-Tu, People's Republic of China. **LC** PL2614; .P36. **DD** 895.1/45/08.

AT
PAPERS. (1990)-. English. Three times a year. 35.00Aus$; (add 13.50Aus$ postage) other Zealand; (add 16.00Aus$ postage) other. Magpies Magazine, 10 Armagh Street, Victoria Park Western Australia 6100 Australia. **Tel** 011 61 9 4721355, FAX 011 61 9 3618295. **ED** Alf Mappin. **Bk Rev. Ad Acc. Pr Rev. Circ:** 500.
Desc: Historical, comparative and evaluative studies into children's literature.

CN/0891-1908
PAPERS GIVEN AT THE ... ANNUAL CONFERENCE ON EDITORIAL PROBLEMS, UNIVERSITY OF TORONTO. [Pap. given annu. Conf. Ed. Probl. Univ. Toronto]. 10th (1974)-. Monographic series. English. an. $29.50. AMS Press Inc., 56 East 13th Street, New York NY 10003. **Tel** (212)777-4700, FAX (212)995-5413, telex 710 581 2302. **DD** 801. ***Continues** Conference on Editorial Problems. Papers Given at the Conference on Editorial Problems, University of Toronto, 0316-2664.*
Desc: Series of bibliographical and textual studies produced by the Conference on Editorial Problems of the University of Toronto.
Ind/Abst MLA Int. Bibl. Books Artic. Mod. Lang. Lit.

US/0195-7260
PAPERS IN ROMANCE. ***Suspended.*** **See** Linguistics.

●US/1059-1079
PAPERS OF ROBERT TREAT PAINE, THE. (1992)-. English. ir. $50.00 (per volume). Massachusetts Historical Society, 1154 Boylston Street, Boston MA 02215. **Tel** (617)536-1608. **Circ:** 500.

GW/0343-0758
PAPERS ON FRENCH SEVENTEENTH CENTURY LITERATURE. [Pap. Fr. seventeenth century lit.]. **VFOAT** P.F.S.C.L.; PFSCL. No. 1 (1973)-. Periodical. English (French). sa. $25.00 individuals, $33.00 institutions US; $31.00 individuals, $39.00 institutions (surface mail) other. Wolfgang Leiner, Romanisches Seminar, Wilhelmstr 50, W 7400 Tuebingen Fed Rep of Germany. **Tel** 011 49 7071 296135. **ED** Wolfgang Leiner. **LC** PQ243; .P36. **DD** 840/.9/004. Index available. **Bk Rev**, (Qty: 60 per year). **Ad Acc, Adv Mgr:** Editor. **Circ:** 500 (ctrl).
Desc: Publishes articles on 17th century French literature.
Ind/Abst Index Book Rev. Humanit.; MLA Int. Bibl. Books Artic. Mod. Lang. Lit.; Romant. Move.

US/0031-1294
PAPERS ON LANGUAGE & LITERATURE. (PAPERS ON LANGUAGE & LITERATURE : PLL.). [Pap. lang. lit.]. **Added/Corp** Midwest Modern Language Association. **VFOAT** Papers on Language and Literature; PLL; P.L.L. Vol. 2, No. 1 (Winter 1966)-. Periodical. English. Four times a year. $24.00 (individuals), $48.00 (institutions), US; $48.00 (add $3.00 postage) other. Southern Illinois University / Edwardsville Humanities, c/o Jean Vassier, Edwardsville IL 62026-1434. **Tel** (618)692-2119, FAX (618)692-3509. **ED** Brian Abel Ragen and Jack Voller. **LC** PR1; .P3. **DD** 820/.9. Index available in last issue of volume--attached. cum. index. **Bk Rev. Ad Acc. Circ:** 800 (ctrl). available on microfilm and microfiche from University Microfilms International (UMI). Documents available from The Genuine Article, UMI Article Clearinghouse. ***Continues** Papers on English Language & Literature.*
Desc: Literary history, theory, and interpretation; publishes essays dealing with writings in English, American, French, German, Spanish, Russian and other languages. Brief notes and a review essay included.
Ind/Abst Abstr. Engl. Stud.; Acad. Search (July 1993-); Am. Bibliogr. Slavic East Europ. Stud.; Arts Humanit. Citation Index [Full Cov.]; Curr. Contents Arts Humanit.; Expand. Acad. Index (1989-); Humanit. Index; Humanit. Source (Jul. 1993-); Index Book Rev. Humanit.; INFO-SOUTH Abstr.; Lang. Lang. Behav. Abstr.; Lit. Crit. Regist.; Mag. Search; Middle East Abstr. Index; MLA Int. Bibl. Books Artic. Mod. Lang. Lit.; Newsp. Period. Abstr. (1991-); Recent. Publ. Artic.; Res. Alert [Full Cov.]; Romant. Move.; Soc. Plann. Policy Dev. Abstr.

UK
PAPERS READ BEFORE THE SOCIETY. **Main/Corp** English Goethe Society. (1924)-. English. an. University College of London / English, English Goethe Society, Gower Street, London WC1 6BT England.

UK
PAPERS / THE CARLYLE SOCIETY. **Added/Corp** Carlyle Society. (198?)-. English. **LC** PR4432.A2; C375. ***Continues** Occasional Papers (Carlyle Society).*
Ind/Abst MLA Int. Bibl. Books Artic. Mod. Lang. Lit.

AT/1034-9243
PAPERS VICTORIA PARK. **See** Children and Youth Interests.

●AG
PAPIROS DEL SIGLO VEINTE. **VFOAT** Papiros del Siglo 20; Papiros del Siglo XX. Vol. 1, No. 1 (Oct. 1992)-. Periodical. Spanish. mo. 3.00Arg$. Editorial Vinciguerra SRL, Buenos Aires, Argentina. **ED** Lidia Vinciguerra.

BE/0078-9402
PAPYROLOGICA BRUXELLENSIA. Vol. 1 (1962)-. Monographic series. Multiple languages (French, English and German). Price varies per volume. Parc du Cinquantenaire 10, B-1040 Brussels Belgium.

SZ
PAPYRUS BODMER. **Added/Corp** Cologny, Switzerland. Bibliotheca Bodmeriana. Vol. 1 (1954)-. Monographic series. French (Greek, Ancient and Coptic, French). ir. Price varies per volume. Bibliotheca Bodmeriana, 1223 Cologny, Geneva Switzerland. **Bk Rev. Ad Acc.**
Desc: Grecian and Coptic texts (Papyri) of the Christianity. Also Meander's comedies (3).

FR/0767-7138
PARADE SAUVAGE. BULLETIN. (PARADE SAUVAGE.). [Parade sauvage, Bull.]. **Added/Corp** Musee Rimbaud. **VFOAT** Parade Sauvage Bulletin. No. 1 (Feb. 1985)-. Periodical. French. sa. Musee Bibliotheque Rimbaud, BP 490, 08109 Charleville, Mezieres Cedex France.
Ind/Abst MLA Int. Bibl. Books Artic. Mod. Lang. Lit.

IT
PARADIGMA. 1- Jan. 1977-. Periodical. Italian. **LC** PQ4001; .P27.
Ind/Abst BHA : Biblio. Hist. Art.

CN/1182-543X
PARAGRAPH (STRATFORD). (PARAGRAPH : THE CANADIAN FICTION MAGAZINE.). [Paragraph]. Vol. 12, No. 2 (1990)-. Periodical. English. Three times a year (Mar., July, Nov.). 13.08Can$ (individuals); 18.69Can$ (institution). Mercury Press / Ontario, 137 Birmingham Street, Stratford ONT N5A 2T1 Canada. **Tel** (519)273-7083. **DD** C813/.5409. **Bk Rev**, (Qty: 100). **Ad Acc, Adv Mgr:** B. Barber. **Circ:** 1,500. available in microform from University Microfilms International (UMI). ***Continues** Cross-Canada Writers' Magazine., 0838-9624.*
Desc: Interviews, essays, articles, and reviews concerning contemporary Canadian fiction.
Ind/Abst Can. Index; Can. Period. Index (19??-); Curr. Contents Arts Humanit.

VE
PARAPARA. **Added/Corp** Banco del Libro. (19??)-. Periodical. Spanish. sa. Banco Del Libro, Apartado 5893, Caracas 1010 A Venezuela. **Tel** 011 58 2 3323136. **LC** PN1008.2; .P37. **DD** 809/.89282/05.
Ind/Abst Child. Lit. Abstr. (19??-).

GR/1012-0211
PARATERETES : PERIODIKE EKDOSE LOGOU KAI TECHNES, O. (1987)-. Periodical. Greek, Modern. bm (6 issues). $50.00. Parateretes Co, Didotou 39, Athens 106 80 Greece. **Tel** 011 30 1 36 00 658.

AT/0313-6221
PARERGON. **See** Classical Studies.

US/0031-2037
PARIS REVIEW, THE. [Paris rev.]. (Feb. 1953)-. English. Four times a year (Seasonally). $40.00 (individuals), $46.00 (institutions) US; $54.00 (individuals), $61.00 (institutions) others. Paris Review, 45-39 171 Place, Flushing NY 11358-3398. **Tel** (718)539-7085. **ED** George Ames Plimpton. **LC** AP4; .P245. **Bk Rev. Ad Acc. Circ:** 10,500 (ctrl). available on microfilm and microfiche from University Microfilms International (UMI). Documents available from The Genuine Article, UMI Article Clearinghouse.
Desc: Publishes fiction and poetry of various genres, styles or modes.
Ind/Abst Abstr. Engl. Stud.; Acad. Abstr. Full Text Elite (July 1990-); Acad. Abstr. (July 1990-); Acad. Ind. [Computer File] (1987-); Acad. Search (July 1990-); Am. Humanit. Index; Annu. Bibliogr. Engl. Lang. Lit.; Arts Humanit. Citation Index [Full Cov.]; Curr. Contents Arts Humanit.; Expand. Acad. Index (1987-); Humanit. Index; Index Am. Period. Verse; INFO-SOUTH Abstr.; Mag. Search; Newsp. Period. Abstr. (1991-); Res. Alert [Full Cov.]; Soc. Sci. Source (Jul. 1990-); Soc. Sci. Cit. Index [Select. Cov.].

US
PARIS REVIEW, THE. (Feb. 1953)-. Periodical. English. ir. Micromedia Limited, 20 Victoria Street, Toronto Ontario M5C 2N8 Canada. **Tel** (416)362-5211, (800)387-2689, FAX (416)362-6161, telex 06524668. available in print.

CN/0821-3003
PARLONS RAISON (1983). (PARLONS RAISON / DE NALOR.). [Parlons raison]. **VFOAT** Parlons Raison (Meditations). No. 14, (Aug./Sept. 1983)-. Periodical. French. bm. Parlons Raison, CP 241, St-Lambert Quebec J4P 3N8 Canada. **DD** C848/.5408. ***Continues** Meditations. Francais, 0826-0842.*

FI/0031-2320
PARNASSO. [Parnasso]. Vol. 1-. Periodical. Finnish. ir. Valiolehdet OY, Heitalahdenranta 13, Helsinki 18 Finland. **LC** PN9; .P3. **DD** 809. ***Formed by the union of** Ajan Kirja **and** Nakoala.*
Ind/Abst MLA Int. Bibl. Books Artic. Mod. Lang. Lit.

IT
PAROLA LETTERARIA, LA. 1-. Monographic series. Italian. Price varies per volume. N Zanichelli Editore S P A, Via Irnerio 34, 40126 Bologna Italy.

US
PAROLES GELEES : UCLA FRENCH STUDIES. **Added/Corp** University of California, Los Angeles. Dept. of French. French Graduate Students Association (University of California, Los Angeles). Vol. 1 (1983)-. English. an (Oct.). $10.00 (institutions); $8.00 (individuals). Paroles Gelees, UCLA French Department, 405 Hilgard Avenue, Los Angeles CA 90024. **Tel** (213)825-1145.
Ind/Abst MLA Int. Bibl. Books Artic. Mod. Lang. Lit.

II
PARSIANA. Periodical. Multiple languages (English and Gujarati). mo. $35.00. **(Subscription address:** Prints India, 11 Darya Ganj, New Delhi 110002 India.**)**

US/0031-2525
PARTISAN REVIEW (1936). **See** Political Science-Socialism, Communism, Anarchism, Utopianism.

II
PARVAZ. Periodical. Urdu (Urdu). 10.00. Parvaz Pres, Books Market, Ludhyana India. **LC** PK2151; .P37.

US/0278-0828
PASSAGES NORTH. **Added/Corp** Bay Area Writers' Guild (Escanaba, Mich.). (1979)-. Periodical. English. Twice a year (Jan. & July). $10.00 (one year), $18.00 (two years). Passages North, c/o Ben Mitchell, Kalamazoo College, 1200 Academy Street, Kalamazoo MI 49007. **Tel** (616)337-7331. **ED** Elinor Benedict. **Ad Acc. Circ:** 2,000.
Desc: High quality fiction and poetry in tabloid size with graphic arts.
Ind/Abst Am. Humanit. Index; Index Am. Period. Verse.

FR/0031-2711
PASSERELLE, LA. (Winter 1970)-. Periodical. French. qt. Pierre Bearn, 60 rue Monsieur le Prince, Paris France. **Tel** 326 22 73. **ED** Pierre Bearn. **LC** AP20; .P346.
Desc: Literary journal written by a single author defending a humane literary style and philosophy. Sponsored by the Academie Francaise.

FR
PAUL VALERY. 1- 1974-. French. 40.00F. Lettres Modernes Minard, 45 rue de Saint Andre, 14123 Fleury Surrey Orne France. **Tel** 011 33 31 844706. **LC** PN3; .R4 subser; PQ2643.A26. **DD** 848/.9/1209 S; 848/.9/1209.

US/0031-3262
PAUNCH. [Paunch]. (1963)-. Periodical. English. ir. $10.00 (individuals), $12.00 (institutions). Arthur Efron, 123 Woodward Avenue, Buffalo NY 14214. **Tel** (716)836-7332. **ED** Arthur Efron. **LC** PN2; .P38. **DD** 805.
Ind/Abst Abstr. Engl. Stud.; Annu. Bibliogr. Engl. Lang. Lit.; Index Am. Period. Verse; Lit. Crit. Regist.; MLA Int. Bibl. Books Artic. Mod. Lang. Lit.

US/0162-0061
PAWN REVIEW, THE. ***Ceased.*** Vol. 1 (Jan. 1976)-Vol. 9 (Sept. 1985). Periodical. English. sa. The Pawn Review, 2903 Windsor Road, Austin TX 78703. **Tel** (512)471-9113. **ED** Thomas Zigal. **Bk Rev. Circ:** 500.
Desc: Literary.

SZ/1013-1191
PEAKE STUDIES. Vol. 1, No. 1 (Autumn 1988)-. Periodical. English. sa. $12.00. G Peter Winnington, Les 3 Chasseurs, CH-1413 Orzens Vaud Switzerland. **Tel** +41 21 88 777 21, FAX +41 21 88 779 76. **ED** G Peter Winnington. Index available. **Bk Rev. Ad Acc. Circ:** 250.
Desc: Prints articles and reviews books relevant to the life and work of Mervyn Peake (1911-1968).
Ind/Abst MLA Int. Bibl. Books Artic. Mod. Lang. Lit.

US/0031-3696
PEBBLE (CRETE). ***Ceased.*** (PEBBLE.). [Pebble]. No. 1 (Autumn 1968)-?. Periodical. English. qt. The Best Cellar Press, 118 South Boswell Avenue, Crete NE 68333. **LC** PS580; .P42. **DD** 811/.5/408.
Ind/Abst Index Am. Period. Verse.

US/1045-7836
PEGASUS (NORWALK, CONN.). (PEGASUS.). (1988)-. Periodical. English (Greek, Modern). Six times a year. $15.00 one year; $28.00 two years; $39.00 three years. Pegasus Publishing Company, 30 Plymouth Avenue, Norwalk CT 06851. **DD** 949.

CC
PEI-CHING WEN HSUEH. VFOAT Beijing Wenxue. Vol. 10, (1980)-. Periodical. Chinese. mo. $17.80. **(Subscription address:** China International Book Trading Corporation, PO Box 399, Library Service Department, Beijing 100044 People's Republic of China.**)** **LC** NX8.C45; P43. **DD** 895.1/09/005. ***Continues*** *Pei-Ching Wen I.*
Desc: Covers Chinese literature.

CC
PEI FANG WEN HSUEH. VFOAT Beifang Wenxue. (July 1978)-. Periodical. Chinese. mo. $27.36. **(Subscription address:** China International Book Trading Corporation, PO Box 399, Library Service Department, Beijing 100044 People's Republic of China.**)** **LC** PL2513; .P43. **DD** 895.1/09/005. ***Continues*** *Hei-Lung-Chiang Wen I.*

US/0097-496X
PEMBROKE MAGAZINE, THE. Added/Corp Pembroke State University. North Carolina Arts Council. Pembroke State College. No. 1 (1969)-. English. an (Mar.). $5.00 US, Canada and Mexico; $5.50 other. Pembroke State University, Box 60, Pembroke NC 28372. **Tel** (919)521-4214, Ext. 246. **ED** Shelby Stephenson, (919)521-6358. **LC** PS1; .P45. **DD** 810/.8/005. Index available. **Bk Rev. Ad Acc. Circ:** 500. available on microfilm and microfiche from University Microfilms International (UMI).
Desc: Publishes writers from Third World cultures and various countries, as well as local North Carolina writers of all ages and preoccupations.
Ind/Abst Am. Humanit. Index; Index Am. Period. Verse; MLA Int. Bibl. Books Artic. Mod. Lang. Lit.

UK
PEN INTERNATIONAL. Added/Corp PEN. Unesco. **VFOAT** P.E.N. International; Bulletin of Selected Books. Vol. 32, No. 1 (1982)-. Periodical. English (French). Twice a year (Apr. & Oct.). £6.00. International Pen, 9/10 Charterhouse Building, Goswell Road, London EC1M 7AT England. **Tel** 011-44-71-253-4308, FAX 011-44-71-253-5711. **ED** Peter Day. **LC** Z1035.A1; P34. **DD** 028.1. **Bk Rev**, (Qty: 35). **Circ:** 1,600. ***Continues*** *International P.E.N. Bulletin of Selected Books, 0020-823X.*
Desc: Features articles, short stories, poetry and information from P.E.N. center.
Ind/Abst Middle East Abstr. Index.

US/8756-5668
PENNSYLVANIA REVIEW (PITTSBURGH, PA.), THE. (THE PENNSYLVANIA REVIEW.). **Added/Corp** University of Pittsburgh. Dept. of English. Writing Program. Vol. 1, No. 1 (Spring 1985)-. Periodical. English. sa. $10.00 (one year) $18.00 (wo years). University of Pittsburgh Department of English, 526 Cathedral of Learning, Pittsburgh PA 15260. **Tel** (412)624-0026. **ED** Julie Parson-Nesbitt. **DD** 810. **Bk Rev**, (Qty: (4-5 per year)). **Ad Acc. Circ:** 1,000 (ctrl).
Desc: Publishing the finest fiction, poetry and essays. Also featuring book reviews in feature issues. Contributors have included Maxine Kumin, Gordon Fish, Linda Pastan, Paul West, and Joyce Carol Oates.
Ind/Abst Index Am. Period. Verse.

US/0149-0516
PEQUOD. [Pequod]. Vol. 1 (Spring 1974)-. Periodical. English. ir. $21.00 (three issues) institutions; $13.50 (six issues) individuals; $42.00 institutions. National Poetry Foundation, University of Maine, 305 Neville Hall, Orono ME 04469. **Tel** (207)581-3814. **(Subscription address:** Mark Rudman, 817 Westend Avenue, New York, NY 10025, telephone: (212)998-8828**)** **ED** Mark Rudman. **LC** PN6010.5; .P46. **DD** 808.8/004.
Desc: Publishes work in contemporary literature. It introduces to its readers translations by known and unknown writers as well as work by previously unpublished poets, essayists and fiction writers. Some of the authors in the recent issues include Michaelangelo Antonioni, Russell Banks, Louise Gluck, Sharon Olds, Charles Tomlinson, and Derek Walcott.
Ind/Abst Am. Bibliogr. Slavic East Europ. Stud.; Index Am. Period. Verse; MLA Int. Bibl. Books Artic. Mod. Lang. Lit.

US/1070-0358
PERCEPTIONS (TOLEDO, OH.). (PERCEPTIONS.). [Perceptions]. (1988)-. Periodical. English. qt (Mar., June, Sep., Dec.). $12.00 US; $15.00 Canada and Mexico; $24.00 other. Perceptions, PO Box 2731, Toledo OH 43606-0731. **DD** 811. **Bk Rev**, (Qty: 4). **Circ:** 250. available on an online database from Compuserve.
Desc: Celebrates the nature of sensuality. Each issue is filled with short stories, fantasy, reviews, poetry, commentary, photos and artwork.

US
PERSEA. V. 1- 1977-. English. $3.95. Persea Books Inc, 60 Madison Avenue, New York NY 10010-1506. **LC** PN6010.5; .P48. **DD** 808.8.

FR/0338-2338
PERSPECTIVES MEDIEVALES. No. 1 (June 1975)-. French. an. 140.00F France; 160.00F other. Societe de Langue et de Litterature Medievales Doc et Doil, M JC Vallecalle, 01310 Buellas France. **Tel** 33 1 74242093. **ED** Roger Bellon (editor's address: 5 Place Degent, 38160 Saint Marcellin Frane; editor's phone: 33 1 76640671). **Bk Rev**, (Qty: 1). **Pr Rev. Circ:** 350.
Desc: Articles about French medieval literature and language, repertory and abstracts of all French thesis, book reviews, papers of the annual conference of the Society de Langue et Litterature Medievales Doc et Doil.

RU
PERSPEKTIVA. (1983)-. Russian. an. Izdatelstvo Sovetskii Pisatel, Ulitsa Vorovskogo 11, 121069 Moscow Russia. **LC** PN849.R9; P38.

CN/0835-9628
PERSUASIONS. OCCASIONAL PAPERS (VICTORIA). (PERSUASIONS. OCCASIONAL PAPERS.). **Added/Corp** Jane Austen Society of North America. No. 1 (1984)-. Monographic series. English. ir. Price varies per volume. Jane Austen Society of North America, 860 North Lake Shore Drive, Chicago IL 60611. **Tel** FAX (312)266-0081. **ED** Gene Koppel. **Circ:** 3,000.
Desc: Contains scholarly articles on the life and writings of Jane Austen.

CN/0821-0314
PERSUASIONS (VICTORIA). (PERSUASIONS.). [Persuasions]. **Added/Corp** Jane Austen Society of North America. Issue No. 2 (Dec. 16, 1980)-. Periodical. English. an. $15.00 (comes with membership). Jane Austen Society of North America, 860 North Lake Shore Drive, Chicago IL 60611. **Tel** FAX (312)266-0081. **ED** Rene Koppel. **LC** PR4036; .A15. **DD** 823/.7. Index available. **Pr Rev. Circ:** 2,500 (ctrl). ***Continues*** *Persuasion (Victoria, B.C.).*
Desc: Devoted to Jane Austen, her life, literature and times.
Ind/Abst MLA Int. Bibl. Books Artic. Mod. Lang. Lit.

CN/0700-9194
PETIT ALMANACH DES LETTRES, LE. No. 1- Nov. 1976-. Periodical. French. bm. Editions De L'Aurore, 1651 Reu St. Denis, Montreal Quebec H2X 3K4. **DD** C840/.5.

HU/0524-8906
PETOFI IRODALMI MUZEUM EVKONYVE, A. [Petofi Irod. Muz. evkv.]. **Main/Corp** Petofi Irodalmi Muzeum (Budapest, Hungary). (19??)-. Periodical. Hungarian (summaries and/or abstracts in French and English). an. **LC** PH3002; .B8. **DD** 894.51.
Ind/Abst MLA Int. Bibl. Books Artic. Mod. Lang. Lit.

US
PETROGLYPH. See Natural History.

NQ/0031-6652
PEZ Y LA SERPIENTE, EL. See The Arts.

II
PHALGU : PHALGU SAHITYA SAMSADARA MUKHAPATRA. Periodical. Oriya (Oriya). ir. Rs20.00. Sri Raghunandan Panigrahi, Sri Krushna Bhavan, Neelakanth Nagar, Berhampur-760003, Ganjam (Orissa) India. **ED** Bauribandhu Sahu and Nikhilananda Panigrahi. **LC** PK2574.5; .P48. Index available. cum. index. **Bk Rev. Ad Acc. Circ:** 1,100 (ctrl).
Desc: Publishes history, culture, myths and legends of India plus creative and neo-classical literature.

US/1052-4878
PHILOMEL (PHILADELPHIA, PA.). (PHILOMEL / THE LITERARY MAGAZINE OF THE PHILOMATHEAN SOCIETY.). [Philomel]. **Added/Corp** University of Pennsylvania. Philomathean Society. (Spring 1981)-. Periodical. English. an (April). $4.00. Philomathean Society, University of Pennsylvania, Box H College Hall, Philadelphia PA 19104. **Tel** (215)898-8907. **DD** 810. **Ad Acc. Circ:** 4,000 (ctrl). ***Continues*** *Era (University of Pennsylvania. Philomathean Society).*
Desc: A literary omnibus of fiction, poetry, essays of a general nature, and interviews.

US/0276-0886
PHILOSOPHICAL SPECULATIONS IN SCIENCE FICTION & FANTASY. VFOAT Philosophical Speculations. **VAT** Philosophical Speculations in Science Fiction and Fantasy. Vol. 1, No. 1 (Mar. 1981)-. Periodical. English. qt. Burning Bush Publications, PO Box 7708, Newark DE 19711.

US/0190-0013
PHILOSOPHY AND LITERATURE. See Philosophy.

US
PHOENIX. English. $5.00 (single issues) US; $6.50 (single issues) other. Division of Arts & Letters, Northeastern State University, Tahlequah OK 74464. **ED** Joan Shaddox Isom.
Ind/Abst Index Am. Period. Verse.

KO
PHOENIX. See Linguistics.

AT/0819-3606
PHOENIX REVIEW. Added/Corp Australian National University. Dept. of English. No. 1 (Summer 1986/87)-. Periodical. English (French). Three times a year. 24.00Aus$ (institution); 20.00Aus$ (individual). Anutech Pty Limited, GPO Box 4, Canberra Act, 2601 Australia. **Tel** 011 61 6 2492479, FAX 011 61 6 2575088. ***Continues*** *Helix, 0155-9044.*

AT/0813-7846
PIED PIPER. See Children and Youth Interests.

US/0275-357X
PIEDMONT LITERARY REVIEW. ***Ceased.*** Periodical. English. qt. Piedmont Literary Society, PO Box 3656, Danville VA 24543. **Tel** (804)793-0956. **ED** Gail White. **Bk Rev. Ad Acc. Circ:** 400 (ctrl).
Desc: Poetry and short stories. A newsletter that contains contests, markets and tips for writers.

FR/0294-0086
PIERRE JEAN JOUVE. VFOAT Serie Pierre Jean Jouve; Jouve. (1982)-. Monographic series. French. ir. Price varies per volume. Lettres Modernes Minard, 45 rue de Saint Andre, 14123 Fleury-sur-Orne France. **Tel** 011 33 31 844706, FAX 011 33 31 844809. **LC** PQ2619.O78; Z72.

US/0362-5214
PIG IRON. [Pigiron]. 1975. Periodical. English. an. $10.00 US; $12.00 other. Pig Iron Press, PO Box 237, Youngstown OH 44501. **Tel** (216)783-1269. **ED** Jim Villani, Rose Sayre and Naton Leslie. **LC** PS615; .P44. **DD** 811/.5/08. Index available. cum. index. **Pr Rev. Circ:** 1,500.
Desc: Series of theme anthologies in the popular arts: science fiction, surrealism, sports, psychology, military, feminism, political, the Third World, and labor.
Ind/Abst Am. Humanit. Index; Index Am. Period. Verse.

US/0895-9706
PINTER REVIEW, THE. [Pinter rev.]. **Added/Corp** University of Tampa. Harold Pinter Society (U.S.). Vol. 1, No. 1 (1987)-. English. an (Aug.). $15.00 (individuals), $25.00 (institutions) Comes with Harold Pinter Society Membership. Harold Pinter Society, 512 North Park Street, Catco Ann Hall, Columbus OH 43215. **Tel** (614)461-1382. **ED** Francis Gillen and Steven H. Gale. **LC** PR6066.I53; Z74. **DD** 822/.914. **Bk Rev.**
Desc: Intended to provide Harold Pinter Society members with a means of communicating and asking for information related to the work of Harold Pinter.
Ind/Abst MLA Int. Bibl. Books Artic. Mod. Lang. Lit.

RU/0554-2065
PISATEL I ZHIZN / LITERATURNYI INSTITUT IMENI A. M. GORKOGO SOIUZA PISATELEI SSSR. Added/Corp Literaturnyi Institut Imeni A.M. Gorkogo. No. 1 (1961)-. Russian. ir. Izdatelstvo Moskovskogo Universiteta, K-9 Ulitsa Gertsena 5/7, Moscow Russia. **Tel** (301)881-5973. **LC** PG2900; .P5. **DD** 891.7/09.

US/1054-6340
PITTSBURGH QUARTERLY : A MAGAZINE FOR CREATIVE FICTION, POETRY & NONFICTION, THE. [Pittsbg. q.]. Vol. 1, No. 1 (Winter 1991)-. Periodical. English. qt. $12.00 US; $14.00 Canada. Frank Correnti, 36 Haberan Avenue, Pittsburgh PA 15211-2144. **LC** WMLC 91/726. **DD** 808.

UK
PLAIN TEXTS SERIES / ANGLO-NORMAN TEXT SOCIETY. 1-. Monographic series. English. ir. Price varies per volume.

US
PLAINSONGS. English. Three times a year (January, May, October). $9.00. Hastings College, Department of English, Hastings NE 68902. **Tel** (402)463-2402 ext 352. **ED** Dwight C Marsh. **Pr Rev.**

Circ: 300 (ctrl).
Desc: A varied collection of poetry of all kinds, preferably one to two pages in length.
Ind/Abst Index Am. Period. Verse.

BU/0032-0528
PLAMUK. **Added/Corp** Suiuz na Bulgarskite Pisateli. (1957)-. Periodical. Bulgarian. mo. DM154.00. **(Subscription address:** Kubon & Sagner, ABT Zeitschriftenimport, D 80328 Munich Germany.) **LC** AP58.B8; P55.
Ind/Abst MLA Int. Bibl. Books Artic. Mod. Lang. Lit.

GR/1105-2473
PLANODION. (1986)-. Greek, Modern. sa. Dr5000.00 institutions; Dr4000.00 individuals. Planodion, G Mistriotou 23, Athens 112 55 Greece. **Tel** 22 84 403. **ED** Yannis Patilis. (Last issue of each volume). cum. index. **Bk Rev**, (Qty: 10-15). **Pr Rev. Circ:** 2,000 (ctrl).
Desc: Contains short stories, essays, anthologies, book reviews, comments and criticism on the cultural life.

US
PLAYS & PLAYWRIGHTS. **Added/Corp** International Society of Dramatists. **VAT** Plays and Playwrights. Vol. 1 (1986)-. English. an. $31.45. International Society of Dramatists, PO Box 1310, Miami FL 33153. **Tel** (305)674-0538. Index available. cum. index. **Ad Acc.**

US/0736-0711
PLAYS IN PROCESS. ***Ceased.*** **See** Theater.

US/0885-6680
PLAZA (CAMBRIDGE, MASS.). ***Ceased.*** (PLAZA.). [Plaza]. (1977)-(19??). Periodical. Spanish. sa. **LC** PQ7074.5; .P53. **DD** 860.8/0973/05.
Ind/Abst MLA Int. Bibl. Books Artic. Mod. Lang. Lit.

FR/0295-1630
PLEINE MARGE. **See** The Arts-Art.

IT
PLOT. No. 1 (Jun 1991)-. Periodical. Italian. bm.

US/0048-4474
PLOUGHSHARES. [Ploughshares]. (Sept. 1971)-. Periodical. English. Three times a year (Fall, Winter, & Spring). $19.00 (individuals), $22.00 (institutions) US; $24.00 (individuals), $27.00 (institutions). Ploughshares, Emerson College, 100 Beacon Street, Boston MA 02116. **Tel** (617)926-9875, (617)578-8753. **ED** Dewitt Henry, Don Lee, Joyce Reseroff and David Daniel. **LC** NX1; .P57. **DD** 700/.9/04. Index available. cum. index. **Bk Rev. Ad Acc. Circ:** 3,800. available on magnetic tape, an online database, and CD-ROM; available on microfilm and microfiche from University Microfilms International (UMI). Documents available from The Genuine Article, UMI Article Clearinghouse.
Desc: New poetry, fiction, essays edited on a revolving basis by professional writers to reflect different and contrasting points of view.
Ind/Abst Acad. Search (July 1993-); Am. Bibliogr. Slavic East Europ. Stud.; Am. Humanit. Index; Annu. Bibliogr. Engl. Lang. Lit.; Arts Humanit. Citation Index (19??-19??) [Full Cov.]; Curr. Contents Arts Humanit.; Expand. Acad. Index (1989-); Humanit. Index; Humanit. Source (Jul. 1993-); Index Am. Period. Verse; INFO-SOUTH Abstr.; Lit. Crit. Regist.; Mag. Search; MLA Int. Bibl. Books Artic. Mod. Lang. Lit.; Newsp. Period. Abstr. (1990-); Res. Alert [Full Cov.].

CY/0554-3363
PNEUMATIKE KYPROS. [Pneum. Kupros]. (1960)-. Periodical. Greek, Modern. mo. **LC** PA5639.8; .P63.
Ind/Abst MLA Int. Bibl. Books Artic. Mod. Lang. Lit.

●US/1057-932X
POBEREZE (PHILADELPHIA, PA.). **See** Ethnic Interests.

PL/0079-3302
POCZNIK KOMISJI HISTORYCZNOLITERACKIEJ. (ROCZNIK KOMISJI HISTORYCZNOLITERACKIEJ / POLSKA AKADEMIA NAUK, ODDZIA W KRAKOWIE, KOMISJA HISTORYCZNOLITERACKA.). **Added/Corp** Polska Akademia Nauk. Oddzia w Krakowie. Komisja Historycznoliteracka. (1963)-. Polish (summaries and/or abstracts in French and Russian). an. Zakad Narodowy Im Ossolinskich We Wrocawiu, Krakowskie Przedmiescie 7, 00 068 Warsaw Poland.
Ind/Abst MLA Int. Bibl. Books Artic. Mod. Lang. Lit.

GW
PODIUM. **Main/Corp** Podium (Association). 1- Apr. 1971-. Periodical. German.

RU
PODVIG (PERIODICAL). (PODVIG.). (19??)-. Periodical. Russian. Six times a year. $89.95. Izdatelstvo Molodaia Gvardiia, Novodmitrovskaya Ul., 5A, 125015 Moscow Russia. **Tel** 095-285-0830. **(Subscription address:** East View Publications Inc., 3020 Harbor Lane North, Suite 110, Minneapolis MN 55447.) **LC** PG3273; .P53.

US/0276-3737
POE MESSENGER, THE. [Poe messenger]. **Added/Corp** Poe Foundation. Vol. 1, No. 1 (Autumn 1969)-. Periodical. English. an. $5.00. Poe Foundation Inc., 1914 E Main Street, Richmond VI 23223. **Tel** (804)648-5523. **LC** PS2631; .P625. **DD** 818/.309.
Ind/Abst Am. Humanit. Index (199?-).

SZ/0378-0643
POESIE (BASEL, SWITZERLAND). (POESIE : ZEITSCHRIFT FUER LITERATUR.). **VFOAT** Zeitschrift fur Literatur. German. qt. Poesie, Postfach 1849, CH-4001 Basel Switzerland.

NE/0303-4178
POETICA (MUNCHEN). (POETICA.). [Poetica]. Vol. 1 (Jan. 1967)-. Periodical. German. qt. DM156.00. Wilhelm Fink Verlag, Ohmstrasse 5, D 80802 Munich Germany. **Tel** 011 49 89 348017, 348018. **(Subscription address:** Ferdinand Schoeningh Verlag, Postfach 2540, D 33055 Paderborn Germany) **ED** Karlheinz Stierle. **LC** P3; .P6. cum. index. **Bk Rev. Ad Acc. Circ:** 750 (ctrl). Documents available from The Genuine Article.
Desc: Interdisciplinary studies in international literature including articles on general problems of theory, criticism and history plus original contributions from German, English, Romance, Slavonic and classical literature.
Ind/Abst Abstr. Engl. Stud.; Arts Humanit. Citation Index [Full Cov.]; MLA Int. Bibl. Books Artic. Mod. Lang. Lit.; Res. Alert [Full Cov.]; Romant. Move.

US/0333-5372
POETICS TODAY. [Poetics today]. **Added/Corp** Makhon Ha-Yisreeli Le-Poetikah Ve-Semyotikah Al-Shem Porter. Vol. 1, No. 1/2 (Autumn 1979)-. Periodical. English. qt (4 issues). $76.00 (institutions), $32.00 (individuals) US; $88.00 (institutions), $44.00 (individuals) other. Duke University Press, PO Box 90660, Durham NC 27708-0660. **Tel** (919)687-3600, (919)688-5134 (orders), FAX (919)688-4574, telex 802829. **ED** Itamar Even-Zohar. **LC** PN1039; .P63. **DD** 801/.95/05. **[CCC].** Index available. **Bk Rev. Ad Acc. Circ:** 1,100 (ctrl). available on microfilm and microfiche from University Microfilms International (UMI). Documents available from The Genuine Article.
Desc: An international journal for theory and analysis of literature and communication.
Ind/Abst Abstr. Anthropol.; Am. Bibliogr. Slavic East Europ. Stud.; Arts Humanit. Citation Index [Full Cov.]; Book Rev. Index (1984-); Child. Lit. Abstr. (19??-); Curr. Contents Arts Humanit.; Film Lit. Index (19??-); MLA Int. Bibl. Books Artic. Mod. Lang. Lit.; Res. Alert [Full Cov.]; Romant. Move.; Soc. Plann. Policy Dev. Abstr.; Soc. Sci. Cit. Index [Select. Cov.].

US/0149-9831
POETS AND AUTHORS. Periodical. English. an. Harlo Press, 16721 Hamilton Avenue, Detroit MI 48203. **Tel** (313)864-1529. **LC** PS536.2; .H37. **DD** 810/.8/0054. ***Continues*** *Harlo's Anthology of Modern-Day Poets and Authors, 0090-2632.*

GW
POGGENDORFFS BIOGRAPHISCH LITERARISCHES HANDWOERTERBUCH DER EXAKTEN NATURWISSENSCHAFTEN. (19??)-. Monographic series. German. ir. Price varies per volume. Akademie-Verlag GmbH, Muehlenstrasse 33 34, D 13162 Berlin Germany. **Tel** 011 49 30 47889300, FAX 011 49 30 47889357. **(Subscription address:** VCH Publishers Inc., 303 Northwest 12th Avenue, Journals Department, Deerfield FL 33442.)

FR
POLAR. No 1 (1990)-. Periodical. French. qt. Rivages, 27 Rue de Fleurus, 75006 Paris France. **LC** IN PROCESS.

US
POLITICAL QUOTATIONS : A COLLECTION OF NOTABLE SAYINGS ON POLITICS FROM ANTIQUITY THROUGH 1988. **See** Political Science.

CN/1183-5214
PORTAL (NANAIMO). (PORTAL.). [Portal]. **Added/Corp** Malaspina College. Dept. of Creative Writing. (Spring 1991)-. English. $3.95 per year. Malaspina College, Department of Creative Writing, 900 5th Street, Nanaimo British Columbia V9R 5S5 Canada. **DD** C810.8/092379.

US/0885-7121
PORTLAND REV. (1981). (PORTLAND REVIEW.). [Portland rev.]. Vol. 27, No. 1 (Fall/Winter Quarter 1981)-. Periodical. English. Twice a year. $10.00. Center for Population Research and Census, Portland State University, PO Box 751, Portland OR 97207. **Tel** (503)725-3922, FAX (503)725-5199. **ED** Nancy Row and Ken Angelo. **DD** 808. cum. index. **Bk Rev. Ad Acc. Circ:** 10,000. ***Continues*** *International Portland Review, 0278-2952.*
Ind/Abst Index Am. Period. Verse.

GW
POSTILLA BOHEMICA. **Added/Corp** Konstanzer Hus-Gesellschaft. **VFOAT** Postylla Bohemica. (1972)-. Periodical. German (Czech and English). qt.
Ind/Abst MLA Int. Bibl. Books Artic. Mod. Lang. Lit.

NE/0923-0483
POSTMODERN STUDIES. [Postmod. stud.]. (1988)-. Monographic series. English. ir. Editions Rodopi BV, Keizersgracht 302-304, 1016 Ex Amsterdam Netherlands. **Tel** 011 31 20 6227507, FAX 011 31 20 380948. **UDC** 82.09. Index available.
Ind/Abst MLA Int. Bibl. Books Artic. Mod. Lang. Lit.

US/1041-9926
POTATO EYES. No. 1 (Spring/Summer 1989)-. Periodical. English. Twice a year. $11.00 (one year), $19.00 (two years), $27.00 (three years) US; $12.00 (one year), $21.00 (two years), $30.00 (three years) Canada; $16.00 (one year), $29.00 (two years), $47.00 (three years) other. Nightshade Press, PO Box 76, Troy ME 04987. **Tel** (207)948-3427. **ED** Carolyn Page. **DD** 810. **Bk Rev**, (Qty: 8). **Pr Rev. Circ:** 700.
Desc: A literary arts journal focusing primarily on talent from the Appalachian Chain. Contents include poetry, short stories, art and reviews.

CN/0228-3344
POTBOILER (RICHMOND). (POTBOILER.). [Potboiler]. Vol. 1, No. 1 (July 1980)-. Periodical. English. $2.25 each number. Potboiler Magazine, 8471 Bennet Road, Richmond BC V6Y 1N6. **DD** C813/.0876.

CN/0226-0840
POTTERSFIELD PORTFOLIO, THE. [Pottersfield portf.]. No. 1 (1979/80)-. English. sa. 14.02Can$ Canada; 15.00Can$ other. The Pottersfield Portfolio, 151 Ryan Court, Fredericton NB E3A 2Y9 Canada. **Tel** (506)472-9251. **ED** Peggy Amirault, Barb Cottrell, Donalee Moulton-Barrett. **DD** C810/.8/09715. **Ad Acc. Circ:** 3,000.
Desc: Devoted exclusively to new writing from Atlantic Canada; includes well-established and less well-known writers, and seeks out and encourages serious beginning writers. Represents the region in its rich diversity by publishing writers of many backgrounds, from all parts of all four provinces. Strives to appeal to a popular audience with the large glossy format, and it is expanding its distribution.
Ind/Abst Am. Humanit. Index; Can. Index; Index Am. Period. Verse.

PL/0079-4791
PRACE POLONISTYCZNE. [Pr. polonist.]. **Added/Corp** Towarzystwo Literackie Imienia Adama Mickiewicza. Oddzia w lodzi. Uniwersytet lodzki. Wydzia Filologiczny. Odzkie Towarzystwo Naukowe. (1937)-. Polish. an. Price on Request. **(Subscription address:** ARS Polona, PO Box 1001, 00068 Warsaw Poland.) **LC** PG7001; .P7. **DD** 891.8/5/09. cum. index.
Ind/Abst MLA Int. Bibl. Books Artic. Mod. Lang. Lit.

UK/0556-1094
PRADALGE. [Pradalge]. **VFOAT** Literaturos Metrastis Pradalge. 1.- 1964-. Periodical. Lithuanian. **LC** PG8713; .P7.
Ind/Abst MLA Int. Bibl. Books Artic. Mod. Lang. Lit.

XR
PRAGUE STUDIES IN ENGLISH. English. ir. Charles University / Univerzita Karlova, Ovocnytrh 5, 116 36 Prague 1 Czech Republic. **Tel** 228441. ***Continues*** *Prispevky k Dejinam Reci a Literatury Anglicke.*

CN/0821-1124
PRAIRIE FIRE (WINNIPEG). (PRAIRIE FIRE.). [Prairie fire]. **Added/Corp** Manitoba Writers Guild. Vol. 4, No. 3 (Jan./Feb 1983)-. Periodical. English. Four times a year (Jan., Mar., June, Sept.). 28.00Can$ (individuals), 36.00Can$ (institutions) US; 24.00Can$ (individuals), 32.00Can$ (institutions) Canada; 30.00Can$ (individuals), 38.00Can$ (institutions) others. Prairie Fire, 100 Arthur Street, Room 423, Winnipeg Manitoba R3B 1H3 Canada. **Tel** (204)943-9066, FAX (201)942-1555. **ED** Andris Taskans. **DD** C810/.8/0054. **Bk Rev**, (Qty: 60). **Ad Acc. Circ:** 1,200. ***Continues*** *Writers News Manitoba, 0707-3852.*
Desc: Challenges writers and readers to walk on the edges. Includes fiction, art, poetry, essays, interviews, translations, plays, film, satire, criticism, reviews, humor, special issues, new and established writers.
Ind/Abst Am. Hist. Life (1986-); Am. Humanit. Index (199?-); Index Am. Period. Verse.

CN/0827-2921
PRAIRIE JOURNAL OF CANADIAN LITERATURE, THE. [Prairie j. Can. lit.]. No. 1 (Fall 1983)-. English. Twice a year (Summer and Winter). 6.00Can$ (individual), 10.00Can$ other, Canada; 14.00Can$ (institution), 16.00Can$ other, Canada. The Prairie Journal of Trust, PO Box 61203 Brentwood, Calgary Alberta T2L 2K6 Canada. **Tel** (403)220-3959. **ED** A. Burke. **DD** C810/.8/09712. Index available (Publish seperately with $6.00 Subscription). **Bk Rev**, (Qty: varies). **Ad Acc. Circ:** 500.
Desc: In the tradition of the small independent press, this is a place where the writer of talent can emerge, a literary magazine devising a new method of writing the new art. Contains interviews and an up-to-date list of books received.
Ind/Abst Can. Index (?-?).

US/0032-6682
PRAIRIE SCHOONER. [Prairie schoon.]. **Added/Corp** Sigma Upsilon. Wordsmith Chapter. University of Nebraska (Lincoln campus) University of Nebraska. Dept. of English. (Jan. 1927)-. Periodical. English. Four times a year. $20.00. Prairie Schooner, 201 Andrews, University of Nebraska, Department of English, Lincoln NE 68588-0334. **Tel** (402)472-3191, (402)472-1812, FAX (402)472-4636. **ED** Hilda Raz. **LC** AP2; .P85285. **DD** 061. Index available. **Bk Rev. Ad Acc. Circ:** 2,000. available on microfilm and microfiche from University Microfilms International (UMI). Documents available from UMI Article Clearinghouse.
Desc: Fiction, poetry, essays, interviews, articles and reviews.
Ind/Abst Acad. Search (July 1993-; Am. Humanit. Index; Annu. Bibliogr. Engl. Lang. Lit.; Book Rev. Index; Expand. Acad. Index (1989-); Humanit. Index; Humanit. Source (Jul. 1993-); Index Am. Period. Verse; Index Book Rev. Humanit.; INFO-SOUTH Abstr.; Lit. Crit. Regist.; Mag. Search; MLA Int. Bibl. Books Artic. Mod. Lang. Lit.; Newsp. Period. Abstr. (1991-); Romant. Move.

NP
PRAKAMPANA. Jhokka 1- April 2030- 1973-. Periodical. Nepali. 31.00 each issue. Premaprasada Ligala, Pulchok Butabal, Butavala Nepal. **LC** PK2598.A2; P718.

NP
PRANGANA. V. 1- April/May 2030- 1973-. Periodical. Nepali. sa. Rs8.00. Ramesa Tivari, 17/350 Tangal Gairidhara, Kathamadaum India. **ED** Ramesa Tivari. **LC** PK2598.A2; P7214.

II
PRASADA (CALCUTTA, INDIA). (PRASADA.). **VFOAT** Prashad. Periodical. Bengali. mo. Rs108.00. Prashad Press and Publications, Calcutta 70001 India. **Tel** 24-3184. **ED** Pronob Kumar Bose. **LC** PK1712.5; .P74. **Bk Rev. Ad Acc. Circ:** 4,200 (ctrl).
Desc: Non political, socio-economic novels.

II
PRASTUTIPARBA. Periodical. Bengali (Bengali). qt. Rs15.00. Kathashilpa, 19 Shyamacharan de Street, Calcutta 700073 India. **LC** PK1712.5; .P75.

NP
PRAYASA. V. 1- 2029- 1972-. Nepali (Nepali). 1.00 each issue. **LC** PK2598.A2; P723.

US/0163-4631
PRECISELY. [Precisely]. (Nov. 1977)-. Periodical. English. **LC** PN2; .P83. **DD** 809.
Ind/Abst MLA Int. Bibl. Books Artic. Mod. Lang. Lit.

PO/0871-0430
PRELO : REVISTA DA IMPRENSA NACIONAL/CASA DA MOEDA. ***Suspended.*** **Added/Corp** Imprensa Nacional-Casa da Moeda. (1983)-(19??). Periodical. Portuguese. qt. Imprensa Nacionalcasa da Moeda, Rua d'Francisco Manuel Melo 5, 1092 Lisbon Portugal. **Tel** 351 1 685684. **LC** PQ9000; .P7. **DD** 869/.09.
Ind/Abst BHA : Biblio. Hist. Art (?-?).

SP
PREMIOS CLARIN Y LARRA / CIENCIAS DE LA INFORMACION. Periodical. Spanish. Editorial Complutense, Donoso Cortes 65 1RA Planta, 28003 Madrid Spain. **Tel** 011 34 1 3946372. **LC** PQ6174; .P73. **DD** 860.8/005. ***Continues*** *Premios Clarin, Larra, Bunuel y Marconi.*

UK/0968-6185
PREMONITIONS ARRETON. [PremonitionsArreton]. (1992)-. Periodical. English. sa. £2.50 per issue. Tony Lee Ed. & Publ., 13 Hazley Combe, Arreton, Isle of Wight, PO30 3AJ England. **Tel** 0983-865668. **Ad Acc.**

NQ
PRENSA LITERARIA, LA. **See** The Arts.

CN/0048-5195
PRESENCE FRANCOPHONE. **Added/Corp** Universite de Sherbrooke. Centre d'Eetude des Litteratures d'Expression Francaise. No. 1 (1970)-. Periodical. French. sa. $25.00 institutions; $20.00 individuals. Universite de Sherbrooke / Francophone, Presence Francophone DLC, Sherbrooke Quebec, J1K 2R1 Canada. **Tel** (819) 821-7266.
Ind/Abst MLA Int. Bibl. Books Artic. Mod. Lang. Lit.; Point Repere (1985-); Soc. Plann. Policy Dev. Abstr.

CN/0226-367X
PRETEXTE (MONTREAL). (PRETEXTE.). [Pretexte]. No. 1- Spring 1980-. Periodical. French. be. Pretexte, A E D E F, Universite de Montreal, Faculte des Arts et des Sciences, Departement d'Etudes Francaises, Salle 8146 rue Jean-Brillant, Montreal Quebec Canada. **DD** C840/.8/092375. ***Supersedes*** *Versance, 0226-3661.*

CN/0711-4966
PRETEXTES (TROIS-RIVIERES). (PRETEXTES.). [Pretextes]. April 1981-. Periodical. French. ir. Free to members. Service d'Information du Cegep de Trois-Rivieres, 3500 rue de Courval, Trois-Rivieres Quebec G9A 5E6 Canada. **DD** C840/.8/092375.

RU
PRIAMURE MOE. (19??)-. Russian. Khabarocshoe Knizhnoe Izdatelstvo, Ulitsa IM Lenina 181, Blagoveshchensk Russia. **LC** PG3504.A48; P74.

US/0364-7609
PRIMAVERA (CHICAGO). (PRIMAVERA. AN ANTHOLOGY OF WOMEN WRITERS AND ARTISTS.). [Primavera]. (1975)-. English. an. $10.05. Primavera an Anthology, 700 East 61st Street, Box 377547, Chicago IL 60637. **Tel** (312)324-5920. **LC** PS508.W7; P75. **DD** 810/.8/09287. **Circ:** 1,000.
Desc: Focuses on the experiences of women. Males and females are to be known has established and unknown writers and literary quality is their most important consideration.
Ind/Abst Am. Humanit. Index; Index Am. Period. Verse.

XV/0351-1189
PRIMERJALNA KNJIZEVNOST. **Added/Corp** Drustvo za Primerjalno Knjizevnost SR Slovenije. Slovensko Drustvo za Primerjalno Knjizevnost. (1978)-. Periodical. Slovenian. sa. **LC** PG1900.A1; P74.
Ind/Abst MLA Int. Bibl. Books Artic. Mod. Lang. Lit.

CN/0032-8790
PRISM INTERNATIONAL. **Added/Corp** University of British Columbia. Dept. of Creative Writing. Vol. 4 (Summer 1964)-. Periodical. English. qt. 22.00Can$ (institutions), 16.00Can$ (individuals). Prism International, Department of Creative Writing, University of British Columbia, E462-1866 Main Mall, Vancouver British Columbia V6T 1W5 Canada. **Tel** (604)228-2514. **ED** P.L. Gabin and M. Logan. **LC** AP5; .P67. cum. index. **Ad Acc. Circ:** 1200. available on microfilm from Xerox; available on microfilm and microfiche from University Microfilms International (UMI). ***Continues*** *Prism, 0380-2345.*
Desc: Publishes fiction, poetry, drama, translation and creative non-fiction by new and established writers from around the world.
Ind/Abst Am. Bibliogr. Slavic East Europ. Stud.; Am. Humanit. Index (1985-1986).

US/0079-5445
PRIZE COLLEGE STORIES. (1961)-. English. an. Random House Inc., 400 Hahn Road, Westminster MD 21157. **Tel** (800)726-0600, (800)733-3000, FAX (800)659-2436. **LC** PZ1; .B44655.

US/0079-5453
PRIZE STORIES. [Prize stories]. (1947)-. English. an. $10.95 (paper bound), $25.00 (hard cover). Bantam Books Doubleday, 1540 Broadway, New York NY 10036. **Tel** (800)323-9872, (212)354-6500. **LC** PZ1; .O11. **DD** 813/.01/08. ***Continues*** *O. Henry Memorial Award Prize Stories.*

RU
PROBLEMY ISTORII KRITIKI I POETIKI REALIZMA. **Added/Corp** Kuibyshevskii Gosudarstvennyi Universitet. (1976)-. Periodical. Russian. 1.00rub. Kuibyshevskii, Gosudarstvennyi Universitet, G Kuibyshev, Ulitsa Adad Pavlova 1, Kuibyshev Russia. **LC** PG2949; .P76.

RU/0134-8876
PROBLEMY METODA I ZHANRA. **Added/Corp** Tomskii Gosudarstvennyi Universitet Imeni V.V. Kuibysheva. (19??)-. Periodical. Russian. 1.57rub each issue. Izdatelstvo Tomskogo Universiteta / Tomsk State University, Prospekt Lenina 36, 634050 Tomsk Russia. **Tel** 23-44-65, FAX 22-24-66, telex 128258. **LC** PG2900; .P73.

RU
PROBLEMY SOVETSKOI LITERATURY, METOD, ZHANR, KHARAKTER. **Added/Corp** Moskovskii Gosudarstvennyi Pedagogicheskii Institut Imeni V.I. Lenina. Vol. 1 (1978)-. Periodical. Russian. 1.00rub each issue. **LC** PG3021; .P6938.

US/0145-8493
PROCEEDINGS OF THE AMERICAN ACADEMY AND INSTITUTE OF ARTS AND LETTERS. ***Title Change.*** **See** The Arts.

UK/0143-0610
PROCEEDINGS OF THE ... CONVENTION. **Main/Corp** Dorothy L. Sayers Historical and Literary Society. Convention. (1981)-. Proceedings. English. Twelve times a year. £5.00 UK; $10.00 US. Dorothy L Sayers Society, 92 Wickham Hill, Hurstpierpoint West Sussex BN6 9NR England. **(Subscription address:** Rose Cottage, Malthouse Lane, Hurstpierpoint, West Sussex BN6 9JY England telephone: 011 44 273-833444**) LC** PR6037.A95; Z643. **DD** 823/.912. Index available. cum. index. **Bk Rev. Circ:** 100 (ctrl). available on audiocassette. ***Continues*** *Dorothy L. Sayers Historical and Literary Society. Seminar. Proceedings of the Seminar.*

US/0272-8710
PROCEEDINGS OF THE PMR CONFERENCE. **See** Classical Studies.

IE
PROCEEDINGS OF THE ROYAL IRISH ACADEMY. **Main/Corp** Royal Irish Academy. 3rd Ser., V. 1, No. 1 (Dec. 1888)-. Proceedings. English. an. £100.50 (complete set). Royal Irish Academy, 19 Dawson Street, Dublin 2 Ireland. **Tel** 011 353 1 762570. ***Formed by the union of*** *Proceedings of the Royal Irish Academy. Science. Royal Irish Academy* ***and*** *Proceedings of the Royal Irish Academy. Polite Literature and Antiquities. Royal Irish Academy.*
Ind/Abst Int. Civil Eng. Abstr.; Numis. Lit.; Soft. Abstr. Eng.; Stat. Theory Method Abstr. (1959-1963); Zentralbl. Math. Ihre Grenzgeb.

US/0735-9381
PROCESSED WORLD. [Process. world]. (19??)-. Periodical. English. ir. $15.00 US & Canada; $25.00 other. Processed World, 41 Sutter Street, Suite 1829, San Francisco CA 94104. **Tel** (415)626-2979. **LC** Discard. Index available. **Bk Rev. Circ:** 3,500.
Ind/Abst Altern. Press Index.

IT
PROMETHEUS. Vol. 1 (1975)-. Periodical. Italian (English and French). tq. L30000 Italy. Franco Angeli Riviste SRL, Viale Monza 106, 20127 Milan Italy. **Tel** 011 39 2 2827651, 011 39 2 289562. Index available (Bound in Sept. issue).

US/0272-9601
PROOFTEXTS. [Prooftexts]. **VAT** Proof Texts. Vol. 1, No. 1 (Jan. 1981)-. Periodical. English. Three times a year (January, May, and Sept.). $51.50 US; $56.10 Canada & Mexico; $56.40 other. Johns Hopkins University Press, 2715 North Charles Street, Baltimore MD 21218-4319. **Tel** (410)516-6987, FAX (410)516-6968. **(Subscription address:** John Hopkins University Press, Journals Publishing Division, PO Box 19966, Baltimore MD 21211.**) ED** Alan Mintz and David Roskies. **LC** PJ5001; .P76. **DD** 892.4/09. **[CCC]. Bk Rev. Ad Acc. Circ:** 900. available on microfilm and microfiche from University Microfilms International (UMI). Documents available from The Genuine Article.
Desc: Covers the literary heritage of the Jewish people.
Ind/Abst Abstr. Engl. Stud.; Am. Bibliogr. Slavic East Europ. Stud.; Arts Humanit. Citation Index [Full Cov.]; Curr. Contents Arts Humanit.; Index Book Rev. Relig.; Index Jew. Period.; Int. Zeitschriftenschau Bibelwissenschaft Grenzgeb.; Lit. Crit. Regist.; MLA Int. Bibl. Books Artic. Mod. Lang. Lit.; New Testam. Abstr.; Old Testam. Abstr.; Relig. Index One Period.; Relig. Theol. Abstr.; Res. Alert [Full Cov.].

US/0734-3027
PROPHETIC VOICES (NOVATO, CALIF.). (PROPHETIC VOICES.). (1983)-. Periodical. English. sa. $14.00. Heritage Trails Press, 94 Santa Maria Drive, Novato CA 94947. **Tel** (415)897-5679.

●PR
PROPOSITO : REVISTA DE LITERATURA, ARTE Y CINE, A. **See** The Arts.

NE
PROPRIETATIBUS LITTERARUM. SERIES DIDACTICA, DE. (1972)-. Periodical. English. ir. Walter de Gruyter Inc. / Hawthorne, 200 Saw Mill River Road, Hawthorne NY 10532. **Tel** (914)747-0110, GERMANY: 011/49/30/260050, FAX (914)747-1326, telex 646677. **(Subscription address:** Germany/ PO Box 110240, 1 Berlin 11**) DD** 370.
Ind/Abst MLA Int. Bibl. Books Artic. Mod. Lang. Lit.

NE/0070-3060
PROPRIETATIBUS LITTERARUM. SERIES MAIOR, DE. 1- 1967-. Monographic series. English (French and German). Price varies per volume. Mouton, PO Box 482, Hague The Netherlands.

NE/0070-3087
PROPRIETATIBUS LITTERARUM. SERIES PRACTICA, DE. (1966)-. Monographic series. English (English and German). ir. Price varies per volume. Walter de Gruyter Inc. / Hawthorne, 200 Saw Mill River Road, Hawthorne NY 10532. **Tel** (914)747-0110, GERMANY: 011/49/30/260050, FAX (914)747-1326, telex 646677. **(Subscription address:** Germany/ PO Box 110240, 1 Berlin 11 Germany**) DD** 800.
Ind/Abst MLA Int. Bibl. Books Artic. Mod. Lang. Lit.

US
PROSCENIUM CHAPBOOKS, THE. No. 1 (1971)-. Monographic series. English. ir. Price varies per volume. Proscenium Press, PO Box 361, Newark DE 19711. **Tel** (302)764-8477.

UK/0144-0357
PROSE STUDIES. Vol. 3, No. 1 (May 1980)-. Periodical. English. Three times a year. $95.00. Frank Cass & Company Ltd, Newbury House, 890-900 Eastern Avenue, Newbury Park, Ilford, Essex IG2 7HH United Kingdom. **Tel** 011 44 81 599 8866, FAX 011 44 81 599

0984, telex 897719. **ED** Ronald Corthell and Thomas N. Corns. **LC** PR750; .P76. **DD** 828/.08. **Ad Acc, Adv Mgr:** Anne Kidson. ***Continues** Prose Studies, 1800-1900.*
Desc: A forum for discussion of the history, theory and criticism of non-fictional prose of all periods. While the journal publishes studies of such recognized genres of nonfiction as autobiography, biography, the sermon, the essay, the letter, the journal, etc.
Ind/Abst Acad. Search (July 1993-); Am. Hist. Life (1983-); Br. Humanit. Index; Humanit. Source (Jul. 1993-); INFO-SOUTH Abstr.; Mag. Search; MLA Int. Bibl. Books Artic. Mod. Lang. Lit.; Romant. Move.

UK/0308-2776
PROSPICE. (1973)-. Periodical. English. Four times a year. £12.50 UK; $25.00 US; £15.00 other. Prospice Publishing Ltd, PO Box 18, Buxton Derbyshire SK17 6YP England. **Tel** (44)538 387368. **ED** J. Green and R. Elkin. **LC** UNC. Index available. cum. index. **Bk Rev. Ad Acc. Circ:** 1,000.
Desc: International literary magazine honoring no single school or style of writing to the exclusion of others. Work in English and translation.

CN/0300-3523
PROTEE. **See** Linguistics.

US/0889-6348
PROTEUS (SHIPPENSBURG, PA.). (PROTEUS.). **Added/Corp** Shippensburg University of Pennsylvania. Vol. 1, No. 1 (Fall 1983)-. Periodical. English. sa (April & October). $10.00. Proteus, Shippensburg University, Shippensburg PA 17257-2299. **Tel** (717)532-1206, FAX (717)532-1253. **ED** Angelo Costanzo, Mary Stewart and Marcia Guild Gibbs (Managing Editor). **LC** AP2; .P76. **DD** 306. cum. index. **Circ:** 4,500 (ctrl). available on microfilm from University Microfilms International (UMI).
Ind/Abst Am. Hist. Life; Arts Humanit. Citation Index; Curr. Contents Arts Humanit.; Hist. Abstr.; MLA Int. Bibl. Books Artic. Mod. Lang. Lit.; PAIS Int. Print; Soc. Sci. Cit. Index [Select. Cov.].

IS
PROZAH. Periodical. Hebrew. $40.00. Prozah, Box 6072, Tel Aviv Israel. **Tel** (03)202823. **ED** Yossi Kraiem. **LC** PJ5038; .P76. **Bk Rev. Ad Acc. Circ:** 5,000 (ctrl).
Desc: Publishes articles on short stories, poetry, theater, cinema, photography, paintings and sculpture.

NZ
PRUDENTIA. Vol. 1, No. 1 (May 1969)-. Periodical. English. Twice a year (May, Nov.). 25.00NZ$. Prudentia University of Auckland, Department of Classics & Ancient, Auckland New Zealand. **Tel** 011 64 7 737999 7624. **ED** Vivienne Cvay. **DD** 913.3/8/038. **Bk Rev. Ad Acc. Pr Rev. Circ:** 200.

PL/0033-2283
PRZEGLAD ORIENTALISTYCZNY. [Prz. orient.]. No. 1 (1952)-. Periodical. Polish (French; table of contents in Russian and French). qt. Price on Request. Panstwowe Wydawn Naukowe, Miodowa 10, PO Box 391, 00251 Warsaw Poland. **LC** PJ9; .P7. cum. index. ***Supersedes** Mysl Karaimska.*
Ind/Abst Am. Hist. Life (1955-1958, 1963-); BHA : Biblio. Hist. Art; Middle East J.

●US/1064-363X
PSYCHOTRAIN (FAYETTEVILLE, ARK.). (PSYCHOTRAIN.). [Psychotrain]. Vol. 1, No. 1 (1992)-. Periodical. English. sa. Hyacinth House Publications, PO Box 120, Fayetteville AK 72702-0120. **DD** 810.

CK/0073-9928
PUBLICACIONES. SERIES MINOR. **See** Linguistics.

BE
PUBLICATIONS - ASBL CENTRE D'HISTOIRE ET D'ART DE LA THUDINIE. **See** History(General).

US/0885-7954
PUBLICATIONS / AUGUSTAN REPRINT SOCIETY. **Added/Corp** Augustan Reprint Society. William Andrews Clark Memorial Library. (19??)-. Monographic series. English. ir (two single, two double issues per year). Price varies per volume. AMS Press Inc., 56 East 13th Street, New York NY 10003. **Tel** (212)777-4700, FAX (212)995-5413, telex 710 581 2302. **ED** David S. Rodes. **LC** UNC. **DD** 808. **Circ:** 700 (ctrl).
Desc: Publishes rare and significant restoration and 18th century works in photographic facsimile, accompanied by scholarly introductions.
Ind/Abst Annu. Bibliogr. Engl. Lang. Lit.; MLA Int. Bibl. Books Artic. Mod. Lang. Lit.

SG/0418-2960
PUBLICATIONS - DAKAR. UNIVERSITE. SECTION DE LANGUES ET LITTERATURES. **See** Linguistics.

UK
PUBLICATIONS OF THE DUGDALE SOCIETY. **Main/Corp** Dugdale Society. Vol. 1 (1921)-. Monographic series. English. ir. Price varies per volume. The Dugdale Society, The Shakespeare Centre, Stratford Avon CV37 6QW England. **Tel** 011 44 0789 204016. Each issue contains an index to its own contents (no volume index)--loose.

UK/0959-3683
PUBLICATIONS OF THE ENGLISH GOETHE SOCIETY. [Publ. Engl. Goethe Soc.]. **Added/Corp** English Goethe Society. Vol. 1-14, (1886-1912); New Series Vol. 1 (1923)-. Periodical. English (German). an (July). £9.00 UK; £11.00 others; $22.00 North America;. University College of London / German, English Goethe Society, Department of German, Gower Street, London WC1 England. **Tel** 011 44 1 3877050. **ED** Frank M. Fowler. **LC** PT2046; .E7. Index available. cum. index. **Circ:** 500 (ctrl).
Desc: Goethe's work and thought and other areas of German literature.
Ind/Abst MLA Int. Bibl. Books Artic. Mod. Lang. Lit.; Romant. Move.

SZ/0079-7812
PUBLICATIONS ROMANES ET FRANCAISES. [Publ. romanes fr.]. (1961)-. Monographic series. French. ir. Librairie Droz SA, 11 rue Massot BP 389, CH 1211 Geneva 12 Switzerland. **Tel** 011 41 22 3466666, FAX 011 41 22 472391. **LC** PC7; .S67p. **[CCC]. *Continues** Publications Societe de Publications Romanes et Francaises.*
Ind/Abst MLA Int. Bibl. Books Artic. Mod. Lang. Lit.

UK
PUBLICATIONS (SCOTTISH TEXT SOCIETY). (SCOTTISH TEXT SOCIETY.). **Added/Corp** Scottish Text Society. **VFOAT** STS; S.T.S.; Scottish Text Society. 1-65 (1884)-New Series, 1 (1911)-New Series, 26 (1930)-; 3rd Series, 1 (1930)-3rd Series, 30 (1956)-; 4th Series, 1 (1963)-. English (Scots). an. £30.00. Scottish Text Society, PO Box 106, c/o Jill Dick, Aberdeen AB9 8ZE Scotland. **Tel** 011 44 224 583777, FAX 011 44 224 583777. **LC** PR8633; .S4. **Bk Rev**, (Qty: 3). **Circ:** 500.
Ind/Abst MLA Int. Bibl. Books Artic. Mod. Lang. Lit.

US/0882-7400
PUBLISHED. [Published]. (1985)-. Periodical. English. Twelve times a year. Platen Publishing Company, 132 Shaker Road, Suite 137, East Long Meadow MA 01028. **Tel** (818)367-9613. **ED** Patricia Begalla. **DD** 810. **Bk Rev. Ad Acc. Circ:** 5,000. ***Continues** Freelancers Newsletter, 0016-0636.*
Desc: Caters to all writers with emphasis on the talented fledgling. Also publishes articles on the craft of writing, research tips and advice from seasoned pros.

US/0738-517X
PUERTO DEL SOL. **Added/Corp** New Mexico State University. Writing Center. (19??)-. Periodical. Multiple languages (English and Spanish). sa (Jan. & Sept.). $7.75 (one year), $15.00 (two years), $25.00 (three years). Puerto Del Sol, Box 3 E/New Mexico State University, Las Cruces NM 88003. **Tel** (505)646-3931. **ED** Kevin McIlvoy. **LC** PS580; .P83. **DD** 810/.8/0054. **Bk Rev. Ad Acc. Circ:** 900.
Desc: Includes book reviews, interviews with Western and Southwestern authors (such as Anaya, Waters, Siko, Hinojosa), poetry and fiction- both conventional and experimental.
Ind/Abst Am. Humanit. Index (-199?); Index Am. Period. Verse.

US/0896-2197
PULITZER PRIZES, THE. Vol. 1 (1987)-. Periodical. English. an. $16.95. Simon & Schuster, 1230 Avenue of the Americas, New York NY 10020. **Tel** (212)698-7000. **LC** PN4722; .P84. **DD** 071/.3/076.

US/0747-7600
PULP VOICES, OR, SCIENCE FICTION VOICES. (PULP VOICES, OR, SCIENCE FICTION VOICES / CONDUCTED BY JEFFREY M. ELLIOT.). [Pulp voices, Sci. fict. voices]. **VFOAT** Pulp Voices. (198?)-. English. ir. Borgo Press, PO Box 2845, San Bernardino CA 92406. **Tel** (714)884-5813, (714)885-1161. **ED** R Reginald. **LC** PS374.S35; S337. **DD** 813/.0876/09. **Circ:** 1,000. ***Continues** Science Fiction Voices, 0164-1093.*
Desc: A collection of interviews with a group of writers or litterateurs, connected with a particular sub-genre or time period.

UK/0143-5531
PULS (LONDON, ENGLAND). (PULS.). Periodical. Polish. qt. $15.00. Puls Publications, BCM Box 697 Kingdom, London WXIN 3XX United Kingdom. **LC** PG7001; .P85.

UK/0033-4278
PUNCH (LONDON). ***Ceased.*** (PUNCH.). [Punch]. **VFOAT** London Charivari. Vol. 1, No. 1 (July 1841)-(April 1992). Periodical. English. wk. Punch Publishers Ltd, Watling Street Bletchley, Milton Keynes MK2 2BW England. **Tel** 0908-71981. **ED** Alan Coren. **LC** AP101; .P8. **DD** 827/.008. **Ad Acc. Circ:** 78,000. available on microfilm and microfiche from University Microfilms International (UMI). Documents available from UMI Article Clearinghouse.
Desc: An absorbing magazine full of English humour and full of fine literary comment by the best English writers.
Ind/Abst Book Rev. Index; Index Period. Artic. Relat. Law; Med. Rev. Dig.; Newsp. Period. Abstr. (1988-1992).

CN/0712-1318
PUNDIT. (THE PUNDIT.). [Pundit]. **Added/Corp** International Save the Pun Foundation. (June 1991)-. Periodical. English. mo. $24.00. International Save the Pun Foundation, PO Box 5040, Station A, Toronto Ontario M5W 1N4 Canada. **Tel** (416)922-1100, FAX (416)922-1100. **ED** Norman Gilbert. **DD** C818/.5407. **Bk Rev**, (Qty: 6). ctrl circ.

II
PURANAM. **Added/Corp** All-India Kasiraja Trust. **VFOAT** Purana. (July 1959)-. Periodical. Multiple languages (English and Sanskrit). Twice a year (Feb., July). All-India Kashiraj Trust, Fort Ramnagar, Varanasi UP India. **(Subscription address:** Prints India, 11 Darya Ganj, New Delhi 110002 India.) **LC** PK2918.P8; P85.

NE/0165-8743
PURDUE UNIVERSITY MONOGRAPHS IN ROMANCE LANGUAGES. **See** Linguistics.

CK
PURO CUENTO (BOGOTA, COLOMBIA). (PURO CUENTO : REVISTA DE IRREALIDADES.). No. 1 (1981)-. Periodical. Spanish. bm. Puro Cuento, Apartado Aereo 6666, Bogota Columbia. **ED** D Sanchez Juliao.

US/0149-7863
PUSHCART PRIZE, THE. 1st- Ed., (1977)-. English. an (Sept.). $29.00. Pushcart Press, PO Box 380, Wainscott NY 11975. **Tel** (516)324-9300. **ED** Bill Henderson. **LC** PS501; .P87. **DD** 810/.8. **Circ:** 10,000.
Desc: An anthology of the work from our small presses.

US/1054-6804
PUTTING OUT : A PUBLISHING RESOURCE GUIDE FOR LESBIAN & GAY WRITERS. [Putt. out]. (1991)-. English. $12.95. Putting Out Books, 2215-R Market Street, Suite 113, San Francisco CA 94114. **DD** 070.

US/0278-1891
PYNCHON NOTES. [Pynchon notes]. (Oct. 1979)-. Periodical. English. Twice a year. $9.00 US and Canada; $12.00 other. University of Wisconsin - Eau Claire, Eau Claire WI 54702-4004. **Tel** (715)826-2639. **ED** Bernard Duyfhuizen; (715)836-3165. **LC** PS3566.Y55; Z82. **DD** 813/.54. **Bk Rev**, (Qty: 6-8). **Ad Acc. Pr Rev. Circ:** 300.
Desc: Dedicated to all aspects of Pynchon's works, and their relations to the contexts of contemporary, American, and comparative literature.
Ind/Abst Abstr. Engl. Stud.; Lit. Crit. Regist.; MLA Int. Bibl. Books Artic. Mod. Lang. Lit.

SI
QAUMI RAJ. V. 1- Jan. 26, 1974-. Periodical. Urdu (Urdu). 5.00. Dairiktoret Janral af Informeshan aind Pablik Rileshanz, Bombay 400032 India. **LC** PK2151; .Q33.

IT
QUADERNI DEL DIPARTIMENTO DI LINGUE E LETTERATURE STRANIERE MODERNE. **Added/Corp** Universita di Genova. Dipartimento di Lingue e Letterature Straniere Moderne. (1987)-. Periodical. Italian (English and French). Piovan Editor, Via Montegrotto 41, 35031 Abano Terme Italy.
Ind/Abst MLA Int. Bibl. Books Artic. Mod. Lang. Lit.

IT
QUADERNI DI LETTERATURE IBERICHE E IBEROAMERICANE. (1983)-. Periodical. Italian (Portuguese and Spanish). Bulzoni Editore Srl, Via dei Liburni 14, 00185 Rome Italy. **Tel** 011 39 6 445-5207, FAX 011 39 6 445-0355.

IT
QUADERNI DI LINGUE E LETTERATURE / UNIVERSIT·A DEGLI STUDI DI PADOVA, FACOLTA DI ECONOMIA E COMMERCIO, ISTITUTO DI LINGUE E LETTERATURE STRANIERE DI VERONA. **Added/Corp** Universita di Padova. Istituto di Lingue e Letterature Straniere di Verona. (1976)-. Italian (English, French and German).
Ind/Abst MLA Int. Bibl. Books Artic. Mod. Lang. Lit.

IT
QUADERNI DI SCHEDE UMANISTICHE. **Added/Corp** Archivio Umanistico Rinascimentale Bolognese. Universita di Bologna. Dipartimento di Italianistica. (1991)-. Monographic series. Italian. sa. L4200000 Itlay; 6800000 other. Clueb Coop Libraria Univ Edi, Bologna Via Marsala 24, 40126 Bologna Italy. **Tel** 011 39 51 220736, 224780, FAX 011 39 51 237758. ***Continues** Schede Umanistiche.*
Desc: Concerned with Italian philology.

CN/0226-8043
QUADERNI D'ITALIANISTICA. [Quad. ital.]. **Added/Corp** Canadian Society for Italian Studies. Vol. 1, No. 1 (Spring 1980)-. Periodical. English (Italian and French). sa (May, Sept.). $24.00 (institutions), $20.00 (individuals) US; $32.00 (institutions), $28.00 (individuals) other. University of Toronto Department of Italian Studies, Toronto Ontario M5S 1A1 Canada. **Tel** (416)978-5573, FAX (416)978-5593. **ED** M. Ciavolella. **LC** PQ4001; .Q35. **DD** 850/.9. **Bk Rev. Ad Acc. Circ:** 500 (ctrl). Documents available from The Genuine Article.
Desc: Devoted to the study of Italian literature, history and culture.
Ind/Abst Arts Humanit. Citation Index [Full Cov.]; Curr. Contents Arts Humanit.; MLA Int. Bibl. Books Artic. Mod. Lang. Lit.; Res. Alert [Full Cov.]; Romant. Move.

IT/0392-873X
QUADERNI UTINENSI. Added/Corp Universita di Udine. Istituto di Filologia Romanza. (1983)-. Periodical. Italian (French; summaries and/or abstracts in English). sa. **LC** DG975.F877; Q33. **DD** 945/.39/005.
Ind/Abst BHA : Biblio. Hist. Art.

IT/0394-2694
QUADERNI VENETI. Added/Corp Centro Interuniversitario di Studi Veneti (Venice, Italy). Vol. 1 (1985)-. Italian (English). sa (June & December). L54000 Italy; L72000 other. Angelo Longo Editore, Via Paolo Costa 33, PO Box 431, 48100 Ravenna Italy. **Tel** 011 39 544 217026, FAX 011 39 544 217026. **ED** Giorgio Padoan. **LC** DG975.V38; Q35. **Circ:** 1,800.
Desc: Studies on Venetian literature, language, history and theater.

FR
QUAI VOLTAIRE, REVUE LITTERAIRE. VFOAT Quai Voltaire. No. 1 (Winter 1991)-. Periodical. French. Three times a year. Editions Quai Voltaire, 68 Rue Mazarine, 75006 Paris France.

US/1053-8496
QUANTA (PITTSBURGH, PA.). (QUANTA [COMPUTER FILE].). [Quanta]. (1989)-. Periodical. English. bm. Free. Quanta Magazine, c/o Daniel K Appelquist, 5440 5th Avenue, Apartment 60, Pittsburgh PA 15232. **(Subscription address:** PostScript subscriptions/ quanta+requests-postscript@andrew.cmu.edu, quanta+requests-postscript@andrew.BITNET; for ASCII subscriptions: quanta+requests-ascii@andrew.cmu.edu, quanta+requests-ascii@andrew.BITNET.**)** **DD** 810.

US
QUANTUM. No. 35 (Spring 1990)-. Periodical. English. Three times a year. $7.00 (one year), $12.00 (two year). Thrust Publications, 8217 Langport Terrace, Gaithersburg MD 20877. **Tel** (202)872-8110. **LC** IN PROCESS. ***Continues*** *Thrust (Adelphi, Md.).*
Ind/Abst Am. Humanit. Index (1990-); Sci. Fict. Fantasy Book Rev. Index.

GW
QUARBER MERKUR. VFOAT QM. (19??)-. Periodical. German. sa.
Ind/Abst Sci. Fict. Fantasy Book Rev. Index.

CN/0033-5266
QUARRY (KINGSTON). (QUARRY.). **Added/Corp** Queen's University (Kingston, Ont.). Vol. 1 (Spring 1952)-. Periodical. English (summaries and/or abstracts in French). Four times a year. $35.25 (institutions), $21.00 (individuals). Quarry Press Inc., PO Box 1061, Kingston Ontario K7L 4Y5 Canada. **Tel** (613)548-8429, FAX (613)548-1556. **ED** Steven Heighton. **Ad Acc, Adv Mgr:** Steve. **Circ:** 900 (ctrl). available on microfilm from Micromedia Limited.
Desc: Publishes new and innovative poetry and fiction by Canadian authors. Committed to discovering new talent on the move. In recent years the magazine has instituted a series of essays on poetics, bridging the gap between critical and creative writing.
Ind/Abst Am. Humanit. Index; Can. Index; Can. Period. Index; Index Am. Period. Verse.

US/0736-4628
QUARRY WEST. [Quarry west]. **Added/Corp** University of California, Santa Cruz. College V. Porter College (University of California, Santa Cruz). No. 5 (1976)-. Periodical. English (Spanish). sa (June & Dec.). $12.00. University of California Porter College, Santa Cruz CA 95064. **Tel** (408)429-2155. **ED** Ken Weisner. **LC** PS501; .Q37. **DD** 810/.8. Index available. **Bk Rev. Ad Acc. Circ:** 800. ***Continues*** *Quarry (Santa Cruz, Calif.), 0033-5266.*
Desc: Poetry, short stories, articles, reviews and art.
Ind/Abst Am. Humanit. Index (199?-).

KE/1018-1555
QUARTERLY INDEX TO PERIODICAL LITERATURE, EASTERN AND SOUTHERN AFRICA. [Q. index period. lit. East. South. Afr.]. **Main/Corp** Library of Congress. Library of Congress Office, Nairobi, Kenya. **Added/Corp** Library of Congress. Library of Congress Office, Nairobi, Kenya. Vol. 1, No. 1 (1991)-. Periodical. English. qt. Free. Library of Congress Office / Kenya, United States Embassy, PO Box 30598, Nairobi Kenya. **LC** Z3503; .Q37; DT365.

US/0893-3103
QUARTERLY (NEW YORK, N.Y. : 1987). (THE QUARTERLY.). [Quarterly]. (Spring 1987)-. Periodical. English. qt. $30.00. Gutter Press, 1600 Bathurst Street, Suite 405, Toronto Ontario, M5P 3H9 Canada. **Tel** (416)980-3099. **LC** PS501; .Q375. **DD** 810/.8.

US/0194-4231
QUARTERLY WEST. [Q. west]. **Added/Corp** University of Utah. No. 1 (Fall 1976)-. Periodical. English. Twice a year (May & Dec.). $11.00 (one year), $20.00 (two years). University of Utah / 317 Olpin Union, Salt Lake City UT 84112. **Tel** (801)581-3938. **ED** Regina Dost and C. F. Pinkerton. **LC** PS501; .Q38. **DD** 810/.8. Index available. **Bk Rev. Ad Acc. Circ:** 1,000.
Desc: Includes poetry, fiction, criticism, interviews with writers, and essays.
Ind/Abst Am. Humanit. Index; Index Am. Period. Verse; West. Hist. Q.

CN/0316-2052
QUEBEC FRANCAIS. [Que fr.]. **Added/Corp** Association Quebecoise des Professeurs de Francais. (Feb. 1971)-. Periodical. French. Four times a year (Feb., May, Aug., Nov.). 22.50Can$ (institutions) Canada; 30.00Can$ (institutions) US; 37.00Can$ (institutions) other; 18.70Can$ (individual) Canada; 26.00Can$ (individual) US; 28.00Can$ (individual) other. Les Publications Quebec Francais, CP 9185, Sainte-Foy Quebec G1V 4B1 Canada. **Tel** (418)527-0809. **LC** F1052; .Q474. **DD** 971.4/005. Index available. **Bk Rev. Ad Acc. Circ:** 8,000 (ctrl).
Desc: Covers education, literature, language and society.
Ind/Abst Point Repere (1983-).

AT/0819-9752
QUEENSLAND WRITER. [Qld. writ.]. (1987)-. Periodical. English. qt. **(Subscription address:** Katherine Davis, Arts Division, PO Box 185, Brisbane QLD 4002 Australia**)** **ED** A Fremd, K Davis. **DD** 808.009943.
Ind/Abst Aust. Educ. Index; Aust. Libr. Inf. Sci. Abstr. (1989-).

US/0277-5360
QUEST STAR. [Quest star]. **VAT** Quest/Star. Vol. 4, No. 1 (Oct. 1981)-. Periodical. English. mo. MW Communications, 247 Fort Pibb Blvd., Pittsburgh PA 15222. **LC** P96.S34; Q4. **DD** 813/.0876/09. ***Continues*** *Questar, 0270-9252.*

FR/0048-6493
QUINZAINE LITTERAIRE, LA. [Quinzaine litt.]. **VFOAT** Quinzaine. No. 1 (March 15, 1966)-. Periodical. French. sm (one issue in Aug.). 425.00F France; 560.00F other; 740.00F (airmail). La Quinzaine Litteraire, 43 rue du Temple, 75004 Paris France. **Tel** 011 33 1 48874858, FAX 011 33 1 48871301. **LC** AP20; .Q53. **DD** 054. cum. index. **Ad Acc. Circ:** 30,000 (ctrl). Documents available from The Genuine Article.
Ind/Abst Arts Humanit. Citation Index [Full Cov.]; Curr. Contents Arts Humanit.; MLA Int. Bibl. Books Artic. Mod. Lang. Lit.; Res. Alert [Full Cov.]; Romant. Move.; Soc. Sci. Cit. Index [Select. Cov.].

US/0273-6705
QUOTE (ATLANTA, GA.). (QUOTE.). [Quote]. Began in 1940. Periodical. English. bw. $33.00. Quote Publ Co, PO Box 815, Las Cruces NM 88004. **Tel** (505)527-0381. **ED** Varese Chambless. **LC** PN6081; .Q65. **DD** 081. Index Available, published separately, free-automatically sent. available on microfilm and microfiche from University Microfilms International (UMI).
Desc: Humor, inspirational, typical digest for speakers, and idea presenters.

SP
RABIDA. Added/Corp Patronato Provincial del V Centenario del Descubrimiento de America (Huelva, Spain). No. 1 (Jun. 1985)-. Periodical. Spanish. sa. **LC** F1401; .R3. **DD** 980/.005.
Ind/Abst Am. Hist. Life (1991-).

CN/0826-5909
RADDLE MOON. (THE RADDLE MOON.). [Raddle moon]. **Added/Corp** University of Victoria (B.C.). English Dept. Creative Writing Programme. (1983)-. Periodical. English (French, Italian and Spanish). Twice a year (Mar. & Nov.). 12.00Can$ (individuals), 17.00Can$ (institutions). The Raddle Moon, 9060 Stephens Street, Vancourver British Columbia V6K 3W5 Canada. **Tel** (604)736-9769. **ED** Susan Clark, Kathryn Macleod, and Jeff Derksen. **LC** PN771 db .R33. **DD** 810.8/0054/05. **Bk Rev. Ad Acc. Circ:** 700 (ctrl). ***Continues*** *From an Island., 0706-8093.*
Desc: Publishes 'new lyric' and language-centered poetry and fiction, poetics, critical and personal essays, translations, photographs and graphics from many countries.
Ind/Abst Can. Period. Index (1990-).

●RU
RADONEZH, VEK XX. VFOAT Radonezh, Vek Dvadtsatyi; Radonezh. (1992)-. Russian.

UN/0033-8591
RADUGA. [Raduga]. **Added/Corp** Soiuz Pisatelei Ukrainy. (1951)-. Periodical. Russian. mo. $99.95. **(Subscription address:** East View Publications Inc., 3020 Harbor Lane North, Suite 110, Minneapolis MN 55447.**)**
Ind/Abst MLA Int. Bibl. Books Artic. Mod. Lang. Lit.

US/0742-2768
RAG MAG (GOODHUE, MINN.). (RAG MAG.). Vol. 2, No. 2 (Fall 1983)-. Periodical. English. Twice a year (Apr., Oct.). $15.00 (institutions); $10.00 (individuals) US; $14.00 (individuals) other. Black Hat Press, PO Box 12, Goodhue MN 55027. **Tel** (612)923-4590. **ED** Beverly Voldseth, (editor's address: 508 2nd Avenue, Goodhue, MN 55027). **Bk Rev**, (Qty: 2-4). **Ad Acc. Circ:** 300. ***Continues*** *Underground Rag Mag.*
Desc: Contains art, poetry, fiction, essays, and reviews of new established authors and artists.
Ind/Abst Am. Humanit. Index (-199?); Index Am. Period. Verse.

IT/0033-8648
RAGGUAGLIO LIBRARIO, IL. **See** Bibliographies.

CN/0712-7871
RAIN FOREST (PORT ALBERNI, B.C.). (RAIN FOREST.). [Rain for.]. Spring 1979-. English. an. $2.00 each volume. Rain Forest, c/o Dorothy Allen, Rain Forest Publishing Committee, Rural Route 1 Port Alberni, British Columbia V9Y 7L5 Canada. **DD** C810/.8/0971134.

II/0448-1690
RAJASTHAN UNIVERSITY STUDIES IN ENGLISH. [Rajasthan Univ. stud. Engl.]. **Main/Corp** Jaipur, India (Rajasthan). University of Rajasthan. English. an. University of Rajasthan Department of English, Jaipur India. **LC** PR1; .J28A. **DD** 820/.9.
Ind/Abst MLA Int. Bibl. Books Artic. Mod. Lang. Lit.

II
RAJASTHANA KE AJANE BRAJABHASHA SAHITYAKARA DARAPANA. Added/Corp Rajasthana Brajabhasha Akadami. **VFOAT** Rajasthana ke Ajane Brajabhasha Sahityakara-Paricai Pothi (Monographa). Vol. 1 (1990)-. Periodical. Braj. Rajasthan Braj Bhasha Academy, C-267 Bhasha Marg, Tilak Nagar, Jaipur-302004 India. **LC** IN PROCESS.

US/0889-1664
RAMBUNCTIOUS REVIEW. (198?)-. Periodical. English. Three times a year. $9.00. Rambunctious Press Inc., 1221 West Pratt Blvd., Chicago IL 60626. **DD** 808.
Ind/Abst Am. Humanit. Index (199?-).

CN/0711-7647
RAMPIKE (TORONTO). (RAMPIKE.). [Rampike]. Vol. 2, No. 1/2 (1982)-. Periodical. English (French; summaries and/or abstracts in French). Three times a year. 16.00Can$ Canada; 18.00Can$ US; 20.00Can$ other. Rampike, 95 Rivercrest Road, Toronto Ontario M6S 4H7 Canada. **Tel** (416)767-6713. **ED** K. Jirgens. **DD** C810/.8/0054. Index available. cum. index. **Bk Rev.** ***Continues*** *Rampike Magazine, 0834-3551.*
Desc: Arts and writing journal featuring select talent from around the world. Features a four-color cover, black and white glossy interior.
Ind/Abst ARTbibliogr. Mod.; Index Am. Period. Verse.

●US/1065-8343
RANDOM REALITIES. (RANDOM REALITIES : RR.). [Random realities]. **Added/Corp** Graphos Fiction Writers Group. **VFOAT** RR. Issue 1 (Summer 1992)-. Periodical. English. sa. $15.00. Random Realities, 5043 Audubon Place, Norcross GA 30093. **DD** 808.

US/1061-6861
RAPPORT (LOS ANGELES, CALIF.). **See** The Arts-Performing Arts.

NE
RAPPORTS HET FRANSE BOEK. Added/Corp Vereniging ter Bevordering van de Studie van het Frans. **VFOAT** Franse Boek. (1971)-. Periodical. French (Dutch). qt. F60.00. Vereniging Bevordering Studie Frans, c/o Dr. E. Verheugd, De Jong Laan 48, 3981 ZJ Bunninck Netherlands. **Tel** 011 31 3405 63602. **ED** S. A. Varga. **Bk Rev. Ad Acc. Circ:** 1,000 (ctrl). ***Continues*** *Het Franse Boek.*
Desc: Accent is laid on book reviews in the domain of French and on articles, that resume briefly, the state of the art of various French disciplines.

US/0275-1607
RARITAN. **See** Literary and Political Reviews.

IT/0557-6857
RASSEGNA DI LETTERATURA TOMISTICA. Added/Corp Pontificia Studiorum Universitas a Sancto Thoma Aquinate in Urbe. Vol. 1 (1966)-. Monographic series. Italian (French). an. Price varies per volume. Herder Editrice e Libreria SRL, Piazza Montecitorio 117-120, 00186 Rome Italy. **Tel** 011 39 6 679 4628, FAX 011 39 6 678 4751. **ED** C. Vansteenkiste. ***Supersedes*** *Bulletin Thomiste.*

Desc: Bibliographic information and review of all publications about St. Thomas Aquinas and Thomism.
Ind/Abst Bibliogr. Mission.

IT/0392-4777
RASSEGNA IBERISTICA. [Rass. iber.]. **Added/Corp** Universita Degli Studi di Venezia. Seminario di Letterature Iberiche e Iberoamericane. (Jan. 1978)-. Periodical. Italian (Portuguese and Spanish). ir. Price varies per volume. Bulzoni Editore Srl, Via dei Liburni 14, 00185 Rome Italy. **Tel** 011 39 6 445-5207, FAX 011 39 6 445-0355. **ED** Franco Meregalli and Giuseppe Bellini. **LC** CB226; .R28. **DD** 909/.046872. **Bk Rev. Ad Acc. Circ:** 500.
Desc: Critiques the latest books and periodicals on Hispano-American subjects and includes two original studies.
Ind/Abst MLA Int. Bibl. Books Artic. Mod. Lang. Lit.

RU
RASSKAZ. (1978)-. Periodical. Russian. an. 1.80rub. Sovremennik, Iartsevskaia 4 Izdatelstvo Sovremennik, 121351 Moscow G-351 Russia. **LC** PG3283; .R237.

NE/0033-9938
RASTER. 1 (April 1967)-. Periodical. Dutch. qt. Fl87.50. De Bezige Bij, PO Box 75184, 1070 AD Amsterdam Netherlands. **Tel** 011 31 20 6735731. **(Subscription address:** I V E C, PO Box 154, 1380 AD WEESP Netherlands.**)**

PK
RAVI. Added/Corp Government College (Lahore, Pakistan). (1906)-. English (Urdu). **LC** PK2151; .R37. **DD** 891/.439/08.
Ind/Abst Annu. Bibliogr. Engl. Lang. Lit.

US/1054-5212
RE ARTS & LETTERS : REAL. See The Arts.

CN/0712-4376
READER'S CHOICE (TORONTO). (READER'S CHOICE.). [Read. choice]. **VFOAT** Readers Choice. Vol. 1, No. 1 (Spring 1982)-. Periodical. English. ir. $3.00 per no. Reader's Choice, PO Box 205 Station S, Toronto Ontario M5M 4L7 Canada. **DD** C813/0108.

US/0034-0464
READERS' GUIDE TO PERIODICAL LITERATURE. See General Interest-Abstracting, Bibliographies and Statistics.

US/1040-3558
READING EDGE (CROWNSVILLE, MD.), THE. See Library and Information Sciences.

US/0882-6196
READING PLUS (NEW YORK, N.Y.). (READING PLUS.). [Read. plus]. Vol. 1 (19??)-. English. an. Peter Lang Publishing, 62 West 45th Street, 4th Floor, New York NY 10036. **Tel** (212)764-1471, (800)770-5264, telex 6973364 PLNY. **ED** Mary A Caws. **DD** 808.
Desc: Interdisciplinary series on thoughts to enhance classical and modern works.

AT/0155-218X
READING TIME. [Read. time]. (1967)-. Periodical. English. qt. 28.00Aus$ (Australia); 38.00Aus$ (other). Childrens Book Council of Australia, PO Box 310, Heidelberg Victoria 3084 Australia. **Tel** 011 61 3 4571905. **DD** 028.52. ***Continues*** *New Books for Boys and Girls.*

GW/0723-0338
REAL (BERLIN, WEST). (THE YEARBOOK OF RESEARCH IN ENGLISH AND AMERICAN LITERATURE : REAL.). [REAL]. **VFOAT** R.E.A.L.; REAL. Vol. 1 (1982)-. English. an. DM171.00 Germany; DM173.00 other. Gunter Narr Verlag, Dishingerweg 5, D 72070 Tuebingen Germany. **Tel** 011 49 7071 78091, FAX (07071)75288. **LC** PR13; .Y42. **DD** 820/.9.
Ind/Abst Annu. Bibliogr. Engl. Lang. Lit.; MLA Int. Bibl. Books Artic. Mod. Lang. Lit.; Romant. Move.

CN
REAPPRAISALS, CANADIAN WRITERS. (19??)-. Monographic series. English. ir. University of Ottawa Press English Department, 175 Waller, Ottawa Ontario K1N 6N5 Canada. **Tel** (613)564-3411. **(Subscription address:** Gaetin Morin Editeur, 171 de Mortagne, Boucherví Que J4B 6G4 Canada.**)**
Ind/Abst MLA Int. Bibl. Books Artic. Mod. Lang. Lit.

FR
RECHERCHES ANGLAISES ET NORD-AMERICAINES : RANAM. VFOAT RANAM. No. 20 (1987)-. French (English). an. 70.00F. Univ Sciences Humaines de Strasbourg, 22 rue Descartes, 67084 Strasbourg Cedex France. **Tel** 88613939. **ED** Andre Bleikasten. **Ad Acc. Circ:** 500 (ctrl). ***Continues*** *Recherches Anglaises et Americaines, 0557-6989.*
Desc: A journal devoted to English and North American studies.
Ind/Abst MLA Int. Bibl. Books Artic. Mod. Lang. Lit.

FR/0769-0886
RECHERCHES SUR DIDEROT ET SUR L'ENCYCLOPEDIE. [Rech. Diderot Encycl.]. **Added/Corp** Societe Diderot. **VFOAT** RDE. No. 1 (Oct. 1986)-. Periodical. French. sa. 237.00F France; 260.00F other. Aux Amateurs de Livres International, 62 Avenue de Suffren, 75015 Paris France. **Tel** 011 33 1 45671838. **LC** PQ1979; .R43. **DD** 034/.1/092.

FR/0765-1155
RECHERCHES SUR L'IMAGINAIRE. [Rech. imagin.]. (1982)-. Monographic series. French. ir. Price varies per volume. Presses de l'Universite D'Angers, 5 rue le Notre, 49045 Angers Cedex 1 France. **Tel** 011 33 41 352100. ***Continues*** *Cahier de Poesie (Angers), 0765-1147.*
Ind/Abst MLA Int. Bibl. Books Artic. Mod. Lang. Lit.

US/0888-4757
RECTANGLE, THE. [Rectangle]. **Added/Corp** Sigma Tau Delta. **VFOAT** Quarterly Rectangle. (1925)-. Periodical. English. sa. Sigma Tau Delta, Executive Secretary, English Department, Northern Illinois University, Dekalb IL 60115. **LC** PS508.C6; R38. **DD** 810/.8/09283.
Ind/Abst Film Lit. Index (19??-).

US/0034-1967
RED CEDAR REVIEW. Added/Corp Michigan State University. Vol. 1 (Spring 1963)-. Periodical. English. sa. $10.00. Michigan State University / Red Cedar Review, 17C Morrill Hall, East Lansing MI 48823. **Tel** (517)355-9656. **ED** Laura Klynstra. **LC** PS501; .R43. **Ad Acc. Circ:** 500.
Desc: Literary magazine covering short fiction, poetry, graphic arts and interviews.

US/0742-454X
RED FOX REVIEW. ***Ceased.*** **VFOAT** Red Fox. V. 1- 1974-?. Periodical. English. an. Mohegan Community College, Mohegan Fine Arts Committee, Norwich CT 06360. **Tel** (203)886-1931. **ED** James Coleman. **Circ:** 750.
Desc: A journal of fiction and poetry- graphics when we can locate some.

US/0887-5715
REDNECK REVIEW OF LITERATURE, THE. Added/Corp Camas Writers' Workshop (Fairfield, Idaho). (1975)-. Periodical. English. Twice a year (Spring and Fall). $15.00 (US); $25.00 (other). Redneck Review, 2919 North Donner Avenue, Milwaukee WI 53211. **Tel** (414)332-6881. **ED** Penelope Reedy. **DD** 810. **Bk Rev**, (Qty: 50-100). **Ad Acc. Circ:** 500.
Desc: Fictions, poetry, essays and drama dealing with the Western American literature.
Ind/Abst Am. Humanit. Index (199?-).

AT/1030-4932
REDOUBT. Added/Corp Canberra College of Advanced Education. School of Communication. No. 1 (Jan. 1988)-. English. Twice a year (April and November). 22.00Aus$ (individuals), 28.00Aus$ (institutions) Australia; 40.00Aus$ other. Canberra College of Advanced Education, PO Box 1, Belconnen Australian Capital Territory 2616 Australia. **Tel** 011 61 6 2012579.

US
REFERENCE GUIDE TO ENGLISH LITERATURE. English. $295.00. St. James Press, PO Box 33477, Detroit MI 48232-5477. **Tel** (800)345-0392.
Desc: Listings of the most important writers in English literature. Entries provide a capsule biography, bibliography of the author's work, further reading lists, and a signed, critical essay on the writer and his/her work.

CN/1184-6305
REFLECTIONS (ORILLIA). (REFLECTIONS / ORILLIA WRITERS' GUILD.). [Reflections]. **Added/Corp** Orillia Writers' Guild.c. (1990)-. English. ir. Orillia Writers' Guild, c/o Mrs. A May Sears, Number 2, 281 Millard Street, Orillia, Ontario L3V 4H2 Canada. **DD** C810.8/09713/17. ***Continues*** *Frieze Frame., 0846-4693.*

GW/0170-8872
REGENSBURGER BEITRAEGE ZUR DEUTSCHEN SPRACH- UND LITERATURWISSENSCHAFT: REIHE B, UNTERSUCHUNGEN. [Regensbg. Beitr. dtsch. Sprach- Lit.wiss., Reihe B, Unters.]. (1975)-. Monographic series. German.
Ind/Abst MLA Int. Bibl. Books Artic. Mod. Lang. Lit.

GW/0344-6786
REIHE DER SCHRIFTEN - FREIES DEUTSCHES HOCHSTIFT. (REIHE DER SCHRIFTEN.). [Reihe Schr. - Freies Dtsch. Hochstift]. **Main/Corp** Freies Deutsches Hochstift (Frankfurt am Main, Germany). (1966)-. Monographic series. German. ir. Price varies per volume. Max Niemeyer Verlag, Postfach 2140, D 72011 Tuebingen Germany. **Tel** 011 49 7071 989494, FAX 011 49 7071 87419. **ED** Detlev Lueders. ***Continues*** *Reihe der Vortrage und Schriften - Freies Deutsches Hochstift, 0344-6824.*
Ind/Abst MLA Int. Bibl. Books Artic. Mod. Lang. Lit.

GW
REIHE SIEGEN. (1977)-. Monographic series. German (English). ir. Universitatsverlag Carl Winter, POB 106140, D 69051 Heidelberg Germany. **Tel** 011 49 6221 770260.
Ind/Abst MLA Int. Bibl. Books Artic. Mod. Lang. Lit.

NE/0925-4757
REINARDUS : YEARBOOK OF THE INTERNATIONAL REYNARD SOCIETY. Added/Corp International Reynard Society. (1988)-. Periodical. English (French and Italian). an. $68.00. John Benjamins BV, Amsteldijk 44, PO Box 75577, 1070 AN Amsterdam Netherlands. **Tel** 011 31 20 6738156, FAX 011 31 20 739773. **(Subscription address:** John Benjamins North America, PO Box 27519, Philadelphia PA 19118-0519.**) ED** Brian Levy, Paul Wackers. **LC** PN690.A6; R44. **DD** 809/.02/05.
Desc: Promotes comparative research in the fields of medieval comic, satirical, didactic, and allegorical literature, with emphasis on beast epic, fable and fabliau, including sources, influences and later developments into the modern period.
Ind/Abst MLA Int. Bibl. Books Artic. Mod. Lang. Lit.

US/0888-3769
RELIGION & LITERATURE. See Religion and Theology.

CC
REN WU. See Biographies.

PR
RENACIMIENTO (RIO PIEDRAS, P.R.). (RENACIMIENTO.). V. 1, No. 1 (Jan./June 1981)-. Periodical. Spanish. sa. $8.00. Apartado 21487, UPR Station, Rio Piedras, Puerto Rico 00931. **LC** PQ7081.A1; R32. **DD** 808.8/998.

CN/0034-429X
RENAISSANCE AND REFORMATION. **See** History(General)-History of Europe.

US/0193-9815
RENAISSANCE AND RENASCENCES IN WESTERN LITERATURE. [Renaiss. renasc. West. lit.]. Vol. 1, No. 1 (Summer 1979)-. Periodical. English. qt. $7.00 US; $9.00 other. Allentown College, Department of English, c/o Wilson F Engel III Editor, Center Valley PA 18034. **LC** PN883; .R46. **DD** 809.
Ind/Abst MLA Int. Bibl. Books Artic. Mod. Lang. Lit.

JA/0388-0796
RENAISSANCE BULLETIN, THE. [Renaiss. bull.]. **Added/Corp** Renaissance Institute. (1974)-. Bulletin. English. an. $32.00. **(Subscription address:** Japan Publications Trading Company, Ltd., PO Box 5030, Tokyo International, Tokyo 100-31 Japan.**) LC** PR411; .R46. **DD** 822/.3/09.
Ind/Abst MLA Int. Bibl. Books Artic. Mod. Lang. Lit.

US/0584-4207
RENAISSANCE PAPERS. [Renaiss. pap.]. (April 23-24, 1954)-. English. an. $20.00. Southeastern Renaissance Conference, English Department, North Carolina State University, Box 8105, Raleigh NC 27695-8105. **Tel** (919)684-2741, FAX (919)515-1836. **ED** B.J. Baines (telephone: (919)515-4152) and G.W. Williams (telephone: (919)684-5827). **LC** CB361; .R42. **DD** 940.2. Index available (irregular). cum. index. **Pr Rev. Circ:** 500 (ctrl).
Desc: A selection of papers read at the annual meeting of the Southeastern Renaissance Conference.
Ind/Abst Abstr. Engl. Stud.; Annu. Bibliogr. Engl. Lang. Lit.; MLA Int. Bibl. Books Artic. Mod. Lang. Lit.

US/0034-4338
RENAISSANCE QUARTERLY. [Renaiss. q.]. **Added/Corp** Renaissance Society of America. Vol. 20 (Spring 1967)-. Academic Scholarly Publication. English. Four times a year (Apr., June, Sept., Nov.). $50.00 (individuals), $65.00 (institutions). Renaissance Society of America, 24 West 12th Street, New York NY 10011. **Tel** (212)998-3797. **DD** 940. **NLM** Z 6207.R4 R393. Index available. cum. index. available on microfilm from Kraus Microform. Documents available from UMI Article Clearinghouse. ***Continues*** *Renaissance News, 0277-903X;* ***Absorbed*** *Studies in the Renaissance, 0081-8658.*
Desc: Covers interdisciplinary Renaissance studies that incorporate reviews and scholarly articles.
Ind/Abst Abstr. Engl. Stud.; Acad. Search (July 1993-); Am. Hist. Life (1972-1974); Annu. Bibliogr. Engl. Lang. Lit.; Arts Humanit. Citation Index [Full Cov.]; BHA : Biblio. Hist. Art; Book Rev. Index; Curr. Contents Arts Humanit.; Expand. Acad. Index (1989-); Humanit. Index; Humanit. Source (Jul. 1993-); INFO-SOUTH Abstr.; Mag. Search; MLA Int. Bibl. Books Artic. Mod. Lang. Lit.; Newsp. Period. Abstr. (1991-); Res. Alert [Full Cov.]; Soc. Sci. Cit. Index [Select. Cov.].

US
RENASCENCE. Added/Corp Usher Society. (Aug. 1945)-. Periodical. English. Four times a year. $25.00 US; $30.00 other; back issues $8.00. Marquette University Press / English Department, 607 North 13th Street,

Milwaukee WI 53233. **Tel** (414)288-6725, FAX (414)288-3300. **ED** Joseph Schwartz. **LC** ML1; .R5. **DD** 780.5.

US/0034-4346
RENASCENCE. ESSAYS ON VALUES IN LITERATURE. [Renascence]. **Added/Corp** Catholic Renascence Society. Vol. 1 (Autumn 1948)-. Periodical. English. Four times a year (Jan., Apr., July, Oct.). $20.00 US; $23.00 other. Marquette University Press, Marquette University, Milwaukee WI 53233. **Tel** (414)288-1564. **(Subscription address:** Renascence, Brooks Hall Room 200, Milwaukee, WI 53233, (414)242-2399**) ED** Joseph Schwartz. **LC** PN2; .R4. Index available. cum. index. **Pr Rev. Circ:** 700. available on microfilm and microfiche from University Microfilms International (UMI). Documents available from The Genuine Article, UMI Article Clearinghouse.
Desc: Essays on values in literature from a Christian perspective.
Ind/Abst Abstr. Engl. Stud.; Acad. Search (July 1993-); Annu. Bibliogr. Engl. Lang. Lit.; Arts Humanit. Citation Index (19??-19??) [Full Cov.]; Curr. Contents Arts Humanit.; Expand. Acad. Index (1989-); Humanit. Index; Humanit. Source (Jul. 1993-); INFO-SOUTH Abstr.; Lit. Crit. Regist.; Mag. Search; MLA Int. Bibl. Books Artic. Mod. Lang. Lit.; Newsp. Period. Abstr. (1990-); Res. Alert [Full Cov.]; Romant. Move.; Abr. Cathol. Period. Lit. Index; Cathol. Period. Lit. Index.

US/0034-4400
RENDEZVOUS (POCATELLO, IDAHO). (RENDEZVOUS : IDAHO STATE UNIVERSITY JOURNAL OF ARTS AND LETTERS.). **Added/Corp** Idaho State University. Vol. 1, No. 1 (Spring 1966)-. Periodical. English. Twice a year (Apr., Dec.). $7.50. Idaho State University, Campus PO Box 8113, Pocatello ID 83209-0009. **Tel** (208)236-2895, FAX (208)236-4000. **ED** Janne Goldbeck (phone: (208)236-2478). **LC** AS30; .R46. **DD** 051. **Bk Rev. Circ:** 200.
Desc: A journal encouraging innovative, speculative and creative work that will generate thoughtful consideration by non-specialists.
Ind/Abst Abstr. Engl. Stud.; Annu. Bibliogr. Engl. Lang. Lit.; MLA Int. Bibl. Books Artic. Mod. Lang. Lit.

HK/0377-3515
RENDITIONS. [Renditions]. **Added/Corp** Chinese University of Hong Kong. Centre for Translation Projects. **VFOAT** I Ts'ung. No. 1 (Autumn 1973)-. Periodical. English (Chinese). Twice a year. $35.00. Research Centre for Translation, Chinese University Hong Kong, Shatin NT Hong Kong. **Tel** 011 852 0 6097399, FAX 011 852 0 6035149. **ED** Dr. Eva Hung; 11 852 0 6097385. **LC** PL2658.E1; R46. **DD** 895.1/0/8. Index available. cum. index. **Ad Acc, Adv Mgr:** Janice K. Wickeri, **Tel** 11 852 0 6097407. **Pr Rev. Circ:** 1,500.
Desc: English translations of classical and modern Chinese literature.
Ind/Abst MLA Int. Bibl. Books Artic. Mod. Lang. Lit.

US
RENEGADE (BLOOMFIELD HILLS). (RENEGADE.). No. 1 (197?)-. Periodical. English. be. $5.90. Renegade, Box 314, Bloomfield Hills MI 48303. **ED** Michael Nowioki and Miriam Jones. **Bk Rev. Ad Acc. Pr Rev. Circ:** 100.
Desc: Publishes poetry, short stories, essays and artwork available.

FR/0989-1773
REPERAGES NANTES. 1988. (REPERAGES.). **Added/Corp** Fondation pour les Arts et les Sciences de la Communication (Nantes). (1988)-. Periodical. French. bm.
Ind/Abst Annu. Bibliogr. Engl. Lang. Lit.

CN/0715-1519
REPERTOIRE DES PRIX LITTERAIRES. [Repert. prix litt.]. No. 1-. French. **DD** 807/.9. ***Continues*** *Guide des Prix Litteraires Decernes au Quebec.*

FR/0987-6030
REPERTOIRE (MONTPELLIER, FRANCE). **See** Encyclopedias and General Reference Books.

GW/0486-4166
REPERTORIEN ZUR DEUTSCHEN LITERATURGESCHICHTE. Vol. 1 (1964)-. Monographic series. German. ir. Price varies per volume. J. B. Metzlersche Verlagsbuchhandling, Kernerstrasse 10 32 41, D-70028 Stuttgart Germany. **Tel** 011 49 711 22902-14, FAX 011 49 711 22902-90. **Bk Rev. Ad Acc. Circ:** 1,000 (ctrl).
Desc: Focuses on historical movements and currents in the history of German literature, often studies through the production of a specific group of writers or through the progress of a literary medium in history.

CR
REPERTORIO AMERICANO. **Added/Corp** Universidad Nacional (Costa Rica). Instituto de Estudios Latinoamericanos. Universidad Nacional (Costa Rica). Escuela de Literatura y Ciencias del Lenguaje. Year 1 (Oct./Dec. 1974)-. Periodical. Spanish. qt. C30.00 Costa Rica; $8.00 other. Administracion Y Canje: Instituto de Estudios Latinoamericanos, Apartado 86, 3000 Heredia Costa Rica. **Tel** 37-6363. **ED** Alfonso Chase. **LC** F1401; .R423. **DD** 980/.005. Index available. cum. index. **Bk Rev. Circ:** 1,300 (ctrl).
Desc: Latin American and Spanish subjects related to literature, linguistics, social sciences, art, education, and philosophy.
Ind/Abst HAPI Hisp. Am. Period. Index.

AG
REPERTORIO LATINOAMERICANO. (Apr. 1975)-. Periodical. Spanish. qt. $15.00. Francisco Bello, Haedo 933 Vicente Lopez, Buenos Aires 1638 Argentina. **Tel** 54 1 404653. **LC** F1408.3; .R44. **DD** 980/.005.
Desc: Latin American literature.
Ind/Abst HAPI Hisp. Am. Period. Index (19??-).

UK/0958-5443
REPORT FOR THE YEAR ... / JANE AUSTEN SOCIETY. [Rep. period ... - Jane Austen Soc.]. **Main/Corp** Jane Austen Society. Began publication in 1944. English. an. Jane Austen Society, Yield House, Overton New Basingstoke Hampshire RG25 3HT England. **LC** PR4036.A1; J32.
Ind/Abst Abstr. Engl. Stud.

US/0197-6923
REPRESENTATIVE AMERICAN SPEECHES. [Represent. Am. speeches]. (1937/1938)-. English. an. Annual subscription to Reference Shelf titles: $62.00 US and Canada; $67.00 other. H W Wilson Company, 950 University Avenue, Bronx NY 10452. **Tel** (800)367-6770, (718)588-8400, FAX (718)590-1617, telex 4990003 HWILSON. **ED** O Peterson. **LC** PS668; .B3. **DD** 815.5082. cum. index.
Desc: Consists of a selection of the previous year's outstanding speeches on diverse topics by statesmen and other eminent figures.

SP
REPUBLICA DE LAS LETRAS : ORGANO DE LA ASOCIACION COLEGIAL DE ESCRITORES DE ESPANO. **Added/Corp** Asociacion Colegial de Escritores de Espana. (19??)-. Periodical. Spanish. qt. Asociacion Colegial de Escritores de Espana, Sagasta 28 5, 28004 Madrid Spain. **LC** PQ6001; .R39. **DD** 860/.9.
Ind/Abst MLA Int. Bibl. Books Artic. Mod. Lang. Lit.

US/0034-5210
RESEARCH IN AFRICAN LITERATURES. [Res. Afr. lit.]. **Added/Corp** University of Texas at Austin. African and Afro-American Studies and Research Center. University of Texas at Austin. African and Afro-American Research Institute. African Studies Association. African Literature Committee. Modern Language Association of America. African Literatures Seminar. African Literature Association. Modern Language Association of America. African Literatures Division. Vol. 1 (Spring 1970)-. Periodical. English (French). qt. $60.00. Indiana University Press, 601 North Morton Street, Bloomington IN 47404. **Tel** (812)855-3830, (800)842-6796. **ED** Richard Bjornson. **LC** PL8010; .R46. **DD** 809/.896. Index available. cum. index. **Bk Rev. Ad Acc. Circ:** 1,000. available on microfilm and microfiche from University Microfilms International (UMI). Documents available from The Genuine Article, UMI Article Clearinghouse.
Desc: Discusses scholarship on African oral and written literatures.
Ind/Abst Abstr. Engl. Stud.; Acad. Search (July 1993-); Arts Humanit. Citation Index [Full Cov.]; Curr. Contents Arts Humanit.; Expand. Acad. Index (1989-); Humanit. Index; Humanit. Source (Jul. 1993-); INFO-SOUTH Abstr.; Mag. Search; MLA Int. Bibl. Books Artic. Mod. Lang. Lit.; Newsp. Period. Abstr. (1991-); Res. Alert [Full Cov.]; Soc. Plann. Policy Dev. Abstr.; Soc. Sci. Cit. Index [Select. Cov.]; Sociol. Abstr.

US/0098-647X
RESEARCH OPPORTUNITIES IN RENAISSANCE DRAMA. [Res. oppor. Renaiss. drama]. **Main/Conf** Modern Language Association Conference on Research Opportunities in Renaissance Drama. (1965)-. English. an. $6.00 (individual); $10.00 (institution). University of Kansas Department of English, c/o Prof. David Bergeron, Lawrence KS 66044. **Tel** (913)864-4798. **LC** PR621; .M75A. **DD** 822/.2/09. ***Continues in part*** *Renaissance Drama, 0486-3739.*
Desc: Contains reports of the Modern Language Association seminars.
Ind/Abst Abstr. Engl. Stud.; Annu. Bibliogr. Engl. Lang. Lit.; MLA Int. Bibl. Books Artic. Mod. Lang. Lit.

II
RESEARCH PAPERS - DEPARTMENT OF TAMIL, UNIVERSITY OF KERALA. **See** Linguistics.

BL
RESENHA DE LIVROS PARA A INFANCIA E JUVENTUDE. **Added/Corp** Fundacao Nacional do Livro Infantil e Juvenil. Vol. 1, No. 1 (1987)-. Portuguese. Four times a year. $12.34. Fundacao Nacional do Livro Infantil e Juvenil, Rua da Imprensa 16 Sala 1008, CEP 20030 Rio De Janeiro RJ Brazil. **Tel** (021)2629130. ***Continues*** *Selecao de Livros Para a Infancia e Juventude.*

FR
RESONNANCES. No. 1-. Periodical. French. 45F single issue. 18 rue Marlot, 51100 Reims France. **LC** PQ1141; .R39. **DD** 840/.8.

US/0162-9905
RESTORATION (KNOXVILLE). (RESTORATION : STUDIES IN ENGLISH LITERARY CULTURE, 1660-1700.). [Restoration]. VOL. 1 (Spring 1977)-. Periodical. English. sa. $10.00 (US); $15.00 (Canada); $15.00 (surface mail), $20.00 (airmail) other. James Madison University College of Letters & Sciences, Harrisonburg VA 22807. **Tel** (703)568-6261, FAX (703)568-3581. **ED** J M Armistead. **LC** PR437; .R47. **DD** 820/.9/004. **Ad Acc. Circ:** 450.
Desc: British and British Colonial culture from 1660-1700, including literature, philosophy, theology, fine arts, theatre, science, and history; to enhance appreciation of Restoration literary culture.
Ind/Abst Am. Hist. Life (1987-); MLA Int. Bibl. Books Artic. Mod. Lang. Lit.; Romant. Move.

NE
REVE JAARBOEK. ***Ceased.*** (1983)-Ceased (19??). Periodical. Dutch. De Prom, PO Box 1, 3740 AA Baarn Netherlands. **LC** PT5881.28.E9; Z85.

US
REVIEW : LATIN AMERICAN LITERATURE AND ARTS. **See** The Arts.

UK/0034-6551
REVIEW OF ENGLISH STUDIES. (THE REVIEW OF ENGLISH STUDIES.). [Rev. Engl. stud.]. Vol. 1, No. 1 (1925)-. Periodical. English. qt. £65.00 UK and Europe; $120.00 other. Oxford University Press, Walton Street, Oxford OX2 6DP England. **Tel** 011 44 865 56767, FAX 011 44 865 267773, telex 837330 OXPRES G. **(Subscription address:** Oxford University Press / USA, Journals Marketing Department, Oxford University Press, 2001 Evans Road, Cary NC 27513.**) ED** R. E. Alton. **LC** PR1; .R4. **DD** 820/.9. **[CCC].** Index available. **Bk Rev. Ad Acc. Circ:** 2,030. available on microfilm and microfiche from University Microfilms International (UMI). Documents available from The Genuine Article, UMI Article Clearinghouse.
Desc: English literature and the English language from the earliest period up to the present day. Articles, notes, reviews of recent books, and a summary of periodical literature are included.
Ind/Abst Abstr. Engl. Stud.; Acad. Abstr. Full Text Elite (July 1990-); Acad. Abstr. (July 1990-); Acad. Ind. [Computer File] (1987-); Acad. Search (July 1990-); Annu. Bibliogr. Engl. Lang. Lit.; Arts Humanit. Citation Index [Full Cov.]; Book Rev. Index; Br. Humanit. Index; Child. Lit. Abstr. (19??-); Curr. Contents Arts Humanit.; Expand. Acad. Index (1987-); Humanit. Index; Humanit. Source (Jul. 1990-); INFO-SOUTH Abstr.; Mag. Search; MLA Int. Bibl. Books Artic. Mod. Lang. Lit.; Newsp. Period. Abstr. (1991-); Res. Alert [Full Cov.]; Romant. Move.; Soc. Plann. Policy Dev. Abstr.

US/0275-6935
REVISION (CAMBRIDGE, MASS.). (RE-VISION.). [ReVision]. **VFOAT** ReVISION. Vol. 1 (Winter 1978)-. Periodical. English. qt. $32.00 (individuals), $53.00 (institutional), add $12.00 (foreign postage). Heldref Publications, 1319 Eighteenth Street Northwest, Washington DC 20036-1802. **Tel** (202)296-6267, (800)365-9753, FAX (202)296-5149. **ED** Jeanne Achterberg, Robert A McDermott, Donald J Rothberg, and Richard T Tarnas. **LC** BF309; .R35. **DD** 150/.19/205. **[CCC]. Ad Acc. Circ:** 4,000. available on microfilm and microfiche from University Microfilms International (UMI).
Desc: An international journal that makes possible an interdisciplinary dialogue between modern science and mysticism. Its goal is to provide a bridge between the ancient and the modern, between nations, cultures, races and religions.
Ind/Abst Altern. Press Index; Psychol. Abstr. (1978-).

GW/0302-8852
REVISOR (AMSTERDAM). (DE REVISOR.). [Revisor]. 1.- V.; Jan. 1974-. Periodical. Dutch. ir. 45.00. Athenaum Verlag GmbH, Adelheidstrabe 2, 6240 Tonigstein TS Germany. **Tel** 06174/3021. **LC** PT5460; .R48.
Ind/Abst MLA Int. Bibl. Books Artic. Mod. Lang. Lit.

SP/0214-4808
REVISTA ALICANTINA DE ESTUDIOS INGLESES. **See** Linguistics.

BL/0101-8248
REVISTA BRASILEIRA DE LINGUA E LITERATURA. **See** Linguistics.

BL/0103-6963
REVISTA BRASILEIRA DE LITERATURA COMPARADA. **Added/Corp** Associacao Brasileira de Literatura Comparada. (Mar 1991)-. Periodical. Portuguese.

CN/0384-8167
REVISTA CANADIENSE DE ESTUDIOS HISPANICOS. [Rev. can. estud. hisp.]. **Added/Corp** Asociacion Canadiense de Hispanistas. Vol. 1 (Autumn

1976)-. Periodical. Spanish (English and French). Three times a year. 30.00Can$. Carleton University / Department of Spanish, Ottawa Ontario K1S 5B6 Canada. **Tel** (613)788-2109. **LC** CB226; .R39. **DD** 860/.9. ***Supersedes*** *Reflexion, 0034-3005.*
Ind/Abst HAPI Hisp. Am. Period. Index; MLA Int. Bibl. Books Artic. Mod. Lang. Lit.; Romant. Move.

SP/0211-5913
REVISTA CANARIA DE ESTUDIOS INGLESES. **See** Linguistics.

CU/0008-7157
REVISTA CASA DE LAS AMERICAS, LA. **Added/Corp** Casa de las Americas. **VFOAT** Casa. (19??)-. Periodical. Spanish. qt. **LC** PN6; .C3. ***Continues*** *Casa de las Americas.*

CL/0048-7651
REVISTA CHILENA DE LITERATURA. [Rev. chil. lit.]. **Added/Corp** Universidad de Chile. Departamento de Espanol. Universidad de Chile. Departamento de Literatura. Vol. 1 (Fall 1970)-. Periodical. Spanish. sa. $40.00. Universidad de Chile / Linguistica, Deptamento de Literatura, Casilla Postal 10136, Santiago Chile. **Tel** 011 52 2 2725978 Ext 42, FAX 011 52 2 2716823. **LC** PQ7900; .R48. **DD** 860. Index available. cum. index. **Pr Rev. Circ:** 600 (ctrl). Documents available from The Genuine Article. ***Supersedes*** *Universidad de Chile. Instituto de Literaturae Chilena. Boletin del Instituto de Literatura Chilena.*
Ind/Abst Arts Humanit. Citation Index [Full Cov.]; Curr. Contents Arts Humanit.; HAPI Hisp. Am. Period. Index; MLA Int. Bibl. Books Artic. Mod. Lang. Lit.; Res. Alert [Full Cov.].

BL
REVISTA DA ACADEMIA GOIANA DE LETRAS. **Main/Corp** Academia Goiana de Letras. Yearly V. 1- 1957-. Portuguese. Academia Goiana de Letras, Avenida Goias 310 S/905, Goiania Brazil. **LC** PQ9502; .A516.

BL
REVISTA DA ACADEMIA PERNAMBUCANA DE LETRAS. **Main/Corp** Academia Pernambucana de Letras. (1901)-. Academic Scholarly Publication. Portuguese. an. CR$8.00. Academia Pernambucana de Letras, Av rui Barbosa 1596 - 6 Racas, Recife Brazil Gracas. **Tel** 011 55 81 268 2211. **ED** Waldemar Lopes. **LC** PQ9502.A59; A3. **Circ:** 100 (ctrl).

US
REVISTA DE ESTUDIOS COLOMBIANOS Y LATINOAMERICANOS / ASOCIACION DE COLOMBIANISTAS NORTEAMERICANOS. **Added/Corp** Association of Northamerican Colombianists. No 11 (1991)-. Periodical. Spanish. sa. Illinois State University / Foreign Languages, Department of Foreign Languages, Normal IL 61761. **LC** PQ8160; .R48. ***Continues*** *Revista de Estudios Colombianos.*
Ind/Abst HAPI Hisp. Am. Period. Index.

PR/0378-7974
REVISTA DE ESTUDIOS HISPANICOS (RIO PIEDRAS, P.R.). **See** Linguistics.

US/0034-818X
REVISTA DE ESTUDIOS HISPANICOS (UNIVERSITY, AL.). **See** Linguistics.

RM
REVISTA DE ISTORIE SI TEORIE LITERARA. SUPLIMENT. (1984)-. Romanian. an. Lei10.00. Colectia Capricorn, Bd Shitu Magureanu Nr 1, Sector 6, COD 70626, Of Postal 1, Bucuresti Romania. **LC** PAR.

CU
REVISTA DE LA BIBLIOTECA NACIONAL JOSE MARTI. **See** Library and Information Sciences.

GT
REVISTA DE LA UNIVERSIDAD DE SAN CARLOS / USAC. **Added/Corp** Universidad de San Carlos de Guatemala. **VFOAT** USAC; USAC, Revista de la Universidad de San Carlos. No. 1 (Mar. 1987)-. Periodical. Spanish. qt.
Ind/Abst HAPI Hisp. Am. Period. Index (19??-).

SP/0034-849X
REVISTA DE LITERATURA. **See** Literature-Abstracting, Bibliographies and Statistics.

VE
REVISTA DE LITERATURA HISPANOAMERICANA. ***Suspended.*** Yearly Vol. 1, No. 1 (July/Dec. 1971)-?. Periodical. Spanish. sa. $7.00. Universidad del Zulia, Apartado 1490, Maracaibo Venezuela. **LC** PQ7081.A1; R39. Index available. **Circ:** 1,000.

AG/0556-6134
REVISTA DE LITERATURAS MODERNAS. ***Suspended.*** **Added/Corp** Universidad Nacional de Cuyo. Instituto de Lenguas y Literaturas Modernas. No. 1 (1956)-(1990). Spanish. an. Editorial Facultad Filosofia, Letras Casilla de Correo 345, 5500 Mendoza Argentina. **Tel** 011 54 61 253010, 234571. **LC** PN695; .R45. ***Continues*** *Estudios Italianos.*
Ind/Abst HAPI Hisp. Am. Period. Index (19??-).

US/0034-9593
REVISTA HISPANICA MODERNA. [Rev. hisp. mod.]. **Added/Corp** Hispanic Institute in the United States. Universidad de Buenos Aires. Instituto de Filologia. Columbia University. Hispanic Institute. Vol. 1, No. 1 (Oct. 1934)-. Periodical. Spanish (English and Portuguese). Twice a year (June & Dec.). $20.00 (individuals); $30.00 (institutions). Hispanic Institute, Columbia University, 612 West 116th Street, New York NY 10027. **Tel** (212)854-8292, (212)854-4187, FAX (212)749-0397. **ED** Susana Redondo de Feldman, Jaime Alazraki and Gonzalo Sobejano. **LC** PQ6001; .R47. **DD** 860.5. Index available (Back issues). **Bk Rev**, (Qty: 22-40). **Pr Rev. Circ:** 1,500 (ctrl). ***Continues in part*** *Hispanic Institute in the United States. Boletin del Instituto de las Espanas.*
Desc: This journal publishes articles, notes, and book reviews on the 19th and 20th century literature of Spain, Portugal, and Latin America.
Ind/Abst Am. Hist. Life (1957-1958); HAPI Hisp. Am. Period. Index; MLA Int. Bibl. Books Artic. Mod. Lang. Lit.; Romant. Move.

US/0034-9631
REVISTA IBEROAMERICANA. [Rev. iberam.]. **Added/Corp** International Institute of Ibero-American Literature. Vol. 1, No. 1 (May 1939)-. Periodical. Spanish (Portuguese). ir (4 issues- sometimes published in double issues). $25.00 (individual), $30.00 (institution) Latin America; $40.00 (individual), $60.00 (institution) other. University of Pittsburgh / Iberoamericana, 1312 C L, Institute of International Literature Iberoamericana, Pittsburgh PA 15260. **Tel** (412)624-5346, FAX (412)624-8505. **ED** Alfredo A Roggiano. **LC** PQ7081.A1; R4. **DD** 860.5. **Bk Rev**. **Ad Acc. Circ:** 2,000 (ctrl). available on microfilm and microfiche from University Microfilms International (UMI). Documents available from The Genuine Article.
Ind/Abst Arts Humanit. Citation Index [Full Cov.]; Curr. Contents Arts Humanit.; HAPI Hisp. Am. Period. Index; MLA Int. Bibl. Books Artic. Mod. Lang. Lit.; Res. Alert [Full Cov.]; Romant. Move.

UY
REVISTA OFICIAL DE LA ASOCIACION GENERAL DE AUTORES DEL URUGUAY. **Main/Corp** Asociacion General de Autores del Uruguay. Spanish. Asociacion General de Autores del Uruguay, Canelones 1130, Montevideo Uruguay. **LC** PQ8510; .A25. ***Continues*** *Asociacion General de Autores del Uruguay. Boletin.*

CL/0035-0451
REVISTA SIGNOS. **See** Linguistics.

US/0890-6998
REVUE CELFAN. (REVUE CELFAN. CELFAN REVIEW.). [Rev. CELFAN]. **Added/Corp** Temple University. Center for the Study of the Francophone Literature of North Africa. **VFOAT** CELFAN Review; RCR. **VAT** Revue Centre d'Etudes sur la Litterature Francophone de l'Afrique du Nord. Vol. 1, No. 1 (Nov. 1981)-. Periodical. English (French). an. $7.50 US & Canada; $10.00 others. Celfan/Dr. Eric Sellin, Tulane University, Department of French & Italian, New Orleans LA 70118. **Tel** (504)865-5115. **ED** Eric Sellin. **LC** PQ3988.N6; R48. **DD** 840. **Bk Rev. Circ:** 150.
Desc: Short articles on the literature of North Africa and literature by French writers from North Africa.
Ind/Abst MLA Int. Bibl. Books Artic. Mod. Lang. Lit.

SZ/0035-1016
REVUE DE BELLES-LETTRES. Periodical. French. Three times a year. 63.00F (Switzerland); 93.00 (other). Medecine et Hygiene, Case Postale 456, CH-1211 Geneve 4 Switzerland. **Tel** 011 41 22 3469355, 011 41 22 3469356. **[CCC].**
Ind/Abst BHA : Biblio. Hist. Art.

FR/0982-6548
REVUE DE BIBLIOLOGIE. **Added/Corp** Societe de Bibliologie et de Schematisation. **VFOAT** Schema et Schematisation. (1986)-. Periodical. French. sa. 130.00F France; 150.00F other. Soc Bibliologie Schematisation, 36 Avunue D Italie Tour Rubis, 75013 Paris France. **Tel** 33 1 45810341, FAX 33 1 45659472. cum. index. ctrl circ. ***Continues*** *Schema et Schematisation, 0586-7606.*

FR/0035-1466
REVUE DE LITTERATURE COMPAREE. [Rev. litt. comp.]. **VFOAT** RLC. 1 Annee, No. 1 (Janv.-Mars 1921)-. Periodical. French (English). qt. $96.00 North America. Societe Nouvelle Didier Erudition, 6 rue de la Sorbonne, 75005 Paris France. **Tel** 011 33 1 43544757, FAX 011 33 1 40517385. **(Subscription address:** PO Box 830350, Birmingham, AL 35283-0350; telephone: (800)633-4931, (205)995-1567 (outside US and Canada); FAX: (205)995-1588**)** **LC** PN851; .R4. cum. index. **Bk Rev**. **Ad Acc. Circ:** 2,500 (ctrl). available on microfiche. Documents available from The Genuine Article.
Desc: The oldest magazine of comparative literature - publishes the comparatist throughout the entire world.
Ind/Abst Abstr. Engl. Stud. (1980-); Annu. Bibliogr. Engl. Lang. Lit.; Arts Humanit. Citation Index (19??-19??) [Full Cov.]; Curr. Contents Arts Humanit.; MLA Int. Bibl. Books Artic. Mod. Lang. Lit.; Res. Alert [Full Cov.]; Romant. Move.; Soc. Sci. Cit. Index [Select. Cov.].

FR/0750-9278
REVUE DES DEUX MONDES (1982). (REVUE DES DEUX MONDES.). [Rev. deux mondes]. (May 1982)-. Periodical. French. Eleven times a year. 538.69F France; 770.00F other. Revue des Deux Mondes, 170 rue de Grenelle, 75007 Paris France. **Tel** 011 33 1 47537110, FAX 47 05 66 74. **(Subscription address:** Revue des Deux Mondes, BP 22, 41354 Vineuil Cedex France.**)** **LC** AP20; .R2437. **DD** 054/.1. **Ad Acc.** available on microfilm and microfiche from University Microfilms International (UMI). ***Continues*** *Nouvelle Revue des Deux Mondes, 0151-914X.*
Desc: Covers literature, politics, history, art, and sciences.
Ind/Abst Am. Hist. Life (1969-1971, 1975-1985); ARTbibliogr. Mod.; MLA Int. Bibl. Books Artic. Mod. Lang. Lit.; Romant. Move. (1982-).

FR/0035-2012
REVUE DES ETUDES AUGUSTINIENNES. **See** Religion and Theology.

FR/0035-2047
REVUE DES ETUDES ITALIENNES. [Rev. etud. ital.]. **Added/Corp** Union Intellectuelle Ffranco-Italienne. Vol. 1-3, (Jan./Mar. 1936)-. Periodical. French. Four times a year. 200.00F France; 210.00F other. University de Paris Grand Palais, Perron Alexander 3, Cours la Reine, F 75008 Paris France. **Tel** 011 33 1 42259640. **ED** Bec Christhan. **LC** PQ4001; .R47. **DD** 850.5. Index available. **Bk Rev. Circ:** 650 (ctrl). Documents available from The Genuine Article. ***Supersedes*** *Etudes Italiennes.*
Desc: This is on italian language and literature.
Ind/Abst Am. Hist. Life (1965-); Arts Humanit. Citation Index (19??-19??) [Full Cov.]; BHA : Biblio. Hist. Art; Curr. Contents Arts Humanit.; MLA Int. Bibl. Books Artic. Mod. Lang. Lit.; Res. Alert [Full Cov.]; Romant. Move.

FR/0373-5737
REVUE DES ETUDES LATINES. **See** Linguistics.

FR/0184-7015
REVUE DES ETUDES MAISTRIENNES. [Rev. etud. maistriennes]. No. 3- 1977-. French. an. Societe Edition Belles Lettres, 95 Boulevard Raspail, 75006 Paris France. **Tel** 011 33 1 45487055, FAX 011 33 1 45449288, telex 200577. ***Continues*** *Etudes Maistriennes, 0337-6702.*

FR/0035-2136
REVUE DES LETTRES MODERNES. (LA REVUE DES LETTRES MODERNES.). [Rev. lett. mod.]. Vol. 1, No. 1 (Feb. 1954)-. Periodical. French. ir (50 issues). Price varies. Lettres Modernes Minard, 45 rue de Saint Andre, 14123 Fleury Surrey Orne France. **Tel** 011 33 31 844706. **LC** PN3; .R4.
Desc: Modern literature.
Ind/Abst Annu. Bibliogr. Engl. Lang. Lit.; MLA Int. Bibl. Books Artic. Mod. Lang. Lit.; Romant. Move.

FR/0180-9423
REVUE DES LETTRES MODERNES. JEAN GIONO, LA. (JEAN GIONO.). 1-. Periodical. French. ir. Lettres Modernes Minard, 45 rue de Saint Andre, 14123 Fleury Surrey Orne France. **Tel** 011 33 31 844706. **LC** PN3; .R4 subser.

FR/0035-2411
REVUE D'HISTOIRE LITTERAIRE DE LA FRANCE. [Rev. hist. litt. Fr.]. **Added/Corp** Societe d'Histoire Litteraire de la France. **VFOAT** Bibliographie de la Litterature Francaise (XVIe-XXe Siecles). Vol. 1 (Jan. 1894)-. Periodical. French. bm. $97.00. Librairie Armand Colin, BP 22, 41354 Vineuil Cedex France. **Tel** 011 33 54 438994. **ED** Rene Pomeau. **LC** PQ2; .R5. **DD** 840/.9. cum. index. Documents available from The Genuine Article.
Ind/Abst Am. Hist. Life (1983-); Arts Humanit. Citation Index [Full Cov.]; BHA : Biblio. Hist. Art; Curr. Contents Arts Humanit.; MLA Int. Bibl. Books Artic. Mod. Lang. Lit.; Res. Alert [Full Cov.]; Romant. Move.; Soc. Sci. Cit. Index [Select. Cov.].

CN/0713-7958
REVUE D'HISTOIRE LITTERAIRE DU QUEBEC ET DU CANADA FRANCAIS. ***Ceased.*** [Rev. hist. litt. Que. Can. fr.]. (1981)-(Nov. 19??). Periodical. French. sa. University of Ottawa Press / 603 Cumberland Avenue, Ottawa Ontario KIN 6N5 Canada. **Tel** (613)745-9356. **DD** C840/.9/9714. ***Continues*** *Histoire Litteraire du Quebec, 0228-8796.*
Desc: Contains French-Canadian literature, Quebec and French-American history and bibliographies.
Ind/Abst MLA Int. Bibl. Books Artic. Mod. Lang. Lit.

FR/0037-9212
REVUE FRANCAISE D'HISTOIRE DU LIVRE. [Rev. fr. hist. livre]. **Added/Corp** Societe des Bibliophiles de Guyenne. Societe Francaise d'Histoire du Livre. (1971)-. French. Four times a year. 260.00F France; 290.00F other. Societes Bibliophiles de Guyenne, 7 rue du Corps, 33075 Bordeaux Cedex France. **Tel** 011 33 57 870447. **LC** Z119; .R47. **DD** 001.55/2. ***Continues*** *Bulletin de la Societe des Bibliophiles de Guyenne.*
Desc: Reference series on French literature and history.
Ind/Abst BHA : Biblio. Hist. Art; Romant. Move.

US/0890-9555
REVUE FRANCOPHONE DE LOUISIANE. **VFOAT** Louisiana Francophone Review. Vol. 1, No. 1 (Spring 1986)-. Periodical. French (English). Twice a year. $12.00 (individuals); $15.00 (institutions). Revue Francophone de Louisiane, PO Box 43331, University of Southwestern Louisiana, Lafayette LA 70504-3331. **Tel** (318)231-6811. **ED** David Barry. **DD** 840. **Bk Rev. Pr Rev. Circ:** 300 (ctrl).
Ind/Abst Annu. Bibliogr. Engl. Lang. Lit.

CN/0715-9994
REVUE FRONTENAC. [Rev. Frontenac]. **Added/Corp** Queen's University (Kingston, Ont.). Dept. of French Studies. **VFOAT** Frontenac Review. No. 1 (1983)-. English (French). an (varies). $10.00Can$. Revue Frontenac, Queens University, Department of French Studiews, Kingston Ontario K7L 3N6 Canada. **Tel** (613)545-2094. **ED** Catherine McGarr. **DD** 809/.03/05. **Bk Rev**, (Qty: 5-10). **Ad Acc. Pr Rev. Circ:** 100 (ctrl).
Ind/Abst MLA Int. Bibl. Books Artic. Mod. Lang. Lit.

FR
REVUE MARIVAUX. **Added/Corp** Societe Marivaux. No 1 (1990)-. French. **LC** PQ2003.Z5; R4.

GW
RICARDA HUCH, STUDIEN ZU IHREM LEBEN UND WERK. **VFOAT** Ricarda Huch; Studien der Ricarda-Huch-Gesellschaft. Vol. 1 (1985)-. German. an. Free (members). Ricarda-Huch-Gesellschaft, 3300 Braunschweig, Bocklinstrasse 30 Germany. **Tel** 0141/332410. **ED** H W Peter. **LC** PT2617.U28; Z944. **DD** 838/.91209/05. Index available. cum. index. **Bk Rev. Ad Acc. Circ:** 10,000 (ctrl).

US/0276-6515
RICHMOND QUARTERLY, THE. ***Suspended.*** (1980)-(19??). Periodical. English. qt. $10.00 (1 year), $18.00 (2 year). The Richmond Quarterly, 2405 Vollmer Road, Richmond VA 23239. **ED** Julia C Killian, (804)288-6914. **LC** F234.R557; R5. **DD** 975.5/451005. **UDC** 975.5; 908.755. **Bk Rev**, (Qty: (as received)). **Circ:** 250. ***Continues*** *Richmond Literature and History Quarterly.*

SP
RILCE : REVISTA DE FILOLOGIA HISPANICA. **Added/Corp** Universidad de Navarra. Facultad de Filosofia y Letras. **VFOAT** Revista del Instituto de Lengua y Cultura Espanolas. Vol. 5 No. 1 (1989)-. Periodical. Spanish. Twice a year (Apr. & Nov.). $30.00. Anuario Filsosfico / Edificio de Bibliotecas / Universidad de Navarra, 31080 Pamplona Spain. **Tel** 011 34 948 252700 Ext 2490, FAX 011 34 948 173650. **LC** PC4008; .R4. Index available. **Bk Rev. Pr Rev. Circ:** 300 (ctrl). ***Continues*** *Revista del Instituto de Lengua y Cultura Espanolas, 0213-2370.*
Desc: Articles and reviews on Spanish and Spanish American literature. Also information on language.

FR/0982-0582
RIO DE LA PLATA. **Added/Corp** Centro de Estudios de Literaturas y Civilizaciones del Rio de la Plata. No. 1 (1985)-. Periodical. Spanish (French). sa. 90.00F Latin America; 140.00F Europe; 150.00F other. Nilda Diaz, CELCIRP, 24 Avenue du Gen Pierre Billotte, F-94000 Creteil France. **Tel** 011 33 1 43770959. **LC** PQ7600; .R56. **DD** 860.9/982/05.
Desc: Covers Spanish language and Argentine literature.
Ind/Abst MLA Int. Bibl. Books Artic. Mod. Lang. Lit.

MC
RIVE DROITE. ***Ceased.*** (1990)-(1992). French. Editions du Rocher, BP 521, Monte Carlo 98015 Monaco. **LC** IN PROCESS.

US/1048-129X
RIVER CITY (MEMPHIS, TENN.). (RIVER CITY.). [River city]. **Added/Corp** Memphis State University. Dept. of English. Vol. 9, No. 1 (Spring 1989)-. Periodical. English. sa. $10.00 institution; $9.00 individual. Memphis State Review, Department of English, Memphis State University, Memphis TN 38152. **Tel** (901)454-4438. **ED** Sharon Bryan. **LC** PS536.2; .M46. **DD** 810.8/0005. **Ad Acc.** ctrl circ. ***Continues*** *Memphis State Review, 0732-2968.*
Desc: Contains poetry, fiction, essays, and interviews.

US/0734-497X
RIVER CITY REVIEW (LOUISVILLE, KY.). ***Ceased.*** (RIVER CITY REVIEW.). [River City rev.]. No. 1 (Fall 1982). Ceased Vol. 4 (1986). Periodical. English. sa. River City Review, PO Box 34275, Louisville KY 40232. **Tel** (502)459-8040. **ED** Richard L Neumayer and Alan Naslund. **Ad Acc. Circ:** 600.
Desc: Modern fiction, poetry, black and white, two-dimensional art and short drama with a strong story line.

US/0149-8851
RIVER STYX. **Added/Corp** Big River Association (Mo.). (1975)-. Periodical. English. Three times a year (Jan., May, & Sept.). $20.00 (one year), $38.00 (two years) individuals; $28.00 (one year), $55.00 (two years) institutions. Big River Association, River Styx Arts Program, 14 South Euclid Avenue, St. Louis MO 63108. **Tel** (314)361-0043. **ED** Jennifer Tahin. **LC** PS501; .R57. **DD** 810/.8. **Ad Acc. Pr Rev. Circ:** 3,000.
Desc: Devoted to multicultural literature and art.
Ind/Abst Am. Humanit. Index (?-199?); Index Am. Period. Verse.

US/0272-9598
RIVERSEDGE. **VAT** Rivers Edge. Vol. 1, No. 1. (Spring 1977)-. Periodical. English (Spanish). Twice a year (Spring and Fall). $12.00. Riversedge Press, 1201 West University Drive, Department of English, Edinburg TX 78539. **Tel** (210)381-3638, FAX (210)381-2177. **ED** Dorey Schmidt, (phone: (210)381-3638). **LC** PS558.T4; R58. **DD** 810/.8/097644. **Pr Rev. Circ:** 300.
Desc: An journal of art, poetry and prose.

US/0889-2326
RIVERSIDE QUARTERLY. [Riverside q.]. Vol. 1 (Aug. 1964)-. Periodical. English. qt (4 issues). $8.00. Riverside Quarterly, PO Box 958, Big Sandy TX 75755. **Tel** (903)636-5505. available on microfilm from University Microfilms International (UMI). ***Supersedes*** *Inside.*
Ind/Abst Am. Humanit. Index (-199?); Annu. Bibliogr. Engl. Lang. Lit.; MLA Int. Bibl. Books Artic. Mod. Lang. Lit.; Sci. Fict. Fantasy Book Rev. Index.

IT/0035-6085
RIVISTA DI CULTURA CLASSICA E MEDIOEVALE. [Riv. cult. class. medioev.]. Vol. 1 (Jan./Apr. 1959)-. Periodical. Italian (English, French, German and Latin). sa (2 issues). L95000 Italy; 140000 other. Gruppo Editoriale Intern SRL, V S Bibiana 30, 56127 Pisa Italy. **Tel** 011 39 50 934242. **LC** PA9; .R55.
Ind/Abst BHA : Biblio. Hist. Art; MLA Int. Bibl. Books Artic. Mod. Lang. Lit.

IT
RIVISTA DI LETTERATURA ITALIANA. v. 1, 1-. Periodical. Italian. Three times a year. L95000, L35000 (per issue) Italy; L150000, L60000 (per issue) other. Via Santa Bibbiana 28, 56100 Pisa Italy. **LC** PQ4001; .R62. **DD** 850/.8. Documents available from The Genuine Article.
Ind/Abst Arts Humanit. Citation Index (19??-19??) [Full Cov.]; Curr. Contents Arts Humanit.; Res. Alert [Full Cov.]; Romant. Move.

IT/0391-2108
RIVISTA DI LETTERATURE MODERNE E COMPARATE. [Riv. lett. mod. comp.]. (1955)-. Periodical. Italian (English, French and German). qt. L70000 Italy; L100000 other. Pacini Editore Srl, Via A Gherardesca 1, 56121 Ospedaletto Pisa Italy. **Tel** 011 39 50 982439. Documents available from The Genuine Article. ***Continues*** *Rivista di Letterature Moderne.*
Ind/Abst Annu. Bibliogr. Engl. Lang. Lit.; Arts Humanit. Citation Index [Full Cov.]; Curr. Contents Arts Humanit.; MLA Int. Bibl. Books Artic. Mod. Lang. Lit.; Res. Alert [Full Cov.]; Romant. Move.

IT/1120-3420
RIVISTA DI STUDI CANADESI. **VFOAT** Canadian Studies Review; Revue d'Etudes Canadiennes. No. 1 (1988)-. Italian (English and French). an. **LC** F1021; .R58. **DD** 971/.005.

CN/0821-3216
RIVISTA DI STUDI ITALIANI. [Riv. studi ital.]. **Added/Corp** University of Toronto. Dept. of Italian Studies. **VFOAT** RSI; R.S.I. Vol. 1, No. 1 (June 1983)-. Academic Scholarly Publication. Italian (English). sa. $30.00 (institutions), $25.00 (individuals). University of Toronto Department of Italian Studies / c/o Anthony Verna, Toronto Ontario M5S 1A1 Canada. **Tel** (416)236-1519, 978-5517. **ED** Anthony Verna. **LC** PQ4001; .R63. **DD** 850/.9. Index available. **Bk Rev. Ad Acc. Circ:** 500 (ctrl).
Desc: A scholarly interdisciplinary journal of Italian language and literature within the context of other European literatures and cultures.
Ind/Abst MLA Int. Bibl. Books Artic. Mod. Lang. Lit.; Romant. Move.

US/0035-7367
ROANOKE REVIEW. **Added/Corp** Roanoke College. English Dept. (Fall 1967)-. Periodical. English. sa (Jan., July). $5.50 (one year), $11.00 (two year). Roanoke College / English Department, Robert Denham, Salem VA 24153. **Tel** (703)375-2365. **LC** PS50; .R6.

US/1062-6999
ROBERT FROST REVIEW, THE. [Robert Frost rev.]. **Added/Corp** Robert Frost Society. **VFOAT** RFR. (Fall 1991)-. Periodical. English. an. $15.00. Winthrop University, Department of English, Rock Hill SC 29733. **Tel** (803)232-4633. **ED** Dr. Earl J. Wilcox. **DD** 813. **Bk Rev**, (Qty: 2-3). **Ad Acc, Adv Mgr:** Jeff Glassen, **Tel** (803)323-4566. **Pr Rev. Circ:** 350.
Desc: An organization whose objective is to promote the study of the life and poetry of Robert Frost. The review contains essays, news items and book reviews that relate to Robert Frost.

US/0146-1419
ROCKBOTTOM. No. 1- Summer 1976-. Periodical. English. qt. $5.00. Mudborn Press, 209 West de la Guerra, Santa Barbara CA 93101. **Tel** (805)962-9996. **LC** PS501; .R63. **DD** 810.

US/0361-1299
ROCKY MOUNTAIN REVIEW OF LANGUAGE AND LITERATURE. [Rocky Mountain rev. lang. lit.]. **Added/Corp** Rocky Mountain Modern Language Association. Vol. 29 (Spring 1975)-. Periodical. English (French, German and Spanish). Twice a year (Mar. & Nov.). $20.00 (individuals); $25.00 (institution) Comes with Rocky Mountain Modern Language Association Membership. Boise State University English Department, 1910 University Drive, Boise ID 83725. **Tel** (208)385-3584, FAX (208)385-4373. **ED** Jan Widmayer, (phone: (208)385-1233). **LC** PB1; .R63a. **DD** 805. **Bk Rev**, (Qty: 40-50). **Ad Acc. Pr Rev. Circ:** 1,200 (ctrl). ***Continues*** *Bulletin of the Rocky Mountain Modern Language Association, 0035-7626.*
Desc: English and foreign language articles, linguistics, popular culture, feminist literary studies, original poetry and short fiction, translations.
Ind/Abst Abstr. Engl. Stud.; Am. Humanit. Index; Annu. Bibliogr. Engl. Lang. Lit.; Book Rev. Index; MLA Int. Bibl. Books Artic. Mod. Lang. Lit.

US/0279-6090
ROD SERLING'S THE TWILIGHT ZONE MAGAZINE. ***Ceased.*** **VFOAT** Twilight Zone Magazine. Vol. 1, No. 1 (April 1981)-Ceased ?. Periodical. English. bm. TZ Publications Inc, 800 Second Avenue, New York NY 10017. **Tel** (212)986-9600. **ED** Tappan King and Peter R Emshwiller. **LC** PS648.F3; R62. **DD** 813/.0876/08. **Bk Rev. Ad Acc. Circ:** 100,000.
Desc: Fantastic fiction and articles in the tradition of Rod Serling's Twilight Zone television series.

NE/0923-0416
RODOPI PERSPECTIVES ON MODERN LITERATURE. [Rodopi perspect. mod. lit.]. (1988)-. Monographic series. English. ir. Price varies per volume. Editions Rodopi BV, Keizersgracht 302-304, 1016 Ex Amsterdam Netherlands. **Tel** 011 31 20 6227507, FAX 011 31 20 380948. **UDC** 82.
Ind/Abst MLA Int. Bibl. Books Artic. Mod. Lang. Lit.

JA
RODOSHA BUNGAKU. June 1979-. Periodical. Japanese. ¥600. Orijin Shuppan Senta, c/o Meja Kagurazaka, 16 Iwatocho, Shinjuku-ku Tokyo 162 Japan. **LC** PL756.L33; R63.

US/0145-5753
ROHMER REVIEW, THE. **Added/Corp** Sax Rohmer Society. (19??)-. Periodical. English. ir. $2.25 (for 3 issues U.S. third class); $2.75 (for 3 issues U.S. first class); $3.00 (for 3 issues others). Robert E. Briney, 4 Forest Avenue, Salem MA 01970. **LC** PS3545.A653; Z8. **DD** 813/.5/2.

FR
ROMAN. ***Ceased.*** No. 1 (Autumn 1982). Ceased with No. 26. Periodical. French. qt. Presses de la Renaissance, 37 Rue du Four, 75006 Paris France. **Tel** 548-59-82. **LC** PQ1271; .R65. **DD** 843/.008. **Circ:** 3,000.

FR/0295-5024
ROMAN 20-50. No. 1 (March 1986)-. Periodical. French. sa.
Ind/Abst MLA Int. Bibl. Books Artic. Mod. Lang. Lit.

CN/0228-0205
ROMANCE. **See** Romance and Adventure.

US
ROMANCE LINGUISTICS & LITERATURE REVIEW. **See** Linguistics.

US
ROMANCE PACKAGE / SPANISH LANGUAGE POPULAR FICTION. **See** Romance and Adventure.

US/0883-1157
ROMANCE QUARTERLY. **See** Linguistics.

RM/0048-8550
ROMANIA LITERARA. **Added/Corp** Uniunea Scriitorilor din Republica Socialista Romania. Uniunea Scriitorilor din Romania. No. 1, (Oct. 10, 1968)-. Periodical. Romanian. wk. DM217.00. **(Subscription address:** Kubon & Sagner, ABT Zeitschriftenimport, D 80328 Munich Germany.) **LC** AP86; .R58.
Desc: Information on Romanian literature.
Ind/Abst Annu. Bibliogr. Engl. Lang. Lit.; MLA Int. Bibl. Books Artic. Mod. Lang. Lit.

US/0035-8118
ROMANIC REVIEW. [Rom. rev.]. **Added/Corp** Columbia University. Dept. of French and Romance

Philology. Columbia University. Dept. of Romance Languages. Vol. 1 (Jan. 1910)-. Periodical. English (French, Spanish and Italian). Four times a year (Jan., Mar., May, Nov.). $45.00 (institutions), $30.00 (individuals), $25.00 (students) US & Canada. Columbia University / Romanic Review, c/o K. Gluckman, 521 Philosophy Hall, New York NY 10027. **Tel** (212)854-3906. **ED** Michael Riffaterre. **LC** PC1; .R7. **DD** 840/.09. **Bk Rev.** **Ad Acc.** **Pr Rev. Circ:** 1200. available on microfilm and microfiche from University Microfilms International (UMI). Documents available from UMI Article Clearinghouse.
Desc: Academic journal of romance languages and literature.
Ind/Abst Acad. Search (July 1993-); Annu. Bibliogr. Engl. Lang. Lit.; Expand. Acad. Index (1989-); Humanit. Index; Humanit. Source (Jul. 1993-); INFO-SOUTH Abstr.; Mag. Search; MLA Int. Bibl. Books Artic. Mod. Lang. Lit.; Newsp. Period. Abstr. (1991-).

BE/0080-3855
ROMANICA GANDENSIA. See Linguistics.

SW/0080-3863
ROMANICA GOTHOBURGENSIA. See Linguistics.

GW/0035-8126
ROMANISCHE FORSCHUNGEN. See Linguistics.

GW
ROMANISTISCHE ARBEITSHEFTE. (19??)-. Monographic series. German. ir. Price varies per volume. Max Niemeyer Verlag, Postfach 2140, D 72011 Tuebingen Germany. **Tel** 011 49 7071 989494, FAX 011 49 7071 87419. **ED** Gustav Ineichen, Bernd Kielhoefer.
Ind/Abst MLA Int. Bibl. Books Artic. Mod. Lang. Lit.

GW/0343-379X
ROMANISTISCHE ZEITSCHRIFT FUER LITERATURGESCHICHTE. See Linguistics.

US/0557-2738
ROMANTIC MOVEMENT. See Literature-Abstracting, Bibliographies and Statistics.

AU/1019-1135
ROMANTIC REASSESSMENT. (SALZBURG STUDIES IN ENGLISH LITERATURE. ROMANTIC REASSESSMENT.). [Romant. reassess.]. **Added/Corp** Universitat Salzburg. Institut fur Englische Sprache und Literatur. **VFOAT** Romantic Reassessment. (1972)-. Monographic series. English.
Ind/Abst MLA Int. Bibl. Books Artic. Mod. Lang. Lit.

FR/0048-8593
ROMANTISME. [Romantisme]. **Added/Corp** Societe des Etudes Romantiques. (1971)-. Periodical. French. Four times a year (Mar., June, Aug., Nov.). Centre de Documentation Universitaire et Societe D Edition D Enseignement Superieur, 88 Boulevard Saint Germain, 75005 Paris France. **Tel** 011 33 1 43252323. Documents available from The Genuine Article.
Desc: Journal about the 19th century art, literature, sciences and technology. All the main currents of ideas of the 19th century.
Ind/Abst Am. Hist. Life (1989-); Arts Humanit. Citation Index [Full Cov.]; BHA : Biblio. Hist. Art; Curr. Contents Arts Humanit.; MLA Int. Bibl. Books Artic. Mod. Lang. Lit.; Res. Alert [Full Cov.]; Romant. Move.; Soc. Sci. Cit. Index [Select. Cov.].

US/0161-682X
ROMANTIST, THE. [Romantist]. **Added/Corp** F. Marion Crawford Memorial Society. No. 1 (1977)-. Periodical. English. ir. F Marion Crawford Memorial Society, Saracinesca House, 3610 Meadowbrook Avenue, Nashville TN 37205. **Tel** (615)292-9695. **ED** John C. Moran, Steve Eng and Jesse F. Knight. **LC** PS1462; .A46. **DD** 808.8/014. Index available (No 1-10, 1977-1986). **Bk Rev.** **Ad Acc. Circ:** 300 (ctrl).
Desc: Modern romanticism with emphasis upon imaginative and fantastic literature. Special section on Francis Marion Crawford (1854-1909).
Ind/Abst Lit. Crit. Regist.; MLA Int. Bibl. Books Artic. Mod. Lang. Lit.

CN/0316-1609
ROOM OF ONE'S OWN. [Room one's own]. Vol. 1 (Spring 1975)-. English. qt. 24.00Can$ (1 year, institutions), 20.00Can$ (1 year), 35.00Can$ (2 year) (individuals) Canada; 35.00Can$ (1 year, institutions), 30.00Can$ (1 year), 45.00Can$ (2 year) (individuals) other. Growing Room Collective, PO Box 46160 Station D, Vancouver British Columbia V6J 5G5 Canada. **DD** C810/.8/0928705. **Bk Rev**, (Qty: 2-4). **Ad Acc. Circ:** 850. available on microfilm (from Toronto : Micromedia).
Desc: Canada's oldest feminist literary magazine; features original fiction, poetry, criticism and reviews by new and established writers. Special issues on writers and themes of interest to women.
Ind/Abst Abstr. Engl. Stud. (1985-); Am. Humanit. Index; Can. Index; MLA Int. Bibl. Books Artic. Mod. Lang. Lit.; Romant. Move.

RU/0320-1031
ROSSIIANE. (1991)-. Periodical. Russian. mo. $79.95. Izdatelstvo Molodaia Gvardiia, Novodmitrovskaya Ul., 5A, 125015 Moscow Russia. **Tel** 095-285-0830. **(Subscription address:** East View Publications Inc., 3020 Harbor Lane North, Suite 110, Minneapolis MN 55447.) **LC** PG3227; .D7. ***Continues** Druzhba (Izd-vo Molodaia Gvardiia).*

CN/0702-7303
ROTHNIUM MAGAZINE. **VAT** Rothnium. V. 1- Apr. 1977-. Periodical. English. $1.25 per no. Cygolian Press, PO Box 471, Owen Sound Ontario N4K 5P7 Canada. **DD** 823/.0876.

●US
ROUNDUP MAGAZINE / WESTERN WRITERS OF AMERICA, THE. **Added/Corp** Western Writers of America. **VFOAT** Round Up. Vol. 1, No. 1 (Sept.-Oct. 1993)-. Periodical. English. bm. $30.00 North America; $35.00 other. Western Writers of America Inc, 416 Bedford, El Paso TX 79922. **Tel** (307)672-0889. **ED** Francis Fugate. **LC** IN PROCESS. **DD** 810. ***Continues** Roundup Quarterly, 1041-5289.*

US/1041-5289
ROUNDUP QUARTERLY, THE. ***Title Change.*** [Roundup q.]. **Added/Corp** Western Writers of America. Vol. 1, No. 1 (Sept. 1988)-(1993). Periodical. English. qt. Western Writers of America Inc, 416 Bedford, El Paso TX 79922. **Tel** (307)672-0889. **ED** Francis Fugate. **LC** PS374.W4; R68. **DD** 810. ***Continues** Roundup, 0035-855X. **Continued by** Roundup Magazine.*
Ind/Abst Book Rev. Index (?-?); West. Hist. Q. (?-?).

US/1056-5841
ROYCROFT REVIEW, THE. See The Arts-Art.

XR
ROZETA : KULTURNI ZAPISNIK RUZE. **Added/Corp** Ruze Ceske Budejovice (Firm). (1991)-. Periodical. Czech.

US/1062-4694
RPCV WRITERS & READERS. [RPCV writ. read.]. **VFOAT** RPCV Writers and Readers. **VAT** Returned Peace Corp Volunteers Writers & Readers. (1991)-. Periodical. English. Six times a year. $12.00. RPCV Writer, c/o Haley Beil, 4 Lodge Pole Road, Pittsford NY 14534. **Tel** (716)223-1155, FAX (716)223-1155. **ED** Marian Haley Beil. **DD** 810. **Bk Rev.** **Ad Acc. Circ:** 400.
Desc: Returned Peace Corps volunteers write about their world.

US/1079-6673
RUBY'S PEARLS ELECMAG. (1991)-. English. mo. Free on request. Ruby's Pearls, 9832-1 Sandler Road, Jacksonville FL 32222. **Tel** (904)573-6269, FAX (904)777-6799. **ED** Del Freeman. available via electronic mail.
Desc: Fiction/humor publication.

CN/0381-1158
RUFANTHOLOGY. V. 1- Winter 1976-. Periodical. English (French). Protestant School Board of Greater Montreal, 6000 Fielding Avenue, Montreal Quebec H3X 1T4 Canada. **DD** C810/.8/09237505.

KO
RUPPO SIDAE. V. 1- (1983)-. Periodical. Korean. W3,300. Silchon Munhaksa, 98-dong 304-ho Panpo Apatu Panpo Pondong Kangnam-ku, Seoul Korea. **LC** PL980.45; .R87.

CN/0822-9600
RUPTURE (TORONTO). (RUPTURE.). [Rupture]. Vol. 1, No. 1 (Summer 1983)-. Periodical. English. qt. $12.00 per no., $30.00 per year. Rupture, PO Box No. 732, Station A, Toronto Ontario M5W 1G2 Canada. **DD** 891/.42/09.

NE/0304-3479
RUSSIAN LITERATURE. Vol. 4-1 (Jan. 1976)-. Monographic series. English (French, German and Russian). Eight times a year (2 vols.). Fl900.00. Elsevier Science Publishers BV, PO Box 211, 1000 AE Amsterdam Netherlands. **Tel** 011 31 20 5803642, FAX 011 31 20 5862696, telex 15682. **ED** N A Nilsson and J van der Eng. **DD** 891.7/005. **[CCC]**. available on microfilm and microfiche from University Microfilms International (UMI). Documents available from The Genuine Article.
Desc: Devoted to special topics of Russian literature with contributions on related subjects in Croatian, Serbian, Czech, Slovak and Polish literatures.
Ind/Abst Arts Humanit. Citation Index [Full Cov.]; Curr. Contents Arts Humanit.; Res. Alert [Full Cov.]; Romant. Move.

●US/1061-1975
RUSSIAN STUDIES IN LITERATURE. [Russ. stud. lit.]. Vol. 28, No. 1 (Winter 1991-92)-. Periodical. English (translations available in Russian). qt (published within seasons). $381.00 US; $421.00 other. M. E. Sharpe Inc., 80 Business Park Drive, Armonk NY 10504. **Tel** (914)273-1800, (800)541-6563, FAX (914)273-2106. **LC** PN2; .S6. **DD** 891. Documents available from The Genuine Article. ***Continues** Soviet Studies in Literature, 0038-5875.*
Ind/Abst Arts Humanit. Citation Index [Full Cov.]; Res. Alert; Soc. Sci. Cit. Index [Select. Cov.].

RU
RUSSKAIA SOVETSKAIA LITERATURA. **Added/Corp** Institut Mirovoi Literatury Imeni A.M. Gorkogo. (1955)-. Academic Scholarly Publication. Russian. an. Izdatelstvo Nauka / Akademiia Nauk, Publishing House of the Russian Academy of Sciences, Leninskii Porspekt 14, 117901 Moscow Russia. **Tel** 011 95 954-21-53, FAX 011 95 938-21-44, telex 411964.

RU/0131-6095
RUSSKAJA LITERATURA (LENINGRAD. 1958). (RUSSKAIA LITERATURA / AKADEMIIA NAUK SSSR, INSTITUT RUSSKOI LITERATURY (PUSHKINSKI DOM).). [Russ. lit.]. **Added/Corp** Institut Russkoi Literatury (Pushkinskii Dom). No. 1 (1958)-. Periodical. Russian. qt. $46.00. **(Subscription address:** Victor Kamkin, 4956 Boiling Brook Parkway, Rockville, MD 20852) cum. index. Documents available from The Genuine Article.
Ind/Abst Annu. Bibliogr. Engl. Lang. Lit.; Arts Humanit. Citation Index (19??-19??) [Full Cov.]; Curr. Contents Arts Humanit.; MLA Int. Bibl. Books Artic. Mod. Lang. Lit.; Res. Alert [Full Cov.].

RU
RUSSKII IAZYK I LITERATURA V UZBEKSKOI SHKOLE. See Linguistics.

US/0222-1543
RUSSKOE VOZROZHDENIE. See Religion and Theology-Eastern Christian Churches.

PL
RUSYCYSTYCZNE STUDIA LITERATUROZNAWCZE. Began in 1977. Periodical. Polish (summaries and/or abstracts in English and Russian). 92.00. Uniwersytet Slaski, Ul Bankowa 14, 40-007 Katowice Poland. **Tel** 59-69-15, FAX 48 32 599-506, telex 0315584 USKPL. **ED** Gabriela Porebina. **LC** PG3015; .R88.

JA
RYUKYU DAIGAKU HO-BUNGAKUBU KIYO : KOKUBUNGAKU RONSHU. **Main/Corp** Ryukyu Daigaku. Ho-Bungakubu. **VFOAT** Bulletin of the College of Law and Literature, University of the Ryukyus: Japanese Literature. Japanese (Japanese). Ryukyu Daigaku Ho-Bungakubu, 1 Shuri Tonokuracho 3-chome, Naha Okinawa 903 Japan. **LC** PL700; .R95A.

UK/0305-9219
SAGA-BOOK. (SAGA BOOK OF THE VIKING SOCIETY FOR NORTHERN RESEARCH / THE VIKING CLUB.). [Saga-book]. **Main/Corp** Viking Society for Northern Research, London. **Added/Corp** Viking Society for Northern Research. **VFOAT** Saga Book of the Viking Society; Saga-Book of the Viking Society for Northern Research; Saga-Book. Vol. 8, Pt. 1 (1913)-. English. an (5-7 issues per volume). £15.00. University College of London / Viking Society, Gower Street, London WC1T 6BT England. **Tel** 011 44 71 380 7176, FAX 011 44 71 380 7750. **ED** A.R. Faulkes, R.M. Perkins, D. Slay and J. Jesch (editors' address: University of Birmingham, Department of English, Birmingham B15 2TT England). Index available. **Bk Rev**, (Qty: 10). **Pr Rev. Circ:** 650 (ctrl). ***Continues** Saga-Book of the Viking Club, 0305-9219.*
Desc: Covers Scandinavian literature, language, history, art and folklore - largely medieval.
Ind/Abst MLA Int. Bibl. Books Artic. Mod. Lang. Lit.

US/1056-2591
SAGARIN REVIEW, THE. (THE SAGARIN REVIEW : THE ST. LOUIS JEWISH LITERARY JOURNAL.). [Sagarin rev.]. **Added/Corp** St. Louis College of Jewish Studies. Central Agency for Jewish Education. Saul Brodsky Jewish Community Library. Vol. 1 (1991)-. English. $4.00. The Sagarin Review, c/o The Saul Brodsky Jewish Community Library, 12 Millstone Campus Drive, St Louis MO 63146-5776. **LC** WMLC 91/2334. **DD** 810.
Ind/Abst Index Jew. Period. (199?-).

IT
SAGGI DI LETTERE ITALIANE. Italian. ir. Casa Editrice Leo S. Olschki, Viuzzo del Pozzetto, Casella Postale 66, 50126 Florence Italy. **Tel** 011 39 55 6530684, FAX 011 39 55 6530214. **ED** V. Branca and C. Ossola. Index available. **Circ:** 100.
Desc: Studies and research in Italian literature.

IT/0581-2917
SAGGI E RICERCHE DI LETTERATURA FRANCESE. **Added/Corp** Pisa. Universita. Istituto di Lingua e Letteratura Francese. Vol. 1 (1960)-. Italian. ir. Price varies. Bulzoni Editore Srl, Via dei Liburni 14, 00185 Rome Italy. **Tel** 011 39 6 445-5207, FAX 011 39 6 445-0355.
Desc: Covers French literature.
Ind/Abst MLA Int. Bibl. Books Artic. Mod. Lang. Lit.

US/0885-5013
SAGUARO. (SAGUARO.). [Saguaro]. **Added/Corp** University of Arizona. Mexican American Studies and Research Center. Vol. 1, No. 1 (1984)-. Spanish (English). ir (Subscriptions are for two years). $10.00 (individuals), $15.00 (institutions) US; $12.00

Literature

(individuals), $17.00 (institutions) other. Mexican American Studies & Research Center, The University of Arizona, Room 315, Tucson AZ 85721. **Tel** (602)621-7551. **ED** T. Gelsinon. **LC** PS508.M4; S28. **DD** 860. **Circ:** 500.
Desc: Mexican American literature: poems, short stories, one-act plays, and creative essays. Publishes works in English, Spanish, and works that are completely bilingual.
Ind/Abst Am. Humanit. Index.

II
SAHITYA. Periodical. Mandingo (Manipuri). Rs5.60. **LC** PL4001.M315; S23.

II
SAHITYA SANKETA. Periodical. Nepali (Nepali). qt. Rs3.00. Nepali Sahitya Adhyayana, Samiti Town Hall, Kalimpong India. **(Subscription address:** Nepali Adhyaan Samity, Llamu Khanson Building, Upper Floor, Reheman Studio, Kalimpong India) **LC** PK2597.5; .S18. Index available. **Bk Rev. Ad Acc. Circ:** 1,000 (ctrl).

II
SAHITYA-SAURABHA. V. 1- Jan. 1972. Periodical. Hindi (Hindi). 20.00. **LC** PK2077; .S27.

II
SAHITYALOCANA. V. 1- Jan. 1973-. Periodical. Hindi (Hindi). 6.00. **LC** PK2030; .S275.

II
SAHITYATIRTHA. Periodical. Bengali (Bengali). an. 6.00. 67 Pathuriaghat Street, Calcutta 700006 India. **LC** PK1700; .S246.

AU
SALZBURG STUDIES IN ENGLISH LITERATURE. Added/Corp Salzburg. Universitat. Institut fur Englische Sprache und Literatur. (19??)-. English. ir. Price varies. Institute Anglistic & Amerikanistik, A-5020 Salzburg, Akademiestrasse Austria.
Ind/Abst Romant. Move.

AU
SALZBURG STUDIES IN ENGLISH LITERATURE. POETIC DRAMA & POETIC THEORY. Added/Corp Universitat Salzburg. Institut fuer Anglistik und Amerikanistik. Universitat Salzburg. Institut fuer Englische Sprache und Literatur. **VFOAT** Poetic Drama & Poetic Theory. (1972)-. Monographic series. English. ir. Price varies per volume. Institute Anglistic & Amerikanistik, A-5020 Salzburg, Akademiestrasse Austria.
Ind/Abst MLA Int. Bibl. Books Artic. Mod. Lang. Lit.

II
SAMADARSI. VFOAT Samadarshi. Periodical. Oriya (Oriya). qt. 2.00. Nilachal Prakashani, Link Road, Cuttack 753009 India. **LC** PK2574.5; .S27.

II
SAMAKALINA BHARATIYA SAHITYA. VFOAT Samkaleen Bharateeya Sahitya. V. 1, No. 1 (July/September 1980)-. Periodical. Hindi (Hindi). qt. Rs16.00. Sahitya Akademi, National Academy of Letters, Rabindra Bhavan, Ferozeshah Road, New Delhi 110001 India. **Tel** 011 91 11 388667. **LC** PK2977.H5; S25.

II
SAMAVETA SVARA. Vol. 1- May 1972-. Periodical. Hindi (Hindi). 5.00. 75 Jawaharlal Nehru Marg 1, New Delhi India. **LC** PK2030; .S29.

II
SAMBODHANA. (19??)-. Periodical. Hindi (Hindi). qt. Rs10.00. Gulfam Khan, Chand Pole, Kankroli 31324 sRjasthan India. **ED** Omar Mewari. **LC** PK2030; .S292. **Circ:** 1,100.

II
SAMIKSHA. (19??)-. Periodical. Hindi (Hindi). qt. $15.00. **(Subscription address:** Prints India, 11 Darya Ganj, New Delhi 110002 India.)

SW/0348-6133
SAMLAREN (UPPSALA). (SAMLAREN.). [Samlaren]. **Added/Corp** Skrifter Utgivna av Svenska Litteratursallskapet. Vol. 1-40, (1880)-. Periodical. Swedish. ir. 180.00F. Almqvist & Wiksell International, PO Box 4627, S-11691 Stockholm Sweden. **Tel** 011-46-8-6408800. **LC** PT9201; .S3.
Ind/Abst Annu. Bibliogr. Engl. Lang. Lit.; MLA Int. Bibl. Books Artic. Mod. Lang. Lit.

GW/0558-3667
SAMMLUNG METZLER. [Samml. Metzler]. Vol. 1 (1961)-. Monographic series. German. ir. Price varies per volume. J. B. Metzlersche Verlagsbuchhandling, Kernerstrasse 10 32 41, D-70028 Stuttgart Germany. **Tel** 011 49 711 22902-14, FAX 011 49 711 22902-90. **Bk Rev. Ad Acc.** ctrl curc.
Desc: Offers scholarly monographs on German authors and their works, from the Middle Ages to the present, considered in the light of style, format, content and characteristics.
Ind/Abst MLA Int. Bibl. Books Artic. Mod. Lang. Lit.

GW
SAMMLUNG PROFILE. See Biographies.

CN/0711-1827
SAMPLINGS. [Samplings]. 1981-. English. an. Free. Samplings, c/o English Department, Peel Board of Education, 73 King Street West, Mississauga Ontario L5B 1H5 Canada. **DD** C810/.8/09282.

II/0558-3764
SAMSKRTAPRATIBHA. See Linguistics.

US/0278-7350
SAMUEL BUTLER NEWSLETTER, THE. Suspended. [Samuel Butler newsl.]. Vol. 2, No. 1 (June 1979)-?. Newsletter. English. qt. $8.00 US; $10.00 other. The Samuel Butler Society, c/o James A Donovan Jr, 4100 Cathedral Avenue NW, Washington DC 20016. **LC** PR4349.B7; Z92. **DD** 828/.809. **Continues** Samuel Butler Society Newsletter, 0161-8806.
Ind/Abst MLA Int. Bibl. Books Artic. Mod. Lang. Lit.

US/1054-6774
SAN DIEGO WRITERS MONTHLY. See Journalism.

CC
SAN WEN. No. 1 (Jan. 1980)-. Periodical. Chinese. mo. $18.85. **(Subscription address:** China International Book Trading Corporation, PO Box 399, Library Service Department, Beijing 100044 People's Republic of China.) **LC** PL2623; .S197. **DD** 895.1/452.

CH
SAN WEN HSUAN. (1981)-. Periodical. Chinese. an. NT$125.00. Chiu Ko Chu Pan She, PO Box 36-445, Taipei Shih Taiwan. **LC** PL3031.T32; S23. **DD** 895.1/45/080951249.

FR
SAND GEORGES 1804-1876 CORRESPONDANCE. (19??)-. French. ir. 6100.00F. Librarie Dunod Solferino, 30 rue Saint Sulpice, 75278 Paris Cedex 06 France. **Tel** 011 33 16 43299430.

CN/0316-5167
SAND PATTERNS. V. 1-. Periodical. English. qt. $1.00 per no. Sand Patterns Publications, PO Box 321, Charlottetown PEI C1A 7K7. **DD** C810/.8/0054.

●US/1061-3579
SANDHILLS REVIEW, THE. [Sandhills rev.]. **Added/Corp** Sandhills Community College. Dept. of Languages. No. 42 (Summer 1992)-. Periodical. English. Twice a year. $14.00. Sandhills Community College, 2200 Airport Road, Pinehurst NC 28374. **Tel** (919)692-6185. **LC** IN PROCESS; PS1; .S25. **DD** 808. **Continues** Sandhills/St. Andrews Review.

PH
SANDS AND CORAL. 1948-. English. an. P75.00 Philippines; $12.00 US. Silliman University, PO Box 606, Dumaguete 6200 Philippines. **ED** Eliseo P Banas. **LC** PR9992.P4; A2. **DD** 820/.8/09599. **Bk Rev. Circ:** 800 (ctrl).
Desc: Contributions accepted from graduate and undergraduate students as well as from faculty members and staff.

II
SANKALANA. 1983-. Periodical. Kannada (Kannada). an. Rs20.00. Printers' Prakashana, 75 Mahatma Gandhi Road, Bangalore 560001 India. **LC** PL4654.5; .S26.

●US/1068-8617
SANTA BARBARA REVIEW. [St. Barbara rev.]. V. 1, No. 1 (Spring/Summer 1993)-. Periodical. English. sa. $17.50 (institutions), $10.00 (individuals). Santa Barbara Review, PO Box 536, Summerland CA 93067. **Tel** (805)969-0861. **ED** Shelly Lowenkopf. **LC** IN PROCESS. **DD** 810.
Desc: Contains fiction, essays, memoirs and poetry.

US/0899-9848
SANTA MONICA REVIEW : SMR. [St. Monica rev.]. **Added/Corp** Santa Monica College (Santa Monica, Calif.). Center for the Humanities. **VFOAT** SMR. (Fall 1988)-. Periodical. English. sa. $7.00 US; $11.00 other. Santa Monica Review, 1900 Pico Boulevard, Santa Monica CA 90405. **Tel** (818)901-7858. **ED** James Krusoe. **LC** PS659; .S33. **DD** 810.8. **Ad Acc. Circ:** 1,400 (ctrl).

CU/0048-9115
SANTIAGO. [Santiago]. **VFOAT** Revista Santiago. Yearly Vol. 1, No. 1 (Dec. 1970)-. Periodical. Spanish. qt. $10.00 US. Ediciones Cubanas, Obispo 527, Altos ESQ Bernaza, CP 10100 Havana Cuba. **Tel** 011 632980, 631942, FAX 011 631011, telex 512337, 6540. **LC** AS71.A1; S26. **DD** 056/.1. **Bk Rev. Ad Acc. Circ:** 10,000. **Continues** Revista (Universidad de Oriente (Santiago de Cuba, Cuba)).
Desc: A cultural, literary and political magazine, with essays, poetry and interviews of outstanding personalities in letters and art; includes book reviews.
Ind/Abst Am. Hist. Life (1973-1977, 1979-).

KO
SARA INNUN ADONG MUNHAK. Periodical. Korean. W2,500. Ingansa, 68 Chungsin-dong Chongno-ku, Seoul Korea. **LC** PL969.5; .S27.

II
SARASVATI-SUSHAMA. Periodical. Multiple languages (English, Hindi and Sanskrit). **LC** PK401.

YU/0036-519X
SAVREMENIK. [Savremenik]. (1955)-. Periodical. Serbo-Croatian (Roman) (Serbo-Croatian (Cyrillic) and Serbo-Croatian (Roman)). mo.
Ind/Abst MLA Int. Bibl. Books Artic. Mod. Lang. Lit.

US
SAYERS REVIEW, THE. V. 1- 1976-. Periodical. English. Three times a year. $7.00 per volume. Christie McMenomy, 3138 Sawtelle Boulevard/#4, Los Angeles CA 90066. **Tel** (310)390-2513. **ED** Christe Ann McMenomy. **Bk Rev. Circ:** 60.
Desc: Articles on the writings and influence of Dorothy L Sayers.
Ind/Abst MLA Int. Bibl. Books Artic. Mod. Lang. Lit.

XR/0036-5351
SBORNIK NARODNIHO MUZEA V PRAZE. RADA C, LITERARNI HISTORIE. [Sb. Nar. Muz. Pr. Rada C, Lit. hist.]. **Added/Corp** Narodni Muzeum v Praze. **VFOAT** Literarni Historie; Historia Litterarum; Acta Musei Nationalis Pragae. Series C, Historia Litterarum. (1956)-. Periodical. Czech (Russian and German; summaries and/or abstracts in English, French, German and Russian). Four times a year. $41.50. **(Subscription address:** Artia Pegas Press Ltd., Palac Metro Narodni Trida 25, 11210 Prague 1 Czech Republic.) **LC** PG5000; .P734.
Ind/Abst Am. Hist. Life (1963-); Art Archaeol. Tech. Abstr.

XR
SBORNIK. RADA C: LITERARNI HISTORIE. Main/Corp Prague. Narodni Muuzeum. **VFOAT** Acta. Historia Litterarum. V. 1- 1956-. Periodical. Czech (table of contents in Russian and English). **LC** PG5000.

BU/0205-2679
SBORNIK ZA NARODNI UMOTVORENIJA I NARODOPIS. See Linguistics.

US/0036-5637
SCANDINAVIAN STUDIES: PUBLICATION OF THE SOCIETY FOR THE ADVANCEMENT OF SCANDINAVIAN STUDY. [Scand. stud.]. **Added/Corp** Society for the Advancement of Scandinavian Study (U.S.). Vol. 16, No. 5 (Feb. 1941)-. Periodical. English. qt. $40.00 North America; $45.00 other. Society for the Advancement of Scandinavian Studies, 3003 JKHB BYU, George Tate, Provo UT 84002. **Tel** (801)378-5598, (801)378-7687, FAX (801)378-4649. **ED** Steven P. Sondrup. **LC** PD1505; .S6. **DD** 439.506273. Index available (Bound in Fourth Issue). **Bk Rev**, (Qty: 100-150). **Ad Acc. Adv Mgr:** W.Reading. **Pr Rev. Circ:** 1,200. available on microfilm. Documents available from The Genuine Article, UMI Article Clearinghouse. **Continues** Scandinavian Studies and Notes.
Ind/Abst Acad. Search (July 1993-); Am. Hist. Life (1963-); Annu. Bibliogr. Engl. Lang. Lit.; Arts Humanit. Citation Index [Full Cov.]; BHA : Biblio. Hist. Art; Child. Lit. Abstr. (19??-); Curr. Contents Arts Humanit.; Expand. Acad. Index (1989-); Humanit. Index; Humanit. Source (Jul. 1993-); INFO-SOUTH Abstr.; Mag. Search; MLA Int. Bibl. Books Artic. Mod. Lang. Lit.; Newsp. Period. Abstr. (1991-); Res. Alert [Full Cov.]; Soc. Sci. Cit. Index [Select. Cov.].

UK/0036-5653
SCANDINAVICA. [Scandinavica]. Vol. 1 (May 1962)-. Periodical. English (French and German). Twice a year (May & Nov.). £17.50 (individuals), £ 25.00 (institutions) UK; $50.00 others;. Norvik Press Ltd., University E Anglia, Subscription Dept., Norwich NR4 7TJ England. **Tel** 011-44-603-56161, FAX 011-44-603-58553. **ED** Janet Garton. **LC** PT7001; .S25. **DD** 839/.5/05. **[CCC]**. Index available. **Bk Rev**, (Qty: 40). **Ad Acc. Circ:** 400. Documents available from The Genuine Article.
Desc: Scandinavian culture and literature of the modern age.
Ind/Abst Am. Hist. Life (1962-); Arts Humanit. Citation Index [Full Cov.]; Curr. Contents Arts Humanit.; MLA Int. Bibl. Books Artic. Mod. Lang. Lit.; Res. Alert [Full Cov.]; Soc. Sci. Cit. Index [Select. Cov.].

DK/0080-6765
SCANDO-SLAVICA. See Linguistics.

DK
SCANDO-SLAVICA. SUPPLEMENTUM. See Linguistics.

US/1058-8612
SCARLET STREET. (SCARLET STREET : THE MAGAZINE OF MYSTERY AND HORROR.). [Scarlet str.]. (19??)-. Periodical. English. qt. R H Enterprises, PO Box 604, Glen Rock NJ 07452. **DD** 813.
Ind/Abst Film Lit. Index (19??-).

US/0740-1965
SCHATZKAMMER DER DEUTSCHEN SPRACHE, DICHTUNG UND GESCHICHTE. [Schatzkamm. dtsch. Sprache Dicht. Gesch.]. **VFOAT** Schatzkammer. (1982)-. Periodical. Multiple languages (German and English). Twice a year (May, Nov.). $20.00. Schatzkammer / University of South Dakota Department of Modern Language, 414 East Clark Street, Vermillion SD 57069. **Tel** (605)677-5490, FAX (605)677-5073. **ED** Donald Pryce and Robert Buchheit. **LC** WMLC 93/3224. Index available (Free). **Bk Rev. Ad Acc. Pr Rev. Circ:** 1,000. ***Continues*** *Schatzkammer der Deutschen Sprachlehre, Dichtung und Geschichte.*
Desc: Poems, short creative works, and translations by German-Americans, reference materials, and reviews of current books are included; for teachers of German at all levels.
Ind/Abst MLA Int. Bibl. Books Artic. Mod. Lang. Lit.; Soc. Plann. Policy Dev. Abstr.

II
SCHOLAR CRITIC. Vol. 1, No. 1 (Jan. 1981)-. Periodical. English. Three times a year. $10.00. Scholar Critic Faculty of English & Foreign Languages, Gandhigram Rural Institute, Gandhigram-624302 DT Madurai Tamilnadu India. **LC** PN2; .S35. **DD** 808.8.

GW
SCHRIFTEN DER GOETHE-GESELLSCHAFT. **Main/Corp** Goethe-Gesellschaft (Weimar, Germany). **Added/Corp** Goethe-Gesellschaft (Weimar, Germany). Vol. 1 (1885)-. Monographic series. German. ir. Price varies per volume. Verlag Hermann Boehlaus Nachfolger, Postfach 260, D 99403 Weimar Germany. **Tel** 011 49 3643 2071, . **LC** PT2045; .G5.
Desc: The contents are comprising texts by Goethe and on Goethe.

GW/0082-3880
SCHRIFTEN DER THEODOR-STORM-GESELLSCHAFT. [Schr. Theodor-Storm-Ges.]. **Main/Corp** Theodor-Storm-Gesellschaft. Vol. 1 (1952)-. German. an (Aug.). DM43.70. Westholsteinische Verlagsanst Boyens & Co., Postfach 1880, D 25738 Heidelberg Germany. **Tel** 011 49 481 68860. **ED** Karl Ernst Laage and Gerd Eversberg. **Circ:** 1,600.
Ind/Abst MLA Int. Bibl. Books Artic. Mod. Lang. Lit.

SZ/0080-7214
SCHWEIZER ANGLISTISCHE ARBEITEN. [Schweiz. angl. Arb.]. **VFOAT** Swiss Studies in English. 1- 1936-. Monographic series. English (German). ir. Price varies per volume. Francke Verlag, Neuengasse 43, Postfach 1445, CH-3001 Bern Switzerland. **Tel** 011/41/31/221715, FAX 011/41/31/221723, telex 911822.
Ind/Abst MLA Int. Bibl. Books Artic. Mod. Lang. Lit.

AT/0314-6677
SCIENCE FICTION. [Sci. fiction]. Vol. 1 (June 1977)-. Periodical. English. Three times a year. 18.00Aus$ (one year), 34.00Aus$ (two years) Australia; 28.00Aus$ (one year), 52.00Aus$ (two years) other. University of Western Australia Department of English, Nedlands Western Australia, 6009 Australia. **Tel** 61 9 4335301, FAX 61 9 3801030, telex AA92992. **ED** Dr. V Ikin (editor's phone: 61 9 3802280). cum. index. **Bk Rev**, (Qty: 10-20). **Ad Acc, Adv Mgr:** same as editor. **Pr Rev. Circ:** 1,000.
Desc: Articles, essays, reviews, and interviews dealing with science fiction, fantasy, and horror literature. Focus mainly on contemporary writing in these areas.
Ind/Abst MLA Int. Bibl. Books Artic. Mod. Lang. Lit.; Sci. Fict. Fantasy Book Rev. Index.

●US/1065-1829
SCIENCE FICTION AGE (HERNDON, VA.). (SCIENCE FICTION AGE.). [Sci. fict. age]. Vol. 1, No. 1 (Nov. 1992)-. Periodical. English. bm. $14.95 (US); $18.95 (other). Sovereign Media, PO Box 749, 487 Carlisle Drive, Herndon VA 22070. **Tel** (703)471-1556. **ED** Scott Edelman. **LC** IN PROCESS. **DD** 808. **Bk Rev. Ad Acc. Circ:** 75,000.

US/1040-192X
SCIENCE FICTION & FANTASY BOOK REVIEW ANNUAL. [Sci. fict. fantasy book rev. annu.]. **VFOAT** Science Fiction and Fantasy Book Review Annual. (1988)-. English. an. $65.00. Greenwood Press Inc., PO Box 5007, Westport CT 06881-5007. **Tel** (203)226-3571, FAX (203)222-1502. **LC** PN3433.8; .S35. **DD** 822/.087609/005.
Ind/Abst Sci. Fict. Fantasy Book Rev. Index.

US/1046-1922
SCIENCE FICTION AND FANTASY BOOK REVIEW INDEX. **See** Literature-Abstracting, Bibliographies and Statistics.

US/0897-1072
SCIENCE FICTION & FANTASY FORUM. [Sci. fict. fantasy forum]. **VFOAT** Science Fiction and Fantasy Forum. (1989)-. Periodical. English. bm. $3.00. SFF Productions, PO Box 138, Woodbury NY 11797-0138. **DD** 809.

US
SCIENCE FICTION AND FANTASY RESEARCH INDEX (PAPER ED.). (SCIENCE FICTION AND FANTASY RESEARCH INDEX.). Vol. 2- 1982-. Periodical. English. an. $185.00. Gale Research Inc., 835 Penobscot Building, Detroit MI 48226. **Tel** (800)877-GALE, (313)961-2242, FAX (313)961-6083, telex TWX 810-221-7086. **ED** H W Hall. ***Continues*** *Science Fiction Research Index (Paper Ed.).*
Desc: Provides over 43,000 author and subject access points to historical and critical books, articles, and essays on science fiction and fantasy literature that have appeared during the period, 1878-1985. Arranged into author and subject sections, there are 19,000 unique bibliographic citations, with 16,000 complete author citations and 27,000 complete subject citations.

US/0195-5365
SCIENCE FICTION CHRONICLE. [Sci. fict. chron.]. (1979)-. Periodical. English. Twelve times a year. $30.00 US; $36.00 Canada; $41.00 others. Andrew I Porter Publishing, PO Box 022730, Brooklyn NY 11202. **Tel** (718)643-9011, FAX (718)643-9011. **ED** Andrew Porter. **Bk Rev. Ad Acc, Adv Mgr:** A. Porter. **Circ:** 6,000. available on microfilm and microfiche from University Microfilms International (UMI). Documents available. ***Continues*** *Starship, 0195-9379.*
Desc: Science fiction news, fantasy news, reviews, letters, market reports, forthcoming book information, convention calendar, awards, columns, editorials, photos. Designed for writers, editors, professionals and readers.
Ind/Abst Book Rev. Index (1985-); MLA Int. Bibl. Books Artic. Mod. Lang. Lit.; Sci. Fict. Fantasy Book Rev. Index.

US/1071-3018
SCIENCE FICTION EYE. [Sci. fict. eye]. (1987)-. Periodical. English. Three times a year. $12.50 US and Canada; $20.00 other. Science Fiction Eye, PO Box 18539, Asheville NC 28814. **Tel** (704)684-5575, FAX (704)684-5779. **ED** Steve Brown. **DD** 813. **Bk Rev**, (Qty: 40-60/year). **Circ:** 4,000.
Ind/Abst Sci. Fict. Fantasy Book Rev. Index.

US/0898-4077
SCIENCE FICTION, FANTASY, & HORROR. [Sci. fict. fantasy horror]. **VFOAT** Science Fiction, Fantasy and Horror. (1986)-. English. an. $50.00. Locus Publications, PO Box 13305, Oakland CA 94661. **Tel** (510)339-9196, FAX (510)339-8144. **ED** Charles N Brown and William G Contento. **LC** Z5917.S36; S298; PN3433.8. **DD** 016.8093/876. **Circ:** 500. ***Continues*** *Science Fiction in Print.*

US/0361-7009
SCIENCE FICTION REVIEW MONTHLY, THE. Periodical. English. mo. $11.00 US & Canada, $16.00 others. Bran Dougal, 56 8th Avenue, New York NY 10014.

CN/0091-7729
SCIENCE-FICTION STUDIES. [Sci. fict. stud.]. **VAT** Science Fiction Studies. Vol. 1 (Spring 1973)-. Periodical. English (summaries and/or abstracts in French). Three times a year (Mar., July, Nov.). $29.50 (institutions). $22.50 (individuals) US; $33.50 (institutions), $25.50 (individuals) all except Canada. Science Fiction Studies, SF-TH, Inc., A. B. Evans, Depauw University, Romance Languages, Greencastle IN 46135-0037. **Tel** (317)658-4758, FAX (317)658-4177. **(Subscription address:** Concordia University, English Department, 7141 Sherbrooke Street W, Montreal Quebec H4B 1R6 Canada) **ED** R. M. Philmus. **LC** PN3448.S45; S34. **DD** 809.3/876. Index available. cum. index. **Bk Rev. Ad Acc. Circ:** 1,050 (ctrl). Documents available from The Genuine Article, UMI Article Clearinghouse.
Desc: An academic journal devoted to the critical appraisal of science fiction including Utopian fiction.
Ind/Abst Abstr. Engl. Stud.; Acad. Search (July 1993-); Am. Humanit. Index; Annu. Bibliogr. Engl. Lang. Lit.; Arts Humanit. Citation Index [Full Cov.]; Book Rev. Index (1988-); Curr. Contents Arts Humanit.; Expand. Acad. Index (1989-); Humanit. Index; Humanit. Source (Jul. 1993-); INFO-SOUTH Abstr.; Lit. Crit. Regist.; Mag. Search; MLA Int. Bibl. Books Artic. Mod. Lang. Lit.; Newsp. Period. Abstr. (1991-); Res. Alert [Full Cov.]; Sci. Fict. Fantasy Book Rev. Index.

US/0882-1348
SCIFANT. **See** Romance and Adventure.

CN/0824-6009
SCINTILLA (TORONTO). (SCINTILLA.). [Scintilla]. Vol. 1 (1984)-. English (French). an. 5.00Can$. Centre for Medieval Studies, 39 Queen's Park Crescent East, Toronto Ontario M5S 1A1 Canada. **Tel** (416)978-4887. **ED** Laurie Cropp, Joanne Findon, Marsha Groves, Monica Sandor and Janet Sands. **DD** 809/.02. **Bk Rev. Ad Acc.**
Desc: Articles published in all areas of medieval studies.

UK
SCOT LIT. **Main/Corp** Association for Scottish Literary Studies. **Added/Corp** Association for Scottish Literary Studies. **VFOAT** ScotLit. No. 1 (March 1989)-. Periodical. English. Twice a year (Spring & Autumn). £50.00 (Comes with Association for Scottish Literary Studies Membership). Association for Scottish Literary Studies, University of Aberdeen, Department of English, Taylor Buildings, Aberdeen AB9 2UB Scotland. **Tel** 011 44 224 272634. **ED** M. Beveridge. **LC** PR8502; .A872. **Ad Acc. Circ:** 3,000 (ctrl). ***Continues*** *ASLS Newsletter.*
Desc: Newsletter for the Association for Scottish Literary Studies.

UK/0957-5499
SCOTLIT ABERDEEN. (SCOTLIT.). (1989)-. Periodical. English (Scots). Twice a year (Spring & Autumn). £50.00. Association for Scottish Literary Studies, University of Aberdeen, Department of English, Taylor Buildings, Aberdeen AB9 2UB Scotland. **Tel** 011 44 224 272634.

UK/0264-2522
SCOTT NEWSLETTER, THE. No. 1 (Autumn 1982)-. Periodical. English. Twice a year (June & Dec.). £6.00. Association for Scottish Literary Studies, University of Aberdeen, Department of English, Taylor Buildings, Aberdeen AB9 2UB Scotland. **Tel** 011 44 224 272634.
Ind/Abst Annu. Bibliogr. Engl. Lang. Lit.

UK/0954-8769
SCOTTISH BOOK COLLECTOR. **See** Publishing.

UK/0080-8024
SCOTTISH GAELIC STUDIES. **See** Linguistics.

UK/0305-0785
SCOTTISH LITERARY JOURNAL. [Scott. lit. j.]. **Added/Corp** Association for Scottish Literary Studies. Vol. 1, (July 1974)-. Academic Scholarly Publication. English (Scots). Twice a year (May, Nov.). £50.00 Scotland; £80.00 US; £102.00 other; £50.00 membership. Association for Scottish Literary Studies, University of Aberdeen, Department of English, Taylor Buildings, Aberdeen AB9 2UB Scotland. **Tel** 011 44 224 272634. **ED** J. H. Alexainder. **LC** PR8514; .S3. **DD** 820/.8/09411. Index available. cum. index. **Bk Rev. Ad Acc. Pr Rev. Circ:** 850 (ctrl). Documents available from The Genuine Article. ***Continues in part*** *Scottish Literary News.*
Desc: A scholarly journal that publishes articles on Scottish literature and Scottish writers of all periods.
Ind/Abst Abstr. Engl. Stud.; Annu. Bibliogr. Engl. Lang. Lit.; Arts Humanit. Citation Index [Full Cov.]; Curr. Contents Arts Humanit.; MLA Int. Bibl. Books Artic. Mod. Lang. Lit.; Res. Alert [Full Cov.].

UK/0952-6439
SCOTTISH LITERARY JOURNAL. SUPPLEMENT. [Scott. lit. j., Suppl.]. **Added/Corp** Association for Scottish Literary Studies. No. 1 (Summer 1975)-. Periodical. English (Scots). Twice a year (Spring & Autumn). £50.00 Scotland; £80.00 US; £102.00 other; £50.00 membership. Association for Scottish Literary Studies, University of Aberdeen, Department of English, Taylor Buildings, Aberdeen AB9 2UB Scotland. **Tel** 011 44 224 272634. **LC** PR8514; .S3 Suppl. **DD** 891.6/3/09. ***Continued in part by*** *Scottish Literary Journal. Year's Work in Scottish Literary and Linguistic Studies.*
Ind/Abst Abstr. Engl. Stud.

UK
SCOTTISH SHORT STORIES. 1973-. English. an. 3.50. Collin's, St James Place, London England. **LC** PZ1.A1; S34; PR8676.

UK/0036-9411
SCOTTISH STUDIES (EDINBURGH). (SCOTTISH STUDIES.). [Scott. stud.]. **Added/Corp** University of Edinburgh. School of Scottish Studies. Vol. 1 (Jan. 1957)-. English (Gaelic (Scots) and Scots). ir. $20.00. University Edinburgh School Scottish Studies, 27 George Square, Edinburgh EH14 1HD Scotland. **Tel** 011 44 31 6503060. **ED** Daphne Hamilton. **LC** AS121; .S35. **DD** 914.1. Index available. cum. index. **Bk Rev. Circ:** 750 (ctrl).
Desc: Oral tradition and transmission, folk tales, literature, material culture, musicology, place, names, social organisation, history, and song.
Ind/Abst Am. Hist. Life (1971-); Anthropol. Index; BHA : Biblio. Hist. Art; Br. Archaeol. Bibliogr.; Br. Humanit. Index; MLA Int. Bibl. Books Artic. Mod. Lang. Lit.

AT/0725-0096
SCRIPSI. **Added/Corp** Scripsi Society. (1981)-. Periodical. English. tq (3 issues). 50.00Aus$ Australia; 60.00Aus$ other. Oxford University Press Australia, GPO Box 2784Y, Melbourne Victoria 3001 Australia. **Tel** 011 61 3 6464200, telex AA 35330. **LC** PN2; .S38. **DD** 808.8/0005. **[CCC].** ***Continues*** *Compass.*
Ind/Abst MLA Int. Bibl. Books Artic. Mod. Lang. Lit.

US
SCRIPTA HUMANISTICA. (19??)-. Monographic series. English. ir. Price varies per volume. Scripta Humanistica, 1383 Kersey Lane, Potomac MD 20854. **Tel** (301)294-7947, 340-1095. **LC** UNC.
Ind/Abst MLA Int. Bibl. Books Artic. Mod. Lang. Lit.

IE/0332-4214
SCRIPTORES LATINI HIBERNIAE. [Scr. Lat. Hiberniae]. (1955)-. Monographic series. Multiple languages. ir. Price varies per volume. Dublin Institute for Advanced Studies, 10 Burlington Road, Dublin 4 Ireland. **Tel** 011 353 1 680748. **DD** 870.0899162 470.0899162.

BE/0036-9772
SCRIPTORIUM. [Scriptorium]. **Added/Corp** Centre d'Etudes des Manuscrits (Brussels, Belgium). Vol. 1 (1947)-. Periodical. English (French, German and Italian). Twice a year (July, Dec.). 5300F. Cultura, Hoenderstraat 22, B 90230 Wetteren Belgium. **Tel** 011 32 91 691595. **ED** F. Lyna and C. Gaspar. **LC** Z108; .S35. **DD** 417.05. **NLM** Z 108 S434. Documents available from The Genuine Article.
Ind/Abst Annu. Bibliogr. Engl. Lang. Lit.; Arts Humanit. Citation Index [Full Cov.]; BHA : Biblio. Hist. Art; Curr. Contents Arts Humanit.; MLA Int. Bibl. Books Artic. Mod. Lang. Lit.; New Testam. Abstr.; Res. Alert [Full Cov.].

CN/0227-5090
SCRIVENER. (SCRIVENER : JOURNAL OF CREATIVE WRITING.). [Scrivener]. **Added/Corp** McGill University. English Literature Association. Vol. 1, No. 1 (Spring 1980)-. Periodical. English. an. 10.00Can$ two years. McGill University, 805 Sherbrooke Street West, Montreal, Quebec H3A 2T6 Canada. **Tel** (514)398-4850. **ED** Ernest Alston and Julie Crawford. **DD** C810/.8/0054. **Bk Rev. Ad Acc. Circ:** 800 (ctrl).
Desc: Publishes new Canadian and American fiction, poetry, reviews, interviews, essays and black and white photography.
Ind/Abst Can. Period. Index (1991-).

US/0147-6629
SEATTLE REVIEW, THE. Added/Corp University of Washington. (Spring 1978)-. English. sa (May, Nov.). $10.00 (1 year), $18.00 (2 year). University of Washington / Padelford Hall, GN30, Seattle WA 98195. **Tel** (206)543-9865. **ED** Donna Gerstenberger. **LC** PS536.2; .S4. **DD** 810/.8. **Ad Acc, Adv Mgr:** J Smith. **Circ:** 750 (ctrl).
Ind/Abst Am. Humanit. Index (19??-).

SZ/0582-3951
SEGES (FRIBOURG). See Linguistics.

US/0885-9574
SELECTED PAPERS FROM THE WEST VIRGINIA SHAKESPEARE AND RENAISSANCE ASSOCIATION. [Sel. papers W. Va. Shakespear. Renaiss. Assoc.]. **Added/Corp** West Virginia Shakespeare and Renaissance Association. West Virginia University. Foundation. (Spring 1976)-. Proceedings. English. an (Spring). $5.00 US; $7.00 other. Marshall University / English, Department of English, Huntington WV 25755-2646. **Tel** (304)696-3155. **ED** Edmund Taft, (phone: (304)696-3155). **LC** PR2887; .W4717. **DD** 822.3/3. **Bk Rev**, (Qty: 1-3). **Pr Rev. Circ:** 120.
Desc: Selections from the annual meeting of the West Virginian Shakespeare and Renaissance Association.
Ind/Abst MLA Int. Bibl. Books Artic. Mod. Lang. Lit.

GW/0170-219X
SEMIOSIS. See Linguistics.

FR
SEMIOSIS (PARIS, FRANCE). (SEMIOSIS.). Vol. 1 (1976)-. Monographic series. French. Price varies per volume. Agis Verlag, Postfach 220, D 76492 Baden Baden Germany.

US/0037-2145
SENECA REVIEW, THE. [Seneca rev.]. **Added/Corp** Hobart Student Association. Hobart College. William Smith College. William Smith Student Association. (May 1970)-. Periodical. English. Twice a year (May and Dec.). $8.00 one year; $15.00 two years. Hobart and William Smith Colleges Press, Box 115, Geneva NY 14456. **Tel** (315)781-3349, FAX (315)781-3348. **ED** Deborah Tall, (phone: (315)781-3364). **LC** PN6010.5; .S45. **DD** 808.8. **Ad Acc. Circ:** 530.
Desc: This publication is about contemporary poetry, translations and essays.
Ind/Abst Am. Humanit. Index; Index Am. Period. Verse.

JA
SENRYU NENKAN. (1972)-. Periodical. Japanese. ¥1500. Yuzankaku, 6-9 Fujimi 2-chome, Chiyoda-ku 102 Tokyo Japan. **LC** PL730; .S45.

JA
SENTEI JIDO TOSHO MOKUROKU. Japanese. Nagoya-shi Jido Tosho Sentei Kyogikai, c/o Nagoya-shi Tsurumai Chuo Toshokan 1-55, Tsurumai 1-chome Showa-ku, Nagoya 466 Japan. **LC** Z1037.8.J3; S42; PN1009.J3.

CN/1181-9677
SEQUELS (TORONTO). (SEQUELS.). [Sequels]. Vol. 1, No. 1 (May 27, 1991)-. Periodical. English. bw. $25.95. Sequels, PO Box 965, Adelaide Post Office, Toronto Ontario M5C 2K3 Canada. **DD** 808.83/872/05.

US/0037-2420
SEQUOIA (STANFORD, CALIF.). (SEQUOIA.). [Sequoia]. **Added/Corp** Stanford University. Associated Students. (Winter 1956)-. Periodical. English. an. $10.00. Storke Student Publications, Storke Publications Building, Stanford CA 94305. **Tel** (415)497-7703. **LC** PS508.C6; S48. **DD** 810/.8.
Ind/Abst Am. Humanit. Index; Index Am. Period. Verse.

IT/0037-2498
SERPE. (LA SERPE.). [Serpe]. **Added/Corp** Associazione Medici Scrittori Italiani. Vol. 1, No. 1 (Sept. 1952)- . Periodical. Italian. qt. L50000 AMSI members (Italy) ; L15000 non-members (Italy); L 30000 (other). Associazione Medici Scrittori Italiani, Via Fabriano 37, 63100 Ascoli Piceno Italy.
Ind/Abst MLA Int. Bibl. Books Artic. Mod. Lang. Lit.

RU
SERVANTESOVSKIE CHTENIIA.
Added/Corp Nauchnyi Sovet po Istorii Mirovoi Kultury (Akademiia Nauk SSSR). Komissiia po Kompleksnomu Izucheniiu Kultury Narodov Pireneiskogo Poluostrova. **VFOAT** Lecturas Cervantinas. (1985)-. Russian (summaries and/or abstracts in Spanish; table of contents in Spanish). ir. Izdatelstvo Nauka St. Petersburg, Mendeleevskaia Liniia 1, 199034 St. Petersburg, B-34 Russia. **Tel** 218-26-12. **LC** PQ6337; .A36.
Desc: Lectures on Cervantes.

UK/0268-117X
SEVENTEENTH CENTURY, THE. See History(General)-History of Europe.

UK/0265-1068
SEVENTEENTH-CENTURY FRENCH STUDIES. Added/Corp Society for Seventeenth-Century French Studies. Vol. 6, (1984)-. English (French). an (Mar.). £8.00. University of East Anglia, Centre for Research in Linguistics, School of Modern Languages, Norwich NR4 7TJ England. **Tel** 011 44 603 592738, FAX 011 44 603 250599. **ED** C. N. Smith. **LC** DC33.4; .S67a. **DD** 944/.033. **Bk Rev. Ad Acc. Pr Rev. Circ:** 325. Documents available from The Genuine Article. ***Continues** Newsletter of the Society for Seventeenth-Century French Studies.*
Desc: Literature, history, thought, music, art history, religion in France in seventeenth century.
Ind/Abst Am. Hist. Life (1989-); Arts Humanit. Citation Index (19??-19??) [Full Cov.]; Curr. Contents Arts Humanit.; MLA Int. Bibl. Books Artic. Mod. Lang. Lit.; Res. Alert [Full Cov.].

US/0037-3028
SEVENTEENTH CENTURY NEWS. [Seventeenth-century news]. **Added/Corp** MLA Discussion Group VI. Milton Society of America. Modern Language Association of America. English VI--Period of Milton Section. Modern Language Association of America. Milton Section. **VFOAT** Seventeenth-Century News; SCN. Vol. 9, No. 1 (Mar. 1951)-. Periodical. English. Four times a year (Mar., May, Aug., Oct.). $9.00 (US & Canada), $13.00 (other) surface mail; $17.00 (US & Canada), $21.00 (other) airmail. Texas A & M University / English, Department of English, College Station TX 77843. **Tel** (409)845-3400, FAX (409)862-2292. **ED** Harrison T. Meserole. **LC** PR1; .S47. Index Bound in First Issue. **Bk Rev. Ad Acc. Circ:** 1,200-1,300. available on microfilm and microfiche from University Microfilms International (UMI). ***Continues** Seventeenth Century News Letter, 0735-7621.*
Desc: Covers all aspects of seventeenth century culture. English, American and European, with emphasis on literature and history.
Ind/Abst Annu. Bibliogr. Engl. Lang. Lit.; Book Rev. Index; MLA Int. Bibl. Books Artic. Mod. Lang. Lit.

US/0893-6889
SEXUALITY AND LITERATURE. [Sex. lit.]. Monographic series. English. ir. Price varies per volume. Peter Lang Publishing, 62 West 45th Street, 4th Floor, New York NY 10036. **Tel** (212)764-1471, (800)770-5264, telex 6973364 PLNY. **ED** John Maynard. **DD** 813. **Pr Rev.**
Desc: Sexual symbolism and themes in literature.

US/0190-3640
SEZ. No. 1 (Winter 1978)-. Monographic series. English. ir. Price varies per volume. Shadow Press, PO Box 8803, Minneapolis MN 55408. **Tel** (612)822-3488. **ED** Jim Dochniak. **Bk Rev. Ad Acc. Circ:** 2,000 (ctrl).
Desc: Multicultural, working class literary magazine. Poetry, fiction, reviews, interviews, and articles on progressive culture. International and regional.
Ind/Abst Am. Humanit. Index (-199?).

●US
SFRA REVIEW. Added/Corp Science Fiction Research Association. **VFOAT** Science Fiction Research Association Review. No. 194 (Jan./Feb. 1992)-. Periodical. English. mo. Science Fiction Research Association, University of North Texas, English Department, Denton TX 76203. **Tel** (817)565-2120. **LC** PS648.S3; S47. ***Continues** SFRA Newsletter.*
Ind/Abst Sci. Fict. Fantasy Book Rev. Index (1992-).

US/1046-5243
SHADOW PLAY. [Shad. play]. No. 1 (Spring 1990)-. Periodical. English. sa. $5.00. Landside Press, RR 1, Box 398, Grand Isle VT 05458. **DD** 811.
Ind/Abst Am. Humanit. Index (199?-).

SA/1011-582X
SHAKESPEARE IN SOUTHERN AFRICA : JOURNAL OF THE SHAKESPEARE SOCIETY OF SOUTHERN AFRICA. See Theater.

GW/0080-9128
SHAKESPEARE JAHRBUCH. ***Title Change.*** [Shakespeare-Jahrb.]. **Added/Corp** Deutsche Shakespeare-Gesellschaft. **VFOAT** Skakespeare-Jahrbuch. **VAT** Skakespeare-Jahrbuch. (1925)-(1992). German (English). an. Verlag Hermann Boehlaus Nachfolger, Postfach 260, D 99403 Weimar Germany. **Tel** 011 49 3643 2071, . **LC** PR2889; .D4. **DD** 822.3/3. cum. index. ***Continues** Jahrbuch der Deutschen Shakespeare-Gesellschaft. **Absorbed by** Deutsche Shakespeare-Gesellschaft West. Jahrbuch - Deutsche Shakespeare-Gesellschaft West.*
Ind/Abst Abstr. Engl. Stud. (1982-); Annu. Bibliogr. Engl. Lang. Lit.; BHA : Biblio. Hist. Art; MLA Int. Bibl. Books Artic. Mod. Lang. Lit.; Romant. Move.

US/0739-6570
SHAKESPEARE ON FILM NEWSLETTER. ***Title Change.*** [Shakespeare film newsl.]. **VFOAT** S.F.N.L.; SFNL. Vol. 1 Dec. (1976)-(1992). Newsletter. English. sa. Nassau Community College Department of English, c/o Bernice W. Kliman, Garden City NY 11530. **Tel** (516)671-1301. **ED** Bernice W Kliman, Kenneth S Rothwell. **DD** 822. Index available. cum. index. **Bk Rev. Ad Acc.** ***Merged into** Shakespeare Bulletin, 0748-2558.*
Ind/Abst Annu. Bibliogr. Engl. Lang. Lit.; MLA Int. Bibl. Books Artic. Mod. Lang. Lit.

US/0037-3222
SHAKESPEARE QUARTERLY. [Shakespear. q.]. **Added/Corp** Folger Shakespeare Library. Shakespeare Association of America. Vol. 1, (Jan. 1950)-. Academic Scholarly Publication. English. qt. $60.00 (institution), $45.00 (individual) US; $65.00 (institution), $50.00 (individual) other. Folger Shakespeare Library, 201 East Capitol Street SE, Washington DC 20003. **Tel** (202)544-4600, FAX (202)544-4623. **ED** Barbara A Mowat. **LC** PR2885; .S63. **DD** 822.3/3. Index available. cum. index. **Bk Rev. Ad Acc. Circ:** 3,800. available on microfilm and microfiche from University Microfilms International (UMI). Documents available from The Genuine Article, UMI Article Clearinghouse. ***Supersedes** Shakespeare Association Bulletin, 0270-8604.*
Desc: Scholarly publication on Shakespearean studies.
Ind/Abst Abstr. Engl. Stud.; Acad. Abstr. Full Text Elite (July 1990-); Acad. Abstr. (July 1990-); Acad. Ind. [Computer File] (1987-); Acad. Search (July 1990-); Annu. Bibliogr. Engl. Lang. Lit.; Arts Humanit. Citation Index [Full Cov.]; BHA : Biblio. Hist. Art; Book Rev. Index (1986-); Curr. Contents Arts Humanit.; Expand. Acad. Index (1987-); Film Lit. Index; Humanit. Index; Humanit. Source (Jul. 1990-); INFO-SOUTH Abstr.; Lit. Crit. Regist.; MLA Int. Bibl. Books Artic. Mod. Lang. Lit.; Newsp. Period. Abstr. (1986-); Res. Alert [Full Cov.]; Soc. Sci. Index.

UK
SHAKESPEARE QUARTO FACSIMILES. See Theater.

JA/0582-9402
SHAKESPEARE STUDIES. Added/Corp Nihon Shieikusupia Kyokai. Vol. 1 (1962)-. English. an. **LC** PR2885; .S54. **DD** 822.3/3.
Ind/Abst Annu. Bibliogr. Engl. Lang. Lit.; MLA Int. Bibl. Books Artic. Mod. Lang. Lit.

US/1045-9456
SHAKESPEARE YEARBOOK. [Shakespeare yearb.]. Vol. 1 (Spring 1990)-. English. ir. $19.95 paper; $29.95 cloth. Edwin Mellen Press, PO Box 450, Lewiston NY 14092. **Tel** (716)754-2788. **LC** PR2885; .S647. **DD** 822.3/3.
Ind/Abst MLA Int. Bibl. Books Artic. Mod. Lang. Lit.

CC
SHAN CHA. (Apr. 1980)-. Periodical. Chinese. Six times a year. $10.33. Science Press, 16 Donghuangchenggen North Street, Beijing 100707, People's Republic of China. **Tel** 011 86 1 4019821, 011 86 1 4010642, FAX 011 86 1 4012180, 011 86 1 4019810, telex 210147. **(Subscription address:** China International Book Trading Corporation, PO Box 399, Library Service Department, Beijing 100044 People's Republic of China.**) LC** PL2515.5.M56; .S53. **DD** 895.1/08. **Bk Rev. Ad Acc. Circ:** 15,000.
Desc: A distinctive journal with national and borderland features, it features national folk literature works and academic theses on research of national literature.

CC
SHAN-HSI WEN HSUEH. VFOAT Shanxi Wenxue. (1982)-. Periodical. Chinese. mo. $27.36. **(Subscription address:** China International Book Trading Corporation, PO Box 399, Library Service

Department, Beijing 100044 People's Republic of China.) **LC** PL3031.S32; S497. **DD** 895.1/09951/17. ***Continues*** *Fen Shui.*

CH
SHAN-TUNG WEN HSUEH. VFOAT Shandong Wenxue. Periodical. Chinese. mo. NT$0.35. Science Press, 16 Donghuangchenggen North Street, Beijing 100707, People's Republic of China. **Tel** 011 86 1 4019821, 011 86 1 4010642, FAX 011 86 1 4012180, 011 86 1 4019810, telex 210147. **LC** PL3031.S34; S52. **DD** 895.1/09/095114.

CC
SHANG-HAI WEN HSUEH. Added/Corp Shang-Hai Wen Hsueh Pien Chi Wei Yuan Hui. **VFOAT** Shanghai Literature; Shanghai Wenxue. (Oct. 1959)-. Periodical. Chinese. Twelve times a year. $38.88. **(Subscription address:** China International Book Trading Corporation, PO Box 399, Library Service Department, Beijing 100044 People's Republic of China.) **ED** Ru Zhi-Juan and Li Zi-Yun. **Bk Rev. Ad Acc. Circ:** 40,000. ***Continues*** *Wen I Yueh Pao.*
Desc: Contains stories, poetry, and literature reviews.

US/0037-329X
SHANTIH. [Shantih]. V. 1- Winter 1971-. Periodical. English. qt. $5.00 per issue. Gottesman Irving, PO Box 1930 Canal Station, New York NY 10013-0872. **ED** Irving Gottlesman. **LC** PN6010.5; .S5. **DD** 808.8/004. **Bk Rev. Ad Acc. Circ:** 2,000 (ctrl).
Desc: Articles covering fiction, poetry and art reviews.

UZ/0488-549X
SHARQ IULDUZI. Added/Corp Uzbekiston Kommunistik Partiiasi. Markazii Komiteti. (19??)-. Periodical. Uzbek. mo. $109.95. **(Subscription address:** East View Publications Inc., 3020 Harbor Lane North, Suite 110, Minneapolis MN 55447.) **LC** WMLC L 83/891; PL56.6; .S53.

CN
SHASHKEVYCHIIANA. See Linguistics.

UK/0037-3346
SHAVIAN (LONDON). (THE SHAVIAN.). [Shavian]. **Added/Corp** Shaw Society, London. No. 1 (Dec. 1953)-. Periodical. English. Eight times a year. £7.00. Shaw Society, 155 North View Road, London N8 7ND England. **Tel** 011 44 81 6902325, 3487411. **ED** T.F. Evans. **Bk Rev**, (Qty: 8-10/yr). **Circ:** 250. available on microfilm and microfiche from University Microfilms International (UMI). ***Supersedes*** *Bernard Shaw Society Bulletin.*
Ind/Abst MLA Int. Bibl. Books Artic. Mod. Lang. Lit.

RU
SHEKSPIROVSKIE CHTENIIA. Added/Corp Akademiia Nauk SSSR. Shekspirovskaia Komissiia. **VFOAT** Shakespeare Readings. (1976)-. Academic Scholarly Publication. Russian. 1.80rub. Izdatelstvo Nauka / Akademiia Nauk, Publishing House of the Russian Academy of Sciences, Leninskii Porspekt 14, 117901 Moscow Russia. **Tel** 011 95 954-21-53, FAX 011 95 938-21-44, telex 411964. **LC** PR2885; .S76. **DD** 822/.33.

CC
SHEN HUA / SHEN HUA. Added/Corp Chi-lin Sheng Chun Chung i Shu Kuan. (19??)-. Periodical. Chinese. mo. RMBY0.30. Shen Hua, Post Office, Chang-Chun Shih, People's Republic of China. **LC** PL2513; .S466. **DD** 895.1/09/005.

US/0037-3583
SHENANDOAH. [Shenandoah]. **Added/Corp** Washington and Lee University. Vol. 1 (Spring 1950)-. Periodical. English. Four times a year (Mar., June, Sept., Dec.). $13.75 US; $17.50 other. Washington Lee University, Box 722, Lexington VA 24450. **Tel** (703)463-8765, FAX (703)463-8945. **ED** Dabney Stuart and Lynn Williams. **LC** AP2; .S528. **DD** 051. Index available (4th iss. in (Dec)). cum. index. **Bk Rev**, (Qty: 4-6). **Ad Acc. Circ:** 1,700 (ctrl). available on microfilm and microfiche from University Microfilms International (UMI). Documents available from The Genuine Article.
Desc: A literary quarterly publishing prize-winning fiction, poetry, essays and reviews to new and established authors.
Ind/Abst Abstr. Engl. Stud.; Am. Humanit. Index (-199?); Annu. Bibliogr. Engl. Lang. Lit.; Arts Humanit. Citation Index [Full Cov.]; Curr. Contents Arts Humanit.; Index Am. Period. Verse; Lit. Crit. Regist.; MLA Int. Bibl. Books Artic. Mod. Lang. Lit.; Res. Alert [Full Cov.]; Romant. Move.

US
SHERLOCK HOLMES. CD-ROM. (19??)-. English. $34.49 US; $39.00 other. Creative Multimedia Corporation, 513 Northwest Avenue, Suite 400, Portland OR 97209. **Tel** (503)241-4351. Index available. cum. index.
Desc: Classic stories of the world's greatest consulting detective.

UK/0037-3621
SHERLOCK HOLMES JOURNAL, THE. Added/Corp Sherlock Holmes Society of London. (1952)-. Periodical. English. Twice a year (July & Dec.). $21.00. Sherlock Holmes Society of London, 3 Outram Road, Southsea Hants D05 1QP England. **Tel** 011 44 705 812104. **ED** Nicholas Utechin (editor's address: Highfield Farm House, 23 Highfield Road, Headington, Oxford England). **LC** PR4623; .A24. **DD** 823/.8. Index available. **Bk Rev. Circ:** 1,500 (ctrl).
Desc: Study of the life, work and times of Sherlock Holmes and Dr. Watson.

US/1040-4937
SHERLOCKIAN TIDBITS. Began in 1987. Periodical. English. qt. $8.00. Arnold Karotkin, 12 Glenwood Road, Upper Montclair NJ 07043. **ED** Arnold Korothn. **DD** 823. **Bk Rev. Circ:** 221.

CC
SHIH CHIEH WEN HSUEH. VFOAT Shijie Wenxue; World Literature. (19??)-. Periodical. Chinese (table of contents in English). Six times a year. $28.64. Science Press, 16 Donghuangchenggen North Street, Beijing 100707, People's Republic of China. **Tel** 011 86 1 4019821, 011 86 1 4010642, FAX 011 86 1 4012180, 011 86 1 4019810, telex 210147. **(Subscription address:** China International Book Trading Corporation, PO Box 399, Library Service Department, Beijing 100044 People's Republic of China.) **ED** Gao Mang. **LC** PN9; .S43. **DD** 809. **Bk Rev. Circ:** 40,000. ***Continues*** *I Wen.*
Desc: Introducing world literature, mostly the modern and the contemporary writers and their works, plus important literary trends and schools, critical essays, cultural exchanges, writers' own accounts, and the newest developments in the literary field.

US/0731-0897
SHIH TAXNG. [Shin tarng.]. **VFOAT** New China. No. 1 (Sept. 1982)-. Periodical. Chinese (English). qt. $9.00. PO Box 993, Athens OH 45701.

CC
SHIH YUEH / SHIYUE. VFOAT Shiyue; Shi Yue. (19??)-. Periodical. Chinese. Six times a year. $29.36 (surface mail); $57.42 (airmail). Science Press, 16 Donghuangchenggen North Street, Beijing 100707, People's Republic of China. **Tel** 011 86 1 4019821, 011 86 1 4010642, FAX 011 86 1 4012180, 011 86 1 4019810, telex 210147. **(Subscription address:** China International Book Trading Corporation, PO Box 399, Library Service Department, Beijing 100044 People's Republic of China.) **LC** PL2513; .S49. **DD** 895.1/09/005.

JA/0911-1557
SHIKYO KENKYU. Added/Corp Shikyogaku Kenkyu Senta. Shikyo Gakkai. **VFOAT** Journal of Shi-Jing. No. 1, (1974)-. Japanese (table of contents in English). Shikyogaku Kenkyu Senta, c/o Waseda, Daigaku Bungakubu Murayama, Kenkyushitsu Toyamacho Shinjuku-ku, Tokyo Japan. **LC** PL2466.Z7; S48.

JA
SHIMANE DAIGAKU HOBUNGAKUBU KIYO. BUNGAKUKA HEN. VFOAT Memoirs of the Faculty of Law and Literature. Literature. Periodical. English (Japanese). Shimane Daigaku Hobungakubu, 1060 Nishi Kawazumachi Matsue-shi, Shimane-ken Japan. **LC** PN9; .S44.

JA
SHIMAZAKI TOSON KENKYU. Added/Corp Shimazaki Toson Kenkyukai. 1st Ed. (1976)-. Periodical. Japanese. Shimazaki Toson Kenkyukai, 4-3 Shibuya, Shibuya 2-chome, Tokyo 150 Japan. **LC** PL816.H55; Z9635. ***Supersedes*** *Fusetsu.*

JA
SHISHA. Spring 1979 Ed.-. Periodical. Japanese. ¥3800. Shogaukkan, 3-1 Hitotsubashi 2, Chiyoda-ku, Tokyo Japan. **LC** PL755.8; .S56.

US/0892-1407
SHOOTING STAR REVIEW. [Shoot. star. rev.]. **VFOAT** Shooting Star. Vol. 1, No. 1 (Spring 1987)-. Periodical. English. qt. $7.50 (students) $10.00 (individuals), $15.00 (institutions). Shooting Star Review, 7123 Race Street, Pittsburgh PA 15208. **Tel** (412)731-7039. **ED** Jerry Ward, Kristin Hunter, and E. Ethelbert Miller. **LC** PS508.N3; S43. **DD** 810.8/0896073/05. **Bk Rev. Ad Acc. Circ:** 1,500 (ctrl).
Desc: Contains fine writing and art about the African American experience.

US
SHORT FICTION BY WOMEN. Issue #1 (Fall 1991)-. Periodical. English. Twice a year. $18.00. Rachel Whalen, PO Box 1254, Old Chelsea Station, New York NY 10011. **Tel** (212)255-4740. **ED** Rachel Whalen. **LC** PN6120.92.W65; S56. **Ad Acc. Circ:** 5,000.
Desc: Publishes original short stories, novel excerpts and short novels by women writers worldwide.

US
SHORT STORY. (1958)-. English.
Ind/Abst Am. Humanit. Index (199?-).

US/1052-648X
SHORT STORY (COLUMBIA, S.C.). (SHORT STORY.). [Short story]. No. 1 (Spring 1990)-. Periodical. English. Twice a year (May, Dec.,). $7.00. Short Story F Iftekharuddin, 80 Fort Brown, Texas Southmost College, Brownsville TX 78520. **Tel** (210)544-8239. **ED** Dr. Farhat Iftekharuddin. **LC** WMLC L 83/9243. **DD** 808. cum. index. **Bk Rev**, (Qty: 2). **Circ:** 100 (ctrl).
Desc: The original short stories, critical essays on and about short stories and short story theories. Book reviews of short story collections and critical works on short stories, and interviews of prominent short story writers.

US/0895-9439
SHORT STORY CRITICISM. [Short story crit.]. **VFOAT** SSC. Vol. 1 (1988)-. English. ir. $85.00. Gale Research Inc., 835 Penobscot Building, Detroit MI 48226. **Tel** (800)877-GALE, (313)961-2242, FAX (313)961-6083, telex TWX 810-221-7086. **ED** David Segal. **LC** PN3373; .S386. **DD** 809.3/1.
Desc: Each volume includes a comprehensive overview of 8-10 short story writers from all nationalities and periods of literary history. Each entry begins with a biographical and critical introduction to the author. The focus is mainly on the short story, with discussions of important collections and widely read individual stories. Every profile presents a chronological historical survey of the critical response to an author's short fiction. Explanatory notes, a complete bibliographical citation, and a further reading list rounds out author entries.

US
SHORT STORY REVIEW, THE. Periodical. English. qt. Short Story Review, PO Box 882108, San Francisco CA 94403. ***Continues*** *Fm. Five.*

JA
SHOSETSU SHINCHO. (1947)-. Periodical. Japanese. mo. $165.00 California; $171.00 other US; $198.00 Europe; $222.00 Asia; $174.00 other. **(Subscription address:** Kinokuniya Company Ltd., 38-1 Sakuragaoka 5, chome Setagaya-ku, Tokyo 156 Japan.) **LC** PL770.A1; S5. ***Continues*** *Shin Sekai.*

CC
SHOU HUO. VFOAT Shouhuo. (July 1957)-. Periodical. Chinese. Six times a year. $27.30. **(Subscription address:** China International Book Trading Corporation, PO Box 399, Library Service Department, Beijing 100044 People's Republic of China.) **LC** PL2513; .S535. **DD** 895.1/08/005.
Desc: Covers Chinese literature.

CN/0229-5776
SI QUE. ***Ceased.*** (SI QUE -- / DEPARTEMENT D'ETUDES FRANCAISES, UNIVERSITE DE MONCTON.). [Si que]. (1974)-No. 6 (19??). French. an. Directeur de si que Dep des Etudes Francaises, Universite de Moncton, Moncton New Brunswick E1A 3E9 Canada. **Tel** (506)858-4050, telex 014-2653. **DD** 840/.9. **Bk Rev.**

II
SIARA. VFOAT Siaar. Periodical. Panjabi. 1.00 single issue. Pasha, Talwandi Salem, Jalandhara India. **LC** PK2650; .A483.

US
SIDE SHOW: AN ANNUAL OF CONTEMPORARY SHORT STORIES. VFOAT Side Show, An Annual of Contemporary Short Stories. (1991)-. English. Somersault Press, PO Box 1428, El Cerrito CA 94530-1428.

CN/0715-3007
SIDETREKKED. (SIDETREKKED : THE STAR TREK ONTARIO FANZINE.). [Sidetrekked]. 1980-. Periodical. English. bm. $5.00. Science Fiction London, 419 Beachwood Avenue, London Ontario N6J 3J9 Canada. **DD** 809.3/876/05.

US/1059-2210
SIDEWALKS (ANOKA, MINN.). (SIDEWALKS.). [Sidewalks]. No. 1 (Aug. 1991)-. Periodical. English. sa. $12.00 (institutions). Tom Heie, PO Box 321, Champlin MN 55316. **DD** 808.

GW/0722-7833
SIEGENER PERIODICUM ZUR INTERNATIONALEN EMPIRISCHEN LITERATURWISSENSCHAFT. VFOAT S.P.I.E.L.; SPIEL. Vol. 1, No. 1 (1982)-. Periodical. German (summaries and/or abstracts in English). sa. Verlag Peter Lang AG, Jupiterstrasse 15, CH-3000 Bern 15 Switzerland. **Tel** 011 41 31 9411122, FAX 011 41 31 321131. **LC** PN4; .S54. **DD** 805.

US/0740-946X
SIGLO XX (LINCOLN, NEB.). (SIGLO XX.). [Siglo XX]. **Added/Corp** Twentieth Century Spanish Association of America. **VFOAT** Siglo Veinte; Twentieth Century; Siglo 20; 20th Century. Vol. 1, No. 1 (Fall 1983)-. Periodical. English (Spanish). sa. $35.00 (one year), $65.00 (two years). Society of Spanish and Spanish-American Studies, Department of Spanish and Portuguese, University of Colorado, Campus Box 278, Boulder CO 80309-0278. **Tel** (303)492-7308, FAX (303)492-3699. **LC** PQ6072; .S49. **DD** 860.9/006/05.
Ind/Abst MLA Int. Bibl. Books Artic. Mod. Lang. Lit.

US
SIGNAL. (SIGNAL : SPECIAL INTEREST GROUP - A NETWORK ON ADOLESCENT LITERATURE.). **Main/Corp** International Reading Association. Special Interest Group on Literature for the Adolescent Reader.

(19??)-. Periodical. English. Three times a year. $12.00. Glassboro State College / SIGNAL, Hawthorn Hall, Glassboro NJ 08028. **Tel** (609)863-6450. **ED** Patricia Kelly. **Bk Rev. Ad Acc. Circ:** 500 (ctrl).

UK/0037-4954
SIGNAL (AMBERLEY). (SIGNAL : APPROACHES TO CHILDREN'S BOOKS.). [Signal]. No. 1 (Jan. 1970)-. Periodical. English. Three times a year (Jan., May, Sep.). £11.25 UK; £22.00 (airmail) other. Thimble Press, Lockwood, Station Road, South Woodchester, Stroud Gloucester, GL5 5EQ England. **Tel** 011 44 453 873716, FAX 011 44 453 878599. **ED** Nancy Chambers. **LC** PN1009.A1; S39. **DD** 025.5/05. Index available.
Desc: Articles on all aspects of children's literature: critical, historical, educational, writing, illustrating and publishing.
Ind/Abst Abstr. Engl. Stud.; Br. Educ. Index; Child. Lit. Abstr. (19??-).

US/1040-4724
SIGNAL (EMMETT, IDAHO), THE. ***Suspended.*** (THE SIGNAL.). (1987)-(19??). Periodical. English. sa. $12.00. Signal, PO Box 67, Emmett ID 83617. **Tel** (208)365-5812. **DD** 810.
Desc: Covers international literature and art, essays, articles, reviews, and interviews. Very broad in scope.

US
SIGNATURE. Periodical. English. ir. $3.00. Sumter High School, Haynsworth Street, Sumter SC 29150. **LC** PS559.S9; S57. **DD** 810/.8/09283.

CN/0843-6290
SIGNATURE : A JOURNAL OF THEORY AND CANADIAN LITERATURE. ***Ceased.*** [Signat. j. theory Can. lit.]. No. 1 (Summer 1989)-No. 5 (Fall 1992). Periodical. English. Twice a year. University of Victoria Department of English, PO Box 3045, Victoria British Columbia V8W 3P4 Canada. **Tel** (604)721-7236. **DD** 801/.95/05.
Ind/Abst Am. Humanit. Index (199?-); MLA Int. Bibl. Books Artic. Mod. Lang. Lit.

FR
SILLAGES. **Added/Corp** Universite de Poitiers. Departement d'Etudes Portugaises et Bresiliennes. (1972)-. French (English, French and Portuguese). ir. 4.50F. Universite de Poitiers, 95 Avenue du Recteur-Pineau, 86022 Poitiers Cedex France. **Tel** 011 33 49453286. **LC** PQ9004; .S54. **DD** 869/.09.

US/0147-6122
SILVER VAIN. [Silver vain]. 1- Spring 1977-. Periodical. English. Three times a year. Pl -Right, PO Box 2366, Park City UT 84060. **LC** PS501; .S5. **DD** 810/.8/0054.

US/0164-1085
SILVERFISH REVIEW. No. 1, (1979)-. Periodical. English. Twice a year (July, & Dec.). $12.00 (individuals); $15.00 (institutions). Silverfish Review, PO Box 3541, Eugene OR 97403. **Tel** (503)344-5060. **ED** Rodger Moody. **LC** PS536.2; .S47. **DD** 810/.8. **Bk Rev**, (Qty: varies). **Ad Acc, Adv Mgr:** R. Moody, **Tel** (503)344-5060. **Circ:** 750.
Desc: A annual chapbook contest for poetry. Included are fiction, interviews, and reviews translation are also showcased.
Ind/Abst Am. Humanit. Index; Index Am. Period. Verse.

US/8755-7517
SIMANTIKA. [Simantika]. **VFOAT** Seemantika. April 1984-. Periodical. Hindi. mo. $20.00. Folklore Institute, PO Box 1142, Berkeley CA 94701. **ED** Ved Prakash Vatuk. **LC** PK2046; .S59. **DD** 891. **Bk Rev. Ad Acc. Circ:** 1,000.
Desc: Articles, poetry, book reviews, and short stories, by Hindi writers world over.

SZ/0259-6415
SIMPLICIANA. (SIMPLICIANA : SCHRIFTEN DER GRIMMELSHAUSEN-GESELLSCHAFT.). [Simpliciana]. **Added/Corp** Grimmelshausen-Gesellschaft. (1973)-. German. ir. Verlag Peter Lang AG, Jupiterstrasse 15, CH-3000 Bern 15 Switzerland. **Tel** 011 41 31 9411122, FAX 011 41 31 321131. **LC** PT1732; .S48. **DD** 833/.5.

US/0731-2016
SIMPLY STATED. ***Ceased.*** No. 8 (July/Aug. 1980)-Ceased ?. Periodical. English. ir. American Institute for Research, 1055 Thomas Jefferson Street NW, Washington DC 20007. **Tel** (202)342-5000. **ED** Robbin M Battison. **Bk Rev. Circ:** 10,000. ***Continues*** *Fine Print.*
Desc: Articles on readability, plain language laws, and research on effective writing.

●CL
SIMPSON 7 : REVISTA DE LA SOCIEDAD DE ESCRITORES DE CHILE. **Added/Corp** Sociedad de Escritores de Chile. **VFOAT** Simpson Siete. Vol. 1 (1992)-. Periodical. Spanish. sa. Sociedad de Escritores de Chile, Almirante Simpson 7, Casillo 4082, Correo Central, Santiago, Chile. **ED** Carlos Olivares.

KO
SIMUNHAK. Periodical. Korean. W3,000. Simunhak Sa, 190 Migun-dong, Sodaemun-ku, Seoul Korea. **LC** PL972.7; .S57.

US/0198-9855
SING HEAVENLY MUSE!. [Sing heaven. muse]. No. 1 (Spring 1978)-. Periodical. English. sa. $21.00 institutions (three issues); $19.00 individuals (three issues). Sing Heavenly Muse, Box 13320, Minneapolis MN 55414. **Tel** (612)340-9777, (612)729-4266. **ED** Sue Ann Martinson. **LC** PS508.W7; S48. **DD** 810/.8/09287. **Circ:** 400.
Desc: A women's publication of poetry and prose.
Ind/Abst Am. Humanit. Index; Index Am. Period. Verse.

US/1055-3401
SINGLE STYLE FOR WRITERS DIALOGUE GROUP. [Single style Writ. Dialogue Group]. **Added/Corp** Writers Dialogue Group. **VFOAT** Single Style. Vol. 1, No. 1 (Jan. 1991)-. Periodical. English. mo. $45.00. Sunday Edition, Box 312, Tiburon CA 94920. **DD** 810.

US/0196-1853
SINISTER WISDOM. **See** Homosexuality.

US/0891-298X
SINK. ***Ceased.*** [Sink]. (1986)-(19??). Periodical. English. an. Sink Press, PO Box 590095, San Francisco CA 94159. **Tel** (415)752-6378. **ED** Spencer Selby. **DD** 810. **Circ:** 250.
Desc: A magazine of innovative, postmodern and language-based poetry and writing.
Ind/Abst Am. Humanit. Index (-19??); Index Am. Period. Verse.

II
SIRALU. Periodical. Assamese (Assamese). mo. 3.00. Sudarshan Prakash, Bamunimaidan Guwahati 781021 India. **LC** PK1560; .A375.

II
SIVAM. Periodical. Hindi (Hindi). mo. Rs20.00. Miss Tripta Tivari, E-114/12 Shivaji Nagar, Bhopal 462006 India. **LC** PK2103.M3; S58.

IC
SKALDSKAPARMAL. (1990)-. Icelandic.

GW/0342-8427
SKANDINAVISTIK. [Skandinavistik]. **Added/Corp** Universitat Kiel. Nordisches Institut. (May 1971)-. Periodical. German. Twice a year (June, & Dec.). DM60.00. Nordisches Institut der Universitaet Kiel, Olshausenstrasse 40, W 2300 Kiel F R Germany. **Tel** 011 49 431 8802323. **LC** DL1; .S54. **DD** 948/.005. Documents available from The Genuine Article.
Ind/Abst Arts Humanit. Citation Index [Full Cov.]; MLA Int. Bibl. Books Artic. Mod. Lang. Lit.; Res. Alert [Full Cov.]; Soc. Sci. Cit. Index [Select. Cov.].

SW/0346-7856
SKRIFTER UTGIVNA AV LITTERATURVETENSKAPLIGA INSTITUTIONEN VID UPPSALA UNIVERSITET. [Skr. utg. Litt.vetensk. inst. Upps. univ.]. (1972)-. Monographic series. Swedish. Price varies per volume. Almqvist & Wiksell International, PO Box 4627, S-11691 Stockholm Sweden. **Tel** 011-46-8-6408800.
Ind/Abst MLA Int. Bibl. Books Artic. Mod. Lang. Lit.

FI/0039-6842
SKRIFTER UTGIVNA AV SVENSKA LITTERATURSALLSKAPET I FINLAND. [Skr. Sven. Litt.sallsk. Finl.]. **Added/Corp** Svenska Litteratursallskapet i Finland. (1886)-. Monographic series. Swedish. **LC** UNC.
Ind/Abst MLA Int. Bibl. Books Artic. Mod. Lang. Lit.

US/0160-7677
SLACKWATER REVIEW, THE. Vol. 1 (Spring 1976)-. Periodical. English. an. $6.00. Confluence Press, Spalding Hall, L-C Campus, Lewiston ID 83501. **Tel** (208)743-0470. **LC** PS1; .S58. **DD** 810/.9/005.

XO/0037-6787
SLAVICA SLOVACA. **See** Linguistics.

XV/0350-6894
SLAVISTICNA REVIJA. **See** Linguistics.

GW/0863-0682
SLB BURIER : NACHRICHTEN AUS DER SACHSISCHEN LANDESBIBLIOTHEK DRESDEN. **VFOAT** Nachrichten aus der Sachsischen Landesbibliothek Dresden Kurier. Vol. 1 (1987)-. Periodical. German. qt. Saechsische Landesbibliothek, Marienallee 12, O-8000 Dresden Germany. **Tel** 52677176. **LC** Z803.S23; S58. **DD** 027.4/09432/142. **Bk Rev.** ctrl circ.

●XO
SLOVAK REVIEW. **Added/Corp** Slovenska Akademia Vied. Ustav Svetovej Literatury. (1992)-. Periodical. English (French and Slovak). sa. DM200.00 Germany; DM236.00 other. Veda, Publishing House of the Slovak Academy of Sciences, Klemensova 19, 814 30 Bratislava Slovakia. **Tel** (7)583-15. **(Subscription address:** Kubon & Sagner, ABT Zeitschriftenimport, D 80328 Munich Germany.) **LC** PG1.; S637. **DD** 491.8/05. ***Formed by the union of*** *Slowakei (Munich, Germany)* ***and*** *Slavica Slovaca.*
Desc: Journal of Slovak philology.

XO/0037-6973
SLOVENSKA LITERATURA. [Slov. lit.]. **Added/Corp** Slovenska Akademia vied. Literarnovedny Ustav SAV. Vol. 1 (1954)-. Periodical. Slovak. bm. DM203.50 Germany; DM243.50 other. Veda, Publishing House of the Slovak Academy of Sciences, Klemensova 19, 814 30 Bratislava Slovakia. **Tel** (7)583-15. **(Subscription address:** Kubon & Sagner, ABT Zeitschriftenimport, D 80328 Munich Germany.) **ED** Dalimir Hajko. **LC** PG5400; .S5. **Bk Rev. Ad Acc. Circ:** 1,250 (ctrl). ***Continues*** *Literarnohistoricky Sbornik Slovenskej Akademie Vied.*
Desc: Covers older classical Slovak literature as well as works and problems of the contemporary Socialistic literature.
Ind/Abst MLA Int. Bibl. Books Artic. Mod. Lang. Lit.

XR
SLOVNIK JAZYKA STAROSLOVENSK'EHO. **See** Linguistics.

RU/0868-4855
SLOVO. **Added/Corp** Gosudarstvennyi Komitet SSSR po Delam Izdatelstv, Poligrafii i Knizhnoi Torgovli. Gosudarstvennyi Komitet Soveta Ministrov RSFSR po Delam Izdatelstv, Poligrafii i Knizhnoi Torgovli. (May 1989)-. Periodical. Russian. mo. $89.95. **LC** Z2495; .V5; PG2900. ***Continues*** *V Mire Knig, 0321-0561.*

RU/0235-4276
SLOVO. **Added/Corp** "Sovremennik" (Firm). Vol. 1, (1988)-. Russian. Sovremennik, Iartsevskaia 4 Izdatelstvo Sovremennik, 121351 Moscow G-351 Russia. **LC** PG2900.A1; S58.

US/0737-1535
SMALL POND MAGAZINE OF LITERATURE, THE. [Small pond mag. lit.]. **VFOAT** Small Pond Magazine; Small Pond. (1964)-. Periodical. English. Three times a year (Feb., June, Oct.). $8.00. Small Pond Magazine, PO Box 664, Stratford CT 06497. **Tel** (203)378-4066. **ED** Napoleon St. Cyr. Index available (every three years). **Bk Rev**, (Qty: 10-15). **Ad Acc. Circ:** 300. available on microfilm from University Microfilms International (UMI). ***Continues*** *Small Pond.*
Desc: Contains poetry, short fiction, prose and opinions.
Ind/Abst Am. Humanit. Index; Index Am. Period. Verse.

US/0360-6074
SMASH. [Smash]. V. 1- 1974-. English. Smash Editorial Offices, 62 West 83rd Street, New York NY 10024. **LC** AP201; .S57. **DD** 051.
Desc: SUMMARY: Includes humorous and informative articles, jokes, games, sports, information, and a poster.

RU
SOBESEDNIK (ANNUAL). (SOBESEDNIK.). Vol. 1 (1981)-. Russian. wk. $114.95. Izdatelstvo Sovremennik, G-351 Iartsevskaia 4, 121351 Moscow Russia. **(Subscription address:** East View Publications Inc., 3020 Harbor Lane North, Suite 110, Minneapolis MN 55447.) **LC** PG2910; .S65. **DD** 891.7/09. ***Continues*** *Sovremennik.*

FR/0985-5939
SOCIOCRITICISM MONTPELLIER. (SOCIOCRITICISM.). [Sociocrit. Montpellier]. (1985)-. Periodical. French (English and Spanish). sa. $50.00 (institutions), $25.00 (individuals). Universite Paul Valery, BP 5043 Route de Mende, 34032 Montpellier, Cedex 1 France. **Tel** 11 33 67 142000, FAX 011 33 67 142052. **UDC** 82-4.

IT
SOCIOLOGIA DELLA LETTERATURA. 1977-. Periodical. Italian. $10.00. C C P 31054000 Intestato A, Bulzoni Editore, Rome Italy. **LC** PN51; .S58213.

RU/0868-8710
SOGLASIE. **Added/Corp** Redaktsionno-Izdatelskii Kompleks "Miloserdie.". No. 1 (Jan. 1991)-. Periodical. Russian. mo. $79.95. VINITI - Vsesoyuznyi Institut Nauchno-Tekhnicheskoi Informatsii, All-Union Scientific and Technical Information Institute, Baltiiskaia Ulitsa 14, 125219 Moscow Russia. **Tel** 238-46-00, FAX 9430060, telex 411160. **(Subscription address:** East View Publications Inc., 3020 Harbor Lane North, Suite 110, Minneapolis MN 55447.) **LC** PG3227.5; .S645.

CN/0709-8863
SOLARIS. [Solaris]. Vol. 5, No. 3 (Aug./Sept. 1979)-. Periodical. French. Four times a year. 20.00Can$ (individuals), 22.00Can$ (institutions) Canada; $23.00 (individuals), $25.00 (institutions) US; 24.00Can$, 27.00Can$ other. Solaris, C P 1589, Villa Marie Quebec J0Z 3WO Canada. **Tel** (819)622-1635. **ED** Luc Pomerleau. **DD** 808.83/876. cum. index. **Bk Rev. Ad**

Acc. Circ: 800. ***Continues*** *Requiem, 0317-5324.*
Desc: Science fiction, fantasy in literature, graphic arts, cinema; essays, reviews, stories and information.

EC
SOLOTEXTOS : REVISTA CULTURAL DEL DEPARTAMENTO DE LITERATURA DE LA CASA DE LA CULTURA ECUATORIANA, NUCLEO DEL AZUAY. **Added/Corp** Casa de la Cultura Ecuatoriana "Benjamin Carrion." Nucleo del Azuay. Departamento de Literature. Casa de la Cultura Ecuatoriana "Benjamin Carrion." Nucleo del Azuay. **VFOAT** Solo Textos. No. 1 (Marzo 1991)-. Periodical. Spanish. sa. Casa de la Cultura Ecuatoriana, Nucleo del Azuay, Aptdo. 01-01-4907, Cuenca, Ecuador. **Tel** 593 2 565808, 565721.

US/0885-6842
SOMETHING ABOUT THE AUTHOR. AUTOBIOGRAPHY SERIES. **Added/Corp** Gale Research Company. **VFOAT** Autobiography Series; SATA Autobiography Series; SAAS; something About the Author Autobiography Series. Vol. 1 (1986)-. English. ir. $83.00. Gale Research Inc., 835 Penobscot Building, Detroit MI 48226. **Tel** (800)877-GALE, (313)961-2242, FAX (313)961-6083, telex TWX 810-221-7086. **ED** Joyce Nakamura. **LC** PN497; .S66. **DD** 028.5/092/2. Index available.
Desc: Contains autobiographical essays by about twenty authors and illustrators of books for young people. Numerous personal photographs, illustrations, and a list of the author's books complement each essay. Each volume contains a cumulative index that lists all essayists in the series.

KO
SOSOL MUNHAK. Periodical. Korean. mo. W24.00. 61-2 Kyonam-dong, Chongno-ku, Seoul 110 South Korea. **LC** PL980.A1; S65.

RU
SOTSIALNYE I GUMANITARNYE NAUKI. SERIIA 7, LITERATUROVEDENIE. ZARUBEZHNAIA LITERATURA. **Added/Corp** Institut Nauchnoi Informatsii po Obshchestvennym Naukam (Rossiiskaia Akademiia Nauk). **VFOAT** Literaturovedenie. Zarubezhnaia Literatura; Zarubezhnaia Literatura. **VAT** Sotsialnye i Gumanitarnye Nauki. Seriia Sem, Literaturovedenie. Zarubezhnaia Literatura. (199?)-. Academic Scholarly Publication. Russian. mo. $79.95. Izdatelstvo Nauka / Akademiia Nauk, Publishing House of the Russian Academy of Sciences, Leninskii Porspekt 14, 117901 Moscow Russia. **Tel** 011 95 954-21-53, FAX 011 95 938-21-44, telex 411964. **(Subscription address:** East View Publications Inc., 3020 Harbor Lane North, Suite 110, Minneapolis MN 55447.**)** **LC** PN9; .O25. ***Continues*** *Obshchestvennye Nauki za Rubezhom. Seriia 7, Literaturovedenie, 0202-2117.*

US
SOUNDINGS EAST. **Added/Corp** Salem State College. Vol. 2 (Spring 1979)-. Periodical. English. Twice a year (Feb. & Aug.). $6.00 US; $12.00 others. Soundings East, Salem State College, Salem MA 01970. **Tel** (508)741-6000. **ED** Jenn Harlon (editor's address: 352 Lafayette Street, English Department, Salem State College, Salem, MA 01970, phone: (508)741-6270). Index available ($3.00 per issue). **Bk Rev. Circ:** 2,000. ***Continues*** *Soundings.*
Desc: Publishes short fiction and poetry; feature poet section, photographs and original illustrations. College literary magazine.

RU
SOUREMENNAIA VOSTOCHNAIA NOVELLA; SBORNIK PEREVODOV. **Added/Corp** Institut Vostokovedeeniia (Akademiia Nauk SSSR) Leningradskii Gosudarstvennyi Universitet Imeni A. Zhdanova. Vol. 1, (1969)-. Academic Scholarly Publication. Russian. 0.42rub. Izdatelstvo Nauka / Akademiia Nauk, Publishing House of the Russian Academy of Sciences, Leninskii Porspekt 14, 117901 Moscow Russia. **Tel** 011 95 954-21-53, FAX 011 95 938-21-44, telex 411964. **LC** PJ486; .S6.

US/0277-335X
SOUTH ATLANTIC REVIEW. **See** Linguistics.

US/0038-3368
SOUTH DAKOTA REVIEW. [S. D. rev.]. **Added/Corp** University of South Dakota. English Dept. University of South Dakota. College of Arts and Sciences. Vol. 1 (Dec. 1963)-. Periodical. English. Four times a year. $16.00 (one year); $25.00 (two years). University of South Dakota English Department, 414 East Clark Street, Vermillion SD 57069. **Tel** (605)677-5229, FAX (605)677-5073. **ED** John R. Milton. **LC** AP2; .S76. **DD** 051. **Bk Rev. Ad Acc. Circ:** 500 (ctrl). available on microfilm and microfiche from University Microfilms International (UMI). Documents available from The Genuine Article.
Desc: Fiction, poetry, essays, critical articles often with emphasis on writers in the American West.
Ind/Abst Abstr. Engl. Stud.; Am. Humanit. Index; Annu. Bibliogr. Engl. Lang. Lit.; Arts Humanit. Citation Index [Full Cov.]; Curr. Contents Arts Humanit.; Index Am. Period. Verse; MLA Int. Bibl. Books Artic. Mod. Lang. Lit.; Res. Alert [Full Cov.].

●US/1062-063X
SOUTH DAKOTA WRITERS. (SOUTH DAKOTA WRITERS: A BOOKWORM CHRONICLE.). (1992)-. English. Free (with SASE). Tesseract Publications, Rural Route 1 Box 27, Fairview SD 57027. **Tel** (605)987-5070, FAX (605)987-5071.

UK
SOUTH EAST ARTS REVIEW. (19??)-. Periodical. English. qt. Free to South East Arts Association members, universities, and libraries. South East Arts, 9-10 Crescent Road, Tunbridge Wells Kent TN1 2LU England. **LC** PR8389.S6245; S66. **DD** 820/.8/099422.

MY/0127-046X
SOUTHEAST ASIAN REVIEW OF ENGLISH. **See** Linguistics.

US
SOUTHEASTERN FRONT. **VFOAT** Front. (1989)-. Periodical. English. ir. Free on request. Southeastern Front Organization, 565 17th Street NW, Cleveland TN 37311. **Tel** (615)479-3244. **ED** Robin Merritt. **Bk Rev. Ad Acc. Circ:** 1,500.

AT/0038-3732
SOUTHERLY. (SOUTHERLY : THE MAGAZINE OF THE AUSTRALIAN ENGLISH ASSOCIATION, SYDNEY.). [Southerly]. **Added/Corp** Australian English Association. English Association. Sydney Branch. (Sept. 1939)-. Periodical. English. Four times a year (Mar., June, Sept., Dec.). 35.00Aus$ Australia; 55.00Aus$ other. English Association / Australia, PO Box 577, Leichhardt NSW 2040 Australia. **Tel** 011 61 2 818 2591. **ED** Professor Elizabeth Webby. **LC** AP7; .S6. **DD** 820/.5. Index available. **Bk Rev. Circ:** 1,000 (ctrl). available on microfilm and microfiche. Documents available from The Genuine Article.
Desc: A review of Australian literature comprising critical articles and reviews and creative writing both fiction and poetry.
Ind/Abst Abstr. Engl. Stud.; Annu. Bibliogr. Engl. Lang. Lit.; APAIS, Aust. Public Aff. Inf. Ser. (1963-); Arts Humanit. Citation Index [Full Cov.]; Child. Lit. Abstr. (19??-); MLA Int. Bibl. Books Artic. Mod. Lang. Lit.; Res. Alert [Full Cov.].

SA/0952-8040
SOUTHERN AFRICAN REVIEW OF BOOKS. **VFOAT** SARB. Vol. 1, No. 1 (July 1987)-. Periodical. English. Six times a year. R90.00. Southern African Review of Books, Sterntalerweg 33, D 89077 ULM Germany. **Tel** 011 49 71 731388272. **LC** PR9350; .S67. **DD** 820.9/8968/05.

US/0743-1406
SOUTHERN CALIFORNIA ANTHOLOGY, THE. [South. Calif. anthol.]. **Added/Corp** University of Southern California. Vol. 1, No. 1 (1983)-. English. an. $7.95. The Southern California Anthology, c/o Master of Professional Writing Program, WPHLT 404/University of Southern California, Los Angeles CA 90089-4034. **Tel** (213)740-3252. **ED** Suzanne Harper and Pamela Main. **LC** PS571.C2; S68. **DD** 810/.8/097949. **Ad Acc. Circ:** 1,000.
Desc: A collection of previously unpublished prose and poetry from established and new authors. Also interviews with well-known writers.

US/0038-4291
SOUTHERN LITERARY JOURNAL, THE. [South. lit. j.]. **Added/Corp** University of North Carolina at Chapel Hill. Dept. of English. Vol. 1 (Autumn 1968)-. Periodical. English. sa. $14.00 (one year), $39.00 (three year) (individual), $17.00 (one year), $48.00 (three year) (institution) US; $17.00 (oen year), $48.00 (three year), (individual), $20.00 (one year), $57.00 (three year), (institution) other. University of North Carolina Press, 116 South Boundary Street, PO Box 2288, Chapel Hill NC 27515-2288. **Tel** (919)966-3561, FAX (919)966-3829. **ED** Louis D. Rubin and Kimball King. **LC** PS261; .S527. **DD** 810.9/975. cum. index. **Circ:** 600 (ctrl). available on microfilm and microfiche from University Microfilms International (UMI). Documents available from The Genuine Article, UMI Article Clearinghouse.
Desc: Essays on Southern literary and intellectual life from colonial times to the present. Includes literary criticism, historical studies and thematic and interpretative analysis.
Ind/Abst Abstr. Engl. Stud.; Acad. Search (July 1993-); Am. Hist. Life (1968-); Annu. Bibliogr. Engl. Lang. Lit.; Arts Humanit. Citation Index [Full Cov.]; Curr. Contents Arts Humanit.; Expand. Acad. Index (1989-); Humanit. Index; Humanit. Source (Jul. 1993-); INFO-SOUTH Abstr.; Lit. Crit. Regist.; Mag. Search; MLA Int. Bibl. Books Artic. Mod. Lang. Lit.; Newsp. Period. Abstr. (1991-); Res. Alert [Full Cov.].

US/1042-6604
SOUTHERN READER. [South. read.]. Vol. 1, No. 1 (Summer 1989)-. Periodical. English. qt. $12.95 (subscription rate), $3.95 (cover price). Guild Bindery Press, Box 2071 Lakeway Station, Paris TN 38242. **Tel** (901)644-9292. **ED** Randall Bedwell. **LC** F209; .S745. **DD** 975/.005. **Ad Acc. Circ:** 7,000.
Desc: Targets academic and nonacademic readers interested in southern culture and history.

US/0038-4534
SOUTHERN REVIEW (BATON ROUGE), THE. (THE SOUTHERN REVIEW.). [South. rev.]. **Added/Corp** Louisiana State University (Baton Rouge, La.). Vol. 1-7, (July 1935-Spring 1942); New Series Vol. 1 (Winter 1965)-. Periodical. English. Four times a year (Jan., Apr., July, Oct.). $18.00 (individuals); $35.00 (institutions). Southern Review, 43 Allen Hall, Louisiana State University, Baton Rouge LA 70803. **Tel** (504)388-5108, FAX (504)388-5098. **ED** James Olney and Dave Smith. **LC** AP2; .S8555. **DD** 051. Index available. cum. index. **Bk Rev. Ad Acc, Adv Mgr:** Joanne Mcmullen, **Tel** (504)388-5108. **Circ:** 3,100. available on microfilm from University Microfilms International (UMI). Documents available from UMI Article Clearinghouse.
Desc: Publishes fiction, poetry, critical essays, interviews, book reviews, and excerpts from works in progress with emphasis on contemporary literature in the United States and abroad, and with special interest in southern culture and history.
Ind/Abst Abstr. Engl. Stud.; Acad. Search (July 1993-); Am. Hist. Life (1969-); Annu. Bibliogr. Engl. Lang. Lit.; Book Rev. Index; Humanit. Index; Humanit. Source (Jul. 1993-); Index Am. Period. Verse; INFO-SOUTH Abstr.; Lit. Crit. Regist.; Mag. Search; MLA Int. Bibl. Books Artic. Mod. Lang. Lit.; Newsp. Period. Abstr. (1991-); Romant. Move.

●US/1065-0156
SOUTHWEST (FLAGSTAFF, AZ.). (SOUTHWEST.). [Southwest]. Vol. 1, No. 1 (Spring 1992)-. Periodical. English. $5.00. Hohokan Flute Player, 3490 South Walkup Drive, Flagstaff AZ 86001. **DD** 808.

US/0891-8619
SOUTHWEST STORYTELLER'S GAZETTE. [Southwest storytell. gaz.]. Vol. 1, No. 1 (Fall 1986)-. Periodical. English. qt. $5.00. Storytellers International Inc, 4703 Club House Lane NW, Suite H-5, Albuquerque NM 87114. **DD** 808.

US/0049-1675
SOUTHWESTERN AMERICAN LITERATURE. [Southwest. Am. lit.]. **Added/Corp** Southwestern American Literature Association. Southwestern Texas State University. Center for the Study of the Southwest. Vol. 1, (Jan. 1971)-. Periodical. English. Twice a year (February and September). $10.00. Southwest Texas State University / Southwest Studies, Center for the Study of the Southwest, c/o Mark Busby, San Marcos TX 78666. **Tel** (512)245-2232. **ED** Mark Busby and Dick Heaberlin. **DD** 810. Index available. **Bk Rev. Ad Acc.** ctrl circ.
Ind/Abst Am. Humanit. Index (199?-); Annu. Bibliogr. Engl. Lang. Lit.

US/0038-4976
SOU'WESTER (EDWARDSVILLE), THE. (THE SOU'WESTER LITERARY MAGAZINE.). **Added/Corp** Southern Illinois University, Edwardsville. English Dept. New Series Vol. 1 (Winter 19??)-. Periodical. English. Three times a year (Jan., June, Oct.). $10.00 (one year); $18.00 (two years). Southern Illinois University / Ewardsvile, Edwardsville Board of Trustees, Edwardsville IL 62026-1438. **Tel** (618)692-3190. **ED** Fred W. Robbins (editor's address: PO Box 1438, Edwardsville, IL 62026). **LC** PS501; .S63. **DD** 810/.8/0054. **Ad Acc. Circ:** 300 (ctrl). ***Continues*** *Sou'Wester Literary Quarterly.*
Desc: Poetry and fiction up to 10,000 words.

RU/0134-4315
SOVETIS HEYMLAND. ***Title Change.*** (SOVETISH HEYMLAND.). [Sov. heyml.]. **Added/Corp** Soiuz Pisatelei SSSR. **VFOAT** Sovetish Heimland; Soviet Homeland. (July/August 1961)-(1993). Periodical. Yiddish (Yiddish; summaries and/or abstracts in English and Russian; table of contents in Russian). mo. **(Subscription address:** Victor Kamkin, 4956 Boiling Brook Parkway, Rockville MD 20852.**)** **LC** DK1; .S5465. Index available in last issue of volume--attached. ***Continued by*** *Di Idishe Gas.*
Ind/Abst MLA Int. Bibl. Books Artic. Mod. Lang. Lit.

LI
SOVETSKAIA LITVA. **Added/Corp** Lietuvos TSR Rasytoju Sajunga. (19??)-. Periodical. Russian. ir. $45.00. **(Subscription address:** Victor Kamkin, 4956 Boiling Brook Parkway, Rockville MD 20852.**)** **LC** PG8771.R1; S6.

RU/0584-5750
SOVREMENNAIA LITERATURA ZA RUBEZHOM. Vol. 1 (1962)-. Periodical. Russian. ir. 2.60rub. Izdatelstvo Sovetskii Pisatel, Ulitsa Vorovskogo 11, 121069 Moscow Russia. **LC** PN777; .S59.

RU
SOZVEZDIE. (19??)-. Russian. 0.55rub (each issue). Mordovskoe Knizhnoe Izdatelstvo, Moskovskaia 115, Saransk Russia. **LC** PG3504.M59; S6.

UK
SPACE. 1-. English. Transatlantic Arts, 80-43 246 Street, Bellerose NY 11426. **LC** PZ1; .S6995; PR1309.S3. **DD** 823/.0876.
Desc: Collection of science fiction stories.

NZ/0313-1459
SPAN. [Span]. **Added/Corp** South Pacific Association for Commonwealth Literature and Language Studies. University of Queensland. **VFOAT** South Pacific Association Newsletter. No. 1 (Oct. 1975)-. Periodical. English. sa (Apr. & Oct.). 40.00Aus$ institutions; 25.00Aus$ individuals. University of Waikato / School of Humanities, Private Bag 3105, Hamilton New Zealand.
Ind/Abst APAIS, Aust. Public Aff. Inf. Ser. (1993-); MLA Int. Bibl. Books Artic. Mod. Lang. Lit.

US/0049-1802
SPANISH TODAY. ***Suspended.*** Suspended (May 1987). Periodical. Spanish (English). bm. $15.00. Cruzada Spanish Publications, PO Box 650909, Miami FL 33165. **Tel** (305)386-5480. **ED** Andres Rivero. **[CCC]. Bk Rev. Ad Acc. Circ:** 10,000 (ctrl). available on microfilm and microfiche from University Microfilms International (UMI).
Desc: An American magazine of Hispanic thought. Informative and useful.

US/0897-4349
SPEAKER REPORT, THE. [Speak. rep.]. **Added/Corp** Speaker Information Service (Fort Lee, N.J.). (Jan. 1988)-. Periodical. English. Ten times a year. $97.00. Speaker Information Service, 177 Main Street, Suite 240, Fort Lee NJ 07024. **Tel** (201)585-4741. **DD** 808.

US/1047-2886
SPECIAL REPORT, FICTION. ***Title Change.*** [Spec. rep. fict.]. **VFOAT** Fiction; Special Report. (Nov. 1988/Jan. 1989)-(199?). Periodical. English. qt. Whittle Communications, 333 Main Avenue, Knoxville TN 37902. **Tel** (615)595-5000, FAX (615)595-5877. **LC** PS501; .S638. **DD** 813/.0108/005. ***Merged with*** *Special Report on Family, 1047-2878; Special Report on Health, 1047-272X; Special Report on Living, 1047-0123; Special Report on Personalities, 1047-286X* ***and*** *Special Report on Sports, 1047-2851* ***to form*** *Special Report (Whittle Communications), 1059-5201.*

NE/0165-084X
SPEKTATOR. [Spektator]. **Added/Corp** Instituut voor Neerlandistiek. Vol. 1 (1972)-. Periodical. Dutch. qt. Fl65.00 (students), Fl140.00 (institutions and libraries), Fl87.50 (regular) Netherlands; Fl70.00 (students), Fl150.00 (institutions and libraries), Fl115.00 (regular) other. Van Gorcum & Company BV, PO Box 43, NL 9400 AA Assen Netherlands. **Tel** 011 31 5920 46846, FAX 011 31 5920 72064.
Ind/Abst MLA Int. Bibl. Books Artic. Mod. Lang. Lit.; Soc. Plann. Policy Dev. Abstr.

IT/0391-4216
SPICILEGIO MODERNO. [Spicilegio mod.]. 1-1972-. Multiple languages (English, French, German and Italian). an. L6.500. Libreria la Goliardica, Piazza Rinascimento 7, 61029 Urbino Italy. **Tel** 39 722 2588. **LC** PN5; .S6.
Ind/Abst MLA Int. Bibl. Books Artic. Mod. Lang. Lit.

BE/0038-7479
SPIEGEL DER LETTEREN. Vol. 1 (Oct. 1956)-. Periodical. Dutch. qt. 1280F. Editions Peeters SA, Bondgenotenlaan 153, BP 41, B-3000 Leuven Belgium. **Tel** 32 16 235170, FAX 32 16 228500, telex 65987 PUL B. **ED** A. Deprez. **LC** PT6000; .S74. Index available. cum. index. **Bk Rev.** ctrl circ. Documents available from The Genuine Article.
Desc: Journal on the history of literature of the low countries and its theory.
Ind/Abst Arts Humanit. Citation Index [Full Cov.]; Curr. Contents Arts Humanit.; MLA Int. Bibl. Books Artic. Mod. Lang. Lit.; Res. Alert [Full Cov.].

CN/0711-4826
SPINDRIFTER, THE. [Spindrifter]. Vol. 1, No. 1 (Mar. 1981)-. Periodical. English. qt. $2.50 each number. Spindrift Writers, Prarsville BC V0R 2S0. **DD** C810/.8/0971134.

US/0364-4014
SPIRIT THAT MOVES US, THE. [Spirit that moves us]. Vol. 2 (Fall 1976)-. Periodical. English. Twice a year. $10.50 (paper); $15.10 (cloth. The Spirit That Moves Us Press, PO Box 720820, Jackson Heights NY 11372-0820. **Tel** (718)426-8788. **ED** Morty Sklar. **LC** PS580; .S69. **DD** 811/.5/408. Index available. cum. index. **Circ:** 3,000. ***Continues*** *Spirit That Moves Us Magazine, 0163-3880.*
Desc: Fiction, poetry, and essays from new and established people.
Ind/Abst Am. Humanit. Index; Index Am. Period. Verse.

US/0095-0459
SPIT IN THE OCEAN. V. 1- 1974-. English. $1.00. Intrepid Trips Information Service, Rt 8 Box 477, Plesant Hill OR 97401. **LC** PS501; .S64. **DD** 810/.8/005.

US/8755-741X
SPITBALL. [Spitball]. Vol. 1, No. 1 (Spring 1981)-. Periodical. English. qt. $16.00. Spitball, 6224 Collegevue, c/o Shannon, Cincinnati OH 45224. **Tel** (513)541-4296. **ED** Mike Shannon. **DD** 810. **Bk Rev**, (Qty: 40). **Ad Acc. Circ:** 1,000 (ctrl).
Desc: Publishes poetry, fiction, and literary prose exclusively about baseball. This periodical reviews every new baseball book. Also sponsors the Casey Award for the best baseball book.

CN/0317-0039
SPLIT LEVEL. Vol. 1 (Oct. 1974)-. Periodical. English. sa. $1.50 per issue. Split Level House, No 1 277 River Avenue, Winnipeg Manitoba R3L 0B5 Canada. **DD** 810/.8/0054.

GW/0038-8475
SPRACHE IM TECHNISCHEN ZEITALTER. **See** Literary and Political Reviews.

SZ/0081-3826
SPRACHE UND DICHTUNG. [Sprache Dicht.]. (1910)-. Monographic series. German. Verlag Paul Haupt, Falkenplatz 11, CH-3001 Bern Switzerland. **Tel** 011 41 31 3012435, FAX 011 41 30 243023, telex 912 906 HAUP CH.
Ind/Abst MLA Int. Bibl. Books Artic. Mod. Lang. Lit.

GW/0724-9713
SPRACHE UND LITERATUR IN WISSENSCHAFT UND UNTERRICHT. **See** Linguistics.

AU/0038-8483
SPRACHKUNST. **See** Linguistics.

GW/0038-8505
SPRACHMITTLER, DER. **See** Linguistics.

US/0891-2378
SPSM&H. [SPSMH]. **VFOAT** SPSM and H. **VAT** Shakespeare, Petrarch, Sidney, Milton and Hopkins. Vol. 1, No. 1 (Jan. 1986)-. Periodical. English. qt. Frederick A Raborg Jr, 329 E Street, Bakersfield CA 93304. **Tel** (805)323-4064. **DD** 810.
Ind/Abst Am. Humanit. Index (199?-).

AT/0816-5432
SPUNTI E RICERCHE. **Added/Corp** University of Melbourne. Dept. of Italian. Vol. 1 (1985)-. English (Italian). an (Dec.). 20.00Aus$ (Australia); 25.00Aus$ (other). Spunte e Ricerche, University of Melbourne, Italian Department, Parkville VIC 3052 Australia. **Tel** 61 3 3446919 7510.
Ind/Abst MLA Int. Bibl. Books Artic. Mod. Lang. Lit.

CN/0383-283X
SQUATCHBERRY JOURNAL, THE. Brew No. 1- June 1975-. Periodical. English. sa. $2.00 each number. Squatchberry Journal, PO Box 205, Geraldton Ontario P0T 1M0 Canada. **DD** C810/.8/0054.

II
SRASHTA. **VFOAT** Sarashta. Periodical. Nepali. bm. 1.50. Paschim Sikkim Sahitya Prakashan Samiti Gejing Bazar, W Sikkim In, Gejinga Bajara India. **ED** Shri Kedar Gurung and Upaman Basnett. **LC** PK2597.5; .S72. Index available. **Bk Rev. Ad Acc. Circ:** 5,000 (ctrl).
Desc: A pure literary and digest type of magazine.

BU/0205-0390
SRAVNITELNO LITERATUROZNANIE / [BULGARSKA AKADEMIIA NA NAUKITE, INSTITUT ZA LITERATURA]. **Added/Corp** Institut za Literatura (Bulgarska Akademiia na Naukite). **VFOAT** Litterature Comparee. Vol. 1, No. 1 (1982)-. Periodical. Bulgarian (summaries and/or abstracts in Multiple languages). sa. 1.67lv each issue. Izdatelstvo na Bulgarskata Akademiia Na Naukite, 6 Rouski Boulevard, Sofia Bulgaria. **Tel** FAX 80 13 41, telex 22267 HEMKIK. **LC** PN851; .S68. **DD** 809.

US/0147-7706
SSI, SHORT STORY INTERNATIONAL. **VFOAT** Short Story International. Vol. 1 (April 1977)-. Periodical. English. Six times a year (Feb., Apr., June, Aug., Oct., Dec.). $24.00. Short Story International, PO Box 405, Great Neck NY 11022. **Tel** (516)466-6091. **ED** Sylvia Tankel. **LC** PZ1.A1; S253; PN6010.5. **DD** 808.83/1. **Circ:** 75,000.
Desc: Contemporary short stories from all lands for the college level adult reader. Stories for pleasurable reading and insight into many cultures around the world.
Ind/Abst Acad. Abstr. (Jan. 1993-); Acad. Search (Jan. 1993-); Mag. Artic. Summar. Elite (Jan. 1993-); Mag. Artic. Summar. CD-ROM (Jan. 1993-); Mag. Search.

CC
SSU-CHUAN WEN HSUEH. **Added/Corp** Chung-kuo Tso Chia Hsieh Hui. Ssu-chuan Fen Hui. **VFOAT** Sichuan Literature. (1991)-. Periodical. Chinese. mo. Ssu-Chuan Wen Hsueh Pien Chi Pu, Chung-Kuo Kuo Chi Tu Shu Mao I Tsung Kung Ssu, PO Box 399, Bejing, People's Republic of China. **LC** PL2513; .S77. ***Continues*** *Hsien Tai Tso Chia.*

US/0896-8276
ST. PAUL'S FAMILY MAGAZINE. **See** The Arts-Art.

SA
STAFFRIDER SERIES. Monographic series. English. qt. Price varies per volume. Raven Press Pty Ltd, 23 O'Riley Road, PO Box 31134, Braamfontein, Johannesburg 2017 South Africa. **Tel** 011 27 11 4033925, FAX (011)339-2439 TELEX 640073, telex 640073. **(Subscription address:** US/ 1185 Avenue of the Americas, New York, NY 10036) **ED** Andries Oliphant. **Bk Rev. Circ:** 3,000.
Desc: Informative, well written description and views of vital issues concerning the future of all South Africans.
Ind/Abst Annu. Bibliogr. Engl. Lang. Lit.

US/1060-4235
STAKE (SAN FRANCISCO, CALIF.), THE. (THE STAKE.). [Stake]. No.1 (1991)-. Periodical. English. $12.00. III Publishing, PO Box 170363, San Francisco CA 94117-0363. **DD** 810.

UK/0952-648X
STAND MAGAZINE. [Stand mag.]. Vol. 24, No. 4, (Autumn 1983)-. Periodical. English. Four times a year (Mar., June, Sept., Dec.). £14.44 UK; £16.00 other; $25.50 US & Canada. Stand Magazine, 179 Wingrove Road, Newcastle on Tyne NE4 9DA England. **Tel** 011 44 91 273 3280. **ED** Jon Silkin, Lorna Tracy and Rodney Pybus. Index available. cum. index. **Bk Rev**, (Qty: 8-10). **Circ:** 4,500 (ctrl). Documents available from The Genuine Article. ***Continues*** *Stand, 0038-9366.*
Desc: Is both British and international and publishes poetry, short stories, reviews, criticism and occasional short plays.
Ind/Abst Abstr. Engl. Stud.; Arts Humanit. Citation Index [Full Cov.]; Book Rev. Index; Curr. Contents Arts Humanit.; Index Am. Period. Verse; Res. Alert [Full Cov.].

SA/0038-9730
STANDPUNTE. [Standpunte]. No. 1 (Dec. 1945)-. Periodical. Afrikaans (Dutch and English). bm.
Ind/Abst Annu. Bibliogr. Engl. Lang. Lit.; MLA Int. Bibl. Books Artic. Mod. Lang. Lit.

US/0886-0750
STANFORD FRENCH AND ITALIAN STUDIES. [Stanf. Fr. Ital. stud.]. **Added/Corp** Stanford University. Dept. of French & Italian. (1975)-. Monographic series. English (French). ir. Price varies per volume. Anma Libri, PO Box 876, Saratoga CA 95070. **Tel** (408)741-0522, 741-1522. **ED** Marc Bertrand. **LC** UNC. **DD** 840. **Ad Acc.**
Desc: University research monographs in French and Italian literature.
Ind/Abst MLA Int. Bibl. Books Artic. Mod. Lang. Lit.

US/0146-2105
STAR-WEB PAPER. No. 1 (1973)-. Periodical. English. $7.00 individuals, $15.00 institutions (per 5 issues). All This & Less Publishers, Regents 509 NMSU, Las Cruces NM 88003.

CN/0228-9326
STARDOCK (OTTAWA). (STARDOCK.). Periodical. English. $1.25 per number. Ottawa Science Fiction Society, PO Box 4601, Stn. E, Ottawa K15 5B3 Canada. **DD** C813/.0876.

US/0893-5211
STARMONT FACSIMILE FICTION. [Starmont facsim. fict.]. (198?)-. Monographic series. English. ir. Price varies per volume. Starmont House, PO Box 851, Mercer Island WA 98040. **Tel** (206)232-848, FAX (206)232-9274. **DD** 813.
Desc: Reproductions of pulp and other classic fantastic literature.

US/0893-5203
STARMONT HARDCOVER COLLECTION. [Starmont hardcover collect.]. (1987)-. Monographic series. English. ir. Price varies per volume. Starmont House, PO Box 851, Mercer Island WA 98040. **Tel** (206)232-848, FAX (206)232-9274. **DD** 813.
Desc: First cloth editions of these classic novels of science fiction and fantasy, tastefully packaged and bound for library circulation.

US/0895-9323
STARMONT POPULAR FICTION. [Starmont pop. fict.]. (1988)-. Monographic series. English. ir. $19.95 (cloth); $9.95 (paper). Starmont House, PO Box 851, Mercer Island WA 98040. **Tel** (206)232-848, FAX (206)232-9274. **DD** 810.
Desc: Great fantasy adventure reprinted from their original sources.

US/0885-0658
STARMONT PULP AND DIME NOVEL STUDIES. (1985)-. Monographic series. English. ir. Price varies per volume. Starmont House, PO Box 851, Mercer Island WA 98040. **Tel** (206)232-848, FAX (206)232-9274.
Desc: Critical monographs on pulp and dime novel authors and themes.

US/0738-0127
STARMONT REFERENCE GUIDE. [Starmont ref. guide]. No. 1- (1983)-. Monographic series. English. ir. Price varies per volume. Starmont House, PO Box 851, Mercer Island WA 98040. **Tel** (206)232-848, FAX (206)232-9274. **DD** 808.

FR/0039-1158
STENDHAL CLUB (GRENOBLE). (STENDHAL CLUB.). [Stendhal club]. No. 1 (Oct. 1958)-. Periodical. French. qt. 362.00F France; 370.00F other. Stendhal Club, 4 rue Lesdiguieres, 38000 Grenoble France. **Tel** 011 33 76 511507. **LC** PQ2436; .S75. **DD** 848/.709. Index available. **Bk Rev.**
Ind/Abst Arts Humanit. Citation Index (19??-19??) [Full Cov.]; BHA : Biblio. Hist. Art; MLA Int. Bibl. Books Artic. Mod. Lang. Lit.; Romant. Move.

●US/1061-6136
STEPHEN CRANE STUDIES. Added/Corp Virginia Polytechnic Institute and State University. Dept. of English. (1992)-. Periodical. English. sa. $20.00 (institutions). Virginia Polytechnic Institute / Department of English, 204 Williams Hall, Blacksburg VA 24061. **Tel** (703)961-7299, (703)961-6501.

US/8750-8974
STING (CENTER SQUARE, PA.). ***Ceased.*** (STING.). Vol. 1, No. 1 (July/Aug. 1984)-?. Periodical. English. bm. Alpine Publications, 1079 Route 202, Bluebell PA 19422. **Tel** (215)277-6342. **ED** C Baker. **LC** E840; .S75. **DD** 909.82.
Desc: Political, humor, and satire.

SW/0491-0869
STOCKHOLM STUDIES IN HISTORY OF LITERATURE. Added/Corp Stockholms Universitet. (1956)-. Monographic series. Multiple languages (English, Spanish, French, German and Swedish). Price varies per volume. Almqvist & Wiksell International, PO Box 4627, S-11691 Stockholm Sweden. **Tel** 011-46-8-6408800. **ED** O. Lindberger and I. Jonsson.

SW/0346-8496
STOCKHOLM STUDIES IN RUSSIAN LITERATURE. (ACTA UNIVERSITATIS STOCKHOLMIENSIS. STOCKHOLM STUDIES IN RUSSIAN LITERATURE.). [Stockh. stud. Russ. lit.]. **VFOAT** Stockholm Studies in Russian Literature. (1974)-. Monographic series. English. Almqvist & Wiksell International, PO Box 4627, S-11691 Stockholm Sweden. **Tel** 011-46-8-6408800. **LC** UNC.

US/0747-6744
STONE LION REVIEW. [Stone lion rev.]. **Added/Corp** Harvard East Asian Graduate Students Colloquium. **VFOAT** Stone Lion. (1978)-. Periodical. English. Twice a year. Stone Lion Review, 2 Divinity Avenue, Cambridge MA 02138. **Tel** (607)547-1422. **ED** Elise A. DeVido. **LC** DS1; .S77. **DD** 950/.05. **Bk Rev. Ad Acc. Circ:** 500.
Desc: The journal wishes to offer a forum for both academic and popular writings in an attempt to reflect the diverse thinking of the community. Includes poetry, prose, interviews, photos, art, etc.

CN/0706-9006
STONEY MONDAY. Issue No. 1- June 1978-. Periodical. English. qt. 0.50Can$ each number. Stoney Monday Collective, 128 Keefer Street, Ottawa K1M 1T5. **DD** C810/.8/0054.

CN/0831-0319
STOP (MONTREAL). (STOP.). [Stop]. Vol. 1, No 1 (1986)-. Periodical. French. Six times a year (Jan., Mar., May, July, Sept., Nov.). 48.00Can$ Canada; 36.00Can$ (individuals), 60.00Can$ (institutions). STOP, Po Box 983, Succursale C, Montreal Quebec H2L 4V2 Canada. **Tel** (514)526-0849. **DD** C843/.54/005. **Ad Acc, Adv Mgr:** Andre Lenelin. **Circ:** 2,000.
Desc: Short stories written by young and/or professional authors.

UK
STORIA (LONDON, ENGLAND). (STORIA.). Periodical. English. sa.

US/0742-2113
STORIES (BOSTON, MASS.). (STORIES.). No. 1 (Sept./Oct. 1982)-. Periodical. English. Three times a year (Jan., Apr., Sept.). $13.50. Stories, 14 Beacon Street, PO Box 1467, East Arlington MA 02174. **Tel** (617)345-1386. **ED** Amy R. Kaufman. **LC** PN6010.5; .S76. **DD** 808.83/1/05. **Ad Acc. Circ:** 5,000.
Desc: Devoted exclusively to the short story, presenting timeless literature by international authors.

US/0895-7592
STORIES (LOS ANGELES, CALIF.). (STORIES.). [Stories]. (1987)-. Periodical. English. qt. $15.00 US; $17.00 Canada and Pan-American nations; $19.00 other. Stories. A Western Storytelling Newsletter, 12600 Woodbine Street, Los Angeles CA 90066. **Tel** (310)398-3701. **ED** Katy Rydell. **DD** 808.

●US/1063-1380
STORIES THAT RHYME EVERY TIME KIDS PAGES. **See** Children and Youth Interests.

US/0039-1999
STORY ART; A MAGAZINE FOR STORYTELLERS. (1930)-. Periodical. English. Four times a year (Jan., Apr., July, Oct.). $10.00. Story Art, 555 Tod Avenue Northwest, Warren OH 44485. **Tel** (216)392-4211. **ED** Helen K. Lea. **Bk Rev**, (Qty: 4). **Circ:** 1,500 (ctrl).
Desc: Periodical containing tellable tales and information concerning becoming an effective storyteller.

CN/0316-0645
STORY SO FAR, THE. VFOAT Story So Four. 1-1971-. English. $3.00. Coach House Press, 401 Huron Street, Toronto Ontario M5S 2G5 Canada. **LC** PZ1.A1; S82. **DD** 818/.005.

US/1045-0831
STORY (VIENNA, AUSTRIA). (STORY.). [Story]. (1931)-. Periodical. English. qt. $19.00 US; $26.00 other. F&W Publications, 1507 Dana Avenue, Cincinnati OH 45207. **Tel** (513)531-2222, FAX (513)531-1843. **(Subscription address:** CDS Agency Hard Copy, PO Box 4966, Des Moines IA 50340.**) ED** Lois Rosenthal. **LC** PZ1.A1; S8. **DD** 808.83/1/08. available on microfilm and microfiche from University Microfilms International (UMI).
Desc: The legendary magazine that first published Salinger, Cheever, Capote, Mailer and others is now the most widely circulated literary magazine published in America. Story's mission is to showcase the finest short stories by the country's most promising new writers. The winner of the 1992 National Magazine Award for Fiction.
Ind/Abst Access (1990-); Am. Humanit. Index (199?-).

GU/1059-7492
STORYBOARD (MANGILAO, GUAM). (STORYBOARD.). [Storyboard]. **Added/Corp** Storyboard Association (Mangilao, Guam). **VFOAT** Story Board. Vol. 1 (1991)-. Periodical. English. $5.00. University of Guam Press, Division of English and Applied Linguistics, Mangilao, Guam 96923. **DD** 808.

US/1041-0708
STORYQUARTERLY (NORTHBROOK, ILL.). (STORYQUARTERLY.). **VFOAT** Story Quarterly. Vol. 1 (1975)-. English. ir. $16.00 US; $20.00 other. Story Quarterly, PO Box 1416, Northbrook IL 60065. **Tel** (312)433-0741. **ED** Barbara S. Nodine, Anne Brashler, Diane Williams, and Melissa Brown Pritchard. **DD** 813. Index available. **Ad Acc. Circ:** 2,500 (ctrl).
Desc: Original short stories, interviews.

US/0889-8812
STORYTELLERS OF SAN DIEGO NEWSLETTER. [Storytell. S. Diego newsl.]. **VFOAT** Newsletter. (1981)-. Newsletter. English. mo. $10.00. Harlynne Geisler, 4182-J Mount Alifan Place, San Diego CA 92111. **DD** 808.

UK
STRAIGHT LINES. Periodical. English. Straight Lines, 30 Mayfield Road, Mosley Birmingham 13 England. **LC** PR1098; .S85. **DD** 820/.5.

CI/0351-0840
STRANI JEZICI. [Strani jez.]. 1 (1972)-. Multiple languages (Serbo-Croatian (Roman)). Four times a year. 10,000 Din Yugoslavia; 20,000 Din other. Skolska Knjiga, PO Box 1039, Masarykova 28, 41001 Zagreb Croatia. **Tel** 011 41 4207842 513 155, telex 21894 YU SKK ZG. **ED** Mirjana Vilke. **LC** PB38.Y8; S76. cum. index. **Bk Rev. Ad Acc.** ctrl circ.
Desc: A favorite journal of many language teachers owning to its approach and short practical articles on all aspects of language teaching methodology. The articles are grouped under headings such as: Linguistics-Methodology, Foreign Language Teaching, Literature, Poetry and Interviews. The articles speak of the practical application of new and tried ideas.
Ind/Abst Lang. Teach.

US/1069-5478
STREET BEAT (PITTSBURGH, PA.). (STREET BEAT.). [Street beat]. Vol. 1, Issue 1 (Fall 1990)-. Periodical. English. qt. $10.00. Community Human Services, 301 Third Avenue, Pittsburgh PA 15222. **Tel** (412)765-3302, FAX (412)765-2646. **ED** Jay Katz (editor's phone: (303)837-9303). **DD** 621. **Ad Acc. Circ:** 3,500.
Desc: First-hand perspectives on homelessness and poverty. Includes opinions, features, poetry, fiction and illustrations.

US/1055-5854
STREET SONGS. [Str. songs]. (1990)-. English. Longstreet Press, 2150 Newmarket Parkway, Suite 102, Marietta GA 30067. **LC** IN PROCESS; PS648.S5; S77. **DD** 819.

US/0747-7287
STRELEC (JERSEY CITY, N.J.). (STRELETS.). [Strelec]. Vol. 1, (Jan. 1984)-. Periodical. Russian. Three times a year. $75.00. Alexander Glezer, 24 Romaine Avenue 2, Jersey City NJ 07306. **ED** Alexander Glezer. **LC** PG3199; .S77. **DD** 891. **Bk Rev. Ad Acc. Circ:** 500 (ctrl).
Desc: Russian unofficial literature and art in USSR, in exile and political reviews.

SW/0282-8006
STRINDBERGIANA. (STRINDBERGIANA / UTGIVEN AV STRINDBERGSSALLSKAPET.). [Strindbergiana]. **Added/Corp** Strindbergssallskapet (Stockholm, Sweden). (1985)-. Periodical. Swedish. **LC** PT9816; .S697. ***Continues*** *Meddelanden Fran Strindbergssallskapet, 0282-9428.*
Ind/Abst MLA Int. Bibl. Books Artic. Mod. Lang. Lit.

US
STROPHES / NATIONAL FEDERATION OF STATE POETRY SOCIETIES, INC. Added/Corp National Federation of State Poetry Societies. (19??)-. Newsletter. English. Four times a year (Jan., Apr., Aug., Oct.). Free (members); $2.00 (individuals) Comes with South Dakota State Poetry Society membership. National Federation of State Poetry Societies, Rural Route 3 Box 348, Alexandria IN 46001. **Tel** (317)754-7082. **ED** Kay Kinnamers. ctrl circ.

IT/0039-2618
STRUMENTI CRITICI. [Strum. crit.]. Vol. 1 (Jan. 1986)-. Periodical. Italian. Three times a year. L68000.00 Italy; L120000.00 (surface mail), L150000.00 (airmail) other. Editrice Turistica SRL, Via Rasella 155, 00187 Rome Italy. **Tel** 011 39 6 4821539. **LC** WMLC L 83/1128.
Ind/Abst Abstr. Engl. Stud.; MLA Int. Bibl. Books Artic. Mod. Lang. Lit.; Romant. Move.

IT/0585-4768
STUDI DI LETTERATURA FRANCESE. [Studi lett. fr.]. **Added/Corp** Universita di Padova. Seminario di Lingue e Letterature Moderne Straniere. Universita di Padova. Istituto di Lingue e Letterature Romanze. Sezione Francese. (1967)-. Periodical. Italian. an. L65000. Casa Editrice Leo S. Olschki, Viuzzo del Pozzetto, Casella Postale 66, 50126 Florence Italy. **Tel** 011 39 55 6530684, FAX 011 39 55 6530214. **LC** PQ5; .S74.
Ind/Abst MLA Int. Bibl. Books Artic. Mod. Lang. Lit.; Romant. Move.

IT/0585-4776
STUDI DI LETTERATURA ISPANO-AMERICANA. (STUDI DI LETTERATURA ISPANO-AMERICANA / UNIVERSITA DEGLI STUDI DI VENEZIA, FACOLTA DI LINGUE E LETTERATURE STRANIERE, SEMINARIO DI LETTERATURE IBERICHE E IBEROAMERICANE.). **Added/Corp** Universita Degli Studi di Venezia. Seminario di Letterature Iberiche e Iberoamericane. Universita Commerciale Luigi Bocconi. Istituto di Letteratura Spagnola e Ispano-Americana. Universita di Milano. Cattedra di Letteratura Ispano-Americana. Vol. 1 (1967)-. Monographic series. Italian (Spanish and Portuguese). ir. Price varies per volume. Cisalpino IST Edit Universitar, via Ferrarese 119 2, 40128 Bologna Italy. **Tel** 011 39 51 370337. **LC** PQ7081.A1; S78. **DD** 860.9/98/05. **Bk Rev. Ad Acc. Circ:** 500.
Ind/Abst HAPI Hisp. Am. Period. Index; MLA Int. Bibl. Books Artic. Mod. Lang. Lit.

IT/0039-2944
STUDI FRANCESI. [Studi fr.]. **Added/Corp** Turin. Universita. Instituto di Lingua e Letteratura Francese. Associazione Universitaria Italo-Francese. Universite de Lyon II. U.E.R. d'Etudes Francaises. (1957)-. Periodical. Italian (English and French). ir (3 issues). L132000 Italy; L150000 Europe; L215000 other. Rosenberg & Sellier, Via Andrea Doria 14, 10123 Turin Italy. **Tel** 011 39 11 8127808, telex 224202 ROSSELI. **ED** Sergio Cigada, Guiseppe di Stafano, Emanuele Kanceff, Gianni Mombello, Mario Richter, Cecillia Rizza, Corrado Rosso and Lionello Sozzi. **LC** PQ5; .S75. cum. index. **Bk Rev. Ad Acc. Circ:** 1,000. Documents available from The Genuine Article.
Desc: French literature.
Ind/Abst Am. Hist. Life (1986-); Arts Humanit. Citation Index [Full Cov.]; Curr. Contents Arts Humanit.; MLA Int. Bibl. Books Artic. Mod. Lang. Lit.; Res. Alert [Full Cov.]; Romant. Move.; Soc. Sci. Cit. Index [Select. Cov.].

IT/0039-2952
STUDI GERMANICI. Added/Corp Istituto Italiano di Studi Germanici. (1935)-. Periodical. German (Italian). Three times a year. L120000. Edizioni Ateneo and Bizzarri Srl, Via Ruggero Bonghi 11 B, 00184 Rome Italy. **Tel** 011 39 6 7593456. **(Subscription address:** Commissionaria Tomassi, Cas Postale 7254, 00100 Rome Italy; phone: 011 39 6 4826073**) LC** PT5; .S78. **DD** 830/.9. **Bk Rev. Circ:** 1,000.
Desc: German language studies and literature.
Ind/Abst MLA Int. Bibl. Books Artic. Mod. Lang. Lit.; Romant. Move.

IT
STUDI GOLDONIANI. No. 1 (1968)-. Italian. ir. Draghi Randi, Via Covour 17-19, Padua Italy. **LC** PQ4698; .A25.
Ind/Abst MLA Int. Bibl. Books Artic. Mod. Lang. Lit.

IT
STUDI ISPANICI. (1976)-. Periodical. Italian (Spanish). an. L300000 Itlay; L400000 other. Giardini Editori Stampatori, Via Santa Bibbiana 28, 56127 Pisa Italy. **Tel** 011 39 50 934242. ***Supersedes*** *Studi Ispanici.*
Ind/Abst MLA Int. Bibl. Books Artic. Mod. Lang. Lit.

IT
STUDI LATINI E ITALIANI / UNIVERSITA DEGLI STUDI "LA SAPIENZA," DIPARTIMENTO DI LINGUE E CULTURE D'ITALIA DALLA LATINITA ALL'ETA CONTEMPORANEA. **Added/Corp** Universita Degli Studi di Roma "La Sapienza." Dipartimento di Lingue e Culture d'Italia Dalla Latinita all'eta Contemporanea. Vol. 1 (1987)-. Periodical. Italian. an. L42000 Italy; L50000 others. Herder Editrice e Libreria SRL, Piazza Montecitorio 117-120, 000186 Rome Italy. **Tel** 011 39 6 6794628. **LC** PC1001; .S83. **DD** 850.9/0005.

IT/0391-8467
STUDI MEDIEVALI (SPOLETO). (STUDI MEDIEVALI.). [Studi mediev.]. New Series, Vol. 1, Issue 1 (1928)-New Series, Vol. 18; New Serie 3 Issue 1 (1960)-. Periodical. Italian (English, French, Spanish and German). Twice a year (June & Dec.). L180000. Centro Italiano di Studi Sull'Alto Medioevo, Palazzo Ancaiani, Piazza della Liberta 12, 06049 Spoleto Italy. **Tel** 011 39 743 220485 or 418, FAX 011 39 743 39107. **ED** Claudio Leonardi. **LC** PN661; .S83. **DD** 809/.02. Index available. cum. index. Documents available from The Genuine Article. ***Continues*** *Nuovi Studi Medievali.*
Desc: A cultural journal which examines and illustrates Medieval civilization of the 6th to the 15th centuries in Europe.
Ind/Abst Arts Humanit. Citation Index [Full Cov.]; BHA : Biblio. Hist. Art; Curr. Contents Arts Humanit.; MLA Int. Bibl. Books Artic. Mod. Lang. Lit.; Res. Alert [Full Cov.]; Soc. Sci. Cit. Index [Select. Cov.].

IT/0585-4962
STUDI MEDIOLATINI E VOLGARI. [Studi mediolat. volg.]. **Added/Corp** Universita di Pisa. Instituto di Filologia Romanzaa. Vol. 1 (1953)-. Italian. an. Pacini Editore Srl, Via A Gherardesca 1, 56121 Ospedaletto Pisa Italy. **Tel** 011 39 50 982439. **LC** PA8035; .P5. **DD** 870/.9/003.
Ind/Abst MLA Int. Bibl. Books Artic. Mod. Lang. Lit.

IT
STUDI PETRARCHESCHI / ACCADEMIA PETRARCA DI LETTERE, ARTI E SCIENZE DI AREZZO. **Added/Corp** Accademia Petrarca di Lettere, Arti e Scienze. Vol. 1 (1948)-. Italian. an. L50000. Editrice Antenore, Via G Rusca 15, 35100 Padua Italy. **Tel** 011 39 49 686566. **LC** PQ4504.A2; S78. **DD** 851/.1. ***Continues*** *Annali Della Cattedra Petrarchesca.*

IT/0081-6256
STUDI TASSIANI. [Studi tassiani]. **Added/Corp** Centro di Studi Tassiani (Bergamo, Italy). (1951)-. Italian. an. L40000.00 Italy; L80000.00 other. Biblioteca Civica Angelo Mai, Piazza Vecchia 15, 24100 Bergamo Italy. **Tel** 011 39 35 240655, FAX 011 3935 240655. **LC** PQ4646; .A36. Index available. **Circ:** 350 (ctrl).
Ind/Abst BHA : Biblio. Hist. Art; MLA Int. Bibl. Books Artic. Mod. Lang. Lit.

SW/0562-2719
STUDIA ANGLISTICA UPSALIENSIA. **See** Linguistics.

UK/0081-6353
STUDIA CELTICA. **See** Linguistics.

BE/0081-6442
STUDIA GERMANICA GANDENSIA. **Added/Corp** Ghent. Rijksuniversiteit. Faculteit der Letteren en Wijsbegeerte. (1959)-. Multiple languages (English, German and Dutch). an. Studia Germanica Gandenica, Rozier 44, B-9000 Ghent Belgium. **Tel** 00-32-91/25.75.71. **ED** G. De Smet. **Circ:** 200.
Desc: Studies on Germanic literature and languages.
Ind/Abst MLA Int. Bibl. Books Artic. Mod. Lang. Lit.

IE/0081-6477
STUDIA HIBERNICA. **See** Linguistics.

IC/0258-3828
STUDIA ISLANDICA. (ISLENZK FRI.). [Stud. isl.]. **VFOAT** Islensk Fri; Studia Islandica. (1937)-. Monographic series. Icelandic (summaries and/or abstracts in English). **LC** UNC.
Ind/Abst MLA Int. Bibl. Books Artic. Mod. Lang. Lit.

HU/0562-2867
STUDIA LITTERARIA. (STUDIA LITTERARIA : COMMUNICATIONES INSTITUTI HISTORIAE LITTERARUM HUNGARICARUM IN UNIVERSITATE SCIENTIARUM DEBRECENIENSI DE LUDOVICO KOSSUTH NOMINATA.). [Stud. litt.]. **Added/Corp** Kossuth Lajos Tudomanyegyetem. Magyar Irodalomtorteneti Intezet. (1963)-. Monographic series. Hungarian (summaries and/or abstracts in English, French, German and Russian). an. **LC** PH3001; .S75.
Ind/Abst MLA Int. Bibl. Books Artic. Mod. Lang. Lit.

PL
STUDIA LITURGICZNE. **Added/Corp** Katolicki Uniwersytet Lubelski. Towarzystwo Naukowe. (19??)-. Periodical. Polish (summaries and/or abstracts in French). Katolickiego Uniwersytetu Lubelskiego, Towrzystwo Naukowe Kul, Ul Chopina 29, Lublin Poland. **LC** BX1977.P7; S78.

US/0161-7222
STUDIA MYSTICA. [Stud. mystica]. Vol. 1 (Spring 1978)-. Periodical. English. an. $34.95 (US) postage included; $37.95 (Canada) postage included. Edwin Mellen Press, PO Box 450, Lewiston NY 14092. **Tel** (716)754-2788. **ED** Robert Boenig. **LC** BL625; .S79. **DD** 291.4/2. Index available. cum. index. **Bk Rev. Ad Acc. Circ:** 400 (ctrl). available on microfilm and microfiche from University Microfilms International (UMI). Documents available from The Genuine Article.
Desc: Studies and expresses the relationship of mystical and aesthetic in all art forms.
Ind/Abst Arts Humanit. Citation Index [Full Cov.]; Curr. Contents Arts Humanit.; Index Book Rev. Relig.; MLA Int. Bibl. Books Artic. Mod. Lang. Lit.; Relig. Index One Period. (1980-); Relig. Theol. Abstr.; Res. Alert [Full Cov.].

CI/0039-3339
STUDIA ROMANICA ET ANGLICA ZAGRABIENSIA. **See** Linguistics.

HU/0418-4572
STUDIA ROMANICA. SERIES LITTERARIA. **Main/Corp** Kossuth Lajos Tudomanyegyetem. No. 1.- 1962-. Periodical. Tankonyvkiado, Szalay u 10 14 Postfiok 20, H 1055 Budapest V Hungary. **LC** PC13.

SW/0562-3022
STUDIA ROMANICA UPSALIENSIA. (ACTA UNIVERSITATIS UPSALIENSIS. STUDIA ROMANICA UPSALIENSIA.). [Stud. Rom. Ups.]. **Added/Corp** Uppsala Universitet. **VFOAT** Studia Romanica Upsaliensia. (1961)-. Monographic series. French (Spanish). Almqvist & Wiksell International, PO Box 4627, S-11691 Stockholm Sweden. **Tel** 011-46-8-6408800. **LC** UNC.
Ind/Abst MLA Int. Bibl. Books Artic. Mod. Lang. Lit.

FI/0781-3333
STUDIA SLAVICA FINLANDENSIA. **See** Linguistics.

PL/0081-6949
STUDIA STAROPOLSKIE. [Stud. staropol.]. **Added/Corp** Instytut Badan Literackich (Polska Akademia Nauk). (1953)-. Monographic series. Polish.
Ind/Abst MLA Int. Bibl. Books Artic. Mod. Lang. Lit.

GW/0174-4410
STUDIEN UND TEXTE ZUR SOZIALGESCHICHTE DER LITERATUR. [Stud. Texte Sozgesch. Lit.]. (1981)-. Monographic series. German. ir. Price varies per volume. Max Niemeyer Verlag, Postfach 2140, D 72011 Tuebingen Germany. **Tel** 011 49 7071 989494, FAX 011 49 7071 87419. **ED** Wolfgang Fruehwald, Georg Jaeger, Dieter Langewiesch, Alberto Martino, Rainer Wohfeil.
Ind/Abst MLA Int. Bibl. Books Artic. Mod. Lang. Lit.

GW/0081-7236
STUDIEN ZUR DEUTSCHEN LITERATUR. [Stud. dtsch. Lit.]. Vol. 1 (1966)-. Monographic series. German. ir. Price varies per volume. Max Niemeyer Verlag, Postfach 2140, D 72011 Tuebingen Germany. **Tel** 011 49 7071 989494, FAX 011 49 7071 87419. **ED** Richard Brinkmann, Wilfried Barner and Conrad Wiedemann.
Desc: Studies on German literature, especially that of the 17th to 20th centuries.
Ind/Abst MLA Int. Bibl. Books Artic. Mod. Lang. Lit.

GW/0340-9023
STUDIEN ZUR LITERATUR DER MODERNE. [Stud. Lit. Mod.]. (1976)-. Monographic series. English (German).
Ind/Abst MLA Int. Bibl. Books Artic. Mod. Lang. Lit.

US/0886-7097
STUDIES IN AMERICAN DRAMA, 1945-PRESENT. ***Suspended.*** **See** Theater.

US/0095-280X
STUDIES IN AMERICAN HUMOR. [Stud. Am. humor]. Vol. 1 - Vol. 3, No. 3 (Apr. 1974-Jan. 1977); New Series Vol. 1 (June 1982)-. Academic Scholarly Publication. English. an. $20.00 Comes with American Humor Studies Association Membership. American Humor Studies Association, Western Oregon State College, Monmouth OR 97361. **Tel** (5030838-8408. **ED** John O. Rosenbolm. **LC** PS430; .S88. **DD** 817/.009. **Bk Rev. Circ:** 600 (ctrl). ***Absorbed*** *American Humor, 0193-7146.*
Desc: Scholarly articles on humor in American Literature.
Ind/Abst Abstr. Engl. Stud.; Am. Hist. Life (1986-); Annu. Bibliogr. Engl. Lang. Lit.; Child. Lit. Abstr. (19??-); Lit. Crit. Regist.; MLA Int. Bibl. Books Artic. Mod. Lang. Lit.

US
STUDIES IN AMERICAN INDIAN LITERATURE. (STUDIES IN AMERICAN INDIAN LITERATURES : NEWSLETTER OF THE ASSOCIATION FOR STUDY OF AMERICAN INDIAN LITERATURES.). [Stud. Am. Indian lit.]. **VFOAT** SAIL Newsletter; S.A.I.L. Newsletter. Vol. 4, No. 1 (Winter 1980)-. Academic Scholarly Publication. English. Four times a year (Mar., June, Sept., Dec.). $35.00 (institutions), $25.00 (individuals). Association for the Study of American Indian Literature / Department of English, Box 112, Richmond VA 23172. **Tel** (804)289-8311, FAX (804)289-8313. **ED** Robert M. Nelson and Rodney Simard. cum. index. **Bk Rev**, (Qty: 20-40). **Ad Acc**, **Adv Mgr:** R.M. Nelson, **Tel** (809)289-8311. **Pr Rev. Circ:** 300. ***Continues*** *Newsletter of the Association for Study of American Indian Literatures.*
Desc: The only scholarly journal in the United States that focuses exclusively on American Indian Literatures. Publishes reviews; interviews; bibliograhies; creative bibliographies including transcription of performances; and scholarly, critical, and theoretical articles on any aspect of Native American Literatures, including traditional oral material in dual-language format or translation, written works and live and media performances of verbal art.
Ind/Abst Am. Humanit. Index; MLA Int. Bibl. Books Artic. Mod. Lang. Lit.

US/0271-9274
STUDIES IN AMERICAN JEWISH LITERATURE (ALBANY, N.Y.). (STUDIES IN AMERICAN JEWISH LITERATURE.). [Stud. Am. Jew. lit.]. No. 1 (1981)-. English. an. $20.00 (individuals), $30.00 (institutions) US; $25.00 (individuals), $35.00 (institutions) others. Studies American Jewish Literature, c/o Daniel Walden, Editor, 117 Burrowes Building, University Park PA 16802. **Tel** (814)865-6381. **ED** Daniel Walden. **LC** PS153.J4; S78. **DD** 810/.9/8924. **Bk Rev. Ad Acc. Pr Rev. Circ:** 200. available on microfilm from University Microfilms International (UMI). ***Continues*** *Studies in American Jewish Literature, 0148-7663.*
Desc: Journal designed to meet the long-felt need for a single publication that examines both the American Jewish writer as well as the American Jewish experience.
Ind/Abst Abstr. Engl. Stud.; Am. Bibliogr. Slavic East Europ. Stud. (19??-19??); Annu. Bibliogr. Engl. Lang. Lit.; Index Jew. Period. (199?-); MLA Int. Bibl. Books Artic. Mod. Lang. Lit.

JA/0385-6100
STUDIES IN AMERICAN LITERATURE (NIHON AMERIKA BUNGAKKAI). (STUDIES IN AMERICAN LITERATURE.). **VFOAT** Amerika Bungaku Kenkyu. English (Japanese). American Literature Society of Japan, c/o Kyoto University, Sakyo Kyoto 606 Japan. **LC** PS1; .S83. **DD** 810/.9.

NE
STUDIES IN ARABIC LITERATURE. (1971)-. Monographic series. English. ir. Price varies per volume. E. J. Brill, Postbus 9000, 2300 PA Leiden Netherlands. **Tel** 011 31 71 312624, FAX 011 31 71 317532, telex 39296 BRILL NL.
Desc: Monographic series covering Arabic literature.

CN/0380-6995
STUDIES IN CANADIAN LITERATURE (FREDERICTON, N.B.). (STUDIES IN CANADIAN LITERATURE.). [Stud. Can. lit.]. **Added/Corp** University of New Brunswick. Dept. of English. **VFOAT** S.C.L.; SCL. Vol. 1, No. 1 (Winter 1976)-. Academic Scholarly Publication. English (French). sa. 22.00Can$ (institutions), 16.00Can$ (individuals) Canada; 26.00Can$ (institutions), 20.00Can$ other. University of New Brunswick Studies in Canadian Literature, Fredericton New Brunswick E3B 5A3 Canada. **Tel** (506)453-4598, FAX (506)453-4599. **ED** Kathleen Scherf. **LC** PR9180; .S88. **DD** 810/.9/971. **Ad Acc, Adv Mgr:** S. Campbell. **Pr Rev. Circ:** 500 (ctrl). available on microfilm from Micromedia Limited; available on an online database.
Desc: Devoted to the scholarly and critical study of Canadian literature of all periods. Each issue contains up to fourteen essays by both established scholars and new young critics.
Ind/Abst Abstr. Engl. Stud.; Am. Hist. Life (1983-); Am. Humanit. Index; Annu. Bibliogr. Engl. Lang. Lit.; Arts Humanit. Citation Index [Full Cov.]; Can. Index; Can. Period. Index; Curr. Contents Arts Humanit.; MLA Int. Bibl. Books Artic. Mod. Lang. Lit.

US/0077-9504
STUDIES IN COMPARATIVE LITERATURE. **Main/Corp** New York University. (1967)-. Monographic series. English. ir. Price varies per volume. Columbia University Press, 136 South Broadway, Irvington NY 10533. **Tel** (914)591-9111.

US/0899-2193
STUDIES IN COMPARATIVE LITERATURE (LUBBOCK, TEX.). (STUDIES IN COMPARATIVE LITERATURE.). [Stud. comp. literature]. **Added/Corp** Texas Tech University. No. 18 (1988)-. Monographic series. English. ir. Price varies per volume. Texas Tech University Press, Administrative Education Room 43, West Basement, Lubbock TX 79409-1037. **Tel** (800)832-4042, (806)742-2982. ***Continues*** *Comparative Literature Symposium. Proceedings, 0084-9103.*
Desc: The purpose of Studies in Comparative Literature is to explore literature of various cultures and linguistic groups in comparison with one another, and to compare literature with other disciplines or fields of study.

US/0163-4143
STUDIES IN CONTEMPORARY SATIRE. [Stud. contemp. satire]. (Spring 1974)-. Periodical. English. an (Jan.). $5.00. Studies in Contemporary Satire, University of Nebraska / Kearney, Kearney NE 68849. **Tel** (308)865-8295, FAX (308)234-8157. **ED** Bedford Sinclair. **LC** PN6149.S2; S78. **DD** 808.87. **Bk Rev**, (Qty: 2/yr). **Ad Acc**. **Pr Rev**. **Circ:** 300 (ctrl).
Desc: Publishes original satiric prose and poetry, critical articles, reviews, and satiric graphics.
Ind/Abst Abstr. Engl. Stud.; MLA Int. Bibl. Books Artic. Mod. Lang. Lit.

US
STUDIES IN ENGLISH AND AMERICAN LITERATURE, LINGUISTICS, AND CULTURE. Vol. 1 (1984)-. Monographic series. English. Camden House Inc, PO Box 4836, Hampden Station, Baltimore MD 21211.
Ind/Abst MLA Int. Bibl. Books Artic. Mod. Lang. Lit.

US/0039-3657
STUDIES IN ENGLISH LITERATURE, 1500-1900. [Stud. Engl. lit. 1500-1900]. **Added/Corp** Rice University. Vol. 1 (Winter 1961)-. Academic Scholarly Publication. English. Four times a year (Feb., May, Aug., Nov.). $30.00 (institutions) US and Puerto Rico; $35.00 (institutions) other; $25.00 individuals. Rice University / Studies in English Literature, PO Box 1892, Houston TX 77251-1892. **Tel** (713)527-4697. **(Subscription address:** Sheridan Press, PO Box 465, Hanover PA 17331.**)** **ED** Robert Patten. **LC** PR1; .S82. **DD** 820/.9. **Bk Rev**. **Ad Acc**. **Circ:** 1,900 (ctrl). available on microfilm and microfiche from University Microfilms International (UMI); available via fax (through Faxpax). Documents available from The Genuine Article, UMI Article Clearinghouse.
Desc: A journal of critical and scholarly studies. Each issue contains a review of the year's scholarship in the area covered by that issue: Winter - English Renaissance; Spring - Renaissance Drama; Summer - 18th Century; Fall - 19th Century.
Ind/Abst Abstr. Engl. Stud.; Acad. Abstr. (July 1990-); Acad. Ind. [Computer File] (1987-); Acad. Search (July 1990-); Am. Hist. Life; Annu. Bibliogr. Engl. Lang. Lit.; Arts Humanit. Citation Index [Full Cov.]; Expand. Acad. Index (1987-); Humanit. Index; Humanit. Source (Jul. 1990-); INFO-SOUTH Abstr.; Lit. Crit. Regist.; Mag. Search; MLA Int. Bibl. Books Artic. Mod. Lang. Lit.; Newsp. Period. Abstr. (1990-); Res. Alert [Full Cov.]; Romant. Move.

JA/0387-3439
STUDIES IN ENGLISH LITERATURE (TOKYO. 1960). (STUDIES IN ENGLISH LITERATURE. EIBUNGAKU KENKYU.). [Stud. Engl. lit.]. **Added/Corp** Nihon Eibungakkai. **VFOAT** Eibungaku Kenkyu. (19??)-. Periodical. English (Japanese). Three times a year. $114.50. **(Subscription address:** Japan Publications Trading Company, Ltd., PO Box 5030, Tokyo International, Tokyo 100-31 Japan.**)** **LC** PR1; .S8. **DD** 820/.9.
Ind/Abst Annu. Bibliogr. Engl. Lang. Lit.; Curr. Contents Arts Humanit.; Humanit. Index; MLA Int. Bibl. Books Artic. Mod. Lang. Lit.

US
STUDIES IN GERMAN LITERATURE, LINGUISTICS AND CULTURE. (19??)-. Monographic series. English. ir. Price varies per volume. Camden House, Drawer 2025, Columbia SC 29202. **Tel** (803)736-9455. **(Subscription address:** Camden House Inc. P. O. Box 4836, Hampden Station, Baltimore, MD 21211, telephone: (410)516-6950 or (800)723-9455**)**
Ind/Abst MLA Int. Bibl. Books Artic. Mod. Lang. Lit.

PL
STUDIES IN HAMITO-SEMITIC. See Linguistics.

US/1043-5794
STUDIES IN ITALIAN CULTURE. LITERATURE IN HISTORY. See Anthropology.

NE
STUDIES IN LITERATURE. English. Humanities Press, 165 1st Avenue, Atlantic Highlands NJ 07716. **Tel** (908)872-1441, (800)221-3845, FAX (908)872-0717, telex 752233. Index available.

DK/0078-3323
STUDIES IN LITERATURE (ODENSE). (STUDIES IN LITERATURE.). **Main/Corp** Odense Universitet. Vol. 1 (1969)-. Monographic series. Danish (summaries and/or abstracts in English). ir. Price varies per volume. Odense University Press, 55 Campusvej, DK-5230 Odense M Denmark. **Tel** 66 15 79 99, FAX 66 15 81 26. **LC** PN35; .O3. **DD** 809.
Desc: Covers Scandinavian, especially Danish, literature.

JA/0913-1507
STUDIES IN MEDIEVAL ENGLISH LANGUAGE AND LITERATURE. See Linguistics.

UK/0738-7164
STUDIES IN MEDIEVALISM. See History(General)-History of Europe.

SW/0283-8494
STUDIES IN MEDITERRANEAN ARCHAEOLOGY AND LITERATURE. POCKET-BOOK. See Archaeology.

US
STUDIES IN MIDDLE EASTERN LITERATURES. No. 1- 1972-. Monographic series. English. ir. Price varies per volume. Bibliotheca Islamica Inc, Box 14474 U Station, Minneapolis MN 55414. **Tel** (612)221-9883.
Desc: Middle Eastern literatures in translation.

US/0888-3904
STUDIES IN MODERN GERMAN LITERATURE. [Stud. mod. Ger. lit.]. (1987)-. Monographic series. English. ir. Price varies per volume. Peter Lang Publishing, 62 West 45th Street, 4th Floor, New York NY 10036. **Tel** (212)764-1471, (800)770-5264, telex 6973364 PLNY. **ED** Peter D G Brown. **DD** 830. **Pr Rev.**
Desc: Presents research in German literary history, analysis, theory and criticism.
Ind/Abst MLA Int. Bibl. Books Artic. Mod. Lang. Lit.

US/0899-9872
STUDIES IN OLD GERMANIC LANGUAGES AND LITERATURES. [Stud. Old Ger. lang. lit.]. English. an. Peter Lang Publishing, 62 West 45th Street, 4th Floor, New York NY 10036. **Tel** (212)764-1471, (800)770-5264, telex 6973364 PLNY. **DD** 430.

US/0039-3738
STUDIES IN PHILOLOGY. See Linguistics.

US/0085-6894
STUDIES IN ROMANCE LANGUAGES (LEXINGTON, KY.). (STUDIES IN ROMANCE LANGUAGES.). [Stud. Roman. lang.]. Vol. 1 (1970)-. Monographic series. English (French and Spanish). ir. Price varies per volume. Harper Collins Publishers, Keystone Industrial Park, Scranton PA 18512. **Tel** (800)242-7737, (800)233-4727, FAX (800)822-4090. **(Subscription address:** The University Press of Kentucky, PO Box 65251, Ithaca, NY 14851**)** **ED** John E. Keller. **LC** UNC. **DD** 440. **Pr Rev**. **Circ:** 750-1,000.
Desc: The series is intended for monographic studies in the romance languages. Principally covering critical and historical studies.
Ind/Abst MLA Int. Bibl. Books Artic. Mod. Lang. Lit.

US/0743-7889
STUDIES IN ROMANTIC AND MODERN LITERATURE. [Stud. romant. mod. lit.]. Vol. 1 (1985)-. Monographic series. English. ir. Price varies per volume. Peter Lang Publishing, 62 West 45th Street, 4th Floor, New York NY 10036. **Tel** (212)764-1471, (800)770-5264, telex 6973364 PLNY. **LC** UNC. **DD** 809.

US/0039-3762
STUDIES IN ROMANTICISM. [Stud. romant.]. **Added/Corp** Boston University. Graduate School. Vol. 1 (Autumn 1961)-. Periodical. English. qt. $55.00 (institution), $20.00 (individual) US. Boston University Scholarly Publications, 881 Commonwealth Avenue, Room 230, Boston MA 02215. **Tel** (617)353-4106. **ED** David Wagenknecht. **LC** PN751; .S8. **DD** 809/.91/4. Index available (bound in 4th issue). **Bk Rev**. **Ad Acc**. available on microfilm and microfiche from University Microfilms International (UMI). Documents available from The Genuine Article, UMI Article Clearinghouse.
Desc: International, interdisciplinary journal of romantic studies.
Ind/Abst Abstr. Engl. Stud.; Acad. Search (Jan. 1993-); Am. Hist. Life (1963-); Annu. Bibliogr. Engl. Lang. Lit.; ARTbibliogr. Mod.; Arts Humanit. Citation Index [Full Cov.]; BHA : Biblio. Hist. Art; Curr. Contents Arts Humanit.; Expand. Acad. Index (1989-); Humanit. Index; Humanit. Source (Jul. 1993-); INFO-SOUTH Abstr.; Lit. Crit. Regist.; Mag. Search; MLA Int. Bibl. Books Artic. Mod. Lang. Lit.; Newsp. Period. Abstr. (1991-); Res. Alert [Full Cov.]; Romant. Move.; Women Stud. Abstr.

NE/0169-0175
STUDIES IN SLAVIC LITERATURE AND POETICS. [Stud. Slav. lit. poet.]. Vol. 1 (1981)-. Monographic series. English. Price varies per volume. Humanities Press, 165 1st Avenue, Atlantic Highlands NJ 07716. **Tel** (908)872-1441, (800)221-3845, FAX (908)872-0717, telex 752233. Index available.
Desc: Studies on Gogol, Dostoevsky and other major figures in Slavic Literature.
Ind/Abst MLA Int. Bibl. Books Artic. Mod. Lang. Lit.

US/1040-5119
STUDIES IN SPECULATIVE FICTION. [Stud. specul. fict.]. No. 1 (1984)-. Monographic series. English. ir. University Microfilms International, 300 North Zeeb Road, Ann Arbor MI 48106-1346. **Tel** (313)761-4700, (800)521-0600 Exts. 2490, 2491, FAX (313)973-1540. **LC** UNC.
Ind/Abst MLA Int. Bibl. Books Artic. Mod. Lang. Lit.

US/0039-3819
STUDIES IN THE LITERARY IMAGINATION. [Stud. literar. imag.]. **Added/Corp** Georgia State University. Dept. of English. Georgia State College. Dept. of English. Vol. 1 (Apr. 1968)-. Periodical. English. Twice a year (Spring & Fall). $10.00 (individuals), $20.00 (institutions) US; $15.00 (individuals), $25.00 (institutions) others. Studies in the Literary Imagination, Department of English, Georgia State University, Atlanta GA 30303. **Tel** (404)651-2900. **ED** Virginia Spencer Carr, R. Barton Palmer, and Matthew Roudane. **LC** PR1; .S84. **DD** 809. available on microfilm and microfiche from University Microfilms International (UMI). Documents available from The Genuine Article, UMI Article Clearinghouse.
Ind/Abst Abstr. Engl. Stud.; Acad. Search (July 1993-); Am. Humanit. Index; Annu. Bibliogr. Engl. Lang. Lit.; Arts Humanit. Citation Index [Full Cov.]; BHA : Biblio. Hist. Art; Child. Lit. Abstr. (19??-); Curr. Contents Arts Humanit.; Expand. Acad. Index (1989-); Film Lit. Index (19??-); Humanit. Index; Humanit. Source (Jul. 1993-); INFO-SOUTH Abstr.; Lit. Crit. Regist.; Mag. Search; MLA Int. Bibl. Books Artic. Mod. Lang. Lit.; Newsp. Period. Abstr. (1991-); Res. Alert [Full Cov.]; Romant. Move.

US/0897-9243
STUDIES IN THE ROMANTIC AGE. [Stud. romant. age]. Vol. 1 (1989)-. Monographic series. English. ir. Price varies per volume. Peter Lang Publishing, 62 West 45th Street, 4th Floor, New York NY 10036. **Tel** (212)764-1471, (800)770-5264, telex 6973364 PLNY. **ED** Charles I. Patterson. **DD** 820. **Pr Rev.**
Desc: Historical and critical works presenting interpretations of primarily major authors and literary currents that appeared between 1770 and 1830.

US/1050-1045
STUDIES IN WEIRD FICTION. [Stud. weird fict.]. **Added/Corp** Necronomicon Press. Vol. 1, No. 1 (Summer 1986)-. Periodical. English. **DD** 810.
Ind/Abst MLA Int. Bibl. Books Artic. Mod. Lang. Lit.; Sci. Fict. Fantasy Book Rev. Index.

●US/1043-8580
STUDIES OF WORLD LITERATURE IN ENGLISH. (1992)-. English. Peter Lang Publishing, 62 West 45th Street, 4th Floor, New York NY 10036. **Tel** (212)764-1471, (800)770-5264, telex 6973364 PLNY.

US/1054-1403
STUDIES ON CERVANTES AND HIS TIMES. [Stud. Cervantes times]. Vol. 1 (1991)-. Monographic series. English. Peter Lang Publishing, 62 West 45th Street, 4th Floor, New York NY 10036. **Tel** (212)764-1471, (800)770-5264, telex 6973364 PLNY. **DD** 860.

US
STUDIES ON LUCETTE DESVIGNES AND THE TWENTIETH CENTURY. **Added/Corp** Societe des Amis de Lucette Desvignes. **VFOAT** SLD. Vol. 1 (1991)-. French (English). New Paradigm Press, 5413 Neilwoods Drive, Knoxville TN 37919. **LC** PQ2664.E84456; Z9.

US/1056-3970
STUDIES ON THEMES AND MOTIFS IN LITERATURE. (1991)-. Monographic series. English. Price varies per volume. Peter Lang Publishing, 62 West 45th Street, 4th Floor, New York NY 10036. **Tel** (212)764-1471, (800)770-5264, telex 6973364 PLNY.

UK/0435-2866
STUDIES ON VOLTAIRE AND THE EIGHTEENTH CENTURY. (STUDIES ON VOLTAIRE AND THE EIGHTEENTH CENTURY / EDITED BY THEODORE BESTERMAN.). [Stud. Voltaire eight. century]. **Added/Corp** Institut et Musee Voltaire. Voltaire Foundation. Vol. 2 (1956)-. Monographic series. English (French). ir. Price varies per volume. Voltaire Foundation, University of Oxford, 99 Banbury Road, Oxford OX2 7RB England. **Tel** 011 44 865 284600, FAX 011 44 865 270740. **ED** Haydn Mason. **LC** PQ2105.A2; S8. Index available. cum. index. ***Continues*** *Travaux sur Voltaire et le Dix-Huitieme Siecle.*
Desc: All aspects of Eighteenth Century culture, literature and history, with particular emphasis upon the European Enlightenment.
Ind/Abst MLA Int. Bibl. Books Artic. Mod. Lang. Lit.; Romant. Move.

RM
STUDII DE LITERATURA ROMANA SI COMPARATA / UNIVERSITATEA DIN TIMISOARA, FACULTATEA DE FILOLOGIE-ISTORIE. **Added/Corp** Universitatea din Timisoara. Facultatea de Filologie-Istorie. Universitatea din Timisoara. Facultatea de Filologie. (1976)-. Periodical. Romanian (summaries and/or abstracts in English, French, German and Russian). **LC** PN9; .S88. **DD** 809.
Ind/Abst Annu. Bibliogr. Engl. Lang. Lit.

RM
STUDII DE LITERATURA UNIVERSALA. **Added/Corp** Societatea de Stiinte Filologice din

Republica Socialista Romaania. (19??)-. Romanian. an. **(Subscription address:** Ilexim Press Department, PO Box 1, 136-1-137, Bucharest, Romania.**)**

SP/0585-766X
STUDIUM (MADRID). (STUDIUM.). [Studium]. **Added/Corp** Estudio General de Teologia (Avila, Spain) Instituto Pontificio de Filosofia de Madrid (Spain) Instituto Pontificio de Teologia de Madrid. Vol. 1/2 (1962)-. Periodical. Spanish. tq. $42.00. Studium, Apartado 61150, 28080 Madrid Spain. **Tel** 011 34 1 3024246. **ED** Vincenzo Cappelletti. **LC** B5; .S8. **Ad Acc. Circ:** 3,000.
Desc: Italian journal of culture and current events.
Ind/Abst BHA : Biblio. Hist. Art; New Testam. Abstr.; Old Testam. Abstr.

GW/0179-2482
STUTTGARTER ARBEITEN ZUR GERMANISTIK. [Stuttg. Arb. Ger.]. **VFOAT** S.A.G. No. 1 (1975)-. Monographic series. Multiple languages (English and German). Price varies per volume. Akademischer Verlag Stuttgart MR Heinz, Steiermarkerstr 132, D-70469 Stuttgart Germany. **Tel** 011 49 711 812413. **ED** Hans-Dieter Heinz. **LC** UNC.
Desc: Monographs, text-books, and editions of German literature (15th century to present) and of general and German linguistics; festschriften and proceedings.
Ind/Abst MLA Int. Bibl. Books Artic. Mod. Lang. Lit.

GW
STUTTGARTER TEXBEITRAGE. No. 1 (1977)-. Monographic series. German. Price varies per volume. Akademischer Verlag Stuttgart MR Heinz, Steiermarkerstr 132, D-70469 Stuttgart Germany. **Tel** 011 49 711 812413.

US/0039-4238
STYLE (FAYETTEVILLE). (STYLE.). [Style]. **Added/Corp** University of Arkansas (Fayetteville Campus) University of Arkansas, Fayetteville. Vol. 1 (Winter 1967)-. Periodical. English. qt. $36.00 (institutions), $24.00 (individuals), $15.00 (students). Northern Illinois University / English, Department of English, Dekalb IL 60115. **Tel** (815)753-6653, (815)753-0611, FAX (815)753-1824. **ED** Harold F Mosher. **LC** PE1; .S89. Index available. **Bk Rev. Ad Acc. Circ:** 600. available on microfilm and microfiche from University Microfilms International (UMI). Documents available from The Genuine Article, UMI Article Clearinghouse.
Desc: Publishes articles, reviews, and bibliographies on stylistics and on the theory and practice of new approaches to literature, especially those dealing closely with texts.
Ind/Abst Abstr. Engl. Stud.; Acad. Search (July 1993-); Am. Bibliogr. Slavic East Europ. Stud.; Arts Humanit. Citation Index [Full Cov.]; Curr. Contents Arts Humanit.; Humanit. Index; Humanit. Source (Jul. 1993-); Index Book Rev. Humanit.; INFO-SOUTH Abstr.; Lang. Lang. Behav. Abstr.; Lit. Crit. Regist.; Mag. Search; MLA Int. Bibl. Books Artic. Mod. Lang. Lit.; Newsp. Period. Abstr. (1991-); Res. Alert [Full Cov.]; Romant. Move.; Soc. Plann. Policy Dev. Abstr.

US/0049-2426
SUB-STANCE. [Sub-stance]. No. 1 (1971)-. Periodical. English (French). Three times a year. $74.00 (one year), $146.00 (two year),$217.00 (three year), institutions; $23.00 (one year), $46.00 (two year), 69.00 (three year) individuals. University of Wisconsin Press, Journal Division, 114 North Murray Street, Madison WI 53715. **Tel** (608)262-4952, FAX (608)262-8909. **ED** Sydney Levy and Michel Pierssens. **LC** PN2; .S82. **DD** 805. **[CCC]**. cum. index. **Bk Rev. Ad Acc. Circ:** 800 (ctrl). available on microfilm and microfiche from University Microfilms International (UMI). Documents available from The Genuine Article.
Desc: An interdisciplinary journal promoting new thoughts by American and European authors which alter the perception of contemporary culture.
Ind/Abst Arts Humanit. Citation Index (19??-19??) [Full Cov.]; Curr. Contents Arts Humanit.; Film Lit. Index; MLA Int. Bibl. Books Artic. Mod. Lang. Lit.; Res. Alert [Full Cov.]; Romant. Move.; Soc. Sci. Cit. Index [Select. Cov.].

II
SUBH-I ADAB. Nov. 1974-. Periodical. Urdu (Urdu). 20.00. Nazir Ahmad Nuri, Mahmood Manzil Gwynne Road, Lakhnau India. **LC** PK2151; .S9.

US/0585-8364
SUCHASNIST. [Sucasnist]. **Added/Corp** Ukrainske Tovarystvo Zakordonnykh Studii (Munich, Germany). **VFOAT** Sucasnist. (1961)-. Periodical. Ukrainian. Twelve times a year. $85.00. Prolog Publishing, PO Box 1084, South Orange NJ 07079. **Tel** (201)414-9877. **LC** AP58.U5; S9. ***Formed by the union of*** *Ukrainska Literaturna Hazeta, 0501-0365* ***and*** *Suchasna Ukraina, 0562-4797.*
Ind/Abst Am. Bibliogr. Slavic East Europ. Stud. (19??-19??); MLA Int. Bibl. Books Artic. Mod. Lang. Lit.

FR/0049-2450
SUD (MARSEILLE). (SUD.). [Sud]. (1970)-. French. Five times a year. 345.00F France; 395.00F other. Sud, 62 rue Sainte, 13001 Marseille France. **Tel** 011 33 91 336068, FAX 011 33 862 280 005.

Desc: The original aim of this journal was to promote and advance poetry, but it has expanded to include all forms of literary expression.

II
SUGANDHA. Periodical. Marathi (Marathi). an. 8.00. Sugandha Prakasana, 271 V Patel Road, Bombay 400004 India. **LC** PK2400; .S83.

SA
SUID-AFRIKAANSE TYDSKRIF VIR AFRIKATALE. **See** Linguistics.

SA
SUID-AFRIKAANSE TYDSKRIF VIR AFRIKATALE. BYBLAD. **Added/Corp** African Language Association of Southern Africa. **VFOAT** South African Journal for African Languages. Supplement; South African Journal of African Languages. Supplement. (1981)-. Afrikaans (English). Four times a year. R76.32 South Africa; $90.00 others. Foundation Education Science & Technology, PO Box 1758, Pretoria 0001 South Africa. **Tel** 011 27 12 3226404, 011 27 12 3225678.

US/0730-305X
SULFUR (PASADENA, CALIF.). (SULFUR.). [Sulfur]. **Added/Corp** California Institute of Technology. Eastern Michigan University. (1981)-. Periodical. English. Twice a year. $14.00 individual, $20.00 institution. Sulfur, 210 Washtenaw Avenue, Ypsilanti MI 48197. **Tel** (313)483-9787, FAX (313)483-9787. **ED** Clayton Eshleman. **LC** PS501; .S84. **DD** 810/.8. **Bk Rev**, (Qty: 15). **Ad Acc, Adv Mgr:** Caryl Eshleman, **Tel** same as publisher. **Circ:** 2,000.
Desc: A literary of the whole art.
Ind/Abst Am. Humanit. Index; Book Rev. Index (1986-); Index Am. Period. Verse.

US/0744-9666
SUN (CHAPEL HILL, N.C.). (THE SUN.). [Sun]. 11th (Nov. 1975)-. Periodical. English. mo. $32.00. The Sun / North Carolina, 107 North Roberson Street, Chapel Hill NC 27516. **Tel** (919)942-5282, FAX (919)932-3101. **ED** Sy Safransky. **LC** AP2; .S952. **DD** 051. **Circ:** 25,000 (ctrl). available on microfilm from University Microfilms International (UMI); available on microfiche. ***Continues*** *Chapel Hill Sun.*
Desc: A journal of ideas, which publishes a wide range of essays, interviews, fiction and poetry.

●US/1062-6387
SUN DANCER REVIEW. (1992)-. Periodical. English. qt. $40.00 (institutions), $20.00 (individuals) US; $50.00 (institutions), $30.00 (individuals) Canada and Mexico; $80.00 (institutions), $40.00 (individuals) other. Curtis Publications Inc., PO Box 23626, Santa Barbara CA 93121. **Bk Rev**, (Qty: (varies)).
Desc: Contains non-fiction, short stories, reviews, essays, poetry, and novel excerpts from both new and experienced writers.

US/0735-7133
SUN DOG. [Sun dog]. **Added/Corp** Florida State University. Poetry/Arts Co-op. Florida State University. Student Writing Association. **VFOAT** Sundog. Vol. 1 (Spring 1979)-. Periodical. English. sa. $8.00 individuals; $10.00 institutions. Florida State University / Sun Dog, 406 Williams Building, Tallahassee FL 32306. **Tel** (904)644-4230. **LC** PS501; .S844. **DD** 810.8/0005.

US/0300-788X
SUN TRACKS. **VFOAT** Suntracks. Began publication with Vol. 1, No. 1 (June 1971)-. Periodical. English. ir. $5.00. Sun Tracks, University of Arizona Press, 1230 North Park Avenue/#102, Tucson AZ 85719. **LC** PS501; .S85. **DD** 810/.8/0054.

CN/0384-8248
SUNYATA (VICTORIA). (SUNYATA.). Vol. 1 (May 1976)-. Periodical. English. qt. $9.00. Sunyata Press, Box 278, Brentwood Bay British Columbia V0S 1A0 Canada. **DD** C810/.8/0054.

FI
SUOMALAIS-UGRILAISEN SEURAN AIKAKAUSKIRJA. **Main/Corp** Suomalais-Ugrilainen Seura. **VFOAT** Journal de la Societe Finno-Ougrienne. Vol. 1 (1886)-. Finnish (German, English and French). ir. Akakeeminen-Kirjakuppa, PO Box 128, 00101 Helsinki Finland. **Tel** 011/358/0/90/12141, FAX +358 0 121 4441, telex 125080 AKAHE SF. **LC** PH1.

FI
SUOMALAISEN KIRJALLISUUDEN SEURAN TOIMITUKSIA. **Added/Corp** Suomalaisen Kirjallisuuden Seura. (18??)-. Monographic series. Finnish.
Ind/Abst MLA Int. Bibl. Books Artic. Mod. Lang. Lit.

US/0739-2419
SUPPLIERS DIRECTORY (COLORADO SPRINGS, COLO.). **See** Religion and Theology.

II
SURA SAURABHA. Periodical. Hindi (Hindi). qt. Rs12.00. Sur Smarak Mandal, 15/230 Bhagatsingh Dvar, Agra 282002 India. **LC** PK1967.9.S9; Z873.

II
SUSA. Periodical. Marathi (Marathi). 2.50. Schroedel Schulbuchverlag, Postfach 810555, Hildesheimer Str 202, 3000 Hannover 81 Germany. **Tel** 011 49 511 83880. **LC** PK2400; .S86.

CI/0350-221X
SUVREMENA METODIKA NASTAVE HRVATSKOGA JEZIKA. **See** Linguistics.

II
SVAKALA. **VFOAT** Swakal. Periodical. Bengali (Bengali). Rs3.00. Provash das Panagarh Bazar, Panagarh, Burdwan 713148 India. **LC** PK1700; .S93.

DK/0106-5378
SVANTEVIT. **See** Linguistics.

SW/0039-6443
SVENSK BOKFORTECKNING. **See** Literature-Abstracting, Bibliographies and Statistics.

SW/0039-663X
SVENSK LITTERATURTIDSKRIFT. [Sven. litteraturtidskr.]. **Added/Corp** Samfundet De Nio. Vol. 1 (1938)-. Periodical. Swedish. Four times a year (Mar., June, Sept., Dec.). $7.70 Sweden; $9.10 others. Professor Knut Ahnland, Parkvagen 50, 183 51 Taby Sweden. **LC** PT9201; .S65. **DD** 839.7/09.
Ind/Abst Annu. Bibliogr. Engl. Lang. Lit.; MLA Int. Bibl. Books Artic. Mod. Lang. Lit.

RU
SVERSTNIKI. (1977)-. Russian. an. 0.75rub. Izdatelstvo Sovremennik, G-351 Iartsevskaia 4, 121351 Moscow Russia. **LC** PG3021; .S835.

XR/0862-8440
SVET LITERATURY. (19??)-. Czech. an. $58.00. John Benjamins BV, Amsteldijk 44, PO Box 75577, 1070 AN Amsterdam Netherlands. **Tel** 011 31 20 6738156, FAX 011 31 20 739773. **(Subscription address:** John Benjamins North America, PO Box 27519, Philadelphia PA 19118-0519.**) ED** Milos Havelka, Jiri Holy, Anna Houskova, Zdenek Hrbata, Pavla Lidmilova, Vladimir Novotny, Martin Prochazka, Zdenek Stribrny.

XR/0039-7075
SVETOVA LITERATURA. [Svet. lit.]. (1956)-. Periodical. Czech. bm.
Ind/Abst Annu. Bibliogr. Engl. Lang. Lit.

US/1045-7682
SWAMP ROOT. [Swamp root]. Vol. 1, No. 1 (Jan. 1988)-. Periodical. English. Three times a year (Apr., Aug., Dec.). $12.00 (individuals), $15.00 (institutions). Swamp Root, Rt 2 Box 1098, Hiwassee One, Jacksboro TN 37757. **Tel** (615)562-7082. **LC** WMLC L 83/6832. **DD** 810.
Ind/Abst Am. Humanit. Index (199?-); Index Am. Period. Verse.

PL/0491-8193
SWIERSZCZYK. (1945)-. Periodical. Polish. Twenty-six times a year. $39.00. **(Subscription address:** ARS Polona, PO Box 1001, 00068 Warsaw Poland.**) UDC** 82-93.

GW
SWIFT STUDIES : THE ANNUAL OF THE EHRENPREIS CENTER. **Added/Corp** Ehrenpreis Institut fuer Swift Studien. Foerderkreis. (1986)-. English. DM67.50, DM40.00 (students). Westfalische Wilhelm University, Johannisstr 12 20, D 48143 Meunster Germany.
Ind/Abst Annu. Bibliogr. Engl. Lang. Lit.; MLA Int. Bibl. Books Artic. Mod. Lang. Lit.

US/1043-1497
SYCAMORE REVIEW. [Sycamore rev.]. **Added/Corp** Purdue University. Dept. of English. Vol. 1, No. 1 (Spring 1989)-. Periodical. English. sa (Jan. & June). $9.00 US; $11.00 other. Sycamore Review, Purdue University, English Department, West Lafayette IN 47907. **Tel** (317)494-3783, FAX (317)494-3780. **ED** Michael S. Manley. **LC** PS501; .S97. **DD** 810.8/0005. Index available. cum. index (for first 5 volumes). **Bk Rev**, (Qty: 6). **Circ:** 1,000.
Desc: A literary journal featuring new and unpublished poetry, fiction, essay, and translation.

AT/0156-5419
SYDNEY STUDIES IN ENGLISH. [Syd. stud. Engl.]. **Added/Corp** University of Sydney. Dept. of English. English Association. Sydney Branch. Vol.1 (1975/76)-. English. an. 8.50Aus$. Sydney Studies in English, University of Sydney Department of English, New South Wales 2006 Australia. **Tel** 011 61 2 692 2432, FAX 011 61 2 692 4203. **ED** G A Wilkes and A P Riemer. **Circ:** 1,200.
Desc: Critical essays on literature and drama.
Ind/Abst Abstr. Engl. Stud.; APAIS, Aust. Public Aff. Inf. Ser. (1985-); MLA Int. Bibl. Books Artic. Mod. Lang. Lit.

Literature

CN/0823-2458
SYMPOSIUM / DEUTSCHKANADISCHE STUDIEN. **Main/Corp** German Canadian Studies (Association). Vol. 1 (1976)-. German (English and French). sa. varies. Etudes Allemandes Departement de Litteratures Langues Modernes, University de Montreal, PO Box 6128 Station A, Montreal Quebec H3C 3J7 Canada. **ED** Karen R Gurttler and Friedhelm Lach. **DD** C830/.9. **Pr Rev. Circ:** 300.
Desc: Proceedings of the symposia on German-Canadian studies published as annals German-Canadian studies.

IT
SYNESIS. *Ceased.* (19??)-No. 2. qt. Istra, Via Brentano 2, 20121 Milan Italy. **(Subscription address:** Istra via Brentano,2, 20121 Milano Italy) Index available. cum. index. **Bk Rev. Circ:** 2,000.

FI/0359-5242
SYNTEESI JYVASKYLA. **VFOAT** Synteesi. (1982)-. Periodical. Finnish. qt. Suomen Taidekasvatuksen Tutkimusseura, Jyvaskylan Yliopiston Taidekasvatuksen Laitos, Jyvaskyla Finland. **UDC** 82. **CODEN** 37.036.
Ind/Abst BHA : Biblio. Hist. Art.

RM/0256-7245
SYNTHESIS (BUCURESTI). (SYNTHESIS.). [Synthesis]. **Main/Corp** Comitetul National Pentru Literatura Comparata. (1974)-. English (French, German, Italian, Russian and Spanish). an. $53.00 North America and Asia; $50.00 Europe; $63.00 other. **(Subscription address:** Orion Press SRL, SPL Independentei 202-A, Bucharest 6 Romania.) **LC** PN855; .C6413.
Ind/Abst Am. Hist. Life (1977-); BHA : Biblio. Hist. Art; Chem Inform; MLA Int. Bibl. Books Artic. Mod. Lang. Lit.

SZ
SZENE. Periodical. German. qt. Deutscher Judo Verband, Redaktion Ippon Segegewaldweg 40, D 12557 Berlin Germany. **Tel** 011 49 711 210770, telex 051 678. **LC** PN2004; .S93.

US/0270-5508
SZIVARVANY. **VFOAT** Rainbow. Vol. 1 (July 1980)-. Periodical. Hungarian. Three times a year. $22.00. Framo Publishing, 561 West Diversey Parkway, Chicago IL 60614. **LC** PH3001; .S94.
Ind/Abst Am. Bibliogr. Slavic East Europ. Stud. (19??-19??).

FR/0761-8239
T.E.M. TEXTE EN MAIN. (TEXTE EN MAIN : TEM.). [T.E.M. Texte en main]. **VFOAT** TEM. Vol. 1 (Spring 1984)-. Periodical. French. Twice a year. 290.00F France; 350.00F other. L'Atelier du Texte Librairie, 2 Place Docteur Leon Martin, 38000 Grenoble France. **Tel** 011 33 76 736684.

FR
TABLE RONDE. CAHIERS, LA. Winter 1973-. Periodical. French. Les Editions de la Table Ronde, France. **LC** PQ1100; .T3. **DD** 840/.8/00914.

VM
TAC PHAM MI. Periodical. Vietnamese. ir. Xunhasaba Exports and Imports, 7 Nguyen Thi Minh Khai Str, Dit 1 Ho Chi Minh City Vietnam. **Tel** 011 84 8 294893, telex 278 XUNHASABA. **LC** PL4378; .A38.

CH
TAI-WAN HSIAO SHUO HSUAN / YEH SHIH-TAO CHU PIEN. **VFOAT** Tai-Wan Hsiao Shuo Nien Hsuan. (1982)-. Periodical. Chinese. an. ¥100. Chien Wei Chu Pan She, PO Box 652555, Taipei Taiwan. **LC** PL3031.T32; T3279. **DD** 895.1/35/080951249.

CH
TAI-WAN SAN WEN HSUAN / CHI CHI CHU PIEN. **VFOAT** Tai-Wan San Wen Nien Hsuan. (1982)-. Periodical. Chinese. **LC** PL3031.T32; T32873. **DD** 895.1/45/080951249.

CH
TAI-WAN SHIH HSUAN / WU SHENG CHU PIEN. Periodical. Chinese. an. NT$90.00. Chien Wei Chu Pan She, PO Box 652555, Taipei Taiwan. **LC** PL3031.T32; T32895. **DD** 895.1/15/080951249.

NZ/0114-4138
TAKAHE CHRISTCHURCH. (TAKAHE.). [Takahe Christch.]. **VFOAT** Takahe Magazine. (1989)-. Periodical. English (Maori). qt. 24.00NZ$ New Zealand; 32.00NZ$ (surface mail); 48.00NZ$ (airmail) North America; 32.00NZ$ (surface mail), 51.50NZ$ (airmail) Europe; 32.00NZ$ (surface mail), 36.00NZ$ (airmail) Australia. Takahe Publishing Collective, PO Box 13-335, Christchurch 1 New Zealand. **Tel** 03-3558-337. **ED** Sandra Arnold, Bernadette Hall, David Howard, Ray Mutton and Tony Scanlan. **DD** _a820.8002. **Ad Acc. Pr Rev. Continues** *Cornucopia (Christchurch), 0113-2644.*
Desc: Aims to promote younger writers by publishing them alongside their established contemporaries.

US/0743-1384
TALK OF THE MONTH. Periodical. English. mo. $120.00. IDHHB Inc, PO Box 370, Nevada City CA 95959. **Tel** (916)477-1116, FAX (916)265-4321. **ED** Linda Corrivean, Della Heywood and Iven Lourie. Index available. cum. index. **Circ:** 200 (ctrl). available on audiocassette.
Desc: Transcriptions of contemporary talks by E.J. Gold and others on topics in metaphysics, transformation, shamanism, mysticism, inner awakening and related practices.

ER
TALLIN. **Added/Corp** Eesti NSV Kirjanike Liit. Estonian S. S. R. Kultuuriministeerium. (1978)-. Periodical. Russian. bm. $17.00. Piarnuskee Shosse, 200001 Estonskaia SSR, 6 Tallin Estonia. **LC** PG3504.E8; T35.

ER
TALLINSKIE TETRADI. (1???)-. Periodical. Russian. ir. 1.20rub. Eesti Raamat / Estonian Book, Parnu Mnt 10, Tallin EE0090 Estonia. **Tel** 0142 443 937. **LC** PG3227; .T28.

NE
TALMON STUDIES IN BIBLICAL LITERATURE. (19??)-. Monographic series. English. ir. Price varies per volume. E. J. Brill, Postbus 9000, 2300 PA Leiden Netherlands. **Tel** 011 31 71 312624, FAX 011 31 71 317532, telex 39296 BRILL NL.

US/1059-3527
TAMPA BAY REVIEW CHAPBOOK SERIES. [Tampa Bay Rev. chapbook ser.]. No. 1 (1991)-. Monographic series. English. $6.00. Tampa Bay Review, Inc., 5458 North Rivershore Drive, Tampa FL 33603. **DD** 810.

NP
TANASENA. **VFOAT** Tansen. V. 1, No. 1 (June/July/August 2035 Sept./Dec. 1978)-. Periodical. Nepali (Nepali). qt (irregular). RS2.00. **LC** PK2598.Z9; P347.

CC
TANG TAI (PEKING, CHINA). (TANG TAI / JEN MIN WEN HSUEH CHU PAN SHE PIEN CHI.). **Added/Corp** Jen Min Wen Hsueh Chu Pan She. **VFOAT** Dang Dai; Dangdai. (July 1979)-. Periodical. Chinese. bm. $23.10. **(Subscription address:** China International Book Trading Corporation, PO Box 399, Library Service Department, Beijing 100044 People's Republic of China.) **LC** PL2250; .T36. **DD** 895.1/09/005.
Desc: Covers Chinese literature.

CC
TANG TAI WEN HSUEH. **VFOAT** Dang Dai Wen Xue. V. 1 (July 1981)-. Periodical. Chinese. qt. RMBY1.00. Kuang-Tung Sheng Hsin Hua Shu Tien, Canton, People's Republic of China. **LC** PN779.C5; T36. **DD** 895.1/08/005.

CC
TANG TAI WEN HSUEH LUN TSUNG / HSI PEI TA HSUEH CHUNG WEN HSI TANG TAI WEN HSUEH YEN CHIU SHIH, HSI PEI TA HSUEH HSUEH PAO PIEN CHI PU PIEN. **VFOAT** Tang Tai Wen Hsueh. Periodical. Chinese. RMBY1.05. Hsin Hua Shu Tien / Shang-Hai Fa Hsing So, Shanghai, People's Republic of China. **LC** PL2291; .T36. **DD** 895.1/09/003. **Continues** *Tang Tai Wen Hseuh (Sian, China).*

●CN/1189-4563
TANGENCE. [Tangence]. (Mar 1992)-. Periodical. French. qt. 28.00Can$ per year. Tangence, 300 Allee des Ursulines, Rimouski Quebec G5L 3A1 Canada. **DD** 840/.5. **Continues** *Urgences., 0226-9554.*

KO
TANGUK MUNHAK. 1982-. Periodical. Korean. W3,500. Tanguk Munhakhoe San 8, Hannam-dong Yongsan-ku, Seoul South Korea. **LC** PL969.8; .T36.

VM/0404-6928
TAP CHI VAN HOC. Periodical. Vietnamese. bm. Xunhasaba Exports and Imports, 7 Nguyen Thi Minh Khai Str, Dit 1 Ho Chi Minh City Vietnam. **Tel** 011 84 8 294893, telex 278 XUNHASABA. **LC** PL4378; .A39.
Ind/Abst Math. Rev.

US/0887-9257
TAPROOT. [Taproot]. **Added/Corp** Suffolk County (N.Y.) Office for the Aging. Taproot Workshops, Inc. Vol. 1, No. 1 (Winter 1974/1975)-. English. Twice a year (Apr., & Nov.). $12.00. State University of New York at Stony Brook, Fine Arts Center 4290, Stony Brook NY 11794. **Tel** (516)632-7250, FAX (516)632-7261. **ED** Philip W. Quigg and Enid Graf. **DD** 810. **Ad Acc. Circ:** 1,500.
Desc: Anthology of senior writing by the most proficient members of the workshops.

NP
TARAKHARA : BHO. JI. SAM. SA. ANERASVAVIYU KO MUKHAPATRA. V. 1, No. 1-. Nepali (Nepali). Rs4.00. Bhojpur District Coordination Committee of all Nepal National Independent Students' Union, Kathmandu Nepal. **LC** PK2598.A2; T37.

RU/0206-4251
TAVAN ATAL. **Added/Corp** Chavash Pisatelesen Soiuze. **VFOAT** Rodnaia Volga. (1931)-. Periodical. Chuvash. mo. $109.95. Izdatelstvo Chuvashskogo Obkoma KPSS, 428019, Cheboksary, Prospekt Ivana Iakoveleva, 13, Cheboksary. **(Subscription address:** East View Publications Inc., 3020 Harbor Lane North, Suite 110, Minneapolis MN 55447.) **LC** PL384.A2; T38.

II
TAY. **VFOAT** Thai. (19??)-. Periodical. Tamil (Tamil). wk. 1.00. K Ravindran, 34 Nelson Manickam Street, Madras 600029 India. **LC** PL4758.45; .T37.

US/0739-0084
TEACHERS & WRITERS. [Teach. writ.]. **Added/Corp** Teachers & Writers Collaborative. **VFOAT** Teachers and Writers. Vol. 13, No. 1 (Sept./Oct. 1981)-. Periodical. English. Five times a year (Sept./Oct., Nov./Dec., Jan./Feb., Mar./Apr., May/June). $15.00 (one year), $26.00 (two years), $37.00 (three years) US; $17.50 (one year), $31.00 (two years), $44.50 (three years) Canada (including postage); $20.00 (one year), $36.00 (two years), $52.00 (three years) other (including postage). Teachers Writers Collaborative, 5 Union Square West, New York NY 10003. **Tel** (212)691-6590. **ED** Ron Padgett. **LC** LB1576; .T373. **DD** 372.6. Index available. cum. index. **Bk Rev. Circ:** 2,000 (ctrl). available on microfilm from University Microfilms International (UMI). **Continues** *Teachers & Writers Magazine, 0146-3381.*
Desc: Publishes articles on all aspects of teaching creative writing. Appropriate for K-12 and college level.
Ind/Abst Curr. Index J. Educ. (March 1990).

●US/1063-5092
TEACHING AND LEARNING LITERATURE WITH CHILDREN AND YOUNG ADULTS. See Education-Teaching and Curriculum.

GW
TEATRO DEL SIGLO DE ORO. ESTUDIOS DE LITERATURA. **VFOAT** Estudios de Literatura. (1984)-. Monographic series. Spanish.
Ind/Abst MLA Int. Bibl. Books Artic. Mod. Lang. Lit.

CN/0712-4627
TECHNOSTYLE. [Technostyle]. Vol. 1, No. 1 (1982). Periodical. English (French). Twice a year. 25.00Can$. CATTW, University of Western Ontario, c/o Department of English, London Ontario N6A 3K7. **ED** Anne Parker. **DD** 808/.0666. **Bk Rev. Pr Rev. Circ:** 150 (ctrl).

US/1061-2254
TEE SHORTS. *Title Change.* [Tee shorts]. **Added/Corp** Art Puppies Shoot Pool (Firm) Blithar (Firm). (1991)-(1992). Monographic series. English. Art Puppies Shoot Pool, 34 Walnut #3, Watertown MA 02172. **Tel** (617)923-8144. **DD** 813. **Continued by** *Cotton Quarterly, 1063-5084.*

PL/0867-0633
TEKSTY DRUGIE. **Added/Corp** Instytut Badan Literackich (Polska Akademia Nauk). (1990)-. Periodical. Polish. bm. **(Subscription address:** ARS Polona, PO Box 1001, 00068 Warsaw Poland.) **LC** PN9; .T44. **Continues** *Teksty, 0324-8208.*

IS
TEL AVIV REVIEW (TEL AVIV, ISRAEL : 1988). *Suspended.* See Religion and Theology-Judaism.

SP
TEMAS DE LA LITERATURA INFANTIL. (19??)-. Spanish. an. 300ptas. INLE, Calle Santiago Rusignol 8, 28040 Madrid Spain. **Tel** 011 34 91 5330802.

US/1055-7644
TEMPORARY CULTURE. [Tempor. cult.]. 5 (Mar. 1991)-. Periodical. English. $5.00 (single issue). Temporary Culture, PO Box 8180, New York NY 10116-4650. **DD** 808. **Continues** *Newsletter of Temporary Culture.*

FR
TEMPS MELES, DOCUMENTS QUENEAU. **VFOAT** Temps Meles. (Spring 1978)-. Periodical. French. qt. $34.00. Andre Blavier, 23 Place du General Jacques, 4800 Verviers Belgium. **Tel** 011 32 87 223385. **Continues** *Temps Meles.*

US/0197-890X
TENDRIL. *Ceased.* [Tendril]. Began with Winter (1977)-Ceased (19??). Periodical. English. Three times a year. Tendril, Box 512, Green Harbor MA 02041. **Tel** (617)834-4137. **ED** George Murphy. **LC** PS615; .T39. **DD** 811/.008. **Ad Acc. Circ:** 1,800.
Desc: Fiction and poetry.
Ind/Abst Am. Humanit. Index (-19??); Index Am. Period. Verse.

MY/0126-6373
TENGGARA. [Tenggara]. No. 1 (1967)-. Multiple languages (English, Indonesian and Malay). sa. £13.00

institutions; £10.00 individuals. Yayasan Penataran Ilmu, Jalan Lapangan Terbang, 50460 Kuala Lumpur Malaysia. **Tel** 011 60 3 2483414. **LC** PJ1; .T45.
Desc: Contributions from writers in Southeast Asian countries.
Ind/Abst MLA Int. Bibl. Books Artic. Mod. Lang. Lit.

IC
TENINGUR. (1985)-. Periodical. Icelandic.
Ind/Abst BHA : Biblio. Hist. Art.

US/0497-2384
TENNESSEE STUDIES IN LITERATURE. [Tenn. stud. lit.]. **Added/Corp** Tennessee Philological Association. University of Tennessee (Knoxville Campus). Vol. 1 (1956)-. Monographic series. English. ir. Price varies per volume. University of Tennessee Press, PO Box 6525, Ithaca NY 14850. **Tel** (800)621-2736, (312)568-1550. **(Subscription address:** University of Chicago Press, 11030 South Langley Avenue, Chicago, IL 60628, telephone: (607)277-2211**)** **LC** PS1; .T43; PS1; .T4 subser. **DD** 809. available on microfilm and microfiche from University Microfilms International (UMI).
Desc: Contains information of papers selected from the 51st annual meeting of the Tennessee Philological Association in 1956.
Ind/Abst Abstr. Engl. Stud.; Am. Humanit. Index; Annu. Bibliogr. Engl. Lang. Lit.; MLA Int. Bibl. Books Artic. Mod. Lang. Lit.; Romant. Move.

UK
TENNYSON SOCIETY MONOGRAPHS. **Added/Corp** Tennyson Society. No. 1 (1969)-. Monographic series. English. Tennyson Society, Free School Lane, Lincoln LN2 1EZ England. **Tel** 44 0522 552866. **LC** PR5579; .T45.
Ind/Abst MLA Int. Bibl. Books Artic. Mod. Lang. Lit.

II
TENOR. (June 1978)-. Periodical. English. sa. M Sivaramkrishna Editor, Tenor 2-2-1137/4/2 Prashantnagar, Hyderabad 500 004 AP India. **Tel** 0842-237026. **ED** M Sivaramkrishna, Alladi Uma, Rama Nair, Sabiha Kamaluddin and Tuton Mukherjee. **LC** PR9480; .T46. **DD** 820/.5. **Bk Rev**. **Ad Acc**. **Circ:** 200.

US/0890-3352
TENSO. (TENSO : BULLETIN OF THE SOCIETE GUILHEM IX.). [Tenso]. **Added/Corp** Societe Guilhem IX. Vol. 1, No. 1 & 2 (1986)-. Bulletin. English (French, Spanish, Italian, German and Catalan). Twice a year (May & Nov.). $20.00 (institutions); $15.00 (individuals); $10.00 (students) US & Canada; $12.00 others. Societe Guilhem IX, E. W. Poe, Tulane University, Department of French & Italian, New Orleans LA 70118. **DD** 849.
Ind/Abst MLA Int. Bibl. Books Artic. Mod. Lang. Lit.

NE/0921-2523
TEORIA LITERARIA, TEXTO Y TEORIA. (1987)-. Monographic series. Spanish (English). ir. Price varies per volume. Editions Rodopi BV, Keizersgracht 302-304, 1016 Ex Amsterdam Netherlands. **Tel** 011 31 20 6227507, FAX 011 31 20 380948. **ED** Iris Zavala. Index available. **Circ:** 500.
Desc: Collects the most important theoretical statements on such topics as: readers and the reading process; intertextuality, metaphor, and semiotics.
Ind/Abst MLA Int. Bibl. Books Artic. Mod. Lang. Lit.

CN/0822-3394
TERMINUS (MONTREAL). (TERMINUS.). [Terminus]. **VFOAT** Revue Terminus. Vol. 1, No. 1 (Feb. 1984)-. Periodical. French. bm. $10.00. Revue Terminus, CP 157 Succursale C, Montreal Quebec H2L 4K1 Canada. **DD** C840/.8/0054.

AT/1031-3001
TERROR AUSTRALIS: THE AUSTRALIAN HORROR & FANTASY MAGAZINE. [Terror Aust.]. (1988)-. Periodical. English. qt. 25.00Aus$ Australia; 31.00Aus$ (surface mail), 37.00Aus$ (airmail) other. R'Lyeh Texts, PO Box A281, Sydney New South Wales 2000 Australia. **Tel** 560-0954. **ED** Leigh D Blackmore, C G C Sequeira and B J Stevens. **DD** 823.305. **Bk Rev**. **Ad Acc**. **Circ:** 300 (ctrl).

CN/0840-4631
TESSERA (BURNABY). (TESSERA : DIALOGUE, CONVERSATION, UNE ECRITURE A DEUX.). [Tessera]. Vol. 5 (Sept. 1988)-. Periodical. English (French). Twice a year (Summer & Winter). 22.00Can$ Canada; 24.00Can$ other. Tessera / Department of English, 350 Stong / York University, 4700 Keele Street, Downsview Ontario M3J 1P3 Canada. **Tel** (416)736-5766, (416)469-1219, FAX (416)736-5412. **ED** Katherine Bintrammer, Anne-Marie Ganthier, Jennifer Henderson and Leanne Moyers. **DD** C810/.8/09287. Index available. cum. index. **Ad Acc**, **Adv Mgr:** Jennifer Henderson. **Circ:** 500 (ctrl).
Desc: A bilingual feminist literary journal publishing experimental writing/criticism informed by post-structuralist theory. Each issue is organized around a single topic with artwork featured. Some attention is paid to the other arts. The first journal in Canada to publish women's writing in both English and French that is informed by post-structuralist theory--experimental, language-centered writing that breaks down traditional boundaries between theory and practice in new modes of writing which foreground the reflexive possibilities of "writing" and the creative possibilities of "criticism". Founded in 1982 as a collective to provide a continuing forum for such theoretically informed writing, it has sustained a dialogue between French and English-speaking women writers and theorists. This interchange at the crossroads of French and American feminist discourses has encouraged innovation in the area of feminist engagement with the symbolic which is one of the most exciting fields of contemporary feminist theory.

IT
TESTI E COMMENTI. **VFOAT** Texts and Commentaries. V. 1 (1975)-. Monographic series. English (Italian). ir. Price varies per volume. Edizioni dell'Ateno, Casella Postale 7216, 00100 Rome Italy. **Tel** 759-3456.

IT
TESTI E DOCUMENTI DE LETTERATURA E DI LINGUA. (1976)-. Monographic series. Italian. Price varies per volume. Salerno Editrice, Via di Donna Olimpia 20, 00152 Rome Italy. **Tel** 011 39 6 58205684 or 688, FAX 06-53-15-688. Index available.

IT
TESTI E STUDI UMANISTICI. 1983-. Monographic series. Italian. Price varies per volume.

IT
TESTO A FRONTE : RIVISTA SEMESTRALE DI TEORIA E PRATICA DELLA TRADUZIONE LETTERARIA. No. 1 (Oct. 1989)-. Periodical. Italian. sa (2 issues). L43000.00 Italy; L65000.00 other. Edizioni Angelo Guerini e Association, Via Amatore Sciesa 7, 20135 Milan Italy. **Tel** 011 39 2 5469589, FAX 011 39 2 55191053. **LC** PN241.A1; T39. **DD** 418/.02/05.

US/0040-4691
TEXAS STUDIES IN LITERATURE AND LANGUAGE. [Texas stud. lit. lang.]. **Added/Corp** University of Texas at Austin. University of Texas. **VFOAT** TSLL. Vol. 1 (Spring 1959)-. Periodical. English. qt. $43.00 (institutions), $26.00 (individuals) US; add $6.00 postage other. University of Texas Press, PO Box 7819, Austin TX 78713. **Tel** (512)471-4531, FAX (512)320-0668, telex 776453 UTEXPRES AUS. **ED** William Scheick and Jerome Bump. **LC** AS30; .T4. **DD** 820.5. **[CCC]**. Index available. **Bk Rev**. **Ad Acc**. **Circ:** 950 (ctrl). available on microfilm and microfiche from University Microfilms International (UMI). Documents available from The Genuine Article, UMI Article Clearinghouse. ***Supersedes** Texas Studies in English, 0364-8656.*
Desc: Journal of literary criticism publishing essays reflecting a variety of critical approaches and covering all periods of literary history.
Ind/Abst Abstr. Engl. Stud.; Acad. Search (July 1993-); Annu. Bibliogr. Engl. Lang. Lit.; Arts Humanit. Citation Index [Full Cov.]; BHA : Biblio. Hist. Art; Child. Lit. Abstr. (19??-); Curr. Contents Arts Humanit.; Expand. Acad. Index (1989-); Humanit. Index; Humanit. Source (Jul. 1993-); INFO-SOUTH Abstr.; Lit. Crit. Regist.; Mag. Search; MLA Int. Bibl. Books Artic. Mod. Lang. Lit.; Newsp. Period. Abstr. (1991-); Res. Alert [Full Cov.]; Romant. Move.; Soc. Plann. Policy Dev. Abstr.; Sociol. Abstr.

US/0892-5186
TEXAS TELLER QUARTERLY NEWSLETTER. **Added/Corp** Texas Storytellers Guild. **VFOAT** Texas Teller. (1986)-. Newsletter. English. bm. $25.00. Tejas Storytelling Association, Box 2806, Denton TX 76202. **Tel** (817)387-8336, FAX (817)387-8336. **ED** Finley Stewart. **DD** 808. **Bk Rev**, (Qty: 6). **Ad Acc**. **Circ:** 500 (ctrl).

US
TEXAS WRITER'S NEWSLETTER. **Added/Corp** Texas Association of Creative Writing Teachers. No. 1 (1974)-. Periodical. English. Twice a year (Spring & Fall). $7.50. Texas Writer Newsletter, Central Texas Studies, PO Box 13016, Denton TX 76203. **Tel** (817)565-2124.

DK/0105-7014
TEXT & KONTEXT. **See** Linguistics.

GW/0040-5329
TEXT + KRITIK. [Text + Krit.]. **VFOAT** Text und Kritik. No. 1 (1963)-. Periodical. German. qt (4 issues). DM63.00. Edition Text & Kritik GmbH, Levelingstrasse 6A, Postfach 800529, D 81605 Munich Germany. **Tel** 011 49 89 432929, FAX 011 49 89 433997. **ED** Heinz Ludwig Arnold. **LC** PN4; .T45. **Ad Acc**. Documents available from The Genuine Article.
Desc: Texts, interpretations and critique. Each volume is dedicated to one contemporary author of the German literature with previously unpublished texts by that author plus interpretation and analysis.
Ind/Abst Arts Humanit. Citation Index [Full Cov.]; Curr. Contents Arts Humanit.; MLA Int. Bibl. Books Artic. Mod. Lang. Lit.; Res. Alert [Full Cov.]; Romant. Move.

GW/0563-3079
TEXTE DES SPATEN MITTELALTERS UND DER FRUHEN NEUZEIT. (1963)-. Monographic series. German. ir. Price varies per volume. Erich Schmidt Verlag GmbH, Postfach 304240, D 10724 Berlin Germany. **Tel** 011 49 30 25008525. **ED** Karl Stackmann and Stanley N Werbow. ***Continues** Texte des Spaten Mittelalters.*
Desc: Literature of the Middle Ages.
Ind/Abst MLA Int. Bibl. Books Artic. Mod. Lang. Lit.

GW/0082-3589
TEXTE UND UNTERSUCHUNGEN ZUR GESCHICHTE DER ALTCHRISTLICHEN LITERATUR. (1883)-. Monographic series. German. ir. Price varies per volume. Akademie-Verlag GmbH, Muehlenstrasse 33 34, D 13162 Berlin Germany. **Tel** 011 49 30 47889300, FAX 011 49 30 47889357. **(Subscription address:** VCH Publishers Inc., 303 Northwest 12th Avenue, Journals Department, Deerfield FL 33442.**)**
Ind/Abst MLA Int. Bibl. Books Artic. Mod. Lang. Lit.

GW/0174-0474
TEXTE ZUR FORSCHUNG. [Texte Forsch.]. (1971)-. Monographic series. German. ir. Wissenschaftliche Buchgesellschaft, Hindenburgstr 40, D 64295 Darmstadt Germany. **UDC** 001.
Ind/Abst MLA Int. Bibl. Books Artic. Mod. Lang. Lit.

FR/0248-4579
TEXTES ET LANGAGES. Periodical. French. Dunod Gauthier Villars, 15 rue Gossin, 92543 Montrouge cedex France. **Tel** 011 33 1 46 56 52 66, FAX 011 33 1 46 57 40 69. **(Subscription address:** Centrale des Revues, 11 rue Gossin, Gauthier Villars, 92543, Montrouge Cedex France**)**
Ind/Abst MLA Int. Bibl. Books Artic. Mod. Lang. Lit.

SZ/0257-4063
TEXTES LITTERAIRES FRANCAIS. [Textes litt. fr.]. (19??)-. Monographic series. French. ir. Price varies per volume. Librairie Droz SA, 11 rue Massot BP 389, CH 1211 Geneva 12 Switzerland. **Tel** 011 41 22 3466666, FAX 011 41 22 472391. **LC** UNC. **Circ:** 600.
Desc: French literature.
Ind/Abst MLA Int. Bibl. Books Artic. Mod. Lang. Lit.

FR/0079-001X
TEXTES PUBLIES PAR L'INSTITUT D'ETUDES SLAVES. **See** Linguistics.

MX/0185-0830
TEXTO CRITICO / CENTRO DE INVESTIGACIONES LINGUISTICO-LITERARIAS. [Texto crit.]. **Added/Corp** Universidad Veracruzana. Centro de Investigaciones Linguistico-Literarias. Vol. 1, No. 1 (June 1975)-. Periodical. Spanish. Twice a year. $25.00. Instituto de Investigaciones Humanisticas, Apartado Postal 369, Xalapa Veracruz Mexico. **Tel** 011 52 281 42656, 011 52 281 52967. **LC** PQ7081.A1; T495. **DD** 860/.9/98. cum. index.
Ind/Abst HAPI Hisp. Am. Period. Index; MLA Int. Bibl. Books Artic. Mod. Lang. Lit.

UK
TEXTUAL PRACTICE. Vol. 1, No. 1 (Spring 1987)-. Periodical. English. Three times a year (Apr., Jun., Oct.). $60.00 (US & Canada); £62.00 (UK); £66.00 (other). Routledge, 11 New Fetter Lane, London EC4P 4EE England. **Tel** 071 583 9855, FAX 071 842 2298. **(Subscription address:** Kinokuniya Company Ltd., 38-1 Sakuragaoka 5, chome Setagaya-ku, Tokyo 156 Japan.**)**
Ind/Abst MLA Int. Bibl. Books Artic. Mod. Lang. Lit.

US/1061-6365
TEXTURE (NORMAN, OKLA.). (TEXTURE.). [Texture]. (1991)-. Periodical. English. bm. $6.00. Texture Press, 3760 Cedar Ridge Drive, Norman OK 73072. **DD** 810.
Ind/Abst Am. Humanit. Index (199?-).

US/1064-2463
THACKERAY NEWSLETTER, THE. [Thackeray newsl.]. **Added/Corp** Mississippi State University. English Dept. (197?)-. Newsletter. English. Twice a year (May & Nov.). $5.00. Mississppi State University / Thackeray Newsletter, Department of English, Drawer E, Mississippi State MS 39762. **Tel** (601)325-3644. **ED** Peter Shillingsburg. **LC** IN PROCESS. **DD** 823. **Circ:** 60.
Desc: Notes and information on William Thackeray.
Ind/Abst Am. Humanit. Index (199?-); Annu. Bibliogr. Engl. Lang. Lit.

CN/0706-5604
THALIA (OTTAWA). (THALIA.). [Thalia]. **Added/Corp** University of Ottawa. Dept. of English. Vol. 1, No. 1 (Spring 1978)-. Periodical. English (French). sa. $22.00 (one year); $42.00 (two year) institutions; $20.00 (one year), $38.00 (two year) individuals. University of Ottawa Department of English, Ottawa Ontario K1N 7N3 Canada. **Tel** (613)230-9505. **ED** J Tavernier-Courbin. **LC** PN6147; .T47. **DD** 809.7. Index available. cum. index. **Bk Rev**. **Ad Acc**. **Circ:** 600 (ctrl). Documents available from The Genuine Article.
Desc: Critical studies on humor in literature, film,

psychology, cartoons, illustrations, literary theory of humor, satire, clinical uses of humor, etc.
Ind/Abst Abstr. Engl. Stud.; Arts Humanit. Citation Index [Full Cov.]; Lit. Crit. Regist.; MLA Int. Bibl. Books Artic. Mod. Lang. Lit.; Res. Alert [Full Cov.]; Romant. Move.

US/1041-4851
THEMA (METAIRIE, LA.). (THEMA.). Vol. 1, No. 1 (Autumn 1988)-. Periodical. English. Three times a year. $16.00. Thema Literary Society, PO Box 74109, Metairie LA 70033. **Tel** (504)568-6268. **ED** Virginia Howard (editor's telephone: (504)887-1263). **DD** 810. **Pr Rev. Circ:** 300.
Desc: Promotes creative thinking by challenging writers to compose stories and poems based on unusual themes.

CK/0040-604X
THESAURUS - INSTITUTO CARO Y CUERVO. See Linguistics.

FR
THESOTHEQUE, LA. Vol. 1 (1978)-. Monographic series. French. Price varies per volume. Librairie Minard, 73 rue de Cardinal Lemoine, 75005 Paris France. **Tel** 011 33 1 43544609.

US
THIRD DEGREE. **Added/Corp** Mystery Writers of America. (1945)-. Periodical. English. mo (except July and Aug.). $65.00 US; $32.50 other (comes with Mystery Writers of America membership). Mystery Writers of America, 17 East 47th Street, Sixth Floor, New York NY 10017. **Tel** (212)888-8171. **ED** Betty Nicholas. **LC** PS1; .T5. **Circ:** 2,500 (ctrl).
Desc: Newsletter of the Mystery Writers of America.

US/0741-5958
THIRD RAIL (LOS ANGELES, CALIF.). (THIRD RAIL.). [Third rail]. No. 1 (1975)-. Periodical. English. an. $12.00. Third Rail, PO Box 46127, Los Angeles CA 90046. **Tel** (415)282-2337. **ED** Uri Hertz. **Bk Rev. Ad Acc. Circ:** 10,000.
Desc: A review of international literature and the arts. Includes poetry, interviews, translation, criticism.
Ind/Abst Am. Humanit. Index; MLA Int. Bibl. Books Artic. Mod. Lang. Lit.

US/0747-9727
THIRTEEN (PORTLANDVILLE, N.Y.). (THIRTEEN.). **VFOAT** 13. (1982)-. Periodical. English. sa. $5.00. M.A.F. Press, Box 392, Portlandville NY 13834.
Ind/Abst Am. Humanit. Index (199?-).

UK/0264-9454
THOMAS HARDY ANNUAL (LONDON, ENGLAND). (THOMAS HARDY ANNUAL.). [Thomas Hardy annu.]. 1982-. Periodical. English. an. $30.00 per issue. Humanities Press, 165 1st Avenue, Atlantic Highlands NJ 07716. **Tel** (908)872-1441, (800)221-3845, FAX (908)872-0717, telex 752233. **DD** 823/.8.
Ind/Abst Abstr. Engl. Stud. (1983-); Annu. Bibliogr. Engl. Lang. Lit.

UK/0268-5418
THOMAS HARDY JOURNAL, THE. [Thomas Hardy j.]. Vol. 1, No. 1 (Jan. 1985)-. Periodical. English. Three times a year. £17.00 UK; £21.00 other. Thomas Hardy Society / England, 59 Yonder Street, Ottery, St Mary Devonshire, EX11 1HF England. **Tel** 011 44 404 813032. ***Formed by the union of** Thomas Hardy Society Review **and** Thomas Hardy Society Newsletter.*
Ind/Abst Annu. Bibliogr. Engl. Lang. Lit.; MLA Int. Bibl. Books Artic. Mod. Lang. Lit.

UK/0082-416X
THOMAS HARDY YEAR BOOK. (THE THOMAS HARDY YEAR BOOK.). [Thomas Hardy year book]. **VFOAT** Thomas Hardy Yearbook. **VAT** Thomas Hardy Yearbook. No. 1 (1970)-. English. an. £5.00. Toucan Press, Lindens, Bascaertils, Guernsey Channel Islands England. **Tel** 011 44 0481-45091. **ED** G. Stevens-Cox. **LC** PR4752; .A4. **DD** 823/.8. **Bk Rev. Ad Acc.** ctrl circ.
Desc: Articles on the life, times and works of Thomas Hardy.
Ind/Abst MLA Int. Bibl. Books Artic. Mod. Lang. Lit.

GW
THOMAS MANN JAHRBUCH. Vol. 1 (1988)-. Periodical. German. an. DM60.00. Vittorio Klostermann, Frauenlobstrasse 22, D 60487 Frankfurt Germany. **Tel** 011 49 69 9708160. **DD** 833/.912.
Ind/Abst MLA Int. Bibl. Books Artic. Mod. Lang. Lit.

SZ/0563-4822
THOMAS MANN STUDIEN. **Added/Corp** Zurich. Eidgenossische Technische Hochschule. Thomas Mann Archiv. Vol. 1 (1967)-. Monographic series. German. ir. Price varies per volume. KG Saur Verlag Bern, Neuengasse 43, CH-3001 Bern Switzerland. **Tel** 011 41 31 447019. **(Subscription address:** Vittorio Klostermann Ges mbH, Frauenlobstr 22, D 60487 Frankfurt Germany.**)**
Ind/Abst MLA Int. Bibl. Books Artic. Mod. Lang. Lit.

GW
THOMAS-MANN-STUDIEN. German. ir. A Francke Verlag GmbH, Postfach 2560, Dischingerweg 5, D 72070 Tuebingen Germany. **Tel** 011 49 7071 78091 or 92.
Ind/Abst MLA Int. Bibl. Books Artic. Mod. Lang. Lit.

US/0276-5683
THOMAS WOLFE REVIEW, THE. [Thomas Wolfe rev.]. **Added/Corp** University of Akron. Dept. of English. Thomas Wolfe Society. Vol. 5, No. 1 (Spring 1981)-. Periodical. English. sa (Mar., Sept.). $10.00. University of Akron / English, Department of English, Akron OH 44325. **Tel** (216)972-7470. **ED** John S. Phillipson. **LC** PS3545.O337; Z8635. **DD** 813/.52. Index available. **Bk Rev. Ad Acc. Pr Rev. Circ:** 800. Documents available from The Genuine Article. ***Continues** Thomas Wolfe Newsletter, 0148-1789.*
Desc: Articles both directly and indirectly about Thomas Wolfe and his family. Occasional poetry.
Ind/Abst Abstr. Engl. Stud.; Am. Humanit. Index; Annu. Bibliogr. Engl. Lang. Lit.; Arts Humanit. Citation Index [Full Cov.]; Curr. Contents Arts Humanit.; Lit. Crit. Regist.; MLA Int. Bibl. Books Artic. Mod. Lang. Lit.; Res. Alert [Full Cov.].

US/0362-2835
THOREAU SOCIETY BOOKLET. [Thoreau Soc. bookl.]. **Main/Corp** Thoreau Society. **Added/Corp** Thoreau Society. Booklet. (19??)-. Monographic series. English. **LC** PS3053; .A22. cum. index.
Ind/Abst Annu. Bibliogr. Engl. Lang. Lit.; MLA Int. Bibl. Books Artic. Mod. Lang. Lit.

US/0040-6406
THOREAU SOCIETY BULLETIN, THE. [Thoreau Soc. bull.]. **Main/Corp** Thoreau Society. **Added/Corp** Thoreau Society. Bulletin. No. 1 (Oct. 1941)-. Bulletin. English. Four times a year. $20.00; Also comes with Thoreau Society Membership. Thoreau Society Inc., Department of English, East Carolina University, Greenville NC 27858. **Tel** (919)757-6675, (919)355-0620, FAX (919)355-5280, (919)757-4889. **ED** Bradley P. Dean. **LC** PS3053; .A23. **Bk Rev**, (Qty: 40). **Pr Rev. Circ:** 1,600 (ctrl). available on microfilm and microfiche from University Microfilms International (UMI).
Desc: Concerning the life, writings, and fame of Henry Thoreau.
Ind/Abst Am. Humanit. Index; Annu. Bibliogr. Engl. Lang. Lit.; MLA Int. Bibl. Books Artic. Mod. Lang. Lit.

US/0145-5575
THORNDYKE FILE, THE. No. 1- Spring 1976-. Periodical. English. sa. $5.00. Box 355, Frederick MD 21701. **LC** PR6011.R43; T46. **DD** 823/.9/12.

US/0886-6481
THOUGHTS FOR ALL SEASONS. [Thoughts all seas.]. **VFOAT** 1984 and Beyond. Vol. 1, No. 1 (Spring 1976)-. Periodical. English. an. $6.25. Thoughts for all Seasons, 11530 Southwest 99th Street, Miami FL 33176. **Tel** (305)598-8599. **ED** Michel P. Richard, Roger Wescott, and Ray Mizer. **DD** 808. **Ad Acc. Pr Rev. Circ:** 1,000.
Desc: To preserve the epigram as a literary form.

US/0275-1410
THREEPENNY REVIEW, THE. [Threepenny rev.]. **VAT** Three Penny Review. Vol. 1 (Winter/Spring 1980)-. Periodical. English. qt. $16.00 US; $30.00 other. Threepenny Review, PO Box 9131, Berkeley CA 94709. **Tel** (510)849-4545, FAX (510)849-4551. **ED** Wendy Lesser. **DD** 810. **Bk Rev. Ad Acc. Circ:** 8,000. available on microfilm from University Microfilms International (UMI).
Desc: A review of the arts featuring poetry, fiction, book, film, theater, dance, music and art reviews by major writers.
Ind/Abst Am. Humanit. Index; Book Rev. Index; Index Am. Period. Verse.

UK/0040-6562
THRESHOLD. ***Ceased.*** **Added/Corp** Lyric Players Theatre. Vol. 1 (Feb. 1957)- Ceased with Vol. 39 (19??). Periodical. English. sa. Thelyric Players Theatre, 55 Ridgeway Street, Belfast BT 9 5FB Ireland. **Tel** (0232)669660. **ED** John Boyd. **LC** AP4; .T435. **DD** 820/.5. Index available. **Bk Rev. Circ:** 600 (ctrl).
Desc: Literary material by Irish writers especially essays, poetry, and short stories.
Ind/Abst Annu. Bibliogr. Engl. Lang. Lit. (?-?).

US/0277-7800
THRESHOLD OF FANTASY. No. 1-. Periodical. English. ir. $2.00 each issue. Fandom Unlimited Enterprises, 3378 Valley Forge Way, San Jose CA 95117. **Tel** (415)960-1151.

●US/1064-0126
THRUST (AUSTIN, TEX.). (THRUST : EXPERIMENTAL AND UNDERGROUND PROSE.). **VFOAT** Experimental and Underground Prose. (1992)-. Periodical. English. sa. $8.00. Thrust, PO Box 1602, Austin TX 78767.

US/1055-0232
THUNDERMUG REPORT. [Thundermug rep.]. Premier Issue (Winter 1991)-. Periodical. English. qt. $5.00 (members of Chambers and Associations in Pacific and Wahkiakum Counties), $30.00 (nonmembers). Tiptoe Literary Service, 110 Wildwood Drive, PO Box 206-876, Naselle WA 98638-0206. **DD** 810.

CN/0824-7579
TIDEPOOL (HAMILTON). (TIDEPOOL.). [Tidepool]. No. 1 (1984)-. English. an. $2.50 (each number). Hamilton Haiku Press, 4 East 23rd Street, Hamilton Ontario L8V 2W6 Canada. **Tel** (416)383-2857. **ED** Herb Barrett. **DD** C811/.04/08. **Circ:** 250.
Desc: Publishes both haiku and short verse. Entry fee for submissions, $10.00.

SW/0282-7913
TIDSKRIFT FOR LITTERATURVETENSKAP. **Added/Corp** Lunds Universitet. Litteraturvetenskapliga Institutionen. **VFOAT** TFL. (1971/1972)-. Periodical. Swedish. Four times a year. Kr130.00. Litteraturventenskapliga Institute, University of Stockholmy, S 106 91 Stockholm Sweden. **Tel** 011 46 46 107000. **LC** PT9201; .T53.
Ind/Abst Annu. Bibliogr. Engl. Lang. Lit.

IO
TIFA SASTRA. Began in 1972?. Periodical. Indonesian. ir. Kelompok Majalah Senat Mahasiswa Fsui, Kompleks Ui Rawamangun Kotakpos 001/Jng, Jakarta Indonesia. **LC** PL5080; .A42.

BE
TIJDSCHRIFT VOOR DE STUDIE VAN DE VERLICHTING EN HET VRIJE DENKEN. (1981)-. Dutch (English, French and German). Four times a year. 600F Belgium; 800F other. Vrije Universiteit Brussel, Centrum voor Studie van de Verlichting en van het Vrije Denken, Pleinlaan 2, B. 416, B 1050 Bruxelles Belgium. ***Continues** Tijdschrift voor de Studie van de Verlichting.*
Ind/Abst Annu. Bibliogr. Engl. Lang. Lit.; Philos. Index.

NE/0168-2148
TIJDSCHRIFT VOOR SKANDINAVISTIEK. See Linguistics.

NE/0165-0890
TIKKER. Dutch. qt. Fl32.25(1-14 copies); Fl22.75 (15 or more). Wolters Noordhoff BV, Postbus 567, 9700 AN Groningen Netherlands. **Tel** 011 31 50 226886, FAX 011 31 50 264866.
Desc: Magazine for youth literature.

US/0896-3878
TIMBUKTU. ***Ceased.*** [Timbuktu]. No. 1, Winter/Spring (1988)-Ceased with Issue 6 (1991). Periodical. English. sa. Timbuktu, PO Box 369, Charlottesville VA 22902. **ED** Keith Smith, Molly Turner and John Moynihan. **DD** 810.
Desc: Eash issue is to present a unique and integrated artifact based on a mythological place or theme.
Ind/Abst Am. Humanit. Index; Index Am. Period. Verse.

US/0739-7003
TINTA (SANTA BARBARA, CALIF.). (TINTA.). **Added/Corp** University of California, Santa Barbara. Dept. of Spanish and Portuguese. Vol. 1, No. 1 (May 1981)-. Periodical. Portuguese (Spanish). an. $2.50. Tinta, University of California, Department of Spanish and Portuguese, Santa Barbara CA 93106. **Tel** (805)961-3161. **ED** Sonia Zuniga-Lomeli. **LC** PQ6001; .T56. **DD** 860/.008. **Bk Rev. Ad Acc. Circ:** 200.
Desc: Publishes original works concerning Latin American and peninsular literature written by graduate students.

RU
TIPOLOGIIA I VZAIMOSVIAZI V RUSSKOI I ZARUBEZHNOI LITERATURE. **Added/Corp** Krasnoiarskii Gosudarstvennyi Pedagogicheskii Institut. Vol. 1 (1976)-. Periodical. Russian. 0.75rub. Redaktsionno-Izdatelskii Otdel, Krasnoiarsk Russia. **LC** PG2981.E8; T55.

IT
TIRATURE. (1991)-. Periodical. Italian. Giulio Einaudi Editore SPA, Via u Biancamanon 1, CP 245-10100 Turin Italy. ***Continues** Pubblico.*

●AT/1038-8400
TIRRA LIRRA. (Spring 1993)-. English. Four times a year (Seasonally). 29.00Aus$. Phoebe Publishing, PO Box 305, Mount Evelyn, VIC 3796 Australia. **Tel** (03)736 1377. **ED** Eva Windisch. Index available. cum. index. **Bk Rev**, (Qty: 4-6). **Ad Acc. Circ:** 800.
Desc: The contemporary magazine on essays, articles, short stories, and poems.

II
TISTA-SUNAKOSA. **VFOAT** Tista Sunkosh. Periodical. Nepali (Nepali). qt. 6.00. Sharada Sanskritik Sangha, Kalchini Out Division, PO Kalchini, Dist Jalpaiguri, Kalchini India. **LC** PK2597.5; .T56.

FR
TITRA. ***Ceased.*** (1993)-(April 1994). French. Twelve times a year. L'Agence Periscoop Multimedia, 12 rue Gilodesque Agropolis, 34080 Montferrier France. **Tel** 011 33 67753229. **ED** Charles Albert Ryng. **Ad Acc, Adv Mgr:** Ryng, **Tel** 67753229. ctrl circ.

UK
TLS, THE TIMES LITERARY SUPPLEMENT INDEX. (19??)-. English. an. $90.10. News International Newspapers Ltd., PO Box 495 Virginia Street, London E1 9XU England. **Tel** 011 44 71 7823000. **(Subscription address:** Research Publications Inc. / Microfilm, 12 Lunar Drive Drawer AB, Woodbridge CT 06525.)

UK/0307-661X
TLS. TIMES LITERARY SUPPLEMENT. **See** Publishing.

RU
TOCHKA OPORY. (19??)-. Russian. Lenizdat, Fontanka 59, St. Petersburg Russia. **LC** PG3505.L5; T63.

FR/1154-5992
TODAY IN ENGLISH PARIS. (TODAY IN ENGLISH.). (1991)-. Periodical. English. mo. 369.00F France; 475.00F other. Bayard Presse, Svc Client, 3 rue Bayard/Dept 2, 75393 Paris Cedex 08 France. **Tel** 011 33 1 44356060, 011 33 1 44356262. **UDC** 802.0.

US/0893-9373
TODAY'S BEST NONFICTION. [Today's best nonfict.]. 1989-. Periodical. English. ir. Reader's Digest, Reader Digest Road, Pleasantville NY 10570. **Tel** (914)241-5000, (800)234-9000. **DD** 810.

KO
TOGIL MUNHAK. **See** Linguistics.

JA/0385-406X
TOHOKU GAKUIN DAIGAKU RONSHU. EIGO, EIBUNGAKU. [Tohoku Gakuin Daigaku ronshu. Eigo, Eibungaku]. **VFOAT** Tohoku Gakuin University Review. Essays and Studies in English Language and Literature; Essays and Studies in English Language and Literature (Sendai). (1961)-. Periodical. Multiple languages. sa. **DD** _a420. ***Continues in part*** *Tohoku Gakuin Daigaku Ronshu.*
Ind/Abst MLA Int. Bibl. Books Artic. Mod. Lang. Lit.

JA
TOKYO-TO HAIKU REMMEI TAIKAI KUSHU. **Main/Corp** Tokyo-to Haiku Remmei. Japanese. Tokyo-To Haiku Remmei, 25-1 Higashi Nakano 1-chome, Nakano-ku 164, Tokyo Japan. **LC** PL759.A1; T64A.

US/1044-1573
TOLSTOY STUDIES JOURNAL. [Tolstoy stud. j.]. **Added/Corp** Tolstoy Society. **VFOAT** TSJ. Vol. 1 (1988)-. Periodical. English. an (Nov.). $15.00 Comes with Tolstoy Society membership. Tolstoy Society / Foreign Department, c/o Kathleen Parthe, University of Rochester, Rochester NY 14637. **Tel** (716)275-4176. **LC** PG3370; .T65. **DD** 891.

CN
TONGIL MUNYE. **VFOAT** Tong Il Korean Literature. V. 1- March 1979-. Periodical. Korean (Korean). Tongil Munye S A, 51 Oakwood Avenue, Toronto Ontario M6H 2V7 Canada. **LC** PL969.8; .T66.

CN
TORONTO MEDIEVAL LATIN TEXTS. **Added/Corp** University of Toronto. Centre for Medieval Studies. Pontifical Institute of Medieval Studies. (1972)-. Monographic series. English (Latin). ir. Price varies per volume. Pontifical Institute of Mediaeval Studies, 59 Queens Park Crescent East, Toronto Ontario M5S 2C4 Canada. **Tel** (416)926-7144, FAX (416)926-7276. **ED** A. G. Rigg.
Desc: Editions of Latin texts based on a single manuscript, covering varied subject matter, intended as teaching texts for medieval Latin.

●CN
TORONTO REVIEW OF CONTEMPORARY WRITING ABROAD, THE. **VFOAT** Toronto Review. Vol. 12, No. 1 (Summer 1993)-. Periodical. English. Three times a year. 18.00Can$. Toronto Review of Contemporary Writing Abroad, PO Box 6996, Station A, Toronto Ontario M5W 1X7 Canada. **Tel** (416)483-7191, FAX (416)486-0706. **ED** M. G. Vassanji. **LC** PK101; .T67. **DD** C810/.8/08914. **Bk Rev**, (Qty: 15-20). **Ad Acc**, **Adv Mgr:** N. Aziz, **Tel** (416)483-7191. **Circ:** 650. available on microfilm. ***Continues*** *Toronto South Asian Review, 0714-3508.*

CN/0714-3508
TORONTO SOUTH ASIAN REVIEW, THE. ***Title Change.*** [Tor. South Asian rev.]. Vol. 1, No. 1 (1982)-Vol. 11, No. 2 (Winter 1993). Periodical. English. Three times a year. Toronto South Asian Review, PO Box 6996 Station A, Toronto Ontario M5W 1X7 Canada. **Tel** (416)483-7191. **ED** M G Vassanji and N Aziz. **LC** PK101; .T67. **DD** C810/.8/08914. cum. index. **Bk Rev.** **Ad Acc.** **Circ:** 500 (ctrl). ***Continued by*** *Toronto Review of Contemporary Writing Abroad.*
Desc: Publishes poetry, fiction, drama and criticism in English and translation; seeks to make more accessible literature that traces some part of its meaning and heritage to the Indian subcontinent. Also, encourages innovative literary forms and discussions on the emerging Canadian culture. Its writers originate from the Indian subcontinent, Africa, the Caribbean and North America.
Ind/Abst Can. Index.

US/1056-8336
TORRE DE PAPEL (IOWA CITY, IOWA). (TORRE DE PAPEL.). [Torre papel]. Vol. 1, No. 1 (Spring 1991)-. Periodical. English. Three times a year. $18.00. Torre de Papel, University of Iowa, 211 SH, Iowa City IA 52442. **DD** 860.

PR/0040-9588
TORRE (RIO PIEDRAS (SAN JUAN), P.R.), LA. (LA TORRE : REVISTA GENERAL DE LA UNIVERSIDAD DE PUERTO RICO.). **Added/Corp** University of Puerto Rico (Rio Piedras Campus). Yearly Vol. 1, No. 1 (Jan./March 1953)-. Periodical. Spanish. qt (4 issues). $28.00 (institution) US. University de Puerto Rico / Oficina de Publicaciones, Apartado 23322 Estacion UPR, San Juan Puerto Rica 00931-1787. **Tel** (809)250-0615, (809)250-0725, (809)250-0725, FAX (809)753-9116. **ED** Arturo Echavarria. **LC** AS74.A1; T6. **DD** 056. Index available (bound in last issue). cum. index. **Bk Rev.** **Ad Acc.** **Pr Rev.** **Circ:** 1,000.
Desc: A learned journal dedicated to literary and linguistic studies with main emphasis on Latin American, Caribbean and Spanish literature.
Ind/Abst Am. Hist. Life (1955-1959, 1969-); MLA Int. Bibl. Books Artic. Mod. Lang. Lit.

FR/0248-496X
TRACES. (19??)-. Periodical. French (French). Four times a year. $22.00. Traces / France, 52 rue Rene Boulanger, 75010 Paris France. **LC** DS101; .T68. **DD** 909/.04924/05.
Ind/Abst Point Repere.

UK/0959-3632
TRAFODION ANRHYDEDDUS GYMDEITHAS Y CYMMRODORION. (THE TRANSACTIONS OF THE HONOURABLE SOCIETY OF CYMMRODORION.). [Trafod. Anrhydeddus Gymd. Cymmrodorion]. **Main/Corp** Honourable Society of Cymmrodorion (London, England). **VFOAT** Trafodion Anrhydeddus Gymdeithas y Cymmrodorion. (1893)-. English. an. £15.00 Honourable Society of Cymmrodorion membership. Honourable Society of Cymmrodorion, 30 Eascastle Street, London W1N 7PD England. **Tel** 011 44 71 6310502. **LC** DA700; .C94. ***Continues in part*** *Cymmrodor.*
Ind/Abst BHA : Biblio. Hist. Art; MLA Int. Bibl. Books Artic. Mod. Lang. Lit.

BE
TRAITS : BULLETIN LITTERAIRE DE LA LIBRAIRIE LIBRIS. Bulletin. French. qt. 300F. Traits, Avenue de la Toison d'Or 29, 1060 Bruxelles Belgium. **LC** Z2403; J7.

GW
TRAJEKT. 1- 1970-. Periodical. German. an. Hinstorff Verlag, Lager Strasse 7, O-2500 Rostock Germany. **Tel** 34441. **LC** PT1141.A2; T73.
Desc: Information of authors and their books which are edited by Hinstorff Verlag.

GR
TRAM : HENA OCHEMA. (Oct. 1971)-. Periodical. Greek, Modern. Tram, Sporadon 1, Thessaloniki TK 546 55 Greece.

UK/0958-5451
TRANSACTIONS OF THE GAELIC SOCIETY OF INVERNESS. **See** Linguistics.

●UK/0968-1361
TRANSLATION AND LITERATURE. **VFOAT** Translation & Literature. Vol. 1 (1992)-. English. an. £39.50 UK & Europe; $75.00 US; £43.50 other. Edinburgh University Press, 22 George Square, Edinburgh EH8 9LF Scotland. **Tel** 011 44 31 650 6207, FAX 011 44 31 662 0053. **ED** Stuart Gillespie. **LC** IN PROCESS; PN241.A1; T73. **Ad Acc**, **Adv Mgr:** Kathryn Maclean.
Desc: Articles, notes and reviews on literary translation of all kinds and periods. Focuses on English literature in its foreign relations.

US/0093-9307
TRANSLATION (NEW YORK). (TRANSLATION.). [Translation]. **Added/Corp** Columbia University. School of the Arts. American Center of P.E.N. Columbia University. Translation Center. Vol. 1 (Winter 1973)-. English. Twice a year (May, Nov.). $18.00 (one year); $34.00 (two years); $44.00 (three years). Translation Center, 412 Dodge, Columbia University, New York NY 10027. **Tel** (212)854-4500, FAX (212)749-0397. **ED** Timothy Sultan. **LC** PN241; .T7. **DD** 418/.02. **Ad Acc**, **Adv Mgr:** Timothy Sultan, **Tel** (212)854-2305. **Circ:** 1,500. available on CD-ROM; available on microfiche.
Desc: Literary journal in which each issue features translations of the literature from a particular country or language.
Ind/Abst Am. Bibliogr. Slavic East Europ. Stud.; Annu. Bibliogr. Engl. Lang. Lit.; Index Am. Period. Verse; Middle East Abstr. Index; MLA Int. Bibl. Books Artic. Mod. Lang. Lit.

US/0737-4836
TRANSLATION REVIEW. **See** Linguistics.

FR
TRAVAUX DE LINGUISTIQUE ET DE PHILOLOGIE. (1988)-. French. an. CDU & Sedes Reunis SA, 88 Boulevard Saint Germain, 75005 Paris France. ***Continues in part*** *Travaux de Linguistique et de Litterature, 0082-6057.*
Ind/Abst MLA Int. Bibl. Books Artic. Mod. Lang. Lit.

FR/0995-6794
TRAVAUX DE LITTERATURE : T.L. **VFOAT** T.L.; TL. Vol. 1 (1988)-. French. an. Societe Edition Belles Lettres, 95 Boulevard Raspail, 75006 Paris France. **Tel** 011 33 1 45487055, FAX 011 33 1 45449288, telex 200577. ***Continues in part*** *Travaux de Linguistique et de Litterature, 0082-6057.*
Ind/Abst MLA Int. Bibl. Books Artic. Mod. Lang. Lit.

FR
TRAVAUX / UNIVERSITE JEAN MONNET-SAINT-ETIENNE, CENTRE INTERDISCIPLINAIRE D'ETUDE ET DE RECHERCHE SUR L'EXPRESSION CONTEMPORAINE. **See** Linguistics.

BL/0101-9570
TRAVESSIA. No. 1 (Second Semester 1980)-. Periodical. Portuguese (Spanish, French, English and Italian). sa. $10.00. Editora da UFSC, Caixa Postal 476, 88000 Florianopolis SC Brazil. **Tel** (0482)339408. **ED** Zahide Muzart. **LC** PQ9500; .T73. **DD** 869/.08/0981. **Bk Rev.** **Circ:** 800.
Desc: Publishes papers on Brazilian literature. Generally, each issue is devoted to a special topic and includes the following features: critical articles on the subject, an updated bibliography, and reviews of recent publications.
Ind/Abst MLA Int. Bibl. Books Artic. Mod. Lang. Lit.

US/0041-2171
TREE. No. 1 (1970)-. Periodical. English. sa. $20.00. Tree Books, PO Box 9005, Berkeley CA 94709. **ED** David Meltzer.

CN/0710-4375
TREELINE. [Treeline]. 1981-. English. ir (as funding is available). $7.95 (each volume) U.S. Treeline, Box 1000, Fort St John British Columbia V1G 4G2 Canada. **Tel** (604)785-6981, telex 036-75193. **ED** Maidie Hilmo and Harry Morgan. **DD** C810/.8/092379. **Circ:** 2,000.
Desc: Includes stories, poems, and plays by local creative writers, old-timers and children in the Northern third of British Columbia, as well as by visiting Canadian writers.

AG
TRIBUNA LITERARIA. (19??)-. Periodical. Spanish. Rivadavia 4213, 1205 Capital Federal, Buenos Aires Argentina. **LC** PQ7600; .T74. **DD** 860.

GW/0721-4294
TRIERER STUDIEN ZUR LITERATUR. [Trier. Stud. Lit.]. (1979)-. Monographic series. German.
Ind/Abst MLA Int. Bibl. Books Artic. Mod. Lang. Lit.

●US/1062-2527
TRINITY FORUM READING, THE. [Trinity Forum read.]. **Added/Corp** Trinity Forum. (Spring 1992)-. Monographic series. English. qt. Price varies per volume. Trinity Forum, 9587 Bronte Drive, Burke VA 22015. **DD** 810.

II
TRIPURA DARPANA. Periodical. Bengali (Bengali). an. Rs10.00. Tripura Darpan Office Agartala, Tripura India. **LC** PK1717.T75; T75.

US/0041-3097
TRIQUARTERLY / NORTHWESTERN UNIVERSITY. [TriQuarterly]. **Added/Corp** Northwestern University (Evanston, Ill.). **VFOAT** TriQuarterly. Vol. 1, No. 1 (Fall 1958)-. Periodical. English. Three times a year. $30.00 US and Canadian institutions; $34.00 other institutions; $20.00 individual; $25.00 other. Triquarterly Magazine, 2020 Ridge Avenue NW, Evanston IL 60208. **Tel** (708)491-7614, FAX (708)467-2096. **ED** Reginald Gibbons. **LC** PS508.C6; T7. **DD** 805. Index available. cum. index. **Bk Rev.** **Ad Acc.** **Circ:** 3,500 (ctrl). available on microfilm and microfiche from University Microfilms International (UMI). Documents available from The Genuine Article, UMI Article Clearinghouse.
Desc: Triquarterly Magazine is an international journal of art, writing, and cultural inquiry published at Northwestern University. The emphasis of the magazine is on new fiction and poetry, and includes essays, book reviews, photography, and art.
Ind/Abst Acad. Abstr. Full Text Elite (July 1990-); Acad. Abstr. (July 1990-); Acad. Ind. [Computer File] (1987-); Acad. Search (July 1990-); Am. Hist. Life (1964-1977); Am. Bibliogr. Slavic East Europ. Stud.; Am. Humanit. Index; Annu. Bibliogr. Engl. Lang. Lit.; Arts Humanit. Citation Index [Full Cov.]; Book Rev. Index (1986-); Curr. Contents Arts Humanit.; Expand. Acad. Index (1987-); Humanit. Index; Humanit. Source (Jul. 1990-); Index Am.

Period. Verse; INFO-SOUTH Abstr.; Lit. Crit. Regist.; Mag. Search; MLA Int. Bibl. Books Artic. Mod. Lang. Lit.; Newsp. Period. Abstr. (1990-); Res. Alert [Full Cov.]; Soc. Sci. Cit. Index [Select. Cov.].

US/0360-3385
TRISTANIA. [Tristania]. Vol. 1 (Nov. 1975)-. Periodical. Multiple languages (English, French and German). Twice a year (Autumn & Spring). $49.95 (latest volume). Edwin Mellen Press, PO Box 450, Lewiston NY 14092. **Tel** (716)754-2788. **LC** PN57.T8; T74. **DD** 841/.1/09351. **Bk Rev. Circ:** 500.
Ind/Abst MLA Int. Bibl. Books Artic. Mod. Lang. Lit.

CN/0829-4275
TROIS. [Trois]. Vol. 1, No 1, (1985). Periodical. French. Three times a year. 25.00Can$ (one year), 50.00Can$ (two year) institutions Canada; 32.00Can$ (one year), 64.00Can$ (two year) institutions other; 20.00Can$ (one year), 40.00Can$ (two year) individuals Canada; 27.00Can$ (one year), 54.00Can$ (two year) individuals other. SODEP, 815 rue Ontario Est, Bureau 202, Montreal Quebec H21 1P1 Canada. **Tel** (514)523-7724, (514)525-2606, FAX (514)523-9401. **DD** C840/.8.

UK
TROLLOPIANA. Added/Corp Trollope Society. No. 1, (1988)-. Periodical. English. qt. Free to members of the Trollope Society. Trollope Society, 9A North St. Clapham, London SW4 0HN United Kingdom. **Tel** 011 44 71 7206789, 011 44 71 9241146.
Desc: Publication covering English fiction.

FR/0761-2591
TROPISMES / CENTRE DE RECHERCHES ANGLO-AMERICAINES.
Added/Corp Universite de Paris X: Nanterre. Centre de Recherches Anglo-Americaines. (19??)-. French.
Ind/Abst MLA Int. Bibl. Books Artic. Mod. Lang. Lit.

RU/0253-259X
TRUDY OTDELA DREVNERUSSKOJ LITERATURY. AKADEMIJA NAUK SSSR; INSTITUT RUSSKOJ LITERATURY. PUSKINSKIJ DOM. (TRUDY OTDELA DREVNERUSSKOI LITERATURY.). [Tr. otd. drevneruss. lit., Akad. Nauk SSSR; Inst. russ. lit., Puskin. dom]. **Added/Corp** Institut Literatury (Pushkinskii Dom). Otdel Drevnerusskoi Literatury. Institut Russkoi Literatury (Pushkinskii Dom). Otdel Drevnerusskoi Literatury. Vol. 1 (1934)-. Russian. an. Izdatelstvo Nauka St. Petersburg, Mendeleevskaia Liniia 1, 199034 St. Petersburg, B-34 Russia. **Tel** 218-26-12. **(Subscription address:** Victor Kamkin, 4956 Boiling Brook Parkway, Rockville, MD 20852) **LC** PG2950; .A5.
Ind/Abst MLA Int. Bibl. Books Artic. Mod. Lang. Lit.

US/1061-3587
TRUDY'S TIME-PERIODS. [Trudy's time-periods]. (1991)-. English. qt. $32.95. Trudy's Time-Periods, 1700 Ranch Drive, Richmond VA 23229-4906. **DD** 813.

CN/0823-1508
TRUE NORTH / DOWN UNDER. [True north, down under]. (1983)-. English. an. True North / Down Under, PO Box 55, Lantzville British Columbia V0R 2H0 Canada. **DD** C810/.8/0054.

JA/0286-9675
TSUKUBA CHUGOKU BUNKA RONSO / TSUKUBA DAIGAKU CHUGOKU BUNKA KENKYU PUROJEKUTO. VFOAT Chu Po Chung-Kuo Wen Hua Lun Tsung; Tsukuba Sinological Studies. Periodical. Chinese (Japanese). Tsukuba Daigaku Chugoku Bunka Kenkyu Purojekuto, c/o Tskukba Daigaku Bungei, Gengo Gakukei Sakura-Mura Niihari-gun, Ibaraki-ken 305 Japan.

CC
TUAN PIEN HSIAO SHUO HSUAN (PEKING, CHINA). (TUAN PIEN HSIAO SHUO HSUAN.). 1980-. Chinese. an. RMBY1.75. Jen Min Wen Hsueh Chu Pan She, Hsin Hua Shu Tien Pei-Ching Fa Hsing So Pei-Ching, Beijing, People's Republic of China. **LC** PL2653; .T8456.

CC
TUAN PIEN HSIAO SHUO NIEN PIEN. 1980-. Chinese. an. RMBY1.69. Chiang-Su Sheng, Hsin Hua Shu Tien, Nan-Ching, People's Republic of China. **LC** PL2653; .T8458. **DD** 895.1/301/08.

GW/0171-7235
TUBINGER STUDIEN ZUR DEUTSCHEN LITERATUR. (1976)-. Monographic series. German.
Ind/Abst MLA Int. Bibl. Books Artic. Mod. Lang. Lit.

PL/0035-9602
TUCH LITERACKI (KRAKOW, POLAND). (RUCH LITERACKI.). [Ruch lit.]. **Added/Corp** Polska Akademia Nauk. Oddzia w Krakowie. Komisja Historycznoliteracka. Towarzystwo Literackie Imienia Adama Mickiewicza. Vol. 1, No. 1 (July/Oct. 1960)-. Periodical. Polish. bm. $48.00. **(Subscription address:** ARS Polona, PO Box 1001, 00068 Warsaw Poland.) **LC** PG7001; .R8. ***Continues*** *Ruch Literacki.*
Ind/Abst MLA Int. Bibl. Books Artic. Mod. Lang. Lit.

US
TUCUMCARI LITERARY REVIEW. (1988)-. Periodical. English. bm. $12.00 US; $20.00 other. Tucumcari Literary Review, 3108 West Bellevue Avenue, Los Angeles CA 90026. **Tel** (310)413-0789. **ED** Troxey Kemper and Neoma Reed. **Circ:** 100.
Desc: Covers literature, poetry, fiction, nostalgia, and nonfiction.

US/0564-4380
TULANE STUDIES IN ROMANCE LANGUAGES AND LITERATURE. [Tulane stud. Roman. lang. lit.]. **Added/Corp** Tulane University. Dept. of French and Italian. Tulane University. Dept. of Spanish and Portuguese. No. 1 (1966)-. Monographic series. English. ir. Price varies per volume. Newcomb College, Tulane University, Art Department, New Orleans LA 70118. **Tel** (504)865-5000. **ED** Gloria Harris. **LC** UNC. **DD** 440. **Ad Acc.**
Desc: These volumes deal with literature from the Middle Ages through the 20th century.
Ind/Abst Abstr. Engl. Stud.; MLA Int. Bibl. Books Artic. Mod. Lang. Lit.

SW/0041-4034
TULIMULD. [Tulimuld]. **Added/Corp** Eesti PEN-Klubi. (1950)-. Periodical. Estonian. qt. Kr73.00. Tulimuld Sweden, 222-38 Lund Sweden. **Tel** 119690. **ED** B. Kangro. **LC** AP95.E4; T8. **Bk Rev. Circ:** 1,000.
Desc: Cultural magazine publishing poetry, short stories, book reviews, articles on art and literature in Estonian language.
Ind/Abst MLA Int. Bibl. Books Artic. Mod. Lang. Lit.

US/0732-7730
TULSA STUDIES IN WOMEN'S LITERATURE. [Tulsa stud. women's lit.]. **Added/Corp** University of Tulsa. Vol. 1, No. 1 (Spring 1982)-. Academic Scholarly Publication. English. Twice a year. $14.00 US; $16.00 other (institution). The University of Tulsa, c/o Linda Frazier, 600 South College Avenue, Tulsa OK 74104. **Tel** (918)631-2503, FAX (918)584-0623. **ED** Linda Frazier. **LC** PN471; .T84. **DD** 809/.89287. Index available ($2.00). cum. index. **Bk Rev. Ad Acc. Circ:** 500 (ctrl). Documents available from The Genuine Article, UMI Article Clearinghouse.
Desc: The only scholarly journal in the world devoted solely to women's literature. Includes articles and reviews on women's writing, from all times and places.
Ind/Abst Abstr. Engl. Stud. (1982-); Acad. Search (July 1993-); Am. Hist. Life (1989-); Annu. Bibliogr. Engl. Lang. Lit.; Arts Humanit. Citation Index [Full Cov.]; Book Rev. Index; Child. Lit. Abstr. (19??-); Expand. Acad. Index (1989-); Humanit. Index; Humanit. Source (Jul. 1993-); INFO-SOUTH Abstr.; MLA Int. Bibl. Books Artic. Mod. Lang. Lit.; Newsp. Period. Abstr. (1991-); Res. Alert [Full Cov.]; Romant. Move.; Soc. Sci. Cit. Index [Select. Cov.]; Stud. Women Abstr.; Women Stud. Abstr.

CH
TUNG FANG (HANG-CHOU SHIH, CHINA). (TUNG FANG.). **VFOAT** Dongfang. Periodical. Chinese. NT$1.00. Science Press, 16 Donghuangchenggen North Street, Beijing 100707, People's Republic of China. **Tel** 011 86 1 4019821, 011 86 1 4010642, FAX 011 86 1 4012180, 011 86 1 4019810, telex 210147. **LC** PL2250; .T86. **DD** 895.1/08/005.

CH
TUNG HUA. VFOAT Tonghua; Tong Hua; Tung Hua Tsung Kan. 1 (May 1980)-. Periodical. Chinese. NT$0.85. Hsin Hua Shu Tien / Tien-Chin, Tien-Chin Shih, People's Republic of China. **LC** PZ10.24; T78.

SP/0213-4373
TURIA. Added/Corp Instituto de Estudios Turolenses. **VFOAT** Turia Revista Cultural. No. 1 (1985)-. Periodical. Spanish. **LC** PN695; .T87. **DD** 809/.005.

US/0896-5951
TURNSTILE (NEW YORK, N.Y.). (TURNSTILE.). [Turnstile]. Vol. 1 (Winter 1988)-. Periodical. English. sa. $15.00 US; $17.00 Canada; $21.00 other. Turnstile Press, 175 Fifth Avenue, Suite 2348, New York NY 10010. **ED** Amit Shah. **LC** WMLC 93/1794. **DD** 810. **Ad Acc. Circ:** 2,500.
Desc: Literary magazine featuring short stories, poetry, essays, and interviews.
Ind/Abst Am. Humanit. Index; Index Am. Period. Verse.

US/0146-2083
TUUMBA. (Aug. 1976)-. Monographic series. English (English). Price varies per volume. Tuumba Press, PO Box 1075, Willits CA 95490. **LC** PS642; .T88. **DD** 813/.008.

RU
TVERDYI ZNAK. (1991)-. Periodical. Russian. qt. **LC** PG3227.5; .T843.

RU
TVORCHESTVO A. P. CHEKHOVA. **See** Linguistics.

US
TWAYNE'S MASTERWORK STUDIES. No. 1 (1986)-. Monographic series. English. ir. Price varies per volume. Macmillan Publishing Company, 100 Front Street, Box 500, Riverside NJ 08075-7500. **Tel** (800)257-5755, (609)461-6500, FAX (609)461-7070.
Ind/Abst MLA Int. Bibl. Books Artic. Mod. Lang. Lit.

US/0496-6015
TWAYNE'S UNITED STATES AUTHORS SERIES. [Twayne's U.S. authors ser.]. **VFOAT** United States Authors Series; TUSAS. (1961)-. Monographic series. English. ir. Price varies per volume. Macmillan Publishing Company, 100 Front Street, Box 500, Riverside NJ 08075-7500. **Tel** (800)257-5755, (609)461-6500, FAX (609)461-7070. **LC** UNC. **DD** 810.
Ind/Abst MLA Int. Bibl. Books Artic. Mod. Lang. Lit.

US/0564-5603
TWAYNE'S WORLD AUTHORS SERIES. [Twayne's world authors ser.]. **VFOAT** World Authors Series; TWAS. (1966)-. Monographic series. English. ir. Price varies per volume. Macmillan Publishing Company, 100 Front Street, Box 500, Riverside NJ 08075-7500. **Tel** (800)257-5755, (609)461-6500, FAX (609)461-7070. **LC** UNC. **DD** 800.
Ind/Abst MLA Int. Bibl. Books Artic. Mod. Lang. Lit.

US/0897-7844
TWENTIETH CENTURY AMERICAN JEWISH WRITERS. [Twent. century Am. Jew. writ.]. **VFOAT** 20th Century American Jewish Writers. Vol. 1 (1989)-. Monographic series. English. ir. Price varies per volume. Peter Lang Publishing, 62 West 45th Street, 4th Floor, New York NY 10036. **Tel** (212)764-1471, (800)770-5264, telex 6973364 PLNY. **DD** 808.

US
TWENTIETH-CENTURY CHILDREN'S WRITERS. English. $123.00. St. James Press, PO Box 33477, Detroit MI 48232-5477. **Tel** (800)345-0392.
Desc: Reflects the developments in the genre and changes in critical opinion during the last five years.

US
TWENTIETH-CENTURY CRIME AND MYSTERY WRITERS. English. $123.00. St. James Press, PO Box 33477, Detroit MI 48232-5477. **Tel** (800)345-0392.
Desc: Provides a unique source on the most influential English-language writers of one of the most popular and enduring fiction genres ever.

US
TWENTIETH-CENTURY ROMANCE & HISTORICAL WRITERS. English. $123.00. St. James Press, PO Box 33477, Detroit MI 48232-5477. **Tel** (800)345-0392.
Desc: Provides biographies, bibliographies, and criticism on 500 English-language writers of this century. Includes romance and historical novels, short stories, plays, and other publications.

US
TWENTIETH-CENTURY SCIENCE-FICTION WRITERS. English. $123.00. St. James Press, PO Box 33477, Detroit MI 48232-5477. **Tel** (800)345-0392.
Desc: Encompasses a vast range of information on more than 600 writers in this increasingly popular genre.

US/0496-6058
TWENTIETH CENTURY VIEWS. VFOAT 20th Century Views. (19??)-. Monographic series. English. ir. Price varies per volume. Maxwell Macmillan Professional Business Division, 910 Sylvan Avenue, Englewood Cliffs NJ 07632-3310. **Tel** (800)431-9025. **(Subscription address:** Maxwell McMillan, P. O. Box 41264, Philadelphia, PA 19162, telephone: (800)288-4745) **LC** UNC. **DD** 800.
Ind/Abst MLA Int. Bibl. Books Artic. Mod. Lang. Lit.

US
TWENTIETH-CENTURY WESTERN WRITERS. English. $123.00. St. James Press, PO Box 33477, Detroit MI 48232-5477. **Tel** (800)345-0392.
Desc: Includes the great fiction writers from this century whose works are set in or relate to the American frontier experience or embody that experience in a modern setting.

NE
TWILIGHT WORLD. (1993)-. English. bm. Free. Richard Karsmakers, Looplantsoen 50, NL-3523 GV Utrecht Netherlands. **Tel** 011 31 0 30 887482. **ED** Richard Karsmakers. ***Continues*** *Twilight Zone.*
Desc: Online (E-Mail), fiction magazine. Genres included are mostly humorous, science fiction and fantasy.

PL/0041-4727
TWORCZOSC. [Tworczosc]. **Added/Corp** Zwiazek Literatow Polskich. Vol. 1 (Aug. 1945)-. Periodical. Polish. mo. Price on Request. **(Subscription address:** ARS Polona, PO Box 1001, 00068 Warsaw Poland.) **LC** PG7001; .T876.
Ind/Abst Annu. Bibliogr. Engl. Lang. Lit.; MLA Int. Bibl. Books Artic. Mod. Lang. Lit.

CC
TZU HSUEH. V. 1, Nov. 1981-. Periodical. Chinese. RMBY0.90. Hsin Hua Shu Tien / Shang-Hai Fa Hsing So, Shanghai, People's Republic of China. **LC** PL2336; .T96. **DD** 895.1/104.

CC
TZU LIU. **VFOAT** Ziliu Shuangyuekan. (19??)-. Periodical. Chinese. bm. Post Office / China, People's Republic of China. **LC** PL2513; .T95. **DD** 895.1/09/005.

CN/0226-3440
U. C. REVIEW. [U.C. rev.]. **Main/Corp** University College, Toronto, Ont. **VFOAT** University College Literary Review. **VAT** University College Review. English. an. U C Review University College, University of Toronto, Toronto Ontario M5S 1A1 Canada. **DD** C810/.8/092379.

US/0892-6530
U.S. RAG. ***Ceased.*** [U.S. rag]. **VFOAT** US Rag. **VAT** United States Rag. (1986)-Ceased Vol. 1 No. 6. Periodical. English. bm. US Rag, 567 Oakland Avenue #104, Oakland CA 94611. **DD** 817.

US/0738-4009
UBU REPERTORY THEATER PUBLICATIONS. **See** Theater.

US/1055-5293
UFPSS FRIENDSHIP. [UFPSS friendsh.]. **VAT** United Federation of Planets and Star Systems Friendship. Vol. 1 No. 1 (1991)-. Periodical. English. qt. $20.00 (U.S.), $25.00 (Canada). Infinite Savant Publishing / California, PO Box 2321, Van Nuys CA 91404. **LC** PS648.S3; U33. **DD** 813/.0876208/005.

HU/0133-5332
UJ FORRAS. **Added/Corp** Komarom Megye (Hungary). Tanacs. Komarom-Esztergom Megye (Hungary). Onkormanyzat. (1971)-. Periodical. Hungarian. Ten times a year. $15.00. **(Subscription address:** Kultura, PO Box 149, H 1389 Budapest 62 Hungary (phone: 011 36 1 359370)) **LC** DB975.K6; U37. ***Continues*** *Forras (Tatabanya, Hungary), 0324-4032.*

UN/0130-5263
UKRAINSKA MOVA I LITERATURA V SHKOLI. [Ukr. mova lit. sk.]. **Added/Corp** Ukraine. Ministerstvo Osvity. Vol. 13 (Sept. 1963)-. Periodical. Ukrainian. mo. $99.95. **(Subscription address:** East View Publications Inc., 3020 Harbor Lane North, Suite 110, Minneapolis MN 55447.) **LC** PG3903; .U54. ***Formed by the union of*** *Ukrainska Mova V Shkoli* ***and*** *Literatura V Shkoli.*
Ind/Abst MLA Int. Bibl. Books Artic. Mod. Lang. Lit.

UN
UKRAINSKE LITERATUROZNAVSTVO. Periodical. Ukrainian. **LC** PG3900.
Ind/Abst MLA Int. Bibl. Books Artic. Mod. Lang. Lit.

FR
UKRAINSKYI VISNYK. **VFOAT** Ukrainian Herald. (1970)-. Periodical. Ukrainian. **LC** DK508.A2; U696.
Ind/Abst Hum. Rights Intern. Rep.

RU
ULAGASHEVSKIE CHTENIIA / GORNO-ALTAISKII NAUCHNO-ISSLEDOVATELSKII INSTITUT ISTORII, IAZYKA I LITERATURY. **Added/Corp** Gorno-Altaiskii Nauchno-Issledovatelskii Institut Istorii, Iazyka i Literatury. Vol. 1 (1979)-. Russian. **LC** PL43.5; .U38.

US/0747-8011
ULULA. (ULULA. UNIVERSITY OF GEORGIA.). [Ulula]. **Added/Corp** University of Georgia. Dept. of Romance Languages. No. 1 (1984)-. English (French, Portuguese and Spanish). an. $4.00. Michigan State University Department of Romance and Classical Languages, c/o Joseph Snow, East Lansing MI 48824. **Tel** (517)355-8350, FAX (517)336-3844. **ED** James Chesnut, Francisco J Penas-Bermejo, John A Ross, Helen Thompson, and Carmen Yerpes-Brown. **DD** 440. **Bk Rev**.
Desc: Graduate students are invited to submit critical contributions, short fiction, poetry, and translations, MLA style.
Ind/Abst MLA Int. Bibl. Books Artic. Mod. Lang. Lit.

●US/1068-3267
UNDISCOVERED COUNTRIES JOURNAL. (1993)-. Periodical. English. bm (6 issues). $23.95 US; $29.95 other. Undiscovered Countries Journal, 9792 Edmonds Way, Suite 252, Edmonds WA 98020. **Tel** (206)672-9040. **ED** Michael Breckenridge. **Bk Rev**, (Qty: 12). **Ad Acc**, **Adv Mgr:** Gary Breckenridge. **Circ:** 1000.
Desc: Reports on science news and space exploration. Also includes science fiction articles, Star Trek news, and studies of Trek Klingon language.

BL/0101-8698
UNILETRAS. [Uniletras]. (1979)-. Periodical. Portuguese. Departamento de Letras Universidade Estadual de Ponta Grossa / Departamento de Letras, Praca Santos Andrade S/No 84.100, Ponta Grossa PR Brazil. **Tel** 0422.243966. **UDC** 801.
Ind/Abst Soc. Plann. Policy Dev. Abstr.

BL
UNILETRAS : REVISTA DO DEPARTAMENTO DE LETRAS DA UEPG. **Added/Corp** Universidade Estadual de Ponta Grossa. Departamento de Letras. (19??)-. Periodical. Portuguese (English). an. Free. Departamento de Letras Universidade Estadual de Ponta Grossa / Departamento de Letras, Praca Santos Andrade S/No 84.100, Ponta Grossa PR Brazil. **Tel** 0422.243966. **ED** Raul Jose Sozim. **LC** PN9; .U53. **DD** 805. **Circ:** 800 (ctrl).
Desc: Essays on language, linguistics, and literary sciences. Publishing short stories and poems.

II/0041-6762
UNILIT (SECUNDERABAD). (UNILIT.). [Unilit]. **Added/Corp** Visvasahiti (Secunderabad, India). (July 1961)-. Periodical. English. qt. **LC** PN2; .U55.
Ind/Abst MLA Int. Bibl. Books Artic. Mod. Lang. Lit.

SA/0041-5359
UNISA ENGLISH STUDIES. [Unisa Engl. stud.]. **Main/Corp** University of South Africa. Dept. of English. **Added/Corp** University of South Africa. Dept. of English. English Studies. **VAT** University of South Africa English Studies. Vol. 1 (Mar. 1968)-. Periodical. English. sa. $9.00. University of South Africa, PO Box 392, Pretoria 0001 South Africa. **Tel** 011 27 12 4298468, FAX 011 (27)12 429 3321, telex (59)350068+. **ED** Shirley G. Kossick. **LC** PR1; .S67a. **DD** 820/.9. **Bk Rev**. **Circ:** 3,000 (ctrl).
Desc: Devoted mainly to articles on literary criticism and theory.
Ind/Abst Annu. Bibliogr. Engl. Lang. Lit.; Lit. Crit. Regist.; MLA Int. Bibl. Books Artic. Mod. Lang. Lit.

US
UNIVERSE. 1990-. English. $19.95. **ED** Editors: 1990- R. Silverberg and K. Haber. **LC** PS648.S3; U39. **DD** 813/.0876208/005. ***Continues*** *Universe (Doubleday and Company, Inc.), 0276-1033.*

US/1048-9576
UNIVERSITY OF HARTFORD STUDIES IN LITERATURE. (UNIVERSITY OF HARTFORD STUDIES IN LITERATURE : UHSL.). [Univ. Hartford stud. lit.]. **Added/Corp** University of Hartford. **VFOAT** UHSL. Vol. 21, No. 1 (1989)-. Periodical. English. Three times a year. $7.50 (individuals), $9.00 (institutions). University of Hartford, 200 Bloomfield Avenue, English Department, West Hartford CT 06117. **Tel** (203)768-4574. **LC** PN2; .H3. **DD** 809. available on microfilm and microfiche from University Microfilms International (UMI). ***Continues*** *Studies in Literature, 0196-2280.*
Ind/Abst Abstr. Engl. Stud.; Am. Humanit. Index (199?-); Annu. Bibliogr. Engl. Lang. Lit.; MLA Int. Bibl. Books Artic. Mod. Lang. Lit.

US/0278-310X
UNIVERSITY OF MISSISSIPPI STUDIES IN ENGLISH, THE. [Univ. Miss. stud. Engl.]. **Added/Corp** University of Mississippi. Dept. of English. New Series Vol. 1 (1980)-. English. an. $20.00. University of Mississippi College of Liberal Arts, University MS 38677. **Tel** (601)232-7439. **ED** Benjamin Fisher. **LC** PR5.M5; A55. **DD** 820/.9. **Bk Rev**. **Pr Rev**. **Circ:** 300. available on microfilm from University Microfilms International (UMI). ***Continues*** *Studies in English (University of Mississippi. Dept. of English).*
Desc: Articles published on any aspects of study of American or British literature.
Ind/Abst Abstr. Engl. Stud.; Annu. Bibliogr. Engl. Lang. Lit.; MLA Int. Bibl. Books Artic. Mod. Lang. Lit.; Romant. Move.

CN
UNIVERSITY OF TORONTO ITALIAN STUDIES. **Added/Corp** University of Toronto. (1986)-. Monographic series. English.
Ind/Abst MLA Int. Bibl. Books Artic. Mod. Lang. Lit.

CN/0708-4382
UNIVERSITY OF TORONTO REVIEW. V. 1- 1977-. English. an. 4.00Can$ Canada; $4.00 US. University of Toronto Review, University of Toronto, 12 Hart House Circle, Toronto Ontario M5S 1A6 Canada. **Tel** (416)978-4911. **ED** David Alfred Kinnear. **DD** C810/.8/092379. **Circ:** 2,500.
Desc: Dedicated to the publishing of significant new literary talents beside the work of major figures like Frye and Heeney.

CN/0082-5336
UNIVERSITY OF TORONTO ROMANCE SERIES. [Univ. Tor. rom. ser.]. **Added/Corp** University of Toronto. Vol. 1 (1949)-. Monographic series. English (French). ir. Price varies per volume. University of Toronto Press, 5201 Dufferin Street, Downsview Ontario M3H 5T8 Canada. **Tel** (416)667-7781, (416)667-7782, FAX (416)667-7803. **LC** UNC.
Desc: A series of studies in the area of romance languages.
Ind/Abst MLA Int. Bibl. Books Artic. Mod. Lang. Lit.

CN/0042-0352
UNIVERSITY OF WINDSOR REVIEW, THE. ***Title Change.*** **Main/Corp** University of Windsor. **Added/Corp** University of Windsor. (19??)-Vol. 26 No. 2 (1993). Periodical. English. sa. University of Windsor Office of the Dean of Arts, Windsor Ontario N9B 3P4 Canada. **Tel** (519)253-4232 ext. 2332. **ED** Joseph A. Quinn. **Bk Rev**. **Circ:** 400 (ctrl). available on microfilm and microfiche from University Microfilms International (UMI). ***Continued by*** *Windsor Review.*
Desc: Covers short fiction, poetry, and reviews.
Ind/Abst Abstr. Engl. Stud.; Am. Hist. Life (1965-1985); Am. Humanit. Index; Annu. Bibliogr. Engl. Lang. Lit.; Can. Index; Can. Period. Index; MLA Int. Bibl. Books Artic. Mod. Lang. Lit.; Romant. Move.

US/0749-4149
UNIVERSITY STUDIES IN MEDIEVAL AND RENAISSANCE LITERATURE. [Univ. stud. Mediev. Renaiss. lit.]. Vol. 1-. Periodical. English. Peter Lang Publishing, 62 West 45th Street, 4th Floor, New York NY 10036. **Tel** (212)764-1471, (800)770-5264, telex 6973364 PLNY. **DD** 809.

RM
UNIVERSUL CARTII / REVISTA LUNARA A MINISTERULUI CULTURII. **Added/Corp** Romania. Ministerul Culturii. (1991)-. Periodical. Romanian. mo. DM116.00. Ministerul Culturii, Piata Pressei Libere nr. 1, 71341 Bucharest 1 Romania. **Tel** 617-33-06. **(Subscription address:** Kubon & Sagner, ABT Zeitschriftenimport, D 80328 Munich Germany.) **LC** Z2923; .U54.

US
UNSHAVED TRUTHS. (199?)-. English. qt. $3.50 per issue. Unshaved Truths, 2507 Roehampton Drive, Austin TX 78745-6964. **ED** Jon Lebkowsky.

GW/0083-4564
UNTERSUCHUNGEN ZUR DEUTSCHEN LITERATURGESCHICHTE. [Unters. dtsch. Lit.gesch.]. Vol. 1 (1962)-. Monographic series. German. ir. Price varies per volume. Max Niemeyer Verlag, Postfach 2140, D 72011 Tuebingen Germany. **Tel** 011 49 7071 989494, FAX 011 49 7071 87419. **DD** 830.
Desc: Monographs on German literature.
Ind/Abst MLA Int. Bibl. Books Artic. Mod. Lang. Lit.

GW/0083-4580
UNTERSUCHUNGEN ZUR SPRACH- UND LITERATURGESCHICHTE DER ROMANISCHEN VOLKER. **Added/Corp** Akademie der Wissenschaften und der Literatur, Mainz. Kommission fuer Romanische Philologie. (1959)-. Monographic series. German. ir. Price varies per volume. Franz Steiner Verlag GmbH, Postfach 101061, D 70009 Stuttgart Germany. **Tel** 011 49 0711 2582372, FAX 011 49 0711 2582290, telex 723636 daz d.
Desc: Monographs about romance literatures and languages.

US/0747-931X
UNVEILING. [Unveiling]. Vol. 2, No. 1 (Sept.-Nov. 1984)-. Periodical. English (Spanish). qt. $9.00. Unveiling, PO Box 170, Rockefeller Center Station, New York NY 10185. **Tel** (718)746-2007. **ED** Ismael Lorenzo. **DD** 860. **Bk Rev**. **Ad Acc**. **Circ:** 2,000. ***Continues*** *Unveiling Cuba, 0747-9328.*
Desc: A literary magazine in English and Spanish whose purpose is to disseminate the work of Cuban writers who could not publish in their own country.

US/1069-8051
UPSOUTH (BOWLING GREEN, KY.). (UPSOUTH.). [Upsouth]. (May 1993)-. Periodical. English. mo. Free. Upsouth Inc., 3627 Hammett Hill Road, Bowling Green KY 42101. **Tel** (502)843-8018. **ED** Galen Smith. **DD** 282. **Bk Rev**. ctrl circ.
Desc: Covers the interests of and issues concerning the Catholic writers of the South.

US/0886-2168
UPSTART CROW, THE. Vol. 1, No. 1 (Fall 1978)-. Periodical. English. an (Dec.). $7.00 US; $10.00 Canada & Mexico; $12.00 other. Clemson University, Department of English, 801 Strode Tower, Clemson SC 29634. **Tel** (803)656-3151. **LC** PR2885; .U67. **DD** 822.3/3. **Pr Rev**.
Ind/Abst MLA Int. Bibl. Books Artic. Mod. Lang. Lit.

PK
URDU. **See** Linguistics.

PK/0042-1065
URDU NAMAH. Periodical. Urdu (Urdu). **LC** AP95.U7; U73.

US/0362-7012
US 1 WORKSH. (US 1 WORKSHEETS.). [US 1 worksh.]. **Added/Corp** US 1 Poets' Cooperative. **VFOAT** US1 Worksheets. **VAT** United States One Worksheets. (19??)-. English. ir. $5.00. US 1 Poets Cooperative, 21 Lake Drive, Roosevelt NJ 08555. **Tel** (609)448-5096. **LC** PS501; .U16. **DD** 810/.8/005. **Circ:** 400.
Desc: High quality literary magazine, publishing fiction and poetry.
Ind/Abst Index Am. Period. Verse (19??-).

NE/0042-1235
US WURK. **See** Linguistics.

US/0171-726X
UTAH STUDIES IN LITERATURE AND LINGUISTICS. [Utah stud. lit. linguist.]. No. 1 (1974)-. Monographic series. English (German, French and Spanish). ir. Price varies per volume. Verlag Peter Lang AG, Jupiterstrasse 15, CH-3000 Bern 15 Switzerland. **Tel** 011 41 31 9411122, FAX 011 41 31 321131.
Ind/Abst Annu. Bibliogr. Engl. Lang. Lit.; MLA Int. Bibl. Books Artic. Mod. Lang. Lit.

US/1045-991X
UTOPIAN STUDIES. **See** Political Science-Socialism, Communism, Anarchism, Utopianism.

NE/0167-8175
UTRECHT PUBLICATIONS IN GENERAL AND COMPARATIVE LITERATURE. **VFOAT** Utrechtse Publikaties voor Algemene Literatuurwetenschap; UPAL; U.P.A.L. Vol. 1 (1962)-. Monographic series. Dutch (summaries and/or abstracts in English, French and German). ir. Price varies per volume. John Benjamins BV, Amsteldijk 44, PO Box 75577, 1070 AN Amsterdam Netherlands. **Tel** 011 31 20 6738156, FAX 011 31 20 739773. **(Subscription address:** John Benjamins North America, PO Box 27519, Philadelphia PA 19118-0519.**) ED** Douwe Fokkema, Joost Kloek, Sophie Levie and Willie van Peer. ***Continues*** *Regesten van de Aanwinsten.*

NE/0566-4640
UTRECHTSE PUBLIKATIES VOOR ALGEMENE LITERATUURWETENSCHAP. [Utrechtse publ. alg. lit.wet.]. (1962)-. Monographic series. Dutch. ir. **UDC** 82.
Ind/Abst MLA Int. Bibl. Books Artic. Mod. Lang. Lit.

II
UTTARA VARSHIKA. Gujarati (Gujarati). 3.00. **LC** PK1855; .U87.

RU/0473-8675
UVRES ET OPINIONS. **Added/Corp** Soiuz Pisatelei SSSR. (1959)-. Periodical. French. mo. **(Subscription address:** Victor Kamkin, 4956 Boiling Brook Parkway, Rockville MD 20852.**) LC** AP20; .O3. ***Supersedes*** *Litterature Sovietique.*

NR/0189-2320
UWA NDI IGBO. **VFOAT** Journal of Igbo Life and Culture. No. 1 (June 1984)-. Periodical. Niger-Kordofanian (English and Igbo). sa.

UZ
UZBEK TILI VA ADABIETI MASALALARI. VOPROSY UZBEKSKOGO IAZYKA I LITERATURY. ***Title Change.*** **See** Linguistics.

UZ/0134-2258
UZBEK TILI VA ADABIETI / UZBEKISTON SSR FANLAR AKADEMIIASI, A.S. PUSHKIN NOMIDAGI TIL VA ADABIET INSTITUTI. **See** Linguistics.

RU
V SELSKOM KLUBE. Vol. 1 (1969)-. Periodical. Russian. an. Izdatelstvo Iskusstvo, Vorotnikovskii Pereulok 11, 103009 Moscow Russia. **LC** PG3255.A42; .V2.

II/0970-9916
VAGARTHA (NEW DELHI). (VAGARTHA.). [Vagartha]. **Added/Corp** Joshi Foundation. Vol. 1 (Apr. 1973)-. Periodical. English. qt. **LC** PK5416; .V33. **DD** 809/.8954.
Ind/Abst MLA Int. Bibl. Books Artic. Mod. Lang. Lit.

US/1047-0913
VAN HOC (GARDEN GROVE, CALIF.). (VAN HOC.). [Van Hoc]. **VFOAT** Tap Chi Van Hoc. (1986)-. Periodical. Vietnamese. Twelve times a year. $42.00 US; $43.29 Canada; $43.36 other. Van Hoc, PO Box 1359, Garden Grove CA 92642. **ED** Trinh y Thu (editor's phone: (714)556-2714). **LC** PL4378.; .A46. **DD** 895. **Circ:** 1,000 (ctrl). ***Continues*** *Van Hoc Nghe Thuat, 0885-128X.*

VM
VAN NGHE. **Added/Corp** Hoi Lien Hiep Van Hoc Nghe Thuat Viet-Nam. (19??)-. Periodical. Vietnamese. wk. Xunhasaba Exports and Imports, 7 Nguyen Thi Minh Khai Str, Dit 1 Ho Chi Minh City Vietnam. **Tel** 011 84 8 294893, telex 278 XUNHASABA. **LC** PL4378; .A47.

US/0275-7672
VANDERBILT STREET REVIEW. Vol. 4 (1983)-. English. an. $5.65. Vanderbilt Street Review, 911 West Vanderbilt Street, Stephensville TX 76401. **Tel** (817)968-4267. **ED** Natrelle Young. **Bk Rev. Ad Acc. Circ:** 400. ***Continues*** *Vanderbilt Review of Prose and Poetry.*
Desc: Contemporary short stories, poetry and essays.

LV/0506-4120
VARAVIKSNE. [Varaviksne]. **VFOAT** Raduga. (1967)-. Latvian. an. Liesma / Flame Publishing House, Aspazijas Bulv 24, Riga Latvia 1455. **Tel** 3712 223 063. **LC** PG9000; .V36.
Ind/Abst MLA Int. Bibl. Books Artic. Mod. Lang. Lit.

TU
VARLIK. (1934)-. Periodical. Turkish. mo. $50.00. Varlik Yayinevi Cagaloglu, Yokusu 40, Ankara Caddesi, 34440 Istanbul Turkey. **Tel** 011 90 1 5226924. **ED** Yasar Nabi Nayr. **Bk Rev. Ad Acc. Circ:** 5,000.
Desc: Covers literature, poetry and the arts.

UK/0505-0448
VECTOR (READING). (VECTOR.). **Added/Corp** British Science Fiction Association. (Summer 1958)-. Periodical. English. bm. £8.00 UK; $13.70 other. British Science Fiction Association, C O 269 Wykeham Road, Reading RG6 1PL England. **Tel** 011 44 734 318022. **ED** Kev McVeigh and Boyd Parkinson. Index available ($1.50). **Bk Rev. Ad Acc. Circ:** 1,100.
Desc: Reviews, interviews and analysis of science fiction and fantasy literature from a British perspective.
Ind/Abst Sci. Fict. Fantasy Book Rev. Index (19??-).

US
VENUS. Vol. 1, No. 1 (June 1944)-. Periodical. English. qt.
Ind/Abst Aquat. Sci. Fish. Abstr. (Computer File); Helminthol. Abstr. (1991-).

US/0730-9708
VERANO, UN. **Added/Corp** Latino Youth (Organization). (Summer 1978)-. Periodical. English. an. $2.50. Latino Youth Alternative H/S, 1919 West Cullerton, Chicago IL 60608. **Tel** (312)829-0178.
Desc: Journal of literature and art.

US/1060-3700
VERB (ATLANTA, GA.). (VERB [SOUND RECORDING].). [Verb]. Winter (1991)-. Periodical. English. qt. $38.00. Verb, PO Box 8336, Atlanta GA 30306. **DD** 813.

GW/0067-592X
VEROFFENTLICHUNGEN DER ABTEILUNG FUER SLAVISCHE SPRACHEN UND LITERATUREN DES OSTEUROPA-INSTITUTS (SLAVISCHES SEMINAR) AN DER FREIEN UNIVERSITAT BERLIN. [Veroff. Abt. Slav. Sprachen Lit. Osteur.-Inst., Slav. Semin., Freien Univ. Berl.]. **Added/Corp** Freie Universitat Berlin. Osteuropa-Institut. **VFOAT** Slavistische Veroffentlichungen. (1953)-. Monographic series. German. Otto Harrassowitz Verlag, Taunusstrasse 14, Postfach 2929, D-65019 Wiesbaden Germany. **Tel** 011 49 611 5300, FAX 530570, telex 4186 135 OH D.
Ind/Abst MLA Int. Bibl. Books Artic. Mod. Lang. Lit.

IT/0506-7715
VERRI, IL. [Verri]. (1952)-. Periodical. Italian. qt. L80000 (Italy); L100000 (other). Enrico Mucchi Editore SRL, Via Emilia Est 1527, 41100 Modena Italy. **Tel** 011 39 59 374094, FAX 059/374096. cum. index.
Ind/Abst MLA Int. Bibl. Books Artic. Mod. Lang. Lit.

NE
VERSLAG OVER HET JAAR ... / STICHTING FONDS VOOR DE LETTEREN. **Main/Corp** Stichting Fonds voor de Letteren (Netherlands). Dutch. an. **LC** PT5083; .S75A.

BE
VERSLAGEN EN MEDEDELINGEN - KONINKLIJKE ACADEMIE VOOR NEDERLANDSE TAAL - EN LETTERKUNDE. **See** Linguistics.

US/0091-7257
VERTEX (LOS ANGELES). (VERTEX.). V. 1- Apr. 1973-. Periodical. English. bm. $6.00. 8060 Melrose Avenue, Los Angeles CA 90046. **LC** PZ1; .V45; PS648.S3. **DD** 813/.0876.

RU
VES SVET. (19??)-. Russian. 1.02rub. Izdatelstvo Molodaia Gvardiia, Novodmitrovskaya Ul., 5A, 125015 Moscow Russia. **Tel** 095-285-0830. **LC** PN6065.R9; V47.

NE
VESTDIJK KRONIEK. **VFOAT** Vestdijkkroniek. No. 1 (1973)-. Periodical. Dutch. ir. Fl45.00 (libraries). H. Gianotten, Heesterbospad 61, 4841 LZ Prinsenbeek, Netherlands. **Tel** 011 31 13 425050. **Circ:** 780.
Desc: Dedicated to the work of the Dutch author Vestdijk.

US/0504-0779
VETERANS' VOICES. **Added/Corp** Women in Communications, Inc. Greater Kansas City Professional Chapter. Theta Sigma Phi. Greater Kansas City Professional Chapter. Hospitalized Veterans Writing Project. (1952)-. Periodical. English. Three times a year. $8.00 hospitalized veterans; $15.00 other. Hospitalized Veterans Writing Project, 5920 Nall/Room 102, Mission KS 66202. **Tel** (913)432-1214. **ED** Margaret Clark. **LC** PS508.V45; V48. **DD** 810/.8/0920697. **Circ:** 5,000.
Desc: Works by patients in veterans administration medical centers; writing as therapy, an all volunteer project; prose and poetry.

US/0147-8184
VIA (BERKELEY). (VIA.). No. 1- May 1976-. Periodical. English (Portuguese and Spanish). sa. $6.00. University of Berkeley, 103 Sproul Hall, Berkeley CA 94720. **LC** PN1; .V5. **DD** 805.
Ind/Abst Archit. Period. Index.

CE
VICAKSANA. Periodical. Sinhalese (Sinhalese). **LC** PK2850; .A443.

AT/0158-3921
VICTORIAN FICTION RESEARCH GUIDES. [Vic. fict. res. guides]. **Added/Corp** University of Queensland. Dept. of English. (1979)-. Monographic series. English. qt. 40.00Aus$. University of Queensland / Department of English, St. Lucia QLD 4067 Australia. **Tel** 011 61 7 3772147, FAX 3719578. **LC** UNC. **DD** 823/.8/09.
Ind/Abst MLA Int. Bibl. Books Artic. Mod. Lang. Lit.

US/1060-1503
VICTORIAN LITERATURE & CULTURE. [Vic. lit. cult.]. **Added/Corp** Browning Institute. Vol. 19 (1991)-. Periodical. English. an. $47.50. AMS Press Inc., 56 East 13th Street, New York NY 10003. **Tel** (212)777-4700, FAX (212)995-5413, telex 710 581 2302. **LC** PR4229; .B77a. **DD** 820/9/003/05. ***Continues*** *Browning Institute. Studies, 0092-4725.*

US/0042-5206
VICTORIAN POETRY. [Vic. poetry]. **Added/Corp** West Virginia University. Vol. 1, (Jan. 1963)-. Periodical. English. Four times a year (Mar., June, Sept., Dec.). $30.00 (institutions) $18.00 (individuals) US and Canada; $35.00 (institutions), $23.00 (individuals) other. West Virginia University Department of English, PO Box 6296, Morgantown WV 26506-6296. **Tel** (304)293-3107, FAX (304)293-5380. **ED** Dr. Hayden Ward. **LC** PR500; .V5. Index available. cum. index. **Bk Rev**, (Qty: 6). **Ad Acc, Adv Mgr:** Dr. H. Ward. **Pr Rev. Circ:** 1,240. available on microfilm and microfiche from University Microfilms International (UMI). Documents available from The Genuine Article, UMI Article Clearinghouse.
Desc: Literary criticism of nineteenth century British and colonial poetry.
Ind/Abst Abstr. Engl. Stud.; Acad. Search (July 1993-); Annu. Bibliogr. Engl. Lang. Lit.; Arts Humanit. Citation Index [Full Cov.]; Child. Lit. Abstr. (19??-); Curr. Contents Arts Humanit.; Humanit. Index; Humanit. Source (Jul. 1993-); Index Book Rev. Humanit.; INFO-SOUTH Abstr.; Lit. Crit. Regist.; Mag. Search; MLA Int. Bibl. Books Artic. Mod. Lang. Lit.; Newsp. Period. Abstr. (1991-); Res. Alert [Full Cov.]; Romant. Move.

CN/0848-1512
VICTORIAN REVIEW. [Vic. rev.]. **Added/Corp** Victorian Studies Association of Western Canada. **VFOAT** Journal of the Victorian Studies Association of Western Canada. Vol. 15, No. 1 (Spring 1989)-. Periodical. English. Twice a year (July, & Dec.). $25.00 North America; $30.00 others. Victorian Studies Association of West Canada, University of Lethbridge, 4401 University Drive, Lethbridge Alberta T1K 3M4 Canada. **Tel** (403)329-2611. **ED** Dr. C. Hosgood (editor's address: Department of History, University of Lethbridge, Lethbridge Alberta T1K 3M4 Canada, phone: (403)329-2543). **LC** PR461; .V53. **Bk Rev. Ad Acc. Pr Rev. Circ:** 250. ***Continues*** *Newsletter of the Victorian Studies Association of Western Canada, 0703-5500.*
Ind/Abst MLA Int. Bibl. Books Artic. Mod. Lang. Lit.

US/0042-5222
VICTORIAN STUDIES. [Vic. stud.]. **Added/Corp** Modern Language Association of America. Victorian Literature Group. Vol. 1 (Sept. 1957)-. Periodical. English. qt. $45.00. Indiana University Press, 601 North Morton Street, Bloomington IN 47404. **Tel** (812)855-3830, (800)842-6796. **ED** Don Gray. **LC** PR1; .V5. **DD** 820/.9/008. **Bk Rev. Ad Acc. Circ:** 3,000 (ctrl). available on microfilm and microfiche from University Microfilms International (UMI). Documents available from The Genuine Article, UMI Article Clearinghouse.
Desc: Study of English culture of the Victorian period, comparative literature, social and political history, and the histories of education, philosophy, fine arts, economics, law, and science.
Ind/Abst Abstr. Engl. Stud.; Acad. Search (July 1993-); Am. Hist. Life (1957-); Annu. Bibliogr. Engl. Lang. Lit.; Arts Humanit. Citation Index [Full Cov.]; BHA : Biblio. Hist. Art; Book Rev. Index; Child. Lit. Abstr. (19??-); Curr. Contents Arts Humanit.; Expand. Acad. Index (1989-); Humanit. Index; Humanit. Source (Jul. 1993-); Index Book Rev. Humanit.; INFO-SOUTH Abstr.; Lit. Crit. Regist.; Mag. Search; MLA Int. Bibl. Books Artic. Mod. Lang. Lit.; Newsp. Period. Abstr. (1990-); Recent. Publ. Artic.; Ref. Sources; Res. Alert [Full Cov.]; RILA, Int. Rep. Lit. Art; Romant. Move.; Soc. Sci. Humanit. Index; Soc. Sci. Cit. Index [Select. Cov.]; SportSearch.

US/0275-8660
VICTORIAN STUDIES BULLETIN. [Vic. stud. bull.]. **Added/Corp** Northeast Victorian Studies Association. City University of New York. Victorian Committee. Vol. 1 (Feb. 1977)-. Bulletin. English. qt (Mar., June, Oct., Dec.). $7.00 institutions; $5.00 individuals. Victorian Studies Bulletin, 24 Centre Street Avenue, Woodmere NY 11598. **Tel** (516)569-6910. **ED** Leonard Beaky and Robert McLeon. **DD** 909. **Circ:** 400.
Desc: A newsletter describing current and forthcoming events in Victorian studies.

AU/0001-799X
VIERTELJAHRESSCHRIFT. [Vierteljahresschr. - Adalbert-Stifter-Inst. landes Oberosterr.]. **Main/Corp** Adalbert Stifter-Institut des Landes Oberosterreich. Periodical. German (French and English). qt. Adalbert Stifter Institut, Untere Donaulaende 6, A-4020 Linz Austria. **LC** PT2525.Z4; A15. cum. index.
Ind/Abst MLA Int. Bibl. Books Artic. Mod. Lang. Lit.

UK/0954-0881
VIGIL. Issue 1 (June 1988)-. English. Three times a year. £3.50 UK; $7.50 North America; £5.00 other. The Gillingham Bookroom, Somdor House/Suite 5, Station Road, Gillingham Dorset SP8 4QA England. **Tel** 0747-51552. **ED** John Howard. **Bk Rev. Ad Acc. Circ:** 250. available on microfilm from University Microfilms International (UMI). ***Continues** Period Piece & Paperback.*
Desc: Seeks to generate enthusiasm for excellence of standards in contemporary literature and language. Each issue presents a selection of poetry and short stories complemented by articles on the theory and practice of literature.

NE/0042-6032
VIGILIAE CHRISTIANAE. ***Ceased.*** [Vigiliae christ.]. Vol. 1 (Jan. 1947)-(1992). Periodical. English (French and German). qt. E. J. Brill, Postbus 9000, 2300 PA Leiden Netherlands. **Tel** 011 31 71 312624, FAX 011 31 71 317532, telex 39296 BRILL NL. **ED** J C M van Winden. **LC** BR66; .V5. **[CCC]. Bk Rev. Ad Acc. Circ:** 850 (ctrl). Documents available from The Genuine Article.
Desc: Contains articles and short notes of a historical, cultural, linguistic or philological nature on early Christian literature written after the new testament, as well as on Christian epigraphy and archaeology. Church and dogmatic history are only dealt with as they relate to social history; byzantine and medieval literature are treated as far as they exhibit continuity with the early Christian period.
Ind/Abst Arts Humanit. Citation Index [Full Cov.]; BHA : Biblio. Hist. Art (?-?); Curr. Contents Arts Humanit.; Index Book Rev. Relig. (19??-199?); MLA Int. Bibl. Books Artic. Mod. Lang. Lit.; New Testam. Abstr.; Relig. Index One Period. (19??-199?); Relig. Theol. Abstr.; Res. Alert [Full Cov.].

NP
VIJAYA. V. 1- 2030- 1973-. Nepali (Nepali). 2.00 single issue. Vijaya Parivara, Vijay Parivar Vijaypur 11, Dharana Nepal. **LC** PK2598.A2; V44.

PK
VIMAN DAIJIST. Periodical. Urdu. mo. Mussarat Aziz, Gardi Building, Nepar Road, Lahor Pakistan. **LC** PK2151; .V55.

UK/0264-5564
VINAVER STUDIES IN FRENCH. (1984)-. Monographic series. English. Francis Cairns, c/o Leeds University, Department of Classic Leeds, West Yorkshire LS2 9JT England. **Tel** 0532-333538.
Ind/Abst MLA Int. Bibl. Books Artic. Mod. Lang. Lit.

NO/0042-6288
VINDUET. [Vinduet]. **Added/Corp** Gyldendal Norsk Forlag. **VFOAT** Gyldendals Tidskrift for Litteratur. Vol. 1, (Aug. 1947)-. Periodical. Norwegian. Four times a year (Mar., June, Sept., Dec.). kr324.45 (individuals), kr389.45 (institutions); kr375.00 Europe; kr90.00 (students). Gyldendal Norsk Forlag, Postboks 6860 St. Olvas Plass, N 0130 Oslo 1 Norway. **Tel** 011 47 2 200710. **(Subscription address:** Forlagsentralen Tidsskriftavd, PO Box 150, Fursuet 1001 Oslo, 1 Norway**) LC** PN9; .V55. **DD** 808.8. cum. index. **Bk Rev. Circ:** 4,500 (ctrl).
Desc: Concerned mainly with literature, presenting new and established authors, foreign or Norwegian. Includes book reviews, interviews and poetry.
Ind/Abst Annu. Bibliogr. Engl. Lang. Lit.; MLA Int. Bibl. Books Artic. Mod. Lang. Lit.

US/0504-426X
VIRGINIA ENGLISH BULLETIN. See Linguistics.

II
VISHAYA VASTU. Vol. 1 No. 1 (July/Aug/Sept 1980)-. Periodical. Hindi (Hindi). qt. Rs15.00. Vishayavastu Karyalays, J-11/7 Rajouri Garden, New Delhi 110027 India. **LC** PK2040.5; .V49.

US
VISIONS-INTERNATIONAL. (19??)-. English. Three times a year (Feb., June, Oct.). $15.00 (one year), $29.00 (two year), $45.00 (three year) US; $18.00 (one year), $35.00 (two year), $54.00 (three year) other. Black Buzzard Press, 1110 Seaton Lane, Falls Church VA 22046-3920. **Tel** (703)241-8626. **ED** Bradley R. Strahan. Index available. cum. index. **Bk Rev**, (Qty: 30). **Circ:** 750. ***Continues** Visions The International Magazine of Illustrated Poetry, 0194-1690.*
Desc: A forum combining the creative energies of the world's poets and artists. Among the many fine poets are Ted Hughes, James Dickey, Marge Piercy, Marilyn Hacker, Allen Ginsberg, Andre Codrescu, Medbh McGuckian, Dennis Scott, Jared Carter and Eugene Ionescuu. Among the artists are Claese Oldenberg, Mary Fitzgerald and M L'Abbe.
Ind/Abst Humanit. Index.

UN/0131-2561
VITCYZNA (KIIV). (VITCHYZNA : LITERATURNO-KHUDOZHNII ZHURNAL SPILKY RADIANSKYKH PISMENNYKIV UKRAINY.). [Vitcyzna]. **Added/Corp** Spilka Radianskykh Pysmennykiv Ukrainy. (1946)-. Periodical. Ukrainian. mo. ***Continues** Ukrainska Literatura.*
Ind/Abst MLA Int. Bibl. Books Artic. Mod. Lang. Lit.

II
VIVECANA (BOMBAY, INDIA). (VIVECANA.). V. 1, No. 1 (January/March 1982)-. Periodical. Gujarati (Gujarati). qt. S N D T University, Bombay 400020 India. **LC** PK1850; .A46.

●US/1064-153X
VIZ (HATTIESBURG, MISS.). (VIZ : THE HUB CITY NEWS/REVIEW, GLOBAL CAFE JOURNAL.). [Viz]. (1992)-. Periodical. English. bm. $15.00. Viz, PO Box 1584, Hattiesburg MS 39403. **DD** 813.

RU
VOENNYE STRANITSY. (1991)-. Russian.

US/0160-4201
VOICE OF YOUTH ADVOCATES. (VOICE OF YOUTH ADVOCATES : VOYA.). [Voice youth advocates]. **VFOAT** VOYA. Vol. 1 (April 1978)-. Periodical. English. bm (Feb., Apr., June, Aug., Oct., Dec.). $32.50 US; $37.50 other. Scarecrow Press Inc., 52 Liberty Street, PO Box 4167, Metuchen NJ 08840. **Tel** (908)548-8600, (800)537-7107. **LC** Z718.5; .V65. **DD** 027.62/605. **Bk Rev. Ad Acc. Circ:** 4,000. available on microfilm and microfiche from University Microfilms International (UMI).
Desc: Articles, bibliographies on library information services to adolescents, reviews of materials for, about, and by adolescents.
Ind/Abst Book Rev. Index; Child. Lit. Abstr. (19??-); Curr. Lit. Fam. Plan.; Libr. Inf. Sci. Abstr.; Libr. Lit.; Sci. Fict. Fantasy Book Rev. Index.

US/1048-292X
VOICES IN ITALIAN AMERICANA. (VOICES IN ITALIAN AMERICANA : VIA.). [Voices Ital. Am.]. **VFOAT** VIA. Vol. 1, No. 1 (Spring 1990)-. Periodical. English. sa. $27.50 (institutions), $20.00 (individuals) US; $30.00 other. Purdue University / Foreign Languages, 1359 Stanley Coulter Hall, West Lafayette IN 47907. **Tel** (317)494-7691, (317)494-3839, FAX (317)494-3660. **ED** Anthony J Tamburri, Paolo A Giordano and Fred L Gardaphe. **LC** E184.I8; V64. **DD** 973/.0451. **Bk Rev**, (Qty: 14). **Ad Acc, Adv Mgr:** A J Tamburri, **Tel** (317)494-3839. **Circ:** 200.
Desc: A semiannual literary and cultural review devoted to the dissemination of information concerning the contributions of and about Italian Americans to the cultural and art worlds of North America. Each issue will be divided into three major sections: creative works, essays, and reviews.

CN/0840-4003
VOICES (SURREY). (VOICES : NEW WRITERS FOR NEW READERS.). [Voices]. **Added/Corp** Lower Mainland Society for Literacy and Employment. Vol. 1, No. 1 (Fall 1988)-. Periodical. English. qt. $12.00. Voices, 9260 140 Street, Surrey, British Columbia, V3V 5Z4 Canada. **Tel** (604)584-5424, FAX (604)584-0251. **ED** Calvin Wharton, Manging Editor. **DD** C810/.8/0920632.

CN/0318-9201
VOIX ET IMAGES. [Voix images]. **VFOAT** Etudes Quebecoises. Vol. 1 (Sept. 1975)-. French. Three times a year. 22.93Can$ Quebec; 24.77Can$ rest of Canada; 26.50Can$ other. University que Mont Svc Publications, CP 8888, Succursale A, Montreal Quebec H3C 3P8 Canada. **Tel** (514)987-7747, (514)987-4851. **LC** PQ3900; .V63. **DD** C840/.9/005. **Circ:** 900 (ctrl). Documents available from The Genuine Article. ***Supersedes** Voix et Images du Pays, 0318-921X.*
Desc: Exclusively studies of Quebec literature. An open journal dealing with modern theories (semiology, study of narratives, psycho-critique) as well as the history of literature.
Ind/Abst Arts Humanit. Citation Index (19??-) [Full Cov.]; Can. Period. Index (19??-); Curr. Contents Arts Humanit. (19??-); MLA Int. Bibl. Books Artic. Mod. Lang. Lit. (19??-); Point Repere (1983-); Res. Alert (19??-) [Full Cov.].

RU
VOPROSY IZUCHENIIA I PREPODAVANIIA SOVETSKOI LITERATURY. See Education-Teaching and Curriculum.

RU/0042-8795
VOPROSY LITERATURY. [Vopr. lit.]. **Added/Corp** Akademiia Nauk SSSR. Institut Mirovoi Literatury im. A.M. Gorkogo. Soiuz Pisatelei SSSR. Vol. 1 (1957)-. Periodical. Russian. Six times a year. $77.00. Izdatelstvo Izvestiia, Pl. Pushkina 5, 103798 Moscow Russia. **(Subscription address:** Victor Kamkin, 4956 Boiling Brook Parkway, Rockville, MD 20852**) LC** PN9; .V6.
Ind/Abst Annu. Bibliogr. Engl. Lang. Lit.; MLA Int. Bibl. Books Artic. Mod. Lang. Lit.

UN
VOPROSY LITERATURY NARODOV SSSR. Added/Corp Odeskyi Derzhavnyi Universytet Imeni I.I. Mechnykova. Vol. 1 (1975)-. Russian. 0.72rub. Izdatelskoe Obedinenie Vyshcha Shkola / Ukraine, Odessa Ostrovidova 64, Kiev Ukraine. **LC** PN849.R9; V58.

UN/0507-3871
VOPROSY RUSSKOI LITERATURY. Added/Corp Lvivskyi Derzhavnyi Universytet im. Iv. Franka. No. 1 (1966)-. Periodical. Russian. ir.
Ind/Abst MLA Int. Bibl. Books Artic. Mod. Lang. Lit.

LV
VOPROSY SIUZHETOSLOZHENIIA. Added/Corp Daugavpils, Latvia (City). Pedagogiskais Instituts. Krievu un Arzemju Literaturas Katedra. (1969)-. Russian. Zvaigzne / Star Publishing House, K Valdemara Iela 105, Riga Latvia 1013. **Tel** 3712 372 396. **LC** PN218; .V66.
Desc: Covers Russian literature with emphasis on plots, drama and the novel.

MX
VORTICE. Added/Corp Grupo Literario Vortice. No. 1 (1943)-. Periodical. Spanish. bm.
Ind/Abst HAPI Hisp. Am. Period. Index.

US/1052-8814
VOX MAGAZINE (NEW YORK, N.Y. 1990). (VOX MAGAZINE.). [Vox mag.]. **VFOAT** Vox. Vol. 1, No. 1 (Winter 1991)-. Periodical. English. bm. $14.00. Vox Publishing, 171 Madison Avenue/Suite 980, New York NY 10016. **Tel** (212)889-6365. **LC** IN PROCESS. **DD** 808. **Ad Acc. Circ:** 20,000.
Desc: Editorial includes poetry, interviews and art.

US
VOYEUR, THE. Added/Corp Open Window Society. Vol. 1 (Dec. 1974)-. Periodical. English. mo. $4.00. Open Window Society, 566 Laguardia Place, New York NY 10012.

RU
VOZVRASHCHENIE. (1991)-. Russian. ir. $89.95. Izdatelstvo Sovetskii Pisatel, Ulitsa Vorovskogo 11, 121069 Moscow Russia. **LC** PG3227.5; .V697.

RU
VREMENNIK PUSHKINSKOI KOMISSII / AKADEMIIA NAUK SSSR, OTDELENIE LITERATURY I IAZYKA PUCHKINSKAIA KOMMISSIIA. Main/Corp Akademiia Nauk SSSR. Pushkinskai A Komissiia. (1962)-. Russian. an. Izdatelstvo Nauka / Akademiia Nauk, Publishing House of the Russian Academy of Sciences, Leninskii Porspekt 14, 117901 Moscow Russia. **Tel** 011 95 954-21-53, FAX 011 95 938-21-44, telex 411964. **(Subscription address:** East View Publications Inc., 3020 Harbor Lane North, Suite 110, Minneapolis MN 55447.**) LC** PG3350.A1; A513. ***Supersedes** Pushkin.*

NE
VRIJE FRIES, DE. Added/Corp Fries Genootschap van Geschied-, Oudheid- en Taalkunde te Leeuwarden. Fries Genootschap van Geschied-, Oudheid- en Taalkunde te Leeuwarden. Fryske Akademy. (1837)-. Friesian. an. Fl35.38 Netherlands; Fl37.50 other. Fryske Akademy, Postbus 54, 8900 AB Leeuwarden Netherlands. **Tel** 011 31 58 131414. **LC** DJ401.F5; F9.
Ind/Abst BHA : Biblio. Hist. Art.

RU
VSTRECHA. (19??)-. Periodical. Russian. Six times a year. $99.95. **(Subscription address:** East View Publications Inc., 3020 Harbor Lane North, Suite 110, Minneapolis MN 55447.**)**

SZ
VWA. See Literature-Poetry.

CC
WAI KUO WEN HSUEH YEN CHIU (WU-CHANG, HUPEH PROVINCE, CHINA). (WAI KUO WEN HSUEH YEN CHIU.). **VFOAT** Studies in Foreign Literature; Waiguo Wenxue Yanjiu; Foreign Literature Studies. Began in 1978. Periodical. Chinese. qt. RMBY0.70. Science Press, 16 Donghuangchenggen North Street, Beijing 100707, People's Republic of China. **Tel** 011 86 1 4019821, 011 86 1 4010642, FAX 011 86 1 4012180, 011 86 1 4019810, telex 210147. **LC** PN9; .W35. **DD** 809.

CC
WAI KUO WEN HSUEH / [PEI-CHING WAI KUO YU HSUEH YUAN, WAI KUO WEN HSUEH YEN CHIU SO]. **Added/Corp** Pei-Ching Wai Kuo Yu Hsueh Yuan. Wai Kuo Wen Hsueh Yen Chiu So. **VFOAT** Foreign Literatures. (19??)-. Periodical. Chinese. mo. RMBY0.84. Chung-Kuo Kuo Chi Tu Shu Mao I Tsung Kung SSU, PO Box 2820, Beijing, People's Republic of China. **Tel** 23724. **LC** PN779.C5; W34. **DD** 809/.04.
Ind/Abst MLA Int. Bibl. Books Artic. Mod. Lang. Lit.

US/0737-0679
WALT WHITMAN QUARTERLY REVIEW. [Walt Whitman q. rev.]. **Added/Corp** University of Iowa. University of Iowa. Graduate College. University of Iowa. Dept. of English. **VFOAT** WWQR. Vol. 1, No. 1 (June 1983)-. Periodical. English. qt (Mar., June, Sept., Dec.). $20.00 (institution), $15.00 (individual). University of Iowa, 308 English/Philosophy Building, Iowa City IA 52242. **Tel** (319)335-5650, (319)335-0592. **ED** Ed Folsom and William White. **LC** PS3229; .W39. **DD** 811/.3. cum. index. **Bk Rev. Ad Acc. Circ:** 525 (ctrl). available on microfilm and microfiche from University Microfilms International (UMI). Documents available from The Genuine Article. ***Continues*** *Walt Whitman Review.*
Desc: Literary journal containing Whitman studies.
Ind/Abst Am. Humanit. Index; Annu. Bibliogr. Engl. Lang. Lit.; Arts Humanit. Citation Index [Full Cov.]; Curr. Contents Arts Humanit.; Lit. Crit. Regist.; MLA Int. Bibl. Books Artic. Mod. Lang. Lit.; Res. Alert [Full Cov.].

US/0083-713X
WALTER PRESCOTT WEBB MEMORIAL LECTURES. (1968)-. Monographic series. English. ir. Price varies per volume. Texas A & M University Press, Drawer C, College Station TX 77843. **Tel** (409)845-1436, (800)826-8911. **DD** 040.
Desc: Subject matter is on the broad field of history.

NE/0923-4764
WAPITI MAASTRICHT. (WAPITI.). [Wapiti Maastricht]. (1989)-. Periodical. Dutch. Eleven times a year. Fl59.50. Europese Jeugdbladen Pers BV, Postbus 88, 3410 CB Lopik Netherlands. **Tel** 011 31 03485 4312. **UDC** 82-9.

US/1046-6967
WAR, LITERATURE, AND THE ARTS. [War lit. arts]. **Added/Corp** United States Air Force Academy. Dept. of English. **VFOAT** WLA. Vol. 1, No. 1 (Spring 1989)-. Periodical. English. Twice a year (Spring & Fall). $10.00 (individuals); $20.00 (institutions). US Air Force Academy English Department, Colorado Springs CO 80840. **Tel** (719)472-3930, (719)472-4207, FAX (719)472-3135. **ED** Col. Donald Anderson. **LC** PN56.W3; W34. **DD** 700. Index available (Fall issue). cum. index. **Bk Rev**, (Qty: 6). **Ad Acc, Adv Mgr:** Donald Anderson. **Pr Rev. Circ:** 200.
Desc: Multidisciplinary journal addressing the relationship of war and the arts.
Ind/Abst Am. Humanit. Index (199?-); Lit. Crit. Regist.; MLA Int. Bibl. Books Artic. Mod. Lang. Lit.

US/0083-7210
WARD-PHILLIPS LECTURES IN ENGLISH LANGUAGE AND LITERATURE. **See** Linguistics.

UK/0269-0055
WASAFIRI. **Added/Corp** Association for the Teaching of Caribbean, African, Asian and Associated Literatures. Vol. 1, No. 1 (Autumn 1984)-. Periodical. English. Twice a year. £16.00 (institutions), £12.00 (individuals) UK; £20.00 (institutions), £16.00 (individuals) other. Wasafiri, PO Box 195, Canterbury Kent CT2 7XB England. **Tel** 011 44 71 7753120. **ED** Susheila Nasta. **Bk Rev**, (Qty: 40-45 per year). **Ad Acc. Circ:** 1,000.
Desc: A journal of African, Asian, and Caribbean literature for readers, teachers, and students.

CN/0043-0412
WASCANA REVIEW. [Wascana rev.]. **Added/Corp** University of Saskatchewan. Regina Campus. Dept. of English. Vol. 1 (1966)-. Academic Scholarly Publication. English. sa. 10.00Can$ Canada; 12.00Can$ other. University of Regina Department of English, Regina Saskatchewan S4S 0A2 Canada. **Tel** (306)585-4140. **ED** Kathleen Wall. **Bk Rev. Circ:** 250 (ctrl).
Desc: Literary criticism of scholarly standards and knowledgeable articles on the theatre, the visual arts and music. Reviews of current books.
Ind/Abst Abstr. Engl. Stud.; Am. Humanit. Index; MLA Int. Bibl. Books Artic. Mod. Lang. Lit.

US/0043-0455
WASHINGTON AND JEFFERSON LITERARY JOURNAL. **Added/Corp** Washington and Jefferson College, Washington, Pa. (1966)-. Periodical. English. an. $1.00. Washington & Jefferson College, 45 S Lincoln Dr., Washington PA 15301. **Tel** (412)222-4400. **DD** 810.

US/0163-903X
WASHINGTON REVIEW. **See** The Arts.

●MW
WASI : [BULLETIN]. **Added/Corp** Writers Advisory Services International Writers and Artists Services International. **VFOAT** Writers Advisory Services International; Writers and Artists Services International; WASI Writer. Vol. 3, No. 2 (June 1992)-. Periodical. English. sa. ***Continues*** *WASI Writer.*

CN/0228-1937
WASTELANDS. [Wastelands]. No. 1 Autumn 1980-. Periodical. English. qt. $6.50. Wastelands, PO Box 300 Station A, Ottawa Ontario J1B 8V3 Canada. **DD** C810/.8/0054.

US/0275-9748
WDS FORUM. ***Title Change.*** [WDS forum]. **Added/Corp** Writer's Digest School. **VAT** Writer's Digest School Forum. (19??)-(19??). Periodical. English. qt. Writer's Digest Books, 1507 Dana Avenue, Cincinnati OH 45207. **Tel** (513)531-2222, (800)289-0963, FAX (513)531-4744. **ED** Kirk Polking. **DD** 808. **Circ:** 13,000 (ctrl). ***Continued by*** *Writer's Forum (Cincinnati, Ohio), 1057-0756.*
Desc: Articles on fiction and nonfiction writing technique plus news of students and faculty.

US
WEB, THE. **Added/Corp** Ohio State University. Center for Language, Literature, and Reading. **VFOAT** Wonderfully Exciting Books. Vol. 1, No. 1 (Fall 1976)-. Periodical. English. Three times a year. $10.00. Ohio State University / College of Education, 174 Arps Hall, 1945 North High Street, Columbus OH 43210-3407. **Tel** (614)292-3407, FAX (614)292-8052. cum. index.

US/1055-6907
WEB (SANTA CRUZ, CALIF.), THE. (THE WEB : CELEBRATING CHILDREN'S LITERATURE.). [Web]. Vol. 1, No. 1 (Spring 1991)-. Periodical. English. qt. $3.00. Wendy E Betts, PO Box 401, Santa Cruz CA 95061-0401. **DD** 808.

AT
WEBBER'S. (Spring 1989)-. English. sa. 10.00Aus$ (one year), 20.00Aus$ (two year) Australia; 15.00Aus$ (one year), 30.00Aus$ (two year) other. Webbers Booksellers, 15 McKillop St, Melbourne Victoria 3000 Australia. **Tel** 03 670 2418, FAX 03 670 2559. **ED** Joanna Kenny. **Bk Rev**, (Qty: 4).
Desc: Publishes original short stories, poetry, and essays particularly those with a local flavor.

US/0363-1230
WEBSTER REVIEW. [Webster rev.]. **Added/Corp** Webster College. Vol. 1, No. 1 (Spring 1974)-. Periodical. English. an. $5.00 US; $6.00 other. Webster Review, Webster University, 470 East Lockwood, Webster Groves MO 63119. **Tel** (314)432-2657. **ED** Nancy Schapiro. **LC** PN6010.5; .W4. **DD** 808.8. **Circ:** 1,000.
Desc: Publishes contemporary international stories, poems, essays and interviews. Emphasizes translations of the above from all languages into English.
Ind/Abst Am. Humanit. Index; Index Am. Period. Verse.

CN/0702-4894
WEE GIANT. V. 1- Autumn 1977-. Periodical. English. Three times a year. $1.25 each number. Wee Giant Press, 178 Bond Street North, Hamilton Ontario L8S 3W6 Canada. **DD** C810/.8/0054.

AU/0043-2199
WEIMARER BEITRAEGE. (1955)-. Periodical. German. Four times a year. S1150.20. Passagen Verlag GES MBH, Walfischgasse 15/14, A 1010 Vienna Austria. **Tel** 011 43 1 5137761, FAX 011 43 1 5126327. **(Subscription address:** Minerva Wissenschaftl Buchhdlg, Sachsenplatz 4 6, Postfach 88, A 1201 Vienna Austria.) **UDC** 82. **CODEN** 82.01.
Ind/Abst Soc. Sci. Cit. Index [Select. Cov.].

GW/0323-4223
WEIMARER BEITRAEGE. [Weimarer Beitr.]. **Added/Corp** Nationale Forschungs- und Gedenkstatten der Klassischen Deutschen Literatur in Weimar. (1955)-. Periodical. German. qt. DM1150.20. Passagen Verlag GES MBH, Walfischgasse 15/14, A 1010 Vienna Austria. **Tel** 011 43 1 5137761, FAX 011 43 1 5126327. **ED** Peter Engelmann. **LC** PT3; .W38. Index available. **Bk Rev**, (Qty: 75). **Ad Acc, Adv Mgr:** Mr. Winkler. **Circ:** 700. Documents available from The Genuine Article.
Ind/Abst Arts Humanit. Citation Index [Full Cov.]; BHA : Biblio. Hist. Art; Curr. Contents Arts Humanit.; MLA Int. Bibl. Books Artic. Mod. Lang. Lit.; Res. Alert [Full Cov.].

US/0898-5073
WEIRD TALES. [Weird tales]. (1923)-. Periodical. English. Four times a year (Seasonally). $16.00 US, $20.00 Canada & Mexico, $22.00 others (four issues). Terminus Publishing Co. Inc., 123 Crooked Lane, King of Prussia PA 19406. **Tel** (215)275-4463. **ED** Darrell Schweitzer. **LC** PS509.F3; W44. **DD** 813/.0876/08. **Bk Rev. Ad Acc, Adv Mgr:** Carol Adams. **Acid Free. Circ:** 9,500.
Desc: Every issue features great new fiction by leading authors in horror and fantasy fiction.
Ind/Abst Sci. Fict. Fantasy Book Rev. Index.

US/8755-7452
WEIRDBOOK. **See** Romance and Adventure.

UK/0263-1776
WELLSIAN (EDWALTON, NOTTINGHAMSHIRE : 1976). (THE WELLSIAN.). New Ser., No. 1 (1976)-. English. £10.00. HG Wells Society / Department of English, Nene Coll Moulton, Northampton NNZ 7AL United Kingdom. **Tel** 011 44 604 735500 ext. 2133. **ED** Michael Drape. **Bk Rev. Ad Acc. Circ:** 500. ***Continues*** *H.G. Wells Society Journal.*
Ind/Abst MLA Int. Bibl. Books Artic. Mod. Lang. Lit.

US/1045-2974
WELLSPRING (LONG LAKE, MINN.). (WELLSPRING : SOURCE OF AWARD-WINNING FICTION.). [Wellspring]. (Summer/Fall 1989)-. Periodical. English. Twice a year (June, Dec.). $8.00 (one year); $15.00 (two years). Castalia Bookmakers Inc, 777 Tonkawa Road, Long Lake MN 55356. **Tel** (612)471-9259. **DD** 813.

NE/0043-2539
WELT DES ISLAMS, DIE. **See** Religion and Theology-Islam, Bahaism, Theosophy.

CH
WEN HSUEH CHIEH. **VFOAT** Literary Taiwan; Wen Hsueh Chieh Chi Kan. Vol. 1-. Periodical. Chinese. qt. NT$90.00. Chung Hui Chu Pan She 8, Lane 3, Ling Ya Chu Cheng I Road, Kao-Hsiung Shih Taiwan. **LC** PL3031.T3; W456. **DD** 895.1/08.

CC
WEN HSUEH LUN TSUNG / HO-NAN SHENG SHE HUI KO HSUEH YUAN, WEN HSUEH YEN CHIU SO, HO-NAN SHENG WEN HSUEH HSUEH HUI PIEN. 1 (Dec. 1983)-. Periodical. Chinese. qt. RMBY0.84. Hsin Hua Shu Tien / Ho-Nan Sheng China, People's Republic of China. **LC** PN595.C6; W445. **DD** 809.

CC
WEN HSUEH YUEH PAO (CHANG-SHA SHIH, CHINA). (WEN HSUEH YUEH PAO.). 1984-4 (April 1984)-. Periodical. Chinese. mo. RMBY120,000. Chung-Kuo Kuo Chi Tu Shu Mao I Tsung Kung SSU, PO Box 2820, Beijing, People's Republic of China. **Tel** 23724. **ED** Ren Guangchun, Wang Yiping. **LC** PL2250; .W3727. **DD** 895.1/09. **Bk Rev. Ad Acc. Circ:** 50,000. ***Continues*** *Hsiang-Chiang Wen Hsueh.*
Desc: A comprehensive magazine carrying mainly novels, essays, poetry, and literature reviews, etc. and is well circulated nation-wide.

US/1045-0491
WE'RE LIVING IN FUNNY TIMES. [We're living funny times]. **VFOAT** We are Living in Funny Times; Funny Times. No. 1 (Nov. 21, 1985)-. Periodical. English. mo. $17.50 (one year), $28.50 (two year). Funny Times, 3108 Scarborough Road, Cleveland Heights OH 44118. **Tel** (216)371-8600. **DD** 817.

US/0149-6441
WEST BRANCH. (1977)-. Periodical. English. Twice a year (May, Nov.). $7.00 (one year), $11.00 (two year), $16.00 (three year). Bucknell University / English Department, Bucknell Hall, Lewisburg PA 17837. **Tel** (717)524-1853. **ED** Karl Patten and Robert Taylor. **LC** PN6010.5; .W47. **DD** 808.81/05. Index available. **Bk Rev. Circ:** 500.
Desc: Poetry and fiction of the highest quality.
Ind/Abst Am. Humanit. Index; Index Am. Period. Verse.

CN/1182-4271
WEST COAST LINE. [West coast line]. **Added/Corp** Simon Fraser University. Dept. of English. **VFOAT** West Coast; Westcoast. Vol. 24, No. 1 (Spring 1990)-. Periodical. English. Three times a year. $30.00 (institution), $20.00 (individual). West Coast Line, The Editor, 2027 E Acad Annex Simon Fraser, Burnaby British Columbia, V5A 1S6 Canada. **Tel** (604)291-4287. **LC** AP2; .W395. **DD** C810.8/09711. available on microfilm and microfiche from University Microfilms International (UMI). ***Continues*** *West Coast Review, 0043-311X.*
Ind/Abst Am. Humanit. Index (19??-); Can. Period. Index (19??-).

CN/1183-2681
WEST FORTY-NINTH. [West forty-ninth]. **Added/Corp** Vancouver Community College. Langara Campus. Vol. 1, No. 1 (1991)-. Periodical. English. sa. Limited free distribution. Vancouver Community College, Langara Campus, #7-8415 Granville Street, Vancouver British Columbia V6P 4Z9 Canada. **DD** C810.8/0054.

US/0890-9024
WEST HILLS REVIEW. ***Suspended.*** [West Hills rev.]. Vol. 1 (Fall 1979)-(19??). Periodical. English. an. $5.00 (plus $1.00 postage). Walt Whitman Birthplace, 246 Old Walt Whitman Road, Huntington Station NY 11746. **Tel** (516)427-5240. **ED** William Fahey. **LC** PS3229; .W47. **DD** 811/.3. **Bk Rev. Circ:** 500.
Desc: Poetry, prose, art and photography in the tradition of Walt Whitman.
Ind/Abst Am. Humanit. Index (-19??).

AT/0043-342X
WESTERLY. [Westerly]. (1956)-. Periodical. English. qt. 24.00Aus$ (1 year), 42.00Aus$ (2 year) Australia;

26.00Aus$ (1 year), 46.00Aus$ (2 year) other. Centre for Studies in Australian Literature, English Department, Nedlands Western Australia 6009 Australia. **Tel** 09 380 2101, FAX 09 380 1030, telex AA92992. **ED** Bruce Bennett, Dennis Haskell, Peter Cowan, Delys Bird. **LC** AP7; .W46. **DD** 820/.5. **[CCC]**. Index available. **Bk Rev. Ad Acc. Circ:** 1,000 (ctrl). Documents available from The Genuine Article.
Desc: Aims at a general intelligent audience wishing to keep abreast of contemporary Australian writing. Publishes lively poems, stories, articles, reviews from Australia and overseas, especially southeast Asia.
Ind/Abst Abstr. Engl. Stud.; Annu. Bibliogr. Engl. Lang. Lit.; APAIS, Aust. Public Aff. Inf. Ser. (1963-); Arts Humanit. Citation Index [Full Cov.]; Curr. Contents Arts Humanit.; MLA Int. Bibl. Books Artic. Mod. Lang. Lit.; Res. Alert [Full Cov.]; Romant. Move.; Soc. Sci. Cit. Index [Select. Cov.].

US/0043-3462
WESTERN AMERICAN LITERATURE. [West. Am. lit.]. **Added/Corp** Western Literature Association. Colorado State University. Dept. of English and Modern Literature. Utah State University. Vol. 1 (Spring 1966)-. Periodical. English. Four times a year. $30.00 US; $31.00 other. Utah State University / English Department, Logan UT 84322-3200. **Tel** (801)797-1603, FAX (801)797-4099. **ED** Thomas J. Lyon. **LC** PS271; .W46. **DD** 810.9/978. Index available (February). **Bk Rev**, (Qty: 140/year). **Ad Acc. Pr Rev. Circ:** 1,200. available on microfilm and microfiche from University Microfilms International (UMI). Documents available from The Genuine Article.
Desc: Dedicated to the study and enjoyment of Western regional literature.
Ind/Abst Abstr. Engl. Stud.; Am. Hist. Life (1966-); Am. Humanit. Index; Annu. Bibliogr. Engl. Lang. Lit.; Arts Humanit. Citation Index [Full Cov.]; Book Rev. Index; Chicano Index; Curr. Contents Arts Humanit.; Film Lit. Index; Index Book Rev. Humanit.; Lit. Crit. Regist.; MLA Int. Bibl. Books Artic. Mod. Lang. Lit.; Ref. Sources; Res. Alert [Full Cov.]; Soc. Sci. Cit. Index [Select. Cov.]; West. Hist. Q.; Women Stud. Abstr.

US/0043-3845
WESTERN HUMANITIES REVIEW. [West. humanit. rev.]. **Added/Corp** Utah Humanities Research Foundation. University of Utah. Dept. of English. Vol. 3 (Jan. 1949)-. Periodical. English. qt. $20.00 (individuals), $26.00 (institutions) US and Canada; $30.00 other. University of Utah / OSH 341, University of Utah, Salt Lake City UT 84112. **Tel** (801)581-6070. **ED** Barry Weller, Larry Levis, Elizabeth Tornes. **LC** AP2; .W426. **DD** 979. cum. index. **Bk Rev. Ad Acc. Circ:** 1,200 (ctrl). available on microfilm and microfiche from University Microfilms International (UMI). Documents available from The Genuine Article. ***Continues** Utah Humanities Review.*
Desc: Articles on the humanities, fiction, poetry, book reviews.
Ind/Abst Abstr. Engl. Stud.; Am. Hist. Life (1963-1980); Am. Humanit. Index; Annu. Bibliogr. Engl. Lang. Lit.; Arts Humanit. Citation Index [Full Cov.]; Book Rev. Index; Curr. Contents Arts Humanit.; Film Lit. Index; Index Am. Period. Verse; Lit. Crit. Regist.; Med. Rev. Dig.; Middle East Abstr. Index; MLA Int. Bibl. Books Artic. Mod. Lang. Lit.; Res. Alert [Full Cov.]; Romant. Move.; West. Hist. Q.

US/0192-1355
WESTERN ILLINOIS REGIONAL STUDIES. ***Ceased.*** **See** History(General)-History of North, South, and Central America.

US/1057-9559
WESTMINSTER REVIEW (NEW WILMINGTON, PA.), THE. (THE WESTMINSTER REVIEW.). [Westminst. rev.]. **Added/Corp** Westminster College (New Wilmington, Pa.). Vol. 1, No. 1 Dec. (1991)-. Periodical. English. sa. $8.00. Dawn Valley Press of Westminster College, Box 102, Westminster College, New Wilmington PA 16172. **DD** 810. ***Continues** Sunrust Magazine, 0741-0271.*

US/0192-5865
WHEELWRIGHTINGS. Added/Corp Hansoms of John Clayton (Society). (197?)-. Periodical. English. Three times a year. $9.00. Hansoms of John Clayton, 4010 Devon Lane, Peoria IL 61614. **Tel** (309)688-2639. **ED** Robert C. Burr. **LC** PR4623; .A28. **DD** 823/.8. **Bk Rev. Circ:** 150 (ctrl).
Desc: Articles, pastiches, poetry, and book reviews, relating to Sherlock Holmes.

CN/0318-1065
WHETSTONE (LETHBRIDGE). (WHETSTONE.). [Whetstone]. **Added/Corp** University of Lethbridge. (1971)-. English. sa (Apr., Nov.). 10.00Can$ one year, 18.00Can$ two year, 26.00Can$ three year. University of Lethbridge, English Department, 4401 University Drive, Lethbridge Alberta T1K 3M4 Canada. **Tel** (403)329-2490, (403)329-2111. **ED** David Cooper and Mary Jane Tallon. **Circ:** 250.
Desc: Fiction, artwork and poetry by new and established artists.

CN/0712-8991
WHITE WALL REVIEW. [White wall rev.]. **Added/Corp** Ryerson Literary Society. Vol. 1 No. 1 (Spring 1976)-. English. an. 5.00Can$, 3.00Can$ students (add $1.00 for postage). White Wall Review, Oakham House, 63 Gould Street, Toronto Ontario M5B 1E9 Canada. **Tel** (416)977-1045. **ED** Lena Friesen and Cara Scott. **DD** C810/.8/0054. **Circ:** 500 (ctrl).
Desc: Since 1975, publishes the work of writers and artists, mainly from across Canada, but also from the United States and overseas. Includes plays, short stories, poems, essays, artwork, photographs and music.
Ind/Abst Can. Period. Index (1990-).

CN/0229-0804
WHIZ FUNNIES. Vol. 1, No. 1 (Oct. 1977)-. Periodical. English. $0.50 each number. Whiz Funnies, 616-415 Edison Avenue, Winnipeg Manitoba R2G 0M3 Canada. **DD** C810/.8/0054.

CN/0715-9366
WHO'S WHO IN CANADIAN LITERATURE. [Who's who Can. lit.]. (1983/1984)-. Directory. English (French). be (every two years). 35.00Can$. Reference Press, PO Box 70, Teeswater Ontario N0G 2S0 Canada. **Tel** (519)392-6634. **ED** Gordon Ripley and Anne Mercer. **LC** PR9189.6; .W47. **DD** 809/.8971. **Pr Rev. Circ:** 1,200.
Desc: A regularly-updated biographical reference to living Canadian poets, novelists, playwrights, short story writers, children's writers, critics and editors.

GW/0722-916X
WHO'S WHO IN THE ARTS AND LITERATURE. 3rd Ed. (1982)-. English. Who's Who Intl Red Series, Bottroper Str 20, Postfach 103244, W4300 Essen 1 Germany. ***Formed by the union of** Who's Who in Literature (Worthsee, Germany), 0170-7051 **and** Who's Who in the Arts.*

AT
WHO'S WHO OF AUSTRALIAN WRITERS. (19??)-. Directory. English. ir. $80.00. D. W. Thorpe, A Reed Reference Publishing Company, A Subsidiary of Reed International Books Australia, 18 Salmon Street, Port Melbourne, Victoria 3207 Australia. **Tel** 011 61 3 6451511, FAX 011 61 3 6453981, telex 39476.
Desc: Offers information on living Australian writers and editors of fiction, nonfiction, poetry, plays, textbooks, and radio and TV scripts.

GW
WIELAND-STUDIEN. Added/Corp Wieland-Archiv (Biberach an der Riss, Germany). **VFOAT** Wieland Studien. (1991)-. German. Jan Thorbecke Verlag GmbH and Company, Karlstrasse 10, Postfach 546, D 72482 Sigmaringen Germany. **Tel** 011 49 7571 728100, FAX 011 07571-728-280, telex 732534. **LC** PT2569; .W54.

AU
WIENER ARBEITEN ZUR DEUTSCHEN LITERATUR. (1970)-. Monographic series. German.
Ind/Abst MLA Int. Bibl. Books Artic. Mod. Lang. Lit.

US/0897-2982
WILKIE COLLINS SOCIETY JOURNAL. [Wilkie Collins Soc. j.]. **Added/Corp** Wilkie Collins Society. Vol. 1 (1981)-. Periodical. English. an. $10.00. Wilkie Collins Society, 1307 F Street, Davis CA 95616. **Tel** (916)756-6454. **LC** PR4496; .A18. **DD** 823/.8.
Ind/Abst MLA Int. Bibl. Books Artic. Mod. Lang. Lit.

US/0197-663X
WILLA CATHER PIONEER MEMORIAL NEWSLETTER. [Willa Cather Pioneer Meml. newsl.]. **Main/Corp** Willa Cather Pioneer Memorial and Educational Foundation. **Added/Corp** Willa Cather Pioneer Memorial and Educational Foundation. Newsletter. Vol. 19, No. 4 (Winter 1975)-. Newsletter. English. Four times a year. $15.00. Willa Cather Pioneer Memorial, 326 North Webster Street, Red Cloud NE 68970. **Tel** (402)746-2653. ***Continues** Newsletter (Willa Cather Pioneer Memorial and Educational Foundation).*
Ind/Abst MLA Int. Bibl. Books Artic. Mod. Lang. Lit.

US/1048-8618
WILLA CATHER YEARBOOK, THE. [Willa Cather yearb.]. Vol. 1 (1991)-. English. $19.95 (paperbound), $29.95 (casebound). Edwin Mellen Press, PO Box 450, Lewiston NY 14092. **Tel** (716)754-2788. **LC** PS3505.A87; Z4588. **DD** 813/.52.

●US/1065-9080
WILLA / WOMEN IN LITERATURE AND LIFE ASSEMBLY. Added/Corp National Council of Teachers of English. Women in Literature and Life Assembly. (1992)-. Periodical. English. $10.00. Women in Literature and Life Assembly, PO Box 224, Ruston LA 71272.

US/0740-6789
WILLAMETTE JOURNAL OF THE LIBERAL ARTS, THE. **See** The Arts.

US/0361-2481
WIND (PIKEVILLE, KY.). (WIND.). [Wind]. **VFOAT** Wind/Literary Journal; Wind Literary Journal; Wind Magazine. Vol. 1, No. 1 (Spring 1971)-. Periodical. English. sa. $8.00 (institutions), $7.00 (individuals) US; $12.00 foreign. Wind Magazine, Route 1/Box 809K, Pikeville KY 41501. **Tel** (606)631-1129. **ED** Quentin R Howard. **LC** PS501; .W55. **DD** 810/.8/10054. **Bk Rev. Circ:** 400.
Desc: An eclectic literary periodical published two times yearly containing poetry, short stories and book reviews from small presses, beginners and established poets and writers.
Ind/Abst Am. Humanit. Index (-199?); Index Am. Period. Verse.

US/0275-2166
WINDOW (BETHESDA, MD.). (WINDOW.). 1 (Spring 1976)-. Periodical. English. qt. $2.50 each issue. Window Press, 7005 Westmoreland Drive, Takoma Park MD 20912. **LC** PS1; .W55A. **DD** 810/.8.

US/1055-1719
WINDOW ON THE ARTS, LITERATURE, AND SOCIETY, THE. **See** The Arts.

CN/0822-2363
WINDSCRIPT. [Windscript]. **Added/Corp** Saskatchewan Writers' Guild. Vol. 1 (Sept. 1983)-. Periodical. English. sa. 8.00Can$ (one year), 12.00Can$ (two years). Saskatchewan Writers Guild, PO Box 1154, Regina SASK S4P 3R9 Canada. **Tel** (306)757-6310. **DD** C810/.8/09283. **Ad Acc. Circ:** 3,500.
Desc: Magazine of Saskatchewan High School literary and visual art.

CN
WINDSOR REVIEW. (19??)-. English (French). Twice a year. 19.95Can$ (individuals); 29.95Can$ (institutions). University of Windsor Office of the Dean of Arts, Windsor Ontario N9B 3P4 Canada. **Tel** (519)253-4232 ext. 2332.

GW/0084-0467
WIRKUNG DER LITERATUR. [Wirk. Lit.]. (1969)-. German. ir. CH Beck Verlagsbuchhandlung, D 80791 Munich Germany. **Tel** 011 49 89 381891.
Ind/Abst MLA Int. Bibl. Books Artic. Mod. Lang. Lit.

US/0084-053X
WISCONSIN CHINA SERIES. No. 1-. Monographic series. English. ir. Price varies per volume. University of Wisconsin / 748 Van Hise Hall, Madison WI 53706. **Tel** (608)262-2291. **ED** William H Nienhauser Jr. **Bk Rev. Ad Acc. Circ:** 300.
Desc: A journal on Chinese literature, modern and traditional.

US
WISCONSIN REGIONAL WRITER. Added/Corp Wisconsin Regional Writers Association. (19??)-. Periodical. English. qt. $10.00. Wisconsin Regional Writer, 1303 Dauphin Road, De Pere WI 54115. **Tel** (608)838-8616.

US/0043-6631
WISCONSIN REVIEW (OSHKOSH). (WISCONSIN REVIEW.). (19??)-. Periodical. English. Three times a year. $8.00. University of Wisconsin-Oshkosh, 308 Radford Hall, Box 158, Oshkosh WI 54901. **Tel** (414)424-2267. **ED** Valerie Jahus. **LC** AP2; .W688. **DD** 051. **Bk Rev. Circ:** 2,000 (ctrl).
Desc: We publish poetry in all forms, fiction to 5000 words, reviews, interviews, articles of literary interest and artwork that is suitable for offset printing.

US
WISCONSIN STUDIES IN LITERATURE. Added/Corp Wisconsin Council of Teachers of English. No. 1,(1964). Periodical. English. **LC** PR1; .W5.

CN/0382-0246
WITCH AND THE CHAMELEON, THE. 1- Aug. 1974-. Periodical. English. $1.00 per number. A. Bankier, Apartment 6, 2 Paisley Avenue South, Hamilton Ontario, L8S 1T7. **DD** 823/.08/76.

US/0891-1371
WITNESS (FARMINGTON HILLS, MICH.). (WITNESS.). **Added/Corp** Center for the Study of the Child. Oakland Community College. Vol. 1, No. 1 (Spring 1987)-. Periodical. English. sa. $18.00 (institution); $12.00 (individual). Witness, Peter Stein, Oakland Community College, 27055 Orchard Lake Road, Farmington Hills MI 48334. **Tel** (313)471-7740. **ED** Peter Stine. **LC** AP2; .W72. **DD** 940.53/15/03924005. **Ad Acc. Circ:** 2,800 (ctrl).
Desc: A journal of fictional essays and poetry that highlight the role of the writer as a witness to the times.
Ind/Abst Index Am. Period. Verse.

●US/1061-4583
WITZ (PENNGROVE, CALIF.). (WITZ.). (1992)-. Periodical. English. Three times a year. $21.00. Syntax Projects for the Arts, PO Box 1059, Penngrove CA 94951. **Tel** (707)224-3337, FAX (707)769-0880. **ED** Christopher Reiner. **Bk Rev**, (Qty: 20 per year). **Circ:** 200.
Desc: Essays, interviews and book reviews of contemporary innovative writing, authors, and literary movements.

GW/0724-956X
WOLFENBUTTELER ABHANDLUNGEN ZUR RENAISSANCEFORSCHUNG. **See** History(General)-History of Europe.

GW/0340-6318
WOLFENBUTTELER BAROCK-NACHRICHTEN. [Wolfenb. Barock-Nachr.]. **Added/Corp** Herzog August Bibliothek Internationaler Arbeitskreis fur Deutsche Barockliteratur. (1974)-. Periodical. German. qt. Dr. Ernst Hauswedell & Co. Verlag, Rosenbergstrasse 113, D 70193 Stuttgart Germany. **Tel** 011 49 711 638265.
Ind/Abst BHA : Biblio. Hist. Art; MLA Int. Bibl. Books Artic. Mod. Lang. Lit.

KO
WOLGAN MUNHAK. **VFOAT** Munhak. Periodical. Korean. W6,000. Wolgan Munhak, 110 Insa-dong, Chongno-ku, Seoul South Korea. **LC** PL950.2; .W64.

AT/0313-6485
WOMAN WRITER. [Women writ.]. (1975)-. Periodical. English. bm. 10.00Aus$. Society of Women Writers, 13 B. Peel Road, O'Connor 6163 W.A., Australia. **Tel** (09)33 2321. **ED** Barb Clews. **DD** _a806.294. **Bk Rev**, (Qty: 6). **Circ:** 650 (ctrl). ***Continues*** *Newsletter - Society of Women Writers. Australia, 0313-6477.*

US/0147-1759
WOMEN & LITERATURE. ***Ceased.*** [Women lit.]. **VAT** Women and Literature. Vol. 3 (Spring 1975)-Vol. 7 (1979); New Series Vol. 1 (1980)-Ceased with Vol. 4 (199?). English. an. Holmes and Meier Publishers Inc, 160 Broadway, Suite 900 East Wing, New York NY 10038. **Tel** (212)374-0100. **ED** Janet Todd. **LC** PN481; .W65. **DD** 809/.933/52. available on microfilm and microfiche from University Microfilms International (UMI). ***Continues*** *Mary Wollstonecraft Journal, 0193-7103.*
Desc: The annual bibliography of women and literature appears in the fall issue of each volume.
Ind/Abst Abstr. Engl. Stud.; Am. Humanit. Index (-199?); Annu. Bibliogr. Engl. Lang. Lit.; Humanit. Index; MLA Int. Bibl. Books Artic. Mod. Lang. Lit.; Romant. Move.; Stud. Women Abstr.; Women Stud. Abstr.

●US/1056-4535
WOMEN WRITERS OF ITALY. (1992)-. Monographic series. English. Price varies per volume. Peter Lang Publishing, 62 West 45th Street, 4th Floor, New York NY 10036. **Tel** (212)764-1471, (800)770-5264, telex 6973364 PLNY.

CN/0714-3257
WORD LOOM. [Word loom]. (Winter 1981/82)-. Periodical. English. sa. 10.00Can$. Word Loom, Box 31, 242 Montrose Street, Winnipeg Manitoba R3M 3M7 Canada. **DD** 820/.8/00914. Index available.

CN/1180-5145
WORD (ST. JOHN'S). **See** Journalism.

US/1054-8823
WORLD LETTER (IOWA CITY, IOWA). (WORLD LETTER.). [World lett.]. Vol. 1, No. 1 (1991)-. Periodical. English. ir. $7.00 US; $8.00 Canada. Jon Cone, 2726 East Court Street, Iowa City IA 52245. **DD** 810.
Ind/Abst Am. Humanit. Index (199?-).

US/0196-3570
WORLD LITERATURE TODAY. (WORLD LITERATURE TODAY.). [World lit. today]. **Added/Corp** University of Oklahoma. Vol. 51 (Winter 1977)-. Periodical. English. qt (Feb., May, Aug., Nov.). $30.00 (one year), $50.00 (two year), individuals; $40.00 (one year), $64.00 (two year) libraries and institutions. University of Oklahoma / 110 Monnet Hall, PO Box 787, Norman OK 73019-0375. **Tel** (405)325-4531, FAX (405)325-7495. **(Subscription address:** World Literature Today 630 Parrington Oval Room 110, Norman, OK 73019 (405)325-4531**)** **ED** Djelal Kadir. **LC** Z1007; .B717. **DD** 028.1. Index available. **Bk Rev**, (Qty: 1000 a year). **Ad Acc. Circ:** 3,000 (ctrl). available on microfilm and microfiche from University Microfilms International (UMI). Documents available from The Genuine Article, UMI Article Clearinghouse. ***Continues*** *Books Abroad, 0006-7431.*
Desc: Reviews of the latest fiction, drama, poetry, critism, and literary biography from 50 languages.
Ind/Abst Abstr. Engl. Stud.; Acad. Search (July 1993-); Am. Bibliogr. Slavic East Europ. Stud.; Annu. Bibliogr. Engl. Lang. Lit.; Arts Humanit. Citation Index [Full Cov.]; Book Rev. Digest; Book Rev. Index; Curr. Contents Arts Humanit.; Expand. Acad. Index (1989-); HAPI Hisp. Am. Period. Index; Humanit. Index; Humanit. Source (Jul. 1993-); INFO-SOUTH Abstr.; Mag. Search; Middle East Abstr. Index; MLA Int. Bibl. Books Artic. Mod. Lang. Lit.; Newsp. Period. Abstr. (1991-); Res. Alert [Full Cov.]; Romant. Move.; Soc. Sci. Cit. Index [Select. Cov.].

US/1043-8343
WORLD REPORT (WHITESTONE, N.Y.). (WORLD REPORT / COUNCIL ON NATIONAL LITERATURES.). **Added/Corp** Council on National Literatures. **VFOAT** Council on National Literatures World Report; CNL/World Report; CNL/WR. (1985)-. English. an. $35.00 membership US; $45.00 membership other. Council on National Literatures, PO Box 81, Whitestone NY 11357. **Tel** (718)767-8380, FAX (718)767-8380. **LC** PN851; .W67. **DD** 809/.005. ***Continues*** *Quarterly World Report (Whitestone, N.Y.), 0145-6873.*
Ind/Abst MLA Int. Bibl. Books Artic. Mod. Lang. Lit.

US/8756-0631
WORLD'S WORD. [World's word]. Vol. 1 (Winter 1983)-. Periodical. English (Multiple languages). qt. Free. World's Word, c/o J P C da Silva, Room F-718/The World Bank, Washington DC 20433. **DD** 808.

US/0043-9401
WORMWOOD REVIEW, THE. [Wormwood rev.]. **VFOAT** WR. Vol. 1, (Winter 1960)-. Periodical. English. Four times a year ((2) in July & (2) Dec.). $10.00 one year; $20.00 two years; $30.00 three years. Wormwood Books and Magazines, PO Box 4698, Stockton CA 95208-0840. **Tel** (209)466-8231. **ED** Marvin Malone. **LC** PS580; .W67. **DD** 811/.5/408. Index available. cum. index. **Bk Rev**, (Qty: 60). **Circ:** 700. available on microfilm and microfiche from University Microfilms International (UMI).
Desc: Publishes traditional to experimental poetry and prose-poems communicating the human situation in modern society. Includes small press reviews.
Ind/Abst Am. Humanit. Index; Index Am. Period. Verse.

US/0196-4682
WPA, WRITING PROGRAM ADMINISTRATION. **Added/Corp** Council of Writing Program Administrators (U.S.). **VFOAT** Writing Program Administration. (19??)-. English. sa. $25.00. Council of Writing Program Administrators, Miami University, English Department, Oxford OH 45056. **Tel** (801)750-3547. **ED** Christine A Hult. **LC** PE1404; .W18. **DD** 808/.042/05. Index available. cum. index. **Bk Rev. Ad Acc. Pr Rev. Circ:** 600.
Desc: A journal for those who administer writing programs in American and Canadian colleges and universities. Especially interested in articles on topics pertinent to writing program administrators, for example; establishing and maintaining a cohesive writing program, training staff, testing and evaluating students, etc.
Ind/Abst Curr. Index J. Educ. (March 1990); Lit. Crit. Regist.

CN/0316-3768
WRIT (TORONTO). (WRIT.). **Added/Corp** Innis College. No. 1 (1970)-. English. an. 20.00Can$ Canada; $20.00 other. Writ Magazine, Two Sussex Avenue, Toronto Ontario, M5S 1J5 Canada. **Tel** (416)978-4871, (416)978-7023, FAX (416)978-5503. **ED** Roger Greenwald. Index available. **Ad Acc. Circ:** 600. ***Supersedes*** *On The Bias, 0316-3776.*
Desc: Poetry, fiction and translations of high quality.
Ind/Abst Index Am. Period. Verse.

CN/1182-901X
WRITE ANGLES. **See** Journalism.

US
WRITE NOW!. English. bm. $9.00 US; $12.00 Canada. Right Here Publications, Box 1014, Huntington IN 46750. **Tel** (219)356-4223. **ED** Emily Jean Carroll. **Bk Rev. Ad Acc. Circ:** 300.
Desc: Newsletter for writers, poets, small press, and self publishers.

US/0884-6049
WRITE TO FAME. [Write fame]. Vol. 1, No. 1 (Nov. 1985)-. Periodical. English. mo. $12.00 US; $16.00 Canada. Keith Publications, PO Box 248, Youngtown AZ 85363. **DD** 810.

II
WRITER AND ILLUSTRATOR : QUARTERLY JOURNAL OF THE ASSOCIATION OF WRITERS AND ILLUSTRATORS FOR CHILDREN. Vol. 1, No. 1 (Oct./Dec. 1981)-. Periodical. English. qt. $6.00. Nehru House, 4 Bahadur Shah Zafar Marg, New Delhi India 110002.

US/0043-9517
WRITER (BOSTON). (WRITER.). [Writ.]. Vol. 1 (April 1887)-. Periodical. English. mo. $27.00 (one year); $50.00 (two years); $74.00 (three years). Writer Inc, 120 Boylston Street, Boston MA 02116-4615. **Tel** (617)423-3157. **ED** Sylvia K. Burack. **LC** PN101; .W7. **DD** 808/.025/05. Index available. **Bk Rev. Ad Acc. Circ:** 56,400. available on microfilm and microfiche from University Microfilms International (UMI). Documents available from UMI Article Clearinghouse, Magazine Collection.
Desc: Today's best-selling writers discuss dialogue, plotting, characterization, suspense, romantic fiction; non-fiction writers cover interviewing, research, finding good subjects, how and when to query, turning personal experience into salable articles and books. Editors and literary agents, and experts on copyright, manuscript preparation and author's rights realistically discuss business side.
Ind/Abst Acad. Abstr. Full Text Elite (June 1984-) [Full Txt.]; Acad. Abstr. (June 1984-); Acad. Search (June 1987-); Annu. Bibliogr. Engl. Lang. Lit.; Gen. Period. Index (1985-); Humanit. Source (Jul. 1993-) [Full Txt.]; Index Am. Period. Verse; INFO-SOUTH Abstr.; Mag. Artic. Summar. Elite (June 1987-) [Full Txt.]; Mag. Artic. Summar. Select (June 1984-) [Full Txt.]; Mag. Artic. Summar. CD-ROM (June 1984-); Mag. Express (1986-) [Full Txt.]; Mag. Index Plus (1989-); Mag. Index Sel. Microfiche (1986-) [Full Txt.]; Mag. Index. Sel. (1986-); Mag. Search; Newsp. Period. Abstr. (1986-); Read. Guide Abstr. Select Ed.; Read. Guide Period. Lit.; Resource/One Ondisc; Mag. Index (1978-); TOM Gen. Index (1985-) [Full Txt.]; Vocat. Search (June 1987-) [Full Txt.].

US/0510-9671
WRITERS AT WORK. 1st- Series. English. ir. Viking Press, 40 West 23rd Street, New York NY 10010. **LC** PN453; .W73. **DD** 809.

US/0043-9525
WRITER'S DIGEST, THE. [Writ. dig.]. Vol. 1, No. 4 (Mar. 1921)-. Periodical. English. Twelve times a year. $24.00 US; $34.00 other. F&W Publications, 1507 Dana Avenue, Cincinnati OH 45207. **Tel** (513)531-2222, FAX (513)531-1843. **(Subscription address:** CDS Agency Hard Copy, PO Box 4966, Des Moines IA 50340.**)** **ED** Bruce Woods. **LC** PN101; .W82. **Bk Rev. Ad Acc. Circ:** 187,277. available on microfiche from University Microfilms International (UMI). Documents available from UMI Article Clearinghouse. ***Continues*** *Successful Writing.*
Desc: Features practical how-to instruction in writing and selling fiction, nonfiction, poetry, scripts and other freelance material, interviews with bestselling authors and influential editors, in-depth reports on equipment and materials for writers, and current listings of publishers seeking editorial material.
Ind/Abst Acad. Search (July 1993-); Access (1979-); Annu. Bibliogr. Engl. Lang. Lit.; Expand. Acad. Index (1992-); Gen. Period. Index (1985-); Index Inf.; Mag. Index Plus (1989-); Mag. Search; Newsp. Period. Abstr. (1989-); Pop. Period. Index; Read. Guide Period. Lit.; Mag. Index (1978-)(1977-).

US/1057-0756
WRITER'S FORUM (CINCINNATI, OHIO). (WRITER'S FORUM : A PUBLICATION FOR STUDENTS, FACULTY, AND FRIENDS OF WRITER'S DIGEST SCHOOL.). [Writer's forum]. **Added/Corp** Writer's Digest School (Cincinnati, Ohio). Vol. 22, No. 1 (Summer 1991)-. Periodical. English. qt. $10.00. Writer's Forum, PO Box 12291, Cincinnati OH 45212-0291. **DD** 807. ***Continues*** *WDS Forum, 0275-9748.*

US/0163-9072
WRITERS FORUM (COLORADO SPRINGS). (WRITERS FORUM.). [Writ. forum]. **Added/Corp** University of Colorado at Colorado Springs. **VFOAT** Riverrun; Rocky Mountain Writers Forum. (Spring 1974)-. Periodical. English. an. $8.95. University of Colorado Writers Forum, PO Box 7150, Colorado Springs CO 80933-7150. **Tel** (719)599-4023, 593-3155. **ED** Alex Blackburn. **LC** PS561; .W7. **DD** 810/.8/0054. Index available. **Circ:** 1,000. available on microfiche.
Desc: Fiction, poetry, some literary criticism. Features contemporary American literature with emphasis on serious Western literature.
Ind/Abst Am. Humanit. Index; Index Am. Period. Verse.

US/0891-8759
WRITERS' JOURNAL (SAINT PAUL, MINN.). (WRITERS' JOURNAL.). [Writ. j.]. **Added/Corp** Inkling Publications, Inc. Vol. 8, No. 1 (Jan./Feb. 1987)-. Periodical. English. bm. $14.97 US; $27.97 Canada; $38.97 other. Minnesota Ink, 27 Empire Drive, St Paul MN 55103. **Tel** (612)225-1306. **DD** 808. **Bk Rev. Ad Acc. Circ:** 10,000. ***Continues*** *Inkling Journal.*

US/1054-2299
WRITER'S NETWORK, THE. **See** Journalism.

US
WRITER'S NEWSLETTER. ***Ceased.*** **VFOAT** Writer's News Letter. (July/Aug. 1977)-?. Newsletter. English. bm. Writers Newsletter, High Point Mountain Road, West Shokan NY 12494. **Tel** (914)657-8092.

US/0043-955X
WRITER'S NOTES & QUOTES. **VAT** Writer's Notes and Quotes. (195?)-. Periodical. English. qt. Writers Notes & Quotes, 142 West Bookdale Place, Fullerton CA 92632. ***Continues*** *Amateur Notes & Quotes.*

US/1057-0772
WRITER'S WORLD (BIG STONE GAP, VA.). **See** Journalism.

US/0084-2737
WRITER'S YEARBOOK. **See** Journalism.

US/1053-7937
WRITING ABOUT WOMEN. (WRITING ABOUT WOMEN : FEMINIST LITERARY STUDIES.). [Writ. women]. Vol. 1 (1991)-. Monographic series. English. Peter Lang Publishing, 62 West 45th Street, 4th Floor, New York NY 10036. **Tel** (212)764-1471, (800)770-5264, telex 6973364 PLNY. **DD** 808.

●US/1062-3434
WRITING FOR OUR LIVES. [Writ. lives]. Vol. 1, No. 1 (Spring/Summer 1992)-. Periodical. English. sa. $7.50. Running Deer Press, 647 North Santa Cruz Avenue, The Annex, Los Gatos CA 95030. **DD** 810.

●US/1060-4448
WRITING IN OHIO. [Writ. Ohio]. 1st ed. (1992)-. Periodical. English. be. $10.95. Writer's World Press, PO Box 24684, Cleveland OH 44121. **DD** 808.

CN/0714-413X
WRITING IN PEEL. [Writ. Peel]. **Added/Corp** Peel (Ont. : Regional Municipality). Board of Education. Issue 7 (June 1980); Vol. 2, No. 1 (April 1982)-. Periodical. English. sa. Limited free distribution. Peel Board of Education, 5650 Hurontario Street, Mississauga Ontario L5R 1C6 Canada. **DD** C810/.8/09282. ctrl circ.

●US/1065-6154
WRITING IT RIGHT. See Journalism.

US/1064-6051
WRITING ON THE EDGE. [Writ. edge]. **Added/Corp** University of California, Davis. Campus Writing Center. **VFOAT** Hypertext on the Edge; WOE. Vol. 1, No. 1 (Fall 1989)-. Periodical. English. Twice a year. $15.00, ($12.00 for students) US; add $15.00 postage other. Writing on the Edge, Campus Writing Center, University of California, Davis CA 95616. **Tel** (916)752-4170. **ED** John Boe and Margaret Eldred. **LC** IN PROCESS; PE1404; .W758. **DD** 808. **Ad Acc, Adv Mgr:** Margaret Eldred. **Pr Rev. Circ:** 400.
Desc: Concerned with writing and the teaching of writing. Aimed at college composition teachers. Publishes interviews with writers and composition scholars as well as articles, personal essays, poetry, short fiction, and humor focused on writing or the teaching of writing.

CN/0712-1385
WRITING (TORONTO). (WRITING.). [Writing]. **VFOAT** Ecrits. **VAT** Ecrits (Toronto). '81-. Periodical. English (French). an. Writing, Information and Publications Department, Toronto Board of Education, 155 College Street, Toronto Ontario M5T 1P6 Canada. **DD** C811/.540809283.

US
WRITINGS ... FROM THE GREAT PLAINS. V. 1, No. 2- Spring 1978-. Periodical. English. sa. Panhandle Press, PO Box 1246, Scottsbluff NE 69361-1246. **Tel** (308)632-8624.

CH
WU HSIA SHIH CHIEH. (Mar. 1959)-. Periodical. Japanese (English, French, German, Chinese and Russian). Three times a year. $100.00. 7-13 Hsin Chieh/2nd Floor, Hong Kong Hong Kong. **Tel** 07746-5-7071. **ED** Masaaki Yamamoto. **LC** PL2653; .W78. **Circ:** 2,000 (ctrl).

CH
WU MING WEN HSUEH. Periodical. Chinese. bm. NT$0.30. Post Office, Tsang-Chou Shih, People's Republic of China. **LC** PL2452; .W8. **DD** 895.1/05.

CN/0824-2178
X-IT. [X-it]. **VFOAT** X-IT Magazine. **VAT** Exit (St. John's). Vol. 1, No. 1 (Jan./June 1984)-. Periodical. English. sa. $2.00 each issue. X-It, PO Box 102, St John's Newfoundland A1C 5H5 Canada. **DD** C810/.8/0054.

US/0748-6189
XALMAN; ALMA CHICANA DE AZTLAN. [Xalman]. Periodical. Spanish. Xalman, 601 East Montecito Street, Santa Barbara CA 93103. **LC** PS508.M4; X34.

SI/0438-0797
XIN SHENG. (HSIN SHENG.). First published in March 1972-. Periodical. Chinese. $0.30 single issue. Chinese Language and Literary Society, Nanyang University, Jurong Road 22, Singapore. **LC** AP95.C4; H7447.

CN/0828-5608
XYZ (MONTREAL, QUEBEC). (XYZ: LA REVUE DE LA NOUVELLE.). [XYZ]. **VFOAT** XYZ; Revue De La Nouvelle. Vol. 1, No. 1, Spring (1985)-. Periodical. French. qt. 23.00 Can$ (one year), 42.00 Can$ (two year) institutions Canada; 28.00 Can$ (one year), 52.00 Can$ (two year) institutions all other; 20.00 Can$ (one year), 36.00 Can$ (two year) individuals Canada; 25.00 Can$ (one year), 48.00 Can$ (two year) individuals other. SODEP, 815 rue Ontario Est, Bureau 202, Montreal Quebec H21 1P1 Canada. **Tel** (514)523-7724, (514)525-2606, FAX (514)523-9401. **DD** C843/.01/089714.

CN/0701-8894
YA HOTLINE. See Children and Youth Interests.

CC
YA-LU CHIANG. **VFOAT** Yalujiang. Periodical. Chinese. mo. $9.18. Science Press, 16 Donghuangchenggen North Street, Beijing 100707, People's Republic of China. **Tel** 011 86 1 4019821, 011 86 1 4010642, FAX 011 86 1 4012180, 011 86 1 4019810, telex 210147. **LC** PL2303; .Y27.

PK
YAD-I BAIZA : ASRI ADAB MEN JADID RAVIYYON KA TARJUMAN. (1991)-. Periodical. Urdu. mo.

US
YALE LITERARY MAGAZINE, THE. **VFOAT** Excommunicate; Yale Lit. Vol. 1, Issue 1 (Spring 1989)-. Periodical. English. sa. **LC** PS501; .Y342. ***Continues*** *Yale Literary Magazine, 0044-0108.*
Desc: Writing's by and for the students of Yale university.

US/0044-0108
YALE LITERARY MAGAZINE (1979), THE. ***Title Change.*** (THE YALE LITERARY MAGAZINE.). [Yale lit. mag.]. Vol. 148-May (1979)-(198?). Periodical. English. qt. Yale Literary Magazine, 6015 78th Street, Elmhurst NY 11373. **Tel** (203)624-8400. **ED** Andrei Navrozov. **LC** PS501; .Y34. **DD** 810/.5. **Circ:** 10,000. available on microfilm and microfiche from University Microfilms International (UMI). ***Continues*** *Yale Lit, 0196-7738.* ***Continued by*** *Yale Literary Magazine (New Haven, Conn. : 1989).*

US/0084-3482
YALE STUDIES IN ENGLISH. See Linguistics.

JA/0513-4846
YAMATO BUNKA. **Added/Corp** Yamato Bunkakan. No. 1 (March 1951)-. Periodical. Japanese. sa. $161.00. **(Subscription address:** Japan Publications Trading Company, Ltd., PO Box 5030, Tokyo International, Tokyo 100-31 Japan.**)**

JA
YASO / CHUGOKU BUNGEI KENKYUKAI. **Added/Corp** Chugoku Bungei Kenkyukai (Osaka, Japan). **VFOAT** Yeh Tsao. Fall Edition (1970)-. Periodical. Japanese. Saika Shorin, c/o Toei Building, 2-kai 17 Suemori-dori 4, Chigusa-ku 464 Japan. **LC** PL2250; .Y37.

SZ
YEARBOOK OF COMPARATIVE AND GENERAL LITERATURE. English (French). an. price varies per issue. Librairie Droz SA, 11 rue Massot BP 389, CH 1211 Geneva 12 Switzerland. **Tel** 011 41 22 3466666, FAX 011 41 22 472391. **ED** Indiana University.
Desc: Contains information on comparative literature.

IT/0826-9661
YEARBOOK OF ITALIAN STUDIES. [Yearb. Ital. stud.]. **Added/Corp** Italian Cultural Institute (Montreal, Quebec). (1971)-. Monographic series. English. ir. Price varies per volume. Casalini Libri, Via Benedetto da Malano 3, 50014 Fiesole Italy. **Tel** 011 39 55 599941, FAX 011 39 55 598895. **ED** A. Dandrea, D. Della Terza, F. Fido and P. D. Stewart. **LC** DG401; .Y4.
Desc: Intends to establish a closer cultural bond between Italy and North America, by providing a meeting ground for scholars in Canada and the US actively involved in Italian studies and those Italian scholars who, having spent some time in the universities of the North American continent, are aware of the intellectual interests of their colleagues on the other side of the ocean.
Ind/Abst MLA Int. Bibl. Books Artic. Mod. Lang. Lit.

UK
YEARBOOK OF THE SOCIETY FOR PIRANDELLO STUDIES, THE. See Theater.

US
YEAR'S BEST FANTASY AND HORROR. **VFOAT** Fantasy and Horror. 1st Ed. (1990)-. English. $14.95. St. Martin's Press, 175 Fifth Avenue, New York NY 10010. **Tel** (800)221-7945, (212)982-3900, FAX (212)777-6359. **ED** E Datlow and T Windling. **DD** 823/.0876608. ***Continues*** *Year's Best Fantasy.*

US/0741-0212
YEAR'S BEST MYSTERY & SUSPENSE STORIES, THE. **VFOAT** Year's Best Mystery and Suspense Stories; Mystery and Suspense Stories. (1982)-. English. an. $16.95. Walker and Company, 435 Hudson Street, New York NY 10014. **Tel** (212)727-8300. **ED** E. D. Hoch. **LC** PZ1; .B446588; PS648.D4; Y43. **DD** 813/.0872/08. ***Continues*** *Best Detective Stories of the Year, 0067-625X.*
Desc: Features the previous year's short stories. Also includes lists of award winners, best mystery and suspense novels of 1985, bibliography, necrology and an honor roll.

US/0743-1740
YEAR'S BEST SCIENCE FICTION (NEW YORK, N.Y.), THE. (THE YEAR'S BEST SCIENCE FICTION.). [Year's best sci. fict.]. **VFOAT** Science Fiction. 1st Annual Collection-. English. an. $9.95 paperback, $17.95 hardcover. Bluejay Books, 130 West 42nd Street, Room 514, New York NY 10036. **LC** PS648.S3; Y43. **DD** 813/.0876/08.

UK/0084-4144
YEAR'S WORK IN ENGLISH STUDIES. (THE YEAR'S WORK IN ENGLISH STUDIES.). [Year's work Engl. stud.]. **Added/Corp** English Association. Vol. 1 (1920)-. English. ir. $140.00. Humanities Press, 165 1st Avenue, Atlantic Highlands NJ 07716. **Tel** (908)872-1441, (800)221-3845, FAX (908)872-0717, telex 752233. **ED** Laurel Brake, Susan Brock, David Burnley, Maureen Moran and John Theime. **LC** PE58; .E6. **[CCC].** available on microfilm and microfiche from University Microfilms International (UMI).
Desc: Team of scholars summarizes and evaluates all significant books and articles relating to study of English language and literature during the year. Comprehensive and worldwide in scope.
Ind/Abst Br. Humanit. Index; Humanit. Index; MLA Int. Bibl. Books Artic. Mod. Lang. Lit.

US/0742-6224
YEATS. [Yeats]. Vol. 1 (1983)-. English. an. $42.50. University of Michigan Press, PO Box 1104, Ann Arbor MI 48106. **Tel** (313)764-4392. **ED** Richard J. Finneran. **LC** PR5906; .A16. **DD** 821/.8. **Circ:** 1,000 (ctrl).
Desc: Volumes present all extant versions of manuscripts of W. B. Yeats' works and offer the greatest possible fidelity in transcription. Photographic facsimiles supplement texts.
Ind/Abst MLA Int. Bibl. Books Artic. Mod. Lang. Lit.

UK/0278-7687
YEATS ANNUAL (LONDON, ENGLAND). (YEATS ANNUAL.). [Yeats annu.]. No. 1 (1982)-. English. ir. Macmillan Distribution Ltd, Houndsmill Basingstoke, Hampshire RG21 2XS England. **Tel** 011 44 256 29242. **ED** Warwick Gould. Index available.
Desc: Publishes work in the field of Yeats scholarship from around the world.
Ind/Abst MLA Int. Bibl. Books Artic. Mod. Lang. Lit.

CN/0704-5700
YEATS ELIOT REVIEW. [Yeats Eliot rev.]. **VFOAT** YER. Vol. 5, No. 1 (Spring 1978)-. Periodical. English. qt. $14.00 (institutions), $12.00 (individuals) US and Canada; $18.00 (institutions), $16.00 (individuals) other. Yeats Eliot Review, Department of English, 2801 South University Avenue, Little Rock AR 72204. **Tel** (501)569-3160. **LC** PS3509.L43; Z96. **DD** 821/.912/09. ***Continues*** *T. S. Eliot Review, 0318-6342.*
Ind/Abst Abstr. Engl. Stud.; Am. Humanit. Index; Annu. Bibliogr. Engl. Lang. Lit.; Child. Lit. Abstr. (19??-); MLA Int. Bibl. Books Artic. Mod. Lang. Lit.

US/0361-8552
YELLOW BRICK ROAD (TEMPE, ARIZ.). (YELLOW BRICK ROAD.). [Yellow brick road]. (19??)-. Periodical. English. Three times a year. $3.00 (individuals), $4.50 (institutions). Emerald City Press, 107 W 7th Street, Tempe AZ 85281. **Tel** (602)882-9409. **DD** 810.
Ind/Abst Index Am. Period. Verse.

US/0736-9212
YELLOW SILK. (Fall 1981)-. Periodical. English. Four times a year. $38.00 US; $46.00 other. Verygraphics, PO Box 6374, Albany CA 94706. **Tel** (510)644-4188. **ED** Lily Pond. Index available. **Bk Rev. Ad Acc, Adv Mgr:** Shelly Hebert. **Circ:** 16,000. available on microfilm from University Microfilms International (UMI).
Desc: Contains fiction, poetry, essays, reviews, and fine-arts in erotic material.
Ind/Abst Am. Humanit. Index (-199?); Index Am. Period. Verse.

US
YELLOWBACK LIBRARY. **VFOAT** Yellow Back Library. Periodical. English. mo. $24.00. Yellowback Press, PO Box 36172, Des Moines IA 50315-2258. **Tel** (515)280-6756. **ED** Gil O'Gara. Index available. cum. index. **Bk Rev. Ad Acc. Circ:** 400 (ctrl).
Desc: For enthusiasts of series literature. Contains articles on series fiction, dime novels, news of the industry, and author interviews. A friendly exchange among students, dealers, and collectors of series books.

IS
YERUSHOLAYMER ALMANAKH. **VFOAT** Jerushalaimer Almanach. 2/3- 1974-. Yiddish. an. $8.00 US. Eygens, Shederot Eshkol 12/6, Yerushalayim Israel. **LC** PJ5161.5; .A48. **Bk Rev. Circ:** 600. ***Continues*** *Almanakh: Yidishe Shrayber Fun Yerusholaim.*
Ind/Abst MLA Int. Bibl. Books Artic. Mod. Lang. Lit.

US/0364-4308
YIDDISH. [Yiddish]. Vol. 1 (Summer 1973)-. Periodical. English. Four times a year. $15.00 (individuals), $20.00 (institutions) US & Canada; $18.00 (individuals), $25.00 (institutions) others. Queens College, Political Science Department, 65-30 Kissena Boulevard, Flushing NY 11367. **Tel** (718)520-7000. **ED** Joseph C. Landis. **LC** PJ5120; .A385. **DD** 839/.09/05. Index available. **Bk Rev. Ad Acc. Circ:** 600 (ctrl). Documents available from The Genuine Article.
Desc: Accepts articles on Yiddish literature, language, folklore, the cultural context of Yiddish and translations of literature and criticism from Yiddish into English.
Ind/Abst Am. Bibliogr. Slavic East Europ. Stud. (19??-19??); Arts Humanit. Citation Index [Full Cov.];

Literature

Curr. Contents Arts Humanit.; Index Jew. Period. (199?-); MLA Int. Bibl. Books Artic. Mod. Lang. Lit.; Res. Alert [Full Cov.].

US/0044-0426
YIDDISHE KULTUR. **Added/Corp** Ikuf (Association). **VFOAT** Yidishe Kultur. Vol. 1 (Nov. 1938)-. Periodical. Yiddish. Eight times a year. $24.00. Kiddisher Kultur Farbound Inc., 1123 Broadway Room 203, New York NY 10010. **Tel** (212)691-0708. **ED** Itche Goldberg. **LC** AP91; .Y53. **DD** 305. **Circ:** 2,000.
Ind/Abst MLA Int. Bibl. Books Artic. Mod. Lang. Lit.

US/0084-4217
YIVO BLETER. (YIVO BLETER : HODESH-SHRIFT FUN YIDISHN VISNSHAFTLEKHN INSTITUT.). [Yivo bleter]. **Added/Corp** Yivo Institute for Jewish Research. **VFOAT** Jiwobleter. (1931)-. Yiddish (summaries and/or abstracts in English). ir.
Ind/Abst Am. Hist. Life (1966-).

KO
YONGHAK NONJIP. See Linguistics.

KO
YOSONG MUNHAK. 1st Vol. (Jan. 1984)-. Periodical. Korean. W3,500 each issue. Chonyewon 569 Socho-dong Kangnam-ku, Seoul Korea. **LC** PL950.2; .Y67.

US/0741-7594
YOUNG AUTHOR'S MAGAZINE. See Journalism.

US/1061-4966
YOUNG INDIANA JONES CHRONICLES, THE. **Ceased.** Summer (1992)-Fall (1992). Periodical. English. qt. Welsh Publishing Group Inc., 300 Madison Avenue, New York NY 10017. **Tel** (212)687-0680, FAX (212)986-5849.

CN/1182-4980
YOUNG VOICES, YOUR VOICES. [Young voices your voices]. **Added/Corp** North York Public Library (Ont.). Youth Services Committee. (1989)-. English. North York Public Library, 5126 Yonge Street, Willowdale Ontario M2N 5N9 Canada. **Tel** (416)395-5613, FAX (416)395-5668. **DD** C811/.54. **Continues** Young Voices (Willowdale, Ont.)., 0714-4431.

CN/0712-1768
YOUTH (FREDERICTON, N.B.). (YOUTH.). [Youth]. English. an. Free. Youth New Brunswick Teachers Association, PO Box 752, Fredericton New Brunswick E3B 5R6 Canada. **DD** C810/.8/092375. ctrl circ. **Continues** Students' Creative Writing, 0712-1776.

CH
YU WEN YUEH KAN. See Linguistics.

US/0098-3640
YUGNTRUF. [Yugntruf]. No. 1, (Nov. 1964)-. Yiddish. ir (Published 2-3 times a year). $18.00. Yugntruf Inc, 200 West 72nd Street, Suite 40, New York NY 10023. **Tel** (212)654-8540. **ED** David Braun. **LC** PJ5111; .Y83.
Bk Rev, (Qty: varies). **Ad Acc. Circ:** 2,000.
Desc: Young adult oriented articles, neons and fiction in Yiddish on various aspects of Yiddish-speaking Jewish life.
Ind/Abst MLA Int. Bibl. Books Artic. Mod. Lang. Lit.

II
YUGOPAYOGI. **VFOAT** Jugopajogi. Periodical. Oriya (Oriya). mo. 2.00. B Das 43 Shitalatala Lane, Post Hind Motor, 712233 Dist Huguli India. **LC** PK2574.5; .Y83.

PL/0084-4411
Z DZIEJOW FORM ARTYSTYCZNYCH W LITERATURZE POLSKIEJ. [Dziej. form artyst. lit. pol.]. Vol. 1-. Monographic series. Polish. Price varies per volume. Zaklad Narodowy Im Ossolinskch, Ul Szewska 37, Wroclaw Poland. **LC** PG7001; .Z15.
Ind/Abst MLA Int. Bibl. Books Artic. Mod. Lang. Lit.

US/0892-9696
Z MISCELLANEOUS. [Z misc.]. Vol. 1, No. 1 (March 1987)-. Periodical. English. bm. $15.00 (libraries) US; $27.00 (libraries) Canada; $45.00 (libraries) Europe. Again & Again Press, Box 20041, New York NY 10028. **Tel** (212)886-0255. **ED** Charles Fabrizio, Esther M Leiper, and Laurel Speer. **DD** 810. Index available (libraries only). **Bk Rev. Circ:** 300.
Desc: A literary journal containing poetry, fiction, non-fiction, and artwork.

II
ZABAN O ADAB : BIHAR URDU AKADMI KA SIHMAHI JARIDAH. **VFOAT** Zoban O Adab; Zoban-O-Adab. Periodical. Urdu. qt. 24.00. Bihar Urdu Academy, 6-A Rajindar Nagar, Patna 800001 India. **LC** PK2151; .Z26.

PL/0084-4446
ZAGADNIENIA RODZAJOW LITERACKICH. [Zag. rodzajow lit.]. **Added/Corp** Odzkie Towarzystwo Naukowe. Wydzia I.--Jezykoznawstwa, Nauki o Literaturze i Filozofii.

VFOAT Voprosy Literaturnykh Zhanrov; Problemes des Genres Litteraires. Vol. 1, No. 1 (1958)-. Polish (English). sa. Price on Request. **(Subscription address:** ARS Polona, PO Box 1001, 00068 Warsaw Poland.**) LC** PN1; .Z23.
Ind/Abst Abstr. Engl. Stud.; Annu. Bibliogr. Engl. Lang. Lit.; MLA Int. Bibl. Books Artic. Mod. Lang. Lit.; Romant. Move.

US
ZAMLUNGEN. No. 1 (Jan.-March 1954)-. Periodical. Yiddish. qt. Jewish Writers Organization YKUF, PO Box 178 Cooper Station, New York NY 10003. **LC** PJ5111; .Z3. **DD** 839/.09/08.

RU
ZARUBEZHNYI VOSTOK. (1989)-. Monographic series. Russian. an. Price varies per volume. **LC** WMLC 91/4036. **Continues** Vostochnyi Almanakh (Moscow, R.S.F.S.R. : 1973).

UN
ZBIRNYK PRATS ... NAUKOVYKH SHEVCHENKIVSKIKH KONFERENTSII / AKADEMIIA NAUK UKRAINSSKOI RSR, INSTYTUT LITERATURY IM. T.H. SHEVCHENKA. **Added/Corp** Instytut Literatury im. T.H. Shevchenka. **VFOAT** Zbirnyk Prats ... Naukovoi Shevchenkivskoi Konferentsii. (1954)-. Ukrainian.
Ind/Abst MLA Int. Bibl. Books Artic. Mod. Lang. Lit.

XV/0350-848X
ZBORNIK FILOZOFSKE FAKULTETE / UNIVERZA V LJUBLJANI, FILOZOFSKA FAKULTETA. **Added/Corp** Univerza v Ljubljani. Filozofska Fakulteta. **VFOAT** Recueil de Travaux de la Faculte des Lettres de Ljubljana. (1950)-. Serbo-Croatian (Roman) (summaries and/or abstracts in English and Russian; table of contents in English, French and Russian).
Ind/Abst BHA : Biblio. Hist. Art.

YU/0084-5183
ZBORNIK ISTORIJE KNJIZEVNOSTI. [Zb. istor. knjizev.]. **VFOAT** Recueil des Travaux de l'Histoire de la Litterature. Vol. 8-. Serbo-Croatian (Cyrillic) (summaries and/or abstracts in French, German and English). ir. varies. Sprska Akademija Nauka I Umetnosti, Knez Mihailova 35, Belgrad Yugoslavia. **Tel** 187-144. **LC** PG1400; .S682. **Circ:** 1,000. **Continues** Zbornik Istorije Knjizevnosti.
Ind/Abst MLA Int. Bibl. Books Artic. Mod. Lang. Lit.

●RU/0131-3266
ZDES I TEPER. (1992)-. Russian. **LC** PG3227.5; .Z347.

GW/0341-0137
ZEITSCHRIFT DER DEUTSCHEN MORGENLANDISCHEN GESELLSCHAFT. See Linguistics.

AU/0323-4096
ZEITSCHRIFT DER SAVIGNY-STIFTUNG FUER RECHTSGESCHICHTE. ROMANISTISCHE ABTEILUNG. (1880)-. Periodical. German. an. DM352.00. Boehlau Verlag GmbH & Co KG, Sachsenplatz 4 6 PF 87, A 1201 Vienna Austria. **Tel** 011 43 222 3302427. **(Subscription address:** Minerva Wissenschaftl Buchhdlg, Sachsenplatz 4 6, Postfach 88, A 1201 Vienna Austria.**) UDC** 34. **Continues in part** Zeitschrift fuer Rechtsgeschichte, 0323-8377.

GW/0044-2305
ZEITSCHRIFT FUER ANGLISTIK UND AMERIKANISTIK. Ceased. [Z. Angl. Am.]. Vol. 1, (1953)-(1994). Periodical. English. Four times a year. Langenscheidt KG, Crellestra 28-30, D 10827 Berlin Germany. **Tel** 011 49 30 7800020, telex 183175 LUGBL. **LC** PR1; .Z4. **DD** 820/.9. Index available in last issue of volume--attached. Documents available from The Genuine Article.
Ind/Abst Abstr. Engl. Stud.; Annu. Bibliogr. Engl. Lang. Lit.; Arts Humanit. Citation Index [Full Cov.]; Chicano Index; Curr. Contents Arts Humanit.; Lang. Teach.; MLA Int. Bibl. Books Artic. Mod. Lang. Lit.; Res. Alert [Full Cov.]; Romant. Move.; Soc. Plann. Policy Dev. Abstr.; Soc. Sci. Cit. Index [Select. Cov.]; Sociol. Abstr. (?-?).

GW/0084-5302
ZEITSCHRIFT FUER CELTISCHE PHILOLOGIE. See Linguistics.

GW/0044-2518
ZEITSCHRIFT FUER DEUTSCHES ALTERTUM UND DEUTSCHE LITERATUR. See Linguistics.

GW/0044-2747
ZEITSCHRIFT FUER FRANZOESISCHE SPRACHE UND LITERATUR. See Linguistics.

SZ
ZEITSCHRIFT FUER GERMANISTIK NEUE FOLGE. (1991)-. German. tq. 140.00F. Verlag Peter Lang AG, Jupiterstrasse 15, CH-3000 Bern 15 Switzerland. **Tel** 011 41 31 9411122, FAX 011 41 31 321131. **Continues** Zeitschrift fuer Germanistik, 0323-7982.

GW/0084-5388
ZEITSCHRIFT FUER PAPYROLOGIE UND EPIGRAPHIK. **VFOAT** ZPE. Vol. 1 (1967)-. German (English, French and Italian). Dr. Rudolf Habelt GmbH, Postfach 150104, D 53040 Bonn Germany. **Tel** 011 49 228 232015. **LC** PA3339; .Z45. **[CCC].** cum. index.
Ind/Abst Numis. Lit.

CN/0824-3492
ZEST (NELSON). (ZEST.). [Zest]. Periodical. English. $2.50 each number. Zest, PO Box 339, Station P, Toronto Ontario M5S 2S8 Canada. **DD** C810/.8/0054.

FR
ZESZYTY LITERACKIE : ZL. VFOAT ZL; Z.L.; Cahiers Litteraires. 1 (Winter 1983)-. Periodical. Polish (French). qt (Jan., Apr., July, Oct). 336.93F institutions France; 330.00 other institutions; 215.48 individuals France; 220.00F other. Cahiers Litteraires, BP 234, 75464 Paris, Cedex 10 France. **Tel** 011 33 1 42463253. **(Subscription address:** Macwire Diffusion, 41 rue Saint Augustin, 75002 Paris France.**) LC** PG7001; .Z39. **DD** 891.8/5/008. Index available. **Bk Rev. Ad Acc. Circ:** 3,000 (ctrl).
Desc: Polish and East European literature.

PL
ZESZYTY PRASOZNAWCZE. Vol. 1- No. 1-; (1960)-. Periodical. Polish (summaries and/or abstracts in English, Russian and French). qt. Price on request. Biuro Kolporta Zu Wydawnictw Zagranicznych Ruch, Ul Wronia 23, Warsaw Poland. **LC** PN4705; .P68. **Continues** Prasa Wspoczesna I Dawna.
Ind/Abst Soc. Plann. Policy Dev. Abstr.; Sociol. Abstr. (?-?).

KZ/0134-3580
ZHULDYZ. Added/Corp Qazaqstan Zhazushylar Odaghynyng. (1928)-. Periodical. Kazakh. mo. $129.95. **(Subscription address:** East View Publications Inc., 3020 Harbor Lane North, Suite 110, Minneapolis MN 55447.**) LC** WMLC L 83/3645; PL65.K46; Z58.

GW/0930-8997
ZIBALDONE (MUNCHEN). (ZIBALDONE.). [Zibaldone]. Vol. 1 (April 1986)-. Periodical. German (Italian). sa.

BN/0514-776X
ZIVOT (SARAJEVO). (ZIVOT; CASOPIS ZA KNJIZEVNOST I KULTURU.). [Zivot]. (Oct 1952)-. Periodical. Serbo-Croatian (Roman). mo. **LC** AP56; .Z48.
Ind/Abst Annu. Bibliogr. Engl. Lang. Lit.; MLA Int. Bibl. Books Artic. Mod. Lang. Lit.

VE/0044-4987
ZONA FRANCA. Suspended. [Zona fr.]. (Sept. 1964)-Suspended (199?). Periodical. Spanish. sm. Zona Franca, Apartado Postal 76978, Caracas 1070 Venezuela. **LC** PN6; .Z66. **DD** 860/.8.
Ind/Abst MLA Int. Bibl. Books Artic. Mod. Lang. Lit.

US/0162-1904
ZONE (BROOKLYN). (ZONE.). (1977)-. Periodical. English. ir. Zone Press, PO Box 194 Bay Station, Brooklyn NY 11235. **Tel** (212)499-3349. **LC** PS501; .Z65A. **DD** 810/.8.
Ind/Abst Am. Humanit. Index.

US/1051-6867
ZORA NEALE HURSTON FORUM, THE. (THE ZORA NEALE HURSTON FORUM : OFFICIAL PUBLICATION OF THE ZORA NEALE HURSTON SOCIETY.). [Zora Neale Hurston forum]. **Added/Corp** Zora Neale Hurston Society. Vol. 1 (Fall 1986)-. Periodical. English. Twice a year (Spring & Fall). $15.00. Zora Neale Hurston Forum, Morgan St University, Box 550 Sheffey, Baltimore MD 21239. **Tel** (410)319-3435. **LC** PS3515.U789; Z965. **DD** 813/.52.
Ind/Abst MLA Int. Bibl. Books Artic. Mod. Lang. Lit.

SW
ZURCHER BEITRAGE ZUR DEUTSCHEN LITERATUR- UND GEISTESGESCHICHTE. Ceased. No. 1 (1948)-(1993-completed series). Monographic series. German. ir. Artemis Verlag Auslieferung, Zeltweg 48, CH-8032 Zurich Switzerland. **Tel** 01 2521100.
Ind/Abst MLA Int. Bibl. Books Artic. Mod. Lang. Lit.

●US/1060-9571
ZUZU'S PETALS QUARTERLY. [Zuzu's petals q.]. **VFOAT** Zuzu's Petals; ZPQ. Vol. 1, Issue 1 (Winter/Spring 1992)-. Periodical. English. qt. $17.00. Devonshire Cream Tea Press, PO Box 4476, Allentown PA 18105-4476. **DD** 810.

Literature —Abstracting, Bibliographies and Statistics

NE/0514-4787
ZWOLSE DRUKKEN EN HERDRUKKEN VOOR DER MAATSCHAPPIJ DER NEDERLANDSE LETTERKUNDE TE LEIDEN. No. 1 (1953)-. Dutch. Maatschappy der Ned Letterkunde, Rapenburg 70-74, Leiden Netherlands. **DD** 839.

US/8756-5633
ZYZZYVA. [Zyzzyva]. Vol. 1, No. 1 (Spring 1985)-. Periodical. English. qt. $28.00 (1 year), $48.00 (2 year) (individual), $36.00 (1 year), $72.00 (2 year) (institutional) US; $48.00 (1 year) (individual) other. Zyzzyva, 41 Sutter Street/Suite 1400, San Francisco CA 94104. **Tel** (415)255-1282, (415)775-9594, FAX (415)255-1144. **ED** Howard Junker. **LC** PS561; .Z98. **DD** 810.8/0979/05. Index available. **Ad Acc. Circ:** 3900.
Desc: Covers west coast writers, artists, and excerpts from forthcoming books from west coast publishers. Also includes black and white photographs and graphic art.
Ind/Abst Am. Humanit. Index; Index Am. Period. Verse.

ABSTRACTING, BIBLIOGRAPHIES AND STATISTICS

US/0161-0376
AEB, ANALYTICAL & ENUMERATIVE BIBLIOGRAPHY. [AEB, Anal. enumer. bibliogr.]. **Added/Corp** Bibliographical Society of Northern Illinois. Northern Illinois University. Dept. of English. **VFOAT** Analytical & Enumerative Bibliography. **VAT** AEB. Analytical and Enumerative Bibliography. Vol. 1 (Jan. 1977)-. Periodical. English. qt. $12.00 (individuals); $17.00 (institutions). Bibliographical Society of Northern Illinois, Northern Illinois University, Department of English, Dekalb IL 60115-2868. **Tel** (815)753-6634. **ED** William P. Williams. **LC** Z1007; .A115. **DD** 016.05. **Bk Rev**, (Qty: 45). **Ad Acc. Pr Rev. Circ:** 250.
Desc: Articles, notes and reviews on bibliography, textual criticism, and book history, especially in relation to English and American literature.
Ind/Abst Abstr. Engl. Stud.; Am. Humanit. Index; Annu. Bibliogr. Engl. Lang. Lit.; Index Book Rev. Humanit. (1985-); Lit. Crit. Regist.; MLA Int. Bibl. Books Artic. Mod. Lang. Lit.; Ref. Sources.

BL
ANAIS DA BIBLIOTECA NACIONAL. **Main/Corp** Rio de Janeiro. Biblioteca Nacional. **Added/Corp** Brazil. Ministerio da Educacao e Saude Publica. Rio de Janeiro. Biblioteca Nacional. Annaes. Vol. 1 (1876)-. Portuguese. **LC** Z1675; .R58. cum. index.
Ind/Abst HAPI Hisp. Am. Period. Index.

US/0743-2410
ANDREJ BELYJ SOCIETY NEWSLETTER, THE. [Andrej Belyj Soc. newsl.]. **Added/Corp** Andrej Belyj Society. No. 1 (1982)-. Newsletter. English. an. Andrej Belyj Society, Texas A & M University, Department of M C Languages, College Station TX 77843. **Tel** (409)693-3704. **ED** Olga Muller Cooke. **Ad Acc. Circ:** 100.
Desc: Abstracts, letters, bibliographies.

UK/0066-3786
ANNUAL BIBLIOGRAPHY OF ENGLISH LANGUAGE AND LITERATURE. (ANNUAL BIBLIOGRAPHY OF ENGLISH LANGUAGE AND LITERATURE / EDITED FOR THE MODERN HUMANITIES RESEARCH ASSOCIATION BY A.C. PAUES.). [Annu. bibliogr. Engl. lang. lit.]. **Added/Corp** Modern Humanities Research Association. Vol. 4 (1923)-. Abstracting/Indexing Service. English. an. $256.00. W. S. Maney and Son Ltd., Hudson Road, Leeds LS9 7DL England. **Tel** 011 44 532 497481, FAX 011 44 532 486983. **(Subscription address:** W.S. Maney & Son Limited, PO Box YR7, Leeds, LS9 7UU England.**) LC** Z2011; .M69. Index available (Free). **Continues** Bibliography of English Language and Literature.
Desc: The aim of the journal is to record all publications on English language and literature throughout the world.

US/0066-4626
ANTARCTIC BIBLIOGRAPHY. Vol. 1 (1965)-. Bibliography. English. ir. Must order direct. Superintendent of Documents, US Government Printing Office, Washington DC 20402. **Tel** (202)275-3328, FAX (202)786-2377. **LC** Z6005.P7; A55. **NLM** Z 6005.P7 A627. **CODEN** AABBA. cum. index. available on CD-ROM.
Desc: Presents abstracts and indexes of current Antarctic literature.

PE
ANUARIO BIBLIOGRAFICO PERUANO. **Added/Corp** Biblioteca Nacional (Peru). (1943)-. Spanish. ir. Price varies. Biblioteca Nacional de Peru, Apartado 2335, Lima Peru. **Tel** 011 51 14 287698. **LC** Z1851; .A5. **DD** 015.85. **NLM** Z 1851 A636.

SP/0523-1760
BIBLIOGRAFIA ESPANOLA (MADRID, SPAIN : 1958). (BIBLIOGRAFIA ESPANOLA.). **Added/Corp** Instituto Bibliografico Hispanico. Spain. Servicio Nacional de Informacion Bibliografica. (1958)-. Periodical. Spanish. mo. 18000ptas Spain; 20000ptas other. Bibliolibria Biblioteca Nacion, Paseo de Recoletos 20, 28001 Madrid Spain. **Tel** 011 34 1 5778707. **LC** Z2685; .B583. **NLM** Z 2685 B581. **Absorbed** Boletin del Deposito Legal de Obras Impresas.

XO
BIBLIOGRAFIA LITERARNEJ VEDY A UMELECKEJ LITERATURY. KNIHY. **VFOAT** Bibliografia Literarnej Vedy a Umeleckej Literatury. Seria A, Knihy. 1977-. Slovak. an. kcs38.00. **LC** Z2138.L5; B49; PG5423. **DD** 016.8918/7/08.

YU/0523-2201
BIBLIOGRAFIJA JUGOSLAVIJE. KNJIGE, BROSURE I MUZIKALIJE. See Music.

US/0006-1255
BIBLIOGRAPHIC INDEX. [Bibliogr. index]. **Added/Corp** H.W. Wilson Company. Vol. 1 (1937/1942)-. Abstracting/Indexing Service. English. sa (April and August). Priced on the Service Basis. H W Wilson Company, 950 University Avenue, Bronx NY 10452. **Tel** (800)367-6770, (718)588-8400, FAX (718)590-1617, telex 4990003 HWILSON. **ED** Laurel Cooley. **LC** Z1002; .B595. **DD** 016.016. available on an online database from WILSONLINE; available on diskette from WILSONSEARCH.
Desc: Index to bibliographies published in English, Germanic and Romance languages. Covers books, pamphlets and periodicals.

GW
BIBLIOGRAPHIE DER DEUTSCHEN SPRACH- UND LITERATURWISSENSCHAFT. Vol. 9 (1969)-. Monographic series. German. ir. Price varies per volume. Vittorio Klostermann, Frauenlobstrasse 22, D 60487 Frankfurt Germany. **Tel** 011 49 69 9708160. **LC** Z2231; .B5. **Continues** Bibliographie der Deutschen Literaturwissenschaft.

GW/0523-2465
BIBLIOGRAPHIE DER FRANZOSISCHEN LITERATURWISSENSCHAFT. **VFOAT** Bibliographie d'Histoire Litteraire Francaise. No. 1-1956/58-. Periodical. German. an. DM296.00. Vittorio Klostermann, Frauenlobstrasse 22, D 60487 Frankfurt Germany. **Tel** 011 49 69 9708160. **ED** Klapp. **LC** Z2171; .B56.

GE/0006-1409
BIBLIOGRAPHIE DER UBERSETZUNGEN DEUTSCHSPRACHIGER WERKE. Ceased. **Added/Corp** Deutsche Buecherei (Germany). Vol. 1 (1954)-Ceased (Dec. 1990). German. ir. Deutscher Judo Verband, Redaktion Ippon Segewaldweg 40, D 12557 Berlin Germany. **Tel** 011 49 711 210770, telex 051 678. **LC** Z2234.T7; B5. **NLM** Z 2225 B582. cum. index.

FR
BIBLIOGRAPHIE DES AUTEURS MODERNES DE LANGUE FRANCAISE. Vol. 1 (1801/1927)-. French. Chronique des Lettres Francais, 33 rue de Verneuil, 75007 Paris France. **ED** Par Hector Talvart et Joseph Place. **LC** Z2171; .T16.

GW/0523-2767
BIBLIOGRAPHIEN ZUR DEUTSCHEN LITERATUR DES MITTELALTERS. [Bibliogr. dtsch. Lit. mittelalt.]. No. 1 (1966)-. Monographic series. German. ir. Price varies per volume. Erich Schmidt Verlag GmbH, Postfach 304240, D 10724 Berlin Germany. **Tel** 011 49 30 25008525. **ED** Ulrich Pretzel and Wolfgang Bachofer. **Bk Rev. Ad Acc.** ctrl circ.
Desc: Bibliographies on German literature of Middle Ages.
Ind/Abst MLA Int. Bibl. Books Artic. Mod. Lang. Lit.

US/0742-6860
BIBLIOGRAPHIES AND INDEXES IN AMERICAN LITERATURE. [Bibliogr. indexes Am. lit.]. No. 1-. English. ir. Greenwood Press Inc., PO Box 5007, Westport CT 06881-5007. **Tel** (203)226-3571, FAX (203)222-1502. **DD** 016.

US/0749-470X
BIBLIOGRAPHIES OF MODERN AUTHORS (SAN BERNARDINO, CALIF.). (BIBLIOGRAPHIES OF MODERN AUTHORS.). [Bibliogr. mod. authors]. (1984)-. Monographic series. English. ir. Price varies per volume. Borgo Press, PO Box 2845, San Bernardino CA 92406. **Tel** (714)884-5813, (714)885-1161. **ED** Robert Reginald. **DD** 800. Index available. **Circ:** 500.
Desc: Comprehensive bibliographies listing all works by and about a particular writer. Includes short works as well as public appearances and work in progress, chronology and index.

US
BIBLIOGRAPHY OF AMERICAN LITERATURE. Ceased. Vol. 1 (1955)- Series Complete (199?). Bibliography. English. ir. Yale University Press, PO Box 209040, New Haven CT 06520. **Tel** (203)432-0940, (800)987-7323, FAX (203)432-0948.

IS/0334-309X
BIBLIOGRAPHY OF MODERN HEBREW LITERATURE IN TRANSLATION. See Literature.

DK/0067-7213
BIBLIOGRAPHY OF OLD NORSE-ICELANDIC STUDIES. Added/Corp Kongelige Bibliotek (Denmark). Vol. 1 (1963)-. Bibliography. Danish. an. Price varies. Det Kongelige Bibliotek, Postboks 2149, 1016 Kobenhavn K Denmark. **Tel** 011 45 33 930111, FAX 011 45 33 329846, telex 15009. **ED** Bekker-Nielsen Hans. **LC** Z2556; .B5. **DD** 016.91003/175/396. **Circ:** 600.

GW/0067-7884
BIBLIOTHECA BIBLIOGRAPHICA AURELIANA. Vol. 1 (1959)-. Monographic series. German (French, English, Italian and Dutch). ir. Price varies per volume. Verlag Valentin Koerner GmbH, Postfach 304, D-76482 Baden Baden Germany. **Tel** 011 49 7221 22423. **Circ:** 1,000.
Desc: Bibliographies in all fields of book history, catalogs, and monographs.

GW
BIBLIOTHEK. **Main/Corp** Literarischer Verein in Stuttgart. Periodical. German. cum. index. **Ad Acc. Circ:** 900.
Desc: Editions of old German literary texts 800 to 1,600.

SW/0005-2833
BOKREVY. (1970)-. Periodical. Swedish. qt. KR516.40. Bibliotekstjanst AB, Box 200, S-221 00 Lund Sweden. **Tel** 011 46 46 180000. **LC** Z1035.5; .B64.

MX/0185-2027
BOLETIN BIBLIOGRAFICO MEXICANO. [Bol. bibliogr. mex.]. Vol. 1, No. 1 (Jan. 1940)-. Periodical. Spanish. bm. $15.00. Libreria Porrua Hermanos CIA, Apartado M 7990, 06020 Mexico DF Mexico. **Tel** 011/52/5/7025467. **LC** Z1415; .B65. **DD** 015.72. **NLM** Z 1415 B688.
Ind/Abst Am. Hist. Life (1956).

US/0006-7520
BOOKS OF THE SOUTHWEST. [Books Southwest]. **Added/Corp** University of Arizona. Library. University of California, Los Angeles. Library. No. 1 (June 1957)-. Periodical. English. mo. $36.00 (US & Canada) institutions; $24.00 (US & Canada) individuals; $60.00 (other). Books of the Southwest, PO Box 40850, Tucson AZ 85717. **Tel** (602)326-3533. **ED** W David Laird, phone# (602)326-3533. **LC** Z1251.S8; B6; F786. **DD** 016.979. **Bk Rev**, (Qty: 700-1,000 per year). **Circ:** 500.
Desc: Publishes only reviews of materials about the Southwest of the United States.

FR/0074-1388
BULLETIN BIBLIOGRAPHIQUE DE LA SOCIETE INTERNATIONALE ARTHURIENNE. [Bull. bibliogr. Soc. int. arthur.]. **Main/Corp** International Arthurian Society. **Added/Corp** International Arthurian Society. Bibliographical Bulletin of the International Arthurian Society. **VFOAT** Bibliographical Bulletin of the International Arthurian Society; Arthurian Bibliographical Bulletin; Bulletin Bibliographique Arthurienne. (1949)-. Bulletin. French (English, French and German). an. $18.00. International Arthurian Society, Dalhousie University, Department of French, H. R. Runte, Halifax Nova Scotia B3H 3J5 Canada. **Tel** (902)494-2430. **ED** Keith Busby. **LC** Z8045; .I5. **DD** 016.809/93351. Index available. **Circ:** 1,400 (ctrl).
Desc: Research, articles, bibliography, membership list, society news.
Ind/Abst MLA Int. Bibl. Books Artic. Mod. Lang. Lit.

XR/0007-7712
BYZANTINOSLAVICA. [Byzantinoslavica]. **Added/Corp** Ceskoslovenska Akademie Ved. Kabinet pro Studia Recka, Rimska a Latinska. Slovansky Ustav v Praze. Byzantologicka Komise. Ceskoslovenska Akademie Ved. Slovansky Ustav. Ceskoslovenska Akademie Ved. Ustav Dejin Evropskych Socialistickych Zemi. Ceskoslovenska Akademie Ved. Ustav Dejin Vychodni Evropy. Vol. 1 (1929)-. Periodical. Czech (English, French, German, Russian and Italian). Twice a year. $149.00. John Benjamins BV, Amsteldijk 44, PO Box 75577, 1070 AN Amsterdam Netherlands. **Tel** 011 31 20 6738156, FAX 011 31 20 739773. **(Subscription address:** John Benjamins North America, PO Box 27519,

Philadelphia PA 19118-0519.) **ED** Vladimir Vavrinek. **LC** CB231; .B9. Documents available from The Genuine Article.
Desc: This publication features papers, news, reviews, and a detailed bibliography of contemporary international byzantinological publications. The bibliography is structured according to the individual branches of byzantinological research.
Ind/Abst Arts Humanit. Citation Index (19??-19??) [Full Cov.]; BHA : Biblio. Hist. Art; MLA Int. Bibl. Books Artic. Mod. Lang. Lit.; Numis. Lit.; Res. Alert [Full Cov.].

CN
CANADIAN SHORT STORY INDEX.
English. ir. 45.00Can$. Reference Press, PO Box 70, Teeswater Ontario N0G 2S0 Canada. **Tel** (519)392-6634.
Desc: A subject, author and title index to thousands of short stories and novellas written by Canadians and published in collections and anthologies.

IT
CATALOGO DEI PERIODICI ITALIANI.
(1981)-. Periodical. Italian. ir. Editrice Bibliografica, Viale Vittoria Veneto 24, 20124 Milan Italy. **Tel** 011 39 2 29006965, FAX 011 39 2 654624. **LC** Z6956.I8; C18; PN5247.P4. **DD** 055/.1.

XR
CESKA LITERARNI VEDA. BOHEMISTIKA. VFOAT Bohemistika. Czech. **LC** Z2138.L5; C383; PG5000.

XR
CESKA LITERARNI VEDA : NESLOVANSKE LITERATURY. 1974-. Czech (German and French). an. Ustav Pro Ceskov A Svetovou Literaturu CSAV, Strahovske Nadvori 132, Prague Czech Republic. **Tel** 532556. **LC** Z6519; .B5; PN695. Index available. cum. index. available on microfilm. ***Continues*** *Bibliografie Literarnevednych Occidentalik V Ceskem Tisku.*

US
CHILDREN'S BOOKS IN PRINT. SUBJECT GUIDE. Added/Corp R.R. Bowker Company. **VFOAT** Subject Guide; Subject Guide to Children's Books in Print. (1989)-. English. an. $145.00. R R Bowker, A Reed Reference Publishing Company, Part of Reed International PLC, PO Box 31, 121 Chanlon Drive, New Providence NJ 07974. **Tel** (908)464-6800, (800)521-8110, FAX (908)665-6688, telex 138-755. available on magnetic tape and CD-ROM. ***Continues*** *Subject Guide to Children's Books in Print, 0000-0167.*
Desc: Information by subject for every available fiction and nonfiction children's book in print.

UK/0306-2015
CHILDREN'S LITERATURE ABSTRACTS. Added/Corp International Federation of Library Associations. Sub-Section on Library Work with Children. No. 1 (May 1973)-. Abstracting/Indexing Service. English. Four times a year (Mar., June, Sept., Dec.). $30.00 US; $32.00 Canada; $33.00 other. Childrens Literature Abstracts, 5906 Fairlane Drive, Austin TX 78757-4417. **Tel** (512)454-1799. **ED** Gillian Adams. **LC** Z1037; .C5446; PN1009.A1. **DD** 028.52. Index available. cum. index (every 3 to 5 years). **Circ:** 350.
Desc: A bibliographical journal listing articles on the subject of literature for children.

US
CRITICAL BIBLIOGRAPHY OF FRENCH LITERATURE, A. (1947)-. Periodical. English. ir. Price varies per volume. Syracuse University Press, 1600 Jamesville Avenue, Syracuse NY 13210. **Tel** (315)443-1870.
Desc: A multi-volume annotated bibliography of French literature covering the 16th through the 20th Centuries. The focus is primarily on literature but other humanistic disciplines are also included.

US/0011-300X
CUMULATIVE BOOK INDEX, THE. Added/Corp H.W. Wilson Company. (1899)-. English. mo (except Aug.). Sold on the Service Basis. H W Wilson Company, 950 University Avenue, Bronx NY 10452. **Tel** (800)367-6770, (718)588-8400, FAX (718)590-1617, telex 4990003 HWILSON. **ED** Nancy Wong. **LC** Z1219; .M78. Index available. cum. index. **Pr Rev.** ctrl circ. available on an online database from WILSONLINE; available on CD-ROM from WILSONDISC; available on magnetic tape from WILSONTAPE; available on diskette from WILSONSEARCH; available on microfilm from University Microfilms International (UMI).
Desc: An international bibliography of books in English, arranged in a single alphabet; provides information on reprints and editions, includes a directory of publishers.

US/0011-300X
CUMULATIVE BOOK INDEX. CD-ROM. English. mo (except Aug.). $1295.00. H W Wilson Company, 950 University Avenue, Bronx NY 10452. **Tel** (800)367-6770, (718)588-8400, FAX (718)590-1617, telex 4990003 HWILSON. **ED** Nancy Wong. Index available. cum. index. ctrl circ. available on diskette from WILSONSEARCH; available on magnetic tape from WILSONTAPE; available in print; available on an online database from WILSONLINE.
Desc: International author, subject and title index of approximately 60,000 books published in the English language. Government publications and pamphlets are excluded.

DK/0070-2714
DANIA POLYGLOTTA. Added/Corp Copenhagen. Kongelige Bibliotek. (1969)-. English. ir. Dansk BiblioteksCenter AS, Tempovej 7-11, DK-2750 Ballerup, Denmark. **Tel** 011 45 42974000. **ED** Sven Jacobsen and Jan William Rasmussen. **LC** Z2561; .D162. **Circ:** 400 (ctrl). ***Supersedes*** *Dania Polyglotta.*
Desc: National bibliography of Danish books printed abroad and regional bibliography of literature on Denmark in non-Danish languages.

GW
DDR-PERIODICA. VAT Deutsche Democratische Republik-Periodica. German (English, French and Russian). an. Free. Democratische Republik-Periodica, Leninstrasse 16, Postfach 160, 710 Leipzig Germany. **Tel** 71370. **LC** Z6956.G3; D14; PN5214.P4. **Circ:** 28,000.
Desc: General catalogue of periodicals and serial publications from the German Democratic Republic.

US/0011-8869
DENVER QUARTERLY. See Literature.

US/0014-083X
ESSAY AND GENERAL LITERATURE INDEX. [Essay gen. lit. index]. **Added/Corp** H.W. Wilson Company. Vol. 1 (1900)-. English. sa (with 12 monthly buying guides that preview books to be indexed). $120.00 US and Canada; $130.00 other. H W Wilson Company, 950 University Avenue, Bronx NY 10452. **Tel** (800)367-6770, (718)588-8400, FAX (718)590-1617, telex 4990003 HWILSON. **ED** Juliette Yaakor. **LC** AI3; .E752. **DD** 080.1/6; 016. Index available. cum. index. **Bk Rev.** ctrl circ. available on an online database from WILSONLINE; available on CD-ROM from WILSONDISC; available on diskette from WILSONSEARCH; available on magnetic tape from WILSONTAPE.
Desc: Provides access to essays and articles in English language essay collections and anthologies. Emphasis is on social sciences and humanities.

US/0014-083X
ESSAY AND GENERAL LITERATURE INDEX. CD-ROM. English. an. $695.00. H W Wilson Company, 950 University Avenue, Bronx NY 10452. **Tel** (800)367-6770, (718)588-8400, FAX (718)590-1617, telex 4990003 HWILSON. **ED** Juliette Yaakor. Index available. cum. index. **Bk Rev.** ctrl circ. available on diskette from WILSONSEARCH; available on magnetic tape from WILSONTAPE; available in print; available on an online database from WILSONLINE.
Desc: Author-subject index to collections of essays and works of a composite nature that have general reference value, particularly in the humanities and social sciences.

US/0191-9199
FRENCH 17. [Fr. 17]. **VFOAT** French Seventeen. No. 26- 1978-. English. an. $4.50. Professor J D Vedvik, Department of Foreign Languages, Colorado State University, Fort Collins CO 80523. **LC** Z2172; .M6; PQ241. **DD** 016.84/09/004. ***Continues*** *Bibliography of French Seventeenth Century Studies.*

US/0085-0888
FRENCH XX BIBLIOGRAPHY. [Fr. XX bibliogr.]. **Added/Corp** French Institute-Alliance Francaise de New York. French Institute in the United States. Camargo Foundation. **VFOAT** French Twenty Bibliography. **VAT** French 20 Bibliography. Vol. 5, No. 21 (1969)-. English. ir (Spring). $88.00. Associated University Press, 440 Forsgate Drive, Cranbury NJ 08512. **Tel** (609)655-4770. **ED** Douglas W. Alden. **LC** Z2173; .F7; PQ305. **DD** 016.8409. **Circ:** 1,200. ***Continues*** *French 7 Bibliography, 0362-0255.*
Desc: Critical and biographical references to French literature since 1885.

US/0361-9729
GIRLS & BOYS TOGETHER. VAT Girls and Boys Together. English. $1.00. Feminist Book Mart, 162-11 Ninth Avenue, Whitestone NY 11357. **LC** Z1035; .G57; PN1009.A1. **DD** 028.52.

US/0090-9130
INDEX OF AMERICAN PERIODICAL VERSE. [Index Am. period. verse]. (1971)-. Abstracting/Indexing Service. English. an. $59.50. Scarecrow Press Inc., 52 Liberty Street, PO Box 4167, Metuchen NJ 08840. **Tel** (908)548-8600, (800)537-7107. **ED** James D Anderson, Rafael Catala, and James V Romano (editors' address: PO Box 38, New Brunswick NJ 08903). **LC** Z1231.P7; I47. **DD** 016.811/5/4. **Circ:** 3,000.
Desc: Indexes over 5,900 poets and translators, and over 16,500 poems; over 300 periodicals are covered.

UK
INDEX OF ISLAMIC LITERATURE. Added/Corp Islamic Foundation (Great Britain). **VFOAT** Muslim World Book Review Index of Islamic Literature. (198?)-. Abstracting/Indexing Service. English. qt. £20.00 (individuals), £30.00 (institutions) UK; £28.00 (individuals), £38.00 (institutions) other. Islamic Foundation Publishing Unit, Unit 9/Old Dunlop Factory, 62 Evington Valley Road, Leicester LE5 5LJ England. **Tel** 011 44 533 734860, FAX 011 44 533 244946, telex 341539 ISLAMF G. **ED** M M Ahsan. Index available. cum. index. **Bk Rev. Ad Acc. Circ:** 1,000.
Desc: Aspires both to inform and stimulate the lay readers as well as the scholars through in-depth reviews, short introductions and select bibliographies.

UK
INDEX TO BRITISH LITERARY BIBLIOGRAPHY. 1 (1969)-. Monographic series. English. ir. Price varies per volume. Oxford University Press, Walton Street, Oxford OX2 6DP England. **Tel** 011 44 865 56767, FAX 011 44 865 267773, telex 837330 OXPRES G. **(Subscription address:** Oxford University Press / USA, Journals Marketing Department, Oxford University Press, 2001 Evans Road, Cary NC 27513.) **ED** T. E. Howard-Hill.

CN
INDEX TO CANADIAN POETRY IN ENGLISH. English. 45.00Can$. Reference Press, PO Box 70, Teeswater Ontario N0G 2S0 Canada. **Tel** (519)392-6634.
Desc: An expanded edition of the author-title-subject-firstline index first published in 1984.

UK/0020-7950
INTERNATIONAL MEDIEVAL BIBLIOGRAPHY. (1967)-. Bibliography. English. Twice a year (Mar., Sept.,). £175.00 UK, £181.00 others, $303.50 US (hardbound); £160.00 UK, £164.50 others, $277.50 US (paperbound). University of Leeds School of History, Leeds LS2 9JT England. **Tel** 011 44 532 333616, FAX 0532 342759, telex 556473. **ED** Simon N. Forde. **LC** Z6203; .I63. **DD** 016.914/03/1. Index available. **Ad Acc. Circ:** 600.
Desc: Bibliography covering periodical literature, acts and collected essays published throughout the world on all areas of scholarly work on the European Middle Ages.
Ind/Abst Annu. Bibliogr. Engl. Lang. Lit.; Br. Archaeol. Bibliogr.

HU/0021-1486
IRODALOMTORTENETI KOZLEMENYEK. [Irodtort. kozl.]. **Added/Corp** Magyar Tudomanyos Akademia. Irodalomtorteneti Intezet. Magyar Irodalomtorteneti Tarsasag. Magyar Tudomanyos Akademia. Irodalomtudomanyi Intezet. **VFOAT** ITK. (1891)-. Academic Scholarly Publication. Hungarian (summaries and/or abstracts in French). Six times a year. $36.00. Akademiai Kiado, Publishing House of the Hungarian Academy of Sciences, Prielle Kornelia u. 19-35, H-1117 Budapest Hungary. **Tel** 011 36 1 1811991, FAX 011 36 1 1811991, telex 22-6228 AKNYO H. **(Subscription address:** Kultura, Hungarian Foreign Trading Company, PO Box 149, H-1389 Budapest Hungary) **ED** T. Komlovszki. Index available. **Bk Rev. Circ:** 1,250 (ctrl).
Desc: History of Hungarian literature.
Ind/Abst MLA Int. Bibl. Books Artic. Mod. Lang. Lit.

IT/0021-2881
ITALIAN BOOKS AND PERIODICALS. Added/Corp Italy. Servizi delle Informazioni e della Proprieta Letteraria, Artistica e Scientifica. Italy. Ufficio della Proprieta Letteraria, Artistica e Scientifica. Italy. Ministero per i beni Culturali e Ambientali. Divisione Editoria. Vol. 1, No. 1 (Jan. 1958)-. Periodical. English (French, German and Spanish). Three times a year. L36000 Italy; L55000 others;. Istituto Poligrafico Zecca Stato, Piazza Verdi 10, 00198 Rome Italy. **Tel** 011 39 6 85082307, 011 39 6 85082221. **LC** Z2345; .I89. **NLM** Z 2345 I86.
Ind/Abst MLA Int. Bibl. Books Artic. Mod. Lang. Lit.

US
JUNIOR BOOK AWARDS. Main/Corp Boys' Clubs of America. English. **LC** Z1037; .B8. **DD** 028.5.

JA
KOKUBUNGAKU KENKYU SHIRYOKAN ZO CHIKUJI KANKOBUTSU MOKUROKU. Main/Corp Kokubungaku Kenkyu Shiryokan. **VFOAT** Catalog of Periodicals Acquired in the National Institute of Japanese Literature. 1977-. Japanese. an. Kokubungaku Kenkyu Shiryokan, 16-10 Yutakamachi 1-chome, Shinagawa-ku 142, Tokyo Japan. **Tel** (03)785-7131. **LC** Z6958.J3; K64A; PN5407.P4.
Desc: Each issue includes a section for serials in non-Japanese languages, arranged alphabetically.

JA
KOKUBUNGAKU KENKYU SHIRYOKAN ZO MAIKURO SHIRYO MOKUROKU / HENSHU, KOKUBUNGAKU KENKYUU SHIRYOKAN SEIRI ETSURANBU. Main/Corp Kokubungaku Kenkyu Shiryokan. **VFOAT** Maikuro Shiryo Mokuroku; Catalog of Japanese Manuscripts and Printed Books in Microform. Japanese. Kokubungaku Kenkyu Shiryokan, 16-10 Yutakamachi 1-chome, Shinagawa-ku 142, Tokyo Japan. **Tel** (03)785-7131. **LC** Z3308.L5; K62A; PL523.

JA
KOMABANO: KAMPO. Japanese. Tokyo-To Kindai Bungaku Hakubutsukan, 3-55 Komaba 4, Meguro-ku 153, Tokyo Japan. **LC** Z3308.L5; K68; PL700.

SW
KOMMUNAL LITTERATURTJANST. (19??)-. Periodical. Swedish. bm. $26.62. Bibliotekstjanst AB, Box 200, S-221 00 Lund Sweden. **Tel** 011 46 46 180000. **LC** Z7164.L8; K65.

FR/0024-0761
LEMOUZI. See Folklore.

IT/1121-0753
LETTERATURA ITALIANA. AGGIORNAMENTO BIBLIOGRAFICO. [Lett. Ital., Aggiorn. bibliogr.]. **VFOAT** L.I.A.B. (1991)-. Periodical. Italian. sa. L350000 Italy; L400000 other. Alcione Edizioni SRL, Corso Italia 31, CP 554, 34121 Trieste Italy. **Tel** 011 39 40 366069. **ED** Benedetto Aschero. **UDC** 01 :850.

AG
LITERATURA ARGENTINA; REVISTA BIBLIOGRAFICA, LA. V. 1- (No. 1-); Sept. (1928)-. Periodical. Spanish. mo. **ED** L J Rosso. **LC** Z1615; .L77. **DD** 015.82.

KO/1225-0090
MUNHON CHONGBO / THE LITERARY INFORMATION. ***Title Change.*** **Added/Corp** Kungnip Chungang Tosogwan (Seoul, Korea). **VFOAT** The Literary Information. Vol 1 (1972)-(1993). Periodical. Korean (English). mo. Kungnip Chungang Tosogwan, 100-177 1-ka Hoehyon-dong Chung-ku, Seoul Korea. **Tel** 753-8536. **LC** Z3316; .M86. ***Formed by the union of*** *Chongchaek Charyo Sokpo* ***and*** *Chulpanmul Nappon Wolbo.* ***Continued by*** *Nappon Wolbo (Seoul, Korea : 1994), 1227-5247.*

US/1052-9438
NEW YORK REVIEW OF SCIENCE FICTION, THE. See Literature.

●US/1068-4468
NIGHT SONGS. [Night songs]. No. 1 (Winter 1992)-. Periodical. English. qt. $3.00. Gothic Press, PO Box 80051, 4998 Perkind Rd, Baton Rouge LA 70808-3043. **Tel** (504)766-2906. **ED** Gary W. Crawford. **DD** 811. **Circ:** 50.

RU
NOVAIA OTECHESTVENNAIA LITERATURA PO OBSHCHESTVENNYM NAUKAM. LITERATUROVEDENIE / ROSSIISKAIA AKADEMIIA NAUK, INSTITUT NAUCHNOI INFORMATSII PO OBSHCHESTVENNYM NAUKAM. ***Title Change.*** **Added/Corp** Institut Nauchnoi Informatsii po Obshchestvennym Naukam (Rossiiskaia Akademiia Nauk). **VFOAT** Literaturovedenie. (1992)-(1992). Academic Scholarly Publication. Russian. mo. Izdatelstvo Nauka / Akademiia Nauk, Publishing House of the Russian Academy of Sciences, Leninskii Porspekt 14, 117901 Moscow Russia. **Tel** 011 95 954-21-53, FAX 011 95 938-21-44, telex 411964. **LC** Z6513; .N67; PN583. ***Continues*** *Novaia Sovetskaia Literatura po Obshchestvennym Naukam. Literaturovedenie.* ***Merged with*** *Novaia Inostrannnaia Literatura po Obshchestvennym Naukam. Literaturovedenie* ***to form*** *Novaia Literatura po Sotsialnym i Gumanitarnym Naukam. Literaturovedenie.*

DK/0106-035X
NOVELLEREGISTER. **Added/Corp** Bibliotekscentralen (Denmark). **VFOAT** Novelle Register. Began in 1971. Danish. an. **LC** Z5917.S5; N68; PN3373. **DD** 016.80883/1.

US/0094-5943
READER'S ADVISER, THE. [Read. advis.]. 10th Ed. (1964)-. English. ir (published approximately every six years). $500.00 (6 volume set). R R Bowker, A Reed Reference Publishing Company, Part of Reed International PLC, PO Box 31, 121 Chanlon Drive, New Providence NJ 07974. **Tel** (908)464-6800, (800)521-8110, FAX (908)665-6688, telex 138-755. **DD** 011. ***Continues*** *Reader's Adviser and Bookman's Manual.*
Desc: Provides intriguing capsule profiles of its authors plus annotated bibliographies (with prices) of selected in-print works by and about them.

SP/0034-849X
REVISTA DE LITERATURA. [Rev. lit.]. **Added/Corp** Instituto "Miguel de Cervantes.". Vol. 1, No. 1 (Jan./March 1952)-. Periodical. Spanish. Twice a year (June & Dec.). 2300ptas Spain; 3450ptas other. Consejo Superior Investigacion Cientificas (CSIC), Vitruvio 8, 28006 Madrid Spain. **Tel** 011 34 1 5612833, FAX 011 34 1 4113077, telex 42182. **LC** PN6; .R48. **Bk Rev.** Documents available from The Genuine Article. ***Formed by the union of*** *Cuadernos de Literatura (Madrid, Spain)* ***and*** *Revista Bibliografica y Documental.*
Desc: Approaches the study of literature from a traditional historically investigative perspective, moving methodologically forward to a theoretically based exegesis. Includes monographs, bibliographic notes, and unpublished texts.
Ind/Abst Am. Hist. Life (1963-1966); Arts Humanit. Citation Index (19??-19??) [Full Cov.]; Curr. Contents Arts Humanit.; MLA Int. Bibl. Books Artic. Mod. Lang. Lit.; Res. Alert [Full Cov.]; Romant. Move. (1963-1966).

US/0557-2738
ROMANTIC MOVEMENT. [Romant. mov.]. (1964)-. Abstracting/Indexing Service. English (French, German, Spanish and Italian). an. $60.00. Locust Hill Press, PO Box 260, West Cornwall CT 06796. **Tel** (203)672-0060, FAX (203)672-4968. **ED** David V. Erdman. **LC** Z6514.R6; R63; PN603. **DD** 016.809/9145. **Bk Rev. Circ:** 500.
Desc: Editors scour a formidable list of journals in search of articles germane to romantic studies, and provide listings and annotations for the same as they are uncovered.

US/1046-1922
SCIENCE FICTION AND FANTASY BOOK REVIEW INDEX. (SCIENCE FICTION AND FANTASY BOOK REVIEW INDEX : SFFBRI.). [Sci. fict. fantasy book rev. index]. **VFOAT** SFFBRI. Vol. 15 (1984)-. Abstracting/Indexing Service. English. an. $10.00. H.W. Hall, 3608 Meadow Oaks Lane, Bryan TX 77801. **Tel** (409)845-2316. **ED** H.W. Hall. **DD** 813. **Circ:** 300. ***Continues*** *Science Fiction Book Review Index.*
Desc: Index to book reviews of science fiction and fantasy books.

CN/0826-3310
SELECTIONS - MODERN LANGUAGES SERVICES BRANCH (RICHMOND). ***Ceased.*** (SELECTIONS.). [Sel. -Mod. Lang. Serv. Branch]. No. 1 (Mar. 1983)-(1992). Periodical. English. ir. **DD** 011.62. available in microform from University Microfilms International (UMI).
Ind/Abst Account. Tax Datab. (1986-) [Full Txt.].

US
SERIF SERIES, THE. ***Ceased.*** No. 42 (1983)-?. Monographic series. English. ir. Kent State University Press / Ohio, Kent OH 44242. **Tel** (216)672-7913. **ED** Leanne West.
Desc: A series of books of checklists and bibliographies focused mainly on American and English authors.

US/0360-9774
SHORT STORY INDEX. (1974)-. English. an (with quinquennial cumulations). $90.00 US and Canada; $100.00 other. H W Wilson Company, 950 University Avenue, Bronx NY 10452. **Tel** (800)367-6770, (718)588-8400, FAX (718)590-1617, telex 4990003 HWILSON. **LC** Z5917.S5; C62. **DD** 016.80883/1. ***Absorbed*** *Short Story Index. Supplement, 0098-3756.*
Desc: Provides indexing coverage of short stodies published in collections or in periodicals indexed by Readers' Guide or Humanities Index.

US
SHORT TITLE CATALOG OF BOOKS PRINTED IN ENGLAND, SCOTLAND, IRELAND, WALES, AND BRITISH AMERICA AND OF ENGLISH BOOKS PRINTED IN OTHER COUNTRIES. (19??)-. Catalog. English. ir. Price varies per volume. Modern Language Association of America, 10 Astor Place, New York NY 10003-6981. **Tel** (212)614-6382, FAX (212)477-9863. **ED** Donald Wing. **Acid Free.**
Desc: Contains over 75,000 entries, covering all known printed materials, except serials, in English from 1641 to 1700.

US/0000-0159
SUBJECT GUIDE TO BOOKS IN PRINT. **Added/Corp** R.R. Bowker Company. **VFOAT** Books in Print. Subject Guide; Subject Guide. Vol. 1 (1957)-. English. an. $315.00. R R Bowker, A Reed Reference Publishing Company, Part of Reed International PLC, PO Box 31, 121 Chanlon Drive, New Providence NJ 07974. **Tel** (908)464-6800, (800)521-8110, FAX (908)665-6688, telex 138-755. **LC** Z1215; .P973. **DD** 015.73. **NLM** Z 1215 S941. **[CCC].**
Desc: Helps to find the latest books on everything from gentrification to immunodiagnosis.

FI/0355-001X
SUOMEN KIRJALLISUUS. **Added/Corp** Helsingin Yliopisto. Kirjasto. **VFOAT** Finlands Litteratur; The Finnish National Bibliography; Litterature Finnoise. (1877)-. Periodical. Finnish. an. Fmk700.00. Valtion Painatuskeskus, PO Box 516, SF 00101 Helsinki Finland. **Tel** 011 358 0 5660266. **LC** Z2520; .S95.

SW/0039-6443
SVENSK BOKFORTECKNING. (SVENSK BOKFORTECKNING. THE SWEDISH NATIONAL BIBLIOGRAPHY.). **Added/Corp** Kungliga Biblioteket (Sweden). Bibliografiska Institutet. **VFOAT** Swedish National Bibliography. (Jan. 1953)-. Bibliography. Swedish (English). Six times a year. Kr1980.00. Tidnings AB Svensk Bokhandel, Sveavaegen 52 Gatan, PO Box 45150, S 111 34 Stockhom Sweden. **Tel** 011 46 8 243145. **LC** Z2625; .S952. **NLM** Z 2625 S969. ***Supersedes*** *Svensk Bokforteckning; Arskatalog for Svenska Bokhandeln, 0349-442X.*
Ind/Abst Annu. Bibliogr. Engl. Lang. Lit.

POETRY

IO
80 I.E. DELAPAN PULUH, BUKU PUISI. Indonesian. 250. N/A Horison, Jalan Gereja Theresia 47, Jakarta Indonesia. **LC** PL5086; .D44.

US/8756-7636
AAG-AAG. [Aag-aag]. **VFOAT** AAG AAG. Periodical. English. be. $2.00 per issue. Two Magpie Press, PO Box 177, Kendrick ID 83537. **DD** 811.

US
ABOVE THE BRIDGE MAGAZINE. Vol. 1, No. 6 (Nov./Dec. 1985)-. Periodical. English. mo. $13.00. Above the Bridge Magazine, PO Box 416, Marquette MI 49855. **Tel** (906)942-7486. **LC** WMLC 93/1753. ***Continues*** *Above the Bridge.*

US/0361-1663
ABRAXAS (MADISON). (ABRAXAS.). (1968)-. Periodical. English (Hungarian, Polish, French, Chinese, Spanish and Portuguese). ir. $16.00. Abraxas Press Inc, 2518 Gregory Street, Madison WI 53711. **Tel** (608)238-0175. **ED** Ingrid Swanberg. **LC** PS325; .A27. **DD** 811/.008. Index available. **Circ:** 600.
Desc: Publishes poetry from the full range of contemporary work, including poetry in translation, as well as essays, criticism and reviews of small press poety books.
Ind/Abst Am. Humanit. Index; Index Am. Period. Verse.

FR
ACTION POETIQUE. **Added/Corp** Action Poetique (Group). (1955)-. Periodical. French. qt. 195.89F France; 300.00F other. Action Poetique, 87 rue Voltaire, 92800 Puteaux France. **Tel** 011 33 42 041474. **Bk Rev. Ad Acc.**

UK
ACUMEN MAGAZINE. **VFOAT** Acumen. No. 1 (Apr. 1985)-. English. Twice a year (Apr. & Oct.). $25.00. Acumen Magazine, 6 The Mount, Higher Furzeham, Brizon South Devon TQ5 8QY England. **Tel** 011 44 803 8051098. **LC** PR1227; .A295. **DD** 821.008/005.

UK/0002-0796
AGENDA (LONDON). (AGENDA.). [Agenda]. **VFOAT** Agenda Magazine. Vol. 1, No. 1 (Jan. 1959)-. Periodical. English. qt. £24.00 (UK), £26.00 (other) institution; £18.00 (UK), £20.00 (other) individual. Agenda, 5 Cranbourne Court, Albert Bridge Road, London SW11 4PE England. **Tel** 11-44-71-2280700. **ED** William Cookson and Peter Dale. **Bk Rev. Ad Acc. Circ:** 1,000. available on microfilm and microfiche from University Microfilms International (UMI). Documents available from The Genuine Article. ***Continues*** *Four Pages.*
Desc: A magazine of poetry and criticism. Special issues on individual poets and themes. Includes regular articles on neglected poets and translation of poets of all ages.
Ind/Abst Abstr. Engl. Stud.; Annu. Bibliogr. Engl. Lang. Lit.; Arts Humanit. Citation Index [Full Cov.]; Curr. Contents Arts Humanit.; MLA Int. Bibl. Books Artic. Mod. Lang. Lit.; Res. Alert [Full Cov.].

CN/0044-6947
AIR (VANCOUVER). (AIR.). [Air]. 1 (Jan. 71)-. Periodical. English. bm. Air, Box 48688 Station Bentall B7X 1A0 Canada. **DD** C811/.54/08.

UK/0002-3728
AKROS. Began publication in 1966. Periodical. English. Akros Publications, 25 Johns Road, Radcliffe on Tr, Nottingham NG12 2GW England. **ED** Duncan Glen.

LE
AL-UDISSIH. **VFOAT** Odyssee. Periodical. Arabic. mo. £L100.00. S B 144, Junih Lebanon. **LC** PJ7631; .U36.

SP
ALBA : REVISTA DE POESIA. Spanish (English, Italian and French). Three times a year. 3.000ptas Spain; 4.500ptas Europe; 6.000ptas North America. Editorial el Paisaje / Aranguren, La Penorra 8-2, 48850 Aranguren Spain. **Tel** (94) 639 07 74. **ED** Jose Antonio Crespo. **Bk Rev. Ad Acc. Circ:** 1,500.

CN/0318-5753
AMBER (DARTMOUTH). (AMBER.). **Added/Corp** Scotian Pen Guild. Vol. 1 (April 1973)-. Periodical. English. qt. Scotian Pen Guild, Box 173, Dartmouth Nova Scotia, B2Y 3Y3 Canada. ***Supersedes*** *Pegasus, 0031-4072.*

UK/0002-6972
AMBIT. **VFOAT** Ambit Magazine. No. 1 (Summer 1959)-. Periodical. English. Four times a year (Jan., Apr., July, Oct.). £20.00 UK; £22.00 other; $40.00 US & Canada. Ambit, 17 Priory Gardens, London N6 4QY

England. **Tel** 011 44 81 340 3566. **ED** Martin Bax. **LC** PR1098; .A44. **DD** 820./8. Index available (Price $2.00). cum. index (No. 101). **Bk Rev.** **Ad Acc.** **Circ:** 2,000. available on microfilm from University Microfilms International (UMI).
Desc: A journal of new poetry, short stories, artwork and reviews.

US/0360-3709
AMERICAN POETRY REVIEW, THE. [Am. poetry rev.]. Vol. 1 (Nov./Dec. 1972)-. Periodical. English. bm (6 issues). $15.00 (one year), $27.00 (two year), $38.00 (three year) US, Guam, Puerto Rico, US Virgin Islands; $18.00 (one year), $33.00 (two year), $47.00 (three year) other. The American Poetry Review, 1721 Walnut Street, Philadelphia PA 19103. **Tel** (215)496-0439. **ED** David Bonanno, Stephen Berg and Arthur Vogelsang. **LC** PS580; .A44. **Bk Rev.** **Ad Acc.** **Circ:** 23,000. available on microfilm and microfiche from University Microfilms International (UMI). Documents available from The Genuine Article, UMI Article Clearinghouse.
Desc: The most comprehensive periodical of poetry, essays, reviews, supplements, columns, and fiction in America. Six times a year, tabloid, featuring folios of poetry by American and European poets - columns by poets and prose writers - essays by various writers - book reviews - younger poets - retrospective reviews.
Ind/Abst Abstr. Engl. Stud.; Acad. Ind. [Computer File] (1992-); Acad. Search (July 1993-); Am. Humanit. Index; Annu. Bibliogr. Engl. Lang. Lit.; Arts Humanit. Citation Index [Full Cov.]; Book Rev. Index; Child. Lit. Abstr. (19??-); Curr. Contents Arts Humanit.; Expand. Acad. Index (1989-); Humanit. Index; Humanit. Source (Jul. 1993-); Index Am. Period. Verse; INFO-SOUTH Abstr.; Lit. Crit. Regist.; Mag. Search; MLA Int. Bibl. Books Artic. Mod. Lang. Lit.; Newsp. Period. Abstr. (1991-); Res. Alert [Full Cov.].

AG
ANFORA (BUENOS AIRES, ARGENTINA). (ANFORA.). (1986)-. Periodical. Spanish. qt. Agenica Periodistica CID, Avenida de Mayo 666, Capital Federal, Argentina. **Tel** 30 2471. **ED** Sebastian Dozo Labat. **Circ:** 2,000.

UK/0143-8050
ANGEL EXHAUST. Periodical. English. £1.50. Islington Press, 59 Ilford House, Dove Road, London N1 3NA England. **LC** PR1170; .A55. **DD** 821/.914/08.

US/0272-4359
ANOTHER CHICAGO MAGAZINE. **See** Literature.

JA
ANTHOLOGY. English. ¥1000 Japan; Free in US; $5.00 other. Ikuta Press, 1-5-3 Sumiyoshi-Yamate, Higashinada-ku 658, Kobe Japan. **Tel** (078)822-1329. **ED** Yoko Danno. **LC** PR9515.6; .A54. **DD** 811/.008/0952. **Circ:** 500.
Desc: Publishes poetry of the contributors living in Japan and abroad.

US/0196-2221
ANTHOLOGY OF MAGAZINE VERSE AND YEARBOOK OF AMERICAN POETRY (1980). ***Suspended.*** (ANTHOLOGY OF MAGAZINE VERSE AND YEARBOOK OF AMERICAN POETRY.). [Anthol. mag. verse yearb. Am. poetry]. **VFOAT** Anthology of Magazine Verse. 1980-(?). Periodical. English. an. $37.50. Monitor Book Company Inc, PO Box 9078, Palm Springs CA 92263-7078. **Tel** (619)323-2270. **ED** Alan F Pater. **LC** PN6099.6; .A57. **DD** 811/.008. **Bk Rev.** ctrl circ. ***Continues*** *Anthology of Magazine Verse for ..., 0270-3904.*
Desc: Part I is a collection of poetry published in magazines during each year. Part II contains bibliographical material covering the world of poetry in all categories each year.

BL
ANUARIO DE POETAS DO BRASIL. 1976-. Portuguese. Folha Carioca Editora, rua Joao Cardoso 23 Cep 20.000, Rio de Janeiro Brazil. **LC** PQ9650; .A58.

●US/1072-9232
APEX OF THE M. (1994)-. English. be. $6.00 single issues; $10.00 (individuals), $15.00 (institutions). M Press, PO Box 247, Buffalo NY 14213-0247. **ED** Lew Daly, Alan Gilbert, Kristin Prevallet, and Pam Rehm. **Bk Rev**, (Qty: 2). **Pr Rev.** **Acid Free.** **Circ:** 1,000.
Desc: This journal of contemporary poetry and poetics information.

US/0003-6765
APPLE (SPRINGFIELD). (APPLE.). No. 1- Summer 1967-. English. $1.25 single issue. D. Curry, Box 2271, Springfield IL 62705. **LC** PS580; .A66. **DD** 811/.5/408. available on microfilm and microfiche from University Microfilms International (UMI).

CK
AQUARIMANTIMA. Vol. 1 (Oct/Dec 1973)-. Periodical. Spanish. Apartado Aereo 3845, Medellin Colombia. **LC** PQ8174; .A765.

UK/0003-7303
AQUARIUS. No. 1 (1969)-. Periodical. English. ir (1 issue). £2.50. Aquarius, Flat 10, Room A 116, Sutherland Avenue, London W9 England. **Tel** 011 44 71 289 4338. **LC** PR1170; .A7.

CN/0705-6397
ARC (OTTAWA). (ARC.). **Added/Corp** Carleton University. Dept. of English. (Spring 1978)-. Periodical. English. Twice a year (Apr. and Oct.). 20.00Can$ Canada; 25.00Can$ US; 28.00Can$ other. Arc / Canada, PO Box 7368, Ottawa Ontario K1L 8E4 Canada. **Tel** (613)993-2303. **ED** John Barton and Nadine McInnis. **LC** PR9190.5; .A72. **DD** 811.009/005. **Bk Rev**, (Qty: 4-8). **Pr Rev.** **Circ:** 600. available on microfiche from Micromedia Limited.
Desc: Publishes poetry and poetry-related criticism, reviews, and articles with particular but not exclusive reference to Canada.
Ind/Abst Can. Index.

AU
ARCHIV FUER LITERATUR UND VOLKSDICHTUNG. **See** Literature.

HU/0572-4082
ARION (BUDAPEST, HUNGARY). (ARION.). (1966)-. Hungarian (English, French, German, Hungarian and Russian). an. International Publications Service, 114 East 32nd Street, New York NY 10016. **LC** PN1010; .A74. **DD** 894/.511/08.
Ind/Abst Curr. Contents Arts Humanit.

US/1043-3848
ARS LYRICA. [Ars lyrica]. **Added/Corp** Lyrica Society (U.S.). Vol. 1, No. 1 (Winter/Spring 1981)-. English. ir. Lyrica Society, 90 Church Street, St Guildford CT 06437. **Tel** (203)453-1503. **DD** 782.
Ind/Abst MLA Int. Bibl. Books Artic. Mod. Lang. Lit.

II
ART AND POETRY TODAY. **See** The Arts-Art.

SP
ATALAYA CULTURAL : REVISTA DE POESIA, ARTE Y LITERATURA. Spanish (English, French and Portuguese). Three times a year. 3000ptas Spain; 4500ptas Europe; 6000ptas North America. Editorial el Paisaje / Aranguren, La Penorra 8-2, 48850 Aranguren Spain. **Tel** (94) 639 07 74. **ED** Agustin Garcia Alonso. **Bk Rev.** **Ad Acc.**

CN/0709-9592
ATHANOR (WESTMOUNT). (ATHANOR.). V. 1- Nov. 1979-. Periodical. English. qt. $1.00 per no. Athanor, PO Box 562, Victoria Station, Westmount Quebec H3Z 2Y6 Canada. **DD** C811/.5408.

AT
AUSTRALIAN POETRY. ***Ceased.*** Vol. 1 (1941)-(19??). English. an. South Head Press, The Market Place, Berrima New South Wales 2577 Australia. **Tel** 011 61 48 711421. **LC** PR9551.A1. **DD** 821.91082.

AT/1035-8803
AUSTRALIAN WRITER'S JOURNAL, THE. [Aust. writ. j.]. (1991)-. Periodical. English. Twice a year (Summer & Winter). 14.00Aus$. Murlysdar Publishing Australia, PO Box 994, Mandurah WA 6210 Australia. **Tel** 011 61 9 5821418. **ED** Joan Lane. **DD** 820.8. ***Continues*** *The New Decade, 1035-9656.*
Desc: A collection of poetry, short stories and plays by the Australian writers. Specializes in new and beginners writers.

US/0899-3750
AVEC (PENNGROVE, CALIF.). **See** Literature.

II/0376-5296
AVEGA. Hindi (Hindi). Rs5.00. 64 Biharilal Marg, Ratalama India. **LC** PK2057; .A83.

FR
BARBACANE, LA. Began in 1965. Periodical. French. sa. 50 single issue. Chateau de Banaguil, 500 Fumel, Saint-Front-Sur-Lemance 47 France. **LC** PQ1184; .B28. **DD** 800.

US/0005-8661
BELOIT POETRY JOURNAL, THE. [Beloit poet. j.]. **Added/Corp** Beloit College. Vol. 1, No. 1 (Fall 1950)-. Periodical. English. Four times a year (Jan., Mar., June, Sept.). $18.00 (one year), $49.50 (three years). Beloit Poetry Journal, Box 154, Rural Free Delivery 2, Ellsworth ME 04605. **Tel** (207)667-5598. **ED** Marion K Stocking. **LC** PS301; .B43. **DD** 811/.008. Index available. cum. index. **Bk Rev**, (Qty: 35). **Pr Rev.** **Circ:** 1,700. available on microfilm.
Desc: Publishes new poems regardless of length, school, form, subject, or the reputation of the poet; reviews books by and about poets, and issues occasional books of special interest.
Ind/Abst Am. Humanit. Index; Annu. Bibliogr. Engl. Lang. Lit.; Index Am. Period. Verse.

US/1040-5763
BEST AMERICAN POETRY, THE. [Best Am. poet.]. (1988)-. English. $9.95 (paperback). Macmillan Publishing Company, 100 Front Street, Box 500, Riverside NJ 08075-7500. **Tel** (800)257-5755, (609)461-6500, FAX (609)461-7070. **LC** PS615; .B474. **DD** 811.008.

US/1058-9910
BEST OF KERVIN FONDREN, THE. **VFOAT** Poetry Showcase. (1991)-. English. $6.00. Kervin Fondren, PO Box 370171, Birmingham AL 35237. ***Continues*** *Passages to Freedom, 1055-0682.*

SP
BILAKABIDE : REVISTA DE POESIA. Spanish (English). qt. 4.500ptas Spain; 7.000ptas North America; 6.000ptas other. Editorial el Paisaje / Aranguren, La Penorra 8-2, 48850 Aranguren Spain. **Tel** (94) 639 07 74. **ED** Agustin Garcia Alonso. **Bk Rev.** **Ad Acc.** **Circ:** 3,000 (ctrl).

US/1047-2258
BIRMINGHAM POETRY REVIEW. [Birm. poet. rev.]. **VFOAT** BPR. No. 1 (Fall/Winter 1988)-. Periodical. English. Twice a year (June & Dec.). $3.00. Birmingham Poetry Review / Department of English, University of Alabama at Birmingham, c/o Dr. Collins, Birmingham AL 35294. **Tel** (205)934-4250. **ED** Robert Collins and Randy Blythe (phone: (205)934-8573). **DD** 811. Index available. cum. index. **Bk Rev**, (Qty: 3-6). **Circ:** 600.
Desc: Publishes contemporary poetry, regardless of style or subject matter.

US/0197-7768
BITS. No. 1- Jan. 1975-. Periodical. English. sa. **ED** R Wallace. **LC** PS580; .B57. **DD** 811/.008.

US
BITTER OLEANDER. V. 1- 1975-. Periodical. English. Three times a year. $5.00. Bitter Oleander Press, 310 Bradford Parkway, Syracuse NY 13224. **LC** PN6099.6; .B58. **DD** 808.81/04/05.

US/0006-3908
BITTERROOT. ***Ceased.*** No. 1 (Fall 1962)-Ceased No.100. Periodical. English. qt. Bitterroot, PO Box 489, Menke Katz Editor, Spring Glen NY 12483.
Ind/Abst Am. Humanit. Index.

US/0733-0073
BLACK WILLOW. **VFOAT** Black Willow Poetry. 1 (Fall '82)-. Periodical. English. sa. $4.00. Black Willow, 3214 Sunset Avenue, Norristown PA 19403.

US/0737-9269
BLIND ALLEYS. Vol. 1, No. 1 (Spring/Summer 1982)-. Periodical. English. sa. $13.00. Blind Alleys, 7th Son Press, PO Box 13224, Baltimore MD 21203. **ED** Glenford H Cummings, Charles Lynch, Aissatou Mijiza and Michael S Weaver. **LC** PS615; .B56. **DD** 811/.008. **Bk Rev.** **Ad Acc.** **Circ:** 500.
Desc: A literary magazine devoted to all genres, art and music.

US/0197-7016
BLUE UNICORN. Vol. 1 (Oct. 1977)-. Periodical. English. Three times a year (Feb., June, Oct.). $14.00. Blue Unicorn, 22 Avon Road, Kensington CA 94707. **Tel** (510)526-8439. **ED** Ruth G. Iodice, Harold Witt and Daniel J. Langton. **LC** PS580; .B58. **DD** 811/.008. **Circ:** 500 (ctrl).
Desc: We publish the poetry that is being written today, including work by established and new writers, in both traditional forms and free verse.
Ind/Abst Am. Humanit. Index.

US/0741-5028
BLUEFISH. ***Ceased.*** [Bluefish]. Vol.1, No. 1 (Autumn 1983). Periodical. English. sa. Bluefish, Box 1601, Southampton NY 11968. **LC** PS615; .B58. **DD** 811/.008.

BN/0352-1044
BOOKS IN BOSNIA AND HERZEGOVINA. **See** Literature.

●US/1065-0342
BORDERLANDS (AUSTIN, TEX.). (BORDERLANDS : TEXAS POETRY REVIEW.). **VFOAT** Border Lands. (1992)-. Periodical. English. sa. $14.00 (individuals), $16.00 (institutions). Borderlands, PO Box 49818, Austin TX 78765. **ED** Dorothy Barnett, Lynn Gilbert, D'Arcy Randall. **Bk Rev.**
Desc: Publishes work aware of the other, the different, the separate from oneself - whether in the landscape, the social context, the ecosphere, the realm of spirit, or the stream of time.

CN/0823-2679
BOREAL INTERNATIONAL. [Boreal int.]. Periodical. Spanish. Boreal International, PO Box 262 Victoria Station, Montreal Quebec H3Z 2V5 Canada. **DD** C861/.64/08. ***Continues*** *Boreal, 0006-7717.*

US/1052-1569
BRIDGE (OAK PARK, MICH.), THE. **See** Literature.

US/0007-4128
BULLETIN BAUDELAIRIEN. **Added/Corp** W.T. Bandy Center for Baudelaire Studies. Vol. 1 (Aug.

1965)-. Bulletin. French (English). Twice a year (Apr., Dec.). $10.00. Vanderbilt University / Box 6325, Station B, Nashville TN 37235. **Tel** (615)322-6900, FAX (615)343-6909. **ED** James S. Patty and Claude Pichois. **LC** PQ2191.Z5; B77. **DD** 841. **Circ:** 300.
Desc: Short document-based studies concerning the life and works of Charles Baudelaire.
Ind/Abst BHA : Biblio. Hist. Art; MLA Int. Bibl. Books Artic. Mod. Lang. Lit.; Romant. Move.

FR/0997-3907
BULLETIN D'ETUDES PARNASSIENNES ET SYMBOLISTES. **Added/Corp** Association Lyonnaise pour le Developpement des Relations Universitaires Internationales. (Spring 1988)-. Bulletin. French. sa. ***Continues*** *Bulletin des Etudes Parnassiennes, 0244-9315.*
Ind/Abst MLA Int. Bibl. Books Artic. Mod. Lang. Lit.

NE/0167-6520
BUMPER. **See** Literature.

CN/1181-8697
BYWORDS (OTTAWA). (BYWORDS : POETRY & OTTAWA LITERARY EVENTS.). [Bywords]. Vol. 1, No. 1 (Nov. 1990)-. Periodical. English. mo. Limited free distribution. Bywords, c/o University of Ottawa, English Department, 175 Waller Street, Ottawa, Ontario K1N 6N5 Canada. **DD** C811/.5408/0971384.

NE/0165-0858
BZZLLETIN. [Bzzlletin]. (1972)-. Periodical. Dutch. Eight times a year. Fl72.50 Holland, Belgium, & Luxemburg; Fl105.00 other. Bzzlletin, Laan van Meerdervoort 10, 2517 AJ Den Haag Netherlands. **Tel** 070-3632934, FAX 070-3631932. **ED** Koos Hageraats. Index available. **Ad Acc. Circ:** 6,000.

US/0007-9537
CAFE SOLO. [Cafe solo]. No. 1 (1969)-. English (Spanish). qt. $30.00 (one year), $55.00 (two years), $80.00 (three years). Solo Press, PO Box 2814, Atascadero CA 93423. **Tel** (805)466-3083. **ED** Glenna Luschei. **DD** 810. **Bk Rev. Circ:** 500 (ctrl).
Ind/Abst Am. Humanit. Index (-199?).

FR
CAHIERS MAYNARD. **Added/Corp** Societe des Amis de Maynard. No. 7 (1977)-. Periodical. French. an. Association des Amis Maynard, La Petite Riviere Epire, 49170 Savennieres France. **LC** PQ1820.M3; C33. **DD** 841/.4; B. ***Continues*** *Societe des Amis de Maynard. Cahier - Association des Amis de Maynard.*

US/0890-7269
CALIBAN (ANN ARBOR, MICH.). (CALIBAN.). [Caliban]. (1986)-. Periodical. English. sa (June and Dec.). $24.00 institution, $14.00 individual. Caliban, PO Box 561, Laguna Beach CA 92652. **LC** PN6101; .C34. **DD** 811/.5408.

SP
CALIOPE Y POLIMNIA : REVISTA DE POESIA Y CUENTOS. Spanish (English, French and Italian). Two issues per month. 2500ptas Spain; 4000ptas Europe; 3000ptas other. Editorial el Paisaje / Aranguren, La Penorra 8-2, 48850 Aranguren Spain. **Tel** (94) 639 07 74. **ED** Agustin Garcia Alonso. **Bk Rev. Ad Acc. Circ:** 4,600 (ctrl).

CN/0383-1574
CANADIAN POETRY ANNUAL, THE. 1976-. English. an. $2.95 per no. Musson Book Company, 30 Lesmill Road, Don Mills Ontario M3B 2T6 Canada. **DD** C811/.5/408.

CN/0704-5646
CANADIAN POETRY (LONDON, ONT.). (CANADIAN POETRY.). [Can. poetry]. No. 1 (Fall/Winter 1977)-. Academic Scholarly Publication. English. sa. 18.00Can$ (1 year), 36.00Can$ (2 year), 54.00Can$ (3 year). University of Western Ontario Department of English, Room 173, London Ontario N6A 3K7 Canada. **Tel** (519)673-1164. **ED** D M R Bentley. **LC** PR9190.2; .C35. **DD** 811/.009/971; C811/.009. **Bk Rev. Ad Acc. Circ:** 400.
Desc: Scholarly and critical journal devoted to the study of poetry from all periods in Canada.
Ind/Abst Abstr. Engl. Stud.; Am. Humanit. Index; Annu. Bibliogr. Engl. Lang. Lit.; Can. Index (?-?); Can. Lit. Index (1985-1986); Can. Period. Index (19??-); Index Book Rev. Humanit.; MLA Int. Bibl. Books Artic. Mod. Lang. Lit.

US/0094-9167
CAPE ISLAND SOUND. V. 1- Spring 1974-. Periodical. English. qt. $4.00. PO Box 242, Cape May NJ 08204. **LC** PS580; .C36. **DD** 811/.5/408.

US/0146-2199
CAPE ROCK, THE. **Added/Corp** Southeast Missouri State University. Vol. 10, No.2 (Summer 1975)-. Periodical. English. sa. $5.00 US; $5.50 Canada; $6.00 other. Southeast Missouri State College, Department of English, Cape Girardeau MO 63701. **Tel** (314)651-2636. **ED** Harvey Hecht. cum. index. **Circ:** 500. ***Continues*** *Cape Rock Journal.*
Desc: Poetry journal with black and white photography. Pays $100.00 for photography, $200.00 for top poem, in each issue.
Ind/Abst Am. Humanit. Index; Index Am. Period. Verse.

AG
CARTA DE OLIVER, LA. No. 1 (1990)-. Periodical. English (Spanish). Three times a year. La Carta de Oliver, Avda Maipu 927, PB "C" (1638), Vte. Lopez, Pcia, Buenos Aires, Argentina.

SP
CASTRO, EL. Spanish. qt. 4000ptas Spain; 8000ptas North America; 7000ptas other. Editorial El Paisaje, Entre los Rios 10, 24760 Castrocalbon Leon Spain. **(Subscription address:** El Castro, Entre los Rios 10, 24760- Castrocalbon Leon Espana**) ED** Agustin Garcia Alonso. Index available. cum. index. **Bk Rev. Ad Acc. Circ:** 6,000 (ctrl).
Desc: Contains novels, poems, biographies, theatre and cultural information.

●US/1065-9250
CATHAY. [Cathay]. (1992)-. Periodical. English. Paradigm Press / Rhode Island, 11 Slater Avenue, Providence RI 02906. **DD** 808.

●US/1062-6379
CAT'S EAR. [Cat's ear]. Vol. 1, No. 1 (Spring 1992)-. Periodical. English. Three times a year. $5.00 individuals; $10.00 institutions. Galliard Group Publishers, Box 946, Kirksville MO 63501. **Tel** (816)627-2210. **ED** Tim Rolands. **DD** 808. **Ad Acc. Circ:** 100.
Desc: Literary publication that strives to unite the public with academia.

US
CENTERING. **Added/Corp** Michigan State University. Dept. of American Thought and Language. (1973)-. Periodical. English. an. $5.00. Michigan State University / Bessey Hall, East Lansing MI 48824-1033. **Tel** (517)355-2400. **ED** F. Richard Thomas. **Circ:** 300.
Desc: Devotes entire issues to one poet.

SP
CERVANTES : REVISTA DE POESIA E INFORMACION CULTURAL. Spanish. Three times a year. 5.000ptas Spain; 7.000ptas Europe; 6.000ptas other. Ediciones Cervantes, Apartado Postal 1049, 48080 Bilbao Spain. **ED** Agustin Garcia Alonso. **Bk Rev. Ad Acc. Circ:** 1,000.

US/0163-5603
CHICOREL INDEX TO POETRY IN ANTHOLOGIES AND COLLECTIONS IN PRINT. **VFOAT** Poetry in Print in Anthologies and Collections. 1st Ed. (1974)-. English. $125.00. American Library Publishing Corporation, PO Box 2014, Sedona AZ 86336. **Tel** (602)284-1162. **ED** Marietta S. Chicorel. **LC** PN1022; .C55. **DD** 808.81/001/6.
Desc: Lists poems in anthologies by author, title, translator, editor and anthologies with complete contents.

CC
CHING NIEN SHIH TAN. **VFOAT** Qingnianshitan. First published in 1983. Periodical. Chinese. bm. RMBY0.40. Kuang-Tung Sheng Hsin Hua Shu, Tien Kuang-chou Shih, People's Republic of China. **LC** PL2543; .C5348. **DD** 895.1/15.

US
CHOOMIA. V. 1-. Periodical. English. Three times a year. $3.00. Choomia, PO Box 107, Framingham MA 01701. **LC** PS615; .C53. **DD** 811/.5/08.

CH
CHUNG-HUA SHIH HSUEH. First published in April 1983. Periodical. Chinese. qt. $1.50. Chung-Hua Shih Hsueh Yueh, Kan She 22-3, 88 Lane Hsin Sheng N Road, Section 2, Taipei Shih Taiwan. **LC** PL2307; .C622. **DD** 895.1/1/009. ***Continues*** *Chung-Hua Shih Kan.*

US/0009-6849
CIMARRON REVIEW. [Cimarron rev.]. **Added/Corp** Oklahoma State University. No. 1- (Sept. 1967)-. Periodical. English. Four times a year (Jan., Apr., July, Oct.). $12.00 one year; $30.00 two year. Cimarron Review, 205 Morrill Hall, Oklahoma State University, Stillwater OK 74078-0135. **Tel** (405)744-9476, FAX (405)744-6326. **ED** Gordon Weaver. **LC** AS36; .O4414. cum. index. **Bk Rev**, (Qty: 8). **Circ:** 750. available on magnetic tape, an online database, and CD-ROM; available on microfilm and microfiche from University Microfilms International (UMI).
Desc: Publishes poetry, fiction, and essays of serious literary quality. Frequent international features.
Ind/Abst Am. Humanit. Index; Annu. Bibliogr. Engl. Lang. Lit.; Index Am. Period. Verse; MLA Int. Bibl. Books Artic. Mod. Lang. Lit.

US
CINCINNATI POETRY REVIEW. **VFOAT** CPR; C.P.R. (Spring 1975)-. Periodical. English. Twice a year. $9.00 (two year subscription). Cincinnati Poetry Review, Department of English 069, University of Cincinnati, Cincinnati OH 45221. **Tel** (513)475-4484. **ED** Dallas Wiebe. **Circ:** 1,100 (ctrl).
Desc: Original contemporary poetry.
Ind/Abst Am. Humanit. Index; Index Am. Period. Verse.

US
CIRCLE; A PERIODICAL OF REVERSIBLE POETRY. Vol. 1, No. 1 (Summer 1973)-. Periodical. English. ir. Circle Forum, PO Box 176, Portland OR 97207.

US
CIRCULO POETICO. **Added/Corp** Circulo de Cultura Panamericano. No. 1 (1971)-. Periodical. English (Spanish). an. $10.00. Circulo de Cultura Panamerican, 16 Malvern Place, Verona NJ 07044. **Tel** (201)239-3125. **ED** Ana H. Raggi. **LC** PQ7084; .C487. **Circ:** 800.

UK
CIVIL SERVICE POETRY. English. an. EMMA, Arden House, Sunny Point, Walton-on-Naze Essex CP14 8LD England.

SP
CLARIN : REVISTA DE CULTURA. Spanish (Italian, Arabic, English and French). mo. 6000ptas Spain; 1200ptas North America; 1100ptas other. Editorial El Paisaje, Entre los Rios 10, 24760 Castrocalbon Leon Spain. **(Subscription address:** Ofinina Central: Editorial"El Paisaje", c/o Arangoiti, 8-2o Izqda., 48850-ARANGUREN (Vizcaya) Spain**) ED** Agustin Garcia Alonso. **Bk Rev. Ad Acc. Circ:** 5,000 (ctrl).
Ind/Abst PROMT.

IT
CLASSICO GIALLO. (19??)-. Italian. L135200 Italy; L166400 others. Arnoldo Mondadori Editore, UFF Cont Abbonamenti, 20090 Segrate MI Italy. **Tel** 011 39 2 75422015, telex 320457 MONDMI I.

US/1061-737X
CLUTCH (FRANKFORT, KY.). **See** Literary and Political Reviews.

US/0161-486X
COLUMBIA, A MAGAZINE OF POETRY AND PROSE. **See** Literature.

US/0277-7770
CONNECTICUT POETRY REVIEW, THE. Vol. 1, No. 1 (Fall/Winter 1981/82)-. Periodical. English. an. $2.00. PO Box 3783, Amity Station, New Haven CT 06525-0783.
Ind/Abst Am. Humanit. Index; Index Am. Period. Verse.

US/0197-6796
CONTACT II. [Contact II]. **VFOAT** Contact/II; Contact 2; Contact Two. Vol. 1, No. 1 (Nov./Dec. 1976)-. Periodical. English. Twice a year. Contact II, PO Box 451 Bowling Green Station, New York NY 10004. **Tel** (212)674-0911. **ED** Maurice Kenney and J.G. Gosciak. **LC** PS615; .C64. **DD** 811/.54/08. **Bk Rev. Ad Acc. Circ:** 2,500 (ctrl).
Desc: Reviews of poetry, notes on poets, literary events and regional literary centers and includes anthologies of poets from different parts of America.
Ind/Abst Am. Humanit. Index; Index Am. Period. Verse.

UK
CONTEMPORARY POETS. (1969)-. English. ir. $135.00. Gale Research Inc., 835 Penobscot Building, Detroit MI 48226. **Tel** (800)877-GALE, (313)961-2242, FAX (313)961-6083, telex TWX 810-221-7086.
Desc: Represents the most famous works of living English and American poets. Includes bibliographical, biographical, and critical information .

US/0734-4260
CONTEMPORARY POETS OF AMERICA. [Contemp. poets Am.]. 1979-. English. an. $7.50. Dorrance & Company, Inc., Cricket Terrace Center, Ardmore PA 19003. **LC** PS615; .C67. **DD** 811/.008.

CN/0831-9502
CONTEMPORARY VERSE TWO. [Contemp. verse 2]. **VFOAT** CV 2; Contemporary Verse Two. **VAT** Contemporary Verse Two (1985). Vol. 9, No. 1 (Summer 1985)-. Periodical. English (French). Four times a year (Vol. changes in the summer). 20.00Can$ (individuals), 36.00Can$ (institutions) Canada; 24.00Can$ (individuals), 40.00Can$ (institutions) others. Contemporary Verse Two, PO Box 3062, Winnipeg Manitoba R3C 4E5 Canada. **Tel** (204)949-1365. **ED** Jane Casey, Keith L. Fulton, Naomi Guilbert, Laurelle Harris, Diane McGifford, Uma Parameswaran, and Patricia Rawson. **DD** C811/.54/09. **Bk Rev. Circ:** 600. ***Continues*** *CV II, Contemporary Verse/Two, 0319-6879.*
Desc: A feminist poetry journal that strives to promote strengthen and unify women. This work is by both women and men, a forum for social action and change.
Ind/Abst Can. Period. Index (19??-19??).

BE/0577-1757
COURRIER DU CENTRE INTERNATIONAL D'ETUDES POETIQUES. **Main/Corp** Centre International d'Etudes Poetiques. **Added/Corp** Maison International de la Poesie, Brussels. Biennales Internationales de Poesie. (1955)-. Monographic series. French. Four times a year (Mar., June, Sept., Dec.). 1200F. Centre International d'Etudes Poetiques, 4 Boulevard de l'Empereur, 1000 Brussels Belgium. **Tel** 011 32 2 519-5580. **ED**

Pierre-Yves Soucy. Index available. cum. index. **Pr Rev. Circ:** 1,000 (ctrl).
Ind/Abst MLA Int. Bibl. Books Artic. Mod. Lang. Lit.

US/0162-7201
CQ, CONTEMPORARY QUARTERLY. ***Suspended.*** **VFOAT** Contemporary Quarterly. Vol. 1, No. 4 (Autumn/Winter 1976/77)-?. Periodical. English. qt. $8.00. CQ Contemporary Quarterly, PO Box 41110, Los Angeles CA 90041. **LC** PS501; .C18. **DD** 811/.008. ***Continues*** *CQ.*

US/0011-0841
CRAZYHORSE (LITTLE ROCK, ARK.). (CRAZY HORSE.). [Crazyhorse]. **Added/Corp** Southwest Minnesota State College. American Language Skills Program. Crazyhorse Association. **VFOAT** Crazyhorse. (1969)-. Periodical. English. Twice a year. $10.00 (one year), $18.00 (two years), $27.00 (three years). Crazyhorse Association, University of Arkansas at Little Rock, English Department, 2801 S University, Little Rock AR 72204. **Tel** (501)569-3160. **ED** Zabelle Stodola. **LC** PS580; .C73. **DD** 811./5/408. **Bk Rev**, (Qty: 2/yr). **Ad Acc. Pr Rev. Circ:** 1,000 (ctrl).
Desc: Publishes poetry, fiction, and criticism. Past contributors include Frederick Busch, Raymond Carver, Michael Cimino, Andre Dubus, Richard Hugo, Galway Kinnel, Denise Levertov, and Bobbie Ann Mason.
Ind/Abst Am. Humanit. Index; Index Am. Period. Verse.

US/8756-0291
CREEPING BENT. No. 1 (Fall 1984)-. Periodical. English. sa (2 issues). $7.00. Creeping Bent, 433 West Market Street, Bethlehem PA 18018. **Tel** (215)691-3548, (215)758-4998. **ED** Jospeh P. Lucia. **DD** 811. **Bk Rev. Circ:** 250.

CN/1180-193X
CRITICAL MASS (HALIFAX). (CRITICAL MASS.). [Crit. mass]. Vol. 1, No. 1 (Spring 1990)-. Periodical. English. sa (Feb., Aug.). 10.00Can$ individuals, 15.00Can$ institutions. Critical Mass, c/o Department of English, Dalhousie University, Halifax, Nova Scotia B3H 3J5 Canada. **Tel** (902)424-3384. **ED** Brent Raycroft. **DD** 809/.005. **Bk Rev**, (Qty: 3-6). **Circ:** 50.
Desc: This publication is a journal of literary studies which includes essays, reviews, and poetry by graduate students of Canadian universities.

CN/0318-6075
CROSS COUNTRY. VAT Crosscountry. No. 1- Winter 1975-. Periodical. English. Three times a year. $8.00 two years. Cross Country Press, 2365 Hampton Avenue No 7, Montreal Quebec H4A 2K5 Canada. **DD** C811'.5'408.

US
CROSSCURRENTS. Added/Corp University of Puget Sound. Associated Student Body. **VFOAT** Cross Currents. (19??)-. English. an.
Ind/Abst Am. Hist. Life (1984-).

US/0731-7980
CUMBERLAND POETRY REVIEW. Vol. 1, No. 1 (Winter 1981)-. Periodical. English. sa (May & Oct.). $17.00 (institutions), $14.00 (individuals) US; $23.00 other. Cumberland Poetry Review, PO Box 120128, Acklen Station, Nashville TN 37212. **Tel** (615)371-9078. **ED** Ingram Bloch, C.B. Darrell, S.B. Darrell, Malcolm Glass, Jeanne Gore, Thomas Heine, Laurence Lerner, Anthonly Lombardy, Alison Touster-Reed, and Eva Touster. **LC** PS580; .C85. **DD** 811/.008. **Circ:** 500.
Desc: Devoted to fine poetry and criticism, presents poets of diverse origins to a widespread audience. No restrictions are placed on form, subject or style. Aims to support the poet's effort to keep up the language.
Ind/Abst Am. Humanit. Index (-199?); Index Am. Period. Verse.

CN/1188-1631
CUMULUS (WOOD MOUNTAIN). (CUMULUS.). [Cumulus]. Vol. 1, No. 1 (Fall 1991)-. Periodical. English. sa. $8.00 per year. Windspeak Press, Box 99, Wood Mountain Saskatchewan S0H 4L0 Canada. **DD** C810.8/005.

CN/0315-9914
DA VINCI. VFOAT Davinci. No. 1- Winter 1973-. Periodical. English. Three times a year. Vechicule Press, POB 125 Station La Cite, Montreal Quebec H2X 2M0 Canada. **DD** C811/.5/405.

US/0084-9529
DACOTAH TERRITORY. V. 1- Jan. 1971-. Periodical. English. **DD** 811/5/408.
Ind/Abst Index Am. Period. Verse (-1980).

US/0191-7722
DALMO'MA. Vol. 1 (July 1976)-. Periodical. English (Chinese and Aztec). ir. Dalmo'ma, PO Box 646, Port Townsend WA 98368. **Tel** (206)386-4943. **ED** Michael Daley, Finn Wilcox and Jeremiah Gorgline. **LC** PS591.I55; D34. **DD** 811/.5/408. **Pr Rev. Circ:** 1,000.
Desc: Periodical of "literature and responsibility" of Northwest writing.

US
DAVIS' ANTHOLOGY OF NEWSPAPER VERSE. VFOAT Newspaper Verse; Yearbook of Newspaper Poetry. (1919)-. Periodical. English. an. **ED** A.S. Davis. **LC** PS593.F7; D3. **DD** 811.50822.

US/1049-0892
DEAD OF NIGHT. See Romance and Adventure.

PL
DEBIUTY POETYCKIE ... ANTOLOGIA. VFOAT Debiuty Poetyckie. (1973)-. Polish. an. **LC** PG7137; .D43.

●US/1066-2197
DEFINED PROVIDENCE. [Defin. provid.]. **VFOAT** Providence Defined. Vol. 1, No. 1 (Fall/Winter 1992)-. Periodical. English. sa. $10.00 (institutions), $8.00 (individuals), $4.50 (sample issue). Defined Providence, PO Box 16143, Rumford RI 02916. **ED** Gary J. Whitehead. **DD** 811. **Bk Rev. Circ:** 500.
Desc: A poetry magazine devoted to publishing well crafted poetry by new and established writers, reviews of new poetry books, essays on poetry, and interviews with poets.

US/0011-7951
DELOS. [Delos]. (1988)-. Periodical. English. sa. $15.00 (one year), $25.00 (two year) individual; $20.00 (one year), $35.00 (two year) institution. Center for World Literature Inc, Box 2880, College Park MD 20740. **Tel** (301)779-0194. **ED** Harold Hanson. **LC** PN241.A1; D4. **DD** 428/.02. **Pr Rev. Circ:** 400. available on microfilm from University Microfilms International (UMI).

RU/0418-6176
DEN POEZII (LENINGRAD). (DEN POEZII.). (1966)-. Russian. an. Izdatelstvo Sovetskii Pisatel, Ulitsa Vorovskogo 11, 121069 Moscow Russia. **LC** PG3505.L5; D4. ***Continues in part*** *Den Poezii.*

●US/1061-6039
DEVELOPING YOUR CREATIVE WRITING STYLE AND LEARNING THE CRAFT OF WRITING. See Literature.

US/0733-9615
DEVIL'S MILLHOPPER, THE. (May 1978)-. English. Twice a year. $5.00 (1 year), $9.00 (2 year) US; $6.00 (1 year), $11.00 (2 year) other. University of South Carolina at Aiken / College of Humanities, 171 University Parkway, Aiken SC 29801. **Tel** (803)641-3239. **ED** Stephen Gardner. **Circ:** 600. ***Continues*** *Local Muse, 0733-9682.*

GW
DICHTER UBER IHRE DICHTUNGEN. ***Ceased.*** (1???)-Series complete. Monographic series. German. Heimeran Verlag, Postfach 400824, 8000 Munich Germany. **DD** 800.

US/0164-1492
DICKINSON STUDIES. ***Ceased.*** [Dickinson stud.]. No. 34 (Dec. 1978)-No. 86 (1993). Periodical. English. sa. Frederick L Morey, 1330 Mass Avenue Northwest, Apartment 503, Washington DC 20005. **Tel** (202)638-1671. **ED** F Morey. **LC** Z8230.5; .E44. **DD** 016.811/4. cum. index. **Bk Rev**, (Qty: 6). **Ad Acc. Pr Rev. Circ:** 250 (ctrl). Documents available from The Genuine Article. ***Continues*** *Emily Dickinson Bulletin, 0046-1881.*
Desc: Emily Dickinson criticism.
Ind/Abst Annu. Bibliogr. Engl. Lang. Lit.; Arts Humanit. Citation Index [Full Cov.]; Curr. Contents Arts Humanit.; MLA Int. Bibl. Books Artic. Mod. Lang. Lit. (1986-); Res. Alert [Full Cov.].

NE/0921-6111
DIEPZEE. (1983)-. Periodical. Dutch. bm. Fl31.00. Wolters Noordhoff BV, Postbus 567, 9700 AN Groningen Netherlands. **Tel** 011 31 50 226886, FAX 011 31 50 264866. **UDC** 839.31.

US
DIRECTORY OF POETRY PUBLISHERS. 1st. Ed. (1985/1986)-. Directory. English. an (July). $18.95. Dustbooks, PO Box 100, Paradise CA 95969. **Tel** (916)877-6110. **ED** Len Fulton and Ellen Ferber. **LC** Z286.P63; D57. **DD** 070.5/025. **Ad Acc. Circ:** 2,000.
Desc: Alphabetical listing of 2100 presses and magazines that publish poetry. With subject and regional indexing.

US/0364-359X
DRAGONFLY (PORTLAND). See Literature.

US/1062-3612
DRY CRIK REVIEW. [Dry crik rev.]. **Added/Corp** Dry Crik Press. **VFOAT** Dry Crik Review of Contemporary Cowboy Poetry. (Winter 1991)-. Periodical. English. qt. $20.00. Dry Crik Press, PO Box 51, Lemon Cove CA 93244. **DD** 810.

US/1052-4789
DUSTY DOG CHAPBOOK SERIES. [Dusty dog chapb. ser.]. No. 1 (1991)-. Periodical. English. Three times a year. $8.00. John Pierce, PO Box 1103, Zuni NM 87327. **DD** 811.

●GW/0944-5277
E.T.A. HOFFMANN-JAHRBUCH : MITTEILUNGEN DER E.T.A. HOFFMANN-GESELLSCHAFT. Added/Corp E.T.A. Hoffmann-Gesellschaft. **VFOAT** ETA Hoffmann Jahrbuch. (1993)-. Periodical. German. an. DM84.00. ETA Hoffmann-Gesellschaft, Nonnenbruecke 1, D 96047 Bamberg Germany. **LC** PT2361.Z49; E15. ***Continues*** *E.T.A. Hoffmann-Gesellschaft. Mitteilungen der E.T A. Hoffmann-Gesellschaft e.V., 0073-2885.*
Ind/Abst BHA : Biblio. Hist. Art; MLA Int. Bibl. Books Artic. Mod. Lang. Lit.

●US/1064-4970
EARTH BOUND. [Earth bound]. **VFOAT** Earthbound. Vol. 1, Issue 1 (Apr. 1992)-. Periodical. English. qt. $20.00. S. D. Dibble, 1455 Valence Drive, Glendale CA 91208. **DD** 811.

CN/0226-6253
ECRITIQUE. [Ecritique]. V. 1- Oct. 1978!-. Periodical. French. Three times a year. 0.75Can$ per no. CEGEP, De St-Jerome 455 rue Fournier, St Jerome Quebec J7Z 4V2 Canada. **DD** C840/.8/092375.

UK
EDITOR'S CHOICE. English. Regency Press, 43 New Oxford Street, London WCIA 1BH England. **LC** PR1227; .E34. **DD** 821/.9/108.

US/0731-0382
EMBERS (GUILFORD, CONN.). (EMBERS.). [Embers]. (1979)-. Periodical. English. sa. $11.00. Embers, PO Box 404, Guilford CT 06437. **Tel** (203)453-2328. **ED** Katrina Van Tassel, Charlotte Garrett Currier and Mark Johnston. **DD** 811. **Circ:** 500.
Desc: Contains previously unpublished poetry with emotional intensity, a rhythmic quality, and originality of expression.
Ind/Abst Am. Humanit. Index.

US/0271-5023
EN PASSANT, POETRY. [En passant poetry]. Periodical. English. sa. $3.50. 4612 Sylvanus Drive, Wilmington DE 19803. **LC** PS580; .E5. **DD** 811/.54/08. ***Continues*** *En Passant Poetry Quarterly, 0363-3780.*
Ind/Abst Index Am. Period. Verse.

UK/0013-9394
ENVOI. No. 1-. Periodical. English. Three times a year. £6.00 UK; $11.50 (surface mail), $14.00 (airmail) US; £6.75 (surface mail), £8.25 (airmail) other. Envoi Publications, Pen Ffordd, Newport, Fishguard, Dyfed SA42 0QT United Kingdom. **Tel** (0239)820285. **ED** Anne Lewis-Smith. **LC** PR1225; .E65. **DD** 821/.008. **Bk Rev. Ad Acc. Circ:** 700 (ctrl).
Desc: Publishes new poetry and reviews. All poems submitted with SAE receive a free criticism from the editorial panel of thirty poets.

SP
EQUIVALENCIAS. Added/Corp Fundacion Fernando Rielo. **VFOAT** Equivalences. (Winter 1982)-. Periodical. English (Spanish). an. $13.00. Fernando Rielo Foundation, 143-48 84th Drive, Briarwood NY 11435. **Tel** (718)526-3694, FAX (718)526-3694, . **ED** Justo Jorge Padron (editor's address: 102, 2B, 28009 Madrid Spain; editor's phone: 34 1 575-4091). **LC** PN1010; .E69. **DD** 808.81/005. **Bk Rev. Circ:** 1,000.
Desc: International multilingual poetry journal, published in Spanish and English. Publishes only previously unpublished poems from poets around the world.
Ind/Abst MLA Int. Bibl. Books Artic. Mod. Lang. Lit.

CN/0706-0556
ESPLUMOIR, L'. V. 1- Feb. 1979-. Periodical. French. mo. $10.00. Cercle Litteraire Esoterique, Bureau 208, 9408 Rue Viau, Montreal Quebec H1R 3B5 Canada. **DD** C841/.5/408. ***Supersedes*** *Solitude-Inflexion; Soliture-Inflexion.*

CN/0700-365X
ESTUAIRE. No. 1 (May 1976)-. Periodical. French. Four times a year. 32.00Can$ instutions Canada; 24.00Can$ (one year), 36.00Can$ (two year), 50.00Can$ (three year) individuals Canada; 35.00Can$ all others. Estuaire, Box 337 Succursale Outremont, Montreal Quebec H2V 4N1 Canada. **Tel** (819)379-9813. **ED** Gerald Gaudet and Gaston Bellemare. **DD** C841/.5/4005. **Bk Rev**, (Qty: 50-75/yr). **Ad Acc. Circ:** 700.
Desc: Publication of poetry, interviews, poems, and chronicles

SZ
ETUDES BAUDELAIREINNES. BIBLIOGRAPHIE. 1973-. French (English). ir. varies. Editions de la Baconniere SA, 19 Avenue du College, Case Postale 185, CH-2017 Boudry Switzerland. **Tel** (038)42 10 04. **ED** Marc Eifeldinger, Claude Pichois. **Circ:** 1,000. ***Separated from*** *Bulletin Baudelairien, 0007-4128.*

Literature —Poetry

Desc: Intended as a meeting point for critics. Publishes studies, comments and documents that contribute to deepen our knowledge of Baudelaire.

US/0014-4770
EXPERIMENT. V. 1- Apr. 1944-. Periodical. English. ir. $13.00. Experiment, 6565 Windmere Road, Seattle WA 98105. **Tel** (202)527-4172. **ED** Carol Ely Harper. **LC** PS301. **DD** 811.505. **Bk Rev. Ad Acc.**
Desc: Original and intellectual, in content and form.

US/0740-7823
EXQUISITE CORPSE. Added/Corp Culture Shock Foundation. Vol. 1, No. 1 (Jan. 1983)-. Periodical. English. ir. $25.00. Publications Unit English Department, Fairchild 110, Illinois State University, Normal IL 61761-6901. **Tel** (309)438-3024. **ED** Andrei Codrescu (Editor's address: PO Box 25051, Baton Rouge, LA 70894, phone: (504)388-2823). **LC** PN771; .E97. **DD** 808.81/005. **Bk Rev,** (Qty: 12-16). **Circ:** 1,500.
Desc: Features poetry, criticisms, essays, reviews, translations, photographs, art, polemics, letters, and reports from many countries.

UK/0531-6243
EXTRA VERSE. Periodical. English. ir. Extra Verse, 18 Gt Percy St Islington, London WC 1 England.

SP
FARO DEL POETA : REVISTA TRIMESTRAL DE POESIA. Spanish. 4000ptas Spain; 6000ptas Europe; 5000ptas other. Editorial el Paisaje / Aranguren, La Penorra 8-2, 48850 Aranguren Spain. **Tel** (94) 639 07 74. **ED** Agustin Garcia Alonso. **Bk Rev. Ad Acc.** ctrl circ.

US/1041-4886
FEDERAL POET, THE. [Fed. poet]. (19??)-. Periodical. English. qt. $10.00. The Federal Poet, PO Box 65400, Washington Sq Sta, Washington DC 20035. **Tel** (301)589-0810. **ED** Miles David Moore. **DD** 811. **Circ:** 150.
Desc: Contains original poems written by members of The Federal Poet.

US
FIELD CONTEMPORATY POETRY AND POETICS. English. ir. $12.00 (US); $13.00 (Canada & Pan American Nations); $14.00 (other). Oberlin College, Press C, Rice Hall, Oberlin OH 44074. **Tel** (216)775-8408, FAX (216) 775-8124.

US/0015-0657
FIELD (OBERLIN, OHIO). (FIELD.). [Field]. **Added/Corp** Oberlin College. No. 1 (Fall 1969)-. Periodical. English. sa (May, Nov.). $12.00 (one year), $20.00 (two year) US; $13.50 (one year), $23.00 (two year) other. Oberlin College, Press C, Rice Hall, Oberlin OH 44074. **Tel** (216)775-8408, FAX (216) 775-8124. **ED** Friebert and Young. **LC** PN6099.6; .F5. **DD** 808.81/04. Index available. cum. index. **Bk Rev. Ad Acc. Circ:** 2,200 (ctrl).
Desc: Contemporary poetry and poetics; also symposia and translations.
Ind/Abst Am. Bibliogr. Slavic East Europ. Stud.; Index Am. Period. Verse; MLA Int. Bibl. Books Artic. Mod. Lang. Lit.

US/0147-1686
FLOATING ISLAND. [Float. isl.]. 1 (Spring 1976)-. English. ir (issued every three to five years). $15.00. Floating Island Publications, PO Box 516, Point Reyes Station CA 94956. **Tel** (415)663-1181. **ED** Michael Sykes. **LC** PS580; .F56. **DD** 811/.5/408. Index available. cum. index. **Circ:** 2,000.
Desc: An occasional anthology of poetry, fiction, photography and graphic arts, large format, with photographs in folio format on coated stock.

US/0742-2466
FLORIDA REVIEW (ORLANDO, FLA.), THE. (THE FLORIDA REVIEW.). **Added/Corp** University of Central Florida. Florida Technological University. Vol. 1, (1972)-. Periodical. English. ir (Varies). $9.00 one year; $13.00 two years. Florida Review, University of Central Florida, Department of English, Orlando FL 32816. **Tel** (407)923-2038. **ED** Russell Kesler (phone: (407)823-2212). **Bk Rev,** (Qty: 6 - 10). **Pr Rev. Circ:** 650.
Desc: Comtemporary fiction, poetry, and critical reviews of the american poetry.
Ind/Abst Am. Humanit. Index; Index Am. Period. Verse.

CN/0714-9093
FOUR BY FOUR (MONTREAL, QUEBEC). (FOUR BY FOUR.). No. 1 (Sept. 1982)-. Periodical. English. $5.00. Villeneuve Publications, 4647 Hutchinson Street, Montreal Quebec H2V 4N4 Canada. **DD** C811/.5408.

US/1041-0945
FREE LUNCH. [Free lunch]. (1989)-. Periodical. English. Three times a year. $10.00 US; $13.00 other. Free Lunch Arts Alliance, 27301 Ventossa, Mission Viejo CA 92691. **Tel** (714)661-7073. **ED** Ron Offen. **DD** 811. **Ad Acc. Circ:** 600.
Desc: Poetry journal of literary quality poetry.

JA
FUKUSHIMA-KEN TANKA SENSHU. Added/Corp Fukushima-ken Kajinkai. (19??)-. Japanese. an. Fukushima-Ken Kajinkai, c/o Shiraki Aza Miyaminami, 108 Osamachi Tadano, Koriyama-shi Japan. **LC** PL758.A1; F84.

SP
GACETA POETICA : REVISTA TRIMESTRAL DE POESIA. Spanish. 3.000ptas Spain; 6.000ptas Europe; 4.500ptas other. Editorial el Paisaje / Aranguren, La Penorra 8-2, 48850 Aranguren Spain. **Tel** (94) 639 07 74. **ED** Agustin Garcia Alonso. **Bk Rev. Ad Acc. Circ:** 2,000 (ctrl).

US/0730-5206
GALLERY WORKS. (19??)-. English. sa (Feb. & Sept.). $8.00 (one year), $13.00 (two years), $20.00 (three years). La Salle University, 1900 West Olney Avenue, Philadelphia PA 19141. **Tel** (215)951-1145, 951-1600, FAX (215)951-1488. **LC** Discard; PS325; .G355.
Ind/Abst Am. Humanit. Index (-199?).

IT
GALLO SILVESTRE, IL. Italian. sa. L40000.00. Protagon Editori Toscani, Via Di Ficareto 29, 53100 Siena Italy. **Tel** 011 39 577 55359.

BL
GANDAIA. Periodical. Portuguese. Rua Dr Noguchi, 271 Casa 6 Ramos, Rio de Janeiro Brazil. **LC** PQ9658; .G35. **DD** 869/.1.

AU
GANGAN BUCH. VFOAT Ganganbuch; Gangan Jahrbuch. (198?)-. German. an. Stadt Graz, Stadtarchiv, Hans-Sachs-Gasse 1, A-8010 Graz, Austria. **LC** PT1175; .G36. **DD** 831/.91408/005. **Continues** Gangan Jahrbuch.

US/1058-532X
GAS (SAN CARLOS, CALIF.). Suspended. (GAS : HIGH OCTANE POETRY.). [Gas]. (Winter 1990)- Suspended (199?). Periodical. English. qt. $40.00 (institutions), $30.00 (individuals). Gas, 1369 Woodland, San Carlos CA 94070. **Tel** (415)508-9234. **LC** IN PROCESS. **DD** 811.

US
GEGENSCHEIN. VFOAT Gegenschein Quarterly; GQ. No. 1 (1972)-. Periodical. English. qt. $5.00. 350 East 9th Street/5, New York NY 10003. **LC** PS580; .G43. **DD** 811/.5/405.

JA
GENDAI HAIKU NENKAN. Added/Corp Gendai Haiku Kyokai (Japan). (19??)-. Japanese. an. ¥6000. Gendai Haiku Kyokai, 6-10 Soto Kanda, 4 Chiyoda-ku, Tokyo-to Japan. **LC** PL759.A1; G436.

CN/0704-6286
GERMINATION. Vol. 1, (Spring 1976)-. Periodical. English. ir. $7.00. Owls Head Press, 428 Yale Avenue, Riverview NB E1B 2B5 Canada. **Tel** (506)386-1687. **ED** Allan Cooper and Leigh Faulkner. **DD** C811/.5/408. **Bk Rev. Ad Acc. Circ:** 500.
Desc: Publishes new, innovative Canadian poets, and work by established world-renowned writers such as Eugenio Montale and Robert Bly. Each issue contains two popular prose departments: "Letters to Young Poets," where established poets give advice and encouragement to beginning writers; and "Ways In: Articles on Contemporary Poetry and Poetics".
Ind/Abst Index Am. Period. Verse.

IT
GIALLO MONDADORI. (19??)-. Italian. L208000 Italy; L244400 others. Arnoldo Mondadori Editore, UFF Cont Abbonamenti, 20090 Segrate MI Italy. **Tel** 011 39 2 75422015, telex 320457 MONDMI I.

AT/0817-4148
GIPPSLAND WRITER. [Gippsl. writ.]. (1986)-. Periodical. English. qt. J R P Publishers, 14 Stirling Avenue, Traralgon 3844 Australia. **DD** 820.8003.

US/0145-6792
GLASSWORKS. V. 1- Fall 1975-. Periodical. English. Three times a year. $6.00. Glassworks, 74 Claradon Lane, Staten Island NY 10305-2809. **LC** PS580; .G55. **DD** 811/.5/405.

UK
GLOBAL TAPESTRY. (1971)-. Periodical. English. ir. £7.50 UK; £9.00 US. Global Tapestry Journal, Spring Bank, Longsight Road, Colster Green, Blackburn, Lancs. BB1 9EU England. **Tel** Blackburn 249128. **ED** Dave Cunliffe. **Bk Rev. Ad Acc. Pr Rev. Circ:** 1,000 to 1,500 (variable). available on microfilm.
Desc: Innovative writing, short story and novel extracts. Exciting creativity. New and old wave poetry. Book, magazine, record, tape, video and poetry gig reviews.

US/0145-7780
GRAHAM HOUSE REVIEW. Vol. 1 (Summer 1976)-. Periodical. English. an. $7.50. Colgate University Press, PO Box 5000, Hamilton NY 13346. **LC** PS580; .G72. **DD** 811/.5/408.
Ind/Abst Am. Humanit. Index; Index Am. Period. Verse.

US
GRANGER'S INDEX TO POETRY. (1904)-. Periodical. English. ir. $199.00. Columbia University Press, 136 South Broadway, Irvington NY 10533. **Tel** (914)591-9111.

US
GREEN HORSE FOR POETRY, THE. V. 1- 1973-. Periodical. English. ir. Bowling Green State University / Creative Writing Program, Bowling Green OH 43403.

US
GRILLED FLOWERS. Vol. 1, No. 1 (Spring 1976)-. Periodical. English. ir. University of Arizona Poetry Center, c/o Logbridge-Rhodes, PO Box 3254, Durango CO 81301.

US/0743-7242
GROLIER POETRY PRIZE. Vol. 1 (1984)-. English. an. $5.00. Ellen la Forge Memorial Poetry Foundation Inc, 6 Plympton Street, Cambridge MA 02138. **Tel** (617)547-4908. **ED** Louisa Solano. **LC** PS615; .G76. **DD** 811/.008. **Pr Rev. Circ:** 400 (ctrl).
Desc: Open to all poets who have not published either a vanity, small press, trade, or chapbook of poetry.

US
GROVE: CONTEMPORARY POETRY AND TRANSLATION. Added/Corp Pitzer College. No. 1, (Summer 1975)-. Periodical. English. sa. Pitzer College, English Department, Claremont Colleges, Claremont CA 91711. **Tel** (909)626-8511.

PR/0017-498x
GUAJANA. Vol. 1 (1962)-. Periodical. Spanish. qt.

US/0190-2253
GUSTO (BRONX). (GUSTO.). (197?)-. Periodical. English. $5.00 (4 issues). M Karl Kulikowski, 2960 Philip Avenue, Bronx NY 10465.
Desc: Information on American poetry.

GW
HAIDE-ANZEIGER. SONDERAUSGABE, DER. VFOAT DHA-S. Vol. 1 June 1986-. Periodical. German.

US
HAIKU REVIEW. (1980)-. Periodical. English. be. $5.00 (two years) US & Canada; $8.00 (two years) other. High Coo Press, Route 1, Battle Ground IN 47920. **Tel** (317)567-2596.
Ind/Abst MLA Int. Bibl. Books Artic. Mod. Lang. Lit.

US/1074-0228
HALF TONES TO JUBILEE. Main/Corp Pensacola Junior College Department of English. (198?)-. English. an (Published in Sept./Oct.). $4.00 (one year), $7.00 (two year), $10.00 (three year). Pensacola Junior College, 1000 College Boulevard, Pensacola FL 32504. **Tel** (904)484-1418, (904)484-2550. **Circ:** 500.

US/0190-6135
HAMPDEN-SYDNEY POETRY REVIEW, THE. Periodical. English. sa. Tom O'Grady, PO Box 126, Hampden Sydney VA 23943. **Supersedes** Maryland Poetry Review.
Ind/Abst Index Am. Period. Verse.

US/0440-2316
HANGING LOOSE. [Hang. loose]. (Fall 1966)-. Periodical. English. tq (Jan., June, Oct.). $15.00. Hanging Loose, 231 Wyckoff Street, Brooklyn NY 11217. **Tel** (617)576-1292. **ED** Robert Hershon (phone: (212)206-8465) and Ron Schreiber (phone: (617)576-1292). **LC** PS580; .H36. **DD** 811/.008. Index available (Every 12 issues, at $5.00 per index). cum. index. **Circ:** 2,000. available on microfilm and microfiche from University Microfilms International (UMI). **Continues** Things (New York, N.Y.), 0563-4660.
Desc: Featuring new and veteran poets and fiction writers. Every issue contains original art or photography work and each issue features a section of high school age writers.
Ind/Abst Am. Humanit. Index; Index Am. Period. Verse.

US/0046-6832
HAPPINESS HOLDING TANK. No. 1- Oct. 1970-. Periodical. English. qt. $3.50. Happiness Holding Tank, 1790 Grand River, Okemos MI 48864. **LC** PS615; .H34. **DD** 811/.5/408.

PE/0440-2987
HARAUI. Yearly V. 1, No. 1 (September 1963)-. Periodical. Spanish. ir. Director Francisco Carrillo, Bolivia 174, Chosica Peru. **LC** PN6108; .H37. **DD** 861./008/0985.

US
HARPOON. V. 1- 1979-. Periodical. English. Three times a year. $7.00. Harpoon, PO Box 2581, Anchorage AK 99510. **Tel** (907)334-8324.

CN/0826-0133
HEJIRA (MONTREAL, QUEBEC). (HEJIRA.). [Hejira]. V. 1, No. 1 (Dec. 1983)-. Periodical. English. mo. $1.00 per no. M Berg Porter's Office, Arts Building, McGill University, Montreal Quebec Canada. **DD** C811/.54/092379.

Literature —Poetry

II
HELICON. Periodical. English. Rs10.00. 10/3C Nepal Bhattacharya Street, Calcutta 26 India. **LC** PN1010; .H45. **DD** 808.81.

US/0164-145X
HIGGINSON JOURNAL. Ceased. (1978)-(1993). Periodical. English. sa. Dr Frederick L Morey, 4508 38th Street, Brentwood MD 20722. **LC** PS580; .H54. cum. index. **Continues** Higginson Journal of Poetry, 0147-040X.
 Ind/Abst Annu. Bibliogr. Engl. Lang. Lit.

US/0018-2036
HIRAM POETRY REVIEW, THE. [Hiram poet. rev.]. **Added/Corp** Hiram College. English Dept. No. 1 (Fall/Winter 1966)-. Periodical. English. Twice a year (Jan., and June). $8.00 US; $10.00 Canada & Mexico; $12.00 other. Hiram Poetry Review, PO Box 162, Hiram OH 44234. **Tel** (216)569-5330, FAX (216)569-5831. **ED** Hale Chatfield and Carol Donley, (phone: (216)569-5331). **LC** PS580; .H56. **DD** 811/.5/05. **Bk Rev. Pr Rev. Circ:** 350. available on microfilm and microfiche from University Microfilms International (UMI).
 Desc: This seeks to discover America's Poets.
 Ind/Abst Am. Humanit. Index; Index Am. Period. Verse.

US
HOO-DOO. (1972)-. English. ir. Energy Earth Communications, PO Box 1141, Galveston TX 77553. **Tel** (409)762-8018.

SP/0212-9442
HORA DE POESIA. (1978)-. Periodical. Spanish (English, French, German, Catalan, Portuguese and Italian). sa (June, Dec.). $49.00. Hora de Poesia, Hipolito Lazaro 19-23 Esc A, 08025 Barcelona Spain. **Tel** 011 34 3 213-3040. **ED** Rosa Lentini Chao. **LC** PQ6075; .H67. Index available (Published separately - free with subscription). cum. index. **Bk Rev. Ad Acc. Circ:** 2,000 (ctrl).
 Desc: General poetry of Spain and different nationalities: England, France, Italy and Germany. Criticisms, essays, and edits from well known authors.

US/0888-3521
HOWLING DOG. See Literature.

CH
HSU SHIH SHIH TSUNG KAN. VFOAT Hsu Shih Shih; Xushishicongkan. V. 1, (June 1980)-. Periodical. Chinese. NT$0.51. Hsing Hua Shu Tien, Cheng-Chou Shih, People's Republic of China. **LC** PL2519.N47; H78. **DD** 895.1/15/08.

PE
HUESO HUMERO. See The Arts.

●US/1065-6421
HUNGRY POET, THE. (1992)-. Periodical. English. qt. $10.00. The Hungry Poet, 2601 McBride Lane, Suite 94, Santa Rosa CA 95403.

DK/0018-8093
HVEDEKORN. (HVEDEKORN; TIDSSKRIFT FOR LITTERATUR OG GRAFIK.). (1927)-. Periodical. English. qt. kr225.00 Denmark. Borgens Forlag A/S, Valbygardsvej 33, DK2500 Valby Denmark. **Tel** 31-462100, FAX 36-441488. **ED** Poul Borum and Line Storm. cum. index. **Continues** Klinte.
 Desc: Covers Danish art and literature.

KO
HWANGTO / HWANGTO SI TONGIN. Periodical. Korean. W500. Paeyongsa, 1-48 Sinmunno Chongno-ku, Seoul 110 Korea. **LC** PL974.A1; H92.

IT
I POVERI, STRENNA POETICA VERONESE. VFOAT I Poveri; Strenna Poetica Veronese. Italian. an.

US/0163-0954
ICARUS. Suspended. Vol. 1 (Summer 1973)-Suspended with Fall 1977 issue. Periodical. English. qt. $30.55. Icarus Press, PO Box 8, Riderwood MD 21139. **ED** M Diorio. **LC** PS580; .I26. **DD** 811/.5/408.

AT/1032-1640
IDIOM 23. See Literature.

US/1058-6962
ILR JOURNAL, THE. [ILR j.]. **Added/Corp** Northwestern University (Evanston, Ill.). Institute for Learning in Retirement. **VAT** Institute for Learning in Retirement Journal. Vol. 1 (1991)-. Periodical. English. $10.00. Northwestern University / ILR, Institute for Learning in Retirement, Andersen Hall, Room 1-117, 2003 Sheridan Road, Evanston IL 60208-2650. **DD** 811.

US/0884-819X
IMAGES (DAYTON, OHIO). Ceased. (IMAGES.). [Images]. Vol. 1 (1974)-Vol. 14, No 3 (19??). Periodical. English. Three times a year. Wright State University English Department, Dayton OH 45431. **Tel** (513)873-2443. **ED** Gary Pacernick. **DD** 811. **Circ:** 2,000.
 Desc: An inexpensive tabloid that publishes the best of contemporary poetry and graphics.
 Ind/Abst Am. Humanit. Index; Can. Index (?-?); Index Am. Period. Verse.

US/0747-489X
IMAGINE (BOSTON, MASS.). (IMAGINE.). [Imagine]. Vol. 1, No. 1 (Summer 1984)-. Periodical. English (Multiple languages; translations available in Spanish). sa. $12.00 (one year), $18.00 (two year) institutions, $8.00 (one year), $14.00 (two year) individuals. Imagine Publishers Inc, 89 Mass Ave., Suite 270, Boston MA 02215. **Tel** (617)267-2592. **ED** Tino Villanueva and Luis Alberto Urrea. **LC** PS591.M49; I48. **DD** 861. **Bk Rev. Circ:** 1,500 (ctrl).
 Desc: Accepts texts in any language provided same are accompanied by the corresponding translations into either English or Spanish.
 Ind/Abst Index Am. Period. Verse; MLA Int. Bibl. Books Artic. Mod. Lang. Lit.

US/1055-0038
IN THE COMPANY OF POETS. [In co. poets]. Vol. 1, No. 1 (Jan./Feb. 1991)-. English. bm. $16.00. In the Company of Poets, ITCOP, PO Box 10786, Oakland CA 94610. **DD** 811.

CN
INDEX TO CANADIAN POETRY IN ENGLISH. See Literature-Abstracting, Bibliographies and Statistics.

II
INDIAN VERSE. Vol. 1 (Winter 1973)-. Periodical. English. qt. $4.00. 9/3 Tamer Lane, Calcutta-9 India. **LC** PK2978.E5; I5. **DD** 821/.005.

CN/0712-6069
INFLUX (MONTREAL, QUEBEC). (INFLUX.). [Influx]. Mar. 1981-. French. an. $2.00 per volume. Influx, CP 595 Depot North, Montreal Quebec H2X 3M6. **DD** C841/.54/08092375.

UK/0951-0427
INKSHED. (1986)-. English. Inkshed, 387 Beverly Road, Hull HU5 1LS England. **ED** Lesli Markham and Anthony Smith.

CN/0714-2870
INKSTONE. [Inkstone]. **Added/Corp** Toronto Haiku Workshop. Vol. 1, No. 1 (Summer 1982)-. Periodical. English. Four times a year. Inkstone Press, PO Box 67 Station H, Toronto Ontario M4C 5H7 Canada. **Tel** (416)531-5688. **ED** Keith Southward, Marshall Hryciuk, and Louise Fletcher. **DD** C811/.0408. **Bk Rev. Circ:** 100 (ctrl).
 Desc: Reviews and articles on subjects related to Haiku.

US/1056-1420
INNER SOUND OF LIFE, THE. [Inner sound life]. Vol. 1, No. 1 (Mar. 1991)-. Periodical. English. mo. $60.00. Marquet-Dubois Enterprises, PO Box 88, Aurora CO 80040-0088. **DD** 811.

IT
INONIJA. Ceased. No. 1 (1987)-(1992). Periodical. Italian. sa.

CN/0711-4648
INSTANT (THEATRE DU GANOUE). (INSTANT : UNE PRODUCTION DU THEATRE DU GANOUE.). [Instant]. **VAT** Instant de Parole. Vol. 1; 1980-. French. an. $5.00 per volume. Instant, c/o Theatre du Ganoue, St-Prosper, Beauce-Sud Quebec Canada. **DD** C841/.5408.

US/0888-2452
INTERIM (LAS VEGAS, NEV.). (INTERIM.). [Interim]. Vol. 5, No. 1 (Spring 1985)-. Periodical. English. Twice a year (Apr., Nov.). $14.00. Interim NV, University of Nevada, Department of English, Las Vegas NV 89154. **Tel** (702)739-3172. **DD** 811. **Continues** Interim, 0020-5478.
 Ind/Abst Index Am. Period. Verse.

CN/0227-5414
INTERNATIONAL HOPKINS ASSOCIATION NEWSLETTER, THE. [Int. Hopkins Assoc. newsl.]. **VFOAT** IHA Newsletter. No. 1 (Summer 1979)-. Newsletter. English. an. Free to members. International Hopkins Association, 81 Mary Street, St. Michael College, Toronto Ontario M5S 1J4 Canada. **Tel** (416)926-1300. **ED** Richard F Giles. **DD** 821/.8. **Circ:** 175.
 Desc: Newsletter on books, videos, conferences, posters, activities, etc., by and about G M Hopkins and his circle.

US/0538-8228
INTERNATIONAL JOURNAL OF SLAVIC LINGUISTICS AND POETICS. See Linguistics.

US/0363-9128
INTERNATIONAL POETRY REVIEW (GREENSBORO, N.C.). (INTERNATIONAL POETRY REVIEW.). [Int. poet. rev.]. (1975)-. Periodical. English. Twice a year (Spring and Fall). $15.00 (institutions); $10.00 (individuals). Department of Romance Languages, University of North Carolina at Greensboro, Greensboro NC 27412-5001. **Tel** (910)334-5655. **ED** Mark Smith-Soto. **DD** 811. **Circ:** 250.
 Desc: Contemporary poetry intransaltion (with pricing original) and original languages poetry.

US/0748-9676
INTERNATIONAL UNIVERSITY POETRY QUARTERLY, THE. Added/Corp International University Press. Vol. 1, No. 1 (Winter 1974)-. Periodical. English. qt. $200.00. International Universities Press Inc., 59 Boston Post Road, PO Box 1524, Madison CT 06443-1524. **Tel** (203)245-4000, FAX (203)245-0775, telex 282986 IUP BK. **ED** John Wayne Johnston. ctrl circ.

●UK
INTERNATIONAL WHO'S WHO IN POETRY AND POETS' ENCYCLOPAEDIA. Added/Corp International Biographical Centre. **VFOAT** Poets' Encyclopaedia. 7th Ed. (1993/94)-. Monographic series. English. ir. Price varies per volume. International Biographical Center, 3 Regal Lane Soham, Ely Cambridge CB7 5BA England. **Tel** 011 44 71 353 721091, FAX 011 44 71 353 721839, telex 81584. **LC** PN452; .I56. **Separated from** International Authors' and Writers' Who's Who, 0143-8263.

CN/0704-7290
INTRINSIC. No. 1- Summer 1977-. Periodical. English. ir. $3.00. Intrinsic, Box 485 Station P, Toronto Ontario M5S 2T1 Canada. **DD** C811/.5/408.

US/0147-4936
INVISIBLE CITY. No. 1 (Feb. 1971)-. Periodical. English. ir. $5.00. Red Hill Press, PO Box 2853, San Francisco CA 94126. **LC** PN6099.6; .I58. **DD** 811/.5/408.

CN/0227-0773
ISLAND (LANTZVILLE). Suspended. (ISLAND.). [Island]. 1971-?. Periodical. English. Three times a year. 11.61Can$. Island / Canada, Box 256, Lantzville British Columbia, V0R 2H0 Canada. **Tel** (604)390-3508. **ED** John Marshall. **DD** C811/.5408. **Bk Rev. Circ:** 550.
 Desc: Canadian literary journal, poetry, prose, interviews, reviews.

US/0732-5886
ISLE SONANTE, L'. 1 (Winter 1982)-. Periodical. French (English). Three times a year. $24.00. l'Isle Sonante, 473 Manoagian Hall/Wayne State University, Detroit MI 48202. **LC** PQ1170.E6; I84. **DD** 841/.008.

US/0749-0291
JAMES DICKEY NEWSLETTER. [James Dickey newsl.]. **Added/Corp** DeKalb Community College. Vol. 1, No. 1 (Fall 1984)-. Newsletter. English. Twice a year (Apr., and Sept.). $5.00 (individuals); $10.00 (institutions). James Dickey Newsletter, 2101 Womack Road, DeKalb Community College, Dunwoody GA 30338. **Tel** (404)551-3162. **ED** J. M. Pair. **LC** PS3507.I267; Z73. **DD** 811/.54. Index available. cum. index. **Bk Rev. Ad Acc.** ctrl circ.
 Ind/Abst Am. Humanit. Index (199?-); MLA Int. Bibl. Books Artic. Mod. Lang. Lit.

US/0098-2199
JOHN BERRYMAN STUDIES. Vol. 1 (Jan. 1975)-. English. qt. $5.00. 805 West First Avenue, Derry PA 15627. **LC** PS3503.E744; Z6. **DD** 811/.5/4.

CN/0705-1328
JOURNAL OF CANADIAN POETRY. Vol. 1 (Winter 1978)-. Academic Scholarly Publication. English (French). an (June). 12.95Can$ (one year), 25.00Can$ (two years), 33.00Can$ (three years); 16.30Can$ (one year), 28.35Can$ (two years), 36.35Can$ (three years) US; 16.80Can$ (one year), 28.85Can$ (two years), 36.85Can$ (three years) other. Borealis Press, 9 Ashburn Drive, Ottawa Ontario K2E 6N4 Canada. **Tel** (613)224-6837, FAX (613)829-7783. **ED** David Staines. **LC** PR9190.25; .J68a. **DD** C811/.009. **Bk Rev. Ad Acc, Adv Mgr:** Glenn Clever, **Tel** (613)224-6837. **Pr Rev. Circ:** 1,000 (ctrl).
 Desc: Scholarly research and criticism of the poetry of Canada from its origins to the present, and review in each issue of previous year's significant books and Canadian poetry.
 Ind/Abst Can. Index (?-?); MLA Int. Bibl. Books Artic. Mod. Lang. Lit.

US/0363-4205
JOURNAL OF NEW JERSEY POETS. [J. N. J. poets]. **Added/Corp** County College of Morris. Fairleigh Dickinson University (Florham-Madison Campus). Dept. of English. Fairleigh Dickinson University (Florham-Madison Campus). Creative Writing Program. Vol. 1 (Spring 1976)-. Periodical. English. Twice a year (Fall and Summer). $7.00. County College of Morris, Route 10 Center Grove Road, Department English, Randolph NJ 07869. **Tel** (201)328-5471. **ED** Sander Zulauf, North Peterson, Sara Pfaffenroth, Peter Williams and Donna Burton. **LC** PS549.N5; J6. **DD** 811/.008. **[CCC]. Bk Rev,** (Qty: 2-4 per year). **Pr Rev. Circ:** 700 (ctrl).
 Desc: A periodical publishing new poetry by New Jersey poets (poets working, or living in, or from New Jersey--i.e., poets who've done time here).
 Ind/Abst Index Am. Period. Verse.

Literature — Poetry

US/0889-3675
JOURNAL OF POETRY THERAPY. See Psychology.

PK
JOURNAL OF THE ENGLISH LITERARY CLUB, THE. **Added/Corp** University of Peshawar. English Literary Club. University of Peshawar. Dept. of English. (1957)-. Periodical. English.
Ind/Abst Annu. Bibliogr. Engl. Lang. Lit.

JA
JUSHO KAJIN SHIRIZU. (19??)-. Periodical. Japanese. ¥1000. Tanka Koron Sha, 18-4 Yamatocho 2 Nakano-ku, Tokyo 165 Japan. **LC** PL758.A1; J87.

US/1052-3758
JUST BETWEEN US. [Just between us]. Vol. 1, No. 1 (April 1989)-. Periodical. English. qt. $36.00. Marqret-Dubois Enterprises, 2918 East Indian School Road, Phoenix AZ 85016-6320. **DD** 811.

II
KALO SURAJA. Periodical. Gujarati (Gujarati). ir. 1.00. **LC** PK1856; .K24.

US/0022-8990
KARAMU (CHARLESTON, ILL.). See Literature.

II
KAVI INDIA. (19??)-. Periodical. English. Four times a year. Rs10.00 India; Rs11.00 Europe; Rs12.00 others. Kavi, PO Box 694, Government Printing Office, Bombay India. **LC** PR9494.5.I5; K38. **DD** 821. **Continues** Kavi.

II
KAVILOKA. Periodical. Gujarati (Gujarati). 8.00. Bacubhai Ravata, Kumar Printery, 1454 Raipur, Amadavada India. **LC** PK1852; .K3.

NP
KAVITA (NEPALA RAJAKIYA PRAJNA-PRATISHTHANA : 1979). (KAVITA.). Punahpravesanka 1 (July, August, Pausha 2036 Oct., Nov., Dec. Periodical. Nepali (Nepali). ir. Rs12.00. Nepal Rajakiya, Prajna-Pratishthan Prajna Bhavan Kamaladi, Kathmandu Nepal. **LC** PK2598.A2; K36. **Continues** Kavita (Nepala Rajakiya Prajna-Pratishthana : 1964).

US/0022-9555
KAYAK (SANTA CRUZ). (KAYAK.). [Kayak]. (Autumn 1964)-. Periodical. English. qt. $3.00. **LC** PS580; .K39. **DD** 811/.5/408. available on microfilm and microfiche from University Microfilms International (UMI).
Ind/Abst Am. Humanit. Index (-199?); Index Am. Period. Verse.

JA
KIKAN HAIKU. **VFOAT** Haiku. No. 1 (Oct. 1973)-. Periodical. Japanese. ¥1000. Chuo Shoin, 8 Saneicho Shinjuku-ku, Tokyo Japan. **ED** Horii Shunichiro. **LC** PL759.A1; K53.

JA
KISEKI. **Added/Corp** Asaka Tankakai. (19??)-. Periodical. Japanese. Asaka Tankakai, c/o Koriyama Shiyakusho, 23-7 Asahi 1-chome, Koriyama Japan. **LC** PL887.K67; K57.

BA
KITABAT. See Literature.

US/0194-424X
KUDZU (CAYCE). (KUDZU.). No. 1- July 1977-. Periodical. English. qt. $4.00. Kudzu, Box 22502, Jackson MS 39205. **LC** PS580; .K82. **DD** 811/.008.

NR/0331-4545
KUKA. **Added/Corp** Ahmadu Bello University. Dept. of English. Vol. 1, No. 1 (1977)-. English. an. **LC** WMLC L 83/402. **Continues** Mirror (Zaria, Nigeria).
Ind/Abst MLA Int. Bibl. Books Artic. Mod. Lang. Lit.

US/0193-7820
LA-BAS. [La-bas]. Began in 1976. Periodical. English. bm. La-Bas, PO Box 431, College Park MD 20740. **Tel** (301)864-6921. **LC** PS580; .L3.

SZ
LADINIA. No. 1 (1977)-. Periodical. Raeto-Romance (German and Italian). an. L30000 Italy; L35000 other. Istituto Ladin Micura, 39030 San Martino, de Tor Italy. **Tel** 011 39 474 523320. **ED** Lois Craffomara.

US/1046-2724
LEDGE, THE. (THE LEDGE : POETRY & PROSE MAGAZINE.). [Ledge]. **VFOAT** Ledge Poetry and Prose Magazine. Ledge Magazine. Vol. 1, No. 1 (June 1988)-. Periodical. English. Three times a year. $13.50. 64-65 Cooper Avenue, Glendale NY 11385. **Tel** (718)366-5169. **ED** Timothy Monaghan. **DD** 810. **Ad Acc.** **Circ:** 450.
Desc: All types and forms of well-written poetry by both young and little known or established writers.

CN/0823-5112
LEVRES URBAINES. [Levres urbaines]. 1-. Periodical. French. bm. $10.00 for 4 months. Levres Urbaines, 3760 Av Parc la Fontaine, Montreal Quebec H2L 3M4 Canada. **DD** C841.54/08.

CN/0024-2020
LIBERTE (MONTREAL). (LIBERTE.). [Libert.]. Vol. 1 (Jan./Feb. 1959)-. Periodical. French. bm (6 issues). 40.00Can$ (institutions), 30.00Can$ (individuals) Canada; 45.00Can$ (institutions), 35.00Can$ (individuals) other. Liberte / Montreal, CP 399, Succursal Outremont, Montreal Quebec H2V 4N3 Canada. **Tel** (514)598-8457, **FAX** (514)524-3145. **ED** Francois Hebert. **LC** AP21; .L46. Index available. cum. index. **Bk Rev.** (Qty: 20). **Circ:** 1,200 (ctrl). available on microfilm and microfiche from University Microfilms International (UMI). Documents available from The Genuine Article.
Ind/Abst Arts Humanit. Citation Index [Full Cov.]; Can. Period. Index; Curr. Contents Arts Humanit.; MLA Int. Bibl. Books Artic. Mod. Lang. Lit.; Point Repere (1983-); Res. Alert [Full Cov.].

●US/1064-8186
LIGHT (CHICAGO, ILL.). See Literature.

US/0147-121X
LIGHT (NEW YORK. 1973). (LIGHT.). Vol 1 (1973)-. English. $3.00 (3 issues). Box 1105 Stuyvesant Station, New York NY 10009. **LC** PS580; .L5. **DD** 811/.5/408.

US/0743-913X
LIGHT YEAR (CLEVELAND, OHIO). **Ceased.** (LIGHT YEAR.). [Light year]. 1984-?. English. be. Bits Press, Department of English, Case Western Reserve University, Cleveland OH 44106. **Tel** (216)795-2810. **ED** Robert Wallace. **LC** PS595.H8; L54. **DD** 811/.07/08. **Circ:** 2,600.
Desc: The annual of light verse and funny poems, edited by Robert Wallace.
Ind/Abst Index Am. Period. Verse.

US/0278-0933
LIPS (MONTCLAIR, N.J.). (LIPS.). No. 1-. Periodical. English. Three times a year. $12.00 (libraries), $9.00 (individuals) US; $15.00 (libraries), $12.00 (individuals) other. Lips, PO Box 1345, Montclair NJ 07042. **Tel** (201)662-1303. **ED** Laura Boss. **Ad Acc.** **Circ:** 1,000 (ctrl).
Desc: Award winning poetry magazine. Includes poems by Allen Ginsberg, Marge Piercy, Ishmael Reed, Michael Benedikt and David Ignatow.
Ind/Abst Index Am. Period. Verse.

UK
LITTLE WORD MACHINE, THE. No. 1 (1972)-. Periodical. English. qt. £4.00 UK; £7.00 other. Little Word Machine Publications, 5 Beech Terrace, Undercliffe Bradford BD3 0PY West York England.

US/1056-7089
LIVE POETS. [Live poets]. **Added/Corp** Live Poets Society. Vol. 1, Issue 1 (1991)-. Periodical. English. $15.00. Live Poets Society, PO Box 391, Islip NY 11751. **DD** 811.

US
LIVING POETS LIBRARY. (1972)-. Monographic series. English. ir. Price varies per volume. Dragon Teeth Press, 7700 Wentworth Springs Road, Georgetown CA 95634.

US
LOFTY TIMES. (1972)-. Periodical. English. ir. $12.00. Poetry Project / St. Marks Church, 10th Street & 2nd Avenue, New York NY 10003. **Tel** (212)674-0910. **ED** Tim Dlugos. **Bk Rev.** **Ad Acc.** **Circ:** 5,000.
Desc: News, information, ideas, and reviews by, for, and about poets from America's most active poetry center.

US
LONG ISLAND POETRY COLLECTIVE NEWSLETTER, THE. **Main/Corp** Long Island Poetry Collective. **Added/Corp** Long Island Poetry Collective - Long Island Poetry Collective. (197?)-. Newsletter. English. Six times a year. $18.00. Long Island Poetry Collective, PO Box 773, Huntington NY 11743. **Tel** (516)691-2376. **ED** Pat Nesbitt. **Bk Rev.** **Ad Acc.** **Circ:** 300 (ctrl).
Desc: We are a poetry information journal. Calendar for Long Island, NYC Area. Extensive poetry markets listings (USA and abroad) and reviews. Occasional contests.

US/0897-6481
LUCIDITY. [Lucidity]. (1986)-. Periodical. English. qt. $7.00 US, (add $1.00 for postage) other. Lucidity, 2711 Watson, Houston TX 77009. **Tel** (713)869-6028. **ED** Ted O Badger. **DD** 811. **Circ:** 230.
Desc: A platform for contemporary understandable english poetry of various styles and subjects.

US/0024-7820
LYRIC (CHRISTIANSBURG, VA.), THE. (THE LYRIC.). [Lyric]. **Added/Corp** Lyric Foundation. Poets' Club (Norfolk, Va.) (1921)-. Periodical. English. qt. $10.00 (one year), $19.00 (two year), $27.00 (three year). Lyric, 307 Dunton Drive Southwest, Blacksburg VA 24060. **Tel** (703)552-3475. **ED** Leslie Mellichamp. **LC** PS301; .L78. Index available. cum. index. **Circ:** 950. available on photocopies; available on phonorecord (from the Library of Congress for the blind or physically handicapped).
Desc: Poetry only. Prefer rhymed verse, traditional forms, 35 lines or so, up-beat, occasionally humorous, no grievances or current political/social problems. Accessible on at least second reading.

US
MADISON REVIEW, THE. See Literature.

US/0047-5432
MADRONA. **Ceased.** Vol. 1 (1971)-(19??). Periodical. English. Three times a year. Madrona, PO Box 67E07, Los Angeles CA 90067-1407.
Ind/Abst Fish Rev. (?-?); Wildl. Rev. (?-?).

US/8755-8785
MAGAZINE OF SPECULATIVE POETRY, THE. [Mag. specul. poet.]. Vol. 1 No. 1 (Winter 1984)-. Periodical. English. qt. $11.00. Mark Rich, PO Box 564, Beloit WI 53511. **ED** Roger Dutcher and Mark Rich. **DD** 811. **Bk Rev.** **Ad Acc.** **Circ:** 200.
Desc: The equivalent in poetry to speculative fiction which was the confluence of post-modernism and science fiction in the late sixties, early seventies.

TI
MAHFIL (TUNIS, TUNISIA). (AL-MAHFIL / JAMIYAT ITTIHAD AL-SHUARA AL-SHABIYIN.). **Added/Corp** Jamiyat Ittihad Al-Shuara Al-Shabiyin (Tunis, Tunisia). Vol. 1, No. 1 (1981)-. Periodical. Arabic. bm. 2.00TD. Majallat Al-Mahfil, 5 Nahj Zarqun, S B 178, Tunis Tunisia. **LC** PJ8254; .M26.

GW/0076-2784
MAINZER REIHE, DIE. Vol. 1 (1956)-. Monographic series. German. ir. Price varies per volume. Verlag Hase & Koehler, Postfach 2269, D-55012 Mainz Germany. **Tel** 011 49 6131 232334. **DD** 830. **Bk Rev.**
Desc: The members of the academy have the possibility to publish manuscripts and poetry.

PR/1050-835X
MAIRENA (RIO PIEDRAS, SAN JUAN, P.R.). (MAIRENA.). [Mairena]. **Added/Corp** Instituto de Cultura Puertorriquena. Vol. 1, No. 2; Spring (1979)-. Periodical. Spanish. sa. $15.00 (institutions), $6.00 (individuals). Mairena/Revista Critica Poesia, Penasco 1656 Paradise Hills, San Juan, PR 00926. **Tel** (809)250-8197. **ED** Manuel de la Puebla, **LC** PQ7420; .M34. **DD** 861/.008. **Ad Acc.** **Circ:** 1,000 (ctrl).
Desc: A journal of poetry: creation and criticism. Accepts studies and book reviews of poetry and individual poems.
Ind/Abst Index Am. Period. Verse (-1982).

TI
MAJALLAT AL-SHIR. **Added/Corp** Tunisia. Wizarat al-Shuun al-Thaqafiyah. **VFOAT** Shir. Vol. 1, No. 1 (1982)-. Periodical. Arabic. qt. **LC** PN1010; .M24.

II
MALAYALAM LITERARY SURVEY. V. 1- Jan. 1977-. Academic Scholarly Publication. English (English). Rs12.00. Kerala Sahitya Akademi, Town Hall Road, Trichur 680 001 India. **LC** PL4718; .A34. **DD** 894/.812/09. **Bk Rev.** **Ad Acc.** **Circ:** 1,000.
Desc: Publishes scholarly articles on various branches of Malayalam literature and language.

US/0885-9205
MANHATTAN POETRY REVIEW. [Manhattan poet. rev.]. **VFOAT** MPR. (19??)-. Periodical. English. Twice a year. $10.00 (one year); $18.00 (two years). Manhattan Poetry Review, 36 Sutton Place South 11D, New York NY 10022. **Tel** (212)355-6634. **LC** WMLC 93/1352. **DD** 811.
Ind/Abst Index Am. Period. Verse.

US/0275-6889
MANHATTAN REVIEW (NEW YORK, N.Y. : 1980), THE. (THE MANHATTAN REVIEW.). [Manhattan rev.]. Vol. 1, No. 1 (Spring 1980)-. Periodical. English. Twice a year. Philip Fried, 440 Riverside Drive/Suite 45, New York NY 10027. **Tel** (212)932-1854. **ED** Philip Fried. **LC** PN1010; .M27. **DD** 811/.008. **Bk Rev.** **Ad Acc.** **Circ:** 500 (ctrl).
Desc: Poetry interviews with poets from different countries; mixture of American and foreign work; relation of poetry to other fields.
Ind/Abst Am. Humanit. Index; Index Am. Period. Verse.

SP/0303-1152
MANO EN EL CAJON, LA. (LA MANO EN EL CAJON; POESIA.). [Mano cajon]. Began in 1970. Periodical. Spanish. qt. 100. Independencia 321 5, 2A Barcelona Spain. **LC** PQ6174.95; .M36.

SP
MANUSCRITOS POETICOS. Spanish. qt. 4000ptas Spain; 8000ptas North America; 7000ptas other. Editorial El Paisaje, Entre los Rios 10, 24760 Castrocalbon Leon Spain. **(Subscription address:** Manusritos Poeticos, c/o Entre los Rios 10, 24760 CASTROBALBON (Leon) **ED** Agustin Garcia Alonso. **Bk Rev.** **Ad Acc.** ctrl circ.
Desc: Articles on poetry.

Literature — Poetry

JA
MANYO. Added/Corp Nara Kenritsu Kashiwara Toshokan. **VFOAT** Manyo Bunko Nempo. (19??)-. Periodical. Japanese. Nara Kenritsu Kashiwara Toshokan, 50 Unebicho 634, Kashiwara Japan. **LC** PL728.15.A1; M34.

PE
MANZANA MORDIDA, LA. No. 1 (Set de 1975)-. Periodical. Spanish. sa. Esther Festini, 1486 Magdalena del Mar, Lima 17 Peru. **LC** PQ8448; .M36. **DD** 861/.008/0985.

CN/0384-093X
MARSH & MAPLE. Added/Corp Scotian Pen Guild. (1974)-. Periodical. English. qt. 2.00Can$. Scotian Pen Guild, Box 173, Dartmouth Nova Scotia B2Y 3Y3 Canada. **DD** C810/.5.

US/0892-807X
MARYLAND POETRY REVIEW (BROOKLANDVILLE, MD.). (MARYLAND POETRY REVIEW.). Added/Corp Maryland Poetry and Literary Society. Vol. 1, No. 1 (1986)-. Periodical. English. Three times a year. Free to members. Maryland Poetry and Literary Society, Maryland Poetry Review, PO Box 1385, Brooklandville MD 21022. **DD** 811. **Ind/Abst** Am. Humanit. Index (199?-).

US/8755-7266
MATRIX (URBANA, ILL.). (MATRIX.). [Matrix]. Began in 1976. English. an. Red Herring Press, 1209 West Oregon Street, Urbana IL 61801. **DD** 811.

US
MERIDIAN. Vol. 1, No. 1 (Mar. 1980)-. Periodical. English. mo.
Ind/Abst Geogr. Abstr. Phys. Geogr. (?-?); Geogr. Abstr. Human Geogr.

UK/0306-3461
MERIDIAN POETRY MAGAZINE. Periodical. English. qt £0.30 each issue. Rondo Publications, 10 Pall Mall, Liverpool England L3 6HJ. **LC** PR1170; .M47. **DD** 821/.9/1408.

CN/0704-5719
MESSIEURS, MES AMOURS. V. 1- Feb. 1978-. Periodical. French. mo. $2.75 each number. Les Entreprises Normand Vaughan, CP 274 Wuccursale M, Montreal Quebec H1V 3M3. **DD** C841/.5/4080353.

US/0026-2773
MICROMEGAS (CEDAR FALLS, IOWA). (MICROMEGAS.). Periodical. Vol. 1, No. 1 (1965)-. Periodical. English. sa. $5.00. University of Northern Iowa Department of Modern Languages, C/O Richard Fehlman, Cedar Falls IA 50614-0504. **Tel** (319)273-2729. **ED** Frederic Will. **DD** 808.

US/0745-8738
MIDWEST POETRY REVIEW. (198?)-. Periodical. English. qt (Jan., Apr., July, Oct.). $20.00 US; $25.00 Canada; $30.00 other. Midwest Poetry Review, Box 4776, Rock Island IL 61201. **Tel** (319)391-1874. **ED** Tom Tilford and Hugh Ferguson. **Bk Rev**, (Qty: 4). ctrl circ.
Desc: Committed to the cause of poetry only, with related commentary and critiques. The goal is to deliver a publication that will encourage and inspire the reader to produce more and better poetry.

US
MILL HUNK HERALD, THE. Ceased. **VFOAT** Punching Out With: The Mill Hunk Herald. (Feb. 1979)-(1992). Periodical. English. qt. Mill Hunk Herald, 916 Middle Street, Pittsburgh PA 15212. **Tel** (412)321-4767. **ED** Larry Evans. **Bk Rev. Circ:** 8,000 (ctrl).
Desc: Contains the views, stories, and poetry of working people.
Ind/Abst Altern. Press Index (-1992).

US/8756-1549
MIND IN MOTION. [Mind motion]. Issue 1, (Spring 1985)-. Periodical. English. Four times a year (Seasonally). $14.00 North America; $18.00 other. Mind in Motion Publications, PO Box 118, Apple Valley CA 92307. **Tel** (6190248-6512. **ED** Celeste Goyer. **DD** 810. **Circ:** 350.
Desc: A magazine of poetry and short prose.

US
MIRRORS : INTERNATIONAL HAIKU FORUM. (1988)-. English (Japanese, German, Dutch and French). Twice a year. $10.00 US and $12.00 overseas surface mail; $20.00 other. International Haiku Spirit, Box 1250, Gualala CA 95445. **Tel** (707)882-2226. **ED** Jane Reichhold. **Bk Rev**, (Qty: 20-30/year). **Ad Acc. Pr Rev. Acid Free.** ctrl circ.
Desc: Publishes haiku, tanka, renga and haibun.

●US/1061-5296
MISNOMER (PRESTONBURG, KY.). (MISNOMER.). [Misnomer]. Vol. 1, No. 1 (Spring 1992)-. Periodical. English. sa. $8.00. Creeker Press, Box 1395, Prestonburg KY 41653. **DD** 811.

CN/0318-2088
MISTRAL. 1975-. English. qt. Mistral, 6023 Bliss Street, Halifax Nova Scotia B3H 2A8 Canada. **DD** C811/.5/405.
Desc: A magazine of poetry and stories by Halifax writers.

CN/0823-1605
MJP. MONTREAL JOURNAL OF POETICS. (MJP.). Series 2, No. 1 (Fall/Winter 1982)-. English. Free to members, $10.00 institutions. MJP, S Morrissey, R R #2, Huntingdon Quebec J0S 1H0 Canada. **Tel** (514)264-4304. **ED** Stephen Morrissey. **DD** 808.1/05. Index available. cum. index. **Bk Rev. Circ:** 150 (ctrl).
Continues Montreal Journal of Poetics, 0228-0388.
Desc: A periodical of book reviews and articles on contemporary poetry with special emphasis on Canadian poets and poetry.

US/0026-7821
MODERN HAIKU. [Mod. Haiku]. Vol. 1, No. 1 (Winter 1969)-. Periodical. English. Three times a year (Feb., June, Oct.). $14.85 US; $17.85 other. Modern Haiku, PO Box 1752, Madison WI 53701. **Tel** (608)233-2738. **ED** Robert Spiess. **LC** PS593.H3; M6. **DD** 811/.04. Index available. **Bk Rev**, (Qty: 35). **Circ:** 700.
Desc: Foremost international English language haiku journal. Publishes haiku, haiku book reviews and articles on haiku aesthetics.
Ind/Abst Am. Humanit. Index (1984-); Index Book Rev. Humanit. (1984-).

US
MODERN POETS IN TRANSLATION SERIES. Monographic series. English. Price varies per volume. Kosmos, 381 Arlington Street, San Francisco CA 94131.

RU
MOLODAIA GVARDIIA. (19??)-. Russian. mo. $89.95. Izdatelstvo Molodaia Gvardiia, Novodmitrovskaya Ul., 5A, 125015 Moscow Russia. **Tel** 095-285-0830. **(Subscription address:** East View Publications Inc., 3020 Harbor Lane North, Suite 110, Minneapolis MN 55447.**)**

RU
MOLODAIA POEZIIA. (19??)-. Russian. Izdatelstvo Sovetskii Pisatel, Ulitsa Vorovskogo 11, 121069 Moscow Russia.

CN/0823-8944
MONTREAL NOW!. [Montr. now]. 1st Quarter (1984)-. Periodical. English (French). qt. 10.00Can$ Canada; 17.67Can$ other. Montreal Now, 1A St. Etienne Street, Quebec H9X 1E8 Canada. **Tel** (514)457-3422. **DD** C841/.54/08.

US/0099-0264
MOONS AND LION TAILES. V. 1-. Monographic series. English. qt. Price varies per volume. Permanent Press, Lake Street Station, Box 8434, Minneapolis MN 55408. **LC** PN6099.6; .M66. **DD** 811/.5/408. available on microfilm and microfiche from University Microfilms International (UMI).

US/0882-147X
MORNING COFFEE CHAPBOOK SERIES. [Morning coffee chapb.]. (19??)-. Monographic series. English. ir. Price varies per volume. Coffee House Press, PO Box 546, West Branch IA 52358. **Tel** (319)643-2604. **LC** UNC. **DD** 811.

US/0027-2604
MOUNTAIN TROUBADOUR, THE. [Mt. troubad.]. Added/Corp Poetry Society of Vermont. Vol. 1 (Aug. 1956)-. Periodical. English. sa (May and Oct.). $4.00. Poetry Society of Vermont, PO Box 102, Belmont VT 05730. **Tel** (802)259-2575. **ED** Jeanne M. Douglas. **DD** 811. **Circ:** 250-300.

US/0145-0042
MOUTH OF THE DRAGON. No. 1 (May 1974)-. Periodical. English. qt. $6.00. Andrew Bifrost Publ, 342 East 15th Street, New York NY 10003. **Tel** (212)673-6025. **LC** PS595.H65; M68. **DD** 811/.5/4080352.

KO
MOYANGCHON. **VFOAT** Moyang Munhak Tongin Sahwajip. Periodical. Korean. W2,500. Mirae Munhaksa, 45-12 1-Ka Wonhyoro Yongsan-ku, Seoul Korea. **LC** PL974.A1; M69.

US/0740-1205
MR. COGITO. **VFOAT** Mister Cogito. Vol. 1, No. 1 (Fall 1973)-. Periodical. English. Three times a year. $9.00. Robert A Davies, Pacific University, Humanities, Forest Grove OR 97116. **Tel** (503)226-4135, (503)233-8131. **ED** John M Gogol and Robert A Davies. **LC** PS615; .M7. **DD** 811.008/005. **Bk Rev**, (Qty: 1-3). **Circ:** 400 (ctrl).
Desc: Poetry in English and in translation, line drawings.

US/0090-4953
MULBERRY. [Mulberry]. No. 1- Nov. 1972-. Periodical. English. bm. $6.00. Mulberry, 2070 Yale Station, New Haven CT 06520. **LC** PS580; .M85. **DD** 811/.5/408.

KO
MUNHAK : KYONGBUSON. Periodical. Korean. 350. 724-6 Taemyong-dong, Taegu Korea. **LC** PL974.A1; M85.

US/1071-1686
N.Y. CITY POETRY CALENDAR. (NEW YORK CITY POETRY CALENDAR.). **VFOAT** Poetry Calendar. (19??)-. Periodical. English. mo (10 issues - not published in July or Aug.). $15.00. New York City Poetry Calendar, 60 East 4th Street, Apartment 21, New York NY 10003. **Tel** (212)475-7110. **ED** Sharon Mattlin. **Circ:** 10,000. available on an online database from Grist.
Desc: Provides information on poetry workshops, poetry readings and other literary activities.

US/0162-9085
NAHUATZEN, EL. 1-. Periodical. English. sa. $6.00. University of Iowa / Nahuatzen, El Nahuatzen, Lowell Jaeger Editor, 310 Calvin Hall, Iowa City IA 52242. **LC** PS591 .M49; N3. **DD** 811/.008/0897.

KO
NARU SIJIP / NARU MUNHAKHOE. V. 1-Series (1981)-. Periodical. Korean. W1,500. Hanguk Munhaksa, 195 Kwanhun-dong, Chongno-ku, Seoul Korea. **LC** PL974.A1; N37.

JA
NENKAN GENDAI SHISHU. (19??)-. Periodical. Japanese. ¥3000. Ninkan Gendai Shishu Henshu Iinkai, c/o Geifu Shoin, Bunkyo Shogaku Building, 15-4 Hongo 1 Bunkyo-ku, Tokyo Japan. **LC** PL763.8; .N45.

GW/0933-2367
NEUE KERAMIK. (198?)-. Periodical. German (summaries and/or abstracts in English). bm. DM66.00. Neue Keramik GMBH, Unter Den Eichen 90, D 12205 Berlin, Germany. **Tel** 011 49 030 8312953, FAX 011 49 030 8316281. **ED** Gustav Weiss. **LC** NK3930; .N48. **DD** 730/.05. Index available (Bound in twelfth issue). cum. index. **Bk Rev. Ad Acc.** ctrl circ.

CN/0832-932X
NEW CANADIAN REVIEW. Ceased. See Literature.

UK
NEW CHATTO POETS. (1986)-. English. ir. Chatto and Windus, 42 William IV Street, London WE2N 4DF England.

JA
NEW CICADA. (19??)-. English. Twice a year (Mar. & Sept.). Y1000.00 Japan; $6.00 other. Tadao Okazaki, 40 Il Kubo Hobora, Fukushima 960 06 Japan. **Tel** 011 81 245754226.
Desc: Introducing to the world the true definition of haiku, a classical poetry form representing Japanese literature and religion.

SA/0028-4459
NEW COIN POETRY. Added/Corp South African Poetry Society. **VFOAT** New Coin. Vol. 1 (Jan. 1965)-. Periodical. English. sa (June and December). $15.50. Institute for Study English in Africa, Rhodes University, Box 94, Grahamstown 6140 South Africa. **Tel** 011 27 461 26093, FAX 011 27 461 25642, telex 244219. **Bk Rev. Circ:** 400.
Desc: Longest-surviving Southern African poetry magazine in continuous publication. Encourages new poetry of merit.
Ind/Abst Annu. Bibliogr. Engl. Lang. Lit.

US/0028-4467
NEW COLLAGE MAGAZINE. **VFOAT** New Collage. Vol. 1 (1970)-. Periodical. English. Three times a year. $6.00. New Collage Press, 5700 North Trail, Sarasota FL 34243. **Tel** (813)359-4360. **ED** A MCA Miller (editor's phone: (813)645-3842). Index available. cum. index. **Bk Rev**, (Qty: Varies). **Circ:** 1,000.
Desc: Poetry with clear focus and strong imagery; contemporary slants on traditional prosodies. Some interviews, book reviews and graphics.

UK
NEW HEADLAND POETRY MAGAZINE. (19??)-. Periodical. English. 27 Brook Road, Epping England. **LC** PR1170; .N48. **DD** 821/.9/1408.

UK/0548-6505
NEW POETRY. No. 28- 1975-. Periodical. English. qt. £3.00. Workshop Press, Accounts Department, 99 Pole Barn Lane, Frinton on Sea Essex CO13 9NQ England. **LC** PR1170; .N4842. **DD** 821/.005. Continues Workshop New Poetry.

UK
NEW POETS. English. $7.00. Regency Press, 43 New Oxford Street, London WC1A 1BH England. **LC** PR1227; .N43. **DD** 821/.9/1408.

CN/0827-2425
NEW POET'S HANDBOOK / THE LEAGUE OF CANADIAN POETS. [New poet's handb.]. Spring 1984-. English. an. 6.00Can$. League of Canadian Poets, 24 Ryerson Avenue, Toronto Ontario M5T 2P3 Canada. **Tel** (416) 363-5047, FAX (416)860-0826. **ED** John Wilson and Marvyne Jenoff. **DD** 808.1/023/71. **Circ:** 3,000 (ctrl).
Desc: A helpful tool for poets interested in launching themselves into the market place. Rich with advice on publishers and publishing.

US/0277-2752
NEW POETS SERIES, THE. (1970)-. Monographic series. English. Twice a year. Price varies per volume. New Poets Series, 541 Piccadilly Road, Baltimore MD 21204. **Tel** (410)321-2863. **ED** Clarinda Harriss Lott. cum. index. **Circ:** 750.
Desc: Publishes first books by outstanding younger poets who have not previously had a collection of their work published.

US/0735-4584
NEW VOICES IN AMERICAN POETRY. [New voices Am. poetry]. (19??)-. Periodical. English. an. $16.25. Vantage Press, 516 West 34th Street, New York NY 10001. **Tel** (212)736-1767. **LC** PS615; .N42. **DD** 811/.008.

US/0028-7482
NEW YORK QUARTERLY : NYQ, THE. **Added/Corp** New York Quarterly Poetry Review Foundation. New York Quarterly Foundation. National Poetry Foundation (U.S.). **VFOAT** NYQ. No. 1 (Winter 1970)-. Periodical. English. Three times a year (Mar., Jun., Oct.). $15.00 (individual), $25.00 (library) US; $20.00 (individual), $30.00 (library) other. National Poetry Foundation, University of Maine, 305 Neville Hall, Orono ME 04469. **Tel** (207)581-3814. **ED** William Packard. **LC** PS580; .N48. **DD** 811/.5/408. cum. index. **Ad Acc. Circ:** 700.
Desc: Contemporary poetry and some editorial commentary.
Ind/Abst Abstr. Engl. Stud.

CN/0319-6658
NEWSLETTER - EXECUTIVE COMMITTEE, LEAGUE OF CANADIAN POETS. **Main/Corp** League of Canadian Poets. **VFOAT** Museletter. No. 13 Fall/Winter (1974)-. Newsletter. English. Six times a year. 25.00Can$. League of Canadian Poets, 24 Ryerson Avenue, Toronto Ontario M5T 2P3 Canada. **Tel** (416) 363-5047, FAX (416)860-0826. **ED** Dolores Ricketts and John Oughton. **DD** C811/.006/271. **Ad Acc. Circ:** 400 (ctrl). ***Continues*** *Poetry Canada, 0316-036X.*
Desc: A comprehensive publication on and about poetry in Canada.

CN/0712-6239
NEWSLETTER / MONTREAL POETS' INFORMATION EXCHANGE. [Newsl. - Montr. Poets' Inf. Exch.]. **Added/Corp** Montreal Poets' Information Exchange. **VFOAT** Bulletin. (1976)-. Newsletter. English (French). mo. $10.00. Montreal Poets Information Exchange, 4050 MacKenzie, Chomedey Laval Quebec H7W 1M5 Canada. **DD** 808.1/05.

UK
NEWSLETTER / W.H. AUDEN SOCIETY. **Added/Corp** W.H. Auden Society. No. 1 (Apr. 1988)-. Newsletter. English. sa. $12.00. W H Auden Society, 78 Clarendon Road, c/o K Bucknell, London W11 2HW England. **Tel** 011 44 71 727 1020. **ED** Nicholas Jenkins. **Bk Rev. Ad Acc. Circ:** 200 (ctrl).
Desc: News of the life and works of poet W H Auden.

JA
NIHON KAIKO SHI SHI. **Added/Corp** Nihon KaikÂo Shinjinkai. (19??)-. Periodical. Japanese. qt. Nihon Kaiko Shijinkai, 3-2 Higashi Komagata 4, Sumida-ku 130 Tokyo Japan. **LC** PL757.A1; N53.

●US/1061-0480
NOCTILUCA (NORWOOD, MASS.). (NOCTILUCA : AN INTERNATIONAL MAGAZINE OF POETRY.). [Noctiluca]. Vol. 1, Issue 1 (Spring 1992)-. Periodical. English. sa. $10.00 (3 issues). Noctiluca, 10 Hillshire Lane, Norwood MA 02062-3009. **DD** 811.

MX/0188-2848
NORTE (MEXICO, D.F.). (NORTE.). [Norte]. **Added/Corp** Frente de Afirmacion Hispanista (Mexico). (1929)-. Periodical. Spanish. Six times a year (Feb., Apr., June, Aug., Oct., Dec.). $40.00. Frente de Afirmacion Hispanista, Lago Ginebra 47C, Mexico 11320 DF Mexico. **Tel** 5411546. **LC** F1201; .N6. **DD** 972/.003. **Circ:** 1,000.
Desc: Anthologies of poems by specific symbols.
Ind/Abst Am. Hist. Life (1963-1964, 1971-1974); MLA Int. Bibl. Books Artic. Mod. Lang. Lit.

CN/0822-0808
NORTHERN LIGHTS (CHELMSFORD). (NORTHERN LIGHTS.). [North. lights]. Began with 1969 issue. English. an. $2.50. Northern Ontario Council Teachers of English, PO Box 278, Chelmsford Ontario P0M 1L0 Canada. **Tel** (705)855-3967. **ED** Don Scott. **DD** C811/.54/0809282. **Bk Rev. Circ:** 2,000 (ctrl).
Desc: An anthology of verse written by students from grade 1 to 13 in Northern Ontario schools.

AT/0314-989X
NORTHERN PERSPECTIVE. See Literature.

US
NOSTOC MAGAZINE. English. ir. $8.00. Arts End Books, Box 162, Newton MA 02168. **ED** Marshall Brooks. **LC** PN2; .N63. **DD** 810/.8. **Bk Rev. Ad Acc. Circ:** 500.
Desc: We publish good contemporary poetry and short fiction.

FR/0294-4030
NOUVELLE TOUR DE FEU, LA. [Nouv. Tour feu]. No. 1 (Feb. 1982)-. Periodical. French. Four times a year (Jan., Apr., July, Oct.). 170.62F France; 200.00F other. Editions du Soleil Natal, c/o M. Herault, 8 Bis rue Lormier, 91580 Etrechy France. **Tel** 011 33 60 802433, 011 33 60 947272. **ED** Eolivious Olu Soleil. **LC** PQ1184; .N63. **DD** 841/.008. **Bk Rev. Ad Acc. Circ:** 800 (ctrl). ***Continues*** *Tour de Feu.*
Desc: Special numbers on great poets, contemporary poetry, criticism, and art reports.

BL
NOVA POESIA BRASILEIRA, A. **Added/Corp** Concurso Raimundo Correa de Poesia. Vol. 1 (1983)-. Portuguese. Shogun Editora E Arte Ltda, Caixa Postal 43.021, CEP 22052 Rio de Janeiro Brazil.

BL
NOVOS POETAS DO CEARA; ANTOLOGIA, OS. (1970)-. Portuguese. H Galeno, Casa de Juvenal Galeno, Fortaleza Brazil. **LC** PQ9691.C42; A15.

US/0885-5919
OCCASIONAL REVIEW (SAN JOSE, CALIF.), THE. (THE OCCASIONAL I.E. OCCASIONAL REVIEW.). [Occas. rev.]. Periodical. English. Realities Library, 1976 Waverly Avenue, San Jose CA 95122. **DD** 811.
Ind/Abst MLA Int. Bibl. Books Artic. Mod. Lang. Lit.

US/0146-9118
OCCURRENCE. English. John Wilson, 928 Pine Street Apartment 12B, Philadelphia PA 19107. **LC** PS580; .O25. **DD** 811/.5/05.

CN/1183-2029
ODYSSEY (TORONTO. 1991). (ODYSSEY.). [Odyssey]. Vol. 1, No. 1 (Jan. 20, 1991)-. Periodical. English. qt. Free. C Schandl, Suite 1711, World Trade Centre, Phase 1, 10 Yonge Street, Toronto Ontario M5E 1R4 Canada. **DD** C811//5408/005.

●US/1056-5035
ORACLE POETRY. [Oracle poet.]. **Added/Corp** Association of African Writers. Vol. 1, No. 1 (Spring 1992)-. Periodical. English. Four times a year. $30.00 (institutions); $25.00 (individuals) Comes with Association of African Writers membership. Rising Star Publishing, 2105 Amherst Road, Hyattsville MD 20783. **Tel** (301)422-2665. **DD** 811.

UK/0030-4425
ORBIS (YOULGREAVE, DERBYSHIRE). (ORBIS.). **Added/Corp** International Poetry Society. (July 1969)-. Periodical. English. Four times a year. $30.00. Orbis International Quarterly, 199 The Long Shot, Nuneaton Warwickshire England. **Tel** 011 44 203 327440, 011 44 23 385551. **ED** Mike Shields. **Bk Rev. Ad Acc. Circ:** 1,000. ***Absorbed*** *Scrip (Chesterfield, Derbyshire), 0036-9659.*
Desc: A wide variety of poetry, prose and features aimed at general readers as well as literary specialists. Very suitable for libraries, colleges, schools, writers and groups.
Ind/Abst Mag. Search.

US/0030-5804
ORPHIC LUTE. (THE ORPHIC LUTE.). Vol. 1- (June/July 1958)-. Periodical. English. qt. $10.00 US; (add $8.00 postage) other. Patricia Doherty Hinnebusch, 526 Paul Place, Los Alamos NM 87544. **Tel** (505)662-4032. **ED** Patricia Doherty Hinnebusch, (tel)505-672-3116. **Circ:** 250.
Desc: Features brief lyric poetry (3 to 40 lines) that is highly compressed and coherent.

US/0095-019X
OSIRIS (SCHENECTADY, N.Y.). (OSIRIS.). [Osiris]. No. 1 (1972)-. Periodical. English (French and German). sa (June, Dec.). $12.00 US; $14.00 Canada; $15.00 other. OSIRIS, PO Box 297, Deerfield MA 01342. **Tel** (413)774-4027, FAX (413)774-6629. **ED** Andrea Moorhead. **LC** WMLC 93/1797. **Ad Acc. Circ:** 750.
Desc: An international multi-lingual journal publishing contemporary poetry and graphics in English, French, Spanish and Italian, and other texts in a bilingual format.
Ind/Abst Am. Humanit. Index; Curr. Contents Arts Humanit.; Curr. Contents Soc. Behav. Sci.; Index Am. Period. Verse.

UK
OUTPOSTS POETRY QUARTERLY. No. 133 (Summer 1982)-. Periodical. English. qt (Mar., Jun., Sep., Dec.). £12.00 (1 year), £22.00 (2 year) UK; $26.00 (1 year), $48.00 (2 year) other. Hippopotamus Press, 22 Whitewell Road/ Frome, Somerset BA11 4EL England. **Tel** 011 44 373 66653. ***Continues*** *Outposts (Blackpool, Lancashire).*

UK
OXFORD POETRY (OXFORD, OXFORDSHIRE). (OXFORD POETRY.). Vol. 1, No. 1 (June 1983)-. Periodical. English. Three times a year. £7.50. Oxford Poetry / Magdalen College, Oxford OX1 4AU England. **Tel** 011 44 865 276000. **ED** Kate Reeves. **Bk Rev. Ad Acc, Adv Mgr:** Kate Reeves. **Circ:** 200 (ctrl).
Desc: Publishes the work of younger poets writing in Great Britain as well as other English speaking countries throughout the world. Also features interviews with recognized poets and critics. Sponsors translation competitions.

BG
PADABALI. 1 (Vol. 1387 Jan. 1980!)-. Periodical. Nepali (Bengali). **LC** PK1714; .P3.

US/0094-1964
PAINTBRUSH (LARAMIE). (PAINTBRUSH.). [Paintbrush]. No. 1 (Spring 1974)-. English. Twice a year (Spring & Fall). $9.00 (individuals); $12.00 (institutions). Northeast Missouri State University, Division of Fine Arts, Kirksville MO 63501. **Tel** (816)785-4442. **ED** Ben Bennani. **LC** PN6099.6; .P33. **DD** 808.81. Index available. cum. index. **Bk Rev**, (Qty: 2-5/yr). **Ad Acc. Circ:** 500 (ctrl).
Desc: News and information on poetry, translations and letters.
Ind/Abst Am. Humanit. Index; Index Am. Period. Verse; MLA Int. Bibl. Books Artic. Mod. Lang. Lit.

US/0362-7969
PAINTED BRIDE QUARTERLY, THE. Vol.1 (Fall 1973). Periodical. English. qt. $20.00 (one year), $40.00 (two year), $60.00 (three year) US; $22.00 Canada; $25.00 other. Painted Bride Art Center, 230 Vine Street, Philadelphia PA 19106. **Tel** (215)925-9914. **ED** Teresa Leo. **LC** PS580; .P33. **DD** 811/.5/408. **Bk Rev**, (Qty: 4/yr). **Ad Acc, Adv Mgr:** Jerry Haging. **Circ:** 100 (ctrl).
Desc: We wish to publish poetry, short fiction, essays, and reviews, from new as well as established writers.
Ind/Abst Am. Humanit. Index; Index Am. Period. Verse.

CN/0822-1561
PALMARES - ALL CANADA POETRY CONTESTS. (PALMARES.). Summer 83-. Periodical. English (French and Spanish). qt. Free. All Canada Poetry Contests, PO Box 5752, Station F, Ottawa Ontario K2C 3M1 Canada. **DD** C811/.54/08.

US/0738-8705
PANHANDLER, THE. (THE PANHANDLER : A REGIONAL JOURNAL / PRODUCED BY THE UNIVERSITY OF WEST FLORIDA'S WRITERS WORKSHOP.). **Added/Corp** University of West Florida. Writers Workshop. Vol. 1, No. 1 (1976)-. English. sa (Jan.& June). $10.00 (one year), $18.00 (two year) individuals; $12.00 (one year), $22.00 (two year) institution. University of West Florida, English Department, Pensacola FL 32514. **Tel** (904)474-2923.
Ind/Abst Am. Humanit. Index (199?-).

US/0048-3028
PARNASSUS : POETRY IN REVIEW. [Parnass., Poet. rev.]. Vol. 1 (Fall/Winter 1972)-. Periodical. English. sa. $46.00 (institutions) US; $54.00 (insstitutions) other. Poetry in Review Foundation, 41 Union Square West, Room 804, New York NY 10003. **Tel** (212)463-0889, (212)787-3569. **ED** Herbert Leibowitz. **LC** PN6099.6; .P36. **DD** 809.1. Index available. cum. index. **Bk Rev**, (Qty: 40 per year). **Ad Acc. Circ:** 2,500. available on microfilm and microfiche from University Microfilms International (UMI). Documents available from The Genuine Article, UMI Article Clearinghouse.
Desc: Poetry magazine devoted to in-depth essay-length reviewing of American and international poetry. Discusses important international and domestic poetry publications and is often used in writing workshops and English departments. Each issue features original poetry, art, fiction and memoirs as well.
Ind/Abst Abstr. Engl. Stud.; Acad. Search (Jan. 1993-); Am. Bibliogr. Slavic East Europ. Stud.; Am. Humanit. Index; Arts Humanit. Citation Index (19??-19??) [Full Cov.]; Book Rev. Index; Curr. Contents Arts Humanit.; Expand. Acad. Index (1989-); Humanit. Index; Humanit. Source (Jul. 1993-); INFO-SOUTH Abstr.; Lit. Crit. Regist.; Mag. Search; MLA Int. Bibl. Books Artic. Mod. Lang. Lit.; Newsp. Period. Abstr. (1991-); Res. Alert [Full Cov.].

US/1043-3325
PARTING GIFTS. [Parting gifts]. Vol. 1, No. 1 (Summer 1988)-. Periodical. English. sa. $6.00 North America; $10.00 other. March Street Press, 3006 Stonecutter Terrace, Greensboro NC 27405. **ED** Robert Bixby. **DD** 811. **Circ:** 100.
Desc: High quality, short literary fiction and poetry.

US/0031-2649
PASQUE PETALS. Vol. 1, No. 1 (May 1926)-. Periodical. English. mo (except Aug. and Nov.). $15.00. South Dakota State Poetry Society Inc, Verlyss Jacobson, Box 398, Lennox SD 57039-0398. **Tel** (605)647-2447. **ED** Barbara Stevens. **LC** PS571.S8; P29. Index available. cum. index. **Bk Rev. Circ:** 250.
Desc: Only use poetry 44 lines long, or less; all types with no rough language; good taste is the criteria.

CN/0847-0561
PAWN TO INFINITY. [Pawn infinity]. Vol. 1, No. 1 (Autumn 1990)-. Periodical. English. ir. $2.50 per year. Pawn to Infinity, c/o M.D. Genereux, Box 33, 2050 Claremont Avenue, Montreal, Quebec H3Z 2P8 Canada. **DD** C811/.5408.

US/0031-4307
PENINSULA POETS. Added/Corp Poetry Society of Michigan. (19??)-. Periodical. English. sa (Apr. and Oct.). $12.00. Poetry Society of Michigan, 1422 Maycroft Road, Lansing MI 48917. **Tel** (517) 323-4725. **ED** Joye Giroux. **Circ:** 300.
Desc: Publication of Poetry Society of Michigan, a non-profit organization.

SP
PENORRA : REVISTA TRIMESTRAL DE POESIA, LA. Spanish. qt. 3.000ptas Spain; 6.000ptas North America; 4.500ptas other. Editorial el Paisaje / Aranguren, La Penorra 8-2, 48850 Aranguren Spain. **Tel** (94) 639 07 74. **ED** Agustin Garcia Alonso. **Bk Rev. Ad Acc. Circ:** 3,500 (ctrl).

US/1056-4888
PHASE AND CYCLE. [Phase cycle]. Vol. 1, No. 1 (Winter 1988)-. Periodical. English. sa. $5.00 US; $8.00 other. Phase and Cycle Press, 3537 East Prospect, Ft Collins CO 80525. **Tel** (303)482-7573. **ED** Loy Banks. **DD** 811. **Circ:** 200.
Desc: Poetry magazine.

US/1045-0904
PHOEBE (ONEONTA, N.Y.). See Women's Interests.

●CN/1191-8632
PHOENIX (WATERLOO). (PHOENIX.). [Phoenix]. **Added/Corp** University of Waterloo. Federation of Students. Creative Arts Board. University of Waterloo. Arts Student Union. University of Waterloo. (1992)-. English. an. Limited free distribution. Arts Student Union, Creative Arts Board, Federation of Students, Campus Centre, Room 235 ,, University of Waterloo, Waterloo, Ontario, N2L 3G1. **DD** C810.8/092379. ***Continues*** *Online (Waterloo, Ont.), 0836-2807.*

DK/0107-6442
PIST PROTTA. [Pist protta]. (1981)-. Periodical. Danish. **DD** 705.
Ind/Abst BHA : Biblio. Hist. Art.

US/0554-2324
PIVOT (STATE COLLEGE, PA.). (PIVOT.). **Added/Corp** Pennsylvania State University. Poetry Workshop. (1951)-. English. an. $7.00 US; $10.00 other. Pivot Associates, 221 South Barnard Street, State College PA 16801. **Tel** (814)238-8887. **ED** Georgia McElhaney.

US/0730-6172
PLAINS POETRY JOURNAL. [Plains poetry j.]. No. 1 (1982)-. Periodical. English. qt. $9.00 US and Canada. Stronghold Press, PO Box 2337, Bismarck ND 58502. **Tel** (701)258-2747. **ED** Jane Greer. **LC** WMLC L 83/6463. **Circ:** 550.
Desc: Contains modern formalist poetry.
Ind/Abst Am. Humanit. Index.

US/0275-0074
PLAINSONG (BOWLING GREEN, KY.). (PLAINSONG.). Vol. 1, No. 1 (Spring 1979)-. Periodical. English. ir. $7.00. Plainsong Inc., PO Box 8245, West Kentucky University, Bowling Green KY 42101. **Tel** (502)781-3468.

US/0277-1098
PLAY THE RED. [Play red]. Vol. 1, No. 1 (Fall 1981)-. Periodical. English. $3.00 single issue. Sisyphus Press, 192 Spring Street, New York NY 10012. **LC** PS301; .P53.

CN/0840-707X
PLOWMAN (BROOKLIN). (THE PLOWMAN.). [Plowman]. Issue No. 1 (Nov. 1988)-. Periodical. English. Four times a year. 10.00Can$. The Plowman, PO Box 414, Whitby Ontario L1N 5S4 Canada. **Tel** (416)688-7803. **ED** Tony Scavetta, Randy Hall, David Wood. **DD** C811/.54/08. **Bk Rev. Ad Acc. Circ:** 15,000 (ctrl).
Desc: Publishes works on the holocaust, religion and more.

US/0032-1885
POEM. [Poem]. **Added/Corp** Huntsville Literary Association (Huntsville, Ala.). No. 1 (Nov. 1967)-. Periodical. English. sa. $10.00. Huntsville Literary Association, PO Box 919, Huntsville AL 35804. **Tel** (205)536-9038. **ED** N F Dillard. **LC** PS580; .P6. Index available. cum. index. **Bk Rev. Ad Acc. Circ:** 400 (ctrl).
Desc: Brief lyric poems, compressed and intense with a high degree of verbal and dramatic tension.
Ind/Abst Index Am. Period. Verse.

●US/1063-1666
POEM FINDER ON DISC. (POEM FINDER ON DISC H.[COMPUTER FILE].). [Poem finder disc]. **Added/Corp** Roth Publishing, Inc. **VFOAT** Poem Finder; Poem Finder on Disc. (1992)-. English. Twice a year. $395.00 (regular); $600.00 (network version 2 8 workstation); $1,100.00 (network version 9 50 workstations). Roth Publishing Inc, PO Box 406, Great Neck NY 11022. **Tel** (516)466-3676, (800)899-7684, FAX (516)829-7746. **(Subscription address:** Roth Publishing Inc., 185 Great Neck Road, Great Neck NY 11021.**) LC** PN1022; .P6. **DD** 808.

CN/0048-4520
POEMES INEDITS. VFOAT Inedits. V. 1- June 1970-. Periodical. French. ir. J. Royer, 198, AV. Royale, Ile d'Orleans, Comte Montmorency, Quebec.

FR
POEMONDE. (Autumn 1978)-. Periodical. French. sa. Claude Herviant, 16 rue Beccaria, 75012 Paris France. **Tel** 011 33 1 43445564.

BL
POESIA. Yearly V. 1- Dec. 1977-. Periodical. Portuguese. Clube de Poesicude Sao Paulo, rua Barao de Itapetininga, 262 30 S 305, Sao Paulo Brazil. **LC** PN1010; .P494. **DD** 808.81.

VE
POESIA. Added/Corp Universidad de Carabobo. Departamento de Literatura. Vol. 1 No. 1 (1971)-. Periodical. Spanish. bm. Departemento de Literatura de la U C, Apdo 3052, El Trigal, Valencia Edo Carabobo Venezuela. **LC** PN1010; .P4943.
Ind/Abst MLA Int. Bibl. Books Artic. Mod. Lang. Lit.

VE/0032-1893
POESIA DE VENEZUELA. No 1 (May/June. 1963)-. Periodical. Spanish (English and French). Three times a year (Jan., May, Sept.). Free. Poesia de Venezuela, Apartado Postal 1114, Caracas 1010 A Venezuela. **Tel** 011 58 2 744361. **LC** PQ8544; .P63. **DD** 861.

SP
POESIA (MADRID, SPAIN). (POESIA.). **Added/Corp** Spain. Direccion General de Difusion Cultural. Spain. Ministerio de Cultura. (March 1978)-. Periodical. Spanish. Three times a year. 7000ptas. Ministerio de Cultura Libreria, C Abdon Terradas 7, 28015 Madrid Spain. **Tel** 011 34 1 5448569. **LC** PN1010; .P4942. ***Continues*** *Poesia Hispanica.*

FR/0048-4555
POESIE; LA POESIE FRANCAISE DE BELGIQUE. (1970)-. Periodical. French. ir. Sodis, 128 Ave Marechal Lattre Tassig, 77400 Lagny France. **Tel** 011 33 1 64305557.

FR/0752-272X
POESIE (PARIS, FRANCE : 1984). (POESIE.). **Added/Corp** Maison de la Poesie (Paris, France). Vol. 1 (Jan./Feb. 1984)-. Periodical. French. Five times a year (Feb., Apr., June, Oct., Dec.). 323.21F France; 350.00F other. Poesie Maison de la Poesie, 228 Bd Raspail, 75014 Paris France. **Tel** 011 33 1 43202888. **LC** PQ1141; .P64. **DD** 841/.91/08.
Ind/Abst Romant. Move.

FR/0048-4563
POESIE PRESENTE. Vol. 1 (May 1971)-. Periodical. French. Four times a year. 250.00F France; 290.00F other. Rougerie Editeur, Mortemart, 873330 France. **Tel** 33 55 680093. **ED** Rene Rougerie. **LC** PQ1160; .P63.

GW
POESIEALBUM. (19??)-. Periodical. German. Twelve times a year. LKG Leipziger Kommissions & Grossbuchhandel, Leninstrasse 16, Postfach 520, D 04005 Leipzig, Germany. **Tel** 011 49 341 71370.
Desc: Presents a contemporary author from the GDR or from abroad, a poet of world literature or a classic of literature.

II/0032-194X
POET. Added/Corp World Poetry Society. Vol. 1 (1960)-. Periodical. English. Twelve times a year. $25.00 (one year); $40.00 (two years); $55.00 (three years). World Poetry Society, 118 Dr Seethapathi Nagar, Madras 42 India. **Tel** 011 91 11 2350186. **ED** Krishna Srinivas. **Bk Rev.** available in microform.
Desc: Devoted to poetry from all countries of the world.

US/0032-1958
POET AND CRITIC (AMES, IOWA). (POET AND CRITIC.). [Poet crit.]. **Added/Corp** Iowa State University. Dept. of English and Speech. Iowa State University. Dept. of English. **VFOAT** Poet & Critic. Vol. 1, No. 1 (Fall 1964)-. Periodical. English. Three times a year (Jan., May, Oct.). $18.00 US; $21.00 other. Iowa State University English Department, 203 Ross Hall, Ames IA 50011. **Tel** (515)294-2180, FAX (515)292-3348. **ED** Neal Bowers. **LC** PS501; .P64. **Bk Rev. Circ:** 500 (ctrl). available on microfilm and microfiche from University Microfilms International (UMI). ***Continues*** *Poet & Critic (Lafayette, Ind.), 0032-1958.*
Desc: Poetry and criticisms.
Ind/Abst Abstr. Engl. Stud.; Index Am. Period. Verse.

US/0032-1966
POET LORE. [Poet lore]. Vol. 1- Jan. 1889-. Periodical. English. qt. $15.00 (individuals), $24.00 (institutions). The Writers Center, 7815 Old Georgetown Road, Bethesda MD 20814. **Tel** (301)654-8664. **ED** Philip K Jason. **LC** PN2; .P7. **DD** 808.805. Index available. cum. index. **Bk Rev**, (Qty: 10 per year). **Ad Acc. Pr Rev. Circ:** 700 (ctrl). available on magnetic tape, an online database, and CD-ROM; available on microfilm and microfiche from University Microfilms International (UMI).
Desc: Each issue spotlights, with informative, lively reviews, new volumes of poetry, particularly small press publications. Presents the work of both new and established writers.
Ind/Abst Am. Bibliogr. Slavic East Europ. Stud.; Index Am. Period. Verse.

US/0190-6682
POET PEU A PEU, THE. VFOAT Poet. Periodical. English. an. D I Nemeth, 2314 West 6th Street, Mishawaka IN 46544. **ED** Doris I Nemeth. **LC** PS615; .P622. **DD** 811/.008.

US/0748-4062
POET (SHREVEPORT, LA.), THE. (THE POET.). [Poet]. Vol. 1, No. 1 (Fall 1984)-. Periodical. English. Four times a year (Jan., Apr., July, Oct.). $20.00. Cooper House Publishing Inc., PO Box 54947, Oklahoma City OK 73154. **Tel** (404)949-2020. **ED** Peggy Cooper. **DD** 811. cum. index. **Bk Rev**, (Qty: varies). **Ad Acc, Adv Mgr:** P. Cooper. **Circ:** 5,000-7,000 (ctrl).
Desc: Dedicated to exciting reading, writing, teaching and publishing for hundreds of new and experienced writers, poets, teachers and students all across the USA and abroad. Loaded with not only poetry but articles for and by teachers.

II/0970-2830
POETCRIT MARANDA. [PoetcritMaranda]. (1988)-. Periodical. English. sa. $15.00. **(Subscription address:** Prints India, 11 Darya Ganj, New Delhi 110002 India.**) UDC** 8.09.

IT
POETI A GRADARA. 1970/71-. Italian. 6.000. Eura Press, Via Lazzaro Papi 15, Milan 20135 Italy. **Tel** (02)5460353. **LC** PQ4214; .P556. **Circ:** 1,500.

US
POETIC JUSTICE : CONTEMPORARY AMERICAN POETRY. English. ir. $10.00. 8220 Rayford Drive, Los Angeles CA 90045. **ED** Alan Engebretsen.
Ind/Abst Index Am. Period. Verse.

CN/0708-9562
POETIC LICENCE (CALGARY). (POETIC LICENCE.). Began publication in March 1978?. Periodical. English. bm. $1.50 per no., $9.00 per year. Poetic Licence, PO Box 3810 Station B, Calgary Alberta T2M 4N6 Canada. **DD** C811/.5/408.

JA
POETICA. (Apr. 1974)-. Periodical. English. sa. $110.50. **(Subscription address:** Japan Publications Trading Company, Ltd., PO Box 5030, Tokyo International, Tokyo 100-31 Japan.**)**
Ind/Abst Romant. Move.

GW
POETICA; ZEITSCHRIFT FUER SPRACH- UND LITERATURWISSENSCHAFT. (Jan. 1967)-. German.
Ind/Abst Annu. Bibliogr. Engl. Lang. Lit.; Curr. Contents Arts Humanit.

US/1043-0814
POETICS. (POETICS : THE NEWSLETTER OF GREAT LAKES POETRY PRESS.). Newsletter. English. Three times a year. Great Lakes Press, Box 56703, Harwood Heights IL 60656. **Tel** FAX (312)631-3697 (ALSO). **DD** 811. **Ad Acc. Circ:** 10,000 (ctrl).
Desc: Covers contemporary American poetry.

NE/0304-422X
POETICS (AMSTERDAM). (POETICS.). [Poetics]. Vol. 1 (1971)-. Academic Scholarly Publication. English (French and German). bm (1 volume). Fl467.00. Elsevier Science Publishers BV, PO Box 211, 1000 AE Amsterdam Netherlands. **Tel** 011 31 20 5803642, FAX 011 31 20 5862696, telex 15682. **ED** S J Schmidt and C J van Rees. **LC** PN45; .P58. **DD** 801. **[CCC].** cum. index. available on microfilm and microfiche from University Microfilms International (UMI). Documents available from The Genuine Article.
Desc: An international forum for theoretical research on literature.
Ind/Abst Abstr. Engl. Stud.; Arts Humanit. Citation Index [Full Cov.]; Curr. Contents Arts Humanit.; MLA Int. Bibl.

Books Artic. Mod. Lang. Lit.; Res. Alert [Full Cov.]; Soc. Plann. Policy Dev. Abstr.; Soc. Sci. Cit. Index [Select. Cov.].

FR/0032-2024
POETIQUE. [Poetique]. (1970)-. Periodical. French. Four times a year (Feb., May, Aug., Nov.). 323.21F France, 375.00F others (surface mail); 390.00F (airmail). Editions du Seuil, 27 rue Jacob, 75261 Paris Cedex 06 France. **Tel** 011 33 1 69092409 or, 40465050. **(Subscription address:** Editions du Sueil Altek Data, 49 rue de la Vanne, 92129 Montrouge CDX France.**) LC** PN3; .P64. **DD** 809. **[CCC].** Documents available from The Genuine Article.
Ind/Abst Arts Humanit. Citation Index [Full Cov.]; Curr. Contents Arts Humanit.; MLA Int. Bibl. Books Artic. Mod. Lang. Lit.; Res. Alert [Full Cov.]; Romant. Move.

UK/0032-2040
POETRY & AUDIENCE. VAT Poetry and Audience. (195?)-. Academic Scholarly Publication. English. be. £4.00. University of Leeds School of English, Leeds LS2 9JT England. **Tel** 011 44 532 334739, FAX 0532 334774, telex 556473 UNILDS 9. **ED** Antony Rowland. **Bk Rev**, (Qty: 51). **Ad Acc. Circ:** 280. Documents available from BLDSC.
Desc: Publishes new poetry alongside the work of established poets. Past contributors include Seamus Heaney, Ted Hughs, Philip Larkin and Stevie Smith.

AT/0032-2059
POETRY AUSTRALIA. [Poet. Aust.]. Vol. 1, No. 1 (1964)-. Periodical. English. qt. 20.00Aus$. South Head Press, The Market Place, Berrima New South Wales 2577 Australia. **Tel** 011 61 48 711421. **ED** John Millett. **LC** PR9548; .P6. **Bk Rev. Circ:** 2,000.
Desc: Australian journal for first instance publication of poetry and criticism. Quality is the only criterion, no prejudice as to subject matter, form, or technique or length. Has published Swedish, Italian, bilingual French, as well as general and other issues.
Ind/Abst Abstr. Engl. Stud. (1980-); MLA Int. Bibl. Books Artic. Mod. Lang. Lit.

UK/0551-1690
POETRY BOOK SOCIETY BULLETIN.
Main/Corp Poetry Book Society. No. 1 (May 1955)-. Bulletin. English. qt. £17.50 UK; £25.50 other. The Poetry Book Society Ltd, 21 Earls Court Square, London SW5 9DE England. **Tel** (01)244-9792. **LC** PR604; .P63A. **DD** 821/.912/09. **Circ:** 1,900 (ctrl).
Desc: Britain's only poetry book club. All major titles at substantial discount.

US/0032-2032
POETRY (CHICAGO). (POETRY.). [Poetry]. **Added/Corp** Modern Poetry Association. Vol. 1 (Oct. 1912)-. Periodical. English. mo. $27.00 (1 year), $49.00 (2 year), $69.00 (3 year) institutions; $25.00 (1 year), $45.00 (2 year), $64.00 (3 year) individuals. Modern Poetry Association, 60 West Walton Street, Chicago IL 60610. **Tel** (312)280-4870. **ED** Joseph Parisi. **LC** PS301; .P6. **DD** 811/.005. **[CCC].** Index available. cum. index. **Bk Rev. Ad Acc. Circ:** 7,000. available on microfilm and microfiche from University Microfilms International (UMI). Documents available from The Genuine Article, UMI Article Clearinghouse.
Desc: Presents articles on American poetry.
Ind/Abst Abstr. Engl. Stud.; Acad. Ind. [Computer File] (1984-); Acad. Search (July 1993-); Access (1980-); Am. Humanit. Index; Arts Humanit. Citation Index [Full Cov.]; Book Rev. Digest; Book Rev. Index; Curr. Contents Arts Humanit.; Gen. Period. Index (1985-); Humanit. Source (Jul. 1993-); Index Am. Period. Verse; Mag. Index Plus (1989-); Newsp. Period. Abstr. (1988-); Pop. Period. Index; Read. Guide Period. Lit.; Res. Alert [Full Cov.]; Mag. Index (1977-).

US/1052-4851
POETRY CRITICISM. (POETRY CRITICISM : EXCERPTS FROM CRITICISM OF THE WORKS OF THE MOST SIGNIFICANT AND WIDELY STUDIED POETS OF WORLD LITERATURE.). [Poet. crit.]. **Added/Corp** Gale Research Inc. Vol. 1 (1991)-. Periodical. English. sa (December). $80.00. Gale Research Inc., 835 Penobscot Building, Detroit MI 48226. **Tel** (800)877-GALE, (313)961-2242, FAX (313)961-6083, telex TWX 810-221-7086. **ED** Drew Kalasky. **LC** PN1010; .P499. **DD** 809.1/005.
Desc: Presents overviews of 8-10 major poets from all time periods, from around the world. A fully illustrated guide to the poets most frequently discussed and studied in high school and undergraduate college courses. Each entry contains a biographical sketch, a wide variety of critical commentaries, and sources for additional reading. For easy access, entries are arranged alphabetically by poet.

US
POETRY DIMENSION ANNUAL. Vol. 4, (1976)-. Monographic series. English. ir. Price varies per volume. Rowman & Littlefield Publishing Inc., 8705 Bollman Place, Savage MD 20763. **Tel** (301)306-0400. **ED** Homer Dickens. ***Continues** Poetry Dimension; A Living Record of the Poetry Year.*
Desc: This seventh annual monograph includes among many others, memorable new poems by Alan Sillitoe, Roy Fisher and Peter Redgrove.

UK
POETRY DURHAM. Added/Corp University of Durham. Dept. of English. No. 1 (Summer 1982)-. Periodical. English. Three times a year (Apr., July, Sept.). £4.50 UK; £18.00 other. University of Durham / Department of English, Poetry Durham, Durham DH1 3JT England. **ED** David Hartnett, Michael O'Neal and Garett Reeves. **Bk Rev. Ad Acc. Circ:** 600.

US/0197-4009
POETRY EAST. [Poetry east]. No. 1 (1980)-. English. Twice a year. $12.00 US; $13.00 Canada; $20.00 other. Poetry East, 802 West Belden Avenue, Chicago IL 60614-3214. **Tel** (312)362-5114, (312)362-8889, FAX (312)362-5684. **ED** Richard Jones. **LC** PN1271; .P6. **DD** 808.81/05. Index available. cum. index. **Bk Rev. Ad Acc. Circ:** 1,800 (ctrl).
Desc: An international magazine of poetry, criticism, translations, interviews and art. Features special issues on such topics as: surrealism, political poems, visual arts, etc.
Ind/Abst Am. Humanit. Index (199?-); Index Am. Period. Verse.

US/0737-4747
POETRY FLASH. (19??)-. Periodical. English. Twelve times a year. $15.00 (individuals); $16.00 (institutions). Poetry Flash, PO Box 4172, Berkeley CA 94704. **Tel** (415)525-5476. **ED** Joyce Jenkins. Index available. **Bk Rev. Ad Acc. Circ:** 15,000 (ctrl).
Desc: Dedicated to covering the entire spectrum of literary styles and schools. Offers reviews of books, magazines, performances and readings. Interviews, poetry, and essays on topics of interest to writers are included. Covers the general literary scene in California and lists regional, national, and international events.
Ind/Abst Am. Humanit. Index (19??-).

UK/0477-0943
POETRY FROM OXFORD. (1953)-. English.

●US/1062-9386
POETRY IN PENNSYLVANIA. (1992)-. Periodical. English. $6.95. Peter Wamback, 2200 Walnut Street, Harrisburg PA 17103.

US/0736-3966
POETRY INDEX ANNUAL. ***Title Change.*** (POETRY INDEX ANNUAL / PREPARED BY THE EDITORIAL BOARD, GRANGER BOOK CO., INC.). [Poet. index annu.]. **Added/Corp** Granger Book Co. Editorial Board. (1982)-(19??). English. an. Roth Publishing Inc, PO Box 406, Great Neck NY 11022. **Tel** (516)466-3676, (800)899-7684, FAX (516)829-7746. **LC** PN1022; .P63. **DD** 808.81/0016. ***Merged into** Poem Finder on Disc.*
Desc: Title, author, first line, and key-line subject index to poetry published in anthologies each year.

IE/0332-2998
POETRY IRELAND REVIEW, THE.
Added/Corp Poetry Ireland (Group). No. 1 (Spring 1981)-. Periodical. English (Irish). Four times a year (Feb., May, Sept., Nov.). 16.00p Ireland & UK; 24.00p (surface mail), 36.00p (airmail) other. Poetry Ireland, Subscription Department, 44 Upper Mount Street, Dublin 2 Ireland. **Tel** 011/44/10/3531610320, FAX 010 353 1 6610320. **ED** Bt Boran, (phone: 010.353.1.6610320). **LC** PR1170; .P64. cum. index. **Bk Rev**, (Qty: 40-50). **Ad Acc, Adv Mgr:** Niamh Morris, **Tel** (353)1-610320. **Pr Rev. Circ:** 1,000 (ctrl).
Desc: Seeks to reflect contemporary poetry being written in Ireland and abroad. Aims to create a forum for international poetry through the unique central geographic and non-aligned position of Ireland vis-a-vis the old and new worlds.

US/0275-1739
POETRY/LA. ***Suspended.*** **VFOAT** Poetry LA. **VAT** Poetry Los Angeles. No. 1 (Fall/Winter 1980)-(19??). Periodical. English. sa. $8.00. Poetry/LA, PO Box 84271, Los Angeles CA 90073. **Tel** (310)472-6171. **ED** Helen Friedland. **LC** PS1; .P63. **DD** 811/.008.
Desc: Poems of literary value by Los Angeles area poets without prior restraint on subject, style, or length.
Ind/Abst Am. Humanit. Index (-19??).

US/0730-8868
POETRY MAG, A. [Poetry mag]. No. 1 (Feb. 1982)-. Periodical. English. qt. $8.00 individuals, $10.00 institutions. Teri Fontaine, 39 Linden Place, Brookline MA 02146.

US
POETRY MAILING LIST, THE. Periodical. English. ir. The Poetry Mailing List, 18 Cheshire Place, Staten Island NY 10301.

CN/0843-2287
POETRY MARKETS FOR CANADIANS. (POETRY MARKETS FOR CANADIANS / THE LEAGUE OF CANADIAN POETS.). [Poet. mark. Can.]. **Added/Corp** League of Canadian Poets. 3rd. Edition (1987)-. Periodical. English. ir. Price varies. League of Canadian Poets, 24 Ryerson Avenue, Toronto Ontario M5T 2P3 Canada. **Tel** (416) 363-5047, FAX (416)860-0826. **ED** James Deahl. **LC** IN PROCESS. **DD** 070.5/2/0971. Index available. **Circ:** 3,000 (ctrl). ***Continues** Poetry Markets in Canada, 0826-4708.*
Desc: Catalogue of poetry markets in Canada and throughout the world, plus suggestions on how to approach them.

AT/0314-6855
POETRY MONASH. Added/Corp Monash University, Melbourne. English Dept. (197?)-. Periodical. English. Three times a year. 9.00Aus$. Monash University, English Department, c/o Dr Dennis Davison, Clayton Victoria 3168 Australia. **Tel** 03 565 2135. **ED** Lynette Wilson. **Circ:** 150.
Desc: Poems written by the writers of the Monash University only.

CN/0822-9937
POETRY MONTREAL. [Poetry Montr.]. No. 1 (Feb. 1984)-. Periodical. English. mo. $1.00 per no. Poetry Montreal, 1-3358 Lorne Avenue, Montreal Quebec H2X 2A6 Canada. **DD** C811/.54/0809714281.

CN/0821-5790
POETRY 'N' PROSE. [Poetry prose]. Periodical. English. bm. $6.00 Canada and US; $7.00 other. Ahnene Publications, Box 3638, Station C, Ottawa Ontario K1Y 4J7 Canada. **DD** C811/.5408.

US
POETRY NEWSLETTER. No. 1 (Dec. 1971)-. Periodical. English. an. $3.00. Temple University / English Department, College of Liberal Arts, Anderson Hall 939, Philadelphia PA 19122. **Tel** (215)204-7539, (215)204-7000. **ED** Richard O'Connell.

JA/0032-2105
POETRY NIPPON. Added/Corp Poetry Society of Japan. (19??)-. Periodical. English. qt. ¥3500 Japan; $29.00 US. Poetry Society of Japan, 5-11 Nagaikecho, Showaku Nagoya 466 Japan. **Tel** (052)833-5724. **(Subscription address:** Japan Publications Trading Company, Ltd., PO Box 5030, Tokyo International, Tokyo 100-31 Japan.**) ED** Yorifumi Yaguchi. **LC** PL757.A1; P64. **DD** 895.6/1/005. cum. index. **Bk Rev. Ad Acc. Circ:** 500. available on microfiche.
Desc: Translation of Japanese poetry. poems by Japanese and foreigners, book reviews, poetics, essays on poets and poetry news home and abroad.

US/0032-2113
POETRY NORTHWEST. [Poetry northwest]. **Added/Corp** University of Washington. (June 1959)-. Periodical. English. qt. $10.00 US; $12.00 other. University of Washington / Seattle, Washington, 4045 Brooklyn Avenue Northeast, JA-15, Seattle WA 98105. **Tel** (206)543-5900, (206)543-2992, FAX (206)685-3234. **ED** Prof David Wagoner, (206)543-5900. **LC** AP2; .P746. **DD** 811/.005. **Circ:** 800.
Desc: Poetry from poets of the USA and other countries.
Ind/Abst Am. Humanit. Index (-199?); Index Am. Period. Verse.

US
POETRY: PEOPLE. (19??)-. English. an.

US/0554-3983
POETRY PILOT. [Poet. pilot]. **Added/Corp** Academy of American Poets. (Aug. 1959)-. Periodical. English. Six times a year. $25.00 Comes with Academy of American Poets Contributing membership. Academy of American Poets, 584 Broadway, Suite 1208, New York NY 10012. **Tel** (212)274-0343. **ED** David Austin. **LC** PS301; .P653. **DD** 811. **Ad Acc. Circ:** 2,800 (ctrl).
Desc: Each issue contains news of Academy activities and other literary events, as well as a poetry contest and a selection of poems, with commentary, by a distinguished poet.

●US
POETRY PROJECT NEWSLETTER, THE.
Added/Corp St. Mark's Church In-the-Bowery (New York, N.Y.). Poetry Project. Vol. 145 (Apr./May 1992)-. Newsletter. English. ***Continues** Poetry Project.*

CN/0381-6591
POETRY TORONTO. ***Ceased.*** [Poetry Tor.]. No. 69 (Sept. 1981)-?. Periodical. English. mo. Poetry Toronto, 217 Northwood Drive, Willowdale Ontario M2M 2K5 Canada. **Tel** (416)222-4690. **ED** Maria Jacobs. **DD** C811/.54/080971354. **Bk Rev. Ad Acc. Circ:** 800 (ctrl). ***Continues** Poetry Toronto Newsletter, 0381-6591.*
Desc: Small magazine listing literary events (readings, workshops, radio, TV programs) in the greater Toronto area. Features several new and established poets each month. One of its regular columns is "The Poet As..." in which poets paint a portrait of themselves engaged in a poetry-associated activity.

UK/0032-2202
POETRY WALES. [Poetry Wales]. **Added/Corp** Welsh Arts Council. Vol. 1 (Spring 1965)-. Periodical. English (Welsh). Four times a year (Mar., June, Sept., Dec.). £12.00 UK; £18.00 other. Seren Books/Poetry Wales, First Floor 2 Wyndham Street, Bridgend CF31 1EF Wales. **Tel** 011 44 656 767834, FAX 011 44 0656 767834. **ED** Richard Poole. **LC** PR8954.5; .P64. Index available. cum. index. **Bk Rev**, (Qty: 40). **Circ:** 1,000. Documents available from The Genuine Article.
Desc: Poetry and articles about poetry, mostly with a Welsh interest. Also reviews of new poetry, critical books and biographies of poets.

Ind/Abst Abstr. Engl. Stud.; Arts Humanit. Citation Index [Full Cov.]; Curr. Contents Arts Humanit.; Res. Alert [Full Cov.].

US/0891-6136
POETS & WRITERS. [Poets writ.]. **Added/Corp** Poets & Writers, Inc. **VFOAT** Poets and Writers; Poets & Writers Magazine; Poets and Writers Magazine. Vol. 15, Issue 1 (Jan./Feb. 1987)-. Periodical. English. Six times a year. $18.00 US, $29.70 Mexico, $40.00 Europe & North Africa, 46.70 others (individuals); $25.00 US, $36.70 Mexico, $47.00 Europe & North Africa, $53.70 others (institutions). Poets & Writers Inc., 72 Spring Street, New York NY 10012. **Tel** (212)226-3586. **ED** Daryln Brewer. **LC** PS129; .C55. **DD** 810/.9. **Ad Acc. Circ:** 12,000 (ctrl). available on microfilm and microfiche from University Microfilms International (UMI). ***Continues** Coda, 0091-5645.*
Desc: Includes interviews with poets and fiction writers as well as essays written by well-known authors, with news about the publishing community and coverage of political issues of interest to writers.
Ind/Abst Child. Lit. Abstr. (19??-).

US
POETS AT WORK. English. $16.00. Jesse Poet Publications, RD 1, Portersville PA 16051. **Ad Acc. Circ:** 320.
Desc: Contains poetry submitted by subscribers who write a 20 line minimum in good taste.

●US/1065-836X
POET'S GUILD. [Poet's guild]. Vol. 1 Issue 1 (1992)-. Periodical. English. qt. $3.00 (non-members). Sutton Publications, Box 9772, Chattanooga TN 37412-0772. **DD** 808.

US
POET'S HANDBOOK. (1989)-. Periodical. English. an. $9.95. Fine Arts Press, 1311-A Broadway, PO Box 3491, Knoxville TN 37927. **ED** Lincoln B Young. **Circ:** 2,000.
Desc: Lists the complete addresses of over 1500 publishers of poetry, and types of poems they are seeking, and the amount of payment offered by each.

US/0883-5470
POET'S MARKET. [Poet's mark.]. (1986)-. English. an (published Sept. of the prior year). $19.95. Writer's Digest Books, 1507 Dana Avenue, Cincinnati OH 45207. **Tel** (513)531-2222, (800)289-0963, FAX (513)531-4744. **ED** Judson Jerome. **LC** PN1059.M3; P59. **DD** 070.5/025/73.
Desc: Contains 1,700 listings that provide detailed analysis of the markets. Interviews with successful poets offer advice and inspiration to poets.

US/0146-3136
POETS ON. Vol. 1 (Winter 1977)-. Periodical. English. sa (Jan., June). $8.00 (one year), $15.00 (two year) US; $9.00 (one year), $17.00 (two year) Canada; $10.00 (one year), $19.00 (two year) other. Poets On, 29 Loring Avenue, Mill Valley CA 94941. **Tel** (415)381-2824. **ED** Ruth Daigon. **Pr Rev. Circ:** 500 (ctrl).
Desc: A theme-oriented poetry magazine interested in well-crafted poetry that explores basic human concerns.
Ind/Abst Am. Humanit. Index.

UK
POET'S VOICE (BATH, SOMERSETSHIRE), THE. (THE POET'S VOICE.). (19??)-. Periodical. English. Three times a year. £12.26. The Poet's Voice, 12 Dartmouth Avenue, Bath England. **ED** Fred Beake.
Desc: Presents an almost uniquely broad picture of English poetry as it is today. Includes a substantial retrospective on lesser known poets of merit.

UN/0130-8483
POEZIJA (KIIV). (POEZIIA.). [Poezija]. (1968)-. Periodical. Ukrainian. sa. **LC** PG3917; .P6. **DD** 891.7/91/008.
Ind/Abst MLA Int. Bibl. Books Artic. Mod. Lang. Lit.

PL/0032-2237
POEZJA. ***Ceased.*** [Poezja]. (1965)-?. Periodical. Polish. mo. **(Subscription address:** ARS Polona, PO Box 1001, 00068 Warsaw Poland.**)** **LC** PN1010; .P78. **DD** 891.8/51/008.
Ind/Abst MLA Int. Bibl. Books Artic. Mod. Lang. Lit.

FR/0032-2369
POINTS ET CONTREPOINTS. New Series, No. 13 April 1951-. Periodical. French. 45.00. Editions de la Revue Moderne, 14 rue de l'Armorique, Paris 15E France. ***Continues** Points et Contrepoints-Ronsard.*
Ind/Abst Romant. Move.

US/0738-6400
POLIS (BOSTON, MASS.). (POLIS.). [Polis]. (1979)-. English. an. $3.00 Single Issue. Mark Katzman, PO Box 938, Provincetown MA 02657. **DD** 810.

US/0163-3872
PORCH. V. 1- Spring 1977-. Periodical. English. qt. $7.00. Porch Publications, 5310 E, Taylor J Cervantes, Phoenix AZ 85008. **LC** PS615; .P66. **DD** 811/.008.

FR/0152-0032
POSIE I.E. POESIE. No. 1 (1977)-. Periodical. French (English, Spanish, German and Italian). qt. 210.58F France; 235.00F other. Edition Belin, 8 rue Ferou, 75278 Paris Cedex 06 France. **Tel** 011 33 1 46342142, FAX (1)43 25 18 29. **ED** Maree Claude Brossollet and Michel Deguy. **LC** PN1010; .P497. **DD** 808.81. **Circ:** 1,000.
Ind/Abst MLA Int. Bibl. Books Artic. Mod. Lang. Lit.

US/0091-7230
POT-HOOKS & HANGERS. Vol. 1 (Summer 1973)-. Periodical. English. sa. $2.50. Pot-Hooks & Hangers, PO Box 718, Old Chelsea Station, New York NY 10014. **LC** PS580; .P67. **DD** 811/.5/405.

US/0196-5913
PUDDING MAGAZINE. **Added/Corp** National Association for Poetry Therapy (U.S.). Ohio Valley Region Training Center and Library. **VFOAT** Pudding. (1980)-. Periodical. English. Three times a year. $15.75 US; $25.75 other. Pudding Magazine, 60 North Main Street, Johnstown OH 43031. **Tel** (614)967-6060. **ED** Jennifer Welch Bosueld, Doug Swisher and Steve Abbott. **Bk Rev. Circ:** 2,000. ***Continues** Pudding.*
Desc: Poetry and articles on applied poetry and other arts in the human services. Features better known small press poets and psychological poetry. Sponsors readings, chapbooks, competitions, tutorials, anthologies, workshops, seminars, criticism.

US
QUARTERLY REVIEW OF LITERATURE. POETRY SERIES. **VFOAT** QRL Contemporary Poetry Series; Poetry Series; Contemporary Poetry Series. Vol. 30 (1991)-. English. Quarterly Review of Literature, 26 Haslet Avenue, Princeton NJ 08540. **Tel** (609)921-6976. **LC** AP2; .Q29. ***Continues** Poetry Series (Princeton, N.J.), 0748-0865.*
Ind/Abst Am. Humanit. Index (199?-); Humanit. Source (Jan. 1988-).

US/0148-0162
RACCOON. ***Ceased.*** No. 1 (May 1977)-(19??). Periodical. English. ir. Ion Books/Raccoon, PO Box 111327, Memphis TN 38111-1327. **Tel** (901)323-8858. **ED** David Spicer. **LC** PS615; .R3. **DD** 811/.5/408. **[CCC]. Bk Rev. Ad Acc. Circ:** 1,000 (ctrl).
Desc: Includes contemporary poetry and criticism.
Ind/Abst Am. Humanit. Index (-199?).

US/0147-0396
REBIS CHAPBOOK SERIES, THE. No. 1-. Monographic series. English. Price varies per volume. Allegany Mountain Press, 111 North 10th Street, Olean NY 14760. **Tel** (716)372-0935.

SP
REDUCCIONS. 1 (Jan. 1977)-. Catalan. ir. 1.200. Llibreria la Tralla, C Riera 7, Vic Spain. **LC** PN1010; .R4. **DD** 849/.91/008.

CN/0225-2104
REENBOU. [Reenbou]. No. 1- Dec. 1979-. Periodical. English (Italian, German, Spanish, Portuguese and French). $3.00 each number, $11.00 for 4 issues. B Mogridge, Reenbou, c/o German Department, Carleton University, Ottawa Ontario K2S 5B6 Canada. **DD** 808.81/04/05.

BL
REVISTA DE POESIA E CRITICA. Yearly V. 1- No. 1- ; July 1976-. Periodical. Portuguese. CLS 415 - Bloco B - Lote 2 Sobreloja, Brasilia Brazil. **LC** PQ9561; .R48.

UK/0268-5981
RIALTO, THE. No. 1 (Autumn 1984)-. Periodical. English. Three times a year (Dec/Jan., Apr., Aug.). £8.00 UK; £11.00 Europe; £15.00 US; £15.50 other. The Rialto, 32 Grosvenor Road, Norwich NR2 2PZ England. **Circ:** 2,000.
Desc: A first-rate literary magazine, very lively, with a keen eye open for fresh contributors, and willing to go out to find them.

US/0148-3730
ROAD/HOUSE. No. 1- Fall 1975-. Periodical. English. sa. $1.50. Road/House Press, 900 West 9th Street, Belvidere IL 61008. **Tel** (815)544-9581. **ED** Todd Moore. **LC** PS580; .R6. **DD** 811/.5. **Circ:** 100 (ctrl).
Desc: Features one poet's work in each issue.

US/0892-6956
ROHWEDDER. [RohWedder]. **VFOAT** Roh Wedder. (1986)-. Periodical. English (German). Twice a year. $10.00 (individuals), $15.00 (institutions) two years. Rough Weather Press, PO Box 29490, Los Angeles CA 90029. **DD** 700.
Ind/Abst Am. Humanit. Index; Index Am. Period. Verse.

US/0163-0687
ROOF. V. 1- Summer 1976-. Periodical. English. qt. $16.00. Segue Press, 300 Bowery, New York NY 10012. **LC** PS580; .R66.

SP
ROSA CUBICA. No. 1 (Winter 1988)-. Periodical. Spanish. qt.

US/0483-4240
ROUND QUARTER SERIES OF NEW POETS & ARTISTS. **VFOAT** Round Quarter Series of New Poets and Artists; Intro-Round Quarter Series; Intro Round Quarter Series. No. 1 (1952)-. Monographic series. English. Price varies per volume. **LC** WMLC 90/0963.

GW/0933-9094
RUCKERT ZU EHREN : EINE SCHRIFTENREIHE DER RUCKERT-GESELLSCHAFT. Vol. 1 (1988)-. Monographic series. German. Price varies per volume. Otto Harrassowitz Verlag, Taunusstrasse 14, Postfach 2929, D-65019 Wiesbaden Germany. **Tel** 011 49 611 5300, FAX 530570, telex 4186 135 OH D.

US/0147-1163
RUFUS, THE. [Rufus]. **VFOAT** RUFUS Poetry. **VAT** The Raise Us Fools Up Serenely. V. 1- Fall 1972-. Periodical. English. Three times a year. $5.00. Gyst Publications, Box 16, Pasadena CA 91102. **LC** PS580; .R84. **DD** 811/.5/05.

US/0735-4665
SAGETRIEB. [Sagetrieb]. Vol. 1, No. 1 (Spring 1982)-. Periodical. English. Three times a year. $18.00 (individual), $35.00 (library) US; $23.00 (individual), $40.00 (library) other. National Poetry Foundation, University of Maine, 305 Neville Hall, Orono ME 04469. **Tel** (207)581-3814. **ED** Burton Hatlen. **LC** PS301; .S24. **DD** 811/.5/09. Index available. **Bk Rev. Ad Acc. Circ:** 334.
Desc: A journal devoted to poets in the imagist/objectivist tradition.
Ind/Abst Abstr. Engl. Stud.; Am. Humanit. Index; MLA Int. Bibl. Books Artic. Mod. Lang. Lit.

JA
SAITO MOKICHI TSUIBO KASHU. No. 1-. Japanese. Kaminoyama Shiritsu Saito Mokichi Kinenkan, Aza Benten 1421, Kitamachi, Kaminoyama-shi 999-31 Japan. **LC** PL758.A1; S25.

US/0196-2884
SAN FERNANDO POETRY JOURNAL. (Spring 1979)-. Periodical. English. qt. $10.00. Kent Publications, 18301 Halsted Street, Northridge CA 91324.
Ind/Abst Am. Humanit. Index.

US
SAND CASTLES. Vol. 1 (June 1969)-. Periodical. English. qt.

US/0271-2342
SARCOPHAGUS. Periodical. English. sa. $5.00. Ashford Press RRI, Box 128, Ashford CT 06278.

CN/0080-6560
SASKATCHEWAN POETRY BOOK. **Added/Corp** Saskatchewan Poetry Society. (1937)-. Periodical. English. Saskatchewan Poetry Society, 3104 College Avenue, Regina Saskatchewan S4T 1V7 Canada. **Tel** 522-6321. **DD** C811/.5/05. **Bk Rev. Circ:** 600. ***Supersedes** Saskatchewan Poetry Year Book.*
Desc: Contains short biographic notes on the poets, celebrating our 50th year as a society.

GW
SCHILLERS WERKE. (19??)-. German. ir. Price varies per volume. Verlag Hermann Boehlaus Nachfolger, Postfach 260, D 99403 Weimar Germany. **Tel** 011 49 3643 2071, . **(Subscription address:** BDK Buecherdienst GmbH, Postfach 900120, D 51111 Cologne Germany**)**

US/0092-9425
SCHIST (WILLIMANTIC). (SCHIST.). No. 1- Fall 1973-. English. $5.00 for 4 issues. PO Box 257, Willimantic CT 06226. **LC** PS615; .S26. **DD** 811/.5/408.

AT/0313-685x
SCOPP : SATURDAY CENTRE OF PROSE & POETRY. **Main/Corp** Saturday Centre. **VFOAT** Saturday Centre of Prose & Poetry. **VAT** Saturday Centre of Prose and Poetry. (19??)-. Periodical. English. Three times a year. 7.50Aus$. Saturday Centre, PO Box 140, Cammeray New South Wales 2062 Australia. ***Supersedes** Saturday Club Book of Poetry.*

US/0095-1730
SEEMS. No. 1 (Autumn 1971)-. English. ir. $16.00 (4 issues). Seems, c/o Karl Elder, Lakeland College, Sheboygan WI 53081. **Tel** (414)565-1276. **ED** Karl Elder. **LC** PS501; .S43. **DD** 810/.8/005. **Circ:** 350-750.
Desc: Contemporary poetry and fiction.
Ind/Abst Am. Humanit. Index (-199?).

IT
SEGRETISSIMO. (19??)-. Italian. L124800 Italy; L156000 others. Arnoldo Mondadori Editore, UFF Cont Abbonamenti, 20090 Segrate MI Italy. **Tel** 011 39 2 75422015, telex 320457 MONDMI I.

US/0883-9565
SEMI-ANNUAL BOOKLIST. [Semi-annu. booklist]. **VFOAT** Semiannual Booklist. (Fall 1984)-. English. sa. Academy of American Poets, 584 Broadway,

Literature —Poetry

Suite 1208, New York NY 10012. **Tel** (212)274-0343. **ED** David Austin. **LC** Z1231.P7; A32A; PS325. **DD** 016.811/008. **Circ:** 2,800 (ctrl). **Continues** Academy of American Poets. Semi-Annual Checklist of Poetry, 0147-1414.
 Desc: Comprehensive listing of newly published books of poetry and other books by and about poets.

FR/0559-4871
SEQUENCES. (SEQUENCES; REVUE FRANCAISE DE POESIE CONTEMPORAINE.). (1958)-. French. an. 236.97F France; 250.00F other. Jean Grassin Editeur, 50 rue Rodier, 75009 Paris France. **ED** Jean Grassin. **LC** PQ1160; .S46. **DD** 841/.008. **Bk Rev. Ad Acc. Circ:** 500.
 Desc: Cloth-bound for the library collection of French contemporary poetry.

RU
SERDTSE ROSII. VFOAT Poeticheskii Sbornik Serdtse Rossii. Vol. 1 (1978)-. Russian. **(Subscription address:** Victor Kamkin, 4956 Boiling Brook Parkway, Rockville MD 20852.**)**

US
SERENDIPTY / NEWSLETTER FOR THE SOUTH DAKOTA STATE POETRY SOCIETY. Main/Corp South Dakota State Poetry Society. **VFOAT** Serendipty Newsletter. (19??)-. Newsletter. English. qt. $15.00 US; $20.00 other. South Dakota State Poetry Society Inc, Verlyss Jacobson, Box 398, Lennox SD 57039-0398. **Tel** (605)647-2447. **ED** Barbara Stevens. Index available. cum. index. **Circ:** 250.
 Desc: Poetry and art mostly of South Dakotans or members of South Dakota State Poetry Society.

US/0146-695X
SEVEN STARS. VFOAT Seven Stars Poetry. Periodical. English. mo. Realities Library, 1976 Waverly Avenue, San Jose CA 95122.

US/0037-5969
SEVENTIES, THE. No. 1 (Spring 1972)-. Periodical. English. $3.00 four issues. Robert BLY, 308 First Street, Moose Lake MN 55767. **Tel** (612)339-1952. **LC** PN1010; .F52. **DD** 808/.81/04. available on microfilm from University Microfilms International (UMI).
 Supersedes Sixties, 0583-4570.

●US/1061-3919
SHANGRI-LA (WASHINGTON, D.C.). (SHANGRI-LA). [Shangri-la]. Vol. 1, No. 1 (Jan. 1992)-. Periodical. English. mo $50.00. Shangri-La Press, 4306 17th Street NW, Washington DC 20011. **DD** 811.

CN/1193-8315
SHARED VOICES. [Shar. voices]. **Added/Corp** Canadian Authors Association. Niagara Branch. Vol. 7 (1991)-. English. Canadian Authors Association, 275 Slater Street, Suite 500, Ottawa, Ontario K1P 5H9 Canada. **Tel** (613)233-2846, **FAX** (613)235-8237. **DD** C811/.5408/0971338. **Continues** There Is., 0823-3276.

US/0146-3985
SHELL (WABAN). (SHELL.). Fall/Winter 1976-. Periodical. English. qt. 362 Waban Avenue, Waban MA 02168. **LC** PS580; .S44. **DD** 811/.5/408.

CH
SHIH HSUAN (TAIPEI, TAIWAN). (SHIH HSUAN / CHANG MO PIEN.). **VFOAT** Nieu tu Shih Hsuan. 1982-. Chinese. an. $130.00. Erh Ya Chu Pan She, PO Box 30-190, Taipei Taiwan. **LC** PL3031.T32; S519. **DD** 895.1/15/080951249.

CC/0583-0230
SHIH KAN. Added/Corp Chung-kuo Tso Chia Hsieh Hui. **VFOAT** Shikan. (Jan. 1957)-. Periodical. Chinese. mo. $17.80. **(Subscription address:** China International Book Trading Corporation, PO Box 399, Library Service Department, Beijing 100044 People's Republic of China.**) LC** PL2543; .S5364. **DD** 895.1/15/09.
 Desc: Contains Chinese poetry.

JA
SHIKAI. (June 1960)-. Periodical. Japanese. mo. ¥200. 1-106 Nijigaoka Nishi Jutaku Chikusa-ku, Nagoya Japan. **LC** PN1010; .S555.

US/0894-606X
SHIRIM. [Shirim]. Vol. 1 (Fall 1982)-. Periodical. English. Twice a year (June & Dec.). $7.00. Shirim, 4611 Vesper Avenue, Sherman Oaks CA 91403. **Tel** (818)906-7600. **ED** Marc Dworkin. **DD** 831. **Circ:** 700.
 Desc: Publishes poetry that reflects various life styles, attitudes and emotions of Jewish living. This journal has published some of America's finest poets.
 Ind/Abst Index Jew. Period.

US/0360-912X
SHOCKS. No. 1- 1972-. English. $10.00. Momo's Press, Box 14061, San Francisco CA 94114. **LC** PS285.S3; S54. **DD** 811/.5/405.

SP
SI (MADRID, SPAIN). (SI.). **VFOAT** Si (Boletin Bello Espanol) del Andaluz Universal; Si del Andaluz Universal. (July 1925)-. Spanish. Si, Entonces, Apartado de Correos 761, 43080 Tarragona Spain.

YU
SIGNAL. Began with Sept./Nov. 1970 issue. Multiple languages (Serbo-Croatian (Roman) and English). **LC** PN6110.C77; S5.

KO
SIMSANG. VFOAT Image. V. 1- Dec. 1973-. Periodical. Korean. 2500. 13-12 Kwanchol-dong Chongno-ku. **LC** PN1010; .S56.

US/1044-8934
SINGLE HOUND. (THE SINGLE HOUND : THE POETRY AND IMAGE OF EMILY DICKINSON.). [Single hound]. Vol. 1, No. 1 (May 1989)-. Periodical. Twice a year (May, Nov.). $20.00 US; $23.00 other. Single Hound, Box 598, Newmarket NH 03857. **Tel** (603)659-2685. **ED** Andrew P. Leibs. **DD** 811. **Bk Rev. Pr Rev. Circ:** 100. available on diskette (3.5 inch).
 Desc: Literary journal dealing with the poetry and life of Emily Dickinson.
 Ind/Abst MLA Int. Bibl. Books Artic. Mod. Lang. Lit.

CN/0700-4834
SKY LETTERS. Vol. 1 (1977)-. Periodical. English. ir. $3.10. Sunyata Press, Box 278, Brentwood Bay British Columbia V0S 1A0 Canada. **DD** C811/.5/408.

US/0749-0771
SLIPSTREAM (NIAGARA FALLS, N.Y.). (SLIPSTREAM.). (1981)-. English. Twice a year. $7.50. Slipstream Publications, Box 2071 New Market Station, Niagara Falls NY 14301. **Tel** (716)282-2616. **LC** Discard.
 Ind/Abst Index Am. Period. Verse.

UK/0143-1412
SLOW DANCER. 1 (Late 1977)-. Periodical. English. $2.00 (4 issues). Slow Dancer Press, 58 Rutland Road, West Bridgford, Nottingham NG2 5DG England. **Tel** 0602-821518. **ED** John Harvey. **LC** PR1170; .S58. **DD** 821/.008. **Circ:** 500.
 Desc: An international magazine of English language poetry.

US/0161-5270
SMALL FARM, THE. No. 1- Mar. 1975-. Periodical. English. sa. $4.00. PO Box 563, Jefferson City TN 37760. **ED** J D Marison. **LC** PS580; .S55. **DD** 811/.5/408.

US/1054-1632
SNAIL'S PACE REVIEW : A BIANNUAL LITTLE MAGAZINE OF CONTEMPRARY POETRY, THE. [Snail's pace rev.]. Vol. 1, No. 1 (Spring 1991)-. Periodical. English. sa. $10.00 (institutions). Snail's Pace Review, RR #2, Box 363, Brownell Road, Cambridge NY 12816. **DD** 811.
 Ind/Abst Am. Humanit. Index (199?-).

US/0272-6459
SO & SO. VFOAT So and So. (19??)-. Periodical. English. sa. So & So Magazine, 1730 Carleton, Berkeley CA 94703. **Tel** (510)548-6116.

US
SOCIETY OF CHRISTIAN POETS DIRECTORY. Added/Corp Society of Christian Poets (U.S.). **VFOAT** Directory. (19??)-. Directory. English. **LC** PS5; .S6517. **DD** 811/.006/073.

CN/0822-4226
SONG (TORONTO). (SONG : NGUYET-SAN THONG-TIN VAN-NGHE.). [Song]. V. 1 (April 6, 1982)-. Periodical. Vietnamese. mo. 34.00Can$. Song, PO Box 317 Station H, Toronto Ontario M4C 5J2 Canada. **Tel** (416)421-4073. **ED** Chuong Tang Nguyen. **LC** AP95.V55; S65. **DD** 059/.95922. **Bk Rev. Ad Acc. Circ:** 4,000 (ctrl).
 Desc: News, stories, and poems.

US/0887-2074
SOUTH COAST POETRY JOURNAL. (SOUTH COAST POETRY JOURNAL : SCPJ.). [South coast poet.j.]. **Added/Corp** California State University, Fullerton. English Dept. **VFOAT** SCPJ. No. 1 (Spring 1986)-. Periodical. English (French and Spanish). Twice a year (Jan. & July). $10.00 (individuals), $12.00 (institutions). California State University / Fullerton Foundation, English Department, Fullerton CA 92634. **Tel** (714)773-3163. **ED** John J. Brugaletta. **DD** 811. **Ad Acc, Adv Mgr:** Jennifer Boyle, **Tel** (909)985-2959. **Circ:** 450.
 Desc: Previously unpublished poetry. Includes poetry published with poems in their original languages, and original art.
 Ind/Abst Am. Humanit. Index (-199?).

US/0885-0720
SOUTH FLORIDA POETRY REVIEW. Suspended. [South Fla. poet. rev.]. Suspended (Fall 1992). Periodical. English. Three times a year. PO Box 7072, Hollywood FL 33081. **DD** 811.

AT/0038-3732
SOUTHERLY. See Literature.

US/0038-447X
SOUTHERN POETRY REVIEW. [South. poet. rev.]. **Added/Corp** University of North Carolina at Charlotte. English Dept. North Carolina State University. School of Liberal Arts. Vol. 5, No. 1 (Fall 1964)-. Periodical. English. Twice a year (Apr., Nov.). $8.00 US; $10.00 other. Southern Poetry Review, Department of English, University of North Carolina, Charlotte NC 28223. **Tel** (704)547-4225. **ED** Ken McLaurin (phone: (704)547-4336). **LC** PS580; .S66. **DD** 811/.008. **Bk Rev,** (Qty: 6-8). **Circ:** 1,000. available on microfilm and microfiche from University Microfilms International (UMI). **Continues** Impetus (De Land, Fla.).
 Desc: Not a regional magazine, though we function naturally as an outlet for new southern talent. We emphasize variety and intensity. No restrictions on style, content or length.
 Ind/Abst Am. Humanit. Index; Annu. Bibliogr. Engl. Lang. Lit.; Index Am. Period. Verse.

UK
SPANNER. See The Arts-Art.

II
SPARK. English. $1.00 each issue. SMT Sadhona Adhikari, 81 Raja Basanta Roy Road, Calcutta 70029 India. **LC** PK5461; .S67. **DD** 891/.4.

US/1062-0478
SPARROW. [Sparrow]. (July 1991)-. Periodical. English. Sparrow Press, 103 Waldon Street, West Lafayette IN 47906. **Tel** (317)743-1991. **DD** 811. **Continues** Sparrow Poverty Pamphlets, 0885-9477.

SZ/0038-7274
SPEKTRUM. Ceased. Ceased with Vol. 33, Iss.132 Dec. (1991). Periodical. German. qt. Knebel Sven, Radaktion Spektrum Napfgasse 4, CH-8001 Zurich Switzerland. **Tel** 01/8531474. **ED** Sven Knebel. **Bk Rev. Circ:** 1,000 (ctrl).
 Desc: International quarterly publication for poetry and original graphics.
 Ind/Abst Am. Hist. Life (1970-1973).

US/0038-7347
SPENSER NEWSLETTER. [Spenser newsl.]. **Added/Corp** University of Western Ontario. Dept. of English. Renaissance Society of America. University of Massachusetts (Amherst campus). Dept. of English Holyoke Community College. Vol. 1 (1970)-. Newsletter. English. Three times a year. $6.50 North America; $11.00 other. Kansas State University / English, 122 Denison Hall, English Department, Manhattan KS 66506. **Tel** (913)532-6011 ext 16, **FAX** (913)532-7004. **ED** Jerome S. Dees. Index available. **Bk Rev. Circ:** 520. available on microfilm and microfiche from University Microfilms International (UMI).
 Desc: Edmund Spenser's career, poetry, art and related aspects of Renaissance history and culture.
 Ind/Abst Annu. Bibliogr. Engl. Lang. Lit.; Index Book Rev. Humanit.

US/0195-9468
SPENSER STUDIES. [Spenser stud.]. (1980)-. English. an. $45.00. AMS Press Inc., 56 East 13th Street, New York NY 10003. **Tel** (212)777-4700, **FAX** (212)995-5413, telex 710 581 2302. **ED** Patrick Cullen and Thomas P. Roche Jr. **LC** PR2362; .A45. **DD** 821.3.
 Desc: Historical investigations and critical studies on Spenser and other poets of the English Renaissance.
 Ind/Abst Annu. Bibliogr. Engl. Lang. Lit.; MLA Int. Bibl. Books Artic. Mod. Lang. Lit.

US/0038-7584
SPIRIT (SOUTH ORANGE). (SPIRIT.). **Added/Corp** Seton Hall University, South Orange, New Jersey. Dept. of English. Catholic Poetry Society of America. Vol. 1 (Mar. 1934)-. Periodical. English. an. $4.00 US; $7.00 other. Seton Hall University, South Orange NJ 07079. **Tel** (201)761-9388. **ED** David Rogers (editor's phone: (201)761-9000). **LC** PS301; .S6. **DD** 811.505. **Bk Rev. Ad Acc. Circ:** 600. available on microfilm from University Microfilms International (UMI).
 Desc: Poetry and criticism of poetry.
 Ind/Abst Annu. Bibliogr. Engl. Lang. Lit.; Index Am. Period. Verse; MLA Int. Bibl. Books Artic. Mod. Lang. Lit.; Abr. Cathol. Period. Lit.; Cathol. Period. Lit. Index.

US
SPOON RIVER POETRY REVIEW. (19??)-. English. Twice a year (two double issues per year). $12.00 (individuals), $15.00 (institutions) US; $18.00 others. Spoon River Poetry Review, Illinois State University, Department of English, Normal IL 61761. **Tel** (309)438-7906. **ED** Dr. Lucia Getsi (phone:

Literature —Poetry

(309)438-7906). **Bk Rev**, (Qty: 4-6). **Ad Acc**, **Adv Mgr:** Jean Lee, **Tel** (309)438-3024. **Pr Rev** **Circ:** 850. **Continues** Spoon River Quarterly, 0738-8993.
Desc: National and international journal of poetry.

US/0735-6889
SPRING (NEW YORK, N.Y. : 1982). (SPRING : THE JOURNAL OF THE E. E. CUMMINGS SOCIETY.). [Spring]. Vol. 1, No. 1 (Apr. 1981)-. Periodical. English. qt. $10.00. D V Forrest Editor, 88 Central Park West IW, New York NY 10023. **Tel** (914)967-4193. **ED** David V Forrest. **LC** PS3505.U334; .Z86. **DD** 811/.52. cum. index. **Ad Acc**. **Circ:** 120 (ctrl).
Desc: The informal and authentic journal of articles news and related to the poetpainter/author/playwright, with accounts of meetings involving discussion, dining etc.

US/1063-8377
STANZA (MEDFORD, N.J.). (STANZA [COMPUTER FILE] : THE ONLINE POETRY MAGAZINE.). [Stanza]. Issue #1 (Nov. 1991)-. Periodical. English. mo. Free. Stanza, 22 Ligntning Drive, Medford NJ 08055-9752. **DD** 811.
Desc: Mode of access: GEnie.

US/0090-4171
STATIONS. (Fall 1972)-. Periodical. English. ir. $4.00 (three issues). Membrane Press, PO Box 5431, Milwaukee WI 53211. **LC** PS501; .S7. **DD** 811/.5/408.

US/0081-5462
STEPPENWOLF. No. 1- Winter 1965/66-. English. Three times a year. Steppenwolf, Box 31773, Omaha NE 68131. cum. index. available on microfilm from University Microfilms International (UMI).

RU
STIKHI, STIKHI. Vol. 1 (1967)-. Russian. Izdatelstvo Iskusstvo, Vorotnikovskii Pereulok 11, 103009 Moscow Russia. **LC** PG3233; .S76.

US
STONE, THE. V. 1- 1967-). Periodical. English. ir. Greenpeace, 125 Beach #44, Santa Cruz CA 95060.

US/0146-1397
STONE COUNTRY. **Ceased.** [Stone ctry.]. 1974-Ceased Nov. 1989. Periodical. English. sa. Stone Country, PO Box 132, Menemsha MA 02552. **Tel** (617)693-5832. **ED** Judith Neeld. **LC** PS580; .S78. **DD** 811/.008. Index available. **Bk Rev**. **Ad Acc**. **Circ:** 900. **Continues** Patterns.
Ind/Abst Am. Humanit. Index; Index Am. Period. Verse.

US/0095-4489
STUDIES IN BROWNING AND HIS CIRCLE. See Biographies.

US/1043-5751
STUDIES IN GERARD MANLEY HOPKINS. [Stud. Gerard Manley Hopkins]. (1990)-. Monographic series. English. ir. Price varies per volume. Peter Lang Publishing, 62 West 45th Street, 4th Floor, New York NY 10036. **Tel** (212)764-1471, (800)770-5264, telex 6973364 PLNY. **DD** 821.

LE
TAHAWWULAT. **VFOAT** Tahaoulat. No. 1 (Summer 1983)-. Periodical. Arabic. $60.00. Tahaoulat, BP 113/6043, Beyrouth Lebanon. **LC** PJ7541; .T34.

US/0749-5994
TALISMAN (COLUMBUS, OHIO). (TALISMAN.). [Talisman]. Vol. 1, No. 1 (Summer '84)-. Periodical. English. sa. $5.50. Box 1117, Hoboken NJ 07030. **DD** 811.
Ind/Abst Am. Humanit. Index; Index Am. Period. Verse.

US/0898-8684
TALISMAN (HOBOKEN, N.J.). (TALISMAN.). [Talisman]. No. 1 (Fall 1988)-. Periodical. English. Twice a year (Feb. and Aug.). $15.00 (institutions), $11.00 (individuals); add $2.00 postage other. Talisman, PO Box 1117, Hoboken NJ 07030. **Tel** (201)798-9093. **ED** Edward Foster. **LC** PS325; .T34. **DD** 811. **Bk Rev**, (Qty: 6). **Ad Acc**, **Adv Mgr Tel** same as publisher. **Circ:** 1,000.
Desc: Each issue centers on the poetry and poetics of a major contemporary poet and includes a selection of new work by other important contemporary writers.
Ind/Abst MLA Int. Bibl. Books Artic. Mod. Lang. Lit.

US
TAMARACK (AUSTERLITZ, N.Y.). **Suspended.** (TAMARACK : JOURNAL OF THE EDNA ST. VINCENT MILLAY SOCIETY.). **Added/Corp** Edna St. Vincent Millay Society. Periodical. English. an. Elizabeth Barnett, 8A Chauncy Street 5, Cambridge MA 02138. **Tel** (617)547-5970. **LC** PS3525.I495; Z84. **DD** 811/.52.
Ind/Abst MLA Int. Bibl. Books Artic. Mod. Lang. Lit.

CC
TANG TAI SHIH TZU. V. 1 (July 1981)-. Periodical. Chinese. qt. RMBY0.32. Hua Cheng Chu Pan She, Hsin Hua Shu Tien, Kuang-Chou Kuang-Tung, People's Republic of China. **LC** PL2543; .T34. **DD** 895.1/15/008.

JA
TANKA GENDAI. Vol. 1 (1977)-. Periodical. Japanese. mo. ¥480. Tanka Shimbun Sha, 43-9 Koenji Minami 4, Suginami-ku 166 Tokyo Japan. **LC** PL758.A1; 136.

US
TANSY (LAWRENCE, KAN. : 1976). (TANSY.). (1976)-. Periodical. English. sa. price varies per volume. John Morits, Rt 4 Box 279, Lawrence KS 66044.

US
TAPJOE. **VFOAT** Talapus Anthology. English. Twice a year. $6.00 (one year), $10.00 (two year). TAPJOE, PO Box 104, Grangeville ID 83530-0104. **ED** Noah Farnsworth, Lisa Therrell, Steve McConnell, Rich Haydon, and Rik Smith. **Circ:** 200.
Desc: Poetry with a slant towards nature, the environment, and social issues.

US/0740-9141
TAR RIVER POETRY. [Tar River Poet.]. **Added/Corp** East Carolina University. Vol. 18, No. 1 (Fall 1978)-. Periodical. English. Twice a year (May, November). $5.00 per issue; $10.00 one year; $18.00 two year. East Carolina University Poetry, Department of English, General Classroom Building, Greenville NC 27834. **Tel** (919)757-6041. **ED** Peter Makuck, (phone: (919)757-6580). **LC** PS558.N8; T37. **DD** 811.008/005. Index available (with 10th annual issue). cum. index. **Bk Rev**, (Qty: 6). **Circ:** 1,000. **Continues** East Carolina University Poetry Forum Series.
Desc: Publishes original poetry, reviews of contemporary books of poetry, interviews with poets, essays, etc.
Ind/Abst Am. Humanit. Index (-199?); Index Am. Period. Verse.

IT/0394-3518
TAVERNA DE AUERBACH, LA. Vol. 1, No. 1 (Autumn 1987)-. Periodical. Italian. Three times a year. L35.000 Italy; $35.00 other. Taverna di Auerbach, Via Colleprata 374, 03011 Alatri Italy 450047. **Tel** 0775 440691, **FAX** 0775 450096. **ED** Giovanni Fontana. **Bk Rev**. **Ad Acc**. **Circ:** 1,000.

UK
TENNYSON SOCIETY MONOGRAPHS. See Literature.

UK
TENTH DECADE. (1990)-. Periodical. English. tq. Ninth Decade, 12 Stevenage Road, London SW6 6ES England. **Continues** Ninth Decade, 0264-6773.

US/0094-162X
TENTH MUSE, THE. English. sa. The Tenth Muse, 2942 West 5th Street, Brooklyn NY 11224. **LC** PS580; .T45. **DD** 811/.5/408.

●US/1061-9887
TEXTURE MINIATURE. [Texture miniat.]. #1-(1992)-. Periodical. English. Three times a year. $3.00 (single issue). Texture Press, 3760 Cedar Ridge Drive, Norman OK 73072. **DD** 811.

UK/0307-9562
THAMES POETRY. **Suspended.** Vol. 1, No. 1 (Winter 1976)-?. Periodical. English. sa. Thames Poetry, 160 High Road, Wealdstone Harrow, Middlesex HA3 7AX England.

CN/0823-3276
THERE IS. **Title Change.** [There is]. **Added/Corp** Canadian Authors Association. Niagara Branch. (1983)-(198?). English. an. Canadian Authors Association, 275 Slater Street, Suite 500, Ottawa, Ontario K1P 5H9 Canada. **Tel** (613)233-2846, FAX (613)235-8237. **DD** C811/.080971338. **Ad Acc**. **Circ:** 250. **Continued by** Shared Voices, 1193-8315.
Desc: Each year submissions of poetry from the Niagara region are invited and selections made by a judge for inclusion in the anthology.

US/0198-800X
THIRD EYE. (19??)-. Periodical. English. Three times a year. $2.50. The Third Eye, 189 Kewin Drive, Kenmore NY 14223. **Tel** (716)832-4097.

US/0362-4846
THREE RIVERS POETRY JOURNAL. **Ceased.** [Three rivers poetry j.]. (1973)-(1993). Monographic series. English. sa. Three River Press, PO Box 21, Carnegie Mellon University, Pittsburgh PA 15213. **LC** PS580; .T54. **DD** 811/.5/405. available on microfilm from University Microfilms International (UMI).
Ind/Abst Index Am. Period. Verse.

CN/0823-6399
TICKLEACE. [TickleAce]. (1977)-. Periodical. English. sa. $7.00 Canada; $10.00 other. Tickleace, PO Box 4276, St John's Newfoundland A1C 6C4 Canada. **ED** Carmelita McGrath and Bruce Porter. **DD** C811/.54/0809718. **Circ:** 400.
Desc: Exists primarily, but not exclusively, to promote the work of poets and fiction writers in the province of Newfoundland and Labrador. Special encouragement is given to new writers, but quality submissions are welcomed from anyone, anywhere.

US
TINDERBOX. 197 -. Periodical. English. qt. 334 Molasses Lane, Mt Pleasant SC 29464. **ED** A R Cabaniss.

JA
TOCHI SHISHU. **Added/Corp** Hiroshima Shijinkai. (19??)-. Periodical. Japanese. ¥1000. Hiroshima Shijinkai, 5633 Kaita Kaita-cho Aki-gun Hiroshima-ken, Kaito-cho Japan. **LC** PL886.H52; T6.

KO
TONGGANG SI / TONGGANG SI TONGINHOE. 1-. Periodical. Korean. W2,500. Tonggang Si Tonginhoe, 34 Hap-dong Sodaemun-ku, Seoul Korea. **LC** PL974.A1; T655.

US
TOP STORIES. **Suspended.** No. 1-?. Periodical. English. Top Stories, 228 7th Avenue, New York NY 10011. **Tel** (212)989-3869.

CN/0495-9701
TOWER (HAMILTON). (TOWER POETRY MAGAZINE.). **Added/Corp** Tower Poetry Society. (1952)-. Periodical. English. Twice a year (Summer & Winter). 8.00Can$ US & Canada; 9.50Can$ others. Tower Poetry Society, 18 Ogilvie Street, Dundas Publishing Library, Dundas ONT Canada L9H 2S@. **Tel** (416)545-5274. **ED** Joanna Lawson. **DD** C811/.5/408. **Circ:** 200.
Desc: Poetry from contributors worldwide.

SP
TREBEDE : REVISTA DE POESIA. Spanish (English). Three times a year. 4000ptas Spain; 8000ptas North America; 7000ptas other. Ediciones Alamo Verde, Entre los Rios 10, 24760- Castrocalbon Leon Espana. (**Subscription address:** Revista TREBEDE, Entre los Rios, 10, 24760-Castrocalbon) **ED** Emilio Garcia Ranz. **Bk Rev**. **Ad Acc**. **Circ:** 3,600 (ctrl).
Desc: Contains poetry, literature and cultural information.

UK
TREBLE POETS. (1974)-. Monographic series. English. ir. Price varies per volume. Chatto and Windus, 42 William IV Street, London WE2N 4DF England. **LC** UNC. **DD** 821/.914/08.

●US/1064-2625
UNIVERSAL ACADEMIA. [Univers. acad.]. **Added/Corp** Universal Academy (Washington, D.C.). Vol. 1, No. 1 (May 20, 1992)-. Periodical. English. wk. $200.00. Universal Acadamia, 223 G Street SW, Washington DC 20024. **DD** 811.

US/0049-5557
UNMUZZLED OX. [Unmuzz. ox]. Vol. 1 (Nov. 1971)-. Periodical. English. Four times a year. $20.00 US; $40.00 other. Unmuzzled Ox Nss, 105 Hudson Street, Room 311, New York NY 10013. **Tel** (212)226-7170. **ED** Michael Andre. **LC** PS580; .U54. **DD** 811/.5/405. **Bk Rev**. **Ad Acc**. **Circ:** 5,000.
Desc: Magazine of poetry, art, and politics.
Ind/Abst Am. Humanit. Index; Index Am. Period. Verse.

CN/0225-3577
UP FRONT. [Up front]. V. 1- Sept./Oct. 1979-. Periodical. English. $1.00 each number. Up Front, 90 Cherry Street, Box 519, Johnstown PA 15907.

IT
URANIA. (19??)-. Italian. L104000 Italy; L135200 others. Arnoldo Mondadori Editore, UFF Cont Abbonamenti, 20090 Segrate MI Italy. **Tel** 011 39 2 75422015, telex 320457 MONDMI I.

US/0146-8510
UROBOROS. (19??-). Periodical. English. ir. $4.00. Allegany Mountain Press, 111 North 10th Street, Olean NY 14760. **Tel** (716)372-0935.

FR/0153-9620
VAGABONDAGES. Began with June 1978 issue. Periodical. French. ir (ten no. a year). 165F. Atelier Marcel Jullian, 3 rue Seguier, 75006 Paris France. **LC** PQ1160; .V34. **DD** 841/.008.

Literature —Poetry

CN/0228-782X
VANCOUVER POETRY CENTRE NEWSLETTER. [Vanc. Poetry Cent. newsl.]. **VAT** From the West: Vancouver Poetry Centre Newsletter. Newsletter. English. Vancouver Poetry Centre, 3504 Bella Vista Street, Vancouver British Columbia V5N 3W9 Canada. **DD** C810/.9/0054.

US/0268-3830
VERSE (OXFORD, OXFORDSHIRE). (VERSE.). Issue 1-Issue 6 (1984)-Vol. 3, No. 3 (Nov. 1986)-. Periodical. English. tq (Jan., May, Oct.). $21.00 institutions, $15.00 individuals. William and Mary, English Department, PO Box 8795, Williamsburg VA 23187-8795. **Tel** (804)221-3922. **ED** Henry Hart.
Desc: An international poetry journal that has published special issues on Elizabeth Bishop, James Merrill, John Ashbery, Donald Justice, Amy Clampitt, New Formalism, Language Poets, Irish Poetry. The magazine prints reviews and essays on contemporary poets. Seamus Heaney, Galway Kinnell, Donald Hall, and other well-known poets appear in Verse.
Ind/Abst Am. Humanit. Index; Index Am. Period. Verse.

US
VISIONS-INTERNATIONAL. See Literature.

US/0042-8280
VOICES INTERNATIONAL. Added/Corp South and West, Inc. Vol.1, (Spring 1966)-. Periodical. English. Four times a year (Feb., Apr., July, Oct.). $10.00 (one year), $18.00 (two year), US; $15.00 (one year), $25.00 (two year), other. Clovita Rice-Editor, 1115 Gillette Drive, Little Rock AR 72207. **Tel** (501)225-0166. **ED** Clovita Rice. **Circ:** 300 (ctrl).
Desc: This magazine looks for exceptional quality poetry that is memorable due to the idea and presentation (poems with strong imagery, new ideas, significant statements).

IS
VOICES ISRAEL. Vol. 6 (Aug. 1978)-. Periodical. English. an. $15.00. Voices Israel, Box 5780, 46101 Herzlia Israel. **Tel** 052-552411. **LC** PR9510.45; .V64. **DD** 821/.008/05694. **Ad Acc. Circ:** 400. available on diskette. **Continues** Voices (Haifa, Israel).
Desc: A poetry anthology in English published in Israel taking in poetry from all over the world.

US/0095-5388
VOYAGES TO THE INLAND SEA. 1- 1971-. English. ir. $8.00 regular edition, $15.00 signed edition. University of Wisconsin / Murphy Library, Center of Contemporary Poetry, Lacrosse WI 54601. **Tel** (608)785-8511. **ED** John Judson. **LC** PS301; .V65. **DD** 811/.5/408.
Desc: Features two or three poets with midwestern connections, with poems, essays, and bibliographies by each.

US/0888-5257
VSTRECI (PHILADELPHIA, PA.). (VSTRECHI : ALMANAKH.). [Vstreci]. (1983)-. Periodical. Russian. an. $11.00 US; $12.00 Canada; $13.00 other. Vstrechi, 7738 Woodbiene Avenue, Philadelphia PA 19151. **Tel** (215)477-6172. **ED** Valentina Sinkevich. **LC** PG3542; .P47. **DD** 891. **Pr Rev. Circ:** 500. **Continues** Perekrestki, 0160-5534.
Desc: Work of Russian poets who live outside of their country.

SZ
VWA. VFOAT V.W.A. No. 1 (Spring 1983)-. Periodical. French (Spanish and Italian). Three times a year. 50.00F. Revue Litteraire, Case postale 172, CH-2301 La Chaux-de-Fonds Switzerland. **Tel** (039)282418, (039)283730. **ED** P Antonietti, P Marthaler and M Palomo. **LC** PQ1141; .V87. **Circ:** 800. available on magnetic tape (No. 4).
Ind/Abst MLA Int. Bibl. Books Artic. Mod. Lang. Lit.

US/0148-7132
WALLACE STEVENS JOURNAL, THE. [Wallace Stevens j.]. **Added/Corp** Wallace Stevens Society. Vol. 1 (Spring 1977)-. Periodical. English. sa. $25.00 institutions; $20.00 (one year), $35.00 (two year) individuals. Wallace Stevens Journal, Clarkson University, John N Serio, Potsdam NY 13699-5750. **Tel** (315)268-3987, **FAX** (315)268-3983. **ED** John N Serio. **Bk Rev.** (Qty: 10). **Ad Acc. Pr Rev. Circ:** 650.
Desc: Criticism on the poetry of Wallace Stevens with book reviews, bibliography, poetry, and news.
Ind/Abst Abstr. Engl. Stud.; Am. Humanit. Index (199?-); Annu. Bibliogr. Engl. Lang. Lit.; Index Book Rev. Humanit. (1985-); Lit. Crit. Regist.; MLA Int. Bibl. Books Artic. Mod. Lang. Lit.

US/0197-4777
WATERWAYS (NEW YORK, N.Y.). (WATERWAYS.). **Added/Corp** Ten Penny Players. Vol. 1 (June 1980)-. Periodical. English. mo ((except August)). $20.00 (1 year); $40.00 (2 year); $60.00 (3 year). Waterways, 393 St Pauls Avenue, Staten Island NY 10304. **Tel** (718)442-7429, **FAX** (718)442-4978. **ED** Barbara Fisher and Richard Spiegel. **DD** 811. Index available ($5.00). **Circ:** 150. **Supersedes** New York State Waterways Project, 0195-718X.
Desc: Poetry, primarily American contemporary, theme issues.

US
WAVES. V. 1- Fall 1978-. Periodical. English. $6.00. Route 2, Shepherd MI 48883. **ED** E Torgerson.

US
WESLEYAN NEW POETS. English. ir. University Press of New England, 23 South Main Street, Hanover NH 03755. **Tel** (800)421-1561, (603)643-7110, **FAX** (603)643-1540. **Separated from** Wesleyan Poetry Program.

US
WESLEYAN POETRY. English. ir. University Press of New England, 23 South Main Street, Hanover NH 03755. **Tel** (800)421-1561, (603)643-7110, **FAX** (603)643-1540. **Separated from** Wesleyan Poetry Program.

US
WESLEYAN POETRY IN TRANSLATION. English. ir. University Press of New England, 23 South Main Street, Hanover NH 03755. **Tel** (800)421-1561, (603)643-7110, **FAX** (603)643-1540. **Separated from** Wesleyan Poetry Program.

US
WESLEYAN POETRY PROGRAM, THE. Title Change. (1959)-(19??). English. sa. University Press of New England, 23 South Main Street, Hanover NH 03755. **Tel** (800)421-1561, (603)643-7110, **FAX** (603)643-1540. **ED** Eliza Childs, Peter Potter and Margaret Klumpp. **Split into** Wesleyan New Poets and Wesleyan Poetry Wesleyan Poetry in Translation.

US
WHITE PINE. V. 1- 1974-. Periodical. English. qt. White Pine, 15 Mount Vernon Avenue, Buffalo NY 14210. **Tel** (716)825-8671.

US/0894-8488
WILLIWAW. Ceased. [Williwaw]. (1987)-?. Periodical. English. sa. Williwaw, PO Box 607, Brockport NY 14420. **DD** 811.

US/0043-5716
WINDLESS ORCHARD, THE. [Wind. orchard]. (Feb. 1970)-. Periodical. English. ir. $10.00 (one year), $29.00 (three years). Windless Orchard, c/o Robert Novak, English Department, Indiana Purdue University, Fort Wayne IN 46805. **Tel** (219)483-6845. **ED** Robert Novak. **LC** PS580; .W55. **DD** 811/.5/408. **Bk Rev. Pr Rev. Circ:** 300. available on microfilm and microfiche from University Microfilms International (UMI).
Desc: Contemporary poetry: original verse and criticism.
Ind/Abst Am. Humanit. Index; Index Am. Period. Verse.

US/0195-6183
WOMAN POET. (WOMAN POET / WOMEN-IN-LITERATURE, INCORPORATED.). [Woman poet]. **Added/Corp** Women-in-Literature, Incorporated (U.S.). Vol. 1 (1980)-. English. ir. $19.95 (Vol. 1-4), each for hardcover; $22.95 for paperback. Women in Literature Inc, PO Box 60550, Reno NV 89506. **Tel** (702)972-1671. **ED** Elaine Dallman. **[CCC]. Circ:** 5,000.
Desc: Each of these anthology studies have 2 to 3 leading womens poets of this region with previously unpublished poems, critical responses, interviews, narrative biographies and photos. Thirty additional poets have been included.
Ind/Abst Am. Humanit. Index (-199?).

US/0275-6773
WOOD IBIS. [Wood ibis]. 1- 1975-. Periodical. English. ir. Place of Herons Press, Box 1952, Austin TX 78768.

US/8756-5277
WORCESTER REVIEW, THE. [Worcest. rev.]. **Added/Corp** Worcester County Poetry Association. (1972)-. Periodical. English. an. price varies per volume. The Worcester County Poetry Association, 6 Chatham Street, Worcester MA 01609. **Tel** (508)797-4770. **DD** 811.
Desc: Publishes primarily poetry but also includes articles about poetry, critical work with a New England connection, fiction, photography and artwork.

US/0043-8154
WORLD (NEW YORK, N.Y. : 1967), THE. (THE WORLD.). No. 1 (1967)-. Periodical. English. ir. Poetry Project / St. Marks Church, 10th Street & 2nd Avenue, New York NY 10003. **Tel** (212)674-0910. **ED** Jessica Hagedorn and Deborah Artman. **Bk Rev. Ad Acc. Circ:** 4,000 (ctrl). **Continues** The Poetry Project Newsletter.
Desc: Publishes poetry, fiction, performance text, book reviews and essays by established and emerging writers; also publishes a list of recommended noteworthy books and small press magazines.

US/0043-9401
WORMWOOD REVIEW, THE. See Literature.

US/0043-9525
WRITER'S DIGEST, THE. See Literature.

CN/0706-1889
WRITING (NELSON). (WRITING.). [Writing (Nelson)]. **Added/Corp** David Thompson University Centre. Writing Program. No. 1 (Summer 1980)-. Periodical. English (French). Three times a year. 18.00Can$ (individuals), 23.00Can$ (institutions) US; 20.00Can$ (individuals), 25.00Can$ (institutions) others. Writing Magazine, Box 69609 Station K, Vancouver British Columbia V5K 4W7 Canada. **Tel** (604)875-0615, (604)688-6001. **ED** Colin Browne. **DD** C810/.8/0054. **Circ:** 750.
Desc: Canadian literary magazine that actively searches out new writing; innovative work with intelligence and heart that's not afraid to challenge its readers. The finest in poetry, prose fiction and poetics. Subscribers and contributors hail from across Canada, the United States and Europe.
Ind/Abst Can. Period. Index (1990-).

●US/1062-8770
WRITING RIGHT NEWSLETTER. [Writ. right newsl.]. (Jan. 1992)-. Newsletter. English. mo. $30.00. Elmwood Park Publishing Company, Po Box 35132, Elmwood Park IL 60635. **DD** 808.

US/0146-0463
XANADU (WANTAGH). (XANADU.). [Xanadu]. **Added/Corp** Long Island Poetry Collective. Vol. 1 (Oct. 1975)-. Periodical. English. an. $5.00. Long Island Poetry Collective, PO Box 773, Huntington NY 11743. **Tel** (516)691-2376. **ED** Anne-Ruth E. Baehr, Mildred M. Jeffrey, Barbara Lucas and Pat Fisher. **LC** WMLC L 83/6786. **Ad Acc. Circ:** 500.

CN/1050-5334
XENOPHILIA. 1990-. English. Omega Cat Press, 904 Old Town Court, Cupertino CA 95014.

US/1058-420X
XIB (SAN DIEGO, CALIF.). (XIB.). [Xib]. Issue No 1 (Spring 1991)-. Periodical. English. qt. $8.00. XIB Publications, PO Box 262112, San Diego CA 92126. **DD** 811.

CH
YA-CHOU HSIEN TAI SHIH CHI / PAI TI, CHEN, CHIEN-WO HO PIEN. Vol. 1 (1982). Periodical. Chinese (Japanese and Korean). an. NT$200.00. Shih Pao Wen Hua Chu Pan Shih Yeh Yu Hsien Kung Ssu, 132 Ta Li Chieh, Taipei Taiwan. **LC** PJ356; .Y3. **DD** 895.

US
YALE LITERARY MAGAZINE, THE. See Literature.

US/0084-3458
YALE SERIES OF YOUNGER POETS, THE. Added/Corp Yale University. Vol. 1 (1919)-. Monographic series. English. ir (Apr.). Price varies per volume. Yale University Press, Box 209040, New Haven CT 06520. **Tel** (203)432-0940, (800)987-7323, **FAX** (203)432-0948. **LC** UNC. **DD** 811/.008.

US
YEARBOOK OF CONTEMPORARY POETRY, THE. (1936)-. English. Avon Books, PO Box 767, Dresden TN 38225. **Tel** (800)238-0658, (800)762-0779 outside of Tennessee. **ED** Margaret Nelson. **LC** PS614; .Y4. **DD** 811.50822.
Desc: Includes biographical notes and Books of poetry published in 1935.

US/0890-2917
YEARBOOK OF LANGLAND STUDIES, THE. [Yearb. Langland stud.]. **VFOAT** YLS. Vol. 1 (1987)-. Periodical. English. an (Oct.). $30.00. Colleagues Press Inc, PO Box 4007, East Lansing MI 48823. **Tel** (517)337-2929. **ED** J.A. Alford. **LC** PR2015; .Y43. **DD** 821. **Bk Rev. Ad Acc. Pr Rev. Circ:** 500.
Ind/Abst MLA Int. Bibl. Books Artic. Mod. Lang. Lit.

US
YOUNG AMERICA SINGS... ANTHOLOGY OF PRIVATE SECONDARY SCHOOL POETRY. **Added/Corp** National High School Poetry Association. (1942)-. English. National High School Poetry Association, Box 218, Agoura CA 91301. **LC** PS591.S3; Y57. **DD** 811.50822.

IT/0393-2362
ZETA (UDINE). (ZETA.). [Zeta]. (1979)-. Italian (English, French and German).
Ind/Abst MLA Int. Bibl. Books Artic. Mod. Lang. Lit.